The Jewish Study Bible

JEWISH PUBLICATION SOCIETY

TANAKH TRANSLATION

CONTRIBUTORS

Yairah Amit: *Judges*   Shimon Bar-Efrat: *First and Second Samuel*

Ehud Ben Zvi: *The Twelve Minor Prophets*   Edward Breuer: *Post-medieval Jewish Interpretation*

Yaakov Elman: *Classical Rabbinic Interpretation*   Esther Eshel: *The Bible in the Dead Sea Scrolls*

Steven E. Fassberg: *Languages of the Bible*   Michael V. Fox: *Proverbs*   Nili S. Fox: *Numbers*

Stephen A. Geller: *The Religion of the Bible*   Leonard J. Greenspoon: *Jewish Translations of the Bible*

Daniel Grossberg: *Lamentations*   Mayer Gruber: *Job*

Jonathan Klawans: *Concepts of Purity in the Bible*   Jon D. Levenson: *Genesis*

Bernard M. Levinson: *Deuteronomy*   Peter Machinist: *Ecclesiastes*

Carol Meyers: *Joshua*   Hindy Najman: *Ezra, Nehemiah, Early Nonrabbinic Interpretation*

Jordan S. Penkower: *The Development of the Masoretic Bible*   Stefan C. Reif: *The Bible in the Liturgy*

Adele Reinhartz: *Ruth, Jewish Women's Scholarly Writings on the Bible*

David Rothstein: *First and Second Chronicles*   Baruch J. Schwartz: *Leviticus*

Avigdor Shinan: *The Bible in the Synagogue*   Uriel Simon: *The Bible in Israeli Life*

Benjamin D. Sommer: *Isaiah, Inner-biblical Interpretation*

S. David Sperling: *Modern Jewish Interpretation*   David Stern: *Midrash and Jewish Interpretation*

Elsie Stern: *The Song of Songs*   Marvin A. Sweeney: *Jeremiah, Ezekiel*

Jeffrey H. Tigay: *Exodus*   Hava Tirosh-Samuelson: *The Bible in the Jewish Philosophical Tradition*

Barry D. Walfish: *Medieval Jewish Interpretation*   Lawrence M. Wills: *Daniel*

Elliot R. Wolfson: *The Bible in the Jewish Mystical Tradition*   Ziony Zevit: *First and Second Kings*

Adele Berlin: *Introduction: What Is The Jewish Study Bible?* [with Marc Zvi Brettler]; *Psalms* [with Marc Zvi Brettler]; *Esther; Introduction to the Essays* [with Marc Zvi Brettler]; *Historical and Geographical Background to the Bible* [with Marc Zvi Brettler]; *Textual Criticism of the Bible* [with Marc Zvi Brettler]; *The Modern Study of the Bible* [with Marc Zvi Brettler]; *Reading Biblical Poetry*

Marc Zvi Brettler: *Introduction: What Is The Jewish Study Bible?* [with Adele Berlin]; *Torah; Nevi'im; Kethuvim; Psalms* [with Adele Berlin]; *Introduction to the Scrolls; Introduction to the Essays* [with Adele Berlin]; *Historical and Geographical Background to the Bible* [with Adele Berlin]; *Textual Criticism of the Bible* [with Adele Berlin]; *The Canonization of the Bible; The Modern Study of the Bible* [with Adele Berlin]

THE JEWISH STUDY BIBLE

Adele Berlin and Marc Zvi Brettler

EDITORS

Michael Fishbane

CONSULTING EDITOR

Jewish Publication Society
TANAKH *Translation*

OXFORD
UNIVERSITY PRESS

OXFORD
UNIVERSITY PRESS

Oxford New York

Auckland Bangkok Buenos Aires Cape Town Chennai
Dar es Salaam Delhi Hong Kong Istanbul Karachi Kolkata
Kuala Lumpur Madrid Melbourne Mexico City Mumbai
Nairobi São Paulo Shanghai Taipei Tokyo Toronto

Published by Oxford University Press, Inc.
198 Madison Avenue, New York, New York 10016

www.oup.com

Oxford is a registered trademark of Oxford University Press

Printed in the United States of America

3 5 7 9 10 8 6 4 2

Contents

Maps and Diagrams

Color Maps follow the last page of the Index

Introduction: What Is "The Jewish Study Bible"?

MORE THAN TWENTY-FIVE CENTURIES have passed since an anonymous Jewish poet wrote an elaborate and lengthy prayer that included this exclamation:

O how I love your teaching!

It is my study all day long (Ps. 119.97).

These two themes—the love for Torah (teaching) and dedication to the study of it—have characterized Jewish reading and interpretation of the Bible ever since. The love is the impetus for the study; the study is the expression of the love. Indeed the intensity with which Jews have examined this text through the centuries testifies both to their love of it—a love combined with awe and deep reverence—and to their intellectual curiosity about it. That tradition of impassioned intellectual engagement continues to the present day.

The tradition of biblical interpretation has been a constant conversation, at times an argument, among its participants; at no period has the text been interpreted in a monolithic fashion. If anything marks Jewish biblical interpretation it is the diversity of approaches employed and the multiplicity of meanings produced. This is expressed in the famous rabbinic saying: "There are seventy faces to the Torah" (*Num. Rab.* 13.15 and parallels), meaning that biblical texts are open to seventy different interpretations, with seventy symbolizing a large and complete number. Thus, there is no official Jewish interpretation of the Bible. In keeping with this attitude, the interpreters who contributed to this volume have followed a variety of methods of interpretation, and the editors have not attempted to harmonize the contributions, so an array of perspectives is manifest. In addition, we do not claim any privileged status for this volume; we can only hope that it will find its place among the myriad Jewish interpretations that have preceded and will follow. We hope that Jewish readers will use this book as a resource to better understand the multiple interpretive streams that have informed, and continue to inform, their tradition. We also hope that *The Jewish Study Bible* will serve as a compelling introduction for students of the Bible from other backgrounds and traditions, who are curious about contemporary academic Jewish biblical interpretation.

Jews have been engaged in reading and interpreting the Bible, or Tanakh, since its inception. Even before the biblical canon was complete, some of its early writings were becoming authoritative, and were cited, alluded to, and reworked in later writings, which themselves would become part of the Bible. Jewish biblical interpretation continued in various forms in early translations into Greek and Aramaic, in the Dead Sea Scrolls, in rabbinic literature, and in medieval and modern commentaries; it continues in the present. We therefore have kept in mind two overarching goals in the commissioning and editing of the study materials in this volume. The first goal is to convey the best of modern academic scholarship on the Bible, that is, scholarship that reflects the way the Bible is approached in the university. This desire comes from a strong conviction that this approach does not undermine Judaism, as leading figures of previous generations had argued, but can add significant depth to Jewish belief and values. The second goal is to reflect, in as broad a fashion as possible, the range of Jewish engagement with the Bible over the past two and a half millennia. The breadth of this engagement, as well as its depth, should not be underestimated. In fact, as a group, the contributors reflect divergent Jewish commitments and beliefs, which infuse their commentaries. They employ state-of-the-art scholarship and a wide range of modern approaches; at the same time, they are sensitive to Jewish readings of the Bible, to classical Jewish interpretation, and to the place of the Bible in Jewish life. In this respect they are actually quite "traditional," in that Jewish interpreters have a long history of drawing on ideas and methods from the non-Jewish world in which they lived and incorporating them into Jewish writings.

Although there is no single notion of Jewish biblical interpretation, our contributors share some commonalities:

• They view the Tanakh as complete in itself, not as a part of a larger Bible or a prelude to the New Testament. For all of them, the Tanakh is "the Bible," and for this reason *The Jewish Study Bible* uses the terms "Tanakh" and "the Bible" interchangeably.

• We avoid the term "Hebrew Bible," a redundancy in the Jewish view. Jews have no Bible but the "Hebrew Bible." (Some Christians use "Hebrew Bible," a sensitive substitute for "Old Testament," to distinguish it from the Greek Bible, or New Testament.)

• They take seriously the traditional Hebrew (Masoretic) text of the Bible.

• They take cognizance of and draw upon traditional Jewish interpretation, thereby placing themselves in the larger context of Jewish exegesis.

• They point out where biblical passages have influenced Jewish practice.

• They call attention to biblical passages that are especially meaningful in the life of the Jewish community.

Just as there is no one Jewish interpretation, there is no authorized Jewish translation of the Bible into English. In fact, translation has always been less important in Jewish communal life than in Christian communities, because public liturgical readings from the Bible have always been in Hebrew, a language understood until recent centuries by many within the community. For Jews, the official Bible is the Hebrew Masoretic Text; it has never been replaced by an official translation (like the Vulgate, for instance, which is the official Bible of the Roman Catholic Church). Nevertheless, because many Jews since postbiblical times did not understand biblical Hebrew, translations into vernacular languages were made. For contemporary English-speaking Jews, the best and most widely read Jewish translation is the most recent one commissioned and published by the Jewish Publication Society, begun in 1955 and completed in 1982, with revisions to the earlier books incorporated in the 1985 edition, and with a revised and corrected second edition in 1999. That second edition of the translation (NJPS *Tanakh*) serves as the basis for this volume.

There is no single way to read through the Bible—this is reflected in the variety of orders found for the biblical books in manuscripts and rabbinic texts. In fact, some may prefer first to read background material about the Bible, and only then to read the text. For this reason, we have taken an expansive approach in offering numerous essays that explore many aspects of the Bible and its intepretation. Some of these are of the type found in other study Bibles, exploring issues such as canon, the history of the biblical period, and modern methods of studying the Bible. Others reflect the specific interests of *The Jewish Study Bible*, including essays on the history of the Jewish interpretation of the Bible, Jewish Bible translation, midrash, and the Bible in the Jewish philosophical, mystical, and liturgical traditions. Each essay is self-standing, and there is often overlap between them. As a whole, however, they convey the important place of the Bible within Judaism, and many of the varieties of uses that this text has found throughout the ages. We hope that, along with the annotations, these essays will introduce a wide audience to the world of Jewish tradition as it relates to the Bible. (A brief introduction to the essays, pp. 1827–28, sets out their arrangement and aims in greater detail.)

For each book of the Bible, our contributors have provided an introduction that sets it in its context—its original setting, so far as that can be determined; the wider corpus of which it is a part; its genre; and its place within Judaism—and provides an overview of the issues involved in reading it. Like many traditional rabbinic texts, the main text, here the NJPS translation, is surrounded by commentary, or more precisely annotations, often quite extensive, that comment on specific points in the text but also bring the reader back to the larger issues raised in the introduction and elsewhere. These annotations frequently refer to other portions of the biblical text, and further insight can be gained by checking these references and reading those texts and their associated annotations.

Besides the essays described above, the volume has further information. A timeline lists rulers in the land of Israel and the surrounding empires during the biblical period. A chart of weights and measures gives modern approximations to the quantities specified at various points in the text (these are usually explained in the annotations as well). A table of chapter/verse numbering differences between the Hebrew text and standard, non-Jewish English translations, will be of help to those who come to this volume from a different translation tradition. A list of biblical readings provides the citations of texts for use in the synagogue. A glossary, explaining technical terms in biblical studies, various literary terms, and numerous words specific to the Jewish interpretive tradition, provides further information for the technical vocabulary that was sometimes unavoidable. An index to the entirety of the study materials—book introductions, annotations, and essays—keyed by page number, facilitates pursuing particular topics through the full range of the study materials. Finally, a set of full-color maps and a map index present geographical background for the events detailed in the text, the annotations, and the historical essays.

ACKNOWLEDGMENTS

In order to produce a work of this length and complexity, many people must play a role. We especially wish to thank Dr. Ellen Frankel, chief executive and editor-in-chief of the Jewish Publication Society, who first suggested this publishing project to Oxford University Press, and Prof. Michael Fishbane, the academic advisor to JPS, who participated in the initial planning and whose scholarly dedication both to the biblical text and to the tradition of Jewish interpretation served as a model for our endeavors. We are grateful to JPS, and particularly to the Board of Trustees of the Society, for agreeing to make their translation available for this study edition.

We are also mindful of all the scholarship that has gone before us, and on which we have relied throughout the volume. In particular, we have followed the model of the *New Oxford Annotated Bible*, and have, with the permission of Oxford University Press, adapted some of the excellent auxiliary materials in that work for use in this one. The introductory essays to the three canonical groups, *Torah, Nevi'im,* and *Kethuvim* are expanded versions of the essays written for the *Annotated:* "The Pentateuch" (Marc Z. Brettler), "The Historical Books" (Marc Z. Brettler), "The Poetical and Wisdom Books" (Marc Z. Brettler), and "The Prophetic Books" (Carol A. Newsom). The essay on "The Canonization of the Bible" is adapted from the essay "The Canons of the Bible" (Marc Z. Brettler and Pheme Perkins). The essay on "Textual Criticism of the Bible" is adapted from "Textual Criticism" by Michael D. Coogan and Pheme

Perkins. The essay on "The Modern Study of the Bible" is adapted from "The Interpretation of the Bible: From the Nineteenth to the Mid-twentieth Centuries" (Michael D. Coogan) and "Contemporary Methods in Biblical Study" (Carol A. Newsom). The essay on "The Historical and Geographical Background to the Bible" is partly based on "The Ancient Near East" (Michael D. Coogan), "The Persian and Hellenistic Periods" (Carol A. Newsom), and "The Geography of the Bible" (Michael D. Coogan).

In addition, the editors would especially like to thank:

The editorial staff at Oxford University Press in New York, especially Jennifer Grady and Miriam Gross, who handled the complex and demanding editorial process with care; James R. Getz, Jr., and Sheila Reeder, who checked many cross references and other internal matters in manuscript and made numerous improvements in the study materials; Leslie Phillips, who designed the volume and oversaw the producton process; Katrina Gettman, who copyedited the manuscript and imposed order on our many and varied editorial decisions; Peachtree Editorial and Proofreading Service, who proofread the entire text and kept the process on schedule; Kate Mertes, who prepared the index to the study materials; and Christopher B. Wyckoff, who drew up the bibliography in "Translations of Primary Sources." We are particularly thankful for the guidance, erudition, and encouragement of Donald Kraus, executive editor in the Bible department at Oxford University Press, U.S.A.; he conceived this volume, and his creative and experienced hand may be seen on every page. We also thank the contributors, from whom we have learned so much, and hope that they will be pleased with the whole, to which each contributed an invaluable part. Both editors, coming from different perspectives, have read every word of every annotation and essay, often more than once. Our editing sessions became wonderful opportunities for serious discussion between ourselves and with our contributors on a wide range of fundamental issues in biblical and Jewish studies. We invite our readers to partake of the fruits of this productive collaboration, the seventy faces of the Torah that await them in this volume.

We are completing our work on this volume as we approach the holiday of Shavuʻot, the time when, according to postbiblical Jewish tradition, the Torah was given to Moses. The volume is being published close to the holiday of Simḥat Torah, the Rejoicing of the Torah, when the annual liturgical reading cycle of the Torah is completed and immediately begun again. As we have worked on this Bible for the last three years, we have gained even greater respect and appreciation for the "gift" of the Bible and for the never-ending, ever-renewing Jewish interpretive traditions. We share with even more profound conviction the sentiment of the psalmist with whose words we opened this introduction:

> O how I love your teaching!
> It is my study all day long.

ADELE BERLIN
MARC ZVI BRETTLER
June 2003
Sivan 5762

Preface to the 1985 JPS Edition

THIS TRANSLATION OF TANAKH, THE HOLY SCRIPTURES, produced by the Jewish Publication Society, was made directly from the traditional Hebrew text into the idiom of modern English. It represents the collaboration of academic scholars with rabbis from the three largest branches of organized Jewish religious life in America. Begun in 1955, the ongoing translation was published in three main stages: *The Torah* in 1962, *The Prophets (Nevi'im)* in 1978, and *The Writings (Kethuvim)* in 1982. These three volumes, with revisions, are now brought together in a complete English *Tanakh (Torah-Nevi'im-Kethuvim)*, the latest link in the chain of Jewish Bible translations.

ON THE HISTORY OF BIBLE TRANSLATION

Bible translation began about 2200 years ago, in the 3rd century BCE, as the large Jewish population of Alexandria, Egypt, came under the influence of Hellenism. When the Greek language replaced Hebrew and Aramaic as their vernacular, and the Torah in its Hebrew original was no longer commonly understood, a translation into Greek was made for the Jewish community of Alexandria. This translation came to be known as the Septuagint, Latin for "seventy," because of the legend that the committee of translators numbered seventy-two, six elders from each of the twelve tribes of Israel.

In the last few centuries BCE, the Jews who lived to the north and east of Judea also found the Hebrew Bible difficult to understand, for their spoken language had become largely Aramaic. Translations into Aramaic, first of the Torah and then of the rest of the Bible, became known as the Targums.

The Septuagint and the Targums are not only the oldest translations of the Bible but also the most influential. Down to our own day, virtually every Christian translation has followed the methods of the Jewish translators who created the Septuagint, and generally followed their renderings of the Hebrew as well. The Christian translators also were influenced by the interpretation of the Hebrew text set forth in the Targums (much of it in oral form at the time) and by the writings of the Jewish philosopher-interpreter Philo of Alexandria (died about 45 CE).

The forerunners and leaders of the Renaissance and the Reformation (14th–15th centuries), and especially Martin Luther and William Tyndale (16th century), made use of Latin translations of the classic Jewish commentators Rashi, Ibn Ezra, and Kimḥi (11th–13th centuries), whose works were imbued with the direct knowledge of the Targums. Luther was greatly indebted to Nicholas of Lyre (1270–1349), who had adopted Rashi's exegesis for his Latin Bible commentary. Rashi's influence on all authorized and most unofficial English translations of the Hebrew Bible becomes evident when Tyndale's dependence on Luther is considered. Tyndale is central to many subsequent English translations: the King James Version of 1611, the (British) Revised Version of 1881–1885, the American Standard Version of 1901, and especially the Revised Standard Version of 1952.

Alongside the close, literal method of Bible translation, the earliest Jewish translators were also influenced by the widely held view that, along with the Written Law (*torah she-bikhtav*), God had given Moses on Mount Sinai an Oral Law (*torah she-be'al peh*) as well; so that to comprehend God's Torah fully and correctly, it was essential to make use of both. Thus, when a translation of the Hebrew Bible into the Judeo-Arabic vernacular was deemed necessary for Jewry in Moslem countries toward the end of the first millennium, the noted philologian, philosopher, and community leader Saadia Gaon (882–942) produced a version that incorporated traditional Jewish interpretation but was not based on word-for-word translation; at the same time, it was a model of clarity and stylistic elegance. The present version is in the spirit of Saadia.

With the growth of Christianity in the 1st century, the Church adopted the Septuagint as its Bible, and the Septuagint was translated into the languages of the various Christian communities. As Greek began to give way to Latin in the Roman empire, it was only a matter of time before a Latin translation of Scripture became the recognized Bible of the Church. The Church father Jerome (ca. 340–420) produced the official Latin version. Drawing on Jewish tradition and consulting Jewish teachers, he achieved what came to be known as the Vulgate, the Bible in the language of the common people. The Vulgate, the Bible of European Christianity until the Reformation, is clearly the most significant Bible translation after the Septuagint.

With the rise of Protestantism in Europe, scholars within this movement set themselves the task of making the Bible available in the various vernaculars of the time. By 1526 the first parts of two notable translations began to appear: Martin Luther's in German and William Tyndale's in English. The latter, by way of several subsequent revisions, became the King James Version of 1611. The more modern English versions—such as *The Holy Scriptures* by the American rabbi Isaac Leeser (1855), the (British) Revised Version (1881–1885), the American Standard Version (1901), the Jewish Publication Society's *The Holy Scriptures* (1917), and the (American) Revised Standard Version (1952)—made extensive use of the King James.

ON THE MAKING OF THE NEW TRANSLATION

After World War II, when the Jewish Publication Society began to consider a new edition of the Bible, the idea of a modest revision of the 1917 translation met with resistance, and the concept of a completely new translation gradually took hold. The proposed translation would reproduce the Hebrew idiomatically and reflect contemporary scholarship, thus laying emphasis upon intelligibility and correctness. It would make critical use of the early rabbinic and medieval Jewish commentators, grammarians, and philologians and would rely on the traditional Hebrew text, avoiding emendations. The need for this new translation was the focus of the Jewish Publication Society's annual meeting in 1953. Later that year the Society announced its intention to proceed with the project, and in 1955 the committee of translators began their task.

Harry M. Orlinsky, Professor of Bible at Hebrew Union College–Jewish Institute of Religion (New York), was asked to serve as editor-in-chief for the new translation, along with H. L. Ginsberg, Professor of Bible at the Jewish Theological Seminary, and Ephraim A. Speiser, Professor of Semitic and Oriental Languages at the University of Pennsylvania, as fellow editors. Associated with them were three rabbis: Max Arzt, Bernard J. Bamberger, and Harry Freedman, representing the Conservative, Reform, and Orthodox branches of organized Jewish religious life. Solomon Grayzel, editor of the Jewish Publication Society, served as secretary of the committee.

The committee profited much from the work of previous translators; the present rendering, however, is essentially a new translation. A few of its characteristics may be noted. The committee undertook to follow faithfully the traditional Hebrew text, but there were certain points at which footnotes appeared necessary: (1) where the committee had to admit that it did not understand a word or passage; (2) where an alternative rendering was possible; (3) where an old rendering, no longer retained, was so well known that it would very likely be missed, in which case the traditional translation was given in the name of "Others" (usually referring to the Society's version of 1917); (4) where the understanding of a passage could be facilitated by reference to another passage elsewhere in the Bible; and (5) where important textual variants are to be found in some of the ancient manuscripts or versions of the Bible.

The translators avoided obsolete words and phrases and, whenever possible, rendered Hebrew idioms by means of their normal English equivalents. For the second person singular, the modern "you" was used instead of the archaic "thou," even when referring to the Deity ("You"). A further obvious difference between this translation and most of the older ones is in the rendering of the Hebrew particle *waw*, which is usually translated "and." Biblical Hebrew demanded the frequent use of the *waw*, but in that style it had the force not only of "and" but also of "however," "but," "yet," "when," and any number of other such words and particles, or none at all that can be translated into English. Always to render it as "and" is to misrepresent the Hebrew rather than be faithful to it. Consequently, the committee translated the particle as the sense required, or left it untranslated.

The chapter and verse divisions found in the printed Bible are indispensable as a system of precise reference, but they do not always coincide with the organic divisions of the text. The chapter divisions, whose origin is neither ancient nor Jewish but medieval Christian, sometimes join or separate the wrong paragraphs, sentences, or even parts of sentences. The verse divisions, though considerably older and of Jewish origin, sometimes join together parts of different sentences or separate from each other parts of the same sentence. The translation of Saadia Gaon often does not correspond to our chapter divisions, which did not exist in his day. More noteworthy is the readiness with which he joined separate verses of the Hebrew text (whose authority he did not question) into single sentences when the sense required it. Thus, in joining Genesis 7.24 and 8.1 into a single sentence, or combining the last part of 1 Kings 6.38 with 7.1, the present translation is following the example of Saadia. The attentive reader will discover other instances in which the translators have followed what they considered to be the logical units of meaning even when they did not coincide with the conventional chapters and verses. The latter, however, are marked and numbered throughout.

The preface to the first edition of *The Torah* was dated September 25, 1962, Erev Rosh Ha-Shanah 5723. A second edition, incorporating some changes by the translators, came out five years later. The committee also produced translations of *The Five Megilloth and Jonah* (1969), *Isaiah* (1973), and *Jeremiah* (1974). The latter two books and Jonah were incorporated, with some corrections and revisions, into the complete translation of *The Prophets (Nevi'im)*. For this volume, which was published in 1978, Professor Ginsberg served as editor, in association with Professor Orlinsky. Whereas Professor Orlinsky had initially prepared a draft translation of the entire Torah, individual members of the committee undertook to prepare a draft of an entire prophetic book or part of a book; but, as in translating the Torah, everyone had an opportunity to criticize the draft and to offer detailed suggestions at periodic committee sessions, which were presided over by Rabbi Bamberger. Differences of opinion were settled by majority vote.

In preparing the translation of *The Prophets,* the translators faced a recurring problem that deserves special mention. The prophetic books contain many passages whose meaning is uncertain. Thus, in order to provide an intelligible rendering, modern scholars have resorted to emending the Hebrew text. Some of these emendations derive from the ancient translators, especially of the Septuagint and the Targums, who had before them a Hebrew text that sometimes differed from today's traditional text. Where these ancient versions provide no help, some scholars have made conjectural emendations of their own. Many modern English versions contain translations of emended texts, sometimes without citing any departure from the traditional Hebrew text.

Like the translation of *The Torah,* the present translation of the prophetic books adheres strictly to the traditional Hebrew text; but where the text remains obscure and an alteration provides marked clarification, a footnote is offered with a rendering of the suggested emendation. If the emendation is based on one or two ancient versions, they are mentioned by name; if more than two versions agree, they are summed up as "ancient versions." Conjectural emendations are introduced by "Emendation yields." Sometimes, however, it was deemed sufficient to offer only a change of vowels, and such modifications are indicated by "Change of vocalization yields." In all cases, the emendation is given in a footnote, which may be readily disregarded by those who reject it on either scholarly or religious grounds. The only exceptions involve such changes in grammatical form as those, say, from second person to third or from singular to plural. In such rare instances, the change is incorporated in the text, and the traditional Hebrew is translated in a footnote.

The committee of translators for *The Writings (Kethuvim),* the third part of the Hebrew Bible, was set up by the Jewish Publication Society in 1966. It consisted of Moshe Greenberg, now Professor of Bible at the Hebrew University, Jonas C. Greenfield, then Professor of Semitic Languages at the Hebrew University, and Nahum M. Sarna, then Professor of Biblical Studies at Brandeis University, in association with Rabbis Saul Leeman, Martin S. Rozenberg, and David

Shapiro of the Conservative, Reform, and Orthodox movements. Chaim Potok, then editor of the Society, served as secretary of the committee.

The present English rendering of *Kethuvim,* like *Torah* and *Nevi'im,* is based on the traditional Hebrew text—its consonants, vowels, and syntactical divisions—although the traditional accentuation occasionally has been replaced by an alternative construction. Following the approach of the original committee, the entire gamut of biblical interpretation, ancient and modern, Jewish and non-Jewish, has been consulted, and, whenever possible, the results of modern study of the languages and cultures of the ancient Near East have been brought to bear on the biblical text. In choosing between alternatives, however, just as antiquity was not in itself a disqualification, so modernity was not in itself a recommendation. Divergences of the present translation from recent renderings reflect the committee's judgment that certain innovations, though interesting, are too speculative for adoption in the present state of knowledge. The as-yet-imperfect understanding of the language of the Bible, or what appears to be some disorder in the Hebrew text, makes sure translation of many passages impossible. This uncertainty in *Kethuvim* is indicated in a note, and, where the Hebrew text permits, alternative renderings have been offered. However, emendations of the text of *Kethuvim*—except for the five *Megilloth*—were not proposed, and notes were kept to a minimum.

Some passages in *Kethuvim* are identical or very similar to passages in *Torah* and *Nevi'im.* The rendering of these passages in *Kethuvim* generally follows the wording in the earlier books; on occasion, however, owing to various considerations, divergences in style and translation will be found. For example, in the presentation of the poetry of the Psalms, it was deemed fitting, because of their liturgical use, to indicate the thought units through appropriate indentation. The text of *Kethuvim* frequently presented the translators with extraordinary difficulties, for it is hardly possible to convey in English the fullness of the Hebrew, with its ambiguities, its overtones, and the richness that it carries from centuries of use. Still, it was their goal to transmit something of the directness, the simplicity, and the uniquely Israelite expressions of piety that are so essential to the sublimity of the Hebrew Bible.

The committee's translation of *The Psalms* appeared in 1973; of *The Book of Job,* in 1980. The two were incorporated, with revisions, into the complete translations of *The Writings (Kethuvim),* which appeared in 1982.

For this one-volume English edition of *Tanakh,* the translation of *The Torah,* first published twenty years earlier, underwent more revision than the more recent publications of *The Prophets* and *The Writings.* A number of the changes had already been projected in *Notes on the New Translation of the Torah,* edited by Harry M. Orlinsky and published by the Society in 1969. Subsequent research on the text has led to further revisions in the translation of *Torah* and some revisions in *Nevi'im* as well.

Ephraim Speiser, of the original committee, died in June 1965. Max Arzt, also an active member of the original committee, died in 1975, when the work of translating the prophetic books was almost complete. Since the appearance of *The Prophets* and *The Writings,* Bernard J. Bamberger, Solomon Grayzel, and Harry Freedman have also passed on.* Their memory, and their scholarship, will be for a blessing.

The Jewish Publication Society joins the members of the committees of translators in the hope that the results of their labors will find favor with God and man.

The Jewish Publication Society
September 15, 1985
ערב ראש השנה תשמ"ו

---

*Deceased and lamented since 1985: H. L. Ginsberg, Harry Orlinsky, and Jonas Greenfield.

Alphabetical Listing of the Books of the Bible

Hebrew Transliteration

Although we have tried to be consistent and simple in transliteration, we have kept certain standard or traditional spellings to avoid confusion.

CHARACTER	TRANSLITERATION		CHARACTER	TRANSLITERATION
א	ʾ		מ	m
בּ בּ	b, v		נ	n
ג	g		ס	s
ד	d		ע	ʿ
ה	h		פּ פ	p, f
ו	v		צ	tz
ז	z		ק	k, q
ח	ḥ		ר	r
ט	t		שׂ	s
י	y		שׁ	sh
כּ כ	k, kh		ת	t
ל	l			

Guide to Abbreviations and Terms

Abbreviations Used for the Books of the Bible

Amos	Amos	Hos.	Hosea	Mic.	Micah
1 Chron.	Chronicles, First	Isa.	Isaiah	Nah.	Nahum
2 Chron.	Chronicles, Second	Jer.	Jeremiah	Neh.	Nehemiah
Dan.	Daniel	Job	Job	Num.	Numbers
Deut.	Deuteronomy	Joel	Joel	Obad.	Obadiah
Eccl.	Ecclesiastes	Jonah	Jonah	Prov.	Proverbs
Esth.	Esther	Josh.	Joshua	Ps(s).	Psalms
Exod.	Exodus	Judg.	Judges	Ruth	Ruth
Ezek.	Ezekiel	1 Kings	Kings, First	1 Sam.	Samuel, First
Ezra	Ezra	2 Kings	Kings, Second	2 Sam.	Samuel, Second
Gen.	Genesis	Lam.	Lamentations	Song	Song of Songs
Hab.	Habakkuk	Lev.	Leviticus	Zech.	Zechariah
Haggai	Hag.	Mal.	Malachi	Zeph.	Zephaniah

Abbreviations and Terms Used in the Footnotes to the Translation

Akkadian	An ancient Semitic language spoken in Mesopotamia; its chief dialects were Babylonian and Assyrian.
Aquila	A 2nd-century convert to Judaism who made a literal translation of the Bible into Greek.
Berakhot	One of the treatises of the Mishnah and the Talmud.
Cf.	A reference to another version, or to a cognate language, that justified the translation adopted.
Heb.	The Hebrew word or phrase in transliteration, especially when necessary to point out a pun, homonym, or the like. *Heb.* is also used to indicate the literal wording for which a superior rendering was employed; see Genesis 46.23, note *a*, or 49.9, note *a*. An example of a somewhat different type may be seen at Exodus 21.22, note *c*.
Ibn Ezra	Rabbi Abraham Ibn Ezra, a Bible commentator and grammarian who lived in Spain in the 12th century.
I.e.	An explanation, to avoid adding words to the text, in order to clarify the translation; see Exodus 22.29, note *d*.
Kethib	The way a word, usually unvocalized, is written in the Bible; see *qere*.

Kimhi	Rabbi David Kimhi (Radak), a Bible commentator and grammarian who lived in southern France in the late 12th and early 13th centuries.
Lit.	For the literal translation of a word or phrase that was given an idiomatic or some-what free translation in the text; see Genesis 30.27, note *f*, and 30.38, *a*; or 43.21, note *a*, and 43.34, note *b*; or Deuteronomy 18.1, note *b* (where the Hebrew and English cannot agree in number).
Masorah	The text of the Bible as transmitted, with vowel signs and accents.
Meaning of Heb. uncertain	Where the translation represents the best that the committee could achieve with an elusive or difficult text. In some cases the text may be unintelligible because of corruption.
Mishnah	The code of Jewish law prepared by Rabbi Judah ha-Nasi about 200 CE. The word is usually followed by the name of the relevant treatise.
Moved up	Where clarity required the shifting of a word or phrase within a verse or from one verse to another; see Genesis 10.14, note *b*.
Or	Indicates an alternative reading that the committee found almost as acceptable as the one adopted for the text.
Others	Indicates a well-known traditional translation, especially if it was used in the older (1917) JPS version, that the committee does not find acceptable even as an alternate reading.
Peshitta	A translation of the Bible into Syriac, parts of which are said to have been made in the 1st century CE.
Qere	The way the Masorah requires a word to be read, especially when it diverges from the *kethib*.
Qumran	The site of the caves where Bible manuscripts were found in 1949–1950. The manu-scripts are identified by such symbols as 4QSam*a* (for manuscript *a* of Samuel, found in the fourth cave of Qumran); 1QIs*a* (for manuscript *a* of Isaiah found in the first cave of Qumran).
Rashbam	Rabbi Shmuel ben Meir, a grandson of Rashi, who commented on the Torah.
Rashi	Rabbi Shlomo Yitzhaki, the best-known Jewish commentator on the Bible. He lived in France at the end of the 11th century.
Saadia	A *gaon*, i.e., a head of a Babylonian talmudic academy, in the early part of the 10th century. His works include the famous translation of the Bible into Arabic.
See	Frequently used in place of *cf.*, but usually intended to begin a note attached to an-other passage in the Bible.
Septuagint	The oldest Jewish translation of the Bible, into Greek. The Torah translation dates from the 3rd century BCE; other books of the Bible were translated somewhat later.
Syriac	See *Peshitta*.
Targum	A Jewish translation of the Bible into Aramaic, a language once widely spoken in western Asia, of which Syriac was a later development.
Ugaritic	A language of inscriptions found at Ras Shamra, on the Syrian coast, in the second millennium BCE. Both the language and its literature have shed much light on the Hebrew Bible.
Vulgate	The Latin translation of the Bible made by the Church father Jerome about the year 400 CE. It became the official Bible of the Roman Catholic Church.

Abbreviations Used in the Annotations, Introductions, and Essays

Abr.	Philo, *On the Life of Abraham*
AEL	*Ancient Egyptian Literature*. M. Lichtheim. 3 vols. Berkeley, 1971–1980
Ag. Ap.	Josephus, *Against Apion*
ANEP	*The Ancient Near East in Pictures Relating to the Old Testament.* J. B. Pritchard, ed. Princeton, 1954
ANET	*Ancient Near Eastern Texts Relating to the Old Testament.* J. B. Pritchard, ed. Princeton, 1969

Ant.	Josephus, *Antiquities of the Jews*
ʿArak.	ʿArakhin (Talmudic Tractate)
Aram.	Aramaic (language)
ʾAvot R. Nat.	ʾAvot of Rabbi Nathan
A. Z.	ʿAvodah Zarah (Talmudic Tractate)
b.	Babylonian Talmud
b.	born
B. Bat.	Bava Batra (Talmudic Tractate)
B. K.	Bava Kamma (Talmudic Tractate)
B. M.	Bava Metziʿa (Talmudic Tractate)
BCE	before the Common Era (= BC)
Bek.	Bekhorot (Talmudic Tractate)
Ber.	Berakhot (Talmudic Tractate)
Bik.	Bikkurim (Talmudic Tractate)
c.	century
ca.	circa
CD	Cairo Genizah copy of the *Damascus Document*
CE	Common Era (= AD)
cf.	compare
ch, chs	chapter, chapters
col(s)	column(s)
cu	cubit(s)
D	Deuteronomic or Deuteronomistic source (of the Torah)
d.	died
Det.	Philo, *Quod deterius potiori insidari soleat, That the Worse Attacks the Better*
E	Elohist or Elohistic source (of the Torah)
e.g.	*exempli gratia,* for example
ed.	editor, edited by
ʿEd.	ʿEduyyot
ʿEruv.	ʿEruvin (Talmudic Tractate)
Esd.	Esdras
esp.	especially
et al.	*et alii,* and others
etc.	*et cetera,* and the rest
ff.	following
fol.	folio
Frg. Tg.	Fragmentary Targum
Git.	Gittin (Talmudic Tractate)
Gk	Greek (language)
H	Holiness Collection (or Code or Legislation)
Hag.	Hagigah (Talmudic Tractate)
Hal.	Hallah (Talmudic Tractate)
HB	Hebrew Bible
Heb	Hebrew (language)
Hev	Hever, Nahal
Hor.	Horayot (Talmudic Tractate)
HUBP	Hebrew University Bible Project
HUC	Hebrew Union College
Hul.	Hullin (Talmudic Tractate)
i.e.	*id est,* that is
ibid.	*ibidem,* in the same place
intro.	introduction, introductory
J	Jahwist or Yahwist source (of the Torah)
JPS	Jewish Publication Society
JTS	Jewish Theological Seminary

Jub.	Jubilees
J. W.	Josephus, *Jewish War*
Ker.	*Keritot* (Talmudic Tractate)
Ketub.	*Ketubbot* (Talmudic Tractate)
kg	kilogram(s)
Kid.	*Kiddushin* (Talmudic Tractate)
Kil.	*Kil'ayim* (Talmudic Tractate)
KJV	King James Version
km	kilometer(s)
Kod.	*Kodoshim* (Talmudic Order)
lit.	literally
L.A.B.	*Liber antiquitatum biblicarum* (Pseudo-Philo)
LXX	Septuagint
m	meter(s)
m.	Mishnah
Ma'as.	*Ma'aserot* (Talmudic Tractate)
Ma'as. S.	*Ma'aser Sheni* (Talmudic Tractate)
Macc.	Maccabees
Mak.	*Makkot* (Talmudic Tractate)
Maks.	*Makhshirin* (Talmudic Tractate)
Mas	Masada
Matt.	Matthew (gospel)
Meg.	*Megillah* (Talmudic Tractate)
Me'il.	*Me'ilah*
Mek.	*Mekhilta* (midrashic text on Exodus)
Menah.	*Menahot* (Talmudic Tractate)
mi	mile(s)
Mid.	*Middot* (Talmudic Tractate)
Midr. + book	*Midrash + biblical book (e.g., Midr. Prov. = Midrash Proverbs)*
Mikv.	*Mikva'ot* (Talmudic Tractate)
MMT	*Miqsat Ma'ase ha-Torah* (a Dead Sea Scroll)
Mo'ed Kat.	*Mo'ed Katan* (Talmudic Tractate)
Mos.	Philo, *On the Life of Moses*
ms, mss	manuscript, manuscripts
MT	Masoretic Text
n., nn.	annotation(s)
Nash.	*Nashim* (Talmudic Order)
Naz.	*Nazir* (Talmudic Tractate)
Ned.	*Nedarim* (Talmudic Tractate)
Neg.	*Nega'im* (Talmudic Tractate)
Nez.	*Nezikin* (Talmudic Order)
Nid.	*Niddah* (Talmudic Tractate)
NJPS	*Tanakh: The Holy Scriptures: The New JPS Translation according to the Traditional Hebrew Text*
NRSV	New Revised Standard Version
'Ohal.	*'Ohalot* (Talmudic Tractate)
op. cit.	*opere citato*, in the work cited
Opif.	Philo, *De opificio mundi, On the Creation of the World*
'Or.	*'Orlah* (Talmudic Tractate)
P	Priestly source (of the Torah)
p., pp.	page, pages
Pes.	*Pesahim* (Talmudic Tractate)
Pesik. Rab.	*Pesikta Rabbati*
Pesik. Rav Kah.	*Pesikta de Rav Kahana*
Pirqe R. El.	*Pirqe Rabbi Eliezer*

pl.	plural
Post.	Philo, *On the Posterity of Cain*
Q	manuscripts found at Qumran (Dead Sea Scrolls)
QG	Philo, *Questions and Answers on Genesis*
q.v.	*quod vide,* which see
R	redactor(s)
R.	Rabbi
RB	Rabbinic Bible *(Miqra'ot Gedolot)*
Rab.	*Rabbah* (book + Rabbah, e.g., Gen. Rab. = Genesis Rabbah)
Rosh Hash.	Rosh Ha-Shanah (Talmudic Tractate)
RSV	Revised Standard Version
Sacr.	Philo, *On the Sacrifices of Cain and Abel*
Sanh.	*Sanhedrin* (Talmudic Tractate)
sg.	singular
Shab.	*Shabbat*
Shek.	*Shekalim* (Talmudic Tractate)
Shev.	*Shevi'it* (Talmudic Tractate)
Shevu.	*Shevu'ot* (Talmudic Tractate)
Sir.	The Wisdom of Jesus ben Sirach (Ecclesiasticus)
Sot.	*Sotah* (Talmudic Tractate)
SP	Samaritan Pentateuch
s.v.	*sub verbum,* under the heading
t.	*Tosefta*
Ta'an.	*Ta'anit* (Talmudic Tractate)
Tanḥ.	*Tanḥuma* (midrashic text on the Torah)
Tehar.	*Teharot* (Talmudic Order)
Tem.	*Temurah* (Talmudic Tractate)
Ter.	*Terumot* (Talmudic Tractate)
Tg.	Targum
Tg. Jon.	*Targum Jonathan*
Tg. Onk.	*Targum Onkelos*
Tg. Ps.-J.	*Targum Pseudo-Jonathan*
T. Yom	*Tevul Yom* (Talmudic Tractate)
'Uk.	*'Uktzin* (Talmudic Tractate)
v., vv.	verse, verses
Vg	Vulgate
Virt.	Philo, *On the Virtues*
viz.	*videlicet,* namely
vs.	versus
VTE	Vassal Treaty of Esarhaddon
y.	Jerusalem Talmud
Yad.	*Yadayim* (Talmudic Tractate)
Yebam.	*Yebamot* (Talmudic Tractate)
Yoma	*Yoma* (Talmudic Tractate)
Wisd.	The Wisdom of Solomon
Zera.	*Zera'im* (Talmudic Order)
Zevaḥ.	*Zevaḥim* (Talmudic Tractate)
‖	parallel
§	section

Note: In chapter/verse references, or following a verse number, the letter "a" means the first section of the verse, "b" means the second section, and so on.

The Jewish Study Bible

JEWISH PUBLICATION SOCIETY

TANAKH TRANSLATION

תורה

TORAH

Terminology, Contents, and Traditional Views of Authorship

THE TERM TORAH, "TEACHINGS, INSTRUCTION," derives from the root *y-r-h*, "to shoot (an arrow)," and thus etymologically refers to that which "hits the mark." Jewish tradition, from the late biblical period on, uses "Torah" to refer to the first section of the Bible, the books Genesis, Exodus, Leviticus, Numbers, and Deuteronomy. These books are also called "The Five Books of Moses" or the "Pentateuch," which derives (via Latin) from the Greek *penta* (five) *teuchoi* (books). As early as the 1st century CE, these five books were written on one long scroll, signaling that they are one unit. Unlike other canonical divisions, where there is significant debate within and between different religious traditions (see the essay on "Canonization," pp. 2072–77), both Jewish and Christian traditions view the books Genesis through Deuteronomy in this order as a single unit, standing first in the Bible. The unanimity of tradition and the initial placement of these five books reflect their significant place within religious life. In Judaism, the Torah is accorded the highest level of sanctity, above that of the other books of the Bible.

Despite their traditional perception as a unity, it is not so obvious how these five books cohere. They certainly do not form a single book in the modern sense, with a single author; modern scholarship has persuasively argued that each of these books is composite, reflecting many traditions and sources (see below). While the plot progresses chronologically, from the creation of the world to the end of the wandering in the wilderness, a large part of this story is retold in Deuteronomy. Moreover, the story does not end here, but continues into the book of Joshua and beyond. While Moses is the central human character in much of the Torah, he is introduced only in ch 2 of Exodus, and is absent from all of Genesis. There are several major themes, including the early development of Israel as a people, the covenant between God and Israel, and the promise of the land; but none of these is present throughout the Torah and all continue beyond it. Theme alone does not define what the Torah is. In fact, if this final theme of promise of the land and its fulfillment is determinative, we should speak of the Hexateuch, the six books of Genesis through Joshua, rather than the Pentateuch or Torah.

The Hebrew terms *torah* and *torat moshe* ("the Torah of Moses"), already in use in late biblical literature to describe what is later called the Torah, offer a better clue to the nature and unity of these books. *Torah* is often understood as "law," and indeed this is one of its frequent meanings in the Bible, as in Exod. 12.49: "There shall be one law [Heb *torah*] for the citizen and for the stranger who dwells among you." Law is a predominant genre of the Torah, which contains not only the Decalogue in Exod. ch 20 and Deut. ch 5, but extensive legal collections in Exod. chs 21–23, Lev. chs 17–26, and Deut. chs 12–26, as well as selected laws within various narratives, such as the law of circumcision in the narrative about Abraham in Gen. ch 17 and the law concerning inheritance of the land by women in Num. ch 36, embedded within a section about the possession of the land. Many narrative sections also contain material that is of legal significance. For example, the first creation story in Genesis culminates with the "creation" of the Sabbath (Gen. 2.2–3), though this would only be legislated in Exod. ch 16, and then as part of the Decalogue, in Exod. 20.8–11. Similarly, the story of the construction of the Tabernacle (Exod. chs 25–40), a temporary temple for God in the wilderness, is not narrated for its own sake, but as an introduction to the various laws of sacrifice, narrated at the beginning of Leviticus, the book that immediately follows these chapters.

Yet "law" is not the only possible translation of *torah*, and the Torah should not be typified as a book of law. The Heb term *torah* also means "instruction" or "teaching," as in Prov. 1.8, "My son, heed the discipline of your father, / And do not forsake the instruction [Heb *torah*] of your mother." Teaching is not confined to law; indeed narratives or stories are as effective a medium of instruction. Given the predominance of narrative in significant portions of the Torah, especially in Genesis, the beginning of Exodus, and Numbers, it is best to understand the biblical term *torat moshe*, the earliest extant term for these five books, as "the instruction of Moses." This instruction was realized through narratives and laws, which together elucidate the proper norms of living and the relationship between God and the world. That the Torah is more than a set of laws is made explicit in the comments of Rashi, the great Jewish medieval interpreter, who, quoting earlier sources, defends the fact that Torah begins with the stories of Genesis rather than with the laws of Exodus.

The terms *torat moshe*, and *torat (ha)elohim/Yhvh*, "God's/the LORD's torah, are found predominantly in various late biblical sections and books, such as Ezra, Nehemiah, and Chronicles. These phrases suggest that the Torah was then understood to be a divine revelation mediated by Moses, as explicitly stated in Ezra 7.6 (cf. Neh. 8.1), "The Torah of Moses which the LORD God of Israel had given." The Torah in the time of Ezra is more or less identical to the Torah as it now exists. It is significant, however, that these terms for it never appear in the Torah itself, suggesting that in the Torah, the word *torah* never refers to the Torah. In fact, the Torah does not explicitly suggest that it was compiled by Moses himself. (The phrase "the Torah" in passages such as Deut. 4.44, "This is the *torah* that Moses set before the Israelites," never refers to the complete Torah.)

After the books came to be viewed as authoritative, it was natural that they should be considered a coherent body of writing given by God through one special "author," Moses. In several places, the Bible suggests that Moses stayed on Mount Sinai for forty days and forty nights (Exod. 24.18; 34.28; Deut. 9.9; 10.10). Clearly, this was too long a time for short

legal collections such as Exod. chs 21–23 to have been conveyed to him, and thus traditions developed that Moses received the entire written Torah from God at that point; according to the classical rabbis, Moses simultaneously received the oral law, which served
as the authoritative interpretation of the written law. In other words, the concept of the divinely inspired Torah expanded to include the Written Torah and all that would derive
from it. The Written Torah, according to all rabbinic sources (which are followed by the
early church), included events before the time of Moses—the book of Genesis, which thus
represents God's authoritative narration to Moses of the early history of the world and of
Abraham and his family—and the death of Moses. Some rabbinic sources suggest that the
final chapter of the Torah, Deut. ch 34, which narrates the death of Moses, was dictated by
God to Moses, who wrote it with his tears. The view that the Torah is the divine word mediated by Moses was the standard view through the Renaissance.

This view is explicitly contradicted by the Torah's narrative, as was sometimes (though
rarely) recognized in the Middle Ages. Thus, Abraham Ibn (son of) Ezra, a 12th-century
CE exegete, noted that Gen. 12.6 states that "The Canaanites were *then* in the land." The
word "then" suggests that when the author of this passage wrote it, the Canaanites were
no longer in the land. In other words, the text must have been written after the time of
Moses, because during Moses' time the Canaanites were still in the land. A small number
of other places that suggest authorship later than Moses were pointed out by a few medieval scholars, but these were not systematized into a thesis which could challenge the
dominant view concerning Moses' authorship of the Torah.

Modern Source Theories

SLOWLY, WITH THE RISE OF RATIONALISM, particularly as associated with figures such as
Thomas Hobbes (1588–1679) and Benedict (Baruch) Spinoza (1632–1677), the view that the
Torah was a unified whole, written by Moses, began to be questioned. (For additional information on this development, see "Modern Jewish Interpretation," pp. 1908–19, and
"Modern Study of the Bible," pp. 2084–96.) This culminated in the development of the
model of the Documentary Hypothesis in the 19th century, according to which the Torah
(or Hexateuch) is comprised of four main sources or documents which were edited or
redacted together: J, E, P, and D. Each of these sources or documents is embedded in a (relatively) complete form in the current Torah, and is typified by vocabulary, literary style,
and theological perspective.

J and E are so called after the names for God that each of them uses in Genesis: J uses
the name "Yahveh" (German "Jahwe," hence "J"), translated in NJPS as "Lord," though it
is really a personal name whose exact meaning is unknown; E prefers to call the deity
"Elohim" (translated "God"), an epithet which also serves as the generic term for God or
gods in the Bible. P, which also uses "Elohim," is an abbreviation for the Priestly material
and D refers to the Deuteronomist, primarily in Deuteronomy.

The difference in divine names, however, is not the main criterion used by scholars
suggesting that the Torah is not a unified composition. Much more significant are do

and contradictions, in both narrative and legal material. For example, it has long been noted that Gen. chs 1–3 twice narrate the creation of the world. People are created first in 1.27—"And God created man in His image, in the image of God He created him; male and female He created them"—and then again in 2.7—"The LORD God formed man from the dust of the earth. He blew into his nostrils the breath of life, and man became a living being." Furthermore, the second creation account does not simply mirror or repeat the first, but differs from the first in both outline and detail. Gen. 1.1–2.3, the first account, narrates the creation of a highly symmetrical world by a very powerful deity who creates through the word. In this story, for example, man and woman are created together (1.27) after the creation of the land animals (1.25). In contrast, the second story, in 2.4–3.24, suggests that man was created (2.7), then the animals (2.19), and then woman (2.21–22). Its focus is on the creation of humanity, not of the entire physical world, and God anthropomorphically "forms" various beings, rather than creating them through the spoken word. Thus, these are two separate stories, written by two authors, representing different worldviews about the nature of creation, humanity, and God.

The two creation stories appear as two totally separate blocks of material in 1.1–2.3 and 2.4–3.24. In several cases, however, the sources do not appear in distinct, long blocks but are intertwined. This is the case in the flood story, a combination of J and P. According to P, two of each type of animal shall come into the ark (Gen. 6.19–20), but J says that of the clean animals, seven pairs shall come in, and of the unclean, one pair (Gen. 7.2). Similarly, the story of the plague of blood (Exod. 7.14–24) contains two accounts which are intertwined; in one (J), Moses is the protagonist, and the blood only affects the Nile (e.g., vv. 17–18), while in the other (P), Aaron appears as well, and the flood affects all Egyptian water sources (e.g., vv. 19, 24). In such cases, the narratives are combined with great skill, though careful attention to plot and vocabulary help to discern the original building blocks or sources of the story in its final form.

In addition to narrative, the legal material in the Torah is also the product of several sources. For example, slave laws concerning the Hebrew or Israelite slave are found in the Torah in Exod. 21.1–6, Lev. 25.39–46, and Deut. 15.12–18. These laws cannot be reconciled in a straightforward fashion since they represent three different notions of slavery. Most significant is the way in which Exodus differentiates between the treatment of a male and female slave, whereas Deuteronomy insists that they should both be treated similarly. While Exodus and Deuteronomy agree that a slave who loves his master may opt to remain a slave "for life" (Exod. 21.6) or "in perpetuity" (Deut. 15.17), Lev. ch 25 insists that slavery of Israelites does not really exist, since slaves must be treated "as a hired or bound laborer," and they may only serve "until the jubilee year" (v. 40). Such legal differences are surprising once we are open to the hypotheses that the Bible is composite, and the different legal collections reflect norms or ideals of different groups living in different time periods. Traditional Jewish interpretation, on the other hand, reconciles these various traditions through a process of harmonization, by assuming, for example, that "for life" or "in perpetuity" should in these cases be interpreted as "until the jubilee year."

It is possible to trace distinctive styles and theological notions that typify individual Torah sources. For example, the J source is well known for its highly anthropomorphic God, who has a close relationship with humans, as seen in Gen. 2.4–3.24, which includes, for example, a description of God "moving about [or walking] in the garden" (3.8) and says that God "made garments of skins for Adam and his wife, and clothed them" (3.21). On the other hand, in E, the Elohist source, God is more distant from people, typically communicating with them by dreams or via intermediaries, such as heavenly messengers (NJPS "angels") and prophets. The P or Priestly source is characterized by a strong interest in order and boundaries (see Gen. ch 1), as well as an overriding concern with the priestly family of Aaron and the Temple-based religious system. D, or Deuteronomy, is character-ized by a unique hortatory or preaching style, and insists strongly that God cannot be seen, as in this source's description of revelation: "The LORD spoke to you out of the fire; you heard the sound of words but perceived no shape—nothing but a voice" (Deut. 4.12). This explains why this source, uniquely, insists that God does not physically dwell in the Temple or Tabernacle; rather, the Temple is "the site where the LORD your God will choose to establish His name" (Deut. 12.11 and elsewhere). D also emphasizes that this one God must be worshipped in one place only (see esp. Deut. ch 12); this place is understood to be Jerusalem.

The narrative sources J, E, P, and D also have legal collections associated with them. The Covenant Collection (see Exod. 24.7) in Exod. 20.19–23.33 is associated with J or E. The Holiness Collection of Lev. chs 17–26 is so named because of its central injunction (Lev. 19.2), "You shall be holy, for I the LORD your God am holy." Though not composed by the Priestly author (P), it represents Priestly theology. The Deuteronomic law collection appears in Deut. chs 12–26. These blocks of material were called "codes" by earlier schol-ars; since the blocks are neither complete nor organized for the law court, however, as a "code" might be, the term "collection" is more suitable.

Critical biblical scholarship, through the latter part of the 20th century, was quite confi-dent in dating each of these Torah sources along with the legal collections that they incor-porated. Thus, J was seen as the earliest collection, often dated to the period of David and Solomon in the 10th century BCE, followed by E, which was often associated with the Northern Kingdom. D was connected to the reform of King Josiah in the late 7th century, and P was seen as deriving from the 6th century. The arguments for these specific dates were in some cases tinged with anti-Semitism, because they tended to devalue rabbinic Judaism, seeing it as a degeneration of the more ideal, early Hebrew religion. There was also an element of Christian supersessionism among some source critics: Biblical Israel is held in high esteem; early Judaism (in the late biblical and postbiblical periods) is not, for it was to be superseded by Christianity. For this reason, many Jewish scholars have until recently shied away from source-critical models.

Scholars now agree that the reasons usually given for assigning these dates to the indi-vidual sources are problematic, and a lively debate has developed concerning such funda-mental issues as the relative order of these sources and the extent to which any of them are as early as previous scholars had suggested. The existence of E as a complete source has been questioned as well, especially since E first appears well after the beginning of the Torah and is very difficult to disentangle from J after the beginning of Exodus. Thus, many scholars now talk of JE together as an early narrative source, incorporating diverse traditions. Additionally, most scholars no longer see each source as representative of a single author writing at one particular time but recognize that each may reflect a long historical period within a single group or "school." Thus, it is best to speak of streams or strands of tradition and to contrast their basic underpinnings, rather than to speak of sources reflecting a single author, period, and locale. For example, despite the unraveling of a consensus on the exact date of the sources, it is still valid to contrast the Deuteronomic view of Israel's fundamental, intrinsic holiness—as seen, for example, in Deut. 7.6, "For you are a people consecrated [holy] to the Lord your God"—with the Priestly view, articulated most clearly in the Holiness Collection (H), which suggests that Israel must aspire to holiness—as in Lev. 19.2, "You shall be holy." These fundamental differences cannot easily be reconciled, suggesting that despite certain problems with the classical source-critical method, certain elements of source criticism remain useful alongside other methods of analyzing biblical texts.

Compilation and Redaction of the Torah

WE DO NOT KNOW HOW THESE VARIOUS SOURCES and legal collections, which now comprise the Torah, came together to form a single book. Scholars have posited an editor or series of editors or redactors, conveniently called R, who combined the various sources, perhaps in several stages, over a long time. Certainly not all ancient Israelite traditions were preserved in the Torah. Much was probably lost. Without knowing what was lost, we cannot suggest how and why the redactor(s), R, made their selection and by what principles they ordered their materials. It must suffice to note that in contrast to modern editing, which works toward articulating a single viewpoint, the redaction of the Torah, like the editing of other ancient works, did not create a purely consistent, singular perspective but incorporated a variety of voices and perspectives.

The ultimate result of this redaction, most likely completed during the Babylonian exile (586–538 BCE) or soon thereafter in the early Persian period, was the creation of a very long book, narrating what must have been felt to be the formative period of Israel, from the period of the creation of the world through the death of Moses. The events narrated in Gen. chs 1–11 describing the creation of the world and its population by many nations serve as an introduction to the singling out of one nation, Israel. The stories of Abraham, Isaac, and Jacob, the ancestors of Israel, form the national prehistory. Israel comes into existence as a nation in Exodus, and the foremost events of its national history are the exodus from Egypt, the revelation at Sinai, and the coming to the promised land. These events are central to Exodus-Deuteronomy.

The ancient Near Eastern world produced no other work of comparable length in the span of time its narrative covers or in the inclusiveness of the literary genres and sources

incorporated into it. This extensive and inclusive nature of the Torah creates a fundamental and interesting problem for biblical interpreters. Should we concentrate on interpreting
the individual sources, on hearing the voices of the component parts of the text before
they were redacted together? Or should we follow the traditional way in which the Bible
was read for many centuries before the rise of modern source criticism, and focus on the
final product, an approach that has been called holistic reading? In the annotations of the
biblical books that follow we will aim for a balance, maintaining our critical stance toward
the sources but never forgetting that it is their combination into a whole that has preserved them and given them meaning. We will show how meaning may be uncovered by
looking both at the early building blocks of the text, and at the text in its final, redacted
form.   [MARC ZVI BRETTLER]

בראשית

Genesis

THE BOOK OF GENESIS RECEIVED its English name from the Greek translation of the Heb word *toledot*, which is used thirteen times in Genesis and is translated as "story" (2.4), "record" (5.1), or "line" (10.1). In Heb, it is known, like many books in the Tanakh, by its first word, *bereishit*, which means, "In the beginning." Genesis is indeed a book about beginnings—the beginning of the natural world, the beginning of human culture, and the beginning of the people Israel, whose story occupies most of this book and will dominate the rest of the Torah. In the ancient Near Eastern world in which Israel emerged, beginnings were deemed to be crucial, for the origins of things were thought to disclose their character and purpose. In Genesis, the origins of Israel—the people known later as the "Jews"—lie in a mysterious promise of God to a Mesopotamian whose name is Abram (changed in ch 17 to "Abraham"). The essence of the promise is that He will make of him a great nation, bless him abundantly, and grant him the land of Canaan. Ostensibly absurd when it first comes, the promise faces one obstacle after another throughout the course of Genesis—principally, the barrenness of Abraham's primary wife (and of other matriarchs in the next two generations) and the murderous fraternal rivalry among his descendants. And yet, by the end of Genesis, all the obstacles notwithstanding, the twelve tribes that make up the people Israel have indeed come into existence, an Israelite effectively rules a superpower (Egypt), and the promise of the land, though far from fulfillment (which comes about only in the book of Joshua), is anything but forgotten.

The book of Genesis is thus, in more senses than one, a primary source for Jewish theology. It presents its ideas on the relationship of God to nature, to the human race in general, and to the people Israel in particular in ways that are, however, foreign to the expectations of most modern readers. It is therefore all too easy to miss the seriousness and profundity of its messages. For the vehicle through which Genesis conveys its worldview is neither the theological tract nor the rigorous philosophical proof nor the confession of faith. That vehicle is, rather, narrative. The theology must be inferred from stories, and the lived relationship with God takes precedence over abstract theology. Those who think of stories (including mythology) as fit only for children not only misunderstand the thought-world and the literary conventions of the ancient Near East; they also condemn themselves to miss the complexity and sophistication of the stories of Genesis. For these are narratives that have evoked interpretation upon interpretation from biblical times into our own day and have occupied the attention of some of the keenest thinkers in human history.

One aspect of narrative in Genesis that requires special attention is its high tolerance for different versions of the same event, a well-known feature of ancient Near Eastern literature, from earliest times through rabbinic midrash. The book presents, for example, two accounts of Abram/Abraham's attempting to pass his wife off as his sister (12.10–20; 20.1–18; cf. 26.1–11), two accounts of God's making a covenant with him (ch 15 and 17), and two accounts of how Jacob's name was changed to Israel (32.23–33; 35.9–15). In these instances, most modern biblical scholars see different antecedent documents that editors (known as redactors) have combined to give us the text now in our hands. This could not have happened, however, if the existence of variation were seen as a serious defect or if rigid consistency were deemed essential to effective storytelling. Rather, the redactors have chosen a different approach, refusing to discard many variants as inauthentic or inaccurate, instead treating the different versions as sequential events in the same longer story. The result is a certain measure of repetition, to be sure, but the repetition is in the service of a sophisticated presentation of themes with variations in a book rich in narrative analogy, revealing echo, and suggestive contrast. For the Rabbis of Talmudic times and their successors through the centuries, the exploration of those subtle literary features provided an indispensable insight not only into the first book of the Torah (the most sacred part of the Tanakh) but also into the mind of God Himself.

The book is composed of four major sections: 1.1–11.26, the primeval story; 11.27–25.18, the story of Abraham; 25.19–36.43, the Jacob cycle; and 37.1–50.26, the story of Joseph. (There is little independent narrative about Isaac, the second patriarch.)

The first section, the primeval history, takes us from the creation of the world through the birth of Abram's father nineteen generations later. Its stories are short, loosely strung together, and connected only by genealogies that identify the generation in which the action takes place. There is, however, an overriding theme: the spread of human wickedness, the refusal of humankind to accept their creaturely status, as they seek to blur the all-important boundary between the human and the divine and, as a result, bring catastrophe upon themselves. The center of attention is God, who is portrayed rather anthropomorphically and speaks directly and frequently to human beings, condemning or sparing, announcing His judgment or His merciful forbearance.

Largely because of its focus on creation, the primeval history exhibits a number of contacts with Mesopotamian mythology. The account of creation with which Genesis opens (1.1–2.3), for example, has affinities with *Enuma elish,* a Babylonian epic, which tells how one god, Marduk, attained supremacy over the others and created the world by splitting his aquatic enemy in half. The story of Adam and Eve's sin in the garden of Eden (2.25–3.24) displays similarities with *Gilgamesh,* an epic poem that tells how its hero lost the opportunity for immortality and came to terms with his humanity. And the story of Noah (6.5–9.17) has close connections with *Atrahasis,* a Mesopotamian story in which the gods send a flood to wipe out the human race, with the exception of one man from whom humankind begins afresh (the story was eventually incorporated into *Gilgamesh* as well). In each case, the biblical narrator has adapted the Mesopotamian forerunner to Israelite theology. The primeval history thus evidences both the deep continuities and the striking points of discontinuity of biblical Israel with its Mesopotamian antecedents and contemporaries.

In the story of Abraham (11.27–25.11), the narrative has become more continuous. Abraham dominates almost every episode. Seeing him in a wide variety of situations, we have a sense of his personality and of the human dimension of the events that God has mysteriously set into motion. Whereas God's relationship to human beings in the primeval history is marked mostly (but not exclusively) by judgment, expulsion, and exile, in the story of Abraham the dominant notes are the contrasting ones of blessing and promise, especially the promise of the land. But the narrative does not spare us the knowledge that while the blessings and promises are as yet unrealized, Abraham's family have their moments of anguish and even ugliness. God, portrayed for the most part less anthropomorphically than in the primeval history, overcomes the obstacles to His promises and blessings, so that Abraham finally acquires both the son from whom the promised nation shall descend and a foothold in the promised land. The LORD accomplishes this partly through palpable miracles and partly through His silent guidance of the course of human events. As the story of Abraham unfolds, its human protagonist, despite some arguably serious lapses, gradually assumes the role of the ideal religious person—obedient to God's commands (even at the cost of the most painful sacrifice), faithful even when the promise seems impossible, gracious, generous, and hospitable, yet committed to justice and compassion even to the point of firmly (if deferentially) questioning God's counsel.

The stories in the Jacob cycle (25.19–36.43) are even more connected and less self-contained than those in the story of Abraham. Here, we are entitled to speak not simply of a general theme, like the theme of blessing and promise in the Abraham story (which continues in this section), but of a plot as well. In its broadest outlines, the plot has to do with how the second son acquires his older brother's superior status and the attendant rights to the Abrahamic promise, yet eventually reconciles with the brother he has wronged and emerges legitimately as the patriarch from whom the people Israel takes its name. Various types of trickery play a major role as this plot develops. The human dimension is more central here than in the Abraham narrative, and the resourcefulness of the protagonists, especially Jacob himself and his mother Rebekah, proportionately more important. Accordingly, God speaks less frequently and intervenes less dramatically. Indeed, His presence is less available and assumes an eerie cast ("Surely the LORD is present in this place, and I did not know it!" [28.16]).

The closing section of the book of Genesis, the story of Joseph (37.1–50.26), represents a narrative so coherent and so continuous that it has justly been termed a novella. Indeed, it offers the deepest psychological portraits and the most subtle and complex plot in Genesis and constitutes one of the gems of biblical prose narrative. Whereas in the first section of Genesis, the primeval history, God booms forth His pronouncements, in this last section

He does not speak at all, with the exception of one apparition to Jacob while he is still in Canaan (46.1–4). Rather, He communicates through dreams (in which, significantly, He does not appear) and, more importantly, through people, especially Joseph's God-given wisdom to interpret dreams and to administer effectively. Here, even more than in the Jacob cycle, God works through the ambivalent and devious designs of flawed human beings, providentially bringing good out of human evil and arranging "the survival of many people" (50.20)—including the brothers who, seething with resentment, once plotted Joseph's death and enslavement but now graciously accept subordination to the younger brother who has saved their lives.

How much history lies behind the story of Genesis? Because the action of the primeval story is not represented as taking place on the plane of ordinary human history and has so many affinities with ancient mythology, it is very far-fetched to speak of its narratives as historical at all. In the cases of the succeeding three large sections of the book, the matter is more complicated, for scholars continue to sift the evidence and to debate the question. Although enormous amounts of data about ancient Mesopotamia, Canaan, and Egypt have been uncovered over the last two centuries, no evidence has turned up that establishes that Abraham, (his son) Isaac, Jacob, or Joseph existed. At best, we can speak of accurate local color, although this may mean only that the Israelites knew something about the lands in which they placed their legendary forebears (see "Historical and Geographical Background to the Bible," pp. 2048–62). Negative evidence, however, is not necessarily evidence of a negative, and historians are likely to continue examining the reports of Israel's Mesopotamian origins and Egyptian sojourn for the foreseeable future.

The authorship of Genesis is a similarly controversial issue, although here the consensus among critical scholars is somewhat more secure (see "Modern Study of the Bible," pp. 2084–96). The book itself names no one as its author, and makes no claim to be divinely revealed or inspired (though it does contain many reports of divine speech). When other biblical books refer to a Torah of Moses, they cite legal texts, and there is no reason to think that Genesis formed part of the corpus so designated. Indeed, there are several indications that the Genesis narrative assumes a post-Mosaic narrator without embarrassment (see the comments on 12.6, 14.14, and 36.31). In Second Temple and rabbinic Judaism, however, Genesis is treated as part of the Torah of Moses. Despite a number of demurrals on a few particular passages by major rabbis in the Middle Ages, this became the consensus of the tradition. Historical-critical scholarship, however, has identified three main sources, which it denotes with the symbols J, E, and P, that have been woven together to produce Genesis (see "Torah," pp. 1–7). The relationship of compositional history to religious faith is not a simple one. If Moses is the human author of Genesis, nothing ensures that God is its ultimate Author. If J, E, P, and various equally anonymous redactors are its human authors, nothing ensures that God is not its ultimate Author.

[JON D. LEVENSON]

BERE'SHIT   בראשית

1 When God began to create[a] heaven and earth—[2] the earth being unformed and void, with darkness over the surface of the deep and a wind from[b] God sweeping over the water—[3] God said, "Let there be light"; and there was light. [4] God saw that the light was good, and God separated the light from the darkness. [5] God called the light Day, and the darkness He called Night. And there was evening and there was morning, a first day.[c]

[6] God said, "Let there be an expanse in the midst of the water, that it may separate water from water." [7] God made the expanse, and it separated the water which was below the expanse from the water which was above the expanse. And it was so. [8] God called the expanse Sky. And there was evening and there was morning, a second day.

[9] God said, "Let the water below the sky be gathered into one area, that the dry land may appear." And it was

a Others "In the beginning God created."
b Others "the spirit of."   c Others "one day."

1.1–2.3: Creation in seven days. The book of Genesis—and thus the Bible itself—opens with an account of creation that is extraordinary for its austerity. Other ancient Near Eastern evocations of God's (or the gods') world-ordering activity, including many in the Bible itself (e.g., Ps. 104), provide high drama and graphic description of the events and their protagonists (even the LORD). Gen. 1.1–2.3, however, is utterly devoid of sensory detail. This eerie abstractness, combined with the highly schematic and formulaic structure of the narrative, conveys a sense of the awe-inspiring majesty and inviolable sovereignty of the God on whom the narrative is unswervingly focused. This narrative is structured by a pattern of seven days, six in which God accomplishes all His creative labors, and one in which He rests in regal repose, blessing and hallowing that climactic day. The correlations between things created on the various days exhibit a high degree of symmetry (diagram, below). The first three days describe the creation of generalities or domains; the next three chronicle the creation of the specifics or the inhabitants of the domains in the same order. Creation comes to its culmination, however, only in the one day that has no counterpart, the Sabbath ("Shabbát" in modern Heb, or "Shábbes" in the Eastern European pronunciation), here observed by God above and not yet enjoined upon His people Israel (who first hear of it in Exodus 16). The organization of time into seven-day units has become so familiar and so widespread that it is easy to forget that unlike the month (which in the Bible is lunar) and the year (which in the Bible never moves too far from its solar base), the biblical week corresponds to no astronomical event. The notion that seven signifies completeness and that things come to their fit conclusion on the seventh day did, however, have wide resonance in the ancient Near Eastern world in which Israel emerged, and that idea doubtless stands in the background of our passage. The role of the number seven in 1.1–2.3 extends, in fact, beyond the obvious division of the acts of creation into a seven-day sequence. For example, the expression, *And God saw that* [something He made] *was good* or *very good* occurs seven times, but not on every day of the primordial week. Missing on the second and seventh, it appears twice on the adjacent third and sixth days (1.10, 12, 25, 31). Similarly, the word "God" occurs exactly thirty-five times (i.e., five times seven) in our passage, and the section devoted to the seventh day (2.1–3) has exactly thirty-five words in the Heb. The organization of the process of creation into a sequence of seven days is familiar to most readers not only from the opening of the Tanakh but also from the Sabbath commandment of the Decalogue in Exod. 20.8–11. But we must not forget that this connection is far from universal in the Tanakh. In fact, most biblical descriptions of creation know nothing of a seven-day sequence

SABBATH	
DAY 7 (2.1–3)	
LAND AND PLANTS	LAND ANIMALS AND HUMANS
DAY 3 (1.9–13)	DAY 6 (1.24–31)
SKY (*separating waters above from waters below*)	FISH/BIRDS
DAY 2 (1.6–8)	DAY 5 (1.20–23)
LIGHT	LIGHTS (*i.e., sun, moon, and stars*)
DAY 1 (1.1–5)	DAY 4 (1.14–19)

so. [10] God called the dry land Earth, and the gathering of waters He called Seas. And God saw that this was good. [11] And God said, "Let the earth sprout vegetation: seed-bearing plants, fruit trees of every kind on earth that bear fruit with the seed in it." And it was so. [12] The earth brought forth vegetation: seed-bearing plants of every kind, and trees of every kind bearing fruit with the seed in it. And God saw that this was good. [13] And there was evening and there was morning, a third day.

[14] God said, "Let there be lights in the expanse of the sky to separate day from night; they shall serve as signs for the set times—the days and the years; [15] and they serve as lights in the expanse of the sky to shine upon the earth." And it was so. [16] God made the two great lights, the greater light to dominate the day and the lesser light to dominate the night, and the stars. [17] And God set them in the expanse of the sky to shine upon the earth, [18] to dominate the day and the night, and to separate light from darkness. And God saw that this was good. [19] And there was evening and there was morning, a fourth day.

[20] God said, "Let the waters bring forth swarms of living creatures, and birds that fly above the earth across the expanse of the sky." [21] God created the great sea monsters, and all the living creatures of every kind that creep, which

(e.g., Ps. 104; Prov. 8.22–31), and most texts about the Sabbath (including the version of the Decalogue in Deut. 5.12–15) make no reference to creation. The suspicion arises that 1.1–2.3 derives from a distinct school of thought, one that dates to a relatively late period in the history of Israelite religion. On the basis of these considerations, and a multitude of others, critical scholars attribute the passage to the P (for "Priestly") source. And God does function here in ways reminiscent of a "kohen" (priest), giving blessings, for example (1.22, 28; 2.3; cf. Lev. 9.22–23; Num. 6.22–27), and consecrating the Sabbath (2.3; cf. Ezek. 44.24). The concern shown in this story for order and clear boundaries typifies the Priestly corpus. More importantly, the creation of the world in 1.1–2.3 bears several striking resemblances to the construction of the Tabernacle mandated in Exod. chs 25–31 and executed in Exod. chs 35–40 (e.g.,

see Gen. 2.1–3; Exod. 39.32, 42–43)—the prototype of the Jerusalem Temple and the focus of the priestly service of the LORD. Note that other ancient Near Eastern creation stories conclude with the construction of a temple for the creation god. In the Tanakh, the world is sometimes seen as the LORD's temple, and the Temple as a microcosm (e.g., Isa. 66.1–2). **1:** A tradition over two millennia old sees 1.1 as a complete sentence: "In the beginning God created the heavens and the earth." In the 11th century, the great Jewish commentator Rashi made a case that the verse functions as a temporal clause. This is, in fact, how some ancient Near Eastern creation stories begin—including the one that starts at 2.4b. Hence the translation, *When God began to create heaven and earth.* **2:** This clause describes things just before the process of creation began. To modern people, the opposite of the created order is "nothing," that is, a

vacuum. To the ancients, the opposite of the created order was something much worse than "nothing." It was an active, malevolent force we can best term "chaos." In this verse, chaos is envisioned as a dark, undifferentiated mass of water. In 1.9, God creates the dry land (and the Seas, which can exist only when water is bounded by dry land). But in 1.1–2.3, water itself and darkness, too, are primordial (contrast Isa. 45.7). In the midrash, Bar Kappara upholds the troubling notion that the Torah shows that God created the world out of preexistent material. But other rabbis worry that acknowledging this would cause people to liken God to a king who had built his palace on a garbage dump, thus arrogantly impugning His majesty (*Gen. Rab.* 1.5). In the ancient Near East, however, to say that a deity had subdued chaos is to give him the highest praise. **3–5:** Since the sun is not created until the fourth day (1.14–19), the light of the first three days is of a different order from what we know. A midrash teaches that when God saw the corruption of the generations of the flood and of the tower of Babel, He hid that primordial light away for the benefit of the righteous in the world-to-come (*b. Ḥag.* 12a). Other ancient Near Eastern myths similarly assume the existence of light before the creation of the luminaries. **6–8:** The word translated *expanse* refers to a piece of metal that has been hammered flat. Here, the function of the sky is to separate the waters above (which fall as rain) from the subterranean waters (which rise as springs; see 7.11). **16:** The sun and moon are created only on the fourth day and are not named, but referred to only as *the greater light* and *the lesser light.* This may be an implicit polemic against the worship of astral bodies (see 2 Kings 23.5). **21:** A similar point can be made about the creation of *the great sea monsters* on the fifth day. In some ancient myths—and biblical texts as well (see Ps. 74.12–17; Job 26.5–14)—creation results from the slaying of a sea the waters brought forth in swarms, and all the winged birds of every kind. And God saw that this was good. ²² God blessed them, saying, "Be fertile and increase, fill the waters in the seas, and let the birds increase on the earth." ²³ And there was evening and there was morning, a fifth day.

²⁴ God said, "Let the earth bring forth every kind of living creature: cattle, creeping things, and wild beasts of every kind." And it was so. ²⁵ God made wild beasts of every kind and cattle of every kind, and all kinds of creeping things of the earth. And God saw that this was good. ²⁶ And God said, "Let us make man in our image, after our likeness. They shall rule the fish of the sea, the birds of the sky, the cattle, the whole earth, and all the creeping things that creep on earth." ²⁷ And God created man in His image, in the image of God He created him; male and female He created them. ²⁸ God blessed them and God said to them, "Be fertile and increase, fill the earth and master it; and rule the fish of the sea, the birds of the sky, and all the living things that creep on earth."

²⁹ God said, "See, I give you every seed-bearing plant that is upon all the earth, and every tree that has seed-bearing fruit; they shall be yours for food. ³⁰ And to all the animals on land, to all the birds of the sky, and to everything that creeps on earth, in which there is the breath of life, [I give] all the green plants for food." And it was so. ³¹ And God saw all that He had made, and found it very good. And there was evening and there was morning, the sixth day.

2 The heaven and the earth were finished, and all their array. ² On the seventh day God finished the work that He had been doing, and He ceased^a on the seventh day from all the work that He had done. ³ And God blessed the seventh day and declared it holy, because on it God ceased from all the work of creation that He had done.

a Or "rested."

monster. Isa. 27.1 uses the same word to describe the frightening sea monster that the LORD will kill at the end of time. **26–28:** The plural construction *(Let us . . .)* most likely reflects a setting in the divine council (cf. 1 Kings 22.19–22; Isa. ch 6; Job chs 1–2): God the King announces the proposed course of action to His cabinet of subordinate deities, though He alone retains the power of deci-

sion. The midrash manifests considerable uneasiness with God's proposal to create something so capable of evil as human beings are. Playing on Ps. 1.6, one midrash reports that God told his ministering angels only of "the way of the righteous" and hid from them "the way of the wicked" (*Gen. Rab.* 8.4). Another one reports that while the angels were debating the proposal among

themselves, God took the matter in hand. "Why are you debating?" he asked them. "Man has already been created!" (*Gen. Rab.* 8.5). Whereas the earth and the waters (at God's command) bring forth the plants, fish, birds, and other animals (1.12, 20, 24), humankind has a different origin and a different character. In the ancient Near East, the king was often said to be the "image" of the god and thus to act with divine authority. So here, the creation of humanity in God's *image* and *likeness* carries with it a commission to rule over the animal kingdom (1.26b, 28b; cf. Ps. 8.4–9). Some have seen in that commission a license for ecological irresponsibility. The fact is, however, that the Tanakh presents humanity not as the owner of nature but as its steward, strictly accountable to its true Owner (see Lev. 25.23–24). This theology is one source of the important institutions of the sabbatical and jubilee years (see Exod. 23.10–11; Lev. ch 25). Whereas the next account of human origins (Gen. 2.4b–24) speaks of God's creation of one male from whom one female subsequently emerges, Gen. ch 1 seems to speak of groups of men and women created simultaneously. The division of humankind into two sexes is closely associated with the divine mandate to *Be fertile and increase*. In Jewish law, this is a positive commandment, although it is obligatory only on Jewish men, not women (*b. Yebam.* 65b). **29–30:** Humankind, animals, and birds all seem originally meant to be neither vegetarians nor carnivores, but frugivores, eating the seeds of plants and trees. **2.1–3:** In the Jewish liturgy, this passage serves as an introduction to the kiddush, the prayer over wine to sanctify the Sabbath that is recited just before the first meal of the holy day, on Friday night (see Exod. 20.8–11). It also appears in the traditional Friday evening service. The passage is characterized by the type of repetition that suggests it might have served as a liturgy already in antiquity.

⁴Such is the story of heaven and earth when they were created.

When the LORD God made earth and heaven—⁵when no shrub of the field was yet on earth and no grasses of the field had yet sprouted, because the LORD God had not sent rain upon the earth and there was no man to till the soil, ⁶but a flow would well up from the ground and water the whole surface of the earth—⁷the LORD God formed man*ᵃ* from the dust of the earth.*ᵇ* He blew into his nostrils the breath of life, and man became a living being.

⁸The LORD God planted a garden in Eden, in the east, and placed there the man whom He had formed. ⁹And from the ground the LORD God caused to grow every tree that was pleasing to the sight and good for food, with the tree of life in the middle of the garden, and the tree of knowledge of good and bad.

¹⁰A river issues from Eden to water the garden, and it then divides and becomes four branches. ¹¹The name of the first is Pishon, the one that winds through the whole land of Havilah, where the gold is. (¹²The gold of that land is good; bdellium is there, and lapis lazuli.*ᶜ*) ¹³The name of the second river is Gihon, the one that winds through the whole land of Cush. ¹⁴The name of the third river is Tigris, the one that flows east of Asshur. And the fourth river is the Euphrates.

a Heb. ʾadam.
b Heb. ʾadamah.
c Others "onyx"; meaning of Heb. shoham uncertain.

2.4–25: The creation of Adam and Eve. Whereas 1.1–2.3 presented a majestic God-centered scenario of creation, 2.4–25 presents a very different but equally profound story of origins. This second account of creation is centered more on human beings and familiar human experiences, and even its deity is conceived in more anthropomorphic terms. Source critics attribute the two accounts to different documents (P and J, respectively) later combined into the Torah we now have. The classical Jewish tradition tends to harmonize the discrepancies by intertwining the stories, using the details of one to fill in the details of the other. Even on the source-critical reading, however, the contrast and interaction of the two creation accounts offer a richer understanding of the relationship of God to humankind than we would have if the accounts were read in isolation from each other. **4:** The Jewish textual tradition places a major break between 2.3 and 2.4, rather than in the middle of v. 4, where many modern interpreters put it, and for good reason. If the latter verse, or even its first half (2.4a), is read with 1.1–2.3, then several of the multiples of seven in 1.1–2.3, of which we gave a sample above (see intro. to 1.1–2.3), disappear. Most likely, 2.4a is an editorial linkage between the two accounts of creation. **5–6:** For the first time, we see the Tetragrammaton (YHVH) or the four-letter proper name of the God of Israel, the pronunciation of which rabbinic law forbids categorically. The name is conventionally rendered in English as "LORD" and in Heb as "Adonai" (in prayer and in liturgical reading of Scripture) or "ha-Shem" (in other contexts). The use of this name is one of several features that cause source critics to attribute this second creation account to the J source. Note that the expression "heaven and earth" (1.1; 2.4a) now appears in the reverse order ("earth and heaven"), as befits the more earth-centered character of this story. Whereas in the first account of creation the primordial problem was too much water, requiring God to split the waters and create dry land (1.6–7, 9–10), here the problem is too little water. The variation may reflect the difference between the situation in Babylonia, in which the saline waters of the sea threatened human life, and a setting in the land of Israel, where a deficiency of water was (and is) a constant threat. **7:** Here, man has a lowlier origin than in the parallel in 1.26–28. He is created not in the image of God but from the dust of the earth. But he also has a closer and more intimate relationship with his Creator, who blows the breath of life into him, transforming that lowly, earth-bound creature into a living being. In this understanding, the human being is not an amalgam of perishable body and immortal soul, but a psychophysical unity who depends on God for life itself. **8–11:** The root of *Eden* denotes fertility. Where the wondrously fertile garden was thought to have been located (if a realistic location was ever conceived) is unclear. The Tigris and Euphrates are the two great rivers of Mesopotamia (now found in modern Iraq). But the Pishon is unidentified, and the only Gihon in the Bible is a spring in Jerusalem (1 Kings 1.33, 38). Adam is conceived as a farmer, and work—albeit in an exceedingly easy form, given the miraculous fertility of Eden—is part of the divine plan.

15 The LORD God took the man and placed him in the garden of Eden, to till it and tend it. 16 And the LORD God commanded the man, saying, "Of every tree of the garden you are free to eat; 17 but as for the tree of knowledge of good and bad, you must not eat of it; for as soon as you eat of it, you shall die."

18 The LORD God said, "It is not good for man to be alone; I will make a fitting helper for him." 19 And the LORD God formed out of the earth all the wild beasts and all the birds of the sky, and brought them to the man to see what he would call them; and whatever the man called each living creature, that would be its name. 20 And the man gave names to all the cattle and to the birds of the sky and to all the wild beasts; but for Adam no fitting helper was found. 21 So the LORD God cast a deep sleep upon the man; and, while he slept, He took one of his ribs and closed up the flesh at that spot. 22 And the LORD God fashioned the rib that He had taken from the man into a woman; and He brought her to the man. 23 Then the man said,

> "This one at last
> Is bone of my bones
> And flesh of my flesh.
> This one shall be called Woman,[a]
> For from man[b] was she taken."

24 Hence a man leaves his father and mother and clings to his wife, so that they become one flesh.

25 The two of them were naked,[c] the man and his wife, yet they felt no shame. 3 1 Now the serpent was the shrewdest of all the wild beasts that the LORD God had made. He said to the woman, "Did God really say: You shall not eat of any tree of the garden?" 2 The woman replied to the serpent, "We may eat of the fruit of the other trees of the garden. 3 It is only about fruit of the tree in the

---

a Heb. 'ishshah.
b Heb. 'ish.
c Heb. 'arummim, play on 'arum "shrewd" in 3.1.

16–17: *Knowledge of good and bad* may be a merism, a figure of speech in which polar opposites denote a totality (like *heaven and earth* in 1.1). But *knowledge* can have an experiential, not only an intellectual, sense in biblical Heb, and "good and bad" can mean either "weal and woe" or "moral good and moral evil." The forbid-

den tree offers an experience that is both pleasant and painful; it awakens those who partake of it to the higher knowledge and to the pain that both come with moral choice. **18–24:** Man's fulfillment requires companionship. As a talmudic rabbi observes about v. 18, "Even though a man has several sons, it is forbidden to him to be

without a wife" (*b. Yebam.* 61b). The LORD's creation of woman from man emphasizes the close connection between them and lays the groundwork for the understanding of marriage (and its association with procreation) in v. 24. The creation of the woman after the man and from a part of his body need not imply the subordination of women to men. According to Ramban (Naḥmanides, a great 13th-century Spanish rabbi), the point of v. 24 is that men are to be different from the males of the animal world, who mate and move on to the next partner: A man "wishes [his wife] to be with him always." Promiscuity is thus a degradation of God's intentions in creating human beings male and female. It is interesting that although polygamy is amply attested in the Tanakh, v. 24 indicates that the ideal, Edenic condition is monogamy (see also Mal. 2.14–16; Prov. 5.15–23).

2.25–3.24: Disobedience, knowledge, exile. 2.25–3.1a: That the primal couple were nude (Heb "'arummim") but not ashamed attests to their innocence but also to their ignorance. It contrasts with the shrewd ("'arum") nature of the snake who will tempt them into losing both. Unlike some later Jewish and Christian literature, Genesis does not identify the talking snake with Satan or any other demonic being. **3.1b–3:** His question is tricky and does not admit of a yes-or-no answer. The woman, who has never heard the commandment directly (2.16–17), paraphrases it closely. Why she adds the prohibition on touching the fruit is unclear. A talmudic rabbi sees here an illustration of the dictum that "he who adds [to God's words] subtracts [from them]" (*b. Sanh.* 29a). Another rabbinic source presents a more complicated explanation. In relaying the prohibition to his wife, Adam has obeyed the rabbinic principle that one should "make a [protective] hedge for the Torah" (*m. 'Avot* 1.1). Tragically, this praiseworthy act gave the snake his opening. He middle of the garden that God said: 'You shall not eat of it or touch it, lest you die.' " 4 And the serpent said to the woman, "You are not going to die, 5 but God knows that as soon as you eat of it your eyes will be opened and you will be like ᵃ divine beings who know ᵃ good and bad." 6 When the woman saw that the tree was good for eating and a delight to the eyes, and that the tree was desirable as a source of wisdom, she took of its fruit and ate. She also gave some to her husband, and he ate. 7 Then the eyes of both of them were opened and they perceived that they were naked; and they sewed together fig leaves and made themselves loincloths.

8 They heard the sound of the LORD God moving about in the garden at the breezy time of day; and the man and his wife hid from the LORD God among the trees of the garden. 9 The LORD God called out to the man and said to him, "Where are you?" 10 He replied, "I heard the sound of You in the garden, and I was afraid because I was naked, so I hid." 11 Then He asked, "Who told you that you were naked? Did you eat of the tree from which I had forbidden you to eat?" 12 The man said, "The woman You put at my side—she gave me of the tree, and I ate." 13 And the LORD God said to the woman, "What is this you have done!" The woman replied, "The serpent duped me, and I ate." 14 Then the LORD God said to the serpent,

"Because you did this,
More cursed shall you be
Than all cattle
And all the wild beasts:
On your belly shall you crawl
And dirt shall you eat
All the days of your life.
15   I will put enmity
Between you and the woman,
And between your offspring and hers;
They shall strike at your head,
And you shall strike at their heel."
16 And to the woman He said,
"I will make most severe
Your pangs in childbearing;
In pain shall you bear children.
Yet your urge shall be for your husband,
And he shall rule over you."
17 To Adam He said, "Because you did as your wife said and ate of the tree about which I commanded you, 'You shall not eat of it,'

a-a Others "God, who knows."

"touched the tree with his hands and his feet, and shook it until its fruits dropped to the ground," thus undermining the credibility of God's entire commandment in the woman's mind (ʾAvot. R. Nat. A,1). **4–5:** The serpent impugns God's motives, attributing the command to jealousy. Whereas in the first creation account human beings are God-like creatures exercising dominion (1.26–28), here their ambition to be like God or like divine beings is the root of their expulsion from Eden. **6:** The fatal progression in the woman's mind begins with the physical (*eating*), moves to the aesthetic (*a delight to the eyes*), and culminates in the intellectual (*a source of wisdom*). The progression may reflect the process of rationalization to which she succumbed just before she engaged in humanity's first act of disobedience. **7:** As the serpent had predicted (v. 5), their eyes are opened, and they have enhanced knowledge (v. 7). **8–17:** But with the new knowledge comes the shame of nudity that they had lacked in their childlike innocence (vv. 10–11; cf. 2.25), a symbol of a much more encompassing sense of guilt and an ominous estrangement between God and the primal couple. The man lamely attempts to pass the buck to his wife, and thus, also to the God who put her at his side (v. 12). She, with more credibility, blames the serpent (v. 13). **14–19:** The LORD God then reverses the order and punishes the malefactors in the order of their misdeeds. The serpent is to lose his legs, slither in the dirt, and suffer from the hostility of human beings (vv. 14–15). The woman will suffer pain in childbirth, experience sexual desire for her husband, yet be subordinate to him (v. 16). The man, for having obeyed her rather than God, will toil over unproductive soil all the days of his life, until the ground from which he was taken reabsorbs him (vv. 17–19; cf. 2.7). The primal couple have left the magical garden of their childhood and their innocence and entered into the harsh world of adulthood and

Cursed be the ground because of you;
By toil shall you eat of it
All the days of your life:

18 Thorns and thistles shall it sprout for you.
But your food shall be the grasses of the field;

19 By the sweat of your brow
Shall you get bread to eat,
Until you return to the ground—
For from it you were taken.
For dust you are,
And to dust you shall return."

20 The man named his wife Eve,ᵃ because she was the mother of all the living.ᵇ 21 And the LORD God made garments of skins for Adam and his wife, and clothed them.

22 And the LORD God said, "Now that the man has become like one of us, knowing good and bad, what if he should stretch out his hand and take also from the tree of life and eat, and live forever!" 23 So the LORD God banished him from the garden of Eden, to till the soil from which he was taken. 24 He drove the man out, and stationed east of the garden of Eden the cherubim and the fiery ever-turning sword, to guard the way to the tree of life.

4 Now the man knewᶜ his wife Eve, and she conceived and bore Cain, saying, "I have gainedᵈ a male child with the help of the LORD." 2 She then bore his brother Abel. Abel became a keeper of sheep, and Cain became a tiller of the soil. 3 In the course of time, Cain brought an offering to the LORD from the fruit of the soil; 4 and Abel, for his part, brought the choicest of the firstlings of his flock. The LORD paid heed to Abel and his offering, 5 but to Cain

a Heb. hawwah.   b Heb. hay.
c Heb. yadaʻ, often in a sexual sense.   d Heb. qanithi, connected with "Cain."

mortal and banishes him from the garden in which the tree of life was found. The cherubim are supernatural beings who sometimes act as protectors of sacred items or places (e.g., Exod. 25.17–22; 1 Kings 8.6–7). The stance of jealousy about His status and anxiety about human beings' acquiring immortality is not the only one taken by the God of Israel. Prov. 3.18 asserts that the tree of life, in the form of Wisdom (therein personified as a woman), remains available to "those who grasp her." The Rabbis identified wisdom with Torah and could therefore cite Prov. 3.18 in support of their characteristic affirmation that Torah "gives life to those who practice it, in this world and in the world-to-come" (m. 'Avot 6.7). In Judaism, the estrangement caused by the innate human appetite for evil does not require an act of messianic redemption to be healed. Rather, the practice and study of Torah renew intimacy with the God of Israel and lead to eternal life. "The Holy One (blessed be He) created the Evil Inclination; He created Torah as its antidote" (b. B. Bat. 16a).

4.1–16: The first murder. This story of the LORD's preference for the younger brother and the older brother's resentment and exile looks both back to the episode in the garden of Eden and forward to other stories of mysterious divine preference, sibling rivalry, and exile later in the book of Genesis (chs 21, 27, 37). **1:** The verb translated knew may have the sense of "had known" in this context. Rashi thinks the conception of Cain occurred in the garden of Eden before his parents had sinned. **3–5:** The Torah does not say why the LORD accepted Abel's offering, but not Cain's. Perhaps we are to infer that Abel offered his with greater devotion (the choicest of the firstlings as opposed to the fruit of the soil). Alternately, the episode may evidence the high regard for shepherds and the pastoral life manifest, for example, in the early life of national heroes such as Jo-

its painful realities. **20–21:** God's clothing the naked indicates that His anger was not the last word in the divine-human relationship. The Jewish ethical tradition finds in this unmerited kindness a paradigm for human behavior, as well. "Great are acts of kindness," a talmudic rabbi remarks, "for the Torah begins with an act of kindness and ends with an act of kindness"—it begins with God's clothing the naked and ends with His burying the dead (Moses) (Deut.

34.6) (b. Soṭ. 14a). **22–24:** Neither the first nor the second account of creation portrays humankind as created immortal. Nor does the punishment of v. 19, which speaks of Adam's returning to the ground from which he was taken, mean that he would have lived forever, had it not been for his disobedience. In this passage, the LORD, alarmed at the very real, God-like status that the man has suddenly attained, resolves to deny him the opportunity to make himself im-

and his offering He paid no heed. Cain was much distressed and his face fell. ⁶ And the LORD said to Cain,

"Why are you distressed,
And why is your face fallen?
⁷ᵃ Surely, if you do right,
There is uplift.
But if you do not do right
Sin couches at the door;
Its urge is toward you,
Yet you can be its master."

⁸ Cain said to his brother Abelᵇ . . . and when they were in the field, Cain set upon his brother Abel and killed him. ⁹ The LORD said to Cain, "Where is your brother Abel?" And he said, "I do not know. Am I my brother's keeper?" ¹⁰ Then He said, "What have you done? Hark, your brother's blood cries out to Me from the ground! ¹¹ Therefore, you shall be more cursed than the ground,ᶜ which opened its mouth to receive your brother's blood from your hand. ¹² If you till the soil, it shall no longer yield its strength to you. You shall become a ceaseless wanderer on earth."

¹³ Cain said to the LORD, "My punishment is too great to bear! ¹⁴ Since You have banished me this day from the soil, and I must avoid Your presence and become a restless wanderer on earth—anyone who meets me may kill me!" ¹⁵ The LORD said to him, "I promise, if anyone kills Cain, sevenfold vengeance shall be taken on him." And the LORD put a mark on Cain, lest anyone who met him should kill him. ¹⁶ Cain left the presence of the LORD and settled in the land of Nod, east of Eden.

¹⁷ Cain knew his wife, and she conceived and bore Enoch. And he then founded a city, and named the city after his son Enoch. ¹⁸ To Enoch was born Irad, and Irad begot Mehujael, and Mehujaelᵈ begot Methusael, and Methusael begot Lamech. ¹⁹ Lamech took to himself two wives: the name of the one was Adah, and the name of the other was Zillah. ²⁰ Adah bore Jabal; he was the ancestor of those who dwell in tents and amidst herds. ²¹ And the name of his brother was Jubal; he was the ancestor of all who play the lyre and the pipe. ²² As for Zillah, she bore Tubal-cain, who forged all implements of copper and iron. And the sister of Tubal-cain was Naamah.

a Meaning of verse uncertain.
b Ancient versions, including the Targum, read "Come, let us go out into the field."
c See 3.17.
d Heb. Mehijael.

seph, Moses, and David. Like Abel, however, all the latter—and many others chosen by God in the Tanakh (e.g., Isaac, Jacob, and Solomon)—were younger brothers. The story of Cain and Abel thus demonstrates a theme widespread in the Tanakh: the difference between God's will and human conventions, such as primogeniture. In this text, the emphasis falls, however, not on the reasons for God's preference, but on Cain's fatal and culpable refusal to reconcile himself to it. **7:** The end of the verse is strikingly reminiscent of the words of God to Eve in 3.16, just as Cain's punishment in 4.11–12 recalls Adam's in 3.17–19. It is possible that the story of Cain and Abel itself once served as an account of the primal sin and the expulsion from paradise. **9:** The LORD's question to Cain recalls that to Adam in 3.9. In both cases, He asks about more than location. Cain's flippant answer offends against the Torah's ethic of responsibility for one's kinsman and neighbor (e.g., Lev. 19.16; Deut. 21.1–9). **13–15:** Although murder is a capital offense in biblical law (e.g., Exod. 21.12), the LORD yields to Cain's plea and protects him from the fate he inflicted on Abel. The irony is pungent: The man who could not tolerate God's inscrutable grace now benefits from it. A midrash sees Cain as the first penitent and attributes his pardon to his repentance (*Gen. Rab.* 22.13).

4.17–26: The growth of culture. This highly compressed passage may be an epitome of well-known legends that have not survived. The emergence of occupations and technologies that it records is reminiscent of the Mesopotamian tradition about the pre-flood sages who founded the basic institutions of civilization. The culminating v. 26 speaks of what is, in the Jewish view, the most important of these: the proper worship of the true God. This comes not from the line of Cain, but from Adam and Eve's third son, Seth. The poem of Lamech in vv. 23–24 continues the

23 And Lamech said to his wives,
"Adah and Zillah, hear my voice;
O wives of Lamech, give ear to my speech.
I have slain a man for wounding me,
And a lad for bruising me.
24   If Cain is avenged sevenfold,
Then Lamech seventy-sevenfold."

25 Adam knew his wife again, and she bore a son and named him Seth, meaning, "God has ᵃprovided me withᵃ another offspring in place of Abel," for Cain had killed him. 26 And to Seth, in turn, a son was born, and he named him Enosh. It was then that men began to invoke the LORD by name.

5 This is the record of Adam's line.—When God created man, He made him in the likeness of God; 2 male and female He created them. And when they were created, He blessed them and called them Man.—3 When Adam had lived 130 years, he begot a son in his likeness after his image, and he named him Seth. 4 After the birth of Seth, Adam lived 800 years and begot sons and daughters. 5 All the days that Adam lived came to 930 years; then he died.

6 When Seth had lived 105 years, he begot Enosh. 7 After the birth of Enosh, Seth lived 807 years and begot sons and daughters. 8 All the days of Seth came to 912 years; then he died.

9 When Enosh had lived 90 years, he begot Kenan. 10 After the birth of Kenan, Enosh lived 815 years and begot sons and daughters. 11 All the days of Enosh came to 905 years; then he died.

12 When Kenan had lived 70 years, he begot Mahalalel. 13 After the birth of Mahalalel, Kenan lived 840 years and begot sons and daughters. 14 All the days of Kenan came to 910 years; then he died.

15 When Mahalalel had lived 65 years, he begot Jared. 16 After the birth of Jared, Mahalalel lived 830 years and begot sons and daughters. 17 All the days of Mahalalel came to 895 years; then he died.

18 When Jared had lived 162 years, he begot Enoch. 19 After the birth of Enoch, Jared lived 800 years and begot sons and daughters. 20 All the days of Jared came to 962 years; then he died.

21 When Enoch had lived 65 years, he begot Methuselah. 22 After the birth of Methuselah, Enoch walked with God 300 years; and he begot sons and daughters. 23 All the

dark theme of violence associated with his ancestor Cain and attests to the increasing evil of the human race.

5.1–32: The ten generations from Adam to Noah. This genealogy can be seen, in part, as the parallel to the list in 4.17–26. Note the similarity or identity of many of the names in the two genealogies: Cain/Kenan, Enoch/Enoch, Irad/Jared, Mehujael/Mehalalel, Methusael/Methuselah, Lamech/Lamech. Even if these figures were originally thought to be descendants of Cain, ch 5 treats them all as descendants of Seth. Cain's line will not survive the flood, and the people Israel will emerge from the lineage of the younger son's replacement (4.25), not from that of the murderous first-born son of Adam. **1–3:** The ostensibly natural process of procreation has high theological import: It continues the creation of human beings in God's likeness (1.26–28). **5:** The enormous life spans of Adam and his antediluvian descendants find a parallel in the Sumerian King List, a very ancient Mesopotamian text, in which the pre-flood kings rule much longer than those who came afterward (the longest reign was 65,000 years). The underlying conception is that things proceeded on a grander scale in those days. These life spans are thus akin to the biblical allusions to primordial giants or heroes (e.g., 6.4; Deut. 2.20–21). **21–23:** Significantly, Enoch occupies the seventh position and lives only 365 years (suggesting a connection with the solar cycle). Like Noah (6.9), he *walked with God,* though the meaning of the statement that *God took him* is unclear. Rashi thinks it means that God caused his death prematurely to spare him from sinning. It is possible that Enoch's earthly life, like Elijah's (2 Kings 2.11–12), ended without death. **29:** The allusion to 3.17 is one of several indications that Noah is the new Adam—a righteous antidote to the wickedness of the father of universal mankind. Remarked an early

a-a Or "established for me"; Heb. shath, connected with "Seth."

days of Enoch came to 365 years. [24]Enoch walked with God; then he was no more, for God took him.

[25]When Methuselah had lived 187 years, he begot Lamech. [26]After the birth of Lamech, Methuselah lived 782 years and begot sons and daughters. [27]All the days of Methuselah came to 969 years; then he died.

[28]When Lamech had lived 182 years, he begot a son. [29]And he named him Noah, saying, "This one will provide us relief[a] from our work and from the toil of our hands, out of the very soil which the LORD placed under a curse." [30]After the birth of Noah, Lamech lived 595 years and begot sons and daughters. [31]All the days of Lamech came to 777 years; then he died.

[32]When Noah had lived 500 years, Noah begot Shem, Ham, and Japheth.

NOTE NUMBERS

6 When men began to increase on earth and daughters were born to them, [2]the divine beings[b] saw how beautiful the daughters of men were and took wives from among those that pleased them.—[3]The LORD said, "My breath shall not abide[c] in man forever, since he too is flesh; let the days allowed him be one hundred and twenty years."—[4]It was then, and later too, that the Nephilim appeared on earth—when the divine beings cohabited with the daughters of men, who bore them offspring. They were the heroes of old, the men of renown.

[5]The LORD saw how great was man's wickedness on earth, and how every plan devised by his mind was nothing but evil all the time. [6]And the LORD regretted that He had made man on earth, and His heart was saddened. [7]The LORD said, "I will blot out from the earth the men whom I created—men together with beasts, creeping things, and birds of the sky; for I regret that I made them." [8]But Noah found favor with the LORD.

NOAH　　　　　　　　　　　　　　　　　　נח

[9]This is the line of Noah.—Noah was a righteous man; he was blameless in his age; Noah walked with God.—[10]Noah begot three sons: Shem, Ham, and Japheth.

[11]The earth became corrupt before God; the earth was

---

a Connecting Noah with Heb. niḥam "to comfort"; cf. 9.20 ff.
b Others "the sons of God."　　c Meaning of Heb. uncertain.

---

rabbi, "When a righteous person comes into the world, goodness comes into the world" (b. Sanh. 113b). **31:** The suspicious figure of 777 is undoubtedly related to (the Cainite) Lamech's mention of

"sevenfold" and "seventy-sevenfold" in 4.24.

6.1–8: The prelude to the flood. 1–4: This brief narrative reads like a condensation of a much longer,

---

well-known myth. It records yet another breach of the all-important boundary between the divine and the human (vv. 1–2) and explains why human beings no longer attain to the great ages of their primordial forebears (v. 3). It also explains the origin of the Nephilim (v. 4), the preternatural giants that Israelite tradition thought once dwelt in the land (Num. 13.31–33). **5–8:** Whereas in ch 1 God seven times "saw" what He had made and pronounced it "good," this passage reports that He *saw how great was man's wickedness* and *regretted that He had made man.* The flood narrative that ensues, a characteristically Israelite adaptation of a well-known and widespread Mesopotamian story, emphasizes human immorality as the provocation for the cataclysm. Most strikingly, the narrator depicts God's heart as *saddened.* The sudden mention of Noah (v. 8)—whose Heb name ("n-ḥ") is "favor" ("ḥ-n") spelled backwards—indicates that human perversion and divine grief will not be the last word.

6.9–9.17: The flood: corruption, destruction, re-creation, covenant. 6.9–10: The mention of Noah's righteousness and blamelessness serves as a counterpoint to the reports of human wickedness and lawlessness that both precede and follow it (vv. 1–7, 11–13). **8:** The *favor* that *Noah found . . . with the* LORD derives, in part or in whole, from his lonely role as the one moral man in an immoral society. As such, he also serves as the one who provides relief from the LORD's curse, as his father predicted when he named him (5.29). **11–16:** The word translated *ark* occurs only in the flood story of Genesis and in the account of Moses' mother's effort to save her baby by putting him in the Nile in Exod. 2.3 (where the term is rendered "basket"). Noah foreshadows Moses, even as Moses, removed from the water, foreshadows the people Israel, whom he leads to safety through the death-dealing sea that drowns their oppressors filled with lawlessness. 12 When God saw how corrupt the earth was, for all flesh had corrupted its ways on earth, 13 God said to Noah, "I have decided to put an end to all flesh, for the earth is filled with lawlessness because of them: I am about to destroy them with the earth. 14 Make yourself an ark of gopher wood; make it an ark with compartments, and cover it inside and out with pitch. 15 This is how you shall make it: the length of the ark shall be three hundred cubits, its width fifty cubits, and its height thirty cubits. 16 Make an opening for daylight in the ark, and ᵃ-terminate it within a cubit of the top.-ᵃ Put the entrance to the ark in its side; make it with bottom, second, and third decks.

17 "For My part, I am about to bring the Flood—waters upon the earth—to destroy all flesh under the sky in which there is breath of life; everything on earth shall perish. 18 But I will establish My covenant with you, and you shall enter the ark, with your sons, your wife, and your sons' wives. 19 And of all that lives, of all flesh, you shall take two of each into the ark to keep alive with you; they shall be male and female. 20 From birds of every kind, cattle of every kind, every kind of creeping thing on earth, two of each shall come to you to stay alive. 21 For your part, take of everything that is eaten and store it away, to serve as food for you and for them." 22 Noah did so; just as God commanded him, so he did.

7 Then the LORD said to Noah, "Go into the ark, with all your household, for you alone have I found righteous before Me in this generation. 2 Of every clean animal you shall take seven pairs, males and their mates, and of every animal that is not clean, two, a male and its mate; 3 of the birds of the sky also, seven pairs, male and female, to keep seed alive upon all the earth. 4 For in seven days' time I will make it rain upon the earth, forty days and forty nights, and I will blot out from the earth all existence that I created." 5 And Noah did just as the LORD commanded him.

6 Noah was six hundred years old when the Flood came, waters upon the earth. 7 Noah, with his sons, his wife, and his sons' wives, went into the ark because of the waters of the Flood. 8 Of the clean animals, of the animals that are

a-a Meaning of Heb. uncertain.

---

protect its passengers from the cataclysm, the ark symbolizes the tender mercies and protective grace with which God envelopes the righteous even in the harshest circumstances.

6.17–22: Further introduction and a pledge. 18: This v. records the first mention of *covenant* ("berit") in the Tanakh. In the ancient Near East, a covenant was an agreement that the parties swore before the gods, and expected the gods to enforce. In this case, God is Himself a party to the covenant, which is more like a pledge than an agreement or contract (this was sometimes the case in the ancient Near East as well). The covenant with Noah will receive longer treatment in 9.1–17. **19–20:** This contradicts 7.2, in which the LORD instructs Noah to take seven pairs of the clean animals and two of the unclean ("clean" and "unclean" refer to ritual categories and not to hygiene; the terminology of "pure" and "impure" would be less misleading). Critical scholars explain the contradiction by attributing 6.19–20 to the Priestly source (P) but 7.2 to the J. Only the latter reports Noah's sacrifice when he emerges from the ark (8.20–21). If there were only one pair of each animal, this sacrifice would lead to the counterproductive result that the species offered would thereby become extinct. The source-critical explanation receives corroboration from the use of *God* in 6.9–22 but "LORD" in 7.1–5, and from the rest of the flood story, which suggests that two slightly differing stories have been interwoven. Traditional commentators have other explanations, for example, that *two* in 6.19 means "at least two" (Rashi) or that a pair of each species would come of their own accord, but Noah would later have to capture seven of the "clean" species to use for the sacrifice (Ramban).

7.1–23: The flood comes. 4: The forty days and forty nights of rainfall here and in v. 12 conflict with the one hundred fifty days of

---

(Exod. chs 14–15). The great biblical tale of redemption occurs first in a shorter, universal form, then in a longer, particularistic one. **14–16:** The cubit being roughly one and a half feet, the ark mea-

sures about 150 m × 25 m × 15 m (450 ft × 75 ft × 45 ft). Unlike other ancient boats, it is entirely enclosed, with the exception of the *opening for daylight* (v. 16). Covered *inside and out with pitch* (v. 14) to not clean, of the birds, and of everything that creeps on the ground, ⁹two of each, male and female, came to Noah into the ark, as God had commanded Noah. ¹⁰And on the seventh day the waters of the Flood came upon the earth.

¹¹In the six hundredth year of Noah's life, in the second month, on the seventeenth day of the month, on that day

All the fountains of the great deep burst apart,
And the floodgates of the sky broke open.

(¹²The rain fell on the earth forty days and forty nights.) ¹³That same day Noah and Noah's sons, Shem, Ham, and Japheth, went into the ark, with Noah's wife and the three wives of his sons—¹⁴they and all beasts of every kind, all cattle of every kind, all creatures of every kind that creep on the earth, and all birds of every kind, every bird, every winged thing. ¹⁵They came to Noah into the ark, two each of all flesh in which there was breath of life. ¹⁶Thus they that entered comprised male and female of all flesh, as God had commanded him. And the LORD shut him in.

¹⁷The Flood continued forty days on the earth, and the waters increased and raised the ark so that it rose above the earth. ¹⁸The waters swelled and increased greatly upon the earth, and the ark drifted upon the waters. ¹⁹When the waters had swelled much more upon the earth, all the highest mountains everywhere under the sky were covered. ²⁰Fifteen cubits higher did the waters swell, as the mountains were covered. ²¹And all flesh that stirred on earth perished—birds, cattle, beasts, and all the things that swarmed upon the earth, and all mankind. ²²All in whose nostrils was the merest breath of life, all that was on dry land, died. ²³All existence on earth was blotted out—man, cattle, creeping things, and birds of the sky; they were blotted out from the earth. Only Noah was left, and those with him in the ark.

²⁴And when the waters had swelled on the earth one **8** hundred and fifty days, ¹God remembered Noah and all the beasts and all the cattle that were with him in the ark, and God caused a wind to blow across the earth, and the waters subsided. ²The fountains of the deep and the floodgates of the sky were stopped up, and the rain from the sky was held back; ³the waters then receded steadily from the earth. At the end of one hundred and fifty days the waters diminished, ⁴so that in the seventh month, on the seventeenth day of the month, the ark came to rest on the mountains of Ararat. ⁵The waters went on diminishing until the tenth month; in the tenth month, on the first of the month, the tops of the mountains became visible.

swelling waters in v. 24. Once again, critical scholars detect a difference between J and P, respectively.

7.24–8.22: The flood ends.
8.1: The statement that *God remembered Noah* is the turning point of the whole flood narrative, marking the triumph of mercy over judgment. It recalls other incidents in the Torah in which God remembers and rescues: remembering Abraham and thus saving his nephew Lot from death in Sodom (19.29); remembering Rachel and thus rescuing her from the humiliation of infertility (30.22); and, most importantly, remembering "His covenant with Abraham and Isaac and Jacob" and finally saving Israel from enslavement to Pharaoh (Exod. 2.23–25). Here, too, the remembrance at issue is associated with God's reliable faithfulness to His covenant (7.18). **4:** *The mountains of Ararat* refers to the hill country of ancient Urartu, a country in eastern Asia Minor occupying parts of what is now Turkey, Iraq, Armenia, and Iran (cf. 2 Kings 19.37; Jer. 51.27). Contrary to a common misimpression, the Tanakh knows of no individual mountain named "Ararat."

⁶ At the end of forty days, Noah opened the window of the ark that he had made ⁷ and sent out the raven; it went to and fro until the waters had dried up from the earth. ⁸ Then he sent out the dove to see whether the waters had decreased from the surface of the ground. ⁹ But the dove could not find a resting place for its foot, and returned to him to the ark, for there was water over all the earth. So putting out his hand, he took it into the ark with him. ¹⁰ He waited another seven days, and again sent out the dove from the ark. ¹¹ The dove came back to him toward evening, and there in its bill was a plucked-off olive leaf! Then Noah knew that the waters had decreased on the earth. ¹² He waited still another seven days and sent the dove forth; and it did not return to him any more.

¹³ In the six hundred and first year, in the first month, on the first of the month, the waters began to dry from the earth; and when Noah removed the covering of the ark, he saw that the surface of the ground was drying. ¹⁴ And in the second month, on the twenty-seventh day of the month, the earth was dry.

¹⁵ God spoke to Noah, saying, ¹⁶ "Come out of the ark, together with your wife, your sons, and your sons' wives. ¹⁷ Bring out with you every living thing of all flesh that is with you: birds, animals, and everything that creeps on earth; and let them swarm on the earth and be fertile and increase on earth." ¹⁸ So Noah came out, together with his sons, his wife, and his sons' wives. ¹⁹ Every animal, every creeping thing, and every bird, everything that stirs on earth came out of the ark by families.

²⁰ Then Noah built an altar to the LORD and, taking of every clean animal and of every clean bird, he offered burnt offerings on the altar. ²¹ The LORD smelled the pleasing odor, and the LORD said to Himself: "Never again will I doom the earth because of man, since the devisings of man's mind are evil from his youth; nor will I ever again destroy every living being, as I have done.

²²　　So long as the earth endures,
　　　Seedtime and harvest,
　　　Cold and heat,
　　　Summer and winter,
　　　Day and night
　　　Shall not cease."

9 God blessed Noah and his sons, and said to them, "Be fertile and increase, and fill the earth. ² The fear and the dread of you shall be upon all the beasts of the earth and upon all the birds of the sky—everything with which the earth is astir—and upon all the fish of the sea; they are

13: At some point in Israelite tradition, the first day of the first month (which occurs in the spring, two weeks before Passover) must have served as New Year's Day. In rabbinic law, it is listed, in fact, as one of four New Year's Days, the most familiar being the autumnal holiday known today as Rosh Ha-Shanah (*m. Rosh Hash.* 1.1). It is significant that in the Tanakh, the first day of the first month is the day that the Tabernacle—the portable temple of the wilderness period—goes up (Exod. 40.2, 17). For the Mesopotamian epic known as *Enuma elish,* which was associated with a New Year's festival, the date celebrates both the creation of the world from the severed body of the creator god's aquatic enemy and the raising of a palace to the victorious creator. In Gen. ch 8, too, the world is, as it were, being created anew from the watery chaos that had undone God's original work of creation. A new beginning is at hand, with Noah as the new Adam.

20–22: Nothing would seem more natural to a biblical Israelite who had survived a life-threatening crisis than to offer a sacrifice to the God of his salvation (v. 20). In this case, the sacrifice appeases the LORD (cf. Num. 17.8–15), who thus moves from anger at human beings to acceptance of them in their weakness. The correspondence of v. 21, at the end of the flood narrative, with 6.5, at its beginning, is striking: Human beings have not improved. "Harsh indeed is the Evil Inclination," goes a saying in the Talmud that quotes v. 21, "for even its own Creator called it *evil.*" (*b. Kid.* 30b). Yet God will spare them nonetheless, and the rhythm of human life goes on (v. 22).

9.1–17: The covenant with Noah. Having rescued the righteous remnant from the lethal waters, God now makes a covenant with them, just as He will with the people Israel at Sinai after enabling them to escape across the Sea of Reeds (Exod. chs 14–15, 19). The closest parallel to our passage, however, is Gen. 17 (the covenant with given into your hand. ³ Every creature that lives shall be yours to eat; as with the green grasses, I give you all these. ⁴ You must not, however, eat flesh with its life-blood in it. ⁵ But for your own life-blood I will require a reckoning: I will require it of every beast; of man, too, will I require a reckoning for human life, of every man for that of his fellow man!

6   Whoever sheds the blood of man,
            By man shall his blood be shed;
            For in His image
            Did God make man.

⁷ Be fertile, then, and increase; abound on the earth and increase on it."

⁸ And God said to Noah and to his sons with him, ⁹ "I now establish My covenant with you and your offspring to come, ¹⁰ and with every living thing that is with you—birds, cattle, and every wild beast as well—all that have come out of the ark, every living thing on earth. ¹¹ I will maintain My covenant with you: never again shall all flesh be cut off by the waters of a flood, and never again shall there be a flood to destroy the earth."

¹² God further said, "This is the sign that I set for the covenant between Me and you, and every living creature with you, for all ages to come. ¹³ I have set My bow in the clouds, and it shall serve as a sign of the covenant between Me and the earth. ¹⁴ When I bring clouds over the earth, and the bow appears in the clouds, ¹⁵ I will remember My covenant between Me and you and every living creature among all flesh, so that the waters shall never again become a flood to destroy all flesh. ¹⁶ When the bow is in the clouds, I will see it and remember the everlasting covenant between God and all living creatures, all flesh that is on earth. ¹⁷ That," God said to Noah, "shall be the sign of the covenant that I have established between Me and all flesh that is on earth."

¹⁸ The sons of Noah who came out of the ark were Shem, Ham, and Japheth—Ham being the father of Canaan. ¹⁹ These three were the sons of Noah, and from these the whole world branched out.

²⁰ Noah, the tiller of the soil, was the first to plant a vineyard. ²¹ He drank of the wine and became drunk, and he

hances mankind's status relative to the animals: The animals shall be afraid of them, and God licenses humans to use them for food (vv. 2–3). The only qualification is that the *blood*, which the Tanakh identifies with the life-force (Lev. 17.11, 14; Deut. 12.23), must be drained out first. This is the origin of kashering, the Jewish practice of salting meat so as to absorb the blood before cooking. **5–6:** *By man* in v. 6 may be more accurately rendered as "in compensation for a human being." Human life is sharply distinguished from animal life; the idea that human beings are created in the image of God (1.26–27) requires a higher degree of respect for human life. In the Talmud, v. 5 is interpreted as a prohibition of killing oneself (*b. B. K.* 91b), and v. 6 is cited in support of the prohibition of abortion (*b. Sanh.* 57b). Jewish law strictly forbids suicide and allows abortion only in extreme situations and never for the purpose of birth control. **8–17:** In the Talmud, it is taught that "descendants of Noah"—that is, universal humanity—are obligated by seven commandments: (1) to establish courts of justice, (2) to refrain from blaspheming the God of Israel, as well as from (3) idolatry, (4) sexual perversion, (5) bloodshed, and (6) robbery, and (7) not to eat meat cut from a living animal (*b. Sanh.* 56a). Whereas Jews have hundreds of commandments in addition to these seven (traditionally, 613 altogether), Gentiles who observe the "seven commandments of the descendants of Noah" can meet with God's full approval.

9.18–28 The sin of Ham and the cursing of Canaan. 20–21: The ancient Rabbis saw in Noah an object lesson about the dangers of intoxication (*Gen. Rab.* 36.4), but whether the first person to grow grapes should have foreseen the degrading consequences of excessive alcohol consumption is unclear. In any event, mentioning the failures of its human heroes is characteristic of the Tanakh; only God is perfect, and even He is at times the

Abraham), also ascribed to P. In each case, God makes an *everlasting covenant* or "pact" (9.16; 17.13, 19) memorialized by a distinctive *sign*, the rainbow in the case of Noah (9.12, 13, 17) and circum-

cision in the case of Abraham and the Jewish people who, he is promised, shall descend from him (17.11). **1–4:** V. 1 repeats the charge to primordial humanity (1.28) verbatim (if only in part), but then en-uncovered himself within his tent. 22 Ham, the father of Canaan, saw his father's nakedness and told his two brothers outside. 23 But Shem and Japheth took a cloth, placed it against both their backs and, walking backward, they covered their father's nakedness; their faces were turned the other way, so that they did not see their father's nakedness. 24 When Noah woke up from his wine and learned what his youngest son had done to him, 25 he said,

> "Cursed be Canaan;
> The lowest of slaves
> Shall he be to his brothers."

26 And he said,

> "Blessed be the LORD,
> The God of Shem;
> Let Canaan be a slave to them.
>
> 27   May God enlarge[a] Japheth,
> And let him dwell in the tents of Shem;
> And let Canaan be a slave to them."

28 Noah lived after the Flood 350 years. 29 And all the days of Noah came to 950 years; then he died.

10 These are the lines of Shem, Ham, and Japheth, the sons of Noah: sons were born to them after the Flood.

2 The descendants of Japheth: Gomer, Magog, Madai, Javan, Tubal, Meshech, and Tiras. 3 The descendants of Gomer: Ashkenaz, Riphath, and Togarmah. 4 The descendants of Javan: Elishah and Tarshish, the Kittim and the Dodanim.[b] 5 From these the maritime nations branched out. [These are the descendants of Japheth][c] by their lands—each with its language—their clans and their nations.

a Heb. yapht, play on Heb. yepheth "Japheth."
b Septuagint and 1 Chron. 1.7 "Rodanim."   c Cf. vv. 20 and 31.

son, so will his own fourth son, Canaan (10.6), be cursed (Gen. Rab. 36.7). V. 23, however, suggests that the words *saw his father's nakedness* are better taken literally. If so, Ham violated two norms highly stressed in both the Tanakh and rabbinic Judaism, the ethic of bodily modesty and the norm to honor and respect one's parents. **25–27:** The cursing of Canaan may be intended, in part, to explain why non-Israelite slaves do not have to be emancipated (e.g., Lev. 25.39–46). Understanding Japheth to be Greece, an early rabbi cited v. 27 in defense of his ruling that scriptural scrolls may be written (other than in Heb) only in Greek: "May the beauty ('yefifut') of Japheth ('yefet') be in the tents of Shem" (b. Meg. 9b).

10.1–32: The seventy nations of the world. As if in fulfillment of God's command to Noah and his sons to "Be fertile and increase, and fill the earth" (9.1), the three sons of Noah rapidly engender nations that *branched out over the earth* (v. 32). The fluidity of identity, which allows a name to refer both to an individual and to a nation, is characteristic of the Tanakh and especially prominent in Genesis. This table of nations, strikingly universal in scope, represents an early exercise in ethnography. But, as in biblical genealogies generally, political relationships are at least as important as ethnicity and linguistic affinity in establishing lines of descent. Thus, the Canaanites are classed with Egypt (*Mizraim*) as Hamites (v. 6), though the geographic and linguistic relations of the Canaanites ought to put them in the same class as Israel (who have not yet emerged), the class of Shemites. The genealogy probably reflects the political reality that for a long time prior to the emergence of Israel, Egypt had dominated Canaan. Race in our contemporary sense of the term is not a basis for human division in Gen. ch 10, and no mention of physical characteristics is made. **3:** *Ashkenaz* refers to the Scythians, who occupied the

target of protest (e.g., see 18.22–33). **22–24:** This perplexing passage serves as an explanation of the sexual perverseness that Israelite culture sometimes thought to be typical of the Canaanites (cf. Lev. 18.3–4, 24–30). Note that it is Canaan who is cursed (Gen. 9.25), although Ham perpetuated the atrocity. The author (or perhaps a redactor) softens the contradiction by twice pointing out that Ham is *the father of Canaan* (vv. 18, 22). The identity of the act in question is

murky. "To uncover the nakedness" of a man means to have sexual relations with his wife (e.g., Lev. 20.11). This makes Ham guilty of incest. In Lev. 20.17, the less common expression "to see the nakedness" means to have sex. This would make Ham guilty of homosexual rape. In an effort to explain why Canaan is cursed for Ham's sin, on the other hand, the midrash sees Ham as castrating his father. Just as Ham prevented Noah from ever having a fourth

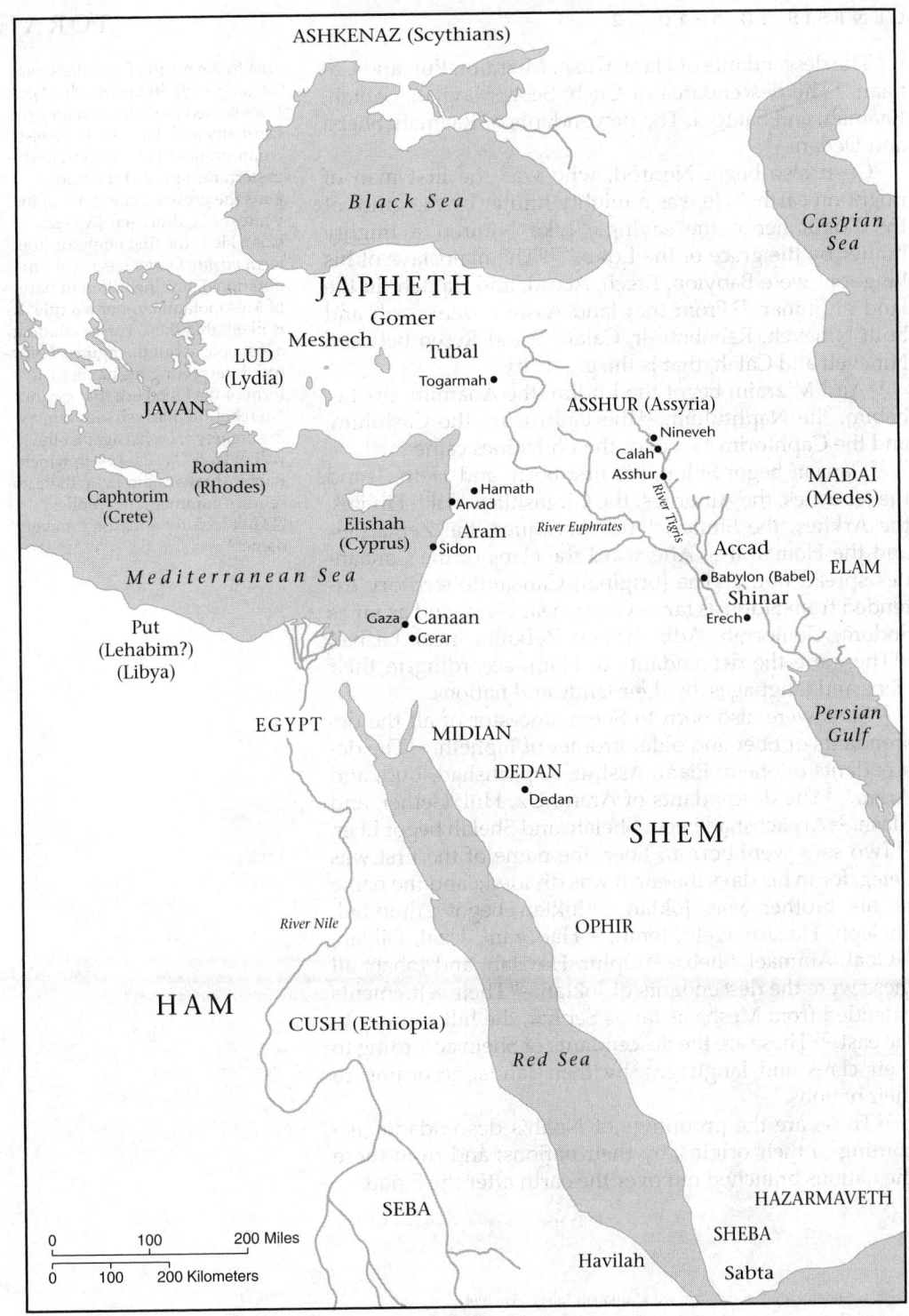

The table of nations. Only places that can be identified with probability are shown.

⁶The descendants of Ham: Cush, Mizraim, Put, and Canaan. ⁷The descendants of Cush: Seba, Havilah, Sabtah, Raamah, and Sabteca. The descendants of Raamah: Sheba and Dedan.

⁸Cush also begot Nimrod, who was the first man of might on earth. ⁹He was a mighty hunter by the grace of the LORD; hence the saying, "Like Nimrod a mighty hunter by the grace of the LORD." ¹⁰The mainstays of his kingdom were Babylon, Erech, Accad, and Calneh ͣ in the land of Shinar. ¹¹From that land Asshur went forth and built Nineveh, Rehoboth-ir, Calah, ¹²and Resen between Nineveh and Calah, that is the great city.

¹³And Mizraim begot the Ludim, the Anamim, the Lehabim, the Naphtuhim, ¹⁴the Pathrusim, the Casluhim, and the Caphtorim, ͤ whence the Philistines came forth.

¹⁵Canaan begot Sidon, his first-born, and Heth; ¹⁶and the Jebusites, the Amorites, the Girgashites, ¹⁷the Hivites, the Arkites, the Sinites, ¹⁸the Arvadites, the Zemarites, and the Hamathites. Afterward the clans of the Canaanites spread out. (¹⁹The [original] Canaanite territory extended from Sidon as far as Gerar, near Gaza, and as far as Sodom, Gomorrah, Admah, and Zeboiim, near Lasha.) ²⁰These are the descendants of Ham, according to their clans and languages, by their lands and nations.

²¹Sons were also born to Shem, ancestor of all the descendants of Eber and older brother of Japheth. ²²The descendants of Shem: Elam, Asshur, Arpachshad, Lud, and Aram. ²³The descendants of Aram: Uz, Hul, Gether, and Mash. ²⁴Arpachshad begot Shelah, and Shelah begot Eber. ²⁵Two sons were born to Eber: the name of the first was Peleg, for in his days the earth was divided; ͨ and the name of his brother was Joktan. ²⁶Joktan begot Almodad, Sheleph, Hazarmaveth, Jerah, ²⁷Hadoram, Uzal, Diklah, ²⁸Obal, Abimael, Sheba, ²⁹Ophir, Havilah, and Jobab; all these were the descendants of Joktan. ³⁰Their settlements extended from Mesha as far as Sephar, the hill country to the east. ³¹These are the descendants of Shem according to their clans and languages, by their lands, according to their nations.

³²These are the groupings of Noah's descendants, according to their origins, by their nations; and from these the nations branched out over the earth after the Flood.

area to the north of the Black Sea (cf. Jer. 51.27). In the Middle Ages, Jews reused the term to refer to Germany and, later, to the Jewish communities of central and northeastern Europe. **8–12:** Nimrod joins the growing company of inventors of culture (cf. 4.17–22; 9.20). He is the first emperor (the term *mighty hunter* has royal connotations), uniting different parts of Mesopotamia under his rule. It is likely that these verses allude to a lost epic about the figure of Nimrod. Interpreting his name as a form of the Heb verb that means "to rebel," a midrash sees him as the archetypal rebel against the will of God *(Tg. Ps.-J.)*—to which Rabbi Abraham Ibn Ezra, the 12th-century commentator, replies, "Don't look for a reason for every name"!

---

a Heb. we-khalneh, *better vocalized* we-khullanah "all of them being."

b I.e., the Cretans; moved up for the sake of clarity; cf. Amos 9.7.

c Heb. niphlegah, *play on "Peleg."*

11 Everyone on earth had the same language and the same words. ² And as they migrated from the east, they came upon a valley in the land of Shinar and settled there. ³ They said to one another, "Come, let us make bricks and burn them hard."—Brick served them as stone, and bitumen served them as mortar.—⁴ And they said, "Come, let us build us a city, and a tower with its top in the sky, to make a name for ourselves; else we shall be scattered all over the world." ⁵ The LORD came down to look at the city and tower that man had built, ⁶ and the LORD said, "If, as one people with one language for all, this is how they have begun to act, then nothing that they may propose to do will be out of their reach. ⁷ Let us, then, go down and confound their speech there, so that they shall not understand one another's speech." ⁸ Thus the LORD scattered them from there over the face of the whole earth; and they stopped building the city. ⁹ That is why it was called Babel,ᵃ because there the LORD confoundedᵇ the speech of the whole earth; and from there the LORD scattered them over the face of the whole earth.

¹⁰ This is the line of Shem. Shem was 100 years old when he begot Arpachshad, two years after the Flood. ¹¹ After the birth ofᶜ Arpachshad, Shem lived 500 years and begot sons and daughters.

¹² When Arpachshad had lived 35 years, he begot Shelah. ¹³ After the birth of Shelah, Arpachshad lived 403 years and begot sons and daughters.

¹⁴ When Shelah had lived 30 years, he begot Eber. ¹⁵ After the birth of Eber, Shelah lived 403 years and begot sons and daughters.

¹⁶ When Eber had lived 34 years, he begot Peleg. ¹⁷ After the birth of Peleg, Eber lived 430 years and begot sons and daughters.

¹⁸ When Peleg had lived 30 years, he begot Reu. ¹⁹ After the birth of Reu, Peleg lived 209 years and begot sons and daughters.

²⁰ When Reu had lived 32 years, he begot Serug. ²¹ After the birth of Serug, Reu lived 207 years and begot sons and daughters.

²² When Serug had lived 30 years, he begot Nahor. ²³ After the birth of Nahor, Serug lived 200 years and begot sons and daughters.

²⁴ When Nahor had lived 29 years, he begot Terah.

a I.e., "Babylon."
b Heb. balal "confound," play on "Babel."
c Lit. "After he begot," and so throughout.

11.1–9: The tower of Babel. Whereas ch 10 presents post-flood humanity as divided into nations, "each with its language" (v. 5), 11.1–9 attributes the emergence of linguistic difference to an act of Promethean hubris on the part of a humankind still unwilling to accept subordination to their Creator. **4:** Since the narrative serves as an account of how Babylon got its name, the ambition of the builders to erect *a tower with its top in the sky* is properly compared with the prideful boast of the king of Babylon, "I will climb to the sky; / Higher than the stars of God / I will set my throne. . . . I will match the Most High" (Isa. 14.13–14). In our passage, one senses both astonishment at the advanced technological level of Babylonian culture and a keen sense that technology poses grave dangers when it is not accompanied by reverence for God. **5:** A nice touch: Human beings erect the highest building they can, but even to see it, the LORD must descend from His heavenly dwelling. **7:** As in 1.26, the plural (*Let us*) probably reflects an address to the divine council. **8–9:** Human disunity and exile are not God's final wish, however, as the next chapter shows. Whereas the builders of Babel sought "to make a name for [them]selves" on their own, the LORD, in the next ch, promises to make Abram's "name great" Himself (12.2). And whereas they feared being "scattered all over the world" (11.4), the LORD calls Abram out of Mesopotamia and promises him a land of his own (12.1, 7). Whereas the builders of Babel are cursed with an inability to understand each other (11.7, 9), the LORD blesses not only Abram but all those who bless him (12.2–3).

11.10–32: Ten generations from Shem to Abram. The text rapidly works its way from Noahide humankind to the particular subject that will dominate the rest of the Torah: God's dealing with the people Israel, descended from Abram and thus from Shem. Compared to

25 After the birth of Terah, Nahor lived 119 years and begot sons and daughters.

26 When Terah had lived 70 years, he begot Abram, Nahor, and Haran. 27 Now this is the line of Terah: Terah begot Abram, Nahor, and Haran; and Haran begot Lot. 28 Haran died in the lifetime of his father Terah, in his native land, Ur of the Chaldeans. 29 Abram and Nahor took to themselves wives, the name of Abram's wife being Sarai and that of Nahor's wife Milcah, the daughter of Haran, the father of Milcah and Iscah. 30 Now Sarai was barren, she had no child.

31 Terah took his son Abram, his grandson Lot the son of Haran, and his daughter-in-law Sarai, the wife of his son Abram, and they set out together from Ur of the Chaldeans for the land of Canaan; but when they had come as far as Haran, they settled there. 32 The days of Terah came to 205 years; and Terah died in Haran.

LEKH LEKHA

לֶךְ לְךָ

12 The LORD said to Abram, "Go forth from your native land and from your father's house to the land that I will show you.

2   I will make of you a great nation,
       And I will bless you;
       I will make your name great,
       And you shall be a blessing.[a]
3   I will bless those who bless you
       And curse him that curses you;
       And all the families of the earth
       Shall bless themselves by you."

4 Abram went forth as the LORD had commanded him, and Lot went with him. Abram was seventy-five years old when he left Haran. 5 Abram took his wife Sarai and his brother's son Lot, and all the wealth that they had amassed, and the persons that they had acquired in Haran; and they set out for the land of Canaan. When they

a I.e., a standard by which blessing is invoked; cf. v. 3 end.

the previous genealogical list in ch 5, which recorded the pre-flood figures, this one displays longevities that are markedly shorter. In fact, they tend to decrease over the generations, and the ages at which these men beget their first-born sons are generally realistic. At least two of the personal names listed here, Serug and Nahor, are known from Mesopotamian literature as place names. **31–32:** The idea that Abram began his trek to Canaan together with his father contradicts the impression one receives from 12.1, wherein Abram leaves his "father's house" to go to an unnamed land that turns out, of course, to be Canaan (cf. 15.7). Source critics solve the problem by assigning vv. 31–32 to P, but the account of Abram's leaving his "father's house" for Canaan to J. The more traditional approach would be to speak of two stages to Abram's trek, the first from Ur to Haran with Terah, the second from Haran to Canaan without him. Note that if one computes the life span of 205 years given for Terah in v. 32 with other numbers in the life of Abram—born when his father is seventy (v. 26), seventy-five when he left Haran (12.4)—then Terah lived for sixty years after Abram's departure. The difference between the narrative order and the chronological order provides Rashi with the basis for pungent observation: "The wicked are called 'dead' even in their lifetime" (according to Josh. 24.2, Terah was an idolater).

12.1–9: The command and the promise to Abram. 1–3: The universalism that marked Gen. chs 1–11 having now failed, the LORD begins anew, singling out one Mesopotamian—in no way distinguished from his peers as yet—and promising to make of him *a great nation,* not numbered in the seventy nations of ch 10. What the LORD promises Abram (his name is changed to "Abraham" only in ch 17)—land, numerous offspring, and blessing—constitutes to a large extent a reversal of some of the curses on Adam and Eve—exile, pain in childbirth, and uncooperative soil (3.16–24). The twin themes of land and progeny inform the rest of the Torah. In Gen. ch 12, these extraordinary promises come like a bolt from the blue, an act of God's grace alone; no indication has been given as to why or even whether Abram merits them. In 22.15–18, they will be reinterpreted as the LORD's condign response to Abraham's great act of obedience when he proved willing to sacrifice his beloved son, Isaac. In Second Temple and rabbinic sources, various details of Abraham's early life are filled in, and he sometimes appears as the first monotheist, discovering the one true God even before God calls him.

arrived in the land of Canaan, 6 Abram passed through the land as far as the site of Shechem, at the terebinth of Moreh. The Canaanites were then in the land.

7 The Lord appeared to Abram and said, "I will assign this land to your offspring." And he built an altar there to the Lord who had appeared to him. 8 From there he moved on to the hill country east of Bethel and pitched his tent, with Bethel on the west and Ai on the east; and he built there an altar to the Lord and invoked the Lord by name. 9 Then Abram journeyed by stages toward the Negeb.

10 There was a famine in the land, and Abram went down to Egypt to sojourn there, for the famine was severe in the land. 11 As he was about to enter Egypt, he said to his wife Sarai, "I know[a] what a beautiful woman you are. 12 If the Egyptians see you, and think, 'She is his wife,' they will kill me and let you live. 13 Please say that you are my sister, that it may go well with me because of you, and that I may remain alive thanks to you."

14 When Abram entered Egypt, the Egyptians saw how very beautiful the woman was. 15 Pharaoh's courtiers saw her and praised her to Pharaoh, and the woman was taken into Pharaoh's palace. 16 And because of her, it went well with Abram; he acquired sheep, oxen, asses, male and female slaves, she-asses, and camels.

17 But the Lord afflicted Pharaoh and his household with mighty plagues on account of Sarai, the wife of Abram. 18 Pharaoh sent for Abram and said, "What is this you have done to me! Why did you not tell me that she was your wife? 19 Why did you say, 'She is my sister,' so that I took her as my wife? Now, here is your wife; take her and be-gone!" 20 And Pharaoh put men in charge of him, and they sent him off with his wife and all that he possessed.

a Or "You"; cf. the second person feminine form -ti in Judg. 5.7; Jer. 2.20; Mic. 4.13, etc.

6: The statement that *The Canaan-ites were then in the land* poses an obstacle to the doctrine of Mosaic authorship, since the Canaanites were still firmly in control of the land when Moses died. Ibn Ezra suggests that the Canaanites may have taken the land from some prior occupants, and "if not, [this verse] has a great secret." The "great secret," according to Joseph Bonfils, a commentator on Ibn Ezra, was that "Joshua or another of the other prophets wrote it. . . . And since we are to have trust in the words of tradition and the prophets," Bonfils concludes, "what should I care whether it was Moses or another prophet who wrote it, since the words of all of them are true and inspired?" (*Tzafenat Paʿaneaḥ*)

12.10–20: Exile and danger. No sooner has Abram been promised the land and taken his tour of it than the promise is thrown into great danger. In the extreme and life-threatening circumstance of famine, Abram leaves Canaan for Egypt, a land that had a reputation in the Israelite mind for sexual impropriety (e.g., Gen. ch 39; Lev. ch 18; Ezek. 23.1–3, 8, 19, 21, 27). Although Abram is sometimes chastised for passing his beautiful wife off as his sister, it is hard to see how Sarai (whose name be-comes "Sarah" in ch 17) would have fared better if he died at the hands of the lecherous and adul-terous Egyptians. Ramban, how-ever, makes a powerful theological criticism of Abram, observing that the patriarch "committed a great sin inadvertently" by not trusting in God's protection, leaving the promised land, and subjecting his righteous wife to the possibility of sexual victimization. This, Ramban remarks, will be the cause of his descendants' painful exile in Egypt (Ramban on 12.10). **17:** The Lord's infliction of plagues on Pharaoh foreshadows the story of the exodus. Indeed, Abram's expe-rience in 12.10–20 pre-enacts major themes of his descendants' experi-ence at the end of Genesis and in exodus: descent into Egypt be-cause of famine, the death (feared or realized) of the male and sur-vival of the female (cf. Exod. 1.15–22), discussions with Phar-aoh, plagues, release, and the ac-quisition of great wealth (cf. Exod. 12.35). "None of the events that happened to the father failed to happen to the descendants" (Ram-ban on 12.10, based on *Gen. Rab.* ad loc.). The wife-sister motif, in this instance ascribed to J, recurs with King Abimelech of Gerar in Pharaoh's place in ch 20 (ascribed to E) and with Isaac and Rebekah, instead of Abraham and Sarah, confronting Abimelech in 26.6–11 (again attributed to J). Thus, no one source repeats the story with the same couple and the same king.

The geography of the ancestral narratives. Places associated with a particular ancestor are highlighted with a star, and the initial of the ancestor follows the place name: A(braham), I(saac), or J(acob).

13 From Egypt, Abram went up into the Negeb, with his wife and all that he possessed, together with Lot. ²Now Abram was very rich in cattle, silver, and gold. ³And he proceeded by stages from the Negeb as far as Bethel, to the place where his tent had been formerly, between Bethel and Ai, ⁴the site of the altar that he had built there at first; and there Abram invoked the LORD by name.

⁵Lot, who went with Abram, also had flocks and herds and tents, ⁶so that the land could not support them staying together; for their possessions were so great that they could not remain together. ⁷And there was quarreling between the herdsmen of Abram's cattle and those of Lot's cattle.—The Canaanites and Perizzites were then dwelling in the land.—⁸Abram said to Lot, "Let there be no strife between you and me, between my herdsmen and yours, for we are kinsmen. ⁹Is not the whole land before you? Let us separate:[a] if you go north, I will go south; and if you go south, I will go north." ¹⁰Lot looked about him and saw how well watered was the whole plain of the Jordan, all of it—this was before the LORD had destroyed Sodom and Gomorrah—all the way to Zoar, like the garden of the LORD, like the land of Egypt. ¹¹So Lot chose for himself the whole plain of the Jordan, and Lot journeyed eastward. Thus they parted from each other; ¹²Abram remained in the land of Canaan, while Lot settled in the cities of the Plain, pitching his tents near Sodom. ¹³Now the inhabitants of Sodom were very wicked sinners against the LORD.

¹⁴And the LORD said to Abram, after Lot had parted from him, "Raise your eyes and look out from where you are, to the north and south, to the east and west, ¹⁵for I give all the land that you see to you and your offspring forever. ¹⁶I will make your offspring as the dust of the earth, so that if one can count the dust of the earth, then your offspring too can be counted. ¹⁷Up, walk about the land, through its length and its breadth, for I give it to you." ¹⁸And Abram moved his tent, and came to dwell at the terebinths of Mamre, which are in Hebron; and he built an altar there to the LORD.

14 Now, when King Amraphel of Shinar, King Arioch of Ellasar, King Chedorlaomer of Elam, and King Tidal of Goiim ²made war on King Bera of Sodom, King Birsha of Gomorrah, King Shinab of Admah, King Shemeber of Zeboiim, and the king of Bela, which is Zoar, ³all the latter joined forces at the Valley of Siddim, now the Dead

13.1–18: Lot and Abram separate. Abram's childlessness (11.30) has raised the suspicion that the "great nation" that God promises to make of him will descend, biologically, from his nephew Lot, whom he may have adopted (11.31; 12.5). Now, the blessing on Abram having worked too well, so to speak, the land cannot support the huge flocks that the two kinsmen have acquired, and they must separate. **8–13:** Abram is characteristically generous and conciliatory, offering Lot the first choice of land (vv. 8–9). Lot, by contrast, is self-interested and immediately selects what he mistakenly takes to be the best. The narrator's comparison of his portion to *the garden of the LORD*, a place of disobedience and curse, and to Egypt, a place of exile and oppression, suggests the short-sightedness of Lot's choice (v. 10). His settling near the archetypal sinners of Sodom contrasts with Abram, who faithfully *remained in the land of Canaan* (vv. 12–13). **14–18:** Whereas Lot "raised his eyes" (v. 10, translated here as "looked about him"), Abram does not do likewise until the LORD so instructs him (v. 14). Whereas Lot "chose for himself" land that the LORD would, in his own lifetime, destroy utterly (v. 11; 19.23–25), the LORD *gives* Abram and his progeny the land of Canaan *forever* (v. 15). And whereas Lot pitches his tent near the arch-sinners of Sodom (vv. 12–13), Abram dwells in Hebron and builds an altar to the God he serves. This contrast of the two kinsmen, with Lot serving as a foil for his uncle, will appear again in chs 18–19.

14.1–24: Abram's heroic campaign. 1–9: Both in content and in style, ch 14 is very different from the rest of the story of Abram/Abraham. Its depiction of him as a warrior is unusual. Vv. 1–9 read like an excerpt from a battle report in an ancient Near Eastern royal inscription. Whether or not this indicates a historical basis for the campaigns reported here has been a matter of debate. Although most

a Lit. *"Please separate from me."*

Sea.[a] [4] Twelve years they served Chedorlaomer, and in the thirteenth year they rebelled. [5] In the fourteenth year Chedorlaomer and the kings who were with him came and defeated the Rephaim at Ashteroth-karnaim, the Zuzim at Ham, the Emim at Shaveh-kiriathaim, [6] and the Horites in their hill country of Seir as far as El-paran, which is by the wilderness. [7] On their way back they came to En-mishpat, which is Kadesh, and subdued all the territory of the Amalekites, and also the Amorites who dwelt in Hazazon-tamar. [8] Then the king of Sodom, the king of Gomorrah, the king of Admah, the king of Zeboiim, and the king of Bela, which is Zoar, went forth and engaged them in battle in the Valley of Siddim: [9] King Chedorlaomer of Elam, King Tidal of Goiim, King Amraphel of Shinar, and King Arioch of Ellasar—four kings against those five.

[10] Now the Valley of Siddim was dotted with bitumen pits; and the kings of Sodom and Gomorrah, in their flight, threw themselves into them, while the rest escaped to the hill country. [11] [The invaders] seized all the wealth of Sodom and Gomorrah and all their provisions, and went their way. [12] They also took Lot, the son of Abram's brother, and his possessions, and departed; for he had settled in Sodom.

[13] A fugitive brought the news to Abram the Hebrew, who was dwelling at the terebinths of Mamre the Amorite, kinsman of Eshkol and Aner, these being Abram's allies. [14] When Abram heard that his kinsman had been taken captive, he mustered his retainers,[b] born into his household, numbering three hundred and eighteen, and went in pursuit as far as Dan. [15] At night, he and his servants deployed against them and defeated them; and he pursued them as far as Hobah, which is north of Damascus. [16] He brought back all the possessions; he also brought back his kinsman Lot and his possessions, and the women and the rest of the people.

[17] When he returned from defeating Chedorlaomer and the kings with him, the king of Sodom came out to meet him in the Valley of Shaveh, which is the Valley of the King. [18] And King Melchizedek of Salem brought out bread and wine; he was a priest of God Most High.[c] [19] He blessed him, saying,

> "Blessed be Abram of God Most High,
> Creator of heaven and earth.
> [20] And blessed be God Most High,
> Who has delivered your foes into your hand."

And [Abram] gave him a tenth of everything.

of the nations mentioned can be identified, confirmation of the individuals involved has not been forthcoming. Note that the names of the four Canaanite kings are arranged in two sets of alliterating pairs, Bera-Birsha, Shinab-Shemeber (v. 2), and that at least the names of the kings of Sodom and Gomorrah seem to be symbolic (Bera = "in evil," Birsha = "in wickedness"). **12–13:** The narrowing of the vast international perspective to Lot and Sodom and the mention of Abram's dwelling *at the terebinths of Mamre* connect this anomalous narrative to the previous chapter (cf. 13.10–13, 18). Why Abram is called *the Hebrew* (if this is the correct translation) is unclear. In the Tanakh, the term seems to refer to an ethnic group (e.g., 39.14; Exod. 1.19; Jonah 1.9). Here, the ethnic group not having as yet appeared, it may be anachronistic. **14:** It is surprising that Abram has 318 retainers. Although the previous stories have mentioned his rapid acquisition of wealth (12.16; 13.2), he remains a humbler and more vulnerable figure throughout the other narratives and is never again portrayed with his own army. Sensing the anomaly, an ancient rabbi identifies the 318 retainers with Abram's steward, Eliezer (15.2) alone, the letters of whose name, if assigned numerical equivalents, total 318 (*Gen. Rab.* 43.2). Since the town of Dan did not acquire that name until long after Abram's time (Josh. 19.47; Judg. 18.27–29), *Dan* here is also anachronistic, reflecting the situation of a much later (human) author. **16:** Separated from Abram, Lot is weak and despoiled (v. 12). Rejoined with Abram (through the latter's heroism), he is restored and recovers his property (cf. 12.3; 19.29). **18–20:** The blessing on Abram of Melchizedek, king of Salem (probably Jerusalem, cf. Ps. 76.3), abruptly interrupts the approach of the king of Sodom, which resumes in v. 21. The term *God Most High* is known from Ugaritic texts of the Late Bronze Age (Ugarit was a Canaanite city along the coast of

---

a Heb. "Salt Sea."   *b Meaning of Heb. ḥanikh uncertain.*   *c Heb. El 'Elyon.*

21 Then the king of Sodom said to Abram, "Give me the persons, and take the possessions for yourself." 22 But Abram said to the king of Sodom, "I swear[a] to the LORD, God Most High, Creator of heaven and earth: 23 I will not take so much as a thread or a sandal strap of what is yours; you shall not say, 'It is I who made Abram rich.' 24 For me, nothing but what my servants have used up; as for the share of the men who went with me—Aner, Eshkol, and Mamre—let them take their share."

15 Some time later, the word of the LORD came to Abram in a vision. He said,
"Fear not, Abram,
I am a shield to you;
Your reward shall be very great."
2 But Abram said, "O Lord GOD, what can You give me, seeing that I shall die childless, [b-and the one in charge of my household is Dammesek Eliezer!"-b] 3 Abram said further, "Since You have granted me no offspring, my steward will be my heir." 4 The word of the LORD came to him in reply, "That one shall not be your heir; none but your very own issue shall be your heir." 5 He took him outside and said, "Look toward heaven and count the stars, if you are able to count them." And He added, "So shall your offspring be." 6 And because he put his trust in the LORD, He reckoned it to his merit.

7 Then He said to him, "I am the LORD who brought you out from Ur of the Chaldeans to assign this land to you as a possession." 8 And he said, "O Lord GOD, how shall I know that I am to possess it?" 9 He answered, "Bring Me a three-year-old heifer, a three-year-old she-goat, a three-

---

a Lit. "lift up my hand."   b-b Meaning of Heb. uncertain.

---

what is now Syria). There it is applied to the god El, with whom the LORD is often equated in the Tanakh (e.g., 33.20; Num. 23.8). *God Most High* is itself a not uncommon epithet of the LORD (e.g., Ps. 47.3). That a foreigner should recognize and revere the God of Israel is not unusual in Genesis, though it is so in much of the rest of the Tanakh. The account of Abram's interaction with the priest-king of Salem may have served to establish the antiquity of Israel's holiest site and the priestly and royal dynasties associated with it. (Jerusalem/Salem is never again mentioned by name in the Torah.) **21–24:** Refusing the Sodomite king's offer to split the booty, Abram again displays his generosity and his graciousness. In v. 22, he employs the liturgical language Melchizedek introduced in v. 19, only this time explicitly equating *God Most High* with the LORD, as Melchizedek did not. Vv. 22–24 underscore Abram's exemplary faith in God: In Abram's view, the true hero of the victorious campaign is not himself, but the LORD.

15.1–21: The LORD promises Abram an heir and a land. This ch falls into two sections, the first

(vv. 1–6) focused on God's promise to provide Abram with an heir who will be his own son, and the second (vv. 7–20) on God's covenantal pledge to redeem Abram's descendants from enslavement abroad and to give them a land. Note that in each section, Abram raises a question that expresses some doubt about the promise (vv. 2–3, 8), and in each case the LORD responds with a renewed promise of staggering proportions (vv. 5, 13, 18–20). **2–3:** These difficult verses (v. 3 reads like a gloss on v. 2) may imply that Abram had adopted Eliezer, on the presumption, of course, that he would have no children of his own. In any event, the mention of Abram's childlessness draws our attention again to Sarai's infertility (11.30) and to the pointlessness of all Abram's recent financial and military success in the absence of a son from whom the promised "great nation" (12.2) can descend. **6:** With nothing more than an extravagant reiteration of the promise of offspring, Abram drops his question and trusts in the LORD. "And thus you find," observes an ancient midrash about this verse, "that our father Abraham inherited this world and the world-to-come only as a reward for the faith that he had" (*Mek. of Rabbi Ishmael, beshallaḥ* 7). In the Tanakh, faith does not mean believing in spite of the evidence. It means trusting profoundly in a person, in this case the personal God who has reiterated His promise. **7:** The resemblance to the beginning of the Decalogue (Exod. 20.2) further reinforces the sense that Abraham's life foreshadows that of his descendants, the people of Israel, whose enslavement in Egypt and subsequent exodus is about to be predicted (15.13–14). **9–11:** The ritual of cutting animals in half and passing between them is found both in the Bible and in Mesopotamia. The parallel in Jer. 34.17–22 makes it likely that the essence of the ritual is a self-curse: Those walking between the pieces will be like the dead animals if they violate the covenant. In the year-old ram, a turtledove, and a young bird." ¹⁰He brought Him all these and cut them in two, placing each half opposite the other; but he did not cut up the bird. ¹¹Birds of prey came down upon the carcasses, and Abram drove them away. ¹²As the sun was about to set, a deep sleep fell upon Abram, and a great dark dread descended upon him. ¹³And He said to Abram, "Know well that your offspring shall be strangers in a land not theirs, and they shall be enslaved and oppressed four hundred years; ¹⁴but I will execute judgment on the nation they shall serve, and in the end they shall go free with great wealth. ¹⁵As for you,

You shall go to your fathers in peace;
You shall be buried at a ripe old age.

¹⁶And they shall return here in the fourth generation, for the iniquity of the Amorites is not yet complete."

¹⁷When the sun set and it was very dark, there appeared a smoking oven, and a flaming torch which passed between those pieces. ¹⁸On that day the LORD made a covenant with Abram, saying, "To your offspring I assign this land, from the river of Egypt to the great river, the river Euphrates: ¹⁹the Kenites, the Kenizzites, the Kadmonites, ²⁰the Hittites, the Perizzites, the Rephaim, ²¹the Amorites, the Canaanites, the Girgashites, and the Jebusites."

16 Sarai, Abram's wife, had borne him no children. She had an Egyptian maidservant whose name was Hagar. ²And Sarai said to Abram, "Look, the LORD has kept me from bearing. Consort with my maid; perhaps I shall have a son[a] through her." And Abram heeded Sarai's request. ³So Sarai, Abram's wife, took her maid, Hagar the Egyptian—after Abram had dwelt in the land of Canaan ten years—and gave her to her husband Abram as concubine. ⁴He cohabited with Hagar and she conceived; and when she saw that she had conceived, her mistress was lowered in her esteem. ⁵And Sarai said to Abram, "The wrong done me is your fault! I myself put my maid in your bosom; now that she sees that she is pregnant, I

---

a Lit. "be built up," play on ben "son" and banah "build up."

---

case at hand, remarkably, it is the LORD, symbolized by the "smoking oven" and "flaming torch" (15.17) who invokes the self-curse, and nothing is said about any covenantal obligations that Abram is to fulfill. This type of covenant is called a covenant of grant, which is a reward for past loyalty, and does not involve any obliga-

tions upon the grantee. The same pattern is prominent in texts about the covenant with David (2 Sam. 7.8–16; Ps. 89.20–37). **12–16:** The good news that has marked Abram's previous interactions with God here gives way to a dark prophecy of his offspring's separation from the promised land and enslavement in Egypt. Like

the birds of prey swooping toward the carcasses of the severed animals (v. 11), horrors will befall the people Israel, but Israel will go free and return to the land. *Amorites* in v. 16 is used as a general term for all the Canaanite nations. They lose the land not only because of the LORD's promise to Abram, but also because of their own sin (cf. Lev. 18.24–30). **18–21:** These are the maximal borders of the promised land given in the Tanakh. They encompass, for example, much more territory than the borders specified in Num. 34.1–12, and may reflect an ideal that was never realized. The expression "river of Egypt" is unparalleled. It may refer to an eastern arm of the Nile or to the Wadi el-Arish, a body of water between the Negev and the Sinai Peninsula. The Heb words for "river" and for "wadi" are very similar.

16.1–16: A tale of two women. 1–3: God's uncompromising reiterations of the promise of offspring in the previous chapter (15.4–5, 13–16, 18) render Sarai's infertility all the more problematic: ten years in Canaan but still no child! Nothing in the promises given to Abram to date having specified the matriarch of the great nation to come, Sarai takes matters into her own hands and, in accordance with documented ancient Near Eastern practice, offers her slave woman as a surrogate mother. Abram (who might have solved his problem by divorcing Sarai but stayed with her nonetheless) accepts. **4:** Given the high estimation of motherhood in biblical culture, the status of Sarai and Hagar now reverses. Among the four things at which "the earth shudders," according to the book of Proverbs, is "a slave-girl who supplants her mistress" (Prov. 30.23). **5–6:** Sarai demands justice from Abram, and he gives her a carte blanche. A midrash sees in Sarai's behavior an object lesson in the dangers of litigiousness: Had she not been so single-mindedly and insensitively preoccupied in am lowered in her esteem. The Lord decide between you and me!" ⁶Abram said to Sarai, "Your maid is in your hands. Deal with her as you think right." Then Sarai treated her harshly, and she ran away from her.

⁷An angel of the Lord found her by a spring of water in the wilderness, the spring on the road to Shur, ⁸and said, "Hagar, slave of Sarai, where have you come from, and where are you going?" And she said, "I am running away from my mistress Sarai."

⁹And the angel of the Lord said to her, "Go back to your mistress, and submit to her harsh treatment." ¹⁰And the angel of the Lord said to her,

> "I will greatly increase your offspring,
> And they shall be too many to count."

¹¹The angel of the Lord said to her further,

> "Behold, you are with child
> And shall bear a son;
> You shall call him Ishmael,ᵃ
> For the Lord has paid heed to your suffering.

12
> He shall be a wild ass of a man;
> His hand against everyone,
> And everyone's hand against him;
> He shall dwell alongside of all his kinsmen."

¹³And she called the Lord who spoke to her, "You Are El-roi,"ᵇ by which she meant, ᶜ"Have I not gone on seeing after He saw me!"⁻ᶜ ¹⁴Therefore the well was called Beer-lahai-roi;ᵈ it is between Kadesh and Bered.—¹⁵Hagar bore a son to Abram, and Abram gave the son that Hagar bore him the name Ishmael. ¹⁶Abram was eighty-six years old when Hagar bore Ishmael to Abram.

17 When Abram was ninety-nine years old, the Lord appeared to Abram and said to him, "I am El Shaddai.ᵉ Walk in My ways and be blameless. ²I will establish My covenant between Me and you, and I will make you exceedingly numerous."

³Abram threw himself on his face; and God spoke to him further, ⁴"As for Me, this is My covenant with you: You shall be the father of a multitude of nations. ⁵And

---

a I.e., "God heeds."   b Apparently "God of Seeing."
c-c Meaning of Heb. uncertain.
d Apparently "the Well of the Living One Who sees me."
e Traditionally rendered "God Almighty."

---

demanding justice for herself, her life span would have equaled Abram's. Instead, whereas he lived to 175, she died at 127 (25.7; 23.1) (*Gen. Rab.* 45.5). **7–9:** The flight of the oppressed slave into the wilderness, only to meet a divine being there, foreshadows again the experience of the exodus, prophesied in the previous chapter (15.13–14; cf. Exod. 3.1–2). But this time the oppressor is Israelite, the slave is Egyptian, and the angel of the Lord commands the escapee to return to her cruel mistress and *submit to her harsh treatment*. God's sympathy with the oppressed is potent in the Tanakh, but so is his election of Israel, and it is the latter that trumps in this instance. **10–12:** But God does take note of Hagar's suffering and rewards her with the Abrahamic blessing of *offspring . . . too many to count* (cf. 13.16; 15.5). Indeed, her high-spirited and militarily formidable son will bear the name Ishmael ("God heeds/heeded") as testimony to the Lord's concern about her affliction. **13–14:** The basis for Hagar's exclamation at the end of v. 13 is the idea that one who sees a divine being must die (cf. Exod. 33.20; Judg. 13.22).

17.1–27: An everlasting covenant with Abraham and a promise about Sarah. Source critics identify ch 17 as the P(riestly) version of the covenant with Abraham (of which the J version appears in ch 15). Nothing in ch 17 indicates any awareness that the covenant mandated therein has, in fact, already been established two chapters earlier. In our chapter, the two chief innovations are that the covenant acquires a sign (circumcision, v. 10) and that it is Sarah who, despite her advanced age, shall bear the promised son (vv. 15–16, 19). The closest parallel to ch 17 in style and diction is 9.1–17, the account of the covenant with Noah. **1:** *El Shaddai* is believed to have originally meant "God, the One of the Mountain" and thus to have expressed the association of a deity with his mountain abode well known in Canaanite literature (cf. the "Lord, Him of Sinai" in Judg. 5.5). In the Priestly conception, the four-letter name translated as Lord was disclosed only in the time of Moses (Exod 6.2–3), and El Shaddai was the name by which God revealed Himself to the patriarchs. **5:** The change of name here and in v. 15 signifies a change in destiny: The childless couple you shall no longer be called Abram, but your name shall be Abraham,[a] for I make you the father of a multitude of nations. 6 I will make you exceedingly fertile, and make nations of you; and kings shall come forth from you. 7 I will maintain My covenant between Me and you, and your offspring to come, as an everlasting covenant throughout the ages, to be God to you and to your offspring to come. 8 I assign the land you sojourn in to you and your offspring to come, all the land of Canaan, as an everlasting holding. I will be their God."

9 God further said to Abraham, "As for you, you and your offspring to come throughout the ages shall keep My covenant. 10 Such shall be the covenant between Me and you and your offspring to follow which you shall keep: every male among you shall be circumcised. 11 You shall circumcise the flesh of your foreskin, and that shall be the sign of the covenant between Me and you. 12 And throughout the generations, every male among you shall be circumcised at the age of eight days. As for the home-born slave and the one bought from an outsider who is not of your offspring, 13 they must be circumcised, home-born, and purchased alike. Thus shall My covenant be marked in your flesh as an everlasting pact. 14 And if any male who is uncircumcised fails to circumcise the flesh of his foreskin, that person shall be cut off from his kin; he has broken My covenant."

15 And God said to Abraham, "As for your wife Sarai, you shall not call her Sarai, but her name shall be Sarah.[b] 16 I will bless her; indeed, I will give you a son by her. I will bless her so that she shall give rise to nations; rulers of peoples shall issue from her." 17 Abraham threw himself on his face and laughed, as he said to himself, "Can a child be born to a man a hundred years old, or can Sarah bear a child at ninety?" 18 And Abraham said to God, "O that Ishmael might live by Your favor!" 19 God said, "Nevertheless, Sarah your wife shall bear you a son, and you shall name him Isaac;[c] and I will maintain My covenant with him as an everlasting covenant for his offspring to come. 20 As for Ishmael, I have heeded you.[d] I hereby bless him. I will make him fertile and exceedingly numerous. He shall be the father of twelve chieftains, and I will make of him a great nation. 21 But My covenant I will maintain with Isaac, whom Sarah shall bear to you at this season next year." 22 And when He was done speaking with him, God was gone from Abraham.

will become the ancestors of many nations, including royal dynasties (v. 6). **9–14:** Just as the rainbow is the sign of the Noahide covenant (9.12–17), so is circumcision the sign of the Abrahamic covenant. It thus becomes a matter of the highest importance in Judaism. A Second Temple source reports that when the Seleucid King Antiochus IV prohibited circumcision (a favorite target of anti-Semites), Jewish mothers chose martyrdom over neglect of the commandment (1 Macc. 1.60–61). Rabbinic law requires that a (healthy) Jewish boy be circumcised on the eighth day of his life (v. 12) even if it is the Sabbath. Although arguments for the hygienic value of circumcision have been made since the mid-19th century, the Torah knows nothing of these and sees circumcision ("berit milah") as a religious duty incumbent only on Jews. The procedure of hygienic circumcision is not identical to that performed by a "mohel" (ritual circumciser) in a "berit milah." **15–22:** Unlike its parallel in ch 15 (J), the P account of the Abrahamic covenant specifies Sarah as the mother of the promised son, and thus makes her indispensable to the fulfillment of the promise to her husband. The natural impossibility of her giving birth at 90 (not to mention her lifelong infertility) only highlights the supernatural character of Isaac and the nation descended from him (v. 17). Ishmael, however, is not dispossessed. Whereas only Isaac inherits the covenant (and its attendant promise of land), Ishmael inherits a large measure of the Abrahamic promise (vv. 20–21; 12.2). Like his nephew Jacob (35.22b–26), he will become the patriarch of a twelve-tribe confederation and thus the father of *a great nation* (v. 20; cf. 25.12–18; 12.2).

---

a Understood as "father of a multitude."   b I.e., "princess."
c Heb. Yiṣḥaq, from ṣaḥaq, "laugh."   d Heb. shemaʿtikha, play on "Ishmael."

23 Then Abraham took his son Ishmael, and all his homeborn slaves and all those he had bought, every male in Abraham's household, and he circumcised the flesh of their foreskins on that very day, as God had spoken to him. 24 Abraham was ninety-nine years old when he circumcised the flesh of his foreskin, 25 and his son Ishmael was thirteen years old when he was circumcised in the flesh of his foreskin. 26 Thus Abraham and his son Ishmael were circumcised on that very day; 27 and all his household, his homeborn slaves and those that had been bought from outsiders, were circumcised with him.

VA-YERA'   וירא

18 The LORD appeared to him by the terebinths of Mamre; he was sitting at the entrance of the tent as the day grew hot. 2 Looking up, he saw three men standing near him. As soon as he saw them, he ran from the entrance of the tent to greet them and, bowing to the ground, 3 he said, "My lords,a if it please you, do not go on past your servant. 4 Let a little water be brought; bathe your feet and recline under the tree. 5 And let me fetch a morsel of bread that you may refresh yourselves; then go on— seeing that you have come your servant's way." They replied, "Do as you have said."

6 Abraham hastened into the tent to Sarah, and said, "Quick, three seahs of choice flour! Knead and make cakes!" 7 Then Abraham ran to the herd, took a calf, tender and choice, and gave it to a servant-boy, who hastened to prepare it. 8 He took curds and milk and the calf that had been prepared and set these before them; and he waited on them under the tree as they ate.

9 They said to him, "Where is your wife Sarah?" And he replied, "There, in the tent." 10 Then one said, "I will return to you next year,b and your wife Sarah shall have a son!" Sarah was listening at the entrance of the tent, which was behind him. 11 Now Abraham and Sarah were old, advanced in years; Sarah had stopped having the periods of women. 12 And Sarah laughed to herself, saying, "Now that I am withered, am I to have enjoyment—with my husband so old?" 13 Then the LORD said to Abraham, "Why did Sarah laugh, saying, 'Shall I in truth bear a child, old as I am?' 14 Is anything too wondrous for the LORD? I will return to you at the same season next year, and Sarah shall have a son." 15 Sarah lied, saying, "I did not laugh," for she was frightened. But He replied, "You did laugh."

18.1–19.37: The conception of Isaac and the destruction of Sodom. Chs 18 and 19 display a chiastic structure (ABB'A'): 18.1–15 is the annunciation of Isaac's conception (A); 18.16–33 is the announcement of Sodom's destruction (B); 19.1–29 reports the destruction of Sodom (B'); and 19.30–38 reports Moab's and Ammon's conception (A'). In the process, Abraham emerges again as a heroic figure, one who deeply reveres God yet politely demands justice from Him. Lot is once again (as in ch 13) a foil for Abraham— self-interested, passive, and, finally, victimized. **18.1–2:** The relationship of the LORD to the men is unclear. Perhaps, as in some Canaanite literature, we are to imagine a deity accompanied by his two attendants (cf. 22.2). **3–8:** Note the contrast between Abraham's self-deprecating language (*a little water, a morsel*) and the enormous efforts to which he goes to serve his guests. **9–18:** Source analysis identifies this as the J parallel to the annunciation of Isaac's birth in ch 17 (P). Note that in 17.17 it is Abraham, whereas in 18.12 it is Sarah, who laughs (and thus gives Isaac his name). **13:** The LORD's citation to Abraham of Sarah's monologue in the preceding verse is not quite accurate (*old as I am* as opposed to *with my husband so old*). "Great is peace," remarks a rabbi in the Talmud about this point, "for even the Holy One (blessed be He) made a change on account of it," sparing the couple the discord that might have come had Abraham known Sarah's true thought (*b. B. M.* 87a).

---

a Or "My Lord."   b Cf. Gen. 17.21; 2 Kings 4.16–17.

16 The men set out from there and looked down toward Sodom, Abraham walking with them to see them off. 17 Now the LORD had said, "Shall I hide from Abraham what I am about to do, 18 since Abraham is to become a great and populous nation and all the nations of the earth are to bless themselves by him? 19 For I have singled him out, that he may instruct his children and his posterity to keep the way of the LORD by doing what is just and right, in order that the LORD may bring about for Abraham what He has promised him." 20 Then the LORD said, "The outrage of Sodom and Gomorrah is so great, and their sin so grave! 21 I will go down to see whether they have acted altogether according to the outcry that has reached Me; if not, I will take note."

22 The men went on from there to Sodom, while Abraham remained standing before the LORD. 23 Abraham came forward and said, "Will You sweep away the innocent along with the guilty? 24 What if there should be fifty innocent within the city; will You then wipe out the place and not forgive it for the sake of the innocent fifty who are in it? 25 Far be it from You to do such a thing, to bring death upon the innocent as well as the guilty, so that innocent and guilty fare alike. Far be it from You! Shall not the Judge of all the earth deal justly?" 26 And the LORD answered, "If I find within the city of Sodom fifty innocent ones, I will forgive the whole place for their sake."

27 Abraham spoke up, saying, "Here I venture to speak to my Lord, I who am but dust and ashes: 28 What if the fifty innocent should lack five? Will You destroy the whole city for want of the five?" And He answered, "I will not destroy if I find forty-five there." 29 But he spoke to Him again, and said, "What if forty should be found there?" And He answered, "I will not do it, for the sake of the forty." 30 And he said, "Let not my Lord be angry if I go on: What if thirty should be found there?" And He answered, "I will not do it if I find thirty there." 31 And he said, "I venture again to speak to my Lord: What if twenty should be found there?" And He answered, "I will not destroy, for the sake of the twenty." 32 And he said, "Let not my Lord be angry if I speak but this last time: What if ten should be found there?" And He answered, "I will not destroy, for the sake of the ten."

33 When the LORD had finished speaking to Abraham, He departed; and Abraham returned to his place.

19 The two angels arrived in Sodom in the evening, as Lot was sitting in the gate of Sodom. When Lot saw them, he rose to greet them and, bowing low with his face

16–33: In this section, God treats Abraham as a prophet (cf. 20.7), disclosing His plans to him (vv. 17–21; cf. Amos 3.7), and Abraham, like one of the prophets of Israel, eloquently demands justice from God (vv. 23–25; cf. Jer. 12.1–4) and pleads for mercy (Gen. 18.26–32; cf. Amos 7.1–6). 24: Notice that Abraham's demand is not that the guilty be punished and the innocent spared, but rather that the LORD *forgive* [the entire city] *for the sake of the innocent . . . who are in it.* The point is made more explicit in v. 26. The underlying theology maintains that the righteous effect deliverance for the entire community. This idea, found elsewhere in the Tanakh (e.g., Jer. 5.1), is prominent in rabbinic literature, where it underlies the notion of the thirty-six righteous individuals for whose sake the world endures. Other biblical texts such as Ezek. 14.12–23; ch 18, however, insist upon individual responsibility and retribution. 27: Recognizing the sovereignty of God and his own subordinate status, Abraham speaks with great deference and scrupulously avoids chutzpah (also in vv. 30–32). The Talmud remarks about this verse, "The Holy One (blessed be He) said to Israel, I deeply love you, for even when I give you abundant greatness, you make yourselves small before Me. I gave greatness to Abraham, and he said *I who am but dust and ashes*" (b. Ḥul. 89a). 19.1–3: The contrast between Abraham and Lot (discussed above, on ch 13) continues. Whereas Abraham sees the LORD (18.1), Lot sees only His two angelic attendants (19.1). Whereas Abraham runs to greet his visitors (18.2), Lot only rises (19.1). Whereas Abraham offers a sumptuous feast (18.6–8), Lot offers *unleavened bread* (19.3).

to the ground, ²he said, "Please, my lords, turn aside to your servant's house to spend the night, and bathe your feet; then you may be on your way early." But they said, "No, we will spend the night in the square." ³But he urged them strongly, so they turned his way and entered his house. He prepared a feast for them and baked unleavened bread, and they ate.

⁴They had not yet lain down, when the townspeople, the men of Sodom, young and old—all the people to the last man—gathered about the house. ⁵And they shouted to Lot and said to him, "Where are the men who came to you tonight? Bring them out to us, that we may be intimate with them." ⁶So Lot went out to them to the entrance, shut the door behind him, ⁷and said, "I beg you, my friends, do not commit such a wrong. ⁸Look, I have two daughters who have not known a man. Let me bring them out to you, and you may do to them as you please; but do not do anything to these men, since they have come under the shelter of my roof." ⁹But they said, "Stand back! The fellow," they said, "came here as an alien, and already he acts the ruler! Now we will deal worse with you than with them." And they pressed hard against the person of Lot, and moved forward to break the door. ¹⁰But the men stretched out their hands and pulled Lot into the house with them, and shut the door. ¹¹And the people who were at the entrance of the house, young and old, they struck with blinding light, so that they were helpless to find the entrance.

¹²Then the men said to Lot, "Whom else have you here? Sons-in-law, your sons and daughters, or anyone else that you have in the city—bring them out of the place. ¹³For we are about to destroy this place; because the outcry against them before the LORD has become so great that the LORD has sent us to destroy it." ¹⁴So Lot went out and spoke to his sons-in-law, who had married his daughters, and said, "Up, get out of this place, for the LORD is about to destroy the city." But he seemed to his sons-in-law as one who jests.

¹⁵As dawn broke, the angels urged Lot on, saying, "Up, take your wife and your two remaining daughters, lest you be swept away because of the iniquity of the city." ¹⁶Still he delayed. So the men seized his hand, and the hands of his wife and his two daughters—in the LORD's mercy on him—and brought him out and left him outside the city. ¹⁷When they had brought them outside, one said, "Flee for your life! Do not look behind you, nor stop anywhere in the Plain; flee to the hills, lest you be swept away." ¹⁸But Lot said to them, "Oh no, my lord! ¹⁹You

4–5: The story in Judg. 19.10–30 is quite possibly patterned after this episode. The wrong that the men of Sodom attempt involves not only the sin of homosexual conduct (defined as an "abhorrence" in Lev. 18.22), but also a gross violation of the conventions of hospitality. According to one opinion in the Mishnah, a lack of generosity is characteristic of Sodom, as epitomized in the saying, "What is mine is mine; what is yours is yours" (*m. ʾAvot* 5.10; cf. Ezek. 16.46–50). **7–8:** Lot's offer of his two daughters is surely connected to the tragicomic scene at the end of the chapter when they get him drunk and engage in incestuous relations with him (19.30–38). **10:** Lot's passivity is patent and contrasts with Abraham's daring challenge to God's justice in the previous chapter (18.22–33). Gen. 19.29 will make it explicit that Lot's escape is owing not to his own deeply irresolute character, but to God's reliable commitment to Abraham. **14:** Whereas Abraham, taking the impending destruction with the utmost seriousness, functions prophetically in hopes of averting the catastrophe, Lot is taken for a buffoon even by his own sons-in-law and cannot save them. Since Lot's two daughters mentioned in v. 8 are unmarried, these sons-in-law are either engaged to them (so the Vulgate and Rashi) or married to two other daughters, who die in the conflagration along with their husbands. **15–22:** Lot's weakness and inconstancy would have done him in, had it not been for *the LORD's mercy on him* (v. 16). His weakness and self-interest, however, result in the sparing of one town (vv. 18–22), whereas Abraham's audacious and principled intervention (18.22–33) proved unable to save anyone.

have been so gracious to your servant, and have already shown me so much kindness in order to save my life; but I cannot flee to the hills, lest the disaster overtake me and I die. ²⁰ Look, that town there is near enough to flee to; it is such a little place! Let me flee there—it is such a little place—and let my life be saved." ²¹ He replied, "Very well, I will grant you this favor too, and I will not annihilate the town of which you have spoken. ²² Hurry, flee there, for I cannot do anything until you arrive there." Hence the town came to be called Zoar.^a

²³ As the sun rose upon the earth and Lot entered Zoar, ²⁴ the LORD rained upon Sodom and Gomorrah sulfurous fire from the LORD out of heaven. ²⁵ He annihilated those cities and the entire Plain, and all the inhabitants of the cities and the vegetation of the ground. ²⁶ Lot's^b wife looked back,^c and she thereupon turned into a pillar of salt.

²⁷ Next morning, Abraham hurried to the place where he had stood before the LORD, ²⁸ and, looking down toward Sodom and Gomorrah and all the land of the Plain, he saw the smoke of the land rising like the smoke of a kiln.

²⁹ Thus it was that, when God destroyed the cities of the Plain and annihilated the cities where Lot dwelt, God was mindful of Abraham and removed Lot from the midst of the upheaval.

³⁰ Lot went up from Zoar and settled in the hill country with his two daughters, for he was afraid to dwell in Zoar; and he and his two daughters lived in a cave. ³¹ And the older one said to the younger, "Our father is old, and there is not a man on earth to consort with us in the way of all the world. ³² Come, let us make our father drink wine, and let us lie with him, that we may maintain life through our father." ³³ That night they made their father drink wine, and the older one went in and lay with her father; he did not know when she lay down or when she rose. ³⁴ The next day the older one said to the younger, "See, I lay with Father last night; let us make him drink wine tonight also, and you go and lie with him, that we may maintain life through our father." ³⁵ That night also they made their father drink wine, and the younger one went and lay with him; he did not know when she lay down or when she rose.

³⁶ Thus the two daughters of Lot came to be with child by their father. ³⁷ The older one bore a son and named him Moab;^d he is the father of the Moabites of today. ³⁸ And the younger also bore a son, and she called him Ben-ammi;^e he is the father of the Ammonites of today.

26: The report of the fate of Lot's wife serves as an explanation for salt formations still evident in the vicinity of the Dead Sea. **30–38:** This passage has strong affinities with the story of Ham's sin in 9.20–27. Here, however, it is possible to construct a defense of Lot's daughters on the grounds that they genuinely and plausibly believed that the human race would die out unless they bore children from the one surviving male, their hapless father (vv. 31–32). The passage is partly a comic inversion of the opening of this two-chapter section, which centers on the unlikely birth of a son to Sarah (18.1–15). Note the similarity of Sarah's remark "with my husband so old" (18.12) and the older daughter's words, *our father is old* (19.31). Gen. 19.30–38 provides an unflattering account of the origins of two of Israel's traditional enemies, the Moabites and the Ammonites (cf. Deut. 23.4–7). Nonetheless, a midrash sees in these acts the origins of two of the great mothers of Israel, the Moabite Ruth, ancestor of King David (Ruth 4.13–22), and the Ammonite Naamah, wife of King Solomon and mother of his successor King Rehoboam (1 Kings 14.21). "I found David" (Ps. 89.21), a rabbi observed. "Where did He find him?—in Sodom!" A seed of messianic redemption thus lies in the squalid events of Gen. 19.30–38 (*Gen. Rab.* 41.4).

20.1–17: Abraham and Sarah in Abimelech's court. Attributed by source criticism to the Elohist (E), this episode parallels the accounts of Abram and Sarai in Pharaoh's court in 12.10–20 and of Isaac and Rebekah in Abimelech's court in 26.1–11 (both ascribed to J). In this version, the emphasis lies on points of law and ethics and on the motivation of the protagonists, and the moral and psychological situation is much more complex than in either of the parallel narratives. **3–7:** Even though Abimelech has not consummated his relationship with Sarah (v. 6), he is still culpable for abducting another

---

^a Connected with miṣʿar *"a little place," v. 20.*　　^b Lit. "His."　　^c Lit. "behind him."
^d As though me-ʾab *"from (my) father."*　　^e As though "son of my (paternal) kindred."

20 Abraham journeyed from there to the region of the Negeb and settled between Kadesh and Shur. While he was sojourning in Gerar, ²Abraham said of Sarah his wife, "She is my sister." So King Abimelech of Gerar had Sarah brought to him. ³But God came to Abimelech in a dream by night and said to him, "You are to die because of the woman that you have taken, for she is a married woman." ⁴Now Abimelech had not approached her. He said, "O Lord, will You slay people even though innocent? ⁵He himself said to me, 'She is my sister!' And she also said, 'He is my brother.' When I did this, my heart was blameless and my hands were clean." ⁶And God said to him in the dream, "I knew that you did this with a blameless heart, and so I kept you from sinning against Me. That was why I did not let you touch her. ⁷Therefore, restore the man's wife—since he is a prophet, he will intercede for you—to save your life. If you fail to restore her, know that you shall die, you and all that are yours."

⁸Early next morning, Abimelech called his servants and told them all that had happened; and the men were greatly frightened. ⁹Then Abimelech summoned Abraham and said to him, "What have you done to us? What wrong have I done that you should bring so great a guilt upon me and my kingdom? You have done to me things that ought not to be done. ¹⁰What, then," Abimelech demanded of Abraham, "was your purpose in doing this thing?" ¹¹"I thought," said Abraham, "surely there is no fear of God in this place, and they will kill me because of my wife. ¹²And besides, she is in truth my sister, my father's daughter though not my mother's; and she became my wife. ¹³So when God made me wander from my father's house, I said to her, 'Let this be the kindness that you shall do me: whatever place we come to, say there of me: He is my brother.' "

¹⁴Abimelech took sheep and oxen, and male and female slaves, and gave them to Abraham; and he restored his wife Sarah to him. ¹⁵And Abimelech said, "Here, my land is before you; settle wherever you please." ¹⁶And to Sarah he said, "I herewith give your brother a thousand pieces of silver; this will serve you as vindication^a before all who are with you, and you are cleared before everyone." ¹⁷Abraham then prayed to God, and God healed Abimelech and his wife and his slave girls, so that they bore children; ¹⁸for the LORD had closed fast every womb of the household of Abimelech because of Sarah, the wife of Abraham.

man's wife (v. 3). V. 7 implies that he may still harbor erotic aspirations toward Sarah and may lack a full understanding of just who Abraham is. **8:** The servants' fear gives the lie to Abraham's attempt at self-exoneration on the grounds that "there is no fear of God in this place" (v. 11). **9–10:** The image of a Gentile king righteously upbraiding an Israelite prophet (v. 7) for the latter's moral failures is a fine comic inversion of our expectations. **12:** Abraham tries a new line of defense based on a semantic ambiguity: Since *sister* can mean "half-sister" (e.g., Lev. 18.9), he really was not lying. But was Sarah even his half-sister? On the plain sense of the biblical text, there is no evidence that she was. Ibn Ezra thinks that with this claim, Abraham simply "put Abimelech off according to the need of the moment." A midrash, however, identifies Iscah, Abraham's niece (11.29), with Sarah and thus makes Abraham's father Sarah's grandfather (*b. Meg.* 14a). Since "father" in ancient Heb could also mean grandfather (e.g., 28.13), this midrash serves to validate Abraham's defense. Ramban notes that even if Sarah really was Abraham's half-sister, Abraham was still in the wrong for not mentioning the vastly more important point that she was his wife. **17:** "Pray" in biblical Heb very often denotes intercession. Abraham is the first person called a prophet in the Bible, and here functions as a prophetic intercessor, as God predicted he would in v. 7. **18:** This conclusion is less surprising than it first seems. It is consistent with 12.17, which speaks of the LORD's afflicting "Pharaoh and his household with mighty plagues" in the analogous situation. It also correlates with the harsh tone that God takes when He first confronts Abimelech in 20.3. Though God recognizes the king's innocence, He also takes special measures to ensure that no untoward act occurs (v. 6).

a Lit. "a covering of the eyes"; meaning of latter half of verse uncertain.

21 The LORD took note of Sarah as He had promised, and the LORD did for Sarah as He had spoken. ²Sarah conceived and bore a son to Abraham in his old age, at the set time of which God had spoken. ³Abraham gave his newborn son, whom Sarah had borne him, the name of Isaac. ⁴And when his son Isaac was eight days old, Abraham circumcised him, as God had commanded him. ⁵Now Abraham was a hundred years old when his son Isaac was born to him. ⁶Sarah said, "God has brought me laughter; everyone who hears will laugh with[a] me." ⁷And she added,

> "Who would have said to Abraham
> That Sarah would suckle children!
> Yet I have borne a son in his old age."

⁸The child grew up and was weaned, and Abraham held a great feast on the day that Isaac was weaned.

⁹Sarah saw the son whom Hagar the Egyptian had borne to Abraham playing. ¹⁰She said to Abraham, "Cast out that slave-woman and her son, for the son of that slave shall not share in the inheritance with my son Isaac." ¹¹The matter distressed Abraham greatly, for it concerned a son of his. ¹²But God said to Abraham, "Do not be distressed over the boy or your slave; whatever Sarah tells you, do as she says, for it is through Isaac that offspring shall be continued[b] for you. ¹³As for the son of the slave-woman, I will make a nation of him, too, for he is your seed."

¹⁴Early next morning Abraham took some bread and a skin of water, and gave them to Hagar. He placed them over her shoulder, together with the child, and sent her away. And she wandered about in the wilderness of Beer-sheba. ¹⁵When the water was gone from the skin, she left the child under one of the bushes, ¹⁶and went and sat down at a distance, a bowshot away; for she thought, "Let me not look on as the child dies." And sitting thus afar, she burst into tears.

¹⁷God heard the cry of the boy, and an angel of God

---

a Lit. "for."   b Lit. "called."

and three in Canaan after Isaac's birth (25.7). The period of his life in which Abraham lived with the promise unfulfilled, though the shortest, is the pivotal and central one and occupies the most space in the narrative.

21.9–21: The expulsion of Ishmael and Hagar. This passage closely parallels ch 16. Source criticism accounts for this by attributing ch 16 to J, but 21.9–21 to E. Note that the J-name ("LORD") never appears here; the E-name ("God") is used throughout. **9:** *Playing* is another pun on Isaac's name (cf. 17.17; 18.12; 19.14; 26.8). Ishmael was "Isaacing," or "taking Isaac's place." **10:** Sarah's omission of the names of the two individuals who have aroused her jealousy indicates the depth of her contempt. **12:** Yet it is Sarah's protection of Isaac's rights, rather than Abraham's solicitude for Ishmael, that mediates God's will in this tragic situation (cf. ch 27). In the Talmud, this is cited as evidence that Sarah was a prophet (*b. Meg.* 14a). God's command to Abraham to *do as she says* uses the same term with which He rebuked Adam for obeying Eve in 3.17— only with the opposite intent. **13:** Like 17.20 (and 21.18), this verse stresses that Isaac does not altogether displace Ishmael (whatever Sarah's designs). Ishmael inherits a substantial portion of the promise to his father Abraham. **14:** There is room to wonder just how far Abraham expected Hagar and Ishmael to travel before the bread and skin of water gave out. Did he not realize that by provisioning them so slimly, he was putting them in mortal danger? Ibn Ezra, surmising that Sarah must have determined the provisions, concludes that had Abraham done otherwise, he would have violated God's command. **15–16:** The narrator presupposes a child small enough to be carried by his mother. But since Ishmael was 13 before Isaac was even conceived (17.25), and Isaac's weaning, which likely occurred at 3, has already taken place (21.8), Ishmael

21.1–8: The promise to Sarah fulfilled at last. With its heavy emphasis on God's fulfillment of His promise of a son to Sarah and Abraham (vv. 1–2) and its note that the father circumcised his son on the eighth day in accordance with God's command (v. 3), this passage marks a major turning point in the story. Despite seemingly insurmountable obstacles (including Abimelech's abduction

of Sarah in the previous chapter), things have gone according to plan. A midrash reports that it was on Rosh Ha-Shanah that *The LORD took note of Sarah* (*b. Rosh Hash.* 11a); Gen. ch 21 is thus the Torah reading for the first day of Rosh Ha-Shanah. **5:** Abraham's life divides into seven periods of 25 years each: three of them in Mesopotamia (12.4), one in Canaan without the promised son (21.5), called to Hagar from heaven and said to her, "What troubles you, Hagar? Fear not, for God has heeded the cry of the boy where he is. [18]Come, lift up the boy and hold him by the hand, for I will make a great nation of him." [19]Then God opened her eyes and she saw a well of water. She went and filled the skin with water, and let the boy drink. [20]God was with the boy and he grew up; he dwelt in the wilderness and became a bowman. [21]He lived in the wilderness of Paran; and his mother got a wife for him from the land of Egypt.

[22]At that time Abimelech and Phicol, chief of his troops, said to Abraham, "God is with you in everything that you do. [23]Therefore swear to me here by God that you will not deal falsely with me or with my kith and kin, but will deal with me and with the land in which you have sojourned as loyally as I have dealt with you." [24]And Abraham said, "I swear it."

[25]Then Abraham reproached Abimelech for the well of water which the servants of Abimelech had seized. [26]But Abimelech said, "I do not know who did this; you did not tell me, nor have I heard of it until today." [27]Abraham took sheep and oxen and gave them to Abimelech, and the two of them made a pact. [28]Abraham then set seven ewes of the flock by themselves, [29]and Abimelech said to Abraham, "What mean these seven ewes which you have set apart?" [30]He replied, "You are to accept these seven ewes from me as proof that I dug this well." [31]Hence that place was called Beer-sheba,[a] for there the two of them swore an oath. [32]When they had concluded the pact at Beer-sheba, Abimelech and Phicol, chief of his troops, departed and returned to the land of the Philistines. [33][Abraham] planted a tamarisk at Beer-sheba, and invoked there the name of the LORD, the Everlasting God. [34]And Abraham resided in the land of the Philistines a long time.

22 Some time afterward, God put Abraham to the test. He said to him, "Abraham," and he answered, "Here I am." [2]And He said, "Take your son, your favored one, Isaac, whom you love, and go to the land of Moriah, and offer him there as a burnt offering on one of the

a I.e., "well of seven" or "well of oath."

is at least 16. In an analysis informed by source criticism, the problem is easily explained, since the present narrative stems from E, but the chronology from P. Calcu-

lating Ishmael's age as 27, a midrash takes a different tack: Sarah had cast the evil eye on him and made him ill, thus incapable of walking (*Gen. Rab.* 53.12).

21.22–34: Abimelech and Abraham make a pact. The focus shifts from the promise of offspring, on whose fulfillment the chapter has so far focused, to the promise of land, as Abraham acquires rights to wells he has dug. Abimelech appears here as another important figure who recognizes Abraham's special status and prospers as a result (cf. 14.18–20; 23.6–16). The passage has close affinities with 26.26–31.

22.1–19: Abraham's last and greatest test. This magnificently told story, known in Judaism as the "'Akedah" ("binding"), is one of the gems of biblical narrative. It also comes to occupy a central role in rabbinic theology and eventually to be incorporated into the daily liturgy. Jewish tradition regards the 'Akedah as the tenth and climactic test of Abraham, the first Jew. **1:** There is no good English equivalent for the Heb "hineni," translated in this verse as *Here I am.* The term indicates readiness, alertness, attentiveness, receptivity, and responsiveness to instructions. It serves as a kind of refrain throughout the 'Akedah. Abraham employs it in answer to God here, to Isaac in v. 7 (where it is rendered as "Yes"), and to the angel of the LORD in v. 11. **2:** The order of the Heb is "your son, your favored one, the one whom you love, Isaac" and indicates increasing tension. Not only is Isaac the son upon whom Abraham's life has centered; he also loves him. If Abraham did not love Isaac, the commandment to sacrifice him would not have constituted much of a test. The expression *go to* ("lekh-lekha"), which otherwise occurs only in 12.1, the initial command to Abraham, ties this narrative to the beginning of Abraham's dealings with God. Note also the parallel of *on one of the heights that I will point out to you* with "to the land that I will show you" (12.1). The location of Moriah (here the name of a land, not a mountain) is unknown. The late biblical book of Chronicles calls the Temple Mount in Jerusalem "Moriah" (2 Chroniheights that I will point out to you." ³ So early next morning, Abraham saddled his ass and took with him two of his servants and his son Isaac. He split the wood for the burnt offering, and he set out for the place of which God had told him. ⁴ On the third day Abraham looked up and saw the place from afar. ⁵ Then Abraham said to his servants, "You stay here with the ass. The boy and I will go up there; we will worship and we will return to you."

⁶ Abraham took the wood for the burnt offering and put it on his son Isaac. He himself took the firestone*a* and the knife; and the two walked off together. ⁷ Then Isaac said to his father Abraham, "Father!" And he answered, "Yes, my son." And he said, "Here are the firestone and the wood; but where is the sheep for the burnt offering?" ⁸ And Abraham said, "God will see to the sheep for His burnt offering, my son." And the two of them walked on together.

⁹ They arrived at the place of which God had told him. Abraham built an altar there; he laid out the wood; he bound his son Isaac; he laid him on the altar, on top of the wood. ¹⁰ And Abraham picked up the knife to slay his son. ¹¹ Then an angel of the LORD called to him from heaven: "Abraham! Abraham!" And he answered, "Here I am." ¹² And he said, "Do not raise your hand against the boy, or do anything to him. For now I know that you fear God, since you have not withheld your son, your favored one, from Me." ¹³ When Abraham looked up, his eye fell upon a*b* ram, caught in the thicket by its horns. So Abraham went and took the ram and offered it up as a burnt offering in place of his son. ¹⁴ And Abraham named that site

---

a Lit. "fire."

b Reading 'eḥad with many Heb. mss. and ancient versions; text 'aḥar "after."

---

cles 3.1), perhaps on the understanding that the ʿAkedah is the foundation legend for the service of God that took place there. **3:** The verse resembles 21.14. The expulsion of Ishmael in the preceding chapter and the ʿAkedah have much in common, but the latter is the more wrenching, since Abraham is directly commanded to sacrifice his son, and the angelic intervention (vv. 11–12) is thus more surprising. Some have wondered why Abraham, who protested God's apparent decision to destroy the innocent with the guilty in Sodom (18.22–32), here

obeys without objection. The essence of the answer is that the context in ch 18 is forensic, whereas the context of the ʿAkedah is sacrificial. A sacrifice is not an execution, and in a sacrificial context the unblemished condition of the one offered does not detract from, but rather commends, the act. **5:** Abraham may be concealing the truth from his servants (lest they prevent him from carrying out God's will), from Isaac (lest he flee), and from himself (lest the frank acknowledgement of his real intention cause his resolve to break). Alternately, he may be ex-

pressing his profound trust in God's promise, casting his faith and hope as a prediction. **6:** The image of Isaac's carrying the wood on which he is to be burned adds enormous power to the story. A midrash relates this to a Roman (not Jewish) method of execution that was sometimes used on Jewish martyrs: "It is like a person who carries his cross on his own shoulder" (*Gen. Rab.* 56.3). **7:** Our ignorance of Isaac's age makes it difficult to interpret his poignant question. Most rabbinic commentators see him as an adult and thus a willing participant in his own sacrifice—the prototype, that is, of the Jewish martyr. **8:** The same possibilities that we outlined for v. 5 apply here as well. The verse ends with the same Heb words with which v. 6 ends. Even after their exchange, father and son still have a single resolve: "the one to bind, and the other to be bound; the one to sacrifice, and the other to be sacrificed" (*Gen. Rab.* 56.3). **12:** In the Tanakh, the "fear of God" denotes an active obedience to the divine will. God is now able to call the last trial of Abraham off because Abraham has demonstrated that this obedience is uppermost for him, surpassing even his paternal love for Isaac. **13:** The substitution of a male sheep for the firstborn son has parallels in the ancient Near East and foreshadows the story of the paschal lamb (Exod. 12.1–42). Contrary to a widespread misperception, however, the story is not about the superiority of animal to human sacrifice, nor is it a polemic against human sacrifice. Note that God commands the sacrifice of Isaac at the beginning of the story (v. 22.2) and commends and rewards Abraham for being willing to carry it through at the end (vv. 12, 15–18). A midrash has Abraham praying that God "see the blood of this ram as if it were the blood of my son Isaac, the entrails of this ram as if they were the entrails of my son Isaac" (*Gen. Rab.* 56.9). **14:** The name of the otherwise unattested site plays on Abraham's words in v. 8. This enigmatic verse may connect the site of the ʿAkedah

Adonai-yireh,[a] whence the present saying, "On the mount of the Lord there is vision."[b]

[15] The angel of the Lord called to Abraham a second time from heaven, [16] and said, "By Myself I swear, the Lord declares: Because you have done this and have not withheld your son, your favored one, [17] I will bestow My blessing upon you and make your descendants as numerous as the stars of heaven and the sands on the seashore; and your descendants shall seize the gates of their foes. [18] All the nations of the earth shall bless themselves by your descendants, because you have obeyed My command." [19] Abraham then returned to his servants, and they departed together for Beer-sheba; and Abraham stayed in Beer-sheba.

[20] Some time later, Abraham was told, "Milcah too has borne children to your brother Nahor: [21] Uz the first-born, and Buz his brother, and Kemuel the father of Aram; [22] and Chesed, Hazo, Pildash, Jidlaph, and Bethuel"— [23] Bethuel being the father of Rebekah. These eight Milcah bore to Nahor, Abraham's brother. [24] And his concubine, whose name was Reumah, also bore children: Tebah, Gaham, Tahash, and Maacah.

ḤAYYEI SARAH

חיי שרה

23 Sarah's lifetime—the span of Sarah's life—came to one hundred and twenty-seven years. [2] Sarah died in Kiriath-arba—now Hebron—in the land of Canaan; and Abraham proceeded to mourn for Sarah and to bewail her. [3] Then Abraham rose from beside his dead, and spoke to the Hittites, saying, [4] "I am a resident alien among you; sell me a burial site among you, that I may remove my dead for burial." [5] And the Hittites replied to Abraham, saying to him, [6] "Hear us, my lord: you are the elect of God among us. Bury your dead in the choicest of our burial places; none of us will withhold his burial place from you for burying your dead." [7] Thereupon Abraham

---

a I.e., "the Lord will see"; cf. v. 8.   b Heb. Behar Adonai yera'eh.

---

to the Temple mount (see v. 2 n.). **15–18:** The second angelic address conveys the Lord's final blessing on Abraham, picking up the language of several earlier addresses (cf. 12.3; 13.16; 15.5). Only this time, the earlier promises are reinterpreted as a consequence of the 'Akedah. Much Jewish prayer calls upon God to remember the 'Akedah for the benefit of Abra-

ham's descendants. **19:** Too much should not be made of the omission of Isaac. The story closes where it opened (v. 1): with the focus on Abraham alone.

22.20–24: The children of Nahor. Like Abraham's as yet unborn grandson, Jacob/Israel (35.22b–26), his brother Nahor becomes the patriarch of eight chil-

dren by his primary wife and four by his secondary wife. Rebekah, who will marry Isaac and thus become the second matriarch of Israel, is the only person of her generation mentioned here (v. 23). One senses that the promise of descendants reiterated and reinterpreted in v. 17 is already on its way to fulfillment. Note the near-identity of v. 17b with the blessing on Rebekah in 24.60.

23.1–20: Abraham acquires a burial ground. After the climactic episode of the 'Akedah, all Abraham's actions are in the nature of putting his affairs in order. In ch 23, he acquires a burial plot for Sarah. In the next chapter, he arranges for a wife for Isaac, and in ch 25, he decrees the distribution of his assets and passes away. **2:** Hebron, in the hill country of Judah, 20 miles south-southwest of Jerusalem, was also the first seat of David's kingship (2 Sam. 2.1–4; 5.1–5). Its principal claim upon the Jewish imagination over the centuries is owing to the biblical reports that not only Sarah but also Abraham, Isaac and Rebekah, and Jacob and Leah are buried there (Gen. 23.19; 35.27; 49.29–32; 50.13). **3:** The "Hittites" mentioned here probably have no connection to the Indo-European peoples with that name who ruled a mighty empire based in what is now eastern Turkey in the second millennium BCE. Rather, they are more likely to be one of the Canaanite nations (cf. 10.15; 15.20). **4–6:** The tension in the story lies in Abraham's contradictory status. On the one hand, he is but a *resident alien* without hereditary land-rights or a secure place in the social and legal order. On the other, he is *the elect of God* (v. 5), to whom the whole land has been promised. Elsewhere in the Tanakh, the entire people Israel is described as resident aliens, living on land owned by God (Lev. 25.23), and the same terms are used to describe the transience of human life and the unworthiness of human beings in the face of God's bounty (2 Chron. 29.15). **7–8:** As a "resident alien," Abrabowed low to the people of the land, the Hittites, [8] and he said to them, "If it is your wish that I remove my dead for burial, you must agree to intercede for me with Ephron son of Zohar. [9] Let him sell me the cave of Machpelah that he owns, which is at the edge of his land. Let him sell it to me, at the full price, for a burial site in your midst."

[10] Ephron was present among the Hittites; so Ephron the Hittite answered Abraham in the hearing of the Hittites, all who entered the gate of his town,[a] saying, [11] "No, my lord, hear me: I give you the field and I give you the cave that is in it; I give it to you in the presence of my people. Bury your dead." [12] Then Abraham bowed low before the people of the land, [13] and spoke to Ephron in the hearing of the people of the land, saying, "If only you would hear me out! Let me pay the price of the land; accept it from me, that I may bury my dead there." [14] And Ephron replied to Abraham, saying to him, [15] "My lord, do hear me! A piece of land worth four hundred shekels of silver—what is that between you and me? Go and bury your dead." [16] Abraham accepted Ephron's terms. Abraham paid out to Ephron the money that he had named in the hearing of the Hittites—four hundred shekels of silver at the going merchants' rate.

[17] So Ephron's land in Machpelah, near Mamre—the field with its cave and all the trees anywhere within the confines of that field—passed [18] to Abraham as his possession, in the presence of the Hittites, of all who entered the gate of his town.[a] [19] And then Abraham buried his wife Sarah in the cave of the field of Machpelah, facing Mamre—now Hebron—in the land of Canaan. [20] Thus the field with its cave passed from the Hittites to Abraham, as a burial site.

24 Abraham was now old, advanced in years, and the LORD had blessed Abraham in all things. [2] And Abraham said to the senior servant of his household, who had charge of all that he owned, "Put your hand under my thigh [3] and I will make you swear by the LORD, the God of heaven and the God of the earth, that you will not take a wife for my son from the daughters of the Canaanites among whom I dwell, [4] but will go to the land of my birth and get a wife for my son Isaac." [5] And the servant said to him, "What if the woman does not consent to follow me to this land, shall I then take your son back to the land from which you came?" [6] Abraham answered him, "On no account must you take my son back there! [7] The

ham probably needed the approval of *the people of the land* (a local council) before he could approach a landowner. **10–16:** It would not behoove Abraham, as "the elect of God" (v. 5) and a man of exemplary generosity and hospitality (13.8–9; 18.1–8), to accept a gift (cf. 14.23–24). It is hard to know what the field and its cave were worth on the market. Compared to the 17 shekels that Jeremiah pays to redeem ancestral land (Jer. 32.9), the price of 400 shekels that Abraham paid (v. 16) seems exorbitant, and thus Ephron's statement in v. 15 seems disingenuous.

24.1–67: Abraham procures a proper wife for Isaac. This sophisticated and beautifully wrought narrative constitutes the longest chapter in Genesis. In certain important ways, it functions as Abraham's deathbed scene, recapitulating the promise that impelled him on his course and foreshadowing events in the life of his grandson Jacob/Israel, eponymous ancestor of the Jewish people. **2:** The rabbinic tradition assumes that Abraham's *senior servant* is Eliezer, but the latter is never termed a "servant" (15.2–4), and precise identification of the man, unnamed throughout the story, is unnecessary. *Thigh* seems to be a euphemism for the male organ (cf. 46.26; Exod. 1.5). Perhaps by touching it, the person swearing the oath calls sterility or loss of children upon himself, should he violate it. The parallel in Gen. 47.29 suggests that ch 24 once functioned as Abraham's last request. **3:** Intermarriage with the Canaanites, a lethal threat to Abraham's identity and destiny, is strictly forbidden in Deut. 7.1–4. The prohibition is extended to intermarriage with other groups in Ezra chs 9–10. **4:** The phrasing rather precisely recalls God's original commandment to Abraham in 12.1 (cf. 24.7, 38, 40). Similarly, Rebekah's consent ("I will [go]," v. 58) recalls God's first word to Abraham in that same verse, "Go." Rebekah thus becomes a kind of

a I.e., all his fellow townsmen.

LORD, the God of heaven, who took me from my father's house and from my native land, who promised me on oath, saying, 'I will assign this land to your offspring'— He will send His angel before you, and you will get a wife for my son from there. ⁸ And if the woman does not consent to follow you, you shall then be clear of this oath to me; but do not take my son back there." ⁹ So the servant put his hand under the thigh of his master Abraham and swore to him as bidden.ᵃ

¹⁰ Then the servant took ten of his master's camels and set out, taking with him all the bounty of his master; and he made his way to Aram-naharaim, to the city of Nahor. ¹¹ He made the camels kneel down by the well outside the city, at evening time, the time when women come out to draw water. ¹² And he said, "O LORD, God of my master Abraham, grant me good fortune this day, and deal graciously with my master Abraham: ¹³ Here I stand by the spring as the daughters of the townsmen come out to draw water; ¹⁴ let the maiden to whom I say, 'Please, lower your jar that I may drink,' and who replies, 'Drink, and I will also water your camels'—let her be the one whom You have decreed for Your servant Isaac. Thereby shall I know that You have dealt graciously with my master."

¹⁵ He had scarcely finished speaking, when Rebekah, who was born to Bethuel, the son of Milcah the wife of Abraham's brother Nahor, came out with her jar on her shoulder. ¹⁶ The maiden was very beautiful, a virgin whom no man had known. She went down to the spring, filled her jar, and came up. ¹⁷ The servant ran toward her and said, "Please, let me sip a little water from your jar." ¹⁸ "Drink, my lord," she said, and she quickly lowered her jar upon her hand and let him drink. ¹⁹ When she had let him drink his fill, she said, "I will also draw for your camels, until they finish drinking." ²⁰ Quickly emptying her jar into the trough, she ran back to the well to draw, and she drew for all his camels.

²¹ The man, meanwhile, stood gazing at her, silently wondering whether the LORD had made his errand successful or not. ²² When the camels had finished drinking, the man took a gold nose-ring weighing a half-shekel,ᵇ and two gold bands for her arms, ten shekels in weight. ²³ "Pray tell me," he said, "whose daughter are you? Is there room in your father's house for us to spend the night?" ²⁴ She replied, "I am the daughter of Bethuel the son of Milcah, whom she bore to Nahor." ²⁵ And she went

Abraham-figure in her own right. Abraham's dispatch of his senior servant back to his native land and his kinfolk brings his story full circle and ensures his legacy will continue in the next generation.
14: Rashi points out the aptness of the sign that the servant requests: The woman appropriate to marry into Abraham's household must practice the extraordinary kindness and generosity characteristic of her future father-in-law.
20: Rebekah's running to serve the visitor (who has not yet introduced himself) recalls Abraham's response to the visit of the unidentified men in 18.6–7.

a Lit. "about this matter."   b Heb. beqaʿ.

on, "There is plenty of straw[a] and feed at home, and also room to spend the night." 26 The man bowed low in homage to the LORD 27 and said, "Blessed be the LORD, the God of my master Abraham, who has not withheld His steadfast faithfulness from my master. For I have been guided on my errand by the LORD, to the house of my master's kinsmen."

28 The maiden ran and told all this to her mother's household. 29 Now Rebekah had a brother whose name was Laban. Laban ran out to the man at the spring— 30 when he saw the nose-ring and the bands on his sister's arms, and when he heard his sister Rebekah say, "Thus the man spoke to me." He went up to the man, who was still standing beside the camels at the spring. 31 "Come in, O blessed of the LORD," he said, "why do you remain outside, when I have made ready the house and a place for the camels?" 32 So the man entered the house, and the camels were unloaded. The camels were given straw and feed, and water was brought to bathe his feet and the feet of the men with him. 33 But when food was set before him, he said, "I will not eat until I have told my tale." He said, "Speak, then."

34 "I am Abraham's servant," he began. 35 "The LORD has greatly blessed my master, and he has become rich: He has given him sheep and cattle, silver and gold, male and female slaves, camels and asses. 36 And Sarah, my master's wife, bore my master a son in her old age, and he has assigned to him everything he owns. 37 Now my master made me swear, saying, 'You shall not get a wife for my son from the daughters of the Canaanites in whose land I dwell; 38 but you shall go to my father's house, to my kindred, and get a wife for my son.' 39 And I said to my master, 'What if the woman does not follow me?' 40 He replied to me, 'The LORD, whose ways I have followed, will send His angel with you and make your errand successful; and you will get a wife for my son from my kindred, from my father's house. 41 Thus only shall you be freed from my adjuration: if, when you come to my kindred, they refuse you—only then shall you be freed from my adjuration.'

42 "I came today to the spring, and I said: O LORD, God of my master Abraham, if You would indeed grant success to the errand on which I am engaged! 43 As I stand by the spring of water, let the young woman who comes out to draw and to whom I say, 'Please, let me drink a little water from your jar,' 44 and who answers, 'You may drink,

30: Laban's instantaneous notice of the jewelry suggests the materialism and stinginess that he will display in dealing with his own son-in-law, Jacob (29.27; 31.14–16, 33–43) and contrasts with his sister's innate generosity.

a Heb. teben, *shredded straw, which in the East is mixed with feed; cf. v. 32.*

and I will also draw for your camels'—let her be the wife whom the Lord has decreed for my master's son.' 45 I had scarcely finished praying in my heart, when Rebekah came out with her jar on her shoulder, and went down to the spring and drew. And I said to her, 'Please give me a drink.' 46 She quickly lowered her jar and said, 'Drink, and I will also water your camels.' So I drank, and she also watered the camels. 47 I inquired of her, 'Whose daughter are you?' And she said, 'The daughter of Bethuel, son of Nahor, whom Milcah bore to him.' And I put the ring on her nose and the bands on her arms. 48 Then I bowed low in homage to the Lord and blessed the Lord, the God of my master Abraham, who led me on the right way to get the daughter of my master's brother for his son. 49 And now, if you mean to treat my master with true kindness, tell me; and if not, tell me also, that I may turn right or left."

50 Then Laban and Bethuel answered, "The matter was decreed by the Lord; we cannot speak to you bad or good. 51 Here is Rebekah before you; take her and go, and let her be a wife to your master's son, as the Lord has spoken." 52 When Abraham's servant heard their words, he bowed low to the ground before the Lord. 53 The servant brought out objects of silver and gold, and garments, and gave them to Rebekah; and he gave presents to her brother and her mother. 54 Then he and the men with him ate and drank, and they spent the night. When they arose next morning, he said, "Give me leave to go to my master." 55 But her brother and her mother said, "Let the maiden remain with us ᵃsome ten days;ᵃ then you may go." 56 He said to them, "Do not delay me, now that the Lord has made my errand successful. Give me leave that I may go to my master." 57 And they said, "Let us call the girl and ask for her reply." 58 They called Rebekah and said to her, "Will you go with this man?" And she said, "I will." 59 So they sent off their sister Rebekah and her nurse along with Abraham's servant and his men. 60 And they blessed Rebekah and said to her,

"O sister!
May you grow
Into thousands of myriads;
May your offspring seize
The gates of their foes."

61 Then Rebekah and her maids arose, mounted the camels, and followed the man. So the servant took Rebekah and went his way.

47: The servant reverses the order of events given in vv. 22–23 to give Rebekah's family the impression that it was her pedigree rather than her character that most commended her. **50:** The appearance of Bethuel here is very strange, since everywhere else in the chapter it is his son, Laban, sometimes together with the girl's mother, who conducts the negotiations (vv. 28–29, 53, 55, 59). Rabbi David Kimḥi (Radak), the great 13th-century Provençal scholar, suggests that Bethuel was aged and the management of the household had fallen upon Laban. **60:** The near-identity of the last two lines with the latter words of the angel after the ʿAkedah (end of 22.17) reinforces the appropriateness of Rebekah for Abraham's son and the providential nature of the match.

a-a Lit. "days or ten."

⁶²Isaac had just come back from the vicinity of Beer-lahai-roi, for he was settled in the region of the Negeb. ⁶³And Isaac went out walkingᵃ in the field toward evening and, looking up, he saw camels approaching. ⁶⁴Raising her eyes, Rebekah saw Isaac. She alighted from the camel ⁶⁵and said to the servant, "Who is that man walking in the field toward us?" And the servant said, "That is my master." So she took her veil and covered herself. ⁶⁶The servant told Isaac all the things that he had done. ⁶⁷Isaac then brought her into the tent of his mother Sarah, and he took Rebekah as his wife. Isaac loved her, and thus found comfort after his mother's death.

25 Abraham took another wife, whose name was Keturah. ²She bore him Zimran, Jokshan, Medan, Midian, Ishbak, and Shuah. ³Jokshan begot Sheba and Dedan. The descendants of Dedan were the Asshurim, the Letushim, and the Leummim. ⁴The descendants of Midian were Ephah, Epher, Enoch,ᵇ Abida, and Eldaah. All these were descendants of Keturah. ⁵Abraham willed all that he owned to Isaac; ⁶but to Abraham's sons by concubines Abraham gave gifts while he was still living, and he sent them away from his son Isaac eastward, to the land of the East.

⁷This was the total span of Abraham's life: one hundred and seventy-five years. ⁸And Abraham breathed his last, dying at a good ripe age, old and contented; and he was gathered to his kin. ⁹His sons Isaac and Ishmael buried him in the cave of Machpelah, in the field of Ephron son of Zohar the Hittite, facing Mamre, ¹⁰the field that Abraham had bought from the Hittites; there Abraham was buried, and Sarah his wife. ¹¹After the death of Abraham, God blessed his son Isaac. And Isaac settled near Beer-lahai-roi.

¹²This is the line of Ishmael, Abraham's son, whom Hagar the Egyptian, Sarah's slave, bore to Abraham. ¹³These are the names of the sons of Ishmael, by their names, in the order of their birth: Nebaioth, the first-born of Ishmael, Kedar, Adbeel, Mibsam, ¹⁴Mishma, Dumah, Massa, ¹⁵Hadad, Tema, Jetur, Naphish, and Kedmah. ¹⁶These are the sons of Ishmael and these are their names by their villages and by their encampments: twelve chieftains of as many tribes.—¹⁷These were the years of the life of Ishmael: one hundred and thirty-seven years; then he breathed his last and died, and was gathered to his kin.—

65: Everywhere else in the chapter, *my master* refers to Abraham, and Isaac has been called "his/my master's son." Perhaps Abraham has died while his steward was on his sacred mission. If so, the events narrated in 25.1–18 had happened beforehand.

25.1–18: Abraham's death and descendants. Abraham's descendants are here mentioned in the reverse order of their ancestors' births: first the many descendants of Keturah, then Isaac, and, lastly, the line of Ishmael, Abraham's first-born son. This puts Isaac in the central position, and it is he alone who inherits his father's estate, Abraham having honorably discharged his obligations to his other sons through gifts (vv. 5–6). **1:** Nothing more is known about the mysterious Keturah. A midrash identifies her with Hagar and explains the name on the grounds that Hagar was "perfumed ('mekuteret') with commandments and good deeds" (*Gen. Rab.* 61.4). **6:** It is possible that *by concubines* is better translated "by concubinage" and thus refers only to the sons of Keturah listed in v. 2. Rabbi Samuel ben Meir (Rashbam, northern France, 12th century) thinks the *concubines* are Hagar and Keturah. **7:** If Abraham was 100 when Isaac was born (21.5), Isaac 60 when Esau and Jacob were born (26.26), and Abraham died at 175 (25.7), then Abraham passed away only when his twin grandsons were 15. This suggests that the notice of Abraham's death is premature here. Source critics resolve the problem by attributing the chronology to P, but the bulk of the ancestral narrative to J. See 11.31–32 n.

---

a Others "to meditate"; meaning of Heb. uncertain.
b Or "Hanoch."

18 They dwelt from Havilah, by Shur, which is close to Egypt, all the way to Asshur; they camped alongside all their kinsmen.

TOLEDOT   תולדות

19 This is the story of Isaac, son of Abraham. Abraham begot Isaac. 20 Isaac was forty years old when he took to wife Rebekah, daughter of Bethuel the Aramean of Paddan-aram, sister of Laban the Aramean. 21 Isaac pleaded with the LORD on behalf of his wife, because she was barren; and the LORD responded to his plea, and his wife Rebekah conceived. 22 But the children struggled in her womb, and she said, "If so, why do I exist?"*a* She went to inquire of the LORD, 23 and the LORD answered her,

> "Two nations are in your womb,
> Two separate peoples shall issue from your body;
> One people shall be mightier than the other,
> And the older shall serve the younger."

24 When her time to give birth was at hand, there were twins in her womb. 25 The first one emerged red, like a hairy mantle all over; so they named him Esau.*b* 26 Then his brother emerged, holding on to the heel of Esau; so they named him Jacob.*c* Isaac was sixty years old when they were born.

27 When the boys grew up, Esau became a skillful hunter, a man of the outdoors; but Jacob was a mild man who stayed in camp. 28 Isaac favored Esau because *d*he had a taste for game;*-d* but Rebekah favored Jacob. 29 Once when Jacob was cooking a stew, Esau came in from the open, famished. 30 And Esau said to Jacob, "Give me some of that red stuff to gulp down, for I am famished"—which is why he was named Edom.*e* 31 Jacob said, "First sell me your birthright." 32 And Esau said, "I am at the point of death, so of what use is my birthright to me?" 33 But Jacob said, "Swear to me first." So he swore to him, and sold his birthright to Jacob. 34 Jacob then gave Esau bread and lentil stew; he ate and drank, and he rose and went away. Thus did Esau spurn the birthright.

26 There was a famine in the land—aside from the previous famine that had occurred in the days of Abraham—and Isaac went to Abimelech, king of the Philistines, in Gerar. 2 The LORD had appeared to him and said, "Do not go down to Egypt; stay in the land which I point out to you. 3 Reside in this land, and I will be with you and bless you; I

25.19–34: Birth and birthright. This passage tells of the birth of Esau and Jacob, and of the former's ominous sale of his status as first-born to the latter. **21:** Rebekah's barrenness puts her again in line of succession to her late mother-in-law, Sarah (cf. 24.67), though the narrative about Rebekah is much more compressed and much less complex than the corresponding story of Sarai/Sarah (cf. ch 16). The "barren mother" is a common motif in special birth stories. Compare also Rachel (Gen. ch 30) and Hannah (1 Sam. ch 1). A midrash sees in God's response to Isaac's plea an object lesson in the power of prayer to move God from anger to mercy (*b. Yebam.* 64a). **25:** In addition to the pun on *Seir* and "se'ar" ("hair"), there is also a play on *red* ("'admoni") and "Edom," another name for Esau and the kingdom descended from him. (See translator's note *b* and 36.9.) **26:** Jacob's naming (as usual in the Tanakh) is based on a folk etymology. "Jacob" probably derives from "y-'-k-b-'-l," "may God protect." **27:** To the ancient Israelite, Esau's hunting, like his hairiness, suggested uncouthness and even a certain degree of danger. The uncouthness is also apparent in his blunt speech and impulsive behavior in the ensuing tale (vv. 30–34). **28:** Once again, the mother mediates God's preference (cf. 21.9–13; Mal. 1.2–5). The father seems blind to the higher purpose (cf. Gen. 27.1–45). God's favoring the younger son is already familiar from the story of Cain and Abel (4.4–5) and, in a different way, Ishmael and Isaac (21.12), and will be a prominent feature of the story of Joseph (37.3).

26.1–33: Episodes in the life of Isaac. In comparison with the two larger-than-life figures who are his father (Abraham) and his son (Jacob), there is remarkably little narrative about Isaac. Indeed, he generally appears passive and, in places, even comic (e.g., 26.8–9; 27.18–23). Gen. 26.1–33 is the only collection of biblical narrative cen-

---

a *Meaning of Heb. uncertain.*   b *Synonym of "Seir," play on Heb. se'ar "hair."*
c *Play on Heb. 'aqeb "heel."*   d-d *Lit. "game was in his mouth."*
e *Play on Heb. 'adom "red."*

will assign all these lands to you and to your heirs, fulfilling the oath that I swore to your father Abraham. [4] I will make your heirs as numerous as the stars of heaven, and assign to your heirs all these lands, so that all the nations of the earth shall bless themselves by your heirs—[5] inasmuch as Abraham obeyed Me and kept My charge: My commandments, My laws, and My teachings."

[6] So Isaac stayed in Gerar. [7] When the men of the place asked him about his wife, he said, "She is my sister," for he was afraid to say "my wife," thinking, "The men of the place might kill me on account of Rebekah, for she is beautiful." [8] When some time had passed, Abimelech king of the Philistines, looking out of the window, saw Isaac fondling his wife Rebekah. [9] Abimelech sent for Isaac and said, "So she is your wife! Why then did you say: 'She is my sister?' " Isaac said to him, "Because I thought I might lose my life on account of her." [10] Abimelech said, "What have you done to us! One of the people might have lain with your wife, and you would have brought guilt upon us." [11] Abimelech then charged all the people, saying, "Anyone who molests this man or his wife shall be put to death."

[12] Isaac sowed in that land and reaped a hundredfold the same year. The LORD blessed him, [13] and the man grew richer and richer until he was very wealthy: [14] he acquired flocks and herds, and a large household, so that the Philistines envied him. [15] And the Philistines stopped up all the wells which his father's servants had dug in the days of his father Abraham, filling them with earth. [16] And Abimelech said to Isaac, "Go away from us, for you have become far too big for us."

[17] So Isaac departed from there and encamped in the wadi of Gerar, where he settled. [18] Isaac dug anew the wells which had been dug in the days of his father Abraham and which the Philistines had stopped up after Abraham's death; and he gave them the same names that his father had given them. [19] But when Isaac's servants, digging in the wadi, found there a well of spring water, [20] the herdsmen of Gerar quarreled with Isaac's herdsmen, saying, "The water is ours." He named that well Esek,[a] because they contended with him. [21] And when they dug another well, they disputed over that one also; so he named it Sitnah.[b] [22] He moved from there and dug yet another well, and they did not quarrel over it; so he called it Rehoboth, saying, "Now at last the LORD has granted us ample space[c] to increase in the land."

trally devoted to the middle patriarch. **1–5:** Here, the LORD affirms the continuity of Isaac with his father, whose experience he in part relives (vv. 1–2; cf. 12.10; 20.1–18). Isaac will fall heir to the Abrahamic promise of offspring, blessing, and land (vv. 3–5; cf. 12.1–3, 7; 15.5). V. 5 may be a reference to the 'Akedah (cf. 22.15–18), the only explicit one in the Tanakh outside of ch 22. In Judaism, Abraham is generally thought to have exemplified not only faith in God and love for Him but also meticulous obedience to His commands. Traditional commentators differ, however, on the extent of the *charge, commandments, laws,* and *teachings* that Abraham had observed, to his son's benefit (v. 5). Rashi, following strong rabbinic precedents (e.g., *b. Yoma* 28b), thinks that Abraham observed all categories of Jewish law, even the Oral Torah. His grandson, Rashbam, more dedicated to the plain sense, thinks that Abraham observed only those commandments that had been communicated to him in Genesis or that human reason can intuit without revelation. **6–11:** This is the last of the three stories of a patriarch's attempting unsuccessfully to pass his wife off as his sister (cf. 12.10–20; 20.1–18), and the only one in which the matriarch is never brought into the foreign king's quarters. A note of comedy relieves its blandness in comparison with the other two when Abimelech sees Isaac ("yitzḥaq") "fondling" ("metzaḥeq") Rebekah and draws the all too obvious conclusion (vv. 8–9). Is Isaac here overconfident, careless, or foolish? **12–33:** The image of Isaac as a landholder and farmer (v. 12) is in tension with the picture of him as a semi-nomad (cf. v. 17). His acquisition of vast wealth (vv. 13–14) underscores the continuity with his father (cf. 12.5, 16; 13.2), just as the ensuing conflict with the Philistines (vv. 15–22) recalls the prologue to the separation of Abraham and Lot (13.5–7). Most historians consider the reference to Philistines here (and in v. 1)

---

a I.e., "contention."   b I.e., "harassment."
c Heb. hirḥib, connected with "Rehoboth."

23 From there he went up to Beer-sheba. 24 That night the LORD appeared to him and said, "I am the God of your father Abraham. Fear not, for I am with you, and I will bless you and increase your offspring for the sake of My servant Abraham." 25 So he built an altar there and invoked the LORD by name. Isaac pitched his tent there and his servants started digging a well. 26 And Abimelech came to him from Gerar, with Ahuzzath his councilor and Phicol chief of his troops. 27 Isaac said to them, "Why have you come to me, seeing that you have been hostile to me and have driven me away from you?" 28 And they said, "We now see plainly that the LORD has been with you, and we thought: Let there be a sworn treaty between our two parties, between you and us. Let us make a pact with you 29 that you will not do us harm, just as we have not molested you but have always dealt kindly with you and sent you away in peace. From now on, be you blessed of the LORD!" 30 Then he made for them a feast, and they ate and drank.

31 Early in the morning, they exchanged oaths. Isaac then bade them farewell, and they departed from him in peace. 32 That same day Isaac's servants came and told him about the well they had dug, and said to him, "We have found water!" 33 He named it Shibah;ª therefore the name of the city is Beer-sheba to this day.

34 When Esau was forty years old, he took to wife Judith daughter of Beeri the Hittite, and Basemath daughter of Elon the Hittite; 35 and they were a source of bitterness to Isaac and Rebekah.

27 When Isaac was old and his eyes were too dim to see, he called his older son Esau and said to him, "My son." He answered, "Here I am." 2 And he said, "I am old now, and I do not know how soon I may die. 3 Take your gear, your quiver and bow, and go out into the open and hunt me some game. 4 Then prepare a dish for me such as I like, and bring it to me to eat, so that I may give you my innermost blessing before I die."

5 Rebekah had been listening as Isaac spoke to his son

---

a As though "oath."

---

anachronistic, since the Philistines did not arrive in Canaan until about 1200 BCE. The dispute about the wells and the covenant-making ceremony that resolves it (vv. 17–33) are highly reminiscent of King Abimelech's previous dealing with Isaac's father in

21.22–32. Incidentally, nothing in this episode, or in the rest of the chapter, gives any indication that the couple's twins have already been born (25.21–26), and one can imagine that the episode once stood elsewhere.

26.34–35: Esau intermarries. Source critics attribute these verses to P and see them as the prologue to 27.46–28.9, the Priestly explanation for Jacob's flight to his uncle's homestead. In the genealogical notice in 36.2–4, Elon's daughter is not Basemath but Adah; Basemath is the daughter of Ishmael, not Elon; and Judith is absent altogether. Esau's intermarriages are a jarring contrast to Abraham's strenuous effort to find a wife for Isaac from within the clan (ch 24) and demonstrate Esau's unworthiness to serve as the next figure in the patriarchal line.

27.1–45: Jacob acquires Esau's blessing. This story, one of the masterpieces of biblical narrative artistry, exhibits both charming comedy and intense pathos. Jacob, having purchased his brother's status of first-born in a questionable fashion (25.29–34), acquires his paternal blessing as well. He does so in a way that advances the divine plan but also utilizes deceit and brings hardship on all involved. **1–4:** Gen. 25.28 has already established Isaac's preference for Esau, who, as the first-born son (27.19), should receive his father's prime blessing anyway. Isaac's instruction to hunt him some game recalls the rather shallow reason for his favoring the uncouth Esau. There may also be a notion here that eating will fortify his innermost self, that is, his life-force ("nefesh," v. 4) so that he may impart a more powerful blessing to his son. Since Isaac is blind, this chapter emphasizes his other senses. He identifies "Esau" by touching his hands, tasting him through a kiss, and smelling his clothing. His sense of hearing tells him that something may be amiss. Esau's response to his aged father's summons, *Here I am* (v. 1), recalls the refrain of the 'Akedah (22.1, 7, 11), another but very different story of a loving father and the near-loss of his beloved son. **5–13:** Once again, it is the mother who arranges the fulfillment of the divine plan, to the benefit of the second-born son, and in a manner

Esau. When Esau had gone out into the open to hunt game to bring home, [6]Rebekah said to her son Jacob, "I overheard your father speaking to your brother Esau, saying, [7]'Bring me some game and prepare a dish for me to eat, that I may bless you, with the LORD's approval, before I die.' [8]Now, my son, listen carefully as I instruct you. [9]Go to the flock and fetch me two choice kids, and I will make of them a dish for your father, such as he likes. [10]Then take it to your father to eat, in order that he may bless you before he dies." [11]Jacob answered his mother Rebekah, "But my brother Esau is a hairy man and I am smooth-skinned. [12]If my father touches me, I shall appear to him as a trickster and bring upon myself a curse, not a blessing." [13]But his mother said to him, "Your curse, my son, be upon me! Just do as I say and go fetch them for me."

[14]He got them and brought them to his mother, and his mother prepared a dish such as his father liked. [15]Rebekah then took the best clothes of her older son Esau, which were there in the house, and had her younger son Jacob put them on; [16]and she covered his hands and the hairless part of his neck with the skins of the kids. [17]Then she put in the hands of her son Jacob the dish and the bread that she had prepared.

[18]He went to his father and said, "Father." And he said, "Yes, which of my sons are you?" [19]Jacob said to his father, "I am Esau, your first-born; I have done as you told me. Pray sit up and eat of my game, that you may give me your innermost blessing." [20]Isaac said to his son, "How did you succeed so quickly, my son?" And he said, "Because the LORD your God granted me good fortune." [21]Isaac said to Jacob, "Come closer that I may feel you, my son—whether you are really my son Esau or not." [22]So Jacob drew close to his father Isaac, who felt him and wondered. "The voice is the voice of Jacob, yet the hands are the hands of Esau." [23]He did not recognize him, because his hands were hairy like those of his brother Esau; and so he blessed him.

[24]He asked, "Are you really my son Esau?" And when he said, "I am," [25]he said, "Serve me and let me eat of my son's game that I may give you my innermost blessing." So he served him and he ate, and he brought him wine and he drank. [26]Then his father Isaac said to him, "Come close and kiss me, my son"; [27]and he went up and kissed him. And he smelled his clothes and he blessed him, saying, "Ah, the smell of my son is like the smell of the fields that the LORD has blessed.

[28]   "May God give you
     Of the dew of heaven and the fat of the earth,

that is morally offensive to a high degree (cf. 21.9–13). It is curious, however, that in seeking to allay her favored son's worry (vv. 11–13), Rebekah never mentions the prenatal oracle that announced the LORD's preference for the younger twin (25.23). Rashbam thinks it was trust in that oracle that enabled her to discount the curse Jacob fears. But note that the Tanakh gives no indication that Jacob ever saw his mother alive again after this disquieting episode. **18–27:** The passage is full of suspense and high drama, as Isaac uses his senses of touch, hearing, taste, and smell to ascertain that it is Esau rather than an impersonator who is serving him the tasty game. There is probably also a note of broad humor in vv. 22–23. Should not a blind man have put more trust in his hearing than in his touch, and just how hairy was Esau that the skin of a goat could be mistaken for his hands? Jacob's answer in v. 20 beautifully encapsulates the dual causation that drives this narrative. On the one hand, he is lying to his father. On the other, he is expressing, perhaps unwittingly, the fact that it is God's preference, not his father's, that has arranged his unlikely success.

Abundance of new grain and wine.

29   Let peoples serve you,
And nations bow to you;
Be master over your brothers,
And let your mother's sons bow to you.
Cursed be they who curse you,
Blessed they who bless you."

30 No sooner had Jacob left the presence of his father Isaac—after Isaac had finished blessing Jacob—than his brother Esau came back from his hunt. 31 He too prepared a dish and brought it to his father. And he said to his father, "Let my father sit up and eat of his son's game, so that you may give me your innermost blessing." 32 His father Isaac said to him, "Who are you?" And he said, "I am your son, Esau, your first-born!" 33 Isaac was seized with very violent trembling. "Who was it then," he demanded, "that hunted game and brought it to me? Moreover, I ate of it before you came, and I blessed him; now he must remain blessed!" 34 When Esau heard his father's words, he burst into wild and bitter sobbing, and said to his father, "Bless me too, Father!" 35 But he answered, "Your brother came with guile and took away your blessing." 36 [Esau] said, "Was he, then, named Jacob that he might supplant me[a] these two times? First he took away my birthright and now he has taken away my blessing!" And he added, "Have you not reserved a blessing for me?" 37 Isaac answered, saying to Esau, "But I have made him master over you: I have given him all his brothers for servants, and sustained him with grain and wine. What, then, can I still do for you, my son?" 38 And Esau said to his father, "Have you but one blessing, Father? Bless me too, Father!" And Esau wept aloud. 39 And his father Isaac answered, saying to him,

"See, your abode shall [b]enjoy the fat of the earth
And [-b] the dew of heaven above.
40   Yet by your sword you shall live,
And you shall serve your brother;
But when you grow restive,
You shall break his yoke from your neck."

41 Now Esau harbored a grudge against Jacob because of the blessing which his father had given him, and Esau said to himself, "Let but the mourning period of my father come, and I will kill my brother Jacob." 42 When the words of her older son Esau were reported to Rebekah, she sent for her younger son Jacob and said to him, "Your brother Esau is consoling himself by planning to kill you. 43 Now,

29: Jacob's mastery over his brothers (the plural need not be taken literally) is probably connected to King David's subjection of the Edomites (2 Sam. 8.13–14). Note also the Abrahamic resonance of the end of the verse (cf. Gen. 12.3). **34–35:** The pathos is palpable, and the sympathy for Esau is in marked contrast to exilic and postexilic literature in which Esau/Edom epitomizes evil and betrayal (e.g., Ps. 137.7; Jer. 49.7–22; Obadiah; Isa. 34.5; 63.1–6). In rabbinic and medieval Jewish literature, he becomes a cipher for the Roman empire and then Christendom, and the highly pejorative portrayal of him there reflects the painful experience of the Jews at the hands of those powers. **36:** *Birthright* ("bekhora") and *blessing* ("berakha") have the same three consonants. Though continuing to believe passionately in the chosenness of Jacob/Israel, the prophet Jeremiah sees in Jacob's deceit a paradigm of the chosen people at their worst and just cause for God's impending punishment (Jer. 9.3–8). **37:** The reversal of the order of fertility and domination of vv. 28–29 reflects the reversal of Esau's expectations. **39–40:** Like Ishmael (17.20; 21.13, 18), Esau receives a blessing that is formidable but inferior to his younger brother's. The prophecy of Esau's breaking free from subjugation to Jacob may be connected to Edom's successful rebellions in the 9th or 8th centuries (2 Kings 8.20–22; 2 Chron. 28.17). **41–45:** Esau's murderous grudge (v. 41) recalls the incident of Cain and Abel (4.3–8); less directly, Rebekah's intervention foreshadows tragic events in the life of David (2 Sam. 14.1–24, esp. vv. 4–7).

a Heb. 'aqab, *connected with "Jacob."*
b-b Others *"be away from the fat of the earth and from."*

my son, listen to me. Flee at once to Haran, to my brother Laban. ⁴⁴Stay with him a while, until your brother's fury subsides—⁴⁵until your brother's anger against you subsides—and he forgets what you have done to him. Then I will fetch you from there. Let me not lose you both in one day!"

⁴⁶Rebekah said to Isaac, "I am disgusted with my life because of the Hittite women. If Jacob marries a Hittite **28** woman like these, from among the native women, what good will life be to me?" ¹So Isaac sent for Jacob and blessed him. He instructed him, saying, "You shall not take a wife from among the Canaanite women. ²Up, go to Paddan-aram, to the house of Bethuel, your mother's father, and take a wife there from among the daughters of Laban, your mother's brother, ³May El Shaddaiᵃ bless you, make you fertile and numerous, so that you become an assembly of peoples. ⁴May He grant the blessing of Abraham to you and your offspring, that you may possess the land where you are sojourning, which God assigned to Abraham."

⁵Then Isaac sent Jacob off, and he went to Paddan-aram, to Laban the son of Bethuel the Aramean, the brother of Rebekah, mother of Jacob and Esau.

⁶When Esau saw that Isaac had blessed Jacob and sent him off to Paddan-aram to take a wife from there, charging him, as he blessed him, "You shall not take a wife from among the Canaanite women," ⁷and that Jacob had obeyed his father and mother and gone to Paddan-aram, ⁸Esau realized that the Canaanite women displeased his father Isaac. ⁹So Esau went to Ishmael and took to wife, in addition to the wives he had, Mahalath the daughter of Ishmael son of Abraham, sister of Nebaioth.

VA-YETSE'   ויצא

¹⁰Jacob left Beer-sheba, and set out for Haran. ¹¹He came upon a certain place and stopped there for the night, for the sun had set. Taking one of the stones of that place, he put it under his head and lay down in that place. ¹²He had a dream; a stairwayᵇ was set on the ground and its top reached to the sky, and angels of God were going up and down on it. ¹³And the LORD was standing beside him and He said, "I am the LORD, the God of your father Abraham and the God of Isaac: the ground on which you are lying I will assign to you and to your offspring. ¹⁴Your descendants shall be as the dust of the earth; you shall spread out

---

a See note at 17.1.   b Or "ramp"; others "ladder."

27.46–28.9: Isaac blesses Jacob (again) and Jacob departs. Most source-critical analysts view this passage as the continuation of 26.34–35 and thus see in it the P version of Isaac's blessing of Jacob and the latter's flight to his uncle Laban (27.1–45 is attributed to J). In this version, Jacob does not flee for his life from a brother he has swindled; rather, he dutifully follows the family tradition of finding a wife from within the clan, rather than intermarrying, as Esau had done. Appended to 27.1–45, however, our passage takes on a new and more complex meaning. The distaste for Hittite women (26.34–35) that Isaac and Rebekah both truly share becomes the pretext for her saving her favorite son from his vindictive brother's rage. **28.3:** On El Shaddai, see 17.1 n. **8–9:** It seems fitting that the one nonfavored older brother (a hunter, 25.27) marries into the immediate family of the other (a bowman, 21.20). A midrash points out that Esau's attempt at rectification missed the point: "If he had put out the first wives, [he would have been all right]. But *in addition to the wives he had*—one source of pain upon another!" (*Gen. Rab.* 67.13). Mahalath is missing from the list of Esau's wives in 36.2–3, where Basemath is Ishmael's daughter (cf. 26.34).

28.10–22: Jacob's dream at Bethel. This passage, which according to most source critics is a combination of J and E, is the continuation of 27.45, and records Jacob's first direct encounter with God. In a dream, he sees a "stairway" or ramp of the sort with which Mesopotamian temple towers (ziggurats) were equipped and atop which the deity was thought to appear to communicate to his worshippers (28.12). The LORD assures Jacob that he will inherit the patriarchal promise, thus demonstrating that, however deceitfully it was gotten, Isaac's blessing on him conforms to God's will and that Jacob's exile will be temporary (vv. 13–15). Waking, Jacob re-to the west and to the east, to the north and to the south. All the families of the earth shall bless themselves by you and your descendants. [15] Remember, I am with you: I will protect you wherever you go and will bring you back to this land. I will not leave you until I have done what I have promised you."

[16] Jacob awoke from his sleep and said, "Surely the LORD is present in this place, and I did not know it!" [17] Shaken, he said, "How awesome is this place! This is none other than the abode of God, and that is the gateway to heaven." [18] Early in the morning, Jacob took the stone that he had put under his head and set it up as a pillar and poured oil on the top of it. [19] He named that site Bethel;[a] but previously the name of the city had been Luz.

[20] Jacob then made a vow, saying, "If God remains with me, if He protects me on this journey that I am making, and gives me bread to eat and clothing to wear, [21] and if I return safe to my father's house—the LORD shall be my God. [22] And this stone, which I have set up as a pillar, shall be God's abode; and of all that You give me, I will set aside a tithe for You."

29 Jacob [b]resumed his journey[b] and came to the land of the Easterners. [2] There before his eyes was a well in the open. Three flocks of sheep were lying there beside it, for the flocks were watered from that well. The stone on the mouth of the well was large. [3] When all the flocks were gathered there, the stone would be rolled from the mouth of the well and the sheep watered; then the stone would be put back in its place on the mouth of the well.

[4] Jacob said to them, "My friends, where are you from?" And they said, "We are from Haran." [5] He said to them, "Do you know Laban the son of Nahor?" And they said, "Yes, we do." [6] He continued, "Is he well?" They answered, "Yes, he is; and there is his daughter Rachel, coming with the flock." [7] He said, "It is still broad daylight, too early to round up the animals; water the flock and take them to pasture." [8] But they said, "We cannot, until all the flocks are rounded up; then the stone is rolled off the mouth of the well and we water the sheep."

[9] While he was still speaking with them, Rachel came with her father's flock; for she was a shepherdess. [10] And

a I.e., "house of God."   b-b Lit. "lifted up his feet."

Mic. 5.12). Nonetheless, Moses sets up twelve of them at the foot of Mount Sinai (Exod. 24.4), and Joshua erects one in the temple at Shechem (Josh. 24.26). Ibn Ezra (here and on Deut. 16.22) thinks that sacred pillars were prohibited only if they were erected to the honor of other gods. More likely is a midrash that sees in the practice a vestige of an early form of worship that was later proscribed altogether (*Sifre Deut.* 146; see also Rashi on Deut. 16.22). **19:** Given the importance of Bethel in Israelite worship and the positive evaluation of it in several biblical texts (e.g., Judg. 20.18, 26–28; 21.2–4; 1 Sam. 7.16), it is appropriate that its foundation should be attributed to the patriarch Jacob. Nonetheless, after King Jeroboam I established a temple there to rival the one in Jerusalem, some texts loyal to the latter saw in Bethel a hotbed of idolatry and condemned it roundly (e.g., 1 Kings 12.25–13.34). Our passage presumes that it was the site of a legitimate temple. **22:** Jacob's pledge of a tithe at Bethel may thus have functioned as a counterpoint to Abraham's gift of a tithe at Salem (Jerusalem) in 14.20.

29.1–30: Jacob marries twice. In a scene remarkably similar to the one in ch 24, when Abraham's servant finds a wife for Isaac, Jacob no sooner arrives in Haran than he encounters Laban's daughter, Rachel, and begins the negotiations to marry her. But this time things do not go smoothly, and Jacob the trickster must drink a hefty dose of his own bitter medicine. **3:** The implication is that it would take the collective strength of all the shepherds to roll the rock off the well. Jacob, energized by the sight of his cousin, will soon do so alone (v. 10). **6:** The immediate appearance of Rachel recalls that of Rebekah in 24.15 and again suggests a hidden hand behind the events. **10:** The future bridegroom's heroism at the well foreshadows Moses' scene of the victimized daughters of Reuel in Exod. 2.16–22.

alizes the awesomeness of the place and consecrates it as a sanctuary (vv. 16–19), vowing to give God a tithe if He protects him as He has promised (vv. 20–22).

18: The Tanakh frequently associates sacred pillars, an important element of ancient worship, especially in Canaan, with idolatry (e.g., Deut. 12.3; 16.22; Hos. 10.1–2;

when Jacob saw Rachel, the daughter of his uncle[a] Laban, and the flock of his uncle Laban, Jacob went up and rolled the stone off the mouth of the well, and watered the flock of his uncle Laban. [11] Then Jacob kissed Rachel, and broke into tears. [12] Jacob told Rachel that he was her father's kinsman, that he was Rebekah's son; and she ran and told her father. [13] On hearing the news of his sister's son Jacob, Laban ran to greet him; he embraced him and kissed him, and took him into his house. He told Laban all that had happened, [14] and Laban said to him, "You are truly my bone and flesh."

When he had stayed with him a month's time, [15] Laban said to Jacob, "Just because you are a kinsman, should you serve me for nothing? Tell me, what shall your wages be?" [16] Now Laban had two daughters; the name of the older one was Leah, and the name of the younger was Rachel. [17] Leah had weak eyes; Rachel was shapely and beautiful. [18] Jacob loved Rachel; so he answered, "I will serve you seven years for your younger daughter Rachel." [19] Laban said, "Better that I give her to you than that I should give her to an outsider. Stay with me." [20] So Jacob served seven years for Rachel and they seemed to him but a few days because of his love for her.

[21] Then Jacob said to Laban, "Give me my wife, for my time is fulfilled, that I may cohabit with her." [22] And Laban gathered all the people of the place and made a feast. [23] When evening came, he took his daughter Leah and brought her to him; and he cohabited with her.— [24] Laban had given his maidservant Zilpah to his daughter Leah as her maid.—[25] When morning came, there was Leah! So he said to Laban, "What is this you have done to me? I was in your service for Rachel! Why did you deceive me?" [26] Laban said, "It is not the practice in our place to marry off the younger before the older. [27] Wait until the bridal week of this one is over and we will give you that one too, provided you serve me another seven years." [28] Jacob did so; he waited out the bridal week of the one, and then he gave him his daughter Rachel as wife.—[29] Laban had given his maidservant Bilhah to his daughter Rachel as her maid.—[30] And Jacob cohabited with Rachel also; indeed, he loved Rachel more than Leah. And he served him another seven years.

[31] The LORD saw that Leah was unloved and he opened her womb; but Rachel was barren. [32] Leah conceived and bore a son, and named him Reuben;[b] for she declared, "It

a Lit. "his mother's brother."
b Understood as "See a son."

12: Rachel's running to Laban recalls Rebekah's (24.28) and adds to our mounting suspicion that she is to be the next matriarch of the chosen family. But, as we shall soon see, things are not so simple. **18:** This is one of the very few explicit references to romantic love in the Tanakh. Interestingly, the subject of one of the others is Jacob's father, Isaac, who loved Rebekah (24.67). **25–26:** *What is this you have done to me?* echoes Pharaoh's and Abimelech's indignation after Abraham and Isaac tried to pass their wives off as their sisters (12.18; 20.9; 26.10). Jacob's accusation of deceit is richly ironic in light of his own deceit in passing himself off as his older brother (27.35). Similarly, Laban's answer in v. 26 is an exquisitely ironic reaffirmation of the principle that Jacob has violated in buying Esau's birthright (25.29–34) and defrauding him of his father's highest blessing (27.1–45). Having acquired his older brother's birthright for a bowl of lentils, he now proves unable to acquire the woman he loves even with seven years of harsh labor (31.38–41). A remarkable midrash in the Talmud speaks of Rachel's selflessness and her concern to spare her unloved older sister humiliation. Jacob, the midrash reports, had given Rachel certain tokens by which he could identify her, lest her deceitful father succeed in substituting Leah. Worried that her sister would then be put to shame in her wedding bed, she handed the tokens over to Leah. In reward for Rachel's self-effacement, the midrash concludes, King Saul was numbered among her descendants (*b. Meg.* 13b).

29.31–30.24: The origins of the tribes of Israel. This passage accounts for the birth of twelve of Jacob's thirteen children and eleven of his twelve sons. Only Benjamin, who will be born after the return to Canaan (35.16–20), is missing from the roster of the eponymous ancestors of the twelve tribes of Israel (in some lists, Levi is missing, and Joseph means: 'The LORD has seen[a] my affliction'; it also means: 'Now my husband will love me.' "[b] 33 She conceived again and bore a son, and declared, "This is because the LORD heard[c] that I was unloved and has given me this one also"; so she named him Simeon. 34 Again she conceived and bore a son and declared, "This time my husband will become attached[d] to me, for I have borne him three sons." Therefore he was named Levi. 35 She conceived again and bore a son, and declared, "This time I will praise[e] the LORD." Therefore she named him Judah. Then she stopped bearing.

30 When Rachel saw that she had borne Jacob no children, she became envious of her sister; and Rachel said to Jacob, "Give me children, or I shall die." 2 Jacob was incensed at Rachel, and said, "Can I take the place of God, who has denied you fruit of the womb?" 3 She said, "Here is my maid Bilhah. Consort with her, that she may bear on my knees and that through her I too may have children." 4 So she gave him her maid Bilhah as concubine, and Jacob cohabited with her. 5 Bilhah conceived and bore Jacob a son. 6 And Rachel said, "God has vindicated me;[f] indeed, He has heeded my plea and given me a son." Therefore she named him Dan. 7 Rachel's maid Bilhah conceived again and bore Jacob a second son. 8 And Rachel said, [g-]"A fateful contest I waged[-g] with my sister; yes, and I have prevailed." So she named him Naphtali.

9 When Leah saw that she had stopped bearing, she took her maid Zilpah and gave her to Jacob as concubine. 10 And when Leah's maid Zilpah bore Jacob a son, 11 Leah said, "What luck!"[h] So she named him Gad. 12 When Leah's maid Zilpah bore Jacob a second son, 13 Leah declared, "What fortune!"[i] meaning, "Women will deem me fortunate." So she named him Asher.

14 Once, at the time of the wheat harvest, Reuben came upon some mandrakes in the field and brought them to his mother Leah. Rachel said to Leah, "Please give me some of your son's mandrakes." 15 But she said to her, "Was it not enough for you to take away my husband, that you would also take my son's mandrakes?" Rachel re-

appears as two tribes, Ephraim and Manasseh. See 48.5–7 n.).
29.31: As in the case of Hagar (16.10–12; 21.17–18), God shows compassion to the unfavored mate, thus partly equalizing the disparity between her and her co-wife. Barrenness, in some instances a punishment (e.g., 2 Sam. 6.20–23), serves in Rachel's case to place her in succession to Sarah and Rebekah (11.30; 25.21). **32–35:** The names Leah gives her first three sons communicate her deep distress at not being the preferred wife. In Heb, *The LORD has seen my affliction* (v. 32) is close to the message of the angel to Hagar, "For the LORD has paid heed to your suffering" (16.11). **30.1:** The theme of bad relations between a fertile co-wife and a barren one, with the latter as their husband's favorite, appears in more developed form in the story of Hannah in 1 Sam. ch 1. **2:** The question *Can I take the place of God?* reappears in 50.19 (where it is translated, "Am I a substitute for God?"). There, probably not coincidentally, it is Rachel's first-born who asks it, and in a context of reconciliation of siblings once riven by jealousy. **3:** The words *that through her I too may have children* is another connection to the story of Hagar (16.2). Ancient Near Eastern evidence suggests that placing a child on one's knees represents acknowledgment of that child as one's own. **14–18:** The mandrake, a plant with purplish flowers and branching roots, was thought to have aphrodisiac properties (cf. Song of Songs 7.14). The bitterness of Leah's tragic position as the wife Jacob never wanted and never loved is especially poignant in vv. 15–16. She has to bargain with her sister to hire her husband just to sleep with her.

a *Heb.* ra'ah, *connected with the first part of "Reuben."*
b *Heb.* ye'ehabani, *connected with the last part of "Reuben."*
c *Heb.* shamaʿ, *connected with "Simeon."*
d *Heb.* yillaweh, *connected with "Levi."*
e *Heb.* 'odeh, *connected with "Judah."*
f *Heb.* dananni, *connected with "Dan."*
g-g *Heb.* naphtule . . . naphtalti, *connected with "Naphtali." Lit. "A contest of God . . ."*
h *Kethib* begad; *the* qere *reads* ba gad *"luck has come"; connected with "Gad."*
i *Heb.* be'oshri, *connected with "Asher."*

plied, "I promise, he shall lie with you tonight, in return for your son's mandrakes." [16] When Jacob came home from the field in the evening, Leah went out to meet him and said, "You are to sleep with me, for I have hired you with my son's mandrakes." And he lay with her that night. [17] God heeded Leah, and she conceived and bore him a fifth son. [18] And Leah said, "God has given me my reward[a] for having given my maid to my husband." So she named him Issachar. [19] When Leah conceived again and bore Jacob a sixth son, [20] Leah said, "God has given me a choice gift;[b] this time my husband will exalt me,[c] for I have borne him six sons." So she named him Zebulun. [21] Last, she bore him a daughter, and named her Dinah.

[22] Now God remembered Rachel; God heeded her and opened her womb. [23] She conceived and bore a son, and said, "God has taken away[d] my disgrace." [24] So she named him Joseph, which is to say, "May the LORD add[e] another son for me."

[25] After Rachel had borne Joseph, Jacob said to Laban, "Give me leave to go back to my own homeland. [26] Give me my wives and my children, for whom I have served you, that I may go; for well you know what services I have rendered you." [27] But Laban said to him, "If you will indulge me,[f] I have learned by divination that the LORD has blessed me on your account." [28] And he continued, "Name the wages due from me, and I will pay you." [29] But he said, "You know well how I have served you and how your livestock has fared with me. [30] For the little you had before I came has grown to much, since the LORD has blessed you wherever I turned. And now, when shall I make provision for my own household?" [31] He said, "What shall I pay you?" And Jacob said, "Pay me nothing! If you will do this thing for me, I will again pasture and keep your flocks: [32] let me pass through your whole flock today, removing from there every speckled and spotted animal—every dark-colored sheep and every spotted and speckled goat. Such shall be my wages. [33] In the future when you go over my wages, let my honesty toward you testify for me: if there are among my goats any that are not speckled or spotted or any sheep that are not dark-colored, they got there by theft." [34] And Laban said, "Very well, let it be as you say."

[35] But that same day he removed the streaked and spot-

22: What Rachel does with the mandrakes she buys is strangely unreported. One expects them to play a role in her overcoming her infertility, but it is God alone who is given credit for that. His remembering her underscores her favored status (cf. 8.1). On the basis of a word for "remembering" in Lev. 23.24 (translated "commemorated"), the Talmud dates Rachel's conceiving (as well as Sarah's [see 21.1–8 n.] and Hannah's) to Rosh Ha-Shanah (b. Rosh Hash. 11a). The matriarchs thus play a prominent role in the traditional Rosh Ha-Shanah liturgy.

30.25–43: Jacob grows wealthy. After strained negotiations about payment for Jacob's services, Laban agrees to his son-in-law's terms, but then tries to cheat him anyway. Jacob outsmarts Laban, cleverly arranging for the rapid proliferation of his own share of the flocks. **25–26:** The underlying assumption seems to be that Jacob had accepted the status of an indentured servant. Thus, he could not leave without his master's permission, and his wives and children would belong to the master (Exod. 21.2–4; cf. Gen. 31.43). The verb translated *Give me leave* serves as the standard term for manumission in the story of the exodus (e.g., Exod. 4.23). **27:** Even Laban, ascertaining the divine will by a method that is later prohibited (Lev. 19.26; Deut. 18.10), can see that Jacob is a graced person who brings good luck to those around him (cf. 2 Sam. 6.12). According to Deut. 15.12–15, the master is obligated to endow his newly manumitted indentured servant liberally. **35–42:** Laban proves his offer to have been in bad faith, but Jacob overcomes the trickery with a clever technique of his own. The basis for Jacob's actions in vv. 37–42 is the folkloristic belief that what animals see while mating determines the appearance of their young. Thus, when the goats (which are ordinarily dark in the Near East) see *the white of the shoots* (v. 37; the word for *white* is the same as Laban's name), they con-

---

a *Heb.* sekhari, *connected with "Issachar."*　　b *Heb.* zebadani . . . zebed.
c *Heb.* yizbeleni; *others "will dwell with me."*　　d *Heb.* 'asaph.
e *Heb.* yoseph.　　f *Lit.* "If I have found favor in your eyes."

ted he-goats and all the speckled and spotted she-goats—every one that had white on it—and all the dark-colored sheep, and left them in the charge of his sons. [36] And he put a distance of three days' journey between himself and Jacob, while Jacob was pasturing the rest of Laban's flock.

[37] Jacob then got fresh shoots of poplar, and of almond and plane, and peeled white stripes in them, laying bare the white of the shoots. [38] The rods that he had peeled he set up in front of the goats[a] in the troughs, the water receptacles, that the goats came to drink from. Their mating occurred when they came to drink, [39] and since the goats mated by the rods, the goats brought forth streaked, speckled, and spotted young. [40] But Jacob dealt separately with the sheep; he made these animals face the streaked or wholly dark-colored animals in Laban's flock. And so he produced special flocks for himself, which he did not put with Laban's flocks. [41] Moreover, when the sturdier[b] animals were mating, Jacob would place the rods in the troughs, in full view of the animals, so that they mated by the rods; [42] but with the feebler[c] animals he would not place them there. Thus the feeble ones[c] went to Laban and the sturdy to Jacob. [43] So the man grew exceedingly prosperous, and came to own large flocks, maidservants and menservants, camels and asses.

31 Now he heard the things that Laban's sons were saying: "Jacob has taken all that was our father's, and from that which was our father's he has built up all this wealth." [2] Jacob also saw that Laban's manner toward him was not as it had been in the past. [3] Then the LORD said to Jacob, "Return to the land of your fathers where you were born, and I will be with you." [4] Jacob had Rachel and Leah called to the field, where his flock was, [5] and said to them, "I see that your father's manner toward me is not as it has been in the past. But the God of my father has been with me. [6] As you know, I have served your father with all my might; [7] but your father has cheated me, changing my wages time and again.[d] God, however, would not let him do me harm. [8] If he said thus, 'The speckled shall be your wages,' then all the flocks would drop speckled young; and if he said thus, 'The streaked shall be your wages,' then all the flocks would drop streaked young. [9] God has taken away your father's livestock and given it to me.

a Lit. "flocks."
b Or "early-breeding."
c Or "late-breeding."
d Lit. "ten times."

ceive kids with patches of white. Similarly, Jacob positioned the sheep (which are normally white) in view of the *streaked or wholly dark-colored animals* (v. 40), so that they would bear lambs with dark patches. Thus was the master trickster Laban finally and justly tricked, and thus did Jacob, by the blessing of God and by his own ingenuity, achieve the wealth that had been characteristic of his grandfather and father as well (13.2; 26.13–14). The refugee is becoming a patriarch.

31.1–54: Jacob breaks free of Laban. This chapter marks the final resolution of the even more difficult relationship between the emerging patriarch and his selfish and duplicitous father-in-law. Jacob first persuades his wives to leave their father (vv. 1–16) and then contends with Laban's accusations, making a few of his own along the way (vv. 22–42). Finally, at Laban's suggestion, the two make a nonaggression pact, solemnly delimiting the terms of their separation and the boundary between their territories (vv. 43–54). **1:** The complaint of Laban's sons (who are mentioned only here) echoes Esau's charge in 27.36. In this case, however, Jacob will not only receive divine validation of his behavior, but also vigorously defend its legality (vv. 36–42). **3:** The verse recalls the LORD's words to Jacob in 28.15, when he first set out for Haran, and thus suggests that He has indeed been protecting the chosen son of Isaac during his long and painful sojourn outside the promised land all along. Functioning as bookends around the story of Jacob in Haran, these two verses illustrate the principle that, in the psalmist's words, "The LORD will guard your going and your coming/now and forever" (Ps. 121.8). **4–13:** Jacob here presents a different account of the increase in his flocks from the one that appears in 30.25–43. Source criticism can explain the divergence through the attribution of this text to E, whereas 30.25–43 is J. Note that

10 "Once, at the mating time of the flocks, ªI had a dream in which I saw ª that the he-goats mating with the flock were streaked, speckled, and mottled. 11 And in the dream an angel of God said to me, 'Jacob!' 'Here,' I answered. 12 And he said, 'Note well that all the he-goats which are mating with the flock are streaked, speckled, and mottled; for I have noted all that Laban has been doing to you. 13 I am the God of Beth-el, where you anointed a pillar and where you made a vow to Me. Now, arise and leave this land and return to your native land.' "

14 Then Rachel and Leah answered him, saying, "Have we still a share in the inheritance of our father's house? 15 Surely, he regards us as outsiders, now that he has sold us and has used up our purchase price. 16 Truly, all the wealth that God has taken away from our father belongs to us and to our children. Now then, do just as God has told you."

17 Thereupon Jacob put his children and wives on camels; 18 and he drove off all his livestock and all the wealth that he had amassed, the livestock in his possession that he had acquired in Paddan-aram, to go to his father Isaac in the land of Canaan.

19 Meanwhile Laban had gone to shear his sheep, and Rachel stole her father's household idols. 20 Jacob ᵇ·kept Laban the Aramean in the dark,·ᵇ not telling him that he was fleeing, 21 and fled with all that he had. Soon he was across the Euphrates and heading toward the hill country of Gilead.

22 On the third day, Laban was told that Jacob had fled. 23 So he took his kinsmen with him and pursued him a distance of seven days, catching up with him in the hill country of Gilead. 24 But God appeared to Laban the Aramean in a dream by night and said to him, "Beware of attempting anything with Jacob, good or bad."

25 Laban overtook Jacob. Jacob had pitched his tent on the Height, and Laban with his kinsmen encamped in the hill country of Gilead. 26 And Laban said to Jacob, "What did you mean by keeping me in the dark and carrying off my daughters like captives of the sword? 27 Why did you flee in secrecy and mislead me and not tell me? I would have sent you off with festive music, with timbrel and lyre. 28 You did not even let me kiss my sons and daughters good-by! It was a foolish thing for you to do. 29 I have it in my power to do you harm; but the God of your father said to me last night, 'Beware of attempting anything with

31.4–13 always uses the E-name (God) and that v. 13 seems to be a variant of v. 3. Reading the two texts as part of one now unified document presents us with two options: Is Jacob here dissembling to his wives in order to make himself look innocent, or is he giving a profound theological interpretation of the events that happened in the previous chapter on a human plane? **14–16:** Rachel and Leah refer to the institution of the bride-price, a gift that the groom paid his fiancee's father; this text suggests that in some cases it ultimately went to the bride herself. Laban, they complain (in agreement for once), has consumed the bride-price (probably in the form of Jacob's labor) without concern for them, in effect disowning them. **19–21:** Concerning these household idols, see 1 Sam. 19.13. "Stealing" (the Heb has a wider range of meaning than the English), in any event, is a recurrent theme in this chapter and points to one of its major ironies. Whereas Jacob vigorously defends himself against the charge that he defrauded Laban (vv. 8–12, 39), he, in fact, had "to steal the mind of Laban the Aramean" (see translators' note b-b) in order to effect his getaway. Unbeknownst to him, his wife had indeed stolen her father's household idols. Given Laban's own deceit (29.21–28), the phrase "stole the mind of Laban the Aramean" constitutes a delicious wordplay. In Heb, "mind" ("lev") sounds like "Laban" ("lavan"), and "Aramean" ("ªarami") sounds like "deceive" ("rima").

a-a Lit. "I raised my eyes and saw in a dream, behold."
b-b Lit. "stole the mind of Laban the Aramean"; similarly in v. 26.

Jacob, good or bad.' ³⁰ Very well, you had to leave because you were longing for your father's house; but why did you steal my gods?"

³¹ Jacob answered Laban, saying, "I was afraid because I thought you would take your daughters from me by force. ³² But anyone with whom you find your gods shall not remain alive! In the presence of our kinsmen, point out what I have of yours and take it." Jacob, of course, did not know that Rachel had stolen them.

³³ So Laban went into Jacob's tent and Leah's tent and the tents of the two maidservants; but he did not find them. Leaving Leah's tent, he entered Rachel's tent. ³⁴ Rachel, meanwhile, had taken the idols and placed them in the camel cushion and sat on them; and Laban rummaged through the tent without finding them. ³⁵ For she said to her father, "Let not my lord take it amiss that I cannot rise before you, for the period of women is upon me." Thus he searched, but could not find the household idols.

³⁶ Now Jacob became incensed and took up his grievance with Laban. Jacob spoke up and said to Laban, "What is my crime, what is my guilt that you should pursue me? ³⁷ You rummaged through all my things; what have you found of all your household objects? Set it here, before my kinsmen and yours, and let them decide between us two.

³⁸ "These twenty years I have spent in your service, your ewes and she-goats never miscarried, nor did I feast on rams from your flock. ³⁹ That which was torn by beasts I never brought to you; I myself made good the loss; you exacted it of me, whether snatched by day or snatched by night. ⁴⁰ Often,ᵃ scorching heat ravaged me by day and frost by night; and sleep fled from my eyes. ⁴¹ Of the twenty years that I spent in your household, I served you fourteen years for your two daughters, and six years for your flocks; and you changed my wages time and again.ᵇ ⁴² Had not the God of my father, the God of Abraham and the Fearᶜ of Isaac, been with me, you would have sent me away empty-handed. But God took notice of my plight and the toil of my hands, and He gave judgment last night."

⁴³ Then Laban spoke up and said to Jacob, "The daughters are my daughters, the children are my children, and the flocks are my flocks; all that you see is mine. Yet what can I do now about my daughters or the children they have borne? ⁴⁴ Come, then, let us make a pact, you and I, that there may be a witness between you and me."

32: According to a midrash, it was Jacob's well-intentioned curse that brought about his beloved Rachel's premature death (*Gen. Rab.* 74.4; see 35.16–20). **33–35:** Note the two-fold satire, against the miserly Laban, vainly rummaging through his own family's tents, and against the household idols themselves, escaping detection only because of Rachel's menstrual period. In the purity system of the Torah, anything on which a menstruant has sat communicates impurity (Lev. 15.22). Whereas Laban refers to his *gods,* the narrator is careful to call them *household idols* (Heb "terafim"). And whereas Laban is fiercely devoted to his *gods,* it is God who has stripped him of his wealth and given it to his daughters (v. 16). Note also the connection of Laban's "rummaging" ("mishesh") and Isaac's "feeling" ("mash") Jacob in 27.21–22. In each case, Jacob escapes detection, but in each case he also pays a steep price. **39:** By the standards of the law in Exod. 22.12, Jacob went beyond his obligations when he made good *that which was torn by beasts.* **44:** Witness ("ʿed") may involve a pun on a similar Semitic word ("ʿad") that means a "pact" or "covenant"; here, it may even be a variant of it. If the word does mean *witness,* the reference is unclear. Most likely, it is God Himself who is to play that role, as in v. 50.

---

a Lit. "I was."   b Lit. "ten times."   c Meaning of Heb. paḥad uncertain.

45 Thereupon Jacob took a stone and set it up as a pillar. 46 And Jacob said to his kinsmen, "Gather stones." So they took stones and made a mound; and they partook of a meal there by the mound. 47 Laban named it Yegar-sahadutha,ᵃ but Jacob named it Gal-ed.ᵇ 48 And Laban declared, "This mound is a witness between you and me this day." That is why it was named Gal-ed; 49 and [it was called] Mizpah, because he said, "May the LORD watchᶜ between you and me, when we are out of sight of each other. 50 If you ill-treat my daughters or take other wives besides my daughters—though no one else be about, remember, God Himself will be witness between you and me."

51 And Laban said to Jacob, "Here is this mound and here the pillar which I have set up between you and me: 52 this mound shall be witness and this pillar shall be witness that I am not to cross to you past this mound, and that you are not to cross to me past this mound and this pillar, with hostile intent. 53 May the God of Abraham and the god of Nahor"—their ancestral deities—"judge between us." And Jacob swore by the Fearᵈ of his father Isaac. 54 Jacob then offered up a sacrifice on the Height, and invited his kinsmen to partake of the meal. After the meal, they spent the night on the Height.

32 Early in the morning, Laban kissed his sons and daughters and bade them good-by; then Laban left on his journey homeward. 2 Jacob went on his way, and angels of God encountered him. 3 When he saw them, Jacob said, "This is God's camp." So he named that place Mahanaim.ᵉ

VA-YISHLAḤ

וישלח

4 Jacob sent messengers ahead to his brother Esau in the land of Seir, the country of Edom, 5 and instructed them as follows, ᶠ"Thus shall you say, 'To my lord Esau, thus says your servant Jacob:ᶠ I stayed with Laban and remained until now; 6 I have acquired cattle, asses, sheep, and male and female slaves; and I send this message to my lord in the hope of gaining your favor.' " 7 The messengers returned to Jacob, saying, "We came to your brother Esau; he himself is coming to meet you, and there are four hun-

47: The narrative gives a folk etymology for Gilead (v. 23), a mountainous area in Transjordan, southeast of the Sea of Galilee (Kinneret). 1 Kings 22.1–38 and 2 Kings 9.14–15 report wars between Israelites and Arameans over one of its major cities in the 9th century BCE. Gen. 31.44–54 may reflect a pact between these two peoples. Laban's giving Gal-ed an Aramaic name is a wonderful little touch. According to the Talmud, one should not esteem the Aramaic language lightly, for, as these two words show, it appears in the Torah itself (y. Sot. 7.7).

32.1–3: A good-bye and a revelation. 1: Laban omits kissing Jacob, in pointed contrast to their initial encounter (29.13). 3: Retrospectively, this verse recalls Jacob's experience at Bethel on his way to Laban (28.10–22). Cf. especially 28.17, "This is none other than the abode of God." Prospectively, the name Mahanaim, understood as "two camps," anticipates Jacob's precautionary division of his entourage in 32.8–9.

32.4–22: Jacob prepares to meet Esau. 4: Messengers is the same Heb word as "angels" in v. 2. The term communicates a premonition that, however fearful the encounter with Esau may seem, God's protective grace will not depart from Jacob. 7: The mention of Esau's 400 men underscores Jacob's vulnerability. For all his wives, offspring, slaves, and animals, he lacks the military might of the brother he has wronged. Things are looking grim.

a Aramaic for "the mound (or, stone-heap) of witness."
b Heb. for "the mound (or, stone-heap) of witness," reflecting the name Gilead, v. 23.
c Heb. yiṣeph, associated with Mizpah.
d Meaning of Heb. paḥad uncertain.
e Connected with Heb. maḥaneh, "camp."
f-f Or "Thus you shall say to my lord Esau, 'Thus says your servant Jacob: . . .' "

dred men with him." 8 Jacob was greatly frightened; in his anxiety, he divided the people with him, and the flocks and herds and camels, into two camps, 9 thinking, "If Esau comes to the one camp and attacks it, the other camp may yet escape."

10 Then Jacob said, "O God of my father Abraham and God of my father Isaac, O LORD, who said to me, 'Return to your native land and I will deal bountifully with you'! 11 I am unworthy of all the kindness that You have so steadfastly shown Your servant: with my staff alone I crossed this Jordan, and now I have become two camps. 12 Deliver me, I pray, from the hand of my brother, from the hand of Esau; else, I fear, he may come and strike me down, mothers and children alike. 13 Yet You have said, 'I will deal bountifully with you and make your offspring as the sands of the sea, which are too numerous to count.' "

14 After spending the night there, he selected from what was at hand these presents for his brother Esau: 15 200 she-goats and 20 he-goats; 200 ewes and 20 rams; 16 30 milch camels with their colts; 40 cows and 10 bulls; 20 she-asses and 10 he-asses. 17 These he put in the charge of his servants, drove by drove, and he told his servants, "Go on ahead, and keep a distance between droves." 18 He instructed the one in front as follows, "When my brother Esau meets you and asks you, 'Whose man are you? Where are you going? And whose [animals] are these ahead of you?' 19 you shall answer, 'Your servant Jacob's; they are a gift sent to my lord Esau; and [Jacob] himself is right behind us.' " 20 He gave similar instructions to the second one, and the third, and all the others who followed the droves, namely, "Thus and so shall you say to Esau when you reach him. 21 And you shall add, 'And your servant Jacob himself is right behind us.' " For he reasoned, "If I propitiate him with presents in advance, and then face him, perhaps he will show me favor." 22 And so the gift went on ahead, while he remained in camp that night.

23 That same night he arose, and taking his two wives, his two maidservants, and his eleven children, he crossed the ford of the Jabbok. 24 After taking them across the stream, he sent across all his possessions. 25 Jacob was left alone. And a man wrestled with him until the break of dawn. 26 When he saw that he had not prevailed against him, he wrenched Jacob's hip at its socket, so that the socket of his hip was strained as he wrestled with him. 27 Then he said, "Let me go, for dawn is breaking." But he answered, "I will not let you go, unless you bless me." 28 Said the other, "What is your name?" He replied,

10–13: Jacob's prayer opens and closes with quotations of those promises of God that the looming confrontation with Esau threatens (vv. 10, 13). V. 11 expresses his humility and his gratitude for previous favors, and v. 12 asks for deliverance, appealing to God's mercy. A talmudic rabbi, however, is critical of Jacob on the grounds that one should never put himself in a dangerous place and then ask that a miracle be performed (*b. Shab.* 32a). The danger should be avoided, if at all possible. **17–22:** The word *face* (Heb "panim") occurs seven times in this passage (in some instances, it is translated as *ahead* and the like). This suggests a connection with Peniel (vv. 31–32) and underscores the association of Esau with the mysterious figure with whom Jacob is about to wrestle (cf. 33.10).

32.23–33: Jacob wrestles with a divine being. The fateful encounter at the Jabbok is one of the best-known episodes in the life of Jacob, but also surely the most enigmatic. **23–25:** Peniel is on the north bank of the *Jabbok* (the wadi Zerka). Why Jacob returned there after fording his wives and children is unclear. In the Talmud, it is suggested that he had returned to retrieve some little jars he had forgotten there (*b. Ḥul.* 91a). In any case, his solitude and lack of property recall his status when he first fled his brother's wrath, before God had showered His bounty upon him (28.11). **25:** The identity of the *man* is as unclear as his reason for attacking Jacob (cf. Exod. 4.24–26). In the Tanakh, God and angels can appear in human form, as in 18.2 (cf. 19.1); Josh. 5.13–15; Judg. 13.6, 10. Jacob's mysterious adversary is surely supernatural, and most traditional Jewish commentators have taken him to be angelic. A well-known midrash sees him as the "patron angel of Esau" and thus interprets this episode as a warning to all future enemies of the Jewish people: "Your patron angel could not withstand him [i.e., Jacob/Israel] and you seek to attack his descen-

"Jacob." ²⁹Said he, "Your name shall no longer be Jacob, but Israel, for you have striven[a] with [b-]beings divine and human,[-b] and have prevailed." ³⁰Jacob asked, "Pray tell me your name." But he said, "You must not ask my name!" And he took leave of him there. ³¹So Jacob named the place Peniel,[c] meaning, "I have seen a divine being face to face, yet my life has been preserved." ³²The sun rose upon him as he passed Penuel, limping on his hip. ³³That is why the children of Israel to this day do not eat the thigh muscle that is on the socket of the hip, since Jacob's hip socket was wrenched at the thigh muscle.

33 Looking up, Jacob saw Esau coming, accompanied by four hundred men. He divided the children among Leah, Rachel, and the two maids, ²putting the maids and their children first, Leah and her children next, and Rachel and Joseph last. ³He himself went on ahead and bowed low to the ground seven times until he was near his brother. ⁴Esau ran to greet him. He embraced him and, falling on his neck, he kissed him; and they wept. ⁵Looking about, he saw the women and the children. "Who," he asked, "are these with you?" He answered, "The children with whom God has favored your servant." ⁶Then the maids, with their children, came forward and bowed low; ⁷next Leah, with her children, came forward and bowed low; and last, Joseph and Rachel came forward and bowed low; ⁸And he asked, "What do you mean by all this company which I have met?" He answered, "To gain my lord's favor." ⁹Esau said, "I have enough, my brother; let what you have remain yours." ¹⁰But Jacob said, "No, I pray you; if you would do me this favor, accept from me this gift; for to see your face is like seeing the face of God, and you have received me favorably. ¹¹Please accept my present which has been brought to you, for God has favored me and I have plenty." And when he urged him, he accepted.

a Heb. saritha, connected with first part of "Israel."
b-b Or "God (Elohim, connected with second part of 'Israel') and men."
c Understood as "face of God."

draw attention to its underlying rationale (m. Ḥul. 7.6). In other words, the prohibition did not come into force until the revelation on Sinai.

33.1–20: The reconciliation of Jacob and Esau. The keynotes of this ch are Jacob's obsequiousness and Esau's gracious forbearance. The murderous revenge that the former had feared (32.12) and the latter had vowed (27.41) thus averted, Jacob succeeds in effecting a definitive separation from his brother and maintaining his own distinctive identity. **1–2:** Jacob graphically reaffirms his preference for Rachel (now extended to her son Joseph), which once caused so much ill will between his wives (29.31–30.21). His preference for Joseph will be the cause of the next tear in the fabric of familial relations. It will nearly result in his beloved son's death (ch 37). **3:** Sevenfold prostration appears in the Amarna Letters (14th century BCE) as a gesture of homage to one's suzerain. The scene reverses the dominance of Jacob over Esau prophesied in 25.23 and 27.29, 37. **4:** *He kissed him* is missing in the Septuagint, an ancient Greek translation of the Torah produced by Jewish scholars in Egypt. In the Masoretic Text (the traditional rabbinic version codified in the late first millennium CE), dots appear over the phrase, probably to indicate its doubtful status in the manuscript tradition. One midrash interprets the dots to mean that, uncharacteristically, Esau felt compassion for Jacob and kissed him wholeheartedly. Another midrash, however, thinks that Esau intended to "bite" ("nashakh") rather than to "kiss" ("nashak") his brother, but God hardened Jacob's neck, foiling his brother's deceitful attack (Gen. Rab. 78.9). **9:** *Enough* ("rav") may echo the prophecy that "the older ('rav') shall serve the younger" (25.23). Esau, confronted with his brother's conspicuous obeisance, renounces any claim to his younger brother's property. **11:** *Accept my present* can also be

dants?" (Gen. Rab. 77.3). **29:** The scientific etymology of *Israel* is unclear, a good guess being "[The God] El rules." The folk etymology in this verse appears again in Hos. 12.4. **30:** Cf. Exod. 3.13–14; Judg. 13.18. *He took leave of him* could also be rendered "he blessed him." If so, Jacob wins his blessing after all. **33:** The Rabbis saw this norm,

unparalleled in the Tanakh, as a commandment ("mitzvah") and thus an indispensable element of the Jewish dietary system ("kashrut"). A majority position in the Mishnah maintains that this "mitzvah" was first announced when the Torah was given on Mount Sinai and only written down in its current location to

12 And [Esau] said, "Let us start on our journey, and I will proceed at your pace." 13 But he said to him, "My lord knows that the children are frail and that the flocks and herds, which are nursing, are a care to me; if they are driven hard a single day, all the flocks will die. 14 Let my lord go on ahead of his servant, while I travel slowly, at the pace of the cattle before me and at the pace of the children, until I come to my lord in Seir."

15 Then Esau said, "Let me assign to you some of the men who are with me." But he said, "Oh no, my lord is too kind to me!" 16 So Esau started back that day on his way to Seir. 17 But Jacob journeyed on to Succoth, and built a house for himself and made stalls for his cattle; that is why the place was called Succoth.ᵃ

18 Jacob arrived safe in the city of Shechem which is in the land of Canaan—having come thus from Paddan-aram—and he encamped before the city. 19 The parcel of land where he pitched his tent he purchased from the children of Hamor, Shechem's father, for a hundred *kesitahs*.ᵇ 20 He set up an altar there, and called it El-elohe-yisrael.ᶜ

34 Now Dinah, the daughter whom Leah had borne to Jacob, went out to visit the daughters of the land. 2 Shechem son of Hamor the Hivite, chief of the country, saw her, and took her and lay with her by force. 3 Being strongly drawn to Dinah daughter of Jacob, and in love with the maiden, he spoke to the maiden tenderly. 4 So Shechem said to his father Hamor, "Get me this girl as a wife."

5 Jacob heard that he had defiled his daughter Dinah; but since his sons were in the field with his cattle, Jacob kept silent until they came home. 6 Then Shechem's father Hamor came out to Jacob to speak to him. 7 Meanwhile Jacob's sons, having heard the news, came in from the field. The men were distressed and very angry, because he had committed an outrage in Israel by lying with Jacob's daughter—a thing not to be done.

8 And Hamor spoke with them, saying, "My son Shechem longs for your daughter. Please give her to him

a Meaning "stalls," "huts," "booths."
b Heb. qesiṭah, a unit of unknown value.
c "El, God of Israel."

neys to Succoth. He once again succeeds in securing his independence from the larger family, thus maintaining the distinctive identity of his lineage against the threat of assimilation into the surrounding nations. **20:** Through this confession El, the supreme Canaanite deity, is identified as the God of Israel.

34.1–31: The rape of Dinah. No sooner does Jacob succeed in separating from Esau (33.12–17) than a new threat to the distinctive identity of his family emerges when a Canaanite prince seeks to marry the daughter of Jacob whom he has raped. And no sooner is an old rent in the family healed through the reconciliation of Jacob and Esau (33.1–11) than a new one opens when Simeon and Levi defy their father and avenge the crime against their sister. **1–2:** Given the extraordinary lengths to which the chosen family has gone to preserve its identity, Dinah's departure from her family's quarters is ominous. In the event, though she goes out "to see" (here rendered *to visit*), she is the one seen, with tragic consequences. Shechem is the name not only of her rapist (and then lover), but also of an important Canaanite city. The book of Joshua concludes with Joshua's making a covenant with Israel at Shechem (Josh. ch 24). Interestingly, there is no account of Israel's having taken the city by force of arms during the conquest of the land recounted in Joshua and Judges. It is possible that complex ethnic and political history lies behind the powerful tale in Gen. ch 34. **2:** Some scholars suggest that the final verb refers to improper sexual relations, in this case nonmarital sex, and not specifically rape. **3:** Without justifying his crime, the narrative builds up considerable sympathy for Shechem. **8–12:** According to biblical law (and strong Assyrian precedents), a man who rapes an unattached woman must pay a fine to her father, marry her, and forfeit the right to divorce her (Deut. 22.28–29). On the other hand, bibli-

translated as "take my blessing." Jacob acknowledges the truth in Esau's charge that "he has taken away my blessing" (27.35–36) and offers amends. It is precisely God's

generosity toward the chosen son that enables him to be generous, in turn, to his unchosen brother. **14:** Jacob never comes to his brother in Seir, but instead jourin marriage. ⁹Intermarry with us: give your daughters to us, and take our daughters for yourselves: ¹⁰You will dwell among us, and the land will be open before you; settle, move about, and acquire holdings in it." ¹¹Then Shechem said to her father and brothers, "Do me this favor, and I will pay whatever you tell me. ¹²Ask of me a bride-price ever so high, as well as gifts, and I will pay what you tell me; only give me the maiden for a wife."

¹³Jacob's sons answered Shechem and his father Hamor—speaking with guile because he had defiled their sister Dinah—¹⁴and said to them, "We cannot do this thing, to give our sister to a man who is uncircumcised, for that is a disgrace among us. ¹⁵Only on this condition will we agree with you; that you will become like us in that every male among you is circumcised. ¹⁶Then we will give our daughters to you and take your daughters to ourselves; and we will dwell among you and become as one kindred. ¹⁷But if you will not listen to us and become circumcised, we will take our daughter and go."

¹⁸Their words pleased Hamor and Hamor's son Shechem. ¹⁹And the youth lost no time in doing the thing, for he wanted Jacob's daughter. Now he was the most respected in his father's house. ²⁰So Hamor and his son Shechem went to the ᵃpublic place⁻ᵃ of their town and spoke to their fellow townsmen, saying, ²¹"These people are our friends; let them settle in the land and move about in it, for the land is large enough for them; we will take their daughters to ourselves as wives and give our daughters to them. ²²But only on this condition will the men agree with us to dwell among us and be as one kindred: that all our males become circumcised as they are circumcised. ²³Their cattle and substance and all their beasts will be ours, if we only agree to their terms, so that they will settle among us." ²⁴All ᵇ⁻who went out of the gate of his town⁻ᵇ heeded Hamor and his son Shechem, and all males, ᵇ⁻all those who went out of the gate of his town,⁻ᵇ were circumcised.

²⁵On the third day, when they were in pain, Simeon and Levi, two of Jacob's sons, brothers of Dinah, took each his sword, came upon the city unmolested, and slew all the males. ²⁶They put Hamor and his son Shechem to the sword, took Dinah out of Shechem's house, and went away. ²⁷The other sons of Jacob came upon the slain and plundered the town, because their sister had been defiled. ²⁸They seized their flocks and herds and asses, all that was inside the town and outside; ²⁹all their wealth, all

cal law strictly forbids the marriage of an Israelite to a Hivite (Deut. 7.1–5), and the patriarchs have gone to great lengths to avoid intermarriage (Gen. ch 24; 27.46–28.9). From the perspective of these (later) laws, a happy resolution to the love-struck Shechem's dilemma is impossible. **13–17:** In this ch, the sons of Jacob have already become adults, and the perspective is that of a later period in the national history (e.g., "he had committed an outrage in Israel," v. 7). Their devious proposal seems to be that the Israelites and the Hivites enter into a covenant, an act that is prohibited in the Torah as inevitably an inducement to break faith with the Lord (Exod. 23.27–33). **23:** Hamor and Shechem change the terms of the offer so as to appeal to their kinsmen. Now the projected deal is said to enrich the townsmen at the expense of Jacob and his family. **26:** Were the Hivites holding Dinah as a hostage throughout the elaborate negotiations? Or had she stayed in Shechem's house voluntarily, recognizing that he had done what the law required (see vv. 8–12 n.) and that the marriage prospects for a raped woman were not good (cf. 2 Sam. 13.12–16)? **27–29:** *Other* does not appear in the Heb of v. 27, and it is unclear whether Simeon and Levi were involved in the plundering. The Bible commends those who abstain from plunder in situations of righteous war (e.g., Deut. 13.13–19; 1 Sam. 15.13–26; Esth. 9.10, 15, 16). Given the emphasis Hamor and Shechem had placed on material benefits (vv. 34.10–12, 23), however, and the fact that the whole episode began with an act of violence (v. 2), the plundering of their town exemplifies the widespread biblical principle that the punishment fit the crime (e.g., Deut. 19.16–21). That Simeon and Levi *slew all the males* when the latter *were in pain* from an operation on their male organs manifests the same principle. **31:** Appropriately, this tragic and ambiguous tale ends with a question, not an assertion. There

a-a Lit. "gate."   b-b I.e., all his fellow townsmen.

their children, and their wives, all that was in the houses, they took as captives and booty.

30 Jacob said to Simeon and Levi, "You have brought trouble on me, making me odious among the inhabitants of the land, the Canaanites and the Perizzites; my men are few in number, so that if they unite against me and attack me, I and my house will be destroyed." 31 But they answered, "Should our sister be treated like a whore?"

35 God said to Jacob, "Arise, go up to Bethel and remain there; and build an altar there to the God who appeared to you when you were fleeing from your brother Esau." 2 So Jacob said to his household and to all who were with him, "Rid yourselves of the alien gods in your midst, purify yourselves, and change your clothes. 3 Come, let us go up to Bethel, and I will build an altar there to the God who answered me when I was in distress and who has been with me wherever I have gone." 4 They gave to Jacob all the alien gods that they had, and the rings that were in their ears, and Jacob buried them under the terebinth that was near Shechem. 5 As they set out, a terror from God fell on the cities round about, so that they did not pursue the sons of Jacob.

6 Thus Jacob came to Luz—that is, Bethel—in the land of Canaan, he and all the people who were with him. 7 There he built an altar and named the site El-bethel,ᵃ for it was there that God had revealed Himself to him when he was fleeing from his brother.

8 Deborah, Rebekah's nurse, died, and was buried under the oak below Bethel; so it was named Allon-bacuth.ᵇ

9 God appeared again to Jacob on his arrival from Paddan-aram, and He blessed him. 10 God said to him,

"You whose name is Jacob,
You shall be called Jacob no more,
But Israel shall be your name."

Thus He named him Israel.

11 And God said to him,
"I am El Shaddai.ᶜ
Be fertile and increase;

a "The God of Bethel."
b Understood as "the oak of the weeping."
c Cf. 17.1.

is room to question the two brothers' zeal here. The same men who kill for the sake of the family's honor (against their father's wishes) in ch 34 consent to have

their own little brother slain or sold into slavery in ch 37. Gen. 49.5-7, in which Jacob curses the anger of Simeon and Levi, explicitly condemns these brothers

for their excessive zeal, and explains the curious fates of the tribes of Simeon (which was absorbed into Judah) and Levi (which became the clerical tribe, without land).

35.1-28: Jacob and his household return to Bethel and travel in the promised land. Marked by three deaths (Deborah, Rachel, and Isaac) and one birth (Jacob's last child, Benjamin), this disjointed chapter provides closure to one phase of Jacob's life and prepares the way for his next set of trials, the apparent loss of Joseph and all that it involves (chs 37-50). **1-7:** This passage functions as a kind of fulfillment to Jacob's vow in 28.20-22. God's protection has indeed been with him, and he is about to return safely to his father's house. **2:** The actions Jacob commands to his entourage are associated with preparations for ritual service (e.g., Num. 19.7-8) and with a deepened and renewed consecration to the one God (cf. Josh. 24.14). **5:** This verse may be the conclusion to the tale told in ch 34. **8:** Nothing else is known about this Deborah. The story of her death serves as an etymology for the name of what must have been a well-known landmark. A different story suggests that a tree in the same region is named after the more famous Deborah, a heroine of the book of Judges (Judg. 4.4-5). A midrash, ingeniously connecting *oak* (Heb "ʾalon") with a form of the Greek word for "other" ("alon"), reports that while still mourning Rebekah's nurse, Jacob received the news of another death, that of Rebekah herself (*Gen. Rab.* 81.5)—an event strangely unreported in the Torah. Another midrash gives a reason: Her funeral was held at night so that "everybody would not say, Cursed be the breasts that suckled a person like this [i.e., her wicked son Esau]" (*Tanḥ., ki-tetze* 4). **9-13:** These verses are characterized by the vocabulary of P. Vv. 9-10 are the Priestly version of the change of Jacob's name that J reports in 32.28-29.

A nation, yea an assembly of nations,
Shall descend from you.
Kings shall issue from your loins.

12   The land that I assigned to Abraham and Isaac
I assign to you;
And to your offspring to come
Will I assign the land."

¹³ God parted from him at the spot where He had spoken
to him; ¹⁴ and Jacob set up a pillar at the site where He had
spoken to him, a pillar of stone, and he offered a libation
on it and poured oil upon it. ¹⁵ Jacob gave the site, where
God had spoken to him, the name of Bethel.

¹⁶ They set out from Bethel; but when they were still
some distance short of Ephrath, Rachel was in childbirth,
and she had hard labor. ¹⁷ When her labor was at its hard-
est, the midwife said to her, "Have no fear, for it is another
boy for you." ¹⁸ But as she breathed her last—for she was
dying—she named him Ben-oni;ᵃ but his father called him
Benjamin.ᵇ ¹⁹ Thus Rachel died. She was buried on the
road to Ephrath—now Bethlehem. ²⁰ Over her grave Jacob
set up a pillar; it is the pillar at Rachel's grave to this day.
²¹ Israel journeyed on, and pitched his tent beyond Migdal-eder.

²² While Israel stayed in that land, Reuben went and lay
with Bilhah, his father's concubine; and Israel found out.

Now the sons of Jacob were twelve in number. ²³ The
sons of Leah: Reuben—Jacob's first-born—Simeon, Levi,
Judah, Issachar, and Zebulun. ²⁴ The sons of Rachel: Joseph and Benjamin. ²⁵ The sons of Bilhah, Rachel's maid:
Dan and Naphtali. ²⁶ And the sons of Zilpah, Leah's maid:
Gad and Asher. These are the sons of Jacob who were born
to him in Paddan-aram.

²⁷ And Jacob came to his father Isaac at Mamre, at Kiriath-arba—now Hebron—where Abraham and Isaac had
sojourned. ²⁸ Isaac was a hundred and eighty years old
²⁹ when he breathed his last and died. Heᶜ was gathered to
his kin in ripe old age; and he was buried by his sons Esau
and Jacob.

36 This is the line of Esau—that is, Edom.
² Esau took his wives from among the Canaanite
women—Adah daughter of Elon the Hittite, and Oholibamah daughter of Anah daughter of Zibeon the Hiviteᵈ—
³ and also Basemath daughter of Ishmael and sister of Ne-

14–15: This is the third time Jacob
names Bethel. The passage seems
to be a variant of 28.18–19, which
it more closely resembles than
35.7. The source analysis of v. 7
and vv. 14–15 is more uncertain
than usual. **18:** According to
1 Sam. 10.2, the tomb of Rachel
was in the territory of Benjamin,
as befits this account of her death,
and not near Bethlehem, which is
in Judah. Similarly, in Jer. 31.15,
Rachel is depicted as weeping for
her children in Ramah, a Benjaminite city (Josh. 18.21–28).
Ephrathah/Bethlehem and Judah,
however, attained high status because of their later association with
David (e.g., Ruth 4.11–12, 18–22),
and this may have contributed to
the identification of Rachel's tomb
with the site mentioned in this
verse. **22a:** The details are missing,
and the text breaks off abruptly
mid-verse (49.4 seems to allude to
the same episode), suggesting that
some material has been lost, or
that there is more to say about this
episode. A son's having intercourse with his father's concubine
was a declaration of rebellion
(2 Sam. 16.20–22; 1 Kings 2.13–25).
Eager to protect the good names of
all involved, a midrash denies that
the report of Reuben's sin is to be
taken literally (e.g., b. Shab. 55b).
28: Abraham's life span of 175
years (25.7) and Isaac's of 180 suggest a pattern: $175 = 7 \times 5^2$, and
$180 = 5 \times 6^2$. Following that progression, Jacob should live 147
years (= 3×7^2), and so he does
(47.28)!

**36.1–43: The descendants of
Esau.** This chapter consists of several overlapping but not altogether
consistent genealogies, most likely
compiled from a variety of
sources. Its placement here is perhaps owing to the list of Jacob's
twelve sons in 35.22b–26; it also
serves to divide the Jacob cycle
from the Joseph story. The generation of Rebekah and Isaac's twins
is now passing, and the focus for
the rest of Genesis will lie on
Jacob's troubled descendants
alone. The attention given to
Esau's family here suggests con-

---

a Understood as "son of my suffering (or, strength)."
b I.e., "son of the right hand," or "son of the south."
c Lit. "Isaac."   d Cf. v. 20, "Horite."

baioth. [4] Adah bore to Esau Eliphaz; Basemath bore Reuel; [5] and Oholibamah bore Jeush, Jalam, and Korah. Those were the sons of Esau, who were born to him in the land of Canaan.

[6] Esau took his wives, his sons and daughters, and all the members of his household, his cattle and all his livestock, and all the property that he had acquired in the land of Canaan, and went to another land because of his brother Jacob. [7] For their possessions were too many for them to dwell together, and the land where they sojourned could not support them because of their livestock. [8] So Esau settled in the hill country of Seir—Esau being Edom.

[9] This, then, is the line of Esau, the ancestor of the Edomites, in the hill country of Seir.

[10] These are the names of Esau's sons: Eliphaz, the son of Esau's wife Adah; Reuel, the son of Esau's wife Basemath. [11] The sons of Eliphaz were Teman, Omar, Zepho, Gatam, and Kenaz. [12] Timna was a concubine of Esau's son Eliphaz; she bore Amalek to Eliphaz. Those were the descendants of Esau's wife Adah. [13] And these were the sons of Reuel: Nahath, Zerah, Shammah, and Mizzah. Those were the descendants of Esau's wife Basemath. [14] And these were the sons of Esau's wife Oholibamah, daughter of Anah daughter of Zibeon: she bore to Esau Jeush, Jalam, and Korah.

[15] These are the clans of the children of Esau. The descendants of Esau's first-born Eliphaz: the clans Teman, Omar, Zepho, Kenaz, [16] Korah, Gatam, and Amalek; these are the clans of Eliphaz in the land of Edom. Those are the descendants of Adah. [17] And these are the descendants of Esau's son Reuel: the clans Nahath, Zerah, Shammah, and Mizzah; these are the clans of Reuel in the land of Edom. Those are the descendants of Esau's wife Basemath. [18] And these are the descendants of Esau's wife Oholibamah: the clans Jeush, Jalam, and Korah; these are the clans of Esau's wife Oholibamah, the daughter of Anah. [19] Those were the sons of Esau—that is, Edom—and those are their clans.

[20] These were the sons of Seir the Horite, who were settled in the land: Lotan, Shobal, Zibeon, Anah, [21] Dishon, Ezer, and Dishan. Those are the clans of the Horites, the descendants of Seir, in the land of Edom. [22] The sons of Lotan were Hori and Hemam; and Lotan's sister was Timna. [23] The sons of Shobal were these: Alvan, Manahath, Ebal, Shepho, and Onam. [24] The sons of Zibeon were these: Aiah[a] and Anah—that was the Anah

siderable fraternal feeling for him (cf. Deut. 23.8), which clashes with later biblical and postbiblical attitudes toward him. See 27.34–35 n. **2–3:** See 26.34–35 n.; 28.8–9 n. **6–8:** The passage is reminiscent of the separation of Abraham and Lot in 13.5–13 and serves a similar purpose. **9–14:** This list provides the names of Esau's sons and their sons in turn. Amalek's conception by a concubine may be a disparagement related to his identity as the ruthless enemy of the people Israel and their God (Exod. 17.8–16; Deut. 25.17–19). **12:** If the notice about Timna is not an interpolation, then Amalek's being reckoned a descendant of Adah is probably related to the institution of surrogate motherhood attested in 16.1–2; 29.3–13. **15–19:** The individuals in vv. 9–14 are here listed as the eponymous heads of the Edomite clans. **20–30:** This is a list of the individuals and the clans of Seir the Horite. According to Deut. 2.12, a group called *Horites* inhabited the land of Seir before the descendants of Esau wiped them out. The exact identity of these Horites—whether, for example, they are the same as the "Hurrians" known from cuneiform sources—is still a matter of debate. Note that Zibeon (vv. 20, 24) appears in v. 2 as the name of a Hivite. **24:** Nothing more is known about Anah's enigmatic discovery. The report reads like an allusion to a story well known to the original listeners.

a Heb. "and Aiah."

who discovered the hot springs[a] in the wilderness while pasturing the asses of his father Zibeon. 25 The children of Anah were these: Dishon and Anah's daughter Oholibamah. 26 The sons of Dishon[b] were these: Hemdan, Eshban, Ithran, and Cheran. 27 The sons of Ezer were these: Bilhan, Zaavan, and Akan. 28 And the sons of Dishan were these: Uz and Aran.

29 These are the clans of the Horites: the clans Lotan, Shobal, Zibeon, Anah, 30 Dishon, Ezer, and Dishan. Those are the clans of the Horites, clan by clan, in the land of Seir.

31 These are the kings who reigned in the land of Edom before any king reigned over the Israelites. 32 Bela son of Beor reigned in Edom, and the name of his city was Dinhabah. 33 When Bela died, Jobab son of Zerah, from Bozrah, succeeded him as king. 34 When Jobab died, Husham of the land of the Temanites succeeded him as king. 35 When Husham died, Hadad son of Bedad, who defeated the Midianites in the country of Moab, succeeded him as king; the name of his city was Avith. 36 When Hadad died, Samlah of Masrekah succeeded him as king. 37 When Samlah died, Saul[c] of Rehoboth-on-the-river succeeded him as king. 38 When Saul died, Baal-hanan son of Achbor succeeded him as king. 39 And when Baal-hanan son of Achbor died, Hadar succeeded him as king; the name of his city was Pau, and his wife's name was Mehetabel daughter of Matred daughter of Me-zahab.

40 These are the names of the clans of Esau, each with its families and locality, name by name: the clans Timna, Alvah, Jetheth, 41 Oholibamah, Elah, Pinon, 42 Kenaz, Teman, Mibzar, 43 Magdiel, and Iram. Those are the clans of Edom—that is, of Esau, father of the Edomites—by their settlements in the land which they hold.

VA-YESHEV　　　　　　　　　　　　　　וישב

37 Now Jacob was settled in the land where his father had sojourned, the land of Canaan. 2 This, then, is the line of Jacob:

At seventeen years of age, Joseph tended the flocks with his brothers, as a helper to the sons of his father's wives Bilhah and Zilpah. And Joseph brought bad reports of them to their father. 3 Now Israel loved Joseph best of all his sons, for he was the child of his old age; and he had made him an ornamented tunic.[d] 4 And when his brothers

---

a Meaning of Heb. yemim uncertain.
b Heb. Dishan; but cf. vv. 21, 25, 28, and 30, and 1 Chron. 1.41.
c Or "Shaul."
d Or "a coat of many colors"; meaning of Heb. uncertain.

31–39: None of the kings listed here succeeded his father, and different capitals are given for different rulers. It is likely that the *kings* listed here were more like the non-dynastic leaders known as "judges" in the biblical book of that name. **31:** The reference to kings reigning in Israel is difficult to reconcile with the traditional attribution of Genesis to Moses, who died long before the monarchy. Ibn Ezra, who is elsewhere open to the idea of post-Mosaic passages, defends the traditional doctrine by identifying Moses himself as the first Israelite king (also in Deut. 33.5)—a title he never holds in the Tanakh, however. **40–43:** The ch closes with another list of Edomite clans, overlapping with vv. 15–19, but not identical with it.

37.1–36: Joseph's brothers sell him into slavery. Ch 37 begins the story of Joseph, a figure who dominates most of the remaining narrative in Genesis. In structure, the Joseph story is quite different from the preceding material centering on Abraham, Isaac, and Jacob. Whereas the latter takes the form, predominantly, of small, self-contained passages, the story of Joseph resembles a coherent novella, with a subtle and well-crafted plot. Its theology, too, is different. Whereas the patriarchal narrative is replete with appearances of God or His messengers, and oracles from them, Joseph never sees or hears God or His messengers (the only direct revelation in these chs comes to Jacob, in 46.1–4). Rather, God works here in a hidden way, secretly guiding the course of human events, even bringing good out of human evil (50.20). Lastly, whereas the stories of Abraham, Isaac, and Jacob take place in Canaan and Mesopotamia, the novella of Joseph and his brothers takes place mostly in Egypt. The events that result in the return to the promised land will begin only after Joseph's death. Many of these special characteristics of the Joseph story are found in wisdom literature (see pp. 1276–77). **1–3:** The order of presentation is saw that their father loved him more than any of his brothers, they hated him so that they could not speak a friendly word to him.

5 Once Joseph had a dream which he told to his brothers; and they hated him even more. 6 He said to them, "Hear this dream which I have dreamed: 7 There we were binding sheaves in the field, when suddenly my sheaf stood up and remained upright; then your sheaves gathered around and bowed low to my sheaf." 8 His brothers answered, "Do you mean to reign over us? Do you mean to rule over us?" And they hated him even more for his talk about his dreams.

9 He dreamed another dream and told it to his brothers, saying, "Look, I have had another dream: And this time, the sun, the moon, and eleven stars were bowing down to me." 10 And when he told it to his father and brothers, his father berated him. "What," he said to him, "is this dream you have dreamed? Are we to come, I and your mother and your brothers, and bow low to you to the ground?" 11 So his brothers were wrought up at him, and his father kept the matter in mind.

12 One time, when his brothers had gone to pasture their father's flock at Shechem, 13 Israel said to Joseph, "Your brothers are pasturing at Shechem. Come, I will send you to them." He answered, "I am ready." 14 And he said to him, "Go and see how your brothers are and how the flocks are faring, and bring me back word." So he sent him from the valley of Hebron.

When he reached Shechem, 15 a man came upon him wandering in the fields. The man asked him, "What are you looking for?" 16 He answered, "I am looking for my brothers. Could you tell me where they are pasturing?" 17 The man said, "They have gone from here, for I heard them say: Let us go to Dothan." So Joseph followed his brothers and found them at Dothan.

18 They saw him from afar, and before he came close to them they conspired to kill him. 19 They said to one another, "Here comes that dreamer! 20 Come now, let us kill him and throw him into one of the pits; and we can say, 'A savage beast devoured him.' We shall see what comes of his dreams!" 21 But when Reuben heard it, he tried to save

could not say 'Shalom' to him." **5:** Like the "bad reports [that] he brought to his father" (v. 2), his telling his brothers the dream evidences Joseph's immaturity and lack of foresight—both of which will be dramatically remedied as his tale unfolds. **8:** In each of the three pairs of dreams in the Joseph story, one dream focuses on grain or grain products (40.16–19; 41.5–7). The brothers see only dominance in Joseph's own first dream, missing altogether the symbolism of the grain imagery. When they do bow down to him, it will be in supplication that he—who has grain when they do not—will feed them (42.6–7). **9–11:** Joseph tells his first dream to the brothers alone, the second to his brothers and his father. Similarly, his brothers come to Egypt alone and bow down to him (42.6); only afterwards does Jacob come (46.6) and bow to his son (47.31). Jacob is doubly incredulous of the dream, perhaps because it appears to mention Rachel, who has already died giving birth to Benjamin (35.16–20). In the Talmud, a rabbi observes that this illustrates the rule that only part of any given dream comes true, not the whole (*b. Ber.* 55a). Rashi, on the other hand, cites a midrash that identifies Joseph's mother with Bilhah, Rachel's slave and surrogate (*Gen. Rab.* 44.11). Some modern scholars have speculated that the second dream presupposes an earlier form of the story, in which Rachel had not yet passed away. **12–13:** Joseph's response, *I am ready* ("hineni"), recalls instances in which the same Heb word appears in contexts in which earlier fathers were about to lose, or seemed about to lose, their favored sons (22.1, 7, 11; 27.1). **14:** *How your brothers are,* lit. "the shalom of your brothers," is telling, given the absence of "shalom" in the family (see v. 4 n.). Shechem being quite a distance from Hebron, there is room to wonder why Jacob did not foresee danger, even before his beloved son reached his angry brothers. Eventually, Joseph does reach Shechem in peace—after his death

revealing—Jacob, Joseph, his brothers. Joseph is caught between his doting father and his envious siblings. Although he is the first-born son of Jacob's preferred wife, Rachel (30.22–24), his older brothers have stationed him with the

sons of the slave women (30.3–13), the lowest ranking siblings. Like his dreams (vv. 5–11), this contradiction may foreshadow the radical reversal of Joseph's status. **4:** The end of the verse can be translated more literally as, "they him from them. He said, "Let us not take his life." [22] And Reuben went on, "Shed no blood! Cast him into that pit out in the wilderness, but do not touch him yourselves"—intending to save him from them and restore him to his father. [23] When Joseph came up to his brothers, they stripped Joseph of his tunic, the ornamented tunic that he was wearing, [24] and took him and cast him into the pit. The pit was empty; there was no water in it.

[25] Then they sat down to a meal. Looking up, they saw a caravan of Ishmaelites coming from Gilead, their camels bearing gum, balm, and ladanum to be taken to Egypt. [26] Then Judah said to his brothers, "What do we gain by killing our brother and covering up his blood? [27] Come, let us sell him to the Ishmaelites, but let us not do away with him ourselves. After all, he is our brother, our own flesh." His brothers agreed. [28] When Midianite traders passed by, they pulled Joseph up out of the pit. They sold Joseph for twenty pieces of silver to the Ishmaelites, who brought Joseph to Egypt.

[29] When Reuben returned to the pit and saw that Joseph was not in the pit, he rent his clothes. [30] Returning to his brothers, he said, "The boy is gone! Now, what am I to do?" [31] Then they took Joseph's tunic, slaughtered a kid, and dipped the tunic in the blood. [32] They had the ornamented tunic taken to their father, and they said, "We found this. Please examine it; is it your son's tunic or not?" [33] He recognized it, and said, "My son's tunic! A savage beast devoured him! Joseph was torn by a beast!" [34] Jacob rent his clothes, put sackcloth on his loins, and observed mourning for his son many days. [35] All his sons and daughters sought to comfort him; but he refused to be comforted, saying, "No, I will go down mourning to my son in Sheol." Thus his father bewailed him.

[36] The Midianites,[a] meanwhile, sold him in Egypt to Potiphar, a courtier of Pharaoh and his chief steward.

38 About that time Judah left his brothers and camped near a certain Adullamite whose name was Hirah. [2] There Judah saw the daughter of a certain Canaanite whose name was Shua, and he married her and cohabited with her. [3] She conceived and bore a son, and he

a Heb. "Medanites."

his nervous dependents (43.29–34). **26–27:** It is Judah's advice that is ultimately heeded, reflecting the importance of this brother elsewhere in the Joseph story. **28:** In its current form, the text mentions both Ishmaelite caravaneers (v. 25) and *Midianite traders*, just as it mentions two different attempts to save Joseph's life, one by Reuben (vv. 21–22, 29–30) and one by Judah (vv. 26–28). Although arguments have been made that Midianites and Ishmaelites are the same group (cf. Judg. 8.24), many modern scholars think the explanation lies in source analysis: Reuben and the Midianites derive from the E version of the story, and Judah and the Ishmaelites from the J version, though it is difficult to find complete J and E versions throughout the narrative. In the story in its current form, it is unclear who is the subject of *pulled* in v. 28—the brothers or the *Midianite traders*. One could argue that if it is the latter, Joseph's brothers truly do not know what became of him. But the idea that it was the Midianites rather than the brothers who sold him to the Ishmaelites cannot explain the reports that it is the Midianites who bring him to Egypt (v. 36; cf. 39.1). **30:** Reuben's cry is strikingly similar to Rachel's lament in Jer. 31.15. **31:** There is a certain poetic justice to the brothers' cruel deception of their father, since Jacob had used kids to deceive his own father (27.5–23). **35:** That Jacob *refused to be comforted* recalls what is said of Rachel in Jer. 31.15, in a lament for the lost members of the nation. See 37.30 n.

38.1–30: Judah and Tamar. This chapter, which treats the origins of the Judahite clans (cf. Num. 26.19–22), is, on the one hand, independent of the novella of Joseph in which it now appears. Note that Judah lives apart from his brothers and already has grown children when the tale begins. On the other hand, a number of verbal and thematic connections to the Joseph story bespeak the exquisite fitness of its placement therein.

(Josh. 24.32)! **23:** The clothing and unclothing of Joseph mark pivotal moments in the course of the narrative (cf. 37.3; 39.15–18; 41.14, 42). **25:** The brothers' meal displays their extraordinary callousness and insensitivity to human life (cf. Esth. 3.15). Later, the tables turn, and Joseph arranges a meal in which he is the master, and they, named him Er. ⁴She conceived again and bore a son, and named him Onan. ⁵Once again she bore a son, and named him Shelah; he was at Chezib when she bore him.

⁶Judah got a wife for Er his first-born; her name was Tamar. ⁷But Er, Judah's first-born, was displeasing to the Lord, and the Lord took his life. ⁸Then Judah said to Onan, "Join with your brother's wife and do your duty by her as a brother-in-law,ᵃ and provide offspring for your brother." ⁹But Onan, knowing that the seed would not count as his, let it go to wasteᵇ whenever he joined with his brother's wife, so as not to provide offspring for his brother. ¹⁰What he did was displeasing to the Lord, and He took his life also. ¹¹Then Judah said to his daughter-in-law Tamar, "Stay as a widow in your father's house until my son Shelah grows up"—for he thought, "He too might die like his brothers." So Tamar went to live in her father's house.

¹²A long time afterward, Shua's daughter, the wife of Judah, died. When ᶜhis period of mourning was over,ᶜ Judah went up to Timnah to his sheepshearers, together with his friend Hirah the Adullamite. ¹³And Tamar was told, "Your father-in-law is coming up to Timnah for the sheepshearing." ¹⁴So she took off her widow's garb, covered her face with a veil, and, wrapping herself up, sat down at the entrance to Enaim,ᵈ which is on the road to Timnah; for she saw that Shelah was grown up, yet she had not been given to him as wife. ¹⁵When Judah saw her, he took her for a harlot; for she had covered her face. ¹⁶So he turned aside to her by the road and said, "Here, let me sleep with you"—for he did not know that she was his daughter-in-law. "What," she asked, "will you pay for sleeping with me?" ¹⁷He replied, "I will send a kid from my flock." But she said, "You must leave a pledge until you have sent it." ¹⁸And he said, "What pledge shall I give you?" She replied, "Your seal and cord, and the staff which you carry." So he gave them to her and slept with her, and she conceived by him. ¹⁹Then she went on her way. She took off her veil and again put on her widow's garb.

²⁰Judah sent the kid by his friend the Adullamite, to redeem the pledge from the woman; but he could not find her. ²¹He inquired of the people of that town, "Where is the cult prostitute, the one at Enaim, by the road?" But they said, "There has been no prostitute here." ²²So he returned to Judah and said, "I could not find her; moreover,

8: The duty in question, known in English as "levirate marriage," is spelled out in Deut. 25.5–10. If a man dies childless, his brother is obligated to marry his widow, and her first son is reckoned as the offspring of the deceased. In Deuteronomy, the surviving brother can decline and undergo a procedure that the Rabbis named "ḥalitzah," but Gen. ch 38 presupposes a stage in the history of the law in which "ḥalitzah" is still unknown (cf. Ruth 4.5–6). Today, levirate marriage is discouraged and "ḥalitzah" is substituted among traditionally observant Ashkenazic Jews. Some Sephardic groups still practice levirate marriage. **9:** Onan would have to expend his own resources to support a child that is legally someone else's, and the child, as the heir to a first-born son, would displace Onan in the line of inheritance to boot. **11:** Judah's loss of two sons and reluctance to surrender the third foreshadows the tragic situation of Jacob, who will soon lose Joseph and Simeon (or so it will appear to him) and refuse to surrender Benjamin, as he must if the family is to survive (42.36–38). **14–15:** The use of a disguise in pursuit of a purpose that conforms to the will of God (and, in this case, religious law) recalls Jacob's deceit in ch 27. **17:** Note the echo of the preceding ch, where a kid also played a key role in deceiving a parent (37.31–35). **21:** *Cult prostitute* and *prostitute* are the same word in Heb; many scholars doubt that cultic prostitution as it is usually understood existed in ancient Israel. A different term underlies "harlot" in vv. 15, 24.

ᵃ Cf. Deut. 25.5.   ᵇ Lit. "spoil on the ground."   ᶜ-ᶜ Lit. "he was comforted."
ᵈ Cf. Enam, Josh. 15.34. Others "in an open place" or "at the crossroad."

the townspeople said: There has been no prostitute here." ²³ Judah said, "Let her keep them, lest we become a laughingstock. I did send her this kid, but you did not find her."

²⁴ About three months later, Judah was told, "Your daughter-in-law Tamar has played the harlot; in fact, she is with child by harlotry." "Bring her out," said Judah, "and let her be burned." ²⁵ As she was being brought out, she sent this message to her father-in-law, "I am with child by the man to whom these belong." And she added, "Examine these: whose seal and cord and staff are these?" ²⁶ Judah recognized them, and said, "She is more in the right than I, inasmuch as I did not give her to my son Shelah." And he was not intimate with her again.

²⁷ When the time came for her to give birth, there were twins in her womb! ²⁸ While she was in labor, one of them put out his hand, and the midwife tied a crimson thread on that hand, to signify: This one came out first. ²⁹ But just then he drew back his hand, and out came his brother; and she said, "What a breach[a] you have made for yourself!" So he was named Perez. ³⁰ Afterward his brother came out, on whose hand was the crimson thread; he was named Zerah.[b]

39 When Joseph was taken down to Egypt, a certain Egyptian, Potiphar, a courtier of Pharaoh and his chief steward, bought him from the Ishmaelites who had brought him there. ² The LORD was with Joseph, and he was a successful man; and he stayed in the house of his Egyptian master. ³ And when his master saw that the LORD was with him and that the LORD lent success to everything he undertook, ⁴ he took a liking to Joseph. He made him his personal attendant and put him in charge of his household, placing in his hands all that he owned. ⁵ And from the time that the Egyptian put him in charge of his household and of all that he owned, the LORD blessed his house for Joseph's sake, so that the blessing of the LORD was upon everything that he owned, in the house and outside. ⁶ He left all that he had in Joseph's hands and, with him there, he paid attention to nothing save the food that he ate. Now Joseph was well built and handsome.

⁷ After a time, his master's wife cast her eyes upon Jo-

a Heb. pereṣ   b I.e., "brightness," perhaps alluding to the crimson thread.

stances of this expression in the Tanakh. Recognition (the same word in Heb) is a major theme in the Joseph story (see also 42.7–8).
26: Tamar's actions are justified in Judah's eyes, and in the eyes of the author. She ensured that the family line of Judah was preserved. A midrash in the Talmud sees Judah's Heb name (which includes every letter of the four-letter name of the LORD) as a reward for his public confession of wrongdoing in this episode (*b. Sot.* 10b). According to 1 Chron. 4.21, Shelah named his first son Er, suggesting that Judah did finally release him to the first Er's widow, Tamar.
27–30: The birth story of Perez and Zerah is highly reminiscent of that of Jacob and Esau in 25.21–26. It is from Perez that King David was descended, as reported, for example, in Ruth (Ruth 4.18–22), a book with striking similarities to Gen. ch 38 (see also Ruth 4.11–12).

39.1–23: Joseph in Potiphar's house. Genesis rejoins the story of Joseph after the digression of ch 38. The bulk of ch 39 centers on the hero's resistance to seduction and the ensuing false accusation of the spurned matron. It shows remarkable similarities to an Egyptian tale, "The Story of Two Brothers." Although some dependence is likely, the biblical narrative adapts its prototype to characteristic Israelite theological and ethical convictions. **39.1–6a:** As in ch 37, which speaks of Jacob's preference for Joseph (vv. 3–4), so here the latter is the beneficiary of a mysterious favor, this time from the LORD. One senses that, unbeknownst to all at the time, Jacob's favoritism for the son of his old age had been the medium for a higher purpose. Like Laban (30.27–30), Potiphar benefits mightily from association with this descendant of Abraham. **6–7:** Good looks are often a sign of divine favor in the Tanakh (e.g., 1 Sam. 9.2; 16.12), but here they set the one who bears them up for a potentially catastrophic temptation. A midrash, finding it difficult to believe that Joseph was altogether innocent, likens him to one

24: Tamar's ostensible capital offense is not prostitution, but adultery (see Deut. 22.23–24), since she is still in a state akin to betrothal to Judah's family. Adultery is the false charge in the next ch as well (39.7–18). **25:** *Examine these* is identical in the Heb to "Please examine it" in the previous chapter (37.32). These are, in fact, the only two in-seph and said, "Lie with me." ⁸But he refused. He said to his master's wife, "Look, with me here, my master gives no thought to anything in this house, and all that he owns he has placed in my hands. ⁹He wields no more authority in this house than I, and he has withheld nothing from me except yourself, since you are his wife. How then could I do this most wicked thing, and sin before God?" ¹⁰And much as she coaxed Joseph day after day, he did not yield to her request to lie beside her, to be with her.

¹¹One such day, he came into the house to do his work. None of the household being there inside, ¹²she caught hold of him by his garment and said, "Lie with me!" But he left his garment in her hand and got away and fled outside. ¹³When she saw that he had left it in her hand and had fled outside, ¹⁴she called out to her servants and said to them, "Look, he had to bring us a Hebrew to dally with us! This one came to lie with me; but I screamed loud. ¹⁵And when he heard me screaming at the top of my voice, he left his garment with me and got away and fled outside." ¹⁶She kept his garment beside her, until his master came home. ¹⁷Then she told him the same story, saying, "The Hebrew slave whom you brought into our house came to me to dally with me; ¹⁸but when I screamed at the top of my voice, he left his garment with me and fled outside."

¹⁹When his master heard the story that his wife told him, namely, "Thus and so your slave did to me," he was furious. ²⁰So Joseph's master had him put in prison, where the king's prisoners were confined. But even while he was there in prison, ²¹the LORD was with Joseph: He extended kindness to him and disposed the chief jailer favorably toward him. ²²The chief jailer put in Joseph's charge all the prisoners who were in that prison, and he was the one to carry out everything that was done there. ²³The chief jailer did not supervise anything that was in Joseph'sᵃ charge, because the LORD was with him, and whatever he did the LORD made successful.

40 Some time later, the cupbearer and the baker of the king of Egypt gave offense to their lord the king of Egypt. ²Pharaoh was angry with his two courtiers, the

---

ᵃ Lit. "his."

"who would stand in the market place, put make-up around his eyes, straighten up his hair, and swing his heels." Mrs. Potiphar's proposition was thus a punish-

ment for his narcissism and machismo (*Gen. Rab.* 87.3).
8–9: Joseph's pointed deference to his *master* stands in striking contrast with his dreams of domi-

nance in 37.5–11. One senses that the brash and unreflective teenager of ch 37 has matured into a more responsible man, with the appropriate humility. Joseph's mention of *God* is his first. No one mentioned the deity in the previous two chs. **12:** The garment left *in her hand* (also in v. 13) contrasts with Potiphar's placing "in his hands all that he owned" (v. 4). The use of a garment as fraudulent evidence recalls Joseph's brothers' displaying the bloodstained tunic to their father (37.31–33) and contrasts with Tamar's truthful presentation to Judah of his "seal and cord and staff" (38.25–26). Note the telling contrast between the woman who attempts to dishonor her marriage without success (Mrs. Potiphar) and the woman who, also acting boldly and seductively, succeeds in implementing the law and thus ensures the survival of her family (Tamar). **14:** Her clever phrasing suggests a hope to profit from her staff's resentment of a foreigner and perhaps of their boss as well (*he had to bring us a Hebrew*). Here she sides with her servants (*bring us*), whereas in v. 17 she sides with her husband ("whom you brought into our house"), although in both cases she blames him for introducing Joseph into the household. **17–18:** Now she blames Joseph primarily, and her husband only indirectly. Note that here (as in v. 15) she describes the garment that was left "in her hand" (v. 12) as *with me,* instead, subtly disguising her true involvement. **19–23:** The tale ends where it began (v. 2), with an affirmation of God's presence in Joseph's affairs and the success it brings. Even in prison, the young man who had been second in rank in his family (37.3) and second in rank in the chief steward's household (vv. 4–6) achieves the same status, when the warden puts him in charge of the other prisoners.

40.1–23: Joseph the dream interpreter. In this chapter, we hear of the second of the three pairs of dreams that mark pivotal mo-

chief cupbearer and the chief baker, ³ and put them in custody, in the house of the chief steward, in the same prison
house where Joseph was confined. ⁴ The chief steward assigned Joseph to them, and he attended them.

When they had been in custody for some time, ⁵ both of
them—the cupbearer and the baker of the king of Egypt,
who were confined in the prison—dreamed in the same
night, each his own dream and each dream with its own
meaning. ⁶ When Joseph came to them in the morning, he
saw that they were distraught. ⁷ He asked Pharaoh's
courtiers, who were with him in custody in his master's
house, saying, "Why do you appear downcast today?"
⁸ And they said to him, "We had dreams, and there is no
one to interpret them." So Joseph said to them, "Surely
God can interpret! Tell me [your dreams]."

⁹ Then the chief cupbearer told his dream to Joseph. He
said to him, "In my dream, there was a vine in front of me.
¹⁰ On the vine were three branches. It had barely budded,
when out came its blossoms and its clusters ripened into
grapes. ¹¹ Pharaoh's cup was in my hand, and I took the
grapes, pressed them into Pharaoh's cup, and placed the
cup in Pharaoh's hand." ¹² Joseph said to him, "This is its
interpretation: The three branches are three days. ¹³ In
three days Pharaoh will pardon youᵃ and restore you to
your post; you will place Pharaoh's cup in his hand, as
was your custom formerly when you were his cupbearer.
¹⁴ But think of me when all is well with you again, and do
me the kindness of mentioning me to Pharaoh, so as to
free me from this place. ¹⁵ For in truth, I was kidnapped
from the land of the Hebrews; nor have I done anything
here that they should have put me in the dungeon."

¹⁶ When the chief baker saw how favorably he had interpreted, he said to Joseph, "In my dream, similarly, there
were three openwork basketsᵇ on my head. ¹⁷ In the uppermost basket were all kinds of food for Pharaoh that a
baker prepares; and the birds were eating it out of the basket above my head." ¹⁸ Joseph answered, "This is its interpretation: The three baskets are three days. ¹⁹ In three days
Pharaoh will lift off your head and impale you upon a
pole; and the birds will pick off your flesh."

²⁰ On the third day—his birthday—Pharaoh made a
banquet for all his officials, and he singled outᶜ his chief
cupbearer and his chief baker from among his officials.
²¹ He restored the chief cupbearer to his cupbearing, and

ments in Joseph's life. The first
pair (37.5–11) were Joseph's own,
and their interpretation came not
from him, but from his outraged
brothers and incredulous father.
Taken for dreams of kingship, they
nearly result in the dreamer's
death and leave him in slavery
(37.18–28). Joseph decodes the second set of dreams himself, through
a hitherto unmentioned God-given
talent. They treat of the same po-
larity, favor from the king (v. 13),
reminiscent of the nearly lethal
favor Joseph received from his father (37.3), on the one hand, and
death, on the other (v. 19). **8:** *Surely
God can interpret!* may imply a critique of divination practices
prominent in the ancient world.
The contrast between Joseph, with
his God-given talent for dream interpretation, and the bankruptcy
of the Egyptian magicians is more
pronounced in the next chapter,
which deals with Pharaoh's
dreams (41.8). The theme foreshadows Moses and Aaron's decisive confrontation with Pharaoh's
magicians in Exod. chs 7–11 (see
esp. Exod. 8.15). **16–19:** The chief
baker altogether misses the key
point that Joseph's gift for interpretation depends on the grace of
God. Instead, he imagines that it is
all a matter of technique: Similar
dreams must lead to similar interpretations (not an unreasonable
expectation in light of the other
pairs in 37.5 and 41.1–32). But Joseph notices a crucial detail that
the chief baker has missed: Not
Pharaoh but birds eat from the
basket on his head. Having missed
God's grace, the chief baker will be
denied Pharaoh's as well.

---

a Lit. "lift up your head."
b Others "baskets with white bread" or "white baskets"; meaning of Heb. ḥori uncertain.
c Lit. "lifted the head of."

he placed the cup in Pharaoh's hand; [22] but the chief baker he impaled—just as Joseph had interpreted to them.

[23] Yet the chief cupbearer did not think of Joseph; he forgot him.

MIKKETS   מקץ

41 After two years' time, Pharaoh dreamed that he was standing by the Nile, [2] when out of the Nile there came up seven cows, handsome and sturdy, and they grazed in the reed grass. [3] But presently, seven other cows came up from the Nile close behind them, ugly and gaunt, and stood beside the cows on the bank of the Nile; [4] and the ugly gaunt cows ate up the seven handsome sturdy cows. And Pharaoh awoke.

[5] He fell asleep and dreamed a second time: Seven ears of grain, solid and healthy, grew on a single stalk. [6] But close behind them sprouted seven ears, thin and scorched by the east wind. [7] And the thin ears swallowed up the seven solid and full ears. Then Pharaoh awoke: it was a dream!

[8] Next morning, his spirit was agitated, and he sent for all the magicians of Egypt, and all its wise men; and Pharaoh told them his dreams, but none could interpret them for Pharaoh.

[9] The chief cupbearer then spoke up and said to Pharaoh, "I must make mention today of my offenses. [10] Once Pharaoh was angry with his servants, and placed me in custody in the house of the chief steward, together with the chief baker. [11] We had dreams the same night, he and I, each of us a dream with a meaning of its own. [12] A Hebrew youth was there with us, a servant of the chief steward; and when we told him our dreams, he interpreted them for us, telling each of the meaning of his dream. [13] And as he interpreted for us, so it came to pass: I was restored to my post, and the other was impaled."

[14] Thereupon Pharaoh sent for Joseph, and he was rushed from the dungeon. He had his hair cut and changed his clothes, and he appeared before Pharaoh. [15] And Pharaoh said to Joseph, "I have had a dream, but no one can interpret it. Now I have heard it said of you that for you to hear a dream is to tell its meaning." [16] Joseph answered Pharaoh, saying, "Not I! God will see to Pharaoh's welfare."

[17] Then Pharaoh said to Joseph, "In my dream, I was standing on the bank of the Nile, [18] when out of the Nile came up seven sturdy and well-formed cows and grazed in the reed grass. [19] Presently there followed them seven other cows, scrawny, ill-formed, and emaciated—never

41.1–57: Joseph interprets Pharaoh's dreams and becomes vizier. Vv. 1–32 deal with the last of the three pairs of dreams in the Joseph story, the dreams of Pharaoh. Vv. 33–57 detail Joseph's unsolicited recommendation of a course to enable Egypt to survive the crisis, and then report the king's enthusiastic appointment of the young Hebrew man to implement his own policy. **1–7:** Pharaoh's dreams revert to the pattern of the first pair, Joseph's own (37.5–11), in that they both mean the same thing (v. 32) and deal with the triumph of the weak over the strong. And like the intervening pair, those of the chief cupbearer and chief baker (40.9–22), each of the two dreams deals with themes of good fortune and ill, in that order. **8:** See 40.8 n. The inability of the pagan magicians to interpret dreams and accurately predict the future is developed at greater length in Dan. ch 2, a narrative influenced by the Joseph story. Cf. Isa. 41.21–24. **14:** The Heb word for *dungeon* (also in 40.15) is the same as that for the "pit" into which Joseph's brothers threw him in 37.20, 22, 24, 28. The chief cupbearer's belated act of remembrance has suddenly reversed Joseph's repeated descents—into the pit, into Egypt, into prison. The pattern is familiar from prayers of thanksgiving (e.g., Ps. 30, esp. vv. 4, 10). For the fourth time, Joseph's clothes are changed (the previous instances are in 37.3, 23; 39.12), this time (like the first) as a sign of elevation. **16:** See 39.8–9 n.

had I seen their likes for ugliness in all the land of Egypt! ²⁰ And the seven lean and ugly cows ate up the first seven cows, the sturdy ones; ²¹ but when they had consumed them, one could not tell that they had consumed them, for they looked just as bad as before. And I awoke. ²² In my other dream, I saw seven ears of grain, full and healthy, growing on a single stalk; ²³ but right behind them sprouted seven ears, shriveled, thin, and scorched by the east wind. ²⁴ And the thin ears swallowed the seven healthy ears. I have told my magicians, but none has an explanation for me."

²⁵ And Joseph said to Pharaoh, "Pharaoh's dreams are one and the same: God has told Pharaoh what He is about to do. ²⁶ The seven healthy cows are seven years, and the seven healthy ears are seven years; it is the same dream. ²⁷ The seven lean and ugly cows that followed are seven years, as are also the seven empty ears scorched by the east wind; they are seven years of famine. ²⁸ It is just as I have told Pharaoh: God has revealed to Pharaoh what He is about to do. ²⁹ Immediately ahead are seven years of great abundance in all the land of Egypt. ³⁰ After them will come seven years of famine, and all the abundance in the land of Egypt will be forgotten. As the land is ravaged by famine, ³¹ no trace of the abundance will be left in the land because of the famine thereafter, for it will be very severe. ³² As for Pharaoh having had the same dream twice, it means that the matter has been determined by God, and that God will soon carry it out.

³³ "Accordingly, let Pharaoh find a man of discernment and wisdom, and set him over the land of Egypt. ³⁴ And let Pharaoh take steps to appoint overseers over the land, and organize^a the land of Egypt in the seven years of plenty. ³⁵ Let all the food of these good years that are coming be gathered, and let the grain be collected under Pharaoh's authority as food to be stored in the cities. ³⁶ Let that food be a reserve for the land for the seven years of famine which will come upon the land of Egypt, so that the land may not perish in the famine."

³⁷ The plan pleased Pharaoh and all his courtiers. ³⁸ And Pharaoh said to his courtiers, "Could we find another like him, a man in whom is the spirit of God?" ³⁹ So Pharaoh said to Joseph, "Since God has made all this known to you, there is none so discerning and wise as you. ⁴⁰ You shall be in charge of my court, and by your command shall all my people be directed;^b only with respect to the

33–36: Unlike the implication of Joseph's own two dreams (37.5–11), the domination of the weak over the strong is not the last word. Foresight and prudence, Joseph tells Pharaoh, can enable the land to survive catastrophe. As things turn out, the survival of Egypt will have a more particular meaning as well: It foreshadows and enables the healing of the rift between Joseph and his brothers. **40:** Joseph is once again second in rank. See 39.19–23 n. Joseph will indeed rule, just as his brothers feared (37.8, 10–11), but with this crucial qualification: His rule will be rooted not in sheer power, but in the benefit he provides to the less fortunate. This corresponds to an ideal of kingship widespread in the ancient Near East, in which the king is the rescuer and servant of the people (cf. Judg. 11.4–11).

---

a Others "take a fifth part of"; meaning of Heb. uncertain.
b Others "order themselves" or "pay homage"; meaning of Heb. yishshaq uncertain.

throne shall I be superior to you." [41] Pharaoh further said to Joseph, "See, I put you in charge of all the land of Egypt." [42] And removing his signet ring from his hand, Pharaoh put it on Joseph's hand; and he had him dressed in robes of fine linen, and put a gold chain about his neck. [43] He had him ride in the chariot of his second-in-command, and they cried before him, "Abrek!"[a] Thus he placed him over all the land of Egypt.

[44] Pharaoh said to Joseph, "I am Pharaoh; yet without you, no one shall lift up hand or foot in all the land of Egypt." [45] Pharaoh then gave Joseph the name Zaphenath-paneah;[b] and he gave him for a wife Asenath daughter of Poti-phera, priest of On. Thus Joseph emerged in charge of the land of Egypt.—[46] Joseph was thirty years old when he entered the service of Pharaoh king of Egypt.—Leaving Pharaoh's presence, Joseph traveled through all the land of Egypt.

[47] During the seven years of plenty, the land produced in abundance. [48] And he gathered all the grain of [c]the seven years that the land of Egypt was enjoying,[c] and stored the grain in the cities; he put in each city the grain of the fields around it. [49] So Joseph collected produce in very large quantity, like the sands of the sea, until he ceased to measure it, for it could not be measured.

[50] Before the years of famine came, Joseph became the father of two sons, whom Asenath daughter of Poti-phera, priest of On, bore to him. [51] Joseph named the first-born Manasseh, meaning, "God has made me forget[d] completely my hardship and my parental home." [52] And the second he named Ephraim, meaning, "God has made me fertile[e] in the land of my affliction."

[53] The seven years of abundance that the land of Egypt enjoyed came to an end, [54] and the seven years of famine set in, just as Joseph had foretold. There was famine in all lands, but throughout the land of Egypt there was bread. [55] And when all the land of Egypt felt the hunger, the people cried out to Pharaoh for bread; and Pharaoh said to all the Egyptians, "Go to Joseph; whatever he tells you, you shall do."—[56] Accordingly, when the famine became severe in the land of Egypt, Joseph laid open all that was within, and rationed out grain to the Egyptians. The famine, however, spread over the whole world. [57] So all

42: This is Joseph's fifth and final change of clothes. See v. 41.14 n. **45:** In Egyptian, *Asenath* means "the one who belongs to (the goddess) Neith." Since Jewish law does not recognize any marriage between a Jew and a Gentile (see 26.34–35 n.), Jewish tradition came to interpret Asenath as the prototypical convert to Judaism. Her powerful story is told at length in an important Hellenistic novella, "Joseph and Asenath." Rabbinic tradition identifies her father, Poti-phera, with the Potiphar of ch 39 (*b. Sot.* 13b), but this is unlikely. **51:** Saved by the cupbearer's act of remembrance (vv. 9–13), Joseph nonetheless gives his first-born son a name that celebrates forgetfulness. The family history that he has repressed will, however, return to confront him with great force in the next chapter (42.8–9). **52:** Fertility in the land of affliction will eventually prove a mixed blessing. "When the Israelites were fertile and prolific, . . . a new king arose over Egypt who did not know Joseph" (Exod. 1.7–8) and sought to inflict upon them the fate decided for Joseph in Gen. ch 37: enslavement and death (Exod. 1.9–12, 15–22).

a Others "Bow the knee," as though from Heb. barakh "to kneel"; perhaps from an Egyptian word of unknown meaning.

b Egyptian for "God speaks; he lives," or "creator of life."

c-c Lit. "the seven years that were in the land of Egypt."

d Heb. nashshani, connected with "Manasseh" (Menashsheh).

e Heb. hiphrani, connected with "Ephraim."

the world came to Joseph in Egypt to procure rations, for the famine had become severe throughout the world.

42 When Jacob saw that there were food rations to be had in Egypt, he[a] said to his sons, "Why do you keep looking at one another? 2 Now I hear," he went on, "that there are rations to be had in Egypt. Go down and procure rations for us there, that we may live and not die." 3 So ten of Joseph's brothers went down to get grain rations in Egypt; 4 for Jacob did not send Joseph's brother Benjamin with his brothers, since he feared that he might meet with disaster. 5 Thus the sons of Israel were among those who came to procure rations, for the famine extended to the land of Canaan.

6 Now Joseph was the vizier of the land; it was he who dispensed rations to all the people of the land. And Joseph's brothers came and bowed low to him, with their faces to the ground. 7 When Joseph saw his brothers, he recognized them; but he acted like a stranger toward them and spoke harshly to them. He asked them, "Where do you come from?" And they said, "From the land of Canaan, to procure food." 8 For though Joseph recognized his brothers, they did not recognize him. 9 Recalling the dreams that he had dreamed about them, Joseph said to them, "You are spies, you have come to see the land in its nakedness." 10 But they said to him, "No, my lord! Truly, your servants have come to procure food. 11 We are all of us sons of the same man; we are honest men; your servants have never been spies!" 12 And he said to them, "No, you have come to see the land in its nakedness!" 13 And they replied, "We your servants were twelve brothers, sons of a certain man in the land of Canaan; the youngest, however, is now with our father, and one is no more." 14 But Joseph said to them, "It is just as I have told you: You are spies! 15 By this you shall be put to the test: unless your youngest brother comes here, by Pharaoh, you shall not depart from this place! 16 Let one of you go and bring your brother, while the rest of you remain confined, that your words may be put to the test whether there is truth in you. Else, by Pharaoh, you are nothing but spies!" 17 And he confined them in the guardhouse for three days.

18 On the third day Joseph said to them, "Do this and you shall live, for I am a God-fearing man. 19 If you are honest men, let one of you brothers be held in your place of detention, while the rest of you go and take home rations for your starving households; 20 but you must bring

a Lit. "Jacob."

42.1–38: The first reunion of Joseph and his brothers. In this chapter, Joseph and his brothers meet again, though in radically different and, in fact, reversed roles from the ones in which we last saw them (ch 37). Now, just as he has dreamt, it is they who are the subordinates, and, moreover, he is the only one who recognizes the situation. Joseph reenacts his brothers' mistreatment of him, only with them now as the victims—and with a dose of mercy altogether missing in ch 37 (with the exception of Reuben's botched attempt to rescue him). **3–4:** Once again, Jacob shows preference for a son of Rachel (cf. 37.3). As the events unfold, Benjamin, Joseph's only full brother and the youngest of the brood, serves as Joseph's alter ego. **6:** Their prostration fulfills the dreams of 37.5–11. Little did anyone suspect at the time, however, that their prostration would be in supplication for their very lives or that Joseph would keep them from death. **9:** *To see the land in its nakedness* recalls the episode in ch 39, in which Joseph is unfairly accused (and convicted) of a sexual crime (see 9.22–24 n.). **11:** The first clause is truer than the brothers recognize; the second remains to be established; only the third is straightforward fact. **13–14:** Having lied to their father about Joseph's fate (37.31–33), the brothers now find themselves unable to convince Pharaoh's vizier of the truth. The Heb of the clause *and one is no more* echoes Reuben's cry of desperation in 37.30 (cf. 42.36). **15–17:** By reaffirming the specialness of the favored son, Joseph's test requires the brothers to confront anew the factor that led them to commit their infamous crime. Having taken one "child of [Jacob's] old age" (37.3) away from his father on the basest motivation, they must now persuade the old man to give up his stand-in (cf. 44.20) in the interest of life itself. Similarly, their imprisonment reenacts Joseph's own fate after they sold or abandoned him (39.1, 20).

me your youngest brother, that your words may be veri-
fied and that you may not die." And they did accordingly.
21 They said to one another, "Alas, we are being punished
on account of our brother, because we looked on at his anguish, yet paid no heed as he pleaded with us. That is why
this distress has come upon us." 22 Then Reuben spoke up
and said to them, "Did I not tell you, 'Do no wrong to the
boy'? But you paid no heed. Now comes the reckoning for
his blood." 23 They did not know that Joseph understood,
for there was an interpreter between him and them. 24 He
turned away from them and wept. But he came back to
them and spoke to them; and he took Simeon from among
them and had him bound before their eyes. 25 Then Joseph
gave orders to fill their bags with grain, return each one's
money to his sack, and give them provisions for the journey; and this was done for them. 26 So they loaded their
asses with the rations and departed from there.

27 As one of them was opening his sack to give feed to
his ass at the night encampment, he saw his money right
there at the mouth of his bag. 28 And he said to his brothers, "My money has been returned! It is here in my bag!"
Their hearts sank; and, trembling, they turned to one another, saying, "What is this that God has done to us?"

29 When they came to their father Jacob in the land of
Canaan, they told him all that had befallen them, saying,
30 "The man who is lord of the land spoke harshly to us
and accused us of spying on the land. 31 We said to him,
'We are honest men; we have never been spies! 32 There
were twelve of us brothers, sons by the same father; but
one is no more, and the youngest is now with our father in
the land of Canaan.' 33 But the man who is lord of the land
said to us, 'By this I shall know that you are honest men:
leave one of your brothers with me, and take something
for your starving households and be off. 34 And bring your
youngest brother to me, that I may know that you are not
spies but honest men. I will then restore your brother to
you, and you shall be free to move about in the land.' "

35 As they were emptying their sacks, there, in each
one's sack, was his money-bag! When they and their father saw their money-bags, they were dismayed. 36 Their
father Jacob said to them, "It is always me that you bereave: Joseph is no more and Simeon is no more, and now
you would take away Benjamin. These things always happen to me!" 37 Then Reuben said to his father, "You may
kill my two sons if I do not bring him back to you. Put him
in my care, and I will return him to you." 38 But he said,
"My son must not go down with you, for his brother is
dead and he alone is left. If he meets with disaster on the

21–22: Just as his brothers saw only domination (and not deliverance) in his dreams (37.5–11), so here they see only punishment, never suspecting the larger design that will lead to survival and reconciliation (45.5; 50.20). **24:** As Leah's second son (29.31–33), Simeon is the appropriate hostage for Benjamin, Rachel's second son (35.18). His name echoes the Heb of "paid no heed" in 42.21, 22. **25:** Joseph's returning their silver (which was weighed out and used as money for much of the biblical period) deftly symbolizes the movement of the whole chapter: The brothers are getting what they gave! **34:** *I will then restore your brother to you* (not reported in vv. 18–20) refers most immediately to Simeon, but unbeknownst to the brothers (and perhaps even to Joseph himself at this point), the release of Benjamin will result in the restoration of Joseph as well. **35:** Practitioners of source criticism tend to see this verse as a variant of vv. 27–28, with the latter as the secondary passage (note that the brothers say nothing about any returned money in vv. 29–34). The supplementation (if such it was) was aided by the difference between the two variants: vv. 27–28 speak literally of only one brother, whereas v. 35 speaks of all of them. **36–38:** Reuben once again proves ineffectual (cf. 37.18–30; 42.22). A midrash paraphrases Jacob's decline of Reuben's offer this way: "This is a foolish first-born son! Are your sons not my sons?" (*Gen. Rab.* 91.9). The theme of the loss of two sons—Jacob's and Reuben's—recalls ch 38, in which Judah loses two sons and withholds the third. Reuben's foolish offer thus sets the stage for Judah's successful interventions in 43.8–14 and 44.18–34.

journey you are taking, you will send my white head down to Sheol in grief."

43 But the famine in the land was severe. [2] And when they had eaten up the rations which they had brought from Egypt, their father said to them, "Go again and procure some food for us." [3] But Judah said to him, "The man warned us, [a-]'Do not let me see your faces[-a] unless your brother is with you.' [4] If you will let our brother go with us, we will go down and procure food for you; [5] but if you will not let him go, we will not go down, for the man said to us, [a-]'Do not let me see your faces[-a] unless your brother is with you.'" [6] And Israel said, "Why did you serve me so ill as to tell the man that you had another brother?" [7] They replied, "But the man kept asking about us and our family, saying, 'Is your father still living? Have you another brother?' And we answered him accordingly. How were we to know that he would say, 'Bring your brother here'?"

[8] Then Judah said to his father Israel, "Send the boy in my care, and let us be on our way, that we may live and not die—you and we and our children. [9] I myself will be surety for him; you may hold me responsible: if I do not bring him back to you and set him before you, I shall stand guilty before you forever. [10] For we could have been there and back twice if we had not dawdled."

[11] Then their father Israel said to them, "If it must be so, do this: take some of the choice products of the land in your baggage, and carry them down as a gift for the man—some balm and some honey, gum, ladanum, pistachio nuts, and almonds. [12] And take with you double the money, carrying back with you the money that was replaced in the mouths of your bags; perhaps it was a mistake. [13] Take your brother too; and go back at once to the man. [14] And may El Shaddai dispose the man to mercy toward you, that he may release to you your other brother, as well as Benjamin. As for me, if I am to be bereaved, I shall be bereaved."

[15] So the men took that gift, and they took with them double the money, as well as Benjamin. They made their way down to Egypt, where they presented themselves to Joseph. [16] When Joseph saw Benjamin with them, he said to his house steward, "Take the men into the house; slaughter and prepare an animal, for the men will dine with me at noon." [17] The man did as Joseph said, and he brought the men into Joseph's house. [18] But the men were

a-a Lit. "Do not see my face."

43.1–34: The brothers' second trip to Egypt. Chs 43–45 repeat the pattern of ch 42, only with variations, greater detail, and much greater emotional tension. Once again, the brothers depart for Egypt, approach Joseph fearfully, find themselves subjected to a frightening test of their honesty as well as accusations of deceit, and once again they return to their father. Ch 43 records, first, Judah's persuasion of a reluctant Jacob to release his beloved Benjamin and, second, the ensuing encounter of Joseph and his brothers—this time all eleven of them. **6–8:** Jacob, to whom the brothers once lied about Joseph (37.31–35), now accuses them of telling too much of the truth. The brothers are, in fact, still lying, though with a more benign intention. For, according to 42.9–13, they volunteered the information about their youngest brother. **9:** *Surety* (Heb "'arav'") recalls the "pledge" ("'eravon'") that Judah offered Tamar in 38.17. In this speech, Judah persuades his father, who believes he has lost two sons, to surrender the third—exactly the act that he had dangerously sought to avoid in ch 38. The commercial terminology is especially apt on the lips of the son that suggested his brother be sold (37.26–27). **11:** As in 37.21–30, Judah's plan succeeds where Reuben's had failed (42.37–38). This is another indication that one function of the Joseph story is to explain why Joseph (the dominant tribe of the North) and Judah (the royal tribe of the South) became more important than Reuben (the first-born). See 1 Chron. 5.1–2. The *balm* and *ladanum* (a fragrant resin) recall the commodities conveyed by the Ishmaelite caravan in 37.25. Once again, Jacob's beloved son is being brought to Egypt—only this time with his father's knowledge and consent and as a sign (unknown to all but Joseph) of healing rather than estrangement.

frightened at being brought into Joseph's house. "It must be," they thought, "because of the money replaced in our bags the first time that we have been brought inside, as a pretext to attack us and seize us as slaves, with our pack animals." 19 So they went up to Joseph's house steward and spoke to him at the entrance of the house. 20 "If you please, my lord," they said, "we came down once before to procure food. 21 But when we arrived at the night encampment and opened our bags, there was each one's money in the mouth of his bag, our money in full.ᵃ So we have brought it back with us. 22 And we have brought down with us other money to procure food. We do not know who put the money in our bags." 23 He replied, "All is well with you; do not be afraid. Your God, the God of your father, must have put treasure in your bags for you. I got your payment." And he brought out Simeon to them.

24 Then the man brought the men into Joseph's house; he gave them water to bathe their feet, and he provided feed for their asses. 25 They laid out their gifts to await Joseph's arrival at noon, for they had heard that they were to dine there.

26 When Joseph came home, they presented to him the gifts that they had brought with them into the house, bowing low before him to the ground. 27 He greeted them, and he said, "How is your aged father of whom you spoke? Is he still in good health?" 28 They replied, "It is well with your servant our father; he is still in good health." And they bowed and made obeisance.

29 Looking about, he saw his brother Benjamin, his mother's son, and asked, "Is this your youngest brother of whom you spoke to me?" And he went on, "May God be gracious to you, my boy." 30 With that, Joseph hurried out, for he was overcome with feeling toward his brother and was on the verge of tears; he went into a room and wept there. 31 Then he washed his face, reappeared, and—now in control of himself—gave the order, "Serve the meal." 32 They served him by himself, and them by themselves, and the Egyptians who ate with him by themselves; for the Egyptians could not dine with the Hebrews, since that would be abhorrent to the Egyptians. 33 As they were seated by his direction, from the oldest in the order of his seniority to the youngest in the order of his youth, the men looked at one another in astonishment. 34 Portions were served them from his table; but Benjamin's portion was severalᵇ times that of anyone else. And they drank their fill with him.

23: Joseph's steward senses the hand of a beneficent providence in these strange events. Much to their surprise, the brothers' honesty works to their advantage. It even restores one lost brother, the hostage Simeon. **30–31:** Joseph's emotion is described as more intense here than in 42.24. The harsh self-presentation of Pharaoh's vizier is rapidly yielding to the Hebrew man's love of father and brothers. **32:** It is unclear why Egyptians would find it abhorrent to dine with Hebrews. The phenomenon is probably connected to the reports that Egyptians found shepherds to be "abhorrent" (46.34; cf. Exod. 8.22), a tradition lacking historical corroboration. **33–34:** Joseph no sooner reaffirms the principle of seniority—the brothers are amazed that the Egyptian vizier knows their order of birth—than he reenacts the favoritism for the youngest that once proved so problematic to the family. This time, however, the brothers show no resentment. This meal contrasts poignantly with the meal to which the brothers sat down after throwing Joseph into the pit (37.25; see also 42.21).

---

a Lit. "by its weight."   b Lit. "five."

44

Then he instructed his house steward as follows, "Fill the men's bags with food, as much as they can carry, and put each one's money in the mouth of his bag. ²Put my silver goblet in the mouth of the bag of the youngest one, together with his money for the rations." And he did as Joseph told him.

³With the first light of morning, the men were sent off with their pack animals. ⁴They had just left the city and had not gone far, when Joseph said to his steward, "Up, go after the men! And when you overtake them, say to them, 'Why did you repay good with evil? ⁵It is the very one from which my master drinks and which he uses for divination. It was a wicked thing for you to do!' "

⁶He overtook them and spoke those words to them. ⁷And they said to him, "Why does my lord say such things? Far be it from your servants to do anything of the kind! ⁸Here we brought back to you from the land of Canaan the money that we found in the mouths of our bags. How then could we have stolen any silver or gold from your master's house! ⁹Whichever of your servants it is found with shall die; the rest of us, moreover, shall become slaves to my lord." ¹⁰He replied, "Although what you are proposing is right, only the one with whom it is found shall be my slave; but the rest of you shall go free."

¹¹So each one hastened to lower his bag to the ground, and each one opened his bag. ¹²He searched, beginning with the oldest and ending with the youngest; and the goblet turned up in Benjamin's bag. ¹³At this they rent their clothes. Each reloaded his pack animal, and they returned to the city.

¹⁴When Judah and his brothers reentered the house of Joseph, who was still there, they threw themselves on the ground before him. ¹⁵Joseph said to them, "What is this deed that you have done? Do you not know that a man like me practices divination?" ¹⁶Judah replied, "What can we say to my lord? How can we plead, how can we prove our innocence? God has uncovered the crime of your servants. Here we are, then, slaves of my lord, the rest of us as much as he in whose possession the goblet was found." ¹⁷But he replied, "Far be it from me to act thus! Only he in whose possession the goblet was found shall be my slave; the rest of you go back in peace to your father."

VA-YIGGASH   ויגש

¹⁸Then Judah went up to him and said, "Please, my lord, let your servant appeal to my lord, and do not be impatient with your servant, you who are the equal of Pharaoh. ¹⁹My lord asked his servants, 'Have you a father or an-

44.1–17: The incident of the silver goblet. This passage recalls Joseph's clandestine return of his brothers' money to their sacks (42.25–38), except this time Joseph specifically targets Jacob's favored son (and Joseph's stand-in), Benjamin (absent in the prior episode). This seems to be a test: Will the older ten brothers jettison Benjamin when his presence becomes inconvenient, as they once did Joseph, or have they finally learned the painful lesson about family solidarity and filial obedience? **5:** *It is the very one from which my master drinks* seems abrupt. An ancient Jewish translation (the Septuagint) gives evidence that a second question, "Why have you stolen my silver goblet?" once followed the one at the end of v. 4. In contrast to other passages in the Torah (Lev. 19.26; Num. 23.23; Deut. 18.10–11), divination (fortune-telling) is not here condemned (cf. 30.27). The practice suggests Joseph's ominous dreams, the immediate cause of his brothers' selling him into slavery, and the silver of the goblet recalls the "twenty pieces of silver" they received for selling him (37.18–28). **7–9:** The accusation strikingly recalls Laban's charge that Jacob had stolen his household icons (31.25–37). The latter's defense, "anyone with whom you find your gods shall not remain alive!" (31.32) is probably connected to Rachel's premature death giving birth to Benjamin (35.16–20). Here, too, the curse involves death for the malefactor, but it also entails slavery for the rest of the brothers (44.9). Not coincidentally, death and slavery were the two punishments that the brothers plotted to inflict on Joseph in 37.18–28. **14–17:** Judah again assumes the leading position (see 43.11 n.). Having devised the plan to sell Joseph into slavery (37.26–27), he now offers to accept slavery upon himself and his brothers rather than abandon Benjamin, as he (and they, with the exception of the ineffectual Reuben) had once callously and criminally abandoned Joseph. **17:** Joseph forces his older brothers to face other brother?' 20 We told my lord, 'We have an old father, and there is a child of his old age, the youngest; his full brother is dead, so that he alone is left of his mother, and his father dotes on him.' 21 Then you said to your servants, 'Bring him down to me, that I may set eyes on him.' 22 We said to my lord, 'The boy cannot leave his father; if he were to leave him, his father would die.' 23 But you said to your servants, 'Unless your youngest brother comes down with you, do not let me see your faces.' 24 When we came back to your servant my father, we reported my lord's words to him.

25 "Later our father said, 'Go back and procure some food for us.' 26 We answered, 'We cannot go down; only if our youngest brother is with us can we go down, for we may not ªshow our faces to the manª unless our youngest brother is with us.' 27 Your servant my father said to us, 'As you know, my wife bore me two sons. 28 But one is gone from me, and I said: Alas, he was torn by a beast! And I have not seen him since. 29 If you take this one from me, too, and he meets with disaster, you will send my white head down to Sheol in sorrow.'

30 "Now, if I come to your servant my father and the boy is not with us—since his own life is so bound up with his—31 when he sees that the boy is not with us, he will die, and your servants will send the white head of your servant our father down to Sheol in grief. 32 Now your servant has pledged himself for the boy to my father, saying, 'If I do not bring him back to you, I shall stand guilty before my father forever.' 33 Therefore, please let your servant remain as a slave to my lord instead of the boy, and let the boy go back with his brothers. 34 For how can I go back to my father unless the boy is with me? Let me not be witness to the woe that would overtake my father!"

45 Joseph could no longer control himself before all his attendants, and he cried out, "Have everyone withdraw from me!" So there was no one else about when Joseph made himself known to his brothers. 2 His sobs were so loud that the Egyptians could hear, and so the news reached Pharaoh's palace.

3 Joseph said to his brothers, "I am Joseph. Is my father still well?" But his brothers could not answer him, so dumfounded were they on account of him.

4 Then Joseph said to his brothers, "Come forward to me." And when they came forward, he said, "I am your brother Joseph, he whom you sold into Egypt. 5 Now, do

a-a Lit. "see the man's face."

and, moreover, to accept the special place that Benjamin (Joseph's alter ego) has in his father's heart.

44.18–45.28: The turning point. With all apparently lost and Benjamin about to enter into slavery (and Jacob about to die as a result), Judah again assumes the lead role, with results that amaze all concerned. **18:** "Va-Yiggash," translated here as *went up,* appears also in the introduction to Abraham's bold intercession for Sodom in 18.23 (where it is rendered "came forward"). Both Judah's speech and Abraham's exhibit a delicate balance of deference and assertion, and both succeed in moving the addressee from judgment to mercy. Abraham's argument, however, rests on the possibility that there is an innocent minority in the evil city (18.23–32), whereas Judah makes no argument for Benjamin's innocence (even if he believed in it, he could hardly make the case without incriminating Joseph or his staff). Instead, he appeals to the vizier's compassion for the foreigners' father and courageously offers himself in Benjamin's stead. **30–31:** Judah is unwittingly accusing Pharaoh's vizier of killing his own father, catching Joseph in his own stratagem. **32–33:** See 43.9 n., where the same verb ("'arav," "pledged himself") appears. **33:** Judah offers to take the place of Benjamin, who takes the place of Joseph (vv. 27–28). The brother responsible for selling Joseph into slavery (37.26–27) now freely offers himself as a slave to Joseph in order to save Jacob's life. Things have come full circle, and the long-standing and nearly fatal rift in the family is about to be healed. **45.4–8:** Joseph no sooner reminds his brothers of their great sin (v. 4) than he renounces retribution, interpreting the events that have overtaken the House of Israel as he had interpreted Pharaoh's dreams (41.25–36): God has arranged things so that the disaster (though very real and very painful) is not the last word. The last word is a word of life, not death (vv. 5–8;

not be distressed or reproach yourselves because you sold me hither; it was to save life that God sent me ahead of you. [6] It is now two years that there has been famine in the land, and there are still five years to come in which there shall be no yield from tilling. [7] God has sent me ahead of you to ensure your survival on earth, and to save your lives in an extraordinary deliverance. [8] So, it was not you who sent me here, but God; and He has made me a father to Pharaoh, lord of all his household, and ruler over the whole land of Egypt.

[9] "Now, hurry back to my father and say to him: Thus says your son Joseph, 'God has made me lord of all Egypt; come down to me without delay. [10] You will dwell in the region of Goshen, where you will be near me—you and your children and your grandchildren, your flocks and herds, and all that is yours. [11] There I will provide for you—for there are yet five years of famine to come—that you and your household and all that is yours may not suffer want.' [12] You can see for yourselves, and my brother Benjamin for himself, that it is indeed I who am speaking to you. [13] And you must tell my father everything about my high station in Egypt and all that you have seen; and bring my father here with all speed."

[14] With that he embraced[a] his brother Benjamin around the neck and wept, and Benjamin wept on his neck. [15] He kissed all his brothers and wept upon them; only then were his brothers able to talk to him.

[16] The news reached Pharaoh's palace: "Joseph's brothers have come." Pharaoh and his courtiers were pleased. [17] And Pharaoh said to Joseph, "Say to your brothers, 'Do as follows: load up your beasts and go at once to the land of Canaan. [18] Take your father and your households and come to me; I will give you the best of the land of Egypt and you shall live off the fat of the land.' [19] And you are bidden [to add], 'Do as follows: take from the land of Egypt wagons for your children and your wives, and bring your father here. [20] And never mind your belongings, for the best of all the land of Egypt shall be yours.' "

[21] The sons of Israel did so; Joseph gave them wagons as Pharaoh had commanded, and he supplied them with provisions for the journey. [22] To each of them, moreover, he gave a change of clothing; but to Benjamin he gave three hundred pieces of silver and several[b] changes of clothing. [23] And to his father he sent the following: ten he-asses laden with the best things of Egypt, and ten she-asses laden with grain, bread, and provisions for his fa-

cf. 50.19–21). *Father to Pharaoh* (v. 8) has some parallels in Egyptian, and seems to denote Joseph's office of vizier and head counselor. *Ruler over the whole land of Egypt* echoes the brothers' angry and incredulous question in 37.8 ("Do you mean to rule over us?"). **9:** *Come down to me* recalls Jacob's plaintive words in 37.35, "I will go down mourning to my son in Sheol." Now he goes down to Joseph not in Sheol, but in Egypt, over which the once rejected son now rules by the grace of God. **14:** The scene is highly reminiscent of the reconciliation of Esau and Jacob in 33.4. **22:** Joseph's giving extra clothing to Benjamin recalls Jacob's giving him an "ornamental tunic" in 37.3. The fraternal reconciliation does not mean that the old favoritism has come to an end and all the brothers are equal. It means, rather, that all concerned are now at last able to live with and accept the favoritism with grace and good will. **24:** Rashi thinks the plain sense is that the brothers should refrain from blaming each other for the sale of Joseph and for defaming him so as to make him hateful to them—not bad advice in light of past experience (42.22).

a Lit. "fell on."   *b* Lit. "five"; cf. 43.34.

ther on the journey. ²⁴ As he sent his brothers off on their way, he told them, "Do not be quarrelsome on the way."

²⁵ They went up from Egypt and came to their father Jacob in the land of Canaan. ²⁶ And they told him, "Joseph is still alive; yes, he is ruler over the whole land of Egypt." His heart went numb, for he did not believe them. ²⁷ But when they recounted all that Joseph had said to them, and when he saw the wagons that Joseph had sent to transport him, the spirit of their father Jacob revived. ²⁸ "Enough!" said Israel. "My son Joseph is still alive! I must go and see him before I die."

46 So Israel set out with all that was his, and he came to Beer-sheba, where he offered sacrifices to the God of his father Isaac. ² God called to Israel in a vision by night: "Jacob! Jacob!" He answered, "Here." ³ And He said, "I am God, the God of your father. Fear not to go down to Egypt, for I will make you there into a great nation. ⁴ I Myself will go down with you to Egypt, and I Myself will also bring you back; and Joseph's hand shall close your eyes."

⁵ So Jacob set out from Beer-sheba. The sons of Israel put their father Jacob and their children and their wives in the wagons that Pharaoh had sent to transport him; ⁶ and they took along their livestock and the wealth that they had amassed in the land of Canaan. Thus Jacob and all his offspring with him came to Egypt: ⁷ he brought with him to Egypt his sons and grandsons, his daughters and granddaughters—all his offspring.

⁸ These are the names of the Israelites, Jacob and his descendants, who came to Egypt.

Jacob's first-born Reuben; ⁹ Reuben's sons: Enoch,ᵃ Pallu, Hezron, and Carmi. ¹⁰ Simeon's sons: Jemuel, Jamin, Ohad, Jachin, Zohar, and Saulᵇ the son of a Canaanite woman. ¹¹ Levi's sons: Gershon, Kohath, and Merari. ¹² Judah's sons: Er, Onan, Shelah, Perez, and Zerah—but Er and Onan had died in the land of Canaan; and Perez's sons were Hezron and Hamul. ¹³ Issachar's sons: Tola, Puvah, Iob, and Shimron. ¹⁴ Zebulun's sons: Sered, Elon, and Jahleel. ¹⁵ Those were the sons whom Leah bore to Jacob in Paddan-aram, in addition to his daughter Dinah. Persons in all, male and female: 33.ᶜ

¹⁶ Gad's sons: Ziphion, Haggi, Shuni, Ezbon, Eri, Arodi, and Areli. ¹⁷ Asher's sons: Imnah, Ishvah, Ishvi, and Beriah, and their sister Serah. Beriah's sons: Heber and Malchiel. ¹⁸ These were the descendants of Zilpah, whom

46.1–7: Jacob sets out for Egypt. With Jacob's departure for Egypt, the tale of Joseph rejoins the patriarchal story from which it separated when Joseph was sold into slavery in ch 37. At the same time, these verses look forward to the next seemingly inseparable challenge to the House of Israel, the affliction in Egypt. **2–4:** God's only speech in chs 37–50 reiterates the promise to Abraham and Isaac (cf. 12.2–3; 26.2–5), assuring Jacob that his departure from the promised land will not void God's commitment to his forebears. *I Myself will also bring you back* (v. 4) looks forward to the exodus and underscores the fact that, as the Passover *Haggadah* puts it, "Our father Jacob did not come down to strike roots in Egypt but only to sojourn there." *Joseph's hand shall close your eyes* (v. 4) means that Joseph will lovingly attend to his father's needs at the moment of the latter's death.

46.8–27: Joseph's household. A list of Jacob's children and grandchildren interrupts the account of his journey to Egypt. **12:** The mention of Er and Onan who *died in the land of Canaan* indicates that the list was once independent of its current role as a census of the Israelites *who came to Egypt* (v. 8). **15:** The figure 33 requires that Er and Onan be counted but Dinah be excluded, despite the unambiguous expression *male and female.* If we replace Judah's two deceased sons with Dinah, we arrive at a figure of 32 descendants of Leah— exactly twice the number of her handmaiden Zilpah (v. 18). The symmetry with Rachel, who has twice as many descendants as her handmaiden Bilhah (vv. 22, 25), commends this interpretation. In order to reach 33, we must then count Jacob himself in the census. A midrash solves the problem by postulating that Moses' mother, Jochebed (Exod. 6.20), was born between the city walls as her parents entered Egypt (i.e., she was counted before she was named)—hence the plural "daughters" in v. 7 (b. B. Bat. 123b).

ᵃ Or "Hanoch."   ᵇ Or "Shaul."   ᶜ Including Jacob.

Laban had given to his daughter Leah. These she bore to Jacob—16 persons.

19 The sons of Jacob's wife Rachel were Joseph and Benjamin. 20 To Joseph were born in the land of Egypt Manasseh and Ephraim, whom Asenath daughter of Poti-phera priest of On bore to him. 21 Benjamin's sons: Bela, Becher, Ashbel, Gera, Naaman, Ehi, Rosh, Muppim, Huppim, and Ard. 22 These were the descendants of Rachel who were born to Jacob—14 persons in all.

23 Dan's son:ª Hushim. 24 Naphtali's sons: Jahzeel, Guni, Jezer, and Shillem. 25 These were the descendants of Bilhah, whom Laban had given to his daughter Rachel. These she bore to Jacob—7 persons in all.

26 All the persons belonging to Jacob who came to Egyptᵇ—his own issue, aside from the wives of Jacob's sons—all these persons numbered 66. 27 And Joseph's sons who were born to him in Egypt were two in number. Thus the total of Jacob's household who came to Egypt was seventy persons.ᶜ

28 He had sent Judah ahead of him to Joseph, to point the way before him to Goshen. So when they came to the region of Goshen, 29 Joseph orderedᵈ his chariot and went to Goshen to meet his father Israel; he presented himself to him and, embracing him around the neck, he wept on his neck a good while. 30 Then Israel said to Joseph, "Now I can die, having seen for myself that you are still alive."

31 Then Joseph said to his brothers and to his father's household, "I will go up and tell the news to Pharaoh, and say to him, 'My brothers and my father's household, who were in the land of Canaan, have come to me. 32 The men are shepherds; they have always been breeders of livestock, and they have brought with them their flocks and herds and all that is theirs.' 33 So when Pharaoh summons you and asks, 'What is your occupation?' 34 you shall answer, 'Your servants have been breeders of livestock from the start until now, both we and our fathers'—so that you may stay in the region of Goshen. For all shepherds are abhorrent to Egyptians."

47 Then Joseph came and reported to Pharaoh, saying, "My father and my brothers, with their flocks and herds and all that is theirs, have come from the land of Canaan and are now in the region of Goshen." 2 And selecting

27: Seventy persons, seventy was considered a perfect number. The quest for progeny—the fulfillment of the promise to Abraham—is now complete. The opening verses of Exodus will recapitulate the numbering of Jacob's family and continue the narrative with the quest for the land promised to Abraham.

46.28–30: The reunion of father and son. The narrative of Jacob's journey to Egypt resumes after the census of vv. 8–27. Having seen for himself that his beloved son lives and that his own life has been fulfilled beyond his wildest dreams, the elderly Jacob is at last prepared to accept his death (contrast 37.35; 42.38).

46.31–47.12: Audience with Pharaoh. Joseph carefully prepares his family for an audience in the royal court. He presents his brothers and then his father to the king of Egypt (the family members make their appearances in the same order as in his dreams in 37.5–11). 46.34: Goshen is a fertile region in the eastern delta of the Nile. It is unclear why all shepherds are abhorrent to Egyptians. Pharaoh has herds of his own (47.6). Some scholars connect this with a late folk etymology of "Hyksos" associated with the Egyptian word for "shepherd." The Hyksos were a Syro-Palestinian group who ruled Lower Egypt about 1680–1540 BCE.

a Heb. "sons."
b Not including Joseph and Joseph's two sons.
c Including Jacob and Joseph.
d Lit. "hitched."

a few[a] of his brothers, he presented them to Pharaoh.
3 Pharaoh said to his brothers, "What is your occupation?"
They answered Pharaoh, "We your servants are shepherds,
as were also our fathers. 4 We have come," they told Pharaoh, "to sojourn in this land, for there is no pasture for your
servants' flocks, the famine being severe in the land of Canaan. Pray, then, let your servants stay in the region of Goshen." 5 Then Pharaoh said to Joseph, "As regards your father and your brothers who have come to you, 6 the land of
Egypt is open before you: settle your father and your
brothers in the best part of the land; let them stay in the region of Goshen. And if you know any capable men among
them, put them in charge of my livestock."

7 Joseph then brought his father Jacob and presented
him to Pharaoh; and Jacob greeted Pharaoh. 8 Pharaoh
asked Jacob, "How many are the years of your life?" 9 And
Jacob answered Pharaoh, "The years of my sojourn [on
earth] are one hundred and thirty. Few and hard have
been the years of my life, nor do they come up to the life
spans of my fathers during their sojourns." 10 Then Jacob
bade Pharaoh farewell, and left Pharaoh's presence.

11 So Joseph settled his father and his brothers, giving
them holdings in the choicest part of the land of Egypt, in
the region of Rameses, as Pharaoh had commanded. 12 Joseph sustained his father, and his brothers, and all his
father's household with bread, down to the little ones.

13 Now there was no bread in all the world, for the
famine was very severe; both the land of Egypt and the
land of Canaan languished because of the famine. 14 Joseph gathered in all the money that was to be found in the
land of Egypt and in the land of Canaan, as payment for
the rations that were being procured, and Joseph brought
the money into Pharaoh's palace. 15 And when the money
gave out in the land of Egypt and in the land of Canaan,
all the Egyptians came to Joseph and said, "Give us bread,
lest we die before your very eyes; for the money is gone!"
16 And Joseph said, "Bring your livestock, and I will sell to
you against your livestock, if the money is gone." 17 So
they brought their livestock to Joseph, and Joseph gave
them bread in exchange for the horses, for the stocks of
sheep and cattle, and the asses; thus he provided them
with bread that year in exchange for all their livestock.
18 And when that year was ended, they came to him the
next year and said to him, "We cannot hide from my lord
that, with all the money and animal stocks consigned to

47.9: Since Jacob dies at 147
(47.28), he has two periods of seventeen years with Joseph, the first
seventeen of the latter's life (37.2)
and the last seventeen of his own.
See 25.7 n.; 35.28 n. **10:** *Bade . . .
farewell* can also be translated
"blessed." The theme that contact
with the family of Abraham results
in blessing for Gentiles (or at least
for those Gentiles who treat them
well) is widespread in Genesis
(12.3; 22.18; 26.4; 28.14; 30.27–30;
39.5, 23).

**47.13–27: Joseph saves and en-
slaves the Egyptians.** This passage
describes the progressive impoverishment of the Egyptian population, Joseph's rescue of them
through skillful administration,
and, finally and most troublingly,
his enslavement of them to Pharaoh. The tables have indeed
turned: The man who was brought
to Egypt as a slave now reduces
the Egyptians to slavery, all the
while, however, saving their lives,
just as he saved the lives of his
own family. The cruelty of
Joseph's enslavement of Egypt
does not seem to bother the
narrator. When Joseph died,
however, and "a new king arose
over Egypt who did not know
Joseph" (Exod. 1.8), the House
of Israel found themselves
once again on the wrong end
of the enslavement process.

a Lit. "five."

my lord, nothing is left at my lord's disposal save our persons and our farmland. ¹⁹Let us not perish before your eyes, both we and our land. Take us and our land in exchange for bread, and we with our land will be serfs to Pharaoh; provide the seed, that we may live and not die, and that the land may not become a waste."

²⁰So Joseph gained possession of all the farm land of Egypt for Pharaoh, every Egyptian having sold his field because the famine was too much for them; thus the land passed over to Pharaoh. ²¹And he removed the population town by town,ª from one end of Egypt's border to the other. ²²Only the land of the priests he did not take over, for the priests had an allotment from Pharaoh, and they lived off the allotment which Pharaoh had made to them; therefore they did not sell their land.

²³Then Joseph said to the people, "Whereas I have this day acquired you and your land for Pharaoh, here is seed for you to sow the land. ²⁴And when harvest comes, you shall give one-fifth to Pharaoh, and four-fifths shall be yours as seed for the fields and as food for you and those in your households, and as nourishment for your children." ²⁵And they said, "You have saved our lives! We are grateful to my lord, and we shall be serfs to Pharaoh." ²⁶And Joseph made it into a land law in Egypt, which is still valid, that a fifth should be Pharaoh's; only the land of the priests did not become Pharaoh's.

²⁷Thus Israel settled in the country of Egypt, in the region of Goshen; they acquired holdings in it, and were fertile and increased greatly.

VA-YEHI   ויחי

²⁸Jacob lived seventeen years in the land of Egypt, so that the span of Jacob's life came to one hundred and forty-seven years. ²⁹And when the time approached for Israel to die, he summoned his son Joseph and said to him, "Do me this favor, place your hand under my thigh as a pledge of your steadfast loyalty: please do not bury me in Egypt. ³⁰When I lie down with my fathers, take me up from Egypt and bury me in their burial-place." He replied, "I will do as you have spoken." ³¹And he said, "Swear to me." And he swore to him. Then Israel bowed at the head of the bed.

48 Some time afterward, Joseph was told, "Your father is ill." So he took with him his two sons, Manasseh and Ephraim. ²When Jacob was told, "Your son Jo-

ª Meaning of Heb. uncertain.

21: The Masoretic Text seems to refer to a forced transfer of the rural population as part of the program of nationalization of the farmland. Other versions evidence a slightly variant wording with a very different meaning: "He made the population into slaves." **27:** Whereas the Egyptians lose their land to Pharaoh because of Joseph's administrative policy, the Israelites acquire holdings through the generosity of Pharaoh, grateful for Joseph's managerial skills. Similarly, the fertility and increase of Israel contrasts with the devastation and impoverishment of the Egyptians, once again underscoring the special role of the former in God's designs.

47.28–48.22: Jacob's deathbed adoption of Joseph's sons. As befits a deathbed scene, this passage looks both to the past and to the future. Jacob gives a retrospective of his experience of the patriarchal promise and his loss of his favored wife, Rachel (48.3–7), but he also makes Joseph promise to bury him in the promised land (47.29–30), thus reiterating and deepening familial devotion to the patrimony of which they have yet to take possession. Similarly, Jacob's blessing of Joseph's two sons, in the reverse of the birth order (48.8–20), looks back to his own supplanting of his older brother early in life (25.22–33; 27.1–45), but it also authorizes the establishment of Ephraim and Manasseh in the twelve-tribe league that was to be biblical Israel **47.28:** See 35.28 n. **29–30:** The scene recalls that of 24.2–9. Once again the patriarchal promise is at risk, and once again an ailing and aged patriarch solemnly undertakes to reconnect with the family tradition. **31:** The meaning of Jacob/Israel's bowing is unclear (cf. 1 Kings 1.47). If he bows to Joseph, he fulfills the second of the latter's two predictive dreams (37.9–10). **48.3:** On El Shaddai, see 17.1 n. **5–7:** Jacob adopts his two grandsons born in Egypt, explaining this by reference to his affection for their departed grandmother, Rachel. This pro-seph has come to see you," Israel summoned his strength and sat up in bed.

3 And Jacob said to Joseph, "El Shaddai appeared to me at Luz in the land of Canaan, and He blessed me, 4 and said to me, 'I will make you fertile and numerous, making of you a community of peoples; and I will assign this land to your offspring to come for an everlasting possession.' 5 Now, your two sons, who were born to you in the land of Egypt before I came to you in Egypt, shall be mine; Ephraim and Manasseh shall be mine no less than Reuben and Simeon. 6 But progeny born to you after them shall be yours; they shall be recorded instead*a* of their brothers in their inheritance. 7 I [do this because], when I was returning from Paddan, Rachel died, to my sorrow, while I was journeying in the land of Canaan, when still some distance short of Ephrath; and I buried her there on the road to Ephrath"—now Bethlehem.

8 Noticing Joseph's sons, Israel asked, "Who are these?" 9 And Joseph said to his father, "They are my sons, whom God has given me here." "Bring them up to me," he said, "that I may bless them." 10 Now Israel's eyes were dim with age; he could not see. So [Joseph] brought them close to him, and he kissed them and embraced them. 11 And Israel said to Joseph, "I never expected to see you again, and here God has let me see your children as well."

12 Joseph then removed them from his knees, and bowed low with his face to the ground. 13 Joseph took the two of them, Ephraim with his right hand—to Israel's left—and Manasseh with his left hand—to Israel's right—and brought them close to him. 14 But Israel stretched out his right hand and laid it on Ephraim's head, though he was the younger, and his left hand on Manasseh's head—thus crossing his hands—although Manasseh was the first-born. 15 And he blessed Joseph, saying,

> "The God in whose ways my fathers Abraham and
>   Isaac walked,
> The God who has been my shepherd from my
>   birth to this day—

16
> The Angel who has redeemed me from all harm—
> Bless the lads.
> In them may my name be recalled,
> And the names of my fathers Abraham and Isaac,
> And may they be teeming multitudes upon the
>   earth."

17 When Joseph saw that his father was placing his right hand on Ephraim's head, he thought it wrong; so he took

motes them to the status of tribal founders and makes his favored wife their mother in place of the Egyptian priest's daughter Asenath (41.50–52). Moreover, the end of v. 5 seems to mean that Ephraim and Manasseh will become the senior tribes, replacing Reuben and Simeon, both of whom earn their father's censure (34.30; 35.22; 49.3–7; cf. 1 Chron. 5.1). V. 6 stipulates that any other children that Joseph has or will have (the Tanakh lists no others) shall be classified under Ephraim and Manasseh and not hold the status of the sons of Jacob. Note that whereas some lists of the twelve include Joseph and the clerical tribe Levi (e.g., Deut. 27.12–13), others omit Levi and divide Joseph into Ephraim and Manasseh (e.g., Num. 1.5–15). **8:** Israel's question is odd, since he has just spoken about Ephraim and Manasseh in considerable detail and with no deficit of clarity. The problem disappears if v. 8 is seen as the continuation of v. 2, and vv. 3–7 (which employ classic P language) are understood as an interpretation. In the text as it comes to us, however, the effect of v. 8 is to suggest that the aged Israel is confused and forgetful, somewhat like his own father in ch 27. If so, this time the suggestion proves wrong (vv. 17–20)! **10:** Cf. 27.1. **17–20:** Both tribes became important, though it is from Ephraim that Moses' successor Joshua, the prophet Samuel, and Jeroboam I, the founder of the Northern Kingdom (Israel) all hailed (Num. 13.8; 1 Sam. 1.1; 1 Kings 11.26). In fact, "Ephraim" eventually became another name for the Northern Kingdom itself (e.g., Hos. 5.3; Isa. 7.1–17).

a Lit. "under the name."

hold of his father's hand to move it from Ephraim's head to Manasseh's. [18] "Not so, Father," Joseph said to his father, "for the other is the first-born; place your right hand on his head." [19] But his father objected, saying, "I know, my son, I know. He too shall become a people, and he too shall be great. Yet his younger brother shall be greater than he, and his offspring shall be plentiful enough for nations." [20] So he blessed them that day, saying, "By you shall Israel invoke blessings, saying: God make you like Ephraim and Manasseh." Thus he put Ephraim before Manasseh.

[21] Then Israel said to Joseph, "I am about to die; but God will be with you and bring you back to the land of your fathers. [22] And now, I assign to you one portion[a] more than to your brothers, which I wrested from the Amorites with my sword and bow."

49 And Jacob called his sons and said, "Come together that I may tell you what is to befall you in days to come.

2   Assemble and hearken, O sons of Jacob;
     Hearken to Israel your father:

3   Reuben, you are my first-born,
     My might and first fruit of my vigor,
     Exceeding in rank
     And exceeding in honor.

4   Unstable as water, you shall excel no longer;
     For when you mounted your father's bed,
     You brought disgrace—my couch he mounted!

5   Simeon and Levi are a pair;
     Their weapons are tools of lawlessness.

6   Let not my person be included in their council,
     Let not my being be counted in their assembly.

a Meaning of Heb. shekhem _uncertain; others "mountain slope."_

20: Jacob's words are used in the blessing that a Jewish father traditionally bestows upon his sons just before the first Sabbath meal (Friday night). In the case of daughters, the tradition devised a functional equivalent that does not actually appear in the Tanakh: "God make you like Sarah, Rebekah, Rachel, and Leah." In both cases, the Aaronic blessing follows (Num. 6.24–26). **22:** _One portion more than to your brothers_ probably

refers to the "double portion" that the first-born son inherits (Deut. 21.17). The word for _portion_ ("shekhem") in this difficult verse puns on the name of (the city) Shechem. Note that Shechem appears as a Manassite clan in Josh. 17.2 but as an Ephraimite city in Josh. 20.7.

49.1–28: Jacob's tribal sayings. Although the prose superscription has Jacob speaking to his sons

themselves (v. 1), the content of the poetry that follows applies to the tribes descended from these twelve men. The closest parallel to this collection of tribal sayings is thus Deut. ch 33, in which Moses blesses most of the tribes just before he dies. A more distant parallel is Judg. 5.14–18, in which the judge, Deborah, and her general, Barak, sing of the courage of some of the tribes and the failure of others in a time of military crisis. Like Judg. 5.14–18, and unlike the Blessing of Moses, however, 49.1–28 interlaces commendation and condemnation. Rich in wordplays impossible to capture in English as well as cryptic phrasings and rare expressions (including unusual, and probably very ancient, divine names), Jacob's tribal sayings have long provoked disagreements among interpreters. There are also considerable variations in wording among the ancient versions. The collection of sayings is organized according to the tribal mothers, in the order of Leah, Zilpah (her handmaiden), Bilhah (Rachel's handmaiden), and Rachel (29.31–30.24; 35.16–19). The first four Leah tribes—Reuben, Simeon, Levi, and Judah—appear in the order of their births, as do those descended from Rachel— Joseph and Benjamin. But whereas in the narrative the sons of the handmaidens appear in the order of Dan, Naphtali, Gad, Asher, and are followed by Leah's last two sons, Issachar and Zebulun, in the tribal sayings of ch 49 the order is Zebulun, Issachar, Dan, Gad, Asher, Naphtali. **4:** The allusion is probably to the event cryptically reported in 35.22. Although Reuben, as the first-born tribe, may once have been important, it has left little mark in biblical history. The Blessing of Moses regards it as small and in danger of extinction (Deut. 33.6), and the Song of Deborah chastises it for its indecision (Judg. 5.15b–16; see Gen. 42.36–38 n.). **5–7:** _Simeon and Levi are a pair_ only in Gen. ch 34, where they also suffer their father's rebuke (v. 30). The dividing and scattering predicted here probably

For when angry they slay men,
And when pleased they maim oxen.

7 Cursed be their anger so fierce,
And their wrath so relentless.
I will divide them in Jacob,
Scatter them in Israel.

8 You, O Judah, your brothers shall praise;
Your hand shall be on the nape of your foes;
Your father's sons shall bow low to you.

9 Judah is a lion's whelp;
On prey, my son, have you grown.
He crouches, lies down like a lion,
Like ᵃthe king of beasts⁻ᵃ—who dare rouse him?

10 The scepter shall not depart from Judah,
Nor the ruler's staff from between his feet;
So that tribute shall come to himᵇ
And the homage of peoples be his.

11 He tethers his ass to a vine,
His ass's foal to a choice vine;
He washes his garment in wine,
His robe in blood of grapes.

12 ᶜHis eyes are darker than wine;
His teeth are whiter than milk.⁻ᶜ

13 Zebulun shall dwell by the seashore;
He shall be a haven for ships,
And his flank shall rest on Sidon.

14 Issachar is a strong-boned ass,
Crouching among the sheepfolds.

15 When he saw how good was security,
And how pleasant was the country,
He bent his shoulder to the burden,
And became a toiling serf.

16 Dan shall govern his people,
As one of the tribes of Israel.

a-a Heb. labi, *another word for "lion."*
b *Shiloh, understood as* shai loh *"tribute to him," following Midrash; cf. Isa. 18.7. Meaning of Heb. uncertain; lit. "Until he comes to Shiloh."*
c-c *Or "His eyes are dark from wine,
   And his teeth are white from milk."*

stick or club of any military commander or tribal leader (cf. Num. 21.18, where the word rendered here as *ruler's staff* is translated as the "maces" of "the nobles of the people"). V. 10 has traditionally been viewed as a messianic prophecy in both the Jewish and Christian traditions. Some commentators, beginning as early as the Aramaic translation known as *Targum Onkelos,* read the word rendered here as *tribute . . . to him* as "his due" (Heb "shelo"): God shall uphold His promise to Judah even till the royal figure comes to claim the dominion that is his due. Ibn Ezra, on the other hand, considers it possible to retain the traditional wording, "Shiloh," in place of "shai loh" (*tribute . . . to him*). Reading *shall come* in the sense of "shall come down," like the setting sun (in Lev. 22.7, the verb is translated "sets"), he connects this verse to Ps. 78, which reports that God "forsook the tabernacle of Shiloh," "did choose the tribe of Judah" and "David, His servant" (vv. 60, 68, 70; see 1 Sam. 3.19–4.22; Jer. 7.12–15). **11–12:** The images suggest preternatural fertility, prosperity, and vigor. According to Rabbi Ovadiah Sforno, an Italian commentator of the 16th century, the messianic king rides an *ass* rather than a horse because it is God who wages the wars by which he comes to rule, "and he will become king in peace" (cf. Zech. 4.6b; 9.9). **13:** The boundaries of Zebulun in Josh. 19.10–15 suggest that it was an inland tribe, but perhaps this was not always the case. **15:** The pronouncement on Issachar seems to be a criticism. It is a strong, but lazy, tribe that became *a toiling serf,* presumably for Canaanites in the northern regions that were its home (cf. Judg. 1.33). There is probably a play here on the tribe's name (as if it were "ʾish sakhar," "hired man"). Influenced by 1 Chron. 12.33, the midrash reconceives Issachar's service as the teaching of Torah and the rendering of halakhic (i.e., legal) rulings (*Gen. Rab.* 99.10). **16:** *Govern* ("yadin") puns on the tribe's name ("dan").

refers to Simeon's absorption into Judah and Levi's redefinition as a priestly tribe, without land of its own (Deut. 18.1–2). **8–10:** The preeminence of Judah (v. 8; cf. 27.29) is doubtless associated with King David's derivation from that tribe (see 38.27–30 n.). *Scepter* and *ruler's staff* may thus be royal symbols, although they can also designate the

17   Dan shall be a serpent by the road,
      A viper by the path,
      That bites the horse's heels
      So that his rider is thrown backward.

18   I wait for Your deliverance, O LORD!

19   Gad shall be raided by raiders,
      But he shall raid at their heels.

20   Asher's bread shall be rich,
      And he shall yield royal dainties.

21   Naphtali is a hind let loose,
      Which yields lovely fawns.

22   ᵃJoseph is a wild ass,
      A wild ass by a spring
      —Wild colts on a hillside.⁻ᵃ

23   Archers bitterly assailed him;
      They shot at him and harried him.
24   Yet his bow stayed taut,
      And his armsᵇ were made firm
      By the hands of the Mighty One of Jacob—
      There, the Shepherd, the Rock of Israel—
25   The God of your father who helps you,
      And Shaddai who blesses you
      With blessings of heaven above,
      Blessings of the deep that couches below,
      Blessings of the breast and womb.
26   ᶜThe blessings of your father
      Surpass the blessings of my ancestors,
      To the utmost bounds of the eternal hills.⁻ᶜ
      May they rest on the head of Joseph,
      On the brow of the elect of his brothers.

27   Benjamin is a ravenous wolf;
      In the morning he consumes the foe,ᵈ
      And in the evening he divides the spoil."

28 All these were the tribes of Israel, twelve in number, and
this is what their father said to them as he bade them

18: This verse seems to be a devout interpolation unrelated to the context (cf. Ps. 119.166). It contains the only mention of the four-letter name of God (LORD) in ch 49. 19: The Heb plays repeatedly on Gad's name. 20: The *royal dainties* may have been served to Canaanite kings (cf. Judg. 1.32, on Naphtali; and vv. 14–15 n., above). 22: Like Judah (v. 9), Issachar (v. 14), Naphtali (v. 21), and Benjamin (v. 27), Joseph is described as an animal. (Even if the alternative suggested in the translation note is accepted, the image is still one of fertility and vigor.) 23–24: Like the rest of the tribal sayings, the image of Joseph under assault relates to the subsequent history of the tribe. It also recalls, however, Joseph's brothers' early hostility in the preceding narrative (ch 37). 24: The unusual titles of the deity, *The Mighty One of Jacob* (or "Bull of Jacob"), *the Shepherd,* and *the Rock of Israel,* may attest to an early date and Canaanite affinities. 25: *Shaddai* is presumably a variant of El Shaddai (see 17.1 n.). 26: The term *my ancestors* ("horay") is otherwise unattested. The Septuagint and the parallels in Deut. 33.15 and Hab. 3.6 suggest that the word is actually "mountains" ("harerei") and that the word after it ("ʿad") means not "to," but "ancient." *Utmost bounds* ("taʾavat"), another unique term, is then more plausibly derived from a root associated with "desire" ("ʾvh"). If this reconstruction were to be accepted, the first sentence would read: "The blessings of your father / Surpass the blessings of the ancient mountains / That which is most desired in the eternal hills." 28: And so, just before he leaves this world, Jacob has bidden farewell to the twelve tribes of Israel—the people promised to his grandfather long ago (12.2), the people that against all odds and in the face of multiple and formidable challenges, external and internal, has now, by the grace of God, come into existence, the people that at long last stands united as it faces the new challenges that lie ahead.

a-a Others "Joseph is a fruitful bough,
          A fruitful bough by a spring,
          Its branches run over a wall."
b Heb. "the arms of his hands."
c-c Meaning of Heb. uncertain.
d Meaning of Heb. uncertain; others "booty."

farewell, addressing to each a parting word appropriate to him.

²⁹ Then he instructed them, saying to them, "I am about to be gathered to my kin. Bury me with my fathers in the cave which is in the field of Ephron the Hittite, ³⁰ the cave which is in the field of Machpelah, facing Mamre, in the land of Canaan, the field that Abraham bought from Ephron the Hittite for a burial site—³¹ there Abraham and his wife Sarah were buried; there Isaac and his wife Rebekah were buried; and there I buried Leah—³² the field and the cave in it, bought from the Hittites." ³³ When Jacob finished his instructions to his sons, he drew his feet into the bed and, breathing his last, he was gathered to his people.

50 Joseph flung himself upon his father's face and wept over him and kissed him. ² Then Joseph ordered the physicians in his service to embalm his father, and the physicians embalmed Israel. ³ It required forty days, for such is the full period of embalming. The Egyptians bewailed him seventy days; ⁴ and when the wailing period was over, Joseph spoke to Pharaoh's court, saying, "Do me this favor, and lay this appeal before Pharaoh: ⁵ 'My father made me swear, saying, "I am about to die. Be sure to bury me in the grave which I made ready for myself in the land of Canaan." Now, therefore, let me go up and bury my father; then I shall return.' " ⁶ And Pharaoh said, "Go up and bury your father, as he made you promise on oath."

⁷ So Joseph went up to bury his father; and with him went up all the officials of Pharaoh, the senior members of his court, and all of Egypt's dignitaries, ⁸ together with all of Joseph's household, his brothers, and his father's household; only their children, their flocks, and their herds were left in the region of Goshen. ⁹ Chariots, too, and horsemen went up with him; it was a very large troop.

¹⁰ When they came to Goren ͣ ha-Atad, which is beyond the Jordan, they held there a very great and solemn lamentation; and he observed a mourning period of seven days for his father. ¹¹ And when the Canaanite inhabitants of the land saw the mourning at Goren ha-Atad, they said, "This is a solemn mourning on the part of the Egyptians." That is why it was named Abel-mizraim,ᵇ which is beyond the Jordan. ¹² Thus his sons did for him as he had in-

a Or "the threshing floor of."
b Interpreted as "the mourning of the Egyptians."

49.29–50.26: The deaths of Jacob and Joseph. The book of Genesis draws to a rapid close with accounts of the deaths of Jacob and Joseph. The overall mood is marked by reverence for these larger-than-life figures and awareness that the promise that started their ancestor Abraham on his fateful journey (12.1–3) has now, amazingly, been largely fulfilled. Only two discordant notes are sounded: the anxiety of Joseph's brothers that their erstwhile victim will seek revenge now that he is no longer accountable to his father (50.15–21), and Joseph's last words, which draw attention to the fact that the Israelites in Egypt, for all their material comfort, do not yet possess the land of Israel, and the solemn promise of God to grant Abraham, Isaac, and Jacob the land thus remains unfulfilled (50.24–25). Joseph allays his brothers' anxiety by affirming God's mysterious providential design, which can bring good out of human evil (50.20–21). Similarly, by affirming the reliability of God's sworn promise to the patriarchs, he expresses his firm faith that their exile will end (50.24–25). **49.33:** *He drew his feet into the bed* closes the action begun in 48.2, when he "sat up in bed." The intervening material is thus presented as Jacob's last will and testament. **50.2–3:** The embalming and the periods of mourning follow Egyptian rather than Israelite custom. Jewish law forbids embalming (and cremating). The body must, instead, be interred in such a way that it will "return to the ground from which [it was] taken" (Gen. 3.19). **10:** It is unclear why the state procession approached Hebron by way of Transjordan. Perhaps vv. 10–11 derive from a lost tradition that did not locate Jacob's grave in the cave of Machpelah, as vv. 12–13 do, but spoke of an interment at the otherwise unattested site of Goren ha-Atad. Whether this is the case or not, the itinerary foreshadows the route Israel takes after their miraculous escape from Egypt, when they entered Canaan from structed them. ¹³His sons carried him to the land of Canaan, and buried him in the cave of the field of Machpelah, the field near Mamre, which Abraham had bought for a burial site from Ephron the Hittite. ¹⁴After burying his father, Joseph returned to Egypt, he and his brothers and all who had gone up with him to bury his father.

¹⁵When Joseph's brothers saw that their father was dead, they said, "What if Joseph still bears a grudge against us and pays us back for all the wrong that we did him!" ¹⁶So they sent this message to Joseph, "Before his death your father left this instruction: ¹⁷So shall you say to Joseph, 'Forgive, I urge you, the offense and guilt of your brothers who treated you so harshly.' Therefore, please forgive the offense of the servants of the God of your father." And Joseph was in tears as they spoke to him.

¹⁸His brothers went to him themselves, flung themselves before him, and said, "We are prepared to be your slaves." ¹⁹But Joseph said to them, "Have no fear! Am I a substitute for God? ²⁰Besides, although you intended me harm, God intended it for good, so as to bring about the present result—the survival of many people. ²¹And so, fear not. I will sustain you and your children." Thus he reassured them, speaking kindly to them.

²²So Joseph and his father's household remained in Egypt. Joseph lived one hundred and ten years. ²³Joseph

adoption (cf. 30.3; 48.12). Not surprisingly, therefore, in Judg. 5.14 Machir appears as a tribe of Israel. **24–25:** *Will surely take notice/has taken notice* (both are "pakod yifkod" in Heb) came to fulfillment in Exod. 3.16, when the LORD instructs Moses to declare to the "elders of Israel" that "I have taken note" ("pakod pakadti") of "you and what is being done to you in Egypt." In fact, it is none other than Moses himself who carries out Joseph's charge. The Mishnah finds in this an illustration of the important rabbinic principle, "By the measure by which a person metes out, it shall be meted out to him." Because "Joseph went up to bury his father" (50.7), Moses, generations later (as reported in Exod. 13.19) "took with him the bones of Joseph" (*m. Sot.* 1.7, 9). Ultimately, those bones were buried in Shechem (Josh. 24.32), the very city to which Jacob had sent Joseph, then a brash teenager, at the beginning of this astonishing tale of discord and reconciliation in the family that bears God's promise (37.13).

Transjordan (Num. 33.1–49; Josh. ch 3). As God had promised (46.4), Jacob, in short, is given his own personal exodus. The Talmud derives from this verse the institution of "shiv'ah," the seven days of most intense mourning incumbent upon Jews who have lost close kin (*y. Mo'ed Kat.* 3.5). Unlike the situation here, however, "shiv'ah" begins after burial. **15:** Cf. 27.41. **16–17:** No such words appear on the lips of Jacob himself. On the basis of this, a rabbi in the Talmud ruled that "it is permissible for a person to modify a statement in the interest of peace." Another rabbi maintained that one was required to do so (*b. Yebam.* 65b). The brothers' lie is defensible because of the good relations it ensured—a result that Jacob, on a plain-sense reading, surely desired. **18–21:** From Joseph's

dreams in 37.5–11, one might have suspected that the enslavement of Joseph's brothers to him would indeed occur and be, in fact, the last word in this complex and suspenseful novella. As they sold him into slavery (37.25–28), so would he (who had already enslaved the Egyptians, 47.13–26) enslave them. In fact, Joseph adheres to the ethic that forbids an Israelite to "take vengeance or bear a grudge" (Lev. 19.18). His rationale rests on the idea that the malignant intentions of human beings can realize the benign intentions of God. The people Israel, ironically, survives the worldwide famine because Joseph's brothers sold him into slavery (50.19–20; cf. 30.2 n.). **22:** *One hundred and ten years* appears in Egyptian sources as the ideal life span (cf. 6.3; Ps. 90.10). **23:** *Born upon Joseph's knees* implies lived to see children of the third generation of Ephraim; the children of Machir son of Manasseh were likewise born upon Joseph's knees. 24 At length, Joseph said to his brothers, "I am about to die. God will surely take notice of you and bring you up from this land to the land that He promised on oath to Abraham, to Isaac, and to Jacob." 25 So Joseph made the sons of Israel swear, saying, "When God has taken notice of you, you shall carry up my bones from here."

26 Joseph died at the age of one hundred and ten years; and he was embalmed and placed in a coffin in Egypt.

Exodus

THE ENGLISH NAME OF EXODUS derives from the Greek title *Exodos*, short for *Exodos Aigyptou*, "Departure from Egypt," used in the Septuagint. The Hebrew title, *Sefer ve'eleh shemot*, "the book of 'And these are the names' " (usually abbreviated to *Shemot*, "Names"), is based on the opening words of the book.

Exodus, in its present form, is not an independent book, but part of the Torah which narrates the story of Israel from the creation of the world through the death of Moses. The Torah in its final form is divided into five separate books simply because ancient scrolls could not contain a work of that length. Nevertheless, the books were not divided arbitrarily but at natural transition points. Exodus begins where the Hebrews grow from a family into a nation (1.1–7; cf. v. 9), and it ends on the first day of the new year following the exodus from Egypt as the sanctuary is erected and the divine Presence takes up Its abode in the Israelites' midst. The opening section (1.1–6, which recapitulates Gen. 46.8–27) and the closing section (40.36–38, which anticipates Num. 9.15–23) look as if they were composed after the subdivision to serve as prologue and epilogue, marking the book as a distinct subunit within the Torah. Thematically, the book marks the transition from God's promises of progeny, land, and a permanent relationship with Israel (e.g., Gen. chs 12–15; 17.1–8) to the fulfillment of these promises, beginning with the Israelites' phenomenal growth, the exodus, and the covenant at Sinai (Exod. 1.1–7; 12.1–36; chs 19–24).

Exodus is arguably the most important book in the Bible since it presents the seminal events in Israel's history and the definitive institutions of its religion, themes that have reverberated through all subsequent Jewish and Western history. These include Pharaoh's enslavement of the Israelites, the leadership of Moses, the beginnings of prophecy, the revelation of God's name YHVH to Moses, the ten plagues, the Pesaḥ ("Passover") festival, the splitting and crossing of the sea, the manna, the revelation of the Decalogue at Mount Sinai, the covenant formally constituting Israel as God's people, the first of the Torah's law collections and rules about the Sabbath and sacrificial worship, the sin of the golden calf, and the construction of the sanctuary.

Structure and Focus

THE BOOK FALLS ROUGHLY INTO FOUR MAIN SECTIONS: (1) enslavement and liberation
(1.1–15.21), during which Israel and Egypt come to "know" the LORD and His name; (2)
the journey to Sinai (15.22–17.16), marked by a series of dangers, Israelite complaints, and
deliverance by God; (3) covenant and lawgiving at Sinai (18.1–24.18), featuring the public
revelation of God; and (4) the sanctuary and the golden calf (chs 25–40), dealing with the
authorized and unauthorized ways of securing God's presence and worshipping Him.
The beginning point of (2) is not certain, and all or part of (2) could be seen as belonging
to (1).

The narrative in Exodus focuses on the paradigmatic significance of the events and on
celebrating them rather than on historical details. The names of the pharaohs—so important for historians—are nowhere mentioned, although those of the midwives who demonstrated "fear of God" are (1.15). Emphasized instead is the contest of wills between
Pharaoh, who does not know YHVH (5.2), and YHVH Himself, who is determined to show
Egypt, Israel, and the world that He is YHVH and what that means (7.5; 9.16; 14.4; etc.):
that He is incomparable (8.6); that He is present in the world (8.18); that the earth is His
(9.29). The book points out the lessons of the events, to be repeated to subsequent generations, and ordains commemorative rites to celebrate them (10.2; chs 12–13). The narrative
is full of the miraculous, such as the plagues against Egypt and the atmospherics at Sinai.
Later, Deuteronomy would declare that the exodus and the revelation at Sinai "clearly
demonstrate . . . that the LORD alone is God in heaven above and on earth below; there is
no other" (Deut. 4.32–39).

Historicity

THE BOOK'S INATTENTION to historical details has left historians grasping at bits of inci-
dental information, and at indirect evidence from ancient Egypt, that might permit dating
of the exodus or assessment of its historicity. None of the biblical narratives in their
current form is contemporary with the events they describe, though they have roots in
earlier oral tradition. Nor is there reference to an exodus in contemporary Egyptian
sources. Such a reference is not really to be expected, however: Egyptian royal inscriptions
avoided mentioning setbacks unless they were followed by victories, and administrative
records from the time and place of the exodus have mostly perished. Still, some data
suggest that there is a plausible historical kernel to the story. Northwestern Semites of the
same ethno-linguistic stock as the Hebrews, from Canaan, Transjordan, and Syria, had for
centuries migrated to Egypt, especially the eastern Nile delta, for food and water during
times of famine, as the Bible reports of Abraham and later of Jacob and his family, who
settled in the eastern delta (1.8 n.; 8.18 n.). Others were brought there as slaves captured
by the Egyptian army during raids. Egyptian documents refer to all of them as "Asiatics,"
rather than the specific ethnic groups to which they belong (e.g., Hebrew/Israelite,
Moabite, Phoenician; some mention people called Ḥapiru, but they are probably not

Hebrews; see 1.15 n.). Some Asiatics served as domestic or state slaves, the latter in royal building projects, like the Hebrews. According to the biblical account, the Hebrew slaves worked on the construction of the city of Rameses (1.11). If there is a historical kernel to the story, the Pharaoh who enslaved them was Rameses II (1279–1213 BCE), the greatest builder in ancient Egypt, who built the city named after himself as his new capital, in the eastern delta. Rameses also built a series of forts in the delta to secure Egypt's borders; this is perhaps reflected in the biblical Pharaoh's concern about foreign invasion (1.10). While we have no extrabiblical record of the ten plagues or of a mass escape of slaves from Egypt, natural disasters did take place periodically (though so many in rapid succession is implausible), and mass escapes of slaves are known from elsewhere in the ancient world, such as the revolt of 100,000 slaves in Italy led by Spartacus. The fact that "Moses" is an Egyptian name (a common element in such Egyptian names as Thutmosis and Rameses) is consistent with the Israelites having spent time in Egypt. If the Pharaoh of the enslavement was Rameses II, the Pharaoh under whom the Israelites left Egypt may have been his son, Merneptah (1213–1203 BCE), one of whose inscriptions claims a victory over "Israel," described as a nonsedentary people somewhere in the vicinity of Canaan, an encounter that would have taken place after the exodus. This makes sense chronologically since archeological evidence probably suggests that the Israelites appeared in Canaan around the beginning of the Iron Age (ca. 1200 BCE). None of this proves that the exodus happened, but it does indicate that the outline of the story, of Hebrews migrating to Egypt during a famine and being enslaved there under Rameses II, and later leaving under Moses, during or by the time of Merneptah, is not inherently implausible. Moreover, if the Israelites had invented their history, it seems more likely that they would have portrayed themselves as the original inhabitants of their land rather than as interlopers with a humiliating background as slaves.

Composition and Date

MODERN CRITICAL SCHOLARSHIP has shown that Exodus, like the Torah as a whole and some other ancient literature as well, was composed by one or more redactors weaving together several earlier written versions of the same events (see "Torah," pp. 1–7). These versions often disagreed with each other about ideology or the course of events. Their preservation side by side has led modern scholars to conclude that the redactor(s) was/were fundamentally conservative. Perhaps they believed all the traditions valid, perhaps even inspired, and therefore preserved them with minimal revision even if that left inconsistencies, non sequiturs, and redundancies. For example, in Exodus 6.3 God tells Moses that He did not make Himself known to the patriarchs by the name YHVH, but according to Genesis 15.7 He did. Within Exodus itself, Moses' father-in-law has different names in 2.18; 3.1; 4.18, and the description of the Tent of Meeting in 33.7–11 is inconsistent with, and oblivious to, both the immediately surrounding narrative and the description of the differently described Tent in chs 25–31 and 35–40. Inconsistencies such as these have alerted scholars to the presence of different sources, and characteristic variations in vocabulary and ideas have guided them in identifying the sources from which various components stem. Most easily identified is the Priestly document (P), the source of sections of chs 1–24 and most of chs 25–31 and 35–40, although recently scholars have found signs of the Holiness Document (H) there as well. P is also found in some of the narratives of the book, but there it shares space with material from the Yahwist (J) and Elohist (E) sources. J and E can sometimes, but not always, be distinguished. They were likely combined into a single narrative before being joined with P, so scholars often speak simply of the JE (or early narrative) source. Some also believe that there are some sections that are Deuteronomic, that is, related to ideas found in Deuteronomy. In numerous cases it is clear that we are dealing with an amalgam of two or three sources, though we cannot fully disentangle them (see introductory comments to chs 19–24 and 31.18–34.35).

Once the components of the text have been assigned as best they can be to their original sources, the differing views of those sources emerge. For example, J represents the oppression of the Israelites as corvée (forced) labor (1.11), P as full enslavement (1.13–14); arranging them in sequence, the redactor indicates that these were two successive stages of oppression. According to J the Israelites lived in Goshen, apart from the Egyptians (9.26); according to E they lived side by side with them (3.22). P (6.2) and E (3.13–15) hold that the name Yhvh was first revealed to Moses, while J believes that it was known earlier (Gen. 15.7). The patterned sequence of ten plagues noted at 7.14–10.29 was shaped by the redactor, who wove together material from J, P, and possibly E, which each had fewer, partly overlapping, partly different, plagues. The sources all represent the events at Mount Sinai very differently. For example, P reports neither a public revelation, the conclusion of a covenant, nor a golden calf episode. All that happened on the mountain was that God's Presence rested there in a cloud and Moses entered the cloud and privately received the instructions for the sanctuary (19.1–2a; 24.15–31.18a); all other lawgiving took place later in the Tabernacle, starting in Leviticus ch 1. It was J and E that reported the covenant, the visual (J) and auditory (E) manifestations of God, the proclamation of the Decalogue and the other covenant laws, and the breach of the covenant in the golden calf episode (chs 19–24; 32–34). It was the redactor(s) who wove all of these varying and conflicting details together in their present order, making them represent different stages of the events. The care and literary skill of the redactor(s) is nicely illustrated by the patterning of the plagues (7.14–10.29) and the location of the golden calf episode between the instructions for the sanctuary and their execution (31.18–32.35 n.). Whether or not the redactors believed that the inconsistencies could be harmonized is unclear. The contradictions and redundancies, however, had an important effect on later Judaism because they encouraged—in fact, forced—readers to create fine distinctions and nonliteral interpretations to enable them to coexist (*Thirteen Hermeneutic Rules of Rabbi Ishmael*, no. 13; *Thirty-two Hermeneutic Rules of Rabbi Eliezer ben Rabbi Jose the Galilean*, no. 15; Saadia, *Book of Beliefs and Opinions*, ch 7), thus paving the way in Judaism for innovations in theology and law.

Exodus and the Jewish Tradition

MANY OF THE FUNDAMENTAL BELIEFS and practices of Judaism are rooted in Exodus. The first of the book's two central events, the exodus itself, is recounted daily in Jewish prayers. It and the other central event, the proclamation of the Decalogue at Mount Sinai, are celebrated and retold on Jewish festivals every year, the exodus on the festival of Pesaḥ, whose rituals, including the Seder, are based on the rules prescribed in chs 12–13, and the proclamation of the Decalogue (ch 20) on the festival of Shavuot. The two festivals are known, respectively, as *zeman ḥerutenu,* "the time of our freedom," and *zeman matan toratenu,* "the time when our Torah was given." The inextricable link between them, ex-pressed in the fact that Pesaḥ begins a fifty-day countdown to Shavuot (see Lev. 23.15–21), proclaims that the freedom attained on the former only reaches fulfillment with the laws received on the latter. These two festivals plus Sukkot, the Feast of Booths, constitute the three "Pilgrimage Festivals" *(shalosh regalim)* of the Jewish religious calendar. Two other rituals that began as commemorations of the exodus are daily wearing of tefillin (13.9–10 n.) and the redemption of first-born sons *(pidyon haben,* 13.13 n.).

The exodus also served to orient Jewish festivals increasingly toward God's actions in history, in contrast to polytheistic festivals which focused on the gods' actions in nature. The role of Pesaḥ and the Feast of Unleavened Bread as commemorations of the exodus completely eclipsed their presumed earlier significance as spring festivals (12.6–14 n., 14–20 n.). Sukkot, although essentially an agricultural festival, also comes to commemo-rate the Israelites' dwelling in booths following the exodus (Lev. 23.43). At least since Second Temple times Shavuot—in the Torah an entirely agricultural festival—has been recognized as commemorating the giving of the Torah at Mount Sinai. Theologically, God's manifestation as Israel's redeemer at the exodus has fortified Jewish belief in re-demption even in the throes of oppression.

Fundamental principles of Judaism based on Exodus are the belief that the relationship between God and the Jewish people is defined by the covenant *(berit)* established between them at Mount Sinai (chs 19; 24) and the belief that God gave the Torah there, ordaining the Jewish way of life (chs 19–24). The momentous encounter with God at Sinai is, for Judaism, the defining moment in Jewish history, the moment when God came down on earth and spoke to all Jews, present and future, giving them His rules for life, which they accepted enthusiastically (20.16; 24.3, 7 n.). These laws (according to rabbinic belief both the Written Torah and its oral interpretation were communicated simultaneously) became the basis of all of Judaism: "Moses received Torah—written and oral—at Sinai and passed it on" down through the generations *(Pirkei ʾAvot* 1.1). Because these laws were presented to the entire people (21.1 n.), it became the duty of every Jew, not just an intellectual elite, to study them. Finally, the Thirteen Attributes of God, recited on various occasions in Jewish liturgy, are based on the attributes that God reveals to Moses in 34.6–7.

The first laws that God proclaimed to the Israelites were the Decalogue (20.2–14), or-daining laws both "between humankind and God" and "between one human being and another." Three of the laws in the first group became defining characteristics of Judaism which Jews have defended, often with their lives: the requirement to worship only the LORD (YHVH) and have no other gods, the requirement to have no idols, and the requirement to observe the Sabbath. Of the latter it has been said that "Even more than the Jews kept the Sabbath, the Sabbath preserved the Jews," as the Zionist philosopher Aḥad Ha-ʿAm (Asher Ginzberg, 1856–1927) observed.

The exodus has reverberated down through world history. Many early American settlers understood their flight from Europe and settlement in America as a new exodus, and later, Benjamin Franklin and Thomas Jefferson recommended that the great seal of the United States depict Moses leading the Israelites across the parted sea as a symbol of the American experience. African-Americans in the United States, hoping for freedom in the 19th century and fighting for civil rights in the 20th century, likewise saw themselves as reliving the Israelite experience. In the 1970s and 1980s, the mass departure of hundreds of thousands of Jews from the Soviet Union was known as "Operation Exodus." The exodus has clearly resonated strongly in Western history.   [JEFFREY H. TIGAY]

SHEMOT   שמות

1 These are the names of the sons of Israel who came to Egypt with Jacob, each coming with his household: 2 Reuben, Simeon, Levi, and Judah; 3 Issachar, Zebulun, and Benjamin; 4 Dan and Naphtali, Gad and Asher. 5 The total number of persons that were of Jacob's issue came to seventy, Joseph being already in Egypt. 6 Joseph died, and all his brothers, and all that generation. 7 But the Israelites were fertile and prolific; they multiplied and increased very greatly, so that the land was filled with them.

8 A new king arose over Egypt who did not know Joseph. 9 And he said to his people, "Look, the Israelite people are much too numerous for us. 10 Let us deal shrewdly with them, so that they may not increase; otherwise in the event of war they may join our enemies in fighting against us and ªrise from the ground."ª 11 So they set taskmasters

a-a Meaning perhaps from their wretched condition, cf. Hos. 2.2; or "gain ascendancy over the country." Others "get them up out of the land."

God's blessings and promises in Genesis, especially to the patriarchs (Gen. 1.20, 28; 9.1, 7; 17.2; 18.18; 28.14; 48.4), implying that these ancestral promises were now being fulfilled by God, who was causing the Israelites' proliferation and thwarting Pharaoh's attempts to check it.

1.8–22: The oppression. 8: This may refer to the rise of the 19th Dynasty, particularly Rameses II (ca. 1279–1213 BCE). This dynasty, founded by military officers, sought to protect Egypt's vulnerable coast and northeastern and northwestern borders from the Sea Peoples, the Libyans, and infiltrators from the Sinai, and to protect access to Egypt's empire in western Asia. Given the Israelites' background in Canaan and current residence in Goshen (8.18 n.), adjacent to the Sinai, Pharaoh may have feared that they would ally with invaders from that direction. **11–22:** Pharaoh's attempts to check the Israelite proliferation unfold in four stages, increasingly more oppressive: subjection to corvée (forced or draft) labor (vv. 11–12), slavery (vv. 13–14), a secret attempt to murder newborn boys (vv. 15–21), and a public at-

1.1–2.22: Prologue. These chs set the stage for the exodus by telling how the family of Jacob grew into a people in Egypt and fell into bondage (as God foretold in Gen. 15.13), and how Moses, the human agent of their deliverance, arose. It is composed of a combination of early narrative sources (JE) and P material.

1.1–7: Transition from Genesis. A recapitulation of Gen. 46.8–27 (cf. Gen. 35.23–26) leads to the account of how Jacob's family grew in Egypt from seventy individuals (a number signifying perfect completion) to a huge population—indeed, from a family to a nation. **7:** Many terms in this v. (and in vv. 12 and 20) are also used in over them to oppress them with forced labor; and they built garrison cities[a] for Pharaoh: Pithom and Rameses. [12] But the more they were oppressed, the more they increased and spread out, so that the [Egyptians] came to dread the Israelites.

[13] The Egyptians ruthlessly imposed upon the Israelites [14] [b-]the various labors that they made them perform. Ruthlessly[-b] they made life bitter for them with harsh labor at mortar and bricks and with all sorts of tasks in the field.

[15] The king of Egypt spoke to the Hebrew midwives, one of whom was named Shiphrah and the other Puah, [16] saying, "When you deliver the Hebrew women, look at the birthstool:[c] if it is a boy, kill him; if it is a girl, let her live." [17] The midwives, fearing God, did not do as the king of Egypt had told them; they let the boys live. [18] So the king of Egypt summoned the midwives and said to them, "Why have you done this thing, letting the boys live?" [19] The midwives said to Pharaoh, "Because the Hebrew women are not like the Egyptian women: they are vigorous. Before the midwife can come to them, they have given birth." [20] And God dealt well with the midwives; and the people multiplied and increased greatly. [21] And because the midwives feared God, He established households[d] for them. [22] Then Pharaoh charged all his people, saying, "Every boy that is born you shall throw into the Nile, but let every girl live."

2 A certain man of the house of Levi went and married a Levite woman. [2] The woman conceived and bore a son; and when she saw how beautiful he was, she hid him for

---

a Others "store cities."
b-b Brought up from the end of the verse for clarity.
c More exactly, the brick or stone supports used by Egyptian women during childbirth.
d Meaning of Heb. batim uncertain.

---

tempt to do the same (v. 22). The presentation of these as four successive, intensifying stages is the work of the redactor who drew them from the earlier sources J (corvée), P (slavery), and perhaps E (one or both attempts at infanticide). **11:** Pharaoh hopes to check the Israelites' proliferation by exhausting them. *Taskmasters,* foremen of corvée contingents (1 Kings 5.27–28). *Garrison cities,* rather "store cities" of a type that usually served military purposes (1 Kings 9.19; 2 Chron. 8.4–6; 17.12–13; 32.27–28). *Pithom and*

Rameses stood at strategic points guarding the entry to Egypt from the north and northeast. *Pithom,* Egyptian Pir-Atum, "House of (the god) Atum," was probably Tel e-Retabeh or Tel el-Maskhutah in the Wadi Tumilat, the entrance to Egypt from the Sinai Peninsula; both sites have archeological remains from the time of Rameses II. The city of Rameses was Pir-Rameses-Meri-Amon, "House of Rameses, beloved of [the god] Amon," capital of the delta region under the 19th and part of the 20th dynasties (1292–1137 BCE). It occu-

pied a very large area that extended over Kantir and Khataana and other nearby sites. Seti I (1294–1279) built a summer palace there, and it was considerably expanded by Rameses II. **13–14:** *Ruthlessly imposed . . . labors,* reduced them to full slavery (Lev. 25.39–46). **15:** *Hebrew,* an old term for Israelites, usually used when contrasting Israelites with other peoples (Gen. 14.13; 39.14, 17; 40.15; Exod. 21.2; Deut. 15.12); it is not normally used after the time of David. A relationship with the groups known as 'Apiru (sometimes spelled Ḫapiru) in ancient Near Eastern sources has been suggested, but the connection is problematic since the latter refers to a social class of outcasts, whereas "Hebrew" refers to an ethnic group. *Hebrew midwives,* the phrase could mean "midwives to the Hebrews" or midwives who were Hebrew. The former interpretation, found in LXX, Josephus, Abravanel, and Judah he-Ḥasid, understands them as righteous Gentiles; hence their motive is said to be fear of God (v. 17) rather than loyalty to their people. **16:** Killing the males and leaving only females would eliminate potential Israelite military power. Pharaoh's efforts are of no avail, as women thwart him (v. 17) and rescue Israel's future deliverer (2.1–10). *Birthstool,* parturient women sat or crouched on a seat of stone or bricks. **17:** *Fearing God,* restrained by an awareness that murder would bring divine retribution. **22:** *Throw into the Nile,* rather "expose in the Nile," that is, to be floated in baskets down the Nile where the babies would sink and drown. This attempt also fails. Ironically, the Nile will become the means by which Moses is saved and raised by Pharaoh's own daughter (2.1–10), and drowning will become the means of Pharaoh's ultimate defeat (Exod. 14.28).

2.1–22: The origins of Moses.

2.1–10: Moses' infancy. The story of Moses' birth and Pharaoh's attempted infanticide may be a relathree months. ³ When she could hide him no longer, she got a wicker basket for him and caulked it with bitumen and pitch. She put the child into it and placed it among the reeds by the bank of the Nile. ⁴ And his sister stationed herself at a distance, to learn what would befall him.

⁵ The daughter of Pharaoh came down to bathe in the Nile, while her maidens walked along the Nile. She spied the basket among the reeds and sent her slave girl to fetch it. ⁶ When she opened it, she saw that it was a child, a boy crying. She took pity on it and said, "This must be a Hebrew child." ⁷ Then his sister said to Pharaoh's daughter, "Shall I go and get you a Hebrew nurse to suckle the child for you?" ⁸ And Pharaoh's daughter answered, "Yes." So the girl went and called the child's mother. ⁹ And Pharaoh's daughter said to her, "Take this child and nurse it for me, and I will pay your wages." So the woman took the child and nursed it. ¹⁰ When the child grew up, she brought him to Pharaoh's daughter, who made him her son. She named him Moses,^a explaining, "I drew him out of the water."

¹¹ Some time after that, when Moses had grown up, he went out to his kinsfolk and witnessed their labors. He saw an Egyptian beating a Hebrew, one of his kinsmen. ¹² He turned this way and that and, seeing no one about, he struck down the Egyptian and hid him in the sand. ¹³ When he went out the next day, he found two Hebrews fighting; so he said to the offender, "Why do you strike your fellow?" ¹⁴ He retorted, "Who made you chief and ruler over us? Do you mean to kill me as you killed the Egyptian?" Moses was frightened, and thought: Then the matter is known! ¹⁵ When Pharaoh learned of the matter, he sought to kill Moses; but Moses fled from Pharaoh. He arrived^b in the land of Midian, and sat down beside a well.

¹⁶ Now the priest of Midian had seven daughters. They came to draw water, and filled the troughs to water their father's flock; ¹⁷ but shepherds came and drove them off. Moses rose to their defense, and he watered their flock. ¹⁸ When they returned to their father Reuel, he said, "How

---

a Heb. Mosheh *from Egyptian for "born of"; here associated with* mashah *"draw out."*
b Lit. *"sat" or "settled."*

---

pitch, but was found and later became king. In an Egyptian story, the god Horus was endangered as an infant by the god Seth and was hidden (but not abandoned) in a papyrus thicket of the Nile delta by his mother Isis to save him. In the biblical story, Moses is exposed as a ruse. **1:** Moses' parents, nameless here, are identified in a different source (6.16–20; P) as Amram and his aunt Jochebed. **2–4:** *The woman conceived and bore a son:* As the subsequent narrative indicates, this was not the couple's first child. This episode knows of an older sister, (v. 4ff.), and other passages recognize an older brother, Aaron (e.g., 4.14; 6.20; 7.7). All the actions to thwart Pharaoh's decree are taken by women—Moses' mother and sister, the midwives (1.17), and Pharaoh's daughter (2.5–10); the Hebrew men have been reduced to inactivity. **4:** *His sister,* elsewhere named Miriam (15.20; Num. 26.59). **7–9:** This sister contrives to return Moses temporarily to his mother's care by means of a wetnursing agreement (such agreements are known from ancient Near Eastern documents). **10:** *Moses* is an Egyptian name meaning "gave birth"; it is a shortened form of names compounded with names of deities, such as Thut-mose and Rameses, meaning "Thut/Ra gave birth (to this child)." Here, in a popular etymology typical of biblical and other ancient Near Eastern literature, it is interpreted as if it were derived from Heb "m-sh-h," "draw out" (cf. Isa. 63.11).

2.11–22: Moses' young adulthood. In the first two episodes (vv. 11–12, 13–14) Moses plays the royal role of defending his people and adjudicating among them (cf. 1 Sam. 8.5, 20), and in the third he defends foreigners and strangers (vv. 16–17), showing that his passion for justice makes no distinctions between nations. **11:** *An Egyptian,* presumably one of the taskmasters (1.11). **15:** Midian, a region in northwest Arabia. **18:** *Their father Reuel,* Moses' father-in-law is called Jethro in 3.1

---

tively late addition to the tradition; the following narratives about the exodus show no awareness of them (e.g., 2.23 and 6.6 are aware only of bondage), and they are never mentioned elsewhere in the

Bible. This story has parallels in birth legends of other heroes, some of which pre-date the Bible, such as Sargon of Akkad who in infancy was born in secret and exposed in a river in a reed basket sealed with is it that you have come back so soon today?" ¹⁹ They answered, "An Egyptian rescued us from the shepherds; he even drew water for us and watered the flock." ²⁰ He said to his daughters, "Where is he then? Why did you leave the man? Ask him in to break bread." ²¹ Moses consented to stay with the man, and he gave Moses his daughter Zipporah as wife. ²² She bore a son whom he named Gershom,ᵃ for he said, "I have been a stranger in a foreign land."

²³ A long time after that, the king of Egypt died. The Israelites were groaning under the bondage and cried out; and their cry for help from the bondage rose up to God. ²⁴ God heard their moaning, and God remembered His covenant with Abraham and Isaac and Jacob. ²⁵ God looked upon the Israelites, and God took notice of them.

3 Now Moses, tending the flock of his father-in-law Jethro, the priest of Midian, drove the flock into the wilderness, and came to Horeb, the mountain of God. ² An angel of the LORD appeared to him in a blazing fire out of a bush. He gazed, and there was a bush all aflame, yet the bush was not consumed. ³ Moses said, "I must turn aside to look at this marvelous sight; why doesn't the bush burn up?" ⁴ When the LORD saw that he had turned aside to look, God called to him out of the bush: "Moses! Moses!" He answered, "Here I am." ⁵ And He said, "Do not come closer. Remove your sandals from your feet, for the place on which you stand is holy ground. ⁶ I am," He said, "the

---

a Associated with ger sham, "a stranger there."

(Jether in 4.18) and elsewhere, and Hobab son of Reuel in Num. 10.29 and Judg. 4.11. These different names reflect different ancient traditions. **19:** An Egyptian, so Moses must have seemed because of his clothing and speech. **22:** Since Moses was raised as an Egyptian, it is only in Midian that he begins to feel the sense of alienness that his kinsfolk have experienced in Egypt.

2.23–25: Prelude to redemption. Pharaoh's death clears the way for Moses' return to Egypt (4.19). The Israelites' outcry rises up to God, who takes note of it and remembers His commitments to their ancestors. *His covenant* refers both to

God's promise of nationhood and territory in Canaan and the promise to free Israel after a long period of servitude (12.1–3; 15.13–20; 17.1–14; Gen. 26.2–5; 46.3–4). God's resolve to carry out these commitments is put into effect immediately, starting with His appearance to Moses in the burning bush (3.7–10).

3.1–22: Moses' call and departure for Egypt. The current narrative is the result of an artful combination of the two early sources, J and E. This is intimated by the different names used for God in 3.4a and b, but the clearest indication is the fact that 3.9–15 seem intrusive: vv. 9, 10, and 15a are redundant with,

respectively, vv. 7, 18b, and 16a; the people never ask for God's name as Moses expects in v. 13; and vv. 10 and 18 describe the goal of Moses' mission to Pharaoh differently and use different terms for the Egyptian king. Vv. 16–18 in fact read like a direct continuation of v. 8. The consistent use of the name "God" ('elohim) in 3.9–15 identifies its source as E; the remainder of this section is mostly from J with a few other passages from E (such as vv. 1, 4b, 6b, and 20b). By incorporating material from both sources the redactor preserved important themes, such as the explanation of God's name in v. 14 (E) and the fact that God both "appeared" to Moses (3.2, 16; 4.1, 5, from J) and "sent" him (vv. 10, 12–15, from E).

3.1–10: God appears to Moses and gives him his charge. The burning bush is both a means of attracting Moses' attention and a manifestation of God's presence. **1:** *Horeb,* alternate name for Mount Sinai (in E and in Deuteronomy). It is generally thought to be located in the Sinai Peninsula, though some believe it is in northwest Arabia, near Midian. Its designation *mountain of God* may indicate that it was already considered a sacred place, or it may be anticipatory. The first possibility may gain support from Egyptian inscriptions of the 14th century BCE that refer to an area, apparently in this region, as "land of the nomads, Yahwe"; this might also be understood as "land of the nomads who worship Yahwe." **2:** *An angel of the LORD,* a manifestation of God. Angels (lit. "messengers") usually take human form, but this one takes the form of *fire,* a substance evocative of the divine because it is insubstantial yet powerful, dangerous, illuminating, and purifying. (For God's manifestation in, and comparison to, fire, see also Gen. 15.17; Exod. 19.18; Deut. 4.24; Ps. 104.4; Ezek. 1.27.) **6:** *The God of Abraham, the God of Isaac, and the God of Jacob:* This phrase later became the way that God is addressed in the 'Amidah prayer.

God of your father, the God of Abraham, the God of Isaac, and the God of Jacob." And Moses hid his face, for he was afraid to look at God.

7 And the LORD continued, "I have marked well the plight of My people in Egypt and have heeded their outcry because of their taskmasters; yes, I am mindful of their sufferings. 8 I have come down to rescue them from the Egyptians and to bring them out of that land to a good and spacious land, a land flowing with milk and honey, the region of the Canaanites, the Hittites, the Amorites, the Perizzites, the Hivites, and the Jebusites. 9 Now the cry of the Israelites has reached Me; moreover, I have seen how the Egyptians oppress them. 10 Come, therefore, I will send you to Pharaoh, and you shall free My people, the Israelites, from Egypt."

11 But Moses said to God, "Who am I that I should go to Pharaoh and free the Israelites from Egypt?" 12 And He said, "I will be with you; that shall be your sign that it was I who sent you. And when you have freed the people from Egypt, you shall worship God at this mountain."

13 Moses said to God, "When I come to the Israelites and say to them, 'The God of your fathers has sent me to you,' and they ask me, 'What is His name?' what shall I say to them?" 14 And God said to Moses, "Ehyeh-Asher-Ehyeh."ᵃ He continued, "Thus shall you say to the Israelites, 'Ehyehᵇ sent me to you.' " 15 And God said further to Moses, "Thus shall you speak to the Israelites: The LORD,ᶜ the God of your fathers, the God of Abraham, the God of Isaac, and the God of Jacob, has sent me to you:

a Meaning of Heb. uncertain; variously translated: "I Am That I Am"; "I Am Who I Am"; "I Will Be What I Will Be"; etc.

b Others "I Am" or "I Will Be."

c The name YHWH (traditionally read Adonai "the LORD") is here associated with the root hayah "to be."

The repetition of "God" before each patriarch is explained in 'Etz Yosef, a commentary on the Jewish prayerbook, as meaning that, like the patriarchs, each person should believe in God on the basis of personal investigation, not merely tradition. He was afraid to look at God: Although the Bible assumes that God has a physical (usually humanlike) form, many passages suggest that seeing Him would be too awesome for humans to survive (Gen. 32.31; Exod. 19.21; 33.20–23; Judg. 13.22; Isa. 6.5; exceptions include Exod. 24.10–11;

Num. 12.8; Deut. 34.10; Ezek. 1.26–28). Later Jewish philosophers, most notably Maimonides, held that God does not in fact have a physical form and that the biblical passages in question are meant as metaphors. 8: A land flowing with milk and honey, a proverbial expression of the fertility of the land of Israel, representing the products of animals and the earth, of herders and farmers ("honey" refers primarily to the nectar of fruit, especially of dates, figs, and grapes). The Canaanites . . . : The Bible offers several slightly differ-

ent lists of peoples who lived in the promised land prior to the Israelites. (Cf., e.g., Gen. 10.15–20; Num. 13.29; Deut. 7.1.) 10: I will send you: As a prophet, Moses' primary role is to serve as God's emissary. Phrases with "send" ("sh-l-ḥ") typify the selection of prophets (e.g., Isa. 6.8; Jer. 1.7).

3.11–4.17: Moses raises five objections to his assignment (3.11, 13; 4.1, 10, 13), but God overcomes each. Prophets are often reluctant to accept their commission; cf. Jer. 1. 12: I will be with you: The verb be (" 'ehyeh") anticipates the etymology of the divine name in v. 14. That shall be your sign, or, "this shall be your sign." It is unclear whether the sign is God's presence with Moses, the fact that He sent him, or the future return to Horeb and worship there. 13: Not having been raised among his own people, Moses (like Pharaoh in 5.2) is ignorant of their God's name and fears he will lack credibility with them. He is told God's name, which the people evidently knew already, though 6.3 implies otherwise. (Source critics assign 6.3 to the Priestly source, while 3.9–15 are said to be from E.) 14: God's proper name, disclosed in the next verse, is YHVH (spelled "yod-heh-vav-heh" in Heb; in ancient times the "vav" was pronounced "w"). But here God first tells Moses its meaning: Ehyeh-Asher-Ehyeh, probably best translated as "I Will Be What I Will Be," meaning "My nature will become evident from My actions." (Compare God's frequent declarations below, that from His future acts Israel and Egypt "shall know that I am the LORD [YHVH]," as in 7.5; 10.2; etc.) Then He answers Moses' question about what to say to the people: "Tell them: 'Ehyeh' ("I Will Be," a shorter form of the explanation) sent me." This explanation derives God's name from the verb "h-v-h," a variant form of "h-y-h," "to be." Because God is the speaker, He uses the first-person form of the verb. 15: The LORD: The Heb states God's name, YHVH, meaning (according to v.

This shall be My name forever,
This My appellation for all eternity.

16 "Go and assemble the elders of Israel and say to them: the LORD, the God of your fathers, the God of Abraham, Isaac, and Jacob, has appeared to me and said, 'I have taken note of you and of what is being done to you in Egypt, 17 and I have declared: I will take you out of the misery of Egypt to the land of the Canaanites, the Hittites, the Amorites, the Perizzites, the Hivites, and the Jebusites, to a land flowing with milk and honey.' 18 They will listen to you; then you shall go with the elders of Israel to the king of Egypt and you shall say to him, 'The LORD, the God of the Hebrews, manifested Himself to us. Now therefore, let us go a distance of three days into the wilderness to sacrifice to the LORD our God.' 19 Yet I know that the king of Egypt will let you go only because of a greater might. 20 So I will stretch out My hand and smite Egypt with various wonders which I will work upon them; after that he shall let you go. 21 And I will dispose the Egyptians favorably toward this people, so that when you go, you will not go away empty-handed. 22 Each woman shall borrow from her neighbor and the lodger in her house objects of silver and gold, and clothing, and you shall put these on your sons and daughters, thus stripping the Egyptians."

4 But Moses spoke up and said, "What if they do not believe me and do not listen to me, but say: The LORD did not appear to you?" 2 The LORD said to him, "What is that in your hand?" And he replied, "A rod." 3 He said, "Cast it on the ground." He cast it on the ground and it became a snake; and Moses recoiled from it. 4 Then the LORD said to Moses, "Put out your hand and grasp it by the tail"—he put out his hand and seized it, and it became a rod in his hand—5 "that they may believe that the LORD, the God of their fathers, the God of Abraham, the God of Isaac, and the God of Jacob, did appear to you."

6 The LORD said to him further, "Put your hand into your bosom." He put his hand into his bosom; and when he took it out, his hand was encrusted with snowy scales![a] 7 And He said, "Put your hand back into your bosom."—He put his hand back into his bosom; and when he took it out of his bosom, there it was again like the rest of his body.—8 "And if they do not believe you or pay heed to the first sign, they will believe the second. 9 And if they are not convinced by both these signs and still do not heed you, take some water from the Nile and pour it on the dry

14): "He Will Be." The LORD is actually a translation of "'adonai" (lit. "my Lord") because that is what Jews now pronounce whenever the consonants YHVH appear. YHVH was probably originally pronounced "Yahweh," but in Second Temple times, as an expression of reverence, Jews began to avoid uttering it, substituting "'adonai" and other surrogates. (As a reminder to do so, in printed Hebrew Bibles the consonants are accompanied by the vowels of the surrogate words, leading to such hybrid English forms as Jehovah [i.e., "Yehovah" or the consonants Y-H-V-H with the vowels from "'adonai"].) **18:** The Egyptians are known to have granted to their workers time off for worship. The request may be simply to test Pharaoh's disposition, or to deceive the tyrant (cf. the deception commanded by God in 1 Sam. 16.1–3). **22:** *Borrow,* better, "request." The text need not imply deception, but a favor God will cause the Egyptians to bestow upon the departing Israelites (see v. 21). Cf. God's promise in Gen. 15.14. Some commentators see this as Egyptian compensation for the Israelites' slave labor, or treatment in accord with Deut. 15.13–14 (*Jub.* 48.18; Philo, *Mos.* 141; *b. Sanh.* 91a; Bahya). **4.1–9:** Three supernatural signs will confirm that Moses was indeed sent by God. All are ominous, portending harm for Egypt if it resists. **6:** The snowy encrustation looks like the skin disease that renders a person impure. (On "leprosy," see Lev. 13.2ff. n.) **9:** *Blood* here is a sign for the Israelites, in contrast to the plague in ch 7. **10:** *Slow of speech and . . . tongue,* encumbered with a speech impediment. **13–17:** Moses' continued resistance, after God has answered all his concerns, causes God to lose patience, but even then He further modifies His plan to accommodate Moses: Aaron will go as Moses' spokesman. No matter what, success will depend on God being "with" the spokesman (v. 15). **16:** Aaron shall speak Moses' words, just as the

a Cf. Lev. 13.2–3.

ground, and it—the water that you take from the Nile—will turn to blood on the dry ground."

10 But Moses said to the LORD, "Please, O Lord, I have never been a man of words, either in times past or now that You have spoken to Your servant; I am slow of speech and slow of tongue." 11 And the LORD said to him, "Who gives man speech? Who makes him dumb or deaf, seeing or blind? Is it not I, the LORD? 12 Now go, and I will be with you as you speak and will instruct you what to say." 13 But he said, "Please, O Lord, make someone else Your agent."ª 14 The LORD became angry with Moses, and He said, "There is your brother Aaron the Levite. He, I know, speaks readily. Even now he is setting out to meet you, and he will be happy to see you. 15 You shall speak to him and put the words in his mouth—I will be with you and with him as you speak, and tell both of you what to do—16 and he shall speak for you to the people. Thus he shall serve as your spokesman, with you playing the role of Godᵇ to him, 17 and take with you this rod, with which you shall perform the signs."

18 Moses went back to his father-in-law Jetherᶜ and said to him, "Let me go back to my kinsmen in Egypt and see how they are faring."ᵈ And Jethro said to Moses, "Go in peace."

19 The LORD said to Moses in Midian, "Go back to Egypt, for all the men who sought to kill you are dead." 20 So Moses took his wife and sons, mounted them on an ass, and went back to the land of Egypt; and Moses took the rod of God with him.

21 And the LORD said to Moses, "When you return to Egypt, see that you perform before Pharaoh all the marvels that I have put within your power. I, however, will stiffen his heart so that he will not let the people go. 22 Then you shall say to Pharaoh, 'Thus says the LORD: Israel is My first-born son. 23 I have said to you, "Let My son go, that he may worship Me," yet you refuse to let him go. Now I will slay your first-born son.' "

24 At a night encampment on the way, the LORD encountered him and sought to kill him. 25 ᵉ So Zipporah took a flint and cut off her son's foreskin, and touched his legs with it, saying, "You are truly a bridegroom of blood to me!" 26 And when He let him alone, she added, "A bridegroom of blood because of the circumcision."

a Lit. "send through whomever You will send."
b Cf. 7.1.   c I.e., Jethro.
d Lit. "whether they are still alive."   e Meaning of vv. 25–26 uncertain.

prophet speaks God's words (cf. 7.1).

4.18–31: Moses returns to Egypt.
20: *The rod of God* with which Moses will perform some of the signs and plagues (v. 17; cf. vv. 2–4; 7.20; 9.23; 10.13; 17.5, 9). This designation suggests that it was given him by God. *Sons,* Gershom and Eliezer (2.22; 18.3–5). **21:** *I . . . will stiffen his heart,* make him unyielding, impermeable to reason. As in v. 23 and 7.3, God here speaks of the final stage of the confrontation with Pharaoh (see 9.12; 10.1, 20, 27; 11.10; 14.4, 8, 17). He does not stiffen Pharaoh's heart initially, but only after Pharaoh has done so himself many times (7.13, 14, 22; 8.11, 15, 28; 9.7, 34, 35). Then God punishes Pharaoh in kind, depriving him of the freedom to change his mind and escape further punishment. The process is drawn out so that God's power can be made abundantly clear (7.3–5; 10.1–2). **22:** *Thus says the LORD:* This is the formula with which a messenger introduces the words of the One who sent him (Gen. 32.5; 45.9; Exod. 5.10; etc.). It is commonly used by prophets, reflecting the prophet's role as God's messenger. The designation of Israel as YHVH's *first-born son* reflects God's special attachment to Israel. **23:** *I will slay your first-born son:* In the Torah God punishes or rewards offspring for their parents' actions. This is part of the ancient view of families as organic units. (See 20.5–6 n.) **24–26:** This episode, possibly abridged from a fuller, clearer version, is extraordinarily puzzling because the motive for God's attack is unclear, the pronouns are equivocal, and Zipporah's remarks are enigmatic. **25:** Here circumcision seems to have apotropaic (magically protective) power, and by touching her son's foreskin to Moses' "legs" (genitals?), Zipporah saved him. The saving power of the bloody foreskin may foreshadow the protective role of the blood on the Israelites' doorposts on the eve of the exodus (12.7, 13, 22–23). *Bridegroom of blood,* cognates of Heb

27 The LORD said to Aaron, "Go to meet Moses in the wilderness." He went and met him at the mountain of God, and he kissed him. 28 Moses told Aaron about all the things that the LORD had committed to him and all the signs about which He had instructed him. 29 Then Moses and Aaron went and assembled all the elders of the Israelites. 30 Aaron repeated all the words that the LORD had spoken to Moses, and he performed the signs in the sight of the people, 31 and the people were convinced. When they heard that the LORD had taken note of the Israelites and that He had seen their plight, they bowed low in homage.

5 Afterward Moses and Aaron went and said to Pharaoh, "Thus says the LORD, the God of Israel: Let My people go that they may celebrate a festival for Me in the wilderness." 2 But Pharaoh said, "Who is the LORD that I should heed Him and let Israel go? I do not know the LORD, nor will I let Israel go." 3 They answered, "The God of the Hebrews has manifested Himself to us. Let us go, we pray, a distance of three days into the wilderness to sacrifice to the LORD our God, lest He strike us with pestilence or sword." 4 But the king of Egypt said to them, "Moses and Aaron, why do you distract the people from their tasks? Get to your labors!" 5 And Pharaoh continued, a-"The people of the land are already so numerous,-a and you would have them cease from their labors!" b

6 That same day Pharaoh charged the taskmasters and foremen of the people, saying, 7 "You shall no longer provide the people with straw for making bricks as heretofore; let them go and gather straw for themselves. 8 But impose upon them the same quota of bricks as they have been making heretofore; do not reduce it, for they are shirkers; that is why they cry, 'Let us go and sacrifice to our God!' 9 Let heavier work be laid upon the men; let them keep at it and not pay attention to deceitful promises."

10 So the taskmasters and foremen of the people went out and said to the people, "Thus says Pharaoh: I will not give you any straw. 11 You must go and get the straw yourselves wherever you can find it; but there shall be no decrease whatever in your work." 12 Then the people scattered throughout the land of Egypt to gather stubble for straw. 13 And the taskmasters pressed them, saying, "You must complete the same work assignment each day as

"ḥatan," *bridegroom*, mean "protect" in Akkadian and Arabic, and "circumcise" in Arabic. **31:** The theme that God has taken note of Israel's plight ends the episode, just as it opened it in 2.23–25 and 3.7.

5.1–6.1. The first encounter with Pharaoh. The ensuing narrative of the plagues and the defeat of the Egyptians in chs 6–15 may be viewed as God's answer to Pharaoh's contemptuous question, *Who is the LORD?* (v. 2). **5.1:** Here and in v. 3 Moses and Aaron request only a leave for worship, as instructed by God in 3.18. **3:** *Lest He strike us*, a reason Pharaoh should understand; failure to worship the deity would lead to punishment. **5:** This v. is best understood on the assumption that the Samaritan reading ("m'm" instead of MT "'m") is correct: Pharaoh claims that the Israelites already outnumber the Egyptians, and if they cease their labors they will increase even more—the very thing he sought to prevent by enslaving them (1.9–14). **7–8:** Bricks were made of Nile mud mixed with sand and straw gathered from harvested fields and chopped. Egyptian documents refer to daily brickmaking quotas and, in one case, to a lack of straw. Pharaoh's new requirement was a severe additional hardship. **9:** *Deceitful promises*, of liberation, by Moses and Aaron. **10:** The *foremen of the people*, Israelites whom the Egyptian taskmasters placed in charge of the Israelite laborers.

a-a Samaritan "Even now they are more numerous than the people of the land," i.e., than the native population (cf. Gen. 23.7).
b See 1.5–11.

when you had straw." [14] And the foremen of the Israelites, whom Pharaoh's taskmasters had set over them, were beaten. "Why," they were asked, "did you not complete the prescribed amount of bricks, either yesterday or today, as you did before?"

[15] Then the foremen of the Israelites came to Pharaoh and cried: "Why do you deal thus with your servants? [16] No straw is issued to your servants, yet they demand of us: Make bricks! Thus your servants are being beaten, when the fault is with your own people." [17] He replied, "You are shirkers, shirkers! That is why you say, 'Let us go and sacrifice to the LORD.' [18] Be off now to your work! No straw shall be issued to you, but you must produce your quota of bricks!"

[19] Now the foremen of the Israelites found themselves in trouble because of the order, "You must not reduce your daily quantity of bricks." [20] As they left Pharaoh's presence, they came upon Moses and Aaron standing in their path, [21] and they said to them, "May the LORD look upon you and punish you for making us loathsome to Pharaoh and his courtiers—putting a sword in their hands to slay us." [22] Then Moses returned to the LORD and said, "O Lord, why did You bring harm upon this people? Why did You send me? [23] Ever since I came to Pharaoh to speak in Your name, he has dealt worse with this people; and still You have not delivered Your people."

6 Then the LORD said to Moses, "You shall soon see what I will do to Pharaoh: he shall let them go because of a greater might; indeed, because of a greater might he shall drive them from his land."

VA-'ERA'   ואֵרָא

[2] God spoke to Moses and said to him, "I am the LORD. [3] I appeared to Abraham, Isaac, and Jacob as El Shaddai, but I did not make Myself known to them by My name יהוה.[a] [4] I also established My covenant with them, to give them the land of Canaan, the land in which they lived as sojourners. [5] I have now heard the moaning of the Israelites because the Egyptians are holding them in bondage, and I have remembered My covenant. [6] Say, therefore, to the Israelite people: I am the LORD. I will free you from the labors of the Egyptians and deliver you from their bondage. I will redeem you with an outstretched arm and through extraordinary chastisements. [7] And I will take

a *This divine name is traditionally not pronounced; instead,* Adonai, *"(the) LORD," is regularly substituted for it.*

6.1: *Drive them:* Ultimately Pharaoh will be forced to expel the Israelites as quickly as possible (12.31–33).

6.2–7.13: God's promises and Moses' mission reaffirmed. The vindication of God's name is the main theme of the plagues. This section, from the P source, is a variant of 3.1–6.1 (from JE), partly inconsistent and redundant with it. For example, the introduction of God's name and the promise of liberation (6.2–8) duplicate 3.7–15; Moses is to demand unconditional release (6.11, 13; 7.2), not merely three days' religious leave (3.18; 5.1); and Moses uses a different idiom to describe his speech impediment (6.12, 30; contrast 4.10). In its present context, however, this section reads as a response to the challenges of ch 5. **6.2:** God begins His reply to Moses (and to the people in v. 6) and concludes it in v. 8, by identifying Himself with the name that conveys His full power ("to know that He is YHVH" [6.7; 7.5] means to experience or witness His power [1 Kings 20.13, 28; Isa. 52.6; Jer. 9.2]). The people are thus reassured of the power and authority that guarantee His promises. **3:** YHVH is the same God who, under the name of El Shaddai, made a covenant with Israel's ancestors (see v. 4 and cf. Gen. 17.1–8; 28.3–4; 35.11–12; 48.3–4), and He now intends to fulfill that covenant. *But I did not make Myself known to them by My name YHVH:* They did not experience the full power that is expressed by the name YHVH, as Israel now will. From a critical point of view, this statement is inconsistent with such vv. as Gen. 15.7; 28.13; it is another indication that different sources underlie the present narrative. One source (J) holds that the name YHVH was first known in the days of Enosh (Gen. 4.26), while others (E and P) hold that it was first revealed in the days of Moses. **7:** *I will take you to be My people, and I will be your God:* This refers to the covenant that will be established at Mount Sinai (cf. El Shaddai's covenant promise you to be My people, and I will be your God. And you shall know that I, the LORD, am your God who freed you from the labors of the Egyptians. [8] I will bring you into the land which I swore[a] to give to Abraham, Isaac, and Jacob, and I will give it to you for a possession, I the LORD." [9] But when Moses told this to the Israelites, they would not listen to Moses, their spirits crushed by cruel bondage.

[10] The LORD spoke to Moses, saying, [11] "Go and tell Pharaoh king of Egypt to let the Israelites depart from his land." [12] But Moses appealed to the LORD, saying, "The Israelites would not listen to me; how then should Pharaoh heed me, a man of impeded speech!" [13] So the LORD spoke to both Moses and Aaron in regard to the Israelites and Pharaoh king of Egypt, instructing them to deliver the Israelites from the land of Egypt.

[14] The following are the heads of their respective clans.

The sons of Reuben, Israel's first-born: Enoch[b] and Pallu, Hezron and Carmi; those are the families of Reuben. [15] The sons of Simeon: Jemuel, Jamin, Ohad, Jachin, Zohar, and Saul[c] the son of a Canaanite woman; those are the families of Simeon. [16] These are the names of Levi's sons by their lineage: Gershon, Kohath, and Merari; and the span of Levi's life was 137 years. [17] The sons of Gershon: Libni and Shimei, by their families. [18] The sons of Kohath: Amram, Izhar, Hebron, and Uzziel; and the span of Kohath's life was 133 years. [19] The sons of Merari: Mahli and Mushi. These are the families of the Levites by their lineage.

[20] Amram took to wife his father's sister Jochebed, and she bore him Aaron and Moses; and the span of Amram's life was 137 years. [21] The sons of Izhar: Korah, Nepheg, and Zichri. [22] The sons of Uzziel: Mishael, Elzaphan, and Sithri. [23] Aaron took to wife Elisheba, daughter of Amminadab and sister of Nahshon, and she bore him Nadab and Abihu, Eleazar and Ithamar. [24] The sons of Korah: Assir, Elkanah, and Abiasaph. Those are the families of the Korahites. [25] And Aaron's son Eleazar took to wife one of Putiel's daughters, and she bore him Phinehas. Those are the heads of the fathers' houses of the Levites by their families.

[26] It is the same Aaron and Moses to whom the LORD said, "Bring forth the Israelites from the land of Egypt, troop by troop." [27] It was they who spoke to Pharaoh king

a Lit. "raised My hand."
b Or "Hanoch"; cf. on Gen. 46.9.
c Or "Shaul"; cf. on Gen. 46.10.

in Gen. 17.7, 8 and those in Lev. 26.12; Jer. 31.33; Hos. 2.25). The expression of this relationship ("take" and "be someone's x") is modeled on idioms for marrying and adopting (Gen. 4.19; Exod. 2.10; Deut. 24.1–2; 2 Sam. 7.14), implying the intimate nature of the intended relationship between God and Israel. (Marriage and the parent-child relationship are used as metaphors for the relationship between God and Israel in many biblical passages, e.g., Exod. 4.22; Deut. 14.2; Isa. 54.5–7; 62.5; Jer. 2.2;. 3.19, 22; Hos. ch 2.) *And you shall know that I, the LORD, am your God:* See v. 2 n.

6.14–27: The pedigree of Moses and Aaron. This is apparently an extract from a larger genealogy (cf. Gen. 46.8–11; Num. 3.17–39; 26.5–14, 57–60), beginning with the descendants of Jacob's first two sons (see Exod 1.2; Gen. 29.32–34), but only for the sake of showing the place of his third son, Levi, the ancestor of Moses and Aaron. Levi's descendants are listed in detail, particularly Aaron and his immediate successors as high priest (v. 25). The rest of the tribes are omitted here as they are not pertinent to identifying Moses and Aaron. **20:** *His father's sister:* Marriage with an aunt, apparently legitimate in Amram's time, is forbidden in Lev. 18.12–13. Jochebed must have been a much younger sister of Kohath. *Aaron and Moses:* Miriam (Num. 26.59) is omitted as the list names only men, apart from the mothers of the most prominent individuals. **21:** *Korah,* see Num. ch 16. **22:** *Mishael, Elzaphan,* see Lev. 10.4. **23:** *Nadab and Abihu,* see Lev. 10.1–5. **25:** *Eleazar,* Aaron's successor, Num. 20.26–28. *Phinehas,* Eleazar's successor and ancestor of the subsequent high priests; see Num. 25.1–13. **26:** *Troop by troop:* The Israelites would not leave Egypt as fleeing slaves but as an army marching to the promised land in military formation (7.4; 12.17; 18.21b; Num. 1.52; etc.). In order to pick up the narrative following the genealogical digression, 6.28–30 and 7.1–2 of Egypt to free the Israelites from the Egyptians; these are the same Moses and Aaron. 28 For when the LORD spoke to Moses in the land of Egypt 29 and the LORD said to Moses, "I am the LORD; speak to Pharaoh king of Egypt all that I will tell you," 30 Moses appealed to the LORD, saying, "See, I am of impeded speech; how then should Pharaoh heed me!"

7 The LORD replied to Moses, "See, I place you in the role of God to Pharaoh, with your brother Aaron as your prophet.[a] 2 You shall repeat all that I command you, and your brother Aaron shall speak to Pharaoh to let the Israelites depart from his land. 3 But I will harden Pharaoh's heart, that I may multiply My signs and marvels in the land of Egypt. 4 When Pharaoh does not heed you, I will lay My hand upon Egypt and deliver My ranks, My people the Israelites, from the land of Egypt with extraordinary chastisements. 5 And the Egyptians shall know that I am the LORD, when I stretch out My hand over Egypt and bring out the Israelites from their midst." 6 This Moses and Aaron did; as the LORD commanded them, so they did. 7 Moses was eighty years old and Aaron eighty-three, when they made their demand on Pharaoh.

8 The LORD said to Moses and Aaron, 9 "When Pharaoh speaks to you and says, 'Produce your marvel,' you shall say to Aaron, 'Take your rod and cast it down before Pharaoh.' It shall turn into a serpent." 10 So Moses and Aaron came before Pharaoh and did just as the LORD had commanded: Aaron cast down his rod in the presence of Pharaoh and his courtiers, and it turned into a serpent. 11 Then Pharaoh, for his part, summoned the wise men and the sorcerers; and the Egyptian magicians, in turn, did the same with their spells; 12 each cast down his rod, and they turned into serpents. But Aaron's rod swallowed their rods. 13 Yet Pharaoh's heart stiffened and he did not heed them, as the LORD had said.

14 And the LORD said to Moses, "Pharaoh is stubborn; he

a Cf. 4.16.

recapitulate 6.9–13. **7.3–5:** See 4.21. *The Egyptians shall know that I am the LORD:* God's "signs and marvels" will answer Pharaoh's contemptuous declaration that he does "not know the LORD" (5.2). **9:** *Produce your marvel,* produce evidence corroborating that you were sent by a god. The marvel is one of those Moses used to convince the

people of his divine mission (4.1–5). **11–13:** Since Pharaoh's magicians are able to duplicate this marvel (vv. 7–12a), he is unimpressed. Nonetheless, this early confrontation foreshadows the eventual outcome of the contest between Moses and Aaron and the Egyptian magicians. The magicians use "their spells" (v. 11; 7.22),

conventional magic; while Aaron works silently, relying not on his own power or on magical technique, but on an unknown power that he identifies as the LORD, whose superiority is shown when Aaron's serpent overcomes those of the magicians.

7.14–10.29: The first nine plagues. There are ten plagues in all, though the Bible nowhere states the number. Source analysis indicates that the narrative is drawn from the J, E, and P sources, which differed in the number of plagues and their details. Indications of this are, for example, inconsistencies regarding whether Aaron or Moses is to bring about the first plague and the nature of the gesture that will initiate it (7.17, 19), whether the first two plagues will involve the Nile only or all the waters of Egypt (7.17, 19, 21, 28; 8.1), and the different terms used for Pharaoh's obstinacy, "stiffening his heart" (7.22; 8.15; 9.12, 35; 10.20, 27; 11.10) and "stubbornness [lit. heaviness] of heart" (8.11, 28; 9.7, 34; rendered "harden" in 10.1). The redactor has skillfully woven the sources into three triads, each with a consistent pattern, followed by a capstone tenth plague. In introducing the first plague of each triad, God tells Moses the main lesson that triad will teach (7.17; 8.18; 9.14). The first two plagues of each triad are preceded by warnings to Pharaoh, while the third is not. Before the first plague in each group God sends Moses to Pharaoh in the morning, saying "station yourself before [Pharaoh]," and before the second he says "Go to Pharaoh" without specifying the time of day. All the plagues in the first triad are brought on by an action of Aaron; in the second triad, the first two are brought about directly by God and the third by Moses; in the third triad, all are brought on by an action of Moses. These nine plagues resemble calamities known within nature (many are attested in ancient Near Eastern literature), but their patterns, their timing and rapid succession, and refuses to let the people go. [15] Go to Pharaoh in the morning, as he is coming out to the water, and station yourself before him at the edge of the Nile, taking with you the rod that turned into a snake. [16] And say to him, 'The LORD, the God of the Hebrews, sent me to you to say, "Let My people go that they may worship Me in the wilderness." But you have paid no heed until now. [17] Thus says the LORD, "By this you shall know that I am the LORD." See, I shall strike the water in the Nile with the rod that is in my hand, and it will be turned into blood; [18] and the fish in the Nile will die. The Nile will stink so that the Egyptians will find it impossible to drink the water of the Nile.' "

[19] And the LORD said to Moses, "Say to Aaron: Take your rod and hold out your arm over the waters of Egypt—its rivers, its canals, its ponds, all its bodies of water—that they may turn to blood; there shall be blood throughout the land of Egypt, even in vessels of wood and stone." [20] Moses and Aaron did just as the LORD commanded: he lifted up the rod and struck the water in the Nile in the sight of Pharaoh and his courtiers, and all the water in the Nile was turned into blood [21] and the fish in the Nile died. The Nile stank so that the Egyptians could not drink water from the Nile; and there was blood throughout the land of Egypt. [22] But when the Egyptian magicians did the same with their spells, Pharaoh's heart stiffened and he did not heed them—as the LORD had spoken. [23] Pharaoh turned and went into his palace, paying no regard even to this. [24] And all the Egyptians had to dig round about the Nile for drinking water, because they could not drink the water of the Nile.

[25] When seven days had passed after the LORD struck the Nile, [26] the LORD said to Moses, "Go to Pharaoh and say to him, 'Thus says the LORD: Let My people go that they may worship Me. [27] If you refuse to let them go, then I will plague your whole country with frogs. [28] The Nile shall swarm with frogs, and they shall come up and enter your palace, your bedchamber and your bed, the houses of your courtiers and your people, and your ovens and your kneading bowls. [29] The frogs shall come up on you and on your people and on all your courtiers.' "

8 And the LORD said to Moses, "Say to Aaron: Hold out your arm with the rod over the rivers, the canals, and the ponds, and bring up the frogs on the land of Egypt." [2] Aaron held out his arm over the waters of Egypt, and the frogs came up and covered the land of Egypt. [3] But the magicians did the same with their spells, and brought frogs upon the land of Egypt.

their announcement and removal by Moses show that they are not a random succession of natural events but the purposeful workings of divine power. The tenth plague stands by itself: Moses, still in Pharaoh's presence following the ninth plague, receives word from God and warns Pharaoh immediately of the final plague, one that will be manifestly supernatural, unlike anything known in human experience.

7.14–8.15: The first three plagues. In this triad, the Egyptians will begin to experience the LORD's power. **7.14–24: The first plague: blood. 17:** Like Israel in 6.7 and Moses in 7.5, Pharaoh is now told what the coming events will show, though he will grasp the lesson by fits and starts and more slowly than his courtiers will. **17–18:** This plague is far more ominous than the sign in 4.9 because here the river itself— the deified source of Egypt's life— is affected. **22:** The magicians' ability to duplicate the plague can only make matters worse for the Egyptians, but it again (see 7.11–13) convinces Pharaoh that nothing but magic is involved, so he remains unmoved. **7.25–8.11: The second plague: frogs.**

4 Then Pharaoh summoned Moses and Aaron and said, "Plead with the LORD to remove the frogs from me and my people, and I will let the people go to sacrifice to the LORD." 5 And Moses said to Pharaoh, "You may have this triumph over me: for what time shall I plead in behalf of you and your courtiers and your people, that the frogs be cut off from you and your houses, to remain only in the Nile?" 6 "For tomorrow," he replied. And [Moses] said, "As you say—that you may know that there is none like the LORD our God; 7 the frogs shall retreat from you and your courtiers and your people; they shall remain only in the Nile." 8 Then Moses and Aaron left Pharaoh's presence, and Moses cried out to the LORD in the matter of the frogs which He had inflicted upon Pharaoh. 9 And the LORD did as Moses asked; the frogs died out in the houses, the courtyards, and the fields. 10 And they piled them up in heaps, till the land stank. 11 But when Pharaoh saw that there was relief, he became stubborn and would not heed them, as the LORD had spoken.

12 Then the LORD said to Moses, "Say to Aaron: Hold out your rod and strike the dust of the earth, and it shall turn to lice throughout the land of Egypt." 13 And they did so. Aaron held out his arm with the rod and struck the dust of the earth, and vermin came upon man and beast; all the dust of the earth turned to lice throughout the land of Egypt. 14 The magicians did the like with their spells to produce lice, but they could not. The vermin remained upon man and beast; 15 and the magicians said to Pharaoh, "This is the finger of God!" But Pharaoh's heart stiffened and he would not heed them, as the LORD had spoken.

16 And the LORD said to Moses, "Early in the morning present yourself to Pharaoh, as he is coming out to the water, and say to him, 'Thus says the LORD: Let My people go that they may worship Me. 17 For if you do not let My people go, I will let loose ᵃswarms of insectsᵃ against you and your courtiers and your people and your houses; the houses of the Egyptians, and the very ground they stand on, shall be filled with swarms of insects. 18 But on that day I will set apart the region of Goshen, where My people dwell, so that no swarms of insects shall be there, that you may know that I the LORD am in the midst of the land. 19 And I will make a distinctionᵇ between My people and your people. Tomorrow this sign shall come to pass.' " 20 And the LORD did so. Heavy swarms of insects invaded Pharaoh's palace and the houses of his courtiers; through-

8.4: Despite the magicians' duplication of the plague (which, again, makes matters worse), this time Pharaoh apparently realizes that his magicians cannot end the plague, and therefore that the LORD is behind it. This is the first of several partial or temporary concessions by Pharaoh, each of which is soon withdrawn (see also vv. 21, 24; 9.27–28; 10.8-11, 16–17, 24–28). **6:** Allowing Pharaoh to specify the time for removing the frogs should reinforce the lesson of the LORD's unique power: He can end a plague at the very moment specified. **8.12–15: The third plague: vermin.** The Heb term refers to some small insect, such as mosquitoes or lice. **14–15:** The magicians' inability to duplicate this plague leads them to explicitly recognize that this is not magic but divine power.

8.16–9.12: The second three plagues. In this triad God applies the punishments only to the Egyptians and not to the Israelites (8.18–19; 9.4, 6–7; cf. 9.11), showing that He is "in the midst of the land," directing events closely and discriminatingly. **8.16–28: The fourth plague. 17:** *Swarms of insects*, the meaning of Heb "ʿarov" is uncertain. **18:** *The region of Goshen*, the area in the eastern part of the Nile delta (near the Sinai peninsula), where Joseph had settled his family (Gen. 46.29, 34; 47.6; 50.8; see map, p. 130).

a-a Others "wild beasts."   b Meaning of peduth uncertain.

out the country of Egypt the land was ruined because of the swarms of insects.

21 Then Pharaoh summoned Moses and Aaron and said, "Go and sacrifice to your God within the land." 22 But Moses replied, "It would not be right to do this, for what we sacrifice to the LORD our God is untouchable to the Egyptians. If we sacrifice that which is untouchable to the Egyptians before their very eyes, will they not stone us! 23 So we must go a distance of three days into the wilderness and sacrifice to the LORD our God as He may command us." 24 Pharaoh said, "I will let you go to sacrifice to the LORD your God in the wilderness; but do not go very far. Plead, then, for me." 25 And Moses said, "When I leave your presence, I will plead with the LORD that the swarms of insects depart tomorrow from Pharaoh and his courtiers and his people; but let not Pharaoh again act deceitfully, not letting the people go to sacrifice to the LORD."

26 So Moses left Pharaoh's presence and pleaded with the LORD. 27 And the LORD did as Moses asked: He removed the swarms of insects from Pharaoh, from his courtiers, and from his people; not one remained. 28 But Pharaoh became stubborn this time also, and would not let the people go.

9 The LORD said to Moses, "Go to Pharaoh and say to him, 'Thus says the LORD, the God of the Hebrews: Let My people go to worship Me. 2 For if you refuse to let them go, and continue to hold them, 3 then the hand of the LORD will strike your livestock in the fields—the horses, the asses, the camels, the cattle, and the sheep—with a very severe pestilence. 4 But the LORD will make a distinction between the livestock of Israel and the livestock of the Egyptians, so that nothing shall die of all that belongs to the Israelites. 5 The LORD has fixed the time: tomorrow the LORD will do this thing in the land.' " 6 And the LORD did so the next day: all the livestock of the Egyptians died, but of the livestock of the Israelites not a beast died. 7 When Pharaoh inquired, he found that not a head of the livestock of Israel had died; yet Pharaoh remained stubborn, and he would not let the people go.

8 Then the LORD said to Moses and Aaron, "Each of you take handfuls of soot from the kiln, and let Moses throw it toward the sky in the sight of Pharaoh. 9 It shall become a fine dust all over the land of Egypt, and cause an inflammation breaking out in boils on man and beast throughout the land of Egypt." 10 So they took soot of the kiln and appeared before Pharaoh; Moses threw it toward the sky,

21–24: Pharaoh weakens further and begins to recognize God, saying *Plead, then, for me.* He makes partial concessions but will not grant all that is asked. **22:** *Untouchable to the Egyptians:* This may be related to the Egyptian aversion mentioned in Gen. 43.32, but whether Moses means what he says or is being evasive is unclear. **24:** *Do not go very far,* less than *a distance of three days* (v. 23). **9.1–7: The fifth plague: pestilence.** Some type of deadly epidemic affecting livestock, perhaps anthrax. **9.8–12: The sixth plague: boils.** A severe skin inflammation (cf. Deut. 28.27).

and it caused an inflammation breaking out in boils on man and beast. [11] The magicians were unable to confront Moses because of the inflammation, for the inflammation afflicted the magicians as well as all the other Egyptians. [12] But the LORD stiffened the heart of Pharaoh, and he would not heed them, just as the LORD had told Moses.

[13] The LORD said to Moses, "Early in the morning present yourself to Pharaoh and say to him, 'Thus says the LORD, the God of the Hebrews: Let My people go to worship Me. [14] For this time I will send all My plagues upon your person, and your courtiers, and your people, in order that you may know that there is none like Me in all the world. [15] I could have stretched forth My hand and stricken you and your people with pestilence, and you would have been effaced from the earth. [16] Nevertheless I have spared you for this purpose: in order to show you My power, and in order that My fame may resound throughout the world. [17] Yet you continue to thwart[a] My people, and do not let them go! [18] This time tomorrow I will rain down a very heavy hail, such as has not been in Egypt from the day it was founded until now. [19] Therefore, order your livestock and everything you have in the open brought under shelter; every man and beast that is found outside, not having been brought indoors, shall perish when the hail comes down upon them!' " [20] Those among Pharaoh's courtiers who feared the LORD's word brought their slaves and livestock indoors to safety; [21] but those who paid no regard to the word of the LORD left their slaves and livestock in the open.

[22] The LORD said to Moses, "Hold out your arm toward the sky that hail may fall on all the land of Egypt, upon man and beast and all the grasses of the field in the land of Egypt." [23] So Moses held out his rod toward the sky, and the LORD sent thunder and hail, and fire streamed down to the ground, as the LORD rained down hail upon the land of Egypt. [24] The hail was very heavy—fire flashing in the midst of the hail—such as had not fallen on the land of Egypt since it had become a nation. [25] Throughout the land of Egypt the hail struck down all that were in the open, both man and beast; the hail also struck down all the grasses of the field and shattered all the trees of the field. [26] Only in the region of Goshen, where the Israelites were, there was no hail.

[27] Thereupon Pharaoh sent for Moses and Aaron and said to them, "I stand guilty this time. The LORD is in the right, and I and my people are in the wrong. [28] Plead with

9.13–10.29: The third triad of plagues. The unprecedented character of the plagues in this triad shows the incomparability of the LORD who causes them (9.14, 18; 10.6, 14). **9.13–35: The seventh plague: hail. 16:** One of God's aims in prolonging the confrontation is to show the Egyptians the consequences of resisting His authority and to make Himself known to the world. See also 10.1–2. **20:** Some Egyptians have come to understand God's power, but others still resist, along with Pharaoh (vv. 21, 30, 34; 10.1). **25:** The first plague that takes human life (cf. vv. 19–21); it represents an escalation of the plagues. **27–28:** Now Pharaoh ca-

a Others "exalt yourself over."

the Lord that there may be an end of God's thunder and of hail. I will let you go; you need stay no longer." [29] Moses said to him, "As I go out of the city, I shall spread out my hands to the Lord; the thunder will cease and the hail will fall no more, so that you may know that the earth is the Lord's. [30] But I know that you and your courtiers do not yet fear the Lord God."—[31] Now the flax and barley were ruined, for the barley was in the ear and the flax was in bud; [32] but the wheat and the emmer[a] were not hurt, for they ripen late.—[33] Leaving Pharaoh, Moses went outside the city and spread out his hands to the Lord: the thunder and the hail ceased, and no rain came pouring down upon the earth. [34] But when Pharaoh saw that the rain and the hail and the thunder had ceased, he became stubborn and reverted to his guilty ways, as did his courtiers. [35] So Pharaoh's heart stiffened and he would not let the Israelites go, just as the Lord had foretold through Moses.

BO'   בא

10 Then the Lord said to Moses, "Go to Pharaoh. For I have hardened his heart and the hearts of his courtiers, in order that I may display these My signs among them, [2] and that you may recount in the hearing of your sons and of your sons' sons how I made a mockery of the Egyptians and how I displayed My signs among them—in order that you may know that I am the Lord." [3] So Moses and Aaron went to Pharaoh and said to him, "Thus says the Lord, the God of the Hebrews, 'How long will you refuse to humble yourself before Me? Let My people go that they may worship Me. [4] For if you refuse to let My people go, tomorrow I will bring locusts on your territory. [5] They shall cover the surface of the land, so that no one will be able to see the land. They shall devour the surviving remnant that was left to you after the hail; and they shall eat away all your trees that grow in the field. [6] Moreover, they shall fill your palaces and the houses of all your courtiers and of all the Egyptians—something that neither your fathers nor fathers' fathers have seen from the day they appeared on earth to this day.' " With that he turned and left Pharaoh's presence.

[7] Pharaoh's courtiers said to him, "How long shall this one be a snare to us? Let the men go to worship the Lord their God! Are you not yet aware that Egypt is lost?" [8] So Moses and Aaron were brought back to Pharaoh and he said to them, "Go, worship the Lord your God! Who are the ones to go?" [9] Moses replied, "We will all go, young

pitulates completely. **29:** *The earth is the Lord's:* He controls nature. **10.1–20: The eighth plague: locusts,** one of the most devastating natural disasters (see Joel chs 1–2). **1–2:** An extension of the idea of 9.16, but noting explicitly that the real point of the plagues is so that the Israelites, not only the Egyptians, will appreciate the Lord's power. **5:** *The surviving remnant,* particularly the wheat and emmer of 9.32. **7–11:** Now all of Pharaoh's courtiers are convinced and urge him to submit. When he hears Moses' terms, he offers only a partial concession.

_____
a A kind of wheat.

and old: we will go with our sons and daughters, our flocks and herds; for we must observe the LORD's festival." [10] But he said to them, "The LORD be with you the same as I mean to let your children go with you! Clearly, you are bent on mischief. [11] No! You menfolk go and worship the LORD, since that is what you want." And they were expelled from Pharaoh's presence.

[12] Then the LORD said to Moses, "Hold out your arm over the land of Egypt for the locusts, that they may come upon the land of Egypt and eat up all the grasses in the land, whatever the hail has left." [13] So Moses held out his rod over the land of Egypt, and the LORD drove an east wind over the land all that day and all night; and when morning came, the east wind had brought the locusts. [14] Locusts invaded all the land of Egypt and settled within all the territory of Egypt in a thick mass; never before had there been so many, nor will there ever be so many again. [15] They hid all the land from view, and the land was darkened; and they ate up all the grasses of the field and all the fruit of the trees which the hail had left, so that nothing green was left, of tree or grass of the field, in all the land of Egypt. [16] Pharaoh hurriedly summoned Moses and Aaron and said, "I stand guilty before the LORD your God and before you. [17] Forgive my offense just this once, and plead with the LORD your God that He but remove this death from me." [18] So he left Pharaoh's presence and pleaded with the LORD. [19] The LORD caused a shift to a very strong west wind, which lifted the locusts and hurled them into the Sea of Reeds;[a] not a single locust remained in all the territory of Egypt. [20] But the LORD stiffened Pharaoh's heart, and he would not let the Israelites go.

[21] Then the LORD said to Moses, "Hold out your arm toward the sky that there may be darkness upon the land of Egypt, a darkness that can be touched." [22] Moses held out his arm toward the sky and thick darkness descended upon all the land of Egypt for three days. [23] People could not see one another, and for three days no one could get up from where he was; but all the Israelites enjoyed light in their dwellings.

[24] Pharaoh then summoned Moses and said, "Go, worship the LORD! Only your flocks and your herds shall be left behind; even your children may go with you." [25] But Moses said, "You yourself must provide us with sacrifices and burnt offerings to offer up to the LORD our God; [26] our own livestock, too, shall go along with us—not a hoof

10.21–29: The ninth plague: darkness. Since the darkness "can be touched" (v. 21), it may reflect a "hamsin," the hot southerly wind from the Sahara desert, carrying unusually dense concentrations of sand and dust that block out sunlight. **24–26:** Pharoah will permit the people to go but not their flocks, as if to undermine the purpose for which the Israelites are leaving—to sacrifice, which requires animals from the flocks. Moses counters by demanding that Pharaoh provide the sacrificial animals from his own livestock, and also insists that the Israelite livestock also go with them. Moses seeks Pharaoh's total capitulation to God.

a Traditionally, but incorrectly, "Red Sea."

shall remain behind: for we must select from it for the worship of the LORD our God; and we shall not know with what we are to worship the LORD until we arrive there." 27 But the LORD stiffened Pharaoh's heart and he would not agree to let them go. 28 Pharaoh said to him, "Be gone from me! Take care not to see me again, for the moment you look upon my face you shall die." 29 And Moses replied, "You have spoken rightly. I shall not see your face again!"

11 And the LORD said to Moses, "I will bring but one more plague upon Pharaoh and upon Egypt; after that he shall let you go from here; indeed, when he lets you go, he will drive you out of here one and all. 2 Tell the people to borrow, each man from his neighbor and each woman from hers, objects of silver and gold." 3 The LORD disposed the Egyptians favorably toward the people. Moreover, Moses himself was much esteemed in the land of Egypt, among Pharaoh's courtiers and among the people.

4 Moses said, "Thus says the LORD: Toward midnight I will go forth among the Egyptians, 5 and every first-born in the land of Egypt shall die, from the first-born of Pharaoh who sits on his throne to the first-born of the slave girl who is behind the millstones; and all the first-born of the cattle. 6 And there shall be a loud cry in all the land of Egypt, such as has never been or will ever be again; 7 but not a dog shall snarl[a] at any of the Israelites, at man or

a Others "move (or whet) his tongue."

28–29: Moses only partially quotes Pharaoh, acknowledging that they will never again meet, but undermining Pharaoh's claim that it is Moses who will die.

11.1–13.16: The tenth plague, the exodus, and commemorative festivals. The composite nature of this section is indicated by differences in the ritual instructions (e.g., 13.3–10 n.), discontinuities in the narrative, and verbal and other links to the various sources in the Torah. Source critics agree that one component of this section is from the Priestly source (11.9–12.20; 12.28, 40–41; 12.43–13.2); they disagree over which parts of the remainder belong to J, E, and (in some views) D. The most puzzling issue is the premature location of 12.14–20: God refers to the exodus in the past tense (v. 17a), though the event does not occur until vv. 37–41, and He commands that the day be commemorated by eating unleavened bread for a week, though the reason for doing so does not occur until vv. 34 and 39. Vv. 21–27 (J) are unaware of this command: When Moses conveys God's instructions about the pesaḥ sacrifice, he tells the people instead to commemorate the event in the future by reenacting the sacrifice. He informs them of the seven-day festival of unleavened bread only later in 13.3–10, after the text explains why the people ate unleavened bread on the day of the exodus. The redactor's reason for placing vv. 14–20 right

after vv. 1–13 (both units are from P), despite the resultant disturbance of the continuity, was evidently his desire to fuse the festival of unleavened bread and the pesaḥ offering—originally separate rites (see 12.14–20 n.)—into a single holiday with the same date (vv. 6, 18). He may have believed that the fact that the meal accompanying the pesaḥ offering included unleavened bread implied that they are part of the same festival, as if the Feast of Unleavened Bread commemorated the fact that the people ate matzah with the pesaḥ offering (v. 8).

11.1–10: The announcement of the tenth plague. The final and decisive plague would be a virulent epidemic (Ps. 78.50) of preternatural specificity, causing the sudden death of all first-born Egyptians. This plague corresponds to the Egyptians' murder of the Hebrew baby boys (1.22; the Egyptian people's cooperation with Pharaoh's decree is implied by 2.2–3). Exod. 4.22–23 explains it as measure-for-measure punishment for Pharaoh's refusal to free Israel, God's "first-born." 11.1: He will drive you out, see 6.1. 2–3: See 3.22. Much esteemed, held in awe because of the power he has displayed. 4–8: Although God does not tell Moses the nature of the final plague in vv. 1–3, according to the present form of the narrative Moses already knew it from God's words in 4.22–23. To make the narrative read more clearly, the Samaritan Pentateuch has Moses quote those words to Pharaoh here, and it also copies vv. 4–7 into God's words in vv. 1–3. According to that reading, then, in vv. 4–7 Moses is telling Pharaoh what God previously told him. Such additions to smooth out the narrative are typical of the Samaritan Pentateuch, and are also found in some Dead Sea Scrolls. 6–7: This plague manifests the probative qualities of the second and third triads of plagues: It will be unprecedented (9.18; 10.6, 14), and God will make a distinction between Egypt and Israel (see 8.18–19; 9.4, 6–7)—signs of the beast—in order that you may know that the LORD makes a distinction between Egypt and Israel.

8 "Then all these courtiers of yours shall come down to me and bow low to me, saying, 'Depart, you and all the people who follow you!' After that I will depart." And he left Pharaoh's presence in hot anger.

9 Now the LORD had said to Moses, "Pharaoh will not heed you, in order that My marvels may be multiplied in the land of Egypt." 10 Moses and Aaron had performed all these marvels before Pharaoh, but the LORD had stiffened the heart of Pharaoh so that he would not let the Israelites go from his land.

12 The LORD said to Moses and Aaron in the land of Egypt: 2 This month shall mark for you the beginning of the months; it shall be the first of the months of the year for you. 3 Speak to the whole community of Israel and say that on the tenth of this month each of them shall take a lamb[a] to a family, a lamb to a household. 4 But if the household is too small for a lamb, let him share one with a neighbor who dwells nearby, in proportion to the number of persons: you shall contribute for the lamb according to what each household will eat. 5 Your lamb shall be without blemish, a yearling male; you may take it from the sheep or from the goats. 6 You shall keep watch over it until the fourteenth day of this month; and all the assembled congrega-

a Or "kid." Heb. seh means either "sheep" or "goat"; cf. v. 5.

unique divine power beyond the event. 6: Loud cry, measure-for-measure punishment for causing the outcry of the Israelites (2.23). 7: Not a dog shall snarl: In contrast to the loud cry among the Egyptians, peace and quiet will prevail among the Israelites. 10: The LORD had stiffened the heart of Pharaoh: See 4.21 n.

12.1–28: Preparations for the exodus. Israel is to prepare for the coming redemption with a sacrificial banquet while the final plague is occurring and is to commemorate the event in the future on its anniversary by eating unleavened bread for a week and reenacting the banquet. This banquet became the prototype of the postbiblical Seder, the festive meal at which the exodus story is retold and expounded each year to this day on

the holiday of Pesaḥ (Passover), as explained below. 2: Since the exodus will be commemorated on its anniversary every year (vv. 6, 17–18), the preparatory instructions begin with the calendar. Henceforth the year will commence with the month of the exodus, and months will be referred to by ordinal numbers rather than names (see v. 18; 16.1; 19.1; Lev. 23.24; etc.). Since the numbers will mean essentially "in the Xth month since we gained freedom," every reference to a month will commemorate the redemption. The first month (later called Nisan [Esth. 3.7; Neh. 2.1]—these later month names were borrowed from the Babylonian calendar during the exile) corresponds to March or April. In Jewish practice, this is the beginning of the liturgical year; it was also the beginning of the Bab-

ylonian year. The calendar year, starting with Rosh Ha-Shanah (the New Year holiday, in the seventh month!), begins in Tishri (September or October). (The older, nature-based, names of a few months are mentioned in 13.4; Deut. 16.1; 1 Kings 6.1, 37, 38; 8.2.) Because vv. 1–20 deal with the month in which Pesaḥ falls and with preparations for the holiday, they are read as an additional Torah portion on the Sabbath preceding the month of Nisan, or on the first of Nisan if it is a Sabbath, and that Sabbath is called Shabbat ha-Ḥodesh, "the Sabbath of the passage beginning 'This month.' " The rest of the ch, which includes the observance of the first Pesaḥ and the exodus, is read on the first day of Pesaḥ. 5: Without blemish, a standard requirement of sacrificial animals (Lev. 22.17–25; Deut. 15.21; 17.1; cf. Mal. 1.6–8). 6–14: Some of the vv. about the sacrifice reflect a different view of the tenth plague from that in the rest of the narrative. In the rest of the narrative, God Himself slays the Egyptian first-born; no special measures are necessary to protect the Israelites (11.4–7; 12.29; 13.15). But in some of the vv. about the sacrifice God is accompanied by "the Destroyer," an angel of death who presumably kills the Egyptians on God's command (v. 23; cf. Gen. 19.13–14; 2 Sam. 24.16; 2 Kings 18.35; 1 Chron. 21.15); the Israelites must apply the blood of the sacrifice to their doorways to prevent the plague from harming them (vv. 7, 13, 22 and 23), although no such measures were needed to protect them from the earlier plagues (8.18; 9.4, 6, 26—all from J; 10.23, E); in v. 22 God warns all Israelites (not just the first-born) to remain indoors; in v. 23 He "protects" their houses from the Destroyer; and again in v. 27 He "protects" and "saves" them, presumably from the Destroyer. From these details scholars have conjectured that the sacrifice was not an original part of the narrative about the plagues but was based on an older shepherds' rite observed on a spring night (perhaps the night before they set tion of the Israelites shall slaughter it at twilight. ⁷They shall take some of the blood and put it on the two door-posts and the lintel of the houses in which they are to eat it. ⁸They shall eat the flesh that same night; they shall eat it roasted over the fire, with unleavened bread and with bitter herbs. ⁹Do not eat any of it raw, or cooked in any way with water, but roasted—head, legs, and entrails—over the fire. ¹⁰You shall not leave any of it over until morning; if any of it is left until morning, you shall burn it.

¹¹This is how you shall eat it: your loins girded, your sandals on your feet, and your staff in your hand; and you shall eat it hurriedly: it is a passover offering[a] to the LORD. ¹²For that night I will go through the land of Egypt and strike down every first-born in the land of Egypt, both man and beast; and I will mete out punishments to all the gods of Egypt, I the LORD. ¹³And the blood on the houses where you are staying shall be a sign for you: when I see the blood I will pass over[b] you, so that no plague will destroy you when I strike the land of Egypt.

¹⁴This day shall be to you one of remembrance: you shall celebrate it as a festival to the LORD throughout the

a Or "protective offering"; Heb. pesaḥ.   b Or "protect" (Heb. pasaḥ); cf. v. 11, note a.

played as a token of the roasted meat, and the story of the exodus, accompanied by rabbinic interpretations, is expounded, based on vv. 26–27 and 13.8. (The provisions of vv. 10 and 11 are not reenacted.) **10:** The sacrifice must be used only for its sacred purpose; hence no leftovers may be saved for eating later. **11:** The Israelites are to eat while prepared to leave on a moment's notice. *Passover offering*, Heb "pesaḥ," which originally referred only to the sacrifice. Later it became the name of the entire festival, including the seven days of the Festival of Unleavened Bread ("Ḥag ha-Matzot"), originally a separate holiday. In most European languages it is also the name of Easter (as in French "Pâques"). The translation "passover" (and hence the English name of the holiday) is probably incorrect. The alternative translation "protective offering" is more likely; see v. 13. **12:** *Mete out punishments to all the gods of Egypt:* This probably means that the Egyptians' idols would be destroyed in the course of the plague (Tg. Ps.-J.; Mek.), just as the Philistine idol Dagon is smashed, and other plagues inflicted on the Philistines, in 1 Sam. ch 5 (Ibn Ezra), and just as Assyrian armies sometimes smashed the idols of conquered cities (2 Kings 19.18). **13:** *Pass over* (Heb "pasaḥ"): The use of this verb in Isa. 31.5, "Like the birds that fly, even so will the LORD of Hosts shield Jerusalem, shielding and saving, protecting ("p-s-ḥ") and rescuing," favors the translation "protect." So does context in v. 23 of the present ch. **14–20:** The Feast of Unleavened Bread. The haste of the Israelites' departure from Egypt would leave them no time to bake leavened bread (see vv. 34, 39). In the future, their annual week-long self-deprivation of leavened bread will serve as a reminder that God so overwhelmed the Egyptians that the latter ultimately hastened the departure of the slaves they had earlier refused to free. As it does here, the Torah usually speaks of this festival as something distinct and separate from the pesaḥ sac-

out for summer pasture) when shepherds believed they were endangered by demons who could be warded off by remaining indoors and applying blood to their entrances. This view of the sacrifice and its blood as apotropaic (magically protective) is consistent with its Heb name, "pesaḥ," "protection"; see v. 11. According to this theory, the Israelites inherited this rite from their pastoral ancestors (see Gen. 46.32) but, because of its proximity in the calendar to the time of the exodus, they reinterpreted it as a memorial of the exodus and introduced it into the narrative of the tenth plague. Gradually they abandoned its demonological-apotropaic aspects in favor of its meaning as a commemoration of the exodus. Traces of this process are visible here: Of the vv. attributed to a source other than P, only v. 23 implies that the Destroyer does the killing; vv. 27 and 29 say that God did the killing, but v. 27, in stating that God "protected" and "saved" the Israelites' houses, preserves a trace

of the older tradition that it was the Destroyer. In vv. attributed to P (12–13), only God does the killing; the Destroyer becomes merely a destructive plague, and the blood is merely a sign to identify Israelite houses (like the red cord in Josh. 2.12, 18, 19), not an apotropaic substance. **6:** *Keep watch*, to prevent it from becoming blemished or escaping during the interval. **8:** *Bitter herbs* are pungent condiments (popular among pastoral nomads) and *unleavened bread* (Heb "matzah," bread that has not risen) frequently accompanied sacrifices (29.2; Lev. 2.4–5; 6.9; 7.12; Judg. 6.19–21; etc.; leavened bread was forbidden with most sacrifices: Exod. 23.18; 34.25; Lev. 2.11; 6.10). Following the prescription of vv. 24–27, this banquet is reenacted annually at the Seder, the liturgical banquet which includes the eating of unleavened bread, bitter herbs ("maror," interpreted as recalling the bitterness of slavery; romaine lettuce or horseradish are commonly used), and other symbolic foods. A roasted shankbone is disages; you shall celebrate it as an institution for all time. [15] Seven days you shall eat unleavened bread; on the very first day you shall remove leaven from your houses, for whoever eats leavened bread from the first day to the seventh day, that person shall be cut off from Israel.

[16] You shall celebrate a sacred occasion on the first day, and a sacred occasion on the seventh day; no work at all shall be done on them; only what every person is to eat, that alone may be prepared for you. [17] You shall observe the [Feast of] Unleavened Bread, for on this very day I brought your ranks out of the land of Egypt; you shall observe this day throughout the ages as an institution for all time. [18] In the first month, from the fourteenth day of the month at evening, you shall eat unleavened bread until the twenty-first day of the month at evening. [19] No leaven shall be found in your houses for seven days. For whoever eats what is leavened, that person shall be cut off from the community of Israel, whether he is a stranger or a citizen of the country. [20] You shall eat nothing leavened; in all your settlements you shall eat unleavened bread.

[21] Moses then summoned all the elders of Israel and said to them, "Go, pick out lambs for your families, and slaughter the passover offering. [22] Take a bunch of hyssop, dip it in the blood that is in the basin, and apply some of

rifice rather than part of the same holiday (see vv. 24–27, 43–49; 13.3–9; 23.15; 34.18; Lev. 23.5–6; Num. 9.1–14; 28.16–17; see also Ezra 6.19–22; 2 Chron. 35.17; only Deut. 16.1–8, 16; Ezek. 45.21; and 2 Chron. 30.2, 5, 13, 15 describe them as a single festival). This has led to the theory that the pesaḥ sacrifice and the Feast of Unleavened Bread have separate origins, the former pastoral (see vv. 6–14 n.) and the latter agrarian. The avoidance of leaven in favor of unleavened bread—"bread of distress" (Deut. 16.3)—suggests that the latter may have begun as a rite of abstinence, perhaps expressing anxiety over the success of the coming grain harvest. The two rites were eventually brought together because of their proximity in the calendar and because unleavened bread was also eaten with the pesaḥ sacrifice (v. 8). In this view, then, the Festival of Unleavened Bread became a commemoration of the exodus because, like the pesaḥ sacrifice, it was observed at the time of year when the exodus took place. In the Bible, any agrarian significance the festival once had has been set aside in favor of its meaning as a commemoration of the exodus. **15:** *Unleavened bread:* The "matzah" was probably similar to the flat unleavened bread like pita that Bedouin still bake on embers. In earlier times it was disk-shaped and less thin than now. *Leaven* refers to leavening agents, such as sourdough or yeast, while *leavened bread* is any food prepared from dough to which a leavening agent was added to make it rise faster. According to rabbinic halakhic exegesis the prohibition covers any leavened product of wheat, barley, spelt, rye, or oats; in traditional Ashkenazic practice, rice, millet, corn, and legumes are also forbidden. *Remove leaven from your houses:* In traditional Jewish practice, the home is cleansed of leavened products in preparation for Pesaḥ and, on the night before the Seder, a few pieces of bread or other leavened products are hidden and "found" in a ceremonial search; the next morning the pieces are burned. Halakhic exegesis construes Deut. 16.4 to mean "no leaven *of yours* shall be seen," meaning that only leaven belonging to Jews must be eliminated. Leavened goods sold to non-Jews for the duration of the festival may be kept and stored out of sight in one's home. This avoids the economic hardship that would result from the destruction of large quantities of leavened goods. *Cut off:* The probable meaning is that God will cut him off (see Lev. 17.10; 20.1–6; 23.29–30), that is, cause him to die early and childless. This is the punishment for noncircumcision and cultic and sexual sins (v. 19; 30.33, 38; 31.14; Gen. 17.14; Lev. 7.20, 21, 25, 27; 17.4, 9, 14; 18.29; 19.8; 20.1–6, 17, 18; 22.3, 29; Num. 9.13; 19.13, 20) that are committed "defiantly" (Num. 15.30–31). **16:** The sacredness of these days is to be expressed by ceasing from work, as on the Sabbath (20.8–11; cf. Gen. 2.2–3), except that, on the festival, food may be cooked (contrast 16.23). **17:** Since the text reads lit. "You shall observe the unleavened bread," an especially stringent interpretation holds that the grain should be carefully guarded from the time it is harvested, or at least from the time it is ground into flour, to ensure that there is no fermentation. Matzah made in this way is called "matzah shemurah," "guarded matzah." **18:** Since holy days begin and end in the evening (Lev. 23.32), the festival lasts from the evening at the end of the fourteenth day through the evening at the end of the twenty-first day. **19:** *Stranger,* a foreigner residing among the Israelites. Although strangers are not obligated to offer a pesaḥ sacrifice (v. 48), they may not eat leavened food during the festival. This is perhaps to prevent them from accidentally contaminating Israelites' food with leaven, since bread was sometimes baked in shared or communal ovens (Lev. 26.26; Jer. 37.21; Neh. 3.11;

the blood that is in the basin to the lintel and to the two doorposts. None of you shall go outside the door of his house until morning. 23 For when the LORD goes through to smite the Egyptians, He will see the blood on the lintel and the two doorposts, and the LORD will pass over*a* the door and not let the Destroyer enter and smite your home.

24 "You shall observe this as an institution for all time, for you and for your descendants. 25 And when you enter the land that the LORD will give you, as He has promised, you shall observe this rite. 26 And when your children ask you, 'What do you mean by this rite?' 27 you shall say, 'It is the passover sacrifice*b* to the LORD, because He passed over*a* the houses of the Israelites in Egypt when He smote the Egyptians, but saved our houses.'"

The people then bowed low in homage. 28 And the Israelites went and did so; just as the LORD had commanded Moses and Aaron, so they did.

29 In the middle of the night the LORD struck down all the first-born in the land of Egypt, from the first-born of Pharaoh who sat on the throne to the first-born of the captive who was in the dungeon, and all the first-born of the cattle. 30 And Pharaoh arose in the night, with all his courtiers and all the Egyptians—because there was a loud cry in Egypt; for there was no house where there was not someone dead. 31 He summoned Moses and Aaron in the night and said, "Up, depart from among my people, you and the Israelites with you! Go, worship the LORD as you said! 32 Take also your flocks and your herds, as you said, and begone! And may you bring a blessing upon me also!"

33 The Egyptians urged the people on, impatient to have them leave the country, for they said, "We shall all be dead." 34 So the people took their dough before it was leavened, their kneading bowls wrapped in their cloaks upon their shoulders. 35 The Israelites had done Moses' bidding and borrowed from the Egyptians objects of sil-

a See v. 13, note b.　　b See v. 11, note a.

12.38). **23:** *Pass over*, rather, "protect" (see above, v. 13 n.). *Destroyer*, see introductory comment to vv. 6–14. The tradition that an angelic figure served as God's agent in the exodus and subsequent events is also reflected in 14.19; 23.20–23 (see also the plan announced by God in 32.34 and 33.2 but withdrawn in 33.14; Num. 20.16; Josh. 5.13–15; Judg. 2.1–5; and Ps. 78.49). This tradition is rejected in other passages which hold that God was the only actor, using no intermediary (Exod. 33.14–15; Deut. 4.37; 7.1 [based on but modifying Exod. 23.20]; 32.12; see also the probably original text of Isa. 63.9 reflected in the readings of the ancient versions). This disagreement was still alive in talmudic times and led to the well-known midrashic passage quoted in the *Haggadah* which declares that Is-

rael was taken out of Egypt by God personally, "not by means of an angel." This declaration indicates that the Rabbis, like the authors of the biblical verses denying a role to angels, considered the tradition of angelic involvement incompatible with absolute monotheism. **24:** *Observe this:* According to talmudic tradition (*m. Pes.* 9.5) only the sacrifice itself is to be repeated annually, not the rites accompanying it in vv. 3, 7, 10–11, 23. Ibn Ezra accepts this tradition on authority but observes that one would not infer this from the text itself. **26–27:** Here and in 13.8, 14–15 and Deut. 6.20–25, the Torah anticipates that children will ask what the various commemorative rites and other laws mean (see also Josh. 4.21–24). The Israelites are to use these questions as opportunities to teach loyalty to God by explaining what He did for them. The religious value of such lessons about the past accounts for why much of the Bible is devoted to past events and for the theological viewpoint of biblical historiography. A midrashic elaboration of these passages about children figures prominently in the *Haggadah* as part of the answer to the children's Four Questions about the unique procedures at the Seder banquet. It explains that the wording of the question in each passage reflects a different type of personality.

12.29–42: The tenth plague and the exodus. 31–33: Pharaoh and his people press the Israelites to leave (see also v. 39). Cf. 6.1; 11.1. **31:** *As you said,* 3.18; 5.3; 7.16. Pharaoh is granting no more than Moses asked, three days' leave for worship (only in 14.5 does he realize they mean to leave for good, though he suspected that earlier [8.24; 10.10]). **32:** *May you bring a blessing upon me also,* i.e., leave with your cattle to worship the LORD (v. 31) with sacrifice, as you said (3.18; 5.3, 8, 17; 8.4, 21–25; 10.25–26), and when you sacrifice and ask for His blessing (see 20.21 end; Lev. 9.22), ask Him to bless ver and gold, and clothing. [36] And the LORD had disposed the Egyptians favorably toward the people, and they let them have their request; thus they stripped the Egyptians.

[37] The Israelites journeyed from Rameses to Succoth, about six hundred thousand men on foot, aside from children. [38] Moreover, a mixed multitude went up with them, and very much livestock, both flocks and herds. [39] And they baked unleavened cakes of the dough that they had taken out of Egypt, for it was not leavened, since they had been driven out of Egypt and could not delay; nor had they prepared any provisions for themselves.

[40] The length of time that the Israelites lived in Egypt was four hundred and thirty years; [41] at the end of the four hundred and thirtieth year, to the very day, all the ranks of the LORD departed from the land of Egypt. [42] That was for

oppression predicted in Gen. 15.13 (JE or E), assuming that the oppression began thirty years after Israel arrived in Egypt. Gen.15.16 (also JE or E), however, states that the Israelites would return in the fourth generation (of living there), a statement compatible with the fact that Moses is the great-grandson of Levi, who went down to Egypt (Exod. 6.16–20). If a generation is the period between a man's birth and the birth of his first child, these two passages are hard to reconcile: Even assuming a generation of forty years (although twenty to twenty-five is more likely), four generations would be no more than 160 years. The Septuagint, the Samaritan Pentateuch, and midrashic traditions (*Seder Olam* 1 and 3; *Mek. R. Shimon bar Yohai*, p. 34 at 12.40; *Mek. Pisḥa* 14 [Horovitz p. 50]; *Pirqe R. El.* 48, p. 114a) minimize the problem by including in these figures the time the patriarchs lived in Canaan, starting with the covenant of Gen. ch 15 or the birth of Isaac, though that is not what our v. or Gen. ch 15 says. **41:** *The ranks of the LORD:* The Israelites are organized as an army, their goal being the conquest of Canaan; cf. v. 51 and 13.18 and their designation as "men on foot," that is, infantry, in v. 37. **42:** *Vigil,* Heb "shimurim." Although derivatives of the root "sh-m-r," "watch, guard, observe" are common (they occur five other times in this ch, vv. 6, 17 twice, 24, 25), this form is unparalleled in the Bible. In rabbinic Heb it means "guarding, care." If that is the meaning here, this v. may represent an interpretation of the term "pesaḥ" (see vv. 11, 13 n.). The sense would be that God guarded the Israelites from the Destroyer on the night of the exodus and will guard them against malevolent forces on the anniversaries of this night (thus *Tg. Ps.-J.* and *b. Pes.* 109b; in that case the v. is a vestige of a magical notion that this date is particularly dangerous, as in the presumed shepherds' belief mentioned in vv. 6–14 n.). Possibly, the term has different nuances and different subjects in

me as well. Pharoah may have a specific blessing—cessation of the tenth plague—in mind (cf. 8.4, 24; 9.28; 10.17), but in any case his plea indicates that his capitulation to the LORD is complete. **35–36:** See 3.22. **37:** *From Rameses to Succoth:* On *Rameses,* the capital, see 1.11. *Succoth* was the name of both a place and a region in the eastern Nile delta, in or near the land of Goshen where the Israelites lived (see 8.18 and map, p. 130). An Egyptian letter from the period of Pharaoh Seti II (1204–1198 BCE) indicates that the place Succoth was one day's journey from the palace, which was presumably in Rameses. On the reasons for the Israelites following this route, see 13.17 n. *Six hundred thousand men,* a round number; see also Num. 11.21; Num. 1.46 and 2.32 give the number more precisely as 603,550 (Num. 3.39 adds 22,000 Levites). According to Exod. 38.26 and Num. 1.46–47, these figures refer to men of military age, twenty and older. Adding women and children yields a population of at least two and a half million. Some scholars believe that in census contexts the word translated *thousand* ("'elef") does not have numerical significance but means "clan" or "squad" (as in Num. 1.16; Judg. 6.15; 1 Sam. 10.19; and elsewhere), in which case the number of people need

not be that high, but it is clear from 38.24–26 and other passages that individuals, not groups, are being counted. This number certainly accords with Exodus' assertions that the Israelites in Egypt were extraordinarily prolific (1.7–12), though the land of Goshen and later the Sinai peninsula could not have sustained such a population. The number probably originated in hyperbole, perhaps as an expansion of the common 600-man military unit (14.7; Judg. 18.11; 1 Sam. 13.15; 23.13; etc.). Comparably, the Haggadah inflates the number of plagues from ten to fifty, and Arabian Bedouin often magnify numbers by factors of ten. Note also the thousand-fold population growth wished for by Moses (Deut. 1.11) and the 3-million-person army attributed to Kirta, the king of the city-state of Ugarit. **38:** *Mixed multitude,* non-Israelites, most likely members of other enslaved groups in Egypt. Egyptian texts and art show the presence of such groups, including Semites and Nubians. **39:** In their haste, the Israelites made unleavened bread because it can be made quickly (for that reason, it is made for unexpected guests [Gen. 19.3; Judg. 6.19; 1 Sam. 28.24], as Arab peasants still do). **40–41:** The figure of 430 years of Israelite residence in Egypt (P) is compatible with the 400 years of slavery and

the LORD a night of vigil to bring them out of the land of
Egypt; that same night is the LORD's, one of vigil for all the
children of Israel throughout the ages.

43 The LORD said to Moses and Aaron: This is the law of
the passover offering: No foreigner shall eat of it. 44 But
any slave a man has bought may eat of it once he has been
circumcised. 45 No bound or hired laborer shall eat of it.
46 It shall be eaten in one house: you shall not take any of
the flesh outside the house; nor shall you break a bone of
it. 47 The whole community of Israel shall offer it. 48 If a
stranger who dwells with you would offer the passover to
the LORD, all his males must be circumcised; then he shall

each clause; e.g., it was a night of
God's protection of Israel at the exodus, so in the future it will be a
night of Israel's observance of the
pesaḥ sacrifice. The translation
"vigil" implies that it was a night
of God's vigilance, protecting Israel (or of Israel's vigilance waiting for God to deliver them [tak-
ing "for the LORD a night of vigil"
as "a night of waiting for the
LORD"]), and in the future it will
be a night of wakefulness for Israel
to offer the pesaḥ sacrifice ("a
night of vigil in honor of the
LORD").

Probable exodus route according to the Bible

be admitted to offer it; he shall then be as a citizen of the country. But no uncircumcised person may eat of it. ⁴⁹There shall be one law for the citizen and for the stranger who dwells among you.

⁵⁰And all the Israelites did so; as the LORD had commanded Moses and Aaron, so they did.

⁵¹That very day the LORD freed the Israelites from the land of Egypt, troop by troop.

13 The LORD spoke further to Moses, saying, ²"Consecrate to Me every first-born; man and beast, the first issue of every womb among the Israelites is Mine."

12.43–51: Seven supplementary rules about the pesaḥ offering (vv. 43b, 44, 45, 46a, 46b, 47, 48–49). V. 50, which recapitulates v. 28, implies that these instructions were given before the Israelites departed. They define who is eligible to take part in the pesaḥ offering and other details concerning it. Those instructions pertaining to foreigners, "strangers" (resident aliens), and slaves and employees of Israelites seem, like those in vv. 24–27, to apply primarily to the future, after Israel settles in the promised land, rather than to their circumstances in Egypt; note particularly that once circumcised the stranger becomes "as a citizen of the country" (of Israel). **43:** *Foreigner,* Heb "ben nekhar," a non-Israelite; normally used of foreigners living or visiting in the land of Israel temporarily, usually for business. It is contrasted with "stranger" ("ger"), which refers to a long-term foreign resident. Here it could also refer to Egyptians or other foreigners in Egypt on friendly terms with the Israelites (cf. Isa. 56.3). Because the pesaḥ sacrifice is integrally connected with Israel's national experience of the exodus, those who do not identify with Israelites and their experience are ineligible to partake of it. Likewise, according to Lev. 23.42, only native Israelites are obligated to dwell in booths, another rite that commemorates Israel's national experience. **44–45:** The implications of the pesaḥ sacrifice being a family-household cere-

mony (vv. 3, 4, 7, 27, 46). **44:** Privately owned foreign slaves, as members of the household, may partake if they are circumcised in accordance with Gen. 17.12–13. **45:** *Bound or hired laborer:* This phrase (lit. "resident and hireling") is better taken as a hendiadys meaning "resident hireling" (as in Lev. 22.10; 25.6, 40), a long-term hired hand who lives on his employer's property. He is not integrated into his employer's household. If a foreigner, he is ineligible for the pesaḥ; if an Israelite, the verse seems to imply that he should partake of his own family's pesaḥ sacrifice, not that of his employer. **46:** All those sharing the same lamb were to eat it together and to remain indoors. See vv. 4, 7, 22–23. *Break a bone of it,* to eat the marrow. **47:** Offering the pesaḥ sacrifice is incumbent on all Israelites, like the obligation to eat nothing leavened during the festival (vv. 15, 19; cf. Num. 9.11). **48–49:** Resident aliens, though they must abstain from leaven (v. 19), are not obligated to offer a pesaḥ sacrifice but may do so voluntarily. They must first undergo circumcision. Then they may make the offering and become "as a citizen of the country," at least for purposes of this offering. This is not a full religious conversion—the stranger's motivation is to make a pesaḥ offering, not to become an Israelite—but since circumcision is a sign of the covenant, and the sacrifice celebrates the exodus, he must first become a

quasi-Israelite in order to identify with Israel's defining national experience. If so, this ceremony is unique in the Bible; there is no other reference to a formal procedure for converting foreigners to Israelites, even quasi-Israelites. Foreigners normally became Israelites only by marriage or the informal, generations-long process of ethnic assimilation that resulted from living in the land. By the rabbinic period, a procedure for religious conversion, including circumcision of males, was created and the Heb word for stranger, "ger," acquired the meaning "proselyte." Since the idea of strangers joining Israel is explicitly mentioned in exilic or postexilic passages (Isa. 14.1; 56.3–8; Ezek. 47.22–23), it is possible that the present passage is also from that period. **49:** *One law for the citizen and for the stranger,* see also Lev. 24.22; Num. 9.14; 15.14–16, 29. In each of these instances strangers and Israelites follow the same specific procedure (cf. Lev. 7.7); it is not a general rule covering all cases. In later halakhic exegesis, when "ger" ("stranger") is understood as "proselyte," this v. is understood as prescribing equality between proselytes and born Jews with respect to all the laws of the Torah (*Mek. Pisḥa* 14, end). **51:** This v. recapitulates v. 40, indicating that the digression in vv. 43–49 is concluded and the narrative resumes.

13.1–16: Further commemorative rituals. 2: The first issue of humans and domestic animals is holy and reserved for the LORD; they must be given to Him or redeemed. According to Gen. 4.4, the sacrifice of firstling cattle goes back to the beginning of the human race when Abel brought "the choicest of the firstlings of his flock" as a gift to the Lord. In vv. 12–15 this practice is given a new raison d'etre as a commemoration of God's slaying the first-born of Egypt and sparing those of Israel at the time of the exodus. *The first issue of every womb* defines *first-born* as the first-born of the mother,

³ And Moses said to the people,

"Remember this day, on which you went free from Egypt, the house of bondage, how the LORD freed you from it with a mighty hand: no leavened bread shall be eaten. ⁴ You go free on this day, in the month*ᵃ* of Abib. ⁵ So, when the LORD has brought you into the land of the Canaanites, the Hittites, the Amorites, the Hivites, and the Jebusites, which He swore to your fathers to give you, a land flowing with milk and honey, you shall observe in this month the following practice:

⁶ "Seven days you shall eat unleavened bread, and on the seventh day there shall be a festival of the LORD. ⁷ Throughout the seven days unleavened bread shall be eaten; no leavened bread shall be found with you, and no leaven shall be found in all your territory. ⁸ And you shall explain to your son on that day, 'It is because of what the LORD did for me when I went free from Egypt.'

⁹ "And this shall serve you as a sign on your hand and as a reminder on your forehead*ᵇ*—in order that the Teaching of the LORD may be in your mouth—that with a mighty hand the LORD freed you from Egypt. ¹⁰ You shall keep this institution at its set time from year to year.

¹¹ "And when the LORD has brought you into the land of

---

a Or "on the new moon."   b Lit. "between your eyes."

---

not the father. **3–10:** The festival of Unleavened Bread, repeating 12.14–20. Because of this duplication and some conflicting details (such as the use here of a name instead of a number for the first month, and the emphasis only on the seventh day and not on the first as well), scholars assign this paragraph to the J source and 12.14–20 to the P source. **4:** *The month of Abib:* The old name of the first month (12.2), now called Nisan. "'Aviv" means "new ears of grain"; this month begins when immature ears of grain have begun to grow on the stalks. The alternative translation "on the new moon of Abib" is based on the preceding phrase "on this day," which seems to refer to a specific date (see also Deut. 16.1). If that is the meaning, this may be a variant tradition that the exodus occurred, and was celebrated, on the first day of the month rather than the fourteenth and fifteenth. **5:** See 3.8. **8:** See 12.26–27. *Explain,* Heb "vehi-

gadta," lit. "tell, relate." The Rabbis derived the injunction to relate the story of the exodus at the Seder from this v., and the name of the text recited at the Seder, "Haggadah shel Pesaḥ" ("The Pesaḥ narrative"; Haggadah for short) from this verb. *What the LORD did for me:* Because every future Israelite is to speak thus, the Rabbis inferred that "In every generation one should look upon himself as if he personally had gone out of Egypt. . . . It was not only our ancestors whom the Holy One, Blessed is He, redeemed, but also us along with them" (Haggadah). The effect is that every individual Jew will identify personally with the exodus experience. **9–10:** *This shall serve you as a sign:* It is not clear what shall serve as a sign: either something mentioned in the preceding vv. or in the second half of the present v. One or several of these things must be remembered well so that the LORD's teaching will be remembered well. The

same interpretation applies to v. 16: The sacrifice or redemption of the first-born (vv. 12–15) is to be "as a sign . . . and as a frontlet" (see translators' note *b*). As noted by Rashbam, "sign," "memorial," and "frontlet" are here used metaphorically to indicate that these things are to be remembered well (cf. the metaphoric use of other ornaments and items of apparel in Isa. 62.3; Jer. 13.11; Prov. 6.21; 7.3; and elsewhere). In neither case does "it shall be a sign," represent an additional observance beyond those mentioned in vv. 2–8 and 12–15. In Deut. 6.8 and 11.18, however, the same phrases are used literally to indicate that God's words are to be "bound" as a sign on the arm and as a frontlet on the forehead, and this is accompanied by the injunction to write those words on the doorposts and city gates. In that context, the command is meant literally. Jewish tradition reinterpreted Exod. 13.9 and 16 in line with Deuteronomy, and took all four passages as referring to tefillin or phylacteries, small leather capsules fastened to the forehead and the upper arm by leather straps, and containing the paragraphs in which these vv. appear (Exod. 13.1–10, 11–16; Deut. 6. 5–9; 11.13–21). In talmudic times they were worn throughout the day on weekdays (that is, not on the Sabbath or festivals); today they are usually worn only during weekday morning prayers. **10:** *This institution,* the eating of unleavened bread. *At its set time:* According to Naḥmanides, this v. is the basis of the practice of creating leap years by periodically adding an extra month at the end of a lunar year to adjust it to the longer solar year so that the festival falls "at its set time," that is, in the spring. This is done in order to delay the festival in years when it would otherwise occur before spring arrives (Hayim Dov Shevel, "Sefer ha-mitsvot leha-Rambam . . . 'im hasagot ha-Ramban" [Jerusalem: Mosad Harav Kook, 1981], pp. 26–27). **11–16:** The sacrifice and redemption of first-borns. **12–13:** See also 22.28–29; 34.19–20;

the Canaanites, as He swore to you and to your fathers, and has given it to you, [12] you shall set apart for the LORD every first issue of the womb: every male firstling that your cattle drop shall be the LORD's. [13] But every firstling ass you shall redeem with a sheep; if you do not redeem it, you must break its neck. And you must redeem every first-born male among your children. [14] And when, in time to come, your son asks you, saying, 'What does this mean?' you shall say to him, 'It was with a mighty hand that the LORD brought us out from Egypt, the house of bondage. [15] When Pharaoh stubbornly refused to let us go, the LORD slew every first-born in the land of Egypt, the first-born of both man and beast. Therefore I sacrifice to the LORD every first male issue of the womb, but redeem every first-born among my sons.'

[16] "And so it shall be as a sign upon your hand and as a symbol[a] on your forehead that with a mighty hand the LORD freed us from Egypt."

BE-SHALLAH   בשלח

[17] Now when Pharaoh let the people go, God did not lead them by way of the land of the Philistines, although it was nearer; for God said, "The people may have a change of heart when they see war, and return to Egypt." [18] So God led the people roundabout, by way of the wilderness at the Sea of Reeds.

Now the Israelites went up armed[b] out of the land of

a Others "frontlet."
b Meaning of Heb. ḥamushim uncertain.

Lev. 27.27; Num. 18.15–18; Deut. 15.19–23 for further, and in some cases conflicting, details. **12:** *Set apart,* for sacrifice (v. 15). *Shall be the LORD's,* that is, sacrificed. **13:** *Every firstling ass:* Asses are domestic animals, but are impure and may not be sacrificed (cf. Lev. 27.26; Num. 18.15); hence the owner must redeem an ass by sacrificing a sheep in its place or breaking its neck (a nonsacrificial method of slaughter). *Among your children:* Since humans may not be sacrificed, they must be redeemed from the priests. Based on Num. 18.16, the ceremony, called "Pidyon ha-ben" ("Redemption of the Son"), takes place on the thirty-first day after birth (or the next day if that is a Sabbath or major holiday). The son is "re-deemed" by giving a "kohen" (a descendant of the priestly family) five units of the local currency (e.g., five dollars). The money is generally returned to the father or donated to charity. Sons whose parents are the offspring of a kohen or a Levite, and sons born by Caesarian section or after the birth of a daughter or a miscarriage are not redeemed. **16:** *Symbol,* the translation "frontlet" (i.e., headband), is preferable. The headband was the characteristic headdress in Canaan and nearby lands in biblical times, as illustrated in Egyptian and Assyrian art.

13.17–15.21. The crossing of the sea. The final episode of God's defeat of the Egyptians. God lures

Egypt to a crushing blow so as to "gain glory through Pharaoh and all his host" and show them that "I am the LORD" (14.4, 18). The Sabbath on which this pericope is read in the annual Torah reading cycle is known as Shabbat Shirah, the "Sabbath of the Song," referring to the poem of 15.1–18. It is also read on the seventh day of Pesaḥ, when, according to tradition, the crossing of the sea took place. See also v. 18 n. **13.17:** *By way of the land of the Philistines,* or "by The Way to the Land of the Philistines" (the name of the road)—in either case, the route leading from Egypt to Philistia in southern Canaan (see map, p. 130). This is presumably the route, called "The Ways of Horus" by the Egyptians, that ran parallel to the Mediterranean coast, from Zilu (Sile) to Gaza, and was the shortest route to Canaan (along it an army could reach Gaza in nine or ten days). If the exodus took place in the 13th century BCE, the reference to the Philistines is anachronistic, since the Philistines were among the "Sea Peoples" who migrated to the Levant from the Aegean region and did not settle in southern Canaan until the early 12th century. *Have a change of heart,* as they do in 14.11–12. *When they see war,* either with the Canaanites in the promised land or the Egyptian forces stationed in Zilu (Sile) and the other fortresses Egypt maintained all along the Ways of Horus in the 13th century BCE to protect its access to Canaan. To avoid demoralization, God leads the Israelites via the difficult southerly route through the marshy lakeland of the eastern delta to Sukkot and thence to the wilderness. **18:** *By way of the wilderness,* or, "by The Way to the Wilderness"— toward the Sinai wilderness. *At the Sea of Reeds,* Heb "yam suf," an unidentified body of water, probably in the Isthmus of Suez, the strip of land, lakes, and marshes between the Gulf of Suez and the Mediterranean (the strip traversed by the Suez Canal today). See map, p. 130. The same name is used for the Gulf of Eilat

Egypt. ¹⁹ And Moses took with him the bones of Joseph, who had exacted an oath from the children of Israel, saying, "God will be sure to take notice of you: then you shall carry up my bones from here with you."

²⁰ They set out from Succoth, and encamped at Etham, at the edge of the wilderness. ²¹ The LORD went before them in a pillar of cloud by day, to guide them along the way, and in a pillar of fire by night, to give them light, that they might travel day and night. ²² The pillar of cloud by day and the pillar of fire by night did not depart from before the people.

14 The LORD said to Moses: ² Tell the Israelites to turn back and encamp before Pi-hahiroth, between Migdol and the sea, before Baal-zephon; you shall encamp facing it, by the sea. ³ Pharaoh will say of the Israelites, "They are astray in the land; the wilderness has closed in on them." ⁴ Then I will stiffen Pharaoh's heart and he will pursue them, that I may gain glory through Pharaoh and all his host; and the Egyptians shall know that I am the LORD.

And they did so.

⁵ When the king of Egypt was told that the people had fled, Pharaoh and his courtiers had a change of heart about the people and said, "What is this we have done, releasing Israel from our service?" ⁶ He ordered[a] his chariot and took his men with him; ⁷ he took six hundred of his picked chariots, and the rest of the chariots of Egypt, with officers[b] in all of them. ⁸ The LORD stiffened the heart of Pharaoh king of Egypt, and he gave chase to the Israelites. As the Israelites were departing defiantly,[c] ⁹ the Egyptians gave chase to them, and all the chariot horses of Pharaoh,

a See on Gen. 46.29.
b Heb. shalish; originally "third man on royal chariot"; hence "adjutant," "officer."
c Lit. "with upraised hand."

[23.31; Deut. 1.40; etc.], a branch of the Red Sea. **19:** See Gen. 50.24–25. According to Josh. 24.32, Joshua buried Joseph in Shechem (modern Nablus; see Color Map 1). **20:** *Etham*, an unidentified place, perhaps at the eastern end of the Wadi Tumilat, where the wadi meets the wilderness, near Lake Timsah (see map, p. 130). (Cf. Num. 33.8, "the wilderness of Etham.") **21:** *The LORD went before them in a pillar of cloud . . . and in a pillar of fire:* The two pillars were probably one, a columnar cloud

enveloping a fire that was visible through it only in the dark. Hence 14.24 refers to a single "pillar of fire and cloud" at daybreak, when the fire was still partly visible as the cloud gradually became opaque. Their role here may reflect the ancient practice of carrying a burning, smoking brazier at the head of an army or caravan to indicate the line of march by day and night. See further at 14.19. **22:** For an exception to this statement, see 14.19. According to P, once the Tabernacle was erected,

the pillar or cloud and fire remained above it even when directing the Israelites' march (Exod. 40.33–38; Num. 9.15–23; 10.11–12, 34). (For a reflection of this image in United States history, see the intro. to Exodus.)

14.1–31: The crossing of the Sea of Reeds. The compositeness of this narrative is indicated by inconsistencies and redundancies. For example, God's stiffening Pharaoh's heart to chase the Israelites (vv. 8–9) is redundant after Pharaoh has already decided to give chase (vv. 5–7). V. 19a says that the angel leading the Israelites moves to their rear, while 19b says that it was the cloud. V. 21b (through "dry ground") presents a relatively naturalistic picture of God causing a strong wind to blow back the waters of the sea, while the remainder of the v. and v. 22 present a more miraculous picture of the sea splitting, with the waters forming walls on either side of the Israelites. Source critics assign the components of the narrative to J, E, and P. By skillfully combining the sources, the redactor has harmonized the differences so as to show, for example, that Pharaoh's independent decision to pursue the Israelites is, in a mysterious way, carrying out God's plan (cf. v. 4), that the cloud is indeed the angel, and that God used the natural means of the wind to carry out His miraculous splitting of the sea. **2:** *Pi-hahiroth* cannot be clearly identified with any known Egyptian toponym. *Migdol* ("watchtower") figures in several toponyms in and near the eastern delta. An Egyptian letter (see 12.37 n.) mentions one apparently in or near the Sinai desert not far from Wadi Tumilat. *Baal-zephon* must refer to a site at which the Canaanite deity of that name was worshipped in Egypt. Several in the eastern delta region are known. **4:** *Gain glory,* more lit. "weightiness," honor, authority, by punishing those who disobey Him. *The Egyptians shall know that I am the* LORD, see 6.2 n. **5:** Only now do the his horsemen, and his warriors overtook them encamped by the sea, near Pi-hahiroth, before Baal-zephon.

¹⁰ As Pharaoh drew near, the Israelites caught sight of the Egyptians advancing upon them. Greatly frightened, the Israelites cried out to the LORD. ¹¹ And they said to Moses, "Was it for want of graves in Egypt that you brought us to die in the wilderness? What have you done to us, taking us out of Egypt? ¹² Is this not the very thing we told you in Egypt, saying, 'Let us be, and we will serve the Egyptians, for it is better for us to serve the Egyptians than to die in the wilderness'?" ¹³ But Moses said to the people, "Have no fear! Stand by, and witness the deliverance which the LORD will work for you today; for the Egyptians whom you see today you will never see again. ¹⁴ The LORD will battle for you; you hold your peace!"

¹⁵ Then the LORD said to Moses, "Why do you cry out to Me? Tell the Israelites to go forward. ¹⁶ And you lift up your rod and hold out your arm over the sea and split it, so that the Israelites may march into the sea on dry ground. ¹⁷ And I will stiffen the hearts of the Egyptians so that they go in after them; and I will gain glory through Pharaoh and all his warriors, his chariots and his horsemen. ¹⁸ Let the Egyptians know that I am LORD, when I gain glory through Pharaoh, his chariots, and his horsemen."

¹⁹ The angel of God, who had been going ahead of the Israelite army, now moved and followed behind them; and the pillar of cloud shifted from in front of them and took up a place behind them, ²⁰ and it came between the army of the Egyptians and the army of Israel. Thus there was the cloud with the darkness, and it cast a spell[a] upon the night, so that the one could not come near the other all through the night.

²¹ Then Moses held out his arm over the sea and the LORD drove back the sea with a strong east wind all that night, and turned the sea into dry ground. The waters were split, ²² and the Israelites went into the sea on dry ground, the waters forming a wall for them on their right and on their left. ²³ The Egyptians came in pursuit after them into the sea, all of Pharaoh's horses, chariots, and horsemen. ²⁴ At the morning watch, the LORD looked down upon the Egyptian army from a pillar of fire and cloud, and threw the Egyptian army into panic. ²⁵ He locked[b] the wheels of their chariots so that they moved forward with difficulty. And the Egyptians said, "Let us

Egyptians realize that the Israelites have left for good (see 12.31). **11–12:** The Israelites' continual complaining in the wilderness, a dominant theme of the Torah, is introduced here. (See 15.24; 16.2–3; 17.2–3; Num. 11.4–6; 14.2–3; 16.13–14; 20.2–5, 13; 21.4–5; Deut. 1.27–28.) **12:** *We told you in Egypt:* No such comment is recorded earlier, but the Samaritan Pentateuch adds it after 6.9. (See 11.4–8 n.) **15–31:** Some believe that the action of the sea corresponds to the rising and falling tides or shallow waters being blown back by wind in the southern part of the isthmus, or a combination of both. A document from Mari, in Syria, reports that an army escaped across a river one night at low tide and the pursuing army was prevented from overtaking them when the tide later rose again. In the present case the heavy Egyptian chariots became mired in the mud and were engulfed by the returning waters. The text, however, claims that miraculously the waters were split and stood up like walls (vv. 16, 22, 29). **19:** The first clause of the v. (from the E source) says that the angel of God was at the head of the Israelites; the next clause (from J) indicates that the pillar of cloud led them, while 13.21 (also J) says that it was the LORD in the cloud. These three statements picture the divine manifestation in different ways (cf. 3.2 n.). **20:** *Cast a spell,* turned it totally dark so that the Egyptians could not approach the Israelites (cf. 10.22–23a; Josh. 24.7). *The one could not come near the other all through the night:* According to a midrashic interpretation, this refers to the angels, who sought to sing a hymn to God as the Egyptians were drowning; God rebuked them, saying: "While my creatures are drowning in the sea you would sing a hymn?!" showing that He does not rejoice in the death of the wicked (b. *Sanh.* 39b, prompted either by the similar phraseology in Isa. 6.3 or by an interpretation of "k-r-v" ["come near"] as a term for prayer). **25:** *Locked:* They became stuck in the mud.

a *From root 'rr, "cast a spell" or "curse." Others "and it lit up."*
b *From root 'sr, with several ancient versions. Others "took off."*

flee from the Israelites, for the LORD is fighting for them against Egypt."

26 Then the LORD said to Moses, "Hold out your arm over the sea, that the waters may come back upon the Egyptians and upon their chariots and upon their horsemen." 27 Moses held out his arm over the sea, and at daybreak the sea returned to its normal state, and the Egyptians fled at its approach. But the LORD hurled the Egyptians into the sea. 28 The waters turned back and covered the chariots and the horsemen—Pharaoh's entire army that followed them into the sea; not one of them remained. 29 But the Israelites had marched through the sea on dry ground, the waters forming a wall for them on their right and on their left.

30 Thus the LORD delivered Israel that day from the Egyptians. Israel saw the Egyptians dead on the shore of the sea. 31 And when Israel saw the wondrous power which the LORD had wielded against the Egyptians, the people feared the LORD; they had faith in the LORD and His servant Moses.

15 Then Moses and the Israelites sang this song to the LORD. They said:

I will sing to the LORD, for He has triumphed
   gloriously;
Horse and driver He has hurled into the sea.
2   The LORD^a is my strength and might;^b
He is become my deliverance.
This is my God and I will enshrine^c Him;
The God of my father, and I will exalt Him.
3   The LORD, the Warrior—
LORD is His name!

a *Heb.* Yah.   b *Others "song."*
c *Others "glorify."*

31: *Feared:* No longer frightened of the Egyptians (v. 10), they were awe-struck at God's power. *Had faith,* i.e., trusted, now that their fears were proven groundless. "Faith" in the Bible regularly means trust, rather than belief in the existence of God or assent to a doctrine. *His servant Moses:* The people now realize that Moses is truly God's servant. Cf. Num. 12.7–8; Deut. 34.10.

15.1–21: The Song at the Sea, a lyric poem, sung as a hymn, celebrating God's defeat of Egypt at the sea. Rich in imagery, hyperbole, and poetic license, it expresses the unrestrained enthusiasm of the Israelites over their miraculous rescue from disaster. Formally it is divided into three sections, each ending with a simile followed by a bicolon addressed to God in which the opening phrase is repeated in the second colon (vv. 5b–6, 10b–11, 16a–b), and a conclusion (vv. 17–18). In terms of content, however, the sections are an introduction (vv. 1–3), the de-

feat of Pharaoh's forces (vv. 4–12), God's guidance of Israel to the promised land and the Temple Mount and the terrified reaction of its inhabitants and neighbors (vv. 13–17), and a coda acclaiming His eternal rule (v. 18). The general plot of the poem—God's control of the sea followed by the building of His sanctuary and the acclamation of His kingship—and some of its vocabulary allude to passages in other biblical poems that tell of His primordial defeat of the sea and assumption of kingship (e.g., Pss. 74.12–16; 89.10–14; 93), which themselves hark back to ancient Near Eastern myths about the storm god's defeat of the sea god followed by the building of his palace/temple. The language and style of the poem are archaic and share many features with Ugaritic poetry of the Late Bronze Age, suggesting that it is one of the oldest poems in the Bible. On the other hand, the mention of Philistia (v. 14; see 13.22 n.) and the Temple imply a date later than the putative date of the exodus, probably in the early monarchic period. In Jewish prayer, the entire poem is recited every morning in the preliminary prayers, and vv. 11 and 18 are recited following the Shema prayer morning and evening, as part of the daily acceptance of God's kingship, the Jewish declaration of allegiance to God. **2:** The first half of this v. also appears in Isa. 12.2 and Ps. 118.14, suggesting that it was a liturgical saying. *I will enshrine Him,* another interpretation of the enigmatic Heb verb is "glorify" or "beautify Him," from which a midrash derived the duty of beautifying religious objects used in His worship, such as the sukkah, tallit, shofar, and Torah scroll; another midrash takes the verb as meaning "show His beauty" by imitating His compassion (*Mek. Shirta,* 3; *b. Shab.* 133b; *Torah Temimah). The God of my father,* see 3.6. **3:** *The LORD, the Warrior,* see 14.14, 25. One of the various metaphors applied to God. The warrior metaphor was frequently applied to deities in the ancient world, reflecting the con-

4   Pharaoh's chariots and his army
     He has cast into the sea;
     And the pick of his officers
     Are drowned in the Sea of Reeds.

5   The deeps covered them;
     They went down into the depths like a stone.

6   Your right hand, O LORD, glorious in power,
     Your right hand, O LORD, shatters the foe!

7   In Your great triumph You break Your opponents;
     You send forth Your fury, it consumes them like
          straw.

8   At the blast of Your nostrils the waters piled up,
     The floods stood straight like a wall;
     The deeps froze in the heart of the sea.

9   The foe said,
     "I will pursue, I will overtake,
     I will divide the spoil;
     My desire shall have its fill of them.
     I will bare my sword—
     My hand shall subdue them."

10   You made Your wind blow, the sea covered
          them;
     They sank like lead in the majestic waters.

11   Who is like You, O LORD, among the celestials;[a]
     Who is like You, majestic in holiness,
     Awesome in splendor, working wonders!

12   You put out Your right hand,
     The earth swallowed them.

13   In Your love You lead the people You redeemed;
     In Your strength You guide them to Your holy
          abode.

14   The peoples hear, they tremble;
     Agony grips the dwellers in Philistia.

15   Now are the clans of Edom dismayed;
     The tribes of Moab—trembling grips them;
     All the dwellers in Canaan are aghast.

16   Terror and dread descend upon them;
     Through the might of Your arm they are still as
          stone—

---

a Others "mighty."

viction that victory is in reality an achievement of God, not of human warriors. Cf. Deut. 20.4; 1 Sam. 17.47; Zech. 4.6. LORD is His name: That is, YHVH ("'adonai") is His name (see 3.15). This declaration reflects the further fulfillment of God's promises that all would come to know that "I am the LORD" (see 5.1–6 n., 6.2 n.). **6:** Your right hand: In this poem Moses' arm, so prominent in the prose narrative of ch 14 (vv. 16, 21, 26, 27), is not mentioned. Only God's role—the ultimate reality behind the event—is celebrated. In this re-spect the poem is a forerunner of the Haggadah, which mentions only God, never Moses. **7:** It consumes them like straw: Although the Egyptians drowned, the image here is of fire burning them. In vv. 6b and 7a God "shatters" and "breaks" the enemy. **8:** The blast of Your nostrils, a metaphor for the wind of 14.21. **9:** Desire, i.e., appetite. **10:** After all the enemy's boasts, God sinks them in an instant. **11:** Celestials, lit. "gods." Exclamations of God's uniqueness among the "gods" (2 Sam. 7.22; 1 Kings 8.23; Ps. 86.8) proclaim Him the greatest power in the universe. They go back to ancient Near Eastern polytheistic prototypes (cf. Jethro in 18.11). Later texts and interpretations retain the term "gods" vestigially to refer to the celestial or supernatural beings that surround God in the manner of a royal court—that is, the "host of heaven," including the sun, moon, stars, spirits, winds, flames, seraphs, and angels (Deut. 4.35–39; Pss. 86.10; 96.4–5; 135.5, 15–17). The translation "celestials" invokes the latter concept so that the verse conforms more closely to the modern sense of monotheism, but whether this ancient poem is referring to angelic beings or actual gods is debated. **13:** Love, Heb "ḥesed," better rendered "faithfulness." It refers to acts of kindness that are expected between parties in a relationship—husband and wife, parents and children, relatives, and allies—and to reciprocation of kindness (Gen. 40.14; Deut. 7.9; 1 Sam. 20.8; 2 Sam. 9.1; 10.2). Here, as frequently, it refers to God's covenantal faithfulness to Israel (2.24; 6.4–8; cf. 20.6; 34.6, 7). To Your holy abode, to the destination mentioned in v. 17, the land of Israel (cf. the sequence of events in Ps. 78.53–55) and/or the Temple Mount in Jerusalem (2 Sam. 15.25; Isa. 33.20); cf. Jer. 25.30; 31.23. **14–16:** Terrified by the power God exercised against Egypt on Israel's behalf, the Canaanites and neighboring nations are petrified at Israel's approach (cf. Josh. 2.9–11). **16:** Still as stone, like the Egyptians, who sank

Till Your people cross over, O LORD,
Till Your people cross whom You have ransomed.

17   You will bring them and plant them in Your own
           mountain,
       The place You made to dwell in, O LORD,
       The sanctuary, O LORD, which Your hands
           established.
18   The LORD will reign for ever and ever!

¹⁹ For the horses of Pharaoh, with his chariots and horsemen, went into the sea; and the LORD turned back on them
the waters of the sea; but the Israelites marched on dry
ground in the midst of the sea.

²⁰ Then Miriam the prophetess, Aaron's sister, took a
timbrel in her hand, and all the women went out after her
in dance with timbrels. ²¹ And Miriam chanted for them:

Sing to the LORD, for He has triumphed gloriously;
Horse and driver He has hurled into the sea.

²² Then Moses caused Israel to set out from the Sea of
Reeds. They went on into the wilderness of Shur; they
traveled three days in the wilderness and found no water.
²³ They came to Marah, but they could not drink the water

led by Miriam who summons them, or all the Israelites, to sing God's praises (either the hymn of vv. 1–18 or a refrain). *Miriam the prophetess:* This title could refer to Miriam's recitation of the hymn, or part of it (cf. 1 Chron. 25.1–3) or to her prophetic status mentioned in Num. 12.2. The activities of Deborah the prophetess also include singing a hymn praising God for a victory (Judg. 4.4; 5), while Huldah delivers a prophetic oracle (2 Kings 22.14; cf. Ezek. 13.17; Joel 3.1; Neh. 6.14).

15.22–17.16: Challenges in the wilderness. Four episodes in which the Israelites face typical dangers of the wilderness: shortages of food and water and attack by marauders. In the face of the shortages the people grumble against Moses and Aaron. God responds to their complaints without anger or punishment, perhaps because they have not previously seen His ability to meet their material needs, or because these incidents occur before the covenant at Sinai at which God promised to meet such needs (23.25). Having seen God's ability to defeat armies (14.30–31), they do not complain (as in 14.10–12) when the Amalekites attack.

15.22–27: Complaints (14.11–12 n.) about food and water recur throughout the wilderness wanderings. See 16.2–3; 17.2–3; Num. 11.4–6; 16.13–14; 20.2–5; 21.4–5. **22:** *The wilderness of Shur,* east of the Isthmus of Suez, apparently named for the defensive wall ("shur") that the Egyptians erected to prevent incursions from the east. *Three days . . . no water:* The midrash, which interprets "water" as Torah (since Torah is as essential for well-being as water), infers that it was three days without Torah that made the people rebellious, and holds that the practice of reading the Torah in the synagogue every Sabbath, Monday, and Thursday was instituted so that three days would not pass without Torah (*Mek. Beshallah, Vayassa',* 1; b. B. K. 82a). **23:** *Marah,* lit. "bitter."

"like a stone" (v. 5). *Cross over:* This refers either to Israel's passing these nations (excepting the Canaanites) on its way to Canaan (Deut. 2.8, 18) or crossing the Jordan into the land (Josh. 1.11; 4.1). *Ransomed,* i.e., redeemed. **17:** *Plant them,* permanently settle them (Amos 9.15; Pss. 44.3; 80.9). *In Your own mountain:* "Mountain" refers to the promised land, which is mountainous (Deut. 3.25; Isa. 11.9; 57.13; Ps. 78.54), but "God's mountain" often refers to the Temple Mount as well (Isa. 2.3; Ezek. 20.40; Zech. 8.3; Ps. 24.3), and the following phrases *the place You made to dwell in* and *the sanctuary . . .* clearly refer to that. The v. blends the concepts of the promised land and the Temple Mount: The Israelites, settled throughout the land with the Temple in the center, are pictured as dwelling around the Temple in which God dwells in their midst (cf. Exod. 25.8; 29.45–46; 1 Kings

6.13; Ezek. 37.25–28). This climactic verse indicates that the conquest of the promised land will not be an end in itself. The redemption will culminate when the Temple is built and Israel dwells there in the presence of God. *You made . . . Your hands established:* As in the victory over Egypt and the conquest of the promised land (vv. 6, 16b–17a), human agency in building the Temple (1 Kings chs 6–8, esp. 8.13) is ignored. In a theological sense it is God who will build the Temple (cf. Ps. 78.69). **18:** God's kingship is acclaimed here because the Temple, as His palace ("heikhal," 1 Kings 6.3, 5, and elsewhere), symbolizes His kingship. This is the first explicit mention of the common biblical metaphor "God is king." **20–21:** In keeping with the custom of women celebrating the victor after a battle (Judg. 11.34; 1 Sam. 18.6), the women dance and play music, of Marah because it was bitter; that is why it was named Marah.[a] 24 And the people grumbled against Moses, saying, "What shall we drink?" 25 So he cried out to the LORD, and the LORD showed him a piece of wood; he threw it into the water and the water became sweet.

There He made for them a fixed rule, and there He put them to the test. 26 He said, "If you will heed the LORD your God diligently, doing what is upright in His sight, giving ear to His commandments and keeping all His laws, then I will not bring upon you any of the diseases that I brought upon the Egyptians, for I the LORD am your healer."

27 And they came to Elim, where there were twelve springs of water and seventy palm trees; and they encamped there beside the water.

16 Setting out from Elim, the whole Israelite community came to the wilderness of Sin, which is between Elim and Sinai, on the fifteenth day of the second month after their departure from the land of Egypt. 2 In the wilderness, the whole Israelite community grumbled against Moses and Aaron. 3 The Israelites said to them, "If only we had died by the hand of the LORD in the land of Egypt, when we sat by the fleshpots, when we ate our fill of bread! For you have brought us out into this wilderness to starve this whole congregation to death."

4 And the LORD said to Moses, "I will rain down bread for you from the sky, and the people shall go out and gather each day that day's portion—that I may thus test them, to see whether they will follow My instructions or not. 5 But on the sixth day, when they apportion what they have brought in, it shall prove to be double the amount they gather each day." 6 So Moses and Aaron said to all the Israelites, "By evening you shall know it was the LORD

a I.e., "bitter."

Brackish pools and wells are common in deserts (cf. the "Bitter Lakes" in the Isthmus of Suez). Assuming that the Israelites are now heading south, the site could be Bir el-Murrah, Arabic for "Bitter Well," nine miles east of Suez, or the oasis Ein Hawarah, 75 km (47 mi) southeast of Suez, near Wadi Amarah which has a similar sounding name. **25:** *A piece of wood,* or a branch with its foliage. Even today, Bedouin sweeten brackish water with shrubs that cause the salt to sink to the bot-

tom. *There He made for them a fixed rule, and there He put them to the test:* The context suggests that this enigmatic sentence refers to the next v. and means that God told Israel the conditions of their future relationship, against which they will be tested (see 16.4; Deut. 8.2, 16). The promise in v. 26, which also implies a warning, is prompted by Israel's grumbling against Moses, God's servant (14.31), which contained the seeds of rebellion against God Himself (cf. 16.8). **26:** *The diseases that I*

brought upon the Egyptians, such as the sixth plague, skin inflammation (9.8–11). *Healer:* This quality of God, with its implicit warning of punishment by disease, is prompted by His purifying the water of its bitterness, which was regarded as "healing" the water (the same verb is translated "make wholesome" in 2 Kings 2.22; Ezek. 47.8, 9, 11). **27:** *Elim,* possibly Wadi Gharandel, the best-watered site in western Sinai, about 15 km (9 mi) south of Ein Hawarah, or Uyun Musa, 12 km (7.5 mi) southwest of Bir el-Murrah, which has a palm grove and twelve springs even today.

16.1–36: Provision of food in the wilderness. This narrative is generally assigned to the Priestly source, but redundancies (such as God's two responses to the people's complaint [vv. 4–5 and 11–12]) and difficulties in the order (vv. 6–8 presuppose vv. 9–12) suggest the presence of a second source (JE) as well. Another episode in which God provides quail, which also refers to the manna, appears in Num. ch 11; it is in part a doublet of this episode. **1–3:** A month after the exodus (Num. 33.3), having left the oasis of Elim and run low on food, the Israelites turn on Moses and Aaron and begin to idealize life in Egypt (cf. 14.11–12; Num. 11.5). **4:** The people's need for food is real, but their accusatory complaint portends rebellion, so God determines to provide food subject to rules that test their obedience and trust (vv. 19–20, 25–29). **5:** When it is apportioned, the manna collected on the sixth day will miraculously double and suffice for the next day as well. Cf. Lev. 25.20–22. *Apportion:* Halakhic exegesis assigns the Heb word its more common meaning, "prepare," and infers a general rule that cooked food for the Sabbath must be prepared before the Sabbath (b. Shab. 117b; b. Pes. 47b; b. Betzah 2b; see also v. 23). **6–7:** Divinely provided food and the appearance of God's Presence will remind the people that, contrary to their charge in v. 3, it was who brought you out from the land of Egypt; [7] and in the morning you shall behold the Presence[a] of the LORD, because He has heard your grumblings against the LORD. For who are we that you should grumble against us? [8] Since it is the LORD," Moses continued, "who will give you flesh to eat in the evening and bread in the morning to the full, because the LORD has heard the grumblings you utter against Him, what is our part? Your grumbling is not against us, but against the LORD!"

[9] Then Moses said to Aaron, "Say to the whole Israelite community: Advance toward the LORD, for He has heard your grumbling." [10] And as Aaron spoke to the whole Israelite community, they turned toward the wilderness, and there, in a cloud, appeared the Presence of the LORD.

[11] The LORD spoke to Moses: [12] "I have heard the grumbling of the Israelites. Speak to them and say: By evening you shall eat flesh, and in the morning you shall have your fill of bread; and you shall know that I the LORD am your God."

[13] In the evening quail appeared and covered the camp; in the morning there was a fall of dew about the camp. [14] When the fall of dew lifted, there, over the surface of the wilderness, lay a fine and flaky substance, as fine as frost on the ground. [15] When the Israelites saw it, they said to one another, "What is it?"[b]—for they did not know what it was. And Moses said to them, "That is the bread which the LORD has given you to eat. [16] This is what the LORD has commanded: Gather as much of it as each of you requires to eat, an *omer* to a person for as many of you as there are; each of you shall fetch for those in his tent."

[17] The Israelites did so, some gathering much, some little. [18] But when they measured it by the *omer*, he who had gathered much had no excess, and he who had gathered little had no deficiency: they had gathered as much as they needed to eat. [19] And Moses said to them, "Let no one leave any of it over until morning." [20] But they paid no attention to Moses; some of them left of it until morning, and it became infested with maggots and stank. And Moses was angry with them.

[21] So they gathered it every morning, each as much as he needed to eat; for when the sun grew hot, it would

Ezek. 1.26–28). But since this is to happen *in the morning*, Rashi holds that this v. does not refer to the theophany of vv. 9–10 but to the manna, which appeared in the morning (vv. 8, 12–13). In that case *the Presence of the LORD* refers to an act of providence or miracle that manifests His power, as in Num. 14.22; Ps. 96.3. **8:** *Flesh . . . bread,* in the form of quail and manna (v. 13). **9–10:** *Advance toward the LORD,* perhaps toward the pillar of cloud/fire (13.21–22). If so, *there, in a* [or "the"] *cloud, appeared the Presence of the LORD* would seem to mean that His fiery Presence became more visible within the cloud. **12:** *You shall know that I the LORD am your God:* See 7.5 n. **13:** *Quail:* Quail migrating, often in great numbers, between Africa and Europe in the spring and fall often drop exhausted in the Sinai and are caught by hunters. This experience was repeated in Num. 11.31–32 but did not become a regular occurrence as did the manna. The quail were not a supernatural phenomenon, but their timely appearance at God's promise was an act of divine providence. **14:** *A fine and flaky substance,* named manna in v. 31. If this has a natural explanation, it is probably the sweet, edible honeydew (still called "manna" in Arabic) found in parts of the Sinai in June and July. Scale insects and plant lice ingest the sap of tamarisk trees and excrete it onto the branches, from which it crystallizes and falls to the ground as sticky solids. Bedouin use it as a sweetener. If this was the manna, the miracle was that it arrived just when the Israelites needed it, that enough was produced to feed the entire people but never more than an *'omer* (about 2.3 liters, 2.1 quarts [dry measure]) per person daily, that it doubled on the sixth day and did not appear on the Sabbath, and that contrary to its natural pattern it appeared year-round. **16:** *Omer:* See v. 36. **19:** Using up the manna before morning shows trust that God will provide more the next day (hence Moses' anger in v. 20). **21–30:** The Sabbath. Since God observes the Sabbath, He will

---

a Others "glory."   *b Heb. man hu; others "It is manna."*

God, not Moses and Aaron, who took them from Egypt (cf. 15.6 n., 17.17 n.) and that their complaints are really against Him. *The Presence of the LORD,* the visual form in

which God appears to humans, usually described as fiery or as enveloped in cloud or fire (v. 10; 24.17; 40.34–38), though sometimes as a human form (33.18, 22;

melt. 22 On the sixth day they gathered double the amount of food, two *omers* for each; and when all the chieftains of the community came and told Moses, 23 he said to them, "This is what the LORD meant: Tomorrow is a day of rest, a holy sabbath of the LORD. Bake what you would bake and boil what you would boil; and all that is left put aside to be kept until morning." 24 So they put it aside until morning, as Moses had ordered; and it did not turn foul, and there were no maggots in it. 25 Then Moses said, "Eat it today, for today is a sabbath of the LORD; you will not find it today on the plain. 26 Six days you shall gather it; on the seventh day, the sabbath, there will be none."

27 Yet some of the people went out on the seventh day to gather, but they found nothing. 28 And the LORD said to Moses, "How long will you men refuse to obey My commandments and My teachings? 29 Mark that the LORD has given you the sabbath; therefore He gives you two days' food on the sixth day. Let everyone remain where he is: let no one leave his place on the seventh day." 30 So the people remained inactive on the seventh day.

31 The house of Israel named it manna;[a] it was like coriander seed, white, and it tasted like wafers[b] in honey. 32 Moses said, "This is what the LORD has commanded: Let one *omer* of it be kept throughout the ages, in order that they may see the bread that I fed you in the wilderness when I brought you out from the land of Egypt." 33 And Moses said to Aaron, "Take a jar, put one *omer* of manna in it, and place it before the LORD, to be kept throughout the ages." 34 As the LORD had commanded Moses, Aaron placed it before the Pact,[c] to be kept. 35 And the Israelites ate manna forty years, until they came to a settled land; they ate the manna until they came to the border of the land of Canaan. 36 The *omer* is a tenth of an *ephah*.

---

a *Heb.* man.
b *Meaning of Heb.* ṣappiḥith *uncertain.*   c *Others* "Testimony."

---

cf. Num. 11.8. *And all that is left put aside . . . :* This means either "cook today for two days, and save what you don't eat today for tomorrow" (Rashi) or "cook what you will eat today and eat the rest raw tomorrow" (Ibn Ezra). **28:** *Refuse to obey My commandments . . . :* Unless this means simply that they refused to believe that there would be no manna on the Sabbath, it must mean that they violated the implicit command not to go out for manna on the Sabbath (vv. 25b–26) or the explicit command to eat the manna that was kept overnight (v. 25a). **29:** *Given you the sabbath:* God has given the Sabbath, previously holy only to Him (Gen. 2.1–3), as a gift to Israel. *Let no one leave his place,* to gather manna. Rabbinic exegesis saw here a broader prohibition on all Sabbath travel and inferred that one may not walk more than 2,000 cubits (roughly 1,000 meters, 3,000 feet) beyond the city limits on the Sabbath. This distance (based on Num. 35.5) is called the "Sabbath boundary" ("teḥum shabbat"). **31:** *Named it manna* (Heb "man"), playfully reinterpreting their original question, "what (Heb 'man') is it?" (v. 15), as a declaration, "it is 'man.'" In essence, then, the term means "whatchamacallit" and expresses the manna's unprecedented character in Israelite experience. *Tasted:* Num. 11.8, a different tradition, says "it tasted like rich cream" and notes various ways to prepare it. This gave rise to the rabbinic tradition that the manna had many different tastes, suiting the palate of each person. **32–34:** One day's portion of manna is to be preserved as a future reminder of God's care for the Israelites in the wilderness. Cf. Lev. 23.42–43. **34:** *Before the Pact,* before the Ark of the Pact (25.10–22), P's term for the Ark of the Covenant (Num. 10.33; Josh. 3.6); the suggestion is that the jar of manna stored in front of the Ark could be taken out to show to future generations. **35:** *Until they came to the border of the land of Canaan,* see Josh. 5.10–12. **36:** *Ephah,* about 23 liters (21 quarts).

not provide manna on the seventh day but will provide a double portion on the sixth day and Israel will observe the Sabbath as well. The Sabbath, having been "created" in Gen. ch 2, is first revealed to Israel here. **22:** See v. 5 n. *Told Moses,* of the mysterious fact that the day's yield turned out to be *double the amount of food* (Heb "leḥem mishneh," lit. "double the bread"). This v. is the source of the Jewish custom of placing two loaves of bread (called "leḥem mishneh") on the table at the main Sabbath and festival meals. **23:** *Day of rest . . . sabbath,* Heb "shabbaton . . . shabbat." Both Heb terms literally refer to "cessation" of activity. The seventh day is a day of cessation from normal labor (20.10), such as gathering and cooking food, because it is a holy day of cessation to God: He does not provide manna on it because He ceased creative activity on it, blessed it and declared it holy (Gen. 2.1–3). *Bake . . . and boil . . . :*

17 From the wilderness of Sin the whole Israelite community continued by stages as the LORD would command. They encamped at Rephidim, and there was no water for the people to drink. [2] The people quarreled with Moses. "Give us water to drink," they said; and Moses replied to them, "Why do you quarrel with me? Why do you try the LORD?" [3] But the people thirsted there for water; and the people grumbled against Moses and said, "Why did you bring us up from Egypt, to kill us and our children and livestock with thirst?" [4] Moses cried out to the LORD, saying, "What shall I do with this people? Before long they will be stoning me!" [5] Then the LORD said to Moses, "Pass before the people; take with you some of the elders of Israel, and take along the rod with which you struck the Nile, and set out. [6] I will be standing there before you on the rock at Horeb. Strike the rock and water will issue from it, and the people will drink." And Moses did so in the sight of the elders of Israel. [7] The place was named Massah[a] and Meribah,[b] because the Israelites quarreled and because they tried the LORD, saying, "Is the LORD present among us or not?"

[8] Amalek came and fought with Israel at Rephidim. [9] Moses said to Joshua, "Pick some men for us, and go out and do battle with Amalek. Tomorrow I will station myself on the top of the hill, with the rod of God in my hand." [10] Joshua did as Moses told him and fought with Amalek, while Moses, Aaron, and Hur went up to the top of the hill. [11] Then, whenever Moses held up his hand, Israel prevailed; but whenever he let down his hand, Amalek prevailed. [12] But Moses' hands grew heavy; so they took a stone and put it under him and he sat on it, while

a I.e., "Trial."　　b I.e., "Quarrel."

17.1–7: The incident at Massah and Meribah. 1: *Rephidim,* the last station before Sinai (19.2; Num. 33.14–15) and, to judge from v. 6, near Sinai. **2:** *Why do you quarrel with me? Why do you try the LORD?* Cf. 16.8. *Try,* i.e., test, demanding proof that God was present among them and controlling the events (see v. 7; cf. 8.18; Deut. 7.21; 31.17; Josh. 3.10). **3:** Cf. 16.3b. **5–6:** Moses is to take some of the elders, perhaps as witnesses, and set out for *Horeb* (Sinai), "the mountain of God" (3.1), to obtain water. Apparently the water would flow from Horeb back to Rephidim via a

wadi (cf. 32.20; Deut. 9.21). *Strike the rock:* In the Sinai there are limestone rocks from which small amounts of water drip, and a blow to their soft surface can expose a porous inner layer containing water. A similar but enigmatic episode, with differences suggesting that it was an oral variant of this one, appears in Num. 20.2–13 (mostly from P in its present form). According to talmudic legend, the water came from the "Well of Miriam" which henceforth accompanied the Israelites on their journeys through the wilderness; it was given to them because of

Miriam's merits and named after her (*Seder Olam* 5; *t. Sot.* 11.1, 8; *b. Ta'an.* 9a). **7:** *The place,* Rephidim, not Horeb. *Massah and Meribah,* meaning "The Place of Testing and Quarreling." These names, playing on the verbs "quarrel" and "try" used in v. 2, became bywords for Israel's lack of trust in God (Deut. 6.16; 9.22; Ps. 95.8).

17.8–16: The attack of the Amalekites. The Amalekites are depicted as marauding nomads living in the Negev and Sinai. In later times they periodically raided and pillaged Israel and joined other enemies in threatening to wipe Israel out (Judg. 3.13; 6.3–5; 30.1; 1 Sam. 30.1–2; Ps. 83.4–9). This passage is read in the synagogue on Purim because Haman, the arch anti-Semite who sought to exterminate all the Jews in the Persian empire, was an Agagite, a descendant of the Amalekite king Agag (cf. Esth. 3.1; 1 Sam. 15.32). In later Jewish tradition Amalek came to symbolize anti-Semites in general. **8:** *Fought with Israel:* According to Deut. 25.18 this was a sneak attack on the defenseless weak lagging at the rear, which showed that Amalekites had no fear of God or conscience (see 1.17 n.). **9:** *Joshua,* Moses' attendant and eventual successor who led the Israelites in conquering the promised land. See 24.13; 33.11; Num. 11.28; 27.15–23; Deut. 1.38; ch 31. **10:** *Hur,* a public figure, associated again with Aaron in 24.14; possibly the Hur who was Bezalel's grandfather (31.2). **11:** *Whenever Moses held up his hand* [or "hands," v. 12]: a gesture of uncertain meaning, perhaps to raise his staff and focus God's power against the enemy (7.20; 14.16; cf. Josh. 8.18–26) or a sign of triumph (see 14.8, translators' note; Deut. 32.27; Mic. 5.8). In any case, the victory is not won by military efforts alone. The *Mekhilta,* sensitive to the impression that Moses is (magically?) controlling the battle (he acts without divine command), states that his hands directed the Israelites' thoughts to God in heaven who gave them victory (*Mek.,*

Aaron and Hur, one on each side, supported his hands; thus his hands remained steady until the sun set. ¹³ And Joshua overwhelmed the people of Amalek^a with the sword.

¹⁴ Then the LORD said to Moses, "Inscribe this in a document as a reminder, and read it aloud to Joshua: I will utterly blot out the memory of Amalek from under heaven!" ¹⁵ And Moses built an altar and named it Adonai-nissi.^b ¹⁶ He said, "It means, 'Hand upon the throne^c of the LORD!' The LORD will be at war with Amalek throughout the ages."

YITRO   יתרו

18 Jethro priest of Midian, Moses' father-in-law, heard all that God had done for Moses and for Israel His people, how the LORD had brought Israel out from Egypt. ² So Jethro, Moses' father-in-law, took Zipporah, Moses' wife, after she had been sent home, ³ and her two sons—of whom one was named Gershom, that is to say, "I have been a stranger^d in a foreign land"; ⁴ and the other was named Eliezer,^e meaning, "The God of my father was my help, and He delivered me from the sword of Pharaoh." ⁵ Jethro, Moses' father-in-law, brought Moses' sons and wife to him in the wilderness, where he was encamped at the mountain of God. ⁶ He sent word to Moses, "I, your father-in-law Jethro, am coming to you, with your wife and her two sons." ⁷ Moses went out to meet his father-in-law; he bowed low and kissed him; each asked after the other's welfare, and they went into the tent.

⁸ Moses then recounted to his father-in-law everything that the LORD had done to Pharaoh and to the Egyptians for Israel's sake, all the hardships that had befallen them on the way, and how the LORD had delivered them. ⁹ And Jethro rejoiced over all the kindness that the LORD had shown Israel when He delivered them from the Egyptians. ¹⁰ "Blessed be the LORD," Jethro said, "who delivered you from the Egyptians and from Pharaoh, and who delivered the people from under the hand of the Egyptians. ¹¹ Now I know that the LORD is greater than all gods,

---

a Lit. "Amalek and his people."   b I.e., "The LORD is my banner."
c Meaning of Heb. kes uncertain.   d Heb. ger.   e Lit. "(My) God is help."

---

morial altars are also mentioned in Gen. 33.20; 35.7; Josh. 22.26–27; Judg. 6.24. **16:** *Hand upon the throne of the LORD:* The anomalous Heb word rendered "throne" may be an error for "banner" (that is, battle standard), which would make the connection to v. 15 clearer. This difficult phrase is possibly an oath formula meaning "I swear by the LORD's throne/banner."

18.1–27: The visit of Jethro. The fact that v. 3 seems unaware of 2.22, and that Moses' father-in-law was called Reuel in that episode (2.16–22, from J), suggests that this episode is drawn from a different source; the predominance of the name "God" ("'elohim") here and other details indicate that it is E.

18.1–12: Jethro's arrival. 1: *Jethro,* see 2.18 n. **2:** This source assumes that Zipporah and the children (2.21–22; 4.20) had been sent back from Egypt to Midian. **4:** This is the first we hear of Eliezer's name. *Delivered me from the sword of Pharaoh,* see 2.15. **5:** *At the mountain of God,* Sinai/Horeb (3.1). Since Israel does not reach Sinai until 19.2, this episode evidently took place afterwards. This is also implied by the context in Deut. 1.6–17 and by the presumption in Exod. 24.14b that the pre-Jethro judicial system is still in place, with Aaron and Hur substituting for Moses. Thus, this passage is not where it belongs chronologically. Talmudic sages recognized that the Torah sometimes narrates events out of their chronological sequence for literary or rhetorical purposes ("there is no earlier or later in the Torah"). Radak suggested that the Torah's aim was to juxtapose Jethro's visit with the attack of the Amalekites (17.8–16) so as to contrast the Midianites' friendliness with the Amalekites' enmity as a guide for future dealings with these two nations (Radak at Judg. 1.16; see 1 Sam. 15.5–7). **11:** *Now I know:* In a further fulfillment of the LORD's aim that all come to know His name and acknowledge Him (see 5.1–6.1 n.; 6.2 n.; 14.4; 15.3), Jethro recognizes His superiority, though

---

Amalek 1). **14:** This event, too, is to be memorialized (cf. 12.14, 26–27; 13.3, 8–9, 14–16; 16.32–34), both in writing and orally (cf. Deut. 25.17). This is the first time writing is mentioned among the Israelites. *Document,* a scroll or an

inscription. *I will utterly blot out,* cf. Num. 24.20. In Deut. 25.19 Israel is commanded to wipe out the Amalekites, apparently acting as God's agents. **15:** The event is also commemorated with a monument, in the shape of an altar. Named meᵃ"yes, by the result of their very schemes against [the people]."⁻ᵃ ¹²And Jethro, Moses' father-in-law, brought a burnt offering and sacrifices for God; and Aaron came with all the elders of Israel to partake of the meal before God with Moses' father-in-law.

¹³Next day, Moses sat as magistrate among the people, while the people stood about Moses from morning until evening. ¹⁴But when Moses' father-in-law saw how much he had to do for the people, he said, "What is this thing that you are doing to the people? Why do you act[b] alone, while all the people stand about you from morning until evening?" ¹⁵Moses replied to his father-in-law, "It is because the people come to me to inquire of God. ¹⁶When they have a dispute, it comes before me, and I decide between one person and another, and I make known the laws and teachings of God."

¹⁷But Moses' father-in-law said to him, "The thing you are doing is not right; ¹⁸you will surely wear yourself out, and these people as well. For the task is too heavy for you; you cannot do it alone. ¹⁹Now listen to me. I will give you counsel, and God be with you! You represent the people before God: you bring the disputes before God, ²⁰and enjoin upon them the laws and the teachings, and make known to them the way they are to go and the practices they are to follow. ²¹You shall also seek out from among all the people capable men who fear God, trustworthy men who spurn ill-gotten gain. Set these over them as chiefs of thousands, hundreds, fifties, and tens, and ²²let them judge the people at all times. Have them bring every major dispute to you, but let them decide every minor dispute themselves. Make it easier for yourself by letting

a-a Meaning of Heb. uncertain.　　b Lit. "sit" as magistrate; cf. v. 13.

he does not renounce other gods (contrast Naaman in 2 Kings 5.15, 17). The Torah does not expect Gentiles to become monotheists (see Deut. 4.19), only to recognize the LORD's superiority and authority when He asserts it, as in the case of Egypt. The ideal of universal monotheism first appears in the classical prophets (Jer. 16.19–20; Zech. 14.9). Neither the prophets nor Jewish tradition call for conversion to Judaism of Gentiles, even monotheistic Gentiles, though later Jewish tradition—characteristically reading the Bible through the prism of the prophets—believed that Jethro did abandon idolatry (*Exod. Rab.* 1.32) and, going even further, became a Jew (*Tg. Ps.-J. Exod.* 18.6, 27; *Tanḥ.* Buber *Yitro*, 5). *Yes, by the result of . . .*, i.e., "Yes, they perished as the result of. . . ." **12:** *A burnt offering and sacrifices:* A burnt offering was entirely burnt as a tribute to God on the altar (Lev. ch 1). The *sacrifice* (short for "sacrifice of well-being," Lev. 3.1) was partly burnt, but most of it was eaten by the donor and guests at a sacrificial meal (v. 12; cf. 24.5, 9–11; 32.6; Deut. 12.27; 27.7).

18.13–27: The organization of a judiciary, also related (with variations) in Deut. 1.9–18. Remarkably, the judicial institution was ascribed to a priest of the Midianites, a nation with whom the Israelites later had hostile relations. **13:** *As magistrate,* better, "to judge" the people's disputes. **15:** *To inquire of God:* Moses would either consult God for a verdict (cf. 22.8) or decide based on prior rulings by God (cf. the laws generated by Moses' continued consultation with God in Lev. 24.10–23; Num. 9.1–14; 15.32–36; chs 27, 36). The judicial role of the prophets Deborah and Samuel (Judg. 4.4–5; 1 Sam. 7.15–17) may also have involved oracular consultation of God. **19:** *And God be with you:* Jethro may be either praying or promising that if Moses follows his advice, God will grant him success (= "you will be able to bear up," v. 23), or he may mean "and if God agrees" (= "and God so commands you," v. 23). **19–22:** Jethro advises Moses to continue consulting God in cases without legal precedent, but to make the resulting *laws and . . . teachings* (v. 20) public, to reduce the need for adjudication and enable him to delegate authority to officials who could judge most remaining cases, leaving only the difficult ones for him (cf. Deut. 17.8–13). **21:** Jethro defines the ideal qualities of character required of judges. *Fear God,* men of conscience (1.17 n.). *Trustworthy men,* or "men of truth." *Spurn ill-gotten gain,* unsusceptible to bribes (23.8). In recounting this event in Deut. 1.13, 15, Moses lists intellectual qualifications. Maimonides, in defining the qualifications for judges, holds that the qualities of both lists, character as well as intellect, are required (*Hilkhot Sanh.* 2.7). *Chiefs of thousands, hundreds, fifties, and tens:* These are military ranks, consistent with the fact that the Israelites are organized as an army (12.41 n.) and have just fought a battle (17.8–16). Military officers sometimes held judicial responsibilities in the ancient Near East. **22:** *Major,* according to v. 26, "difficult." **23:** *And God so com-*

them share the burden with you. 23 If you do this—and God so commands you—you will be able to bear up; and all these people too will go home unwearied."

24 Moses heeded his father-in-law and did just as he had said. 25 Moses chose capable men out of all Israel, and appointed them heads over the people—chiefs of thousands, hundreds, fifties, and tens; 26 and they judged the people at all times: the difficult matters they would bring to Moses, and all the minor matters they would decide themselves. 27 Then Moses bade his father-in-law farewell, and he went his way to his own land.

19 On the third new moon after the Israelites had gone forth from the land of Egypt, on that very day, they entered the wilderness of Sinai. 2 Having journeyed from Rephidim, they entered the wilderness of Sinai and encamped in the wilderness. Israel encamped there in front of the mountain, 3 and Moses went up to God. The LORD called to him from the mountain, saying, "Thus shall you say to the house of Jacob and declare to the children of Israel: 4 'You have seen what I did to the Egyp-

---

mands you, i.e., authorizes you to follow this suggestion. **27:** According to Num. 10.29–32, from a different source, Moses sought to persuade Jethro to remain with the Israelites and share God's bounty with them in the promised land, but he declined.

Chs 19–24: The theophany, covenant, and laws at Sinai. The momentous encounter with God at Sinai is, for the Torah, the defining and seminal moment in Israel's relationship with God. Nevertheless, it is extraordinarily difficult to follow. It was transmitted in multiple versions that differed about the nature of the event and what God communicated to the people. The text clearly combines material from J, E, and P, but the relative paucity of identifying characteristics in several vv. has made it more difficult than usual to reach a consensus about which source they belong to. The combination of these sources, based on the redactor's perception that they are all true, resulted in significant tensions within the narrative. For example, according to 19.9, the theophany was to be auditory: The

people would hear God speaking to Moses, although it is not clear what they would hear. According to v. 19 it was a dialogue (possibly consisting of vv. 20–25), but 20.1 says that it was the Decalogue. In contrast, in 19.11 God speaks of a visual rather than auditory theophany, although in v. 21 He warns against the people trying "to gaze." The account of Moses' writing and communicating the laws during the covenant ceremony in 24.3 and 7 apparently refers to the laws of 20.19–23.33 and seems unaware of the Decalogue; only in 24.12 does God summon him to receive the stone tablets, which played no role in the covenant just concluded (24.3–8). Moses' reports in 19.8b and 9b are redundant, as are God's two descents to the mountain (19.18a, 20a), while "Come up to the LORD" (24.1) is a non sequitur since Moses has already done so (20.18). Despite, or perhaps because of, these tensions, the narrative has great power, expressing the multifaceted, ambiguous nature of revelation.

19.1–25: The theophany. 1–2: The anomalous order (contrast 16.1)

seems designed to foreground the date because of the historic significance of what will happen at Sinai. *The third new moon,* the new moon of Sivan, counting the new moon of Nisan as the first (12.2 n.). The Israelites will remain at Sinai for just short of a year (Num. 10.11). *The wilderness of Sinai,* the wilderness surrounding Mount Sinai, where Moses' mission had begun (see 3.1 and n.). The arrival there heralds the fulfillment of God's promise to Moses (3.12). **3–6:** God announces the purpose, first revealed in 6.6–7, toward which everything has led: Having redeemed Israel, as promised, He proposes a covenant relationship, as promised in 6.7. This relationship is modeled on ancient royal covenants, in which a citizenry accepted a king, and on suzerainty treaties, in which a weaker king accepted a more powerful one as his suzerain. The covenant proposed here goes beyond the one established with Israel's ancestors (Gen. chs 15, 17). Here, God imposes specific, detailed obligations and, in return, promises Israel an especially close relationship with Him. This covenant, along with the earlier one, became the basis on which Judaism defined its relationship with God. As befits the solemnity of the proposal, much of God's statement is in a quasi-poetic style, marked by parallelism and metaphors. According to the final form of the text, the terms of the covenant—which is formally established in 24.7–8—are the Decalogue (20.2–14) and the "Book of the Covenant" (20.19–23.33). **3:** *House of Jacob,* the Israelites, Jacob's descendants (1.1–5). According to *Mek. Baḥodesh* 2, this phrase refers specifically to the women, while *the children of Israel* refers to the men. **4:** God reminds Israel of what He has already done, since in the ancient Near East a suzerain's prior benefactions to a vassal, such as delivering him from enemies, are the vassal's motivation to accept a treaty with him (cf. 20.2–3). *You have seen:* The premise of the covenant is Israel's national experience.

tians, how I bore you on eagles' wings and brought you to Me. [5] Now then, if you will obey Me faithfully and keep My covenant, you shall be My treasured possession among all the peoples. Indeed, all the earth is Mine, [6] but you shall be to Me a kingdom of priests and a holy nation.' These are the words that you shall speak to the children of Israel."

[7] Moses came and summoned the elders of the people and put before them all that the Lord had commanded him. [8] All the people answered as one, saying, "All that the Lord has spoken we will do!" And Moses brought back the people's words to the Lord. [9] And the Lord said to Moses, "I will come to you in a thick cloud, in order that the people may hear when I speak with you and so trust you ever after." Then Moses reported the people's words to the Lord, [10] and the Lord said to Moses, "Go to the people and warn them to stay pure[a] today and tomorrow. Let them wash their clothes. [11] Let them be ready for the third day; for on the third day the Lord will come down, in the sight of all the people, on Mount Sinai. [12] You shall set bounds for the people round about, saying, 'Beware of going up the mountain or touching the border of it. Who-

a Cf. v. 15.

From biblical times on, Jewish belief has been based primarily on Jewish historical experience rather than speculative thought. *On eagles' wings:* God led Israel swiftly and safely through the wilderness, like an eagle training its young to fly, catching them on its back when they tire or fall. Cf. Deut. 32.11–12. *To Me,* to Mount Sinai/Horeb, "the mountain of God." **5:** *Treasured possession,* Heb "segulah" is personal property: the private property of a king, as distinct from that used for public purposes (1 Chron. 29.3; Eccl. 2.8), or of economic dependents, such as a wife's nest egg or the "peculium" of a son or slave. One's personal stake in his private property gives it the connotation of something "treasured." Although God owns all things, if Israel accepts His covenant He will cherish Israel because of His personal relationship with it. A Hittite king described one of his vassals by this term, and an ancient Syrian royal seal describes the king as the servant, beloved, and treasure of

the gods. **5b–6a:** Although all the (peoples of the) world are mine, if you obey My covenant it is you who shall be My *kingdom of priests and a holy nation:* enjoying the status of priests, close to God and sacrosanct (Deut. 26.19; 28.9; and esp. Isa. 61.6; 62.12; for "holy meaning sacrosanct and inviolable," see Jer. 2.3). Deuteronomy (Deut. 7.1–6; 14.2, 21) and later Jewish tradition converted this from a promise to a responsibility (noblesse oblige) requiring the entire Jewish people, not just the priests, to live by a code of holiness—God's commandments—and to serve as priests, bringing knowledge of Him to the world. **7:** *All that the Lord had commanded him,* in vv. 3–6. **8:** Although they have not yet heard the terms of the covenant, the people willingly and unanimously accept God's proposal and promise to obey Him, as they reconfirm twice in 24.3, 7. **8b–13:** Vv. 8b–9a and 9b–13 seem to be alternative versions of Moses' report to God and God's

reply. According to 8b–9a, God replied by telling Moses, privately, that He would come and speak to Moses in the people's hearing in order to confirm Moses' credibility. According to vv. 9b–13 He told Moses to prepare the people for His coming appearance, but did not divulge its purpose (cf. 20.17). **9a:** *In order that the people may hear when I speak with you and so trust you ever after:* Once the people personally overhear God and Moses conversing (v. 19b), they will be convinced once and for all that Moses really is God's prophet. This conviction, first instilled in 4.1–9 and 14.31, is essential for their acceptance of all the rest of the Torah, which God communicates through Moses after the people decline to hear Him directly following the Decalogue (20.16). In classical Jewish thought, the fact that the entire nation witnessed God speaking to Moses is the definitive evidence that the Torah is from God (Judah Halevi, *Kuzari* 1:87–88; Maimonides, *Hilkhot Yesodei Hatorah* 8:1), though according to Saadia Gaon, this demonstration of the truth of Judaism was only a stopgap until the Jewish people could derive the same lesson by the slower process of reasoning (*Beliefs and Opinions,* Introductory Treatise, sec. 6). **9b–13:** God's descent to the mountain will turn it into a holy place and it will accordingly have to be safeguarded from impurity and encroachment by zones of increasingly restricted access, like the Tabernacle. **10:** *Warn them to stay pure,* lit. "purify them," possibly meaning "have them purify themselves"—by laundering (cf. Lev. 11.25, 28, 40, etc.), abstaining from sexual relations (v. 15), and possibly by bathing as well (2 Sam. 11.2, 4). **11:** Purification the day before witnessing a manifestation of God's power is also prescribed in Num. 11.18; Josh. 3.5; cf. Josh. 7.13. Here an extra day is prescribed because of the momentousness of the event. *Come down,* from His dwelling-place in heaven. **12:** *Set bounds,* temporarily (see v. 13b). Cf. 3.5; Josh. 5.15. *Whoever touches the* ever touches the mountain shall be put to death: [13] no hand shall touch him, but he shall be either stoned or shot; beast or man, he shall not live.' When the ram's horn a-sounds a long blast,-a they may go up on the mountain."

[14] Moses came down from the mountain to the people and warned the people to stay pure, and they washed their clothes. [15] And he said to the people, "Be ready for the third day: do not go near a woman."

[16] On the third day, as morning dawned, there was thunder, and lightning, and a dense cloud upon the mountain, and a very loud blast of the horn; and all the people who were in the camp trembled. [17] Moses led the people out of the camp toward God, and they took their places at the foot of the mountain.

[18] Now Mount Sinai was all in smoke, for the LORD had come down upon it in fire; the smoke rose like the smoke of a kiln, and the whole mountain[b] trembled violently. [19] The blare of the horn grew louder and louder. As Moses spoke, God answered him in thunder. [20] The LORD came down upon Mount Sinai, on the top of the mountain, and the LORD called Moses to the top of the mountain and Moses went up. [21] The LORD said to Moses, "Go down, warn the people not to break through to the LORD to gaze, lest many of them perish. [22] The priests also, who come near the LORD, must stay pure, lest the LORD break out against them." [23] But Moses said to the LORD, "The people cannot come up to Mount Sinai, for You warned us saying, 'Set bounds about the mountain and sanctify it.' " [24] So the LORD said to him, "Go down, and come back together with Aaron; but let not the priests or the people

a-a Meaning of Heb. uncertain.
b Some Hebrew manuscripts and the Greek read "all the people"; cf. v. 16.

structions in vv. 10–13, infers that not regarding women as part of the active community reflects Moses' own, male-centered, viewpoint, not God's. For a more inclusive view of women, see Deut. 29.10; 31.12. **16:** *Thunder . . . lightning . . . dense cloud . . . :* The arrival of God (v. 18) is heralded by these awesome forces of nature serving like a king's outrunners (2 Sam. 15.1; 1 Kings 1.5) and by a *loud blast of the horn.* See also 1 Kings 19.11–13; Hab. 3.3–5; Pss. 18.8–16; 68.9–10. Outside the Bible these phenomena also appear in theophanies, particularly of storm gods. In Israelite tradition, although the LORD is no mere storm god, these motifs were taken over to describe the overwhelming power and majesty of the direct experience of the divine. **18:** *The LORD had come down upon it in fire,* see 3.2 n. *Like the smoke of a kiln,* cf. Gen. 19.28. **19:** *As Moses spoke, God answered him:* The Heb verbs are iterative, indicating that Moses kept speaking and God kept answering him; what the people overheard was a dialogue. Its contents are not specified (it cannot be the dialogue of vv. 20–24 since Moses conveyed its contents to the people [v. 25], and it cannot be the Decalogue since that is a monologue; in the present context, however, the redactor may have believed it was one of those). *In thunder,* in a thunderous voice; cf. Pss. 18.14; 29.3–9; Job 40.9. **21–24:** Further instructions to prevent the people from encroaching and dying. **21:** *Lest many of them perish,* see 3.6 n.; 33.20; cf. Num. 4.20; 1 Sam. 6.19. **22:** Even the priests *who come near the LORD* when performing their sacrificial duties (28.43; Ezek. 44.13) *must stay pure,* or "purify themselves," like the rest of the people. Although priests will later have access to the sanctuary, at the theophany they are restricted like the rest of the people. *Break out,* strike them down; cf. 2 Sam. 6.8. **23:** *Sanctify it,* treat it like a sanctuary, by the restrictions specified above. **24:** *Come back together with Aaron:* The summit of the mountain, like the Holy of Holies, is ac-

mountain *shall be put to death,* like unauthorized persons who encroach upon the sanctuary (Num. 3.10, 38). **13:** Since violators become subject to death for touching the holy mountain (cf. Num. 4.15; 1 Chron. 13.10), they must be executed by methods that do not require touching them, lest they infect their executioners with its fatal holiness. *Shot,* by arrow. *When the ram's horn sounds a long blast, they may go up on the mountain:* It is never reported that this happened. The v. could mean that a final,

long blast of the trumpet will later indicate when God has left the mountain and it is safe for people to go up; alternately, it reflects a different tradition that did not believe that contact with the mountain was deadly. **15:** *Do not go near a woman:* Sexual relations produce ritual impurity, which disqualifies one from entering the sanctuary (Lev. 15.18; 1 Sam. 21.5–6). Some modern Jewish feminist exegesis, noting that this clause is clearly addressed to the men only and that it was not part of God's in-break through to come up to the LORD, lest He break out against them." [25] And Moses went down to the people and spoke to them.

20 God spoke all these words,[a] saying: [2] I the LORD am your God who brought you out of the land of Egypt, the house of bondage: [3] You shall have no other gods besides Me.

[4] You shall not make for yourself a sculptured image, or

a Tradition varies as to the division of the Commandments in vv. 2–14, and as to the numbering of the verses from 13 on.

cessible only to Moses (25.22; 26.33; Lev. 16.3). **25:** *Spoke to them:* He told them what God had said in vv. 21–24.

20.1–14: The Decalogue. The Decalogue, Heb "'aseret hadevarim," lit. "ten words," i.e., "statements" (see 34.28; Deut. 4.13; 10.4) is the initial stipulation of the covenant. ("Decalogue," from the Latin for "ten words," or "ten statements," is a more literal rendition of Heb than "Ten Commandments.") They are addressed directly to the people. No punishments are stated; obedience is motivated not by fear of punishment but by God's absolute authority and the people's desire to live in accordance with His will. The belief that God is the author of the laws is a distinctive feature of biblical law. Elsewhere in the ancient Near East the laws were believed to be the product of human minds, particularly the king. While Mesopotamian kings claimed to have learned the principles of truth and justice from the gods, they themselves turned those principles into specific laws. Implicit in this biblical view is that God is Israel's king, hence its legislator. This elevated the status of law beyond matters of practicality and endowed it with sanctity. Obedience to law—civil no less than moral and ritual law—became a religious duty; obedience made one holy and crimes were sins, a flouting of God's authority. The items in the Decalogue are arranged in two groups. Duties to God come first. Each commandment in this group

contains the phrase, "the LORD your God." The second group contains duties toward fellow humans, which are depicted as being of equal concern to God. The first five are accompanied by explanatory comments or exhortations. The remaining five, as widely recognized ethical requirements, need no such support. Exod. 34.28 and Deut. 4.13 and 10.4 all refer to "Ten Commandments," but do not clarify how these should be divided to reach that number, and this issue was debated in antiquity, and continues to be disputed. The translation follows the view of Philo, Josephus, and some talmudic sources. The Decalogue is repeated in Deut. 5.6–17 with a few variations, especially in the Sabbath commandment. **1:** The addressee is not specified. The present sequence of the narrative suggests that it was the people, as stated in Deut. 5.4 and 19, but according to Deut. 5.5 and, possibly, Exod. 20.15–18, God spoke only to Moses, who later communicated His words to the people. Talmudic exegesis resolves the inconsistency by explaining that the people heard the first two commandments, in which God speaks in the first person, directly from God and the remainder, in which God is spoken of in the third person, via Moses (b. Mak. 24a). **2–3:** The first commandment. **2:** *I the LORD am your God:* This v. lacks an imperative verb and is not itself a commandment but an introduction to the entire Decalogue. The LORD identifies Himself by name to solemnly indicate that His author-

ity stands behind the following stipulations. His authority derives from His freeing Israel from bondage (cf. 19.4 n.). This v. also serves as the motive clause for the first commandment (v. 3), explaining that since the LORD alone freedIsrael from Egypt, He alone is Israel's God, and the worship of other gods is prohibited (cf. Judg. 6.8–10; Ps. 81.9–11). This is a central doctrine of biblical religion, which is based on the historical experience of the Israelites (see 19.4 n.). The logic is that of covenants, which establish an exclusive relationship: A subject population or king may have only one sovereign or suzerain, and ancient oaths of allegiance and treaties explicitly prohibit subjects and vassals from accepting another. As noted (19.4 n.), subjects entered into such relationships because of the past benefactions of the king or suzerain, such as delivering them from enemies. The covenant was thus an apt metaphor for Israel's exclusive relationship with YHVH because of the exodus. Although this v. lacks an imperative verb, and thus cannot be called a commandment, later Jewish tradition interpreted it as a command in itself requiring belief in God (Maimonides, *Hilkhot Yesodei Hatorah* 1:6; *Sefer Hamitsvot*, positive no. 1; Ramban) or belief that the LORD alone is God (Ibn Ezra). **3:** *You shall have no other gods:* This is not a theological statement denying the existence of other gods (such as Deut. 4.35–39) but a behavioral injunction ruling out worship of the other beings and objects known as gods (see 15.11 n.). This prohibition, banning the worship of all but one deity, was unique. Polytheism was inherently tolerant of the worship of many gods since no single god was believed to control all the phenomena of nature that are vital to human life. *Besides Me,* in addition to Me. Israelites tempted to worship other gods would not abandon the LORD but would worship others in addition to Him **4–6:** The second commandment. **4:** *A sculptured image:* Only images made for any likeness of what is in the heavens above, or on the earth below, or in the waters under the earth. [5] You shall not bow down to them or serve them. For I the LORD your God am an impassioned God, visiting the guilt of the parents upon the children, upon the third and upon the fourth generations of those who reject Me, [6] but showing kindness to the thousandth generation of those who love Me and keep My commandments.

[7] You shall not ªswear falsely byª the name of the LORD your God; for the LORD will not clear one who swears falsely by His name.

[8] Remember the sabbath day and keep it holy. [9] Six days

a-a Others "take in vain."

worship (v. 5) are prohibited. Non-idolatrous statues of certain creatures were permitted, such as the cherubs (Exod. 25.18–20) and the oxen supporting the water tank in Solomon's Temple (1 Kings 7.25); see also Num. 21.8–9. *What is in the heavens above,* such as birds (Deut. 4.17), the sun, moon, and stars, or other members of God's heavenly retinue (see 15.11 n.). Not even an idol of the LORD is permitted. *On the earth below,* such as animals (Deut. 4.17–18a) or sacred trees (Exod. 34.13). *In the waters under the earth,* i.e., in oceans, lakes, and rivers. The surface of the earth is conceived as standing or floating on a huge body of water which surrounds it in the form of oceans and breaks through to the earth's surface in the form of lakes, springs, and rivers. For the reasons for this commandment, see vv. 19–20; Deut. 4.9–18. **5:** *An impassioned God:* This is a warning against provoking God's jealous indignation—the rage felt by one whose prerogatives are given to another (cf. Isa. 42.8; 48.11). God's reaction reflects His emotional tie with Israel, described metaphorically by the prophets as a marital bond (see 6.7 n.). Hence, worship of other gods is as repugnant as adultery (34.15–16; Ezek. ch 16) and God's response, like that of an aggrieved husband, is jealousy (see the use of this term ["k-n-ʾ"] in Prov. 6.34). In the biblical view, this is an aspect of His passionate involvement with human beings

and no more a character flaw than is human jealousy over marital infidelity. But postbiblical commentators found the implications of divine jealousy troubling, and Maimonides interpreted the term as merely an anthropomorphism based on the necessity of borrowing terms from human experience to describe God based on His actions: "[In reality, His punitive actions] are in accordance with the guilt of those who are to be punished, and not the result of any emotion; for He is above all defect!" (*Guide of the Perplexed,* 1.54). *Visiting the guilt of the parents upon the children:* God does not punish the idolater alone, but his descendants as well, just as He rewards descendants for their ancestors' loyalty and obedience. This view of divine retribution as extending to descendants corresponds to the concept of family solidarity in ancient societies, especially those with a tribal background, like Israel. It is stated most starkly in 34.7 and Num. 14.18. Here, the phrases *of those who reject Me* and *of those who love Me* (v. 6) modify it to indicate that God punishes or rewards descendants for ancestral sins and virtues only if they act as their ancestors did. For further, outright rejection of transgenerational retribution, see Deut. 24.16; Jer. 31.29–30; Ezek. 18.1–20. *Upon the third and . . . fourth generations:* That is, upon grandchildren and great-grandchildren—the descendants the guilty are likely to see in

their own lifetimes. This indicates that the punishment of descendants is intended as a deterrent to, and punishment of, their ancestors, not a transfer of guilt to the descendants in their own right. *Those who reject Me:* A polytheistic Israelite would not literally reject the LORD but would worship Him together with other gods or, at worst, ignore Him, but since He demands total fidelity, worshipping another god alongside Him is tantamount to rejection. **6:** *Showing kindness,* better, "keeping faith" or "dealing faithfully." On Heb "ḥesed" see 15.13 n. This v. assures Israel, which is covenanted to God, that He will faithfully reciprocate its devotion and obedience. *To the thousandth generation,* infinitely. God's favor far exceeds His wrath, which extends only to the third and fourth generation. *Those who love Me,* those who are loyal to Me. In biblical Heb, "love" includes the loyalty of allies and of a vassal toward his suzerain (1 Sam. 18.1, 3; 20.17; 1 Kings 5.15). **7:** The third commandment. *Swear falsely by the name of the LORD:* Assertions in court, in public affairs, and even in ordinary conversation were often backed up with conditional self-curses that would take effect if the swearer's assertion were false or his promise unfulfilled. Typical formulations were: "By the life of the LORD, I will (or will not) . . . ," or, "May the LORD do such and such to me if I did (or if I didn't) . . ." The swearer proved his sincerity by invoking punishment from God, who cannot be deceived or evaded. A false oath would show contempt for God by implying that the swearer does not fear His punishment. Cf. Lev. 19.12. *Will not clear,* will not leave unpunished. **8–11:** The fourth commandment. The first three prohibit acts of disrespect for God; this requires a positive act of honoring Him. This is the longest commandment in the Decalogue, indicating the sabbath's importance as one of the quintessential expressions of loyalty to God. **8:** *Sabbath,* See 16.23 n. *Keep it holy,* withdraw it from common use (by you shall labor and do all your work, ¹⁰but the seventh day is a sabbath of the LORD your God: you shall not do any work—you, your son or daughter, your male or female slave, or your cattle, or the stranger who is within your settlements. ¹¹For in six days the LORD made heaven and earth and sea, and all that is in them, and He rested on the seventh day; therefore the LORD blessed the sabbath day and hallowed it.

¹²Honor your father and your mother, that you may long endure on the land that the LORD your God is assigning to you.

¹³You shall not murder.

You shall not commit adultery.

You shall not steal.

You shall not bear false witness against your neighbor.

¹⁴You shall not covet your neighbor's house: you shall not covet your neighbor's wife, or his male or female slave, or his ox or his ass, or anything that is your neighbor's.

desisting from labor [v. 10]) and reserve it for a special purpose associated with God. Dedication to God was expressed by visits to sanctuaries and prophets (2 Kings 4.23; Isa. 1.13; 66.23), by special sacrifices and other activities in the Temple (Num. 28.9–10; Lev. 24.8), by the recitation of a special psalm for the day (Ps. 92), and by a joyous atmosphere (Hos. 2.13; Isa. 58.13; Lam. 2.6). **10:** *A sabbath of the LORD your God:* Since He observes the Sabbath (Gen. 2.2; Exod. 16.21–30) it must be used for His purposes, not one's own (cf. Isa. 58.13). *You shall not do any work,* defined by various biblical passages to include gathering food and fuel, kindling fire, agriculture, and business activities (16.23–30; 34.21; 35.3; Num. 15.32–36; Amos 8.5; Jer. 17.21–22; Neh. 13.15–21). The Rabbis defined more precisely what kinds of work fell under this prohibition, identifying thirty-nine categories (e.g., weaving, hammering, writing) based on the inference that the activities performed in constructing the Tabernacle—forbidden on the Sabbath—exemplified the definition of "work" (Exod. 31.13–17; 35.2; *m. Shab.* 7.2; *b. Shab.* 49b). *Your male or female slave:* This one day a week the ser-

vant is treated as the master's equal. *The stranger,* the resident alien (12.19 n., 43 n.). Cf. 23.12. The text reads lit. "your stranger," which implies that the resident alien was, at least in some cases, dependent on a specific individual. **11:** Keeping the Sabbath holy honors God by emulating His actions at the time of creation (Gen. 2.1–3; cf. Exod. 21.17). In place of this explanation of the origin of the Sabbath, the Decalogue in Deuteronomy states its purpose of providing rest to servants and cites the exodus as the reason for observing it (Deut. 5.14–15). **12:** The fifth commandment. Honoring one's parents is a counterpart to the honor due God; it forms a bridge between duties toward God and toward humans. *Honor:* One aspect of this duty is respect, which includes obedience and forbids hitting, insulting and behaving disrespectfully toward them, and misappropriating their property (21.15, 17; Lev. 20.9; Deut. 27.16; Prov. 30.17). Another is caring for them when they are infirm, as recognized in the Talmud: "What is honoring? Providing them food and drink, clothing and covers, and taking them in and out" (*b. Kid.* 31b). *That you may long*

endure on the land: This does not refer to personal longevity. Ancient Near Eastern legal documents make children's right to inherit their parents' property contingent on honoring them by providing and caring for them. Here God applies this condition on a national scale: The right of future generations of Israelites to inherit the land of Israel from their parents is contingent upon honoring them. **13:** The sixth through tenth commandments. *You shall not murder:* This refers to illicit killing. The King James Version's "thou shalt not kill" is too broad; it implies that even capital punishment and war are prohibited, whereas the Torah sometimes mandates these. *You shall not commit adultery:* In the Bible this refers to voluntary sexual relations between a married or engaged woman and a man other than her husband. It did not refer to the extramarital relations of a married man (in polygamous societies a wife might share her husband with other wives and did not have an exclusive right to him). The Torah views adultery as a sin against God (Gen. 20.6; 39.9; cf. Ps. 51.6; Prov. 2.7) and a capital crime (Lev. 20.10; Deut. 22.22–27). *You shall not steal:* Although *b. Sanh.* 86a, followed by some modern scholars, holds that this refers to stealing of persons, i.e. kidnapping (21.16), the plain sense is, as Ibn Ezra recognized, that the commandment refers to theft. *You shall not bear false witness:* This covers both false accusation and false testimony in court. False accusation is a means of depriving one's fellow of what belongs to him, as when the accuser falsely claims ownership of something in another's possession and the accused cannot disprove it (cf. 22.8). The penalty for false testimony is described in Deut. 19.16–21. **14:** *You shall not covet:* Some view this as an ethical exhortation to master the kinds of impulses that would lead to violation of the preceding commandments, but the Heb verb sometimes refers to having designs on a desired object, perhaps even to scheming or ma-

15 All the people witnessed the thunder and lightning, the blare of the horn and the mountain smoking; and when the people saw it, they fell back and stood at a distance. 16 "You speak to us," they said to Moses, "and we will obey; but let not God speak to us, lest we die." 17 Moses answered the people, "Be not afraid; for God has come only in order to test you, and in order that the fear of Him may be ever with you, so that you do not go astray." 18 So the people remained at a distance, while Moses approached the thick cloud where God was.

19 The LORD said to Moses:
Thus shall you say to the Israelites: You yourselves saw

neuvering to acquire it (see especially 34.24). Hence, the sense could be "do not scheme to acquire. . . ." *Your neighbor's house:* that is, "household," which the second clause explicates as consisting of wife, servants, and livestock. In Deut. 5.18, which places the wife in the first clause and house, field, servants, and cattle in the second, "house" means dwelling. The wording in Exodus reflects conditions when the Israelites lived as nomadic herders without real estate (Gen. 12.5, 16; 26.14; Num. 16.30, 32; Deut. 11.6); Deut. refers to the kinds of property people will own after settlement in Canaan.

20.15–18: The people's response to the theophany. 15: Since the people do not refer to God's words but only to *the thunder and lightning,* etc. (cf. 19.16–19), Ramban infers that this scene took place before God spoke the Decalogue. **16:** Moses' office and authority as prophet are now made permanent at the people's request (cf. Deut. 5.19–28; 18.15–19). The circumstances explain why God continued to communicate to Israel through prophets rather than directly. *You speak to us,* anything further that God says. If this scene preceded the Decalogue, the people (who already know that God will proclaim laws [19.5]) mean that Moses should hear the Decalogue by himself and convey it to them. *Lest we die:* They fear that

auditory contact with God may be as lethal as visual contact (3.6 n.; 19.21 n.). **17:** *In order to test you:* It is not clear what is tested. Another possible translation is "to give you an experience (of Him)" (M. Greenberg), meaning that the theophany would give the people a vivid, sensory experience of God. This interpretation fits the rest of the v., *That the fear of Him may be ever with you, so that you do not go astray,* namely the experience would instill "fear of God," a deterrent to sin (1.17 n.; cf. Deut. 5.26). **18:** *Moses approached the thick cloud where God was:* to hear either the Decalogue or further instructions (20.19–23.33), depending on when this scene took place.

20.19–23.33: The Book of the Covenant (or Covenant Code or Collection) lays out the terms of the covenant in detail, beginning with a law about idolatry and proper worship (20.19–23), followed by a series of civil and criminal laws (21.1–22.16) and then a collection of ethical and religious exhortations concluding with further laws about worship (22.17–23.19), and an epilogue containing promises of reward for fidelity and warnings about idolatry (23.20–33). These laws may reflect a settled society of farmers and herders in premonarchic times (since the highest official of whom they are aware is the chieftain, not the king; 22.27 n.). Like the laws of

the Torah as a whole, they are not a complete, systematic code. Practical details of how to apply the law are rarely spelled out, and areas such as commerce, real estate, marriage, inheritance, and government are mentioned barely or not at all. Apparently only part of the existing laws have been selected, perhaps to illustrate certain ideal principles of justice and religion. Other areas and details of enforcement must have been governed by the oral law, courts, and administrative agencies. These details became the subject of the Oral Torah in rabbinic times, embodied in the Mishnah, Talmud, and halakhic midrashim. The Book of the Covenant (for this term, see Exod. 24.7, translated "the record of the covenant") constitutes the first of four major collections of law in the Torah. The others (in addition to the brief variant of the Book of the Covenant in 34.11–26) are the Priestly laws (primarily Exod. chs 25–40, most of Leviticus, and the laws in Numbers), the Holiness Collection (Lev. chs 17–26), and the Deuteronomic laws (Deut. 11.31–28.69). Unlike most narratives, the law collections were not blended by a redactor into a single, integrated whole but were left separate. The resolution of their discrepancies is a fundamental feature of rabbinic exegesis.

20.19–23: The altar. All of the Torah's law collections begin with laws contrasting forbidden, pagan means of worship with permitted ones at a proper place of worship (see also chs 25–31 in contrast to Exod. 32 [see introductory comment to 31.18–32.35]; Lev. ch 17; Deut. ch 12). **19–21:** Since Israel has seen that God communicates with them directly from heaven without the use of idols (which idolaters use to draw the gods close), they should not make idols to secure His presence and blessing but instead build Him an altar, offer sacrifices, and invoke His name. Cf. the similar argument in Deut. 4.9–18. **19:** *I spoke to you from the very heavens:* This v. (probably from E, which distances God from that I spoke to you from the very heavens: ²⁰ With Me, therefore, you shall not make any gods of silver, nor shall you make for yourselves any gods of gold. ²¹ Make for Me an altar of earth and sacrifice on it your burnt offerings and your sacrifices of well-being,ᵃ your sheep and your oxen; in every place where I cause My name to be mentioned I will come to you and bless you. ²² And if you make for Me an altar of stones, do not build it of hewn stones; for by wielding your tool upon them you have profaned them. ²³ Do not ascend My altar by steps, that your nakedness may not be exposed upon it.

MISHPATIM　　　　　　　　　　　　　משפטים

21 These are the rules that you shall set before them: ² When you acquire a Hebrew slave, he shall serve six years; in the seventh year he shall go free, without payment. ³ If he came single, he shall leave single; if he had a wife, his wife shall leave with him. ⁴ If his master gave

---

a Others "peace-offering." Meaning of shelamin uncertain.

---

human beings and avoids anthropomorphism) contradicts ch 19, according to which God came down onto Mount Sinai (19.3, 9, 11, 18, 20, 21, from J). The midrash reconciled the contradiction by inferring from Deut. 4.36 that God spoke from heaven and only the fire and His power were on earth; another view is that He lowered the heavens to the top of Mount Sinai (Mek. Baḥodesh 9; Rashi). **20:** *With Me, therefore, you shall not make any gods of silver, nor shall you make for yourselves any gods of gold,* to draw God close and secure His blessings (v. 21b). Idolatry assumes that the deity is somehow present in (though not limited to) its image and available to bless its worshippers. Israel is to eschew such means and instead follow the instructions in the next v. **21:** *In every place:* This law permits numerous places of sacrifice (Maimonides, *Sefer Hamitzvot,* positive commandment no. 20); contrast the later restriction of sacrifice to a single site in Deut. ch 12. *Where I cause My name to be mentioned:* The Heb is problematic; the original reading was probably "In every place where you invoke My name," as implied by the Peshitta,

Targum Neofiti, and the *Fragmentary Targum.* Invoking God's name refers to calling upon Him in worship. *I will come to you and bless you:* Altars, instead of idols, will serve as the locus and symbol of God's presence, as does the altar in 24.4–8. **22:** *And if you make for Me an altar of stones:* An exception to the requirement that the altar be made of earth (v. 21); perhaps the clause has in mind locations where the soil is sandy and cannot be packed firmly, but stones are available. *Do not build it of hewn stones; for by wielding your tool upon them you have profaned them:* The stones must be in their natural state, uncut. Cf. Deut. 27.5–6. The reason for the prohibition is uncertain. The Mishnah explains that "iron was created to shorten man's days [through its use in weapons], while the altar was created to lengthen man's days [by means of sacrifice]: what shortens may not rightly be lifted up against what lengthens" (*m. Mid.* 3:4). Rashbam suggests that the prohibition on cutting the stones is to preclude the temptation to carve images on them. **23:** *Do not ascend My altar by steps, that your nakedness may not be exposed upon it:* The altar must ei-

ther be low or, if built on a platform, have a ramp rather than stairs to climb onto it, lest one's private parts be exposed beneath the skirtlike garments that were worn. According to later Priestly legislation, when the Tabernacle was built, the priests were required to wear undergarments for this reason (28.42).

21.1–22.16: Civil and criminal laws to establish a just society, the purpose for which, according to Gen. 18.19, God chose Abraham and his descendants. The Torah's strong emphasis on law led to the important place that law and its study have in Judaism. The casuistic formulation of these laws ("if / when x happens, [then] y shall happen") is typical of all the ancient Near Eastern legal collections, and several laws are notably similar to their counterparts in those collections and later Arabic law, but they also display uniquely Israelite values, as in the treatment of murder and crimes against property and the concern for slaves and strangers. **21.1:** Teaching the laws to the entire people is practically unparalleled in the ancient world. See further, "Exodus and the Jewish Tradition" in intro. to Exodus. **2–6:** Manumission of indentured servants. Biblical law deals with two types of bondsmen: Israelite ("Hebrew"; see 1.15 n.) slaves, who are really indentured servants, and full slaves. Hebrew slaves (v. 2) must be freed after six years; full, lifelong slavery is in principle limited to foreigners (Deut. 15.12–18; Lev. 25.39–55). Both types were domestic slaves living in their owners' homes (see 12.44 n.), not members of slave gangs working on plantations. Biblical law and ethical teachings require humane treatment of slaves, based on the shared humanity of master and servant (Job 31.13–15) and the Israelites' own experience as slaves (Deut. 5.15; 15.15; 16.12; 24.18, 22). *When you acquire a Hebrew slave:* An indigent Israelite might indenture himself or a member of his household to obtain support him a wife, and she has borne him children, the wife and her children shall belong to the master, and he shall leave alone. [5] But if the slave declares, "I love my master, and my wife and children: I do not wish to go free," [6] his master shall take him before God.[a] He shall be brought to the door or the doorpost, and his master shall pierce his ear with an awl; and he shall then remain his slave for life.

[7] When a man sells his daughter as a slave, she shall not be freed as male slaves are. [8] If she proves to be displeasing to her master, who designated her for himself, he must let her be redeemed; he shall not have the right to sell her to outsiders, since he broke faith with her. [9] And if he designated her for his son, he shall deal with her as is the practice with free maidens. [10] If he marries another, he must not withhold from this one her food, her clothing, or her conjugal rights.[b] [11] If he fails her in these three ways, she shall go free, without payment.

[12] He who fatally strikes a man shall be put to death. [13] If he did not do it by design, but it came about by an act of God, I will assign you a place to which he can flee.

[14] When a man schemes against another and kills him treacherously, you shall take him from My very altar to be put to death.

[15] He who strikes his father or his mother shall be put to death.

---

a Others "to the judges."   b Or "ointments."

(see Lev. 25.39, 47), and a convicted thief who could not make restitution would be sold to raise the money to pay it (Exod. 22.2). Debtors and members of their households might also be seized to work off defaulted loans (2 Kings 4.1; Neh. 5.1–6); it is questionable whether the Torah permits this, but in any case the present law would have the effect of limiting debt servitude. *In the seventh year he shall go free,* so, too, Deut. 15.12. According to the Babylonian laws of Hammurabi (par. 117; in M. Roth, *Law Collections from Mesopotamia and Asia Minor,* p. 103 = *Context of Scripture* 2, p. 343), debt servants went free after three years. Lev. 25.10, 40–41 prescribe an entirely different system: All Hebrew slaves go free simultaneously in the jubilee year no matter how long they have served. **5:** The servant might become attached to his master or the family he has established in the master's household, or consider security in subservience preferable to the financial risks of independence. **6:** *Before God . . . to the door or the doorpost,* either at a sanctuary near the master's home or before some symbol of God kept at the master's door. *Pierce his ear:* This may symbolize the servant's obligation to have his ear permanently open to hear his master's orders or (see Deut. 15.17) permanent attachment to the master's house. The midrash saw the ceremony as symbolic: The ear, which heard God say that Israelites are His servants and may not be sold into permanent servitude (Lev. 25.42), is punished for electing to remain a servant to a human master (*b. Kid.* 22b). *For life:* According to halakhic interpretation, for the rest of the master's life, unless a jubilee year (Lev. ch 25) comes first; even if the servant chooses to remain with the master, he does not remain beyond the jubilee (*Mekhilta,* Nezikin 2). This reconciles Exod. ch 21 with Lev. ch 25. **7–11:** According to Deut. 15.12–18, females sold into slavery go free, like males, after six years. The present law deals with a special case, that of a father selling his minor daughter for the purpose of marriage or concubinage in the purchaser's family. (Similar arrangements are known from the ancient Near East, where a poor father might arrange for his daughter's adoption by a well-to-do family in order to ensure a marriage for her.) Since the sale is for marriage, it is not terminated after six years, but the purchaser must meet certain conditions. If he reneges on these conditions (either those of v. 10 or those of vv. 8–10), she goes free. *Conjugal rights,* or "ointments," or "lodging." **12–32:** Crimes against persons. **12–14:** Capital punishment for murder. Unlike ancient Near Eastern and Arabic law, the Bible does not permit compensation of the victim's family for economic loss instead of capital punishment (Num. 35.31). Human life is sacred and beyond economic value, according to Gen. 1.26; 9.6 because of man's creation in the divine image. **13–14:** In tribal societies lacking strong central authority the kinship group is the primary defender of its members. When a person is killed a kinsman is obliged to "redeem" the blood by slaying the killer (2 Sam. 3.27–30). Such "blood-vengeance" was originally exacted even if the killing was accidental. This v. limits it to deliberate murder and allows the accidental killer to seek refuge from the victim's kin at an altar or perhaps other places of sanctuary until a court can determine whether he acted intentionally (see the development of this idea in Num. 35.9–34; Deut. 19.1–13; Josh. ch 20). Originally in the ancient world the innocent and guilty alike could claim sanctuary; this v. subjects the institution to a moral criterion. **15:** Obedience toward parents is considered the

16 He who kidnaps a man—whether he has sold him or is still holding him—shall be put to death.

17 He who insults[a] his father or his mother shall be put to death.

18 When men quarrel and one strikes the other with stone or fist, and he does not die but has to take to his bed—19 if he then gets up and walks outdoors upon his staff, the assailant shall go unpunished, except that he must pay for his idleness and his cure.

20 When a man strikes his slave, male or female, with a rod, and he dies there and then,[b] he must be avenged. 21 But if he survives a day or two, he is not to be avenged, since he is the other's property.

22 When men fight, and one of them pushes a pregnant woman and a miscarriage results, but no other damage ensues, the one responsible[c] shall be fined according as the woman's husband may exact from him, the payment to be based on reckoning.[d] 23 But if other damage ensues, the penalty shall be life for life, 24 eye for eye, tooth for tooth, hand for hand, foot for foot, 25 burn for burn, wound for wound, bruise for bruise.

26 When a man strikes the eye of his slave, male or female, and destroys it, he shall let him go free on account of his eye. 27 If he knocks out the tooth of his slave, male or female, he shall let him go free on account of his tooth.

28 When an ox gores a man or a woman to death, the ox

---

a Or "reviles."   b Lit. "under his hand."
c Heb. "he."   d Others "as the judges determine."

---

cornerstone of all order and authority, especially in a tribal, patriarchal society like ancient Israel. In the Laws of Hammurabi (par. 195; in Roth, *Law Collections*, p. 120 = *Context*, p. 348) a son who strikes his father is punished by cutting off his hand. The biblical law applies to both parents. The death penalty suggests that the Bible regards this crime as posing a severe danger to society. **16:** The primary purpose of kidnapping was to enslave the victim. See also Deut. 24.7, where some details differ. **17:** *Insults:* The Heb verb (lit. "treat lightly") has a wide range of meanings from "disrespect" to "revile, treat contemptuously, curse." The death penalty may be meant only rhetorically as a deterrent (cf. Deut. 21.18–21), though if the verb means "curse" it may be meant literally because of the potentially serious consequences that cursing was thought to entail. **18–19:** This law and the next provide a rule of thumb for assessing the killer's motive: immediate death from a fight or disciplinary beating is presumptive evidence of murderous intent and calls for capital punishment, but death following temporary recovery, and a lingering death, are not. *Idleness,* income lost during convalescence. *Cure:* From this clause the Rabbis determined that the Bible permits medical care and people should not refuse it on the grounds that their injury or illness is the will of God and that the cure must come from Him alone (*b. B. K.* 85a, Rashi and tosafot). **20–21:** This law and vv. 26–27 protect slaves from extreme corporal punishment. They do not distinguish between Hebrew slaves and others. **21:** *Since he is the other's property:* That is, the slave is the master's property. This means either that the master was within his rights to punish the slave corporally, or that (in addition to the slave's lingering death) his investment in the slave makes it unlikely that he would have intentionally killed him. **22:** *Other damage* to the woman. *Based on reckoning:* perhaps reckoning the age of the fetus, but both this translation and the alternative "as the judges determine" are questionable. Halakhic exegesis infers that, since the punishment is monetary rather than execution, the unborn fetus is not considered a living person and feticide is not murder (cf. 12–14 n.); hence, abortion is permitted when necessary to save the mother (Rashi and Yad Ramah to *b. Sanh.* 72b; see also Gen. 9.5–6 n.). **23–25:** *Life for life, eye for eye:* This is the "lex talionis," measure-for-measure punishment by which the law strives to make punishment for death or injury fit the crime perfectly. See Deut. 19.21 and esp. Lev. 24.17–21. It may not be an obligatory requirement (Num. 35.31 implies that for injuries other than death an indemnity could be accepted instead; Josephus, *Ant.* 4.280) but a limitation of vengeance: It may not exceed the original injury (contrast Gen. 4.23). Talmudic loose construction of the law considered the equitable application of talion impossible and inferred that it requires the assailant to pay damages corresponding to the severity of the injury (*m. B. K.* 8.1; *b. B. K.* 83b–84a). In Mesopotamia, perpetrators were originally required to pay monetary indemnities; later, talion was imposed when the victim was a member of the upper class. Biblical law is the same for all classes. **28–32:** These laws have especially close parallels in Babylonian law (Laws of Eshnunna, pars. 53–55; Laws of Hammurabi pars. 250–252; in Roth, *Law Collections*, pp. 67, 128 = *Context of Scripture* 2, pp. 335, 350), suggesting that the Bible might have bor-shall be stoned and its flesh shall not be eaten, but the owner of the ox is not to be punished. ²⁹ If, however, that ox has been in the habit of goring, and its owner, though warned, has failed to guard it, and it kills a man or a woman—the ox shall be stoned and its owner, too, shall be put to death. ³⁰ If ransom is laid upon him, he must pay whatever is laid upon him to redeem his life. ³¹ So, too, if it gores a minor, male or female, [the owner] shall be dealt with according to the same rule. ³² But if the ox gores a slave, male or female, he shall pay thirty shekels of silver to the master, and the ox shall be stoned.

³³ When a man opens a pit, or digs a pit and does not cover it, and an ox or an ass falls into it, ³⁴ the one responsible for the pit must make restitution; he shall pay the price to the owner, but shall keep the dead animal.

³⁵ When a man's ox injures his neighbor's ox and it dies, they shall sell the live ox and divide its price; they shall also divide the dead animal. ³⁶ If, however, it is known that the ox was in the habit of goring, and its owner has failed to guard it, he must restore ox for ox, but shall keep the dead animal.

^{37a} When a man steals an ox or a sheep, and slaughters it or sells it, he shall pay five oxen for the ox, and four sheep **22** for the sheep.—¹ If the thief is seized while tunneling,^b and he is beaten to death, there is no bloodguilt in his case. ² If the sun has risen on him, there is bloodguilt in that case.—He^c must make restitution; if he lacks the means, he shall be sold for his theft. ³ But if what he stole—whether ox or ass or sheep—is found alive in his possession, he shall pay double.

a *This constitutes chap. 22.1 in some editions.*
b *I.e., under a wall for housebreaking.*   c *I.e., the thief of 21.37.*

and the stoning of the ox treats the slave's death like that of freemen (v. 28). Perhaps in this case the slave is a foreigner, and the master, acting in lieu of the slave's absent family, has agreed to accept a ransom as in v. 30. This case differs from v. 30 by setting a fixed amount for the ransom, perhaps because a slave has a market value (thirty silver shekels is the price of a slave in several documents from Nuzi).

21.33–22.16: Crimes against property. 21.34: *He . . . shall keep the dead animal,* which has some value. Thus the owner of the dead animal receives full restitution, but no more, and the person who dug the pit can recover some of his costs. **35–36:** If the goring was an unpredictable accident, both parties share in the loss, but if the owner of the goring ox was negligent, he must make full restitution. **37:** This law continues in 22.2b–3. It establishes the principle that a thief (whose action was direct, intentional, and intended for profit) owes the victim more than restitution. **22.1–2a:** These vv., set between hyphens, are a separate law, interposed here for an unknown reason. *There is no bloodguilt in his case,* i.e., if the circumstances are such that the homeowner has reason to fear for his or his family's life, such as where the thief is not visible to witnesses. But if he catches the thief in broad daylight, when the thief would presumably fear detection and not risk killing anybody, the homeowner is guilty of homicide. In the absence of danger to life, there is no right to kill a thief. **2b–3:** These vv. continue 21.37. *He shall be sold for his theft,* to raise funds to pay restitution and the fine. According to the Laws of Hammurabi, a thief who is unable to make restitution is executed (par. 8; in Roth, *Law Collections,* p. 82 = *Context* 2, p. 337). Mesopotamian law often prescribes death for property offenses (Laws of Hammurabi, pars. 6–13, 21–22; in Roth, *Law Collections,* pp. 82–85 = *Context* 2, pp. 337–38). Biblical law, which considers human life

rowed and revised them. **28:** *The ox shall be stoned:* Stoning, otherwise used only for humans, treats the ox as a criminal because it has killed a human (see Gen. 9.5). This and the avoidance of the ox's flesh express abhorrence at its taking of a human life. The owner is not punished because the accident was unpredictable. **29:** If the owner ignored warnings that the ox had previously gored, he is executed for criminal negligence. The penalties in these vv. are not paralleled in Babylonian law, where nothing is done to the ox and the owner is only required to pay damages. V. 30 permits this if the victim's

family agrees because his responsibility was only indirect and unintentional (contrast Num. 35.31). **31:** *According to the same rule* apparently means that if the ox kills somebody's child, it is still the owner who is executed and not his child (cf. Deut. 24.16), as would apparently have been done as a form of talion under Babylonian law (cf. Laws of Hammurabi pars. 209–210, 229–230; in Roth, *Law Collections,* pp. 122, 125 = *Context* 2, pp. 348, 349). **32:** The anomalous prescription of monetary compensation for killing a human being is puzzling since v. 20 prescribes capital punishment for killing a slave

⁴When a man lets his livestock loose to graze in another's land, and so allows a field or a vineyard to be grazed bare, he must make restitution for the impairment*a* of that field or vineyard.

⁵When a fire is started and spreads to thorns, so that stacked, standing, or growing*b* grain is consumed, he who started the fire must make restitution.

⁶When a man gives money or goods to another for safe-keeping, and they are stolen from the man's house—if the thief is caught, he shall pay double; ⁷if the thief is not caught, the owner of the house shall depose before God*c* that he has not laid hands on the other's property. ⁸In all charges of misappropriation—pertaining to an ox, an ass, a sheep, a garment, or any other loss, whereof one party alleges, "This is it"—the case of both parties shall come before God: he whom God declares guilty shall pay double to the other.

⁹When a man gives to another an ass, an ox, a sheep or any other animal to guard, and it dies or is injured or is carried off, with no witness about, ¹⁰an oath before the Lord shall decide between the two of them that the one has not laid hands on the property of the other; the owner must acquiesce, and no restitution shall be made. ¹¹But if [the animal] was stolen from him, he shall make restitution to its owner. ¹²If it was torn by beasts, he shall bring it as evidence; he need not replace what has been torn by beasts.

¹³When a man borrows [an animal] from another and it dies or is injured, its owner not being with it, he must make restitution. ¹⁴If its owner was with it, no restitution need be made; but if it was hired, he is entitled to the hire.

¹⁵If a man seduces a virgin for whom the bride-price has not been paid,*d* and lies with her, he must make her his

a Lit. "excellence."   b Lit. "field."   c See note on 21.6.
d So that she is unmarried; cf. Deut. 20.7; 22.23 ff.

them. **9–12:** (b) But if he was asked to keep cattle, which roam in the field, extra precautions are expected and if they are stolen (v. 11) he is held negligent and must pay for the loss. If, however, the loss was unpreventable, he may establish this by oath (v. 10) or by producing the carcass (v. 12; cf. Amos 3.12; Gen. 31.39). **13–14a:** (c) If the bailee borrowed an animal for his own use, since all the benefit is his, he assumes liability for whatever causes its death or injury unless its owner was with it, presumably because the owner would then be expected to protect it. **14b:** This may introduce a fourth case: (d) where the bailee has hired the animal and any damage to it is covered by the fee. The Talmud identifies these four types of bailee as the unpaid and paid guardians, the borrower and the hirer, and holds that their different degrees of liability depend on the benefit each receives or expects from the arrangement (*m. B. M.* 7.8 and Gemara). **8:** This covers the case when, in these or other circumstances, a man claims to have identified his possessions among another's (such as the bailee's); the matter is to be decided by an oracle, such as the Urim and Thummim (28.29–30; cf. Josh. 7.14–18; 1 Sam. 14.37–42). **9:** *Carried off,* captured in war or a raid, as distinct from being stolen. **10:** *An oath before the Lord:* The use of the Tetragrammaton suggests that this law was drawn from a different source than vv. 7–8, which use "God." **13:** *And it dies or is injured,* rather, "and it is injured and dies" or "and it is injured or dies." **15:** *For whom the bride-price has not been paid:* Betrothal normally consisted of paying a bride-price to a girl's father (Gen. 34.12; Deut. 20.7). Seduction of an unbetrothed virgin diminishes her chances of marriage and her father may never receive the bride-price (hence this law's inclusion with economic damages; if the girl is already betrothed the seduction counts as adultery, Deut. 22.23–27). Her seducer must make good on both losses. Contrast the case of rape, Deut. 22.28–29.

beyond economic value (vv. 12–14 n.), never does. **4–5:** Damaging another's field or crops. V. 4 continues the theme of theft. The owner of the livestock must make restitution, either by replacing the crop or by giving the owner another field. *For the impairment* [rather: "from the best part"] *of that field or vineyard:* Whatever the quality of the damaged field or crops, the damages are assessed as if they were of the highest quality. **5:** If a fire spreads accidentally, the one who started it must repay only the actual value of the loss.

6–14: When property is lost or damaged while in another's care, liability depends on the degree of responsibility implicitly assumed by the bailee. The comments below list the four main cases, followed by comments on other matters. **6–7:** (a) In the case of small movables deposited for safekeeping, since the bailee is expected simply to keep them in his house without taking precautions beyond those he takes with his own property, if they are stolen he may clear himself with an oath (20.7 n.) that he did not misappropriate wife by payment of a bride-price. [16] If her father refuses to give her to him, he must still weigh out silver in accordance with the bride-price for virgins.

[17] You shall not tolerate[a] a sorceress.

[18] Whoever lies with a beast shall be put to death.

[19] Whoever sacrifices to a god other than the LORD alone shall be proscribed.[b]

[20] You shall not wrong a stranger or oppress him, for you were strangers in the land of Egypt.

[21] You shall not ill-treat any widow or orphan. [22] If you do mistreat them, I will heed their outcry as soon as they cry out to Me, [23] and My anger shall blaze forth and I will put you to the sword, and your own wives shall become widows and your children orphans.

[24] If you lend money to My people, to the poor among you, do not act toward them as a creditor; exact no interest from them. [25] If you take your neighbor's garment in pledge, you must return it to him before the sun sets; [26] it is his only clothing, the sole covering for his skin. In what else shall he sleep? Therefore, if he cries out to Me, I will pay heed, for I am compassionate.

[27] You shall not revile God, nor put a curse upon a chieftain among your people.

[28] You shall not [c]put off the skimming of the first yield of your vats.[c] You shall give Me the first-born among your sons. [29] You shall do the same with your cattle and your flocks: seven days it[d] shall remain with its mother; on the eighth day you shall give it to Me.

---

a Lit. "let live."   b See Lev. 27.29.
c-c Meaning of Heb. uncertain.   d I.e., the male first-born.

22.17–23.19: Ethical and religious exhortations. 17: *Sorceress*, a practitioner of malevolent magic (usually a woman but males are banned in Deut. 18.10), which is punished severely because it was deemed dangerous and antisocial. The Bible does not deny the efficacy of magic, but bans it as rebellion against God (Deut. 18.9–15). **18:** See Lev. 18.23; 20.15–16; Deut. 27.21. **19:** *Proscribed*, executed. This law applies only to Israelites; only they are subject to the first commandment (Exod. 20.3) and punished for violating it. Cf. 18.11 n.; Deut. 4.19–20; 32.8–9. (The Canaanites are punished for abominable rituals, such as child sacrifice [Lev. 18.24–29; Deut 12.31; 20.18], not for idolatry per se.)

20–26: Resident aliens (12.19 n., 43 n.), the poor, widows, and orphans are often mentioned together because, lacking social or family protection, they are vulnerable to exploitation. The duty of treating these groups fairly and compassionately is reiterated frequently (e.g., 20.10; 23.6, 9, 12; Lev. 19.33–34; 23.22; Deut. 1.16; 10.18–19; 24.17–22; 27.19). Concern for foreigners, not found in other ancient Near Eastern law collections, grows out of Israel's consciousness of being foreigners in Egypt. **24:** Charitable loans to countrymen who have fallen on hard times. Lending to them is a moral obligation and must be done without further increasing the borrower's poverty by requir-

ing interest, which could be ruinous (rates of 20 to 50 percent were common in the ancient Near East). Loans to foreigners were not subject to this rule, since visiting foreigners were normally businessmen. If they borrowed, it was for business and not to survive poverty. **22:** *I will heed their outcry,* cf. v. 25. God is the ultimate patron of the powerless and He will punish those who mistreat them. This warning may imply that human government was not well equipped to protect their rights and that God was their only recourse. Cf. Deut. 24.13, 15. **23:** Measure-for-measure punishment, a very common principle in the Bible. **25–26:** *Take . . . in pledge,* rather, as noted by Rashi, "seize . . . as collateral." Creditors might legally seize property from defaulting debtors to induce them to repay. The poorest debtors might have nothing left but the cloaks they slept in (Amos 2.8; Job 22.6). In such circumstances, the present law subordinates the creditor's right to repayment to the welfare of the debtor. See also Deut. 24.6, 10–13, 17. *You must return it to him before the sun sets* each day, to sleep in, and he will return it to you in the morning. **27:** *Revile,* cf. Lev. 24.10–16; Job 2.9. *Chieftain,* of a clan or tribe, the highest human authority prior to the monarchy. The two offenses covered by this v. are mentioned together in 1 Kings 21.10, 13, where "chieftain" is reasonably construed as applying to the king and the law is (falsely) enforced. **28–29:** The first fruits of the soil and first-born animals (13.2) must be given to God, thereby acknowledging Him as the source of the land's fertility and the true owner of its produce. **28:** The uncertain nouns refer to the first wine and oil, and possibly to the first grain as well (see also Num. 18.27; Deut. 22.9). *Give Me the first-born among your sons,* see 13.2, 12–13. Here no provision for redemption is mentioned. **29:** On first-born animals, see 13.2, 12–13. This is a humane law, respecting the mother-child relationship among animals. See also 23.19;

30 You shall be holy people to Me: you must not eat flesh torn by beasts in the field; you shall cast it to the dogs.

23 You must not carry false rumors; you shall not join hands with the guilty to act as a malicious witness: 2 You shall neither side with the mighty[a] to do wrong—you shall not give perverse testimony in a dispute so as to pervert it in favor of the mighty[a]—3 nor shall you show deference to a poor man in his dispute.

4 When you encounter your enemy's ox or ass wandering, you must take it back to him.

5 When you see the ass of your enemy lying under its burden and would refrain from raising[b] it, you must nevertheless raise it with him.

6 You shall not subvert the rights of your needy in their disputes. 7 Keep far from a false charge; do not bring death on those who are innocent and in the right, for I will not acquit the wrongdoer. 8 Do not take bribes, for bribes blind the clear-sighted and upset the pleas of those who are in the right.

9 You shall not oppress a stranger, for you know the feelings of the stranger, having yourselves been strangers in the land of Egypt.

10 Six years you shall sow your land and gather in its yield; 11 but in the seventh you shall let it rest and lie fallow. Let the needy among your people eat of it, and what they leave let the wild beasts eat. You shall do the same with your vineyards and your olive groves.

a Others "multitude."
b For this use of the verb ʿzb, cf. Neh. 3.8, 34. For the whole verse see Deut. 22.4.

Lev. 22.27–28; Deut. 22.6–7. **30:** *You shall be holy people to me:* The prohibition of eating torn flesh, and the related one in Deut. 14.21, are addressed to priests in Lev. 22.8 and Ezek. 44.31. The present v. requires all Israelites to maintain a quasi-priestly level of holiness (cf. Lev. 19.2). *You must not eat flesh torn by beasts:* Only properly slaughtered animals may be eaten by Israelites. The word for "torn" (Heb "terefah") is the source of the postbiblical Heb term "taref" (in English [from Yiddish] "treif"), referring to any animal or food that does not conform to the Jewish dietary laws. Food that does conform is termed in postbiblical Heb "kasher," "fit," "proper" ("kosher" in Yiddish and English); the sys-

tem of dietary laws as a whole is called "kashrut."

23.1–3: These vv. and vv. 6–8 concern judicial procedures. **1:** Cf. 20.13; Lev. 19.11, 16; Deut. 19.15–21. **2:** *So as to pervert it in favor of the mighty:* The ambiguity of the Heb permitted this to be construed as a separate, positive command meaning "follow the majority" in determining the law. As a jurisprudential principle this meant that, in general, judicial rulings and legal questions are be decided not simply by invoking the literal interpretation of the Torah nor by invoking new revelations, but by flexible interpretation (loose construction) of the Torah, based on the circumstances, as de-

termined by a majority of competent sages (b. Ḥul. 11a; y. Sanh. 4:2, p. 22a). **3:** This v. and Lev. 19.15 presume that the Bible's concern for the poor will be internalized, and warn against taking it to an unjust extreme: It is wrong to favor the powerful in a trial, and also wrong to favor the poor. **4–5:** One must assist others facing difficulty or possible economic loss (Deut. 22.1–4), even a personal enemy. **4:** *Ox or ass,* the usual beasts of burden; according to the halakhah the obligation applies to any animal (m. B. K. 5.7; b. B. K. 54b). *Wandering:* Since much of the population was engaged in herding and animals were used for transport, it was common to come upon strays (cf. 1 Sam. 9.3, 20). **5:** A pack animal might collapse or lose its balance under its load. The fastest way to raise it was for two people to lift the load simultaneously, one on each side of the animal. Talmudic sages hold that this commandment is meant to benefit the animal as well as its owner, citing it as the basis of the obligation to prevent animals from suffering (called "tzaʿar baʿalei ḥayim") (b. B. M. 32a-b). **6–9:** Another group of exhortations concerning the weak (cf. 22.20–26). **6:** You must not rule unfairly against the poor in a trial. **7:** *The wrongdoer,* the judge or witness who causes the death of the innocent. **8:** *Bribes,* lit. "gifts" (Prov. 21.14; perhaps 17.8). This could refer to a payoff to influence judges (see Deut. 27.25; Isa. 5.23; Prov. 17.23) or to a fee charged by judges merely for hearing cases (Isa. 1.23; Mic. 3.11; cf. 7.3). *For bribes blind the clear-sighted,* see also Deut. 16.19. The explanation is in a poetic style resembling that of wisdom literature; cf. Eccl. 7.7. *Upset the pleas of those who are in the right,* i.e., influence the judge against the claims of the innocent party. **9:** See 22.20. This v. may be repeated here because strangers, who lack kin to protect their rights, are at a disadvantage in courts composed of local or tribal elders (cf. Ps. 127.5). **10–19:** The religious calendar and related requirements. Vv. 10–12

¹² Six days you shall do your work, but on the seventh day you shall cease from labor, in order that your ox and your ass may rest, and that your bondman and the stranger may be refreshed.

¹³ Be on guard concerning all that I have told you. Make no mention of the names of other gods; they shall not be heard on your lips.

¹⁴ Three times a year you shall hold a festival for Me: ¹⁵ You shall observe the Feast of Unleavened Bread—eating unleavened bread for seven days as I have commanded you—at the set time in the month^a of Abib, for in it you went forth from Egypt; and none shall appear before Me empty-handed; ¹⁶ and the Feast of the Harvest, of the first fruits of your work, of what you sow in the field; and the Feast of Ingathering at the end of the year, when you gather in the results of your work from the field. ¹⁷ Three times a year all your males shall appear before the Sovereign, the LORD.

a See note at 13.4.

and 14–17 deal with requirements that occur at fixed intervals.
10–13: The sabbatical fallow year (cf. Lev. 25.1–7, 20–22) and the Sabbath day. In line with the theme of vv. 1–9, only their social and humanitarian goals are stated here; Exod. 16.23; 20.10; Lev. 25.2, 4 describe both as "a sabbath of the LORD," indicating their religious significance. According to Deut. 15.1–3, debts were also remitted in the seventh year, possibly because debts commonly came due at harvest time, when farmers realized their income, and there would be no harvest in the seventh year. Neh. 10.32 mentions both fallowing and debt cancellation in the seventh year. **13:** *Be on guard . . . :* This may be intended as a conclusion to all the preceding laws and exhortations (21.1–23.12) or to the mostly negative commandments in 22.17–23.12 (or just 23.1–12) before turning to the laws of worship in vv. 14–19. Or, in view of its position between v. 12 and the next clause, it may mean: Remember not only the Sabbath, but all of the first four commandments (20.2–11) and have nothing to do with any other god. Note the similar sequence of commands in Lev.

19.3–4 followed by laws about worship in vv. 5–8 (cf. Exod. 34.17 followed by vv. 18–23). *Make no mention . . . :* That is, do not invoke other gods in worship (cf. 20.21); instead, worship the LORD, as prescribed in vv. 14–19. This warning is especially pertinent to the agricultural festivals mentioned in those vv., since several non-Israelite deities mentioned in the Bible were closely associated with fertility. The Bible teaches that the LORD alone controls nature. **14–17:** The festivals mark the two agricultural seasons. The Feast of Unleavened Bread and the Feast of the Harvest, respectively, precede and follow the spring grain harvest, while the Feast of Ingathering occurs in the fall when the new grain and wine are stored away for the winter. See also 34.18–26; Lev. ch 23; Num. 9.1–14; chs 28–29; Deut. 16.1–17. **15:** In Jewish tradition *the Feast of Unleavened Bread* (see 12.14–20 n.), which commemorates the exodus, is called "zeman ḥerutenu," "the time of our freedom." The Bible does not connect it to the harvest, which follows the festival, but in the popular mind eating primitive, unleavened bread was possibly perceived as a

type of abstinence expressing anxiety about the success of the coming harvest. *The month of Abib,* see 13.4 n. Lev. 23.6 gives a specific date, the fifteenth of the month. *As I have commanded you,* see 12.14–20, 34, 39. *None shall appear before Me empty-handed:* All must bring offerings. This is emphasized in connection to this festival here since no new agricultural produce is ready. In Deut. 16.16–17 this obligation is explicitly applied to all three festivals. **16:** *The Feast of the Harvest,* also called "the day of the first fruits" (of the grain harvest, Num. 28.26) and "the Feast of Weeks" ("Shavu'ot," 34.22), because it is observed exactly seven weeks after the harvest begins (Lev. 23.15–21; Deut. 16.10). Because of the later tradition that this festival falls on the anniversary of the giving of the Torah, it is also known as "zeman matan toratenu," "the time when our Torah was given." Here it is an agricultural festival only, and is not connected to the previous Feast of Unleavened Bread. *The Feast of Ingathering,* at the end of the summer, celebrates the gathering of the processed grain and new wine into storage for the coming year, the goal of all the preceding agricultural activities. It is also known as "the Feast of Booths" ("Sukkot," Lev. 23.34; Deut. 16.13), after the practice of dwelling in booths during the festival (Lev. 23.42; Neh. 8.14, 17), or simply "the Feast," meaning "the festival par excellence" (1 Kings 8.2, 65; Ezek. 45.25; Neh. 8.14). In Jewish tradition it is also called "zeman simḥatenu," "the time of our rejoicing," because it was the most joyous festival, coming at a time when the bounty of the harvest was manifest. *At the end of the year,* at the close of the agricultural year. Cf. 34.22. According to Lev. 23.34, 39 the festival begins on the fifteenth day of the seventh month (September-October). **17:** *All your males:* The obligation is limited to males, probably because pregnant and nursing women could not travel to distant sanctuaries. *Appear before . . . the LORD,* visit a sanc-

¹⁸You shall not offer the blood of My sacrifice with anything leavened; and the fat of My festal offering shall not be left lying until morning.

¹⁹The choice first fruits of your soil you shall bring to the house of the LORD your God.

You shall not boil a kid in its mother's milk.

²⁰I am sending an angel before you to guard you on the way and to bring you to the place that I have made ready. ²¹Pay heed to him and obey him. Do not defy him, for he will not pardon your offenses, since My Name is in him; ²²but if you obey him and do all that I say, I will be an enemy to your enemies and a foe to your foes.

²³When My angel goes before you and brings you to the Amorites, the Hittites, the Perizzites, the Canaanites, the Hivites, and the Jebusites, and I annihilate them, ²⁴you

tuary in any of the country's temple cities (34.24; Deuteronomy 31.11; 1 Sam. 1.22; Isa. 1.12). Deut. later limited this to a single sanctuary (Deut. 12.4–14; 16.2–7; cf. 2 Kings 23.21–23; 2 Chron. ch 30). This clause probably originally read "see the face of the LORD," meaning to visit Him and pay Him homage at His sanctuary. The reading was probably changed to prevent the impression that God could literally be seen there. God's designation as *the Sovereign* (see also 34.23; cf. Zech. 14.16) emphasizes that He is Israel's king, and therefore His subjects must appear before Him regularly to acknowledge His sovereignty, just as subjects of a human suzerain were required to do. **18–19:** These rules about offerings and food seem to apply both year-round and also specifically to the festivals just mentioned. **18:** Leavened bread was forbidden with most sacrifices (12.8 n.), and several types of sacrifice must be consumed before morning (29.34; Lev. 7.15; 22.30), but 12.8, 10 apply both rules to the "pesaḥ" sacrifice in particular, as does 34.25b to the second rule. *The fat of* [the] *festal offering* refers to the fat on the entrails of sacrificial animals; it is burnt as part of the sacrifice, and eating it is forbidden (Lev. 3.17; 7.23, 25; 17.6). **19:** *First fruits,* see 22.28–29 n. Farmers probably brought first-fruit offerings at various times of the year,

according to when each species was harvested, but in v. 16 the practice is mentioned particularly in connection with the Feast of the Harvest. See also Lev. 23.16–20; Num. 28.26; Deut. 26.1–11. *You shall not boil a kid in its mother's milk:* Meat boiled in sour milk ("leben") was probably considered a delicacy, as it is by Arabs, since it is tastier and more tender than meat boiled in water. As noted by Philo (*Virt.* 143–144), Ibn Ezra, and Rashbam, this law is similar to the rules that forbid acts of insensitivity against animals such as slaughtering cattle on the same day as their young, sacrificing cattle in their first week, and taking a mother bird along with her fledglings or her eggs (22.29; Lev. 22.27–28; Deut. 22.6–7). It is therefore likely that it also applied to lambs and calves, kids being mentioned only because goats were the most common type of cattle or because their meat is most in need of tenderizing and flavoring. Jewish law construes this rule broadly, forbidding cooking or eating any domestic cattle with the milk or milk products of any domestic cattle. Supplementary regulations also prohibited eating fowl or game with milk and required the use of separate utensils for milk and meat, including their products (Maimonides, *Hilkhot Ma'akhalot 'Asurot,* ch 9). The association of this rule with the festivals is prob-

ably due to the fact that meat was eaten infrequently but was part of festival meals. Since in Israel goats begin to give birth in the fall, the Feast of Ingathering was probably the one at which kids were typically eaten.

23.20–33: Conclusion. The Book of the Covenant (see 24.7) concludes with an epilogue containing promises of the reward for fidelity to the preceding laws. This is comparable to ancient Near Eastern treaties, which conclude with promises and warnings about the consequences of fidelity to or betrayal of the treaty, though here (contrast Lev. ch 26 and Deut. ch 28) only rewards are described. The final exhortations against idolatry (vv. 24, 32–33) hark back to the book's first law (20.19–20) and the beginning of the Decalogue (20.2–6). **20:** *Angel,* lit. "messenger," "emissary" (from God); see 3.2 n. and 12.23 n. *To guard you,* cf. 14.19; 33.2; Gen. 24.7; 48.16. *The place that I have made ready,* the promised land. **21:** The angel will instruct and chastise the people on God's behalf since God's *Name is in him,* that is, God's presence and authority are manifest in him (3.2 n.). Cf. Judg. 2.1–4. **22:** A classic expression of a treaty relationship in which the parties agree that the enemy of one is the enemy of the other. Cf. Gen. 12.3; Ps. 139.21–22. **24–26:** Cf. 34.11–17; Num. 33.52; Deut. 7.5, 25–26. Victors sometimes worshipped the gods of the nations they defeated, believing that they had abandoned their people to enable the victor to triumph (2 Chron. 25.14; cf. 1 Sam. 5.2). **24:** *Follow their practices,* i.e. (according to Deut. 12.2–4, 29–31), adapt Canaanite rituals for worshipping the LORD. Israel may not even take Canaanite idols as booty (2 Sam. 5.21) but must *tear them down:* At Hazor archeologists found a statue with its head deliberately chopped off in the stratum likely destroyed by the incoming Israelites. *Pillars,* stones erected for a cultic purpose, whether plain or engraved with images of a deity or its symbols.

shall not bow down to their gods in worship or follow their practices, but shall tear them down and smash their pillars to bits. 25 You shall serve the LORD your God, and He will bless your bread and your water. And I will remove sickness from your midst. 26 No woman in your land shall miscarry or be barren. I will let you enjoy the full count of your days.

27 I will send forth My terror before you, and I will throw into panic all the people among whom you come, and I will make all your enemies turn tail[a] before you. 28 I will send a plague[b] ahead of you, and it shall drive out before you the Hivites, the Canaanites, and the Hittites. 29 I will not drive them out before you in a single year, lest the land become desolate and the wild beasts multiply to your hurt. 30 I will drive them out before you little by little, until you have increased and possess the land. 31 I will set your borders from the Sea of Reeds to the Sea of Philistia, and from the wilderness to the Euphrates; for I will deliver the inhabitants of the land into your hands, and you will drive them out before you. 32 You shall make no covenant with them and their gods. 33 They shall not remain in your land, lest they cause you to sin against Me; for you will serve their gods—and it will prove a snare to you.

24 Then He said to Moses, "Come up to the LORD, with Aaron, Nadab and Abihu, and seventy elders of Israel, and bow low from afar. 2 Moses alone shall come

a Lit. "back."   b Others "hornet"; meaning of Heb. uncertain.

Apparently they were thought to embody the presence of a deity, either by representing it or serving as its residence (cf. Gen. 28.16–22; 2 Kings 3.2; 10.27). Sacrifices were offered to them and they were treated like idols. Although they were sometimes used in the worship of the Lord (Gen. 28.16–22; 21.13; 35.14; cf. Isa. 19.19; Hos. 3.4), Deut. 16.22 bans even such use because of their associations with idolatry. **25–26:** These are rewards typically promised in ancient treaties; see also Lev. 26.3–10; Deut. 11.13–15, 21; 28.1–13. **27:** *My terror,* a divinely induced panic, here reified as in Gen. 35.5; 1 Sam. 14.15; Isa. 24.17; Jer. 48.44. Alternatively, in view of the following verb, "My terror" might refer to God's fearsome aura, comparable to the fearsome aura of

Mesopotamian gods and kings which overwhelms their enemies; cf. Isa. 2.10, 19, 21. *Throw into panic,* rather, "rout" (14.24; Deut. 7.23; Josh. 10.10; Judg. 4.15; 1 Sam. 7.10; Esth. 9.24). **28:** *Plague,* better, "hornets" or "wasps," meaning either that ferocious swarms of wasps will chase the Canaanites or that God will induce a panic or frenzy like that caused by wasps and cause the Canaanites to flee. **31:** Starting at a line running *from the Sea of Reeds* (here the Gulf of Eilat, 13.18 n.) *to the Sea of Philistia* (the Mediterranean off the coast of Philistia—roughly the Gaza Strip today), Israel's territory will extend *from the* (Sinai-Negev) *wilderness* in the south *to the Euphrates* in the northeast (see also Gen. 15.18; Deut. 1.7; 11.24; Josh. 1.4); other passages in the Torah place the

northern boundary in Lebanon's Bekaa Valley in Lebanon (Num. 13.21; 34.8). *You will drive them out,* see also 33.2; 34.11 (cf. Lev. 18.25b, 28; Num. 33.52–55; Josh. 24.12, 18; Judg. 6.9). According to Deut. 7.2, 16; 20.15–18, however, the Canaanites are to be killed. Jewish exegesis resolves the inconsistency by holding that the Canaanites were given the option of fighting, emigrating, or remaining in the land as forced laborers, provided they accept the seven Noahide laws (Gen. 9.8–17 n.) (Maimonides, *Hilkhot Melakhim* 6.5). Historically speaking, there was probably no policy of either expulsion or extermination. Archeological evidence and passages such as Josh. 15.63; 16.10; 17.12–13; Judg. 1.19, 27–36; 1 Kings 9.20–21 indicate that Canaanites remained in the land. Driving out or killing the Canaanites are both probably late, theoretical reconstructions. **32:** *Covenant,* conditions under which the Canaanites or their idolatry could remain. **33:** *Lest they cause you to sin . . . ,* cf. 34.15–16; Deut. 7.3–4. According to Deut. 20.18 the danger is that the Canaanites would influence Israelites to adopt their abhorrent rites, such as child sacrifice and various occult practices (Deut. 12.31; 18.9–12). According to Genesis and Leviticus, God will expel the Canaanites because of immorality, occult practices, and child sacrifice (see Gen. 9.22–27; 15.16; 19.4–5; Lev. chs 18, 20).

24.1–18: The covenant ceremony. The covenant proposed in 19.4–6 is formally established when Moses reads its terms to the people in the course of a blood rite in which they ratify its terms, followed by a sacrificial meal for the leaders in the presence of God. The sequence of events is hard to follow because of the interweaving of conflicting versions of the narrative (see chs 19–24, introductory comment), though the ch as a whole is organized to suggest that different groups, according to their status, ascended the mountain to different levels. Vv. 1–2 (*Come up . . .*) interrupt the preceding narrative, since near the LORD; but the others shall not come near, nor shall the people come up with him."

³ Moses went and repeated to the people all the commands of the LORD and all the rules; and all the people answered with one voice, saying, "All the things that the LORD has commanded we will do!" ⁴ Moses then wrote down all the commands of the LORD.

Early in the morning, he set up an altar at the foot of the mountain, with twelve pillars for the twelve tribes of Israel. ⁵ He designated some young men among the Israelites, and they offered burnt offerings and sacrificed bulls as offerings of well-being to the LORD. ⁶ Moses took one part of the blood and put it in basins, and the other part of the blood he dashed against the altar. ⁷ Then he took the record of the covenant and read it aloud to the people. And they said, "All that the LORD has spoken ᵃwe will faithfully do!"-ᵃ ⁸ Moses took the blood and dashed it on the people and said, "This is the blood of the covenant that the LORD now makes with you concerning all these commands."

⁹ Then Moses and Aaron, Nadab and Abihu, and seventy elders of Israel ascended; ¹⁰ and they saw the God of

a-a Lit. "we will do and obey."

20.18 shows that Moses was already on the mountain when he received the laws of 20.19–23.33. The immediate sequel to that narrative is 24.3–8, followed by vv. 12–15a and 18b (from E). Vv. 1–2 and 9–11, in which Moses is called up to God, are the sequel to 19.25; they are from J, while 15b–18a—the sequel of 19.1–2—are from P. There are differences in detail between these groups of vv. In J, Moses is to be accompanied part way by the priests and elders (vv. 1–2, 9); in E he is apparently accompanied part way by Joshua (13–14; cf. 32.17) but leaves the elders, Aaron and Hur, behind; while in P (vv. 15b–18a) he seems not to be accompanied at any time. J does not tell of any lawgiving; to it the event at Sinai was a visual encounter with God, experienced in differing degrees by the people, the leaders, and Moses, and the covenant was established by a meal (24.1–2, 9–11; cf. 19.11, 18, 21). E, preserved more fully, tells of a primarily auditory experience,

the establishment of the covenant by a blood rite and ratification of the "Book of the Covenant," and Moses' ascent to receive the tablets of the Decalogue (19.9, 16, 19; chs 20–23; 24.3–8, 12–15a). To P the event consisted primarily of Moses going up on the mountain to receive the instructions for constructing the Tabernacle (chs 25–31) in which God will dwell among the Israelites and give Moses laws, and where they will worship Him; He also gave Moses the "Pact" to put in the Ark (25.8, 22; 29.38–46; 31.18). **1–2:** The summons is answered, and this scource is continued in vv. 9–11. *Nadab and Abihu*, 6.23 n. For the various zones of permitted access cf. 19.12, 24. **3:** *Repeated to the people*, as they had requested in 20.16 and as God had commanded in 21.1. After hearing the specific terms of the covenant, the people repeat the assent they first expressed in 19.8. *All the commands of the LORD*, 20.19–23.33. *All the people answered with one voice*, the slightly

redundant language emphasizes the unanimity of their assent, as in 19.8. *We will do*, as they promised in 20.16. **4:** Once the people assent to the terms of the covenant, Moses prepares for a ceremony formally establishing it. In the ceremony the *altar* (cf. 20.21) and *twelve pillars* will represent, respectively, God and Israel. These pillars are not cultic as in 23.24. **5:** *Young men*, perhaps the firstborns (Rashi; Targum) assisting Moses. Apparently E, like P (28.1), assumes that the Aaronide priestly order has not yet been established (J, in vv. 1, 9 and 19.22, assumes otherwise). Priests' assistants are called "young men" in 1 Sam. 2.13–18; 3.1. *Burnt offerings . . . offerings of well-being*, 18.12 n. **6–8:** Dashing the blood on the altar and on the people (v. 8) joins God and Israel in the covenant. Here the altar represents God, as in 20.21; cf. Ps. 42.3–4; 1 Kings 8.22, 31, 54; 2 Kings 18.22; Isa. 19.19 (cf. Gen. 15.17, where a torch and smoking oven represent God in a covenant ceremony). Establishing a covenant by the parties sharing blood, each other's or that of an animal, is attested in many places; Aeschylus describes a covenant in which the parties dip their hands in the blood of a slaughtered animal (Aeschylus, *Seven Against Thebes*, 43–48). **7:** *Record*, i.e., a scroll or a stone inscription (cf. Deut. 27.2–3, 8), containing, apparently, 20.19–23.33. On the basis of this phrase, the legal collection of 20.19–23.33 is called the Book of the Covenant. *We will faithfully do:* The most literal translation would be "we will do and listen," and the midrash inferred from this that the people trusted God so thoroughly that they committed themselves to obeying His commands before they even heard their contents (b. *Shab.* 88a). **8:** *On the people,* perhaps, on the pillars representing the people. **9:** See v. 1. **10:** For this unique occasion the people's leaders and representatives are granted a visual experience of God. Later Jewish writers, who believed that God is not visible, held that the experi-

Israel: under His feet there was the likeness of a pavement of sapphire, like the very sky for purity. [11] Yet He did not raise His hand against the leaders[a] of the Israelites; they beheld God, and they ate and drank.

[12] The LORD said to Moses, "Come up to Me on the mountain and wait there, and I will give you the stone tablets with the teachings and commandments which I have inscribed to instruct them." [13] So Moses and his attendant Joshua arose, and Moses ascended the mountain of God. [14] To the elders he had said, "Wait here for us until we return to you. You have Aaron and Hur with you; let anyone who has a legal matter approach them."

[15] When Moses had ascended the mountain, the cloud covered the mountain. [16] The Presence of the LORD abode on Mount Sinai, and the cloud hid it for six days. On the seventh day He called to Moses from the midst of the cloud. [17] Now the Presence of the LORD appeared in the sight of the Israelites as a consuming fire on the top of the mountain. [18] Moses went inside the cloud and ascended the mountain; and Moses remained on the mountain forty days and forty nights.

TERUMAH   תרומה

25 The LORD spoke to Moses, saying: [2] Tell the Israelite people to bring Me gifts; you shall accept gifts for Me from every person whose heart so moves him. [3] And these are the gifts that you shall accept from them:

---

a Meaning of Heb. ʾaṣilim uncertain.

---

ence was not literally visual but was either an intellectual perception (Maimonides, *Guide*, 1.4) or a prophetic vision such as those in Isa. 6.1 and Ezek. ch 1 (Ibn Ezra). The Bible does not deny that God is visible, but the text is reticent about describing Him. By focusing on what was *under His feet*, it seems to suggest that the leaders did not see God directly but from below, through a transparent sapphire- (or rather, lapis-lazuli-) colored pavement. Cf. Ezek. 1.26–28; 10.1–2. This lapis-lazuli pavement is the floor of God's palace, and also explains why the sky is blue. **11:** *He did not raise His hand:* Despite their seeing God, no harm befell them; see 3.6 n. *They ate and drank:* A well-attested way of celebrating the establishment of a covenant; see Gen. 26.28–30; 31.54;

and the ceremony reaffirming the covenant in Deut. 27.1–8; cf. the parallelism in Obad. 7 and Ps. 41.10. In covenants between humans both parties share the meal. Here, one of the parties, God, does not eat, and Moses and the leaders merely eat in His presence. **12:** In addition to the Book of the Covenant (v. 7), the Israelites would receive two tablets containing the Decalogue inscribed by God Himself (31.18; 32.16) as a monument to their revelation at Sinai. Stone was normally used only for permanent inscriptions, such as royal and ceremonial inscriptions, boundary inscriptions, and treaties. The tablets may have resembled a square stone tablet containing a 7th-century BCE Aramaic decree. Two such tablets, 15 or 16 inches square and inscribed

on both sides (like the Decalogue, 32.16), could have contained the entire Decalogue. This shape is consistent with Jewish tradition and early Christian art, which conceived of the tablets as rectangular. The tablets with curved tops, familiar today, reflect later Roman practice, and were first introduced in Christian art around the 11th century. *With the teachings and commandments,* according to 34.28, the Decalogue. The Heb can also be construed as *"and the teachings and commandments,"* which midrashic exegesis took to mean the rest of the written Torah (or of the Bible) plus the Oral Torah; in other words, all were given to Moses at Mount Sinai (*b. Ber.* 5a; *Lekaḥ Tov; Midrash HaGadol*). **13:** *Joshua* (17.9 n.) apparently accompanied Moses part way (see v. 14; cf. 32.17). **14:** *Aaron and Hur,* 17.10 n. They are to perform Moses' duties in his absence (18.16a). **15:** *The cloud,* in which God's Presence is manifest; see 13.21 n., 22 n. **16:** *The Presence of the LORD,* 16.6–7 n. This *Presence* is the main manifestation of the divine in Priestly thought. *Abode on Mount Sinai:* The main thrust of the instructions in chs 25–32 is the construction of the Tabernacle (Heb "mishkan," lit. "abode") to which God will transfer His abode (40.34–38) and accompany Israel; see 25.8, where "dwell" should be rendered "abide" to indicate that it is the same Heb verb (sh-k-n) as here. The Tabernacle, in other words, is essentially a portable Mount Sinai, the locus of God's presence. **17:** On the appearance of God's Presence, see 16.6–7 n.

25.1–31.17: Instructions for building the Tabernacle (see diagram, p. 164) **and inaugurating the priesthood.** The sanctuary will enable God to abide among the Israelites henceforth, and will be the place from which He issues commands for Israel (25.22 n.). It will also be the place of sacrificial worship (v. 30; 29.38–42; Lev. chs 1–7), where the priests officiate daily (29.9–12, 21, 29); but its main purpose is for the benefit of Israel, that gold, silver, and copper; [4]blue, purple, and crimson yarns, fine linen, goats' hair; [5]tanned ram skins,[a] dolphin[b] skins, and acacia wood; [6]oil for lighting, spices for the anointing oil and for the aromatic incense; [7]lapis lazuli[c] and other stones for setting, for the ephod and for the breastpiece.

a Others "rams' skins dyed red."
b Or "dugong"; meaning of Hebrew taḥash uncertain.
c Cf. Gen. 2.12 and note.

they may experience God's guiding presence, and not for the benefit of God, who has no need for sacrifice (see also 29.42b–46 n.). In contrast, an important purpose of sanctuaries in polytheistic religions was to serve as places where worshippers feed the gods. Like Mount Sinai (19.9b–13 n.), the sanctuary will have three carefully delimited zones of holiness and restricted access. They are, in descending order of holiness: (a) the "Holy of Holies," where the Ark and Tablets of the Covenant are kept, (b) its antechamber, "the Holy Place"—both of these inside the Tent of Meeting, the Tabernacle proper—and (c) the surrounding courtyard. Nonpriests will be admitted only to the courtyard (c); the Holy Place (b) will be accessible only to priests and Moses; and the Holy of Holies (a) only to High Priest, and that only on the Day of Atonement (Lev. 16.2; whether Moses may enter the Holy of Holies is unclear; see below, 25.22 n.). In all cases, access will be limited to those who are ritually pure (cf. Lev. 12.4; Num. 5.3; 2 Chron. 23.19). These restrictions will protect the Ark, above which God's Presence is situated (25.22 n.), from impurity so that the Tabernacle will remain fit for His Presence (Lev. 15.31; 20.3). The materials used in constructing the Tabernacle, its paraphernalia, and the priestly vestments reflect its varying levels of holiness: the closer to the Ark and the Holy of Holies, the more precious the materials. For example, all the furniture in the Tent of Meeting is made of gold or wood overlaid with gold, while the altar and laver outside in the courtyard are overlaid or made with bronze; the fabric directly covering the Tent of Meeting is made of fine twisted linen and blue, purple, and crimson yarns, while the layers of fabric above that one are made of less precious fabrics; the outer vestments of Aaron, who ministers inside the Tent, are made of gold thread, blue, purple, and crimson yarns and fine twisted linen, while the garments of the other priests, who officiate only in the courtyard, are made mostly of linen. The instructions for the Tabernacle fall into

The structure of the Tabernacle

⁸And let them make Me a sanctuary that I may dwell among them. ⁹Exactly as I show you—the pattern of the Tabernacle and the pattern of all its furnishings—so shall you make it.

two main sections: The Tabernacle structure and its contents (25.10–27.19) and its activities (27.20–30.38). These are preceded by an introduction (25.1–9) and followed by two paragraphs dealing with the builders of the Tabernacle (31.1–11) and suspending its construction on Sabbaths (31.12–17). These instructions, and the narrative of their implementation in chs 35–40, are drawn from the Priestly source (P), with some additions from the Holiness Collection (H; see comments on Lev. chs 17–26). In many respects they echo the Priestly account of creation in Gen. 1.1–2.4a: The instructions are divided into seven separate divine commands, culminating in the Sabbath (see 25.1; 30.11, 17, 22, 34; 31.1, 12), the lampstand holds seven candles (25.37), Aaron wears seven sacral vestments (28.1–39), the account of the building of the Tabernacle culminates in several allusions to the creation account (compare 39.32 to Gen. 2.1, 3; 39.43 to Gen. 1.31; and 40.33 to Gen. 2.2), and the Tabernacle is completed on New Year's day (40.17). See comments to 39.32, 43; 40.16, 33. The Priestly Tabernacle instructions are an unexpected sequel to 24.12–18, according to which Moses was summoned to receive the stone tablets (24.12, E) which the present order of the text delays for seven chs until 31.18. In the present sequence it seems that God's first order of business was to arrange for the housing of the tablets (the role of the Tabernacle according to 25.10–16 n.; 38.21), but Rashi holds that the Tabernacle instructions were actually not given until after the entire golden calf episode was concluded (Rashi at 31.18, following *Tanḥ. Ki Tissa* 31). For a likely reason for the present sequence, see the introductory comments to 31.18–34.35. To modern readers, the quantity of detail of this sec-

tion and much of the end of Exodus, which repeats, with minor variations, the execution of these commands, seems excessive. The key is found in 25.8, "And let them make Me a sanctuary that I may dwell among them." The indwelling of God, along with the blessing and protection that this offers, is crucial for the well-being of the community; thus it is crucial to construct a "house" to exact divine specifications. There is significant scholarly debate concerning the existence of the Tabernacle. Some believe that some form of the First Temple is being described, and that it is historically retrojected into the period of the wanderings to give it legitimacy. Others note that aspects of the Tabernacle's architecture are paralleled in second millennium Egypt and Syria (Mari) and that portable shrines are attested among Arab tribes, and suggest that at least in broad strokes, the Tabernacle here reflects a recollection of a premonarchic sanctuary, perhaps one that antedates the settlement of the Israelites in Canaan.

25.1–9: Introduction. 1: *The L*ORD *spoke to Moses,* while he was on Mount Sinai (24.18). For the Priestly author, the instructions for the Tabernacle, rather than laws, are given on Sinai. **2:** *Gifts . . . from every person whose heart so moves him:* The Tabernacle is to be built entirely of voluntary gifts from the entire community. **3:** *Gold, silver, and copper,* for the Tabernacle paraphernalia and the priestly vestments. The metal of which each object is made will depend on its proximity to the Holy of Holies. *Copper,* more likely bronze. **4–5:** *Blue, purple, and crimson yarns, fine linen, goats' hair, tanned ram skins, dolphin skins,* the finest fabrics, for the Tabernacle curtains, hangings, and covers, and the priests' vestments. As with the

metals, these are listed in descending order of quality, and the material of which an item is made depends on its proximity to the Holy of Holies. *Blue, purple,* bluish- and reddish-purple colors manufactured from fluid obtained from the murex snails found in abundance along the Mediterranean coast north of Acco, also called Acre (the ancient name of the region, "Phoenicia," is related to Greek "phoinix," "purple," "crimson"). *Dolphin skins,* more likely, dyed sheep or goat leather. *Acacia wood,* for the frame of the Tabernacle, its furniture and carrying-poles. **8:** *Sanctuary:* The sanctuary is referred to by three main terms, each expressing different aspects of it: "mikdash" ("sanctuary"), lit. "holy place," "sanctum," referring to its sacred dimension; "mishkan" ("Tabernacle"), lit. "abode," referring to it as God's dwelling (v. 9 and frequently); and "'ohel mo'ed" ("Tent of Meeting"), referring to it as an oracle site, the place where God would communicate with Moses (29.42–43; 30.6, 36; cf. 33.7–11; 25.22 n.; cf. 29.46 n.). "Sanctuary" refers to the entire compound described below—the covered structure and the courtyard surrounding it. "Tabernacle" and "Tent of Meeting" sometimes refer to the entire compound and at other times only the covered structure (see also 26.1; 27.19). *That I may dwell among them,* rather, "that I may abide among them," the same verb as that used in 24.16. This verb and the Heb word for Tabernacle ("mishkan"; see above) are from the same root, as is "Shekhinah," the term for the divine Presence in later Jewish tradition. **9:** God showed Moses either "blueprints," pictures, or a model of the Tabernacle. This information is repeated in connection with the table and the lampstand, the Tabernacle structure, and the sacrificial altar and its utensils (v. 40; 26.30; 27.8; Num. 8.4; cf. 1 Chron. 28.11–19; Ezek. chs 40–42). The Tabernacle is not to be a product of human creativity but must conform exactly to divine specifications ("One cannot ap-

10 They shall make an ark of acacia wood, two and a half cubits long, a cubit and a half wide, and a cubit and a half high. 11 Overlay it with pure gold—overlay it inside and out—and make upon it a gold molding round about. 12 Cast four gold rings for it, to be attached to its four feet, two rings on one of its side walls and two on the other. 13 Make poles of acacia wood and overlay them with gold; 14 then insert the poles into the rings on the side walls of the ark, for carrying the ark. 15 The poles shall remain in the rings of the ark: they shall not be removed from it. 16 And deposit in the Ark [the tablets of] the Pact which I will give you.

17 You shall make a cover of pure gold, two and a half cubits long and a cubit and a half wide. 18 Make two cherubim of gold—make them of hammered work—at the two ends of the cover. 19 Make one cherub at one end and the other cherub at the other end; of one piece with the cover shall you make the cherubim at its two ends. 20 The cherubim shall have their wings spread out above, shielding the cover with their wings. They shall confront each other, the faces of the cherubim being turned toward the cover. 21 Place the cover on top of the Ark, after depositing inside the Ark the Pact that I will give you. 22 There I will meet with you, and I will impart to you—from above the cover, from between the two cherubim that are on top of the Ark of the Pact—all that I will command you concerning the Israelite people.

proach God except by [the ways that] He commands" [Judah Halevi, *Kuzari* 3.23; cf. 1.79, 98, 99]).

25.10–27.19: The Tabernacle structure and its contents.
25.10–49: The furnishings of the building. The furnishings of both chambers of the Tabernacle building—the Holy of Holies and the Holy Place—are to be of solid gold or overlaid with gold. **10–16: The Ark.** The instructions begin with the Ark (Heb "'aron," lit. "chest"). The Ark will hold the "Pact," the two tablets containing the Decalogue (31.18). For that reason it will be placed in the innermost chamber of the Tabernacle, the "Holy of Holies" (meaning "the holiest" chamber; 26.31–44). As the container of the Pact, the Ark is the heart of the Tabernacle, which is called "the Tabernacle [lit. the

Abode] of the Pact" in 38.21, as if the main purpose of the Tabernacle is to serve as the housing for the Pact (Rashbam at v. 10). It is significant that the heart of the sanctuary is a symbol of God's law, rather than an image as was the case in non-Israelite sanctuaries. In postbiblical Judaism the Torah scroll, housed in the Holy Ark (see below) and carried in procession around the synagogue, came to symbolize God's Presence, and the study of the Torah's laws and teachings became one of the primary means of access to Him. (Nowadays the term "Ark," more fully "Holy Ark" ["'aron kodesh"], is used of the wall cabinet that houses the Torah scrolls in the synagogue.) **10:** *Cubits:* The Ark's dimensions were 1.25 m long, .75 m wide, and .75 m high (3.75 ft by 2.25 ft by 2.25 ft). **16:** Cf. 1 Kings 8.9.

25.17–22: The Ark cover. The Ark is to be covered with a lid made of gold hammered into the shape of two cherubs standing on a base. Cherubs are not the chubby, naked, winged boys known from medieval art, but winged composite creatures (cf. Ezek. 1.6–11; 10.14–22). Various types of such creatures are known from ancient Near Eastern art, such as winged sphinxes, with lions' bodies, eagles' wings, and human faces (sometimes with a second, animal face), and winged anthropoids with eagles' wings and birds' heads. Such creatures, frequently in pairs, often serve as protective spirits for kings, their palaces and thrones. Images of royal thrones with cherubs sculpted on their sides, several of which were found in Canaan and ancient Israel, are consistent with v. 22, which indicates that God would be present between the cherubs. They suggest that the Ark cover represented God's throne (cf. 1 Sam. 4.4; 2 Sam. 6.2; 2 Kings 19.15; Pss. 80.2; 99.1) and the Ark itself His footstool. The symbolism thus represents God as King and the Holy of Holies as the literal seat of divine government. This symbolism is consistent with the fact that architecturally the Tabernacle resembles a royal residence, particularly the royal tent in Egyptian military camps. It also is similar in structure to temples of surrounding nations. **20:** Unlike the cherubs flanking royal thrones, and the free-standing cherubs in Solomon's Temple (1 Kings 6.23–27), the Tabernacle cherubs face each other. **21:** Treaties were often stored in sanctuaries in the presence of the deities who would enforce their observance. In some cases treaties and other documents are explicitly said to be placed beneath the deity's feet; this is consistent with the conception of the Ark as God's footstool. **22:** See 29.42–43; 30.36; Num. 7.89; 17.19; and cf. Lev. 16.2, 13. Appropriately, the place where the first revelation is stored will serve as the site of future revelations. The text expresses this by paronomasia (punning),

23 You shall make a table of acacia wood, two cubits long, one cubit wide, and a cubit and a half high. 24 Overlay it with pure gold, and make a gold molding around it. 25 Make a rim of a hand's breadth around it, and make a gold molding for its rim round about. 26 Make four gold rings for it, and attach the rings to the four corners at its four legs. 27 The rings shall be next to the rim, as holders for poles to carry the table. 28 Make the poles of acacia wood, and overlay them with gold; by these the table shall be carried. 29 Make its bowls, ladles, jars and jugs with which to offer libations; make them of pure gold. 30 And on the table you shall set the bread of display, to be before Me always.

31 You shall make a lampstand of pure gold; the lampstand shall be made of hammered work; its base and its shaft, its cups, calyxes, and petals shall be of one piece. 32 Six branches shall issue from its sides; three branches from one side of the lampstand and three branches from the other side of the lampstand. 33 On one branch there shall be three cups shaped like almond-blossoms, each with calyx and petals, and on the next branch there shall be three cups shaped like almond-blossoms, each with calyx and petals; so for all six branches issuing from the lampstand. 34 And on the lampstand itself there shall be four cups shaped like almond-blossoms, each with calyx and petals: 35 a calyx, of one piece with it, under a pair of branches; and a calyx, of one piece with it, under the second pair of branches, and a calyx, of one piece with it, under the last pair of branches; so for all six branches issuing from the lampstand. 36 Their calyxes and their stems shall be of one piece with it, the whole of it a single hammered piece of pure gold. 37 Make its seven lamps—the lamps shall be so mounted as to give the light on its front side—38 and its tongs and fire pans of pure gold. 39 It shall be made, with all these furnishings, out of a talent of pure gold. 40 Note well, and follow the patterns for them that are being shown you on the mountain.

since the Heb words for "Pact" ("ʿedut") and "meet" ("noʿad") sound alike (though they are from different roots), as if to say that the site of the Pact ("ʿedut") is the site of meeting ("noʿad"). Whether Moses enters the Holy of Holies or listens to God from the Holy Place (Sforno at Lev. 1.1) is debated.

25.23–40: The table and lampstand. The furnishings of the antechamber, the Holy Place. **23–30:** The *table* was to hold the "bread of display," that is, "the Bread of the (Divine) Presence" (also called "shewbread"), explained as bread placed "before (that is, in the presence of) God." It consisted of twelve loaves placed on the table every Sabbath and replaced a week later and then eaten by the priests (see Lev. 24.5–9; cf. Num. 4.7; 1 Sam.

21.4–7; 1 Chron. 9.32). Ancient Near Eastern art often shows tables holding gifts of food before enthroned royalty and deities. In Mesopotamian ritual, curtains were drawn around the image of the deity and the table when sacrificial food was brought in for the deity to eat. It is significant that here the table is in the antechamber, separated from the Holy of Holies by the curtain (26.31–35). This partition between God and the Table makes it clear that the bread of display is not actually consumed by God but is only a token gift—this is also underlined by the fact that it was eaten by priests. That its purpose was display, not consumption, is also indicated by the fact that it is replaced weekly, not daily as elsewhere in the ancient Near East. See also vv. 31–40 n. and 30.9 n. **31–40:** The *lampstand* ("menorah") for illuminating the interior of the Holy Place each night (27.20–21). Its location in the antechamber indicates that the light is for the benefit of the officiating priests, not God. With its central shaft and three branches emerging from each side it resembled a stylized tree, possibly symbolizing fertility or the sustenance of life. It held seven *lamps* (v. 37), i.e., cups to hold the oil and wicks (it is debated whether six of these were on the branches or all seven were on the central shaft). The seven-branched lampstand later became a popular Jewish symbol in synagogues, tombs, and amulets, and today it is a symbol of the State of Israel. According to the Talmud it is forbidden to make exact replicas of the menorah except for the Tabernacle or the Temple (*b. Rosh Hash.* 24a–b); hence synagogue menorahs have six or eight branches instead of seven, although this prohibition is not always observed. **40:** Cf. v. 9 n.

26 As for the Tabernacle,[a] make it of ten strips of cloth; make these of fine twisted linen, of blue, purple, and crimson yarns, with a design of cherubim worked into them. [2] The length of each cloth shall be twenty-eight cubits, and the width of each cloth shall be four cubits, all the cloths to have the same measurements. [3] Five of the cloths shall be joined to one another, and the other five cloths shall be joined to one another. [4] Make loops of blue wool on the edge of the outermost cloth of the one set; and do likewise on the edge of the outermost cloth of the other set: [5] make fifty loops on the one cloth, and fifty loops on the edge of the end cloth of the other set, the loops to be opposite one another. [6] And make fifty gold clasps, and couple the cloths to one another with the clasps, so that the Tabernacle becomes one whole.

[7] You shall then make cloths of goats' hair for a tent over the Tabernacle; make the cloths eleven in number. [8] The length of each cloth shall be thirty cubits, and the width of each cloth shall be four cubits, the eleven cloths to have the same measurements. [9] Join five of the cloths by themselves, and the other six cloths by themselves; and fold over the sixth cloth at the front of the tent. [10] Make fifty loops on the edge of the outermost cloth of the one set, and fifty loops on the edge of the cloth of the other set. [11] Make fifty copper clasps, and fit the clasps into the loops, and couple the tent together so that it becomes one whole. [12] As for the overlapping excess of the cloths of the tent, the extra half-cloth shall overlap the back of the Tabernacle, [13] while the extra cubit at either end of each length of tent cloth shall hang down to the bottom of the two sides of the Tabernacle and cover it. [14] And make for the tent a covering of tanned ram skins, and a covering of dolphin skins above.

[15] You shall make the planks for the Tabernacle of acacia wood, upright. [16] The length of each plank shall be ten cubits and the width of each plank a cubit and a half. [17] Each plank shall have two tenons, parallel[b] to each other; do the same with all the planks of the Tabernacle. [18] Of the planks of the Tabernacle, make twenty planks on the south[c] side: [19] making forty silver sockets under the twenty planks, two sockets under the one plank for its two tenons and two sockets under each following plank for its two tenons; [20] and for the other side wall of the Tabernacle, on the north side, twenty planks, [21] with their forty silver sockets, two

---

a Here the lowest of the covers of the Tabernacle.
b Meaning of Heb. meshullaboth uncertain.
c Heb. uses two terms for "south."

26.1–37: The Tabernacle structure. The Holy of Holies and the Holy Place will be housed in a structure of gold-overlaid wood roofed with four layers of material. **1–6:** *The Tabernacle* (lit. "abode"): Here, apparently, this term means the lowest, innermost layer of the covers (cf. v. 6); it is so called because as the layer closest to the Ark it is the "abode" proper (Rashbam). It is to be made of the finest materials: *fine twisted linen, of blue, purple, and crimson yarns, with a design of cherubim worked into them,* corresponding to the cherubs on the Ark cover. Because it is contiguous with the Holy of Holies and the Holy Place, the clasps holding its sections together are to be made of gold. **7–13:** The *tent over the Tabernacle,* the second layer, is to be made of less precious material, goats' hair, and its clasps are to be made of *copper* (rather, bronze; v. 11). **14:** The upper layer is to be made of the least expensive of the Tabernacle materials, tanned ram skins and "dolphin skins" (see 25.5 n.). These constitute two separate layers (39.34), making four in all. **15–30:** The wooden structure, made of vertical planks of gold-overlaid acacia wood stabilized by silver sockets, or bases, and gold-overlaid wooden bars held in place by gold rings. The structure, with its opening facing east, was 30 cubits (15 m, 45 ft) long and 10 cubits (5 m, 15 ft) high and wide (see 25.10 n.). Silver is probably chosen for the sockets despite the fact that the planks are inside the Tabernacle because gold is not strong enough to support the planks. **30:** See 25.9 n. **31–35:** The curtain ("parokhet") for the Holy of Holies, again made of the finest materials and decorated with cherubs because of its contiguity with the Holy of Holies (cf. vv. 1–6 n.). The same Heb term is now used for the curtain that covers the Holy Ark in synagogues. The *blue, purple, and crimson yarns* must have been woollen since only wool could be dyed successfully in ancient times. Hence the curtain, which also contained *linen,* consisted of a combination of sockets under the one plank and two sockets under each following plank. ²² And for the rear of the Tabernacle, to the west, make six planks; ²³ and make two planks for the corners of the Tabernacle at the rear. ²⁴ ᵃThey shall match at the bottom, and terminate alike at the top inside one ring;⁻ᵃ thus shall it be with both of them: they shall form the two corners. ²⁵ Thus there shall be eight planks with their sockets of silver: sixteen sockets, two sockets under the first plank, and two sockets under each of the other planks.

²⁶ You shall make bars of acacia wood: five for the planks of the one side wall of the Tabernacle, ²⁷ five bars for the planks of the other side wall of the Tabernacle, and five bars for the planks of the wall of the Tabernacle at the rear to the west. ²⁸ The center bar halfway up the planks shall run from end to end. ²⁹ Overlay the planks with gold, and make their rings of gold, as holders for the bars; and overlay the bars with gold. ³⁰ Then set up the Tabernacle according to the manner of it that you were shown on the mountain.

³¹ You shall make a curtain of blue, purple, and crimson yarns, and fine twisted linen; it shall have a design of cherubim worked into it. ³² Hang it upon four posts of acacia wood overlaid with gold and having hooks of gold, [set] in four sockets of silver. ³³ Hang the curtain under the clasps, and carry the Ark of the Pact there, behind the curtain, so that the curtain shall serve you as a partition between the Holy and the Holy of Holies. ³⁴ Place the cover upon the Ark of the Pact in the Holy of Holies. ³⁵ Place the table outside the curtain, and the lampstand by the south wall of the Tabernacle opposite the table, which is to be placed by the north wall.

³⁶ You shall make a screen for the entrance of the Tent, of blue, purple, and crimson yarns, and fine twisted linen, done in embroidery. ³⁷ Make five posts of acacia wood for the screen and overlay them with gold—their hooks being of gold—and cast for them five sockets of copper.

27 You shall make the altar of acacia wood, five cubits long and five cubits wide—the altar is to be

---

a-a *Meaning of Heb. uncertain.*

---

cubits (10 m, 30 ft) from the entrance. Since the entire structure is 30 cubits (15 m, 45 ft) from front to back, the Holy Place occupies its eastern two-thirds and the Holy of Holies the westernmost third. The latter, then, is a perfect cube, 10 cubits (5 m, 15 ft) wide, long, and tall. **35:** On the location of the table and the lampstand *outside the curtain,* see 25.23–30 n.; 25.31–40 n. **36–37:** The *screen for the entrance of the Tent* (here *Tent* means the Tabernacle structure). It is made of the same fine materials as the "parokhet" but, since it is not contiguous with the Holy of Holies, it is not adorned with cherubs, its sockets are of a less valuable metal (copper [bronze] rather than silver), and it is *done in embroidery*— apparently a less sophisticated weave than that used for the "parokhet."

27.1–19: The altar and the courtyard. Just as chs 25–26 first described the main contents of the Tabernacle and then the Tabernacle structure, the text now describes the most important object placed in the courtyard—the altar—and then the courtyard itself. Since all of this is outside the Tabernacle structure, it is mostly made of less precious materials: The altar, its utensils, and the posts and sockets supporting the courtyard wall are made of bronze and bronzed wood, and the hangings are made of *fine twisted linen* but without blue, purple, or crimson. **1–8:** *The altar:* This is the main altar on which animal and grain offerings were burnt and wine offerings (libations) were poured. It is called "the altar of burnt offering" (30.28), after the type of offering made on it twice daily (29.38–43)—though in fact it is used for all types of offering (Lev. chs 1–7). It is also called "the copper [rather, bronze] altar" (38.30). Sacrifice is regarded as an expression of honor and gratitude and a means of purification and expiation, not a way of feeding God; God derives from it only the "pleasing odor" (29.18, 25, 41; Lev. 1.9 n.), an expression perhaps

---

fabrics that the laity are forbidden to wear (Lev. 19.19; Deut. 22.11) precisely because it is reserved for sacred use. See also 28.6, 15. **33:** *Under the clasps,* the clasps holding together the two halves of

the innermost cover (v. 6). Since this cover is 40 cubits (20 m, 60 ft) from front to back (including the part that hangs over the back of the structure), the clasps, and hence the curtain, are placed 20 square—and three cubits high. [2] Make its horns on the four corners, the horns to be of one piece with it; and overlay it with copper. [3] Make the pails for removing its ashes, as well as its scrapers, basins, flesh hooks, and fire pans—make all its utensils of copper. [4] Make for it a grating of meshwork in copper; and on the mesh make four copper rings at its four corners. [5] Set the mesh below, under the ledge of the altar, so that it extends to the middle of the altar. [6] And make poles for the altar, poles of acacia wood, and overlay them with copper. [7] The poles shall be inserted into the rings, so that the poles remain on the two sides of the altar when it is carried. [8] Make it hollow, of boards. As you were shown on the mountain, so shall they be made.

[9] You shall make the enclosure of the Tabernacle:

On the south side,[a] a hundred cubits of hangings of fine twisted linen for the length of the enclosure on that side— [10] with its twenty posts and their twenty sockets of copper, the hooks and bands of the posts to be of silver. [11] Again a hundred cubits of hangings for its length along the north side—with its twenty posts and their twenty sockets of copper, the hooks and bands of the posts to be of silver. [12] For the width of the enclosure, on the west side, fifty cubits of hangings, with their ten posts and their ten sockets. [13] For the width of the enclosure on the front, or east side, fifty cubits: [14] fifteen cubits of hangings on the one flank, with their three posts and their three sockets; [15] fifteen cubits of hangings on the other flank, with their three posts and their three sockets; [16] and for the gate of the enclosure, a screen of twenty cubits, of blue, purple, and crimson yarns, and fine twisted linen, done in embroidery, with their four posts and their four sockets. [17] All the posts round the enclosure shall be banded with silver and their hooks shall be of silver; their sockets shall be of copper. [18] The length of the enclosure shall be a hundred cubits, and the width fifty throughout; and the height five cubits—[with hangings] of fine twisted linen. The sockets shall be of copper: [19] all the utensils of the Tabernacle,[b] for all its service, as well as all its pegs and all the pegs of the court, shall be of copper.

a Cf. note at 26.18.
b I.e., of the Tabernacle enclosure; the furnishings inside were of gold.

meant literally or perhaps to indicate God's pleasure at the worshipper's devotion. That the sacrificial altar is located outside the Tabernacle building, and that none of the sacrifices are ever taken inside where God's presence abides, nicely expresses the idea that the sacrifices are not His food (cf. 25.23–30 n., 31–40 n.; 30.9 n.). **2:** *Horns,* horn-like projections pointing vertically at the upper corners of the altar (see also 30.2–3). Horned altars have been found by archeologists at several sites in Israel and elsewhere. They are an essential part of the altar: The blood of the "sin offering" is daubed on them (29.12; Lev. 4.29–30), and those seeking asylum at the altar (21.13–14 n.) would grasp them (1 Kings 1.50; 2.28). Their significance is not known, though Ps. 118.27 mentions tying sacrifices to them. **8:** *Hollow:* Unlike the case of the incense altar (30.3), no top is mentioned here, indicating that there was an open space inside the four walls of this altar. It may, then, have resembled in a general way the pit altars used by the Samaritans. It would have been very difficult, however, for the priests to reach down over the sides (which were 3 cubits = 1.5 m, 4.5 ft high [v. 1]) to handle the sacrifice at the bottom of such an open space, and the heat of the sacrificial fire would probably have damaged the bronzed wooden structure. It is traditionally assumed that, in keeping with the requirement of 20.21, the empty space was filled with earth each time the Israelites encamped, producing an earthen altar on which the sacrifices would be burnt (*Tg. Jon.;* Rashi; Rashbam). **9–19:** *The enclosure* of the Tabernacle (that is, its courtyard) will be 100 by 50 cubits (50 by 25 m, 150 by 75 ft) and five cubits (2.5 m, 7.5 ft) high—half as high as the Tabernacle itself (26.16). **13–16:** The eastern wall will have a 20-cubit-wide opening (10 m, 30 ft), shielded by a screen of the same width, to serve as its entrance. The screen will be made of the same quality materials as the

TETSAVVEH

תצוה

20 You shall further instruct the Israelites to bring you clear oil of beaten olives for lighting, for kindling lamps regularly. ²¹ Aaron and his sons shall set them up in the Tent of Meeting, outside the curtain which is over [the Ark of] the Pact, [to burn] from evening to morning before the LORD. It shall be a due from the Israelites for all time, throughout the ages.

28 You shall bring forward your brother Aaron, with his sons, from among the Israelites, to serve Me as priests: Aaron, Nadab and Abihu, Eleazar and Ithamar, the sons of Aaron. ² Make sacral vestments for your brother Aaron, for dignity and adornment. ³ Next you shall instruct all who are ^askillful, whom I have endowed with the gift of skill,^{-a} to make Aaron's vestments, for consecrating him to serve Me as priest. ⁴ These are the vest-

a-a Lit. "wise of heart, whom I have filled with a spirit of wisdom."

screen for the entrance of the Tent (v. 36) which it faces, except for its bronze rather than gold overlay. **19:** *The Tabernacle:* Here this means the courtyard.

27.20–30.38: The Tabernacle activities. After describing most of the fixed, permanent items of the sanctuary structure made of the materials listed in 25.3–5, the text turns to items made from the materials listed in 25.6–7. These items are described along with the activities (particularly the regular ["tamid"], daily priestly activities) performed with them: oil for the lamps (of 25.31–40) that are kindled regularly, the vestments worn by the priests when officiating (and hence also their ordination), culminating in the regular daily sacrifices (chs 28–29), the incense altar and the incense burned on it regularly (30.1–10, 34–38), the census (30.11–16), the laver where the priests would wash before officiating (30.17–21), and the sacred anointing oil (30.22–33). The shift in subject matter from sacred objects to activities is reflected in the fact that in Jewish liturgical practice a new weekly Torah portion ("Tetzaveh," "You shall . . . instruct") begins here.

27.20–21: Oil for the lamps. 20: *Further instruct the Israelites to bring you clear oil:* In addition to the original request (25.6), oil will have to be requested regularly since, unlike the materials used to construct the sanctuary (25.3–5), the oil supply is depletable. *For kindling lamps* (those of 25.31–40; see Lev. 24.4) *regularly,* every evening, to burn until morning (v. 21; Lev. 24.3–4; cf. 1 Sam. 3.3). In current Jewish practice this command is emulated by suspending a lamp from the ceiling in the synagogue above and in front of the Torah Ark. The lamp is called the "ner tamid," "eternal light," based on an alternative parsing of the Heb words for *lamps regularly.* This lamp identifies the synagogue as a "miniature sanctuary" (Ezek. 11.16) and serves as a symbol that the divine Presence accompanies the Jewish people (b. *Shab.* 22b). **21:** *Aaron and his sons,* the priests (28.1). According to 30.8; Lev. 24.3; Num. 8.2–3, only Aaron was to kindle the lamps; his sons—if their mention is not a scribal error—may have assisted him with the preparations. *Tent of Meeting,* see 25.8 n.

Chs 28–29: The priests. Having mentioned the priests in 27.21, the

text turns to their identity, their vestments, and their ordination.

28.1–43: The priestly vestments. *Bring forward:* This is to take place after the sanctuary is constructed (29.4; Lev. 8.6). *Aaron, with his sons,* 6.23; 24.1. The priesthood will be hereditary (29.8). The Bible never explains why Aaron was granted the priesthood. Later Jewish tradition praises him as a lover of peace who encouraged reconciliation and who brought people near to Torah (*Pirkei 'Avot* 1.12). One midrash holds that he was granted the privilege of wearing the Urim and Thummim over his heart (v. 29) because instead of being jealous of Moses' greater stature he "rejoiced in his heart" (4.14, literal translation; *Tanḥ., Shemot* 27). Another credits his receipt of the high priesthood to his employing delaying tactics when the Israelites decided to make the golden calf (*Exod. Rab.* 37.2). **2:** Aaron's *sacral vestments . . . for dignity and adornment* number seven in all, the six listed here plus a frontlet (vv. 36–38). An eighth item, *breeches* (vv. 42–43), is listed separately because they are neither visible nor sacral (contrast Lev. 16.4). These garments will be worn by the priests when officiating (Lev. 6.3; Ezek. 42.14; 44.17–19). No footwear is mentioned; 30.19 implies that they officiated barefoot (Naḥmanides; cf. 3.5; Josh. 5.14; *Exod. Rab.* 2, end), as their descendants still do nowadays when reciting the priestly benediction (Num. 6.24–26) in the synagogue. The four main vestments mentioned first are listed in order from the outermost to the innermost: the breastpiece, which was attached to the front of the ephod, the ephod itself, the robe, and the tunic (see 29.5; cf., with a slight difference, Lev. 8.7–8). **3:** *Skillful . . . skill:* Artistic skills, no less than intellectual ones, are recognized as forms of wisdom. *Gift,* lit. "spirit." Extraordinary skills are gifts from God. *For consecrating him to serve Me:* Placing these vestments on Aaron (and his sons) will be a constitutive part of their ordination ments they are to make: a breastpiece, an ephod, a robe, a fringed[a] tunic, a headdress, and a sash. They shall make those sacral vestments for your brother Aaron and his sons, for priestly service to Me; [5] they, therefore, shall receive the gold, the blue, purple, and crimson yarns, and the fine linen.

[6] They shall make the ephod of gold, of blue, purple, and crimson yarns, and of fine twisted linen, worked into designs. [7] It shall have two shoulder-pieces attached; they shall be attached at its two ends. [8] And the decorated band that is upon it shall be made like it, of one piece with it: of gold, of blue, purple, and crimson yarns, and of fine twisted linen. [9] Then take two lazuli stones and engrave on them the names of the sons of Israel: [10] six of their names on the one stone, and the names of the remaining six on the other stone, in the order of their birth. [11] On the two stones you shall make seal engravings—the work of a lapidary—of the names of the sons of Israel. Having bordered them with frames of gold, [12] attach the two stones to the shoulder-pieces of the ephod, as stones for remembrance of the Israelite people, whose names Aaron shall carry upon his two shoulder-pieces for remembrance before the LORD.

[13] Then make frames of gold [14] and two chains of pure gold; braid these like corded work, and fasten the corded chains to the frames.

[15] You shall make a breastpiece of decision,[b] worked into a design; make it in the style of the ephod: make it of gold, of blue, purple, and crimson yarns, and of fine twisted linen. [16] It shall be square and doubled, a span in length and a span in width. [17] Set in it mounted stones, in four rows of stones. The first row shall be a row of [c]car-

---

a Others "checkered."   b See v. 30 below; others "judgment."
c The identity of several of these twelve stones is uncertain.

---

ceremony (v. 41; 29.1–9; Lev. 8.7–9, 13; Num. 29.26, 28). **5:** *They, therefore, shall receive,* those with artistic skill (v. 3). The finest materials called for in 25.3–4 shall be given to the artisans to make the priestly vestments. These will be made of the same materials as the most sacred parts of the sanctuary itself. **6–38:** Aaron's sacral vestments. **6–30:** The ephod (vv. 6–12) and the breastpiece (vv. 15–30). The order of these two items is the reverse of that given in v. 4, but in essence the two constitute a unit both

physically, since the breastpiece is attached to the ephod (vv. 22–28), and functionally, since both are involved in ascertaining the divine will. Elsewhere the term ephod (and cognates in other Semitic languages) refers to a garment of uncertain appearance (1 Sam. 2.18; 2 Sam. 6.14) and also to a device carried by priests and used to determine God's will (1 Sam. 2.28; 14.3; 23.6, 9–12; 30.7–8). Here it is clearly a garment, and the divinatory device— the breastpiece containing the

Urim and Thummim (vv. 15–30)— is attached to it. Using the Urim and Thummim to determine God's will is one of the most important functions of the priest. Because of the importance of this function and Aaron's access to the interior of the sanctuary, the ephod and the breastpiece are, like it, made of the most precious materials (vv. 6, 15) including the sacred mixture of wool and linen (26.31 n.); cf. 39.29. **9–12:** The inscriptions on the epaulets of the ephod. **9:** *Lazuli,* translation not certain. **10:** *In the order of their birth,* see Gen. 29.32–30.24; 35.16–18. **11:** *Seal engravings—the work of a lapidary,* cf. v. 21. The stones are to be inscribed by the technique used by lapidaries who engraved people's names on gems and other stones to be used as seals. **12:** *For remembrance . . . before the LORD:* This phrase evokes the formula of ancient graffiti and votive inscriptions that pray that "so-and-so may be remembered (for good) before the deity." The ancients sought by various means to make the gods mindful of them: by placing votive statues of themselves in an attitude of prayer in sanctuaries—a method forbidden in the Bible—by donating ritual objects inscribed with their names to sanctuaries, and by writing graffiti praying for remembrance by the deity. Most reminiscent of the present v. are seals inscribed with both the owner's name and a prayer for divine blessing. Some of these are written in positive rather than mirror-writing and hence were not intended as functional seals; they were likely placed in sanctuaries to secure divine remembrance. Thus, each time Aaron entered the sanctuary wearing these inscriptions he not only represented the Israelites but carried before God an implicit prayer on their behalf. **15–30:** The *breastpiece of decision,* a pouch, approx. 24 cm (9 in) square and attached to the ephod, containing *the instrument of decision* (v. 30). **17–20:** The inscribed stones on the breastpiece function as do the inscribed epaulets (vv. 9–12). The translation nelian, chrysolite, and emerald; [18] the second row: a turquoise, a sapphire, and an amethyst; [19] the third row: a jacinth, an agate, and a crystal; [20] and the fourth row: a beryl, a lapis lazuli, and a jasper. They shall be framed with gold in their mountings. [21] The stones shall correspond [in number] to the names of the sons of Israel: twelve, corresponding to their names. They shall be engraved like seals, each with its name, for the twelve tribes.

[22] On the breastpiece make braided chains of corded work in pure gold. [23] Make two rings of gold on the breastpiece, and fasten the two rings at the two ends of the breastpiece, [24] attaching the two golden cords to the two rings at the ends of the breastpiece. [25] Then fasten the two ends of the cords to the two frames, which you shall attach to the shoulder-pieces of the ephod, at the front. [26] Make two rings of gold and attach them to the two ends of the breastpiece, at its inner edge, which faces the ephod. [27] And make two other rings of gold and fasten them on the front of the ephod, low on the two shoulder-pieces, close to its seam above the decorated band. [28] The breastpiece shall be held in place by a cord of blue from its rings to the rings of the ephod, so that the breastpiece rests on the decorated band and does not come loose from the ephod. [29] Aaron shall carry the names of the sons of Israel on the breastpiece of decision over his heart, when he enters the sanctuary, for remembrance before the LORD at all times. [30] Inside the breastpiece of decision you shall place the Urim and Thummim,[a] so that they are over Aaron's heart when he comes before the LORD. Thus Aaron shall carry the instrument of decision for the Israelites over his heart before the LORD at all times.

[31] You shall make the robe of the ephod of pure blue.[b] [32] The opening for the head shall be in the middle of it; the opening shall have a binding of woven work round about—it shall be like the opening of a coat of mail—so that it does not tear. [33] On its hem make pomegranates of blue, purple, and crimson yarns, all around the hem, with bells of gold between them all around: [34] a golden bell and a pomegranate, a golden bell and a pomegranate, all around the hem of the robe. [35] Aaron shall wear it while

a Meaning of these two words uncertain. They designate a kind of oracle; cf. Num. 27.21.
b Others "all of blue."

of the names of the twelve stones is not certain. **21:** *Engraved like seals,* see v. 11 n. **29:** See v. 12 n. **30:** *Urim and Thummim . . . the instrument of decision:* The Urim and Thummim was a device for ob-

taining God's *decision* on important questions on which human judgment was found inadequate, such as military actions, allocation of land, legal verdicts in the absence of evidence, and choice of

leaders (Num. 27.21; 1 Sam. 14.37–42 [see v. 41 translators' note *a-a*]; Ezra 2.63; cf. Exod. 22.8 n.; Josh. 7.14–18; Judg. 1.1–2; 20.18; 1 Sam. 10.20–22; 2 Sam. 2.1; 5.23–24). It apparently consisted of two or more lots (Prov. 16.33) which the priest drew out of the breastpiece and which signified a positive, negative, or noncommittal answer to a question or indicated a particular message (see esp. 1 Sam. 14.41 with translators' note *a-a*). *Urim and Thummim* may have been the names of the lots. Derivation of these terms from Heb "'or," "light," and "tom," "completeness, perfection, integrity," is suggestive but far from certain. *Thus Aaron shall carry the instrument of decision for the Israelites . . . before the LORD at all times:* This may indicate that the Urim and Thummim were consulted only in the sanctuary. **31–35:** *The robe of the ephod* indicates that it is part of the same unit as the ephod and the breastpiece of decision; they would all be worn together. Its shape seems to resemble an ankle-length sleeveless shirt, and its single color, with no gold or linen admixture, indicates its lesser importance than the two outer items. **33:** The robe's most distinctive feature is its hemline with dyed wool pomegranate-shaped tassels and golden bells. Pomegranates—a well-known symbol of fertility—were a popular artistic motif in ancient Israel and adorned Solomon's Temple in several places (1 Kings 7.42; 2 Kings 25.17; Jer. 52.23; 2 Chron. 3.16; 4.13). A small ivory pomegranate, containing an inscription in Heb script of the First Temple period, came to light in Jerusalem in 1979; the inscription, plausibly restored, seems to say "Belonging to the Tem[ple of the Lor]d, holy to the priests." **35:** The purpose of the bells is not clear. The ominous explanation *that he may not die* may indicate that the bells were apotropaic devices to protect the priest from demons that are widely believed to haunt thresholds (cf. Gen. 4.7; the rites mentioned in 1 Sam. 5.5 and Zeph. 1.9 may have originated in a similar officiating, so that the sound of it is heard when he comes into the sanctuary before the LORD and when he goes out—that he may not die.

36 You shall make a frontlet of pure gold and engrave on it the seal inscription: "Holy to the LORD." 37 Suspend it on a cord of blue, so that it may remain on the headdress; it shall remain on the front of the headdress. 38 It shall be on Aaron's forehead, that Aaron may take away any sin arising from the holy things that the Israelites consecrate, from any of their sacred donations; it shall be on his forehead at all times, to win acceptance for them before the LORD.

39 You shall make the fringed tunic of fine linen.
You shall make the headdress of fine linen.
You shall make the sash of embroidered work.

40 And for Aaron's sons also you shall make tunics, and make sashes for them, and make turbans for them, for dignity and adornment. 41 Put these on your brother Aaron and on his sons as well; anoint them, and ordain them[a] and consecrate them to serve Me as priests.

42 You shall also make for them linen breeches to cover

---

a Lit. "and fill their hands."

---

belief); that is why the sound must be heard when the priest leaves the sanctuary as well as when he enters. If that was the original purpose it seems to have been abandoned by the Bible, which gives similar warnings with the requirements that the priests wear underpants and wash their hands and feet before ministering (v. 43; 30.20–21); this suggests that these items and actions are expressions of respect for God: One does not approach Him unannounced, unwashed, or immodestly dressed. In any case, all such warnings reflect the potential lethality of the sanctuary and its contents (19.21 n., 22 n.; see also 30.33, 37; Lev. 10.6, 9; 16.2, 13; Num. 4.15, 19–20; 17.28; 18.3, 22). **36–38:** The *frontlet* (lit. "blossom, flower," perhaps indicating its shape; it is called a "diadem" in 29.6 and both terms are used in 39.30 and Lev. 8.9) was attached to the front of Aaron's *headdress* (v. 39). The frontlet functions in relation to sin that might occur in the sanctuary because of imperfections or impurities in the Israel-

ites' sacrifices. Aaron, by wearing the inscription "Holy to the Lord"—presumably meaning that he is sacrosanct and hence protected by God from harm (19.5b–6a n.)—will be able to expiate any such sin and eliminate it. Coming as it does after the bells (and pomegranates) on Aaron's hem that may have originated as apotropaic devices, it is noteworthy that the frontlet is called "blossom, flower" and is worn on Aaron's forehead, since in Mesopotamian iconography the most common apotropaic headornament (worn even by gods for their own protection) is the rosette, a blossom-shaped decoration worn on the forehead, and that it is held in place by a blue cord, since blue is frequently used in apotropaic devices. Here, however, the text says that *Aaron*—not the frontlet—[shall] *take away . . . sin* and that his wearing it is *to win acceptance for* Israel *before the* LORD—indicating that Aaron will take away sin because wearing the frontlet pleases God, not because it

has any inherent apotropaic power. **39:** In addition to the preceding vestments, Aaron was to wear a *fringed tunic of fine linen* ("of woven work" according to 39.27) under them, a *headdress* of unknown appearance, and an ornate *sash* which, like the ephod and the breastpiece, was made of the sacred mixture of wool and linen (39.29). Since the sash was an emblem of office (Isa. 22.21) and ornate in appearance, it was naturally to be worn over Aaron's other vestments (29.5–9). **40:** The other priests have three vestments, similar to the last three of Aaron's vestments but simpler, reflecting their lower status: *tunics* ("of fine linen, of woven work," 39.27), like Aaron's, but not fringed; *sashes*, whether identical to Aaron's or simpler depends on whether 39.29 refers only to Aaron's sash or to those of all the priests; and *turbans* (translation uncertain, but presumably different in appearance from Aaron's *headdress*), also made of fine linen (39.28) but lacking a frontlet. In contrast to Aaron's vestments which are made of materials used in the interior of the sanctuary, those of the other priests, possibly excluding their sashes, match the material of the courtyard hangings (linen, 27.9). **41:** That is: Robe the priests in their vestments and then anoint them and ordain them, thereby consecrating them as priests; see 29.1–37, introductory n. *Anoint:* Sacred anointing oil is to be poured on Aaron's head and sprinkled on his sons (29.7, 21) to sanctify them for their duties (29.21; 30.22–33). *Ordain:* lit. "fill their hand," an expression that probably originated in an induction ceremony in which a symbol of office was placed in the inductee's hand. Conceivably it refers to the temporary placement of parts of the "ordination offering" in the priests' hands (29.24; see Lev. 8.22–29 n.), but it may be no more than an idiom here. **42–43.** The priests' *breeches*, that is, underpants, are separated from the list of sacral vestments by v. 41 because they are not sacral their nakedness; they shall extend from the hips to the thighs. [43] They shall be worn by Aaron and his sons when they enter the Tent of Meeting or when they approach the altar to officiate in the sanctuary, so that they do not incur punishment and die. It shall be a law for all time for him and for his offspring to come.

29 This is what you shall do to them in consecrating them to serve Me as priests: Take a young bull of the herd and two rams without blemish; [2] also unleavened bread, unleavened cakes with oil mixed in, and unleavened wafers spread with oil—make these of choice wheat flour. [3] Place these in one basket and present them in the basket, along with the bull and the two rams. [4] Lead Aaron and his sons up to the entrance of the Tent of Meeting, and wash them with water. [5] Then take the vestments, and clothe Aaron with the tunic, the robe of the ephod, the ephod, and the breastpiece, and gird him with the decorated band of the ephod. [6] Put the headdress on his head, and place the holy diadem upon the headdress. [7] Take the anointing oil and pour it on his head and anoint him. [8] Then bring his sons forward; clothe them with tunics [9] and wind turbans upon them. And gird both Aaron and his sons with sashes. And so they shall have priesthood as their right for all time.

You shall then ordain Aaron and his sons. [10] Lead the bull up to the front of the Tent of Meeting, and let Aaron and his sons lay their hands upon the head of the bull. [11] Slaughter the bull before the LORD, at the entrance of the Tent of Meeting, [12] and take some of the bull's blood and put it on the horns of the altar with your finger; then pour out the rest of the blood at the base of the altar. [13] Take all the fat that covers the entrails, the protuberance on the liver, and the two kidneys with the fat on them, and turn them into smoke upon the altar. [14] The rest of the flesh of the bull, its hide, and its dung shall be put to the fire outside the camp; it is a sin offering.

[15] Next take the one ram, and let Aaron and his sons lay their hands upon the ram's head. [16] Slaughter the ram, and take its blood and dash it against all sides of the altar. [17] Cut up the ram into sections, wash its entrails and legs,

unique to priests (robing with the vestments, anointing with holy oil, and the ordination sacrifice [28.41]) constitute their consecration; the other parts (washing and the first two sacrifices) are preparatory. The performance of the ceremony is narrated in Lev. chs 8–9; cf. Exod. 40.12–16. **3:** *Present them,* "before the LORD" (v. 23), probably before the altar (Deut. 26.4, 10). **4:** *Entrance of the Tent of Meeting,* the courtyard in front of the Tent. *Wash them with water,* as part of the process of purification (Lev. chs 14–17). **5–6:** For the vestments, see ch 28. Only those that have ceremonial significance are mentioned here; that the priests would put on their breeches (28.42–43) goes without saying. **7:** *Anointing oil,* 30.22–33; *anoint,* 28.41 n. **9b–14:** The purification offering (Heb "ḥaṭa't"; for this translation, rather than "sin offering" [v. 14], see Lev. 4.3 n.) follows the procedure prescribed in Lev. ch 4; cf. Num. 15.22–31. On the purpose of this type of offering, see introductory notes to Lev. 4.1–5.26; 4.1–35; chs 12–25; 16.1–34; 15.31 n. Here the altar is purified (v. 12), either from impurities stemming from its builders and the donors of its materials and (since purification offerings normally purge impurities stemming from the individuals who bring them) from the priests. **10:** *Lay their hands upon the head of the bull:* The meaning of the act is uncertain; it may identify Aaron and his sons as the ones on whose behalf the sacrifice is being made. For another view, see Lev. 1.4 n. **12:** *Take some of the bull's blood and put on the horns of the altar:* The animal's blood serves as the purifying agent, the "detergent" in purification offerings. Applying the blood to the horns of the altar (27.2)—its vulnerable extremities representing all of the altar—purifies the altar (cf. Ezek. 43.20). *Pour out the rest of the blood at the base of the altar,* Lev. 4.4–11 n. **13:** Lev. 3.3–4 n. **14:** Lev. 4.11; 6.23 (see n.). *Sin offering,* better, "purification offering" (see Lev. 4.3 n.). **15–18:** The burnt offering, following the procedure prescribed in

vestments and hence not part of the ordination ceremony (cf. 29.5 n.); they are purely functional, to prevent exposure of the genitals. Evidently breeches were not regularly worn by men, hence the need to require them for priests. See 20.23 n. **43:** *To officiate,* to offer sacrifices (Ezek. 44.15; 2 Chron. 29.11). *And die,* v. 35 n.

29.1–37: The consecration of the priests. This ceremony consists of six parts: washing, robing, and anointing the priests and three sacrifices. The three elements that are and put them with its quarters and its head. [18] Turn all of the ram into smoke upon the altar. It is a burnt offering to the LORD, a pleasing odor, an offering by fire to the LORD.

[19] Then take the other ram, and let Aaron and his sons lay their hands upon the ram's head. [20] Slaughter the ram, and take some of its blood and put it on the ridge[a] of Aaron's right ear and on the ridges of his sons' right ears, and on the thumbs of their right hands, and on the big toes of their right feet; and dash the rest of the blood against every side of the altar round about. [21] Take some of the blood that is on the altar and some of the anointing oil and sprinkle upon Aaron and his vestments, and also upon his sons and his sons' vestments. Thus shall he and his vestments be holy, as well as his sons and his sons' vestments.

[22] You shall take from the ram the fat parts—the broad tail, the fat that covers the entrails, the protuberance on the liver, the two kidneys with the fat on them—and the right thigh; for this is a ram of ordination. [23] Add one flat loaf of bread, one cake of oil bread, and one wafer, from the basket of unleavened bread that is before the LORD. [24] Place all these on the palms of Aaron and his sons, and offer them as an elevation offering before the LORD. [25] Take them from their hands and turn them into smoke upon the altar with the burnt offering, as a pleasing odor before the LORD; it is an offering by fire to the LORD.

[26] Then take the breast of Aaron's ram of ordination and offer it as an elevation offering before the LORD; it shall be your portion. [27] You shall consecrate the breast that was offered as an elevation offering and the thigh that was offered as a gift offering from the ram of ordination—from that which was Aaron's and from that which was his sons'—[28] and those parts shall be a due for all time from

a Or "lobe."

Lev. ch 1. See the comments there. **19–34:** The ordination offering. This is the most elaborate offering, completing the priests' consecration by further anointment and then ordaining them. It follows the procedure for offering sheep as "sacrifices of well-being" (18.12 n.) prescribed in Lev. 3.6–11 and 7.11–34 with modifications specific to this occasion. **20:** As in the case of applying blood to the horns of the altar (v. 12), vulnerable extremities of the priests, representing

their entire bodies, are daubed with blood, apparently to purge them of impurity (cf. v. 33 and the similar rite in Lev. 14.14–20, 25–31). *Dash the rest of the blood against every side of the altar,* a standard procedure in sacrifices (see Lev. 1.5 n.). **21:** The mixture of blood from the altar and anointing oil makes the priests and their garments holy; the anointing oil because that is its function (30.25–30) and the blood because being on the altar has made it holy (v. 37b).

and capable of transmitting holiness to anything it touches (Hazzekuni; see Lev. 6.11 n.). **22:** The fat parts of the sacrifice of well-being are burnt on the altar, as prescribed in Lev. 3.9–11. *And the right thigh; for this is a ram of ordination:* The right thigh of a sacrifice of well-being is normally given to the officiating priest (Lev. 7.32–33), but not in the case of an ordination offering. **23:** Sacrifices of well-being commonly include grain offerings (Lev. 7.11–13; cf. Lev. ch 2; Exod. 12.8). These, too, are normally eaten by the officiating priest (Lev. ch 2; 6.7–11; 7.14), but when, as on the present occasion, the offering is on his own behalf, it is burnt on the altar (Lev. 6.12–16). *Unleavened bread:* As v. 2 indicates, all the items mentioned in this v. must be unleavened, as is the case with most grain offerings (12.8 n.; Lev. 2.11–12; 6.9–10). **24:** Moses is to place these items in the priests' hands, to indicate that they are from them (Lev. 7.30; Num. 6.19–20) and then cause them to *offer* (lit. "elevate") *them as an elevation offering:* a gesture indicating that the offering is donated to God (Lev. 7.30 n.). **25:** *With the burnt offering,* of vv. 15–18. The combination of burnt offerings and sacrifices of well-being is very common (10.25; 18.12; 20.21; 24.5; 32.6; Lev. 17.8; etc.). The former is given entirely to God, while parts of the latter are eaten by the donor, guests, and the priests. **26:** *Your portion:* Since the priests' consecration is not yet complete and Moses is officiating in their stead, he is to receive the portion that will in the future go to them (vv. 27–28). **27–28:** A parenthetic note indicating that the disposition of the ram is to be the precedent for all future sacrifices of well-being, with one exception: both the *breast . . . and* (unlike the present occasion, v. 22) the right *thigh* shall be given to the priests (Lev. 7.34–35; 10.15). **28:** In addition to the fat parts, which are burnt (vv. 22, 25), the breast and right thigh of sacrifices of well-being are also donated by the people to God, who assigns them to the Israelites to Aaron and his descendants. For they are a gift; and so shall they be a gift from the Israelites, their gift to the LORD out of their sacrifices of well-being.

29 The sacral vestments of Aaron shall pass on to his sons after him, for them to be anointed and ordained in. 30 He among his sons who becomes priest in his stead, who enters the Tent of Meeting to officiate within the sanctuary, shall wear them seven days.

31 You shall take the ram of ordination and boil its flesh in the sacred precinct; 32 and Aaron and his sons shall eat the flesh of the ram, and the bread that is in the basket, at the entrance of the Tent of Meeting. 33 These things shall be eaten only by those for whom expiation was made with them when they were ordained and consecrated; they may not be eaten by a layman, for they are holy. 34 And if any of the flesh of ordination, or any of the bread, is left until morning, you shall put what is left to the fire; it shall not be eaten, for it is holy.

35 Thus you shall do to Aaron and his sons, just as I have commanded you. You shall ordain them through seven days, 36 and each day you shall prepare a bull as a sin offering for expiation; you shall purge the altar by performing purification upon it, and you shall anoint it to consecrate it. 37 Seven days you shall perform purification for the altar to consecrate it, and the altar shall become most holy; whatever touches the altar shall become consecrated.

38 Now this is what you shall offer upon the altar: two yearling lambs each day, regularly. 39 You shall offer the one lamb in the morning, and you shall offer the other lamb at twilight. 40 There shall be a tenth of a measure of choice flour with a quarter of a *hin* of beaten oil mixed in, and a libation of a quarter *hin* of wine for one lamb; 41 and you shall offer the other lamb at twilight, repeating with it the meal offering of the morning with its libation—an of-

consecration of the priests and the altar is to go on for a week. Cf. Ezek. 43.25–26; 2 Chron. 7.9. *Shall become consecrated:* Once the altar is sanctified, its holiness will become contagious. As in the case of other sanctuary furniture and parts of certain sacrifices, anything that touches it will likewise become holy and unfit for ordinary activity and will become the property of the sanctuary. See 30.29; Lev. 6.11 n., 20; Num. 17.1–4 (Ezek. 44.19; 46.20 holds that even people can become consecrated in this way).

29.38–42: The obligatory daily offering. Now that the altar and priests have been sanctified, the text again (as in vv. 27–30) turns to the future, describing the regular daily offering for which the priests are now fit (cf. Ezek. 43.18–27). This offering, made twice daily and known as the "tamid" ("regular" [sacrifice], Dan. 8.11), became the core of the sacrificial system (Num. 28.3–8). With this the text resumes the theme of regular ("tamid") rites begun in 27.20–21. The "tamid" offering consists of the simple staples of the Israelites' diet: the meat of lambs (the least expensive meat), wheat, oil, and wine. No attempt is made to provide delicacies or sumptuous quantities as would befit God's greatness (contrast the royal diet in 1 Kings 5.2–3). This reflects the token nature of biblical sacrifice, expressive of the worshippers' attitude, as distinct from actually feeding God (27.1–8 n.). **39:** *In the morning . . . at twilight:* In the priestly calendar, the day began in the morning. **40:** Cf. Lev. 6.12–16. *A tenth of a measure,* a tenth of an "'efah" measure, about 2.3 liters (2.1 dry quarts); see 16.36 n. *Hin,* a liquid measure of uncertain size (possibly about a gallon, in which case a quarter of a "hin" would be a liter or a quart). *Libation:* Libations of wine often accompany burnt and well-being offerings (Lev. 23.13, 18, 27; Num. 15.1–12; Num. 28–29; 2 Kings 6.13, 15), though no independent libation is prescribed. **41:** *An offering by fire for a pleasing odor to the LORD:* Lev.

the priests for their maintenance. **29–30:** A second parenthetic note: The robing of the high priest and the seven-day duration of the ceremony (v. 35) shall be the precedent for the ordination of future high priests. **31–33:** The consecration continues: The remainder of the ram is cooked and eaten, along with the remainder of the unleavened bread, by the priests in the courtyard. **31:** *The sacred precinct,* lit. "in a holy place," either anywhere in the court or in a specific

part of it, perhaps the area between the altar and the Tent of Meeting (cf. Lev. 6.9, 19; 8.31). **33:** *They may not be eaten by a layman, for they are holy,* a blanket rule concerning the sacrificial portions assigned to the priests (Lev. 22.10–16). Cf. 30.31–33. **34:** This rule also applies to other sacrifices of well-being, namely the pesaḥ and other festival offerings (12.10; 23.28; 34.25; Lev. 7.15; 22.30; contrast 7.16–17; 19.6). **35–37:** The fering by fire for a pleasing odor to the LORD, [42] a regular burnt offering throughout the generations, at the entrance of the Tent of Meeting before the LORD.

For there I will meet with you, and there I will speak with you, [43] and there I will meet with the Israelites, and it shall be sanctified by My Presence. [44] I will sanctify the Tent of Meeting and the altar, and I will consecrate Aaron and his sons to serve Me as priests. [45] I will abide among the Israelites, and I will be their God. [46] And they shall know that I the LORD am their God, who brought them out from the land of Egypt that I might abide among them, I the LORD their God.

30 You shall make an altar for burning incense; make it of acacia wood. [2] It shall be a cubit long and a cubit wide—it shall be square—and two cubits high, its horns of one piece with it. [3] Overlay it with pure gold: its top, its sides round about, and its horns; and make a gold

1.9 n. **42:** *At the entrance of the Tent of Meeting:* i.e., at the altar in the courtyard.

29.42b–46: The divine Presence in the sanctuary. The sanctuary will be ready to serve its various functions as the site of divine-human communication, as a sanctuary, and as the locus of God's Presence among the Israelites. In this climactic passage, all these functions are alluded to by the verbs (each occurring at least twice) from which the three main terms for the sanctuary (25.8) are derived—thereby explaining these terms. God will *meet* ("ʾivaʿed," "noʿad") there with Moses and Israel, echoing "Tent of Meeting" ("ʾohel moʿed"), it will be *sanctified* ("nikdash," "kadesh," echoing "mikdash," "sanctuary"), and God will *abide* ("shakhan") there, echoing "abode" ("mishkan"). That these goals are mentioned after the regular daily sacrifice may reflect the idea that sacrificial worship is the means by which God is drawn to the sanctuary (20.21 n.). Notably, however, sacrifice is presented as a means, not as a goal in itself. The sanctuary is for the benefit of Israel, not God (see introductory note to 25.1–31.17).
42b–43: *For there I will meet with*

you . . . , see 25.22. The threefold repetition of "there" emphasizes that it is the sanctuary that will become the regular place of communication between God and Israel. **43:** The ordination ceremony will culminate in a theophany in which God's Presence will appear at the Tent of Meeting in the sight of the entire people (Lev. 9.4, 6, 23–24), thus sanctifying it by His Presence (cf. also 40.34). *I will meet* [Heb "noʿadti"] *with the Israelites:* This statement is unexpected since elsewhere God meets only with Moses (Num. 17.19) (although the first "you" in v. 42 and the one in Num. 17.19 are in the plural, the Septuagint and Samaritan Pentateuch and some Heb manuscripts read the singular, consistent with the second "you"). One wonders, therefore, whether the text did not originally read "I shall make Myself known ("nodaʿti") to the Israelites"; cf. Ezek. 20.5, 9; 36.23.
44: Perhaps this refers to God's sending fire to consume the offerings on the altar (Lev. 9.24), meaning that the fire sanctified the altar and the sanctuary, and hence the priests who made the offerings. But this v. and v. 43 seem redundant and inconsistent with vv. 21, 36–37 and 30.29–30 which state that it is Moses who will sanctify

the sanctuary, the altar, and the priests by sacrifice and anointment. This has led to the suggestion that vv. 42b–46 are not from the Priestly source but stem from the "Holiness Collection" ("H") in which God regularly concludes His statements with "I, the LORD your/their God," and which holds that it is God who sanctifies the priests and the sanctuary (Lev. 21.15, 23; 2.16). If that is the case, the aim of the interpolation is apparently to override the message of vv. 21, 36–37; 30.29–30 by indicating that sacrifice and anointment are not efficacious by themselves; the real source of sanctification is God. **45–46:** These concluding vv. echo the promises of 25.8 and 6.7, tying the exodus narrative and the Tabernacle instructions into one overarching structure of meaning: With the Tabernacle finished God will abide among the Israelites, as promised in 25.8, and fulfill His covenant with them by being their God, as promised in 6.7, and the Israelites will understand that these were the ultimate purpose of the exodus: *that I might abide among them.* Although reminiscent of 6.7b, this v. diverges from it by emphasizing the ultimate goal of the exodus: not only freedom from servitude but living in the presence of God. In this respect the goal of the exodus is already achieved even before reaching the promised land. This might explain why the Torah is complete without the depiction of the conquest in the book of Joshua—it is the indwelling of the divine Presence, rather than the conquest of the land that culminates the exodus. According to 15.17 (see also 6.8), however, the same goal will be achieved in the promised land when the Temple is built (15.17 n.).

30.1–31.17: Supplementary instructions concerning the sanctuary. This section begins with instructions for constructing the incense altar, taking a census, constructing the laver, and for compounding the anointing oil and sacred incense (ch 30). These five molding for it round about. ⁴And make two gold rings for it under its molding; make them on its two side walls, on opposite*ᵃ* sides. They shall serve as holders for poles with which to carry it. ⁵Make the poles of acacia wood, and overlay them with gold.

⁶Place it in front of the curtain that is over the Ark of the Pact—in front of the cover that is over the Pact—where I will meet with you. ⁷On it Aaron shall burn aromatic incense: he shall burn it every morning when he tends the lamps, ⁸and Aaron shall burn it at twilight when he lights the lamps—a regular incense offering before the LORD throughout the ages. ⁹You shall not offer alien incense on it, or a burnt offering or a meal offering; neither shall you pour a libation on it. ¹⁰Once a year Aaron shall perform purification upon its horns with blood of the sin offering of purification; purification shall be performed upon it once a year throughout the ages. It is most holy to the LORD.

KI TISSA'   כי תשא

¹¹The LORD spoke to Moses, saying: ¹²When you take a census of the Israelite people according to their enrollment, each shall pay the LORD a ransom for himself on

a Lit. "its two."

Holies, flanked by the table and the lampstand (40.5, 22–26). The burning of incense on it was, like the activities performed on the table and lampstand, one of the regular ("tamid"), daily activities of the Tabernacle (27.20–30.38 n.; 27.20 n.). It was .5 m (1.5 ft) square and 1 m (3 ft) high. Numerous incense altars, some with horns as prescribed here, have been found among archeological remains from ancient Israel and elsewhere. Burning incense was common in ancient religions. Since here it is part of the complex of daily activities inside the Holy Place that includes kindling lamps (v. 7), it is perhaps regarded as a natural feature of a courtly residence, creating a pleasing aroma inside. Maimonides holds that it is to counteract the stench of the animals being slaughtered and sacrificed (*Guide of the Perplexed* 3.45). **9:** *Alien,* unauthorized, compounded with a formula different from that prescribed in vv. 34–36. *Or a burnt offering or a meal offering; neither shall you pour a libation on it:* No food or drink offerings may be made inside the Tent. Only the "bread of display," which is eaten by the priests, is presented there. This shows again that the offerings are tokens but are not consumed by God. See 25.23–30 n.; 29.38–42 n. **10:** *Once a year,* on the Day of Atonement (Lev. 16.16; cf. 4.18; *m. Yoma* 5.5).

30.11–16: Census. Apparently this regulation is placed here because the census involves collecting silver that will be used for the construction of the Tabernacle (v. 16) and because the donations serve as "expiation" (vv. 15–16), thus creating a link with v. 10 where "purification" is expressed by the same Heb word ("kaper"/"kipurim"; see Lev. 4.3 n.). The juxtaposition of this law to the incense altar may also have been prompted by the apotropaic function (i.e., one that averts ill consequences) of the census donation in preventing a plague (v. 12), since incense sometimes has an apotropaic function (Num. 17.11–13). Censuses were

supplementary instructions are followed by the designation of the chief artisans for the entire construction project and a final injunction to suspend all construction and manufacture on the Sabbath (31.1–17). There are phraseological similarities among the five subsections of ch 30, and their order could be due to the fact that first three deal with items made, respectively, of gold, silver, and bronze (see 25.1–31.17 n.) and that items two through five employ materials acquired from special contributions, not those donated by the public at large or in response to the initial appeal (25.2–7; 35.4–9): silver from the census levy (v. 13), the bronze for the laver "from the mirrors of the women who performed tasks at the entrance of the Tent" (38.8), and the spices and oil from the chieftains (35.27–28). It is unclear, however, why all these items appear after 29.42b–46, which seems to conclude the manufacturing instruc-

tions. Why were the incense altar and the laver not mentioned earlier along with the other items in, respectively, the Holy Place (25.23–40; 26.35) and the courtyard (27.1–19) where they will stand, and why do the census, the anointing oil, and the incense appear here? In subsequent lists of the contents of the Tabernacle, the incense altar, the laver, the anointing oil, and the incense are listed in their proper physical or functional location (30.26–28; 31.7–11; 35.11–19; 39.33–40; 40.1–15, 18–33). Their location here indicates that the material was organized according to principles that elude us and, perhaps, that they were added to this text (though not necessarily composed) at a later date.

30.1–10: The incense altar. This altar would stand in the Holy Place and was, accordingly, overlaid with gold. Its importance is indicated by its location directly in front of the curtain of the Holy of being enrolled, that no plague may come upon them through their being enrolled. ¹³ This is what everyone who is entered in the records shall pay: a half-shekel by the sanctuary weight—twenty *gerahs* to the shekel—a half-shekel as an offering to the LORD. ¹⁴ Everyone who is entered in the records, from the age of twenty years up, shall give the LORD's offering: ¹⁵ the rich shall not pay more and the poor shall not pay less than half a shekel when giving the LORD's offering as expiation for your persons. ¹⁶ You shall take the expiation money from the Israelites and assign it to the service of the Tent of Meeting; it shall serve the Israelites as a reminder before the LORD, as expiation for your persons.

¹⁷ The LORD spoke to Moses, saying: ¹⁸ Make a laver of copper and a stand of copper for it, for washing; and place it between the Tent of Meeting and the altar. Put water in it, ¹⁹ and let Aaron and his sons wash their hands and feet [in water drawn] from it. ²⁰ When they enter the Tent of Meeting they shall wash with water, that they may not die; or when they approach the altar to serve, to turn into smoke an offering by fire to the LORD, ²¹ they shall wash their hands and feet, that they may not die. It shall be a law for all time for them—for him and his offspring—throughout the ages.

normally taken for purposes of military (14 n.; Num. 1.2–3; 2 Sam. 24.9) or other forms of public service (Num. 4.2–3, 22–23, 29–30; 1 Chron. 23.24–32), land distribution (Num. 26.52) and redistribution, and taxation (known from ancient Mari). The link with expiation is evidently due to popular fear that counting people or listing their names might expose them to supernatural danger (Rashi; cf. 2 Sam. 24.1–15; 2 Chron. 21.1–14). Hence when a census was necessary, a payment would be made to "ransom" the lives of those counted and protect them from danger (cf. Num. 31.48–50). The same fear is known from many places in the world and evidently underlies the talmudic dictum not to count Israelites directly; where counting is necessary, objects representing each person, such as ostraca, are counted (*b. Yoma* 22b; Maimonides, *Temidin* 4.4). This practice survives in a

Jewish custom for determining whether a prayer quorum ("minyan") of ten is present: ten words of a biblical verse, rather than numbers, are applied to those being counted. Similarly, in the present case Rashi holds that it is the half-shekels, not the people, that are to be counted, which would explain why all must pay the same amount (v. 15); that would be the only way to infer the number of people from the total collected. Although this regulation applies only when a census is taken, in Second Temple times it became the basis of an annual impost for maintaining the Temple (possibly reflected in 2 Chron. 24.4–10 [cf. 2 Kings 12.12–25]). The details are spelled out in the talmudic tractate *Shekalim*. Since the payment was due in the month of Adar (early spring), in order to announce it the present law, called "the Section concerning Shekels" (*Parashat Shekalim*), was added to

the weekly Torah reading on the Sabbath of, or preceding, the New Moon of Adar (*m. Meg.* 3.4), and the Sabbath is called "the Sabbath of Shekels" (*Shabbat Shekalim*). Nowadays half of the common currency (e.g., one half-dollar) is collected on Purim, which falls in Adar, and the proceeds are used for the support of synagogues and the poor. **12:** *Ransom,* a payment made to escape death or physical punishment (21.30; Prov. 6.35). **13:** *Half-shekel,* of silver (38.25–26). The shekel was the standard weight. *By the sanctuary weight:* There were different types of shekel, varying in weight: the standard shekel, weighing ca. 11.4 grams, or .4 oz and possibly the same as the "shekel at the going merchant's weight" (Gen. 23.16), the "sanctuary shekels" (as here), and the "shekel by the royal weight" (2 Sam. 14.26). **14:** *From the age of twenty years up,* i.e., of military age (Num. 1.3; etc.). The envisioned censuses would be for military purposes, since the Israelites were organized as an army (12.41 n.). **16:** *Assign it to the service of the Tent of Meeting,* rather, "for the (construction) work on the Tent of Meeting." See 35.21 n. and, for the use to which the silver would be put, 38.25–28. The items made with the silver will stand in the sanctuary *as a reminder before the LORD, as expiation,* that is, for favorable remembrance (28.12 n.) which, by expiating, will prevent a plague. Cf. Num. 31.50, 54.

30.17–21: The laver, a basin containing water for washing, is to be placed between the sacrificial altar and the Tent. Before entering the Tent or offering sacrifices (activities just mentioned in 29.38–42; 30.7–8) the priests must wash their hands and feet (28.4 n.), with which they touch the sacrifices, the sanctuary, and its ground. Talmudic sources describe this as "sanctifying" the hands and feet (*m. Yoma* 3.2). Ramban explains it as an act of respect for God. **18:** *Copper,* rather, bronze, like the other items in the courtyard. For the

22 The LORD spoke to Moses, saying: 23 Next take choice spices: five hundred weight of solidified[a] myrrh, half as much—two hundred and fifty—of fragrant cinnamon, two hundred and fifty of aromatic cane, 24 five hundred—by the sanctuary weight—of cassia, and a *hin* of olive oil. 25 Make of this a sacred anointing oil, a compound of ingredients expertly blended, to serve as sacred anointing oil. 26 With it anoint the Tent of Meeting, the Ark of the Pact, 27 the table and all its utensils, the lampstand and all its fittings, the altar of incense, 28 the altar of burnt offering and all its utensils, and the laver and its stand. 29 Thus you shall consecrate them so that they may be most holy; whatever touches them shall be consecrated. 30 You shall also anoint Aaron and his sons, consecrating them to serve Me as priests.

31 And speak to the Israelite people, as follows: This shall be an anointing oil sacred to Me throughout the ages. 32 It must not be rubbed on any person's body, and you must not make anything like it in the same proportions; it is sacred, to be held sacred by you. 33 Whoever compounds its like, or puts any of it on a layman, shall be cut off from his kin.

34 And the LORD said to Moses: Take the herbs stacte, onycha, and galbanum—these herbs together with pure frankincense; let there be an equal part of each. 35 Make them into incense, a compound expertly blended, refined, pure, sacred. 36 Beat some of it into powder, and put some before the Pact in the Tent of Meeting, where I will meet with you; it shall be most holy to you. 37 But when you make this incense, you must not make any in the same proportions for yourselves; it shall be held by you sacred to the LORD. 38 Whoever makes any like it, to smell of it, shall be cut off from his kin.

31 The LORD spoke to Moses: 2 See, I have singled out by name Bezalel son of Uri son of Hur, of the tribe of Judah. 3 I have endowed him with a divine spirit of skill, ability, and knowledge in every kind of craft; 4 to make designs for work in gold, silver, and copper, 5 to cut stones for setting and to carve wood—to work in every kind of craft. 6 Moreover, I have assigned to him Oholiab son of Ahisamach, of the tribe of Dan; and I have also granted skill to all who are skillful, that they may make everything that I have commanded you: 7 the Tent of Meeting, the Ark for the Pact and the cover upon it, and all the furnishings of the Tent; 8 the table and its utensils,

source of this bronze, see 38.8. **20:** *That they may not die,* 28.35 n.

30.22–33: The sacred anointing oil. The formula of the sacred anointing oil is now given, along with the instruction that it is to be used to sanctify the sanctuary and all its other furniture as well. It is to be a fragrant compound of olive oil and the finest spices, and because it is sacred to the LORD it may be used only for the stated purpose, not for everyday hygienic and cosmetic anointing; nor may it be duplicated or used by laymen. **29:** *Whatever touches them shall be consecrated,* 29.35–37 n. **33:** *Cut off from his kin,* 12.15 n.; 28.35 n.

30.34–38: The sacred incense, to be burned on the incense altar (vv. 1–10). Like the anointing oil, it is sacred to the LORD and may not be duplicated and used for any other purpose. **36:** *Put some before the Pact:* See v. 6.

31.1–11: The master builders. Having completed all the instructions for the sanctuary, God designates two master builders to be in charge of executing His plans, Bezalel and his associate Oholiab from the tribes of Judah and Dan, respectively. The construction is supervised and executed by skilled people from all the tribes (v. 6b), not just priests and Levites. **2:** *Hur,* possibly, but not necessarily, the Hur mentioned in 17.11 and 24.14. **3:** *Divine spirit,* 28.3 n. **7:** *Ark for the Pact,* 25.10–16 n.

a Others "flowing."

the pure lampstand[a] and all its fittings, and the altar of incense; [9] the altar of burnt offering and all its utensils, and the laver and its stand; [10] the service[b] vestments, the sacral vestments of Aaron the priest and the vestments of his sons, for their service as priests; [11] as well as the anointing oil and the aromatic incense for the sanctuary. Just as I have commanded you, they shall do.

[12] And the LORD said to Moses: [13] Speak to the Israelite people and say: Nevertheless, you must keep My sabbaths, for this is a sign between Me and you throughout the ages, that you may know that I the LORD have consecrated you. [14] You shall keep the sabbath, for it is holy for you. He who profanes it shall be put to death: whoever does work on it, that person shall be cut off from among his kin. [15] Six days may work be done, but on the seventh day there shall be a sabbath of complete rest, holy to the LORD; whoever does work on the sabbath day shall be put to death. [16] The Israelite people shall keep the sabbath, observing the sabbath throughout the ages as a covenant for all time: [17] it shall be a sign for all time between Me and the people of Israel. For in six days the LORD made heaven and earth, and on the seventh day He ceased from work and was refreshed.

a Or "lampstand of pure gold."   b Others "plaited."

11: *Just as I have commanded you, they shall do:* The design is entirely God's (25.9 n.), the artisans merely follow God's blueprint. This explains why they are designated only after the construction plans are given.

31.12–17: The Sabbath. The last of the seven divine commands about building the sanctuary concerns the seventh day of the week, the Sabbath (20.8–11; cf. 25.1–31.17 n.). Thus far, the instructions concerned a holy place; now the instructions emphasize the importance of a holy time. As God created a holy time after constructing the world, Israel must observe that holy time even while constructing the sanctuary. Suspending construction on the Sabbath indicates that holy time is more important than holy space. **13:** *Nevertheless,* notwithstanding the instructions to construct the sanctuary. *My sabbaths:* Since the Sabbath belongs to God (20.10 n.),

observing it serves as *a sign between Me and you* indicating to Israel that God has consecrated them, making them His people, dedicated to His service and sacrosanct to Him (19.5b–6a n.). The notion of *a sign* is key to Priestly thinking about the Sabbath—it is not merely a day of rest. **14:** Because the Sabbath is God's and holy to Him (vv. 13, 15), it must also be holy to Israel (20.8 n.) like the sanctuary and its parts (30.29). Hence, profaning it—treating it as unholy, common—is no less a capital crime than encroaching on the sanctuary (28.35 n.) or Mount Sinai (19.12). *Put to death,* Num. 15.32–36. *Work,* 20.10 n. *Cut off,* 12.15 n.; 28.35 n. **15:** *Rest,* 16.23 n. **16–17:** The Sabbath serves as a sign of Israel's relationship with God because it commemorates God's own actions and, in observing it, Israel follows His example (Gen. 2.1–3; for emulating God, cf. Lev. 19.2); as such, in Priestly thinking, it is also *a cov-*

enant for all time. And was refreshed, 25.11 n.

31.18–34.35: The violation and restoration of the covenant. See also Deut. 9.8–10.11 (where the order of the events differs); Ps. 106.19–23. Like chs 19–24, this pericope, with its inconsistencies, nonsequiturs, and redundancies, shows evidence of being based on multiple sources that differ about the course of the events. In 32.7, e.g., God renounces punishment, but in v. 35 He punishes the people, though Aaron is excepted despite his acknowledged complicity (vv. 21–24). Moses' request in 33.15 that God accompany Israel personally is redundant, since God already promised that in v. 14. God's promise to do wonders in 34.10 is not a direct answer to Moses' plea that He go in Israel's midst (v. 9). The description in 33.7–11 about what Moses regularly did with "the tent" interrupts his dialogue with God, and the surrounding narrative (32.30; 34.2, 4, 28–29) is oblivious to it. What is more, although the tent is here regularly in use, and is called the Tent of Meeting (v. 7), it is very different from the tent of the same name in chs 25–31, which is not erected until ch 40 (see 33.7–11 n.). It likely represents a non-Priestly variant tradition about the Tent and was placed here because its location outside the camp seemed compatible with God's alienation from the people in ch 32. It seems unlikely that its author, who writes that God and Moses spoke "face to face" (33.11), even if meant figuratively, was the same one who wrote that Moses may not see God's face (v. 20). God's words about making a covenant in 34.10, 27 give no indication that they refer to the restoration of a prior covenant, and 34.27–28 give confusing information about which document is the basis of the covenant—vv. 11–26 (a doublet, with contextually inexplicable variations, of 23.12–33) or the Decalogue. It is plausible to conjecture that ch 34 contains what was originally a parallel account of the original Sinai covenant, and

18 When He finished speaking with him on Mount Sinai, He gave Moses the two tablets of the Pact, stone tablets inscribed with the finger of God.

32 When the people saw that Moses was so long in coming down from the mountain, the people gathered against Aaron and said to him, "Come, make us a god who shall go before us, for that man Moses, who brought us from the land of Egypt—we do not know what has happened to him." 2 Aaron said to them, "Take off the gold rings that are on the ears of your wives, your sons, and your daughters, and bring them to me." 3 And all the people took off the gold rings that were in their ears and brought them to Aaron. 4 This he took from them and a-cast in a mold,-a and made it into a molten calf. And they exclaimed, b-"This is your god,-b O Israel, who brought you

a-a Cf. Zech. 11.13 (beth hayyoṣer, "foundry"); others "fashioned it with a graving tool."
b-b Others "These are your gods."

that the redactor, confronted with both accounts, reinterpreted this account as describing the covenant's renewal. This section clearly combines material from J, E, P, and perhaps other hands as well, but, as in the case of chs 19–24, there is wide disagreement about which passages belong to which source.

31.18–32.35: The golden calf episode. The location of the Tabernacle instructions prior to the golden calf episode is puzzling (see introductory comments to 25.1–31.17). The present order of the text, by giving precedence to the Tabernacle as the divinely authorized means of securing God's Presence among the people, shows that the calf is a perverted, humanly devised means of doing the same thing (see 32.4 n.), already forbidden in 20.4–5, 20. The connection between the two is highlighted by a sequence of events that parallels God's instructions for the Tabernacle and the people's response: The people command Aaron to make them a god, Aaron responds with a public appeal for gold, all the people bring him the gold, he makes the calf with it, builds an altar and offers sacri-

fices, and the people celebrate (cf. chs 25–31; 35.4–9, 20–29; 36.8–38.20; Lev. chs 8–9). The people's celebration of the calf also bears an ironic resemblance to the covenant ceremony in ch 24: An altar is built, burnt offerings and sacrifices of well-being are made, and the people eat and drink (cf. 24.4–5, 10–11). Their declaration that the calf is the God who brought them out of Egypt contrasts ironically with God's declaration that it is through the Tabernacle that He will abide among the Israelites and they will know that He is their God who brought them out of Egypt (29.45–46). In fact, the calf leads to the annulment of the covenant (v. 19 n.) and to God's refusal to abide among the people (33.3, 5), and threatens their very existence (32.10). The present arrangement conveys these messages and shows that the people's generous and obedient response to the Tabernacle instructions (chs 35–39, especially 36.3–7; 39.42–43) is a sign of their repentance, while God's Presence entering the Tabernacle (40.34–38) is a sign of His forgiveness. The narrative has similarities to the account of the golden calves that Jeroboam (the

first king of the Northern Kingdom) erected in Bethel and Dan (1 Kings 12.25–33), and some scholars believe that the Exodus narrative is a pejorative recasting of a northern legend about the origin of Jeroboam's calves. The original northern legend would have viewed the making of the calf positively, as a pedestal or mount for God (not as an idol; 32.4 n.), and would have invoked it to legitimize Jeroboam's calves. The manufacture of golden calves was seen as idolatry, and the story about Aaron's calf was revised to characterize the phenomenon as sinful from the outset and, at the same time, show the legitimacy of the Jerusalem Temple and the illegitimacy of the northern sanctuaries at Bethel and Dan. **31.18:** The Masoretic paragraph system starts this episode here (unlike the medieval ch divisions, which start it at 32.1), highlighting the outrage of the people's behavior: At the very moment that God was giving Moses the Tablets of the Pact, which forbids idolatry (20.4–5), the people were demanding just that (see also Deut. 9.8–13). In modern terms, "the ink was not yet dry" on the covenant when the people violated it. **32.1:** With Moses now gone for forty days (24.18), the people (see v. 28 n.) fear that he has disappeared, and since he had been their sole conduit to God they ask Aaron to make them a "god" to lead them in his stead (Radak at 1 Kings 12.28). Although most commentators believe that they mean "god" literally, it is more likely that they mean it as a metonymy for something that would serve as a new means of securing God's Presence. See v. 4 n. *That man Moses:* In the people's view, Moses disappeared because he was a mortal; that is why they want a "god" to replace him. **3:** *Gold rings,* 3.22; 11.2–3; 12.35–36. **4:** *Cast in a mold,* rather, as Rashi notes, "tied them in a garment (or bag)" (2 Kings 5.23). *And made it into a molten calf,* from the melted earrings. *And they exclaimed, "This is your God, O Israel, who brought you out of the land of Egypt":* As out of the land of Egypt!" ⁵When Aaron saw this, he built an altar before it; and Aaron announced: "Tomorrow shall be a festival of the Lord!" ⁶Early next day, the people offered up burnt offerings and brought sacrifices of well-being; they sat down to eat and drink, and then rose to dance.

⁷The Lord spoke to Moses, "Hurry down, for your people, whom you brought out of the land of Egypt, have acted basely. ⁸They have been quick to turn aside from the way that I enjoined upon them. They have made themselves a molten calf and bowed low to it and sacrificed to it, saying: 'This is your god, O Israel, who brought you out of the land of Egypt!' "

⁹The Lord further said to Moses, "I see that this is a stiffnecked people. ¹⁰Now, let Me be, that My anger may blaze forth against them and that I may destroy them, and make of you a great nation." ¹¹But Moses implored the Lord his God, saying, "Let not Your anger, O Lord, blaze forth against Your people, whom You delivered from the land of Egypt with great power and with a mighty hand. ¹²Let not the Egyptians say, 'It was with evil intent that He delivered them, only to kill them off in the mountains and annihilate them from the face of the earth.' Turn from Your blazing anger, and renounce the plan to punish Your people. ¹³Remember Your servants, Abraham, Isaac, and Israel, how You swore to them by Your Self and said to them: I will make your offspring as numerous as the stars

God normally refers to Israel as "My people" "whom I brought out of Egypt" (3.7; 29.46). Here He feels alienated from them and speaks of them as Moses' people, much as an exasperated parent may refer to a misbehaving child as the other spouse's child. Contrast Moses' language in vv. 11 and 33.13. **9:** *Stiffnecked,* obstinate. The Heb idiom is close in meaning to English "headstrong." **10:** *Let Me be:* God implies that Moses can restrain Him from destroying Israel. Midrashic commentaries understand this as a hint for Moses to do just that by praying on Israel's behalf and making the case for sparing them. Prophets frequently and appropriately play this intercessory role (1 Sam. 12.23; Jer. 18.20; Ezek. 22.30–31; Ps. 106.23; cf. Gen. 18.17–32). *Make of you a great nation:* God would fulfill His promise to the patriarchs to make their descendants a great nation through Moses and his descendants.
11–14: Moses mounts a multifaceted plea: Israel is God's own people on whose behalf He has invested much effort; destroying His own people will injure His reputation among other nations; and He has a sworn obligation to the Israelites' ancestors, who were His loyal servants. In Jewish practice this passage and 34.1–10 are read in the synagogue on the public fast days that commemorate national disasters or near-disasters. **11:** *Your people, whom You delivered from the land of Egypt:* Here Moses counters God's disassociation of Himself from Israel in v. 7. All the effort that God has invested in Israel would be for naught if He were to destroy them. **12:** Moses' most daring argument: annihilating Israel would damage God's reputation in the world. He would appear diabolical and lose the stature that He had gained from the exodus. This suggests that God cares about His reputation. **13:** By destroying the Israelites God would, furthermore, violate His oath to the patriarchs to give them countless descendants and eternal possession of the promised land (Gen. 12.7; 13.15–16; 15.5; 17.7–8).

Rashbam notes, the people cannot be so foolish as to believe that the resultant image is the God who had brought them out of Egypt. They must view it either as an image that represents Him and will attract His Presence (20.20 n.) or as a pedestal on which He will stand invisibly (cf. the cherub throne, 25.17–22 n.). Images of calves and bulls in these roles have been found in archeological excavations in Israel and neighboring lands. The Heb reads lit. "These are your gods," and "brought" is also plural, as is the verb for "go" and "lead" in vv. 1 and 23. Since Heb "'elohim," "god/God," is itself grammatically plural in form even when its meaning is singular, it is on occasion accompanied by a plural verb, as in Josh. 24.19; 2 Sam. 7.23. But since the plural verb is also found in Jeroboam's nearly identical words about the

two calves he made (1 Kings 12.28), it seems possible that, in the putative northern legend underlying our account, the people's words were originally singular and that the plural form is part of the pejorative recasting of the legend, highlighting their similarity to Jeroboam's and characterizing the people's request as idolatrous and polytheistic from the outset. **5:** *A festival of the Lord:* Since the image does not represent a different god, the people are not in violation of the Decalogue's prohibition against worshiping other gods but rather, as v. 8 indicates, the prohibition of making and worshiping idols (20.4–5). **6:** *Dance,* cf. vv. 18–19, where singing and dancing are both mentioned. The people are honoring the calf as they had honored God in 15.20–21. **7:** *Your people, whom you brought out of the land of Egypt:*

of heaven, and I will give to your offspring this whole land of which I spoke, to possess forever." ¹⁴ And the LORD renounced the punishment He had planned to bring upon His people.

¹⁵ Thereupon Moses turned and went down from the mountain bearing the two tablets of the Pact, tablets inscribed on both their surfaces: they were inscribed on the one side and on the other. ¹⁶ The tablets were God's work, and the writing was God's writing, incised upon the tablets. ¹⁷ When Joshua heard the sound of the people in its boisterousness, he said to Moses, "There is a cry of war in the camp." ¹⁸ But he answered,

"It is not the sound of the tune of triumph,
Or the sound of the tune of defeat;
It is the sound of song that I hear!"

¹⁹ As soon as Moses came near the camp and saw the calf and the dancing, he became enraged; and he hurled the tablets from his hands and shattered them at the foot of the mountain. ²⁰ He took the calf that they had made and burned it; he ground it to powder and strewed it upon the water and so made the Israelites drink it.

²¹ Moses said to Aaron, "What did this people do to you that you have brought such great sin upon them?" ²² Aaron said, "Let not my lord be enraged. You know that this people is bent on evil. ²³ They said to me, 'Make us a god to lead us; for that man Moses, who brought us from the land of Egypt—we do not know what has happened to him.' ²⁴ So I said to them, 'Whoever has gold, take it off!' They gave it to me and I hurled it into the fire and out came this calf!"

²⁵ Moses saw that the people were out of control—since Aaron had let them get out of control—so that they were a menace^a to any who might oppose them. ²⁶ Moses stood

---

a Others "an object of derision."

(Heb "ḥarut") *upon the tablets:* In a verbal play, a midrash interprets the text as if it read "(there was) freedom ("ḥerut") upon the tablets," explaining that no one is free except one who studies the Torah (*Pirkei ʾAvot* 6.2). Ironically, subjugation to law is viewed as bringing true freedom. **17–18:** Joshua, waiting for Moses part-way up the mountain (24.13 n.), hears the people's noise but misjudges its nature, but Moses discerns that it is singing. The Heb word for singing ("ʿanot") is the same one used for Miriam's singing of God's praises in 15.21, again suggesting that the people are honoring the calf as they had honored God (v. 6 n.). **19:** Breaking the tablets expresses not only Moses' rage but (as in Mesopotamian law) the annulment of the covenant, since its most fundamental condition has been violated. His action is the equivalent of tearing up a contract. **20:** Rabbinic exegesis, followed by some modern scholars, takes the forced drinking as a kind of ordeal designed to identify the guilty, comparable to the "waters of bitterness" ritual for testing the suspected adulteress (Num. 5.11–31; *b. A. Z.* 44a). Ramban suggests that making the people drink the water with the powdered ashes of the calf would degrade the idol further by turning it into human waste. **21:** Moses demands an accounting of Aaron because he had left him in charge (24.14). **24:** *Out came this calf!:* Aaron denies responsibility for making the calf; it made itself. Some see here evidence for a version of the story in which the calf was created supernaturally (which supports the view that the story was originally an approving one), like midrashim that describe how the Tabernacle and Solomon's Temple, respectively, erected and built themselves (e.g., *Exod. Rab.* 52.4) and a Ugaritic myth that tells how Baal's palace was built by firing silver and gold for six days (D. Pardee in W. W. Hallo and K. L. Younger, eds., *The Context of Scripture* 1.261). **26:** *Whoever is for*

Even Israel's violation of the conditional covenant made at Sinai (19.5–6) would not justify destroying Israel, since the earlier covenant with the patriarchs was unconditional and irrevocable (Gen. 17.7; Deut. 4.31). Moses' invocation of the patriarchs became the precedent for the postbiblical idea of the "merit of the ancestors" ("zekhut ʾavot") in Jewish prayers. Going beyond the idea that God rewards later generations for their ancestors' merits (20.6), and the notion that the ancestral *promise* may never be broken, this concept holds that even when Israel lacks merit—as in the present case—its ancestors' merits can sustain it and God may grant mercy for their sake. **14:** God's agreement not to destroy the people responds to Moses' plea in v. 12, but not to the request to bring Israel to the promised land in v. 13 (see v. 34). In fact, full reconciliation will require several further pleas by Moses. See v. 34; 33.12–17; 34.9. **15:** *Bearing the two tablets of the Pact,* which he has just received (31.18). **16:** *Incised* up in the gate of the camp and said, "Whoever is for the LORD, come here!" And all the Levites rallied to him. 27 He said to them, "Thus says the LORD, the God of Israel: Each of you put sword on thigh, go back and forth from gate to gate throughout the camp, and slay brother, neighbor, and kin." 28 The Levites did as Moses had bidden; and some three thousand of the people fell that day. 29 And Moses said, "Dedicate yourselvesᵃ to the LORD this day—for each of you has been against son and brother—that He may bestow a blessing upon you today."

30 The next day Moses said to the people, "You have been guilty of a great sin. Yet I will now go up to the LORD; perhaps I may win forgiveness for your sin." 31 Moses went back to the LORD and said, "Alas, this people is guilty of a great sin in making for themselves a god of gold. 32 Now, if You will forgive their sin [well and good]; but if not, erase me from the record which You have written!" 33 But the LORD said to Moses, "He who has sinned against Me, him only will I erase from My record. 34 Go now, lead the people where I told you. See, My angel shall go before you. But when I make an accounting, I will bring them to account for their sins."

35 Then the LORD sent a plague upon the people, ᵇ-for what they did with the calf that Aaron made.-ᵇ

33 Then the LORD said to Moses, "Set out from here, you and the people that you have brought up from

a Lit. "fill your hands."
b-b Meaning of Heb. uncertain.

the LORD: As far as Moses is concerned, whatever the intention of its worshippers, worshipping an image is tantamount to worshipping another god and must be opposed by those who are loyal to the LORD. The Levites, Moses' fellow tribesmen, step forward. This story thus justifies the Levites' later important cultic role (see v. 29 n.). **27:** With Israel's fate in the balance (v. 30), Moses orders the Levites, in God's name, to summarily execute the guilty, not sparing even their own kin. **29:** The Heb is difficult. Taking the verbs as past tense (thus LXX), the v. may mean that by their action the Levites have dedicated themselves to God's service. In view of the idiom "fill the hand" (28.41 n.) the v. may mean, "Today you have

ordained yourselves/been *ordained* for the service of the LORD . . . and so have brought a blessing upon yourselves (or: He has granted you a blessing) today." This has been seen as referring to the Levites' future role as sanctuary attendants (Num. 1.48–54; chs 3–4), but in P texts in the Torah only priests are ordained, and according to Deut. 10.8 it was at this time that God chose the Levites for their future priestly role. Deut. holds, contrary to P (Exod. 28.1), that all Levites, not only descendants of Aaron, may be priests (Deut. 18.1–8); the present non-P narrative may share that view. Having battled illegitimate worship, the Levites are made the ministers of legitimate worship. See also Deut. 33.8–10. **30:** *Perhaps*

I may win forgiveness for your sin: From God's incomplete response in v. 14 Moses realizes that He has not yet forgiven the people. Moses wants more than their survival. **32:** *Erase me from the record which You have written,* i.e., "the book of life" (or, "the book of the living," Ps. 69.29; cf. Isa. 4.3), a notion (based on Mesopotamian tablets of life and destiny written by the gods) developed in much detail in the postbiblical liturgy for Rosh Ha-Shanah and Yom Kippur. Moses demands that his own life be taken if God will not forgive Israel. According to Ramban, he means that if God will not forgive Israel, He should take Moses' life in Israel's place. In either case, Moses here goes beyond his earlier refusal to supplant Israel (v. 10 n.). **33–34:** God declines both of Moses' requests: He will not take Moses' life or waive further punishment of the people. He does agree that the people may proceed to the promised land, but led only by an angel (23.20 n.), not Himself personally. **35:** Punishment was not limited to those directly involved in worshipping the calf but, in keeping with the concept of collective responsibility, strikes "the people," i.e., others as well (Num. 25.8–9; Josh. 7.1–5, 24–26).

33.1–6: The LORD's further displeasure. 1–3: Explaining what He meant in 32.34, God's reference to *the people that you* (Moses) *have brought up from the land of Egypt* indicates that He is still alienated from Israel. Despite the similarity of His words in v. 2 to His promise in 20.20–23, vv. 3b–5 make clear that here the promise of angelic guidance is punitive: God Himself will not accompany a rebellious people. The people's misguided attempt to secure God's Presence and guidance (32.1) has backfired, and God's plan to abide among the people in the Tabernacle (25.8; 29.45–46) is implicitly withdrawn. All of Moses' efforts in chs 33–34 are directed toward ending this alienation and restoring God's direct Presence among the people, and he succeeds step by step; see the land of Egypt, to the land of which I swore to Abraham, Isaac, and Jacob, saying, 'To your offspring will I give it'—²I will send an angel before you, and I will drive out the Canaanites, the Amorites, the Hittites, the Perizzites, the Hivites, and the Jebusites—³a land flowing with milk and honey. But I will not go in your midst, since you are a stiffnecked people, lest I destroy you on the way."

⁴When the people heard this harsh word, they went into mourning, and none put on his finery.

⁵The LORD said to Moses, "Say to the Israelite people, 'You are a stiffnecked people. If I were to go in your midst for one moment, I would destroy you. Now, then, leave off your finery, and I will consider what to do to you.'" ⁶So the Israelites remained stripped of the finery from Mount Horeb on.

⁷Now Moses would take the Tent and pitch it outside the camp, at some distance from the camp. It was called the Tent of Meeting, and whoever sought the LORD would go out to the Tent of Meeting that was outside the camp. ⁸Whenever Moses went out to the Tent, all the people would rise and stand, each at the entrance of his tent, and gaze after Moses until he had entered the Tent. ⁹And when Moses entered the Tent, the pillar of cloud would descend and stand at the entrance of the Tent, while He spoke with Moses. ¹⁰When all the people saw the pillar of cloud poised at the entrance of the Tent, all the people would rise and bow low, each at the entrance of his tent. ¹¹The LORD would speak to Moses face to face, as one man speaks to another. And he would then return to the camp; but his attendant, Joshua son of Nun, a youth, would not stir out of the Tent.

¹²Moses said to the LORD, "See, You say to me, 'Lead this people forward,' but You have not made known to me whom You will send with me. Further, You have said, 'I have singled you out by name, and you have, indeed, gained My favor.' ¹³Now, if I have truly gained Your favor, pray let me know Your ways, that I may know You and continue in Your favor. Consider, too, that this nation is Your

moves the site for communicating with Him outside the camp and (v. 12) resumes his dialogue with Him. Since this tent is also called "the Tent of Meeting," scholars consider it part of a variant tradition (found also in Num. 11.16–30; 12.4–13; Deut. 31.14–15) which sees the "Tent of Meeting" not as a sanctuary or a place of sacrifice, as does P (chs 25–31, 35–40), but purely as an oracle-site. Kept outside the camp, it is tended by Joshua rather than priests, and anybody who wants to consult God may come to it. God does not abide in it but descends to it in a pillar of cloud to converse with Moses *face to face, as one man speaks to another* (v. 11), rather than by voice only from between the cherubs (25.27; Num. 7.89). The statement that Moses *would . . . pitch* [the Tent] *outside the camp* supports the theory that this passage was not originally part of the present context; it indicates that Moses would regularly pitch the Tent outside the camp, not inside the camp as P requires (Num. 2.2, 17); cf. Num. 11.26, 30; 12.4. **7:** *Tent of Meeting:* The explanation that *whoever sought the LORD* would resort to the Tent is consistent with the etymology of the name (25.8 n.). **11:** *Face to face,* cf. Num. 12.8; Deut. 34.10. Even if meant figuratively, this is incompatible with vv. 20–22, which is from a different source. *Would not stir out of the Tent,* cf. 1 Sam. 3.3, 15.

33.12–23: Moses pleads with God. 12: *You have not made known to me whom You will send with me,* perhaps alluding to the fact that the angel of God mentioned in v. 2 does not seem to have the same authority as the one promised in 23.21–22. **13:** *Let me know Your ways,* Your ways in dealing with humankind, meaning—as indicated by God's response in 34.6–7 and Ps. 103.7–13—the principles by which you deal with human sin. God had said that the angel would be unforgiving (23.21). What is God's own way? *Consider, too, that this nation is Your people:* Perhaps: What is Your way,

vv. 14, 17; 34.1, 10. In the present, redacted form of Exodus, with this narrative (from J and E) followed by chs 35–40 (P), Moses' crowning success is the resumption of plans to build God's abode among the people in chs 35–40. **2–3a:** *The*

Canaanites . . . milk and honey, 3.8 n.

33.7–11: The Tent of Meeting moved outside the camp. As a consequence of God's refusal to abide among the people, Moses people." ¹⁴ And He said, ᵃ⁻"I will go in the lead and will⁻ᵃ lighten your burden." ¹⁵ And he said to Him, "Unless You go in the lead, do not make us leave this place. ¹⁶ For how shall it be known that Your people have gained Your favor unless You go with us, so that we may be distinguished, Your people and I, from every people on the face of the earth?"

¹⁷ And the Lᴏʀᴅ said to Moses, "I will also do this thing that you have asked; for you have truly gained My favor and I have singled you out by name." ¹⁸ He said, "Oh, let me behold Your Presence!" ¹⁹ And He answered, "I will make all My goodness pass before you, and I will proclaim before you the name Lᴏʀᴅ, ᵇ⁻and the grace that I grant and the compassion that I show.⁻ᵇ ²⁰ But," He said, "you cannot see My face, for man may not see Me and live." ²¹ And the Lᴏʀᴅ said, "See, there is a place near Me. Station yourself on the rock ²² and, as My Presence passes by, I will put you in a cleft of the rock and shield you with My hand until I have passed by. ²³ Then I will take My hand away and you will see My back; but My face must not be seen."

34 The Lᴏʀᴅ said to Moses: "Carve two tablets of stone like the first, and I will inscribe upon the tablets the words that were on the first tablets, which you shattered. ² Be ready by morning, and in the morning come up to Mount Sinai and present yourself there to Me, on the top of the mountain. ³ No one else shall come up with you, and no one else shall be seen anywhere on the

a-a Lit. "My face will go and I will."
b-b Lit. "and I will grant the grace that I will grant and show the compassion that I will show."

considering that Israel is Your own people? (32.7 n., 11 n.; cf. v. 16 below). **14:** *I will go in the lead and will lighten your burden:* Rather: "I personally will go and will deliver you to safety." "Deliver to a safe haven" is a common meaning of the second verb (Deut. 3.20; 25.19). This is essentially the role God had promised the angel would play in v. 2 and 23.20–23, and is therefore a further concession to Moses, though he has not yet agreed to go in Israel's midst (34.9). **15:** *Unless You go in the lead:* Rather, "unless you personally go," as in v. 14. **16:** A preferable translation would be: "For how shall it be known

that I have gained Your favor—I and Your people—unless You go with us, so that we may be distinguished—I and Your people—from every people on the face of the earth?" Moses insists that Israel enjoy the same favor that he does and reiterates that it is God's people. The proof of divine favor is to be led by God Himself, not by an intermediary. **18:** Emboldened by God's favorable reply, Moses supplements his request to know God's ways (v. 13) with a request to behold God's Presence (16.6–7 n.), that is, to know Him visually as well (see vv. 20–23). He seeks total familiarity with God.

19–23: God replies to both of Moses' requests: He will let him know His ways (v. 19) and grant him a partial visual experience, but a full visual experience would be fatal (vv. 20–23). **19:** *Proclaim . . . the name Lᴏʀᴅ:* God will disclose all the qualities embodied in His name, Yʜᴠʜ (3.14 n.; 6.2 n.); this is fulfilled in 34.6–7. According to rabbinic exegesis, the name Yʜᴠʜ ("Lᴏʀᴅ") expresses God's attribute of mercy while "God" ("ʾelohim") expresses His attribute of strict justice, but as 34.6–7 shows, the name Yʜᴠʜ expresses both attributes (cf. 34.13). *And the grace that I grant and the compassion that I show:* Better, "but I shall grant grace to whom I will and shall be merciful to whom I will." Notwithstanding His gracious qualities, God remains sovereign and decides whom or whether to forgive. Justice may not be viewed as automatic. **20:** See 3.6 n.; cf. 24.10 n. According to Num. 12.8, Moses sees God's "likeness" (Heb "temunah," which appears in poetic parallelism with "face" in Ps. 17.15). This may represent a different tradition than the present v., or it may represent a later stage in Moses' relationship with God. **21:** *On the rock,* On the top of Mount Sinai. **22–23:** *My hand . . . My back . . . My face:* As noted in the comment to 3.6, the Bible assumes that God has a human form; but that seeing Him would be too awesome for humans to survive.

34.1–35: Restoration of the covenant. Exod. 34.1–10, containing the list of God's attributes and the phrase "Pardon our iniquity and our sin, and take us for Your own!" (v. 9), is part of the Torah reading on public fast days. **1:** God now prepares to formally restore the covenant by replacing the broken tablets (32.19 n.). But whereas the first tablets were made by God (32.16), these would be man-made, though inscribed by God. Sforno infers from the difference that God did not forgive Israel completely. **3:** As when the terms of the covenant were first proclaimed, access mountain; neither shall the flocks and the herds graze at the foot of this mountain."

⁴ So Moses carved two tablets of stone, like the first, and early in the morning he went up on Mount Sinai, as the LORD had commanded him, taking the two stone tablets with him. ⁵ The LORD came down in a cloud; He stood with him there, and proclaimed the name LORD. ⁶ The LORD passed before him ᵃand proclaimed: "The LORD! the LORD!⁻ᵃ a God compassionate and gracious, slow to anger, abounding in kindness and faithfulness, ⁷ extending kindness to the thousandth generation, forgiving iniquity, transgression, and sin; yet He does not remit all punishment, but visits the iniquity of parents upon children and children's children, upon the third and fourth generations."

⁸ Moses hastened to bow low to the ground in homage, ⁹ and said, "If I have gained Your favor, O Lord, pray, let the Lord go in our midst, even though this is a stiffnecked people. Pardon our iniquity and our sin, and take us for Your own!"

¹⁰ He said: I hereby make a covenant. Before all your people I will work such wonders as have not been wrought on all the earth or in any nation; and all the people ᵇwho are with youᵇ shall see how awesome are the LORD's deeds which I will perform for you. ¹¹ Mark well what I command you this day. I will drive out before you the Amorites, the Canaanites, the Hittites, the Perizzites, the Hivites, and the Jebusites. ¹² Beware of making a cove-

a-a Or "and the Lord proclaimed: The LORD! a God compassionate," etc.; cf. Num. 14.17–18.
b-b Lit. "in whose midst you are."

to the mountain is restricted (cf. 19.12, 21–24) in preparation for God's descending to it (v. 5). **5–7:** God grants both of Moses' requests, passing His Presence before him (33.22) and proclaiming His ways (33.13). *The name LORD* [Yʜvʜ], that is, the attributes it represents. These attributes include both magnanimity (vv. 6–7a) and justice (v. 7b; cf. v. 14). *Kindness and faithfulness,* rather, "steadfast faithfulness" (Heb "ḥesed" [15.13 n.; 20.6 n.] and "ʾemet"), extending Himself to those in covenant with Him; cf. Ps. 25.10 (rendered "steadfast love"). **7:** *Extending kindness . . . visits the iniquity . . . ,* 20.5–6 n. This v.

closely parallels the latter but it reverses the order, giving precedence to God's magnanimous attributes in response to Moses' plea for pardon. At the same time, its characterization of transgenerational reward and punishment is unconditional, unlike that in 20.5–6 which limits it to descendants who follow their ancestors' ways. God's sovereign right to dispense reward and punishment is not bound by the limits He imposes on human justice (Deut. 24.16). *Yet He does not remit all punishment,* Num. 14.19. God never entirely waives punishment, although it may be deferred, even to a later generation (see esp. 1 Kings

21.29). **8–9:** Ignoring God's punitive attributes, Moses invokes His magnanimous attributes and pleads that He cancel His refusal to go in Israel's midst (vv. 3, 5) and forgive its sin. *Take us for Your own,* reestablish Israel as His own people. The Heb means "take us (back) as your inalienable hereditary property," a metaphor frequently applied to Israel to express God's attachment to them (Deut. 4.20; 9.29), "since a person's personal property and his portion are dear to him" (Saadia Gaon, *Book of Beliefs and Opinions,* 2:11). Moses' ignoring of God's punitive qualities became a precedent in the Bible and in later Jewish practice, both of which frequently recite only God's magnanimous attributes (e.g., Jonah 4.2; Joel 2.23; Ps. 86.15; and esp. Neh. 9.17–18, which refers to the golden calf episode; Ps. 25.4–11 is virtually a commentary on the magnanimous attributes), reflecting a firm belief that God is more magnanimous than punitive (Ezek. 18.23, 32). Jewish tradition reads the list of God's magnanimous qualities as His "Thirteen Attributes." It is recited as a prayer for forgiveness on various holidays, fast days, and other penitential occasions, especially the Days of Awe (the High Holidays). **10:** God will (re)establish the covenant. He will lead Israel to the promised land with unprecedented miracles (cf. 9.13–10.29 n.). In return, Israel is to obey the following terms. **11–26:** In view of the people's recent religious sin, these terms restate their religious duties; they are a variant—in some details stricter—of the pertinent section of the Book of the Covenant (23.12–33; see comments there). In light of the people's sin of idolatry, the order in the parallel section in ch 23 is reversed, presenting the laws against idolatry first and in greater detail (vv. 11–17 ‖ 23.20–33) and then the religious calendar (vv. 18–26 ‖ 23.12–19). **11:** Cf. 23.23, 31b. **12–13:** An expanded list (based on 23.32–33) of Canaanite cult objects that must be destroyed. *Sacred posts,* Heb nant with the inhabitants of the land against which you are advancing, lest they be a snare in your midst. [13] No, you must tear down their altars, smash their pillars, and cut down their sacred posts; [14] for you must not worship any other god, because the LORD, whose name is Impassioned, is an impassioned God. [15] You must not make a covenant with the inhabitants of the land, for they will lust after their gods and sacrifice to their gods and invite you, and you will eat of their sacrifices. [16] And when you take wives from among their daughters for your sons, their daughters will lust after their gods and will cause your sons to lust after their gods.

[17] You shall not make molten gods for yourselves.

[18] You shall observe the Feast of Unleavened Bread— eating unleavened bread for seven days, as I have commanded you—at the set time of the month[a] of Abib, for in the month of Abib you went forth from Egypt.

[19] Every first issue of the womb is Mine, from all your livestock that drop a male[b] as firstling, whether cattle or sheep. [20] But the firstling of an ass you shall redeem with a sheep; if you do not redeem it, you must break its neck. And you must redeem every first-born among your sons.

None shall appear before Me empty-handed.

[21] Six days you shall work, but on the seventh day you shall cease from labor; you shall cease from labor even at plowing time and harvest time.

[22] You shall observe the Feast of Weeks, of the first fruits of the wheat harvest; and the Feast of Ingathering at the turn of the year. [23] Three times a year all your males shall appear before the Sovereign LORD, the God of Israel. [24] I will drive out nations from your path and enlarge your territory; no one will covet your land when you go up to appear before the LORD your God three times a year.

[25] You shall not offer the blood of My sacrifice with anything leavened; and the sacrifice of the Feast of Passover shall not be left lying until morning.

[26] The choice first fruits of your soil you shall bring to the house of the LORD your God.

You shall not boil a kid in its mother's milk.

[27] And the LORD said to Moses: Write down these com-

---

a See note at 13.4.   b Heb. tizzakhar, form uncertain.

"'asherah," a wooden object standing at a place of worship. It was a natural or artificial tree, an image, a tree trunk, or a pole (Deut. 16.21; Judg. 6.25–32; 1 Kings 21.3, 7). It may have been regarded as a sym-

bol of the Canaanite goddess Asherah or of the protection, fertility, or nourishment worshippers hoped to receive from a deity. **14:** Exod. 23.24 is restated in the more comprehensive terms of 20.3,

5, including the prohibition of worshipping *any* other god and the warning against provoking God's indignation (20.5 n.). This passage goes beyond 20.5 in stating that the LORD's very *name* is *Impassioned*, meaning that jealous indignation (20.5 n.) is another of the qualities embodied in His name or essence (33.19). This is possibly a play on the name YHVH, equating its root "h-v-h" with "h-w-y" used in Arabic with the meaning "passion." **15–16:** This explains v. 12, warning that Canaanites remaining in the land would, especially through intermarriage, seduce the Israelites into participating in their idolatry (cf. Num. 25.1–3). **17:** *You shall not make molten gods for yourselves,* essentially a restatement of 20.4 in terms relevant to the present circumstances (32.4, 8). **18–26:** Since in worshipping the calf the Israelites created an illicit religious festival (32.5), the calendar of legitimate festivals and related obligations is restated. **18:** Cf. 23.14–15. **19–20a:** A digression prompted by the connection of dedicating the first-born with the exodus; cf. 13.2, 11–15 and cf. 22.28–29. **20b:** *None shall appear before Me empty-handed,* continuing v. 18; cf. 23.15b. **21:** A further digression, prompted by the mention of the harvest in the next v. *Even at plowing time and harvest time:* The Sabbath (cf. 23.12) takes precedence even at the busiest time of the agricultural year, as it does when building the Tabernacle (31.12–17; 35.2–3). **22:** Cf. 23.16. *The Feast of Weeks* is another name for the Feast of the Harvest. According to Lev. 23.15–16 and Deut. 16.9–10 it is observed seven weeks ("the weeks appointed for reaping," Jer. 5.24) after the Feast of Unleavened Bread. **23:** *Three times a year,* on the three pilgrimage festivals (23.14–17 n.; Deut. 16.16). See 23.17. **24:** The people need have no fear of an attack on their homes when they leave for the festivals (23.17 n.). *Covet,* rather, have designs on, scheme against (20.14). **25–26:** See 12.6–11, 21–26; 23.18–19. **27:** The commandments just received are to form the basis mandments, for in accordance with these commandments I make a covenant with you and with Israel.

28 And he was there with the LORD forty days and forty nights; he ate no bread and drank no water; and he wrote down on the tablets the terms of the covenant, the Ten Commandments.

29 So Moses came down from Mount Sinai. And as Moses came down from the mountain bearing the two tablets of the Pact, Moses was not aware that the skin of his face was radiant, since he had spoken with Him. 30 Aaron and all the Israelites saw that the skin of Moses' face was radiant; and they shrank from coming near him. 31 But Moses called to them, and Aaron and all the chieftains in the assembly returned to him, and Moses spoke to them. 32 Afterward all the Israelites came near, and he instructed them concerning all that the LORD had imparted to him on Mount Sinai. 33 And when Moses had finished speaking with them, he put a veil over his face.

34 Whenever Moses went in before the LORD to speak with Him, he would leave the veil off until he came out; and when he came out and told the Israelites what he had been commanded, 35 the Israelites would see how radiant the skin of Moses' face was. Moses would then put the veil back over his face until he went in to speak with Him.

VA-YAKHEL   ויקהל

35 Moses then convoked the whole Israelite community and said to them:

These are the things that the LORD has commanded you to do: 2 On six days work may be done, but on the seventh day you shall have a sabbath of complete rest, holy to the

the divine Presence is surrounded by a radiant luminosity (a concept also found in Mesopotamian literature, where it is called "fearsome radiance"). Thus, from his lengthy and intense encounter with God, Moses' face came to reflect the divine radiance. In this way, the golden calf episode ends with the theme with which it began: Moses' role as Israel's conduit to God, which the people feared they had lost (32.1 n.), is reaffirmed and he is shown to be more than a common "man" (32.1). **29:** *Radiant,* Heb "karan," from "keren," "horn," in the sense of projection, emanation, as in Hab. 3.4 ("rays"). In the Vulgate, Jerome, in an over-etymological translation, rendered "was horned," although he knew from the Septuagint that the meaning was figurative. Nevertheless, his translation led to the image of Moses with horns in medieval and Renaissance art (see esp. Michelangelo's Moses), and eventually, coupled with the notion of Satan's horns, to the anti-Semitic belief that Jews have horns.

Chs 35–40: The construction of the Tabernacle and God's entrance into it. The people's change of heart following their rebellion is shown by their punctilious obedience to God's commands, highlighted by near verbatim correspondence between the instructions in chs 25–31 and their execution in 35–40, and by the recurring phrase "as the LORD had commanded Moses" in 38.32, 42, 43 and ch 39, and by their enthusiasm, indicated by recurrent references in ch 35 to their hearts and spirits moving them to give, to their freewill offerings (35.29; 36.3), and by their giving so much that they had to be stopped (36.3–7). In these chs the LXX has a slightly different order than the Hebrew.

35.1–3: The Sabbath reiterated. Moses begins with the Sabbath, the same subject with which God's instructions concluded in 31.12–17. It is an appropriate introduction to a section in which the word

of the restored covenant. **28:** *Forty days and forty nights,* as when he received the first tablets (24.18). *Ate no bread and drank no water:* During his private, intimate encounter with God Moses was beyond human needs and concerns (contrast 24.9–11). *He wrote down on the tablets the terms of the covenant, the Ten Commandments:* In view of v. 1 and Deut. 10.4 this seems to mean that God wrote down the Decalogue, so that two covenant documents—vv. 11–26 and the Decalogue—resulted from this encounter, just as the terms of the earlier covenant included both the Decalogue and the Book of the Covenant (24.4, 7–8, 12; 31.18). But

in the immediate context *he wrote* is most naturally construed as referring to Moses and *the terms of the covenant* as referring to the terms mentioned in vv. 11–26; this explains why some scholars call these verses the Cultic Decalogue. Their identification as the Decalogue—which God was to write on the tablets (v. 1)—is puzzling. The present text appears to combine two different traditions about what the terms of the covenant were. **29–35:** Not only was Moses beyond human needs while with God (v. 27 n.), but his face came to radiate an awe-inspiring light. According to passages such as Ezek. 1.27–28; Hab. 3.4; Ps. 104.2,

LORD; whoever does any work on it shall be put to death. [3] You shall kindle no fire throughout your settlements on the sabbath day.

[4] Moses said further to the whole community of Israelites:

This is what the LORD has commanded: [5] Take from among you gifts to the LORD; everyone whose heart so moves him shall bring them—gifts for the LORD: gold, silver, and copper; [6] [a] blue, purple, and crimson yarns, fine linen, and goats' hair; [7] tanned ram skins, dolphin skins, and acacia wood; [8] oil for lighting, spices for the anointing oil and for the aromatic incense; [9] lapis lazuli and other stones for setting, for the ephod and the breastpiece.

[10] And let all among you who are skilled come and make all that the LORD has commanded: [11] the Tabernacle, its tent and its covering, its clasps and its planks, its bars, its posts, and its sockets; [12] the ark and its poles, the cover, and the curtain for the screen; [13] the table, and its poles and all its utensils; and the bread of display; [14] the lampstand for lighting, its furnishings and its lamps, and the oil for lighting; [15] the altar of incense and its poles; the anointing oil and the aromatic incense; and the entrance screen for the entrance of the Tabernacle; [16] the altar of burnt offering, its copper grating, its poles, and all its furnishings; the laver and its stand; [17] the hangings of the enclosure, its posts and its sockets, and the screen for the gate of the court; [18] the pegs for the Tabernacle, the pegs for the enclosure, and their cords; [19] the service vestments for officiating in the sanctuary, the sacral vestments of Aaron the priest and the vestments of his sons for priestly service.

[20] So the whole community of the Israelites left Moses' presence. [21] And everyone who excelled in ability and everyone whose spirit moved him came, bringing to the LORD his offering for the work of the Tent of Meeting and for all its service and for the sacral vestments. [22] Men and women, all whose hearts moved them, all who would make an elevation offering of gold to the LORD, came bringing brooches, earrings, rings, and pendants[b]—gold objects of all kinds. [23] And everyone who had in his possession blue, purple, and crimson yarns, fine linen, goats' hair, tanned ram skins, and dolphin skins, brought them; [24] everyone who would make gifts of silver or copper brought them as gifts for the LORD; and everyone who had in his possession acacia wood for any work of the service brought that. [25] And all the skilled women spun with their

"work" (Heb "mela'khah") appears twenty-one more times.

3: *You shall kindle no fire throughout your settlements on the sabbath day:* Rabbinic exegesis holds that this prohibition does not forbid letting a previously kindled fire burn on the Sabbath, so long as it is not refueled on the Sabbath. The Karaite Jewish sect, however, took the law to prohibit the use even of a previously kindled fire and spent the Sabbath in darkness.

35.4–29: The call for donations and craftspeople and the people's response. 10–19: The contents of the Tabernacle are listed in more systematic order than in chs 25–31 (see introductory n. to 30.1–31.17). **21:** *For the work of the Tent of Meeting and for all its service,* rather, "for the work on the Tent of Meeting, all the labor on it." The materials contributed were for the construction of the Tabernacle, not for the worship that would be conducted there afterwards. Heb "'avodah," translated "service" here and in 27.19; 30.16; 35.24; 36.1, 3, 5; 39.40, is better rendered "labor" (referring to construction). See esp. 36.1 where the "'avodah," performed by nonpriests, cannot refer to the worship service, which was conducted by the priests. **22:** *Elevation offering,* 29.24 n. *Gold objects of all kinds:* The jewelry given by the Egyptians is now used to obey rather than violate God's commands (contrast 32.2–3). **25–26:** *And all the skilled women spun:* Spinning was woman's work.

---

a See 25.4 ff. and the notes there.　　*b Meaning of Heb.* kumaz *uncertain.*

own hands, and brought what they had spun, in blue, purple, and crimson yarns, and in fine linen. ²⁶ And all the women who excelled in that skill spun the goats' hair. ²⁷ And the chieftains brought lapis lazuli and other stones for setting, for the ephod and for the breastpiece; ²⁸ and spices and oil for lighting, for the anointing oil, and for the aromatic incense. ²⁹ Thus the Israelites, all the men and women whose hearts moved them to bring anything for the work that the LORD, through Moses, had commanded to be done, brought it as a freewill offering to the LORD.

³⁰ And Moses said to the Israelites: See, the LORD has singled out by name Bezalel, son of Uri son of Hur, of the tribe of Judah. ³¹ He has endowed him with a divine spirit of skill, ability, and knowledge in every kind of craft ³² and ᵃhas inspired himᵃ to make designs for work in gold, silver, and copper, ³³ to cut stones for setting and to carve wood—to work in every kind of designer's craft— ³⁴ and to give directions. He and Oholiab son of Ahisamach of the tribe of Dan ³⁵ have been endowed with the skill to do any work—of the carver, the designer, the embroiderer in blue, purple, crimson yarns, and in fine linen, **36** and of the weaver—as workers in all crafts and as makers of designs. ¹ Let, then, Bezalel and Oholiab and all the skilled persons whom the LORD has endowed with skill and ability to perform expertly all the tasks connected with the service of the sanctuary carry out all that the LORD has commanded.

² Moses then called Bezalel and Oholiab, and every skilled person whom the LORD had endowed with skill, everyone who excelled in ability, to undertake the task and carry it out. ³ They took over from Moses all the gifts that the Israelites had brought, to carry out the tasks connected with the service of the sanctuary. But when these continued to bring freewill offerings to him morning after morning, ⁴ all the artisans who were engaged in the tasks of the sanctuary came, each from the task upon which he was engaged, ⁵ and said to Moses, "The people are bringing more than is needed for the tasks entailed in the work that the LORD has commanded to be done." ⁶ Moses thereupon had this proclamation made throughout the camp: "Let no man or woman make further effort toward gifts for the sanctuary!" So the people stopped bringing: ⁷ their efforts had been more than enough for all the tasks to be done.

⁸ Then all the skilled among those engaged in the work made the Tabernacle of ten strips of cloth, which they

35.30–36.1: The appointment of the master builders. The translation correctly ignores the ch break (a medieval innovation; there is none in the Heb text) since Moses' announcement continues through 36.1. **35.30:** Moses informs the public of Bezalel and Oholiab's appointment. The Talmud, interpreting "see" as meaning "do you agree?" inferred that one must not appoint a public leader without first consulting the public (b. Ber. 54a with Rashi). **34:** *And to give directions,* to instruct others in these skills.

36.2–7: The overabundance of donations. 3: *Continued,* even after the work began; see v. 4. The commencement of the work is related in v. 8.

36.8–38.20: The construction of the Tabernacle. As in 35.10–19, the contents are listed in a more systematic order than earlier.

36.8–37: The Tabernacle structure. See 26.1–37. **35:** *The curtain* for the entrance to the Holy of Holies (26.31–33).

a-a *Moved up from v. 34 for clarity.*

made of fine twisted linen, blue, purple, and crimson yarns; into these they worked a design of cherubim. ⁹ The length of each cloth was twenty-eight cubits, and the width of each cloth was four cubits, all cloths having the same measurements. ¹⁰ They joined five of the cloths to one another, and they joined the other five cloths to one another. ¹¹ They made loops of blue wool on the edge of the outermost cloth of the one set, and did the same on the edge of the outermost cloth of the other set: ¹² they made fifty loops on the one cloth, and they made fifty loops on the edge of the end cloth of the other set, the loops being opposite one another. ¹³ And they made fifty gold clasps and coupled the units^a to one another with the clasps, so that the Tabernacle became one whole.

¹⁴ They made cloths of goats' hair for a tent over the Tabernacle; they made the cloths eleven in number. ¹⁵ The length of each cloth was thirty cubits, and the width of each cloth was four cubits, the eleven cloths having the same measurements. ¹⁶ They joined five of the cloths by themselves, and the other six cloths by themselves. ¹⁷ They made fifty loops on the edge of the outermost cloth of the one set, and they made fifty loops on the edge of the end cloth of the other set. ¹⁸ They made fifty copper clasps to couple the Tent together so that it might become one whole. ¹⁹ And they made a covering of tanned ram skins for the tent, and a covering of dolphin skins above.

²⁰ They made the planks for the Tabernacle of acacia wood, upright. ²¹ The length of each plank was ten cubits, the width of each plank a cubit and a half. ²² Each plank had two tenons, parallel^b to each other; they did the same with all the planks of the Tabernacle. ²³ Of the planks of the Tabernacle, they made twenty planks for the south side,^c ²⁴ making forty silver sockets under the twenty planks, two sockets under one plank for its two tenons and two sockets under each following plank for its two tenons; ²⁵ and for the other side wall of the Tabernacle, the north side, twenty planks, ²⁶ with their forty silver sockets, two sockets under one plank and two sockets under each following plank. ²⁷ And for the rear of the Tabernacle, to the west, they made six planks; ²⁸ and they made two planks for the corners of the Tabernacle at the rear. ^{29d} They matched at the bottom, but terminated as one at the top into one ring;^d they did so with both of them at the two corners. ³⁰ Thus there were

---

a Lit. "strip of cloth," here used collectively.
b See note at 26.17.
c See note at 26.18.
d-d See note at 26.24.

eight planks with their sockets of silver: sixteen sockets, two under each plank.

31 They made bars of acacia wood, five for the planks of the one side wall of the Tabernacle, 32 five bars for the planks of the other side wall of the Tabernacle, and five bars for the planks of the wall of the Tabernacle at the rear, to the west; 33 they made the center bar to run, halfway up the planks, from end to end. 34 They overlaid the planks with gold, and made their rings of gold, as holders for the bars; and they overlaid the bars with gold.

35 They made the curtain of blue, purple, and crimson yarns, and fine twisted linen, working into it a design of cherubim. 36 They made for it four posts of acacia wood and overlaid them with gold, with their hooks of gold; and they cast for them four silver sockets.

37 They made the screen for the entrance of the Tent, of blue, purple, and crimson yarns, and fine twisted linen, done in embroidery; 38 and five posts for it with their hooks. They overlaid their tops and their bands with gold; but the five sockets were of copper.

37 Bezalel made the ark of acacia wood, two and a half cubits long, a cubit and a half wide, and a cubit and a half high. 2 He overlaid it with pure gold, inside and out; and he made a gold molding for it round about. 3 He cast four gold rings for it, for its four feet: two rings on one of its side walls and two rings on the other. 4 He made poles of acacia wood, overlaid them with gold, 5 and inserted the poles into the rings on the side walls of the ark for carrying the ark.

6 He made a cover of pure gold, two and a half cubits long and a cubit and a half wide. 7 He made two cherubim of gold; he made them of hammered work, at the two ends of the cover: 8 one cherub at one end and the other cherub at the other end; he made the cherubim of one piece with the cover, at its two ends. 9 The cherubim had their wings spread out above, shielding the cover with their wings. They faced each other; the faces of the cherubim were turned toward the cover.

10 He made the table of acacia wood, two cubits long, one cubit wide, and a cubit and a half high; 11 he overlaid it with pure gold and made a gold molding around it. 12 He made a rim of a hand's breadth around it and made a gold molding for its rim round about. 13 He cast four gold rings for it and attached the rings to the four corners at its four legs. 14 The rings were next to the rim, as holders for the poles to carry the table. 15 He made the poles of acacia wood for carrying the table, and overlaid them

37.1–9: The Ark and its cherub-cover. See 25.10–22. These would stand in the Holy of Holies.

37.10–28: The table, the lamp-stand, and the incense altar. See 25.23–40; 31.1–10. These would stand in the Holy Place. Note that the incense altar is not separated from the other items that it would stand with as it is in 31.1–10.

with gold. [16] The utensils that were to be upon the table—its bowls, ladles, jugs, and jars with which to offer libations—he made of pure gold.

[17] He made the lampstand of pure gold. He made the lampstand—its base and its shaft—of hammered work; its cups, calyxes, and petals were of one piece with it. [18] Six branches issued from its sides: three branches from one side of the lampstand, and three branches from the other side of the lampstand. [19] There were three cups shaped like almond-blossoms, each with calyx and petals, on one branch; and there were three cups shaped like almond-blossoms, each with calyx and petals, on the next branch; so for all six branches issuing from the lampstand. [20] On the lampstand itself there were four cups shaped like almond-blossoms, each with calyx and petals: [21] a calyx, of one piece with it, under a pair of branches; and a calyx, of one piece with it, under the second pair of branches; and a calyx, of one piece with it, under the last pair of branches; so for all six branches issuing from it. [22] Their calyxes and their stems were of one piece with it, the whole of it a single hammered piece of pure gold. [23] He made its seven lamps, its tongs, and its fire pans of pure gold. [24] He made it and all its furnishings out of a talent of pure gold.

[25] He made the incense altar of acacia wood, a cubit long and a cubit wide—square—and two cubits high; its horns were of one piece with it. [26] He overlaid it with pure gold: its top, its sides round about, and its horns; and he made a gold molding for it round about. [27] He made two gold rings for it under its molding, on its two walls—on opposite sides—as holders for the poles with which to carry it. [28] He made the poles of acacia wood, and overlaid them with gold. [29] He prepared the sacred anointing oil and the pure aromatic incense, expertly blended.

38 He made the altar for burnt offering of acacia wood, five cubits long and five cubits wide—square—and three cubits high. [2] He made horns for it on its four corners, the horns being of one piece with it; and he overlaid it with copper. [3] He made all the utensils of the altar—the pails, the scrapers, the basins, the flesh hooks, and the fire pans; he made all these utensils of copper. [4] He made for the altar a grating of meshwork in copper, extending below, under its ledge, to its middle. [5] He cast four rings, at the four corners of the copper grating, as holders for the poles. [6] He made the poles of acacia wood and overlaid them with copper; [7] and he inserted the poles into the rings on the side walls of the altar, to carry it by them. He made it hollow, of boards.

37.29: The anointing oil and the incense. See 30.22–37. The incense is mentioned here because it would be burnt on the incense altar. The anointing oil is mentioned with it by association, since it too is a compound.

38.1–8: The altar of burnt offering and the laver. See 27.1–8; 30.17–21. These would stand in the courtyard. Note that they are not separated from each other as they were when first mentioned. **8:** The laver is not made from the copper (bronze) donated by the general public (vv. 29–31) but from a separate gift from *the women who performed tasks at the entrance of the Tent of Meeting:* The same class of women is mentioned in 1 Sam. 2.22 but there is no indication of what they did. The Heb phrase translated *performed tasks* refers to the Levites performing physical labor in Num. 4.23; 8.24. This notice is doubly enigmatic since the Tent has not yet been erected. It indicates some role for women in connection with the Tabernacle (see 35.22).

38.9–20: The enclosure. See 27.9–19.

8 He made the laver of copper and its stand of copper, from the mirrors of the women who performed tasks[a] at the entrance of the Tent of Meeting.

9 He made the enclosure:

On the south[b] side, a hundred cubits of hangings of fine twisted linen for the enclosure—10 with their twenty posts and their twenty sockets of copper, the hooks and bands of the posts being silver.

11 On the north side, a hundred cubits—with their twenty posts and their twenty sockets of copper, the hooks and bands of the posts being silver.

12 On the west side, fifty cubits of hangings—with their ten posts and their ten sockets, the hooks and bands of the posts being silver.

13 And on the front side, to the east, fifty cubits: 14 fifteen cubits of hangings on the one flank, with their three posts and their three sockets, 15 and fifteen cubits of hangings on the other flank—on each side of the gate of the enclosure[c]—with their three posts and their three sockets.

16 All the hangings around the enclosure were of fine twisted linen. 17 The sockets for the posts were of copper, the hooks and bands of the posts were of silver, the overlay of their tops was of silver; all the posts of the enclosure were banded with silver.—18 The screen of the gate of the enclosure, done in embroidery, was of blue, purple, and crimson yarns, and fine twisted linen. It was twenty cubits long. [d]Its height—or width—was five cubits, like that of[d] the hangings of the enclosure. 19 The posts were four; their four sockets were of copper, their hooks of silver; and the overlay of their tops was of silver, as were also their bands.—20 All the pegs of the Tabernacle and of the enclosure round about were of copper.

PEKUDEI פקודי

21 These are the records of the Tabernacle, the Tabernacle of the Pact, which were drawn up at Moses' bidding—the work of the Levites under the direction of Ithamar son of Aaron the priest. 22 Now Bezalel, son of Uri son of Hur, of the tribe of Judah, had made all that the LORD had commanded Moses; 23 at his side was Oholiab son of Ahisamach, of the tribe of Dan, carver and designer, and embroiderer in blue, purple, and crimson yarns and in fine linen.

24 All the gold that was used for the work, in all the

38.21–31: The tally of materials. A tally of donations was being made as they were given (cf. 36.3–7). (Egyptian art shows metal being weighed and recorded before being used by the artisans [*ANEP* no. 133].) The items are listed in descending order of value. The list is not balanced. It includes the total of all the gold donated by the general public and used throughout the sanctuary, but does not identify the specific items made with it. On the other hand, it tallies, and specifies the items made with, the silver acquired from the census (30.11–16), but not that given in the general donation (35.24; it is not known what was done with the latter, since the former was used for everything that is supposed to be made of silver [26.19–32; 27.10–11, 17]). In contrast to the silver, it tallies, and specifies articles made with, the copper/bronze given in the general donation (35.25), but not that obtained from the women's mirrors (38.8). For the fabrics in 39.1 (if they are part of this list), no quantities are given at all. **21:** *These are the records,* better, "this is the tally." *The Tabernacle of the Pact,* 25.10–16 n. *The work of the Levites:* They conducted the tally. *Under the direction of Ithamar son of Aaron the priest:* The later censuses were also under priestly supervision (Num. 1.2–3, 17–18; 26.1–3, 63). *Ithamar* (6.23; 28.1) would later supervise some of the Levites in their porterage duties (Num. 4.28, 33; 7.8). **22–23:** The cooperation of Bezalel and Oholiab was necessary for the Levites to supervise how the metals were used.

---

a *Meaning of Heb. uncertain.*   b *Cf. note at 26.18.*

c *Which accounts for the remaining 20 cubits; cf. v. 18.*

d-d *Meaning of Heb. uncertain.*

work of the sanctuary—the elevation offering of gold—came to 29 talents[a] and 730 shekels by the sanctuary weight. 25 The silver of those of the community who were recorded came to 100 talents and 1,775 shekels by the sanctuary weight: 26 a half-shekel[b] a head, half a shekel by the sanctuary weight, for each one who was entered in the records, from the age of twenty years up, 603,550 men. 27 The 100 talents of silver were for casting the sockets of the sanctuary and the sockets for the curtain, 100 sockets to the 100 talents, a talent a socket. 28 And of the 1,775 shekels he made hooks for the posts, overlay for their tops, and bands around them.

29 The copper from the elevation offering came to 70 talents and 2,400 shekels. 30 Of it he made the sockets for the entrance of the Tent of Meeting; the copper altar and its copper grating and all the utensils of the altar; 31 the sockets of the enclosure round about and the sockets of the gate of the enclosure; and all the pegs of the Tabernacle and all the pegs of the enclosure round about.

39 Of the blue, purple, and crimson yarns they also[c] made the service vestments for officiating in the sanctuary; they made Aaron's sacral vestments—as the LORD had commanded Moses.

2 The ephod was made[d] of gold, blue, purple, and crimson yarns, and fine twisted linen. 3 They hammered out sheets of gold and cut threads to be worked into designs among the blue, the purple, and the crimson yarns, and the fine linen. 4 They made for it attaching shoulder-pieces; they were attached at its two ends. 5 The decorated band that was upon it was made like it, of one piece with it; of gold, blue, purple, and crimson yarns, and fine twisted linen—as the LORD had commanded Moses.

6 They bordered the lazuli stones with frames of gold, engraved with seal engravings of the names of the sons of Israel. 7 They were set on the shoulder-pieces of the ephod, as stones of remembrance for the Israelites—as the LORD had commanded Moses.

8 The breastpiece was made in the style of the ephod: of gold, blue, purple, and crimson yarns, and fine twisted linen. 9 It was square; they made the breastpiece doubled—a span in length and a span in width, doubled. 10 They set in it four rows of stones. The first row was a

25–26: When this census was carried out is unclear since none is ordered until a month after the sanctuary was completed (Num. 1.1, 18; see Exod. 40.2, 17). 26: Half-shekel: Stone weights inscribed with this term in Heb script ("beka'," a different term than that used in 30.13, 15) have been found in excavations. 603,550 men, men of military age, excluding the Levites. See Num. 1.46; 2.32. 30: The copper altar, the main sacrificial altar, overlaid with copper (27.1–8).

39.1–31: The making of the priestly vestments. See ch 28. 1: The first half of this v. may belong with the tally of materials in 29.21–31.

a A talent here equals 3,000 shekels.
b Heb. beqa'.
c See 36.8.
d Here and elsewhere in this chapter the singular active verb (lit. "he made") is used impersonally.

row of ᵃcarnelian, chrysolite, and emerald; ¹¹the second row: a turquoise, a sapphire, and an amethyst; ¹²the third row: a jacinth, an agate, and a crystal; ¹³and the fourth row: a beryl, a lapis lazuli, and a jasper. They were encircled in their mountings with frames of gold. ¹⁴The stones corresponded [in number] to the names of the sons of Israel: twelve, corresponding to their names; engraved like seals, each with its name, for the twelve tribes.

¹⁵On the breastpiece they made braided chains of corded work in pure gold. ¹⁶They made two frames of gold and two rings of gold, and fastened the two rings at the two ends of the breastpiece, ¹⁷attaching the two golden cords to the two rings at the ends of the breast-piece. ¹⁸They then fastened the two ends of the cords to the two frames, attaching them to the shoulder-pieces of the ephod, at the front. ¹⁹They made two rings of gold and attached them to the two ends of the breastpiece, at its inner edge, which faced the ephod. ²⁰They made two other rings of gold and fastened them on the front of the ephod, low on the two shoulder-pieces, close to its seam above the decorated band. ²¹The breastpiece was held in place by a cord of blue from its rings to the rings of the ephod, so that the breastpiece rested on the decorated band and did not come loose from the ephod—as the LORD had commanded Moses.

²²The robe for the ephod was made of woven work, of pure blue.ᵇ ²³The opening of the robe, in the middle of it, was like the opening of a coat of mail, with a binding around the opening, so that it would not tear. ²⁴On the hem of the robe they made pomegranates of blue, purple, and crimson yarns, twisted. ²⁵They also made bells of pure gold, and attached the bells between the pomegran-ates, all around the hem of the robe, between the pome-granates: ²⁶a bell and a pomegranate, a bell and a pome-granate, all around the hem of the robe for officiating in—as the LORD had commanded Moses.

²⁷They made the tunics of fine linen, of woven work, for Aaron and his sons; ²⁸and the headdress of fine linen, and the decorated turbans of fine linen, and the linen breeches of fine twisted linen; ²⁹and sashes of fine twisted linen, blue, purple, and crimson yarns, done in embroi-dery—as the LORD had commanded Moses.

³⁰They made the frontlet for the holy diadem of pure gold, and incised upon it the seal inscription: "Holy to the LORD." ³¹They attached to it a cord of blue to fix it upon the headdress above—as the LORD had commanded Moses.

a See note at 28.17.   b See note at 28.31.

³² Thus was completed all the work of the Tabernacle of the Tent of Meeting. The Israelites did so; just as the Lord had commanded Moses, so they did.

³³ Then they brought the Tabernacle to Moses, with the Tent and all its furnishings: its clasps, its planks, its bars, its posts, and its sockets; ³⁴ the covering of tanned ram skins, the covering of dolphin skins, and the curtain for the screen; ³⁵ the Ark of the Pact and its poles, and the cover; ³⁶ the table and all its utensils, and the bread of display; ³⁷ the pure lampstand,ᵃ its lamps—lamps in due order—and all its fittings, and the oil for lighting; ³⁸ the altar of gold, the oil for anointing, the aromatic incense, and the screen for the entrance of the Tent; ³⁹ the copper altar with its copper grating, its poles and all its utensils, and the laver and its stand; ⁴⁰ the hangings of the enclosure, its posts and its sockets, the screen for the gate of the enclosure, its cords and its pegs—all the furnishings for the service of the Tabernacle, the Tent of Meeting; ⁴¹ the service vestments for officiating in the sanctuary, the sacral vestments of Aaron the priest, and the vestments of his sons for priestly service. ⁴² Just as the Lord had commanded Moses, so the Israelites had done all the work. ⁴³ And when Moses saw that they had performed all the tasks—as the Lord had commanded, so they had done—Moses blessed them.

40 And the Lord spoke to Moses, saying: ² On the first day of the first month you shall set up the Tabernacle of the Tent of Meeting. ³ Place there the Ark of the Pact, and screen off the ark with the curtain. ⁴ Bring in the table and lay out its due setting; bring in the lampstand and light its lamps; ⁵ and place the gold altar of incense before the Ark of the Pact. Then put up the screen for the entrance of the Tabernacle.

a See note at 31.8.

Tabernacle). The section ends with Moses inspecting ("seeing") everything that was made and blessing the people (cf. Gen. 1.31; 2.3; see v. 43 n. regarding phraseology), and the Tabernacle is completed on New Year's day (40.17). See also 40.11 n. All of these allusions reflect the view that the sanctuary and the world mirror each other and that actions of the priests officiating in the sanctuary mirror God's actions in creating the world (note esp. the role of dividing/discriminating ["havdel"] in creation and in the priests' duties, Gen. 1.4, 6, 14; Lev. 10.10). *The Tabernacle of the Tent of Meeting:* This designation (see also v. 40) combines the two main terms for the sanctuary, expressing its two main functions. See 25.8 n. **34:** *And the curtain for the screen,* the screen at the entrance to the Holy of Holies (26.31–33). *The curtain,* for the entrance to the Holy of Holies (26.31–33). **38:** *The altar of gold,* the incense altar, overlaid with gold (31.1–9). **39:** *The copper altar,* the main sacrificial altar (27.1–8). **43:** *And when Moses saw that they had performed all the tasks,* lit. "And Moses saw all the work, and behold . . ." echoing Gen. 1.31, lit. "And God saw all that He had made, and behold . . ." "Work" (Heb "mela'khah") is the term used for God's work of creation in Gen. 2.2–3 (see also introductory note to 35.2–3). *Moses blessed them,* another echo of the Priestly creation account, though here it is Moses who blesses; cf. Gen. 1.22, 28; 2.3.

39.32–43: The completion and inspection of the Tabernacle's components. This section begins and ends by indicating that everything was made exactly as God had commanded. See chs 35–40 n. As in 35.10–19; 36.8–38.20, the contents of the Tabernacle are listed in a more systematic order than earlier. **32:** *Thus was completed all the work of the Tabernacle of the Tent of Meeting:* The phraseology (see also 40.33 n.) alludes to the completion of the creation of the world in Gen.

2.1, 3, one of several echoes of the Priestly source's account of creation here in the Priestly account of the creation of the Tabernacle (see 25.1–31.17 n.). The leitmotif of this section, mentioned seven times, that each item was made exactly "as the Lord had commanded Moses" echoes the sevenfold repetition of the formula "and there/it was (so)" in Gen. ch 1, indicating that all happened as God commanded (see also vv. 17–33 with reference to setting up the

40.1–16: Instructions for setting up and consecrating the Tabernacle and the priests. Only Moses can set up the components of the Tabernacle because only he has been shown visually how the Tabernacle is to look (25.9 n.). He must also perform certain priestly tasks because the priests are not yet consecrated and eligible to perform them (vv. 4, 23, 25, 27).

40.1–8: The Tabernacle. 2: *On the first day of the first month,* an appropriate date for beginning the sanc-

⁶ You shall place the altar of burnt offering before the entrance of the Tabernacle of the Tent of Meeting. ⁷ Place the laver between the Tent of Meeting and the altar, and put water in it. ⁸ Set up the enclosure round about, and put in place the screen for the gate of the enclosure.

⁹ You shall take the anointing oil and anoint the Tabernacle and all that is in it to consecrate it and all its furnishings, so that it shall be holy. ¹⁰ Then anoint the altar of burnt offering and all its utensils to consecrate the altar, so that the altar shall be most holy. ¹¹ And anoint the laver and its stand to consecrate it.

¹² You shall bring Aaron and his sons forward to the entrance of the Tent of Meeting and wash them with the water. ¹³ Put the sacral vestments on Aaron, and anoint him and consecrate him, that he may serve Me as priest. ¹⁴ Then bring his sons forward, put tunics on them, ¹⁵ and anoint them as you have anointed their father, that they may serve Me as priests. This their anointing shall serve them for everlasting priesthood throughout the ages.

¹⁶ This Moses did; just as the LORD had commanded him, so he did.

¹⁷ In the first month of the second year, on the first of the month, the Tabernacle was set up. ¹⁸ Moses set up the Tabernacle, placing its sockets, setting up its planks, inserting its bars, and erecting its posts. ¹⁹ He spread the tent over the Tabernacle, placing the covering of the tent on top of it—just as the LORD had commanded Moses.

²⁰ He took the Pact and placed it in the ark; he fixed the poles to the ark, placed the cover on top of the ark, ²¹ and brought the ark inside the Tabernacle. Then he put up the curtain for screening, and screened off the Ark of the Pact—just as the LORD had commanded Moses.

²² He placed the table in the Tent of Meeting, outside the curtain, on the north side of the Tabernacle. ²³ Upon it he laid out the setting of bread before the LORD—as the LORD had commanded Moses. ²⁴ He placed the lampstand in the Tent of Meeting opposite the table, on the south side of the Tabernacle. ²⁵ And he lit the lamps before the LORD—as the LORD had commanded Moses. ²⁶ He placed the altar of gold in the Tent of Meeting, before the curtain. ²⁷ On it he burned aromatic incense—as the LORD had commanded Moses. ²⁸ Then he put up the screen for the entrance of the Tabernacle. ²⁹ At the entrance of the Tabernacle of the Tent of Meeting he placed the altar of burnt offering. On it he offered up the burnt offering and the meal offering—as the LORD had commanded Moses. ³⁰ He placed the laver

tuary service. **4:** *Its due setting,* i.e., the bread of display (25.30 n.).

40.9–16: Consecrating the Tabernacle and the priests. See 30.26–30; 29.4–9. **9:** *Consecrate it . . . so that it shall be holy,* lit. "make it holy . . . so that it shall be holy." This phrase in this context, with its allusions to the creation story (39.32 n.) reminds one of God's consecrating the seventh day ("declared it holy" is the same Heb word) in Gen. 2.3. **16:** *This Moses did,* referring to the instructions in vv. 1–15, which Moses carries out in two stages: He sets up the Tabernacle in vv. 17–33 and consecrates it and the priests in Lev. 8.1–13. *Just as the LORD had commanded him, so he did:* A slightly different form of this statement appears seven times in vv. 17–33.

40.17–33a: Setting up the Tabernacle. 27: There is no explicit command for Moses to burn the incense or offer the sacrifices (v. 29), but his doing so is consistent with God's commands that he perform the other priestly duties of laying out the bread and lighting the lamps (vv. 4, 23, 25) prior to the priests' consecration. The reference to Moses approaching the altar in vv. 31–32 must refer to the same pre-consecration period.

between the Tent of Meeting and the altar, and put water in it for washing. [31] From it Moses and Aaron and his sons would wash their hands and feet; [32] they washed when they entered the Tent of Meeting and when they approached the altar—as the LORD had commanded Moses. [33] And he set up the enclosure around the Tabernacle and the altar, and put up the screen for the gate of the enclosure.

When Moses had finished the work, [34] the cloud covered the Tent of Meeting, and the Presence of the LORD filled the Tabernacle. [35] Moses could not enter the Tent of Meeting, because the cloud had settled upon it and the Presence of the LORD filled the Tabernacle. [36] When the cloud lifted from the Tabernacle, the Israelites would set out, on their various journeys; [37] but if the cloud did not lift, they would not set out until such time as it did lift. [38] For over the Tabernacle a cloud of the LORD rested by day, and fire would appear in it[a] by night, in the view of all the house of Israel throughout their journeys.

40.33b–38: The divine Presence enters the Tabernacle: With the Tabernacle complete, God's Presence (16.6–7 n.) leaves Mount Sinai and takes up Its abode amidst the Israelites, fulfilling the promise of 29.43, 45 and signifying the complete repair of the rupture between God and Israel occasioned by the golden calf. From there God will communicate with Moses from now on (Lev. 1.1) and will accompany the Israelites on their journeys (24.16 n.; 25.1–31.17 n.).
33: *When Moses had finished the work,* another echo of creation; see Gen. 2.2. *The cloud,* in which God's Presence is manifest; see 13.21 n., 22 n.; 24.15. As it covered Mount Sinai, it now covers the Tabernacle, where it will remain to guide Israel. For the appearance of fire within it at night, see 13.21 n.
36–38: These vv. look ahead to Israel's future journeys accompanied by God (Num. 9.15–23; 10.11–28). The narrative will resume in Leviticus with God's call to Moses from the Tent (Lev. 1.1) and the consecration of the priests in Lev. chs 8–9. But at this point Exodus ends, allowing the reader to contemplate the phenomenon of God dwelling on earth with a symbol of His Presence in full view of the Israelites (cf. 1 Kings 8.27).

_____
a *I.e., in the cloud.*

וִיקְרָא

Leviticus

LEVITICUS, THE THIRD BOOK OF THE TORAH, is traditionally called *vayikra'* ("and He [the LORD] called," but see 1.1 n.), after the first word in the book. It was also called *torat kohanim*, "instruction of (or 'for') the priests" in rabbinic times, hence its Greek name *Levitikon*, "things pertaining to the Levites" (i.e., the priests, who are of the tribe of Levi), referring to the book's main concern with commandments connected with the worship of God, for which the priests were responsible.

Context

LEVITICUS IS PART OF A LONG NARRATIVE, extending from Exodus ch 25 to Numbers ch 10, that may be called "When the Tabernacle Stood at Sinai." It begins with God's instructions to Moses to provide a portable residence (called a *mishkan*, "Tabernacle," lit. "dwelling," or *mikdash*, "holy place") for the divine Presence (the LORD's *kavod*) and to consecrate his brother Aaron and the latter's sons as priests. The Tabernacle was also the place for God to meet regularly with Moses to impart His laws (Exod. 25.22); thus it is also called the *'ohel mo'ed*, "Tent of Meeting." The Tabernacle and all its appurtenances were manufactured at the foot of Mount Sinai; the divine Presence took up residence; the priests were consecrated and sacrificial worship commenced; the laws were conveyed; the priests, Levites, and remaining tribes were mustered and arranged and instructions for the journey to Canaan were given; and finally the Israelites departed from Sinai on their journey to Canaan.

The Tabernacle narrative stands at the center of the Torah, and although it takes up almost a third of the Torah, it covers a timespan of less than one year. This indicates its crucial importance. All the institutions that ultimately shaped Israel's national and religious existence—the law, the priesthood, the forms of Temple worship and the tribal foundation of its society—are said to have been ordained and established during this brief period in Israel's history.

According to the story that emerges from the Torah as a whole, the Tabernacle narrative is a stage in Israel's sojourn at Sinai, interwoven with the theophany and proclamation of the Decalogue (Exod. chs 19–20), the giving of the laws and the covenant ceremony (Exod. chs 21–24), the giving of the two sets of tablets, and the incident of the golden calf

(Exod. chs 32–34). However, according to the critical theory that separates the Torah into sources which were originally distinct and independent (see "Modern Study of the Bible," pp. 2084–96), the literary source that contained the Tabernacle narrative called the Priestly document, or P, contained none of these other events. In P's view, only the events recounted by the Tabernacle narrative took place. The centrality of the Tabernacle narrative is therefore far more pronounced in P than in the redacted Torah, since, in P, only in connection with the arrival of the divine Presence to dwell among the Israelites was a code of law given and the social structure established; no other theophany or covenant preceded it and no sin of collective apostasy followed.

Content and Structure

LEVITICUS IS THE DIRECT CONTINUATION of what precedes it at the end of Exodus, and the narrative at the end of Leviticus continues directly into Numbers. Ch 1 takes up the story from the time the divine Presence enters the Tabernacle, on the first day of Nisan (the first month, in the spring) in the year following the exodus (Exod. ch 40). From within, God calls to Moses and imparts to him, in a series of encounters (Lev. chs 1–27), His laws and commandments. Since Numbers begins on the first day of 'Iyar (the second month) in the same year (Num. 1.1), it emerges that the entire book of Leviticus covers but one month.

The first group of laws, on sacrifice (chs 1–7), are given on the first day of the month, the day the Presence entered the Tabernacle (see 7.37–38). Then, interrupting the law-giving, is the consecration of the priesthood (ch 8), the dedication of the Tabernacle (ch 9), and the crime and immediate death of Aaron's sons (10.1–7, 12–20). The law-giving resumes as Moses is given the commandments concerning permitted and forbidden foods (ch 11), the purification and atonement following physical defilement (chs 12–15), the annual "Day of Atonement" (ch 16), prohibitions of profane slaughter and blood (ch 17), sexual crimes (chs 18, 20), miscellaneous regulations assuring Israel's holiness (ch 19), the sanctity of the priests (ch 21), the qualifications for sacrificial animals (ch 22), the weekly Sabbath and annual festivals (ch 23), the oil for the Tabernacle lamp (24.1–4), and the showbread (24.5–9). Again the law-giving is briefly interrupted, this time to recount the crime of the blasphemer and his execution (24.10–16, 23). It concludes with the laws of the sabbatical and jubilee years, including laws of slavery and property rights (25.1–26.2), a lengthy speech promising reward for compliance and punishment for failure to obey (26.3–45), and a summarizing caption (26.46). Then the laws of vows and tithes (ch 27) are appended and the caption is repeated (27.34).

The two narratives that interrupt the laws lead to brief legal sections. Thus following the crime of Nadab and Abihu, Moses clarifies for Aaron and his surviving sons the law regulating the proper disposal of sacrificial offerings (10.12–19); and while pronouncing sentence upon the blasphemer, God also imparts the laws of damages, governed by the eye-for-eye principle (24.17–22).

The complex interaction of narrative and law displayed in Leviticus is the defining literary feature of the Torah and of the Priestly document in particular. Both are narrative works, but the purpose of the narrative is to provide the literary framework, and thus the historical rationale and theological explanation, for the laws and commandments which are embedded within the narrative.

Composition

MODERN BIBLE SCHOLARS AGREE that all of Leviticus belongs to the Priestly source (P). If, however, the Torah is treated as a unified whole, the laws and narratives belonging to the Priestly source must be reconciled and harmonized with the non-Priestly material, so that they all interact and complement each other. This is done by traditional Jewish interpretation, and also by modern scholars who hold that the Priestly source was composed as a supplement to the non-Priestly sources. This commentary, however, believes that the Priestly work does not interact on any primary level with the non-Priestly material, so its main aim is to demonstrate the uniqueness of the Priestly tradition by pointing out the contrast between P and the other sources. The harmonistic approach will be illustrated only for the purpose of comparison and to explain the basis of traditional Jewish interpretations.

Date

THE BOOK OF LEVITICUS, like the other books of the Torah, came into existence as a defined literary entity no earlier than the time of the Babylonian exile in the 6th century. On the date of P there is much disagreement. This commentary will espouse the view that the Priestly source was the product of learned scribes of the Jerusalemite priesthood of the last centuries of the Judean kingdom and that it took shape in two phases, the Holiness Legislation (H) (chs 17–26) being added to the Priestly work in the final years before the exile.

Leviticus and Judaism

THE STUDY OF THE LAWS in Leviticus stood at the center of rabbinic learning, and the halakhic midrash on Leviticus was called simply *Sifra*, or "the Book." It was customary for small children to begin their study of the Bible with Leviticus. The traditional explanation for this is that "the pure" (i.e., children) should be engaged in the study of purity (i.e., the laws of purification and atonement). A more likely reason is that Leviticus contains most of the laws which the Jew is commanded to observe on a regular basis, and it was only natural that the child's program of study should begin with the practical knowledge required for the life of *mitzvot* (commandments).

Even after the destruction of the Temple and the cessation of sacrificial worship and Temple ritual, Leviticus remains at the foundation of Jewish life. Among the institutions still central to Judaism which have their biblical origins in Leviticus are most of the dietary laws (the permitted and forbidden animals, and the blood prohibition); many of the festival rituals; most of the laws regulating sex, marriage, and family purity; and the commandments governing the seventh year, still applicable in the land of Israel. Moreover, the religious life of the congregation, centered upon the synagogue and the daily prayers offered at fixed times and in precisely ordained ritual forms, is a direct outgrowth of, and according to rabbinic tradition a substitute for, the Temple ritual as envisioned in Leviticus.

Another aspect of the heritage of Leviticus that has become normative in Judaism is its unique theology of the performance of *mitzvot*. Leviticus teaches that the ritual commandments and the ethical or social ones (in rabbinic terms: *mitzvot* between a human being and God and *mitzvot* between fellow human beings) are equally important and equally valid. To be precise, there is really no such thing as a *mitzvah* pertaining solely to interpersonal relations; the love of one's neighbor is a divine command (see 19.18), and every offense against one's fellow human being desecrates the name of God. This idea, which has taken shape and developed over the centuries and has ultimately become a central pillar of Jewish religious thought, derives directly from the book of Leviticus, where it is summed up in a single verse: "You shall each revere his mother and his father, and keep My sabbaths: I the LORD am your God" (19.3).

Finally, nowhere outside of Leviticus is there a clearer articulation of the reason for the Jewish people's existence. God has entered into a relationship with the Israelites so that they might perpetually sanctify His name. Their role in the world, and in history, is to attest to His existence, to publicize His oneness, and to advertise His greatness. This they are commanded to do by worshipping Him and keeping His laws. When they fail to do so, His name is profaned, that is, His fame is diminished and His reputation tarnished; when they live up to this charge and duty, He and His name are sanctified. This statement, explicit in 22.31–33 and implicit throughout the book, has remained fundamental to Jewish belief and consciousness throughout all generations.   [BARUCH J. SCHWARTZ]

VA-YIKRA'   ויקרא

1 The LORD called to Moses and spoke to him from the Tent of Meeting, saying: [2] Speak to the Israelite people, and say to them:

When any of you presents an offering of cattle to the LORD, [a-]he shall choose his[-a] offering from the herd or from the flock.

a-a Lit. "you shall offer your."

1.1–3.17: Gift offerings. Chs 1–3 are a single, uninterrupted divine speech. The theme is "gift offerings," expressed in the word "'isheh," "food gift," used in each ch to characterize the offering prescribed (see 1.9 n.). Gift offerings, as distinct from expiatory sacrifices (treated in chs 4–5), express

the worshipper's desire to present something to the LORD as a token of love and reverence. The Rabbis referred to them as "nedavah," "voluntary offerings," since they could be made at will—in fulfillment of vows, at private visits to the sanctuary, in supplication in times of distress, in gratitude for

deliverance from danger or harm, or simply in a spontaneous urge to pay homage to God. Each of the subsections corresponds to one of the three types of gift offering: the burnt offering (ch 1), the cereal offering (ch 2), and the sacrifice of well-being (ch 3). While the burnt offering and cereal offering also figure prominently in the ordained public rituals performed by the priests on specified occasions, the sacrifice of well-being belongs almost entirely to the realm of individual piety.

1.1–17: Burnt offerings from the herd and flock. As with the other offerings in chs 1–3, only some of the procedures are detailed here. Some have already been given with the instructions for the

³ If his offering is a burnt offering from the herd, he shall make his offering a male without blemish. He shall bring it to the entrance of the Tent of Meeting, for acceptance in his behalf before the LORD. ⁴ He shall lay his hand upon the head of the burnt offering, that it may be acceptable in his behalf, in expiation for him. ⁵ The bull shall be slaughtered before the LORD; and Aaron's sons, the priests, shall offer the blood, dashing the blood against all sides of the

---

consecration ceremonies (Exod. 29.15–18), and others are implicit in the instructions for other sacrifices. The text economizes, preferring not to repeat material found in other contexts. The defining feature of the burnt offering is that none of the meat is eaten; it is burned on the altar in its entirety. This makes it the gift-offering par excellence. The text does not specify the circumstances that might occasion a burnt offering, but Noah's sacrifices of thanksgiving or propitiation after the flood (Gen. 8.20), Abraham's near-sacrifice of Isaac (Gen. ch 22), Balaam's sacrifices entreating divine vision (Num. 23.15; etc.), Saul's sacrifices before battle (1 Sam. 13.12), and Job's sacrifices of atonement for his sons' hypothetical sins (Job 1.5), among many others, were burnt offerings. Since it also comprised the central component of the statutory public offerings, the altar in the Tabernacle court is called "the altar of the offering" (Exod. 30.28; etc.). **1:** This is connected to the P narrative at the end of Exodus, so it should be translated "and it [the Presence of the LORD (Exod. 40.35)] called out to Moses." After it filled the Tabernacle, the Presence called to Moses from within. A distinction is made between the Presence, which called, and the LORD Himself, who spoke; this is similar to the first encounter with God experienced by the prophet Ezekiel (Ezek. 1.28–2.1ff.). *Tent of Meeting,* one of the names for the Tabernacle; see the intro. **2: The heading for chs 1–3.** According to the Masoretic accents, the v. should be translated as two separate provisions. The first, "When any of you presents

an offering, [it must be] to the LORD," is the basic postulate of all Israelite worship: Sacrifices are to be made to the LORD alone. The second goes on to stipulate: "He shall make his offering of livestock, that is, from the herd or from the flock." This preserves the original intent of the second half of the v.: Offerings must be of livestock. Later, when the laws allowing burnt offerings from fowl (vv. 14–17) and cereal offerings (2.1–16) were added, the v. was understood to mean that when one wished to sacrifice livestock, the choice was limited to domestic animals. *Any of you:* Heb "'adam," "human being," refers to male and female alike (see Gen. 1.27; 5.2, also P). In P opportunities for individual worship are identical for male and female; only the public ritual was confined to males, namely, the Aaronic priesthood. See also 6.1–6; 7.8. **3–9:** Making a burnt offering from the herd. Instructions follow for a third type of burnt offering, made from fowl (vv. 14–17). The fowl offering, which does not fit the explicit provision "you shall choose your offering from the herd or from the flock" (v. 2), was apparently not part of the original text. The offerer is responsible for acquiring the proper animal (see 22.17–20), bringing it to the Tabernacle entrance, placing his hand upon its head as an act of presentation, slaughtering it, removing the hide and flaying the animal. The priest performs the remaining actions: presenting the blood, dashing some of it around the altar in the Tabernacle courtyard, placing the quarters, head, and suet on the altar fire, washing the entrails

and legs and placing them too on the altar, and seeing that all the flesh is "turned into smoke," that is, consumed completely until nothing but ashes remain. **3:** *An offering,* Heb "korban," a term expressing the notion of something presented (from Heb "k-r-b," "near") in homage. It does not mean "sacrifice" in the sense of "giving something up." *Burnt offering,* Heb "'olah," from the verb "'-l-h," "go up, ascend"; the distinguishing visible feature of all altar sacrifices was the smoke ascending heavenward. *For acceptance in his behalf:* Central to all gift-offerings is the worshipper's need to know that the deity has accepted his gift; this is consistently referred to as "ratzon," "acceptance" (see 22.17–20). **4:** *Lay his hand,* to signify the transfer of ownership of the animal to the deity. *Acceptable,* correctly: "accepted"; see 7.18; 19.5–8; 22.17–30. *In expiation for him,* Heb "kiper," often translated "atone," has two meanings in P: "decontaminate [the sacred precincts] of sin or defilement" (see 4.1–5.26 n.) and "serve as ransom or payment [for one's life]" (see 17.11 n.). The latter seems to be intended here; that is why it is mentioned along with the hand-laying ritual: The moment ownership of the animal is transferred to the deity, it is accepted as payment, i.e., as a substitute for the worshipper himself. The lay person's private burnt offering would then be one way of symbolically offering oneself to God. The Rabbis ruled that the burnt offering be given in expiation for the failure to carry out performative commandments. **5:** *The bull shall be slaughtered,* better, [the offerer] shall slaughter the bull. This is not strictly a part of the ritual in that no sacral significance was attached to the animal's death. Heb "sh-ḥ-t" implies that the slaughter is performed by slitting the throat, but since the Bible provides no details, rabbinic tradition held that the specifics were communicated orally by God to Moses. *Offer the blood . . . against all sides of the altar:* This is a symbolic method of offer-altar which is at the entrance of the Tent of Meeting. [6] The burnt offering shall be flayed and cut up into sections. [7] The sons of Aaron the priest shall put fire on the altar and lay out wood upon the fire; [8] and Aaron's sons, the priests, shall lay out the sections, with the head and the suet, on the wood that is on the fire upon the altar. [9] Its entrails and legs shall be washed with water, and the priest shall turn the whole into smoke on the altar as a burnt offering, an offering by fire of pleasing odor to the LORD.

[10] If his offering for a burnt offering is from the flock, of sheep or of goats, he shall make his offering a male without blemish. [11] It shall be slaughtered before the LORD on the north side of the altar, and Aaron's sons, the priests, shall dash its blood against all sides of the altar. [12] When it has been cut up into sections, the priest shall lay them out, with the head and the suet, on the wood that is on the fire upon the altar. [13] The entrails and the legs shall be washed with water; the priest shall offer up and turn the whole into smoke on the altar. It is a burnt offering, an offering by fire, of pleasing odor to the LORD.

[14] If his offering to the LORD is a burnt offering of birds, he shall choose his offering from turtledoves or pigeons. [15] The priest shall bring it to the altar, pinch off its head, and turn it into smoke on the altar; and its blood shall be drained out against the side of the altar. [16] He shall remove its crop with its contents,[a] and cast it into the place of the ashes, at the east side of the altar. [17] The priest shall tear it open by its wings, without severing it, and turn it into smoke on the altar, upon the wood that is on the fire. It is a burnt offering, an offering by fire, of pleasing odor to the LORD.

2 When a person presents an offering of meal to the LORD, his offering shall be of choice flour; he shall pour oil upon it, lay frankincense on it, [2] and present it to

---

a Others "feathers."

---

ing the blood to the LORD. **6:** *Shall be flayed* by the offerer. The division of labor is clear: The offerer is responsible for the mundane tasks of transferring ownership of the animal and transforming it from a living animal into food fit for consumption; the priests are responsible for the sacred tasks of dashing the blood and offering the flesh as a gift to the LORD. **7:** *Fire* here, as in many passages, probably means burning coals. The priests were re-

quired to maintain a constant altar fire on the altar (see 6.6). **9:** *An offering by fire:* Heb "'isheh" is not derived from "'esh," "fire," but from a root meaning "gift." Thus a better translation is "food gift," since the word denotes burnt offerings, cereal offerings, and sacrifices of well-being. It is not used for the purification and reparation offerings, as the latter are not gifts but rituals of expiation. *Of pleasing odor to the LORD:* P's unique anthro-

pomorphism attributes to God the sensual, carnal pleasure derived from inhaling the fragrant odor of roasting meat while at the same time denying that He actually consumes it as food. Similarly, P portrays God's Presence as abiding within the Tabernacle, but offerings presented to Him are turned into smoke and ascend heavenward. The LORD's contrasting human and supernatural traits, as well as His opposite attributes of immanence and transcendence, exist in P side by side. **10–13:** A burnt offering from the flock (sheep and goats) is like offerings from the herd (cattle). **14–17:** Making a burnt offering from fowl, presumably for those who could not afford a sacrifice of livestock. The birds that qualify as offerings, turtledoves and pigeons, are the two types of domesticated fowl used for human consumption. The particulars of the procedure stem from the nature of fowl and its small size. The wingspread is left intact so that the carcass placed upon the altar will not appear ridiculously small. **16:** The first part of the v. should be translated "He shall remove its feathers and its excrement." These are to be cast into the ash-heap alongside the altar.

2.1–16: The offering of grain. Instructions for the "minḥa" (see also 6.7–16). The word means tribute paid to a superior (e.g., Gen. 32.14, 22; etc.) or a ruler (e.g., Judg. 3.15ff.; 1 Sam. 10.27), and is used in non-Priestly texts to refer to sacrifices in general, e.g., Cain and Abel's offerings (Gen. 4.3–5) and the offerings at the Shiloh sanctuary (1 Sam. 2.17). This expresses the basic notion underlying the sacrificial system: that the Israelites, as a people and as individuals, are expected to offer to God regular tokens of His lordship over them. P uses the term in a specific sense of "offering made of grain." This ch interrupts the original sequence of burnt offering and well-being offering; it was introduced here to provide an opportunity for even the poorest Israelite

Aaron's sons, the priests. The priest shall scoop out of it a handful of its choice flour and oil, as well as all of its frankincense; and this token portion he shall turn into smoke on the altar, as an offering by fire, of pleasing odor to the Lord. ³ And the remainder of the meal offering shall be for Aaron and his sons, a most holy portion from the Lord's offerings by fire.

⁴ When you present an offering of meal baked in the oven, [it shall be of] choice flour: unleavened cakes with oil mixed in, or unleavened wafers spread with oil.

⁵ If your offering is a meal offering on a griddle, it shall be of choice flour with oil mixed in, unleavened. ⁶ Break it into bits and pour oil on it; it is a meal offering.

⁷ If your offering is a meal offering in a pan, it shall be made of choice flour in oil.

⁸ When you present to the Lord a meal offering that is made in any of these ways, it shall be brought to the priest who shall take it up to the altar. ⁹ The priest shall remove the token portion from the meal offering and turn it into smoke on the altar as an offering by fire, of pleasing odor to the Lord. ¹⁰ And the remainder of the meal offering shall be for Aaron and his sons, a most holy portion from the Lord's offerings by fire.

¹¹ No meal offering that you offer to the Lord shall be made with leaven, for no leaven or honey may be turned into smoke as an offering by fire to the Lord. ¹² You may bring them to the Lord as an offering of choice products;[a]

a Exact meaning of Heb. uncertain.

the flesh of animals, is by definition a *pleasing odor*, whereas in non-Priestly texts it is assumed that the addition of fragrant spice renders the offering pleasing (see Isa. 1.13; 43.23; Jer. 6.20; 17.26; 41.5; Ps. 141.2). **3:** *A most holy portion*, Heb "kodesh kodashim" (see also v. 10), a term applied to the purification offering and the reparation offering as well, but not to the burnt offering. Gradation of sanctity or holiness (see 6.11), thought of as an effusion of the divine Presence varying in degree, is an essential aspect of the Tabernacle and its worship. The most holy among the food gifts are those of which a portion is eaten by the priests but not by the worshippers. **8–10:** The procedure for the prepared "minḥa." The three types in vv. 4–7 are offered in the same manner as the uncooked type. **8–9:** *Take it up to the altar:* Before the *token portion* is removed, the entire offering is symbolically presented to the deity. This gives ritual expression to the fact that the cakes, loaves, or wafers were prepared for God and not simply brought from the supply of foods kept at home for common consumption. **11–12:** The prohibition of leaven. In the Heb v. 11a is a general prohibition of "ḥametz," leavened cakes or loaves, while v. 11b gives the details: In order to prevent fermentation, neither "se'or," the leavening agent (sourdough) nor "devash," *honey*, may be used in any of the Lord's food gifts (see 1.9 n.) Though both date-honey and the honey of bees are leavening agents, in the Bible "devash" is almost always the honey of fruits (see Gen. 43.11; Deut. 8.8; 2 Chron. 31.5; etc.). There is nothing intrinsically unacceptable about leaven and honey; they may be offered (v. 12) but not placed on the altar. Rather it is the fermentation of the grain offering specifically that is prohibited, most likely for practical reasons, so that the preparation, offering, and eating of food gifts would all take place within a short period of time and in proximity to the altar. The preparation of leavened cakes

to make a freewill offering, from grain. The "minḥa" also figures prominently among the statutory public offerings, accompanying the burnt offerings made each morning and evening. The public "minḥa" (see Exod. 29.40; 40.29; Num. 28.5; etc.), especially that which was a part of the daily evening sacrifice, eventually gave its name to the afternoon prayer, known since rabbinic times as the "minḥa" prayer. **1–8:** Types of grain offering. The two essential ingredients are semolina of wheat and [olive] oil; these give it its character of a food gift (the oil was also necessary to facilitate the burning). Several variations exist. The uncooked mixture (v. 1) requires the addition of frankincense, so it is the most costly. The remaining types, requiring no

frankincense, involve some preparation of unleavened cakes: oven-baked (as loaves or wafers, v. 4), griddle-toasted (and crumbled, vv. 5–6), and pan-fried (v. 7); see also 7.9–10. The grain offering is prepared by the worshipper and presented in its entirety to the priest. Unlike the burnt offering, however, only an "'azkara," a "reminder" or token portion, is placed on the altar; the remainder is eaten by the priest (see 6.11; 7.9); God thus gives the priests the "leftover" portions of his own food gift (see 6.10). The "'azkara" of the uncooked "minḥa" includes the frankincense, all of which belongs to the deity. **2:** *Offering by fire*, see 1.9 n. *Of pleasing odor*, see 1.9 n. As v. 9 confirms, this is not simply the result of the frankincense. In P, the "minḥa" itself, like but they shall not be offered up on the altar for a pleasing odor. ¹³ You shall season your every offering of meal with salt; you shall not omit from your meal offering the salt of your covenant with God; with all your offerings you must offer salt.

¹⁴ If you bring a meal offering of first fruits to the LORD, you shall bring new ears parched with fire, grits of the fresh grain, as your meal offering of first fruits. ¹⁵ You shall add oil to it and lay frankincense on it; it is a meal offering. ¹⁶ And the priest shall turn a token portion of it into smoke: some of the grits and oil, with all of the frankincense, as an offering by fire to the LORD.

3 If his offering is a sacrifice of well-being[a]— If he offers of the herd, whether a male or a female, he shall bring before the LORD one without blemish. ² He shall lay his hand upon the head of his offering and slaughter it at the entrance of the Tent of Meeting; and Aaron's sons, the priests, shall dash the blood against all sides of the altar. ³ He shall then present from the sacrifice of well-being, as an offering by fire to the LORD, the fat

---

a Others "peace offering." Exact meaning of shelamim uncertain.

---

would take much longer. The presentation of ready-made loaves of bread is known outside of P (1 Sam. 10.3; 21.5; 22.13). **13:** The requirement to salt the grain offering is a corollary of this: Salt is an anti-fermentation agent and would impede natural leavening. *The salt of your covenant:* Heb "berit," *covenant,* is used here in the sense of imposed obligation, and simply means that the salting of offerings is to be observed perpetually. *With all your offerings . . . offer salt:* Characteristically, the Rabbis took this summary to mean that animal offerings as well, and not only the "minha," required salting; this eventually became normative. In commemoration of this, Jewish custom requires salt on the table. **14–16:** A final type of "minha" is described, *a meal offering of first fruits.* This gift offering of grain, before it has fully matured and before flour can be produced from it, is prepared and offered in the same way as the uncooked offering, and provides a means for approaching God the moment one's grain begins to

ripen, when the natural impulse to make an offering is strongest.

3.1–17: The sacrifice of well-being. V. 1a introduces the possibility of offering a third type of gift offering, namely, the sacrifice of well-being; vv. 1b–5 lay out the procedure for making such an offering if the animal is taken from the herd; vv. 6–16 lay out the procedure if the animal is from the flock (v. 6a)—either a sheep (vv. 7–11) or a goat (vv. 12–16). This follows the basic outline of ch 1. The prohibition of suet and blood (v. 17) ends the ch. **1:** *A sacrifice of well-being:* Heb consists of two components: "zevaḥ" denotes a sacrifice of a slaughtered animal of which the offerer partakes in a festive meal; in P this is the only way in which the eating of meat is permitted (see 17.3–7). Several interpretations have been suggested for the word "shelamim." The translation "sacrifice of well-being" reflects the fact that in P a "zevaḥ" offered by the individual is an expression of joy, gladness, gratitude, or relief; see 7.11–17 n.

Additional regulations concerning the "shelamim" sacrifice are given in 7.11–38; 19.5–8; 22.21–30. The distinctive feature is that only the blood and token fatty portions of the animal are placed on the altar, and only certain prescribed portions of the meat are eaten by the priests; most of the animal is eaten by the offerer and invited guests as a festive meal "in the LORD's presence." Well-being offerings are thus the natural expression of gladness, the worshipper celebrating by feasting in the presence of God in acknowledgment of His loving-kindness. The feast is a sacrifice because ownership of the animal is first transferred to God, after which the portions eaten by the priest and the worshipper are considered to have been given to them by God—much as a king is sustained by the tribute provided by his subjects, yet the subjects are nevertheless honored to be invited to dine at the royal table. **1b–5:** The procedure for a "shelamim" sacrifice from the herd. The animal may be male or female. The tasks of the worshipper are similar to those for a burnt offering (1.3–9). No mention is made of the distribution of the remainder of the animal (see 7.11ff.) since the sole interest of this ch is the manner in which the food-gift is presented to the deity. **2:** *Shall dash the blood against . . . the altar,* as an offering; see 1.5 n. **3–4:** The LORD's portion of the sacrifice. Fatty portions of slaughtered animals were considered to be the richest, tastiest morsels. Best of all are the layers of suet (Heb "ḥelev," translated as "fat"), the hard, subcutaneous fatty tissue surrounding the internal organs; therefore these portions would be assigned to God. That which is "too good" for mortals might logically be assumed to be a proper repast for a deity. Burning suet also provides a dense smoke of sweet, meaty fragrance, suggesting that pleasure is derived from it by a transcendent divine being. Biblical tradition is thus unanimous that the suet of sacrificial flesh is offered to the deity (below, v. 16; see also that covers the entrails and all the fat that is about the entrails; [4] the two kidneys and the fat that is on them, that is at the loins; and the protuberance on the liver, which he shall remove with the kidneys. [5] Aaron's sons shall turn these into smoke on the altar, with the burnt offering which is upon the wood that is on the fire, as an offering by fire, of pleasing odor to the LORD.

[6] And if his offering for a sacrifice of well-being to the LORD is from the flock, whether a male or a female, he shall offer one without blemish. [7] If he presents a sheep as his offering, he shall bring it before the LORD [8] and lay his hand upon the head of his offering. It shall be slaughtered before the Tent of Meeting, and Aaron's sons shall dash its blood against all sides of the altar. [9] He shall then present, as an offering by fire to the LORD, the fat from the sacrifice of well-being: the whole broad tail, which shall be removed close to the backbone; the fat that covers the entrails and all the fat that is about the entrails; [10] the two kidneys and the fat that is on them, that is at the loins; and the protuberance on the liver, which he shall remove with the kidneys. [11] The priest shall turn these into smoke on the altar as food, an offering by fire to the LORD.

[12] And if his offering is a goat, he shall bring it before the LORD [13] and lay his hand upon its head. It shall be slaughtered before the Tent of Meeting, and Aaron's sons shall dash its blood against all sides of the altar. [14] He shall then present as his offering from it, as an offering by fire to the LORD, the fat that covers the entrails and all the fat that is about the entrails; [15] the two kidneys and the fat that is on them, that is at the loins; and the protuberance on the liver, which he shall remove with the kidneys. [16] The priest shall turn these into smoke on the altar as food, an offering by fire, of pleasing odor.

All fat is the LORD's. [17] It is a law for all time throughout the ages, in all your settlements: you must not eat any fat or any blood.

4 The LORD spoke to Moses, saying: [2] Speak to the Israelite people thus:

When a person unwittingly incurs guilt in regard to any of the LORD's commandments about things not to be done, and does one of them—

made each morning and evening; the assumption is that it is either being burned, or at least its remains are smouldering, on the altar fire at all times. For *the wood,* see 6.1ff. *Pleasing odor,* see 1.9 n.
6–16: The procedure for a "shelamim" sacrifice from the flock. Sheep and goats are treated separately because only sheep possess the heavy fat-tail which, like suet, needs to be removed and added to the portions placed upon the altar. **16:** *All fat,* better, "all suet," as explained above. However, the words *all fat [is]* are evidently a scribal error, copied unintentionally from the next v. (where they are translated "any fat"); v. 16 should conclude "of pleasing odor to the LORD" just like vv. 5 and 11. **17:** What belongs to the LORD is not to be eaten by humans, thus, all blood and suet are prohibited. The details of the blood prohibition are given in 17.10–16; for elaboration on the prohibition of suet, see 7.22–27. This prohibition is appropriately placed here, since, according to P, the "shelamim" offering is the one occasion on which lay people would have eaten the flesh of domestic livestock.

4.1–5.26: The purification and reparation offerings. Chs 4–5 present three speeches of God to Moses (4.1–5.13; 5.14–19; 5.20–26). The first contains the laws concerning the "hata't" or purification offering; the second and third give regulations governing the "'asham" or reparation offering. This completes instructions for the five types of occasional sacrifice. The sacrifices in these two chs do not reflect the individual's voluntary resolve to serve God, but are occasioned by specific violations or wrongdoing. The Rabbis therefore called these sacrifices "hova": debts, penalites incurred. Such sacrificial rituals are said to "atone" (Heb "kiper"), traditionally understood as amends for wrongdoing. Atonement, in this view, is a sort of payment made to propitiate an angry deity and be reconciled with him. However, Heb "kiper," actually means "wipe clean," and

1 Sam. 2.15–16; Deut. 32.38; Isa. 1.11; 34.6; 43.24; Ezek. 44.7, 15). In addition to the suet, two organs— the *kidneys* and *the protuberance on the liver* (the caudate lobe)—are offered to God; these are surrounded by so much fatty tissue that they are considered as suet. **3:** *Entrails,* i.e., intestines. **4:** *Loins* (Heb "kesalim"), better, "sinews." **5:** *With the burnt offering . . . on the fire:* The public burnt offering is

³If it is the anointed priest who has incurred guilt, so that blame falls upon the people, he shall offer for the sin of which he is guilty a bull of the herd without blemish as a sin offeringᵃ to the LORD. ⁴He shall bring the bull to the entrance of the Tent of Meeting, before the LORD, and lay

a So traditionally; more precisely "offering of purgation."

the atoning act consists of the application of the blood of the animal to the sanctuary as a whole and to the objects within it. This is strikingly reminiscent of Mesopotamian ritual texts where the root "k-p-r" is used to refer to the ritual cleansing of temples. It follows that "atonement" in P is actually a type of expiation by which the divine abode is ritually purged of contamination that has accumulated there. According to P, this contamination comes from the Israelites' bodily impurities (see chs 12–15) and from certain acts of wrongdoing that they commit. It defiles the sanctuary and, if allowed to collect there, threatens the community's collective existence. "Atonement," which is really Temple purification, is thus of critical importance (see 15.31 n.). Chs 4–5 provide basic instructions for sacrificial atonement initiated by, and performed on behalf of, individual offending parties as the need arises; these are the basis for regulations regarding public rituals of atonement and atonement for bodily impurities in later chs. The order of chs 1–5 is also significant. In Israel's cultic system, the natural impulse to petition and to worship (chs 1–3) is primary, while the obligation to expiate (chs 4–5), i.e., to purge the sacred of impurities, is the result of circumstance.

4.1–35: The purification offering. If an Israelite has inadvertently transgressed a prohibition (v. 2), a "ḥaṭa't" or purification offering (see below, v. 3) must be made (vv. 3–35). The details differ according to the identity of the guilty party, the main distinction pertaining to the objects to which the blood is applied. Since the more severe the contamination,

the more deeply it penetrates the sacred sphere, the instructions regarding where the blood is to be applied are an exact indication of the severity of the impurity or sin for which atonement is being made. This determines the division of the ch into two main sections. The first section (vv. 3–21) speaks of offenses that have brought guilt upon the community. The transgression may be committed by the high priest (vv. 3–12) or by "the whole community of Israel" (vv. 13–21); in both cases the purgation of the interior of the Tabernacle is required and a bull, the largest sacrificial animal, is slaughtered. The second section (vv. 22–35) pertains to offenses that have not resulted in communal guilt; these require only the purgation of the outer sphere, by applying blood to the altar in the Tabernacle court. The type of animal used varies according to the social status of the individual. Ch 16 completes this picture: Deliberate sins penetrate to the inner sanctum; see 16.11–17. Additional regulations concerning the "ḥaṭa't" are given in 6.17–23; see also 10.16–20. A variant tradition is found in Num. 15.22–31. **2:** A person, Heb "nefesh," "a living being" (see 17.10 n.), male or female. Unwittingly incurs guilt, better, "sins inadvertently." "Sin" (Heb "ḥaṭa'") basically means to err, to miss the mark, and the qualifier "bishgagah," "in error," makes it clear that the offender did not know the act was prohibited. A basic postulate of Israelite thought is that inadvertent acts are just as harmful as deliberate ones, the need to atone for them just as real, and the desire to do so, once they are realized, greater. Any of the LORD's commandments: Since in P

the overwhelming majority of commandments belong to the category of prohibited acts, "commandment" in P is essentially defined as a prohibition, and "sin" is primarily an act of commission, not of omission. **3–12:** The purification offering of the high priest. In P the high priest is not a public official, a teacher or a leader (contrast the role of Joshua in Zech. 3.3–7), but rather a divinely designated, sacred representative of the Israelite people. His entire function is ceremonial. In his person, dressed in the priestly vestments, he represents the body politic (see esp. Exod. 28.9–12), serving within God's earthly abode, paying uninterrupted homage to the enthroned deity on behalf of the Israelite tribes, and calling attention to their needs in the twice-daily regimen of worship. He is also the sole officiant in the annual Day of Atonement ceremonies (ch 16), which means he is the only person ever to enter the inner sanctum. **3:** The anointed priest: He alone has the sacred anointing oil poured on his head at his investiture (Exod. 29.7; Lev. 8.12; 21.10). He is also called "the high priest" (Heb "ha-kohen ha-gadol" [Num. 35.25, 28; Josh. 20.6]), short for "the highest priest among his brothers" (Lev. 21.10), which parallels the Ugaritic "rb khnm," and "[ha-]kohen ha-rosh," "the head priest" (e.g., 2 Kings 25.18). Incurred guilt, better, "sinned"; see above, v. 2. So that blame falls upon the people: Corporate guilt for the crimes of leaders is assumed elsewhere in the Bible. In this case, because the high priest is the representative of the people, his sins of commission are accounted to the people as a whole, and since he serves on their behalf in the innermost sphere of sanctity, his misdeeds contaminate the Tabernacle interior by his very presence there. For the sin of which he is guilty, better, "for the sin which he committed." A sin offering: This is the usual translation of "ḥaṭa't," associating it with "ḥeṭ'," "sin, misdeed" and "ḥaṭa'," "to sin, err" (see above). The noun his hand upon the head of the bull. The bull shall be slaughtered before the LORD, [5] and the anointed priest shall take some of the bull's blood and bring it into the Tent of Meeting. [6] The priest shall dip his finger in the blood, and sprinkle of the blood seven times before the LORD, in front of the curtain of the Shrine. [7] The priest shall put some of the blood on the horns of the altar of aromatic incense, which is in the Tent of Meeting, before the LORD; and all the rest of the bull's blood he shall pour out at the base of the altar of burnt offering, which is at the entrance of the Tent of Meeting. [8] He shall remove all the fat from the bull of sin offering: the fat that covers the entrails and all the fat that is about the entrails; [9] the two kidneys and the fat that is on them, that is at the loins; and the protuberance on the liver, which he shall remove with the kidneys—[10] just as it is removed from the ox of the sacrifice of well-being. The priest shall turn them into smoke on the altar of burnt offering. [11] But the hide of the bull, and all its flesh, as well as its head and legs, its entrails and its dung—[12] all the rest of the bull—he shall carry to a clean place outside the camp, to the ash heap, and burn it up in a wood fire; it shall be burned on the ash heap.

[13] If it is the whole community of Israel that has erred and the matter escapes the notice of the congregation, so that they do any of the things which by the LORD's commandments ought not to be done, and they realize their guilt—[14] when the sin through which they incurred guilt

is actually derived, however, from the verb "ḥite'," "purge, decontaminate" (8.15; 9.15; 14.49, 52; Num. 8.21; 19.12, 13, 20; 31.19–20, 23; Ezek. 43.22–23; 45.18; Ps. 51.9) which is virtually synonymous with "kiper," "atone" (see also Exod. 29.36; Ezek. 43.20), and so the preferred translation is "purification offering"; note also the "ḥaṭa't"-water (Num. 8.7), which means "water of purification." **4–12:** The procedure. The high priest is both the offerer and the officiant. The requirement to *lay his hand upon the head of the bull* here too symbolically transfers ownership of the animal to the deity. Having slaughtered the bull *before the LORD*, i.e., "in the LORD's presence," at *the entrance of the Tent of Meeting*, the priest begins the sprinkling of blood in order to cleanse the areas that have become contaminated. Here and in the

next subsection (see vv. 17–18a), the priest is to bring some of the blood into the Tabernacle's outer sanctum. The sevenfold sprinkling of blood toward the curtain (see Exod. 26.31–33) and the application of blood on the horns (rounded protuberances) of the incense altar (see Exod. 30.1–10) serve to purify the entire outer sanctum. The remaining blood is poured out at the base of the sacrificial altar in the court, that is, drained onto the ground since it is not a sacrifice, but kept within the sacred precincts since it has been consecrated. After this, the fatty portions of the bull are turned into smoke upon the altar just as is done with sacrifices of well-being (see 3.3–4). Significantly, though the LORD's portion of the sacrificial animal is presented to Him in the customary way, it is not called a "gift" nor is it said to be of pleas-

ing odor (but see v. 31). Further, the remaining meat of the animal is not eaten by anyone; it is rather incinerated along with the refuse, outside the camp upon the ash-heap. On this total disposal of the animal's flesh, see 6.23 and 10.16–20. **13–21:** The community's purification offering. The ritual is the same as the one preceding, except for the fact that since the offense has been committed by the community as a whole, the offerer is *the congregation,* represented by *the elders of the community* who perform the hand-laying gesture on behalf of the people. Rabbinic tradition found the notion that the *whole community* might sin spontaneously to be farfetched, and also rejected the idea that if only some, even a majority, of the population sinned the entire community was obligated to atone. They therefore interpreted the case as one in which the High Court errs in instructing the community how to behave and the latter commits the resulting offense. **13:** *The whole community of Israel that has erred and the matter escapes the notice of the congregation:* The entire community has somehow performed an act thought at the time to be innocuous but subsequently determined to have been in violation of a prohibition, for instance, laboring on a day which they were unaware had been proclaimed sacred. *And they realize their guilt:* This may result from the reinvestigation of past actions spurred by pangs of conscience, or even from some form of suffering suspected to be a divine punishment or warning (see also vv. 22 and 27; the phrase is implicit in the previous section). **14:** *When the sin . . . becomes known,* better, "or the sin they committed becomes known"; (similarly the opening clauses of vv. 23 and 28). Alternatively, the offense may come to one's attention as a result of information learned from others. Atonement in P is possible only when the realization of wrongdoing and the feeling of guilt move the offender to remorse and to an active desire to rid the sanctuary of the result-becomes known, the congregation shall offer a bull of the herd as a sin offering, and bring it before the Tent of Meeting. ¹⁵ The elders of the community shall lay their hands upon the head of the bull before the LORD, and the bull shall be slaughtered before the LORD. ¹⁶ The anointed priest shall bring some of the blood of the bull into the Tent of Meeting, ¹⁷ and the priest shall dip his finger in the blood and sprinkle of it seven times before the LORD, in front of the curtain. ¹⁸ Some of the blood he shall put on the horns of the altar which is before the LORD in the Tent of Meeting, and all the rest of the blood he shall pour out at the base of the altar of burnt offering, which is at the entrance of the Tent of Meeting. ¹⁹ He shall remove all its fat from it and turn it into smoke on the altar. ²⁰ He shall do with this bull just as is done with the [priest's] bull of sin offering; he shall do the same with it. Thus the priest shall make expiation for them, and they shall be forgiven. ²¹ He shall carry the bull outside the camp and burn it as he burned the first bull; it is the sin offering of the congregation.

²² In case it is a chieftain who incurs guilt by doing unwittingly any of the things which by the commandment of the LORD his God ought not to be done, and he realizes his guilt—²³ or the sin of which he is guilty is brought to his knowledge—he shall bring as his offering a male goat without blemish. ²⁴ He shall lay his hand upon the goat's head, and it shall be slaughtered at the spot where the burnt offering is slaughtered^a before the LORD; it is a sin offering. ²⁵ The priest shall take with his finger some of the blood of the sin offering and put it on the horns of the altar of burnt offering; and the rest of its blood he shall pour out at the base of the altar of burnt offering. ²⁶ All its fat he shall turn into smoke on the altar, like the fat of the sacrifice of well-being. Thus the priest shall make expiation on his behalf for his sin, and he shall be forgiven.

²⁷ If any person from among the populace^b unwittingly incurs guilt by doing any of the things which by the LORD's commandments ought not to be done, and he realizes his guilt—²⁸ or the sin of which he is guilty is brought to his knowledge—he shall bring a female goat without blemish as his offering for the sin of which he is guilty. ²⁹ He shall lay his hand upon the head of the sin offering, and the sin offering shall be slaughtered at the place of the burnt offering. ³⁰ The priest shall take with his finger some of its blood and put it on the horns of the altar of burnt offering; and all the rest of its blood he shall pour out at the

ing contamination. **20:** *Thus the priest shall make expiation for them, and they shall be forgiven:* Though this summary result clause (cf. vv. 26, 31, 35) is absent from the first section, it must be understood there too. In P, forgiveness is not a grace to be hoped for; it is rather the promised result of the completed atonement process. When, following the realization and remorse, the sacred sphere has been rid of the contamination one's act has caused, one is assured that no further consequences will result. **21:** *As he burned the first bull,* i.e., the bull described in the previous subsection; the two rituals would not necessarily be performed on the same occasion. **22–35:** The remaining purification offerings. The misdeeds of individual commoners and even of tribal chieftains are their own. Their severity is less than that of the sins of the high priest or the community, their contaminating force penetrates less deeply, and so the blood of the animal is applied to the horns of the sacrificial altar that stood in the Tabernacle court. The instructions regarding the disposal of the meat in these three subsections is spelled out in 6.19, 22–23, and its rationale is provided in 10.17. **22–23:** *And he realizes his guilt—or the sin . . . is brought to his knowledge:* The translation here and in vv. 27–28 reflects more accurately the two possible ways in which the offending party is eventually moved to atone; see vv. 13–14. **31:** *For a pleasing odor to the* LORD: This phrase appears nowhere else in reference to the atoning sacrifices and is indeed out of place; many scholars believe it to be a scribal error. **35:** *Over the* LORD's *offering by fire,* better, "on top of (or along with) the LORD's food gifts" (see 1.9); i.e., together with the other offerings smouldering on the altar. This proves that the purification offering itself is not a food gift; see chs 4–5 n.

---

a Cf. 1.11.   b Lit. "people of the country."

base of the altar. ³¹ He shall remove all its fat, just as the fat is removed from the sacrifice of well-being; and the priest shall turn it into smoke on the altar, for a pleasing odor to the LORD. Thus the priest shall make expiation for him, and he shall be forgiven.

³² If the offering he brings as a sin offering is a sheep, he shall bring a female without blemish. ³³ He shall lay his hand upon the head of the sin offering, and it shall be slaughtered as a sin offering at the spot where the burnt offering is slaughtered. ³⁴ The priest shall take with his finger some of the blood of the sin offering and put it on the horns of the altar of burnt offering, and all the rest of its blood he shall pour out at the base of the altar. ³⁵ And all its fat he shall remove just as the fat of the sheep of the sacrifice of well-being is removed; and this the priest shall turn into smoke on the altar, over the LORD's offering by fire. Thus the priest shall make expiation on his behalf for the sin of which he is guilty, and he shall be forgiven.

5 If a person incurs guilt—
When he has heard a public imprecation^a and—although able to testify as one who has either seen or learned of the matter—he does not give information, so that he is subject to punishment;

² Or when a person touches any unclean thing—be it the carcass of an unclean beast or the carcass of unclean cattle or the carcass of an unclean creeping thing—and the fact has escaped him, and then, being unclean, he realizes his guilt;

³ Or when he touches human uncleanness—any such uncleanness whereby one becomes unclean—and, though he has known it, the fact has escaped him, but later he realizes his guilt;

⁴ Or when a person utters^b an oath to bad or good purpose—whatever a man may utter in an oath—and, though he has known it, the fact has escaped him, but later he realizes his guilt in any of these matters—

⁵ when he realizes his guilt in any of these matters, he shall confess that wherein he has sinned. ⁶ And he shall bring as his penalty to the LORD, for the sin of which he is

a *Namely, against one who withholds testimony.*   b *Lit. "utters with his lips."*

5.1–13: Further instructions on the purification offering. Next comes a specific list of wrongs that require atonement by means of the "ḥaṭaʾt" sacrifice. No instructions for performing the sacrifice are given; the listener is to rely on the

previous ch. The rest of the section provides for the sacrifice of two fowl by a person who cannot afford an animal from the flock (vv. 7–10) and for a "ḥaṭaʾt" of a grain offering by the person of even more limited means. These

adjustments gave the sacrifice its rabbinic name of "korban ʿole ve-yored," "graduated offering"—but see below (vv. 7–13 n.). **1–4:** The cases. The situations requiring sacrifice are: (a) A person has refrained from coming forward with testimony about some matter to which he was an eyewitness or about which he has indirect knowledge, even though a public imprecation, solemnly adjuring all that have knowledge about the matter to speak up, has been heard (v. 1); (b) a person has neglected to cleanse himself of a secondary impurity within the prescribed time period (see 11.4–8, 24–40), or (c) of corpse-contamination (see Num. 19.10a–22) of which he was originally aware but subsequently forgot, only later realizing his negligence (vv. 2–3); (d) a person has sworn verbally to perform some action but subsequently forgot to do so, only to realize his negligence at some later date. This list differs greatly from the general stipulation in ch 4. The cases aim to counter the notion that duties weaken with time and eventually cease to exist ("forget it and it will simply go away"). In P's view, the opposite is the case: Severity of negligence, whether of physical impurity or of moral or legal obligation, intensifies the longer it lasts. **1:** *Incurs guilt,* rather, "sins"; see 4.2. *So that he is subject to punishment,* actually, "and he bears his sin." Protracted negligence is an objective guilt that continues to weigh upon the sinner until the appropriate measures are taken to be rid of it; see 7.18. **2:** *The carcass of an unclean beast or . . . cattle,* correctly "of an unclean animal"; see 7.21; 11.40. *And then, being unclean, he realizes his guilt,* correctly: "though he had been unclean, and then he realizes his guilt." An emendation yields the more logical: "the fact escaped him, though he had known it, and then he realizes his guilt." **5–6:** The procedure. Unique to these four cases is the requirement that the guilty party supplement his realization and remorse with verbal confession. P's idea is thus that verbalizing what guilty, a female from the flock, sheep or goat, as a sin of-fering; and the priest shall make expiation on his behalf for his sin.

7 But if his means do not suffice for a sheep, he shall bring to the LORD, as his penalty for that of which he is guilty, two turtledoves or two pigeons, one for a sin offer-ing and the other for a burnt offering. 8 He shall bring them to the priest, who shall offer first the one for the sin offering, pinching its head at the nape without severing it. 9 He shall sprinkle some of the blood of the sin offering on the side of the altar, and what remains of the blood shall be drained out at the base of the altar; it is a sin offering. 10 And the second he shall prepare as a burnt offering, ac-cording to regulation. Thus the priest shall make expia-tion on his behalf for the sin of which he is guilty, and he shall be forgiven.

11 And if his means do not suffice for two turtledoves or two pigeons, he shall bring as his offering for that of which he is guilty a tenth of an *ephah* of choice flour for a sin offering; he shall not add oil to it or lay frankincense on it, for it is a sin offering. 12 He shall bring it to the priest, and the priest shall scoop out of it a handful as a token portion of it and turn it into smoke on the altar, with the LORD's offerings by fire; it is a sin offering. 13 Thus the priest shall make expiation on his behalf for whichever of these sins he is guilty, and he shall be forgiven. It shall be-long to the priest, like the meal offering.

14 And the LORD spoke to Moses, saying:
15 When a person commits a trespass, being unwittingly remiss about any of the LORD's sacred things, he shall

Perhaps the use of flour in some Mesopotamian purification cere-monies has cleared the way for its admission to Israel's cult, at least in this one case.

5.14–26: The reparation offering. Two concluding sections (vv. 14–19 and 20–26) convey the regulations concerning the other atonement offering, the *"'asham,"* required when trespass against the sacred sphere, deliberate or uninten-tional, has taken place. The first section prescribes the sacrifice in cases of trespass against sacred objects and the sacred domain (vv. 14–16) and in cases of undis-covered violations (vv. 17–19). In the second section the obligation is extended to instances of false oath in property offenses. Since the verb *"'-sh-m"* often means "to be guilty" or "realize one's guilt" (see 4.13 n.; 5.17, 23, 24 n.), the *"'asham"* sacrifice is generally translated "guilt offering." Its lit-eral meaning, however, is "to incur liability," and *"'asham"* as a noun denotes the payment of damages (Num. 5.7–8; 1 Sam. 6.3–4, 8; see also Lev. 5.6). This fact, along with the importance attached by P, as well as in the Mesopotamian cultic texts, to the need to guard against misuse of the sacred and to make reparations when this has oc-curred, make it preferable to trans-late "reparation offering." Further cases requiring the reparation of-fering are found in 14.10–14; 19.21–22; Num. 6.12. Additional regulations appear in 7.1–7. **15:** *Trespass,* or "sacrilege"; Heb "ma'al." The Tabernacle and its furnishings and appurtenances, as well as offerings and gifts that have been presented to it, are sacrosanct; their misuse or misap-propriation is a crime against the deity Himself. See also 22.14. *Con-vertible . . . by the sanctuary weight:* According to this translation, the animal need not be sacrificed; it may be converted into its mone-tary equivalent. Another possibil-ity is that the ram, which is to be offered in every case, must be one whose value is symbolically com-mensurate with that of the misap-

one ought to have done but failed to do is part of expiation. In later Jewish tradition, verbal confession of all sin, whether communal or individual, became an essential requirement for atonement.
7–13: Unlike the allowances made in 1.14–17 and 2.1–16, which serve to alleviate the poor person's sense of being excluded, the reason for the concessions here is that the sa-cred precincts must be decontami-nated and sin must be eradicated from Israel's midst. It is not clear why the necessity to provide a means for the poor Israelite to atone for sin should be restricted to the four cases enumerated here. Perhaps these vv. are a subscript to the entire "hata't" section, apply-

ing equally to 4.27–35. **7–10:** If the offender cannot afford a sheep or goat, he is to bring two birds. One serves as the "hata't" itself, sup-plying the blood to cleanse the altar; the other is presented as a burnt offering. The burnt offering does not atone; rather it provides for the altar a respectable amount of flesh (in place of the fatty por-tions of the "hata't") which would otherwise be negligible. See also 12.8; 14.22–31. **10:** *According to reg-ulation,* according to the procedure outlined in 1.14–17. **11–13:** The possibility of substituting a cereal offering for an animal is remark-able here, since the essential step in the "hata't" procedure is the application of blood to the altar.

bring as his penalty to the Lord a ram without blemish from the flock, convertible into payment in silver by the sanctuary weight, as a guilt offering. ¹⁶He shall make restitution for that wherein he was remiss about the sacred things, and he shall add a fifth part to it and give it to the priest. The priest shall make expiation on his behalf with the ram of the guilt offering, and he shall be forgiven.

¹⁷And when a person, without knowing it, sins in regard to any of the Lord's commandments about things not to be done, and then realizes his guilt, he shall be subject to punishment. ¹⁸He shall bring to the priest a ram without blemish from the flock, or the equivalent,ᵃ as a guilt offering. The priest shall make expiation on his behalf for the error that he committed unwittingly, and he shall be forgiven. ¹⁹It is a guilt offering; he has incurred guilt before the Lord.

²⁰The Lord spoke to Moses, saying: ²¹When a person sins and commits a trespass against the Lord by dealing deceitfully with his fellow in the matter of a deposit or a pledge,ᵇ or through robbery, or by defrauding his fellow, ²²or by finding something lost and lying about it; if he swears falsely regarding any one of the various things that one may do and sin thereby—²³when one has thus sinned and, realizing his guilt, would restore that which he got through robbery or fraud, or the deposit that was entrusted to him, or the lost thing that he found, ²⁴or anything else about which he swore falsely, he shall repay the principal amount and add a fifth part to it. He shall pay it to its owner when he realizes his guilt. ²⁵Then he shall bring to the priest, as his penalty to the Lord, a ram without blemish from the flock, or the equivalent,ᶜ as a guilt offering. ²⁶The priest shall make expiation on his behalf before the Lord, and he shall be forgiven for whatever he may have done to draw blame thereby.

TSAV   צו

6 The Lord spoke to Moses, saying: ²Command Aaron and his sons thus:

This is the ritual of the burnt offering: The burnt offer-

---

a I.e., in currency; cf. v. 15.
b Meaning of Heb. uncertain.
c I.e., in currency; cf. v. 15.

17–19: The case is unclear. The circumstances are almost identical to those requiring the "ḥaṭaʾt" in ch 4, the only difference being the words "without knowing it" in v. 17, repeated in v. 18. Perhaps the offender, though he feels guilty of something, never becomes fully aware of what he has done; the "unknown sin" is a common motif in ancient religion. The Rabbis suggest that if the offender eventually becomes aware of his offense, he will be obligated to bring a ḥaṭaʾt as well. But why make a reparation offering if no sacrilege has taken place? There is no persuasive solution to the text in its given form. **17:** *He shall be subject to punishment,* correct to "and bears his sin"; see 5.1; 7.18. **18:** *Or the equivalent,* see v. 15. **20–26:** The "ʾasham" for fraud. Defrauding one's fellow over property disputes is an act of sacrilege when a false oath using God's name has been sworn. The misuse of the divine name is probably the most common form of desecration of the sacred, since every Israelite has immediate access to it at all times (see 24.10–13). The restitution and fine are paid to the injured party, while the sacrificial expiation is made as above. This law is supplemented by Num. 5.5–8. **25:** *Or the equivalent,* see v. 15.

Chs 6–7. These chs complete the sacrificial instructions conveyed to Moses on the first of Nisan. They are transmitted in five speeches (6.1–11; 6.12–16; 6.17–7.21; 7.22–27; 7.28–36) and followed by a typical P caption summing up the whole of chs 1–7 (7.37–38). Each of the five types of sacrifice prescribed in chs 1–5 is taken up again, with added regulations. Each new topic is introduced by the phrase "this is the 'torah' of . . . ," i.e., "these are the instructions regarding . . ." (6.2; 6.7; 6.18; 7.1; 7.11). Some suggest that while chs 1–5 are addressed to the lay Israelite, chs 6–7 are addressed to the priests. More accurately, in contrast to chs 1–5, which outline who offers what sort of sacrifice and how this is done, the primary purpose of chs 6–7 is

---

propriated sacred property. This would also account for the name of the offering. **16:** *Restitution . . . add a fifth part:* The payment of damages in addition to restitution is common to biblical and Near

Eastern law. *The priest shall make expiation on his behalf:* It may be presumed that this is accomplished through the blood application as performed with the "ḥaṭaʾt," but this is not certain.

ing itself shall remain where it is burned upon the altar all night until morning, while the fire on the altar is kept going on it. [3] The priest shall dress in linen raiment, with linen breeches next to his body; and he shall take up the ashes to which the fire has reduced the burnt offering on the altar and place them beside the altar. [4] He shall then take off his vestments and put on other vestments, and carry the ashes outside the camp to a clean place. [5] The fire on the altar shall be kept burning, not to go out: every morning the priest shall feed wood to it, lay out the burnt offering on it, and turn into smoke the fat parts of the offerings of well-being. [6] A perpetual fire shall be kept burning on the altar, not to go out.

[7] And this is the ritual of the meal offering: Aaron's sons shall present it before the LORD, in front of the altar. [8] A handful of the choice flour and oil of the meal offering shall be taken from it, with all the frankincense that is on the meal offering, and this token portion shall be turned into smoke on the altar as a pleasing odor to the LORD. [9] What is left of it shall be eaten by Aaron and his sons; it shall be eaten as unleavened cakes, in the sacred precinct; they shall eat it in the enclosure of the Tent of Meeting. [10] It shall not be baked with leaven; I have given it as their portion from My offerings by fire; it is most holy, like the sin offering and the guilt offering. [11] Only the males among Aaron's descendants may eat of it, as their due for all time throughout the ages from the LORD's offerings by fire. Anything that touches these shall become holy.

[12] The LORD spoke to Moses, saying: [13] This is the offer-

---

to spell out precisely how the sacrifice is to be apportioned and disposed of following the altar ritual (see 7.35–36 n.). The three passages addressed specifically to the priesthood (6.1, 12, 17) are a logical subcategory.

6.1–6: The burnt offering. This refers to the burnt offering of the individual, discussed in 1.3–13, and not the "tamid" or daily burnt offering (Exod. 29.38 and elsewhere). Two regulations are added here: the stipulation that the flesh may burn throughout the night but by morning the ash should be removed (v. 2) and the instructions for the ash removal by the priest (vv. 3–4). A corollary follows: The fire on the altar must be kept burning at all times (vv. 5–6). Since

none of the flesh is eaten, these two regulations are the counterpart of the corresponding instructions for distribution and consumption given below for the remaining types of sacrifice. **2:** *Command Aaron and his sons* because handling the flesh of the burnt offering is their task. *This is the ritual of,* better, "these are the instructions concerning"; Heb "torah" means "body of instruction pertaining to." **3:** *The priest,* not necessarily the high priest. *In linen raiment, with linen breeches next to his body,* see Exod. 28.39–43. Since collecting the ashes involves contact with the high degree of sanctity attached to the altar, linen vestments are required. In order to exit the sphere of the sacred, however, nonsacred vestments must be

worn. **4:** *A clean place:* Since the ashes derive from a sacred offering, they must be disposed of in a ritually pure spot. **5–6:** The altar fire, once ignited (see 9.24), must never be allowed to die out; it serves as a perpetual sign that the enshrined deity is being worshipped constantly. Later tradition derived from this v. the obligation to supply a regular "wood offering" to keep the altar aflame; see Neh. 10.35; 13.31.

6.7–11: The grain offering. Further instructions concerning the "minḥah" of the individual, prescribed in 2.1–13. They include (vv. 7–9a) a restatement of 2.2–3 and 2.9–10, along with the precise regulations regarding the priests' preparation and consumption of the "minḥah" and the consequences of the sacred portions of the offering coming into contact with the laity. **7:** *Ritual,* see v. 2, above. **9b–10a:** The prohibition of leaven (see 2.11) is here extended specifically to the priests' portion of the "minḥah." *In the sacred precinct . . . of the Tent of Meeting,* within the Tabernacle courtyard. Offerings of the highest degree of sanctity could not leave the sacred precincts. **10–11:** The priests' portion of the sacrifice is not a gift from the person who presents the offering. Rather, the entire sacrifice is a gift to the LORD, who graciously "shares" it with the priests for their service (see 2.1–10; 7.34). **10, 11:** *Offerings by fire,* see 1.9. *It is most holy,* see 2.3. **11:** *Only the males,* more precisely, "any male." The priests' portions of most holy offerings may be eaten only by priests qualified to offer them; namely, males. Female members of the priestly families are permitted to eat the meat of the well-being sacrifices. *Anything that touches these shall become holy:* Direct contact with any of the most holy food-gifts of the LORD communicates holiness, conceived of as a contagious, dynamic effervescence of the deity's Presence which renders whatever comes into contact with it holy. See also v. 20; Exod. 29.37; 30.29; Num. 17.1–4.

ing that Aaron and his sons shall offer to the LORD on the occasion of his[a] anointment: a tenth of an *ephah* of choice flour as a regular meal offering, half of it in the morning and half of it in the evening, [14] shall be prepared with oil on a griddle. You shall bring it well soaked, and offer it as a meal offering of baked slices,[b] of pleasing odor to the LORD. [15] And so shall the priest, anointed from among his sons to succeed him, prepare it; it is the LORD's—a law for all time—to be turned entirely into smoke. [16] So, too, every meal offering of a priest shall be a whole offering: it shall not be eaten.

[17] The LORD spoke to Moses, saying: [18] Speak to Aaron and his sons thus: This is the ritual of the sin offering: the sin offering shall be slaughtered before the LORD, at the spot[c] where the burnt offering is slaughtered: it is most holy. [19] The priest who offers it as a sin offering shall eat of it; it shall be eaten in the sacred precinct, in the enclosure of the Tent of Meeting. [20] Anything that touches its flesh shall become holy; and if any of its blood is spattered upon a garment, you shall wash the bespattered part in the sacred precinct. [21] An earthen vessel in which it was boiled shall be broken; if it was boiled in a copper vessel, [the vessel] shall be scoured and rinsed with water. [22] Only the males in the priestly line may eat of it: it is most holy. [23] But no sin offering may be eaten from which any blood is brought into the Tent of Meeting for expiation in the sanctuary; any such shall be consumed in fire.

7 This is the ritual of the guilt offering: it is most holy. [2] The guilt offering shall be slaughtered at the spot where the burnt offering is slaughtered, and the blood

a *Or "their."*
b *Meaning of Heb.* tuphine *uncertain.*
c *Cf. 1.11.*

6.12–16: The grain offering of the priest. The "minḥah" of the high priest, half to be offered each morning and the other half each evening (v. 13), is incumbent upon the high priest's successors for all time (v. 15). These regulations are appended here as an exception to the preceding lay grain offering, since the priestly offering is turned into smoke in its entirety. The priest does not receive a share of his own gift. **13:** *Aaron and his sons,* i.e., the first high priest and his successors; see v. 15. *On the occa-*

sion of his anointment, most likely "from the time of his anointment [onward]." *A regular meal offering,* better: "as a grain offering, perpetually." **16:** Like the high priest, lesser priests too receive no share of a "minḥah" they offer on their own behalf. *Shall be a whole offering,* more precisely: "shall be turned completely into smoke."

6.17–23: Further instructions concerning the purification offering ("ḥaṭaʾt"). For the types and procedure see 4.1–5.13. The paragraph

stipulates where the "ḥaṭaʾt" is to be slaughtered, defines its degree of sanctity, prescribes who may eat of its flesh and where (vv. 18–19, 22), and sets forth the ramifications of contact with the sacrificial flesh (vv. 20–21). It concludes by spelling out the crucial distinction between the eaten "ḥaṭaʾt" and the burned one (v. 23); see 10.16–20 n. **18:** *Ritual,* see v. 2 n. *At the spot,* see 1.11. *Sin offering,* see 4.3 n. **19, 22:** These vv. refer to the eaten "ḥaṭaʾt" (see v. 23 n.), and seem to contradict each other. The simplest resolution is that the flesh must be eaten and the officiating priest is entitled to it (see also 7.7, 14); he may, however, share it with other male members of the priesthood (see v. 11 n.). A single priest could hardly eat all of it, likely consumed within the space of a single day (see 10.19; cf. 7.15). **20:** *Shall become holy,* see v. 11 n. **20b–21:** These vv. confirm that the purification offering removes impurity by absorbing it. As a result, whatever flesh and blood have not been disposed of by consumption or burning communicate impurity to objects with which they come in contact, requiring them to be cleansed. **23:** As explained in ch 4 n., there are two types of purification offering: those whose blood purges the interior of the Tabernacle and those whose blood decontaminates the courtyard. Here the implications are spelled out. The flesh of the "ḥaṭaʾt" for severe offenses may not be eaten; it must be burned. That of the "ḥaṭaʾt" for less severe offenses and impurities must be eaten; thus the impurity is disposed of and the purification process made complete (see 10.16–20).

7.1–10: Further instructions concerning the reparation offering ("ʾasham") **and priestly share.** See 5.14–26. **1:** *Ritual,* see 6.2. *Guilt offering,* see 5.14–26 n. *It is most holy,* see 2.3. **2:** See 1.11. **2b–5a:** These details are not mentioned in connection with the "ʾasham" in 5.14–26, though they are included in the ritual prescribed for other sacrifices in chs 1–5 (e.g., 3.2b–5;

shall be dashed on all sides of the altar. ³ All its fat shall be offered: the broad tail; the fat that covers the entrails; ⁴ the two kidneys and the fat that is on them at the loins; and the protuberance on the liver, which shall be removed with the kidneys. ⁵ The priest shall turn them into smoke on the altar as an offering by fire to the LORD; it is a guilt offering. ⁶ Only the males in the priestly line may eat of it; it shall be eaten in the sacred precinct: it is most holy.

⁷ The guilt offering is like the sin offering. The same rule applies to both: it shall belong to the priest who makes expiation thereby. ⁸ So, too, the priest who offers a man's burnt offering shall keep the skin of the burnt offering that he offered. ⁹ Further, any meal offering that is baked in an oven, and any that is prepared in a pan or on a griddle, shall belong to the priest who offers it. ¹⁰ But every other meal offering, with oil mixed in or dry, shall go to the sons of Aaron all alike.

¹¹ This is the ritual of the sacrifice of well-being that one may offer to the LORD:

¹² If he offers it for thanksgiving, he shall offer together with the sacrifice of thanksgiving unleavened cakes with oil mixed in, unleavened wafers spread with oil, and cakes of choice flour with oil mixed in, well soaked. ¹³ This offering, with cakes of leavened bread added, he shall offer along with his thanksgiving sacrifice of well-being. ¹⁴ Out of this he shall offer one of each kindᵃ as a gift to the LORD; it shall go to the priest who dashes the blood of the offering of well-being. ¹⁵ And the flesh of his thanksgiving sacrifice of well-being shall be eaten on the day that it is offered; none of it shall be set aside until morning.

¹⁶ If, however, the sacrifice he offers is a votive or a freewill offering, it shall be eaten on the day that he offers his sacrifice, and what is left of it shall be eaten on the morrow. ¹⁷ What is then left of the flesh of the sacrifice shall be consumed in fire on the third day. ¹⁸ If any of the flesh of his sacrifice of well-being is eaten on the third day,

a Lit. "offering."

---

of 5.11 and the "minḥah" of the suspected adulteress (Num. 5.15).

7.11–34: Instructions for the sacrifice of well-being. See ch 3. **11–21:** As explained in 3.1 n., the meat of the well-being offering is eaten primarily by the offerer and his guests in a sacred meal. There are three types of well-being offerings; the distinctions are reflected also in 19.5–8 and 22.29–30. **11:** *Ritual,* see 6.2. **12–15:** The first type, the "todah" or sacrifice of thanksgiving, is offered according to Ps. 107 (and rabbinic law) by one who has recovered from illness, been rescued from danger, or returned safely from a journey. It is accompanied by prayers of thanksgiving, proclaiming to all present the beneficence of God enjoyed by the offerer. Mandated by happy circumstance, it is more of an obligation than a voluntary offering. It is accompanied by leavened cakes and wafers; one of each type is presented to the officiating priest. The meat is to be consumed by the following morning. **16–18:** The second and third types, here lumped together but distinguished in 22.21–23, are the "neder" or votive offering, obligatory in that it is made in fulfillment of a vow, though the vow itself was undertaken freely, and the "nedavah" or freewill offering, entirely an act of spontaneous devotion. No loaves are required and two days are allowed for the consumption of the meat. The burning of uneaten meat prescribed in v. 17 applies to the thanksgiving offering as well but would take place on the second day. **18:** Violating the time restriction invalidates the sacrifice retroactively. *It shall not be acceptable,* more precisely: "it shall not be accepted." See 1.3, 4; 19.5–8; 22.17–30. An *offensive thing,* Heb "pigul," meaning uncertain; perhaps "foul" or "desecrated." *Shall bear his guilt,* lit. "shall bear his sin"; see 5.1. P uses this phrase to mean that the act of wrongdoing remains with the individual until he has cleansed himself of it or, if this is impossible (as with particularly heinous misdeeds) or he fails

---

4.7–10; etc.). **3:** *The broad tail,* included since the animal prescribed for the "'asham" offering is a ram (5.15, 18, 25); see 3.6–16 n. **5:** *Offering by fire,* see 1.9 n. This is the only time this term is used of expiatory sacrifices; probably it refers to the portions given to the LORD and not to the sacrifice as a whole. **6–7:** As is the case with the "ḥaṭa't" (6.19ff.), only male priests

are eligible to eat the meat of the "'asham." The officiating priest receives the meat and may share it with other male priests. **8–10:** The discussion of most holy sacrifices is concluded, with remaining details regarding the distribution of the priestly portions; v. 8 supplements 1.3–13 and 6.1–6, and vv. 9–10 supplement 2.1–13 and 6.7–11. **10:** *Dry,* the cereal "ḥaṭa't"

it shall not be acceptable; it shall not count for him who offered it. It is an offensive thing, and the person who eats of
it shall bear his guilt.

¹⁹ Flesh that touches anything unclean shall not be
eaten; it shall be consumed in fire. As for other flesh, only
he who is clean may eat such flesh. ²⁰ But the person who,
in a state of uncleanness, eats flesh from the Lord's sacrifices of well-being, that person shall be cut off from his
kin. ²¹ When a person touches anything unclean, be it
human uncleanness or an unclean animal or any unclean
creature,ᵃ and eats flesh from the Lord's sacrifices of well-
being, that person shall be cut off from his kin.

²² And the Lord spoke to Moses, saying: ²³ Speak to the
Israelite people thus: You shall eat no fatᵇ of ox or sheep or
goat. ²⁴ Fat from animals that died or were torn by beasts
may be put to any use, but you must not eat it. ²⁵ If anyone
eats the fat of animals from which offerings by fire may be
made to the Lord, the person who eats it shall be cut off
from his kin. ²⁶ And you must not consume any blood, either of bird or of animal, in any of your settlements.
²⁷ Anyone who eats blood shall be cut off from his kin.

²⁸ And the Lord spoke to Moses, saying: ²⁹ Speak to the
Israelite people thus: The offering to the Lord from a sacrifice of well-being must be presented by him who offers
his sacrifice of well-being to the Lord: ³⁰ his own hands
shall present the Lord's offerings by fire. He shall present
the fat with the breast, the breast to be elevated as an elevation offering before the Lord; ³¹ the priest shall turn the
fat into smoke on the altar, and the breast shall go to
Aaron and his sons. ³² And the right thigh from your sacrifices of well-being you shall present to the priest as a
gift; ³³ he from among Aaron's sons who offers the blood
and the fat of the offering of well-being shall get the right
thigh as his portion. ³⁴ For I have taken the breast of eleva-

a Heb. sheqeṣ, lit. "abomination"; several mss. and ancient versions read shereṣ "swarming things."

b I.e., hard, coarse fat (suet); cf. 3.3–5.

world, but it is more probable that
"cutting off" is extirpation, i.e., the
eventual total extinction of one's
line, by whatever means God sees
fit. **21:** *Any unclean creature,* referring only to the carcasses of impure animals; for the question this
poses, see 5.2; 11.40. **22–27:** Elaborating on the brief stipulation of
3.17; the *fat* mentioned here is suet
(see 3.3–4 and translators' note *b*).
Eating the suet of permitted animals, whether sacrificed or not,
just as ingesting their blood (v. 26;
see also 17.10–16), is prohibited.
The Israelite is commanded to abstain from the "food" of the Lord
even when no sacrifice is made.
24: *Animals,* i.e., domestic animals,
named in the previous v., that
have not been slaughtered as sacrifice but rather have been killed by
beasts or died of themselves. Their
meat, according to P, may be eaten
(see 11.40 n.; 17.15–16 n.; 22.8 n.),
but since no sacrificial ritual has
taken place, no sanctity attaches to
the meat, so household use of the
suet is permissible. *Torn by beasts,*
Heb "terefah," which in postbiblical phraseology became a term for
all prohibited foods. **25:** *Offerings
by fire,* see 1.9 n. **26–27:** The blood
prohibition of 3.17 is also repeated
in this context; see 17.10–16.
28–34: The distribution of the
well-being sacrifice. The altar portions are presented by the worshipper to be turned by the priest
into smoke (see 3.3–5a). The
priests' share of the well-being sacrifice is treated last. As elsewhere,
the priests' portion is perceived as
a gift from God (see v. 34), not
from the offerer, as remuneration
for their service and in compensation for their having been given
no land (see also Num. 18.8–24).
30: *Elevation offering,* Heb "tenu-
fah." The ritualized transfer of
ownership from the offerer to the
deity. The Rabbis understood the
presentation ritual as waving
the offering back and forth, but
the translation "elevation," also
known from ancient times as well
as from the depiction of the rite in
an ancient Egyptian relief, is more
accurate. *Offerings by fire,* see 1.9 n.
34: *Breast of elevation offering and*

to do so, until he has suffered its
consequences. **19–21:** Sacred meat
that comes into contact with a
source of impurity may not be
eaten. Further, if an impure individual, or one who has contracted
impurity by means of direct contact, eats of the sacrificial meat, he
is subject to the penalty of extirpation. **20, 21:** *Shall be cut off from his*

kin: This threat recurs throughout
the Priestly writings and is applied
to many crimes committed against
the sacred. Traditional commentators correctly understood that it
implies a penalty inflicted by God
and not a form of ostracism or excommunication. They often saw it
as death by divine agency or the
denial of eternal bliss in the next

tion offering and the thigh of gift offering from the Israelites, from their sacrifices of well-being, and given them to Aaron the priest and to his sons as their due from the Israelites for all time.

35 Those shall be the perquisites[a] of Aaron and the perquisites of his sons from the LORD's offerings by fire, once they have been inducted[b] to serve the LORD as priests; 36 these the LORD commanded to be given them, once they had been anointed, as a due from the Israelites for all time throughout the ages.

37 Such are the rituals of the burnt offering, the meal offering, the sin offering, the guilt offering, the offering of ordination, and the sacrifice of well-being, 38 with which the LORD charged Moses on Mount Sinai, when He commanded that the Israelites present their offerings to the LORD, in the wilderness of Sinai.

8 The LORD spoke to Moses, saying: 2 Take Aaron along with his sons, and the vestments, the anointing oil, the bull of sin offering, the two rams, and the basket of unleavened bread; 3 and assemble the whole community at the entrance of the Tent of Meeting. 4 Moses did as the LORD commanded him. And when the community was assembled at the entrance of the Tent of Meeting, 5 Moses said to the community, "This is what the LORD has commanded to be done."

6 Then Moses brought Aaron and his sons forward and washed them with water. 7 He put the tunic on him,

---

a Lit. "anointment," i.e., accruing from anointment.   b Lit. "brought forward."

---

the thigh of gift offering: Deut. 18.3, which assigns to the priests "the shoulder, cheeks and the stomach," has a different view of the priests' portions. Rabbinic law reconciled the two passages by interpreting Deut. ch 18 as referring to nonsacrificial meat slaughtered for food.

7.35–36: Summary. A summary of chs 6–7 in their entirety: The two chs refer primarily to the apportionment of the sacrificial offerings in general, and in particular to the priests' share. **35:** Perquisites, Heb "mishhah," a rare word (see also Num. 18.8, there vocalized as "moshhah"), meaning the priests' due, their assigned portion. **35:** Offerings by fire, see 1.9 n.;

here alone it refers to all the sacrifices.

7.37–38: Overall summary. A summary of chs 1–7, closing the account of what was communicated to Moses on the first day of Nisan. **37:** Offering of ordination: These rituals were included in the instructions given to Moses before the building of the Tabernacle (Exod. ch 29) and will be introduced in ch 8 (see 8.22–29). Their inclusion in the caption is puzzling. **38:** When, on 1 Nisan. On Mount Sinai: As is clear from in the wilderness of Sinai at the end of the v., this phrase means "[in the Tabernacle which stood] at [the foot of] Mount Sinai"; see also 25.1; 26.46; 27.34.

8.1–36: The consecration of Aaron and his sons. Aaron and his sons are consecrated to the priesthood. According to P, God, many months earlier, had informed Moses that Aaron and his sons were to become His priests (Exod. ch 28), and outlined the details of this ceremony (Exod. ch 29). Now the consecration is to take place. Most of the ch (vv. 6–30) thus consists of a past-tense repetition of Exod. ch 29 with minor differences and the added refrain "as the LORD had commanded Moses." The ceremony of induction into the priesthood consists of five elements. (1) Investiture: The priests are clothed for the first time in the garments required to perform their service (vv. 7–9, 13). (2) Invocation: The priests present a burnt offering (vv. 18–21). (3) Consecration: The blood of a ram of offering is smeared on the priests' bodies (vv. 22–24a). (4) "Filling the hands": The priests receive for the first time their allotted share of the sacrifices; they offer a portion to the LORD (vv. 26–29) and eat the remaining meat and loaves (v. 31). (5) Anointment: The priests are anointed with the sacred oil, infusing them with holiness (vv. 12, 30). Afterwards the priests remain within the Tabernacle for seven full days, completing their consecration (vv. 31–36). Three preparatory rituals are also performed, each at the appropriate moment. Before their investiture the priests must be bathed (v. 6); before the first sacrifices to be offered in the divine abode are made, the Tabernacle and its furnishings must be anointed (vv. 10–11); before being used, the altar must be purified (vv. 15–17). The latter two rituals sanctify the Tabernacle itself; its consecration thus takes place simultaneously with that of the priests. **2:** The vestments, see Exod. chs 28, 39. The anointing oil, see Exod. 30.22–33; 37.29. The bull of sin offering (see 4.3), the two rams, and the basket of unleavened bread, as already prescribed in Exod. 29.1–2. **7–9:** The outer "garments" of the high priest are marks of "dignity and adornment" (Exod. 28.2) and girded him with the sash, clothed him with the robe, and put the ephod on him, girding him with the decorated band with which he tied it to him. [8] He put the breastpiece on him, and put into the breastpiece the Urim and Thummim.[a] [9] And he set the headdress on his head; and on the headdress, in front, he put the gold frontlet, the holy diadem—as the LORD had commanded Moses.

[10] Moses took the anointing oil and anointed the Tabernacle and all that was in it, thus consecrating them. [11] He sprinkled some of it on the altar seven times, anointing the altar, all its utensils, and the laver with its stand, to consecrate them. [12] He poured some of the anointing oil upon Aaron's head and anointed him, to consecrate him. [13] Moses then brought Aaron's sons forward, clothed them in tunics, girded them with sashes, and wound turbans upon them, as the LORD had commanded Moses.

[14] He led forward the bull of sin offering. Aaron and his sons laid their hands upon the head of the bull of sin offering, [15] and it was slaughtered. Moses took the blood and with his finger put some on each of the horns of the altar, cleansing the altar; then he poured out the blood at the base of the altar. Thus he consecrated it in order to make expiation upon it.

[16] Moses then took all the fat that was about the entrails, and the protuberance of the liver, and the two kidneys and their fat, and turned them into smoke on the altar. [17] The rest of the bull, its hide, its flesh, and its dung, he put to the fire outside the camp—as the LORD had commanded Moses.

[18] Then he brought forward the ram of burnt offering. Aaron and his sons laid their hands upon the ram's head, [19] and it was slaughtered. Moses dashed the blood against all sides of the altar. [20] The ram was cut up into sections and Moses turned the head, the sections, and the suet into smoke on the altar; [21] Moses washed the entrails and the legs with water and turned all of the ram into smoke. That was a burnt offering for a pleasing odor, an offering by fire to the LORD—as the LORD had commanded Moses.

[22] He brought forward the second ram, the ram of ordination. Aaron and his sons laid their hands upon the ram's head, [23] and it was slaughtered. Moses took some of its blood and put it on the ridge[b] of Aaron's right ear, and on the thumb of his right hand, and on the big toe of his right foot. [24] Moses then brought forward the sons of Aaron, and put some of the blood on the ridges of their right ears, and on the thumbs of their right hands, and on

appurtenances of the daily regimen of perpetual worship, each one having a specific ritual function as enumerated in Exod. 28.12, 30, 35, 38. **8:** *Urim and Thummim,* see Exod. 28.30. **10–13:** In P, the anointing of persons and objects infuses them with holiness (see 6.11). Anointing Aaron and his sons (v. 30) transforms them into God's personal servants; they belong permanently to the sphere of the divine. All contact with the nonsacred is restricted and any contact with the impure is potentially fatal and must be avoided (see 21.1–15). **12:** *Upon Aaron's head,* see 4.3. **13:** The *tunics, sashes,* and *turbans* of Aaron's sons are for "dignity and adornment" (Exod. 28.40); they (and probably Aaron as well) also wore breeches for modesty (Exod. 28.42). **14–17:** The purification offering of the high priest, a bull, is offered and its parts are disposed of (see 4.3–12). This decontaminates the sacred sphere, in particular the altar, of the impurities that have collected there prior to the induction of the priests and the inauguration of worship. *Sin offering,* purification offering; see 4.3. **15:** *Thus . . . to make expiation upon it,* better, "and made expiation upon it." **18–21:** The first "food gift" to be presented is a burnt offering (see 1.3–9); it invokes the deity and summons His presence. Prior to the consummation of the induction ceremony, Aaron is the individual offerer, while Moses assumes the role of priest. **19:** *And it was slaughtered,* by Aaron; see 1.5. **22–29:** The central feature of the induction ceremony, translated here as ordination, is in Heb "milu'im," "filling," an ellipsis for "filling the hand" (see v. 33; 16.32; 21.10; also Exod. 28.41; 29.3ff.; 32.29; Judg. 17.5, 12; etc.). This phrase, also attested in Akkadian, expresses the priests' entitlement to their allotted portions of the sacrifices. Along with the "filling" comes the added consecration ritual of daubing some of the ram's blood upon Aaron and his sons and on the altar. **23:** *Ear . . . thumb . . . big toe,* probably the extremities

a *See note on Exod. 28.30.*   b *Or "lobe."*

the big toes of their right feet; and the rest of the blood Moses dashed against every side of the altar. 25 He took the fat—the broad tail, all the fat about the entrails, the protuberance of the liver, and the two kidneys and their fat—and the right thigh. 26 From the basket of unleavened bread that was before the LORD, he took one cake of unleavened bread, one cake of oil bread, and one wafer, and placed them on the fat parts and on the right thigh. 27 He placed all these on the palms of Aaron and on the palms of his sons, and elevated them as an elevation offering before the LORD. 28 Then Moses took them from their hands and turned them into smoke on the altar with the burnt offering. This was an ordination offering for a pleasing odor; it was an offering by fire to the LORD. 29 Moses took the breast and elevated it as an elevation offering before the LORD; it was Moses' portion of the ram of ordination—as the LORD had commanded Moses.

30 And Moses took some of the anointing oil and some of the blood that was on the altar and sprinkled it upon Aaron and upon his vestments, and also upon his sons and upon their vestments. Thus he consecrated Aaron and his vestments, and also his sons and their vestments.

31 Moses said to Aaron and his sons: Boil the flesh at the entrance of the Tent of Meeting and eat it there with the bread that is in the basket of ordination—as I commanded:[a] Aaron and his sons shall eat it; 32 and what is left over of the flesh and the bread you shall consume in fire. 33 You shall not go outside the entrance of the Tent of Meeting for seven days, until the day that your period of ordination is completed. For your ordination will require seven days. 34 Everything done today, the LORD has commanded to be done [seven days], to make expiation for you. 35 You shall remain at the entrance of the Tent of Meeting day and night for seven days, keeping the LORD's charge—that you may not die—for so I have been commanded.

36 And Aaron and his sons did all the things that the LORD had commanded through Moses.

SHEMINI   שמיני

9 On the eighth day Moses called Aaron and his sons, and the elders of Israel. 2 He said to Aaron: "Take a calf of the herd for a sin offering and a ram for a burnt offering, without blemish, and bring them before the LORD. 3 And speak to the Israelites, saying: Take a he-goat for a sin offering; a calf and a lamb, yearlings without blemish,

of the body represent the whole. **25–29:** One of each of the loaves and cakes, along with the *right thigh*, is symbolically placed in the hands of the ordinands. They in turn present them to the LORD by elevating them (see 7.30) and then have them turned into smoke on the altar; priests do not receive a portion of their own offerings (see 6.12–15; 6.16). However, one of the priestly portions, the breast, is treated differently. As Moses serves on this occasion in the role of priest, he performs the elevation and receives the breast as his "priest's share" of the sacrificial meat. **30:** The sanctifying oil, previously poured on Aaron's head (v. 12), is now applied to the person of Aaron and his sons. It is mixed with blood from the altar and is sprinkled, rather than smeared, on them, completing his consecration and accomplishing theirs. **31–36:** The newly ordained priests may now eat of the sacred meat and bread, making sure to consume it all and to observe the time restriction (see Exod. 29.34). They then remain within the Tabernacle for seven days of "milu'im." Exod. 29.30 also ordains that the "milu'im" ritual be repeated when a new high priest is installed. **33:** *Your ordination will require seven days*, lit. "he [Moses] will fill your hands for seven days"; i.e., the ceremony of vv. 22–29 will be repeated on each of the next six days (see Exod. 29.35–37). **34:** *Everything done today*, all of the purification and ordination rituals. *Make expiation for you*, specifically, purge the altar of impurities that accrue there during the seven-day period that you are in such close proximity to it. **35:** If the priests fail to keep *the LORD's charge* and exit the Tabernacle during the critical first seven days of their priesthood, the contact between their heightened state of sanctity and the realm of the nonsacred will be fatal.

9.1–10.20: The Day of Revelation and the transgression of Aaron's sons. Chs 9 and 10 comprise one unit recounting the events of the

---

a Or, vocalizing ṣuwwethi, *"I have been commanded"; cf. below, vv. 35 and 10.13.*

for a burnt offering; [4] and an ox and a ram for an offering of well-being to sacrifice before the LORD; and a meal offering with oil mixed in. For today the LORD will appear to you."

[5] They brought to the front of the Tent of Meeting the things that Moses had commanded, and the whole community came forward and stood before the LORD. [6] Moses said: "This is what the LORD has commanded that you do, that the Presence of the LORD may appear to you." [7] Then Moses said to Aaron: "Come forward to the altar and sacrifice your sin offering and your burnt offering, making expiation for yourself and for the people; and sacrifice the people's offering and make expiation for them, as the LORD has commanded."

[8] Aaron came forward to the altar and slaughtered his calf of sin offering. [9] Aaron's sons brought the blood to him; he dipped his finger in the blood and put it on the horns of the altar; and he poured out the rest of the blood at the base of the altar. [10] The fat, the kidneys, and the protuberance of the liver from the sin offering he turned into

---

eighth day. In the Heb text no new division occurs at 10.1. After Aaron and his sons have been ordained, Moses orders them to perform their first sacrificial service in preparation for the appearance of the divine Presence (9.1–6). This consists of a number of offerings, including a well-being offering made on behalf of the entire people in celebration of the great event (9.7–23a). When the deity's Presence manifests itself in the sight of the people, signaling that He is pleased with their worship and has agreed to abide in the shrine they have built for Him, the people burst into rejoicing (9.23b–24). At the very moment that the inauguration of Israel's cult seems to have reached its auspicious climax, however, two of Aaron's sons commit a blatant act of sacrilege, overstepping the strictly prescribed bounds of acceptable worship (10.1). The LORD sanctifies His name by striking them down on the spot (10.2–3), and the surviving members of the priestly family are forbidden to mourn their demise (10.4–7). They are reminded of their sacred charge—to keep the sacred

separate from the nonsacred (10.8–11)—and told to continue the day's ceremonies (10.12–15). When Moses discovers that they have deviated from the normal manner of disposing of the "ḥaṭaʾt" meat, he is incensed (10.16–18); it takes some convincing before he agrees that their act was justified (10.19–20). **1–6:** After their seven-day seclusion, Aaron and his sons are told to emerge from the Tabernacle and to begin preparations for the Revelation Day ritual. Moses has them prepare the offerings they will make and tells Aaron to order the people, represented by the elders (see 4.15), to prepare the sacrifices that will be offered on their behalf. Thus the high priest takes up, for the first time, his crucial role of informing the Israelite people of their cultic duties. **1:** The eighth day, beginning with the first day of the seven-day ordination. **2:** Sin offering, purification offering; see 4.3. Here too the purification of the Tabernacle is necessary before acts of worship can begin. Burnt offering: The first gift the priests offer the LORD is a sublime act of devotion and serves also as an act of attraction, invoking the

deity's presence. **3:** The people too are to offer a purification offering, confirming that in P all are responsible for eradicating impurities from the divine abode; see ch 4. **4:** One of the few occasions on which a well-being offering ("shelamim"; see ch 3) is made by the public (see also 23.19). Since all will be present for the manifestation of the divine Presence shortly to occur, all will celebrate the joyous event in the appropriate manner, partaking of a sacred repast in God's presence. Meal offering, "minḥah" or grain offering; see ch. 2. One of each of the three types of gift offerings (see 1.1–3.17 n.) is to be made by the people, inaugurating the perpetual regimen of worship. For today the LORD will appear to you: This is echoed in v. 6 by "[in order] that the Presence of the LORD may appear to you," confirming Rashi's view that the purpose of these rituals is to bring about the theophany, i.e., to induce the divine Presence to make its appearance. **5:** And the whole community came forward, i.e., after having collected the prescribed materials, presumably so instructed by the elders. **6:** Moses said: "This is what the LORD has commanded," see also v. 7, "as the LORD has commanded." But nowhere is it recounted that God issued these commands, so most commentators assume that the text economizes for the sake of brevity. Rabbinic tradition acknowledges that Moses often commanded in the name of the LORD actions about which he had received no prior orders (e.g., Exod. 19.15; 32.27; elsewhere in P this occurs in Num. 30.2), implying that Moses' prophetic intuition was tantamount to explicit divine authority. Note that v. 21 says that the offerings were made "as Moses had commanded." **7:** And for the people: This apparently refers to the second purification offering, subsequently to be made on behalf of the people (see vv. 3, 15–16). The Septuagint here reads "and for your house" (i.e., Aaron's family). **8–14:** The priests' purification and burnt offerings are made in accordance with their prescribed rituals.

smoke on the altar—as the LORD had commanded Moses; [11] and the flesh and the skin were consumed in fire outside the camp. [12] Then he slaughtered the burnt offering. Aaron's sons passed the blood to him, and he dashed it against all sides of the altar. [13] They passed the burnt offering to him in sections, as well as the head, and he turned it into smoke on the altar. [14] He washed the entrails and the legs, and turned them into smoke on the altar with the burnt offering.

[15] Next he brought forward the people's offering. He took the goat for the people's sin offering, and slaughtered it, and presented it as a sin offering like the previous one. [16] He brought forward the burnt offering and sacrificed it according to regulation. [17] He then brought forward the meal offering and, taking a handful of it, he turned it into smoke on the altar—in addition to the burnt offering of the morning.[a] [18] He slaughtered the ox and the ram, the people's sacrifice of well-being. Aaron's sons passed the blood to him—which he dashed against every side of the altar—[19] and the fat parts of the ox and the ram: the broad tail, the covering [fat], the kidneys, and the protuberances of the livers. [20] They laid these fat parts over the breasts; and Aaron[b] turned the fat parts into smoke on the altar, [21] and elevated the breasts and the right thighs as an elevation offering before the LORD—as Moses had commanded.

[22] Aaron lifted his hands toward the people and blessed them; and he stepped down after offering the sin offering, the burnt offering, and the offering of well-being. [23] Moses and Aaron then went inside the Tent of Meeting. When they came out, they blessed the people; and the Presence of the LORD appeared to all the people. [24] Fire came forth from before the LORD and consumed the burnt offering and the fat parts on the altar. And all the people saw, and shouted, and fell on their faces.

a See Exod. 29.38–46.　　b This word moved up from v. 21 for clarity.

15–21: The people's sacrifices are offered, again following the logical sequence: purification, then the burnt offering and grain offering (since it too is in the "most-holy" category; see 6.10), and finally the well-being offering which is to constitute the sacred feast of celebration. **15:** *Like the previous one:* The text does not state specifically (as it did above regarding the priests' "hata't") what was done with the meat; this omission prepares us for what is to follow (10.16–20). **17:** Unlike the "minhah" of the individual (2.3, etc.; 6.9–11), this public one is offered in its entirety (as is the priest's; 6.16). *The burnt offering of the morning,* apparently the daily burnt offering prescribed in Exod. 29.38–39 (= Num. 28.3–4), indicating that its regular practice has already commenced (see Exod. 40.29). **18–21:** Though the ritual of the "shelamim" is per-

formed meticulously, the celebration to follow will be aborted. **22–24:** Some rabbinic commentators suggest that Aaron's initial blessing was a plea for God to appear, consisting of the priestly blessing prescribed in Num. 6.22–27 (which includes the words "May the LORD shine His face upon you" and "May the LORD lift up His face toward you"). When this was not answered, Aaron realized he had been found wanting, either in his priestly abilities, in which case he needed to enter the Tabernacle for instruction, or in his personal merits, in which case he needed Moses to pray on his behalf. After Moses accompanied him into the Tabernacle and the situation was rectified, the subsequent blessing pronounced by two of them (consisting of the words of Ps. 90.17) was answered and the LORD appeared. This interpretation is fanciful. Taken in context, the vv. indicate two separate acts. In Aaron's first blessing he asks the LORD to deal favorably with the people; he and Moses then enter the Tabernacle and invite the deity to emerge, after which they bless the people again—this time praying on their behalf that God favor them all with His manifest Presence—to which the LORD then responds by making His long-awaited appearance. **22:** *Lifted his hands toward the people,* to convey to them the blessings he has solicited on their behalf from God. *Stepped down:* The author anachronistically assumes the later Temple with which he is familiar, in which the altar would have been raised high above the ground; the Tabernacle altar was a portable one and was but three cubits (1.5 m, about 4.5 ft) high (Exod. 27.1). **23–24:** The Presence appears in the entrance of the Tabernacle and divine fire emerges from within, igniting the altar fire and consuming the sacrificial portions arrayed there. At this the people cry out, an expression of joy, and fall prostrate, a mark of obeisance. The non-Priestly narratives too tell of a theophany at Sinai/Horeb (Exod. chs 19–20;

10 Now Aaron's sons Nadab and Abihu each took his fire pan, put fire in it, and laid incense on it; and they offered before the LORD alien fire, which He had not enjoined upon them. [2] And fire came forth from the LORD and consumed them; thus they died a-at the instance of-a the LORD. [3] Then Moses said to Aaron, "This is what the LORD meant when He said:

Through those near to Me I show Myself holy,
And gain glory before all the people."
And Aaron was silent.

[4] Moses called Mishael and Elzaphan, sons of Uzziel the uncle of Aaron, and said to them, "Come forward and carry your kinsmen away from the front of the sanctuary to a place outside the camp." [5] They came forward and carried them out of the camp by their tunics, as Moses had ordered. [6] And Moses said to Aaron and to his sons Eleazar and Ithamar, "Do not b-bare your heads-b and do not rend your clothes, lest you die and anger strike the whole community. But your kinsmen, all the house of Israel, shall bewail the burning that the LORD has wrought. [7] And so do not go outside the entrance of the Tent of Meeting, lest you die, for the LORD's anointing oil is upon you." And they did as Moses had bidden.

a-a Others "before."   b-b Or "dishevel your hair."

24.1–15a). The Priestly counterpart of these accounts relates nothing of a thunderous voice booming out from heaven and proclaiming the Decalogue or of a fiery descent of the LORD in the sight of all the people on the mountain. For P the theophany began with the arrival of the divine Presence at Sinai (Exod. 24.15–18a) where it lingered until the Israelites finished building the Tabernacle. It continued with the entrance of the divine Presence to dwell in its abode (Exod. 40.34–35), and reaches its culmination here. **10.1–3:** The sin and death of Nadab and Abihu follow directly (see 9.1–10.20 n.). **1:** *Fire pan,* a metal utensil with a handle used for offering smoking incense. *Fire,* Heb "'esh" here means kindling material; see also Num. 17.2, 11. The brothers placed unlit coals (or wood for kindling) in the pans, in order to attract the divine fire to light them (see 1 Kings 18.38). *Offered,* i.e., presented, "brought near"; *alien fire,*

unauthorized coals. They thus prepared an incense offering upon kindling of their own. *Which He had not enjoined upon them:* No offering of incense had been ordered; the only legitimate incense offerings are those made daily, by the high priest, upon the sacred altar (see Exod. 30.7–8). In public worship, only what is prescribed is legitimate; what is not is sacrilege. The Rabbis and medieval commentators thought otherwise, incredulous at the idea that God had struck down two young priests for a "mere" ritual offense, especially since it seemed to stem from a sincere, though perhaps overenthusiastic, desire to serve the LORD. They therefore suggested other reasons for the severe fate suffered by the two (such as drunkenness, celibacy, arrogant impatience for Moses and Aaron to die, or neglect of their sacred obligations). In biblical thought, however, ritual crimes are dire. Further, the sin of the two brothers was not simply

that they went too far in their misguided super-piety. Rather, they acted in utter disregard for the deity. God intended that the manifestation of His Presence would ignite the altar fire, marking His acceptance of His people's devotion. Their intent was for the divine fire to ignite their own pans; that is, they were attempting to arrogate control of the deity to themselves. **2:** *Fire came forth from the LORD,* from the Holy of Holies; similarly 9.24. The sacrilege of Nadab and Abihu evokes a spontaneous response: Crimes of trespass upon the sacred are automatically fatal. **3:** *This is what the LORD meant:* The reference may be to Exod. 29.42; otherwise one must assume that the statement was made at an earlier point but recorded only here. *Those near to Me,* perhaps more simply, "those who come too near to Me." *Show Myself holy . . . gain glory:* Frequently in biblical thought, God's holiness is displayed, and His glory made manifest, in the swift and unrelenting punishment of those who offend His majesty. **4–5:** The corpses must be removed immediately; to allow such a potent source of contamination to remain in contact with the most sacred sphere would be particularly dangerous. **5:** *By their tunics:* Direct physical contact with the bodies is also avoided. **6–7:** Mourning rituals, as well as contact with the dead, are forbidden to priests (21.1–6, 10–12). The surviving priests are warned that if they compound the offense of Nadab and Abihu with further ritual infraction their fate will be no less severe, and the community too will be placed in jeopardy; see 4.3. Their first concern must be to prevent the holy from being defiled and the service of the deity from being disrupted. *Bare your heads,* correctly "dishevel your heads [i.e., your hair]"; a bared head was not a sign of mourning. *Shall bewail the burning that the LORD has wrought:* The death of Aaron's sons is all the more tragic for the fact that it was deserved. Although the officiating priests are forbidden to display any outward

8 And the LORD spoke to Aaron, saying: 9 Drink no wine or other intoxicant, you or your sons, when you enter the Tent of Meeting, that you may not die. This is a law for all time throughout the ages, 10 for you must distinguish between the sacred and the profane, and between the unclean and the clean; 11 and you must teach the Israelites all the laws which the LORD has imparted to them through Moses.

12 Moses spoke to Aaron and to his remaining sons, Eleazar and Ithamar: Take the meal offering that is left over from the LORD's offerings by fire and eat it unleavened beside the altar, for it is most holy. 13 You shall eat it in the sacred precinct, inasmuch as it is your due, and that of your children, from the LORD's offerings by fire; for so I have been commanded. 14 But the breast of elevation offering and the thigh of gift offering you, and your sons and daughters with you, may eat in any clean place, for they have been assigned as a due to you and your children from the Israelites' sacrifices of well-being. 15 Together with the fat of fire offering, they must present the thigh of gift offering and the breast of elevation offering, which are to be elevated as an elevation offering before the LORD, and which are to be your due and that of your children with you for all time—as the LORD has commanded.

16 Then Moses inquired about the goat of sin offering, and it had already been burned! He was angry with Eleazar and Ithamar, Aaron's remaining sons, and said, 17 "Why did you not eat the sin offering in the sacred area? For it is most holy, and He has given it to you to remove the guilt of the community and to make expiation for them before the LORD. 18 Since its blood was not brought inside the sanctuary,ᵃ you should certainly have eaten it in the sanctuary, as I commanded." 19 And Aaron spoke to Moses, "See, this day they brought their sin offering and their burnt offering before the LORD, and such things have befallen me! Had I eaten sin offering today, would the LORD have approved?" 20 And when Moses heard this, he approved.

11 The LORD spoke to Moses and Aaron, saying to them: 2 Speak to the Israelite people thus:
These are the creatures that you may eat from among all the land animals: 3 any animal that has true hoofs, with clefts through the hoofs, and that chewsᵇ the cud—such

a As is done in the case of the most solemn offerings; see 4.3–21; 16.11–17.
b Lit. "brings up."

manifestations of grief, the people at large are under no such restriction (but see 19.27–28).
8–10: Priests need to maintain sobriety in order to discharge their sacred tasks, not only their ritual duties but also priestly instruction, which require the ability to make precise distinctions and rulings. This parenthetical passage, which seems out of place here, could well serve as the introduction to the remainder of Leviticus, in which the priestly tasks of distinguishing *between the sacred and the profane, and between the unclean and the clean* are described. **12–16:** Internal feelings notwithstanding, Aaron, Elazar, and Ithamar are to continue as though nothing has occurred. The priests' portions of the well-being offerings are given to them; they, and their families, may eat the meat later in the day and perhaps the next day as well (see 7.15–16). The festive repast to be held by the people (see 9.18–21) following the day's ceremonies was probably canceled. **16–20:** Diligently keeping track that each of the day's offerings has been handled properly, Moses finally arrives at the people's "ḥata᾽t" (9.15). Since this, though public, was performed for preventive purification, its blood, unlike that for a communal offense (4.13–21), was not brought into the Tabernacle interior. Yet, Moses discovers, Aaron and his surviving sons, instead of eating the meat, have had it burned, in apparent violation of 6.23. Aaron's response means that what has occurred is a one-time exception in light of the tragic circumstances; no ritual reform has been attempted nor is there any dispute as to the proper procedure. Thus is Moses' apprehension put to rest.

11.1–47: Laws regulating the consumption of flesh. Communication of laws to Moses now resumes. The Priestly doctrine of prohibited and permitted foodstuffs derives from the belief that human beings, having dominion over the world and all it contains, are permitted, since the flood, to eat all vegetation and all (nonhuyou may eat. 4 The following, however, of those that either chew the cud or have true hoofs, you shall not eat: the camel—although it chews the cud, it has no true hoofs: it is unclean for you; 5 the daman—although it chews the cud, it has no true hoofs: it is unclean for you; 6 the hare—although it chews the cud, it has no true hoofs: it is unclean for you; 7 and the swine—although it has true hoofs, with the hoofs cleft through, it does not chew the cud: it is unclean for you. 8 You shall not eat of their flesh or touch their carcasses; they are unclean for you.

9 These you may eat of all that live in water: anything in water, whether in the seas or in the streams, that has fins and scales—these you may eat. 10 But anything in the seas or in the streams that has no fins and scales, among all the

man) meat. There is but one stipulation: Humans must not consume an animal's blood along with its flesh. All this, P believes, has been known since the time of Noah (Gen. 9.1–4). Now, however, Moses is informed that the Israelite people are to be subject to a host of additional restrictions. These extend to all five categories of the animal kingdom: (a) large land animals (vv. 2–8), (b) beings that dwell in the water (vv. 9–12), (c) fowl (vv. 13–19), (d) flying insects (vv. 20–23), and (e) small land animals (vv. 41–42). Each category is subdivided into those animals that Israelites may eat and those that they may not. The criteria of division are present in nature itself: The distinction between forbidden and permitted meat, while incumbent upon Israelites alone, is a part of creation as reflected in Gen. 1.1–2.4. This is similar to the Sabbath: Though it was sanctified at creation, its observance was obligatory only for the Israelites. By maintaining a set of dietary restrictions corresponding to the distinctions held to be present in the natural world, the Israelites, in Priestly thought, are kept holy, that is, separate from the remainder of humanity (vv. 44–45; see also 20.25–26) and within the inner circle of proximity to the divine. In both categories of land animals (a and e), an additional dimension exists: Contact with the carcasses of the prohibited animals also

communicates impurity. Though this is mentioned briefly in (a) (vv. 4, 7, 8), its ramifications are detailed in the vv. preceding (e) (vv. 24–40). This ch anticipates the next four (chs 12–15), in which the issue of impurity and the need to eradicate it will be taken up in full. The laws of permitted and forbidden meat (also in briefer form in Deut. 14.3–20) constitute only a portion of the biblical dietary laws. Elsewhere in P are prohibitions of blood and suet (3.16–17; 7.22–27; 17.10–14; see also 19.26); outside of P too blood is prohibited (Deut. 12.16, 23–24). The non-Priestly laws also forbid Israelites to eat carrion (Exod. 22.30; Deut. 14.21), which P does not accept (see vv. 39–40 n.), and prohibit cooking a kid in its mother's milk (Exod. 23.19; 34.26; Deut. 14.21), which P does not mention. Together with the law of slaughter, traditionally believed to have been communicated to Moses orally (see 1.5 n.), these laws provide the biblical basis for the laws of "kashrut" practiced to this day. **1:** These laws are communicated to Aaron along with Moses, in view of the priests' responsibility for scrupulously maintaining the prescribed distinctions; see 10.10–11. **2–8:** Category (a): large land animals. It is assumed that domestic livestock (cattle, sheep, and goats) may be eaten; since these animals are fit for sacrifice, they are obviously permitted. In

Priestly law, however, domestic livestock may only be eaten as sacrificial meat (see 17.3–8). Therefore the text here must be dealing with nondomestic animals, as is the case throughout the ch. These vv. establish that Israelites may eat the meat of other large land animals only if they resemble domestic livestock, i.e., if they possess the latter's characteristics. They are listed in Deut. 14.5: the deer, the gazelle, the roebuck, the wild goat, the ibex, the antelope, the mountain sheep. There, however, they are equated with the domestic ones, since Deuteronomic law disagrees with P, permitting the non-sacrificial slaughter of cattle, sheep, and goats as well. **3:** *Has true hoofs . . . chews the cud:* These characteristics have no intrinsic or symbolic significance; they are simply the distinguishing features of cattle, sheep, and goats and therefore serve as a simple means for identifying other permitted animals. **4–7:** The three illustrations—the *camel,* the *daman,* and the *swine*—serve as further indication that nondomestic animals are intended. Their inclusion shows that one characteristic is not enough; only animals that both ruminate and have cloven hooves are permitted. Swine are not singled out here. *Unclean:* In addition to being forbidden as food, the meat of these animals communicates impurity. This is elaborated upon below (see vv. 24–28). **8:** *You shall not eat of their flesh or touch their carcasses,* probably equivalent to the parallel v. 11 "you shall not eat of their flesh [and you shall avoid] (see v. 10 n.) their carcasses." Throughout P contact with sources of impurity is not forbidden; it is to be avoided when possible, and when it has occurred purification is mandatory but no misdeed has been committed (see chs 12–15). As is clear from vv. 24ff., this applies here as well. **9–12:** Category (b): water creatures. The Israelites may eat the flesh of beings that populate the waters only if they have the characteristics peculiar to fish. **9–10:** *Fins and scales:* The water creatures divide into two swarming things of the water and among all the other living creatures that are in the water—they are an abomination for you [11] and an abomination for you they shall remain: you shall not eat of their flesh and you shall abominate their carcasses. [12] Everything in water that has no fins and scales shall be an abomination for you.

[13] The following[a] you shall abominate among the birds—they shall not be eaten, they are an abomination: the eagle, the vulture, and the black vulture; [14] the kite, falcons of every variety; [15] all varieties of raven; [16] the ostrich, the nighthawk, the sea gull; hawks of every variety; [17] the little owl, the cormorant, and the great owl; [18] the white owl, the pelican, and the bustard; [19] the stork; herons of every variety; the hoopoe, and the bat.

[20] All winged swarming things that walk on fours shall be an abomination for you. [21] But these you may eat among all the winged swarming things that walk on fours: all that have, above their feet, jointed legs to leap with on the ground—[22] of these you may eat the following:[a] locusts of every variety; all varieties of bald locust; crickets of every variety; and all varieties of grasshopper. [23] But all other winged swarming things that have four legs shall be an abomination for you.

[24] And the following shall make you unclean—whoever touches their carcasses shall be unclean until evening, [25] and whoever carries the carcasses of any of them shall wash his clothes and be unclean until evening—[26] every animal that has true hoofs but without clefts through the hoofs, or that does not chew the cud. They are unclean for you; whoever touches them shall be unclean. [27] Also all animals that walk on paws, among those that walk on fours, are unclean for you; whoever touches their carcasses shall be unclean until evening. [28] And anyone who carries their carcasses shall wash his clothes and remain unclean until evening. They are unclean for you.

a *A number of these cannot be identified with certainty.*

groups: fish, thought of as the "proper" or normal form of maritime life, and all others, *all the swarming things of the water.* Those in the former group are easily identified by the two features characteristic of fish; those in the latter are forbidden. **10–12:** *Abomination* (Heb "sheketz"), *abominate* (Heb "sh-k-tz"), in this ch refer specifically to forbidden animals. Perhaps *you shall abominate* and *an abomination for you* mean that al-

though there is nothing intrinsically loathsome about these animals, the Israelite is to abhor them simply because they are prohibited. But *abominate* may be too strong and in P may mean "avoid." Unlike forbidden land creatures, forbidden water creatures and flying creatures do not communicate impurity. **13–19:** Category (c): fowl. This section does not provide a set of distinguishing markings to identify

the permitted species; it simply enumerates the prohibited ones, implying that all others are allowed. Rabbinic tradition attempted to supply the missing key, suggesting that the prohibited fowl are all birds of prey; the permitted fowl are nonpredators. This category may be analogous to (a): It is taken for granted that the turtledove and the pigeon are permitted since they are fit for the altar; the list of forbidden fowl would then be an enumeration of all known fowl that are dissimilar in their appearance and habits to the fowl used in sacrifice. *The eagle, the vulture, . . . :* Some of the translations are uncertain. **20–23:** Category (d): flying insects, *winged swarming things.* Those with jointed legs above their feet for leaping on the ground are permissible. These are named; all others, as stressed by the repetition in v. 23, are forbidden. Unlike the previous categories, here the basic category itself is forbidden; only insects that diverge from the characteristics of the category and resemble birds more than insects may be eaten. **24–40:** These parenthetical vv. interrupt the flow, introducing a series of laws pertaining to impurities generated or communicated by the flesh of creatures mentioned in (a) and (e). This is anticipated by, and elaborates on, what has preceded, but since v. 41 is the direct continuation of v. 23, it seems most likely that these vv. are secondary. Perhaps they were inserted here, instead of after (e) which would have been more natural, in order for v. 43 to follow vv. 41–42 directly. **24–25:** The superscription and its explanation: The carcasses of the following creatures communicate impurity by direct contact and carrying. The impurity is minor; only a brief time, until sunset, followed by laundering (and, presumably, bathing) is needed for it to dissipate. **26–28:** Elaborating on (a). The first to be mentioned (v. 26) whose impurity was noted above (vv. 3–8); to these, such animals such as bears, dogs and cats, which would not be eaten in any

29 The following[a] shall be unclean for you from among the things that swarm on the earth: the mole, the mouse, and great lizards of every variety; 30 the gecko, the land crocodile, the lizard, the sand lizard, and the chameleon. 31 Those are for you the unclean among all the swarming things; whoever touches them when they are dead shall be unclean until evening. 32 And anything on which one of them falls when dead shall be unclean: be it any article of wood, or a cloth, or a skin, or a sack—any such article that can be put to use shall be dipped in water, and it shall remain unclean until evening; then it shall be clean. 33 And if any of those falls into an earthen vessel, everything inside it shall be unclean and [the vessel] itself you shall break. 34 As to any food that may be eaten, it shall become unclean if it came in contact with water;[b] as to any liquid that may be drunk, it shall become unclean if it was inside any vessel.[c] 35 Everything on which the carcass of any of them falls shall be unclean: an oven or stove shall be smashed. They are unclean and unclean they shall remain for you. 36 However, a spring or cistern in which water is collected shall be clean, but whoever touches such a carcass in it shall be unclean. 37 If such a carcass falls upon seed grain that is to be sown, it is clean; 38 but if water is put on the seed and any part of a carcass falls upon it, it shall be unclean for you.

39 If an animal that you may eat has died, anyone who touches its carcass shall be unclean until evening; 40 anyone who eats of its carcass shall wash his clothes and remain unclean until evening; and anyone who carries its carcass shall wash his clothes and remain unclean until evening.

41 All the things that swarm upon the earth are an abomination; they shall not be eaten. 42 You shall not eat,

a A number of these cannot be identified with certainty.
b I.e., if the food then came in contact with the carcass of any animal named in vv. 29–30.
c I.e., a vessel that had become contaminated by such contact.

case and are therefore omitted above, are added (v. 27). The opening statement is then repeated (v. 28). **29–38:** Anticipating (e) (vv. 41–42). The realities of life are such that the carcasses of small land animals are not only likely to come into direct contact with humans, thus communicating impurity directly; they are especially likely to come into contact with foodstuffs, vessels and utensils, seeds, and water supply.

31–35: Like humans who have contracted this impurity and are governed by the rule in vv. 24–25 (see v. 31), articles of wood and leather require washing and the lapse of one day in order for the impurity to dissipate (v. 32). Earthen vessels that have absorbed impurity cannot be cleansed (v. 33). Liquid in vessels becomes impure if the unclean animal has fallen in (v. 34b), but sources of fresh water, while not

cleansing the unclean animal, remain pure and do not communicate impurity, since they are constantly washing it away (v. 36). Dry foodstuffs are not susceptible to impurity, but are if they have been moistened by water (v. 34a). **34:** If it came in contact with water: This translation is misleading; the water does not render it unclean. Rather, it becomes capable of contracting impurity if, prior to coming in contact with the unclean object, it is moistened at any time by water; see v. 38. **35:** An oven or stove shall be smashed: These too are of earthenware; earthenware, being porous, thoroughly absorbs impurity and cannot be cleansed. **37–38:** Seed and grain, like foodstuffs, are not susceptible to impurity until they come into contact with water; thenceforth contact with an unclean animal renders them unclean. **39–40:** These vv. confirm that according to P "nevelah," the meat of an animal that has died by itself rather than being slaughtered, is permitted as long as the animal is one that may be eaten. Impurity results and must be remedied, but no sin has been committed. Elsewhere in P this is extended to "terefah," the meat of an animal that has been "torn," i.e., killed by another beast; see 17.15–16. In P, only priests are commanded to abstain from "nevelah" and "terefah"; see 17.15–16 and 22.8. **39:** An animal that you may eat: Above, and in 5.2 and 7.21, it is only the meat of unclean animals that communicates impurity. Here, and in 17.15–16 (see also 7.23) the meat of permitted animals does so as well. It may be possible to reconcile this conflict; perhaps the carcass and flesh of an unclean animal (which may not be eaten) communicates impurity no matter how the animal has died, whereas that of permitted animals does so only if the animal has died on its own or been killed by a beast (though it may be eaten, see above); if it has been slaughtered, no impurity results. **41–42:** Category (e): small land animals. Like (d), the category per se is prohibited, but here there are no ex-among all things that swarm upon the earth, anything that crawls on its belly, or anything that walks on fours, or anything that has many legs; for they are an abomination. ⁴³ You shall not draw abomination upon yourselves through anything that swarms; you shall not make yourselves unclean therewith and thus become unclean. ⁴⁴ For I the LORD am your God: you shall sanctify yourselves and be holy, for I am holy. You shall not make yourselves unclean through any swarming thing that moves upon the earth. ⁴⁵ For I the LORD am He who brought you up from the land of Egypt to be your God: you shall be holy, for I am holy.

⁴⁶ These are the instructions concerning animals, birds, all living creatures that move in water, and all creatures that swarm on earth, ⁴⁷ for distinguishing between the unclean and the clean, between the living things that may be eaten and the living things that may not be eaten.

TAZRIA‘   תזריע

12 The LORD spoke to Moses, saying: ²Speak to the Israelite people thus: When a woman at childbirth[a] bears a male, she shall be unclean seven days; she shall be

---

a Heb. tazria‘, lit. "brings forth seed."

---

ceptions. The only permitted land animals are thus domestic livestock and fowl and those which resemble them, and a few exceptions to the general rule prohibiting all others, namely the explicitly named types of flying insects. **43–45:** The conclusion of the instructions stresses the aim of the food restrictions. By restricting consumption of meat to clean animals, the Israelites sanctify themselves and become *holy;* for the idea expressed by these terms see 11.1–47 n. **43:** *Draw abomination upon yourselves:* Heb actually means "make your throats loathsome," a straightforward way of saying "eat that which is loathsome." **45:** *Who brought you up from the land of Egypt to be your God,* see 26.13 n. *You shall be holy, for I am holy,* see 19.2. **46–47:** This typically Priestly caption, like 7.37–38, summarizes what precedes it.

Chs 12–15: Disposal of impurity. The next four chs prescribe how to dispose of the types of impurity

indentified by the Priestly tradition. "Impurity" (Heb "tum'ah") is often translated as contamination, defilement, pollution, or uncleanness. In P "tum'ah" is like an atmospheric layer or coating, enveloping the impure person or object. Though invisible, it is believed to be quite real; though amorphous it is substantive. Its causes are four: human corpses, carcasses of animals, fluxes of life fluids, and a specific condition known as "tzara‘at" (see chs 13–14). The common denominator is that all these are manifestations of death, or more precisely, of the escape of the forces of life. Thus the corpse and the carcass, out of which life may be thought to "leak," defile; similarly semen, menstrual fluid, the blood lost in childbirth, and other genital discharge (though not human waste, which has nothing to do with the escape of life, and not blood, apparently because it is the purifying agent) defile as well. The disease or condition known as "tzara‘at"

too is thought of as a form of gradually escaping life (see Num. 12.12). Impurity is distinct from its causes: Corpses, carcasses, fluids, and "tzara‘at" are not the defilement itself; rather, they produce the defilement, by process of spontaneous generation. We may compare "tum'ah" to a miasma, an aura of invisible vapors, expanding to fill available space and polluting all that it touches, contagiously contaminating persons and objects with which they come into contact and communicating to them various degrees of indirect (secondary or tertiary) impurity, which in turn needs to be disposed of. Unlike similar notions found outside the Bible, "tum'ah" in P is not demonic, not created by or connected with evil spirits or malicious deities. Neither is it the same as modern notions of dirt or filth, or of infection. Rather, it is a simple fact of life, a part of nature; certain phenomena in the created world are empirically sources of impurity. These phenomena are not necessarily bad; there is nothing morally repugnant about a human corpse or the carcass of an animal, there is nothing sinful about menstruation or sexual intercourse, and there is no evil in a genital flux or a disease of the skin. For this reason, nowhere in the Priestly law is there a prohibition of the lay Israelite's becoming "tame'" per se; people and objects routinely and unavoidably contract impurity at all times. The grievous and dangerous sin connected with impurity is rather that of remaining impure, of failing to dispose of impurity once one has contracted it, thereby allowing it to spread and to come into contact with the sacred, i.e., the sanctuary and its furnishings. For "tum'ah," as pictured by Priestly thought, is drawn irresistibly to the sacred sphere, which is particularly vulnerable to its penetration, and there it accumulates. If this goes unchecked, i.e., if too much of this odious matter collects in the divine abode, the divine Presence will depart and then Israel is doomed (see 15.31 n.). Only priests, who unclean as at the time of her menstrual infirmity.—³ On the eighth day the flesh of his foreskin shall be circumcised.— ⁴ She shall remain in a state of blood purification* for thirty-three days: she shall not touch any consecrated thing, nor enter the sanctuary until her period of purification is completed. ⁵ If she bears a female, she shall be unclean two weeks as during her menstruation, and she shall remain in a state of blood purification* for sixty-six days.

⁶ On the completion of her period of purification, for ei-

---

a Meaning of Heb. uncertain.

---

are in constant contact with the sacred sphere, are explicitly cautioned to shun all but the most unavoidable impurity; lay Israelites are under no such obligation; they are simply required to attend conscientiously to its disposal. Three elements effect the disposal of impurity: the passage of time, cleansing (usually in water), and the purification offering. The first two purify the individual, the third purges the sanctuary. The minor types of impurity require only the bathing of the impure individual and the laundering of clothing, after which the impurity dissipates on its own by nightfall. Contamination of the Tabernacle by such minor impurities is negligible and is presumably cleansed by routine public offerings. Major impurities, on the other hand, directly contaminate the Tabernacle. When they occur, in addition to the passage of time and cleansing, a "hata't" sacrifice must be made on behalf of the impure individual, in order to eradicate the impurity that he has caused to accumulate in the Tabernacle. Later tradition tended to adopt a less literal, more practical view of biblical "tum'ah," and often reinterpreted it symbolically. Further, by rejecting the idea that impurity is drawn to the sanctuary from afar, the Rabbis made it less of a concern—only those who planned actually to visit the Temple need worry about purifying themselves. Ultimately "tum'ah" became simply an arbitrarily decreed ritual "state." In biblical teaching, in contrast to its later interpretation, impurity

is not simply a condition; it is real.

12.1–8: Impurity after childbirth. Neither procreation nor childbirth is sinful. Like other bodily impurities, the defilement attached to childbirth has no moral significance whatsoever; it is a fact of nature. As the text explicitly says, the woman who has given birth needs to be purified *from her flow of blood* (v. 7). The observable discharge of heavy, dark fluid ("lochia rubra"), which lasts for a number of days, followed by a lighter flow ("lochia blanca") which may last for a number of weeks, provides the empirical explanation of the two phases of her purification. In order to prescribe unified legislation, these two approximate periods are standardized into the "round" numbers seven and forty used throughout the Bible, which are then doubled (see v. 5). The ch outlines the stages of the mother's purification if a male child has been born (vv. 2–4), explains how they differ if a female child is born (v. 5), and prescribes how the mother is obligated to see to the purification of the sanctuary, whether she is a person of means (vv. 6–7) or not (v. 8). **2:** *She shall be unclean seven days:* During the first phase the mother is severely unclean; her impurity penetrates to the sphere of the sacred, requiring her to offer a "hata't." This, however, she cannot do until she is completely purified, several weeks later (vv. 6–7a). *Unclean as at the time of her menstrual infirmity:* In addition to the fact that her impurity con-

taminates the sanctuary from afar, the regulations pertaining to the parturient are identical to those pertaining to the menstruant, as given in 15.19–24. She communicates minor impurity to whatever and whomever she touches by direct or almost direct contact. **3:** Circumcision is not a stage in the purification process. It is noted here by association; mention of the seventh day of a male child's life quite naturally calls to mind the event of the eighth day. Halakhic exegesis also notes that since the command of circumcision was given not to Moses but to Abraham (Gen. 17.9–14), it needed to be repeated here, in the context of the giving of the law to Israel in the wilderness, in order to be valid. **4:** *In a state of blood purification,* lit. "in the blood of becoming pure," that is, she will continue to observe some discharge, and thus remain impure to a lesser degree, before becoming fully purified. *Thirty-three days:* The number thirty-three, which has no significance, when combined with the first seven days yields forty, a "round" number of purification days. *Not touch any consecrated thing,* better, "anything holy." During the second phase, she continues to contaminate sacred objects and the sanctuary, but only by direct contact, no longer from afar; she no longer communicates impurity to the nonsacred (to other humans or objects) at all. Thus she is permitted to resume relations with her husband in this second phase. Rabbinic law is more stringent, requiring a longer period of time; see also 15.19. **5:** The reason the length of each phase is doubled when a female child is born is difficult to determine. Modern medicine recognizes no difference between the postpartum genital flow of the mother of a boy and that of the mother of a girl. The ancients, however, may have believed there was a difference, or they may have noted that there is occasionally vaginal flow from the infant girl herself and viewed this as necessitating a longer purification by the mother. **6–7a:** The *expi-*

ther son or daughter, she shall bring to the priest, at the entrance of the Tent of Meeting, a lamb in its first year for a burnt offering, and a pigeon or a turtledove for a sin offering.[a] [7] He shall offer it before the LORD and make expiation on her behalf; she shall then be clean from her flow of blood. Such are the rituals concerning her who bears a child, male or female. [8] If, however, her means do not suffice for a sheep, she shall take two turtledoves or two pigeons, one for a burnt offering and the other for a sin offering. The priest shall make expiation on her behalf, and she shall be clean.

13 The LORD spoke to Moses and Aaron, saying: [2] When a person has on the skin of his body a swelling, a rash, or a discoloration, and it develops into a scaly affection on the skin of his body, it shall be reported[b] to Aaron the priest or to one of his sons, the priests. [3] The priest shall examine the affection on the skin of his body:

a See note at 4.3.   b Or "he shall be brought."

ation, that is, decontamination of the sanctuary, is accomplished elsewhere by means of the "ḥaṭa᾽t" sacrifice (see ch 4). Uniquely, the mother is also required to offer a burnt offering (see ch 1), though generally this is not needed for expiation. It may be an expression of thanks or a required gesture of obeisance. **6:** *Sin offering,* correctly, purification offering (see 4.3); no sin has been committed. **7b:** The summary caption. **8:** An appended provision made for the woman who cannot afford the costly sacrifice (see 5.7–10 n.). Here the concern is to ensure that every parturient, even the poorest, performs her expiation, so that the divine abode is cleansed.

13.1–14.57: Impurity caused by "tzaraʿat." These two chs are a unit (see summary at 14.54–57), prescribing the elimination of the impurity caused by "tzaraʿat." This has sometimes been translated as "leprosy" (or "leprous affection"), but the disease today called leprosy (Hanson's disease) was not known in biblical times and the description given in the Bible is not consistent with it. Further,

since "tzaraʿat" afflicts not only humans but also fabrics (13.47–59) and building materials (14.33–47), it cannot be identified with a single pathology. The distinctive symptom of "tzaraʿat" in humans is scale-like eruptions of the skin. Though most similar to psoriasis and vitiligo, not all of the symptoms correspond. Lacking modern microbiology, the Bible referred to conditions with similar outward manifestations by a single name. "Tzaraʿat" in fabrics and building materials are types of mildew. The Bible does not view disease per se as defiling. Only those having "tzaraʿat" or abnormal genital fluxes (see 15.1–33 n., 15.1–15, 25–30) are considered to be impure. "Tzaraʿat," seen as a gradual erosion of the skin, was thought to culminate, unless the patient recovered, in the ultimate disintegration of the flesh, which was taken as a manifestation of the gradual escape of life. The person afflicted with it was looked upon as potentially dead (see Num. 12.12), death itself having begun to consume his body (Job 18.13). This "leakage" of life, according to P, creates impurity (see

chs 12–15 n.). For the steps necessary to dispose of the impurity lest it spread to the sanctuary, the priest, in his sacred role of distinguishing the pure from the impure (see 10.10; cf. 11.47) is given the task of "diagnosing" "tzaraʿat" in humans, fabrics, and buildings. But the priest is not a physician, and has no role in the healing process; the commands detail only the procedure to be followed, and the information necessary, for him to determine if the lesion is "tzaraʿat" or not. If it is, purification and expiation are prescribed; if not, the priest pronounces it clean. In the Bible, the onset and progress of disease, its persistence or eventual disappearance, are essentially outside of human control. In other biblical books "tzaraʿat" is seen as a divine penalty (e.g., Num. 12.10; 2 Kings 15.5). Rabbinic thought agreed, suggesting that the person afflicted with "tzaraʿat" (the "metzoraʿ") was being punished thereby for the sin of slander (the same consonants in Heb: "motzi raʿ"). But none of this is expressed here. P seems to view "tzaraʿat" quite matter-of-factly as a feature of the natural world created by God, like unclean animals, gonorrhea, and menstruation. No moral judgment is passed on the afflicted individuals, who are accountable only if they fail to attend to the prompt eradication of impurity once the disease has disappeared. **13.1:** As in 11.1, the laws are communicated to Aaron as well as Moses, reflecting the central role of the priest in what follows. **1–46:** Each set of symptoms is taken up separately, and directions are provided in order to determine whether "tzaraʿat" is present or not. If it is not, the priest declares the person pure. If it is, the person is declared impure until such time as the affliction is healed and the purification rituals have been completed (ch 14). If a conclusive diagnosis cannot be made, seven-day waiting periods ensue, after which the condition is examined again. **2–8:** *A swelling, a rash, or a discoloration* (better: "shiny mark"): These are immediately if hair in the affected patch has turned white and the affection appears to be deeper than the skin of his body, it is a leprous affection;[a] when the priest sees it, he shall pronounce him unclean. [4] But if it is a white discoloration on the skin of his body which does not appear to be deeper than the skin and the hair in it has not turned white, the priest shall isolate the affected person for seven days. [5] On the seventh day the priest shall examine him, and if the affection has remained unchanged in color and the disease has not spread on the skin, the priest shall isolate him for another seven days. [6] On the seventh day the priest shall examine him again: if the affection has faded and has not spread on the skin, the priest shall pronounce him clean. It is a rash; he shall wash his clothes, and he shall be clean. [7] But if the rash should spread on the skin after he has presented himself to the priest and been pronounced clean, he shall present himself again to the priest. [8] And if the priest sees that the rash has spread on the skin, the priest shall pronounce him unclean; it is leprosy.

[9] When a person has a scaly affection, it shall be reported[b] to the priest. [10] If the priest finds on the skin a white swelling which has turned some hair white, with [c]a patch of undiscolored flesh[c] in the swelling, [11] it is chronic leprosy on the skin of his body, and the priest shall pronounce him unclean; he need not isolate him, for he is unclean. [12] If the eruption spreads out over the skin so that it covers all the skin of the affected person from head to foot, wherever the priest can see—[13] if the priest sees that the eruption has covered the whole body—he shall pronounce the affected person clean; he is clean, for he has turned all white. [14] But as soon as undiscolored flesh appears in it, he shall be unclean; [15] when the priest sees the undiscolored flesh, he shall pronounce him unclean. The undiscolored flesh is unclean; it is leprosy. [16] But if the undiscolored flesh again turns white, he shall come to the priest, [17] and the priest shall examine him: if the affection has turned white, the priest shall pronounce the affected person clean; he is clean.

[18] When an inflammation appears on the skin of one's body and it heals, [19] and a white swelling or a white discoloration streaked with red develops where the inflammation was, he shall present himself to the priest. [20] If the

deemed to be "tzara'at" if the two symptoms in v. 3 are present. Otherwise a seven-day quarantine commences, after which, if the condition has spread or if the two symptoms appear, it is pronounced to be "tzara'at." If not, a second seven-day period is observed; during it, if the condition spreads the afflicted person must immediately report back to the priest and be pronounced unclean. At the end of the second week, a final check is made: If the affection has faded it is deemed to be merely a rash and the person is pronounced clean; if at that time, or subsequently, it has spread or the two symptoms have appeared, it is deemed "tzara'at." **3:** *A leprous affection,* Heb "tzara'at"; better, "scale disease" (see above) or "surface affection." **4:** *Shall isolate the affected person:* This quarantine is not aimed at arresting the spread of the disease, but is an attempt to contain the spread of an intolerable amount of severe impurity in case "tzara'at" is present. **9–11:** *A scaly affection:* This is immediately deemed to be "tzara'at" if it shows the three symptoms given in v. 3; no period of waiting is needed. **10:** *Undiscolored flesh,* lit. "raw" or "living" flesh. It appears where scales have rubbed off, indicating that the disease is still active. **11–13:** The spreading of the scales to the entire body rather than deepening and causing erosion in specific spots indicates that healing is under way and the person is pronounced pure. **14–17:** *Undiscolored flesh,* see v. 10. Its reappearance indicates the disease has not yet healed; that is established only when the "raw" flesh again turns white and remains so. **18–23:** A boil that heals and is followed by a white swelling or a whitish-reddish mark is deemed on sight to be "tzara'at" if the two symptoms outlined in v. 20 are present. If they are not, a seven-day waiting period is observed, after which, if the condition has spread, it is pronounced "tzara'at"; otherwise the person is pronounced pure.

---

a Heb. *ṣaraʿath is used for a variety of diseases. Where a human being is declared unclean by reason of ṣaraʿath, the traditional translation "leprosy" has been retained without regard to modern medical terminology.*

b *See note a at 13.2.*

c-c *Others "quick raw flesh."*

priest finds that it appears lower than the rest of the skin and that the hair in it has turned white, the priest shall pronounce him unclean; it is a leprous affection that has broken out in the inflammation. ²¹ But if the priest finds that there is no white hair in it and it is not lower than the rest of the skin, and it is faded, the priest shall isolate him for seven days. ²² If it should spread in the skin, the priest shall pronounce him unclean; it is an affection. ²³ But if the discoloration remains stationary, not having spread, it is the scar of the inflammation; the priest shall pronounce him clean.

²⁴ When the skin of one's body sustains a burn by fire, and the patch from the burn is a discoloration, either white streaked with red, or white, ²⁵ the priest shall examine it. If some hair has turned white in the discoloration, which itself appears to go deeper than the skin, it is leprosy that has broken out in the burn. The priest shall pronounce him unclean; it is a leprous affection. ²⁶ But if the priest finds that there is no white hair in the discoloration, and that it is not lower than the rest of the skin, and it is faded, the priest shall isolate him for seven days. ²⁷ On the seventh day the priest shall examine him: if it has spread in the skin, the priest shall pronounce him unclean; it is a leprous affection. ²⁸ But if the discoloration has remained stationary, not having spread on the skin, and it is faded, it is the swelling from the burn. The priest shall pronounce him clean, for it is the scar of the burn.

²⁹ If a man or a woman has an affection on the head or in the beard, ³⁰ the priest shall examine the affection. If it appears to go deeper than the skin and there is thin yellow hair in it, the priest shall pronounce him unclean; it is a scall, a scaly eruption in the hair or beard. ³¹ But if the priest finds that the scall affection does not appear to go deeper than the skin, yet there is no black hair in it, the priest shall isolate the person with the scall affection for seven days. ³² On the seventh day the priest shall examine the affection. If the scall has not spread and no yellow hair has appeared in it, and the scall does not appear to go deeper than the skin, ³³ the person with the scall shall shave himself, but without shaving the scall; the priest shall isolate him for another seven days. ³⁴ On the seventh day the priest shall examine the scall. If the scall has not spread on the skin, and does not appear to go deeper than the skin, the priest shall pronounce him clean; he shall wash his clothes, and he shall be clean. ³⁵ If, however, the scall should spread on the skin after he has been pronounced clean, ³⁶ the priest shall examine him. If the scall has spread on the skin, the priest need not look for yellow

24–28: A *burn* displaying the symptoms is subjected to the same scrutiny and diagnostic procedure as boils (vv. 19–23). **29–37:** *On the head or in the beard,* i.e., on the scalp or in the flesh beneath the beard. A mark appearing here is immediately deemed "tzara'at" if it is a "scall" (Heb "netek," detachment), that is, hairs have become detached from their follicles, and both of the symptoms described in v. 30 are present. If they are not, the person is reexamined after a seven-day quarantine, after which, if both symptoms fail to appear and the condition has not spread, the procedures given in vv. 33–37 are carried out. The presence of yellow hair is not necessary to prove the presence of "tzara'at" if the condition has spread, but the presence of dark hair in the scall is a sure sign of healing.

hair: he is unclean. [37] But if the scall has remained unchanged in color, and black hair has grown in it, the scall is healed; he is clean. The priest shall pronounce him clean.

[38] If a man or a woman has the skin of the body streaked with white discolorations, [39] and the priest sees that the discolorations on the skin of the body are of a dull white, it is a tetter broken out on the skin; he is clean.

[40] If a man loses the hair of his head and becomes bald, he is clean. [41] If he loses the hair on the front part of his head and becomes bald at the forehead, he is clean. [42] But if a white affection streaked with red appears on the bald part in the front or at the back of the head, it is a scaly eruption that is spreading over the bald part in the front or at the back of the head. [43] The priest shall examine him: if the swollen affection on the bald part in the front or at the back of his head is white streaked with red, like the leprosy of body skin in appearance, [44] the man is leprous; he is unclean. The priest shall pronounce him unclean; he has the affection on his head.

[45] As for the person with a leprous affection, his clothes shall be rent, his head shall be left bare,[a] and he shall cover over his upper lip; and he shall call out, "Unclean! Unclean!" [46] He shall be unclean as long as the disease is on him. Being unclean, he shall dwell apart; his dwelling shall be outside the camp.

[47] When an eruptive affection occurs in a cloth of wool or linen fabric, [48] in the warp or in the woof of the linen or the wool, or in a skin or in anything made of skin; [49] if the affection in the cloth or the skin, in the warp or the woof, or in any article of skin, is streaky green[b] or red, it is an eruptive affection. It shall be shown to the priest; [50] and the priest, after examining the affection, shall isolate the affected article for seven days. [51] On the seventh day he shall examine the affection: if the affection has spread in the cloth—whether in the warp or the woof, or in the skin, for whatever purpose the skin may be used—the affection is a malignant eruption; it is unclean. [52] The cloth—whether warp or woof in wool or linen, or any article of skin—in which the affection is found, shall be burned, for it is a malignant eruption; it shall be consumed in fire. [53] But if the priest sees that the affection in the cloth—whether in warp or in woof, or in any article of skin—has not spread, [54] the priest shall order the affected article washed, and he shall isolate it for another seven days.

a See note at 10.6.
b Or "yellow."

38–39: *Streaked with white discolorations,* better, "shiny white marks." This supplements vv. 2–8, providing a method for determining if the mark is merely a "tetter" or white patch. **40–44:** Normal baldness is not a sign of "tzara'at." If, however, it is accompanied by the symptoms given in v. 43, it is immediately deemed to be "tzara'at" and no waiting period is required. **44–46:** These vv. detail the behavior required of the person found to have "tzara'at" of any type from the moment the diagnosis is certain until he or she is cured, after which the instructions given in ch 14 are followed. **45:** *His head shall be left bare,* better, "[the hair of] his head shall be disheveled"; this, together with the rending of garments, is a sign of mourning (see 10.6), appropriate for a person diagnosed with a disease equivalent to death itself. Covering of the upper lip was also a sign of mourning (see Ezek. 24.17, 22). *He shall call out, "Unclean! Unclean!"* to warn others that the impurity (not the disease) is contagious. **46:** *He shall dwell apart:* Since he remains removed from society, no details regarding how his impurity is transmitted to other persons and objects are given. Most likely the person with "tzara'at" also contaminates whatever is under the same roof; therefore he must dwell apart. His impurity also defiles the sacred, from afar, which is why he will need to perform expiation when he is able (see 14.19). *Outside the camp:* This refers to the wilderness period; in later periods, outside the city (see 2 Kings 7.3). **47–58:** Types of mildew or mold in fabrics that cause erosion and destruction were yet another manifestation of the same leakage of life-force that is the source of all impurity in P and are therefore also "tzara'at." As with humans, the fabric suspected of impurity is isolated for seven days; if the condition has spread the suspicion is confirmed. If not, the fabric is cleaned and isolated for seven more days. If the affection has not spread and has begun to clear up the fabric is pro-

55 And if, after the affected article has been washed, the priest sees that the affection has not changed color and that it has not spread, it is unclean. It shall be consumed in fire; it is a fret,[a] whether on its inner side or on its outer side. 56 But if the priest sees that the affected part, after it has been washed, is faded, he shall tear it out from the cloth or skin, whether in the warp or in the woof; 57 and if it occurs again in the cloth—whether in warp or in woof—or in any article of skin, it is a wild growth; the affected article shall be consumed in fire. 58 If, however, the affection disappears from the cloth—warp or woof—or from any article of skin that has been washed, it shall be washed again, and it shall be clean.

59 Such is the procedure for eruptive affections of cloth, woolen or linen, in warp or in woof, or of any article of skin, for pronouncing it clean or unclean.

METSORA'　　　　　　　　　　　　　　　מצרע

14 The LORD spoke to Moses, saying: 2 This shall be the ritual for a leper at the time that he is to be cleansed.

When it has been reported[b] to the priest, 3 the priest shall go outside the camp. If the priest sees that the leper has been healed of his scaly affection, 4 the priest shall order two live clean birds, cedar wood, crimson stuff, and hyssop to be brought for him who is to be cleansed. 5 The priest shall order one of the birds slaughtered over fresh water in an earthen vessel; 6 and he shall take the live bird, along with the cedar wood, the crimson stuff, and the hyssop, and dip them together with the live bird in the blood of the bird that was slaughtered over the fresh water. 7 He shall then sprinkle it seven times on him who is to be

a Meaning of Heb. peḥeteth uncertain.　　　b Cf. note a at 13.2.

nounced pure; otherwise it is deemed to have "tzaraʿat." Fabrics with confirmed cases cannot be "cured," and must be destroyed promptly; they cannot be purified through a ritual. This explains why these vv., which would perhaps read more naturally after 14.32, are placed here, before the laws prescribing the purification of persons and objects that have been cured. **55:** *Whether on its inner side or on its outer side,* Heb is identical to v. 42 "the bald part in the front or at the back of the head" and is translated appropriately to the context. Most likely these words

are a scribal error and should be deleted. **59:** *Procedure,* better, "instructions" (Heb "torat"; see 6.2). This summary caption refers only to vv. 47–58; the entire "tzaraʿat" section is summed up at 14.54–57. **14.1–32:** Resuming 13.46, these vv. prescribe the steps required of the person cured to dispose of the impurity he has created. Anthropologically and sociologically these rituals have been seen as rites of passage, marking the return of the outcast to normal life in human society and in God's presence. Rabbinic interpretation, which tended to view the person afflicted as

under divine sanction for wrongdoing, generally explained these rituals as acts of contrition, penance, and thanksgiving. In fact, however, they are for ridding the person and the environment of the impurity that has been generated, and the afflicted person is under no disapprobation unless he or she fails to carry them out. **2–3:** The process begins when the priest has examined the afflicted person and declared him cured. The cure itself is God's affair; the priest's task begins where God's ends. **2:** *This shall be the ritual for,* better, "these are the instructions concerning"; see 6.2. A *leper* (Heb "metzoraʿ," i.e., a person afflicted with "tzaraʿat"); see 13.3 and 13.1–14.57 n. **3–20:** The purification of the "metzoraʿ" and the expiation, in three stages. **3–7:** Stage one takes place outside the camp as soon as the priest pronounces the afflicted person cured. Its purpose is to rid the person of the impurity that has enveloped the physical body during the ailment. The purging agent is the blood of the first of two birds. This is the only instance in which purifying blood is applied to a human. The sprinkling of the reconstituted blood of the red heifer on the person contaminated by contact with a corpse (Num. ch 19) is the closest parallel and further indicates the close connection between "tzaraʿat" and death. The second bird is kept alive and set free to carry off the impurity, like the scapegoat on the annual Day of "Atonement" (or Purification); see ch 16. **4:** *Live,* i.e., wild birds, that live in the open country. *Clean birds,* see 11.13–19. *Cedar wood, crimson stuff,* agents of purification throughout biblical and ancient Near Eastern tradition. *Hyssop,* used for dipping and sprinkling, and therefore associated with purification (Ps. 51.9). **5:** *Over fresh water in an earthen vessel,* to dilute the substance, so that there is a sufficient quantity that may easily be sprinkled. **7:** The two birds are considered one entity. Thus the impurity, after being removed by the blood of the slaughtered bird, cleansed of the eruption and cleanse him; and he shall set the live bird free in the open country. 8 The one to be cleansed shall wash his clothes, shave off all his hair, and bathe in water; then he shall be clean. After that he may enter the camp, but he must remain outside his tent seven days. 9 On the seventh day he shall shave off all his hair— of head, beard, and eyebrows. When he has shaved off all his hair, he shall wash his clothes and bathe his body in water; then he shall be clean. 10 On the eighth day he shall take two male lambs without blemish, one ewe lamb in its first year without blemish, three-tenths of a measure of choice flour with oil mixed in for a meal offering, and one *log* of oil. 11 These shall be presented before the LORD, with the man to be cleansed, at the entrance of the Tent of Meeting, by the priest who performs the cleansing.

12 The priest shall take one of the male lambs and offer it with the *log* of oil as a guilt offering, and he shall elevate them as an elevation offering before the LORD. 13 The lamb shall be slaughtered at the spot in the sacred area where the sin offering and the burnt offering are slaughtered.ª For the guilt offering, like the sin offering, goes to the priest; it is most holy. 14 The priest shall take some of the blood of the guilt offering, and the priest shall put it on the ridge of the right ear of him who is being cleansed, and on the thumb of his right hand, and on the big toe of his right foot. 15 The priest shall then take some of the *log* of oil and pour it into the palm of his own left hand. 16 And the priest shall dip his right finger in the oil that is in the palm of his left hand and sprinkle some of the oil with his finger seven times before the LORD. 17 Some of the oil left in his palm shall be put by the priest on the ridge of the right ear of the one being cleansed, on the thumb of his right hand, and on the big toe of his right foot—over the blood of the guilt offering. 18 The rest of the oil in his palm the priest shall put on the head of the one being cleansed. Thus the priest shall make expiation for him before the LORD. 19 The priest shall then offer the sin offering and make expiation for the one being cleansed of his uncleanness. Last, the burnt offering shall be slaughtered, 20 and the priest shall offer the burnt offering and the meal offering on the altar, and the priest shall make expiation for him. Then he shall be clean.

21 If, however, he is poor and his means are insufficient, he shall take one male lamb for a guilt offering, to be elevated in expiation for him, one-tenth of a measure of choice flour with oil mixed in for a meal offering, and a *log*

is believed to be transferred to the second, live bird which is then dispatched, thereby permanently disposing of it. **8–9:** Stage two, on the seventh day, consists of the cleansing of the individual. That cleansing is not sufficient in itself, but must be preceded by the removal and disposal rituals and the lapse of a seven-day period, indicates the severity of this impurity. **10–20:** In stage three, on the eighth day, the "metzoraʿ" makes his offerings. **12:** *Guilt offering:* The presence of an "ʾasham" sacrifice (see 5.14–26), its prominence evidenced among other things by the elevation ritual, is a mystery, since being afflicted with "tzaraʿat" is not an obvious trespass against the sacred. One theory is that the "metzoraʿ" is under the strong presumption of having committed sacrilege; otherwise why would he have been stricken (see 2 Chron. 26.16–19)? Another possibility is that the inherent sanctity of the Israelite individual (see 19.2) has been compromised, though this would be unexpected in this portion of the book (see 19.1–37 n.). Perhaps the "ʾasham" is brought simply to provide blood for the final removal of residual impurity a week after the initial decontamination. **14–18:** The smearing of consecrated oil in addition to the blood of the "ʾasham" sacrifice apparently adds a measure of sanctification to the purification process. **19:** *Sin offering,* i.e., purification offering (see ch 4), by means of which the "metzoraʿ" rids the sacred sphere of the impurity that has accumulated there during the course of his illness. **20:** *The burnt offering and the meal offering:* These complete the full set of offerings by the "metzoraʿ." These acts of homage express rejoining the society of living Israelites engaged in the worship of the LORD. *Then he shall be clean:* This sums up the entire process; it does not mean that the offerings purify the person. **21–32:** The provisions for the healed "metzoraʿ" of modest means; see 5.7–13 n.; 12.8 n. Note that the "ʾasham" lamb (v. 12) is not reducible even in this

ª *See 1.11; 4.24.*

of oil; 22 and two turtledoves or two pigeons, depending on his means, the one to be the sin offering and the other the burnt offering. 23 On the eighth day of his cleansing he shall bring them to the priest at the entrance of the Tent of Meeting, before the LORD. 24 The priest shall take the lamb of guilt offering and the *log* of oil, and elevate them as an elevation offering before the LORD. 25 When the lamb of guilt offering has been slaughtered, the priest shall take some of the blood of the guilt offering and put it on the ridge of the right ear of the one being cleansed, on the thumb of his right hand, and on the big toe of his right foot. 26 The priest shall then pour some of the oil into the palm of his own left hand, 27 and with the finger of his right hand the priest shall sprinkle some of the oil that is in the palm of his left hand seven times before the LORD. 28 Some of the oil in his palm shall be put by the priest on the ridge of the right ear of the one being cleansed, on the thumb of his right hand, and on the big toe of his right foot, over the same places as the blood of the guilt offering; 29 and what is left of the oil in his palm the priest shall put on the head of the one being cleansed, to make expiation for him before the LORD. 30 He shall then offer one of the turtledoves or pigeons, depending on his means— 31 whichever he can afford—the one as a sin offering and the other as a burnt offering, together with the meal offering. Thus the priest shall make expiation before the LORD for the one being cleansed. 32 Such is the ritual for him who has a scaly affection and whose means for his cleansing are limited.

33 The LORD spoke to Moses and Aaron, saying:

34 When you enter the land of Canaan that I give you as a possession, and I inflict an eruptive plague upon a house in the land you possess, 35 the owner of the house shall come and tell the priest, saying, "Something like a plague has appeared upon my house." 36 The priest shall order the house cleared before the priest enters to examine the plague, so that nothing in the house may become unclean; after that the priest shall enter to examine the house. 37 If, when he examines the plague, the plague in the walls of the house is found to consist of greenish[a] or reddish streaks[b] that appear to go deep into the wall, 38 the priest shall come out of the house to the entrance of the house, and close up the house for seven days. 39 On the seventh day the priest shall return. If he sees that the plague has spread on the walls of the house, 40 the priest shall order the stones with the plague in them to be pulled out and

case (see v. 24). **33–53:** Mildew or rot in the walls of a house. Since the condition resembled "tzaraʿat" in humans, it was believed to be a manifestation of the same deadly leakage of life. *Greenish or reddish streaks . . . deep into the wall* (v. 37) are deemed on sight to be "tzaraʿat," but the measures taken depend on the reexamination of the house after a seven-day quarantine. If the condition has spread, the affected stones and plaster are removed and replaced. (If it has not spread, perhaps another week of quarantine follows; the text is silent.) If it returns, the house must be demolished and the materials disposed of, since the condition has pervaded the entire dwelling. Otherwise the "tzaraʿat" is determined to have run its course and the priest pronounces the house to be clean. To eradicate the impurity that has accumulated, a ritual similar to the first stage in the purification of the affected human (vv. 3–7) is performed (vv. 49–53). **36:** Once the priest determines that "tzaraʿat" is present, everything in the house susceptible to contamination will be declared impure. To prevent this, the house is cleared in advance and the foods and objects that have been removed remain under the presumption of purity. Rabbinic interpretation correctly recognized that this is designed to prevent undue economic hardship. **46–47:** The impurity is contagious during the week of quarantine. **53:** *Make expiation for,* Heb "kiper" is used anomalously here (see 16.1–34 n.) to refer to the decontamination of a person. No purification of the sacred sphere is prescribed, since if the "tzaraʿat" is deemed severe the house is destroyed before the impurity spreads to the sanctuary. **54–57:** Concluding subscription to chs 13–14. *Ritual,* better, "instructions"; see 6.2.

---

a Or "yellowish."   *b* Meaning of Heb. sheqaʿaruroth *uncertain.*

cast outside the city into an unclean place. [41] The house shall be scraped inside all around, and the coating[a] that is scraped off shall be dumped outside the city in an unclean place. [42] They shall take other stones and replace those stones with them, and take other coating and plaster the house.

[43] If the plague again breaks out in the house, after the stones have been pulled out and after the house has been scraped and replastered, [44] the priest shall come to examine: if the plague has spread in the house, it is a malignant eruption in the house; it is unclean. [45] The house shall be torn down—its stones and timber and all the coating on the house—and taken to an unclean place outside the city.

[46] Whoever enters the house while it is closed up shall be unclean until evening. [47] Whoever sleeps in the house must wash his clothes, and whoever eats in the house must wash his clothes.

[48] If, however, the priest comes and sees that the plague has not spread in the house after the house was replastered, the priest shall pronounce the house clean, for the plague has healed. [49] To purge the house, he shall take two birds, cedar wood, crimson stuff, and hyssop. [50] He shall slaughter the one bird over fresh water in an earthen vessel. [51] He shall take the cedar wood, the hyssop, the crimson stuff, and the live bird, and dip them in the blood of the slaughtered bird and the fresh water, and sprinkle on the house seven times. [52] Having purged the house with the blood of the bird, the fresh water, the live bird, the cedar wood, the hyssop, and the crimson stuff, [53] he shall set the live bird free outside the city in the open country. Thus he shall make expiation for the house, and it shall be clean.

[54] Such is the ritual for every eruptive affection—for scalls, [55] for an eruption on a cloth or a house, [56] for swellings, for rashes, or for discolorations—[57] to determine when they are unclean and when they are clean.

Such is the ritual concerning eruptions.

15 The LORD spoke to Moses and Aaron, saying: [2] Speak to the Israelite people and say to them:

When any man has a discharge issuing from his member,[b] he is unclean. [3] The uncleanness from his discharge shall mean the following—whether his member runs with the discharge or is stopped up so that there is no dis-

15.1–33: Impurity from bodily discharges. Concluding the laws of purification from bodily impurities, this ch deals with defilement caused by the flow of life fluids from the genital organs: semen, menstrual fluid, and the discharge accompanying gonorrhea or urethral infection. They are treated as facts of nature: some normal, some abnormal. The only sin connected with them is failure to purify oneself from them. The ch is arranged chiastically. Section (a) speaks of abnormal discharge from a male (vv. 2b–15) and parallels section (e), which speaks of abnormal discharge from a female (vv. 25–30). These are severe impurities; since they reach the sacred sphere, their bearers must make purification offerings to decontaminate the sanctuary after they have been cleansed. Section (b) speaks of normal discharge from a male, i.e., the emission of semen (vv. 16–17); this parallels section (d), which speaks of normal discharge from a female; i.e., menstruation (vv. 19–24). These are lesser impurities; they require only the cleansing of the individual which, if performed promptly, arrests any possible contamination of the sacred. At the center is section (c) (v. 18), which deals with the impurity contracted during sexual intercourse by both males and females. **1:** *Moses and Aaron*, see 11.1; 13.1. **2b–15:** Abnormal discharge in a male; the symptoms are consistent with urethral infections of various types and not only gonorrhea. In biblical times it was not known that these ailments are transmitted by sexual contact. **2:** *His member,* lit. "his flesh" (see translators' note b), a euphemism; see v. 19.

---

a Lit. "dust," "mud."   *b* Lit. "flesh."

charge, his uncleanness means this: ⁴Any bedding on which the one with the discharge lies shall be unclean, and every object on which he sits shall be unclean. ⁵Anyone who touches his bedding shall wash his clothes, bathe in water, and remain unclean until evening. ⁶Whoever sits on an object on which the one with the discharge has sat shall wash his clothes, bathe in water, and remain unclean until evening. ⁷Whoever touches the body of the one with the discharge shall wash his clothes, bathe in water, and remain unclean until evening. ⁸If one with a discharge spits on one who is clean, the latter shall wash his clothes, bathe in water, and remain unclean until evening. ⁹Any means for riding that one with a discharge has mounted shall be unclean; ¹⁰whoever touches anything that was under him shall be unclean until evening; and whoever carries such things shall wash his clothes, bathe in water, and remain unclean until evening. ¹¹If one with a discharge, without having rinsed his hands in water, touches another person, that person shall wash his clothes, bathe in water, and remain unclean until evening. ¹²An earthen vessel that one with a discharge touches shall be broken; and any wooden implement shall be rinsed with water.

¹³When one with a discharge becomes clean of his discharge, he shall count off seven days for his cleansing, wash his clothes, and bathe his body in fresh water; then he shall be clean. ¹⁴On the eighth day he shall take two turtledoves or two pigeons and come before the LORD at the entrance of the Tent of Meeting and give them to the priest. ¹⁵The priest shall offer them, the one as a sin offering and the other as a burnt offering. Thus the priest shall make expiation on his behalf, for his discharge, before the LORD.

¹⁶When a man has an emission of semen, he shall bathe his whole body in water and remain unclean until evening. ¹⁷All cloth or leather on which semen falls shall be washed in water and remain unclean until evening. ¹⁸And if a man has carnal relations with a woman, they shall bathe in water and remain unclean until evening.

¹⁹When a woman has a discharge, her discharge being

self of it. **11:** *Touches another person,* i.e., with his hands (which have probably come into contact with his genitals). *Without having rinsed his hands in water:* In rabbinic law this too was taken to mean immersion, thus equating it with the washing required in the preceding cases. **12:** See 11.31–35. **13–15:** The impurity is severe; thus it lasts for seven days after the condition has passed, after which the final cleansing of the man takes place. Then, when he is finally rid of his impurity and may approach the divine abode, the "ḥaṭa't" is offered and the sacred area decontaminated. **14:** *Two turtledoves or two pigeons,* see 5.7–10 n.; 12.8 n. Here, however, the two birds are prescribed for all, not just for those too poor to offer livestock; for the reason, see v. 29 n. **16–17:** See also Deut. 23.10–12; 1 Sam. 20.26; here, however, the law is not restricted to involuntary nocturnal emission. The emission of semen per se, deliberate or accidental, during intercourse or not, creates a minor impurity which, after cleansing, is gone by nightfall. **17:** Being minor, this impurity is not communicated to others by contact, but it is communicated to objects (and perhaps persons too) if the semen itself touches them. **18:** As a function of the previous section and serving as a transition to the next. Sexual intercourse defiles both participants; their impurity, after cleansing, lasts until nightfall. **19–24:** The menstruant. According to this ch, everyday nonsexual contact with the menstruating woman merely confers a minor impurity which, after cleansing, dissipates by nightfall. Even sexual intercourse with the menstruant is not forbidden; although it communicates a more severe impurity lasting seven days (v. 24), if the necessary purification takes place no sin has been committed. Thus the law in 18.19, forbidding sexual relations with a menstruant on pain of "karet" (see 7.20), directly contradicts this ch. Jewish tradition not only accepted the stricter view, forbidding intercourse with the menstruant, but

4–12: The communication of impurity by direct or indirect contact. The details provided here and in vv. 19–27 are given in this ch only, to be applied by appropriate analogy in other cases of bodily impurity of similar degree; see, e.g., 12.2 and 13.46 n. Secondary impurity is less severe than that borne by the affected person himself; after washing (traditionally understood

to mean immersion) and laundering it dissipates by nightfall and does not spread to the sacred sphere. It is taken for granted that contact with impure persons will occur in the normal course of everyday life. Unclean individuals are not "off limits," but since contact with them communicates minor impurity, the necessary measures must be taken to rid one-blood from her body, she shall remain in her impurity seven days; whoever touches her shall be unclean until evening. 20 Anything that she lies on during her impurity shall be unclean; and anything that she sits on shall be unclean. 21 Anyone who touches her bedding shall wash his clothes, bathe in water, and remain unclean until evening; 22 and anyone who touches any object on which she has sat shall wash his clothes, bathe in water, and remain unclean until evening. 23 Be it the bedding or be it the object on which she has sat, on touching it he shall be unclean until evening. 24 And if a man lies with her, her impurity is communicated to him; he shall be unclean seven days, and any bedding on which he lies shall become unclean.

25 When a woman has had a discharge of blood for many days, not at the time of her impurity, or when she has a discharge beyond her period of impurity, she shall be unclean, as though at the time of her impurity, as long as her discharge lasts. 26 Any bedding on which she lies while her discharge lasts shall be for her like bedding during her impurity; and any object on which she sits shall become unclean, as it does during her impurity: 27 whoever touches them shall be unclean; he shall wash his clothes, bathe in water, and remain unclean until evening.

28 When she becomes clean of her discharge, she shall count off seven days, and after that she shall be clean. 29 On the eighth day she shall take two turtledoves or two pigeons, and bring them to the priest at the entrance of the Tent of Meeting. 30 The priest shall offer the one as a sin offering and the other as a burnt offering; and the priest shall make expiation on her behalf, for her unclean discharge, before the LORD.

31 You shall put the Israelites on guard against their uncleanness, lest they die through their uncleanness by defiling My Tabernacle which is among them.

32 Such is the ritual concerning him who has a discharge: concerning him who has an emission of semen and becomes unclean thereby, 33 and concerning her who is in menstrual infirmity, and concerning anyone, male or female, who has a discharge, and concerning a man who lies with an unclean woman.

ʾAḤAREI MOT   אחרי מות

16 The LORD spoke to Moses after the death of the two sons of Aaron who died when they drew too close to the presence of the LORD. 2 The LORD said to Moses:

Tell your brother Aaron that he is not to come at will[a]

---

a Lit. "at any time."

interpreted the latter law in such a way as to prohibit other forms of physical contact with her as well. The need to comply with 18.19 led to the survival of the laws restricting marital relations to the days between menstrual cycles, forbidding physical contact with menstruating women and requiring the monthly immersion of the wife ("tohorat hamishpaḥah") in Jewish law. The case is unique among the purification laws in the Bible, virtually all of which fell into disuse after the destruction of the Temple. **19:** *Blood,* menstrual fluid was thought to be blood. *Body,* a euphemism; see v. 2. *Seven days,* approximating the maximum number of days each month during which most women menstruate. Rabbinic law, however, on the analogy of v. 28, determined that the seven "clean" days commence after the actual flow has ceased. **25–30:** Paralleling 2b–15, above, but taking into account a second possibility as well: menstrual flow that lasts beyond its normal duration. **29:** The inexpensive animals are prescribed since prolonged menstrual flow or irregular discharges are relatively frequent, so requiring livestock would impose economic hardship and the purification of the sanctuary would be neglected. By simple analogy birds are prescribed for males as well in v. 14. **31:** The rationale for all of the purification laws in P; see chs 12–15 n. *Lest they die through their uncleanness:* The "death" is the collective destruction of Israel *by defiling My Tabernacle which is among them.* Failing to eradicate defilement causes it to collect in the divine abode, leading to its abandonment by the deity. See also 16.16; Num. 5.3; 19.13, 20. Rabbinic tradition reinterpreted this and similar passages to mean that the divine abode would be defiled only if the unclean person entered it; thus it severed the laws of purification from their biblical moorings.

16.1–34: Purging the Tabernacle annually. The preceding chs have established that sins and bodily into the Shrine behind the curtain, in front of the cover that is upon the ark, lest he die; for I appear in the cloud over the cover. ³ Thus only shall Aaron enter the Shrine: with a bull of the herd for a sin offering and a ram for a burnt offering.—⁴ He shall be dressed in a sacral linen tunic, with linen breeches next to his flesh, and be girt with a linen sash, and he shall wear a linen turban. They are sacral vestments; he shall bathe his body in water and then put them on.—⁵ And from the Israelite community he shall take two he-goats for a sin offering and a ram for a burnt offering.

⁶ Aaron is to offer his own bull of sin offering, to make expiation for himself and for his household. ⁷ Aaronᵃ shall take the two he-goats and let them stand before the Lord

---

a Moved up from v. 8 for clarity.

---

impurities contaminate the Tabernacle. Regular atonement for unintentional sin and the routine eradication of impurity eliminate as much of both types of defilement as possible. Yet, since not all unintentional wrongs are discovered and not everyone is diligent about atonement, a certain amount of defilement remains. In particular, deliberate crimes, which contaminate the inner sanctum where the divine Presence itself is said to dwell, are not expurgated by the regular atonement rituals. This ch thus provides the instructions for purging the inner sanctum along with the rest of the Tabernacle once a year, so that defilement does not accumulate. It logically follows the laws of purification (chs 12–15), as they conclude with the statement that only by preventing the spread of impurity can the Israelites ensure God's continual presence among them (15.31). The annual purification ritual, briefly alluded to in Exod. 30.10, is to be performed on the tenth day of the seventh month (v. 29). Elsewhere (23.27, 28; 25.9) this day is referred to as "yom hakippurim"—often translated as "Day of Atonement," with the verb "kiper," "atone," being used in the sense of "decontaminate [the sacred precincts] of sin or defilement" (see 1.4; 4.1–5.26 n.). This day is found only in the Priestly

calendar of sacred times (23.26–32; see also Num. 29.7–11). Sanctuary purification rites are known in the ancient Near East outside of Israel. The biblical Day of Atonement, while unique in its conceptual and ritual complexity and in its nondemonic view of defilement, shares with them the specific ritual aim of decontaminating the sanctuary. It also, however, brings about a sort of purification of the Israelite people, since the thorough eradication and disposal of their sins and impurities serves as a personal and communal catharsis. Further, the people have a role in the process: vv. 29–34a prescribe that they must observe a fast and a cessation of labor. The Israelites emerge from this day secure in the knowledge that the equilibrium in their relationship with God has been restored and "all is forgiven." This too is expressed by the text: "For on this day atonement shall be made for you to cleanse you of all your sins; you shall be clean before the Lord" (v. 30). Long after the original notion that God threatened to abandon His people if His abode became impure had receded, the Day of Atonement, as an annual occasion for repentance and forgiveness, continued to have crucial importance. Even since the destruction of the Temple, when fasting, prayer, and penitence are all that survive of the day's ritual,

it has remained a central feature of the liturgical year in Jewish tradition. **1:** *After the death of the two sons of Aaron,* related in 10.1–2. Some have assumed a connection between the offense of Aaron's sons and the annual purgation, suggesting either that the priest is cautioned not to repeat their actions or that the purgation was necessitated by their deaths or their dire sins. But the narrator probably means that this ch was actually imparted to Moses immediately after Revelation Day, while chs 11–15, conveyed to Moses later in the month, have been placed here so that the reader may correctly grasp what is meant by "the uncleanness . . . of the Israelites" in v. 16 and understand why the Tabernacle needs to be purged (see 16.1–34 n.). **2:** *At will,* lit. "at any time." Only once a year may Aaron or his successor enter the inner sanctum. *The Shrine behind the curtain, in front of the cover that is upon the ark,* the inner sanctum, known as the "holy of holies" and here called "haqodesh," "the holy place." *Lest he die; for I appear in the cloud over the cover:* How Aaron is to avoid death when purging the inner sanctum is explained in vv. 12–13. **3–22:** The thorough purification of the Tabernacle, focusing on the inner sanctum. **4:** Since the tasks to be performed on Purification Day are for purgation, not for worship, the priest is to remove the vestments worn for the daily service and to don simple linen garments, which, when soiled by the sprinkling of blood, are easily laundered. **5–22:** The ritual includes the following components: (a) a slaughtered *bull,* to serve as a purification offering on behalf of the high priest and his household (cf. 4.3–12); (b) a slaughtered *goat* to serve as a purification offering on behalf of the Israelite people; (c) a live *goat,* to carry away the transgressions of the Israelites to the wilderness; (d) two burnt offerings, one on Aaron's own behalf and the other on behalf of the people. **7–10:** The use of the two goats is similar to that of the two birds in 14.4–7, 49–53. The lottery deter-at the entrance of the Tent of Meeting; [8] and he shall place lots upon the two goats, one marked for the LORD and the other marked for Azazel. [9] Aaron shall bring forward the goat designated by lot for the LORD, which he is to offer as a sin offering; [10] while the goat designated by lot for Azazel shall be left standing alive before the LORD, to make expiation with it and to send it off to the wilderness for Azazel.

[11] Aaron shall then offer his bull of sin offering, to make expiation for himself and his household. He shall slaughter his bull of sin offering, [12] and he shall take a panful of glowing coals scooped from the altar before the LORD, and two handfuls of finely ground aromatic incense, and bring this behind the curtain. [13] He shall put the incense on the fire before the LORD, so that the cloud from the incense screens the cover that is over [the Ark of] the Pact, lest he die. [14] He shall take some of the blood of the bull and sprinkle it with his finger over the cover on the east side; and in front of the cover he shall sprinkle some of the blood with his finger seven times. [15] He shall then slaughter the people's goat of sin offering, bring its blood behind the curtain, and do with its blood as he has done with the blood of the bull: he shall sprinkle it over the cover and in front of the cover.

[16] Thus he shall purge the Shrine of the uncleanness and transgression of the Israelites, whatever their sins; and he shall do the same for the Tent of Meeting, which abides with them in the midst of their uncleanness. [17] When he goes in to make expiation in the Shrine, nobody else shall be in the Tent of Meeting until he comes out.

When he has made expiation for himself and his household, and for the whole congregation of Israel, [18] he shall go out to the altar that is before the LORD and purge it: he shall take some of the blood of the bull and of the goat and apply it to each of the horns of the altar; [19] and the rest of the blood he shall sprinkle on it with his finger seven

Ark of] the Pact, the platform upon which the two winged cherubs stand, serving as a throne for the divine Presence which hovers above it (Exod. 25.10–22). The incense is placed on the coals to create a cloud of smoke, preventing Aaron from viewing the deity. The blood is sprinkled in front of the throne and behind it, purging the area most vulnerable to contamination. **15–16a:** Aaron's second entry into the inner sanctum, to expiate for the transgressions and impurities of the people. The blood of the goat is sprinkled in the same way as that of the bull. **16:** *Of the uncleanness:* A better translation is "of the impurities of the Israelites and, among all their sins, of their deliberate transgressions"; see v. 22 n. **16b:** The cleansing of the inner sanctum is followed by the purification of the outer sanctum. Probably the procedure in 4.6–7a and 4.17–18a is intended, performed first with the blood of the bull and then with that of the goat. *The Tent . . . abides,* better, "the Tent of Meeting of the One who abides." **17:** The first half of the v. confirms that in the outer sanctum too Aaron is to be alone (translate "the holy place" instead of *the Shrine*); the second half sums up the cleansing of the Tabernacle. **18–19a:** The next step: purging the altar. *The altar that is before the LORD:* Rabbinic interpretation took this to mean the incense altar located in the inner sanctum. The words *he shall go out* would thus refer to Aaron's exiting the inner sanctum. But the v. would then be out of place, and the summary vv. 20 and 33 distinguish between the inner sanctum, the outer sanctum, and the altar. It is preferable to explain *he shall go out* as meaning "he shall exit the Tent of Meeting." The altar is the sacrificial altar that stood in the courtyard, the purgation of the incense altar having been accomplished already (see v. 16b). **19:** *And consecrate it:* The translation reflects the rabbinic midrash, according to which the altar was not only purged but reconsecrated for the coming year, but the word "vekidesho" stands

mines at random how each goat is to be used. **8:** *Azazel:* The Rabbis cleverly divided this name into two words "'ez 'azel," "the goat that goes away," from which the traditional "scapegoat" is derived. It literally means "fierce god" and as intimated by the medieval exegete Abraham Ibn Ezra is evidently the name of a demon or deity believed to inhabit the wilderness. Thus the sins of the people are symbolically cast into the realm beyond civilization, to

become the property of a being who is the antithesis of the God of Israel. Though Azazel accepts the goat bearing Israel's sins as a sacrifice to him, this is no disloyalty to God since He Himself commands it, as Naḥmanides (Ramban) says: It is as though a king ordered "Give a portion [of this feast] to my servant so-and-so." **11–14:** Aaron's first entry into the inner sanctum, to expiate for his own transgressions and impurities. **13:** *The cover that is over [the* times. Thus he shall cleanse it of the uncleanness of the Israelites and consecrate it.

20 When he has finished purging the Shrine, the Tent of Meeting, and the altar, the live goat shall be brought forward. 21 Aaron shall lay both his hands upon the head of the live goat and confess over it all the iniquities and transgressions of the Israelites, whatever their sins, putting them on the head of the goat; and it shall be sent off to the wilderness through a designated[a] man. 22 Thus the goat shall carry on it all their iniquities to an inaccessible region; and the goat shall be set free in the wilderness.

23 And Aaron shall go into the Tent of Meeting, take off the linen vestments that he put on when he entered the Shrine, and leave them there. 24 He shall bathe his body in water in the holy precinct and put on his vestments; then he shall come out and offer his burnt offering and the burnt offering of the people, making expiation for himself and for the people. 25 The fat of the sin offering he shall turn into smoke on the altar.

26 He who set the Azazel-goat free shall wash his clothes and bathe his body in water; after that he may reenter the camp.

27 The bull of sin offering and the goat of sin offering whose blood was brought in to purge the Shrine shall be taken outside the camp; and their hides, flesh, and dung shall be consumed in fire. 28 He who burned them shall wash his clothes and bathe his body in water; after that he may re-enter the camp.

29 And this shall be to you a law for all time: In the seventh month, on the tenth day of the month, you shall practice self-denial; and you shall do no manner of work, neither the citizen nor the alien who resides among you. 30 For on this day atonement shall be made for you to cleanse you of all your sins; you shall be clean before the

a Meaning of Heb. ʿitti uncertain.

___

before of the uncleanness of the Israelites and means "and purge it." 20–22: Having removed the impure material from the inner and outer sanctums, Aaron now transfers it to the live goat for dispatch to the wilderness. The transfer is accomplished by placing both hands on the goat's head and making verbal declaration of the people's sins. Rabbinic law, reinterpreting the term "vekiper," "he shall make expiation" in vv. 6 and 11, added two more confes-sions to the Day of Atonement ritual. 21: Lay both his hands: Elsewhere single-hand leaning (e.g., 1.4) reflects designation of an animal; the gesture here is one of transfer to the animal. 22: All their iniquities, rather, "all the intentional sins and deliberate transgressions of the Israelites among all their sins." The impurities (see v. 16) have disappeared, eradicated by the blood of the "ḥataʾt" offerings. Deliberate sins, however, are indestructible; they can

only be sent away, in the hope that they may never return. The idea is that intentional acts of wrongdoing, once committed, can never really be undone. 23–28: The remaining offerings, the cleansing of Aaron, the removal of the contaminated garments, the disposal of the flesh, and the purification of those who have become secondarily defiled as a result of their roles in the ritual. 29–34a: The rituals are to be performed on a specific date, annually, in perpetuity, by Aaron's successors in the high priesthood, accompanied by a community-wide fast and cessation of labor, observed by citizen and alien alike (see 23.26–32). 29: Practice self-denial, lit. "deprive your throats," i.e., fast (see Isa. 58.3, 5). The translation reflects the halakhic midrash, according to which "nefesh" is used in the sense of "self"; based on this the Rabbis decreed additional forms of self-affliction besides the abstinence from food and drink indicated explicitly by the text. Citizen, Heb "ʾezraḥ," "native," referring to the Israelite born in the land of Israel of bona fide Israelite ancestry. The alien who resides among you: The "ger," or resident alien, is a person of non-Israelite ancestry residing more or less permanently in the land of Israel. He is not considered a descendant of the Canaanite peoples, since they are believed to have been evacuated (see 18.24–30). Rabbinic tradition understands the "ger" as a proselyte or convert, but this is anachronistic; neither religious conversion nor gradual assimilation is contemplated anywhere in P. Laws pertaining to the "ger" appear throughout the remaining chs of Leviticus and elsewhere in the Priestly law; see, e.g., 17.8, 10, 12, 15; 18.26; 19.33–36; 24.16 n.; 25.47–54 n. The "ger" is not required to worship Israel's God but may do so voluntarily; thus the "ger" is not obligated to observe the performative commands, but must comply with all prohibitions, and must observe the laws of fairness and justice (see 24.17–22). The Israelite must refrain from op-

LORD. 31 It shall be a sabbath of complete rest for you, and you shall practice self-denial; it is a law for all time. 32 The priest who has been anointed and ordained to serve as priest in place of his father shall make expiation. He shall put on the linen vestments, the sacral vestments. 33 He shall purge the innermost Shrine; he shall purge the Tent of Meeting and the altar; and he shall make expiation for the priests and for all the people of the congregation.

34 This shall be to you a law for all time: to make atonement for the Israelites for all their sins once a year.

And Moses did as the LORD had commanded him.

17 The LORD spoke to Moses, saying: 2 Speak to Aaron and his sons and to all the Israelite people and say to them:

This is what the LORD has commanded: 3 if anyone of the house of Israel slaughters an ox or sheep or goat in the

commands what was only implicit in the earlier stratum of P, namely, that Israel's compliance with God's expectations in these areas impinges on the sacred no less than the maintenance of the institutions of worship. Among the unique characteristics of H are its distinct rationale for the blood prohibition (see 17.10–12), its peculiar understanding of sacrificial atonement (17.11), its strict prohibition of sexual relations with the menstruating woman (18.19), the new meaning it instills into the concept of impurity (18.24–30), its incorporation of popular ritual into the observance of the holy days (23.1–44), its detailed exploration of the full ramifications of God's lordship over His people and land (25.1–55), and its explicit historicization of the Priestly promise of divine indwelling and threat of divine abandonment (26.3–45).

pressing or exploiting the "ger." **31:** *A sabbath of complete rest for you,* see 23.30 n.

Chs 17–26. Scholars agree that chs 17–26, along with some other passages in Leviticus and elsewhere in P, belong to a literary stratum distinct from the remainder of the Priestly work. Although this section is not structurally differentiated from the rest, and does echo and supplement the ritual and sacral regulations in P in many ways, on substantive and stylistic grounds it appears to have been composed by Priestly authors other than those responsible for the remainder of P. Its most characteristic feature is a concern for holiness. Throughout Priestly thought, holiness is conceived of as an effervescence of the Presence of the LORD. It infuses everything with which it comes into contact (see 6.11; 8.10–13), transforming it into the designated "personal" property of the deity. In these chs we hear for the first time that holiness is not confined to the realm of the Tabernacle and priesthood; rather, the Israelite people as a whole can and must attain holiness (chs 19–20). This section also contains legislation concerning the holiness of the priests and of sacred offerings (chs 21–22), the an-

nual festivals, here called holy times (ch 23), the holiness of the name of God (ch 24), and the holiness of the fiftieth year (ch 25). Implied also is the holiness of the land of Israel (chs 18 and 26). Holiness as the all-encompassing theme of these chs has given them their name, the Holiness Legislation (or Holiness Code or Collection), or H. While earlier critics believed H to be more ancient than P, many scholars now think that H was added to, and is therefore probably later than, the kernel of the Priestly document. If so, the addition of the Holiness Collection to the preexisting Priestly document marks an important development in Priestly tradition and thought. The earlier Priestly work reflects the idea that the commandments given by God to the Israelites at Sinai were concerned solely with worship and the maintenance of the purity of the divine abode; all else was a matter of universal morality but not the stuff of divine legislation for Israel. The H chs constitute a transformation; they claim that the laws given to Israel at Sinai included civil and criminal legislation and pertained to every sphere of interpersonal relationships and social behavior as well as ritual activity. H thereby makes explicit through specific

17.1–16: Slaughter and blood. Three laws are communicated to Moses: the prohibition of common, or "profane," slaughter of domestic livestock (vv. 3–7), the prohibition of sacrifice outside of the Tabernacle (vv. 8–9), and the prohibition of "eating" any blood (vv. 10–12). The third law draws in its wake two corollaries: the requirement to drain the blood of wild animals killed for food (vv. 13–14), and the need to dispose of the impurity one contracts from eating carrion (vv. 15–16). All five sections are thus concerned with proper disposal of the blood of slain animals. They derive from P's view of the commands given to Noah and his descendants in Gen. 9.1–7 (see 11.1–47 n.), and they supplement the laws of sacrifice in chs 1–7, the dietary laws given in ch 11, and the laws of purification given in chs 12–15. **2:** *To Aaron and his sons and to all the Israelite people:* As the laws commanded here require specific activity on the part of the priests, Aaron and his sons are singled out, but the laws in the ch apply to the people as a whole. **3–4:** *Ox or sheep or goat:* Since animals from the herd camp, or does so outside the camp, [4] and does not bring it to the entrance of the Tent of Meeting to present it as an offering to the LORD, before the LORD's Tabernacle, bloodguilt shall be imputed to that man: he has shed blood; that man shall be cut off from among his people. [5] This is in order that the Israelites may bring the sacrifices which they have been making in the open—that they may bring them before the LORD, to the priest, at the entrance of the Tent of Meeting, and offer them as sacrifices of well-being to the LORD; [6] that the priest may dash the blood against the altar of the LORD at the entrance of the Tent of Meeting, and turn the fat into smoke as a pleasing odor to the LORD; [7] and that they may offer their sacrifices no more to the goat-demons after whom they stray. This shall be to them a law for all time, throughout the ages.

[8] Say to them further: If anyone of the house of Israel or of the strangers who reside among them offers a burnt offering or a sacrifice, [9] and does not bring it to the entrance of the Tent of Meeting to offer it to the LORD, that person shall be cut off from his people.

[10] And if anyone of the house of Israel or of the strangers who reside among them partakes of any blood, I will set My face against the person who partakes of the blood, and I will cut him off from among his kin. [11] For the life of the flesh is in the blood, and I have assigned it to you for making expiation for your lives upon the altar; it is the blood, as life, that effects expiation. [12] Therefore I say

mons thought to inhabit the open fields and desolate regions. Now that the Tabernacle cult is established, any further activity of this sort is an unpardonable sin. *A law for all time, throughout the ages:* The law is thus irreconcilable with that in Deut. 12.15, 20–27, according to which, after the Temple is built, it will become permissible to slaughter and eat livestock anywhere without making an offering. Though the law in H seems oppressive, it may not be entirely utopian. It imposes no restriction on the consumption of permitted nondomestic livestock (see 11.1–8), fowl, fish, or flying creatures (11.9–23). It is also conceivable that blemished sheep and cattle, not fit for the altar (22.21–24), might be slaughtered for food. The law in Deuteronomy ultimately became normative in Judaism. **8–9:** Having established that all domestic livestock may be consumed only after having been presented as "shelamim" offerings, the law commands that all offerings must be made at the Tabernacle; anyone presenting a sacrifice elsewhere is threatened with the "karet" penalty (see 7.20–21). The Priestly legislator clearly has in mind a single legitimate sanctuary, agreeing with Deut. ch 12 in its demand that all sacrificial worship be centralized in one location, but disagreeing on whether nonsacrificial slaughter may be practiced after the centralization has been accomplished. **8:** *The strangers who reside among them,* Heb "ger" ("resident alien"); see 16.29. **10–12:** The blood prohibition. See Gen. 9.4; Lev. 3.17; 7.26–27. Deuteronomy also records this prohibition (Deut. 12.16, 23–24; 15.23). H offers its peculiar rationale for this law (see vv. 11-12 n.). **10:** *Partakes of any blood,* lit. "eats" any blood. The act referred to is that of eating meat without first draining the blood. *I will set My face,* I will give it My personal, undivided and immediate attention (26.17). For this phrase, along with the active form of the threat of "karet" (see 7.20–21), both characteristic of H, see 20.3, 5, 6; cf. 23.30. **11–12:** H's

and flock are fit for the altar, they are considered as belonging to God. Thus, according to this law, the Israelites may not simply slaughter domestic livestock for food; they are required to offer them as a sacrifice of well-being ("shelamim"; see 3.1–17 and 7.11–34), after which they may partake of the offerers' share of the flesh. **4:** *Bloodguilt . . . he has shed blood:* In P's view, until the time of the flood it was a capital crime to shed the blood of any animal; thereafter it was permissible as long as the blood was not ingested (Gen. 9.3–4). Now that the Tabernacle has been erected, Israelites may slay sheep and cattle for food only as well-being offerings; if they fail to present the animal as an offering, it is as if they had slain the animal in the antediluvian period when such an act was considered murder. *Shall be cut off,* see

7.20–21. **5–7:** These three vv. are spoken only for Moses' ears, and they provide the actual rationale for the prohibition. **5:** *The sacrifices . . . in the open:* This rests on the Priestly belief that the worship of the LORD began with the establishment of the Israelite cult at Sinai and until then the LORD was never worshipped. (The stories of sacrifices in Genesis and the first part of Exodus—such as those offered by Cain and Abel, by Noah after the flood and by the patriarchs— all belong to the non-Priestly material.) Heretofore, any slaughter of domestic livestock has been meaningless, "in the open"—in the Rabbis' phrase, "profane" or common slaughter. **7:** *That they may offer their sacrifices no more to the goat-demons:* Conceptually, however, the nonsacrificial slaughter of domestic livestock actually is a sacrifice—not to God but to the de-to the Israelite people: No person among you shall partake of blood, nor shall the stranger who resides among you partake of blood.

13 And if any Israelite or any stranger who resides among them hunts down an animal or a bird that may be eaten, he shall pour out its blood and cover it with earth. 14 For the life of all flesh—its blood is its life. Therefore I say to the Israelite people: You shall not partake of the blood of any flesh, for the life of all flesh is its blood. Anyone who partakes of it shall be cut off.

15 Any person, whether citizen or stranger, who eats what has died or has been torn by beasts shall wash his clothes, bathe in water, and remain unclean until evening; then he shall be clean. 16 But if he does not wash [his clothes] and bathe his body, he shall bear his guilt.

18 The Lord spoke to Moses, saying: 2 Speak to the Israelite people and say to them:
I the Lord am your God. 3 You shall not copy the prac-

unique rationale for the blood prohibition (intended like vv. 5–7 for Moses' ears alone) differs from that implied in 3.17 and 7.26–27, where blood, like suet, is God's food. It differs too from that given in Deut. 12.16, 23–24, where ingesting the animal's meat along with its "life" is inherently improper. Here, since the blood of sacrificial offerings has been assigned to the altar as ransom (see below), the blood of all flesh is strictly forbidden. **11:** *The life of the flesh is in the blood:* Since loss of blood brings about swift death, it would be natural to assume that the life-force (Heb "nefesh," lit. "gullet" but often figuratively "life-force") is contained in the blood. *For making expiation for your lives,* better, "to serve as ransom for your lives"; see 1.4 n. This too is unique to H; sacrificial atonement is not the decontamination of the sacred precincts but rather a symbolic payment in exchange for one's life which would otherwise be forfeit. **13–14:** In order to prevent the ingestion of the blood of nondomestic quadrupeds (which may be eaten if they conform to the stipulations of 11.3) and fowl (those not listed in 11.13–19), which would presumably be

hunted, the Israelite is commanded to drain out the blood on the ground. *Cover it with earth:* Jewish tradition viewed this as a command in its own right; some interpreters saw it as a symbolic way of returning the "life" of the animal, i.e., its blood, to God. But the explicit reason for the draining and covering of the blood is to prevent its being eaten. **15–16:** As mentioned in 7.24, permitted animals that have not been slaughtered as sacrifice but rather have died of themselves ("nevelah") or were killed by beasts ("terefah") may be eaten, although, as stated in 11.40, impurity results. This law is repeated here because it is an exception to the blood prohibition. When the blood of a permitted animal has cooled and coagulated within it, it no longer contains the animal's "nefesh" (see v. 11) and may be eaten. In opposition, the non-Priestly law collections prohibit the eating of "nevelah" (Deut. 14.21) and "terefah" (Exod. 22.30). The opposing views share the idea that refraining from "nevelah" and "terefah" is a mark of sanctity. Since according to the non-Priestly sources all Israelites are on an equal plane of sanctity, all must avoid "nevelah" and

"terefah." In P, only priests are so commanded (22.8), while lay Israelites are not. This opinion is held by Ezekiel as well (Ezek. 44.31). In the Priestly view, there are different grades of holiness and only the priests, who belong to the innermost sphere of sanctity, must observe the restriction. Rabbinic law accepts the stricter view, and even uses the term "terefah" as a general designation for all prohibited ("nonkosher") food. **15:** *Citizen or stranger,* see 16.29.

18.1–30: The Abominations of the Canaanites. A list of prohibited sexual unions (vv. 6–23), including incestuous relationships (vv. 6–18), and the prohibition of sacrificing children to Molech (v. 21). These laws, rather than merely being proclaimed, are presented as part of a speech warning the Israelites not to practice the "abominations" characteristic of the peoples of Egypt and Canaan lest they suffer their dire fate. H thus conveys the idea that refraining from forbidden sexual practices and child sacrifice, no less than the scrupulous maintenance of the purity of the divine abode as emphasized by the earlier part of P, is the key to Israel's national survival in its land. This ch is read in the synagogue at the afternoon service on the Day of Atonement, a practice for which various interpretations have been suggested. **2–5:** The introductory vv. lay the groundwork for what will follow. To survive, Israel must shun the practices of Egypt and Canaan and adhere only to God's commands. **2:** *I the Lord am your God,* better, "I am the Lord your God" (or "I am Yhvh your God"). This formula (with variations) is one of the hallmarks of H's style; here it sets up the contrast between "My rules/ laws" and those of Egypt and Canaan. **3:** *The practices of the land of Egypt . . . or of the land of Canaan:* The Egyptians and Canaanites are characterized in biblical tradition, particularly P, by rampant sexual licentiousness and perversion. This, however, does not emerge from Canaanite and Egyptian litertices of the land of Egypt where you dwelt, or of the land of Canaan to which I am taking you; nor shall you follow their laws. 4 My rules alone shall you observe, and faithfully follow My laws: I the LORD am your God.

5 You shall keep My laws and My rules, by the pursuit of which man shall live: I am the LORD.

6 None of you shall come near anyone of his own flesh to uncover nakedness: I am the LORD.

7 a-Your father's nakedness, that is, the nakedness of your mother, you shall not uncover; she is your mother— you shall not uncover her nakedness.

8 Do not uncover the nakedness of your father's wife;-a it is the nakedness of your father.

9 The nakedness of your sister—your father's daughter or your mother's, whether born into the household or out-side—do not uncover their nakedness.

10 The nakedness of your son's daughter, or of your daughter's daughter—do not uncover their nakedness; for their nakedness is yours.b

11 The nakedness of your father's wife's daughter, who

---

a-a A man and his wife are one flesh (Gen. 2.24), even if he should die or divorce her.
b Meaning uncertain.

---

ature, and it is now thought that the biblical writers used this accusation as a means of stigmatizing Israel's cultural rivals (in the guise of long-extinct enemies) by attributing to them the most heinous crimes. Thus they provided moral justification for the displacement of the Canaanites, while at the same time polemicizing against such practices in Israelite society itself. *Nor shall you follow their laws:* The midrash took these words as an indication that the Egyptians and the Canaanites actually had laws requiring these sexual practices (*Sifre Aḥare Mot Perek* 18 parshah 8 [8]). **5:** *By the pursuit of which man shall live,* better, "which, if a person follows, he/she will live," most simply understood as the converse of vv. 24–30, which detail how violation of these laws leads to collective death and to "karet" for the individual. Here too rabbinic law introduced a legislative import into an originally nonlegislative phrase, interpreting that one must *"live by them [but do not die by them]*," and ruling that all the laws of the Torah (except idola-

try, incest, and bloodshed) are set aside if their observance will endanger the preservation of human life (*b. Sanh.* 74a). **6–23:** *My laws and My rules* mentioned in v. 5 are now spelled out. **6:** *Anyone of his own flesh,* the extended family; see 25.49; cf. 21.2. *Uncover nakedness,* "uncover the sexual organ." This term is used throughout vv. 6–19 (see also 20.11, etc.) to denote sexual intercourse. It focuses on the shamelessness of engaging in sexual relations with a member of one's family in flagrant disregard for the repulsion that viewing the nakedness of a close relative was thought to arouse. In postbiblical terminology, the phrase "uncover nakedness," ("gilui 'arayot") losing its literal meaning, became the standard term for incest, and the word "nakedness" became a euphemism for a forbidden sexual partner or act. **7–18:** The list of prohibited sexual unions extends over four generations, with the male addressed in the text placed in the second. All female members of his immediate family who might be the object of his sexual

desire during his adulthood are named. (a) Directly related women: in the generation preceding, his mother (v. 7) and stepmother (v. 8); in his own generation, his sister (v. 9); in the vertical line, his granddaughter (v. 10). (There is no satisfactory explanation for the omission of the daughter.) Supplementing the immediate relatives is the step-sister, pronounced here to be of the same degree as a true sister (v. 11). (b) Indirectly related women: in the generation preceding, his true aunt (vv. 12–13) and his aunt by marriage, pronounced here to be of the same degree (v. 14); in the next generation, his daughter-in-law (v. 15); in his own generation, his brother's wife. (c) Women related to each other: mother and daughter, grandmother and granddaughter (v. 17); sisters (v. 18). It cannot be determined whether analogous prohibitions, such as one's mother's brother's wife and one's niece, are implied or not. **7:** *Your father's nakedness, that is, the nakedness of your mother:* A woman's sexual organs are permitted only to her husband; by engaging in intercourse with the wife of one's close relation one commits a crime against the male relation as well. **9:** *Your father's daughter or your mother's,* referring specifically to the half-sister. The full sister may be supplied by inference since she is in both categories; see v. 14. *Whether born into the household or outside,* better: whether belonging (now) to the household of the parent to which you (now) belong or to another household. **10:** *For their nakedness is yours,* obscure. **11:** *She is your sister:* Similarly "she is your aunt" (v. 14), meant figuratively; the step-sister and uncle's wife are declared to be on the same level as blood-relations. **14:** *Your aunt:* The legislator would thus view Amram's marriage to his aunt (Exod. 6.20) as an improper act. Similarly Abraham's marriage to his half-sister (Gen. 20.12), which violates v. 9, and Jacob's marriage to Rachel and Leah (Gen. 29.16–28), which violates v. 18, but these marriages are re-was born into your father's household—she is your sister; do not uncover her nakedness.

12 Do not uncover the nakedness of your father's sister; she is your father's flesh.

13 Do not uncover the nakedness of your mother's sister; for she is your mother's flesh.

14 Do not uncover the nakedness of your father's brother: do not approach his wife; she is your aunt.

15 Do not uncover the nakedness of your daughter-in-law: she is your son's wife; you shall not uncover her nakedness.

16 a-Do not uncover the nakedness of your brother's wife; it is the nakedness of your brother.-a

17 Do not uncover the nakedness of a woman and her daughter; nor shall you marry her son's daughter or her daughter's daughter and uncover her nakedness: they are kindred; it is depravity.

18 Do not marry a woman as a rival to her sister and uncover her nakedness in the other's lifetime.

19 Do not come near a woman during her period of uncleanness to uncover her nakedness.

20 Do not have carnal relations with your neighbor's wife and defile yourself with her.

21 Do not allow any of your offspring to be offered up to Molech, and do not profane the name of your God: I am the LORD.

22 Do not lie with a male as one lies with a woman; it is an abhorrence.

a-a A man and his wife are one flesh (Gen. 2.24), even if he should die or divorce her.

counted only in the non-Priestly sources. **16:** *Your brother's wife:* In direct opposition to the levirate law in Deut. 25.5–9. Rabbinic law resolved the conflict by viewing the latter as an exception: Intercourse with one's sister-in-law is prohibited in every case except that described in Deuteronomy. The midrash even suggests that the two laws were spoken in the same utterance, so that the general rule and the exception would become known at one and the same time (*Mek. de R. Yishmael, Yitro, ba-Hodesh 7* [Horowitz-Rabin, p. 229]; *Sifre Ki Tetze* 223 [Finkelstein, p. 266]). **17:** *Nor shall you marry,* Heb "tikkaḥ," "take" (so v. 18) does not always refer to marrriage (see 20.17, 21), and may refer to

sexual contact in general. Since the rhetorical aim of the ch is to enumerate the abhorrent sexual practices of the Canaanites, perhaps illicit unions too are contemplated. The halakhic tradition understood the entire series as a table of prohibited marriages, and legal systems throughout the Jewish and Christian worlds have based the impediments to lawful marriage on it. **18:** *A woman as a rival to her sister,* see 1 Sam. 1.6. See v. 14 n. above. *In the other's lifetime:* After the death of one sister, however, it might be considered meritorious to marry the other. **19–23:** Additional sexual prohibitions, arranged as follows: (a) intercourse with women, first, one's own wife, when menstruating

(v. 19), second, another's wife (v. 20); (b) nonprocreative intercourse, first, with a male (v. 22), second, with an animal (v. 23a); (c) intercourse in which no human seed is emitted, i.e., between a woman and a beast (v. 23b). **19:** See 15.19–24 n. This stricter law is probably an indication of H's espousal of popular tradition, viewing the menstruating woman as taboo, overriding P's concern with purely formal, technical definitions according to which menstruation is no different from any other bodily impurity. **20:** The adultery prohibition is included here since it too was thought to be characteristic of the Canaanites. *Defile yourself:* Note the wider sense of "defile" in H; in the strict, Priestly sense all sexual intercourse is defiling (see 15.18). **21:** The inclusion in this ch of the prohibition of Molech sacrifice (see 20.2–5 n.) is unexpected. Apparently H shares the view of Deut. 12.31; 18.9–12 that child sacrifice was among the abominable practices for which the Canaanites were expelled from their land, so he adds it to the list of sexual offenses which he believes are equally responsible. Other biblical texts confirm that it was in fact practiced in Israel at certain times during the monarchy (see 2 Kings 16.3; 17.17; 21.6; 23.10; Isa. 30.33; 57.9; Jer. 7.31; 19.5; 32.35; Ezek. 16.21; 23.37; Ps. 106.37–38), and this accounts for the Torah sources' having attributed it to the Canaanites: to serve as a warning for Israel. **22:** Biblical and ancient Near Eastern culture was not familiar with homosexuality in the sense of a defined sexual orientation or lifestyle (according to the biblical evidence David and Jonathan had no sexual relationship). It acknowledges only the occasional act of male anal intercourse, usually as an act of force associated with humiliation, revenge, or subjection (for the biblical examples see Gen. 19.4–5; Judg. 19.22). Of the biblical legal collections only H mentions it (here and in 20.13), declaring it to be an abominable act and a capital offense. It seems that

²³ Do not have carnal relations with any beast and defile yourself thereby; and let no woman lend herself to a beast to mate with it; it is perversion.

²⁴ Do not defile yourselves in any of those ways, for it is by such that the nations that I am casting out before you defiled themselves. ²⁵ Thus the land became defiled; and I called it to account for its iniquity, and the land spewed out its inhabitants. ²⁶ But you must keep My laws and My rules, and you must not do any of those abhorrent things, neither the citizen nor the stranger who resides among you; ²⁷ for all those abhorrent things were done by the people who were in the land before you, and the land became defiled. ²⁸ So let not the land spew you out for defiling it, as it spewed out the nation that came before you. ²⁹ All who do any of those abhorrent things—such persons shall be cut off from their people. ³⁰ You shall keep My charge not to engage in any of the abhorrent practices that were carried on before you, and you shall not defile yourselves through them: I the LORD am your God.

H views all sexual acts that are not potentially procreative as aberrant. **24–30:** The concluding exhortation, extrapolating from *abhorrence* in v. 22 and from the defilement mentioned in vv. 19 and 20, speaks of defilement as a destructive force emanating from all of the acts mentioned. These acts *defile* those who commit them, and this in turn defiles the land of Canaan which then spits out its inhabitants. This is the automatic reaction of the land of Canaan to abominations, no matter who commits them, Canaanites or Israelites. The intent of the exhortation is to say that what was, will be, unless the listeners themselves prevent it. *The nations that I am casting out before you:* The Egyptians, mentioned in v. 3, have disappeared from view; the focus is entirely on the Canaanites. See also 20.23. **25:** *Spewed out,* lit. "vomited"; not actions performed upon the land by attackers from outside but rather performed by the land upon its population. As recognized by the midrash, "the land of Israel is not like the rest of the earth in that it does not sustain those who commit [sexual] offenses" (*Sifre* to v. 28 [*Kod.* 11:14], mistakenly placed in the *Sifra* at 20.22 because

of similarity to the v. there). The land is so sensitive to the criminal behavior of its inhabitants that when abominable acts are performed, "defiling" the land, it ceases to yield its bounty and its population is forced to emigrate. Of course, as the previous v. confirms, God has imbued the land of Israel with its delicate constitution. This is unique to H; elsewhere in the Torah it is presumed that the pre-Israelite inhabitants of Canaan were either destroyed or expelled by the conquering Israelites. **26:** *Neither the citizen nor the stranger who resides among you,* see 16.29. **28:** *Spewed out the nation that came before you:* Unique also is the idea that the evacuation of Canaan has already occurred. **29:** Not only is the national fate sealed by failing to avoid the abominations, each perpetrator is punished with "karet" (see 7.20, 21).

19.1–37: Holiness of individuals. Commands pertaining to virtually every area of Israelite life; there is no such thing as a command pertaining merely to relations between human beings ("ben 'adam laḥavero"); every commanded or prohibited action affects the sacred realm and is in the category of

laws between God and human beings ("ben 'adam lamakom"). The ch expresses this by presenting an admixture of laws from every sphere—from worship to fairness in commerce, from legal proceedings to reverence for the Temple, from idolatry and the avoidance of pagan practices to family relations, from the use of the name of God in oaths to support for the needy, from the sanctity of first fruits to theft and fraud—all on equal footing; punctuating the separate paragraphs with the repeated refrain *I am the LORD* or *I the LORD am your God,* which is approximately equivalent to "because I, the LORD, say so." The opening and closing vv. (2 and 37) provide the key to meaning: *You shall be holy, for I, the LORD your God, am holy* (v. 2). *You shall faithfully observe all My laws and all My rules: I am the LORD* (v. 37). These vv. resemble two that occur alongside each other in the next ch, 20.7–8. Only through faithful observance of God's commands can the Israelite fulfill the sacred charge of being holy. This is repeated in Num. 15.39–40, recited every morning and evening as part of the Shema prayer, where the function of the fringe on the tallit is that one may "look at it and recall all the commandments of the LORD and observe them. . . . Thus you shall be reminded to observe all My commandments and be holy to your God." Through this miscellany of laws H expresses the idea that through the performance of all commanded deeds and the avoidance of all prohibited actions, all Israelites are able to absorb the effusion of the divine Presence in their midst (see 6.11) and be holy. A number of rabbinic and modern interpreters, noting that the prohibitions of idolatry (v. 4), theft and falsehood (v. 11), and false witness (v. 12), along with the command to keep the Sabbath and to revere one's mother and father (v. 3), are included in this collection, have suggested that this ch is the Priestly version of the Decalogue (see Exod. ch 20; Deut. ch 5). This is unlikely. The Priestly literature

KEDOSHIM   קְדֹשִׁים

19 The LORD spoke to Moses, saying: [2] Speak to the whole Israelite community and say to them:

You shall be holy, for I, the LORD your God, am holy.

[3] You shall each revere his mother and his father, and keep My sabbaths: I the LORD am your God.

[4] Do not turn to idols or make molten gods for yourselves: I the LORD am your God.

[5] When you sacrifice an offering of well-being to the LORD, sacrifice it so that it may be accepted on your behalf. [6] It shall be eaten on the day you sacrifice it, or on the day following; but what is left by the third day must be consumed in fire. [7] If it should be eaten on the third day, it is an offensive thing, it will not be acceptable. [8] And he who eats of it shall bear his guilt, for he has profaned what is sacred to the LORD; that person shall be cut off from his kin.

[9] When you reap the harvest of your land, you shall not reap all the way to the edges of your field, or gather the gleanings of your harvest. [10] You shall not pick your vineyard bare, or gather the fallen fruit of your vineyard; you shall leave them for the poor and the stranger: I the LORD am your God.

[11] You shall not steal; you shall not deal deceitfully or falsely with one another. [12] You shall not swear falsely by My name, profaning the name of your God: I am the LORD.

[13] You shall not defraud your fellow. You shall not commit robbery. The wages of a laborer shall not remain with you until morning.

is completely unfamiliar with the Decalogue tradition; there is no logical explanation for the missing commands; and the six scattered parallels are outweighed by the remainder of ch 19, which does not resemble the Decalogue at all. **2:** *You shall be holy, for I, the* LORD *your God, am holy:* This is the caption; what follows is its elaboration. Later interpreters often took it as a general command to emulate divine attributes such as compassion and forgiveness ("imitatio dei"). But "holy" in the Bible does not refer to superior moral qualities. God's holiness is His essential "otherness," His being separate from all that is not divine; humans are not called upon to be holy in this sense (the text does not say "as

I am holy"). Holiness in humans, as in time, space, objects, and speech, is the state of belonging to the deity, being designated God's "personal" property. In the non-Priestly tradition Israel is holy simply by virtue of having been chosen (see Exod. 19.5–6; Deut. 7.6; 14.2, 21). In Priestly thought, holiness is the desired result of an effusion of God's immanent Presence (see Exod. 29.43), which, according to H, Israel must actively absorb by performing the commandments. **3:** The legislative part of the ch leads with a command pertaining to the ethical realm, reverence for parents, alongside one obviously belonging to the sacred sphere, the Sabbath, together with the formulaic *I the*

LORD *am your God. Revere:* The Rabbis correctly sensed that this differs from "honor" in Exod. 20.12 and Deut. 5.16; the Decalogue refers to the do's; this v. refers to the don'ts. *And keep My sabbaths,* see 23.3. **5–8:** See 7.11–21. This refers to the well-being offerings of the votive and freewill types (see 7.16–18; 22.21–23). The third type of well-being offering, that of thanksgiving (see 7.12–15) is mentioned in 22.29–30, marking the close of this section of H (chs 19–22). **7:** *It is an offensive thing,* see 7.18. *It will not be acceptable,* correctly, "it will not be accepted." See 1.3; 7.18 n.; 22.17–30. **8:** *He has profaned what is sacred to the* LORD: This theme connects the passage with the holiness motif. *Cut off from his kin,* see 7.20, 21. **9–10:** Four prohibitions, two in the field and two in the vineyard. The first in each pair is observed while reaping, the second during ingathering. All lead up to *you shall leave them for the poor and the stranger.* The command to care for the needy is fulfilled by inaction. *I the* LORD *am your God* transforms social legislation into a sacred act. Cf. Deut. 24.19–21. *The stranger,* see 16.29. **11–18:** Four two-v. paragraphs, each one ending with *I am the* LORD, indicating that decency and honesty, ostensibly pertaining to interpersonal affairs, are in fact divine concerns. All four deal with matters of conscience: Since all of the crimes are to some degree committed in secret, their perpetrators imagine that they will go undetected. The progression is from the crimes most difficult to conceal to those which can never be proven and whose victims have no remedy whatsoever, leaving detection and punishment in the hands of God alone. **11–12:** Falsehood in commerce and its ramifications; see 5.20–26. Theft naturally leads to deceit, denial, and cover-up; these are likely to be aggravated by false oath, thus profaning the sacred name of God, so God becomes a party to what began as a purely civil matter. **13–14:** Taking unfair advantage. The first v. prohibits fraud, extor-

14 You shall not insult the deaf, or place a stumbling block before the blind. You shall fear your God: I am the LORD.

15 You shall not render an unfair decision: do not favor the poor or show deference to the rich; judge your kinsman fairly. 16 Do not a-deal basely with-a your countrymen. Do not b-profit by-b the blood of your fellow: I am the LORD.

17 You shall not hate your kinsfolk in your heart. Reprove your kinsman butc incur no guilt because of him. 18 You shall not take vengeance or bear a grudge against your countrymen. Love your fellow as yourself: I am the LORD.

19 You shall observe My laws.

You shall not let your cattle mate with a different kind; you shall not sow your field with two kinds of seed; you shall not put on cloth from a mixture of two kinds of material.

20 If a man has carnal relations with a woman who is a slave and has been designated for another man, but has not been redeemed or given her freedom, there shall be an indemnity; they shall not, however, be put to death, since

a-a Others "go about as a talebearer among"; meaning of Heb. uncertain.
b-b Lit. "stand upon"; precise meaning of Heb. phrase uncertain.
c Exact force of we- uncertain.

tion, and withholding wages from the defenseless laborer; the second, speaking metaphorically and not of those literally deaf or blind, extends the principle to include exploitation of others by capitalizing on their ignorance or vulnerability. **14:** *You shall fear your God:* The victims of such exploitation may never know how they have been used; fear of God is the only real sanction (see also v. 32 as well as 25.17, 36, 43). As noted by the Rabbis, this phrase occurs when compliance is a matter of conscience rather than legal enforcement. **15–16:** Perversion of justice. The first v. speaks directly of the corruption of judicial proceedings on the part of judges. A better rendering of v. 16 is: "Do not spread [false] rumors among your countrymen [to have unjust charges brought against a person]; do not stand by the blood of your fellow [i.e., ignore bloodshed, thus preventing charges from being brought against the perpetrator]."

15: *Render an unfair decision,* lit. "commit distortion in judgment"; see v. 35. **17–18:** Pent-up hatred and its consequences. The two vv. are a unit, better rendered: "Do not hate your kinsfolk in your heart, rather, reprove your kinsman so as to incur no guilt because of him. In other words: Do not take vengeance or bear a grudge against your countrymen, rather, love your fellow as yourself." The first v. prohibits one whose fellow has wronged him from keeping his resentment inside instead of informing the wrongdoer of his action, lest the bottled-up hatred result in incurring guilt. The second v. explains: Such bearing of grudges results ultimately in vengeance, while by refraining from this course one treats his fellow with the same "love," i.e., understanding and forgiveness, one normally extends toward one's own shortcomings. Traditional interpretation tended to treat each phrase as a general command in

its own right. For instance the words *reprove your kinsman* were seen as obligating competent persons to chastise their fellow Israelites for failings in their religious and ethical duties and returning them to the path of righteousness (b. ʿArak. 16 b and many other places). Most notably, *love your fellow as yourself* was generalized in Jewish and Christian tradition to serve as a brief encapsulation of the Torah's ethics (e.g., b. Shab. 31a; Matt. 22.34–40) and as a blanket command covering all ethical duties not specifically mentioned (e.g., Maimonides *Yad ʾAvelut* 14:1; Matt. 19.16–19). **18:** *I am the LORD:* In the Priestly worldview, ethical behavior is a religious act only when performed as an act of obedience to God. **19:** *My laws:* "ḥukkotay" should be understood here more literally as "the boundaries I have fixed in the natural world"; cf. Isa. 5.14; Jer. 5.22; 33.25; Job 38.33). As explained in ch 11, according to P's view Israel is to maintain the distinctions present in the created order. *Different kind, two kinds,* Heb "kilʾayim," used in the parallel law in Deut. 22.9 as well. *Mixture,* Heb "shaʿatnez." However, wool and linen are woven together in the priestly vestments (Exod. 28.6; 39.29) and in the fringes (tzitzit) Israelites are obligated to place in their clothing (Num. 15.37–40). The "unnatural" mixture is therefore taboo for mundane use but not for sacred garments. **20–22:** If one's female slave is *designated* for marriage to another man, sexual relations with her are illicit. Only by legal technicality (since the woman is not yet free, she is not strictly "betrothed" in the legally binding sense) are the two exempt from the death penalty mandated for adultery (see 20.10 n.) but the offense against God must be expiated. The "ʾasham" sacrifice is prescribed (see 5.14–26) even though no desecration of the sacred has taken place, because the "hataʾt" sacrifice (see 4.1–35) does not atone for deliberate acts. **20:** *There shall be an indemnity:* This translation is uncertain. A simpler one is:

she has not been freed. ²¹ But he must bring to the entrance of the Tent of Meeting, as his guilt offering to the LORD, a ram of guilt offering. ²² With the ram of guilt offering the priest shall make expiation for him before the LORD for the sin that he committed; and the sin that he committed will be forgiven him.

²³ When you enter the land and plant any tree for food, you shall regard its fruit as forbidden.ª Three years it shall be forbiddenª for you, not to be eaten. ²⁴ In the fourth year all its fruit shall be set aside for jubilation before the LORD; ²⁵ and only in the fifth year may you use its fruit—that its yield to you may be increased: I the LORD am your God.

²⁶ You shall not eat anything with its blood. You shall not practice divination or soothsaying. ²⁷ You shall not round off the side-growth on your head, or destroy the side-growth of your beard. ²⁸ You shall not make gashes in your flesh for the dead, or incise any marks on yourselves: I am the LORD.

²⁹ Do not degrade your daughter and make her a harlot, lest the land fall into harlotry and the land be filled with depravity. ³⁰ You shall keep My sabbaths and venerate My sanctuary: I am the LORD.

³¹ Do not turn to ghosts and do not inquire of familiar spirits, to be defiled by them: I the LORD am your God.

³² You shall rise before the aged and show deference to the old; you shall fear your God: I am the LORD.

³³ When a stranger resides with you in your land, you shall not wrong him. ³⁴ The stranger who resides with you shall be to you as one of your citizens; you shall love him as yourself, for you were strangers in the land of Egypt: I the LORD am your God.

³⁵ You shall not falsify measures of length, weight, or ca-

---

a *Heb. root 'rl, commonly "to be uncircumcised."*

"a distinction shall be made."
23–25: The fruit of a tree is off-limits for the first three years, and offered to the LORD in the fourth; only then may it be eaten. **23:** *You shall regard its fruit as forbidden,* lit. "treat it as uncircumcised." Figuratively speaking, the fruit tree is to be regarded as though sealed off from use. **24:** *Set aside,* Heb "kodesh," a sacred or "holy" object, thus connecting this law with the theme of the ch as a whole. The text does not state how the fruit is to be set aside and what is to be done with it. *For jubilation before the LORD,* see Judg. 9.27.

25: *That its yield to you may be increased:* Abstaining from the first three years' fruit will result not in material loss but rather in divine blessing. **26–28:** From context it appears that *You shall not eat anything with its blood,* which refers to eating meat without having drained the blood (see 17.10–14; 1 Sam. 14.32–35), must, like the two prohibitions that follow, be associated with pagan forms of divination and magic. The acts prohibited in the next two vv. are extreme expressions of grief and mourning (see Deut. 14.1–2; 1 Kings 18.28); as they are associated with conjuring

up dead spirits and the gods of the netherworld, they are not to be copied from the pagan peoples. Similar restrictions are placed on priests (see 21.5). **29:** *Degrade,* lit. "profane." This is the opposite of holiness. **30–32:** These three vv. mark the close of the main section of the unit, returning to the themes with which it opened and adding to them. **30:** *Keep My sabbaths,* corresponding to v. 3a. *Venerate My sanctuary,* i.e., do not trespass the bounds of the sacred. The verb corresponds to that used in the second law in 3a. This v. occurs again in 26.2. **31:** *Do not turn to,* corresponding to v. 4. *Ghosts . . . familiar spirits,* Heb "'ov" and "yide'oni," mentioned throughout the Bible as spirits conjured up by necromancers. Biblical tradition admits that this method of gaining knowledge of the occult is effective (see 1 Sam. 28.3–25) but places it strictly off-limits for Israelites; see 20.6, 27; cf. Deut. 18.9ff. **32:** *Rise . . . show deference to the old,* corresponding to v. 3a. *You shall fear your God,* see v. 14 n. **33–36:** These vv. make up the appendix, extending two of the laws mentioned in the main body of the ch to the "ger" or resident alien (see 16.29). Elsewhere in P, when the law is extended to include the strangers, it is to enable them to perform positive commands if they desire or to obligate them to observe prohibitions. Here, the purpose is to obligate the Israelite to treat the "ger" with the same decency he is required to show his fellow Israelite. **33–34:** Reinterpreting and extending the law in v. 18 to the resident alien. *Love* of the "ger" is manifest in treating him as a citizen, though he is not one, in financial dealings. **33:** *Wrong him,* the sense is "cheat him in commerce." **34:** *For you were strangers in the land of Egypt:* The prohibition of exploiting the "ger" is logically grounded in Israel's own experience; see Exod. 22.20; 23.9; Deut. 10.19. **35–36:** Extending the law in v. 15, "do not commit distortion in judgment," by employing "mishpat," "judgment," in its additional pacity. ³⁶ You shall have an honest balance, honest weights, an honest *ephah*, and an honest *hin*.

I the LORD am your God who freed you from the land of Egypt. ³⁷ You shall faithfully observe all My laws and all My rules: I am the LORD.

20 And the LORD spoke to Moses: ² Say further to the Israelite people:

Anyone among the Israelites, or among the strangers residing in Israel, who gives any of his offspring to Molech, shall be put to death; the people of the land shall pelt him with stones. ³ And I will set My face against that man and will cut him off from among his people, because he gave of his offspring to Molech and so defiled My sanctuary and profaned My holy name. ⁴ And if the people of the land should shut their eyes to that man when he gives of his offspring to Molech, and should not put him to death, ⁵ I Myself will set My face against that man and his kin, and will cut off from among their people both him and all who follow him in going astray after Molech. ⁶ And if any person turns to ghosts and familiar spirits and goes astray after them, I will set My face against that person and cut him off from among his people.

meaning of "correct portion." These two vv. likely also refer to the "ger," warning the Israelite not to take advantage of the alien's lack of familiarity with local weights and measures. A similar law, not connected with "gerim" specifically, appears in Deut. 25.13–16. **36:** *Ephah,* a dry measure, about 23 liters (21 quarts); *hin,* a liquid measure, a little less than 4 liters (1 gallon). *I the LORD am your God who freed you from the land of Egypt:* The elongated self-assertion formula (cf. for instance 26.13) signals the end of the ch; it also indicates that this paragraph is connected with the one preceding. **37:** Concluding summation; see 19.1–37 n.

20.1–27: Molech worship and sexual crimes. A single speech, introduced in v. 1 and divided into four parts: (a) penalties for Molech worship (vv. 2–5); (b) exhortation (vv. 7–8); (c) a series of prescribed penalties for sexual and other crimes (vv. 9–21); (d) exhortation (vv. 22–26). Two appendices, dealing with conjuring up the spirits of the dead, have been placed at the conclusions of sections (a) and (d), respectively (vv. 6 and 27). Sacrifice to Molech and sexual crimes were treated at length in ch 18 as direct commands ("Do not uncover the nakedness of . . ."), while here they are phrased conditionally ("If a man [commits such-and-such], he shall [suffer such-and-such punishment]"). Many commentators have therefore assumed that this ch provides the punishments for the crimes given in ch 18. But this is unlikely for many reasons. Several of the acts prohibited in ch 18 are missing (intercourse with one's mother, granddaughter, half-sister, step-granddaughter, and wife's sister). Conversely, this ch mentions crimes not included in ch 18 (cursing one's parents and consulting spirits). Even some of the parallels are not exact: 20.14, 17, 18 do not quite correspond to the commands in 18.9, 17, 19. Further, according to 18.29 all the crimes enumerated are punished by "karet," whereas this ch mentions "karet" in a few cases only, and prescribes capital punishment in the others. Finally, the very existence of two separate chs devoted to one theme, with an entire ch standing between them, indicates that the two chapters were composed separately. The compilers of H, in their endeavor to include as much legislation as possible, preserved and included overlapping and contradictory compositions without harmonization. This illustrates the reverence ancient authors had for texts that they inherited from earlier bearers of tradition. **2–5:** *Molech* is the Heb for an ancient Near Eastern deity associated with the netherworld. Biblical tradition is unanimous that the worship of Molech consisted of the sacrifice of children, and there is evidence that this cult of death was occasionally practiced in Israel, and that at times Israelites engaged in child sacrifice. In 18.21 this monstrous crime is included among the "abominations" which caused (and will again cause) the land of Canaan to spew out its inhabitants. **2–3:** Sacrificing to Molech is a capital offense. The *people of the land* (which may refer to a designated body of citizens) are required to see the death by stoning of the perpetrators. In addition, God will personally attend to the eventual extinction of their line ("karet," see 7.20, 21). *Defiled My sanctuary:* Sacrifices to Molech were not made in the LORD's sanctuary; rather, the contamination of God's abode results from this crime wherever it is committed. *Profaned My holy name,* by attributing salvific power to another deity, or by imagining that the God of Israel desires the sacrifice of children. **4–5:** If those charged with prosecuting the criminal neglect their duty, God will extend the "karet" threat to the perpetrator's larger family and all those who *follow him in going astray after Molech.* **6:** *Ghosts and familiar spirits,* see 19.31. In v. 27 the death penalty is prescribed for those who "have" ghosts and familiar spirits. Thus the "providers" are punished by death, and the "consumers" are

⁷You shall sanctify yourselves and be holy, for I the LORD am your God. ⁸You shall faithfully observe My laws: I the LORD make you holy.

⁹If anyone insults his father or his mother, he shall be put to death; he has insulted his father and his mother—his bloodguilt is upon him.

¹⁰If a man commits adultery with a married woman, committing adultery with another man's wife, the adulterer and the adulteress shall be put to death. ¹¹If a man lies with his father's wife, it is the nakedness of his father that he has uncovered; the two shall be put to death—their bloodguilt is upon them. ¹²If a man lies with his daughter-in-law, both of them shall be put to death; they have committed incest—their bloodguilt is upon them. ¹³If a man lies with a male as one lies with a woman, the two of them have done an abhorrent thing; they shall be put to death—their bloodguilt is upon them. ¹⁴If a man marries a woman and her mother, it is depravity; both he and they shall be put to the fire, that there be no depravity among you. ¹⁵If a man has carnal relations with a beast, he shall be put to death; and you shall kill the beast. ¹⁶If a woman approaches any beast to mate with it, you shall kill the woman and the beast; they shall be put to death—their bloodguilt is upon them.

¹⁷If a man marries his sister, the daughter of either his father or his mother, so that he sees her nakedness and she sees his nakedness, it is a disgrace; they shall be excommunicated[a] in the sight of their kinsfolk. He has uncovered the nakedness of his sister, he shall bear his guilt. ¹⁸If a man lies with a woman in her infirmity and uncovers her nakedness, he has laid bare her flow and she has exposed her blood flow; both of them shall be cut off from among their people. ¹⁹You shall not uncover the nakedness of your mother's sister or of your father's sister, for that is laying bare one's own flesh; they shall bear their guilt. ²⁰If a man lies with his uncle's wife, it is his uncle's nakedness that he has uncovered. They shall bear their guilt: they shall die childless. ²¹If a man marries the wife of his brother, it is indecency. It is the nakedness of

a Lit. "cut off."

grace"), and it is uncertain why only some vv. contain such characterizations and others do not. These and other features of the text indicate that this ch, like the remainder of H, was not composed to be studied as a precise legal document but rather as an exhortation, with all the rhetorical technique and emotional expression that this entails. **9:** *Insults,* Heb "curses." *His bloodguilt is upon him:* This phrase, here and in the following vv., emphasizes that although the crime was not one of bloodshed, the guilty parties have indeed incurred the death penalty and the executioners are not accountable. **10:** *Adultery* is defined as sexual relations between any man, married or single, and a woman betrothed or married to someone else. Both parties to the crime are guilty; see Deut. 22.22. **11:** See 18.8. **12:** See 18.15. *They have committed incest,* Heb "tevel," taken to mean "improper mixing." **13:** See 18.22. **14:** See 18.17, where the formulation is "a woman and her daughter." **15–16:** See 18.23. **17:** See 18.9. *Marries,* see 18.17 n.; here too the Heb "yikaḥ," "takes," may suggest a sexual relationship. *They shall be excommunicated,* Heb (see translators' note a) simply says "shall be cut off," precisely as in the "karet" threat in the next v. and throughout the Priestly law (see 7.20, 21). *He shall bear his guilt,* for this phrase, used also in vv. 19 and 20, see 5.1; 7.18. **18:** See 15.19–24 n. and 18.19 n. *In her infirmity,* during her menstrual period; see 12.2; 15.33. **19:** *You shall not uncover the nakedness,* see 18.12, 13. This v. abandons the conditional formulation found throughout this ch and reverts to the "you shall not" formulation of ch 18. **20:** *Uncle's wife:* This may include the wife of the mother's brother as well as the wife of the father's brother mentioned specifically in 18.14. *They shall die childless:* This penalty, found here and in the next v., is probably a specific form of "karet" (see 7.20, 21), since the childless person's line is thereby made extinct. **21:** See 18.16.

punished by "karet." **7–8:** See ch 19. These two vv. provide the transition to the second set of laws in the ch. **9–21:** The series of penalties for severe crimes. For those in vv. 9–16 the death penalty is prescribed, with burning mentioned as the method in one case (v. 14). For the remainder, "karet" (see 7.20, 21) is either pronounced (vv. 17–18) or implied (vv. 19–21). It is unclear why particular punishments are legislated for particular offenses. Many of the terms used to characterize the crimes are unclear (e.g., "depravity," "dishis brother that he has uncovered; they shall remain childless.

²² You shall faithfully observe all My laws and all My regulations, lest the land to which I bring you to settle in spew you out. ²³ You shall not follow the practices of the nation that I am driving out before you. For it is because they did all these things that I abhorred them ²⁴ and said to you: You shall possess their land, for I will give it to you to possess, a land flowing with milk and honey. I the LORD am your God who has set you apart from other peoples. ²⁵ So you shall set apart the clean beast from the unclean, the unclean bird from the clean. You shall not draw abomination upon yourselves through beast or bird or anything with which the ground is alive, which I have set apart for you to treat as unclean. ²⁶ You shall be holy to Me, for I the LORD am holy, and I have set you apart from other peoples to be Mine.

²⁷ A man or a woman who has a ghost or a familiar spirit shall be put to death; they shall be pelted with stones—their bloodguilt shall be upon them.

'EMOR   אמר

21 The LORD said to Moses: Speak to the priests, the sons of Aaron, and say to them:

None shall defile himself for any [dead] person among his kin, ² except for the relatives that are closest to him: his mother, his father, his son, his daughter, and his brother; ³ also for a virgin sister, close to him because she has not married, for her he may defile himself. ⁴ But he shall not defile himself ᵃ as a kinsman by marriage,ᵃ and so profane himself.

---

a-a Lit. "as a husband among his kin"; meaning uncertain.

22–26: The concluding exhortation returns briefly (vv. 22–24) to the themes of 18.24–30, adding the description of the land of Canaan as *a land flowing with milk and honey.* It then (vv. 25–26) introduces the motif of "setting apart": As God has separated Israel from the nations, they must separate clean from unclean foods, and thus be *holy.* Since *holy* means set apart, the text is saying that in order to be holy (*to be Mine*, v. 26) they are required to act accordingly (*So you shall set apart*, v. 25). Vv. 25–26 resemble 11.43–45 and would read well as an alternate conclusion to ch 11. **27:** The appendix, evidently

a secondary addition to the ch; see v. 6.

21.1–22.32: Worship and holiness. Whereas earlier chs were concerned with the proper procedure for sacrifice (chs 1–7, 17) and with the prompt disposal of impurity (chs 11–16), this section revolves primarily around holiness, that of the priests (ch 21) and that of sacrificial offerings (22.1–16). The sacred, which belongs to the divine sphere and has been "saturated" with holiness (see 6.11 n.), is vulnerable to attack; it is subject to desecration if it is not kept apart from impurity, disqualifying im-

perfections, and unauthorized contact or use. Desecration of the holy redounds to God, profaning His abode and His holy name, and brings disastrous consequences in its wake. The second topic, arising from the mention of disqualifying blemishes, is that of the acceptance of offerings, first mentioned in 1.3–4 (see also 7.18; 19.5–8). The chs consist of five speeches to Moses, the first four of which he is to convey to Aaron and his sons: (a) avoiding the desecration of the priests (21.1–15); (b) avoiding the desecration of the sanctuary and the offerings by contact with defective priests (21.16–24); (c) avoiding the desecration of the sanctuary and the sacred offerings by contact with impure priests and consumption by ineligible persons (22.1–16); (d) offerings deemed unacceptable due to physical defect or pagan origin (22.17–25); (e) offerings deemed unacceptable because of time factors, and concluding vv. of a general nature (22.26–33).

21.1–15: The holiness of the priesthood. 1–4: The priests, in contrast to the lay Israelite, must stay clear of avoidable impurity and must refrain from nearing the sacred when they become unavoidably impure since they are holy in the highest degree. Thus, while lay Israelites may come into contact with a corpse as long as they dispose of their impurity afterwards (see Num. ch 19), priests may not do so, unless it be in order to mourn the death of a blood relative—in which case they must, of course, avoid contact with the sacred until they have been cleansed. **2:** *The relatives that are closest to him,* a narrower group than those denoted by the phrase "anyone of his own flesh" in 18.6; 25.49. **2–3:** *His mother, his father,* etc.: In Jewish tradition, this (along with the wife, who is not mentioned but was supplied exegetically) is the basis for the list of relatives for whom one is required to observe the statutory mourning periods. **4:** *Defile himself as a kinsman by marriage:* Others translate

5 They shall not shave smooth any part of their heads, or cut the side-growth of their beards, or make gashes in their flesh. 6 They shall be holy to their God and not profane the name of their God; for they offer the LORD's offerings by fire, the food of their God, and so must be holy.

7 They shall not marry a woman defiled by harlotry, nor shall they marry one divorced from her husband. For they are holy to their God 8 and you must treat them as holy, since they offer the food of your God; they shall be holy to you, for I the LORD who sanctify you am holy.

9 When the daughter of a priest defiles herself through harlotry, it is her father whom she defiles; she shall be put to the fire.

10 The priest who is exalted above his fellows, on whose head the anointing oil has been poured and who has been ordained to wear the vestments, shall not bare his head[a] or rend his vestments. 11 He shall not go in where there is any dead body; he shall not defile himself even for his father or mother. 12 He shall not go outside the sanctuary and profane the sanctuary of his God, for upon him is the distinction of the anointing oil of his God, Mine the LORD's. 13 He may marry only a woman who is a virgin. 14 A widow, or a divorced woman, or one who is degraded by harlotry—such he may not marry. Only a virgin of his own kin may he take to wife—15 that he may not profane his offspring among his kin, for I the LORD have sanctified him.

16 The LORD spoke further to Moses: 17 Speak to Aaron and say: No man of your offspring throughout the ages who has a defect shall be qualified to offer the food of his God. 18 No one at all who has a defect shall be qualified: no man who is blind, or lame, or [b]has a limb too short or too long;[b] 19 no man who has a broken leg or a broken

a See note at 10.6.   b-b Or "mutilated or has a limb too long."

(see 18.6–23) and the latter as a woman born of such a relationship, or of a union between a priest and a woman prohibited to him. Halakhah derives the prohibition of marriage between a priest and a proselyte from this phrase. **8:** The repeated rationale, including a reference to God's own holiness. **9:** The lay Israelite too is forbidden to allow his daughter to engage in harlotry (19.29). The priest's daughter, however, is a more serious case; her father's sanctity would thereby be desecrated, and the offense is therefore a capital one. **10–14:** The high priest is subject to even stricter safeguards against possible desecration, since he is required to enter the Tabernacle daily. He must refrain even from benign expressions of grief, and may not contract corpse contamination even in order to mourn for a close relative (similarly the Nazirite; see Num. 6.6). Further, he must marry a virgin; even a widow (whom a lesser priest may marry, presumably because her husband has been dead long enough to nullify any suspicion of paternity) is off-limits; since another man's seed has entered her at some time in her life, the high priest's union with her is thought to desecrate his own seed. Ezekiel forecasts that in the rebuilt Temple all priests will be subject to the same restrictions (Ezek. 44.22–26); halakhah maintained the Torah's leniency. **10:** *On whose head,* see 4.3 n. *Bare his head,* better: dishevel his head [i.e., his hair]; see 10.6. *Or rend his vestments,* see 10.6. **14:** *Of his own kin,* i.e., of priestly descent. In contrast Ezekiel permits the priest to marry any virgin of the seed of Israel (44.22). Here the halakhah follows Ezekiel, once again adopting the more lenient view. **15:** *Have sanctified,* better, "sanctify him," reflecting Priestly thought, where God sanctifies constantly by His very presence (Exod. 29.43–44; see also v. 8 above; Exod. 31.13; Lev. 20.8; 22.9, 16, 32; cf. Ezek. 37.28). **16–24:** Physical defects, broadly defined as the absence or permanent mal-

this difficult phrase literally: "a 'master' [i.e., a priest] must not defile himself for his kinsmen," a recapitulation of v. 1b. **5:** Desecration of the priest results also from observing the widespread rituals of mourning detailed here; see 10.6–7. According to 19.27–28 these expressions of grief are also forbidden to lay Israelites. **6:** The rationale for the preceding. The priests must maintain the sanctity with which they, like the Tabernacle and its furnishings, have been imbued (see 8.10–13). Since they offer the deity food gifts, any desecration of their persons would profane the name of God. *Offerings by fire,* see 1.9. **7:** The holiness of the priests is held to be genetically transmitted; they may marry only women about whom there can be no suspicion of the presence of another man's seed. See v. 14 n. *A woman defiled by harlotry,* lit. "a harlotrous woman and one defiled," taken by most exegetes as two distinct categories. Traditionally, the former is defined as a woman who has had prohibited intercourse arm; 20 or who is a hunchback, or a dwarf, or who has a growth in his eye, or who has a boil-scar, or scurvy, or crushed testes. 21 No man among the offspring of Aaron the priest who has a defect shall be qualified to offer the LORD's offering by fire; having a defect, he shall not be qualified to offer the food of his God. 22 He may eat of the food of his God, of the most holy as well as of the holy; 23 but he shall not enter behind the curtain or come near the altar, for he has a defect. He shall not profane these places sacred to Me, for I the LORD have sanctified them.

24 Thus Moses spoke to Aaron and his sons and to all the Israelites.

22 The LORD spoke to Moses, saying: 2 Instruct Aaron and his sons to be scrupulous about the sacred donations that the Israelite people consecrate to Me, lest they profane My holy name, Mine the LORD's. 3 Say to them:

Throughout the ages, if any man among your offspring, while in a state of uncleanness, partakes of any sacred donation that the Israelite people may consecrate to the LORD, that person shall be cut off from before Me: I am the LORD. 4 No man of Aaron's offspring who has an eruption or a discharge[a] shall eat of the sacred donations until he is clean. If one touches anything made unclean by a corpse, or if a man has an emission of semen, 5 or if a man touches any swarming thing by which he is made unclean or any human being by whom he is made unclean—whatever his uncleanness—6 the person who touches such shall be unclean until evening and shall not eat of the sacred donations unless he has washed his body in water. 7 As soon as the sun sets, he shall be clean; and afterward he may eat of the sacred donations, for they are his food. 8 He shall not eat anything that died or was torn by beasts, thereby becoming unclean: I am the LORD. 9 They shall keep My charge, lest they incur guilt thereby and die for it, having committed profanation: I the LORD consecrate them.

10 No lay person shall eat of the sacred donations. No bound or hired laborer of a priest shall eat of the sacred donations; 11 but a person who is a priest's property by purchase may eat of them; and those that are born into his household may eat of his food. 12 If a priest's daughter

a See chapters 13 and 15.

formation of external parts of the human body in its "completed," adult, male form, disqualify the priest from offering the sacred food gifts to God. Though he may not officiate, the defective priest remains a priest, as this is a fact of birth, and is entitled to eat the priestly portions of the sacrificial flesh. **21:** See 1.9. **23:** The specific

ineligibility of the defective priest, i.e., the prohibition of approaching the altar and beyond, may indicate the precise rationale for the law. According to Priestly teaching, the human being is made in the image of the deity (Gen. 1.26–27; 5.1). The priest, as God's palace servant, profanes the abode of the deity if he cannot adequately reflect the divine form; only the fully formed specimens of the image of God can serve in His earthly habitation. *These places sacred to Me,* "mikdashay," lit. "My sanctuaries." This does not, however, indicate that P or H accepted a decentralized cult with multiple sanctuaries (see also 26.31 n.) *Have sanctified,* as in v. 15, "sanctify them."

22.1–16. Desecration of the offerings. Even minor impurities desecrate the sacred (vv. 2–9); moreover, the consumption of sacred flesh by nonpriests desecrates it (vv. 10–16). **2:** *Be scrupulous about,* lit. "keep away from [whenever they are impure]." This v. thus provides the caption for vv. 2–9. *Lest they profane My holy name:* Allowing impurity to come into contact with the sacred profanes the divine name, since the divine abode and the food gifts of the deity are thereby treated as though they were common. *Mine the LORD's,* better, "I am the LORD [who commands this]." **3–7:** Contact impurities (see ch 11) and bodily impurities (see chs 13–15). **3:** *Shall be cut off,* see 7.20, 21. **4:** *Until he is clean,* as stipulated by the laws that apply in each case. **7:** *Sun sets:* The rule applies to vv. 4b–6 (see 11.24, etc.; 15.17). **8:** See 11.39–40; 17.15–16 n. **9:** *And die for it:* Death is depicted as the automatic and inevitable consequence of desecrating the sacred; see 10.2 n. **10–16:** The portions of the sacrificial offerings whose consumption is restricted to the priests are considered among the most sacred; contact between them and the lay person leads to their desecration. Nonpriests in the priest's employ, and the daughters of priests, may eat of them only as marries a layman, she may not eat of the sacred gifts; [13] but if the priest's daughter is widowed or divorced and without offspring, and is back in her father's house as in her youth, she may eat of her father's food. No lay person may eat of it: [14] but if a man eats of a sacred donation unwittingly, he shall pay the priest for the sacred donation, adding one-fifth of its value. [15] But [the priests] must not allow the Israelites to profane the sacred donations that they set aside for the LORD, [16] or to incur guilt requiring a penalty payment, by eating such sacred donations: for it is I the LORD who make them sacred.

[17] The LORD spoke to Moses, saying: [18] Speak to Aaron and his sons, and to all the Israelite people, and say to them:

When any man of the house of Israel or of the strangers in Israel presents a burnt offering as his offering for any of the votive or any of the freewill offerings that they offer to the LORD, [19] it must, to be acceptable in your favor, be a male without blemish, from cattle or sheep or goats. [20] You shall not offer any that has a defect, for it will not be accepted in your favor.

[21] And when a man offers, from the herd or the flock, a sacrifice of well-being to the LORD for an explicit[a] vow or as a freewill offering, it must, to be acceptable, be without blemish; there must be no defect in it. [22] Anything blind, or injured, or maimed, or with a wen, boil-scar, or scurvy—such you shall not offer to the LORD; you shall not put any of them on the altar as offerings by fire to the LORD. [23] You may, however, present as a freewill offering an ox or a sheep with a limb extended or contracted; but it will not be accepted for a vow. [24] You shall not offer to the LORD anything [with its testes] bruised or crushed or torn or cut. You shall have no such practices[b] in your own land, [25] nor shall you accept such [animals] from a foreigner for offering as food for your God, for they are mutilated, they have a defect; they shall not be accepted in your favor.

[26] The LORD spoke to Moses, saying: [27] When an ox or a sheep or a goat is born, it shall stay seven days with its mother, and from the eighth day on it shall be acceptable as an offering by fire to the LORD. [28] However, no animal

a Or "unspecified" or "extraordinary"; meaning of Heb. lephalle uncertain.
b I.e., mutilations.

long as they are formally a part of the priest's household. **14:** On unwitting desecration of the sacred, see also 5.14–16. **15–16:** These vv. make it clear that actively preserving the boundaries between the sacred and the profane is the responsibility of the priests; see also 10.10.

22.17–25: Animals unfit for sacrifice. The disqualifying defects of a priest, just covered, and of a potential offering are analogous, but their ramifications are not. Whereas defective priests must not approach the altar lest they desecrate the sacred, they are not thereby excluded from the priesthood per se and may eat sacred flesh. Deformed animals do not cause desecration, but are simply not accepted and the person's sacrifice is deemed not to have been offered. For the underlying idea that what is placed on God's table must be without defect, see Mal. 1.6–14. **17–20:** The disqualifying blemishes in the burnt offering; see 1.3 n. **19:** *Acceptable,* see 1.3–4; 7.18 n. **21–23:** The disqualifying blemishes in the well-being sacrifice. From this passage it becomes evident that the votive offering is of a greater sanctity since all of the blemishes enumerated disqualify it, whereas the freewill offering, in which the deformities mentioned in v. 23 are acceptable, is of a lesser sanctity. Taken along with 7.12–18, these vv. confirm that the hierarchy of the three classes is "todah" (thanksgiving offering), "neder" (votive offering),"nedavah" (freewill offering), in descending order. **24:** Animals with defective or mutilated genitalia; this v. appears to pertain to all sacrificial animals. *No such practices in your own land:* The Rabbis took this as a general prohibition of castrating animals, even outside of the sacrificial context (b. Ḥag. 14b; b. Shab. 110b).

22.26–33: Rules of acceptability. The fifth and final speech of the section, containing three laws pertaining to the acceptability of sacrificial animals as a function of the time factor and concluding with a general exhortation. **26–27:** From the context (see also Exod. 22.29), an animal is not considered fit for sacrifice until it is viable, i.e., has safely gotten beyond the stage of a newborn and is a creature in its own right. **27:** *Offering by fire,* see 1.9. **28:** In contrast to the preceding, the humane concern seems to be the only plausible explanation for this restriction; see Exod. 23.19 (= 34.26; Deut. 14.21) from the herd or from the flock shall be slaughtered on the same day with its young.

29 When you sacrifice a thanksgiving offering to the LORD, sacrifice it so that it may be acceptable in your favor. 30 It shall be eaten on the same day; you shall not leave any of it until morning: I am the LORD.

31 You shall faithfully observe My commandments: I am the LORD. 32 You shall not profane My holy name, that I may be sanctified in the midst of the Israelite people—I the LORD who sanctify you, 33 I who brought you out of the land of Egypt to be your God, I the LORD.

23 The LORD spoke to Moses, saying: 2 Speak to the Israelite people and say to them:

These are My fixed times, the fixed times of the LORD, which you shall proclaim as sacred occasions.

3 On six days work may be done, but on the seventh day there shall be a sabbath of complete rest, a sacred occasion. You shall do no work; it shall be a sabbath of the LORD throughout your settlements.

and Deut. 22.6–7. All of the Torah law collections thus exhibit the same motif. It is not clear whether it expresses the sense that animals have emotional attachment to their young and experience distress at their fate or whether the aim is to sensitize humans to avoid unnecessary cruelty. **29–30:** See 7.12–15. Together with 19.5–8, these vv. are a repetition of 7.12–18. **31–33:** Elsewhere in the Holiness Legislation we have been told that compliance with the commandments enables the Israelites to absorb the holiness of God (19.2, 37; 20.7–8). This hortatory conclusion expresses the converse: that the failure to obey the commandments desecrates the name of God. This is only logical: The purpose of Israel's existence is to sanctify God's name, that is, to attest to His existence, to publicize His oneness, and to advertise His greatness, by worshipping Him and by keeping His laws. Their failure to do so has the opposite effect: His name is profaned, that is, His fame is diminished and His reputation tarnished.

23.1–44: Sacred times. God conveys to Moses, in five speeches,

the laws of the weekly Sabbath and the annual holy days. Each of the Torah law collections contains a calendar of annual festivities, and most include a Sabbath law (some mention the Sabbath more than once). The command to abstain from labor on the Sabbath is found in all the collections, as is the tradition of festivals coinciding with the major events in the agricultural year: the early grain ripening, the reaping of the first produce, and the final ingathering. Some of the names of the festivals are shared by more than one law collection, as is the intrinsic connection between the springtime "matzot" festival and the commemorative "pesah" offering. The collections also agree that a central feature of at least some of the festivals is the "hag," which means "pilgrimage" (later called "ʿaliyah" or "ascent"), namely, the obligation to appear before the LORD. Despite these similarities, the Sabbath laws and festival calendars found in the separate law collections differ in many ways. Tradition managed to combine all of the legislation into a coherent whole, creatively reconciling the contradictions and interpreting each re-

peated passage as providing some further detail. Critical scholarship generally views each version of the festival calendar as reflecting a stage in the historical development of the festivals. The laws in this ch provide a glimpse of the unique Priestly vision of the Sabbath and festivals. They are "sacred times," i.e., dates set apart from the remainder of the calendar and designated as "belonging to" the deity. Like sacred objects, persons, areas, and utterances, they may not be treated as common. Thus, only in P are the festivals, like the Sabbath, days of cessation from work, since engaging in daily activity (that is, labor) would amount to the desecration of the holy, which Priestly law, especially H, is at such pains to prevent. Further, in the Priestly view, though the festivals are determined by the agricultural year, they are primarily God's special occasions. Thus they are days on which He is worshipped—by His priests, in His abode—in a manner exceeding the daily routine. The literary structure of the ch reflects these two features. It is organized as a calendar of precise dates on which a cessation from labor is to be observed and a special "food-gift" offered to the LORD. Another Priestly festival calendar appears in Num. chs 28–29; that calendar is primarily concerned with the required offerings. **1–2:** The caption. The terms *fixed times of the LORD* and *sacred occasions* express the underlying idea for the festival legislation. *Which you shall proclaim:* The translation reflects the rabbinic tradition (*b. Rosh Hash.* 24a) that the dates of the festivals are determined by the Israelites, i.e., the proclamation of the New Moon and the introduction of the intercalated month, upon which the entire calendar depends, are the responsibility of the Sages. **3:** The weekly Sabbath. In the Priestly version of history, the weekly "shabbat" (lit. "cessation") was consecrated at creation (see Gen. 2.1–3) but was not implemented until the Israelites had become a people, the Tabernacle was ready to be erected, and the

4 These are the set times of the LORD, the sacred occasions, which you shall celebrate each at its appointed time: 5 In the first month, on the fourteenth day of the month, at twilight, there shall be a passover offering to the LORD, 6 and on the fifteenth day of that month the LORD's Feast of Unleavened Bread. You shall eat unleavened bread for seven days. 7 On the first day you shall celebrate a sacred occasion: you shall not work at your occupations. 8 Seven days you shall make offerings by fire to the LORD. The seventh day shall be a sacred occasion: you shall not work at your occupations.

9 The LORD spoke to Moses, saying: 10 Speak to the Israelite people and say to them:

When you enter the land that I am giving to you and you reap its harvest, you shall bring the first sheaf of your harvest to the priest. 11 He shall elevate the sheaf before the LORD for acceptance in your behalf; the priest shall elevate it on the day after the sabbath. 12 On the day that you elevate the sheaf, you shall offer as a burnt offering to

worship of the LORD was about to be inaugurated there (Exod. 31.12–17; 35.1–3). The Sabbath law is repeated several times in H (Lev. 19.3, 30; 26.2; see also Num. 15.32–36). In the non-Priestly literature the Sabbath and festivals are two distinct topics; only Priestly law, with its notion of sacred times, calls the Sabbath holy and mentions it alongside the festivals (see also Exod. 34.21, the location of which may have been influenced by this text). **4:** The repetition of the caption (see v. 2) gives the impression that the inclusion of the weekly Sabbath among the "sacred times" was not part of an earlier version of the ch. See v. 38 n. **5–8:** The annual "pesaḥ" sacrifice, which is not a sacred occasion but which immediately precedes the first of these, the "matzot" pilgrimage. The historical explanation for each, the connection between the two, and the details of their observance, including the abstention from leaven, are given by P in Exod. ch 12; here only those aspects relevant to the calendar of "sacred occasions" are mentioned. **5:** *The first month,* see Exod. 12.2. *On the fourteenth day of the month, at twilight:*

The date of the evening is that of the preceding day (see v. 32; Exod. 12.18); only in postbiblical tradition was the method reversed and evenings given the date of the following day. *A passover offering,* "pesaḥ" (see Exod. 12.11–13) is the name of the sacrifice made in commemoration of the exodus; in postbiblical Judaism it became the name of the ensuing festival. **6:** *Feast,* Heb "ḥag," "pilgrimage." In the non-Priestly calendars there are three annual pilgrimages: the pilgrimage of Unleavened Bread ("ḥag ha-matzot"), the pilgrimage of Harvest ("katzir"), also called Weeks ("shavuʿot") and the pilgrimage of Ingathering ("ḥag ha'asif") or Booths ("sukkot"). Here and in Num. 28.26–31 there are only two, and "shavuʿot" is observed as a sacred occasion but not as a pilgrimage. In addition, in the non-Priestly tradition, the three pilgrimages are an absolute requirement, incumbent upon all males (Exod. 23.14, 17; 34.23–24; Deut. 16.16); in P, no such unqualified obligation is present. Those who do not make the pilgrimages must, however, observe the cessation from labor on the days designated as holy. *You shall eat unleav-*

ened bread: Nowhere does P provide the rationale for this; the non-Priestly traditions explain it as a commemoration of the haste in which the Israelites left Egypt (see Exod. 12.39; Deut. 16.3). The Priestly tradition thus preserves the agricultural origin of the eating of "matzot" in the early spring, marking the very beginning of the barley harvest. *For seven days:* The eating of unleavened bread lasts seven days; the pilgrimage, unlike "sukkot" (see vv. 34, 39–40) does not. According to Exod. 13.6 only the seventh day was observed as a pilgrimage; in our text it appears that the pilgrimage was observed on the first day, the day after the "pesaḥ" offering, followed by six more days of eating unleavened bread; this is stated explicitly in Deut. 16.7–8. **7:** *You shall not work at your occupations:* This phrase recurs in vv. 8, 21, 25, 35, 36, prohibiting labor on the fully sacred festival days. It differs from the phrase "You shall do no work" used with regard to the weekly Sabbath and the Day of Atonement in vv. 3, 28, 30. Relying on Exod. 12.16, Ramban interpreted the difference to mean that labors required for the preparation of food are permissible on festival days but not on the Sabbath and Day of Atonement. **8:** *Offerings by fire,* see 1.9 n. *The seventh day:* The observance of the first and last days of the festival as full holy days, which became normative Jewish practice, is peculiar to the Priestly tradition (see vv. 36, 39; Exod. 12.16; Num. 28.25; 29.35). **9–22:** The second speech contains a lengthy set of instructions for the rituals commencing after the "matzot" festival and culminating seven weeks later with the second of the sacred occasions. **9–14:** The presentation (lit. "elevation"; see 7.30 n.) of the "ʿomer," or first sheaf of the new barley harvest, with its accompanying offerings, performed each year to secure the deity's blessing for the new crops. **11:** *For acceptance in your behalf,* see 1.3–4; 7.18; 19.5; 22.19. *On the day after the sabbath:* This phrase (appearing also in v. 15) became a the Lord a lamb of the first year without blemish. [13] The meal offering with it shall be two-tenths of a measure of choice flour with oil mixed in, an offering by fire of pleasing odor to the Lord; and the libation with it shall be of wine, a quarter of a *hin*. [14] Until that very day, until you have brought the offering of your God, you shall eat no bread or parched grain or fresh ears;[a] it is a law for all time throughout the ages in all your settlements.

[15] And from the day on which you bring the sheaf of elevation offering—the day after the sabbath—you shall count off seven weeks. They must be complete: [16] you must count until the day after the seventh week—fifty days; then you shall bring an offering of new grain to the Lord. [17] You shall bring from your settlements two loaves of bread as an elevation offering; each shall be made of two-tenths of a measure of choice flour, baked after leavening, as first fruits to the Lord. [18] With the bread you shall present, as burnt offerings to the Lord, seven yearling lambs without blemish, one bull of the herd, and two rams, with their meal offerings and libations, an offering by fire of pleasing odor to the Lord. [19] You shall also offer one he-goat as a sin offering and two yearling lambs as a sacrifice of well-being. [20] The priest shall elevate these— the two lambs[b]—together with the bread of first fruits as an elevation offering before the Lord; they shall be holy to the Lord, for the priest. [21] On that same day you shall hold a celebration; it shall be a sacred occasion for you; you shall not work at your occupations. This is a law for all time in all your settlements, throughout the ages.

[22] And when you reap the harvest of your land, you shall not reap all the way to the edges of your field, or

a *I.e., of the new crop.*   b *Meaning of Heb. uncertain.*

major source of controversy in talmudic times (*Sifra 'Emor* 12:4; *b. Menaḥ.* 66a). The Pharisaic sages, claiming that the word "sabbath" is used here in its nonspecific, literal sense ("cessation") but does not indicate the weekly Sabbath day, vehemently asserted that the "'omer" is presented on the day after the day of rest at the beginning of the "matzot" pilgrimage, namely, the sixteenth of Nisan; otherwise the definite article in the phrase *"the* sabbath" would have no referent. Though this view has been accepted by Jewish tradition, the more natural sense of the phrase is that the ceremony was to

take place on the first day of the week (Sunday) following the pilgrimage. This was the view of the Boethusians as well as the Qumran sect, while the Samaritans and the Karaites held that the Sunday during the "matzot" pilgrimage was intended. **14:** As the presentation of the "'omer" marks the beginning of the new harvest, partaking of the new grain is prohibited until the ceremony has taken place. **15–22:** The new-grain ("first fruits"; see v. 20) offering, performed seven weeks later. **15–16:** The precise counting of seven weeks is required in order for the cessation from labor ob-

served by the population at large, wherever they are, to coincide with the Temple observances prescribed, since in P this festival is not marked by a pilgrimage (see v. 6). Only with the acceptance of the rabbinic interpretation of "the day after the sabbath" (see v. 11) and the establishment of the calendar did it become possible to specify a fixed date (6 Sivan) for this holy day; prior to this the fiftieth day would have fallen on a different date each year. The counting later became a ceremony in its own right, called, in commemoration of the sheaf of barley presented at its start, the "Counting of [i.e., from] the 'omer." The counting of seven weeks is also prescribed in Deut. 16.9, and even gives its name ("shavu'ot," "Weeks") to the festival observed at its conclusion (vv. 10 and 16; see also Exod. 34.22), but there it is to enable each landowner to determine the appropriate day for his own family's visit to the Temple. Here it has no name, but Num. 28.26 calls it "yom ha-bikkurim," "the Day of First Fruits" (see v. 20) and describes it further as "your Weeks." The connection of "shavu'ot" with the giving of the Torah at Sinai is not found in biblical tradition; it was derived by the Rabbis, who held that the dates coincide. **17–20:** The offerings presented on the fiftieth day (in addition to those enumerated in Num. 28.26–31). They consist of a unique offering of two leavened loaves called the "bread of first fruits" (see v. 20), in thanks for the new grain harvest and accompanied by appropriate additional offerings. Among the latter are two yearling lambs offered as a wellbeing offering ("shelamim"). This is the only such offering made on behalf of the public, functioning here as a communal offering of thanksgiving. **20:** *First fruits:* The word "fruit" is misleading; the reference here is to the new crop of wheat (see Exod. 23.16; 34.22) from which these loaves are produced; see also 2.14–17. **21:** *On that same day,* see vv. 15–16 n. **22:** A partial quotation from 19.9–10, added gather the gleanings of your harvest; you shall leave them for the poor and the stranger: I the LORD am your God.

23 The LORD spoke to Moses, saying: 24 Speak to the Israelite people thus: In the seventh month, on the first day of the month, you shall observe complete rest, a sacred occasion commemorated with loud blasts. 25 You shall not work at your occupations; and you shall bring an offering by fire to the LORD.

26 The LORD spoke to Moses, saying: 27 Mark, the tenth day of this seventh month is the Day of Atonement. It shall be a sacred occasion for you: you shall practice self-denial, and you shall bring an offering by fire to the LORD; 28 you shall do no work throughout that day. For it is a Day of Atonement, on which expiation is made on your behalf before the LORD your God. 29 Indeed, any person who does not practice self-denial throughout that day shall be cut off from his kin; 30 and whoever does any work throughout that day, I will cause that person to perish from among his people. 31 Do no work whatever; it is a law for all time, throughout the ages in all your settlements. 32 It shall be a sabbath of complete rest for you, and you shall practice self-denial; on the ninth day of the month at evening, from evening to evening, you shall observe this your sabbath.

33 The LORD spoke to Moses, saying: 34 Say to the Israelite people:

here by association to the context of harvest-time. **23–25:** The third speech ordains the sacred occasion observed on the first day of the seventh month. The beginning of the seventh month marks the beginning of the agricultural year and opens the season of holy days culminating two weeks later in the Ingathering pilgrimage. The non-Priestly calendars are unfamiliar with this observance. **24:** *Commemorated with loud blasts,* correctly, "remembrance by shouting"; compare "a day of shouting" [NJPS: "a day when the horn is sounded"] in the parallel law in Num. 29.1. The Priestly literature contains a number of observances to remind God of the Israelite people (Exod. 28.12, 29; 30.16; Num. 31.54). These may be compared to the rainbow, designated by God as a reminder (to Himself!) of His promise to preserve humanity (Gen. 9.14–16).

Num. 10.9–10 states that this is the function of the trumpet blasts sounded when Israel is in distress, to call their plight to God's attention and secure His assistance, or when celebrating festivals, New Moons, and appointed seasons. The annual "Day of Shouting" would thus be envisaged by the Priestly tradition as a day of Israel's crying out to God, to remind Him that they are His people and to secure His aid. In later tradition this observance developed in several directions. Though "teru'ah" literally means "raise a cry, shout," it is used in Num. 10.5–10 in conjunction with the sounding of trumpets, and in Lev. 25.9 in reference to the ram's horn. This led to the conclusion that here too the sound is to be made by the ram's horn or shofar. With the eventual adoption of the autumnal New Year as the pri-

mary one, the first day of the seventh month in the vernal calendar became New Year's Day ("Rosh Ha-Shanah"). Since, in the cultural milieu of the ancient Near East, the heralding of the New Year was particularly associated with celebrations of kingship, Rosh Ha-Shanah became, among other things, a day to mark God's sovereignty as king. Finally, since it opens a period leading up to the annual Day of Atonement (see ch 16; 23.26–32), Rosh Ha-Shanah became invested with the significance of the latter, and now marks the beginning of Judaism's annual ten-day penitential period. **26–32:** The Day of Atonement, also unknown outside of Priestly literature. On this day the Tabernacle is purged of the accumulated impurities and transgressions of the Israelite people (ch 16). The cessation of labor, which serves (along with the fast) to effect the purification and atonement rituals performed, marks this day too as holy time, a "sacred occasion," thus incorporating it into the annual cycle of such dates. **27:** *Practice self-denial,* fast; see 16.29 n. **28:** *For it is a Day of Atonement,* see 16.30. **29–30:** See 7.20, 21; 17.10. **32:** *A sabbath of complete rest,* a phrase used only of the Sabbath (v. 3; Exod. 31.15; 35.2) and the Day of Atonement (see also 16.31), highlighting the strict and total abstention required in order for the atonement rituals to be effective. **32:** *On the ninth day of the month at evening, from evening to evening,* see v. 5. *Sabbath,* cessation from labor. **33–42:** The final speech, containing the laws for the "sukkot" festival and the concluding captions. **34:** *Feast,* "pilgrimage"; see v. 6. *Booths,* Heb "sukkot," "huts" serving as makeshift, temporary shelters while laboring in the field or vineyard for several days at a time (see Isa. 1.8). The autumn pilgrimage is so named because its long duration—seven full days—necessitates the erection of such shelters to accommodate the many pilgrims during their stay in the Temple city (see vv. 43–44 n.). Notably, the texts which do not spec-

On the fifteenth day of this seventh month there shall be the Feast of Booths[a] to the LORD, [to last] seven days. [35] The first day shall be a sacred occasion: you shall not work at your occupations; [36] seven days you shall bring offerings by fire to the LORD. On the eighth day you shall observe a sacred occasion and bring an offering by fire to the LORD; it is a solemn gathering:[b] you shall not work at your occupations.

[37] Those are the set times of the LORD that you shall celebrate as sacred occasions, bringing offerings by fire to the LORD—burnt offerings, meal offerings, sacrifices, and libations, on each day what is proper to it—[38] apart from the sabbaths of the LORD, and apart from your gifts and from all your votive offerings and from all your freewill offerings that you give to the LORD.

[39] Mark, on the fifteenth day of the seventh month, when you have gathered in the yield of your land, you shall observe the festival of the LORD [to last] seven days: a complete rest on the first day, and a complete rest on the eighth day. [40] On the first day you shall take the product of hadar[c] trees, branches of palm trees, boughs of leafy[d] trees, and willows of the brook, and you shall rejoice before the LORD your God seven days. [41] You shall observe it as a festival of the LORD for seven days in the year; you shall observe it in the seventh month as a law for all time, throughout the ages. [42] You shall live in booths seven days; all citizens in Israel shall live in booths, [43] in order that future generations may know that I made the Israelite

a Others "Tabernacles."

b Precise meaning of Heb. ʿasereth uncertain.

c Others "goodly"; exact meaning of Heb. hadar uncertain. Traditionally the product is understood as "citron."

d Meaning of Heb. aboth uncertain.

ify that the fall pilgrimage lasts for seven days (Exod. 23.16; 34.22) do not call it sukkot, whereas vv. 39 and 42, as well as Num. 29.12, refer to it as "the pilgrimage of the LORD"—the pilgrimage par excellence. Rabbinic tradition too called it simply "ḥag." 36: On the eighth day: As distinct from the "matzot" observance, the concluding holy day is added to the first seven. Apparently, the pilgrimage is to last seven days, while on the eighth day, not called a "ḥag" but simply a "sacred occasion," a cessation from labor is to be observed by all—those who do not make the pilgrimage, those who do so but return home for the eighth day, and those who remain an additional day. The eighth day is unknown outside of the Priestly tradition. A solemn gathering, Heb "ʿatzeret" (see Isa. 1.13; Joel 2.15; Amos 5.21; etc); this day is therefore later called "shemini ʿatzeret," "the solemn gathering of the eighth [day]." In Deut. 16.8 "ʿatzeret" is used for the solemnities on the final day of the "mat-

zot" festival. Both apparently refer to local festive gatherings, as distinct from the pilgrimage to the Temple-city denoted by the word "ḥag." 37–38: A summary caption. 38: Apart from the sabbaths of the LORD: The Sabbath law in v. 3 was not originally part of the ch; see v. 4 n. 39–43: The closing section repeats the date and length of the pilgrimage, and the cessation of labor on the first and eighth days. Here, however, in place of the refrain "you shall offer food gifts to the LORD" are the additional observances of the festival. Since these are not sacrificial rites performed by the priests but are rather observed by the public at large, during their week-long visit to the Temple-city, they are not included in what comes before the caption in vv. 37–38. 39: Observe the festival, lit. "make a pilgrimage"; see v. 6. 40: The "taking" of the four species of branches and boughs is evidently a ritual of joyous acknowledgment of the current year's agricultural abundance. It may also have been a form of supplication for the next year's rainfall, expected to begin at this period of the year; in later times it was so interpreted. In Neh. 8.14–15 the branches were used for the construction of the booths, while according to rabbinic practice, they were gathered together in a bouquet and waved. Product, Heb "peri," "fruit"; possibly also boughs or branches. Of hadar trees, lit. "majestic" or beautiful trees (see translators' note c). Though no specific identification can be determined, ancient tradition (b. Sukkah 31a) ruled that the fruit of the citron (the "ʾetrog") is to be used. Boughs of leafy trees, traditionally, the myrtle. You shall rejoice, mentioned only here, a stark contrast to Deuteronomy, where rejoicing on the pilgrimages is mentioned several times (Deut. 16.11, 14, 15). 41: As a festival, "as a pilgrimage"; see v. 6. 43–44: Dwelling in booths for the seven days of the pilgrimage is here prescribed as a requirement, incumbent upon the entire population. The rationale differs from the people live in booths when I brought them out of the land of Egypt, I the LORD your God.

⁴⁴ So Moses declared to the Israelites the set times of the LORD.

24 The LORD spoke to Moses, saying: ² Command the Israelite people to bring you clear oil of beaten olives for lighting, for kindling lamps regularly. ³ Aaron shall set them up in the Tent of Meeting outside the curtain of the Pact [to burn] from evening to morning before the LORD regularly; it is a law for all time throughout the ages. ⁴ He shall set up the lamps on the pureᵃ lampstand before the LORD [to burn] regularly.

⁵ You shall take choice flour and bake of it twelve loaves, two-tenths of a measure for each loaf. ⁶ Place them on the pureᵃ table before the LORD in two rows, six to a row. ⁷ With each row you shall place pure frankincense, which is to be a token offeringᵇ for the bread, as an offering by fire to the LORD. ⁸ He shall arrange them before the LORD regularly every sabbath day—it is a commitment for all time on the part of the Israelites. ⁹ They shall belong to Aaron and his sons, who shall eat them in the sacred precinct; for they are his as most holy things from the LORD's offerings by fire, a due for all time.

¹⁰ There came out among the Israelites one whose mother was Israelite and whose father was Egyptian. And a fight broke out in the camp between that half-Israeliteᶜ

---

a See note at Exod. 31.8.   b See Lev. 2.2.   c Lit. "the son of an Israelite woman."

---

one suggested above (see v. 34 n.) and is obscure. It is an attempt to historicize the central observance of the pilgrimage, suggesting that it commemorates the period of dwelling in the presence of the LORD's abode, the Tabernacle, in the wilderness. The notion that God housed the Israelites in booths in the wilderness is not attested elsewhere.

24.1–9: Oil and loaves. A divine speech containing two laws. The first law (vv. 2–4), instructions for the oil for the Tabernacle lampstand, is almost a repetition of Exod. 27.20–21; the second (vv. 5–9), the procedure for the loaves to be displayed on the table in the Tabernacle, completes the

legislation of Exod. 25.23–30. Both laws pertain to the ritual acts performed by the high priest regularly, inside the Tabernacle, and constituting a perpetual (Heb "tamid") display of worship. The daily lighting and tending of the lampstand is also mentioned in Exod. 30.7–8, in the context of the high priest's incense offering, the third component of the ritual complex. The laws relating to daily Tabernacle routine may supplement the preceding ch, which details the calendar of perpetually recurring special occasions. **2–3:** See Exod. 27.20–21. **4:** The instructions for fashioning the Tabernacle lampstand ("menorah") in Exod. 25.31–40 do not explain how the lampstand is to be used. The

legislation here clarifies the command to have light burn from evening to morning in the Tabernacle (Exod. 27.20–21). *The pure lampstand*, an ellipsis meaning "the lampstand made of pure gold"; see Exod. 25.31, 39; 31.8; 37.17; 39.37; Num. 8.4. **5–9:** The twelve loaves, known as the "show bread" or "Bread of Presence," are a symbolic offering, displayed but not sacrificed. They represent the twelve tribes of Israel and suggest dramatically their constant devotion to the deity enthroned in their midst. In the Priestly Tabernacle, the deity is enshrined in the inner sanctum, but the furnishings and the acts of devotion performed upon them all belong to the outer sanctum, and the partition dividing the two realms is never breached. Thus God, even as His Presence dwells among the Israelites, is perceived as separate from them and noncorporeal. *The pure table*, i.e., "the table overlaid with pure gold"; see Exod. 25.24; 37.11. **7, 9:** *Offering(s) by fire*, better, "food gifts" (see 1.9 n.) **8:** *Every sabbath day:* The weekday morning entry of the high priest into the Tabernacle consisted of offering incense and tending the lampstand; on the Sabbath, the removal and replacement of the twelve display loaves is added. **9:** The loaves, having absorbed permanent, contagious sanctity from their close contact with the deity's Presence, can neither be discarded nor eaten by the laity. Conceptually, the loaves are a gift made by the Israelite people to the LORD, who gives it to the priests in recognition of their service (see 6.10–11).

24.10–23: The blasphemer. The report of an extraneous event interrupts the giving of the laws. A similar interruption is found in ch 10. In both cases, the resolution of the unforeseen situation requires direct divine intervention, and both times this leads to a brief legal discussion arising from the events (10.12–19; 24.17–22). Most significantly, both passages tell of flagrant crimes committed by individual Israelites in violation of the and a certain Israelite. [11] The son of the Israelite woman pronounced the Name in blasphemy, and he was brought to Moses—now his mother's name was Shelomith daughter of Dibri of the tribe of Dan—[12] and he was placed in custody, until the decision of the LORD should be made clear to them.

[13] And the LORD spoke to Moses, saying: [14] Take the blasphemer outside the camp; and let all who were within hearing lay their hands upon his head, and let the whole community stone him.

[15] And to the Israelite people speak thus: Anyone who blasphemes his God shall bear his guilt; [16] if he also pronounces the name LORD, he shall be put to death. The whole community shall stone him; stranger or citizen, if he has thus pronounced the Name, he shall be put to death.

[17] If anyone kills any human being, he shall be put to death. [18] One who kills a beast shall make restitution for it:

divinely imposed order established in the preceding chs: the crime of Nadab and Abihu against the indwelling deity, and the crime of the blasphemer against the sacred Name. Thus, both strata of the Priestly work, P and H (see ch 17), tell of a primal sin occurring shortly after the revelation of God, upsetting what should have been an untroubled relationship between God and His people and necessitating immediate action. The motif is also found in the non-Priestly tradition (Exod. 32–34; Deut. 9–10). **10:** *Half-Israelite:* The case was initially puzzling because of the blasphemer's mixed ancestry, but v. 16 renders the decision that both Israelites (citizens) and resident aliens were equally liable for blasphemy. **11:** *Pronounced the Name in blasphemy:* Merely uttering YHVH is not a crime in P; throughout the Bible this is a normal and even commendable action. Nor is uttering God's name in falsehood or "in vain," prohibited in the Decalogue (Exod. 20.7 ‖ Deut. 5.11), a case of blasphemy. Blasphemy consists of cursing God (see Exod. 22.27; 1 Kings 21.10–13), that is, uttering an imprecation against Him in which His name is included ("May such-and-such befall YHVH"). As the divine Name is the one sacred "object" that can be

used, or misused, by anyone at any time (see 5.20–26 n.), it is only logical that in the Holiness Legislation this is a sacrilege par excellence. **12–13:** The blaphemer is apprehended and held in custody until Moses seeks and receives oracular instruction from God (probably by means of the "'urim" on Aaron's breastplate; see Exod. 28.15, 30). Moses' inability to render a decision before consulting God occurs three more times in P, in the accounts of the second Passover, the Sabbath wood-gatherer, and the daughters of Zelophehad (Num. 9.1–14; 15.32–36; 27.1–11), and in all four cases the remedy for a specific circumstance becomes a permanent law applicable for future generations as well. **14:** The laying-on of hands (see 16.21) transfers to the blasphemer the guilt that the listeners have incurred by hearing the desecration of the sacred Name. This guilt will be eradicated along with the offender, who is stoned as an expression of the community's collective horror and its urgent need to be rid of the instrument of desecration. **15–16:** The legal decision is now generalized for future use. **15:** *Blasphemes his God . . . also pronounces the name LORD,* lit. "curses his God and pronounces the name of YHVH"; thus, one who maligned

God or invoked evil upon Him without actually pronouncing the Tetragrammaton would be exempt from the death penalty, since no actual desecration of the sacred Name would have taken place. **16:** *Stranger or citizen,* see 16.29. The logical counterpart to the "ger" or resident alien, familiar in the author's own period, would have been a non-Israelite accompanying the Israelites in the wilderness. In the author's mind such persons would have been the offspring of Israelite women and Egyptian men, conceived and born while still in Egypt (the non-Priestly tradition probably agrees; see Exod. 12.38). Such a person is cast in the central role of the narrative in order to establish the legal principle that the desecration of YHVH's name is a capital offense by definition, whether performed by an Israelite or a "ger." The Bible's principle of patrilineal descent would consider such a person Egyptian rather than Israelite. **17–22:** This short collection of laws is parenthetical and the narrative flow of vv. 10–16 continues, and concludes, in v. 23. It has been inserted here in accord with H's principle that laws pertaining to wrongs committed against one's fellow are the stuff of divine commands only if they impinge on the realm of the sacred. This brief law collection has a simple theme: With regard to the talionic or measure-for-measure ("eye-for-eye") rule in crimes and damages, the resident alien has precisely the same obligation as the citizen (v. 22). God's laws of fairness and justice are to be observed throughout the land where His Presence, with the holiness it effuses, resides. Unlike the obligation to worship Him, which rests upon Israel alone, the obligation to make fair restitution applies wherever God's Presence dwells. The similar statement in the law of the blasphemer (v. 16) accounts for the addition of this section here. **17:** See Gen. 9.6; Num. 35.31–34; outside of P: Exod. 21.12. The laws of asylum for unintentional homicide are designed to circumvent the life for life. ¹⁹ If anyone maims his fellow, as he has done so shall it be done to him: ²⁰ fracture for fracture, eye for eye, tooth for tooth. The injury he inflicted on another shall be inflicted on him. ²¹ One who kills a beast shall make restitution for it; but one who kills a human being shall be put to death. ²² You shall have one standard for stranger and citizen alike: for I the LORD am your God.

²³ Moses spoke thus to the Israelites. And they took the blasphemer outside the camp and pelted him with stones. The Israelites did as the LORD had commanded Moses.

BE-HAR   בהר

25 The LORD spoke to Moses on Mount Sinai: ² Speak to the Israelite people and say to them:

When you enter the land that I assign to you, the land shall observe a sabbath of the LORD. ³ Six years you may sow your field and six years you may prune your vineyard and gather in the yield. ⁴ But in the seventh year the land shall have a sabbath of complete rest, a sabbath of the LORD: you shall not sow your field or prune your vineyard. ⁵ You shall not reap the aftergrowth of your harvest or gather the grapes of your untrimmed vines; it shall be a year of complete rest for the land. ⁶ But you may eat whatever the land during its sabbath will produce—you, your male and female slaves, the hired and bound laborers who

death penalty when it is patently unethical; see in P Num. 35.9–33. **18:** Restitution can always be made for destruction of livestock; see Exod. 21.33–37. **19–20:** On the law of talion, or "eye-for-eye" principle, for bodily harm, see Exod. 21.23–25, where monetary compensation equivalent to the damages is meant (see v. 22). Rabbinic law interprets our text and Deut. 19.21 in the same fashion, but from the formulation of v. 20 it would seem that in Leviticus the literal sense is intended. **21:** The recapitulation indicates the end of the interpolated section and reemphasizes the legal distinction between human life and the life of animals. **23:** The narrative resumes and concludes: The people carry out the instructions given to Moses in v. 14.

25.1–26.46. As the end of the the first month of the second year after the exodus approaches (see

Num 1.1), the law-giving at Sinai draws to a close. During the first three weeks of the second month, some additional laws will be communicated (see Num. chs 5, 6; 8.23–26; 9.1–14; 10.1–10), but most of what is presented as divine communication to Moses during that period will consist of instructions for the journey to commence on the twentieth of the month. Thus, chs 25 and 26 mark the final stage of the law-giving. This is evident from the content of 26.3–45 and stated explicitly in the concluding verse (26.46). (Ch 27 is chronologically displaced.) Chs 25 and 26 contain two integrally connected sections, the laws of the sabbatical and jubilee (25.1–26.2) and the speech of promise and threat (26.3–45). The theme of the first section is God's ownership of the land of Israel and the Israelites' status as hired tenants on His estate; the second details the wages promised to the tenants if they ac-

quiesce in all the Landowner's demands and the measures He will take if they do not, culminating, if necessary, in their being evicted from His property. By combining two speeches into one, the longest in Leviticus, with the legal section flowing directly into the concluding exhortation, the author establishes this connection.

25.1–55: Sabbatical and jubilee laws. 1: *On Mount Sinai:* Midrashic interpretation took this to mean that the divine speech recorded here was communicated to Moses during one of his visits to the top of the mountain. In P, however, Moses ascended Sinai only once, for the sole purpose of receiving the instructions for the Tabernacle and the priesthood. Thus here the words "behar sinay" mean "at (not on) Mount Sinai," i.e., [in the Tabernacle which stood] at [the foot of] Mount Sinai; see 7.38. **2:** *Assign to you,* correctly, "give you" as in 14.34. **2–7:** The sabbatical year. The command to "release and abandon" the produce of the seventh year appears in Exod. 23.11; the purpose there is to allow the poor to gather and eat what the owner leaves behind. The year of release in Deuteronomy also highlights social concerns, but it pertains to the cancellation of debts rather than the produce of the land (Deut. 15.1–6). Here, uniquely, it is forbidden to work the land in the seventh year, while its produce may be gathered and eaten—by the landholder. In Priestly law the poor are provided for by other measures (19.9–10; 23.22). **2:** *A sabbath of the LORD:* Only here is the seventh year called "shabbat of the LORD," thus making it equivalent to the other appointed times and sacred occasions of the LORD (see ch 23). **4:** *Sabbath of complete rest, a sabbath of the LORD,* similarly with regard to the weekly Sabbath and the Day of Atonement; see 23.32 n. **5:** *Aftergrowth,* plants that spring up on their own, without deliberate sowing. **6:** Normal, wholesale reaping and harvesting is not permitted; rather, the landholder may gather

live with you, [7] and your cattle and the beasts in your land
may eat all its yield.

[8] You shall count off seven weeks of years—seven times
seven years—so that the period of seven weeks of years
gives you a total of forty-nine years. [9] Then you shall
sound the horn loud; in the seventh month, on the tenth
day of the month—the Day of Atonement—you shall
have the horn sounded throughout your land [10] and you
shall hallow the fiftieth year. You shall proclaim release[a]
throughout the land for all its inhabitants. It shall be a jubilee[b] for you: each of you shall return to his holding and
each of you shall return to his family. [11] That fiftieth year
shall be a jubilee for you: you shall not sow, neither shall
you reap the aftergrowth or harvest the untrimmed vines,
[12] for it is a jubilee. It shall be holy to you: you may only
eat the growth direct from the field.

[13] In this year of jubilee, each of you shall return to his
holding. [14] When you sell property to your neighbor,[c] or

---

a Others "liberty."   b Heb. yobel, "ram" or "ram's horn."
c I.e., fellow Israelite; see v. 46.

---

as needed in order to feed his own
household, and his livestock may
graze. **8–22:** The jubilee year. It is
not known whether the jubilee
was ever observed in actual practice. There is no mention of the jubilee in biblical history of First
Temple times, and according to
the Rabbis it was not observed
in Second Temple times at all
(b. 'Arak. 32 b). There are, however, indications that a fifty-year
cycle was employed in the calendar in ancient times; traditions
of calculating the jubilees survived beyond the biblical period.
The primary law of the jubilee
(vv. 8–13) introduces its frequency
and onset, its inauguration, its
sanctity, and its two central features: the land release and the release of indentured persons. This
is followed by a brief section detailing the implications for the sale
of real estate between jubilees
(vv. 14–17). The law then promises
prosperity and security as reward
for faithful observance (vv. 18–19)
and concludes by reassuring the
uneasy that God will provide
(vv. 20–22). **8:** Weeks of years, lit.
"sabbaths of years"; "shabbat" in
the sense of "week"is common in

later Heb. **9:** The fiftieth year follows the seventh sabbatical
(though rabbinic tradition records
other views as well). Unlike the
seventh year, which is called a
"shabbat" but not referred to as
holy, it is sacred. It is inaugurated
in the seventh month since the autumnal New Year, which later became dominant in the Jewish calendar but has biblical roots, is the
start of the agricultural cycle (see
Exod. 23.16; 34.22). On the tenth
day of the month—the Day of Atonement: Perhaps the tenth of the
month was thought of, as it was
in later times, as the conclusion
of the New Year's celebrations.
10: Release, Heb "deror"; see
Isa. 61.1; Jer. 34.8; Ezek. 46.17. A
related term is known from Mesopotamia, where it indicates the
general release proclaimed occasionally by kings in order to create
or restore economic stability. This
second aspect of the jubilee, the release of indentured persons, is detailed in vv. 39–46. Jubilee: Ancient
translators drew an artificial connection between Heb "yovel" and
the similar sounding Latin "jubi-
lare," "shout for joy"; thus the
English "jubilee" suggests the idea

of jubilation not present in the
Heb. Outside of the Priestly literature "yovel" indicates a ram
(Josh. 6.4–6) or a ram's horn
(Exod. 19.13), and since the fiftieth
year is inaugurated by the sounding of the ram's horn (v. 9), some
feel that this has given its name to
the institution. But the word "shofar" rather than "yovel" is mentioned in v. 9, and throughout the
ch (and in 27.17–24; Num. 36.4) is
used to denote what takes place
during the fiftieth year and not the
manner in which the year is heralded. "Yovel" here seems to be
derived from "y-b-l," "bring" and
to mean "sending forth, home-
bringing" or simply liberation, as
reflected in LXX and realized in
the 12th century by Abraham Ibn
Ezra. Each of you shall return to his
holding: The basic postulate of the
jubilee, from which the legislation
in this ch (and that in 27.17–24;
Num. 36.4) derives, is that once
the Israelites have entered Canaan,
the land is divided up (by lot, see
Num. 33.54) in perpetuity. The
land of Canaan is not the Israelites' property, it is rather a "holding" ("'ahuzah"; see 14.34;
Gen. 17.8; 48.4; Deut. 32.49); so are
the plots of land held by each
tribe, clan, and family. Collectively
and individually, these holdings
are not theirs to buy, sell, and reap-
portion. The Israelites are mere
leaseholders, tenants on the divine
estate, and the holdings God has
parceled out to them are inalienable. Though the ultimate effect of
this far-reaching legislation may
be social, the pervasive concern is
religious, indeed theocentric. The
jubilee, like the Sabbath and festivals, is an assertion of God's exclusive proprietorship and dominion,
designed to keep the Israelites
constantly aware that they are His
indentured servants (vv. 42, 55).
Once again the law-giver expresses the idea that social legislation is included among God's
commands only insofar as it impinges on the sacred; see notes to
chs 17–26, 18, 19; 24.17–22. **11:** See
vv. 5–6. Since the fiftieth year always follows a sabbatical year, a
two-year cessation of agricultural

buy any from your neighbor, you shall not wrong one another. [15] In buying from your neighbor, you shall deduct only for the number of years since the jubilee; and in selling to you, he shall charge you only for the remaining crop years: [16] the more such years, the higher the price you pay; the fewer such years, the lower the price; for what he is selling you is a number of harvests. [17] Do not wrong one another, but fear your God; for I the LORD am your God.

[18] You shall observe My laws and faithfully keep My rules, that you may live upon the land in security; [19] the land shall yield its fruit and you shall eat your fill, and you shall live upon it in security. [20] And should you ask, "What are we to eat in the seventh year, if we may neither sow nor gather in our crops?" [21] I will ordain My blessing for you in the sixth year, so that it shall yield a crop sufficient for three years. [22] When you sow in the eighth year, you will still be eating old grain of that crop; you will be eating the old until the ninth year, until its crops come in.

[23] But the land must not be sold beyond reclaim, for the land is Mine; you are but strangers resident with Me. [24] Throughout the land that you hold, you must provide for the redemption of the land.

[25] If your kinsman is in straits and has to sell part of his holding, his nearest redeemer[a] shall come and redeem what his kinsman has sold. [26] If a man has no one to redeem for him, but prospers and acquires enough to redeem with, [27] he shall compute the years since its sale, refund the difference to the man to whom he sold it, and return to his holding. [28] If he lacks sufficient means to recover it, what he sold shall remain with the purchaser until the jubilee; in the jubilee year it shall be released, and he shall return to his holding.

[29] If a man sells a dwelling house in a walled city, it may be redeemed until a year has elapsed since its sale; the redemption period shall be a year. [30] If it is not redeemed before a full year has elapsed, the house in the walled city

---

a I.e., the closest relative able to redeem the land.

---

activity is entailed. **14–17:** *Buying* and *selling* of land in Canaan is actually a matter of leasing until the jubilee. **17:** *Wrong:* i.e., cheat, by deceitfully inflating the price. *But fear your God,* see 19.14 n.; 25.36. **20:** *And should you ask:* Though the issue should properly have arisen after v. 7, it applies even more urgently here; see below. **21–22:** The people are told to trust in God and do as commanded. The promise given is most easily understood elliptically. Crops sown in the fall of the sixth year and reaped in the spring will suffice for (1) the remainder of that year and (2) the entire seventh year. In the fall of the eighth year new crops may be sown, so the grain from the sixth year will suffice until the spring of the eighth, two years altogether. And if the eighth year is a jubilee, the produce of the sixth year will last until (3) the spring of the ninth year, when the crops sown in the fall following the jubilee come in, a total of three years. **23–55:** While the jubilee effects a general, universal release, throughout the years leading up to it society must provide for the restoration of property and liberty whenever possible; the jubilee is the last resort. The basic law stating this (vv. 23–24) is followed by a series of specific cases spelling out its specific ramifications. **23:** *But,* better, "Furthermore"; that is, in addition to all of the above and prior to it. *Strangers resident,* see 16.29. **24:** *Redemption:* In the Bible this term retains its literal, commercial sense, as in reclaiming a pawned item or mortgaged property. One who has lost his property or liberty must be enabled to regain it. This obligation is twofold: It devolves upon the buyer, who is required to allow the person in question to repurchase property or liberty, and upon the kinsmen of the person in question, who must assist if the means to do so do not suffice. Otherwise the jubilee, when it eventually arrives, effects the redemption by default. Speaking of God as Israel's "Redeemer" is thus a metaphor. Since Israel is God's near kinsman, when Israel is in distress it is God's veritable obligation to come to its aid and make whatever efforts are necessary in order to extricate it from its predicament. **25–28:** An Israelite is forced to sell (i.e., lease) a portion of an ancestral heritage. Prior to the jubilee, the buyer must enable the seller, or a kinsman acting on the seller's behalf, to reclaim at a price calculated in view of the number of years remaining until the jubilee. But even if neither the seller nor the kinsmen can come up with the necessary cash, the sale remains in effect only until the jubilee. **29–34:** The only exception to the above is the sale (i.e., lease) of strictly urban property. The seller and the kinsmen have but one year to come up with the redemption price; if they default, the sale is final. But even here, several exceptions are enumerated.

shall pass to the purchaser beyond reclaim throughout the ages; it shall not be released in the jubilee. 31 But houses in villages that have no encircling walls shall be classed as open country: they may be redeemed, and they shall be released through the jubilee. 32 As for the cities of the Levites, the houses in the cities they hold—the Levites shall forever have the right of redemption. 33ª Such property as may be redeemed from the Levites—houses sold in a city they hold—shall be released through the jubilee; for the houses in the cities of the Levites are their holding among the Israelites. 34 But the unenclosed land about their cities cannot be sold, for that is their holding for all time.

35 If your kinsman, being in straits, comes under your authority, and you hold him as though a resident alien, let him live by your side: 36 do not exact from him advance or accrued interest,ᵇ but fear your God. Let him live by your side as your kinsman. 37 Do not lend him your money at advance interest, or give him your food at accrued interest. 38 I the LORD am your God, who brought you out of the land of Egypt, to give you the land of Canaan, to be your God.

39 If your kinsman under you continues in straits and must give himself over to you, do not subject him to the treatment of a slave. 40 He shall remain with you as a hired or bound laborer; he shall serve with you only until the jubilee year. 41 Then he and his children with him shall be free of your authority; he shall go back to his family and return to his ancestral holding.—42 For they are My servants, whom I freed from the land of Egypt; they may not give themselves over into servitude.—43 You shall not rule over him ruthlessly; you shall fear your God. 44 Such male and female slaves as you may have—it is from the nations round about you that you may acquire male and female slaves. 45 You may also buy them from among the children

a Meaning of first half of verse uncertain.
b I.e., interest deducted in advance, or interest added at the time of repayment.

35–37: According to the simplest interpretation, the impoverished Israelite may have no recourse but to enter the kinsman's household and become a dependent. The kinsman, however, is commanded to refrain from exacting interest on the sustenance provided, so that the poor relative may save enough to regain economic independence. The prohibition of interest, which outside of the Priestly law is universal (Exod. 22.24; Deut. 23.20–21) and stems from explicitly humanitarian concerns, is restricted here to the live-in relative attempting to redeem property or liberty. Here, the land of Canaan is God's estate, and the command for the tenants to behave charitably toward one another derives from this. **38:** A transitional verse concluding the laws of land release; the remainder of the ch deals with the release of indentured persons. **39–46:** In contrast to the picture emerging from the non-Priestly law collections (see Exod. 21.2–11 n.; Deut. 15.12–18 n.), the Priestly legal tradition recognizes no Israelite slavery as such. What appears to be servitude is not; an Israelite forced to become indentured to another Israelite has the status of a hired laborer. Moreover, this servitude is temporary, and the option of remaining in slavery forever, available in the non-Priestly codes, is not provided. **39:** *Continues*, not reflected in the Heb. The dependent relative, in a dire situation, may become a kinsman's indentured laborer even without the prior, dependent stage. **40:** *Only until the jubilee year:* Logical, but not explicit, is the possibility that the indentured servant may save enough to redeem himself before the jubilee arrives or that his kinsmen may help him to do so. **41:** This v. indicates that the servitude envisaged was subsequent to the sale of property. When the jubilee arrives, the servants are released from their servitude and their ancestral property is released from its buyers, so persons and lands are reunited. *And his children with him:* Here, in contrast to Exod. 21.3–4, even children born during the long years of servitude do not become the property of the employer. **42–43:** Israelites, like landholdings in Canaan, are divine property; thus they are released in the jubilee. Israelites are servants of God alone: He took them out of Egypt not in order to make them free but to make them slaves—of His own. This idea has practical as well as theological implications: Indentured Israelites may not be exploited or treated with the harshness with which a master may legitimately treat actual slaves. **44–46:** These vv. make clear that the Priestly law has no principled objection to slavery per se. Non-Israelites may be enslaved, and they and their progeny become the permanent property of their master. **44:** *The nations round about you:* According to the picture of history envisaged by H, the land of Canaan itself will have of aliens resident among you, or from their families that are among you, whom they begot in your land. These shall become your property: ⁴⁶ you may keep them as a possession for your children after you, for them to inherit as property for all time. Such you may treat as slaves. But as for your Israelite kinsmen, no one shall rule ruthlessly over the other.

⁴⁷ If a resident alien among you has prospered, and your kinsman being in straits, comes under his authority and gives himself over to the resident alien among you, or to an offshoot of an alien's family, ⁴⁸ he shall have the right of redemption even after he has given himself over. One of his kinsmen shall redeem him, ⁴⁹ or his uncle or his uncle's son shall redeem him, or anyone of his family who is of his own flesh shall redeem him; or, if he prospers, he may redeem himself. ⁵⁰ He shall compute with his purchaser the total from the year he gave himself over to him until the jubilee year; the price of his sale shall be applied to the number of years, as though it were for a term as a hired laborer under the other's authority. ⁵¹ If many years remain, he shall pay back for his redemption in proportion to his purchase price; ⁵² and if few years remain until the jubilee year, he shall so compute: he shall make payment for his redemption according to the years involved. ⁵³ He shall be under his authority as a laborer hired by the year; he shall not rule ruthlessly over him in your sight. ⁵⁴ If he has not been redeemed in any of those ways, he and his children with him shall go free in the jubilee year. ⁵⁵ For it is to Me that the Israelites are servants: they are My servants, whom I freed from the land of Egypt, I the LORD your God.

26 You shall not make idols for yourselves, or set up for yourselves carved images or pillars, or place figured ͣ stones in your land to worship upon, for I the LORD am your God. ² You shall keep My sabbaths and venerate My sanctuary, Mine, the LORD's.

BE-ḤUKKOTAI   בחקתי

³ If you follow My laws and faithfully observe My commandments, ⁴ I will grant your rains in their season, so

---

ͣ Meaning of Heb. maskith uncertain.

been evacuated of its former inhabitants (see 18.24–30), so non-Israelite slaves can only be purchased from foreign nations. **47–54:** The Israelite forced to sell (i.e., indenture) himself to a non-Israelite is entitled to redeem himself; moreover, the members of his immediate and even extended family are obligated to make every effort to redeem him if he cannot redeem himself. As with landholdings (see vv. 14–17), the redemption price depends on the number

of years remaining until the jubilee, since at that time the Israelite will be released in any case. **47:** *Resident alien,* see. 16.29. It is assumed that the "ger" must, and can be compelled to, comply with the law requiring Israelite self-redemption or the release of the Israelite when the jubilee arrives. *An offshoot of an alien's family,* mentioned only here, but clearly indicating that in the Priestly view the "ger" does not eventually become an Israelite by assimilation, much less by conversion (unknown in biblical times). Rather, though he and his descendants may dwell and prosper in the land of Israel, they retain their non-Israelite status. For P, the only Israelites are the biological descendants of Jacob. **54:** *He and his children with him,* see v. 41. **55:** Repeating the rationale of v. 42, pertinent here and serving to conclude the corpus of jubilee legislation.

26.1–46: Promise and threat. **1–2:** The ch division misinterprets these two vv. as the introduction to what follows, but they are in fact the conclusion to what precedes. They echo commands in ch 19; v. 1 elaborates on 19.4, and v. 2 repeats 19.30. They act as concluding refrains, expressing three of the basic concerns of the Holiness legislation and signaling the end of its body of laws. **3–45:** The promise of reward and the threat of divine chastisement. By analogy to Deut. ch 28 and the treaty curses found in Mesopotamian texts, scholars generally refer to this section as the "blessings and curses" of the Holiness Legislation. But neither "bless" nor "curse" appears in the text, nor does the idea that these terms imply. **3–13:** The reward for compliance: God will give the Israelites peace and prosperity, safety from wild beasts, population increase, and victory over their enemies. Further, He will give them the security that comes from the certain knowledge that all this is assured them. The aim of the exodus will be accomplished: Israel will become God's people, that is, His loyal servants;

that the earth shall yield its produce and the trees of the field their fruit. ⁵ Your threshing shall overtake the vintage, and your vintage shall overtake the sowing; you shall eat your fill of bread and dwell securely in your land.

⁶ I will grant peace in the land, and you shall lie down untroubled by anyone; I will give the land respite from vicious beasts, and no sword shall cross your land. ⁷ You shall give chase to your enemies, and they shall fall before you by the sword. ⁸ Five of you shall give chase to a hundred, and a hundred of you shall give chase to ten thousand; your enemies shall fall before you by the sword.

⁹ I will look with favor upon you, and make you fertile and multiply you; and I will maintain My covenant with you. ¹⁰ You shall eat old grain long stored, and you shall have to clear out the old to make room for the new.

¹¹ I will establish My abode in your midst, and I will not spurn you. ¹² I will be ever present in your midst: I will be your God, and you shall be My people. ¹³ I the LORD am your God who brought you out from the land of the Egyptians to be their slaves no more, who broke the bars of your yoke and made you walk erect.

¹⁴ But if you do not obey Me and do not observe all these commandments, ¹⁵ if you reject My laws and spurn

first to be aimed at bringing Israel's national existence to an end (as in Deuteronomy), is finally revealed to be yet another attempt at making Israel walk the straight and narrow. This stage, entailing destruction and exile, will culminate in Israel's remorse; when this occurs God will remember His covenant and try once again to implement His plan of abiding in their midst and ruling over them. The effect of this diatribe is complex. On the one hand, it rains down upon the listener an unending barrage of fire and brimstone. The very contemplation of the horrors described forces the individual to consider the consequences of acting against the will of a God so uncompromising and so powerful. On the other hand, it casts God not in the role of the petty tyrant exacting retaliation for each infringement but rather as the undeterred ruler, patient but far from passive, who realizes that He may not achieve His end immediately and that severe measures may be necessary. God is pictured here as compelled to give repeated second chances, since He is bound and determined to have His way and cannot simply give up. In Priestly thought, the covenant cannot ever become null and void. **15:** *Reject, spurn,* lit. graphic expressions of distaste: "you will find disgusting and your throat will vomit up"; see vv. 11, 30, 43, 44. *So that you do not observe all My commandments:* This is not a gradual abandonment of God's laws after a period during which they were obeyed (as in Deuteronomy), but rather an initial, wholesale rejection of the commandments and successive attempts by God to "try again" to beat Israel into submission. Thus it is incorrect to speak of repentance here, since repentance consists of the return to former righteousness. *And you break My covenant:* This seems inconsistent with the Priestly view that the covenant is God's to keep (or break), not Israel's; only in the non-Priestly tradition is the covenant thought to be mutual. Probably, as in Gen. 17.14, the idea is that by refusing

He will take up residence in their midst, enshrined in the earthly abode which they will fashion for Him, and reign over them as their liege Lord. **3:** *If you follow My laws,* all the laws that have been conveyed, from the beginning of Leviticus. **5:** *Threshing shall overtake the vintage, and your vintage shall overtake the sowing:* There will be so much grain that threshing will continue into late summer, when the vines are picked; this will continue until early spring when sowing begins. See Amos 9.13. **9:** *Maintain My covenant:* In P this means "uphold My promise." In Priestly tradition the covenant is the commitment made by God to Abraham (Gen. 17.4–8) and repeated to Moses (Exod. 6.2–8): to make Israel numerous and to give them the land of Canaan as a hereditary holding (see 25.10 n.). **11:** *Spurn,* see v. 15. **13:** *To be their slaves no more,* for the implication, see 25.42, 55. *Broke the bars:*

Though God's purpose in bringing Israel out of Egyptian slavery was to make them His own slaves, in the course of doing so He did indeed break their yoke and enable them to walk erect. The point is to remind them what He is capable of doing for them if they comply with His wishes. **14–45:** The results of noncompliance. As in Deut. ch 28, considerably more space is given to the threats than the promises; but in direct contrast to Deut. 11.13–17 (recited daily as part of the Shema) and 28.15–68, the disasters threatened here are not punishments. Rather they are warnings arranged as a series of successive attempts to discipline the Israelites, that is, to force them into obedience. Each stage demonstrates an example of the sort of deadly disaster God may let loose upon them if they persist in their refusal to obey. Even the final stage, though it includes the element of vengeance and seems at

My rules, so that you do not observe all My commandments and you break My covenant, [16] I in turn will do this to you: I will wreak misery upon you—[a]consumption and fever, which cause the eyes to pine and the body to languish; you shall sow your seed to no purpose, for your enemies shall eat it. [17] I will set My face against you: you shall be routed by your enemies, and your foes shall dominate you. You shall flee though none pursues.

[18] And if, for all that, you do not obey Me, I will go on to discipline you sevenfold for your sins, [19] and I will break your proud glory. I will make your skies like iron and your earth like copper, [20] so that your strength shall be spent to no purpose. Your land shall not yield its produce, nor shall the trees of the land yield their fruit.

[21] And if you remain hostile toward Me and refuse to obey Me, I will go on smiting you sevenfold for your sins. [22] I will loose wild beasts against you, and they shall bereave you of your children and wipe out your cattle. They shall decimate you, and your roads shall be deserted.

[23] And if these things fail to discipline you for Me, and you remain hostile to Me, [24] I too will remain hostile to you: I in turn will smite you sevenfold for your sins. [25] I will bring a sword against you to wreak vengeance for the covenant; and if you withdraw into your cities, I will send pestilence among you, and you shall be delivered into enemy hands. [26] When I break your staff of bread, ten women shall bake your bread in a single oven; they shall dole out your bread by weight, and though you eat, you shall not be satisfied.

[27] But if, despite this, you disobey Me and remain hostile to Me, [28] I will act against you in wrathful hostility; I, for My part, will discipline you sevenfold for your sins. [29] You shall eat the flesh of your sons and the flesh of your daughters. [30] I will destroy your cult places and cut down your incense stands, and I will heap your carcasses upon your lifeless fetishes.

I will spurn you. [31] I will lay your cities in ruin and make your sanctuaries desolate, and I will not savor your pleasing odors. [32] I will make the land desolate, so that your enemies who settle in it shall be appalled by it.

a *Precise nature of these ills is uncertain.*

to obey God's commands the Israelites move God to abrogate His promise. **16–17:** The first attempt. An onslaught of diseases, followed by enemy incursions upon Israel's territory and despoliation of her crops. The fear instilled by the oc-cupier's force will become so all-pervasive that the Israelites will "flee though none pursues." **16:** *Misery,* better: "shock." **18–20:** The second attempt. If the measures described do not suc-ceed, they will be followed by the withholding of rain and the result-ant crop failure. **18:** *Sevenfold for your sins,* an expression signifying the maximum punishment. **21–22:** The third attempt; the re-verse of v. 6. Wild beasts are one of God's four weapons of destruction in Ezek. 14.12–23. **23:** *Hostile,* un-certain; it should probably be un-derstood to mean something like "uncaring, indifferent"; see v. 24. **23–26:** Sword, pestilence, and famine, the three other divine judgments mentioned in Ezek. ch 14. Typically all three occur to-gether, the latter two being the horrrible results of the siege brought about by the former. Yet they are three separate phenom-ena, bringing the total number of measures employed by God to pressure His people into compli-ance to seven, commonly used in biblical literature to express com-pleteness. **24:** *I too will remain hos-tile to you:* He will treat them as they have treated Him. The mutu-ality is telling: God requires Israel's obedience the same way that they require His providence and kindness; if they withhold what He demands, He will do likewise. **26:** *Staff of bread,* what one leans upon in order to remain erect; see Isa. 3.1. **27–33:** The final blow. The enemy's siege of Israel's towns will culminate in the worst of its horrors, cannibalism result-ing from dire famine (a trope in ac-counts of siege). It will end with the utter destruction of the towns, followed by desolation of the land and the dispersion of the popula-tion. **28:** *Wrathful hostility,* see v. 21. **30:** The invading enemy will de-stroy all the local shrines and cul-tic objects in its path, the very exis-tence of which is a symptom of Israel's widespread, ongoing in-subordination. The image of heap-ing the carcasses of slaughtered Is-raelites upon the lifeless idols of the false deities they worshipped is a particularly ironic instance of poetic justice. *I will spurn you:* The translation makes this the begin-ning of a new thought, but this is not warranted. For the meaning of the phrase see v. 15 n. **31:** *Sanctuar-ies:* The existence of multiple local

33 And you I will scatter among the nations, and I will unsheath the sword against you. Your land shall become a desolation and your cities a ruin.

34 Then shall the land make up for its sabbath years throughout the time that it is desolate and you are in the land of your enemies; then shall the land rest and make up for its sabbath years. 35 Throughout the time that it is desolate, it shall observe the rest that it did not observe in your sabbath years while you were dwelling upon it. 36 As for those of you who survive, I will cast a faintness into their hearts in the land of their enemies. The sound of a driven leaf shall put them to flight. Fleeing as though from the sword, they shall fall though none pursues. 37 With no one pursuing, they shall stumble over one another as before the sword. You shall not be able to stand your ground before your enemies, 38 but shall perish among the nations; and the land of your enemies shall consume you.

39 Those of you who survive shall be heartsick over their iniquity in the land of your enemies; more, they shall be heartsick over the iniquities of their fathers; 40 and they shall confess their iniquity and the iniquity of their fathers, in that they trespassed against Me, yea, were hostile to Me. 41 When I, in turn, have been hostile to them and have removed them into the land of their enemies, then at last shall their obdurate[a] heart humble itself, and they shall atone for their iniquity. 42 Then will I remember My covenant with Jacob; I will remember also My covenant with Isaac, and also My covenant with Abraham; and I will remember the land.

a Others "uncircumcised"; lit. "blocked."

whom will survive the enemy assault. They will be persecuted by their captors and consumed by fear of dangers real and imagined; finally they will simply cease to exist. **39:** *Those of you who survive:* The repetition of the phrase (see v. 36) indicates that only a fraction of those who survive to go into exile will also survive the tribulations of the exile itself. After a few generations, hardly any will be left even of these. *Be heartsick over,* correctly, "will rot away because of," become fewer and fewer with the passage of time. The repeated refusal of earlier generations to obey God's commands will be the cause of the misery of later ones. **40–42:** At last, the remaining survivors will consider the cause of what has happened, will realize it was their own (and their ancestors' own) obduracy that caused their plight, and God will respond appropriately. *Confess:* It is not the ceremonial, ritual confession that accompanies sacrificial atonement (as in 16.21; Num. 5.7) that is predicted; in their exilic condition the remnant of the Israelite people will simply acknowledge their guilt and that of their ancestors, and this contrition will suffice. **41:** *Obdurate heart,* lit. "uncircumcised heart." *Atone for,* better, "make full restitution for." When they finally take upon themselves the commitment to comply with God's demands, the slate will be wiped clean of the accumulated guilt. **42:** *Then will I remember My covenant:* This event, to take place at some future time, is a fitting conclusion to the Priestly history of the nation of Israel, which begins when God hears Israel's cry in bondage and is moved to remember His covenant (Exod. 6.5). In the predicted future, He will hear not their cry of misery but their confession of guilt; recalling His promise to the patriarchs, He will try again to implement His plan. *Jacob . . . Isaac . . . Abraham:* The inverted order may express the gradual motion of God's recollection backwards in history. In P, God gives His promise to Abraham in Gen. 17.4–8 and reiterates

sanctuaries is another manifestation of Israel's chronic disobedience. See 17.8–9 n. **33:** *And I will unsheath the sword against you,* "after you," as you go into exile. *Your land shall become a desolation and your cities a ruin:* The enemies who will have by then settled in their land (v. 32) are not pictured as rebuilding it. **34–35:** Israel's sustained failure to obey God's commands will necessarily have included the repeated nonobservance of the sabbatical year (25.2–7). But when Israel goes into exile and its land is deserted with none to work it, it will have a permanent "sabbath" and be repaid the rest it was denied. Rabbinic

tradition interpreted these vv. more literally, viewing restitution for the land's missed sabbaths as the actual purpose of the exile and taking the sin of ignoring the sabbatical year as its specific cause. The plain sense of the text does not imply this, however. In contrast to the Deuteronomic doctrine that Israel's demise will have a particular cause, the worship of foreign deities, this ch insists that it is the nonobservance of the totality of the commandments that will bring about the horrible fate described. **36–38:** After focusing momentarily on the land, the speaker now returns to the fate of the dispersed former inhabitants, not all of

43 For the land shall be forsaken of them, making up for its sabbath years by being desolate of them, while they atone for their iniquity; for the abundant reason that they rejected My rules and spurned My laws. 44 Yet, even then, when they are in the land of their enemies, I will not reject them or spurn them so as to destroy them, annulling My covenant with them: for I the Lord am their God. 45 I will remember in their favor the covenant with the ancients, whom I freed from the land of Egypt in the sight of the nations to be their God: I, the Lord.

46 These are the laws, rules, and instructions that the Lord established, through Moses on Mount Sinai, between Himself and the Israelite people.

27 The Lord spoke to Moses, saying: 2 Speak to the Israelite people and say to them: When anyone explicitly[a] vows to the Lord the equivalent for a human being, 3 the following scale shall apply: If it is a male from twenty to sixty years of age, the equivalent is fifty shekels of silver by the sanctuary weight; 4 if it is a female, the equivalent is thirty shekels. 5 If the age is from five years to twenty years, the equivalent is twenty shekels for a male and ten shekels for a female. 6 If the age is from one month to five years, the equivalent for a male is five shekels of silver, and the equivalent for a female is three shekels of silver. 7 If the age is sixty years or over, the equivalent is fifteen shekels in the case of a male and ten shekels for a female. 8 But if one cannot afford the equivalent, he shall be presented before the priest, and the priest shall assess him; the priest shall assess him according to what the vower can afford.

a Cf. note at Lev. 22.21.

it to Jacob in Gen. 35.11–12. No surviving P text tells of His repeating it to Isaac, but Isaac passes it on to Jacob (Gen. 28.1–4). **43:** Eloquently elaborating on the end of v. 42, the v. describes God thinking of His abandoned estate. **45:** *The covenant with the ancients, whom I freed from the land of Egypt:* Nowhere in P is God explicitly said to have made a covenant with the generation of the exodus. The reference is not to the Sinai events, as these are not called a covenant in P. The promise made to Abraham, Isaac, and Jacob was,

however, communicated to the generation of the exodus as well, by Moses; see Exod. 6.6–9. *I, the Lord,* better, "I am the Lord"; cf. 18.2; ch 19. **46:** The caption to the Priestly account of the law-giving in the Tabernacle; cf. 7.37–38; see 25.1. *On Mount Sinai, see 25.1.*

27.1–34: Monetary and other dedications. The laws in this ch prescribe how monetary and other dedications are made to the sanctuary, the values or method for determining them, and whether or not such dedications may be re-

deemed. If the dedication is of land or property, the effect of the jubilee release on its value is prescribed. Objects that belong intrinsically to God and those that have been irrevocably consecrated cannot be dedicated; in the case of tithes, however, redemption is possible. Voluntary contributions might be made by anyone, at any time, as spontaneous acts of devotion. Besides constituting the most important source of revenue for the Temple, they allowed individual Israelites to achieve a sense that the regimen of public worship performed by the priests was being conducted on their behalf. The placement of this ch after the concluding caption in 26.46 can be explained on literary grounds. Since a section of the ch (vv. 16–24) is dependent upon the laws of land tenure, it would have been unclear if it had been placed before ch 25. On the other hand, placing this ch between chs 25 and 26 would have interrupted their thematic continuity. Wishing to keep distinct topics of legislation separate and at the same time to make the laws as intelligible as possible, the author occasionally saw the need to stray somewhat from the order in which he imagined the laws were conveyed to Moses, taking care not to hide this from the reader (see also 16.1 n.). **2–8:** A vow to dedicate the value of a human being. The person wishes to make a significant monetary contribution to the upkeep of the sanctuary. Through the procedure described, a purely fiscal transaction takes on the character of the ultimate act of devotion, that of consecrating oneself or a member of one's household to the Lord. Thus biblical religion preserves vicariously the notion of self-consecration without requiring one actually to sacrifice oneself. **3–7:** The scale is evidently based on size and strength, and thus on potential productivity in terms of physical labor. It is not indicative of any social hierarchy. **8:** If a poor person wishes to "dedicate" himself or a member of his family, the scale is flexible, in con-

⁹ If [the vow concerns] any animal that may be brought as an offering to the LORD, any such that may be given to the LORD shall be holy. ¹⁰ One may not exchange or substitute another for it, either good for bad, or bad for good; if one does substitute one animal for another, the thing vowed and its substitute shall both be holy. ¹¹ If [the vow concerns] any unclean animal that may not be brought as an offering to the LORD, the animal shall be presented before the priest, ¹² and the priest shall assess it. Whether ªhigh or low,ª whatever assessment is set by the priest shall stand; ¹³ and if he wishes to redeem it, he must add one-fifth to its assessment.

¹⁴ If anyone consecrates his house to the LORD, the priest shall assess it. Whether ªhigh or low,ª as the priest assesses it, so it shall stand; ¹⁵ and if he who has consecrated his house wishes to redeem it, he must add one-fifth to the sum at which it was assessed, and it shall be his.

¹⁶ If anyone consecrates to the LORD any land that he holds, its assessment shall be in accordance with its seed requirement: fifty shekels of silver to a *ḥomer* of barley seed. ¹⁷ If he consecrates his land as of the jubilee year, its assessment stands. ¹⁸ But if he consecrates his land after the jubilee, the priest shall compute the price according to the years that are left until the jubilee year, and its assessment shall be so reduced; ¹⁹ and if he who consecrated the land wishes to redeem it, he must add one-fifth to the sum at which it was assessed, and it shall pass to him. ²⁰ But if he does not redeem the land, and the land is sold to another, it shall no longer be redeemable: ²¹ when it is released in the jubilee, the land shall be holy to the LORD, as land proscribed; it becomes the priest's holding.

²² If he consecrates to the LORD land that he purchased,

a-a Lit. "good or bad."

trast to the previous section. **9–13:** Vows to donate animals. Animals are of two types: those fit for the altar (vv. 9–10) and those which may not be sacrificed (vv. 11–13). In the former category, once dedicated to the sanctuary, the pledged animal must be brought in fulfillment of the vow and may not be substituted, and the consequence of substitution is that both animals are dedicated. Animals in the latter category, since they cannot be sacrificed, can be dedicated only in order to be sold by the sanctuary for their monetary value. Unlike persons, animals must have their values fixed ad hoc by the priest. The consecration of an animal not fit for sacrifice may sound strange, but the aim of this system is to enable anyone to devote a portion of his wealth to the upkeep of the divine abode. A person whose wealth consists, say, of asses rather than of herds of sheep is thus not disenfranchised. **12–13:** *Whether high or low:* The priest's assessment is final, i.e., it is valid for the outside buyer or for the donor *if he wishes to redeem it;* i.e., if, instead of donating the animal, he would prefer to make his contribution and also

keep the animal, he may pay a 20 percent surcharge (compare 5.16, 24). This would apply also to persons wishing to extricate themselves from vows they regret having made. It is not clear whether this option exists for animals in both categories or only for nonsacrificial ones. **14–15:** Similarly, one may chose to dedicate his house, that is, to donate it to the sanctuary for sale, or, if his primary intention is actually to make a monetary contribution in the amount of his home, he may effect this by dedicating the house and redeeming it for silver, adding 20 percent to the price that has been fixed. **16–24:** Dedication of fields. These too may be donated for sale, the proceeds going to the sanctuary treasury, or the donor may redeem them at a 20 percent surcharge, with proper adjustment for the number of years remaining until the jubilee. **16:** *Any land that he holds,* any portion of the land belonging to his ancestral holding. *In accordance with its seed requirement:* The sale price is thus a function of size, which is constant, whereas fixing it in accordance with how much it has produced in past years would be a function of divine blessing, which may change from one year, or from one owner, to the next. *Fifty shekels of silver:* Probably one shekel per year; maximally fifty, if the jubilee is 50 years away. *A ḥomer of barley seed,* a measure of seed equal to the normal load carried by an ass; see Ezek. 45.11. It was about 230 liters (a little more than 6.5 bushels). **17:** *Its assessment stands,* see v. 12. **20–21:** The original holder's right to reclaim his land expires when the Temple treasury has sold it to another or when the jubilee arrives, whichever comes first. *When it is released in the jubilee,* in the former case. If not sold to another person, it remains the property of the Temple. *The land shall be holy to the LORD:* Since the whole point of the jubilee is that the land is the LORD's property, land that has been dedicated to the LORD obviously remains His when the next jubilee comes, the proprietorship which is not land of his holding, [23] the priest shall compute for him the proportionate assessment up to the jubilee year, and he shall pay the assessment as of that day, a sacred donation to the LORD. [24] In the jubilee year the land shall revert to him from whom it was bought, whose holding the land is. [25] All assessments shall be by the sanctuary weight, the shekel being twenty *gerahs.*

[26] A firstling of animals, however, which—as a firstling—is the LORD's, cannot be consecrated by anybody; whether ox or sheep, it is the LORD's. [27] But if it is of unclean animals, it may be ransomed as its assessment, with one-fifth added; if it is not redeemed, it shall be sold at its assessment.

[28] But of all that anyone owns, be it man or beast or land of his holding, nothing that he has proscribed for the LORD may be sold or redeemed; every proscribed thing is totally consecrated to the LORD. [29] No human being who has been proscribed can be ransomed: he shall be put to death.

[30] All tithes from the land, whether seed from the ground or fruit from the tree, are the LORD's; they are holy to the LORD. [31] If anyone wishes to redeem any of his tithes, he must add one-fifth to them. [32] All tithes of the herd or flock—of all that passes under the shepherd's

passing to the priests. As land proscribed, see vv. 28–29. **22–24:** Dedication of purchased fields, i.e., lands that will revert to their original owners at the jubilee. The donor is not donating something of his own, and he does not have the option of transferring ownership to the sanctuary for sale to a third party. Purchased fields thus, like humans (vv. 3–8), may be consecrated only by donating their monetary value, as assessed by the priest, and in the jubilee they revert to their original owner. **25:** All assessments: This applies to all of the preceding legislation. The sanctuary weight, better: the sacred shekel, i.e., the official shekel in use in the sanctuary treasury (about 11.5 grams, less than half an ounce). Twenty gerahs, see Exod. 30.13; Num. 3.47; 18.16. **26–33:** A set of restrictions on the above: objects that cannot be consecrated to the LORD since they belong to Him already. **26–27:** A firstling of livestock may not be

dedicated, as it belongs to the LORD by definition (see Exod. 13.2; 22.28–29; 34.19; Num. 3.40 ff.; Deut. 15.19–20). Firstlings of the flock and herd must be sacrificed and cannot be redeemed; firstlings of nonsacrificial animals may be redeemed or sold. The law here differs from the non-Priestly regulation in Exod. 13.13; 34.20, according to which impure animals must be exchanged for a lamb or destroyed. **27:** Ransomed, Heb "padah," usually synonymous with "ga'al," "redeem." Since they are the property of God, the person is not regaining ownership of them but gaining it for the first time. **28–29:** The second restriction: proscribed things (Heb "herem"). This term is used outside of the Priestly writings for those condemned to destruction, such as defeated military enemies, those guilty of idolatry, and persons who fail to comply with the terms of a communal oath (the so-called "ban") requiring all to

"do or die." It refers also to the spoils confiscated from those so condemned, consisting of animals, which were also destroyed, and inanimate objects, which were probably reserved for the sanctuary. Such items are "off-limits" and their taboo nature is contagious. Further, this destruction or confiscation of spoils is said to be for the LORD. This indicates that the obligation to condemn, destroy, and despoil is a divinely sanctioned one, and implies that the destroyed persons and animals are, like the silver and gold confiscated for the sanctuary, a form of offering to God. This passage seems to mean another type of "herem": the "proscribing" by an individual (rather than by the community or God) of an object by pledging that no use would ever be made of it and that it would become the permanent property of the LORD, with no option to sell, redeem, or exchange. **28:** Be it man or beast, see next v. Totally consecrated, Heb "kodesh kodashim," "most holy" (see also 2.3, etc.). Consistent with Priestly thought and law, such objects are here deemed to be sacred; since they have been made immutably so, they are called "most holy." The use of the term is not entirely consistent with its use elsewhere. **29:** The text shockingly says that one may sentence oneself, one's slave, or a household member under one's authority to death as a consecration to the LORD, and once this is done there is no reprieve or remedy. Commentators have interpreted the text differently, but there is little basis for this. **30–33:** Tithes constitute the third and final restriction: They belong to God already and cannot be dedicated. **30–31:** It is not clear whether this tithe, which belongs to the LORD, is in addition to the crop tithe assigned to the Levites in Num. 18.21ff. for their upkeep, or whether our ch views all crop tithes as a tax given to the central sanctuary. **32–33:** A tithe of herds and flocks is not mentioned elsewhere in the Torah. According to 1 Sam. 8.15–17, kings are notorious for imposing such tithes as a staff, every tenth one—shall be holy to the LORD. ³³ He must not look out for good as against bad, or make substitution for it. If he does make substitution for it, then it and its substitute shall both be holy: it cannot be redeemed.

³⁴ These are the commandments that the LORD gave Moses for the Israelite people on Mount Sinai.

form of taxation. **33:** *He must not look out for good as against bad:* He must offer the tenth sheep to pass under the staff, without regard to its size or quality. *Make substitution,* see vv. 9–13 n. **34:** The caption of 26.46 is repeated in abbreviated form; see 27.1–34 n. *On Mount Sinai,* explained at 7.38; 25.1.

בְּמִדְבַּר

Numbers

THE FOURTH BOOK OF THE TORAH, Numbers, recounts memorable events of the Israelite wanderings from Sinai, God's mountain, to the plains of Moab, just opposite the promised land. Thus, Numbers continues the story begun in Exodus and continued in Leviticus of the escape from Egyptian servitude, the desert journey to Mount Sinai, the revelation at Sinai and giving of the law, and the building of the Tabernacle with instruction on its operation. The Hebrew name of this book, *Bemidbar*, "in the wilderness [of Sinai]," taken from the fifth Hebrew word in chapter 1, reflects this theme. In contrast, the English name, Numbers, derives from the Greek translation, the Septuagint, which titled the book after the censuses mentioned in the first four chapters. This Greek name reflects an earlier Hebrew name for the book, well-attested in classical rabbinic sources, from a period when books of the Torah were named thematically rather than after one of their initial words.

Numbers is a complex collection of texts containing an assortment of interwoven literary genres: historical narratives, legal texts, ritual prescriptions, and poetic folk traditions. Its final form reflects a long and intricate literary history. Modern critical scholarship—based on stylistic, linguistic, and contextual criteria—identifies separate sources underlying the final version of the book. (See essay "Modern Study of the Bible," pp. 2084–96.) Primarily, the texts derive from various layers of the Priestly school (P), with additional texts from the two older narrative sources, the Yahwist (J) and Elohist (E). The predominant Priestly material often functions to expand, supplement, or recast ideologically the earlier (JE) texts to fit the agenda of Priestly circles. The lengthy Balaam pericope (chs 22–24) in its entirety stands untouched by the Priestly writer and may represent the hand of yet another author(s), neither J, E, or P. Jewish tradition, on the other hand, views the seemingly disparate texts in Numbers as a single work written by Moses. Although critical scholarship does not recognize Mosaic authorship, it has begun to emphasize the merits of a holistic approach, one that studies the parts in the context of the whole.

The book of Numbers can easily be divided by subject and other criteria into several primary units; these can be further subdivided into smaller sections and subsections. It is, however, often difficult to determine the relationship between contiguous segments. Based on geographical criteria and ideological motifs, three major units can be distinguished, reflecting a literary sandwich of sorts: (1) the final encampment at Sinai and preparation to resume the wilderness trek (1.1–10.10); (2) the generation-long march in the desert from Sinai to Moab (10.11–22.1); (3) the encampment on the plains of Moab and preparation to enter Canaan (22.2–36.13). Unit one marks the period when Israel, with God's law in hand, readies itself for the desert march to its final destination. This is the first time that the people enter the wilderness while they are bonded by covenant to the LORD. The wanderings in the second unit form a bridge between the first and last units. The slave generation dies in the desert and a new generation matures. In unit three this new generation prepares to embark on a journey once more, this time to enter the promised land as a free-born national entity.

The Final Encampment at Sinai

THE THEME OF THIS UNIT (1.1–10.10) centers on the organization of the Israelite camp around the Tabernacle and the maintenance of cult purity within the camp, assuring God's presence in the Tabernacle. Thus the material is mainly prescriptive. The first section of the unit opens with a census of eligible military-age males and an election of tribal chieftains (1.1–46). A description of duties for the military-exempt Levites follows (1.47–54). Next is a diagram of the traveling tribal camp (2.1–34). Much space is devoted to the roles of the Levites, who are stationed closest to the Tabernacle, performing guard duty there, making sure that no non-priests approach the Tabernacle. Topics include the consecration of the Levites in place of first-born Israelites, two Levite censuses, and a detailed outline of the familial relationships of the Levitical clans and their duties (chs 3–4).

The next sections shift focus from camp organization to the maintenance of camp purity. Conditions for removal and readmission of persons who have become impure are delineated (parts of ch 5). Laws regarding Nazirite vows and the formula for the priestly blessing follow (ch 6). The next few sections focus again on the Tabernacle and its functionaries: the initiatory gifts brought by the tribal chieftains to the sanctuary (ch 7); the procedure for lighting the lampstand (menorah); and the purification of the Levites (ch 8). The last section of unit one (9.1–10.10) discusses the final preparations for departure from Sinai. Israel celebrates the first Passover in the wilderness, and Moses makes provisions for ritually impure persons to celebrate a second Passover one month later. Directives concerning the fire-cloud, to guide Israel's travels, and the silver trumpets, to herald movement of the camp divisions, conclude the unit.

The Generation-long March in the Desert from Sinai to Moab

THIS MIDDLE UNIT (10.11–22.1) is composed of narratives woven into a story line interspersed by sacrificial law, injunctions against certain transgressions, and expiation processes. A recurring cycle of murmuring and rebellion against the authority of God and Moses, by individuals or by the community as a whole, characterizes this unit. Even Miriam, Aaron, and Moses have moments of disloyalty to God. In certain cases, where rebellion by a few persons is contagious to the group or where it is enacted by the leadership, punishment is severe.

The unit opens with a description of the camp's departure (10.11–36) followed by a litany of grievances and their resolutions (11.1–35). After the first complaint God responds with deadly fire; Moses then successfully intercedes on Israel's behalf. This cycle repeats in one form or another. Eventually Moses appoints seventy elders to relieve his burden, but displays of disloyalty continue, even among the community leaders. Miriam and Aaron criticize Moses on account of his Cushite wife while ultimately protesting against his unique status as prophet (ch 12). The mood of rebellion intensifies in the spy episode (chs 13–14). Israel sides with the ten spies who declare Canaan unconquerable and ponder returning to Egypt, and God reacts by condemning the entire exodus generation to death in the wilderness. Soon thereafter a Levite named Korah and his followers stage a rebellion against Moses and Aaron (chs 16–17). Finally, in frustration, Moses and Aaron defy God (20.1–13). For their hubris God, in an unexpected decree, bars Moses and Aaron from entering the promised land.

Interspersed between these accounts of human infidelity and divine retribution are prescriptive passages detailing ordinances regarding sacrifices and purification (chs 15, 19), and the duties and privileges of priests and Levites (ch 18), including the commandment for Israelites to attach tzitzit (fringes) to their garments (15.37–41). At the end of unit two Israel emerges from the wilderness to face the peoples inhabiting Transjordan. Not surprisingly, the rulers of those small kingdoms deny Israel passage through their territory. Nevertheless, Israel moves ever closer to its final destination, and prevails in encounters with her enemies (20.14–21.35).

Encampment on the Plains of Moab and Preparation to Enter Canaan

UNIT THREE (22.2–36.13) finds the Israelites encamped on the eastern side of the Jordan opposite Jericho, their destination within visible reach. This unit, like the previous two, is composed of narrative and legal material; it also contains lengthy poetic folk traditions. The theme centers on the new Israelite community's final preparation to inherit the land of Canaan. As such, much of the legal material here focuses on inheritance.

The first section, composed of narrative and poetry, is the story of the Moabite king Balak and the prophet Balaam whom he hires to curse the Israelites (chs 22–24). God thwarts Balaam's mission, turning the intended curse into a blessing. Israel's apostasy at Baal-peor follows (25.1–18); the plague that God inflicts upon the sinners eliminates the last members of the exodus generation.

The opening of chapter 26 is an alternate juncture for the end of unit two and the beginning of unit three. With the demise of the older generation and the crossing into Canaan imminent, Moses conducts a second census and apportions the land to the tribes (ch 26). The Levitical clans, who are not allotted landholdings, are counted separately. Arising from the process of apportioning land is the special case of Zelophehad's daughters, who petition for the right of women to inherit when there are no male heirs (27.1–11). That case is followed by the succession of Joshua (27.12–23). Next is an insertion of ritual prescriptions establishing the cultic calendar and governing the daily, new moon, Sabbath, and festival offerings (28.1–30.1). The section ends with a discussion on the annulment of vows and oaths. Following a statement that men are bound by their vows and oaths comes a list of conditions under which women's vows can be annulled (30.2–17). The narrative resumes with a war against the Midianites, allegedly in retaliation for their seduction of the Israelites at Baal-peor (ch 31).

Having routed her enemies in Transjordan, Israel begins the settlement process. The tribes of Reuben and Gad ask to receive a portion of land on the eastern side of the Jordan (ch 32). Part of the tribe of Manasseh settles there as well. A summary of the wilderness itinerary that highlights key events follows (33.1–49). The next narrative section continues where the previous one left off (32.42); having appropriated land to two and a half tribes in Transjordan, Moses reformulates the division of Canaan among the remaining nine and a half tribes (33.50–35.8). As part of the process, he defines the boundaries of Canaan and assigns Levitical towns in place of tribal land for Levites.

Unit three ends with several final prescriptions (35.9–36.13). Moses designates six cities of refuge, three of which are across the Jordan River, in the land about to be conquered; furthermore he distinguishes between involuntary and deliberate homicide. The last section outlines marriage regulations for female heirs, using the case of Zelophehad's daughters as a model. The issue of land inheritance projects into the future since it is significant only after the land of Israel is settled. The book of Numbers ends by stating that the precepts in this unit were enjoined upon the Israelites "on the steppes of Moab, at the Jordan near Jericho." This phrase forms an inclusio with the last phrase of the second unit (22.1), a transition between units two and three.

[NILI S. FOX]

BE-MIDBAR   במדבר

1 On the first day of the second month, in the second year following the exodus from the land of Egypt, the LORD spoke to Moses in the wilderness of Sinai, in the Tent of Meeting, saying:
² Take a census of the whole Israelite community by the clans of ªits ancestral houses,ª listing the names, every male, head by head. ³ You and Aaron shall record them by their groups, from the age of twenty years up, all those in Israel who are able to bear arms. ⁴ Associated with you shall be a man from each tribe, each one the head of his ancestral house.
⁵ These are the names of the men who shall assist you:
From Reuben, Elizur son of Shedeur.
6   From Simeon, Shelumiel son of Zurishaddai.
7   From Judah, Nahshon son of Amminadab.
8   From Issachar, Nethanel son of Zuar.
9   From Zebulun, Eliab son of Helon.

a-a *I.e., of its tribes.*

1.1–46: First Israelite census and appointment of tribal chieftains: Numbers opens with the Israelites still encamped at the base of Mt. Sinai (1.1–10.10). They already have received the laws, constructed the portable Tabernacle, and been instructed on formal worship procedures and regulated observances both for priests and lay persons (Exod. chs 20–31; 34–40; Lev. chs 1–27). Now they must be organized into a mobile war camp to resume their travels in the wilderness and in readiness to meet any foes along the way. Ch 1 begins with a census. **2:** The purpose of a census is to determine military strength or potential taxation revenues (cf. 2 Sam. ch 24), though later Jewish interpretation suggests that God counts Israel because they are dear to Him (see Rashi). All males 20 years and older are eligible for military duty, and tribal chieftains who function

10   From the sons of Joseph:

      from Ephraim, Elishama son of Ammihud;

      from Manasseh, Gamaliel son of Pedahzur.

11   From Benjamin, Abidan son of Gideoni.

12   From Dan, Ahiezer son of Ammishaddai.

13   From Asher, Pagiel son of Ochran.

14   From Gad, Eliasaph son of Deuel.

15   From Naphtali, Ahira son of Enan.

16 Those are the elected of the assembly, the chieftains of their ancestral tribes: they are the heads of the contingents of Israel.

17 So Moses and Aaron took those men, who were designated by name, 18 and on the first day of the second month they convoked the whole community, who were registered by the clans of their ancestral houses—the names of those aged twenty years and over being listed head by head. 19 As the LORD had commanded Moses, so he recorded them in the wilderness of Sinai.

20 They totaled as follows:

The descendants of Reuben, Israel's first-born, the registration of the clans of their ancestral house, as listed by name, head by head, all males aged twenty years and over, all who were able to bear arms—21 those enrolled from the tribe of Reuben: 46,500.

22 Of the descendants of Simeon, the registration of the clans of their ancestral house, their enrollment as listed by name, head by head, all males aged twenty years and over, all who were able to bear arms—23 those enrolled from the tribe of Simeon: 59,300.

24 Of the descendants of Gad, the registration of the clans of their ancestral house, as listed by name, aged twenty years and over, all who were able to bear arms—25 those enrolled from the tribe of Gad: 45,650.

26 Of the descendants of Judah, the registration of the clans of their ancestral house, as listed by name, aged twenty years and over, all who were able to bear arms—27 those enrolled from the tribe of Judah: 74,600.

28 Of the descendants of Issachar, the registration of the clans of their ancestral house, as listed by name, aged twenty years and over, all who were able to bear arms—29 those enrolled from the tribe of Issachar: 54,400.

30 Of the descendants of Zebulun, the registration of the clans of their ancestral house, as listed by name, aged twenty years and over, all who were able to bear arms—31 those enrolled from the tribe of Zebulun: 57,400.

32 Of the descendants of Joseph:

Of the descendants of Ephraim, the registration of the clans of their ancestral house, as listed by name, aged

as census supervisors are appointed, one from each tribe. A separate census is taken of the Levites who are exempt from military service (ch 3; 26.57–62). **5–15:** Heading the list of chieftains is the representative of Reuben, Jacob's first-born son, though elsewhere in Numbers, Judah is typically listed first. The other sons follow Reuben in chronological order of birth with Leah's sons first, Rachel's second, and the concubines' last. None of the names on the list contains a theophoric element, that is, a element with the name of God as prefix ("yeho-" or "yo-") or suffix ("-yahu" or "-yah"). In the latter period of the monarchy such names are commonplace (e.g., Jehoiada, Zechariah). **20–46:** The census figures for each tribe, with a grand total of 603,550, are vastly inflated by any realistic standards. The final tally, however, is generally consistent in the biblical literature (cf. Exod. 12.37; 38.26; Num. 11.21; 26.51). Earlier biblical scholars posited that this number reflected a census at a later period, perhaps under David, but this is incorrect. **27:** *Judah* has the largest number, reflecting its later importance.

twenty years and over, all who were able to bear arms— [33] those enrolled from the tribe of Ephraim: 40,500.

[34] Of the descendants of Manasseh, the registration of the clans of their ancestral house, as listed by name, aged twenty years and over, all who were able to bear arms— [35] those enrolled from the tribe of Manasseh: 32,200.

[36] Of the descendants of Benjamin, the registration of the clans of their ancestral house, as listed by name, aged twenty years and over, all who were able to bear arms— [37] those enrolled from the tribe of Benjamin: 35,400.

[38] Of the descendants of Dan, the registration of the clans of their ancestral house, as listed by name, aged twenty years and over, all who were able to bear arms— [39] those enrolled from the tribe of Dan: 62,700.

[40] Of the descendants of Asher, the registration of the clans of their ancestral house, as listed by name, aged twenty years and over, all who were able to bear arms— [41] those enrolled from the tribe of Asher: 41,500.

[42] [Of] the descendants of Naphtali, the registration of the clans of their ancestral house as listed by name, aged twenty years and over, all who were able to bear arms— [43] those enrolled from the tribe of Naphtali: 53,400.

[44] Those are the enrollments recorded by Moses and Aaron and by the chieftains of Israel, who were twelve in number, one man to each ancestral house. [45] All the Israelites, aged twenty years and over, enrolled by ancestral houses, all those in Israel who were able to bear arms— [46] all who were enrolled came to 603,550.

[47] The Levites, however, were not recorded among them by their ancestral tribe. [48] For the LORD had spoken to Moses, saying: [49] Do not on any account enroll the tribe of Levi or take a census of them with the Israelites. [50] You shall put the Levites in charge of the Tabernacle of the Pact, all its furnishings, and everything that pertains to it: they shall carry the Tabernacle and all its furnishings, and they shall tend it; and they shall camp around the Tabernacle. [51] When the Tabernacle is to set out, the Levites shall take it down, and when the Tabernacle is to be pitched, the Levites shall set it up; any outsider who encroaches shall be put to death. [52] The Israelites shall encamp troop by troop, each man with his division and each under his standard. [53] The Levites, however, shall camp around the Tabernacle of the Pact, that wrath may not strike the Israelite community; the Levites shall stand guard around the Tabernacle of the Pact.

[54] The Israelites did accordingly; just as the LORD had commanded Moses, so they did.

1.47–54: Levites are charged with the Tabernacle. This is part one of a lengthy, detailed outline of Levitical duties (continued in chs 3–4). Being exempt from military service, the Levites are charged with guarding the Tabernacle as well as dismantling it for travel and erecting it when encamped. As such, their position in the layout of the camp is closest to the Tabernacle. Rabbinic midrash (*Num. Rab.* 1.12) attributes their prestigious responsibilities to a reward they receive for remaining loyal to God by not having participated in the golden calf worship (Exod. 32.25–29).

2 The LORD spoke to Moses and Aaron, saying: ²The Israelites shall camp each with his standard, under the banners of their ancestral house; they shall camp around the Tent of Meeting at a distance.

³Camped on the front, or east side: the standard of the division of Judah, troop by troop.
    Chieftain of the Judites: Nahshon son of Amminadab.
      ⁴His troop, as enrolled: 74,600.
5   Camping next to it:
    The tribe of Issachar.
    Chieftain of the Issacharites: Nethanel son of Zuar.
      ⁶His troop, as enrolled: 54,400.
7   The tribe of Zebulun.
    Chieftain of the Zebulunites: Eliab son of Helon. ⁸His
    troop, as enrolled: 57,400.
⁹The total enrolled in the division of Judah: 186,400, for all troops. These shall march first.

¹⁰On the south: the standard of the division of Reuben, troop by troop.
    Chieftain of the Reubenites: Elizur son of Shedeur.
      ¹¹His troop, as enrolled: 46,500.
12   Camping next to it:
    The tribe of Simeon.
    Chieftain of the Simeonites: Shelumiel son of Zurishaddai. ¹³His troop, as enrolled: 59,300.
14   And the tribe of Gad.
    Chieftain of the Gadites: Eliasaph son of Reuel.
      ¹⁵His troop, as enrolled: 45,650.
¹⁶The total enrolled in the division of Reuben: 151,450, for all troops. These shall march second.

¹⁷Then, midway between the divisions, the Tent of Meeting, the division of the Levites, shall move. As they camp, so they shall march, each in position, by their standards.

¹⁸On the west: the standard of the division of Ephraim, troop by troop.
    Chieftain of the Ephraimites: Elishama son of Ammihud. ¹⁹His troop, as enrolled: 40,500.
20   Next to it:
    The tribe of Manasseh.
    Chieftain of the Manassites: Gamaliel son of Pedahzur. ²¹His troop, as enrolled: 32,200.
22   And the tribe of Benjamin.
    Chieftain of the Benjaminites: Abidan son of Gideoni.
      ²³His troop, as enrolled: 35,400.

2.1–34: The plan of the camp. The camp blueprint, according to God's instruction, situates the Tabernacle in the center surrounded by the twelve tribes. Each tribe is assigned a location in this military-style camp. **2:** Each tribal group marches and camps with its *standard, under the banners* of its ancestral house. The meaning of the Heb term "degel" is uncertain. It may refer to a standard, probably with an attached banner or flag bearing the insignia of the tribe. Medieval commentators suggest that the tribal animal totem is depicted on the banner (Ibn Ezra) or that a colored cloth corresponding to the color of the tribe's stone on the priest's breastplate hangs from the banner (Rashi). Alternately, "degel" may refer to a military unit, a subdivision of the tribe. Levites and priests are not assigned a position in this account (see ch 3), and the Joseph tribe is broken into his two sons, Ephraim and Manasseh (see Gen. 48.1–20) to reach the number twelve. **3–31:** The twelve tribes are arranged to form a square camp of four divisions with three tribes in each. The Leah tribes are situated to the east and south of the Tabernacle; Gad, a son of Leah's maidservant Zilpah, replaces Levi. Benjamin and Joseph's sons Ephraim and Manasseh, the Rachel tribes, take their position west of the Tabernacle. The remaining concubine tribes are located to the north. Judah's eastern position facing the Tabernacle entrance is a mark of the tribe's distinction as the progenitor of the Davidic royal house (see Gen. 49.10). Each of the four camp divisions has a designated leading tribe; the choice is based on traditions regarding attributes of Jacob's sons (Gen. ch 49).

²⁴ The total enrolled in the division of Ephraim: 108,100 for all troops. These shall march third.

²⁵ On the north: the standard of the division of Dan, troop by troop.
Chieftain of the Danites: Ahiezer son of Ammishaddai. ²⁶ His troop, as enrolled: 62,700.
²⁷ Camping next to it:
The tribe of Asher.
Chieftain of the Asherites: Pagiel son of Ochran. ²⁸ His troop, as enrolled: 41,500.
²⁹ And the tribe of Naphtali.
Chieftain of the Naphtalites: Ahira son of Enan. ³⁰ His troop, as enrolled: 53,400.
³¹ The total enrolled in the division of Dan: 157,600. These shall march last, by their standards.

³² Those are the enrollments of the Israelites by ancestral houses. The total enrolled in the divisions, for all troops: 603,550. ³³ The Levites, however, were not recorded among the Israelites, as the Lord had commanded Moses.

³⁴ The Israelites did accordingly; just as the Lord had commanded Moses, so they camped by their standards, and so they marched, each with his clan according to his ancestral house.

3 This is the line of Aaron and Moses at the time that the Lord spoke with Moses on Mount Sinai. ² These were the names of Aaron's sons: Nadab, the first-born, and Abihu, Eleazar and Ithamar; ³ those were the names of Aaron's sons, the anointed priests who were ordained for priesthood. ⁴ But Nadab and Abihu died ᵃ by the will of ᵃ the Lord, when they offered alien fire before the Lord in the wilderness of Sinai; and they left no sons. So it was Eleazar and Ithamar who served as priests in the lifetime of their father Aaron.

⁵ The Lord spoke to Moses, saying: ⁶ Advance the tribe of Levi and place them in attendance upon Aaron the priest to serve him. ⁷ They shall perform duties for him and for the whole community before the Tent of Meeting, doing the work of the Tabernacle. ⁸ They shall take charge of all the furnishings of the Tent of Meeting—a duty on behalf of the Israelites—doing the work of the Tabernacle. ⁹ You shall assign the Levites to Aaron and to his sons: they are formally assigned to him from among the Israelites. ¹⁰ You shall make Aaron and his sons responsible for

32–34: These summary verses repeat the census grand total of ch 1, adding the information about the military organization, which, after all, is the purpose of the census. The concluding v. confirms that subsequently the Israelites camped and marched according to this plan (Num. 10.14–28). Such summary verses at the end of a unit typify Priestly literature, which also emphasizes that God's command was fulfilled exactly (v. 34).

3.1–51: The first Levite census, their ranking, and special roles. This is the first of three Levite censuses (ch 4; 26.57–62). The tribe of Levi is divided into clans; each bears the name of a son of Gershon, Kohath, or Merari, Levi's three sons. Preserving the genealogy of the Levites and especially that of the Aaronite priests is of great importance to the Priestly writer(s). P considers the Aaronites as the sole legitimate priestly line. Non-Aaronite Levites function in subordinate roles to the priests. Any challenge to Aaron's divinely ordained authority is summarily crushed (see Korah rebellion, chs 16–17). **1–3:** *This is the line of Aaron and Moses:* It is most unusual for Aaron's name to precede Moses'; elsewhere this occurs only in other genealogical texts of the P source (Exod. 6.20; Num. 26.59; 1 Chron. 5.29; 23.13). Rashi notes that Aaron's sons are named but not Moses', and he concludes that Moses is, figuratively, the father of Aaron's sons as well because he (Moses) taught them Torah on the day God spoke to him on Mt. Sinai. **4:** A reference to the obscure incident described in Lev. ch 10. **5–10:** The main role of the Levites is guard duty. They are charged with guarding the Tabernacle from non-priestly encroachers while it is stationary and guarding its furnishings during travel. The purview of the priests is the interior of the Tabernacle, its sacred objects, and performing the rites associated with them. *Any outsider,* that is, a non-priest, is forbidden contact with the holy place or holy

a-a Others "before."

observing their priestly duties; and any outsider who encroaches shall be put to death.

¹¹ The LORD spoke to Moses, saying: ¹² I hereby take the Levites from among the Israelites in place of all the first-born, the first issue of the womb among the Israelites: the Levites shall be Mine. ¹³ For every first-born is Mine: at the time that I smote every first-born in the land of Egypt, I consecrated every first-born in Israel, man and beast, to Myself, to be Mine, the LORD's.

¹⁴ The LORD spoke to Moses in the wilderness of Sinai, saying: ¹⁵ Record the Levites by ancestral house and by clan; record every male among them from the age of one month up. ¹⁶ So Moses recorded them at the command of the LORD, as he was bidden. ¹⁷ These were the sons of Levi by name: Gershon, Kohath, and Merari. ¹⁸ These were the names of the sons of Gershon by clan: Libni and Shimei. ¹⁹ The sons of Kohath by clan: Amram and Izhar, Hebron and Uzziel. ²⁰ The sons of Merari by clan: Mahli and Mushi.

These were the clans of the Levites within their ancestral houses:

²¹ To Gershon belonged the clan of the Libnites and the clan of the Shimeites; those were the clans of the Gershonites. ²² The recorded entries of all their males from the age of one month up, as recorded, came to 7,500. ²³ The clans of the Gershonites were to camp behind the Tabernacle, to the west. ²⁴ The chieftain of the ancestral house of the Gershonites was Eliasaph son of Lael. ²⁵ The duties of the Gershonites in the Tent of Meeting comprised: the Tabernacle,ᵃ the tent, its covering, and the screen for the entrance of the Tent of Meeting; ²⁶ the hangings of the enclosure, the screen for the entrance of the enclosure which surrounds the Tabernacle, the cords thereof, and the altar— all the service connected with these.

²⁷ To Kohath belonged the clan of the Amramites, the clan of the Izharites, the clan of the Hebronites, and the clan of the Uzzielites; those were the clans of the Kohathites. ²⁸ All the listed males from the age of one month up came to 8,600, attending to the duties of the sanctuary. ²⁹ The clans of the Kohathites were to camp along the south side of the Tabernacle. ³⁰ The chieftain of the ancestral house of the Kohathite clans was Elizaphan son of Uzziel. ³¹ Their duties comprised: the ark, the table, the lampstand, the altars, and the sacred utensils that were used with them, and the screenᵇ—all the service connected with these. ³² The head chieftain of the Levites was

articles, on penalty of death. Only the sanctified priests may enter the sacred space of the Tabernacle. Naḥmanides (Ramban) compares the boundaries of the Tabernacle with the bounds set for Mt. Sinai when Moses ascends the mountain to receive the law (Exod. 19.12). **11–13:** Another role of the Levites is to replace first-born Israelites who are consecrated to God. Levites serve the priests *in place* of Israelite first-born males, who by birth are destined to minister to God. The dedication of Samuel to Eli at Shiloh reflects this practice (1 Sam. 1.10–11, 24–28). Rabbinic interpretation understands the substitution by Levites as an indication that originally first-born children were sacrificed to the deity, comparable to the offering of first-born animals (Exod. 13.2; Lev. 27.26–27; Num. 8.17; 18.15–16), but no proof exists for that assumption. **14–39:** The first census of Levites states that they are counted from the age of one month up, the age of a viable infant; contrast the Israelite census from age 20 up in 1.3, the age of military conscription. The various clans of Gershonites, Kohathites, and Merarites are numbered and assigned a position from which to guard the Tabernacle: the west side, south side, and north side, respectively; the priests are stationed at the eastern entrance. The specific duties of each clan are also delineated.

ᵃ *See note on Exod. 26.1.*   ᵇ *I.e., the screening curtain; cf. 4–5.*

Eleazar son of Aaron the priest, in charge of those attending to the duties of the sanctuary.

33 To Merari belonged the clan of the Mahlites and the clan of the Mushites; those were the clans of Merari. 34 The recorded entries of all their males from the age of one month up came to 6,200. 35 The chieftain of the ancestral house of the clans of Merari was Zuriel son of Abihail. They were to camp along the north side of the Tabernacle. 36 The assigned duties of the Merarites comprised: the planks of the Tabernacle, its bars, posts, and sockets, and all its furnishings—all the service connected with these; 37 also the posts around the enclosure and their sockets, pegs, and cords.

38 Those who were to camp before the Tabernacle, in front—before the Tent of Meeting, on the east—were Moses and Aaron and his sons, attending to the duties of the sanctuary, as a duty on behalf of the Israelites; and any outsider who encroached was to be put to death. 39 All the Levites who were recorded, whom at the LORD's command Moses and Aaron recorded by their clans, all the males from the age of one month up, came to 22,000.

40 The LORD said to Moses: Record every first-born male of the Israelite people from the age of one month up, and make a list of their names; 41 and take the Levites for Me, the LORD, in place of every first-born among the Israelite people, and the cattle of the Levites in place of every first-born among the cattle of the Israelites. 42 So Moses recorded all the first-born among the Israelites, as the LORD had commanded him. 43 All the first-born males as listed by name, recorded from the age of one month up, came to 22,273.

44 The LORD spoke to Moses, saying: 45 Take the Levites in place of all the first-born among the Israelite people, and the cattle of the Levites in place of their cattle; and the Levites shall be Mine, the LORD's. 46 And as the redemption price of the 273 Israelite first-born over and above the number of the Levites, 47 take five shekels per head—take this by the sanctuary weight, twenty gerahs to the shekel— 48 and give the money to Aaron and his sons as the redemption price for those who are in excess. 49 So Moses took the redemption money from those over and above the ones redeemed by the Levites; 50 he took the money from the first-born of the Israelites, 1,365 sanctuary shekels. 51 And Moses gave the redemption money to Aaron and his sons at the LORD's bidding, as the LORD had commanded Moses.

40–51: Although Levites function as substitutes for first-born Israelites, apparently the Levite population is short by 273 of the number of Israelite first-borns. The excess children are redeemed with a payment to the priests of five shekels per head. The numbers here are problematic as well; it is difficult to understand how the number of first-born children from all the tribes was nearly equivalent to the number of Levites; this would assume that each mother had a huge number of children. **47:** *By the sanctuary weight, twenty gerahs to the shekel:* Two standards of weights coexisted in ancient Israel, the sanctuary weight (Exod. 30.13, 24; Lev. 5.15; Num. 7.13) and the royal weight (2 Sam. 14.26). The gloss "twenty gerahs" specifies the number of small units of weight in the lighter sanctuary shekel. The royal shekel (24 gerahs), also known as the shekel of the king, is widely attested in the archeological record. A gerah was about .5 gm; the royal shekel was about 11.5 gm, the sanctuary shekel about 9.5 gm (less than .5 oz.).

4 The Lord spoke to Moses and Aaron, saying: ²Take a [separate] census of the Kohathites among the Levites, by the clans of their ancestral house, ³from the age of thirty years up to the age of fifty, all who are subject to service, to perform tasks for the Tent of Meeting. ⁴This is the responsibility of the Kohathites in the Tent of Meeting: the most sacred objects.

⁵At the breaking of camp, Aaron and his sons shall go in and take down the screening curtain and cover the Ark of the Pact with it. ⁶They shall lay a covering of dolphin ͣ skin over it and spread a cloth of pure blue on top; and they shall put its poles in place.

⁷Over the table of display they shall spread a blue cloth; they shall place upon it the bowls, the ladles, the jars, and the libation jugs; and the regular bread shall rest upon it. ⁸They shall spread over these a crimson cloth which they shall cover with a covering of dolphin skin; and they shall put the poles in place.

⁹Then they shall take a blue cloth and cover the lampstand for lighting, with its lamps, its tongs, and its fire pans, as well as all the oil vessels that are used in its service. ¹⁰They shall put it and all its furnishings into a covering of dolphin skin, which they shall then place on a carrying frame.

¹¹Next they shall spread a blue cloth over the altar of gold and cover it with a covering of dolphin skin; and they shall put its poles in place. ¹²They shall take all the service vessels with which the service in the sanctuary is performed, put them into a blue cloth and cover them with a covering of dolphin skin, which they shall then place on a carrying frame. ¹³They shall remove the ashes from the [copper] altar and spread a purple cloth over it. ¹⁴Upon it they shall place all the vessels that are used in its service: the fire pans, the flesh hooks, the scrapers, and the basins—all the vessels of the altar—and over it they shall spread a covering of dolphin skin; and they shall put its poles in place.

¹⁵When Aaron and his sons have finished covering the sacred objects and all the furnishings of the sacred objects at the breaking of camp, only then shall the Kohathites come and lift them, so that they do not come in contact with the sacred objects and die. These things in the Tent of Meeting shall be the porterage of the Kohathites.

¹⁶Responsibility shall rest with Eleazar son of Aaron the

4.1–49: The second Levite census and delineation of Levite duties. The second census of Levites is restricted to the work force between the ages of 30 and 50, who transport the Tabernacle's structural parts, its curtains, and its sacred objects during travel in the wilderness. Responsibilities for specific components of the Tabernacle are divided among the Levitical clan groups. **4–20:** The most important components of the Tabernacle are dealt with first. Since the Levites are not empowered to handle these sacred objects or even view them, on pain of death, those objects, including the Ark, are first wrapped by priests. Coverings of different material and color distinguish the sacred objects transported by the Kohathite clans. The Ark of the Covenant, the most sacred article, is covered with three cloths. The Ark is considered the divine throne of God (1 Sam. 4.4; 2 Sam. 6.2), who in Priestly literature is envisioned as dwelling in the Tabernacle itself (contrast Deut. 12). For that reason the Ark is sometimes brought into battle (1 Sam. ch 4). According to a rabbinic midrash, the earthly Ark is a counterpart of the heavenly throne (*Num. Rab.* 4:13).

a See note at Exod. 25.5.

priest for the lighting oil, the aromatic incense, the regular meal offering, and the anointing oil—responsibility for the whole Tabernacle and for everything consecrated that is in it or in its vessels.

¹⁷ The LORD spoke to Moses and Aaron, saying: ¹⁸ Do not let the group of Kohathite clans be cut off from the Levites. ¹⁹ Do this with them, that they may live and not die when they approach the most sacred objects: let Aaron and his sons go in and assign each of them to his duties and to his porterage. ²⁰ But let not [the Kohathites] go inside and ᵃwitness the dismantling of the sanctuary,ᵃ lest they die.

NASO'   נשא

²¹ The LORD spoke to Moses: ²² Take a census of the Gershonites also, by their ancestral house and by their clans. ²³ Record them from the age of thirty years up to the age of fifty, all who are subject to service in the performance of tasks for the Tent of Meeting. ²⁴ These are the duties of the Gershonite clans as to labor and porterage: ²⁵ they shall carry the cloths of the Tabernacle, the Tent of Meeting with its covering, the covering of dolphin skin that is on top of it, and the screen for the entrance of the Tent of Meeting; ²⁶ the hangings of the enclosure, the screen at the entrance of the gate of the enclosure that surrounds the Tabernacle, the cords thereof, and the altar, and all their service equipment and all their accessories; and they shall perform the service. ²⁷ All the duties of the Gershonites, all their porterage and all their service, shall be performed on orders from Aaron and his sons; you shall make them responsible for attending to all their porterage. ²⁸ Those are the duties of the Gershonite clans for the Tent of Meeting; they shall attend to them under the direction of Ithamar son of Aaron the priest.

²⁹ As for the Merarites, you shall record them by the clans of their ancestral house; ³⁰ you shall record them from the age of thirty years up to the age of fifty, all who are subject to service in the performance of the duties for the Tent of Meeting. ³¹ These are their porterage tasks in connection with their various duties for the Tent of Meeting: the planks, the bars, the posts, and the sockets of the Tabernacle; ³² the posts around the enclosure and their sockets, pegs, and cords—all these furnishings and their service: you shall list by name the objects that are their porterage tasks. ³³ Those are the duties of the Merarite clans, pertaining to their various duties in the Tent of

21–28: The Gershonite clans are responsible for transporting the four layers of tent curtains. They are supervised by Aaron's son Ithamar. **29–33:** The Merarites, the third group of clans, are charged with carrying the structural parts of the Tabernacle. Ithamar oversees their duties as well. **34:** *The chieftains of the community:* The tribal leaders assist Moses and Aaron in recording the Levite census; this also connects ch 4 to ch 1.

---

a-a Others "look at the sacred objects even for a moment."

Meeting under the direction of Ithamar son of Aaron the priest.

34 So Moses, Aaron, and the chieftains of the community recorded the Kohathites by the clans of their ancestral house, 35 from the age of thirty years up to the age of fifty, all who were subject to service for work relating to the Tent of Meeting. 36 Those recorded by their clans came to 2,750. 37 That was the enrollment of the Kohathite clans, all those who performed duties relating to the Tent of Meeting, whom Moses and Aaron recorded at the command of the LORD through Moses.

38 The Gershonites who were recorded by the clans of their ancestral house, 39 from the age of thirty years up to the age of fifty, all who were subject to service for work relating to the Tent of Meeting—40 those recorded by the clans of their ancestral house came to 2,630. 41 That was the enrollment of the Gershonite clans, all those performing duties relating to the Tent of Meeting whom Moses and Aaron recorded at the command of the LORD.

42 The enrollment of the Merarite clans by the clans of their ancestral house, 43 from the age of thirty years up to the age of fifty, all who were subject to service for work relating to the Tent of Meeting—44 those recorded by their clans came to 3,200. 45 That was the enrollment of the Merarite clans which Moses and Aaron recorded at the command of the LORD through Moses.

46 All the Levites whom Moses, Aaron, and the chieftains of Israel recorded by the clans of their ancestral houses, 47 from the age of thirty years up to the age of fifty, all who were subject to duties of service and porterage relating to the Tent of Meeting—48 those recorded came to 8,580. 49 Each one was given responsibility for his service and porterage at the command of the LORD through Moses, and each was recorded as the LORD had commanded Moses.

5 The LORD spoke to Moses, saying: 2 Instruct the Israelites to remove from camp anyone with an ªeruption or a discharge-ª and anyone defiled by a corpse. 3 Remove male and female alike; put them outside the camp so that they do not defile the camp of those in whose midst I dwell.

4 The Israelites did so, putting them outside the camp; as the LORD had spoken to Moses, so the Israelites did.

5 The LORD spoke to Moses, saying: 6 Speak to the Israelites: When a man or woman commits any wrong toward a

a-a *See Lev. 13, 15.*

5.1–31: Laws of purity and the role of the priests. Priestly tasks include responsibilities over worldly as well as sacred matters; in the ancient world the two were inseparable. Laws concerned with the maintenance of religious purity inside the Israelite camp reflect this ideology, and the purity of the camp was essential if the Israelites wanted God to continue dwelling in their midst. This explains why these regulations immediately follow the instructions for the proper organization and transport of the wilderness camp (chs 1–4). **1–4:** The sacred status of the Tabernacle, which sits in the center of the camp, necessitates that the entire area within the bounds of the camp preserve a state of cultic (religious) purity. According to the Priestly writer(s), contact with impurity is contagious to both persons and objects. Therefore, that which is in a state of impurity must be removed from the camp, lest it pollute the holiness of the sanctuary and endanger the Presence of God. The most dangerous conditions, those marked by severe impurity, require a seven-day purification process (Lev. chs 13–16; Num. ch 19). They include persons with certain skin diseases, abnormal sexual discharges, menstruating women, or those who are defiled by a corpse. **5–10:** Lev. ch 5 details the "'asham," or guilt offering, and the expiation processes for transgressions that require this category of sacrifices. Here in Numbers two provisions supplement the guilt offering for sins involving robberies and accompanying false oaths: (1) A confession must precede the act of restitution; (2) if the injured party has no living relative the reparation payment goes to the officiating priest (as does the meat from the expiatory sacrifice).

fellow man, thus breaking faith with the Lord, and that person realizes his guilt, [7] he shall confess the wrong that he has done. He shall make restitution in the principal amount and add one-fifth to it, giving it to him whom he has wronged. [8] If the man has no kinsman[a] to whom restitution can be made, the amount repaid shall go to the Lord for the priest—in addition to the ram of expiation with which expiation is made on his behalf.[b] [9] So, too, any gift among the sacred donations that the Israelites offer shall be the priest's. [10] And each shall retain his sacred donations: each priest shall keep what is given to him.

[11] The Lord spoke to Moses, saying: [12] Speak to the Israelite people and say to them:

If any man's wife has gone astray and broken faith with him [13] in that a man has had carnal relations with her unbeknown to her husband, and she keeps secret the fact that she has defiled herself without being forced, and there is no witness against her—[14] but a fit of jealousy comes over him and he is wrought up about the wife who has defiled herself; or if a fit of jealousy comes over one and he is wrought up about his wife although she has not defiled herself—[15] the man shall bring his wife to the priest. And he shall bring as an offering for her one-tenth of an *ephah* of barley flour. No oil shall be poured upon it and no frankincense shall be laid on it, for it is a meal offering of jealousy, a meal offering of remembrance which recalls wrongdoing.

[16] The priest shall bring her forward and have her stand before the Lord. [17] The priest shall take sacral water in an earthen vessel and, taking some of the earth that is on the floor of the Tabernacle, the priest shall put it into the water. [18] After he has made the woman stand before the Lord, the priest shall bare the woman's head[c] and place upon her hands the meal offering of remembrance, which is a meal offering of jealousy. And in the priest's hands shall be the water of bitterness [d]that induces the spell.[-d] [19] The priest shall adjure the woman, saying to her, "If no man has lain with you, if you have not gone astray in defilement while married to your husband, be immune to harm from this water of bitterness that induces the spell. [20] But if you have gone astray while married to your husband and have defiled yourself, if a man other than your husband has had carnal relations with you"—

11–31: The ordeal, or more correctly, the trial of the suspected adulteress, is a means of allaying or confirming the fears of a husband that his wife was unfaithful. Marital infidelity by the woman is a grave offense because it threatens the purity of the lineage. Adultery is defined as involving sexual contact between a married woman and a man other than her husband, and is a capital crime (Lev. 20.10). (Since Israel was a polygynous society, sexual contact between a married man and an unmarried woman was not considered adultery, although it was not encouraged.) When conclusive evidence is lacking, judgment and subsequent punishment is left in the hands of the divine. Water ordeals of varying types are attested from the ancient Near East. In the Babylonian Laws of Hammurabi, §132, (18th century BCE), one method of determining the guilt or innocence of a suspected adulteress is the river ordeal, in which the woman is thrown into the water and her fate is left to the river god. According to the Mishnah, the biblical ordeal for a suspected adulteress was suspended after the destruction of the Second Temple, one reason being the uncontrollable number of cases of adultery (*m. Sot.* 9.9). The episode of the suspected adulteress is narrated here for two reasons: The ritual utilizes earth from the floor of the Tabernacle (v. 17), the focus of the previous chapter, and the ritual, like the guilt offering, is connected to broken faith (see vv. 6, 12). **12:** If a man's wife *has gone astray:* The initial sin of the woman may be a violation of the marriage oath. Rashi understands it as the woman having gone mad. **14:** The reason for the husband's jealousy is not stated but may be that his wife is pregnant and he questions the paternity of the child. **15–26:** The husband brings a menial meal offering, and the priest prepares a mixture of sacral water, dust from the sanctuary floor, and ink rubbed off the inscription of the curse for the woman to drink. Most importantly, the priest ad-

---

a Lit. "redeemer."   b Cf. Lev. 5.15 f.
c See note at Lev. 10.6.   d-d Meaning of Heb. uncertain.

21 here the priest shall administer the curse of adjuration to the woman, as the priest goes on to say to the woman— "may the LORD make you a curse and an imprecation among your people, as the LORD causes your thigh to sag and your belly to distend; 22 may this water that induces the spell enter your body, causing the belly to distend and the thigh to sag." And the woman shall say, "Amen, amen!"

23 The priest shall put these curses down in writing and rub it off into the water of bitterness. 24 He is to make the woman drink the water of bitterness that induces the spell, so that the spell-inducing water may enter into her to bring on bitterness. 25 Then the priest shall take from the woman's hand the meal offering of jealousy, elevate the meal offering before the LORD, and present it on the altar. 26 The priest shall scoop out of the meal offering a token part of it and turn it into smoke on the altar. Last, he shall make the woman drink the water.

27 Once he has made her drink the water—if she has defiled herself by breaking faith with her husband, the spell-inducing water shall enter into her to bring on bitterness, so that her belly shall distend and her thigh shall sag; and the woman shall become a curse among her people. 28 But if the woman has not defiled herself and is pure, she shall be unharmed and able to retain seed.

29 This is the ritual in cases of jealousy, when a woman goes astray while married to her husband and defiles herself, 30 or when a fit of jealousy comes over a man and he is wrought up over his wife: the woman shall be made to stand before the LORD and the priest shall carry out all this ritual with her. 31 The man shall be clear of guilt; but that woman shall suffer for her guilt.

6 The LORD spoke to Moses, saying: 2 Speak to the Israelites and say to them: If anyone, man or woman, explicitly[a] utters a nazirite's vow, to set himself apart for the LORD, 3 he shall abstain from wine and any other intoxicant; he shall not drink vinegar of wine or of any other intoxicant, neither shall he drink anything in which grapes have been steeped, nor eat grapes fresh or dried. 4 Throughout his term as nazirite, he may not eat anything that is obtained from the grapevine, even seeds or skin.[b]

5 Throughout the term of his vow as nazirite, no razor shall touch his head; it shall remain consecrated until the completion of his term as nazirite of the LORD, the hair of

a See note at Lev. 22.21.
b Meaning of Heb. ḥarṣannim and zag uncertain.

ministers the woman's oath and utters the curse that takes effect if she is guilty. **18:** *Water of bitterness* seems to refer to the bitter taste of the water, which contains ink and dust, probably mixed with ashes fallen to the sanctuary floor from the altar. Alternatively, the "bitterness" can refer to the punishment, apparently a distended uterus, a possible miscarriage, and ultimate infertility (so medieval commentators). A third interpretation translates the Heb term "hamarim" as "instructing," derived from a different verbal root ("y-r-h"). Thereby, the waters reveal the woman's innocence or guilt. **21:** This v. repeats the curse; it can be explained as an interpolation that adds God to the formula. **22:** *The woman shall say, "Amen, amen!"*: Amen or twice amen is an affirmation of truth often attached to oaths (Deut. 27.15–26; Neh. 5.13). An archeological discovery of a letter from the 7th century BCE that records the petition of an Israelite worker to his officer, uses "Amen" to affirm the truth of the worker's statement. Oaths and curses similar in formula to those uttered in this biblical case are known from ancient Near Eastern treaties. In the case of the biblical adulteress, as well as in some non-biblical examples, the function of the water mixture is to effectuate the oath. **27–28:** These vv. repeat the two possible results of the trial. **29–31:** *This is the ritual,* or instruction, "Torah." Priestly legislation often concludes with these types of summary statements (see concluding verses in Lev. chs 7, 11, 15).

6.1–21: Vow of the Nazirite. By taking the vow of a Nazirite an Israelite consecrates himself or herself to God for a limited time period, becoming a type of lay priest, with restrictions similar to those of priests. The vow entails a number of restrictions to the person's lifestyle: abstaining from fermented drinks and grape products; abstaining from cutting the hair; and abstaining from coming in contact with the dead. (This explains why Samson, who was a his head being left to grow untrimmed. ⁶Throughout the term that he has set apart for the Lord, he shall not go in where there is a dead person. ⁷Even if his father or mother, or his brother or sister should die, he must not defile himself for them, since ª·hair set apart for his God·ª is upon his head: ⁸throughout his term as nazirite he is consecrated to the Lord.

⁹If a person dies suddenly near him,ᵇ defiling his consecrated hair, he shall shave his head on the day he becomes clean; he shall shave it on the seventh day. ¹⁰On the eighth day he shall bring two turtledoves or two pigeons to the priest, at the entrance of the Tent of Meeting. ¹¹The priest shall offer one as a sin offering and the other as a burnt offering, and make expiation on his behalf for the guilt that he incurred through the corpse. That same day he shall reconsecrate his head ¹²and rededicate to the Lord his term as nazirite; and he shall bring a lamb in its first year as a penalty offering. The previous period shall be void, since his consecrated hair was defiled.

¹³This is the ritual for the nazirite: On the day that his term as nazirite is completed, heᶜ shall be brought to the entrance of the Tent of Meeting. ¹⁴As his offering to the Lord he shall present: one male lamb in its first year, without blemish, for a burnt offering; one ewe lamb in its first year, without blemish, for a sin offering; one ram without blemish for an offering of well-being; ¹⁵a basket of unleavened cakes of choice flour with oil mixed in, and unleavened wafers spread with oil; and the proper meal offerings and libations.

¹⁶The priest shall present them before the Lord and offer the sin offering and the burnt offering. ¹⁷He shall offer the ram as a sacrifice of well-being to the Lord, together with the basket of unleavened cakes; the priest shall also offer the meal offerings and the libations. ¹⁸The nazirite shall then shave his consecrated hair, at the entrance of the Tent of Meeting, and take the locks of his consecrated hair and put them on the fire that is under the sacrifice of well-being.

¹⁹The priest shall take the shoulder of the ram when it has been boiled, one unleavened cake from the basket, and one unleavened wafer, and place them on the hands of the nazirite after he has shaved his consecrated hair. ²⁰The priest shall elevate them as an elevation offering before the Lord; and this shall be a sacred donation for the priest, in addition to the breast of the elevation offering

Nazirite, was not supposed to cut his hair.) The Rabbis explain that the passage on Nazirite vows follows the section on the suspected adulteress to teach that abstinence from drink is commendable, since drinking intoxicants can lead to adultery (*b. Sot.* 2a). Modern critical approaches connect the sections by their emphasis on the key roles of the priests. **9–12:** Contamination by a corpse requires shaving the hair and following the purification process outlined in ch 19. After purification, the Nazirite restarts his or her original vow timetable. Defilement of a Nazirite affects the consecrated hair rather than the person. **18:** The significance of the hair is also apparent at the completion ceremony, at which time it is burnt in the fire underneath (the pot of) the Nazirite's sacrifice of well-being. Hair offerings are known from ancient practices in the Aegean. **13–20:** The rites that the Nazirite undergoes at the completion of the vow not only commemorate the fulfillment of the vow but function as a transitional ritual that allows the person to return to his or her former status. In this Priestly passage, the role of the priest in the ceremony is central to the discussion of the Nazirite. These verses concern a Nazirite for a prescribed period of time; Judg. ch 13 depicts Samson as a lifetime Nazirite, with similar restrictions.

---

a-a Others "his consecration unto God."   b Cf. Num. 19.14–16.
c Or "it," i.e., the consecrated hair; cf. v. 19.

and the thigh of gift offering. After that the nazirite may drink wine.

21 Such is the obligation of a nazirite; except that he who vows an offering to the LORD of what he can afford, beyond his nazirite requirements, must do exactly according to the vow that he has made beyond his obligation as a nazirite.

22 The LORD spoke to Moses: 23 Speak to Aaron and his sons: Thus shall you bless the people of Israel. Say to them:

24 The LORD bless you and protect you!

25 The LORD ᵃ-deal kindly and graciously with you!-ᵃ

26 The LORD ᵇ-bestow His favor-ᵇ upon you and grant you peace!ᶜ

27 Thus they shall link My name with the people of Israel, and I will bless them.

7 On the day that Moses finished setting up the Tabernacle, he anointed and consecrated it and all its furnishings, as well as the altar and its utensils. When he had anointed and consecrated them, 2 the chieftains of Israel, the heads of ancestral houses, namely, the chieftains of the tribes, those who were in charge of enrollment, drew nearᵈ 3 and brought their offering before the LORD: six draught carts and twelve oxen, a cart for every two chieftains and an ox for each one.

When they had brought them before the Tabernacle,

a-a Others "make His face to shine upon thee and be gracious to thee."
b-b Others "lift up His countenance."
c Or "friendship."   d Cf. Exod. 14.10.

6.22–27: The priestly blessing. Another duty of priests is to bless the community of Israel (Lev. 9.22–23; Deut. 10.8; 21.5) or individual Israelites (1 Sam. 2.20) in the name of the LORD. The three-part blessing here invokes God's mercy and favor toward the children of Israel for the sake of their general well-being, "shalom." Each of the three parts is longer than the preceding one, emphasizing the overflowing of blessing that is hoped for. Ibn Ezra connects Aaron's blessing of Israel at the dedication of the Tabernacle (Lev. 9.22–23) to the priestly blessing in Numbers. An interpretive version of the priestly blessing, contained in the sectarian literature of the Dead Sea Scrolls, ex-pands the biblical text to more clearly define the particulars of God's blessing (1QS 2.2–4). **25:** *Deal kindly* is more literally "shine His face," a sign of favor. Similarly in v. 26, *bestow his favor* is "raise His head." The Bible often refers to God in such anthropomorphic terms. **27:** The prescription to place God's name upon Israel may refer to amulets inscribed with the name of the LORD worn around the neck. This interpretation is supported by the discovery in a Jerusalem tomb of two silver amulets incised with slightly shorter versions of the priestly benediction in Numbers. These First Temple–period amulets testify to the antiquity of the blessing. The priestly blessing has been pre-served to modernity in Jewish liturgy as part of the "'Amidah" and in the blessing recited by parents for their children on Friday night. *And I will bless them:* The Heb actually reads, "and I will bless you (plural)." Ibn Ezra correctly explains that "you" refers to the priests; the priests bless Israel and God in turn blesses the priests.

7.1–89: Final preparation for the operation of the Tabernacle cult. After the organization of the camp and the relegation of duties to the Levites and priests, Moses consecrates the Tabernacle and its implements and outfits it with supplies necessary for its operation. The consecration of the altar repeats the account in Lev. chs 8–9, expanding the narrative in Leviticus by adding the chieftains' gifts. The tribal chieftains bring joint gifts, representing all Israel equally (cf. Exod. 30.15), as well as gifts from their separate tribes. Joint initiatory gifts for the sanctuary consist of six carts and twelve oxen. The carts and oxen are given to the Gershonite and Merarite Levitic clans for transporting the portable Tabernacle. The Kohathites do not receive carts because they must carry the sacred objects on their shoulders. Individual chieftains bring their tribe's gifts and dedication offerings for twelve consecutive days, one chieftain per day. The insertion of this information at this point fits with the previous assignment of Levitic tasks and the appointment of tribal heads. **1:** Anointing the Tabernacle and its implements with oil as an act of consecration is an ancient Near Eastern practice. In the Bible, a comparable act is performed by Jacob at Bethel when he anoints the pillar that he erects to mark the holiness of the site. Jacob then designates the pillar as a future shrine (Gen. 28.18–22). **2:** According to Rashi, the chieftains of Israel are the same officers who were in charge of the slaves in Egypt and beaten on their (the Israelites') account (see Exod. 5.14, where they are called "foremen"). Now they

4 the LORD said to Moses: 5 Accept these from them for use in the service of the Tent of Meeting, and give them to the Levites according to their respective services.

6 Moses took the carts and the oxen and gave them to the Levites. 7 Two carts and four oxen he gave to the Gershonites, as required for their service, 8 and four carts and eight oxen he gave to the Merarites, as required for their service—under the direction of Ithamar son of Aaron the priest. 9 But to the Kohathites he did not give any; since theirs was the service of the [most] sacred objects, their porterage was by shoulder.

10 The chieftains also brought the dedication offering for the altar upon its being anointed. As the chieftains were presenting their offerings before the altar, 11 the LORD said to Moses: Let them present their offerings for the dedication of the altar, one chieftain each day.

12 The one who presented his offering on the first day was Nahshon son of Amminadab of the tribe of Judah. 13 His offering: one silver bowl weighing 130 shekels and one silver basin of 70 shekels by the sanctuary weight, both filled with choice flour with oil mixed in, for a meal offering; 14 one gold ladle of 10 shekels, filled with incense; 15 one bull of the herd, one ram, and one lamb in its first year, for a burnt offering; 16 one goat for a sin offering; 17 and for his sacrifice of well-being: two oxen, five rams, five he-goats, and five yearling lambs. That was the offering of Nahshon son of Amminadab.

18 On the second day, Nethanel son of Zuar, chieftain of Issachar, made his offering. 19 He presented as his offering: one silver bowl weighing 130 shekels and one silver basin of 70 shekels by the sanctuary weight, both filled with choice flour with oil mixed in, for a meal offering; 20 one gold ladle of 10 shekels, filled with incense; 21 one bull of the herd, one ram, and one lamb in its first year, for a burnt offering; 22 one goat for a sin offering; 23 and for his sacrifice of well-being: two oxen, five rams, five he-goats, and five yearling lambs. That was the offering of Nethanel son of Zuar.

24 On the third day, it was the chieftain of the Zebulunites, Eliab son of Helon. 25 His offering: one silver bowl weighing 130 shekels and one silver basin of 70 shekels by the sanctuary weight, both filled with choice flour with oil mixed in, for a meal offering; 26 one gold ladle of 10 shekels, filled with incense; 27 one bull of the herd, one ram, and one lamb in its first year, for a burnt offering; 28 one goat for a sin offering; 29 and for his sacrifice of well-being: two oxen, five rams, five he-goats, and five yearling lambs. That was the offering of Eliab son of Helon.

are rewarded. **10:** *Dedication offering for the altar:* In Heb "ḥanukah" is the term for the opening dedication of a house, temple, or altar (cf. Deut. 20.5; 1 Kings 8.63; 2 Chron. 7.9). Similarly, the holiday of Hanukkah celebrates the purification and rededication of the Jerusalem Temple by the Maccabees (1 Macc. 4.36–61). The Torah reading for Hanukkah is taken from this chapter in Numbers. **12:** *Judah,* as most important, is mentioned first.

30 On the fourth day, it was the chieftain of the Reubenites, Elizur son of Shedeur. 31 His offering: one silver bowl
weighing 130 shekels and one silver basin of 70 shekels by
the sanctuary weight, both filled with choice flour with oil
mixed in, for a meal offering; 32 one gold ladle of 10
shekels, filled with incense; 33 one bull of the herd, one
ram, and one lamb in its first year, for a burnt offering;
34 one goat for a sin offering; 35 and for his sacrifice of well-
being: two oxen, five rams, five he-goats, and five yearling
lambs. That was the offering of Elizur son of Shedeur.

36 On the fifth day, it was the chieftain of the Simeonites,
Shelumiel son of Zurishaddai. 37 His offering: one silver
bowl weighing 130 shekels and one silver basin of 70
shekels by the sanctuary weight, both filled with choice
flour with oil mixed in, for a meal offering; 38 one gold
ladle of 10 shekels, filled with incense; 39 one bull of the
herd, one ram, and one lamb in its first year, for a burnt offering; 40 one goat for a sin offering; 41 and for his sacrifice
of well-being: two oxen, five rams, five he-goats, and five
yearling lambs. That was the offering of Shelumiel son of
Zurishaddai.

42 On the sixth day, it was the chieftain of the Gadites,
Eliasaph son of Deuel. 43 His offering: one silver bowl
weighing 130 shekels and one silver basin of 70 shekels by
the sanctuary weight, both filled with choice flour with oil
mixed in, for a meal offering; 44 one gold ladle of 10
shekels, filled with incense; 45 one bull of the herd, one
ram, and one lamb in its first year, for a burnt offering;
46 one goat for a sin offering; 47 and for his sacrifice of well-
being: two oxen, five rams, five he-goats, and five yearling
lambs. That was the offering of Eliasaph son of Deuel.

48 On the seventh day, it was the chieftain of the Ephraimites, Elishama son of Ammihud. 49 His offering: one silver bowl weighing 130 shekels and one silver basin of 70
shekels by the sanctuary weight, both filled with choice
flour with oil mixed in, for a meal offering; 50 one gold
ladle of 10 shekels, filled with incense; 51 one bull of the
herd, one ram, and one lamb in its first year, for a burnt offering; 52 one goat for a sin offering; 53 and for his sacrifice
of well-being: two oxen, five rams, five he-goats, and five
yearling lambs. That was the offering of Elishama son of
Ammihud.

54 On the eighth day, it was the chieftain of the Manassites, Gamaliel son of Pedahzur. 55 His offering: one silver
bowl weighing 130 shekels and one silver basin of 70
shekels by the sanctuary weight, both filled with choice
flour with oil mixed in, for a meal offering; 56 one gold
ladle of 10 shekels, filled with incense; 57 one bull of the

herd, one ram, and one lamb in its first year, for a burnt offering; [58] one goat for a sin offering; [59] and for his sacrifice
of well-being: two oxen, five rams, five he-goats, and five
yearling lambs. That was the offering of Gamaliel son of
Pedahzur.

[60] On the ninth day, it was the chieftain of the Benjaminites, Abidan son of Gideoni. [61] His offering: one silver
bowl weighing 130 shekels and one silver basin of 70
shekels by the sanctuary weight, both filled with choice
flour with oil mixed in, for a meal offering; [62] one gold
ladle of 10 shekels, filled with incense; [63] one bull of the
herd, one ram, and one lamb in its first year, for a burnt offering; [64] one goat for a sin offering; [65] and for his sacrifice
of well-being: two oxen, five rams, five he-goats, and five
yearling lambs. That was the offering of Abidan son of
Gideoni.

[66] On the tenth day, it was the chieftain of the Danites,
Ahiezer son of Ammishaddai. [67] His offering: one silver
bowl weighing 130 shekels and one silver basin of 70
shekels by the sanctuary weight, both filled with choice
flour with oil mixed in, for a meal offering; [68] one gold
ladle of 10 shekels, filled with incense; [69] one bull of the
herd, one ram, and one lamb in its first year, for a burnt offering; [70] one goat for a sin offering; [71] and for his sacrifice
of well-being: two oxen, five rams, five he-goats, and five
yearling lambs. That was the offering of Ahiezer son of
Ammishaddai.

[72] On the eleventh day, it was the chieftain of the Asherites, Pagiel son of Ochran. [73] His offering: one silver bowl
weighing 130 shekels and one silver basin of 70 shekels by
the sanctuary weight, both filled with choice flour with oil
mixed in, for a meal offering; [74] one gold ladle of 10
shekels, filled with incense; [75] one bull of the herd, one
ram, and one lamb in its first year, for a burnt offering;
[76] one goat for a sin offering; [77] and for his sacrifice of well-
being: two oxen, five rams, five he-goats, and five yearling
lambs. That was the offering of Pagiel son of Ochran.

[78] On the twelfth day, it was the chieftain of the Naphtalites, Ahira son of Enan. [79] His offering: one silver bowl
weighing 130 shekels and one silver basin of 70 shekels by
the sanctuary weight, both filled with choice flour with oil
mixed in, for a meal offering; [80] one gold ladle of 10
shekels, filled with incense; [81] one bull of the herd, one
ram, and one lamb in its first year, for a burnt offering;
[82] one goat for a sin offering; [83] and for his sacrifice of well-
being: two oxen, five rams, five he-goats, and five yearling
lambs. That was the offering of Ahira son of Enan.

[84] This was the dedication offering for the altar from the

chieftains of Israel upon its being anointed: silver bowls, 12; silver basins, 12; gold ladles, 12. ⁸⁵ Silver per bowl, 130; per basin, 70. Total silver of vessels, 2,400 sanctuary shekels. ⁸⁶ The 12 gold ladles filled with incense—10 sanctuary shekels per ladle—total gold of the ladles, 120.

⁸⁷ Total of herd animals for burnt offerings, 12 bulls; of rams, 12; of yearling lambs, 12—with their proper meal offerings; of goats for sin offerings, 12. ⁸⁸ Total of herd animals for sacrifices of well-being, 24 bulls; of rams, 60; of he-goats, 60; of yearling lambs, 60. That was the dedication offering for the altar after its anointing.

⁸⁹ When Moses went into the Tent of Meeting to speak with Him, he would hear the Voice addressing him from above the cover that was on top of the Ark of the Pact between the two cherubim; thus He spoke to him.

BE-HA‘ALOTEKHA   בהעלתך

8 The LORD spoke to Moses, saying: ² Speak to Aaron and say to him, "When you mount^a the lamps, let the seven lamps give light at the front of the lampstand." ³ Aaron did so; he mounted the lamps at the front of the lampstand, as the LORD had commanded Moses.—⁴ Now this is how the lampstand was made: it was hammered work of gold, hammered from base to petal. According to the pattern that the LORD had shown Moses, so was the lampstand made.

⁵ The LORD spoke to Moses, saying: ⁶ Take the Levites from among the Israelites and cleanse them. ⁷ This is what you shall do to them to cleanse them: sprinkle on them water of purification, and let them go over their whole body with a razor, and wash their clothes; thus they shall be cleansed. ⁸ Let them take a bull of the herd, and with it a meal offering of choice flour with oil mixed in, and you take a second bull of the herd for a sin offering. ⁹ You shall bring the Levites forward before the Tent of Meeting. Assemble the whole Israelite community, ¹⁰ and bring the Levites forward before the LORD. Let the Israelites lay their hands upon the Levites, ¹¹ and let Aaron designate^b the Levites before the LORD as an elevation offering from the Israelites, that they may perform the service of the LORD. ¹² The Levites shall now lay their hands upon the heads of the bulls; one shall be offered to the LORD as a sin offering and the other as a burnt offering, to make expiation for the Levites.

a Cf. Exod. 25.37.   b Lit. "elevate."

84–88: A typically Priestly summary of the account. **89:** This appended v. reiterates how Moses communicates with God in the Tent of Meeting, the portable site for revelation where God dwells (Exod. 25.17–22; Lev. 9.23). God's name is not mentioned but is substituted by *the Voice,* a term that is the precursor of the rabbinic "bat kol," "daughter of the voice," or "echo," signifying a divine voice from the heavens.

8.1–4: Lighting the lampstand. Several passages in Exodus (25.31–40; 27.20–21; 30.7–8; 37.17–24; 40.4) and one in Leviticus (24.1–4) deal with the construction and lighting instructions for the lampstand (menorah). Here the instructions are fulfilled. Lighting the lampstand inside the Tabernacle is a logical conclusion to 7.89, where Moses enters the Tent of Meeting and communicates with God. Ibn Ezra explains the textual placement as a lesson that God's word also comes at night, necessitating the light to burn day and night. **2:** *Let the seven lamps give light at the front of the lampstand:* The lamps are positioned on the stand facing forward, northward, to cast light on the altar and the table with showbread situated in front of the menorah. Seven-spouted ceramic lamps excavated from the shrine at Dan, dating to the First Temple period, are shaped differently; they are circular with spouts for wicks projecting in all directions. **4:** The unit concludes in typically Priestly fashion, that God's command was executed exactly.

8.5–26: Cleansing of the Levites. The duties of the Levites are explicated in the previous chs. Here they undergo rites of ritual purification so that they can handle the Tabernacle and its contents. **7:** Cleansing entails being sprinkled with water of purification (fresh water mixed with the ashes of the red cow; see ch 19), shaving the entire body, and washing one's clothing. **9–16:** These preparatory rituals are followed by sacrifices

13 You shall place the Levites in attendance upon Aaron and his sons, and designate them as an elevation offering to the Lord. 14 Thus you shall set the Levites apart from the Israelites, and the Levites shall be Mine. 15 Thereafter the Levites shall be qualified for the service of the Tent of Meeting, once you have cleansed them and designated them as an elevation offering. 16 For they are formally assigned to Me from among the Israelites: I have taken them for Myself in place of all the first issue of the womb, of all the first-born of the Israelites. 17 For every first-born among the Israelites, man as well as beast, is Mine; I consecrated them to Myself at the time that I smote every first-born in the land of Egypt. 18 Now I take the Levites instead of every first-born of the Israelites; 19 and from among the Israelites I formally assign the Levites to Aaron and his sons, to perform the service for the Israelites in the Tent of Meeting and to make expiation for the Israelites, so that no plague may afflict the Israelites ᵃ-for coming-ᵃ too near the sanctuary.

20 Moses, Aaron, and the whole Israelite community did with the Levites accordingly; just as the Lord had commanded Moses in regard to the Levites, so the Israelites did with them. 21 The Levites purified themselves and washed their clothes; and Aaron designated them as an elevation offering before the Lord, and Aaron made expiation for them to cleanse them. 22 Thereafter the Levites were qualified to perform their service in the Tent of Meeting, under Aaron and his sons. As the Lord had commanded Moses in regard to the Levites, so they did to them.

23 The Lord spoke to Moses, saying: 24 This is the rule for the Levites. From twenty-five years of age up they shall participate in the work force in the service of the Tent of Meeting; 25 but at the age of fifty they shall retire from the work force and shall serve no more. 26 They may assist their brother Levites at the Tent of Meeting by standing guard, but they shall perform no labor. Thus you shall deal with the Levites in regard to their duties.

9 The Lord spoke to Moses in the wilderness of Sinai, on the first new moon of the second year following the exodus from the land of Egypt, saying: 2 Let the Israelite people offer the passover sacrifice at its set time: 3 you shall offer it on the fourteenth day of this month, at twilight, at its set time; you shall offer it in accordance with all its rules and rites.

a-a Lit. "when the Israelites come."

and a laying-on-of-hands ceremony in front of the Tent of Meeting. In a gesture reminiscent of laying hands upon the heads of sacrificial animals (8.12), a group of Israelite representatives lay their hands on the Levites as Aaron designates them (the Levites) as an elevation offering from Israel. These rituals officially separate the Levites from other Israelites and dedicate them to God's service. **23–26:** The last vv. of this section specify the age limits for Levitic duties. The starting age for joining the Levite work force, age 25, conflicts with the starting age for being counted in the census, age 30 (ch 4). This suggests that the Priestly material in Numbers has a complex history, though rabbinic interpretation harmonizes the conflicting numbers by surmising that between the ages of 25 and 30 Levites function as assistants and only at age 30 are they counted as full-fledged members of the work force.

9.1–14: First Passover in the wilderness. Israel observed the first Passover in Egypt just prior to the exodus (Exod. ch 12). Now, one year later, as Israel prepares to depart from Sinai, it celebrates the first Passover in the wilderness. Here the Passover is bound to the Sinaitic covenant, including the laws of ritual purity that must be observed inside the camp in the presence of the Tabernacle. The time-bound obligation to partake of the Passover sacrifice presents a legal problem for Israelites who are ritually impure from contact with a corpse. The issue is resolved with the designation of an alternate Passover, one month later, for persons in a state of impurity or on a distant journey. According to the Chronicler, King Hezekiah (late 8th century bce) also postponed one Passover to the second month. In that case, not enough priests were in a state of purity and those Israelites residing in the north needed time to assemble in Jerusalem (2 Chron. 30). Passover is the only festival or ritual for which a "make-up" is

⁴Moses instructed the Israelites to offer the passover sacrifice; ⁵and they offered the passover sacrifice in the first month, on the fourteenth day of the month, at twilight, in the wilderness of Sinai. Just as the LORD had commanded Moses, so the Israelites did.

⁶But there were some men who were unclean by reason of a corpse and could not offer the passover sacrifice on that day. Appearing that same day before Moses and Aaron, ⁷those men said to them,ᵃ "Unclean though we are by reason of a corpse, why must we be debarred from presenting the LORD's offering at its set time with the rest of the Israelites?" ⁸Moses said to them, "Stand by, and let me hear what instructions the LORD gives about you."

⁹And the LORD spoke to Moses, saying: ¹⁰Speak to the Israelite people, saying: When any of you or of your posterity who are defiled by a corpse or are on a long journey would offer a passover sacrifice to the LORD, ¹¹they shall offer it in the second month, on the fourteenth day of the month, at twilight. They shall eat it with unleavened bread and bitter herbs, ¹²and they shall not leave any of it over until morning. They shall not break a bone of it. They shall offer it in strict accord with the law of the passover sacrifice. ¹³But if a man who is clean and not on a journey refrains from offering the passover sacrifice, that person shall be cut off from his kin, for he did not present the LORD's offering at its set time; that man shall bear his guilt.

¹⁴And when a stranger who resides with you would offer a passover sacrifice to the LORD, he must offer it in accordance with the rules and rites of the passover sacrifice. There shall be one law for you, whether stranger or citizen of the country.

¹⁵On the day that the Tabernacle was set up, the cloud covered the Tabernacle, the Tent of the Pact; and in the evening it rested over the Tabernacle in the likeness of fire until morning. ¹⁶It was always so: the cloud covered it, appearing as fire by night. ¹⁷And whenever the cloud lifted from the Tent, the Israelites would set out accordingly; and at the spot where the cloud settled, there the Israelites would make camp. ¹⁸At a command of the LORD the Israelites broke camp, and at a command of the LORD they made camp: they remained encamped as long as the cloud stayed over the Tabernacle. ¹⁹When the cloud lingered over the Tabernacle many days, the Israelites observed the LORD's mandate and did not journey on. ²⁰At

scheduled; this is because of the importance of the festival as an acknowledgment of God's role as redeemer from Egypt. **10:** *Defiled by a corpse or are on a long journey:* Both of these exemptions require further definition. According to the Rabbis, corpse defilement is inclusive of all other impurities; the distance that qualifies as a long journey from the Temple is debated. **14:** Observance of the Passover is mandatory both for Israelites and resident aliens, though according to Exod. 12.48, only circumcised resident aliens may partake.

9.15–23: The divine fire-cloud. This passage is strategically placed just prior to Israel's resumption of the desert march which was interrupted by their encampment at Sinai (Exod. 19.1–Num. 10.1). The fire-cloud, God's manifestation to Israel, guides the movement of the traveling camp as a cloud by day and a fire at night. When the fire-cloud descends over the Tabernacle, Israel camps; when it rises, Israel marches (also Exod. 40.36–38). The cloudy fiery aura of the LORD is a divine feature also found in non-Israelite societies; it arrives over the Tabernacle once that structure is completed (v. 15) and serves as a sign of divine favor. In other Priestly writings this divine fire is called "kavod," God's Presence or glory (Exod. 24.16–17; 2 Chron. 7.3). In the account of the burning bush (Exod. ch 3) and Ezekiel's vision of the divine chariot (Ezek. ch 1), God also manifests Himself as, or from within, fire.

ᵃ Lit. "him."

such times as the cloud rested over the Tabernacle for but a few days, they remained encamped at a command of the LORD, and broke camp at a command of the LORD. 21 And at such times as the cloud stayed from evening until morning, they broke camp as soon as the cloud lifted in the morning. Day or night, whenever the cloud lifted, they would break camp. 22 Whether it was two days or a month or a year—however long the cloud lingered over the Tabernacle—the Israelites remained encamped and did not set out; only when it lifted did they break camp. 23 On a sign from the LORD they made camp and on a sign from the LORD they broke camp; they observed the LORD's mandate at the LORD's bidding through Moses.

10 The LORD spoke to Moses, saying: 2 Have two silver trumpets made; make them of hammered work. They shall serve you to summon the community and to set the divisions in motion. 3 When both are blown in long blasts,ᵃ the whole community shall assemble before you at the entrance of the Tent of Meeting; 4 and if only one is blown, the chieftains, heads of Israel's contingents, shall assemble before you. 5 But when you sound short blasts,ᵃ the divisions encamped on the east shall move forward; 6 and when you sound short blasts a second time, those encamped on the south shall move forward. Thus short blasts shall be blown for setting them in motion, 7 while to convoke the congregation you shall blow long blasts, not short ones. 8 The trumpets shall be blown by Aaron's sons, the priests; they shall be for you an institution for all time throughout the ages.

9ᵇ⁻When you are at warᵇ in your land against an aggressor who attacks you, you shall sound short blasts on the trumpets, that you may be remembered before the LORD your God and be delivered from your enemies. 10 And on your joyous occasions—your fixed festivals and new moon days—you shall sound the trumpets over your burnt offerings and your sacrifices of well-being. They shall be a reminder of you before your God: I, the LORD, am your God.

11 In the second year, on the twentieth day of the second month, the cloud lifted from the Tabernacle of the Pact 12 and the Israelites set out on their journeys from the wilderness of Sinai. The cloud came to rest in the wilderness of Paran.

13 When the march was to begin, at the LORD's com-

10.1–10: The silver trumpets. The trumpets, like the fire-cloud, summon the Israelite divisions to march. Together, the fire-cloud and trumpets appeal to the senses of hearing and sight. Similarly, both senses are invoked in the revelation at Sinai by thunder, lightning, and dense cloud cover (Exod. 19.16). Usually an animal horn, a shofar, is used to signal the people to assemble for religious or military purposes (i.e., Lev. 25.9; Judg. 3.27). Trumpets, presumably of metal, are attested in a number of biblical texts, primarily of Priestly authorship. Only trumpets explicitly manufactured of silver are mentioned in this text. Trumpets play a significant role in the postbiblical *War Scroll*, a description of the eschatological war found among the Dead Sea Scrolls. 9–10: In wartime, the sound of the trumpets alerts God that Israel is in trouble; at festivals, the sound of the trumpets is a reminder that Israel stands before God, no doubt as a blessing. The Rabbis used the final verse in this section as the foundation on which they constructed the three-part "Musaf" (additional prayer) of Rosh Ha-Shanah. *I, the LORD, am your God* stands for God's kingship ("malkhuyot"—kingship); *you shall sound the trumpets* stands for trumpets or horns ("shofarot"— related to the shofar or ram's horn); *they shall be a reminder of you before your God* stands for memorials ("zikhronot"— remembrance).

10.11–12.16: The march from Sinai to the desert of Paran. 10.11–28: Order of march. The second major literary unit in Numbers begins here. (The chapter numbers in our Bibles date from the 13th century CE, so it is not surprising that a major unit may begin in the middle of a chapter.) It starts with the Israelite departure from Sinai to resume their journey through the wilderness. The four camp divisions travel in a single column while maintaining the same order as in camp. The division of Judah leads, reflecting

ᵃ Meaning of Heb. uncertain.   b-b Meaning of Heb. uncertain.

mand through Moses, [14] the first standard to set out, troop by troop, was the division of Judah. In command of its troops was Nahshon son of Amminadab; [15] in command of the tribal troop of Issachar, Nethanel son of Zuar; [16] and in command of the tribal troop of Zebulun, Eliab son of Helon.

[17] Then the Tabernacle would be taken apart; and the Gershonites and the Merarites, who carried the Tabernacle, would set out.

[18] The next standard to set out, troop by troop, was the division of Reuben. In command of its troop was Elizur son of Shedeur; [19] in command of the tribal troop of Simeon, Shelumiel son of Zurishaddai; [20] and in command of the tribal troop of Gad, Eliasaph son of Deuel.

[21] Then the Kohathites, who carried the sacred objects, would set out; and by the time they arrived, the Tabernacle would be set up again.

[22] The next standard to set out, troop by troop, was the division of Ephraim. In command of its troop was Elishama son of Ammihud; [23] in command of the tribal troop of Manasseh, Gamaliel son of Pedahzur; [24] and in command of the tribal troop of Benjamin, Abidan son of Gideoni.

[25] Then, as the rear guard of all the divisions, the standard of the division of Dan would set out, troop by troop. In command of its troop was Ahiezer son of Ammishaddai; [26] in command of the tribal troop of Asher, Pagiel son of Ochran; [27] and in command of the tribal troop of Naphtali, Ahira son of Enan.

[28] Such was the order of march of the Israelites, as they marched troop by troop.

[29] Moses said to Hobab son of Reuel the Midianite, Moses' father-in-law, "We are setting out for the place of which the LORD has said, 'I will give it to you.' Come with us and we will be generous with you; for the LORD has promised to be generous to Israel."

[30] "I will not go," he replied to him, "but will return to my native land." [31] He said, "Please do not leave us, inasmuch as you know where we should camp in the wilderness and can be our guide.[a] [32] So if you come with us, we will extend to you the same bounty that the LORD grants us."

[33] They marched from the mountain of the LORD a distance of three days. The Ark of the Covenant of the LORD traveled in front of them on that three days' journey to

a Lit. "eyes."

yet again the importance of this tribe; they are followed by the Gershonites and Merarites who carry the structural parts of the Tabernacle. The division of Reuben is next, followed by the Kohathites with the sacred objects. In that way the structure of the Tabernacle can be reassembled by the time the sanctuary objects reach an encampment stop. The last two divisions, those led by Ephraim and then Dan, bring up the rear. **29–32:** From this point until the end of ch 12 the narrative style and contents reflect the writing of the JE source(s). The focus switches to the story of the journey, without the features that characterize the Priestly source: genealogical lists, lengthy discussions of priestly laws, and ritual regulations. At the outset of the march, Moses persuades his father-in-law to help guide Israel through the wilderness. **29:** *Hobab son of Reuel the Midianite:* In Exodus, the name of Moses' father-in-law appears as Reuel (2.18) or Jethro (18.1ff). One of those names, Reuel, may be his Midianite clan name (Gen. 36.17). Some scholars think that Hobab (Jethro), who was a priest of Midian, was a worshipper of the LORD and that Moses actually adopted this deity as Israel's God after learning of Him from his father-in-law. These scholars refer to the theophoric place-name YHW' in the Sinai which is mentioned in an Egyptian text (14th century), as well as biblical references that the LORD came from that region (Deut. 33.2; Judg. 5.4; Hab. 3.3). As a biblical prooftext they also use Jethro's exclamation to Moses that "the LORD is greater than all gods" (Exod. 18.11). This is highly hypothetical. In the latter statement, however, Jethro may simply be reacting in awe to Israel's redemption from Egypt. In any case, Hobab (Jethro) is welcome in the Israelite camp. **33–36:** According to this JE tradition, the Ark travels in front of the Israelite camp rather than in its midst (cf. vv. 11–28). It is striking that the two different traditions about the place of the Ark are juxtaposed so closely to seek out a resting place for them; 34 and the LORD's cloud kept above them by day, as they moved on from camp.

35 When the Ark was to set out, Moses would say:

Advance, O LORD!

May Your enemies be scattered,

And may Your foes flee before You!

36 And when it halted, he would say:

aReturn, O LORD,

You who are Israel's myriads of thousands!-a

11 The people took to complaining bitterly before the LORD. The LORD heard and was incensed: a fire of the LORD broke out against them, ravaging the outskirts of the camp. 2 The people cried out to Moses. Moses prayed to the LORD, and the fire died down. 3 That place was named Taberah,b because a fire of the LORD had broken out against them.

4 The riffraff in their midst felt a gluttonous craving; and then the Israelites wept and said, "If only we had meat to eat! 5 We remember the fish that we used to eat free in Egypt, the cucumbers, the melons, the leeks, the onions, and the garlic. 6 Now our gullets are shriveled. There is nothing at all! Nothing but this manna to look to!"

7 Now the manna was like coriander seed, and in color it was like bdellium. 8 The people would go about and gather it, grind it between millstones or pound it in a mortar, boil it in a pot, and make it into cakes. It tasted like rich cream.c 9 When the dew fell on the camp at night, the manna would fall upon it.

10 Moses heard the people weeping, every clan apart, each person at the entrance of his tent. The LORD was very

a-a Others "Return, O LORD, unto the
      ten thousands of the families of Israel!"
b From root b'r, "to burn."   c Lit. "cream of oil (or, fat)."

each other, but this typifies the Torah (compare, e.g., the two conflicting creation accounts that open Genesis). Ibn Ezra and Ramban reconcile this contradiction by suggesting that initially, to alleviate Israel's fears, the Ark led the group. 35–36: The song of the Ark, evidently part of a Mosaic tradition, is a type of victory song praising God as a divine warrior, the defender of Israel. Its insertion here may be related to the first word of the song, "binsoa'," which picks up on the key word of this subsection, "travel" (of the Ark). Here the Ark can be understood as God's chariot. This poem is preserved in Jewish tradition in the liturgy as part of the Torah service. 36: Myriads of thousands is an epithet of the LORD as a warrior similar to the more common biblical epithet LORD of Hosts (1 Sam. 17.45; Isa. 1.24; 21.10; Zeph. 2.9).

11.1–35: Murmuring in the wilderness. As the Israelites resume their long trek in the wilderness, they fall into a pattern of complaining. After each incident God reacts by punishing the people, essentially because the grievances reflect disloyalty to the Sinaitic covenant. Moses responds to God's action by interceding on Israel's behalf—this is a typical role of biblical prophets (see, e.g., Jer. 7.16; 11.14; 14.11). The biblical writer preserves the incident in the collective memory of Israel by naming the location after the event that occurred there. This cycle repeats in one form or another throughout the wanderings. Two complaint stories are found in this chapter. 1–3: The grievance in the first case is not specified, but God's punishment, deadly fire, is mentioned. The place name, Taberah, recalls the punishment by fire, and might be connected to the manifestation of God as fire in ch 9. Clearly, there is an intended lesson for Israel, but it is not heeded and the murmuring continues. 4–35: The second incident is far more detailed and complex. It originates from the camp's non-Israelite contingent which joined the Israelites in the exodus (Exod. 12.38). The people crave a more varied diet than just manna, like the one they claim was available in Egypt. As commonly happens, the complaints of a few are echoed by the entire group. This larger section seems to combine two originally independent stories concerning the quail and the seventy elders. 4–5: If only we had meat. . . . we remember the fish: Meat may actually refer to fish, a cheap and ample food from the Nile. Why the Israelites do not slaughter animals from their herds (Exod. 12.38; Num. 32.1) is not explained in the text. 7–9: Manna is described here as a rich and tasty food suitable for various modes of preparation. This positive depiction of manna underscores the unjustified complaints of the people. Some scholars identify the manna with the edible sap of the tamarisk tree that forms flaky sweet pellets in conjunction with the activity of plant lice. Its description here differs from Exod. 16.31; this is reconangry, and Moses was distressed. [11] And Moses said to the Lord, "Why have You dealt ill with Your servant, and why have I not enjoyed Your favor, that You have laid the burden of all this people upon me? [12] Did I conceive all this people, did I bear them, that You should say to me, 'Carry them in your bosom as a nurse carries an infant,' to the land that You have promised on oath to their fathers? [13] Where am I to get meat to give to all this people, when they whine before me and say, 'Give us meat to eat!' [14] I cannot carry all this people by myself, for it is too much for me. [15] If You would deal thus with me, kill me rather, I beg You, and let me see no more of my wretchedness!"

[16] Then the Lord said to Moses, "Gather for Me seventy of Israel's elders of whom you have experience as elders and officers of the people, and bring them to the Tent of Meeting and let them take their place there with you. [17] I will come down and speak with you there, and I will draw upon the spirit that is on you and put it upon them; they shall share the burden of the people with you, and you shall not bear it alone. [18] And say to the people: ᵃPurify yourselvesᵃ for tomorrow and you shall eat meat, for you have kept whining before the Lord and saying, 'If only we had meat to eat! Indeed, we were better off in Egypt!' The Lord will give you meat and you shall eat. [19] You shall eat not one day, not two, not even five days or ten or twenty, [20] but a whole month, until it comes out of your nostrils and becomes loathsome to you. For you have rejected the Lord who is among you, by whining before Him and saying, 'Oh, why did we ever leave Egypt!' "

[21] But Moses said, "The people ᵇwho are with meᵇ number six hundred thousand men; yet You say, 'I will give them enough meat to eat for a whole month.' [22] Could enough flocks and herds be slaughtered to suffice them? Or could all the fish of the sea be gathered for them to suffice them?" [23] And the Lord answered Moses, ᶜ"Is there a limit to the Lord's power?ᶜ You shall soon see whether what I have said happens to you or not!"

[24] Moses went out and reported the words of the Lord to the people. He gathered seventy of the people's elders and stationed them around the Tent. [25] Then the Lord came down in a cloud and spoke to him; He drew upon the spirit that was on him and put it upon the seventy elders. And when the spirit rested upon them, they ᵈspoke in ecstasy,ᵈ but did not continue.

[26] Two men, one named Eldad and the other Medad,

ciled in classical Jewish thought by suggesting that the manna could take on various flavors (see, e.g., *m. Yoma* 75a). **10–35:** Utterly frustrated, Moses questions his heavy burden of leadership and his ability to succeed at it. He is ready to die if no relief comes. The point of this episode, including Moses' desire to satisfy the people, is to elicit divine solutions for the problems. Most important is the appointment of seventy elders to assist Moses. The judicial roles of Israel's elders are legitimated for all time because of their endowment with Moses' spirit. Simultaneously, this scene affirms Moses' human traits and limitations. God's solution to the meat crisis differs from an earlier rendition of the story. In Exod. ch 16, quail and manna are God's gift to Israel; here in Numbers the wording of their grievance bespeaks their desire to return to Egypt, clearly a rejection of God that warrants punishment. Therefore, when the quail finally arrive, many people become fatally ill from gorging themselves with meat. Appropriately, the place name for this event becomes Kibroth-hattaavah, "burials of the craving." **26–29:** This account is connected to the broader story since both involve the transmission of some of Moses' "spirit" to other individuals (vv. 17, 26; cf. v. 31 which uses the same Heb word "ruah" in its other sense of "wind"). This story may reflect an ancient debate concerning whether there is only one legitimate prophet at a time, as assumed perhaps by Deut. 18.15–18, or if there may be many prophets in a single era.

---

a-a *I.e., as for a sacrificial meal.*   b-b *Lit. "in whose midst I am."*
c-c *Lit. "Is the Lord's hand too short?"*   d-d *Others "prophesied."*

had remained in camp; yet the spirit rested upon them—they were among those recorded, but they had not gone out to the Tent—and they ᵃ·spoke in ecstasy·ᵃ in the camp. 27 A youth ran out and told Moses, saying, "Eldad and Medad are acting the prophet in the camp!" 28 And Joshua son of Nun, Moses' attendant from his youth, spoke up and said, "My lord Moses, restrain them!" 29 But Moses said to him, "Are you wrought up on my account? Would that all the LORD's people were prophets, that the LORD put His spirit upon them!" 30 Moses then reentered the camp together with the elders of Israel.

31 A wind from the LORD started up, swept quail from the sea and strewed them over the camp, about a day's journey on this side and about a day's journey on that side, all around the camp, and some two cubits deep on the ground. 32 The people set to gathering quail all that day and night and all the next day—even he who gathered least had ten ḥomers—and they spread them out all around the camp. 33 The meat was still between their teeth, nor yet chewed,ᵇ when the anger of the LORD blazed forth against the people and the LORD struck the people with a very severe plague. 34 That place was named Kibroth-hattaavah,ᶜ because the people who had the craving were buried there.

35 Then the people set out from Kibroth-hattaavah for Hazeroth.

12 When they were in Hazeroth, 1 Miriam and Aaron spoke against Moses because of the Cushite woman he had married: "He married a Cushite woman!" 2 They said, "Has the LORD spoken only through Moses? Has He not spoken through us as well?" The LORD heard it. 3 Now Moses was a very humble man, more so than any other man on earth. 4 Suddenly the LORD called to Moses, Aaron, and Miriam, "Come out, you three, to the Tent of Meeting." So the three of them went out. 5 The LORD came down in a pillar of cloud, stopped at the entrance of the Tent, and called out, "Aaron and Miriam!" The two of them came forward; 6 and He said, "Hear these My words: ᵈ·When a prophet of the LORD arises among you, I·ᵈ make Myself known to him in a vision, I speak with him in a dream. 7 Not so with My ser-

a-a Others "prophesied."
b Meaning of Heb. yikkareth uncertain.
c I.e., "the graves of craving."
d-d Meaning of Heb. uncertain. Others "If there be a prophet among you, I the LORD."

12.1–16: Miriam and Aaron speak against Moses. Miriam and Aaron, like other Israelites, are subject to complaining. Their grievance against Moses is founded on two issues: his wife, and more seriously, his authority. This narrative continues the themes from the previous ch, namely, prophecy and the questioning of Moses' leadership capabilities and his limitations. The first objection that Miriam and Aaron raise is to Moses' marriage to a Cushite woman; the second questions his special role as a prophet. Moses remains silent in the face of these accusations so that God takes up his defense. The message of the narrative is clear: God chose Moses to be His unique prophet and no one, not even other key Israelite leaders, may challenge that decision. Miriam's severe punishment underscores the point and makes clear that any other who arise to challenge Moses are doomed from the start. **1:** *He married a Cushite woman:* Moses' wife Zipporah is Midianite (Exod. 2.21). Two explanations are possible: (1) This reference is to Zipporah, "Cushan" being part of Midian (Hab. 3.7); (2) Moses married a second woman in Egypt, a Nubian (= Cush). The latter is more plausible since Nubia was part of the Egyptian empire and dark-skinned women were considered beautiful, as reflected in the Targum's rendition of Cushite as "beautiful." **3:** Moses' attribute of humility is underscored as praiseworthy. It stands in stark contrast to Miriam's and Aaron's arrogance. **6–8:** These poetic vv. show an introverted, triangular-shaped, literary structure with v. 7 as the climax. God distinguishes Moses' prophetic privileges from those accorded any other prophet. Moses can speak to God directly, in live dialogue rather than in dreams or visions. God is at His most anthropomorphic in these verses. **10:** *Snow-white scales:* This disease is mentioned in Lev. ch 13 as one causing severe impurity that requires a seven-day purification process. It was previously identified as leprosy, but recent thinking vant Moses; he is trusted throughout My household. [8] With him I speak mouth to mouth, plainly and not in riddles, and he beholds the likeness of the LORD. How then did you not shrink from speaking against My servant Moses!" [9] Still incensed with them, the LORD departed.

[10] As the cloud withdrew from the Tent, there was Miriam stricken with snow-white scales![a] When Aaron turned toward Miriam, he saw that she was stricken with scales. [11] And Aaron said to Moses, "O my lord, account not to us the sin which we committed in our folly. [12] Let her not be as one dead, who emerges from his mother's womb with half his flesh eaten away." [13] So Moses cried out to the LORD, saying, "O God, pray heal her!"

[14] But the LORD said to Moses, "If her father spat in her face, would she not bear her shame for seven days? Let her be shut out of camp for seven days, and then let her be readmitted." [15] So Miriam was shut out of camp seven days; and the people did not march on until Miriam was readmitted. [16] After that the people set out from Hazeroth and encamped in the wilderness of Paran.

SHELAḤ-LEKHA   שלח לך

13 The LORD spoke to Moses, saying, [2] "Send men to scout the land of Canaan, which I am giving to the Israelite people; send one man from each of their ancestral tribes, each one a chieftain among them." [3] So Moses, by the LORD's command, sent them out from the wilderness of Paran, all the men being leaders of the Israelites. [4] And these were their names:

From the tribe of Reuben, Shammua son of Zaccur.
[5]   From the tribe of Simeon, Shaphat son of Hori.
[6]   From the tribe of Judah, Caleb son of Jephunneh.
[7]   From the tribe of Issachar, Igal son of Joseph.
[8]   From the tribe of Ephraim, Hosea[b] son of Nun.
[9]   From the tribe of Benjamin, Palti son of Rafu.
[10]   From the tribe of Zebulun, Gaddiel son of Sodi.
[11]   From the tribe of Joseph, namely, the tribe of
        Manasseh, Gaddi son of Susi.
[12]   From the tribe of Dan, Ammiel son of Gemalli.
[13]   From the tribe of Asher, Sethur son of Michael.

a Cf. Lev. 13.2–3.   b Or "Hoshea."

stood the name of the skin condition, "metzoraʿ," as indicative of its cause, the sin of slander, "motziʾ shem raʿ" ("uttering an evil name") (*Lev. Rab.* 16.1–6). They conclude that Miriam and not Aaron was punished because she instigated the gossip and vocalized it, as indicated by the feminine gender of the verb *spoke* in 12.1, and the placement of Miriam before Aaron. Ibn Ezra speculates that Aaron was silent or simply agreed. **13:** *"O God, pray heal her!"*: Moses' brief plea for Miriam is an example of biblical prose prayer. The terseness of Moses' prayer may reflect his disappointment with his siblings. Prayer expressed in poetic style, used for more public or ceremonial occasions, is far more common in the Bible; for example, Hannah's lengthy prayer of thanksgiving after Samuel's birth (1 Sam. ch 2). **14:** *If her father spat in her face:* Apparently, this is an act of rebuke that entails shame plus seven days of banishment. Usually the purpose of spitting is to shame someone, but the custom of banishment is unknown (cf. Deut. 25.9). Seclusion outside the camp is undoubtedly related to a notion of impurity.

13.1–33: The scouts' expedition and report. The goal of this expedition is two-fold: to assess the strength of the indigenous population and the strongholds in which they reside, and to investigate the productivity of the land. This narrative is a conflation of at least two traditions that reflect different sources (JE and P). Discrepancies in the story revolve around two issues: What area of Canaan is scouted and how many scouts bring a positive report. In the earlier JE version the scouts reconnoiter the southern portion of Canaan (13.17); Caleb alone recommends that Israel proceed with the conquest (13.30). The Priestly account expands the scouting expedition over the entire land of Canaan (13.21); it adds Joshua as a spokesman for undertaking the conquest (14.6–9). **1–15:** Moses

rejects this in favor of curable skin diseases, since persons afflicted with this condition in the Bible are often cured after being quarantined. Furthermore, the symptoms of the disease do not correlate with leprosy (Hansen's disease). Disease, in general, was believed to be divine retribution for sin (2 Sam. 3.29). The Rabbis under-

14 From the tribe of Naphtali, Nahbi son of Vophsi.

15 From the tribe of Gad, Geuel son of Machi.

16 Those were the names of the men whom Moses sent to scout the land; but Moses changed the name of Hosea[a] son of Nun to Joshua.

17 When Moses sent them to scout the land of Canaan, he said to them, "Go up there into the Negeb and on into the hill country, 18 and see what kind of country it is. Are the people who dwell in it strong or weak, few or many? 19 Is the country in which they dwell good or bad? Are the towns they live in open or fortified? 20 Is the soil rich or poor? Is it wooded or not? And take pains to bring back some of the fruit of the land."—Now it happened to be the season of the first ripe grapes.

21 They went up and scouted the land, from the wilderness of Zin to Rehob, at Lebo-hamath.[b] 22 They went up into the Negeb and came to Hebron, where lived Ahiman, Sheshai, and Talmai, the Anakites.—Now Hebron was founded seven years before Zoan of Egypt.—23 They reached the wadi Eshcol, and there they cut down a branch with a single cluster of grapes—it had to be borne on a carrying frame by two of them—and some pomegranates and figs. 24 That place was named the wadi Eshcol[c] because of the cluster that the Israelites cut down there.

25 At the end of forty days they returned from scouting the land. 26 They went straight to Moses and Aaron and the whole Israelite community at Kadesh in the wilderness of Paran, and they made their report to them and to the whole community, as they showed them the fruit of the land. 27 This is what they told him: "We came to the land you sent us to; it does indeed flow with milk and honey, and this is its fruit. 28 However, the people who inhabit the country are powerful, and the cities are fortified and very large; moreover, we saw the Anakites there. 29 Amalekites dwell in the Negeb region; Hittites, Jebusites, and Amorites inhabit the hill country; and Canaanites dwell by the Sea and along the Jordan."

30 Caleb hushed the people before Moses and said, "Let us by all means go up, and we shall gain possession of it, for we shall surely overcome it."

31 But the men who had gone up with him said, "We cannot attack that people, for it is stronger than we." 32 Thus they spread calumnies among the Israelites about the land they had scouted, saying, "The country that we traversed and scouted is one that devours its settlers. All

chooses tribal leaders, presumably those trained for such a mission. Some rabbis take note of the fact that Moses chooses the scouts rather than asking God to do it (by lot). They attribute the ill-fated scouting expedition to Moses, assuming that God could foresee the scouts' sin (*Num. Rab.* 16.4). **16:** Moses emends Joshua's name, Hosea (13.8), by adding the prefix "ye," possibly a theophoric element associated with the Israelite God. In the sources of the names of the tribal leaders, only Joshua's name bears such an element. **22:** The gloss added to the mention of Hebron stresses the antiquity of that city which was David's capital for the first seven years of his reign (1 Kings 2.11). Zoan, the Egyptian capital city of Tanis, was (re)built at the same time as Jerusalem. **23:** Grapes, pomegranates, and figs are late summer fruits. **24:** This is an etiological account (origin story) for the name of the wadi, Eshcol—in Heb, a cluster of grapes. **22, 28, 33:** Anakites, or giants, are mentioned in several texts (Deut. 2.11; Josh. 11.21–22). An etiological account for the Nephilim is found in Gen. 6.1–4. The reference to Anakites in Joshua notes that even after the conquest some survived in Philistine cities (11.22). David's adversary Goliath, a Philistine from Gath, is depicted as a giant (1 Sam. 17.4) descended from a group of giants from Raphah (1 Chron. 20.5–6). The tall headdresses of the Philistines may have contributed to their gigantic image. More importantly, the report of giants in the land makes the Canaanites more intimidating. **27:** *Flow with milk and honey:* This biblical phrase describing the promised land (also Exod. 3.8, 17) has been preserved in Jewish tradition to modernity. Honey most likely refers to "honey" made of dates, since bee's honey was relatively rare (see Prov. 25.16). **29:** For the indigenous population of Canaan, see the table of nations in Gen. 10.15–20; there is tremendous variability in the lists of these nations found in various texts.

---

a Or "Hoshea."   b Others "the entrance to Hamath."   c I.e., "cluster."

the people that we saw in it are men of great size; [33] we saw the Nephilim[a] there—the Anakites are part of the Nephilim—and we looked like grasshoppers to ourselves, and so we must have looked to them."

14 The whole community broke into loud cries, and the people wept that night. [2] All the Israelites railed against Moses and Aaron. "If only we had died in the land of Egypt," the whole community shouted at them, "or if only we might die in this wilderness! [3] Why is the LORD taking us to that land to fall by the sword? Our wives and children will be carried off! It would be better for us to go back to Egypt!" [4] And they said to one another, "Let us [b]head back for[b] Egypt."

[5] Then Moses and Aaron fell on their faces before all the assembled congregation of the Israelites. [6] And Joshua son of Nun and Caleb son of Jephunneh, of those who had scouted the land, rent their clothes [7] and exhorted the whole Israelite community: "The land that we traversed and scouted is an exceedingly good land. [8] If the LORD is pleased with us, He will bring us into that land, a land that flows with milk and honey, and give it to us; [9] only you must not rebel against the LORD. Have no fear then of the people of the country, for they are our prey:[c] their protection has departed from them, but the LORD is with us. Have no fear of them!" [10] As the whole community threatened to pelt them with stones, the Presence of the LORD appeared in the Tent of Meeting to all the Israelites.

[11] And the LORD said to Moses, "How long will this people spurn Me, and how long will they have no faith in Me despite all the signs that I have performed in their midst? [12] I will strike them with pestilence and disown them, and I will make of you a nation far more numerous than they!" [13] But Moses said to the LORD, "When the Egyptians, from whose midst You brought up this people in Your might, hear the news, [14] they will tell it to the inhabitants of that land. Now they have heard that You, O LORD, are in the midst of this people; that You, O LORD, appear in plain sight when Your cloud rests over them and when You go before them in a pillar of cloud by day and in a pillar of fire by night. [15] If then You slay this people to a man, the nations who have heard Your fame will say, [16] 'It must be because the LORD was powerless to bring that people into the land He had promised them on oath that He slaugh-

---

a See Gen. 6.4.

b-b Lit. "set the head and return to"; cf. Neh. 9.17. Others "Let us make a captain and return to."

c Lit. "food (or, bread)."

30: The place of Judah is again emphasized, as Caleb the Judaean (see v. 6) is represented as the faithful scout. **32:** Canaan as a country that devours its settlers may refer to the land's infertility. More likely, however, the metaphor alludes to the results of frequent warfare (cf. Ezek. 36.13–14).

14.1–45: Aftermath of the scouting expedition. In the continuous cycle of rebellions, this one constitutes the most serious. The ten scouts who incite the populace advocate abandoning Israel's ultimate goal, to settle the promised land. The fear they instill in the Israelites supersedes the memory of Egyptian oppression. This extreme display of faithlessness before God exacts the ultimate punishment, forty years of wandering in the desert and the death of the exodus generation. **4:** *Let us head back:* This phrase can also be translated, "Let us appoint a leader," indicating that the Israelites were ready to replace Moses and return to Egypt under new leadership. **6–10:** Rending the garment is a sign of mourning that has survived in modern times, albeit a ribbon sometimes substitutes for an article of clothing. Joshua and Caleb are not only frustrated by the negative report of the other scouts but they fear God's harsh punishment, as evidenced by their plea to the people not to rebel against God. The imminence of Israel's rebellion is apparent by the people's intent to stone Moses and Aaron, and probably also Joshua and Caleb (cf. Exod. 17.4). *The Presence of the LORD* (v. 10) is God's typical manner of manifestation in Priestly material. **11–19:** Here God is prepared to eradicate all Israel save Moses (cf. Exod. 32.10). He offers to create a new people from the descendants of Moses. Moses' initial argument centers on preserving God's reputation among the nations (cf. Ezek. 36.16–36; 39.21–29); his second argument appeals to God's attribute of mercy (see Exod. 34.6–7 in the context of the second set of Decalogue tered them in the wilderness.' ¹⁷ Therefore, I pray, let my Lord's forbearance be great, as You have declared, saying,ᵃ ¹⁸ 'The LORD! slow to anger and abounding in kindness; forgiving iniquity and transgression; yet not remitting all punishment, but visiting the iniquity of fathers upon children, upon the third and fourth generations.' ¹⁹ Pardon, I pray, the iniquity of this people according to Your great kindness, as You have forgiven this people ever since Egypt."

²⁰ And the LORD said, "I pardon, as you have asked. ²¹ Nevertheless, as I live and as the LORD's Presence fills the whole world, ²² none of the men who have seen My Presence and the signs that I have performed in Egypt and in the wilderness, and who have tried Me these manyᵇ times and have disobeyed Me, ²³ shall see the land that I promised on oath to their fathers; none of those who spurn Me shall see it. ²⁴ But My servant Caleb, because he was imbued with a different spirit and remained loyal to Me—him will I bring into the land that he entered, and his offspring shall hold it as a possession. ²⁵ Now the Amalekites and the Canaanites occupy the valleys. Start out, then, tomorrow and march into the wilderness by way of the Sea of Reeds."ᶜ

²⁶ The LORD spoke further to Moses and Aaron, ²⁷ "How much longer shall that wicked community keep muttering against Me? Very well, I have heeded the incessant muttering of the Israelites against Me. ²⁸ Say to them: 'As I live,' says the LORD, 'I will do to you just as you have urged Me. ²⁹ In this very wilderness shall your carcasses drop. Of all of you who were recorded in your various lists from the age of twenty years up, you who have muttered against Me, ³⁰ not one shall enter the land in which I sworeᵈ to settle you—save Caleb son of Jephunneh and Joshua son of Nun. ³¹ Your children who, you said, would be carried off—these will I allow to enter; they shall know the land that you have rejected. ³² But your carcasses shall drop in this wilderness, ³³ while your children roam the wilderness for forty years, suffering for your faithlessness, until the last of your carcasses is down in the wilderness. ³⁴ You shall bear your punishment for forty years, corresponding to the number of days—forty days—that you scouted the land: a year for each day. Thus you shall know what it means to thwart Me. ³⁵ I the LORD have spoken: Thus will I do to all that wicked band that has banded together against Me: in this very wilderness they shall die to the last man.' "

tablets). The long prayer of Moses after the entire nation sins grievously stands in marked contrast to his short prayer on behalf of his sister in 12.13.
18: *Visiting the iniquity of fathers upon children,* a quotation of the divine attributes found in the Decalogue (Exod. 20.5–6; Deut. 5.9–10) and in Exod. 34.6–7. **20–38:** God reduces the people's punishment: The entire nation will not be wiped out immediately, but the current generation will not inherit Canaan. The rebellious adult generation will perish in the desert according to their wish (14.2).
21, 28: *As I live* is an oath formula. **36–37:** The ten scouts who incited the rebellion with their negative report die in a plague on the spot. **39–45:** The people attempt to invade Canaan either because they regret their previous behavior and lack of trust in God, or because they hope to reverse God's decree. In any case, the invasion fails and they are defeated. The writer's message here is clear: Without God's blessing and Presence (accompanying the Ark) conquest is impossible. The function of the Ark in the military camp is also emphasized in the passage. **45:** *Hormah* means destruction; thus the site name.

a Cf. Exod. 34.6–7.   b Lit. "ten"; cf. note at Gen. 31.41.
c See note at Exod. 10.19.   d Lit. "raised My hand."

36 As for the men whom Moses sent to scout the land, those who came back and caused the whole community to mutter against him by spreading calumnies about the land—37 those who spread such calumnies about the land died of plague, by the will of the LORD. 38 Of those men who had gone to scout the land, only Joshua son of Nun and Caleb son of Jephunneh survived.

39 When Moses repeated these words to all the Israelites, the people were overcome by grief. 40 Early next morning they set out toward the crest of the hill country, saying, "We are prepared to go up to the place that the LORD has spoken of, for we were wrong." 41 But Moses said, "Why do you transgress the LORD's command? This will not succeed. 42 Do not go up, lest you be routed by your enemies, for the LORD is not in your midst. 43 For the Amalekites and the Canaanites will be there to face you, and you will fall by the sword, inasmuch as you have turned from following the LORD and the LORD will not be with you."

44 Yet defiantly[a] they marched toward the crest of the hill country, though neither the LORD's Ark of the Covenant nor Moses stirred from the camp. 45 And the Amalekites and the Canaanites who dwelt in that hill country came down and dealt them a shattering blow at Hormah.

15 The LORD spoke to Moses, saying: 2 Speak to the Israelite people and say to them:

When you enter the land that I am giving you to settle in, 3 and would present an offering by fire to the LORD from the herd or from the flock, be it burnt offering or sacrifice, in fulfillment of a vow explicitly uttered,[b] or as a freewill offering, or at your fixed occasions, producing an odor pleasing to the LORD:

4 The person who presents the offering to the LORD shall bring as a meal offering: a tenth of a measure of choice flour with a quarter of a hin of oil mixed in. 5 You shall also offer, with the burnt offering or the sacrifice, a quarter of a hin of wine as a libation for each sheep.

6 In the case of a ram, you shall present as a meal offering: two-tenths of a measure of choice flour with a third of a hin of oil mixed in; 7 and a third of a hin of wine as a libation—as an offering of pleasing odor to the LORD.

8 And if it is an animal from the herd that you offer to the LORD as a burnt offering or as a sacrifice, in fulfillment of a vow explicitly uttered or as an offering of well-being, 9 there shall be offered a meal offering along with the animal: three-tenths of a measure of choice flour with half a

15.1–41: A variety of laws. The narrative of the forty years in the wilderness is interrupted here by the insertion of legal material. Medieval commentators suggest that the placement of the laws, immediately following the condemnation of the adult generation to death in the desert, reiterates God's promise that the children will indeed inherit Canaan, thus the introduction to the first two sets of laws; *When you enter the land* (vv. 2, 18). The first set of laws deals with accompaniments to the sacrifices: meal, oil, and wine (vv. 1–16). These are followed by the bread dough offering, "ḥalah" (vv. 17–21), and then by those sacrifices required for individual or communal inadvertent violations of any law (vv. 22–31). The delineation of laws is interrupted by a case study that contrasts the preceding type of violations. That case entails extreme, willful breaking of the law through the desecration of the Sabbath (vv. 32–36). The prescriptive passages resume with the commandment to wear fringes, tzitzit, on one's garment (vv. 37–41). The purpose of the fringes, to remind the wearer of God's laws, clearly ties into the previous case of the Sabbath breaker. Ibn Ezra maintains that the fringes are worn on the outer everyday garment, in addition to the prayer shawl, for that explicit purpose. **3–16:** Animal burnt offerings and offerings of well-being are accompanied by a grain and oil mixture and wine (Lev. chs 1–3) reminiscent of a complete meal. In the case of sacrifices, the meal is for the deity. Although the Bible describes these offerings as *producing an odor pleasing to the LORD*, it never states that God actually eats them. **5:** *Hin* is an Egyptian measure equal to approximately 4 liters (1 gal).

a Meaning of Heb. uncertain.   b See note at Lev. 22.21.

hin of oil mixed in; [10] and as libation you shall offer half a *hin* of wine—these being offerings by fire of pleasing odor to the LORD.

[11] Thus shall be done with each ox, with each ram, and with any sheep or goat, [12] as many as you offer; you shall do thus with each one, as many as there are. [13] Every citizen, when presenting an offering by fire of pleasing odor to the LORD, shall do so with them.

[14] And when, throughout the ages, a stranger who has taken up residence with you, or one who lives among you, would present an offering by fire of pleasing odor to the LORD—as you do, so ªshall it be done by [15] the rest of the congregation.ª There shall be one law for you and for the resident stranger; it shall be a law for all time throughout the ages. You and the stranger shall be alike before the LORD; [16] the same ritual and the same rule shall apply to you and to the stranger who resides among you.

[17] The LORD spoke to Moses, saying: [18] Speak to the Israelite people and say to them:

When you enter the land to which I am taking you [19] and you eat of the bread of the land, you shall set some aside as a gift to the LORD: [20] as the first yield of your baking,*b* you shall set aside a loaf as a gift; you shall set it aside as a gift like the gift from the threshing floor. [21] You shall make a gift to the LORD from the first yield of your baking, throughout the ages.

[22] If you unwittingly fail to observe any one of the commandments that the LORD has declared to Moses—[23] anything that the LORD has enjoined upon you through Moses—from the day that the LORD gave the commandment and on through the ages:

[24] If this was done unwittingly, through the inadvertence of the community, the whole community shall present one bull of the herd as a burnt offering of pleasing odor to the LORD, with its proper meal offering and libation, and one he-goat as a sin offering. [25] The priest shall make expiation for the whole Israelite community and they shall be forgiven; for it was an error, and for their error they have brought their offering, an offering by fire to the LORD and their sin offering before the LORD. [26] The whole Israelite community and the stranger residing among them shall be forgiven, for it happened to the entire people through error.

[27] In case it is an individual who has sinned unwittingly, he shall offer a she-goat in its first year as a sin offering.

14–16: In most matters, including sacrificial matters (except for the paschal lamb, see Exod. 12.48), the resident alien must be treated as the native Israelite. **17–21:** The dough offering is the first part of the dough prepared in the kneading basin, somewhat analogous to the first-fruits offering, though the latter is a once-a-year event (Lev. 19.24–25; 23.10–11). The dough is given to the priest; in turn, the homes of the Israelites are blessed (cf. Ezek. 44.30). According to the Rabbis in the Talmud, this "ḥalah" offering brings blessings to the nonfarmer as well because it constitutes his labor (*b. Shab.* 32b). The sweet Sabbath bread is called "ḥalah" after this custom. **22–31:** This section continues the previous one. Sacrifices for inadvertent violations are applicable to all laws (for more details, see Lev. ch 4). **29:** *One ritual,* more correctly, "one law" ("torah") applies to both Israelites and alien residents. Breaking a law has a negative effect on the "terra sancta," therefore an expiation is required of all inhabitants. **30–31:** Defiant, willful violation of ritual law cannot be expiated in the manner of an inadvertent sin. "Karet," the cutting off of a person, is a punishment enacted by the divine. What constitutes the punishment is not defined here but can be gleaned from other biblical passages which indicate punishments affecting both the sinner and his progeny (e.g., Mal. 2.12; Ps. 109.13). Traditional Jewish interpretation includes childlessness, early death, and/or the death of the soul together with the body at the time of death. **32–36:** The case of the wood gatherer is distinct from the above. It illustrates a most severe violation of ritual law, the desecration of the Sabbath which is a capital offense, here punished by stoning (cf. Exod. 31.14). It is possible that Moses here asks God what to do because earlier legislative texts note that the punishment is death, but are unclear about whether it should be carried out by people or God (Exod. 31.14–15). **35–36:** God

---

a-a Meaning of Heb. uncertain.   *b Meaning of Heb. ʿarisah uncertain.*

²⁸ The priest shall make expiation before the LORD on behalf of the person who erred, for he sinned unwittingly, making such expiation for him that he may be forgiven. ²⁹ For the citizen among the Israelites and for the stranger who resides among them—you shall have one ritual for anyone who acts in error.

³⁰ But the person, be he citizen or stranger, who acts defiantly^a reviles the LORD; that person shall be cut off from among his people. ³¹ Because he has spurned the word of the LORD and violated His commandment, that person shall be cut off—he bears his guilt.

³² Once, when the Israelites were in the wilderness, they came upon a man gathering wood on the sabbath day. ³³ Those who found him as he was gathering wood brought him before Moses, Aaron, and the whole community. ³⁴ He was placed in custody, for it had not been specified what should be done to him. ³⁵ Then the LORD said to Moses, "The man shall be put to death: the whole community shall pelt him with stones outside the camp." ³⁶ So the whole community took him outside the camp and stoned him to death—as the LORD had commanded Moses.

³⁷ The LORD said to Moses as follows: ³⁸ Speak to the Israelite people and instruct them to make for themselves fringes on the corners of their garments throughout the ages; let them attach a cord of blue to the fringe at each corner. ³⁹ That shall be your fringe; look at it and recall all the commandments of the LORD and observe them, so that you do not follow your heart and eyes in your lustful urge. ⁴⁰ Thus you shall be reminded to observe all My commandments and to be holy to your God. ⁴¹ I the LORD am your God, who brought you out of the land of Egypt to be your God: I, the LORD your God.

KORAH   קרח

16 Now Korah, son of Izhar son of Kohath son of Levi, ^bbetook himself,^{-b} along with Dathan and Abiram sons of Eliab, ^cand On son of Peleth—descendants of Reuben^{-c}—² to rise up against Moses, together with two hun-

a Lit. "with upraised hand."   b-b Lit. "took"; meaning of Heb. uncertain.
c-c According to Num. 26.5, 8–9, Eliab was son of Pallu, son of Reuben.

Himself sentences the violator. Stoning signifies the serious nature of the infraction, which is an affront to the entire community.
37–41: The fringes or tassels on the corners of the outer garments

call the Israelites to action regarding the fulfillment of the commandments. Remembering, Heb "zakhar," is often a verb of action rather than simply thought (e.g., Gen. 8.1; 30.22; Exod. 12.14). In an-

tiquity, fringes were common on Canaanite and Mesopotamian dress. Prophets from the Babylonian city of Mari legitimated their oracles before the king by sending a fringe from their garment, which is a symbolic way of sending part of themselves, like a signature. The imprinting of fringes on clay tablets, like the touching of the fringe of the prayer shawl to the Torah today when one is called to the Torah during its reading, is a way of verifying or endorsing the written document. Like garments and hair, fringes are considered part of the individual's identity, and by giving them to the ruler, a person is pledging his loyalty. It is no accident that the violet-blue wool cord that must be attached to the fringes (according to P) is identical to the cord that hangs from the priest's headdress (Exod. 28.37). The tzitzit on the garments of Israelites identifies them as being holy to God and symbolically connects them to the priests. Thereby, Israelites pledge their loyalty to God as well as to the priests who oversee the laws (cf. the nonspecific garment fringes called "gedilim" [lit. "twisted threads"] in Deut. 22.12). Modern prayer shawls, tallit (sing.), and the small tallit, worn daily under the shirt by observant Jews, no longer require a violet-blue cord for their tzitzit. That aspect of the commandment was suspended in talmudic times because of the scarcity and expense of the blue dye derived from the murex snail. Most likely because of the reference "to observe all My commandments," this paragraph came to be recited daily as part of the Shema prayer (see Deut. 6.4).
41: The redemption from Egyptian slavery is often employed as grounds for Israelite allegiance to God (Exod. 6.7; 20.2–3; Lev. 11.45; Deut. 26.17–19).

16.1–35: The rebellions of Korah and Dathan and Abiram. These rebellions against the divinely appointed leadership of Moses and Aaron constitute public defiance that requires swift and harsh retri-

dred and fifty Israelites, chieftains of the community, chosen in the assembly, men of repute. [3] They combined
against Moses and Aaron and said to them, "You have
gone too far! For all the community are holy, all of them,
and the LORD is in their midst. Why then do you raise
yourselves above the LORD's congregation?"

[4] When Moses heard this, he fell on his face.[a] [5] Then he
spoke to Korah and all his company, saying, "Come morning, the LORD will make known who is His and who is
holy, and will grant him access to Himself; He will grant
access to the one He has chosen. [6] Do this: You, Korah and
all your[b] band, take fire pans, [7] and tomorrow put fire in
them and lay incense on them before the LORD. Then the
man whom the LORD chooses, he shall be the holy one.
You have gone too far, sons of Levi!"

[8] Moses said further to Korah, "Hear me, sons of Levi. [9] Is
it not enough for you that the God of Israel has set you
apart from the community of Israel and given you access to
Him, to perform the duties of the LORD's Tabernacle and to
minister to the community and serve them? [10] Now that He
has advanced you and all your fellow Levites with you, do
you seek the priesthood too? [11] Truly, it is against the LORD
that you and all your company have banded together. For
who is Aaron that you should rail against him?"

[12] Moses sent for Dathan and Abiram, sons of Eliab; but
they said, "We will not come! [13] Is it not enough that you
brought us from a land flowing with milk and honey to
have us die in the wilderness, that you would also lord it
over us? [14] c-Even if you had-c brought us to a land flowing
with milk and honey, and given us possession of fields
and vineyards, should you gouge out those men's eyes?[d]
We will not come!" [15] Moses was much aggrieved and he
said to the LORD, "Pay no regard to their oblation. I have
not taken the ass of any one of them, nor have I wronged
any one of them."

[16] And Moses said to Korah, "Tomorrow, you and all
your company appear before the LORD, you and they and
Aaron. [17] Each of you take his fire pan and lay incense on
it, and each of you bring his fire pan before the LORD, two
hundred and fifty fire pans; you and Aaron also [bring]
your fire pans." [18] Each of them took his fire pan, put fire
in it, laid incense on it, and took his place at the entrance
of the Tent of Meeting, as did Moses and Aaron. [19] Korah

a Perhaps in the sense of "his face fell."
b Lit. "his."
c-c Lit. "You have not even."
d "Those men's" is a euphemism for "our"; cf. 1 Sam 29.4. Gouging out the eyes was punishment for runaway slaves and rebellious vassals; cf. 2 Kings 25.4–7; Jer. 39.4–7, 52.7–11.

bution. Like other rebellions in the
wilderness, these begin with a few
individuals and spread to the community at large. At least two insurrection stories are interwoven by
the redactor. One involves Korah,
a Kohathite Levite who demands a
share in the Aaronite priesthood;
the second has three Reubenites,
two brothers, Dathan and Abiram,
and a third individual, On, question the authority of Moses. The
rebel leaders assemble followers.
Defiance of Moses is clearly tied to
miseries of the wilderness experience and doubts surrounding the
eventual settlement of Canaan. On
the other hand, the challenge of
Aaron deals with the legitimacy of
the priests' exclusive position vis-
à-vis the Levites, who had a secondary role in the cult that was
much less prestigious than the
priestly role. Both situations are resolved by divine wrath. In the case
of Dathan and Abiram, they, their
families, and all their possessions
are literally swallowed up by the
earth. In a twist of fate, they who
had refused to *come (up)* to Moses
(v. 12), *went down* into the earth
(v. 33). Korah's contingent is first
offered a test to settle the matter
of the priesthood for all time.
For their punishment, they who
had sought the right to make
fire for God's offerings are consumed themselves by divine fire.
1: *Descendants of Reuben:* This story
may help to explain why the tribe
of Reuben, the first-born, was supplanted by Judah. In fact, Ibn Ezra
maintains that Reubenites challenged Moses because he did not
give them their just due as descendants of Jacob's first-born. Instead
he chose Joshua, an Ephraimite of
the House of Joseph, as his assistant. **2:** Two hundred and fifty Israelite chieftains join the uprising
against Moses (v. 2), though later
these chieftains are connected to
the Levites who challenge Aaron
(v. 35). This is a clear example of a
redactor tightly weaving two separate accounts. **3:** *All the community
are holy:* Korah's group argues
against the notion that only the
priests are sanctified to perform religious rituals. The fact that Korah

gathered the whole community against them at the entrance of the Tent of Meeting.

Then the Presence of the LORD appeared to the whole community, [20] and the LORD spoke to Moses and Aaron, saying, [21] "Stand back from this community that I may annihilate them in an instant!" [22] But they fell on their faces and said, "O God, Source[a] of the breath of all flesh! When one man sins, will You be wrathful with the whole community?"

[23] The LORD spoke to Moses, saying, [24] "Speak to the community and say: Withdraw from about the abodes of Korah, Dathan, and Abiram."

[25] Moses rose and went to Dathan and Abiram, the elders of Israel following him. [26] He addressed the community, saying, "Move away from the tents of these wicked men and touch nothing that belongs to them, lest you be wiped out for all their sins." [27] So they withdrew from about the abodes of Korah, Dathan, and Abiram.

Now Dathan and Abiram had come out and they stood at the entrance of their tents, with their wives, their children, and their little ones. [28] And Moses said, "By this you shall know that it was the LORD who sent me to do all these things; that they are not of my own devising: [29] if these men die as all men do, if their lot be the common fate of all mankind, it was not the LORD who sent me. [30] But if the LORD brings about something unheard-of, so that the ground opens its mouth and swallows them up with all that belongs to them, and they go down alive into Sheol, you shall know that these men have spurned the LORD." [31] Scarcely had he finished speaking all these words when the ground under them burst asunder, [32] and the earth opened its mouth and swallowed them up with their households, all Korah's people and all their possessions. [33] They went down alive into Sheol, with all that belonged to them; the earth closed over them and they vanished from the midst of the congregation. [34] All Israel around them fled at their shrieks, for they said, "The earth might swallow us!"

[35] And a fire went forth from the LORD and consumed the two hundred and fifty men offering the incense.

17 The LORD spoke to Moses, saying: [2] Order Eleazar son of Aaron the priest to remove the fire pans—for they have become sacred—from among the charred remains; and scatter the coals abroad. [3][b] [Remove] the fire pans of those who have sinned at the cost of their lives,

and his followers are proven wrong demonstrates that popular holiness attached to the tzitzit (15.40) still renders wearers subordinate to priests. The people's holiness derives from their obligation to follow the commandments (Lev. 19.2). **8–11:** Moses rebukes Korah and the Levites for not being satisfied with their God-appointed positions as guardians of the Tabernacle. Their sin is challenging God's authority rather than that of Aaron. **13–14:** The rebels call Egypt a land flowing with milk and honey, thus attributing the bounty of the promised land to Egypt, the land of enslavement. **15:** Moses defends his conduct as an honorable leader. The prophet Samuel responds similarly when the Israelites demand that a king replace him (1 Sam. 12.3). The prayer for their punishment sharply contrasts with Moses' other prayers for the nation's forgiveness. **16–18:** It is not specified that the fire which burnt the incense in the Levites' fire pans was taken from the altar. Thus, their sin may be compounded by the use of unauthorized *fire* (cf. Nadab and Abihu, Lev. 10.1–2). **20–22:** Apparently God is ready to annihilate Israel. Moses and Aaron appeal to God as creator of humanity (v. 22a) and appeal to His sense of justice: Sin must be punished individually rather than communally (v. 22b; see Ezek. ch 18). **33:** *Sheol* is the underworld, the place where the dead, both the righteous and the sinners, dwell (1 Kings 2.6; Isa. 14.9–20). **35:** Korah is not mentioned as having died in the LORD's fire, although it is implied that he did (cf. 26.10, Korah perishes with Dotham and Amiram). The phrase *a fire went forth from the LORD and consumed* is used in Lev. 10.2 as well, in reference to Nadab and Abihu, thereby connecting these two units that focus on improper worship of God.

17.1–18.7: The aftermath of Korah's insurrection. This ch continues the previous story, tying up some loose ends. First, the copper fire pans of the Levites, which

a Lit. "God."   *b* Meaning of parts of verse uncertain.

and let them be made into hammered sheets as plating for the altar—for once they have been used for offering to the LORD, they have become sacred—and let them serve as a warning to the people of Israel. ⁴Eleazar the priest took the copper fire pans which had been used for offering by those who died in the fire; and they were hammered into plating for the altar, ⁵as the LORD had ordered him through Moses. It was to be a reminder to the Israelites, so that no outsider—one not of Aaron's offspring—should presume to offer incense before the LORD and suffer the fate of Korah and his band.

⁶Next day the whole Israelite community railed against Moses and Aaron, saying, "You two have brought death upon the LORD's people!" ⁷But as the community gathered against them, Moses and Aaron turned toward the Tent of Meeting; the cloud had covered it and the Presence of the LORD appeared.

⁸When Moses and Aaron reached the Tent of Meeting, ⁹the LORD spoke to Moses, saying, ¹⁰"Remove yourselves from this community, that I may annihilate them in an instant." They fell on their faces. ¹¹Then Moses said to Aaron, "Take the fire pan, and put on it fire from the altar. Add incense and take it quickly to the community and make expiation for them. For wrath has gone forth from the LORD: the plague has begun!" ¹²Aaron took it, as Moses had ordered, and ran to the midst of the congregation, where the plague had begun among the people. He put on the incense and made expiation for the people; ¹³he stood between the dead and the living until the plague was checked. ¹⁴Those who died of the plague came to fourteen thousand and seven hundred, aside from those who died on account of Korah. ¹⁵Aaron then returned to Moses at the entrance of the Tent of Meeting, since the plague was checked.

¹⁶The LORD spoke to Moses, saying: ¹⁷Speak to the Israelite people and take from them—from the chieftains of their ancestral houses[a]—one staff for each chieftain of an ancestral house: twelve staffs in all. Inscribe each man's name on his staff, ¹⁸there being one staff for each head of an ancestral house; also inscribe Aaron's name on the staff of Levi. ¹⁹Deposit them in the Tent of Meeting before the Pact, where I meet with you. ²⁰The staff of the man whom I choose shall sprout, and I will rid[b] Myself of the incessant mutterings of the Israelites against you.

²¹Moses spoke thus to the Israelites. Their chieftains

a I.e., of their tribes.
b Meaning of Heb. wahashikkothi uncertain.

were exposed to divine fire, must be preserved since they are sacred. Second, the Israelites who question the fate of their rebel leaders are punished by plague. Third, the absolute divinely ordained authority of the Aaronide Levites is confirmed in the test of the staffs. Fourth, the Aaronide priests and their Levite subordinates take all sanctuary responsibilities and consequences of misconduct upon themselves. **17.3–5:** The fire pans rescued from the conflagration become copper plating for the altar, thereby serving as a *warning* sign, a visible *reminder,* aimed at stopping future would-be encroachers on the Tabernacle. The same Heb terms are used to describe the function of the tefillin (phylacteries) in Exod. 13.9, and the rainbow at the end of the flood story, though in that account God is the one being reminded (Gen. 9.12–17). These words refer to an action or object that is of symbolic rather than intrinsic significance. **6–15:** The Israelite community blames Moses and Aaron for the death of their leaders, here called *the LORD's people,* so Moses and Aaron must act to show that God is responsible. It is thus Aaron's expiation ritual that halts the plague. Similarly, David stops a plague by building an altar and offering a sacrifice on it (2 Sam. 24.18–25). The efficacy of ritual is apparent in both accounts. **16–26:** By collecting a staff from each tribal chieftain, the election of the tribe of Levi for sanctuary duties and the Aaronides as priests is reconfirmed. Aaron's name is inscribed on the staff of Levi, thus affirming his clan's status among the Levites. The contest, however, is not to determine who among the Levites can function as priests, as that issue was already settled with the death of Korah's group. **19:** *In the Tent of Meeting before the Pact:* The staffs are placed in front of the deity, or more correctly at His throne, the Ark. **23:** Aaron's staff not only sprouts but it produces blossoms which in turn develop into almonds overnight. The sprouting of a staff or pillar for the gave him a staff for each chieftain of an ancestral house, twelve staffs in all; among these staffs was that of Aaron. 22 Moses deposited the staffs before the LORD, in the Tent of the Pact. 23 The next day Moses entered the Tent of the Pact, and there the staff of Aaron of the house of Levi had sprouted: it had brought forth sprouts, produced blossoms, and borne almonds. 24 Moses then brought out all the staffs from before the LORD to all the Israelites; each identified and recovered his staff.

25 The LORD said to Moses, "Put Aaron's staff back before the Pact, to be kept as a lesson to rebels, so that their mutterings against Me may cease, lest they die." 26 This Moses did; just as the LORD had commanded him, so he did.

27 But the Israelites said to Moses, "Lo, we perish! We are lost, all of us lost! 28 Everyone who so much as ventures near the LORD's Tabernacle must die. Alas, we are doomed to perish!"

18 The LORD said to Aaron: You and your sons and the ancestral house under your charge shall bear any guilt connected with the sanctuary; you and your sons alone shall bear any guilt connected with your priesthood. 2 You shall also associate with yourself your kinsmen the tribe of Levi, your ancestral tribe, to be attached to you and to minister to you, while you and your sons under your charge are before the Tent of the Pact.ª 3 They shall discharge their duties to you and to the Tent as a whole, but they must not have any contact with the furnishings of the Shrine or with the altar, lest both they and you die. 4 They shall be attached to you and discharge the duties of the Tent of Meeting, all the service of the Tent; but no outsider shall intrude upon you 5 as you discharge the duties connected with the Shrine and the altar, that wrath may not again strike the Israelites.

6 I hereby take your fellow Levites from among the Israelites; they are assigned to you in dedication to the LORD, to do the work of the Tent of Meeting; 7 while you and your sons shall be careful to perform your priestly duties in everything pertaining to the altar and to what is behind the curtain. I make your priesthood a service of dedication; any outsider who encroaches shall be put to death.

8 The LORD spoke further to Aaron: I hereby give you charge of My gifts, all the sacred donations of the Israelites; I grant them to you and to your sons as a perquisite,ᵇ

a Meaning of latter part of verse uncertain.
b See note at Lev. 7.35.

purpose of identifying a hero or priest is also known from Herodotus (IV.67–68). Almonds are considered among the choicest products of Canaan (Gen. 43.11). **25:** Aaron's staff is placed in the sanctuary as a warning sign, like the copper plating of fire pans on the altar. Alternatively, Aaron's staff was kept as a memorial attesting God's choice of Aaron (Rashi). **27–28:** The people fear that even approaching the Tabernacle could constitute encroachment and result in death. **18.1:** God speaks to Aaron directly rather than through Moses (only in this ch and in Lev. 10.8). The priests are responsible to keep other priests who are in a state of cultic impurity out of the sanctuary (Exod. 28.43; 30.20; Lev. 10.9; 16.2; 21.23). **2–5:** Levite guard duties concerning the Tabernacle and its contents protect the Israelites from the consequences of encroachment. These verses also contain a popular or folk etymology of Levites: They are the cultic functionaries who are *attached* to (vv. 2 and 4, from the root "l-v-h") the priests.

18.8–32: Compensation for the priests and Levites. This section, which by and large repeats Priestly legislation found in other books of the Torah, continues the subject of the previous section by delineating a system of compensation for priestly and Levitic services. In their responsibilities vis-à-vis the Tabernacle, religious functionaries work on behalf of the people, who, in turn, support them and their families. Regular tax revenues designated for the sanctuary satisfy those needs. Naturally, those holding the highest status and charged with the most sacred duties, the priests, are allocated the most desirable gifts, those marked "holy to the LORD, for the priests" (Lev. 23.20). Priestly portions are divided into two categories *most sacred* and *sacred*, and accordingly, are designated for consumption by only pure males in the sacred precinct, and by their female relatives living at home, re-a due for all time. ⁹ This shall be yours from the most holy sacrifices, ᵃthe offerings by fire:ᵃ every such offering that they render to Me as most holy sacrifices, namely, every meal offering, sin offering, and guilt offering of theirs, shall belong to you and your sons. ¹⁰ You shall partake of them as most sacred donations: only males may eat them; you shall treat them as consecrated.ᵇ

¹¹ This, too, shall be yours: the gift offeringsᶜ of their contributions, all the elevation offerings of the Israelites, I give to you, to your sons, and to the daughters that are with you, as a due for all time; everyone of your household who is clean may eat it.

¹² All the best of the new oil, wine, and grain—the choice parts that they present to the Lord—I give to you. ¹³ The first fruits of everything in their land, that they bring to the Lord, shall be yours; everyone of your household who is clean may eat them. ¹⁴ Everything that has been proscribed in Israelᵈ shall be yours. ¹⁵ The first issue of the womb of every being, man or beast, that is offered to the Lord, shall be yours; but you shall have the first-born of man redeemed, and you shall also have the firstling of unclean animals redeemed. ¹⁶ Take as their redemption price,ᵉ from the age of one month up, the money equivalent of five shekels by the sanctuary weight, which is twenty gerahs. ¹⁷ But the firstlings of cattle, sheep, or goats may not be redeemed; they are consecrated. You shall dash their blood against the altar, and turn their fat into smoke as an offering by fire for a pleasing odor to the Lord. ¹⁸ But their meat shall be yours: it shall be yours like the breast of elevation offering and like the right thigh.

¹⁹ All the sacred gifts that the Israelites set aside for the Lord I give to you, to your sons, and to the daughters that are with you, as a due for all time. It shall be an everlasting covenant of saltᶠ before the Lord for you and for your offspring as well. ²⁰ And the Lord said to Aaron: You shall, however, have no territorial share among them or own any portion in their midst; I am your portion and your share among the Israelites.

²¹ And to the Levites I hereby give all the tithes in Israel as their share in return for the services that they perform, the services of the Tent of Meeting. ²² Henceforth, Israelites shall not trespass on the Tent of Meeting, and thus incur guilt and die: ²³ only Levites shall perform the ser-

a-a Meaning of Heb. uncertain; lit. "from the fire."
b Or "they are consecrated for your use."
c Cf. Lev. 7.29 ff.   d See Lev. 27.28.
e I.e., for human first-born; cf. Num. 3.44 ff. For animals see Exod. 34.19 f.
f See Lev. 2.13.

spectively. A statement regarding these priestly emoluments is found in the writings of the prophet Ezekiel, himself a priest (44.29–30). The Levites, on the other hand, receive the tithes. **9–10:** *Most sacred* includes that part of purification (NJPS "sin") and guilt offerings which is not burnt (see Lev. 6.1–7.10). **11–18:** "Sacred" is a much larger category which includes the following: portions of nonsacrificial gifts and elevation offerings (see Lev. 7.11–38); offerings of first fruits, grain, wine, and oil (see Exod. 23.16–19; Lev. 2.14; 23.17–18; Deut. 18.4; 26.1–11); anything proscribed or dedicated that becomes the property of the Lord under the law of "ḥerem" (the ban; see Lev. 27.21, 28–29; Deut. 7.26; Josh. chs 6–7); all human and animal first-born males, both those to be redeemed—man and animals unfit for sacrifice—and those animals sacrificed (see Exod. 13.2, 11–13; 22.28; 34.19–20; Lev. 27.1–13; Deut. 12.17; 14.23; 15.19–23). **16:** For the values of the sanctuary weight, the shekel, and *"gerah"* see 3.47 n. **19:** *An everlasting covenant of salt:* Salt, a valuable food preservative, is symbolic of the permanence of the covenant agreement. It is used with sacrifices (Lev. 2.13; 2 Chron. 13.5). Based on this v., the Rabbis maintain that the covenant between the priests and God is eternal, even following the destruction of the Temple and the end of the sacrificial system (*Lev. Rab.* 24.2). This explains why in some contemporary groups of Judaism, the priests retain certain privileges, such as blessing the congregation (see 6.22–27) or being called first to the Torah. **20:** *I am your portion:* The personal name Hilkiah, "Yah (the Lord) is my portion," which is the name of several priests (2 Kings 22.10; Ezra 7.1; 1 Chron. 5.39; and on the personal seal of a priest), reflects the sense of this phrase. **21–24:** Laws concerning tithes are outlined in Lev. 27.30–32 and Deut. 12.17–19; 14.22–29. **25–32:** Levites are compensated for their service by the tithes. They are required to donate to the vices of the Tent of Meeting; others[a] would incur guilt. It is the law for all time throughout the ages. But they shall have no territorial share among the Israelites; 24 for it is the tithes set aside by the Israelites as a gift to the LORD that I give to the Levites as their share. Therefore I have said concerning them: They shall have no territorial share among the Israelites.

25 The LORD spoke to Moses, saying: 26 Speak to the Levites and say to them: When you receive from the Israelites their tithes, which I have assigned to you as your share, you shall set aside from them one-tenth of the tithe as a gift to the LORD. 27 This shall be accounted to you as your gift. As with the new grain from the threshing floor or the flow from the vat, 28 so shall you on your part set aside a gift for the LORD from all the tithes that you receive from the Israelites; and from them you shall bring the gift for the LORD to Aaron the priest. 29 You shall set aside all gifts due to the LORD from everything that is donated to you, from each thing its best portion, the part thereof that is to be consecrated.

30 Say to them further: When you have removed the best part from it, you Levites may consider it the same as the yield of threshing floor or vat. 31 You and your households may eat it anywhere, for it is your recompense for your services in the Tent of Meeting. 32 You will incur no guilt through it, once you have removed the best part from it; but you must not profane the sacred donations of the Israelites, lest you die.

ḤUKKAT   חקת

19 The LORD spoke to Moses and Aaron, saying: 2 This is the ritual law that the LORD has commanded:

Instruct the Israelite people to bring you a red cow without blemish, in which there is no defect and on which no yoke has been laid. 3 You shall give it to Eleazar the priest. It shall be taken outside the camp and slaughtered in his

a Lit. "they."

priests one-tenth of the tithes that they collect, however. Thus, Levites are obligated to pay tithes like other Israelites; only priests are exempt. This final section of the ch is an addition or amendment to the law in Leviticus.

19.1–22: Ritual of purification with the ashes of a red cow. Contamination through contact with a corpse, or any part thereof,

whether by actual touch or through proximity in an enclosed space, is considered a severe impurity (cf. 5.1–4) requiring a complex purification process. While impurities in general are discussed elsewhere (Lev. chs 11–15), the process of erasing corpse pollution is delineated only here (and briefly in 31.19–24 in connection with combat). Contaminated persons or objects must be cleansed lest they

communicate their contagious state to other humans or objects within the camp and ultimately defile the sanctuary. Classical Judaism understands the term "ḥukah" (NJPS *ritual law*, v. 2), as a law that defies rational explanation. However, the types of procedures described here have parallels in ancient Near Eastern literature, and may be understood using anthropological understandings of how rituals function. The seven-day purification process involves a type of "ḥata't," a purification offering. The affected person or object is sprinkled on the third and seventh day with a prepared mixture of fresh water and the ashes of a red cow, cedar wood, hyssop plant, and red dye. Essentially on the principle of sympathetic magic, the red-colored ash mixture absorbs the corpse pollution. (Note also how blood functions as a type of "ritual detergent" in Lev. ch 16.) This particular rite renders this ritual unique in biblical practices, one reason being that those officiating at the cleansing contract a measure of impurity in the process of performing it. Ch 19 consists of two subsections. The first, vv. 1–13, contains instructions on the preparation of the ashes and the mixture. It also details the purification procedure for persons preparing the concoction. The second part, vv. 14–22, details conditions that qualify persons or objects to undergo this rite and the actual sprinkling ritual. Failure to undergo this process is subject to "karet," divine retribution (vv. 13, 20). **2:** *Ritual law:* The Rabbis derive justification for this seemingly peculiar rite, over which the nations of the world taunt Israel, by this reference to law, "Torah." *A red cow:* Red, symbolic of blood, ensures the efficacy of the rite. The ashes of a cow rather than a bull are used for individuals (cf. Deut. 21.1–9); the bull "ḥata't" is used for the high priest and the community (Lev. 4.1–21; 16.11). Generations have puzzled over the color of this cow. The best explanation is that it is a brown, or red-presence. [4] Eleazar the priest shall take some of its blood with his finger and sprinkle it seven times toward the front of the Tent of Meeting. [5] The cow shall be burned in his sight—its hide, flesh, and blood shall be burned, its dung included—[6] and the priest shall take cedar wood, hyssop, and crimson stuff, and throw them into the fire consuming the cow. [7] The priest shall wash his garments and bathe his body in water; after that the priest may reenter the camp, but he shall be unclean until evening. [8] He who performed the burning shall also wash his garments in water, bathe his body in water, and be unclean until evening. [9] A man who is clean shall gather up the ashes of the cow and deposit them outside the camp in a clean place, to be kept for water of lustration[a] for the Israelite community. It is for cleansing. [10] He who gathers up the ashes of the cow shall also wash his clothes and be unclean until evening.

This shall be a permanent law for the Israelites and for the strangers who reside among you.

[11] He who touches the corpse of any human being shall be unclean for seven days. [12] He shall cleanse himself with it[b] on the third day and on the seventh day, and then be clean; if he fails to cleanse himself on the third and seventh days, he shall not be clean. [13] Whoever touches a corpse, the body of a person who has died, and does not cleanse himself, defiles the LORD's Tabernacle; that person shall be cut off from Israel. Since the water of lustration was not dashed on him, he remains unclean; his uncleanness is still upon him.

[14] This is the ritual: When a person dies in a tent, whoever enters the tent and whoever is in the tent shall be unclean seven days; [15] and every open vessel, with no lid fastened down, shall be unclean. [16] And in the open, anyone who touches a person who was killed[c] or who died naturally, or human bone, or a grave, shall be unclean seven days. [17] Some of the ashes[d] from the fire of cleansing shall be taken for the unclean person, and fresh water shall be added to them in a vessel. [18] A person who is clean shall take hyssop, dip it in the water, and sprinkle on the tent and on all the vessels and people who were there, or on him who touched the bones or the person who was killed or died naturally or the grave. [19] The clean person shall sprinkle it upon the unclean person on the third day and on the seventh day, thus cleansing him by the seventh day. He[e] shall then wash his clothes and bathe in water, and at

dish-brown cow with no spots of other color on it. **6–10:** The priest who oversees the incineration of the cow, and the persons who conduct the various tasks associated with it, become unclean. **9:** *It is for cleansing:* The translation of "hata't" reflects the fact that this is not a sacrifice in the true sense of a sin offering which is made on the altar inside the camp. **14:** Pollution from a corpse seems to be airborne. **16:** Any portion of a corpse is defiling. Contact with sacred objects defiles them permanently. King Josiah used human ashes to desecrate illegitimate altars and other cult objects and to invalidate sacred space in perpetuity (2 Kings chs 22–23). **17:** *Fresh water,* lit. "living water," is water running from its source rather than taken from a storage unit (cf. Lev. 14.5, 50). In postbiblical Jewish law such running water must be used in the mikveh or ritual bath. **20:** The sin of defiling the sanctuary only applies if a contaminated Israelite or foreign resident does not undergo this cleansing process. Priests, on the other hand, are restricted to contact with a corpse of immediate family members (Lev. 21.1–4). The consequences of defiling the sanctuary are severe: God will abandon it when it becomes sufficiently defiled (see Ezek. chs 1–11). The biblical Day of Atonement ritual (Lev. ch 16) is a purification ritual, which cleanses the sanctuary from accumulated impurities or pollution.

---

a Lit. "water for impurity."   b I.e., the ashes, as in v. 9.
c Lit. "slain by the sword."   d Lit. "earth" or "dust."
e I.e., the person being cleansed.

nightfall he shall be clean. 20 If anyone who has become unclean fails to cleanse himself, that person shall be cut off from the congregation, for he has defiled the LORD's sanctuary. The water of lustration was not dashed on him: he is unclean.

21 That shall be for them a law for all time. Further, he who sprinkled the water of lustration shall wash his clothes; and whoever touches the water of lustration shall be unclean until evening. 22 Whatever that unclean person touches shall be unclean; and the person who touches him shall be unclean until evening.

20 The Israelites arrived in a body at the wilderness of Zin on the first new moon,ᵃ and the people stayed at Kadesh. Miriam died there and was buried there.

2 The community was without water, and they joined against Moses and Aaron. 3 The people quarreled with Moses, saying, "If only we had perished when our brothers perished at the instance of the LORD! 4 Why have you brought the LORD's congregation into this wilderness for us and our beasts to die there? 5 Why did you make us leave Egypt to bring us to this wretched place, a place with no grain or figs or vines or pomegranates? There is not even water to drink!"

6 Moses and Aaron came away from the congregation to the entrance of the Tent of Meeting, and fell on their faces. The Presence of the LORD appeared to them, 7 and the LORD spoke to Moses, saying, 8 "You and your brother Aaron take the rod and assemble the community, and before their very eyes order the rock to yield its water. Thus you shall produce water for them from the rock and provide drink for the congregation and their beasts."

9 Moses took the rod from before the LORD, as He had commanded him. 10 Moses and Aaron assembled the congregation in front of the rock; and he said to them, "Listen, you rebels, shall we get water for you out of this rock?"

a Of the fortieth year; cf. Num. 33.36–38.

20.1–13: The sin of Moses and Aaron. Chs 20–21 continue the wilderness narrative. This section opens with the Israelites at Kadesh. According to the Priestly writer(s) this marks the end of the 40-year period in the desert, which was spent primarily in northern Sinai. In contrast, the JE tradition places this stop early in the 40-year march, claiming that Israel traveled only one to two years in the

Sinai, with the balance of the 40 years being spent in the wilderness of Edom and Moab en route to the crossing at the Jordan River. (32.8 states that the spies were distracted from Kadesh; 13.26 records the spies' return to the Israelite camp at Kadesh. The punishment of 40 years of wandering follows their report. Num. 14.25 instructs the Israelites to head for the Red Sea immediately, then cross into

the wilderness of Edom.) Vv. 1–13 comprise the first of three subsections of ch 20. This part recounts Miriam's death, Israel's murmuring to Moses and Aaron over a water shortage, Moses' and Aaron's handling of the crisis, and their tragic banning from entering Canaan. Actually, the incident involving water is the second of its kind, explained as either P's version of the JE account of a water shortage at Massah and Meribah (Exod. 17.1–7) or simply a second crisis over water. In the Exodus narrative God instructs Moses to hit the rock with his rod to bring forth water. In the Priestly version in Numbers, Moses and Aaron are to speak to the rock in front of the Israelites (v. 8). When Moses strikes the rock instead of speaking to it, God, in an unexpected move, hands down the ultimate punishment to His appointed leaders. Puzzled by the apparent harshness of God's verdict, biblical scholars past and present as well as students of the Bible have tried to reconcile Moses' and Aaron's punishment with their sin (see v. 10). The deaths of Aaron and, especially, Moses in Transjordan overlooking the promised land have become a symbol epitomizing the human condition. **1:** *On the first new moon:* This is the first month of the fortieth year according to 33.38, which places Kadesh before Aaron's death in the fifth month of that year. Some rabbinic traditions connect Miriam to water, and find significance in the juxtaposition of Miriam's death (v. 1) to the absence of water (*Song of Songs Rab.* 4.12). **10:** "*Shall we get water for you out of this rock?*": Striking the rock, as in the Exodus version, does not seem to account for the gravity of Moses' sin, even though according to some interpretations, it constitutes public disobedience of God's instructions, which in itself is punishable. Another, more plausible, interpretation is found among medieval commentators who focus on the pronoun "we" in "shall we get water." By attributing the act of drawing water from a rock to him-

11 And Moses raised his hand and struck the rock twice with his rod. Out came copious water, and the community and their beasts drank.

12 But the LORD said to Moses and Aaron, "Because you did not trust Me enough to affirm My sanctity in the sight of the Israelite people, therefore you shall not lead this congregation into the land that I have given them." 13 Those are the Waters of Meribah[a]—meaning that the Israelites quarrelled with the LORD—through which He affirmed His sanctity.

14 From Kadesh, Moses sent messengers to the king of Edom: "Thus says your brother Israel: You know all the hardships that have befallen us; 15 that our ancestors went down to Egypt, that we dwelt in Egypt a long time, and that the Egyptians dealt harshly with us and our ancestors. 16 We cried to the LORD and He heard our plea, and He sent a messenger[b] who freed us from Egypt. Now we are in Kadesh, the town on the border of your territory. 17 Allow us, then, to cross your country. We will not pass through fields or vineyards, and we will not drink water from wells. We will follow the king's highway, turning off neither to the right nor to the left until we have crossed your territory."

18 But Edom answered him, "You shall not pass through us, else we will go out against you with the sword." 19 "We will keep to the beaten track," the Israelites said to them, "and if we or our cattle drink your water, we will pay for it. We ask only for passage on foot—it is but a small matter." 20 But they replied, "You shall not pass through!" And Edom went out against them in heavy force, strongly armed. 21 So Edom would not let Israel cross their territory, and Israel turned away from them.

22 Setting out from Kadesh, the Israelites arrived in a body at Mount Hor. 23 At Mount Hor, on the boundary of the land of Edom, the LORD said to Moses and Aaron,

a I.e., "Quarrel"; cf. Exod. 17.7 and note b there.   b Or "angel."

self and Aaron, Moses, standing before Israel, fails to credit the miracle to God; this is particularly significant because in vv. 4–5 the nation seems to attribute the exodus to Moses and Aaron rather than to God. The distinction carries theological implications in light of the Bible's need to show the superiority of Israel's God over Pharaoh and the gods of Egypt (Exod. ch 5–12). Of significance is an Egyptian inscription on a roadside rock temple in the eastern desert dedicated by Pharaoh Seti I (late 14th century) to his gods: "He (god) has made water come forth for me from the mountain."

20.14–21: Confrontation with Edom. Since the Israelites fail to enter Canaan from the south (14.40–45) they now plan to cut through the territory of Edom, follow the main road north to Moab, and then cross the Jordan from the east. Moses twice petitions the ruler of Edom for permission to cross his country, emphasizing Israel's misfortunes as he appeals for sympathy. But the Edomites deny Israel access to their territory and confront them with a large military force. Israel must circumvent the entire region of Edom by detouring south to the Red Sea and marching around the eastern border of Edom. It is this detour that according to the JE tradition took thirty-eight years to complete. A variant version in Deuteronomy recalls that Israel did indeed march through Edom (2.1–8). **14:** *Your brother Israel* may refer to Edom's relationship to Jacob (Gen. 25.24–26), a legacy reflected in certain laws (Deut. 23.8). On the other hand, in the ancient Near East "brother" signifies someone of equal status. Here Moses may be indicating that the two groups, the Edomites and Israelites, are essentially of equal status and should therefore practice a "brother" relationship when dealing with each other. **17:** *The king's highway* is an important ancient trade route leading from Damascus to the delta in Egypt via Elath.

20.22–29: Aaron's death. The Priestly narrative continues with the transference of the office of high priest to Eleazar and the death of Aaron on Mount Hor. Mount Hor is also the site of Aaron's death according to 33.38 and Deut. 32.50; but in Deut. 10.6 he dies at Moserah. The two geographical names, both of disputed locales, may actually refer to the same site. For P it is important to record in detail Eleazar's inheritance of his father's priestly garments along with his office. The fact that all Israel mourned Aaron for thirty days, instead of the customary seven (Gen. 50.10; 1 Sam. 31.13), reflects his stature in the community. Moses is also mourned for thirty days (Deut. 34.8). In later Jewish law, these are reconciled by having a more stringent period of seven

24 "Let Aaron be gathered to his kin: he is not to enter the land that I have assigned to the Israelite people, because you disobeyed my command about the waters of Meribah. 25 Take Aaron and his son Eleazar and bring them up on Mount Hor. 26 Strip Aaron of his vestments and put them on his son Eleazar. There Aaron shall be gathered *unto the dead."*-a

27 Moses did as the LORD had commanded. They ascended Mount Hor in the sight of the whole community. 28 Moses stripped Aaron of his vestments and put them on his son Eleazar, and Aaron died there on the summit of the mountain. When Moses and Eleazar came down from the mountain, 29 the whole community knew that Aaron had breathed his last. All the house of Israel bewailed Aaron thirty days.

21 When the Canaanite, king of Arad, who dwelt in the Negeb, learned that Israel was coming by the way of Atharim,b he engaged Israel in battle and took some of them captive. 2 Then Israel made a vow to the LORD and said, "If You deliver this people into our hand, we will proscribec their towns." 3 The LORD heeded Israel's plea and delivered up the Canaanites; and they and their cities were proscribed. So that place was named Hormah.d

4 They set out from Mount Hor by way of the Sea of Reedse to skirt the land of Edom. But the people grew restive on the journey, 5 and the people spoke against God and against Moses, "Why did you make us leave Egypt to

a-a Lit. "and die."

b Meaning of Heb. ha-ʾatharim uncertain. Targum and other ancient versions render "the way [taken by] the scouts."

c I.e., utterly destroy, reserving no booty except what is deposited in the Sanctuary; see Josh. 6.24.

d Connected with heḥerim "to proscribe."   e See Exod. 10.19 note.

success (14.43–45); a fruitless encounter with Edomites is also mentioned (20.14–21). In this ch, the confrontations with the inhabitants on the borders of Canaan proper mark a turning point in Israel's fortunes. With God at their side, their victories preview coming events during the conquest of Canaan. Two ancient poems are preserved in this section. **1–3:** This encounter with Canaanites in the northern Negev in the region of Arad seems to be an alternate tradition concerning the naming of Hormah (14.43–45). In this version, God ends up by championing Israel's cause after the people vow to proscribe the enemy as "ḥerem," utter destruction with the booty dedicated to the sanctuary. **1:** *King of Arad:* Archeological excavations show no evidence of a settlement at Arad in the second millennium. Probably, a writer living at a later time, when Israelite Arad was inhabited, assumed that during the exodus period a Canaanite king resided there. On Hormah, see 14.45. **4–9:** This incident is the final recurrence of wilderness murmuring. Complaints again center around a lack of water and poor food. The bronze serpent as an apotropaic (evil-averting, from Greek "turn from") symbol seems to be the etiological account for the bronze serpent, Neḥushtan, which was worshipped in Jerusalem until the late 8th century when King Hezekiah destroyed it (2 Kings 18.4). Winged serpents associated with the divine are attested in Isaiah (6.6–7; 14.20–30) and elsewhere in the ancient Near East. In Egypt, the uraeus, an amulet of an upreared cobra, symbolized kingship and divinity. It was worn on the pharaoh's forehead and was believed to protect him with its fiery saliva. A serpent attached to a staff brings to mind the caduceus symbol of the modern medical profession. **4:** This verse continues 20.21; *from Mount Hor* is a Priestly interpolation. *The Sea of Reeds* here must refer to the Red Sea (see map on p. 130). **5:** Once again, the people revolt against God and Moses.

days of mourning followed by a period of moderate mourning that lasts for an additional twenty-three days. According to a midrashic tradition, Aaron was loved by the people because he was a harbinger of peace, especially between husband and wife (ʾAvot R. Nat. 12).

21.1–22.1: The final events of the wilderness experience. This ch consists of four subsections. The first and last focus on Israel's encounters with different ethnic groups that inhabit the eastern Negev and Transjordan; the middle two recount events on this part of the journey. These travels end the wilderness period bringing the Israelites from Kadesh-barnea to the eastern bank of the Jordan River in Moab just opposite Canaan. The Deuteronomistic History calculates that period as thirty-eight years (Deut. 2.13–15). Previously, Israel had met an armed group of indigenous people when attempting to invade Canaan from the south, but without die in the wilderness? There is no bread and no water, and we have come to loathe this miserable food." ⁶ The LORD sent *seraph*ᵃ serpents against the people. They bit the people and many of the Israelites died. ⁷ The people came to Moses and said, "We sinned by speaking against the LORD and against you. Intercede with the LORD to take away the serpents from us!" And Moses interceded for the people. ⁸ Then the LORD said to Moses, "Make a *seraph*ᵃ figure and mount it on a standard. And if anyone who is bitten looks at it, he shall recover." ⁹ Moses made a copper serpent and mounted it on a standard; and when anyone was bitten by a serpent, he would look at the copper serpent and recover.

¹⁰ The Israelites marched on and encamped at Oboth. ¹¹ They set out from Oboth and encamped at Iye-abarim, in the wilderness bordering on Moab to the east. ¹² From there they set out and encamped at the wadi Zered. ¹³ From there they set out and encamped beyond the Arnon, that is, in the wilderness that extends from the territory of the Amorites. For the Arnon is the boundary of Moab, between Moab and the Amorites. ¹⁴ Therefore the Book of the Wars of the LORD speaks of ᵇ". . . Waheb in Suphah, and the wadis: the Arnon ¹⁵ with its tributary wadis, stretched along the settled country of Ar, hugging the territory of Moab . . ."

¹⁶ And from there to Beer,ᶜ which is the well where the LORD said to Moses, "Assemble the people that I may give them water." ¹⁷ Then Israel sang this song:

Spring up, O well—sing to it—
18   The well which the chieftains dug,
        Which the nobles of the people started
        With maces, with their own staffs.

And from Midbarᵈ to Mattanah, ¹⁹ and from Mattanah to Nahaliel, and from Nahaliel to Bamoth, ²⁰ and from Bamoth to the valley that is in the country of Moab, at the peak of Pisgah, overlooking the wasteland.ᵉ

²¹ Israel now sent messengers to Sihon king of the Amorites, saying, ²² "Let me pass through your country. We will not turn off into fields or vineyards, and we will not drink water from wells. We will follow the king's highway until we have crossed your territory." ²³ But Sihon would not let Israel pass through his territory. Sihon gathered all his people and went out against Israel in the wilderness. He came

This *miserable food* refers to the manna. **6:** *Seraph serpents*, based on the verb, means "burning serpents," because of their poisonous bite. **9:** *A copper serpent* more likely refers to one made of bronze, a copper-tin alloy. Heb "neḥoshet" (copper) resembles the word for snake, "naḥash." Rabbinic interpreters were disturbed by the magical nature of this cure, and suggested that it was the glance of the afflicted to their father in heaven, rather than the snake, which effected the cure (*b. Rosh Hash.* 29a, cited in Rashi).
10–20: This subsection summarizes Israel's trek through Transjordan (cf. 33.41–49); another similar list is found in 33.1–49. **14:** *Book of the Wars of the LORD* is a reference to an ancient collection, not extant, probably epic poems describing Israel's battles (cf. Book of Jashar in Josh. 10.13; 2 Sam. 1.18).
17–18: The song of the well celebrates God providing Israel with water (cf. Song at the Sea, Exod. 15.1–18; Song of Deborah, Judg. ch 5). It is an etiology for the toponym Beer, "well" (v. 16).
21.21–22.1: The conquest narrative actually begins here with Israel's triumph over two Amorite kinglets in Transjordan. Accounts of victories in Transjordan provide the backdrop for settlement in that region by the tribes of Reuben, Gad, and half of Manasseh. **21.21–32:** Israel must conquer the Amorite king Sihon in order to advance. The territory ruled by Sihon is in Moab; apparently it has changed hands.

───────────────

a Cf. Isa. 14.29; 30.6. Others "fiery"; exact meaning of Heb. saraph uncertain.
b The quotation that follows is a fragment; text and meaning are uncertain.
c Lit. "well."   *d* Septuagint "the well" (= Beer); cf. v. 16.   *e* Or "Jeshimon."

to Jahaz and engaged Israel in battle. ²⁴ But Israel put them to the sword, and took possession of their land, from the Arnon to the Jabbok, as far as [Az] of the Ammonites, for Az^a marked the boundary of the Ammonites. ²⁵ Israel took all those towns. And Israel settled in all the towns of the Amorites, in Heshbon and all its dependencies.

²⁶ Now Heshbon was the city of Sihon king of the Amorites, who had fought against a former king of Moab and taken all his land from him as far as the Arnon. ²⁷ Therefore the bards would recite:

^b"Come to Heshbon; firmly built
And well founded is Sihon's city.

28 For fire went forth from Heshbon,
Flame from Sihon's city,
Consuming Ar of Moab,
The lords of Bamoth^c by the Arnon.

29 Woe to you, O Moab!
You are undone, O people of Chemosh!
His sons are rendered fugitive
And his daughters captive
By an Amorite king, Sihon."

30^d Yet we have cast them down utterly,
Heshbon along with Dibon;
We have wrought desolation at Nophah,
Which is hard by Medeba.

³¹ So Israel occupied the land of the Amorites. ³² Then Moses sent to spy out Jazer, and they captured its dependencies and dispossessed the Amorites who were there.

³³ They marched on and went up the road to Bashan, and King Og of Bashan, with all his people, came out to Edrei to engage them in battle. ³⁴ But the LORD said to Moses, "Do not fear him, for I give him and all his people and his land into your hand. You shall do to him as you did to Sihon king of the Amorites who dwelt in Heshbon." ³⁵ They defeated him and his sons and all his people, until no remnant was left him; and they took possession **22** of his country. ¹ The Israelites then marched on and encamped in the steppes of Moab, across the Jordan from Jericho.

27–30: The ballad of Heshbon celebrates Sihon's conquest of Moabite territory. Various theories have been proposed as to why it is preserved in the Bible. According to the Rabbis, it justifies Israel's defeat of Sihon (*Num. Rab.* 19.30). Israel was prohibited from provoking the Moabites to battle (Deut. 2.9). **29:** *Chemosh* is the national god of the Moabites. **33–35:** The record of the victory over Og king of the Bashan region (see map on p. 498) parallels Deut. 3.1–2. In this encounter God directs the military action. **22.1:** This v., which also contextualizes the subsequent Balaam pericope, is a postscript to ch 21.

a Septuagint "Jazer," cf. v. 32. Others "for the boundary of the Ammonites was strong."
b The meaning of several parts of this ancient poem is no longer certain.
c Cf. vv. 19 and 20 and Num. 22.21.
d Meaning of verse uncertain. Alternatively:
"Their dominion is at an end
From Heshbon to Dibon
And from Nashim to Nophah,
Which is hard by Medeba."

BALAK בלק

2 Balak son of Zippor saw all that Israel had done to the Amorites.

3 Moab was alarmed because that people was so numerous. Moab dreaded the Israelites, 4 and Moab said to the elders of Midian, "Now this horde will lick clean all that is about us as an ox licks up the grass of the field."

Balak son of Zippor, who was king of Moab at that time, 5 sent messengers to Balaam son of Beor in Pethor, which is by the Euphrates,ᵃ in the land of his kinsfolk, to invite him, saying, "There is a people that came out of Egypt; it hides the earth from view, and it is settled next to me. 6 Come then, put a curse upon this people for me, since they are too numerous for me; perhaps I can thus defeat them and drive them out of the land. For I know that he whom you bless is blessed indeed, and he whom you curse is cursed."

7 The elders of Moab and the elders of Midian, ᵇ versed in divination,ᵇ set out. They came to Balaam and gave him Balak's message. 8 He said to them, "Spend the night here, and I shall reply to you as the LORD may instruct me." So the Moabite dignitaries stayed with Balaam.

a Lit. "the River."
b-b Lit. "with divination in their power (hand)."

22.2–24.25: The story of the seer Balaam. Inserted into the narrative of Israel's final preparation to enter Canaan is the story of the Moabite king Balak and the prophet Balaam whom he hires to curse Israel into oblivion. This independent composition, possibly originating from a different scribal circle than those associated with other portions of Numbers, is composed of narrative and poetry. It is inserted at this juncture, the beginning of Israel's period of encampment in Moab, because the outcome of Balak's scheme determines if Israel will inherit the promised land. The account is a contest in the divine realm between the God of Israel and those supernatural elements available to Balak. At times amusing, and somewhat mocking of the non-Israelite prophet, the message of this pericope is serious: The intent of the LORD reigns supreme and cannot be superseded. Even the

powers of a well-known non-Israelite prophet are ultimately controlled by God. In the end nothing in Balaam's four oracles exacts a curse upon Israel; in fact, his prophecies function in reverse, blessing Israel and cursing her enemies. The biblical traditions are not consistent in their assessment of Balaam's intentions. In Deuteronomy (23.4–7) and Joshua (24.9–10) it is God who reverses Balaam's actual intent. Num. 31.16 blames Balaam for Israel's apostasy at Baal-peor (ch 25), implying that he previously sought to curse them. The memory preserved in the writings of the 8th-century BCE prophet Micah (6.5) is more compatible with most of the favorable Num. chs 22–24 accounts. Postbiblical literature is divided as well in evaluations of Balaam (cf. Tg. Num. chs 22–24; Num. Rab. 14.20). A visionary named Balaam is attested outside the Bible, on a frag-

mentary inscription on wall plaster (late 9th to 8th century) from a temple at Deir ʿAlla in Transjordan, which records the night vision of a certain Balaam. The seer Balaam may have been a legendary character of antiquity or a real person well known in the region.

The complete biblical story of Balaam is composed of several subsections: (1) Balak hires Balaam to curse Israel (22.2–40). Within this narrative is inserted the tale of Balaam and his talking she-ass (22.21–35). (2) Balaam's first oracle (22.41–23.10); (3) Balak's response and Balaam's second oracle (23.11–24); (4) Balak's response and Balaam's third oracle (23.25–24.9); (5) Balak's response and Balaam's fourth oracle; their departure (24.10–25). Each subsection containing an oracle is composed of narrative followed by a poem (the oracle). If read detached from the narrative, the four poems connect to tell the story in poetic form. The entire poem may thus derive from an older independent source. Like much biblical poetry, this poem contains many words and phrases that are obscure or possibly have become corrupted over time.

22.2–40: Balak hires Balaam to curse Israel. 4: *The elders of Midian* refers to the leaders of Midianite groups who lived in Moab (cf. Gen. 36.35). **5:** *Balaam son of Beor in Pethor:* The seer of the Deir ʿAlla inscription bears the same name and patronymic. The place name Pethor, Balaam's home, is identified as a site on the Sajur River in Aram (Syria) some 400 miles from Moab. **6–7:** Balaam apparently has a reputation not only as a seer, but also as a diviner who can effectuate curses. The elders of Moab and Midian, sent to fetch him, are versed in divinatory techniques. Execration texts on pottery cursing rulers of Canaanite cities are known from Egypt (early 2nd millennium). Prophets from the same period are mentioned in letters from the Mesopotamian city-state of Mari. **8–21:** The biblical writer

9 God came to Balaam and said, "What do these people want of you?" 10 Balaam said to God, "Balak son of Zippor, king of Moab, sent me this message: 11 Here is a people that came out from Egypt and hides the earth from view. Come now and curse them for me; perhaps I can engage them in battle and drive them off." 12 But God said to Balaam, "Do not go with them. You must not curse that people, for they are blessed."

13 Balaam arose in the morning and said to Balak's dignitaries, "Go back to your own country, for the LORD will not let me go with you." 14 The Moabite dignitaries left, and they came to Balak and said, "Balaam refused to come with us."

15 Then Balak sent other dignitaries, more numerous and distinguished than the first. 16 They came to Balaam and said to him, "Thus says Balak son of Zippor: Please do not refuse to come to me. 17 I will reward you richly and I will do anything you ask of me. Only come and damn this people for me." 18 Balaam replied to Balak's officials, "Though Balak were to give me his house full of silver and gold, I could not do anything, big or little, contrary to the command of the LORD my God. 19 So you, too, stay here overnight, and let me find out what else the LORD may say to me." 20 That night God came to Balaam and said to him, "If these men have come to invite you, you may go with them. But whatever I command you, that you shall do."

21 When he arose in the morning, Balaam saddled his ass and departed with the Moabite dignitaries. 22 But God was incensed at his going; so an angel of the LORD placed himself in his way as an adversary.

He was riding on his she-ass, with his two servants alongside, 23 when the ass caught sight of the angel of the LORD standing in the way, with his drawn sword in his hand. The ass swerved from the road and went into the fields; and Balaam beat the ass to turn her back onto the road. 24 The angel of the LORD then stationed himself in a lane between the vineyards, with a fence on either side. 25 The ass, seeing the angel of the LORD, pressed herself against the wall and squeezed Balaam's foot against the wall; so he beat her again. 26 Once more the angel of the LORD moved forward and stationed himself on a spot so narrow that there was no room to swerve right or left. 27 When the ass now saw the angel of the LORD, she lay down under Balaam; and Balaam was furious and beat the ass with his stick.

28 Then the LORD opened the ass's mouth, and she said to Balaam, "What have I done to you that you have beaten

makes it clear that the Israelites are a blessed people. In this account, which views Balaam postively, his words and actions are bound to God's will and no reward of riches can enable him to counter it.

22–35: This episode of Balaam and the she-ass derives from a different tradition that contradicts the favorable view of Balaam expressed by the main story (contrast esp. v. 20). In this version God is angry with the prophet (v. 22) and in turn depicts the donkey as the actual visionary. Balaam becomes the object of mockery: He is portrayed as being blind to divine will; it is the ass that sees what the seer cannot. **22:** *As an adversary:* In the Bible the term "satan" is used attributively (1 Sam. 29.4), or when personified it refers to a divine being who answers to God (Job 1.6–12; 1 Chron. 21.1), rather than to an independent entity who is God's adversary ("Satan"). The concept only later developed into the "Devil." **36–40:** Balak offers a sacrifice of well-being, which is eaten by Balaam and his entourage.

me these three times?" 29 Balaam said to the ass, "You have made a mockery of me! If I had a sword with me, I'd kill you." 30 The ass said to Balaam, "Look, I am the ass that you have been riding all along until this day! Have I been in the habit of doing thus to you?" And he answered, "No."

31 Then the LORD uncovered Balaam's eyes, and he saw the angel of the LORD standing in the way, his drawn sword in his hand; thereupon he bowed ᵃright down to the ground.ᵃ 32 The angel of the LORD said to him, "Why have you beaten your ass these three times? It is I who came out as an adversary, for the errand is obnoxiousᵇ to me. 33 And when the ass saw me, she shied away because of me those three times. If she had not shied away from me, you are the one I should have killed, while sparing her." 34 Balaam said to the angel of the LORD, "I erred because I did not know that you were standing in my way. If you still disapprove, I will turn back." 35 But the angel of the LORD said to Balaam, "Go with the men. But you must say nothing except what I tell you." So Balaam went on with Balak's dignitaries.

36 When Balak heard that Balaam was coming, he went out to meet him at Ir-moab, which is on the Arnon border, at its farthest point. 37 Balak said to Balaam, "When I first sent to invite you, why didn't you come to me? Am I really unable to reward you?" 38 But Balaam said to Balak, "And now that I have come to you, have I the power to speak freely? I can utter only the word that God puts into my mouth."

39 Balaam went with Balak and they came to Kiriath-huzoth.

40 Balak sacrificed oxen and sheep, and had them served to Balaam and the dignitaries with him. 41 In the morning Balak took Balaam up to Bamoth-baal. From there he could see a portion of the people.

23 Balaam said to Balak, "Build me seven altars here and have seven bulls and seven rams ready here for me." 2 Balak did as Balaam directed; and Balak and Balaam offered up a bull and a ram on each altar. 3 Then Balaam said to Balak, "Stay here beside your offerings while I am gone. Perhaps the LORD will grant me a manifestation, and whatever He reveals to me I will tell you." And he went off alone.ᶜ

---

a-a Lit. "and prostrated himself to his nostrils."
b Precise meaning of Heb. uncertain.
c Others "to a bare height"; exact meaning of Heb. shephi uncertain.

22.41–23.10: Balaam's first oracle.
23.1: Seven is a magical number in the Bible, often signaling complete perfection (cf. Josh. 6.4; 1 Kings 18.43; 2 Kings 5.10, 14), and is frequent in Northwest Semitic literature. In connection with sacrifices the number seven corresponds to the seven bulls and seven rams which God commands Job's friends to offer (Job 42.8). Balaam's offerings seem to invoke the deity's message. Ibn Ezra notes the frequency of the number seven in the cultic calendar.

⁴God manifested Himself to Balaam, who said to Him, "I have set up the seven altars and offered up a bull and a ram on each altar." ⁵And the LORD put a word in Balaam's mouth and said, "Return to Balak and speak thus."

⁶So he returned to him and found him standing beside his offerings, and all the Moabite dignitaries with him. ⁷He took up his theme, and said:

> From Aram has Balak brought me,
> Moab's king from the hills of the East:
> Come, curse me Jacob,
> Come, tell Israel's doom!
> 8 How can I damn whom God*ᵃ* has not damned,
>   How doom when the LORD has not doomed?
> 9 As I see them from the mountain tops,
>   Gaze on them from the heights,
>   There is a people that dwells apart,
>   Not reckoned among the nations,
> 10 Who can count the dustᵇ of Jacob,
>   Numberᶜ the dust-cloud of Israel?
>   May I die the death of the upright,ᵈ
>   May my fate be like theirs!

¹¹Then Balak said to Balaam, "What have you done to me? Here I brought you to damn my enemies, and instead you have blessed them!" ¹²He replied, "I can only repeat faithfully what the LORD puts in my mouth." ¹³Then Balak said to him, "Come with me to another place from which you can see them—you will see only a portion of them; you will not see all of them—and damn them for me from there." ¹⁴With that, he took him to Sedehzophim,ᵉ on the summit of Pisgah. He built seven altars and offered a bull and a ram on each altar. ¹⁵And [Balaam] said to Balak, "Stay here beside your offerings, while I seek a manifestation yonder."

¹⁶The LORD manifested Himself to Balaam and put a word in his mouth, saying, "Return to Balak and speak thus." ¹⁷He went to him and found him standing beside his offerings, and the Moabite dignitaries with him. Balak asked him, "What did the LORD say?" ¹⁸And he took up his theme, and said:

> Up, Balak, attend,
> Give ear unto me, son of Zippor!

8: The deity name "El," probably short for "Elohim," God, appears in parallel construction to the Tetragrammaton (YHVH). Some scholars believe that the designations refer to two separate deities, El being the Canaanite high God also worshipped by Israel. **8:** This is a poetic variant of the idea expressed in prose in 22.18. More extensive prose and poetic variants of the same story are found in Exod. chs 14–15 and Judg. chs 4–5. **10:** Balak's fear that the Israelite multitude will be triumphant (22.3) is confirmed already in Balaam's first oracle. *Who can count the dust of Jacob* reverberates the patriarchal blessing (Gen. 13.16). This English translation assumes a textual error, that the single Heb word "umispar" ("and the number of") should be read as two words: "umiy safar" ("[who can] number"). The parallelism of the verse supports this emendation.

23.11–24: The second oracle. 11–17: Sandwiched between the poems of the first and second oracles is a narrative section containing reactions to the initial poem. In a dialogue between Balak and Balaam, Balak expresses shock at Balaam's blessing of Israel; Balaam responds with a disclaimer to his own words. Balak then attempts to elicit a curse from Balaam by having the prophet view the Israelite camp from a less threatening angle. Fresh sacrifices need to be offered to attain another vision. The narrator is mocking Balak, who fails to understand that God's desire may not be contravened in this manner. **18–24:** The poem of the second oracle underscores the message of the first. Emphasis is placed on God's constancy in general and specifically in connection with His devotion to Israel's welfare. Other gods may be capricious, subject to human manipulation through magic, but the LORD is not.

---

a Heb. El, as often in these poems.   *b Cf. Gen. 13.16.*   *c Lit. "and the number of."*
d Heb. yesharim, a play on yeshurun (Jeshurun in Deut. 32.15), a name for Israel.
e Or "Lookout Point."

19 God is not man to be capricious,
Or mortal to change His mind.
Would He speak and not act,
Promise and not fulfill?

20 My message was to bless:
When He blesses, I cannot reverse it.

21 No harm is in sight for Jacob,
No woe in view for Israel.
The LORD their God is with them,
And their King's acclaim in their midst.

22 God who freed them from Egypt
Is for them like the hornsᵃ of the wild ox.

23 Lo, there is no augury in Jacob,
No divining in Israel:ᵇ
Jacob is told at once,
Yea Israel, what God has planned.ᶜ

24 Lo, a people that rises like a lion,
Leaps up like the ᵈking of beasts,ᵈ
Rests not till it has feasted on prey
And drunk the blood of the slain.

25 Thereupon Balak said to Balaam, "Don't curse them and don't bless them!" 26 In reply, Balaam said to Balak, "But I told you: Whatever the LORD says, that I must do." 27 Then Balak said to Balaam, "Come now, I will take you to another place. Perhaps God will deem it right that you damn them for me there." 28 Balak took Balaam to the peak of Peor, which overlooks the wasteland.ᵉ 29 Balaam said to Balak, "Build me here seven altars, and have seven bulls and seven rams ready for me here." 30 Balak did as Balaam said: he offered up a bull and a ram on each altar.

24 Now Balaam, seeing that it pleased the LORD to bless Israel, did not, as on previous occasions, go in search of omens, but turned his face toward the wilderness. 2 As Balaam looked up and saw Israel encamped tribe by tribe, the spirit of God came upon him. 3 Taking up his theme, he said:

ᶠWord of Balaam son of Beor,
Word of the man whose eye is true,ᵍ

22: The redemption from Egypt is cited as evidence of God's power and allegiance to Israel. **24:** The simile of a lion previews Israel's military victories and kingdom in Canaan (cf. Gen. 49.9–10).

23.25–24.9: The third oracle.
23.25–24.2: In this second narrative segment between oracles, Balak, in distress, wants to abandon cursing Israel if that will nullify the blessing. The foolish Moabite king, in contrast to the seer, is not resigned to God's will as a fait accompli. Sacrifices are offered for the third time from yet another location. This time Balaam does not search for omens in the process of seeking divine spirit, implying that he did so previously. **2:** For the first time Balaam views the entire Israelite camp (cf. 22.41; 23.13). **3–4:** Balaam opens this oracle with self-praise. He considers himself a true prophet of God.

---

a Lit. "eminences," used figuratively.
b Cf. Deut. 18.10–15.
c Or, "Else would it be told to Jacob, / Yea to Israel, what God has planned."
d-d Heb. 'ari, another term for "lion."
e Cf. note on 21.20.
f Some of the poetic portions of this chapter are unclear.
g Others "whose eye is (or, eyes are) open"; meaning of Heb. uncertain.

4   Word of him who hears God's speech,
    Who beholds visions from the Almighty,
    Prostrate, but with eyes unveiled:
5   How fair are your tents, O Jacob,
    Your dwellings, O Israel!
6   Like palm-groves that stretch out,
    Like gardens beside a river,
    Like aloes planted by the LORD,
    Like cedars beside the water;
7   Their boughs drip with moisture,
    Their roots[a] have abundant water.
    Their king shall rise above Agag,
    Their kingdom shall be exalted.
8   God who freed them from Egypt
    Is for them like the horns[b] of the wild ox.
    They shall devour enemy nations,
    Crush their bones,
    And smash their arrows.
9   They crouch, they lie down like a lion,
    Like the king of beasts;[c] who dare rouse them?
    Blessed are they who bless you,
    Accursed they who curse you!

10 Enraged at Balaam, Balak struck his hands together. "I called you," Balak said to Balaam, "to damn my enemies, and instead you have blessed them these three times! 11 Back with you at once to your own place! I was going to reward you richly, but the LORD has denied you the reward." 12 Balaam replied to Balak, "But I even told the messengers you sent to me, 13 'Though Balak were to give me his house full of silver and gold, I could not of my own accord do anything good or bad contrary to the LORD's command. What the LORD says, that I must say.' 14 And now, as I go back to my people, let me inform you of what this people will do to your people in days to come." 15 He took up his theme, and said:

    Word of Balaam son of Beor,
    Word of the man whose eye is true,
16 Word of him who hears God's speech,
    Who obtains knowledge from the Most High,
    And beholds visions from the Almighty,
    Prostrate, but with eyes unveiled:
17 What I see for them is not yet,
    What I behold will not be soon:

a Lit. "and its seed."   b See note at 23.22.
c Heb. labi, another word for "lion"; cf. note at 23.24.

4: *The Almighty* (also v. 16): Heb "shadai" is an epithet of God common in the patriarchal stories (e.g., Gen. 17.1; 28.3; 35.11). Its likely meaning, "high," is related to the Akkadian term for mountain. **5:** This idyllic portrayal of the Israelites in their homes is noted in the midrash. In Jewish liturgy this line begins the daily morning service, since *tents* and *dwellings* are understood to refer to the synagogue. **6–7:** The depiction of lush vegetation contrasts with the wilderness background of Balaam's view of Israel's encampment (24.1). **7:** *Agag* is the king of Amalek at the time of Saul's reign (1 Sam. 15.8). Saul's victory is foretold here, suggesting to many scholars a date for the text in the monarchic period. **8–9:** The oracle ends by returning to the lion imagery at the end of the previous oracle (23.24), and reiterating the promise to the patriarchs that anyone who blesses Israel will be blessed in turn, but anyone who curses her is himself cursed (Gen. 12.3; 27.29).

24.10–25: The fourth oracle. 10–14: Balak's reaction to Balaam's third oracle is one of outrage, no doubt exacerbated by the pronouncement that he who curses Israel will be cursed in turn. Balak sends Balaam home. **10:** *Balak struck his hands together:* This is a gesture of anguish and anger (cf. Ezek. 6.11; 21.19, 22; 22.13; Lam. 2.15). **15–25:** Before returning to his home, Balaam utters one more oracle, this one containing a prophecy about Moab's future and that of Israel's other enemies. A very common pattern in biblical literature, followed here, is the 3–4 pattern, where the fourth element is climactic. **17:** This v. predicts the destruction of Moab by an Israelite king. Either David or Omri qualifies (2 Sam. 8.2; the Mesha [or Moabite] Stone). This v. played a significant role in the 2nd century CE, when the star (Heb "kokhav") was connected by some to Bar Kosba, a Jewish leader who headed an unsuccessful revolt against Rome in 132–35. Based on

A star rises from Jacob,
A scepter comes forth from Israel;
It smashes the brow of Moab,
The foundation of[a] all children of Seth.

18   Edom becomes a possession,
Yea, Seir a possession of its enemies;
But Israel is triumphant.

19   A victor issues from Jacob
To wipe out what is left of Ir.

20 He saw Amalek and, taking up his theme, he said:
A leading nation is Amalek;
But its fate is to perish forever.

21 He saw the Kenites and, taking up his theme, he said:
Though your abode be secure,
And your nest be set among cliffs,

22   Yet shall Kain[b] be consumed,
When Asshur takes you captive.

23 He took up his theme and said:
Alas, who can survive except God has willed it!

24   Ships come from the quarter of Kittim;
They subject Asshur, subject Eber.
They, too, shall perish forever.

25 Then Balaam set out on his journey back home; and
Balak also went his way.

25 While Israel was staying at Shittim, the people
[c]profaned themselves by whoring[c] with the Moabite women, 2 who invited the people to the sacrifices for
their god. The people partook of them and worshiped that
god. 3 Thus Israel attached itself to Baal-peor, and the
LORD was incensed with Israel. 4 The LORD said to Moses,

a Samaritan "the pate of," cf. Jer. 48.45; others "breaks down."
b I.e., the Kenites.
c-c Others "began to commit harlotry."

this verse, some sages renamed
this leader as Bar Kokhba, "the son
of the star," and viewed him as a
messianic figure (see esp. y.Taʿan.
68d). The revolt was a miserable
failure. 18–24: Balaam predicts the
conquest of several national or ethnic groups, including Edomites,
Amalekites, and Midianites. Kittim, people from Cyprus, are mentioned as invaders into the region

of Syria and Mesopotamia; the historical setting for this is unclear. In
the Dead Sea Scrolls, "Kittim" represents the Romans. 25: The narrative ends with Balaam and Balak
returning home, the latter's mission having failed.

25.1–19: Worship of Baal-peor
and its aftermath. Ch 25 continues
the narrative begun in 22.1, which

was interrupted by the insertion of
the story of Balak and Balaam.
While encamped on the plains of
Moab awaiting crossing into Canaan, Israelite men mingle with
local, non-Israelite women. As
predicted in warnings to Israel
(Exod. 34.16; cf. 1 Kings 11.1–6),
marriage with idolaters leads to
idolatry, in this case worship of the
local god Baal-peor. This chapter
can be divided into three smaller
segments: vv. 1–5, 6–9, and 10–19.
Scholars often attribute the latter
two segments to a Priestly expansion of the first five verses, a JE account. In P's rendition, the role of
Phinehas, Aaron's grandson, is
central in the expiation process of
the sin (vv. 7–18), even supersed-
ing that of Moses. Furthermore, it
offers historical support for the divine appointment of the Aaronide
priesthood. Memory of Israel's
apostasy of Baal-peor and subsequent punishment is preserved in
several biblical accounts outside
the book of Numbers (cf. Deut. 4.3;
Josh. 22.17; Hos. 9.10; Ps. 106.28).
1: Ramban suggests that it was
Balaam's evil advice that provoked the incident. Otherwise,
he reasons, why would the Israelites have killed Balaam (31.8)?
2–3: Ps. 106 identifies the sacrificial feast as a ritual associated with
a funerary cult. Baal-peor is the
local manifestation of the fertility
storm-god Baal, the high god of
Canaanite religion; Peor is a geographic name previously mentioned in the Balaam saga (23.28;
also Deut. 3.29). The calf image
that Israel fashioned of gold and
then worshiped at Sinai (Exod.
ch 32) is a common representation
of the deity Baal, apparently, as
well as the LORD in the sanctuaries
of Dan and Bethel (see 1 Kings
12.28–29). 4: Take all the ringleaders
and have them publicly impaled.
Ringleaders is an interpretive translation of the Heb. A literal understanding, "all the heads of the people," implies that the leadership,
both guilty individuals and innocent ones, are liable for the
people's action. Their execution
and subsequent public impalement is to serve as expiation for

"Take all the ringleaders[a] and have them publicly[b] impaled before the LORD, so that the LORD's wrath may turn away from Israel." [5] So Moses said to Israel's officials, "Each of you slay those of his men who attached themselves to Baal-peor."

[6] Just then one of the Israelites came and brought a Midianite woman over to his companions, in the sight of Moses and of the whole Israelite community who were weeping at the entrance of the Tent of Meeting. [7] When Phinehas, son of Eleazar son of Aaron the priest, saw this, he left the assembly and, taking a spear in his hand, [8] he followed the Israelite into the chamber and stabbed both of them, the Israelite and the woman, through the belly. Then the plague against the Israelites was checked. [9] Those who died of the plague numbered twenty-four thousand.

PINHAS   פינחס

[10] The LORD spoke to Moses, saying, [11] "Phinehas, son of Eleazar son of Aaron the priest, has turned back My wrath from the Israelites by displaying among them his passion for Me, so that I did not wipe out the Israelite people in My passion. [12] Say, therefore, 'I grant him My pact of friendship. [13] It shall be for him and his descendants after him a pact of priesthood for all time, because he took impassioned action for his God, thus making expiation for the Israelites.' "

[14] The name of the Israelite who was killed, the one who was killed with the Midianite woman, was Zimri son of Salu, chieftain of a Simeonite ancestral house. [15] The name of the Midianite woman who was killed was Cozbi daughter of Zur; he was the tribal head of an ancestral house in Midian.

[16] The LORD spoke to Moses, saying, [17] "Assail the Midianites and defeat them—[18] for they assailed you by the trickery they practiced against you—because of the affair of Peor and because of the affair of their kinswoman Cozbi, daughter of the Midianite chieftain, who was killed at the time of the plague on account of Peor."

26 [19] When the plague was over, [1] the LORD said to Moses and to Eleazar son of Aaron the priest, [2] "Take a census of the whole Israelite community from

a Lit. "heads of the people."   b Others "in face of the sun."

Israel's violation of the Sinaitic covenant, which prohibits foreign worship. Similarly, Saul's sons are executed and publicly impaled for their father's violation of a treaty with the Gibeonites (2 Sam. 21.1–14). In that case, a drought, attributed to the violation of the oath, ends when the princes' deaths appease the deity. In both cases, extreme measures need to be taken to control the divine wrath. **5:** Moses seems to intercede here (cf. 11.2; 14.13–19; 16.22), instructing Israel's officials to slay only the guilty (cf. the role of the Levites in Exod. 32.25–29). **6–9:** The Israelite man is later identified as Zimri son of Salu, a chieftain of Simeon (v. 14); the woman is Cozbi daughter of Zur, a Midianite chief (v. 15). Thus, both are influential members of their respective communities. **6:** For the association of Midianites and Moabites (v. 1), see 22.4 n. **8:** *The chamber,* Heb "ha-kubah," probably refers to a tent (also in Arabic) that is part of the cultic area, rendering the transgression as pagan worship. No evidence exists, however, for any act of cultic prostitution. **9:** Those who died in the plague would have included any remnant of the exodus generation (26.64–65). **10–13:** God rewards Phinehas's zealous act, which appeases His wrath and makes expiation for Israel (cf. Aaron's act, 17.11–12), with a *pact of friendship* guaranteeing divine protection (cf. Isa. 54.10; Ezek. 34.25; 37.26). A *pact of priesthood for all time* reiterates the eternal and exclusive election of the Aaronides to the priesthood (chs 16–17). **16–19:** God's command that Israel take vengeance on the Midianites for their part in the apostasy of Baal-peor is realized in the continuation of this account in ch 31, where v. 1 completes the verse fragment of 25.19 (for the association of Midianites and Moabites, see 22.4 n.). Thus, chs 26–30 have been placed here secondarily.

26.1–65: The second census. Initially, the Israelites were counted at Sinai prior to their forty-year wilderness trek (ch 1). That population consisted of the exodus generation. This second census takes place after the death of that entire population (26.64). Levites are again numbered separately (cf. 3.14–39). The statistics of the second census are necessary for determining the allotment of the land of Canaan (see Josh. chs 14–19), the

the age of twenty years up, by their ancestral houses, all Israelites able to bear arms." [3] [a]So Moses and Eleazar the priest, on the steppes of Moab, at the Jordan near Jericho, gave instructions about them, namely, [4] those from twenty years up, as the LORD had commanded Moses.

The descendants of the Israelites who came out of the land of Egypt were:

[5] Reuben, Israel's first-born. Descendants of Reuben: [Of] Enoch,[b] the clan of the Enochites; of Pallu, the clan of the Palluites; [6] of Hezron, the clan of the Hezronites; of Carmi, the clan of the Carmites. [7] Those are the clans of the Reubenites. The persons enrolled came to 43,730.

[8] [c]Born to[c] Pallu: Eliab. [9] The sons of Eliab were Nemuel, and Dathan and Abiram. These are the same Dathan and Abiram, chosen in the assembly, who agitated against Moses and Aaron as part of Korah's band when they agitated against the LORD. [10] Whereupon the earth opened its mouth and swallowed them up with Korah—when that band died, when the fire consumed the two hundred and fifty men—and they became an example. [11] The sons of Korah, however, did not die.

[12] Descendants of Simeon by their clans: Of Nemuel, the clan of the Nemuelites; of Jamin, the clan of the Jaminites; of Jachin, the clan of the Jachinites; [13] of Zerah, the clan of the Zerahites; of Saul,[d] the clan of the Saulites. [14] Those are the clans of the Simeonites; [persons enrolled:] 22,200.

[15] Descendants of Gad by their clans: Of Zephon, the clan of the Zephonites; of Haggi, the clan of the Haggites; of Shuni, the clan of the Shunites; [16] of Ozni, the clan of the Oznites; of Eri, the clan of the Erites; [17] of Arod, the clan of the Arodites; of Areli, the clan of the Arelites. [18] Those are the clans of Gad's descendants; persons enrolled: 40,500.

[19] [c]Born to[c] Judah: Er and Onan. Er and Onan died in the land of Canaan.

[20] Descendants of Judah by their clans: Of Shelah, the clan of the Shelanites; of Perez, the clan of the Perezites; of Zerah, the clan of the Zerahites. [21] Descendants of Perez: of Hezron, the clan of the Hezronites; of Hamul, the clan of the Hamulites. [22] Those are the clans of Judah; persons enrolled: 76,500.

[23] Descendants of Issachar by their clans: [Of] Tola, the clan of the Tolaites; of Puvah, the clan of the Punites; [24] of Jashub, the clan of the Jashubites; of Shimron, the clan of the Shimronites. [25] Those are the clans of Issachar; persons enrolled: 64,300.

subject of the end of this chapter (vv. 52–56). This chapter also precedes a major battle, the war against the Midianites (ch 31), since a count of military-age males is required in preparation for this battle and for others planned in the conquest of Canaan. **1–4:** The instructions for the second census, like the first, come directly from God who addresses both Moses and the current high priest (cf. 1.1–3). **5–51:** The Israelites are numbered by tribes, excluding Levi. Each tribe's total is derived from the sum of its clans. Whereas clan chieftains are named in connection with the first census (1.5–15), the names of the clans appear in the account of the second census. Some scholars attempt to understand these vast, unrealistic numbers symbolically. **9–11:** These verses recall the fate of the Reubenites Dathan and Abiram who were part of the Korah rebellion (chs 16–17). Similar short notices are sometimes placed in the genealogies that open Chronicles.

---

a Meaning of parts of vv. 3 and 4 uncertain.   b Or "Hanoch."
c-c Or "descendants of."   d Or "Shaul."

26 Descendants of Zebulun by their clans: Of Sered, the clan of the Seredites; of Elon, the clan of the Elonites; of Jahleel, the clan of the Jahleelites. 27 Those are the clans of the Zebulunites; persons enrolled: 60,500.

28 The sons of Joseph were Manasseh and Ephraim—by their clans.

29 Descendants of Manasseh: Of Machir, the clan of the Machirites.—Machir begot Gilead.—Of Gilead, the clan of the Gileadites. 30 These were the descendants of Gilead: [Of] Iezer, the clan of the Iezerites; of Helek, the clan of the Helekites; 31 [of] Asriel, the clan of the Asrielites; [of] Shechem, the clan of the Shechemites; 32 [of] Shemida, the clan of the Shemidaites; [of] Hepher, the clan of the Hepherites.—33 Now Zelophehad son of Hepher had no sons, only daughters. The names of Zelophehad's daughters were Mahlah, Noah, Hoglah, Milcah, and Tirzah.—34 Those are the clans of Manasseh; persons enrolled: 52,700.

35 These are the descendants of Ephraim by their clans: Of Shuthelah, the clan of the Shuthelahites; of Becher, the clan of the Becherites; of Tahan, the clan of the Tahanites. 36 These are the descendants of Shuthelah: Of Eran, the clan of the Eranites. 37 Those are the clans of Ephraim's descendants; persons enrolled: 32,500.

Those are the descendants of Joseph by their clans.

38 The descendants of Benjamin by their clans: Of Bela, the clan of the Belaites; of Ashbel, the clan of the Ashbelites; of Ahiram, the clan of the Ahiramites; 39 of Shephupham, the clan of the Shuphamites; of Hupham, the clan of the Huphamites. 40 The sons of Bela were Ard and Naaman: [Of Ard,] the clan of the Ardites; of Naaman, the clan of the Naamanites. 41 Those are the descendants of Benjamin by their clans; persons enrolled: 45,600.

42 These are the descendants of Dan by their clans: Of Shuham, the clan of the Shuhamites. Those are the clans of Dan,ᵃ by their clans. 43 All the clans of the Shuhamites; persons enrolled: 64,400.

44 Descendants of Asher by their clans: Of Imnah, the clan of the Imnites; of Ishvi, the clan of the Ishvites; of Beriah, the clan of the Beriites. 45 Of the descendants of Beriah: Of Heber, the clan of the Heberites; of Malchiel, the clan of the Malchielites.—46 The name of Asher's daughter was Serah.—47 These are the clans of Asher's descendants; persons enrolled: 53,400.

48 Descendants of Naphtali by their clans: Of Jahzeel, the clan of the Jahzeelites; of Guni, the clan of the Gunites;

29–34: The tribe of Manasseh increases in size more than any other tribe (five tribes decrease in number), almost doubling its population (cf. 1.34–35). Five Manassite clan names (Iezer [= Abiezer], Helek, Asriel, Shechem, and Shemida) and two names of Zelophehad's daughters (Noah and Hoglah) appear as place names on the Samaria Ostraca pottery sherds from the 8th century BCE inscribed as receipts for wine and oil, which were excavated in the remains of the palace complex at Samaria. Thus, it is possible that the names mentioned in this chapter do not refer to actual individuals, but to geographical regions whose connection is expressed through genealogical language. **33:** The legal implications of the inheritance of Zelophehad's daughters are discussed in 27.1–11; 36.1–12.

a Meaning of parts of vv. 42 and 43 uncertain.

⁴⁹of Jezer, the clan of the Jezerites; of Shillem, the clan of the Shillemites. ⁵⁰Those are the clans of the Naphtalites, clan by clan; persons enrolled: 45,400.

⁵¹This is the enrollment of the Israelites: 601,730.

⁵²The Lord spoke to Moses, saying, ⁵³"Among these shall the land be apportioned as shares, according to the listed names: ⁵⁴with larger groups increase the share, with smaller groups reduce the share. Each is to be assigned its share according to its enrollment. ⁵⁵The land, moreover, is to be apportioned by lot; and the allotment shall be made according to the listings of their ancestral tribes. ⁵⁶Each portion shall be assigned by lot, whether for larger or smaller groups."

⁵⁷This is the enrollment of the Levites by their clans: Of Gershon, the clan of the Gershonites; of Kohath, the clan of the Kohathites; of Merari, the clan of the Merarites. ⁵⁸These are the clans of Levi: The clan of the Libnites, the clan of the Hebronites, the clan of the Mahlites, the clan of the Mushites, the clan of the Korahites.—Kohath begot Amram. ⁵⁹The name of Amram's wife was Jochebed daughter of Levi, who was born to Levi in Egypt; she bore to Amram Aaron and Moses and their sister Miriam. ⁶⁰To Aaron were born Nadab and Abihu, Eleazar and Ithamar. ⁶¹Nadab and Abihu died when they offered alien fire before the Lord.—⁶²Their enrollment of 23,000 comprised all males from a month up. They were not part of the regular enrollment of the Israelites, since no share was assigned to them among the Israelites.

⁶³These are the persons enrolled by Moses and Eleazar the priest who registered the Israelites on the steppes of Moab, at the Jordan near Jericho. ⁶⁴Among these there was not one of those enrolled by Moses and Aaron the priest when they recorded the Israelites in the wilderness of Sinai. ⁶⁵For the Lord had said of them, "They shall die in the wilderness." Not one of them survived, except Caleb son of Jephunneh and Joshua son of Nun.

27 The daughters of Zelophehad, of Manassite family—son of Hepher son of Gilead son of Machir son of Manasseh son of Joseph—came forward. The names of the daughters were Mahlah, Noah, Hoglah, Milcah, and Tirzah. ²They stood before Moses, Eleazar the priest, the

ancient Near Eastern divination practice; according to several biblical passages, God controls the results (Josh. 18.8; 19.51; 1 Sam. 10.20–24; 14.41).

26.57–62: The Levites are numbered for the third time (cf. chs 3–4). They are listed separately because they do not serve in the military, nor do they receive a portion of land. They are, however, assigned Levitical towns (see 35.1–8), the number of which is determined by the size of the group. **58–59:** These verses trace the genealogy of Moses and Aaron, Israel's leaders. **61:** For the episode surrounding the death of Nadab and Abihu, see Lev. 10.1–3. **63–65:** The ch ends by stating that God's punishment of the wilderness generation was fulfilled, preparing the way for the death of Moses and the conquest of the land.

27.1–11: The case of Zelophehad's daughters. A specific case is used here to introduce a revision to the laws of inheritance. The special case of Zelophehad, who died leaving daughters but no sons, already appears in 26.33 in the census record of his clan. The detailed account that follows in ch 27 and continues in ch 36 addresses questions surrounding this case and uses it to explore more generally female inheritance of property in Israel, a patriarchal society. In contrast, ancient texts from Mesopotamia, Syria, and Egypt attest to inheritance rights of women even in the presence of male heirs. Underlying the discussion in Numbers is the biblical precept that the ancestral lands in question are divinely granted in perpetuity and may not be alienated from their original tribes or families (see Lev. 25.25–34; 1 Kings 21.1–19). **1–4:** Zelophehad's daughters present the arguments for their case. **2:** *At the entrance of the Tent of Meeting,* a location in the camp analogous to the city gate of permanent settlements where courts convened (cf. Jer. 26.10; Ruth 4.1). **3:** *Korah's faction,* see ch 16. *But*

51: The total of 601,730 indicates a net loss of 1,820 males aged 20 and up (cf. 603,550 in 1.46). **52–56:** Here are the directions for apportioning the land of Canaan.

The size of each tribal territory is determined by the population of the tribe; the geographical area, however, is assigned to the tribes by lot. Casting lots is a common chieftains, and the whole assembly, at the entrance of the Tent of Meeting, and they said, ³ "Our father died in the wilderness. He was not one of the faction, Korah's faction, which banded together against the LORD, but died for his own sin; and he has left no sons. ⁴ Let not our father's name be lost to his clan just because he had no son! Give us a holding among our father's kinsmen!"

⁵ Moses brought their case before the LORD.

⁶ And the LORD said to Moses, ⁷ "The plea of Zelophehad's daughters is just: you should give them a hereditary holding among their father's kinsmen; transfer their father's share to them.

⁸ "Further, speak to the Israelite people as follows: 'If a man dies without leaving a son, you shall transfer his property to his daughter. ⁹ If he has no daughter, you shall assign his property to his brothers. ¹⁰ If he has no brothers, you shall assign his property to his father's brothers. ¹¹ If his father had no brothers, you shall assign his property to his nearest relative in his own clan, and he shall inherit it.' This shall be the law of procedure for the Israelites, in accordance with the LORD's command to Moses."

¹² The LORD said to Moses, "Ascend these heights of Abarim and view the land that I have given to the Israelite people. ¹³ When you have seen it, you too shall be gathered to your kin, just as your brother Aaron was. ¹⁴ For, in the wilderness of Zin, when the community was contentious, you disobeyed My command to uphold My sanctity in their sight by means of the water." Those are the Waters of Meribath-kadesh,ᵃ in the wilderness of Zin.

¹⁵ Moses spoke to the LORD, saying, ¹⁶ "Let the LORD, Source of the breath of all flesh, appoint someone over the community ¹⁷ ᵇ who shall go out before them and come in before them, and who shall take them out and bring them in,ᵇ so that the LORD's community may not be like sheep that have no shepherd." ¹⁸ And the LORD answered Moses, "Single out Joshua son of Nun, an inspired man, and lay your hand upon him. ¹⁹ Have him stand before El-

---

ᵃ See note at 20.13.

ᵇ-ᵇ I.e., who shall lead them in all matters and whom they shall follow in all matters.

---

with the person gathering stubble on the Sabbath (15.32–36).
8–11: Granting the women's request is a divine decision, and this presents an opportunity to expand on the particular case by offering a hierarchical list of potential heirs, thereby establishing a legal principle. Num. 36.1–13 will further clarify that since the women actually *transfer* the patrimony to future male heirs, they are bound by certain marriage requirements.

27.12–23: The transfer of leadership to Joshua. Key to the success of Israel's inheritance of Canaan is the succession of Moses by a competent and worthy leader. The role is filled by Joshua, one of two spies who gave a positive report claiming that Canaan can be conquered (chs 13–14). Certain other texts as well (e.g., Exod. 17.9–14; 24.13; Num. 11.28) also prepare the reader for the role that Joshua would play as Moses' successor. **12–14:** The beginning of the narrative suggests that Moses is about to die in fulfillment of God's punishment (20.12; cf. Aaron's death and Eleazar's assumption of leadership of the priesthood, 20.22–29). His death, however, is postponed to Deut. ch 34. **12:** Mount Nebo, the site of Moses' death (Deut. ch 34) is part of the heights of Abarim (33.47; Deut. 32.49). **15–17:** Moses requests that God appoint his successor. In this period, national leadership, unlike the priesthood, is not hereditary. Moses' own descendants were not suitable for leadership (see Judg. 18.30 n.). **18–23:** Joshua's investiture is witnessed by Eleazar the priest and the entire community, probably to avoid challenges to the legitimacy of his authority. **18:** *An inspired man,* lit. "a man in whom there is spirit," anticipates the transfer of Mosaic attributes to Joshua. *Lay your hand* [*hands,* v. 23] *upon him,* for the purpose of transferring *authority* (v. 20). The spirit may refer to prophetic ability (see 1 Kings 22.21–23), and the ritual may express Moses' transferring his prophetic abilities to Joshua. The rite of laying hands is em-

---

[*Zelophehad*] *died for his own sin,* difficult to interpret. It may refer to the condemnation of Zelophehad as part of the entire sinful exodus generation (14.29) or imply an assumed transgression explaining his lack of male heirs (cf. 1 Kings 1.17–18). Traditional Jewish commentary makes the latter connection. **4:** *Let not our father's name be lost:* Preserving a person's name is of tantamount importance and clearly connected to his estate (Deut. 25.5–6) **5:** Moses brings this difficult case before God (Deut. 1.17), as he did earlier eazar the priest and before the whole community, and commission him in their sight. 20 Invest him with some of your authority, so that the whole Israelite community may obey. 21 But he shall present himself to Eleazar the priest, who shall on his behalf seek the decision of the Urim before the LORD. By such instruction they shall go out and by such instruction they shall come in, he and all the Israelites, the whole community."

22 Moses did as the LORD commanded him. He took Joshua and had him stand before Eleazar the priest and before the whole community. 23 He laid his hands upon him and commissioned him—as the LORD had spoken through Moses.

28 The LORD spoke to Moses, saying: 2 Command the Israelite people and say to them: Be punctilious in presenting to Me at stated times *the offerings of food due Me,-* as offerings by fire of pleasing odor to Me.

3 Say to them: These are the offerings by fire that you are to present to the LORD:

As a regular burnt offering every day, two yearling lambs without blemish. 4 You shall offer one lamb in the morning, and the other lamb you shall offer at twilight. 5 And as a meal offering, there shall be a tenth of an *ephah* of choice flour with a quarter of a *hin* of beaten oil mixed in— 6 the regular burnt offering instituted at Mount Sinai*b*—an offering by fire of pleasing odor to the LORD.

7 The libation with it shall be a quarter of a *hin* for each lamb, to be poured in the sacred precinct as an offering of fermented drink*c* to the LORD. 8 The other lamb you shall offer at twilight, preparing the same meal offering and libation as in the morning—an offering by fire of pleasing odor to the LORD.

9 On the sabbath day: two yearling lambs without blemish, together with two-tenths of a measure*d* of choice flour with oil mixed in as a meal offering, and with the proper libation—10 a burnt offering for every sabbath, in addition to the regular burnt offering and its libation.

a-a Lit. "My offering, My food."
b Exod. 29.38–41.   *c* I.e., wine.   *d* I.e., of an ephah.

ployed for animals as well as persons (Lev. 16.21; Num. 8.10). Contrast the transfer of power from Elijah to Elisha (2 Kings 2.9–15). Jewish tradition refers to the ceremony of rabbinic ordination as "semikhah," the laying of hands. **21:** *Seek the decision of the Urim:*

The Urim and Thummim (here abbreviated) are consulted as an oracle (1 Sam. 14.41 [LXX]; 28.6). According to the Priestly tradition, they fit into a pouch of the breastplate worn by the high priest (Exod. 28.30; Lev. 8.8), many scholars believe that they were cast like

dice to answer yes-or-no questions. Clearly, Joshua cannot commune directly with God as does Moses.

28.1–30.1: Calendar of the public cult. Chs 28–29 are an insertion into the narrative consisting of ritual prescriptions that delineate the daily, Sabbath, new moon, and festival schedule of offerings. The variety and number of sacrificial animals vary, but all are males: bulls, rams, lambs, and goats. Meal offerings and wine libations are also part of the formulas. Num. 28.1–15 deals with daily, weekly, and monthly sacrifices. Num. 28.16–29.38 is an outline of the annual cycle of festivals, beginning with Passover in the first month and ending with Sukkot in the seventh month. The Numbers calendar expands on the calendar in Lev. ch 23, also a product of the Priestly tradition, by adding the daily and new moon rituals. A third, non-Priestly calendar, Deut. 16.1–17, describes the three main pilgrimage festivals (Passover, Feast of Weeks, Feast of Booths) in conjunction with the requirement of a central sanctuary. The Numbers complete cultic calendar is a guide for ritual observances required of a settled community, especially those rites pertaining to harvest festivals. Therefore, it is included in the text at a point prior to the Israelite crossing into Canaan. **28.2:** *Offerings of food due Me,* lit. "My food," designates sacrifices as divine food. This notion pervades the ancient Near East, where food was placed daily at mealtime before statues of deities. Vestiges of such beliefs appear in the Bible (Gen. 8.20–21). In Priestly writings, however, anthropomorphic concepts of God are generally absent, although the pleasing odor of offerings to the Lord is commonly mentioned (Lev. 21.6; Num. 15.3–13); it is unclear if this should be understood literally, or is vestigial, and should be understood metaphorically. **3–8:** The daily offering, "tamid," is the standard to which the special holy day sacrifices are added. **9–10:** The Sabbath

¹¹On your new moons you shall present a burnt offering to the LORD: two bulls of the herd, one ram, and seven yearling lambs, without blemish. ¹²As meal offering for each bull: three-tenths of a measure of choice flour with oil mixed in. As meal offering for each ram: two-tenths of a measure of choice flour with oil mixed in. ¹³As meal offering for each lamb: a tenth of a measure of fine flour with oil mixed in. Such shall be the burnt offering of pleasing odor, an offering by fire to the LORD. ¹⁴Their libations shall be: half a *hin* of wine for a bull, a third of a *hin* for a ram, and a quarter of a *hin* for a lamb. That shall be the monthly burnt offering for each new moon of the year. ¹⁵And there shall be one goat as a sin offering to the LORD, to be offered in addition to the regular burnt offering and its libation.

¹⁶In the first month, on the fourteenth day of the month, there shall be a passover sacrifice to the LORD, ¹⁷and on the fifteenth day of that month a festival. Unleavened bread shall be eaten for seven days. ¹⁸The first day shall be a sacred occasion: you shall not work at your occupations. ¹⁹You shall present an offering by fire, a burnt offering, to the LORD: two bulls of the herd, one ram, and seven yearling lambs—ᵃsee that they areᵃ without blemish. ²⁰The meal offering with them shall be of choice flour with oil mixed in: prepare three-tenths of a measure for a bull, two-tenths for a ram; ²¹and for each of the seven lambs prepare one-tenth of a measure. ²²And there shall be one goat for a sin offering, to make expiation in your behalf. ²³You shall present these in addition to the morning portion of the regular burnt offering. ²⁴You shall offer the like daily for seven days as food, an offering by fire of pleasing odor to the LORD; they shall be offered, with their libations, in addition to the regular burnt offering. ²⁵And the seventh day shall be a sacred occasion for you: you shall not work at your occupations.

²⁶On the day of the first fruits, your Feast of Weeks, when you bring an offering of new grain to the LORD, you shall observe a sacred occasion: you shall not work at your occupations. ²⁷You shall present a burnt offering of pleasing odor to the LORD: two bulls of the herd, one ram, seven yearling lambs. ²⁸The meal offering with them shall be of choice flour with oil mixed in, three-tenths of a measure for a bull, two-tenths for a ram, ²⁹and one-tenth for each of the seven lambs. ³⁰And there shall be one goat for expiation in your behalf. ³¹You shall present them—ᵃsee that they areᵃ without blemish—with their libations, in addition to the regular burnt offering and its meal offering.

offering doubles the daily one. Cf. the larger Sabbath offering described by the prophet Ezekiel (46.4–5). The Sabbath labor prohibition is mentioned in Leviticus (23.3) but not in Numbers. **11–15:** The sacrificial animals offered on the new moon parallel those offered on other festivals, though their number varies (cf. Ezekiel 46.6–7). They include a goat purification (NJPS "sin") offering, which the Rabbis connect to the purification of the sanctuary (*m. Shevuʿot* 1.4–5). **16–25:** Passover is the first festival of the cultic calendar (Exod. 12.2) and marks the beginning of the barley harvest. The holy day on which the Passover sacrifice ("pesaḥ") is offered is distinct from the seven-day Festival of Unleavened Bread ("matzot"); in other words, we have a festival complex of an evening festival (Pesaḥ) followed immediately by a seven-day Matzot festival. Neither here nor in Leviticus (23.5–8) is the commemoration of the exodus from Egypt mentioned, though it is noted elsewhere (Exod. 23.15; Deut. 16.1–3). Biblical records of Passover celebrations in the preexilic period are associated with the reigns of two Judean kings, Hezekiah (2 Chron. 30.1–27) and Josiah (2 Kings 23.21–23; 2 Chron. 35.1–19); Ezra the scribe notes that the returning exiles in the Persian period celebrated Passover (Ezra 6.19–22). **26–31:** The Feast of Weeks, celebrated seven weeks from Passover, marks the wheat harvest. No calendrical date is given here (contrast Lev. 23.15–21), perhaps because the new grain might ripen at different times in different years. In Priestly writings, including Ezekiel, it is not considered a pilgrimage festival. The Deuteronomist, however, does count the Feast of Weeks as one of three pilgrimage festivals (Deut. 16.16). **26:** *First fruits* refers to the new crop of wheat and perhaps the grapes and olives used in preparation of the offering (Lev. 23.17).

---

a-a Lit. *"they shall be to you."*

29 In the seventh month, on the first day of the month, you shall observe a sacred occasion: you shall not work at your occupations. You shall observe it as *-a day when the horn is sounded.-a 2 You shall present a burnt offering of pleasing odor to the LORD: one bull of the herd, one ram, and seven yearling lambs, without blemish. 3 The meal offering with them—choice flour with oil mixed in—shall be: three-tenths of a measure for a bull, two-tenths for a ram, 4 and one-tenth for each of the seven lambs. 5 And there shall be one goat for a sin offering, to make expiation in your behalf—6 in addition to the burnt offering of the new moon with its meal offering and the regular burnt offering with its meal offering, each with its libation as prescribed, offerings by fire of pleasing odor to the LORD.

7 On the tenth day of the same seventh month you shall observe a sacred occasion when you shall practice self-denial. You shall do no work. 8 You shall present to the LORD a burnt offering of pleasing odor: one bull of the herd, one ram, seven yearling lambs; see that they are*b without blemish. 9 The meal offering with them—of choice flour with oil mixed in—shall be: three-tenths of a measure for a bull, two-tenths for the one ram, 10 one-tenth for each of the seven lambs. 11 And there shall be one goat for a sin offering, in addition to the sin offering of expiation and the regular burnt offering with its meal offering, each with its libation.

12 On the fifteenth day of the seventh month, you shall observe a sacred occasion: you shall not work at your occupations.—Seven days you shall observe a festival of the LORD.—13 You shall present a burnt offering, an offering by fire of pleasing odor to the LORD: Thirteen bulls of the herd, two rams, fourteen yearling lambs; they shall be without blemish. 14 The meal offerings with them—of choice flour with oil mixed in—shall be: three-tenths of a measure for each of the thirteen bulls, two-tenths for each of the two rams, 15 and one-tenth for each of the fourteen lambs. 16 And there shall be one goat for a sin offering—in addition to the regular burnt offering, its meal offering and libation.

17 Second day: Twelve bulls of the herd, two rams, fourteen yearling lambs, without blemish; 18 the meal offerings and libations for the bulls, rams, and lambs, in the quantities prescribed; 19 and one goat for a sin offering—in addition to the regular burnt offering, its meal offering and libations.

29.1–6: The new moon of the seventh month is like a sabbath of new moon celebrations. According to the earlier covenant collection in Exodus, the seventh month marks the transition between the end and the beginning of the agricultural year (Exod. 23.16). Jewish tradition adopted the new moon of the seventh month as the start of the new year, Rosh Ha-Shanah. The oddity of having the new year begin in the seventh month comes from the fact that two calendrical systems are reflected in the Bible: one in which the year begins in the fall (Tishri), and one beginning in the spring (Nisan), as the Babylonian year did. We have here a hybrid: the year beginning in the fall but the month named according to the spring beginning. The sounding of the horn (v. 1), the shofar, is still practiced on Rosh Ha-Shanah. The shofar differs from the metal trumpets sounded by the priests (10.2–10). **7–11:** In Leviticus (23.27) the tenth day of the seventh month is called "yom ha-kippurim," the Day of Atonement. It is designated as a Sabbath of complete rest (Lev. 16.31; 23.32). For the priestly expiation rites associated with it, see Lev. 16.29–34. **7:** *Self-denial* elsewhere refers to fasting (Isa. 58.3–5; Ps. 35.13), as observed by Ibn Ezra. **12–34:** This festival, lasting from the fifteenth to the twenty-first day of the seventh month is also known by more descriptive names: Feast of Booths, "sukkot" (Lev. 23.34; Deut. 16.13) and Feast of Ingathering (Exod. 23.16; 34.22). A far larger amount of livestock is offered on this festival than on any other, perhaps reflecting its importance. For the nonsacrificial rituals, like that of the "lulav," palm bough, see Lev. 23.33–36, 39–43. King Solomon celebrated Sukkot, called "the Feast," at the time he dedicated the Temple (2 Chron. 7.8–10). Judeans in the Persian period observed Sukkot at the bidding of Ezra (Neh. 8.14–18). In more modern times, the Pilgrims modeled their thanksgiving celebration in the New World after this biblical harvest festival.

a-a Or "a day of festivity." b See note at 28.19.

20 Third day: Eleven bulls, two rams, fourteen yearling lambs, without blemish; 21 the meal offerings and libations for the bulls, rams, and lambs, in the quantities prescribed; 22 and one goat for a sin offering—in addition to the regular burnt offering, its meal offering and libation.

23 Fourth day: Ten bulls, two rams, fourteen yearling lambs, without blemish; 24 the meal offerings and libations for the bulls, rams, and lambs, in the quantities prescribed; 25 and one goat for a sin offering—in addition to the regular burnt offering, its meal offering and libation.

26 Fifth day: Nine bulls, two rams, fourteen yearling lambs, without blemish; 27 the meal offerings and libations for the bulls, rams, and lambs, in the quantities prescribed; 28 and one goat for a sin offering—in addition to the regular burnt offering, its meal offering and libation.

29 Sixth day: Eight bulls, two rams, fourteen yearling lambs, without blemish; 30 the meal offerings and libations for the bulls, rams, and lambs, in the quantities prescribed; 31 and one goat for a sin offering—in addition to the regular burnt offering, its meal offering and libations.

32 Seventh day: Seven bulls, two rams, fourteen yearling lambs, without blemish; 33 the meal offerings and libations for the bulls, rams, and lambs, in the quantities prescribed; 34 and one goat for a sin offering—in addition to the regular burnt offering, its meal offering and libation.

35 On the eighth day you shall hold a solemn gathering;ª you shall not work at your occupations. 36 You shall present a burnt offering, an offering by fire of pleasing odor to the LORD; one bull, one ram, seven yearling lambs, without blemish; 37 the meal offerings and libations for the bull, the ram, and the lambs, in the quantities prescribed; 38 and one goat for a sin offering—in addition to the regular burnt offering, its meal offering and libation.

39 All these you shall offer to the LORD at the stated times, in addition to your votive and freewill offerings, be

30 they burnt offerings, meal offerings, libations, or offerings of well-being. 1 So Moses spoke to the Israelites just as the LORD had commanded Moses.

MATTOT   מטות

2 Moses spoke to the heads of the Israelite tribes, saying: This is what the LORD has commanded:

3 If a man makes a vow to the LORD or takes an oath imposing an obligationᵇ on himself, he shall not break his pledge; he must carry out all that has ᶜcrossed his lips.ᶜ

---

a See note at Lev. 23.36.   b Or "a prohibition."
c-c Lit. "come out of his mouth."

35–38: An eighth day of Sukkot, characterized as a concluding solemn gathering, may have been originally a distinct holy day, as indicated by the contradiction between v. 12, *seven days,* and v. 35, *On the eighth day.* This gives rise to significant confusion in Jewish legal texts concerning the nature and status of the eighth day. **39:** A Priestly summary verse. Public cult observances are required in addition to private votive or freewill offerings. Examples of the latter include Elkanah's family sacrifice at the Shiloh shrine (1 Sam. 1.3–6) and Absalom's fulfillment of a vow in Hebron (2 Sam. 15.7–8). **30.1:** This subscript statement, common in Priestly literature, attests to the fact that the LORD's instructions were carried out (cf. 5.4).

30.2–17: Annulling women's vows and oaths. The section of cult regulations begun in ch 28 ends with the subject of the annulment of vows and oaths. This topic connects to the aforementioned votive and freewill offerings (29.39), which most often constitute the pledge. A sworn statement in the name of God defines the seriousness of the pledge (Exod. 20.7; Deut. 5.11). Vow and oath obligations differ from each other in that a vow is conditional. It binds the devotee only after God fulfills the requested blessing. For example, Jacob vows to erect a shrine at Bethel if God delivers him safely from the wrath of his brother (Gen. 28.20, 22); Jephthah vows to sacrifice whatever comes out first from his house if he returns having defeated the Ammonites (Judg. 11.30–31); and Hannah vows to dedicate her son to sanctuary service if she conceives (1 Sam. 1.11). **3:** This initial statement affirms the obligation of men to any vows and oaths they take (Deut. 23.22–24). This case is simple: Since all men are independent, they are thus responsible for their vows. The rest of the chapter deals with women's vows; the status of these depends on the status of the woman, particularly if she is de-

4 If a woman makes a vow to the LORD or assumes an obligation while still in her father's household by reason of her youth, 5 and her father learns of her vow or her self-imposed obligation and offers no objection, all her vows shall stand and every self-imposed obligation shall stand. 6 But if her father restrains her on the day he finds out, none of her vows or self-imposed obligations shall stand; and the LORD will forgive her, since her father restrained her.

7 If she should marry while her vow or the commitment[a] to which she bound herself is still in force, 8 and her husband learns of it and offers no objection on the day he finds out, her vows shall stand and her self-imposed obligations shall stand. 9 But if her husband restrains her on the day that he learns of it, he thereby annuls her vow which was in force or the commitment[a] to which she bound herself; and the LORD will forgive her.—10 The vow of a widow or of a divorced woman, however, whatever she has imposed on herself, shall be binding upon her.—11 So, too, if, while in her husband's household, she makes a vow or imposes an obligation on herself by oath, 12 and her husband learns of it, yet offers no objection—thus failing to restrain her—all her vows shall stand and all her self-imposed obligations shall stand. 13 But if her husband does annul them on the day he finds out, then nothing that has crossed her lips shall stand, whether vows or self-imposed obligations. Her husband has annulled them, and the LORD will forgive her. 14 Every vow and every sworn obligation of self-denial may be upheld by her husband or annulled by her husband. 15 If her husband offers no objection from that day to the next, he has upheld all the vows or obligations she has assumed: he has upheld them by offering no objection on the day he found out. 16 But if he annuls them after [the day] he finds out, he shall bear her guilt.

17 Those are the laws that the LORD enjoined upon Moses between a man and his wife, and as between a father and his daughter while in her father's household by reason of her youth.

31 The LORD spoke to Moses, saying, 2 "Avenge the Israelite people on the Midianites; then you shall be gathered to your kin."

3 Moses spoke to the people, saying, "Let men be picked out from among you for a campaign, and let them fall upon Midian to wreak the LORD's vengeance on Midian.

a Lit. "utterance of her lips."

pendent on a man, that is, under his legal authority, specifically her father or husband. **4–13:** The discussion turns to the responsibility of women regarding such promises. Four cases are presented: (1) The vow or oath of a young woman (but presumably not a minor) living in her father's house and under his authority (vv. 4–6); (2) The vow or oath of a married woman made while still in her father's house but now under the authority of her husband (vv. 7–9); (3) The vow of a widow or divorced woman (v. 10); (4) The vow or oath of a widowed or divorced woman made prior to her husband's death or before their divorce (vv. 11–13). Nullification of a woman's vows and oaths is only possible if the woman is in a state of dependency, either on her father or husband. Independent women, such as widows or divorcees, who take on these obligations are bound to them in the same way as men. These laws suggest that a woman's vows and oaths required validation by a male if she was legally dependent on him. The Dead Sea Scrolls, however, placed almost equal weight on the oaths of adult females and limited a husband's or father's right of annulment to oaths and vows which transgress the laws of the Torah (CD 16.10–12). **14–16:** A husband (or father) who annuls a woman's vow or oath outside the prescribed parameters bears the woman's guilt and is liable for punishment. Problems arising from vows made in error or haste prompted the Rabbis to assert that four kinds of vows were not binding: vows of incitement; vows of exaggeration; vows made in error; and vows of constraint (*m. Ned.* 3.1). **17:** This v. formally concludes these legal prescriptions.

31.1–54: War of vengeance against the Midianites. Ch 31 consists of narrative that picks up from the end of ch 25 (see 25.19 n.). The divine command to defeat the Midianites in retaliation for their seduction of the Israelites at Baal-peor (25.17–18) is realized in this

4 You shall dispatch on the campaign a thousand from every one of the tribes of Israel."

5 So a thousand from each tribe were furnished from the divisions of Israel, twelve thousand picked for the campaign. 6 Moses dispatched them on the campaign, a thousand from each tribe, with Phinehas son of Eleazar serving as a priest on the campaign, equipped with the sacred utensils[a] and the trumpets for sounding the blasts. 7 They took the field against Midian, as the LORD had commanded Moses, and slew every male. 8 Along with their other victims, they slew the kings of Midian: Evi, Rekem, Zur, Hur, and Reba, the five kings of Midian. They also put Balaam son of Beor to the sword.

9 The Israelites took the women and children of the Midianites captive, and seized as booty all their beasts, all their herds, and all their wealth. 10 And they destroyed by fire all the towns in which they were settled, and their encampments. 11 They gathered all the spoil and all the booty, man and beast, 12 and they brought the captives, the booty, and the spoil to Moses, Eleazar the priest, and the whole Israelite community, at the camp in the steppes of Moab, at the Jordan near Jericho.

13 Moses, Eleazar the priest, and all the chieftains of the community came out to meet them outside the camp. 14 Moses became angry with the commanders of the army, the officers of thousands and the officers of hundreds, who had come back from the military campaign. 15 Moses said to them, "You have spared every female! 16 Yet they are the very ones who, at the bidding of Balaam, induced[b] the Israelites to trespass against the LORD in the matter of Peor, so that the LORD's community was struck by the plague. 17 Now, therefore, slay every male among the children, and slay also every woman who has known a man carnally; 18 but spare every young woman who has not had carnal relations with a man.

19 "You shall then stay outside the camp seven days; every one among you or among your captives who has slain a person or touched a corpse shall cleanse himself on the third and seventh days. 20 You shall also cleanse every cloth, every article of skin, everything made of goats' hair, and every object of wood."

21 Eleazar the priest said to the troops who had taken part in the fighting, "This is the ritual law that the LORD has enjoined upon Moses: 22 Gold and silver, copper, iron, tin, and lead—23 any article that can withstand fire—these you

a Perhaps the Urim; cf. 27.21.
b Meaning of Heb. hayu . . . limsor uncertain.

ch, which opens with a call to battle (for the association of Midianites and Moabites, see 22.4 n.). The brevity and somewhat legendary nature of the war account point to several issues of real concern underlying the lengthy chapter, which integrates several laws mentioned in the book, and adduces some new ones. Clearly evident is the Priestly writer's agenda: the key military role of the priesthood; the fate of male and female captives in a holy war; ritual purification of soldiers and booty; and the taxation of spoils for the sanctuary. Thus, the main focus is not the battle, but the legal precedents that it sets. **4:** *A thousand from every one of the tribes:* The term "'elef" can also refer to "division" (a military unit), hence twelve divisions. **6:** *Phinehas son of Eleazar* the high priest serves as the military priest (cf. 25.7–8; Deut. 20.2–4). According to the midrash (*Num. Rab.* 22.4), Phinehas was assigned this role so that he could finish the sacred task he began when he smote the Midianite woman in the affair of Baal-peor (25.1–9). *The sacred utensils* are not specified but probably include the Ark (1 Sam. 4.3–11) and the Urim and Thummim (1 Sam. 14.41; 28.6). The *trumpets* are mentioned earlier in 10.1–10. **7:** *Slew every male:* Total annihilation is an expression of victory not to be taken literally. It is a common propagandistic statement in ancient Near Eastern battle accounts. **8:** *Put Balaam son of Beor to the sword:* According to this tradition (also v. 16) he is killed for his association with the Midianites, through whom he incited the Israelites to the apostasy of Baal-peor (see 22.2–24.25 n.). **15–18:** Only young girls who are virgins are left alive and presumably taken captive (Deut. 20.14; 21.10–14). Since lineage was determined patriarchally, they do not pose the danger of producing Midianite sons who can avenge their fathers. **19–24:** Soldiers returning from battle as well as captives must be purified from corpse defilement; this recalls ch 19. In addition, shall pass through fire and they shall be clean, except that they must be cleansed with water of lustration; and anything that cannot withstand fire you must pass through water. ²⁴ On the seventh day you shall wash your clothes and be clean, and after that you may enter the camp."

²⁵ The LORD said to Moses: ²⁶ "You and Eleazar the priest and the family heads of the community take an inventory of the booty that was captured, man and beast, ²⁷ and divide the booty equally between the combatants who engaged in the campaign and the rest of the community. ²⁸ You shall exact a levy for the LORD: in the case of the warriors who engaged in the campaign, one item in five hundred, of persons, oxen, asses, and sheep, ²⁹ shall be taken from their half-share and given to Eleazar the priest as a contribution to the LORD; ³⁰ and from the half-share of the other Israelites you shall withhold one in every fifty human beings as well as cattle, asses, and sheep—all the animals—and give them to the Levites, who attend to the duties of the LORD's Tabernacle."

³¹ Moses and Eleazar the priest did as the LORD commanded Moses. ³² The amount of booty, other than the spoil that the troops had plundered, came to 675,000 sheep, ³³ 72,000 head of cattle, ³⁴ 61,000 asses, ³⁵ and a total of 32,000 human beings, namely, the women who had not had carnal relations.

³⁶ Thus, the half-share of those who had engaged in the campaign [was as follows]: The number of sheep was 337,500, ³⁷ and the LORD's levy from the sheep was 675; ³⁸ the cattle came to 36,000, from which the LORD's levy was 72; ³⁹ the asses came to 30,500, from which the LORD's levy was 61. ⁴⁰ And the number of human beings was 16,000, from which the LORD's levy was 32. ⁴¹ Moses gave the contributions levied for the LORD to Eleazar the priest, as the LORD had commanded Moses.

⁴² As for the half-share of the other Israelites, which Moses withdrew from the men who had taken the field, ⁴³ that half-share of the community consisted of 337,500 sheep, ⁴⁴ 36,000 head of cattle, ⁴⁵ 30,500 asses, ⁴⁶ and 16,000 human beings. ⁴⁷ From this half-share of the Israelites, Moses withheld one in every fifty humans and animals; and he gave them to the Levites, who attended to the duties of the LORD's Tabernacle, as the LORD had commanded Moses.

⁴⁸ The commanders of the troop divisions, the officers of thousands and the officers of hundreds, approached Moses. ⁴⁹ They said to Moses, "Your servants have made a check of the warriors in our charge, and not one of us is missing. ⁵⁰ So we have brought as an offering to the LORD

their metal implements must be cleansed by fire, a new law.

22–23: This process of cleansing vessels and other objects is perpetuated, with adaptations, in the Jewish tradition of preparing kitchen utensils for Passover.

25–30: A similar practice concerning distribution of booty is noted in 1 Sam. 30.22–31; both cases, by different authors, are intended as illustrative precedents.

28–30: A form of the laws concerning tithing, detailed in ch 18, is carried out. **31–47:** The amount of booty recorded here, including the share designated for the sanctuary, is fantastic by any standards.

48–54: Conducting a census not initiated by God was believed to provoke divine anger (see 2 Sam. ch 24 where God in anger incites David to take a census that results in a plague). To avert that possibility, the army commanders donate precious articles of gold to God as a ransom for the Israelites (cf. Exod. 30.12). **54:** *As a reminder:* The gold ransom is used in the Tent of Meeting as a continual ritual reminder (Exod. 30.16). This recalls the earlier fire pans, which serve the same purpose (17.5).

such articles of gold as each of us came upon: armlets, bracelets, signet rings, earrings, and pendants,[a] that expiation may be made for our persons before the LORD." [51] Moses and Eleazar the priest accepted the gold from them, all kinds of wrought articles. [52] All the gold that was offered by the officers of thousands and the officers of hundreds as a contribution to the LORD came to 16,750 shekels.—[53] But in the ranks, everyone kept his booty for himself.—[54] So Moses and Eleazar the priest accepted the gold from the officers of thousands and the officers of hundreds and brought it to the Tent of Meeting, as a reminder in behalf of the Israelites before the LORD.

32 The Reubenites and the Gadites owned cattle in very great numbers. Noting that the lands of Jazer and Gilead were a region suitable for cattle, [2] the Gadites and the Reubenites came to Moses, Eleazar the priest, and the chieftains of the community, and said, [3] "Ataroth, Dibon, Jazer, Nimrah, Heshbon, Elealeh, Sebam, Nebo, and Beon—[4] the land that the LORD has conquered for the community of Israel is cattle country, and your servants have cattle. [5] It would be a favor to us," they continued, "if this land were given to your servants as a holding; do not move us across the Jordan."

[6] Moses replied to the Gadites and the Reubenites, "Are your brothers to go to war while you stay here? [7] Why will you turn the minds of the Israelites from crossing into the land that the LORD has given them? [8] That is what your fathers did when I sent them from Kadesh-barnea to survey the land. [9] After going up to the wadi Eshcol and surveying the land, they turned the minds of the Israelites from invading the land that the LORD had given them. [10] Thereupon the LORD was incensed and He swore, [11] 'None of the men from twenty years up who came out of Egypt shall see the land that I promised on oath to Abraham, Isaac, and Jacob, for they did not remain loyal to Me— [12] none except Caleb son of Jephunneh the Kenizzite and Joshua son of Nun, for they remained loyal to the LORD.' [13] The LORD was incensed at Israel, and for forty years He made them wander in the wilderness, until the whole generation that had provoked the LORD's displeasure was gone. [14] And now you, a breed of sinful men, have replaced your fathers, to add still further to the LORD's wrath against Israel. [15] If you turn away from Him and He abandons them once more in the wilderness, you will bring calamity upon all this people."

32.1–42: Settlement of Transjordan. The settlement process begins. Since the Israelites had already routed a number of their enemies in Transjordan (21.21–35; 31.1–12), the tribes of Reuben and Gad consider it prudent to settle that land with their families and livestock. Subsequently, half the tribe of Manasseh also settles east of the Jordan River. The narrative in this ch primarily serves to legitimate Israelite occupation of land outside Canaan proper (see also Josh. ch 22). A nonbiblical text, the Mesha (Moabite) Stone (9th century BCE), confirms Gadite occupation of Ataroth—a town assigned to that tribe in 32.34—since antiquity. **1–5:** These introductory vv. provide a backdrop for the narrative. **3:** The cities of Gad and Reuben are more fully discussed in vv. 34–38; variant traditions about each tribe's holdings are found elsewhere (cf. Josh. 13.17–23). **6–15:** Moses interprets Gad's and Reuben's request as a sign that they are unwilling to fight in the conquest of Canaan, comparing them with the ten scouts who disheartened Israel in the wilderness (chs 13–14). **15:** Moses fears for the fate of Israel on account of the actions of Gad and Reuben (cf. Josh. 22.16–19; Judg. 5.16–17); this v. assumes corporate responsibility, where a serious infraction by part of the nation endangers the nation as a whole.

a See note at Exod. 35.22.

16 Then they stepped up to him and said, "We will build here sheepfolds for our flocks and towns for our children. 17 And we will hasten[a] as shock-troops in the van of the Israelites until we have established them in their home, while our children stay in the fortified towns because of the inhabitants of the land. 18 We will not return to our homes until every one of the Israelites is in possession of his portion. 19 But we will not have a share with them in the territory beyond the Jordan, for we have received our share on the east side of the Jordan."

20 Moses said to them, "If you do this, if you go to battle as shock-troops, at the instance of the LORD, 21 and every shock-fighter among you crosses the Jordan, at the instance of the LORD, until He has dispossessed His enemies before Him, 22 and the land has been subdued, at the instance of the LORD, and then you return—you shall be clear before the LORD and before Israel; and this land shall be your holding under the LORD. 23 But if you do not do so, you will have sinned against the LORD; and know that your sin will overtake you. 24 Build towns for your children and sheepfolds for your flocks, but do what you have promised."

25 The Gadites and the Reubenites answered Moses, "Your servants will do as my lord commands. 26 Our children, our wives, our flocks, and all our other livestock will stay behind[b] in the towns of Gilead; 27 while your servants, all those recruited for war, cross over, at the instance of the LORD, to engage in battle—as my lord orders."

28 Then Moses gave instructions concerning them to Eleazar the priest, Joshua son of Nun, and the family heads of the Israelite tribes. 29 Moses said to them, "If every shock-fighter among the Gadites and the Reubenites crosses the Jordan with you to do battle, at the instance of the LORD, and the land is subdued before you, you shall give them the land of Gilead as a holding. 30 But if they do not cross over with you as shock-troops, they shall receive holdings among you in the land of Canaan."

31 The Gadites and the Reubenites said in reply, "Whatever the LORD has spoken concerning your servants, that we will do. 32 We ourselves will cross over as shock-troops, at the instance of the LORD, into the land of Canaan; and we shall keep our hereditary holding across the Jordan."[c]

33 So Moses assigned to them—to the Gadites, the Reubenites, and the half-tribe of Manasseh son of Joseph—the kingdom of Sihon king of the Amorites and the kingdom

17: *Shock-troops:* Gad and Reuben commit to frontline action as vanguard troops. The modern Heb "ḥalutz," a pioneer who settled the land of Israel in the early 20th century, is derived from this word, specifically from the idea that they are the vanguard of settling the land. 20–22: *At the instance of the LORD,* lit. "before the LORD": Moses repeats this phrase emphasizing Gad's and Reuben's commitment to march in front of the Ark. In the wilderness the Ark leads (cf. 10.33). 22: *You shall be clear before the LORD:* Freedom from obligation in legal terms indicates that the Gadites and Reubenites took an oath (Gen. 24.8). 28: Moses instructs Joshua about the obligation of the Transjordanian tribes because the conquest will take place under Joshua's leadership. 31–32: The Gadites and Reubenites repeat their acceptance of the terms. 33: Moses assigns Gad, Reuben, and half the tribe of Manasseh the lands of conquered kings (21.21–35) as their inheritance (see map on p. 498). Settlement of Manasseh in Transjordan first appears here, perhaps indicating a secondary addition, although one attested elsewhere (Deut. 3.12–16; Josh. 13.29–31).

a Meaning of Heb. hushim uncertain.
b Lit. "there."　　c I.e., in Transjordan.

of King Og of Bashan, the land with its various cities and the territories of their surrounding towns. ³⁴ The Gadites rebuilt Dibon, Ataroth, Aroer, ³⁵ Atroth-shophan, Jazer, Jogbehah, ³⁶ Beth-nimrah, and Beth-haran as fortified towns or as enclosures for flocks. ³⁷ The Reubenites rebuilt Heshbon, Elealeh, Kiriathaim, ³⁸ Nebo, Baal-meon—some names being changed—and Sibmah; they gave [their own] names to towns that they rebuilt.ᵃ ³⁹ The descendants of Machir son of Manasseh went to Gilead and captured it, dispossessing the Amorites who were there; ⁴⁰ so Moses gave Gilead to Machir son of Manasseh, and he settled there. ⁴¹ Jair son of Manasseh went and captured ᵇtheir villages,⁻ᵇ which he renamed Havvoth-jair.ᶜ ⁴² And Nobah went and captured Kenath and its dependencies, renaming it Nobah after himself.

MASE'EI   מסעי

33 These were the marches of the Israelites who started out from the land of Egypt, troop by troop, in the charge of Moses and Aaron. ² Moses recorded the starting points of their various marches as directed by the LORD. Their marches, by starting points, were as follows:

³ They set out from Rameses in the first month, on the fifteenth day of the first month. It was on the morrow of the passover offering that the Israelites started out defiantly,ᵈ in plain view of all the Egyptians. ⁴ The Egyptians meanwhile were burying those among them whom the LORD had struck down, every first-born—whereby the LORD executed judgment on their gods.

⁵ The Israelites set out from Rameses and encamped at Succoth. ⁶ They set out from Succoth and encamped at Etham, which is on the edge of the wilderness. ⁷ They set out from Etham and turned about toward Pi-hahiroth, which faces Baal-zephon, and they encamped before Migdol. ⁸ They set out from Peneᵉ-hahiroth and passed through the sea into the wilderness; and they made a three-days' journey in the wilderness of Etham and encamped at Marah. ⁹ They set out from Marah and came to Elim. There were twelve springs in Elim and seventy palm trees, so they encamped there. ¹⁰ They set out from Elim and encamped by the Sea of Reeds.ᶠ ¹¹ They set out from the Sea of Reeds and encamped in the wilderness of Sin. ¹² They set out from the wilderness of Sin and en-

39–42: In contrast to other tribes, Manassites conquer a portion of their inheritance on their own. A tradition in Judg. 10.4 ascribes the origin of Havvoth-jair to a later period.

33.1–49: A comprehensive wilderness itinerary. This record encompasses the itinerary of Israel's travels from their point of departure in Egypt to their final encampment in Transjordan (42 stations; see map on p. 130). Notably, some toponyms appear here for the first time, being absent from accounts of the exodus in other biblical texts (see Deut. chs 1–3 for another summary). The literary style of the itinerary, the repetition of campsite names, and the highlighting of events in those places closely resemble extant military records from the ancient Near East, especially from Assyria. Accordingly, the notation in this Priestly source that Moses *recorded the starting points of their various marches* (v. 2) fits the genre. Some scholars, however, consider ch 33 a composite text extracted from other portions of Numbers, Exodus, and Deuteronomy. As in the census in ch 26, at some points small expansions appear here (e.g., vv. 38–39). **3–5:** On Rameses, see Exod. 12.37. **6–7:** For Succoth and Etham (= Shur in Exod. 15.22), see Exod. 13.20. **8:** For the incident at Marah, see Exod. 15.23–25. **9–10:** For Elim, see Exod. 15.27. **11–12:** For the story of the manna in the wilderness of Sin, see Exod. ch 16.

---

a Cf. vv. 41, 42.   b-b Or "the villages of Ham"; cf. Gen. 14.5.

c I.e., "the villages of Jair."   d See note at Exod. 14.8.

e Many Hebrew manuscripts and ancient versions read "Pi."

f See note at Exod. 10.19.

camped at Dophkah. [13] They set out from Dophkah and encamped at Alush. [14] They set out from Alush and encamped at Rephidim; it was there that the people had no water to drink. [15] They set out from Rephidim and encamped in the wilderness of Sinai. [16] They set out from the wilderness of Sinai and encamped at Kibroth-hattaavah. [17] They set out from Kibroth-hattaavah and encamped at Hazeroth. [18] They set out from Hazeroth and encamped at Rithmah. [19] They set out from Rithmah and encamped at Rimmon-perez. [20] They set out from Rimmon-perez and encamped at Libnah. [21] They set out from Libnah and encamped at Rissah. [22] They set out from Rissah and encamped at Kehelath. [23] They set out from Kehelath and encamped at Mount Shepher. [24] They set out from Mount Shepher and encamped at Haradah. [25] They set out from Haradah and encamped at Makheloth. [26] They set out from Makheloth and encamped at Tahath. [27] They set out from Tahath and encamped at Terah. [28] They set out from Terah and encamped at Mithkah. [29] They set out from Mithkah and encamped at Hashmonah. [30] They set out from Hashmonah and encamped at Moseroth. [31] They set out from Moseroth and encamped at Bene-jaakan. [32] They set out from Bene-jaakan and encamped at Hor-haggidgad. [33] They set out from Hor-haggidgad and encamped at Jotbath. [34] They set out from Jotbath and encamped at Abronah. [35] They set out from Abronah and encamped at Ezion-geber. [36] They set out from Ezion-geber and encamped in the wilderness of Zin, that is, Kadesh. [37] They set out from Kadesh and encamped at Mount Hor, on the edge of the land of Edom.

[38] Aaron the priest ascended Mount Hor at the command of the LORD and died there, in the fortieth year after the Israelites had left the land of Egypt, on the first day of the fifth month. [39] Aaron was a hundred and twenty-three years old when he died on Mount Hor. [40] And the Canaanite, king of Arad, who dwelt in the Negeb, in the land of Canaan, learned of the coming of the Israelites.[a]

[41] They set out from Mount Hor and encamped at Zalmonah. [42] They set out from Zalmonah and encamped at Punon. [43] They set out from Punon and encamped at Oboth. [44] They set out from Oboth and encamped at Iyeabarim, in the territory of Moab. [45] They set out from Iyim and encamped at Dibon-gad. [46] They set out from Dibongad and encamped at Almon-diblathaim. [47] They set out from Almon-diblathaim and encamped in the hills of Abarim, before Nebo. [48] They set out from the hills of Ab-

14: At Rephidim Moses brought forth water by striking the rock; Israel was attacked there by Amalek (Exod. ch 17). **15:** Sinai still cannot be identified with any degree of certainty. Accounts of events associated with Mount Sinai begin in Exod. ch 19. **16–17:** For Kibroth-hattavah and Hazeroth, see 11.34–35. **18–29:** The toponyms listed in these vv. are unattested elsewhere. **30–34:** For these sites, see Deut. 10.6–7. **36:** In non-Priestly sources Kadesh was an early stop on the wilderness trek (cf. 13.26; Deut. 2.14). **37–39:** Aaron's death, a memorable event for the Priestly writer, is described here in detail with the addition of the date and his age (cf. 20.22–29). **38:** *At the command of the LORD*, lit. "at the mouth of the LORD." Rashi (following *b. B. Bat.* 17a) comments that Aaron dies by the divine kiss, as does Moses (Deut. 34.5). **40:** Cf. 21.1–3. **41–42:** These are two unknown toponyms. **41–49:** The location of these sites, although not all are known, suggest a route through Edomite and Moabite territory, in keeping with Deuteronomy (chs 2–13) but contra Num. 20.19–21. **49:** Abel-shittim is the site from which Israel crosses the Jordan River into Canaan in Josh. 3.1.

a See 21.1–3.

arim and encamped in the steppes of Moab, at the Jordan near Jericho; [49] they encamped by the Jordan from Beth-jeshimoth as far as Abel-shittim, in the steppes of Moab.

[50] In the steppes of Moab, at the Jordan near Jericho, the LORD spoke to Moses, saying: [51] Speak to the Israelite people and say to them: When you cross the Jordan into the land of Canaan, [52] you shall dispossess all the inhabitants of the land; you shall destroy all their figured[a] objects; you shall destroy all their molten images, and you shall demolish all their cult places. [53] And you shall take possession of the land and settle in it, for I have assigned the land to you to possess. [54] You shall apportion the land among yourselves by lot, clan by clan: with larger groups increase the share, with smaller groups reduce the share. Wherever the lot falls for anyone, that shall be his. You shall have your portions according to your ancestral tribes. [55] But if you do not dispossess the inhabitants of the land, those whom you allow to remain shall be stings in your eyes and thorns in your sides, and they shall harass you in the land in which you live; [56] so that I will do to you what I planned to do to them.

34 The LORD spoke to Moses, saying: [2] Instruct the Israelite people and say to them: When you enter the land of Canaan, this is the land that shall fall to you as your portion, the land of Canaan with its various boundaries:

[3] Your southern sector shall extend from the wilderness of Zin alongside Edom. Your southern boundary shall start on the east from the tip of the Dead Sea. [4] Your boundary shall then turn to pass south of the ascent of Akrabbim and continue to Zin, and its limits shall be south of Kadesh-barnea, reaching Hazar-addar and continuing to Azmon. [5] From Azmon the boundary shall turn toward the Wadi of Egypt and terminate at the Sea.[b]

[6] For the western boundary you shall have the coast of the Great Sea;[b] that shall serve as your western boundary.

[7] This shall be your northern boundary: Draw a line from the Great Sea to Mount Hor; [8] from Mount Hor draw a line to Lebo-hamath,[c] and let the boundary reach Zedad. [9] The boundary shall then run to Ziphron and terminate at Hazar-enan. That shall be your northern boundary.

a See note at Lev. 26.1.
b I.e., the Mediterranean Sea.
c See note at 13.21.

33.50–35.8: Instructions on the conquest and division of Canaan. The final task before crossing into Canaan is to delineate the boundaries of the land so that it can be divided among the nine-and-a-half tribes that will inhabit it. The Levites, who are not allotted tribal territory, are provided with towns and pastureland within the holdings of the other tribes. A repetition of the method by which the land will be apportioned (26.52–56) and, more importantly, the command to utterly destroy the indigenous Canaanite population together with its religious objects and shrines (33.50–56) precede instructions relating to the division of Canaan. **33.50–56:** The eradication of the Canaanites and their cult is a divine command. Failure to do so will result in the demise of Israel (cf. Deut. 7.16; Josh. 23.13). **52:** *Figured objects* may refer to stone images in relief (cf. Lev. 26.1). Such objects have been uncovered in archeological excavations from Syria to Israel. *Their cult places,* Heb "bamah," high place, is difficult to define but probably refers to a shrine smaller than a full-scale temple with an elevated cult platform, like those uncovered in archeological excavations at Megiddo and Tel Dan. **34.1–15:** The exact boundaries of the promised land are delineated from south to north, the direction corresponding to the scouting account (13.21). Scholars have observed a correlation between the Levantine territory under Egyptian control at the end of the 13th century and the borders as defined in vv. 3–12 (cf. Josh. 15.1–12; Ezek. 47.13–20). The large size of Israel's domain is clearly idealized. **3–5:** Israel's territory begins at the southern tip of the Dead Sea, extending in a southern arc through Kadesh-barnea and west to the Mediterranean Sea at the Brook of Egypt, Wadi El-ʿArish (see map on p. 469). **6–9:** From the west it extends northward. The northernmost border, at Hazar-enan, is tentatively identified with the oasis of Qayatein 70 miles northeast of Damascus. **7–8:** *Mount Hor* is not

10 For your eastern boundary you shall draw a line from Hazar-enan to Shepham. 11 From Shepham the boundary shall descend to Riblah on the east side of Ain; from there the boundary shall continue downward and abut on the eastern slopes of the Sea of Chinnereth.ᵃ 12 The boundary shall then descend along the Jordan and terminate at the Dead Sea.

That shall be your land as defined by its boundaries on all sides.

13 Moses instructed the Israelites, saying: This is the land you are to receive by lot as your hereditary portion, which the LORD has commanded to be given to the nine and a half tribes. 14 For the Reubenite tribe by its ancestral houses, the Gadite tribe by its ancestral houses, and the half-tribe of Manasseh have already received their portions: 15 those two and a half tribes have received their portions across the Jordan, opposite Jericho, on the east, the orient side.

16 The LORD spoke to Moses, saying: 17 These are the names of the men through whom the land shall be apportioned for you: Eleazar the priest and Joshua son of Nun. 18 And you shall also take a chieftain from each tribe through whom the land shall be apportioned. 19 These are the names of the men: from the tribe of Judah: Caleb son of Jephunneh. 20 From the Simeonite tribe: Samuelᵇ son of Ammihud. 21 From the tribe of Benjamin: Elidad son of Chislon. 22 From the Danite tribe: a chieftain, Bukki son of Jogli. 23 For the descendants of Joseph: from the Manassite tribe: a chieftain, Hanniel son of Ephod; 24 and from the Ephraimite tribe: a chieftain, Kemuel son of Shiphtan. 25 From the Zebulunite tribe: a chieftain, Elizaphan son of Parnach. 26 From the Issacharite tribe: a chieftain, Paltiel son of Azzan. 27 From the Asherite tribe: a chieftain, Ahihud son of Shelomi. 28 From the Naphtalite tribe: a chieftain, Pedahel son of Ammihud.

29 It was these whom the LORD designated to allot portions to the Israelites in the land of Canaan.

35 The LORD spoke to Moses in the steppes of Moab at the Jordan near Jericho, saying: 2 Instruct the Israelite people to assign, out of the holdings apportioned to them, towns for the Levites to dwell in; you shall also assign to the Levites pasture land around their towns. 3 The towns shall be theirs to dwell in, and the pasture shall be for the cattle they own and all their other beasts. 4 The

the site in the region of Edom where Aaron died (20.22; 33.38). **10–12:** The border then extends south around the eastern banks of the Sea of Galilee and further southward along the Jordan River to the Dead Sea. **14–15:** These vv. serve as a reminder that Reuben, Gad, and half of Manasseh received land in Transjordan. **16–29:** New tribal chieftains, with the exception of Caleb (13.6), are appointed to assist Eleazar the priest and Joshua in allotting portions of land to the nine-and-a-half remaining tribes. The tribal chieftains are listed here more or less in an order corresponding to the geographical tribal distribution in Canaan, from south to north. For the delineation of each tribe's territory, see Josh. chs 15–19. **35.1–8:** Each tribe must allocate land from its holdings for the Levites. The towns and pastureland apportioned to the Levites by each tribe is proportional to the size of its tribal territory. These instructions diverge from the division of the 48 Levitical towns among the tribes in Joshua (21.1–40), where nine of the tribes allocate four towns each, Judah gives eight, Simeon one, and Naphtali three. **4–5:** Pastureland extends from the town 1000 cubits (1 cubit = approximately .5 meter [18 in]) in all directions, thereby forming a square of at least 2000 × 2000 cubits, depending on the town size. **6:** The mention of *cities of refuge* serves as a bridge to the following unit.

a I.e., the Sea (or Lake) of Galilee.　　b Or "Shemuel."

town pasture that you are to assign to the Levites shall extend a thousand cubits outside the town wall all around. ⁵You shall measure off two thousand cubits outside the town on the east side, two thousand on the south side, two thousand on the west side, and two thousand on the north side, with the town in the center. That shall be the pasture for their towns.

⁶The towns that you assign to the Levites shall comprise the six cities of refuge that you are to designate for a manslayer to flee to, to which you shall add forty-two towns. ⁷Thus the total of the towns that you assign to the Levites shall be forty-eight towns, with their pasture. ⁸In assigning towns from the holdings of the Israelites, take more from the larger groups and less from the smaller, so that each assigns towns to the Levites in proportion to the share it receives.

⁹The LORD spoke further to Moses: ¹⁰Speak to the Israelite people and say to them: When you cross the Jordan into the land of Canaan, ¹¹you shall provide yourselves with places to serve you as cities of refuge to which a manslayer who has killed a person unintentionally may flee. ¹²The cities shall serve you as a refuge from the avenger,ᵃ so that the manslayer may not die unless he has stood trial before the assembly.

¹³The towns that you thus assign shall be six cities of refuge in all. ¹⁴Three cities shall be designated beyond the Jordan, and the other three shall be designated in the land of Canaan: they shall serve as cities of refuge. ¹⁵These six cities shall serve the Israelites and the resident aliens among them for refuge, so that anyone who kills a person unintentionally may flee there.

¹⁶Anyone, however, who strikes another with an iron object so that death results is a murderer; the murderer must be put to death. ¹⁷If he struck him with a stone toolᵇ that could cause death, and death resulted, he is a murderer; the murderer must be put to death. ¹⁸Similarly, if the object with which he struck him was a wooden toolᵇ that could cause death, and death resulted, he is a murderer; the murderer must be put to death. ¹⁹The blood-avenger himself shall put the murderer to death; it is he who shall put him to death upon encounter. ²⁰So, too, if he pushed him in hate or hurled something at him on purpose and death resulted, ²¹or if he struck him with his hand in enmity and death resulted, the assailant shall be

35.9–34: Cities of refuge and laws governing intentional and unintentional homicide. Different traditions concerning accidental homicide and the cities of refuge are found in Exod. 21.12–14; Deut. 4.41–43; 19.1–13, and Josh. ch 20. **9–15:** Levitical towns also serve another purpose. Six (of the 48) designated towns, three in Transjordan and three in Canaan, function as places of asylum for perpetrators of involuntary manslaughter. **12:** *The avenger*, lit. "redeemer," is a kinsman of the victim who is obligated (vv. 19–27) to avenge (or restore) the lost blood of the slain family member with the blood of the murderer. **15:** Aliens are offered asylum like Israelites. These laws, while protecting persons from unjustified vengeance, clearly reflect the Priestly concern over bloodshed as a source of defilement of the land (vv. 33–34). **16–23:** Listed are concrete examples that distinguish intentional from unintentional homicide; as is typical of the Bible and ancient Near Eastern law, specific cases rather than general principles are adduced.

a Lit. "redeemer," i.e., next of kin; cf. note at Lev. 25.25.
b Lit. "of the hand."

put to death; he is a murderer. The blood-avenger shall put the murderer to death upon encounter.

²²But if he pushed him without malice aforethought or hurled any object at him unintentionally, ²³or inadvertently[a] dropped upon him any deadly object of stone, and death resulted—though he was not an enemy of his and did not seek his harm—²⁴in such cases the assembly shall decide between the slayer and the blood-avenger. ²⁵The assembly shall protect the manslayer from the blood-avenger, and the assembly shall restore him to the city of refuge to which he fled, and there he shall remain until the death of the high priest who was anointed with the sacred oil. ²⁶But if the manslayer ever goes outside the limits of the city of refuge to which he has fled, ²⁷and the blood-avenger comes upon him outside the limits of his city of refuge, and the blood-avenger kills the manslayer, there is no bloodguilt on his account. ²⁸For he must remain inside his city of refuge until the death of the high priest; after the death of the high priest, the manslayer may return to his land holding.

²⁹Such shall be your law of procedure throughout the ages in all your settlements.

³⁰If anyone kills a person, the manslayer may be executed only on the evidence of witnesses; the testimony of a single witness against a person shall not suffice for a sentence of death. ³¹You may not accept a ransom for the life of a murderer who is guilty of a capital crime; he must be put to death. ³²Nor may you accept ransom in lieu of flight to a city of refuge, enabling one to return to live on his land before the death of the priest. ³³You shall not pollute the land in which you live; for blood pollutes the land, and the land can have no expiation for blood that is shed on it, except by the blood of him who shed it. ³⁴You shall not defile the land in which you live, in which I Myself abide, for I the LORD abide among the Israelite people.

36 The family heads in the clan of the descendants of Gilead son of Machir son of Manasseh, one of the Josephite clans, came forward and appealed to Moses and the chieftains, family heads[b] of the Israelites. ²They said, "The LORD commanded my lord to assign the land to the Israelites as shares by lot, and my lord was further commanded by the LORD to assign the share of our kinsman Zelophehad to his daughters. ³Now, if they marry persons from another Israelite tribe, their share will be cut off from our ancestral portion and be added to the portion of

a Lit. "without seeing."   b I.e., tribal heads.

24: *The assembly* probably refers to the court of elders (cf. 11.16–25). **25:** Apparently, court is not held in cities of refuge. The death of the high priest seems to atone accidental homicide. Cf. other purgings of impurity and sin by the high priest in his lifetime (Lev. 16.16–22). For the ritual of anointing the high priest, see Lev. 21.10. **26–28:** The perpetrator of involuntary manslaughter is only protected from the blood avenger inside the city of refuge. **30–34:** These vv., only loosely connected to the preceding, outline the procedure for convicting and punishing persons guilty of intentional homicide. **30:** At least two witnesses are required in capital cases (cf. Deut. 17.6). **31:** In cases of intentional homicide monetary compensation is explicitly prohibited. It does not compensate for the victim's lost blood as does the death of the killer (cf. Deut. 21.1–9). Biblical law differs in this respect from practices among other ancient Near Eastern societies, especially the Hittites, where monetary restitution to the family of the victim was an option. Thus, murder in the Bible was seen as a crime beyond an offense against the family of the deceased. **33–34:** The notion that bloodshed and other transgressions pollute the land, thereby endangering its inhabitants with divine wrath, is common in the Bible (see Gen. 4.10–12; Lev. 18.28; 2 Sam. 21.1–14; Ezek. 36.17–19; Hos. 4.2–3).

36.1–13: Marriage of Zelophehad's daughters. Previously, the case of Zelophehad's daughters elicited divine permission for females to inherit in the absence of male heirs (27.1–11). This ch, which completes the third unit of Numbers as well as of the entire book, addresses practical issues arising from female inheritance of land. It balances two important, but potentially conflicting principles: the right of women to inherit land in certain special circumstances and the idea of not alienating land from its original tribe or clan. The narrative provides legal the tribe into which they marry; thus our allotted portion will be diminished. ⁴And even when the Israelites observe the jubilee, their share will be added to that of the tribe into which they marry, and their share will be cut off from the ancestral portion of our tribe."

⁵So Moses, at the LORD's bidding, instructed the Israelites, saying: "The plea of the Josephite tribe is just. ⁶This is what the LORD has commanded concerning the daughters of Zelophehad: They may marry anyone they wish, provided they marry into a clan of their father's tribe. ⁷No inheritance of the Israelites may pass over from one tribe to another, but the Israelites must remain bound each to the ancestral portion of his tribe. ⁸Every daughter among the Israelite tribes who inherits a share must marry someone from a clan of her father's tribe, in order that every Israelite may keep his ancestral share. ⁹Thus no inheritance shall pass over from one tribe to another, but the Israelite tribes shall remain bound each to its portion."

¹⁰The daughters of Zelophehad did as the LORD had commanded Moses: ¹¹Mahlah, Tirzah, Hoglah, Milcah, and Noah, Zelophehad's daughters, were married to sons of their uncles, ¹²marrying into clans of descendants of Manasseh son of Joseph; and so their share remained in the tribe of their father's clan.

¹³These are the commandments and regulations that the LORD enjoined upon the Israelites, through Moses, on the steppes of Moab, at the Jordan near Jericho.

---

mandment. In cases where a woman is already married to a man from a different tribe, any property she stands to inherit from her father subsequently must go to another relative. **5:** The validity of the clan elders' case evokes divine justice, as did the case of Zelophehad's daughters (27.6). **10–12:** The narrative concludes with the marriage of Zelophehad's daughters according to the conditions of the law. **13:** This v. is a postscript to the preceding laws, those commanded by God while Israel was encamped in Moab (22.1), and is not a concluding formula encompassing the book as a whole. Its form is typical of Priestly literature (e.g., Lev. 26.46; 27.34).

instruction for heiresses so that their marriage will not result in the transfer of ancestral tribal lands from one tribe to another. Some scholars, citing the marriage of Zelophehad's daughters to their first cousins, maintain that originally the real concern centered on the preservation of clan holdings, rather than those of the larger tribal unit. The discussion of the distribution of permanent tribal holdings in chs 32 and 34 may account for the placement of this explanatory text to 27.1–11 following ch 34. **1–4:** These vv. outline the potential problem surrounding female inheritance of property. **1:** The opening of the narrative parallels that of 27.1–11. **3–4:** The property still passes through the male line, the daughter's possession being interim. As a result of Israel's patrilineal and patrilocal system, a consequence of the daughter's marriage is that the property permanently passes to the husband's tribe via the inheritance of her sons. **4:** *Jubilee:* According to the Priestly system, every fiftieth year all sold land reverts to its original owner (see Lev. 25.8–16; 27.16–24). The jubilee law does not apply in this case since the land is inherited, not sold. **5–9:** These vv. contain broader stipulations for heiress marriages that preserve tribal holdings. The redundancy in vv. 7 and 9 pertaining to the inviolability of tribal estates prompted Ramban to view v. 9 as a separate com-

דברים

Deuteronomy

DEUTERONOMY MAY WELL BE the first book to pose the problem of modernity. Its authors struggled with issues conventionally viewed as exclusively modern ones, such as the historical distance between past and present, the tension between tradition and the needs of the contemporary generation, and the distinction between divine revelation and human interpretation. Seen from this perspective, ancient Israel's Deuteronomy becomes a remarkably contemporary text, one that challenges its readers to rethink their assumptions about time, about Scripture, and about religion. Of course, Deuteronomy is also a deeply traditional text that, more than any other book of the Bible, provides the foundation of Judaism. The religious conviction that God made a covenant with Israel at Sinai and that the Torah embodies the terms of that covenant originates with Deuteronomy. Many familiar Jewish ritual objects, like the mezuzah, the tefillin, and the tzitzit (fringed garment), come from Deuteronomy, as does Judaism's most important prayer, the Shema (6.4–9). But the Shema is more than a prayer. Judaism understands its recitation to be a binding legal act in which individuals pledge their commitment to Torah. By reciting the Shema, the congregation in the synagogue brings the plot of Deuteronomy to life in the present, as it enacts and renews that oath of allegiance to God that, it believes, Israel first vowed on the plains of Moab.

The story begins just as the Israelites, encamped on the plains of Moab, stand poised finally to enter the promised land. The entry into Canaan would provide the long-awaited climax of the story that had begun with the promises to the ancestors in Genesis, and whose fulfillment had been delayed by the enslavement in Egypt and the wandering in the wilderness. Now, on the eve both of his death and of the nation's entry into the land without him, Moses, portrayed as Deuteronomy's speaker, arrests the narrative action in order to deliver a series of three speeches, grouped together as a long valedictory address. He reviews the nation's history, expounds upon their laws, and instructs them about the importance of loyalty to God. He also adjures the nation to uphold this combination of law and theological instruction as a covenant upon the plains of Moab, one that supplements the one previously sworn at Horeb (Deuteronomy's name for Sinai; 28.69). Only after the conclusion of these discourses and a following appendix (chs 31–34) does the overall narrative line resume with the account of the nation's entry into Canaan in Joshua and Judges.

The Historical Context and Literary Background

THE ENGLISH NAME OF THE BOOK, based on the Septuagint (see 17.18 n.), means "second law." That title reflects the perspective that Deuteronomy is a Mosaic rehearsal of law that was previously given in Exod. chs 19–23. Despite this perspective and the text's own self-presentation, Deuteronomy is likely not Mosaic in origin. More probably, the core of the book was written sometime during the 7th century BCE by educated scribes associated with Jerusalem's royal court. It has been long recognized that there are very striking similarities between the distinctive religious and legal requirements of Deuteronomy and the account of the major religious reform carried out by King Josiah in 622 BCE. That reform had been inspired by the discovery in the Temple of a "scroll of the Teaching" (2 Kings 22.8). Josiah's reform restricted all sacrificial worship of God to Jerusalem and removed foreign elements from the system of worship (technically, the "cultus"); it culminated in the celebration of the first nationally centralized Passover at the Temple in Jerusalem (2 Kings chs 22–23). So strongly do these royal initiatives correspond to the distinctive requirements of Deuteronomy that scholars have long identified the "scroll of the Torah" discovered in Josiah's Temple as Deuteronomy, and thus have assigned the book a 7th-century date.

Josiah's reform, with some form of Deuteronomy as its catalyst, was much more a revolution than a simple return to older forms of worship. Previously, it was entirely legitimate to sacrifice to God throughout the land, as did Abraham at Shechem and Bethel (Gen. 12.7–8); Jacob at Bethel (Gen. 35.1–7); Samuel at Mitzpah, Ramah, Gilgal, and Bethlehem (1 Sam. 7.9, 17; 9.11–14; 10.8; 16.1–5); and Elijah upon Mount Carmel (1 Kings 18.20–46). Indeed, even earlier biblical law, associated with the revelation at Sinai, stipulated that God would grant blessing "in every place where I cause My name to be mentioned" (Exod. 20.21). Deuteronomy challenged that older norm, prohibiting sacrifice "at any [or, every] place" and restricting it to a single site, understood to be Jerusalem (Deut. 12.13–14). In this way, Deuteronomy's self-presentation, whether as an explication of (1.1–5) or as a supplement to (28.69) the prior covenant, does not address the extent to which Deuteronomy actually challenges and revises earlier law.

The historical background of Josiah's reforms was the increasing threat of imperial domination. The Northern Kingdom of Israel had fallen under the Neo-Assyrian invasion a scant century before (722 BCE; 2 Kings ch 17). Continuing Assyrian incursions down the coastal littoral had all but reduced Judah to a rump-state (2 Kings 18.13). In a desperate bid to preserve the nation's autonomy, Hezekiah had already made a pact with Assyria (2 Kings 18.13–18). Subsequently, Judah's political and religious independence seemed to hover uncertainly between the threats presented by Assyria and resurgent Babylon (2 Kings 20.12–15). The resulting military allegiances led to religious syncretism, as Judean officials introduced various foreign forms of worship into the Temple (2 Kings 16.10–20; 21.1–6).

In this context, Josiah's religious reforms represented an important bid for Judean cultural, political, and religious autonomy. The monarch extended his reforms into the area of the former Northern Kingdom of Israel and thus implicitly into territory under Assyrian control (2 Kings 23.15–20). Deuteronomy, apparently written sometime during this historical crisis, likewise reflects the desire to preserve Judean cultural and religious integrity. Its authors had the conviction that older conventions of worship and social organization were no longer viable. If the religion of Yahweh was to survive the crisis, renewal and adaptation were necessary. Deuteronomy's legal corpus (chs 12–26) provides a comprehensive program for cultural renewal. It addresses worship; the festival calendar; the major institutions of public life (justice, kingship, priesthood, prophecy); criminal, family, and civil law; and ethics. The law is presented as a covenant between God and nation, which the people take an oath to uphold, upon penalty of sanctions, while maintaining unconditional loyalty to their God. That covenant structure closely corresponds to the Neo-Assyrian state treaties that have been recovered from this period, the most famous of which is the Vassal Treaty of Esarhaddon (672 BCE). At a number of points, the authors of Deuteronomy seem consciously to have patterned their covenant after this treaty tradition, which they could have known either directly or in Aramaic translation. From this perspective, Deuteronomy represents a counter-treaty: Its authors turned the weapon of imperialism into a bid for freedom, shifting its oath of loyalty from the Assyrian overlord to their divine sovereign.

Thus tutored in international treaty conventions, the authors of Deuteronomy elsewhere reveal their knowledge of two additional important literary genres from the ancient Near East: the legal collection (15.1–18 n.; 17.8–13 n., 14–20 n.; 22.13–23.1 n.) and wisdom literature (1.13 n.; 4.2 n.). Moreover, they also employed a convention of authorship familiar in their time. They did not directly attach their name to their composition or write in their own voice. Instead, they attributed their composition to a prestigious figure from the past. By employing "Moses" as their spokesperson, they established a link with tradition at precisely the time when tradition, for the sake of survival, had to be transformed. This convention of ascribing a text to an ancient personage, called "pseudepigraphy," is well known in the literature of the Second Temple period; examples include *Jubilees, 4 Ezra,* the *Testament of Abraham,* and (among the Dead Sea Scrolls) the *Temple Scroll.*

The Layers of Tradition

DEUTERONOMY PRESERVES SEVERAL LAYERS of tradition within itself: The structure of three different discourses with an appendix already suggests a process of literary growth. That growth is closely connected to the gradual formation of the Hebrew Bible. To appreciate what is involved, it helps imaginatively to turn the clock back to the time before there was an assembled, complete Bible as we now know it.

1. When Deuteronomy was first promulgated, it would not have been part of any larger whole. Instead, it would have been complete by itself as a "scroll of the torah" (i.e., the "scroll of the Teaching" in 2 Kings 22.8). It would have consisted primarily of some form of most of the laws of chs 12–26, framed by a relatively simple introduc-

tion and conclusion. This form of Deuteronomy presented itself as a treaty concluded between the nation and its God in a formal ceremony whereby each citizen took an oath of loyalty under penalty of strict sanctions (28.1–46). This was very likely the preexilic form of Deuteronomy.

2. At a later stage, presumably sometime during the exile (586–538 BCE), Deuteronomy would have been incorporated into the Deuteronomistic History (Joshua through 2 Kings) to serve as its introduction. At this point, the "Deuteronomistic" editors would have given the book its present literary frame (1.1–4.40, chs 31–34), while also adding to the legal corpus, selectively tying its promises or expectations to the later historical material (see 12.8 n.). Expansions in Deuteronomy that reflect the Babylonian exile may derive from this stage (i.e., 4.25–31; 28.47–56; 30.1–10).

3. At a still later point, in the postexilic period, Priestly editors appended Deuteronomy to the newly formed Pentateuch, to serve as its conclusion. Ironically, the decision to conclude the Pentateuch with Deuteronomy separated the overall narrative plan of Genesis through Numbers from its logical fulfillment in an account of the conquest of the land. This narrative climax was delayed until Joshua.

The insertion of Deuteronomy into these larger literary units makes an important theological statement. Following the insertion of Deuteronomy into the story of the promise of the land to the patriarchs, the enslavement in Egypt, the exodus, and the wilderness wandering, Deuteronomy's last chapter (ch 34) brings to a close both the book and the Torah. But that formal conclusion now separates not only Moses but also the reader from access to the land whose covenantal promise was the basis of the entire narrative (Gen. 12.1). Early on, from the vantage point of the Judean hills, Abram viewed the panorama of that promised land, as it extended in every direction of the compass (Gen. 13.14–17). But at the end of his life he was constrained to bargain for a small plot of land where he might bury his wife, Sarah (Gen. 23.1–20): poignant testimony that Abraham never gained possession of the land promised him. So too, now, closing the circle, does the Torah conclude with a panorama that symbolizes dislocation and loss, as Moses looks out over Canaan from the heights of Mount Pisgah. Prohibited from entering the very promised land to which he successfully led his people, he finds his only access in that forlorn prospect.

As with Abraham and Moses, so, too, the reader. Ancient editors have deliberately defined the Torah as a literary unit so as, first, to accommodate the addition of Deuteronomy and, second, to sever it from its logically expected fulfillment. The possession of the land is diverted instead into the next literary unit, which is to say, into the future. So profound a reconfiguration both of the patriarchal promise and of the overall plot is conceivable only in light of the historical experience of exile, which profoundly called the possession of the land into question. Had possession of the land remained central to the covenant, Israelite religion would have collapsed. The fulfillment of the Torah is thus redactionally redefined as obedience to the requirements of covenantal law rather than the acquisition of a finite possession.

The Transformation of Deuteronomy in the Second Temple Period

IN BIBLICAL NARRATIVE, THE TORAH crosses the symbolic geographic divide of the Jordan, carried, in the Ark of the Covenant, upon the shoulders of the Levitical priests (Deut. 31.25; Josh. 3.14–17). So did the text of Deuteronomy cross the historical divide of the Babylonian exile, borne on the shoulders of the multiple Jewish communities that survived the exile and that developed their distinct identities thereafter. This crucial transition from the First Temple to the Second Temple periods, from preexilic Israelite religion to postexilic religion, represents a major pivot in the history of Israelite literature, thought, and belief. The wrenching force of that transition, as institutions and assumptions underwent profound transformations, created "stress fractures" in the text of Deuteronomy. In many cases, preexilic religious and legal norms became unintelligible to these postexilic communities. Therefore in the process of teaching and translating Deuteronomy, they were forced to translate not only the language of the text but also its ideas: from one language into another, from one historical period into another, from one set of assumptions into another. Sometimes this overlay of postexilic ideas may interfere with understanding the original meaning of the text, even though that overlay now represents the conventional way that Deuteronomy has come to be read and understood. Such cases require attention in the annotations.

As a broader model for understanding such issues, it would be helpful to view the religion of Israel reflected by Deuteronomy in the preexilic period as in many ways a "Near Eastern" religion. This applies preeminently to the original theology of the text, which, like all religions of its time and place, viewed its god as presiding over a "divine council" of lesser deities (5.7 n.; 6.4 n.). From this perspective, texts like the Shema called for exclusive loyalty to God, without thereby denying the existence of other deities, just as Near Eastern treaties required that a vassal swear allegiance to a single political monarch (6.4–9 n.). But once radical monotheism became the Jewish norm in the Second Temple period, under the influence of exilic prophecy, the original "Israelite" view gradually became "foreign" and unintelligible. The Shema could only be understood as affirming the later "truth" of Jewish monotheism. This authentically Israelite religious language seems to have become so alien that the Hebrew text was "corrected" in several cases to bring it into conformity with later Jewish theology (32.8 n; 32.43 n.).

The same issue applies to law. In certain cases, the preexilic authors of Deuteronomy clearly followed Near Eastern procedures. For example, they required the immediate, summary execution of those disloyal to God, as if under the emergency conditions of martial law (13.10 n.). In the Second Temple period, however, this breach of Deuteronomy's own requirement for due process (17.2–7 n.) was understandably seen as contradicting the norms of Jewish law! The text was therefore read and taught as if the requirement for execution were to take place only after the due process that, in fact, it originally bypassed. As a next step, this originally oral legal interpretation of the law was introduced into the text of the law, when Deuteronomy was translated into Greek for the Jewish community of Alexandria (in the Septuagint, ca. 225 BCE). The conscientious translator could do no less, since that revision of the law was what the law "had" to mean, lest the Torah here contradict Jewish law!

Just as the Septuagint updates the Hebrew in light of later Jewish law, elsewhere the reverse may hold true. On occasion, the Greek version retains classical views of preexilic Israelite religion that have been updated or corrected in the standardized Masoretic Text of the Bible (see notes at 28.69; 32.8; 32.43). In such cases, the Septuagint or the Dead Sea Scrolls may open a window into the original meaning of a passage that has been lost in the Masoretic Text. The commentary will therefore take these ancient textual "witnesses" to the text into account, in the hope of recovering what Deuteronomy's original authors sought to say. Since the NJPS translation follows the Masoretic Hebrew version, which is familiar from synagogue worship, it should simply be pointed out that these additional versions are themselves part of Jewish history. Unfortunately, at the level of popular culture, it is often no longer recognized that the Septuagint was a Jewish translation, one prepared for the thriving Jewish community of Alexandria. In translating the Bible into their living language of Greek, that community saw the Torah as also telling their story. Thus, where Deuteronomy's Hebrew refers to the "horror" of foreign invasion as punishment for national wrongdoing, the Septuagint reinterprets that punishment as the contemporary truth of "diaspora" (28.25 n.). The multiple Judaisms of the Second Temple period each had their own way of reading Deuteronomy, and thus of having Moses include them in his oration.

Deuteronomy and Interpretation

DEUTERONOMY REWARDS THE ATTENTION of contemporary readers and thinkers, whether religiously committed or secular, whether Jewish or non-Jewish. The modernity of Deuteronomy is that it does not permit itself to be read literally or passively. It challenges its readers actively to confront the problem of the relation between divine revelation and human interpretation, even as it breaks down the conventional boundaries between Scripture and tradition. It makes paradox central to its structure. As the book narrates the story of its formation, it also anticipates its prior existence as a complete literary work (31.1–34.12 n.). Interpretation is directly and indirectly a theme of Deuteronomy (1.5 n.). At many points, the authors of Deuteronomy reinterpret earlier laws and narratives (6.1–3 n.). Moreover, the process of the book's editing intentionally preserves conflicting perspectives on a full range of key issues central to Israelite religion: on whether the revelation of the Decalogue at Sinai/Horeb was direct or required the mediation of Moses (5.5 n.); on the stature of Moses relative to other prophets (34.10 n.); on the nature of divine punishment for sin (5.9–10 n.; 7.10 n.); on whether God rules as head of a pantheon or is the only God who exists (see notes at 4.15–31, 35; and 32.8); and even on Deuteronomy's own setting in time and place (see notes at 1.1; 2.12; and 3.11). There is no facile "air-brushing" away of this interplay of perspectives, which in effect reflects an ongoing ancient debate about fundamental religious assumptions. There is finally, for Deuteronomy, no access to

God in the covenant without joining this debate. The reader of Deuteronomy must become, like the authors of Deuteronomy, an interpreter.

Outline and Structure of Deuteronomy

I. The first discourse of Moses (1.1–4.43)
    A. Editorial headnote (1.1–5)
    B. Historical review (1.6–3.29)
    C. Exhortation to obey the Torah (4.1–40)
    D. Appendix: cities of refuge in Transjordan (4.41–43)
II. The second discourse of Moses (4.44–28.68)
    A. Introduction (4.44–49)
    B. The revelation of the Decalogue at Sinai/Horeb (5.1–30)
    C. Preamble to the laws: the requirement of loyalty to God (6.1–11.32)
        1. Validation of Mosaic instruction as revealed upon Horeb (6.1–3)
        2. A sermon on the first commandment of the Decalogue (6.4–25)
        3. The war of conquest (7.1–26)
        4. The temptation to pride and self-sufficiency in the land (8.1–20)
        5. The already broken and renewed covenant (9.1–10.11)
        6. Obedience as the condition for prosperity in the land (10.12–11.32)
    D. The legal corpus (12.1–26.15)
        1. Centralization and purification of sacrificial worship (12.1–13.1)
        2. The requirement for unconditional loyalty (13.2–19)
        3. The obligations of holiness (14.1–29)
        4. Remission of debts and manumission of slaves (15.1–18)
        5. Sacrifice of firstlings (15.19–23)
        6. The festival calendar (16.1–17)
        7. Laws of public officials (16.18–18.22)
            a. The organization of justice (16.18–17.13)
            b. The law of the king (17.14–20)
            c. The Levitical priesthood (18.1–8)
            d. The Mosaic prophet (18.9–22)
        8. Cities of refuge (19.1–13)
        9. Boundary markers (19.14)
        10. The integrity of the judicial system (19.15–21)
        11. Rules for waging holy war (20.1–20)
        12. Atonement for an unsolved murder (21.1–9)
        13. Miscellaneous criminal, civil, and family laws (21.10–25.19)
        14. Concluding liturgies (26.1–15)
    E. Formal conclusion: the reciprocity of the covenant (26.16–19)
    F. Ceremonies at Shechem upon entry to land (27.1–26; cf. 11.29–32)
    G. The consequences of obedience or disobedience: blessing or curse (28.1–68)

III. The third discourse of Moses: the ratification ceremony for the covenant on the plains of Moab (28.69–30.20)

A. Editorial heading: the relation between Moab and Horeb (28.69)

B. Didactic review of Israel's history (29.1–8)

C. Imprecation to ensure loyalty to the covenant (29.9–28)

D. Reassurance of restoration (30.1–10)

E. The accessibility of Torah (30.11–14)

F. The necessity of choice (30.15–20)

IV. The death of Moses and the formation of the Torah (31.1–34.12)

A. Moses makes arrangements for his death (31.1–29)

B. The Song of Moses (31.30–32.44)

C. Double conclusion to the Song (32.45–47)

D. Moses commanded to die (32.48–52)

E. The Blessing of Moses (33.1–29)

F. The death of Moses (34.1–12)

[BERNARD M. LEVINSON]

DEVARIM   דברים

1 These are the words that Moses addressed to all Israel on the other side of the Jordan.—ªThrough the wilderness, in the Arabah near Suph, between Paran and Tophel, Laban, Hazeroth, and Di-zahab, ²it is eleven days from Horeb to Kadesh-barnea by the Mount Seir route.—³ It was in the fortieth year, on the first day of the eleventh month, that Moses addressed the Israelites in accordance with the instructions that the LORD had given him for them, ⁴after he had defeated Sihon king of the Amorites, who dwelt in Heshbon, and King Og of Bashan, who dwelt at Ashtaroth [andᵇ] Edrei. ⁵On the other side of the Jordan, in the land of Moab, Moses undertook to expound this Teaching. He said:

a The rest of this verse and v. 2 are unclear; cf. v. 19 and Num. 33.16–36.
b Cf. Josh. 12.4; 13.12, 31.

1.1–4.43: The first discourse of Moses. This first of Deuteronomy's three discourses has two subsections: an historical retrospective (1.6–3.29) and a sermon on the importance of obeying Torah (4.1–40). An editorial headnote (1.1–5) and appendix (4.41–43) frame the discourse. **1.1–5: Editorial headnote.** Refers to Moses in the third person, attributes the book to him, and locates the book historically and geographically. **1:** On the other side of the Jordan, designating the land east of the Jordan River (Transjordan), where the Israelites have stopped, awaiting entry to the land. That geographical frame of reference places the speaker west of the Jordan and thus already in Canaan. According to the narrative line, however, the Israelites have not yet reached the promised land and Moses never does. From this and similar anachronisms, a small number of medieval Jewish commentators already recognized that not all of the Torah could be attributed to Moses (see also 2.12 n.; 3.11 n.); this is the modern consensus as well. The Arabah, the rift valley that includes the Jordan River and stretches south from the Dead Sea through Eilat and the Red Sea into Africa. The places mentioned cannot be identified with certainty. **2:** Eleven days implies a scathing indictment of the nation. As a result of their rebellion in the desert (Num. chs 13–14), it actually took them thirty-eight years, eight months, and twenty days to reach this point after they first broke camp (Num. 10.11). Horeb (Exod. 3.1; 17.6; 33.6) is Deuteronomy's term for the mount of revelation. "(Mount) Sinai," in contrast, is the more standard term used by the Yahwistic and Priestly writers elsewhere in the Torah (see Exod. 19.11; 34.29); it occurs in Deuteronomy only at 33.2. **4:** Num. 21.21–35. **5:** Expound seems intentionally ambiguous about whether

⁶ The LORD our God spoke to us at Horeb, saying: You have stayed long enough at this mountain. ⁷ Start out and make your way to the hill country of the Amorites and to all their neighbors in the Arabah, the hill country, the Shephelah,ᵃ the Negeb, the seacoast, the land of the Canaanites,ᵇ and the Lebanon, as far as the Great River, the river Euphrates. ⁸ See, I place the land at your disposal. Go, take possession of the land that the LORD swore to your fathers, Abraham, Isaac, and Jacob, to assign to them and to their heirs after them.

⁹ Thereupon I said to you, "I cannot bear the burden of you by myself. ¹⁰ The LORD your God has multiplied you until you are today as numerous as the stars in the sky.— ¹¹ May the LORD, the God of your fathers, increase your numbers a thousandfold, and bless you as He promised you.—¹² How can I bear unaided the trouble of you, and the burden, and the bickering! ¹³ Pick from each of your tribes men who are wise, discerning, and experienced, and I will appoint them as your heads." ¹⁴ You answered me and said, "What you propose to do is good." ¹⁵ So I took your tribal leaders, wise and experienced men, and appointed them heads over you: chiefs of thousands, chiefs of hundreds, chiefs of fifties, and chiefs of tens, and officials for your tribes. ¹⁶ I charged your magistrates at that time as follows, "Hear out your fellow men, and decide justly between any man and a fellow Israelite or a stranger. ¹⁷ You shall not be partial in judgment: hear out low and high alike. Fear no man, for judgment is God's. And any matter that is too difficult for you, you shall bring to me and I will hear it." ¹⁸ Thus I instructed you, at that time, about the various things that you should do.

ᵃ Others "Lowland."   ᵇ I.e., Phoenicia.

Moses here proclaims new religious teachings, not previously heard, or simply explicates material already proclaimed. *This Teaching,* lit. "this torah" (4.8, 44; 27.3, 8, 26; 28.58, 61; 29.20, 28; 30.10; 31.9, 11, 12; 32.46). The word designates not only the combination of ritual, civil, family, and ethical law found in chs 12–26, but also the religious instructions of chs 5–11. Here, as elsewhere in Deuteronomy, the reference is not to the entire Torah, but specifically to Deuteronomy itself.

1.6–3.29: Historical review. Moses rehearses the exodus, revelation at Horeb, and rebellion in the desert for the generation who arose after these events and did not directly witness them, so that they may understand what brought them to the present moment. At a number of points, this narrative diverges from that of Exodus–Numbers. **6:** The original of the divine command quoted has not been preserved (cf. Num. ch 10). **7:** *Amorites,* as at Gen. 15.16, seems to be used generically for the family of nations who are the original inhabitants of Canaan, rather than technically to designate one of those nations (contrast Gen. 15.19–21; Exod. 3.8, 17). *The Shephelah* is the region of foothills between the hill country on the east and the *seacoast* on the west. *The Negeb* is the semi-arid region south of the hill country. *Great River:* The ideal borders of the Israelite empire extended to the *Euphrates* (Gen. 15.18), the northern limit of David's conquests (2 Sam. 8.3). **8:** *See . . . at your disposal:* With this binding oral proclamation, God symbolically displays the land and transfers its legal title to Israel (similarly, Gen. 13.14–15).

1.9–18: Leadership institutionalized. This account combines and reinterprets two previous accounts of the creation of a military-judicial system to share the burden of leadership (compare vv. 9–12 with Num. 11.14–17 and vv. 13–17 with Exod. 18.13–27). This new version places the institutionalization of leadership after the departure from Sinai rather than before it and omits the important advisory role of Jethro, the non-Israelite (contrast Exod. ch 18). **10:** *Stars in the sky,* thus fulfilling the promises to the ancestors (Gen. 15.5; 22.17; 26.4; Exod. 32.13). **11:** *God of your fathers:* Deuteronomy's normal phrase is "the LORD your/our God" (i.e., vv. 6, 10, 19–21; 6.1, 4, 10). This departure from that formula ties this new generation to its past by recalling God's earlier promises (Gen. 26.24; 32.10; Exod. 3.6). **13:** *Wise* (contrast Exod. 18.21), an attribute regularly stressed by Deuteronomy (4.6; 32.29), suggesting the influence of wisdom literature upon its authors. *Experienced,* lit. "knowing," continuing the emphasis upon wisdom as a criterion for leadership. **16:** *Stranger,* better, "resident alien," a legal term that refers to the non-Israelite who lives in the community without title to land and who is therefore economically vulnerable. Deuteronomy insists upon a single law that applies to Israelite and non-Israelite alike (5.14; 10.18–19; 14.29; 16.11; 24.14, 17, 19–21). **17:** Similarly, 16.18–20.

¹⁹ We set out from Horeb and traveled the great and terrible wilderness that you saw, along the road to the hill country of the Amorites, as the LORD our God had commanded us. When we reached Kadesh-barnea, ²⁰ I said to you, "You have come to the hill country of the Amorites which the LORD our God is giving to us. ²¹ See, the LORD your God has placed the land at your disposal. Go up, take possession, as the LORD, the God of your fathers, promised you. Fear not and be not dismayed."

²² Then all of you came to me and said, "Let us send men ahead to reconnoiter the land for us and bring back word on the route we shall follow and the cities we shall come to." ²³ I approved of the plan, and so I selected twelve of your men, one from each tribe. ²⁴ They made for the hill country, came to the wadi Eshcol, and spied it out. ²⁵ They took some of the fruit of the land with them and brought it down to us. And they gave us this report: "It is a good land that the LORD our God is giving to us."

²⁶ Yet you refused to go up, and flouted the command of the LORD your God. ²⁷ You sulked⁰ in your tents and said, "It is because the LORD hates us that He brought us out of the land of Egypt, to hand us over to the Amorites to wipe us out. ²⁸ᵇ⁻What kind of place⁻ᵇ are we going to? Our kinsmen have taken the heart out of us, saying, 'We saw there a people stronger and taller than we, large cities with walls sky-high, and even Anakites.'"

²⁹ I said to you, "Have no dread or fear of them. ³⁰ None other than the LORD your God, who goes before you, will fight for you, just as He did for you in Egypt before your very eyes, ³¹ and in the wilderness, where you saw how the LORD your God carried you, as a man carries his son, all the way that you traveled until you came to this place. ³² Yet for all that, you have no faith in the LORD your God, ³³ who goes before you on your journeys—to scout the place where you are to encamp—in fire by night and in cloud by day, in order to guide you on the route you are to follow."

³⁴ When the LORD heard your loud complaint, He was angry. He vowed: ³⁵ Not one of these men, this evil generation, shall see the good land that I swore to give to your fathers—³⁶ none except Caleb son of Jephunneh; he shall see it, and to him and to his descendants will I give the land on which he set foot, because he remained loyal to the LORD.

³⁷ Because of you the LORD was incensed with me too, and He said: You shall not enter it either. ³⁸ Joshua son of

1.19–46: From Horeb to Kadesh: A retelling, with significant variations, of the spies' reconnaissance of the land (Num. ch 13), the people's complaining of God's inability to fulfill the promises made to Israel's ancestors (Num. 14.1–38), and the abortive attempt to penetrate Canaan from the south despite the divine command not to do so (Num. 14.39–45; cf. 21.1–3). **28:** *Anakites,* see Num. 13.22, 33 n. **30:** Exod. 14.14. **33:** *Fire . . . cloud,* see Exod. 13.21–22 n. **34–36:** See Num. 14.28–30. **37:** Here Moses is not punished for his own sin (contrast Num. 20.10–13; 27.12–23). Instead, the narrator presents Moses as innocent and as vicariously bearing the punishment due Israel for its sin (see 3.24–28).

---

a Precise meaning of Heb. uncertain.   *b-b Lit. "Where."*

Nun, who attends you, he shall enter it. Imbue him with strength, for he shall allot it to Israel. [39] Moreover, your little ones who you said would be carried off, your children who do not yet know good from bad, they shall enter it; to them will I give it and they shall possess it. [40] As for you, turn about and march into the wilderness by the way of the Sea of Reeds.

[41] You replied to me, saying, "We stand guilty before the LORD. We will go up now and fight, just as the LORD our God commanded us." And you all girded yourselves with war gear and recklessly[a] started for the hill country. [42] But the LORD said to me, "Warn them: Do not go up and do not fight, since I am not in your midst; else you will be routed by your enemies." [43] I spoke to you, but you would not listen; you flouted the LORD's command and willfully marched into the hill country. [44] Then the Amorites who lived in those hills came out against you like so many bees and chased you, and they crushed you at Hormah in Seir. [45] Again you wept before the LORD; but the LORD would not heed your cry or give ear to you.

2 [46] Thus, after you had remained at Kadesh [b]all that long time,[b] [1] we marched back into the wilderness by the way of the Sea of Reeds, as the LORD had spoken to me, and skirted the hill country of Seir a long time.

[2] Then the LORD said to me: [3] You have been skirting this hill country long enough; now turn north. [4] And charge the people as follows: You will be passing through the territory of your kinsmen, the descendants of Esau, who live in Seir. Though they will be afraid of you, be very careful [5] not to provoke them. For I will not give you of their land so much as a foot can tread on; I have given the hill country of Seir as a possession to Esau. [6c]What food you eat you shall obtain from them for money; even the water you drink you shall procure from them for money.[c] [7] Indeed, the LORD your God has blessed you in all your undertakings. He has watched over your wanderings through this great wilderness; the LORD your God has been with you these past forty years: you have lacked nothing.

[8] We then moved on, away from our kinsmen, the descendants of Esau, who live in Seir, away from the road of the Arabah, away from Elath and Ezion-geber; and we marched on in the direction of the wilderness of Moab. [9] And the LORD said to me: Do not harass the Moabites or

2.1–25: The circuit via Transjordan. 1–8a: Num. 20.14–21. From Kadesh Israel turned south through the Arabah to the Gulf of Aqaba in order to go around Edom (Num. 21.4; cf. 33.47–49). **4:** *Descendants of Esau,* see Gen. 36.1. **8a:** *Elath,* see 1 Kings 9.26. *Ezion-geber,* see Num. 33.35. **8b–25:** Num. 21.4–20, significantly revised. Turning along the brook Zered (modern Wadi el-Hasa), which formed Edom's southern boundary, Israel detoured through the wilderness of Moab toward the Amorite kingdom of Sihon. **9:** Moab and Ammon (v. 19) were traditionally related through Lot (Gen. 19.36–38).

---

a Meaning of Heb. uncertain.　　b-b Lit. "many days, like the days that you remained."
c-c Or "You may obtain food from them to eat for money; and you may also procure water from them to drink for money."

provoke them to war. For I will not give you any of their land as a possession; I have assigned Ar as a possession to the descendants of Lot.—

10 It was formerly inhabited by the Emim, a people great and numerous, and as tall as the Anakites. 11 Like the Anakites, they are counted as Rephaim; but the Moabites call them Emim. 12 Similarly, Seir was formerly inhabited by the Horites; but the descendants of Esau dispossessed them, wiping them out and settling in their place, just as Israel did in the land they were to possess, which the LORD had given to them.—

13 Up now! Cross the wadi Zered!

So we crossed the wadi Zered. 14 The time that we spent in travel from Kadesh-barnea until we crossed the wadi Zered was thirty-eight years, until that whole generation of warriors had perished from the camp, as the LORD had sworn concerning them. 15 Indeed, the hand of the LORD struck them, to root them out from the camp to the last man.

16 When all the warriors among the people had died off, 17 the LORD spoke to me, saying: 18 You are now passing through the territory of Moab, through Ar. 19 You will then be close to the Ammonites; do not harass them or start a fight with them. For I will not give any part of the land of the Ammonites to you as a possession; I have assigned it as a possession to the descendants of Lot.—

20 It, too, is counted as Rephaim country. It was formerly inhabited by Rephaim, whom the Ammonites call Zamzummim, 21 a people great and numerous and as tall as the Anakites. The LORD wiped them out, so that [the Ammonites] dispossessed them and settled in their place, 22 as He did for the descendants of Esau who live in Seir, when He wiped out the Horites before them, so that they dispossessed them and settled in their place, as is still the case.*a* 23 So, too, with the Avvim who dwelt in villages in the vicinity of Gaza: the Caphtorim, who came from Crete,*b* wiped them out and settled in their place.—

24 Up! Set out across the wadi Arnon! See, I give into your power Sihon the Amorite, king of Heshbon, and his land. Begin the occupation: engage him in battle. 25 This day I begin to put the dread and fear of you upon the peoples everywhere under heaven, so that they shall tremble and quake because of you whenever they hear you mentioned.

10–12: These verses are slightly indented, setting them off from the rest of the passage so as to mitigate the anachronistic post-conquest perspective (see v. 12 n.). 10–11: *Emim, Rephaim* (cf. v. 20; 3.11–13), names reflecting the legendary view that the aboriginal inhabitants of the land were fearsome giants. 12: *Horites,* see Gen. 36.20 n. *As Israel did . . . to possess:* Here the Israelite conquest of the land is represented as already having been completed, conflicting with the attribution to Moses and the narrative setting in Transjordan, prior to the conquest. The anachronism reflects the date of composition of this section (see 1.1 n.; 3.11 n.). 13: *Wadi,* a seasonal stream that dries up in the summer. 14: Fulfilling God's angry oath (1.34–35; Num. 14.28–30). Without the death of the generation of the exodus, here marked as accomplished, there can be no entry into the promised land. 15: *Hand of the LORD,* thus indicating that they did not die merely of old age or natural causes. The imagery inverts the standard idea of holy war: God had turned against Israel rather than fighting on its behalf (32.30 n.; see 3.22; 7.1–5; 12.29–31; 20.1–20). 20: Cf. vv. 10–11 n., Gen. 14.5. 23: *Caphtorim . . . Crete* refers to the conquest of the coastal plain by Sea Peoples such as Philistines shortly after 1200 BCE (see Gen. 10.14; Amos 9.7). 24: *Arnon,* see Num. 21.13–14.

a Lit. "until this day."   b Heb. "Caphtor."

26 Then I sent messengers from the wilderness of Kedemoth to King Sihon of Heshbon with an offer of peace, as follows, 27 "Let me pass through your country. I will keep strictly to the highway, turning off neither to the right nor to the left. 28 What food I eat you will supply for money, and what water I drink you will furnish for money; just let me pass through*—29 as the descendants of Esau who dwell in Seir did for me, and the Moabites who dwell in Ar—that I may cross the Jordan into the land that the LORD our God is giving us."

30 But King Sihon of Heshbon refused to let us pass through, because the LORD had stiffened his will and hardened his heart in order to deliver him into your power—as is now the case. 31 And the LORD said to me: See, I begin by placing Sihon and his land at your disposal. Begin the occupation; take possession of his land.

32 Sihon with all his men took the field against us at Jahaz, 33 and the LORD our God delivered him to us and we defeated him and his sons and all his men. 34 At that time we captured all his towns, and we doomed*b* every town—men, women, and children—leaving no survivor. 35 We retained as booty only the cattle and the spoil of the cities that we captured. 36 From Aroer on the edge of the Arnon valley, including the town*c* in the valley itself, to Gilead, not a city was too mighty for us; the LORD our God delivered everything to us. 37 But you did not encroach upon the land of the Ammonites, all along the wadi Jabbok and the towns of the hill country, just as the LORD our God had commanded.

3 We made our way up the road toward Bashan, and King Og of Bashan with all his men took the field against us at Edrei. 2 But the LORD said to me: Do not fear him, for I am delivering him and all his men and his country into your power, and you will do to him as you did to Sihon king of the Amorites, who lived in Heshbon.

3 So the LORD our God also delivered into our power King Og of Bashan, with all his men, and we dealt them such a blow that no survivor was left. 4 At that time we captured all his towns; there was not a town that we did not take from them: sixty towns, the whole district of Argob, the kingdom of Og in Bashan—5 all those towns were fortified with high walls, gates,*d* and bars—apart from a great number of unwalled towns. 6 We doomed

26–37: The victory over *Sihon,* whose capital was at Heshbon. The earlier source in Num. 21.21–32 is here supplemented and revised. **30:** See Exod. 4.21 n. **34:** *Doomed,* see 7.2 n. **37:** The river *Jabbok* makes a wide bend south and thus forms the western border of Ammon (3.16).

3.1–11: The victory over Bashan (Num. 21.33–35). **1:** *Edrei,* on the extreme south border of *Bashan;* see Num. 21.33.

a Lit. "with my feet."
b I.e., placed under ḥerem, which meant the annihilation of the population. Cf. note c at Num. 21.2; Josh. 6.24.
c Meaning of Heb. uncertain.   d I.e., two-leaf doors.

them as we had done in the case of King Sihon of Heshbon; we doomed every town—men, women, and children—⁷and retained as booty all the cattle and the spoil of the towns.

⁸Thus we seized, at that time, from the two Amorite kings, the country beyond the Jordan, from the wadi Arnon to Mount Hermon—⁹Sidonians called Hermon Sirion, and the Amorites call it Senir—¹⁰all the towns of the Tableland and the whole of Gilead and Bashan as far as Salcahᵃ and Edrei, the towns of Og's kingdom in Bashan. ¹¹Only King Og of Bashan was left of the remaining Rephaim. His bedstead, an iron bedstead, is now in Rabbah of the Ammonites; it is nine cubits long and four cubits wide, by ᵇ‍the standard cubit!‍ᵇ

¹²ᶜAnd this is the land which we apportioned at that time: The part from Aroer along the wadi Arnon, with part of the hill country of Gilead and its towns, I assigned to the Reubenites and the Gadites. ¹³The rest of Gilead, and all of Bashan under Og's rule—the whole Argob district, all that part of Bashan which is called Rephaim country—I assigned to the half-tribe of Manasseh. ¹⁴Jair son of Manasseh received the whole Argob district (that is, Bashan) as far as the boundary of the Geshurites and the Maacathites, and named it after himself: Havvoth-jairᵈ—as is still the case. ¹⁵To Machir I assigned Gilead. ¹⁶And to the Reubenites and the Gadites I assigned the part from Gilead down to the wadi Arnon, the middle of the wadi being the boundary, and up to the wadi Jabbok, the boundary of the Ammonites.

¹⁷ᵉ[We also seized] the Arabah, from the foot of the slopes of Pisgah on the east, to the edge of the Jordan, and from Chinnereth down to the sea of the Arabah, the Dead Sea.

¹⁸At that time I charged you,ᶠ saying, "The LORD your God has given you this country to possess. You must go as shock-troops, warriors all, at the head of your Israelite kinsmen. ¹⁹Only your wives, children, and livestock—I know that you have much livestock—shall be left in the towns I have assigned to you, ²⁰until the LORD has granted your kinsmen a haven such as you have, and they too have taken possession of the land that the LORD your God is assigning them, beyond the Jordan. Then you may return each to the homestead that I have assigned to him."

11: The oversized bed of Og, one of the legendary Rephaim (2.10–11), was a "museum piece" in Rabbah, a city on the Ammonite border. The emphasis that this bed *is now* there places the historical perspective of the narrator, and thus of Deuteronomy's composition, long after the events here recounted (1.1 n.; 2.12 n.). A *cubit* was about 44 cm (17.5 in.). **12–22:** The allotment of tribal territories in Transjordan (Num. ch 32; Josh. ch 13). **14:** Num. 32.41. **17:** The territory included the eastern part of the Jordan Valley or

---

a Others "Salecah" or "Salchah."

b-b Lit. "by a man's forearm."

c Vv. 12–13 proceed from south to north; vv. 14–16 from north to south.

d I.e., "villages of Jair."   e Continuing vv. 8–10; cf. 4.47–49.

f I.e., the two and a half tribes.

21 I also charged Joshua at that time, saying, "You have seen with your own eyes all that the LORD your God has done to these two kings; so shall the LORD do to all the kingdoms into which you shall cross over. 22 Do not fear them, for it is the LORD your God who will battle for you."

VA-ʾETḤANNAN   ואתחנן

23 I pleaded with the LORD at that time, saying, 24 "O Lord GOD, You who let Your servant see the first works of Your greatness and Your mighty hand, You whose powerful deeds no god in heaven or on earth can equal! 25 Let me, I pray, cross over and see the good land on the other side of the Jordan, that good hill country, and the Lebanon." 26 But the LORD was wrathful with me on your account and would not listen to me. The LORD said to me, "Enough! Never speak to Me of this matter again! 27 Go up to the summit of Pisgah and gaze about, to the west, the north, the south, and the east. Look at it well, for you shall not go across yonder Jordan. 28 Give Joshua his instructions, and imbue him with strength and courage, for he shall go across at the head of this people, and he shall allot to them the land that you may only see."

29 Meanwhile we stayed on in the valley near Beth-peor.

4 And now, O Israel, give heed to the laws and rules that I am instructing you to observe, so that you may live to enter and occupy the land that the LORD, the God of your fathers, is giving you. 2 You shall not add anything to what I command you or take anything away from it, but keep the commandments of the LORD your God that I enjoin upon you. 3 You saw with your own eyes what the LORD did in the matter of Baal-peor, that the LORD your God wiped out from among you every person who followed Baal-peor; 4 while you, who held fast to the LORD your God, are all alive today.

5 See, I have imparted to you laws and rules, as the LORD my God has commanded me, for you to abide by in

---

ment and broadening its significance. Admonitions to obedience (vv. 1, 40) frame the unit, which systematically contrasts: obedience (vv. 5–24)/disobedience (vv. 25–31); remembering/forgetting (vv. 9, 23); the LORD/other gods (vv. 7, 34); Israel's revealed Torah/the laws of other nations (vv. 8, 28); and God/idols (vv. 12–20). The central lesson is that the correct worship of God is aniconic: Images (whether of God or of natural phenomena) should play no role in Israelite religion. This becomes so strong a theme that idolatry, in and of itself, is asserted to be the cause of the nation's exile from its land (vv. 25–31). The explicit reference to exile suggests that the unit is a late theological explanation for the Babylonian exile (586–538 BCE). The focus on idolatry as the basis for the divine punishment diverges significantly from the perspective elsewhere that views failure to heed "all his [God's] commandments and decrees" as the cause of exile (28.15; cf. 28.1, 45, 58–59).

4.1–4: The incident at Baal-peor (Num. 25.1–9) **is recalled** to emphasize the importance of fidelity to God and the dire consequences of worshipping other gods. **2:** This admonition not to alter the Torah, whether by addition or subtraction (cf. 13.1), parallels similar admonitions in wisdom literature (Prov. 30.6; Eccl. 3.14; 12.12–13; Sir. 42.21; cf. Revelation 22.18–19). It seems to originate in ancient Near Eastern literature (Egyptian wisdom literature; Babylonian law codes; Neo-Assyrian state treaties; cf. 1 Maccabees 8.30). **3:** *Followed*, see 6.14 n. **5–8:** The Torah as Israel's "wisdom." The author here challenges the prevailing Near Eastern idea that wisdom was a royal prerogative. Whereas, for example, the ancient Babylonian Laws of Hammurabi (ca. 1755 BCE) praised the "just decisions" of its "wise" king (cols 47.1; 4.7), here it is rather the nation Israel who will be internationally renowned as "wise" for its "just"

Arabah. **22:** The whole story of the exodus, wilderness journey, and invasion of Canaan is governed by the conventions of holy war, whereby God is a divine warrior who engages in battle on behalf of Israel. **23–29:** Num. 27.12–23. **24:** *No god . . . can equal:* The assertion of God's superior power, relative to other gods *in heaven*, assumes the existence of other gods (5.7 n; 6.4 n.; 32.8 n.; Exod. 15.11;

Ps. 89.5–8). For the later perspective of monotheism, see 4.35 n. **26:** On the vicarious suffering of Moses, see 1.37 n. **27:** Mount *Pisgah*, see 34.1 n.

4.1–40: Exhortation to obey the Torah. While preceding the Decalogue in narrative terms (5.6–18), this unit provides a historically later theological reflection upon it, focusing on the second command-the land that you are about to enter and occupy. ⁶Observe them faithfully, for that will be proof of your wisdom and discernment to other peoples, who on hearing of all these laws will say, "Surely, that great nation is a wise and discerning people." ⁷For what great nation is there that has a god so close at hand as is the LORD our God whenever we call upon Him? ⁸Or what great nation has laws and rules as perfect as all this Teaching that I set before you this day?

⁹But take utmost care and watch yourselves scrupulously, so that you do not forget the things that you saw with your own eyes and so that they do not fade from your mind as long as you live. And make them known to your children and to your children's children: ¹⁰The day you stood before the LORD your God at Horeb, when the LORD said to me, "Gather the people to Me that I may let them hear My words, in order that they may learn to revere Me as long as they live on earth, and may so teach their children." ¹¹You came forward and stood at the foot of the mountain. The mountain was ablaze with flames to the very skies, dark with densest clouds. ¹²The LORD spoke to you out of the fire; you heard the sound of words but perceived no shape—nothing but a voice. ¹³He declared to you the covenant that He commanded you to observe, the Ten Commandments; and He inscribed them on two tablets of stone. ¹⁴At the same time the LORD commanded me to impart to you laws and rules for you to observe in the land that you are about to cross into and occupy.

¹⁵For your own sake, therefore, be most careful—since you saw no shape when the LORD your God spoke to you

laws (vv. 6, 8). See also 29.29 n. and 30.11–14 n. **7–8:** Israel is distinguished both by its God and by its law: The two ideas are interlocked. **7:** God is *close at hand,* both in having entered history on behalf of Israel and in revealing His will as Torah (30.14). **8:** The laws are *perfect* (lit. "righteous"), not only in their morality but also as embodying the will of God. This Israelite idea of law as divine revelation diverges from Near Eastern views of law as royal wisdom (see 5.1–30 n.).

4.9–14: The revelation at Sinai/Horeb (Exod. chs 19–20; Deut. ch 5) is recalled in order to instruct the present generation,

who did not experience it. **9:** The paired injunctions not to *forget* the powerful experience of God's actions and to educate *your children,* so that the past becomes "present" also to them, represent a prominent aim of Deuteronomy: to overcome the historical distance of the past and to maintain it as a source of identity (vv. 23, 25; 6.2, 7, 20–25; 8.11; 9.7; 31.13; 32.18). *You saw,* and the following "you stood" (v. 10) are highly paradoxical assertions. Neither is literally true: The actual generation of the exodus had died off and been replaced by this new one, who had experienced none of the events here being recounted (2.14–15 n.). This paradoxical structure of thought, whereby

Moses addresses those who had not witnessed the events as if they had, while insisting that they inculcate the events to posterity, is central to Deuteronomy's theology of history (5.3–4, 20; 11.7; 29.13–14). This develops further in postbiblical Judaism to the idea that all Jews, past, present, and future, were at Sinai. **10:** *My words,* here, the Decalogue ("Ten Commandments"; v. 13; 10.4). Elsewhere, however, the reference to God's "words" designates the legal corpus of chs 12–26 (12.28). *Revere* (lit. "fear"): This important Deuteronomic characterization for the proper relation between the nation and God seems to originate with wisdom literature (Prov. 1.7; Job 28.28). **11:** The manifestation of a god ("theophany") was often associated with disturbances of nature in Ugaritic (Canaanite) literature (see 5.1–30 n.). This motif was taken over by Israelite writers and applied to God (Exod. 19.16–19; 20.15; Pss. 18.7–15; 29.3–9). **12:** *Shape* (also vv. 15; "likeness" vv. 16, 23, 25), directly alluding to the second commandment of the Decalogue (5.8 = Exod. 20.4). **13:** A subtle reinterpretation of Sinai: The specification of that event as one where God proclaimed the *Ten Commandments* occurs only here, at 10.4, and at Exod. 34.28. There is no special number of or name for the commandments (lit. "words") in Exod. chs 19–20 or Deut. ch 5. The rationale for *two tablets of stone* (as at 5.19) derives from ancient Near Eastern state treaties, whereby both sovereign and vassal would retain a separate copy of the treaty. The popular image of a single tablet with a double arch misunderstands that historical context.

4.15–31: Reinterpretation of the second commandment. The Decalogue concedes the existence of other gods, while prohibiting Israel from worshipping them (5.7; cf. 32.8; Exod. 15.11; Ps. 82.1). It then separately prohibits the making of images (5.8). The distinction between those two commandments is dissolved here. The exisat Horeb out of the fire—[16] not to act wickedly and make for yourselves a sculptured image in any likeness whatever: the form of a man or a woman, [17] the form of any beast on earth, the form of any winged bird that flies in the sky, [18] the form of anything that creeps on the ground, the form of any fish that is in the waters below the earth. [19] And when you look up to the sky and behold the sun and the moon and the stars, the whole heavenly host, you must not be lured into bowing down to them or serving them. These the LORD your God allotted to other peoples everywhere under heaven; [20] but you the LORD took and brought out of Egypt, that iron blast furnace, to be His very own people, as is now the case.

[21] Now the LORD was angry with me on your account and swore that I should not cross the Jordan and enter the good land that the LORD your God is assigning you as a heritage. [22] For I must die in this land; I shall not cross the Jordan. But you will cross and take possession of that good land. [23] Take care, then, not to forget the covenant that the LORD your God concluded with you, and not to make for yourselves a sculptured image in any likeness, against which the LORD your God has enjoined you. [24] For the LORD your God is a consuming fire, an impassioned God.

[25] When you have begotten children and children's children and are long established in the land, should you act wickedly and make for yourselves a sculptured image in any likeness, causing the LORD your God displeasure and vexation, [26] I call heaven and earth this day to witness against you that you shall soon perish from the land that you are crossing the Jordan to possess; you shall not long endure in it, but shall be utterly wiped out. [27] The LORD will scatter you among the peoples, and only a scant few of you shall be left among the nations to which the LORD will drive you. [28] There you will serve man-made gods of wood and stone, that cannot see or hear or eat or smell.

[29] But if you search there for the LORD your God, you will find Him, if only you seek Him with all your heart and soul—[30] when you are in distress because all these things have befallen you and, in the end, return to the LORD your God and obey Him. [31] For the LORD your God is a compassionate God: He will not fail you nor will He let you perish; He will not forget the covenant which He made on oath with your fathers.

[32] You have but to inquire about bygone ages that came before you, ever since God created man on earth, from one end of heaven to the other: has anything as grand as this

tence of other gods is no longer conceivable; the sole focus is the prohibition against idols. Here and elsewhere (see v. 19 n.), key ideas in Deuteronomy are reinterpreted from a later theological perspective; such passages therefore represent a later textual layer within Deuteronomy that dates to the exilic period. **16b–19a:** This catalogue follows the order of creation in Gen. ch 1 in reverse order, consistent with an ancient scribal practice when quoting an earlier text. **18:** *Waters below the earth,* seas, rivers, and lakes. Ancient cosmology conceived the earth to be a disk floating on such waters (cf. Gen. 1.9). **19:** *Sun . . . heavenly host:* This polemic against astral cults may reflect images derived from the Neo-Assyrian pantheon that were brought into the Jerusalem Temple by Manasseh but removed by Josiah (2 Kings 21.5; 23.4–5; Jer. 8.2). The idea of idols or of celestial phenomena literally being worshipped sharply distorts ancient Near Eastern religion, which regarded such phenomena as visible manifestations or emblems of a deity, not as themselves alive or divine. This polemic, with the idea that God *allotted* the celestial phenomena to other nations while reserving Israel as "his very own people" (v. 20; cf. 7.6 n.), reinterprets the earlier biblical idea that God, as head of the pantheon, assigned other nations to the supervision of lesser gods but retained Israel as "His allotment" (lit. "His very own possession"; 32.8–9). The author de-animates those gods, reducing them to lifeless celestial objects. **21:** See 1.37 n. **26:** *Heaven . . . witness,* similarly, 30.19; 31.28; 32.1; Isa. 1.2; 44.23; Pss. 69.35; 96.11. **27–28:** These verses allude to the exile of conquered populations, a policy used effectively by the Assyrians and the Babylonians.

4.32–40: Continuation of the double focus on the uniqueness of God's revelation to Israel and of the covenant He made with the nation. This passage fits best in the historical context of the Babyloever happened, or has its like ever been known? 33 Has any people heard the voice of a god speaking out of a fire, as you have, and survived? 34 Or has any god ventured to go and take for himself one nation from the midst of another by prodigious acts, by signs and portents, by war, by a mighty and an outstretched arm and awesome power, as the LORD your God did for you in Egypt before your very eyes? 35 a-It has been clearly demonstrated to you-a that the LORD alone is God; there is none beside Him. 36 From the heavens He let you hear His voice to discipline you; on earth He let you see His great fire; and from amidst that fire you heard His words. 37 And because He loved your fathers, He chose their heirs after them; He Himself,ᵇ in His great might, led you out of Egypt, 38 to drive from your path nations greater and more populous than you, to take you into their land and assign it to you as a heritage, as is still the case. 39 Know therefore this day and keep in mind that the LORD alone is God in heaven above and on earth below; there is no other. 40 Observe His laws and commandments, which I enjoin upon you this day, that it may go well with you and your children after you, and that you may long remain in the land that the LORD your God is assigning to you for all time.

41 Then Moses set aside three cities on the east side of the Jordan 42 to which a manslayer could escape, one who unwittingly slew a fellow man without having been hostile to him in the past; he could flee to one of these cities and live: 43 Bezer, in the wilderness in the Tableland, belonging to the Reubenites; Ramoth, in Gilead, belonging to the Gadites; and Golan, in Bashan, belonging to the Manassites.

44 This is the Teaching that Moses set before the Israelites: 45 these are the decrees, laws, and rules that Moses addressed to the people of Israel, after they had left Egypt, 46 beyond the Jordan, in the valley at Beth-peor, in the land of King Sihon of the Amorites, who dwelt in Heshbon, whom Moses and the Israelites defeated after they had left Egypt. 47 They had taken possession of his country and that of King Og of Bashan—the two kings of the Amorites—which were on the east side of the Jordan 48 from Aroer on the banks of the wadi Arnon, as far as Mount Sion,ᶜ that is, Hermon; 49 also the whole Arabah on the east side of the Jordan, as far as the Sea of the Arabah, at the foot of the slopes of Pisgah.

nian exile (see v. 35 n.). **33:** This alludes to the normal expectation that no human can look directly upon God and survive (Gen. 16.13; 32.30; Exod. 3.6; 19.21; 33.20). **34:** *Prodigious acts . . . portents* refers to the signs performed by Moses and Aaron in Egypt, including the plagues, to persuade Pharaoh to release Israel (Exod. 7.3; 8.19; 10.1, 2; 11.9, 10). **35:** *There is none beside Him:* This affirmation of full or radical monotheism (contrast v. 7; 5.7) corresponds to the thought of the contemporaneous Second Isaiah (Isa. 43.10–13; 44.6–8; 45.6–7, 22).

4.41–43: An appendix: the cities of refuge to be established in Transjordan (cf. Num. 35.9–15; Josh. 20.8). Since Deuteronomy's law concerned with these cities (ch 19) does not refer to this passage, these verses are most likely an editorial appendix composed after the completion of ch 19. Similar disconnected appendices often appear in the Bible at the conclusion of longer literary units (e.g., Lev. ch 27).

4.44–28.68: The second discourse of Moses. 4.44–49: Introduction. Cf. 1.1–5. **49:** *Sea of the Arabah,* the Dead Sea.

a-a Lit. "You have been shown to know."
b Lit. "With His face (or Presence)"; cf. note at Exod. 33.14. c Cf. "Sirion," 3.9.

5 Moses summoned all the Israelites and said to them: Hear, O Israel, the laws and rules that I proclaim to you this day! Study them and observe them faithfully! ² The LORD our God made a covenant with us at Horeb. ³ It was not with our fathers that the LORD made this covenant, but with us, the living, every one of us who is here today. ⁴ Face to face the LORD spoke to you on the mountain out of the fire— ⁵ I stood between the LORD and you at that time to convey the LORD's words to you, for you were afraid of the fire and did not go up the mountain—saying:

5.1–30: The revelation of the Ten Commandments at Sinai/Horeb. The Decalogue is distinctive in the context of ancient Near Eastern literature and religion, transforming the literary conventions of both theophany and law. In Ugaritic myth, for example, the manifestation of a god was accompanied by disturbances of nature like thunder, lightning, and earthquake. But the same phenomena here (Exod. 19.16–19; 20.15) simply provide the dramatic background for Israel's distinctive infusion of moral law into the older theophany tradition. Similarly, several ancient Mesopotamian legal collections (most famously, the Laws of Hammurabi, 1755 BCE) were attributed to a human monarch. King Hammurabi sought in his legal corpus to embody the cosmic principles of justice and equity. In the Decalogue, by contrast, law derives from God and represents divine will. As a result, law and ethics provide the foundation for the nation's covenantal relationship to God. This revision of Near Eastern literary convention is underscored by the markedly public nature of the divine revelation at Sinai/ Horeb. Previously, neither theophany nor law was public and universally accessible. In this account, however, God reveals Himself to the whole nation, including non-Israelites (Exod. 12.38), cutting across boundaries of gender, race, and class.

The literary form of the Decalogue is also significant. It differs from the casuistic "if [infraction]— then [punishment]" form standard to both biblical law (Exod. chs 21–23) and Near Eastern law. That form, which seeks to mete out equitable punishment, nonetheless presupposes a status quo in which infraction of the law is inevitable. The Decalogue's prohibitions, in contrast, are "apodictic" (universal and absolute). The "thou shalt not" form in effect stipulates, "You must never!" The intent is to transform society by creating a moral community in which murder, theft, etc. cease to exist. Equally meaningful is the literary structure of the Decalogue, with one pentad of laws directed toward God and one toward the neighbor. Obedience to God's will (vv. 6–16) here demands active respect for the integrity of the neighbor (vv. 17–18). The Decalogue thus ties love of God inextricably together with love of neighbor: There is no separation of one's religious duties to God from one's moral commitments as a member of the divinely created community. Further, the direct address to the entire nation is grammatically unusual. It employs a singular rather than the expected plural form of "you" to stress that God directly addresses each former slave as an individual human being.

The chapter emphasizes that there is no access to God or revelation without mediation and interpretation (vv. 5, 25–29). The editing drives that point home. It preserves two mutually independent viewpoints about whether God spoke directly to the people, with them standing on the mountain (v. 4), or only through the mediation of Moses, while the people remained at the foot of the moun-

tain (v. 5 n.). Similarly, there seems to be a disagreement about the terror involved in hearing the divine voice directly (vv. 21–22). That the editing of the chapter preserves this play of perspectives requires the attentive reader to join that ancient debate about the nature of revelation.

5.1–5: Making the past present. 3: *Not with our fathers . . . but with us* contrasts literally with the earlier emphasis that the generation who experienced these events has now died off (2.14–15). The aim is to overcome the limits of historical time and place through participation in the covenant, which makes revelation "present" (see 4.9 n.; 29.13–14 n.). *Our fathers* may refer either to the exodus generation (2.14–15 n.) or to the patriarchs Abraham, Isaac, and Jacob (1.11 n.). **5:** NJPS sets off the entire sentence (except for the final word) within dashes to suggest that it intends merely to clarify the preceding verse. More likely, the statement neither continues nor supplements v. 4 but presents an alternative perspective inconsistent with v. 4. *I stood between the LORD and you,* contrast "Face to face" (v. 4). *To convey the LORD's words to you,* contrast "Face to face the LORD spoke" (v. 4). *You . . . did not go up the mountain* (lit. "up on the mountain") contradicts v. 4, "the LORD spoke to you on the mountain." *Saying* provides the original transition from the end of v. 4 directly to the Decalogue.

5.6–18: The Decalogue. The narrative of the Decalogue affirms that God wrote "Ten Words" or statements on two stone tablets and gave them to Moses following the revelation at Horeb (4.13; 10.4). The actual enumeration, however, of the text of the Decalogue into ten commandments is complicated because there are more than ten verbs expressing commands. Because of the ambiguity, three different divisions of the text emerged in ancient Judaism as shown in the chart on p. 376.

⁶ᵃI the LORD am your God who brought you out of the land of Egypt, the house of bondage: ⁷You shall have no other gods beside Me.

⁸You shall not make for yourself a sculptured image, any likeness of what is in the heavens above, or on the

a Tradition varies as to the divisions of the Commandments in vv. 6–18 and the numbering of the verses. Cf. Exod. 20.1, note a.

The text's punctuation for synagogue worship preserves each of the three different systems simultaneously: (1) The cantillation marks that accompany the text for oral chanting (in Yiddish, the "trope") include an "upper" set (above the line), organizing the text according to the conventional rabbinic division; and (2) the "lower" set of cantillation marks (below the line), which reflects the sequence of Hellenistic Judaism. (3) The system of open and closed paragraphs, which divides the final prohibition (v. 18) into two separate laws, is reflected in the later Roman Catholic and Protestant enumeration.

Within the narrative frame, Deuteronomy's authors present the Decalogue as a precise reprise of that found in Exod. 20.2–14. This presentation is complicated by the fact that the text actually diverges in several places from the Exodus version. The most substantial inconsistency lies in the motivation given for the command to observe the Sabbath (see vv. 12–15 n.). Deuteronomy also expands the command to honor the mother and father (v. 16) and presents a slightly different version of the prohibition on coveting (see v. 18 n.). Other factors also challenge any simple reading of the narrative's claim. Whereas what follows the Decalogue in Exodus is the Book of the Covenant (Exod. chs 21–23), here, what follows is a legal collection that, while patterned after the Book of the Covenant, at key points sharply contradicts it (e.g., 12.13–14 n.; 15.12–18 n.). These and other inconsistencies suggest that the reuse of the Decalogue serves to anchor Deuteronomy's

religious and legal innovations (chs 12–26) to the tradition of divine revelation at Sinai/Horeb. But by borrowing the authority of tradition for their new legal compilation, Deuteronomy's authors displace the earlier, competing collection of law: the Book of the Covenant (see further 6.1–3 n.).

At the time of Deuteronomy's composition, it is almost certain that the book of Exodus and the book of Deuteronomy existed independently of one another. However, once Second Temple period editors integrated both into a single literary work, subsequent generations of readers had to struggle to make sense of how the one Torah contained two mutually inconsistent Decalogues! The Rabbis developed elaborate interpretive strategies in order to resolve the inevitable difficulties that resulted. Their exegetical model presupposed that the Torah had a single author and that it was free of contradiction. On that basis, for example, the two different formulations of the Sabbath commandment were resolved by arguing that God had spoken both simultaneously (see v. 12 n.). Similarly, the inconsistency in the narrative frame about whether God spoke directly to the people or only through the mediation of Moses (see v. 5 n.), coupled with the abrupt change from first-person to third-person reference to God in the Decalogue (see v. 11 n.), was resolved by suggesting that God Himself spoke only the first two commandments while Moses spoke the rest on behalf of God, because the people complained of their fear of God (5.20–24). In contrast to this model of interpretation that "harmo-

nizes" inconsistencies, modern critical scholarship presupposes that the Torah represents the work of multiple authors and editors who lived at different times and places. Consequently, the editorial "seams" implicitly recognized by the ancient Rabbis are explained in different ways. For example, the inconsistency in the Decalogue's narrative frame about whether revelation was direct or indirect probably points to the intentional splicing together of originally different traditions, each of which is here honored. The two different versions of the Decalogue most likely derive from two different historical contexts and communities.

5.7: This first commandment takes for granted the existence of other gods; its concern is only to ensure Israel's exclusive loyalty to YHVH. This perspective, called "monolatry," is found frequently within Deuteronomy (see 6.4; 32.8–9, 43; 33.2–3, 27). The idea of monolatry is often expressed by representing YHVH as the ruler of the divine council (see 32.8 n.; Pss. 82; 89.6–8; cf. Exod. 15.11). That perspective almost certainly represents an earlier form of Israelite religion. Ancient Near Eastern sources similarly envision a chief god ruling over a council of other gods. During the Babylonian exile, perhaps under the influence of Second Isaiah, a very different understanding developed. Radical "monotheism" affirms God's greatness, not by portraying Him as more powerful than other gods but, instead, by denying the existence of other deities altogether (see 4.15–31 n; Isa. 43.10–12; 44.6–8; 45.5–6, 14, 18–19, 22). Once that perspective became normative in the period following the exile, the earlier view was no longer intelligible. As a result, in the process of reading, preaching, and translating the biblical text, Second Temple Jewish communities sometimes read the later perspective of monotheism into texts that actually had in mind the earlier idea of God as ruling a divine council (see v. 9 n.; 6.4 n.; 32.8 n.).

earth below, or in the waters below the earth. ⁹ You shall not bow down to them or serve them. For I the LORD your God am an impassioned God, visiting the guilt of the parents upon the children, upon the third and upon the fourth generations of those who reject Me, ¹⁰ but showing kindness to the thousandth generation of those who love Me and keep My commandments.

That original theology has also become unavailable to most contemporary readers, since many of the translations found in synagogue prayer books employ euphemisms to "explain away" the biblical text's clear references to other gods. **9:** *You shall not bow down to them or serve them:* As it stands, the grammar of the text is illogical. The two references to "them" require a plural antecedent. The intended reference cannot be to the immediately previous v. 8, which refers only to "a sculptured image," in the singular. The grammatical difficulty suggests that, at an earlier stage of the text, v. 9 directly continued v. 7, which prohibits the Israelites from expressing their allegiance to "other gods," in the plural. The sequence of thought in the original form of the Decalogue would thus have prohibited allegiance to other gods (v. 7) by bowing down to them in worship (v. 9). Under the impact of later prophetic thought, the standard pre-exilic idea of monolatry became inconceivable and the existence of deities other than YHVH was denied (see previous note). The "other gods" of older texts were reinterpreted as mere lifeless "idols" (see Isa. 40.18–20; 44.9–20). On the basis of such an association, the original direct connection between vv. 6–7 and v. 9 (prohibiting first allegiance to and then worship of other gods) was severed by the later theological perspective represented by v. 8, with its prohibition merely of a "sculptured image." *Serve:* The same verb is translated "worship" at 13.3. The variation reflects the word's two different basic meanings. The first is "to perform a service or labor" (Exod. 21.2; Num. 3.7–8). The second is "to make sacrificial offerings to a deity," whether to God (Exod. 3.12; 4.23; 13.5) or to other gods (Deut. 7.16; 12.2, 30). Here the latter meaning is clearly intended. A postbiblical sermonic interpretation of this commandment is preserved by the word's grammatically impossible vocalization (see also 13.3; Exod. 20.5; 23.24; the vocalization of the Bible dates from the second half of the first millennium CE). The Masoretic Text implies that the prohibition warns: "You shall not be enslaved by them." This theological vocalization unites the word's two meanings: False worship leads to slavery (4.28); only in the worship of YHVH is there freedom (5.6; Lev. 25.55; 26.13). The daily recitation of the Decalogue in the developing liturgy of the Second Temple period provides the context for such ongoing interpretive activity, here witnessed by the formal vocalization of the text. The same understanding appears in a phylactery from Qumran (1Q13). *Visiting the guilt of the parents upon the children:* Punishment for sins against God extends across three generations. This principle of di-

		THE ANALYSIS OF THE "TEN" COMMANDMENTS IN DEUTERONOMY 5.6–18	
COMMAND	RABBINIC JUDAISM	HELLENISTIC JUDAISM AND CHURCH FATHERS	CATHOLIC/LUTHERAN
1	Self-Identification of God as separate command (v. 6)	Other Gods (vv. 6–7)	Other Gods + Images (vv. 6–10)
2	Other Gods + Images (vv. 7–10)	Images (vv. 8–10)	False Oath (v. 11)
3	False Oath (v. 11)	False Oath (v. 11)	Sabbath (vv. 12–15)
4	Sabbath (vv. 12–15)	Sabbath (vv. 12–15)	Parents (v. 16)
5	Parents (v. 16)	Parents (v. 16)	Murder (v. 17)
6	Murder (v. 17)	Murder (v. 17)	Adultery (v. 17)
7	Adultery (v. 17)	Adultery (v. 17)	Theft (v. 17)
8	Theft (v. 17)	Theft (v. 17)	False Witness (v. 17)
9	False Witness (v. 17)	False Witness (v. 17)	Coveting Wife (v. 18)
10	Coveting (v. 18)	Coveting (v. 18)	Coveting Property (v. 18)

¹¹ You shall not swear falsely by the name of the LORD your God; for the LORD will not clear one who swears falsely by His name.

¹² Observe the sabbath day and keep it holy, as the LORD your God has commanded you. ¹³ Six days you shall labor and do all your work, ¹⁴ but the seventh day is a sabbath of the LORD your God; you shall not do any work—you, your son or your daughter, your male or female slave, your ox or your ass, or any of your cattle, or the stranger in your settlements, so that your male and female slave may rest as you do. ¹⁵ Remember that you were a slave in the land of Egypt and the LORD your God freed you from there with a mighty hand and an outstretched arm; therefore the LORD your God has commanded you to observe the sabbath day.

¹⁶ Honor your father and your mother, as the LORD your God has commanded you, that you may long endure, and that you may fare well, in the land that the LORD your God is assigning to you.

¹⁷ You shall not murder.

You shall not commit adultery.

You shall not steal.

You shall not bear false witness against your neighbor.

¹⁸ You shall not covet your neighbor's wife. You shall not crave your neighbor's house, or his field, or his male or female slave, or his ox, or his ass, or anything that is your neighbor's.

---

vine vicarious punishment contrasts sharply with the Israelite norm for civil and criminal law, which restricts punishment to the agent alone (24.16). Later layers of tradition challenged this theological principle of divine justice (see 7.10 n.; Jer. 31.29–30; Ezek. ch 18). **10:** *Kindness* or "grace," loyalty of action as an expectation of the covenant (2 Sam. 7.15: "favor"; Hos. 6.6: "goodness"). *Who love Me* employs the technical language of Near Eastern treaties, whereby "love" refers to the loyalty the vassal owes to the sovereign. See also 6.14 n. **11:** The intent is to prohibit careless use of the divine name in the context of swearing an oath ("May God do X to me unless I do Y"); such oaths were viewed as dangerous and legally binding (see Judg. 11.29–40). *The LORD your God:* The grammatical perspective here shifts from direct reference to

God by God Himself (i.e., "those who love Me and keep My commandments"; v. 10) to a reference to God in relation to Israel by a third party ("your God"). Using different paradigms, both ancient rabbinic interpreters and modern scholars have sought to explain this shift. In the context of rabbinic interpretation, the inconsistency was resolved by claiming that it was only the first two commandments that God revealed directly to the people (in the first person). In response to the people's fear (v. 5), Moses then mediated the remaining commandments to the people, now logically referring to God in the third person (*b. Mak.* 24a; *b. Hor.* 8a). More likely, the explanation for the shift lies in the nature of the text as divine decree: Many Near Eastern royal inscriptions reflect the same inconsistency in the monarch's reference to

himself. The shift may also point to different layers of composition. **12:** *Observe,* contrast Exod. 20.8, "Remember." Faced with two different versions of the Decalogue, rabbinic interpretation held that God uttered both versions simultaneously: " 'Observe' and 'Remember' in a single utterance" (*b. Shevu.* 20b). This interpretation recurs in the hymn for Sabbath eve, "Lekha Dodi." *As the LORD . . . commanded you:* A reference to the Decalogue of Exodus. The ostensibly precise repetition nonetheless here diverges from the original (Exod. 20.8). The Decalogue embeds the perspective of Moses as speaker, whose reference to God's prior proclamation now itself becomes part of the revelation. **14:** The law equally benefits slaves and non-Israelites (1.16 n.; 15.15; 16.11; 24.17). **15:** Contrast the rationale provided for the Sabbath at Exod. 20.11. Deuteronomy here, as elsewhere, emphasizes the exodus as a central motivation for religious and social practices, though how and why the Sabbath might be connected to the exodus are open to interpretation. **16:** See v. 12 n. *And that you may fare well* is absent from the Exodus version (Exod. 20.12). This motivational phrase is typical of Deuteronomy's exhortations to obedience (4.40; 5.26; 6.3, 18; 12.25, 28; 22.7). **17:** The prohibition against adultery in the Decalogue is absolute. The Decalogue has transformed the ancient Near Eastern breach of the contractual rights of the woman's husband (see Laws of Hammurabi §129) into an offense against both God and the larger community. Biblical law here removes the wife from the disposal of the husband and grants her the status of legal person (see 22.22 n.). **18:** *Wife . . . house,* contrast the order "house . . . wife" in the Exodus Decalogue (Exod. 20.14). There the sequence suggests that "house" is the inclusive term, with the following list (wife, slave, ox, or ass) serving to itemize its contents. Consistent with their view elsewhere, the authors of Deuteronomy here completely

¹⁹ The LORD spoke those words—those and no more—to your whole congregation at the mountain, with a mighty voice out of the fire and the dense clouds. He inscribed them on two tablets of stone, which He gave to me. ²⁰ When you heard the voice out of the darkness, while the mountain was ablaze with fire, you came up to me, all your tribal heads and elders, ²¹ and said, "The LORD our God has just shown us His majestic Presence, and we have heard His voice out of the fire; we have seen this day that man may live though God has spoken to him. ²² Let us not die, then, for this fearsome fire will consume us; if we hear the voice of the LORD our God any longer, we shall die. ²³ For what mortal ever heard the voice of the living God speak out of the fire, as we did, and lived? ²⁴ You go closer and hear all that the LORD our God says, and then you tell us everything that the LORD our God tells you, and we will willingly do it."

²⁵ The LORD heard the plea that you made to me, and the LORD said to me, "I have heard the plea that this people made to you; they did well to speak thus. ²⁶ May they always be of such mind, to revere Me and follow all My commandments, that it may go well with them and with their children forever! ²⁷ Go, say to them, 'Return to your tents.' ²⁸ But you remain here with Me, and I will give you the whole Instruction—the laws and the rules—that you shall impart to them, for them to observe in the land that I am giving them to possess."

²⁹ Be careful, then, to do as the LORD your God has commanded you. Do not turn aside to the right or to the left: ³⁰ follow only the path that the LORD your God has enjoined upon you, so that you may thrive and that it may go well with you, and that you may long endure in the land you are to possess.

separate family law from property law. They invert the earlier sequence, placing the wife first. By removing her altogether from the list of other chattels, they establish that the law does not regard the woman as merely one commodity among others comprising a "house" (see also 22.22–23.1 n.). This is consisent with Deuteronomy's general view of women.

5.19–30: Moses as mediator. While the Decalogue was given directly to the people (v. 4; 4.10–13), the rest of the laws were mediated to the people by Moses, at their plea (v. 22–24; 4.14). **19–23:** See 4.33; cf. Exod. 20.15–18. **19:** *The LORD spoke . . . at the mountain . . . out of the fire,* lit. "The LORD spoke . . . on the mountain out of the fire." The more precise translation of the Hebrew shows its exact correspondence to v. 4: "Face to face the LORD spoke to you on the mountain out of the fire . . ." The Decalogue is thus set in a precise literary frame, with both verses affirming the direct nature of the divine revelation. In this view, God spoke the Decalogue directly to Israel without the mediation of Moses. *Those and no more,* lit. "He did not add [anything more]." There is no source for this comment in Exod. ch 20. The authors of Deuteronomy here seem to be arguing that the Covenant Collection, which immediately follows the Decalogue in Exodus, was not included in the revelation at Sinai/Horeb. The phrase thus makes way for the presentation of the laws of Deuteronomy alone as the further words of God to Moses at Sinai/Horeb. **20–24:** This section expands Exod. 20.15–18, while also revising that narrative in several key aspects. The editor here recognizes the existence of the two mutually inconsistent traditions about the Decalogue: that it was spoken directly by God to the people (vv. 4, 19); that it was mediated by Moses (v. 5). In this section, he establishes a compromise between the two views: While the Decalogue was proclaimed by God directly, thereafter all law was mediated by Moses. The editor's careful reuse and expansion of Exod. 20.15–18 facilitates this attempt to reconcile the conflicting perspectives. **22:** *Let us not die:* The people's anxiety explains their request that Moses serve as mediator. The emphasis upon the mortal threat of the divine voice conflicts, however, with the affirmation of safety in v. 21. Therefore this verse is less a continuation of the previous one than an alternative to it, consistent with the idea of divine revelation in v. 5. *If we hear . . . any longer:* This formulation presupposes that God has already spoken to them directly. The Exodus source, however, does not presuppose God's prior speech. Its formulation is unconditional and absolute: "Let God not speak to us, lest we die" (Exod. 20.16). Deuteronomy's editor has added "any longer" in order to adapt the verse to the new context. It now supports the editorial compromise: God spoke (only) the Decalogue directly; Moses mediated (only) the following legal material. **25–30:** The idea that Moses mediates between God and the people will be used in two ways: (1) to justify the laws that Moses subse-

6 And this is the Instruction—the laws and the rules—that the LORD your God has commanded [me] to impart to you, to be observed in the land that you are about to cross into and occupy, ² so that you, your children, and your children's children may revere the LORD your God and follow, as long as you live, all His laws and commandments that I enjoin upon you, to the end that you may long endure. ³ Obey, O Israel, willingly and faithfully, that it may go well with you and that you may increase greatly [in] ᵃ·a land flowing with milk and honey,·ᵃ as the LORD, the God of your fathers, spoke to you.

⁴ Hear, O Israel! The LORD is our God, the LORD alone.ᵇ ⁵ You shall love the LORD your God with all your heart

a-a *According to Ibn Ezra this phrase connects with the end of v. 1.*
b *Cf. Rashbam and Ibn Ezra; see Zech. 14.9. Others "The LORD our God, the LORD is one."*

quently propounds as revelation (chs 12–26); (2) to justify the institution of "Mosaic" prophecy (18.15–22). **28:** *Instruction,* lit. "commandment." Note the deliberate allusion to this verse in 6.1 (see 6.1–3 n.).

6.1–11.32: The requirement of loyalty to God. A sermonic preamble to the laws of chs 12–26. **6.1–3:** Introduction, validating Mosaic instruction as revealed upon Horeb. NJPS correctly follows the standard chapter division and recognizes that this paragraph begins a new literary unit. Whereas Moses speaks about the past in ch 5, as he recalls the revelation at Horeb, he now shifts into the present, to explain the significance of that revelation for the new generation whom he addresses in Moab. The Masoretic division of the text follows a different scheme, regarding 5.19–6.3 as a single paragraph. That organization attempts to show that there is no "break" whatsoever between Horeb and Moab. It maintains that "the laws and rules" that God originally proclaimed to Moses subsequent to the revelation on Sinai/Horeb (5.28) are identical to "the laws and the rules" (6.1; 12.1) of the following sermon (chs 6–11) and legal code (chs 12–26). That claim, however, runs counter to the tradition found in Exodus, whereby the

Book of the Covenant (Exod. chs 21–23)—not Deuteronomy's laws—records the "rules" that God spoke to Moses on the mountain (Exod. 21.1; 24.3). The attribution of the following sermon and law corpus to Sinaitic revelation by Deuteronomy's authors thus reuses the earlier tradition in order to lend authority to Deuteronomy's new vision of law and religion. The entire Mosaic reprise of ostensibly earlier law is therefore more sophisticated than at first evident, since repetition here entails competition, as Deuteronomy seeks to displace the Book of the Covenant. Accordingly, while the present chapter division is formally correct, the Masoretic division preserves an important insight into the original aims of the text's authors. The sophistication of their literary strategy should not be underestimated. The *Temple Scroll* from Qumran, and the laws in the pseudepigraphic book of *Jubilees* similarly present sectarian law as deriving from Sinaitic revelation. The development during the early rabbinic movement (ca. 70–300 CE) of the doctrine of Oral Torah as a tradition that originates in revelation at Mount Sinai also corresponds to this model. **1:** *And,* marking the transition from past retrospective about Horeb (chs 4–5) to the speaker's addressing the Israelites in the

present, in Moab, about the requirements of the covenant. *The Instruction . . . occupy:* The Hebrew is nearly identical to 5.28. The precise repetition of terminology is important. It legitimates the entire second discourse—both *the Instruction* (chs 6–11) and *the laws and the rules* (the legal corpus of chs 12–26; see 12.1)—as originating in direct divine revelation from God on Horeb (5.28). **2:** *Revere,* see 4.10 n.

6.4–25: A sermon on the first commandment of the Decalogue, incorporating direct allusions to it: vv. 4 and 14 refer to 5.7; vv. 12, 21, 23 refer to 5.6; v. 15 ("impassioned God") refers to 5.9; vv. 5 and 17 refer to 5.10. **4–9: The Shema.** These verses form the first paragraph of the important Jewish prayer called the Shema, after its first word, Heb for "Hear!" During the late Second Temple period, this prayer rose to special prominence both in the synagogue liturgy and in individual piety, a position that it still maintains. Strikingly, Deuteronomy itself gives no indication that this passage is theologically central or liturgically important. Nor do any of the biblical passages that incorporate liturgical prayer refer to it (see Ezra 3.10–11; Neh. ch 9; 1 Chron. 16.7–36; 2 Chron. 5.11–14; 7.3); its formal recitation is not attested until late in the Second Temple period. The centrality of this text is likely the result of early rabbinic interpretation of the requirement to "recite [these words] . . . when you lie down and when you get up" (vv. 6–7). This interpretation led to recitation of the Shema twice daily, in the morning and evening. A similar injunction to "recite . . . these My words" is found at 11.18–19. Because of the double reference to "these words," the prayer was formally defined as including both paragraphs (6.4–9; 11.13–21). A third paragraph was also added (Num. 15.37–41): the requirement to wear a garment whose fringes (tzitzit) provide a further context for reflection upon Torah and fulfilling its precepts.

and with all your soul and with all your might. ⁶Take to heart these instructions with which I charge you this day. ⁷Impress them upon your children. Recite them when you stay at home and when you are away, when you lie down and when you get up. ⁸Bind them as a sign on your hand

Modern readers regard the Shema as an assertion of monotheism, a view that is anachronistic. In the context of ancient Israelite religion, it served as a public proclamation of exclusive loyalty to Yhvh as the sole Lord of Israel. Subsequently, as the Shema became incorporated into the synagogue liturgy, its recitation was also given legal significance. The prayer was regarded as a legally binding oath to carry out the requirements of the Torah. Through the liturgical recitation of the Shema the worshipper thus reenacts, twice daily, the original covenant ratification ceremony that, in the narrative of Deuteronomy, took place on the plains of Moab.

4–5: The Shema, with its call for complete personal devotion to God, became normative for the various Judaisms of the Second Temple period; in fact, these verses were cited by Jesus as the "first" of all commandments (Mark 12.29–30). **4:** *The Lord . . . alone:* NJPS correctly departs from the more familiar translation, "The Lord [Yhvh] our God, the Lord is one" (see translators' note *b*, end). Each of the two interpretations is theoretically possible because, in Hebrew, it is possible to form a sentence by simply joining a subject and a predicate, without specifying the verb "to be." The Hebrew here thus allows either "Yhvh, our God, Yhvh *is* one" or "Yhvh *is* our God, Yhvh alone." The first, older translation, which makes a statement about the unity and the indivisibility of God, does not do full justice to this text (though it makes sense in a later Jewish context as a polemic against Christianity). The verse makes not a quantitative argument (about the number of deities) but a qualitative one, about the nature of the relationship between God and

Israel. Almost certainly, the original force of the verse, as the medieval Jewish exegetes in translators' note *b* recognized, was to demand that Israel show exclusive loyalty to *our God,* Yhvh—but not thereby to deny the existence of other gods! In this way, it assumes the same perspective as the first commandment of the Decalogue, which, by prohibiting the worship of other gods, presupposes their existence (see 5.7 n.). Once true monotheism became the norm in the Second Temple period, this earlier perspective became unintelligible. Second Temple readers and translators of the Shema were thus forced to read this and similar passages in a way that made them consistent with the normative monotheism (see 32.8 n.; cf. 4.15–31 n.; 5.9 n.). That process of reinterpretation is already evident in the Septuagint's translation (3rd century BCE): "the Lord is one." As the basis for most subsequent translations, that reading is the source for the common understanding of the verse. *Alone:* The traditional translation (see translators' note *b*) preserves the normal use of Hebrew "ʾeḥad," "one," which may have contributed to interpreting the Shema as a declaration of monotheism. But what it might mean to say that God is "one" is unclear, since that is not the same as affirming that there is only one God (Isa. 44.6; 45.5–7, 14, 18, 21; 46.9). Nor is it likely that the verse intends to clarify that there is only one Yhvh, as opposed to many Yhvhs, since there was no difficulty in recognizing that different manifestations of a divinity could derive from a single god (Exod. 6.3). NJPS thus properly understands "ʾeḥad" to mean "alone," i.e., "exclusively." This interpretation receives support in the prophet Zechariah's interpreta-

tion of this verse: "In that day there shall be one Lord with one name" (Zech. 14.9 and translators' note *d*). **5:** *Love,* see 5.10 n. The paradox of commanding a feeling (as in Lev. 19.17–18) is resolved with the recognition that covenantal "love" does not refer to internal sentiment or to private emotion. The focus is, instead, upon loyalty of action toward both deity and neighbor (see 5.1–30 n.). *With all your soul:* This phrase, in rabbinic interpretation, meant that one should be willing to give one's life for God. This interpretation led to the practice of reciting the Shema on one's deathbed or in the midst of acts of martyrdom. *Might:* Heb "meʾod" is elsewhere an adverb meaning "very" or "exceedingly." It is used as a noun only here and in the Deuteronomistic description of King Josiah, which cites this verse in order to portray Josiah as the paragon of obedience to Torah (2 Kings 23.25). While the word's basic meaning is "might" or "strength," it was understood as "wealth" or "property" both at Qumran (CD 9.11; 12.10) and in early rabbinic literature (*Tg. Jon.; Sifre*). The two interpretations each call for full commitment to God, whether psychological or practical; both are preserved in the Mishnah (*m. Ber.* 9.5). **6:** *These instructions,* lit. "these words," as at 11.19. **7:** *Impress them,* in the sense of "teach them incisively"; similarly, "teach them" (11.19). *Recite them:* This translation reflects the formal liturgical recitation of the prayer, a ritual that is postbiblical. The original idea of the Hebrew is rather to "speak about them" (see also Ps. 119.13, 46): to be mindful of and discuss the laws of the Torah. *When you lie down and when you get up,* originally, a merism signifying that one should always reflect upon these Deuteronomic teachings. Rabbinic interpretation, however, understands the phrase to refer literally to two distinct times: "in the evening" and "in the morning." On that basis, the Shema is formally recited twice daily. So important is this obligation that the and let them serve as a symbol[a] on your forehead;[b] [9] inscribe them on the doorposts of your house and on your gates.

[10] When the LORD your God brings you into the land that He swore to your fathers, Abraham, Isaac, and Jacob, to assign to you—great and flourishing cities that you did not build, [11] houses full of all good things that you did not fill, hewn cisterns that you did not hew, vineyards and olive groves that you did not plant—and you eat your fill, [12] take heed that you do not forget the LORD who freed you from the land of Egypt, the house of bondage. [13] Revere only the LORD your God and worship Him alone, and swear only by His name. [14] Do not follow other gods, any gods of the peoples about you—[15] for the LORD your God in your midst is an impassioned God—lest the anger of the LORD your God blaze forth against you and He wipe you off the face of the earth.

a Others "frontlet"; cf. Exod. 13.16.   b Lit. "between your eyes"; cf. Exod. 13.9.

Mishnah (the formal compilation of rabbinic law) begins with a debate about how to fulfill it properly: "From what time in the evening should one recite the Shema?" (m. Ber. 1.1).
6.8: Bind them: This law, literally interpreted, provides the basis for the Jewish convention of binding tefillin (phylacteries) upon the arm and forehead. Tefillin have been found at Qumran, and it is clear that their use dates from at least the second century BCE. The Samaritan and some manuscripts of the Septuagint, however, understood the law metaphorically. There was thus clearly a debate within Second Temple Judaism about the correct interpretation of this prescription: whether literally to bind an object or symbolically to take instruction to heart (Exod. 13.9, 16; Prov. 3.3; 6.21; 7.3). Both perspectives have merit, but since the instructions to write upon the doorposts are intended literally (see v. 9 n.), it is possible, even likely, that the authors of Deuteronomy expected their audience to wear portions of the text upon the body. There is archeological evidence for such a practice. Inscribed silver amulets (with the text on, not in, them) that date to

the 7th and 6th centuries BCE have been found at Jerusalem. Similar amulets are depicted in Egyptian and Mesopotamian art and literature. Such amulets, however, were likely worn as magic charms in order to ward off evil. In Deuteronomy, the objects have a different function: The text is worn to express the wearer's dedication and obedience to Torah. In refocusing the purpose of wearing texts upon the body, Deuteronomy thus takes over an established practice but completely transforms its meaning. The same subordination of older custom to Deuteronomic Torah occurs elsewhere; see 6.9 n.; 12.13–19 n.; 17.14–20 n.; 18.15–22 n. Ironically, the Greek translation "phylakterion" (the source of "phylactery") actually means "amulet," suggesting the connection with magic that was rejected by the authors of Deuteronomy. Sign: Based on the archeological evidence, it seems that the texts would originally have been inscribed on metal and displayed in full view. Only later, in the Second Temple period, did the practice develop of enclosing the text in small leather cases. According to rabbinic custom, the texts placed in the tefillin always included the

four biblical passages that refer to the practice (Exod. 13.3–10, 11–16; Deut. 6.4–9; 11.13–21), though the tefillin found at Qumran sometimes contain different passages, including the Decalogue and other passages.
9: Doorposts: The doorways of houses and temples were regarded in Israel and the ancient Near East as important transitional spaces in which religious-legal ceremonies were performed and where divine images might be stored (see Exod. 12.7, 21–23; 21.6; Isa. 57.8). The practice of inscribing these liminal spaces with cultic or religious invocations is also well known throughout the ancient Near East. Deuteronomy adopts that custom but subordinates the doorway, as a religiously significant space, to the authority of Deuteronomic law. Originally, the words were to be directly displayed on the doorposts, as can be seen from the stone plaques inscribed with the words of the Decalogue found outside ancient Samaritan dwellings. By the late Second Temple period, as evidenced at Qumran, the texts were written on parchment, placed in small boxes (mezuzot), and affixed to the doorpost. The texts placed in the mezuzot varied: All contained this passage (vv. 4–9) and Deut. 11.13–21. Samaritan mezuzot also contained the Decalogue. At Qumran, the Decalogue and Deut. 10.12–11.12 were sometimes added.

6.10–11: The list land . . . houses . . . cisterns . . . olive groves (cf. Josh. 24.13; Neh. 9.24–25) defines the elements of an established civilization, which Israel is about to both inherit and become. **12:** The threat of forgetting and the risk of apostasy are repeatedly stressed (4.9–14 n.; 8.11–20; 32.18; cf. 5.26; Hos 2.5–13). **14:** Do not follow, lit. "do not go after," employs the technical language of Neo-Assyrian state treaties, which were concerned to ensure that the vassal show obedience and commitment to the suzerain alone. Deuteronomy redeploys that language, originally used in the context of in-

¹⁶ Do not try the Lord your God, as you did at Massah.^a ¹⁷ Be sure to keep the commandments, decrees, and laws that the Lord your God has enjoined upon you. ¹⁸ Do what is right and good in the sight of the Lord, that it may go well with you and that you may be able to possess the good land that the Lord your God promised on oath to your fathers, ¹⁹ and that all your enemies may be driven out before you, as the Lord has spoken.

²⁰ When, in time to come, your children ask you, "What mean the decrees, laws, and rules that the Lord our God has enjoined upon you?"^b ²¹ you shall say to your children, "We were slaves to Pharaoh in Egypt and the Lord freed us from Egypt with a mighty hand. ²² The Lord wrought before our eyes marvelous and destructive signs and portents in Egypt, against Pharaoh and all his household; ²³ and us He freed from there, that He might take us and give us the land that He had promised on oath to our fathers. ²⁴ Then the Lord commanded us to observe all these laws, to revere the Lord our God, for our lasting good and for our survival, as is now the case. ²⁵ It will be therefore to our merit before the Lord our God to observe faithfully this whole Instruction, as He has commanded us."

7 When the Lord your God brings you to the land that you are about to enter and possess, and He dislodges many nations before you—the Hittites, Girgashites, Amorites, Canaanites, Perizzites, Hivites, and Jebusites, seven nations much larger than you—² and the Lord your God delivers them to you and you defeat them, you must doom them to destruction: grant them no terms and give

a Cf. Exod. 17.1–7.   b Septuagint and rabbinic quotations read "us."

ternational diplomacy, in a new context: the covenant with Israel in which YHWH functions as divine suzerain. **16:** *Try . . . Massah:* For the incident and the Hebrew pun, see Exod. 17.2–7; see also Matthew 4.7. **20:** The Passover service ("Haggadah") includes this and similar didactic questions (Exod. 12.21–27; 13.1–10, 11–16) in the section about the Four Sons. **22:** See 4.34 n.

7.1–10.11: Risks to covenantal faith upon entering the land. The first issue is that Israel enters an already inhabited land, whose greater population and worship apparatus it must confront (ch 7).

Thereafter, successful habitation carries its own risks: complacency and loss of historical memory (ch 8).

7.1–26: The war of conquest. Two topics are treated: (1) the command to destroy the original occupants of Canaan (vv. 1–3, 6, 17–24); and (2) the command not to worship their gods (vv. 4–5, 7–15, 25–26). The editors join the two themes at v. 16. **1:** A number of factors combine to imply that this list is primarily an after-the-fact literary compilation rather than an historical portrayal. The identity, sequence, and number of the peoples included in the "table

of nations" vary considerably (Gen. 15.19–21; Exod. 3.8, 17; 13.5; 23.23; 33.2; 34.11; Deut. 20.17; Josh. 3.10; 9.1; 11.3; 12.8; 24.11; Judg. 3.5; 1 Kings 9.20; Ezra 9.1; Neh. 9.8; 2 Chron. 8.7). *Hittites* (e.g., Gen. 23.10; 25.9; 49.29–30; 50.13; Num. 13.29) are presented as one of the original inhabitants of Canaan, in contrast to the historically important Hittite empire which flourished in Anatolia, in central Turkey, ca. 1700–1200 BCE. The *Jebusites,* the pre-Israelite inhabitants of Jerusalem, retained control of the city until it was conquered by David several centuries after the period in which the conquest is set (2 Sam. 5.6–7). The latter narrative implies that this law was never implemented. The ideal number *seven,* which signifies completion or totality (Gen. ch 1; the plague list of Pss. 78.44–51 and 105.28–36 in contrast to Exod. chs 7–12), suggests that the enumeration may be artificial. The number of peoples included in the "table" elsewhere in the Bible varies considerably: twelve, seven, six, or fewer. **2:** This requirement for destruction is anomalous in several ways. Earlier sources contemplate only the expulsion of these groups (Exod. 23.27–33; cf. 34.11). The definition and requirements of the "ban" vary considerably throughout the Bible: total destruction of people and property (here; 13.15–17; 20.16–17; 1 Sam. 15.3); sparing of property (2.34–35; 3.6–7); sparing of women, children, and property (20.10–14). Finally, other narratives, which seem far more realistic, speak of the failure to carry out the conquest except in very limited areas and the use of conquered populations for labor (Josh. chs 15–17; Judg. ch 1; 3.1–6). These factors suggest that the law of the ban is an anachronistic literary formulation. It first arose centuries after the settlement; it was never implemented because there was no population extant against whom it could be implemented. Its polemic is directed at internal issues in 6th century Judah. Often the authors of Deuteronomy use the term "Canaanite" rhetorically to stigmatize them no quarter. ³ You shall not intermarry with them: do not give your daughters to their sons or take their daughters for your sons. ⁴ For they will turn your children away from Me to worship other gods, and the LORD's anger will blaze forth against you and He will promptly wipe you out. ⁵ Instead, this is what you shall do to them: you shall tear down their altars, smash their pillars, cut down their sacred posts, and consign their images to the fire.

⁶ For you are a people consecrated to the LORD your God: of all the peoples on earth the LORD your God chose you to be His treasured people. ⁷ It is not because you are the most numerous of peoples that the LORD set His heart on you and chose you—indeed, you are the smallest of peoples; ⁸ but it was because the LORD favored you and kept the oath He made to your fathers that the LORD freed you with a mighty hand and rescued you from the house of bondage, from the power of Pharaoh king of Egypt.

⁹ Know, therefore, that only the LORD your God is God, the steadfast God who keeps His covenant faithfully to the thousandth generation of those who love Him and keep His commandments, ¹⁰ but who instantly requites with destruction those who reject Him—never slow with those who reject Him, but requiting them instantly. ¹¹ Therefore, observe faithfully the Instruction—the laws and the rules—with which I charge you today.

'EKEV   עקב

¹² And if you do obey these rules and observe them carefully, the LORD your God will maintain faithfully for you the covenant that He made on oath with your fathers: ¹³ He will favor you and bless you and multiply you; He

7.6–16: The meaning of Israel's covenantal relationship to God. **6:** *For* suggests that the verse originally continued v. 3, since it provides the rationale for total separation from the Canaanites, not for the destruction of their cult sites. This verse, repeated at 14.2, summarizes Deuteronomy's view of Israel's relation to God. *Consecrated*, lit., "set aside as separate," as is clear here. *Chose*, the precondition of Israel's elected status. *His treasured people* (14.2 n.; 26.18; Exod. 19.5; Mal. 3.17; Ps. 135.4), designating Israel as the exclusive property of God; similarly, 4.20, using a different Hebrew word. The term originates in Near Eastern treaty language for the special relationship of vassal to overlord. **9–11:** A sermon on the second commandment that radically revises its meaning. The reuse of key phrases and inversion of the order of punishment and blessing in 5.9–10 mark the citation. **9:** *Keeps His covenant faithfully:* NJPS translates the same phrase as "showing kindness" at 5.10 (see note). **10:** *Instantly requites . . . requiting them instantly:* Note the ABB'A' frame, at whose center in the key idea that God is *never slow.* The idea here is that the sinner is punished directly, as already recognized by Rashi (cf. NRSV "in their own person"). At issue is the rejection of the norm of vicarious or transgenerational punishment as previously propounded in the Decalogue (5.9 = Exod. 20.5; cf. Exod. 34.7; Num. 14.18). Instead, the sermon argues for individual retribution, as in criminal law (24.16), while deleting any reference to the transmission of punishment across generations. There is a similar rejection of transgenerational punishment in Jer. 31.27–30; Ezek. 18.1–4; it is nevertheless quite remarkable that Deuteronomy here directly polemicizes against the Decalogue. **12–14:** The blessings of fertility do not come from the nature gods of Canaan but from Israel's God (see Hos. ch 2). Natural fertility is here made contingent upon obedience to the covenant. **13:** *Calving . . . lambing*

older forms of Israelite religion that they no longer accept (see v. 5 n.; 16.22 n.; 18.9–14 n.). *Doom them to destruction,* or "place under the ban," or "devote." That which is "devoted" is set aside for divine use and denied to humans. The war of conquest, as a holy war, should not be one where the individual profits through plunder (see 12.29–31 n.; 13.14 n.; 20.1–20 n.; Josh. ch 7). The law addresses apostasy as opposed to ethnicity; it is directed against apostate Israelites in 8.20; 13.15–17. **3:** This prohibition against intermarriage does not fit easily after v. 2, suggesting several layers of editing. It is also inconsistent with 21.10–14, which

seems more likely to reflect the original policy. **5:** See Exod. 34.13. *Pillars:* stone monuments that marked places where God appeared and were thus originally legitimate in worship (Gen. 35.14; Exod. 24.4; Hos. 3.4). Only subsequently were they prohibited as alien (Exod. 23.24; 34.13; Lev. 26.1; Deut. 12.3; 16.22; 2 Kings 18.4). *Sacred posts,* Heb "'Asherim." The singular, "'Asherah," preserves the name of an important Canaanite goddess known from Ugarit (1 Kings 18.19); here the word designates merely the tree, wooden pole, or image that represented her (16.21; Judg. 6.25, 26, 28).

will bless the issue of your womb and the produce of your soil, your new grain and wine and oil, the calving of your herd and the lambing of your flock, in the land that He swore to your fathers to assign to you. ¹⁴ You shall be blessed above all other peoples: there shall be no sterile male or female among you or among your livestock. ¹⁵ The LORD will ward off from you all sickness; He will not bring upon you any of the dreadful diseases of Egypt, about which you know, but will inflict them upon all your enemies.

¹⁶ You shall destroy all the peoples that the LORD your God delivers to you, showing them no pity. And you shall not worship their gods, for that would be a snare to you. ¹⁷ Should you say to yourselves, "These nations are more numerous than we; how can we dispossess them?" ¹⁸ You need have no fear of them. You have but to bear in mind what the LORD your God did to Pharaoh and all the Egyptians: ¹⁹ the wondrous acts that you saw with your own eyes, the signs and the portents, the mighty hand, and the outstretched arm by which the LORD your God liberated you. Thus will the LORD your God do to all the peoples you now fear. ²⁰ The LORD your God will also send a plagueᵃ against them, until those who are left in hiding perish before you. ²¹ Do not stand in dread of them, for the LORD your God is in your midst, a great and awesome God.

²² The LORD your God will dislodge those peoples before you little by little; you will not be able to put an end to them at once, else the wild beasts would multiply to your hurt. ²³ The LORD your God will deliver them up to you, throwing them into utter panic until they are wiped out. ²⁴ He will deliver their kings into your hand, and you shall obliterate their name from under the heavens; no man shall stand up to you, until you have wiped them out.

²⁵ You shall consign the images of their gods to the fire; you shall not covet the silver and gold on them and keep it for yourselves, lest you be ensnared thereby; for that is abhorrent to the LORD your God. ²⁶ You must not bring an abhorrent thing into your house, or you will be proscribed like it; you must reject it as abominable and abhorrent, for it is proscribed.

8 You shall faithfully observe all the Instruction that I enjoin upon you today, that you may thrive and increase and be able to possess the land that the LORD promised on oath to your fathers. ² Remember the long way that the LORD your God has

(28.4, 18, 51), originally two Ugaritic fertility deities; the second, "Astarte," is named at 1 Kings 11.5. **15:** Cf. Exod. 15.26.

7.17–26: Israel need not fear nations more powerful than it since, according to the idea of the holy war, God "is in your midst" in battle (v. 21; 6.15; cf. 20.1–4). These verses echo ideas found in Exod. 23.20–33. **20:** *Plague,* see Exod. 23.27–28 n.; Josh. 24.12. **22:** Abbreviating Exod. 23.29–30; contrast Deut. 9.3.

8.1–20: The temptation to pride and self-sufficiency in the land. Moses warns the people that success in Canaan will tempt them to forget the wilderness lesson of complete dependence upon God. **1–10:** An appeal to Israel's memory: In the wilderness God sustained the people daily (Exod. 12.37–17.16; Num. chs 11–14).

---

a Others "hornet"; meaning of Heb. uncertain. Cf. note at Exod. 23.28.

made you travel in the wilderness these past forty years, that He might test you by hardships to learn what was in your hearts: whether you would keep His commandments or not. [3] He subjected you to the hardship of hunger and then gave you manna to eat, which neither you nor your fathers had ever known, in order to teach you that man does not live on bread alone, but that man may live on anything that the LORD decrees. [4] The clothes upon you did not wear out, nor did your feet swell these forty years. [5] Bear in mind that the LORD your God disciplines you just as a man disciplines his son. [6] Therefore keep the commandments of the LORD your God: walk in His ways and revere Him.

[7] For the LORD your God is bringing you into a good land, a land with streams and springs and fountains issuing from plain and hill; [8] a land of wheat and barley, of vines, figs, and pomegranates, a land of olive trees and honey; [9] a land where you may eat food without stint, where you will lack nothing; a land whose rocks are iron and from whose hills you can mine copper. [10] When you have eaten your fill, give thanks to the LORD your God for the good land which He has given you.

[11] Take care lest you forget the LORD your God and fail to keep His commandments, His rules, and His laws, which I enjoin upon you today. [12] When you have eaten your fill, and have built fine houses to live in, [13] and your herds and flocks have multiplied, and your silver and gold have increased, and everything you own has prospered, [14] beware lest[a] your heart grow haughty and you forget the LORD your God—who freed you from the land of Egypt, the house of bondage; [15] who led you through the great and terrible wilderness with its seraph[b] serpents and scorpions, a parched land with no water in it, who brought forth water for you from the flinty rock; [16] who fed you in the wilderness with manna, which your fathers had never known, in order to test you by hardships only to benefit you in the end—[17] and you say to yourselves, "My own power and the might of my own hand have won this wealth for me." [18] Remember that it is the LORD your God who gives you the power to get wealth, in fulfillment of the covenant that He made on oath with your fathers, as is still the case.

[19] If you do forget the LORD your God and follow other gods to serve them or bow down to them, I warn you this day that you shall certainly perish; [20] like the nations that the LORD will cause to perish before you, so shall you perish—because you did not heed the LORD your God.

3: *Manna,* see Exod. ch 16; Num. 11.7–8. **5:** Suffering is here interpreted as discipline, as in a parent's correction of a child (Hos. ch 11); like many others in Deuteronomy, this idea reflects the influence of wisdom literature (see Prov. 3.11–12; cf. Deut. 1.13 n.; 4.2 n.; 4.5–8 n.; 4.10 n.; 11.2). **10:** *When you have eaten your fill, give thanks to the* LORD *your God* serves as the rabbinic justification for reciting the grace after meals (*b. Ber.* 21a).

8.11–20: The peril of prosperity. 11: A bold equation between *the* LORD, on the one hand, and the legal corpus (*His commandments . . . rules . . . laws . . . today*), on the other. Disobedience to Deuteronomy's laws becomes tantamount to forgetting God and transgressing the first commandment (see v. 19 n.). **15:** *Water . . . from the flinty rock,* Exod. 17.1–7; Num. 20.2–13; Ps. 114.8. **19:** *Follow,* see 6.14 n. *Other gods . . . serve . . . bow down to,* citing the first and second commandments of the Decalogue (5.7, 9). **20:** *Like the nations:* Here Israel is itself placed under the ban if it commits apostasy (see 7.1–26 n.). *Cause to perish . . . perish:* The same word is used to underscore the precise "measure-for-measure" nature of the punishment. Israel's election (7.6 n.) grants no exemption from upholding the law. Rightful habitation in the promised land, like its fertility (7.12–14 n.), depends upon covenantal obedience, not ethnic identity (7.2 n.).

---

a Heb. pen *moved down from v. 12 for clarity.*   *b See note at Num. 21.6.*

9 Hear, O Israel! You are about to cross the Jordan to go in and dispossess nations greater and more populous than you: great cities with walls sky-high; ² a people great and tall, the Anakites, of whom you have knowledge; for you have heard it said, "Who can stand up to the children of Anak?" ³ Know then this day that none other than the LORD your God is crossing at your head, a devouring fire; it is He who will wipe them out. He will subdue them before you, that you may quickly dispossess and destroy them, as the LORD promised you. ⁴ And when the LORD your God has thrust them from your path, say not to yourselves, "The LORD has enabled us to possess this land because of our virtues"; it is rather because of the wickedness of those nations that the LORD is dispossessing them before you. ⁵ It is not because of your virtues and your rectitude that you will be able to possess their country; but it is because of their wickedness that the LORD your God is dispossessing those nations before you, and in order to fulfill the oath that the LORD made to your fathers, Abraham, Isaac, and Jacob.

⁶ Know, then, that it is not for any virtue of yours that the LORD your God is giving you this good land to possess; for you are a stiffnecked people. ⁷ Remember, never forget, how you provoked the LORD your God to anger in the wilderness: from the day that you left the land of Egypt until you reached this place, you have continued defiant toward the LORD.

⁸ At Horeb you so provoked the LORD that the LORD was angry enough with you to have destroyed you. ⁹ I had ascended the mountain to receive the tablets of stone, the Tablets of the Covenant that the LORD had made with you, and I stayed on the mountain forty days and forty nights, eating no bread and drinking no water. ¹⁰ And the LORD gave me the two tablets of stone inscribed by the finger of God, with the exact words that the LORD had addressed to you on the mountain out of the fire on the day of the Assembly.

¹¹ At the end of those forty days and forty nights, the LORD gave me the two tablets of stone, the Tablets of the Covenant. ¹² And the LORD said to me, "Hurry, go down from here at once, for the people whom you brought out of Egypt have acted wickedly; they have been quick to stray from the path that I enjoined upon them; they have made themselves a molten image." ¹³ The LORD further said to me, "I see that this is a stiffnecked people. ¹⁴ Let Me alone and I will destroy them and blot out their name from under heaven, and I will make you a nation far more numerous than they."

9.1–10.11: The already broken and renewed covenant. God does not give the land to the people as a reward for righteousness, for in the wilderness they acted rebelliously. **9.2:** See Num. 13.22, 33. **4–5:** Victory will be given in the holy war because (negatively) Canaan has been irrevocably corrupted by the actions of its present occupants and because (positively) of God's enduring commitment to the promises made to Israel's ancestors. **6–24:** The historical record shows that Israel has been rebellious since the exodus (Ezek. 20.5–8; contrast Jer. 2.2–3; Hos. 2.14–20). **8–10:** Exod. 24.12–18; 31.18. **11–21:** Exod. ch 32, revised. **17:** *Smashing them,* not simple anger but a legal ceremony to confirm breach of treaty. **22:** Num. 11.1–3; Exod. 17.1–7; and Num. 11.31–34. **23:** Num. chs 13–14. **25–29:** A paraphrase of Exod. 32.11–14. Deuteronomy portrays Moses as the ideal prophet (34.10–12); he intercedes for the people and vicariously suffers for them (1.37 n.; cf. Isa. ch 53).

15 I started down the mountain, a mountain ablaze with fire, the two Tablets of the Covenant in my two hands. 16 I saw how you had sinned against the LORD your God: you had made yourselves a molten calf; you had been quick to stray from the path that the LORD had enjoined upon you. 17 Thereupon I gripped the two tablets and flung them away with both my hands, smashing them before your eyes. 18 I threw myself down before the LORD—eating no bread and drinking no water forty days and forty nights, as before—because of the great wrong you had committed, doing what displeased the LORD and vexing Him. 19 For I was in dread of the LORD's fierce anger against you, which moved Him to wipe you out. And that time, too, the LORD gave heed to me.—20 Moreover, the LORD was angry enough with Aaron to have destroyed him; so I also interceded for Aaron at that time.—21 As for that sinful thing you had made, the calf, I took it and put it to the fire; I broke it to bits and ground it thoroughly until it was fine as dust, and I threw its dust into the brook that comes down from the mountain.

22 Again you provoked the LORD at Taberah, and at Massah, and at Kibroth-hattaavah.

23 And when the LORD sent you on from Kadesh-barnea, saying, "Go up and take possession of the land that I am giving you," you flouted the command of the LORD your God; you did not put your trust in Him and did not obey Him.

24 As long as I have known you, you have been defiant toward the LORD.

25 When I lay prostrate before the LORD ᵃthose forty days and forty nights,ᵃ because the LORD was determined to destroy you, 26 I prayed to the LORD and said, "O Lord GOD, do not annihilate Your very own people, whom You redeemed in Your majesty and whom You freed from Egypt with a mighty hand. 27 Give thought to Your servants, Abraham, Isaac, and Jacob, and pay no heed to the stubbornness of this people, its wickedness, and its sinfulness. 28 Else the country from which You freed us will say, 'It was because the LORD was powerless to bring them into the land that He had promised them, and because He rejected them, that He brought them out to have them die in the wilderness.' 29 Yet they are Your very own people, whom You freed with Your great might and Your outstretched arm."

10 Thereupon the LORD said to me, "Carve out two tablets of stone like the first, and come up to Me on

10.1–11: The second ascent of the mountain (this narrative is abstracted at Exod. 34.1–4, 27–28). **1–3:** These verses rest on a tradition that Moses made the Ark and put the stone tablets in it (1 Kings 8.9).

a-a Lit. "the forty days and forty nights that I lay prostrate."

the mountain; and make an ark of wood. ²I will inscribe on the tablets the commandments that were on the first tablets that you smashed, and you shall deposit them in the ark."

³I made an ark of acacia wood and carved out two tablets of stone like the first; I took the two tablets with me and went up the mountain. ⁴The Lord inscribed on the tablets the same text as on the first, the Ten Commandments that He addressed to you on the mountain out of the fire on the day of the Assembly; and the Lord gave them to me. ⁵Then I left and went down from the mountain, and I deposited the tablets in the ark that I had made, where they still are, as the Lord had commanded me.

⁶From Beeroth-bene-jaakanᵃ the Israelites marched to Moserah. Aaron died there and was buried there; and his son Eleazar became priest in his stead. ⁷From there they marched to Gudgod,ᵇ and from Gudgod to Jotbath, a region of running brooks.

⁸At that time the Lord set apart the tribe of Levi to carry the Ark of the Lord's Covenant, to stand in attendance upon the Lord, and to bless in His name, as is still the case. ⁹That is why the Levites have received no hereditary portion along with their kinsmen: the Lord is their portion, as the Lord your God spoke concerning them.

¹⁰I had stayed on the mountain, as I did the first time, forty days and forty nights; and the Lord heeded me once again: the Lord agreed not to destroy you. ¹¹And the Lord said to me, "Up, resume the march at the head of the people, that they may go in and possess the land that I swore to their fathers to give them."

¹²And now, O Israel, what does the Lord your God demand of you? Only this: to revere the Lord your God, to walk only in His paths, to love Him, and to serve the Lord your God with all your heart and soul, ¹³keeping the Lord's commandments and laws, which I enjoin upon you today, for your good. ¹⁴Mark, the heavens ᶜto their uttermost reachesᶜ belong to the Lord your God, the earth and all that is on it! ¹⁵Yet it was to your fathers that the Lord was drawn in His love for them, so that He chose you, their lineal descendants, from among all peoples—as is now the case. ¹⁶Cut away, therefore, the thickening about your hearts and stiffen your necks no more. ¹⁷For the Lord your God is ᵈGod supreme and Lord

---

a Lit. "wells of Bene-jaakan"; cf. Num. 33.31–32.
b "Hor-haggidgad" in Num. 33.32–33.   c-c Lit. "and the heaven of heavens."
d-d Lit. "the God of gods and the Lord of lords."

6–9: An editorial insertion; vv. 6–7 seem to quote a wilderness itinerary from the Priestly literature (cf. Num. 33.30–38). **6:** Num. 20.22–29. **8:** Exod. 32.25–29. The Levites' role is to bear the Ark (Num. 4.4–15), to *stand in attendance,* i.e., conduct the sacrificial services (Num. ch 18), and to *bless* the people (Num. 6.22–27). **9:** See 12.12 n.; 18.2 n.

10.12–11.32: Obedience as the condition for prosperity in the land. This section provides the climax and conclusion of the historical review found in 8.1–10.11. **10.12–13:** A striking transformation of the Decalogue. Earlier, breach of the first and second Decalogue commandments, with their focus specifically on God, had been redefined and equated with failing to "keep His commandments . . . rules . . . and . . . laws" (8.11 n.). Now obedience to God is similarly redefined as compliance with the fixed *commandments and laws* (v. 13) of Deuteronomy, i.e., the laws of chs 12–26 (see 28.15, 45). **13:** *Keeping,* the precise antithesis of 8.11. The sequence *love . . . keeping . . . commandments* (vv. 12–13) cites 5.10. **16:** *Cut away . . . the thickening about your hearts* (lit. "circumcise . . . the foreskin of your heart") means to open oneself to God (Lev. 26.41); no distinction is intended between mind, will, and emotion. The metaphorical formulation, which challenges any attempt to reduce Deuteronomy to narrow "legalism," corresponds to prophetic ideals (cf. Jer. 4.4; 31.33). **17–18:** Integrity in the administration of court justice (v. 17; cf. 1.17; 16.19) and protection of the marginalized (v. 18) are together given a theological foundation, making the remarkable argument that human social ethics amounts to "imitatio dei." Ensuring justice in court and defending the marginalized were conventional royal prerogatives (Laws of Hammurabi prologue; Ps. 72.4). Deuteronomy contemplates no such role for the monarch (17.14–20 n.). Instead, it is here God who protects the rights of the supreme,-d the great, the mighty, and the awesome God, who shows no favor and takes no bribe, [18] but upholds the cause of the fatherless and the widow, and befriends the stranger, providing him with food and clothing.—[19] You too must befriend the stranger, for you were strangers in the land of Egypt.

[20] You must revere the LORD your God: only Him shall you worship, to Him shall you hold fast, and by His name shall you swear. [21] He is your glory and He is your God, who wrought for you those marvelous, awesome deeds that you saw with your own eyes. [22] Your ancestors went down to Egypt seventy persons in all; and now the LORD your God has made you as numerous as the stars of heaven.

11 Love, therefore, the LORD your God, and always keep His charge, His laws, His rules, and His commandments.

[2] aTake thought this day that it was not your children, who neither experienced nor witnessed the lesson of the LORD your God—

His majesty, His mighty hand, His outstretched arm; [3] the signs and the deeds that He performed in Egypt against Pharaoh king of Egypt and all his land; [4] what He did to Egypt's army, its horses and chariots; how the LORD rolled back upon them the waters of the Sea of Reeds when they were pursuing you, thus destroying them b-once and for all;-b [5] what He did for you in the wilderness before you arrived in this place; [6] and what He did to Dathan and Abiram, sons of Eliab son of Reuben, when the earth opened her mouth and swallowed them, along with their households, their tents, and every living thing in their train, from amidst all Israel—

[7] but that it was you who saw with your own eyes all the marvelous deeds that the LORD performed.

[8] Keep, therefore, all the Instruction that I enjoin upon you today, so that you may have the strength to enter and take possession of the land that you are about to cross into and possess, [9] and that you may long endure upon the soil that the LORD swore to your fathers to assign to them and to their heirs, a land flowing with milk and honey.

[10] For the land that you are about to enter and possess is not like the land of Egypt from which you have come. There the grain you sowed had to be watered by your own labors,c like a vegetable garden; [11] but the land you

marginalized, entering history to do so (cf. Exod 3.7–10; similarly Philippians 2.5–8). Love of neighbor thus originates in divine action as ethics receives a theological foundation. In its use of the consecutive adjectives *the great, the mighty, and the awesome* to describe God, this section echoes the style of Mesopotamian royal inscriptions, but projects these royal attributes on to God. This phrase becomes significant in later Judaism when it is quoted as part of the first blessing of the daily statutory prayer ("'Amidah").
18–19: *Stranger . . . strangers,* better, "resident alien" in both cases; see 1.16 n. The Israelite is not urged simply to love an unfamiliar fellow Israelite. Instead, the Israelite is adjured to love and identify with the non-Israelite. Just as justice must be rendered to Israelite and alien alike (see 1.16 n.), so must "love" reach across national or ethnic lines (cf. Lev. 19.33–34). **18:** *Befriends* (lit., "loves"): Note the concrete expression of love in action and service (see 5.10 n.; 6.5 n.). **19:** *For you were,* see Exod. 23.9. **22:** *Seventy persons* (Gen. 46.27; Exod. 1.5), here a stereotypical number expressing completeness, comes first in the Hebrew, emphasizing Israel's miraculous transformation into a nation. *Stars of heaven,* see 1.10 n.

11.1–32: Loyalty to the covenant provides the condition for life in Canaan. The punishments and rewards in this section are predominantly addressed to a plural "you," stressing communal rather than individual responsibility. **2:** The frequent phrase *this day* in Deuteronomy emphasizes the contemporaneity of the covenant (see 5.3 n.). *Lesson,* see 8.5 n. **4:** See Exod. ch 14. **6:** The address is based upon the early tradition of the revolt of Dathan and Abiram (Num. ch 16). There is no mention of Korah's rebellion (Num. 16.3–11), which was very likely added to the narrative in Numbers by the Priestly school after this abstract was made. **10–12:** The Nile valley must be irrigated

a *Syntax of Heb. uncertain.*   b-b *Lit. "to this day."*   c *Lit. "by your foot."*

are about to cross into and possess, a land of hills and valleys, soaks up its water from the rains of heaven. [12] It is a land which the LORD your God looks after, on which the LORD your God always keeps His eye, from year's beginning to year's end.

[13] If, then, you obey the commandments that I enjoin upon you this day, loving the LORD your God and serving Him with all your heart and soul, [14] I[a] will grant the rain for your land in season, the early rain and the late. You shall gather in your new grain and wine and oil—[15] I[a] will also provide grass in the fields for your cattle—and thus you shall eat your fill. [16] Take care not to be lured away to serve other gods and bow to them. [17] For the LORD's anger will flare up against you, and He will shut up the skies so that there will be no rain and the ground will not yield its produce; and you will soon perish from the good land that the LORD is assigning to you.

[18] Therefore impress these My words upon your [b]very heart:[b] bind them as a sign on your hand and let them serve as a [c]symbol on your forehead,[c] [19] and teach them to your children—reciting them when you stay at home and when you are away, when you lie down and when you get up; [20] and inscribe them on the doorposts of your house and on your gates—[21] to the end that you and your children may endure, in the land that the LORD swore to your fathers to assign to them, as long as there is a heaven over the earth.

[22] If, then, you faithfully keep all this Instruction that I command you, loving the LORD your God, walking in all His ways, and holding fast to Him, [23] the LORD will dislodge before you all these nations: you will dispossess nations greater and more numerous than you. [24] Every spot on which your foot treads shall be yours; your territory shall extend from the wilderness to the Lebanon and from the River—the Euphrates—to the Western[d] Sea. [25] No man shall stand up to you: the LORD your God will put the dread and the fear of you over the whole land in which you set foot, as He promised you.

RE'EH   ראה

[26] See, this day I set before you blessing and curse: [27] blessing, if you obey the commandments of the LORD your God that I enjoin upon you this day; [28] and curse, if you do not obey the commandments of the LORD your God, but turn away from the path that I enjoin upon you this day and

through human effort; Canaan depends upon seasonal rainfall. The difference is mentioned to stress Israel's dependence upon God, who gives and withholds rain (Amos 4.7–8), as well as the fundamental sanctity of the land of Israel. **14:** *I,* God (see translators' note *a*). Moses as speaker here shifts from referring to God in the third person to speaking directly on God's behalf, in the first person (see 28.20 n.). The *early rain* comes at the end of the summer dry season (October–November); the *late* comes in the spring (March–April). **16–17:** See 7.12–14 n. **18–21:** See 6.6–9 n. **24:** *Every spot . . . yours,* a legal ritual that effected transfer of title by pacing out the perimeter of the territory (see 25.9 n.; Gen. 13.17). The territory is described in terms of the ideal limits of David's empire (see 1.7 n.). **26–32:** The two ways (see ch 28; 30.15–20). **26:** *Curse,* the sanctions for violating a treaty, which a vassal assumes in a sworn oath (see 28.15–68). **28:** *Follow,* see 6.14 n.

---

a I.e., the LORD; Samaritan reads "He."   b-b Lit. "heart and self."
c-c See notes on 6.8.   d I.e., Mediterranean.

follow other gods, ªwhom you have not experienced.ªª
29 When the LORD your God brings you into the land that
you are about to enter and possess, you shall pronounce
the blessing at Mount Gerizim and the curse at Mount
Ebal.—30 Both are on the other side of the Jordan, beyond
the west road that is in the land of the Canaanites who
dwell in the Arabah—near Gilgal, by the terebinths of
Moreh.

31 For you are about to cross the Jordan to enter and possess the land that the LORD your God is assigning to you.
When you have occupied it and are settled in it, 32 take
care to observe all the laws and rules that I have set before
you this day.

12 These are the laws and rules that you must carefully observe in the land that the LORD, God of
your fathers, is giving you to possess, as long as you live
on earth.

2 You must destroy all the sites at which the nations you
are to dispossess worshiped their gods, whether on lofty
mountains and on hills or under any luxuriant tree. 3 Tear
down their altars, smash their pillars, put their sacred
posts to the fire, and cut down the images of their gods,
obliterating their name from that site.

4 Do not worship the LORD your God in like manner,
5 but look only to the site that the LORD your God will

---

a-a *I.e., who have not proved themselves to you; cf. Hos. 13.4.*

29–30: These verses represent an editorial intrusion. Previously, *blessing . . . and the curse* identify the benefits of covenantal obedience and the sanctions for breach of covenant (vv. 26–28; 28.2, 15). That theme is the expected climax of this chapter. Here, "blessing" and "curse" are restricted to a series of positive and negative sayings shouted from mounts *Gerizim and . . . Ebal,* in anticipation of ch 27. *Gerizim,* on the south, and *Ebal,* on the north, flank the pass guarded by the city of Shechem in the central hill country. This geographic restriction fits poorly in a chapter otherwise directed to the entire land (vv. 22–25; 31–32). **30:** *The terebinths of Moreh,* at Shechem (see Gen. 12.6). **31–32:** Transition to the legal corpus. **32:** *Take care to observe . . . laws and rules,* cited chiastically at 12.1

("laws . . . rules . . . carefully observe") to effect the transition from the literary frame of Deuteronomy (chs 1–11) into the laws (chs 12–26).

12.1–26.15: The legal corpus, the core of Deuteronomy's transformation of Israelite religion. For the topical organization, see introduction.

12.1–13.1: Centralization and purification of the sacrificial worship, distinguishing Deuteronomic law and theology. These two requirements radically transformed Israelite religion, which in its formative stages, like all religions of antiquity, viewed sacrifice as indispensable to honor and to communicate with the deity. Historically, they are associated with the reform movements of King

Hezekiah (2 Kings 18.3–6, 22; 727/715–698/687) and, especially, of King Josiah (2 Kings chs 22–23; 640–609 BCE). The chapter requires the removal of foreign elements from the cultus (the system of sacrificial worship of God). It also centralizes the cultus by restricting sacrifice to a single, exclusively legitimate sanctuary. Four paragraphs (vv. 2–7, 8–12, 13–19, 20–28) each contain the centralization command; a fifth paragraph (vv. 29–31), concerned with cultic purification, vividly warns of the consequences of introducing alien worship into the Israelite system. An editorial superscription (v. 1) and conclusion (13.1) frame the unit, as each urges obedience. **1:** *Earth,* more accurately, "land." **12.2–7:** Israel must violently reject the Canaanite precedent of worshipping God at multiple sanctuaries distributed throughout the land; instead, no matter where the members of the covenant live, they must travel to the single, legitimate sanctuary. **2:** *You:* The chapter alternates between primarily plural (vv. 1–12) and primarily singular (vv. 13–31). This unexplained grammatical shift, combined with six repetitions of the command for cultic centralization (vv. 5, 11, 14, 18, 21, 26), suggests a complex compositional history. *Destroy:* Similar commands to destroy all implements associated with the worship of foreign gods are found at Exod. 23.23–24; 34.11–14; Deut. 7.5. *Lofty mountains . . . luxuriant tree,* formulaic language of the school of Deuteronomy for Canaanite sanctuaries, also known as "high places" (1 Kings 3.2; 2 Kings 16.4). Such sanctuaries were not only used to worship alien deities, however. During the monarchy, God could also be worshipped at such locations (1 Kings 3.4). **5:** *The site that the LORD . . . will choose:* This frequent formula consistently refers to Jerusalem, where Solomon built the Temple. Since Jerusalem played no role in Israel's history until David conquered it, made it his capital, and brought the Ark of the Covenant there (2 Sam. 5.6–6.19), the city cannot choose amidst all your tribes as His habitation, to establish His name there. There you are to go, ⁶ and there you are to bring your burnt offerings and other sacrifices, your tithes and contributions,ᵃ your votive and freewill offerings, and the firstlings of your herds and flocks. ⁷ Together with your households, you shall feast there before the LORD your God, happy in all the undertakings in which the LORD your God has blessed you.

⁸ You shall not act at all as we now act here, every man as he pleases, ⁹ because you have not yet come to the allotted haven that the LORD your God is giving you. ¹⁰ When you cross the Jordan and settle in the land that the LORD your God is allotting to you, and He grants you safety from all your enemies around you and you live in security, ¹¹ then you must bring everything that I command you to the site where the LORD your God will choose to establish His name: your burnt offerings and other sacrifices, your tithes and contributions,ᵃ and all the choice votive offerings that you vow to the LORD. ¹² And you shall rejoice before the LORD your God with your sons and daughters and with your male and female slaves, along with the Levite in your settlements, for he has no territorial allotment among you.

¹³ Take care not to sacrifice your burnt offerings in any place you like, ¹⁴ but only in the place that the LORD will choose in one of your tribal territories. There you shall sacrifice your burnt offerings and there you shall observe all that I enjoin upon you. ¹⁵ But whenever you desire, you may slaughter and eat meat in any of your settlements, according to the blessing that the LORD your God has granted you. The unclean and the clean alike may partake of it, as of the gazelle and the deer.ᵇ ¹⁶ But you must not partake of the blood; you shall pour it out on the ground like water.

a Lit. "the contribution(s) of your hands."
b I.e., animals that may be eaten (cf. 14.5; Lev. 11.1 ff.), but not sacrificed (Lev. 1.1 ff.).

be named explicitly without undermining the literary form of Deuteronomy as a Mosaic address. *To establish His name there:* Deuteronomy rejects the common older idea that a nation's God would inhabit the Temple (contrast 1 Kings 8.12–13). Thus, *as His habitation* would better be translated "to establish it" (the divine name), indicating possession and special relationship. **6:** A list of different types of sacrificial offerings. *Burnt offer*ings is a technical term for a type of sacrifice where all of the animal's flesh was burnt on the altar (v. 27; Lev 1.3–17). *Other sacrifices* refers to offerings where portions of the animal were assigned to the priests or shared by the worshippers (v. 27; 18.1–3; Lev. ch 3; 7.29–36). **12.8–12:** This paragraph understands centralization of worship as part of a divine plan that awaits future fulfillment. The idea here that sacrificial worship at multiple sanctuaries was intended from the beginning to have limited temporal validity differs from the viewpoint of Exod. 20.21, where it is chronologically unconditional. **8:** *Every man as he pleases,* lit. "each person doing what is right in his own eyes" in the absence of a central authority; a negative judgment, as in Judg. 17.6; 21.25. **9–10:** *Allotted haven* is a typical Deuteronomic term for the land as a whole. These verses designate territorial security as the precondition for the inauguration of centralization. This condition was fulfilled, according to the Deuteronomistic historian, only with David's conquest of Jerusalem, which then allowed the construction of the Temple (2 Sam. 7.1, 11; 1 Kings 8.56; cf. Josh. 21.43–45). **12:** Since *the Levites* were not assigned land (see Josh. 13.14; cf. Ezek. 44.28), they had to depend upon voluntary offerings (see 10.9; 18.2 n.).

12.13–19: This section, the earliest in the chapter, is concentrically arranged in a chiasm, a literary device frequently used by the authors and editors of antiquity to structure diverse material in an ABC:C'B'A' pattern (diagram on p. 393). **13–16:** The paragraph introduces two important distinctions in Israelite religion, each of which was revolutionary. **13–14:** The first distinction is between sacrificial worship *any place* (i.e., at sites scattered throughout the land), which is here rejected as illegitimate, and legitimate sacrifice performed at a single sanctuary, *the place that the LORD will choose* (v. 14). The prohibition of sacrifice at multiple sites marks a dramatic contrast with the nation's previous norms. It was formerly common to erect altars and sacrifice to God throughout the land (Gen. 12.7; 35.1–7; 1 Sam. 7.17; 1 Kings 18.20–46); indeed, earlier biblical law assures God's blessing at multiple sacrificial altars: "in every place" (Exod. 20.21). **14–16:** The second distinction is between the ritual sacrifice of animals at an altar and the secular slaughter of domestic animals for

17 You may not partake in your settlements of the tithes of your new grain or wine or oil, or of the firstlings of your herds and flocks, or of any of the votive offerings that you vow, or of your freewill offerings, or of your contributions.ᵃ 18 These you must consume before the LORD your God in the place that the LORD your God will choose—you and your sons and your daughters, your male and female slaves, and the Levite in your settlements—happy before the LORD your God in all your undertakings. 19 Be sure not to neglect the Levite as long as you live in your land.

20 When the LORD enlarges your territory, as He has promised you, and you say, "I shall eat some meat," for you have the urge to eat meat, you may eat meat whenever you wish. 21 If the place where the LORD has chosen to establish His name is too far from you, you may slaughter any of the cattle or sheep that the LORD gives you, as I have instructed you; and you may eat to your heart's content in your settlements. 22 Eat it, however, as the gazelle and the deer are eaten: the unclean may eat it together with the clean. 23 But make sure that you do not partake of the blood; for the blood is the life, and you must not consume the life with the flesh. 24 You must not partake of it; you must pour it out on the ground like water: 25 you

a Lit. "the contribution(s) of your hands."

food. Prior to Deuteronomy, that distinction almost certainly did not exist. The existence of multiple altars throughout the land made it easy to comply with the requirement that the slaughter of a domestic animal should take place upon an altar, on the base of which its blood would be spilled in devotion to God (Lev. 17.1–9). This requirement lies behind the condemnation of Saul's troops for slaughtering domestic animals "on the ground," without an altar (1 Sam. 14.31–35). The prohibition

of all local altars, however, created a real difficulty for those living in any of your settlements (v. 15), without easy access to the central sanctuary. In order that those far from the Temple could continue to eat meat, the legislator sought a legal precedent for the innovation of permitting the slaughter of domestic animals without performing that slaughter at an altar. The precedent employed was, paradoxically, the convention that applied to wild game such as the gazelle and . . . deer (v. 15). Although

permissible for consumption, these animals could not be sacrificed (note translators' note b). Accordingly, Priestly law allowed the slaughter of wild game in the open field: i.e., away from an altar. (Later rabbinic law also provides specific rules concerning how any animal should be slaughtered, seeking to prevent suffering.) The one condition imposed was not to consume the animal's blood but to "pour out its blood and cover it with earth" (Lev. 17.13). Deuteronomy's legislator applies that model to domestic animals, which may now—paradoxically in contravention of Priestly norms (Lev. 17.3–7)—similarly be slaughtered throughout the land, on condition that their blood is not consumed but poured out on the ground like water (v. 16). Blood was accorded special status because it symbolized the vitality and "life" of animals and humans (v. 23; 15.23; Gen. 9.4–5; Lev. 17.14; 19.26). Ritually pure and impure alike (the unclean and the clean) may now eat meat slaughtered under the new regulations (v. 15; contrast Lev. 7.19–21). **17:** Tithes, see 14.22–29 n. **12.20–28:** This section repeats the permission for secular slaughter. It presents it in a new light, however, now explaining it as a necessary consequence of the expansion of Israel's boundaries and resulting distance from the cultic shrine. The assumption of a 7th century date for the composition of Deuteronomy would imply that the paragraph's future formulation reflects an after-the-fact explanation. **23–27:** Although secular slaughter does not require an altar, common to it and the rules for sac-

CHIASTIC STRUCTURE OF 12.13–19

v. 13	Take care not (Heb "hishamer lekha pen")		A
v. 14	but only ("ki 'im") + centralization		B
v. 15	But ("rak") + secular slaughter		C
v. 16	But ("rak") + secular slaughter		C'
v. 18	But rather ("ki 'im"; not translated) + centralization		B'
v. 19	Be sure not ("hishamer lekha pen")		A'

must not partake of it, in order that it may go well with you and with your descendants to come, for you will be doing what is right in the sight of the LORD.

²⁶ But such sacred and votive donations as you may have ᵃ·shall be taken by youᵃ to the site that the LORD will choose. ²⁷ You shall offer your burnt offerings, both the flesh and the blood, on the altar of the LORD your God; and of your other sacrifices, the blood shall be poured out on the altar of the LORD your God, and you shall eat the flesh.

²⁸ Be careful to heed all these commandments that I enjoin upon you; thus it will go well with you and with your descendants after you forever, for you will be doing what is good and right in the sight of the LORD your God.

²⁹ When the LORD your God has cut down before you the nations that you are about to enter and dispossess, and you have dispossessed them and settled in their land, ³⁰ beware of being lured into their ways after they have been wiped out before you! Do not inquire about their gods, saying, "How did those nations worship their gods? I too will follow those practices." ³¹ You shall not act thus toward the LORD your God, for they perform for their gods every abhorrent act that the LORD detests; they even offer up their sons and daughters in fire to their gods. ¹ Be careful to observe only that which I enjoin upon you: neither add to it nor take away from it.

²If there appears among you a prophet or a dream-diviner and he gives you a sign or a portent, ³ saying, "Let us follow and worship another god"—whom you have not experiencedᵇ—even if the sign or portent that he

a-a Lit. "you shall pick up and come."   b See note on 11.28.

rifice are special procedures for handling the animal's blood (see vv. 13–16 n.). In neither case may the blood ever be consumed by humans. Slaughter requires the blood to be poured on the ground (vv. 23–25). Similarly, the rules for each of the two main types of animal sacrifice direct the blood away from human consumption (v. 27). With *burnt offerings, both the flesh and the blood* are offered to God on the altar (see v. 6 n.). With *your other sacrifices*, the blood is directed *on the altar*, at or upon its base.
28: *Commandments*, lit. "words."
12.29–31: Here the focus shifts to purification of worship. **30:** The

new covenant requires that Israelites not imitate the more established sacrificial practices of the Canaanites, by whose antiquity the newcomers might be *lured*. Elsewhere, the corruption of Israelite religion is presented as resulting from the attractions of marital contract (7.1–5, 25) or political treaty (Exod. 23.33; 34.12). **31:** *Offer up their sons and their daughters in fire:* The Canaanites are accused of child sacrifice (see 2 Kings 3.27; 23.10; Jer. 19.5–6), elsewhere associated with the deity Molech (Lev. 18.2; 20.2–5). This practice may have entrenched itself during the monarchy, with a cult

center in the Hinnom Valley, just southwest of Jerusalem (2 Kings 23.10; Jer. 7.31; 19.5–6). The historical evidence for such practices, however, remains disputed.

13.1: NJPS, following the Masoretic paragraph divisions, correctly regards this verse as the conclusion to ch 12; contrast the standard chapter and verse numbers, which were first added to the Hebrew text in the 13th century CE. The demarcation of the unit is here important. In form, ch 12 is thus framed by an inclusio (see next note) that urges fidelity to law and tradition, even though, in its content, the unit has just profoundly transformed both. *Be careful to observe*, the same idiom found at 12.1 (also 11.32), frames the unit with an inclusio. Moreover, *Neither add to it nor take away from it* reflects an ancient Near Eastern scribal formula that was often included in the epilogue of treaties, inscriptions, or law collections to protect them from being defaced, altered, or written over. Although the admonition may begin a section (4.2), more frequently, as here, it serves as an ending marker or "colophon" to conclude the literary unit (Prov. 30.6; Eccl. 3.14; cf. Revelation 22.18–19).

13.2–19: The requirement for unconditional loyalty to God. Three hypothetical test cases introduced by "if," each of which requires a difficult choice between competing social or personal commitments and allegiance to Israel's God. In the first case (vv. 2–6), a prophet or interpreter of dreams, symbolizing powerful religious authority, invites the citizen to worship other gods and thereby betray God by committing apostasy. The second test case (vv. 7–12) presents the incitement to apostasy as coming from an intimate family member, spouse, or close friend. The third case (vv. 13–19) concerns the successful conversion to apostasy of an entire city. In each instance, the crime is capital, and the citizen must act decisively by executing the prophet or dream interpreter named to you comes true, ⁴ do not heed the words of that prophet or that dream-diviner. For the Lᴏʀᴅ your God is testing you to see whether you really love the Lᴏʀᴅ your God with all your heart and soul. ⁵ Follow none but the Lᴏʀᴅ your God, and revere none but Him; observe His commandments alone, and heed only His orders; worship none but Him, and hold fast to Him. ⁶ As for that prophet or dream-diviner, he shall be put to death; for he urged disloyalty to the Lᴏʀᴅ your God—who freed you from the land of Egypt and who redeemed you from the house of bondage—to make you stray from the path that the Lᴏʀᴅ your God commanded you to follow. Thus you will sweep out evil from your midst.

⁷ If your brother, ᵃ your own mother's son,⁻ᵃ or your son or daughter, or the wife of your bosom, or your ᵇ⁻closest friend⁻ᵇ entices you in secret, saying, "Come let us worship other gods"—whom neither you nor your fathers have experienced ᶜ—⁸ from among the gods of the peoples around you, either near to you or distant, anywhere from one end of the earth to the other: ⁹ do not assent or give heed to him. Show him no pity or compassion, and do not shield him; ¹⁰ but take his life. Let your hand be the first

a-a Samaritan reads, "the son of your father or the son of your mother."
b-b Lit. "your friend who is as yourself."   c See note on 11.28.

(v. 6), killing the family member, spouse, or friend (v. 10), or conducting a war of attrition against a town of fellow citizens (v. 16). The literary model for these requirements is found in ancient Near Eastern treaties, which stipulated that vassals subject to a suzerain owed absolute loyalty to that suzerain and his designated successor. Political conspiracy had to be reported and was punishable by death. The author of this chapter has transformed that treaty requirement into a demand for absolute covenantal loyalty to Israel's divine suzerain.

13.2–6: While Deuteronomy presents Moses as the founder of Israelite prophecy, establishing both its standard (18.15–22) and its pinnacle (34.10–12), the book is nonetheless concerned to regulate prophecy. No other Torah law collection legislates concerning the prophet. Deuteronomy does so twice, in each case requiring the execution of the prophet who con-

travenes Deuteronomy's Torah (vv. 1–5; 18.19–22) and thus subordinating prophecy to covenantal law. At the same time, Deuteronomy sharply reworks the role of the prophet. Older forms of charismatic revelation (*dream, sign or a portent*), once the touchstone of the legitimate prophet and employed by Moses himself, now become suspect. No longer is the power to perform signs the test of a prophet's legitimacy (contrast v. 2 with 34.11–12; Exod. 4.1–9, 21; 1 Kings 18.20–40). The true prophet will now proclaim Torah (18.18). **2:** As a mediator of divine communications, *a prophet or a dream-diviner* (lit. "a prophet or dreamer of dreams") would by definition command public credibility and authority, making it the more difficult to resist his incitement to apostasy. *Dream-diviner:* Predicting the future by dream interpretation was one of the most common techniques of divination (Gen. 37.5–10; Num. 12.6; Jer.

23.25; Joel 3.1). The two sources of religious authority identified here correspond closely to the nearly contemporary Neo-Assyrian Vassal Treaty of Esarhaddon (672 BCE), which requires loyalty even in the face of conspiracy from "your brothers, your sons, your daughters, or from the mouth of a prophet, an ecstatic, or an inquirer of oracles" (§10). *Signs* or *portents* were also used by legitimate prophets to authenticate their proclamations (34.11; Exod. 4.1–9, 21; 7.9; Judg. 6.17). **3:** *Follow . . . another god:* The incitement to apostasy is formulated in the language of Neo-Assyrian treaties; see 6.14 n. *Worship*, specifically, with sacrifice; see 5.9 n. **6:** *Disloyalty*, as betrayal of the divine suzerain to whom covenant loyalty is owed. *Sweep out evil from your midst:* a formula that emphasizes the community's obligation to eliminate particularly offensive religious transgressions (e.g., 17.7, 12; 19.19; 21.21).

13.7–12: The possible conflict between love of family, spouse, or friend—exclusive loyalty to God (cf. Luke 14.26). **7:** *In secret*, i.e., in private, without witnesses. *Your own mother's son* (lit. "the son of your mother"), that is, "your full brother." In the context of Second Temple Judaism, the law was read as incomplete because of its asymmetrical formulation. Seeking to fill the perceived gap in the law, the Samaritan, the Septuagint, and fragments of Deuteronomy found at Qumran add: "the son of your father" (in translators' note a-a), so that it would include both the full and the half-brother. The addition no longer understands the original intent of this law, which demands that the addressee choose between loyalty to God and loyalty to the closest possible member of the immediate family. Thus, the Masoretic version preserves the better reading by restricting the focus to the full brother. **10:** *But take his life*, lit. "But you shall surely kill him." This verb is almost never used for a standard judicial execution. Here it demands that the inciter should be killed on the spot. Only the religious emergency of a grave threat against him to put him to death, and the hand of the rest of the people thereafter. ¹¹ Stone him to death, for he sought to make you stray from the LORD your God, who brought you out of the land of Egypt, out of the house of bondage. ¹² Thus all Israel will hear and be afraid, and such evil things will not be done again in your midst.

¹³ If you hear it said, of one of the towns that the LORD your God is giving you to dwell in, ¹⁴ that some scoundrels from among you have gone and subverted the inhabitants of their town, saying, "Come let us worship other gods"—whom you have not experienced—¹⁵ you shall investigate and inquire and interrogate thoroughly. If it is true, the fact is established—that abhorrent thing was perpetrated in your midst—¹⁶ put the inhabitants of that town to the sword and put its cattle to the sword. Doom it and all that is in it to destruction: ¹⁷ gather all its spoil into the open square, and burn the town and all its spoil as a holocaust to the LORD your God. And it shall remain an everlasting ruin, never to be rebuilt. ¹⁸ Let nothing that has been doomed stick to your hand, in order that the LORD may turn from His blazing anger and show you compassion, and in His compassion increase you as He promised your fathers on oath—¹⁹ for you will be heeding the LORD your God, obeying all His commandments that I enjoin upon you this day, doing what is right in the sight of the LORD your God.

14 You are children of the LORD your God. You shall not gash yourselves or shave the front of your heads because of the dead. ² For you are a people consecrated to the LORD your God: the LORD your God chose you from among all other peoples on earth to be His treasured people.

to the covenant, requiring urgent action, explains this type of summary execution (see also Exod. 32.27; Num. 25.5; Ezek. 9.6; cf. Lev. 20.15–16). Similar requirements for summarily executing traitors may be found in the Neo-Assyrian loyalty treaties that serve as a partial literary source for this chapter. Historically, the requirement for unconditional loyalty to YHVH, at all costs, modeled after the political treaty's similar demand for loyalty to the suzerain, accounts for the law's stringency. Nonetheless, compliance with the law conflicts with Deuteronomy's own require-

ment for due process (17.2–7 n.; 19.15; similarly, Num. 35.30). Later editors therefore added another layer to bring the law into conformity with the normal protocol for a public, judicial execution (v. 11 n.). In the Second Temple period, the law could only be taught and understood in that light: as consistent with the standard requirement that any execution require a prior legal conviction based upon the testimony of two witnesses. The Septuagint embeds that later reinterpretation of the law into its translation of the initial command: "You shall report."

11: *Stone:* Stoning was reserved for a particular class of offenses regarded as violating the community's fundamental values or sources of authority: apostasy or treason (here; 17.2–7; Lev. 20.2; Josh. 7.10–26; 1 Kings 21.8–14), blasphemy (Lev. 24.13–23), defying parental authority (21.18–21; 22.20–21), betraying marriage (22.23–24). Each of these offenses is prohibited by the Decalogue (5.6–7, 11, 16, 17). This form of punishment compelled the entire community to act collectively to repudiate the offense.

13.14: *Scoundrels,* lit., "sons of worthlessness," or "children of Belial" (KJV), a very strong derogatory term. **16–18:** In the sphere of clan life, little could be more horrifying and socially divisive than to have to "join battle with our kinsmen" (Judg. 20.23). Nonetheless, the infidelity of the entire town represents so significant a betrayal of the covenant that its entire population must be placed under the same ban as that otherwise reserved for the Canaanite population (7.1–6, 25–26; 12.29–30; 20.16–18). **17:** Normally in antiquity, new occupants would rebuild cities after their military destruction, right on top of the *ruin* (Heb "tel"). The word yields the term for the city-mounds that remain visible throughout the Near East, where archeological digs are conducted. In cases of particular cataclysm, the mounds sometimes were not rebuilt, and served as visible reminders of the destruction (Josh. 8.28; Jer. 26.18; 49.2; Mic. 3.12).

14.1–29: The obligations of holiness. 1–21: The special status that the covenant grants Israel as *a people consecrated to the* LORD entails special obligations upon them, one focus of which is dietary. The affirmation of holiness (vv. 2, 21) therefore frames the list of permitted and prohibited foods (vv. 3–21). That the nation's holiness requires special selectivity regarding food is also evident in earlier biblical law (the "holy" of Exod. 22.30). **1:** *Children of the* LORD, the first of

³You shall not eat anything abhorrent. ⁴These are the animals that you may eat: the ox, the sheep, and the goat; ⁵ᵃthe deer, the gazelle, the roebuck, the wild goat, the ibex, the antelope, the mountain sheep, ⁶and any other animal that has true hoofs which are cleft in two and brings up the cud—such you may eat. ⁷But the following, which do bring up the cud or have true hoofs which are cleft through, you may not eat: the camel, the hare, and the daman—for although they bring up the cud, they have no true hoofs—they are unclean for you; ⁸also the swine—for although it has true hoofs, it does not bring up the cud—is unclean for you. You shall not eat of their flesh or touch their carcasses.

⁹These you may eat of all that live in water: you may eat anything that has fins and scales. ¹⁰But you may not eat anything that has no fins and scales: it is unclean for you.

¹¹You may eat any clean bird. ¹²The following you may not eat: ᵃthe eagle, the vulture, and the black vulture; ¹³the kite, the falcon, and the buzzard of any variety; ¹⁴every variety of raven; ¹⁵the ostrich, the nighthawk, the sea gull, and the hawk of any variety; ¹⁶the little owl, the great owl, and the white owl; ¹⁷the pelican, the bustard, and the cormorant; ¹⁸the stork, any variety of heron, the hoopoe, and the bat.

¹⁹All winged swarming things are unclean for you: they may not be eaten. ²⁰You may eat only clean winged creatures.

a A number of these creatures cannot be identified with certainty.

three metaphors used in vv. 1–2 to emphasize the special relation between God and Israel. The divine parent has special custody for the child (Exod. 2.22–23; Hos. 1.10) but, equally, special indignation at wrongdoing (32.5–6, 19–20; Isa. 1.2). *Gash . . . shave . . . dead:* Gashing and head shaving were customary mourning rituals within Israel and the larger Near East (1 Kings 18.28; Jer. 16.6–7; 41.4–5; 47.5; Amos 8.10). The rationale for their prohibition (see also Lev. 19.27–28; 21.1–6) may be their association with foreign religion. More likely, such rituals were associated with ancestor worship or cults of the dead, an aspect of Israelite popular religion rejected by Deuteronomy (see 18.10–11). **2:** *For you are a people consecrated to the LORD:* Just as priests observe

more stringent purity rules than other Israelites, so must Israel distinguish itself from other nations by observing the special requirements of the Torah. This second metaphor of election departs from the idea of Israel's status found in the other biblical legal collections. Both the Book of the Covenant and the Holiness Collection understand the nation's holiness as a goal to be achieved in the future ("you shall be": Exod. 22.30; Lev. 19.2). In contrast, Deuteronomy affirms Israel's present status as already holy. *His treasured people:* The third metaphor is political. Just as the monarch is entitled to a "private hoard" of treasure not in the public domain (1 Chron. 29.3), so does God single Israel out for a special relationship. Both the second and third metaphors *(conse-*

crated; treasured people) derive from God's affirmation just prior to Sinai (Exod. 19.5–6).

14.3–21: The word "kosher" is never used in the Bible in reference to food. Nor is there in the Torah a comprehensive set of rules, similar to the later rabbinic system of kashrut, which covers permitted and nonpermitted foods, combinations of foods, means of preparation, rules for slaughter, etc. Deuteronomy nevertheless begins to build toward such a system. In contrast to Priestly law (Lev. ch 11), it brings together a list of creatures that may or may not be eaten (vv. 3–20), which it combines with laws implicitly concerned with slaughter and food preparation (v. 21). Deuteronomy's dietary restrictions abridge and revise the more detailed list of permitted and prohibited foods provided by the Priestly source (Lev. 11.2–23). For example, contrast the land animals prohibited by vv. 7–9 with the fuller list, including individual explanations, of Lev. 11.4–8. Similarly, vv. 9–10 offer a précis of Lev. 11.9–12; and v. 19 issues a blanket prohibition against insects in contrast to the lengthy distinctions between permitted and prohibited insects of Lev. 11.20–23. This textual relationship, where Deuteronomy uses and revises Priestly material, is highly unusual; by and large, it seems unaware of these texts. The classification of creatures as permitted or nonpermitted employs unexplained criteria to establish three basic divisions of species: creatures of the land (Deut. 14.1–8), water (vv. 9–10), or air (vv. 11–20). The same tripartite division occurs in the Priestly creation account (Gen. 1.20–25). Species that fail to satisfy the defining characteristics established for each category are not permitted: the pig (v. 8) and shellfish (v. 10). It is important to recognize that the classification system reflects the desire to imprint a human system of categorization upon nature and is based on a concern for systematic order rather than on hygiene or health. Thus, the term *unclean* (v. 8) does

21 You shall not eat anything that has died a natural death; give it to the stranger in your community to eat, or you may sell it to a foreigner. For you are a people consecrated to the LORD your God.

You shall not boil a kid in its mother's milk.

22 You shall set aside every year a tenth part of all the yield of your sowing that is brought from the field. 23 You shall consume the tithes of your new grain and wine and oil, and the firstlings of your herds and flocks, in the presence of the LORD your God, in the place where He will choose to establish His name, so that you may learn to revere the LORD your God forever. 24 Should the distance be too great for you, should you be unable to transport them, because the place where the LORD your God has chosen to establish His name is far from you and because the LORD your God has blessed you,ᵃ 25 you may convert them into money. Wrap up the money and take it with you to the place that the LORD your God has chosen, 26 and spend the money on anything you want—cattle, sheep, wine, or other intoxicant, or anything you may desire. And you shall feast there, in the presence of the LORD your God, and rejoice with your household.

27 But do not neglect the Levite in your community, for he has no hereditary portion as you have. 28 ᵇ-Every third year-ᵇ you shall bring out the full tithe of your yield of that year, but leave it within your settlements. 29 Then the Levite, who has no hereditary portion as you have, and the stranger, the fatherless, and the widow in your settlements shall come and eat their fill, so that the LORD your God may bless you in all the enterprises you undertake.

15 ᶜ-Every seventh year-ᶜ you shall practice remission of debts. 2 This shall be the nature of the remission: every creditor shall remit the due that he claims from his fellow; he shall not dun his fellow or kinsman, for the re-

a I.e., with abundant crops.
b-b Lit. "After a period of three years"; cf. Deut. 26.12.
c-c Cf. 14.28.

not imply that an animal is dirty. Ritually "impure" conveys the idea more clearly. **21:** *Anything that has died a natural death:* Israelites may not eat carrion (Exod. 22.30) or any other animal that is not slaughtered according to Deuteronomy's stringent requirement that the blood be drained (12.16, 23–25). The motivation is not hy-

giene but the enforcement of rules for slaughter. Carrion may therefore be donated to resident aliens or sold to foreigners, since the laws of slaughter apply only to Israelites. *Boil a kid:* This law is repeated three times in the Torah (here; Exod. 23.19; 34.26). The rabbinic assumption that no law in the Bible is redundant led to the

postbiblical generalization that prohibited the consumption of meat and milk products together. On its own terms, the law seems to have had a more restricted application. It originally applied specifically to the pilgrimage festival offerings (Exod. 23.19; 34.26). Deuteronomy now reinterprets it as a general law of food preparation. Philo viewed it as directing the mind away from the body; Maimonides viewed it as directed against idolatry. Some moderns have viewed the prohibition as directed against Canaanite religious rituals; others view it as concerned to prevent the abuse of animals.

14.22–29: The requirement to *set aside every year a tenth* of crops and livestock as a tax or honorarium paid to a monarch is common (Gen. 14.20; 28.22; 1 Sam. 8.15, 17). Here the rule signifies that Israel is God's steward, working but not owning God's land. **23:** The standard rules of the tithe (Lev. 27.30–33; Num. 18.21–32; cf. Exod. 22.29) are revised to direct offerings to the single sanctuary. Later rabbinic norms for tithing do not recognize this, and attempt to harmonize these various laws. *You shall consume:* Whereas Deuteronomy assigns the tithe to the landholder, Lev. 27.30 directs it to the sanctuary and Num. 18.21 to the Levites. **24:** In light of centralization, sanctified crops (designated for the sanctuary) may be converted *into money* (v. 25) to facilitate the journey. That *firstlings* (v. 23) may also be sold for cash is at variance with Lev. 27.32. *Distance be too great,* as in 12.21 ("too far"). **28–29:** *Every third year* the tithe is shifted away from the central sanctuary to focus on the needs of the disadvantaged and the marginalized in the local community, to ensure that they too may *eat their fill.*

15.1–18: Remission of debts (vv. 1–11) **and manumission of slaves** (vv. 12–18). On accession to the throne, ancient Near Eastern rulers would sometimes grant one-time cancellation of debts, return land confiscated by the crown, and mission proclaimed is of the LORD. ³ You may dun the foreigner; but you must remit whatever is due you from your kinsmen.

⁴ There shall be no needy among you—since the LORD your God will bless you in the land that the LORD your God is giving you as a hereditary portion—⁵ if only you heed the LORD your God and take care to keep all this Instruction that I enjoin upon you this day. ⁶ For the LORD your God will bless you as He has promised you: you will extend loans to many nations, but require none yourself; you will dominate many nations, but they will not dominate you.

⁷ If, however, there is a needy person among you, one of your kinsmen in any of your settlements in the land that the LORD your God is giving you, do not harden your heart and shut your hand against your needy kinsman. ⁸ Rather, you must open your hand and lend him sufficient for whatever he needs. ⁹ Beware lest you harbor the base thought, "The seventh year, the year of remission, is approaching," so that you are mean to your needy kinsman and give him nothing. He will cry out to the LORD against you, and you will incur guilt. ¹⁰ Give to him readily and have no regrets when you do so, for in return the LORD your God will bless you in all your efforts and in all your undertakings. ¹¹ For there will never cease to be needy ones in your land, which is why I command you: open your hand to the poor and needy kinsman in your land.

servitude, an ancient form of bankruptcy (see Lev. 25.13–55 for a similar sequence). Slavery and manumission serve as rich theological metaphors for both Jews and Christians (see Lev. 25.42, 55; Romans 6.20–23; Philippians 2.5–8).

15.1–6: Cancellation of debts. **1:** *Seventh year:* This law presupposes the requirement of the Book of the Covenant that agricultural land should be permitted to lie fallow each "seventh year" (Exod. 23.10–11). **2:** *Remission,* using the same verb found in Exod. 23.11 for "lie fallow," but now reapplying that agricultural requirement to command the cancellation of all existing debts. **3:** The utopian requirement is restricted to fellow citizens. In not canceling the debts of foreigners, the legislator makes a concession to the pragmatic concerns of the creditor. **4:** *There shall be no needy,* or, "no poor." Note the contrast between this unconditional utopian affirmation and the pragmatism of v. 7.

15.7–11: An appeal to conscience, anticipating the problem of implementing and enforcing such a law. **9:** *Cry . . . guilt.* The law has no judicial penalty or sanction. The neighbor's appeal is to the divine judge for enforcement (similarly, 24.15; Exod. 22.22–23).

15.12–18: Manumission: This law adjusts the older laws regulating male (Exod. 21.2–6) and female slaves (Exod. 21.7–11) in four significant ways. (1) It rejects separate procedures for the female bondservant and creates a single law that applies to both genders, strikingly abrogating the older law (contrast v. 17b with Exod. 21.7b)! (2) It secularizes the procedure for a slave who voluntarily relinquishes the right to freedom (vv. 16–17) by eliminating the former requirement that the ceremony take place "before God," i.e., at one of the now prohibited local sanctuaries or before the household deities (Exod. 21.6). (3) The master must now grant the slave a gift (vv. 13–14) rather than simply releasing him or her empty-handed (contrast Exod. 21.2). (4) In the

free indentured slaves. That custom, Akkadian "duraru," is reflected in the Hebrew "deror," "jubilee" or "release," of Lev. 25.10; Isa. 61.1; Jer. 34.15, 17. Deuteronomy's conception of the covenant between Israel and God entails a similar fresh start in which prior economic obligations are canceled at the initiative of the divine monarch. Now, however, it is not financial obligations to a privileged monarch that are canceled. Instead, the covenant requires the wealthy to forgive the debts of the poor! Moreover, this remission of debts and still unpaid labor contracts is no longer to be a voluntary, one-time act but a covenantal obligation that recurs every seven years. This blueprint for social justice is highly idealistic. By providing specific mechanisms to

eliminate poverty and financial inequality every seven years, Deuteronomy seeks to prevent economic injustice from becoming entrenched in society.

There is evidence that the authors are aware of the gap between this aspiration and worldly convention: Perspectives that are idealistic (v. 4) and pragmatic (v. 11) alternate in the chapter. For reflections of the injustices at issue, see Amos 2.6–8; Jer. 34.8–22; Ezek. 18.16–18; Job 24.9; Neh. 5.1–13. In the concern for social justice, the chapter reworks earlier laws found in the Book of the Covenant (Exod. chs 21–23), adjusting their requirements to the innovation of centralization of worship. The sequence of the paragraphs reflects increasingly severe stages of financial distress: from debt to indentured

¹²If a fellow Hebrew, man or woman, is sold to you, he shall serve you six years, and in the seventh year you shall set him free. ¹³When you set him free, do not let him go empty-handed: ¹⁴Furnish him out of the flock, threshing floor, and vat, with which the LORD your God has blessed you. ¹⁵Bear in mind that you were slaves in the land of Egypt and the LORD your God redeemed you; therefore I enjoin this commandment upon you today.

¹⁶But should he say to you, "I do not want to leave you"—for he loves you and your household and is happy with you—¹⁷you shall take an awl and put it through his ear into the door, and he shall become your slave in perpetuity. Do the same with your female slave. ¹⁸When you do set him free, do not feel aggrieved; for in the six years he has given you double the service of a hired man. Moreover, the LORD your God will bless you in all you do.

¹⁹You shall consecrate to the LORD your God all male firstlings that are born in your herd and in your flock: you must not work your firstling ox or shear your firstling sheep. ²⁰You and your household shall eat it annually before the LORD your God in the place that the LORD will choose. ²¹But if it has a defect, lameness or blindness, any serious defect, you shall not sacrifice it to the LORD your God. ²²Eat it in your settlements, the unclean among you no less than the clean, just like the gazelle and the deer. ²³Only you must not partake of its blood; you shall pour it out on the ground like water.

16 Observe the month^a of Abib and offer a passover sacrifice to the LORD your God, for it was in the month^a of Abib, at night, that the LORD your God freed

a Cf. Exod. 13.4; 23.15; 34.18.

Book of the Covenant, there is no connection between the manumission law (Exod. 21.2–6) and the land sabbatical law (Exod. 23.10–11). Nor should one be expected. Logically, the year of manumission would not be uniform through the land but would vary with each household, depending upon when a slave began to labor. By conjoining the two originally separate laws, Deuteronomy creates a single year of release that now applies to both remission of debts (vv. 1–6) and manumission (vv. 12–18). Deuteronomy thus transforms manumission, which

used to be based in the individual household, into a year of universal liberty (see also Lev. ch 25). That perspective lies behind Zedekiah's last-ditch attempt to curry divine favor by implementing this law on the eve of the Babylonian invasion of Jerusalem in 587 BCE, with a universal emancipation of slaves (Jer. 34.6–22). And whereas the legislator of Deuteronomy can only appeal to individual moral conscience to urge obedience (v. 18), Jeremiah explains the Babylonian destruction as divine punishment for Jerusalem's citizens' reneging on the law by immedi-

ately reenslaving those whom they freed (Jer. 34.11–22). With national exile thus made the penalty for infringement, setting slaves free every seven years becomes, in this view, a central requirement of the covenant. The delay of manumission to the fiftieth year in the Holiness Collection may reflect the difficulty of implementing this idealistic law (Lev. 25.39–44). **12:** *Is sold,* alternately, "sells himself," expressing the two alternative ways of understanding the contractual and economic nature of this slavery, which is not based on race, nationality, or religion. The court might require that a thief, unable to repay a theft, "be sold," i.e., indenture his labor to compensate the victim (Exod. 21.37–22.3). Alternatively, if overcome by debt, a serf might "sell himself," i.e., assign his labor to repay a loan (Lev. 25.39–44). **14–15:** The gift provided the manumitted slave recalls and reenacts the nation's own manumission by God from slavery in Egypt. **18:** As in vv. 8–10, an appeal to conscience that anticipates the difficulty of enforcing a law that lacks judicial sanction.

15.19–23: Sacrifice of firstlings. Older religious convention required that each first-born male domestic animal be offered as a sacrifice to God at one of the local sanctuaries (Exod. 13.1–2, 11–16; 22.28–29; 34.19–20). The author now adjusts that law to the new one stipulating a single sanctuary. **19:** *Not work,* so as to reserve the animal for God. **20:** *Before the LORD* refers to sacrifice at an altar, which now requires a pilgrimage to the central sanctuary of Jerusalem, *the place that the LORD will choose.* **21–23:** Blemished first-born livestock need not be taken to the central sanctuary. They may be slaughtered locally, *in your settlements,* following the requirements for secular slaughter (12.15–16, 21–25).

16.1–17: The festival calendar. Deuteronomy strikingly transforms older religious celebrations in order to accommodate them you from Egypt. ² You shall slaughter the passover sacrifice for the LORD your God, from the flock and the herd, in the place where the LORD will choose to establish His name. ³ You shall not eat anything leavened with it; for seven days thereafter[a] you shall eat unleavened bread, bread of distress—for you departed from the land of Egypt hurriedly—so that you may remember the day of your departure from the land of Egypt as long as you live. ⁴ For seven days no leaven shall be found with you in all your territory, and none of the flesh of what you slaughter on the evening of the first day shall be left until morning.

⁵ You are not permitted to slaughter the passover sacrifice in any of the settlements that the LORD your God is giving you; ⁶ but at the place where the LORD your God will choose to establish His name, there alone shall you slaughter the passover sacrifice, in the evening, at sundown, the time of day when you departed from Egypt. ⁷ You shall cook and eat it at the place that the LORD your God will choose; and in the morning you may start back on your journey home. ⁸ After eating unleavened bread six days, you shall hold a solemn gathering[b] for the LORD your God on the seventh day: you shall do no work.

a Lit. "upon it."   b See note at Lev. 23.36.

required that the observance be redirected to the central sanctuary (vv. 2, 6–7). Now made into a pilgrimage festival, the older blood ritual in the doorway of the private home—the defining act of the original Passover observance—is no longer mentioned. The new observance then merges with the Festival of Unleavened Bread, which was also celebrated in early spring. Traces of the separate identity of Passover and Unleavened Bread remain evident in their distinct dates and naming in Lev. 23.5, 6; Num. 28.16, 17–25. **1:** *Abib* (lit. "new ear of grain"), in early spring, when ears of barley, the first crop, began to ripen (Exod. 13.4; 23.15; 34.18). It was originally the first month of the Hebrew calendar (Exod. 12.2); later this month was called by the Babylonian month name "Nisan." **2:** *From the flock and the herd* expands the earlier restriction of the paschal offering to "a lamb . . . from the sheep or from the goats" (Exod. 12.4–5, 21). **3:** *For seven days:* This section, through v. 4a, splices the seven-day observance of the Festival of Unleavened Bread (Exod. 12.14–20; 23.15) into the one-day observance of Passover (vv. 1–3a, 4b–7). **7:** *Cook:* more accurately, "boil," like other standard sacrifices (Exod. 29.1; Lev. 6.21; 8.31; Num. 6.19; 1 Sam. 2.13, 15; Zech. 14.21). This prescription is at odds with the earlier stipulation that the paschal offering be "roasted by fire," not "boiled in water" (Exod. 12.8–9; Hebrew). The Passover is now being treated as a standard sacrifice. These two mutually inconsistent laws are harmonized at 2 Chron. 35.13, where the Hebrew paradoxically reads: "They boiled the Passover offering by fire, according to the law." **8:** *After eating unleavened bread six days:* The Hebrew reads simply, "For six days you shall eat unleavened bread." The NJPS rendering, *"after . . . six days,"* results in an eight-day total for the festivals of Passover and Unleavened Bread, modeled after the Priestly version of the calendar: 1 day (Passover) + 6 days (Unleavened Bread) + 1 day (the

to its requirement for centralization of worship. Previously, each male Israelite was commanded to undertake three pilgrimages to "appear before the LORD," i.e., to make an offering at one of the multiple local sanctuaries (v. 16; Exod. 23.14–18). The Hebrew term for these important events in ancient Israel's religious calendar is "Ḥag" (as in the still common greeting, "Ḥag Sameaḥ"). Often translated as "feasts" (v. 16; Exod. 23.14), the original idea is "pilgrimage festival." As a consequence of restricting sacrifice to a single, central sanctuary, Deuteronomy redirects the required pilgrimage from the prohibited local sanctuaries (v. 5) to the central one, *the place where the LORD will choose* (vv. 2, 6, 7, 11, 15, 16; 12.17–18). These three festivals were Unleavened Bread (Heb "Matzot"), Harvest, and Ingathering (Exod. 23.14–17; 34.18, 23). Deuteronomy renames the latter two "Weeks" (v. 10; Heb "Shavu'ot") and "Booths" (v. 13;

Heb "Sukkot"), which remain their current names.

16.1–8: The blend of Passover and the Festival of Unleavened Bread is the most remarkable section of this calendar. Passover was originally a separate observance, celebrated within the family or clan. Since it did not require a sacrifice at the sanctuary, it was not included among the three pilgrimage festivals (Exod. 23.14–17; 34.18, 21–23). Instead, it was distinguished by a nighttime slaughter of a sheep or goat in the doorway of the house, where the blood was smeared to demarcate the house as Israelite (Exod. 12.7, 21–22). First performed to protect the Israelites in Egypt from the plague against the first-born, the ritual thereafter annually commemorated Israel's deliverance from that plague (Exod. 12.1–13, 21–28). But Deuteronomy's restriction of sacrifice to the single sanctuary prohibited Passover from being observed locally (v. 5) and

9 You shall count off seven weeks; start to count the seven weeks when the sickle is first put to the standing grain. 10 Then you shall observe the Feast of Weeks for the LORD your God, offering your freewill contribution according as the LORD your God has blessed you. 11 You shall rejoice before the LORD your God with your son and daughter, your male and female slave, the Levite in your communities, and the stranger, the fatherless, and the widow in your midst, at the place where the LORD your God will choose to establish His name. 12 Bear in mind that you were slaves in Egypt, and take care to obey these laws.

13 After the ingathering from your threshing floor and your vat, you shall hold the Feast of Booths for seven days. 14 You shall rejoice in your festival, with your son and daughter, your male and female slave, the Levite, the stranger, the fatherless, and the widow in your communities. 15 You shall hold a festival for the LORD your God seven days, in the place that the LORD will choose; for the LORD your God will bless all[a] your crops and all your undertakings, and you shall have nothing but joy.

a Lit. "you in all."

solemn gathering); see Lev. 23.3–8. In contrast, Deuteronomy intended to fuse the two holidays into a single seven-day observance.

16.9–12: The Festival of Weeks (Exod. 34.22; Lev. 23.15–16; Num. 28.26), originally, as the earliest name signifies, the "Festival of Harvest" (Exod. 23.16), celebrated in May–June. In postbiblical Judaism, the festival came to be associated with the revelation at Mount Sinai (Exod. chs 19–20). The idea underlies the New Testament narrative of the Holy Spirit's activity at "Pentecost" (Acts 2.1; cf. 20.16; 1 Corinthians 16.8), the Greek term for which reflects the calculation of "fifty days" (Lev. 23.16). **9:** *Start to count the seven weeks when the sickle is first put to the standing grain:* The date of this festival is not a fixed date set by the calendar but is based upon the cycle of the agricultural year. The seven-week period delays the celebration until the safe conclusion of the harvest, a precarious period when the im-

portant crop might be damaged by natural forces. This kind of calculation implies that different parts of the land might celebrate the festival on different dates. This ambiguity gave rise to a chain of successive interpretations in Second Temple literature that attempted to clarify the precise date of the festival. The first of these attempts may well be that of the Holiness Collection, which dates the seven weeks "from the day on which you bring the sheaf of elevation offering— the day after the sabbath" (Lev. 23.15). But that calculation remains ambiguous, since the "sabbath" to which the text refers is not identified. Contextually, "the day after the sabbath" refers to the first Sunday after the first ripe sheaf of grain is harvested, but precisely that absence of a specific date for Weeks led to sectarian disagreement in Second Temple times over when to observe it. Pharisees understood the sabbath in question simply as a reference to the Passover, no matter on which day of the week it fell; Sadducees re-

garded it as the Sabbath during the week of Passover/Unleavened Bread; and the Qumran community viewed it as the Sabbath of the following week. The proliferation of sects in the Second Temple period may well reflect, in part, the mutually exclusive interpretations of different groups who struggled to resolve the Bible's calendrical ambiguities. **11:** *With your son and daughter:* The command to rejoice before God at the central sanctuary specifies the inclusion of women (as v. 14; 12.12, 18). That the wife is not named separately in the list implies that the law regards the male and female adult citizen as equals. Contrast the more formulaic vv. 16–17, which is slavishly adopted from its source in Exodus. *Slave . . . widow:* The marginalized and the disadvantaged are also included in this comprehensive list. *Stranger,* better, "resident alien," see 10.18–19 n.

16.13–15: The Feast of Booths. Curiously, the law provides no explanation for the name of the festival, which is elsewhere called "Ingathering" (Exod. 23.16; 34.22), reflecting its origins as the fall harvest festival. The Holiness Collection fills in this gap with the sermon-like explanation that the name recalls how God "made the Israelite people live in booths when I brought them out of the land of Egypt" (Lev. 23.43). But that explanation is inconsistent with the narrative tradition that the Israelites lived in tents during the wilderness sojourn (Num. 11.10; 16.27; 25.8). More likely, the name reflects the agricultural custom of farmers erecting temporary shelters in the fields during the summer while the grapes, olives, and other crops are tended and then harvested (see Isa. 1.8). **15:** *Seven days:* Deuteronomy's observance differs from that of the Holiness Collection, which requires a total of eight days (Lev. 23.36, 40). Moreover, Deuteronomy does not require that the first and the final days of the festival involve a "holy convocation" or "solemn assembly,"

¹⁶Three times a year—on the Feast of Unleavened Bread, on the Feast of Weeks, and on the Feast of Booths—all your males shall appear before the LORD your God in the place that He will choose. They shall not appear before the LORD empty-handed, ¹⁷but each with his own gift, according to the blessing that the LORD your God has bestowed upon you.

SHOFETIM   שפטים

¹⁸You shall appoint magistrates and officials for your tribes, in all the settlements that the LORD your God is giving you, and they shall govern the people with due justice. ¹⁹You shall not judge unfairly: you shall show no partiality; you shall not take bribes, for bribes blind the eyes of the discerning and upset the plea of the just. ²⁰Justice,

when work was prohibited (Lev. 23.35–36).

16.16–17: The formulaic summary ("colophon") reuses the conclusion of the older festival calendar in the Book of the Covenant (Exod. 23.17), which it now updates to specify that the three annual pilgrimages must be to the central sanctuary, *the place that He will choose.* Two elements, however, reflect older assumptions inconsistent with the rest of this chapter: Passover (vv. 1–8) is not mentioned, and the pilgrimage requirement is directed to *all your males* (as Exod. 23.17), despite the gender inclusivity of vv. 11, 14.

16.18–18.22: Laws of public officials. Although western political theory is normally traced back to ancient Athens, this section is remarkable for providing what seems to be the first blueprint for a constitutional system of government. The carefully thought-out plan is designed to ensure that no single branch of government and no single religious institution should have sole power. Each is brought into relationship to the others and, more importantly, each is made subordinate to the one true authority: the Torah of Deuteronomy. Even institutions that might justifiably claim absolute authority—whether political, as in the case of the king (see Ps. 2.6–7),

or religious, as in the case of the prophet (see Exod. 3.10–12)—are integrated into Deuteronomy's comprehensive vision. It is unlikely that the ambitious program envisioned by this draft constitution was ever fully implemented. Upon the return from exile, when Judah regained some measure of political autonomy under Persian rule, different religious and political priorities preempted this blueprint. There is a great deal of scholarly disagreement about the precise dating of this section: how much to ascribe to the original legislation of Deuteronomy, associated with the Josianic period shortly before the exile, and how much may derive from the Babylonian exile itself, as Judean thinkers reflected on their national history and mapped out a new model of society, structured by Torah. Most likely, an original Josianic layer underwent elaboration during the exile.

In its organization, this section addresses the full range of public officials in the judicial, executive, and religious branches: the local and the central courts (16.18–17.13), kingship (17.14–20), the Levitical priesthood (18.1–8), and prophecy (18.9–22). Although the focus on public officials ostensibly marks a significant change from the previous section's focus on the sacrificial system (12.1–16.17), the concern of the leg-

islator in both sections is consistent: the impact of centralization of worship upon all spheres of life. The desire to bridge from the first section to the new one explains the puzzling way in which ritual laws (16.21–17.1) seem to intrude between two paragraphs concerned with justice (16.18–20, 17.2–7). By means of the repetition, the editor provides a transition into the new section, while establishing the underlying unity of both areas of community life:

A   Cultus (12.1–16.17)
B   Justice (16.18–20)
A' Cultus (16.21–17.1)
B' Justice (17.2–7, 17.8–13)

16.18–17.13: The organization of justice. 16.18–20: Deuteronomy here establishes a professionalized local judiciary. **18:** *Settlements,* lit., "gates," Deuteronomy's metaphor for the local sphere (12.15, 17, 21; 16.5), as distinguished from the central sanctuary. Here the metaphor takes on an additional meaning, because the city gate served as the location where justice was traditionally dispensed by the village elders (Job 29.7; Ruth 4.1, 11; Lam. 5.14). By appointing professional *magistrates and officials* to just that location, while leaving the elders unmentioned, Deuteronomy significantly contracts the elders' sphere of authority, if not altogether eliminating it. The professionalization of the judicial system thus entails a disruption of traditional patterns of clan authority. The elders are mentioned elsewhere in the legal corpus as involved with judicial matters (21.1–9, 19; 22.15, 25.7). These references may preserve an older perspective; otherwise, they show how the elders' role in justice has now been restricted to family and marital law. **19:** *You shall not judge unfairly:* This admonition to the judges, sometimes called a "Mirror for Magistrates," quotes Exod. 23.6a (where the same verb is translated "subvert"). *For bribes blind the eyes of the discerning* (lit. "of the wise"): The older law of Exod. 23.8, which refers to "the clear-sighted" as being blinded by justice shall you pursue, that you may thrive and occupy the land that the LORD your God is giving you.

²¹ You shall not set up a sacred post—any kind of pole beside the altar of the LORD your God that you may make—²² or erect a stone pillar; for such the LORD your God detests.

17 You shall not sacrifice to the LORD your God an ox or a sheep that has any defect of a serious kind, for that is abhorrent to the LORD your God.

² If there is found among you, in one of the settlements that the LORD your God is giving you, a man or woman who has affronted the LORD your God and transgressed His covenant—³ turning to the worship of other gods and bowing down to them, to the sun or the moon or any of the heavenly host, something I never commanded—⁴ and you have been informed or have learned of it, then you shall make a thorough inquiry. If it is true, the fact is established, that abhorrent thing was perpetrated in Israel, ⁵ you shall take the man or the woman who did that wicked thing out to the public place, and you shall stone them, man or woman, to death.—⁶ A person shall be put to death only on the testimony of two or more[a] witnesses; he must not be put to death on the testimony of a single witness.—⁷ Let the hands of the witnesses be the first against him to put him to death, and the hands of the rest of the people thereafter. Thus you will sweep out evil from your midst.

⁸ If a case is too baffling for you to decide, be it a controversy over homicide, civil law, or assault—matters of dis-

a Lit. "three."

---

bribery, is revised in light of Deuteronomy's stress upon wisdom. The failure of Samuel's sons to meet this standard of judicial probity (1 Sam. 8.3) is viewed by the Deuteronomistic historian as the justification for the establishment of the monarchy (1 Sam. 8.5).

16.21–17.1: Prohibitions against Canaanite cultic objects (7.5; 12.3; Exod. 34.13). **16.21:** *Sacred post* or *"'Asherah,"* see 7.5 n. Archeological evidence suggests that this Canaanite goddess may also have been popular in Israel. **16.22:** See 7.5 n. **17.1:** This verse broadens the prohibition against sacrificing

blemished firstlings (15.21) into a general law of sacrifice.

17.2–7: Local justice. Because of the extent to which this law so closely overlaps with 13.7–12, both in its wording and in the topic of apostasy by an individual, many scholars have viewed it as out of place and as belonging to ch 13. That is incorrect. Whereas the theme of ch 13 is incitement, at issue here are the procedures and the jurisdiction of the local courts. Under the professionalized judiciary (16.18), the law grants the local courts maximal autonomy, enabling them to try even capital

cases and to address religious matters (the accusation of apostasy). Just one essential condition is imposed: that a trial be conducted according to strictly rational standards that assure empirical proof for the verdict. Thus v. 4 provides the procedures to put a vague rumor *(you have been informed)* to the formal test of *a thorough inquiry* in order to verify its truth. The law stipulates the criteria necessary to establish judicial "proof": *the testimony of two or more witnesses* (v. 6). This law may be the first place in the Bible, historically speaking, where norms of justice regarding witness law were established. (Scholars normally date the Priestly source, and thus the parallel requirement of more than one witness in Num. 35.30, later than Deuteronomy.) The power of this law is that it rejects the summary execution in the case of incitement required by Deut. 13.7–12. By stipulating that *he must not be put to death on the testimony of a single witness* (v. 6b), the law seeks to impose rigorous requirements for evidence even in cases of apostasy. The older law is then subordinated to the new standard of justice: No longer is the execution carried out by the single witness ("your hand," 13.10); rather the agents carrying out the execution are now plural: *the hands of the witnesses* (v. 7). **2:** *A man or a woman:* The law views the woman as a legally responsible individual. The viewpoint in marriage and family law differs, however (see 22.13–29). **3:** Contravening the Decalogue (5.8–9); see 4.19; 2 Kings 23.5; Jer. 8.2. **6:** A travesty of the condition for *two or more witnesses* occurs in the kangaroo court set up by Jezebel to execute Naboth (1 Kings 21.10, 13). The prohibition against execution on the basis of testimony by a *single witness* is also found at 19.15–16; Num. 35.30.

17.8–13: Justice at the central sanctuary. In the pre-Deuteronomic period, the local sanctuaries served a judicial function in addition to providing a place for the sacrificial worship of God. In legal pute in your courts—you shall promptly repair to the place that the LORD your God will have chosen, ⁹and appear before the levitical priests, or the magistrate in charge at the time, and present your problem. When they have announced to you the verdict in the case, ¹⁰you shall carry out the verdict that is announced to you from that place that the LORD chose, observing scrupulously all their instructions to you. ¹¹You shall act in accordance with the instructions given you and the ruling handed down to you; you must not deviate from the verdict that they announce to you either to the right or to the left. ¹²Should a man act presumptuously and disregard the priest charged with serving there the LORD your God, or the magistrate, that man shall die. Thus you will sweep out evil from Israel: ¹³all the people will hear and be afraid and will not act presumptuously again.

¹⁴If, after you have entered the land that the LORD your God has assigned to you, and taken possession of it and settled in it, you decide, "I will set a king over me, as do all the nations about me," ¹⁵you shall be free to set a king over yourself, one chosen by the LORD your God. Be sure to set as king over yourself one of your own people; you must not set a foreigner over you, one who is not your kinsman. ¹⁶Moreover, he shall not keep many horses or

cases where there was an absence either of physical evidence or of witnesses, no court could make a ruling. Such cases were remanded to divine jurisdiction at the local sanctuary on the assumption that God could determine guilt or innocence without being bound by empirical criteria. The parties to the dispute would swear a judicial oath at the altar, symbolically "before God" (19.17; 1 Kings 8.31–32; see also Exod. 21.6). In special circumstances, a priest might conduct a judicial ordeal (Num. 5.11–31). In both cases, Israelite judicial procedures conform closely to those evident in ancient Babylonian legal collections like The Laws of Hammurabi (§§9, 23, 266, 281) or the Laws of Eshnunna. Deuteronomy's prohibition of the local sanctuaries (ch 12) therefore created an important local judicial void. The intent of these two laws (17.2–7, 8–13) is to fill the void. Deuteronomy grants the local courts absolute judicial autonomy, extending even to capital cases and to religious matters, on condition that all such cases meet the standard of sufficient evidence (17.2–7). Cases that do not meet that empirical standard, and that once would have been remanded to the local sanctuary for divine resolution, must now be remanded instead to the central sanctuary (17.8–13). Deuteronomy is thus completely consistent in its transformation of sacrifice and in its revolution of the judicial system. The local sphere is completely secularized (12.15–16, 20–25; 17.2–7); the central sanctuary provides the sole legitimate context for either sacrifice (12.13–14, 26–27; 16.2, 5–7a) or divine resolution of ambiguous legal cases (17.8–13). **8:** *Too baffling for you to decide,* going beyond what is possible for human knowledge to resolve. *A controversy over homicide,* when it is unclear whether the defendant is guilty of murder or manslaughter (Exod. 21.12–14; Num. 35.16–23).

In each of these pairs, the distinction is between premeditated and unintentional offenses. **9:** The tribunal at the sanctuary includes both priestly and lay members, assuming that *the magistrate* refers to a secular official (as in 19.17). The account of Jehoshaphat's setting up tribunals throughout Judah composed of lay and clerical judges reflects this law (2 Chron. 19.5–11).

17.14–20: The law of the king. Deuteronomy's conception of the kingship entails an extraordinary restriction of royal authority. Whereas generally Near Eastern monarchs like Hammurabi themselves promulgated law, here the monarch is subject to the law and required to read the Torah daily (v. 19). Conventionally the monarch was assigned a crucial role in the administration of justice, serving as a court of last appeal to defend the rights of the oppressed (Ps. 72.1–4). Deuteronomy remarkably denies the king any role whatsoever in justice, granting the local courts and the central sanctuary complete jurisdiction. The king is also denied his customary Near Eastern role in supervising the public cultus. This law far more emphasizes what the king may not do than what he may do. The remarkable subordination of the king to *this Teaching* (v. 18)— Deuteronomic Torah—thus envisions something like a constitutional monarchy. This notion exists in some tension to the views of the Deuteronomic historian, who returns the king to his public religious function as Josiah leads the national Passover celebration (2 Kings 23.21–23), and to the royalist concerns of the Chronicler. **14:** *As do all the nations,* see 1 Sam. 8.5. **16–18:** The offenses specified here allude to the warnings against royal autocracy outlined at the very founding of the monarchy (1 Sam. 8.10–18). They almost certainly presuppose Solomon's trade in horses (1 Kings 10.26–29) and his multiple marital alliances with foreign wives (1 Kings 11.1–8). The Deuteronomistic historian under-send people back to Egypt to add to his horses, since the LORD has warned you, "You must not go back that way again." [17] And he shall not have many wives, lest his heart go astray; nor shall he amass silver and gold to excess.

[18] When he is seated on his royal throne, he shall have a copy of this Teaching written for him on a scroll by[a] the levitical priests. [19] Let it remain with him and let him read in it all his life, so that he may learn to revere the LORD his God, to observe faithfully every word of this Teaching as well as these laws. [20] Thus he will not act haughtily toward his fellows or deviate from the Instruction to the right or to the left, to the end that he and his descendants may reign long in the midst of Israel.

18 The levitical priests, the whole tribe of Levi, shall have no territorial portion with Israel. They shall live only off the LORD's offerings by fire as their[b] portion, [2] and shall have no portion among their brother tribes: the LORD is their portion, as He promised them.

---

a Nuance of Heb. milliphne uncertain.   b Lit. "its," i.e., the tribe's.

---

stood those marriages to lead to religious syncretism and the corruption of Israelite religion (1 Kings 11.1–8), with the breakup of the united monarchy the divine punishment for these transgressions (1 Kings 11.9–13). **16:** *People,* lit. "the people," i.e., the Israelites. *Back to Egypt to add to his horses:* The reference is difficult. Elsewhere, the idea of Israel's returning to Egypt implies divine punishment and the reimposition of slavery (28.68; Hos. 8.13; 9.3). But here that idea is combined with a veiled critical reference to Judah's attempt to forge a military alliance with Egypt against Assyria in 701 BCE, when Isaiah challenged "those who go down to Egypt for help/And rely upon horses!" (Isa. 31.1). *Since the LORD has warned you,* see 28.68 n. **18:** The law requires the king to be subject to the law, not above it. The common status of the monarch throughout the ancient Near East as promulgator of the law (as in the Laws of Hammurabi) and as enjoying a special relationship with the divinity (so also Ps. 2) might suggest that the king would be exempt from the law's require-

ments. To emphasize its rejection of that norm, Deuteronomy requires the king to have a *copy of this Teaching written for him:* The king must daily read the law that limits his powers. The literal Hebrew phrase, "a copy of this Teaching (torah)," provides the basis for one of the two ancient Jewish designations of the book. One title is "Sefer Devarim," "The Book of Words," short for "The Book of 'These are the Words . . . '" (based on 1.1). That title follows the common ancient Near Eastern convention of naming books after their opening phrase or incipit. The second ancient rabbinic title, based on this phrase, was "Mishneh Torah" (*Sifre* §160). This was translated into Greek by Philo and the Septuagint as "Deuteronomion" and is the source of the book's familiar English title, "Deuteronomy." That title, however, is based on a misunderstanding of this phrase in 17.18 as referring to Deuteronomy as a whole.

18.1–8: The Levitical priesthood. Centralization of worship also had an impact upon the Israelite priesthood, to which the legislator now

turns. Deuteronomy provides a concise "job description" of the priesthood (vv. 1–5) and then addresses the impact of centralization upon its livelihood (vv. 6–8). **1:** The phrase *levitical priests* marks a distinctively Deuteronomic conception of the priesthood, one that significantly differs from that found in the Priestly literature, where "the priests" and "the Levites" are separate from one another. The Priestly source establishes a hierarchy within the tribe of Levi between the direct descendants of Aaron and the rest of the tribe (Num. ch 18). Only the Aaronides are technically called "priests" and thereby permitted to officiate at the altar before God (Num. 18.5, 7). For their support they are assigned the priestly share of the sacrificial offerings brought by Israelites to the sanctuary (Num. 18.8–20). In contrast, the remainder of the tribe, the "Levites," serve the priests and are prohibited from officiating at the altar (Num. 18.3–4, 6). For their support, they receive the tithes of produce and cattle. In turn, they pay a tithe of what they have received to the priests (Num. 18.21–31). Deuteronomy's approach is very different. There is no genealogical hierarchy within the tribe; all are deemed equally Levitical priests and are eligible to serve at the altar and to receive sacrifices. The emphatic appositional phrase, *the whole tribe of Levi,* seems to rule out precisely the hierarchy presupposed by Num. ch 18. It should be stressed, however, that continuing scholarly debate about the dating of the Priestly source makes it very difficult to establish the relative dating and sequence of these two diverging approaches to the priesthood. **2:** They *shall have no portion:* Levi does not participate in the tribal land distribution at the time of the conquest (see Josh. 13.14; Ezek. 44.28). Without their own land allocation, the tribe has no independent means of agricultural support or income. As an alternative, *the LORD is their portion:* God grants them a share of the sacrificial offer-

3 This then shall be the priests' due from the people: Everyone who offers a sacrifice, whether an ox or a sheep, must give the shoulder, the cheeks, and the stomach to the priest. 4 You shall also give him the first fruits of your new grain and wine and oil, and the first shearing of your sheep. 5 For the LORD your God has chosen him and his descendants, out of all your tribes, to be in attendance for service in the name of the LORD for all time.

6 If a Levite would go, from any of the settlements throughout Israel where he has been residing, to the place that the LORD has chosen, he may do so whenever he pleases. 7 He may serve in the name of the LORD his God like all his fellow Levites who are there in attendance before the LORD. 8 They shall receive equal shares of the dues, a-without regard to personal gifts or patrimonies.-a

9 When you enter the land that the LORD your God is giving you, you shall not learn to imitate the abhorrent practices of those nations. 10 Let no one be found among you who consigns his son or daughter to the fire, or who is an augur, a soothsayer, a diviner, a sorcerer, 11 one who

a-a Meaning of Heb. uncertain.

ings brought to the sanctuary. This system in effect made the Levitical priests completely dependent upon other Israelites for their support. The system must have run into difficulty because the priest-prophet Ezekiel allocates land both to the priests and the Levites in his vision of the future restoration of Judah after the exile (Ezek. 48.10–14). **3:** These specific portions of the sacrificial offerings are reserved for the priests. The abuse of this privilege by the greedy sons of Eli led to divine punishment (1 Sam. 2.12–17, 22–36). **5:** *To be in attendance for service* refers technically to officiating at the altar. **6–8:** While rejecting any genealogical hierarchy within the tribe, the law anticipates a geographical one and seeks to prevent it. **6:** With Deuteronomy's prohibition of local altars (12.8–12; 13–15), the Levites serving at those altars would face sudden unemployment. With no independent landholding as a means of support, the local Levite would thus become completely destitute. Accordingly,

if a Levite would go, from any of the settlements to the central sanctuary in Jerusalem, seeking to serve there as a priest, he must be provided for. **7:** The concern is to guarantee the country Levite equal access to the altar. This admonition correctly anticipates that the Levites who had long been stationed at the Jerusalem Temple would hardly welcome such newcomers, fearing that their own income and power would be threatened. The emphasis that each displaced Levite *may serve in the name of the LORD his God* implies that the countryside altars prohibited by Deuteronomy were not entirely devoted to Canaanite cults, as 12.2–4 asserts. They clearly included sanctuaries officiated over by a priesthood loyal to the God of Israel. **8:** *Equal shares*, the choice meats, grains, and oil assigned the tribe in vv. 3–4. The Deuteronomistic historian, while narrating the accomplishments of Josiah's reform, concedes that the priests at the Temple failed to implement this requirement. The displaced countryside

Levites thus became second-class citizens, able to eat only "unleavened bread" (2 Kings 23.9).

18.9–22: The Mosaic prophet. This section divides into two main paragraphs. The first condemns various types of divination as illegitimate and associates them with the Canaanites (vv. 9–14). The second establishes a uniquely Israelite model of prophecy, patterned after Moses, which understands the prophet to mediate God's word to the people (vv. 15–22). **9–14:** Just as the legal corpus prohibits forms of sacrificial worship that it condemns as Canaanite (12.1–4, 29–31; also 7.1–6, 25–26; Exod. 23.24; 34.11–16), so here does it prohibit certain forms of divination, which are repeatedly branded as Canaanite, almost as a refrain (vv. 9, 12, 14). In each case, Deuteronomy consistently requires its own alternative: here, prophecy rather than divination; previously, centralization of worship rather than multiple altar sites (12.5–7). At the same time, the condemnation of the rejected practices as Canaanite warrants further consideration. Strikingly, when divination or necromancy are elsewhere mentioned and even challenged (in sources that do not depend upon this list), there is no accusation or hint that they are foreign or not efficacious. They seem completely Israelite (1 Sam. 28.3–25; Isa. 8.19–22; 29.4). The same applies to the rejected forms of sacrificial worship (see 12.14 n.; 16.21 n.). Indeed, in the seventh century, the generally accepted date of Deuteronomy's composition (see introduction), the Canaanites would no longer have been a live issue. Most likely the authors of the legal corpus represented prior norms as "Canaanite" in order to gain acceptance for their trenchant critique of Israelite popular religion. **10:** *Consigns . . . to the fire*: It is unclear if this refers to child sacrifice, and if so, why this law is included in this context. *Who is an augur, a soothsayer . . .* : The AB sequence of these two initial terms is reversed at the end of the list, in the B'A' of casts spells, or one who consults ghosts or familiar spirits, or one who inquires of the dead. ¹²For anyone who does such things is abhorrent to the LORD, and it is because of these abhorrent things that the LORD your God is dispossessing them before you. ¹³You must be wholehearted with the LORD your God. ¹⁴Those nations that you are about to dispossess do indeed resort to soothsayers and augurs; to you, however, the LORD your God has not assigned the like.

¹⁵The LORD your God will raise up for you a prophet from among your own people, like myself; him you shall heed. ¹⁶This is just what you asked of the LORD your God at Horeb, on the day of the Assembly, saying, "Let me not hear the voice of the LORD my God any longer or see this wondrous fire any more, lest I die." ¹⁷Whereupon the LORD said to me, "They have done well in speaking thus. ¹⁸I will raise up a prophet for them from among their own people, like yourself: I will put My words in his mouth and he will speak to them all that I command him; ¹⁹and if anybody fails to heed the words he speaks in My name, I Myself will call him to account. ²⁰But any prophet who presumes to speak in My name an oracle that I did not command him to utter, or who speaks in the name of other gods—that prophet shall die." ²¹And should you ask yourselves, "How can we know that the oracle was not spoken by the LORD?"—²²if the prophet speaks in the name of the LORD and the oracle does not come true, that oracle was not spoken by the LORD; the prophet has uttered it presumptuously: do not stand in dread of him.

"soothsayers and augurs" (v. 14), thereby providing the long list of vv. 10–14 with a frame. The list provides the most comprehensive compilation of such activities in the Bible (Exod. 22.17; Lev. 19.30–31; 20.6, 27; Isa. 8.19). It is no longer possible precisely to identify each of the prohibited forms of divination. Indeed, because the list is so comprehensive, it is unclear whether each term represented a distinct activity still known to the author or whether the list represents more of a scholastic compilation. *Sorcerer* reflects the standard Akkadian term for magic ("kishpu"). **11:** *Who consults ghosts or familiar spirits . . . dead:* necromancy, or conjuring the dead (1 Sam. 28.7–15; Isa. 29.4). Popular religion in antiquity devoted ex-

tensive attention to communicating with the dead, especially with ancestors, as do many contemporary religions. **12:** *Abhorrent:* This condemnation of necromancy as obnoxious to God is remarkable for what is not said. There is no claim that it is ineffective. The Deuteronomistic historian narrates the ability of the witch of Endor to raise Samuel's ghost on demand (1 Sam. 28.7–25). **15–22:** Deuteronomy transforms prophecy, viewing the prophet as the spokesperson of Torah (see 13.2–6 n.) and defining Moses as the paradigmatic prophet. **15:** *The LORD . . . will raise up:* The continuity of prophecy is assured by means of divine election. Other offices achieve their continuity by means of professional training and

appointment (as with the judges of 16.18–20; 17.2–13), or dynastically (the king of 17.14–20), or by tribal membership (the Levitical priesthood of vv. 1–8). That God alone appoints the prophet makes the prophet independent of all institutions and able to challenge them. *A prophet*, while grammatically singular, is distributive in its meaning: "I will repeatedly raise up for you a prophet." More than one prophet is clearly intended. A much later Jewish reinterpretation that was accepted by the Christian church (John 1.21, 45; 6.14; 7.40; Acts 3.22; 7.37) understands the verse to promise a single, messianic prophet at the end of time. *Like myself:* At Horeb (5.20–30), Moses established the distinctively Israelite model of prophecy as mediating God's word to the people. This model contrasts with the prophet as diviner (vv. 9–14), where the prophet does not represent the God of Israel and where the supernatural communication about the future bears no relation to covenantal law. Thus the prophet, like the king (17.15), should be *from among your own people.* **16–17:** See 5.20–28; Exod. 20.16–18. **18:** The prophet's oracles do not originate from other deities, from dead spirits, from skilled manipulation of objects, or from the prophet's own reflections. God instead affirms, *I will put My words in his mouth.* The prophet reiterates the word of Israel's God. That metaphorical promise is reused in the call narrative of Jeremiah (Jer. 1.9) and then dramatically enacted in Ezekiel's call, where the metaphor is taken literally (Ezek. 2.9–3.3). **20:** Having established an Israelite model of prophecy, the law provides two criteria to distinguish true from false prophecy. The first is that the prophet should speak exclusively on behalf of God, and report only God's words. Breach of that rule is a capital offense (Jer. 28.12–17). **21–23:** The second criterion makes the fulfillment of a prophet's oracle the measure of its truth. That approach attempts to solve a critical problem: If two prophets each

19 When the LORD your God has cut down the nations whose land the LORD your God is assigning to you, and you have dispossessed them and settled in their towns and homes, ² you shall set aside three cities in the land that the LORD your God is giving you to possess. ³ You shall survey the distances, and divide into three parts the territory of the country that the LORD your God has allotted to you, so that any manslayer may have a place to flee to.—⁴ Now this is the case of the manslayer who may flee there and live: one who has killed another

claim to speak on behalf of God yet make mutually exclusive claims—(1 Kings 22.6 versus v. 17; Jer. 27.8 versus 28.2)—how may one decide which prophet speaks the truth? The solution offered is not free of difficulty. If a false prophet is distinguished by the failure of his oracle to come true, then making a decision in the present about which prophet to obey becomes impossible. Nor can this criterion easily be reconciled with 13.3, which concedes that the oracles of false prophets might come true. Finally, the prophets frequently threatened judgment, hoping to bring about repentance (Jer. ch 7; 26.1–6). If the prophet succeeds, and the people repent and thereby avert doom (Jonah chs 3–4), one would assume the prophet to be authentic, since he has accomplished God's goal of repentance. Yet according to the criteria here (but contrast Jer. 28.9), the prophet who accomplished repentance is nonetheless a false prophet, since the judgment oracle that was proclaimed remains unfulfilled. These texts, with their questions and differences of opinion on such issues, reflect the vigorous debate that took place in Israel about prophecy.

19.1–13: Cities of refuge. Under the old system of clan justice, the kin of a homicide victim assumed the burden of killing the slayer to avenge the death. Deuteronomy limits but cannot eradicate that older system. In cases of murder, the capital punishment is not carried out by the state but by the kinsman ("the blood-avenger,"

v. 12; Num. 35.19, 21). Similarly, while the law can insist that unintentional homicide is not a capital crime, it cannot simply declare the person innocent. It must also provide a city to serve as sanctuary where the avenging kinsman may not enter. The law concedes that it can provide no protection should the avenger overtake the unintentional slayer before he reaches sanctuary (v. 6; cf. Num. 35.26–28).

The literary model for the law may be found in the Book of the Covenant, which stipulated that criminal homicide was a capital crime but exempted unintentional homicide: "He who fatally strikes a man shall be put to death. If he did not do it by design, but it came about by an act of God, I will assign you a place to which he can flee" (Exod. 21.12–13). But should that person have committed murder rather than manslaughter, "you shall take him from My very altar to be put to death" (Exod. 21.14). The coordination of these two laws establishes that the "place" of refuge refers specifically to the "altar" of the sanctuary (so also 1 Kings 1.49–53; 2.28–35). The same Hebrew word ("place" or "site") also designates the altar in 12.5, 11, 13, 18, 21, 26; Exod. 20.21.

Once centralization declared those local altars illegitimate, Deuteronomy had to update the law of sanctuary. Simply shifting the location of sanctuary from the local to the central sanctuary was clearly not feasible, since the distance for the trip would jeopardize the person needing protection (v. 6). Instead, Deuteronomy retains the

local setting of the law but secularizes the site of refuge. No longer the altar but three neutral "cities" are designated to fill the void, with provision made for an additional three when necessary (vv. 8–9). Even the language of the older law is updated. According to the older law, the accidental homicide takes place when "the god deflected his [the slayer's] hand" (Exod. 21.13, lit.). But that attribution of the accident to the agency of a generic god, following an archaic formula inherited from Near Eastern law, is no longer acceptable even as a cliché of speech. The scrupulous authors of Deuteronomy eliminate the superstitious element and redefine the accident neutrally: "the ax head flies off the handle" (v. 5).

The later Deuteronomistic introduction to the book (4.44) provides a concise summary of the law but understands the six cities to refer to three in Transjordan and three in Israel (4.41–44), rather than as all within the land, three in the present and three in the future (vv. 2, 8–9). The Priestly source correctly recognizes the original cultic basis of the law, which had been rooted in the local altars. It accepts Deuteronomy's designation of the city as the new sanctuary site but defines those cities as belonging to the Levites (Num. 35.6). It extends the law to non-Israelites and follows 4.41–44 in concluding that three of the six cities are located in Transjordan (Num. 35.13–15). Josh. 20.7–8 reconciles these different reflections of the law of asylum while narrating its enactment at the time of the settlement, following the enumeration of 4.41–44 while conforming to Num. 35.9–34 in selecting cities assigned to the Levites.

19.1: For the formulaic introduction, see 12.29. **4:** *Who may flee there,* more literally, "where he might flee (there)," an exact citation of the older law that requires revision (Exod. 21.13b; translated "to which he can flee" in NJPS). Whereas the law in Exodus refers specifically to the altar at the local sanctuary as the site of refuge, Deuteronomy redefines the word unwittingly, without having been his enemy in the past. [5] For instance, a man goes with his neighbor into a grove to cut wood; as his hand swings the ax to cut down a tree, the ax-head flies off the handle and strikes the other so that he dies. That man shall flee to one of these cities and live.—[6] Otherwise, when the distance is great, the blood-avenger, pursuing the manslayer in hot anger, may overtake him and kill him; yet he did not incur the death penalty, since he had never been the other's enemy. [7] That is why I command you: set aside three cities.

[8] And when the LORD your God enlarges your territory, as He swore to your fathers, and gives you all the land that He promised to give your fathers—[9] if you faithfully observe all this Instruction that I enjoin upon you this day, to love the LORD your God and to walk in His ways at all times—then you shall add three more towns to those three. [10] Thus blood of the innocent will not be shed, bringing bloodguilt upon you in the land that the LORD your God is allotting to you.

[11] If, however, a person who is the enemy of another lies in wait for him and sets upon him and strikes him a fatal blow and then flees to one of these towns, [12] the elders of his town shall have him brought back from there and shall hand him over to the blood-avenger to be put to death; [13] you must show him no pity. Thus you will purge Israel of the blood of the innocent,[a] and it will go well with you.

[14] You shall not move your countryman's landmarks, set up by previous generations, in the property that will be allotted to you in the land that the LORD your God is giving you to possess.

[15] A single witness may not validate against a person any guilt or blame for any offense that may be committed; a case can be valid only on the testimony of two witnesses or more.[b] [16] If a man appears against another to testify ma-

---

a Cf. Num. 35.33–34.   b See note at 17.6.

---

so that, in the new context, it now refers to one of the three "cities" of vv. 2–3. (The same cited phrase also occurs in the Hebrew of v. 3.) **5:** *Shall flee to one of these cities:* The same key phrase is now explicitly amended to include the city reference. **6:** *When the distance is great:* The formula marks Deuteronomy's updating of older law; see 14.24. *In hot anger,* lit. "for his heart is incensed." If the kinsman kills the slayer while in hot pursuit, the law is powerless. **8:** *En-*

larges your territory: This formula provides a means for updating older law to address present realities (see 12.20; Exod. 34.24). It does so by casting the provision for change as intended from the beginning, rather than something that takes place after the fact. **10:** *Blood of the innocent,* a bold conception of innocence. The law insists that wrongfully killing someone who has unintentionally committed homicide—yet who is innocent of murder—would itself constitute

murder! *Bloodguilt:* Spilling innocent blood defiles the land (see Num. 35.33–34; Deut. 21.1–9). **12:** *Brought back from there,* secularizing the original law of Exod. 21.14, "You shall take him from My very altar." *Hand him over to the blood-avenger to be put to death.* The law here regulates but does not replace the clan-based system of justice, surrendering the murderer to the kinsman to serve as executioner.

19.14: Boundary marker. The sacrosanct status of a *landmark* (lit. "boundary marker") was a legal tradition in the ancient Near East (see 27.17; Isa. 5.8; Hos. 5.10; Job 24.2; Prov. 22.28). The verse also marks a topical boundary within the legal corpus and provides a transition marker. In the next law, the legislator will conclude the section devoted to the impact of centralization upon justice.

19.15–21: The integrity of the judicial system. This section, whose theme is the public order (16.18–19.21), began with a law that required probity on the part of the newly established judges (16.18–20). The section therefore appropriately concludes with a law that demands corresponding integrity from witnesses. The two laws thus frame the unit with an inclusio that emphasizes the honesty required of all participants in the judicial system. The same emphasis, symbolizing the legal collection's commitment to justice, is also evident in Near Eastern law (Laws of Hammurabi §§1–5). **15:** *Validate against a person any guilt or blame for any offense:* Heb is even more insistent on the universal application of this law, repeating the "any" before each of the three nouns. *A case can be valid . . . two witnesses or more,* broadening the specific focus of 17.6 on capital crimes: "A person shall be put to death only on the testimony of two or more witnesses." That principle is here made a universal requirement for justice. It prohibits hearsay or spurious accusation (one person's word against another's) from having any legal liciously and gives false testimony against him, [17] the two parties to the dispute shall appear before the LORD, before the priests or magistrates in authority at the time, [18] and the magistrates shall make a thorough investigation. If the man who testified is a false witness, if he has testified falsely against his fellow, [19] you shall do to him as he schemed to do to his fellow. Thus you will sweep out evil from your midst; [20] others will hear and be afraid, and such evil things will not again be done in your midst. [21] Nor must you show pity: life for life, eye for eye, tooth for tooth, hand for hand, foot for foot.

20 When you take the field against your enemies, and see horses and chariots—forces larger than yours— have no fear of them, for the LORD your God, who brought you from the land of Egypt, is with you. [2] Before you join battle, the priest shall come forward and address the troops. [3] He shall say to them, "Hear, O Israel! You are about to join battle with your enemy. Let not your courage falter. Do not be in fear, or in panic, or in dread of them. [4] For it is the LORD your God who marches with you to do battle for you against your enemy, to bring you victory." [5] Then the officials shall address the troops, as follows:

force whatsoever. **17:** *Before the LORD,* testimony before the altar at the central sanctuary (12.7; 14.23; 17.8–13). **19:** *You shall do to him* [the false witness] *as he schemed to do to his fellow:* This reciprocal formulation of justice is called "talion," the technical term for "measure for measure" or "an eye for an eye." That principle is elsewhere employed in the context of bodily injury or homicide (Exod. 21.23–25; Lev. 24.17–21). It distinguishes crimes against the person (which require talion) from property crimes (where alone financial compensation is permitted). By applying the principle of talion to the category of crimes against the judicial system, the legislators here seek to ensure the integrity of the law by using the highest sanction available to them (see also Laws of Hammurabi §§1–5).

20.1–20: Rules for waging holy war. In contrast to the other biblical legal collections, which include only brief sections concerning military engagement (Exod. 23.23–33;

34.11–16; Num. 34.50–56), Deuteronomy, reflecting a literary setting of Israel about to enter the land, concerns itself extensively with the laws of holy war. Underlying this theology of holy war is the idea that Israel's God joins the fray as a divine warrior and directly confronts the adversary on behalf of the nation. God's presence in the military camp imposes additional purity requirements upon the people (23.11–15). Although wars of conquest would normally be waged for the sake of empire building and profit, Israel's holy war is fought for religious reasons: to extirpate iniquity and to create a covenantal community organized by divine law (Lev. 18.24–29; 20.22–24). Accordingly, the usual seizing of plunder—property, animals, and humans—is prohibited (7.25b; 13.15–17). Throughout the Near East, the kinds of spoils taken in war would include men, for their labor, and women, for labor and child-rearing (v. 11). For that reason, the rules for holy war must stipulate that no prisoners be

taken (vv. 16–18; 7.1–5). All the normal spoils of war had to be devoted exclusively to God, like the sacrificial "holocaust" offering (13.17) from which neither priest nor lay Israelite could take any portion (see 12.23–27 n.). Contemporary inscriptions like the Moabite or Mesha Stone (ca. 850 BCE) establish that similar theologies of holy war were shared by a number of nations. In the case of Deuteronomy, it is important to recognize that the conception of the conquest as a holy war represents, paradoxically, a highly schematized idealization, formulated half a millennium after the settlement, at a time when ethnic Canaanites would already long have assimilated into the Israelite population. (See 18.9–14 n.) **1:** *When you take the field against your enemies:* This introductory formula enables the editor to group a series of various laws loosely together (21.10–14; cf. 23.9–14; 24.5). *Horses and chariots:* The adversary is superior both in numbers and in military equipment (see Exod. 14.9; 15.4; Josh. 11.4). *Forces* (lit. "people"): Deuteronomy imagines both Israel and the adversary less as a professionally organized army than as an entire nation arrayed for a common purpose. This conception, also reflected in the conquest account in Joshua, is an idealization about the past that is inconsistent with earlier accounts, which represent the settlement as a series of initiatives by individual tribes who achieved very restricted penetration into the land, and who did not act in concert as a unified nation (Judg. 1.18–20, 27–36). The ideal national perspective outlined by Deuteronomy lies behind the account in Joshua. *Have no fear of them, for the LORD your God . . . is with you:* The narrator, in this introductory formula, summarizes the priest's oracle of military reassurance in vv. 3–4. **3–4:** See 9.1–3; 31.3–6; cf. Exod. 14.14, 25; 15.1–4. **5–9:** A reverse muster, designed to thin the ranks. The primary intent is to remove conscripts who may have competing priorities because they are in a transitional state: about to

"Is there anyone who has built a new house but has not dedicated it? Let him go back to his home, lest he die in battle and another dedicate it. ⁶ Is there anyone who has planted a vineyard but has never harvested it? Let him go back to his home, lest he die in battle and another harvest it. ⁷ Is there anyone who has paid the bride-price for a wife,ᵃ but who has not yet married her? Let him go back to his home, lest he die in battle and another marry her." ⁸ The officials shall go on addressing the troops and say, "Is there anyone afraid and disheartened? Let him go back to his home, lest the courage of his comrades flag like his." ⁹ When the officials have finished addressing the troops, army commanders shall assume command of the troops.

¹⁰ When you approach a town to attack it, you shall ᵇ offer it terms of peace.ᵇ ¹¹ If it responds peaceably and lets you in, all the people present there shall serve you at forced labor. ¹² If it does not surrender to you, but would join battle with you, you shall lay siege to it; ¹³ and when the LORD your God delivers it into your hand, you shall put all its males to the sword. ¹⁴ You may, however, take as your booty the women, the children, the livestock, and everything in the town—all its spoil—and enjoy the use of the spoil of your enemy, which the LORD your God gives you.

¹⁵ Thus you shall deal with all towns that lie very far

---

a Thereby making her his wife legally, even though the marriage has not yet taken place.
b-b Or "call on it to surrender."

---

officially begin living in a house that is awaiting occupation; about to make a first harvest; about to complete an engagement with marriage and consummation (vv. 5–7). The importance of "taking possession of" house, vineyard, and wife is evident in their inclusion also in the curses for disobedience (28.30), where they signify dispossession by the enemy. The sequence of the three together symbolizes the home as an entirety. **5:** *Dedicated* (or "inaugurated"): Although Solomon's dedication of the Temple is narrated (1 Kings ch 8), there are no specific rituals of home dedication recorded in the Bible. The parallel curse employs "live" (28.30). **6:** *Harvested it,* lit. "profaned it"; Priestly law stipulated that newly planted fruit trees were only avail-

able for common use in the fifth year (Lev. 19.23–25). **7:** *Paid the bride-price . . . married:* Marriage was a two-step process; see NJPS translators' note *a*; 22.23–27 n. *Wife:* For the order in which "wife" follows "house," see Exod. 20.14. The wife comes first at 5.18; 28.30. **8:** *Comrade:* The Hebrew employs "brother," to which Deuteronomy frequently, and distinctively, gives the meaning "fellow citizen." The same word is elsewhere translated "a fellow Hebrew" (15.12). **11:** The use of a defeated people for *forced labor* was widespread. The earliest narratives within the Deuteronomistic History establish that the Israelites employed the indigenous population of Canaan as such a resource (Judg. 1.27–36). So important was it to the monarchy that David's cabinet included an offi-

cial responsible for "forced labor" (2 Sam. 20.24). **15–18:** *Thus you shall deal with all towns that lie very far from you:* The law now retroactively restricts the preceding rules of engagement (vv. 10–14), which tolerate the taking of captives as "forced labor," so that they apply only to foreign wars. That restriction comes unexpectedly and contradicts the unconditional formulation of v. 10, which imposed no geographical restriction. Moreover, the stipulation that the indigenous population of Canaan should uniformly be exterminated is inconsistent both with the earliest narratives of the settlement and with the administrative list of the monarchy (see v. 11 n.). Most likely, therefore, the law sanctioning the negotiation of peace treaties and the taking of captives (vv. 10–14) originally applied to warfare within Canaan. It preserves the earliest rules of engagement and more closely reflects the actual course of events. The geographical restriction imposed upon the law—nowhere within the law itself but only from the perspective of vv. 15–16—allows the editor to preserve the venerated older law by giving it a new application. The formulaic prohibition against taking prisoners (see 7.1–6; 12.29–31) thus represents a later addition reflecting the 7th century theology of Deuteronomy. The rationale for the literary fiction may be an ex post facto ideal of religious purity at the very historical moment that Judah was in fact a vassal state paying tribute to Assyria (2 Kings 18.7–19.35). **15:** The *nations hereabout* refers to the Canaanites. With that turn of language, the narrator places himself in the land of Canaan (as at 1.1). According to the narrative, however, the nation has not yet entered the land and Moses died before entering Canaan (34.5). Similar anachronisms (2.12b; 3.11; 34.5; Gen. 12.6b) led a few medieval Jewish biblical commentators, like Abraham Ibn Ezra (1089–1164 CE), to recognize that both Deuteronomy and the Torah include substantial post-Mosaic material.

from you, towns that do not belong to nations hereabout. 16 In the towns of the latter peoples, however, which the LORD your God is giving you as a heritage, you shall not let a soul remain alive. 17 No, you must proscribe[a] them— the Hittites and the Amorites, the Canaanites and the Perizzites, the Hivites and the Jebusites—as the LORD your God has commanded you, 18 lest they lead you into doing all the abhorrent things that they have done for their gods and you stand guilty before the LORD your God.

19 When in your war against a city you have to besiege it a long time in order to capture it, you must not destroy its trees, wielding the ax against them. You may eat of them, but you must not cut them down. Are trees of the field human to withdraw before you into the besieged city? 20 Only trees that you know do not yield food may be destroyed; you may cut them down for constructing siege-works against the city that is waging war on you, until it has been reduced.

21 If, in the land that the LORD your God is assigning you to possess, someone slain is found lying in the open, the identity of the slayer not being known, 2 your elders and magistrates shall go out and measure the distances from the corpse to the nearby towns. 3 The elders of the town nearest to the corpse shall then take a heifer which has never been worked, which has never pulled in a yoke; 4 and the elders of that town shall bring the heifer down to an everflowing wadi, which is not tilled or sown. There, in the wadi, they shall break the heifer's neck. 5 The priests, sons of Levi, shall come forward; for the LORD your God has chosen them to minister to Him and to pronounce blessing in the name of the LORD, and every lawsuit and case of assault[b] is subject to their ruling. 6 Then all the elders of the town nearest to the corpse shall wash their hands over the heifer whose neck was broken in the

a See Lev. 27.29.
b Cf. 17.8. Or "skin affection"; cf. 24.8.

There are similar cases involving corpses found between two cities in older Near Eastern law (Laws of Hammurabi §§23–24; Hittite Laws §6), where the primary focus is to clarify whether financial liability exists. Here, in contrast, the sole concern is to atone for the spilled blood of the victim. The law shows evidence of several stages of literary reworking, making it difficult to recover the exact meaning of its rituals. 1: In the open, a technical term, meaning beyond the legal jurisdiction of any particular town (see 22.23, 25). The reference implies the absence of witnesses to identify the culprit. 2: For the judicial role of the elders in cases of homicide, see 19.12; 21.18–21; for the magistrates, see 16.18 n. Measure the distances in order to establish legal jurisdiction, as in the Hittite Laws §6. 3: Never been worked . . . never pulled in a yoke: The heifer's immaturity and physically intact state symbolize the human victim's innocence (similarly, Num. 19.2). 4: Everflowing wadi, lit. "with reliable water" (Amos 5.24), in contrast to unreliable seasonal streams (Jer. 15.18). Break the heifer's neck, nonsacrificial slaughter; sacrifice requires ritual slitting of the throat (see Exod. 13.13; 34.20). 5: The priests, sons of Levi were not mentioned among the officials of v. 2 and play no subsequent role in the law. Their inclusion therefore seems like a later addition, perhaps prompted by the prayer. Every lawsuit and case of assault contrasts with 17.9, where the Levitical priests, officiating at the central sanctuary, had jurisdiction only in cases that could not be resolved locally. The NJPS translation is correct as it stands. The alternative translation mentioned in translators' note b is valid only when the word here properly translated "assault" is combined with another word specifying "skin" (as at 24.8). 6: Wash their hands over the heifer, with no laying on of hands, thus entailing no ritual transfer of culpability from the elders to the animal (contrast Lev. 16.21–22). Instead, the ritual seems symbolically to contrast this

16: In the towns of the latter peoples refers to the Canaanites. 17: You must proscribe them: The Hebrew phrase is elsewhere translated as "doom . . . to destruction" (7.2; 13.16; see also translators' note a). 19–20: Wars often involved the kind of "scorched earth policy" prohibited here (2 Kings 3.19, 25). 20: Siegeworks were regularly built against walled cities (1 Sam. 20.15; 2 Kings 25.1). Remnants of Roman siegeworks (70–74 CE) remain visible at Masada.

21.1–9: Atonement for an unsolved murder. Since a murder victim's blood tainted the land (Gen. 4.10; Num. 35.33–34), it was imperative to "purge Israel of the blood of the innocent" (19.13). This law therefore addresses the difficulty of how to do so when the perpetrator cannot be identified.

wadi. [7] And they shall make this declaration: "Our hands did not shed this blood, nor did our eyes see it done. [8] Absolve, O LORD, Your people Israel whom You redeemed, and do not let guilt for the blood of the innocent remain among Your people Israel." And they will be absolved of bloodguilt. [9] Thus you will remove from your midst guilt for the blood of the innocent, for you will be doing what is right in the sight of the LORD.

KI TETSE'   כי תצא

[10] When you take the field against your enemies, and the LORD your God delivers them into your power and you take some of them captive, [11] and you see among the captives a beautiful woman and you desire her and would take her to wife, [12] you shall bring her into your house, and she shall trim her hair, pare her nails, [13] and discard her captive's garb. She shall spend a month's time in your house lamenting her father and mother; after that you may come to her and possess her, and she shall be your wife. [14] Then, should you no longer want her, you must release her outright. You must not sell her for money: since you had your will of her, you must not enslave her.

[15] If a man has two wives, one loved and the other unloved, and both the loved and the unloved have borne him sons, but the first-born is the son of the unloved one—[16] when he wills his property to his sons, he may not treat as first-born the son of the loved one in disregard of the son of the unloved one who is older. [17] Instead, he must accept the first-born, the son of the unloved one, and allot to him a double portion[a] of all he possesses; since he is the first fruit of his vigor, the birthright is his due.

a Lit. two-thirds.

---

slaughter with that of the human victim. **7:** *Our hands . . . nor did our eyes see it done:* The formula extends the notion of responsibility from direct (*our hands*) to indirect: mere failure to avert or report a witnessed crime (cf. Lev. 5.1). **8:** *Absolve, O LORD:* The extended ritual of vv. 3–6 has no intrinsic efficacy; prayer is the means of absolution. *Your people Israel:* The verse's double reference to the nation drives home that the frame of reference is no longer the "elders of the town nearest to the corpse" (v. 6) but the people's collective responsibility (19.10, 13). The prayer

has a chiastic structure: "Absolve . . . your people Israel . . . your people Israel . . . will be absolved" (AB:B'A'). *And they will be absolved,* better, "so that they may be absolved." The verse's literary symmetry and grammar together establish that absolution ultimately depends upon divine action, not human ritual.

21.10–25.19: Miscellaneous criminal, civil, and family laws. The following laws are concerned with individual family, civil, and ethical issues; in comparison, the preceding section was more broadly con-

cerned with the system of worship, the judicial procedures, and the public administration of the nation as a whole. Laws extending legal protection to women in contexts where they would otherwise be disenfranchised concern female captives (21.10–14), the property rights of the less-favored wife (21.15–17), and false charges of infidelity (22.13–19).

21.10–14: Legal obligations toward female captives. In light of 20.10–18, the law would apply only to female captives taken in wars outside of the land; most likely, however, it also applied to the Canaanite population (20.15–18 n.). Female war captives routinely became concubines of their captors. This law regulates that convention and accords such women dignity and protection against enslavement. **12–13:** The rituals provide both captive and captor means to effect a transition from one status to another. **13:** *A month's time,* the full mourning period, as for Aaron and Moses (Num. 20.29; Deut. 34.8). *Lamenting:* Contextually it is unclear whether the captive's parents actually died in the war or are mourned as lost to her because of her captivity. The prescribed time to grieve implies legal respect for the female captive as a person. **13:** *Come to her* sexually; consummation provides the legal means for her to become *your wife.* **14:** Manumission to protect female concubines from being sold as slaves is also prescribed at Exod. 21.7–8. *Had your will of her,* more specifically, "violated her" sexually (22.24, 29; Gen. 34.2; Judg. 19.24; 2 Sam. 13.12).

21.15–17: Legal protection of the less-favored wife. The law uses the norm of primogeniture (Gen. 25.29–34; Laws of Hammurabi §§165–70) to protect the son of the less-favored wife from disinheritance. **17:** *Double portion,* two-thirds (see Zech. 13.8), leaving one third for the other son. *The birthright,* the technical legal term for the preferential share of the inheri-

18 If a man has a wayward and defiant son, who does not heed his father or mother and does not obey them even after they discipline him, 19 his father and mother shall take hold of him and bring him out to the elders of his town at the public place of his community. 20 They shall say to the elders of his town, "This son of ours is disloyal and defiant; he does not heed us. He is a glutton and a drunkard." 21 Thereupon the men of his town shall stone him to death. Thus you will sweep out evil from your midst: all Israel will hear and be afraid.

22 If a man is guilty of a capital offense and is put to death, and you impale him on a stake, 23 you must not let his corpse remain on the stake overnight, but must bury him the same day. For an impaled body is an affront to God: you shall not defile the land that the LORD your God is giving you to possess.

22 If you see your fellow's ox or sheep gone astray, do not ignore it; you must take it back to your fellow. 2 If your fellow does not live near you or you do not know who he is, you shall bring it home and it shall remain with you until your fellow claims it; then you shall give it back to him. 3 You shall do the same with his ass; you shall do the same with his garment; and so too shall you do with anything that your fellow loses and you find: you must not remain indifferent.

4 If you see your fellow's ass or ox fallen on the road, do not ignore it; you must help him raise it.

5 A woman must not put on man's apparel, nor shall a man wear woman's clothing; for whoever does these things is abhorrent to the LORD your God.

tance. Ironically, the foundation narratives concerning Isaac, Jacob, and Joseph subvert the legal norm here affirmed (Gen. 17.15–22; 21.8–14; 27.1–40; 48.8–22).

21.18–21: The rebellious son. The Decalogue requirement to honor the parents (5.16; Exod. 20.12) carries no explicit sanction; here flagrant and sustained disobedience is a capital offense. Nevertheless, the Rabbis (*m. Sanh. 8*) attenuated the force of this law by making the son's violation much more stringent than the text suggests, essentially eliminating cases in which the penalty would apply. The law becomes, then, an ideal law teaching respect for parents. Other Near

Eastern law collections included similar laws but did not require capital punishment (Law of Hammurabi §195). This law concerning sons should be read in tandem with the law concerning daughters in 22.13–21. **18:** *Not heed his father or mother:* The Heb more emphatically ascribes equal authority to each parent: "obey either his father or his mother." *Discipline:* The term extends to physical measures such as flogging (1 Kings 12.11). **19:** *The elders* functioned as judges of family law and held court at the city gate, which served as a public forum (22.15; 25.7; Job. 29.7; Ruth 4.1–2, 11; Lam. 5.14). This system contrasts with the professionalized judiciary established at the same

site (16.18), which may specifically have had jurisdiction over religious and criminal law (17.2–7). **21:** In contrast to 13.14 and 17.4, no investigation is required; only parental testimony. *Stone him,* see 13.10 n.

21.22–23: Treatment of the executed. Public exposure of the corpse of an executed criminal, which was not the norm, was a form of reproach directed against enemies of the state (Josh. 8.29; 10.26; 1 Sam. 31.10; Esth. 9.6–14). Out of respect for the body, to prevent it from serving as carrion (2 Sam. 21.10), this law sets stringent limits to that procedure. The law applies to Israelites and non-Israelites alike (Josh. 8.29; 10.27). **22:** *Impale him on a stake:* The Hebrew phrase may also mean death caused by hanging from a tree or gallows, or suspending someone who has already been executed from a pole or gallows (Josh. 10.26; Esth. 9.11–14).

22.1–12: Various moral and religious responsibilities of citizenship. The rationale for the sequence and selection of these laws is often unclear.

22.1–4: Moral duties toward the neighbor. Two laws (vv. 1–3, 4) that develop, in sequence, two corresponding laws from the earlier Covenant Collection. **1–3:** The earlier law governing the return of wandering animals (Exod. 21.1–3) is here revised and extended in its application. **1:** *Your fellow's ox,* in contrast to "your enemy's ox" (Exod. 23.4). **3:** *Anything:* The earlier law has now been universalized to apply to any lost property, even that which cannot independently have "gone astray" (v. 1). *You must not remain indifferent:* The law makes a moral appeal to conscience but possesses no legal sanction. **4:** Reworking Exod. 23.5 to emphasize the neighbor, as in v. 1.

22.5–12: Miscellaneous laws. 5: The prohibition against crossdressing likely seeks to maintain

⁶ If, along the road, you chance upon a bird's nest, in any tree or on the ground, with fledglings or eggs and the mother sitting over the fledglings or on the eggs, do not take the mother together with her young. ⁷ Let the mother go, and take only the young, in order that you may fare well and have a long life.

⁸ When you build a new house, you shall make a parapet for your roof, so that you do not bring bloodguilt on your house if anyone should fall from it.

⁹ You shall not sow your vineyard with a second kind of seed, else the crop—from the seed you have sown—and the yield of the vineyard may not be used. ¹⁰ You shall not plow with an ox and an ass together. ¹¹ You shall not wear cloth combining wool and linen.

¹² You shall make tassels on the four corners of the garment with which you cover yourself.

¹³ A man marries a woman and cohabits with her. Then he takes an aversion to her ¹⁴ and makes up charges against her and defames her, saying, "I married this woman; but when I approached her, I found that she was not a virgin." ¹⁵ In such a case, the girl's father and mother shall produce the evidence of the girl's virginity before the elders of the town at the gate. ¹⁶ And the girl's father shall

during certain prayers. *Yourself:* Here, the requirement is not explicitly restricted to males. One side of a rabbinic debate on the issue argued that women, too, are to wear tassels, although the majority view exempted women from this requirement (see *Sifre Numbers* §115; b. *Menaḥ.* 43a).

22.13–23.1: Violations of marriage law. In the ancient Near East, marriage was a contractual relationship. A woman, regarded in terms of her relation to her father or her husband, could not act independently. There was little conception of the woman as a free agent, either in legal or sexual terms. She remained in the household of her father until a suitor paid a bride-price (v. 28–29; Exod. 22.15–16) to compensate the father for the reduction of the household. At that point she became formally engaged in the sense of legally contracted for, although still living "under her father's authority" (v. 21; lit. "in her father's house"). Later, at the marriage feast, the union was consummated (Gen. 29.22–25) and the woman took up residence in the household of her husband. The following laws presuppose these contractual norms and terminology. **13–21: False accusation of breach of marital contract. 13:** *Cohabits with her* to consummate the marriage sexually (as 21.13). *Takes an aversion to her,* cf. 21.15. **14:** *Makes up charges against her:* His reason for using this option to end the relation may well be mercenary. Displeasure with a wife provided grounds for divorce (24.1), but divorce would almost certainly have required the man to provide financial support, as presupposed by the requirement for a "bill of divorce" (24.3; Isa. 50.1; Jer. 3.8; cf. Exod. 21.10) and stipulated by Near Eastern law (Laws of Hammurabi §§137–40). In contrast, the slander, *I found that she was not a virgin,* would entail the refund of the bride-price and payment of a penalty for breach of contract. **15:** The *evidence* sought is the blood-stained cloth of v. 17. For a different approach to a charge of

gender boundaries; a similar concern for boundaries is evident in vv. 10–12. In none of these cases is it possible to recover the original social or religious context and rationale for these laws. **6–7:** The respect for the life of other creatures here parallels that shown for the integrity of the natural environment even in the context of war (20.19–20). Desire to avoid the simultaneous consumption of two generations of the same creature is also evident in other laws (14.21; Exod. 23.19; 34.26; Lev. 22.28). **7:** To elicit compliance, the legislator makes an appeal to enlightened self-interest; as in v. 3, there is no legal sanction for noncompliance. **8:** The *roof* was used as living space (Josh. 2.6; Judg. 3.20–25; 2 Sam. 11.2). *Bloodguilt* defines the negligence in criminal rather than civil terms, with the implication that the offense is capital (see 19.10 n.). For other examples of criminal negligence, see Exod. 21.29 and, also involving liability for faulty construction, Laws

of Hammurabi §229. **9–10:** Corresponding to Lev. 19.19, these laws attempt to maintain specific boundaries between categories seen as incompatible (as in v. 5; 14.3–20). The rationale for the specific examples selected, however, is hard to establish. **9:** *May not be used,* lit. becomes "set apart" or "holy"; that is, not permitted for human consumption. **12:** *Tassels:* No reason is given for this requirement, although the law receives a theological rationale at Num. 15.37–40. Since Neo-Assyrian palace reliefs distinguish royalty by their fringed garments, it may symbolize the application of a royal dress code to the nation as a whole. The command's original intention was that the tassels were to be worn in full view. Only during the persecution of the Middle Ages did the practice develop of wearing tassels (the "tallit katan") underneath the clothing. Based on this law and its parallel in Numbers, rabbinic law requires that a tasseled shawl (tallit) be worn say to the elders, "I gave this man my daughter to wife, but he has taken an aversion to her; [17] so he has made up charges, saying, 'I did not find your daughter a virgin.' But here is the evidence of my daughter's virginity!" And they shall spread out the cloth before the elders of the town. [18] The elders of that town shall then take the man and flog him, [19] and they shall fine him a hundred [shekels of] silver and give it to the girl's father; for the man has defamed a virgin in Israel. Moreover, she shall remain his wife; he shall never have the right to divorce her.

[20] But if the charge proves true, the girl was found not to have been a virgin, [21] then the girl shall be brought out to the entrance of her father's house, and the men of her town shall stone her to death; for she did a shameful thing in Israel, committing fornication while under her father's authority. Thus you will sweep away evil from your midst.

[22] If a man is found lying with another man's wife, both of them—the man and the woman with whom he lay—shall die. Thus you will sweep away evil from Israel.

[23] In the case of a virgin who is ᵃengaged to a manᵃ—if a man comes upon her in town and lies with her, [24] you shall take the two of them out to the gate of that town and stone them to death: the girl because she did not cry for help in the town, and the man because he violated another man's wife. Thus you will sweep away evil from your midst. [25] But if the man comes upon the engaged girl in the open country, and the man lies with her by force, only the man who lay with her shall die, [26] but you shall do

a-a I.e., for whom a bride-price has been paid; see 20.7.

infidelity, see Num. 5.11–31. *Elders of the town at the gate*, see 16.18 n.; 21.19 n. **17:** *The cloth* upon which husband and wife slept upon consummation of the relationship. There is scant medical support for the underlying assumptions: that intercourse would cause the first perforation of the hymen and that such perforation would cause bleeding upon the bedding, which is here held up in public display as legal evidence. **18:** *Flog him*, the same Hebrew word as "discipline him" (21.18); it may refer to flogging or simply to the following fine. **19:** *They shall fine him:* The penalty for his slanderous accusation is financial, although the penalty for her infidelity, if proven

true, is capital (vv. 20–21). This disproportion seriously conflicts with Deuteronomy's requirement that "you shall do to the false witness just as the false witness had meant to do to the other" (19.19). *A hundred shekels*, about 1.1 kg (2.5 lbs), is twice the fine for rape (v. 29). **21:** *Entrance of her father's house*, the very site of the offense. *Stone her to death*, see 13.11 n. *Shameful thing in Israel*, a violation of basic community sexual and religious norms (Gen. 34.7; Josh. 7.15; Judg. 19.23–34; 20.6, 10). *Sweep away evil*, see 13.5 n.

22.22–23.1: Adultery and rape. The editors' placement of these laws suggests their concern to es-

tablish sex and family law as an independent moral category. In so doing, the authors of Deuteronomy depart from the earlier legal system of the Covenant Collection. There, the law of the seduced virgin (Exod. 22.15–16) came at the end of a sequence of property law (Exod. 21.35–22.14), implying that the daughter was seen as an extension of her father's estate. In contrast, the corresponding law found here (22.28–29) concludes a series of similar laws (22.13–23.1); there is no longer any connection to property law (see also 5.18 n.). **22:** Adultery is a violation of the seventh commandment (5.17) and a capital offense (Lev. 18.20; 20.10). *Both of them . . . shall die:* This stipulation makes a sharp contrast with ancient Near Eastern legal norms, which required the adulterer's death but left the fate of the adulterous wife to the disposition of her husband. That the wife is here removed from the authority of the husband defines her as a legal person who is accountable for her actions. **23–27:** Two laws determining the woman's culpability (vv. 23–24) or nonculpability (vv. 25–27) in cases of rape. The distinction hangs upon the expectation of protest to express refusal (v. 24). **23:** *Engaged to a man* (cf. v. 25): This specification of legal status permits the transition from adultery to rape: Although the woman still resides with her father, she is contractually bound to her future husband (see translators' note a-a). *In town*, where there are potential witnesses. The contrast with "in the open country" (v. 25) symbolically determines the availability or unavailability of witnesses who could testify or come to the rescue. Similarly, Middle Assyrian Laws §A 12 (ca. 1076 BCE). **24:** *Cry for help:* The fabrication of such a cry in the false accusation against Joseph therefore has legal significance (Gen. 39.14–15). **25:** The assault *in the open country*, where witnesses are unlikely, suggests planned malice. **26:** *For this case is like:* A distinctive cross-reference to another legal case (19.11–13), used to make an argunothing to the girl. The girl did not incur the death penalty, for this case is like that of a man attacking another and murdering him. [27] He came upon her in the open; though the engaged girl cried for help, there was no one to save her.

[28] If a man comes upon a virgin who is not engaged and he seizes her and lies with her, and they are discovered, [29] the man who lay with her shall pay the girl's father fifty [shekels of] silver, and she shall be his wife. Because he has violated her, he can never have the right to divorce her.

23 No man shall marry his father's former wife, so as ªto remove his father's garment.ª

[2] No one whose testes are crushed or whose member is cut off shall be admitted into the congregation of the LORD.

[3] No one misbegotten[b] shall be admitted into the congregation of the LORD; none of his descendants, even in the tenth generation, shall be admitted into the congregation of the LORD.

[4] No Ammonite or Moabite shall be admitted into the congregation of the LORD; none of their descendants, even in the tenth generation, shall ever be admitted into the

a-a *I.e., lay claim to what his father had possessed. Cf. Lev. 18.8, 20.11; Ezek. 16.8; Ruth 3.9.*

b *Meaning of Heb.* mamzer *uncertain; in Jewish law, the offspring of adultery or incest between Jews.*

ment from analogy. *A man attacking another and murdering him:* This case is determined to be analogous to the one involving premeditated murder. The law understands rape as a criminal assault against the woman rather than as a sex crime. **28–29:** The seizure and rape of a virgin who is not engaged, the enforced marriage, and the prohibition of divorce correspond to Middle Assyrian Laws §A 55. The law also follows the literary model of Exod. 22.16–17, which specifies sexual intercourse with, but not forced rape of, a "virgin who is not engaged." The conflation of the two different models makes it unclear whether or not this law refers to consensual intercourse. **28:** *Seizes her:* The Hebrew word differs from that in v. 25, where force is clearly intended; here it may mean simply "hold" or "handle" (Jer. 2.8). *And lies with her,* as

in Exod. 22.15. The fact of intercourse normally marks legal consummation of a marriage; here it places the woman in a legally ambiguous position, unavailable to others (v. 14). **29:** *Fifty . . . silver:* In contrast to Exod. 22.15–16, the payment to the father does not represent compensation for the loss of the bride-price, which is normally a negotiated amount (Gen. 34.12). As a fixed amount externally imposed by the law, the payment here seems closer to a fine (v. 19), paid for the woman's violation. As in Exod. 22.16, the law requires the man now also legally and contractually to marry the woman by paying the bride-price to the father. In contrast to Exod. 22.16, the father's consent is not sought. Postbiblical Jewish law granted both the father and the daughter the right to refuse such marriages. **23.1:** A transition from

marriage law to the next section, which resembles the previous one in form (prohibition) and content (prohibited sexual relations). The Hebrew chapter division reflects the law's closer connection to what follows. *Father's former wife* presupposes the death of the father and almost certainly refers to the widowed stepmother, not the birth mother (see Lev. 18.7–8). *Remove his father's garment:* The intent is to respect the sexual privacy of the father and to avoid even indirect sexual contact with him (Gen. 9.23–24; 49.4; Lev. 18.8; 20.11).

23.2–9: Restrictions on access to Israel's assembly. *The congregation of the LORD* (v. 2) served as the national governing body, akin to a popular legislature, that was charged with a broad range of judicial, political, and policy matters (Judg. 20.2). **2:** *Testes . . . member:* Thus covering any physical damage to the male genitalia. Deuteronomy here seems to impose the same physiological qualification for membership in the assembly that the Holiness Collection requires of the priesthood (Lev. 21.17–23; see also Deut. 14.2 n.). Alternatively, eunuchs may be here excluded for reasons of their cultural association, since they served as officials in Near Eastern bureaucracies. **3:** *Misbegotten,* the offspring of a marriage viewed as incestuous (see vv. 1, 4; Lev. 18.6–18; translators' note b). *Tenth generation,* see v. 4 n. **4–9:** The restriction on access to Israel's national assembly does not entail denial of residence rights. Those named retain the protection afforded by the legal status of "resident alien" (see 1.16; 5.14; Lev. 19.10, 33–34; 23.22). It is likely, however, that those excluded could not marry within the community, and could not enter the Temple precincts. **4–7:** These laws were reused in the postexilic context to prohibit intermarriage (Ezra chs 9–10; Neh. 13.1–3). **4:** *Ammonite or Moabite,* perhaps introduced after v. 3 because of an older tradition concerning their incestuous origins (Gen. 19.30–38). *Tenth generation,* "forever," as congregation of the LORD, [5] because they did not meet you with food and water on your journey after you left Egypt, and because they hired Balaam son of Beor, from Pethor of Aram-naharaim, to curse you.—[6] But the LORD your God refused to heed Balaam; instead, the LORD your God turned the curse into a blessing for you, for the LORD your God loves you.—[7] You shall never concern yourself with their welfare or benefit as long as you live.

[8] You shall not abhor an Edomite, for he is your kinsman. You shall not abhor an Egyptian, for you were a stranger in his land. [9] Children born to them may be admitted into the congregation of the LORD in the third generation.[a]

[10] When you go out as a troop against your enemies, be on your guard against anything untoward. [11] If anyone among you has been rendered unclean by a nocturnal emission, he must leave the camp, and he must not reenter the camp. [12] Toward evening he shall bathe in water, and at sundown he may reenter the camp. [13] Further, there shall be an area for you outside the camp, where you may relieve yourself. [14] With your gear you shall have a spike, and when you have squatted you shall dig a hole with it and cover up your excrement. [15] Since the LORD your God moves about in your camp to protect you and to deliver your enemies to you, let your camp be holy; let Him not find anything unseemly among you and turn away from you.

[16] You shall not turn over to his master a slave who seeks refuge with you from his master. [17] He shall live with you in any place he may choose among the settlements in your midst, wherever he pleases; you must not ill-treat him.

[18] No Israelite woman shall be a cult prostitute, nor shall any Israelite man be a cult prostitute. [19] You shall not bring the fee of a whore or the pay of a dog[b] into the house

---

a I.e., of residence in Israel's territory.   b I.e., a male prostitute.

---

forward from the rules determining the composition of the assembly to the special rules that apply to the military camp. The focus is no longer on the rules of engagement (20.1–20; 21.10–14) but rather personal hygiene. The theology of holy war assumes God's direct participation in the campaign (7.17–24; 20.4), creating a demand for heightened purity such as was demanded of the entire people at Sinai (Exod. 19.10, 14). Sexual abstinence seems also to have been required (1 Sam. 21.4–5; 2 Sam. 11.8–11; cf. Exod. 19.15). **10–11:** Cf. Lev. 15.16–18. **13:** *Area for you outside the camp,* a latrine. These laws are reused in the Dead Sea Scrolls *(War Scroll; Temple Scroll),* each of which also specifies the exact distance of the latrine from the camp. **15:** *Moves about,* see 20.4; 31.6. *Anything unseemly,* as in 24.1.

23.16–25.19: The heightened moral responsibilities of the covenant community. The text moves forward from membership (vv. 2–9) and military camp rules (vv. 10–15) to broader ethical and religious norms imposed upon Israel.

23.16–17: Prohibition against the return of escaped slaves. The law rejects the almost universal stipulation within ancient Near Eastern law that escaped slaves must be returned to their owner, usually under penalty of death, and that rewards bounty hunters for their return (Laws of Hammurabi §§16–20; Hittite Laws §§22–24). **17:** The extraordinary fivefold repetition of phrases designating the location of residence emphasizes that the entire community must be open to them.

23.18–19: Restrictions on prostitution. These verses presuppose the inevitability of prostitution, while regulating it in such a way as to preserve the Temple's sanctity. **18:** *Cult prostitute:* The translation reflects the widely held belief in the existence of sacred prostitution in Israel and the ancient Near

---

explicitly stated in the Hebrew. **5:** The rationale, which could be a late addition, substantially varies from the earlier report that Israel detoured around Ammon without requesting assistance and received food and water from Moab (2.19, 29, 37). *Balaam,* see Num. chs 22–24. **8:** *Not abhor an Edomite:* The retention of this exhortation is extraordinary, since the Edomites participated in the destruction of

Jerusalem (Ps. 137.7; Obadiah; cf. Amos 1.11). *Kinsman,* through Esau (Gen. 25.24–26; 36.1). *Egyptian:* This equally remarkable injunction must reflect stories about Egypt as a site of sanctuary (Gen. chs 12; 37–50), while managing to overlook the enslavement (26.6; 28.60, 68; Exod. chs 1–15).

23.10–15: Special rules for the military camp. These laws move of the LORD your God in fulfillment of any vow, for both are abhorrent to the LORD your God.

²⁰ You shall not deduct interest from loans to your countrymen, whether in money or food or anything else that can be deducted as interest; ²¹ but you may deduct interest from loans to foreigners. Do not deduct interest from loans to your countrymen, so that the LORD your God may bless you in all your undertakings in the land that you are about to enter and possess.

²² When you make a vow to the LORD your God, do not put off fulfilling it, for the LORD your God will require it of you, and you will have incurred guilt; ²³ whereas you incur no guilt if you refrain from vowing. ²⁴ You must fulfill what has crossed your lips and perform what you have voluntarily vowed to the LORD your God, having made the promise with your own mouth.

²⁵ When you enter another man's vineyard, you may eat as many grapes as you want, until you are full, but you must not put any in your vessel. ²⁶ When you enter another man's field of standing grain, you may pluck ears with your hand; but you must not put a sickle to your neighbor's grain.

24 A man takes a wife and possesses her. She fails to please him because he finds something obnoxious about her, and he writes her a bill of divorcement, hands it to her, and sends her away from his house; ² she leaves his household and becomes the wife of another man; ³ then this latter man rejects her, writes her a bill of divorcement, hands it to her, and sends her away from his house; or the man who married her last dies. ⁴ Then the first husband who divorced her shall not take her to wife again, since

---

East, for which there is scant evidence. Heb "kedesha" here more likely serves as a standard euphemism for the coarser term for a regular prostitute that appears in v. 19. The same alternation between the two terms appears in the narrative of Tamar, whom Judah privately regards as a "whore" but who is publicly referred to as a "kedesha" (Gen. 38.15, 21). The word might better be translated as "one set aside." **19:** *Dog*, in context, the male counterpart to a common female prostitute. To maintain holiness, the law proscribes the donation of income gained from prostitution

to the Temple (cf. Hos. 4.14; Mic. 1.7).

23.20–26: Laws of financial ethics, vows, gathering by the needy. 20–21: As Israelites must not sexually exploit one another (vv. 18–19), so must they avoid economic exploitation. This law builds on Exod. 22.25, which clarifies that, in this economy, lending served primarily as a means of social support for "the poor among you" (similarly Lev. 25.36–37). Charging interest would amount to profiteering from the misfortunes of others. **21:** *Foreigners*, as distinct from the "resident alien"

or "stranger," who fully participated in Israel's social welfare system (5.14; 14.29; 16.11; 24.14, 17, 19, 20, 21; for similar distinctions, see 15.3; Lev. 25.44–45). **22–24:** A *vow* (v. 22) promises payment to God (usually a sacrifice at a temple) for granting a petitioner's request (see 1 Sam. 1.11). The cautious reserve expressed here closely corresponds to wisdom teachings (Eccl. 5.4–6). The precedent of stories like Jephthah's vow (Judg. 11.29–40) trenchantly explains such reserve. For a more positive view, see Ps. 50.14. **25–26:** These rules prohibit exploitation of Deuteronomy's extensive support system for the needy (14.28–29; 24.19–22; 25.4). **26:** *Pluck . . . hand*, to address immediate hunger (illustrated in a later period in Luke 6.1; cf. Matt. 12.1; Mark 2.23).

24.1–22: The chapter, like the previous one, begins with a restriction on marriage and concludes by stipulating care for those in need. **1–4:** This complex law, theologically applied by two prophets (Isa. 50.1; Jer. 3.1, 8), addresses only the specific case of remarriage after divorce to a wife who subsequently married another; it does not prohibit remarriage in general. No general laws of either marriage or divorce survive from ancient Israel; biblical law includes only special cases that raise particular ethical or religious issues. **1:** Male-initiated divorce was the norm, though there is some evidence in the Near East and in the Jewish Elephantine papyri (5th century BCE) of marriage contracts permitting either party to initiate proceedings (cf. Exod. 21.10–11). *He finds . . . about her*, a legal formula used to charge someone with disloyal action or betrayal of trust (1 Sam. 29.3, 6, 8; 2 Kings 17.4; cf. 1 Sam. 12.5). *Obnoxious*, "unseemly" (23.15). It is unclear from the term, whose exact meaning is debated in early Jewish texts, what valid criteria for divorce were. *Bill of divorcement*, legally freeing her to remarry (22.14 n.). **4:** *Since she has been defiled*, not in general, since she is permitted to remarry, she has been defiled[a]—for that would be abhorrent to the LORD. You must not bring sin upon the land that the LORD your God is giving you as a heritage.

5 When a man has taken a bride, he shall not go out with the army or be assigned to it for any purpose; he shall be exempt one year for the sake of his household, to give happiness to the woman he has married.

6 A handmill or an upper millstone shall not be taken in pawn, for that would be taking someone's life in pawn.

7 If a man is found to have kidnapped a fellow Israelite, enslaving him or selling him, that kidnapper shall die; thus you will sweep out evil from your midst.

8 In cases of a skin affection[b] be most careful to do exactly as the levitical priests instruct you. Take care to do as I have commanded them. 9 Remember what the LORD your God did to Miriam on the journey after you left Egypt.[c]

10 When you make a loan of any sort to your countryman, you must not enter his house to seize his pledge. 11 You must remain outside, while the man to whom you made the loan brings the pledge out to you. 12 If he is a needy man, you shall not go to sleep in his pledge; 13 you must return the pledge to him at sundown, that he may sleep in his cloth and bless you; and it will be to your merit before the LORD your God.

14 You shall not abuse a needy and destitute laborer, whether a fellow countryman or a stranger in one of the communities of your land. 15 You must pay him his wages on the same day, before the sun sets, for he is needy and urgently depends on it; else he will cry to the LORD against you and you will incur guilt.

16 Parents shall not be put to death for children, nor children be put to death for parents: a person shall be put to death only for his own crime.

17 You shall not subvert the rights of the stranger or the fatherless; you shall not take a widow's garment in pawn. 18 Remember that you were a slave in Egypt and that the LORD your God redeemed you from there; therefore do I enjoin you to observe this commandment.

19 When you reap the harvest in your field and overlook

a I.e., disqualified for him.   b Cf. Lev. 13.1 ff.   c See Num. 12.10 ff.

but specifically as regards relations with her first husband. **5:** Another of the rules for holy war (20.1–20; 21.10–14; 23.10–15). Newly *married:* Contrast the premarital deferral from service in 20.7. *To give happiness to,* including conjugal joy.

6: The law prohibits oppression in economic relations (like vv. 10–15). *Taken . . . in pawn,* held as collateral for a loan. *Handmill . . . upper millstone:* Like the garment taken as "pledge" in vv. 10–12, they lack significant intrinsic value but are

essential to survival; thus, only as incentive for repayment would they be taken in pawn. The law prohibits such activity as extortion. **7:** Restricts the application of Exod. 21.16 to kidnappers of fellow Israelites; perhaps also an interpretation of Deut. 5.17 (cf. Laws of Hammurabi §14; Hittite Laws §§19–21). **8–9:** *Remember . . . Miriam,* see Num. 12.1–15. *Skin affection,* not leprosy but an unidentified inflammation; see Lev. chs 13–14. **10–13:** Expands upon Exod. 22.25–26 (cf. Amos. 2.8; Prov. 20.16; 22.27; 27.13; Job 22.6). As in Exodus, the *pledge* refers to a garment. The Yavneh Yam inscription, a recently excavated legal petition written on a pottery sherd from the late 7th century BCE, deals with a similar case. **14–15:** See Exod. 22.21–24; Lev. 19.13. Israel's ethics are based upon the conviction that God identifies with and vindicates the oppressed. **14:** The prohibition against economic exploitation applies equally to the non-Israelite; it is not contingent upon ethnicity or nationality (see 1.16 n.). **16:** This law, restricting punishment to the responsible individual, applies specifically to civil and criminal law; it is cited in 2 Kings 14.6. In contrast, collective responsibility for wrongdoing operates in the realm of offenses against God (5.9–10; Exod. 34.7; Num. 16.31–33; Josh. 7.24–25; 2 Sam. 21.1–9). That theological principle was subsequently brought into conformity with the law of individual liability (7.10; Jer. 31.29–30; Ezek. ch 18). **17:** *You shall not subvert the rights,* identical to the comprehensive "You shall not judge unfairly" (16.19). This law, therefore, ensures full judicial protection of the most vulnerable members of the community, the *stranger* (or "resident alien") and the *fatherless. Take . . . in pawn,* better, "seize" or "distrain" to force payment (see Job 24.3). This law accords the *widow* special protection; for day laborers, the garment could be taken but must be returned daily (vv. 10–13). **18:** See 15.15. **19–22:** Lev. 19.9–10; 23.22. The story of Ruth, both widow and alien, presupposes a sheaf in the field, do not turn back to get it; it shall go to the stranger, the fatherless, and the widow—in order that the LORD your God may bless you in all your undertakings. 20 When you beat down the fruit of your olive trees, do not go over them again; that shall go to the stranger, the fatherless, and the widow. 21 When you gather the grapes of your vineyard, do not pick it over again; that shall go to the stranger, the fatherless, and the widow. 22 Always remember that you were a slave in the land of Egypt; therefore do I enjoin you to observe this commandment.

25 When there is a dispute between men and they go to law, and a decision is rendered declaring the one in the right and the other in the wrong—2 if the guilty one is to be flogged, the magistrate shall have him lie down and be given lashes in his presence, by count, as his guilt warrants. 3 He may be given up to forty lashes, but not more, lest being flogged further, to excess, your brother be degraded before your eyes.

4 You shall not muzzle an ox while it is threshing.

5 When brothers dwell together and one of them dies and leaves no son, the wife of the deceased shall not be married to a stranger, outside the family. Her husband's brother shall unite with her: he shall take her as his wife and perform the levir's duty. 6 The first son that she bears shall be accounted to the dead brother, that his name may not be blotted out in Israel. 7 But if the man does not want to marry his brother's widow, his brother's widow shall appear before the elders in the gate and declare, "My husband's brother refuses to establish a name in Israel for his brother; he will not perform the duty of a levir." 8 The elders of his town shall then summon him and talk to him. If he insists, saying, "I do not want to marry her," 9 his brother's widow shall go up to him in the presence of the elders, pull the sandal off his foot, spit in his face, and make this declaration: Thus shall be done to the man who will not build up his brother's house! 10 And he shall go in Israel by the name of "the family of the unsandaled one."

floggings of five to one hundred lashes. The rationale for the restriction is an extrajudicial notion of human dignity: The criminal, despite his judicial status, remains *your brother.* **4:** For similar humane treatment of animals, see 22.6–7; Prov. 12.10. **5–10: Levirate marriage.** Biblical, Near Eastern, and Roman inheritance law assigned special responsibilities to the "husband's brother" (vv. 5–7), for which Hebrew had a special term, "yavam" (cf. Latin "levir"). Should a man die, leaving his widow childless, his brother was expected to marry the widow, thereby continuing the deceased's line (see variations of this law in Gen. 38.8; Ruth 4.5–6). **5:** *Stranger* most likely refers to someone outside of the larger clan. The widow's marriage outside the clan would diminish the landholding of the clan and add it to her husband's, affecting the original equitable division of land among the tribes (Josh. chs 13–21). *Her husband's brother shall unite with her:* This requirement conflicts with the prohibition against incest with the sister-in-law (Lev. 18.16; 20.21). Possibly, as in the Hittite Laws, levirate marriage provided an exception to the normal prohibition of such relations; alternatively, the Holiness Collection's incest laws, which seem to be later, are intended to prohibit the practice altogether. **6:** *The first son* alone here counts to the brother; cf. Gen. 38.8; Ruth 4.5–6. The intent is to mitigate the injustice created by the institution of levirite marriage: The brother who complied with its requirements would effectively disinherit himself. **9:** Legal title was symbolically claimed by walking over the land (11.24 n.; Gen. 13.17); transfer of title therefore entailed passing the *sandal* (Ruth 4.7); and renunciation of title was symbolized by removal of the *sandal.* The intent of the ceremony, with the man passive and spat upon, is public shaming, since the dereliction of duty abandons the brother's wife to the category of those who are economically dependent: "the stranger, the fatherless, and the widow in your

such laws, which assign harvest gleanings to the needy, allowing them to eat without begging for food. **20:** *Beat,* with poles, so as to harvest the olives (Isa. 17.6).

25.1–3: This law imposes a double restriction upon the Near Eastern convention of judicial flogging (22.18 n.), which was also employed for discipline in nonjudi-

cial contexts (21.18 n.; Exod. 21.20; Prov. 10.13; 26.3; 1 Kings 12.14). **2:** First, the sentence must be carried out under the judge's direct supervision: *in his presence,* with the lashes delivered *by* [his] *count.* **3:** Second, the number is restricted to *forty lashes.* No parallel restriction exists in Near Eastern law; the Middle Assyrian Laws stipulate

11 If two men get into a fight with each other, and the wife of one comes up to save her husband from his antagonist and puts out her hand and seizes him by his genitals, 12 you shall cut off her hand; show no pity.

13 You shall not have in your pouch alternate weights, larger and smaller. 14 You shall not have in your house alternate measures, a larger and a smaller. 15 You must have completely honest weights and completely honest measures, if you are to endure long on the soil that the LORD your God is giving you. 16 For everyone who does those things, everyone who deals dishonestly, is abhorrent to the LORD your God.

17 Remember what Amalek did to you on your journey, after you left Egypt—18 how, undeterred by fear of God, he surprised you on the march, when you were famished and weary, and cut down all the stragglers in your rear. 19 Therefore, when the LORD your God grants you safety from all your enemies around you, in the land that the LORD your God is giving you as a hereditary portion, you shall blot out the memory of Amalek from under heaven. Do not forget!

KI TAVO'   כי תבוא

26 When you enter the land that the LORD your God is giving you as a heritage, and you possess it and settle in it, 2 you shall take some of every first fruit of the soil, which you harvest from the land that the LORD your God is giving you, put it in a basket and go to the place where the LORD your God will choose to establish His name. 3 You shall go to the priest in charge at that time and say to him, "I acknowledge this day before the LORD your God that I have entered the land that the LORD swore to our fathers to assign us."

4 The priest shall take the basket from your hand and set it down in front of the altar of the LORD your God.

5 You shall then recite as follows before the LORD your

---

issue may rather be the perceived insult to dignity or to decency (compare Laws of Hammurabi §195). **13–16:** Compare Laws of Hammurabi §108; Lev. 19.35–36; Amos. 8.5. **14:** By fraudulently using two different sets of counterweights—small ones to sell grain but large ones to purchase it—a merchant could turn a tidy profit. **17–19:** The tradition presupposes Exod. 17.8–17, in which the Amalekites, a fierce desert tribe, attacked Israel (cf. Ps 83.4–8). Within later Jewish tradition, these verses play a central role, as Amalek came to symbolize any enemy of the Jews. These verses are read liturgically on the Sabbath before Purim, since according to Jewish tradition, Haman, the evil protagonist of Esther, is an Amalekite (see 1 Sam. 15.8 and Esth. 8.3). **18:** These details are not reflected in Exod. 17.8–17; the Deuteronomic author may have supplied them in order to justify the extirpation of Amalek (v. 19; cf. Exod. 17.14; 1 Sam. 15.2–3). **19:** *Grants you safety,* see 3.20; 12.9–10 n.

26.1–15: Concluding liturgies. Two already prescribed laws (14.22–29) are given a historical and theological foundation (similarly, 16.12, for the Festival of Weeks). **1–11:** The context is the Festival of Weeks (16.9–12), when the Israelite was to make an annual pilgrimage to the central sanctuary, bringing the first fruits of the harvest, to thank God for the land's bounty. **4:** *The priest shall take the basket . . . and set it down in front of the altar,* in contrast to the stipulation, " You shall leave it before the LORD" (v. 10). On that basis, vv. 3–4 may represent a later addition to the text, in order to emphasize the role of the priests in the ceremony. That would account for the absence of reference to the priests elsewhere in the unit; the double tradition about what is recited at the sanctuary (v. 3, vv. 5–10); and the two versions of who is to set the basket before the altar. Thus, v. 5 would originally have continued v. 2. **5:** *My father was a fugitive Aramean:* This verse is de-

---

settlements" (14.29 n.). **10:** *Shall go . . . by the name of,* thus explicitly applying a form of talionic justice (19.19 n.). For refusing to build up the deceased's "name" (vv. 6, 7) and "house" (v. 9), the brother's own *family* (lit. "house") is stigmatized by its new *name.* **11–12:** This law, like the preceding one, deals with threats to reproduction; it provides a corollary to Exod. 21.22–25, where a case involving a pregnant woman is used to de-

velop the law of talion. The rationale for the punishment is difficult. While physical mutilation is characteristic in the Middle Assyrian Laws, it is nowhere else prescribed in the Bible, except in the general formula for talion (19.21; Exod. 21.23–24; Lev. 24.19–20). That formula does not apply here, however, since there can be no symmetry between injury and punishment. Since no physical injury to the male is actually specified, the

God: "My father was a fugitive Aramean. He went down to Egypt with meager numbers and sojourned there; but there he became a great and very populous nation. ⁶The Egyptians dealt harshly with us and oppressed us; they imposed heavy labor upon us. ⁷We cried to the Lord, the God of our fathers, and the Lord heard our plea and saw our plight, our misery, and our oppression. ⁸The Lord freed us from Egypt by a mighty hand, by an outstretched arm and awesome power, and by signs and portents. ⁹He brought us to this place and gave us this land, a land flowing with milk and honey. ¹⁰Wherefore I now bring the first fruits of the soil which You, O Lord, have given me."

You shall leave itᵃ before the Lord your God and bow low before the Lord your God. ¹¹And you shall enjoy, together with the Levite and the stranger in your midst, all the bounty that the Lord your God has bestowed upon you and your household.

¹²When you have set aside in full the tenth part of your yield—in the third year, the year of the titheᵇ—and have given it to the Levite, the stranger, the fatherless, and the widow, that they may eat their fill in your settlements, ¹³you shall declare before the Lord your God: "I have cleared out the consecrated portion from the house; and I have given it to the Levite, the stranger, the fatherless, and the widow, just as You commanded me; I have neither transgressed nor neglected any of Your commandments: ¹⁴ᶜ I have not eaten of it while in mourning, I have not

a *I.e., the basket of v. 4.*   b *See Deut. 14.28–29.*
c *Meaning of first part of verse uncertain.*

no mention of Sinai has suggested to a number of scholars the possibility that the inclusion of the Sinai/Horeb experience in the overall Torah narrative represents a relatively late, secondary addition. Sinai seems to have been incorporated into the larger narrative only in exilic or later texts (Ps. 106; Neh. ch 9). Some scholars have explained this by reasoning that only a minority of the tribes or groups eventually comprising Israel experienced Sinai/Horeb; thus, only at a late stage of the tradition was their experience extended to all Israel and incorporated into the narrative of the Torah. Alternately, this act of thanksgiving commemorates Israel's wondrous transformation from a single, landless, persecuted individual into a populous nation, secure and at home in its land. In this thanksgiving for the double miracle—the individual has now become a nation and those who were homeless now harvest crops from their land—mention of the journey to Sinai to receive the law would have been disruptive and irrelevant. **6:** *Oppressed . . . heavy labor,* see Exod. 1.11–14. **11:** *Enjoy,* or "rejoice" (16.11, 14–15), specifically in a festive meal consumed at the central sanctuary (12.7, 18), which must include *the Levite and the stranger,* for whose benefit (along with other disadvantaged groups) the following law is directed. **12–15:** Produce was tithed annually and consumed by the farmer and his household at the central sanctuary (14.22–27); every third year that tithe was used locally to support the poor (14.28–29). **12:** *The stranger, the fatherless, and the widow,* see 1.16 n.; 14.29 n.; 23.3–8 n., 20 n. **14:** The triple confession of the donor's ritual purity implies that the formula was originally used for donations of produce to God at a sanctuary, where purity would be expected. That formula has now been reused for the donation of food to the poor in a noncultic setting: "in your settlements" (v. 12). *Deposited any of it with the dead:* The duty of the living to care for dead ances-

ployed in the Passover Haggadah (just following the section on the Four Sons) in a famous passage that emphasizes God's miraculous sparing of Israel from a long line of persecutors, beginning with Laban's attack on Jacob (Gen. ch 31). By means of a midrashic reworking of its original meaning, the verse is interpreted to mean "an Aramean sought to destroy my ancestor." That rendering departs from the actual grammar of the verse and almost certainly reflects the politics of the Second Temple period, when the Seleucid empire, which ruled Israel from Syria (198–168 BCE), was referred to obliquely as Laban, the Aramean. The hyperbolic claim in the Haggadah that Laban's oppression of Israel/Jacob was more invidi-

ous than the Egyptian enslavement points to a polemic against the Seleucids, whose policies triggered the Hasmonean revolt (167 BCE). **8–9:** The thanksgiving prayer recited by the pilgrim provides a précis of the main narrative line of the Pentateuch and Joshua (the "Hexateuch"). For that reason, the verses have been seen by some scholars as an ancient confession of faith, or creed, that is older than its present context. Strikingly, this summary of the main events of Israel's religious history makes no mention of the revelation of law at Sinai/Horeb. The same is true for many similar "confessions" in the Bible (see 6.20–24; Josh. 24.2–13; 1 Sam. 12.8; Pss. 78, 105, 136). The existence of such a strong tradition that makes cleared out any of it while I was unclean, and I have not deposited any of it with the dead.[a] I have obeyed the LORD my God; I have done just as You commanded me. [15]Look down from Your holy abode, from heaven, and bless Your people Israel and the soil You have given us, a land flowing with milk and honey, as You swore to our fathers."

[16]The LORD your God commands you this day to observe these laws and rules; observe them faithfully with all your heart and soul. [17]You have affirmed[b] this day that the LORD is your God, that you will walk in His ways, that you will observe His laws and commandments and rules, and that you will obey Him. [18]And the LORD has affirmed[b] this day that you are, as He promised you, His treasured people who shall observe all His commandments, [19]and that He will set you, in fame and renown and glory, high above all the nations that He has made; and that you shall be, as He promised, a holy people to the LORD your God.

27 Moses and the elders of Israel charged the people, saying: Observe all the Instruction that I enjoin upon you this day. [2c]As soon as you have crossed the Jordan into the land that the LORD your God is giving you,

a *No part of the tithe may be left as food for the dead.*
b *Exact nuance of Heb. uncertain.*   c *Construction of vv. 2–4 uncertain.*

specifies His responsibility (to be God) and then identifies His three expectations of Israel. Symmetrically, Israel proclaims (v. 18) one responsibility (to obey the commandments) while then outlining the three responsibilities of God toward Israel (to grant treasured status, election, holiness). This reciprocal model contrasts with the Sinai covenant, which was unilaterally offered by God (Exod. 19.3–6) and unilaterally agreed to by Israel (Exod. 19.8; 24.3, 7). Deuteronomy invokes the language of the Sinai covenant as a model, while revising that model in the process. **18:** *His treasured people,* see 7.6 n.; 14.2 n. *As He promised you,* Exod. 19.5–6. **19:** *High above all the nations,* see 28.13–14 n. *That He has made,* see Exod. 19.5b. *A holy people to the LORD your God* continues the reference to Exod. 19.5–6, while substituting *people* for "nation," which Deuteronomy uses for non-Israelites (12.29). *In fame and renown and glory:* NJPS implies that the accolades will be given to Israel. The Hebrew also allows for the possibility that the honors will go to God because of His action on Israel's behalf (see Jer. 13.11; 33.9).

tors through food offerings at their place of burial was widely assumed in the ancient Near East (see the Ugaritic Aqhat epic) and continued to be held in Second Temple times (Tobit 4.17). Here the practice is not condemned; it is viewed as improper specifically when coming into contact with cultic donations, because the impurity associated with death would render food unfit for donation to the Temple (Lev. 22.2–4). **15:** *From Your holy abode, from heaven* (as in 1 Kings 8.30): The double preposition may point to the correction of an older theology in light of a newer one, following Deuteronomy's older view that only God's name resides in the Temple (12.11; 16.11; 26.2). For the earlier idea, that God Himself inhabits the Temple, see 1 Kings 8.13; cf. Deut. 12.5. *Bless Your people Israel and the soil:* The farmer prays for the blessing of the community and of the land, not directly for fertility or the abundance of his own crops.

26.16–19: Formal conclusion, which presents the legal corpus as a mutually binding relationship between God and Israel. Having just read the law to the people, Moses presents it to them in a formal ratification ceremony (vv. 17–18; cf. 2 Kings 23.1–3). **16:** *Laws and rules . . . observe . . . faithfully* forms an inclusio with 12.1, thus providing the laws of chs 12–26 with an elegant frame to mark their conclusion. **17–18:** *You have affirmed:* The past tense points to a prior action or speech in which each party has proclaimed what is here described. No record of such an event or ceremony survives. Deuteronomy emphasizes that both God and Israel have explicitly assented to the covenant and have affirmed the mutuality of the obligations that each undertakes. God's proclamation (v. 17)

27.1–26: The ceremonies at Shechem. The injunctions of 11.29–32 are here reiterated and detailed. The laws of chs 12–26 are thus framed with ceremonies that connect entry into the land with obedience to Torah. The chapter joins four separate sections that are only loosely connected to one another and to the rest of Deuteronomy. A later editor has aligned the sections with one another, while breaking up the continuity of the Mosaic speech of chs 26 and 28. The resulting digression preserves several competing traditions about how and where the covenant between God and Israel was concluded: at Sinai; or on the plains of Moab; or at Gilgal immediately upon entering the land; or at the important northern shrine of Shechem (see 11.29 n.). **1–8:** This section combines two separate requirements: the raising of plasyou shall set up large stones. Coat them with plaster [3] and inscribe upon them all the words of this Teaching. When you cross over to enter the land that the LORD your God is giving you, a land flowing with milk and honey, as the LORD, the God of your fathers, promised you—[4] upon crossing the Jordan, you shall set up these stones, about which I charge you this day, on Mount Ebal, and coat them with plaster. [5] There, too, you shall build an altar to the LORD your God, an altar of stones. Do not wield an iron tool over them; [6] you must build the altar of the LORD your God of unhewn[a] stones. You shall offer on it burnt offerings to the LORD your God, [7] and you shall sacrifice there offerings of well-being and eat them, rejoicing before the LORD your God. [8] And on those stones you shall inscribe every word of this Teaching most distinctly.

[9] Moses and the levitical priests spoke to all Israel, saying: Silence! Hear, O Israel! Today you have become the people of the LORD your God: [10] Heed the LORD your God and observe His commandments and His laws, which I enjoin upon you this day.

[11] Thereupon Moses charged the people, saying: [12 b] After you have crossed the Jordan, the following shall stand on Mount Gerizim when the blessing for the people is spoken: Simeon, Levi, Judah, Issachar, Joseph, and Benjamin. [13] And for the curse, the following shall stand on Mount Ebal: Reuben, Gad, Asher, Zebulun, Dan, and Naphtali. [14] The Levites shall then proclaim in a loud voice to all the people of Israel:

a Lit. "whole."   b Construction of vv. 12–13 uncertain.

tered-over stones inscribed with the Torah (vv. 1–4, 8), and the construction of a stone altar for sacrifice (vv. 5–7). **1:** Moses is here referred to in the third person, interrupting his first-person address (chs 5–26, 28). *And the elders:* Nowhere else in Deuteronomy do they join Moses in addressing the people; this plural subject does not easily fit the following singular *I*. **2:** *As soon as you have crossed the Jordan . . . you shall set up large stones:* The Deuteronomistic historian understands this command to have been fulfilled at Gilgal, just across the Jordan and less than a mile from Jericho (see Josh. ch 4). *Coat them with plaster,* to serve as a surface for an inscription. Archeology attests the use of plaster-covered inscriptions. **4:** *Mount Ebal,* at over 1,000 m (3,280 ft) high, the tallest mountain in the region, lies in central Canaan, adjacent to the city of Shechem. But that site, more than 50 km (30 mi) from the Jordan, is inconsistent with v. 2 and the beginning of this verse, which each anticipate that the ceremony will take place immediately upon crossing the river. It would be impossible to reach Shechem in a day. The most logical explanation is that Josh. ch 4 points to the original form of these verses, with Gilgal, which later became an important sanctuary (1 Sam. 11.15; Hos. 4.15; 9.15; 12.12; Amos 4.4; 5.5) as the site where Israel complied with this command. That older tradition was then replaced here by the reference to the mountains around Shechem, the chief town of the northern tribes (Josh. 24.1, 32). **5–7:** These verses are an insertion that reinterprets the plastered stones on which the Torah is to be inscribed as an altar of *unhewn stones,* following Exod. 20.22. Such an altar, outside of Jerusalem, conflicts with the centralization requirement of ch 12, further suggesting this tradition's antiquity and its independence from the rest of Deuteronomy. The Deuteronomistic historian understood this law to be fulfilled at Mount Ebal some time after the Israelite entry into the land, following the defeats of Jericho and Ai (Josh. 8.30–35). **8:** *On those stones you shall inscribe every word of this Teaching:* repeats and resumes the key terms of vv. 3–4, thus bracketing the insertion of vv. 5–7. Since the term "law" (Heb "torah") is elastic, there is significant debate in traditional and critical scholarship about what was meant to be written on these stones. **9–10:** This paragraph, which has its own beginning, is independent of what precedes it. **9:** *And the levitical priests,* see v. 1 n.; here too the plural subject is continued by "I" (v. 10). *Today:* The assertion here that Israel becomes God's people just now, in Moab, contrasts with statements that define the bond as previously formed, either at the time of the exodus (Exod. 6.6–7) or at Sinai (4.20; Exod. 19.5–6). **11–13:** A fragment that refers to an ancient covenant ceremony at Shechem, instituted at the command of Moses (Josh. 8.30–35). The antiquity of the tribal list is seen in the facts that Levi is listed as a tribe (Gen. 49.5–7) and that the division of the House of Joseph into Manasseh and Ephraim has not yet occurred (Gen. 49.22–26; contrast Deut. 33.17). The division of the tribes into two groups of six is attested only here. **11:** *Thereupon,* lit., "on that day," without further specification. **12–13:** *Mount Gerizim . . . Mount Ebal:* See 11.29 n. One group of tribes, on Gerizim, proclaims a set of blessings (see 28.1–14); the other, on Ebal, a set of curses (see 28.15–68). **14–26:** De-

15 Cursed be anyone who makes a sculptured or molten image, abhorred by the Lord, a craftsman's handiwork, and sets it up in secret.—And all the people shall respond, Amen.

16 Cursed be he who insults his father or mother.—And all the people shall say, Amen.

17 Cursed be he who moves his fellow countryman's landmark.—And all the people shall say, Amen.

18 Cursed be he who misdirects a blind person on his way.—And all the people shall say, Amen.

19 Cursed be he who subverts the rights of the stranger, the fatherless, and the widow.—And all the people shall say, Amen.

20 Cursed be he who lies with his father's wife, for he has removed his father's garment.ᵃ—And all the people shall say, Amen.

21 Cursed be he who lies with any beast.—And all the people shall say, Amen.

22 Cursed be he who lies with his sister, whether daughter of his father or of his mother.—And all the people shall say, Amen.

23 Cursed be he who lies with his mother-in-law.—And all the people shall say, Amen.

24 Cursed be he who strikes down his fellow countryman in secret.—And all the people shall say, Amen.

25 Cursed be he who accepts a bribe ᵇin the case of the murder ofᵇ an innocent person.—And all the people shall say, Amen.

26 Cursed be he who will not uphold the terms of this Teaching and observe them.—And all the people shall say, Amen.

28 Now, if you obey the Lord your God, to observe faithfully all His commandments which I enjoin upon you this day, the Lord your God will set you high above all the nations of the earth. 2 All these blessings shall come upon you and take effect, if you will but heed the word of the Lord your God:

a See note at 23.1.
b-b I.e., to acquit the murderer; others "to slay."

mary list of rejected actions, making no references to the consequences of the transgressions. **14:** *The Levites:* Deuteronomy's normal term is "levitical priests" (v. 9; 18.1). **15–26:** In context, the twelve curses correspond to the twelve tribes, although this section makes no reference to the tribal division, and the people function as a single entity (v. 14). The resulting incongruence points to the many editorial revisions that this chapter has undergone.

28.1–68: The consequences of obedience or disobedience: blessing or curse. The Mosaic covenant specifies a series of blessings and curses that follow upon national obedience or disobedience to the law. These are modeled after ancient Near Eastern state treaties, in which the consequences of breach of the treaty are spelled out at its conclusion; this chapter has several close parallels to the Vassal Treaty of Esarhaddon (VTE), a Neo-Assyrian treaty dating to 672 BCE. The present strong disproportion between the sections devoted to blessing (vv. 1–14) and to curse (vv. 15–68) most likely reflects the actual historical experience of the Babylonian conquest, deportation, and exile of Judah (597 and 586 BCE), here recast as a prophetic warning. The two appendices which have expanded the section (vv. 47–57, 58–68) each seek to make theological sense of that catastrophe. The two other legal collections of the Torah (the Covenant Collection of Exod. chs 21–23; the Holiness Collection of Lev. chs 17–26) similarly end with exhortations to obedience, accompanied by blessings and curses (Exod. 23.20–33; Lev ch 26), as does the Code of Hammurabi. Here an inclusio frames and defines the blessings section: *if you obey . . . observe faithfully* (vv. 1, 13). **1–2:** The proem emphasizes the conditionality of the elected status of Israel. The repetition of the conditional nature of the fulfillment, *If you obey the Lord your God* (vv. 1 and 2), places a frame around the central idea of divine election of Israel. *Set*

spite the paragraphing in NJPS, v. 14 more likely begins a new section with a very different conception of the ceremony. Here the tribe of Levi alone proclaims a set of prohibited actions and *all the people*— acting in unison and not divided into tribes—respond, *Amen* (see Jer.

11.3–5). There is no list of blessings (cf. v. 12). Nor is "the curse" intended by v. 13—a description of divine punishment for wrongful action, as in 28.15–68—provided. In contrast, the "cursed be" proclamations here employ an unrelated Heb word and stigmatize a sum-

³ Blessed shall you be in the city and blessed shall you be in the country.

⁴ Blessed shall be the issue of your womb, the produce of your soil, and the offspring of your cattle, the calving of your herd and the lambing of your flock.

⁵ Blessed shall be your basket and your kneading bowl.

⁶ Blessed shall you be in your comings and blessed shall you be in your goings.

⁷ The LORD will put to rout before you the enemies who attack you; they will march out against you by a single road, but flee from you by many[a] roads. ⁸ The LORD will ordain blessings for you upon your barns and upon all your undertakings: He will bless you in the land that the LORD your God is giving you. ⁹ The LORD will establish you as His holy people, as He swore to you, if you keep the commandments of the LORD your God and walk in His ways. ¹⁰ And all the peoples of the earth shall see that the LORD's name is proclaimed over you,[b] and they shall stand in fear of you. ¹¹ The LORD will give you abounding prosperity in the issue of your womb, the offspring of your cattle, and the produce of your soil in the land that the LORD swore to your fathers to assign to you. ¹² The LORD will open for you His bounteous store, the heavens, to provide rain for your land in season and to bless all your undertakings. You will be creditor to many nations, but debtor to none.

¹³ The LORD will make you the head, not the tail; you will always be at the top and never at the bottom—if only you obey and faithfully observe the commandments of the LORD your God that I enjoin upon you this day, ¹⁴ and do not deviate to the right or to the left from any of the commandments that I enjoin upon you this day and turn to the worship of other gods.

¹⁵ But if you do not obey the LORD your God to observe faithfully all His commandments and laws which I enjoin

---

a Lit. "seven."　　　b I.e., the LORD recognizes you as His own; cf. Isa. 4.1.

---

you high above all the nations of the earth (see also v. 13): The metaphor, which is also used to denote the elected status of the Davidic dynasty (Ps. 89.28), here denotes the divine election of the nation. The same affirmation of Israel's election appears at 26.19, where it is not conditional; instead, it fulfills God's past promises. Here, in contrast, the nation's elected status is presented as a future promise that is conditional upon obedience. The marked change may well reflect the revision of earlier expectations in light of the catastrophe of exile. **3–6:** The six benedictions have their malediction counterpart at vv. 16–19. The two antonym pairs (vv. 3, 6) provide a frame to the unit. The opposites form a merism to stress totality (like "night and day"); see 6.7 n. **3:** City and *country,* "everywhere," urban and

rural. **4:** *Issue . . . lambing:* For womb, ground, and livestock, obedience to the Torah is rewarded with comprehensive fertility. Fecundity is contingent upon obedience to the covenant—and thus not upon either natural fertility or competing fertility gods (see 7.12–14 n.). **6:** *Comings . . . goings,* whenever and wherever you go. **7:** Military success is conditional upon covenantal obedience rather than strength of arms (9.1–3; Josh. 1.6–8). **9:** *The LORD will establish you . . . if you keep:* The assertion here that the nation's holiness or election is conditional upon obedience represents a remarkable shift from other contexts in Deuteronomy where Israel's holiness is not future but present, and not conditional but unconditional (7.6; 14.2; cf. 26.18). **10:** *The LORD's name is proclaimed over you* signifies a special relationship with God, which includes particular accountability to God and corresponding divine oversight. The formula can apply to either the nation (here; Isa. 63.19; Jer. 14.9; 2 Chron. 7.14) or an individual (Exod. 33.12; Jer. 15.16). **12:** *Store:* In Israelite and Near Eastern cosmology, primordial waters remained above the dome of the sky and were released as rain (Gen. 1.7; 7.11). *Creditor . . . debtor:* For the use of the same image as a metaphor for national sovereignty, see 15.6. **13:** Further metaphors for autonomy, as at 15.6. **14:** *And turn . . . gods,* lit. "to go after other gods to worship them." See 6.14 n.

28.15–68: Consequences of disobedience. This long section has two subsections. The focus of the first (vv. 15–46) is a broad range of misfortunes, extending from infertility of crops, livestock, or the human population through to military defeat. The second unit (vv. 47–68) places its focus specifically on foreign invasion, siege, national defeat, and exile, reversing key components of the covenantal promises and of the nation's history of salvation. By disobeying the covenant, the nation undoes its own history. **15–46:** The first section is framed upon you this day, all these curses shall come upon you and take effect:

16 Cursed shall you be in the city and cursed shall you be in the country.

17 Cursed shall be your basket and your kneading bowl.

18 Cursed shall be the issue of your womb and the produce of your soil, the calving of your herd and the lambing of your flock.

19 Cursed shall you be in your comings and cursed shall you be in your goings.

20 The LORD will let loose against you calamity, panic, and frustration in all the enterprises you undertake, so that you shall soon be utterly wiped out because of your evildoing in forsaking Me. 21 The LORD will make pestilence cling to you, until He has put an end to you in the land that you are entering to possess. 22 The LORD will strike you with ªconsumption, fever, and inflammation, with scorching heat and drought, with blight and mildew; they shall hound you until you perish. 23 The skies above your head shall be copper and the earth under you iron. 24 The LORD will make the rain of your land dust, and sand shall drop on you from the sky, until you are wiped out.

25 The LORD will put you to rout before your enemies; you shall march out against them by a single road, but flee from them by many b roads; and you shall become a horror to all the kingdoms of the earth. 26 Your carcasses shall become food for all the birds of the sky and all the beasts of the earth, with none to frighten them off.

27 The LORD will strike you with the Egyptian inflammation,c with hemorrhoids, boil-scars, and itch, from which you shall never recover.

a Exact nature of these afflictions uncertain.
b Lit. "seven."   c See Exod. 9.9–10.

---

by an ancient editorial device, a chiastic inclusio, whereby the initial sequence AB is repeated at the end of the unit as B'A'. Thus, the sequence in v. 15, *not obey . . . to observe* (A) and *these curses shall come upon you and take effect* (B) is reversed in v. 45 as *these curses shall befall you . . . overtake you* (B', identical in the Hebrew) and *not heed . . . keep the commandments* (A'). **15:** A precise negation of v. 1: Disobedience negates blessing and occasions punishment. *Come upon you and take effect:* The verbs are animate and active; the curses are

almost personified, as if they had agency or acted by themselves to punish those who infringe the covenant (cf. Exod. 12.23). **16–19:** Negating vv. 3–6. **20:** Corresponding to the promise of tripartite blessing for obedience (v. 8: agriculture, activity, and land) stands the triple threat of *calamity, panic, and frustration.* The first term would more accurately be translated "curse," as the precise negation of blessing. The threats summarized by this verse are spelled out in the rest of the section (vv. 21–44). *Me:* Moses speaks on

behalf of God directly: Note the shift to the first person from third person reference to God (as at 7.4; 17.3). The shift takes place in the opposite direction in the Decalogue (cf. 5.6, 11). **21–44:** This section echoes the state treaties imposed by the Neo-Assyrian empire upon its vassal states in order to ensure loyalty and tribute (826–625 BCE). The degree of similarity suggests that the curse section of these state treaties, either directly or by way of Aramaic translation, provided a model for the authors of this chapter to use in describing Israel's relationship to God. According to biblical narratives, Judah was a vassal to the Assyrian empire (2 Kings 18.13–18) and both Neo-Assyrian and Judean officials freely employed Aramaic (2 Kings 18.26–27). **23:** *Copper . . . iron:* See VTE §63–64: "May [the gods] make your ground like iron . . . Just as rain does not fall from a bronze sky. . . ." **25:** The routers of v. 7 become the routed. *You shall become a horror:* The Septuagint reads "you shall become a 'diaspora,' " reinterpreting the Hebrew so as to reflect the historical circumstances of its 3rd century BCE Alexandrian authors. **26:** Deuteronomic law requires even executed criminals to be buried by sundown, lest their corpses become carrion (21.22–23); the abrogation of that religious norm here underscores the punishment's horror (Jer 7.33). **27–35:** The sequence of punishments specified in this section initially seems arbitrary: skin inflammation (v. 27); blindness (vv. 28–29); and loss of wife, house, and property (vv. 30a, 30b, 33). The sequence finds its explanation, however, in VTE §39–43, where each curse is associated with a particular god within the Neo-Assyrian pantheon. The moon god Sin is responsible for leprosy; the sun god Shamash for blindness; and Dilipat (the planet Venus) for rape, dispossession, and pillage by a foreign army. The arrangement of the curses follows the rank of the deities within that pantheon's hierarchy. **27:** *Egyptian*

28 The LORD will strike you with madness, blindness, and dismay.[a] 29 You shall grope at noon as a blind man gropes in the dark; you shall not prosper in your ventures, but shall be constantly abused and robbed, with none to give help.

30 If you pay the bride-price for a wife, another man shall enjoy her. If you build a house, you shall not live in it. If you plant a vineyard, you shall not harvest it.[b] 31 Your ox shall be slaughtered before your eyes, but you shall not eat of it; your ass shall be seized in front of you, and it shall not be returned to you; your flock shall be delivered to your enemies, with none to help you. 32 Your sons and daughters shall be delivered to another people, while you look on; and your eyes shall strain for them constantly, but you shall be helpless. 33 A people you do not know shall eat up the produce of your soil and all your gains; you shall be abused and downtrodden continually, 34 until you are driven mad by what your eyes behold. 35 The LORD will afflict you at the knees and thighs with a severe inflammation, from which you shall never recover—from the sole of your foot to the crown of your head.

36 The LORD will drive you, and the king you have set over you, to a nation unknown to you or your fathers, where you shall serve other gods, of wood and stone. 37 You shall be a consternation, a proverb, and a byword among all the peoples to which the LORD will drive you.

38 Though you take much seed out to the field, you shall gather in little, for the locust shall consume it. 39 Though you plant vineyards and till them, you shall have no wine to drink or store, for the worm shall devour them. 40 Though you have olive trees throughout your territory, you shall have no oil for anointment, for your olives shall drop off. 41 Though you beget sons and daughters, they shall not remain with you, for they shall go into captivity. 42 The cricket shall take over all the trees and produce of your land.

43 The stranger in your midst shall rise above you higher and higher, while you sink lower and lower: 44 he shall be your creditor, but you shall not be his; he shall be the head and you the tail.

45 All these curses shall befall you; they shall pursue you and overtake you, until you are wiped out, because you did not heed the LORD your God and keep the commandments and laws that He enjoined upon you. 46 They shall serve as signs and proofs against you and your offspring for all time. 47 Because you would not serve the

inflammation: inversion of 7.15; see Exod. 9.9–11. **28–29:** Blindness: The Mesopotamian sun god Shamash punishes disobedience by withholding light and vision. Shamash is also the god of justice. Thus, his punishment entails the breakdown of civil order and legal standards: You shall be constantly abused and robbed. **30:** Wife . . . house . . . vineyard: Contrast 20.7, which provides the same conditions for exemption from conscription, in different order. **32:** The sale of the children to foreigners as slaves guarantees their non-return (Gen. 37.25–38). **36:** Both the Neo-Assyrian army (2 Kings ch 17) and the Neo-Babylonian invaders (2 Kings chs 24–25) practiced deportation. **37:** Byword: The nation's fate will become a negative standard that all other peoples will hope to avoid. The opposite idea was central to God's covenant with Abraham, whose people were to become the paradigm of divine providence (Gen. 12.3). **38–42:** Futility curses. The frustration of human labor through infertility of the harvest (caused by insects or other natural enemies) is here presented as punishment for infringement of the covenant, reversing the blessings of vv. 7–14. From this perspective, crop failure is interpreted as divine judgment (Lev. 26.20; Amos 4.7–12). **43–44:** Reversing vv. 12b–13. **45–46:** Summary statement that, in conjunction with vv. 38–44, shows systematically how disobedience undoes blessing: (A) the blessings of agricultural and reproductive fertility (vv. 11–12a) and (B) economic independence and political sovereignty (vv. 12b–13), which result from (C) obedience (vv. 13b–14), are reversed with (A') failure of crops and loss of progeny (vv. 38–42) and (B') political and economic domination by foreigners (vv. 43–44), all of which result from (C') disobedience to the covenant (v. 45). **46:** Signs and proofs, more commonly translated "sign(s) and marvel(s)," as at 29.2. These terms normally specify the miracles performed by God on behalf of Israel at the time of the exo-

---

a Lit. "numbness of heart."   *b* Cf. 20.6.

LORD your God in joy and gladness over the abundance of everything, [48] you shall have to serve—in hunger and thirst, naked and lacking everything—the enemies whom the LORD will let loose against you. He will put an iron yoke upon your neck until He has wiped you out.

[49] The LORD will bring a nation against you from afar, from the end of the earth, which will swoop down like the eagle—a nation whose language you do not understand, [50] a ruthless nation, that will show the old no regard and the young no mercy. [51] It shall devour the offspring of your cattle and the produce of your soil, until you have been wiped out, leaving you nothing of new grain, wine, or oil, of the calving of your herds and the lambing of your flocks, until it has brought you to ruin. [52] It shall shut you up in all your towns throughout your land until every mighty, towering wall in which you trust has come down. And when you are shut up in all your towns throughout your land that the LORD your God has assigned to you, [53] you shall eat your own issue, the flesh of your sons and daughters that the LORD your God has assigned to you, because of the desperate straits to which your enemy shall reduce you. [54] He who is most tender and fastidious among you shall be too mean to his brother and the wife of his bosom and the children he has spared [55] to share with any of them the flesh of the children that he eats, because he has nothing else left as a result of the desperate straits to which your enemy shall reduce you in all your towns. [56] And she who is most tender and dainty among you, so tender and dainty that she would never venture to set a foot on the ground, shall begrudge the husband of her bosom, and her son and her daughter, [57] the afterbirth that issues from between her legs and the babies she bears; she shall eat them secretly, because of utter want, in the desperate straits to which your enemy shall reduce you in your towns.

[58] If you fail to observe faithfully all the terms of this Teaching that are written in this book, to reverence this

---

to the offense: *Because you would not serve . . . (v. 47) you shall have to serve:* Israel is judged by talionic justice ("an eye for an eye"). The formulation works on the double meaning of the key Hebrew word: "to serve" can refer to sacrificial worship of God (13.5) as well as to labor as a servant or slave (see 5.13 n.). God thus redeemed Israel from servitude in Egypt so that, in freedom, they serve Him in the covenant (Lev. 25.42, 55). *Iron yoke,* symbolizing vassal status, as in Jer. chs 27–28. **49–57:** Systematic presentation of foreign conquest, proceeding from invasion (vv. 48–50), to the invaders' plunder and despoiling of the land (v. 51), to crippling siege (v. 52), and culminating in the horrors of starvation that arise from the siege (vv. 53–57). These descriptions of the invader and of the consequences of the siege are based upon the literary model of the Vassal Treaty of Esarhadon. **49–52:** Closely parallels Jer. 5.15–19. **49:** *Like the eagle,* cf. Ezek. 17.3–7; Hab. 1.8. **51:** Contrast the idealistic war laws of 20.19–20, which prohibit occupiers from despoiling the land. **52:** *It shall shut you up . . . until every . . . wall . . . has come down:* The Neo-Assyrian (2 Kings 17.5) and Neo-Babylonian armies (2 Kings 24.3; 25.1–7) employed advanced engineering to mount a siege campaign involving ramparts, battering rams, and catapults. **53–57:** The starvation resulting from the siege causes a complete breakdown of the normal social order, as parents become predators of their children and family members compete for food. For cannibalism under siege conditions, see Lev. 26.29; 2 Kings 6.28–32; Jer. 19.9; Ezek. 5.10; Lam. 2.20; 4.10; and VTE §§47, 69, 71, 75.

28.58–68: Undoing the exodus. The orientation here differs considerably from what precedes; the unit seems to represent a third layer to the chapter. **58:** The Mosaic speaker has thus far urged Israel to obey God's "commandments which I enjoin upon you this day" (v. 1; similarly, vv. 13–14).

---

dus (4.34; 6.22; 7.19; 34.11; Exod. 7.3; 8.19; 10.1–2; 11.9–10). They now threaten instead to immortalize the divine punishment of Israel, as even language is now inverted against the nation.

28.47–57: Scenario of foreign invasion. This unit, outside the frame provided by vv. 15, 45–46, seems like a later appendix. **47:** *Because you would not serve:* Here the

detailed depiction of the future curse is based upon wrongdoing already committed in the past, in contrast to the conditional formulation of v. 15, which presents the disobedience as a future possibility. *Abundance:* The threat that prosperity in the land will cause Israel to forget the source of that comfort is here realized (see 6.11–12; 8.11–20; 33.15, 18). **48:** The punishment corresponds precisely honored and awesome Name, the LORD your God, ⁵⁹ the LORD will inflict extraordinary plagues upon you and your offspring, strange and lasting plagues, malignant and chronic diseases. ⁶⁰ He will bring back upon you all the sicknesses of Egypt that you dreaded so, and they shall cling to you. ⁶¹ Moreover, the LORD will bring upon you all the other diseases and plagues that are not mentioned in this book of Teaching, until you are wiped out. ⁶² You shall be left a scant few, after having been as numerous as the stars in the skies, because you did not heed the command of the LORD your God. ⁶³ And as the LORD once delighted in making you prosperous and many, so will the LORD now delight in causing you to perish and in wiping you out; you shall be torn from the land that you are about to enter and possess.

⁶⁴ The LORD will scatter you among all the peoples from one end of the earth to the other, and there you shall serve other gods, wood and stone, whom neither you nor your ancestors have experienced.ᵃ ⁶⁵ Yet even among those nations you shall find no peace, nor shall your foot find a place to rest. The LORD will give you there an anguished heart and eyes that pine and a despondent spirit. ⁶⁶ The life you face shall be precarious; you shall be in terror, night and day, with no assurance of survival. ⁶⁷ In the morning you shall say, "If only it were evening!" and in the evening you shall say, "If only it were morning!"—because of what your heart shall dread and your eyes shall see. ⁶⁸ The LORD will send you back to Egypt in galleys, by a route which I told you you should not see again. There you shall offer yourselves for sale to your enemies as male and female slaves, but none will buy.

⁶⁹ These are the terms of the covenant which the LORD commanded Moses to conclude with the Israelites in the

a See note at 11.28.

Here, in contrast, Israel must obey *the terms of this Teaching that are written in this book.* How the commandments have already become transformed from oral proclamation into a written text, i.e., Torah in its later sense, is unexplained, since it is not until 31.9, 24 that Moses commands that the Torah be put into writing as a book. Moreover, hitherto the required obedience was to the plural "commandments" (vv. 1, 9, 13, 15, 45). Here, for the first time in the chap-

ter, Israel must obey a codified, single *Teaching. This . . . Name:* distinctively, *Name* stands directly for God (elsewhere in the Torah only Lev. 24.11). The word's special reference is explained by the following *the* LORD, which denotes the Tetragrammaton (YHVH), God's personal name. **59–68:** Consistent with the "book" perspective, the consequences for breach of the written Torah have a different focus than the preceding horrors of foreign invasion. Contra-

vention of the Torah triggers a systematic reversal of the national history, covenantal promises, and theology included in that Torah. The punishment amounts to an anti-Torah that will dissolve the national identity. **59–61:** *Bring back . . . sicknesses:* After the miracle of the exodus, God had promised, if the people obeyed, "I will not bring upon you any of the diseases that I brought upon the Egyptians" (Exod. 15.26). Now the threat implicit in that conditional promise becomes realized (also vv. 21–22, 35; 7.15). **62:** *Stars . . . skies:* God will cancel the promise made to Abraham that his people shall be as numerous as the stars of heaven (Gen. 15.5–6). The covenantal promise of peoplehood (Gen. 12.2) will thus be rescinded. **63:** Dispossession and exile (as in 4.26; Lev. 26.33–39) rescinds the covenantal promise of the land, contravening even the unconditional divine promises of Gen. 12.7 and 13.17. **64:** The double loss of Israel's identity: Dispersion of the population dissolves its political identity, and idol worship dissolves its religious identity. **65–67:** In the absence of the national destiny provided by the covenant, historical existence has no meaning. **68:** Forced return to Egypt, where the former taskmasters now spurn Israel's desperate bid to sell itself back into slavery and thus to undo its own history. For selling oneself into slavery under financial hardship to pay off debts or gain support ("indenture"), see Lev. 25.39. *Route which I told you you should not see again* (cf. 17.16): Although the reference to the "route" or "direction" is unclear, the threat reverses the unconditional promise by Moses at the time of the exodus: "the Egyptians whom you see today you will never see again" (Exod. 14.13). The covenant violations by Israel are so serious that Moses threatens to abrogate that promise.

28.69–30.20: The third discourse of Moses: The ratification ceremony for the covenant on the plains of Moab. Israel is formally land of Moab, in addition to the covenant which He had made with them at Horeb.

29 Moses summoned all Israel and said to them: You have seen all that the LORD did before your very eyes in the land of Egypt, to Pharaoh and to all his courtiers and to his whole country: ² the wondrous feats that you saw with your own eyes, those prodigious signs and marvels. ³ Yet to this day the LORD has not given you a mind to understand or eyes to see or ears to hear.

⁴ I led you through the wilderness forty years; the clothes on your back did not wear out, nor did the sandals on your feet; ⁵ you had no bread to eat and no wine or other intoxicant to drink—that you might know that I the LORD am your God.

⁶ When you reached this place, King Sihon of Heshbon and King Og of Bashan came out to engage us in battle, but we defeated them. ⁷ We took their land and gave it to the Reubenites, the Gadites, and the half-tribe of Manasseh as their heritage. ⁸ Therefore observe faithfully all the terms of this covenant, that you may succeed in all that you undertake.

NITSAVIM   נצבים

⁹ You stand this day, all of you, before the LORD your God—your tribal heads, your elders and your officials, all

adjured to enter the covenant: to swear to obey the laws of chs 12–26 under penalty of the sanctions of ch 28. **28.69–29.28:** A didactic review of Israel's history (29.1–8) precedes an imprecation to ensure loyal adherence to the covenant (vv. 9–28). The people are formally assembled and instructed in the serious consequences of what they are about to undertake. **28.69: Editorial Heading.** NJPS follows the Masoretic textual division, understanding the verse as a colophon that concludes the second discourse of Moses (4.44–28.69). In contrast, most English translations follow the more logical Septuagint system, which regards the verse (as 29.1) as a superscription to the third discourse (29.1–30.20). Similar formulae (*these are the . . .*) are used to introduce the first and second discourses (1.1; 4.45). *The covenant . . . Moab:* This editorial heading provides two new perspectives on the legal corpus. (1) The earlier "laws and rules" (12.1) are now seen as a unified, single *covenant* between God and Israel. This perspective is absent from the legal corpus itself, where the word "covenant" appears only at 17.2. In this third discourse, however, that understanding becomes the norm (see 28.69; 29.8, 11, 13, 20, 24; 31.16, 20). (2) The second new perspective regards the laws of Moab as a covenant *in addition* to the one made at Horeb; the phrase suggests an editor's attempt to work in a later version of a law or narrative alongside an earlier one (Gen. 26.1; Lev. 23.38). This view stylizes Deuteronomy—originally intended as an independent body of law—as now working in tandem with prior law. It is striking that, in other contexts, Deuteronomy does not take the covenant at Horeb into account but presents itself as an independent and autonomous covenant. There is no reference to Horeb in the redundant introductory formulae of 4.44–45 or, more importantly, in the superscription to the legal corpus at 12.1.

29.1–8. Didactic review of Israel's history. 29.1: *You have seen:* As at 5.2–4, Moses addresses the present generation, who are actually one generation removed from the miraculous events, as if they had themselves lived through the exodus and the wilderness wandering. **2:** *Signs . . . marvels,* see 28.46 n. **3:** *Yet to this day,* more accurately, "the LORD has not given you until today." The thrust is to stress informed consent. The admonition creates a tension with the preceding two verses: the addressees who "have seen" The miraculous events (v. 1), which their own "eyes" saw (v. 2), are accused of having lacked *eyes to see.* The castigation reflects the episodes of rebellion (9.7–24). **4–5:** The Mosaic homily reinterprets the wilderness wandering, originally intended as divine punishment of Israel (Num. 14.13–35), and presents it positively, in didactic terms. **4:** *I:* For the intrusion of divine speech into Mosaic speech, see 7.4, 17.3, 28.20, 68. *Clothes . . . feet,* see 8.4. **5:** *You had no bread to eat . . . no wine . . . to drink:* The sense is, "It was not bread that you ate . . . nor wine that you drank." The manna, quail, and water that Israel consumed were supplied by divine providence (8.2–5; Exod. ch 16; Num. 11.4–9, 31–33). *Know:* The miraculous sustenance of Israel in the desert was intended didactically to bring the people to God (8.3). Knowledge here is not abstract speculation but the recognition of God's historical actions on behalf of the nation. *I the LORD am your God,* better, "I, YHVH, am your God" (6.4; Exod. 20.2). **6–7:** See 1.4; 2.26–3.22; Num. 21.21–35.

29.9–28: Imprecation to ensure loyalty to the covenant. 9: *Stand . . . all of you,* in formal array for a public legal ceremony (see the men of Israel, [10] your children, your wives, even the stranger within your camp, from woodchopper to water drawer—[11] to enter into the covenant of the LORD your God, which the LORD your God is concluding with you this day, with its sanctions;[a] [12] to the end that He may establish you this day as His people and be your God, as He promised you and as He swore to your fathers, Abraham, Isaac, and Jacob. [13] I make this covenant, with its sanctions, not with you alone, [14] but both with those who are standing here with us this day before the LORD our God and with those who are not with us here this day.

[15] Well you know that we dwelt in the land of Egypt and that we passed through the midst of various other nations; [16] and you have seen the detestable things and the fetishes of wood and stone, silver and gold, that they keep. [17] Perchance there is among you some man or woman, or some clan or tribe, whose heart is even now turning away from the LORD our God to go and worship the gods of those nations—perchance there is among you a stock sprouting poison weed and wormwood. [18] When such a one hears the words of these sanctions, he may fancy himself immune, thinking, "I shall be safe, though I follow my own willful heart"—to the utter ruin of moist and dry alike.[b] [19] The LORD will never forgive him; rather will the LORD's anger and passion rage against that man, till every sanction recorded in this book comes down upon him, and the LORD blots out his name from under heaven.

[20] The LORD will single them[c] out from all the tribes of Israel for misfortune, in accordance with all the sanctions of the covenant recorded in this book of Teaching. [21] And later generations will ask—the children who succeed you,

a I.e., the curses that violations of the covenant will entail.

b I.e., everything.   c I.e., clan or tribe, v. 17.

Ps. 82.1). *This day,* making the transition from historical review (28.69–29.7) to present adjuration (similarly, VTE §33). **10:** In Deuteronomy, all, including women, are included in the covenantal community. **11:** *Covenant . . . with its sanctions:* This legal formula recurs at v. 13, thus framing the central idea of the covenant: the binding relationship between God and Israel. *Sanctions,* more accurately, "its imprecation" or "its curse" (see translators' note a). Treaty infraction is punished with "all the curses of the covenant" (v. 20,

more accurately translating the same Hebrew terms), which are named and sworn to in advance. As in the colloquial expression that joins a promise ("Cross my heart") to a pronouncement dooming oneself for noncompliance ("and hope to die"), so in the ancient Near East were covenants validated by means of a concluding imprecation (VTE §§37–56, 58–106). On that model, the preceding laws of chs 12–26 represent the treaty stipulations; ch 28, its sanctions; and ch 29, the formal ceremony of the imprecation.

13–14: The covenant binds even future generations (as in VTE §25, 33, 34, 57); consequently, the punishment for infraction of its terms extends to the third and fourth generation (5.9; Exod. 20.5; 34.7). **16–26:** A stark, two-part warning, showing how the attempt even of a single individual secretly to withdraw from the covenant (vv. 16–18) jeopardizes the entire nation (vv. 19–27). **17:** *Turning away,* transferring loyalty from God to other gods (13.6–11; 17.2–7). *Poison weed and wormwood,* Hos. 10.4; Amos 5.7; 6.12. **18:** *Fancy himself immune,* rather than proclaim the imprecation, hoping to escape the sanctions of the covenant. *Moist and dry:* Most likely the paired antonyms designate totality (see 28.3–6 n.), but the exact meaning is lost. **19:** *Passion:* God is described as an "impassioned God" (5.9; Exod. 34.14; with the adjectival form of the same word), referring to His zeal to defend the mutual exclusivity of the covenant relation. *Comes down upon him,* more literally, "will crouch down upon them" (cf. Gen. 4.7), with the imprecation here almost animate. *Blots out his name:* The image is of the erasure of a tablet or scroll (Num. 5.23), given a theological cast based on the Mesopotamian idea that the divine decree of human fate is inscribed in a heavenly book. Erasure from this book, then, symbolizes punishment (9.14; Gen. 6.7; Exod. 17.14; 32.32; 2 Kings 14.27; Ps. 9.6). This early, non-Israelite idea figures prominently in the later Jewish liturgy for Rosh Ha-Shanah (the Jewish New Year) and Yom Kippur (the Day of Atonement). **21–27:** The negative instruction. As the wilderness wandering provided an instructional lesson for the nation (vv. 4–5), so will Israel, now herself transformed into a devastation, provide an object lesson for future generations and other nations. Normally this question-and-answer model, which anticipates the child's question, seeks to provide the rationale for ritual observance with reference to God's redemptive acts and foreigners who come from distant lands and see the plagues and diseases that the LORD has inflicted upon that land, 22 all its soil devastated by sulfur and salt, beyond sowing and producing, no grass growing in it, just like the upheaval of Sodom and Gomorrah, Admah and Zeboiim, which the LORD overthrew in His fierce anger—23 all nations will ask, "Why did the LORD do thus to this land? Wherefore that awful wrath?" 24 They will be told, "Because they forsook the covenant that the LORD, God of their fathers, made with them when He freed them from the land of Egypt; 25 they turned to the service of other gods and worshiped them, gods whom they had not experienced[a] and whom He had not allotted[b] to them. 26 So the LORD was incensed at that land and brought upon it all the curses recorded in this book. 27 The LORD uprooted them from their soil in anger, fury, and great wrath, and cast them into another land, as is still the case."

28 Concealed acts concern the LORD our God; but with overt acts, it is for us and our children ever to apply all the provisions of this Teaching.

30 When all these things befall you—the blessing and the curse that I have set before you—and you take them to heart amidst the various nations to which the LORD your God has banished you, 2 and you return to the LORD your God, and you and your children heed His command with all your heart and soul, just as I enjoin upon you this day, 3 then the LORD your God will restore your fortunes[c] and take you back in love. He will bring you together again from all the peoples where the LORD your God has scattered you. 4 Even if your outcasts are at the ends of the world,[d] from there the LORD your God will gather you, from there He will fetch you. 5 And the LORD

a See note at 11.28.   b See 4.19–20.   c Others "captivity."   d Lit. "sky."

(4.32–38; Exod. 12.25–27; 13.8–10). Reversing that scenario, the lesson here involves divine punishment for breach of covenant (see 1 Kings 9.9). **22:** *Sulfur and salt* were used in antiquity as chemical defoliants by invading armies. *Sodom . . . Zeboiim:* The land's resulting sterility will recall the divine devastation of the proverbial wicked cities located in the arid area around the Dead Sea (Gen. 19.24–25; Isa. 1.9–10). **24:** *The covenant,* conflating the covenants of Horeb and Moab (28.69). **25:** *Gods . . . not allot-*

ted *to them:* As at 32.8–9, the idea is that each nation is allocated its own god, and that YHVH is the God of Israel. As at 5.7–9, the existence of other deities is here conceded. Contrast 4.19, where it is rather only inanimate "stars . . . [that] God allotted," which reinterprets the polytheistic image from the later perspective of monotheism. **27:** *Cast them into another land, as is still the case:* The reference to the present implies that the chapter was composed subsequent to the Babylonian exile of 586 BCE.

28: *Concealed acts* may, as here, refer to acts that God will punish (vv. 17–18); or to future events. More likely, the antithesis rejects religions that define truth in terms of esoteric speculation and restrict access to such truth to a learned few. Instead, the Torah, based upon a public revelation (ch 5) and Mosaic instruction (chs 12–26), is accessible to all. Similarly, Israel's God is "near" and obedience to the revealed Torah constitutes "wisdom" (4.6–7). *For us and our children ever,* tripartite emphasis on lasting open access. *To apply* continues the antithesis: The Torah requires not esoteric speculation but moral and religious action.

30.1–10: Reassurance of restoration. The promise of restoration here contradicts the unconditional denial of divine pardon and the blotting out of Israel's name in 29.19. Indeed, this section, with its emphasis on restoration, does not logically follow ch 29, which urges obedience to the covenant by stressing the seriousness of its sanctions. The unit makes most sense as an insertion that serves the religious needs of a community different from that of the book's original audience (see v. 5 n.). Its literary and theological elegance is difficult to represent in English. The author uses the Heb word "shuv" (which can mean "return," "repent," or "restore") in seven different ways to establish the close bond between human repentance and divine forgiveness: (v. 1) If you *take them to heart . . .* (v. 2) and *return . . .* (v. 3) then the LORD will *restore your fortunes and take you back . . .* (v. 8) Then you shall *again* obey . . . (v. 9) For the LORD will *again* take delight . . . (v. 10) because you *return.* This notion of returning (using "shuv") is central to Deuteronomy 4 as well, and to prophetic literature, and is further developed into the rabbinic doctrine of "teshuvah" or repentance, which replaces the Priestly idea of "kapparah" or atonement. **4:** Contrast Amos 9.2–3. **5:** *Bring you to the land that your fathers possessed:* The your God will bring you to the land that your fathers possessed, and you shall possess it; and He will make you more prosperous and more numerous than your fathers. ⁶ Then the LORD your God will open up*ᵃ* your heart and the hearts of your offspring to love the LORD your God with all your heart and soul, in order that you may live. ⁷ The LORD your God will inflict all those curses upon the enemies and foes who persecuted you. ⁸ You, however, will again heed the LORD and obey all His commandments that I enjoin upon you this day. ⁹ And the LORD your God will grant you abounding prosperity in all your undertakings, in the issue of your womb, the offspring of your cattle, and the produce of your soil. For the LORD will again delight in your well-being, as He did in that of your fathers, ¹⁰ since you will be heeding the LORD your God and keeping His commandments and laws that are recorded in this book of the Teaching—once you return to the LORD your God with all your heart and soul.

¹¹ Surely, this Instruction which I enjoin upon you this day is not too baffling for you, nor is it beyond reach. ¹² It is not in the heavens, that you should say, "Who among us can go up to the heavens and get it for us and impart it to us, that we may observe it?" ¹³ Neither is it beyond the sea, that you should say, "Who among us can cross to the other side of the sea and get it for us and impart it to us, that we may observe it?" ¹⁴ No, the thing is very close to you, in your mouth and in your heart, to observe it.

¹⁵ See, I set before you this day life and prosperity, death and adversity. ¹⁶ For*ᵇ* I command you this day, to love the LORD your God, to walk in His ways, and to keep His commandments, His laws, and His rules, that you may thrive and increase, and that the LORD your God may

---

a Others "circumcise."
b Septuagint reads "If you obey the commandments of the LORD your God, which."

"you" no longer refers to the desert generation whom Moses, according to the narrative, addresses on the plains of Transjordan, as they are about to enter the land (ca. 1220 BCE). Instead, the perspective has shifted to that of the Judean exiles in Babylonia (586–539 BCE), who look forward to returning to the land they once occupied, and from which they have since been displaced. *More numerous,* using the language of the covenantal promise (Gen. 17.2; 22.17). For similar claims that the

future will repeat the past while also surpassing it, see Isa. 42.9; 43.6–20; 51.9–11. **6:** *The LORD . . . will open up* [lit. "circumcise"] *your heart:* God is the agent, in contrast with the previous call for Israel itself to "cut away . . . the thickening about your hearts" (see 10.16 n.). The change in perspective suggests skepticism about the people's ability to effect such a change of heart independently. Still more skepticism is evident in the prophetic vision of a divine "reprogramming" of the human

heart by inscribing the Torah upon it (Jer. 31.31–34; Ezek. 11.19–20; 36.26–27). **7:** The curses are deflected from Israel to the adversary; contrast 28.47, 49, where the foreign nation functions as God's agent to punish Israel for its disobedience. **9:** *Issue . . . offspring . . . produce:* The blessings upon return from exile conform to those promised upon initial entry into the land (28.4). **10:** *Heeding the LORD . . . and keeping His . . . laws that are recorded in this book of the Teaching:* The reference is to the text of Deuteronomy itself, which replaces the live speech of Moses (12.28; 13.1) or prophetic speech (18.18–9) as authoritative revealer of God's word.

30.11–20: The original continuation of ch 29, with two sections: vv. 11–14, 15–20. **11–14: The accessibility of Torah.** Turning their own characteristic imagery against them, the passage challenges the assumptions of Near Eastern wisdom schools about the inaccessibility of divine wisdom and the limits of human knowledge (cf. Job ch 28). **11:** *Surely,* better, "because," logically continuing 29.28 and emphasizing the ready accessibility of the Torah. The NJPS translation is an accommodation to the insertion of vv. 1–10. *This Instruction,* when used in the singular, refers to the Torah as a whole (as at 6.1); the contrasting plural use designates the individual stipulations (v. 10; 4.2, 40; 5.10; 6.17). **12:** See Prov. 30.4. *That we may observe it,* lit. "so that He may proclaim it to us." **14:** *In your mouth:* In antiquity, written texts were normally read, taught, and recited aloud rather than silently (6.7; 31.19, 21; Josh. 1.8). **15–20: The necessity of choice.** If "life" meant only biological life, there would be no choice. The choice is rather between life in the covenant and life not in the covenant. From this viewpoint, biological existence, and even prosperity, if not in the covenant, constitutes death. **16:** *Love . . . walk in His ways:* In the technical language of Near Eastern treaties, "love" means to act loy-

bless you in the land that you are about to enter and possess. [17] But if your heart turns away and you give no heed,
and are lured into the worship and service of other gods,
[18] I declare to you this day that you shall certainly perish;
you shall not long endure on the soil that you are crossing
the Jordan to enter and possess. [19] I call heaven and earth
to witness against you this day: I have put before you life
and death, blessing and curse. Choose life—if you and
your offspring would live—[20] by loving the LORD your
God, heeding His commands, and holding fast to Him.
For thereby you shall have life and shall long endure upon
the soil that the LORD swore to your ancestors, Abraham,
Isaac, and Jacob, to give to them.

VA-YELEKH   וילך

31 [a]Moses went and spoke[-a] these things to all Israel.
[2] He said to them:

*a-a An ancient Heb. ms. and the Septuagint read: "When Moses had finished speak-
ing . . ."; cf. 29.1.*

ally and to honor the commitments of the treaty (6.5 n.).
19: *Heaven and earth to witness,* see
4.26; 32.1 n. *Choose life:* Joshua reiterates the necessity of choice (Josh.
24.15). The didactic use of life and
death suggests the influence of
wisdom teachings upon the authors (Prov. 11.19; 14.27; 18.21; cf.
Jer. 8.3; 21.8).

**31.1–34.12: The death of Moses
and the formation of the Torah.**
With the imprecation of ch 30
marking the conclusion of the
treaty between God and Israel,
Deuteronomy now returns to
Moses, the mediator of the treaty,
as his life draws to a close. The inevitable question of succession is
here given a twofold answer, as
befits the role of Moses as both political and religious leader of Israel. Moses invests Joshua with
leadership in political and military
matters (31.1–8, 14–15, 23; 32.44,
48–52; 34.9), while also "putting
down in writing the words of this
Teaching" (31.24) to instruct the
nation in matters of religion. Deuteronomy thus ends in paradox:
Moses, ostensibly the book's
narrator, narrates his own death
(ch 34); and the book of the Torah,

which is already presupposed
(29.26), nevertheless provides an
account of its own formation
(31.9–13, 24–29). The conclusion of
Deuteronomy also marks, however, the conclusion of the Pentateuch. As they incorporated Deuteronomy into that larger work,
later editors with the background
of the exile contributed their perspectives on the function of the
Torah in the people's life. Finally,
the Pentateuch's literary precedent
of a patriarch's deathbed bequest
and blessing (Gen. chs 27, 48–49)
led to the incorporation of "The
Song of Moses" (32.1–43) and of
"The Blessing of Moses" (ch 33),
each of which may originally have
circulated independently. What results is a heavily "written over"
text that blends several viewpoints. Themes like the Mosaic
appointment of Joshua begin,
then begin again from a different
perspective, and then are continued only after an apparent digression, which marks the insertion of
new material. The editors sought
to incorporate later layers by patterning them after earlier ones,
often repeating their key terms,
while arranging the whole in
an overarching chiastic pattern

(AB:B'A'A"). See diagram on
page 438.

**31.1–29: Moses makes arrange-
ments for his death.** Publicly announcing his imminent death,
Moses invests Joshua with leadership and initiates the writing
down of the Torah, which is to be
taught regularly to the entire people. These two legacies seem independent of each other and suggest
that an earlier narrative, concerned
with the leadership issue, has been
expanded to provide an account of
the formation of the book of Deuteronomy. But, perhaps because of
the importance of each of these
two traditions, and the pivotal role
occupied by Deuteronomy in the
Pentateuch, each tradition is itself
doubled. The chapter is thus quite
complex and contains many layers
of tradition: (a) There is a double
announcement of the imminent
mortality of Moses: v. 1 (at the
initiative of Moses, citing previous divine commandment) and
vv. 14–15 (with no reference to a
previous announcement). (b)
There is a corresponding double
tradition concerning the transfer of
leadership. Although Moses begins a public ceremony in order
himself to appoint the new leader
(vv. 7–8), a variant tradition has
God commission Joshua directly
(vv. 14–15, 23). (c) There is a double tradition concerning what
Moses writes: one of "the words
. . . of this Teaching" (v. 24) and
one of "this poem" (v. 19). Each is
to serve as a "witness" (vv. 21, 26).
The first tradition, which refers to
Deuteronomy, was supplemented
by the second in order to integrate
the following "Song of Moses"
(32.1–43). (d) In the "Song" tradition, Israel's future apostasy is
already a foregone conclusion
(vv. 16–22; 28–29); in the covenant-
making tradition, there is yet hope
that, by taking the law to heart,
Israel might avoid catastrophe
(vv. 9–13, 24–27).

   31.1: *Moses went and spoke:* The
Septuagint and Qumran texts attest an alternate version, "Moses
finished speaking" (see translators'
note *a-a;* in Hebrew, the difference

I am now one hundred and twenty years old, I can no longer ᵃbe active.ᵃ Moreover, the LORD has said to me, "You shall not go across yonder Jordan." ³ The LORD your God Himself will cross over before you; and He Himself will wipe out those nations from your path and you shall dispossess them.—Joshua is the one who shall cross before you, as the LORD has spoken.—⁴ The LORD will do to them as He did to Sihon and Og, kings of the Amorites, and to their countries, when He wiped them out. ⁵ The LORD will deliver them up to you, and you shall deal with them in full accordance with the Instruction that I have enjoined upon you. ⁶ Be strong and resolute, be not in fear or in dread of them; for the LORD your God Himself marches with you: He will not fail you or forsake you.

⁷ Then Moses called Joshua and said to him in the sight

a-a Lit. "come and go."

between the two involves only the transposition of two consonants). The latter reading may make more sense since it creates an exact parallel between this verse and 32.45, each of which marks a transition between two sections of text and

is continued by "and he said to them . . ." (v. 2; 32.46).

2: *I am now one hundred and twenty years old:* The Hebrew places the age first, thus immediately announcing the key issue in the plot. Moses has reached the

maximum age allocated by God to humans (Gen. 6.3); the imminence of death makes it urgent to assure continuity of leadership. *I can no longer be active,* lit. "go out and come in," referring specifically to military leadership (Num. 27.17; 1 Kings 3.7; cf. 2 Sam. 11.1).

2–3: Resumes 1.37–38; 3.27–28. The death of a key leader and the transfer of his authority mark important turning points within the larger context of the Deuteronomistic History and partially follow a common model (cf. Josh. 23.2; 1 Sam. 12.2; 1 Kings 2.1–2). **4:** The successful military campaigns in Transjordan provide assurance in the conquest of Canaan; Moses aims to counter Israel's intimidation (1.27–28; Num. chs 13–14). **5:** *The Instruction that I have enjoined upon you* refers to the ban (7.1–7; 12.29–31; 20.16–18). **7–8:** The speech commissioning Joshua into office includes three formal elements: encouragement *(Be strong and resolute),* description of the task *(for it is you who . . .),*

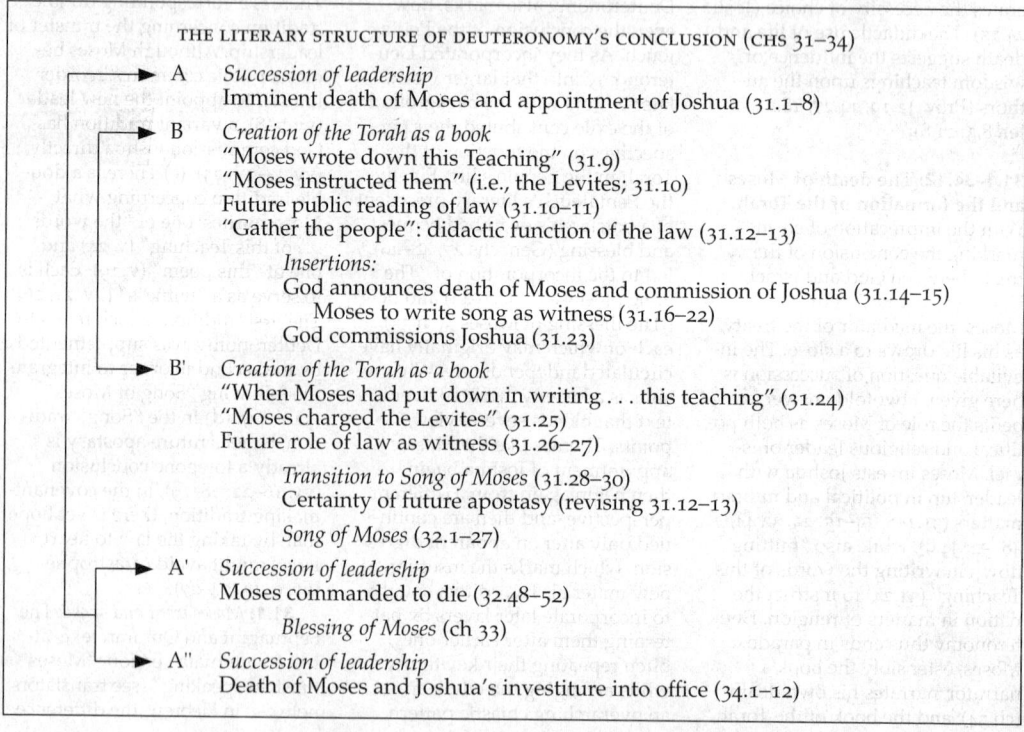

THE LITERARY STRUCTURE OF DEUTERONOMY'S CONCLUSION (CHS 31–34)

A   *Succession of leadership*
    Imminent death of Moses and appointment of Joshua (31.1–8)

B   *Creation of the Torah as a book*
    "Moses wrote down this Teaching" (31.9)
    "Moses instructed them" (i.e., the Levites; 31.10)
    Future public reading of law (31.10–11)
    "Gather the people": didactic function of the law (31.12–13)

      Insertions:
      God announces death of Moses and commission of Joshua (31.14–15)
        Moses to write song as witness (31.16–22)
      God commissions Joshua (31.23)

B'   *Creation of the Torah as a book*
    "When Moses had put down in writing . . . this teaching" (31.24)
    "Moses charged the Levites" (31.25)
    Future role of law as witness (31.26–27)

      Transition to Song of Moses (31.28–30)
      Certainty of future apostasy (revising 31.12–13)

      Song of Moses (32.1–27)

A'   *Succession of leadership*
    Moses commanded to die (32.48–52)

      Blessing of Moses (ch 33)

A"   *Succession of leadership*
    Death of Moses and Joshua's investiture into office (34.1–12)

of all Israel: "Be strong and resolute, for it is you who shall go with this people into the land that the LORD swore to their fathers to give them, and it is you who shall apportion it to them. 8 And the LORD Himself will go before you. He will be with you; He will not fail you or forsake you. Fear not and be not dismayed!"

9 Moses wrote down this Teaching and gave it to the priests, sons of Levi, who carried the Ark of the LORD's Covenant, and to all the elders of Israel.

10 And Moses instructed them as follows: Every seventh year,ᵃ the year set for remission, at the Feast of Booths, 11 when all Israel comes to appear before the LORD your God in the place that He will choose, you shall read this Teaching aloud in the presence of all Israel. 12 Gather the people—men, women, children, and the strangers in your communities—that they may hear and so learn to revere the LORD your God and to observe faithfully every word of this Teaching. 13 Their children, too, who have not had the experience, shall hear and learn to revere the LORD your God as long as they live in the land that you are about to cross the Jordan to possess.

14 The LORD said to Moses: The time is drawing near for you to die. Call Joshua and present yourselves in the Tent of Meeting, that I may instruct him. Moses and Joshua went and presented themselves in the Tent of Meeting. 15 The LORD appeared in the Tent, in a pillar of cloud, the pillar of cloud having come to rest at the entrance of the tent.

16 The LORD said to Moses: You are soon to lie with your fathers. This people will thereupon go astray after the alien gods in their midst, in the land that they are about to enter; they will forsake Me and break My covenant that I made with them. 17 Then My anger will flare up against them, and I will abandon them and hide My countenance from them. They shall be ready prey; and many evils and troubles shall befall them. And they shall say on that day, "Surely it is because our God is not in our midst that these evils have befallen us." 18 Yet I will keep My countenance hidden on that day, because of all the evil they have done in turning to other gods. 19 Therefore, write down this poem and teach it to the people of Israel; put it in their mouths, in order that this poem may be My witness against the people of Israel. 20 When I bring them into the land flowing with milk and honey that I promised on oath to their fathers, and they eat their fill and grow fat and

and assurance of support (the LORD . . . will be with you). **9–13:** The institution of a covenant ceremony to be held every seven years, in the sabbatical year (15.1–11), during the Feast of Booths (16.13–15). **12:** The requirement that the law must be read publicly and taught to the assembled nation specifies the inclusion of women, minors, and non-Israelite resident aliens. The law does not restrict the responsibility to observe the covenant to males (contrast Exod. 19.15). **14:** Tent of Meeting: In the J source, the site outside of the camp where God speaks to Moses, with Joshua in attendance (Exod. 33.7–11). This tent should be distinguished from the Tabernacle of the Priestly literature, located in the center of the Israelite encampment and housing the Ark of the Covenant and the altar (Exod. chs 26–27; Num. 7.1–3; 18.1–7). That I may instruct him: The more standard tradition involves direct commission by Moses at God's command (3.27–28; 34.9; Num. 27.18–23). **15:** The double reference to the pillar of cloud, located both in the Tent (cf. Exod. 30.36; 40.34–35; Lev. 16.2) and at the entrance of the tent (cf. Exod. 33.9–10; Num. 12.5) blends the separate traditions associated with each of the two tents regarding the site of divine communication. **16:** Forsake: The punishment is measure for measure (v. 17). **17:** Our God: Although the word generally has this meaning, the Hebrew could also mean "our gods," which makes sense here. The people will have strayed so far from the covenant that they attribute the resulting divine punishment to other gods. This interpretation explains God's angry response (v. 18).

a See note at 15.1.

turn to other gods and serve them, spurning Me and breaking My covenant, [21] and the many evils and troubles befall them—then this poem shall confront them as a witness, since it will never be lost from the mouth of their offspring. For I know what plans they are devising even now, before I bring them into the land that I promised on oath.

[22] That day, Moses wrote down this poem and taught it to the Israelites.

[23] And He charged Joshua son of Nun: "Be strong and resolute: for you shall bring the Israelites into the land that I promised them on oath, and I will be with you."

[24] When Moses had put down in writing the words of this Teaching to the very end, [25] Moses charged the Levites who carried the Ark of the Covenant of the LORD, saying: [26] Take this book of Teaching and place it beside the Ark of the Covenant of the LORD your God, and let it remain there as a witness against you. [27] Well I know how defiant and stiffnecked you are: even now, while I am still alive in your midst, you have been defiant toward the LORD; how much more, then, when I am dead! [28] Gather to me all the elders of your tribes and your officials, that I may speak all these words to them and that I may call heaven and earth to witness against them. [29] For I know that, when I am dead, you will act wickedly and turn away from the path that I enjoined upon you, and that in time to come misfortune will befall you for having done evil in the sight of the LORD and vexed Him by your deeds.

[30] Then Moses recited the words of this poem to the very end, in the hearing of the whole congregation of Israel:

HA'AZINU   האזינו

32 Give ear, O heavens, let me speak;
Let the earth hear the words I utter!

2   May my discourse come down as the rain,
My speech distill as the dew,
Like showers on young growth,
Like droplets on the grass.[a]

3   For the name of the LORD I proclaim;
Give glory to our God!

4   The Rock!—His deeds are perfect,
Yea, all His ways are just;
A faithful God, never false,
True and upright is He.

---

a I.e., may my words be received eagerly; cf. Job 29.22–23.

22–23: The sequence of *Moses wrote down* (v. 22) and . . . *charged* (v. 23) uses the same key terms as "When Moses had put down in writing . . . Moses charged" (vv. 24–25). The repetition of the paired terms provided a means for editors to insert the section on the song (vv. 16–22). **23:** *And He charged*, lit. "He commanded," with no subject identified. NJPS, by capitalizing the pronoun, indicates the divine reference to clarify that the verse does not continue from v. 22 but directly resumes vv. 14–15.

31.30–32.44: The Song of Moses. The Song is a late insertion that reflects upon Israel's history and almost certainly presupposes the exile. The Song's literary form is a revised and expanded prophetic lawsuit (Isa. ch 1; Jer. ch 2; Mic. ch 6; Ps. 50). The basic structure is as follows: (1) Introduction, with summoning of witnesses (vv. 1–3); (2) Summary accusation of Israel's disloyalty (vv. 4–6); (3) Recital of God's loving actions on Israel's behalf as the basis for the charge (vv. 7–14); (4) Indictment of Israel as disloyal (vv. 15–18); (5) Declaration of the decision to punish Israel (vv. 19–25). At this very point, however, God interrupts His own judicial sentence to recognize a risk to His honor: other nations might conclude that Israel's God was weak should they see Israel destroyed (vv. 26–27). God reverses Himself, cancels the just-pronounced punishment, and decides instead to punish Israel's enemies so as to vindicate Israel (vv. 28–42). The Song concludes with a call for the divine council to praise God for His actions; the call may originate from within the divine council itself (v. 43; similarly, Ps. 29.1). A prose frame links the Song to Deuteronomy by identifying Moses, otherwise unmentioned in the poem, as its speaker (31.30; 32.44). **2:** The reference to *discourse*, and the criticism of Israel as "dull and witless" (v. 6) show how the original prophetic lawsuit has been combined with ideas taken from wisdom literature (Prov. 1.5; 4.2; 7.21). **4:** *Rock*, more

5a　Children unworthy of Him—
　　That crooked, perverse generation—
　　Their baseness has played Him false.
6　Do you thus requite the LORD,
　　O dull and witless people?
　　Is not He the Father who created you,
　　Fashioned you and made you endure!

7　Remember the days of old,
　　Consider the years of ages past;
　　Ask your father, he will inform you,
　　Your elders, they will tell you:
8　When the Most High gave nations their homes
　　And set the divisions of man,
　　He fixed the boundaries of peoples
　　In relation to Israel's numbers.
9　For the LORD's portion is His people,
　　Jacob His own allotment.

10　He found him in a desert region,
　　In an empty howling waste.
　　He engirded him, watched over him,
　　Guarded him as the pupil of His eye.
11　Like an eagle who rouses his nestlings,
　　Gliding down to his young,
　　So did He spread His wings and take him,
　　Bear him along on His pinions;
12　The LORD alone did guide him,
　　No alien god at His side.

13　He set him atop the highlands,
　　To feast on the yield of the earth;
　　He fed him honey from the crag,
　　And oil from the flinty rock,
14　Curd of kine and milk of flocks;
　　With the best[b] of lambs,
　　And rams of Bashan, and he-goats;
　　With the [c]very finest[c] wheat—
　　And foaming grape-blood was your drink.

a Meaning of Heb. uncertain.　　b Lit. "fat."
c-c "kidney fat of."

pantheon of gods ruled by the chief deity (Pss. 82.1; 89.6–8). Israelite authors regularly applied El's title to Israel's God (Gen. 14.18–22; Num. 24.16; Pss. 46.5; 47.3). Even the precise parallelism "Rock" / "'Elyon" (see v. 4; Ps. 78.35) reflects a conventional Ugaritic title for El. *In relation to Israel's numbers* is unintelligible as it stands. The variant attested by the Septuagint and at Qumran, "according to the sons of El" (cf. NRSV), which preserves the mythological reference to *Most High* ("'Elyon") earlier in the verse, makes much more sense. Here, the idea is that the chief god allocates the nations to lesser deities in the pantheon. (A postbiblical notion that seventy angels are in charge of the world's seventy nations echoes this idea.) Almost certainly, the unintelligible reading of the MT represents a "correction" of the original text (whereby God presides over other gods) to make it conform to the later standard of pure monotheism: There are no other gods! The polytheistic imagery of the divine council is also deleted at 32.43; 33.2–3, 7. **9:** *Portion:* This and the following term reflect ancient estate law: Israel is God's special inheritance (4.20; cf. 7.6; 14.2; 26.18). *Own allotment:* NJPS has added *own* in order to avoid the impression that 'Elyon, as head of the pantheon, has assigned Israel to YHVH, as merely a member of the pantheon. The translation suggests that Israel's God, here identified with Elyon, reserves Israel for Himself until the end. The Hebrew permits either reading. **10:** *Found* (Hos. 9.10): Overlooking the traditions about the slavery in Egypt, the Song here traces the beginnings of Israel to the wilderness period, romanticizing its ideal purity (similarly, Hos. 2.14–15; Jer. 2.2–3; contrast Deut. 9.6–7, 22–27; Ezek. ch 20). *Eagle,* as God, as an eagle, tenderly bears Israel as a fledgling (see Exod. 19.4). Ironically, the dietary laws prohibit the eagle as ritually unclean (14.12). **13:** *Highlands,* see Exod. 15.17. **14:** *Curd,* symbolic of extravagant hospitality offered to special guests (Gen.

accurately, "Mountain," a title applied to the high god of ancient Canaanite literature (see v. 8 n.) and to the biblical God (vv. 15, 18, 30, 31, 37; Isa. 44.8; Ps. 78.35). **6:** *Created you,* when God redeemed Israel from Egypt (Exod. 15.16). **8:** *Most High,* or "'Elyon," is the formal title of El, the senior god who presided over the divine council in the Ugaritic literature of ancient Canaan. The reference thus invokes, as do other biblical texts, the Near Eastern convention of a

15 So Jeshurun grew fat and kicked—
  You grew fat and gross and coarse[a]—
  He forsook the God who made him
  And spurned the Rock of his support.

16 They incensed Him with alien things,
  Vexed Him with abominations.

17 They sacrificed to demons, no-gods,
  Gods they had never known,
  New ones, who came but lately,
  [b-]Who stirred not your fathers' fears.[-b]

18 You neglected the Rock that begot you,
  Forgot the God who brought you forth.

19 The LORD saw and was vexed
  And spurned His sons and His daughters.

20 He said:
  I will hide My countenance from them,
  And see how they fare in the end.
  For they are a treacherous breed,
  Children with no loyalty in them.

21 They incensed Me with no-gods,
  Vexed Me with their futilities;[c]
  I'll incense them with a no-folk,
  Vex them with a nation of fools.

22 For a fire has flared in My wrath
  And burned to the bottom of Sheol,
  Has consumed the earth and its increase,
  Eaten down to the base of the hills.

23 I will sweep[a] misfortunes on them,
  Use up My arrows on them:

24 Wasting famine, ravaging plague,
  Deadly pestilence, and fanged beasts
  Will I let loose against them,
  With venomous creepers in dust.

25 The sword shall deal death without,
  As shall the terror within,
  To youth and maiden alike,
  The suckling as well as the aged.

26 [d-]I might have reduced them to naught,[-d]
  Made their memory cease among men,

27 But for fear of the taunts of the foe,
  Their enemies who might misjudge
  And say, "Our own hand has prevailed;

a Meaning of Heb. uncertain.
b-b Meaning of Heb. uncertain; Arabic shaʿara suggests the rendering "Whom your fathers did not know."
c I.e., idols.
d-d Lit. "I said, I will reduce . . ."; meaning of Heb. ʾaphʾehem uncertain.

18.8; Judg. 5.25). **15:** *Jeshurun,* probably meaning "upright," a poetic term for Israel (33.5, 26; Isa. 44.2). **17:** *Demons,* better, "protective spirits," using a word borrowed from Akkadian (also Ps. 106.37). *No-gods:* The language is intentionally sarcastic (see also v. 21). **18:** *The Rock that begot you . . . brought you forth:* The Hebrew much more vividly presents God as going through childbirth: "The Rock who gave birth to you . . . who writhed in labor (to bear) you." The same verb is elsewhere applied to Sarah, who "writhed in labor" to bring Israel forth (so Isa. 51.2, lit.). That God had to suffer labor pains to bear Israel only increases the injustice of Israel's forgetting its divine parent. For the metaphor of God panting as a woman in labor, see Isa. 42.14. Such cases provide an important alternative to the normal masculine imagery associated with God. **21:** *Incensed* refers to the covenant's demand for exclusive loyalty to God (5.8; 6.15; Num. 25.11). Accordingly, the punishment for breach of the covenant metes out precise talionic justice (see 19.19 n.). Heb emphasizes the sarcasm: thus, *with no-gods* and *no-folk. Their futilities,* lit. "their vapors" or "their vanities," even "their vapidities" (Jer. 8.19, "futilities"; 10.15, "delusion"; 16.19, "delusions"; Eccl. 1.2, "futility"). **22:** *Sheol,* the underworld (Gen. 37.25; 1 Sam. 2.6; Ps. 139.8). The abode of all the dead, not a place of damnation like the later idea of hell. **23:** *My arrows,* divine punishments (v. 42; Ezek. 5.16; Pss. 7.14; 18.15; 38.3). **24:** *Ravaging plague* reflects the name of the Ugaritic god of pestilence, thus better, "devoured by Plague." **25:** *Youth . . . maiden,* better, "young man . . . young woman," to emphasize along with *suckling . . . aged* the double merism (28.3–6 n.), which symbolizes the totality of the slaughter. **26–27:** The Song here pivots from judgment of Israel to her vindication at the expense of the foreign invaders. **27:** *For fear:* God has feelings and vulnerabilities (as at Gen. 6.6). *Our own hand*

None of this was wrought by the LORD!"

28ª For they are a folk void of sense,
Lacking in all discernment.

29 Were they wise, they would think upon
this,
Gain insight into their future:

30 "How could one have routed a thousand,
Or two put ten thousand to flight,
Unless their Rock had sold them,
The LORD had given them up?"

31 For their rock is not like our Rock,
ᵇ·In our enemies' ownᶜ estimation.·ᵇ

32 Ah! The vine for them is from Sodom,
From the vineyards of Gomorrah;
The grapes for them are poison,
A bitter growth their clusters.

33 Their wine is the venom of asps,
The pitiless poison of vipers.

34 Lo, I have it all put away,
Sealed up in My storehouses,

35 To be My vengeance and recompense,
At the time that their foot falters.
Yea, their day of disaster is near,
And destiny rushes upon them.

36 For the LORD will vindicate His people
ᵈ·And take revenge forᵈ His servants,
When He sees that their might is gone,
And neither bond nor free is left.

37 He will say: Where are their gods,
The rock in whom they sought refuge,

38 Who ate the fat of their offerings
And drank their libation wine?
Let them rise up to your help,
And let them be a shield unto you!

39 See, then, that I, I am He;
There is no god beside Me.
I deal death and give life;
I wounded and I will heal:
None can deliver from My hand.

40 Lo, I raise My hand to heaven
And say: As I live forever,

a Here, apparently, Moses is the speaker; God resumes in v. 32.
b-b I.e., as everyone must admit.
c For Heb. pelilim see Exod. 21.22; cf. Gen. 48.11.
d-d Cf. Isa. 1.24. Others "and repent Himself concerning."

has prevailed, lit., "our hand is held high" in victory (Num. 33.3, "defiantly"; Ps. 89.14). **28–31:** God's soliloquy is interrupted by another voice that refers to God in the third person and speaks on behalf of Israel (vv. 30–31). The voice is contextually that of Moses (see translators' note a), but it is one that assumes the perspective of scribal wisdom. The section therefore seems to be an addition to the text, separating God's abrupt change of heart (vv. 25–27) from the explicit announcement of judgment upon the foreign nation (vv. 34–38). **28–29:** The insertion here directs against the foreign nation the same critique already made of Israel: God's judgment is justified by the nation's lack of wisdom (vv. 6, 20). **30:** A citation within a citation: The verse, attributed to Israel's enemy, in effect reproaches the foreign nation for failing to understand that it owes its triumph over Israel to God rather than force of arms. The imagery ironically inverts the holy war idea (3.22; 20.1), now turning it against Israel. **32:** Sodom . . . Gomorrah, here symbolizing moral corruption more than ruinous devastation (cf. 29.22 n.). **34:** It, the punishment of the foreign nation, which is about to be announced (vv. 35–42). Put away . . . sealed up refers to the formal legal procedures for rolling and then sealing a witnessed deed or contract with a wax seal, so that the unaltered document can subsequently be introduced into court as evidence (Isa. 8.16; Jer. 32.9–15). **35:** Vengeance, better, "vindication," since the idea is not revenge but justice. **36:** Their might is gone, And neither bond nor free is left: God will act when no one survives who can take charge or provide assistance (2 Kings 14.26; cf. 1 Kings 14.10; 21.21; 2 Kings 9.8). **37–38:** Further sarcasm. **39:** Similar to exilic Second Isaiah (Isa. 41.4; 43.10, 13; 44.6; 45.6–7, 22; 48.12). **40:** I raise my hand, elsewhere translated "I swear," which clarifies the meaning here. God is represented anthropomorphically, as performing the physical gesture that marks a formal legal oath (see

41　When I whet My flashing blade
　　And My hand lays hold on judgment,
　　Vengeance will I wreak on My foes,
　　Will I deal to those who reject Me.
42　I will make My arrows drunk with blood—
　　As My sword devours flesh—
　　Blood of the slain and the captive
　　From the long-haired enemy chiefs.

43　O nations, acclaim His people!
　　For He'll avenge the blood of His servants,
　　Wreak vengeance on His foes,
　　And cleanse the land of His people.[a]

44 Moses came, together with Hosea son of Nun, and recited all the words of this poem in the hearing of the people.
45 And when Moses finished reciting all these words to

---

a Cf. Num. 35.33. Meaning of Heb. uncertain; Ugaritic 'udm't "tears" suggests the rendering "And wipe away His people's tears." Cf. Isa. 25.8.

Exod. 6.8 n.; Num. 14.30; Ezek. 20.5–6, 15, 23, 28, 42; 36.7; 44.12; 47.14; Neh. 9.15). **41:** *Wreak*, lit. "return," in talionic justice. Thus, because of the judicial connotation, *vengeance* gives the wrong idea (v. 35 n.). *Reject Me,* treaty language that refers to disloyal action that violates the covenant. **43:** As it stands, the Hebrew presents numerous difficulties. The opening vocative *O nations* is illogical in this context. The verse demands that the very nations judged guilty of spilling Israel's blood suddenly join in the chorus of those praising Israel—in the moment before their destruction! The expected poetic parallelism (AA'BB', as in v. 2) is absent. Here the second line presents a completely different idea than the first line, rather than repeating it with a variation. The absence of parallelism is not simply a formal stylistic issue: It renders the climax of the poem unintelligible. The incoherence of v. 43 in its present form suggests that the original text has been disrupted. Alternative reflections of the text, as preserved by the LXX and by the Dead Sea Scrolls, restore the

poem's lost coherence. A reconstruction of the original form of the verse is shown in the diagram below. The restoration opens up an entire world of meaning and provides the expected poetic parallelism for the first, second, and third pairs of lines, which is absent in the MT. In the ancient versions, it is logically the "heavens" who are addressed (as in v. 1 and Isa 1.2) and who rejoice with God. That makes more sense than requiring the *nations* illogically to praise Israel. The restoration also shows how the poem's conclusion, "heavens . . . *land*" (v. 43) forms an inclusio with its beginning, "heavens . . . earth" (v. 1). It also continues the mythological imagery of God presiding over the divine council and acting as Divine Warrior (see vv. 8–9 n.; vv. 41–42). Almost certainly, the challenge to monotheism in the original form of the verse is what triggered the attempts to purge the text of polytheistic elements, i.e. the shift from "heavens" to "nations" and the elision of the parallelism, with its reference to plural deities. Note the similar "correction" of the text at v. 8. *Avenge the blood:* These lines present God as divine blood-avenger (cf. 19.6), who removes the stain of Israel's blood from the land by requiting the aggressor for having spilled it (19.11–13). *Cleanse:* The line makes sense as it stands; the textual emendation suggested by NJPS in translators' note a is neither necessary nor linguistically valid. The moral stain on the land can only be "wiped clean" (the word's literal meaning) with the blood of the murderer (Num. 35.33–34; cf. Deut. 21.8): here, the foreign nation. God's position is nonetheless morally ambiguous, since it was God who had sanctioned the foreign invasion as just punishment for Israel's wrongdoing (vv. 19–26).

32.44–47: Double conclusion to the Song. Two originally separate conclusions joined by Deuteronomy's editors. **44:** *All the words . . .* frames the Song of Moses in a perfect inclusio (see 31.30), thus con-

---

ORIGINAL FORM OF 32.43	
RECONSTRUCTED TEXT	NJPS (MASORETIC TEXT)
Rejoice, *O heavens*, with Him!	O nations, acclaim His people!
Worship Him, O every god!	. . . . .
For He'll avenge the blood of His *children*,	For He'll avenge the blood of His *servants*,
Wreak vengeance on His foes;	Wreak vengeance on His foes,
He will repay those who hate him,	. . . . .
And cleanse the land of His people.	And cleanse the land of His people.

all Israel, ⁴⁶he said to them: Take to heart all the words with which I have warned you this day. Enjoin them upon your children, that they may observe faithfully all the terms of this Teaching. ⁴⁷For this is not a trifling thing for you: it is your very life; through it you shall long endure on the land that you are to possess upon crossing the Jordan.

⁴⁸That very day the LORD spoke to Moses: ⁴⁹Ascend these heights of Abarim to Mount Nebo, which is in the land of Moab facing Jericho, and view the land of Canaan, which I am giving the Israelites as their holding. ⁵⁰You shall die on the mountain that you are about to ascend, and shall be gathered to your kin, as your brother Aaron died on Mount Hor and was gathered to his kin; ⁵¹for you both broke faith with Me among the Israelite people, at the waters of Meribath-kadesh in the wilderness of Zin, by failing to uphold My sanctity among the Israelite people. ⁵²You may view the land from a distance, but you shall not enter it—the land that I am giving to the Israelite people.

VE-ZO'T HA-BERAKHAH   וזאת הברכה

33 This is the blessing with which Moses, the man of God, bade the Israelites farewell before he died. ²He said:

---

cluding that unit. **45–47:** A separate section, the original continuation of 31.29 prior to the insertion of the Song. **46:** *All the words,* specifically, the laws of Deuteronomy (31.24); now, following the insertion of the Song, reinterpreted to refer to both. **47:** *Not a trifling thing,* using the same word as the Laws of Hammurabi: "My laws . . . are trifling only to the fool" (Epilogue).

32.48–52: Moses commanded to die. This section repeats the announcement of Moses' death (Num. 27.12–14) and thus joins it to its logical continuation, the narrative of that death (Deut. ch 34). The original connection between these two Priestly sections was broken with Deuteronomy's insertion into the Torah. **49:** *These heights of Abarim to Mount Nebo,* as in the Priestly narrative (Num. 27.12; 33.47); but, according to the Deuteronomistic tradition, Pisgah

(3.27). The two traditions are joined at 34.1. **50:** *You shall die,* lit. "Die . . . !" This unusual imperative establishes that Moses both lives and dies at God's command (34.5 n.). *Gathered to your kin* refers specifically to burial in a family tomb, where the bones of the generations would be gathered together (2 Kings 8.24; 22.20; cf. 1 Kings 13.31). Here the phrase is used metaphorically, since Moses' burial place is unknown (34.6). *Mount Hor,* consistent with the Priestly tradition (Num. 20.22–29; 33.37–39); but, in the Deuteronomistic tradition, "Moserah" (10.6). **51:** *You both broke faith,* see Num. 20.1–13.

33.1–29: The Blessing of Moses. Based upon the literary precedent of a father's blessing of his progeny when death is imminent (Gen. 27.27–29; 48.15–16; 49.1–28; cf. 1 Kings 2.1–4), Moses addresses the tribes, arrayed before him

(29.1, 9; 31.7, 30) as if all Israel were his own progeny, gathered before the deathbed (Gen. 48.2; 49.33). Conforming to the literary model of the blessing, the tribes are primarily addressed in the singular, as if they were individual sons (cf. v. 19). Surprisingly, Deuteronomy makes no reference to the two sons of Moses (Exod. 2.22; 18.3–4; see also 34.6 n.). This poem is clearly an insertion into Deuteronomy, intruding between God's command to Moses to ascend Nebo to prepare for his death (32.49–50) and Moses' compliance (34.1–5).

In its present form the poem was created by editors who have consciously combined several older literary models, in three stages, to create something new. (1) The literary convention of the patriarchal blessing addressed individually to each of the twelve tribes (vv. 6–25) has been (2) embedded in a framing poem, which is rather addressed to a united Israel (vv. 1–5, 26–29). The focus of the framing poem is not on tribal destiny but on YHVH as the Divine Warrior who departs from the distant mountains that are His home. Accompanied by His divine pantheon, God comes to the rescue of His people in a powerful theophany that disturbs nature, defeats foreign adversaries, and results in His proclamation as Divine King, while ensuring His nation's rule. This model goes back to the classical victory hymns to the Divine Warrior (Judg. ch 5, Ps. 18.8–16; Hab. ch 3; cf. Exod. ch 15). That older model has been (3) significantly transformed, however. In vv. 1–4, the expected climax of the divine theophany in the military defeat of the enemy has been totally eclipsed (cf. vv. 26–29), although it is the logical precondition for the proclamation of God as King (v. 5). The editors have instead introduced a new climax: Moses' proclamation of Torah (v. 4 n.). The reference here to Sinai instead of Deuteronomy's usual Horeb (see 1.2 n.) is an attempt by the later editors of the Blessing to integrate Deuteronomy with

The LORD came from Sinai;
He shone upon them from Seir;
He appeared from Mount Paran,
And approached from Ribeboth-kodesh,[a]
Lightning flashing at them from His right.[b]

3c   Lover, indeed, of the people,
Their hallowed are all in Your hand.
They followed in Your steps,
Accepting Your pronouncements,

4   When Moses charged us with the Teaching
As the heritage of the congregation of Jacob.

5   Then He became King in Jeshurun,
When the heads of the people assembled,
The tribes of Israel together.

6   May Reuben live and not die,
Though few be his numbers.

7 And this he said of Judah:
Hear, O LORD the voice of Judah
And restore him to his people.
d-Though his own hands strive for him,-d
Help him against his foes.

---

a Cf. Meribath-kadesh, 32.51.

b Meaning of Heb. mimino 'eshdath uncertain, perhaps a place name.

c The meaning of vv. 3–5 is uncertain. An alternative rendering, with v. 3 apostrophizing Moses, is: ³Then were, O lover of the people, / All His worshippers in your care; / They followed your lead, / Accepted your precepts. / ⁴Moses charged us with the Teaching / As the heritage of the congregation of Jacob. / ⁵Thus was he king in Jeshurun . . .

d-d Better (vocalizing rab with pathah) "Make his hands strong for him." Cf. rabbeh, Judg. 9.29.

---

the other literary sources of the Torah (Exod. chs 19–20; Lev. 25.1; Num. 10.12). The editors have used an inclusio pattern to embed the Blessing (with its focus upon the individual tribes) into the framing hymn to the Divine Warrior (where united Israel is the focus). Thus the chiasm LORD:Jacob:Jeshurun::Jeshurun': Jacob':LORD' (A:B:C::C':B':A'; vv. 2, 4, 5, 26, 28, 29) brackets the inserted Blessing. Older hymns to the Divine Warrior sometimes list the tribes' contributions to the battle (Judg. 5.14–18), facilitating the combination of the two models. Although it draws upon older textual traditions, the poem in its present form is almost certainly exilic or post-exilic. The combina-

tion of two separate literary models and the emphasis on Torah rather than on the Divine Warrior's manifestation in battle suggests the later literary setting. **33.1:** Man of God, a prophet, concerning whom "everything that he says comes true" (1 Sam. 9.6; see also Josh. 14.6; 1 Kings 13.1–32; 17.18, 24; 2 Kings 4.7–41). This term is not used of Moses elsewhere in Deuteronomy. **2:** The LORD came from Sinai; He shone: God's departure from His distant mountain stronghold, dramatically coming to the rescue of His people, closely follows the model of Judg. 5.4; Hab. 3.3. Sinai . . . Seir: The geography intended by the parallelism is anomalous. Normally Sinai is located in the Sinai

Peninsula, south of Israel, while Seir, associated with Edom (Judg. 5.4), lies in the east, in southern Transjordan. And approached from Ribeboth-kodesh: The place name is otherwise unknown; and the alternative in translators' note a, Kadesh, has no connection to God's theophany. The Heb can also be understood (with LXX, Samaritan; cf. NRSV) as "with Him were thousands of holy ones," i.e., the divine council who accompany God into battle (32.8 n.; Pss. 68.18; 89.8). This alternative translation, which only changes the vowels of one word in the MT, (from approached to "with Him,") is to be preferred since it preserves the poem's representation of God as Divine Warrior (see 33.1–29 n.). God similarly ventures forth from Sinai, at the head of a divine host of "thousands upon thousands," to appear in theophany in Ps. 68.18. **3:** Their hallowed, originally, the divine council. The poem's editors seem to have shifted it to refer to Israel (7.6; 14.2, 21; 26.19; 28.9; Lev. 19.2; Num. 16.3) to permit a transition to v. 4. **4:** Moses charged us: Since Moses is himself the speaker (v. 1), the change of perspective is disruptive and suggests that the verse was inserted so as to present the promulgation of Mosaic Torah as the climax of the Divine Warrior's theophany! (See 33.1–29 n.) **5:** Then He became King: Although the subject is not specified, it almost certainly refers to God as Divine King of Israel (Exod. 15.18; Num. 23.21; Judg. 8.22–23; 1 Sam. 8.7; Isa. 33.22; Ps. 29.10). NJPS's capitalized pronoun reflects this interpretation. The idea of God's kingship is central to the Bible, but is rarely explicit in the Torah. Jeshurun, see 32.15 n. **6:** Reuben, who once had the leadership of the first-born (see Gen. 49.3–4), is apparently threatened with extinction, owing to military pressures in Transjordan. (Simeon, Jacob's second-born, is missing from the list entirely.) **7:** Judah, in sore trouble because of an unnamed adversary (perhaps the Philistines), should be helped by other tribes. This depiction con-

8 And of Levi he said:
> Let Your Thummim and Urim
> Be with Your faithful one,
> Whom You tested at Massah,
> Challenged at the waters of Meribah;

9
> Who said of his father and mother,
> "I consider them not."
> His brothers he disregarded,
> Ignored his own children.
> Your precepts alone they observed,
> And kept Your covenant.

10
> They shall teach Your laws to Jacob
> And Your instructions to Israel.
> [a-]They shall offer You incense to savor[-a]
> And whole-offerings on Your altar.

11
> Bless, O Lord, his substance,
> And favor his undertakings.
> Smite the loins of his foes;
> Let his enemies rise no more.

12 Of Benjamin he said:
> Beloved of the Lord,
> He rests securely beside Him;
> Ever does He protect him,
> [b-]As he rests between His shoulders.[-b]

13 And of Joseph he said:
> Blessed of the Lord be his land
> With the bounty of dew[c] from heaven,
> And of the deep that couches below;

14
> With the bounteous yield of the sun,
> And the bounteous crop of the moons;

15
> With the best from the ancient mountains,
> And the bounty of hills immemorial;

16
> With the bounty of earth and its fullness,
> And the favor of the Presence[d] in the Bush.
> May these rest on the head of Joseph,
> On the crown of the elect of his brothers.

17
> Like a firstling bull in his majesty,
> He has horns like the horns of the wild-ox;
> With them he gores the peoples,
> The ends of the earth one and all.

trasts sharply with Gen. 49.8–12. **8–11:** *Levi*, once a warlike tribe (Gen. 49.5–7), is to receive the prerogatives of the priesthood: to teach *law*, or Torah (v. 10), and to officiate at the altar. **8:** *Thummim* and *Urim*, the priestly divination devices (Exod. 28.30; Ezra 2.63). *Massah* and *Meribah*, see Exod. 17.1–7; Num. 20.2–13. **9:** On Levi's zealous loyalty to the covenant, at the expense of *father and mother . . . brothers . . . his own children*, thus complying with 13.7, see Exod. 32.25–29. **13–17:** See Gen. 49.25–26. **16–17:** By ascribing primacy of rule and the status of *firstling* to Joseph, this blessing conflicts with the law affirming the norm of primogeniture (21.15–17). **16:** *Presence in the Bush* refers to Exod. 3.1–6; 19.1–20.21. *Elect* goes back to a time when Joseph (the Northern Kingdom, destroyed in 722 BCE) enjoyed greater prestige than Judah (v. 7). **17:** *Ephraim* and *Manasseh*, the two tribes making up "the house of Joseph" (Gen. 48.13–14).

a-a Lit. "They shall place incense in Your nostril."
b-b Or "He dwells amid his slopes."
c Targum Onkelos and two Hebrew manuscripts read: "With the bounty of heaven above" (me'al for mittal, cf. Gen. 49.25).
d Lit. "Dweller"; cf. Exod. 3.1 ff.

These^a are the myriads of Ephraim,
Those^b are the thousands of Manasseh.

18 And of Zebulun he said:
Rejoice, O Zebulun, on your journeys,
And Issachar, in your tents.
19   They invite their kin to the mountain,
Where they offer sacrifices of success.
For they draw from the riches of the sea
And the hidden hoards of the sand.

20 And of Gad he said:
Blessed be He who enlarges Gad!
Poised is he like a lion
To tear off arm and scalp.
21   ^{c-}He chose for himself the best,
For there is the portion of the revered chieftain,
Where the heads of the people come.
He executed the LORD's judgments
And His decisions for Israel.^{-c}

22 And of Dan he said:
Dan is a lion's whelp
That leaps forth from Bashan.

23 And of Naphtali he said:
O Naphtali, sated with favor
And full of the LORD's blessing,
Take possession on the west and south.

24 And of Asher he said:
Most blessed of sons be Asher;
May he be the favorite of his brothers,
May he dip his foot in oil.
25^d   May your doorbolts be iron and copper,
And your security last all your days.

26   O Jeshurun, there is none like God,
Riding through the heavens to help you,
Through the skies in His majesty.
27^d   The ancient God is a refuge,
A support are the arms everlasting.
He drove out the enemy before you
By His command: Destroy!

18–19: *Zebulun* and *Issachar* will enjoy great influence owing to the resources of the Mediterranean and Lake Chinnereth, later known as the Sea of Galilee (Gen. 49.13). **20–21:** *Gad* occupied the *best* tableland in Transjordan but aided the other tribes in the occupation of Canaan (Num. ch 32). **22:** *Dan*, vigorous as a *lion's whelp*, must here already have migrated from its original tribal allotment on the coastal plain, adjacent to the Philistine pentapolis, to the far north, at the base of Mount Hermon (Judg. ch 18). *Bashan*, in northern Transjordan. **23:** *Naphtali*, located in the region of the Sea of Galilee and the Ginnesar plain, *west* and *south* of Dan. **24–25:** *Asher*, located below Phoenicia, is to be strong and prosperous. **26–29:** The resumption of the hymn to the Divine Warrior (vv. 2–5) and a return to the focus upon *Jeshurun* (v. 26), meaning all *Israel* (v. 28). **26:** Much like the Canaanite storm god Ba'al, Israel's Divine Warrior is represented as riding upon the clouds (Isa. 19.1; Pss. 18.10; 68.33). **27:** As translators' note *d* indicates, the Hebrew is difficult. NJPS's translation, although plausible, seems inconsistent with the emphasis of v. 26 upon God as Divine Warrior. On that basis, the alternate reconstruction of the Hebrew by the NRSV seems more appropriate: "He subdues the ancient gods, shatters the forces of old; he drove out the enemy before you, and said, 'Destroy!' "

a I.e., the one horn.   b I.e., the other horn.
c-c Meaning of Heb. uncertain; cf. vv. 3–5 (with note c) above, and saphun "esteemed" in post-biblical Heb.
d Meaning of Heb. uncertain.

28   Thus Israel dwells in safety,
       Untroubled is Jacob's abode,[a]
       In a land of grain and wine,
       Under heavens dripping dew.
29   O happy Israel! Who is like you,
       A people delivered by the LORD,
       Your protecting Shield, your Sword triumphant!
       Your enemies shall come cringing before you,
       And you shall tread on their backs.

34 Moses went up from the steppes of Moab to Mount Nebo, to the summit of Pisgah, opposite Jericho, and the LORD showed him the whole land: Gilead as far as Dan; [2] all Naphtali; the land of Ephraim and Manasseh; the whole land of Judah as far as the Western[b] Sea; [3] the Negeb; and the Plain—the Valley of Jericho, the city of palm trees—as far as Zoar. [4] And the LORD said to him, "This is the land of which I swore to Abraham, Isaac, and Jacob, 'I will assign it to your offspring.' I have let you see it with your own eyes, but you shall not cross there."

[5] So Moses the servant of the LORD died there, in the land of Moab, at the command of the LORD. [6] He buried him in the valley in the land of Moab, near Beth-peor; and no one knows his burial place to this day. [7] Moses was a hundred and twenty years old when he died; his eyes were undimmed and his vigor unabated. [8] And the Israelites bewailed Moses in the steppes of Moab for thirty days.

The period of wailing and mourning for Moses came to an end. [9] Now Joshua son of Nun was filled with the spirit

---

a Others "fountain."   b I.e., Mediterranean; cf. note at 11.24.

28: As in Ugaritic epic, the theophany of the Divine Warrior and His proclamation as King results in the fertility of the land. **29:** *Tread on their backs,* the standard biblical and Near Eastern symbol of military triumph (Josh. 10.24; Ps. 110.1; also attested in Neo-Assyrian reliefs).

34.1–12: The death of Moses. This chapter highlights the absence of access to Moses, who leaves behind no progeny and whose burial site is unknown. The Torah alone is the enduring Mosaic bequest. After the insertion of the Song of Moses (ch 32) and the Blessing of Moses (ch 33), the chapter directly continues the narrative concerning the death of Moses and the transfer of leadership to Joshua, his successor (ch 31). At another level, however, the chapter also directly continues the narrative thread of Num. ch 27, where God had commanded Moses to "ascend these heights" to survey the promised land before his death, and to "lay your hand" upon Joshua, to transfer the mantle of authority to him (vv. 12, 18). The belated resumption of that narrative, with its two themes of Mosaic death and succession, forms a literary bracket around the book of Deuteronomy, suggesting that editors interrupted the narrative in order to work Deuteronomy into the Torah. **1:** *Went up,* responding to the command of 32.49; Num. 27.12. The verse joins two different traditions about the site of Moses' death: *Mount Nebo,* which is in Transjordan, east of Jericho; and *the summit of Pisgah,* which is slightly to its west, and unmentioned in 32.49. Seeking to preserve both traditions, the editor presents them as if they were the same. **2–3:** The lofty vantage point allows Moses to look northward to the Sea of Galilee (area of the tribal allotment of Dan and *Naphtali*), to the *Western Sea* (the Mediterranean), south to the *Negeb* desert and along the Jordan rift valley as far south as *Zoar* (once located at the southern end of the Dead Sea as one of the "cities of the Plain" and thus likely destroyed; Gen. 14.2, 8; 19.29). **5:** *At the command of the LORD,* see 32.50 n. The unusual formulation greatly honors Moses, who, despite advanced age, does not die of old age nor succumb to physical or intellectual infirmity. **6:** *He buried him:* The clear indication is that God Himself buried Moses, as He Himself sealed Noah into the ark (Gen. 7.16). Instead of Moses' progeny assuming the important legal responsibility of caring for the dead, God undertook it personally. This divine care fits the image of Moses in Deuteronomy. *Beth-peor,* see 3.29; 4.46; Josh. 13.20. *No one knows his burial place,* thus precluding pilgrimages to the site as a shrine. **7:** *A hundred and twenty,* see 31.2 n. **8:** *Thirty days,* so also for Aaron (Num. 20.29). Israel mourns the loss of Moses for the full mourning period stipulated for a parent (21.13). **9:** *Joshua . . . was filled with the spirit of wisdom:* As at 1.13 and 16.18–20, Deuteronomy revises earlier traditions to stress wisdom as the essential qualification of office, and thus what Joshua receives from Moses. In Num. 27.18, Joshua was already "an inspired man" (often associated with prophecy or possession), while Moses was to transfer his "authority" to him. Here "the spirit of wisdom" is what Joshua receives from Moses. *Because Moses* of wisdom because Moses had laid his hands upon him; and the Israelites heeded him, doing as the LORD had commanded Moses.

10 Never again did there arise in Israel a prophet like Moses—whom the LORD singled out, face to face, 11 for the various signs and portents that the LORD sent him to display in the land of Egypt, against Pharaoh and all his courtiers and his whole country, 12 and for all the great might and awesome power that Moses displayed before all Israel.

had laid his hands upon him: as at Num. 27.22–23, a means of transfer of attributes (Lev. 16.21; Num. 8.10–13), here used for investiture into office. **10–12:** An editor eulogizes Moses as marking the pinnacle of prophecy, both because of his direct access to divine revelation and his power to work miracles. This double elevation of Moses to an ideal standard differs from his more human representation elsewhere in the book. The contrast between the two suggests that an editor's later, idealizing retrospective operates here, as Deuteronomy is now worked into the Torah. **10:** *Never again:* Note the discrepancy between the perspective of this verse and the divine promise to Moses that the line of prophetic succession will continue in the future: "I will raise up a prophet for them . . . like yourself" (18.18). *Face to face,* rather than through dreams or visions (13.2); similarly, Exod. 33.11; Num. 12.8–10. Other traditions reject that Moses had such direct access to God (Exod. 33.20–23).

נביאים
NEVI'IM

Terminology and Content

ACCORDING TO JEWISH TRADITION, the second canonical division, Nevi'im or Prophets, is comprised of the eight books Joshua, Judges, Samuel, Kings, Isaiah, Jeremiah, Ezekiel, and the Twelve Minor (in the sense of short) Prophets. Samuel and Kings, which are now each divided into two books, are each considered as a single book in Jewish tradition, though the NJPS translation follows the practice, first found in the Septuagint, of dividing these two long books in half. In the classical rabbinic period, these eight books were seen as a single unit; in the medieval period, these books were divided in half thematically, with Joshua through Kings called the former prophets *(nevi'im rishonim)*, and Isaiah through the Twelve called the latter prophets *(nevi'im 'aharonim)*. The terms "former" and "latter" refer to the placement of these collections within Nevi'im rather than their chronological order since, for example, some of the events narrated in Kings, the fourth book of Nevi'im, transpire later than the events in some of the Twelve Minor Prophets.

It is likely that these eight books were canonized after the Torah, and that at some point the canon was comprised of Torah plus Nevi'im (see "Canonization," pp. 2072-77). It is less certain why the first four books were called "prophets" and how they became part of a larger collection called Nevi'im. Perhaps the collection is named after its last four books, which were seen as the more significant part of the collection. Alternatively, the name Nevi'im reflects an awareness that prophets and prophetic activity play important roles in each of the first four books as well: In the book of Joshua, Joshua is depicted as the prophetic successor to Moses (see esp. ch 1); in Judges oracles are often consulted (e.g., 1.1; 20.18); Samuel the prophet is a central figure of the book that bears his name; and Elijah, Elisha, and several other named and unnamed prophets figure prominently in Kings. Thus, even though Joshua through Kings might be categorized as historical books according to their genre, and are so placed in non-Jewish Bibles, which follow the order of the Septuagint (see the chart on p. 2076), their inclusion in Nevi'im reflects an ancient tradition that reflects the history of canonization rather than a thematic or generic arrangement of the books. Nevertheless, due to their different content and nature, they will be treated separately in this introduction.

—451—

The Historical Books and Historiography

THE BOOKS OF JOSHUA THROUGH KINGS are often categorized as historical texts. Yet the idea that historical writing should capture the events "as they really were," that historians should attempt to write an objective account of the events of the past, is a relatively recent notion which developed in European universities in the 19th century. Before that, history was typically didactic in nature, teaching the readers how to be good citizens or how to lead proper religious lives. Sometimes histories were produced in the royal court, in which case they were apologetic, showing how the king fulfilled his royal duties. Surviving historical documents from the ancient Near East show similar religious and ideological goals. Thus, it should not be surprising that the biblical writers are not primarily interested in the accurate recording of real events; rather, they use narratives about the past to illustrate various issues of significance to their earliest audience, the ancient Israelite community.

It is easiest to understand the biblical notion of history by first focusing on an earlier work, Exodus ch 13. Verse 3 begins: "And Moses said to the people, 'Remember this day, on which you went free from Egypt, the house of bondage.'" This would seem to suggest the importance of history for its own sake. This unit continues, however, with a set of commandments that directly result from this event: "No leavened bread shall be eaten" (v. 3); "seven days you shall eat unleavened bread, and on the seventh day there shall be a festival of the Lord" (v. 6); "no leavened bread shall be found with you, and no leaven shall be found in all your territory" (v. 7); "And you shall explain to your son on that day . . ." (v. 8); "and this shall serve you as a sign on your hand and as a reminder on your forehead" (v. 9); "you shall set apart for the Lord every first issue of the womb: every male firstling that your cattle drop shall be the Lord's" (v. 12). Taken as a whole, this passage indicates that the exodus is not significant as a disembodied historical event, as the beginning of v. 3 might suggest; rather, the exodus is a key occurrence because it serves as the basis for the observance of a central set of laws or norms.

The use of historical material in Psalms is even more instructive, since there these traditions about the past are typically surrounded by a framework which explicitly highlights their theological significance or purpose. For example, in Psalm 78, a particular set of traditions is chosen and shaped so:

> that a future generation might know
> —children yet to be born—
> and in turn tell their children
> that they might put their confidence in God,
> and not forget God's great deeds,
> but observe His commandments,
> and not be like their fathers,
> a wayward and defiant generation,
> a generation whose heart was inconstant,
> whose spirit was not true to God. (vv. 6–8)

Psalm 106 tells how God saved Israel time after time, despite their covenant violations. This is used as an argument to God that they should be rescued again:

> Deliver us, O LORD our God,
> and gather us from among the nations,
> to acclaim Your holy name,
> to glory in Your praise. (v. 47)

Unfortunately, the material collected in Joshua through Kings is not as explicit about its purposes as these psalms or Exodus; for this reason, these books need to be subjected to internal analysis, in order to see what motivations and interests best explain their shape.

The Former Prophets and the Deuteronomistic History

NOT ONLY ARE JOSHUA THROUGH KINGS separated from the "true" prophetic books that follow on the basis of content, but Joshua, Judges, Samuel, and Kings, along with the preceding book of Deuteronomy, fit so well together that it is likely that at some point these five books were edited together as a single work. This work is called by scholars the Deuteronomistic History, meaning the history written under the influence of ideas found in the book of Deuteronomy. This theory has much to commend it: These five books do read as a unified whole from a chronological perspective, narrating a continuous history from the end of the life of Moses through the Babylonian exile (586 BCE), and they share many phrases and ideological notions, such as an insistence on exclusive worship of God and the catastrophic consequences of idolatry, a concern with the centrality of Jerusalem, and a belief in the supremacy of the eternal Davidic dynasty. If this theory is correct, the size of the Deuteronomistic History, and the long period that it depicts, is quite remarkable, especially for an ancient historical work.

Many details of this theory remain debated; some scholars suggest that these books are not quite unified enough to represent the product of a single individual, intellectual school, or movement. For example, the book of Samuel has remarkably few echoes of the language of Deuteronomy, and the book of Kings contains narratives in which the great prophets Elijah and Elisha are legitimately active outside of the Jerusalem Temple (see especially Elijah on Mt. Carmel, 1 Kings ch 18). Scholars have thus suggested various theories concerning successive editions of the Deuteronomistic History, which many believe was begun in the 7th century under the Judean King Josiah (640–609 BCE), but was completed only in the Babylonian exile (586–538 BCE) or later. Some suggest that the lack of unity is due to non-Deuteronomistic material that has been added at a late stage to an earlier Deuteronomistic History. There have also been attempts to isolate narratives which might have preceded the Deuteronomistic History and other sources used by the Deuteronomist(s), and to discern their original purposes before these narratives and sources became integrated into the larger literary work. In sum, this collection has a long and complicated history, so it is impossible to speak of a totally unified purpose or interest in the compilation of the books of Joshua, Judges, Samuel, and Kings. They reflect many different interests and stages of development: pre-Deuteronomic, Deuteronomistic, and later, postexilic concerns. The interests of the individual books of the Deuteronomistic History are thus discussed in the introductory material at the beginning of each book.

The Historical Books and Historicity

THE PROBLEMATIC NATURE OF ALL of these texts as historical documents does not mean that we have no idea of the historical periods that they cover, or that they are entirely useless as historical sources. Each text needs to be weighed individually in terms of its date of composition and its likely goals. Using these criteria, there are reasons to accept the veracity of, for example, the dry notice in 1 Kings 14.25–26 ("In the fifth year of King Rehoboam, King Shishak of Egypt marched against Jerusalem and carried off the treasures of the House of the LORD and the treasures of the royal palace. He carried off everything; he even carried off all the golden shields that Solomon had made"), which might even come from an archival source, and has some confirmation from Egyptian sources. In contrast, there are good reasons to be suspicious of the historicity of the long, detailed, and embellished story of David slaying Goliath in 1 Sam. ch 17; this story uses late biblical Hebrew language, comes from a different source than the surrounding material in Samuel, and is structured like a fairy-tale, in that the poor, short, unexpected hero gets to marry the tall king's daughter by killing the giant who had vilified God. Additionally, 2 Samuel 21.19 reads: "Again there was fighting with the Philistines at Gob; and Elhanan son of Jaare-oregim the Bethlehemite killed Goliath the Gittite, whose spear had a shaft like a weaver's bar." It is much more likely that a short tradition in which Goliath is killed by a relatively unknown figure (Elhanan) would be the source for the long, elaborate tale attributing the same event to the well-known David, rather than vice versa. Thus, the modern historian must subject each text in these Historical Books to the type of internal analysis used on nonbiblical historical texts when external information bearing on the text is lacking.

There are a number of cases where we do have external, ancient Near Eastern written evidence that deals with events depicted in these Historical Books. For example, the events surrounding the siege of Jerusalem by the Assyrian King Sennacherib in 701 BCE are narrated in several Assyrian sources, and are also depicted in the palace reliefs of that king. These sources suggest that part of the terse account in 2 Kings 18.13–16 is quite accurate, while the highly developed continuation of the story in chs 19 and 20, especially the note in 19.35, that the angel of the LORD killed 185,000 Assyrian soldiers in a single night, is most likely imaginative. Similarly, from various Mesopotamian sources, we know of a "house of Omri"; Omri's name is also mentioned on the Moabite Mesha Stele. This confirms the existence of the Northern (Israelite) king mentioned in 1 Kings 16.23–28. However, Kings tells little of his achievements during his twelve years as monarch, other than his building of Samaria and the notice that: "Omri did what was displeasing to the LORD; he was worse than all who preceded him. He followed all the ways of Jeroboam son of Nebat and the sins which he committed and caused Israel to commit, vexing the LORD, the God of Israel, with their futilities" (vv. 25–26). The external sources, however, suggest that Omri was a powerful king who established a significant name for himself through his military activities. This highlights the extreme selectivity of the biblical sources.

Archeological evidence confirms the picture suggested above: There may be some truth (or kernel of truth) to some of the biblical stories, but in their current form, they lack historical veracity, because that is not their prime concern. Recent decades, for example, have seen a remarkable reevaluation of the evidence concerning the conquest of the land of Canaan by Joshua. As more sites have been excavated, there has been a growing consensus that the main story of Joshua, that of a speedy and complete conquest (e.g., Josh. 11.23: "Thus Joshua conquered the whole country, just as the LORD had promised Moses") cannot be upheld by the archeological record, though there are indications of *some* destruction and conquest at the appropriate time. Various events and traditions have been reworked very substantially over time and ultimately included in the Bible in order to substantiate a particular picture of God.

In sum, though Joshua through Kings are often viewed as early historical texts, they should not be viewed as historical in the contemporary sense. Many of these texts do contain the raw materials for a modern historian researching the history of ancient Israel from the time of the conquest through the 6th century BCE or later, but this material can only be teased out using sophisticated and complex tools. This is because these various biblical historians each wrote accounts, sometimes using sources, to illustrate particular perspectives concerning the relationship between God and Israel. These accounts did not remain stagnant, but were changed by later tradents, authors and editors, who revised them in accordance with their beliefs. It is these religious and religio-political perspectives that we must try to appreciate as we study these books; if we read them as we read modern historical accounts, we will misunderstand these texts in the most fundamental way. Thus, given that prophets frequently are depicted as the vehicles of religious and religiopolitical perspectives, "the former prophets" is a suitable name for the first part of this collection.

The Latter Prophets and Their Order

THE BOOKS OF ISAIAH, JEREMIAH, EZEKIEL, AND THE TWELVE are fundamentally different from the previous four books: With the exception of Jonah in the Twelve, they all contain collections of oracles attributed to various prophets, who spoke these oracles publicly to the Israelites. These contrast with the prophets described in the Former Prophets, whose mission was largely private, mostly to kings, and whose prestige was often established through performing unusual ("magical") actions (see esp. Elijah and Elisha, 1 Kings chs 17–19, 21; 2 Kings chs 1–9) rather than through speaking the divine word in elevated rhetorical speeches.

In contrast to the Torah, there is some debate about how these four latter prophetic books should be ordered. The typical manuscript order of the first three, Isaiah, Jeremiah, Ezekiel, reflects chronological ordering. (First) Isaiah was active mostly in the later 8th century, Jeremiah prophesied in the late 7th through the early 6th century, while Ezekiel spoke in the Babylonian exile in the 6th century. The Twelve is then placed last as reflecting prophets working in a diversity of time periods; the latest prophets (Haggai, Zechariah, Malachi) are later than Ezekiel, reflecting the return from exile. A different order is noted in the Babylonian Talmud (*b. B. Bat.* 14b): Jeremiah, Ezekiel, Isaiah, the Twelve. This is explained in terms of offering thematic continuity: The pessimistic Jeremiah follows the destruction noted at the end of Kings, and this is followed by Ezekiel, which opens with destruction and finishes with consolation.

The Nature and Composition of the Prophetic Books

THE PROPHETIC BOOKS ARE UNUSUAL and complex compositions. While the books undoubtedly do preserve authentic words of the prophets in question, we should not think of the prophetic books simply as transcriptions of the words of prophets. Although much remains unknown about the composition of the prophetic books, it is possible to reconstruct a general picture. Scholars generally agree that the poetic materials of most of the prophetic books originated as oral pronouncements by the prophet to a public audience. These oral sayings were subsequently written down, perhaps by the prophet or a disciple. Various circumstances led to the compilation of these original written collections. A reference in Isaiah suggests that oracles might be written down as a form of authentication (Isa. 30.8). The book of Jeremiah describes a situation in which Jeremiah, having been banned from speaking publicly in the Temple, had his assistant Baruch write down a selection of his prophetic words so that they could be taken into the Temple and read to the people (Jer. 36.5–6). When King Jehoiakim destroyed the scroll, Jeremiah had Baruch write out another copy, to which they added additional material (Jer. 36.27–32). This collection may have formed the nucleus of the book of Jeremiah. (Unlike most of the other prophetic books, Ezekiel may have been composed as a written document from the beginning.) It is unclear if what was written was identical to what the prophet recited, or if the prophet or his disciples even at this earliest stage introduced changes, reflecting the difference between the oral form of a publicly recited oracle versus the written form of a scroll.

Once small collections of prophetic oracles and pronouncements were made, they were subject to further editing, rearranging, annotating, and expansion. Like other biblical texts, these prophetic works did not fossilize. In some cases narratives about the prophet were added; these are both autobiographical (e.g., Isa. chs 6, 8; Jer. 1.4–19; 13.1–11; Hos. chs 1–2; Amos 7.1–7) and biographical (e.g., Isa. chs 7, 36–39; Jer. chs 26, 36–44; Hos. ch 3; Amos 7.10–17). The occasions for such editorial activity will have differed, but national crises may have prompted some of this process. Most likely, written collections of the oracles of Amos and Hosea, which were originally addressed to the Northern Kingdom (Israel) were brought to Judah after the fall of the Northern Kingdom in 722 BCE, and edited and circulated there (see Amos 1.1–2 n.). Isaiah of Jerusalem seems to have knowledge of Amos's oracles, and Jeremiah is unquestionably influenced by Hosea. Many of the prophetic books originating before the fall of Judah to the Babylonians in 586 BCE show evidence of editorial additions and reorganizations that reflect the circumstances of exilic and postexilic times. The book of Amos, for example, now includes material that presupposes the fall of Judah (9.11–15). The most dramatic example of the expansion and reworking of prophetic materials is the book of Isaiah. Although it contains extensive material from the 8th-century prophet, chs 40–66 clearly reflect the situation of the Babylonian exile and the subsequent period of the restoration of the Judean community after the exile. Yet even though the book contains materials dating from several centuries, it is unified by a number of motifs, themes, and topics that recur throughout the work.

The complex activity of preserving and developing the prophetic oracle collections reflects a conviction that a prophet's words were not only significant for the circumstance in which they were originally pronounced but potentially relevant for later ones as well. (This notion, which became more significant in the exilic and postexilic period, is very well established in the Dead Sea Scrolls and in later rabbinic literature.) At the same time, the freedom with which later generations could rework the prophetic oracles indicates that the prophets' words did not at first possess the kind of fixed authority that is later associated with canonical Scripture. Although the processes by which the prophetic books came to assume a relatively final form and canonical status are difficult to trace, this probably occurred during the Persian and early Hellenistic periods (the 5th through the 3rd centuries BCE). Most likely, during this time scribal editors added the superscriptions that introduce most of the books, indicating the identity of the prophet (name, father's name, and occasionally other information) and often the kings of Israel or Judah during whose reigns the prophets were active (e.g., Isa. 1.1; Jer. 1.1–3; Hos. 1.1). In addition to editorial additions to the individual prophetic books, the smaller prophetic books (Hosea through Malachi) were arranged and edited to form a group known as "the book of the Twelve," which was copied on a single scroll. By the beginning of the 2nd century BCE Ben Sirach refers to these prophets as "the twelve" (Sir. 49.10). The number twelve is symbolic of the twelve sons of Jacob and the twelve tribes of Israel, and considerable editorial work was required to organize these prophetic materials into a grouping of twelve. In fact, the book of Zechariah consists of three separate collections (chs 1–8, 9–11, 12–14) grouped together editorially. Only the first of these comes from the prophet Zechariah, whereas the other two are anonymous. The final book in the collection, Malachi, is also an anonymous piece, since "Malachi" is not a personal name but a phrase meaning "my messenger," picked up from 3.1 to serve as the name of the prophet in the superscription.

The Phenomenon of Prophecy

THE PHENOMENON OF PROPHECY was widespread in the ancient Near East, and many important themes and genres familiar from biblical prophecy have parallels there. It should be viewed as part of a larger belief in that area that the deity's will is transparent in the world. This may happen through omen interpretation, as was typical in Mesopotamia, or through prophecy, which seems to have been the preferred method in Israel.

Many popular perceptions of biblical prophecy are incorrect. The prophets were not predominantly forecasters of the future, ancient fortune-tellers. Rather, they had a crucial role in critiquing and trying to change society. This could be accomplished through fore-telling the future, but most often these predictions were contingent upon the nation's be-havior. Not all prophets, however, were interested in changing the people's conduct—bib-lical religion sometimes suggested that Israel had gone too far, and must be punished (see esp. Jer. ch 25). In such cases, the main role of the prophet was to assure the nation that their punishment, which derived from God, was deserved.

It is natural to read the prophets, which canonically follow the Torah, in relation to this previous canonical body of writing. Jewish tradition thus typically reads the prophets as interpreters of the Torah, whose role was to make sure that the people adhered to the Torah. Protestant tradition, on the other hand, often emphasized the apparently antino-mian tendencies in such prophecies as Isaiah 1.10–20 or Amos 5.21–25. Neither of these views is correct from a scholarly perspective. Critical biblical scholarship has ascertained that the Torah and Prophets developed simultaneously from a chronological perspective; thus, not all prophets knew all the Torah since the Torah had not yet been canonized by the time that most of the prophets were active. The Protestant view is problematic because it ignores the fact that certain prophetic oracles are very interested in punctilious perfor-mance of particular ritual laws (see esp. Jer. 17.19–27). Furthermore, a close reading of prophets such as Isaiah or Amos suggests that they are not anti-law or anti-Temple, but are rhetorically emphasizing that ritual behavior alone, without proper moral behavior, is insufficient to assure divine blessing.

Many more prophets were active in ancient Israel and Judah than those whose work is represented in the prophetic books of the Bible, and their activities were more varied than these writings suggest. The books of Samuel and Kings provide important additional in-formation. Since our sources are limited, it is difficult to reconstruct the history of proph-ecy. Some of the features are clear, however. The prophet was essentially an intermediary between God and the people, and one of the major functions was that of messenger (Heb mal'akh). Often prophets introduced their communications with a version of the formula typically used by messengers, "thus says the LORD." But prophets might also carry in-quiries from the people to God or make intercession on behalf of the people. In contrast to the priesthood, which was exclusively male, both women and men could be prophets. Women prophets included Deborah (Judg. 4.4) and Huldah (2 Kings 22.14); see also Joel 3.1. Additional aspects of the prophetic role are suggested by the various terms used to identify them. In addition to "prophet" (Heb navi', perhaps meaning "one who is called"), the prophets are identified as seers (Heb ro'eh), visionaries (Heb ḥozeh), and holy men (Heb 'ish 'elohim, lit. "man of God"). It is uncertain if these different titles reflect different types of prophets.

The religious phenomenon of Israelite prophecy can be traced for more than a thousand years, from the premonarchical period to the turn of the era. As one would expect, over such a long period of time the nature and function of prophecy altered in response to changing historical, social, and religious circumstances. Four periods define the major epochs of prophecy: the early monarchical period (11th through 9th centuries), the Assyrian crisis (8th century), the Babylonian crisis (late 7th through early 6th centuries), and the postexilic restoration (mid-6th through mid-5th centuries).

In the earliest period prophets may have been local or itinerant holy men and women who were revered for their special religious powers and who might be consulted for a variety of private inquiries, from locating lost property (1 Sam. 9.1–10) to learning whether a sick child would live or die (1 Kings 14.1–18). Some lived in prophetic communities which cultivated ecstatic forms of religious experience (1 Sam. 19.18–24; 2 Kings 6.1–7); these are called "sons of (the) prophets" in the sense of members of prophetic guilds. Prophets also had the public function of declaring God's will concerning whether the people should go to war (Judg. 4.4–10). The emergence of monarchy in ancient Israel may have changed aspects of the prophets' role. Prophets appear as king-makers and king-breakers, as they announce that God has designated an individual to become king or has rejected a reigning king (1 Sam. 10.1; 15.23; 1 Kings 11.29–39; 14.1–18). Though prophets continued their role in advising about matters of war (1 Kings ch 22), they also served as critics of the king in religious and social affairs. The consolidation of royal power and the foreign religious practices introduced through royal marriages often threatened older tribal institutions and values. The conflict between Elijah, the prophet, and Ahab and Jezebel, the king and queen, illustrates these tensions between prophet and king (1 Kings chs 18–21).

Prophecy appears to have undergone a dramatic change during the 8th century, although this impression may be affected by the change in the nature of the sources of information. From the 8th century onward collections of prophetic oracles are preserved, yet, with the exception of Jeremiah, few extended narratives about prophets exist. It does appear, however, that in this period prophets began to function less as private counselors and critics of kings and more as public figures who influenced opinion through their pronouncements in the Temple courts and in other public places. Prophets of the 8th century (Amos, Hosea, Isaiah, Micah) interpreted international affairs, critiqued complacent religious practices, and condemned the abuses of social justice that accompanied the increasing urbanization and centralization of state power characteristic of the 8th century. The prophetic careers of Hosea, Micah, and Isaiah took place in the shadow of the expansionist Assyrian empire, which eventually put an end to the Northern Kingdom of Israel and subjected Judah to the condition of vassalage. They interpreted these events, however, in terms of the judgment of the LORD, not simply as the success of a powerful Assyrian empire. This perspective allowed Isaiah, for example, to anticipate the ultimate downfall of Assyria because of its overweening arrogance.

The third major period of prophecy occurred during the Babylonian crisis. The prophet Nahum celebrated the defeat of Assyria (612–609 BCE), but the excitement he expressed was soon turned to confusion as Babylonia succeeded Assyria as the dominant empire (see the introduction and notes to Habakkuk and the essay "Historical and Geographical Background," pp. 2048–62). Jeremiah's prophetic career (ca. 627–586) spanned the time from the decline of Assyria through the Babylonian overlordship of Judah, to the revolt and destruction of Judah and the exile of a portion of its population. Although it is difficult to correlate many of his poetic oracles with specific events in this period, the narratives about Jeremiah give a vivid picture of a nation and its leadership deeply conflicted about what political course to follow and the religious significance of the choices that were forced upon it. Even the prophetic community was bitterly divided and gave contradictory advice to the king concerning the will of the LORD (Jer. chs 26–29, 36–44). Overlapping the career of Jeremiah, the prophet Ezekiel (active 593–ca. 571 BCE) was among the Judeans exiled to Babylonia after the revolt of 597 BCE, a decade before the final revolt and the destruction of Jerusalem. Ezekiel's prophetic work was, first, to persuade the exiled Judeans of the inevitability of Jerusalem's destruction, and to justify this event. Following the fall of the city, he began to articulate the theological grounds for conceiving a possible future, including a return of the exiles and a rebuilding of the destroyed Temple. In contrast to most of the prophets who preceded him, Ezekiel drew strongly on Priestly traditions for his categories of thought, forms of speech, and evocative symbols.

The defeat of the Babylonian empire by the Persian king Cyrus in 539 BCE altered political conditions dramatically. Although Judah did not regain its independence but became a part of the Persian empire, Cyrus and his successors authorized the rebuilding of the Temple and of Jerusalem, allowing members of the exiled community in Babylonia who so desired to return to Judah. Thus the prophetic task during this period largely concerned issues of the restoration of the community and its institutions in a context significantly different from that which prevailed during the Israelite and Judean monarchy. The anonymous prophet whose work is found in Isa. chs 40–55 (often called "Second Isaiah") addressed the Babylonian exiles just at the time that Cyrus was engaged in the conquest of Babylonia. Second Isaiah had to persuade the exilic community that unfolding events represented God's action in history, to interpret the significance of Cyrus (God's "anointed" who would rebuild Jerusalem [44.28–45.1]), and to encourage the exiles to return to Jerusalem. The process of rebuilding the Temple (520–515 BCE) provides the context for the prophets Haggai and Zechariah. Zechariah's work in particular suggests this was a time of expectation that perhaps the monarchy might be restored, an event that did not occur. Issues concerning reorganization of the Judean community and tensions regarding economic justice, institutional corruption, and the boundaries of the community are variously reflected in Zechariah, Isa. chs 56–66, and Malachi, prophets who were active in roughly the period 525–475 BCE.

Although prophets in all periods might speak of the dramatic intervention of God in historical events and the consequent transformation of the conditions of life, this type of language seems to have become more common and more vivid in the postexilic prophets (e.g., Isa. chs 56–66, Zechariah, Malachi, Joel, and postexilic additions to earlier prophetic books, such as Isa. chs 24–27). Some of the passages anticipate a war or other cataclysmic event of cosmic proportions that will precede a time of deliverance, peace, and virtual re-creation of the world, themes associated with apocalypticism. Such imagery and the expectations it expresses suggest to some scholars that apocalypticism emerges out of postexilic prophecy. Though it is true that apocalyptic literature is influenced by these prophetic writings and their imagery, apocalyptic cannot simply be understood as an outgrowth of the phenomenon of prophecy.

The book of Daniel, a prophetic book which is found in the Kethuvim (in Christian Bibles it is included among the prophets), is the only book in the Hebrew Bible that could be called an apocalypse. In the latter part of the book, Daniel is the recipient of visions which disclose the future. These vision reports do bear significant similarities to those found in Ezekiel and especially in Zechariah, though their almost allegorical style is quite different. Similarly, although general claims about God's foreknowledge of historical events can be found in Second Isaiah, Daniel's representation of history as predetermined both with respect to its epochal structure and its specific events is strikingly different from the representation of history by the prophets. A clue to the relationship of apocalyptic to prophecy may be found in Dan. ch 9, where Daniel is presented as studying the book of Jeremiah and receiving an angelic interpretation of its significance. As suggested by the representation of Daniel as a technically trained sage, the authors of apocalyptic books, many of which were produced in the Hellenistic period, were perhaps themselves learned scribes who studied and appropriated aspects of the prophetic tradition and combined them with other influences in their attempts to understand the nature of the cosmos and the course of history. The movement from receiving the prophetic word directly, as in the first three periods, to receiving it via an intermediary angel in the fourth period, and of understanding what God wants by studying earlier prophetic texts, would ultimately become responsible for the perception among many in the Second Temple period that prophecy as a living, core institution had died. With the canonization of God's revelation in the form of the written books of the Bible, new revelations through prophets became superfluous. Prophecy was gradually replaced by scriptural study and interpretation, and prophets by scribes, sages, and rabbis.   [MARC ZVI BRETTLER]

יְהוֹשֻׁעַ

Joshua

THE BOOK OF JOSHUA, which derives its title from the name of its chief character, begins after the death of Moses (Deut. ch 34) and continues until the death and burial of Joshua (Josh. 24.29–30). Its narratives recount how Joshua leads the people of Israel across the Jordan River into the land promised to the ancestors, takes possession of that land, divides it among the tribes, and leads them in swearing allegiance to the covenant. Many of these narratives, such as the story of Rahab and the spies and the conquest of Jericho, are well known; others, such as the treaty with the Gibeonites and the land grant to Achsah, are more obscure. Even less familiar are other parts of Joshua: lists of tribal towns and boundaries, and descriptions of rituals.

As the first biblical book following the Torah, Joshua has many features in common with some of those books, especially Deuteronomy. Some passages are nearly direct quotations of texts from Deuteronomy. In addition, just as Deuteronomy is cast as a series of hortatory speeches by Moses, Joshua is replete with declamatory speeches—by Joshua, the leaders, Rahab, the people, and even God. As in Deuteronomy, the focus on the covenant is central to Joshua, with obedience to the covenant a prerequisite for God's blessings.

These similarities and the fact that the land promise of Genesis is only fulfilled in Joshua led many scholars in the 19th and early 20th centuries to speak of the Hexateuch, the first six books of the Bible, comprising Genesis through Joshua. Even more widely accepted now is the idea that, because Deuteronomic features are found throughout the Former Prophets (Joshua to 2 Kings), Joshua in its final form is the result of the compilation of a comprehensive historical work called the Deuteronomistic History, which begins in Deuteronomy and ends in 2 Kings. Such a work might have initially taken shape in the late 7th century BCE, when King Josiah is said to have found a "scroll of the Teaching" and subsequently instituted reforms that reflect Deuteronomic rules and perspectives (see 2 Kings chs 22–23). Because the last events of this "history" take place during the exile, it probably received a final editing in the 6th century BCE. This sequence of redactions may explain some of the duplications and inconsistencies of the book.

Although the completed book may date to the middle of the first millennium BCE, some of its elements may be much older. It clearly draws on materials—such as town lists, battle

stories, and etiologies—that are similar to ancient historiographic and folkloristic traditions known from other ancient Near Eastern cultures of the second and first millennia
BCE. In addition, it contains twelve personal names of non-Israelites (including Rahab,
Jabin, and Adoni-zedek), and these names are attested in Near Eastern documents dating
from or before the period of early Israel.

The reputation of Joshua—the leader and the book—usually is based on the belief that
the land was entirely conquered by Israelites in the early post-Mosaic period. There are
two problems with this view of the narrative, however. First, the book's idea of total acquisition of the land involves carrying out the command to annihilate all the inhabitants
of the land (see, e.g., 6.21); carrying out this *herem*, or "proscription," would have been a
project of genocidal proportions. Second, the intense archeological investigation of virtually all of the places mentioned in Joshua that can be identified with current sites reveals
no pattern of destruction that can be correlated, in either chronology or location, with the
period of early Israel. The moral horror of the first problem may, in fact, be diminished by
the historical data provided by the second. That is, the military and destructive aspects
of the so-called conquest are probably not entirely historical, but rather are literary-
theological constructions to portray the overarching idea of Israelite acquisition of *all* the
land promised to the ancestors. Indeed, most scholars now speak of Israelite settlement in
the land, rather than of conquest, especially because archeology has also shown that
earliest Israel consisted of scores of new villages—settlements of previously unoccupied
territory in the central highlands—rather than rebuilt towns on destroyed Canaanite
strongholds. In this understanding, the *herem* is not historical but rather an ideological expression of the divine ownership of the land being transmitted to the Israelites as the
rightful heirs to their inheritance (*naḥalah*) from the LORD. It also emphasizes that the
Deuteronomistic authors of Joshua felt that the native population of Canaan posed a
serious religious threat, which in theory should be dealt with through annihilation (see
also Deut. 7.2; 20.16–18). That the *herem* was not applied to all these Canaanites is also
suggested by references in Joshua and Judges that non-Israelites did indeed survive in the
land for generations to come.

The structure of the book is straightforward, with an overall division into two parts: The
first twelve chapters present the conquest, and the second twelve describe the apportionment of the land. Within each half there are several units. The conquest part contains an
elaborate account of crossing the Jordan (chs 1–5), followed by military narratives (chs
6–12). The latter focus mainly on the center of the country (chs 6–9), giving only cursory
attention to the south (ch 10) and the north (half of ch 11). The apportionment consists of a
unit delineating tribal lands (chs 13–21) followed by an epilogue of closing speeches and
ceremonies (chs 22–24).

The religious aspects of the book, aside from the overall concern with following God's
teaching, are manifest in several institutions and ceremonies that appear in Joshua. Circumcision and the Passover sacrifice mark the entry to the land and thereby provide didactic value in emphasizing two traditions, introduced in the Torah, that were to become

defining practices of Judaism. Similarly, the important role of the Ark of the Covenant—along with priests, altars, and sacrifices—reflects the integral relationship of the sacral and political in ancient Israelite life. This prominence of the Ark, as the repository of the covenant, foreshadows the centrality of the synagogue Ark (*'aron*), which serves as the repository of the Torah scrolls in later Jewish tradition.

In its frequent usage of Deuteronomistic forms (e.g., speeches), language, and themes, the book of Joshua reveals its didactic intent rather than its interest in accurately depicting the past for its own sake. Furthermore, the telling of Israel's early "history" is not simply to provide a narrative of claim for the land; it also provides a way to make features of the land itself become signals of the past. For example, the numerous etiologies (origin accounts), many of them connected with stone heaps presumably visible on the ancient landscape of the later authors, provide instructional associations for geographic markers.

The continuity with Deuteronomy, and with the Torah in general, is most striking in the way Joshua mirrors aspects of Moses' leadership. Just as Moses led a miraculous crossing of the parted waters of the Reed Sea, so Joshua leads a miraculous crossing of the divided waters of the Jordan. Both leaders send out spies and apportion the land. The exodus itself is thus replicated, to a certain extent, in the experiences of the Israelites described in Joshua. Perhaps most important, the unity of all Israel, exhorted to act in obedience to the Teaching of the LORD, is emphasized in Joshua as in the Torah. This unity will dissipate in the succeeding biblical books. But it is an ideal, along with the concept of an extensive territorial holding with no foreign enclaves, that dominates the book of Joshua. That Israel falls short of the covenant and territorial ideals is alluded to; but it remains for the rest of the Bible to develop those tensions between the ideal and reality.   [CAROL MEYERS]

1 After the death of Moses the servant of the LORD, the LORD said to Joshua son of Nun, Moses' attendant:

2 "My servant Moses is dead. Prepare to cross the Jordan, together with all this people, into the land that I am giving to the Israelites. 3 Every spot on which your foot treads I give to you, as I promised Moses. 4 Your territory shall extend from the wilderness and the Lebanon to the Great River, the River Euphrates [on the east]—the whole Hittite country—and up to the Mediterranean[a] Sea on the west. 5 No one shall be able to resist you as long as you live. As I was with Moses, so I will be with you; I will not fail you or forsake you.

6 "Be strong and resolute, for you shall apportion to this people the land that I swore to their fathers to assign to them. 7 But you must be very strong and resolute to observe faithfully all the Teaching that My servant Moses enjoined upon you. Do not deviate from it to the right or to

1.1–5.12: Preparing to enter the land. 1.1–18: Commissioning Joshua. 1: The announcement of Moses' death connects the book of Joshua to the end of the Torah, for the last chapters of Deuteronomy (32–34) are concerned with the end of Moses' life. The continuity of leadership, originating in the authority of Moses and now manifest in Joshua, was emphasized in the Torah (Num. 27.15–23; Deut. 31.7–8). It was important to rabbinic Judaism as well, as was the connection of the Torah to the subsequent biblical books. Probably for those reasons, the haftarah (prophetic reading) for Simḥat Torah at the conclusion of Sukkot, when chs 33–34 of Deuteronomy are read, is Josh. 1.1–18. **2–18:** The commission is presented in four speeches, one delivered by God (vv. 2–9), two by Joshua (vv. 10–11,

a Heb. "Great."

the left, that you may be successful wherever you go. ⁸ Let not this Book of the Teaching cease from your lips, but recite it day and night, so that you may observe faithfully all that is written in it. Only then will you prosper in your undertakings and only then will you be successful.

⁹ "I charge you: Be strong and resolute; do not be terrified or dismayed, for the LORD your God is with you wherever you go."

¹⁰ Joshua thereupon gave orders to the officials of the people: ¹¹ "Go through the camp and charge the people thus: Get provisions ready, for in three days' time you are to cross the Jordan, in order to enter and possess the land that the LORD your God is giving you as a possession."

¹² Then Joshua said to the Reubenites, the Gadites, and the half-tribe of Manasseh, ¹³ "Remember what Moses the servant of the LORD enjoined upon you, when he said: 'The LORD your God is granting you a haven; He has assigned this territory to you.' ¹⁴ Let your wives, children, and livestock remain in the land that Moses assigned to you ᵃ⁻on this side ofᵃ the Jordan; but every one of your fighting men shall go across armedᵇ in the van of your kinsmen. And you shall assist them ¹⁵ until the LORD has given your kinsmen a haven, such as you have, and they too have gained possession of the land that the LORD your God has assigned to them. Then you may return to the land on the east side of the Jordan, which Moses the servant of the LORD assigned to you as your possession, and you may possess it."

a-a Lit. "across."
b Meaning of Heb. uncertain.

12–15), and one by the people (vv. 16–18). **2–9:** The first speech introduces major themes of the book: crossing the Jordan, acquiring the territory promised to Moses, apportioning the land to the people, and obeying God's teaching as a requisite for success and prosperity. **2–5:** The full extent of the land runs from the *Jordan* on the east to the *Mediterranean Sea* on the west, from the *Lebanon* in the northwest and the *Great River, the River Euphrates,* in the northeast to the *wilderness* in the south. These borders are virtually the same as in the description given by Moses in Deut. 11.24–25. These are ideal borders only, and likely do not re-

flect the land held by Israel either in this period, or in some later time. **2:** *People . . . land* is a juxtaposition that is central to the covenant idea, depicted as originating in the ancestral period and becoming actualized in the era of Joshua. **4:** *The whole Hittite country* does not appear in the parallel description of the land in Deut. 11 or in the Septuagint, the earliest translation of the Bible. It may therefore be a later addition, referring to northern Aram. **5:** *With Moses . . . with you* emphasizes God's presence, essential for success. **6:** The military exhortation to *be strong and resolute,* which occurs three times in this section and again at

the end of ch 1, echoes the language of Deut. 31.6, 7, 23, and also appears in Josh. 10.25. The Vilna Gaon (Elijah ben Solomon Zalman of Vilna, an 18th-century Lithuanian rabbi and biblical commentator) considered "strong" to refer to the body and "resolute" to the emotions, and together they have come to signify the courage necessary for all difficult endeavors. **7–9:** Daily reflections on God's teaching, along with courage, are essential for successful occupation of the land. Many consider these verses as an addition, which reinterprets the earlier idea of strength through military victory as strength through Torah study and obedience. **7:** *Teaching* is the translation here of Heb "torah." It is thus understood to be broader than legislation, whereas Christian translations use "law." Here, as in many places in the Bible, it is unclear if "torah" should be translated as the canonized Torah, or as a set of precanonical "teachings." **8:** *Book* denotes that God's teachings are in written form, though in this period they would have been on a scroll rather than in a book of bound pages (cf. Exod. 24.3–7). Language similar to this verse is also found in Ps. 1.2–3. The opening chapters of Nevi'im and Kethuvim thus both contain references to "torah," emphasizing the significance of Torah within the canon. **10–11:** Joshua gives his first orders. **11:** *Three days* may denote a ritual period before a significant event and is not always to be taken literally (e.g., Gen. 40.13, 19, 20; Exod. 3.18; 19.11). **12–15:** Joshua's second speech is directed to the two-and-a-half Transjordanian tribes. The other nine-and-a-half tribes have helped them take their territory; now they are to cross the Jordan to help those tribes acquire their land (cf. Num. ch 32; Deut. 3.12–20). **14:** *Wives, children, and livestock* are the three parts of a household that are taken as booty in warfare (cf. Deut. 20.14). Mention of them is the first indication that taking the land will involve warfare. The term *fighting men,* used several times (8.3; 10.7) in

16 They answered Joshua, "We will do everything you have commanded us and we will go wherever you send us. 17 We will obey you just as we obeyed Moses; let but the LORD your God be with you as He was with Moses! 18 Any man who flouts your commands and does not obey every order you give him shall be put to death. Only be strong and resolute!"

2 Joshua son of Nun secretly sent two spies from Shittim, saying, "Go, reconnoiter the region of Jericho." So they set out, and they came to the house of a harlot named Rahab and lodged there. 2 The king of Jericho was told, "Some men have come here tonight, Israelites, to spy out the country." 3 The king of Jericho thereupon sent orders to Rahab: "Produce the men who came to you and entered your house, for they have come to spy out the whole country." 4 The woman, however, had taken the two men and hidden them. "It is true," she said, "the men did come to me, but I didn't know where they were from. 5 And at dark, when the gate was about to be closed, the men left; and I don't know where the men went. Quick, go after them, for you can overtake them."—6 Now she had taken them up to the roof and hidden them under some stalks of flax which she had lying on the roof.—7 So the men pursued them in the direction of the Jordan down to the fords; and no sooner had the pursuers gone out than the gate was shut behind them.

8 a-The spies-a had not yet gone to sleep when she came up to them on the roof. 9 She said to the men, "I know that the LORD has given the country to you, because dread of you has fallen upon us, and all the inhabitants of the land are quaking before you. 10 For we have heard how the LORD dried up the waters of the Sea of Reeds for you when you left Egypt, and what you did to Sihon and Og, the two Amorite kings across the Jordan, whom you doomed.b 11 When we heard about it, we lost heart, and no man had any more spirit left because of you; for the LORD your God is the only God in heaven above and on earth

a-a Heb. "They."

b I.e., placed under ḥerem, which meant the annihilation of the inhabitants. Cf. Deut. 2.34 ff.

Joshua to refer to Israelite warriors, likewise anticipates military encounters. **16–18:** The Transjordanian tribes deliver the final speech in ch 1, affirming Joshua as the authoritative successor to Moses.

2.1–24: Reconnaissance: the spies and Rahab. The story of the capture of Jericho in ch 6 is anticipated by the narrative of ch 2, in which two spies are sent to investigate the area west of the Jordan. In commissioning this reconnais-

sance, Joshua reflects the actions of his predecessor Moses, who had earlier sent out spies, according to Num. ch 13. This evidence for the continuity of leadership was important in Jewish tradition and is marked by the fact that the haftarah for Shelaḥ-Lekha (Num. chs 13–15) is Josh. ch 2. **1:** Shittim is the Transjordanian camp of the Israelites and also the setting of the problematic sexual encounter between the Israelites and the Moabite women (Num. 25.1). The mention of Shittim is a fitting introduction to the reconnaissance narrative because of the sexual occupation of the woman who shelters the spies. **2:** Rahab, a harlot of Jericho, is mentioned by name in ch 2 (and again in 6.17, 23, 25), while the spies are not named. The idea of a prostitute as the hero of the narrative was troubling to the Rabbis. Thus she is said (Sifre Num., 78; Zuta'., 75) to have become a pious convert because of her encounter with the spies; she then marries Joshua and becomes the ancestor of nine prophets, including Huldah. In Christian tradition she is reckoned as an ancestor of Jesus (Matt. 1.5) and as an example of living by faith (Hebrews 11.31). An alternate solution, based on a wordplay with "zonah," "harlot"—already found in the Targum and some medieval Jewish commentators— is the claim that Rahab was an innkeeper, who provided food ("mazon"). **2:** Jericho, identified as Tel es-Sultan, is situated about 8 km (five miles) west of the Jordan. Extensive archeological investigations of the site indicate that it was uninhabited at the time of the Israelite settlement in the land; it had probably been destroyed several centuries earlier. **6:** Flax, like other agricultural products, was laid out to dry on the roof. The flat roofs of ancient dwellings were often used for such food-processing activities. **9–13:** In her speech to the spies, Rahab is depicted as having familiarity with the exodus and the battle with the Amorite kings Sihon and Og (Num. ch 21). She also gives voice to what will be the below. 12 Now, since I have shown loyalty to you, swear to me by the LORD that you in turn will show loyalty to my family. Provide me with a reliable sign 13 that you will spare the lives of my father and mother, my brothers and sisters, and all who belong to them, and save us from death." 14 The men answered her, "Our persons are pledged for yours, even to death! If you do not disclose this mission of ours, we will show you true loyalty when the LORD gives us the land."

15 She let them down by a rope through the window—for her dwelling was at the outer side of the city wall and she lived in the actual wall. 16 She said to them, "Make for the hills, so that the pursuers may not come upon you. Stay there in hiding three days, until the pursuers return; then go your way."

17 But the men warned her, "We will be released from this oath which you have made us take 18 [unless,] when we invade the country, you tie this length of crimson cord to the window through which you let us down. Bring your father, your mother, your brothers, and all your family together in your house; 19 and if anyone ventures outside the doors of your house, his blood will be on his head, and we shall be clear. But if a hand is laid on anyone who remains in the house with you, his blood shall be on our heads. 20 And if you disclose this mission of ours, we shall likewise be released from the oath which you made us take." 21 She replied, "Let it be as you say."

She sent them on their way, and they left; and she tied the crimson cord to the window.

22 They went straight to the hills and stayed there three days, until the pursuers turned back. And so the pursuers, searching all along the road, did not find them.

23 Then the two men came down again from the hills and crossed over. They came to Joshua son of Nun and reported to him all that had happened to them. 24 They said to Joshua, "The LORD has delivered the whole land into our power; in fact, all the inhabitants of the land are quaking before us."

3 Early next morning, Joshua and all the Israelites set out from Shittim and marched to the Jordan. They did not cross immediately, but spent the night there. 2 Three

---

scribed," also is used frequently (see 6.17–18). **11:** The designation of the LORD as the *only God in heaven above and on earth below* is rare in the Bible. Calling the LORD the only deity is usually associated with 6th-century BCE prophecy (see Isa. 45.18). **14–22:** The spies pledge loyalty to Rahab, but with conditions that minimize the danger to them. In contrast, Rahab's loyalty to them is absolute; it involves risks and is thus heroic. **15:** *Dwelling . . . in the actual wall* refers to a type of fortification called a casemate wall, one constructed of two separate walls with a space between, which could be left empty or be filled with rubble. It therefore differed from a solid wall by having rooms—often living quarters—between its outer and inner faces. **16:** *Make for the hills,* head westward, where there would be trees and uneven terrain in which the spies might hide. **18:** The *crimson cord* is identified in Jewish tradition with the scarlet thread used to mark the elder of Tamar's twin sons (Gen. 35.28). Rahab's family will be spared because the house will be marked by a red cord, just as the Israelites were spared from the plague of the first-born by marking their homes with red blood (Exod. 12.7, 13). **23–24:** The spies report back to Joshua, relying on Rahab's words rather than on their direct observations, that the land would be theirs to take. **23:** The words *Joshua son of Nun* appear at the end of the spy story as at the beginning (v. 1), thus defining the Rahab narrative as a literary unit. **24:** *Delivered . . . into our power,* lit. "given . . . into our hands," is a phrase used in the ancient Near East to denote that a god is granting victory over enemies.

3.1–5.1: Crossing the Jordan. The story of crossing into the land west of the Jordan is told in several overlapping units (3.1–17; 4.1–9; 4.10–14; 4.15–18; 4.19–5.1), with some of the constituent events anticipated and recounted more than once. The resulting complex narrative may be the result of a redactor

---

characteristic enemy response to the Israelites: *we have heard . . . we lost heart* (see 5.1). Clearly, as in other ancient historical writing, the narrator is speaking by inserting these words into her mouth.

10: The term *doomed,* which occurs fourteen times in Joshua in verbal form, appears for the first time here. It refers to the "ḥerem," or utter destruction of the enemy. The noun form, translated "pro-days later, the officials went through the camp ³and charged the people as follows: "When you see the Ark of the Covenant of the LORD your God being borne by the levitical priests, you shall move forward. Follow it—⁴but keep a distance of some two thousand cubits from it, never coming any closer to it—so that you may know by what route to march, since it is a road you have not traveled before." ⁵And Joshua said to the people, "Purify yourselves,ᵃ for tomorrow the LORD will perform wonders in your midst."

⁶Then Joshua ordered the priests, "Take up the Ark of the Covenant and advance to the head of the people." And they took up the Ark of the Covenant and marched at the head of the people.

⁷The LORD said to Joshua, "This day, for the first time, I will exalt you in the sight of all Israel, so that they shall know that I will be with you as I was with Moses. ⁸For your part, command the priests who carry the Ark of the Covenant as follows: When you reach the edge of the waters of the Jordan, make a halt in the Jordan."

⁹And Joshua said to the Israelites, "Come closer and listen to the words of the LORD your God. ¹⁰By this," Joshua continued, "you shall know that a living God is among you, and that He will dispossess for you the Canaanites, Hittites, Hivites, Perizzites, Girgashites, Amorites, and Jebusites: ¹¹the Ark of the Covenant of the Sovereign of all the earth is advancing before you into the Jordan. ¹²Now select twelve men from the tribes of Israel, one man from each tribe. ¹³When the feet of the priests bearing the Ark of the LORD, the Sovereign of all the earth, come to rest in the waters of the Jordan, the waters of the Jordan—the water coming from upstream—will be cut off and will stand in a single heap."

¹⁴When the people set out from their encampment to cross the Jordan, the priests bearing the Ark of the Cove-

---

a See Exod. 19.10, 15.

---

the Covenant served as a container for the Book of Teaching according to Deut. 31.26. As the potent physical symbol of God's presence among the people, it could be protective in battle (see Num. 10.33–35; 1 Sam. 4.3–5). *The levitical priests*, as bearers of the Ark, may have been a militant group in early Israel (cf. Gen. 49.5–7). **4:** *Two thousand cubits*, about 1,000 m (.625 mile) was the distance needed to separate the people from the powerful sanctity of the Ark. **5:** *Purify yourselves* connotes ritual sanctity, befitting God's presence. The preparations are faintly reminiscent of the preparations for the revelation at Sinai (Exod. 19.9–15). **7:** The statement *the LORD said to Joshua* occurs repeatedly in chs 1–6, indicating that Joshua fully succeeds Moses; and *I will be with you* resumes the promise of the commission in 1.5. **8:** The priests *halt* in the Jordan; this image recurs in vv. 13, 15, 17 and in 4.9–10. **10:** *A living God* is archaic language, perhaps drawn from the identification of the LORD with the Canaanite deity El. It expresses the vitality of God. *Canaanites . . . Jebusites* is a stereotyped listing of the existing population of the land. Similar lists, with varying components, appear frequently in the Bible, often totaling seven groups, thereby signaling the totality of non-Israelite groups (because seven is a symbolic number, representing completeness). Not all of these names can be identified, but the plurality of groups itself may indicate ethnic diversity in the population of Cannan. **12:** *Twelve men* indicates the tribal components of the unified group—all Israel—that figures prominently in Joshua; it anticipates the ceremonial acts of 4.1–9, 20. **13:** *Stand*, in reference to the miraculous piling up of water, is also used for the miraculous halt of the sun's course in 10.13. *Heap* is an unusual term, used elsewhere in the Bible only in references to the parting of the Sea of Reeds (Exod. 15.8; cf. Ps. 78.13). The crossing of the Jordan is thus made parallel to the crossing of the Sea

---

using different sources and being unwilling to eliminate repetitive components.

3.1–17: The Ark and the people cross. The first description of the crossing introduces the religious aspects of the event, represented by the actions of the priests as bearers of the Ark of the Covenant. **1:** *Early next morning*, a phrase meaning that diligent activity is about to begin, recurs at 6.12; 7.16;

8.10. It serves as a formula proclaiming that Joshua is carrying out God's instructions. *The Jordan* symbolizes all the borders of the promised land, and crossing a river into Israel's territory echoes the people's passage through water (the Reed Sea) under the leadership of Moses at the outset of the journey. This strengthens the depiction of Joshua as a new Moses, with great auhority. **2:** Connects with 1.11. **3:** *The Ark of*

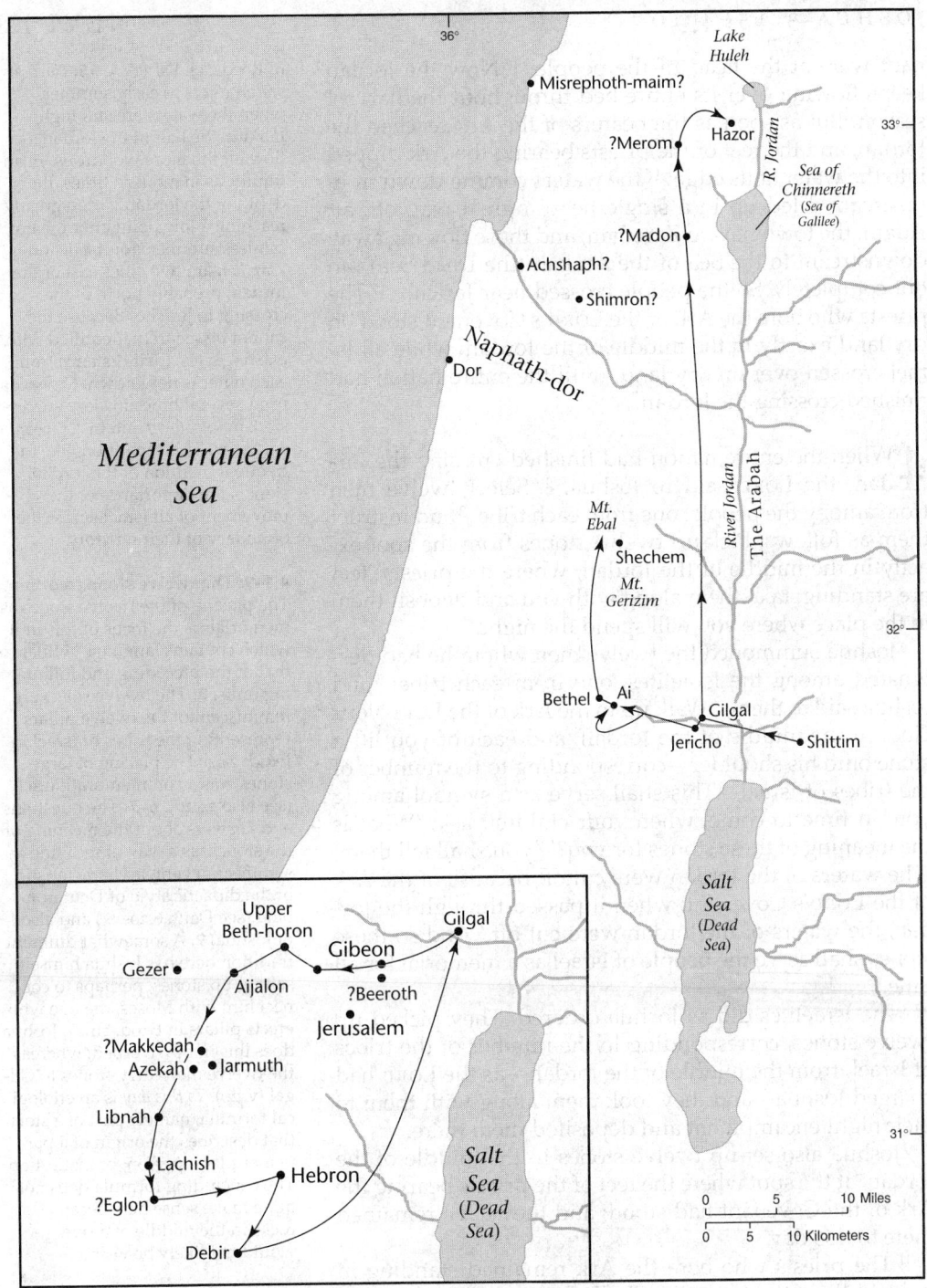

The conquest of Canaan according to the book of Joshua

Labels on the map:

Lake Huleh
Misrephoth-maim?
?Merom
Hazor
R. Jordan
Sea of Chinnereth (Sea of Galilee)
?Madon
Achshaph?
Shimron?
Naphath-dor
Dor
Mediterranean Sea
Mt. Ebal
Shechem
Mt. Gerizim
River Jordan
The Arabah
Bethel
Ai
Gilgal
Jericho
Shittim
Salt Sea (Dead Sea)

Inset map labels:

Upper Beth-horon
Gilgal
Gezer
Gibeon
Aijalon
?Beeroth
Jerusalem
?Makkedah
Azekah
Jarmuth
Libnah
Lachish
?Eglon
Hebron
Debir
Salt Sea (Dead Sea)

0   5   10 Miles
0   5   10 Kilometers

nant were at the head of the people. ¹⁵Now the Jordan keeps flowing over its entire bed throughout the harvest season. But as soon as the bearers of the Ark reached the Jordan, and the feet of the priests bearing the Ark dipped into the water at its edge, ¹⁶the waters coming down from upstream piled up in a single heap a great way off, atᵃ Adam, the town next to Zarethan; and those flowing away downstream to the Sea of the Arabah (the Dead Sea) ran out completely. So the people crossed near Jericho. ¹⁷The priests who bore the Ark of the LORD's Covenant stood on dry land exactly in the middle of the Jordan, while all Israel crossed over on dry land, until the entire nation had finished crossing the Jordan.

4 When the entire nation had finished crossing the Jordan, the LORD said to Joshua, ²"Select twelve men from among the people, one from each tribe, ³and instruct them as follows: Pick up twelve stones from the spot exactly in the middle of the Jordan, where the priests' feet are standing; take them along with you and deposit them in the place where you will spend the night."

⁴Joshua summoned the twelve men whom he had designated among the Israelites, one from each tribe; ⁵and Joshua said to them, "Walk up to the Ark of the LORD your God, in the middle of the Jordan, and each of you lift a stone onto his shoulder—corresponding to the number of the tribes of Israel. ⁶This shall serve as a symbol among you: in time to come, when your children ask, 'What is the meaning of these stones for you?' ⁷you shall tell them, 'The waters of the Jordan were cut off because of the Ark of the LORD's Covenant; when it passed through the Jordan, the waters of the Jordan were cut off.' And so these stones shall serve the people of Israel as a memorial for all time."

⁸The Israelites did as Joshua ordered. They picked up twelve stones, corresponding to the number of the tribes of Israel, from the middle of the Jordan—as the LORD had charged Joshua—and they took them along with them to their night encampment and deposited them there.

⁹Joshua also set up twelve stones in the middle of the Jordan, at the spot where the feet of the priests bearing the Ark of the Covenant had stood; and they have remained there to this day.

¹⁰The priests who bore the Ark remained standing in the middle of the Jordan until all the instructions that the LORD had ordered Joshua to convey to the people had

a So kethib; qere "from."

of Reeds; cf. Ps. 114.3. **15:** *Harvest season* refers to early summer, when the waters are still high, making the halt in the Jordan's flow all the more wondrous. In antiquity, as in modern times, the depth of the Jordan varied greatly, reaching a low point after the hot, rainless summer. **16:** *Adam* and *Zarethan* are two cities east of the Jordan, probably north of the crossing to Jericho. Because they cannot be securely identified with existing sites, their distance from each other is not known. *Crossed* is used several times in close succession: in vv. 16–17 and in 4.1, 9, 11, 13, 22, 23. This repetition, like the frequent mention of the Jordan, signals the importance of the movement of all Israel across the boundary of their territory.

4.1–9: The twelve stone tradition. The placing of the twelve stones as memorials is the focus of this unit, which contains language similar to that of the preceding and following units. **3:** The twelve *stones* are reminiscent of the twelve pillars representing the tribes of Israel in Exod. 24.4. The placing of large stones was a commemorative act (see also 24.27). **6–7:** The questions and answers about the meaning of the stones, as a way of recalling a significant event, is characteristic of the didactic style of Deuteronomy (see Deut. 6.20–24) and also of Joshua. **9:** A somewhat different tradition here has Joshua himself setting up stones, perhaps to connect him with Moses, the one who erects pillars in Exod. ch 24. Joshua does this in the riverbed, whereas the twelve men carry stones to Gilgal (v. 20). *To this day* is an etiological formula, namely part of a story that describes the origin of a particular place, person, or institution. The concluding formula does not quite make sense here because rocks in the middle of a river would not likely be visible.

4.10–14: The people cross. The crossing of the Jordan is reiterated with a strong emphasis on the connection of this event, led by Joshua, with Moses and the exobeen carried out. And so the people speedily crossed over, [a]just as Moses had assured Joshua in his charge to him.[a] [11]And when all the people finished crossing, the Ark of the LORD and the priests advanced to the head of the people.

[12]The Reubenites, the Gadites, and the half-tribe of Manasseh went across armed[b] in the van of the Israelites, as Moses had charged them.[c] [13]About forty thousand shock troops went across, at the instance of the LORD, to the steppes of Jericho for battle.

[14]On that day the LORD exalted Joshua in the sight of all Israel, so that they revered him all his days as they had revered Moses.

[15]The LORD said to Joshua, [16]"Command the priests who bear the Ark of the Pact to come up out of the Jordan." [17]So Joshua commanded the priests, "Come up out of the Jordan." [18]As soon as the priests who bore the Ark of the LORD's Covenant came up out of the Jordan, and the feet of the priests stepped onto the dry ground, the waters of the Jordan resumed their course, flowing over its entire bed as before.

[19]The people came up from the Jordan on the tenth day of the first month, and encamped at Gilgal on the eastern border of Jericho. [20]And Joshua set up in Gilgal the twelve stones they had taken from the Jordan. [21]He charged the Israelites as follows: "In time to come, when your children ask their fathers, 'What is the meaning of those stones?' [22]tell your children: 'Here the Israelites crossed the Jordan on dry land.' [23]For the LORD your God dried up the waters of the Jordan before you until you crossed, just as the LORD your God did to the Sea of Reeds, which He dried up before us until we crossed. [24]Thus all the peoples of the earth shall know how mighty is the hand of the LORD, and you shall fear the LORD your God always."

5 When all the kings of the Amorites on the western side of the Jordan, and all the kings of the Canaanites near the Sea, heard how the LORD had dried up the waters of the Jordan for the sake of the Israelites until they crossed over, they lost heart, and no spirit was left in them because of the Israelites.

[2]At that time the LORD said to Joshua, "Make flint knives and proceed with a second circumcision of the Israelites." [3]So Joshua had flint knives made, and the Israelites were circumcised at Gibeath-haaraloth.[d]

dus. **10:** *Speedily* is reminiscent of the haste of the exodus. **12–13:** The participation of the Transjordanian tribes in the anticipated military events echoes 1.12–13 and again emphasizes Moses' role. **14:** Joshua is *exalted,* as promised in 3.7; he is again compared to Moses.

4.15–18: The priests cross. This unit is largely repetitive in its description of the priests exiting the Jordan, but now the river resumes its flow. **16:** *Pact* is an alternative term for the covenant but appears only here in Joshua (cf. 2 Kings 11.12).

4.19–5.1: The question and answer about the stones, in the last unit of the crossing narrative, emphasizes the didactic role of the story. **4.19:** The *first month* would have been Nisan (formerly Aviv), and the entrance to the land west of the Jordan on the *tenth day* recalls the date when preparations began for the first Passover (Exod. 12.3). **20:** The *twelve stones* are now deposited by Joshua (cf. 4.8). *Gilgal* ("round"), named as the site of the stone deposit, cannot be identified with any certainty. **21:** See a similar didactic question in v. 6. **23:** The exodus analogy is stated directly in this passage, which contains a large number of echoes of the exodus tradition. **24:** *All the peoples* extends the focus from one people, Israel (v. 19), to the non-Israelite world; Israel's crossing gives to other peoples knowledge of the LORD's power (see 2.9–11). **5.1:** Two of the groups of 3.19 represent all the peoples west of the Jordan. *Heard . . . lost heart* resumes 2.9–11 (cf. the opening verse of chs 9–11).

5.2–15: Final preparations for the people and Joshua. Preparations for entering the land are completed by two rituals: circumcision and Passover (5.2–12). The latter is relevant to the selection of these verses (along with 5.13–6.1) as the haftarah for the first day of Passover, when the account of the Passover in Exodus (12.21–51) is

---

a-a *Connection of clause uncertain; cf. Deut. 31.7–8.*   b *Meaning of Heb. uncertain.*
c *See Num. 32.20–22.*   d *I.e., "the Hill of Foreskins."*

⁴This is the reason why Joshua had the circumcision performed: All the people who had come out of Egypt, all the males of military age, had died during the desert wanderings after leaving Egypt. ⁵Now, whereas all the people who came out of Egypt had been circumcised, none of the people born after the exodus, during the desert wanderings, had been circumcised. ⁶For the Israelites had traveled in the wilderness forty years, until the entire nation—the men of military age who had left Egypt—had perished; because they had not obeyed the LORD, and the LORD had sworn never to let them see the land that the LORD had sworn to their fathers to assign to us, a land flowing with milk and honey. ⁷But He had raised up their sons in their stead; and it was these that Joshua circumcised, for they were uncircumcised, not having been circumcised on the way. ⁸After the circumcising of the whole nation was completed, they remained where they were, in the camp, until they recovered.

⁹And the LORD said to Joshua, "Today I have rolled away from you the disgrace of Egypt."ᵃ So that place was called Gilgal,ᵇ as it still is.

¹⁰Encamped at Gilgal, in the steppes of Jericho, the Israelites offered the passover sacrifice on the fourteenth day of the month, toward evening.

¹¹On the day after the passover offering, on that very day, they ate of the produce of the country, unleavened bread and parched grain. ¹²On that same day,ᶜ when they ate of the produce of the land, the manna ceased. The Israelites got no more manna; that year they ate of the yield of the land of Canaan.

¹³Once, when Joshua was near Jericho, he looked up and saw a man standing before him, drawn sword in hand. Joshua went up to him and asked him, "Are you one of us or of our enemies?" ¹⁴He replied, "No, I am cap-

---

a I.e., of the Egyptian bondage.   b Interpreted as "rolling."
c Lit. "on the day after."

---

norm in Judaism. **6:** *Land flowing with milk and honey* is a phrase used many times in the Torah, particularly in Deuteronomy and related literature, but only here in Joshua. In the Torah, the forty years of wandering is attributed to the sin of the spies (Num. ch 13; 14.33), which has been compensated for by the successful mission of the second set of spies in ch 2. **8:** *Nation* ("goy," here and in v. 6), rarely used as a designation for the Israelites (see also 3.17; 4.1), who are usually called a "people" ("ʿam"). *Nation* means a people with a land. **9:** *Disgrace* may signify the lack of circumcision since the exodus, which has been rectified, because "disgrace" is also used for the uncircumcised son of Hamor in Genesis 34.14. *Gilgal* is given a folk etymology, enhancing its didactic role in recounting the crossing of the Jordan. **10:** Offering the *Passover sacrifice* is one more narrative parallel between the exodus and the entrance to the land. *Fourteenth day*, in conformity with Exod. 12.6, gives the circumcised Israelites three days to recover. **11:** *Unleavened bread* is consumed after the Passover offering (a lamb) and may have originally been part of a separate festival derived from farmers, in contrast to the paschal sacrifice, which may derive from shepherds. It too contributes to the exodus connection (Exod. 12.17–20). *Parched grain* is added in anticipation of the "produce of the land" (v. 12), designated in Lev. 23.14 as one of the first fruits of the land. **12:** The cessation of *manna*, the food of wandering, marks the beginning of settled agrarian life.

5.13–15: Joshua's final preparation. 13: Angels are always nameless until the postexilic period, though this unidentified *man standing* is identified as the archangel Michael according to Jewish tradition (*Aggadat Bereshit* 32.64). **14:** The man identifies himself as *captain of the LORD's host*, a military figure that partakes of the imagery of the LORD as a divine warrior with commanding officers of the heavenly hosts (cf. Deut. 33.2;

---

the main Torah reading. Joshua himself is prepared by meeting with the LORD's military commander (5.13–15).

5.2–12: Circumcision and Passover. 5.2: *Second circumcision* may refer to the need to circumcise males who had been born during the wilderness period; the first circumcision would have been that performed in Egypt. As a require-

ment for celebrating the Passover (Exod. 12.48), circumcision, a sign of induction into the Israelite community, is a necessary prelude to the ensuing celebration. **4:** Because of the specification of *military age*, twenty years and older (Num. 1.3), the text is assuming adult circumcision, more typical of peoples practicing this rite than the infant circumcision of the Priestly source (Gen. 17.10–14), which became the tain of the LORD's host. Now I have come!" Joshua threw himself face down to the ground and, prostrating himself, said to him, "What does my lord command his servant?" 15 The captain of the LORD's host answered Joshua, "Remove your sandals from your feet, for the place where you stand is holy." And Joshua did so.

6 Now Jericho was shut up tight because of the Israelites; no one could leave or enter.

2 The LORD said to Joshua, "See, I will deliver Jericho and her king [and her] warriors into your hands. 3 Let all your troops march around the city and complete one circuit of the city. Do this six days, 4 with seven priests carrying seven ram's horns preceding the Ark. On the seventh day, march around the city seven times, with the priests blowing the horns. 5 And when a long blast is sounded on the horn—as soon as you hear that sound of the horn—all the people shall give a mighty shout. Thereupon the city wall will collapse, and the people shall advance, every man straight ahead."

6 Joshua son of Nun summoned the priests and said to them, "Take up the Ark of the Covenant, and let seven priests carrying seven ram's horns precede the Ark of the LORD." 7 And he instructed the people, "Go forward, march around the city, with the vanguard marching in front of the Ark of the LORD." 8 When Joshua had instructed the people, the seven priests carrying seven ram's horns advanced before the LORD, blowing their horns; and the Ark of the LORD's Covenant followed them. 9 The vanguard marched in front of the priests who were blowing the horns, and the rear guard marched behind the Ark, with the horns sounding all the time. 10 But Joshua's orders to the rest of the people were, "Do not shout, do not let your voices be heard, and do not let a sound issue from your lips until the moment that I command you, 'Shout!' Then you shall shout."

11 So he had the Ark of the LORD go around the city and complete one circuit; then they returned to camp and spent the night in camp. 12 Joshua rose early the next day; and the priests took up the Ark of the LORD, 13 while the seven priests bearing the seven ram's horns marched in front of the Ark of the LORD, blowing the horns as they marched. The vanguard marched in front of them, and the rear guard marched behind the Ark of the LORD, with the horns sounding all the time. 14 And so they marched around the city once on the second day and returned to the camp. They did this six days.

15 On the seventh day, they rose at daybreak and

Judg. 5.20; Zech. 9.14). In *prostrating himself*, Joshua acknowledges that the man is a messenger from God. **15:** *"Remove . . . holy"* quotes Exod. 3.5 directly and provides one more connection between Joshua and Moses. This episode seems to end in the middle; it is unclear if something has been lost, or if we are to follow the text's clue and continue to fill in the chapter from Exod. 3.

6.1–12.24: Conquest of Canaanite towns. The Israelite military advance proceeds in three stages: center (6.1–9.27), south (10.1–43), and north (11.1–15). Summaries of conquest (11.16–23; 12.1–24) conclude the account.

6.1–9.27: The central campaign. Taking the central part of the land involves two major victories, Jericho (6.1–27) and Ai (7.1–8.29), followed by a covenant ceremony at Shechem (8.30–35) and an alliance with the Gibeonites (9.1–27).

6.1–27: The destruction of Jericho. The LORD gives specific instructions to Joshua in language combining ritual with warfare. Joshua then carries out the commands, vanquishing Jericho and instituting the "ḥerem," the complete annihilation of the enemy, but, following the promise of ch 2, sparing Rahab and her family. **3:** The *circuit* ploy is a folkloristic element contributing to the rhetoric of conquest. *City* is really a walled town, a much smaller settlement than the term "city" usually implies. Such towns, with their surrounding villages, formed the city-states of Canaanite Palestine (cf. 13.23, 28, etc.). **4:** *Seven* appears 14 times (2 × 7) in ch 6—to indicate days, priests, ram's horns, and circuits of the city. As a biblical idiom for completeness, seven might function as a magical number, but also denotes the totality of the ensuing territorial possession. *Ram's horns,* or shofars, are battle trumpets here (cf. Judg. 6.34) but are more often used to signal worship in the Bible. In Num. 10.9, trumpets play an analogous role. **5:** Archeological research has marched around the city, in the same manner, seven times; that was the only day that they marched around the city seven times. ¹⁶ On the seventh round, as the priests blew the horns, Joshua commanded the people, "Shout! For the LORD has given you the city. ¹⁷ The city and everything in it are to be proscribed for the LORD; only Rahab the harlot is to be spared, and all who are with her in the house, because she hid the messengers we sent. ¹⁸ But you must beware of that which is proscribed, or else you will be proscribed:ᵃ if you take anything from that which is proscribed, you will cause the camp of Israel to be proscribed; you will bring calamity upon it. ¹⁹ All the silver and gold and objects of copper and iron are consecrated to the LORD; they must go into the treasury of the LORD."

²⁰ So the people shouted when the horns were sounded. When the people heard the sound of the horns, the people raised a mighty shout and the wall collapsed. The people rushed into the city, every man straight in front of him, and they captured the city. ²¹ They exterminated everything in the city with the sword: man and woman, young and old, ox and sheep and ass. ²² But Joshua bade the two men who had spied out the land, "Go into the harlot's house and bring out the woman and all that belong to her, as you swore to her." ²³ So the young spies went in and brought out Rahab, her father and her mother, her brothers and all that belonged to her—they brought out her whole family and left them outside the camp of Israel.

²⁴ They burned down the city and everything in it. But the silver and gold and the objects of copper and iron were deposited in the treasury of the House of the LORD. ²⁵ Only Rahab the harlot and her father's family were spared by Joshua, along with all that belonged to her, and she dwelt among the Israelites—as is still the case. For she had hidden the messengers that Joshua sent to spy out Jericho.

²⁶ At that time Joshua pronounced this oath: "Cursed of the LORD be the man who shall undertake to fortify this city of Jericho: he shall lay its foundations at the cost of his first-born, and set up its gates at the cost of his youngest."

²⁷ The LORD was with Joshua, and his fame spread throughout the land.

7 The Israelites, however, violated the proscription: Achan son of Carmi son of Zabdi son of Zerah, of the tribe of Judah, took of that which was proscribed, and the LORD was incensed with the Israelites.

² Joshua sent men from Jericho to Ai, which lies close to

---

a I.e., be put to death; cf. Lev. 27.28–29.

shown that the last *city wall* of Jericho no longer existed at the time of earliest Israel; therefore the story of its conquest may be more symbolic than historical. **17–19:** *Proscribed* denotes the sacral extermination, or "ḥerem," of the enemy, a linking of violence and sanctity common to war ideologies. The destroyed enemy items—people, animals, and objects—are consecrated to the deity who made the victory possible. The "ḥerem" is also mentioned in the Moabite Mesha stele. **19:** *Silver . . . iron* are valuable metal objects and constitute booty for the LORD. **24:** *House of the LORD,* the most common designation for the Jerusalem Temple, is used anachronistically here. **26:** *Cursed . . . be the man,* an imprecation proleptically (i.e., by anticipation) cursing the city's possible rebuilder, is unique in the Bible. The fulfillment of this curse is narrated in 1 Kings 16.34. **27:** This verse is meant to contrast with the following episode, illustrating one of the main themes of the Deuteronomistic History: Following the divine word leads to blessing, while abrogating it leads to curse and punishment.

7.1–8.29: Achan's sin and the destruction of Ai. 7.1–26: Achan's sin. The men of Ai, the next city to be taken, at first overpower the Israelites because one person, Achan, had disobeyed the order to destroy Jericho utterly. **1:** *The LORD was incensed,* describing divine displeasure, appears only once in Joshua in contrast to its frequent presence in Judges. **2:** *Ai* means "The Ruin." The city's name appears very frequently (27 times) in chs 7 and 8, etiologically calling attention to Israel's territorial rights. Archeological research indicates that, like Jericho, the site of Ai (modern et-Tel), located 13 km (8 miles) north of Jerusalem, was uninhabited at the time of earliest Israel. Thus, like the previous story of Jericho, this account is not historically accurate. **3–5:** The attack on Ai does not mention God's presence; the result is a severe routing. **6–15:** An exchange be-

Beth-aven—east of Bethel—with orders to go up and spy out the country. So the men went up and spied out Ai. [3] They returned to Joshua and reported to him, "Not all the troops need go up. Let two or three thousand men go and attack Ai; do not trouble all the troops to go up there, for [the people] there are few." [4] So about three thousand of the troops marched up there; but they were routed by the men of Ai. [5] The men of Ai killed about thirty-six of them, pursuing them outside the gate as far as Shebarim, and cutting them down along the descent. And the heart of the troops [a]sank in utter dismay.[-a]

[6] Joshua thereupon rent his clothes. He and the elders of Israel lay until evening with their faces to the ground in front of the Ark of the LORD; and they strewed earth on their heads. [7] "Ah, Lord GOD!" cried Joshua. "Why did You lead this people across the Jordan only to deliver us into the hands of the Amorites, to be destroyed by them? If only we had been content to remain on the other side of the Jordan! [8] O Lord, what can I say after Israel has turned tail before its enemies? [9] When the Canaanites and all the inhabitants of the land hear of this, they will turn upon us and wipe out our very name from the earth. And what will You do about Your great name?"

[10] But the LORD answered Joshua: "Arise! Why do you lie prostrate? [11] Israel has sinned! They have broken the covenant by which I bound them. They have taken of the proscribed and put it in their vessels; they have stolen; they have broken faith! [12] Therefore, the Israelites will not be able to hold their ground against their enemies; they will have to turn tail before their enemies, for they have become proscribed. I will not be with you any more unless you root out from among you what is proscribed. [13] Go and purify the people. Order them: Purify yourselves for tomorrow. For thus says the LORD, the God of Israel: Something proscribed is in your midst, O Israel, and you will not be able to stand up to your enemies until you have purged the proscribed from among you. [14] Tomorrow morning you shall present yourselves by tribes. Whichever tribe the LORD indicates[b] shall come forward by clans; the clan that the LORD indicates shall come forward by ancestral houses, and the ancestral house that the LORD indicates shall come forward man by man. [15] Then he who is [c]indicated for proscription,[-c] and all that is his, shall be put to the fire, because he broke the Covenant of the LORD and because he committed an outrage in Israel."

tween Joshua (and the elders) and the LORD consists of a complaint and a petition followed by God's explanation and instructions. The setting—in front of the Ark—indicates that the divine presence is understood to dwell in the Ark. Joshua's role as intercessor is similar to that of Moses (e.g., Exod. 32.11–13; Num. 11.11–15; 14.13–19). **6:** *Rent his clothes*, a typical act of penitence as well as mourning. **7:** *Amorites* here represents all the inhabitants of the land (as in 24.15). **11:** *Sinned . . . stolen* indicates that the proscribed vessels belonged to God and that Achan's taking them was theft, a sin violating the covenant. **14:** *Tribes . . . clans . . . ancestral houses* comprise the sociopolitical structure of the Israelites. "Ancestral house," or family household, was the basic unit of society and is understood to represent the extended family and its possessions. *Indicates* probably refers to the casting of lots, a method by which divine decisions were communicated to humans (cf. 14.2).

a-a Lit. *"melted and turned to water."*
b Lit. *"catches."*   c-c Or *"caught in the net."*

16 Early next morning, Joshua had Israel come forward by tribes; and the tribe of Judah was indicated. 17 He then had the clans of Judah come forward, and the clan of Zerah was indicated. Then he had the clan of Zerah come forward by ᵃancestral houses,ᵃ and Zabdi was indicated. 18 Finally he had his ancestral house come forward man by man, and Achan son of Carmi, son of Zabdi, son of Zerah, of the tribe of Judah, was indicated.

19 Then Joshua said to Achan, "My son, pay honor to the LORD, the God of Israel, and make confession to Him. Tell me what you have done; do not hold anything back from me." 20 Achan answered Joshua, "It is true, I have sinned against the LORD, the God of Israel. This is what I did: 21 I saw among the spoil a fine Shinar mantle, two hundred shekels of silver, and a wedge of gold weighing fifty shekels, and I coveted them and took them. They are buried in the ground in my tent, with the silver under it."ᵇ

22 Joshua sent messengers, who hurried to the tent; and there itᵇ was, buried in his tent, with the silver underneath. 23 They took them from the tent and brought them to Joshua and all the Israelites, and displayedᶜ them before the LORD. 24 Then Joshua, and all Israel with him, took Achan son of Zerah—and the silver, the mantle, and the wedge of gold—his sons and daughters, and his ox, his ass, and his flock, and his tent, and all his belongings, and brought them up to the Valley of Achor. 25 And Joshua said, "What calamity you have brought upon us! The LORD will bring calamity upon you this day." And all Israel pelted him with stones. They put them to the fire and stoned them. 26 They raised a huge mound of stones over him, which is still there. Then the anger of the LORD subsided. That is why that place was named the Valley of Achorᵈ—as is still the case.

8 The LORD said to Joshua, "Do not be frightened or dismayed. Take all the fighting troops with you, go and march against Ai. See, I will deliver the king of Ai, his people, his city, and his land into your hands. 2 You shall treat Ai and her king as you treated Jericho and her king; however, you may take the spoil and the cattle as booty for yourselves. Now set an ambush against the city behind it."

3 So Joshua and all the fighting troops prepared for the march on Ai. Joshua chose thirty thousand men, valiant

16–20: The guilty party is identified by lots, through a dramatic selection process involving all Israel, thus intensifying the notion of communal responsibility for adherence to the covenant. **21:** The stolen objects are identified: a garment from Shinar (probably Babylonia), 200 shekels of silver (2.5 kg, 5.9 lbs) and a 50-shekel wedge of gold (about .5 kg, 1.25 lbs). **25:** The reference to *calamity* is foreshadowed by 6.18. *Put them to the fire and stoned them* probably means that the stolen booty was burned and the guilty family stoned. Like severe ritual impurity, Achan's sin had infected the entire household. **26:** *Mound of stones . . . still there:* The didactic function of the narrative is made clear in this etiology. *Valley of Achor* is a wordplay on "to stir up a calamity" ("ʿakhar").

8.1–29: The destruction of Ai.
1–2: Now that the Israelites are purified of Achan's sin, the LORD provides instructions that will assure victory. The annihilation of Ai, however, unlike that of Jericho, will allow for booty. **3–8:** Joshua relays God's instructions but in much greater detail, thus contributing to the drama of the impending event. **3:** *Thirty thousand men,* an impossible number for an ambush, possibly means "thirty, a man from each contingent," or "thirty contingents." The word translated "thousand" can also denote a small military unit, ranging from five to fifteen men per contingent. *Valiant warriors* echoes 1.14 and anticipates 10.7. The Heb is the same in these three verses. **9:** *Bethel,* which became a major city of the Northern Kingdom, is identified with modern Beitun, less than 3.5 km (2 miles) west of Ai. **10–29:** Using brilliant military strategy, the Israelites take Ai and put all its inhabitants to death. A similar strategy is used in Judg. chs 9 and 21. **12:** *Five thousand men* may represent another, smaller ambush; or it may be an alternative designation for the warriors of 8.3. **14:** *Facing the Arabah,* eastward, toward the Jordan Valley.

a-a So some Heb. mss. and some ancient versions; most mss. and editions have "men."
b I.e., the mantle.   c Meaning of Heb. uncertain.
d Connected with ʾakhar "to bring calamity upon"; cf. v. 25.

warriors, and sent them ahead by night. ⁴He instructed them as follows: "Mind, you are to lie in ambush behind the city; don't stay too far from the city, and all of you be on the alert. ⁵I and all the troops with me will approach the city; and when they come out against us, as they did the first time, we will flee from them. ⁶They will come rushing after us until we have drawn them away from the city. They will think, 'They are fleeing from us the same as last time'; but while we are fleeing before them, ⁷you will dash out from your ambush and seize the city, and the LORD your God will deliver it into your hands. ⁸And when you take the city, set it on fire. Do as the LORD has commanded. Mind, I have given you your orders."

⁹Joshua then sent them off, and they proceeded to the ambush; they took up a position between Ai and Bethel— west of Ai—while Joshua spent the night with the rest of the troops.

¹⁰Early in the morning, Joshua mustered the troops; then he and the elders of Israel marched upon Ai at the head of the troops. ¹¹All the fighting force that was with him advanced near the city and encamped to the north of Ai, with a hollow between them and Ai.—¹²He selected about five thousand men and stationed them as an ambush between Bethel and Ai, west of the city. ¹³Thus the main body of the army was disposed on the north of the city, but the far end of it was on the west. (This was after Joshua had ᵃspent the nightᵃ in the valley.ᵇ)— ¹⁴When the king of Ai saw them, he and all his people, the inhabitants of the city, rushed out in the early morning to the ᶜmeeting place,ᶜ facing the Arabah, to engage the Israelites in battle; for he was unaware that a force was lying in ambush behind the city. ¹⁵Joshua and all Israel fled in the direction of the wilderness, as though routed by them. ¹⁶All the troops in the city gathered to pursue them; pursuing Joshua, they were drawn out of the city. ¹⁷Not a man was left in Ai or in Bethel who did not go out after Israel; they left the city open while they pursued Israel.

¹⁸The LORD then said to Joshua, "Hold out the javelin in your hand toward Ai, for I will deliver it into your hands." So Joshua held out the javelin in his hand toward the city. ¹⁹As soon as he held out his hand, the ambush came rushing out of their station. They entered the city and captured it; and they swiftly set fire to the city. ²⁰The men of Ai looked back and saw the smoke of the city rising to the sky; they had no room for flight in any direction.

18: The *javelin* is indicated by a rare word for a weapon that symbolized sovereignty. Joshua holds it out (vv. 18, 26) in a magical gesture reminiscent of Moses' actions (Exod. 14.15–21, 26–27; 17.9–12). Later commentators such as Rashi, disturbed at the magical background of this action, instead viewed it as sign for those ambushing to attack.

---

a-a *So with some mss. (cf. v. 9); most mss. and editions read "marched."*
b *Syriac reads "with the troops"; cf. v. 9.*   c-c *Emendation yields "descent"; cf. 7.5.*

The people who had been fleeing to the wilderness now became the pursuers. ²¹ For when Joshua and all Israel saw that the ambush had captured the city, and that smoke was rising from the city, they turned around and attacked the men of Ai. ²² Now the other [Israelites] were coming out of the city against them, so that they were between two bodies of Israelites, one on each side of them. They were slaughtered, so that no one escaped or got away. ²³ The king of Ai was taken alive and brought to Joshua.

²⁴ When Israel had killed all the inhabitants of Ai who had pursued them into the open wilderness, and all of them, to the last man, had fallen by the sword, all the Israelites turned back to Ai and put it to the sword.

²⁵ The total of those who fell that day, men and women, the entire population of Ai, came to twelve thousand.

²⁶ Joshua did not draw back the hand with which he held out his javelin until all the inhabitants of Ai had been exterminated. ²⁷ However, the Israelites took the cattle and the spoil of the city as their booty, in accordance with the instructions that the LORD had given to Joshua.

²⁸ Then Joshua burned down Ai, and turned it into a mound of ruins for all time, a desolation to this day. ²⁹ And the king of Ai was impaled on a stake until the evening. At sunset, Joshua had the corpse taken down from the stake and it was left lying at the entrance to the city gate. They raised a great heap of stones over it, which is there to this day.

³⁰ At that time Joshua built an altar to the LORD, the God of Israel, on Mount Ebal, ³¹ as Moses, the servant of the LORD, had commanded the Israelites—as is written in the Book of the Teaching of Moses[a]—an altar of unhewn stone upon which no iron had been wielded. They offered on it burnt offerings to the LORD, and brought sacrifices of well-being. ³² And there, on the stones, he inscribed a copy of the Teaching that Moses had written for the Israelites. ³³ All Israel—stranger and citizen alike—with their elders, officials, and magistrates, stood on either side of the Ark, facing the levitical priests who carried the Ark of the LORD's Covenant. Half of them faced Mount Gerizim and half of them faced Mount Ebal, as Moses the servant of the LORD had commanded them of old, in order to bless the people of Israel. ³⁴ After that, he read all the words of the Teaching, the blessing and the curse, just as is written in the Book of the Teaching.[b] ³⁵ There was not a word of all

a See Deut. 27.3–8.   b See Deut. 27.11–28.68.

27: The modification of the "herem," perhaps to prevent another Achan incident, is less liberal than that of Deut. 20.14, where even women and children can be taken as booty, provided the captured town is not in Israelite territory. **28:** *Ruins for all time* echoes the language of Deut. 13.16, contributes to the etymology of Ai, and provides an instructive etiology. **29:** The king of Ai, who has been taken alive, is *impaled on a stake,* a common treatment of a vanquished ruler in the ancient Near East (cf. 10.26–27). The removal of his body at evening may reflect the precept in Deut. 21.23. *Heap of stones . . . to this day,* another etiological proclamation.

8.30–35: Covenant ceremony at Shechem. This section, which narrates the fulfillment by Joshua of Deut. ch 27, interrupts the continuity between 8.29 and 9.1–3. It portrays an event in a location some distance from Jericho and Ai and is similar in theme to ch 24. Its presence here maintains the importance of the Book of the Teaching of Moses in the Joshua narrative (cf. 1.7–8) and also affirms again Joshua's legitimacy as successor to Moses. **30:** *Mount Ebal* is situated opposite Mount Gerizim (v. 33) in the hill country of Ephraim. The important northern city of Shechem (modern Tel Balatah), near Nablus, commands the valley between the two mountains. **31:** The *altar of unhewn stone* fits the guidelines of Exod. 20.22 and fulfills the directive of Moses in Deut. 27.5. *Burnt offerings . . . sacrifices of well-being* replicate the sacrifices ordered by Moses after he wrote all the words of the covenant at Mount Sinai (Exod. 24.3–5). **32:** The *stones,* not the altar stones but rather those intended for the copy of the Teaching to be inscribed on stone when the Israelites cross the Jordan according to Moses' instructions (Deut. 27.2–3). Since these stones could not hold a complete copy of the Torah or even all of Deuteronomy, it is unclear exactly what was written that Moses had commanded that Joshua failed to read in the presence of the entire assembly of Israel, including the women and children and the strangers who accompanied them.

9 When all the kings ᵃ⁻west of⁻ᵃ the Jordan—in the hill country, in the Shephelah, and along the entire coast of the Mediterranean Sea up to the vicinity of Lebanon, the [land of the] Hittites, Amorites, Canaanites, Perizzites, Hivites, and Jebusites—learned of this, ²they gathered with one accord to fight against Joshua and Israel.

³But when the inhabitants of Gibeon learned how Joshua had treated Jericho and Ai, ⁴they for their part resorted to cunning. They set out ᵇ⁻in disguise:⁻ᵇ they took worn-out sacks for their asses, and worn-out waterskins that were cracked and patched; ⁵they had worn-out, patched sandals on their feet, and threadbare clothes on their bodies; and all the bread they took as provision was dry and crumbly. ⁶And so they went to Joshua in the camp at Gilgal and said to him and to the men of Israel, "We come from a distant land; we propose that you make a pact with us." ⁷The men of Israel replied to the Hivites, "But perhaps you live among us; how then can we make a pact with you?"ᶜ

⁸They said to Joshua, "We will be your subjects." But Joshua asked them, "Who are you and where do you come from?" ⁹They replied, "Your servants have come from a very distant country, because of the fame of the LORD your God. For we heard the report of Him: of all that He did in Egypt, ¹⁰and of all that He did to the two Amorite kings on the other side of the Jordan, King Sihon of Heshbon and King Og of Bashan who lived in Ashtaroth. ¹¹So our elders and all the inhabitants of our country instructed us as follows, 'Take along provisions for a trip, and go to them and say: We will be your subjects; come make a pact with us.' ¹²This bread of ours, which we took from our houses as provision, was still hot when we set out to come to you; and see how dry and crumbly it has become. ¹³These wineskins were new when we filled them, and see how they have cracked. These clothes and sandals of ours are worn out from the very long journey." ¹⁴The men ᵇ⁻took [their word] because of⁻ᵇ their provisions, and did not inquire of the LORD. ¹⁵Joshua established friendship with them; he made a pact with them to spare their lives, and the chieftains of the community gave them their oath.

on them. This topic is the subject of much debate and discussion in rabbinic and medieval Jewish commentary. **34:** *The blessing and the curse* typically conclude covenants in the ancient Near East (as Deut. 27.11–13; ch 28; cf. Lev. 26.3–34). **35:** *Women . . . strangers,* indicating the inclusive community required to hear the recitation of the teaching, as in Deut. 31.12.

9.1–27: The treaty with the Gibeonites. Having conquered Ai through a ruse, the Israelites themselves are now tricked by the clever strategy of the Gibeonites. The story that follows both shows the great power of the LORD and explains the origins of a particular class of Temple servants. **1–2:** This introductory statement describes the response—preparation for war—of those who hear of the Israelite victories. The list of people should probably also include the Girgashites, as in 3.10 and 24.11. These verses introduce through contrast the actions of the Gibeonites. **3:** *Gibeon,* identified with modern el-Jib, lies on an important east-west route 9 km (5.5 miles) north of Jerusalem. Its existence during the period of Israelite beginnings is doubtful according to the archeological evidence, but it was an important city during the monarchy. **6:** *Pact,* another translation of "berit," Heb for "covenant." **7:** *Hivites,* a group probably originating in Asia Minor. **9:** The Gibeonites claim to be from a *distant country,* which would mean they would not be subject to the required annihilation of those living in territory promised to Israel (cf. 8.27, Deut. 20.14). *Fame of the LORD,* meaning that the victories of a people are attributed to their god. **10:** The conquest of the Transjordanian kings *Sihon . . . Og,* like the departure from Egypt, arouses dread (as in 2.10; see Num. 21.21–35; Deut. 2.26–3.17). **12–13:** The details of their provisions and clothing, anticipated in vv. 4–5, create vivid dramatic interest. **15:** *Friendship,* Heb "shalom," or "peace."

---

a-a Lit. "across."   b-b Meaning of Heb. uncertain.   c Cf. Deut. 7.2.

¹⁶But when three days had passed after they made this pact with them, they learned that they were neighbors, living among them. ¹⁷So the Israelites set out, and on the third day they came to their towns; these towns were Gibeon, Chephirah, Beeroth, and Kiriath-jearim. ¹⁸But the Israelites did not attack them, since the chieftains of the community had sworn to them by the LORD, the God of Israel. The whole community muttered against the chieftains, ¹⁹but all the chieftains answered the whole community, "We swore to them by the LORD, the God of Israel; therefore we cannot touch them. ²⁰This is what we will do to them: We will spare their lives, so that there may be no wrath against us because of the oath that we swore to them." ²¹And the chieftains declared concerning them, "They shall live!" And they became hewers of wood and drawers of water for the whole community, as the chieftains had decreed concerning them.

²²Joshua summoned them and spoke to them thus: "Why did you deceive us and tell us you lived very far from us, when in fact you live among us? ²³Therefore, be accursed! Never shall your descendants cease to be slaves, hewers of wood and drawers of water for the House of my God." ²⁴But they replied to Joshua, "You see, your servants had heard that the LORD your God had promised His servant Moses to give you the whole land and to wipe out all the inhabitants of the country on your account; so we were in great fear for our lives on your account. That is why we did this thing. ²⁵And now we are at your mercy; do with us what you consider right and proper." ²⁶And he did so; he saved them from being killed by the Israelites. ²⁷That day Joshua made them hewers of wood and drawers of water—as they still are—for the community and for the altar of the LORD, in the place that He would choose.

10 When King Adoni-zedek of Jerusalem learned that Joshua had captured Ai and proscribed it, treating Ai and its king as he had treated Jericho and its king, and that, moreover, the people of Gibeon had come to terms with Israel and remained among them, ²ᵃ⁻he was⁻ᵃ very frightened. For Gibeon was a large city, like one of the royal cities—in fact, larger than Ai—and all its men were warriors. ³So King Adoni-zedek of Jerusalem sent this message to King Hoham of Hebron, King Piram of Jarmuth, King Japhia of Lachish, and King Debir of Eglon: ⁴"Come up and help me defeat Gibeon; for it has come to terms with Joshua and the Israelites."

a-a Heb. "they were."

16–27: The Gibeonite deception is discovered, and the Israelites reluctantly honor their pact, which had been sworn, presumably, in the name of the LORD. The Bible takes such vows very seriously (see Exod. 20.7; Deut. 5.11). Thus, a main theme of this chapter is the conflict between the obligation to obliterate the inhabitants of the land, and the oath promising to allow these people to live. According to 2 Sam. ch 21, Saul violated this promise and put some Gibeonites to death. **17:** The Hivites live in Gibeon and in *Chephirah, Beeroth, and Kiriath-jearim,* three settlements west of Gibeon. **21:** *Hewers of wood and drawers of water* are the menial jobs to which the Gibeonites are assigned as subjects of Israel, despite the idea that even such workers were equal participants in the covenant (Deut. 29.10–11). This eternal assignment is repeated in vv. 23 and 27, underscoring the servitude of the deceivers. **24:** The Gibeonites refer to the "herem" (Deut. 20.16–18). **27:** *As they still are* is an etiological marker. *Place that He would choose* is the typical language of Deuteronomy (e.g., Deut. 12.5–18), anticipating the central and sole place, namely Jerusalem, for sacrificing to the LORD. This oblique reference to Jerusalem offers continuity with the following chapter, which narrates a coalition led by the king of Jerusalem.

10.1–43: Southern campaign. Two units comprise the military encounters leading to the control of the south: vanquishing a coalition of five kings (vv. 1–27); seven other victories (vv. 28–43).

10.1–27: The battle with the five kings. The first unit of the southern campaign is recounted in two parts. First, Joshua and the Israelites honor their pact with Gibeon and rescue them from an Amorite coalition (vv. 1–15). Then the kings of that coalition are captured and executed (vv. 16–27). **10.1–15: Rescuing the Gibeonites.** Led by the king of Jerusalem, a group of five kings, fearing the

5 The five Amorite kings—the king of Jerusalem, the king of Hebron, the king of Jarmuth, the king of Lachish, and the king of Eglon, with all their armies—joined forces and marched on Gibeon, and encamped against it and attacked it. 6 The people of Gibeon thereupon sent this message to Joshua in the camp at Gilgal: "Do not fail your servants; come up quickly and aid us and deliver us, for all the Amorite kings of the hill country have gathered against us." 7 So Joshua marched up from Gilgal with his whole fighting force, all the trained warriors.

8 The LORD said to Joshua, "Do not be afraid of them, for I will deliver them into your hands; not one of them shall withstand you." 9 Joshua took them by surprise, marching all night from Gilgal. 10 The LORD threw them into a panic before Israel: [Joshua] inflicted a crushing defeat on them at Gibeon, pursued them in the direction of the Beth-horon ascent, and harried them all the way to Azekah and Makkedah. 11 While they were fleeing before Israel down the descent from Beth-horon, the LORD hurled huge stones on them from the sky, all the way to Azekah, and they perished; more perished from the hailstones than were killed by the Israelite weapons.

12 On that occasion, when the LORD routed the Amorites before the Israelites, Joshua addressed the LORD; he said in the presence of the Israelites:

> "Stand still, O sun, at Gibeon,
> O moon, in the Valley of Aijalon!"

13   And the sun stood still
            And the moon halted,
            While a nation wreaked judgment on its foes

—as is written in the Book of Jashar.ᵃ Thus the sun halted in midheaven, and did not press on to set, for a whole day; 14 for the LORD fought for Israel. Neither before nor since has there ever been such a day, when the LORD acted on words spoken by a man. 15 Then Joshua together with all Israel returned to the camp at Gilgal.

16 Meanwhile, those five kings fled and hid in a cave at Makkedah. 17 When it was reported to Joshua that the five kings had been found hiding in a cave at Makkedah, 18 Joshua ordered, "Roll large stones up against the mouth of the cave, and post men over it to keep guard over them. 19 But as for the rest of you, don't stop, but press on the

a Presumably a collection of war songs.

and Hebron, are vanquished.
1: *Jerusalem,* appearing here by this name for the first time in the Bible, is depicted in a leadership role among local Amorite city-states. Inhabited by Jebusites, it did not become Israelite until the time of David (see 15.63 and 2 Sam. 5.6–9; Judg. 1.8 is not historical). *Ai . . . Jericho . . . Gibeon* differs from the order of the preceding narratives. **3:** *Debir* as the king's name is problematic, for it is a city name in v. 38. **6:** *Hill country* designates the central highlands, the core of ancient Israel (cf. v. 40); but three of the cities of the coalition (Jarmuth, Lachish, and Eglon) are in the foothills, or Shephelah. **8–10:** *The LORD* is to be directly involved. The mention of *Azekah and Makkedah,* both probably in the southern Shephelah, anticipates the second unit of the southern campaign in which Makkedah figures prominently (vv. 16, 17, 21, 28, 29). **11:** *Descent from Beth-horon,* a pass also known as the Valley of Aijalon (see v. 12), is a major route from the Shephelah to the hill country. *Hailstones,* lit. "large stones," wreak havoc on the enemy. They are understood as divine intervention, and they are echoed by the "large stones" of v. 18. **12:** *Stand still . . . ,* opens an ancient mythic poem, using language similar to that used for the Divine Warrior in Canaanite mythology (cf. Judg. 5.20; Hab. 3.11) and signifying God's miraculous and direct involvement in human affairs. As stated in the following verse, the purpose of this action is for the Israelites to have sufficient time to kill the enemy before the sun set. **13:** *Book of Jashar,* also cited in 2 Sam. 1.18, is one of many biblical references to ancient Heb writings that are no longer extant. **10.16–27: Capturing the kings. 16:** Their forces have been defeated by God, but the *five kings* themselves escape. **17–18:** *Large stones,* same as the "hailstones" of v. 11. The *cave* is first a refuge and then a tomb (v. 27) for the kings, thus serving two functions of caves in ancient Israel.

alliance between Gibeon and Israel, seeks to vanquish Gibeon. The Gibeonites are saved by invoking their pact with the Israelites, who themselves receive help from the LORD; and the kings of certain cities that would be central to later history, such as Jerusalem heels of your enemies and harass them from the rear. Don't let them reach their towns, for the Lord your God has delivered them into your hands." ²⁰ When Joshua and the Israelites had finished dealing them a deadly blow, they were wiped out, except for some fugitives who escaped into the fortified towns. ²¹ The whole army returned in safety to Joshua in the camp at Makkedah; no one so much as snarled[a] at the Israelites. ²² And now Joshua ordered, "Open the mouth of the cave, and bring those five kings out of the cave to me." ²³ This was done. Those five kings—the king of Jerusalem, the king of Hebron, the king of Jarmuth, the king of Lachish, and the king of Eglon—were brought out to him from the cave. ²⁴ And when the kings were brought out to Joshua, Joshua summoned all the men of Israel and ordered the army officers who had accompanied him, "Come forward and place your feet on the necks of these kings." They came forward and placed their feet on their necks. ²⁵ Joshua said to them, "Do not be frightened or dismayed; be firm and resolute. For this is what the Lord is going to do to all the enemies with whom you are at war." ²⁶ After that, Joshua had them put to death and impaled on five stakes, and they remained impaled on the stakes until evening. ²⁷ At sunset Joshua ordered them taken down from the poles and thrown into the cave in which they had hidden. Large stones were placed over the mouth of the cave, [and there they are] to this very day.

²⁸ At that time Joshua captured Makkedah and put it and its king to the sword, proscribing it[b] and every person in it and leaving none that escaped. And he treated the king of Makkedah as he had treated the king of Jericho.

²⁹ From Makkedah, Joshua proceeded with all Israel to Libnah, and he attacked it. ³⁰ The Lord delivered it and its king into the hands of Israel; they put it and all the people in it to the sword, letting none escape. And he treated its king as he had treated the king of Jericho.

³¹ From Libnah, Joshua proceeded with all Israel to Lachish; he encamped against it and attacked it. ³² The Lord delivered Lachish into the hands of Israel. They captured it on the second day and put it and all the people in it to the sword, just as they had done to Libnah.

³³ At that time King Horam of Gezer marched to the help of Lachish; but Joshua defeated him and his army, letting none of them escape.

³⁴ From Lachish, Joshua proceeded with all Israel to

24: Joshua's officers put their *feet on the necks* of the five kings in a symbolic action of conquest (cf. 1 Kings 5.17; Ps. 110.1). Various representations of this action in Mesopotamian royal reliefs indicate that it was an action used widely in the ancient Near East. 25: *Firm and resolute* echoes God's exhortation of 1.7, 9 and signals impending battles. 26: After being killed, the kings are *impaled on five stakes;* the public exposure of corpses is meant to instill fear in other enemies (as in 8.29). 27: *To this very day* signifies an etiology.

10.28–43: Seven additional victories. In repetitive language, the conquest of seven cities is reported (vv. 27–39), followed by a summary of the southern campaign (vv. 40–43). 28: *Proscribing* is specified for four of the cities, and other terms indicate that all are subject to the complete slaughter of the vanquished. The treatment of the *king of Jericho* is not mentioned in the account of the fall of Jericho in ch 6. 31: *Lachish* (modern Tel ed-Duweir), a major site in the southern Shephelah, holds out for two days. There is no mention of the slaughter of its king. 33: *Gezer* is the main site of the central Shephelah. Its king and army are defeated in the field, but the city itself remains a Canaanite stronghold until the time of Solomon (see 16.10; Judg. 1.29; 1 Kings 9.16). 36: *Hebron,* south of Jerusalem, is conquered by Caleb, not Joshua, according to 15.13 (cf. Judg. 1.9). 37: *All its towns,* designating the satellite settlements of an ancient walled city, is used only for Hebron and Debir, both sites in the hill country. 38: The taking of *Debir* is attributed elsewhere to Othniel (15.15–17; Judg. 1.11–13). 39: *As they had done* is used seven times in vv. 28–39, conveying the complete success of the southern campaign. 41–42: In these summary verses, *Joshua,* like the typical ancient Near Eastern ruler, is credited with all the victories, despite other texts with different traditions. 41: *Kadesh-barnea . . . Gibeon* designates the southern

a Cf. Exod. 11.7.
b So several mss.; most mss. and the editions read "them."

Eglon; they encamped against it and attacked it. 35 They captured it on the same day and put it to the sword, proscribing all the people that were in it, as they had done to Lachish.

36 From Eglon, Joshua marched with all Israel to Hebron and attacked it. 37 They captured it and put it, its king, and all its towns, and all the people that were in it, to the sword. He let none escape, proscribing it and all the people in it, just as he had done in the case of Eglon.

38 Joshua and all Israel with him then turned back to Debir and attacked it. 39 He captured it and its king and all its towns. They put them to the sword and proscribed all the people in it. They let none escape; just as they had done to Hebron, and as they had done to Libnah and its king, so they did to Debir and its king.

40 Thus Joshua conquered the whole country:a the hill country, the Negeb, the Shephelah, and the slopes, with all their kings; he let none escape, but proscribed everything that breathed—as the LORD, the God of Israel, had commanded. 41 Joshua conquered them from Kadesh-barnea to Gaza, all the land of Goshen, and up to Gibeon. 42 All those kings and their lands were conquered by Joshua at a single stroke, for the LORD, the God of Israel, fought for Israel. 43 Then Joshua, with all Israel, returned to the camp at Gilgal.

11 When the news reached King Jabin of Hazor, he sent messages to King Jobab of Madon, to the king of Shimron, to the king of Achshaph, 2 and to the other kings in the north—in the hill country, in the Arabah south of Chinnereth, in the lowlands, and in the districtb of Dor on the west; 3 to the Canaanites in the east and in the west; to the Amorites, Hittites, Perizzites, and Jebusites in the hill country; and to the Hivites at the foot of Hermon, in the land of Mizpah. 4 They took the field with all their armies—an enormous host, as numerous as the sands on the seashore—and a vast multitude of horses and chariots. 5 All these kings joined forces; they came and encamped together at the Waters of Merom to give battle to Israel.

6 But the LORD said to Joshua, "Do not be afraid of them; tomorrow at this time I will have them all lying slain before Israel. You shall hamstring their horses and burn their chariots." 7 So Joshua, with all his fighting men, came upon them suddenly at the Waters of Merom, and

a I.e., the whole southern part of Canaan.
b Meaning of Heb. uncertain.

territory, with *Goshen* referring to the northern Negev, not the Egyptian Goshen (Gen. 45.10). **43:** *All Israel* emphasizes that the successful campaign involved the whole people.

11.1–15: Northern campaign. Fewer details are provided for the conquest of the north, revealing the narrator's greater interest in the central and southern regions, a bias that likely reflects Judean authorship. All the northern kings join in one large coalition, which Joshua overcomes through divine intervention. **1:** *Jabin* is called the King of Canaan in Judg. 4.2, underscoring his prominence in the north. *Hazor* (modern Tel el-Qedah), located in upper Galilee on a route controlling trade with Mesopotamia, was a powerful city-state for much of the Bronze Age. *Madon . . . Shimron . . . Achshaph* cannot be securely identified but are presumably in the vicinity of Hazor. Although scholars have proposed various ways of harmonizing this account with Judg. chs 4–5, none of these harmonizations has succeeded because they all tend to treat these narratives as straightforward historical accounts and do not recognize that they are legendary, fictional tales. **2–3:** The inclusiveness of the northern enemy is provided by listing geographical extent and by naming peoples (six groups; as 9.1; cf. 3.9; 24.11). **2:** *Arabah . . . Chinnereth,* Jordan Valley . . . Sea of Galilee. **3:** *Hermon,* a high mountain northeast of the Sea of Galilee. **4:** *Sands on the seashore* uses hyperbole to convey the enormity of the enemy force and recalls God's promise to the ancestors (Gen. 22.17). *Horses and chariots* denote military technology superior to Israelite infantry. **5:** *Waters of Merom* may specify a high plain, suitable for chariot warfare, because "merom" can mean "elevated." **6:** *Hamstring their horses and burn their chariots,* a strategy to remove the Canaanite technological advantage. Hamstringing means cutting the large tendon of a horse's rear leg, thereby dispounced upon them. [8] The LORD delivered them into the hands of Israel, and they defeated them and pursued them all the way to Great Sidon ªand Misrephothmaim,ª and all the way to the Valley of Mizpeh[b] on the east; they crushed them, letting none escape. [9] And Joshua dealt with them as the LORD had ordered him; he hamstrung their horses and burned their chariots.

[10] Joshua then turned back and captured Hazor and put her king to the sword.—Hazor was formerly the head of all those kingdoms.—[11] They proscribed and put to the sword every person in it. Not a soul survived, and Hazor itself was burned down. [12] Joshua captured all those royal cities and their kings. He put them to the sword; he proscribed them in accordance with the charge of Moses, the servant of the LORD. [13] However, all those towns that are still standing on their mounds were not burned down by Israel; it was Hazor alone that Joshua burned down. [14] The Israelites kept all the spoil and cattle of the rest of those cities as booty. But they cut down their populations with the sword until they exterminated them; they did not spare a soul. [15] Just as the LORD had commanded His servant Moses, so Moses had charged Joshua, and so Joshua did; he left nothing undone of all that the LORD had commanded Moses.

[16] Joshua conquered the whole of this region: the hill country [of Judah], the Negeb, the whole land of Goshen, the Shephelah, the Arabah, and the hill country and coastal plain of Israel—[17] [everything] from Mount Halak, which ascends to Seir, all the way to Baal-gad in ᶜthe Valley of the Lebanonᶜ at the foot of Mount Hermon; and he captured all the kings there and executed them.

[18] Joshua waged war with all those kings over a long period. [19] Apart from the Hivites who dwelt in Gibeon, not a single city made terms with the Israelites; all were taken in battle. [20] For it was the LORD's doing to stiffen their hearts to give battle to Israel, in order that they might be proscribed without quarter and wiped out, as the LORD had commanded Moses.

[21] At that time, Joshua went and wiped out the Anakites from the hill country, from Hebron, Debir, and Anab, from the entire hill country of Judah, and from the entire hill country of Israel; Joshua proscribed them and their towns. [22] No Anakites remained in the land of the Israelites; but some remained in Gaza, Gath, and Ashdod.

a-a *Change of vocalization yields "and Misrephoth on the west."*
b *Apparently identical with Mizpah in v. 3.*
c-c *I.e., the valley between the Lebanon and Anti-Lebanon ranges.*

abling it (cf. 2 Sam. 8.4). **8:** The western and eastern extent of the rout. **10:** *Head of all those kingdoms* again suggests Hazor's supremacy in the north. **11–14:** The proscription against the northern coalition involves the burning of Hazor and slaughter of its inhabitants, but only the slaughter of the people and kings of the other cities, with booty allowed. **13:** *Mounds* is the word for "tel," the artificial hill formed by the successive building of settlements over earlier ones. **15:** *Moses . . . Joshua* again conveys the transition of divinely ordained leadership.

11.16–23: Summary of the conquest. The acquisition of all the territory west of the Jordan, except Gibeon, is presented in sweeping terms. "Whole," "all," and "entire"—the same Heb word—appear repeatedly in this section to emphasize the complete extent of the conquest. Yet this section likely incorporates several sources, including v. 18, which contains a different notion of the conquest. **17:** *Mount Halak* (Jebel Halaq) is southeast of Beersheba. *Seir,* a name for the mountain of Edom, east of the Rift Valley. *Baal-gad,* a northern site, possibly Banias on the slopes of Mount Hermon. **18:** The notion that these wars were *waged . . . over a long period* contradicts the tenor of the previous material, and likely reflects another voice in the text. **19:** *Made terms,* lit. "made shalom," a reference to the treaty with Gibeon. **20:** *Stiffen their hearts,* the phrase used to describe God's control over the pharaoh of the exodus (Exod. 4.21, etc.), thereby allowing Moses to succeed as Joshua now has done. **21:** *Anakites,* a name for pre-Israelite inhabitants of Canaan who were renowned for their stature (Num. 13.33; Deut. 9.2). **21:** Mention of the *hill country of Judah . . . Israel* reflects the perspective of the narrator, aware of a southern and a northern kingdom, Judah and Israel. **22:** *Gaza, Gath, and Ashdod,* all Philistine cities, may indicate that the Anakites were related peoples. The giant Goliath

23 Thus Joshua conquered the whole country, just as the LORD had promised Moses; and Joshua assigned it to Israel to share according to their tribal divisions. And the land had rest from war.

12 The following are the local kings whom the Israelites defeated and whose territories they took possession of:

East of the Jordan, from the Wadi Arnon to Mount Hermon, including the eastern half of the Arabah: 2 ªKing Sihon of the Amorites, who resided in Heshbon and ruled over part of Gilead—from Aroer on the bank of the Wadi Arnon and the wadi proper up to the Wadi Jabbok [and] the border of the Ammonites—3 and over the eastern Arabah up to the Sea of Chinnereth and, southward by way of Beth-jeshimoth at the foot of the slopes of Pisgah on the east, down to the Sea of the Arabah, that is, the Dead Sea. 4 Also the territory of King Og of Bashan—one of the last of the Rephaim—who resided in Ashtaroth and in Edrei 5 and ruled over Mount Hermon, Salcah, and all of Bashan up to the border of the Geshurites and the Maacathites, as also over part of Gilead [down to] the border of King Sihon of Heshbon. 6 These were vanquished by Moses, the servant of the LORD, and the Israelites; and Moses, the servant of the LORD, assigned ᵇthat territoryᵇ as a possession to the Reubenites, the Gadites, and the half-tribe of Manasseh.

7 And the following are the local kings whom Joshua and the Israelites defeated on the west side of the Jordan—from Baal-gad in the Valley of the Lebanon to Mount Halak, which ascends to Seir—which Joshua assigned as a possession to the tribal divisions of Israel: 8 in the hill country, in the lowlands, in the Arabah, in the slopes,ᶜ in the wilderness, and in the Negeb—[in the land of] the Hittites, the Amorites, the Canaanites, the Perizzites, the Hivites, and the Jebusites. 9 They were:

	the king of Jericho	1
	the king of Ai, near Bethel,	1
10	the king of Jerusalem	1
	the king of Hebron	1
11	the king of Jarmuth	1
	the king of Lachish	1
12	the king of Eglon	1
	the king of Gezer	1

a Meaning of vv. 2 and 3 uncertain.
b-b Lit. "it."
c I.e., the slopes of Pisgah; cf. 13.20.

was from Gath (1 Sam. 17.4; cf. 2 Sam. 21.19). **23:** *To share . . . divisions,* anticipating the territorial allotments presented in the second half of Joshua. *The land had rest from war* begins the transition to territorial assignments and also links Joshua's defeat of the Anakites with another tradition in which Caleb defeats them (14.6–13).

12.1–24: The vanquished kings. Another summary of Israel's victories includes those of Moses in Transjordan (vv. 1–6) and those of Joshua—summarized (vv. 7–8) and then listed by city (vv. 9–24)—west of the Jordan. This chapter continues the main theme of a complete conquest, but accomplishes this in a different form, using lists.

12.1–6: Moses in Transjordan, a summary based on Num. 21.21–35 and Deut. 2.26–3.17 (cf. Joshua 2.10; 9.10). The cities mentioned, as far as they have been identified with excavated ruins, appear not to have been occupied at the time of Israelite beginnings. Again, the historicity of the narrative appears doubtful. **1:** *Wadi Arnon to Mount Hermon* comprises Ammon, Gilead, and Bashan. The east-west Arnon gorge divides Ammon from Moab to the south. **2:** *Wadi Jabbok,* the east-west gorge separating Ammon from Gilead. **4:** *Bashan,* northern Transjordan, known today as the Golan Heights. *Rephaim,* perhaps a designation for professional chariot warriors, also signified people of great stature (see Deut. 2.20–21). **12.7–8: Joshua's victories,** summarized once more, as in 11.2–3, 16–17. **12.9–24: List of conquered cities.** This list includes more than twice as many cities as those mentioned in the preceding narratives, indicating how selective the narratives are. Of the total of thirty-one cities, only twenty have been securely identified with excavated sites. Of those, only two—Bethel (v. 16) and Hazor (v. 19)—reflect the claims of Joshua: destruction of a city followed by a smaller, presumably Israelite settlement. This discrepancy between text and archeol-

13	the king of Debir	1
	the king of Geder	1
14	the king of Hormah	1
	the king of Arad	1
15	the king of Libnah	1
	the king of Adullam	1
16	the king of Makkedah	1
	the king of Bethel	1
17	the king of Tappuah	1
	the king of Hepher	1
18	the king of Aphek	1
	the king of Sharon	1
19	the king of Madon	1
	the king of Hazor	1
20	the king of Shimron-meron	1
	the king of Achshaph	1
21	the king of Taanach	1
	the king of Megiddo	1
22	the king of Kedesh	1
	the king of Jokneam in the Carmel	1
23	the king of Dor in the district*a* of Dor	1
	the king of Goiim in Gilgal	1
24	the king of Tirzah	1
	Total number of kings	31.

13 Joshua was now old, advanced in years. The LORD said to him, "You have grown old, you are advanced in years; and very much of the land still remains to be taken possession of. ² This is the territory that remains: all the districts of the Philistines and all [those of] the Geshurites, ³ from the Shihor, which is close to Egypt, to the territory of Ekron on the north, are accounted Canaanite, namely, those of the five lords of the Philistines—the Gazites, the Ashdodites, the Ashkelonites, the Gittites, and the Ekronites—and those of the Avvim ⁴ on the south; further, all the Canaanite country from Mearah of the Sidonians to Aphek at the Amorite border ⁵ and the land of the Gebalites, with the whole [Valley of the] Lebanon, from Baal-gad at the foot of Mount Hermon to Lebo-hamath on the east, ⁶ with all the inhabitants of the hill country from the [Valley of the] Lebanon to *b-*Misrephoth-maim,*-b* namely, all the Sidonians. I Myself will dispossess *c-*those nations*-c* for the Israelites; you have only to apportion *d-*their lands*-d* by lot among Israel, as I have commanded you. ⁷ Therefore, divide this territory into heredi-

a Meaning of Heb. uncertain.   b-b See note on 11.8.
c-c Lit. "them."   d-d Lit. "it."

ogy, as for the Transjordanian cities, points to the Joshua narratives as serving ideological purposes rather than preserving historical sequences of events.

13.1–21.43: Tribal land allotments. Having accomplished his first task, taking possession of most of the land, Joshua must now divide it into portions for all the tribes located west of the Jordan. The priest Eleazar and heads of the family households join Joshua in this task, presented in religious as well as sociopolitical terms. The assignment of Transjordanian allotments by Moses is reviewed (ch 13), and the apportionment of the remaining tribal lands follows (chs 14–19). It uses boundary descriptions as well as lists of towns; and brief narratives, integrated into some of the tribal sections, give an instructional quality to the otherwise tedious designations of territory. The final allotments, within tribal possessions, are the cities of refuge (ch 20) and the Levitical cities (ch 21). It is unclear which period, if any, these lists reflect.

13.1–7: The remaining land. Despite the overall picture of complete conquest, these verses acknowledge that some territory, in the southeast and the north, is not yet controlled by Israelites according to the full dimensions of the land in Num. 34.1–12. Other passages in chs 13–21 will similarly acknowledge the presence of uncaptured areas or of foreigners remaining within tribal boundaries (15.63; 16.10; 17.11–13; 19.47). **1:** The beginning of this verse is similar to 23.1. This suggests that the intervening material, dealing with tribal allotments, may be a resumptive repetition, which was inserted secondarily in Joshua. **2:** *Philistines* and *Geshurites* controlled the southwestern coast and the land east of the Sea of Galilee, respectively. These areas became Israelite at the time of the united monarchy (2 Sam. 8.1–2; 3.3). **4–6:** Areas to the north and northeast (i.e., Phoenicia) will be taken for the Israelites by God. **7:** *Heredi-*

tary portions for the nine tribes and the half-tribe of Manasseh."

8 Now the Reubenites and the Gadites, along with ª the other half-tribe, ª had already received the shares which Moses assigned to them on the east side of the Jordan—as assigned to them by Moses the servant of the LORD: 9 from Aroer on the edge of the Wadi Arnon and the town in the middle of the wadi, the entire Tableland [from] Medeba to Dibon, 10 embracing all the towns of King Sihon of the Amorites, who had reigned in Heshbon, up to the border of the Ammonites; 11 further, Gilead, the territories of the Geshurites and the Maacathites, and all of Mount Hermon, and the whole of Bashan up to Salcah—12 the entire kingdom of Og, who had reigned over Bashan at Ashtaroth and at Edrei. (He was the last of the remaining Rephaim.) These were defeated and dispossessed by Moses; 13 but the Israelites failed to dispossess the Geshurites and the Maacathites, and Geshur and Maacath remain among Israel to this day. 14 No hereditary portion, however, was assigned to the tribe of Levi, their portion being the fire offerings of the LORD, the God of Israel, as He spoke concerning them. ᵇ

15 And so Moses assigned [the following] to the tribe of the Reubenites, for their various clans, 16 and it became theirs: The territory from Aroer, on the edge of the Wadi Arnon and the town in the middle of the wadi, up to Medeba—the entire Tableland—17 Heshbon and all its towns in the Tableland: Dibon, Bamoth-baal, Beth-baal-meon, 18 Jahaz, Kedemoth, Mephaath, 19 Kiriathaim, Sibmah, and Zereth-shahar ᶜ in the hill of the valley, ᶜ 20 Beth-peor, the slopes of Pisgah, and Beth-jeshimoth—21 all the towns of the Tableland and the entire kingdom of Sihon, the king of the Amorites, who had reigned in Heshbon. (For Moses defeated him and the Midianite chiefs Evi, Rekem, Zur, Hur, and Reba, who had dwelt in the land as princes of Sihon. 22 Together with the others that they slew, the Israelites put Balaam son of Beor, the augur, to the sword.) 23 The boundary of the Reubenites was the edge of the Jordan. That was the portion of the Reubenites for their various clans—those towns with their villages.

24 To the tribe of Gad, for the various Gadite clans, Moses assigned [the following], 25 and it became their territory: Jazer, all the towns of Gilead, part of the country of the Ammonites up to Aroer, which is close to Rabbah,

a-a Lit. "it."
b See Deut. 18.1.
c-c Emendation yields "in the hill country; and in the Valley . . ."

tary portions is the translation of "naḥalah," a word appearing repeatedly in the allotment chapters, usually as "portion" (e.g., 13.14, 23, 33; 14.2, 3; 15.1, 13, 20; 19.49). A legal term, it designates land as part of an estate; God, the ultimate owner of the land, bestows it on the tribes.

13.8–33: Transjordanian allotments. A general description of the territories across the Jordan (vv. 8–13) and a statement about Levi's lack of territory (v. 14) are followed by a detailed description of the boundaries and cities of the two-and-a-half Transjordanian tribes (vv. 15–32) and another statement about the Levites having no portion (v. 33). This land was rarely controlled by the Israelites but was usually considered within the ideal boundaries of the land (as Deut. 3.12–18). **10–12:** Sihon and Og, Transjordanian rulers said to have been conquered by Moses, are repeatedly mentioned in Joshua (see 12.2–6). **13:** One of several acknowledgements that not all the land was controlled by Israelites. **14:** Levi, a priestly group, lacks its own tribal lands and will be dispersed among the other tribes (ch 21). Fire offerings, sacrifices brought by other Israelites, become the revenues of the officiants. **15:** Reubenites, descendants of Jacob's first-born son, come first here as elsewhere in the Bible (e.g., Gen. 35.23; 46.8, 9; Exod. 1.2). **20:** Beth-peor, a place near the burial spot of Moses (Deut. 34.6). Probably the same as Baal Peor, it is the site of the idolatrous Israelite behavior (Num. ch 25) alluded to in Joshua 22.17. **21:** Midianite, a designation for southern groups controlling desert trade routes. Seen as close to the Israelites at the time of Moses (Exod. 3.1), they are elsewhere Israel's enemies (Judg. chs 7–8). **22:** Balaam . . . the augur, a prophetic figure depicted favorably in Num. chs 22–24, is here said to have been killed by Israelites (cf. Num. 31.8). **23:** Towns with their villages denotes walled settlements with their satellite settlements (cf. 6.3 n.).

26 and from Heshbon to Ramath-mizpeh and Betonim, and from Mahanaim to the border of Lidbir;ᵃ 27 and in the Valley, Beth-haram, Beth-nimrah, Succoth, and Zaphon— the rest of the kingdom of Sihon, the king of Heshbon— down to the edge of the Jordan and up to the tip of the Sea of Chinnereth on the east side of the Jordan. 28 That was the portion of the Gadites, for their various clans—those towns with their villages.

29 And to the half-tribe of Manasseh Moses assigned [the following], so that it went to the half-tribe of Manasseh, for its various clans, 30 and became their territory: Mahanaim,ᵇ all of Bashan, the entire kingdom of Og, king of Bashan, and all of Havvoth-jairᶜ in Bashan, sixty towns; 31 and part of Gilead, and Ashtaroth and Edrei, the royal cities of Og in Bashan, were assigned to the descendants of Machir son of Manasseh—to a part of the descendants of Machir—for their various clans.

32 Those, then, were the portions that Moses assigned in the steppes of Moab, on the east side of the Jordan. 33 But no portion was assigned by Moses to the tribe of Levi; the LORD, the God of Israel, is their portion, as He spoke concerning them.ᵈ

14 And these are the allotments of the Israelites in the land of Canaan, that were apportioned to them by the priest Eleazar, by Joshua son of Nun, and by the heads of the ancestral houses of the Israelite tribes, 2 the portions that fell to them by lot, as the LORD had commanded through Moses for the nine and a half tribes. 3 For the portion of the other two and a half tribes had been assigned to them by Moses on the other side of the Jordan. He had not assigned any portion among them to the Levites; 4 for whereas the descendants of Joseph constituted two tribes, Manasseh and Ephraim, the Levites were assigned no share in the land, but only some towns to live in, with the pastures for their livestock and cattle. 5 Just as the LORD had commanded Moses, so the Israelites did when they apportioned the land.

6 The Judites approached Joshua at Gilgal, and Caleb son of Jephunneh the Kenizzite said to him: "You know what instructions the LORD gave at Kadesh-barnea to Moses, the man of God, concerning you and me. 7 I was forty years old when Moses the servant of the LORD sent me from Kadesh-barnea to spy out the land, and I gave

14.1–5: Introduction to the allotments west of the Jordan. The lands of the other nine-and-a-half tribes are assigned by Joshua, the priest Eleazar, and officials of sub-tribal units through the casting of lots. **1:** *Eleazar* is the priest who presided at Joshua's installation as successor to Moses (Num. 27.15–23). *Heads of the ancestral houses,* denoting leaders of household groups smaller than tribes, appears only here and in 19.51 and 21.1. **2:** Apportionment by *lot* was the standard procedure for assigning undivided inheritances in the ancient Near East. The tribes are thus made co-beneficiaries of God's bequest. This explains the role of Eleazar, who is probably imagined as the official casting lots with the Urim and Thummim (see Ezra 2.63; Neh. 7.65). **4:** *Manasseh and Ephraim,* the sons of Joseph, one of Jacob's twelve sons, each become eponymous ancestors of land-holding tribes to compensate for Levi as a tribe without territory, thus maintaining the total of twelve territorial tribes.

14.6–17.18: Judah and Joseph allotments. Allocation of tribal lands proceeds in stylized format: A narrative framework encloses boundaries and town lists as well as brief stories. The first tribe is Judah (14.6–15.63), which will become the most prominent of all as the biblical story unfolds. The one-and-a-half Joseph tribes are next (chs 16–17); these would be central in the Northern Kingdom. The emphasis on Judah and Joseph, and certain parallels in the structure used to describe them, thus reflect the prominence of the Northern and Southern Kingdoms after the monarchy is divided in the early 10th century (ca. 922 BCE).

14.6–15: Caleb's role. A narrative reviewing deeds of a leading Judahite figure, Caleb, begins the Judahite allotment. It reinforces a main theme of the book: God keeps His word, obedience is rewarded, and through God's power, even the greatest enemies are vanquished. **6:** *Caleb,* one of the

---

ᵃ *Change of vocalization yields "Lo-debar"; cf. 2 Sam. 9.4, 5; 17.27.*

ᵇ *Lit. "from Mahanaim."*

ᶜ *See note on Num. 32.41.*   ᵈ *See Deut. 18.1.*

him a forthright report. [8] While my companions who went up with me took the heart out of the people, I was loyal to the LORD my God. [9] On that day, Moses promised on oath, 'The land on which your foot trod shall be a portion for you and your descendants forever, because you were loyal to the LORD my God.' [10] Now the LORD has preserved me, as He promised. It is forty-five years since the LORD made this promise to Moses, when Israel was journeying through the wilderness; and here I am today, eighty-five years old. [11] I am still as strong today as on the day that Moses sent me; my strength is the same now as it was then, for battle and for activity.[a] [12] So assign to me this hill country as the LORD promised on that day. Though you too heard on that day that Anakites are there and great fortified cities, if only the LORD is with me, I will dispossess them, as the LORD promised."

[13] So Joshua blessed Caleb son of Jephunneh and assigned Hebron to him as his portion. [14] Thus Hebron became the portion of Caleb son of Jephunneh the Kenizzite, as it still is, because he was loyal to the LORD, the God of Israel.—[15] The name of Hebron was formerly Kiriath-arba: [Arba] was the great man among the Anakites.

And the land had rest from war.

15 The portion that fell by lot to the various clans of the tribe of Judah lay farthest south, down to the border of Edom, which is the Wilderness of Zin. [2] Their southern boundary began from the tip of the Dead Sea, from the tongue that projects southward. [3] It proceeded to the south of the Ascent of Akrabbim, passed on to Zin, ascended to the south of Kadesh-barnea, passed on to Hezron, ascended to Addar, and made a turn to Karka. [4] From there it passed on to Azmon and proceeded to the Wadi of Egypt; and the boundary ran on to the Sea. That shall be your southern boundary.

[5] The boundary on the east was the Dead Sea up to the mouth of the Jordan. On the northern side, the boundary began at the tongue of the Sea at the mouth of the Jordan. [6] The boundary ascended to Beth-hoglah and passed north of Beth-arabah; then the boundary ascended to the Stone of Bohan son of Reuben. [7] The boundary ascended [b]from the Valley of Achor to Debir and turned north[b] to Gilgal,[c] facing the Ascent of Adummim which is south of the wadi; from there the boundary continued to the waters of En-shemesh and ran on to En-rogel. [8] Then the boundary ascended into the Valley of Ben-hinnom, along

twelve spies sent out by Moses (Num. chs 13–14), was celebrated for military prowess and loyalty in defeating the formidable Anakites (see 11.21–22). *Kenizzite,* originally a non-Israelite group, perhaps from Edom (Gen. 36.9–11, 15, 42), but later incorporated into the Judahite genealogy (Judg. 1.13). **8:** *Took the heart out,* undermined the morale of the people, who feared the might of the inhabitants of the land. **13:** *Hebron,* in the hills 30 km (19 miles) south of Jerusalem. **15:** *Kiriath-arba,* lit. "Town of the Four," may mean that it once was a small coalition of neighboring settlements. But "Arba" becomes etiologically linked with the Anakites.

15.1–63: Judah's allotment consists of three different types of materials: boundary descriptions (vv. 1–12), a brief narrative about Caleb and Othniel (vv. 13–19), and a list of towns (vv. 20–63) that ends with a notice of the failure to capture Jerusalem.

15.1–12: Judah's boundaries are laid out in a counterclockwise direction: south (vv. 2–4), east (v. 5a), north (vv. 5b–11), and west (12a). A summary statement appears in v. 12b. **1:** *Zin,* northeast of Kadesh-barnea (see Num. 20.1), is probably a region of the northern Negev. **3:** *Hezron,* also the name of a Judahite figure considered the ancestor of most of the families in the hill country of Judah (Gen. 46.12; Num. 26.21; 1 Chron. 2.9–55). **4:** *Wadi of Egypt,* presumably Wadi el-Arish, southwest of Gaza. **6:** *Bohan,* nowhere else listed as a son of Reuben (except 18.17), means "thumb" and may be a topographical feature (thumb-shaped stone) displacing a personal name. **8:** *Jebusites,* implying Jerusalem is not yet Israelite.

---

a Lit. "and to go out and come in."   *b-b* Meaning of Heb. uncertain.
c Apparently identical with Geliloth, 18.17.

the southern flank of the Jebusites—that is, Jerusalem. The boundary then ran up to the top of the hill which flanks the Valley of Hinnom on the west, at the northern end of the Valley of Rephaim. ⁹From that hilltop the boundary curved to the fountain of the Waters of Nephtoah and ran on to the towns of Mount Ephron; then the boundary curved to Baalah—that is, Kiriath-jearim. ¹⁰From Baalah the boundary turned westward to Mount Seir,ª passed north of the slope of Mount Jearim—that is, Chesalon—descended to Beth-shemesh, and passed on to Timnah. ¹¹The boundary then proceeded to the northern flank of Ekron; the boundary curved to Shikkeron, passed on to Mount Baalah, and proceeded to Jabneel; and the boundary ran on to the Sea. ¹²And the western boundary was the edge of the Mediterranean Sea. Those were the boundaries of the various clans of the Judites on all sides.

¹³In accordance with the LORD's command to Joshua, Caleb son of Jephunneh was given a portion among the Judites, namely, Kiriath-arba—that is, Hebron. ([Arba] was the father of Anak.) ¹⁴Caleb dislodged from there the three Anakites: Sheshai, Ahiman, and Talmai, descendants of Anak. ¹⁵From there he marched against the inhabitants of Debir—the name of Debir was formerly Kiriath-sepher—¹⁶and Caleb announced, "I will give my daughter Achsah in marriage to the man who attacks and captures Kiriath-sepher." ¹⁷His kinsman Othniel the Kenizziteᵇ captured it; and Caleb gave him his daughter Achsah in marriage.

¹⁸ᶜWhen she came [to him], she induced himᶜ to ask her father for some property. She dismounted from her donkey, and Caleb asked her, "What is the matter?" ¹⁹She replied, "Give me a present; for you have given me away as Negeb-land;ᵈ so give me springs of water." And he gave her Upper and Lower Gulloth.ᵉ

²⁰This was the portion of the tribe of the Judites by their clans:

²¹The towns at the far end of the tribe of Judah, near the border of Edom, in the Negeb, were: Kabzeel, Eder, Jagur, ²²Kinah, Dimonah, Adadah, ²³Kedesh, Hazor, Ithnan, ²⁴Ziph, Telem, Bealoth, ²⁵Hazor-hadattah, Kerioth-hezron—that is, Hazor—²⁶Amam, Shema, Moladah, ²⁷Hazar-gaddah, Heshmon, Beth-pelet, ²⁸Hazar-shual, Beer-sheba, Biziothiah, ²⁹Baalah, Iim, Ezem, ³⁰Eltolad, Chesil, Hormah, ³¹Ziklag, Madmannah, Sansannah,

15.13–19: Recollections of Caleb and Othniel (see 10.36–39; 14.8–13; this material is repeated with minor variants in Judg. 1.9–15). As already reported, Caleb conquers Hebron. His Kenizzite kinsman takes Debir and marries Caleb's daughter. **15:** *Debir*, south of Hebron, is probably Khirbet Rabûd. **17:** *Achsah*, Caleb's daughter, is a reward for Othniel's victory. She in turn manipulates her father so that she owns well-watered lands (vv. 18–19).

15.20–63: Judah's towns. The list is the longest and most detailed of the tribal town lists, a function of the material available to the author, and reflecting Judah's leading role in the biblical account of ancient Israel—it is the tribe of the Davidic dynasty and the dominant tribe of the Southern Kingdom, Judah. If one includes the two units not yet conquered (the Philistine cities, vv. 45–47; Jerusalem, v. 63), the towns comprise twelve units and probably represent authentic administrative districts established later during the monarchy. **63:** Contrast Judg. 1.21.

---

a Not the Seir of Edom.   b Cf. 14.6, 14.
c-c Meaning of Heb. uncertain. Some Greek mss. read "he induced her"; cf. Judg. 1.14.
d I.e., as a dry land, that is, without a dowry.   e I.e., "springs."

32 ᵃ-Lebaoth, Shilhim,-ᵃ Ain and Rimmon.ᵇ Total: 29ᶜ towns, with their villages.

33 In the Lowland: Eshtaol, Zorah, Ashnah, 34 Zanoah, En-gannim, Tappuah, Enam, 35 Jarmuth, Adullam, Socoh, Azekah, 36 Shaaraim, Adithaim, Gederah, and Gedero-thaim—14ᵈ towns, with their villages.

37 Zenan, Hadashah, Migdal-gad, 38 Dilan, Mizpeh, Jok-theel, 39 Lachish, Bozkath, Eglon, 40 Cabbon, Lahmas, Chithlish, 41 Gederoth, Beth-dagon, Naamah, and Makke-dah: 16 towns, with their villages.

42 Libnah, Ether, Ashan, 43 Iphtah, Ashnah, Nezib, 44 Ke-ilah, Achzib, and Mareshah: 9 towns, with their villages.

45 Ekron, with its dependencies and villages. 46 From Ekron westward, all the towns in the vicinity of Ashdod, with their villages—47 Ashdod, its dependencies and its villages—Gaza, its dependencies and its villages, all the way to the Wadi of Egypt and the edge of the Mediter-ranean Sea.

48 And in the hill country: Shamir, Jattir, Socoh, 49 Dan-nah, Kiriath-sannahᵉ—that is, Debir—50 Anab, Eshtemoh, Anim, 51 Goshen, Holon, and Giloh: 11 towns, with their villages.

52 Arab, Dumah, Eshan, 53 Janum, Beth-tappuah, Aphekah, 54 Humtah, Kiriath-arba—that is, Hebron—and Zior: 9 towns, with their villages.

55 Maon, Carmel, Ziph, Juttah, 56 Jezreel, Jokdeam, Zanoah, 57 Kain, Gibeah, and Timnah: 10 towns, with their villages.

58 Halhul, Beth-zur, Gedor, 59 Maarath, Beth-anoth, and Eltekon: 6 towns, with their villages.ᶠ

60 Kiriath-baal—that is, Kiriath-jearim—and Rabbah: 2 towns, with their villages.

61 In the wilderness: Beth-arabah, Middin, Secacah, 62 Nibshan, Ir-melah,ᵍ and En-gedi: 6 towns, with their vil-lages.

63 But the Judites could not dispossess the Jebusites, the inhabitants of Jerusalem; so the Judites dwell with the Jeb-usites in Jerusalem to this day.

a-a Cf. below 19.6.

b Cf. Ain, Rimmon, 19.7 below, and 1 Chron. 4.32; En-rimmon, Neh. 11.29.

c The number is uncertain. Some of the same towns are listed under Simeon, cf. 19.1–9; so Rashi.

d The number is uncertain. Tappuah and Enam may have been one place; so Rashi on basis of 17.7.

e Emendation yields "Kiriath-sepher"; cf. Septuagint.

f Septuagint adds: Tekoa, Ephrathah—that is, Bethlehem—Peor, Etam, Kulon, Tatam, Sores, Karem, Gallim, Bether, and Manach—11 towns, with their villages.

g Or "the City of Salt."

16

The portion that fell by lot to the Josephites ran from the Jordan at Jericho—from the waters of Jericho east of the wilderness. From Jericho it ascended through the hill country to Bethel. [2] From Bethel it ran to Luz and passed on to the territory of the Archites at Ataroth, [3] descended westward to the territory of the Japhletites as far as the border of Lower Beth-horon and Gezer, and ran on to the Sea. [4] Thus the Josephites—that is, Manasseh and Ephraim—received their portion.

[5] The territory of the Ephraimites, by their clans, was as follows: The boundary of their portion ran from Atrothaddar on the east to Upper Beth-horon, [6] and the boundary ran on to the Sea. And on the north, the boundary proceeded from Michmethath to the east of Taanath-shiloh and passed beyond it up to the east of Janoah; [7] from Janoah it descended to Ataroth and Naarath, touched on Jericho, and ran on to the Jordan. [8] Westward, the boundary proceeded from Tappuah to the Wadi Kanah and ran on to the Sea. This was the portion of the tribe of the Ephraimites, by their clans, [9] together with the towns marked off[a] for the Ephraimites within the territory of the Manassites—all those towns with their villages. [10] However, they failed to dispossess the Canaanites who dwelt in Gezer; so the Canaanites remained in the midst of Ephraim, as is still the case. But they had to perform forced labor.

17

And this is the portion that fell by lot to the tribe of Manasseh—for he was Joseph's first-born. Since Machir, the first-born of Manasseh and the father of Gilead, was a valiant warrior, Gilead and Bashan were assigned to him. [2] And now assignments were made to the remaining Manassites, by their clans: the descendants of Abiezer, Helek, Asriel, Shechem, Hepher, and Shemida. Those were the male descendants of Manasseh son of Joseph, by their clans.

[3] [b]Now Zelophehad son of Hepher son of Gilead son of Machir son of Manasseh had no sons, but only daughters. The names of his daughters were Mahlah, Noah, Hoglah, Milcah, and Tirzah. [4] They appeared before the priest Eleazer, Joshua son of Nun, and the chieftains, saying: "The LORD commanded Moses to grant us a portion among our male kinsmen." So, in accordance with the LORD's instructions, they were granted a portion among their father's kinsmen. [5] Ten districts fell to Manasseh, apart from the lands of Gilead and Bashan, which are across the Jordan. [6] Manasseh's daughters inherited a por-

16.1–17.18: Joseph's allotment (Ephraim and half of Manasseh). The Joseph tribes dominate the Northern Kingdom and thus are presented immediately after Judah. An introductory narrative (16.1–4) treats the Joseph tribes together, and the Ephraimite boundaries are then described (16.5–10). A brief narrative scene relaying the story of several female descendants of Manasseh (17.1–6) precedes the description of Manasseh's borders (17.7–13) and a Josephite complaint about its allotment (17.14–18). Manasseh lacks a town list.

16.1–4: Introductory narrative links Ephraim and half Manasseh and delineates their southern border. **1:** One *lot* for more than one tribe suggests the ambiguity of the Joseph tribes—more than one, less than two.

16.5–10: Ephraim's boundaries, a much less detailed account than for Judah. **10:** *Canaanites . . . in Gezer* resist Israelite control until the time of Solomon (see 10.33 n.; cf. Judg. 1.29).

17.1–6: Manassite clans—male and female. 1: *Manasseh—for he was Joseph's first-born,* in agreement with the tradition in Gen. 48.13–20. *Machir,* Manasseh's oldest son, represents the Transjordanian part of Manasseh, though he is elsewhere associated with events west of the Jordan (Judg. 5.14–17). *Valiant warrior* may be an attempt to provide for Manasseh a hint of heroic deeds, like those of Caleb and Othniel for the Judahites (14.6–13; 15.13–17). **3:** *No sons, but only daughters,* this is noteworthy because the land is typically passed through the male line. **4:** *Appeared* before the leaders, indicating women as well as men had access to certain official decision-making groups. **6:** In this anomalous case, where there are no direct male heirs, the sisters receive a *portion* (cf. Num. 27.1–11; 36.1–12), just as Achsah acquired land.

---

a Meaning of Heb. uncertain.   b Cf. Num. 27.1–11.

tion in these together with his sons, while the land of Gilead was assigned to the rest of Manasseh's descendants.

⁷ The boundary of Manasseh ran from Asher to Michmethath, which lies near Shechem. The boundary continued to the right, toward the inhabitants of En-tappuah.—⁸ The region of Tappuah belonged to Manasseh; but Tappuah, on the border of Manasseh, belonged to the Ephraimites.—⁹ Then the boundary descended to the Wadi Kanah. Those towns to the south of the wadi belonged to Ephraim as an enclave among the towns of Manasseh. The boundary of Manasseh lay north of the wadi and ran on to the Sea. ¹⁰ What lay to the south belonged to Ephraim, and what lay to the north belonged to Manasseh, with the Sea as its boundary. [This territory] was contiguous with Asher on the north and with Issachar on the east. ¹¹ Within Issachar and Asher, Manasseh possessed Beth-shean and its dependencies, Ibleam and its dependencies, the inhabitants of Dor and its dependencies, the inhabitants of En-dor and its dependencies, the inhabitants of Taanach and its dependencies, and the inhabitants of Megiddo and its dependencies: ᵃthese constituted three regions.ᵃ

¹² The Manassites could not dispossess [the inhabitants of] these towns, and the Canaanites stubbornly remained in this region. ¹³ When the Israelites became stronger, they imposed tribute on the Canaanites; but they did not dispossess them.

¹⁴ The Josephites complained to Joshua, saying, "Why have you assigned as our portion a single allotment and a single district, seeing that we are a numerous people whom the LORD has blessed so greatly?" ¹⁵ "If you are a numerous people," Joshua answered them, "go up to the forest country and clear an area for yourselves there, in the territory of the Perizzites and the Rephaim, seeing that you are cramped in the hill country of Ephraim." ¹⁶ "The hill country is not enough for us," the Josephites replied, "and all the Canaanites who live in the valley area have iron chariots, both those in Beth-shean and its dependencies and those in the Valley of Jezreel." ¹⁷ But Joshua declared to the House of Joseph, to Ephraim and Manasseh, "You are indeed a numerous people, possessed of great strength; you shall not have one allotment only. ¹⁸ The hill country shall be yours as well; true, it is forest land, but you will clear it and possess it to its farthest limits. And you shall also dispossess the Canaanites, even though they have iron chariots and even though they are strong."

17.7–13: Manasseh's boundaries are incomplete and irregular, with Ephraimite towns within Manasseh (v. 9), and with Manasseh holding towns of Issachar and Asher (vv. 11–12). As for Ephraim, Canaanites remain and pay tribute to Manasseh (vv. 12–13; cf. Judg. 1.27–28). **7:** *Shechem,* the major city between Mounts Ebal and Gerizim (cf. 8.30–35), will be an asylum town (20.7), a Levitical city (21.21), and the site of the covenant scene of ch 24. **11:** *Dor,* probably not the coastal city of that name. **12:** *These towns,* the ones listed in v. 11, are all located in the Jezreel Valley, an area of great strategic and economic importance and a traditional Canaanite stronghold (see v. 16).

17.14–18: Joseph's complaints. The logic of the Josephite complaint and Joshua's response is vague, suggesting that vv. 14–15 and 16–18 are separate traditions that have not been smoothly combined. The text is problematic in places, but may reflect an old tradition, now known through archaeology, that the earliest Israelite settlements were in the hill country. **15:** *Forest country,* denoting land still heavily forested in early biblical times. **17:** *House of Joseph,* an unusual designation, contrasting with the standard "Josephite" (lit. "children of Joseph") of chs 16–17 and highlighting the importance of the Joseph tribes.

---

a-a Meaning of Heb. uncertain.

18 The whole community of the Israelite people assembled at Shiloh, and set up the Tent of Meeting there. The land was now under their control; ²but there remained seven tribes of the Israelites which had not yet received their portions. ³So Joshua said to the Israelites, "How long will you be slack about going and taking possession of the land which the Lord, the God of your fathers, has assigned to you? ⁴Appoint three men of each tribe; I will send them out to go through the country and write down a description of it for purposes of apportionment, and then come back to me. ⁵They shall divide it into seven parts—Judah shall remain by its territory in the south, and the house of Joseph shall remain by its territory in the north.—⁶When you have written down the description of the land in seven parts, bring it here to me. Then I will cast lots for you here before the Lord our God. ⁷For the Levites have no share among you, since the priesthood of the Lord is their portion; and Gad and Reuben and the half-tribe of Manasseh have received the portions which were assigned to them by Moses the servant of the Lord, on the eastern side of the Jordan."

⁸The men set out on their journeys. Joshua ordered the men who were leaving to write down a description of the land—"Go, traverse the country and write down a description of it. Then return to me, and I will cast lots for you here at Shiloh before the Lord."

⁹So the men went and traversed the land; they described it in a document, town by town, in seven parts, and they returned to Joshua in the camp at Shiloh. ¹⁰Joshua cast lots for them at Shiloh before the Lord, and there Joshua apportioned the land among the Israelites according to their divisions.

¹¹The lot of the tribe of the Benjaminites, by their clans, came out first. The territory which fell to their lot lay between the Judites and the Josephites. ¹²The boundary on their northern rim began at the Jordan; the boundary ascended to the northern flank of Jericho, ascended westward into the hill country and ran on to the Wilderness of Beth-aven. ¹³From there the boundary passed on southward to Luz, to the flank of Luz—that is, Bethel; then the boundary descended to Atroth-addar [and] to the hill south of Lower Beth-horon. ¹⁴The boundary now turned and curved onto the western rim; and the boundary ran southward from the hill on the south side of Beth-horon till it ended at Kiriath-baal—that is, Kiriath-jearim—a town of the Judites. That was the western rim. ¹⁵The southern rim: From the outskirts of Kiriath-jearim, the

18.1–19.51: Allotments to the remaining seven tribes. These portions are described with far less detail than are those of the Judahites and Josephites, clearly the leading groups in ancient Israel.

18.1–10: Survey of the land. Introducing the last accounts of apportionment is the report of a reconnaissance (cf. 2.1; 7.2) of the territory to be divided. **1:** *Shiloh,* mentioned often in this chapter (and also 19.51; 21.2; 22.9, 12), was the major northern sacred site before the monarchy (see 1 Sam. chs 1–4). Modern Khirbet Seilûn, it is in the heart of Ephraim some 30 km (19 miles) north of Jerusalem. *Tent of Meeting,* another term for the portable sanctuary ("mishkan," or "tabernacle") of the wilderness period. **4:** *Write down,* a command assuming some literacy among some Israelites; the general rate of literacy in ancient Israel is debated. **10:** *Lots . . . Lord,* makes the apportionment the result of God's will.

18.11–28: Benjamin's portion. Benjamin is north of Judah and with Judah forms the Southern Kingdom after the monarchy divides. A boundary description (vv. 12–20) precedes the town list (vv. 21–28), which is organized by districts as are the Judahite towns. **28:** *Jerusalem* is a Judahite town in 15.63.

boundary passed westward[a] and ran on to the fountain of the Waters of Nephtoah. [16] Then the boundary descended to the foot of the hill by the Valley of Ben-hinnom at the northern end of the Valley of Rephaim; then it ran down the Valley of Hinnom along the southern flank of the Jebusites to En-rogel. [17] Curving northward, it ran on to En-shemesh and ran on to Geliloth, facing the Ascent of Adummim, and descended to the Stone of Bohan son of Reuben. [18] It continued northward to the edge of the Arabah and descended into the Arabah. [19] The boundary passed on to the northern flank of Beth-hoglah, and the boundary ended at the northern tongue of the Dead Sea, at the southern end of the Jordan. That was the southern boundary. [20] On their eastern rim, finally, the Jordan was their boundary. That was the portion of the Benjaminites, by their clans, according to its boundaries on all sides.

[21] And the towns of the tribe of the Benjaminites, by its clans, were: Jericho, Beth-hoglah, Emek-keziz, [22] Beth-arabah, Zemaraim, Bethel, [23] Avvim, Parah, Ophrah, [24] Chephar-ammonah, Ophni, and Geba—12 towns, with their villages. [25] Also Gibeon, Ramah, Beeroth, [26] Mizpeh, Chephirah, Mozah, [27] Rekem, Irpeel, Taralah, [28] Zela, Eleph, and Jebus[b]—that is, Jerusalem—Gibeath [and] Kiriath:[c] 14 towns, with their villages. That was the portion of the Benjaminites, by their clans.

19 The second lot fell to Simeon. The portion of the tribe of the Simeonites, by their clans, lay inside the portion of the Judites. [2] Their portion comprised: Beer-sheba—or Sheba—Moladah, [3] Hazar-shual, Balah, Ezem, [4] Eltolad, Bethul,[d] Hormah, [5] Ziklag, Beth-marcaboth, Hazar-susah, [6] Beth-lebaoth, and Sharuhen[e]—13 towns, with their villages. [7] Ain, Rimmon, Ether, and Ashan: 4 towns, with their villages—[8] together with all the villages in the vicinity of those towns, down to Baalath-beer [and] Ramath-negeb. That was the portion of the tribe of the Simeonites, by their clans. [9] The portion of the Simeonites was part of the territory of the Judites; since the share of the Judites was larger than they needed, the Simeonites received a portion inside their portion.

[10] The third lot emerged for the Zebulunites, by their clans. The boundary of their portion: Starting at Sarid, [11] their boundary[f] ascended westward to Maralah, touching Dabbesheth and touching the wadi alongside Jok-

19.1–9: Simeon's portion. This brief section indicates that Simeon's territory was eventually incorporated into that of Judah (vv. 1, 9; cf. Judg. 1.3).

19.10–16: Zebulun's portion. The borders (vv. 10–14) and a brief list of towns (v. 15) are given for Zebulun. The area is in southern Galilee and is wedged in among four other tribes.

---

a Emendation yields "eastward."   b Heb. "the Jebusite."
c Emendation yields "and Kiriath-jearim."
d 15.30 reads "Chesil."   e-e 15.32 reads "Shilhim."   f I.e., the southern one.

neam. [12] And it also ran from Sarid along the eastern side, where the sun rises, past the territory of Chisloth-tabor and on to Daberath and ascended to Japhia. [13] From there it ran [back] to the east, toward the sunrise, to Gath-hepher, to Eth-kazin, and on to Rimmon, where it curved to Neah. [14] Then it turned—that is, the boundary on the north—to Hannathon. Its extreme limits[a] were the Valley of Iphtah-el, [15] Kattath, Nahalal, Shimron, Idalah, and Bethlehem: 12 towns, with their villages. [16] That was the portion of the Zebulunites by their clans—those towns, with their villages.

[17] The fourth lot fell to Issachar, the Issacharites by their clans. [18] Their territory comprised: Jezreel, Chesulloth, Shunem, [19] Hapharaim, Shion, Anaharath, [20] Rabbith, Kishion, Ebez, [21] Remeth, En-gannim, En-haddah, and Beth-pazzez. [22] The boundary touched Tabor, Shahazimah, and Beth-shemesh; and their boundary ran to the Jordan: 16 towns, with their villages. [23] That was the portion of the tribe of the Issacharites, by their clans—the towns with their villages.

[24] The fifth lot fell to the tribe of the Asherites, by their clans. [25] Their boundary[b] ran along Helkath, Hali, Beten, Achshaph, [26] Allammelech, Amad, and Mishal; and it touched Carmel on the west, and Shihor-libnath. [27] It also ran[c] along the east side to Beth-dagon, and touched Zebulun and the Valley of Iphtah-el to the north, [as also] Beth-emek and Neiel; [d-]then it ran to Cabul on the north,[-d] [28] Ebron,[e] Rehob, Hammon, and Kanah, up to Great Sidon. [29] The boundary turned to Ramah and on to the fortified city of Tyre; then the boundary turned to Hosah [d-]and it ran on westward to Mehebel,[-d] Achzib, [30] Ummah, Aphek, and Rehob: 22 towns, with their villages. [31] That was the portion of the tribe of the Asherites, by their clans—those towns, with their villages.

[32] The sixth lot fell to the Naphtalites, the Naphtalites by their clans. [33] [f]Their boundary ran from Heleph, Elon-bezaanannim, Adami-nekeb, and Jabneel to Lakkum, and it ended at the Jordan. [34] The boundary then turned westward to Aznoth-tabor and ran from there to Hukok. It touched Zebulun on the south, and it touched Asher on the west, and Judah at the Jordan on the east. [35] Its fortified towns were Ziddim, Zer, Hammath, Rakkath, Chin-

a *I.e., the northwest corner, opposite the starting point, Sarid.*
b *I.e., the southern one.*
c *I.e., from Helkath, v. 25.*
d-d *Meaning of Heb. uncertain.*
e *Some Heb. mss., as well as Josh. 21.30 and 1 Chron. 6.59, read "Abdon."*
f *The geography of vv. 33–35 is unclear in part.*

19.17–23: Issachar's portion. This short account features a list of territories and an attenuated description of its borders between the eastern Jezreel Valley and the Jordan River.

19.24–31: Asher's portion. The town list is integrated with the border description for Asher, which occupies the coastal areas of the western Galilee. That it includes areas of the Phoenician coast up to Sidon and Tyre (vv. 28–29), which never became Israelite, betrays the idealized character of the territorial allotments.

19.32–39: Naphtali's portion. A border description (vv. 33–34) and a town list (vv. 35–38) place Naphtali in the mountainous region of upper and eastern Galilee but do not indicate how far north it extended.

19.40–48: Dan's portion. The last allotment is for the problematic tribe of Dan, which could not take possession of its southeastern allotment (cf. Judg. 1.34). Only a town list is provided (vv. 41–47), along with a brief account of Dan's migration north (cf. Judg. 5.17; 18.1–31). No description of its territory, other than the city Dan, is indicated. **47:** *Leshem,* an alternative form of Laish, is modern Tel Dan/Tel el-Qâdi.

19.49–51: Conclusion to the division of the land. Joshua received an individual portion (vv. 49–50), just as Caleb had (14.6–15). Caleb had fought for Hebron, but Joshua requests a mountainous site that he himself fortifies. A final summation (v. 51), by mentioning the figures of 14.1 and the place of 18.1, closes off the full account of the allotments west of the Jordan. **50:** *Timnath-serah,* probably modern Khirbet Tibnah, southwest of Shechem. Meaning "leftover" portion, it may have earlier been called "Sun's Portion" ("Timnath-heres," in Judges 2.9). **51:** A conclusion formula, referring back to 14.1, thus enclosing the unit about tribal allotment west of the Jordan.

nereth, 36 Adamah, Ramah, Hazor, 37 Kedesh, Edrei, En-hazor, 38 Iron, Migdal-el, Horem, Beth-anath, and Beth-shemesh: 19 towns, with their villages. 39 That was the portion of the tribe of the Naphtalites, by their clans—the towns, with their villages.

40 The seventh lot fell to the tribe of the Danites, by their clans. 41 Their allotted territory comprised: Zorah, Eshtaol, Ir-shemesh, 42 Shaalabbin, Aijalon, Ithlah, 43 Elon, Timnah, Ekron, 44 Eltekeh, Gibbethon, Baalath, 45 Jehud, Bene-berak, Gath-rimmon, 46 Me-jarkon, and Rakkon, at the border near Joppa. 47 But the territory of the Danites slipped from their grasp. So the Danites migrated and made war on Leshem.ᵃ They captured it and put it to the sword; they took possession of it and settled in it. And they changed the name of Leshem to Dan, after their ancestor Dan. 48 That was the portion of the tribe of the Danites, by their clans—those towns, with their villages.

49 When they had finished allotting the land by its boundaries, the Israelites gave a portion in their midst to Joshua son of Nun. 50 At the command of the LORD they gave him the town that he asked for, Timnath-serah in the hill country of Ephraim; he fortified the town and settled in it.

51 These are the portions assigned by lot to the tribes of Israel by the priest Eleazar, Joshua son of Nun, and the heads of the ancestral houses, before the LORD at Shiloh, at the entrance of the Tent of Meeting.

20 When they had finished dividing the land, 1 the LORD said to Joshua: 2 "Speak to the Israelites: Designate the cities of refuge—about which I commanded you through Moses—3 to which a manslayer who kills a person by mistake, unintentionally, may flee. They shall serve you as a refuge from the blood avenger. 4 He shall flee to one of those cities, present himself at the entrance to the city gate, and plead his case before the elders of that city; and they shall admit him into the city and give him a place in which to live among them. 5 Should the blood avenger pursue him, they shall not hand the manslayer over to him, since he killed the other person without intent and had not been his enemy in the past. 6 He shall live in that city until he can stand trial before the assembly, [and remain there] until the death of the high priest who is in office at that time. Thereafter, the manslayer may go back to his home in his own town, to the town from which he fled."

20.1–21.43: Additional portions. Appended to the tribal portions are two allotment units, each setting aside towns within the tribes for special usages. Joshua and others designate towns for asylum (20.1–9) and for Levites (21.1–40), following the instructions of God through Moses (20.2; 21.2; cf. Num. ch 35; Deut. 19.1–13). A conclusion (21.41–43) gives an ideal picture of the acquisition and settlement of all the territories.

20.1–9: Asylum towns. Six towns, three on each side of the river, are assigned to provide refuge for anyone accused of involuntary manslaughter, until the case is tried, for such persons might be the target of blood revenge. The six designated towns are also Levitical towns (21.11, 21, 27, 32, 36, 38). In a fashion that may be typified as proto-rabbinic, the narrative here combines aspects of the laws found in Num. 35.9–29 and Deut. 19.1–10. The main function of this narrative is to explain the existence and function of the Levitical cities, mentioned in the following chapter. **3:** An example of killing *by mistake* is given in Deut. 19.5. *Blood avenger,* lit. a "redeemer (go'el) of blood," was usually a close relative of the slain person (see 2 Sam. 14.2–9). **4:** The *gate* of ancient Israelite towns typically had an adjacent plaza used for civic purposes (see Amos 5.15; Ruth 4.1–12). **6:** *Trial before the assembly* seems to be at odds with the information in v. 4 and may be a separate tradition. *Death of the high priest,* following Num. 35.25, perhaps the occasion for a general amnesty.

ᵃ Called Laish in Judg. 18.7 ff.

The Levitical cities. Cities of refuge are highlighted with a star. The tribal boundaries are shown by a dashed line.

7 So they set aside Kedesh in the hill country of Naphtali in Galilee, Shechem in the hill country of Ephraim, and Kiriath-arba—that is, Hebron—in the hill country of Judah. 8 And across the Jordan, east of Jericho, they assigned Bezer in the wilderness, in the Tableland, from the tribe of Reuben; Ramoth in Gilead from the tribe of Gad; and Golan in Bashan from the tribe of Manasseh. 9 Those were the towns designated[a] for all the Israelites and for aliens residing among them, to which anyone who killed a person unintentionally might flee, and not die by the hand of the blood avenger before standing trial by the assembly.

21 The heads of the ancestral houses of the Levites approached the priest Eleazar, Joshua son of Nun, and the heads of the ancestral houses of the Israelite tribes, 2 and spoke to them at Shiloh in the land of Canaan, as follows: "The Lord commanded through Moses that we be given towns to live in, along with their pastures for our livestock." 3 So the Israelites, in accordance with the Lord's command, assigned to the Levites, out of their own portions, the following towns with their pastures:

4 The [first] lot among the Levites fell to the Kohathite clans. To the descendants of the priest Aaron, there fell by lot 13 towns from the tribe of Judah, the tribe of Simeon, and the tribe of Benjamin; 5 and to the remaining Kohathites [there fell] by lot 10 towns from the clans of the tribe of Ephraim, the tribe of Dan, and the half-tribe of Manasseh.

6 To the Gershonites [there fell] by lot 13 towns from the clans of the tribe of Issachar, the tribe of Asher, the tribe of Naphtali, and the half-tribe of Manasseh in Bashan.

7 [And] to the Merarites, by their clans—12 towns from the tribe of Reuben, the tribe of Gad, and the tribe of Zebulun. 8 The Israelites assigned those towns with their pastures by lot to the Levites—as the Lord had commanded through Moses.

9 From the tribe of the Judites and the tribe of the Simeonites were assigned the following towns, which will be listed by name; 10 they went to the descendants of Aaron among the Kohathite clans of the Levites, for the first lot had fallen to them. 11 To them were assigned in the hill country of Judah Kiriath-arba—that is, Hebron—together with the pastures around it. [Arba was] the father of the Anokites.[b] 12 They gave the fields and the villages of the

21.1–40: Levitical towns. Lacking a discrete tribal portion (Deut. 10.8–9; Josh. 13.14, 33; 18.7), the Levites are to be integrated into all Israel by receiving towns with adjacent pastureland in the territories of all the other tribes. Altogether they are to have forty-eight towns, which are not equally distributed among the tribes. The allocation is made according to the three Levitical clans—Kohathites, Gershonites, and Merarites—and is presented in summary form (vv. 4–8) and then with specified cities (vv. 9–40). **4:** *The Kohathite clans,* the most important priestly group (see Num. 4.4), are associated with Aaron and receive the most towns (twenty-three). **6:** *The Gershonites* receive thirteen towns, indicating they are less prominent than the Kohathites. **7:** *The Merarites,* with twelve towns, are the weakest of the three Levitical groups. **10–11:** A narrative insert, about Hebron and its association with Caleb, adds to Hebron's stature (cf. 14.13–15; 15.13–19).

a Meaning of Heb. uncertain.   b Elsewhere Anakites; cf. Num. 13.22; Deut. 9.2.

town to Caleb son of Jephunneh as his holding. ¹³But to the descendants of Aaron the priest they assigned Hebron—the city of refuge for manslayers—together with its pastures, Libnah with its pastures, ¹⁴Jattir with its pastures, Eshtemoa with its pastures, ¹⁵Holon with its pastures, Debir with its pastures, ¹⁶Ain with its pastures, Juttah with its pastures, and Beth-shemesh with its pastures—9 towns from those two tribes. ¹⁷And from the tribe of Benjamin: Gibeon with its pastures, Geba with its pastures, ¹⁸Anathoth with its pastures, and Almon with its pastures—4 towns. ¹⁹All the towns of the descendants of the priest Aaron, 13 towns with their pastures.

²⁰ᵃAs for the other clans of the Kohathites, the remaining Levites descended from Kohath, the towns in their lot were: From the tribe of Ephraim ²¹they were given, in the hill country of Ephraim, Shechem—the city of refuge for manslayers—with its pastures, Gezer with its pastures, ²²Kibzaim with its pastures, and Beth-horon with its pastures—4 towns. ²³From the tribe of Dan, Elteke with its pastures, Gibbethon with its pastures, ²⁴Aijalon with its pastures, and Gath-rimmon with its pastures—4 towns. ²⁵And from the half-tribe of Manasseh, Taanach with its pastures, and Gath-rimmon with its pastures—2 towns. ²⁶All the towns for the remaining clans of the Kohathites came to 10, with their pastures.

²⁷To the Gershonites of the levitical clans: From the half-tribe of Manasseh, Golan in Bashan—the city of refuge for manslayers—with its pastures, and Beeshterah with its pastures—2 towns. ²⁸From the tribe of Issachar: Kishion with its pastures, Dobrath with its pastures, ²⁹Jarmuth with its pastures, and En-gannim with its pastures—4 towns. ³⁰From the tribe of Asher: Mishal with its pastures, Abdon with its pastures, ³¹Helkath with its pastures, and Rehob with its pastures—4 towns. ³²From the tribe of Naphtali, Kedesh in Galilee—the city of refuge for manslayers—with its pastures, Hammoth-dor with its pastures, and Kartan with its pastures—3 towns. ³³All the towns of the Gershonites, by their clans, came to 13 towns, with their pastures.

³⁴To the remaining Levites, the clans of the Merarites: From the tribe of Zebulun, Jokneam with its pastures, Kartah with its pastures, ³⁵Dimnah with its pastures, and Nahalal with its pastures—4 towns.ᵇ ³⁶From the tribe of Gad, Ramoth in Gilead—the city of refuge for manslayers—

a Explicating v. 5.
b Some mss. and editions add the following (cf. 1 Chron. 6.63–64): "And from the tribe of Reuben: Bezer with its pastures, Jahaz with its pastures, Kedemoth with its pastures, and Mephaath with its pastures—4 towns."

with its pastures, Mahanaim with its pastures, ³⁷ Heshbon with its pastures, and Jazer with its pastures—4 towns in all. ³⁸ All the towns which went by lot to the Merarites, by their clans—the rest of the levitical clans—came to 12 towns. ³⁹ All the towns of the Levites within the holdings of the Israelites came to 48 towns, with their pastures. ⁴⁰ ª Thus those towns were assigned, every town with its surrounding pasture; and so it was with all those towns.

⁴¹ The LORD gave to Israel the whole country which He had sworn to their fathers that He would assign to them; they took possession of it and settled in it. ⁴² The LORD gave them rest on all sides, just as He had promised to their fathers on oath. Not one man of all their enemies withstood them; the LORD delivered all their enemies into their hands. ⁴³ Not one of the good things which the LORD had promised to the House of Israel was lacking. Everything was fulfilled.

22 Then Joshua summoned the Reubenites, the Gadites, and the half-tribe of Manasseh, ² and said to them, "You have observed all that Moses the servant of the LORD commanded you, and have obeyed me in everything that I commanded you. ³ You have not forsaken your kinsmen through the long years down to this day, but have faithfully observed the Instruction of the LORD your God. ⁴ Now the LORD your God has given your kinsmen rest, as He promised them. Therefore turn and go to your homes, to the land of your holdings beyond the Jordan that Moses the servant of the LORD assigned to you. ⁵ But be very careful to fulfill the Instruction and the Teaching that Moses the servant of the LORD enjoined upon you, to love the LORD your God and to walk in all His ways, and to keep His commandments and hold fast to Him, and to serve Him with all your heart and soul." ⁶ Then Joshua blessed them and dismissed them, and they went to their homes.

⁷ To the one half-tribe of Manasseh Moses had assigned territory in Bashan, and to the other Joshua assigned [territory] on the west side of the Jordan, with their kinsmen.ᵇ

Furthermore, when Joshua sent themᶜ off to their homes, he blessed them ⁸ and said to them, "Return to your homes with great wealth—with very much livestock,

---

a Meaning of verse uncertain.
b I.e., the other nine tribes.
c I.e., the two and a half tribes.

21.41–43: General Summary. The LORD is responsible for the Israelites' ability to acquire and settle the land. In claiming totality of conquest, the summary overlooks the reality of continual enemy presence and provides an idealized view of divine trustworthiness: Everything promised was delivered. This is emphasized through the use of the Heb word "kol," "all," six times in these three verses. **41:** *Sworn to their fathers . . . assign to them* echoes the opening promise of 1.6. **42:** A fulfillment of Deut. 12.10. **43:** *House of Israel*, a phrase appearing only here in Joshua, emphasizes Israelite unity.

22.1–24.33: Epilogue. The concluding chapters of Joshua stress faithfulness to the LORD. Ch 22 recounts the return of the Transjordanian warriors and their problematic construction of an altar east of the Jordan; in ch 23, Joshua delivers a final speech; ch 24 describes a covenant ceremony at Shechem (vv. 1–28) and gives burial accounts (vv. 29–33) of three leaders: Joshua, Joseph, and Eleazar. All three chapters include much language and many themes found in Deuteronomy as well as the introduction to Joshua in ch 1.

22.1–34: Return of the Transjordanians. The Jordan represents more than a geographical division between the two-and-a-half and the nine-and-a-half tribes. The warriors return to their homes east of the river (vv. 1–9), where they construct an altar viewed as a violation of the LORD's word (vv. 10–34).

22.1–9: Warriors return. The introduction to the fighting men from across the Jordan in 1.12–18 is here paralleled by Joshua's farewell to them (vv. 2–5), which also emphasizes obedience to the Teaching of Moses and the commandments of the LORD. **3:** *Long years* represents seven years of conquest and seven years of land division, according to the Rabbis (*Seder Olam* 11). **5:** This verse is composed totally with silver and gold, with copper and iron, and with a great quantity of clothing. Share the spoil of your enemies with your kinsmen." ⁹So the Reubenites, the Gadites, and the half-tribe of Manasseh left the Israelites at Shiloh, in the land of Canaan, and made their way back to the land of Gilead, the land of their own holding, which they had acquired by the command of the LORD through Moses. ¹⁰When they came to the region of the Jordan in the land of Canaan, the Reubenites and the Gadites and the half-tribe of Manasseh built an altar there by the Jordan, a great conspicuous altar.

¹¹A report reached the Israelites: "The Reubenites, the Gadites, and the half-tribe of Manasseh have built an altar opposite the land of Canaan, in the region of the Jordan, across from the Israelites." ¹²When the Israelites heard this, the whole community of the Israelites assembled at Shiloh to make war on them. ¹³But [first] the Israelites sent the priest Phinehas son of Eleazar to the Reubenites, the Gadites, and the half-tribe of Manasseh in the land of Gilead, ¹⁴accompanied by ten chieftains, one chieftain from each ancestral house of each of the tribes of Israel; they were every one of them heads of ancestral houses of the contingents of Israel. ¹⁵When they came to the Reubenites, the Gadites, and the half-tribe of Manasseh in the land of Gilead, they spoke to them as follows:

¹⁶"Thus said the whole community of the LORD: What is this treachery that you have committed this day against the God of Israel, turning away from the LORD, building yourselves an altar and rebelling this day against the LORD! ¹⁷Is the sin of Peor, which brought a plague upon the community of the LORD, such a small thing to us? We have not cleansed ourselves from it to this very day; ¹⁸and now you would turn away from the LORD! If you rebel against the LORD today, tomorrow He will be angry with the whole community of Israel. ¹⁹If it is because the land of your holding is unclean, cross over into the land of the LORD's own holding, where the Tabernacle of the LORD abides, and acquire holdings among us. But do not rebel against the LORD, and do not rebel against us by building for yourselves an altar other than the altar of the LORD our God. ²⁰When Achan son of Zerah violated the proscription, anger struck the whole community of Israel; he was not the only one who perished for that sin."

²¹The Reubenites, the Gadites, and the half-tribe of Manasseh replied to the heads of the contingents of Israel: They said, ²²"God, the LORD God! God, the LORD God! He knows, and Israel too shall know! If we acted in rebellion or in treachery against the LORD, do not vindicate us this

of Deuteronomic cliches. For example, *Love the LORD* is Deuteronomic language (Deut. 6.5; 10.12–13; etc.) and appears again in 23.11. *Walk . . . soul* uses Deuteronomic terminology. The emphasis on keeping commandments, for example, appears thirty-seven times in Deuteronomy, including the Shema passage (Deut. 6.4–9).

22.10–34: The problem of the Transjordanian altar. The returning warriors construct an altar as soon as they cross the Jordan, an act seen as unacceptable by the west-of-the-Jordan majority. The Transjordanian tribes provide an acceptable explanation, stressing national unity. **13:** Because *Phinehas* provides priestly leadership for the confrontation and because the focus is on a sacral structure (an altar), many scholars see this as a priestly admonition against illegal ritual sites and acts. **16:** The *treachery* of the altar involves the assumption that it will be used for sacrifice, which would violate the Deuteronomic notion of one altar for sacrifice (Deut. 12.13–14). The sacrilege may be especially serious since the altar is constructed east of the Jordan, and thus is not on territory that is centrally part of the land of Israel. **17:** Recalling the *sin of Peor* (see 13.20 n.) marks the seriousness of their action by comparing it to a particularly grievous sin, where according to the notion of corporate responsibility, the sins of a few can bring punishment to the whole. **19:** The suggestion of *unclean* land across the Jordan may reflect a tendentious perspective, namely, that God's true territory—*the LORD's own holding*—lies west of the Jordan. *Tabernacle,* Tent of Meeting (cf. 18.1). **20:** Recalling *Achan* (ch 7) means remembering the notion of group punishment. *Violated,* or "committed treachery against," uses the same (often Priestly) term as 7.1 (see also 22.16, 22). **25:** The Transjordanians fear discrimination, perhaps rightly so (see Judg. 12.1–6). **28:** As a *witness* (cf. Gen. 31.47–48), the altar—probably made of stones (cf.

day! 23 If we built an altar to turn away from the LORD, if it was to offer burnt offerings or meal offerings upon it, or to present sacrifices of well-being upon it, may the LORD Himself demand [a reckoning]. 24 We did this thing only out of our concern that, in time to come, your children might say to our children, 'What have you to do with the LORD, the God of Israel? 25 The LORD has made the Jordan a boundary between you and us, O Reubenites and Gadites; you have no share in the LORD!' Thus your children might prevent our children from worshiping the LORD. 26 So we decided to provide [a witness] for ourselves by building an altar—not for burnt offerings or [other] sacrifices, 27 but as a witness between you and us, and between the generations to come—that we may perform the service of the LORD before Him[a] with our burnt offerings, our sacrifices, and our offerings of well-being; and that your children should not say to our children in time to come, 'You have no share in the LORD.' 28 We reasoned: should they speak thus to us and to our children in time to come, we would reply, 'See the replica of the LORD's altar,[a] which our fathers made—not for burnt offerings or sacrifices, but as a witness between you and us.' 29 Far be it from us to rebel against the LORD, or to turn away this day from the LORD and build an altar for burnt offerings, meal offerings, and sacrifices other than the altar of the LORD our God which stands before His Tabernacle."

30 When the priest Phinehas and the chieftains of the community—the heads of the contingents of Israel—who were with him heard the explanation given by the Reubenites, the Gadites, and the Manassites, they approved. 31 The priest Phinehas son of Eleazar said to the Reubenites, the Gadites, and the Manassites, "Now we know that the LORD is in our midst, since you have not committed such treachery against the LORD. You have indeed saved the Israelites from punishment by the LORD."

32 Then the priest Phinehas son of Eleazar and the chieftains returned from the Reubenites and the Gadites in the land of Gilead to the Israelites in the land of Canaan, and gave them their report. 33 The Israelites were pleased, and the Israelites praised God; and they spoke no more of going to war against them, to ravage the land in which the Reubenites and Gadites dwelt.

34 The Reubenites and the Gadites named the altar ["Witness"], meaning, "It is a witness between us and them that the LORD is [our] God."

8.31)—was to serve didactic purposes (8.34), as do many other stone heaps in Joshua (e.g., 4.9; 7.25; 8.29; 10.27; 24.27).

a I.e., at Shiloh.

23 Much later, after the LORD had given Israel rest from all the enemies around them, and when Joshua was old and well advanced in years, ²Joshua summoned all Israel, their elders and commanders, their magistrates and officials, and said to them: "I have grown old and am advanced in years. ³You have seen all that the LORD your God has done to all those nations on your account, for it was the LORD your God who fought for you. ⁴See, I have allotted to you, by your tribes, [the territory of] these nations that still remain, and that of all the nations that I have destroyed, from the Jordan to the Mediterranean Sea in the west. ⁵The LORD your God Himself will thrust them out on your account and drive them out to make way for you, and you shall possess their land as the LORD your God promised you.

⁶"But be most resolute to observe faithfully all that is written in the Book of the Teaching of Moses, without ever deviating from it to the right or to the left, ⁷and without intermingling with these nations that are left among you. Do not utter the names of their gods or swear by them; do not serve them or bow down to them. ⁸But hold fast to the LORD your God as you have done to this day.

⁹"The LORD has driven out great, powerful nations on your account, and not a man has withstood you to this day. ¹⁰A single man of you would put a thousand to flight, for the LORD your God Himself has been fighting for you, as He promised you. ¹¹For your own sakes, therefore, be most mindful to love the LORD your God. ¹²For should you turn away and attach yourselves to the remnant of those nations—to those that are left among you—and intermarry with them, you joining them and they joining you, ¹³know for certain that the LORD your God will not continue to drive these nations out before you; they shall become a snare and a trap for you, a scourge to your sides and thorns in your eyes, until you perish from this good land that the LORD your God has given you.

¹⁴"I am now going the way of all the earth. Acknowledge with all your heart and soul that not one of the good things that the LORD your God promised you has failed to happen; they have all come true for you, not a single one has failed. ¹⁵But just as every good thing that the LORD your God promised you has been fulfilled for you, so the LORD can bring upon you every evil thing until He has wiped you off this good land that the LORD your God has given you. ¹⁶If you break the covenant that the LORD your God enjoined upon you, and go and serve other gods and bow down to them, then the LORD's anger will burn

23.1–16: Joshua's final speech. Like Jacob (Gen. 49) and Moses (Deut. ch 33), Joshua delivers a final speech before he dies. His charge, replete with Deuteronomic terminology, celebrates the LORD as the one responsible for conquest and exhorts the people to obey the covenant. This speech may have originally followed 13.1; see 13.1 n. **1:** *Rest* (elsewhere "haven") from enemies, a main theme of Deuteronomy, is promised in 1.13, 15 and proclaimed to have been achieved in 21.42 and 22.4, always as a result of the LORD's acts. **2:** *All Israel,* here perhaps represented by the leaders. **6:** Strength is reflected in Torah observance, as in 1.7–8, which is here applied to all Israel. **7:** *Nations that are left,* acknowledging that all the territory has not yet been acquired (cf. v. 12). *Do not . . . bow down* invokes a fundamental covenant concept, expressed in the Decalogue (Exod. 20.5, Deut. 5.9) and recurring in Deuteronomic texts. **11:** *Love the LORD,* see 22.5 n. **12–13:** The problem of cultural identity and boundaries between groups is manifest in the prohibition of intermarriage (cf. Exod. 34.11–16; Deut. 7.1–4). **13:** Even at this early period of the narrative, immediately after narrating the conquest, the author emphasizes the conditional nature of land tenure. **14:** *Going the way of all the earth* means "to die" and gives Joshua a royal tinge; King David is the only other biblical leader to use this phrase (1 Kings 2.2). **15:** *Good thing . . . evil thing* signifies the blessings and the curses of the covenant. **16:** *Anger will burn* is a euphemism for the LORD striking disobedient people with the deadly plague (cf. Num. 11.33). The notion that Israel will *quickly perish from the good land* if it is disobedient is found in Deut. 4.26; 11.17.

against you, and you shall quickly perish from the good land that He has given you."

24 Joshua assembled all the tribes of Israel at Shechem. He summoned Israel's elders and commanders, magistrates and officers; and they presented themselves before God. [2] Then Joshua said to all the people, "Thus said the LORD, the God of Israel: In olden times, your forefathers—Terah, father of Abraham and father of Nahor—lived beyond the Euphrates and worshiped other gods. [3] But I took your father Abraham from beyond the Euphrates and led him through the whole land of Canaan and multiplied his offspring. I gave him Isaac, [4] and to Isaac I gave Jacob and Esau. I gave Esau the hill country of Seir as his possession, while Jacob and his children went down to Egypt.

[5] "Then I sent Moses and Aaron, and I plagued Egypt with [the wonders] that I wrought in their midst, after which I freed you—[6] I freed your fathers—from Egypt, and you came to the Sea. But the Egyptians pursued your fathers to the Sea of Reeds with chariots and horsemen. [7] They cried out to the LORD, and He put darkness between you and the Egyptians; then He brought the Sea upon them, and it covered them. Your own eyes saw what I did to the Egyptians.

"After you had lived a long time in the wilderness, [8] I brought you to the land of the Amorites who lived beyond the Jordan. They gave battle to you, but I delivered them into your hands; I annihilated them for you, and you took possession of their land. [9] Thereupon Balak son of Zippor, the king of Moab, made ready to attack Israel. He sent for Balaam son of Beor to curse you, [10] but I refused to listen to Balaam; he had to bless you, and thus I saved you from him.

[11] "Then you crossed the Jordan and you came to Jericho. The citizens of Jericho and the Amorites, Perizzites, Canaanites, Hittites, Girgashites, Hivites, and Jebusites fought you, but I delivered them into your hands. [12] I sent a plague[a] ahead of you, and it drove them out before you—[just like] the two Amorite kings—not by your sword or by your bow. [13] I have given you a land for which you did not labor and towns which you did not build, and you have settled in them; you are enjoying vineyards and olive groves which you did not plant.

[14] "Now, therefore, revere the LORD and serve Him with undivided loyalty; put away the gods that your forefa-

24.1–28: Covenant ceremony at Shechem. Cast as another speech of Joshua, this is partly the LORD's review of Israel's history (vv. 2–13). Joshua then convinces the people to choose the LORD, warning them of the consequences if they do not (vv. 14–24). A ceremony cements the covenantal relationship. **1:** *All the tribes*, emphasizing Israelite unity. *Shechem*, a centrally located Ephraimite town, where Joshua had already built an altar (8.30–35) and also a city of refuge and a Levitical city (20.7; 21.21). The ceremony there signifies its importance in Israelite political and religious life. **2–13:** The review of Israel's history includes the ancestral period (vv. 2–4), the escape from Egypt (vv. 5–7), and the acquisition of the land (vv. 8–13). As in Deut. 26.5–9, Sinai is not mentioned. **2–4:** These verses are central to the Haggadah's retelling of the Passover story. **9:** *Balak* and *Balaam*, see 13.22 n. (cf. Num. chs 22–24). **11:** *Amorites . . . Jebusites*, a final listing of the totality of the inhabitants of the land, all seven nations (cf. 3.10). **11–12:** This account of the conquest of Jericho differs from that of ch 6. **12:** *Plague*, sometimes translated "hornet" (see Exod. 23.28; Deut. 7.20) is narrated as a fulfillment of the promise in Deut. 7.20. Its symbolism is uncertain. *Two Amorite kings*, Sihon and Og (12.2, 4; 13.10, 12, 27, 30–31). **14–24:** *Revere the LORD*: A major covenant stipulation (see 4.24) is loyalty to God. *Put away the gods* replicates Jacob's words to his household at Shechem (Gen. 35.2–4); both texts may reflect an ancient purification ritual.

---

a See note at Exod. 23.28.

thers served beyond the Euphrates and in Egypt, and serve the LORD. [15] Or, if you are loath to serve the LORD, choose this day which ones you are going to serve—the gods that your forefathers served beyond the Euphrates, or those of the Amorites in whose land you are settled; but I and my household will serve the LORD."

[16] In reply, the people declared, "Far be it from us to forsake the LORD and serve other gods! [17] For it was the LORD our God who brought us and our fathers up from the land of Egypt, the house of bondage, and who wrought those wondrous signs before our very eyes, and guarded us all along the way that we traveled and among all the peoples through whose midst we passed. [18] And then the LORD drove out before us all the peoples—the Amorites—that inhabited the country. We too will serve the LORD, for He is our God."

[19] Joshua, however, said to the people, "You will not be able to serve the LORD, for He is a holy God. He is a jealous God; He will not forgive your transgressions and your sins. [20] If you forsake the LORD and serve alien gods, He will turn and deal harshly with you and make an end of you, after having been gracious to you." [21] But the people replied to Joshua, "No, we will serve the LORD!" [22] Thereupon Joshua said to the people, "You are witnesses against yourselves that you have by your own act chosen to serve the LORD." "Yes, we are!" they responded. [23] "Then put away the alien gods that you have among you and direct your hearts to the LORD, the God of Israel." [24] And the people declared to Joshua, "We will serve none but the LORD our God, and we will obey none but Him."

[25] On that day at Shechem, Joshua made a covenant for the people and he made a fixed rule for them. [26] Joshua recorded all this in a book of divine instruction. He took a great stone and set it up at the foot of the oak in the sacred precinct of the LORD; [27] and Joshua said to all the people, "See, this very stone shall be a witness against us, for it heard all the words that the LORD spoke to us; it shall be a witness against you, lest you break faith with your God." [28] Joshua then dismissed the people to their allotted portions.

[29] After these events, Joshua son of Nun, the servant of the LORD, died at the age of one hundred and ten years. [30] They buried him on his own property, at Timnath-serah in the hill country of Ephraim, north of Mount Gaash. [31] Israel served the LORD during the lifetime of Joshua and the lifetime of the elders who lived on after Joshua, and who had experienced all the deeds that the LORD had wrought for Israel.

16–18: Because the LORD has performed wonders for them, the people will swear allegiance, knowing full well what that entails. **19:** *Jealous God,* or "El the Jealous" (cf. "the living God," 3.10). God's jealousy typically is cited in contexts of idolatry (Exod. 20.5; 34.14; Deut. 5.9). The results of such behavior are usually disastrous (Deut. 6.15). **22:** *Witnesses* suggests a binding ceremonial act. **25:** *Fixed rule,* lit. "statute and judgment," signifies the contents of the covenant document. The plural is used three times in the same sense in Deut. ch 4 (vv. 5, 8, 14). **26:** *Book of divine instruction,* or "Book of the Teachings of God," expands the language of 1.8 and 8.34 (cf. 8.32; 23.6). *Great stone,* one last example of stones memorializing events (see 22.28 n.).

24.29–33: Epilogue: three burial accounts. 29–31: This is narrated in a slightly different form and order in Judg. 2.7–9. **29:** *Servant of the LORD,* a frequent designation for Moses in Joshua (1.1, 2, 13; 8.31, 33; etc.) but used only here for Joshua himself, a final case where the narrator compares Moses to Joshua, thereby legitimating him. *One hundred and ten years,* ten fewer than for Moses, for whom 120 years signifies Mosaic uniqueness (Deut. 34.7, 10). **30:** *Timnath-serah,* see 19.50 n. **31:** The point seems to be that obedience depends on witnesses who recount God's great power. **32:** *Bones of Joseph* are buried, fulfilling the promise to him in Gen. 50.24–25 (cf. Exod. 13.19). The recollection of this tradition in Genesis, along with the observation that the land promise, a main theme of Genesis, is only fulfilled in Joshua has suggested to some modern scholars that we should speak of the first six books of the Bible together as the Hexateuch ("six books"), namely the Torah (Pentateuch) plus Joshua (see intro.). *Shechem,* where Jacob had bought land and built an altar when he entered the land (Gen. 33.18–20). **33:** The death of *Eleazar,* as punishment for insufficient mourning for

³² The bones of Joseph, which the Israelites had brought up from Egypt, were buried at Shechem, in the piece of ground which Jacob had bought for a hundred *kesitahs*ᵃ from the children of Hamor, Shechem's father, and which had become a heritage of the Josephites.

³³ Eleazar son of Aaron also died, and they buried him on the hill of his son Phinehas, which had been assigned to him in the hill country of Ephraim.

Joshua according to Jewish legend (*b. Shab.* 105b), ends the book with an event of Priestly interest. This interest is central to the Priestly sections of the Torah and is reflected sporadically in Joshua.

---

a See note at Gen. 33.19.

שופטים

Judges*

THE BOOK OF JUDGES is the second of Former Prophets. Its place was determined chronologically—it covers the period after Joshua's death at the end of the book of Joshua and before the anointing of Saul as king in 1 Samuel. The book is named after its central characters, "judges" (typically translated in NJPS as "chieftains"). Although the book ends before the birth of Samuel the prophet, 1 Samuel 8.1, "When Samuel grew old, he appointed his sons judges over Israel," suggests that Samuel and his sons should be considered judges as well.

The judges are mostly shown as tribal leaders who delivered their people from oppression. Some were military leaders (Othniel, Ehud, Barak, Gideon, and Jephthah), some were lone warriors (Shamgar and Samson), and one was both leader and commander (Jephthah). Some judges were prophets (Deborah and Samuel), one was a Nazirite (Samson), some were also priests (Eli and Samuel), or sat in judgment (Deborah and Samuel), while the acts of others are not specified (Tola, Jair, Ibzan, Elon, and Abdon). The term "judge," Hebrew *shofet* (see esp. 2 Sam. 7.11; 2 Kings 23.22; Ruth 1.1; 1 Chron. 17.6, 10), thus covers the range of diverse leaders who flourished in the period prior to the monarchy. It should not be understood in a narrow juridical sense.

The book of Judges does not describe the entire period of the judges, nor is it organized chronologically. It opens in the time of the elders who survived Joshua and concludes with Samson, so the last judges, Eli (1 Sam. 4.18) and Samuel (1 Sam. 7.15–17), now appear in the book of Samuel. The ending of the book of Judges, however, deals with events that took place at the start of the period: the conquest of Dan and the war against Gibeah, both of which are placed in the third generation after the exodus from Egypt (18.30; 20.28). Its nonchronological order shows that the editors' purpose was not only to describe and record the period, but to draw lessons from it. The book's main theme is the inefficacy of the judges, who could only save and affect their people for a limited time; then the people would relapse, would be punished, and would cry to the LORD to save them again. This recurrent theme of sin, punishment, and rescue gives the book a cyclical structure.

The book offers two principal lessons. The first concerns the role of God in history: It

---

* This is the traditional rendering of *shofetim*, which, however, in the text is rendered "chieftains." The corresponding verb *shafat* is usually translated not "judged" but "ruled" or "led."

describes the course of history as an interaction between God and His people, with God heeding His people's cries, and saving them through various judges. The second concerns the type of preferred leader: The judges are not depicted as ideal leaders, and their depiction thus paves the way for the establishment of a more successful political institution, namely the monarchy. The ideal king could confront the people's enemies and prevent anarchy, though the book warns that the king may also be a villain, as in the case of Abimelech, symbolized by the bramble (ch 9).

The book can be divided into three parts. The first is an exposition that describes the background to the rise of the judges (1.1–3.6). The second, main part of the book is devoted largely to the acts of the judges (3.7–16.31). The third, final part describes two episodes: that of Micah's graven image and the shrine built at Dan, and the story of the rape in Gibeah and the subsequent civil war (chs 17–21). These final episodes create the impression that monarchy alone could end the chaotic period of the judges, when "there was no king in Israel; every man did as he pleased" (17.6; 21.25).

The Sages (b. B. Bat. 14b) assumed that the book of Judges was written by the prophet Samuel, who lived not long after the events described. Biblical scholars, however, maintain that this book, like the other historiographic books in the Bible, was written later, and should not be viewed as a unified work of a single author. Scholars suggest that it could only have been written in an established social culture possessing self-consciousness, appropriate institutions, and a receptive public. Scholars distinguish between the judges' stories, which are based on local-tribal traditions of deliverance and which do not interpret events with theological causality, and their frameworks, which depict the deliverer in a broad national context, characterized by a cycle that begins with sin and ends with peace. There is widespread agreement that these frameworks reflect a Deuteronomistic redaction which took the tribal stories, gave them a national-religious character, and fitted the whole into the great Deuteronomistic work that describes the history from the years in the wilderness (the book of Deuteronomy) to the Babylonian exile (the end of the book of Kings). At a later stage, they suggest, post-Deuteronomistic redactors added certain passages, such as the ones about the Canaanite nations that were or were not driven out, in the exposition (1.1–2.5) and the concluding chapters (17–21).

But the assumption that the book of Judges reflects the ideological world of Deuteronomy may not be correct. Deuteronomy's ideology and style are only partly evident in the book of Judges. Deuteronomistic literature criticizes monarchy (Deut. 17.14–20), places prophets above it (Deut. 18.15–19; 1 Kings 12.22–24, etc.), demands centralization of cult (Deut. 12.5–28; 1 Kings 8.16ff, etc.), and depicts the deity as a remote being whose name alone dwells in the Temple (Deut. 12.5; 1 Kings 8.27, etc.). By contrast, the book of Judges has positive expectations from the monarchy, makes scarcely any reference to prophecy and its function of predicting historical events, does not call for the centralization of the cult, and shows God intervening in the events, directly or by means of angels. Moreover, the phrases that are typical of Deuteronomistic literature are concentrated only in the exposition of the book (2.6–3.4). It would seem, therefore, that the main redaction of the book of Judges was completed in the pre-Deuteronomistic stage—namely, in the late 8th or in the 7th century BCE—and that it reflected the shocked mood in Judah after the downfall of the Northern Kingdom of Israel in 722 (see the allusion to exile in 18.30). This would explain the negative portrayal of the northern tribes throughout the book, from the exposition which accuses them of the sin of failing to drive out the local inhabitants, to the final chapters that speak of Mount Ephraim and the shrine at Dan as sinful places. By contrast, the tribe of Judah is depicted in the opening as a tribe which succeeded completely in driving out the local inhabitants and was faithful to the covenant with God. The redaction sought to justify the punishment that befell the Northern Kingdom by showing it as a group of sinful tribes; this theme is evident in each of the sections of the book. The book later was slightly adapted when it became part of the great Deuteronomistic work of Deuteronomy-Kings. Additions from this period or later may include: Deuteronomistic phrases noticeable in the exposition (2.11–19), the text criticizing Gideon for making the ephod (8.27b), and the episode of the concubine in Gibeah (chs 19–21), which is mainly a veiled polemical attack on the house of Saul.

The book of Judges presents itself as covering a period of more than 400 years—111 years of subjugation, and 299 of judgeship and peace (or possibly 319 years, given the uncertainty about the length of Samson's period). These data do not agree either with the chronology of 1 Kings 6.1, according to which 480 years passed from the exodus to the building of the Jerusalem Temple, or with the historical and archeological findings, which suggest that less than 200 years passed from the end of the 13th century, when the hill country was settled, to the latter half of the 11th century BCE and the beginning of the established monarchy. Modern research has abandoned the conservative view, which accepted the bulk of the book of Judges as historically authentic, and has emphasized certain ideological (anti-Northern Kingdom, anti-Saul, pro-Davidic) and literary elements of the book. At the same time, it acknowledges the fact that ancient traditions sometimes preserve some echo of the historical reality. Thus, while some scholars chose not to speak of a "period of the judges" at all, other scholars regard this period—namely, the time of settlement leading up to the monarchy—as a decisive one in the history of the people of Israel, in the course of which groups of settling nomads grew into an established society, developed a sense of national identity with a cultural-religious heritage, and came to form the people of Israel.   [YAIRAH AMIT]

1 After the death of Joshua, the Israelites inquired of the LORD, "Which of us shall be the first to go up against the Canaanites and attack them?" ² The LORD replied, "Let [the tribe of] Judah go up. I now deliver the land into their hands." ³ Judah then said to their brother-tribe Simeon, "Come up with us to our allotted territory and let us attack the Canaanites, and then we will go with you to your allotted territory." So Simeon joined them.

Introduction to the book of Judges (1.1–3.6) **1.1–2.10: The days of the elders.** The period between the death of Joshua and the beginning of the age of the judges is called the days of the elders (cf. 2.7). This period is created to explain how the people, who during the days of Joshua were noted for their loyalty to the LORD, became

⁴When Judah advanced, the LORD delivered the Canaanites and the Perizzites into their hands, and they defeated ten thousand of them at Bezek. ⁵At Bezek, they encountered Adoni-bezek, engaged him in battle, and defeated the Canaanites and the Perizzites. ⁶Adoni-bezek fled, but they pursued him and captured him; and they cut off his thumbs and his big toes. ⁷And Adoni-bezek said, "Seventy kings, with thumbs and big toes cut off, used to pick up scraps under my table; as I have done, so God has requited me." They brought him to Jerusalem and he died there.

⁸The Judites attacked Jerusalem and captured it; they put it to the sword and set the city on fire. ⁹After that the Judites went down to attack the Canaanites who inhabited the hill country, the Negeb, and the Shephelah.

¹⁰The Judites marched against the Canaanites who dwelt in Hebron, and they defeated Sheshai, Ahiman, and Talmai. (The name of Hebron was formerly Kiriath-arba.) ¹¹From there they marched against the inhabitants of Debir (the name of Debir was formerly Kiriath-sepher). ¹²And Caleb announced, "I will give my daughter Achsah in marriage to the man who attacks and captures Kiriath-sepher." ¹³His younger kinsman, Othniel the Kenizzite,ᵃ captured it; and Caleb gave him his daughter Achsah in marriage. ¹⁴ᵇWhen she came [to him], she induced him to ask her father for some property. She dismounted from her donkey, and Caleb asked her, "What is the matter?" ¹⁵She replied, "Give me a present, for you have given me away as Negeb-land; give me springs of water." And Caleb gave her Upper and Lower Gulloth.ᵇ

¹⁶The descendants of the Kenite, the father-in-law of Moses, went up with the Judites from the City of Palms to

a Cf. Josh. 14.6, 14.   b-b Cf. Josh. 15.18–19 and notes.

transformed into one that repeatedly did evil in His eyes. During this period the tribes needed to fight against the nations who remained in the land after Joshua's death. The tribe of Judah did so, but most of the tribes preferred to subjugate the remaining nations and allowed them to remain in their habitations, thereby laying the groundwork for assimilation and sin.

1.1–20: The conquests of Judah. The tribe of *Judah* and the tribe of *Simeon* that *joined them* destroyed the *Canaanites*, with the exception of the inhabitants of the valley, who had iron chariots and therefore could not be destroyed. This presentation shows the preference of Judah, which characterizes the whole passage. **3:** The connection between *Judah* and *Simeon* reflects the geographical-historical reality of assimilation of the tribe of Simeon within Judah's inheritance (Josh. 19.1–9; 15.26–32). **5:** Bezek is mentioned as the site where Saul mustered his army in his first war (1 Sam. 11.8). It is generally identified with Khirbet Ibzik, about 25 km (15 miles) northeast of Shechem. *Adoni-bezek:* Many think that the name of this king is a corruption of Adoni-zedek, who was king of Jerusalem according to Josh. 10.1. The fact that the king was buried in Jerusalem (v. 7) supports this conjecture. **7:** The king's servants took him to die in Jerusalem. **8:** In the description of the conquest of Jerusalem by the Judites, there is no hint that any inhabitants were left. Further on (v. 21), the blame for not dispossessing the Jebusites from Jerusalem is placed on Benjamin, while in Josh. 15.63 it is imposed upon Judah. According to many modern historians, Jerusalem remained a Jebusite enclave until it was conquered by David. **9:** A general summary of Judah's conquests south of Jerusalem. **10:** The biblical *Hebron* is identified with Tel Romeda, 30 km (18 miles) southwest of Jerusalem. The conquest of Hebron and its giants ("Anakites," v. 20) is here attributed to Judah. Other traditions appear in Josh. 10.36–37; 14.6–14, as well as in v. 20 below. Hebron is an important city in the ancestral narratives in Genesis (see esp. Gen. ch 23), and in the early part of David's reign (2 Sam. chs 2–5). **11:** *Debir* is identified with Khirbet Rabud, 15 km (9 miles) southwest of Hebron. **12:** The families of *Caleb* and Kenaz are presented here as part of the tribe of Judah. **13:** The representation of *Othniel* as *younger* than Caleb indicates that Caleb's clan was a more important one. **14:** According to this v., Achsah persuaded Othniel, but further on the negotiation occurs between Achsah and Caleb; hence, many scholars prefer the reading of the Septuagint, according to which Othniel persuaded Achsah. Dismounting from the donkey is a gesture of politeness. **16:** The Kenites were another group integrated into the tribe of Judah. The origins of the connection with them is told through the story of Moses' marriage to Zipporah, daughter of Jethro (Exod. 2.16–22). *The City of Palms:* As the name is applicable to any settlement in the wilderness of Judah; and they went and settled among the people*a* in the Negeb of Arad. ¹⁷ And Judah with its brother-tribe Simeon went on and defeated the Canaanites who dwelt in Zephath. They proscribed it, and so the town was named Hormah.*b* ¹⁸ And Judah captured*c* Gaza and its territory, Ashkelon and its territory, and Ekron and its territory.

¹⁹ The Lᴏʀᴅ was with Judah, so that they took possession of the hill country; but they were not able to dispossess the inhabitants of the plain, for they had iron chariots. ²⁰ They gave Hebron to Caleb, as Moses had promised; and he drove the three Anakites out of there. ²¹ The Benjaminites did not dispossess the Jebusite inhabitants of Jerusalem; so the Jebusites have dwelt with the Benjaminites in Jerusalem to this day.

²² The House of Joseph, for their part, advanced against Bethel, and the Lᴏʀᴅ was with them. ²³ While the House of Joseph were scouting at Bethel (the name of the town was formerly Luz), ²⁴ their patrols*d* saw a man leaving the town. They said to him, "Just show us how to get into the town, and we will treat you kindly." ²⁵ He showed them how to get into the town; they put the town to the sword, but they let the man and all his relatives go free. ²⁶ The man went to the Hittite country. He founded a city and named it Luz, and that has been its name to this day.

²⁷ Manasseh did not dispossess [the inhabitants of] Bethshean and its dependencies, or [of] Taanach and its dependencies, or the inhabitants of Dor and its dependencies, or the inhabitants of Ibleam and its dependencies, or the inhabitants of Megiddo and its dependencies. The Canaanites persisted in dwelling in this region. ²⁸ And when Israel gained the upper hand, they subjected the Canaanites to forced labor; but they did not dispossess them. ²⁹ Nor did Ephraim dispossess the Canaanites who inhabited Gezer; so the Canaanites dwelt in their midst at Gezer.

³⁰ Zebulun did not dispossess the inhabitants of Kitron or the inhabitants of Nahalol; so the Canaanites dwelt in their midst, but they were subjected to forced labor. ³¹ Asher did not dispossess the inhabitants of Acco or the inhabitants of Sidon, Ahlab, Achzib, Helbah, Aphik, and Rehob. ³² So the Asherites dwelt in the midst of the Canaanites, the inhabitants of the land, for they did not dispossess them. ³³ Naphtali did not dispossess the inhabitants of Beth-shemesh or the inhabitants of Beth-anath.

which there are date palms, it is difficult to identify. **18:** *Gaza . . . Ashkelon . . . Ekron:* The conquest of three of the five Philistine royal city-states, which elsewhere were only conquered in the days of David, is here attributed to *Judah.* **20:** Judah gave the city to Caleb and he dispossessed the giants (Anakites), whose names are mentioned in v. 10 above. The story of a struggle with giants appears in the narratives of the conquest (see, e.g., Num. 13.28, 32–33).

1.21–36: The conquests of the northern tribes. The tribes of the north, who here number seven, are mentioned in order from south to north, from Benjamin to Dan, who was forced to leave his inheritance and later settled in the north. This order is similar to that of the whole book, which begins with Ehud the Benjaminite and concludes with the northward wandering of Dan. The northern tribes are represented as responsible for the majority of the failures to take possession of the land. **22–29:** Similar to Judah who conquered Jerusalem, the first conquest of the *House of Joseph* is their central cultic city, *Bethel.* Bethel is identified with the Arab village Beitin, about 20 km (12 miles) north of Jerusalem. **30–33:** The tribes dwelling north of the valley of Jezreel are described as a minority that ruled the Canaanite population. **34–35:** The tribe of Dan did not succeed in taking hold of its inheritance, and was forced into the area of Har-heres near Beth-shemesh. The House of Joseph, unlike Judah who cooperated with Simeon his brother, did not help the tribe of Dan and preferred to subjugate the Amorites as forced labor.

---

a Meaning of Heb. uncertain. Emendation yields "Amalekites"; cf. 1 Sam. 15.6.

b I.e., "Proscribed." Cf. notes at Num. 21.2–3.

c Septuagint reads "But Judah did not capture Gaza . . ." Gaza is in the coastal plain referred to in v. 19.　　d Lit. "watchmen."

But they settled in the midst of the Canaanite inhabitants of the land, and the inhabitants of Beth-shemesh and Beth-anath had to perform forced labor for them.

³⁴ The Amorites pressed the Danites into the hill country; they would not let them come down to the plain. ³⁵ The Amorites also persisted in dwelling in Har-heres, in Aijalon, and in Shaalbim. But the hand of the House of Joseph bore heavily on them and they had to perform forced labor. ³⁶ The territory of the Amorites[a] extended from the Ascent of Akrabbim—from Sela—onward.

2 An angel of the LORD came up from Gilgal to Bochim and said, "I brought you up from Egypt and I took you into the land which I had promised on oath to your fathers. And I said, 'I will never break My covenant with you. ² And you, for your part, must make no covenant with the inhabitants of this land; you must tear down their altars.' But you have not obeyed Me—look what you have done! ³ Therefore, I have resolved not to drive them out before you; they shall become your oppressors,[b] and their gods shall be a snare to you." ⁴ As the angel of the LORD spoke these words to all the Israelites, the people broke into weeping. ⁵ So they named that place Bochim,[c] and they offered sacrifices there to the LORD.

⁶ When Joshua dismissed the people, the Israelites went to their allotted territories and took possession of the land. ⁷ The people served the LORD during the lifetime of Joshua and the lifetime of the older people who lived on after Joshua and who had witnessed all the marvelous deeds that the LORD had wrought for Israel. ⁸ Joshua son of Nun, the servant of the LORD, died at the age of one hundred and ten years, ⁹ and was buried on his own property, at Timnath-heres[d] in the hill country of Ephraim, north of Mount Gaash. ¹⁰ And all that generation were likewise gathered to their fathers.

Another generation arose after them, which had not experienced [the deliverance of] the LORD or the deeds that He had wrought for Israel. ¹¹ And the Israelites did what was offensive to the LORD. They worshiped the Baalim ¹² and forsook the LORD, the God of their fathers, who had brought them out of the land of Egypt. They followed other gods, from among the gods of the peoples around them, and bowed down to them; they provoked the LORD. ¹³ They forsook the LORD and worshiped Baal and the

2.1–5: The assembly in Bochim and the punishment for non-dispossessing. This episode is somewhat obscure. **1:** The *angel* is evidently a prophet sent by the LORD to the city of *Bochim*, i.e., Bethel. This identification is based upon the Septuagint, and upon the connection of Bethel to *weeping* (v. 5; see 20.26, 17–23; 21.2). It was only natural that Bethel, which is identified with the golden calf (1 Kings 12.25–30), was chosen to serve as the place of rebuke to the northern tribes, who violated the covenant and sinned in non-dispossessing.

2.6–3.6: Characterization of the age of the judges. 2.6–10: The first generation of the age of the judges did not know the deliverance of the LORD. **2.11–19:** The period of the judges is characterized by repeating cycles comprised of four stages: the sin of doing evil in the eyes of the LORD (vv. 11–13); punishment by subjugation to the surrounding nations (vv. 14–15), deliverance by judges (v. 16), and the days during which the judges ruled, which were periods of calm following the deliverance (vv. 17–19). Sometimes the people returned to sin during the judge's lifetime, and at others only after his death; in any event the period of sin always returns. Later in the book, the stage of deliverance (see 3.9, etc.) is also preceded by a stage of crying out or turning to the LORD. The absence of this stage here emphasizes the nation's apostasy. This description is rich in repetitions and in Deuteronomistic expressions, suggesting a late editing. **11:** *Baalim:* Baal, whose name means "master," was one of the heads of the Canaanite pantheon. The use of the plural may indicate the existence of a multiplicity of cults of which Baal is the center, or various other kinds of idolatry. **13:** *Ashtaroth:* The name Ashtoreth also appears here in the plural. This goddess, one of the consorts of Baal, was responsible for love and fertility.

a Some Septuagint mss. read "Edomites."

b So Targum and other ancient versions. Meaning of Heb. uncertain.

c I.e., "weepers."   d Some mss. read "Timnath-serah"; cf. Josh. 24.30.

Ashtaroth.[a] [14] Then the LORD was incensed at Israel, and He handed them over to foes[b] who plundered them. He surrendered them to their enemies on all sides, and they could no longer hold their own against their enemies. [15] In all their campaigns, the hand of the LORD was against them to their undoing, as the LORD had declared and as the LORD had sworn to them; and they were in great distress. [16] Then the LORD raised up chieftains who delivered them from those who plundered them. [17] But they did not heed their chieftains either; they went astray after other gods and bowed down to them. They were quick to turn aside from the way their fathers had followed in obedience to the commandments of the LORD; they did not do right. [18] When the LORD raised up chieftains for them, the LORD would be with the chieftain and would save them from their enemies during the chieftain's lifetime; for the LORD would be moved to pity by their moanings because of those who oppressed and crushed them. [19] But when the chieftain died, they would again act basely, even more than [c]the preceding generation[c]—following other gods, worshiping them, and bowing down to them; they omitted none of their practices and stubborn ways.

[20] Then the LORD became incensed against Israel, and He said, "Since that nation has transgressed the covenant that I enjoined upon their fathers and has not obeyed Me, [21] I for My part will no longer drive out before them any of the nations that Joshua left when he died." [22] For it was in order to test Israel by them—[to see] whether or not they would faithfully walk in the ways of the LORD, as their fathers had done—[23] that the LORD had left those nations, instead of driving them out at once, and had not delivered them into the hands of Joshua.

3 [d]These are the nations that the LORD left so that He might might test by them all the Israelites who had not known any of the wars of Canaan, [2] so that succeeding generations of Israelites might be made to experience war— but only those who had not known the [e]former wars:[e] [3] the five principalities[f] of the Philistines and all the Canaanites, Sidonians, and Hivites who inhabited the hill country of the Lebanon from Mount Baal-hermon to Lebo-hamath.[g] [4] These served as a means of testing Israel, to learn whether they would obey the commandments which the LORD had enjoined upon their fathers through Moses.

2.20–3.6: Three answers as to why the nations remained. This is clearly a composite text, reflecting various answers to the central question: Why was the conquest of the indigenous population not complete? **21:** The sins of the period of the judges made the LORD decide not to continue to dispossess the nations. **22–23:** According to a second view, God intended from the outset to leave the nations in order to test Israel and see if they would be loyal to Him. **3.1–2:** According to a third view, incorporated in the previous one, God planned from the outset to leave the other nations in order to allow the Israelites practice in the art of war. **5–6:** The lack of complete annihilation of the local population led to assimilation (see Deut. 7.1–6; 20.16–18), and thus explains the faithlessness of the Israelites in the rest of the book.

3.7–11: Othniel the Kenizzite. The first judge was from Judah, and he waged war against an enemy from the far north, thus lending a national character to the event. The description of the deliverance does not give any details about the war itself, but is rich in terms found elsewhere in the cyclical formulae. This description serves as a transitional stage from the introduction to the specific narratives. Othniel's success is complete, suggesting the preeminence of Judah. **7:** *Asheroth:* The plural indicates a multiplicity of cults. In the Ugaritic pantheon Asherah is the consort of El, the old chief god. The word is used in the Bible both as the name of the goddess and as the term for a cultic object made of wood, which was evidently her symbol (see, e.g., Deut. 16.21–22). **8:** *Cushanrishathaim:* The name is strange. The dual ending *(ayim)* seems intended to suggest a particularly wicked enemy. The name as a whole may be translated as "Dark double-wickedness," and is likely symbolic. *Aram-naharaim:* The land of the family of the two rivers (Tigris and Euphrates), in northeast Syria. Some think that the

---

a *Canaanite female deities.* b Lit. *"plunderers."* c-c Lit. *"their fathers."*
d *The sentence structure of vv. 1–2 is uncertain.*
e-e Lit. *"them formerly."* f Lit. *"lords."* g *See note at Num. 13.21.*

⁵The Israelites settled among the Canaanites, Hittites, Amorites, Perizzites, Hivites, and Jebusites; ⁶they took their daughters to wife and gave their own daughters to their sons, and they worshiped their gods. ⁷The Israelites did what was offensive to the Lord; they ignored the Lord their God and worshiped the Baalim and the Asheroth. ⁸The Lord became incensed at Israel and surrendered them to King Cushan-rishathaim of Aram-naharaim; and the Israelites were subject to Cushan-rishathaim for eight years. ⁹The Israelites cried out to the Lord, and the Lord raised a champion for the Israelites to deliver them: Othniel the Kenizzite, a younger kinsman of Caleb. ¹⁰The spirit of the Lord descended upon him and he became Israel's chieftain. He went out to war, and the Lord delivered King Cushan-rishathaim of Aram into his hands. He prevailed over Cushan-rishathaim, ¹¹and the land had peace for forty years.

When Othniel the Kenizzite died, ¹²the Israelites again did what was offensive to the Lord. And because they did what was offensive to the Lord, the Lord let King Eglon of Moab prevail over Israel. ¹³[Eglon] brought the Ammonites and the Amalekites together under his command, and went and defeated Israel and occupied the City of Palms. ¹⁴The Israelites were subject to King Eglon of Moab for eighteen years.

¹⁵Then the Israelites cried out to the Lord, and the Lord raised up a champion for them: the Benjaminite Ehud son of Gera, a left-handed man. It happened that the Israelites sent tribute to King Eglon of Moab through him. ¹⁶So Ehud made for himself a two-edged dagger, a *gomed* in length, which he girded on his right side under his cloak. ¹⁷He presented the tribute to King Eglon of Moab. Now Eglon was a very stout man. ¹⁸When [Ehud] had finished presenting the tribute, he dismissed the people who had conveyed the tribute. ¹⁹But he himself returned from Pesilim, near Gilgal, and said, "Your Majesty, I have a secret message for you." [Eglon] thereupon commanded, "Silence!" So all those in attendance left his presence; ²⁰and when Ehud approached him, he was sitting alone in his cool upper chamber. Ehud said, "I have a message for you from God"; whereupon he rose from his seat. ²¹Reaching with his left hand, Ehud drew the dagger from his right side and drove it into [Eglon's]ᵃ belly. ²²The fat closed over the blade and the hilt went in after the blade—for he did not pull the dagger out of his belly—and the filthᵇ came out.

a Heb. "his."   b Meaning of Heb. uncertain.

name Aram is a corruption of Edom, which borders Judah, but it is more likely that the intention is to attribute to Othniel from Judah a national war against a powerful distant nation. **10:** *The spirit of the Lord:* This refers to a temporary endowment of power or charisma that allows him to be a successful warrior and leader.

3.12–30: Ehud son of Gera. In this story, the deliverance performed by Ehud the Benjaminite is performed with military tactics, some planned and others improvised. The victory suggests that divine providence stands behind human success. **13:** *The City of Palms:* In this case, unlike 1.16, most commentators, following Josephus, identify this place with Jericho. **16:** *Two-edged dagger:* Ordinary daggers were curved and sharp only on the inner edge. Ehud's dagger, intended for stabbing, was short, perhaps a foot long, and sharpened on both edges, perhaps because he would wield it in his left hand, contrary to the usual practice. **17:** The king's stoutness is emphasized because it complicated the planned assassination, as Ehud had a short sword. The picture of the dagger buried in the fleshy king's abdomen (vv. 21–22) adds to the humorous put-down of Eglon. **18:** *Had finished . . . he dismissed the people:* These expressions create the impression of an elaborate gift-offering ceremony. The time consumed by the ceremony enabled Ehud to become familiar with the place and to create the impression of a submissive subject. Ehud alone remained, thereby obviating the need to reenter the well-guarded palace. **19:** Ehud arrived at Eglon's residence after previously visiting the Pesilim ("idols"), evidently a cultic site with statues of the gods near Gilgal, next to Jericho. **20:** *From God:* Ehud anticipated that, upon hearing God's name, the king would stand up and stretch himself, thereby making it easier to kill him. Eglon expects a divine oracle, but receives a divinely sanctioned stabbing. Some sages emphasized

Mediterranean Sea

Sidon

ARAM (SYRIA)

Kedesh

Hazor

NAPHTALI

Bethlehem

ZEBULUN

ISSACHAR

MANASSEH

MANASSEH

Shechem
Mt. Gerizim
Arumah

Zaphon?
Penuel
Succoth

River Jabbok

GILEAD

EPHRAIM

Ramah

Jogbehah

Bethel
Ophrah
Aijalon
Mizpah

AMMON

DAN

Timnah
Ekron
Zorah
Lehi?

Ashdod

Heshbon

Ashkelon

Gath?

PHILISTIA

River Jordan

Gaza

Dead Sea

R. Arnon

Karkor →

MOAB

AMALEK

0   10   20 Miles

0   10   20 Kilometers

MIDIAN

Harosheth-hagoiim?

Mt. Tabor

Wadi Kishon

Hill of Moreh

V. of Jezreel runstate river

Hill Country of Ephraim

Thebez?

35°   36°   31°   32°

Important cities mentioned in the book of Judges. Square boxes indicate Philistine cities.

23 Stepping out into the vestibule,[a] Ehud shut the doors of the upper chamber on him and locked them. 24 After he left, the courtiers returned. When they saw that the doors of the upper chamber were locked, they thought, "He must be relieving himself in the cool chamber." 25 They waited a long time; and when he did not open the doors of the chamber, they took the key and opened them—and there their master was lying dead on the floor! 26 But Ehud had made good his escape while they delayed; he had passed Pesilim and escaped to Seirah. 27 When he got there, he had the ram's horn sounded through the hill country of Ephraim, and all the Israelites descended with him from the hill country; and he took the lead. 28 "Follow me closely," he said, "for the LORD has delivered your enemies, the Moabites, into your hands." They followed him down and seized the fords of the Jordan against the Moabites; they let no one cross. 29 On that occasion they slew about 10,000 Moabites; they were all robust and brave men, yet not one of them escaped. 30 On that day, Moab submitted to Israel; and the land was tranquil for eighty years.

31 After him came Shamgar [b]son of Anath,[b] who slew six hundred Philistines with an ox-goad. He too was a champion of Israel.

4 The Israelites again did what was offensive to the LORD—Ehud now being dead. 2 And the LORD surrendered them to King Jabin of Canaan, who reigned in Hazor. His army commander was Sisera, whose base was Harosheth-goiim. 3 The Israelites cried out to the LORD; for he had nine hundred iron chariots, and he had oppressed Israel ruthlessly for twenty years.

4 Deborah, wife of Lappidoth, was a prophetess; she led Israel at that time. 5 She used to sit under the Palm of Deborah, between Ramah and Bethel in the hill country of

---

a Meaning of Heb. uncertain.   b-b Or "the Beth-anathite."

---

heroism, such as the story about Samson who smote 1,000 people with the jaw bone of an ass (Judg. 15.15–16; cf. 2 Sam. 23.8). The inclusion of Shamgar among the judges rounds out their number to twelve.

4.1–24: Deborah, Jael, and Barak. Deborah the prophetess, Barak the army commander, and Jael wife of Heber the Kenite, all contributed to achieving delivery from the Canaanite enemy. None of them is called the deliverer, because each of these human figures made only a partial contribution to the victory; in practice, the true deliverer was God (v. 23). In Jewish tradition this story, and the song which follows, constitute the haftarah for "Be-shallaḥ," whose Torah reading relates that the LORD confused the camp of Egypt (cf. Exod. 14.24; Judg. 4.15), that they drowned in the sea until "not one of them remained" (cf. Exod. 14.28; Judg. 4.16), and that Moses and Israel sang a song to the LORD after they saw their salvation (cf. Exod. 15.1–18; Judg. ch 5). The prose account of the defeat of Sisera in ch 4, followed by the song in ch 5, is structurally similar to the prose account of the drowning of the Egyptians in Exod. ch 14, followed by the Song of the Sea in ch 15. **2:** *King Jabin of Canaan,* a problematic phrase found in this story alone (cf. vv. 23–24) since Canaan, which was divided into many royal city-states, was not ruled by a king. The desire to magnify the dimensions of this deliverance may have led to the creation of this idiom. *Who reigned in Hazor:* Jabin is mentioned below (v. 17) as the king of Hazor, which is located in upper Galilee and was known as a very important city (Josh. 11.9). *Sisera:* The origin and meaning of the name are unknown. *Harosheth-goiim:* The place, mentioned only here, has not been identified. The name *Harosheth* seems to be derived from the term "ḥarish," i.e., a plowed area, referring to the flat areas in the Jezreel Valley near Taanach and Megiddo, where Sisera's army encamped

---

the positive aspect in Eglon's behavior, namely, that he stood up out of respect for the LORD, and they considered Ruth the Moabite to be Eglon's daughter, making David one of his descendants (*Ruth Rab.* 2.9). **23:** The architectural details are unclear. **24:** Eglon is indeed relieving himself in that his guts are spilling out. **25:** *Lying dead:* The servants did not sense the murder, as the fat covering the dagger prevented bleeding. They

therefore did not suspect Ehud, who had enough time to escape. **26:** *Seirah,* unidentified site in the hill country of Ephraim. **28:** *The fords of the Jordan,* places that served as river-crossings where the river was shallow. **29:** *Not one of them escaped,* a likely allusion to divine providence. **31:** *Shamgar son of Anath:* The report about Shamgar may be based on his mention in the Song of Deborah (5.6). It is reminiscent of other stories of

Ephraim, and the Israelites would come to her for decisions.

⁶She summoned Barak son of Abinoam, of Kedesh in Naphtali, and said to him, "The LORD, the God of Israel, has commanded: Go, march up to Mount Tabor, and take with you ten thousand men of Naphtali and Zebulun. ⁷And I will draw Sisera, Jabin's army commander, with his chariots and his troops, toward you up to the Wadi Kishon; and I will deliver him into your hands." ⁸But Barak said to her, "If you will go with me, I will go; if not, I will not go." ⁹"Very well, I will go with you," she answered. "However, there will be no glory for you in the course you are taking, for then the LORD will deliver Sisera into the hands of a woman." So Deborah went with Barak to Kedesh. ¹⁰Barak then mustered Zebulun and Naphtali at Kedesh; ten thousand men marched up ᵃ⁻after him;⁻ᵃ and Deborah also went up with him.

¹¹Now Heber the Kenite had separated ᵇ⁻from the other Kenites,⁻ᵇ descendants of Hobab, father-in-law of Moses, and had pitched his tent at Elon-bezaanannim, which is near Kedesh.

¹²Sisera was informed that Barak son of Abinoam had gone up to Mount Tabor. ¹³So Sisera ordered all his chariots—nine hundred iron chariots—and all the troops he had to move from Harosheth-goiim to the Wadi Kishon. ¹⁴Then Deborah said to Barak, "Up! This is the day on which the LORD will deliver Sisera into your hands: the LORD is marching before you." Barak charged down Mount Tabor, followed by the ten thousand men, ¹⁵and the LORD threw Sisera and all his chariots and army into a panic ᶜ⁻before the onslaught of Barak.⁻ᶜ Sisera leaped from his chariot and fled on foot ¹⁶as Barak pursued the chariots and the soldiers as far as Harosheth-goiim. All of Sisera's soldiers fell by the sword; not a man was left.

¹⁷Sisera, meanwhile, had fled on foot to the tent of Jael, wife of Heber the Kenite; for there was friendship between King Jabin of Hazor and the family of Heber the Kenite. ¹⁸Jael came out to greet Sisera and said to him, "Come in, my lord, come in here, do not be afraid." So he entered her tent, and she covered him with a blanket. ¹⁹He said to her, "Please let me have some water; I am thirsty." She opened a skin of milk and gave him some to drink; and she covered him again. ²⁰He said to her, "Stand at the entrance of the tent. If anybody comes and asks you

with his chariot. **6:** *Kedesh in Naphtali,* located in the southeast part of the inheritance of Naphtali, identified with Khirbet Kadish at the foot of Poriyah. *Mount Tabor:* At this mountain, overlooking the Valley of Jezreel from the north, Barak was commanded to gather his army. **7:** *Wadi Kishon,* one of the branches of the Kishon, the most important of the brooks of the Jezreel Valley. This branch flows close to Taanach and Megiddo and is referred to in the song as "Megiddo's waters" (5.19). **8:** *If not, I will not go:* The military leader needs the prophetess as a means of inquiring of the LORD. **9:** *Into the hands of a woman:* This does not enhance the army commander's dignity. The reader assumes that this refers to Deborah, but when reaching the end of the story, realizes that Jael is meant. Thus, Deborah's "prophecy" in this verse is fulfilled. **11:** *Heber the Kenite,* a tribal unit that became separated from the Kenites who were annexed to Judah (1.16). **14:** *The LORD is marching before you:* These words of Deborah indicate the LORD's direct participation in the battle, as the leader going at the head of the army. **15:** *"At the edge of the sword"* (translators' note c-c): These words are appended here from v. 16. Nowhere else in the entire Bible does the LORD throw the enemy into a panic by the sword. **16:** *Not a man was left:* This unrealistic detail alludes to divine intervention (cf. 3.29). **17:** *To the tent of Jael . . . for there was friendship:* Sisera preferred the tent of the Kenites to Harosheth-goiim, because he was convinced that this direction of flight would not occur to his pursuers, due to the friendship between the Kenites and the Israelites. **19:** Even though he asked for water she gave him milk, because of its soothing qualities; Jael wanted to assure that Sisera would sleep deeply. **21:** Here it is revealed that Jael is the woman into whose hands the LORD delivered Sisera (see v. 9). **23:** *God subdued:* The conclusion emphasizes the LORD's central role in accomplish-

---

a-a Lit. "at his feet."
b-b Lit. "from Cain"; cf. 1.16.
c-c Lit. "at the edge of the sword before Barak."

if there is anybody here, say 'No.' " ²¹ Then Jael wife of Heber took a tent pin and grasped the mallet. When he was fast asleep from exhaustion, she approached him stealthily and drove the pin through his temple till it went down to the ground. Thus he died.

²² Now Barak appeared in pursuit of Sisera. Jael went out to greet him and said, "Come, I will show you the man you are looking for." He went inside with her, and there Sisera was lying dead, with the pin in his temple.

²³ On that day God subdued King Jabin of Canaan before the Israelites. ²⁴ The hand of the Israelites bore harder and harder on King Jabin of Canaan, until they destroyed King Jabin of Canaan.

5 On that day Deborah and Barak son of Abinoam sang:

²ᵃ   When ᵇ⁻locks go untrimmed⁻ᵇ in Israel,
        When people dedicate themselves—
        Bless the LORD!

³   Hear, O kings! Give ear, O potentates!
        I will sing, will sing to the LORD,
        Will hymn the LORD, the God of Israel.

⁴   O LORD, when You came forth from Seir,
        Advanced from the country of Edom,
        The earth trembled;
        The heavens dripped,
        Yea, the clouds dripped water,
⁵   The mountains quakedᶜ—
        Before the LORD, Him of Sinai,
        Before the LORD, God of Israel.

a In many parts of this poem the meaning is uncertain.
b-b Apparently an expression of dedication; cf. Num. 6.5.
c Taking nazelu as a by-form of nazollu; cf. Targum.

ing the general victory and the partial contribution of the human figures.

5.1–31: The Song of Deborah. This is a hymn of praise thanking and extolling God for overcoming the enemies that threatened His people. It incorporates calls and addresses expressing the joy of victory and the need to offer thanksgiving. The poem is written in the first person, presented from the viewpoint of the speaker; read-ers in effect sing the song and identify with the speaker. Besides the opening (vv. 2–3) and closing (v. 31a) it consists of three sections. The first (vv. 4–11c) depicts God's theophany, the difficult situation of His people and its hope for sal-vation; the second (vv. 11d–23) portrays the Israelite warriors in contrast with the Canaanite kings; the third (vv. 24–30) focuses upon Jael, who represents victory, con-trasted with Sisera's mother, who represents defeat. Although there are similarities between the song in ch 5 and the story in ch 4, there are also numerous differences: e.g., the story only mentions two tribes who participate in battle, the song mentions at least six; according to the song Sisera headed the Ca-naanite alliance and Jabin is not mentioned. Many scholars believe that the story was composed as an interpretation of the song. Stylisti-cally, the song is in archaic Heb, and is extremely difficult, and in places, perhaps corrupt. It makes use of extensive contrasts and ex-treme transitions: from the LORD's might to Israel's unfortunate situa-tion; from the Israelite tribes to their enemies; from Jael to Sisera's mother. It also conveys an atmo-sphere of spontaneous enthusi-asm. The poem does not mention Judah, Simeon, and Levi, suggest-ing that it was composed in the north. **1:** According to the editor, Deborah and Barak uttered the song in immediate reaction to the joy of victory.

5.2–3: Opening explaining the circumstances of reciting the song. 2: *When locks go untrimmed,* the Heb is difficult. The translation alludes to the phenomenon of Nazirites who dedicated them-selves to warfare wearing long hair (see Num. ch 6). Rashi's inter-pretation, that the phrase refers to disturbances or even disasters that confronted Israel, is preferable. *Dedicate,* volunteer of one's own will. *Bless,* addressed to the people of Israel. **3:** *I will sing . . . :* The rep-etition emphasizes the function of the speaker and strengthens the in-volvement of the person later recit-ing the song.

5.4–5: God's theophany and His influence on the mighty forces of nature. 4: *Seir . . . Edom,* syn-onyms referring to God's revela-tion in the land of Edom, south-east of Judah. On the tradition of God's epiphany there, see Deut. 32.2. **5:** *Quaked,* some interpret the Heb in the sense of flowing, liquid matter. On the connection between earthquakes and liquid imagery, see Amos 9.5.

6   In the days of Shamgar ᵃson of Anath,·ᵃ
In the days of Jael, caravansᵇ ceased,
And wayfarers went
By roundabout paths.

7   Deliverance ceased,
Ceased in Israel,
Till youᶜ arose, O Deborah,
Arose, O mother, in Israel!

8   When they chose new gods,
ᵈ⁻Was there a fighter then in the gates? ·ᵈ
No shield or spear was seen
Among forty thousand in Israel!

9   My heart is with Israel's leaders,
With the dedicated of the people—
Bless the LORD!

10   You riders on tawny she-asses,
You who sit on saddle rugs,
And you wayfarers, declare it!

11   Louder than the ᵉsound of archers,·ᵉ
There among the watering places
Let them chant the gracious acts of the LORD,
His gracious deliverance of Israel.
Then did the people of the LORD
March down to the gates!

12   Awake, awake, O Deborah!
Awake, awake, strike up the chant!
Arise, O Barak;
Take your captives, O son of Abinoam!

13   Then was the remnant made victor over the
mighty,
The LORD's peopleᶠ won my victory over the
warriors.

14   From Ephraim came they whose roots are in
Amalek;

---

a-a Or "the Beth-anathite."   b Or "roads."

c Heb. qamti, archaic second-person singular feminine.

d-d Meaning of Heb. uncertain; others "then was war in the gates."

e-e Or "thunder peals"; meaning of Heb. uncertain.

f Reading 'am (with pathaḥ) Adonai; so many Heb. mss.

**5.6–11c: Description of the diffi-
cult situation in Israel. 6:** *Shamgar,*
see 3.31 n. **7:** *Deliverance ceased:* In
the Aramaic Targum and in traditional exegesis the Heb word "per-
azon" is taken as referring to

"open" cities. People were afraid
to live in towns without a wall,
and fled to fortified cities. *You
arose:* Here the speaker addresses
Deborah; see v. 12. **8:** *New gods:*
The cause of the difficult situation

is the people's abandonment of the
LORD for the gods of Canaan. See
Deut. 32.15–19. *Then:* This word is
repeated five times (vv. 8, 11, 13,
19, 22). Its appearance indicates
various stages in the course of the
war: danger, gathering together,
arrival at the battlefield, war, retreat. *Forty thousand,* an exaggerated typological number, intended
to suggest a war of national dimensions. **9:** *Leaders:* The Heb formula carries the connotation of
legislators. **10:** *You riders . . . :* Only
the wealthy could allow them-
selves to ride specifically on yellowish donkeys. Riding on a donkey was a symbol of wealth; see
10.4 n. **11:** *Sound of archers:* Alternately, the Heb may refer to the
noise made by shepherds while dividing their flocks in order to
water them. The sound of those
who tell God's victories will be
louder than this sound. *His gracious deliverance:* The LORD's deliverance restored confidence.

**5.11d-13: General description of
preparation for war. 11:** *Gates:* The
city gate served as a gathering
place. Those who had left the unwalled cities gathered at the gates
of the fortified cities in order to set
out to battle. **12:** *Strike up the chant:*
Deborah is expected to prophesy
on the eve of the war. *Take your
captives:* On the connection between victory and booty, see v. 30.
13: *Then was the remnant . . . :* The
Heb is difficult. A preferable reading is "Then they went down to
Sarid [a city in the Jezreel Valley]
against the mighty ones [i.e., the
Canaanite kings; see v. 25], the
LORD's people with their warriors."

**5.14–18: Description of the Israel-
ite side.** Most commentators state
that six tribes went to war
(Ephraim, Benjamin, Machir [i.e.,
Manasseh], Zebulun, Issachar and
Naphtali), while four other tribes
(Reuben, Gilead [i.e., Gad and the
other half of Manasseh], Dan and
Asher) refused to join. According
to the interpretation suggested
here, all ten northern tribes participated. **14:** *In Amalek:* This phrase is

After you, your kin Benjamin;
From Machir came down leaders,
From Zebulun such as hold the marshal's staff.
15   And Issachar's chiefs were with Deborah;
As Barak, so was Issachar—
Rushing after him into the valley.

Among the clans of Reuben
Were great decisions of heart.
16   Why then did you stay among the sheepfolds
And listen as they pipe for the flocks?
Among the clans of Reuben
Were great searchings of heart!
17   Gilead tarried beyond the Jordan;
And Dan—why did he linger *by the ships?*-a
Asher remained at the seacoast
And tarried at his landings.
18   Zebulun is a people *b*-that mocked at death,-b
Naphtali—on the open heights.

19   Then the kings came, they fought:
The kings of Canaan fought
At Taanach, by Megiddo's waters—
They got no spoil of silver.
20   The stars fought from heaven,
From their courses they fought against Sisera.
21   The torrent Kishon swept them*c* away,
The raging torrent, the torrent Kishon.

March on, my soul, with courage!

22   Then the horses' hoofs pounded
d-As headlong galloped the steeds.-d

a-a Or "at Onioth," a presumed designation of Dan's region.
b-b Lit. "belittled its life to die."   c I.e., the kings of Canaan (v. 19).
d-d Lit. "From the gallopings, the gallopings of his steeds."

unclear; hence one should adopt the emendation based on the similarity of the Heb letters: "From Ephraim chieftains [went down] to the valley (Heb 'mk; Amalek is 'mlk)." *Your kin:* The collective noun here follows the plural in the Heb, which may be interpreted as: "After you, Benjamin, among your kinfolk." This usage strengthens the sense of Benjamin's large army. Benjamin is mentioned as a fighting tribe in ch 20, in the blessing of Jacob (Gen 49.27), and in the de-

scription of the establishment of the kingdom (2 Sam. ch 11). *Machir:* The first-born son of Manasseh; cf. Josh. 17.1. *Marshal's staff:* the Heb word suggests commanders, who recorded the number of those going to war (see 2 Kings 25.19). **15:** *So was Issachar:* It is strange that Issachar is repeated twice in this v., while Naphtali is absent. It therefore seems likely that it originally read "Naphtali." This conjecture is strengthened by the fact that Barak was from Ke-

desh-Naphtali, and by the affinity of this v. to the description of Naphtali in the blessing of Jacob (Gen. 49.21). *Heart:* The ancients thought of the heart as the center of thinking and wisdom (see, e.g., 1 Kings 3.12). **16:** *Why then:* the Heb "lamah" (why) does not necessarily imply query. Here and in v. 17 it seems preferable to read as a term of negation with an emphatic mem. Thus, it is not a denunciation of Reuben, and later Dan, for not taking part in the battle. A preferable translation, which notes Reuben's participation, is: "You [certainly] did not stay among the sheepfolds . . . !" **17:** *Tarried,* alternately, "dwelled" or "lived," suggesting that even though the inhabitants of Gilead (Gad and the half tribe of Manasseh) lived far away from the locus of events, they took part in them. *And Dan . . . ships,* alternately, "Dan [certainly] did not linger by the ships." The mention of ships is difficult, because the territory of Dan, both in the south and in the north, has no connection to the sea. *Asher:* The tribe Asher, who dwelt on the northern coastal plain, also joined the war. **18:** *Zebulun . . . Naphtali:* These two tribes alone are mentioned as bold warriors. This is why they alone are mentioned in the prose story (ch 4). *Open heights:* The war was in the valley; the expression alludes to Naphtali's inheritance.

5.19–23: The battle. 19: *Kings of Canaan:* Jabin, who is mentioned in the prose story, does not appear here; v. 20 notes Sisera as heading the alliance. *At Taanach, by Megiddo's waters:* The battlefield was between Taanach and one of the tributaries of the Kishon next to Megiddo, in Jezreel Valley, near the ancient international highway connecting Egypt and Mesopotamia (see 4.7). **21:** *The raging torrent:* The Heb is obscure, and an emendation suggests "the brook Kishon came in front of them." *March on:* The joy of victory finds expression as the speaker addresses himself. **22:** A description of the noise of the enemy's horses' feet fleeing

23 "Curse Meroz!" said the angel of the LORD.
   "Bitterly curse its inhabitants,
   Because they came not to the aid of the LORD,
   To the aid of the LORD among[a] the warriors."

24 Most blessed of women be Jael,
   Wife of Heber the Kenite,
   Most blessed of women in tents.
25 He asked for water, she offered milk;
   In a princely bowl she brought him curds.
26 Her [left] hand reached for the tent pin,
   Her right for the workmen's hammer.
   She struck Sisera, crushed his head,
   Smashed and pierced his temple.
27 At her feet he sank, lay outstretched,
   At her feet he sank, lay still;
   Where he sank, there he lay—destroyed.

28 Through the window peered Sisera's mother,
   Behind the lattice she whined:[b]
   "Why is his chariot so long in coming?
   Why so late the clatter of his wheels?"
29 The wisest of her ladies give answer;
   She, too, replies to herself:
30 "They must be dividing the spoil they have found:
   A damsel or two for each man,
   Spoil of dyed cloths for Sisera,
   Spoil of embroidered cloths,
   A couple of embroidered cloths
   Round every neck as spoil."

31 So may all Your enemies perish, O LORD!
   But may His friends be as the sun rising in might!

And the land was tranquil forty years.

6 Then the Israelites did what was offensive to the LORD, and the LORD delivered them into the hands of the Midianites for seven years. ² The hand of the Midianites prevailed over Israel; and because of Midian, the Israelites

a Or "against."   b Or "gazed"; meaning of Heb. uncertain.

from the battle's confusion. **23:** *Meroz*, which has not been identified and whose inhabitants did not join the battle, is cursed. *The warriors:* Here and in v. 13 it speaks of the warriors of Israel who joined the LORD's battle.

5.24–27: Description of the killing of Sisera in Jael's tent. Death at the hands of a woman was considered shameful; cf. 9.54. The appearance of Jael in the poem is not explained; furthermore, the song does not suggest

that Sisera slept, implying instead that Jael struggled with Sisera. The poem describes Sisera's death in slow motion.

5.28–30: Transition to Sisera's house. The mother's apprehension contrasts with the ladies' expectations of booty. This scene, which is not found in the narrative in ch 4, portrays Sisera's demise from a different perspective. **28:** The picture of a woman looking through the window is repeated in the Bible (2 Sam. 6.16; 2 Kings 9.30) and in other ancient Near Eastern texts. **30:** *Dyed cloths . . . embroidered:* The making of dye was expensive; hence colored clothing was expensive, as were garments embroidered with colored threads. Cf. Exod. 26.36. *Every neck:* This seems to refer to the necks of those who took the spoils.

5.31a: Closing. *His friends:* The people of the LORD are compared to the sun, rising with great intensity.

5.31b: Editorial conclusion. These words are not part of the song, but are the closing frame of the Deborah-Barak cycle. In its present location it emphasizes the transition to a new cycle of stories.

6.1–8.28: The cycle of Gideon stories. The description of Gideon's deliverance of the Israelites is divided into two sections, distinctive in subject matter, events, and characterization. The former (6.1–7.23) depicts the period from the people's sin and consequent subjugation to the Midianites until Gideon's victory. This section is rich with miracles, while Gideon is portrayed as a coward requiring divine support. By contrast, the second section (7.24–8.28) is concerned with problems of leadership, there are no miracles, and Gideon is displayed as a charismatic leader. The two sections illustrate the central problem of Judges: What is the preferred leadership? Divine leadership rich in miraculous signs, as in the first section, or human rule, as in the *a*provided themselves with refuges in the caves and strongholds of the mountains.*-a* 3 After the Israelites had done their sowing, Midian, Amalek, and the Kedemites would come up and raid them; 4 they would attack them, destroy*b* the produce of the land all the way to Gaza, and leave no means of sustenance in Israel, not a sheep or an ox or an ass. 5 For they would come up with their livestock and their tents, swarming as thick as locusts; they and their camels were innumerable. Thus they would invade the land and ravage it. 6 Israel was reduced to utter misery by the Midianites, and the Israelites cried out to the Lord.

7 When the Israelites cried to the Lord on account of Midian, 8 the Lord sent a prophet to the Israelites who said to them, "Thus said the Lord, the God of Israel: I brought you up out of Egypt and freed you from the house of bondage. 9 I rescued you from the Egyptians and from all your oppressors; I drove them out before you, and gave you their land. 10 And I said to you, 'I the Lord am your God. You must not worship the gods of the Amorites in whose land you dwell.' But you did not obey Me."

11 An angel of the Lord came and sat under the terebinth at Ophrah, which belonged to Joash the Abiezrite. His son Gideon was then beating out wheat inside a winepress in order to keep it safe from the Midianites. 12 The angel of the Lord appeared to him and said to him, "The Lord is with you, valiant warrior!" 13 Gideon said to him, "Please, my lord, if the Lord is with us, why has all this befallen us? Where are all His wondrous deeds about which our fathers told us, saying, 'Truly the Lord brought us up from Egypt'? Now the Lord has abandoned us and delivered us into the hands of Midian!" 14 The Lord turned to him and said, "Go in this strength of yours and deliver Israel from the Midianites. I herewith make you My messenger." 15 He said to Him, "Please, my lord, how can I deliver Israel? Why, my clan is the humblest in Manasseh, and I am the youngest in my father's household."

a-a Meaning of Heb. uncertain.   *b I.e., by grazing their livestock.*

the entire land was devastated. **5:** *As locusts,* an image emphasizing a large number and severe damage. Cf. Joel 1.6–7. **7–10:** Israel *cried to the Lord,* but this time He delayed the deliverer and sent a prophet to rebuke the people for being ungrateful and violating the covenant.

6.11–24: Gideon's appointment as savior. The account is a stereotypic scene composed of seven stages: meeting (vv. 11–13), presentation of the mission (v. 14), refusal (v. 15), encouragement (v. 16), request for and giving of a sign (vv. 17–22), acknowledgment and fear (v. 23), and further encouragement (v. 24). The appointment of Moses in Exod. 3.1–4.17 has a similar structure, but in a different sequence. **11:** *Ophrah:* There are several other places bearing this name. Ophrah of the Abiezrites (v. 24) is located within the territory of the Abiezer clan, one of the important families in Manasseh, who is mentioned in the Samaria Ostraca from the mid-8th century BCE. *Gideon:* This story offers a folk etymology of his name from the root "g-d-ʿ," "to hack," mentioned in connection with destroying sacred posts (Deut. 7.5). *Winepress:* The winepress, in contrast to a threshing floor, is sunk in the ground, and thus is more effective for hiding the grain from the Midianites. **12:** *Angel:* Angels, or messengers from God, tend to appear as adult human beings; therefore Gideon does not know that he is confronted by an angel. *The Lord is with you:* A conventional formula of blessing and encouragement (Ruth 2.4). *Valiant warrior:* An allusion to the military role that Gideon is expected to play. **13:** The angel alludes to the prophet's rebuke in vv. 7–10. **14:** *The Lord,* as the angel of the Lord. *This strength,* Rashi: "By virtue of the fact that you spoke in defense of my sons." **15:** *Humblest . . . youngest,* a polite refusal characteristic of appointment stories, since Gideon's family is depicted as prosperous (vv. 19, 25, 27; cf. 1 Sam. 9.21). The choice of the

second? Gideon's victory is also mentioned in Isa. 10.26 and Ps. 83.10–13.

6.1–10: Exposition. 1–2: The period of oppression lasted for only seven years, but since it involved subjugation by nomadic tribes with grazing flocks, they succeeded in causing great damage by

destroying all the crops. The Israelites were forced to go into hiding and to conceal their grain in the hills. **3:** *Amalek . . . Kedemites,* wandering tribes from southern and eastern deserts who joined the Midianites. **4:** *Gaza,* located in the southwest of Israel, later marking the boundary of the land (1 Kings 5.4). Its mention here suggests that

16 The LORD replied, "I will be with you, and you shall defeat Midian to a man." 17 And he said to Him, "If I have gained Your favor, give me a sign that it is You who are speaking to me: 18 do not leave this place until I come back to You and bring out my offering and place it before You." And He answered, "I will stay until you return."

19 So Gideon went in and prepared a kid, and [baked] unleavened bread from an ephah of flour. He put the meat in a basket and poured the broth into a pot, and he brought them out to Him under the terebinth. As he presented them, 20 the angel of God said to him, "Take the meat and the unleavened bread, put them on yonder rock, and spill out the broth." He did so. 21 The angel of the LORD held out the staff that he carried, and touched the meat and the unleavened bread with its tip. A fire sprang up from the rock and consumed the meat and the unleavened bread. And the angel of the LORD vanished from his sight. 22 Then Gideon realized that it was an angel of the LORD; and Gideon said, "Alas, O Lord GOD! For I have seen an angel of the LORD face to face."

23 But the LORD said to him, "All is well; have no fear, you shall not die." 24 So Gideon built there an altar to the LORD and called it *a*-Adonai-shalom.*a* To this day it stands in Ophrah of the Abiezrites.

25 That night the LORD said to him: "Take the *b*-young bull*b* belonging to your father and another bull seven years old; pull down the altar of Baal which belongs to your father, and cut down the sacred post which is beside it. 26 Then build an altar to the LORD your God, on *b*-the level ground*b* on top of this stronghold. Take the other bull and offer it as a burnt offering, using the wood of the sacred post that you have cut down." 27 So Gideon took ten of his servants and did as the LORD had told him; but as he was afraid to do it by day, on account of his father's household and the townspeople, he did it by night. 28 Early the next morning, the townspeople found that the altar of Baal had been torn down and the sacred post beside it had been cut down, and that the second bull had been offered on the newly built altar. 29 They said to one

a-a I.e., "The LORD, 'All-is-well.' "   b-b Meaning of Heb. uncertain.

mysterious stranger is an angel is his avoidance of eating; instead he uses the materials from the meal for a cultic ceremony: The meat is a sacrificial offering, the cakes are a meal offering, and the gravy is a substitute for the libation. **21:** The second sign is the appearance of fire from the rock (cf. 13.20; 1 Kings 18.38; etc.) consuming the materials of the meal; the third sign is the miraculous disappearance of the angel. This piling up of signs is later mirrored in the signs that Gideon requests at the end of the ch. **22:** Once Gideon realized that he had seen God's angel, he was afraid that this contact with the divine might prove fatal, since encounter with the divine is typically fraught with danger (see Exod. 20.15; Judg. 13.22). **24:** The name of the altar is related to God's comforting words in v. 23: "All is well."

6.25–32: Gideon wages war against the Baal cult. On the night after his appointment, the LORD commands Gideon to destroy his father's altar of Baal, to cut down the sacred post next to it, and to build an altar to the LORD. Gideon fears the townspeople and works with ten of his servants under cover of darkness. In the morning, after a short investigation, the townspeople want to kill Gideon, but his father prevents them from doing so by saying that, if Baal is god, he can fight his own battles. This story mocks Baal worship, and explains the additional name given to Gideon: Jerubbaal (see v. 32), emphasizing that Gideon did battle with the cult of Baal. **25:** *Another bull seven years old:* The reference to two bulls here, and to the second bull in vv. 26 and 28, is problematic, and may reflect a textual error; therefore, it should be translated: "the bull that had been fattened for seven years." *Sacred post,* symbol of the goddess Asherah (see 3.7 n.). **26:** The building of the LORD's altar in place of Baal's symbolizes the LORD's victory over Baal, who is unable to wage his own battles. **27:** Gideon is shown as a coward, a feature re-

youngest is also a repeated motif (e.g., 1 Sam. 16.11), whose function is to emphasize divine intervention through the unexpected. **17:** *A sign that it is You:* Gideon is skeptical that the messenger is God's angel and asks for proof. **18:** The proof is based upon the belief that

angels do not usually participate in human meals (cf. 13.15; Tobit 12.19). **19:** Prepared from dough that has not risen, *unleavened bread* bakes quickly. *Ephah,* about 23 liters (21 dry quarts), a large quantity, signifying an honorable portion. **20:** The first sign that this another, "Who did this thing?" Upon inquiry and investigation, they were told, "Gideon son of Joash did this thing!" 30 The townspeople said to Joash, "Bring out your son, for he must die: he has torn down the altar of Baal and cut down the sacred post beside it!" 31 But Joash said to all who had risen against him, "Do you have to contend for Baal? Do you have to vindicate him? Whoever fights his battles shall be dead by morning! If he is a god, let him fight his own battles, since it is his altar that has been torn down!" 32 That day they named him*a* Jerubbaal, meaning "Let Baal contend with him, since he tore down his altar."

33 All Midian, Amalek, and the Kedemites joined forces; they crossed over and encamped in the Valley of Jezreel. 34 The spirit of the LORD enveloped Gideon; he sounded the horn, and the Abiezrites rallied behind him. 35 And he sent messengers throughout Manasseh, and they too rallied behind him. He then sent messengers through Asher, Zebulun, and Naphtali, and they came up to meet the Manassites.*b*

36 And Gideon said to God, "If You really intend to deliver Israel through me as You have said— 37 here I place a fleece of wool on the threshing floor. If dew falls only on the fleece and all the ground remains dry, I shall know that You will deliver Israel through me, as You have said." 38 And that is what happened. Early the next day, he squeezed the fleece and wrung out the dew from the fleece, a bowlful of water. 39 Then Gideon said to God, "Do not be angry with me if I speak just once more. Let me make just one more test with the fleece: let the fleece alone be dry, while there is dew all over the ground." 40 God did so that night: only the fleece was dry, while there was dew all over the ground.

7 Early next day, Jerubbaal—that is, Gideon—and all the troops with him encamped above En-harod,*c* while the camp of Midian was in the plain to the north of him, at Gibeath-moreh.*d* 2 The LORD said to Gideon, "You have too many troops with you for Me to deliver Midian into their hands; Israel might claim for themselves the glory due to Me, thinking, 'Our own hand has brought us victory.' 3 Therefore, announce to the men, 'Let anybody who is timid and fearful turn back, *e-*as a bird flies from Mount Gilead.' "*-e* Thereupon, 22,000 of the troops turned back and 10,000 remained.

4 "There are still too many troops," the LORD said to

peated in the first section (until 7.23). **31:** Joash puts Baal to the test in the eyes of his believers. This motif is reminiscent of Elijah's test at Mount Carmel (1 Kings 18.20–40). *By morning,* i.e., of the next day. Joash left time for Baal to act. **32:** *Jerubbaal,* originally a theophoric name, praising Baal as founder. The component "Jeru," repeated in the name "Jerusalem," means to establish. The derivation of the name here as *Let Baal contend . . .* is a folk etymology.

6.33–35: The military mustering. The Midianite army had spread out across the Jezreel Valley; troops from Gideon's father's house were not sufficient, so he called to his assistance his own and the neighboring tribes who were harmed by the Midianites.

6.36–40: The signs of the fleece. Gideon requires additional signs and tests God with two opposite tests, in order to be certain that it was not by chance, but by the LORD's will, that Gideon will deliver Israel. This is the culmination of a ch which has as its theme Gideon's fear.

7.1–8: The three hundred lappers. Gideon's army was reduced from a force of 32,000 warriors to a band of 300 lappers of water, in order to convince the people that the deliverance comes from God. According to rabbinic tradition the lappers were chosen because, unlike those who bent on their knees, they did not bow down to an idol (*Tanḥuma,* ed. Buber, *Toledot* 19; *Yalqut Shim'oni, Judges* 62; 1 Kings 29). According to Josephus the lappers were the cowards. Following this view, which is more likely, Gideon highlights the miracle of the victory by choosing cowards (Josephus, *Ant.,* V.vi.3 [216–17]). **1:** *Plain:* The Midianites encamped on the plain at the feet of Gibeath-moreh, south of Afula. **2:** The concern was that Israel would be haughty and attribute the victory to themselves and not to God (see Deut. 8.17–18). **3:** A call to those fearful of war to re-

a I.e., Gideon.   *b Heb. "them."*   *c Or "the Spring of Harod."*
d Or "the Hill of Moreh."   *e-e Meaning of Heb. uncertain.*

Gideon. "Take them down to the water and I will sift[a] them for you there. Anyone of whom I tell you, 'This one is to go with you,' that one shall go with you; and anyone of whom I tell you, 'This one is not to go with you,' that one shall not go." [5]So he took the troops down to the water. Then the LORD said to Gideon, "Set apart all those who [b-]lap up the water with their tongues like dogs[-b] from all those who get down on their knees to drink." [6]Now those who "lapped" the water into their mouths by hand numbered three hundred; all the rest of the troops got down on their knees to drink. [7]Then the LORD said to Gideon, "I will deliver you and I will put Midian into your hands through the three hundred 'lappers'; let the rest of the troops go home." [8c-]So [the lappers] took the provisions and horns that the other men had with them,[-c] and he sent the rest of the men of Israel back to their homes, retaining only the three hundred men.

The Midianite camp was below him, in the plain. [9]That night the LORD said to him, "Come, attack[d] the camp, for I have delivered it into your hands. [10]And if you are afraid to attack, first go down to the camp with your attendant Purah [11]and listen to what they say; after that you will have the courage to attack the camp." So he went down with his attendant Purah to the outposts of the warriors who were in the camp.—[12]Now Midian, Amalek, and all the Kedemites were spread over the plain, as thick as locusts; and their camels were countless, as numerous as the sands on the seashore.—[13]Gideon came there just as one man was narrating a dream to another. "Listen," he was saying, "I had this dream: There was a commotion[e]—a loaf of barley bread was whirling through the Midianite camp. It came to a tent and struck it, and it fell; it turned it upside down, and the tent collapsed." [14]To this the other responded, "That can only mean the sword of the Israelite Gideon son of Joash. God is delivering Midian and the entire camp into his hands."[f]

[15]When Gideon heard the dream told and interpreted, he bowed low. Returning to the camp of Israel, he shouted, "Come on! The LORD has delivered the Midianite camp into your hands!" [16]He divided the three hundred men into three columns and equipped every man with a ram's horn and an empty jar, with a torch in each jar. [17]"Watch me," he said, "and do the same. When I get to

turn to their homes appears in the laws of war in Deut. 20.8. **6:** The v. seems to be corrupt, the phrase "in their mouth by hand" belongs at its end, as a dog does not lap water by bringing its hand to its mouth.

7.9–15a: The dream of the Midianite soldier and its meaning. Gideon, who remains fearful of battle, is given another encouraging sign. God commands him to go close to the Midianite camp; there he hears a Midianite telling his friend a dream, whose solution signifies their defeat. Gideon thanks God. **13:** A dream was understood by the ancients as revealing God's will. (See esp. Gen. chs 37, 40, 41; Dan. ch 2.) *A commotion—a loaf . . . :* The Midianite dreamer heard a commotion in which a loaf of barley bread whirled through the camp until it knocked over a tent. **14:** The falling of the tent is interpreted as the defeat of Midian, while the barley bread symbolizes Gideon's sword.

7.15b-23: The battle. The battle description consists of three stages: the preparations (vv. 15b–18), the battle itself (vv. 19–22), and the pursuit (v. 23). The description emphasizes the passivity of the (cowardly) fighters, whose only task is to blow the ram's horns, cry out "For the LORD and for Gideon," and watch God's deliverance. **15:** The army is divided into three parts in order to surround the camp. **19:** *Middle watch:* The night is divided into three watches. During the middle watch sleep is strongest; hence, at the time of changing guards, the soldiers are likely to be groggy and to panic at every sound. **20:** In order to emphasize that the sword is the LORD's, Gideon's soldiers are shown as having both their hands occupied: in the right hand the horns to blow, and in the left, the torches, so that all they can do is to shout. **21:** Unlike "real" soldiers, Gideon's soldiers stood at their places while the Midianites

---

a Lit. "smelt."

b-b Actually, using their hands as a dog uses its tongue; see v. 6.

c-c Meaning of Heb. uncertain.   d Lit. "descend upon"; so in vv. 10 and 11.

e Meaning of Heb. uncertain.

f The loaf of bread symbolizes the agricultural Israelites; the tent, the nomadic Midianites.

the outposts of the camp, do exactly as I do. [18] When I and all those with me blow our horns, you too, all around the camp, will blow your horns and shout, 'For the LORD and for Gideon!' "

[19] Gideon and the hundred men with him arrived at the outposts of the camp, at the beginning of the middle watch, just after the sentries were posted. [a]They sounded the horns and smashed the jars that they had with them,[-a] [20] and the three columns blew their horns and broke their jars. Holding the torches in their left hands and the horns for blowing in their right hands, they shouted, "A sword for the LORD and for Gideon!" [21] They remained standing where they were, surrounding the camp; but the entire camp ran about yelling, and took to flight. [22] For when the three hundred horns were sounded, the LORD turned every man's sword against his fellow, throughout the camp, and the entire host fled as far as Beth-shittah and on to Zererah—as far as the outskirts of Abel-meholah near Tabbath.

[23] And now the men of Israel from Naphtali and Asher and from all of Manasseh rallied for the pursuit of the Midianites. [24] Gideon also sent messengers all through the hill country of Ephraim with this order: [b]"Go down ahead of the Midianites and seize their access to the water all along the Jordan down to Beth-barah." So all the men of Ephraim rallied and seized the waterside down to Beth-barah by the Jordan. [25] They pursued the Midianites and captured Midian's two generals, Oreb and Zeeb. They killed Oreb at the Rock of Oreb and they killed Zeeb at the Winepress of Zeeb; and they brought the heads of Oreb and Zeeb from the other side of the Jordan to Gideon.

8 And the men of Ephraim said to him, "Why did you do that to us—not calling us when you went to fight the Midianites?" And they rebuked him severely. [2] But he answered them, "After all, what have I accomplished compared to you? Why, Ephraim's gleanings are better than Abiezer's vintage! [3] God has delivered the Midianite generals Oreb and Zeeb into your hands, and what was I able to do compared to you?" And when he spoke in this fashion, their anger against him abated.

a-a Emendation yields "He sounded the horn and smashed the jar that he had with him."
b Meaning of rest of verse uncertain.

all of Manasseh joined in the chase.

7.24–8.3: The confrontation with Ephraim. Ephraim's warriors were insulted because they were invited to the chase and not to the battle itself, and were concerned for their status among the tribes. Gideon calmed them, preventing a civil war while displaying responsible leadership and diplomatic talent. This story opens the second section, in which there are no divine interventions or miracles, and Gideon is not fearful. **24:** Upon setting out in pursuit, Gideon called the men of Ephraim, imposing upon them responsibility for the pursuit adjacent to their territory. *Beth-barah* has not been identified. Gideon's instruction was to seize all the water sources flowing into the Jordan. **25:** *Rock of . . . :* The places where the Midianite generals were killed, north of Jericho and to the west of the Jordan, are named for them. *The other side of the Jordan,* east of the Jordan. **8.1:** *When you went to fight:* Ephraim's warriors were angry that Gideon did not involve them earlier when he called Manasseh, Asher, and Naphtali (6.35). **2:** *Gleanings,* the grapes that remain after the main part of the harvest has been completed. Gideon explained to the warriors in a diplomatic way that the killing of the two generals was even more important than the battle itself, in which he and his family, the house of Abiezer, had taken part.

called for help and began to flee. **22:** The blowing of 300 horns, coupled with the LORD's intervention, caused the Midianites to kill one another. Those who escaped fled southeast, to the fords of the Jordan. The places mentioned have not been identified. **23:** *The men of Israel . . . rallied:* The fighting units of Naphtali, Asher, and

⁴Gideon came to the Jordan and crossed it. The three hundred men with him were famished, but still in pursuit. ⁵He said to the people of Succoth, "Please give some loaves of bread to the men who are following me, for they are famished, and I am pursuing Zebah and Zalmunna, the kings of Midian." ⁶But the officials of Succoth replied, ᵃ-"Are Zebah and Zalmunna already in your hands,⁻ᵃ that we should give bread to your troops?" ⁷"I swear," declared Gideon, "when the LORD delivers Zebah and Zalmunna into my hands, I'll thresh ᵇ your bodies upon desert thorns and briers!" ⁸From there he went up to Penuel and made the same request of them; but the people of Penuel gave him the same reply as the people of Succoth. ⁹So he also threatened the people of Penuel: "When I come back safe, I'll tear down this tower!"

¹⁰Now Zebah and Zalmunna were at Karkor with their army of about 15,000; these were all that remained of the entire host of the Kedemites, for the slain numbered 120,000 fighting men.ᶜ ¹¹Gideon marched up the road of the tent dwellers, up to east of Nobah and Jogbehah, and routed the camp, which was off guard. ¹²Zebah and Zalmunna took to flight, with Gideonᵈ in pursuit. He captured Zebah and Zalmunna, the two kings of Midian, and threw the whole army into panic.

¹³On his way back from the battle at the Ascent of Heres, Gideon son of Joash ¹⁴captured a boy from among the people of Succoth and interrogated him. The latter drew up for him a list of the officials and elders of Succoth, seventy-seven in number. ¹⁵Then he came to the people of Succoth and said, "Here are Zebah and Zalmunna, about whom you mocked me, saying, ᵃ-'Are Zebah and Zalmunna already in your hands,⁻ᵃ that we should give your famished men bread?' " ¹⁶And he took the elders of the city and, [bringing] desert thorns and briers, he punishedᵉ the people of Succoth with them. ¹⁷As for Penuel, he tore down its tower and killed the townspeople.

¹⁸Then he asked Zebah and Zalmunna, "Those men you killed at Tabor, ᶠ-what were they like?"⁻ᶠ "They looked just like you," they replied, "like sons of a king." ¹⁹"They were my brothers," he declared, "the sons of my mother. As the LORD lives, if you had spared them, I would not kill you." ²⁰And he commanded his oldest son Jether, "Go kill

a-a Lit. "Is the palm of Zebah and Zalmunna in your hand."
b I.e., throw them naked in a bed of thorns and trample them; but exact meaning uncertain.
c Lit. "men who drew the sword." d Heb. "him."
e Meaning of Heb. uncertain; emendation yields "threshed"; cf. v. 7.
f-f Others "Where are they?"

8.4–21: The confrontation with Succoth and Penuel. Gideon, leading 300 men, crosses the Jordan to smite the camp of Midian in the east and to capture Zebah and Zalmunna, the kings of Midian. The inhabitants of the Israelite cities Succoth and Penuel question their ability to defeat the Midianites and refuse to give bread to Gideon's tired troops. After smiting the Midianites, Gideon comes back to severely punish these two towns. In this second confrontation, Gideon is again shown as an authoritative and decisive leader. **5:** *Succoth* is located east of the Jordan, in Gad's territory. It is first mentioned in the tradition of Jacob (Gen. 33.17), and is usually identified with Tel Deir ʿAlla. *Kings of Midian:* Earlier Oreb and Zeeb were described as generals. Both titles refer to heads of tribes. **6:** The response of the Succoth officials indicates that they had not yet heard about Gideon's mighty deeds in the west. **8:** *Penuel* is located east of Succoth, close to it and to Jabbok ford. It is mentioned in the tradition of Jacob (Gen. 32.23–31) and served as the temporary capital of Jeroboam I (1 Kings 12.25). Its identification has not been fixed definitively. **9:** *Tower,* a fortified building that served for defense and observation. **10:** *Karkor,* a desert oasis on the caravan route of pilgrims to Mecca, about 170 km (100 miles) southeast of Amman. The numbers mentioned here are exaggerated, as is the notion that Gideon had a battle so far away. **11:** A nomadic route east of Amman. *Off guard:* The Midianites did not suspect that Gideon and his army would get so far. **17:** Gideon did not threaten to kill the people of the city, but to destroy the tower. Therefore Radak concludes: "Perhaps they were warring with him when he came to destroy the tower." **18:** *Tabor:* Mount Tabor is in the northeastern corner of Jezreel Valley. *Zebah and Zalmunna* relate to Gideon as to a king; their behavior is the opposite of that of Succoth and Penuel. **20:** The description of Jether as fearful is reminiscent of Gideon's them!" But the boy did not draw his sword, for he was timid, being still a boy. ²¹ Then Zebah and Zalmunna said, "Come, you slay us; for strength comes with manhood." So Gideon went over and killed Zebah and Zalmunna, and he took the crescents that were on the necks of their camels.

²² Then the men of Israel said to Gideon, "Rule over us—you, your son, and your grandson as well; for you have saved us from the Midianites." ²³ But Gideon replied, "I will not rule over you myself, nor shall my son rule over you; the Lᴏʀᴅ alone shall rule over you." ²⁴ And Gideon said to them, "I have a request to make of you: Each of you give me the earring he received as booty." (They*a* had golden earrings, for they were Ishmaelites.) ²⁵ "Certainly!" they replied. And they spread out a cloth, and everyone threw onto it the earring he had received as booty. ²⁶ The weight of the golden earrings that he had requested came to 1,700 shekels of gold; this was in addition to the crescents and the pendants and the purple robes worn by the kings of Midian and in addition to the collars on the necks of their camels. ²⁷ Gideon made an ephod of *b-this gold-b* and set it up in his own town of Ophrah. There all Israel went astray after it, and it became a snare to Gideon and his household.

²⁸ Thus Midian submitted to the Israelites and did not raise its head again; and the land was tranquil for forty years in Gideon's time.

a I.e., the Midianites. The author explains that the Midianites wore earrings like the Ishmaelites, who were better known to his contemporaries.
b-b Heb. "it."

---

that the Lᴏʀᴅ raises up the redeemer and therefore He is the ruler. Throughout these vv., the verb used is "to rule" (Heb "m-sh-l"), not "to reign" (Heb "m-l-k").

8.24–28: The golden ephod.
24: The substitution of Ishmaelites, who were descendants of Hagar, for Midianites, who were descendants of Keturah, also appears in the Joseph story (Gen. 37.25–36). The author thereby indicates a relationship between them. Alternatively, the term "Ishmaelites" may be a generic designation for nomadic traders and not a mark of ethnic identity. **25:** Willingness to forgo the booty indicates Gideon's status and influence. **27:** *Ephod:* The ephod is mentioned in various contexts: a means of inquiring of God (1 Sam. 23.6–12), or a part of the priestly garment (Exod. 28.6–8; 1 Sam. 2.18). It seems that the reference here is to a statue intended to commemorate the deliverance, which over the course of time became an object of pagan adulation. The making of the statue is reminiscent of the golden calf story (Exod. 32.2–4). *In his own town of Ophrah:* Ophrah is depicted as Gideon's capital city for those tribes who recognized his leadership. *There all . . . a snare . . . :* The description of Gideon as one who sinned and caused Israel to sin is inappropriate to the whole cycle and to the view that he did good for Israel (8.35; 9.16ff.). Thus, this phrase seems to be an addition by a late editor, who criticized the making of the ephod and wished to justify the murder of Gideon's sons. **28:** *Tranquil for forty years,* a formulaic conclusion (see 5.31b).

---

behavior in the first section, and highlights the changed attitude of Gideon in the second section. **21:** The kings of Midian preferred that Gideon, and not the youth, should kill them, both as a matter of honor and because they wanted to die quickly at the hand of an experienced warrior.

8.22–23: The offer of kingship to Gideon. Gideon's refusal to rule as king is interpreted by scholars in different ways. Some see it as an early text connected to the ideology that God alone may be king; others claim that it is a later interpolation critical of the monarchy; still others suggest that it has nothing to do with this political issue, and Gideon is simply offering a

polite refusal, although the text then depicts him as a king. In the larger context of the Deuteronomistic History, Gideon's refusal may reflect the awareness that Israelite society was not yet ripe for a monarch. If the army of a few tribes should offer kingship to someone, there would likely be civil war, as may be seen from the case of Abimelech in the following ch. **22:** *The men of Israel,* the army of the tribes, which in this case is composed of five: Manasseh, Asher, Zebulun, Naphtali, and Ephraim (6.35; 7.24). *You, your son,* a rule that passes from father to son, that is, a royal dynasty. *You have saved us:* The army sees Gideon and not the Lᴏʀᴅ as their deliverer. **23:** Gideon emphasizes

²⁹So Jerubbaal son of Joash retired to his own house. ³⁰Gideon had seventy sons of his own issue, for he had many wives. ³¹A son was also born to him by his concubine in Shechem, and he named him Abimelech. ³²Gideon son of Joash died at a ripe old age, and was buried in the tomb of his father Joash at Ophrah of the Abiezrites.

³³After Gideon died, the Israelites again went astray after the Baalim, and they adopted Baal-berith as a god. ³⁴The Israelites gave no thought to the LORD their God, who saved them from all the enemies around them. ³⁵Nor did they show loyalty to the house of Jerubbaal-Gideon in return for all the good that he had done for Israel.

9 Abimelech son of Jerubbaal went to his mother's brothers in Shechem and spoke to them and to the whole clan of his mother's family. He said, ²"Put this question to all the citizens of Shechem: Which is better for you, to be ruled by seventy men—by all the sons of Jerubbaal—or to be ruled by one man? And remember, I am your own ^{a-}flesh and blood."^{-a} ³His mother's brothers said all this in his behalf to all the citizens of Shechem, and they were won over to Abimelech; for they thought, "He is our kinsman." ⁴They gave him seventy shekels from the temple of Baal-berith; and with this Abimelech hired some worthless and reckless fellows, and they followed him. ⁵Then he went to his father's house in Ophrah and killed his brothers, the sons of Jerubbaal, seventy men on one stone. Only Jotham, the youngest son of Jerubbaal, survived, because he went into hiding.

⁶All the citizens of Shechem and all Beth-millo convened, and they proclaimed Abimelech king at the terebinth of the pillar^b at Shechem. ⁷When Jotham was in-

---

a-a Lit. "bone and flesh."   b Meaning of Heb. uncertain.

9.1–6: Abimelech's enthronement. Abimelech is depicted as a powerful figure, who became king through his own bloody deception and not by the will of God. He is negatively characterized through the contrast between his actions and those of Gideon. **1:** He first convinces his mother's brothers, then the family of his maternal grandfather, and only afterwards addresses the other city citizens. **2:** His suggestion that being *ruled by seventy men* is an actual possibility is absurd and rhetorical. **4:** *From the temple . . . :* Ancient Near Eastern temples often have large treasuries (cf. 1 Kings 7.51). *Worthless . . . :* Jephthah (11.3) and David (1 Sam. 22.2) also utilized such people at the beginning of their path. **5:** *One stone:* One stone was used for all seventy people, a particularly horrific image. *Jotham,* a theophoric name meaning "God acts with integrity." The name, and perhaps this whole story, are likely symbolic. **6:** *Beth-millo* seems to refer to a quarter of the city that was built upon a filling of earth near Shechem (see v. 20). *The terebinth:* There may be a relationship between this tree and the oak mentioned in the stories of Jacob (Gen. 35.4) and Joshua (Josh. 24.23–27). Many of these stories concerning Shechem are connected to the fact that this city was significant in the Northern Kingdom (see esp. 1 Kings 12.1).

9.7–21: Jotham's parable. Jotham, who was saved from being slaughtered, stood at the top of Mount Gerizim and told the Shechemites a parable (vv. 7–15) and its interpretation (vv. 16–20). The connection between the parable and what it represents is not exact, but this happens with other biblical parables as well (see esp. Jonah 4.6–11). Abimelech, for example, unlike the trees in the parable, was not offered the monarchy, and he and his supporters, unlike the explanation, were not burned by the citizens of Shechem. It seems, therefore, that the parable was an independent anti-monarchic work, but was integrated here to criticize

---

8.29–9.57: The rule of Abimelech. Abimelech was the son of Gideon by his concubine from Shechem, and thus of lower status than his brothers. Unlike his father, he was willing to pay any price to become king. He murdered his brothers, conducted a civil war, and was ultimately killed in battle. His brief and bloody reign marks the failure of the first attempt at monarchy. **8.30:** *Seventy,* a large typological number (cf. 2 Kings 10.1, 7). Having many wives and sons conveys having a significant social position; see 10.4 n.; 12.9, 14.

31: At that time marriage also had political significance; therefore Abimelech is closely tied to his mother's city of Shechem. *Abimelech,* a theophoric name: "God [who is referred to as king] is my father." It is ironic that the person with a name highlighting divine kingship attempts to become the first king of Israel. **33:** *Baal-berith,* also called El-berith (9.46), he had a temple in Shechem (9.3–4). He is not known from other sources. **35:** From here on Gideon is only mentioned by his name Jerubbaal.

formed, he went and stood on top of Mount Gerizim and called out to them in a loud voice. "Citizens of Shechem!" he cried, "listen to me, that God may listen to you.

8 "Once the trees went to anoint a king over themselves. They said to the olive tree, 'Reign over us.' 9 But the olive tree replied, 'Have I, through whom God and men are honored, stopped yielding my rich oil, that I should go and wave above the trees?' 10 So the trees said to the fig tree, 'You come and reign over us.' 11 But the fig tree replied, 'Have I stopped yielding my sweetness, my delicious fruit, that I should go and wave above the trees?' 12 So the trees said to the vine, 'You come and reign over us.' 13 But the vine replied, 'Have I stopped yielding my new wine, which gladdens God and men, that I should go and wave above the trees?' 14 Then all the trees said to the thornbush, 'You come and reign over us.' 15 And the thornbush said to the trees, 'If you are acting honorably in anointing me king over you, come and take shelter in my shade; but if not, may fire issue from the thornbush and consume the cedars of Lebanon!'

16 "Now then, if you acted honorably and loyally in making Abimelech king, if you have done right by Jerubbaal and his house and have requited him according to his deserts—17 considering that my father fought for you and saved you from the Midianites at the risk of his life, 18 and now you have turned on my father's household, killed his sons, seventy men on one stone, and set up Abimelech, the son of his handmaid, as king over the citizens of Shechem just because he is your kinsman—19 if, I say, you have this day acted honorably and loyally toward Jerubbaal and his house, have joy in Abimelech and may he likewise have joy in you. 20 But if not, may fire issue from Abimelech and consume the citizens of Shechem and Beth-millo, and may fire issue from the citizens of Shechem and Beth-millo and consume Abimelech!"

21 With that, Jotham fled. He ran to Beer and stayed there, because of his brother Abimelech.

22 Abimelech held sway over Israel for three years. 23 Then God sent a spirit of discord between Abimelech and the citizens of Shechem, and the citizens of Shechem broke faith with Abimelech—24 to the end that the crime

---

way for an aggressive figure, and that Abimelech is totally useless. **7:** It would have been impossible for the Shechemites to hear things uttered at the top of Mount Gerizim; this is a literary model of uttering from a high place (cf., e.g., 1 Sam. 26.13–14; Num. 23.14). **9:** *God and men are honored:* The oil and the wine (v. 13) were used in the cult and in everyday life. *Wave above,* to supervise, to rule. **14:** *Thornbush,* a barren shrub whose fruit is inedible. **15:** *Shade,* an ironic description, because the thornbush hardly provides shade. *Cedars,* archetypal tall and strong trees. The thornbush warns those interested in his protection that, if they attempt to rebel, his fire will be so powerful that it will consume even the highest and strongest trees. **16:** *Now,* a transitional formula to a new subject, used here to introduce the parable's explanation. **16b–19b:** Many scholars consider this passage to be an addition, intended to strengthen the connection between the Abimelech and Gideon cycles. **21:** *Beer,* an unidentified locale.

9.22: The kingship of Abimelech. *Held sway,* Heb "sarar" may be interpreted as arbitrary rule (translated "lord it over" in Num. 16.13). It is likely significant that the more typical verb "malak," "reigned," is not used. *Over Israel:* This does not refer to all Israel, but to Shechem and its environs, and perhaps to additional areas in the hill country of Ephraim that were interested in kingship. *Three years:* The number indicates a brief reign, and prepares for the description of Abimelech's downfall.

9.23–41: First stage: the first battle in Shechem. The editor explains that Abimelech's fall is a measure-for-measure divine punishment (see also vv. 56–57). **23:** The power of the evil spirit also affects King Saul (1 Sam. 16.14; 18.10). Here the God of justice intervened directly. **24:** The punishment will also fall upon the citizens of Shechem who

---

Abimelech and to inform the reader that when all the trees are interested in having a king, they must beware of the thornbush and look carefully for a suitable tree. The parable is based upon a pattern of three and four, where the

fourth element is different and climactic: three refusals by the useful trees—olive, fig, and grapevine—opposed to the agreement of the fourth, the thornbush. This structure emphasizes that the refusal of the useful trees cleared the committed against the seventy sons of Jerubbaal might be avenged, and their blood recoil upon their brother Abimelech, who had slain them, and upon the citizens of Shechem, who had abetted him in the slaying of his brothers. ²⁵ The citizens of Shechem planted ambuscades against him on the hilltops; and they robbed whoever passed by them on the road. Word of this reached Abimelech.

²⁶ Then Gaal son of Ebed and his companions came passing through Shechem, and the citizens of Shechem gave him their confidence. ²⁷ They went out into the fields, gathered and trod out the vintage of their vineyards, and made a festival. They entered the temple of their god, and as they ate and drank they reviled Abimelech. ²⁸ Gaal son of Ebed said, "Who is Abimelech and who are [we] Shechemites, that we should serve him? ᵃ This same son of Jerubbaal and his lieutenant Zebul once served the men of Hamor, the father of Shechem;ᵃ so why should we serve him? ²⁹ Oh, if only this people were under my command, I would get rid of Abimelech! Oneᵇ would challenge Abimelech, 'Fill up your ranks and come out here!' "

³⁰ When Zebul, the governor of the city, heard the words of Gaal son of Ebed, he was furious. ³¹ He sent messages to Abimelech at Tormahᶜ to say, "Gaal son of Ebed and his companions have come to Shechem and they are incitingᵃ the city against you. ³² Therefore, set out at night with the forces you have with you and conceal yourself in the fields. ³³ Early next morning, as the sun rises, advance on the city. He and his men will thereupon come out against you, and you will do to him whatever you find possible."

³⁴ Abimelech and all the men with him set out at night and disposed themselves against Shechem in four hiding places. ³⁵ When Gaal son of Ebed came out and stood at the entrance to the city gate, Abimelech and the army with him emerged from concealment. ³⁶ Gaal saw the army and said to Zebul, "That's an army marching down from the hilltops!" But Zebul said to him, "The shadows of the hills look to you like men." ³⁷ Gaal spoke up again, "Look, an army is marching down from Tabbur-erez, and another column is coming from the direction of Elon-meonenim." ³⁸ "Well," replied Zebul, "where is your boast, 'Who is Abimelech that we should serve him'? There is the army you sneered at; now go out and fight it!"

a-a Meaning of Heb. uncertain.
b Septuagint reads "I."
c Called "Arumah" in v. 41.

supported Abimelech. **26:** It is difficult to determine whether the name of his father was *Ebed* (Heb for "slave") or whether Gaal was the son of a slave. Gaal was apparently the head of a brigade, similar to Jephthah (11.3) and David (1 Sam. 22.2). Gaal and his men did not intend to settle in Shechem; rather, their services were hired by the citizens of the city for purposes of the battle, just as Achish hired the services of David (1 Sam. 28.1–2). **27:** *They entered the temple* in order to thank their god for the grape harvest. **28:** *Who is . . . and who are . . . :* Gaal incites the citizens by means of his rhetorical questions: Who is Abimelech that he should rule over Shechem, and why should we Shechemites maintain loyalty to him? He represent himself as one of the Shechemites. *Son of Jerubbaal:* Gaal represents Abimelech as a foreigner, mentioning the name of his Israelite father but not of his Shechemite mother. *Lieutenant:* Further on Zebul appears as the ruler of the city (v. 30). *The men of Hamor:* The family of Hamor represents the old Canaanite element in the city (Gen. 34.2), who should not accept this upstart ruler. **29:** *This people,* the people of Shechem. Gaal proposes the Shechemites accept his rule and unite to free the city of the rule of Abimelech and his men. **30:** Abimelech at that time was at Tormah, a corruption of Arumah (see v. 41). Zebul, who remained loyal to Abimelech, secretly sent messengers, informing him that he needed to go to war against Shechem. **34:** *Four hiding places,* in order to surround the city. **36:** *The shadows . . . :* It is difficult to determine whether visibility was poor, whether Zebul wanted to distract Gaal, or whether he was mocking and alluding to the fears of Gaal, who began to understand the severity of the situation. **37:** *From Tabbur-erez:* The expression is also found in Ezek. 38.12. The Septuagint and most commentators interpret it as "the navel of the earth." *Elon-meonenim:* A road named for a sacred terebinth that

³⁹ So Gaal went out at the head of the citizens of Shechem and gave battle to Abimelech. ⁴⁰ But he had to flee before him, and Abimelech pursued him, and many fell slain, all the way to the entrance of the gate. ⁴¹ Then Abimelech stayed in Arumah,^a while Zebul expelled Gaal and his companions and kept them out of Shechem.

⁴² The next day, when people went out into the fields, Abimelech was informed. ⁴³ Taking the army, he divided it into three columns and lay in ambush in the fields; and when he saw the people coming out of the city, he pounced upon them and struck them down. ⁴⁴ While Abimelech and the column^b that followed him dashed ahead and took up a position at the entrance of the city gate, the other two columns rushed upon all that were in the open and struck them down. ⁴⁵ Abimelech fought against the city all that day. He captured the city and massacred the people in it; he razed the town and sowed it with salt.

⁴⁶ When all the citizens of the Tower of Shechem^c learned of this, they went into the tunnel^d of the temple of El-berith.^e ⁴⁷ When Abimelech was informed that all the citizens of the Tower of Shechem had gathered [there], ⁴⁸ Abimelech and all the troops he had with him went up on Mount Zalmon. Taking an ax^f in his hand, Abimelech lopped off a tree limb and lifted it onto his shoulder. Then he said to the troops that accompanied him, "What you saw me do—quick, do the same!" ⁴⁹ So each of the troops also lopped off a bough; then they marched behind Abimelech and laid them against the tunnel, and set fire to the tunnel over their heads. Thus all the people of the Tower of Shechem also perished, about a thousand men and women.

⁵⁰ Abimelech proceeded to Thebez; he encamped at Thebez and occupied it. ⁵¹ Within the town was a fortified tower; and all the citizens of the town, men and women, took refuge there. They shut themselves in, and went up on the roof of the tower. ⁵² Abimelech pressed forward to the tower and attacked it. He approached the door of the tower to set it on fire. ⁵³ But a woman dropped an upper millstone on Abimelech's head and cracked his skull. ⁵⁴ He immediately cried out to his attendant, his armsbearer, "Draw your dagger and finish me off, that they

a Cf. "Tormah" in v. 31.   b Heb. "columns."
c Perhaps identical with Beth-millo of vv. 6 and 20.
d Cf. 1 Sam. 13.6; others "citadel."   e Called "Baal-berith" in v. 4.   f Heb. plural.

9.42–45: Second stage: the second battle in Shechem. There is no explicit justification for the second war and the harsh means taken by Abimelech against the Shechemites. It is directly connected to the depiction of Abimelech in the parable and its explanation: He is a fire that consumes all its environs. **45:** *Sowed it with salt,* a symbolic action intended to signify that the destruction is final and the city would be barren and could not be rebuilt. Assyrian kings behaved in a similar manner. Already in the days of Jeroboam I, however, Shechem is mentioned as a central place (1 Kings 12.1).

9.46–49: Third stage: the battle at the Tower of Shechem. Once again the narrative gives no reason for the war. Here the fire imagery is strengthened, because Abimelech himself made use of fire. On the other hand, he is described as a charismatic, though excessively cruel leader. It would appear that the Tower of Shechem (Heb "migdal shekhem") was not part of Shechem, which had already been destroyed, but was a nearby settlement whose name was Migdalshechem. **46:** *Of this,* the destruction of Shechem. **48:** *Zalmon,* a mountain near Shechem, whose identification is uncertain. *Do the same:* These words are reminiscent of Gideon (7.17).

9.50–54: Fourth stage: the battle of Thebez and Abimelech's death. In this fourth, climactic stage, Abimelech meets his ignominious death (see 2 Sam. 11.20–21). **50:** *Thebez:* Contemporary scholars think that this name is a corruption of Tirzah, located 12 km (7 miles) northeast of Shechem. **51:** *Went up:* They went up on the roof in order to fight by throwing rocks, arrows, and the like. **53:** The Sages (*Tanḥuma,* Buber ed., *Vayera* 51b [102]) emphasize the principle of measure for measure, connecting Abimelech's death from a stone to the stone upon which he slew his brothers. **54:** Abimelech's request to his armor-bearer is similar to

was adjacent to it, where necromancers (Heb "me'onenim") were evidently active. **39:** Many men from Gaal's army fell in the area between the battle location and the city gate. **41:** After his victory Abimelech returned to dwell in *Arumah.*

may not say of me, 'A woman killed him!' " So his attendant stabbed him, and he died. ⁵⁵ When the men of Israel saw that Abimelech was dead, everyone went home.

⁵⁶ Thus God repaid Abimelech for the evil he had done to his father by slaying his seventy brothers; ⁵⁷ and God likewise repaid the men of Shechem for all their wickedness. And so the curse of Jotham son of Jerubbaal was fulfilled upon them.

10 After Abimelech, Tola son of Puah son of Dodo, a man of Issachar, arose to deliver Israel. He lived at Shamir in the hill country of Ephraim. ² He led Israel for twenty-three years; then he died and was buried at Shamir.

³ After him arose Jair the Gileadite, and he led Israel for twenty-two years. (⁴ He had thirty sons, who rode on thirty burros and owned thirty boroughsª in the region of Gilead; these are called Havvoth-jairᵇ to this day.) ⁵ Then Jair died and was buried at Kamon.

⁶ The Israelites again did what was offensive to the LORD. They served the Baalim and the Ashtaroth, and the gods of Aram, the gods of Sidon, the gods of Moab, the gods of the Ammonites, and the gods of the Philistines; they forsook the LORD and did not serve Him. ⁷ And the LORD, incensed with Israel, surrendered them to the Philistines and to the Ammonites. ⁸ That year they battered

a *Imitating the pun in the Heb., which employs* 'ayarim *first in the sense of "donkeys" and then in the sense of "towns."*

b *I.e., "the villages of Jair"; cf. Num. 32.41.*

that of Saul in the battle of Gilboa (1 Sam. 31.4), and emphasizes how even in his death he was concerned for his honor. Yet he is remembered as the one killed by a woman (2 Sam. 11.20–21).

9.55–57: Denouement: the dispersion of the army and the end of the cycle. 55: Upon Abimelech's death, the army that supported him was dispersed, thereby ending the first attempt to establish monarchical rule over Israel. The fall of his kingship showed that in order to assure quiet and stability it is not enough to have a charismatic king who is supported by the army. **56–57:** The story concludes by alluding to the various units that opened it: the murder and the parable.

10.1–5: Consecutive judges: first list. The judges mentioned after Abimelech appear one after another, without intervening periods of sin and punishment; they may therefore be described as consecutive judges. (Other scholars call them "minor judges," because the accounts of their actions are "minor" or short.) The account referring to them does not describe any acts of deliverance, but merely lists the place where they lived, their burial place, the period they were judges, and sometime their descendants and property. Scholars debate whether they are to be seen as a distinct type of judge, or if they were similar to the other judges, but for whatever reasons, less information has been recorded about them. Their appearance

helps create the impression that leadership continuity may prevent return to a period of sin, and thus on the one hand, softens the negative impression created by the kingdom of Abimelech, and on the other, confirms the final conclusion of the book concerning the advantages of monarchy. A second list appears in 12.8–15. Some scholars believe that these two lists were originally joined, and that Jephthah was in the middle of this list, and the expanded Jephthah story now interrupts the list. **1:** *To deliver:* It is not told from whom or how he delivered Israel. *Tola:* This name is connected with the families of the tribe of Issachar (Gen. 46.13; Num. 26.23–25; 1 Chron. 7.1–5). *Shamir . . . Ephraim . . . :* Not identified, but the existence of families from Issachar in the central mountain suggests that they began taking possession there, before they went down to the Jezreel Valley. **3:** Sources outside the book of Judges (Num. 32.41; Deut. 3.14; 1 Chron. 2.22–23) relate this tradition to an earlier Jair, who conquered territory in Gilead. **4:** The large number of offspring and burros indicates his established position. **5:** *Kamon,* located in northern Gilead.

10.6–16: Introduction to the Jephthah cycle. Following Jair the Gileadite no other judge appears, and as a result the people return to sin. The stages of sin, punishment, and crying out that precede Jephthah are particularly detailed and represented as graver than those that preceded it. **6:** The text enumerates seven types of idolatry, concluding by stating that Israel had completely abandoned the worship of the LORD. **7:** The subjugation is also presented as more severe. This time the LORD gave His people to the Philistines in the west and the Ammonites in the east. The reference to the Philistines may also foreshadow the stories of Samson. The sequel of this description focuses on the Ammonites. **8:** *The land of the Amorites:* It follows from the sequel (11.22) that this refers to southern Gilead, the territory lying between the and shattered the Israelites—for[a] eighteen years—all the Israelites beyond the Jordan, in [what had been] the land of the Amorites in Gilead. 9 The Ammonites also crossed the Jordan to make war on Judah, Benjamin, and the House of Ephraim. Israel was in great distress.

10 Then the Israelites cried out to the LORD, "We stand guilty before You, for we have forsaken our God and served the Baalim." 11 But the LORD said to the Israelites, "[I have rescued you] from the Egyptians, from the Amorites, from the Ammonites, and from the Philistines. 12 The Sidonians, Amalek, and Maon[b] also oppressed you; and when you cried out to Me, I saved you from them. 13 Yet you have forsaken Me and have served other gods. No, I will not deliver you again. 14 Go cry to the gods you have chosen; let them deliver you in your time of distress!" 15 But the Israelites implored the LORD: "We stand guilty. Do to us as You see fit; only save us this day!" 16 They removed the alien gods from among them and served the LORD; and He could not bear the miseries of Israel.

17 The Ammonites mustered and they encamped in Gilead; and the Israelites massed and they encamped at Mizpah. 18 The troops—the officers of Gilead—said to one another, "Let the man who is the first to fight the Ammonites be chieftain over all the inhabitants of Gilead."

11 Jephthah the Gileadite was an able warrior, who was the son of a prostitute. Jephthah's father was Gilead; 2 but Gilead also had sons by his wife, and when the wife's sons grew up, they drove Jephthah out. They said to him, "You shall have no share in our father's property, for you are the son of an outsider."[c] 3 So Jephthah fled from his brothers and settled in the Tob country. Men of low character gathered about Jephthah and went out raiding with him.

4 Some time later, the Ammonites went to war against

a Meaning of Heb. uncertain; perhaps "enough for" or "continuing for."
b Septuagint reads "Midian."   c Lit. "another woman."

Rivers Arnon and Jabbok. **10–16:** This time God rebuked His people, and they acknowledged their sin and removed the foreign gods. **10:** *We stand guilty before You:* This v., very close to the book's center, is the only explicit reference to repentance in the entire book, and may be a later addition; elsewhere, the Israelites simply "cry out." **12:** *Maon:* The Maonites were a nomadic tribe in the southwest of Judah (1 Chron. 4.41; 2 Chron. 26.7); therefore their mention here is surprising. In some manuscripts this word is missing, supporting its possible deletion. **16:** It is possible that some ritual action stands behind the activity depicted here and in Gen. 35.1; Josh. 24.23 and 1 Sam. 7.3.

10.17–11.11: Jephthah's appointment. Jephthah, who had been expelled from the inheritance by his brothers, established himself as the head of a band of ruffians in the eastern border area. It seems that his expulsion was with the approval of the elders of Gilead. Thanks to his military experience, and the absence of any other candidate, the elders were forced to ask him to lead the army. But he made his appointment conditional: If he won the war, he would be leader of all the inhabitants of Gilead. The elders agreed and appointed Jephthah before the LORD in Mizpah, not only as commander, but also as chieftain. This story depicts Jephthah similarly to Abimelech, hinting at his problematic rule. The story of Jephthah's appointment and his victory over the Ammonites (11.1–12.7, omitting the story of Jephthah's daughter) is read as the haftarah for the parashah of Ḥukkat (Num. chs 19–21), which describes Israel's war against Sihon king of the Amorites, a subject that arises in the negotiation between Jephthah and the king of the Ammonites. **10.17:** *Mizpah* (which means "outlook") has not been identified. **18:** *The first . . . :* The phrasing emphasizes their despair. The leadership is promised to whoever will dare to fight, and not necessarily to the one who achieves victory. *Chieftain:* a leader whose authority is not only military, but also judicial and administrative. The people are prepared to convey this authority to the one who dares to fight the Ammonites even during the period following the war. **11.1:** According to the Sumerian law of Lipit-Ishtar, when a man has no sons by his wife but does have sons by a harlot, those sons are allowed to inherit his estate. Perhaps a similar law applied in Israel. **2:** Gilead's wife apparently bore him sons after Jephthah's birth. *Outsider,* in this context, a euphemism for a prostitute. **3:** *Tob country,* located in the northeast of Gilead; presumably a border district to which lawbreakers and banished people came. *Men of low character,* see 9.4. **4:** This v. belongs before 10.17.

Israel. ⁵ And when the Ammonites attacked Israel, the elders of Gilead went to bring Jephthah back from the Tob country. ⁶ They said to Jephthah, "Come be our chief, so that we can fight the Ammonites." ⁷ Jephthah replied to the elders of Gilead, "You are the very people who rejected me and drove me out of my father's house. How can you come to me now when you are in trouble?" ⁸ The elders of Gilead said to Jephthah, "Honestly, we have now turned back to you. If you come with us and fight the Ammonites, you shall be our commander over all the inhabitants of Gilead." ⁹ Jephthah said to the elders of Gilead, "[Very well,] if you bring me back to fight the Ammonites and the Lord delivers them to me, I am to be your commander." ¹⁰ And the elders of Gilead answered Jepthah, "The Lord Himself shall be witness between us: we will do just as you have said."

¹¹ Jephthah went with the elders of Gilead, and the people made him their commander and chief. And Jephthah repeated all these terms before the Lord at Mizpah.

¹² Jephthah then sent messengers to the king of the Ammonites, saying, "What have you against me that you have come to make war on my country?" ¹³ The king of the Ammonites replied to Jephthah's messengers, "When Israel came from Egypt, they seized the land which is mine, from the Arnon to the Jabbok as far as the Jordan. Now, then, restore it peaceably."

¹⁴ Jephthah again sent messengers to the king of the Ammonites. ¹⁵ He said to him, "Thus said Jephthah: Israel did not seize the land of Moab or the land of the Ammonites. ¹⁶ When they left Egypt, Israel traveled through the wilderness to the Sea of Reeds and went on to Kadesh. ¹⁷ Israel then sent messengers to the king of Edom, saying, 'Allow us to cross your country.' But the king of Edom would not consent. They also sent a mission to the king of Moab, and he refused. So Israel, after staying at Kadesh, ¹⁸ traveled on through the wilderness, skirting the land of

11.12–28: The negotiation with the king of the Ammonites. Jephthah attempted to prevent war by negotiation, where he questions the Ammonites' motivation for war. Against the argument of the Ammonite king that the territory "from the Arnon to the Jabbok as far as the Jordan" belongs to the Ammonites (v. 13), Jephthah justifies the Israelite conquest by the following arguments: (1) the area under dispute never belonged to Ammon, but to Sihon king of the Amorites (vv. 14–19); (2) Israel was forced to wage war against Sihon because he did not allow them to pass through his land (v. 20); (3) the conquest of Sihon's land was the Lord's will (vv. 21–24); (4) for the past 300 years the Ammonites have not questioned Israelite settlement in these areas (vv. 25–26). Once the king of the Ammonites rejected these arguments, war was inevitable. For a variety of reasons, including the fact that Chemosh (v. 24) is the national god of Moab, not Ammon, and that the story mentions the Moabite King Balak (v. 25), many scholars believe that much of this ch was a separate document concerning Israel and Moab; once this became integrated here, Moab was changed to Ammon—at the beginning and at the end (vv. 12–14, 27–28). The subject is repeated in the Torah (Num. 20.14–21; 33.37–49; Deut. chs 2–3). **13:** *Arnon . . . Jabbok . . . Jordan:* The brook Arnon, which spills into the Dead Sea, marks the southern border of Gilead and the land of Sihon, and the northern boundary of Moab. The Jabbok spills into the Jordan north of the city Adam and divides Gilead into two parts. The western border is the Jordan and the eastern is the desert. Reuben and Dan settled in the land of Sihon. **16:** The narrator describes events from the beginning of the period of wandering briefly, focusing upon those that preceded the conquest of the disputed region. *Kadesh,* Kadesh-barnea, a desert oasis in northern Sinai. **19:** *Heshbon,* located about 10 km (6 miles) north of Medeba, and described as a royal city from

5: *The elders of Gilead:* They are so desperate, they come themselves rather than sending messengers. **6:** *Chief,* in this context, a man of war ("katzin"), whose authority is less than that of the "head" ("ro'sh"). Jephthah understands this adverse proposal, and therefore begins negotiations. **7–9:** From Jephthah's viewpoint the elders are responsible for his expulsion because they did not stop his

brothers. The elders do not deny it and offer him all the authority he asks for. Jephthah, in all fairness, states that he will accept the position only if he is victorious. **10:** The witness of God was usual in Israel (Gen. 31.50; etc.) and divine witnesses are well known from treaties in the ancient Near East. **11:** *Before the Lord,* in a place sanctified to the Lord, such as a temple or an altar.

Edom and the land of Moab. They kept to the east of the land of Moab until they encamped on the other side of the Arnon; and, since Moab ends at the Arnon, they never entered Moabite territory.

19 "Then Israel sent messengers to Sihon king of the Amorites, the king of Heshbon. Israel said to him, 'Allow us to cross through your country to our homeland.' 20 But Sihon would not trust Israel to pass through his territory. Sihon mustered all his troops, and they encamped at Jahaz; he engaged Israel in battle. 21 But the LORD, the God of Israel, delivered Sihon and all his troops into Israel's hands, and they defeated them; and Israel took possession of all the land of the Amorites, the inhabitants of that land. 22 Thus they possessed all the territory of the Amorites from the Arnon to the Jabbok and from the wilderness to the Jordan.

23 "Now, then, the LORD, the God of Israel, dispossessed the Amorites before His people Israel; and should you possess their land? 24 Do you not hold what Chemosh your god gives you to possess? So we will hold on to everything that the LORD our God has given us to possess.

25 "Besides, are you any better than Balak son of Zippor, king of Moab? Did he start a quarrel with Israel or go to war with them?

26 "While Israel has been inhabiting Heshbon and its dependencies, and Aroer and its dependencies, and all the towns along the Arnon for three hundred years, why have you not tried to recover them all this time? 27 I have done you no wrong; yet you are doing me harm and making war on me. May the LORD, who judges, decide today between the Israelites and the Ammonites!"

28 But the king of the Ammonites paid no heed to the message that Jephthah sent him.

29 Then the spirit of the LORD came upon Jephthah. He marched through Gilead and Manasseh, passing Mizpeh of Gilead; and from Mizpeh of Gilead he crossed over [to] the Ammonites. 30 And Jephthah made the following vow to the LORD: "If You deliver the Ammonites into my hands, 31 then whatever comes out of the door of my house to meet me on my safe return from the Ammonites shall be the LORD's and shall be offered by me as a burnt offering."

32 Jephthah crossed over to the Ammonites and attacked them, and the LORD delivered them into his hands. 33 He utterly routed them—from Aroer as far as Minnith, twenty towns—all the way to Abel-cheramim. So the Ammonites submitted to the Israelites.

which Sihon ruled his country. **20:** *Jahaz,* identification uncertain; it is also mentioned in the Moabite Mesha inscription (ll. 18–20). **24:** *Chemosh,* the national god of Moab, mentioned in the Mesha inscription (ll. 5–6, etc.). As noted, the reference to Chemosh, rather than Milcom, the high god of Ammon, indicates the source of this document. **25:** On *Balak,* who wished to curse Israel and ended up blessing them, see Num. 22.2–24.5. **26:** *Aroer:* Located on the northern shore of the Arnon, it marks the southern border of Sihon's kingdom. It is mentioned in the Moabite Mesha inscription as a city he built (l. 26). *Three hundred:* A round and inexact number that has no relation to the length of the period of the judges. The author thought that 300 years had passed from the conquest until Jephthah.

11.29–40: The war and the oath. Before going out to battle Jephthah makes a vow, stating that if the LORD will give him victory, he will make Him an offering of the first thing that comes out of his house. After defeating the Ammonites he returns home, where he is met by his only daughter, who had come out to greet him, and he is forced to carry out his vow. In practice, the brief account of the war is incorporated within the account of the vow, depicted in detail and in a way that emphasizes the tragedy of this fateful, irreversible error. Biblical literature struggles with the norm of offering human sacrifices, which was apparently practiced throughout the First Temple period (2 Kings 21.6; 23.10; Jer. 7.31; etc.). Hence, this incident shows Jephthah in a negative light. Jephthah is, genealogically speaking, a marginal person both in his ancestry and in his progeny. **29:** Jephthah advanced in a northeasterly direction. The places mentioned here and in v. 33 have not been identified. **31:** The formulation of the oath, referring to one coming out of the door of his house, suggests a human rather than animal sacrifice.

[34] When Jephthah arrived at his home in Mizpah, there was his daughter coming out to meet him, with timbrel and dance! She was an only child; he had no other son or daughter. [35] On seeing her, he rent his clothes and said, "Alas, daughter! You have brought me low; you have become my troubler! For I have [a]uttered a vow[-a] to the LORD and I cannot retract." [36] "Father," she said, "you have uttered a vow to the LORD; do to me as you have vowed, seeing that the LORD has vindicated you against your enemies, the Ammonites." [37] She further said to her father, "Let this be done for me: let me be for two months, and I will go with my companions and lament[b] upon the hills and there bewail my maidenhood." [38] "Go," he replied. He let her go for two months, and she and her companions went and bewailed her maidenhood upon the hills. [39] After two months' time, she returned to her father, and he did to her as he had vowed. She had never known a man. So it became a custom in Israel [40] for the maidens of Israel to go every year, for four days in the year, and chant dirges for the daughter of Jephthah the Gileadite.

12 The men of Ephraim mustered and crossed [the Jordan] to Zaphon. They said to Jephthah, "Why did you march to fight the Ammonites without calling us to go with you? We'll burn your house down over you!" [2] Jephthah answered them, "I and my people were in a bitter conflict with the Ammonites; and I summoned you, but you did not save me from them. [3] When I saw that you were no saviors, I risked my life and advanced against the Ammonites; and the LORD delivered them into my hands. Why have you come here now to fight against me?" [4] And Jephthah gathered all the men of Gilead and fought the Ephraimites. The men of Gilead defeated the Ephraimites; for [c]they had said, "You Gileadites are nothing but fugitives from Ephraim—being in Manasseh is like being in Ephraim."[-c] [5] The Gileadites held the fords of the Jordan against the Ephraimites. And when any fugitive from

a-a Lit. "opened my mouth."
b Lit. "descend," i.e., with weeping; cf. Isa. 15.3.
c-c Meaning of Heb. uncertain.

34: *Mizpah:* This is not Mizpeh of Gilead mentioned in v. 29, but is apparently Mizpah which is mentioned in 11.11. **35:** *I cannot retract:* Jephthah and his daughter understand the oath as an obligation that cannot be nullified, since vows were taken very seriously in the biblical period (see Deut. 23.22–23; Prov. 20.25; Eccl. 5.3–4). **37:** *My maidenhood:* I will weep because I will die in my youth, as a childless virgin. **39:** The text shies away from explicitly depicting her sacrifice, which leads some ancient and modern interpreters (e.g.,

Radak) to suggest that she was not actually killed. **40:** The story has an etiological conclusion, explaining a custom that had presumably existed since hoary antiquity: to sing dirges four days a year in memory of Jephthah's daughter. This custom is unattested elsewhere in the Bible.

12.1–7: Jephthah's battle with Ephraim and the conclusion. This story likewise shows Jephthah in a negative light. The men of Ephraim had threatened to burn Jephthah's house because he had not called them to participate in the war against the Ammonites. Jephthah replies that he had attempted to call them in the past, but they refused. He went to war against Ephraim, and this concluded with the death of 42,000 Ephraimites. This conflict mirrors Gideon's conflict with Ephraim (8.1–3) and presents Ephraim negatively in a struggle for inter-tribal hegemony. Within the broader book, this fits the pro-Judean, anti-northern ideology of the editor. (Ephraim is used elsewhere in the Bible to refer to the Northern Kingdom.) While Gideon succeeded in preventing a civil war, Jephthah conducted a bloody conflict. The blocking of the Jordan crossings was a tactic used by Ehud (3.28), but while Ehud made war against the Moabites, Jephthah did so against his own people. These comparisons stress that Jephthah is not fit to lead. **1:** *Zaphon:* This may refer to the settlement Zaphon, located in the territory of Gad near the city of Succoth (Josh. 13.27). **4:** The men of Gilead were insulted by the Ephraimites. According to one interpretation, even the lowest of Ephraim, naming the fugitives, despised the people of Gilead, telling them that they had no importance in Ephraim and Manasseh. Others suggest that the phrase "fugitives of Ephraim" relates to the inhabitants of Gilead as refugees who left the region of Ephraim and Manasseh. **5:** The Gileadites seized the Jordan fords even before the men of Ephraim

Ephraim said, "Let me cross," the men of Gilead would ask him, "Are you an Ephraimite?"; if he said "No," [6] they would say to him, "Then say *shibboleth*"; but he would say *"sibboleth,"* not being able to pronounce it correctly. Thereupon they would seize him and slay him by the fords of the Jordan. Forty-two thousand Ephraimites fell at that time.

[7] Jephthah led Israel six years. Then Jephthah the Gileadite died and he was buried in one of the towns of Gilead.

[8] After him, Ibzan of Bethlehem[a] led Israel. [9] He had thirty sons, and he married off thirty daughters outside the clan and brought in thirty girls from outside the clan for his sons. He led Israel seven years. [10] Then Ibzan died and was buried in Bethlehem.

[11] After him, Elon the Zebulunite led Israel; he led Israel for ten years. [12] Then Elon the Zebulunite died and was buried in Aijalon, in the territory of Zebulun.

[13] After him, Abdon son of Hillel the Pirathonite led Israel. [14] He had forty sons and thirty grandsons, who rode on seventy jackasses. He led Israel for eight years. [15] Then Abdon son of Hillel the Pirathonite died. He was buried in Pirathon, in the territory of Ephraim, on the hill of the Amalekites.

13 The Israelites again did what was offensive to the LORD, and the LORD delivered them into the hands of the Philistines for forty years.

[2] There was a certain man from Zorah, of the stock of Dan, whose name was Manoah. His wife was barren and had borne no children. [3] An angel of the LORD appeared to the woman and said to her, "You are barren and have borne no children; but you shall conceive and bear a son.

a I.e., Bethlehem in Zebulun; cf. Josh. 19.15.

arrived. **6:** The difference in pronunciation, *"sibboleth"* instead of *"shibboleth"* (s/sh) reflected dialectical variation in the different areas of settlement. It is uncertain whether the word "shibboleth" refers to the current of the river (Ps. 69.3) or to sheaves of grain (Gen. 41.5–7). **7:** While Jephthah the commander did indeed save his people from the Ammonites, he did not prove himself as a leader, and his term only lasted six years. The final burial notice is

odd; it would be expected that he was buried in his city, Mizpah.

12.8–15: Consecutive judges: second list. Three consecutive judges appear after Jephthah, suggesting an additional period without sin, punishment, or deliverance. On these judges, see 10.1–5 n. **8:** Except Othniel, who was from Judah, all the judges throughout the book are from northern Israel. Hence, the *Bethlehem* mentioned here is a city in the territory of Zebulun

(Josh. 19.15). **9:** The author wishes to indicate his extensive connections, as marriage was one of the means of creating foreign alliances. **13:** Pirathon is elsewhere mentioned as the city of Benaiah of Pirathon, one of David's warriors (2 Sam. 23.30; 1 Chron. 27.14).

Chs 13–16: The Samson cycle. Samson was different from the other judges. His activity bears a miraculous character, he fights as an individual rather than a commander, and his heroic acts are the result of personal involvement with Philistine women. The stories concerning him are filled with remnants of myth, legends, and folk traditions. On the other hand, he is not portrayed as a giant, and he has a direct connection with God, both through his being a Nazirite and through his prayers. Concluding the stories of the judges with a hero who does not deliver his people but only himself, and who dies in enemy captivity, contributes to the feeling of disappointment with the type of leadership that the judges represent. This bolsters the book's ultimate conclusion, that permanent kingship over all of Israel must be established. This cycle, like the others in the book, comprises originally distinct stories which have been joined together into a largely unified whole.

13.1–25: Samson's birth. The story is reminiscent of other annunciation stories, where God or His messengers appear (Gen. 18.1–15; Judg. 6.11–24; 1 Sam. ch 1; 2 Kings 4.8–37). This story serves as the haftarah for the Torah portion of Naso' (Num. 4.21–7.89), which includes the Nazirite laws (6.1–21), since Samson is depicted as a Nazirite from before his birth. **1:** Subjugation of 40 years is the longest in the book. The absence of the stage of crying out strengthens the impression of distance from the LORD. **2:** *Zorah,* located in the territory of Dan, near the modern kibbutz of that name. Nearby is an altar carved into rock, commonly known as "the altar of Manoah."

⁴Now be careful not to drink wine or other intoxicant, or to eat anything unclean. ⁵For you are going to conceive and bear a son; let no razor touch his head, for the boy is to be a nazirite to God from the womb on. He shall be the first to deliver Israel from the Philistines."

⁶The woman went and told her husband, "A man of God came to me; he looked like an angel of God, very frightening. I did not ask him where he was from, nor did he tell me his name. ⁷He said to me, 'You are going to conceive and bear a son. Drink no wine or other intoxicant, and eat nothing unclean, for the boy is to be a nazirite to God from the womb to the day of his death!' "

⁸Manoah pleaded with the LORD. "Oh, my Lord!" he said, "please let the man of God that You sent come to us again, and let him instruct us how to act with the child that is to be born." ⁹God heeded Manoah's plea, and the angel of God came to the woman again. She was sitting in the field and her husband Manoah was not with her. ¹⁰The woman ran in haste to tell her husband. She said to him, "The man who came to me beforeª has just appeared to me." ¹¹Manoah promptly followed his wife. He came to the man and asked him: "Are you the man who spoke to my wife?" "Yes," he answered. ¹²Then Manoah said, "May your words soon come true! What rules shall be observed for the boy?" ¹³The angel of the LORD said to Manoah, "The woman must abstain from all the things against which I warned her. ¹⁴She must not eat anything that comes from the grapevine, or drink wine or other intoxicant, or eat anything unclean. She must observe all that I commanded her."

¹⁵Manoah said to the angel of the LORD, "Let us detain you and prepare a kid for you." ¹⁶But the angel of the LORD said to Manoah, "If you detain me, I shall not eat your food; and if you present a burnt offering, offer it to LORD."—For Manoah did not know that he was an angel of the LORD. ¹⁷So Manoah said to the angel of the LORD, "What is your name? We should like to honor you when your words come true." ¹⁸The angel said to him, "You must not ask for my name; it is unknowable!"

¹⁹Manoah took the kid and the meal offering and offered them up on the rock to the LORD; ᵇand a marvelous thing happened ᵇ while Manoah and his wife looked on. ²⁰As the flames leaped up from the altar toward the sky, the angel of the LORD ascended in the flames of the altar, while Manoah and his wife looked on; and they flung themselves on their faces to the ground.—²¹The angel of

Stock: The Heb word used here is "family," referring to the entire tribe, as this small tribe consisted of only one family (Num. 26.42). **5:** Samson's Nazirite-hood is exceptional, referred to by the Sages as "the Nazirite-hood of Samson"—namely, even when his hair grew heavy he did not thin it (*m. Naz.* 1.2). The prohibition of drinking wine applies only to his mother. *The first,* the Heb and KJV: "he shall begin," meaning that he will not deliver them fully, but only in a partial manner (Rashi ad loc). **6:** From the woman's report to her husband, she seems to suspect that the man of God was an angel, and therefore did not ask him usual questions, such as his name or where he was from. **7:** *To the day of his death:* The woman does not repeat the angel's words exactly. She focuses upon the prohibitions applied to her, and interprets the partial deliverance as alluding to the premature death of the child. Thus, she creates gaps that cause Manoah to ask for another appearance of the visitor. **8:** *Us:* Manoah wants to be a full partner in the additional visit; he seems to mistrust his wife's report. **9:** Due to the woman's preferred status in birth stories (cf. 2 Kings 4.8–17), the angel, notwithstanding Manoah's request, reappears to the woman, and thereafter Manoah follows his wife. **11:** The observation that Manoah *promptly followed his wife* is unusual in biblical literature, and reflects the role reversal of man and woman in this ch. **12:** *Your words,* i.e., of prophecy. *For the boy:* Manoah asks how to behave regarding the child who is to be born. **13–14:** The angel's answer ignores Manoah's question and only relates to the woman. **15:** Manoah invites the angel to a meal—behavior reminiscent of Gideon's in 6.18. Perhaps the function of the meal is to determine whether he is in fact an angel; alternatively, the text suggests that Manoah has no clue that this man is actually an angel. **16:** The angel, as angels do, refuses to eat and suggests that the goat be offered to the LORD. The second half of this

---

ª Lit. "in the day."   ᵇ⁻ᵇ Meaning of Heb. uncertain.

the LORD never appeared again to Manoah and his wife.—
Manoah then realized that it had been an angel of the
LORD. 22 And Manoah said to his wife, "We shall surely
die, for we have seen a divine being." 23 But his wife said
to him, "Had the LORD meant to take our lives, He would
not have accepted a burnt offering and meal offering from
us, nor let us see all these things; and He would not have
made such an announcement to us."

24 The woman bore a son, and she named him Samson.
The boy grew up, and the LORD blessed him. 25 The spirit
of the LORD first moved him in the encampment of Dan,
between Zorah and Eshtaol.

14 Once Samson went down to Timnah; and while in
Timnah, he noticed a girl among the Philistine
women. 2 On his return, he told his father and mother, "I
noticed one of the Philistine women in Timnah; please get
her for me as a wife." 3 His father and mother said to him,
"Is there no one among the daughters of your own kinsmen and among all our ª people, that you must go and
take a wife from the uncircumcised Philistines?" But Samson answered his father, "Get me that one, for she is the
one that pleases me." 4 His father and mother did not realize that this was the LORD's doing: He was seeking a pretext against the Philistines, for the Philistines were ruling
over Israel at that time. 5 So Samson and his father and
mother went down to Timnah.

When heᵇ came to the vineyards of Timnah [for the first
time], a full-grown lion came roaring at him. 6 The spirit of
the LORD gripped him, and he tore him asunder with his
bare hands as one might tear a kid asunder; but he did not
tell his father and mother what he had done. 7 Then he
went down and spoke to the woman, and she pleased
Samson.

8 Returning the following year to marry her, he turned
aside to look at the remains of the lion; and in the lion's
skeleton he found a swarm of bees, and honey. 9 He
scooped it into his palms and ate it as he went along.

a Heb. "my."   b Heb. "they."

when the sacrifice is offered, while
Manoah and his wife watch.
20: *Altar,* the rock. 21: Only after
the angel disappears does Manoah
understand that God's messenger
had been revealed to them. His
wife already felt this at the first encounter. 22: The view that seeing
the LORD brings death (cf. 6.22 and
elsewhere) causes Manoah to express his fear. 23: Manoah's wife is
logical. She calms him by stating
that if God had wished to kill
them He would not have sent
His angel twice. The narrator's
depiction of Manoah in this ch
supports the Rabbis' observation
that "Manoah was a boorish, ignorant person" (*b. Ber.* 61a). 24a: The
woman gives the infant his name.
Many commentators connect the
name with the sun (Heb "Shim-
shon" [Samson]/"shemesh"
[sun]), seeing in this a mythological allusion. 24b–25: These vv.
summarize Samson's unique
growth and development under
divine protection. *Eshtaol,* near
Zorah.

**14.1–15.20: Samson's marriage to
the Timnite and its consequences.**
Samson's marriage to a Philistine
woman is part of a deliberate divine strategy that might be described as a policy of "pretext," by
which Samson's connection with
Philistine women was intended to
provide him justification for harming the Philistines by a series of
annoyances and not by wars of deliverance. As in wisdom texts, God
acts in mysterious ways that are
not transparent to human observers. 14.1: *Timnah,* located between Beth Shemesh and Ekron.
5: Although Samson went with his
parents, during the journey he left
the main road, so that they did not
know of his struggle with the lion
(v. 6; see also v. 9). Gilgamesh, the
hero of the Babylonian myth, and
Hercules, the Greek mythic hero,
also overcame lions. 8: The removal of honey from the skeleton
of a lion has parallels in the literature of the ancient world. These
two acts provide the material for
the riddle. 9: Samson gave his parents some of the honey, but did not

v. (*for Manoah . . .*) may belong at
the end of v. 15. 17: Manoah continues to examine the angel and
asks for his name. He justifies this
question by stating that he wishes
to honor the messenger once his
tidings are realized. Since angels
do not have names (see Gen.
32.30), this may be Manoah's way

of testing to see if the man is an
angel, or it may be the narrator's
way of suggesting that Manoah is
not very clever, and in contrast to
his wife, still does not realize that
an angel is before him. 18: The
angel refuses to disclose his name.
19–20: The angel behaves in a
miraculous way and disappears

When he rejoined his father and mother, he gave them some and they ate it; but he did not tell them that he had scooped the honey out of a lion's skeleton.

10 So his father came down to the woman, and Samson made a feast there, as young men used to do. 11 When they[a] saw him, they designated thirty companions to be with him. 12 Then Samson said to them, "Let me propound a riddle to you. If you can give me the right answer during the seven days of the feast, I shall give you thirty linen tunics and thirty sets of clothing; 13 but if you are not able to tell it to me, you must give me thirty linen tunics and thirty sets of clothing." And they said to him, "Ask your riddle and we will listen." 14 So he said to them:

"Out of the eater came something to eat,
Out of the strong came something sweet."

For three days they could not answer the riddle.

15 On the seventh[b] day, they said to Samson's wife, "Coax your husband to provide us with the answer to the riddle; else we shall put you and your father's household to the fire; have you invited us here[c] in order to impoverish us?" 16 Then Samson's wife harassed him with tears, and she said, "You really hate me, you don't love me. You asked my countrymen a riddle, and you didn't tell me the answer." He replied, "I haven't even told my father and mother; shall I tell you?" 17 During the rest of the seven days of the feast she continued to harass him with her tears, and on the seventh day he told her, because she nagged him so. And she explained the riddle to her countrymen. 18 On the seventh day, before the sunset, the townsmen said to him:

"What is sweeter than honey,
And what is stronger than a lion?"

He responded:

"Had you not plowed with my heifer,
You would not have guessed my riddle!"

19 The spirit of the LORD gripped him. He went down to Ashkelon and killed thirty of its men. He stripped them and gave the sets of clothing to those who had answered the riddle. And he left in a rage for his father's house.

20 Samson's wife then married one of those who had been his wedding companions.

15 Some time later, in the season of the wheat harvest, Samson came to visit his wife, bringing a kid as a gift. He said, "Let me go into the chamber to my wife."

tell them its source. **10:** The father alone is mentioned here; the mention of Samson's mother at the beginning of the ch may help connect this story, an originally separate narrative (note that Samson is never depicted as a Nazirite in chs 14–15), with the previous ch, in which the mother plays a central role. **11:** *To be with him,* to provide him with companionship, as he was a stranger. **12:** *A riddle:* The proposal of a riddle accompanied by betting was part of the feast entertainment. The postponement of the riddle's solution until the seventh day indicates that Samson was convinced that it could be impossible to solve. **13:** Samson takes upon himself an obligation 30 times greater than that of any other. **14:** Samson's riddle is personal, and could not be solved without knowledge of his earlier acts. **15:** *On the seventh day:* Some versions of the Septuagint suggest the fourth day, which is more likely in context. *Have you invited us here:* The Philistines accuse the bride and her family of collaboration with Samson, with the intent of impoverishing them. **16:** *My countrymen:* This formulation emphasizes the national confrontation: she and her countrymen against Samson. **18:** Samson responds with a riddle. He compares the woman to a heifer and the way of discovering to plowing. Thus he suggests that he knows how they arrived at the solution. His parable is phrased in a poetic formulation identical to the solution that they proposed, thereby concealing his anger and allowing the festive atmosphere to continue. **19:** Samson responds measure for measure, without deviating from the number 30. **20:** After his vengeance, Samson returns to his father's house. It is possible that the marriage had yet to be consummated. **15.2:** *Taken a dislike* may be a technical term for divorce. **3:** In accordance with the policy of pretexts, Samson takes revenge not only against his wife's family, but against the Philistines in general. **4:** The motif of using foxes to damage fields is also known from other

a *I.e., the people of Timnah.* b *Septuagint and Syriac read "fourth."*
c *Reading* halom, *with some Heb. mss. and Targum.*

But her father would not let him go in. 2 "I was sure," said her father, "that you had taken a dislike to her, so I gave her to your wedding companion. But her younger sister is more beautiful than she; let her become your wife instead." 3 Thereupon Samson declared, "Now the Philistines can have no claim against me for the harm I shall do them."

4 Samson went and caught three hundred foxes. He took torches and, turning [the foxes] tail to tail, he placed a torch between each pair of tails. 5 He lit the torches and turned [the foxes] loose among the standing grain of the Philistines, setting fire to stacked grain, standing grain, vineyards, [and]ᵃ olive trees.

6 The Philistines asked, "Who did this?" And they were told, "It was Samson, the son-in-law of the Timnite, who took Samson'sᵇ wife and gave her to his wedding companion." Thereupon the Philistines came up and put her and her fatherᶜ to the fire. 7 Samson said to them, "If that is how you act, I will not rest until I have taken revenge on you." 8 ᵈ·He gave them a sound and thorough thrashing.·ᵈ Then he went down and stayed in the cave of the rock of Etam.

9 The Philistines came up, pitched camp in Judah and spread out over Lehi. 10 The men of Judah asked, "Why have you come up against us?" They answered, "We have come to take Samson prisoner, and to do to him as he did to us." 11 Thereupon three thousand men of Judah went down to the cave of the rock of Etam, and they said to Samson, "You knew that the Philistines rule over us; why have you done this to us?" He replied, "As they did to me, so I did to them." 12 "We have come down," they told him, "to take you prisoner and to hand you over to the Philistines." "But swear to me," said Samson to them, "that you yourselves will not attack me." 13 "We won't," they replied. "We will only take you prisoner and hand you over to them; we will not slay you." So they bound him with two new ropes and brought him up from the rock.

14 When he reached Lehi, the Philistines came shouting to meet him. Thereupon the spirit of the LORD gripped him, and the ropes on his arms became like flax that catches fire; the bonds melted off his hands. 15 He came upon a fresh jawbone of an ass and he picked it up; and with it he killed a thousand men. 16 Then Samson said:

ancient literature (cf. Song 2.15). **6:** The Philistines justify Samson's anger by taking revenge against his wife and her father. **7:** The violence escalates. **8:** *A sound and thorough thrashing:* The exact meaning of the Heb expression, lit. "calf as well as thigh," is not known, but it is clear that the sense is a severe beating. *Etam:* Samson goes to live in the cleft of a rock in Judah, near Zorah; see 1 Chron. 4.3. **9:** Samson's presence in the territory of Judah led the Philistines to apply further pressure on the tribe of Judah. *Lehi,* not identified. The folk etymology of the name, which means "jaw," appears in v. 17. **10–13:** Samson is not afraid of the Philistines, but of an attack by Judah. He therefore makes them take an oath. **15:** The jawbone of the ass was the first chance object that came to his hand. This act of bravery is reminiscent of the heroic acts of Shamgar son of Anath (3.31); cf. 2 Sam. 23.8–23. **16:** Samson does not mention God in his song of victory.

a *So Targum.*
b *Heb.* "his."
c *Many mss. read* "her father's household"; *cf.* 14.15.
d-d *Lit.* "He smote them leg as well as thigh, a great smiting."

"With the jaw of an ass,
Mass upon mass!
With the jaw of an ass
I have slain a thousand men."

[17] As he finished speaking, he threw the jawbone away; hence that place was called Ramath-lehi.[a]

[18] He was very thirsty and he called to the LORD, "You Yourself have granted this great victory through Your servant; and must I now die of thirst and fall into the hands of the uncircumcised?" [19] So God split open the hollow which is at Lehi, and the water gushed out of it; he drank, regained his strength, and revived. That is why it is called to this day "En-hakkore[b] of Lehi."

[20] He led Israel in the days of the Philistines for twenty years.

16 Once Samson went to Gaza; there he met a whore and slept with her. [2][c]The Gazites [learned][d] that Samson had come there, so they gathered and lay in ambush for him in the town gate the whole night; and all night long they kept whispering to each other, "When daylight comes, we'll kill him." [3] But Samson lay in bed only till midnight. At midnight he got up, grasped the doors of the town gate together with the two gateposts, and pulled them out along with the bar. He placed them on his shoulders and carried them off to the top of the hill that is near Hebron.

[4] After that, he fell in love with a woman in the Wadi Sorek, named Delilah. [5] The lords of the Philistines went up to her and said, "Coax him and find out what makes him so strong, and how we can overpower him, tie him

---

a I.e., "Jawbone Heights."   b Understood as "The Spring of the Caller."
c Meaning of parts of verse uncertain.   d Septuagint reads "were told."

18: Samson's thirst is interpreted as a result of the battle, but it also has educational meaning. He realizes that his might and life are dependent upon God's will. *Your servant:* This time, in contrast to the song of victory, Samson represents himself as a servant before his master and admits that the victory came from God. **19:** The etymology connects the name of the spring with Samson's calling upon God (v. 18). **20:** The appearance here of the closing formula, citing the number of years that he judged

Israel, may suggest that the cycle originally ended here. Alternately, it is meant to indicate that the period of his being judge took place between his marriage and the events in ch 16 that led to his death. *In the days of the Philistines:* The emphasis that Samson judged Israel during the period of Philistine rule indicates that his mighty acts did not bring about deliverance or quiet.

16.1–21: Samson's betrayal and capture. Samson's final acts, all of

which are associated with the city of Gaza, end with his death in Philistine captivity. As in all the Samson stories, a woman plays a prominent role. **1–3:** *Gaza:* Samson easily carried off the city gates, leaving the Philistines ashamed and exposed. This explains the Philistines' readiness to pay Delilah any price in order to catch Samson. **2:** The town gate was a fortified structure with numerous rooms. **3:** Against the preparations of the townspeople "the whole night" (repeated twice), the author repeats that already "at midnight" Samson had left. Thus, while they were still waiting to catch him, he was no longer in the place. *To the top of the hill . . . :* The geographical details emphasize the miracle. Samson walked a distance of some 58 km (35 miles), from the lowlands to the mountains, carrying the doors, the gateposts, and the bar on his shoulders. **4–21:** *Delilah:* Delilah exploits Samson's love and, in exchange for a handsome sum, discovers the secret of his strength and betrays him to the Philistines. Samson is taken, blind and humiliated, to a prison in Gaza. Delilah's attempts to uncover the source of his strength are based upon the model of ascending numbers, three and four (see Jotham's parable: 9.8–15). Three times she fails (vv. 6–9, 10–12, 13–14), but in the climactic fourth (vv. 15–21) he reveals his secret to her. In so doing he betrays his destiny and is punished. **4:** *He fell in love:* For the first time we are told that Samson was in love, and the woman is named. This indicates that this time Samson was emotionally involved and was bound to behave differently. *A woman:* It is not mentioned that Delilah was a Philistine. *Wadi Sorek,* adjacent to Zorah and Eshtaol, rather than to the Philistine cities. *Delilah:* The etymology of Delilah may relate to woven braids of hair (Song 7.6), and thus may foreshadow Samson's undoing. **5:** *Each . . . eleven hundred shekels:* Hence Delilah was offered the enormous sum of 5,500 shekels, as there were five Philistine lords, heading the five up, and make him helpless; and we'll each give you eleven hundred shekels of silver."

6 So Delilah said to Samson, "Tell me, what makes you so strong? And how could you be tied up and made helpless?" 7 Samson replied, "If I were to be tied with seven fresh tendons that had not been dried,*a* I should become as weak as an ordinary man." 8 So the lords of the Philistines brought up to her seven fresh tendons that had not been dried. She bound him with them, 9 while an ambush was waiting in her room. Then she called out to him, "Samson, the Philistines are upon you!" Whereat he pulled the tendons apart, as a strand of tow comes apart at the touch of fire. So the secret of his strength remained unknown.

10 Then Delilah said to Samson, "Oh, you deceived me; you lied to me! Do tell me now how you could be tied up." 11 He said, "If I were to be bound with new ropes that had never been used, I would become as weak as an ordinary man." 12 So Delilah took new ropes and bound him with them, while an ambush was waiting in a room. And she cried, "Samson, the Philistines are upon you!" But he tore them off his arms like a thread. 13 Then Delilah said to Samson, "You have been deceiving me all along; you have been lying to me! Tell me, how could you be tied up?" He answered her, "If you weave seven locks of my head into the web."*b* 14 And she pinned it with a peg*c* and cried to him, "Samson, the Philistines are upon you!" Awaking from his sleep, he pulled out the peg, the loom,*d* and the web.

15 Then she said to him, "How can you say you love me, when you don't confide in me? This makes three times that you've deceived me and haven't told me what makes you so strong." 16 Finally, after she had nagged him and pressed him constantly, he was wearied to death 17 and he confided everything to her. He said to her, "No razor has ever touched my head, for I have been a nazirite to God since I was in my mother's womb. If my hair were cut, my strength would leave me and I should become as weak as an ordinary man."

18 Sensing that he had confided everything to her, Delilah sent for the lords of the Philistines, with this message: "Come up once more, for he has confided everything to me." And the lords of the Philistines came up and brought the money with them. 19 She lulled him to sleep on her lap.

cities: Gaza, Ashkelon, Gath, Ekron, and Ashdod. **6:** Evidently, tendons taken from the intestines or sinews of animals. Their being fresh assures their flexibility and makes it more difficult to tear them. **10:** By the second attempt Delilah is angry that Samson misled her. This attempt is reminiscent of the incident at Lehi (15.13–14). **13:** In the third attempt Delilah's tone is more imperious, and Samson reveals the object of his undoing, his hair, but not how it might undo him. Samson's answer is incomplete: It begins with a conditional sentence, but without the second half. The verse may be completed by the LXX. This time the ambush is not mentioned. *Locks:* In this connection and from the continuation (v. 19), we may understand that his hair was divided into seven plaits, which were tied into a braid. *Into the web,* into the threads of the warp of the loom. **14:** *The loom, and the web,* the weave and the threads of the warp, which are part of the loom. **15:** On the fourth attempt, Delilah marshals her femininity and claims that Samson's declarations of love are false. He can convince her that his love is true only by revealing his secret. **16:** This attempt continued during a long time of nagging until Samson felt his life wasn't worth living. This is reminiscent of the woman in 14.16. **19:** As he fell asleep on her lap, she called a man to assist her in cutting his hair, because she was afraid that he might waken.

---

a For use as bowstrings.

b Septuagint adds "and pin it with a peg to the wall, I shall become as weak as an ordinary man. So Delilah put him to sleep and wove the seven locks of his head into the web."

c Septuagint adds "to the wall."

d Meaning of Heb. uncertain.

Then she called in a man, and she had him cut off the seven locks of his head; thus she weakened him[a] and made him helpless: his strength slipped away from him. [20] She cried, "Samson, the Philistines are upon you!" And he awoke from his sleep, thinking he would break loose[b] and shake himself free as he had the other times. For he did not know that the LORD had departed from him. [21] The Philistines seized him and gouged out his eyes. They brought him down to Gaza and shackled him in bronze fetters, and he became a mill slave in the prison. [22] After his hair was cut off, it began to grow back.

[23] Now the lords of the Philistines gathered to offer a great sacrifice to their god Dagon and to make merry. They chanted,

> "Our god has delivered into our hands
> Our enemy Samson."

[24] [c] When the people saw him, they sang praises to their god, chanting,

> "Our god has delivered into our hands
> The enemy who devastated our land,
> And who slew so many of us."

[25] As their spirits rose, they said, "Call Samson here and let him dance for us." Samson was fetched from the prison, and he danced for them. Then they put him between the pillars. [26] And Samson said to the boy who was leading him by the hand, "Let go of me and let me feel the pillars that the temple rests upon, that I may lean on them." [27] Now the temple was full of men and women; all the lords of the Philistines were there, and there were some three thousand men and women on the roof watching Samson dance. [28] Then Samson called to the LORD, "O Lord GOD! Please remember me, and give me strength just this once, O God, to take revenge of the Philistines, if only for one of my two eyes." [29] He embraced the two middle pillars that the temple rested upon, one with his right arm and one with his left, and leaned against them; [30] Samson cried, "Let me die with the Philistines!" and he pulled with all his might. The temple came crashing down on the lords and on all the people in it. Those who were slain by him as he died outnumbered those who had been slain by him when he lived.

[31] His brothers and all his father's household came down and carried him up and buried him in the tomb of his father Manoah, between Zorah and Eshtaol. He had led Israel for twenty years.

16.22–31: Samson's death and burial. The Philistines gathered at Dagon's temple to offer sacrifices and to thank their god for catching Samson. They wanted to entertain themselves by taunting the defeated. Samson turned to the LORD to assist him in having a final vengeance upon the Philistines, by enabling him to overturn the pillars of the temple and all that was within it. Thus, even Samson's death became a pretext for a strike against the Philistines. Members of his tribe took his body and buried him in his father's grave. **22:** The mention of his hair growing back alludes to the renewal of his strength; only in this ch is his strength connected to his "magical" locks. **25:** The Philistines wished to enjoy the sight of Samson humiliated (the Heb text does not explicitly mention dancing). **28:** As in the earlier story, Samson prays (15.18), but this time the prayer is a supplication for vengeance. In En-hakkore (15.19) one could hear in his prayer an element of questioning and even complaint. **29:** One may assume that the pillars were placed closely together. **30:** Samson, upon feeling his strength returning to him, utters a cry of encouragement to himself. **31:** *His brothers,* his compatriots. *He had led . . . :* This refers to the period preceding what is related in ch 16. This phrase returns the reader to 15.20.

---

a *Taking* wattaḥel *as equivalent to* wattaḥal; *cf. vv. 7, 11, and 17.*
b *Meaning of Heb. uncertain.*   c *This verse would read well after v. 25.*

17 There was a man in the hill country of Ephraim whose name was Micah.[a] [2]He said to his mother, "The eleven hundred shekels of silver that were taken from you, so that you uttered an imprecation[b] which you repeated in my hearing—I have that silver; I took it." "Blessed of the LORD be my son," said his mother.[c] [3]He returned the eleven hundred shekels of silver to his mother; but his mother said, "I herewith consecrate the silver to the LORD, transferring it to my son to make a sculptured image and a molten image. I now return it to you." [4]So when he gave the silver back to his mother, his mother took two hundred shekels of silver and gave it to a smith. He made of it a sculptured image and a molten image, which were kept in the house of Micah.

[5]Now the man Micah had a house of God; he had made an ephod and teraphim and he had inducted one of his sons to be his priest. [6]In those days there was no king in Israel; every man did as he pleased.

[7]There was a young man from Bethlehem of Judah, from the clan seat of Judah; he was a Levite and had resided there as a sojourner. [8]This man had left the town of Bethlehem of Judah to take up residence wherever he could find a place. On his way, he came to the house of Micah in the hill country of Ephraim. [9]"Where do you come from?" Micah asked him. He replied, "I am a Levite from Bethlehem of Judah, and I am traveling to take up residence wherever I can find a place." [10]"Stay with me," Micah said to him, "and be a father and a priest to me, and I will pay you ten shekels of silver a year, an allowance of clothing, and your food." [d]The Levite went.[d] [11]The Levite agreed to stay with the man, and the youth became like one of his own sons. [12]Micah inducted the Levite, and the young man became his priest and remained in Micah's

---

a "Micaihu" here and in v. 4.

b Cursing anyone who knew the whereabouts of the silver and did not disclose it; cf. Lev. 5.1; 1 Kings 8.31.

c In order to nullify the imprecation.   d-d Force of Heb. uncertain.

17.1–18.31: Micah's house of God and the temple of Dan. This story, focused upon cultic sites, serves to criticize the period of the judges by representing it as an age of anarchy: "In those days there was no king in Israel; every man did as he pleased." In terms of chronology, the story is set at the beginning of the age of the judges (see 18.30 and the introduction), but is placed at the end of the book to emphasize that the end of the period was similar to its beginning and the judges were unable to correct the situation; hence, the solution is monarchy. In several details, including its setting (cf. 16.31 to 18.2, 8, 11) and the sum of money—1,100 silver shekels (16.5 and 17.3), this story is connected to the Samson cycle. **1–13:** Micah's *house of God:* The account of establishing Micah's house of God reveals the manner in which God was worshipped during the period of the judges: A statue made by means of stolen silver was the center of the cult, and the priest was Micah's son, whom he himself appointed. During this period Levites sought a livelihood; hence Micah hired a Levite and appointed him as priest rather than his son. Some scholars think that Micah's temple in the hill country of Ephraim is an allusion to Bethel, which was connected with Dan, and that the criticism here is of the central temples of the Northern Kingdom. **1:** *Hill country of Ephraim:* The name of Micah's town is not specified, but rather the broad region of the central hill country. Cf. 13.2. **4:** *Two hundred shekels:* His mother said that she had consecrated the money to the LORD, but in practice she only set aside 200 out of 1,100 shekels—this too reflects poorly on the cult center that is ultimately established. *Sculptured image and a molten image:* This may refer to a single article, namely a molten (cast) sculpture. In any event, these are expressions related to pagan worship or worship of the LORD in a pagan manner (see Deut. 27.15; Exod. 20.3; 34.17; etc.). Micah and his mother are described as serving the LORD, but not in the proper way. **5:** *Ephod and teraphim,* means of inquiring of God. *One of his sons,* an illegitimate appointment, as he was not a Levite. **6:** This statement criticizes what precedes it, and serves as a critical introduction to what follows. It also suggests that Micah's specific act is representative of the whole. **7:** A Levite could not be a resident in Judah, but only a temporary sojourner. **8:** *A place,* where he would be able to earn a livelihood. The Levite came to Micah's house to rest from his travels and did not imagine that he would find his livelihood there. **10:** *A father:* Micah promises the Levite a respected position (cf. Gen. 45.8). *Ten shekels . . . a year:* The gap between the annual wage of the Levite and the amount of money stolen by Micah indicates his great shrine. [13] "Now I know," Micah told himself, "that the LORD will prosper me, since the Levite has become my priest."

18 In those days there was no king in Israel, and in those days the tribe of Dan was seeking a territory in which to settle; for to that day no territory had fallen to their lot among the tribes of Israel. [2] The Danites sent out five of their number, from their clan seat at Zorah and Eshtaol—valiant men—to spy out the land and explore it. "Go," they told them, "and explore the land." When they had advanced into the hill country of Ephraim as far as the house of Micah, they stopped there for the night. [3] While in the vicinity of Micah's house, they recognized the speech[a] of the young Levite, so they went over and asked him, "Who brought you to these parts? What are you doing in this place? What is your business here?" [4] He replied, "Thus and thus Micah did for me—he hired me and I became his priest." [5] They said to him, "Please, inquire of God; we would like to know if the mission on which we are going will be successful." [6] "Go in peace," the priest said to them, "the LORD views with favor the mission you are going on." [7] The five men went on and came to Laish. They observed the people in it dwelling carefree, after the manner of the Sidonians, a tranquil and unsuspecting people, with no one in the land to molest them and [b] with no hereditary ruler. [b] Moreover, they were distant from the Sidonians and had no dealings with anybody.

[8] When [the men] came back to their kinsmen at Zorah and Eshtaol, their kinsmen asked them, "How did you fare?" [9] They replied, "Let us go at once and attack them! For we found that the land was very good, and you are sitting idle! Don't delay; go and invade the land and take possession of it, [10] for God has delivered it into your hand. When you come, you will come to an unsuspecting people; and the land is spacious and nothing on earth is lacking there."

[11] They departed from there, from the clan seat of the Danites, from Zorah and Eshtaol, six hundred strong, girt with weapons of war. [12] They went up and encamped at Kiriath-jearim in Judah. That is why that place is called "the Camp of Dan" to this day; it lies west of Kiriath-jearim. [13] From there they passed on to the hill country of Ephraim and arrived at the house of Micah. [14] Here the

wealth. *The Levite went:* This expression seems superfluous and may be an erroneous duplication (dittography) of the words that follow ("the Levite agreed"), which are similar to it in Heb.

18.1–31: The conquest of Dan and the setting up of its temple. The Danites' wandering may reflect the intertribal relations during the period of the judges, the difficult situation of the individual, and the status of the cultic sites. **1:** *In those days . . . :* A truncated version of 17.6, suggesting its critical sequel: "every man did as he pleased." Here too this statement is integrated within the transition from one scene to another, bearing on both what precedes and what follows. The tribe of Dan was forced to leave its territory in the coastal lowlands, near Zorah and Eshtaol, and to seek a new territory, while none of the other tribes came to their help (see 1.34–35; Josh. 19.47). **4:** *Thus and thus . . . :* The narrator abbreviates the information already known from ch 17. **5:** *Inquire of God:* Before carrying out any task it was customary to inquire of God; see 1 Sam. 23.1–13 and the opening v. of Judges. **7:** *Laish,* the former name of Dan (see v. 29), referred to in Josh. 19.47 as Leshem. The description of the city is from the viewpoint of the spies, who emphasized that it was peaceful and isolated, and therefore could easily be conquered. *Distant from . . . :* The Galilee separates Laish and the area of the Sidonians. **9:** *Sitting idle:* The spies criticize the apathy of their tribe and enumerate the virtues of the place and the ease with which it might be conquered. Their enthusiasm is reminiscent of Joshua and Caleb (Num. 14.7ff.). **11:** Six hundred indicates a military unit. See 1 Sam. 30.9. **12:** *Kiriath-jearim,* located on the border of Judah and Benjamin, west of Jerusalem, and identified with Abu-Ghosh. *The Camp of Dan:* The site has not been identified. *To this day,* the days of the author (see v. 30). **14:** *In these houses:* Micah's house was not an isolated house in

---

a Lit. *"voice." The men could tell by his dialect that he came from Judah and was therefore a former neighbor of the Danites; cf. vv. 11–12.*

b-b Meaning of Heb. uncertain.

five men who had gone to spy out the Laish region remarked to their kinsmen, "Do you know, there is an ephod in these houses, and teraphim, and a sculptured image and a molten image? Now you know what you have to do." ¹⁵ So they turned off there and entered the home of the young Levite at Micah's house and greeted him. ¹⁶ The six hundred Danite men, girt with their weapons of war, stood at the entrance of the gate, ¹⁷ while the five men who had gone to spy out the land went inside and took the sculptured image, the ephod, the teraphim, and the molten image. The priest was standing at the entrance of the gate, and the six hundred men girt with their weapons of war, ¹⁸ while those men entered Micah's house and took ᵃ the sculptured image, the molten image, the ephod, and the household gods.ᵃ The priest said to them, "What are you doing?" ¹⁹ But they said to him, "Be quiet; put your hand on your mouth! Come with us and be our father and priest. Would you rather be priest to one man's household or be priest to a tribe and clan in Israel?" ²⁰ The priest was delighted. He took the ephod, the household gods, and the sculptured image, and he joined the people.

²¹ They set out again, placing the children, the cattle, and their household goods in front. ²² They had already gone some distance from Micah's house, when the men in the houses near Micah's mustered and caught up with the Danites. ²³ They called out to the Danites, who turned around and said to Micah, "What's the matter? Why have you mustered?" ²⁴ He said, "You have taken my priest and the gods that I made, and walked off! What do I have left? How can you ask, 'What's the matter'?" ²⁵ But the Danites replied, "Don't do any shouting at us, or some desperate men might attack you, and you and your family would lose your lives." ²⁶ So Micah, realizing that they were stronger than he, turned back and went home; and the Danites went on their way, ²⁷ taking the things Micah had made and the priest he had acquired. They proceeded to Laish, a people tranquil and unsuspecting, and they put them to the sword and burned down the town. ²⁸ There was none to come to the rescue, for it was distant from Sidon and they had no dealings with anyone; it lay in the valley of Beth-rehob.

They rebuilt the town and settled there, ²⁹ and they named the town Dan, after their ancestor Dan who was Israel's son. Originally, however, the name of the town was Laish. ³⁰ The Danites set up the sculptured image for

the hill country of Ephraim, but was located within a settlement whose name is not given. It seems to refer to Bethel (cf. Jer. 4.15). *You know what you have to do,* an agreed signal among conspirators. **15:** *The home of the young Levite,* i.e., the temple in which he serves. **20:** *The priest was delighted:* The narrator probes the Levite's thoughts to represent him as one who prefers his own interest—to be a priest for an entire tribe—over ethics and loyalty. **21:** *In front:* As they wished to protect their property and the weak among them, they placed them in the front, so that the fighting men would serve as a buffer against marauders from the rear. In the case of Jacob, Esau was approaching him, so he behaved in the opposite manner, placing the women and children in the rear. **22:** See v. 14 above. **23:** The Danites' questions were sarcastic, as they knew the real reason. **24:** Micah's answer indicates the depth of divine worship in an improper manner. **28:** *Beth-rehob,* an Aramean kingdom (2 Sam. 10.6) whose locale is unidentified. **30:** *Jonathan . . . :* Here the Levite's identity is revealed, being a grandson of Moses, the third generation from the exodus. The name Moses is obscured and turned into Manasseh (an evil Judean king) by means of a hanging letter "nun" to clear Moses from his grandson's misdeeds. (According to Exod. 2.22, *Gershom* is Moses' son.) *Exile:* This seems to refer to 732 BCE, when Galilee was exiled by Assyria (2 Kings 15.29), or the exile of the Northen Kingdom in 722.

---

a-a Lit. "the sculptured image of the ephod, and the household gods, and the molten image."

themselves; and Jonathan son of Gershom son of Manasseh,[a] and his descendants, served as priests to the Danite tribe until the land went into exile. [31] They maintained[b] the sculptured image that Micah had made throughout the time that the House of God stood at Shiloh.

19 In those days, when there was no king in Israel, a Levite residing at the other end of the hill country of Ephraim took to himself a concubine from Bethlehem in Judah. [2] Once his concubine deserted[c] him, leaving him for her father's house in Bethlehem in Judah; and she stayed there a full four months. [3] Then her husband set out, with an attendant and a pair of donkeys, and went after her to woo her and to win her back. She admitted him into her father's house; and when the girl's father saw him, he received him warmly. [4] His father-in-law, the girl's father, pressed him, and he stayed with him three days; they ate and drank and lodged there. [5] Early in the morning of the fourth day, he started to leave; but the girl's father said to his son-in-law, "Eat something to give you strength, then you can leave." [6] So the two of them sat down and they feasted together. Then the girl's father said to the man, "Won't you stay overnight and enjoy yourself?" [7] The man started to leave, but his father-in-law kept urging him until he turned back and spent the night there. [8] Early in the morning of the fifth day, he was about to leave, when the girl's father said, "Come, have a bite." The two of them ate, dawdling until past noon. [9] Then the man, his concubine, and his attendant started to leave. His father-in-law, the girl's father, said to him, "Look, the day is waning toward evening; do stop for the night. See, the

a Heb. מנשה with נ suspended, indicating an earlier reading "Moses"; cf. Exod. 2.22.
b Meaning of Heb. uncertain.   c Lit. "played the harlot."

31: This v. does not fit the one that precedes it. Shiloh was destroyed in the days of Samuel (1 Sam. chs 4–5), more than 300 years before the Assyrian invasion. It seems that this v. is an editorial addition, introduced to connect the story with the book of Samuel, which begins with the temple of Shiloh (1 Sam. ch 1). The mention of Kiriath-jearim in v. 12 also connects Judges to Samuel (see 1 Sam. 7.1–2).

Chs 19–21: The happenings with Gibeah and Benjamin. This account concerns a brutal rape in the town of Gibeah, following which all the tribes of Israel set out to punish those responsible. The tribe of Benjamin covered for the townspeople, and as a result a war broke out and Benjamin was nearly decimated. After the war, the other tribes arranged for the surviving Benjaminites to marry women from Jabesh-gilead and Shiloh. A distinctive feature of this episode is the anonymity of the figures involved and the focus upon place names. Gibeah, which fails to provide hospitality, is contrasted with the exemplary hospitality of Bethlehem in Judah. Through the

named places and what occurred there the author strongly hints his preference for David from Bethlehem over Saul from Gibeah. Even though the story is framed by the motto "in those days there was no king in Israel" (19.1; 21.25), it seems doubtful that this was intended to concretize anarchy. The story depicts a unified society, sensitive to problems of ethics and serving the LORD. It therefore appears that by using the motto the episode was appended to the book of Judges as an anticipatory hint to the book of Samuel, preparing specifically for the disappointment from Saul of Gibeah and the hope from Bethlehem. The story includes numerous allusions to stories from the Torah and from the early prophets. It likewise raises many strange questions which have no solution (see the commentary)—suggesting that its composition was not completed. Finally, it contains several echoes to the beginning of Judges (see 20.18 and 1.1–2; 21.24 and 2.6), using the literary device of an inclusio to frame the book and bring it to a close.

19.1–30: Between two cities. A concubine from the hill country of Ephraim left her husband and returned to her father's home in Bethlehem in Judah. Her husband came to take her back and enjoyed outstanding hospitality. On the way home they stopped to sleep in Gibeah, where the woman was raped by the townspeople until she died. The husband conveyed this terrible news to all the tribes of Israel. There are many points of similarity between this incident and the earlier story of Sodom (Gen. ch 19); and Gibeah, Saul's city, is thus portrayed as a wicked Sodom. **1:** *Concubine,* a woman in a lower legal status than a wife. **3–9:** The repeated entreaties of the father-in-law, the focus upon the feasts and staying overnight, and the emphasis that the hospitality continued for five days—all these emphasize the generous hospitality offered in Bethlehem in Judah.

day is declining; spend the night here and enjoy yourself. You can start early tomorrow on your journey and head for home."

¹⁰ But the man refused to stay for the night. He set out and traveled as far as the vicinity of Jebus—that is, Jerusalem; he had with him a pair of laden donkeys, and his concubine ᵃ·was with him.·ᵃ ¹¹ Since they were close to Jebus, and the day was very far spent, the attendant said to his master, "Let us turn aside to this town of the Jebusites and spend the night in it." ¹² But his master said to him, "We will not turn aside to a town of aliens who are not of Israel, but will continue to Gibeah. ¹³ Come," he said to his attendant, "let us approach one of those places and spend the night either in Gibeah or in Ramah." ¹⁴ So they traveled on, and the sun set when they were near Gibeah of Benjamin.

¹⁵ They turned off there and went in to spend the night in Gibeah. He went and sat down in the town square, but nobody took them indoors to spend the night. ¹⁶ In the evening, an old man came along from his property ᵇ·outside the town.·ᵇ (This man hailed from the hill country of Ephraim and resided at Gibeah, where the townspeople were Benjaminites.) ¹⁷ He happened to see the wayfarer in the town square. "Where," the old man inquired, "are you going to, and where do you come from?" ¹⁸ He replied, "We are traveling from Bethlehem in Judah to the other end of the hill country of Ephraim. That is where I live. I made a journey to Bethlehem of Judah, and now I am on my way ᶜ·to the House of the LORD,·ᶜ and nobody has taken me indoors. ¹⁹ We have both bruised straw and feed for our donkeys, and bread and wine for me and your handmaid,ᵈ and for the attendant ᵉ·with your servants.·ᵉ We lack nothing." ²⁰ "Rest easy," said the old man. "Let me take care of all your needs. Do not on any account spend the night in the square." ²¹ And he took him into his house. He mixed fodder for the donkeys; then they bathed their feet and ate and drank.

²² While they were enjoying themselves, the men of the town, a depraved lot, had gathered about the house and were pounding on the door. They called to the aged owner of the house, "Bring out the man who has come into your house, so that we can be intimate with him."

a-a *Emendation yields "and his attendant."*
b-b *Lit. "in the field."*
c-c *Meaning of Heb. uncertain; emendation yields "to my home"; cf. v. 29.*
d *I.e., the concubine.*
e-e *I.e., "with us."*

10: There is no external corroboration that Jebus was the previous name of Jerusalem. The name Jerusalem is known from the beginning of the second millenium BCE. **12:** According to 2 Sam. ch 5, Jerusalem was conquered only in the days of David, so that during the period of the judges it was a foreign city. It is mentioned here to emphasize the lack of expectations from an alien city as opposed to the Israelite city of Gibeah. **13:** The mention of Ramah, located 10 km (6 miles) north of Jerusalem, alludes to Samuel, who anointed Saul and David. The mention of these specific cities suggests that they avoid the good cities, associated with David and Samuel, and choose the evil city associated with Saul. **14–21:** The man who hosted the Levite and his company in his house was not from Gibeah but a stranger from the hill country of Ephraim. The mention of this location helps to tie this story to the previous one (18.2, 12, 13). Similarly, in the episode of Sodom it was the stranger Lot who provided hospitality to the strangers (Gen. 19.2–3). **22–26:** The violence of the people of Gibeah is reminiscent of the Sodomites: Both try to break into the host's house and want to sodomize the guests. But while in Sodom the guests were angels, here they were ordinary human beings; hence the different result. The host protected the Levite, offering his own virgin daughter and the concubine. At the end the Levite gave them his concubine, whom they abused all night long, until in the morning she was found dead at the threshold of the house. This description entails many strange features, indicating its relation to the story of Sodom, and on the other hand its incomplete editing. It is strange that the host offers them the concubine, who was a guest. It is strange that the people of Gibeah were satisfied with the concubine and did not insist upon receiving the Levite or the virgin daughter. It is also strange that once the woman fell at the entrance to the house and her hands were on

23 The owner of the house went out and said to them, "Please, my friends, do not commit such a wrong. Since this man has entered my house, do not perpetrate this outrage. 24 Look, here is my virgin daughter, and his concubine. Let me bring them out to you. Have your pleasure of them, do what you like with them; but don't do that outrageous thing to this man." 25 But the men would not listen to him, so the man seized his concubine and pushed her out to them. They raped her and abused her all night long until morning; and they let her go when dawn broke.

26 Toward morning the woman came back; and as it was growing light, she collapsed at the entrance of the man's house where her husband was. 27 When her husband arose in the morning, he opened the doors of the house and went out to continue his journey; and there was the woman, his concubine, lying at the entrance of the house, with her hands on the threshold. 28 "Get up," he said to her, "let us go." But there was no reply. So the man placed her on the donkey and set out for home. 29 When he came home, he picked up a knife, and took hold of his concubine and cut her up limb by limb into twelve parts. He sent them throughout the territory of Israel. 30 And everyone who saw it cried out, "Never has such a thing happened or been seen from the day the Israelites came out of the land of Egypt to this day! Put your mind to this; take counsel and decide."

20 Thereupon all the Israelites—from Dan to Beer-sheba and [from] the land of Gilead—marched forth, and the community assembled to a man before the LORD at Mizpah. 2 All the leaders of the people [and] all the tribes of Israel presented themselves in the assembly of God's people, 400,000 fighting men on foot.—3 The Benjaminites heard that the Israelites had come up to Mizpah.ᵃ—The Israelites said, "Tell us, how did this evil thing happen?" 4 And the Levite, the husband of the murdered woman, replied, "My concubine and I came to Gibeah of Benjamin to spend the night. 5 The citizens of Gibeah set out to harm me. They gathered against me around the house in the night; they meant to kill me, and they ravished my concubine until she died. 6 So I took hold of my concubine and I cut her in pieces and sent them through every part of Israel's territory. For an outrageous act of depravity had been committed in Israel. 7 Now you are all Israelites; produce a plan of action here and now!"

8 Then all the people rose, as one man, and declared,

the threshold no one heard her; were they asleep? 23: *Outrage,* a strong term, used in the context of sexual transgressions (see Gen. 34.7; Deut. 22.21; etc.). 25: The numerous descriptions of time ("all night," "long until morning," "when dawn broke") emphasize the brutality. 27: The Levite's behavior was strange as well. He prepares to leave as though nothing had happened, and upon seeing the concubine's body, he calls her to get up and go. 29: The cutting of the body and the sending of its pieces are also strange. It is meant to recall Saul who divided a pair of cattle (1 Sam. 11.7), but there the purpose is clear: to dramatize what Saul would do to the cattle of those who refused to join him.

20.1–48: The war against Benjamin. Benjamin's refusal to turn over those who were guilty in Gibeah led to a bloody war. On the first two days Israel was defeated, for reasons that are not clear. On the third day they overpowered Benjamin, leaving only 600 people. This description raises problems to which there is no solution, and also relies upon the well-known story of Israel's war against Ai (Josh. chs 7–8). **1:** There is no other unification of this type throughout the book of Judges; this description thus prepares the reader for the establishment of the monarchy in the beginning of the book of Samuel, which follows. **2:** The number 400,000 is exaggerated. **3:** It is strange that the examination of the Levite is only performed once the army had been mustered. **4–11:** The story of the Levite is brief and not entirely truthful; nevertheless, the Israelite side does not feel a need to investigate, but adopts a decision to go to war. **9:** *According to lot:* The casting of lots determines when to go to war and which of the tribes will go first (v. 18). **10:** Ten percent were responsible for the supplies to the combatants. **11–13:** The men of Israel were interested in punishing only the scoundrels from Gibeah, but the tribe of Benjamin did not

a *This sentence is continued at v. 14 below.*

"We will not go back to our homes, we will not enter our houses! ⁹But this is what we will do to Gibeah: [we will wage war] against it according to lot. ¹⁰We will take from all the tribes of Israel ten men to the hundred, a hundred to the thousand, and a thousand to the ten thousand to supply provisions for the troops—ᵃto prepare for their going to Geba in Benjaminᵃ for all the outrage it has committed in Israel." ¹¹So all the men of Israel, united as one man, massed against the town. ¹²And the tribes of Israel sent men through the whole tribeᵇ of Benjamin, saying, "What is this evil thing that has happened among you? ¹³Come, hand over those scoundrels in Gibeah so that we may put them to death and stamp out the evil from Israel." But the Benjaminites would not yield to the demand of their fellow Israelites.

¹⁴So the Benjaminites gathered from their towns to Gibeah in order to take the field against the Israelites. ¹⁵ᶜOn that day the Benjaminites mustered from the towns 26,000 fighting men, mustered apart from the inhabitants of Gibeah; 700 picked men ¹⁶of all this force—700 picked men—were left-handed. Every one of them could sling a stone at a hair and not miss. ¹⁷The men of Israel other than Benjamin mustered 400,000 fighting men, warriors to a man. ¹⁸They proceeded to Bethel and inquired of God; the Israelites asked, "Who of us shall advance first to fight the Benjaminites?" And the LORD replied, "Judah first." ¹⁹So the Israelites arose in the morning and encamped against Gibeah.

²⁰The men of Israel took the field against the Benjaminites; the men of Israel drew up in battle order against them at Gibeah. ²¹But the Benjaminites issued from Gibeah, and that day they struck down 22,000 men of Israel. ²²Now the army—the men of Israel—rallied and again drew up in battle order at the same place as they had on the first day. ²³For the Israelites had gone up and wept before the LORD until evening. They had inquired of the LORD, "Shall we again join battle with our kinsmen the Benjaminites?" And the LORD had replied, "March against them." ²⁴The Israelites advanced against the Benjaminites on the second day. ²⁵But the Benjaminites came out from Gibeah against them on the second day and struck down 18,000 more of the Israelites, all of them fighting men.

²⁶Then all the Israelites, all the army, went up and came to Bethel and they sat there, weeping before the LORD.

agree to turn them over, preferring to fight. **15–17:** The number of combatants from Benjamin is problematic. There is a conflict between the number mentioned here (26,700 fighters) and the number in v. 35 (25,100, with 600 surviving), as well as with vv. 44–47 (25,000, with 600 left). **16:** *Left-handed,* see 3.15. On a group of chosen people from Benjamin who used both hands, see 1 Chron. 12.2. **17:** The number 400,000 seems to include the tenth appointed over the supplies. **18:** *Judah first:* This seems to have been introduced under the influence of the beginning of the book (1.1–2). **19–25:** It would seem that v. 22 ought to appear after v. 23. In the first two battles Israel acted after asking the LORD; nevertheless the Benjaminite warriors killed 40,000 of them. **26–28:** The army of Israel went up a third time to Bethel, where the Ark of God was at that time and where Phinehas son of Eleazar son of Aaron, third generation from the exodus, served as priest. This connects the end of Judges to the end of Joshua (Josh. 24.33), while much of the rest of the story connects it to the following book of Samuel. The army fasted, offered burnt offerings, and inquired of the LORD. God promised that this time He would give Benjamin into their hands.

a-a *Emendation yields "for those who go to requite Gibeah."*
b *Heb. plural.*
c *Meaning of parts of vv. 15 and 16 uncertain.*

They fasted that day until evening, and presented burnt offerings and offerings of well-being to the LORD. 27 The Israelites inquired of the LORD (for the Ark of God's Covenant was there in those days, 28 and Phinehas son of Eleazar son of Aaron the priest ministered before Him in those days), "Shall we again take the field against our kinsmen the Benjaminites, or shall we not?" The LORD answered, "Go up, for tomorrow I will deliver them into your hands."

29 Israel put men in ambush against Gibeah on all sides. 30 And on the third day, the Israelites went up against the Benjaminites, as before, and engaged them in battle at Gibeah. 31 The Benjaminites dashed out to meet the army and were drawn away from the town onto the roads, of which one runs to Bethel and the other to Gibeah. As before, they started out by striking some of the men dead in the open field, about 30 men of Israel.

32 The Benjaminites thought, "They are being routed before us as previously." But the Israelites had planned: "We will take to flight and draw them away from the town to the roads." 33 And while the main body of the Israelites had moved away from their positions and had drawn up in battle order at Baal-tamar, the Israelite ambush was rushing out from its position at Maareh-geba.ᵃ 34 Thus 10,000 picked men of all Israel came to a point south ofᵇ Gibeah, and the battle was furious. Before they realized that disaster was approaching, 35 the LORD routed the Benjaminites before Israel. That day the Israelites slew 25,100 men of Benjamin, all of them fighting men. 36 Then the Benjaminites realized that they were routed.ᶜ Now the Israelites had yielded ground to the Benjaminites, for they relied on the ambush which they had laid against Gibeah. 37 One ambush quickly deployed against Gibeah, and the other ambush advanced and put the whole town to the sword.

38 A time had been agreed upon by the Israelite men with those in ambush: When a huge column of smoke was sent up from the town, 39 the Israelite men were to turn about in battle. Benjamin had begun by striking dead

a Emendation yields "west of Gibeah."

b So many Heb. mss. and Targum; most mss. and the editions read "opposite."

c This sentence is continued by v. 45.

29–47: According to most scholars this story has been expanded and reworked here. Abravanel already wrote: "The verses in this narrative seem to be repeated and inconsistent, and the interpreters did not solve them properly." The material here seems to be a combination of two versions, whose reworking into a single text was not completely successful. Underlying both versions is a combined strategy trick of ambush and decoy, known from Joshua's battle with Ai (Josh. chs 7–8). The function of the ambush was to besiege the city and set fire to it after tempting its inhabitants to chase an Israelite decoy force that would stage a retreat. Once the pursuers saw their city going up in flames, they would lose their fighting spirit, and the pursued would become pursuers. Thus the Benjaminites would find themselves caught between the ambush and the new pursuers, while the city and its protectors were destroyed. While the first version refers to the task of the main Israelite force which encamped at Baal-tamar and was counted neither with the decoy force nor with the ambush, the second version relates to the agreed signal between the decoy force and the ambush. 29: According to vv. 33–34 the main force was east of Gibeah, the ambush west of the city, while the decoy force was opposite the city. 30: This refers to the decoy force alone; see v. 34. 31: To Gibeah: It is preferable to read "to Geba," located east of Gibeah. The choice of two directions of flight divides the pursuing force. About 30 men: The small number of the fallen, in comparison to the first two wars, is evidently influenced by the story of Ai (Josh. 7.5). 33: The main Israelite force had been mustered before in Baal-tamar, whose location has not been identified. 34: Before they realized, i.e., before the Benjaminites realized. 35: See the interpretation of vv. 15–17. 36b: The second version begins here. It emphasizes that the Israelite army, who had relied upon the ambush, placed to the west of Gibeah, waited for a sign to enter into battle, giving the decoy time to lead the inhabitants of Gibeah away from their city. 37: The English translation divides the ambush into two parts, which is unnecessary. It should read: "The ambush quickly deployed against Gibeah and advanced . . ." 38–39a: The Israelite decoy force and the ambush agreed upon a about 30 Israelite men, and they thought, "They are being routed before us as in the previous fighting." ⁴⁰ But when the column, the pillar of smoke, began to rise from the city, the Benjaminites looked behind them, and there was the whole town going up in smoke to the sky! ⁴¹ And now the Israelites turned about, and the men of Benjamin were thrown into panic, for they realized that disaster had overtaken them. ⁴² They retreated before the men of Israel along the road to the wilderness, where the fighting caught up with them; meanwhile those ᵃfrom the townsᵃ were massacring them in it. ⁴³ᵇThey encircled the Benjaminites, pursued them, and trod them down [from] Menuhah to a point opposite Gibeah on the east. ⁴⁴ That day 18,000 men of Benjamin fell, all of them brave men. ⁴⁵ They turned and fled to the wilderness, to the Rock of Rimmon; but [the Israelites] picked off another 5,000 on the roads and, continuing in hot pursuit of them up to Gidom, they slew 2,000 more. ⁴⁶ Thus the total number of Benjaminites who fell that day came to 25,000 fighting men, all of them brave. ⁴⁷ But 600 men turned and fled to

sign—a great cloud of smoke rising from the city—to determine when the pursued would turn into pursuers. **39b:** Cf. this clause to vv. 31–32. **41:** *The Israelites turned about,* the decoy force. **42:** The Benjaminites attempted to escape from the pincer motion of the ambush and the decoy force by fleeing in the direction of the desert, but the war overtook them there as well. *From the towns:* Those who fled from the town of Gibeah were killed in the middle. **43:** The v. is in the form of a (difficult) poem, which may be a remnant of an epic poem in whose center is the victory over Benjamin. Israel surrounded Benjamin and pursued them from a settlement called Nuhah (see 1 Chron. ch 8) until close to Gibeah. **45–47:** Here, the total number of those fallen from Benjamin was 25,000. Six hundred men found shelter in the Rock of Rimmon on the edge of the desert east of Bethel, where they remained for four months.

---

a-a *Meaning of Heb. uncertain; emendation yields "in the town" (i.e., Gibeah).*
b *Meaning of verse uncertain.*

Sites mentioned in connection with the Benjaminite War

the wilderness, to the Rock of Rimmon; they remained at the Rock of Rimmon four months. ⁴⁸ The men of Israel, meanwhile, turned back to the rest of the Benjaminites and put them to the sword—towns, people, cattle—everything that remained. Finally, they set fire to all the towns that were left.

21 Now the men of Israel had taken an oath at Mizpah: "None of us will give his daughter in marriage to a Benjaminite."

² The people came to Bethel and sat there before God until evening. They wailed and wept bitterly, ³ and they said, "O Lord God of Israel, why has this happened in Israel, that one tribe must now be missing from Israel?" ⁴ Early the next day, the people built an altar there, and they brought burnt offerings and offerings of well-being.

⁵ The Israelites asked, "Is there anyone from all the tribes of Israel who failed to come up to the assembly before the Lord?" For a solemn oath had been taken concerning anyone who did not go up to the Lord at Mizpah: "He shall be put to death." ⁶ The Israelites now relented toward their kinsmen the Benjaminites, and they said, "This day one tribe has been cut off from Israel! ⁷ What can we do to provide wives for those who are left, seeing that we have sworn by the Lord not to give any of our daughters to them in marriage?"

⁸ They inquired, "Is there anyone from the tribes of Israel who did not go up to the Lord at Mizpah?" Now no one from Jabesh-gilead had come to the camp, to the assembly. ⁹ For, when the roll of the troops was taken, not one of the inhabitants of Jabesh-gilead was present. ¹⁰ So the assemblage dispatched 12,000 of the warriors, instructing them as follows: "Go and put the inhabitants of Jabesh-gilead to the sword, women and children included. ¹¹ This is what you are to do: Proscribe every man, and every woman who has known a man carnally." ¹² They found among the inhabitants of Jabesh-gilead 400 maidens who had not known a man carnally; and they brought them to the camp at Shiloh, which is in the land of Canaan.ᵃ

¹³ Then the whole community sent word to the Benjaminites who were at the Rock of Rimmon, and offered them terms of peace. ¹⁴ Thereupon the Benjaminites returned, and they gave them the girls who had been spared from the women of Jabesh-gilead. ᵇ But there were not enough of them.·ᵇ

---

a I.e., west of the Jordan, while Jabesh-gilead is east of the Jordan.
b-b Meaning of Heb. uncertain.

48: The army of Israel treated Benjamin like a proscribed Canaanite city (see Deut. 20.16–18), destroying its population, property, and cities.

21.1–14: The war against Jabesh-gilead. The Israelite army had taken an oath at Mizpah (20.1, 3) not to marry their daughters to the Benjaminites and to put to death those who did not join the battle. In order to rehabilitate the remnants of Benjamin, it was necessary to find them wives. Investigation revealed that Jabesh-gilead had not joined the war; therefore it was decided to smite its inhabitants apart from the virgins, and the result was leaving 400 maidens from Jabesh-gilead for those left from Benjamin. This story, which condemns Jabesh-gilead, relates to the story of Israel's war against the Midianites at the time of the wanderings in the desert (Num. ch 31), which combines condemnation of Midian and taking their women captive. The story thus reflects negatively on Jabesh-gilead which, according to the traditions preserved in Samuel, was closely affiliated with Saul (1 Sam. 31.11–13; 2 Sam. 2.4–7; etc.). **1:** From the sequel it follows that at the gathering in Mizpah at the beginning of the war the Israelites took another oath: to put to death those who did not join in the war effort (v. 5). **2:** The people gathered at *Bethel*, which once again serves as a place for weeping (2.1–5; 20.23, 26). **5:** The purpose of the inquiry was to find out who did not participate in the gathering at Mizpah and would be subject to the death penalty, but simultaneously exempt from the oath against giving their daughters to the Benjaminites. **9:** *Jabesh-gilead* is located in the north of Gilead, but has not been precisely identified. **10–11:** Use of the typical number 12,000, in which each 1,000 represents one tribe, as well as of the term *woman who has known a man carnally*, indicates the connection to Num. ch 31. **12:** The maidens were brought to *Shiloh* and not to Mizpah or Bethel because of the

15 Now the people had relented toward Benjamin, for the LORD had made a breach in the tribes of Israel. 16 So the elders of the community asked, "What can we do about wives for those who are left, since the women of Benjamin have been killed off?" 17 For they said, "There must be a saving remnant for Benjamin, that a tribe may not be blotted out of Israel; 18 yet we cannot give them any of our daughters as wives," since the Israelites had taken an oath: "Cursed be anyone who gives a wife to Benjamin!"

19 They said, "The annual feast of the LORD is now being held at Shiloh." (It lies north of Bethel, east of the highway that runs from Bethel to Shechem, and south of Lebonah.)

20 So they instructed the Benjaminites as follows: "Go and lie in wait in the vineyards. 21 As soon as you see the girls of Shiloh coming out to join in the dances, come out from the vineyards; let each of you seize a wife from among the girls of Shiloh, and be off for the land of Benjamin. 22 And if their fathers or brothers come to us to complain, we shall say to them, a-'Be generous to them for our sake! We could not provide any of them with a wife on account of the war, and you would have incurred guilt if you yourselves had given them [wives].' "-a

23 The Benjaminites did so. They took to wife, from the dancers whom they carried off, as many as they themselves numbered. Then they went back to their own territory, and rebuilt their towns and settled in them. 24 Thereupon the Israelites dispersed, each to his own tribe and clan; everyone departed for his own territory.

25 In those days there was no king in Israel; everyone did as he pleased.

a-a Meaning of Heb. uncertain.

sequel, which also takes place in Shiloh. **14:** *Returned:* The surviving men from Benjamin returned from the Rock of Rimmon to their towns, but there were still 200 left without wives.

21.15–25: The abduction at Shiloh. In order to resolve the problem of the 200 additional Benjaminites who were left without wives, the elders of the community suggested that the others circumvent the oath by lying in wait in the vineyards of Shiloh to abduct from there the young women dancing at the feast of the LORD. The motif of stealing women on a festival day is known from Greek (Herodotus) and Roman (Livy) literature. The story connecting Benjamin with Shiloh prepares the ground for the decline of the town's status in the days of Eli and his sons according to the following book of Samuel. **15:** The blow struck to the Benjaminites harmed the overall structure of the Israelite tribes. **19:** *The annual feast:* It is not clear what feast this refers to. According to Josephus this was one of the three pilgrimage festivals, while a rabbinic tradition knows of a similar festival commemorated on the 15th of Av (the fifth month, in the mid-summer) or the Day of Atonement (*m. Ta'an.* 4.8). It may simply refer to a local grape-harvest festival similar to the vintage festival in Shechem (9.27). The detailed geographical description of Shiloh's location is unusual in the Bible. This may be an addition from the period when Shiloh, which is identified with Khirbet Sailun, north of Bethel, was destroyed. **24:** Once a solution had been found, the Israelites left Bethel and returned to their own territories. **25:** The book concludes with the motto that expresses disappointment in the judges and hope in the monarchy. Given the negative associations in the story with Saul, it is the Davidic monarchy to which the book looks forward.

שמואל א

I Samuel

Name and Contents

THE BOOKS OF SAMUEL were originally one book. In the Septuagint it was divided into two, owing to its length, and the Christian tradition followed this division. In Hebrew Bibles used by the Jewish community, this division was not made before the 15th century, under the influence of the Vulgate. Following a pattern found in some other biblical books, which end with the death of a main character, the division in the book of Samuel was made at the point of Saul's death. Thus, 1 Samuel recounts the periods of Eli (chs 1–4), Samuel (chs 5–12), and Saul (chs 13–31); 2 Samuel tells of the reign of David. The work was named after the prophet Samuel (*b. B. Bat.* 14b), because the story of his birth opens the book and he is the principal figure in the first part. He greatly influenced events during his life and even after his death, since he anointed the first two kings, whose actions and fate occupy the major part of the book of Samuel.

The book of Samuel consists chiefly of narratives, which are supplemented with a few songs, lists, and brief notices. Its central concern is with the personal life of the leaders. Their aspirations, feelings, and passions are depicted realistically, displaying negative qualities as well as positive ones. Through the events of their lives the main ideas of the book are expressed. As a rule, human beings, not God, occupy the central stage, their lot being determined by their conduct. God acts behind the scenes, usually refraining from direct, supernatural intervention, shaping individual destinies through the natural course of events.

Samuel, the only person in the Bible whose biography begins before his birth and extends after his death, acted as both judge and prophet. Saul, the first king, who led Israel after Samuel, is depicted in most of the book as an unstable character. When he tries to free himself from Samuel's stern tutelage, a break ensues between the two men, and Saul is rejected in favor of David—the focal figure in both books. David, as opposed to Saul, is generally portrayed in a favorable light. His personality is many-faceted and richer than any other figure in the Bible. He is a strong leader, successful in war and peace, a gifted musician and poet, deeply religious, endowed with a strong sense of justice, respectful and loyal towards Saul. Only in his dealings with his children does he appear weak. He sins, abusing his power, but repents wholeheartedly. At the peak of his reign he receives God's promise that his dynasty will reign forever.

Background

THE BOOK OF SAMUEL describes the transition from the rule of the judges to the monarchic system of government. It tells of the foundation of the monarchy and its early struggles, paying special attention to questions concerning the rights, duties, and restrictions of the kings. It depicts how, through clashes between King Saul and the prophet Samuel, and between King David and the prophet Nathan, a type of kingship emerged that radically differed from the absolute kingship prevalent in the ancient Near East. According to the Bible, kings in Israel were not allowed to do whatever they fancied. They were subject to a higher power and to the rule of law and morality, upheld by the prophets.

The book also deals with the transfer of government from the old leaders to the new. Though hereditary succession was not unknown (see esp. Judg. chs 6–9), the three leaders Eli, Samuel, and Saul were not succeeded by their sons, but by others—each of whom had initially been under the patronage of his predecessor. The transfer was effected smoothly in the case of Eli and Samuel, with difficulty in the case of Samuel and Saul, and with bitter conflict in the case of Saul and David, culminating in Saul's recurring attempts to kill David.

Literary Form

THE BOOK OF SAMUEL is a work of literary art and is best read as such. Though only partly visible in translation, the literary and stylistic features are unmistakable, bearing witness to the book's artistry. The narratives excel in dramatic force and human appeal. Almost all contain a large amount of direct speech, which gives them their vivid character. Some are made up almost exclusively of direct speech; for instance, the narrative of Saul, who went to look for his father's asses and was anointed king of Israel (9.1–10.16). Conversations are usually brief, including only what is essential for the development of the plot. The same holds true for descriptions. Unlike conversations, however, descriptions of people, places, and objects are relatively rare and in many narratives wholly absent. The literary features play an important role in expressing or highlighting the narratives' ideas and values and impressing them on the readers. The book's literary character has no bearing on the question of its historical veracity, since both fact and fiction may be cast in an aesthetic mold. The book, however, should not be understood as a straightforward history of the early monarchic period.

Text

IN THE TRADITIONAL HEBREW TEXT of Samuel a considerable number of corruptions are found, generally resulting from scribal errors. For instance, 13.1 reads "Saul was a year old when he became king and he reigned over Israel two years." It is clear that a number was accidentally omitted before the word "year" ("a" is not expressed in Heb). The number "two" at the end of the sentence is also implausible because it seems quite impossible to accommodate all the events of Saul's kingship within a span of two years (see, e.g., 27.7). In some cases it is possible to correct the Masoretic Text of Samuel with the help of alternative texts. Parallel passages to Samuel, containing partly divergent readings, are found in the book of Psalms and the book of Chronicles. Among the Dead Sea Scrolls fragments of four different manuscripts of Samuel have been discovered, which contain pre-Masoretic texts. The Septuagint and other ancient translations also testify to different readings. In some cases even *Antiquities of the Jews* by Josephus, whose readings are often similar to those of the Septuagint and one of the Dead Sea manuscripts, may be helpful. The following annotations will be based on the Hebrew Masoretic Text and the NJPS translation, but whenever the text seems corrupt, attention will be paid to alternative readings.

Composition

SEVERAL STORIES IN THE BOOK OF SAMUEL occur twice, though in different versions. Cases in point include the stories about the election of Saul (9.15–10.9; 10.20–24), his rejection by Samuel (13.8–14; 15.9–33), David's first meeting with Saul (16.14–23; 17.31–37, 55–58), the killing of Goliath (in one case by David, in the other by Elhanan, 17.40–51; 2 Sam. 21.19), Saul's attempt to kill David by throwing his spear at him (18.10–11; 19.9–10), David's escape from Saul (19.11–12; 20.1–21.1), his taking refuge with Achish (21.11–16; 27.1–28.2; 29.1–11), and his refusal to kill Saul when he had the opportunity to do so (24.1–22; 26.1–25). The origin of the saying, "Is Saul too among the prophets?" is explained twice and in different ways (10.10–12; 19.18–24), and there are two divergent accounts of Saul's death (31.1–7; 2 Sam. 1.3–10).

Different versions of the same story, which are often met with in folk tales, arose, in all likelihood, when these stories were transmitted orally, before they were written down. The double, and sometimes contradictory, stories were probably included in the book of Samuel because they were not seen as different versions of the same story, but as accounts of different events, or because of the light they shed on the protagonists. As for contradictions, these were looked at in a different way from today: Consistency was not considered essential. Besides, the contradictions could always be resolved in one way or another (see, for instance, how the two differing accounts of the killing of Goliath are reconciled in 1 Chron. 20.5).

Jewish sources ascribe the composition of the book of Samuel to Samuel himself (*b. B. Bat.* 14b). But since his death is already recorded in ch 25, the prophets Gad and Nathan, who are mentioned together with Samuel as the authors of a history of David (1 Chron. 29.29), are said to have finished the work (*b. B. Bat.* 15a). In the book of Samuel itself one source is mentioned: the Book of Jashar, from which David's elegy for Saul and Jonathan was taken (2 Sam. 1.18).

Biblical scholarship has posited a plurality of sources. In this respect three main theories have been put forward. First, the book of Samuel is composed of two or three parallel and continuous narrative strands, which run through the whole length of the book (this view was current in the 19th and the beginning of the 20th centuries). Second, the book of Samuel consists of many single, independent narratives. Third, the book of Samuel is a compilation of large thematic units—such as the Ark narrative, the Saul cycle, the history of David's rise, the so-called succession narrative (which continues into the first chapters of Kings)—which are not parallel, but arranged one after the other. Most scholars hold that the book of Samuel was also subjected to a Deuteronomistic redaction (that is, based on the tenets of the book of Deuteronomy), but it is generally agreed that this redaction was much slighter than in the book of Judges or the book of Kings. Some scholars assume a prophetic stratum between the older narrative material and the Deuteronomistic redaction. In any case, many hands have contributed to the formation of the book of Samuel, as is also borne out by the differences in style and narrative method—yet the different elements have generally been integrated into one unified whole.

In its final form the book of Samuel, and particularly the figures of David and Saul, have had a great impact on Jewish and Western thought and art. Many compositions—religious, moral, and political—as well as innumerable works of poetry, drama, narrative prose, painting, sculpture, and music have been influenced by them, and they continue to be a source of inspiration even today.   [SHIMON BAR-EFRAT]

1 There was a man from ª⁻Ramathaim of the Zuphites,⁻ª in the hill country of Ephraim, whose name was Elkanah son of Jeroham son of Elihu son of Tohu son of Zuph, an Ephraimite. ² He had two wives, one named Hannah and the other Peninnah; Peninnah had children, but Hannah was childless. ³ This man used to go up from his town every year to worship and to offer sacrifice to the LORD of Hosts at Shiloh.—Hophni and Phinehas, the two sons of Eli, were priests of the LORD there.

⁴ One such day, Elkanah offered a sacrifice. He used to give portions to his wife Peninnah and to all her sons and daughters; ⁵ but to Hannah he would give one portion ᵇ⁻only—though⁻ᵇ Hannah was his favorite—for the LORD had closed her womb. ⁶ Moreover, her rival, to make her miserable, would taunt her that the LORD had closed her

a-a Heb. "Ramathaim-zophim." In 1.19, 2.11, 7.17, 15.34, 19.18, etc., the town is called Ramah; and 9.5 ff. shows that it was in the district of Zuph.
b-b Meaning of Heb. uncertain.

1.1–2.11a: The vow. The book of Samuel begins with the story of the remarkable birth of Samuel. The story focuses on Samuel's mother, who was barren and so desperate for a child that she vowed to part from it and dedicate it to God, if her prayer for a son were answered. The motif of formerly barren women who give birth to national leaders or ancestors is well attested in the Bible (Sarah, Rebekah, Rachel, Samson's mother; see Gen. 21.1–8; 25.19–26; 30.1–2, 22–24; Judg. 13.2–3, 24), the exceptional birth hinting at divine concern and purpose for the child. The narrative consists of an exposition, which gives details about the persons, the background, and relevant customs, and three parts. The first part takes place at Shiloh, the second at Ramah, and the third at Shiloh again; a final section, which rounds off the story, is embedded within the next narrative, 2.18–21. **1:** The list of Elkanah's ancestors shows that he was of distinguished lineage. **2:** Bigamy was allowed and not uncommon. **3:** The Ark of the LORD was housed in the sanctuary *at Shiloh.* The information concerning the worship every year at Shiloh links the beginning of the book of Samuel with the end of the book of Judges, where a feast of God is mentioned, celebrated every year at Shiloh (Judg. 21.19). Though not figuring in the present story, the two sons of Eli are mentioned because the stories about Samuel are intertwined with those about Eli and his sons (see ch 2). **5:** *One portion only—though:* The Heb may also be interpreted, "one twofold portion—for" (cf. the fivefold portion Joseph gave to Benjamin, Gen. 43.34); this interpretation better explains Peninnah's reaction. **6:** Fertility is understood throughout the womb. [7a]This happened[-a] year after year: Every time she went up to the House of the LORD, the other would taunt her, so that she wept and would not eat. [8]Her husband Elkanah said to her, "Hannah, why are you crying and why aren't you eating? Why are you so sad? Am I not more devoted to you than ten sons?"

[9]After they had eaten and drunk at Shiloh, Hannah rose.[b]—The priest Eli was sitting on the seat near the doorpost of the temple of the LORD.—[10]In her wretchedness, she prayed to the LORD, weeping all the while. [11]And she made this vow: "O LORD of Hosts, if You will look upon the suffering of Your maidservant and will remember me and not forget Your maidservant, and if You will grant Your maidservant a male child, I will dedicate him to the LORD for all the days of his life; and no razor shall ever touch his head."

[12]As she kept on praying before the LORD, Eli watched her mouth. [13]Now Hannah was praying in her heart; only her lips moved, but her voice could not be heard. So Eli thought she was drunk. [14]Eli said to her, "How long will you make a drunken spectacle of yourself? [c]Sober up!"[-c] [15]And Hannah replied, "Oh no, my lord! I am a very unhappy woman. I have drunk no wine or other strong drink, but I have been pouring out my heart to the LORD. [16]Do not take your maidservant for a worthless woman; I have only been speaking all this time out of my great anguish and distress." [17]"Then go in peace," said Eli, "and may the God of Israel grant you what you have asked of Him." [18]She answered, "You are most kind to your handmaid." So the woman left, and she ate, and was no longer downcast. [19]Early next morning they bowed low before the LORD, and they went back home to Ramah.

Elkanah knew[d] his wife Hannah and the LORD remembered her. [20]Hannah conceived, and at the turn of the year bore a son. She named him Samuel,[e] meaning, "I asked the LORD for him." [21]And when the man Elkanah and all his household were going up to offer to the LORD the annual sacrifice and his votive sacrifice, [22]Hannah did not go up. She said to her husband, "When the child is weaned, I will bring him. For when he has appeared before the LORD, he must remain there for good." [23]Her husband Elkanah said to her, "Do as you think best. Stay

Bible as a divine gift. Barrenness was considered a disgrace, causing great distress to the woman concerned (e.g., Gen. 30.1, 22–23). **7:** Peninnah is the opposite of Hannah. Not only does Peninnah have many children, whereas Hannah has none, but Peninnah deliberately hurts her rival, while Hannah refrains from paying back, weeping in silence. **8:** *Am I not more devoted to you than ten sons,* cf. Ruth 4.15. **9:** Though Hannah does not eat, she waits until all have finished their meal. **11:** The structure of Hannah's vow is typical of vows in the Bible: First a condition is stated, and this is followed by a commitment if the condition is fulfilled (cf. Gen. 28.20–22; Judg. 11.30–31). Here the vow is preceded by an invocation of God. Long hair was characteristic of Nazirites, who devoted themselves to God (Num. 6.5). The word "Nazirite" is actually used by the Septuagint in the present v. and by the Dead Sea manuscript 4QSam[a] in v. 22. Samuel is also called a Nazirite in the postbiblical book of Sirach (46.13). **13:** Silent prayer was uncommon. **19:** *They went back home:* This phrase often serves to mark the end of a story or an episode (e.g., 2.11). *The LORD remembered her:* This is shown when Hannah's womb is opened (see v. 11), enabling her to conceive. **20:** The verb "sha'al" (= ask) recurs in the narrative several times, more than is expressed in the translation (see also 2.20). **22:** Weaning used to take place after several years; according to 2 Macc. 7.27 after three years. **24:** *One ephah,* about 23 liters (21 quarts). **27:** Hannah uses the same words as Eli did before (v. 17), to indicate to the priest that his blessing has materialized.

a-a Lit. "Thus he did."
b Septuagint adds "and stood before the LORD."
c-c Lit. "Remove your wine from you."
d Cf. note at Gen. 4.1.
e Connected with sha'ul me'el "asked of God"; cf. vv. 17, 27–28.

home until you have weaned him. May the LORD fulfill ªHis word."ª So the woman stayed home and nursed her son until she weaned him.

²⁴ When she had weaned him, she took him up with her, along with ᵇthree bulls,ᵇ one *ephah* of flour, and a jar of wine. And ᶜthough the boy was still very young,ᶜ she brought him to the House of the LORD at Shiloh. ²⁵ After slaughtering the bull, they brought the boy to Eli. ²⁶ She said, "Please, my lord! As you live, my lord, I am the woman who stood here beside you and prayed to the LORD. ²⁷ It was this boy I prayed for; and the LORD has granted me what I asked of Him. ²⁸ I, in turn, hereby lendᵈ him to the LORD. For as long as he lives he is lent to the LORD." And theyᵉ bowed low there before the LORD.

2 And Hannah prayed:

My heart exults in the LORD;
ᶠI have triumphedᶠ through the LORD.
ᵍI gloatᵍ over my enemies;
I rejoice in Your deliverance.

2   There is no holy one like the LORD,
Truly, there is none beside You;
There is no rock like our God.

3   Talk no more with lofty pride,
Let no arrogance cross your lips!
For the LORD is an all-knowing God;
By Him actions are measured.

4   The bows of the mighty are broken,
And the faltering are girded with strength.
5   Men once sated must hire out for bread;
Men once hungry hunger no more.
While the barren woman bears seven,
The mother of many is forlorn.
6   The LORD deals death and gives life,
Casts down into Sheol and raises up.

2.1–10: Hannah's song, which is similar in style and content to certain psalms (cf. v. 8 with Ps. 113.7–8), expresses thanks and praise to God for a victory over an enemy. It fits neither Hannah's situation nor her personality. Moreover, a king is mentioned in v. 10, whereas at Hannah's time the monarchy had not yet been established in Israel. The song was put in Hannah's mouth because of v. 5, *while the barren woman bears seven,* and because of its general idea, that God often completely reverses the fortunes of human beings, in accordance with their conduct. The idea of reversal is underscored by the contrasts between or within the lines of the parallelisms in the central part of the song. **1:** The horn (see translators' note *f-f*), a symbol of strength (Deut. 33.17), is mentioned in the Heb text both at the beginning and the end of the song, thus stressing the idea of triumph. **2:** The second line prevents understanding the first and third lines as if other gods existed. **3:** Here the enemies are addressed. For the thought that God is all-knowing and that He measures the actions of human beings (and pays them accordingly) see also Prov. 24.12, where the same Heb roots are used as here. **5:** The number *seven* denotes multiplicity, and also has the connotation of perfection. **6–8a:** The LORD is the cause of all changes in life. **6:** *Sheol,* the place beneath the earth, where, according to biblical belief, all people go after death. Sheol differs from the "'olam haba'" (the next world), the belief in which developed in Judaism in the Second Temple period, because in Sheol there is no retribution and all its inhabitants are equal, without regard to their former status or behavior in life. Raising up from Sheol does not refer to resurrection from death—a later belief as well—but to deliverance from near death (see Ps. 30.3–4).

---

a-a *Septuagint and 4QSamª (a Samuel fragment from Qumran) read "the utterance of your mouth." The translators express their thanks to Professor Frank M. Cross, Jr., for graciously making available to them copies of his unpublished Samuel fragments.*

b-b *Septuagint and 4QSamª read "a three-year-old [cf. Gen. 15.9] bull and bread"; cf. v. 25.*

c-c *Meaning of Heb. uncertain.*

d *From the same root as that of the verb rendered "asked for" in v. 20.*

e *Heb. "he"; cf. 2.11. A reading in the Talmud (Berakhot 61a) implies that Elkanah was there.*

f-f *Lit. "My horn is high."*   g-g *Lit. "My mouth is wide."*

7   The LORD makes poor and makes rich;
     He casts down, He also lifts high.
8   He raises the poor from the dust,
     Lifts up the needy from the dunghill,
     Setting them with nobles,
     Granting them seats of honor.
     For the pillars of the earth are the LORD's;
     He has set the world upon them.
9   He guards the steps of His faithful,
     But the wicked perish in darkness—
     For not by strength shall man prevail.

10   The foes of the LORD shall be shattered;
     He will thunder against them in the heavens.

8: *Dust* and *dunghill* are metaphorical for utter degradation. The earth was believed to be flat and resting upon pillars. **9:** *Not by strength,* but by the LORD's providence. **10:** *The ends of the earth,* all peoples, even the most remote ones. *His anointed one* (Heb "mashiah," from which comes the English word "messiah") denotes the king, since kings were anointed with oil. **11a:** See 1.19 n.

2.11b–36: Ascent versus descent. Samuel's ascent is contrasted with the descent of the house of Eli, both processes taking place simultaneously at the sanctuary of

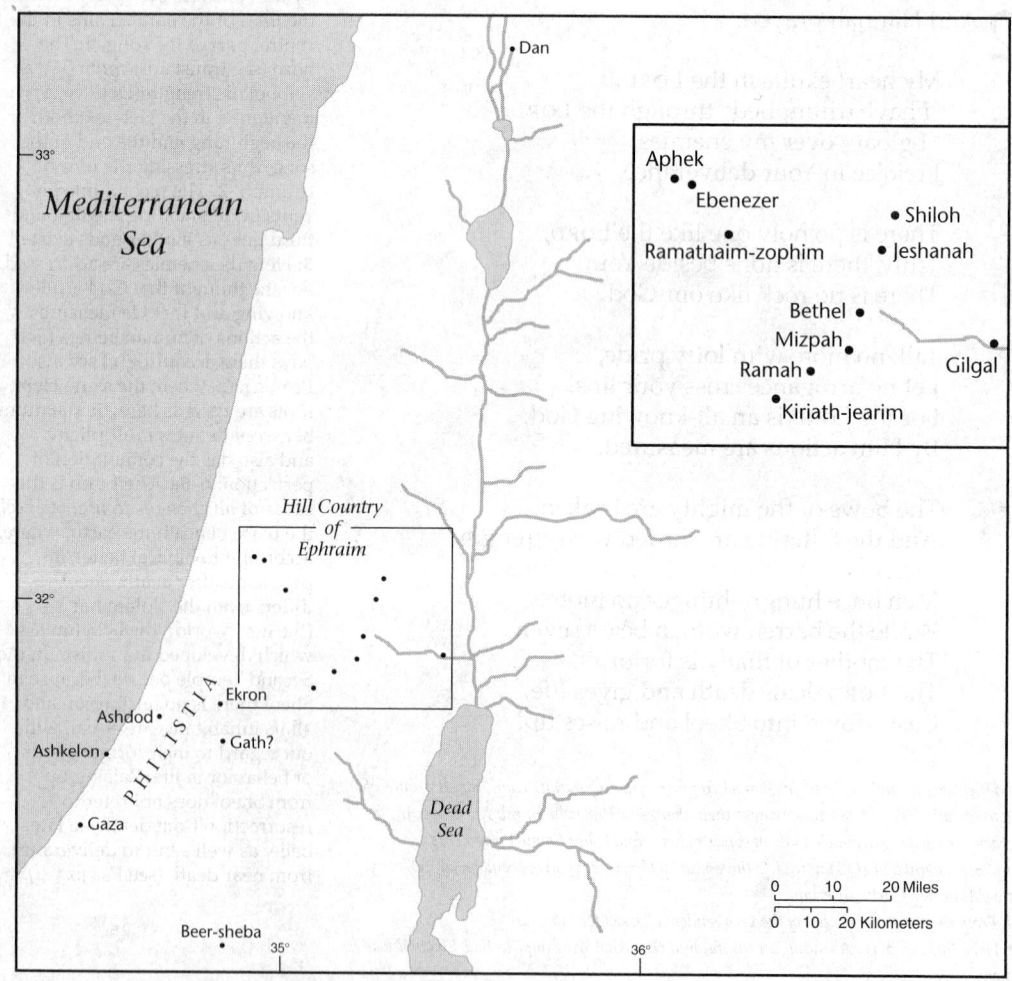

Mediterranean
Sea

33°

• Dan

Aphek
• •
    Ebenezer
•   • Shiloh
Ramathaim-zophim   • Jeshanah

                    Bethel •
                 Mizpah.
            Ramah •   Gilgal
               •
            Kiriath-jearim

Hill Country
of
Ephraim

32°

Ekron
Ashdod •
Ashkelon •   • Gath?

PHILISTIA

• Gaza

Dead
Sea

Beer-sheba
•   35°   36°

| 0 | 10 | 20 Miles |
| 0 | 10 | 20 Kilometers |

The activity of Samuel according to First Samuel

The LORD will judge the ends of the earth.
He will give power to His king,
ᵃ·And triumph to·ᵃ His anointed one.

11 Then Elkanahᵇ [and Hannah] went home to Ramah; and the boy entered the service of the LORD under the priest Eli.

12 Now Eli's sons were scoundrels; they paid no heed to the LORD. 13 This is how the priests used to deal with the people: When anyone brought a sacrifice, the priest's boy would come along with a three-pronged fork while the meat was boiling, 14 and he would thrust it into ᶜthe cauldron, or the kettle, or the great pot, or the small cooking-pot;ᶜ and whatever the fork brought up, the priest would take away ᵈ·on it.·ᵈ This was the practice at Shiloh with all the Israelites who came there. 15 [But now] even before the suet was turned into smoke, the priest's boy would come and say to the man who was sacrificing, "Hand over some meat to roast for the priest; for he won't accept boiled meat from you, only raw." 16 And if the man said to him, "Let them first turn the suet into smoke, and then take as much as you want," he would reply, "No, hand it over at once or I'll take it by force." 17 The sin of the young men against the LORD was very great, for the men treated the LORD's offerings impiously.

18 Samuel was engaged in the service of the LORD as an attendant, girded with a linen ephod. 19 His mother would also make a little robe for him and bring it up to him every year, when she made the pilgrimage with her husband to offer the annual sacrifice. 20 Eli would bless Elkanah and his wife, and say, "May the LORD grantᵉ you offspring by this woman in place of the loan she made to the LORD." Then they would return home. 21 Forᶠ the LORD took note of Hannah; she conceived and bore three sons and two daughters. Young Samuel meanwhile grew up in the service of the LORD.

22 Now Eli was very old. When he heard all that his sons were doing to all Israel, and how they lay with the women who ᵍ·performed tasks·ᵍ at the entrance of the Tent of Meeting, 23 he said to them, "Why do you do such things? I get evil reports about you from the people on all hands.

Shiloh. Most of the space is allotted to the house of Eli, so as to make it clear that leaders who abuse their office and exploit their people will not escape punishment. In the first part (vv. 12–17) the recurring sins of Eli's sons are described; the second part (vv. 22–25) tells of Eli's reprimands to them, which they ignore; and the third part (vv. 27–36) specifies the future punishment to the House of Eli. These parts alternate with short pieces of information about Samuel. **12:** The names of Eli's sons were mentioned at 1.3. It is unusual for a biblical narrator to judge the characters explicitly; here he does so because of the graveness of their sins (see also v. 17). *They paid no heed,* lit. "they did not know." **13–14:** These vv. can be interpreted as describing either an accepted, legitimate custom or sinful and greedy behavior (cf. Lev. 7.34; Deut. 18.3). **15–16:** The priest's boy would demand (raw) meat even before the suet was sacrificed to the LORD. He would also threaten to use force. **18–21:** The conclusion of the previous narrative (1.1–2.11a). An *ephod* is a garment worn by priests and fastened around the waist (see 22.18; 2 Sam. 6.14). **19:** The *little robe* Hannah made every year for Samuel symbolizes her enduring love for him. **20:** *By this woman,* excluding Peninnah. **22:** *And how they lay:* The sin of lying with these women (cf. Exod. 38.8) is mentioned neither before in the narrative nor afterwards by the man of God; in the Dead Sea manuscript 4QSamᵃ and Septuagint this part of the verse does not occur. The *Tent of Meeting* was so called because God used to meet there with Israel (see Exod. 29.42).

a-a Lit. "And will raise the horn of."

b See note e at 1.28.

c-c These vessels have not been distinguished precisely.

d-d Targum and Septuagint add "for himself."

e 4QSamᵃ and Septuagint read "repay."

f 4QSamᵃ reads "And."   g-g Meaning of Heb. uncertain.

24 Don't, my sons! It is no favorable report I hear the people of the LORD spreading about. 25 If a man sins against a man, the LORD may pardon[a] him; but if a man offends against God, who can [a]obtain pardon[-a] for him?" But they ignored their father's plea; for the LORD was resolved that they should die. 26 Young Samuel, meanwhile, grew in esteem and favor both with God and with men.

27 A man of God came to Eli and said to him, "Thus said the LORD: Lo, I revealed Myself to your father's house in Egypt when they were subject to the House of Pharaoh, 28 and I chose them from among all the tribes of Israel to be My priests—to ascend My altar, to burn incense, [and] to carry an ephod[b] before Me—and I assigned to your father's house all offerings by fire of the Israelites. 29 Why, then, do you [c]maliciously trample upon the sacrifices and offerings that I have commanded?[-c] You have honored your sons more than Me, feeding on the first portions of every offering of My people Israel.[d] 30 Assuredly—declares the LORD, the God of Israel—I intended for you and your father's house to remain in My service forever. But now—declares the LORD—far be it from Me! For I honor those who honor Me, but those who spurn Me shall be dishonored. 31 A time is coming when I will break your power and that of your father's house, and there shall be no elder in your house. 32 You will gaze grudgingly[e] at all the bounty that will be bestowed on Israel, but there shall never be an elder in your house. 33 [a]I shall not cut off all your offspring from My altar; [but,] to make your eyes pine and your spirit languish, all the increase in your house shall die as [ordinary] men.[-a] 34 And this shall be a sign for you: The fate of your two sons Hophni and Phinehas—they shall both die on the same day. 35 And I will raise up for Myself a faithful priest, who will act in accordance with My wishes and My purposes. I will build for him an enduring house, and he shall walk before My anointed evermore. 36 And all the survivors of your house shall come and bow low to him for the sake of a money fee and a loaf of bread, and shall say, 'Please, assign me to one of the priestly duties, that I may have a morsel of bread to eat.' "

23–25: Eli's rebuke is concerned with the reports the people spread about and the punishment threatening his sons rather than with their sins. *The LORD was resolved that they should die,* because they were confirmed in their sins (cf. God's hardening of Pharaoh's heart, Exod. 7.3–5). **26:** Samuel's reputation with both God and men is contrasted with that of Eli's sons. **27–36:** The prophecy about the downfall of the house of Eli contains three parts: the election of the house to the priesthood in the past; the abuse of its office in the present; the rejection of the house and the election of a new and faithful house in the future. The word "house," denoting family or dynasty, recurs ten times. It is not stated who will replace the house of Eli. **28:** For the three priestly duties enumerated here see Deut. 33.8–10. **31:** *And there shall be no elder in your house* is repeated in the next v.; in the Dead Sea manuscript 4QSam[a] and Septuagint these words do not occur in the present v. **33:** *Shall die as . . . men:* The Dead Sea manuscript 4QSam[a] and Septuagint read "shall fall by the sword of men." This may refer to the massacre of the priests of Nob (ch 22). **35:** *Faithful* and *enduring:* The Heb uses the same word, indicating that because the priest will be faithful, his house shall be enduring. Possibly the priest meant is Zadok, who replaced Abiathar, a descendant of Eli (1 Kings 2.26–27). *My anointed,* see v. 10 n.

---

a-a *Meaning of Heb. uncertain.*

b *Here a device for obtaining oracles (cf. 14.3; 23.6, 9–12), not a garment as in v. 18 above.*

c-c *Meaning of Heb. uncertain. Emendation yields "gaze [cf. Septuagint] grudgingly upon the sacrifices and offerings which I have commanded" (connecting* ma'on *with* 'oyen, *"keeping a jealous eye"; see 1 Sam. 18.9); cf. v. 32 and note e below.*

d *See vv. 15–16.*

e *Cf. note c-c above.*

3 Young Samuel was in the service of the Lord under Eli. In those days the word of the Lord was rare; prophecy was not widespread. ²One day, Eli was asleep in his usual place; his eyes had begun to fail and he could barely see. ³The lamp of God had not yet gone out, and Samuel was sleeping in the temple of the Lord where the Ark of God was. ⁴The Lord called out to Samuel, and he answered, "I'm coming." ⁵He ran to Eli and said, "Here I am; you called me." But he replied, "I didn't call you; go back to sleep." So he went back and lay down. ⁶Again the Lord called, "Samuel!" Samuel rose and went to Eli and said, "Here I am; you called me." But he replied, "I didn't call, my son; go back to sleep."—⁷Now Samuel had not yet experienced the Lord; the word of the Lord had not yet been revealed to him.—⁸The Lord called Samuel again, a third time, and he rose and went to Eli and said, "Here I am; you called me." Then Eli understood that the Lord was calling the boy. ⁹And Eli said to Samuel, "Go lie down. If you are called again, say, 'Speak, Lord, for Your servant is listening.'" And Samuel went to his place and lay down.

¹⁰The Lord came, and stood there, and He called as before: "Samuel! Samuel!" And Samuel answered, "Speak, for Your servant is listening." ¹¹The Lord said to Samuel: "I am going to do in Israel such a thing that both ears of anyone who hears about it will tingle. ¹²In that day I will fulfill against Eli all that I spoke concerning his house, from beginning to end. ¹³And I declare to him that I sentence his house to endless punishment for the iniquity he knew about—how his sons committed sacrilege ᵃ·at will·ᵃ—and he did not rebuke them. ¹⁴Assuredly, I swear concerning the house of Eli that the iniquity of the house of Eli will never be expiated by sacrifice or offering."

¹⁵Samuel lay there until morning; and then he opened the doors of the House of the Lord. Samuel was afraid to report the vision to Eli, ¹⁶but Eli summoned Samuel and said, "Samuel, my son"; and he answered, "Here." ¹⁷And

a-a Meaning of Heb. uncertain. Septuagint reads "against God."

3.1–4.1a: Revelation. God's revelation to Samuel, which elevates him to the rank of prophet, contains a second message of calamity to the house of Eli. The narrative consists of five parts: an introduction, dialogues between Eli and Samuel, the revelation (in the center), again dialogue between Eli and Samuel, and a conclusion.

1–3: The exposition supplies the background information. Because *the word of the Lord was rare* and *prophecy* (i.e., revelations) *was not widespread,* neither Samuel nor Eli recognizes at first who is calling. In this way an ironic situation is created (dramatic irony). Samuel, who waits upon the almost blind Eli, sleeps near the Ark of God

(from where God's voice is heard, see Exod. 25.22; Num. 7.89). *The lamp of God,* which used to burn from evening to morning (Exod. 27.20–21), *had not yet gone out*—so it is still night. *The Ark of God,* see 4.4 n. **4–9:** In his innocence and humility, it does not enter Samuel's mind that it is God who is calling to him. Though aware that he was mistaken before, he again and again gets up and goes to Eli. By repeating the situation with slight changes, the narrative builds dramatic tension. **6:** To reassure Samuel, Eli fondly adds *my son.* **7:** The v. is inserted at this particular point in order to explain why at the third call the inexperienced Samuel still does not understand who is calling, whereas Eli now realizes that it is the Lord. **10:** Samuel's state of awe causes him not to add "Lord" in his response, as Eli has instructed him to do. **11–14:** In the first half of the revelation God announces His intention to inflict dreadful calamities upon Israel and the house of Eli; in the second half He states the reason why He will do so and will not forgive them. Though repentance is a major theme in the Bible, not all sins may be forgiven. **11:** *Both ears . . . will tingle:* The figure refers to the shock felt at learning of a terrible disaster (see 2 Kings 21.12; Jer. 19.3). **12:** *All that I spoke,* through the man of God (2.27–36). **13:** According to Jewish tradition *at will* is a "scribes' emendation." Initially the Heb text read, "against God" (like Septuagint), but this was changed by the ancient scribes to avoid affronting His dignity. *Not rebuke,* rather, "not restrain." Eli did rebuke his sons (see 2.23–25), though insufficiently. **14:** *Sacrifice or offering* will not atone, as they were trampled upon (2.29). **15:** *He opened the doors:* In spite of his tremendous experience Samuel continues to carry out his daily duties as usual. He does not report the vision to Eli so as not to distress him. **16:** *My son . . . here:* Eli's address and Samuel's response are the same as in the previous night. **17:** *Thus and more* in a formula of adjuration refers to

[Eli] asked, "What did He say to you? Keep nothing from me. a-Thus and more may God do to you-a if you keep from me a single word of all that He said to you!" [18] Samuel then told him everything, withholding nothing from him. And [Eli] said, "He is the LORD; He will do what He deems right."

[19] Samuel grew up and the LORD was with him: He did not leave any of Samuel's[b] predictions unfulfilled. [20] All Israel, from Dan to Beer-sheba, knew that Samuel was trustworthy as a prophet of the LORD. [21] And the LORD continued to appear at Shiloh: the LORD revealed Himself to Samuel at Shiloh with the word of the LORD; [1] and Samuel's word went forth to all Israel.

4 [c]Israel marched out to engage the Philistines in battle; they encamped near Eben-ezer, while the Philistines encamped at Aphek. [2] The Philistines arrayed themselves against Israel; and when the battle was fought,[d] Israel was routed by the Philistines, who slew about four thousand men on the field of battle. [3] When the [Israelite] troops returned to the camp, the elders of Israel asked, "Why did the LORD put us to rout today before the Philistines? Let us fetch the Ark of the Covenant of the LORD from Shiloh; thus He will be present among us and will deliver us from the hands of our enemies." [4] So the troops sent men to Shiloh; there Eli's two sons, Hophni and Phinehas, were in charge of the Ark of the Covenant of God, and they brought down from there the Ark of the Covenant of the LORD of Hosts Enthroned on the Cherubim.

[5] When the Ark of the Covenant of the LORD entered the camp, all Israel burst into a great shout, so that the earth resounded. [6] The Philistines heard the noise of the shouting and they wondered, "Why is there such a loud shouting in the camp of the Hebrews?" And when they learned that the Ark of the LORD had come to the camp, [7] the Philistines were frightened; for they said, "God has come to the camp." And they cried, "Woe to us! Nothing like this

a-a A formula of adjuration.

b Heb. "his."

c Preceding this, Septuagint has "In those days, the Philistines gathered for war against Israel."

d Meaning of Heb. uncertain.

expression *from Dan to Beer-sheba* means from the northern to the southern limit of Israel (see Judg. 20.1). **21a:** The situation at the end of the story is opposed to that at the beginning (v. 1).

4.1b–22: Disaster. In chs 4–6 the Ark of the Covenant is the main subject, and Samuel is not mentioned at all. Ch 4 relates the capture of the Ark by the Philistines, the death of Eli's sons on one day (as predicted in 2.34), and the death of Eli himself. It consists of two parts: the first, located at Eben-ezer, tells of the battles between Israel and the Philistines; the second, at Shiloh, describes the events in the wake of the defeat. **1b:** The *Philistines*—from which the name Palestine was derived in the Hellenistic-Roman period— came from the area of the Aegean Sea and settled on the eastern Mediterranean coast about 1200 BCE. According to the Bible their origin was from Caphtor (Jer. 47.4; Amos 9.7), which is identified with Crete. Archeological excavations in the coastal cities have brought their material culture to light, but little is known of their spiritual culture. Having better fighting equipment, including chariots, they were militarily superior to Israel. **3:** It was not unusual to bring the Ark of the Covenant to the battlefield, as a physical sign of the presence of the LORD (see 2 Samuel 11.11). **4:** The *Ark of the Covenant* was a chest containing the Tablets of the Covenant between the LORD and Israel (Deut. 9.11; 10.5). It was the holiest object in the First Temple, but was absent from the Second Temple. The Ark served as a throne for the LORD of Hosts (= armies). On its cover were two *Cherubim*, probably creatures with the body of a lion or bull, the head of a human, and the wings of an eagle. In the ancient Near East such creatures used to flank royal thrones. **6:** *Hebrews* is the designation of the Israelites by foreigners and by themselves when talking to foreigners (e.g., Exod. 1.15–16, 19). **7–9:** Several voices are cited, mainly expressing fear and de-

harmful occurrences, which the adjurer shrinks from mentioning explicitly. **19–21; 4.1a:** These verses conclude the story. After the first revelation Samuel had many more, and since all his predictions came true, he was recognized as a *trustworthy* prophet (the Heb uses the same adjective rendered as "faithful" at 2.35), in accordance with the criterion of a true prophet in Deut. 18.22. **20:** The has ever happened before. [8] Woe to us! Who will save us from the power of this mighty God? He is the same God who struck the Egyptians with every kind of plague in the wilderness! [9] Brace yourselves and be men, O Philistines! Or you will become slaves to the Hebrews as they were slaves to you. Be men and fight!" [10] The Philistines fought; Israel was routed, and they all fled to their homes. The defeat was very great, thirty thousand foot soldiers of Israel fell there. [11] The Ark of God was captured, and Eli's two sons, Hophni and Phinehas, were slain.

[12] A Benjaminite ran from the battlefield and reached Shiloh the same day; his clothes were rent and there was earth on his head.[a] [13] When he arrived, he found Eli sitting on a seat, waiting beside the road—his heart trembling for the Ark of God. The man entered the city to spread the news, and the whole city broke out in a cry. [14] And when Eli heard the sound of the outcry and asked, "What is the meaning of this uproar?" the man rushed over to tell Eli. [15] Now Eli was ninety-eight years old; his eyes were fixed in a blind stare. [16] The man said to Eli, "I am the one who came from the battlefield; I have just fled from the battlefield." [Eli] asked, "What happened, my son?" [17] The bearer of the news replied, "Israel fled before the Philistines and the troops also suffered a great slaughter. Your two sons, Hophni and Phinehas, are dead, and the Ark of God has been captured." [18] When he mentioned the Ark of God, [Eli] fell backward off the seat beside[b] the gate, broke his neck and died; for he was an old man and heavy. He had been a chieftain of Israel for forty years.

a I.e., as a sign of mourning.   b Meaning of Heb. uncertain.

spair, but, finally, also encouragement. **8:** *God:* The Heb reads "gods" in the plural. The Philistines believe that the Hebrews, like themselves, worship many gods. They are also confused as to the location of the plagues of Egypt. **9:** *Be men,* brave (see 1 Kings 2.2). **10:** *Thirty thousand* seems exaggerated, but brings home the magnitude of the defeat. **11:** *The Ark of God was captured,* in keeping with the ancient custom of taking the statue of the god of the defeated people as booty. **12:** Rent clothes and earth on the head were signs of mourning (see 2 Samuel 1.2). **13:** *Trembling for the Ark of God,* more than for his sons. **17:** The bad news is conveyed in increasing order, seen from Eli's perspective. **18:** *The Ark of God,* see v. 13 n. *Forty years,* a round number (Judg. 3.11; 5.31; 8.28).

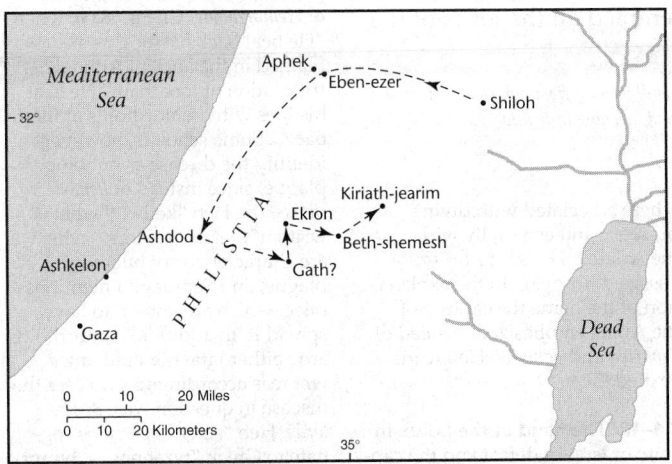

Wanderings of the Ark of the Covenant according to First Samuel

19 His daughter-in-law, the wife of Phinehas, was with child, about to give birth. When she heard the report that the Ark of God was captured and that her father-in-law and her husband were dead, she was seized with labor pains, and she crouched down and gave birth. 20 As she lay dying, the women attending her said, "Do not be afraid, for you have borne a son." But she did not respond or pay heed. 21 She named the boy Ichabod, meaning, "The glory has departed from Israel"—referring to the capture of the Ark of God and to [the death of] her father-in-law and her husband. 22 "The glory is gone from Israel," she said, "for the Ark of God has been captured."

5 When the Philistines captured the Ark of God, they brought it from Eben-ezer to Ashdod. 2 The Philistines took the Ark of God and brought it into the temple of Dagon and they set it up beside Dagon. 3 Early the next day, the Ashdodites found Dagon lying face down on the ground in front of the Ark of the LORD. They picked Dagon up and put him back in his place; 4 but early the next morning, Dagon was again lying prone on the ground in front of the Ark of the LORD. The head and both hands of Dagon were cut off, lying on the threshold; only a-Dagon's trunk was left intact.-a 5 That is why, to this day, the priests of Dagon and all who enter the temple of Dagon do not tread on the threshold of Dagon in Ashdod.

6 The hand of the LORD lay heavy upon the Ashdodites, and He wrought havoc among them: He struck b-Ashdod and its territory-b with hemorrhoids. 7 When the men of Ashdod saw how matters stood, they said, "The Ark of the God of Israel must not remain with us, for His hand has dealt harshly with us and with our god Dagon." 8 They sent messengers and assembled all the lords of the

a-a Meaning of Heb. uncertain.
b-b Meaning of Heb. uncertain. Septuagint reads differently from our Heb. text; it also mentions mice swarming in the Philistine ships and invading their fields. Cf. the mention of "mice" in 6.4, 18; and the note at 6.1.

19–22: The story of Eli's daughter-in-law shows another outcome of the disaster. The report of the calamities is again arranged in increasing order, but now from her perspective. **19:** *She crouched down,* the customary position for childbirth in ancient times. **21–22:** Names were usually given by the mothers. *Ichabod* means "no-glory," or "where is glory." Glory (Heb "kavod") is else-where associated with divine presence and especially with the Ark (e.g., Exod. 24.16–17; Pss. 24.7–10; 79.9). In the explanation of the name the capture of the Ark is emphasized. Instead of *departed* and *gone* the Heb reads "exiled."

5.1–12: The hand of the LORD. In spite of Israel's defeat and the capture of the Ark, the LORD's rule over the Philistines and His superiority to their god are evident and recognized by the Philistines themselves. The narrator takes no interest in the political and military consequences of their victory: their penetration into the heart of the country and the destruction of Shiloh and its sanctuary (see Jer. 7.12–14; Ps. 78.60). He is concerned only with their affliction by the *hand of the LORD* (which is mentioned four times in this ch and three times in the next). The recurrence of the situations in the temple of Dagon and in the Philistine towns shows that the described misfortunes did not happen accidentally. The narrative makes fun of the Philistines. **1:** *Ashdod,* one of the five cities of the Philistines. The others are Gaza, Gath, Ekron, and Ashkelon. **2:** *Dagon,* the Near Eastern god of grain, who was adopted by the Philistines. Placing war trophies in the sanctuary was not uncommon (see 21.10; 31.10). **3–5:** The description of Dagon lying face down on the ground before the Ark makes a mockery of the Philistine god; this is even more pronounced when the fallen god has also lost his head and hands. The mockery extends to the custom not to tread on the threshold because parts of the god have lain on it (cf. Zeph. 1.9). *To this day:* A temple of Dagon stood at Ashdod as late as the Maccabean period (1 Macc. 10.83–84; 11.4). **6:** *Hemorrhoids:* Cf. Ps. 78.66, where "He beat back his foes" is explained in the ancient Aramaic translation of Jonathan: "He beat his foes with hemorrhoids at their back." Some scholars, however, identify the disease as bubonic plague, since instead of *hemorrhoids,* the Heb "ketiv" ("what is written") reads "tumors," which are characteristic of bubonic plague, and Septuagint mentions mice, which are known to have spread it. In addition, hemorrhoids are neither fatal nor epidemic, whereas according to vv. 11–12 the disease in question was. **8:** *The lords,* Heb "seren" (perhaps cognate to Greek "tyrannos" = tyrant), the title of the five Philistine rulers.

Philistines and asked, "What shall we do with the Ark of the God of Israel?" They answered, "Let the Ark of the God of Israel be removed to Gath." So they moved the Ark of the God of Israel [to Gath]. ⁹ And after they had moved it, the hand of the LORD came against the city, causing great panic; He struck the people of the city, young and old, so that hemorrhoids ᵃ-broke out-ᵃ among them. ¹⁰ Then they sent the Ark of God to Ekron. But when the Ark of God came to Ekron, the Ekronites cried out, "They have moved the Ark of the God of Israel to us to slay us and our kindred." ¹¹ They too sent messengers and assembled all the lords of the Philistines and said, "Send the Ark of the God of Israel away, and let it return to its own place, that it may not slay us and our kindred." For the panic of death pervaded the whole city, so heavily had the hand of God fallen there; ¹² and the men who did not die were stricken with hemorrhoids. The outcry of the city went up to heaven.

6 The Ark of the LORD remained in the territory of the Philistines seven months.ᵇ ² Then the Philistines summoned the priests and the diviners and asked, "What shall we do about the Ark of the LORD? Tell us with what we shall send it off to its own place." ³ They answered, "If you are going to send the Ark of the God of Israel away, do not send it away without anything; you must also pay an indemnity to Him. Then you will be healed, and ᶜ-He will make Himself known to you; otherwise His hand will not turn away from you."-ᶜ ⁴ They asked, "What is the indemnity that we should pay to Him?" They answered, "Five golden hemorrhoids and five golden mice, corresponding to the number of lords of the Philistines; for the same plague struck all of youᵈ and your lords. ⁵ You shall make figures of your hemorrhoids and of the mice that are ravaging your land; thus you shall honor the God of Israel, and perhaps He will lighten the weight of His hand upon you and your gods and your land. ⁶ Don't harden your hearts as the Egyptians and Pharaoh hardened their hearts. As you know, when He made a mockery of them, they had to let Israelᵈ go, and they departed. ⁷ Therefore, get a new cart ready and two milch cows that have not borne a yoke; harness the cows to the cart, but take back indoors the calves that follow them. ⁸ Take the Ark of the

6.1–7.1: The Ark's return. The first part of the narrative, located at Ekron, tells about the Philistines' decision to return the Ark to its place; the second part, located at Beth-shemesh, describes the reaction of the people there to the Ark's arrival. **2:** As experts on matters of ritual and predicting the future, *the priests and the diviners* will know how to deal with the Ark. Soothsaying was characteristic of the Philistines according to Isa. 2.6. **3:** Instead of *He will make Himself known to you,* the Dead Sea manuscript 4QSamᵃ and Septuagint read "there will be atonement for you." *His hand:* See 5.1–12 n. **4–5:** The golden hemorrhoids and golden mice correspond to the nature of the plagues; they are a gift to *honor the God of Israel* and to appease Him. *The mice that are ravaging* the land by destroying the grain crops are a blow to Dagon, the god of grain (but see also 5.6 n.). *Upon you,* who are afflicted by disease, *and your gods,* who are deeply humiliated, *and your land,* which is ravaged by mice. **6:** The precedent of Egypt (see also 4.8) serves to convince those Philistines who, believing that their misfortunes happened by chance (see v. 9), are still unwilling to part with their precious trophy. **7:** As a mark of reverence for the Ark, the cart and the cows transporting it should not have been defiled by previous use. Cows were kept for work rather than for milk or meat; milch cows would have young calves and naturally be drawn to them.

a-a *Meaning of Heb. uncertain.*
b *Septuagint continues "and mice invaded their fields"; cf. vv. 4, 5, 18, and note at 5.6.*
c-c *Or "and you will know why His hand would not turn away from you." Meaning of Heb. uncertain.*
d *Heb. "them."*

LORD and place it on the cart; and put next to it in a chest the gold objects you are paying Him as indemnity. Send it off, and let it go its own way. ⁹ Then watch: If it goes up the road to Beth-shemesh, to His own territory, it was He who has inflicted this great harm on us. But if not, we shall know that it was not His hand that struck us; it just happened to us by chance."

¹⁰ The men did so. They took two milch cows and harnessed them to the cart, and shut up their calves indoors. ¹¹ They placed the Ark of the LORD on the cart together with the chest, the golden mice, and the figures of their hemorrhoids. ¹² The cows went straight ahead along the road to Beth-shemesh. They went along a single highroad, lowing as they went, and turning off neither to the right nor to the left; and the lords of the Philistines walked behind them as far as the border of Beth-shemesh.

¹³ The people of Beth-shemesh were reaping their wheat harvest in the valley. They looked up and saw the Ark, and they rejoiced ᵃwhen they saw [it].ᵃ ¹⁴ The cart came into the field of Joshua of Beth-shemesh and it stopped there. They split up the wood of the cart and presented the cows as a burnt offering to the LORD. A large stone was there; ¹⁵ and the Levites took down the Ark of the LORD and the chest beside it containing the gold objects and placed them on the large stone. Then the men of Beth-shemesh presented burnt offerings and other sacrifices to the LORD that day. ¹⁶ The five lords of the Philistines saw this and returned the same day to Ekron.

¹⁷ The following were the golden hemorrhoids that the Philistines paid as an indemnity to the LORD: For Ashdod, one; for Gaza, one; for Ashkelon, one; for Gath, one; for Ekron, one. ¹⁸ᵇAs for the golden mice, their number accorded with all the Philistine towns that belonged to the five lords—both fortified towns and unwalled ᶜvillages, as far asᶜ the great stoneᵈ on which the Ark of the LORD was set down, to this day, in the field of Joshua of Beth-shemesh.

¹⁹ [The LORD] struck at the men of Beth-shemesh because ᵉthey looked into the Ark of the LORD; He struck down seventy men among the people [and] fifty thousand men.ᵉ The people mourned, for He had inflicted a great slaughter upon the population. ²⁰ And the men of Beth-

12: *The cows went straight ahead,* as if they knew the way. *Lowing as they went,* better, "lowing continuously." This seemingly unimportant fact is mentioned in order to show the distress of the cows at being unable to follow their instinctive urge and return to their calves. **13:** Here the viewpoint of the narrative switches to Beth-shemesh, which was the nearest Israelite town. **15:** Only Levites, who had been consecrated to serve the LORD, were allowed to handle the Ark. **18:** Instead of *as far as the great stone,* read as a new sentence: "There still is the great stone" (requiring a small change in the Heb vocalization). **19:** The number *fifty thousand* is far too big for a little town like Beth-shemesh. Read only *seventy,* as in *Antiquities of the Jews* by Josephus. **20:** God's holiness is awesome—approaching the Ark, without being consecrated, involves peril of death (Num. 4.19–20). The Ark cannot return to Shiloh because the town has been destroyed (see 5.1–12 n.).

---

a-a *Septuagint reads "As they met it."*

b *Meaning of vv. 18 and 19 uncertain in part.*

c-c *Emendation yields "villages, as witness there is."*

d *Reading 'eben with some Heb. mss., Septuagint, and Targum, most mss. and editions* 'abel, *"meadow [?]."*

e-e *Force of Heb. uncertain.*

shemesh asked, "Who can stand in attendance on the LORD, this holy God? And to whom shall He go up from us?" 21 They sent messengers to the inhabitants of Kiriath-jearim to say, "The Philistines have sent back the Ark of the LORD. Come down and take it into your keeping."

7 1 The men of Kiriath-jearim came and took up the Ark of the LORD and brought it into the house of Abinadab on the hill; and they consecrated his son Eleazar to have charge of the Ark of the LORD.

2 A long time elapsed from the day that the Ark was housed in Kiriath-jearim, twenty years in all; and all the House of Israel *-yearned after-* the LORD. 3 And Samuel said to all the House of Israel, "If you mean to return to the LORD with all your heart, you must remove the alien gods and the Ashtaroth from your midst and direct your heart to the LORD and serve Him alone. Then He will deliver you from the hands of the Philistines." 4 And the Israelites removed the Baalim and Ashtaroth and they served the LORD alone.

5 Samuel said, "Assemble all Israel at Mizpah, and I will pray to the LORD for you." 6 They assembled at Mizpah, and they drew water and poured it out before the LORD; they fasted that day, and there they confessed that they had sinned against the LORD. And Samuel acted as chieftain of the Israelites at Mizpah.

7 When the Philistines heard that the Israelites had assembled at Mizpah, the lords of the Philistines marched out against Israel. Hearing of this, the Israelites were terrified of the Philistines 8 and they implored Samuel, "Do not neglect us and do not refrain from crying out to the LORD our God to save us from the hands of the Philistines." 9 Thereupon Samuel took a suckling lamb and sacrificed it as a whole burnt offering to the LORD; and Samuel cried out to the LORD in behalf of Israel, and the LORD responded to him. 10 For as Samuel was presenting the burnt offering and the Philistines advanced to attack Israel, the LORD thundered mightily against the Philistines that day. He threw them into confusion, and they were routed by Israel. 11 The men of Israel sallied out of Mizpah and pursued the Philistines, striking them down to a point below Beth-car.

12 Samuel took a stone and set it up between Mizpah

a-a Meaning of Heb. uncertain.

7.2–17: The spiritual leader. After the Ark narrative, in which Samuel was not mentioned at all, the present narrative again focuses on him. Samuel is the last of the judges, but unlike most of his predecessors, he does not deliver Israel from its enemies by military means. His leadership is religious and judicial. The narrative demonstrates that if Israel gets rid of its idols and serves the LORD alone, it will overcome its enemies and live in peace. **2:** *Twenty years,* half a generation. This number fits the chronology of the book of Judges, which is based on periods of forty years, but also twenty and eighty years. **3–4:** *Ashtaroth* (plural), images of Ashtoreth, the main Canaanite goddess (of fertility and love). *Baalim* (plural), images of Baal, the god of heaven and earth, who was the head of the Canaanite pantheon. The removal of foreign deities is also mentioned in Gen. 35.2–4; Josh. 24.23; Judg. 10.16. **5:** There was probably a religious center at *Mizpah,* where the community used to assemble before the LORD (see Judg. 20.1; 1 Sam. 10.17). Samuel, who later became renowned for his success in praying (Jer. 15.1; Ps. 99.6), will beseech the LORD to forgive Israel its sins and deliver them from the Philistines. **6:** The ritual of pouring out water is mentioned nowhere else in the Bible. In the Second Temple period water was poured out on the festival of Sukkot, probably as a request for rain. But here it is done as a request for remission of sins, just as are the prayer, fasting, and confession. Instead of *acted as chieftain,* which suggests a connection to the preceding book of Judges, the Heb may be translated "acted as magistrate" (cf. Moses sitting as magistrate, Exod. 18.13). **9:** According to Jewish traditional interpretation sacrifice was permitted everywhere before there was a central sanctuary. Modern scholarship, however, holds that sacrifice outside the central sanctuary became prohibited only when the law of Deuteronomy, demanding centralization of the cult, was introduced during the reign of King Josiah (640–609 BCE). See notes to Deut. ch 12. **10:** *Thundered:* The LORD uses the forces of nature to help Israel (cf. Judg. 5.20–21). **12:** The recurrence of the name *Eben-ezer* (see 4.1) points to the reversal in the situation: then defeat by the and Shen,[a] and named it Eben-ezer:[b] "For up to now," he said, "the LORD has helped us." 13 The Philistines were humbled and did not invade the territory of Israel again; and the hand of the LORD was set against the Philistines as long as Samuel lived. 14 The towns which the Philistines had taken from Israel, from Ekron to Gath, were restored to Israel; Israel recovered all her territory from the Philistines. There was also peace between Israel and the Amorites.

15 Samuel judged Israel as long as he lived. 16 Each year he made the rounds of Bethel, Gilgal, and Mizpah, and acted as judge over Israel at all those places. 17 Then he would return to Ramah, for his home was there, and there too he would judge Israel. He built an altar there to the LORD.

8 When Samuel grew old, he appointed his sons judges over Israel. 2 The name of his first-born son was Joel, and his second son's name was Abijah; they sat as judges in Beer-sheba. 3 But his sons did not follow in his ways; they were bent on gain, they accepted bribes, and they subverted justice.

4 All the elders of Israel assembled and came to Samuel at Ramah, 5 and they said to him, "You have grown old, and your sons have not followed your ways. Therefore appoint a king for us, to govern us like all other nations." 6 Samuel was displeased that they said "Give us a king to govern us." Samuel prayed to the LORD, 7 and the LORD replied to Samuel, "Heed the demand of the people in everything they say to you. For it is not you that they have rejected; it is Me they have rejected as their king. 8 Like everything else they have done ever since I brought them out of Egypt to this day—forsaking Me and worshiping other gods—so they are doing to you. 9 Heed their demand; but warn them solemnly, and tell them about the practices of any king who will rule over them."

a *Otherwise unknown; perhaps identical with "Jeshanah"; cf. Septuagint; also 2 Chron.* 13.19.
b *I.e., "Stone of Help."*

Philistines, now victory over them (after Israel's return to the LORD). **13:** *The hand of the LORD:* See 5.1–12 n. Contrary to the statement here, which aims at glorifying Samuel, in the ensuing narratives Israel is still in the hands of the Philistines, even in Samuel's lifetime (e.g., 9.16). On the subject of contradictions in the book, see

intro. **14:** *Amorites* is a general designation of the inhabitants of Canaan before the Israelite conquest. Many Amorites remained in the country after the conquest. **15–17:** In order to facilitate the administration of justice Samuel makes yearly rounds of the towns in the central region of the country, going out to the people

instead of requiring them to come to him.

Chs 8–12: The foundation of the monarchy. No less than five chs are devoted to the foundation of the monarchy, which shows the importance attached to the subject. Their attitude towards kingship is not uniform—in chs 8, 10.17–27, and 12 it is negative, in the other chs positive. This reflects ancient controversy concerning the merits of kingship. In biblical scholarship the difference is usually explained by assuming different sources: The pro-monarchic chs 9.1–10.16 and 11 are believed to belong to an older source, the anti-monarchic chs 8, 10.17–27 and 12 to a later one. The materials are arranged artistically: The first and last chs, 8 and 12, contain speeches by Samuel, the second and penultimate ones (9.1–10.16 and 11.1–13) embody narratives having Saul as protagonist, and the middle section (10.17–27) recounts the election of Saul as king.

8.1–22: The request for a king. This narrative is concerned with the advantages and disadvantages of the monarchy. The people desire a strong, centralized government, whereas Samuel warns against the king's violation of individual rights and liberty. God, though disapproving, yields to the wish of the people. The first part of the narrative recounts the people's request, Samuel's appeal to God, and God's reply; the central part contains the "king's practice"; and the last part again tells of the people's request, Samuel's appeal to God and God's reply. **1–3:** Background information regarding the people's request. Like Eli, Samuel is old and his sons are corrupt and unworthy to succeed him. **5:** Cf. Deut. 17.14. In both places it is the example of the nations that appeals to the people. **7:** God's kingship is presumed to be conflicting with human kingship. For God's kingship, see Exod. 15.18; Judg. 8.23. **8:** Just as the people were always ungrateful to God, so they are now to Samuel.

[10] Samuel reported all the words of the LORD to the people, who were asking him for a king. [11] He said, "This will be the practice of the king who will rule over you: He will take your sons and appoint them as his charioteers and horsemen, and they will serve as outrunners for his chariots. [12] He will appoint them as his chiefs of thousands and of fifties; or they will have to plow his fields, reap his harvest, and make his weapons and the equipment for his chariots. [13] He will take your daughters as perfumers, cooks, and bakers. [14] He will seize your choice fields, vineyards, and olive groves, and give them to his courtiers. [15] He will take a tenth part of your grain and vintage and give it to his eunuchs and courtiers. [16] He will take your male and female slaves, your choice [a]young men,[a] and your asses, and put them to work for him. [17] He will take a tenth part of your flocks, and you shall become his slaves. [18] The day will come when you cry out because of the king whom you yourselves have chosen; and the LORD will not answer you on that day."

[19] But the people would not listen to Samuel's warning. "No," they said. "We must have a king over us, [20] that we may be like all the other nations: Let our king rule over us and go out at our head and fight our battles." [21] When Samuel heard all that the people said, he reported it to the LORD. [22] And the LORD said to Samuel, "Heed their demands and appoint a king for them." Samuel then said to the men of Israel, "All of you go home."

9 There was a man of Benjamin whose name was Kish son of Abiel son of Zeror son of Becorath son of Aphiah, a Benjaminite, a man of substance. [2] He had a son whose name was Saul, an excellent young man; no one among the Israelites was handsomer than he; [b]he was a head taller[b] than any of the people.

[3] Once the asses of Saul's father Kish went astray, and Kish said to his son Saul, "Take along one of the servants and go out and look for the asses." [4] He passed into the hill country of Ephraim. He crossed the district of Shalishah, but they did not find them. They passed through the

---

a-a Septuagint reads "cattle."   *b-b Lit. "taller from his shoulders up."*

11–17: The "king's practice" is based on the reality of the ancient Near East, in accordance with the people's request to have a king "like all other nations" (v. 5). It is not meant to enumerate the rights of the king in Israel, but to deter the people from desiring one. The king will load a heavy burden upon all individuals—unlike the existing regime, which rarely interfered with personal life. He will *take*—Samuel repeats this verb many times—their sons to the army, impose corvée (forced labor) upon their sons and daughters, confiscate their lands, levy taxes, and use their property. **11:** *Outrunners* served as bodyguards to the king (see 22.17). **12:** *Chiefs of thousands and of fifties,* cf. Exod. 18.21, 25, where also hundreds and tens are mentioned. **15:** The Heb word translated *eunuchs* can also mean "high officials," which better suits the context. **17:** *Slaves:* As a result of the foregoing the citizens will lose their freedom. **18:** Instead of crying out because of their enemies (Judg. 3.9, 15; 6.6–7; 10.10) they will cry out because of their king, and God who answered their cry in the past will then refrain from answering them. **20:** The people want a king to rule the country in times of peace and lead the army in times of war. *Go out at our head* is a military term (see 18.13). **22:** Because of Samuel's objection the LORD reiterates His command (v. 7), adding explicitly that Samuel appoint a king. Samuel, however, not eager to execute the order, does not transmit this to the people, but tells them to go home.

9.1–10.16: The anointing. The story of the young man who went to search for lost asses and found a kingdom is told vividly. Everything happens in a natural way, yet, as elsewhere in the Bible (see esp. the Joseph story in Genesis), God's directing the course of events is manifested in the "accidental" occurrences. Only thanks to his persevering servant—and against his own intention—does Saul happen to get to Samuel's town, and only thanks to the chance encounter with some girls does he enter the town at the precise moment when Samuel comes out, thus meeting the prophet who will anoint him. The first part of the narrative describes Saul's journey up to his arrival at Samuel's town, the second part tells of the encounter between the two men and of Saul's anointing, and the third part recounts Saul's way back home. The narrative gives a first glimpse of Saul's character before he becomes king. **1–2:** The exposition provides details about the hero. Regarding the list of ances-

The kingdom of Saul according to the book of Samuel. The dashed line shows the approximate outer boundary of his kingdom.

district of Shaalim, but they were not there. They traversed the [entire] territory of Benjamin, and still they did not find them. ⁵When they reached the district of Zuph, Saul said to the servant who was with him, "Let us turn back, or my father will stop worrying about the asses and begin to worry about us." ⁶But he replied, "There is a man of God in that town, and the man is highly esteemed; everything that he says comes true. Let us go there; perhaps he will tell us about the errand on which we set out." ⁷"But if we go," Saul said to his servant, "what can we bring the man? For the food in our bags is all gone, and there is nothing we can bring to the man of God as a present. What have we got?" ⁸The servant answered Saul again, "I happen to have a quarter-shekel of silver. I can give that to the man of God and he will tell us about our errand."—⁹ᵃFormerly in Israel, when a man went to inquire of God, he would say, "Come, let us go to the seer," for the prophet of today was formerly called a seer.—¹⁰Saul said to his servant, "A good idea; let us go." And they went to the town where the man of God lived.

¹¹As they were climbing the ascent to the town, they met some girls coming out to draw water, and they asked them, "Is the seer in town?" ¹²"Yes," they replied. "He is up there ahead of you. ᵇHurry, for he has just come to the town·ᵇ because the people have a sacrifice at the shrine today. ¹³As soon as you enter the town, you will find him before he goes up to the shrine to eat; the people will not eat until he comes; for he must first bless the sacrifice and only then will the guests eat. Go up at once, for you will find him right away." ¹⁴So they went up to the town; and as they were entering the town,ᶜ Samuel came out toward them, on his way up to the shrine.

¹⁵Now the day before Saul came, the LORD had revealed the following to Samuel: ¹⁶"At this time tomorrow, I will send a man to you from the territory of Benjamin, and you shall anoint him ruler of My people Israel. He will deliver My people from the hands of the Philistines; for I have taken note of ᵈMy people,ᵈ their outcry has come to Me."

¹⁷As soon as Samuel saw Saul, the LORD declared to him, "This is the man that I told you would govern My people." ¹⁸Saul approached Samuel inside the gate and

tors cf. 1.1. *Benjamin,* the land of the tribe of Benjamin. **5:** *Zuph,* Samuel's home district (1.1). **6:** *That town,* Ramah. **7:** It was customary to bring some food or presents when making inquiries of a prophet concerning the future or other hidden matters (see 1 Kings 14.3; 2 Kings 8.8–9; Ezek. 13.19). **8:** Were it not for the *quarter-shekel* (a measure of weight, approximately 2.5 gram or a little less than 0.1 oz.) *of silver* the servant happened to possess, Saul and Samuel would not have met. **9:** This explanatory note, which separates Saul's reply from the servant's proposal, is inserted here in order to explain the term "seer" in v. 11 and to provide the background for the expression "come, let us go" (so in the Heb), used by Saul in v. 10. **11:** The source of water was downhill outside the town. **12–13:** Several voices of the girls can be distinguished, all eager to supply more information than asked for. Samuel has come to the town from one of his circuits (7.16–17). Regarding the sacrifice, see 7.9 n. **15–16:** The revelation shows that the "accidental" occurrences were guided by God. The term *ruler* ("nagid") designates in the book of Samuel a governor who is appointed by God, whereas "king" ("melekh") connotes nomination by the people. The repetitions of *My people* here and in v. 17 indicate God's affectionate relationship with Israel. *Their outcry has come to Me,* cf. Exod. 3.9.

a This verse explains the term "seer" in v. 11.

b-b Emendation yields "Hurry, for he has just reached ('attah kayyom ba, so Septuagint) the gate"; cf. v. 18.

c Emendation yields "gate"; cf. v. 18.

d-d Septuagint and Targum read "the plight of My people"; cf. Exod. 3.7.

said to him, "Tell me, please, where is the house of the seer?" 19 And Samuel answered Saul, "I am the seer. Go up ahead of me to the shrine, for you shall eat with me today; and in the morning I will let you go, after telling you whatever may be on your mind. 20 As for your asses that strayed three days ago, do not concern yourself about them, for they have been found. And for whom is all Israel yearning, if not for you and all your ancestral house?" 21 Saul replied, "But I am only a Benjaminite, from the smallest of the tribes of Israel, and my clan is the least of all the clans of the tribe*a* of Benjamin! Why do you say such things to me?"

22 Samuel took Saul and his servant and brought them into the hall, and gave them a place at the head of the guests, who numbered about thirty. 23 And Samuel said to the cook, "Bring the portion which I gave you and told you to set aside." 24 The cook lifted up the thigh and *b*-what was on it,*b* and set it before Saul. And [Samuel] said, *c*-"What has been reserved is set before you. Eat; it has been kept for you for this occasion, when I said I was inviting the people."*c* So Saul ate with Samuel that day. 25 They then descended from the shrine to the town, and *d*-[Samuel] talked with Saul on the roof.

26 Early, at*d* the break of day, Samuel called to Saul on the roof. He said, "Get up, and I will send you off." Saul arose, and the two of them, Samuel and he, went outside. 27 As they were walking toward the end of the town, Samuel said to Saul, "Tell the servant to walk ahead of us"—and he walked ahead—"but you stop here a moment and I will make known to you the word of God."

10 Samuel took a flask of oil and poured some on Saul's*e* head and kissed him, and said, "The LORD herewith *f*-anoints you ruler*f* over His own people. 2 When you leave me today, you will meet two men near the tomb of Rachel in the territory of Benjamin, *c*-at Zelzah,*c* and they will tell you that the asses you set out to look for have been found, and that your father has stopped being concerned about the asses and is worrying about you, saying:

a Heb. plural.

b-b Meaning of Heb. uncertain. Emendation yields "the broad tail."

c-c Meaning of Heb. uncertain.

d-d Meaning of Heb. uncertain. Septuagint reads "They spread a bed for Saul on the roof, and he lay down. At . . ."

e Heb. "his."

f-f Septuagint and Vulgate read "anoints you ruler over His people Israel, and you will govern the people of the LORD and deliver them from the hands of their foes roundabout. And this is the sign for you that the LORD anoints you."

19–20: With each utterance Samuel's answer becomes more astonishing to Saul. *For whom is all Israel yearning,* "hinting to him concerning the kingship" (Rashi). **21:** Saul's reply testifies to his modesty (cf. Gideon's reply, Judg. 6.15). **22–24:** Saul and his servant are the guests of honor. The reservation of the thigh (the best part) for Saul shows that he was expected. **25–26:** The reading of Septuagint (see translators' note d–d) is preferable. People used to sleep on the flat roofs of their homes because of the heat inside. **27:** Saul's anointing must be kept secret because of the Philistines. **10.1:** Anointing effected consecration to office in the name of God (initially it symbolized purification). The king was also designated "the LORD's anointed" (e.g., 24.7; 26.9). **2–6:** The three signs are to convince Saul of the truth of Samuel's words and to persuade him that he will indeed be king. **2:** The tradition that the tomb of Rachel, the ancestress of Saul's tribe Benjamin, was located near Ramah in Benjaminite territory contradicts the tradition that it was near Bethlehem (Gen. 35.19), but is corroborated by Jer. 31.15. **3–4:** From the items intended for the sanctuary of Bethel two loaves of bread will be given to Saul, whose food has run out (9.7). **5:** *The Hill of God* (Gibeah of God) is also called Gibeah of Saul, Gibeah of Benjamin, or just Gibeah. Music served to induce a state of ecstasy (see 2 Kings 3.15). The ecstatic, communal prophets were essentially different from the later literary prophets. **6:** *The spirit of the LORD* manifests itself in some exceptional ability, like prophesying or leadership. **8:** Samuel informs Saul of their relationship right from the beginning: The king is subordinate to the prophet and must follow his instructions. **9:** *Another heart,* another personality. From a simple, diffident peasant Saul is transformed into a charismatic leader. **10–12:** The episode demonstrates that Saul has become *another man* (v. 6). **11:** Here *son of Kish* is not necessar-

'What shall I do about my son?' ³ You shall pass on from there until you come to the terebinth of Tabor. There you will be met by three men making a pilgrimage to God at Bethel. One will be carrying three kids, another will be carrying three loaves of bread, and the third will be carrying a jar of wine. ⁴ They will greet you and offer you two loaves of bread, which you shall accept. ⁵ After that, you are to go on to ᵃthe Hill⁻ᵃ of God, where the Philistine prefects reside. There, as you enter the town, you will encounter a band of prophets coming down from the shrine, preceded by lyres, timbrels, flutes, and harps, and they will be ᵇ⁻speaking in ecstasy.⁻ᵇ ⁶ The spirit of the LORD will grip you, and you will speak in ecstasy along with them; you will become another man. ⁷ And once these signs have happened to you, ᶜ⁻act when the occasion arises,⁻ᶜ for God is with you. ⁸ After that, you are to go down to Gilgal ahead of me, and I will come down to you to present burnt offerings and offer sacrifices of well-being. Wait seven days until I come to you and instruct you what you are to do next."

⁹ As [Saul] turned around to leave Samuel, God gave him another heart; and all those signs were fulfilled that same day. ¹⁰ And when they came there, to ᵃthe Hill,⁻ᵃ he saw a band of prophets coming toward him. Thereupon the spirit of God gripped him, and he spoke in ecstasy among them. ¹¹ When all who knew him previously saw him speaking in ecstasy together with the prophets, the people said to one another, "What's happened to ᵈ⁻the son of Kish?⁻ᵈ Is Saul too among the prophets?" ¹² But another person there spoke up and said, "And who are their fathers?" Thus the proverb arose: "Is Saul too among the prophets?" ¹³ And when he stopped speaking in ecstasy, he entered the shrine.

¹⁴ Saul's uncle asked him and his servant, "Where did you go?" "To look for the asses," he replied. "And when we saw that they were not to be found, we went to Samuel." ¹⁵ "Tell me," said Saul's uncle, "what did Samuel say to you?" ¹⁶ Saul answered his uncle, "He just told us that the asses had been found." But he did not tell him anything of what Samuel had said about the kingship.

¹⁷ Samuel summoned the people to the LORD at Mizpah ¹⁸ and said to them, "Thus said the LORD, the God of Is-

ily slighting (contrast translators' note *d-d*). Kish is a well-known and prosperous citizen, and his son's conduct arouses astonishment. **12:** *And who are their fathers,* a disdainful rhetorical question. The other prophets do not come from distinguished families like Saul, which makes his affiliation with them even more astonishing. *"Is Saul too among the prophets?"* The proverb, whose origin is explained differently at 19.24, expresses surprise at a person who engages in something foreign to him or associates with people unlike himself. **16:** The last sentence may also be translated: "But he did not tell him anything about the kingship, as Samuel had said." In compliance with Samuel's instructions Saul keeps the kingship a secret, even from his close relatives.

10.17–27: The election. The people, convened by Samuel, acclaim—now openly—the king chosen by the LORD. Samuel again expresses his objection to the monarchy, but he does not object to Saul as a person, deeming him most suitable for the office. **17:** On *Mizpah* see 7.5 n. **18–19:** The people are ungrateful. In demanding a king they are rejecting their God (cf. 8.7), who has always saved them.

a-a *Or "Gibeah."*
b-b *Others "prophesying"; cf. Num. 11.25 and note.*
c-c *See 11.5–13.*
d-d *To refer to a person merely as "the son (ben) of . . ." is slighting; cf. 20.27, 30, 31; Isa. 7.4.*

rael: 'I brought Israel out of Egypt, and I delivered you from the hands of the Egyptians and of all the kingdoms that oppressed you.' 19 But today you have rejected your God who delivered you from all your troubles and calamities. For you said, 'No,ª set up a king over us!' Now station yourselves before the LORD, by your tribes and clans."

20 Samuel brought forward each of the tribes of Israel, and the lot indicated the tribe of Benjamin. 21 Then Samuel brought forward the tribe of Benjamin by its clans, and the clan of the Matrites was indicated; and thenᵇ Saul son of Kish was indicated. But when they looked for him, he was not to be found. 22 They inquired of the LORD again, ᶜ"Has anyone else come here?"⁻ᶜ And the LORD replied, "Yes; he is hiding among the baggage." 23 So they ran over and brought him from there; and when he took his place among the people, he stood a head taller than all the people. 24 And Samuel said to the people, "Do you see the one whom the LORD has chosen? There is none like him among all the people." And all the people acclaimed him, shouting, "Long live the king!"

25 Samuel expounded to the people the rules of the monarchy, and recorded them in a document which he deposited before the LORD. Samuel then sent the people back to their homes. 26 Saul also went home to Gibeah, accompanied by ᵈupstanding men⁻ᵈ whose hearts God had touched. 27 But some scoundrels said, "How can this fellow save us?" So they scorned him and brought him no gift. ᵉBut he pretended not to mind.⁻ᵉ

11 Nahash the Ammonite marched up and besieged Jabesh-gilead. All the men of Jabesh-gilead said to Nahash, "Make a pact with us, and we will serve you." 2 But Nahash the Ammonite answered them, "I will make a pact with you on this condition, that everyone's right eye be gouged out; I will make this a humiliation for all Is-

---

a So many Heb. mss. and ancient versions. Other mss. and editions read "to Him."

b Septuagint reads "then he brought up the family of the Matrites by their men and . . ."

c-c Septuagint reads "Has the man come here?"

d-d In contrast to "scoundrels" (v. 27); understanding Heb. ḥayil as the equivalent of bene ḥayil, as read by Septuagint and 4QSamª.

e-e Lit. "But he was as one who holds his peace." Septuagint and 4QSamª read "About a month later," connecting with what follows.

---

the king" marks the acclamation of the king by the people and was part of the coronation ceremony (cf. 2 Samuel 16.16; 1 Kings 1.25, 39; 2 Kings 11.12). **25:** The expression *rules of the monarchy* is in the Heb almost identical to "practice of the king" (8.11). This probably indicates that Samuel repeats and records his previous account of the practice of the king (8.11–17) as a warning and witness for the future (cf. Deut. 31.19–21). But it is also possible that those rules laid down the rights and duties of the monarch, though in that case the narrator would probably have reproduced them. *Before the LORD,* in the sanctuary. **26–27:** Two extreme reactions to Saul's election are recounted: on the one hand warm support from "upstanding men," on the other, scorn from "scoundrels," who do not believe in his ability to help. *This fellow* (lit. "this one"), a contemptuous phrase.

11.1–13: Deliverance. This story demonstrates Saul's ability to assume leadership and help his countrymen. Saul is depicted here after the model of the judges: The spirit of God grips him, he gathers the people, leads them to victory, and delivers them from the neighboring people that oppressed them. The first part of the narrative is located east of the Jordan at Jabesh-gilead, the second part west of the Jordan, mainly at Gibeah, and the third part again east of the Jordan at Jabesh-gilead (see map, p. 576). At the beginning of the narrative the Dead Sea manuscript 4QSamª and Josephus have an additional passage, which supplies the background to the story. The passage relates that Nahash, king of the Ammonites, oppressed the Gadites and the Reubenites, gouging out the right eye of each of them, but 7,000 men escaped and came to Jabesh-gilead. **1:** The Ammonites, who lived east of the Jordan, clashed with the Israelite tribes settled there (Judg. 10.6–11.33). **2:** Gouging out eyes was considered deeply humiliating (Judg. 16.21; 2 Kings 25.7). **4:** Gibeah belonged to Benjamin, and

---

20–21: Finding someone by lot proceeded by narrowing down: First the person's tribe was indicated, then the clan, then the family, and finally the person himself

(cf. Josh. 7.14). **22:** According to Radak, Saul is *hiding among the baggage,* because "he shunned authority." **23:** *A head taller than all the people,* cf. 9.2. **24:** The cry *"Long live* rael." ³ The elders of Jabesh said to him, "Give us seven days' respite, so that we may send messengers throughout the territory of Israel; if no one comes to our aid, we will surrender to you." ⁴ When the messengers came to Gibeah of Saul and gave this report in the hearing of the people, all the people broke into weeping.

⁵ Saul was just coming from the field driving the cattle; and Saul asked, "Why are the people crying?" And they told him about the situation of the men of Jabesh. ⁶ When he heard these things, the spirit of God gripped Saul and his anger blazed up. ⁷ He took a yoke of oxen and cut them into pieces, which he sent by messengers throughout the territory of Israel, with the warning, "Thus shall be done to the cattle of anyone who does not follow Saul and Samuel into battle!" Terror from the LORD fell upon the people, and they came out as one man. ⁸ [Saul] mustered them in Bezek, and the Israelites numbered 300,000, the men of Judah 30,000. ⁹ The messengers who had come were told, "Thus shall you speak to the men of Jabesh-gilead: Tomorrow, when the sun grows hot, you shall be saved." When the messengers came and told this to the men of Jabesh-gilead, they rejoiced. ¹⁰ The men of Jabesh then told [the Ammonites], "Tomorrow we will surrender to you, and you can do to us whatever you please."

¹¹ The next day, Saul divided the troops into three columns; at the morning watch they entered the camp and struck down the Ammonites until the day grew hot. The survivors scattered; no two were left together.

¹² The people then said to Samuel, "Who was it said, 'Shall Saul be king over us?' Hand the men over and we will put them to death!" ¹³ But Saul replied, "No man shall be put to death this day! For this day the LORD has brought victory to Israel."

¹⁴ Samuel said to the people, "Come, let us go to Gilgal and there inaugurate the monarchy." ¹⁵ So all the people went to Gilgal, and there at Gilgal they declared Saul king before the LORD. They offered sacrifices of well-being there before the LORD; and Saul and all the men of Israel held a great celebration there.

12 Then Samuel said to all Israel, "I have yielded to you in all you have asked of me and have set a king over you. ² Henceforth the king will be your leader.

"As for me, I have grown old and gray—but my sons are still with you—and I have been your leader from my youth to this day. ³ Here I am! Testify against me, in the presence of the LORD and in the presence of His anointed

members of that tribe were related to the people of Jabesh (Judg. 21.14). **5:** Saul, not yet inaugurated king, still works in the field. **6:** *The spirit of God,* see 10.6 n. and cf. Judg. 6.34; 11.29; 14.6, 19; 15.14. **7:** Military service was not compulsory, but Saul, with violent threats, manages to recruit the people. For a similar act, also performed at Gibeah, see Judg. 19.29. **8:** Israel and Judah are thought of as different entities. David united them, but after Solomon they divided into two separate states. **10:** *We will surrender to you,* lit. "we will come out to you." This is understood by the Ammonites as "we will surrender," but meant by the people of Jabesh as "we will fight." **11:** During *the morning watch,* the last of the three watches into which the night was divided, sleep is deepest. Saul attacks from three directions (cf. Gideon's tactic, Judg. 7.16ff.). **12–13:** *Who was it said* refers to 10.27. After Saul's imposing victory opposition is tolerated no more, but Saul himself is prepared to forgive.

11.14–12.25: The prophet's address. At the inception of the monarchy Samuel addresses the people, denouncing their request for a king and urging them to obey the LORD, but also trying to secure his own position under the new regime as spiritual authority. The address begins with the vindication of Samuel's past leadership and ends with his continuing task as mediator between God and the people. In its ideas and language it evinces Deuteronomistic influence. **14–15:** After Saul's great achievement the time is fit to inaugurate him as king. Offering sacrifices and holding a *great celebration,* lit. "great rejoicing," were part of the royal inauguration ceremony (1 Kings 1.25, 40; 2 Kings 11.14). **12.2–5:** Samuel asserts—and his assertion is confirmed by the people—that he never abused his office for his own profit (whereas corruption among leaders is widespread), implying that his rejection is unjustified and an act of ingratitude (cf. Num. 16.15). **3:** *His* one: Whose ox have I taken, or whose ass have I taken? Whom have I defrauded or whom have I robbed? From whom have I taken a bribe *a*to look the other way?*a* I will return it to you." [4] They responded, "You have not defrauded us, and you have not robbed us, and you have taken nothing from anyone." [5] He said to them, "The LORD then is witness, and His anointed is witness, *b*to your admission*b* this day that you have found nothing in my possession." They*c* responded, "He is!"

[6] Samuel said to the people, *d*"The LORD [is witness], He who appointed*d* Moses and Aaron and who brought your fathers out of the land of Egypt. [7] Come, stand before the LORD while I cite against you all the kindnesses that the LORD has done to you and your fathers.

[8] "When Jacob came to Egypt,*e* . . . your fathers cried out to the LORD, and the LORD sent Moses and Aaron, who brought your fathers out of Egypt and settled them in this place. [9] But they forgot the LORD their God; so He delivered them into the hands of Sisera the military commander of Hazor, into the hands of the Philistines, and into the hands of the kind of Moab; and these made war upon them. [10] They cried to the LORD, 'We are guilty, for we have forsaken the LORD and worshiped the Baalim and Ashtaroth. Oh, deliver us from our enemies and we will serve You.' [11] And the LORD sent Jerubbaal and Bedan*f* and Jephthah and Samuel, and delivered you from the enemies around you; and you dwelt in security. [12] But when you saw that Nahash king of the Ammonites was advancing against you, you said to me, 'No, we must have a king reigning over us'—though the LORD your God is your King.

[13] "Well, the LORD has set a king over you! Here is the king that you have chosen, that you have asked for. [14] "If you will revere the LORD, worship Him, and obey Him, and will not flout the LORD's command, if both you and the king who reigns over you will follow the LORD your God, [well and good]. [15] But if you do not obey the LORD and you flout the LORD's command, the hand of the LORD will strike you *d*as it did your fathers.*d*

[16] "Now stand by and see the marvelous thing that the LORD will do before your eyes. [17] It is the season of the wheat harvest.*g* I will pray to the LORD and He will send

anointed one, see 2.10 n. **7–12:** The LORD always delivered Israel from its enemies, even when their plight was caused by their own guilt, so there was no need to ask for a king in order to be delivered. **8:** *Cried out to the LORD,* see Exod. 2.23. **9:** The interpretation of the historical events largely conforms to the book of Judges: Deliverance into the hands of the enemies is seen as punishment for forsaking the LORD and worshipping other gods, deliverance from the enemies as the result of returning to Him. *Sisera,* see Judg. 4.2. *Philistines,* see Judg. 13.1. *Moab,* see Judg. 3.12. **10:** *They cried to the LORD . . . ,* see Judg. 10.10. *The Baalim and Ashtaroth,* see 7.3–4 n. **11:** *Jerubbaal,* also called Gideon (see Judg. 7.1). *Bedan,* no judge by that name is known. The Rabbis stated, "Bedan is Samson" (b. *Rosh Hash.* 25a), since Bedan means "in Dan," and Samson belonged to the tribe of Dan. But perhaps Barak should be read (see Judg. 4.6). Alternately, this refers to a judge not mentioned in the extant book of Judges. **12:** The advance of Nahash is not mentioned in ch 8 among the reasons for requesting a king. Moreover, according to the order of the narratives, the request for a king (ch 8) preceded the war against Nahash (ch 11). But according to a passage in the Dead Sea manuscript 4QSam*a* and in Josephus (see 11.1–13 n.), Nahash troubled Israel already before the war at Jabeshgilead. These earlier attacks (together with the Philistine occupation; see 9.16) probably inspired the wish for a strong military leader.

---

a-a Septuagint reads "or a pair of sandals? [cf. Amos 2.6] Testify against me."
b-b Lit. "against you."   c Heb. "he."
d-d Meaning of Heb. uncertain.
e Septuagint adds "the Egyptians oppressed them."
f Septuagint "Barak."
g When thunderstorms do not occur in the land of Israel.

thunder and rain; then you will take thought and realize what a wicked thing you did in the sight of the LORD when you asked for a king."

[18] Samuel prayed to the LORD, and the LORD sent thunder and rain that day, and the people stood in awe of the LORD and of Samuel. [19] The people all said to Samuel, "Intercede for your servants with the LORD your God that we may not die, for we have added to all our sins the wickedness of asking for a king." [20] But Samuel said to the people, "Have no fear. You have, indeed, done all those wicked things. Do not, however, turn away from the LORD, but serve the LORD with all your heart. [21] Do not turn away to follow worthless things, which can neither profit nor save but are worthless. [22] For the sake of His great name, the LORD will never abandon His people, seeing that the LORD undertook to make you His people.

[23] "As for me, far be it from me to sin against the LORD and refrain from praying for you; and I will continue to instruct you in the practice of what is good and right. [24] Above all, you must revere the LORD and serve Him faithfully with all your heart; and consider how grandly He has dealt with you. [25] For if you persist in your wrongdoing, both you and your king shall be swept away."

13 Saul was . . .[a] years old when he became king, and he reigned over Israel two years. [2] Saul picked 3,000 Israelites, of whom 2,000 were with Saul in Michmas[b] and in the hill country of Bethel, and 1,000 with Jonathan in Gibeah of Benjamin; the rest of the troops he sent back to their homes. [3] Jonathan struck down the Philistine prefect in Geba;[c] and the Philistines heard about it. [d] Saul had the ram's horn sounded throughout the land, saying, "Let the Hebrews hear."[-d]

[4] When all Israel heard that Saul had struck down the Philistine prefect, and that Israel had [e-]incurred the wrath of[-e] the Philistines, all the people rallied to Saul at Gilgal. [5] The Philistines, in turn, gathered to attack Israel: 30,000[f] chariots and 6,000 horsemen, and troops as numerous as the sands of the seashore. They marched up and encamped at Michmas, east of Beth-aven.

18: The miracle demonstrates both the anger of the LORD and the power of Samuel's prayer. In the land of Israel rain only falls from the late fall to the early spring. Rain during the harvest in the summer would cause the crop to spoil. **22:** Abandonment of Israel would damage the LORD's *great name* among the nations, who would attribute it to His impotence (cf. Num. 14.15–16; Josh. 7.9). **23:** Samuel, whose authority is reconfirmed by the miracle, will continue to represent the people before God by means of prayer and represent God before the people by means of instruction. **25:** The fate of the people and the king are intertwined.

13.1–14.52: The king's failure and the prince's success. Saul, in his first war against the Philistines, dreads their superior force, whereas Jonathan his son, convinced that God can grant victory "by many or by few" (14.6), takes action and achieves an impressive victory. **1:** This formula—here incomplete—often introduces the reign of kings, e.g., 2 Sam. 2.10; 1 Kings 14.21; 22.42. **2:** Saul sets up a standing army. *Gibeah of Benjamin,* see 10.5 n. **3:** By killing the Philistine prefect Jonathan initiates the revolt. Sounding *the ram's horn* serves to mobilize the *Hebrews.* To incite the Israelites to arms Saul uses the Philistine designation, "Hebrews" (see 4.6 n.). **4:** Saul, as king, is credited with Jonathan's deed. **5:** The Philistine army exceeds the Israelite force by far. Unlike the Israelites, it has chariots, though the numbers mentioned seem greatly exaggerated. The Heb word translated *horsemen* can also mean "horses"; these were used for pulling the chariots, not for riding. *As the sands of the seashore* is a common figure (e.g., Gen. 22.17; Josh. 11.4).

---

a *The number is lacking in the Heb. text; also, the precise context of the "two years" is uncertain. The verse is lacking in the Septuagint.*

b *So in oldest mss.; other mss. and editions read "Michmash" throughout the chapter.*

c *Apparently identical with Gibeah in v. 2.*

d-d *Meaning of Heb. uncertain.*

e-e *Lit. "became malodorous to."*

f *Septuagint and other versions read "three thousand."*

6 a-When the men of Israel saw that they were in trouble—for the troops were hard pressed—the people hid in caves, among thorns, among rocks, in tunnels, and in cisterns. 7 Some Hebrews crossed the Jordan, [to] the territory of Gad and Gilead. Saul was still at Gilgal, and the rest of the people rallied to him in alarm.-ᵃ

8 He waited seven days, the time that Samuel [had set].ᵇ But when Samuel failed to come to Gilgal, and the people began to scatter, 9 Saul said, "Bring me the burnt offering and the sacrifice of well-being"; and he presented the burnt offering. 10 He had just finished presenting the burnt offering when Samuel arrived; and Saul went out to meet him and welcome him. 11 But Samuel said, "What have you done?" Saul replied, "I saw the people leaving me and scattering; you had not come at the appointed time, and the Philistines had gathered at Michmas. 12 I thought the Philistines would march down against me at Gilgal before I had entreated the LORD, so I ᵃ-forced myself-ᵃ to present the burnt offering." 13 Samuel answered Saul, ᶜ-"You acted foolishly in not keeping the commandments that the LORD your God laid upon you! Otherwise-ᶜ the LORD would have established your dynasty over Israel forever. 14 But now your dynasty will not endure. The LORD will seek out a man after His own heart, and the LORD will appoint him ruler over His people, because you did not abide by what the LORD had commanded you."

15 ᵈ-Samuel arose and went up from Gilgal-ᵈ to Gibeahᵉ of Benjamin. Saul numbered the troops who remained with him—about 600 strong. 16 Saul and his son Jonathan, and the troops who remained with them, stayed in Geba of Benjamin, while the Philistines were encamped at Michmas. 17 The raiders came out of the Philistine camp in three columns: One column headed for the Ophrah road that leads to the district of Shual, 18 another column headed for the Beth-horon road, and the third column headed for the borderᶠ road that overlooks the valley of Zeboim toward the desert.

19 No smith was to be found in all the land of Israel, for the Philistines were afraid that the Hebrews would make swords or spears. 20 So all the Israelites had to go down to

8–15a: The episode of Samuel's clash with Saul connects with 10.8, where Samuel explicitly told Saul to wait for him. **9:** It was customary to offer a sacrifice before battle (see 7.10). There are several instances of kings sacrificing, e.g., David (2 Sam. 6.17), Solomon (1 Kings 8.62–64), Jeroboam (1 Kings 13.1). **11–12:** To Samuel's short question, Saul, to justify himself, gives a lengthy answer. **13–14:** Samuel is angry that Saul did not obey him and offered the sacrifice, a task that Samuel, as religious leader, wished to retain for himself. Samuel acknowledges Saul as the political leader of the people, not as the religious one. The words *commandments* and *commanded* are in Heb of the same root as *appoint* (tz-v-h), thus connecting the punishment with the sin according to the principle of measure for measure. *Ruler*, see 9.15–16 n. **15:** Unlike the Septuagint, the Masoretic version fails to record that Saul goes from Gilgal to Gibeah (see v. 16). The omission is probably due to haplography (the copyist's eye skipping from the first *Gilgal* to the second). Samuel refrains from accompanying Saul. **16:** *Geba* and *Michmas* were across from each other, separated by a ravine with precipitous sides. **17–18:** The raiders disperse in different directions in order to devastate the area (cf. 2 Sam. 11.1). **19–22:** The Israelites are inferior to the Philistines not only in number, but also in the quality of their weapons. Not being allowed by the Philistines to manufacture or repair iron tools (the period described coincides with the beginning of the Iron Age), they do not have iron weapons, and are also dependent on the Philistines for the (expensive) maintenance of their agricultural implements.

a-a *Meaning of Heb. uncertain.*

b *So some Heb. mss.; other mss., Septuagint, and Targum read "said." Cf. 10.8.*

c-c *Change of vocalization yields, "You acted foolishly. If you had kept the commandment the LORD your God laid upon you . . ."*

d-d *Septuagint reads here, "Samuel rose and left Gilgal and went his way. The rest of the people followed Saul to meet the soldiers, and they went from Gilgal."*

e *Sometimes called Geba; cf. vv. 3, 16; 14.5.*

f *Septuagint reads "Geba."*

the Philistines to have their plowshares, their mattocks, axes, and colters[a] sharpened. 21[b]The charge for sharpening was a *pim*[c] for plowshares, mattocks, three-pronged forks, and axes, and for setting the goads. 22 Thus on the day of the battle, no sword or spear was to be found in the possession of any of the troops with Saul and Jonathan; only Saul and Jonathan had them.

23 Now the Philistine garrison had marched out to the pass of Michmas.

14 One day, Jonathan son of Saul said to the attendant who carried his arms, "Come, let us cross over to the Philistine garrison on the other side"; but he did not tell his father. 2 Now Saul was staying on the outskirts of Gibeah,[d] under the pomegranate tree at Migron, and the troops with him numbered about 600. 3 Ahijah son of Ahitub brother of Ichabod son of Phinehas son of Eli, the priest of the LORD at Shiloh, was there bearing an ephod.—The troops did not know that Jonathan had gone. 4[e]At the crossing[e] by which Jonathan sought to reach the Philistine garrison, there was a rocky crag on one side, and another rocky crag on the other, the one called Bozez and the other Seneh. 5 One crag was located on the north, near Michmas, and the other on the south, near Geba.

6 Jonathan said to the attendant who carried his arms, "Come, let us cross over to the outpost of those uncircumcised fellows. Perhaps the LORD will act in our behalf, for nothing prevents the LORD from winning a victory by many or by few." 7 His arms-bearer answered him, "Do whatever [f]you like. You go first,[f] I am [g]with you, whatever you decide."[g] 8 Jonathan said, "We'll cross over to those men and let them see us. 9 If they say to us, 'Wait until we get to you,' then we'll stay where we are, and not go up to them. 10 But if they say, 'Come up to us,' then we will go up, for the LORD is delivering them into our hands. That shall be our sign." 11 They both showed themselves to the Philistine outpost and the Philistines said, "Look, some Hebrews are coming out of the holes where they have been hiding." 12 The men of the outpost shouted to

21: The word *pim* occurs only here. Its meaning became clear when stone weights inscribed with this word were unearthed. **22:** *No sword or spear,* made of iron. **14.3:** *Ichabod,* see 4.21. The ephod was a device used by priests for consulting the LORD. **6:** The repetition (see 14.1) serves to resume the thread of the story after the interruption depicting the background (vv. 2–5). *Uncircumcised fellows,* a contemptuous way to refer to the Philistines, who, unlike the Israelites and most peoples in the area, were not circumcised. This was considered a disgrace (cf. Gen. 34.14). **11–12:** The presumptuous Philistines belittle the two Israelites. *Hebrews,* see 4.6 n. *The holes,* see 13.6.

a *Meaning of Heb. uncertain. Septuagint reads "sickle."*
b *Meaning of several terms in this verse uncertain.*
c *I.e., two-thirds of a shekel.*
d *See note e at 13.15.*
e-e *Meaning of Heb. uncertain.*
f-f *Lit. "is in your heart. Incline yourself." Septuagint reads "your heart inclines to."*
g-g *Lit. "with you, according to your heart." Septuagint reads "with you; my heart is like your heart."*

Jonathan and his arms-bearer, "Come up to us, and we'll teach you a lesson." Then Jonathan said to his arms-bearer, "Follow me, for the LORD will deliver them into the hands of Israel." [13] And Jonathan clambered up on his hands and feet, his arms-bearer behind him; [the Philistines] fell before Jonathan, and his arms-bearer finished them off behind him. [14] The initial attack that Jonathan and his arms-bearer made accounted for some twenty men, *within a space about half a furrow long [in] an acre of land.-ª [15] Terror broke out among all the troops both in the camp [and] in the field; the outposts and the raiders were also terrified. The very earth quaked, and a terror from God ensued.

[16] Saul's scouts in Gibeah of Benjamin saw that the multitude was *scattering in all directions.-ᵇ [17] And Saul said to the troops with him, "Take a count and see who has left us." They took a count and found that Jonathan and his arms-bearer were missing. [18] Thereupon Saul said to Ahijah, "Bring the Ark*c of God here"; for the Ark*c of God was at the time amongᵈ the Israelites. [19] But while Saul was speaking to the priest, the confusion in the Philistine camp kept increasing; and Saul said to the priest, "Withdraw your hand." [20] Saul and the troops with him assembled and rushed into battle; they found [the Philistines] in very great confusion, every man's sword turned against his fellow. [21ª] And the Hebrews who had previously sided with the Philistines, who had come up with them in the army [from] round about—they too joined the Israelites-ª who were with Saul and Jonathan. [22] When all the men of Israel who were hiding in the hill country of Ephraim heard that the Philistines were fleeing, they too pursued them in battle. [23] Thus the LORD brought victory to Israel that day.

The fighting passed beyond Beth-aven. [24ᵉ] The men of Israel were distressed-ᵉ that day. For Saul had laid an oath upon the troops: "Cursed be the man who eats any food before night falls and I take revenge on my enemies." So none of the troops ate anything. [25] Everybody came to a ᶠstack of beehivesᶠ where some honey had spilled on the ground. [26] When the troops came to the beehivesᶠ and

13: Jonathan climbs the precipice at a difficult, unexpected site, thus surprising the Philistine outpost. **15:** *The very earth quaked,* lit. "the land trembled," metonymical for "the people trembled." *Terror from God,* immense terror (cf. 11.7; Gen. 35.5). **19:** *Withdraw your hand:* Do not continue consulting the LORD, because, in view of the confusion, there is neither need nor time for it. **21–22:** Israelites who were in the service of the Philistines as well as those who were hiding (13.6) now join Saul's army. **24:** Saul does not want the people to pause in the pursuit of the Philistines, but the result of his curse is that they become faint from hunger (cf. the rash vow of Jephthah, which also afflicted his own child, Judg. 11.30–31).

a-a Meaning of Heb. uncertain.

b-b Lit. "shaken and going thither." Meaning of Heb. uncertain.

c Septuagint reads "ephod," and cf. vv. 3, 23.9, 30.7.

d Heb. "and."

e-e Meaning of Heb. uncertain. Septuagint reads "And all the troops, about 10,000 men, were with Saul; and the battle spread into the hill country of Ephraim. Now Saul committed a rash act."

f-f Meaning of Heb. uncertain; cf. Song of Songs 5.1.

found the flow of honey there, no one put[a] his hand to his mouth, for the troops feared the oath. [27] Jonathan, however, had not heard his father adjure the troops. So he put out the stick he had with him, dipped it into the beehive of honey, and brought his hand back to his mouth; and his eyes lit up. [28] At this one of the soldiers spoke up, "Your father adjured the troops: 'Cursed be the man who eats anything this day.' And so the troops are faint." [29] Jonathan answered, "My father has brought trouble on the people. See for yourselves how my eyes lit up when I tasted that bit of honey. [30] If only the troops had eaten today of spoil captured from the enemy, the defeat of the Philistines would have been greater still!"

[31] They struck down the Philistines that day from Michmas to Aijalon, and the troops were famished. [32] The troops pounced on the spoil; they took the sheep and cows and calves and slaughtered them on the ground, and the troops ate with the blood.[b] [33] When it was reported to Saul that the troops were sinning against the LORD, eating with the blood, he said, "You have acted faithlessly. Roll a large stone over to me today."[c] [34] And Saul ordered, "Spread out among the troops and tell them that everyone must bring me his ox or his sheep and slaughter it here, and then eat. You must not sin against the LORD and eat with the blood." Every one of the troops brought [d]his own ox with him[d] that night and slaughtered it there. [35] Thus Saul set up an altar to the LORD; it was the first altar he erected to the LORD.

[36] Saul said, "Let us go down after the Philistines by night and plunder among them until the light of morning; and let us not leave a single survivor among them." "Do whatever you please," they replied. But the priest said, "Let us approach God here." [37] So Saul inquired of God, "Shall I go down after the Philistines? Will You deliver them into the hands of Israel?" But this time He did not respond to him. [38] Then Saul said, "Come forward, all chief officers of the troops, and find out how this guilt was incurred today. [39] For as the LORD lives who brings victory to Israel, even if it was through my son Jonathan, he shall be put to death!" Not one soldier answered him. [40] And he said to all the Israelites, "You stand on one side, and my son Jonathan and I shall stand on the other." The troops said to Saul, "Do as you please." [41] Saul then said to the

25–27: *Beehives,* rather "honeycombs." The Heb word may also be translated "forest" (in vv. 25–26). Honey was produced by wild bees (see Judg. 14.8–9) and considered a delicacy. **29–30:** Jonathan openly criticizes his father: If the troops had eaten, they would have had more strength to pursue the Philistines. **32–34:** It was forbidden to eat meat with the blood, which was considered to be the life (Lev. 19.26; Deut. 12.23). Accordingly, for meat to be kosher, rabbinic law requires that all traces of blood be meticulously removed. By slaughtering on the ground the blood will not drain out properly and will mix with the meat, whereas by slaughtering on a stone the blood can drain out and flow down, leaving the meat fit for consumption. **36–39:** It was customary to inquire of God before going to battle (Num. 27.21). The lack of response is an indication of guilt. **40–42:** The guilty person was found by means of the Urim and Thummim. These were lots allowing only yes-or-no answers (cf. Saul's questions in v. 37), so the people had to be divided into two groups, one group being indicated at each stage. From the fuller Septuagint reading the method becomes clear: The appearance of Urim meant yes; of Thummim, no (the omission in the Masoretic Text is probably due to haplography, the copyist's eye skipping from the first *Israel* to the last).

a *Meaning of Heb. uncertain.*
b *I.e., without the proper rites.*
c *Septuagint reads "here."*
d-d *Septuagint reads "whatever he had in his possession."*

Lord, the God of Israel, *-"Show Thammim."* Jonathan and Saul were indicated by lot, and the troops were cleared. 42 And Saul said, "Cast the lots between my son and me"; and Jonathan was indicated.

43 Saul said to Jonathan, "Tell me, what have you done?" And Jonathan told him, "I only tasted a bit of honey with the tip of the stick in my hand. I am ready to die." 44 Saul said, "Thus and more may God do:*b* You shall be put to death, Jonathan!" 45 But the troops said to Saul, "Shall Jonathan die, after bringing this great victory to Israel? Never! As the Lord lives, not a hair of his head shall fall to the ground! For he brought this day to pass with the help of God." Thus the troops saved Jonathan and he did not die. 46 Saul broke off his pursuit of the Philistines, and the Philistines returned to their homes.

47 After Saul had secured his kingship over Israel, he waged war on every side against all his enemies: against the Moabites, Ammonites, Edomites, the Philistines, and the kings*c* of Zobah; and wherever he turned he worsted [them]. 48 He was triumphant, defeating the Amalekites and saving Israel from those who plundered it.

49 Saul's sons were: Jonathan, Ishvi,*d* and Malchishua; and the names of his two daughters were Merab, the older, and Michal, the younger. 50 The name of Saul's wife was Ahinoam daughter of Ahimaaz; and the name of his army commander was Abiner*e* son of Saul's uncle Ner. 51 Kish, Saul's father, and Ner, Abner's father, were sons of Abiel.

52 There was bitter war against the Philistines all the days of Saul; and whenever Saul noticed any stalwart man or warrior, he would take him into his service.

15 Samuel said to Saul, "I am the one the Lord sent to anoint you king over His people Israel. Therefore, listen to the Lord's command!

2 "Thus said the Lord of Hosts: I am exacting the penalty for what Amalek did to Israel, for the assault he made upon them on the road, on their way up from Egypt. 3 Now go, attack Amalek, and proscribe*f* all that belongs to him. Spare no one, but kill alike men and women, infants and sucklings, oxen and sheep, camels and asses!"

---

a-a *Meaning of Heb. uncertain. Septuagint reads "Why have You not responded to Your servant today? If this iniquity was due to my son Jonathan or to me, O Lord, God of Israel, show Urim; and if You say it was due to Your people Israel, show Thummim."*

b *Many mss. and Septuagint add "to me."*

c *Septuagint and 4QSam*a *read "king."*

d *The same as Ishbosheth (2 Sam. 2.8) and Eshbaal (1 Chron. 8.33).*

e *Usually "Abner."*   f *See note at Josh. 6.18.*

43: The lack of proportion between the "crime" (Jonathan only *tasted* and just *a bit*) and the punishment is manifest. Jonathan has broken a vow, however, and vows had to be observed unconditionally (Deut. 23.22–24). **44:** *Thus and more,* see 3.17. **45:** *Not a hair of his head shall fall to the ground:* The same hyperbolic expression occurs in 2 Sam. 14.11; 1 Kings 1.52. *Saved,* lit. "redeemed." Although Jonathan did not hear his father's oath, he is considered formally guilty, and therefore has to be redeemed (cf. *Midrash Samuel:* "Israel gave his weight in gold and redeemed him"). Biblical law allows in some cases redemption of the offender (see Exod. 21.30). **46:** The statement that people returned home usually marks the end of a narrative (e.g., 15.34; 26.25). **47–52:** A summary of Saul's kingship, with regard to his wars and family. The Amalekites are mentioned separately, because the war against them will be the subject of the next story.

15.1–35: Rejection. As in 13.8–14 Saul and Samuel clash over the king's insubordination to the prophet, and Samuel tells Saul that his kingship will not abide. But whereas in the earlier narrative the rejection referred to his dynasty, here it applies to Saul himself. There the clash occurred in connection with the war against the Philistines, here against Amalek, a nomadic people to the south of Israel. The Amalekites are regarded in the Bible as vicious adversaries of Israel; in later times the name Amalek came to signify "archenemy of the Jews." **1:** At the beginning of the narrative—without an introduction—Samuel stresses Saul's obligation to obey. **2:** The Amalekites' vile attack upon Israel is described in Exod. 17.8–16; Deut. 25.17–19. **3:** Proscription, practiced by Israel and other peoples in the ancient Near East, was a way of consecrating the fruits of victory to the deity; it meant exterminating all the people and all their belongings, as emphasized in the present v.

⁴Saul mustered the troops and enrolled them at Telaim: 200,000 men on foot, and 10,000 men of Judah. ⁵Then Saul advanced as far as the city of Amalek and ᵃlay in wait⁻ᵃ in the wadi. ⁶Saul said to the Kenites, "Come, withdraw at once from among the Amalekites, that I may not destroy you along with them; for you showed kindness to all the Israelites when they left Egypt." So the Kenites withdrew from among the Amalekites.

⁷Saul destroyed Amalek from Havilah all the way to Shur, which is close to Egypt, ⁸and he captured King Agag of Amalek alive. He proscribed all the people, putting them to the sword; ⁹but Saul and the troops spared Agag and the best of the sheep, the oxen, the second-born,ᵇ the lambs, and all else that was of value. They would not proscribe them; they proscribed only ᵃwhat was cheap and worthless.⁻ᵃ

¹⁰The word of the Lord then came to Samuel: ¹¹"I regret that I made Saul king, for he has turned away from Me and has not carried out My commands." Samuel was distressed and he entreated the Lord all night long. ¹²Early in the morning Samuel went to meet Saul. Samuel was told, "Saul went to Carmel, where he erected a monument for himself; then he left and went on down to Gilgal."

¹³When Samuel came to Saul, Saul said to him, "Blessed are you of the Lord! I have fulfilled the Lord's command." ¹⁴"Then what," demanded Samuel, "is this bleating of sheep in my ears, and the lowing of oxen that I hear?" ¹⁵Saul answered, "They were brought from the Amalekites, for the troops spared the choicest of the sheep and oxen for sacrificing to the Lord your God. And we proscribed the rest." ¹⁶Samuel said to Saul, "Stop! Let me tell you what the Lord said to me last night!" "Speak," he replied. ¹⁷And Samuel said, "You may look small to yourself, but you are the head of the tribes of Israel. The Lord anointed you king over Israel, ¹⁸and the Lord sent you on a mission, saying, 'Go and proscribe the sinful Amalekites; make war on them until you have exterminated them.' ¹⁹Why did you disobey the Lord and swoop down on the spoil ᶜin defiance of the Lord's will?"⁻ᶜ ²⁰Saul said to Samuel, "But I did obey the Lord! I performed the mission on which the Lord sent me: I captured King Agag of Amalek, and I proscribed Amalek, ²¹and the troops took from the spoil some sheep and oxen—the best of what had

4: The numbers are exaggerated; however, the Heb word for "thousand" may refer to a much smaller military unit. **5:** *The city of Amalek,* their main settlement. **6:** The *Kenites* were a nomadic tribe in the south of the country. It is unknown wherein their kindness to the Israelites consisted. According to Judg. 1.16; 4.11, Moses' father-in-law was a Kenite, and he extended help to the Israelites (Exod. 18.1–27; Num. 10.29). **8:** *Agag:* In Esth. 3.1 Haman is called the Agagite. **12:** *Carmel,* a town in the south of Judah. **15:** Saul shifts the blame for the violation of the proscription to the troops, but in the proscription's execution he includes himself *(we).* He also contends that though the choicest animals were spared, this was done for a most worthy purpose. He possibly believes that he has in fact performed the Lord's command. **17:** *You may look small to yourself* (cf. 9.21), but as head of Israel you bear responsibility. **18:** *Sinful,* refers to all Amalekites, those at the time of the exodus as well as those living at the time of Saul. **20–21:** To Samuel's accusation Saul replies by repeating his previous arguments.

---

a-a Meaning of Heb. uncertain.

b Targum and Syriac read "fatlings."

c-c Lit. "and do what was evil in the sight of the Lord."

been proscribed—to sacrifice to the Lord your God at Gilgal." [22] But Samuel said:

"Does the Lord delight in burnt offerings and
sacrifices
As much as in obedience to the Lord's command?
Surely, obedience is better than sacrifice,
Compliance than the fat of rams.
[23] For rebellion is like the sin of divination,
Defiance, like the iniquity of teraphim.[a]
Because you rejected the Lord's command,
He has rejected you as king."

[24] Saul said to Samuel, "I did wrong to transgress the Lord's command and your instructions; but I was afraid of the troops and I yielded to them. [25] Please, forgive my offense and come back with me, and I will bow low to the Lord." [26] But Samuel said to Saul, "I will not go back with you; for you have rejected the Lord's command, and the Lord has rejected you as king over Israel."

[27] As Samuel turned to leave, Saul seized the corner of his robe, and it tore. [28] And Samuel said to him, "The Lord has this day torn the kingship over Israel away from you and has given it to another who is worthier than you. [29] Moreover, the Glory[b] of Israel does not deceive or change His mind, for He is not human that He should change His mind." [30] But [Saul] pleaded, "I did wrong. Please, honor me in the presence of the elders of my people and in the presence of Israel, and come back with me until I have bowed low to the Lord your God." [31] So Samuel followed Saul back, and Saul bowed low to the Lord.

[32] Samuel said, "Bring forward to me King Agag of Amalek." Agag approached him [c]with faltering steps;[c] and Agag said, "Ah, bitter death is at hand!"[b]
[33] Samuel said:

"As your sword has bereaved women,
So shall your mother be bereaved among women."
And Samuel [d]cut Agag down[d] before the Lord at Gilgal.

[34] Samuel then departed for Ramah, and Saul went up to his home at Gibeah of Saul.

[35] Samuel never saw Saul again to the day of his death. But Samuel grieved over Saul, because the Lord regretted that He had made Saul king over Israel. 16 [1] And the Lord said to Samuel, "How long will you grieve over Saul, since I have rejected him as king over Israel? Fill your horn with oil and set out; I am sending you to

22–23: The poetic form of these vv. serves to highlight their significance. They convey the message that right is more important than rite. Samuel is the first in the line of prophets such as Amos, Isaiah, and Micah, who do not attribute paramount importance to sacrifices. Most of the literary prophets demand moral behavior along with ritual; only Jeremiah (7.21–23) resembles Samuel in demanding obedience to the Lord. *The fat of rams,* the best part. *Rebellion* against the Lord is like *the sin of divination* (which is a form of idolatry; see Deut. 18.9–14), both involving turning away from Him. The repetition of *rejected* hints at the principle of measure for measure, the punishment corresponding to the sin. By enthroning Saul the people rejected the Lord as king (8.7); now the Lord rejects Saul as king. **24:** Though now admitting his guilt, Saul still shifts the blame to the troops. **25:** In asking for forgiveness Saul hopes that his rejection will be revoked. **28:** Samuel gives a symbolic interpretation to the tearing of the robe (for a similar interpretation, see 1 Kings 11.30–31; cf. also 1 Sam. 24.5). **29:** This verse seems to contradict vv. 11 and 35. The Lord does occasionally regret His previous decisions, for instance when a person's behavior displeases Him (see Gen. 6.6). Perhaps the sense is that He is not fickle like human beings. **30:** This time Saul does not shift the blame to others, but he still accompanies his confession with a personal request to prevent his public humiliation. **31:** Samuel's compliance with Saul's request does not mean that he has forgiven him. **32:** Instead of *with faltering steps,* the Heb may be translated, "with delight"; and instead of *is at hand,* "has gone away." According to this interpretation Agag expects that the prophet will save his life. Ironically, however, the opposite happens. **33:** Samuel's poetic lines justify Agag's punishment by stressing its correspondence with his sins. **34:** See 14.46 n.

a Idols consulted for oracles; see Ezek. 21.26; Zech. 10.2.
b Meaning of Heb. uncertain.   c-c From root ma'ad, "to falter"; cf. Septuagint.
d-d Meaning of Heb. uncertain.

Jesse the Bethlehemite, for I have decided on one of his sons to be king." ²Samuel replied, "How can I go? If Saul hears of it, he will kill me." The LORD answered, "Take a heifer with you, and say, 'I have come to sacrifice to the LORD.' ³Invite Jesse to the sacrificial feast, and then I will make known to you what you shall do; you shall anoint for Me the one I point out to you." ⁴Samuel did what the LORD commanded. When he came to Bethlehem, the elders of the city went out in alarm to meet him and said, "Do you come on a peaceful errand?" ⁵"Yes," he replied, "I have come to sacrifice to the LORD. Purify yourselves and join me in the sacrificial feast." He also instructed Jesse and his sons to purify themselves and invited them to the sacrificial feast.

⁶When they arrived and he saw Eliab, he thought: "Surely the LORD's anointed stands before Him." ⁷But the LORD said to Samuel, "Pay no attention to his appearance or his stature, for I have rejected him. For not as man sees [does the LORD see];ᵃ man sees only what is visible, but the LORD sees into the heart." ⁸Then Jesse called Abinadab and had him pass before Samuel; but he said, "The LORD has not chosen this one either." ⁹Next Jesse presented Shammah; and again he said, "The LORD has not chosen this one either." ¹⁰Thus Jesse presented seven of his sons before Samuel, and Samuel said to Jesse, "The LORD has not chosen any of these."

¹¹Then Samuel asked Jesse, "Are these all the boys you have?" He replied, "There is still the youngest; he is tending the flock." And Samuel said to Jesse, "Send someone to bring him, for we will not ᵇsit down to eatᵇ until

---

ᵃ These words are preserved in the Septuagint.   ᵇ⁻ᵇ Meaning of Heb. uncertain.

16.1–13: Anointing renewed. In this first story about David he still plays a passive role. Even his name is not mentioned until the last v. His being chosen, though the youngest and least esteemed of eight brothers, agrees with the biblical motif of the younger being preferred to the elder: Abel to Cain (Gen. 4.2–5), Isaac to Ishmael (Gen. 21.9–13), Jacob to Esau (Gen. 27.28–40), Joseph to Reuben (Gen. 37.3–11; 49.3–4, 22–26). This indicates that not seniority, but suitability, is the decisive factor. **1:** Samuel's grieving over Saul links the beginning of this narrative to the end of the previous one. The verb *rejected* evokes not only 15.23, but also 8.7; 10.19; 15.26. The hollow ram's *horn* was used as a vessel. **2:** *He will kill me,* for subversive action. The sacrifice serves to disguise Samuel's mission. **4:** *In alarm,* in fear that the prophet's visit portends evil. **6–7:** Eliab's *stature* reminds Samuel of Saul, who was also tall (9.2; 10.23). But height and outward appearance are unimportant: God, who knows each person from within, has *rejected* Eliab, just as He rejected Saul. **10:** For the names of Jesse's sons, see 1 Chron. 2.13–15; 27.18. **11:** The shepherd who tends the flock is the one suited to tend the people (cf. Ps. 78.70–71). Moses is depicted as a shepherd (Exod. 3.1) and "shep-

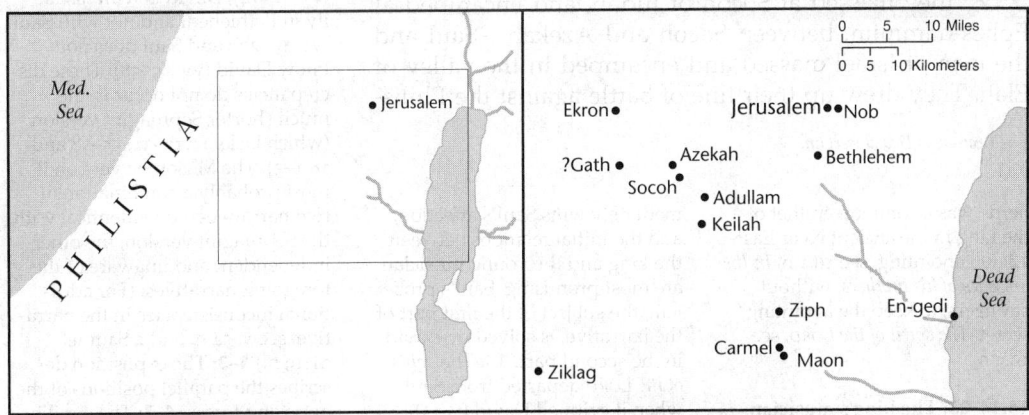

David's early career and his flight from Saul according to the book of Samuel

he gets here." [12] So they sent and brought him. He was ᵃruddy-cheeked, bright-eyed,ᵃ and handsome. And the LORD said, "Rise and anoint him, for this is the one." [13] Samuel took the horn of oil and anointed him in the presence of his brothers; and the spirit of the LORD gripped David from that day on. Samuel then set out for Ramah.

[14] Now the spirit of the LORD had departed from Saul, and an evil spirit from the LORD began to terrify him. [15] Saul's courtiers said to him, "An evil spirit of God is terrifying you. [16] Let our lord give the order [and] the courtiers in attendance on you will look for someone who is skilled at playing the lyre; whenever the evil spirit of God comes over you, he will play itᵃ and you will feel better." [17] So Saul said to his courtiers, "Find me someone who can play well and bring him to me." [18] One of the attendants spoke up, "I have observed a son of Jesse the Bethlehemite who is skilled in music; he is a stalwart fellow and a warrior, sensible in speech, and handsome in appearance, and the LORD is with him." [19] Whereupon Saul sent messengers to Jesse to say, "Send me your son David, who is with the flock." [20] Jesse took ᵃan ass [laden with]ᵃ bread, a skin of wine, and a kid, and sent them to Saul by his son David. [21] So David came to Saul and entered his service; [Saul] took a strong liking to him and made him one of his arms-bearers. [22] Saul sent word to Jesse, "Let David remain in my service, for I am pleased with him." [23] Whenever the [evil] spirit of God came upon Saul, David would take the lyre and play it;ᵃ Saul would find relief and feel better, and the evil spirit would leave him.

17 The Philistines assembled their forces for battle; they massed at Socoh of Judah, and encamped at Ephes-dammim, between Socoh and Azekah. [2] Saul and the men of Israel massed and encamped in the valley of Elah. They drew up their line of battle against the Philis-

a-a Meaning of Heb. uncertain.

manifested in attacks of mental disorder. **16:** Music therapy may be beneficial in relieving mental distress. **18:** The person recommended is not only a skilled musician (cf. Amos 6.5), but excels in many other fields as well. The characterization summarizes David's traits, which will emerge in the following narratives (and which make him suitable to be king). David's depiction as a musician contributed to the tradition that he composed the psalms. **20:** The presents serve to express Jesse's loyalty and to secure a favorable treatment for his son.

17.1–18.5: The shepherd boy and the giant. The story of David and Goliath demonstrates the triumph of faith over physical strength. The detailed description of Goliath's weapons and the rejection of Saul's armor by David serve, together with David's speech before the battle (vv. 45–47), to underscore this idea. Fairy-tale motifs have been incorporated in the narrative: A giant terrifies the community; riches and the king's daughter are promised to him who slays the giant; three elder brothers are unable to do so; and only the youngest and least esteemed brother achieves success by the use of clever, unconventional means. Several details in the narrative are inconsistent with the preceding ch: David and his family are introduced as new characters (vv. 12–14); David is with his family in Bethlehem and not with Saul (vv. 17–20); and Saul does not know David (vv. 55–58). These discrepancies do not occur in the much shorter Septuagint version (which lacks 17.12–31, 55–58 and 18.1–5). The Masoretic version is most probably a combination of two narratives—one identical with the Septuagint version, the other independent and unaware of the foregoing narratives. (For additional inconsistencies in the narrative, see v. 54 n. and 2 Samuel 21.19 n.) **1–3:** The exposition describes the parallel positions of the opposing forces. **4–7:** The equilibrium is disturbed by the appear-

herd" was a common epithet of the king in the ancient Near East. **13:** On anointing, see 10.1 n. *In the presence of his brothers*, without strangers, to keep the anointing secret. *The spirit of the LORD*, see 10.6 n.

16.14–23: The king's musician. David, on arriving at the court, im-

mediately wins Saul's affection, and the initial relations between the king and the young musician are most promising. Saul's problem, the subject of the first part of the narrative, is solved by David in the second part. **14:** The *spirit of the LORD* departed from Saul when it gripped David (v. 13), and in its place came *an evil spirit*, tines, 3 with the Philistines stationed on one hill and Israel stationed on the opposite hill; the ravine was between them. 4 A champion[a] of the Philistine forces stepped forward; his name was Goliath of Gath, and he was six cubits and a span tall. 5 He had a bronze helmet on his head, and wore a breastplate of scale armor, a bronze breastplate weighing five thousand shekels. 6 He had bronze greaves on his legs, and a bronze javelin [slung] from his shoulders. 7 The shaft of his spear was like a weaver's bar, and the iron head of his spear weighed six hundred shekels; and the shield-bearer marched in front of him.

8 He stopped and called out to the ranks of Israel and he said to them, "Why should you come out to engage in battle? I am the Philistine [champion], and you are Saul's servants. Choose[b] one of your men and let him come down against me. 9 If he bests me in combat and kills me, we will become your slaves; but if I best him and kill him, you shall be our slaves and serve us." 10 And the Philistine ended, "I herewith defy the ranks of Israel. Get me a man and let's fight it out!" 11 When Saul and all Israel heard these words of the Philistine, they were dismayed and terror-stricken.

12 David was the son of a certain Ephrathite of Bethlehem in Judah whose name was Jesse. He had eight sons, and in the days of Saul the man was already old, advanced in years.[b] 13 The three oldest sons of Jesse had left and gone with Saul to the war. The names of his three sons who had gone to the war were Eliab the first-born, the next Abinadab, and the third Shammah; 14 and David was the youngest. The three oldest had followed Saul, 15 and David would go back and forth from attending on Saul to shepherd his father's flock at Bethlehem.

16 The Philistine stepped forward morning and evening and took his stand for forty days.

17 Jesse said to his son David, "Take an ephah of this parched corn and these ten loaves of bread for your brothers, and carry them quickly to your brothers in camp. 18 Take these ten cheeses[b] to the captain of their thousand. Find out how your brothers are and bring some token[b] from them." 19 Saul and [c]the brothers[c] and all the men of Israel were in the valley of Elah, in the war against the Philistines.

20 Early next morning, David left someone in charge of the flock, took [the provisions], and set out, as his father Jesse had instructed him. He reached the barricade[b] as the

ance of the Philistine champion, whose height and arms are described in atypical detail. The description of the man's armor and weaponry serves to explain why he caused such great terror among the Israelites and also to contrast him with David, who prevails over him without any military equipment (vv. 39, 45, 50). The custom of champions from both sides fighting each other as representatives of their armies is known from the Bible (2 Samuel 2.14–16) and also from the *Iliad* (3.85–95; 7.66–91), where Trojan and Greek champions—Paris and Menelaus, Hector and Ajax—oppose each other (the Philistines originated from the area of the Aegean; see 4.1b n.). Its purpose was to prevent large-scale fighting of the entire armies. **4:** The name *Goliath* is mentioned only here and in v. 23. Otherwise the man is always called *the Philistine*. Perhaps he was initially anonymous, and his name was added later from 2 Samuel 21.19. *Six cubits and a span,* almost 3 meters (about 9 feet). **5:** *Five thousand shekels:* approximately 60 kg (about 130 pounds). **7:** *Like a weaver's bar:* The comparison refers either to the size of the shaft or to a loop attached to it to facilitate hurling. In the first case, the weaver's bar is the beam to which the warp is fastened in a loom; in the second, it denotes the shaft carrying the eyed strings for separating the threads of the warp. *Six hundred shekels,* about 7 kg (15 pounds). **12:** Instead of *certain* the Heb has "this," which serves to connect the present narrative to the preceding ones, where Jesse was already mentioned. **15:** This v. serves to reconcile this narrative, in which David is at home, with the preceding one, in which he is with Saul. **16:** The protraction of the war necessitates sending food to the warriors. **17:** *Ephah,* about 23 liters (21 quarts). **18:** *Captain of . . . thousand,* officer in charge of a large military unit. **19:** These are probably still the words of Jesse, instructing David where to go (instead of *were,* the Heb may be translated "are"). **20:** *Barricade,*

a Lit. "the man of the space between," i.e., between the armies.
b Meaning of Heb. uncertain.   c-c Heb. "they."

army was going out to the battle lines shouting the war cry. [21] Israel and the Philistines drew up their battle lines opposite each other. [22] David left his baggage with the man in charge of the baggage and ran toward the battle line and went to greet his brothers. [23] While he was talking to them, the champion, whose name was Goliath, the Philistine of Gath, stepped forward from the Philistine ranks and spoke the same words as before; and David heard him.

[24] When the men of Israel saw the man, they fled in terror. [25] And the men of Israel were saying [among themselves], "Do you see that man coming out? He comes out to defy Israel! The man who kills him will be rewarded by the king with great riches; he will also give him his daughter in marriage and grant exemption[a] to his father's house in Israel." [26] David asked the men standing near him, "What will be done for the man who kills that Philistine and removes the disgrace from Israel? Who is that uncircumcised Philistine that he dares defy the ranks of the living God?" [27] The troops told him in the same words what would be done for the man who killed him.

[28] When Eliab, his oldest brother, heard him speaking to the men, Eliab became angry with David and said, "Why did you come down here, and with whom did you leave those few sheep in the wilderness? I know your impudence and your impertinence:[b] you came down to watch the fighting!" [29] But David replied, "What have I done now? I was only asking!" [30] And he turned away from him toward someone else; he asked the same question, and the troops gave him the same answer as before.

[31] The things David said were overheard and were reported to Saul, who had him brought over. [32] David said to Saul, "Let [c]no man's[c] courage fail him. Your servant will go and fight that Philistine!" [33] But Saul said to David, "You cannot go to that Philistine and fight him; you are only a boy, and he has been a warrior from his youth!" [34] David replied to Saul, "Your servant has been tending his father's sheep, and if a lion or[d] a bear came and carried off an animal from the flock, [35] I would go after it and fight it and rescue it from its mouth. And if it attacked me, I would seize it by the beard and strike it down and kill it. [36] Your servant has killed both lion and bear; and that uncircumcised Philistine shall end up like one of them, for he has defied the ranks of the living God. [37] The LORD," David went on, "who saved me from lion and bear will

lit. "circle," the round army camp (cf. 26.5, where the same word is used). **26:** *Uncircumcised,* see 14.6 n. **28:** The eldest brother had great authority in the family, and the younger ones had to obey him. Eliab accuses David of irresponsible behavior, vicious intent, and malice (rather than impudence and impertinence), but David, on the contrary, has acted responsibly (v. 20) and carried out his father's mission faithfully. **34–35:** *If,* the Heb expresses "each time that." Having fought wild animals more than once, David is not inexperienced in fighting strong opponents.

---

a *I.e., freedom from royal levies.*   b *Lit. "badness of heart."*
c-c *Septuagint reads "not my lord's."*   d *Meaning of Heb. uncertain.*

also save me from that Philistine." "Then go," Saul said to David, "and may the Lord be with you!"

38 Saul clothed David in his own garment; he placed a bronze helmet on his head and fastened ᵃ⁻a breastplate on him.⁻ᵃ 39 David girded his sword over his garment. Then he ᵇ⁻tried to walk; but⁻ᵇ he was not used to it. And David said to Saul, "I cannot walk in these, for I am not used to them." So David took them off. 40 He took his stick, picked a fewᶜ smooth stones from the wadi, put them in the pocketᵈ of his shepherd's bag and, sling in hand, he went toward the Philistine.

41 The Philistine, meanwhile, was coming closer to David, preceded by his shield-bearer. 42 When the Philistine caught sight of David, he scorned him, for he was but a boy, ruddy and handsome. 43 And the Philistine called out to David, "Am I a dog that you come against me with sticks?" The Philistine cursed David by his gods; 44 and the Philistine said to David, "Come here, and I will give your flesh to the birds of the sky and the beasts of the field."

45 David replied to the Philistine, "You come against me with sword and spear and javelin; but I come against you in the name of the Lord of Hosts, the God of the ranks of Israel, whom you have defied. 46 This very day the Lord will deliver you into my hands. I will kill you and cut off your head; and I will give ᵉ⁻the carcasses⁻ᵉ of the Philistine camp to the birds of the sky and the beasts of the earth. All the earth shall know that there is a God inᶠ Israel. 47 And this whole assembly shall know that the Lord can give victory without sword or spear. For the battle is the Lord's, and He will deliver you into our hands."

48 When the Philistine began to advance toward him again, David quickly ran up to the battle line to face the Philistine. 49 David put his hand into the bag; he took out a stone and slung it. It struck the Philistine in the forehead; the stone sank into his forehead, and he fell face down on the ground. 50 Thus David bested the Philistine with sling and stone; he struck him down and killed him. David had no sword; 51 so David ran up and stood over the Philistine, grasped his sword and pulled it from its sheath; and with it he dispatched him and cut off his head.

When the Philistines saw that their warrior was dead, they ran. 52 The men of Israel and Judah rose up with a war cry and they pursued the Philistines all the way to

38–39: David has no military experience and is *not used* to wearing armor. **40:** David prefers the simple implements of the shepherd. *Wadi*, a dry streambed. *Sling*, a strip of cloth or leather folded double, in the center of which a stone is placed. The sling is held at the ends and rotated, and then one end is suddenly released, which causes the stone to fly with great force to its target. Exactly hitting the mark requires considerable dexterity (cf. Judg. 20.16). The sling was used by shepherds, hunters, and soldiers. **42:** Cf. 16.12. **43–47:** Delivering speeches before the battle, which is also attested in the *Iliad* (see vv. 4–7 n.), served to strengthen the spirit of one side and demoralize the other. Whereas the Philistine trusts in his arms, David trusts in the Lord of Hosts, the God of the ranks of Israel, who determines *the battle.* **48:** The heavily armed Philistine moves slowly; David runs quickly. **49:** While still at a distance, David hurls the stone at the unsuspecting Philistine. **50–51:** Though killed by the stone, Goliath is finished off with his own sword.

a-a Heb. "clothed him in a breastplate" (cf. v. 5), because a breastplate was combined with a leather jerkin.
b-b Septuagint reads "was unable to walk, for . . ."   c Lit. "five."
d Meaning of Heb. uncertain.   e-e Septuagint reads "your carcass and the carcasses."
f So many Heb. mss. and ancient versions; other mss. and the editions read "to."

Gai[a] and up to the gates of Ekron; the Philistines fell mortally wounded along the road to Shaarim up to Gath and Ekron. [53] Then the Israelites returned from chasing the Philistines and looted their camp.

[54] David took the head of the Philistine and brought it to Jerusalem;[b] and he put his weapons in his own tent.

[55] When Saul saw David going out to assault the Philistine, he asked his army commander Abner, "Whose son is that boy, Abner?" And Abner replied, "By your life, Your Majesty, I do not know." [56] "Then find out whose son that young fellow is," the king ordered. [57] So when David returned after killing the Philistine, Abner took him and brought him to Saul, with the head of the Philistine still in his hand. [58] Saul said to him, "Whose son are you, my boy?" And David answered, "The son of your servant Jesse the Bethlehemite."

18 When [David] finished speaking with Saul, Jonathan's soul became bound up with the soul of David; Jonathan loved David as himself. [2] Saul took him [into his service] that day and would not let him return to his father's house.—[3] Jonathan and David made a pact, because [Jonathan] loved him as himself. [4] Jonathan took off the cloak and tunic he was wearing and gave them to David, together with his sword, bow, and belt. [5] David went out [with the troops], and he was successful in every mission on which Saul sent him, and Saul put him in command of all the soldiers; this pleased all the troops and Saul's courtiers as well. [6] When the [troops] came home [and] David returned from killing the Philistine, [c]the women of all the towns of Israel came out singing and dancing to greet King Saul[c] with timbrels, shouting, and sistrums.[d] [7] The women sang as they danced, and they chanted:

> Saul has slain his thousands;
> David, his tens of thousands!

[8] Saul was much distressed and greatly vexed about the matter. For he said, "To David they have given tens of thousands, and to me they have given thousands. All that he lacks is the kingship!" [9] From that day on Saul kept a jealous eye on David. [10] The next day an evil spirit of God gripped Saul and he began to rave in the house, while David was playing [the lyre], as he did daily. Saul had a

---

a Septuagint reads "Gath"; cf. end of verse.

b I.e., after David's capture of Jerusalem (2 Sam. 5).

c-c Meaning of Heb. uncertain. Septuagint reads "the dancing women came out to meet David from all the towns of Israel."

d Meaning of Heb. uncertain.

54: Since *Jerusalem* was not yet in Israelite hands and David did not yet have his own tent, the v. must be anticipatory (cf. v. 57). **55–58:** Saul inquires about David's father, though in the preceding narrative he is said to have sent a message to Jesse (see 17.1–18.5 n.). In the past a person's identity was mainly determined by his or her ancestry (see Gen. 24.23–24; 1 Sam. 1.1; 9.1; for David's ancestors, see Ruth 4.18–22). **18.1–5:** Jonathan's love for David is expressed practically in the pact between them, and symbolically in the bestowal of the garments and arms—which, however, were also of considerable real value. **5:** *Soldiers,* lit. "men of war," i.e., professional soldiers or perhaps raiders.

18.6–30: Jealousy. David, who after his victory over Goliath is successful in all his undertakings and loved by everyone, including the king's son and daughter, arouses the jealousy and enmity of Saul, who schemes to get rid of his (supposed) rival, but his attempts all fail. Three times the narrative states that David is successful (vv. 5, 14, 30), and three times that Saul fears David because the Lord is with him (vv. 12, 14–15, 28–29). The narrative makes Saul completely transparent by repeatedly and explicitly disclosing his feelings and motives. **6:** For the custom of women greeting the victors with dance and song, see Exod. 15.20–21; Judg. 11.34; 2 Samuel 1.20. **7–8:** *Thousands* and *tens of thousands* are regularly paired in the parallelisms of biblical poetry (e.g., Deut. 32.30; Ps. 91.7), the greater number always appearing in the second line. Thus, although a stereotypical phrase is being used, Saul infers from the order of the numbers that the women praise David more than him. **10:** *The next day:* The indication of time hints at a causal relation between Saul's vexation and his fit of mental disorder. *Rave,* lit. "speak in ecstasy" (see 10.5–6, 10). David *was playing,* see 16.23.

spear in his hand, [11] and Saul threw[a] the spear, thinking to pin David to the wall. But David eluded him twice. [12] Saul was afraid of David, for the LORD was with him and had turned away from Saul. [13] So Saul removed him from his presence and appointed him chief of a thousand, [b]to march at the head of the troops.[-b] [14] David was successful in all his undertakings, for the LORD was with him; [15] and when Saul saw that he was successful, he dreaded him. [16] All Israel and Judah loved David, for he marched at their head.

[17] Saul said to David, "Here is my older daughter, Merab; I will give her to you in marriage; in return, you be my warrior and fight the battles of the LORD." Saul thought: "Let not my hand strike him; let the hand of the Philistines strike him." [18] David replied to Saul, "Who am I and [c]what is my life[-c]—my father's family in Israel—that I should become Your Majesty's son-in-law?" [19] But at the time that Merab, daughter of Saul, should have been given to David, she was given in marriage to Adriel the Meholathite. [20] Now Michal daughter of Saul had fallen in love with David; and when this was reported to Saul, he was pleased. [21] Saul thought: "I will give her to him, and she can serve as a snare for him, so that the Philistines may kill him." So Saul said to David, [d]"You can become my son-in-law even now through the second one."[-d] [22] And Saul instructed his courtiers to say to David privately, "The king is fond of you and all his courtiers like you. So why not become the king's son-in-law?" [23] When the king's courtiers repeated these words to David, David replied, "Do you think that becoming the son-in-law of a king is a small matter, when I am but a poor man of no consequence?" [24] Saul's courtiers reported to him, "This is what David answered." [25] And Saul said, "Say this to David: 'The king desires no other bride-price than the foreskins of a hundred Philistines, as vengeance on the king's enemies.' "—Saul intended to bring about David's death at the hands of the Philistines.—[26] When his courtiers told this to David, David was pleased with the idea of becoming the king's son-in-law. [d]Before the time had expired,[-d] [27] David went out with his men and killed two hundred[e] Philistines; David brought their foreskins and [d]they were counted out[-d] for the king, that he might become the king's son-in-law. Saul then gave him his

13: *Chief of a thousand,* 17.18 n. **17:** Saul is prepared to give his daughter to David as promised (17.25), but he imposes additional conditions. *Warrior,* lit. "man of strength," i.e., of courage. Saul wants David to undertake daring and dangerous exploits. *The battles of the LORD* are in fact the battles of Israel. **18:** David's reply shows his humility. **20:** Michal is the only woman in all biblical narrative of whom it is said that she loves a man (see also v. 28). **25:** Since David is poor (v. 23) he cannot pay the bride-price. *Foreskins:* This would prove that David has killed Philistines, who were not circumcised (see 14.6 n.), and not men of another group. **27:** According to the Masoretic Text David doubles the bride-price, which shows his prowess in battle. He becomes the king's son-in-law at Saul's, not his own, initiative. This position gives him right of succession, though Saul's own sons have precedence.

a *Change of vocalization yields "raised."*
b-b *Lit. "and he went out and came in before the troops."*
c-c *Meaning of Heb. uncertain. Change of vocalization yields "who are my kin."*
d-d *Meaning of Heb. uncertain.*
e *Septuagint reads "one hundred" and cf. 2 Sam. 3.14.*

daughter Michal in marriage. ²⁸When Saul realized that the LORD was with David ᵃand that Michal daughter of Saul loved him,ᵃ ²⁹Saul grew still more afraid of David; and Saul was David's enemy ever after.

³⁰The Philistine chiefs marched out [to battle]; and every time they marched out, David was more successful than all the other officers of Saul. His reputation soared.

19 Saul urged his son Jonathan and all his courtiers to kill David. But Saul's son Jonathan was very fond of David, ²and Jonathan told David, "My father Saul is bent on killing you. Be on your guard tomorrow morning; get to a secret place and remain in hiding. ³I will go out and stand next to my father in the field where you will be, and I will speak to my father about you. If I learn anything, I will tell you." ⁴So Jonathan spoke well of David to his father Saul. He said to him, "Let not Your Majesty wrong his servant David, for he has not wronged you; indeed, all his actions have been very much to your advantage. ⁵He took his life in his hands and killed the Philistine, and the LORD wrought a great victory for all Israel. You saw it and rejoiced. Why then should you incur the guilt of shedding the blood of an innocent man, killing David without cause?" ⁶Saul heeded Jonathan's plea, and Saul swore, "As the LORD lives, he shall not be put to death!" ⁷Jonathan called David, and Jonathan told him all this. Then Jonathan brought David to Saul, and he served him as before.

⁸Fighting broke out again. David went out and fought the Philistines. He inflicted a great defeat upon them and they fled before him. ⁹Then an evil spirit of the LORD came upon Saul while he was sitting in his house with his spear in his hand, and David was playing [the lyre]. ¹⁰Saul tried to pin David to the wall with the spear, but he eluded Saul, so that he drove the spear into the wall. David fled and got away.

That night ¹¹Saul sent messengers to David's home to keep watch on him and to kill him in the morning. But David's wife Michal told him, "Unless you run for your life tonight, you will be killed tomorrow." ¹²Michal let David down from the window and he escaped and fled. ¹³Michal then took the household idol, laid it on the bed, and covered it with a cloth; and at its head she put a net of goat's hair. ¹⁴Saul sent messengers to seize David; but she said, "He is sick." ¹⁵Saul, however, sent back the messengers to see David for themselves. "Bring him up to me in the bed,"

19.1–24: Escape. All three stories in this ch deal with Saul's unconcealed efforts to kill David. Jonathan and Michal prove their love for David by acting in his behalf, opposing their father. **2:** *Tomorrow morning,* the time fixed for killing David. **4:** *Wrong,* lit. "sin against." *Wronged,* lit. "sinned against." **5:** *Incur the guilt of,* lit. "sin by." The repetitions of "sin" emphasize that by killing a man without sin Saul will gravely sin himself. This will contrast with David's behavior later in the book, when he refuses to kill the guilty Saul. **8–10:** David's success again arouses Saul's jealousy (cf. 18.10–11). **11:** *To keep watch,* so that David cannot escape. **13:** Michal risks her life in order to gain time for David and enable him to get farther away. *Household idol,* see Gen. 31.19, 35.

---

a-a Septuagint reads "and that all Israel loved him."

he ordered, "that he may be put to death." 16 When the messengers came, they found the household idol in the bed, with the net of goat's hair at its head. 17 Saul said to Michal, "Why did you play that trick on me and let my enemy get away safely?" "Because," Michal answered Saul, "he said to me: 'Help me get away or I'll kill you.' "

18 David made good his escape, and he came to Samuel at Ramah and told him all that Saul had done to him. He and Samuel went and stayed at Naioth. 19 Saul was told that David was at Naioth in Ramah, 20 and Saul sent messengers to seize David. They[a] saw a band of prophets [b]speaking in ecstasy,[b] with Samuel standing by [c]as their leader;[c] and the spirit of God came upon Saul's messengers and they too began to speak in ecstasy. 21 When Saul was told about this, he sent other messengers; but they too spoke in ecstasy. Saul sent a third group of messengers; and they also spoke in ecstasy. 22 So he himself went to Ramah. When he came to [d]the great cistern at Secu,[d] he asked, "Where are Samuel and David?" and was told that they were at Naioth in Ramah. 23 He was on his way there, to Naioth in Ramah, when the spirit of God came upon him too; and he walked on, speaking in ecstasy, until he reached Naioth in Ramah. 24 Then he too stripped off his clothes and he too spoke in ecstasy before Samuel; and he lay naked all that day and all night. That is why people say, "Is Saul too among the prophets?"

20 David fled from Naioth in Ramah; he came to Jonathan and said, "What have I done, what is my crime and my guilt against your father, that he seeks my life?" 2 He replied, "Heaven forbid! You shall not die. My father does not do anything, great or small, without disclosing it to me; why should my father conceal this matter from me? It cannot be!" 3 David [e]swore further,[e] "Your father knows well that you are fond of me and has decided: Jonathan must not learn of this or he will be grieved. But, as the LORD lives and as you live, there is only a step between me and death." 4 Jonathan said to David, "Whatever you want, I will do it for you."

5 David said to Jonathan, "Tomorrow is the new moon, and I [f]am to sit with the king at the meal. Instead, let[f] me go and I will hide in the countryside until the third[g] evening. 6 If your father notes my absence, you say, 'David

17: Michal lies to her father, telling him that self-preservation prompted her to help her husband to escape, while in fact she acted out of love for David. Her explanation does not account for the deception of her father with the household idol. **18:** David flees north to Samuel, who has anointed him, and not south to his family in Bethlehem, where Saul would probably look for him. **24:** *"Is Saul too among the prophets?"* The origin of this saying was explained differently at 10.10–12. There, following Saul's election, it referred to him in a positive sense; here, after his rejection, it alludes to his disgraceful, degrading behavior.

20.1–21.1: Friendship. The story demonstrates Jonathan's profound friendship for David, in spite of his knowledge that David's success will be at his expense. The narrative consists of four parts. The first part, in Jonathan's house, and the second part, in the open, deal with planning; the third part, in Saul's house, and the fourth, in the open again, tell of the execution of the plans. Like the previous narrative, it shows Saul being deceived by a member of his own family. **1:** The repetitions in David's question express his distress. **2:** Jonathan is unaware of Saul's attempts to kill David (see 19.6). **5:** The *new moon* was celebrated as a festival (see Num. 28.11; 2 Kings 4.23; Isa. 1.13; Amos 8.5), which included a festive meal. In postbiblical times the day lost its importance as festival, but great significance was attached to the Rabbis' official proclamation of the new moon since that determined when festivals would be commemorated. The moon's renewal is still marked in Jewish liturgy by special prayers and by the ceremony of Blessing the Moon, which is performed at night, when the new moon can clearly be seen. *Third,* counting from and including the present day.

a Heb. "He."   b-b Cf. note at 10.5.   c-c Meaning of Heb. uncertain.
d-d Septuagint reads "the cistern of the threshing floor on the bare height."
e-e Septuagint reads "replied to him."
f-f Septuagint reads "will not sit . . . meal. Let . . ."
g Septuagint lacks "third."

asked my permission to run down to his home town, Bethlehem, for the whole family has its annual sacrifice there.' ⁷If he says 'Good,' your servant is safe; but if his anger flares up, know that he is resolved to do [me] harm. ⁸Deal faithfully with your servant, since you have taken your servant into a covenant of the Lord with you. And if I am guilty, kill me yourself, but don't make me go back to your father." ⁹Jonathan replied, "Don't talk like that! If I learn that my father has resolved to kill you, I will surely tell you about it." ¹⁰David said to Jonathan, "Who will tell me if^a your father answers you harshly?" ¹¹Jonathan said to David, "Let us go into the open"; and they both went out into the open.

^{12b}Then Jonathan said to David, "By the Lord, the God of Israel! I will sound out my father at this time tomorrow, [or] on the third day; and if [his response] is favorable for David, I will send a message to you at once and disclose it to you. ¹³But if my father intends to do you harm, may the Lord do thus to Jonathan and more if I do [not] disclose it to you and send you off to escape unharmed. May the Lord be with you, as He used to be with my father. ¹⁴Nor shall you fail to show me the ^cLord's faithfulness,^c while I am alive; nor, when I am dead, ¹⁵shall you ever discontinue your faithfulness to my house—not even after the Lord has wiped out every one of David's enemies from the face of the earth. ¹⁶Thus has Jonathan covenanted with the house of David; and may the Lord requite the enemies of David!"

¹⁷Jonathan, out of his love for David, adjured^d him again, for he loved him as himself. ¹⁸Jonathan said to him, "Tomorrow will be the new moon; and you will be missed when your seat remains vacant.^e ¹⁹So the day after tomorrow, go down ^fall the way^f to the place where you hid ^gthe other time,^g and stay close to the Ezel stone. ²⁰Now I will shoot three arrows to one side of it, as though I were shooting at a mark, ²¹and I will order the boy to go and find the arrows. If I call to the boy, 'Hey! the arrows are on this side of you,' be reassured^h and come, for you are safe and there is no danger—as the Lord lives! ²²But if, instead, I call to the lad, 'Hey! the arrows are beyond you,' then leave, for the Lord has sent you away. ²³As for the promise we made to each other,ⁱ may the Lord be [witness] between you and me forever."

8: *Faithfully*, in accordance with the covenant (see 18.3). *Don't make me go back*, as you did last time (19.7). **11:** *The open*, where one can talk in private (cf. Gen. 31.4). **12:** *Third*, see v. 5 n. **13:** *Thus . . . and more*, see 3.17 n. If Saul's response is favorable, Jonathan will inform David through a messenger; if harmful, Jonathan will come and disclose it himself, because a messenger could reveal David's whereabouts to Saul. *As He used to be with my father*, a hint that David will be king. **14–16:** Jonathan, who deals faithfully with David now, wants David to deal faithfully with him and his offspring in the future. **15:** *My house:* To secure his throne the king of a new dynasty often killed the former king's relatives (1 Kings 15.29; 16.11; 2 Kings 10.11). Jonathan recognizes that David will succeed his father. **17:** Jonathan's motive to help David is his deep love for him, not his desire to secure his and his offspring's future destiny. **23:** *May the Lord be [witness] between you and me:* May the Lord watch over each of us that we keep the covenant

---

a *Meaning of Heb. uncertain.*   b *The meaning of several parts of vv. 12–16 is uncertain.*
c-c *I.e., the faithfulness pledged in the covenant before the* Lord.
d *Septuagint reads "swore to."*   e *At the festal meal.*   f-f *Lit. "very much."*
g-g *Lit. "on the day of the incident"; see 19.2 ff.*   h *Lit. "accept it."*
i *See above, vv. 12–17.*

24 David hid in the field. The new moon came, and the king sat down to partake of the meal. 25 When the king took his usual place on the seat by the wall, Jonathan rose[a] and Abner sat down at Saul's side; but David's place remained vacant. 26 That day, however, Saul said nothing. "It's accidental," he thought. [b-]"He must be unclean and not yet cleansed."[-b] 27 But on the day after the new moon, the second day, David's place was vacant again. So Saul said to his son Jonathan, "Why didn't the son of Jesse[c] come to the meal yesterday or today?" 28 Jonathan answered Saul, "David begged leave of me to go to Bethlehem. 29 He said, 'Please let me go, for we are going to have a family feast in our town and my brother has summoned me to it. Do me a favor, let me slip away to see my kinsmen.' That is why he has not come to the king's table."

30 Saul flew into a rage against Jonathan. "You son of a perverse, rebellious woman!" he shouted. "I know that you side with the son of Jesse—to your shame, and to the shame of your mother's nakedness! 31 For as long as the son of Jesse lives on earth, neither you nor your kingship will be secure. Now then, have him brought to me, for he is marked for death." 32 But Jonathan spoke up and said to his father, "Why should he be put to death? What has he done?" 33 At that, Saul threw[d] his spear at him to strike him down; and Jonathan realized that his father was determined to do away with David. 34 Jonathan rose from the table in a rage. He ate no food on the second day of the new moon, because he was grieved about David, and because his father had humiliated him.

35 In the morning, Jonathan went out into the open for the meeting with David, accompanied by a young boy. 36 He said to the boy, "Run ahead and find the arrows that I shoot." And as the boy ran, he shot the arrows past him. 37 When the boy came to the place where the arrows shot by Jonathan had fallen, Jonathan called out to the boy, "Hey, the arrows are beyond you!" 38 And Jonathan called after the boy, "Quick, hurry up. Don't stop!" So Jonathan's boy gathered the arrows and came back to his master.— 39 The boy suspected nothing; only Jonathan and David knew the arrangement.—40 Jonathan handed the gear to his boy and told him, "Take these back to the town." 41 When the boy got there, David [e-]emerged from his concealment at[-e] the Negeb.[f] He flung himself face down on

(cf. Gen. 31.49). **26:** Ritual impurity prevented one from participating in ritual meals. A frequent cause of impurity was the emission of semen, but in that event one could become pure again in the evening according to the legislation in Lev. 15.16–18. **29:** *My brother has summoned me,* probably the eldest brother (see 17.28 n.). *Slip away,* lit. "escape." **30:** It is clear from Jonathan's answer that he sides with David. This infuriates Saul and causes him to use obscene language. Both *shame* (besides its usual meaning) and *nakedness* denote the genitals. The insult is directed at the son, not the mother. **33:** Saul has no answer to Jonathan's questions, because David has committed no capital crime, so Saul throws his spear at him. **34:** *Grieved,* see v. 3. **38:** Jonathan's words are directed at the boy and David at the same time.

---

a Force of Heb. uncertain; Septuagint "faced him."

b-b Heb. construction unclear.

c See note at 10.11.   d See 18.11 and note.

e-e Lit. "rose up from beside."   f Identical with the "Ezel Stone," v. 19.

the ground and bowed low three times. They kissed each other and wept together; David wept the longer.

⁴²Jonathan said to David, "Go in peace! For we two have sworn to each other in the name of the LORD: 'May

21 the LORD be [witness] between you and me, and between your offspring and mine, forever!' " ¹David then went his way, and Jonathan returned to the town.

²David went to the priest Ahimelech at Nob. Ahimelech came out in alarm to meet David, and he said to him, "Why are you alone, and no one with you?" ³David answered the priest Ahimelech, "The king has ordered me on a mission, and he said to me, 'No one must know anything about the mission on which I am sending you and for which I have given you orders.' So I have ᵃdirected [my] young men toᵃ such and such a place. ⁴Now then, what have you got on hand? Anyᵇ loaves of bread? Let me have them—or whatever is available." ⁵The priest answered David, "I have no ordinary bread on hand; there is only consecrated bread—provided the young men have kept away from women." ⁶In reply to the priest, David said, "I assure you that women have been kept from us, as always. Whenever I went on a mission, even if the journey was a common one, the vessels of the young men were consecrated; all the more then ᶜmay consecrated food be put into their vessels today."ᶜ ⁷So the priest gave him consecrated bread, because there was none there except the bread of display, which had been removed from the presence of the LORD, to be replaced by warm bread as soon as it was taken away.—⁸Now one of Saul's officials was there that day, ᵈdetained before the LORD;ᵈ his name was Doeg the Edomite, Saul's ᵉchief herdsman.ᵉ

⁹David said to Ahimelech, "Haven't you got a spear or sword on hand? I didn't take my sword or any of my weapons with me, because the king's mission was urgent." ¹⁰The priest said, "There is the sword of Goliath the Philistine whom you slew in the valley of Elah; it is over there, wrapped in a cloth, behind the ephod. If you want to take that one, take it, for there is none here but that one." David replied, "There is none like it; give it to me."

¹¹That day David continued on his flight from Saul and

42: See v. 23. **21.1:** This v. serves to mark the end of the story (cf. 26.25).

21.2–10: The helpful priest. David, finding himself, after his hasty flight, without food or weapon, gets consecrated bread and Goliath's sword. **2:** *Ahimelech* was the great-grandson of Eli and brother of Ahijah (see 14.3). *In alarm,* because David, a high army commander, came unaccompanied. **3:** In order to obtain food David lies to Ahimelech. His lie has dire consequences. **5:** *Consecrated bread,* see Leviticus 24.5–9. The bread was renewed once a week, and the old bread was eaten by the priests in the sacred precinct. *Provided the young men have kept away from women:* According to Lev. 15.18 sexual intercourse entails ritual impurity. Ahimelech respectfully refrains from mentioning David himself, but he is of course included in the provision. **6:** Soldiers were prohibited from having sexual relations (as can be inferred from Deut. 23.10–12). Not only the persons but the eating *vessels* as well are ritually pure. **8:** Doeg's presence at the sanctuary is noted because of its importance for the story in the next ch. Foreigners were employed in David's young kingdom (1 Chron. 27.30–31). **10:** The sword of Goliath was kept at the sanctuary as a trophy (cf. 5.1–2; 31.10). Its exact place is described because it will play a role in the next ch. *Ephod,* see 14.3 n.

21.11–16: In Philistia. David flees to the Philistine city of Gath, believing that there he will be out of danger, but he barely succeeds in saving his life. **12:** The song of the women (18.7) has spread to the Philistines (see 29.5), and the courtiers infer from it that David, who features in the song together with Saul, is master of the land—a conclusion not far from that of Saul himself (18.8). **13:** David, understanding that he has been recognized, fears for his life, because the cited song celebrates his victory over the Philistines and par-

a-a Meaning of Heb. uncertain. 4QSamᵇ (cf. Septuagint) reads "made an appointment with [my] young men at . . ."
b Lit. "five."
c-c Meaning of Heb. uncertain in part.
d-d I.e., excluded from the shrine, perhaps because of ritual impurity.
e-e Meaning of Heb. uncertain.

he came to King Achish of Gath. 12 The courtiers of Achish said to him, "Why, that's David, king of the land! That's the one of whom they sing as they dance:

> Saul has slain his thousands;
> David, his tens of thousands."

13 These words worried David and he became very much afraid of King Achish of Gath. 14 So he concealed his good sense from them; he feigned madness ᵃfor their benefit.ᵃ He scratched marks on the doors of the gate and let his saliva run down his beard. 15 And Achish said to his courtiers, "You see the man is raving; why bring him to me? 16 Do I lack madmen that you have brought this fellow to rave for me? Should this fellow enter my house?"

22 David departed from there and escaped to the caveᵇ of Adullam; and when his brothers and all his father's house heard, they joined him down there. 2 Everyone who was in straits and everyone who was in debt and everyone who was desperate joined him, and he became their leader; there were about four hundred men with him. 3 David went from there to Mizpeh of Moab, and he said to the king of Moab, "Let my father and mother come [and stay] with you, until I know what God will do for me." 4 So he ᶜled them toᶜ the king of Moab, and they stayed with him as long as David remained in the stronghold.ᵇ 5 But the prophet Gad said to David, "Do not stay in the stronghold; go at once to the territory of Judah." So David left and went to the forest of Hereth.

6 When Saul heard that David and the men with him had been located—Saul was then in Gibeah, sitting under the tamarisk tree on the height, spear in hand, with all his courtiers in attendance upon him—7 Saul said to the courtiers standing about him, "Listen, men of Benjamin! Will the son of Jesseᵈ give fields and vineyards to every one of you? And will he make all of you captains of thousands or captains of hundreds? 8 Is that why all of you have conspired against me? For no one informs me when my own son makes a pact with the son of Jesse; no one is concernedᵉ for me and no one informs me when my own son has set my servant ᶠin ambushᶠ against me, as is now the case."

ticularly over Goliath, whose origin was from Gath. **14:** *For their benefit*, the Heb can also be interpreted, "[when] in their control." **15:** David's clever ruse succeeds. It is clear that Achish wants David to be expelled (the expulsion is mentioned explicitly at the heading of Ps. 34).

22.1–5: Head of a band. David, as leader of a group of people who fled from the established order, now has a force of his own at his disposal. **1:** The members of David's family, who are in danger from Saul, join David at *Adullam*, situated in the border region between Judah and Philistia. **3:** David takes care of his parents, for whom a fugitive's life would be too strenuous. He probably has family relations in Moab, since his great-grandmother was a Moabite, who married into a family from Bethlehem (Ruth 1.1, 4; 4.17). According to the Bible the relations between Israel and Moab were always hostile, this story being the only exception. **4:** *Stronghold*, probably at Adullam. But perhaps all the "strongholds of the wilderness" (23.14) are meant, and the space of time mentioned refers to all the wanderings of David in the wilderness.

22.6–23: The massacre. This narrative continues the narrative of 21.2–10: All priests and inhabitants of Nob are killed because of Ahimelech's help to David. Saul, fearing David, whom he considers a rebel, wants to set a deterring example. He does not even shrink from sacrilege. In his insanity he suspects everyone of conspiring against him. **6:** *Sitting under the tamarisk tree*, cf. 14.2; Judg. 4.5. *Spear in hand*, as symbol of his rule (see 26.11 n.). **7:** Saul's courtiers belong to his tribe, Benjamin. Kings used to distribute *fields and vineyards* and appoint army officers as signs of personal favor (see 8.12, 14). David, however, is of the tribe of Judah and therefore will not benefit the men of Benjamin. **8:** *My servant:* Saul makes it clear that David is his subordinate.

ᵃ⁻ᵃ Lit. "in their hand"; meaning of Heb. uncertain.

ᵇ The "cave" in v. 1 is referred to as "stronghold" in vv. 4–5; cf. the same variation in 2 Sam. 23.13–14; 1 Chron. 11.15–16.

ᶜ⁻ᶜ Targum and Syriac read "left them with."

ᵈ See note at 10.11.

ᵉ For this meaning of ḥoleh, cf. Amos 6.6.

ᶠ⁻ᶠ Septuagint reads "as an enemy."

⁹Doeg the Edomite, who was standing among the courtiers of Saul, spoke up: "I saw the son of Jesse come to Ahimelech son of Ahitub at Nob. ¹⁰He inquired of the Lord on his behalf and gave him provisions; he also gave him the sword of Goliath the Philistine." ¹¹Thereupon the king sent for the priest Ahimelech son of Ahitub and for all the priests belonging to his father's house at Nob. They all came to the king, ¹²and Saul said, "Listen to me, son*ᵃ* of Ahitub." "Yes, my lord," he replied. ¹³And Saul said to him, "Why have you and the son of Jesse conspired against me? You gave him food and a sword, and inquired of God for him—that he may rise *ᵇ*in ambush*ᵇ* against me, as is now the case."

¹⁴Ahimelech replied to the king, "But who is there among all your courtiers as trusted as David, son-in-law of Your Majesty and *ᶜ*obedient to your bidding,*ᶜ* and esteemed in your household? ¹⁵This is the first time that I inquired of God for him; *ᵈ*I have done no wrong.*ᵈ* Let not Your Majesty find fault with his servant [or] with any of my father's house; for your servant knew nothing whatever about all this." ¹⁶But the king said, "You shall die, Ahimelech, you and all your father's house." ¹⁷And the king commanded the guards standing by, "Turn about and kill the priests of the Lord, for they are in league with David; they knew he was running away and they did not inform me." But the king's servants would not raise a hand to strike down the priests of the Lord. ¹⁸Thereupon the king said to Doeg, "You, Doeg, go and strike down the priests." And Doeg the Edomite went and struck down the priests himself; that day, he killed eighty-five men *ᵉ*who wore the linen ephod.*ᵉ* ¹⁹He put Nob, the town of the priests, to the sword: men and women, children and infants, oxen, asses, and sheep—[all] to the sword.

²⁰But one son of Ahimelech son of Ahitub escaped—his name was Abiathar—and he fled to David. ²¹When Abiathar told David that Saul had killed the priests of the Lord, ²²David said to Abiathar, "I knew that day, when Doeg the Edomite was there, that he would tell Saul. I *ᶠ*am to blame for all the deaths*ᶠ* in your father's house. ²³Stay with me; do not be afraid; for *ᶠ*whoever seeks your life must seek my life also.*ᶠ* It will be my care to guard you."

a See note at 10.11.

b-b Septuagint reads "as an enemy."

c-c Cf. Isa. 11.14; but meaning of Heb. uncertain.

d-d Lit. "Far be it from me!"

e-e Septuagint reads "bearers of the ephod"; cf. note at 2.28.

f-f Meaning of Heb. uncertain.

9: *Doeg the Edomite,* see 21.8. **10:** The giving of provisions and the sword of Goliath to David was reported in 21.7, 10, but no mention was made there of inquiring of the Lord. Either Doeg lied or, more probably, when Ahimelech went behind the ephod to take the sword and unwrap it from its cloth, Doeg imagined that the priest went to inquire of the Lord (see 21.10 n.). **11–13:** Saul summons Ahimelech and all the priests to a trial, accusing them of conspiring. **14–15:** Ahimelech justifies himself, arguing that he aided David because he knew of the latter's esteemed and trusted position at the court and he was not aware that this had changed. **15:** The Heb can also be translated: "Did I begin now to inquire of God for him? Far be it from me!" According to this rendering Ahimelech denies that he inquired of God for David. This seems to be the truth, because otherwise the narrator would not have kept silent on so crucial a fact. **18:** Only Doeg, not being Israelite, is prepared to execute the king's order and kill the priests of the Lord. *Linen ephod,* see 2.18 n. **19:** Compare the enumeration here with the one at 15.3. The similarity of the two lists (there camels are also mentioned, because those animals were kept by the Amalekites, who were desert nomads) suggests that what Saul failed to do to Amalek, though commanded by the Lord, he did to his own town of priests of the Lord. This strongly condemns Saul. **20:** The massacre of the priests may be the fulfillment of the prophecy of 2.33, and the "offspring" mentioned there may refer to Abiathar. This prophecy-fulfillment pattern is frequent in the Deuteronomistic History. **22–23:** David feels responsible for the disaster, and he promises to protect Abiathar's life like his own.

23.1–13: Consulting the Lord. In the preceding narrative Ahimelech was (falsely) accused of having consulted God for David; in the present one Ahimelech's son Abiathar actually and repeatedly con-

23

David was told: "The Philistines are raiding Keilah and plundering the threshing floors." [2] David consulted the LORD, "Shall I go and attack those Philistines?" And the LORD said to David, "Go; attack the Philistines and you will save Keilah." [3] But David's men said to him, "Look, we are afraid here in Judah, how much more if we go to Keilah against the forces of the Philistines!" [4] So David consulted the LORD again, and the LORD answered him, "March down at once to Keilah, for I am going to deliver the Philistines into your hands." [5] David and his men went to Keilah and fought against the Philistines; he drove off their cattle and inflicted a severe defeat on them. Thus David saved the inhabitants of Keilah.

[6] When Abiathar son of Ahimelech fled to David at Keilah, [a]he brought down an ephod with him.[-a]

[7] Saul was told that David had come to Keilah, and Saul thought, "God has delivered[b] him into my hands, for he has shut himself in by entering a town with gates and bars." [8] Saul summoned all the troops for war, to go down to Keilah and besiege David and his men. [9] When David learned that Saul was planning[b] to harm him, he told the priest Abiathar to bring the ephod forward. [10] And David said, "O LORD, God of Israel, Your servant has heard that Saul intends to come to Keilah and destroy the town because of me. [11] Will the citizens of Keilah deliver me into his hands? Will Saul come down, as Your servant has heard? O LORD, God of Israel, tell Your servant!" And the LORD said, "He will." [12] David continued, "Will the citizens of Keilah deliver me and my men into Saul's hands?" And the LORD answered, "They will." [13] So David and his men, about six hundred in number, left Keilah at once and moved about wherever they could. And when Saul was told that David had got away from Keilah, he did not set out.

[14] David was staying [a]in the strongholds of the wilderness [of Judah];[a] he stayed in the hill country, in the wilderness of Ziph. Saul searched for him constantly, but God did not deliver him into his hands. [15] David was once at Horesh in the wilderness of Ziph, when David learned that Saul had come out to seek his life. [16] And Saul's son Jonathan came to David at Horesh and encouraged him in [the name of] God. [17] He said to him, "Do not be afraid: the hand of my father Saul will never touch you. You are going to be king over Israel and I shall be second to you; and even my father Saul knows this is so." [18] And the two of them entered into a pact before the LORD. David remained in Horesh, and Jonathan went home.

sults God for David. Consulting God is a recurring theme in the narratives about Saul and David. When successful, it is a sign that God is with David; when unsuccessful, that He is not with Saul. The first part of this narrative tells of David's deliverance of Keilah, the second part of his escape from Keilah. **1:** The Philistines came at the end of the harvest to plunder the crops (cf. Judg. 6.3). **2–3:** David wants to use his force to help Keilah, but his motley band lacks the courage. **4:** The LORD's second reply, explicitly promising to deliver the Philistines into David's hands, aids in instilling confidence in the men. **5:** *He drove off their cattle:* The Philistines had come with their livestock (cf. Judg. 6.5). **6:** Abiathar's flight to David was already reported in 22.20, before David's rescue of Keilah. *Keilah* here may be the result of dittography. An *ephod* probably contained Urim and Thummim, the means for consulting the LORD. Regarding the technique of consulting the LORD see 14.40–42 n. **7:** The only way to leave the walled town was through the gates, and there David could easily be captured. **11:** David asks two questions, but because it was possible to ask only one at a time, he has to repeat his first question. **12:** Notwithstanding their rescue by David the citizens of Keilah will deliver him into Saul's hands. They greatly fear Saul after he massacred the whole town of Nob because of the help extended to David. **13:** *Six hundred:* According to 22.2 there were about 400 men with David, so meanwhile the number has increased.

23.14–18: Encouragement. Jonathan comes to David's hiding place to encourage him, assuring his friend that eventually he will become king. **14:** *Strongholds,* table mountains with steep sides, providing natural protection. **17:** Saul knows that David will be king, and yet he continues pursuing him, driven by jealousy and enmity. **18:** *A pact* ("berit"),

---

a-a *Meaning of Heb. uncertain.*   b *Meaning of Heb. uncertain.*

19[a]Some Ziphites went up to Saul in Gibeah and said, "David is hiding among us in the strongholds of Horesh, at the hill of Hachilah south of Jeshimon. 20 So if Your Majesty has the desire to come down, come down, and it will be our task to deliver him into Your Majesty's hands." 21 And Saul replied, "May you be blessed of the LORD for the compassion you have shown me! 22 Go now and prepare further. Look around and learn what places he sets foot on [and] who has seen him there, for I have been told he is a very cunning fellow. 23 Look around and learn in which of all his hiding places he has been hiding, and return to me when you are certain. I will then go with you, and if he is in the region, I will search him out among all the clans of Judah."

24 They left at once for Ziph, ahead of Saul; David and his men were then in the wilderness of Maon, in the Arabah, to the south of Jeshimon. 25 When Saul and his men came to search, David was told about it; and he went down to [b]the rocky region[-b] and stayed in the wilderness of Maon. On hearing this, Saul pursued David in the wilderness of Maon. 26 Saul was making his way along one side of a hill, and David and his men were on the other side of the hill. [b]David was trying hard to elude Saul, and Saul and his men were trying to encircle David and his men and capture them,[-b] 27 when a messenger came and told Saul, "Come quickly, for the Philistines have invaded the land." 28 Saul gave up his pursuit of David and went to meet the Philistines. That is why that place came to be called the Rock of Separation.[c]

24 David went from there and stayed in the wildernesses of En-gedi.

2 When Saul returned from pursuing the Philistines, he was told that David was in the wilderness of En-gedi. 3 So Saul took three thousand picked men from all Israel and went in search of David and his men [b]in the direction of the rocks of the wild goats;[-b] 4 and he came to the sheepfolds along the way. There was a cave there, and Saul went in [d]to relieve himself.[-d] Now David and his men were sitting in the back of the cave.

5 David's men said to him, "This is the day of which the LORD said to you, 'I will deliver your enemy into your hands; you can do with him as you please.' " [e]David went and stealthily cut off the corner of Saul's cloak. 6 But after-

stipulating that when David will be king, Jonathan shall rank next to him.

23.19–28: Narrow escape. At the last moment, when his capture by Saul seems unavoidable, David is saved. The first part of the narrative contains the dialogue between Saul and the Ziphites concerning David's capture; the second part relates Saul's pursuit and its unexpected outcome. **19–20:** The Ziphites, in proving their loyalty to Saul, are probably under the impact of the massacre of Nob, whose priests were accused of failing to inform Saul (22.17). **21:** *May you be blessed of the LORD,* a customary blessing (see 15.13; 2 Sam. 2.5; Ps. 115.15). The king, uttering satisfaction at being pitied, makes a sorry figure. **26:** Instead of *trying to encircle,* read "encircling" (*trying* is not expressed in the Heb). David is already encircled by Saul's men and on the verge of being captured, when suddenly the messenger appears. This may be seen as directed by God to save David. **28:** *Rock of Separation,* "because there Saul separated and departed from David" (Abravanel).

24.1–23: Magnanimity. David has the opportunity to kill Saul, but refrains from doing so. When the king falls into his hands, David does not take revenge, but shows himself magnanimous and loyal towards him. In the first part of the narrative the event itself is described; the second part contains a speech by David, stating that he never wronged the king; the third part consists of a speech by Saul, who is impressed by David's generosity. The word "hand(s)" recurs frequently (in the Heb even more than in the translation): Though he has Saul in his hands, David will not raise his hand against him. **4:** *Sheepfolds* were often attached to caves, which provided shelter to the animals from heat and cold. **5:** The LORD's promise cited by David's men has not been mentioned before. It seems that the men interpret Saul's entering the cave as directed by the LORD, in

---

a *The meaning of many parts of 23.19 ff. is uncertain. The events described in 23.19–24.22 are partly paralleled in chapter 26, with variations.*

b-b *Meaning of Heb. uncertain.*   c *Meaning of Heb. uncertain.*

d-d *Lit. "to cover his feet."*   e *Vv. 5b–6 read well after 8a.*

ward [a]David reproached himself[a] for cutting off [b]the corner of Saul's cloak.[b] 7 He said to his men, "The LORD forbid that I should do such a thing to my lord—the LORD's anointed—that I should raise my hand against him; for he is the LORD's anointed." 8 David rebuked[c] his men and did not permit them to attack Saul.

Saul left the cave and started on his way. 9 Then David also went out of the cave and called after Saul, "My lord king!" Saul looked around and David bowed low in homage, with his face to the ground. 10 And David said to Saul, "Why do you listen to the people who say, 'David is out to do you harm?' 11 You can see for yourself now that the LORD delivered you into my hands in the cave today. And though [d]I was urged[d] to kill you, I showed you pity;[e] for I said, 'I will not raise a hand against my lord, since he is the LORD's anointed.' 12 Please, sir,[f] take a close look at the corner of your cloak in my hand; for when I cut off the corner of your cloak, I did not kill you. You must see plainly that I have done nothing evil or rebellious, and I have never wronged you. Yet you are bent on taking my life.13 May the LORD judge between you and me! And may He take vengeance upon you for me, but my hand will never touch you. 14 As the ancient proverb has it: 'Wicked deeds come from wicked men!' My hand will never touch you. 15 Against whom has the king of Israel come out? Whom are you pursuing? A dead dog? A single flea? 16 May the LORD be arbiter and may He judge between you and me! May He take note and uphold my cause, and vindicate me against you."

17 When David finished saying these things to Saul, Saul said, "Is that your voice, my son David?" And Saul broke down and wept. 18 He said to David, "You are right, not I; for you have treated me generously, but I have treated you badly. 19 Yes, you have just revealed how generously you treated me, for the LORD delivered me into your hands and you did not kill me. 20 If a man meets his enemy, does he let him go his way unharmed? Surely, the LORD will reward you generously for [g]what you have done for me this day.[g] 21 I know now that you will become king, and that the kingship over Israel will remain in your hands. 22 So swear to me by the LORD that you will not destroy my de-

order to enable David to strike his pursuer down. David, however, only cuts off the corner of Saul's cloak as proof that he could have killed him. He is not aware that the cutting of the cloak also has symbolic significance, namely, cutting off the kingdom (cf. 15.27–28; 1 Kings 11.29–32). The author may be foreshadowing those later events. **6–7:** According to biblical scholars, vv. 5b–6 should be placed after vv. 7–8a. According to Rashi, since the narrator began to talk about the cutting of the cloak, he finishes the subject, remarking that—some time later—David reproached himself even for having cut the cloak; the narrator then returns to the first subject and reports David's reply to his men. *The LORD's anointed:* Because the king was anointed by a prophet in the name of the LORD, he is inviolable (see 2 Sam. 1.16). **9:** Though persecuted by Saul, David honors the king. **14:** *Wicked deeds come from wicked men,* i.e., not from me. **15:** David designates Saul here *king of Israel* to contrast him with himself, who is as insignificant and harmless as *a dead dog* or (even) *a single flea.* Such expressions of submissiveness were customary in the ancient Near East. **16:** David puts his case in the hands of the LORD. **17:** Saul's question expresses his astonishment. *My son,* in response to "my father" (v. 12, see translators' note), indicates close relationship. **21:** Saul acknowledges that David will be king and that his kingship will endure—as opposed to Saul's kingship. **22:** See 20.15 n.

---

a-a *Lit. "David's heart struck him."*

b-b *So several mss. and ancient versions; cf. v. 5. Most mss. and editions read "Saul's corner."*

c *Meaning of Heb. uncertain.*   d-d *Meaning of Heb. uncertain.*

e *Understanding the Heb. as an ellipsis of* wattaḥos 'eni *(cf., e.g., Deut. 7.16).*

f *Lit. "[my] father," cf. 2 Kings 5.13.*

g-g *Meaning of Heb. uncertain. Emendation yields "the generosity you have shown me."*

scendants or wipe out my name from my father's house." 23 David swore to Saul, Saul went home, and David and his men went up to the strongholds.

25 Samuel died, and all Israel gathered and made lament for him; and they buried him in Ramah, his home.

David went down to the wilderness of Paran.[a]

2 There was a man in Maon whose possessions were in Carmel. The man was very wealthy; he owned three thousand sheep and a thousand goats. At the time, he was shearing his sheep in Carmel. 3 The man's name was Nabal, and his wife's name was Abigail. The woman was intelligent and beautiful, but the man, a Calebite, was a hard man and an evildoer. 4 David was in the wilderness when he heard that Nabal was shearing his sheep. 5 David dispatched ten young men, and David instructed the young men, "Go up to Carmel. When you come to Nabal, greet him in my name. 6 Say [b]as follows: 'To life![b] Greetings to you and to your household and to all that is yours! 7 I hear that you are now doing your shearing. As you know, your shepherds have been with us; we did not harm them, and nothing of theirs was missing all the time they were in Carmel. 8 Ask your young men and they will tell you. So receive these young men graciously, for we have come on a festive occasion. Please give your servants and your son David whatever you can.' "

9 David's young men went and delivered this message to Nabal in the name of David. When they stopped speaking, 10 Nabal answered David's servants, "Who is David? Who is the son of Jesse? There are many slaves nowadays who run away from their masters. 11 Should I then take my bread and my water,[c] and the meat that I slaughtered for my own shearers, and give them to men who come from I don't know where?" 12 Thereupon David's young men retraced their steps; and when they got back, they told him all this. 13 And David said to his men, "Gird on your swords." Each girded on his sword; David too girded on his sword. About four hundred men went up after David, while two hundred remained with the baggage.

14 One of [Nabal's] young men told Abigail, Nabal's wife, that David had sent messengers from the wilderness to greet their master, and that he had spurned[b] them. 15 "But the men had been very friendly to us; we were not

23: See 14.46 n. Saul abandons the pursuit, yet David and his men go up to the *stronghold* (in the Heb the word is in the singular), because they do not trust Saul.

25.1–44: The evil husband and the clever wife. The violent clash between David and the boorish, evil, foolish Nabal is prevented by Nabal's clever wife Abigail, who succeeds in persuading David to refrain from spilling blood. She also alludes to David's future kingship, as did Saul in the preceding narrative. **1:** The note concerning Samuel's death, which has no connection with the following narrative, may have been placed here because it was thought that the death occurred at this juncture (cf. 28.3). **2–3:** The exposition specifies Nabal's wealth even before stating his and his wife's names and qualities. *Carmel,* see 15.12 n. *Calebite:* The clan of Caleb was part of Judah, but Kenizzite in origin (Gen. 15.19; Num. 32.12; Josh. 14.14). **4:** Sheepshearing was an occasion for celebration (see 2 Sam. 13.23). **5:** *Ten young men,* to carry the generous gift David expects to receive as reward for his services. **6:** Before the request itself good wishes are uttered. The Heb may also be translated: "Say: 'So be it (also) next year: May you be well and may your household be well and all that is yours be well!' " **7:** *Your shepherds have been with us,* under our protection. **10:** *"Who is David?":* Nabal's rude reply expresses contempt (cf. Exod. 5.2). By implying that they are runaway slaves he insults both David, who escaped from Saul, and his men, who fled from society. **11:** *My bread and my water,* food and drink in general (Hos. 2.7). **13:** David is determined to use force; girding the swords is mentioned three times. **14:** The narrative's point of view switches to Abigail. **15–16:** The young man (or rather, servant), confirming David's statement (v. 7), specifies the protection Nabal's shepherds received. *They were a wall:* The metaphor denotes defense against marauders.

a Septuagint reads "Maon," cf. v. 2 and 23.24, 25.
b-b Meaning of Heb. uncertain. c Septuagint reads "wine," and cf. v. 18.

harmed, nor did we miss anything all the time that we went about with them while we were in the open. ¹⁶They were a wall about us both by night and by day all the time that we were with them tending the flocks. ¹⁷So consider carefully what you should do, for harm threatens our master and all his household; he is such a nasty fellow that no one can speak to him."

¹⁸Abigail quickly got together two hundred loaves of bread, two jars of wine, five dressed sheep, five *seahs* of parched corn, one hundred cakes of raisin, and two hundred cakes of pressed figs. She loaded them on asses, ¹⁹and she told her young men, "Go on ahead of me, and I'll follow you"; but she did not tell her husband Nabal. ²⁰She was riding on the ass and going down a trail[a] on the hill, when David and his men appeared, coming down toward her; and she met them.—²¹Now David had been saying, "It was all for nothing that I protected that fellow's possessions in the wilderness, and that nothing he owned is missing. He has paid me back evil for good. ²²May God do thus and more to [b]the enemies of[b] David if, by the light of morning, I leave [c]a single male[c] of his."—²³When Abigail saw David, she quickly dismounted from the ass and threw herself face down before[a] David, bowing to the ground. ²⁴Prostrate at his feet, she pleaded, "Let the blame be mine, my lord, but let your handmaid speak to you; hear your maid's plea. ²⁵Please, my lord, pay no attention to that wretched fellow Nabal. For he is just what his name says: His name means 'boor' and he is a boor.

"Your handmaid did not see the young men whom my lord sent. ²⁶I swear, my lord, as the LORD lives and as you live—the LORD who has kept you from seeking redress by blood with your own hands—let your enemies and all who would harm my lord fare like Nabal! ²⁷Here is the present which your maidservant has brought to my lord; let it be given to the young men who are the followers of my lord. ²⁸Please pardon your maid's boldness. For the LORD will grant my lord an enduring house, because my lord is fighting the battles of the LORD, and no wrong is ever to be found in you. ²⁹And if anyone sets out to pur-

a *Meaning of Heb. uncertain.*
b-b *The phrase is intended to avoid the imprecation of David against himself; it is lacking in the Septuagint.*
c-c *Lit. "one who pees against a wall."*

17: *Nasty,* better, "evil" (lit. "good-for-nothing"). Because speaking to Nabal is impossible, the servant appeals to Abigail. **18:** The wise Abigail understands that she has to act quickly in order to anticipate David and that first of all his request must be generously satisfied. *Seahs:* A *seah* was probably about 7 liters (more than 6 quarts). **19:** *Go*

on ahead of me: Abigail wants to placate David before she meets him. **22:** *Thus and more,* see 3.17 n. **23:** Though a wealthy and distinguished woman, Abigail hastens to display profuse gestures of respect to the runaway chieftain. She begins by taking the blame—either for Nabal's behavior or for addressing David. **24–31:** Abigail's speech shows her intelligence and eloquence. She refers throughout to David as *my lord* and to herself as his *handmaid.* In the first part she expresses agreement with David as regards Nabal; in the second part she cautions David that by spilling blood now he will do harm to himself in the future. **24:** *At his feet,* a gesture of pleading (see 2 Kings 4.27; Esth. 8.3). **25:** *Wretched,* better, "evil." Nabal's wife uses the same strong term as Naval's servant (see v. 17 n.), which indicates that she shares his opinion—evidently the common sentiment. *For he is just what his name says:* In the Bible people are aware of the meaning of names. Some names occur that, like Nabal, have unpleasant meanings, e.g., Mahlon and Chilion in Ruth 1.2, whose names mean "sickness" and "destruction." *Boor:* According to Isa. 32.6 the Heb word "naval" denotes a villain, who "leaves the hungry unsatisfied and deprives the thirsty of drink," just as Nabal did to David (see also Prov. 17.7, 21). **26:** *Fare like Nabal,* a hint that Nabal is surely going to die (cf. 2 Sam. 18.32)—therefore David need take no action himself. **27:** *Let it be given to the young men,* a polite expression, implying that the present is too humble for David himself. **28:** *Enduring house:* Abigail knows that David will be king and that his dynasty will endure, because he is fighting *the battles of the LORD* (see 18.17 n.). **29:** *Anyone,* an allusion to Saul, who set out to *pursue* David (23.25; 28; 24.15) and *seek his life* (20.1; 22.23; 23.15). *The life . . . will be bound up in the bundle of life,* a metaphor denoting long life. The LORD's bundle of life was believed to contain the names of the living, similar to His "book of life" sue you and seek your life, the life of my lord will be bound up in the bundle of life in the care of the LORD; but He will fling away the lives of your enemies as from the hollow of a sling. ³⁰ And when the LORD has accomplished for my lord all the good He has promised you, and has appointed you ruler of Israel, ³¹ do not let this be a cause of stumbling and of faltering courage to my lord that you have shed blood needlessly and that my lord sought redress with his own hands. And when the LORD has prospered my lord, remember your maid."

³² David said to Abigail, "Praised be the LORD, the God of Israel, who sent you this day to meet me! ³³ And blessed be your prudence, and blessed be you yourself for restraining me from seeking redress in blood by my own hands. ³⁴ For as sure as the LORD, the God of Israel, lives— who has kept me from harming you—had you not come quickly to meet me, not ᵃa single maleᵃ of Nabal's line would have been left by daybreak." ³⁵ David then accepted from her what she had brought him, and he said to her, "Go up to your home safely. See, I have heeded your plea and respected your wish."

³⁶ When Abigail came home to Nabal, he was having a feast in his house, a feast fit for a king; Nabal was in a merry mood and very drunk, so she did not tell him anything at all until daybreak. ³⁷ The next morning, when Nabal had slept off the wine, his wife told him everything that had happened; and his courage died within him, and he became like a stone. ³⁸ About ten days later the LORD struck Nabal and he died. ³⁹ When David heard that Nabal was dead, he said, "Praised be the LORD who championed my cause against the insults of Nabal and held back His servant from wrongdoing; the LORD has brought Nabal's wrongdoing down on his own head."

David sent messengers ᵇto propose marriage toᵇ Abigail, to take her as his wife. ⁴⁰ When David's servants came to Abigail at Carmel and told her that David had sent them to her to make her his wife, ⁴¹ she immediately bowed low with her face to the ground and said, "Your handmaid is ready to be your maidservant, to wash the feet of my lord's servants." ⁴² Then Abigail rose quickly and mounted an ass, and with five of her maids in attendance she followed David's messengers; and she became his wife.

⁴³ Now David had taken Ahinoam of Jezreel; so both of them became his wives. ⁴⁴ Saul had given his daughter Michal, David's wife, to Palti son of Laish from Gallim.

(Ps. 69.29). In postbiblical times the bundle of life came to signify eternal life in the next world, and therefore the expression is found regularly on Jewish tombstones. *Fling away the lives,* a metaphor denoting the opposite of the preceding one. *The hollow of a sling,* the middle of the sling, where the stone would be placed (see 17.40 n.). **30:** *The good* refers to the enduring house (v. 28). **31:** Refraining from bloodshed is in David's own interest. *Faltering courage,* lit. "faltering of heart," i.e., weakness. *Remember your maid,* rewarding her. **34:** David's present oath annuls his previous one (v. 22). *From harming you:* David refers to Abigail as representative of Nabal's household. **36:** Nabal's feasting shows him to be quite oblivious of any danger. **37:** *His courage,* lit. "his heart." The simile *like a stone* points to paralysis, which was presumably understood as death of the heart, in accordance with the tendency of the Bible to attribute to the heart not only feelings, but also thoughts, traits, and some physical functions (e.g., eating is often described as strengthening the heart). It seems that when Nabal hears what happened and to what terrible danger he was exposed, he suffers a stroke and becomes paralyzed and ten days later he dies. David then proposes marriage to the widow because of her intelligence, beauty, and wealth. **41:** *To wash the feet of my lord's servants,* an expression of extreme politeness and humility. **42:** The five maids are mentioned to show Abigail's economic and social status. **43:** *Jezreel,* near Carmel in southern Judah. **44:** Since Michal was David's wife, Saul had no right to give her to someone else. By doing so he intentionally hurt both David and his daughter, who had deceived him in order to help her husband (19.11–17).

a-a Lit. "one who pees against a wall."   b-b Lit. "and spoke for"; cf. Song of Songs 8.8.

26 ^aThe Ziphites came to Saul at Gibeah and said, "David is hiding in the hill of Hachilah facing Jeshimon." ²Saul went down at once to the wilderness of Ziph, together with three thousand picked men of Israel, to search for David in the wilderness of Ziph, ³and Saul encamped on the hill of Hachilah which faces Jeshimon, by the road. When David, who was then living in the wilderness, learned that Saul had come after him into the wilderness, ⁴David sent out scouts and made sure that Saul had come. ⁵David went at once to the place where Saul had encamped, and David saw the spot where Saul and his army commander, Abner son of Ner, lay asleep. Saul lay asleep inside the barricade^b and the troops were posted around him.

⁶David spoke up and asked Ahimelech the Hittite and Abishai son of Zeruiah, Joab's brother, "Who will go down with me into the camp to Saul?" And Abishai answered, "I will go down with you." ⁷So David and Abishai approached the troops by night, and found Saul fast asleep inside the barricade,^b his spear stuck in the ground at his head, and Abner and the troops sleeping around him. ⁸And Abishai said to David, "God has delivered your enemy into your hands today. Let me pin him to the ground with a single thrust of the spear. I will not have to strike him twice." ⁹But David said to Abishai, "Don't do him violence! No one can lay hands on the LORD's anointed with impunity." ¹⁰And David went on, "As the LORD lives, the LORD Himself will strike him down, or his time will come and he will die, or he will go down to battle and perish. ¹¹But the LORD forbid that I should lay a hand on the LORD's anointed! Just take the spear and the water jar at his head and let's be off." ¹²So David took away the spear and the water jar at Saul's head, and they left. No one saw or knew or woke up; all remained asleep; a deep sleep from the LORD had fallen upon them.

¹³David crossed over to the other side and stood afar on top of a hill; there was considerable distance between them. ¹⁴And David shouted to the troops and to Abner son of Ner, "Abner, aren't you going to answer?" And Abner shouted back, "Who are you to shout at the king?" ¹⁵And David answered Abner, "You are a man, aren't you? And there is no one like you in Israel! So why didn't you keep watch over your lord the king? For one of [our] troops came to do violence to your lord the king. ¹⁶You have not given a good account of yourself! As the LORD

26.1–25: Magnanimity repeated. The present story is similar to the one in ch 24. In both, David has the opportunity to kill Saul, but though urged by his men to do so, he refuses to harm the LORD's anointed. Instead, he takes one object from him to prove that he could have killed him, and when Saul sees this, he expresses regret at having persecuted David. In addition, there are verbal similarities (e.g., the simile in 24.15 and 26.20, and the question in 24.17 and 26.17). It seems that two variants of the same story have been included in the book—probably because of the differences between them (e.g., in one Saul comes to David in a cave by day and David takes a corner of Saul's coat, in the other David comes to Saul in an army camp by night and takes Saul's spear and water jar). The repetition causes David's magnanimity to emerge as a constant character trait. **5:** *Barricade,* see 17.20 n. Saul is surrounded by his troops. **6:** *Ahimelech the Hittite* is not mentioned elsewhere. The Hittite empire had its center in present-day Turkey, but Hittites are also mentioned in the land of Canaan (Gen. 23.3; 26.34; 27.46; 2 Sam. 11.3). *Abishai,* who is willing to accompany David on his dangerous exploit, and his more famous brother *Joab,* David's future army commander, are always designated sons of *Zeruiah,* who was David's sister. **7:** *His spear:* The same spear that Saul used against David can now be used by David against Saul. **9:** See 24.6–7 n. **10:** *Strike him down,* by means of an illness (see 25.38). **11:** The spear, besides being a useful weapon, was a symbol of Saul's kingship (see 13.22; 18.10; 19.9; 20.33; 22.6; 2 Sam. 1.6). A water jar was vitally important in the desert. **12:** In coming close to Saul's head David exposes himself to extreme danger. *No one saw or knew or woke up; all remained asleep:* The repetitiveness serves to ridicule the defective watch. **15:** *A man,* a hero.

a Cf. 23.19 and note.

b Meaning of Heb. uncertain; cf. 17.20.

lives, [all of] you deserve to die, because you did not keep watch over your lord, the LORD's anointed. Look around, where are the king's spear and the water jar that were at his head?"

17 Saul recognized David's voice, and he asked, "Is that your voice, my son David?" And David replied, "It is, my lord king." 18 And he went on, "But why does my lord continue to pursue his servant? What have I done, and what wrong am I guilty of? 19 Now let my lord the king hear his servant out. If the LORD has incited you against me, let Him be appeased[a] by an offering; but if it is men, may they be accursed of the LORD! For they have driven me out today, so that I cannot have a share in the LORD's possession, but am told, 'Go and worship other gods.' 20 Oh, let my blood not fall to the ground, away from the presence of the LORD! For the king of Israel has come out to seek a single flea—as if he were hunting a partridge in the hills."

21 And Saul answered, "I am in the wrong. Come back, my son David, for I will never harm you again, seeing how you have held my life precious this day. Yes, I have been a fool, and I have erred so very much." 22 David replied, "Here is Your Majesty's spear. Let one of the young men come over and get it. 23 And the LORD will requite every man for his right conduct and loyalty—for this day the LORD delivered you into my[b] hands and I would not raise a hand against the LORD's anointed. 24 And just as I valued your life highly this day, so may the LORD value my life and may He rescue me from all trouble." 25 Saul answered David, "May you be blessed, my son David. You shall achieve, and you shall prevail."

David then went his way, and Saul returned home.

27 David said to himself, "Some day I shall certainly perish at the hands of Saul. The best thing for me is to flee to the land of the Philistines; Saul will then give up hunting me throughout the territory of Israel, and I will escape him." 2 So David and the six hundred men with him went and crossed over to King Achish son of Maoch of Gath. 3 David and his men stayed with Achish in Gath, each man with his family, and David with his two wives, Ahinoam the Jezreelite and Abigail wife of Nabal the Carmelite. 4 And when Saul was told that David had fled to Gath, he did not pursue him any more.

5 David said to Achish, "If you please, let a place be

17–18: Saul's question aims at achieving certainty, since in the dark he is unable to see David. David, who politely addresses Saul as *my lord* and calls himself *his servant*, tries to dissuade Saul from pursuing him. Saul again calls David *my son* (see 24.17). **19:** *They have driven me out:* They have compelled me to flee from *the LORD's possession*—i.e., the land of Israel—to a foreign country, where I will be obliged to *worship other gods.* This probably alludes to David's intention to flee to the Philistines (see ch 27) and to the popular belief that each nation has its own god, who rules over that nation's territory (cf. 2 Kings 5.17; 17.24–28). In the land of Israel the LORD must be worshipped, in other countries the local gods. **20:** David begs not to have to die in a foreign country. *King of Israel, a single flea,* see 24.15 n. **21:** Saul, trying to reassure David, again calls him *my son* (see vv. 17 and 25). **22:** David, who does not trust Saul anymore, ignores his invitation and promise. **25:** Saul's final words ever to David are a blessing, assuring him of success. The verbs *achieve* and *prevail* are emphasized in the Heb. The concluding sentence, which marks the end of the story (cf. 21.1), makes it clear that David rejects Saul's call to return to him.

27.1–28.2: In Philistia again. For the second time David flees to Achish and deceives the Philistine king. But whereas the first time (21.11–16) he came alone and was expelled, now he comes at the head of a useful unit of 600 men and is received favorably. **1:** Because David's decision to enter the enemy's service is rather questionable, his considerations are recounted at some length and in his own words. **3:** *Stayed with Achish,* as his vassal. **5:** It was customary for a suzerain to give an estate to his vassal in return for his services. David's aim is to get away from Achish's watchful eyes. **6:** *Ziklag* was evidently crown property at the time of the narrator, during the reign of the kings of Judah—i.e.,

---

a Cf. Amos 5.21.

b So many mss.; other mss. and editions omit.

granted me in one of the country towns where I can live; why should your servant remain with you in the royal city?" 6 At that time Achish granted him Ziklag; that is how Ziklag came to belong to the kings of Judah, as is still the case. 7 The length of time that David lived in Philistine territory was a year and four months.

8 David and his men went up and raided the Geshurites, the Gizrites, and the Amalekites—who were the inhabitants of the region of Olam,ª all the way to Shur and to the land of Egypt.—9 When David attacked a region, he would leave no man or woman alive; he would take flocks, herds, asses, camels, and clothing. When he returned and cameᵇ to Achish, 10 Achish would ask, "Whereᶜ did you raid today?" and David would reply, "The Negebᵈ of Judah," or "the Negeb of the Jerahmeelites," or "the Negeb of the Kenites." 11 David would leave no man or woman alive to be brought to Gath; for he thought, "They might tell about us: David did this." Such was his practice as long as he stayed in the territory of the Philistines. 12 Achish trusted David. He thought: ᵉ"He has aroused the wrath of ᵉ his own people Israel, and so he will be my vassal forever."

28 At that time the Philistines mustered their forces for war, to take the field against Israel. Achish said to David, "You know, of course, that you and your men must march out with my forces." 2 David answered Achish, "You surely know what your servant will do." "In that case," Achish replied to David, "I will appoint you my bodyguard for life."

3 ᶠNow Samuel had died and all Israel made lament for him; and he was buried in his own town of Ramah. And Saul had forbidden [recourse to] ghosts and familiar spirits in the land.

4 The Philistines mustered and they marched to Shunem and encamped; and Saul gathered all Israel, and they encamped at Gilboa. 5 When Saul saw the Philistine force, his heart trembled with fear. 6 And Saul inquired of the LORD, but the LORD did not answer him, either by dreams or by Urimᵍ or by prophets. 7 Then Saul said to his courtiers, "Find me a woman who consults ghosts, so that I can go to her and inquire through her." And his courtiers

a *Septuagint reads "Telam" (cf. "Telaim" in 15.4; and "Telem" in Josh. 15.24).*
b *Change of vocalization yields "brought it"; cf. v. 11.*
c *So some mss. and Targum; Septuagint and 4QSamª read "Whom."*
d *I.e., the part of the Negeb occupied by these clans.*
e-e *Cf. note at 13.4.*
f *The rest of this chapter would read well after chapters 29 and 30.*
g *A kind of oracle; see note at Exod. 28.30 and 1 Sam. 14.41.*

after Solomon and before the Babylonian exile. **8–11:** Achish expects David to make raids on Judah. But David refuses to fight his own people, so he raids non-Israelite tribes and clans. After killing their population so as not to leave witnesses, he lies to Achish about the object of his raids. *The Negeb*, the desert region in the south. The clans of *Jerahmeelites* and *Kenites* were attached to Judah. **28.1–2:** This time lying cannot solve David's problem: how to reconcile his obligations to his suzerain with his unwillingness to fight against Israel. Meanwhile David gives an ambiguous answer to Achish, who, however, interprets it as expressing loyalty. As a sign of his trust, he appoints David to the sensitive office of bodyguard. Here the narrative breaks off, leaving open the question of what course David will take in the impending war.

28.3–25: Prophecy of doom. This narrative, which explains the reason for Saul's imminent defeat and death in the battle against the Philistines, seems misplaced. It would fit better immediately before ch 31, where that battle is described. Moreover, placed there the break between 28.1–2 and ch 29, which clearly belong together, would be avoided. That position would also solve the difficulty that according to 28.4 the Philistines are already at Shunem in the valley of Jezreel, whereas according to 29.1 they are only at Aphek, close to their territory, and from there they march to Jezreel (29.11). The narrative consists of five parts, arranged concentrically around Samuel's prophecy: narrator's report, dialogue between Saul and the necromancer, dialogue between Samuel and Saul, dialogue between Saul and the necromancer, narrator's report. **3:** The exposition mentions two events, which happened previously, but are important for the present story: Samuel's death and Saul's removal of necromancers. **4:** *Shunem* and Mount *Gilboa* lie on opposite sides of the valley of Jezreel. Saul's fear is an indication of his decline. **7:** Since discovering told him that there was a woman in En-dor who consulted ghosts.

8 Saul disguised himself; he put on different clothes and set out with two men. They came to the woman by night, and he said, "Please divine for me by a ghost. Bring up for me the one I shall name to you." 9 But the woman answered him, "You know what Saul has done, how he has banned [the use of] ghosts and familiar spirits in the land. So why are you laying a trap for me, to get me killed?" 10 Saul swore to her by the LORD: "As the LORD lives, you won't get into trouble over this." 11 At that, the woman asked, "Whom shall I bring up for you?" He answered, "Bring up Samuel for me." 12 Then the woman recognized Samuel,[a] and she shrieked loudly, and said to Saul, "Why have you deceived me? You are Saul!" 13 The king answered her, "Don't be afraid. What do you see?" And the woman said to Saul, "I see a divine being coming up from the earth." 14 "What does he look like?" he asked her. "It is an old man coming up," she said, "and he is wrapped in a robe." Then Saul knew that it was Samuel; and he bowed low in homage with his face to the ground.

15 Samuel said to Saul, "Why have you disturbed me and brought me up?" And Saul answered, "I am in great trouble. The Philistines are attacking me and God has turned away from me; He no longer answers me, either by prophets or in dreams. So I have called you to tell me what I am to do." 16 Samuel said, "Why do you ask me, seeing that the LORD has turned away from you and has become your adversary?[b] 17 The LORD has done [c]for Himself[c] as He foretold through me: The LORD has torn the kingship out of your hands and has given it to your fellow, to David, 18 because you did not obey the LORD and did not execute His wrath upon the Amalekites. That is why the LORD has done this to you today. 19 Further, the LORD will deliver the Israelites who are with you into the hands of the Philistines. Tomorrow your sons and you will be with me; and the LORD will also deliver the Israelite forces into the hands of the Philistines."

20 At once Saul flung himself prone on the ground, terrified by Samuel's words. Besides, there was no strength in him, for he had not eaten anything all day and all night. 21 The woman went up to Saul and, seeing how greatly disturbed he was, she said to him, "Your handmaid listened to you; I took my life in my hands and heeded the

the future by legitimate means failed—a bad sign in itself—Saul has recourse to an illegitimate one. It is ironic that he who banned necromancers now consults one himself. **8:** Sheol, the abode of the dead was believed to be beneath the earth. **11:** Though dead, Samuel the prophet is still expected to be able to foretell the future. **12–14:** Apparently only the woman could see the ghost, whereas Saul could only hear him. The appearance of Samuel's ghost is considered to be real—not trickery by the woman or imagination of Saul. The Bible believes in the possibility of sorcery, soothsaying and necromancy, but prohibits them as heathen practices (Deut. 18.9–14). *Wrapped in a robe:* Samuel's robe played a role before; see 2.19; 15.27. **17–18:** See 15.18–19, 28. **19:** *With me,* in Sheol, the underworld (see 2.6 n.). **20:** *He had not eaten,* owing to his depression. **21–24:** In contrast to the stern Samuel, the woman is depicted as concerned for Saul's well-being. She has compassion for him and urges him to eat (she mentions only *a bit of food,* but slaughters *a stall-fed calf* and bakes *cakes*). She uses the argument that because she listened to Saul, he should listen to her in return. Much urging, by the woman as well as by the courtiers, is needed to persuade Saul to eat. **23:** It was customary to sit *on the bed* (or couch) while eating (Ezek. 23.41; Amos 6.4). **25:** Saul and his courtiers leave as soon as they finish eating, before anyone can recognize them.

---

a *Some Septuagint mss. read "Saul."*
b *Meaning of Heb. uncertain.*
c-c *Some mss. and Septuagint read "to you."*

request you made of me. ²²So now you listen to me: Let me set before you a bit of food. Eat, and then you will have the strength to go on your way." ²³He refused, saying, "I will not eat." But when his courtiers as well as the woman urged him, he listened to them; he got up from the ground and sat on the bed. ²⁴The woman had a stall-fed calf in the house; she hastily slaughtered it, and took flour and kneaded it, and baked some unleavened cakes. ²⁵She set this before Saul and his courtiers, and they ate. Then they rose and left the same night.

29 The Philistines mustered all their forces at Aphek, while Israel was encamping at the spring in Jezreel. ²The Philistine lords came marching, each with his units of hundreds and of thousands; and David and his men came marching last, with Achish. ³The Philistine officers asked, "Who are those Hebrews?" "Why, that's David, the servant of King Saul of Israel," Achish answered the Philistine officers. "He has been with me ᵃ˙for a year or more,˙ᵃ and I have found no fault in him from the day he defected until now." ⁴But the Philistine officers were angry with him; and the Philistine officers said to him, "Send the man back; let him go back to the place you assigned him. He shall not march down with us to the battle, or else he may become our adversary in battle. For with what could that fellow appease his master if not with ᵇ˙the heads of these men?˙ᵇ ⁵Remember, he is the David of whom they sang as they danced:

Saul has slain his thousands;
David, his tens of thousands."

⁶Achish summoned David and said to him, "As the LORD lives, you are an honest man, and I would like to have you serveᶜ in my forces; for I have found no fault with you from the day you joined me until now. But you are not acceptable to the other lords. ⁷So go back in peace, and do nothing to displease the Philistine lords."

⁸David, however, said to Achish, "But what have I done, what fault have you found in your servant from the day I appeared before you to this day, that I should not go and fight against the enemies of my lord the king?" ⁹Achish replied to David, "I know; you are as acceptable to me as an angel of God. But the Philistine officers have decided that you must not march out with us to the battle. ¹⁰So rise early in the morning, you and your lord's ser-

29.1–11: The problem solved. This narrative continues 28.1–2. It shows again that God is with David: His problem of how to refrain from fighting against his own people without violating his suzerain's order is solved by the Philistine lords, who mistrust David. The narrative is composed of two rounds of dialogues—the first between the Philistine officers and Achish, the second between Achish and David. **2:** *The Philistine lords,* see 5.8 n. **3:** *Hebrews,* see 4.6 n. **4:** *Angry,* because in the officers' opinion, David endangers them. *The place you assigned him,* Ziklag. *That fellow,* a disdainful phrase. *These men,* the Philistines in front of them. **5:** Like Achish's courtiers (21.12), the Philistine officers base their argument on the song of the Israelite women (18.7), which celebrated David for his glorious victory over the Philistines. **6–7:** Before ordering David back, Achish praises him and stresses his faith in him. It is ironic that Achish has complete confidence in David, who repeatedly deceived him. *As the* LORD *lives:* Achish even swears by the God of David. Polytheistic peoples believed in the power of other peoples' gods (see 4.8). *The other lords,* the Philistine lords adopted the officers' opinion. **8:** David, who is happy not to have to participate in the war, pretends to be offended so as to underscore his (feigned) loyalty to Achish. **9:** *Acceptable to me,* lit. "good in my eyes." Achish intensifies his praise of David, even comparing him to an *angel of God.* The same rather extreme comparison is applied to David—and to no one else—three more times (2 Sam. 14.17, 20; 19.28). **10:** *Your lord's servants:* David's men became Achish's servants together with David himself.

---

a-a *Meaning of phrase uncertain.*
b-b *A euphemism for "our heads."*
c *Lit. "go out and come in."*

vants who came with you—ᵃrise early in the morning,ᵃ and leave as soon as it is light." ¹¹ Accordingly, David and his men rose early in the morning to leave, to return to the land of the Philistines, while the Philistines marched up to Jezreel.

30 By the time David and his men arrived in Ziklag, on the third day, the Amalekites had made a raid into the Negeb and against Ziklag; they had stormed Ziklag and burned it down. ² They had taken the women in it captive, low-born and high-born alike; they did not kill any, but carried them off and went their way. ³ When David and his men came to the town and found it burned down, and their wives and sons and daughters taken captive, ⁴ David and the troops with him broke into tears, until they had no strength left for weeping. ⁵ David's two wives had been taken captive, Ahinoam of Jezreel and Abigail wife of Nabal from Carmel. ⁶ David was in great danger, for the troops threatened to stone him; for all the troops were embittered on account of their sons and daughters.

But David sought strength in the LORD his God. ⁷ David said to the priest Abiathar son of Ahimelech, "Bring the ephod up to me." When Abiathar brought up the ephodᵇ to David, ⁸ David inquired of the LORD, "Shall I pursue those raiders? Will I overtake them?" And He answered him, "Pursue, for you shall overtake and you shall rescue."

⁹ So David and the six hundred men with him set out, and they came to the Wadi Besor, where a halt was made by those who were to be left behind. ¹⁰ David continued the pursuit with four hundred men; two hundred men had halted, too faint to cross the Wadi Besor. ¹¹ They came upon an Egyptian in the open country and brought him to David. They gave him food to eat and water to drink; ¹² he was also given a piece of pressed fig cake and two cakes of raisins. He ate and regained his strength, for he had eaten no food and drunk no water for three days and three nights. ¹³ Then David asked him, "To whom do you belong and where are you from?" "I am an Egyptian boy," he answered, "the slave of an Amalekite. My master abandoned me when I fell ill three days ago. ¹⁴ We had raided the Negeb of the Cherethites, and [the Negeb] of Judah, and the Negeb of Caleb; we also burned down Ziklag." ¹⁵ And David said to him, "Can you lead me down to that

11: *To Jezreel,* where the Israelite army was encamping (v. 1).

30.1–30: Defeat turned into victory. In David's absence the Amalekites raided Ziklag, taking captives and spoil. Thanks to the Philistine lords' distrust, and particularly to Achish's order to leave early in the morning, David arrives home soon enough to be able to overtake the Amalekites and rescue the captives and spoil. The first part of the narrative is devoted to the encounter with the Amalekites, the second part to the distribution of the spoils taken from them. The narrative presents some important contrasts between David and Saul: David successfully consults God, Saul does not; David is victorious in battle, Saul suffers defeat; David rescues all women and children, Saul and his children die, together with many of his troops. The contrasts are highlighted by the fact that David's battle against the Amalekites and Saul's battle against the Philistines took place at approximately the same time (see 2 Sam. 1.1–2). Furthermore, this battle should not have taken place since Saul should have killed all the Amalekites (ch 15). **1:** The Amalekites attacked *Ziklag* (see 27.6), when there were only women and children in the town. **5:** See 25.42–43. **6:** David, as leader, is held responsible for the disaster. **7:** See 23.6 n. **8:** In contrast to Saul (28.6), the LORD answers David, telling him that he will surely *overtake* and *rescue* (these verbs are emphasized in the Heb). **10:** *Too faint:* After marching home from Aphek, the men immediately had to set out again and hurry into the desert in pursuit of the Amalekites. **11–15:** Thanks to the Egyptian boy, David soon discovers the Amalekites and is able to rescue captives and spoil. Because the boy, being ill, was cruelly abandoned by his master, without food or drink, he is prepared to help David—only concerned that he not be killed or delivered to his Amalekite master. **14:** *Cherethites,* Philistines (cf. v. 16; Ezek. 25.16).

---

a-a *Meaning of parts of verse uncertain. Septuagint reads "and go to the place that I have assigned you; and harbor no evil thought in your heart, for you are acceptable to me."*
b *See note at 2.28.*

band?" He replied, "Swear to me by God that you will not kill me or deliver me into my master's hands, and I will lead you down to that band." 16 So he led him down, and there they were, scattered all over the ground, eating and drinking and making merry because of all the vast spoil they had taken from the land of the Philistines and from the land of Judah. 17 David attacked them from *a*before dawn until the evening of the next day; *a* none of them escaped, except four hundred young men who mounted camels and got away. 18 David rescued everything the Amalekites had taken; David also rescued his two wives. 19 Nothing of theirs was missing—young or old, sons or daughters, spoil or anything else that had been carried off—David recovered everything. 20 David took all the flocks and herds, *a*which [the troops] drove ahead of the other livestock; *a* and they declared, "This is David's spoil."

21 When David reached the two hundred men who were too faint to follow David and who had been left at the Wadi Besor, they came out to welcome David and the troops with him; David came forward with the troops and greeted them. 22 But all the mean and churlish fellows among the men who had accompanied David spoke up, "Since they did not accompany us,*b* we will not give them any of the spoil that we seized—except that each may take his wife and children and go." 23 David, however, spoke up, "You must not do that, *c*my brothers, in view of*c* what the LORD has granted us, guarding us and delivering into our hands the band that attacked us. 24 How could anyone agree with you in this matter? The share of those who remain with the baggage shall be the same as the share of those who go down to battle; they shall share alike." 25 So from that day on it was made a fixed rule for Israel, continuing to the present day.

26 When David reached Ziklag, he sent some of the spoil to the elders of Judah *a*[and] to his friends,*a* saying, "This is a present for you from our spoil of the enemies of the LORD." 27 [He sent the spoil to the elders] in Bethel,*d* Ramoth-negeb, and Jattir; 28 in Aroer, Siphmoth, and Eshtemoa; 29 in Racal, in the towns of the Jerahmeelites, and in the towns of the Kenites; 30 in Hormah, Bor-ashan, and Athach; 31 and to those in Hebron—all the places where David and his men had roamed.

The name probably points to their origin from the island of Crete (see 4.1b n). *Caleb,* see 25.2–3 n. *Burned down Ziklag,* in revenge for David's raid (27.8). **15:** The law in the ancient Near East required returning slaves to their masters—Israelite law only being an exception (Deut. 23.16–17). **16:** The feasting Amalekites are completely oblivious of a possible attack. **17:** *The next day* after coming there David attacks from before dawn until evening. **20:** *This is David's spoil,* a sign of the men's gratitude, and a radical reversal of their attitude at the beginning of the narrative (v. 6). **24:** The men who guard the baggage, thereby allowing the others to move swiftly, have contributed to the victory (cf. 25.13). **25:** The narrator explains that a rule existing in his time originated from David's prescription. **26–31:** David sends parts of the spoil to the elders of Judah, to express his gratitude for their help when he roamed through their territory, and to gain their support in the future. All places mentioned were situated in the area of Hebron and Beer-sheba.

a-a Meaning of Heb. uncertain.

b So some mss. and versions; most mss. and editions read "me."

c-c Meaning of Heb. uncertain. Septuagint reads "after."

d Called Bethul in Josh. 19.4.

31

^aThe Philistines attacked Israel, and the men of Israel fled before the Philistines and [many] fell on Mount Gilboa. ² The Philistines pursued Saul and his sons, and the Philistines struck down Jonathan, Abinadab, and Malchishua, sons of Saul. ³ The battle raged around Saul, and ^b·some of the archers·^b hit him, and he ^c·was severely wounded·^c by the archers. ⁴ Saul said to his arms-bearer, "Draw your sword and run me through, so that the uncircumcised may not run me through and make sport of me." But his arms-bearer, in his great awe, refused; whereupon Saul grasped the sword and fell upon it. ⁵ When his arms-bearer saw that Saul was dead, he too fell on his sword and died with him. ⁶ Thus Saul and his three sons and his arms-bearer, ^d·as well as all his men,·^d died together on that day. ⁷ And when the men of Israel ^e·on the other side of the valley and on the other side of the Jordan·^e saw that the men of Israel had fled and that Saul and his sons were dead, they abandoned the towns and fled; the Philistines then came and occupied them.

⁸ The next day the Philistines came to strip the slain, and they found Saul and his three sons lying on Mount Gilboa. ⁹ They cut off his head and stripped him of his armor, and they sent them throughout the land of the Philistines, to spread the news ^f·in the temples of their idols·^f and among the people. ¹⁰ They placed his armor in the temple of Ashtaroth, and they impaled his body on the wall of Bethshan. ¹¹ When ^g·the inhabitants of Jabesh-gilead heard about it—what·^g the Philistines had done to Saul—¹² all their stalwart men set out and marched all night; they removed the bodies of Saul and his sons from the wall of Beth-shan and came^h to Jabesh and burned them there. ¹³ Then they took the bones and buried them under the tamarisk tree in Jabesh, and they fasted for seven days.

31.1–13: Tragic end. Saul, who was anointed king in order to liberate Israel from the Philistines (9.16), dies while being defeated by the Philistines. Not only did he fail in liberating Israel, but at his death the Philistines gained domination over most of the country. Saul's career began with the rescue of Jabesh-gilead (ch 11), and it ended with the men of Jabesh-gilead rescuing his dead body. The first part of the narrative tells of Israel's defeat and Saul's death, the second part of the treatment of his and his sons' corpses. **1:** The narrative takes no interest in the details of the battle, only in its outcome. **4:** A few cases of suicide, mostly committed to escape being killed by the enemy, are recorded in the Bible (Judg. 9.54; 16.30; 2 Sam. 17.23; 1 Kings 16.18). The Bible does not view these suicides negatively, in the way later Judaism would. *The uncircumcised,* a deprecatory designation (see 14.6). Instead of *make sport of,* the Heb may be translated "abuse." The abuse of enemy corpses springs from feelings of rage and hatred towards them. **6:** *All his men,* those close to him; the others fled (Radak). **7:** The people living near the battlefield fled in fear of the Philistines. **10:** *They placed his armor in the temple,* cf. 21.10. *Ashtaroth,* see 7.3. Impalement of corpses was designed to shame and demoralize the enemy. **12:** By their courageous deed, intended to prevent further desecration of the corpses, the men of Jabesh-gilead pay their debt to Saul for the rescue of their city (ch 11). Cremation was not practiced in Israel. In this particular case the flesh was probably burned because it was in a state of decay, and only the bones were buried. **13:** *They fasted,* as an act of mourning. According to the Bible mourning rites were observed *for seven days* (see Gen. 50.10; Job 2.13), and that is still the case in Judaism today (the mourning period is called "shiv'ah," from the Heb word for seven).

---

a 1 Chron. 10 reproduces this chapter, with minor variations.

b-b Meaning of Heb. uncertain. Lit. "the archers, men with the bow."

c-c Construed as hophal form; cf. 1 Kings 2.34.

d-d Lacking in the Septuagint; 1 Chron. 10.6 reads "all his house."

e-e Meaning of Heb. uncertain. 1 Chron. 10.7 reads "in the valley."

f-f Septuagint and 1 Chron. 10.9 read "among their idols."

g-g 1 Chron. 10.11 reads "all [the inhabitants of] Jabesh-gilead heard all that."

h 1 Chron. 10.12 reads "brought them."

שמואל ב

2 Samuel

AS STATED IN THE INTRODUCTION to 1 Samuel, the two books of Samuel are actually one work. For information about the background, literary form, text, and composition of 2 Samuel, see the introduction to 1 Samuel.

The reign of King David is the subject of 2 Samuel, which is composed of three parts. The first part (1.1–8.18) tells of David's rise to power, the second (8.19–20.26) of his sin and the ensuing troubles in his family, and the third (chs 21–24) is an appendix consisting of miscellaneous materials. Both the first and the second part end with a list of David's chief officials (8.16–18; 20.23–26).

David is highly successful in his career. He conquers Jerusalem, makes it his administrative and religious center, liberates Israel definitively from Philistine domination, and even creates an empire. In his personal life, however, he makes serious mistakes, and consequently has to undergo great sufferings.

[SHIMON BAR-EFRAT]

1 After the death of Saul—David had already returned from defeating the Amalekites—David stayed two days in Ziklag. ²On the third day, a man came from Saul's camp, with his clothes rent and earth on his head; and as he approached David, he flung himself to the ground and bowed low. ³David said to him, "Where are you coming from?" He answered, "I have just escaped from the camp of Israel." ⁴"What happened?" asked David. "Tell me!" And he told him how the troops had fled the battlefield, and that, moreover, many of the troops had fallen and

1.1–16: Message of death. This narrative reports David's reaction to the message of Saul's death. The account of Saul's death here disagrees with the account in 1 Sam. ch 31. There it was told that Saul, after begging his arms-bearer to kill him, committed suicide by falling on his sword; here, that Saul, after requesting an unknown Amalekite to kill him, died by the hand of that Amalekite. Some scholars explain the discrepancy by assuming two different sources; others contend that the Amalekite lied (to find favor with David). It is quite possible, however, that the two accounts complement each other. The Amalekite does not say that he killed Saul, but that he *finished him off* (v. 10). Perhaps Saul, close to death after falling upon

his sword, begged the Amalekite to finish him off (regarding the statement in 31.6 that Saul died, cf. 1 Sam. 17.50–51). According to this interpretation, Saul, who failed to kill all the Amalekites and particularly their king (1 Sam. ch 15), is now dispatched himself by an Amalekite. David, at any rate, believes the Amalekite, who brings Saul's crown and armlet as evidence. The Amalekite expects to be rewarded by David for liquidating his enemy, but David puts him to death, and mourns over Saul and Jonathan. **1:** *After the death of Saul,* cf. Josh. 1.1; Judg. 1.1. This formula motivated the division of Samuel into two books at this particular point. *The Amalekites,* see 1 Sam. ch 30. *Ziklag,* see 1 Sam. 27.6. **2:** *His clothes rent and earth on his head,* conventional signs of mourning. **4:** The man's account, conveying the bad news died; also that Saul and his son Jonathan were dead. [5] "How do you know," David asked the young man who brought him the news, "that Saul and his son Jonathan are dead?" [6] The young man who brought him the news answered, "I happened to be at Mount Gilboa, and I saw Saul leaning on his spear, and the chariots and horsemen closing in on him. [7] He looked around and saw me, and he called to me. When I responded, 'At your service,' [8] he asked me, 'Who are you?' And I told him that I was an Amalekite. [9] Then he said to me, 'Stand over me, and finish me off, [a-]for I am in agony and am barely alive.'[-a] [10] So I stood over him and finished him off, for I knew that [a-]he would never rise from where he was lying.[-a] Then I took the crown from his head and the armlet from his arm, and I have brought them here to my lord."

[11] David took hold of his clothes and rent them, and so did all the men with him. [12] They lamented and wept, and they fasted until evening for Saul and his son Jonathan, and for the soldiers of the LORD[b] and the House of Israel who had fallen by the sword. [13] David said to the young man who had brought him the news, "Where are you from?" He replied, "I am the son of a resident alien, an Amalekite." [14] "How did you dare," David said to him, "to lift your hand and kill the LORD's anointed?" [15] Thereupon David called one of the attendants and said to him, "Come over and strike him!" He struck him down and he died. [16] And David said to him, "Your blood be on your own head! Your own mouth testified against you when you said, 'I put the LORD's anointed to death.'"

[17] And David intoned this dirge over Saul and his son Jonathan—[18] [a-]He ordered the Judites to be taught [The Song of the] Bow.[-a] It is recorded in the Book of Jashar.[c]

[19]　　Your glory, O Israel,
　　　　Lies slain on your heights;
　　　　How have the mighty fallen!
[20]　　Tell it not in Gath,
　　　　Do not proclaim it in the streets of Ashkelon,
　　　　Lest the daughters of the Philistine rejoice,
　　　　Lest the daughters of the uncircumcised exult.

[21]　　O hills of Gilboa—
　　　　Let there be no dew or rain on you,
　　　　[d-]Or bountiful fields,[-d]

a-a Meaning of Heb. uncertain.　　b Septuagint reads "Judah."
c See note at Josh. 10.13.
d-d Meaning of Heb. uncertain. Emendation yields "springs from the deep" (cf. Ugaritic shrᶜthmtm, and Gen. 7.11; 8.2).

in increasing order, is similar to the account given to Eli by the man of Benjamin (1 Sam. 4.16–17). **6:** Saul, weak from his mortal wounds, supported himself on his spear, the symbol of his kingship (see 1 Sam. 26.11 n.). The Philistines had chariots, which carried a charioteer and an archer. **10:** The Amalekite justifies his deed: Not only did he fulfill Saul's explicit wish, but he was also sure that Saul had no chance of recovering. *He would never rise from where he was lying,* lit. "he would not live after his falling" (presumably, upon his sword). *Crown,* actually a coronet or band worn on the forehead. It was a symbol of kingship (2 Kings 11.12); the *armlet* here likely serves a similar function. **14:** *To lift your hand and kill the LORD's anointed,* cf. 1 Sam. 24.7; 26.9, 11. **16:** This v. chronologically precedes v. 15. *Your blood be on your own head,* the guilt for your death is entirely yours. *I put the LORD's anointed to death:* David's formulation of the Amalekite's confession reflects his own viewpoint.

1.17–27: David's dirge. Like the first part of the ch, the dirge demonstrates David's deep sorrow over Saul and Jonathan's death. The dirge lacks religious or national motifs. It does not mention God, and the expressions of grief relate to the deaths of Saul and Jonathan only, not to Israel's defeat. Prominent among the dirge's many poetical features—parallelism, metaphor, synecdoche, etc.—is the frequent use of apostrophe, the direct addressing of Israel, (virtual) messengers, the hills of Gilboa, the daughters of Israel, and Jonathan. This device is particularly impressive, because the addressees are unable to hear and respond. The two lines of v. 19 recur, in different form, in v. 25, and the second line also recurs in v. 26, forming a refrain that underscores the contrast between the leaders' courage and their fate. **18:** The difficult word *bow* is not in LXX. Regarding David's instruction that the song be taught, cf. Deut. 31.22 and Ps. 60.1.

For there the shield of warriors lay rejected,
The shield of Saul,
Polished with oil no more.

22   From the blood of slain,
From the fat of warriors—
The bow of Jonathan
Never turned back;
The sword of Saul
Never withdrew empty.

23   Saul and Jonathan,
Beloved and cherished,
Never parted
In life or in death!
They were swifter than eagles,
They were stronger than lions!

24   Daughters of Israel,
Weep over Saul,
Who clothed you in crimson and finery,
Who decked your robes with jewels of gold.

25   How have the mighty fallen
In the thick of battle—
Jonathan, slain on your heights!

26   I grieve for you,
My brother Jonathan,
You were most dear to me.
Your love was wonderful to me
More than the love of women.

27   How have the mighty fallen,
The ᵃ⁻weapons of war⁻ᵃ perished!

2 Sometime afterward, David inquired of the LORD, "Shall I go up to one of the towns of Judah?" The LORD answered, "Yes." David further asked, "Which one shall I go up to?" And the LORD replied, "To Hebron." ² So David went up there, along with his two wives, Ahinoam of Jezreel and Abigail wife of Nabal the Carmelite. ³ David also took the men who were with him, each with his family, and they settled in the towns about Hebron. ⁴ The men of Judah came and there they anointed David king over the House of Judah.

David was told about the men of Jabesh-gilead who

19: *Glory:* The metaphor refers to Saul. **20:** The towns *Gath* and *Ashkelon* stand for all Philistia. *Daughters:* Women used to celebrate victories with song and dance (Judg. 11.34; 1 Sam. 18.6). *Uncircumcised,* see 1 Sam. 14.6 n. **21:** *Gilboa,* see 1 Sam. 31.1, 8. Instead of *bountiful fields,* the Heb may be translated "fields of heights" (the same Heb root in Judg. 5.18), which parallels *hills of Gilboa.* Shields were made of leather, and had to be oiled regularly. **22:** *From the blood . . . from the fat,* i.e., from spilling the blood and the fat. **24:** *Daughters of Israel:* Dirges were conventionally sung by women (Jer. 9.16–19). The clothes and ornaments represent the prosperity brought by Saul. **26:** This v., wholly dedicated to Jonathan, and formulated in the first and second person, is the most direct and personal one in the dirge. David's statement that Jonathan's *love was wonderful* to him *more than the love of women* (for him) does not hint at homosexual relations, but is an expression of deep friendship (regarding this friendship, see 1 Sam. chs 18–20; 23.15–18).

2.1–11: King of Judah. While David reigns over Judah, Ishbosheth, Saul's son, reigns over parts of Israel, which consisted of the other tribes. **1:** After Saul's death David wants to return home from the land of the Philistines, where he fled from Saul's persecutions (1 Sam. ch 27). *Inquired,* most likely by means of the ephod, which contained the Urim and Thummim (1 Sam. 14.42; 23.6, 11). *Hebron* was the principal city of Judah. **2:** *Ahinoam, Abigail,* see 1 Sam. 25.42–43. Both Jezreel and Carmel were near Hebron; thus David is related through his wives to the families in the region. **3:** *The men who were with him,* see 1 Sam. 27.2. **4a:** Through the initiative of the men of Judah David is made king. The gifts he sent to the elders of Judah (1 Sam. 30.26–31) may have contributed to his being chosen. **4b–7:** Besides expressing appreciation for their pious burial of Saul (1 Sam. 31.11–13), David's

a-a I.e., Saul and Jonathan.

buried Saul. [5] So David sent messengers to the men of Jabesh-gilead and said to them, "May you be blessed of the LORD because you performed this act of faithfulness to your lord Saul and buried him. [6] May the LORD in turn show you true faithfulness; and I too will reward you generously because you performed this act. [7] Now take courage and be brave men; for your lord Saul is dead and the House of Judah have already anointed me king over them."

[8] But Abner son of Ner, Saul's army commander, had taken Ish-bosheth[a] son of Saul and brought him across to Mahanaim [9] and made him king over Gilead, the Ashurites,[b] Jezreel, Ephraim, and Benjamin—over all Israel. [10] Ish-bosheth[a] son of Saul was forty years old when he became king of Israel, and he reigned two years. But the House of Judah supported David. [11] The length of time that David reigned in Hebron over the House of Judah was seven years and six months.

[12] Once Abner son of Ner and the soldiers of Ish-bosheth son of Saul marched out from Mahanaim to Gibeon, [13] and Joab son of Zeruiah and the soldiers of David [also] came out.[c] They confronted one another at the pool of Gibeon: one group sat on one side of the pool, and the other group on the other side of the pool. [14] Abner said to Joab, "Let the young men come forward and sport[d] before us." "Yes, let them," Joab answered. [15] They came forward and were counted off, twelve for Benjamin and Ish-bosheth son of Saul, and twelve of David's soldiers. [16] Each one grasped his opponent's head[e] [and thrust] his dagger into his opponent's side; thus they fell together. That place, which is in Gibeon, was called Helkath-hazzurim.[f]

[17] A fierce battle ensued that day, and Abner and the men of Israel were routed by David's soldiers. [18] The three sons of Zeruiah[g] were there—Joab, Abishai, and Asahel. Asahel was swift of foot, like a gazelle in the open field. [19] And Asahel ran after Abner, swerving neither right nor left in his pursuit of Abner. [20] Abner looked back and shouted, "Is that you, Asahel?" "Yes, it is," he called back. [21] Abner said to him, "Turn to the right or to the left, and seize one of our boys and strip off his tunic." But Asahel would not leave off. [22] Abner again begged Asahel, "Stop pursuing me, or I'll have to strike you down. How will I

blessing of the men of *Jabesh-gilead* also has the purpose of persuading them to offer him Saul's throne. **8:** *Abner*, Saul's cousin (1 Sam. 14.50), is the strong man, who dominates *Ish-bosheth*. *Mahanaim*, east of the Jordan. Most of the land west of the Jordan was under Philistine control after their victory at the battle of Mount Gilboa (1 Sam. ch 31). **9:** Ish-bosheth first reigns over Gilead, then gradually extends his rule to the west and the south, and in the last two years rules over all Israel (except Judah). *Ashurites*, probably Asherites (members of the tribe of Asher). **10:** See 1 Sam. 13.1 n.

2.12–32: Civil war. David's men gain victory over Ish-bosheth's men, signaling the ascent of David versus the descent of the house of Saul (cf. 3.1). **13:** *Joab*, see 1 Sam. 26.6 n. Archeological excavations at Gibeon have revealed a deep pool, hewn in the rock. **14:** Single combat between representatives of two opposing armies was not uncommon (see 1 Sam. 17.4–7 n.). Its purpose was to avoid comprehensive fighting of the entire armies. **15:** *Benjamin*, Ish-bosheth's tribe. **17:** Since none of the young men prevailed over his opponent a battle between the armies ensues. **18–24:** The account of the battle focuses on two men: Abner and Asahel. Abner does not want to kill Asahel, but sees no alternative. **21:** *Strip off his tunic*, see Judg. 14.19. **23:** *A backward thrust*, rather "the back end." The butt of the spear was fitted with a metal blade, which would be stuck in the ground (1 Sam. 26.7). **26:** In order to prevent further bloodshed Abner, who has suffered many more losses than Joab, proposes to end hostilities. *Must the sword devour forever*: The same metaphor is used in Deut. 32.42; 2 Sam. 18.8, and elsewhere. **28:** The sounding of the horn signals the cessation of pursuit. **32:** Lying unburied on the battlefield and being a prey to the wild animals was the greatest horror that a warrior could face (cf. 1 Sam. 17.44, 46). Especially great value was attached to burial

---

a Meaning "Man of Shame," deliberately altered from Ish-baal, "man of Baal"; cf. 1 Chron. 8.33; 9.39, and note at 2 Sam. 4.4.   b Meaning of Heb. uncertain.
c Septuagint adds "from Hebron."   d I.e., engage in single combat.
e Septuagint adds "with his hand."
f Meaning perhaps "the Field of the Flints (or Blades)."
g A sister of David, 1 Chron. 2.16.

look your brother Joab in the face?" 23 When he refused to desist, Abner struck him in the belly with ᵃ‑a backward thrust⁻ᵃ of his spear and the spear protruded from his back. He fell there and died on the spot. And all who came to the place where Asahel fell and died halted; 24 but Joab and Abishai continued to pursue Abner. And the sun was setting as they reached the hill of Ammah, ᵃ‑which faces Giah on the road to the wilderness of Gibeon.⁻ᵃ

25 The Benjaminites rallied behind Abner, forming a single company; and they took up a position on the top of a hill. 26 Abner then called out to Joab, "Must the sword devour forever? You know how bitterly it's going to end! How long will you delay ordering your troops to stop the pursuit of their kinsmen?" 27 And Joab replied, "As God lives, ᵇ‑if you hadn't spoken up, the troops would have given up the pursuit of their kinsmen only the next morning."⁻ᵇ 28 Joab then sounded the horn, and all the troops halted; they ceased their pursuit of Israel and stopped the fighting. 29 Abner and his men marched through the Arabah all that night and, after crossing the Jordan, they marched ᵃ‑through all of Bithron⁻ᵃ until they came to Mahanaim. 30 After Joab gave up the pursuit of Abner, he assembled all the troops and found nineteen of David's soldiers missing, besides Asahel. 31 David's soldiers, on the other hand, ᵃ‑defeated the Benjaminites and the men under Abner and killed three hundred and sixty men.⁻ᵃ 32 They bore Asahel away and buried him in his father's tomb in Bethlehem. Then Joab and his men marched all night; day broke upon them in Hebron.

3 The war between the House of Saul and the House of David was long-drawn-out; but David kept growing stronger, while the House of Saul grew weaker.

2 ᶜSons were born to David in Hebron: His first-born was Amnon, by Ahinoam of Jezreel; 3 his second was Chileab, by Abigail wife of Nabal the Carmelite; the third was Absalom son of Maacah, daughter of King Talmai of Geshur; 4 the fourth was Adonijah son of Haggith; the fifth was Shephatiah son of Abital; 5 and the sixth was Ithream, by David's wife Eglah. These were born to David in Hebron.

6 During the war between the House of Saul and the House of David, Abner supported the House of Saul. 7 Now Saul had a concubine named Rizpah, daughter of

in one's father's tomb (see 19.38; 21.14).

3.1–5: Family enlargement, part 1. Through his marriages David enters into relations with many families, one of them a royal one. Numerous wives and children were considered a sign of status. The list mentions only one son, probably the eldest, for each wife. **1:** This v. serves as a link between 2.12–32 and 3.6–39. Only a few details are told concerning the *long-drawn-out* war. **3:** *Geshur,* a small Aramaic kingdom, east of the Sea of Galilee.

3.6–39: The strong army chief. The first part of the narrative deals with Abner's efforts to transfer rule over Israel from Ish-bosheth to David; the second part is concerned with Abner's death. Both parts aim at proving that Abner's murder *was not by the king's will* (v. 37). Thus the first part stresses (three times) that Abner, after being honorably received by David, went away unharmed; the second part, that David intensely mourned Abner's death. Abner's death was disadvantageous to David, because Abner was in the course of making him king over all Israel, whereas it benefitted Joab, who feared that Abner might take his place. **7:** Sexual relations with the king's wife or concubine amounted to claiming the throne (see 16.22; 1 Kings 2.22).

a-a *Meaning of Heb. uncertain.*

b-b *Emendation yields "If you had only spoken up, the troops would already have given up the pursuit of their kinsmen this morning."*

c *The list of David's wives and sons in vv. 2–5 differs somewhat from the parallel list in 1 Chron. 3.1–3. The narrative in v. 1 is resumed in v. 6.*

Aiah; and [Ish-bosheth] said to Abner, "Why have you lain with my father's concubine?" [8] Abner was very upset by what Ish-bosheth said, and he replied, "Am I a dog's head *·from Judah?·* Here I have been loyally serving the House of your father Saul and his kinsfolk and friends, and I have not betrayed you into the hands of David; yet this day you reproach me over a woman! [9] May God do thus and more to Abner if I do not do for David as the LORD swore to him—[10] to transfer the kingship from the House of Saul, and to establish the throne of David over Israel and Judah from Dan to Beer-sheba." [11] [Ish-bosheth] could say nothing more in reply to Abner, because he was afraid of him.

[12] Abner immediately*·* sent messengers to David, saying, *·"To whom shall the land belong?" and to say [further],·* "Make a pact with me, and I will help you and bring all Israel over to your side." [13] He replied, "Good; I will make a pact with you. But I make one demand upon you: Do not appear before me unless you bring Michal daughter of Saul when you come before me." [14] David also sent messengers to Ish-bosheth son of Saul, to say, "Give me my wife Michal, for whom I paid the bride-price[b] of one hundred Philistine foreskins."[c] [15] So Ish-bosheth sent and had her taken away from [her] husband, Paltiel son of Laish. [16] Her husband walked with her as far as Bahurim, weeping as he followed her; then Abner ordered him to turn back, and he went back.

[17] Abner had conferred with the elders of Israel, saying, "You have wanted David to be king over you all along. [18] Now act! For the LORD has said concerning David: *·I will deliver·* My people Israel from the hands of the Philistines and all its other enemies through My servant David." [19] Abner also talked with the Benjaminites; then Abner went and informed David in Hebron of all the wishes of Israel and of the whole House of Benjamin.

[20] When Abner came to David in Hebron, accompanied by twenty men, David made a feast for Abner and the men with him. [21] Abner said to David, "Now I will go and rally all Israel to Your Majesty. They will make a pact with you, and you can reign over all that your heart desires." And David dismissed Abner, who went away unharmed.

[22] Just then David's soldiers and Joab returned from a raid, bringing much plunder with them; Abner was no

8–10: Ish-bosheth's reproach infuriates Abner, who swears to deprive the king of his rule. **8:** *A dog's head:* Comparison to a dog was a common way of expressing contempt (see 9.8; 16.9). Dogs lived in human society as scavengers, not as pets. Abner does not deny Ish-bosheth's accusation. **9:** *Thus and more,* see 1 Sam. 3.17 n. **10:** *From Dan to Beer-sheba,* see 1 Sam. 3.19–21 n. **13:** *Michal daughter of Saul:* David's right to succeed Saul as king is based in part on his marriage to Saul's daughter. **14:** The official request for Michal is made to the king, who, in spite of its political implications, must concede, because Abner demands it. **15:** Michal was given to Paltiel by Saul (1 Sam. 25.44). **16:** Paltiel's weeping brings out the fact that nothing is said about Michal's or David's feelings—their reunion being purely political (see 6.20 n.). **17:** Abner argues that both the people and God wanted David to be king. Regarding David's popularity, see 1 Sam. 18.16. **18:** Since Saul failed to deliver Israel from the hands of the Philistines (see 1 Sam. 9.16), that task passed to David. **19:** Abner even succeeds in persuading *Benjamin,* the tribe of Ish-bosheth (and Abner himself), to replace their king with a non-Benjaminite.

---

a-a Meaning of Heb. uncertain.

b Cf. Exod. 22.15; Deut. 20.7; 22.23–29.

c Cf. 1 Sam. 18.27 (where the number is given as "two hundred").

d-d So many mss. and versions; most mss. and editions have "He has delivered."

longer with David in Hebron, for he had been dismissed and had gone away unharmed. ²³ When Joab and the whole force with him arrived, Joab was told that Abner son of Ner had come to the king, had been dismissed by him, and had gone away unharmed. ²⁴ Joab went to the king and said, "What have you done? Here Abner came to you; why did you let him go? Now he has gotten away! ²⁵ Don't you know that Abner son of Ner came only to deceive you, to learn your comings and goings and to find out all that you are planning?" ²⁶ Joab left David and sent messengers after Abner, and they brought him back from the cistern of Sirah; but David knew nothing about it. ²⁷ When Abner returned to Hebron, Joab took him aside within the gate to talk to him privately;^a there he struck him in the belly. Thus [Abner] died for shedding the blood of Asahel, Joab's^b brother.

²⁸ Afterward, when David heard of it, he said, "Both I and my kingdom are forever innocent before the LORD of shedding the blood of Abner son of Ner. ²⁹ May [the guilt] fall upon the head of Joab and all his father's house. May the house of Joab never be without someone suffering from a discharge or an eruption, or ^{c-}a male who handles the spindle,^{-c} or one slain by the sword, or one lacking bread."—³⁰ Now Joab and his brother Abishai had killed Abner because he had killed their brother Asahel during the battle at Gibeon.—³¹ David then ordered Joab and all the troops with him to rend their clothes, gird on sackcloth, and make lament before^d Abner; and King David himself walked behind the bier. ³² And so they buried Abner at Hebron; the king wept aloud by Abner's grave, and all the troops wept. ³³ And the king intoned this dirge over Abner,

> "Should Abner have died the death of a churl?

³⁴
> Your hands were not bound,
> Your feet were not put in fetters;
> But you fell as one falls
> Before treacherous men!"

And all the troops continued to weep over him.

³⁵ All the troops came to urge David to eat something while it was still day; but David swore, "May God do thus to me and more if I eat bread or anything else before sundown." ³⁶ All the troops ^{e-}took note of it^{-e} and approved, ^{e-}just as all the troops approved everything else the king did.^{-e} ³⁷ That day all the troops and all Israel knew that it was not by the king's will that Abner son of Ner was

24–25: Joab accuses both David and Abner: David, that he let the enemy commander go, and Abner, that he came to spy on David. *Comings and goings,* a military term (cf. translators' note at 1 Sam. 29.6). **27:** Instead of *privately,* the Heb may be translated "misleadingly" (cf. 2 Kings 4.28). Joab strikes Abner in the belly, just as Abner struck Asahel in the belly (2.23). **28–29:** Shedding innocent blood entails punishment by heaven. Therefore David declares that responsibility for the murder does not rest with him, but with Joab. *A discharge,* a venereal disease. *An eruption,* a skin disease. **30:** According to v. 27 Joab alone killed Abner. But instead of the first *killed,* the Dead Sea manuscript 4QSam^a and Septuagint read "lay in wait for," i.e., both Joab and Abishai watched for an opportunity to kill Abner. Whereas Asahel was killed *during the battle,* Abner was killed in peacetime (cf. 1 Kings 2.5). **31:** Joab, the murderer, is obliged to participate in the mourning. Rending clothes and wearing sackcloth were signs of grief. **33–34:** The first line of David's dirge parallels the fourth (*died the death/fell as one falls*), and the second line parallels the third (*your hands/your feet; not bound/not put in fetters*). **35:** Fasting until evening was an expression of mourning (see 1.12).

---

a *Meaning of Heb. uncertain.*   b *Heb. "his."*
c-c *I.e., a man fit only for woman's work.*   d *I.e., in the procession.*
e-e *Meaning of Heb. uncertain.*

killed. [38] And the king said to his soldiers, "You well know that a prince, a great man in Israel, has fallen this day. [39] And today I am weak, even though anointed king; those men, the sons of Zeruiah, are too savage for me. May the LORD requite the wicked for their wickedness!"

4 When [Ish-bosheth] son of Saul heard that Abner had died in Hebron, *he lost heart* and all Israel was alarmed. [2] The son of Saul [had] two company commanders, one named Baanah and the other Rechab, sons of Rimmon the Beerothite—Benjaminites, since Beeroth too was considered part of Benjamin. [3] The Beerothites had fled to Gittaim,[b] where they have sojourned to this day. ([4]Jonathan son of Saul had a son whose feet were crippled. He was five years old when the news about Saul and Jonathan came from Jezreel, and his nurse picked him up and fled; but as she was fleeing in haste, he fell and was lamed. His name was Mephibosheth.[c]) [5] Rechab and Baanah, sons of Rimmon the Beerothite, started out, and they reached the home of Ish-bosheth at the heat of the day, when he was taking his midday rest. [6] [d]So they went inside the house, as though fetching wheat, and struck him in the belly.[d] Rechab and his brother Baanah slipped by, [7] and entered the house while he was asleep on his bed in his bedchamber; and they stabbed him to death. They cut off his head and took his head and made their way all night through the Arabah. [8] They brought the head of Ish-bosheth to David in Hebron. "Here," they said to the king, "is the head of your enemy, Ish-bosheth son of Saul, who sought your life. This day the LORD has avenged my lord the king upon Saul and his offspring."

[9] But David answered Rechab and his brother Baanah, the sons of Rimmon the Beerothite, and said to them, "As the LORD lives, who has rescued me from every trouble: [10] The man who told me in Ziklag that Saul was dead thought he was bringing good news. But instead of rewarding him for the news, I seized and killed him. [11] How much more, then, when wicked men have killed a blameless man in bed in his own house! I will certainly avenge his blood on you, and I will rid the earth of you." [12] David gave orders to the young men, who killed them; they cut off their hands and feet and hung them up by the pool in

39: David explains why he does not punish Joab and Abishai, leaving that to the LORD.

4.1–12: The weak king. After several introductory remarks the narrative first tells of Ish-bosheth's death, and then of David's reaction to it, which is similar to his reaction to Saul's and Abner's death. Because Ish-bosheth's assassination made the way free for David to become king over all Israel, the narrative aims to clear him of all suspicion of complicity. This continues the theme of the initial chapters of 2 Samuel. David had no hand in the death of Saul and his family. **1–2:** *Son of Saul:* The omission of the personal name may express contempt (cf. 1 Sam. 20.27, 30, 31). *Benjaminites*, of the tribe of Ish-bosheth. **3:** After the original inhabitants of Beeroth (see Josh. 9.17ff.) had fled, Benjaminites settled in the town. **4:** Mephibosheth being crippled and therefore considered unfit to be king, no offspring of Saul, except Ish-bosheth, was left who could be king of Israel. **6–7:** V. 6 is largely repeated in v. 7 (the Heb verb at its end means "escaped" rather than *slipped by*). Abravanel explains that either v. 7 adds details about the way Ish-bosheth was murdered or that after striking him in the belly the assassins returned to his house in order to finish him off. It seems, however, that v. 6 is corrupt (cf. the different reading of Septuagint) and superfluous. V. 7 is a perfect continuation of v. 5. **8:** The *enemy . . . who sought your life* is Saul, not Ish-bosheth (in the Heb the word order is "the head of Ish-bosheth son of Saul, your enemy"). Cf. 1 Sam. 20.1; 23.15. **10:** See 1.1–16. **12:** Cutting off hands and feet as well as hanging in a public place (after the execution) were considered extremely humiliating (Judg. 1.6–7; Deut. 21.22–23).

a-a Lit. "his hands weakened"; and so frequently.

b Gittaim was likewise in Benjamin; cf. Neh. 11.31 ff.

c The original form of the name, Merib-baal, is preserved in 1 Chron. 8.34; 9.40. Cf. Ish-bosheth (Eshbaal) in 2 Sam. 2.8, note a. This subject is resumed in chapter 9.

d-d Meaning of Heb. uncertain. Septuagint reads, "And behold, the woman who kept the door of the house was cleaning wheat. She became drowsy and fell asleep."

Hebron. And they took the head of Ish-bosheth and buried it in the grave of Abner at Hebron.

5 ªAll the tribes of Israel came to David at Hebron and said, "We are your own flesh and blood. ² Long before now, when Saul was king over us, it was you who ᵇ⁻led Israel in war;⁻ᵇ and the LORD said to you: You shall shepherd My people Israel; you shall be ruler of Israel." ³ All the elders of Israel came to the king at Hebron, and King David made a pact with them in Hebron before the LORD. And they anointed David king over Israel.

⁴ David was thirty years old when he became king, and he reigned forty years. ⁵ In Hebron he reigned over Judah seven years and six months, and in Jerusalem he reigned over all Israel and Judah thirty-three years.

⁶ The king and his men set out for Jerusalem against the Jebusites who inhabited the region. David was told, "You will never get in here! ᶜEven the blind and the lame will turn you back." (They meant: David will never enter here.)⁻ᶜ ⁷ But David captured the stronghold of Zion; it is now the City of David. ⁸ On that occasion David said, "Those who attack the Jebusites ᶜshall reach the water channel and [strike down] the lame and the blind, who are hateful to David." That is why they say: "No one who is blind or lame may enter the House."⁻ᶜ

⁹ David occupied the stronghold and renamed it the City of David; David also fortified the surrounding area, from the Milloᵈ inward. ¹⁰ David kept growing stronger, for the LORD, the God of Hosts, was with him.

¹¹ ᵉKing Hiram of Tyre sent envoys to David with cedar logs, carpenters, and stonemasons; and they built a palace for David. ¹² Thus David knew that the LORD had established him as king over Israel and had exalted his kingship for the sake of His people Israel.

¹³ After he left Hebron, David took more concubines and wives in Jerusalem, and more sons and daughters were born to David. ¹⁴ These are the names of the children born to him in Jerusalem: ᶠShammua, Shobab, Nathan, and Solomon; ¹⁵ Ibhar, Elishua, Nepheg, and Japhia; ¹⁶ Elishama, Eliada, and Eliphelet.

a The account in vv. 1–3 and 6–10 is to be found also, with variations, in 1 Chron. 11.1–9.
b-b Lit. "led Israel out and in."
c-c Meaning of Heb. uncertain.
d A citadel.
e The account in vv. 11–25 is to be found also, with variations, in 1 Chron. 14.1–16.
f The list in vv. 14–16 is found, in addition to 1 Chron. 14.4–7, in 1 Chron. 3.5–8, with variations.

5.1–5: King of Israel. 1–3: Without effort on his part, the kingdom of Israel is offered to David, just as the kingdom of Judah was seven years earlier. The account emphasizes, right from its beginning, that *all the tribes* favored David. **4–5:** The summary of David's kingship conforms to the summarizing formulas in the book of Kings (e.g., 1 Kings 14.21).

5.6–12: Jerusalem. In order to unite the tribes under his rule, David conquers Jebusite Jerusalem, which separated the southern tribe of Judah from the northern tribes of Israel. **6:** *Jebusites,* one of the peoples of Canaan. *The blind and the lame:* Their function is not clear. Perhaps they were part of a magical procedure or served as living illustration of a curse, expressing: Whoever enters here shall become like them. The Hittites, to whom the Jebusites were possibly related, used to parade a blind and a deaf person before their soldiers, proclaiming: Whoever does evil to the king [and] the queen, let them make him blind, let them make him [deaf]. **8:** *Shall reach,* lit. "and touch." The meaning of the Heb word translated *water channel* is unclear. It may refer to the tunnel (known today as Warren's shaft) that connected the city on the hill with the spring in the valley. In that case, the target may have been cutting off the water supply or entering the city through that tunnel. Cf. 1 Chron. 11.4–6, where neither the blind and the lame nor the water channel are mentioned. *The House,* the Temple. **9:** David makes Jerusalem his capital, probably because of its central location between Judah and Israel, and because it was neutral territory, which had belonged to neither. **11:** *Tyre,* the most important city of Phoenicia. *Cedar* trees, for which Lebanon was famous, made excellent building material.

5.13–16: Family enlargement, part 2. The list complements 3.2–5 (see there).

The kingdom of David according to Second Samuel. The dashed line shows the approximate boundary of the kingdom at its greatest extent.

17[a]When the Philistines heard that David had been anointed king over Israel, the Philistines marched up in search of David; but David heard of it, and he went down to the fastness.[b] 18 The Philistines came and spread out over the Valley of Rephaim. 19 David inquired of the LORD, "Shall I go up against the Philistines? Will You deliver them into my hands?" And the LORD answered David, "Go up, and I will deliver the Philistines into your hands." 20 Thereupon David marched to Baal-perazim, and David defeated them there. And he said, "The LORD has broken through my enemies before me as waters break through [a dam]." That is why that place was named Baal-perazim.[c] 21 The Philistines abandoned their idols there, and David and his men carried them off.

22 Once again the Philistines marched up and spread out over the Valley of Rephaim. 23 David inquired of the LORD, and He answered, "Do not go up, but circle around behind them and confront them at the baca[d] trees. 24 And when you hear the sound of marching in the tops of the baca trees, then go into action, for the LORD will be going in front of you to attack the Philistine forces." 25 David did as the LORD had commanded him; and he routed the Philistines from Geba all the way to Gezer.

6 David again assembled all the picked men of Israel, thirty thousand strong. 2[e] Then David and all the troops that were with him set out from Baalim[f] of Judah to bring up from there the Ark of God to which the Name was attached, the name LORD of Hosts Enthroned on the Cherubim.

3 They loaded the Ark of God onto a new cart and conveyed it from the house of Abinadab, which was on the hill; and Abinadab's sons, Uzza and Ahio, guided the [g]new cart. 4 They conveyed it from Abinadab's house on the hill, [Uzzah walking][h] alongside[-g] the Ark of God and Ahio walking in front of the Ark. 5 Meanwhile, David and all the House of Israel danced before the LORD to [i][the sound of] all kinds of cypress wood [instruments],[-i] with lyres, harps, timbrels, sistrums, and cymbals.

5.17–25: Liberation. David, succeeding where Saul failed, liberates Israel from Philistine domination. **17–18:** The *fastness* may refer to the stronghold mentioned in vv. 7 and 9 (the Heb uses the same word in all these vv.), which was close to the Valley of Rephaim. **19:** See 2.1 n. **20:** *The LORD has broken through my enemies:* An etiological explanation of the name *Baal-perazim.* It seems that "Baal," lit. "master," but also the name of the main Canaanite deity, is here an epithet for the Israelite God. **21:** It was customary to bring one's gods to the battlefield in order to obtain their help (see 1 Sam. 4.3 n.). David's capture of the Philistine idols is a reversal of the situation of 1 Sam. 4.11, when the Ark of the LORD was captured by the Philistines. **23:** *Do not go up,* to the front. **24:** *The sound of marching,* "when a wind will move the tops of the *bacas* so that a sound is heard like the footsteps of marching people" (Ralbag). **25:** Routing the Philistines to *Gezer,* on the border between Israel and Philistia, amounts to expelling them from Israelite territory.

6.1–23: Holiness. David brings the Holy Ark to Jerusalem, making the city not only his administrative, but also his religious, center. Thus Jerusalem becomes the holy city, first in Judaism, where it is still the direction of prayer, and later also in Christianity and Islam, though for different reasons. **1:** *Thirty thousand,* see 1 Sam. 15.4 n. **2:** *The Ark of God,* see 1 Sam. 4.4 n. **3–4:** *A new cart,* see 1 Sam. 6.7 n. *Abinadab,* see 1 Sam. 7.1. The passage from *new* at the end of v. 3 to *hill* in v. 4 is a dittography, repeating (in exactly the same words in the Heb) what was said in v. 3a. Read: "Uzza and Ahio guided the cart, [Uzzah walking] alongside the Ark of God and Ahio walking in front of the Ark." **5:** *To all kinds of cypress wood* is a corruption of "with all their might and with songs" (1 Chron. 13.8), which is similar in Heb writing.

a Vv. 17–25 continue the narrative of v. 3.

b Probably the stronghold of Adullam (cf. 1 Sam. 22.4–5).

c Interpreted as "Baal of Breaches." Cf. 6.8 below, and the name Perez in Gen. 38.29 and note.   d Meaning of Heb. uncertain.

e Vv. 2–12 are found also in 1 Chron. 13.5–14, with variations.

f Identical with Baalah, another name for Kiriath-jearim, where the Ark had been kept (cf. 1 Sam. 6.21; 1 Chron. 13.6; Josh. 15.9).

g-g Septuagint and 4QSam[a] read "cart alongside."   h Cf. vv. 6–7.

i-i Cf. Kimhi; the parallel passage 1 Chron. 13.8 reads "with all their might and with songs."

⁶But when they came to the threshing floor of Nacon, Uzzah reached out for the Ark of God and grasped it, for the oxen had stumbled.ᵃ ⁷The Lord was incensed at Uzzah. And God struck him down on the spot ᵇ-for his indiscretion,-ᵇ and he died there beside the Ark of God. ⁸David was distressed because the Lord had inflicted a breach upon Uzzah; and that place was named Perez-uzzah,ᶜ as it is still called.

⁹David was afraid of the Lord that day; he said, "How can I let the Ark of the Lord come to me?" ¹⁰So David would not bring the Ark of the Lord to his place in the City of David; instead, David diverted it to the house of Obed-edom the Gittite. ¹¹The Ark of the Lord remained in the house of Obed-edom the Gittite three months, and the Lord blessed Obed-edom and his whole household.

¹²It was reported to King David: "The Lord has blessed Obed-edom's house and all that belongs to him because of the Ark of God." ᵈThereupon David went and brought up the Ark of God from the house of Obed-edom to the City of David, amid rejoicing. ¹³When the bearers of the Ark of the Lord had moved forward six paces, he sacrificed ᵉ-an ox and a fatling.-ᵉ ¹⁴David whirled with all his might before the Lord; David was girt with a linen ephod. ¹⁵Thus David and all the House of Israel brought up the Ark of the Lord with shouts and with blasts of the horn.

¹⁶As the Ark of the Lord entered the City of David, Michal daughter of Saul looked out of the window and saw King David leaping and whirling before the Lord; and she despised him for it.

¹⁷They brought in the Ark of the Lord and set it up in its place inside the tent which David had pitched for it, and David sacrificed burnt offerings and offerings of well-being before the Lord. ¹⁸When David finished sacrificing the burnt offerings and the offerings of well-being, he blessed the people in the name of the Lord of Hosts. ¹⁹And he distributed among all the people—the entire multitude of Israel, man and woman alike—to each a loaf of bread, ᵃ-a cake made in a pan, and a raisin cake.-ᵃ Then all the people left for their homes.

²⁰David went home to greet his household. And Michal daughter of Saul came out to meet David and said,

---

ᵃ Meaning of Heb. uncertain.

ᵇ-ᵇ So Targum; 1 Chron. 13.10 reads "because he had laid a hand on the Ark."

ᶜ I.e., "the Breach of Uzzah"; cf. 5.20 and note.

ᵈ Vv. 12b–14 are found, with variations, in 1 Chron. 15.25–27; vv. 15–19a, with variations, in 1 Chron. 15.28–16.3; vv. 19b–20a, with variations, in 1 Chron. 16.43.

ᵉ-ᵉ 4QSamᵃ reads "seven oxen and seven [rams]"; cf. 1 Chron. 15.26.

6–8: Touching the sacred object, loaded with awesome divine power, is fraught with danger (cf. Num. 4.15; 1 Sam. 6.19). David is distressed, because Uzzah only intended to prevent the Ark from slipping down. The fact is, however, that Uzzah came in direct contact with the Ark and therefore he is slain by God. The name *Perez-uzzah* is explained etiologically. **10:** *Obed-edom* may have been one of the Gittites who accompanied David on his way from the Philistine town of Gath (see 15.18). But there were also several places called Gath (meaning "winepress") in Israel. **12:** The report to King David convinces him that the Ark can be a blessing, if only it is handled properly. **13:** This time no cart is mentioned. The bearers were probably priests or Levites (see Num. 7.9; 1 Chron. 15.2). The sacrifices are meant to appease God in case another inadvertent mistake is made (cf. Job 1.5). **14:** The *ephod* was a priestly garment (1 Sam. 2.18–21 n.). **16:** *Michal daughter of Saul* (i.e., daughter of a king) despises her husband *King David*, whose frivolous behavior is unworthy of a king. **17:** The Ark had been in a tent since olden times (Exod. ch 40; Josh. 18.1). **18:** David, sacrificing and blessing in the name of the Lord, exercises priestly functions (see also vv. 13–14). **20:** Honor in Michal's view consists of external dignified behavior; in David's view, of devotion to lofty ideas. But Michal's sarcasm springs from pent-up pain and bitterness. In the past she loved David, helped him to escape, and even deceived her father for his sake (1 Sam. 18.20, 28; 19.11–17). Then Saul gave her to Paltiel, who fervently loved her (2 Sam. 3.15–16). After many years David demanded her back, for utilitarian reasons (see 3.13, 16 n.), and she found herself one of his many wives. There is no hint that David ever loved her. **21:** *Instead of your father:* David taunts Michal in return. **22:** Michal's childlessness may be a punishment by God or the result of David's abstaining from sexual relations with her.

"Didn't the king of Israel do himself honor today—exposing himself today in the sight of the slavegirls of his subjects, as one of the riffraff might expose himself!" [21] David answered Michal, "It was before the LORD who chose me instead of your father and all his family and appointed me ruler over the LORD's people Israel! I will dance before the LORD [22] and dishonor myself even more, and be low in ᵃmy ownᵃ esteem; but among the slavegirls that you speak of I will be honored." [23] So to her dying day Michal daughter of Saul had no children.

7 ᵇWhen the king was settled in his palace and the LORD had granted him safety from all the enemies around him, [2] the king said to the prophet Nathan: "Here I am dwelling in a house of cedar, while the Ark of the LORD abides in a tent!" [3] Nathan said to the king, "Go and do whatever you have in mind, for the LORD is with you."

[4] But that same night the word of the LORD came to Nathan: [5] "Go and say to My servant David: Thus said the LORD: Are you the one to build a house for Me to dwell in? [6] From the day that I brought the people of Israel out of Egypt to this day I have not dwelt in a house, but have moved about in Tent and Tabernacle. [7] As I moved about wherever the Israelites went, did I ever reproach any of the tribal leadersᶜ whom I appointed to care for My people Israel: Why have you not built Me a house of cedar?

[8] "Further, say thus to My servant David: Thus said the LORD of Hosts: I took you from the pasture, from following the flock, to be ruler of My people Israel, [9] and I have been with you wherever you went, and have cut down all your enemies before you. Moreover, I will give you great renown like that of the greatest men on earth. [10] I will establish a home for My people Israel and will plant them firm, so that they shall dwell secure and shall tremble no more. Evil men shall not oppress them any more as in the past, [11] ever since I appointed chieftains over My people Israel. I will give you safety from all your enemies.

"The LORD declares to you that He, the LORD, will establish a houseᵈ for you. [12] When your days are done and you lie with your fathers, I will raise up your offspring after you, one of your own issue, and I will establish his kingship. [13] He shall build a house for My name, and I will

a-a *Septuagint reads "your."*

b *This chapter is found, with variations, also in 1 Chron. 17.*

c *Understanding* shibṭe *as "scepters"; so Kimhi. 1 Chron. 17.6 reads "chieftains"; cf. below, v. 11.*

d *I.e., a dynasty; play on "house" (i.e., Temple) in v. 5.*

There is thus no possibility of uniting the house of Saul and the house of David through a child of David and Michal.

7.1–29: The house. The ch contains a short introduction and two long speeches: one by God and one by David. God objects to David's plan to build Him a house (temple, Heb "bayit"), and announces instead that He will make a house (dynasty, Heb "bayit") for David and that David's son will build Him a house (temple). David first thanks the LORD and then requests that his house (dynasty) may endure forever. Biblical scholars have pointed out many Deuteronomistic characteristics in the ch. **1:** *Palace,* lit. "house." *All the enemies around him:* Either only the Philistines are meant or the ch is not in its proper chronological place, because in the following chs more wars are reported. **2:** *House of cedar,* paneled with precious cedar. **3–7:** Nathan encourages David to carry out his plan, but the LORD objects. Prophets sometimes express their personal feelings, which are not always in accord with God (e.g., Samuel opposed the people's demand for a king, whereas God consented, 1 Sam. 8.6–7). **5:** *Thus said the LORD,* the messenger formula (cf. Gen. 32.4–5), which assures that the following words, spoken by Nathan, are really the LORD's. **6:** *Not dwelt in a house:* In Shiloh, however, there was a House of the LORD (1 Sam. 1.7, 9). But there was also a Tent (Josh. 18.1; 1 Sam. 2.22), which symbolized the idea that the LORD is not restricted to one fixed place. **12:** *Your offspring:* This undoubtedly refers to Solomon. This v. and the following ones, however, have been interpreted in the postbiblical period as referring to the Messiah, who will be of the house of David and whose reign will last forever. **13:** In this verse the two main themes of the ch, the building of the Temple and the establishment of the Davidic dynasty, are joined together. The reason that David's son, rather than David himself, is to build the establish his royal throne forever. [14]I will be a father to him, and he shall be a son to Me. When he does wrong, I will chastise him [a]with the rod of men and the affliction of mortals;[-a] [15]but I will never withdraw My favor from him as I withdrew it from Saul, whom I removed [b]to make room for you.[-b] [16]Your house and your kingship shall ever be secure before you;[c] your throne shall be established forever."

[17]Nathan spoke to David in accordance with all these words and all this prophecy. [18]Then King David came and sat before the LORD, and he said, "What am I, O Lord GOD, and what is my family, that You have brought me thus far? [19]Yet even this, O Lord GOD, has seemed too little to You; for You have spoken of Your servant's house also for the future. [d]May that be the law for the people,[-d] O Lord GOD. [20]What more can David say to You? You know Your servant, O Lord GOD. [21][d]For Your word's sake and of Your own accord[-d] You have wrought this great thing, and made it known to Your servant. [22]You are great indeed, O Lord GOD! There is none like You and there is no other God but You, as we have always heard. [23]And who is like Your people Israel, a unique nation on earth, whom God went and redeemed as His people, winning renown for Himself and doing great and marvelous deeds for them[e] [and] for Your land—[driving out][f] nations and their gods before Your people, whom You redeemed for Yourself from Egypt. [24]You have established Your people Israel as Your very own people forever; and You, O LORD, have become their God.

[25]"And now, O LORD God, fulfill Your promise to Your servant and his house forever; and do as You have promised. [26]And may Your name be glorified forever, in that men will say, 'The LORD of Hosts is God over Israel'; and may the house of Your servant David be established before You. [27]Because You, O LORD of Hosts, the God of Israel, have revealed to Your servant that You will build a house for him, Your servant has ventured to offer this prayer to You. [28]And now, O Lord GOD, You are God and Your words will surely come true, and You have made this gracious promise to Your servant. [29]Be pleased, therefore, to bless Your servant's house, that it abide before You forever; for You, O Lord GOD, have spoken. May Your servant's house be blessed forever by Your blessing."

house for the LORD is given in 1 Kings 5.17 and, somewhat differently, in 1 Chron. 22.8–10: David fought many wars and shed much blood, whereas his son enjoyed peace. *My name* (instead of "Me") serves to exclude the possible misunderstanding that God actually dwells in a house (see Deut. 12.11; 1 Kings 8.27). **14–15:** Like a father his son, the LORD will chastise David's successor but never reject him. **15–16:** The promise that David's dynasty shall last *forever* is not accompanied by any conditions (but see 1 Kings 9.4–7). **18:** David's humility is shared by other leaders in the Bible, including Moses (Exod. 3.11), Gideon (Judg. 6.15), and Saul (1 Sam. 9.21). *Family,* lit. "house." The word "house," Heb "bayit," in its various meanings occurs in the ch 15 times (in the Heb). **21:** *This great thing,* the promise of a lasting dynasty. **23:** *Redeemed,* from slavery in Egypt. *[Driving out],* from the land of Canaan. **24:** The idea that Israel is the LORD's people and that He is Israel's God is central in biblical thought (e.g., Exod. 6.7) and in Judaism in general. **25–29:** After extolling God and His deeds for Israel, David returns to the subject of his own dynasty and prays that God may fulfill His promise *forever* (because sometimes He changes His mind, e.g., 1 Sam. 2.30–31).

a-a I.e., only as a human father would.

b-b Lit. "from before you."

c Septuagint reads "before Me," i.e., "by My favor."

d-d Meaning of Heb. uncertain.

e Heb. "you," apparently denoting Israel.   f So 1 Chron. 17.21.

8 ^aSome time afterward, David attacked the Philistines and subdued them; and David took Metheg-ammah^b from the Philistines. ²He also defeated the Moabites. He made them lie down on the ground and he measured them off with a cord; he measured out two lengths of cord for those who were to be put to death, and one length for those to be spared.^c And the Moabites became tributary vassals of David.

³David defeated Hadadezer son of Rehob, king of Zobah, who was then on his way to restore his monument^d at the Euphrates River. ⁴David captured 1,700 horsemen and 20,000 foot soldiers of his force; and David hamstrung all the chariot horses, except for 100 which he retained. ⁵And when the Arameans of Damascus came to the aid of King Hadadezer of Zobah, David struck down 22,000 of the Arameans. ⁶David stationed garrisons in Aram of Damascus, and the Arameans became tributary vassals of David. The LORD gave David victory wherever he went. ⁷David took the gold shields^e carried by Hadadezer's retinue and brought them to Jerusalem; ⁸and from Betah and Berothai, towns of Hadadezer, King David took a vast amount of copper.

⁹When King Toi of Hamath heard that David had defeated the entire army of Hadadezer, ¹⁰Toi sent his son Joram to King David to greet him and to congratulate him on his military victory over Hadadezer—for Hadadezer had been at war with Toi. [Joram] brought with him objects of silver, gold, and copper. ¹¹King David dedicated these to the LORD, along with the other silver and gold that he dedicated, [taken] from all the nations he had conquered: ¹²from Edom,^f Moab, and Ammon; from the Philistines and the Amalekites, and from the plunder of Hadadezer son of Rehob, king of Zobah.

¹³David gained fame ^gwhen he returned from defeating^g Edom^f in the Valley of Salt, 18,000 in all. ¹⁴He stationed garrisons in Edom—^hhe stationed garrisons in all of Edom ^h—and all the Edomites became vassals of David. The LORD gave David victory wherever he went.

¹⁵David reigned over all Israel, and David executed

---

a This chapter is reproduced, with some variations, in 1 Chron. 18.

b If not a place name, meaning of Heb. uncertain.

c I.e., he repeatedly doomed twice the number he spared.

d On yad in this sense, cf. 18.18; 1 Chron. 18.3; 1 Sam. 15.12. Others "dominion."

e Or "quivers."

f So several mss., Septuagint, and 1 Chron. 18.11–13; and cf. v. 14 below. Printed editions and most mss. read "Aram."

g-g 1 Chron. 18.12 and Ps. 60.1 read differently.

h-h This phrase is lacking in 1 Chron. 18.13.

8.1–14: Expansion. The summary of David's conquests shows him at the height of his power, ruling over a vast territory, from the Euphrates in the northeast to the Egyptian border in the southwest. His success is attributed to divine help, in recognition of which David consecrates to God the spoils from his wars. This ch is the only one in the book that contains no dialogue. **1:** In 5.25 it was told that David expelled the Philistines from Israelite territory; here it is reported that he subjugated them. **2:** In order to explain David's cruel act the Midrash (*Tanhuma*, Buber recension, *Vayera'* 25) asserts that the king of Moab had killed David's parents, who had been entrusted to his care (1 Sam. 22.4). **3:** *Hadadezer* was David's chief opponent. He not only ruled over the Aramean kingdom of Zobah, but also dominated other Aramean territories (see 10.19). The circumstances of Hadadezer's restoring *his monument* are unclear (1 Chron. 18.3 reads "set up his monument"). But the Heb may also be translated "turn his hand" (the same expression in Isa. 1.25; Ezek. 38.12; Amos 1.8), though it is not said against whom. **4:** The word translated *horsemen* may also mean "horses" (as regards the numbers, cf. 1 Chron. 18.4). David *hamstrung* the horses, making them unfit for military use because Israel did not yet employ chariots in its army. **6:** *Garrisons*, rather "prefects," as the Heb word is translated in 1 Sam. 10.5; 13.3–4. **8:** *Copper* was of high value for the production of bronze tools and weapons. **9:** *Hamath* was the capital of a Hittite-Canaanite (i.e., non-Aramean) country, adjacent to Zobah. **10:** By sending his son with precious presents King Toi acknowledges David's supremacy. Instead of *Joram*, the Heb form of the name, 1 Chron. 18.10 reads "Hadoram," which is the Canaanite form. **11:** The silver and gold were later deposited in the Temple (1 Kings 7.51). **14:** *Garrisons*, see v. 6 n.

8.15–18: Administration, part 1. After the summary account of true justice among all his people. [16] Joab son of Zeruiah was commander of the army; Jehoshaphat son of Ahilud was recorder; [17] Zadok son of Ahitub and ᵃAhimelech son of Abiatharᵃ were priests; Seraiahᵇ was scribe; [18] Benaiah son of Jehoiada was ᶜcommander ofᶜ the Cherethites and the Pelethites; and David's sons were priests.

9 David inquired, "Is there anyone still left of the House of Saul with whom I can keep faith for the sake of Jonathan?" [2] There was a servant of the House of Saul named Ziba, and they summoned him to David. "Are you Ziba?" the king asked him. ᵈ"Yes, sir,"ᵈ he replied. [3] The king continued, "Is there anyone at all left of the House of Saul with whom I can keep faith as pledged before God?"ᵉ Ziba answered the king, "Yes, there is still a son of Jonathan whose feet are crippled." [4] "Where is he?" the king asked, and Ziba said to the king, "He is in the house of Machir son of Ammiel, in Lo-debar." [5] King David had him brought from the house of Machir son of Ammiel, at Lo-debar; [6] and when Mephibosheth son of Jonathan son of Saul came to David, he flung himself on his face and prostrated himself. David said, "Mephibosheth!" and he replied, "At your service, sir." [7] David said to him, "Don't be afraid, for I will keep faith with you for the sake of your father Jonathan. I will give you back all the land of your grandfather Saul; moreover, you shall always eat at my table." [8] [Mephibosheth] prostrated himself again, and said, "What is your servant, that you should show regard for a dead dog like me?"

[9] The king summoned Ziba, Saul's steward, and said to him, "I give to your master's grandson everything that belonged to Saul and to his entire family. [10] You and your sons and your slaves shall farm the land for him and shall bring in [its yield] to provide food for your master's grandsonᶠ to live on; but Mephibosheth, your master's grandson, shall always eat at my table."—Ziba had fifteen sons and twenty slaves.—[11] Ziba said to the king, "Your

a-a Emendation yields "Abiathar son of Ahimelech," cf., e.g., 20.25; 1 Sam. 22.20.
b "Sheva" in 20.25; "Shavsha" in 1 Chron. 18.16.
c-c So Targum (cf. 20.23; 1 Chron. 18.17); Heb. "and."   d-d Lit. "Your servant is."
e See 1 Sam. 20.14 and note.   f Septuagint reads "household."

David's foreign enterprises, a brief list of his senior officials follows, which shows that he also concerned himself with the organization of his administration at home. The list marks the conclusion of the first part of 2 Samuel. **15:** The execution of justice is considered

in the Bible to be the king's foremost duty (1 Kings 10.9; Jer. 22.2–3). David is pictured as the ideal king. **18:** *The Cherethites and the Pelethites,* military units of (Philistine) mercenaries, probably serving as David's bodyguard. The Cherethites—i.e., Cretans—are

mentioned together with the Philistines in Ezek. 25.16; Zeph. 2.5. *David's sons were priests:* Apparently David's sons fulfilled priestly functions at the court (cf. 6.18 n. and 20.26), whereas Zadok and Abiathar were the chief priests.

Chs 9–20. These chs, with the addition of 1 Kings chs 1–2, are known as the succession narrative, because the succession to David's throne is believed by many biblical scholars to be their principal subject. Only 1 Kings ch 1 is devoted specifically to that subject, however. Most of the other chs (11–19) are concerned with David's sin and its consequences. The calamities in his family, which are interpreted by the prophet Nathan (12.9–12) as punishment for his crimes, convey the message that kings are not above law and morals. Chs 9–10 provide the background for the main story.

9.1–13: Faithfulness. David, true to his covenant with Jonathan (1 Sam. 20.14–16), shows kindness to Jonathan's son Mephibosheth. **1:** The Heb word "ḥesed," translated *faith,* also means "kindness." **2:** Since the courtiers are unable to answer David's question, they summon Ziba. **3:** *Crippled,* see 4.4 and n. **4:** *Machir son of Ammiel,* one of the notables of Gilead (17.27). **6:** *Mephibosheth:* The original form of the name was "Merib-baal" (see translators' note at 4.4). The element "baal" was changed into "bosheth," meaning "shame" (cf. translators' notes at 2.8 and 11.21). The names of his father and grandfather are mentioned because of their relevance to David's treatment of Mephibosheth (v. 7). His excessive expressions of submissiveness testify to his fear that David will put him to death as a potential pretender to the throne (see 1 Sam. 20.15 n.). **7:** Eating at the king's table, i.e., being maintained by the king, was considered a special favor (1 Kings 2.7; 18.19; 2 Kings 25.29–30). **8:** *A dead dog,* see 3.8 n. **10:** Though a servant, Ziba is clearly well-to-do, keeping servant will do just as my lord the king has commanded him." ᵃ-"Mephibosheth shall eat at my table-ᵃ like one of the king's sons."

¹² Mephibosheth had a young son named Mica; and all the members of Ziba's household worked for Mephibosheth. ¹³ Mephibosheth lived in Jerusalem, for he ate regularly at the king's table. He was lame in both feet.

10 ᵇSome time afterward, the king of Ammon died, and his son Hanun succeeded him as king. ²David said, "I will keep faith with Hanun son of Nahash, just as his father kept faith with me." He sent his courtiers with a message of condolence to him over his father. But when David's courtiers came to the land of Ammon, ³ the Ammonite officials said to their lord Hanun, "Do you think David is really honoring your father just because he sent you men with condolences? Why, David has sent his courtiers to you to explore and spy out the city, and to overthrowᶜ it." ⁴So Hanun seized David's courtiers, clipped off one side of their beards and cut away half of their garments at the buttocks, and sent them off. ⁵When David was told of it, he dispatched men to meet them, for the men were greatly embarrassed. And the king gave orders: "Stop in Jericho until your beards grow back; then you can return."

⁶ The Ammonites realized that they had ᵈincurred the wrath of-ᵈ David; so the Ammonites sent agents and hired Arameans of Beth-rehob and Arameans of Zobah—20,000 foot soldiers—the king of Maacah [with] 1,000 men, and 12,000 men from Tob. ⁷On learning this, David sent out Joab and the whole army—[including] the professional fighters. ⁸The Ammonites marched out and took up their battle position at the entrance of the gate, while the Arameans of Zobah and Rehob and the men of Tob and Maacah took their stand separately in the open. ⁹Joab saw that there was a battle line against him both front and rear. So he made a selection from all the picked men of Israel and arrayed them against the Arameans, ¹⁰and the rest of the troops he put under the command of his brother Abishaiᵉ and arrayed them against the Ammonites. ¹¹[Joab] said, "If the Arameans prove too strong for me, you come to my aid; and if the Ammonites prove too strong for you, I will come to your aid. ¹²Let us be strong and resolute for the

a-a Septuagint reads "And Mephibosheth ate at David's table."
b This chapter is found also in 1 Chron. 19.
c Emendation yields "reconnoiter"; cf. Deut. 1.22; Josh. 2.2–3.
d-d See note at 1 Sam. 13.4.
e Heb. "Abshai."

slaves himself; nevertheless, he now has to work for Mephibosheth. **13:** Mephibosheth moves to Jerusalem in order to eat at the king's table.

10.1–19: War. The account of the war with Ammon serves as background to the next story, which deals with David's sin against Bathsheba and Uriah. The first part of the present account explains the cause of the war, the second part tells of its first stage, which involved both the Ammonites and the Arameans, and the third part reports the second stage, which was conducted against the Arameans only (mentioned in ch 8). David did not initiate the war, but through his victory he gained supremacy in the region (the third stage of the war, against the Ammonites only, is related in chs 11–12). **2:** *Nahash* is mentioned in 1 Sam. 11.1–2. It is unknown of what his *faith* (or "kindness," Heb "hesed") to David consisted. Perhaps there was a treaty between David and Nahash. David's gesture signals that he is willing to continue the good relations with Ammon. **4:** *Hanun*, accepting his officials' opinion, not only expels David's courtiers, but also humiliates them, insulting their dignity. **5:** *Jericho* was on the border between Israel and Ammon. The city had been (almost) empty since Joshua destroyed it; it was rebuilt only during Ahab's reign (1 Kings 16.34). **6:** The enumeration of the countries and the numbers of the fighting men hint at the superiority of the enemy's forces, and thus enhance Joab's victory. **8:** *The gate*, of Rabbah, capital of Ammon. **9:** Joab's position between the Arameans and the Ammonites is extremely hazardous. **11–12:** Joab, in the only speech in the ch, first sets forth his plan of battle based on mutual aid, and then delivers a message of encouragement and faith in God. *Let us be strong and resolute*, lit. "be strong and let us strengthen ourselves." **16:** *Hadadezer*, see 8.3 n.

sake of our people and the land[a] of our God; and the LORD will do what He deems right."

13 Joab and the troops with him marched into battle against the Arameans, who fled before him. 14 And when the Ammonites saw that the Arameans had fled, they fled before Abishai and withdrew into the city. So Joab broke off the attack against the Ammonites, and went to Jerusalem.

15 When the Arameans saw that they had been routed by Israel, they regrouped their forces. 16 Hadadezer[b] sent for and brought out the Arameans from across the Euphrates; they came to Helam, led by Shobach, Hadadezer's[b] army commander. 17 David was informed of it; he assembled all Israel, crossed the Jordan, and came to Helam. The Arameans drew up their forces against David and attacked him; 18 but the Arameans were put to flight by Israel. David killed 700 Aramean charioteers and 40,000 horsemen;[c] he also struck down Shobach, Hadadezer's[d] army commander, who died there. 19 And when all the vassal kings of Hadadezer[b] saw that they had been routed by Israel, they submitted to Israel and became their vassals. And the Arameans were afraid to help the Ammonites any more.

11 At the turn of the year, the season when kings go out [to battle], David sent Joab with his officers and all Israel with him, and they devastated Ammon and besieged Rabbah; David remained in Jerusalem. 2 Late one afternoon, David rose from his couch and strolled on the roof of the royal palace; and from the roof he saw a woman bathing. The woman was very beautiful, 3 and the king sent someone to make inquiries about the woman. He reported, "She is Bathsheba daughter of Eliam [and] wife of Uriah the Hittite." 4 David sent messengers to fetch her; she came to him and he lay with her—she had just purified herself after her period—and she went back home. 5 The woman conceived, and she sent word to David, "I am pregnant." 6 Thereupon David sent a message to Joab, "Send Uriah the Hittite to me"; and Joab sent Uriah to David.

7 When Uriah came to him, David asked him how Joab and the troops were faring and how the war was going. 8 Then David said to Uriah, "Go down to your house and bathe your feet." When Uriah left the royal palace, a pres-

a Lit. "towns."
b Many editions read "Hadarezer . . . Hadarezer's."
c 1 Chron. 19.18 reads "foot soldiers."
d Heb. "his."

11.1–27a: Adultery and murder. The narrative of David's adultery and murder is embedded in the account of the war with Ammon (ch 10; 12.26–31), because the events of the story occur against the background of that war. Uriah's absence from home, which paves the way for the adultery and also necessitates creating an explanation for Bathsheba's pregnancy, is occasioned by the war, as is Uriah's death. The narrative does not try to conceal or mitigate David's sins. The outstanding loyalty of the non-Israelite soldier (Uriah) underscores the perfidy of the Israelite king. It is highly unusual for ancient literature to criticize powerful and successful kings. The way David's behavior is depicted and condemned in the Bible shows the overriding importance it assigns to moral values. Some rabbinic sources tried to clear David from guilt, claiming that he did not commit adultery, since warriors, before setting out to battle, gave their wives (conditional) divorces so that they could remarry in case their husbands should not return; neither was David considered to be guilty of murder, since Uriah was killed in action by the Ammonites (b. Shab. 56a). **1:** The season, the spring. An alternative and more literal translation of v. 1a would be: "It happened when a year had passed since the time that the kings went out [to battle]," i.e., a year after the war of ch 10 took place. Rabbah, modern Amman, the capital of ancient Ammon. **2:** David strolls on the flat roof of his palace in the evening breeze and sees a woman bathing, perhaps to purify herself after her period (v. 4). **3:** Both Bathsheba's father and her husband are mentioned, which is unusual. Uriah was an army officer, and so perhaps was Eliam (see 23.34, 39). David thus commits adultery with the wife of one of his officers and probably the daughter of another. Hittite, see 1 Sam. 26.6 n. **4:** She had just purified herself after her period: This indicates that at this juncture Bathsheba is not pregnant. **7:** David's questions disguise his real intent.

ent from the king followed him. ⁹ But Uriah slept at the entrance of the royal palace, along with the other officers of his lord, and did not go down to his house. ¹⁰ When David was told that Uriah had not gone down to his house, he said to Uriah, "You just came from a journey; why didn't you go down to your house?" ¹¹ Uriah answered David, "The Ark and Israel and Judah are located at Succoth, and my master Joab and Your Majesty's men are camped in the open; how can I go home and eat and drink and sleep with my wife? ᵃ⁻As you live, by your very life,⁻ᵃ I will not do this!" ¹² David said to Uriah, "Stay here today also, and tomorrow I will send you off." So Uriah remained in Jerusalem that day. The next day, ¹³ David summoned him, and he ate and drank with him until he got him drunk; but in the evening, [Uriah] went out to sleep in the same place, with his lord's officers; he did not go down to his home.

¹⁴ In the morning, David wrote a letter to Joab, which he sent with Uriah. ¹⁵ He wrote in the letter as follows: "Place Uriah in the front line where the fighting is fiercest; then fall back so that he may be killed." ¹⁶ So when Joab was besieging the city, he stationed Uriah at the point where he knew that there were able warriors. ¹⁷ The men of the city sallied out and attacked Joab, and some of David's officers among the troops fell; Uriah the Hittite was among those who died.

¹⁸ Joab sent a full report of the battle to David. ¹⁹ He instructed the messenger as follows: "When you finish reporting to the king all about the battle, ²⁰ the king may get angry and say to you, 'Why did you come so close to the city to attack it? Didn't you know that they would shoot from the wall? ²¹ Who struck down Abimelech son of Jerubbesheth?ᵇ Was it not a woman who dropped an upper millstone on him from the wall at Thebez, from which he died? Why did you come so close to the wall?' Then say: 'Your servant Uriah the Hittite was among those killed.'"

²² The messenger set out; he came and told David all that Joab had sent him to say.ᶜ ²³ The messenger said to David, "First the men prevailed against us and sallied out against us into the open; then we drove them back up to the entrance to the gate. ²⁴ But the archers shot at your men from the wall and some of Your Majesty's men fell;

The narrator omits Joab's answers, thus hinting that David is not really interested in them. **8:** David permits Uriah to go to his house, expecting that he will sleep with his wife and thus—unwittingly—cover up the adultery. *Bathe your feet,* as usual after a journey (cf. Gen. 18.4). *A present,* victuals. **9:** *Uriah slept,* but not with his wife and not even in his house. **11:** *The Ark* was taken to the battlefield in the belief that God's presence would ensure victory (cf. 1 Sam. 4.3). *Succoth,* the Heb word means "booths." Probably not the town Succoth is meant, but the simple shelters of the soldiers in the *open* (lit. "field"), as opposed to the comfortable *home* of Uriah. Uriah rejects any amenities that are denied his comrades. *Located at,* lit. "staying in." **13:** *He got him drunk,* hoping that in that state Uriah would sleep with his wife. The expression *did not go down to his (your) house (home)* occurs four times (vv. 9–13), thus emphasizing Uriah's steadfastness. **14:** David trusts Uriah that he will not open the sealed letter. **15:** David's order to *fall back* is not carried out, and other officers are killed along with Uriah. **20–21:** Joab knows that he made a fatal mistake, allowing his men to come close to the city wall. In his instructions to the messenger he couches David's anticipated reaction in the form of a series of rhetorical questions. The first and last questions, being similar (ring composition), contain the main argument, whereas the other questions supply the reasons. Joab should have learned from the precedent of Abimelech, who was killed by a (weak) woman. The message that Uriah was one of the killed, however, instead of increasing the king's rage at the unwarranted death of a loyal officer and comrade, will have the (ironic) effect of calming him down. **23–24:** In order to forestall David's anger the messenger explains that the men came close to the gate in the course of driving the enemy back; and, without waiting for the king's expected angry reaction, he immediately adds that Uriah also

a-a Meaning of Heb. uncertain. Emendation yields "As the LORD lives and as you live" (cf. 1 Sam. 20.3; 25.26; etc.). Lit. "as you live and as your being lives."
b The earlier form is Jerubbaal (another name for Gideon), Judg. 7.1; on -bosheth/besheth for -baal, see note at 2 Sam. 4.4. For the event at Thebez described here, see Judg. 9.35 ff.
c Septuagint continues with a recapitulation of vv. 19–21.

your servant Uriah the Hittite also fell." [25] Whereupon David said to the messenger, "Give Joab this message: 'Do not be distressed about the matter. The sword ᵃalways takes its toll.ᵃ Press your attack on the city and destroy it!' Encourage him!"

[26] When Uriah's wife heard that her husband Uriah was dead, she lamented over her husband. [27] After the period of mourning was over, David sent and had her brought into his palace; she became his wife and she bore him a son.

12 But the LORD was displeased with what David had done, [1] and the LORD sent Nathan to David. He came to him and said, "There were two men in the same city, one rich and one poor. [2] The rich man had very large flocks and herds, [3] but the poor man had only one little ewe lamb that he had bought. He tended it and it grew up together with him and his children: it used to share his morsel of bread, drink from his cup, and nestle in his bosom; it was like a daughter to him. [4] One day, a traveler came to the rich man, but he was loath to take anything from his own flocks or herds to prepare a meal for the guest who had come to him; so he took the poor man's lamb and prepared it for the man who had come to him."

[5] David flew into a rage against the man, and said to Nathan, "As the LORD lives, the man who did this deserves to die! [6] He shall pay for the lamb four times over, because he did such a thing and showed no pity." [7] And Nathan said to David, "That man is you! Thus said the LORD, the God of Israel: 'It was I who anointed you king over Israel and it was I who rescued you from the hand of Saul. [8] I gave you your master's house and possession of your master's wives; and I gave you the House of Israel and Judah; and if that were not enough, I would give you twice as much more. [9] Why then have you flouted the command of the LORD and done what displeases Him? You have put Uriah the Hittite to the sword; you took his wife and made her your wife and had him killed by the sword of the Ammonites. [10] Therefore the sword shall never depart from your House—because you spurned Me by taking the wife of Uriah the Hittite and making her your wife.' [11] Thus said the LORD: 'I will make a calamity

a-a Lit. "consumes the like and the like."

crimes induces the king to repent. **27b:** Explicit judgment of the characters or their actions is rare in the book of Samuel. Here it is attributed to God Himself because of the seriousness of the sins and because the sinner is a king. God's authority is above that of the king and from Him nothing can be concealed. **1–4:** Nathan's parable, presented as a legal case, aims at getting David to pass verdict on himself unwittingly (kings used to perform judicial functions, see 15.2–6 n.). Therefore it closely corresponds to the actual events, but not completely (cf. Jotham's parable in Judg. 9): e.g., whereas the rich man represents David, the poor man Uriah, and the lamb Bathsheba, nobody corresponds to the traveler; moreover, the lamb is slaughtered, instead of being added to the herd. The parable stresses the social aspect of the robbery, the rich man taking the scant property of the poor man. **1:** *The LORD sent,* as against David's frequent sending (11.1, 3, 6, 14, 27). **3:** Nathan stresses the emotional angle: the poor man's touching attachment to his lamb. **5:** *Deserves to die,* an outburst of indignation. Israelite law does not impose the death penalty for robbery. **6:** *Four times over,* in accordance with the law in Exod. 21.37 (Septuagint reads "sevenfold," cf. Prov. 6.31). *Pity:* The same Heb word is translated "loath" in v. 4. It seemed a pity to the rich man to take from his own herd, but he showed no pity for the poor man's only lamb. **7–12:** Nathan's rebuke. **7–9:** David has been ungrateful to the LORD, who gave him everything. **7:** *Thus said the LORD,* the messenger formula (see 7.5 n.), assuring that the following statement derives from God. **8:** *Your master's wives:* Perhaps David took over Saul's wives, though this is nowhere mentioned. **10–12:** The punishments correspond to David's sins: Because he put Uriah to the sword, the sword will never depart from his house (alluding to the violent deaths of Amnon, Absalom, and Adonijah in the following chs), and because he took

died. **25:** Because of Uriah's death, David does not get enraged, and even comforts and encourages Joab. **27a:** *Period of mourning,* see 1 Sam. 31.13 n. Because of Bath-

sheba's pregnancy David cannot wait long.

11.27b–12.25: Repentance. God's stern condemnation of David's rise against you from within your own house; I will take your wives and give them to another man before your very eyes and he shall sleep with your wives under this very sun. [12] You acted in secret, but I will make this happen in the sight of all Israel and in broad daylight.' "

[13] David said to Nathan, "I stand guilty before the Lord!" And Nathan replied to David, "The Lord has remitted your sin; you shall not die. [14] However, since you have spurned ᵃthe enemies ofᵃ the Lord by this deed, even the child about to be born to you shall die."

[15] Nathan went home, and the Lord afflicted the child that Uriah's wife had borne to David, and it became critically ill. [16] David entreated God for the boy; David fasted, and he went in and spent the night lyingᵇ on the ground. [17] The senior servants of his household tried to induce him to get up from the ground; but he refused, nor would he partake of food with them. [18] On the seventh day the child died. David's servants were afraid to tell David that the child was dead; for they said, "We spoke to him when the child was alive and he wouldn't listen to us; how can we tell him that the child is dead? He might do something terrible." [19] When David saw his servants talking in whispers, David understood that the child was dead; David asked his servants, "Is the child dead?" "Yes," they replied.

[20] Thereupon David rose from the ground; he bathed and anointed himself, and he changed his clothes. He went into the House of the Lord and prostrated himself. Then he went home and asked for food, which they set before him, and he ate. [21] His courtiers asked him, "Why have you acted in this manner? While the child was alive, you fasted and wept; but now that the child is dead, you rise and take food!" [22] He replied, "While the child was still alive, I fasted and wept because I thought: 'Who knows? The Lord may have pity on me, and the child may live.' [23] But now that he is dead, why should I fast? Can I bring him back again? I shall go to him, but he will never come back to me."

[24] David consoled his wife Bathsheba; he went to her and lay with her. She bore a son and she named him Solomon. The Lord favored him, [25] and He sent a message through the prophet Nathan; and he was named Jedidiahᶜ at the instance of the Lord.

Uriah's wife, his wives will be taken by another man (Absalom). V. 10b gives the reason for the punishment mentioned in vv. 11–12 (see 16.22). **13:** David, without arguing, frankly and immediately admits his guilt (contrary to Saul, 1 Sam. ch 15). *Remitted,* better "transferred," namely to the young child (see Exod. 34.7). **15:** *The child that Uriah's wife had borne to David:* The wording hints at the adultery. **20:** *The House of the Lord,* the tent that housed the Ark. **21–22:** The courtiers thought that David's fasting and weeping were signs of grief, but David explains that they expressed repentance and supplication, in the hope that the child would yet be saved. **24:** Bathsheba is now designated *his* (David's) *wife,* and he is now sensitive to her feelings (contrary to 11.4).

---

a-a *The phrase is intended to avoid saying "spurned the Lord"; cf. note b-b at 1 Sam. 25.22.*

b *Some Septuagint mss. and 4QSamᵃ add "in sackcloth"; cf. 1 Kings 21.27.*

c *I.e., "Beloved of the Lord."*

26ªJoab attacked Rabbah of Ammon and captured the royal city. 27 Joab sent messengers to David and said, "I have attacked Rabbah and I have already captured ᵇ·the water city.·ᵇ 28 Now muster the rest of the troops and besiege the city and capture it; otherwise I will capture the city myself, and my name will be connected with it." 29 David mustered all the troops and marched on Rabbah, and he attacked it and captured it. 30ᶜThe crown was taken from the head of their kingᵈ and it was placed on David's head—it weighed a talent of gold, and [on it]ᵉ were precious stones. He also carried off a vast amount of booty from the city. 31 He led out the people who lived there and set them to work with saws, iron threshing boards, and iron axes, or assigned them to brickmaking; David did this to all the towns of Ammon. Then David and all the troops returned to Jerusalem.

13 This happened sometime afterward: Absalom son of David had a beautiful sister named Tamar, and Amnon son of David became infatuated with her. 2 Amnon was so distraught because of his [half-]sister Tamar that he became sick; for she was a virgin, and it seemed impossible to Amnon to do anything to her. 3 Amnon had a friend named Jonadab, the son of David's brother Shimah; Jonadab was a very clever man. 4 He asked him, "Why are you so dejected, O prince, morning after morning? Tell me!" Amnon replied, "I am in love with Tamar, the sister of my brother Absalom!" 5 Jonadab said to him, "Lie down in your bed and pretend you are sick. When your father comes to see you, say to him, 'Let my sister Tamar come and give me something to eat. Let her prepare the food in front of me, so that I may look on, and let her serve it to me.' "

6 Amnon lay down and pretended to be sick. The king came to see him, and Amnon said to the king, "Let my sister Tamar come and prepare a couple of cakes in front of me, and let her bring them to me." 7 David sent a message to Tamar in the palace, "Please go to the house of your brother Amnon and prepare some food for him." 8 Tamar went to the house of her brother Amnon, who was in bed. She took dough and kneaded it into cakes in front of him, and cooked the cakes. 9 She took the ᶠpan and set out [the cakes],·ᶠ but Amnon refused to eat and ordered everyone

12.26–31: Conquest. The passage concludes the account of the Ammonite war (ch 10; 11.1). **26:** *The royal city,* probably the citadel with the palace. **27:** *Captured the water city,* controlling the water supply. The final conquest of the city would now be easy. **30:** *A talent,* more than 34 kg (75 pounds). **31:** Setting captives to forced labor was customary in the ancient Near East. *Returned to Jerusalem,* see 1 Sam. 1.19 n.

13.1–22: Rape. The story of Amnon and Tamar is the first of a trilogy, the other two stories relating Absalom's murder of Amnon and Absalom's return from exile. Tamar's rape is seen as punishment for David, corresponding to his adultery: a sexual offense, followed by murder. **1–3:** The exposition supplies the necessary information about the characters. Absalom is the first character introduced, probably because of the central role he has in the following narratives, which describe the developments ensuing from the events in the present story. **1:** Tamar was Absalom's full sister and Amnon's half-sister. **2:** *Impossible:* Being a virgin, she was "chaste at home and did not go out" (Rashi). **5:** Jonadab advises Amnon how to lure Tamar to his home and keep her there for a while, but he does not mention rape. **7:** Apparently each prince had his own house (cf. v. 20).

---

a Vv. 26–29 are abridged in 1 Chron. 20.1b.

b-b Meaning of Heb. uncertain; perhaps the source of the water supply.

c Vv. 30–31 are found also in 1 Chron. 20.2–3.

d Heb. "malkam," perhaps equivalent to "Milcom," the Ammonite deity; cf. 1 Kings 11.5.

e So Targum and 1 Chron. 20.2.   f-f Meaning of Heb. uncertain.

to withdraw. After everyone had withdrawn, [10] Amnon said to Tamar, "Bring the food inside and feed me." Tamar took the cakes she had made and brought them to her brother inside. [11] But when she served them to him, he caught hold of her and said to her, "Come lie with me, sister." [12] But she said to him, "Don't, brother. Don't force me. Such things are not done in Israel! Don't do such a vile thing! [13] Where will I carry my shame? And you, you will be like any of the scoundrels in Israel! Please, speak to the king; he will not refuse me to you." [14] But he would not listen to her; he overpowered her and lay with her by force.

[15] Then Amnon felt a very great loathing for her; indeed, his loathing for her was greater than the passion he had felt for her. And Amnon said to her, "Get out!" [16] She pleaded with him, "Please don't ᵃ-commit this wrong; to send me away would be even worse-ᵃ than the first wrong you committed against me." But he would not listen to her. [17] He summoned his young attendant and said, "Get that woman out of my presence, and bar the door behind her."—[18] She was wearing an ornamented tunic,ᵇ for maiden princesses were customarily dressed ᶜ-in such garments.-ᶜ—His attendant took her outside and barred the door after her. [19] Tamar put dust on her head and rent the ornamented tunic she was wearing; she put her hands on her head,ᵈ and walked away, screaming loudly as she went. [20] Her brother Absalom said to her, "Was it your brother Amnonᵉ who did this to you? For the present, sister, keep quiet about it; he is your brother. Don't brood over the matter." And Tamar remained in her brother Absalom's house, forlorn. [21] When King David heard about all this, he was greatly upset.ᶠ [22] Absalom didn't utter a word to Amnon, good or bad; but Absalom hated Amnon because he had violated his sister Tamar.

[23] Two years later, when Absalom was having his flocks sheared at Baal-hazor near Ephraim, Absalom invited all the king's sons. [24] And Absalom came to the king and said, "Your servant is having his flocks sheared. Would Your Majesty and your retinue accompany your servant?" [25] But the king answered Absalom, "No, my son. We must not all come, or we'll be a burden to you." He urged him,

a-a *Meaning of Heb. uncertain.*

b *See Gen. 37.3 and note.*

c-c *Meaning of Heb. uncertain. Emendation yields "(thus) in olden times," meʿolam.*

d *A gesture of wild grief; cf. Jer. 2.37.*

e *Heb. "Aminon."*

f *Septuagint adds "but he did not rebuke his son Amnon, for he favored him, since he was his first-born"; cf. 1 Kings 1.6.*

11: Amnon tries to persuade Tamar with words, but at the same time he retains his hold of her. **12:** Tamar's long reply, her arguments, her alternative proposal, and her repetitions of *don't*, all attest to her vigorous objection. **13:** Tamar states the shameful consequences of rape for each of them, hoping for her good to arouse Amnon's mercy and to deter him for his own good. Marrying one's half-sister, though forbidden in Lev. 20.17, was apparently not impossible at the time (cf. Gen. 20.12). Tamar's suggestion to speak to the king cannot merely be a stratagem to buy time, because it must be plausible in order to serve its end. **15:** *Get out*, lit. "get up, go"—the exact reversal of Amnon's earlier "come, lie" (v. 11). **16:** Sending Tamar away is *even worse* than the rape, because she will be desolate for life. According to Deut. 22.28–29 and ancient Assyrian law, the rapist must marry the raped woman (in order to secure her material and social position). **17:** *That woman*, a contemptuous expression. Amnon's orders are deeply offending. **19:** Tamar's gestures are all expressions of grief. The rending of *the ornamented tunic* signifies that she is no longer a virgin. **21:** David is *greatly upset*, but he does not act. **22:** *A word*, about the matter.

13.23–39: Vengeance. Absalom murders Amnon to avenge his sister's rape. The murder is a punishment not only for Amnon, but also for David for his murder of Uriah. **23:** Absalom waits *two years* for the right opportunity to kill Amnon, and for Amnon's suspicions to abate. Sheepshearing was an occasion for celebration (cf. 1 Sam. 25.4ff.). **24–27:** In order to prevent suspicion, Absalom first invites the king, expecting that he will decline, and then asks for the crown prince to come instead. David is weak and yields to Absalom's urging.

but he would not go, and he said good-bye to him. 26 Thereupon Absalom said, "In that case, let my brother Amnon come with us," to which the king replied, "He shall not go with you." 27 But Absalom urged him, and he sent with him Amnon and all the other princes.ᵃ

28 Now Absalom gave his attendants these orders: "Watch, and when Amnon is merry with wine and I tell you to strike down Amnon, kill him! Don't be afraid, for it is I who give you the order. Act with determination, like brave men!" 29 Absalom's attendants did to Amnon as Absalom had ordered; whereupon all the other princes mounted their mules and fled. 30 They were still on the road when a rumor reached David that Absalom had killed all the princes, and that not one of them had survived. 31 At this, David rent his garment and lay down on the ground, ᵇ-and all his courtiers stood by with their clothes rent.-ᵇ 32 But Jonadab, the son of David's brother Shimah, said, "My lord must not think that all the young princes have been killed. Only Amnon is dead; for this has been ᶜ-decided by-ᶜ Absalom ever since his sister Tamar was violated. 33 So my lord the king must not think for a moment that all the princes are dead; Amnon alone is dead."

34 Meanwhile Absalom had fled.

The watchman on duty looked up and saw a large crowd coming ᵈ-from the road to his rear,-ᵈ from the side of the hill. 35 Jonadab said to the king, "See, the princes have come! It is just as your servant said." 36 As he finished speaking, the princes came in and broke into weeping; and David and all his courtiers wept bitterly, too.

37 Absalom had fled, and he came to Talmai son of Ammihud, king of Geshur. And [King David] mourned over his son a long time. 38 Absalom, who had fled to Geshur, remained there three years. 39 And ᵉ-King David-ᵉ was pining away for Absalom, for [the king] had gotten over Amnon's death.

14 Joab son of Zeruiah could see that the king's mind was on Absalom; 2 so Joab sent to Tekoa and brought a clever woman from there. He said to her, "Pretend you are in mourning; put on mourning clothes and don't anoint yourself with oil; and act like a woman who

28: *Merry with wine*, drunk. **29:** *Mules* were used by the royal family (18.9; 1 Kings 1.33). The other princes fear that Absalom intends to kill them all. **32–33:** Jonadab understands that Absalom's purpose was not to put the princes out of the way in order to secure the throne for himself, but to take revenge on Amnon. **37:** *Talmai*, Absalom's maternal grandfather (see 3.3 and n.). **39:** Adopting the superior reading of 4QSamᵃ, the beginning of the v. may also be translated: "and the king's wrath (lit. "spirit," as in Eccl. 10.4) towards Absalom was spent." This translation accords better with the following narrative.

14.1–33: Reconciliation. The first part of the narrative describes the ruse used to persuade David to allow Absalom's return from exile; the second part tells of obtaining David's consent to meeting his son. In both parts it is Joab who endeavors to reconcile father and son. **2–3:** The woman is to present a judicial case to David in order to get him, unwittingly, to absolve his son from the death penalty. Like Nathan's parable (12.1–4), the case is similar to the real events, but not identical. The woman must not only describe the case, as Nathan did, but actually perform it—including dressing up. Her cleverness is revealed in her acting as well as her speech, which is submissive, polite, and rich in rhetorical means, such as metaphor and simile. The dialogue between the woman and the king is one of the longest in the Bible.

---

a Septuagint adds "and Absalom made a feast fit for a king."

b-b Septuagint reads "and all his courtiers who were standing by him rent their clothes."

c-c Lit. "determined by the command of."

d-d Emendation yields "down the slope of the Horonaim road. The watchman came and told the king 'I see men coming from the Horonaim road.'" Cf. Septuagint.

e-e Some Septuagint mss. and 4QSamᵃ read "the spirit [ruah] of the king."

has grieved a long time over a departed one. [3] Go to the king and say to him thus and thus." And Joab told her what to say.[a]

[4] The woman of Tekoa came[b] to the king, flung herself face down to the ground, and prostrated herself. She cried out, "Help, O king!" [5] The king asked her, "What troubles you?" And she answered, "Alas, I am a widow, my husband is dead. [6] Your maidservant had two sons. The two of them came to blows out in the fields where there was no one to stop them, and one of them struck the other and killed him. [7] Then the whole clan confronted your maidservant and said, 'Hand over the one who killed his brother, that we may put him to death for the slaying of his brother, [c]even though we wipe out the heir.'[-c] Thus they would quench the last ember remaining to me, and leave my husband without name or remnant upon the earth." [8] The king said to the woman, "Go home. I will issue an order in your behalf." [9] And the woman of Tekoa said to the king, "My lord king, may the guilt be on me and on my ancestral house; Your Majesty and his throne are guiltless." [10] The king said, "If anyone says anything more to you, have him brought to me, and he will never trouble you again." [11] She replied, "Let Your Majesty be mindful of the LORD your God and restrain the blood avenger bent on destruction, so that my son may not be killed." And he said, "As the LORD lives, not a hair of your son shall fall to the ground."

[12] Then the woman said, "Please let your maidservant say another word to my lord the king." "Speak on," said the king. [13] And the woman said, "Why then have you planned the like against God's people? In making this pronouncement, Your Majesty condemns himself in that Your Majesty does not bring back his own banished one. [14] We must all die; we are like water that is poured out on the ground and cannot be gathered up. [d]God will not take away the life of one who makes plans so that no one may be kept banished.[-d] [15] And the reason I have come to say these things to the king, my lord, is that the people have frightened me. Your maidservant thought I would speak to Your Majesty; perhaps Your Majesty would act on his handmaid's plea. [16] For Your Majesty would surely agree to deliver his handmaid from the hands of anyone [who would seek to] cut off both me and my son from the her-

7: The demand to kill the murderer is rooted in the custom of blood vengeance. But acceding to it would worsen the woman's situation, because instead of one dead son she would have two and be left without an heir. *Without name,* see Deut. 25.6; Ruth 4.10. **9:** *The guilt,* for not expiating the blood of the slain (see Num. 35.33). The woman strives for an explicit and binding pardon for the murderer. **11:** *Be mindful of the* LORD, i.e., mention the LORD (in an oath). *Not a hair . . . shall fall to the ground,* see 1 Sam. 14.45 n. **12:** The woman's respectful speech contrasts with the king's curtness. **13:** Absalom's death would be harmful to God's people, Israel. *This pronouncement,* pardoning the woman's fictional son. **14:** *Like water . . . :* Death is irreversible; executing Absalom will not bring Amnon back. *God will not take away the life,* see v. 9 n. **15–17:** Because the king might get angry and punish her, the woman now explains why she deceived David and presented a fictional case to him.

a Lit. "and he put words into her mouth."

b So many mss. and printed editions. Most mss. and printed editions read "said."

c-c Emendation yields "Thus they would destroy the [last] heir and . . ."

d-d Meaning of Heb. uncertain. The apparent sense is: God will not punish you for bringing back the banished Absalom.

itage[a] of God. [17] Your maidservant thought, 'Let the word of my lord the king provide comfort; for my lord the king is like an angel of God, understanding everything, good and bad.' May the LORD your God be with you."

[18] In reply, the king said to the woman, "Do not withhold from me anything I ask you!" The woman answered, "Let my lord the king speak." [19] The king asked, "Is Joab in league with you in all this?" The woman replied, "As you live, my lord the king, [b]it is just as my lord the king says.[b] Yes, your servant Joab was the one who instructed me, and it was he who [c]told your maidservant everything she was to say.[c] [20] It was to conceal the real purpose of the matter that your servant Joab did this thing. My lord is as wise as an angel of God, and he knows all that goes on in the land."

[21] Then the king said to Joab, "I will do this thing. Go and bring back my boy Absalom." [22] Joab flung himself face down on the ground and prostrated himself. Joab blessed the king and said, "Today your servant knows that he has found favor with you, my lord king, for Your Majesty has granted his servant's request." [23] And Joab went at once to Geshur and brought Absalom to Jerusalem. [24] But the king said, "Let him go directly to his house and not present himself to me." So Absalom went directly to his house and did not present himself to the king.

[25] No one in all Israel was so admired for his beauty as Absalom; from the sole of his foot to the crown of his head he was without blemish. [26] When he cut his hair—he had to have it cut every year, for it grew too heavy for him—the hair of his head weighed two hundred shekels by the royal weight. [27] Absalom had three sons and a daughter whose name was Tamar; she was a beautiful woman.

[28] Absalom lived in Jerusalem two years without appearing before the king. [29] Then Absalom sent for Joab, in order to send him to the king; but Joab would not come to him. He sent for him a second time, but he would not come. [30] So [Absalom] said to his servants, "Look, Joab's field is next to mine, and he has barley there. Go and set it on fire." And Absalom's servants set the field on fire. [31] Joab came at once to Absalom's house and said to him, "Why did your servants set fire to my field?" [32] Absalom replied to Joab, "I sent for you to come here; I wanted to send you to the king to say [on my behalf]: 'Why did I leave Geshur? I would be better off if I were still there.

[17:] *Like an angel of God,* an extreme flattery (see 1 Sam. 29.9 n.). **19:** Though the woman was careful not to betray Joab, David understands that it was all his design. **20:** The woman repeats the flattering comparison of David to an angel. **21:** The woman now leaves the stage, and Joab himself appears. **22:** Joab's excessive expressions of gratitude and politeness testify to his fear of punishment for having deceived David. **24:** The king allowed Absalom to return, but has not forgiven him. **26:** Growing and weighing his hair are signs of Absalom's narcissism. *Two hundred shekels,* more than two kg (4.5 pounds). **27:** *Tamar:* Her name is probably mentioned, unlike the sons' names, because she bears the same name as Absalom's sister. **28:** David's prolonged refusal to see Absalom is humiliating and unbearable to him. **30:** Absalom uses violent means to compel Joab to intervene with the king. **32:** Absalom considers himself free of guilt, because the killing of Amnon was justified. **33:** Though the kiss signifies forgiveness, it should be noted that the verse repeatedly uses the designation *the king* instead of "David" or "his father." In addition, there is no mention of any verbal exchange between father and son—after five years of separation! This suggests that the enforced reconciliation is purely formal.

a I.e., people.
b-b Lit. "there is no turning to the right or to the left of what my lord the king says."
c-c See note a above.

Now let me appear before the king; and if I am guilty of anything, let him put me to death!' " [33] Joab went to the king and reported to him; whereupon he summoned Absalom. He came to the king and flung himself face down to the ground before the king. And the king kissed Absalom.

15 Sometime afterward, Absalom provided himself with a chariot, horses, and fifty outrunners. [2] Absalom used to rise early and stand by the road to the city gates; and whenever a man had a case that was to come before the king for judgment, Absalom would call out to him, "What town are you from?" And when he answered, "Your servant is from *such and such a tribe-a* in Israel," [3] Absalom would say to him, "It is clear that your claim is right and just, but there is no one assigned to you by the king to hear it." [4] And Absalom went on, "If only I were appointed judge in the land and everyone with a legal dispute came before me, I would see that he got his rights." [5] And if a man approached to bow to him, [Absalom] would extend his hand and take hold of him and kiss him. [6] Absalom did this to every Israelite who came to the king for judgment. Thus Absalom won away the hearts of the men of Israel.

[7] After a period of forty[b] years had gone by, Absalom said to the king, "Let me go to Hebron and fulfill a vow that I made to the LORD. [8] For your servant made a vow when I lived in Geshur of Aram: If the LORD ever brings me back to Jerusalem, I will worship the LORD."[c] [9] The king said to him, "Go in peace"; and so he set out for Hebron.

[10] But Absalom sent agents to all the tribes of Israel to say, "When you hear the blast of the horn, announce that Absalom has become king in Hebron." [11] Two hundred men of Jerusalem accompanied Absalom; they were invited and went in good faith, suspecting nothing. [12] Absalom also *d-sent [to fetch]-d* Ahithophel the Gilonite, David's counselor, from his town, Giloh, when the sacrifices were to be offered. The conspiracy gained strength, and the people supported Absalom in increasing numbers.

[13] Someone came and told David, "The loyalty of the men of Israel has veered toward Absalom." [14] Whereupon David said to all the courtiers who were with him in Jerusalem, "Let us flee at once, or none of us will escape from

15.1–12: Rebellion. Absalom prepares his rebellion over several years. **1:** The *chariot, horses and fifty outrunners* were signs of kingship (cf. 1 Sam. 8.11). **2–6:** Absalom uses demagogic means to win popular support. Administration of justice was one of the king's main functions (see 12.1–6; 1 Kings 3.16–28; 2 Kings 8.1–6). **7:** *Hebron,* capital of Judah, where David first was king (2.4). Apparently Absalom found among his kinsmen there discontent with David, who became king of all Israel and moved his capital to Jerusalem (cf. 5.9). **8:** Even if he really made the vow in Geshur, he could have fulfilled it long since. **9:** *Go in peace,* but Absalom goes for war. David is naively unaware of his son's real intentions. **11–12:** A sacrificial meal including many guests was part of the royal inauguration ceremony (1 Kings 1.18–19).

15.13–16.14: Flight. David decides not to fortify himself in Jerusalem, but to leave the city. His flight is depicted in a series of scenes, mainly consisting of dia-

a-a *Lit. "one of the tribes."*
b *Some Septuagint mss. and Syriac read "four."*
c *Some Septuagint mss. add "in Hebron."*
d-d *Some Septuagint mss. and 4QSam^a read "sent and summoned."*

Absalom. We must get away quickly, or he will soon overtake us and bring down disaster upon us and put the city to the sword." [15] The king's courtiers said to the king, "Whatever our lord the king decides, your servants are ready." [16] So the king left, followed by his entire household, except for ten concubines whom the king left to mind the palace.

[17] The king left, followed by *all the people,*[a] and they stopped at *the last house.*[b] [18] All *his followers*[c] marched past him, including all the Cherethites and all the Pelethites; and[d] all the Gittites, six hundred men who had accompanied him from Gath, also marched by the king. [19] And the king said to Ittai the Gittite, "Why should you too go with us? Go back and stay with the [new] king, for you are a foreigner and you are also an exile from[e] your country. [20] You came only yesterday; should I make you wander about with us today, when I myself must go wherever I can? Go back, and take your kinsmen with you, [in][f] true faithfulness." [21] Ittai replied to the king, "As the LORD lives and as my lord the king lives, wherever my lord the king may be, there your servant will be, whether for death or for life!" [22] And David said to Ittai, "Then march by." And Ittai the Gittite and all his men and all the children who were with him marched by.

[23] The whole countryside wept aloud as the troops marched by. The king *crossed the Kidron Valley, and all the troops crossed by the road to*[g] the wilderness. [24] Then Zadok appeared, with all the Levites carrying the Ark of the Covenant of God; and they set down the Ark of God until all the people had finished marching out of the city. *Abiathar also came up.*[b] [25] But the king said to Zadok, "Take the Ark of God back to the city. If I find favor with the LORD, He will bring me back and let me see it and its abode. [26] And if He should say, 'I do not want you,' I am ready; let Him do with me as He pleases." [27] And the king said to the priest Zadok, *"Do you understand? You return*[h] to the safety of the city with your two sons, your own son Ahimaaz and Abiathar's son Jonathan. [28] Look, I shall linger in the steppes of the wilderness until word comes from you to inform me." [29] Zadok and Abiathar

logues. **16:** The fact that David leaves *ten concubines* behind discloses his intention soon to return. **17:** *The last house,* probably on the boundary of Jerusalem. **18:** The repetition of *all* shows that among his retinue nobody is disloyal. *Cherethites* and *Pelethites,* see 8.18 n. *Gittites,* mercenaries from the Philistine town of Gath, where David stayed sometime in the past (1 Sam. 27.3). **19–20:** David, forgoing his own interest, shows extraordinary consideration for Ittai and his men. **21:** The double oath reinforces Ittai's declaration of unlimited loyalty. **22:** *The children:* The Gittites had come with their families. **23:** *The Kidron Valley,* the eastern boundary of biblical Jerusalem. **24–29:** Both Zadok and Abiathar are priests, but *Zadok* appears here to be the principal one. **25–26:** David expresses the idea that God's favor is not dependent on the presence or veneration of religious objects. **27–28:** The priests and their sons will be useful as intelligence agents.

a-a Septuagint reads "his courtiers."　　b-b Meaning of Heb. uncertain.
c-c Septuagint reads "the people."　　d Emendation yields "and Ittai and."
e So one Heb. ms. and several ancient versions; most mss. and editions read "to."
f Meaning of Heb. uncertain. Septuagint reads "and may the LORD show you" (cf., e.g., 2.6).
g-g Meaning of Heb. uncertain. Emendation yields "stopped in the Kidron Valley, while all the people marched on before him by way of the Mount of Olives to . . ."
h-h Meaning of Heb. uncertain. Emendation yields "Look, you and Abiathar return."

brought the Ark of God back to Jerusalem, and they stayed there.

30 David meanwhile went up the slope of the [Mount of] Olives, weeping as he went; his head was covered and he walked barefoot. And all the people who were with him covered their heads and wept as they went up. 31 David [was] told that Ahithophel was among the conspirators with Absalom, and he prayed, "Please, O LORD, frustrate Ahithophel's counsel!"

32 When David reached the top, where people would prostrate themselves to God, Hushai the Archite was there to meet him, with his robe torn and with earth on his head. 33 David said to him, "If you march on with me, you will be a burden to me. 34 But if you go back to the city and say to Absalom, 'I will be your servant, O king; I was your father's servant formerly, and now I will be yours,' then you can nullify Ahithophel's counsel for me. 35 You will have the priests Zadok and Abiathar there, and you can report everything that you hear in the king's palace to the priests Zadok and Abiathar. 36 Also, their two sons are there with them, Zadok's son Ahimaaz and Abiathar's son Jonathan; and through them you can report to me everything you hear." 37 And so Hushai, the friend of David, reached the city as Absalom was entering Jerusalem.

16 David had passed a little beyond the summit when Ziba the servant of Mephibosheth came toward him with a pair of saddled asses carrying two hundred loaves of bread, one hundred cakes of raisin, one hundred cakes of figs,ª and a jar of wine. 2 The king asked Ziba, "What are you doing with these?" Ziba answered, "The asses are for Your Majesty's family to ride on, the bread and figs are for the attendants to eat, and the wine is to be drunk by any who are exhausted in the wilderness." 3 "And where is your master's son?" the king asked. "He is staying in Jerusalem," Ziba replied to the king, "for he thinks that the House of Israel will now give him back the throne of his grandfather." 4 The king said to Ziba, "Then all that belongs to Mephibosheth is now yours!" And Ziba replied, "I bow low. Your Majesty is most gracious to me."

5 As King David was approaching Bahurim, a member of Saul's clan—a man named Shimei son of Gera—came out from there, hurling insults as he came. 6 He threw stones at David and all King David's courtiers, while all the troops and all the warriors were at his right and his left. 7 And these are the insults that Shimei hurled: "Get

30: Covering the head and walking barefoot were signs of grief (Jer. 14.3; Esth. 6.12). **31:** David, aware of Ahithophel's wisdom, greatly dreads his counsel to Absalom. **32:** At the very place *where people would prostrate themselves to God* David's prayer (v. 31) is answered: Hushai appears, who will counteract Ahithophel's counsel. *His robe torn and with earth on his head,* see 1.2 n. **33–36:** David assigns Hushai a twofold task: to nullify Ahithophel's counsel, and to supply information right from the heart of the uprising to David's secret agents. **37:** *Friend,* or perhaps "companion," an official title (1 Kings 4.5). **16.1:** *Ziba,* see 9.2. The detailed list of supplies underscores Ziba's gesture of support. **2:** *The attendants,* see 1 Sam. 25.27 n. **3:** *Your master's son,* Mephibosheth, Saul's grandson (9.6). **4:** David believes Ziba, and, wishing to reward him for his support, gives him all the fields he has previously given to Mephibosheth (9.9).

ª Lit. "summer fruit."

out, get out, you criminal, you villain! [8] The Lord is paying you back for all your crimes against the family of Saul, whose throne you seized. The Lord is handing over the throne to your son Absalom; you are in trouble because you are a criminal!"

[9] Abishai son of Zeruiah said to the king, "Why let that dead dog abuse my lord the king? Let me go over and cut off his head!" [10] But the king said, [a]-"What has this to do with you,-[a] you sons of Zeruiah? He is abusing [me] only because the Lord told him to abuse David; and who is to say, 'Why did You do that?'" [11] David said further to Abishai and all the courtiers, "If my son, my own issue, seeks to kill me, how much more the Benjaminite! Let him go on hurling abuse, for the Lord has told him to. [12] Perhaps the Lord will look upon my punishment[b] and recompense me for the abuse [Shimei] has uttered today." [13] David and his men continued on their way, while Shimei walked alongside on the slope of the hill, insulting him as he walked, and throwing stones at him and flinging dirt. [14] The king and all who accompanied him arrived[c] exhausted, and he rested there.

[15] Meanwhile Absalom and all the people, the men of Israel, arrived in Jerusalem, together with Ahithophel. [16] When Hushai the Archite, David's friend, came before Absalom, Hushai said to Absalom, "Long live the king! Long live the king!" [17] But Absalom said to Hushai, "Is this your loyalty to your friend? Why didn't you go with your friend?" [18] "Not at all!" Hushai replied. "I am for the one whom the Lord and this people and all the men of Israel have chosen, and I will stay with him. [19] Furthermore, whom should I serve, if not David's[d] son? As I was in your father's service, so I will be in yours."

[20] Absalom then said to Ahithophel, "What do you advise us to do?" [21] And Ahithophel said to Absalom, "Have intercourse with your father's concubines, whom he left to mind the palace; and when all Israel hears that you have dared the wrath of your father, all who support you will be encouraged." [22] So they pitched a tent for Absalom on the roof, and Absalom lay with his father's concubines [e]-with the full knowledge-[e] of all Israel.—[23] In those days, the advice which Ahithophel gave was accepted like an oracle sought from God; that is how all the advice of Ahithophel was esteemed both by David and by Absalom.

8: Shimei accuses David of having murdered Abner and Ishbaal in order to usurp Saul's throne. The initial chs of 2 Sam. deny this accusation. **9:** *That dead dog,* see 3.8 n. **10:** *Sons of Zeruiah:* David habitually lumps Abishai and Joab, his sister's sons, together (cf. 3.39; 19.23). **11:** David accepts his profound humiliation with resignation. What his son, his *own issue,* is doing to him is much worse than *the Benjaminite*'s abuse. **14:** *There:* According to 17.21–22, David waited near the Jordan.

16.15–17.14: The counselors' contest. The importance of the contest between Ahithophel and Hushai lies in the fact that its outcome will ultimately decide the battle between David and Absalom. **16–19:** Hushai, though known to be *David's friend* (vv. 16–17), tries to win Absalom's confidence. His statements, however, are equivocal. By *the king* (v. 16) either Absalom or David can be meant, and the same applies to the *chosen* one (v. 18). Similarly, the answer to the question in v. 19 can be Absalom or David himself. Finally, *so* (v. 19) can refer to loyal service either to Absalom or to David even while Hushai is in Absalom's employment. Absalom understands that he is meant, but Hushai probably thinks of David. Absalom's answer is not reported, but he turns to Ahithophel for advice. **21:** *Have intercourse,* see 3.7 n. *To mind the palace,* see 15.16. **22:** Absalom's public intercourse with *his father's concubines,* on the very roof from where David observed Bathsheba, is the fulfillment of Nathan's prophecy (12.11–12).

a-a Lit. "What have I and you."
b So kethib; qere "eye." Ancient versions read "suffering."
c Some Septuagint mss. add "at the Jordan."
d Heb. "his."　　e-e Lit. "before the eyes."

17 And Ahithophel said to Absalom, "Let me pick twelve thousand men and set out tonight in pursuit of David. [2] I will come upon him when he is weary and disheartened, and I will throw him into a panic; and when all the troops with him flee, I will kill the king alone. [3] And I will bring back all the people [a]to you; when all have come back [except] the man you are after,[-a] all the people will be at peace." [4] The advice pleased Absalom and all the elders of Israel. [5] But Absalom said, "Summon Hushai the Archite as well, so we can hear what he too has to say." [6] Hushai came to Absalom, and Absalom said to him, "This is what Ahithophel has advised. Shall we follow his advice? If not, what do you say?"

[7] Hushai said to Absalom, "This time the advice that Ahithophel has given is not good. [8] You know," Hushai continued, "that your father and his men are courageous fighters, and they are as desperate as a bear in the wild robbed of her whelps. Your father is an experienced soldier, and he will not spend the night with the troops; [9] even now he must be hiding in one of the pits or in some other place. And if any of them[b] fall at the first attack, whoever hears of it will say, 'A disaster has struck the troops that follow Absalom'; [10] and even if he is a brave man with the heart of a lion, he will be shaken—for all Israel knows that your father and the soldiers with him are courageous fighters. [11] So I advise that all Israel from Dan to Beer-sheba—as numerous as the sands of the sea—be called up to join you, and that you yourself march [c]into battle.[-c] [12] When we come upon him in whatever place he may be, we'll descend on him [as thick] as dew falling on the ground; and no one will survive, neither he nor any of the men with him. [13] And if he withdraws into a city, all Israel will bring ropes to that city and drag [d]its stones[-d] as far as the riverbed, until not even a pebble of it is left." [14] Absalom and all Israel agreed that the advice of Hushai the Archite was better than that of Ahithophel.—The LORD had decreed that Ahithophel's sound advice be nullified, in order that the LORD might bring ruin upon Absalom.

a-a *Meaning of Heb. uncertain. Septuagint reads "to you as a bride comes back to her husband; you seek the life of but one man, and . . ."*
b *Some Septuagint mss. read "the troops" (i.e., Absalom's).*
c-c *Ancient versions read "among them."*
d-d *Heb. "it."*

17.1–3: Ahithophel's second advice is to set out immediately and come upon David while he is weary and not yet organized. Ahithophel, without battle, will kill the king alone and then all the people will turn to Absalom. **1:** *Twelve thousand,* see 1 Sam.

15.4 n. **3:** *When all have come back* is probably a dittography of *and I will bring back all.* Read: "and I will bring back all the people to you; for you are after one man, and all the people will be at peace." **5–6:** Hushai gets the opportunity to nullify Ahithophel's advice. But achieving this is exceedingly difficult, because Ahithophel's counsel is generally highly esteemed (16.23), his present advice has already been accepted by Absalom and all the elders (v. 4), and Hushai is probably still suspected of allegiance to David. **7:** *This time:* Hushai begins with subscribing to the prevailing opinion concerning Ahithophel's advice—only this piece of advice is an exception. **8–13:** Hushai's aim is to buy time for David to rest and organize his defense. In the first part of his speech (vv. 8–10) he shows the shortcomings of Ahithophel's plan: It has no chance of success because of the nature of the opponents, and it is even harmful to Absalom's forces. In the second part (vv. 11–13) he proposes an alternative plan: Thorough preparations must be made, and then Absalom will be able to inflict utter defeat upon David. Hushai's speech excels in the use of rhetorical means, such as metaphor, simile, and hyperbole. **9:** *He must be hiding,* therefore it will be impossible to find him and kill him alone. **10:** Not only Absalom knows his father's courage (v. 8), *all Israel knows* it. **11:** Only quantity can overcome quality—i.e., only by assembling a huge army can Absalom prevail over David's courageous men. Contrary to Ahithophel, who stressed his own role (note the repetitions of "I"), Hushai gives prominence to Absalom's leadership. **14:** Because rejection of Ahithophel's sound advice seemed unthinkable, the narrator ascribes this to the LORD. On the human level, it was Hushai's outstanding rhetorical skill and psychological insight that achieved the rejection of Ahithophel's plan.

15 Then Hushai told the priests Zadok and Abiathar, "This is what Ahithophel advised Absalom and the elders of Israel; this is what I advised. 16 Now send at once and tell David, 'Do not spend the night at the fords of the wilderness, but cross over at once; otherwise the king and all the troops with him will be annihilated.' " 17 Jonathan and Ahimaaz were staying at En-rogel, and a slave girl would go and bring them word and they in turn would go and inform King David. For they themselves dared not be seen entering the city. 18 But a boy saw them and informed Absalom. They left at once and came to the house of a man in Bahurim who had a well in his courtyard. They got down into it, 19 and the wife took a cloth, spread it over the mouth of the well, and scattered groats on top of it, so that nothing would be noticed. 20 When Absalom's servants came to the woman at the house and asked where Ahimaaz and Jonathan were, the woman told them that they had crossed *-a bit beyond the water.*-a They searched, but found nothing; and they returned to Jerusalem.

21 After they were gone, [Ahimaaz and Jonathan] came up from the well and went and informed King David. They said to David, "Go and cross the water quickly, for Ahithophel has advised thus and thus concerning you." 22 David and all the troops with him promptly crossed the Jordan, and by daybreak not one was left who had not crossed the Jordan.

23 When Ahithophel saw that his advice had not been followed, he saddled his ass and went home to his native town. He set his affairs in order, and then he hanged himself. He was buried in his ancestral tomb.

24 David had reached Mahanaim when Absalom and all the men of Israel with him crossed the Jordan. 25 Absalom had appointed Amasa army commander in place of Joab; Amasa was the son of a man named Ithra the b-Israelite, who had married Abigal, daughter of Nahash and sister of Joab's mother Zeruiah.-b 26 The Israelites and Absalom encamped in the district of Gilead. 27 When David reached Mahanaim, Shobi son of Nahash from Rabbath-ammon, Machir son of Ammiel from Lo-debar, and Barzillai the Gileadite from Rogelim 28 presented c couches, basins, and earthenware; also wheat, barley, flour, parched grain, beans, lentils, d-parched grain,-d 29 honey, e-curds, a flock,-e

17.15–29: Recovery. Hushai's triumph over Ahithophel marks a turning point in David's situation. From now on all developments are in David's favor. **15–17:** Using the intelligence chain set up earlier (15.27–28, 35–36), Hushai reports to David and advises him to cross the Jordan immediately, lest *the elders* after all convince Absalom to adopt Ahithophel's plan. *En-Rogel,* a well in the Kidron Valley, not far from Jerusalem. **18–20:** *Bahurim* belonged to Benjamin, the tribe of Saul, and there Shimei cursed David a short while ago (16.5–8). Now in the same place a woman, believing in David, helps his agents in the same way Rahab once helped Joshua's agents (Josh. 2.3–7). **23:** His advice being rejected, Ahithophel commits suicide (see 1 Sam. 31.4 n.), convinced that David will gain the upper hand and execute him as traitor. Now at least he can *set his affairs in order* and be *buried in his ancestral tomb* (see 2.32 n.). **24:** *Mahanaim,* see 2.8. **25:** *Amasa,* like Joab, David's nephew and Absalom's cousin. *Nahash:* According to 1 Chron. 2.16 *Abigal*'s father was Jesse. "Nahash" probably crept in erroneously from v. 27. **27–29:** *Shobi son of Nahash* is probably the brother of Hanun, who was defeated by David (ch 10), *Machir son of Ammiel* accommodated Mephibosheth, Saul's grandson, in his home (9.4–5), and *Barzillai* is presumably the father of Saul's son-in-law (21.8). These men, though close to the royal houses of Ammon and Saul, display their belief in David's kingship. The long list of their gifts demonstrates the extent of their support.

---

a-a Meaning of Heb. uncertain. Targum reads "the Jordan."

b-b Some Septuagint mss. and 1 Chron. 2.12–17 read "Ishmaelite" and give a somewhat different genealogy.

c Brought up from v. 29 for clarity.   d-d Lacking in the Septuagint and Syriac.

e-e Emendation yields "curds from the flock."

and cheese[a] from the herd for David and the troops with him to eat. For they knew that the troops must have grown hungry, faint, and thirsty in the wilderness.

18 David mustered the troops who were with him and set over them captains of thousands and captains of hundreds. [2] David [b]sent out the troops,[b] one-third under the command of Joab, one-third under the command of Joab's brother Abishai son of Zeruiah, and one-third under the command of Ittai the Gittite. And David said to the troops, "I myself will march out with you." [3] But the troops replied, "No! For if some of us flee, the rest will not be concerned about us; even if half of us should die, the others will not be concerned about us. But [c]you are worth ten thousand of us.[c] Therefore, it is better for you to support us from the town." [4] And the king said to them, "I will do whatever you think best."

So the king stood beside the gate as all the troops marched out by their hundreds and thousands. [5] The king gave orders to Joab, Abishai, and Ittai: "Deal gently with my boy Absalom, for my sake." All the troops heard the king give the order about Absalom to all the officers.

[6] The troops marched out into the open to confront the Israelites,[d] and the battle was fought in the forest of Ephraim.[e] [7] The Israelite troops were routed by David's followers, and a great slaughter took place there that day—twenty thousand men. [8] The battle spread out over that whole region, and the forest devoured more troops that day than the sword.

[9] Absalom encountered some of David's followers. Absalom was riding on a mule, and as the mule passed under the tangled branches of a great terebinth, his hair got caught in the terebinth; he [f]was held[f] between heaven and earth as the mule under him kept going. [10] One of the men saw it and told Joab, "I have just seen Absalom hanging from a terebinth." [11] Joab said to the man who told him, "You saw it! Why didn't you kill him [g]then and there?[g] I would have owed you ten[h] shekels of silver and a belt." [12] But the man answered Joab, "Even if I had a

18.1–18: The rebels' downfall.
The battle between the armies of David and Absalom results in Absalom's death. **1:** *Thousands . . . hundreds,* military units (cf. 1 Sam. 29.2). **2:** *Ittai,* see 15.19. **3–4:** The army understands—just as Ahithophel did (17.2–3)—that David is the rebels' only target and his death will decide the battle. *Ten thousand,* see v. 1 n. **5:** *My boy,* notwithstanding his criminal behavior. **9:** Unlike David, Absalom participates in the battle himself, as suggested by Hushai (17.11). *Mule,* see 13.29 n. Absalom, who used to grow his hair and weigh it every year (14.26), is caught by *his hair* (lit. "his head")—indicating that his pride is his undoing. **10–15:** The dialogue between Joab and the man who saw Absalom hanging in the tree underscores Joab's deliberate violation of David's explicit order to deal gently with Absalom. Though Absalom is finally killed by ten armsbearers, responsibility for his death rests with Joab, who gave the order—just as responsibility for Amnon's death, though carried out by attendants, rested with Absalom (13.28–29). Joab was probably driven by concern for the people and the kingdom, but personal feelings—disappointment and anger at Absalom's ingratitude and violence (14.30–31)—may also have been involved.

---

a *Meaning of Heb. uncertain.*

b-b *Some Septuagint mss. read "divided the troops into three."*

c-c *So two Heb. mss., Septuagint, and Vulgate; cf. 1 Kings 1.18 and note. Most mss. and the editions read "Now there are ten thousand like us."*

d *The usual term in this narrative for the supporters of Absalom.*

e *Some Septuagint mss. read "Mahanaim"; cf. 17.24.*

f-f *Meaning of Heb. uncertain. Ancient versions and 4QSam[a] read "was left hanging"; cf. v. 10.*

g-g *Lit. "to the ground."*   h *Some Septuagint mss. and 4QSam[a] read "fifty."*

thousand shekels of silver in my hands, I would not raise a hand against the king's son. For the king charged you and Abishai and Ittai in our hearing, 'Watch over my boy Absalom, [a-]for my sake.'[-a] 13 If I betrayed myself[b]—and nothing is hidden from the king—you would have stood aloof." 14 Joab replied, [c-]"Then I will not wait for you."[-c] He took three darts in his hand and drove them into Absalom's chest. [Absalom] was still alive in the thick growth of the terebinth, 15 when ten of Joab's young arms-bearers closed in and struck at Absalom until he died. 16 Then Joab sounded the horn, and the troops gave up their pursuit of the Israelites; for Joab held the troops in check. 17 They took Absalom and flung him into a large pit in the forest, and they piled up a very great heap of stones over it. Then all the Israelites fled to their homes.—18 Now Absalom, in his lifetime, had taken the pillar which is in the Valley of the King and set it up for himself; for he said, "I have no son to keep my name alive." He had named the pillar after himself, and it has been called Absalom's Monument to this day.

19 Ahimaaz son of Zadok said, "Let me run and report to the king that the LORD has vindicated him against his enemies." 20 But Joab said to him, "You shall not be the one to bring tidings today. You may bring tidings some other day, but you'll not bring any today; for the king's son is dead!" 21 And Joab said to a Cushite, "Go tell the king what you have seen." The Cushite bowed to Joab and ran off. 22 But Ahimaaz son of Zadok again said to Joab, "No matter what, let me run, too, behind the Cushite." Joab asked, "Why should you run, my boy, when you have no news [d-]worth telling?"[-d] 23 "I am going to run anyway." "Then run," he said. So Ahimaaz ran by way of the Plain, and he passed the Cushite.

24 David was sitting between the two gates.[e] The watchman on the roof of the gate walked over to the city wall. He looked up and saw a man running alone. 25 The watchman called down and told the king; and the king said, "If he is alone, he has news to report." As he was coming nearer, 26 the watchman saw another man running; and he called out to the gatekeeper, "There is another man running alone." And the king said, "That one, too, brings news." 27 The watchman said, "I can see that the first one

16: *Sounded the horn,* see 2.28 n. *Held . . . in check,* lit. "spared." **17:** *Flung him into a large pit,* an act of contempt. *A heap of stones,* a sign of disgrace (see Josh. 7.26; 8.29). **18:** The humiliating pile of stones on his grave is an ironic contrast to the glorious memorial that Absalom had set up for himself in the *Valley of the King. No son:* According to 14.27 Absalom had three sons. Radak resolves the contradiction by assuming that they had died. *Absalom's Monument,* not to be confused with the Roman-period tomb bearing that designation today.

18.19–19.9: The sad victory. Joy over the victory is overshadowed by David's grief over Absalom's death. In spite of what Absalom did to him, David loved his son dearly. **19–32:** The detailed account concerning the two runners focuses attention on David's reaction to their messages. **19:** *Ahimaaz,* see 15.27. **20:** Joab fully understands the significance of Absalom's death for David. **21:** *Cushite,* a black person from Cush, the region south of Egypt. **23:** *The Plain,* the Jordan Valley. **24:** The narrative's point of view leaps to Mahanaim, where David is anxiously waiting for news from the battlefield. Cities in biblical times often had two gates one after another, which were connected by a short fortified passageway. **27:** David's reply reflects the view that messenger and message are of the same nature (cf. 1 Kings 1.42).

a-a So some Heb. mss. and ancient versions. Most mss. and editions read "who"—perhaps meaning "whoever you are."

b I.e., by killing Absalom.

c-c Some Septuagint mss. and Targum read "Therefore, I will begin before you."

d-d Meaning of Heb. uncertain.

e I.e., the inner and outer gateways.

runs like Ahimaaz son of Zadok"; to which the king replied, "He is a good man, and he comes with good news." 28 Ahimaaz called out and said to the king, "All is well!" He bowed low with his face to the ground and said, "Praised be the LORD your God, who has delivered up the men who raised their hand against my lord the king." 29 The king asked, "Is my boy Absalom safe?" And Ahimaaz answered, "I saw ⸀a large crowd when Your Majesty's servant Joab was sending your servant off,⸀ but I don't know what it was about." 30 The king said, "Step aside and stand over there"; he stepped aside and waited.

31 Just then the Cushite came up; and the Cushite said, "Let my lord the king be informed that the LORD has vindicated you today against all who rebelled against you!" 32 The king asked the Cushite, "Is my boy Absalom safe?" And the Cushite replied, "May the enemies of my lord the king and all who rose against you to do you harm fare like that young man!" 19 1b The king was shaken. He went up to the upper chamber of the gateway and wept, moaning these words as he went,ᶜ "My son Absalom! O my son, my son Absalom! If only I had died instead of you! O Absalom, my son, my son!"

2 Joab was told that the king was weeping and mourning over Absalom. 3 And the victory that day was turned into mourning for all the troops, for that day the troops heard that the king was grieving over his son. 4 The troops stole into town that day like troops ashamed after running away in battle. 5 The king covered his face and the king kept crying aloud, "O my son Absalom! O Absalom, my son, my son!"

6 Joab came to the king in his quarters and said, "Today you have humiliated all your followers, who this day saved your life, and the lives of your sons and daughters, and the lives of your wives and concubines, 7 by showing love for those who hate you and hate for those who love you. For you have made clear today that the officers and men mean nothing to you. I am sure that if Absalom were alive today and the rest of us dead, you would have preferred it. 8 Now arise, come out and placate your followers! For I swear by the LORD that ifᵈ you do not come out, not a single man will remain with you overnight; and that would be a greater disaster for you than any disaster that has befallen you from your youth until now." 9 So the king

28: *All is well:* Ahimaaz thinks of the battle, whereas David is concerned about Absalom. **29:** Ahimaaz evades David's question. **32:** The Cushite's reply is indirect, but unambiguous, hinting that Absalom was a rebel. **19.1:** David's personal lament, unlike the public laments for Saul and Jonathan (1.19–27) and for Abner (3.33–34), consists mainly of short cries, repeating the beloved's name over and over again. **5:** *Covered his face,* see 15.30 n. **6–9:** While David the father succumbs to his personal grief, Joab threatingly orders him to fulfill his public duties as king. **6:** Joab accuses David of ingratitude to his loyal followers. **7:** Joab's extreme, unjustified accusations are based on half-truths. His aggressive language is probably related to the fact that it was he who killed Absalom. **9:** David yields to Joab, but does not forgive him (see v. 14).

---

a-a *Meaning of Heb. uncertain.*   b *Counted as 18.33 in some versions.*

c *Some Septuagint mss. read "wept."*

d *So Septuagint, 4QSamᵃ, and some other Heb. mss., and an ancient masoretic tradition; ordinary texts omit "if."*

arose and sat down in the gateway; and when all the troops were told that the king was sitting in the gateway, all the troops presented themselves to the king.

Now the Israelites had fled to their homes. 10 All the people throughout the tribes of Israel were arguing: Some said, "The king saved us from the hands of our enemies, and he delivered us from the hands of the Philistines; and just now he had to flee the country because of Absalom. 11 But Absalom, whom we anointed over us, has died in battle; why then do you sit idle instead of escorting the king back?" 12 The talk of all Israel reached the king in his quarters. So King David sent this message to the priests Zadok and Abiathar: "Speak to the elders of Judah and say, 'Why should you be the last to bring the king back to his palace? 13 You are my kinsmen, my own flesh and blood! Why should you be the last to escort the king back?' 14 And to Amasa say this, 'You are my own flesh and blood. May God do thus and more to me if you do not become my army commander permanently in place of Joab!' " 15 So [Amasa] swayed the hearts of all the Judites as one man; and they sent a message to the king: "Come back with all your followers."

16 The king started back and arrived at the Jordan; and the Judites went to Gilgal to meet the king and to conduct the king across the Jordan. 17 Shimei son of Gera, the Benjaminite from Bahurim, hurried down with the Judites to meet King David, 18 accompanied by a thousand Benjaminites. ᵃAnd Ziba, the servant of the House of Saul, together with his fifteen sons and twenty slaves, rushed down to the Jordan ahead of the king 19 while the crossing was being made, to escort the king's family over, and to do whatever he wished. Shimei son of Gera flung himself before the king as he was about to cross the Jordan. 20 He said to the king, "Let not my lord hold me guilty, and do not remember the wrong your servant committed on the day my lord the king left Jerusalem; let Your Majesty give it no thought. 21 For your servant knows that he has sinned; so here I have come down today, the first of all the House of Joseph, to meet my lord the king." 22 Thereupon Abishai son of Zeruiah spoke up, "Shouldn't Shimei be put to death for that—insulting the LORD's anointed?" 23 But David said, ᵇ"What has this to do with you,ᵇ you sons of Zeruiah, that you should cross me today? Should a single Israelite be put to death today? Don't Iᶜ know that

19.10–41: Return. On his flight from Jerusalem David first met his loyal supporters the priests and Hushai, then Mephibosheth's servant Ziba, and finally his opponent Shimei the son of Gera; on his way back the order is reversed—he first meets Shimei, then Mephibosheth himself, and finally his staunch supporter Barzillai. **10–11:** Only the arguments in favor of David are reported. *Israel*, excluding Judah. **12:** *Zadok and Abiathar* were left in Jerusalem in order to transmit information (15.27–29). The men of *Judah*, David's own tribe, probably supported Absalom (see 15.7 n.). **14:** Although *Amasa* was Absalom's army commander (17.25), David appoints him—his nephew—as permanent army commander in place of Joab, because of his anger at Joab for killing Absalom. David knows that Amasa has great influence in Judah. **16:** *Gilgal*, near the Jordan. **17:** *Shimei*, who cursed and insulted David on his flight from Jerusalem (16.5–13), now hurries to make amends and save his life. **18:** The *thousand Benjaminites* are meant to show Shimei's power in his tribe. *Ziba*, see 16.1ff. **20–21:** Shimei couches his plea in most deferential language. *House of Joseph*, a designation of northern Israel as opposed to Judah (see Josh. 18.5). **22–24:** *Abishai*, Joab's brother. His relentless approach (cf. 1 Sam. 26.8ff.; 2 Sam. 16.9ff.) sets off David's moderate attitude. David swears not to put Shimei to death, probably in order to win the support of Benjamin. He does not, however, forgive Shimei (see 1 Kings 2.8–9).

---

a Meaning of parts of the rest of vv. 18 and 19 uncertain.
b-b See note at 16.10.
c Some Septuagint mss. read "you."

today I am again king over Israel?" 24 Then the king said to Shimei, "You shall not die"; and the king gave him his oath.

25 Mephibosheth, the grandson of Saul, also came down to meet the king. He had not pared his toenails, or trimmed his mustache, or washed his clothes from the day that the king left until the day he returned safe. 26 When he a-came [from]-a Jerusalem to meet the king, the king asked him, "Why didn't you come with me, Mephibosheth?" 27 He replied, "My lord the king, my own servant b deceived me. c-Your servant planned to saddle his ass and ride-c on it and go with Your Majesty—for your servant is lame. 28 [Ziba] has slandered your servant to my lord the king. But my lord the king is like an angel of the LORD; do as you see fit. 29 For all the members of my father's family deserved only death from my lord the king; yet you set your servant among those who ate at your table. What right have I to appeal further to Your Majesty?" 30 The king said to him, "You need not speak further. I decree that you and Ziba shall divide the property." 31 And Mephibosheth said to the king, "Let him take it all, as long as my lord the king has come home safe."

32 Barzillai the Gileadite had come down from Rogelin and d-passed on to the Jordan with the king, to see him off at-d the Jordan. 33 Barzillai was very old, eighty years of age; and he had provided the king with food during his stay at Mahanaim, for he was a very wealthy man. 34 The king said to Barzillai, "Cross over with me, and I will provide for you in Jerusalem at my side." 35 But Barzillai said to the king, "How many years are left to me that I should go up with Your Majesty to Jerusalem? 36 I am now eighty years old. Can I tell the difference between good and bad? Can your servant taste what he eats and drinks? Can I still listen to the singing of men and women? Why then should your servant continue to be a burden to my lord the king? 37 d-Your servant could barely cross the Jordan-d with your Majesty! Why should Your Majesty reward me so generously? 38 Let your servant go back, and let me die in my own town, near the graves of my father and mother. But here is your servant Chimham; let him cross with my lord the king, and do for him as you see fit." 39 And the king said, "Chimham shall cross with me, and I will do for him as you see fit; and anything you want me to do, I will do for you."

25–29: *Mephibosheth,* addressing David in most polite language, accuses Ziba of failing to bring his ass and slandering him (16.1–4). He acknowledges the favors David has shown to him (ch 9) and even compares David to an angel of God (see 1 Sam. 29.9 n.), but refrains from mentioning directly that David, unjustly, gave his fields to Ziba. **30:** David understands Mephibosheth's hint. Without investigating who lied, Ziba or Mephibosheth, he decrees that the fields shall be divided. According to the Talmud (*b. Shab.* 56a), David's unjust decision will have repercussions in the future: "When David said to Mephibosheth, you and Ziba shall divide the field, a heavenly voice was heard, saying, Rehoboam and Jeroboam will divide the kingdom." (See 1 Kings ch 12.) The narrator's information in v. 25 makes it clear that Mephibosheth spoke the truth. **32:** *Barzillai,* see 17.27. **35–38:** Rhetorical questions are characteristic of Barzillai's style. **36:** *Good and bad,* in the material, not the moral, sense. **38:** *Chimham,* probably Barzillai's son. **39:** David does not forget his promise (see 1 Kings 2.7).

a-a *So Septuagint. Heb. "entered."*   b *I.e., Ziba (cf. v. 30 and 9.2 ff.).*
c-c *Ancient versions read "Your servant said to him, 'Saddle my ass, that I may ride . . . '"*
d-d *Meaning of Heb. uncertain.*

40a All the troops crossed the Jordan; and when the king was ready to cross, the king kissed Barzillai and bade him farewell; and [Barzillai] returned to his home. 41 The king passed on to Gilgal, with Chimham*b* accompanying him; and all the Judite soldiers and part of the Israelite army escorted the king across.

42 Then all the men of Israel came to the king and said to the king, "Why did our kinsmen, the men of Judah, steal you away and escort the king and his family across the Jordan, along with all David's men?" 43 All the men of Judah replied to the men of Israel, "Because the king is our relative! Why should this upset you? Have we consumed anything that belongs to the king? Has he given us any gifts?" 44 But the men of Israel answered the men of Judah, "We have ten shares in the king, and *c*in David, too, we have more than you.*c* Why then have you slighted us? Were we not the first to propose that our king be brought back?" However, the men of Judah prevailed over the men of Israel.

20 A scoundrel named Sheba son of Bichri, a Benjaminite, happened to be there. He sounded the horn and proclaimed:

"We have no portion in David,
No share in Jesse's son!
Every man to his tent, O Israel!"

2 All the men of Israel left David and followed Sheba son of Bichri; but the men of Judah accompanied their king from the Jordan to Jerusalem. 3 David went to his palace in Jerusalem, and the king took the ten concubines he had left to mind the palace and put them in a guarded place; he provided for them, but he did not cohabit with them. They remained in seclusion until the day they died, in living widowhood.

4 The king said to Amasa, "Call up the men of Judah to my standard, and report here three days from now." 5 Amasa went to call up Judah, but he took longer than the time set for him. 6 And David said to Abishai, "Now Sheba son of Bichri will cause us more trouble than Absalom. So take your lord's servants and pursue him, before he finds fortified towns and *d*eludes us."*d* 7e Joab's men, the Cherethites and Pelethites, and all the warriors, marched out behind him.*e* They left Jerusalem in pursuit of Sheba son

41: *Soldiers, army,* lit. "people" (see vv. 11–12, 16).

19.42–20.22: Rebellion again. Conflict between Israel and Judah leads to Israel's breaking away from David. Civil war and division of the kingdom are prevented by David's swift action, resulting in the rebel's death. **42:** See v. 16. **44:** *Ten shares,* ten times as much (Rashi: "for we are ten tribes"). **20.1:** *A Benjaminite,* from the tribe of Saul. *His tent,* an archaic term for "his home." **2:** Only Judah remains loyal to David. **3:** *The ten concubines,* see 15.16. David does not cohabit with them, because Absalom had slept with them (16.22). **4:** *Amasa,* see 19.14 n. **6:** Because of Amasa's delay in calling up the men of Judah, David, aware of the urgency of action, appoints *Abishai,* Joab's brother, as commander of his personal forces, and not Joab himself, because David is angry with him for killing Absalom. **7:** *The Cherethites and Pelethites,* see 8.18 n. *Behind him,* behind Abishai.

a Meaning of parts of vv. 40–44 uncertain.　　b Heb. Chimham.
c-c Septuagint reads "we are the first-born, rather than you."
d-d Meaning of Heb. uncertain.
e-e Emendation yields "Joab, the Cherethites and Pelethites, and all the warriors marched out behind Abishai."

of Bichri. 8 They were near the great stone in Gibeon when Amasa appeared before them. ᵃ⁻Joab was wearing his military dress, with his sword girded over it and fastened around his waist in its sheath; and, as he stepped forward, it fell out.⁻ᵃ 9 Joab said to Amasa, "How are you, brother?" and with his right hand Joab took hold of Amasa's beard as if to kiss him. 10 Amasa was not on his guard against the sword in Joab's [left] hand, and [Joab] drove it into his belly so that his entrails poured out on the ground and he died; he did not need to strike him a second time.

Joab and his brother Abishai then set off in pursuit of Sheba son of Bichri, 11 while one of Joab's henchmen stood by ᵇ⁻the corpse⁻ᵇ and called out, "Whoever favors Joab, and whoever is on David's side, follow Joab!" 12 Amasa lay in the middle of the road, drenched in his blood; and the man saw that everyone stopped. And when he saw that all the people were stopping, he dragged Amasa from the road into the field and covered him with a garment. 13 Once he was removed from the road, everybody continued to follow Joab in pursuit of Sheba son of Bichri. 14 [Sheba] had passed through all the tribes of Israel up to Abel of ᶜ Beth-maacah; and all the Beerites ᵈ assembled and followed him inside. 15 [Joab's men] came and besieged him in Abel of Beth-maacah; they threw up a siegemound against the city ᵉ⁻and it stood against the rampart.⁻ᵉ

All the troops with Joab were ᶠ⁻engaged in battering the wall,⁻ᶠ 16 when a clever woman shouted from the city, "Listen! Listen! Tell Joab to come over here so I can talk to him." 17 He approached her, and the woman asked, "Are you Joab?" "Yes," he answered; and she said to him, "Listen to what your handmaid has to say." "I'm listening," he replied. 18 And she continued, "In olden times people used to say, ᵃ⁻'Let them inquire of Abel,'⁻ᵃ and that was the end of the matter. 19 I am one of those who seek the welfare of the faithful in Israel. But you seek to bring death upon a mother city in Israel! Why should you destroy the LORD's possession?" 20 Joab replied, "Far be it, far be it from me to destroy or to ruin! 21 Not at all! But a certain man from the hill country of Ephraim, named Sheba son of Bichri, has rebelled against King David. Just hand him

10: Usually the sword is held in the right hand. Joab lets it slip out of its sheath and then snatches it with his left hand. He treacherously kills Amasa in the same way he killed Abner, striking him in the belly (3.27). His motive, then and now, was to get rid of a rival. David never forgave him (see 1 Kings 2.5). **11:** The henchman urges Amasa's men to go over to Joab, who assumed command over the troops pursuing Sheba. **14:** *Abel of Beth-maacah,* a town in the extreme north of Israel. **16:** The *clever woman* of Abel, like her counterpart of Tekoa (ch 14), is endowed with great power of persuasion. **18:** *Let them inquire . . . the end of the matter:* The town of Abel was apparently famous for its wisdom, and its rulings were invariably accepted. **19:** *Mother city,* metropolis. *The LORD's possession,* the people of Israel. **21:** The *hill country of Ephraim* included parts of Benjamin.

a-a Meaning of Heb. uncertain.

b-b Heb. "him."

c Heb. "and." Cf. v. 15 (and "Abel-beth-maacah" in 1 Kings 15.20 and 2 Kings 15.29).

d Emendation yields "Bichrites"; cf. Septuagint.

e-e Meaning of Heb. uncertain. The phrase would read well in the next verse (". . . a clever woman stood on the rampart and shouted . . .").

f-f Lit. "destroying, to topple the wall." Septuagint and Targum read "were planning to topple the wall."

alone over to us, and I will withdraw from the city." The woman assured Joab, "His head shall be thrown over the wall to you." 22 The woman came to all the people with her clever plan; and they cut off the head of Sheba son of Bichri and threw it down to Joab. He then sounded the horn; all the men dispersed to their homes, and Joab returned to the king in Jerusalem.

23 Joab was commander of the whole army [of] Israel; Benaiah son of Jehoiada was commander of the Cherethites and the Pelethites; 24 Adoram*a* was in charge of forced labor; Jehoshaphat son of Ahilud was recorder; 25 Sheva*b* was scribe; and Zadok and Abiathar were priests. 26 Ira the Jairite also served David as priest.

21 There was a famine during the reign of David, year after year for three years. David inquired of the LORD, and the LORD replied, "It is because of the bloodguilt of Saul and [his] house, for he put some Gibeonites to death." 2 The king summoned the Gibeonites and spoke to them.—Now the Gibeonites were not of Israelite stock, but a remnant of the Amorites, to whom the Israelites had given an oath; and Saul had tried to wipe them out in his zeal for the people of Israel and Judah.—3 David asked the Gibeonites, "What shall I do for you? How shall I make expiation, so that you may bless the LORD's own people?" 4 The Gibeonites answered him, "We have no claim for silver or gold against Saul and his household; and we have no claim on the life of any other man in Israel." And [David] responded, "Whatever you say I will do for you." 5 Thereupon they said to the king, "The man who massacred us and planned to *c-*exterminate us, so that we*-c* should not survive in all the territory of Israel—6 let seven of his male issue be handed over to us, and we will impale them before the LORD in *d-*Gibeah of Saul, the chosen of the LORD."*-d* And the king replied, "I will do so."

a So in 1 Kings 12.18 and 2 Chron. 10.18 ("Hadoram"); elsewhere "Adoniram."

b See note b at 8.17.

c-c Meaning of Heb. uncertain.

d-d Emendation yields "at Gibeon, on the mountain of the LORD" (cf. Septuagint and v. 9).

22: *Clever plan,* lit. "cleverness." The woman persuades her people, thus preventing war. *Sounded the horn,* see 2.28 n. *To the king,* to his service.

20.23–26: Administration, part 2. The list of David's senior officials is similar to the list in 8.16–18 (see

annotations there), but probably reflects a later stage in David's reign. The list marks the conclusion of the second part of 2 Samuel. **24:** *Adoram* still functions under Solomon (see translators' note). Since *forced labor* is not mentioned in the first list, it was apparently instituted later. It aroused

fierce opposition, culminating in Adoram's murder (see 1 Kings 12.18). **26:** Cf. 8.18.

Chs 21–24: Appendix. The last four chapters of Samuel include diverse materials. These are somewhat different in character, theological outlook, and language from the main body of the book, and were added later as an appendix. They are arranged in chiastic order: (A) a narrative about a national calamity, (B) short accounts of heroic feats, (C) a poem, (C') a poem, (B') short accounts of heroic feats, with a list of David's heroes, and (A') a narrative about a national calamity. The first narrative looks back to the past, to events that occurred before David's reign; the last narrative points to the future, to the period of David's son Solomon.

21.1–14: Vengeance versus charity. The first part of the narrative tells of the Gibeonites' revenge for Saul's violation of the oath promising them preservation of life; the second part describes the acts of charity to the dead performed by Saul's concubine and David. **1:** The famine was the result of drought. Rain and drought are regarded in the Bible as divine reward and punishment for good or bad behavior (see esp. Deut. 11.13–17). *Put some Gibeonites to death,* lit. "killed the Gibeonites." This act of Saul is mentioned nowhere else. **2:** The *Gibeonites* were a remnant of the *Amorites,* or native Canaanites, who inhabited the country before the Israelite conquest. Joshua swore to them that their lives would be spared (Josh. 9.15). The whole people has to bear, even after many years, the consequences of Saul's sin. *In his zeal:* The narrator explains why Saul broke the oath and *tried* to exterminate the Gibeonites (but did not quite succeed). **3:** The Gibeonites' blessing will annul the curse of the famine. **4:** The Gibeonites, demanding blood vengeance, settle neither for material reparations nor for the death of anyone other than Saul's offspring. **6:** *Gibeah of Saul,* Saul's town (see 1 Sam. 10.5 n.). *The cho-*

7 The king spared Mephibosheth son of Jonathan son of Saul, because of the oath before the LORD between the two, between David and Jonathan son of Saul. 8 Instead, the king took Armoni and Mephibosheth, the two sons that Rizpah daughter of Aiah bore to Saul, and the five sons that Merab[a] daughter of Saul bore to Adriel son of Barzillai the Meholathite, 9 and he handed them over to the Gibeonites. They impaled them on the mountain before the LORD; all seven of them perished at the same time. They were put to death in the first days of the harvest, the beginning of the barley harvest.

10 Then Rizpah daughter of Aiah took sackcloth and spread it on a rock for herself, and she stayed there from the beginning of the harvest until rain from the sky fell on [b]the bodies;[b] she did not let the birds of the sky settle on them by day or the wild beasts [approach] by night. 11 David was told what Saul's concubine Rizpah daughter of Aiah had done. 12 And David went and took the bones of Saul and of his son Jonathan from the citizens of Jabesh-gilead, who had made off with them from the public square of Beth-shan, where the Philistines had hung them up on the day the Philistines killed Saul at Gilboa. 13 He brought up the bones of Saul and of his son Jonathan from there; and he gathered the bones of those who had been impaled. 14 And they buried the bones of Saul and of his son Jonathan[c] in Zela, in the territory of Benjamin, in the tomb of his father Kish. And when all that the king had commanded was done, God responded to the plea of the land thereafter.

15 Again war broke out between the Philistines and Israel, and David and the men with him went down and fought the Philistines; David grew weary, 16 and [d]Ishbi-benob[d] tried to kill David.—He was a descendant of the Raphah;[e] his bronze spear weighed three hundred shekels and he wore new armor.—17 But Abishai son of Zeruiah came to his aid; he attacked the Philistine and killed him. It was then that David's men declared to him on oath, "You shall not go with us into battle any more, lest you extinguish the lamp of Israel!"

18[f] After this, fighting broke out again with the Philistines, at Gob; that was when Sibbecai the Hushathite killed Saph, a descendant of the Raphah.[e] 19 Again there

sen of the LORD, a sarcastic utterance (but see translators' note). **7:** Contrary to Saul, who violated the oath to the Gibeonites, David keeps the oath to Jonathan (1 Sam. 20.14–15, 42). **8:** *Rizpah,* Saul's concubine (3.7). *Merab . . . Adriel,* see 1 Sam. 18.19. **9:** *The mountain before the LORD:* In Gibeah, on the Hill of God, there was a shrine (1 Sam. 10.5). *The barley harvest* began in April. **10:** *Spread it,* pitched it as a tent to protect herself from the scorching sun. *Until rain from the sky fell,* until the beginning of winter. All during the hot summer Rizpah guards the decaying, smelling corpses. **11:** The noble deed of the simple *concubine* provokes David also to perform an act of charity for the dead. **12:** See 1 Sam. 31.10–13. **14:** *In the tomb of his father Kish:* Great value was attached to being buried in one's forefathers' grave (see 2.32 n.). *God responded to the plea of the land* and put an end to the famine.

21.15–22: Heroic feats. The four short accounts of feats performed by David's heroes against Philistine giants resemble each other in content and form. They also show similarities—particularly the third one—with the narrative of David and Goliath (1 Sam. ch 17). All of them tell of single combats. They probably belong to David's early period. **15:** *Went down,* from the mountain region to the plain. **16:** *Ishbi-benob,* a peculiar name, probably resulting from textual corruption. *His bronze spear weighed three hundred shekels,* about 3.5 kg. Cf. 1 Sam. 17.7. **17:** *Abishai,* see 1 Sam. 26.6 n. Regarding the declaration of David's men, compare 18.3. **19:** According to 1 Sam. ch 17 *Goliath of Gath* (i.e., the Gittite), *whose spear had a shaft like a weaver's bar* (1 Sam. 17.7), was killed by David, the Bethlehemite. To resolve the contradiction 1 Chron. 20.5 reads "brother of Goliath." Rashi assumes that David and Elhanan were one and the same person. Probably, however, the killing of the giant Goliath was initially attributed to Elhanan (perhaps the hero mentioned in 23.24), but later

a *So two Heb. mss., many Septuagint mss., and Peshitta; and cf. Targum, Sanhedrin 19b, and 1 Sam. 18.19. Most mss. and the printed editions read "Michal."*
b-b *Heb. "them."*   c *Septuagint adds "and the bones of those impaled."*
d-d *Meaning of Heb. uncertain.*   e *Apparently a race of giants.*
f *This paragraph is found also in 1 Chron. 20.4–8; in part, also in 1QSamᵃ, with some variations.*

was fighting with the Philistines at Gob; and Elhanan son of Jaare-oregim[a] the Bethlehemite killed Goliath the Gittite, whose spear had a shaft like a weaver's bar. [20]Once again there was fighting, at Gath. There was a [b]giant of a man,[b] who had six fingers on each hand and six toes on each foot, twenty-four in all; he too was descended from the Raphah. [21]When he taunted Israel, Jonathan, the son of David's brother Shimei, killed him. [22]Those four were descended from the Raphah in Gath, and they fell by the hands of David and his men.

22 [c]David addressed the words of this song to the LORD, after the LORD had saved him from the hands of all his enemies and from the hands of Saul. [2]He said:

O LORD, my crag, my fastness, my deliverer!
3   O [d]God, the rock[d] wherein I take shelter:
      My shield, my [e]mighty champion,[e] my fortress
            and refuge!
      My savior, You who rescue me from violence!

4   [f]All praise! I called on the LORD,[f]
      And I was delivered from my enemies.

5   For the breakers of Death encompassed me,
      The torrents of Belial[g] terrified me;
6   The snares of Sheol encircled me,
      The coils of Death engulfed me.

7   In my anguish I called on the LORD,
      Cried out to my God;
      In His Abode[h] He heard my voice,
      My cry entered His ears.

8   Then the earth rocked and quaked,
      The foundations of heaven[i] shook—
      Rocked by His indignation.

---

a *Perhaps a duplicate of 'oregim ("weavers") at the end of the verse; meaning of Heb. uncertain. 1 Chron. 20.5 reads "And Elhanan son of Jair killed Lahmi, the brother of Goliath the Gittite."*

b-b *Meaning of Heb. uncertain.*

c *This poem occurs again as Ps. 18, with a number of variations, some of which are cited in the following notes.*

d-d *Lit. "the God of my rock"; Ps. 18.3 "my God, my rock."*

e-e *Lit. "horn of rescue."*

f-f *Construction of Heb. uncertain.*

g *I.e., the netherworld, like "Death" and "Sheol."*

h *Lit. "Temple."*

i *Ps. 18.8 "mountains."*

the more famous David was credited with it. This was facilitated by the fact that the Philistine killed by David was originally anonymous (only in 1 Sam. 17.4, 23, where he is introduced, is his name mentioned; otherwise he is simply designated "the Philistine"). **20:** *Six fingers . . . six toes,* an extraordinary and perhaps frightening phenomenon.

22.1–51: A song of thanksgiving. The song, attributed to David, expresses thanks to the LORD, who delivered the author from mortal danger and granted him victory over his enemies. The song, which abounds in poetical devices, includes the following themes: praise of God (vv. 2–4); the author's plight and cry for help (vv. 5–7); God's appearance (vv. 8–16); God's rescue (vv. 17–20); the reward for the author's righteousness (vv. 21–25); God's ways of requital (vv. 26–28); the power of God's help (vv. 29–32); God's equipping the author for battle (vv. 33–37); the victory over the enemies (vv. 38–43); the author ruler of nations (vv. 44–46); praise of God (vv. 47–51). The song's frame—praise of God—defines its purpose. The same poem, with minor variations, which crept in during the process of transmission, is found in Ps. 18. **1:** The superscription resembles headings in the book of Psalms (see, e.g., Pss. 3, 34, 51), which were added to the songs to connect them with the events in David's life that occasioned their composition. **2–3:** The metaphors, occurring in a long string of epithets, stress God's strength. **5–6:** The author was close to death (see 1 Sam. 2.6 n.). **7:** *Abode:* According to v. 10 God's heavenly abode is meant. **8–16:** God's appearance (theophany) is manifested by terrifying natural phenomena: earthquake, volcanic eruption, and thunderstorm (cf. Exod. 19.16–18; Judg. 5.4–5). God is pictured in anthropomorphic terms.

11: *Cherub,* see 1 Sam. 4.4 n.
21, 25: These vv., framing the passage concerning the author's righteousness, convey the idea that the deliverance is a reward for merit.

9   Smoke went up from His nostrils,
     From His mouth came devouring fire;
     Live coals blazed forth from Him.
10   He bent the sky and came down,
     Thick cloud beneath His feet.
11   He mounted a cherub and flew;
     ᵃ‑He was seen‑ᵃ on the wings of the wind.
12   He made pavilions of darkness about Him,
     Dripping clouds, huge thunderheads;
13   In the brilliance before Him
     Blazed fiery coals.
14   The LORD thundered forth from heaven,
     The Most High sent forth His voice;
15   He let loose bolts, and scattered them;ᵇ
     Lightning, and put them to rout.
16   The bed of the sea was exposed,
     The foundations of the world were laid bare
     By the mighty roaring of the LORD,
     At the blast of the breath of His nostrils.
17   He reached down from on high, He took me,
     Drew me out of the mighty waters;ᶜ
18   He rescued me from my enemy so strong,
     From foes too mighty for me.
19   They attacked me on my day of calamity,
     But the LORD was my stay.
20   He brought me out to freedom,
     He rescued me because He was pleased with me.
21   The LORD rewarded me according to my merit,
     He requited the cleanness of my hands.

22   For I have kept the ways of the LORD
     And have not been guilty before my God;
23   I am mindful of all His rules
     And have not departed from His laws.
24   I have been blameless before Him,
     And have guarded myself against sinning—
25   And the LORD has requited my merit,
     According to my purity in His sight.
26   With the loyal You deal loyally;
     With the blameless hero,ᵈ blamelessly.
27   With the pure You act in purity,
     And with the perverse You are wily.
28   To humble folk You give victory,
     ᵉ‑And You look with scorn on the haughty.‑ᵉ

---

a-a Ps. 18.11 "Gliding."   b I.e., the enemies in v. 4.
c Cf. v. 5.   d Ps. 18.26 "man."
e-e Lit. "And lower Your eyes on the haughty"; Ps. 18.28 "But haughty eyes You humble."

29 You, O Lord, are my lamp;
    The Lord lights up my darkness.
30 With You, I can rush a barrier,[a]
    With my God, I can scale a wall.
31 The way of God is perfect,
    The word of the Lord is pure.
    He is a shield to all who take refuge in Him.
32 Yea, who is a god except the Lord,
    Who is a rock except God—
33 The God, [b]my mighty stronghold,[b]
    Who kept[c] my path secure;
34 Who made my legs like a deer's,
    And set me firm on the[d] heights;
35 Who trained my hands for battle,
    So that my arms can bend a bow of bronze!
36 You have granted me the shield of Your protection
    [e]And Your providence has made me great.[e]
37 You have let me stride on freely,
    And my feet have not slipped.
38 I pursued my enemies and wiped them out,
    I did not turn back till I destroyed them.
39 I destroyed them, I struck them down;
    They rose no more, they lay at my feet.
40 You have girt me with strength for battle,
    Brought low my foes before me,
41 Made my enemies turn tail before me,
    My foes—and I wiped them out.
42 They looked,[f] but there was none to deliver;
    To the Lord, but He answered them not.
43 I pounded them like dust of the earth,
    Stamped, crushed them like dirt of the streets.
44 You have rescued me from the strife of peoples,[g]
    [h]Kept me to be[h] a ruler of nations;
    Peoples I knew not must serve me.
45 Aliens have cringed before me,
    Paid me homage at the mere report of me.
46 Aliens have lost courage
    [e]And come trembling out of their fastnesses.[e]

47 The Lord lives! Blessed is my rock!
    Exalted be God, the rock

29: "The hardship is the darkness and the deliverance is the light" (Radak). **32:** A declaration of monotheism (cf. Isa. 44.8). **34:** The singular of the word translated *the heights* also means "my back" and thence in the plural perhaps "my thighs" (parallel to *my legs*). **46:** *Lost courage,* lit. "wilted." **47:** *Rock,* see vv. 2–3 n.

a Cf. postbiblical *gedudiyyoth* "walls," Aramaic *gudda,* "wall."
b-b Ps. 18.33 "who girded me with might."
c Meaning of Heb. uncertain; Ps. 18.33 "made."
d Taking *bamothai* as a poetic form of *bamoth;* cf. Hab. 3.19; others "my."
e-e Meaning of Heb. uncertain.   f Ps. 18.42 "cried."
g So some mss. and the Septuagint; most mss. and the printed editions "my people."
h-h Ps. 18.44 "made me."

48 Who gives me victory;
The God who has vindicated me
And made peoples subject to me,

49 Rescued me from my enemies,
Raised me clear of my foes,
Saved me from lawless men!

50 For this I sing Your praise among the nations
And hymn Your name:

51 *a*-Tower of victory-*a* to His king,
Who deals graciously with His anointed,
With David and his offspring evermore.

23

These are the last words of David:

*b*The utterance of David son of Jesse,
The utterance of the man *c*-set on high,-*c*
The anointed of the God of Jacob,
d-The favorite of the songs of Israel:-*d*

2 The spirit of the LORD has spoken through me,
His message is on my tongue;

3 The God of Israel has spoken,
The Rock of Israel said concerning me:
"He who rules men justly,
He who rules in*e* awe of God

4 Is like the light of morning at sunrise,
A morning without clouds—
*f*Through sunshine and rain
[Bringing]-*f* vegetation out of the earth."

5 Is not my House established before God?
For He has granted me an eternal pact,
Drawn up in full and secured.
Will He not cause all my success
And [my] every desire to blossom?

6 But the wicked shall all
Be raked aside like thorns;
For no one will take them in his hand.

7 Whoever touches them
Must arm himself with iron
And the shaft of a spear;
And they must be burned up on the spot.

51: *Tower of victory*, cf. Ps. 61.4. But the reading "he accords great victories" (Ps. 18.51) is preferable (in the Heb the difference between the two readings is very slight). *His anointed*, see 1 Sam. 2.10 n. This v. is part of the prayer Grace after Meals.

23.1–7: Last words. Poems containing last words are also attributed to Jacob (Gen. ch 49) and Moses (Deut. ch 33). The present poem, ascribed to David, contrasts the just ruler, who is likened to light and beneficial rain, to the wicked, who are compared to harmful thorns. **1:** *Utterance*, cf. Num. 24.3–4, 15 (in the Heb the same word is used). The rendering *the favorite of the Mighty One of Israel* (translators' note d-d) is preferable because it constitutes a parallel to *the anointed of the God of Jacob* (note the parallelisms in vv. 1–3). *Anointed*, see 22.51. **3:** *Rock*, see 22.47. **5:** The *eternal pact* refers to God's promise of an everlasting dynasty for David (7.16). **6:** *The wicked*, David's opponents.

a-a Kethib and Ps. 18.51 read "He accords wondrous victories."
b Meaning of much of this poem (vv. 1–7) uncertain.
c-c 4QSam*a* reads "God raised up."
d-d Or "The favorite of the Mighty One of Israel"; cf. Exod. 15.2. Others "The sweet singer of Israel."
e So many Heb. mss. Most mss. and the printed editions lack "in."
f-f Meaning of Heb. uncertain.

8 These are the names[a] of David's warriors: Josheb-basshebeth, a Tahchemonite, the chief officer—he is Adino the Eznite; [b][he wielded his spear][b] against eight hundred [c]and slew them[c] on one occasion.

9 Next to him was Eleazar son of Dodo son of Ahohi. He was one of the three warriors with David when they defied the Philistines gathered there for battle. The Israelite soldiers retreated, 10 but he held his ground. He struck down Philistines until his arm grew tired and his hand stuck to his sword; and the LORD wrought a great victory that day. Then the troops came back to him—but only to strip [the slain].

11 Next to him was Shammah son of Age the Ararite. The Philistines had gathered [d]in force[d] where there was a plot of ground full of lentils; and the troops fled from the Philistines. 12 But [Shammah] took his stand in the middle of the plot and defended it, and he routed the Philistines. Thus the LORD wrought a great victory.

13 [d]Once, during the harvest,[d] three of the thirty chiefs went down to David at the cave[e] of Adullam, while a force of Philistines was encamped in the Valley of Rephaim. 14 David was then in the stronghold,[e] and a Philistine garrison was then at Bethlehem. 15 David felt a craving and said, "If only I could get a drink of water from the cistern which is by the gate of Bethlehem!" 16 So the three warriors got through the Philistine camp and drew water from the cistern which is by the gate of Bethlehem, and they carried it back. But when they brought it to David he would not drink it, and he poured it out as a libation to the LORD. 17 For he said, "The LORD forbid that I should do this! Can [I drink][f] the blood of the men who went at the risk of their lives?" So he would not drink it. Such were the exploits of the three warriors.

18 Abishai, the brother of Joab son of Zeruiah, was head of [g]another three.[g] He once wielded his spear against three hundred [c]and slew them.[c] 19 He won a name among the three;[h] since he was the most highly regarded among the three,[h] he became their leader. However, he did not attain to the three.

20 Benaiah son of Jehoiada, from Kabzeel, was [i]a brave soldier[i] who performed great deeds. He killed the two [d][sons] of Ariel of Moab.[d] Once, on a snowy day, he went

23.8–39: The heroes. The first part contains short stories, which are similar to the short accounts of 21.15–22. They also relate heroic feats of individual warriors and refer to David's early period. The second part merely contains the names of David's body of heroes, without their actions. The order is hierarchical: First the exploits of the highest in rank, "the three," are recorded, beginning with the chief officer; then those of two heroes who were prominent among "the thirty"—the main body—but did not attain to "the three"; finally the names of "the thirty" are listed. **8:** *Josheb-basshebeth,* an odd name. Septuagint reads "Ish-bosheth" (or "Ish-baal"). Instead of *he is Adino the Eznite,* 1 Chron. 11.11 reads "he wielded his spear" (see v. 18). Emendation yields "he wielded his ax" (the Semitic word for "ax" is similar in Heb to "the Eznite"). **9:** Instead of *when they defied,* 1 Chron. 11.13 reads "at Pas Dammim when" (note the following *there* and see 1 Sam. 17.1). **11:** Instead of *in force,* mss of Septuagint read "to Lehi," which is almost identical in Heb (note the following *there* and see Judg. 15.9). **13:** *During the harvest,* i.e., in the hot, dry season. *Three,* probably the three heroes mentioned before. **15:** *Bethlehem,* David's hometown. **17:** Drinking the water would be like drinking the blood of the men, who risked their lives. **18:** The reading of Syriac is to be preferred (*another* does not occur in the Heb). **19:** The more plausible "thirty" instead of *three* (twice) is confirmed by v. 23. **20:** *Benaiah,* see 8.18.

a A number of these names, with variations, are found in 1 Chron. 11 and 27.

b-b Preserved in 1 Chron. 11.11; similarly some Septuagint mss. of 2 Sam.

c-c Lit. "slain."   d-d Meaning of Heb. uncertain.

e See note at 1 Sam. 22.1.   f So Septuagint and 1 Chron. 11.19.

g-g Two Heb. mss. and Syriac read "the thirty"; cf. vv. 23–24.

h Emendation yields "thirty."   i-i Heb. "the son of a brave soldier."

down into a pit and killed a lion. 21 He also killed an Egyptian, a huge^a man. The Egyptian had a spear in his hand, yet [Benaiah] went down against him with a club, wrenched the spear out of the Egyptian's hand, and killed him with his own spear. 22 Such were the exploits of Benaiah son of Jehoiada; and he won a name among the three^b warriors. 23 He was highly regarded among the thirty, but he did not attain to the three. David put him in charge of his bodyguard.^c

24 Among the thirty were Asahel, the brother of Joab; Elhanan son of Dodo [from] Bethlehem, 25 Shammah the Harodite, Elika the Harodite, 26 Helez the Paltite, Ira son of Ikkesh from Tekoa, 27 Abiezer of Anathoth, Mebunnai the Hushathite, 28 Zalmon the Ahohite, Maharai the Netophathite, 29 Heleb son of Baanah the Netophathite, Ittai son of Ribai from Gibeah of the Benjaminites, 30 Benaiah of Pirathon, Hiddai of Nahale-gaash, 31 Abi-albon the Arbathite, Azmaveth the Barhumite, 32 Eliahba of Shaalbon, sons of ^dJashen, Jonathan,^d 33 Shammah the Ararite, Ahiam son of Sharar the Ararite, 34 Eliphelet son of Ahasbai son of the Maacathite, Eliam son of Ahithophel the Gilonite, 35 Hezrai the Carmelite, Paarai the Arbite, 36 Igal son of Nathan from Zobah, Bani the Gadite, 37 Zelek the Ammonite, Naharai the Beerothite—the arms-bearer of Joab son of Zeruiah—38 Ira the Ithrite, Gareb the Ithrite, 39 Uriah the Hittite: thirty-seven in all.^e

24 ^fThe anger of the LORD again^g flared up against Israel; and He incited David against them, saying, "Go and number Israel and Judah." 2 The king said to Joab, ^hhis army commander,^h "Make the rounds of all the tribes of Israel, from Dan to Beer-sheba, and take a census of the people, so that I may know the size of the population." 3 Joab answered the king, "May the LORD your God increase the number of the people a hundredfold, while your own eyes see it! But why should my lord king want this?" 4 However, the king's command to Joab and to the officers of the army remained firm; and Joab and the officers of the army set out, at the instance of the king, to take a census of the people of Israel.

a Meaning of Heb. uncertain. 1 Chron. 11.23 reads "a giant of a man."
b Emendation yields "thirty."   c Meaning of Heb. uncertain.
d-d Meaning of Heb. uncertain.   e Septuagint and 1 Chron. 11 differ from the foregoing lists in vv. 8–38, and from each other in the number and forms of the names.
f This chapter is also found, with some variations, in 1 Chron. 21.1–7.
g Cf. above 21.1–14.
h-h 1 Chron. 21.2 reads "and to the officers of the army"; cf. below v. 4.

24–39: Most of the heroes are from Judah, and particularly from the region around Bethlehem. Some are from Benjamin and Ephraim, and the last-named are of foreign origin. **34:** *Ahithophel,* see 15.12. **39:** *Uriah,* see ch 11. *Thirty-seven:* Since only 36 names are mentioned, the name of Joab, who is conspicuous by his absence from the list, should probably be added (both his brothers are included).

24.1–25: Census, plague, and altar. These three topics, which are successively dealt with in the three parts of the narrative, are causally connected. David conducts a census, which is considered a sin. God then punishes Israel with a plague. To put an end to the plague, David erects an altar on the site where later the Temple will be built (2 Chron. 3.1). Though the plague as well as its cessation result from actions by David, they are independently decided upon by God, hinting at both human responsibility and divine sovereignty. **1:** It is unknown what caused God's anger. In order to punish Israel He incites David to number the people, which raises the theological problem of God inciting to sin. The author of 1 Chron. 21.1 solves the problem by replacing God with Satan (a relatively late concept). Radak explains that inciting does not mean commanding, but only putting the idea in David's mind; therefore it remained David's decision whether actually to carry the census out. According to ancient belief counting people exposes them to misfortune. Exod. 30.11–16 requires each counted person to pay expiation money, so "that no plague may come upon them" (Rashi: "for the evil eye rules over counting"). **2:** The census is conducted for military purposes (see v. 9). *From Dan to Beer-sheba,* see 1 Sam. 3.20 n. **3:** Joab's objection serves as counterweight to God's incitement (cf. 1 Chron. 21.3).

⁵ They crossed the Jordan and ᵃencamped at Aroer, on the right side of the town, which is in the middle of the wadi of Gad, and ᵃ [went on] to Jazer. ⁶ They continued to Gilead and to the region of ᵇTahtim-hodshi, and they came to Dan-jaan and around to ᵇ Sidon. ⁷ They went onto the fortress of Tyre and all the towns of the Hivites and Canaanites, and finished at Beer-sheba in southern Judah. ⁸ They traversed the whole country, and then they came back to Jerusalem at the end of nine months and twenty days. ⁹ Joab reported to the king the number of the people that had been recorded: in Israel there were 800,000 soldiers ready to draw the sword, and the men of Judah numbered 500,000.

¹⁰ But afterward David ᶜreproached himself ᶜ for having numbered the people. And David said to the LORD, "I have sinned grievously in what I have done. Please, O LORD, remit the guilt of Your servant, for I have acted foolishly." ¹¹ When David rose in the morning, the word of the LORD had come to the prophet Gad, David's seer: ¹² "Go and tell David, 'Thus said the LORD: I hold three things over you; choose one of them, and I will bring it upon you.' " ¹³ Gad came to David and told him; he asked, "Shall a seven-year famine come upon you in the land, or shall you be in flight from your adversaries for three months while they pursue you, or shall there be three days of pestilence in your land? Now consider carefully what reply I shall take back to Him who sent me." ¹⁴ David said to Gad, "I am in great distress. Let us fall into the hands of the LORD, for His compassion is great; and let me not fall into the hands of men." ᵈ

¹⁵ The LORD sent a pestilence upon Israel from morning ᵇuntil the set time; ᵇ and 70,000 of the people died, from Dan to Beer-sheba. ¹⁶ But when the angel extended his hand against Jerusalem to destroy it, the LORD renounced further punishment and said to the angel who was destroying the people, "Enough! Stay your hand!" The angel of the LORD was then by the threshing floor of Araunah the Jebusite. ¹⁷ When David saw the angel who was striking down the people, he said to the LORD, "I alone am guilty, I alone have done wrong; but these poor sheep, what have they done? Let Your hand fall upon me and my father's house!"

¹⁸ Gad came to David the same day and said to him,

a-a Some Septuagint mss. read "began at Aroer, and from the town, which is . . . Gad, they."

b-b Meaning of Heb. uncertain.

c-c See note at 1 Sam. 24.6.

d Septuagint adds "So David chose the pestilence. It was the time of the wheat harvest."

5–7: The census-takers follow the borderline, beginning in the southeast, going up to the north, from there to the west, and finishing in the south. **11:** *Gad,* first mentioned at 1 Sam. 22.5. **12:** *Thus said the LORD,* see 7.5 n. **13:** Instead of *seven-year,* Septuagint and 1 Chron. 21.12 read "three-year" (note the recurrence of the number three). **14:** The expression *the hands* (lit. "hand") *of the LORD* points to pestilence (cf. Exod. 9.3). **16:** The *angel* is the Destroyer (see Exod. 12.23), who acts on the LORD's orders. The *threshing floor,* a flat area where the grain was removed from the ears and separated from the chaff. It was usually situated outside the city, near the gate. *Araunah,* one of the Jebusites, the Canaanite people who inhabited Jerusalem before David's conquest. **17:** David saw the destroying angel (the people being struck down) before the LORD ordered him to stop (v. 16). Instead of *I alone have done wrong* the Dead Sea manuscript 4QSamᵃ, some mss of Septuagint, and Josephus read: "I the shepherd have caused harm" (cf. 1 Chron. 21.17), in contradistinction to *these poor sheep.* David's pronouncement thus expresses objection to collective punishment, which is felt to be unjust; though it is clear that wrong, as well as wise, decisions of rulers necessarily have repercussions on their peoples. **19:** *David went up:* This indicates that Araunah's threshing floor was higher than David's residence, namely, on the mountain to the north of biblical Jerusalem (cf. 2 Chron. 3.1). **20:** The narrative's point of view switches to Araunah, who receives the king with great respect. **22:** Araunah offers the king everything as a present, a customary part of negotiating in the East (cf. Gen. 23.11). *Threshing boards,* presumably wooden boards, having sharp iron teeth underneath, which were drawn by animals over the ears of grain. **24:** The fact that David paid for the threshing floor and the oxen is strongly emphasized, to indicate that the Temple site was acquired by proper transaction and

"Go and set up an altar to the LORD on the threshing floor of Araunah the Jebusite." [19] David went up, following Gad's instructions, as the LORD had commanded. [20] Araunah looked out and saw the king and his courtiers approaching him.[a] So Araunah went out and bowed low to the king, with his face to the ground. [21] And Araunah asked, "Why has my lord the king come to his servant?" David replied, "To buy the threshing floor from you, that I may build an altar to the LORD and that the plague against the people may be checked." [22] And Araunah said to David, "Let my lord the king take it and offer up whatever he sees fit. Here are oxen for a burnt offering, and the threshing boards and the gear of the oxen for wood. [23] All this, [b]O king,[b] Araunah gives to Your Majesty. And may the LORD your God," Araunah added, "respond to you with favor!"

[24] But the king replied to Araunah, "No, I will buy them from you at a price. I cannot sacrifice to the LORD my God burnt offerings that have cost me nothing." So David bought the threshing floor and the oxen for fifty shekels of silver. [25] And David built there an altar to the LORD and sacrificed burnt offerings and offerings of well-being. The LORD responded to the plea for the land, and the plague against Israel was checked.

duly paid for (cf. Gen. 23). *Fifty shekels*, approximately 0.55 kg (slightly more than 1 pound). 1 Chron. 21.25 considerably magnifies that amount. **25:** *The LORD responded to the plea for the land:* According to v. 16 the LORD, acting independently, had already decided to renounce further punishment before David built the altar. Cf. the similar ending of the narrative about the famine (21.14). The book of Samuel concludes with a pious deed of David: the acquisition and sanctification of the site of the Temple.

a 4QSam[a] and 1 Chron. 21.20 add "Araunah (Ornan) was threshing wheat."
b-b Meaning of Heb. uncertain.

מלכים א

I Kings

KINGS, THE LAST BOOK of the "Former Prophets," relates the history of Israel from the declining days of David (10th century) through the beginning of the Babylonian exile. Its last verses describe the release of Jehoiachin, exiled king of Judah, from prison in Babylonia during the reign of Evil-merodach son of Nebuchadnezzar, an event datable through Babylonian sources to 562–561 BCE.

The division of Kings into two books is first attested in the Septuagint, the Greek version of the Bible, where it is combined with Samuel into a single four-part composition, *Basileiai* ("kingdoms" or "dynasties" or "reigns"). The division of Kings into two books was later followed in the Latin Vulgate version, and was adopted from there to vernacular Bible translations. Classical Jewish sources through the end of the Middle Ages do not make such a division, and it is first attested in Hebrew printed texts from the early 16th century, where it is noted as a division used by foreign translators. In the course of time, however, the division has been universally adopted by Jews as a matter of convention and convenience.

The narrative of Kings falls naturally into three sections followed by two brief appendices. The first section (1 Kings chs 1–11) narrates the circumstances of Solomon's ascent to the throne and describes the source of his wisdom, his reign over all Israel in a united kingdom, and the building and furnishing of the Temple and other structures; it also evaluates his religious behavior. The second section (1 Kings ch 12–2 Kings ch 17) begins by recounting the circumstances under which the northern tribes rejected the authority of Solomon's son, Rehoboam, withdrew from his kingdom (henceforth called Judah), and formed another, called Israel, with a king of their choosing. From that point the narrative provides a synchronistic, overlapping history of the kings of Judah and Israel for almost two centuries until the Northern Kingdom was destroyed by Assyria in 722. The third section (2 Kings 18.1–25.21) describes the reigns of Davidic dynasts in Judah, the Southern Kingdom, until Babylonia conquered Judah, ruined Jerusalem, destroyed the Temple, and executed some and exiled others from among its leading citizens in 586. The first brief appendix (2 Kings 25.22–26) tells of the appointment and assassination of Gedaliah, a native Israelite appointed administrator of Judah by the Babylonians; the second

(2 Kings 25.27–30) appends a notice that Jehoiachin, the exiled king of Judah, was released from a Babylonian prison in the thirty-seventh year of exile.

Kings is not a history in the contemporary sense of the word, that is, a factual description of past events and an explanation for their occurrence that a modern reader might expect. It is, in the main, an extended theological essay written by a person or persons with passionately held beliefs, convinced that the destruction of the Northern Kingdom and the fall of the southern one were due to the misguided policies of their kings. The author described past events selectively, commenting or summarizing them as illustrations of the lessons that he believed they taught.

The author maintained that the LORD, the God of history, made His will known to Israel with regard to specific key issues, that punishments are preceded by warnings through prophets, and that people are responsible for the consequences of their choices. He further maintained that kings were responsible for the fate of their people. For him, it was axiomatic that those ruling over the tribes of Israel were obligated to maintain the centrality of the Jerusalem Temple as the unique place where offerings acceptable to God might be made and to eliminate the illegitimate worship of any deity other than the LORD. The author's composition demonstrated how all northern and most southern kings failed to meet their obligations and how all adversity, from minor disasters to the final catastrophe, followed as a consequence of this failure. Somewhat contradictorily, he also took pains to note that despite this, the divine promise of an eternal dynasty to David (2 Sam. 7.11) was maintained out of God's love for David ("for the sake of David," 1 Kings 11.12; 2 Kings 8.19; 19.34).

The author expressed his axiomatic notions, described Josiah (2 Kings chs 22–23)—whom he regarded as best exemplifying what a king should be—and expressed his theme of the uniqueness of the Jerusalem Temple, in language closely tied to that of Deut. ch 12. Deuteronomy is the only book in the Torah to project an image of the ideal king (Deut. 17.14–20), who bears a striking resemblance to Josiah as depicted in Kings. The author's ideas about how God works in history parallel those of Deut. ch 28. For these reasons, contemporary scholarship refers to the author of Kings as a Deuteronomistic historian, i.e., as one who wrote under the influence and reflecting the concerns and ideology of Deuteronomy. In addition to sharing phrases found in Deuteronomy, the author also developed some unique expressions of his own that are repeatedly used throughout Kings: worshipping foreign gods and serving them (1 Kings 9.6; 16.31; 2 Kings 17.35; 21.3, 21); on every high hill and under every leafy tree (1 Kings 14.23; 2 Kings 16.4; 17.10); idolatry as abhorrent (1 Kings 14.24; 2 Kings 16.3; 21.2, 11); detestable things (1 Kings 11.5, 7; 2 Kings 23.24); the city that the LORD has chosen (1 Kings 8.16, 44, 48; 11.13, 32, 36; 14.21; 2 Kings 21.7; 23.27); to build a House for the name of the LORD (1 Kings 3.2; 5.17, 19; 8.17, 18, 19, 20, 44); to sacrifice and offer at the open shrines (1 Kings 3.2, 3; 22.44; 2 Kings 12.4; 14.4; 15.4, 35; 16.4); to revere the LORD, i.e., serve God from a sense of awe (1 Kings 8.40, 43; 2 Kings 17.32, 33, 34, 39, 41).

The author cites by name three sources to which the original readers might refer for additional information about the kings discussed: Annals of Solomon (1 Kings 11.41); Annals of the Kings of Israel (1 Kings 14.19); Annals of the Kings of Judah (1 Kings 14.20). The formula used by the author to introduce individual kings in the second section of Kings most likely draws regularly on information from the second and third of these sources: "In the _____ year of king _____ son of _____ of Israel/Judah, _____ son of _____ became king of Judah/Israel. He was _____ years old when he began to reign, and he reigned for _____ years. He did what was pleasing/displeasing to the LORD." The source also includes the names of the mothers of the kings of Judah (the queen mother).

Although no scholarly consensus exists concerning the nature of these documents, the author, by mentioning them, challenged readers to deny the veracity of the facts that he was evaluating and interpreting. In addition to these, he had access to documents bearing on the Davidic court (1 Kings chs 1–2) and the history of the Temple (1 Kings chs 6–7; 2 Kings ch 23), as well as to some form of edited materials by and about the prophet Isaiah (2 Kings 19.20–20.11), and to collections of prophetic stories that he interspersed in his narratives about the Northern Kingdom: Ahijah (1 Kings 11.29–14.18), Elijah (1 Kings 17.1– 2 Kings 2.18), Micaiah (1 Kings 22.1–40), and Elisha (2 Kings 2.1–13.21). Although no copies of these sources survive, documents that match each type or genre of document are known from other ancient Near Eastern sources.

The author's sustained lesson about God's justice in history continues through the untimely death of Josiah in 2 Kings 23.25. This death stilled his voice. According to the author's philosophy, Josiah should not have died as he did. The deeds of that good king should have set things right, but did not.

A second person, writing during the Babylonian exile, completed the book through 2 Kings 25.26. This writer attributed Josiah's death and every bad thing that happened subsequently to the sins of King Manasseh, a 7th-century Judean monarch. Passages expressing this notion, combined with a prophetic idea that Israelites as a people bore responsibility for the fate of their kingdoms, were inserted into earlier parts of the book, contradicting the first author's original axiom of royal responsibility (2 Kings 21.10–15; 22.16–17). The second writer continued the narrative, appending terse notices about the last kings but describing only political events, not religious ones. The Annals of Judah are not cited after 2 Kings 24.5 and were most likely not needed; he was noting current events. This writer made no comments and found no lesson to teach in the destruction of Jerusalem.

The combined efforts of the original author and the second writer produced a document relevant to the post-destruction communities in both Judah and Babylonia. Their situation was explained as the outcome not only of the religious policies of their kings, who had violated ancient revealed teachings, but also of the behavior of their own ancestors. The implication of this didactic text was that the very facts of destruction and exile demonstrated the power of God, the validity of His covenant with Israel, and His meticulousness in maintaining it. Therefore, when the punishment of ruin and exile had run its course, His promises of restoration made in Deut. 30.1–5 and by different prophets could reasonably be expected to come to fruition.

At least 25 years after the destruction of Jerusalem, a third person appended a few sentences to the composition, now the last three verses of the book. This person may have hoped that the event recorded, King Jehoiachin's release from prison, was the harbinger of coming changes in the fortunes of his people.

Jewish tradition has maintained, on the basis of statements in the Babylonian Talmud (*b. B. Bat.* 14b–15a), that the prophet Jeremiah, who prophesied from the time of Josiah until the exile, but lived beyond that (Jer. 1.2–3; chs 40–41), wrote Kings. This tradition may be based on the similarities between the final chapter of Kings and Jer. chs 25 and 52. As noted above, however, Kings has a much more complex history, and may not be attributed to a single individual; like most ancient Near Eastern compositions, its author is anonymous.   [ZIONY ZEVIT]

1 King David was now old, advanced in years; and though they covered him with bedclothes, he never felt warm. ² His courtiers said to him, "Let a young virgin be sought for my lord the king, to wait upon Your Majesty and be his attendant;ᵃ and let her lie in your bosom, and my lord the king will be warm." ³ So they looked for a beautiful girl throughout the territory of Israel. They found Abishag the Shunammite and brought her to the king. ⁴ The girl was exceedingly beautiful. She became the king's attendantᵃ and waited upon him; but the king was not intimate with her.

⁵ Now Adonijah son of Haggith ᵇwent about boasting,·ᵇ "I will be king!" He provided himself with chariots and horses,ᶜ and an escort of fifty outrunners. ⁶ His father had never scolded him: "Why did you do that?" He was the

a *Meaning of Heb. uncertain.*
b-b *Or "presumed to think."*
c *Others "horsemen"; meaning of Heb.* parash(im) *not always certain.*

1.1–2.46: How Solomon became king of Israel after David. The first two chapters of Kings detail the turbulent events, most of which transpired in a single day, that resulted in Solomon, one of David's younger sons, ascending the throne of his father. The narrative line continues from 2 Sam. 20.26 and according to many scholars, is the conclusion of the succession narrative.

1.1–4: David weakens with age. David is portrayed as frail and dependent. Others advise him about caring for his essential needs. From 1.1 through 2.10, where his death is mentioned, the narrative implies that David was bedridden; see 1.47. **2:** The warmth of a human body could have been provided by any of David's wives or concubines. Malbim suggests that his advisers didn't want him to be

weakened further by sexual intercourse so they sought a suitable person with whom he would not have intercourse. **3:** *The Shunnamite,* from the town of Shunem, in northern Israel. *Abishag* should not be confused with the woman whose dead son was revived by Elisha in 2 Kings 4.8–37. **4:** *Attendant,* the Heb denotes "caretaker" and nothing more. As a special servant, her presence was ignored by others, e.g., 1.15. Although she was present when David was in undignified circumstances, the author makes a point of indicating that they were not intimate. It is unclear, however, if this was common knowledge.

1.5–53: Adonijah's attempted usurpation of the throne and its aftermath. 5–6: Adonijah outfits himself with royal trappings and embarks on a program modeled after the failed one of his older brother Absalom (see 2 Sam. 15.1), to whom the author compares him, thereby suggesting that he would fail. After the violent deaths of his older brothers Amnon and Absalom, and perhaps the natural death of Chileab, Adonijah was apparently the oldest of David's living sons and the main heir of his personal property (see 2 Sam. 3.2–5). **5:** *I will be king:* There was no tradition of royal primogenione born after Absalom[a] and, like him, was very handsome.

7 He conferred with Joab son of Zeruiah and with the priest Abiathar, and they supported Adonijah; 8 but the priest Zadok, Benaiah son of Jehoiada, the prophet Nathan, Shimei and Rei, and David's own fighting men did not side with Adonijah. 9 Adonijah made a sacrificial feast of sheep, oxen, and fatlings at the Zoheleth stone which is near En-rogel; he invited all his brother princes[b] and all the king's courtiers of the tribe of Judah; 10 but he did not invite the prophet Nathan, or Benaiah, or the fighting men, or his brother Solomon.

11 Then Nathan said to Bathsheba, Solomon's mother, "You must have heard that Adonijah son of Haggith has assumed the kingship without the knowledge of our lord David. 12 Now take my advice, so that you may save your life and the life of your son Solomon. 13 Go immediately to King David and say to him, 'Did not you, O lord king, swear to your maidservant: "Your son Solomon shall succeed me as king, and he shall sit upon my throne"? Then why has Adonijah become king?' 14 While you are still there talking with the king, I will come in after you and confirm your words."

15 So Bathsheba went to the king in his chamber.—The king was very old, and Abishag the Shunammite was waiting on the king.—16 Bathsheba bowed low in homage to the king; and the king asked, "What troubles you?" 17 She answered him, "My lord, you yourself swore to your maidservant by the LORD your God: 'Your son Solomon shall succeed me as king, and he shall sit upon my throne.' 18 Yet now Adonijah has become king, and you,[c] my lord the king, know nothing about it. 19 He has prepared a sacrificial feast of a great many oxen, fatlings, and sheep, and he has invited all the king's sons and Abiathar the priest and Joab commander of the army; but he has not invited your servant Solomon. 20 And so the eyes of all Israel are upon you, O lord king, to tell them who shall succeed my lord the king on the throne. 21 Otherwise, when my lord the king lies down with his fathers, my son Solomon and I will be regarded as traitors."

22 She was still talking to the king when the prophet Nathan arrived. 23 They announced to the king, "The prophet Nathan is here," and he entered the king's presence. Bowing low to the king with his face to the ground, 24 Nathan

ture, nor were there laws governing the transmission of royal authority. Adonijah may have acted not only because he thought that the young Abishag could become pregnant and produce an heir that might be named successor, but also because the incapacitated David was not a reigning presence outside of the palace. **7:** *Joab* and *Abiathar*, supporters of David from his earliest days as an outlaw, may have become disaffected because of the erosion of their influence and prestige as some of their authority was assigned to others. See the list of officials in 2 Sam. 20.23–25. **8:** These were the loyalists of David's party. They would do what David directed. **9:** *En-Rogel*, a spring southeast of Jerusalem in the Kidron Valley, out of sight of the city itself (2 Sam. 17.17). The plan calls for Adonijah to be confirmed king by an oligarchy of a priest, a general, princes, and tribal leaders (vv. 19, 25). **11–27:** Nathan's response to the plan. Nathan's motivation is not clarified by the author, but since he spurs Bathsheba to action by pointing out that her life and that of Solomon are in danger, he may have perceived that his life was in danger also. **12:** *Save your life:* Abravanel proposes that the danger lay in that Adonijah knew about David's promise to Bathsheba (v. 13) and that should he succeed, he would eliminate potential threats to his rule. **13:** The key to Nathan's plan is the oath David swore to her concerning Solomon. There is no earlier mention of this oath. On the basis of 2 Sam. 12.24–25, Radak infers that David swore this oath to Bathsheba after the death of their first child as a way of consoling her. Nathan would subsequently have learned of it from Bathsheba. Some interpreters suggest that Nathan and Bathsheba are taking advantage of David's feebleness to "plant" a memory so that he will act in the manner that they wish. **17–18:** Abravanel highlights the rhetorical flourishes of Bathsheba's calculated presentation: (1) She initiates conversation with an hon-

---

a Thus, Absalom having died, Adonijah was David's oldest living son.

b Lit. "all his brothers sons of the king."

c So many mss. and ancient versions; usual editions "now."

said, "O lord king, ᵃ·you must have said,·ᵃ 'Adonijah shall succeed me as king and he shall sit upon my throne.' ²⁵ For he has gone down today and prepared a sacrificial feast of a great many oxen, fatlings, and sheep. He invited all the king's sons and the army officers and Abiathar the priest. At this very moment they are eating and drinking with him, and they are shouting, 'Long live King Adonijah!' ²⁶ But he did not invite me your servant, or the priest Zadok, or Benaiah son of Jehoiada, or your servant Solomon. ²⁷ Can this decision have come from my lord the king, without your telling your servant who is to succeed to the throne of my lord the king?"

²⁸ King David's response was: "Summon Bathsheba!" She entered the king's presence and stood before the king. ²⁹ And the king took an oath, saying, "As the LORD lives, who has rescued me from every trouble: ³⁰ The oath I swore to you by the LORD, the God of Israel, that your son Solomon should succeed me as king and that he should sit upon my throne in my stead, I will fulfill this very day!" ³¹ Bathsheba bowed low in homage to the king with her face to the ground, and she said, "May my lord King David live forever!"

³² Then King David said, "Summon to me the priest Zadok, the prophet Nathan, and Benaiah son of Jehoiada." When they came before the king, ³³ the king said to them, "Take ᵇ·my loyal soldiers,·ᵇ and have my son Solomon ride on my mule and bring him down to Gihon. ³⁴ Let the priest Zadok and the prophet Nathan anoint him there king over Israel, whereupon you shall sound the horn and shout, 'Long live King Solomon!' ³⁵ Then march up after him, and let him come in and sit on my throne. For he shall succeed me as king; him I designate to be ruler of Israel and Judah." ³⁶ Benaiah son of Jehoiada spoke up and said to the king, "Amen! And may the LORD, the God of my lord the king, so ordain. ³⁷ As the LORD was with my lord the king, so may He be with Solomon; and may He exalt his throne even higher than the throne of my lord King David."

³⁸ Then the priest Zadok, and the prophet Nathan, and Benaiah son of Jehoiada went down with the Cherethites and the Pelethites. They had Solomon ride on King David's mule and they led him to Gihon. ³⁹ The priest Zadok took the horn of oil from the Tent and anointed Solomon. They sounded the horn and all the people shouted, "Long live King Solomon!" ⁴⁰ All the people then

orific, my lord. (2) Going beyond Nathan's words (v. 13), she states that David swore . . . by the LORD your God, so that his words must be considered not an idle promise to her but an oath to God. (3) She quotes and does not paraphrase David's promise, making it immediate in a historical present. (4) She emphasizes David's promise that Solomon would reign in the future so that it contrasts with her description of Adonijah reigning in the present. **28:** Summon Bathsheba: Since Bathsheba was already there (v. 22), this is an indication that different accounts, one with Nathan taking the lead, the other with Bathsheba, have been combined. **30:** In my stead: David repeats the contents of the oath quoted by Bathsheba (v. 17) but purposely misquoted by Nathan (v. 24) to spur David's response. David, however, adds a concluding phrase which, apparently, he remembered but that they had forgotten. Although feeble, he is neither forgetful nor witless. Informed, he proves capable of decisive action. **32–39:** At David's command and under the protection of David's personal guard, the Cherethites and the Pelethites (see v. 38 n.), Solomon is confirmed king by an oligarchy of a priest, a general, and a prophet. The anointing ceremony (cf. 1 Sam. 10.1) takes place by the Gihon spring in the Kidron Valley just below the city wall; all the people by their acclamation confirm the choice. **33:** My mule: Ancient convention disallowed casual use of royal property. David's provision of his own animal confirms that Solomon's accession to the throne is indeed supported by David and is not a partisan act (see v. 44 and Esth. 6.6–11). **38:** Cherethites and the Pelethites, Aegean mercenaries in David's personal service with no ties of loyalty to anybody other than him (see 2 Sam. 8.18; 20.23). The former group may have come from Crete; the origins of the latter are uncertain.

a-a Or (cf. Rashi, Ralbag, Radak) "have you said . . . ?"
b-b Lit. "your lord's men."

marched up behind him, playing on flutes and making merry till the earth was split open by the uproar.

⁴¹Adonijah and all the guests who were with him, who had just finished eating, heard it. When Joab heard the sound of the horn, he said, "Why is the city in such an uproar?" ⁴²He was still speaking when the priest Jonathan son of Abiathar arrived. "Come in," said Adonijah. "You are a worthy man, and you surely bring good news." ⁴³But Jonathan replied to Adonijah, "Alas, our lord King David has made Solomon king! ⁴⁴The king sent with him the priest Zadok and the prophet Nathan and Benaiah son of Jehoiada, and the Cherethites and Pelethites. They had him ride on the king's mule, ⁴⁵and the priest Zadok and the prophet Nathan anointed him king at Gihon. Then they came up from there making merry, and the city went into an uproar. That's the noise you heard. ⁴⁶Further, Solomon seated himself on the royal throne; ⁴⁷further, the king's courtiers came to congratulate our lord King David, saying, 'May God make the renown of Solomon even greater than yours, and may He exalt his throne even higher than yours!' And the king bowed low on his couch. ⁴⁸And further, this is what the king said, 'Praised be the LORD, the God of Israel who has this day provided a successor to my throne, while my own eyes can see it.' " ⁴⁹Thereupon, all of Adonijah's guests rose in alarm and each went his own way.

⁵⁰Adonijah, in fear of Solomon, went at once [to the Tent] and grasped the horns of the altar. ⁵¹It was reported to Solomon: "Adonijah is in fear of King Solomon and has grasped the horns of the altar, saying, 'Let King Solomon first swear to me that he will not put his servant to the sword.' " ⁵²Solomon said, "If he behaves worthily, not a hair of his head shall fall to the ground; but if he is caught in any offense, he shall die." ⁵³So King Solomon sent and had him taken down from the altar. He came and bowed before King Solomon, and Solomon said to him, "Go home."

2 When David's life was drawing to a close, he instructed his son Solomon as follows: ²"I am going the way of all the earth; be strong and show yourself a man. ³Keep the charge of the LORD your God, walking in His ways and following His laws, His commandments, His rules, and His admonitions as recorded in the Teaching of Moses, in order that you may succeed in whatever you undertake and wherever you turn. ⁴Then the LORD will fulfill the promise that He made concerning me: 'If your

50: *Horns of the altar*, projections from each corner of the top surface. Blood of purification sacrifices was usually daubed on the horns. Taking hold of them was a way for an individual who believed himself innocent of any capital crime to claim sanctuary. **51:** *Let King Solomon . . . swear:* Adonijah acknowledges not only that Solomon is king, but that he, Adonijah, is his servant.

2.1–46: Solomon guarantees the throne for himself. 1–12: David counsels Solomon to follow the norms established by God to maintain the promise of an everlasting dynasty, and asks Solomon to execute David's vengeance on Joab, act kindly toward descendants of a former benefactor, and kill one who had insulted him, all on David's behalf. These actions would eliminate Solomon's potential enemies and protect his supporters. **1–4:** The author introduces the theme of a conditional promise to David of a dynasty. There is some tension between this version of the promise and the unconditional promise of 2 Sam. 7.11–16 and the ancient poem in 2 Sam 23.5. The "Teaching ["torah"] of Moses" refers to Deuteronomy (cf. Deut. 4.44–45), which contains instructions about a future king (Deut. 17.14–20).

descendants are scrupulous in their conduct, and walk before Me faithfully, with all their heart and soul, ᵃyour line on the throne of Israel shall never end!'ᵃ

5 "Further, you know what Joab son of Zeruiah did to me, what he did to the two commanders of Israel's forces, Abner son of Ner and Amasa son of Jether: he killed them, shedding ᵇ blood of war in peacetime, staining the girdle of his loins and the sandals on his feet with blood of war.ᶜ ⁶ So act in accordance with your wisdom, and see that his white hair does not go down to Sheol in peace.

7 "But deal graciously with the sons of Barzillai the Gileadite, for they befriended me when I fled from your brother Absalom; let them be among those that eat at your table.ᵈ

8 "You must also deal with Shimei son of Gera, the Benjaminite from Bahurim. He insulted me outrageously when I was on my way to Mahanaim; but he came down to meet me at the Jordan,ᵉ and I swore to him by the LORD: 'I will not put you to the sword.' ⁹ So do not let him go unpunished; for you are a wise man and you will know how to deal with him and send his gray hair down to Sheol in blood."

10 So David slept with his fathers, and he was buried in the City of David. ¹¹ The length of David's reign over Israel was forty years: he reigned seven years in Hebron, and he reigned thirty-three years in Jerusalem. ¹² And Solomon sat upon the throne of his father David, and his rule was firmly established.

13 Adonijah son of Haggith came to see Bathsheba, Solomon's mother. She said, "Do you come with friendly intent?" "Yes," he replied; ¹⁴ and he continued, "I would like to have a word with you." "Speak up," she said. ¹⁵ Then he said, "You know that the kingship was rightly mine and that all Israel wanted me to reign. But the kingship passed on to my brother; it came to him by the will of the LORD. ¹⁶ And now I have one request to make of you; do not refuse me." She said, "Speak up." ¹⁷ He replied, "Please ask King Solomon—for he won't refuse you—to give me Abishag the Shunammite as wife." ¹⁸ "Very well," said Bathsheba, "I will speak to the king in your behalf."

19 So Bathsheba went to King Solomon to speak to him

5: Joab's self-interested acts could not be addressed at the time (2 Sam. 3.27–39; 20.8–10). **7:** Barzillai aided David selflessly during Absalom's revolt (2 Sam. 19.32–40). **8–9:** Shimei cursed David during Absalom's revolt (2 Sam. 16.5–8; 19.22–24). **10–12:** David dies, and Solomon, having served as co-regent with his father for an undisclosed period of time, ascends his father's throne as sole monarch, his authority firmly established, but only in principle. **11:** *Forty years:* Solomon also reigned forty years (11.42). The number may be typological, indicating an indeterminate but long period of time: The catastrophic rain of the deluge lasted forty days and nights (Gen. 7.12), and Israelites were in the desert forty years. **13–23:** Adonijah's incipient insurrection and its aftermath. **17:** Adonijah's request is hardly innocent. He plans to take as wife one who, so far as the public knew, may have been intimate with David. This is tantamount to usurping the throne, as is clear from Solomon's response in v. 22. Compare Absalom's action in 2 Sam. 16.21–22.

a-a Lit. "there shall never cease to be a man of yours on the throne of Israel." Cf. 2 Sam. 7.12–16.

b Meaning of Heb. uncertain.

c I.e., Joab had thus brought bloodguilt on David's house; see 2 Sam. 3.27 and 20.10.

d I.e., for whose maintenance you provide; see 2 Sam. 19.32 ff.

e See 2 Sam. 16.5 ff; 19.17 ff.

about Adonijah. The king rose to greet her and bowed down to her. He sat on his throne; and he had a throne placed for the queen mother, and she sat on his right. ²⁰ She said, "I have one small request to make of you, do not refuse me." He responded, "Ask, Mother; I shall not refuse you." ²¹ Then she said, "Let Abishag the Shunammite be given to your brother Adonijah as wife." ²² The king replied to his mother, "Why request Abishag the Shunammite for Adonijah? Request the kingship for him! For he is my older brother, ^{a-}and the priest Abiathar and Joab son of Zeruiah are on his side."^{-a}

²³ Thereupon, King Solomon swore by the Lord, saying, "So may God do to me and even more, if broaching this matter does not cost Adonijah his life! ²⁴ Now, as the Lord lives, who has established me and set me on the throne of my father David and who has provided him^b with a house, as he promised, Adonijah shall be put to death this very day!" ²⁵ And Solomon instructed Benaiah son of Jehoiada, who struck Adonijah^c down; and so he died.

²⁶ To the priest Abiathar, the king said, "Go to your estate at Anathoth! You deserve to die, but I shall not put you to death at this time, because you carried the Ark of my Lord God before my father David and because you shared all the hardships that my father endured." ²⁷ So Solomon dismissed Abiathar from his office of priest of the Lord—thus fulfilling what the Lord had spoken at Shiloh^d regarding the house of Eli.

²⁸ When the news reached Joab, he fled to the Tent of the Lord and grasped the horns of the altar—for Joab had sided with Adonijah, though he had not sided with Absalom. ²⁹ King Solomon was told that Joab had fled to the Tent of the Lord and that he was there by the altar; so Solomon sent Benaiah son of Jehoiada, saying, "Go and strike him down." ³⁰ Benaiah went to the Tent of the Lord and said to him, "Thus said the king: Come out!" "No!" he replied; "I will die here." Benaiah reported back to the king that Joab had answered thus and thus, ³¹ and the king said, "Do just as he said; strike him down and bury him, and remove guilt from me and my father's house for the blood of the innocent that Joab has shed. ³² Thus the Lord will bring his blood guilt down upon his own head, because, unbeknown to my father, he struck down with the sword two men more righteous and honorable than he—Abner son of

22: Solomon sees through the ploy and responds to her ironically at first. Although the meaning of the end of the verse is unclear, Solomon's mention of Abiathar and Joab indicates that he discerns a potential plot against him. **23–25:** Solomon goes further than his father's advice and has his main rival, Adonijah, killed. **26–27:** Solomon banishes *Abiathar* to Anathoth, a Levitical city north of Jerusalem. The author interprets Solomon's decision as fulfillment of a prophetic oracle delivered against Abiathar's ancestor (1 Sam. 2.30–36). Prophecy and fulfillment is a major theme of the Deuteronomistic History. For the author, events happen on both the human and divine planes simultaneously. Abravanel suggests that Solomon's reason for not executing Abiathar rings hollow; the true reason, unstated in the text, is that Solomon did not want to call down on himself misfortunes such as those that visited Saul after he executed Abiathar's relatives, the priests at Nob (1 Sam. 22.17–19). **28:** *Horns of the altar,* see 1.50 n. **30–31:** *I will die here:* Solomon cleverly misconstrues Joab's intemperate statement as a request which thereby nullifies the sanctuary of the altar. Ostensibly convinced by Solomon's words, Benaiah returns and kills Joab on the spot.

a-a Lit. "And for him and for Abiathar and for Joab son of Zeruiah." Meaning of Heb. uncertain.

b Heb. "me."

c Heb. "him."

d Cf. 1 Sam. 3.14.

Ner, the army commander of Israel, and Amasa son of Jether, the army commander of Judah. ³³ May the guilt for their blood come down upon the head of Joab and his descendants forever, and may good fortune from the LORD be granted forever to David and his descendants, his house and his throne." ³⁴ So Benaiah son of Jehoiada went up and struck him down. And he was buried at his home in the wilderness. ³⁵ In his place, the king appointed Benaiah son of Jehoiada over the army, and in place of Abiathar, the king appointed the priest Zadok.

³⁶ Then the king summoned Shimei and said to him, "Build yourself a house in Jerusalem and stay there—do not ever go out from there anywhere else. ³⁷ On the very day that you go out and cross the Wadi Kidron, you can be sure that you will die; your blood shall be on your own head." ³⁸ "That is fair," said Shimei to the king, "your servant will do just as my lord the king has spoken." And for a long time, Shimei remained in Jerusalem.

³⁹ Three years later, two slaves of Shimei ran away to King Achish son of Maacah of Gath. Shimei was told, "Your slaves are in Gath." ⁴⁰ Shimei thereupon saddled his ass and went to Achish in Gath to claim his slaves; and Shimei returned from Gath with his slaves. ⁴¹ Solomon was told that Shimei had gone from Jerusalem to Gath and back, ⁴² and the king summoned Shimei and said to him, "Did I not adjure you by the LORD and warn you, 'On the very day that you leave and go anywhere else, you can be sure that you will die,' and did you not say to me, 'It is fair; I accept'? ⁴³ Why did you not abide by the oath before the LORD and by the orders which I gave you?" ⁴⁴ The king said further to Shimei, "You know all the wrong, which you remember very well, that you did to my father David. Now the LORD brings down your wrongdoing upon your own head. ⁴⁵ But King Solomon shall be blessed, and the throne of David shall be established before the LORD forever."

⁴⁶ The king gave orders to Benaiah son of Jehoiada and he went out and struck Shimei^a down; and so he died.

Thus the kingdom was secured in Solomon's hands.

3 Solomon allied himself by marriage with Pharaoh king of Egypt. He married Pharaoh's daughter and brought her to the City of David [to live there] until he had finished building his palace, and the House of the LORD, and the walls around Jerusalem. ² The people, however, continued to offer sacrifices at

36–46: *Shimei*, a Benjaminite (Saul's tribe: 1 Sam. 9.1–2), was not only a former enemy of David but also, therefore, a potential enemy of his dynasty in the future. **37:** *Wadi Kidron*, the valley just to the east of the city wall. A wadi is a seasonal watercourse. **46:** Through the death and banishment of internal enemies, in partial fulfillment of David's requests, Solomon secured the reins of power over his kingdom.

3.1–4: Introduction. Brief comments introducing themes and ideas developed later in the book. **1:** After consolidating authority among his own people, Solomon turned to establishing strategic political alliances with neighboring kingdoms through diplomatic marriages. Since Egyptian sources indicate it is unlikely that the actual daughter of a reigning pharaoh would have been given in marriage to a non-Egyptian, "daughter" may refer to a woman closely related to or descended from the royal family. The names of the pharaoh and the woman are not mentioned. She lived in the City of David only until Solomon built her a palace elsewhere. This brief notice anticipates the more detailed versions of Solomon's construction projects (chs 7–8) and also the problems caused by Solomon's foreign wives (ch 11).

a Heb. "him."

the open shrines, because up to that time no house had been built for the name of the LORD. ³ And Solomon, though he loved the LORD and followed the practices of his father David, also sacrificed and offered at the shrines.

⁴ The king went to Gibeon to sacrifice there, for that was the largest shrine; on that altar Solomon presented a thousand burnt offerings. ⁵ At Gibeon the LORD appeared to Solomon in a dream by night; and God said, "Ask, what shall I grant you?" ⁶ Solomon said, "You dealt most graciously with Your servant my father David, because he walked before You in faithfulness and righteousness and in integrity of heart. You have continued this great kindness to him by giving him a son to occupy his throne, as is now the case. ⁷ And now, O LORD my God, You have made Your servant king in place of my father David; but I am a young lad, ᵃ with no experience in leadership.ᵃ ⁸ Your servant finds himself in the midst of the people You have chosen, a people too numerous to be numbered or counted. ⁹ Grant, then, Your servant an understanding mind to judge Your people, to distinguish between good and bad; for who can judge this vast people of Yours?"

¹⁰ The Lord was pleased that Solomon had asked for this. ¹¹ And God said to him, "Because you asked for this—you did not ask for long life, you did not ask for riches, you did not ask for the life of your enemies, but you asked for discernment in dispensing justice—¹² I now do as you have spoken. I grant you a wise and discerning mind; there has never been anyone like you before, nor will anyone like you arise again. ¹³ And I also grant you what you did not ask for—both riches and glory all your life—the like of which no king has ever had. ¹⁴ And I will further grant you long life, if you will walk in My ways and observe My laws and commandments, as did your father David."

¹⁵ Then Solomon awoke: it was a dream! He went to Jerusalem, stood before the Ark of the Covenant of the LORD, and sacrificed burnt offerings and presented offerings of well-being; and he made a banquet for all his courtiers.

¹⁶ Later two prostitutes came to the king and stood before him. ¹⁷ The first woman said, "Please, my lord! This woman and I live in the same house; and I gave birth to a child while she was in the house. ¹⁸ On the third day after I was delivered, this woman also gave birth to a child. We were alone; there was no one else with us in the house, just the two of us in the house. ¹⁹ During the night this

2–3: *Open shrines:* The author is apologetic about Solomon's participation in rites at these places (Heb "bamot"), usually translated "high places," even though Deuteronomy did not prohibit their use until after the construction of the Temple (Deut. 12.4–12). In describing events transpiring after the Temple was built, the author condemns worship at such shrines. Their mention here introduces the next section.

3.4–15: The dream at the large open shrine at Gibeon, northwest of Jerusalem, and four divine grants. **4–5:** The story may be describing a ritual of incubation attested elsewhere in ancient literature. A person seeking guidance would sleep in a sanctuary or holy spot in the hope of a divine visitation in a dream. **9:** *Understanding mind,* Heb "lev shome'a," "listening heart." *Judge,* Heb "lishpot," also connotes leading, guiding, administering, or ruling. **10–14:** The four grants: wisdom, riches, glory, and a long life. A block of narratives, 3.16–10.29, demonstrates how these promises were fulfilled.

3.16–28: The case of the two prostitutes demonstrates Solomon's judicial wisdom.

---

a-a Lit. "do not know to go out and come in"; cf. Num. 27.17.

woman's child died, because she lay on it. 20 She arose in the night and took my son from my side while your maid-servant was asleep, and laid him in her bosom; and she laid her dead son in my bosom. 21 When I arose in the morning to nurse my son, there he was, dead; but when I looked at him closely in the morning, it was not the son I had borne."

22 The other woman spoke up, "No, the live one is my son, and the dead one is yours!" But the first insisted, "No, the dead boy is yours; mine is the live one!" And they went on arguing before the king.

23 The king said, "One says, 'This is my son, the live one, and the dead one is yours'; and the other says, 'No, the dead boy is yours, mine is the live one.' 24 So the king gave the order, "Fetch me a sword." A sword was brought be-fore the king, 25 and the king said, "Cut the live child in two, and give half to one and half to the other."

26 But the woman whose son was the live one pleaded with the king, for she was overcome with compassion for her son. "Please, my lord," she cried, "give her the live child; only don't kill it!" The other insisted, "It shall be neither yours nor mine; cut it in two!" 27 Then the king spoke up. "Give the live child to her," he said, "and do not put it to death; she is its mother."

28 When all Israel heard the decision that the king had rendered, they stood in awe of the king; for they saw that he possessed divine wisdom to execute justice.

4 King Solomon was now king over all Israel. 2 These were his officials:

Azariah son of Zadok—the priest;
3   Elihoreph and Ahijah sons of Shisha—scribes;
     Jehoshaphat son of Ahilud—recorder;
4   Benaiah son of Jehoiada—over the army;
     Zadok and Abiathar—priests;
5   Azariah son of Nathan—in charge of the prefects;
     Zabud son of Nathan the priest—companion of the king;
6   Ahishar—in charge of the palace; and
     Adoniram son of Abda—in charge of the forced labor.

7 Solomon had twelve prefects governing all Israel, who provided food for the king and his household; each had to provide food for one month in the year. 8 And these were their names: Ben-hur, in the hill country of Ephraim; 9 Ben-deker, in Makaz, Shaalbim, Beth-shemesh, and Elon-beth-hanan; 10 Ben-hesed in Arubboth—he governed Socho and all the Hepher area; 11 Ben-abinadab, [in] all of

23: *One says . . . the other says . . . :* Solomon discerns a distinctive pat-tern in each woman's speech: The more loquacious one emphasizes death first while the other empha-sizes life. Solomon intuits who is the mother of the living child and announces it circumspectly.
24–26: Since justice requires a more convincing demonstration of truthfulness, Solomon stages a confrontation in which the pas-sionate public behavior of the mother emphasizing life validates his intuition.

4.1–20: Solomon's bureaucracy for the administration of Israel demonstrates other applications of his wisdom. 2–6: A list of Solomon's high officials. His ad-ministration is more complex than that of David (cf. 2 Sam. 20.23–26) and includes new offices. This list contains some obvious inconsis-tencies: *Azariah son of Zadok* is listed as holding the office of *priest*, as are *Zadok and Abiathar;* the latter was deposed (2.27). It may combine two lists from different periods in Solomon's reign.
7–19: Although the *twelve prefects* correspond to the number of tribes, the territories of some pre-fectures did not follow tribal boundaries. This may have been an attempt by Solomon to weaken the authority of tribal organization in the interest of making Jerusalem more central. Judah is not men-tioned in this list unless the first word of v. 20 is considered the last word of v. 19. The last part of v. 19 would then be translated: "and one prefect who was in the land of Judah." See 5.7–8 on the reason for this division of the kingdom.

Mediterranean Sea

A S H E R

N A P H T A L I

B A S H A N

VIII

IX

ISSACHAR

IV

X

Dor •

Megiddo •

NAPATH-DOR

• Jezreel

Taanach •

V

Beth-shean •

VI

• Ramoth-gilead

G I L E A D

• Hepher

Arubboth •

Abel-meholah •

• Socoh

III

E P H R A I M

I

VII

• Mahanaim

XI

Shaalbim •

Makaz • • Elon

B E N J A M I N

Beth-shemesh •

JERUSALEM

XII

J U D A H

Dead Sea

0   10   20 Miles

0   10   20 Kilometers

33°

32°

31°

35°

36°

Solomon's twelve administrative districts according to First Kings 4

Naphath-dor (Solomon's daughter Taphath was his wife);
12 Baana son of Ahilud [in] Taanach and Megiddo and all
Beth-shean, which is beside Zarethan, below Jezreel—
from Beth-shean to Abel-meholah as far as the other side
of Jokmeam; 13 Ben-geber, in Ramoth-gilead—he governed the villages of Jair son of Manasseh which are in
Gilead, and he also governed the district of Argob which
is in Bashan, sixty large towns with walls and bronze bars;
14 Ahinadab son of Iddo, in Mahanaim; 15 Ahimaaz, in
Naphtali (he too took a daughter of Solomon—Basemath—to wife); 16 Baanah son of Hushi, in Asher and Bealoth;ᵃ 17 Jehoshaphat son of Paruah, in Issachar; 18 Shimei
son of Ela, in Benjamin; 19 Geber son of Uri, in the region
of Gilead, the country of Sihon, king of the Amorites,
and Og, king of Bashan; ᵇ⁻and one prefect who was in the
land.⁻ᵇ

20 Judah and Israel were as numerous as the sands of the
sea; they ate and drank and were content.

5 Solomon's rule extended over all the kingdoms from
the Euphrates to the land of the Philistines and the
boundary of Egypt. They brought Solomon tribute and
were subject to him all his life. 2 Solomon's daily provisions consisted of 30 *kors* of semolina, and 60 *kors* of [ordi-
nary] flour, 3 10 fattened oxen, 20 pasture-fed oxen, and
100 sheep and goats, besides deer and gazelles, roebucks
and ᶜfatted geese.⁻ᶜ 4 For he controlled the whole region
west of the Euphrates—all the kings west of the Euphrates, from Tiphsah to Gaza—and he had peace on all his
borders roundabout. 5 All the days of Solomon, Judah and
Israel from Dan to Beer-sheba dwelt in safety, everyone
under his own vine and under his own fig tree. 6 Solomon
had 40,000 stalls of horses for his chariotry and 12,000
horsemen.

7ᵈAll those prefects, each during his month, would furnish provisions for King Solomon and for all who were
admitted to King Solomon's table; they did not fall short
in anything. 8 They would also, each in his turn, deliver
barley and straw for the horses and the swift steeds to the
places where they were stationed.

9 God endowed Solomon with wisdom and discernment in great measure, with understanding as vast as the

a Or "in Aloth."
b-b Meaning of Heb. uncertain.
c-c Exact meaning of Heb. uncertain.
d Resuming the account begun in 4.2.

20: The author informs readers
that despite the bureaucracy, both
Judah—a term used anachronistically here to refer to what would
become the Southern Kingdom—
and *Israel,* the tribes north of
Judah, lacked nothing and were
content.

**5.1–8: Solomon's income and re-
quirements** for varying luxurious
comestibles are described to
demonstrate his wealth. This attests to the fulfillment of the grant
of riches. **1:** In addition to the
tribal territories, Solomon controlled two large vassal territories:
(1) northeast of Israel, extending
from the Bashan and Golan to the
Euphrates settled by Aramean
groups; (2) the coastland and territories west and southwest of
Judah up to the Egyptian border
settled by tribes originating in
lands bordering the Aegean Sea
lumped together under the name
of one tribe, Palastu, as *Philistines.*
All paid tribute to Solomon directly. **2–4:** Solomon lived lavishly,
ate well, had a large chariotry, and
maintained peace all his days.
These are mentioned here as ad-
mirable accomplishments. **5:** The
author repeats a comment (see
4.20) that Judah and Israel dwelt in
safety and contentment. *Dan to
Beer-sheba,* the traditional northern
and southern limits of the Land of
Israel. **6–8:** Only now does the author explain that the prefects were
responsible for provisioning the
royal household and maintaining
chariotry and *horsemen.* These
verses imply that Solomon developed an organized system of taxation in kind and in labor as well as
a sophisticated approach to logis-
tics. Nothing pejorative is intended by this information. The
author and his readers understood that the institution of the
monarchy had to be supported
(cf. 1 Sam. 8.10–17).

**5.9–7.51: The Temple construc-
tion project.** The author portrays
Solomon using his wisdom,
wealth, and glory in a project for
his God. **5.9–14:** Solomon's great
wisdom, his talent in composing

sands on the seashore. [10] Solomon's wisdom was greater than the wisdom of all the Kedemites and than all the wisdom of the Egyptians. [11] He was the wisest of all men: [wiser] than Ethan the Ezrahite, and Heman, Chalkol, and Darda the sons of Mahol. His fame spread among all the surrounding nations. [12] He composed three thousand proverbs, and his songs numbered one thousand and five. [13] He discoursed about trees, from the cedar in Lebanon to the hyssop that grows out of the wall; and he discoursed about beasts, birds, creeping things, and fishes. [14] Men of all peoples came to hear Solomon's wisdom, [sent] by all the kings of the earth who had heard of his wisdom.

[15] King Hiram of Tyre sent his officials to Solomon when he heard that he had been anointed king in place of his father; for Hiram had always been a friend of David. [16] Solomon sent this message to Hiram: [17] "You know that my father David could not build a house for the name of the LORD his God because of the enemies[a] that encompassed him, until the LORD had placed them under the soles of his feet. [18] But now the LORD my God has given me respite all around; there is no adversary and no mischance. [19] And so I propose to build a house for the name of the LORD my God, as the LORD promised my father David, saying, 'Your son, whom I will set on your throne in your place, shall build the house for My name.' [20] Please, then, give orders for cedars to be cut for me in the Lebanon. My servants will work with yours, and I will pay you any wages you may ask for your servants; for as you know, there is none among us who knows how to cut timber like the Sidonians."

[21] When Hiram heard Solomon's message, he was overjoyed. "Praised be the LORD this day," he said, "for granting David a wise son to govern this great people." [22] So Hiram sent word to Solomon: "I have your message; I will supply all the cedar and cypress logs you require. [23] My servants will bring them down to the sea from the Lebanon; and at the sea I will make them into floats and [deliver them] to any place that you designate to me. There I shall break them up for you to carry away. You, in turn, will supply the food I require for my household." [24] So Hiram kept Solomon provided with all the cedar and cypress wood he required, [25] and Solomon delivered to Hiram 20,000 *kors* of wheat as provisions for his household and [b-]20 *kors*[-b] of beaten oil. Such was Solomon's annual payment to Hiram.

proverbs and poetry, and his knowledge were famous throughout the world. This section is offered as a demonstration that the grant of glory was fulfilled. **10:** *Kedemites,* "people of the east," i.e., perhaps the peoples of Mesopotamia, who, along with *Egyptians,* would represent the great civilizations of the ancient world and their *wisdom.* **11:** *Ethan the Ezrahite* is mentioned in Ps. 89.1; *Heman,* referred to also as the Ezrahite, in Ps. 88.1. *Chalkol and Darda, sons of Mahol* are not known outside of this passage. **13:** *Trees . . . cedar . . . hyssop,* all trees, from the largest to the smallest. *Beasts . . . fishes,* all animals. Solomon's knowledge was encyclopedic. **15:** *Hiram of Tyre,* who had supplied wood for David's palace (2 Sam. 5.11–12), was king of the two leading Phoenician citystates, Sidon and Tyre, north of Israel. The Phoenicians were important sea traders, exporting lumber from the Lebanese hinterland east to Mesopotamia and down the coast to Egypt. **17:** *David could not build:* According to 2 Sam. 7.5–7, the LORD forbade David to build a Temple. **20–31:** International trade in the ancient Near East was a royal monopoly. Solomon guarantees to provide food for Hiram's household annually for an unspecified number of years (vv. 23, 25) in return for cypress and cedar logs, their transport to a Mediterranean landing place, their manufacture on shore into lumber (vv. 19, 22–23), and, apparently, the loan of master masons and stone cutters (vv. 31–32). **25:** *Kor,* the largest dry measure used in Israel, is estimated to have been about 230 liters or 6.5 bushels. The tradition preserved in the Septuagint that Solomon supplied 20,000 "baths" of olive oil, a liquid measure, is preferable to what is found in the MT. A "bath" is estimated to have been 23 liters or 6 gallons.

---

a Heb. "war"; cf. Targum.   b-b Septuagint reads, "20,000 baths."

26 The LORD had given Solomon wisdom, as He had promised him. There was friendship between Hiram and Solomon, and the two of them made a treaty.

27 King Solomon imposed forced labor on all Israel; the levy came to 30,000 men. 28 He sent them to the Lebanon in shifts of 10,000 a month: they would spend one month in the Lebanon and two months at home. Adoniram was in charge of the forced labor. 29 Solomon also had 70,000 porters and 80,000 quarriers in the hills, 30 apart from Solomon's 3,300 officials who were in charge of the work and supervised the gangs doing the work.

31 The king ordered huge blocks of choice stone to be quarried, so that the foundations of the house might be laid with hewn stones. 32 Solomon's masons, Hiram's masons, and the men of Gebal shaped them. Thus the timber and the stones for building the house were made ready.

6 In the four hundred and eightieth year after the Israelites left the land of Egypt, in the month of Ziv—that is, the second month—in the fourth year of his reign over Israel, Solomon began to build the House of the LORD. 2 The House which King Solomon built for the LORD was 60 cubits long, 20 cubits wide, and 30 cubits high. 3 The portico in front of the Great Hall of the House was 20 cubits long—along the width of the House—and 10 cubits deep to the front of the House. 4 ªHe made windows for the House, recessed and latticed. 5 Against the outside wall of the House—the outside walls of the House enclosing the Great Hall and the Shrineᵇ—he built a storied structure; and he made side chambers all around. 6 The lowest story was 5 cubits wide, the middle one 6 cubits wide, and the third 7 cubits wide; for he had provided recesses around the outside of the House so as not to penetrate the walls of the House.

7 When the House was built, only finished stones cut at the quarry were used, so that no hammer or ax or any iron tool was heard in the House while it was being built.

8 The entrance to the middleᶜ [story of] the side chambers was on the right side of the House; and winding stairs led up to the middle chambers, and from the middle chambers to the third story. 9 When he finished building the House, ᵈ⁻he paneled the House with beams and planks of cedar.⁻ᵈ 10 He built the storied structure against the en-

27: Solomon exploits his prerogative to have Adoniram conscript a labor corps of 30,000 workers for work on a rotational basis as lumberjacks in Lebanon. The remaining 150,000 workers may have been paid.

6.1–7.1: Building the Temple. 6.1: Solomon's fourth year, determined on the basis of the chronology of Tyrian kings provided by Josephus and Assyro-Tyrian synchronisms, was 968 BCE. This would date the exodus to 1448 BCE, a date most scholars consider too early. If, however, 480 years are a figurative way of indicating 12 generations, and an actual generation is 25 years, the exodus would be dated to 1268 BCE. The Canaanite month name, Ziv, is the same as "Iyar," the month name adopted by Jews after the Babylonian exile. The second month on a spring-based calendar, it corresponds to April-May. 2: The cubit, a measure of length equal to 0.5 meter or 18 inches. 2–36: The main building was a tripartite, rectangular structure 20 cubits wide consisting of a portico (v. 3) and a main building entered through a doorway (v. 33) divided into a 40-cubit-long entrance hall (v. 17) and a 20-cubit-square inner shrine blocked by chained doors from the hall (vv. 20–21, 31–32). The tripartite floor plan of Solomon's Temple is paralleled by an 8th-century BCE temple excavated at Tel Tainat, while some of its structural and internal designs have parallels in a temple at Ain Dara, both in Syria. 5–8: A three-story store building enveloped the main Temple on three sides, buttressing and protecting it as well as providing some massiveness to the sparse structure.

a Meaning of parts of vv. 4–6 uncertain.

b I.e., the inner sanctuary, designated in v. 16 and elsewhere as the "Holy of Holies."

c Septuagint and Targum read "lowest."

d-d Meaning of Heb. uncertain.

tire House—each story 5 cubits high, so that it encased the House with timbers of cedar.

¹¹ Then the word of the LORD came to Solomon, ¹² "With regard to this House you are building—if you follow My laws and observe My rules and faithfully keep My commandments, I will fulfill for you the promise that I gave to your father David: ¹³ I will abide among the children of Israel, and I will never forsake My people Israel."

¹⁴ When Solomon had completed the construction of the House, ¹⁵ he paneled the walls of the House on the inside with planks of cedar. He also overlaid the walls on the inside with wood, from the floor of the House to the ceiling. And he overlaid the floor of the House with planks of cypress. ¹⁶ Twenty cubits from the rear of the House, he built [a partition] of cedar planks from the floor to the walls;ᵃ he furnished its interior to serve as a shrine, as the Holy of Holies. ¹⁷ ᵇThe front part of the House, that is, the Great

15–22: The interior of the main building was floored, paneled, decorated, and *overlaid . . . with gold* (see also vv. 29–30). Although some consider the author to be exaggerating in this description, the study of almost contemporary ancient Near Eastern culture supports the likelihood of the description. In Mesopotamian documents ranging from about 2400 to 539 BCE different rulers proclaim that they covered the walls and doors of their temples with gold and silver, while Egyptian documents indicate that pharaohs living between 1550 and 1152 did likewise.

a Septuagint reads "rafters."   b Meaning of vv. 17–22 is unclear in part.

The Temple and palace of Solomon according to First Kings

Hall, measured 40 cubits. [18] The cedar of the interior of the House had carvings of gourds and calyxes; it was all cedar, no stone was exposed. [19] In the innermost part of the House, he fixed a Shrine in which to place the Ark of the LORD's Covenant. [20] [a-]The interior of the[-a] Shrine was 20 cubits long, 20 cubits wide, and 20 cubits high. He overlaid it with solid gold; he similarly overlaid [its] cedar altar. [21] Solomon overlaid the interior of the House with solid gold; and he inserted golden chains [b-]into the door of[-b] the Shrine. He overlaid [the Shrine] with gold, [22] so that the entire House was overlaid with gold; he even overlaid with gold the entire altar of the Shrine. And so the entire House was completed.

[23] In the Shrine he made two cherubim of olive wood, each 10 cubits high. [24] [One] had a wing measuring 5 cubits and another wing measuring 5 cubits, so that the spread from wingtip to wingtip was 10 cubits; [25] and the wing-spread of the other cherub was also 10 cubits. The two cherubim had the same measurements and proportions: [26] the height of the one cherub was 10 cubits, and so was that of the other cherub.

[27] He placed the cherubim inside the [c-]inner chamber.[-c] Since the wings of the cherubim were extended, a wing of the one touched one wall and a wing of the other touched the other wall, while their wings in the center of the chamber touched each other. [28] He overlaid the cherubim with gold. [29] All over the walls of the House, of both the inner area and the outer area, he carved reliefs of cherubim, palms, and calyxes, [30] and he overlaid the floor of the House with gold, both the inner and the outer areas.

[31] For the entrance of the Shrine he made doors of olive wood, [d-]the pilasters and the doorposts having five sides.[-d] [32] The double doors were of olive wood, and on them he carved reliefs of cherubim, palms, and calyxes. He overlaid them with gold, hammering the gold onto the cherubim and the palms. [33] For the entrance of the Great Hall, too, he made doorposts of oleaster wood, [d-]having four sides,[-d] [34] and the double doors of cypress wood, each door consisting of two rounded planks. [35] On them he carved cherubim, palms, and calyxes, overlaying them with gold applied evenly over the carvings. [36] He built the inner enclosure of three courses of hewn stones and one course of cedar beams.

23: *Cherubim:* The "im" ending is a Heb plural marker equivalent to English "s" as in "boys." A "cherub" was a mythical, composite animal, often represented with a human face, eagle wings, and a lion's body. Cherubim were considered guardian figures. Solomon not only placed two three-dimensional cherubim in the Holy of Holies, but also had them carved in relief on the two sets of doors in the main building (vv. 32, 35). Cherub images are attested on various ancient Near Eastern artifacts, including carved ivory panels used to decorate furniture from Samaria and on two clay cult stands from excavations at Taanach. They are also known to have been carved into the sides of the throne used by Hiram of Tyre, which is illustrated on his excavated sarcophagus; this may suggest that in the Temple as well the cherubim served as the throne of (the invisible) God. In Jewish tradition they came to symbolize the presence of God. **36:** Israeli archeologists have excavated stone structures and fortification walls in which horizontal courses of wood beams were laid intermittently between courses of stones. These would allow the buildings to absorb earthquake shocks without collapsing. (Many parts of Israel are in active earthquake zones.) In Mesopotamia, layers of reeds were placed between every few courses of brick in the construction of the great ziggurats for the same reason.

a-a I.e., the inner sanctuary, designated in v. 16 and elsewhere as the "Holy of Holies."
b-b Heb. "in front of."
c-c I.e., the Shrine.
d-d Meaning of Heb. uncertain.

[37] In the fourth year, in the month of Ziv, the foundations of the House were laid; [38] and in the eleventh year, in the month of Bul—that is, the eighth month—the House was completed according to all its details and all its specifications. It took him seven years to build it. **7** [1] And it took Solomon thirteen years to build his palace, until his whole palace was completed.

[2] He built the *[a]Lebanon Forest House with four rows[a]* of cedar columns, and with hewn cedar beams above the columns. Its length was 100 cubits, its breadth 50 cubits, and its height 30 cubits. [3] It was paneled above with cedar, with the planks[b] that were above on the 45 columns—15 in each row. [4] And there were three rows of window frames, with three tiers of windows facing each other. [5] All the doorways and doorposts[c] had square frames—with three tiers of windows facing each other.

[6] He made the portico of columns 50 cubits long and 30 cubits wide; [d]the portico was in front of [the columns], and there were columns with a canopy in front of them.[d] [7] He made the throne portico, where he was to pronounce judgment—the Hall of Judgment. It was paneled with cedar from floor to floor.[e]

[8] The house that he used as a residence, in the rear courtyard, back of the portico, was of the same construction. Solomon also constructed a palace like that portico for the daughter of Pharaoh, whom he had married.

[9] All these buildings, from foundation to coping and all the way out to the great courtyard, were of choice stones, hewn according to measure, smooth on all sides.[f] [10] The foundations were huge blocks of choice stone, stones of 10 cubits and stones of 8 cubits; [11] and above were choice stones, hewn according to measure, and cedar wood. [12] The large surrounding courtyard had three tiers of hewn stone and a row of cedar beams, the same as for the inner court of the House of the LORD, and for the portico of the House.

[13] King Solomon sent for Hiram and brought him down from Tyre. [14] He was the son of a widow of the tribe of Naphtali, and his father had been a Tyrian, a coppersmith.

---

a-a *So called because of the rows of cedar columns. Septuagint reads "three rows" instead of "four rows"; cf. v. 3.*

b *Apparently the "planks" connected the columns longitudinally, and the "beams" (v. 2) connected the planks transversely.*

c *Septuagint reads "windows."*

d-d *Meaning of Heb. uncertain.*

e *Syriac reads "rafters."*

f *Lit. "sawed with a saw in the inside and outside."*

37: *Bul*, the eighth month of the Canaanite calendar, was renamed Marḥeshvan by Jews after the Babylonian exile. It corresponds to October–November.

7.1–12: Solomon's palace complex. Having provided details about the seven-year Temple construction project, the author provides similar details about Solomon's thirteen-year public building and palace projects, undertaken only after the Temple was completed (cf. 9.10): the Lebanon Forest House, a large public building containing many wings including a Hall of Judgment and a private throne room (vv. 7–8) and two palaces. These projects, larger and more complex architecturally than the magnificently endowed Temple, intending to accommodate large numbers of people, necessitated pillars. In combination, both projects attest to Solomon's skill as a designer-contractor.

7.13–51: Furnishing the Temple. The author returns to the main line of his narrative. **13–14:** *Hiram*, not the king of Tyre. This Hiram, a bronzeworker living in Tyre, is accounted to the northern tribe of Naphtali through his deceased father. This artisan plays a role similar to that of Bezalel in the construction of the tent-shrine in the wilderness (Exod. 36.1; 37.1). His specialty appears to have been the ability to cast very large, curved and spherical objects (cf. 7.46). *Bronze*, an alloy of (usually) copper and tin. As translators' note a points out, Heb makes no distinction between pure copper and copper alloys such as bronze. Pure copper is too soft, however, to make an effective "pillar." **15–22:** The two specially made bronze pillars, manufactured after the Temple's completion, lacked any structural purpose. Their function may have been symbolically decorative. Artistic reconstructions often represent them as freestanding either near the entrance of the Temple or at the front edge of the portico on the basis of 2 Chron.

He was endowed with skill, ability, and talent for executing all work in bronze.[a] He came to King Solomon and executed all his work. [15] He cast two columns of bronze; one column was 18 cubits high and measured 12 cubits in circumference, [and similarly] the other column. [16] He made two capitals, cast in bronze, to be set upon the two columns, the height of each of the two capitals being 5 cubits; [17] also nets of meshwork with festoons of chainwork for the capitals that were on the top of the columns, seven for each of the two capitals. [18] He made the columns[b] so that there were two rows [of pomegranates] encircling the top of the one network, to cover the capitals that were on the top of the pomegranates;[c] and he did the same for [the network on] the second capital. [19] The capitals upon the columns of the portico were of lily design, 4 cubits high; [20] so also the capitals upon the two columns extended above and next to the bulge[d] that was beside the network. There were 200 pomegranates in rows around the top of the second capital.[e]

[21] He set up the columns at the portico of the Great Hall; he set up one column on the right and named it Jachin, and he set up the other column on the left and named it Boaz. [22] Upon the top of the columns there was a lily design. Thus the work of the columns was completed.

[23] Then he made the tank[f] of cast metal, 10 cubits across from brim to brim, completely round; it was 5 cubits high, and it measured 30 cubits in circumference. [24] There were gourds below the brim completely encircling it—ten to a cubit, encircling the tank; the gourds were in two rows, cast in one piece with it. [25] It stood upon twelve oxen: three facing north, three facing west, three facing south, and three facing east, with the tank resting upon them; their haunches were all turned inward. [26] It was a handbreadth thick, and its brim was made like that of a cup, like the petals of a lily. Its capacity was 2,000 *baths*.

[27] He made the ten laver stands of bronze. The length of each laver stand was 4 cubits and the width 4 cubits, and the height was 3 cubits. [28] The structure of the laver stands was as follows: They had insets,[g] and there were insets within the frames; [29] and on the insets within the frames

3.17. The consonants of the Heb names *Jachin* and *Boaz* may be read as a sentence meaning "May he establish in strength." The pillars may have comprised a visible prayer asking that God care either for the Temple or for the dynasty. (2 Kings 11.14; 23.3 may support the latter interpretation even though they mention only one pillar.) Shrine models excavated in the Levant show such freestanding pillars. **23–26:** The elevated *tank* provided water under pressure so that the priests could wash conveniently without having to draw water from Temple cisterns (2 Chron. 4.6). The Tanakh does not indicate how water was released from the tank or how it was filled. The tank's design, mounted on the back of twelve oxen, actually bulls, facing the cardinal points of the compass, may have been symbolically meaningful. **23:** A comparison of the tank's diameter and circumference indicates that the author used 3 as the value of pi. Assuming the correctness of the diameter, the circumference was almost 31.5 cubits (15 m or 47 ft). **27–39:** Hiram also made ten *lavers* and ten intricately designed rolling *stands* for the washing of sacrificial parts (cf. 2 Chron. 4.6). The inclusion of mythical cherubs along with bulls and lions in the side frames of the stands suggests that they too conveyed some symbolic message (v. 29). Bronze models of such stands have been found in excavations on Cyprus and in Israel.

---

a *Heb.* neḥosheth *means both copper and bronze. In the translation "copper" is ordinarily used to denote the natural product and "bronze" for the artifacts.*

b *Two Heb. mss. read "pomegranates."*

c *About fifty Heb. mss. read "columns."*

d *Lit. "belly"; exact force of Heb. uncertain.*

e *I.e., each of the two capitals.*

f *Lit. "sea."*

g *Emendation yields "frames."*

were lions, oxen, and cherubim. Above the frames was a stand; and both above and below the lions and the oxen were spirals of hammered metal. ³⁰ Each laver stand had four bronze wheels and [two] bronze axletrees. Its four legs had brackets; the brackets were under the laver, cast ᵃ⁻with spirals beyond each.⁻ᵃ ³¹ Its funnel, within the crown, rose a cubit above it; this funnel was round, in the fashion of a stand, a cubit and a half in diameter. On the funnel too there were carvings.

But the insets were square, not round. ³² And below the insets were the four wheels. The axletrees of the wheels were [fixed] in the laver stand, and the height of each wheel was a cubit and a half. ³³ The structure of the wheels was like the structure of chariot wheels; and their axletrees, their rims, their spokes, and their hubs were all of cast metal. ³⁴ Four brackets ran to the four corners of each laver stand; the brackets were of a piece with the laver stand. ³⁵ At the top of the laver stand was a round band half a cubit high, and together with the top of the laver stand; its sides and its insets were of one piece with it. ³⁶ ᵃ⁻On its surface—on its sides—and on its insets [Hiram] engraved cherubim, lions, and palms, as the clear space on each allowed,⁻ᵃ with spirals roundabout. ³⁷ It was after this manner that he made the ten laver stands, all of them cast alike, of the same measure and the same form. ³⁸ Then he made ten bronze lavers, one laver on each of the ten laver stands, each laver measuring 4 cubits and each laver containing forty *baths*.

³⁹ He disposed the laver stands, five at the right side of the House and five at its left side; and the tank he placed on the right side of the House, at the southeast [corner].

⁴⁰ Hiram also made the lavers, the scrapers, and the sprinkling bowls.

So Hiram finished all the work that he had been doing for King Solomon on the House of the LORD: ⁴¹ the two columns, the two globes of the capitals upon the columns; and the two pieces of network to cover the two globes of the capitals upon the columns; ⁴² the four hundred pomegranates for the two pieces of network, two rows of pomegranates for each network, to cover the two globes of the capitals upon the columns; ⁴³ the ten stands and the ten lavers upon the stands; ⁴⁴ the one tank with the twelve oxen underneath the tank; ⁴⁵ the pails, the scrapers, and the sprinkling bowls. All those vessels in the House of the LORD that Hiram made for King Solomon were of bur-

a-a *Meaning of Heb. uncertain.*

nished bronze. ⁴⁶The king had them cast ªin earthen molds,ª in the plain of the Jordan between Succoth and Zarethan. ⁴⁷Solomon left all the vessels [unweighed] because of their very great quantity; the weight of the bronze was not reckoned.

⁴⁸And Solomon made all the furnishings that were in the House of the LORD: the altar, of gold; the table for the bread of display, of gold; ⁴⁹the lampstands—five on the right side and five on the left—in front of the Shrine, of solid gold; and the petals, lamps, and tongs, of gold; ⁵⁰the basins, snuffers, sprinkling bowls, ladles, and fire pans, of solid gold; and the hinge sockets for the doors of the innermost part of the House, the Holy of Holies, and for the doors of the Great Hall of the House, of gold.

⁵¹When all the work that King Solomon had done in the House of the LORD was completed, Solomon brought in the sacred donations of his father David—the silver, the gold, and the vessels—and deposited them in the treasury of the House of the LORD.

8 Then Solomon convoked the elders of Israel—all the heads of the tribes and the ancestral chieftains of the Israelites—before King Solomon in Jerusalem, to bring up the Ark of the Covenant of the LORD from the City of David, that is, Zion. ²All the men of Israel gathered before King Solomon at the Feast,ᵇ in the month of Ethanim—that is, the seventh month. ³When all the elders of Israel had come, the priests lifted the Ark ⁴and carried up the Ark of the LORD. Then the priests and the Levites brought the Tent of Meeting and all the holy vessels that were in the Tent. ⁵Meanwhile, King Solomon and the whole community of Israel, who were assembled with him before the Ark, were sacrificing sheep and oxen in such abundance that they could not be numbered or counted.

⁶The priests brought the Ark of the LORD's Covenant to its place underneath the wings of the cherubim, in the Shrine of the House, in the Holy of Holies; ⁷for the cherubim had their wings spread out over the place of the Ark, so that the cherubim shielded the Ark and its poles from above. ⁸The poles projected so that the ends of the poles were visible in the sanctuary in front of the Shrine, but they could not be seen outside; and there they remain to this day. ⁹There was nothing inside the Ark but the two

48–49: In contrast to the bronze vessels and implements manufactured for use in the courtyard and on the altar in front of the Temple, those intended for use within the Temple itself were made from or covered with gold. The metals themselves indicated gradations of holiness.

8.1–66: Dedicating the Temple. The formal dedication ceremonies consisted of moving the Ark and attendant items from a tent where they had been kept since the days of David, joyful celebration, public sacrifices, prayers, and speeches. The dedication ceremonies took place in the seventh month, *Ethanim*, called "Tishri" after the Babylonian exile. It corresponds to September-October and is the month when the high holidays, Rosh Ha-Shanah (New Year) and Yom Kippur (Day of Atonement) are observed, followed immediately by Sukkot (Tabernacles or Booths). The dedication, eleven months after the completion of the Temple (see 6.37), was scheduled for the feast of Booths, Sukkot (v. 2). **1:** The sacred objects were kept in a tent within the *City of David*. They had to be carried *up* to the Temple, which had been constructed on a hill north of the city. A broad consensus among historians and archeologists maintains that Solomon's Temple was built beneath the platform around the Dome of the Rock and in the surrounding area.

---

a-a Lit. "in the thick of the earth."   *b I.e., of Booths. Cf. Lev. 23.34.*

tablets of stone which Moses placed there at Horeb, when the LORD made [a covenant] with the Israelites after their departure from the land of Egypt.

10 When the priests came out of the sanctuary—for the cloud had filled the House of the LORD 11 and the priests were not able to remain and perform the service because of the cloud, for the Presence of the LORD filled the House of the LORD—12 then Solomon declared:

"The LORD has chosen
To abide in a thick cloud:

13   I have now built for You
A stately House,
A place where You
May dwell forever."

14 Then, with the whole congregation of Israel standing, the king faced about and blessed the whole congregation of Israel. 15 He said:

"Praised be the LORD, the God of Israel, ªwho has fulfilled with deeds the promise He madeª to my father David. For He said, 16 'Ever since I brought My people Israel out of Egypt, I have not chosen a city among all the tribes of Israel for building a House where My name might abide; but I have chosen David to rule My people Israel.'

17 "Now my father David had intended to build a House for the name of the LORD, the God of Israel. 18 But the LORD said to my father David, 'As regards your intention to build a House for My name, you did right to have that intention. 19 However, you shall not build the House yourself; instead, your son, the issue of your loins, shall build the House for My name.'

20 "And the LORD has fulfilled the promise that He made: I have succeededᵇ my father David and have ascended the throne of Israel, as the LORD promised. I have built the House for the name of the LORD, the God of Israel; 21 and I have set a place there for the Ark, containing the covenant which the LORD made with our fathers when He brought them out from the land of Egypt."

22 Then Solomon stood before the altar of the LORD in the presence of the whole community of Israel; he spread the palms of his hands toward heaven 23 and said, "O LORD God of Israel, in the heavens above and on the earth below there is no god like You, who keep Your gracious covenant with Your servants when they walk before You in wholehearted devotion; 24 You who have kept the

a-a Lit. "who spoke with His own mouth . . . and has fulfilled with His own hand."
b Lit. "risen in place of."

10: *The cloud,* a conventional figure indicating divine presence (Exod. 33.9). The author alludes to earlier traditions about the Tabernacle (Exod. 40.34–35). Part of the ritual within the Temple building consisted of incense offerings on the small, golden altar. **12–13:** Since God dwells in *a thick cloud,* Solomon has provided a proper house. The Temple building was dimly illuminated by light entering through apertures high on the wall and by ten lamps. The square, back chamber, where the Ark was kept, was blocked off from the long hall, so that it was always dim.

8.13–66: The prayer of Solomon is filled with phrases that echo Deuteronomy: v. 23, *keep Your gracious covenant* (Deut. 7.9, 12); v. 23, *in the heavens above and on the earth below* (Deut. 4.39); v. 24, *as is now the case* (Deut. 2.30; 4.20; etc.); vv. 30, 39, 43, 49, *Your heavenly abode* (Deut. 26.15); vv. 33, 34, 38, 43, 52, *Your people Israel* (Deut. 21.8; 26.15); v. 36, *which You gave . . . as their heritage* (Deut. 4.21; 15.4; etc.); v. 40, *revere* [the LORD] (Deut. 4.10; 5.26; etc.); v. 42, *mighty hand . . . outstretched arm* (Deut. 4.34; 5.15; etc.); v. 51, *iron furnace* (Deut. 4.20). **13:** *I have built for You* recurs five additional times in Solomon's speeches (vv. 20, 27, 43, 44, 48), sounding a message of personal piety. *A place where You may dwell forever:* The concept expressed here that the Temple is the place where God dwells is qualified by a more abstract conception in v. 29, which portrays the Temple as the place where the divine "name" dwells. This suggests that the prayers in vv. 12–13 and 15–53 are two separate compositions; the latter may have a long history of composition. **22:** In the ancient world, the proper posture for petitionary prayer was standing erect with raised hands. In addition to other biblical descriptions (Exod. 9.29; Isa. 1.15) it is represented in drawings from Israel, Assyria, and Egypt. **25–26:** Solomon introduces his petition by suggesting that insofar as he has met conditions prepromises You made to Your servant, my father David, fulfilling with deeds the promise You made—as is now the case. [25] And now, O LORD God of Israel, keep the further promise that You made to Your servant, my father David: 'Your line on the throne of Israel shall never end, if only your descendants will look to their way and walk before Me as you have walked before Me.' [26] Now, therefore, O God of Israel, let the promise that You made to Your servant my father David be fulfilled.

[27] "But will God really dwell[a] on earth? Even the heavens to their uttermost reaches cannot contain You, how much less this House that I have built! [28] Yet turn, O LORD my God, to the prayer and supplication of Your servant, and hear the cry and prayer which Your servant offers before You this day. [29] May Your eyes be open day and night toward this House, toward the place of which You have said, 'My name shall abide there'; may You heed the prayers which Your servant will offer toward this place. [30] And when You hear the supplications which Your servant and Your people Israel offer toward this place, give heed in Your heavenly abode—give heed and pardon.

[31] "Whenever one man commits an offense against another, and the latter utters an imprecation to bring a curse upon him, and comes with his imprecation before Your altar in this House, [32] oh, hear in heaven and take action to judge Your servants, condemning him who is in the wrong and bringing down the punishment of his conduct on his head, vindicating him who is in the right by rewarding him according to his righteousness.

[33] "Should Your people Israel be routed by an enemy because they have sinned against You, and then turn back to You and acknowledge Your name, and they offer prayer and supplication to You in this House, [34] oh, hear in heaven and pardon the sin of Your people Israel, and restore them to the land that You gave to their fathers.

[35] "Should the heavens be shut up and there be no rain, because they have sinned against You, and then they pray toward this place and acknowledge Your name and repent of their sins, when You answer[b] them, [36] oh, hear in heaven and pardon the sin of Your servants, Your people Israel, after You have shown them the proper way in which they are to walk; and send down rain upon the land which You gave to Your people as their heritage. [37] So, too, if there is a famine in the land, if there is pestilence, blight,

sented by God in the dream at Gibeon (3.14) by building the Temple, God should fulfill His (conditional) promise to David about his descendants (cf. 2.4) which would include guaranteeing Solomon long life. **27–61:** This section begins with a rhetorical question challenging the notion expressed in vv. 12–13 that God now has an actual presence on earth in the Temple (v. 27). Meditative prayers (vv. 28–53) assert that God, truly present in heaven, resides only symbolically on earth in the Temple; nevertheless, prayer should be directed to the Temple (vv. 29, 31, 35, 38, 42). These ideas, couched in phrases and images from Deuteronomy (see Deut. 6.13; 12.4, 11), attempt to harmonize the Deuteronomic notion of divine immanence in the Temple with the contrasting notion of the universal transcendence of God. The whole section may have been inserted into a text that originally continued seamlessly from v. 26 to 62. V. 54 has Solomon praying on his knees, while v. 22 has him standing. V. 55 has him standing to bless the people, something described already in v. 14. In its present context, the section dilutes the aura of God's immanence cast by the materialistic physicality of Solomon's speech (vv. 12–26). V. 34, calling for the restoration of Israel to the land, is most likely an exilic addition to the text.

a 2 Chron. 6.18 adds "with man."
b The Septuagint, with a different vocalization, reads "chastise."

mildew, locusts or caterpillars, or if an enemy oppresses them in any of the settlements of the land.

"In any plague and in any disease, ³⁸ in any prayer or supplication offered by any person among all Your people Israel—each of whom knows his own affliction—when he spreads his palms toward this House, ³⁹ oh, hear in Your heavenly abode, and pardon and take action! Render to each man according to his ways as You know his heart to be—for You alone know the hearts of all men—⁴⁰ so that they may revere You all the days that they live on the land that You gave to our fathers.

⁴¹ "Or if a foreigner who is not of Your people Israel comes from a distant land for the sake of Your name—⁴² for they shall hear about Your great name and Your mighty hand and Your outstretched arm—when he comes to pray toward this House, ⁴³ oh, hear in Your heavenly abode and grant all that the foreigner asks You for. Thus all the peoples of the earth will know Your name and revere You, as does Your people Israel; and they will recognize that Your name is attached to this House that I have built.

⁴⁴ "When Your people take the field against their enemy by whatever way You send them, and they pray to the LORD in the direction of the city which You have chosen, and of the House which I have built to Your name, ⁴⁵ oh, hear in heaven their prayer and supplication and uphold their cause.

⁴⁶ "When they sin against You—for there is no man who does not sin—and You are angry with them and deliver them to the enemy, and their captors carry them off to an enemy land, near or far; ⁴⁷ and then they take it to heart in the land to which they have been carried off, and they repent and make supplication to You in the land of their captors, saying: 'We have sinned, we have acted perversely, we have acted wickedly,' ⁴⁸ and they turn back to You with all their heart and soul, in the land of the enemies who have carried them off, and they pray to You in the direction of their land which You gave to their fathers, of the city which You have chosen, and of the House which I have built to Your name—⁴⁹ oh, give heed in Your heavenly abode to their prayer and supplication, uphold their cause, ⁵⁰ and pardon Your people who have sinned against You for all the transgressions that they have committed against You. Grant them mercy in the sight of their captors that they may be merciful to them. ⁵¹ For they are Your very own people that You freed from Egypt, from the midst of the iron furnace. ⁵² May Your eyes be open to the supplication of Your servant and the supplication of Your people Israel, and may You heed them whenever they call

upon You. 53 For You, O Lord GOD, have set them apart for Yourself from all the peoples of the earth as Your very own, as You promised through Moses Your servant when You freed our fathers from Egypt."

54 When Solomon finished offering to the LORD all this prayer and supplication, he rose from where he had been kneeling, in front of the altar of the LORD, his hands spread out toward heaven. 55 He stood, and in a loud voice blessed the whole congregation of Israel:

56 "Praised be the LORD who has granted a haven to His people Israel, just as He promised; not a single word has failed of all the gracious promises that He made through His servant Moses. 57 May the LORD our God be with us, as He was with our fathers. May He never abandon or forsake us. 58 May He incline our hearts to Him, that we may walk in all His ways and keep the commandments, the laws, and the rules, which He enjoined upon our fathers. 59 And may these words of mine, which I have offered in supplication before the LORD, be close to the LORD our God day and night, that He may provide for His servant and for His people Israel, according to each day's needs— 60 to the end that all the peoples of the earth may know that the LORD alone is God, there is no other. 61 And may you be wholehearted with the LORD our God, to walk in His ways and keep His commandments, even as now."

62 The king and all Israel with him offered sacrifices before the LORD. 63 Solomon offered 22,000 oxen and 120,000 sheep as sacrifices of well-being to the LORD. Thus the king and all the Israelites dedicated the House of the LORD. 64 That day the king consecrated the center of the court that was in front of the House of the LORD. For it was there that he presented the burnt offerings, the meal offerings, and the fat parts of the offerings of well-being, because the bronze altar that was before the LORD was too small to hold the burnt offerings, the meal offerings, and the fat parts of the offerings of well-being.

65 So Solomon and all Israel with him—a great assemblage, [coming] from Lebo-hamath to the Wadi of Egypt[a]— observed the Feast[b] at that time before the LORD our God, seven days and again seven days, fourteen days in all. 66 On the eighth day[c] he let the people go. They bade the king good-bye and went to their homes, joyful and glad of heart over all the goodness that the LORD had shown to His servant David and His people Israel.

8.62–66: Conclusion of the dedication. The attendance of the entire population, and the huge numbers of sacrifices offered, are intended to express the completeness of participation and consecration. Taken literally, they would have required the abandonment of all activity by the entire people for two weeks, and the rate of sacrifice (even assuming non-stop activity) would have been one oxen and six sheep every minute. **64:** *Burnt offerings* (Lev. 1.3–17), those wholly consumed by fire. They are at the initiative of the donor, and serve to expiate any shortcomings not covered by purification or reparatory offerings. *Meal offerings* (Lev. 2.1–16), portions of grain burnt completely. The meal offering was a burnt offering that even poor people could afford (*Lev. Rab.* 8.4). *Offerings of well-being* (Lev. 3.1–16), sacrifice of an animal involving burning its inner organs (entrails, kidney, and liver) and the fat (suet) that is attached to them. These are thanksgiving or celebratory offerings, and the worshipper partakes of the meat that is not burnt.

a I.e., coming from one end of the country to the other.   b I.e., of Booths. Cf. Lev. 23.34.
c I.e., of the second seven-day feast; cf. 2 Chron. 7.8–10.

9 When Solomon had finished building the House of the LORD and the royal palace and everything that Solomon had set his heart on constructing, [2] the LORD appeared to Solomon a second time, as He had appeared to him at Gibeon. [3] The LORD said to him, "I have heard the prayer and the supplication which you have offered to Me. I consecrate this House which you have built and I set My name there forever. My eyes and My heart shall ever be there. [4] As for you, if you walk before Me as your father David walked before Me, wholeheartedly and with uprightness, doing all that I have commanded you [and] keeping My laws and My rules, [5] then I will establish your throne of kingship over Israel forever, as I promised your father David, saying, 'Your line on the throne of Israel shall never end.' [6] [But] if you and your descendants turn away from Me and do not keep the commandments [and] the laws which I have set before you, and go and serve other gods and worship them, [7] then I will sweep[a] Israel off the land which I gave them; I will reject[b] the House which I have consecrated to My name; and Israel shall become a proverb and a byword among all peoples. [8] And [c]as for this House, once so exalted,[c] everyone passing by it shall be appalled and shall hiss.[d] And when they ask, 'Why did the LORD do thus to the land and to this House?' [9] they shall be told, 'It is because they forsook the LORD their God who freed them from the land of Egypt, and they embraced other gods and worshiped them and served them; therefore the LORD has brought all this calamity upon them.' "

[10] At the end of the twenty years[e] during which Solomon constructed the two buildings, the LORD's House and the royal palace—[11] since King Hiram of Tyre had supplied Solomon with all the cedar and cypress timber and gold that he required—King Solomon in turn gave Hiram twenty towns in the region of Galilee. [12] But when Hiram came from Tyre to inspect the towns that Solomon had given him, he was not pleased with them. [13] "My brother," he said, "what sort of towns are these you have given me?" So they were named the land of Cabul,[f] as is still the case. [14] However, Hiram sent the king one hundred and twenty talents of gold.

[15] This was the purpose of the forced labor which Solo-

---

a Lit. "cut."　　　b Lit. "dismiss from My presence."

c-c Targum and some other ancient versions read "and this House shall become a ruin."

d An action performed at the sight of ruin to ward off a like fate from the observer; cf. note at Jer. 18.16.　　　e See 6.38–7.1.　　　f Perhaps taken to mean "as nothing."

9.1–9: The second revelation. This unit harks back to the revelation at Gibeon (ch 3.4–15). God here responds to the dedicatory prayers of Solomon; the narrative leaves unclear when and where this occurred. **2–3:** God indicates that He had consecrated the *House* in response to Solomon's prayers and supplications. This emphasizes that it is His act of will, not Solomon's, that makes the Temple an effective place. **4–9:** Reaffirming the conditionality of the promise to David and his dynasty, God denies Solomon's request of 8.25–26 for a guarantee. For emphasis, God states also that the existence of the Temple itself depends on the proper behavior of Israel. Vv. 6–9 are intended to anticipate the exile of all Israel, of both the kingdoms of Israel and Judah, that at this point in the narrative have not yet come into existence as separate kingdoms.

9.10–10.29: The rest of the deeds of Solomon. This section presents truncated information about various financial and administrative arrangements consequent to Solomon's building projects. **9:10–14:** A final payment for supplies and for *gold*—not mentioned in the earlier contractual arrangements (5.20–31)—to king Hiram was made by Solomon in the form of twenty towns. Despite Hiram's disparaging remark that gave rise to the area being called *Cabul*, he accepted them and remitted a final gold payment to Solomon to cover the difference between the value of the cities and what was owed him. **11:** Josephus reports that they were near Tyre, in western Galilee. **13:** *My brother,* "brother" refers to an equal partner in a treaty. **14:** *Talent,* the equivalent of 3,000 shekels (Exod. 38.25–26), weighed approximately 30 kg (66 pounds). **15–23:** Solomon's labor force. Solomon conducted construction projects in many parts of his kingdom and depended on a combination of conscripted workers under a labor tax system as well as partially enslaved populations. The location of sites mentioned sugmon imposed: It was to build the House of the LORD, his own palace, the Millo,ª and the wall of Jerusalem, and [to fortify] Hazor, Megiddo, and Gezer. (¹⁶Pharaoh king of Egypt had come up and captured Gezer; he destroyed it by fire, killed the Canaanites who dwelt in the town, and gave it as dowry to his daughter, Solomon's wife.) ¹⁷So Solomon fortified Gezer, lower Beth-horon, ¹⁸Baalith, and Tamarᵇ in the wilderness, in the land [of Judah], ¹⁹and all of Solomon's garrison towns, chariot towns, and cavalry towns—everything that Solomon set his heart on building in Jerusalem and in the Lebanon, and throughout the territory that he ruled. ²⁰All the people that were left of the Amorites, Hittites, Perizzites, Hivites, and Jebusites who were not of the Israelite stock—²¹those of their descendants who remained in the land and whom the Israelites were not able to annihilate—of these Solomon made a slave force, as is still the case. ²²But he did not reduce any Israelites to slavery; they served, rather, as warriors and as his attendants, officials, and officers, and as commanders of his chariotry and cavalry.

²³These were the prefects that were in charge of Solomon's works and were foremen over the people engaged in the work, who numbered 550.ᶜ

²⁴As soon as Pharaoh's daughter went up from the City of David to the palace that he had built for her, he built the Millo.ª

²⁵Solomon used to offer burnt offerings and sacrifices of well-being three times a year on the altar that he had built for the LORD, and ᵈhe used to offer incense on the one that was before the LORD. And he kept the House in repair.⁻ᵈ

²⁶King Solomon also built a fleet of ships at Eziongeber, which is near Elothᵉ on the shore of the Sea of Reeds in the land of Edom. ²⁷Hiram sent servants of his with the fleet, mariners who were experienced on the sea, to serve with Solomon's men. ²⁸They came to Ophir; there they obtained gold in the amount of four hundred and twenty talents, which they delivered to King Solomon.

10 The queen of Sheba heard of Solomon's fame, ᶠthrough the name of the LORD,⁻ᶠ and she came to test him with hard questions. ²She arrived in Jerusalem with a very large retinue, with camels bearing spices, a

gests that he felt threatened by Arameans northeast of the Sea of Galilee, Philistines from the coastal plain, and Egyptians from the southwest. The author drew this information from the same source as 5.27–31. **21:** *Slave force* (Heb "mas 'oved") refers to tax paid in labor. V. 22 suggests that the status of non-Israelites under this system differed from that of Israelites; this contradicts 5.27–28. **23:** The names of the prefects are not presented. In 2 Chron. 8.10, their number is given as 250.

9.26–10.22: The outcome of Solomon's additional business dealings with Hiram of Tyre. 9.26–28: Solomon and Hiram undertook a joint venture in a combination of land and sea trade. Hiram provided the seafaring know-how and Solomon granted overland access to the port at *Ezion-geber* on the Gulf of Eilat. From there, both kings had access to the Red Sea and beyond. **28:** *Ophir*, location uncertain. It has been identified with ports or regions in Ethiopia, North Somalia, South Arabia, and even India.

10.1–13: The story of the queen's visit to Solomon continues the theme of wisdom and wealth (3.12–13). It interrupts the report of his trading venture, which continues in 10.14, and was inserted because of its thematic connection to the international business ventures. **1:** *Sheba*, ancient Sabea at the southwest corner of the Arabian peninsula, controlled access into the Sea of Aden from the Red Sea at the Bab el-Mandeb. The story tells that the queen came to meet a potential trading partner. She provided him with her gifts, and he reciprocated.

a *A citadel.*
b *So kethib, cf. Ezek. 47.19, 48.28; qere* Tadmor.
c *Their names are not listed in the text.*
d-d *Meaning of Heb. uncertain.*
e *Elsewhere called Elath.*
f-f *The force of the phrase is uncertain.*

great quantity of gold, and precious stones. When she came to Solomon, she asked him all that she had in mind. [3] Solomon had answers for all her questions; there was nothing that the king did not know, [nothing] to which he could not give her an answer. [4] When the queen of Sheba observed all of Solomon's wisdom, and the palace he had built, [5] the fare of his table, the seating of his courtiers, the service and attire of his attendants, and his wine service, [a] and the burnt offerings that he offered at [a] the House of the LORD, she was left breathless.

[6] She said to the king, "The report I heard in my own land about you and your wisdom was true. [7] But I did not believe the reports until I came and saw with my own eyes that not even the half had been told me; your wisdom and wealth surpass the reports that I heard. [8] How fortunate are your men and how fortunate are these your courtiers, who are always in attendance on you and can hear your wisdom! [9] Praised be the LORD your God, who delighted in you and set you on the throne of Israel. It is because of the LORD's everlasting love for Israel that He made you king to administer justice and righteousness."

[10] She presented the king with one hundred and twenty talents of gold, and a large quantity of spices, and precious stones. Never again did such a vast quantity of spices arrive as that which the queen of Sheba gave to King Solomon.—[11] Moreover, Hiram's fleet, which carried gold from Ophir, brought in from Ophir a huge quantity of *almug* wood [b] and precious stones. [12] The king used the *almug* wood for decorations in the House of the LORD and in the royal palace, and for harps and lyres for the musicians. Such a quantity of *almug* wood has never arrived or been seen to this day.—[13] King Solomon, in turn, gave the queen of Sheba everything she wanted and asked for, in addition to what King Solomon gave her out of his royal bounty. Then she and her attendants left and returned to her own land.

[14] The weight of the gold which Solomon received every year was 666 talents of gold, [15] besides what came from tradesmen, from the traffic of the merchants, and from all the kings of Arabia and the governors of the regions. [16] King Solomon made 200 shields of beaten gold—600 shekels of gold to each shield—[17] and 300 bucklers of beaten gold—three *minas* of gold to each buckler. The king placed them in the Lebanon Forest House.

[18] The king also made a large throne of ivory, and he

11–12: Information about *almug* wood and how it was used dates the Ophir venture to within a few years of Solomon's initial arrangement with Hiram. These verses interrupt the account of the queen's visit.

10.14–29: Solomon's wealth. Extravagant golden furnishings were captured by David from the Aramean king Hadadezer (2 Sam. 8.7). Ancient Near Eastern documents indicate that gold bowls and dishes were given as gifts to royalty while gold shields are mentioned by Assyrian kings as prize spoils of war. Solomon's trade arrangements explain his access to gold. **22:** *A Tarshish fleet* may refer to a type of ship or to the place to which such ships sailed. The fleet was Solomon's, and run independently from ships involved in joint ventures with Hiram. Since the Ophir fleet plied the Red Sea trade, the Tarshish fleet may have competed with Phoenicians around the Mediterranean. Scholars have identified Tarshish with Sardinia or with Tartessus in southern Spain. **23–25:** Solomon's wealth and wisdom helped confer great recognition and honor on him. These verses reprise God's grants to Solomon in 3.12–13 and what was already narrated in 5.14. **26–29:** Solomon used and traded in chariots from Egypt and horses from two small kingdoms in Anatolia, keeping some (9.19) and reselling others to small Hittite kingdoms in North Syria near the Euphrates and to Aramean kingdoms (cf. 2 Sam. 10.19). Information about his arms trade with Arameans brings to the foreground the brief notice in 11.23–25.

a-a 2 Chron. 9.4 reads ". . . and the procession with which he went up to . . ."
b Others "sandalwood."

overlaid it with refined gold. ¹⁹ Six steps led up to the throne, and the throne had a back with a rounded top, and arms on either side of the seat. Two lions stood beside the arms, ²⁰ and twelve lions stood on the six steps, six on either side. No such throne was ever made for any other kingdom.ª

²¹ All King Solomon's drinking cups were of gold, and all the utensils of the Lebanon Forest House were of pure gold: silver did not count for anything in Solomon's days. ²² For the king had a Tarshishᵇ fleet on the sea, along with Hiram's fleet. Once every three years, the Tarshish fleet came in, bearing gold and silver, ivory, apes, and peacocks.

²³ King Solomon excelled all the kings on earth in wealth and in wisdom. ²⁴ All the world came to pay homage to Solomon and to listen to the wisdom with which God had endowed him; ²⁵ and each one would bring his tribute—silver and gold objects, robes, weapons and spices, horses and mules—in the amount due each year.

²⁶ Solomon assembled chariots and horses. He had 1,400 chariots and 12,000 horses, which he stationedᶜ in the chariot towns and with the king in Jerusalem. ²⁷ The king made silver as plentiful in Jerusalem as stones, and cedars as plentiful as sycamores in the Shephelah. ²⁸ Solomon's horses were procured from Mizraimᵈ and Kue. The king's dealers would buy them from Kue at a fixed price. ²⁹ A chariot imported from Mizraimᵈ cost 600 shekels of silver, and a horse 150; these in turn were exported by themᵉ to all the kings of the Hittites and the kings of the Arameans.

11 King Solomon loved many foreign women in addition to Pharaoh's daughter—Moabite, Ammonite, Edomite, Phoenician, and Hittite women, ² from the nations of which the LORD had said to the Israelites, "None of you shall join them and none of them shall join you,ᶠ lest they turn your heart away to follow their gods." Such Solomon clung to and loved. ³ He had seven hundred royal wives and three hundred concubines; and his wives turned his heart away. ⁴ In his old age, his wives turned away Solomon's heart after other gods, and he was not as wholeheartedly devoted to the LORD his God as his father David had been. ⁵ Solomon followed Ashtoreth the god-

11.1–43: The dissolution of Solomon's kingdom. Some of what is narrated here occurred simultaneously with what was presented in chs 1–10. For example, Solomon's marriage to an Ammonite princess occurred while David was alive (14.21). This sugggests that the material is arranged theologically rather than chronologically; the first part narrates the successes of Solomon while he observes the law, while ch 11 is part of a section which narrates his failures that result from abrogating the law. **1:** Solomon's diplomatic marriages reflect the range of his trading ventures and his attempt to secure alliances with kingdoms on his undefined eastern Transjordanian borders: Ammon, Moab, Edom. Malbim notes that the author's choice of words, *loved many foreign women*, denotes a child's lust after objects rather than an adult's love for a particular woman. This invites a contrast between David, whose impetuous acts were sins of youth, and Solomon, who sinned in his old age. **1–3:** Having many wives violated general instructions to the king (Deut. 17.16–17). Foreign wives would introduce their pagan practices into Judah. The author here combines various biblical texts and extends earlier traditions that prohibit intermarriage with specific nations (Exod. 34.11–16; Deut. 7.1–6; 23.4–9). A similar general ban on intermarriage is found in Ezra-Nehemiah, suggesting that this text in Kings is from the latest, exilic edition of the book. **5–8:** Solomon's tolerance of, participation in, and contributions toward foreign worship—corollary activities to his diplomatic marriages—are described and condemned by the author.

a Or "prince"; like Phoenician mamlakt.

b Probably a fleet of large ships.

c So 2 Chron. 1.14; 9.25; Heb. here "led."

d Usually Egypt, here perhaps Muṣru, a neighbor of Kue (Cilicia).

e I.e., Solomon's dealers.

f I.e., in marriage; cf. Deut. 7.3–4; 23.4, 8–9.

dess of the Phoenicians, and Milcom the abomination of the Ammonites.

⁶Solomon did what was displeasing to the LORD and did not remain loyal to the LORD like his father David. ⁷At that time, Solomon built a shrine for Chemosh the abomination of Moab on the hill near Jerusalem, and one for Molech the abomination of the Ammonites. ⁸And he did the same for all his foreign wives who offered and sacrificed to their gods.

⁹The LORD was angry with Solomon, because his heart turned away from the LORD, the God of Israel, who had appeared to him twice ¹⁰and had commanded him about this matter, not to follow other gods; he did not obey what the LORD had commanded. ¹¹And the LORD said to Solomon, ᵃ"Because you are guilty of this ᵃ—you have not kept My covenant and the laws which I enjoined upon you—I will tear the kingdom away from you and give it to one of your servants. ¹²But, for the sake of your father David, I will not do it in your lifetime; I will tear it away from your son. ¹³However, I will not tear away the whole kingdom; I will give your son one tribe, for the sake of My servant David and for the sake of Jerusalem which I have chosen."

¹⁴So the LORD raised up an adversary against Solomon, the Edomite Hadad, who was of the royal family of Edom. ¹⁵When David ᵇwas inᵇ Edom, Joab the army commander went up to bury the slain, and he killed every male in Edom; ¹⁶for Joab and all Israel stayed there for six months until he had killed off every male in Edom. ¹⁷But Hadad,ᶜ together with some Edomite men, servants of his father, escaped and headed for Egypt; Hadad was then a young boy. ¹⁸Setting out from Midian, they came to Paran and took along with them men from Paran. Thus they came to Egypt, to Pharaoh king of Egypt, who gave him a house, assigned a food allowance to him, and granted him an estate. ¹⁹Pharaoh took a great liking to Hadad and gave him his sister-in-law, the sister of Queen Tahpenes, as wife. ²⁰The sister of Tahpenes bore him a son, Genubath. Tahpenes weanedᵈ him in Pharaoh's palace, and Genubath remained in Pharaoh's palace among the sons of Pharaoh. ²¹When Hadad heard in Egypt that David had been laid to rest with his fathers and that Joab the army commander was dead, Hadad said to Pharaoh, "Give me leave to go to my own country." ²²Pharaoh

9–13: God's angry reaction to the actual behavior of a properly informed and warned Solomon (cf. 3.5; 9.2). **10:** Alludes to 9.4–7. **11–13:** The final judgment compromises God's promises to David (2 Sam. 7.16). The kingdom will be torn away, but not the whole kingdom as it was from Saul (1 Sam. 15.28; 28.17–18). *For the sake of . . . David* is a major subtheme of the book (11.34; 15.4; 2 Kings 8.19; 19.34; 20.6). **14–22:** *Adversary,* Heb "satan," related to later English "Satan." *Hadad* of Edom, also connected to the Egyptian court through marriage, threatened Solomon from the east. Solomon's overland caravans from Eilat most likely followed routes in the eastern Sinai to avoid Edomite raiders.

---

a-a Lit. "This is with you."
b-b Emendation yields "defeated"; cf. 2 Sam. 8.13.
c Heb. Adad.   d Septuagint reads "reared."

replied, "What do you lack with me, that you want to go to your own country?" But he said, "Nevertheless, give me leave to go."

23 Another adversary that God raised up against Solomon[a] was Rezon son of Eliada, who had fled from his lord, King Hadadezer of Zobah, 24 when David was slaughtering them. He gathered men about him and became captain over a troop; they went to Damascus and settled there, and they established a kingdom in Damascus. 25 He was an adversary of Israel all the days of Solomon, adding to the trouble [caused by] Hadad; he repudiated [the authority of] Israel and reigned over Aram.

26 Jeroboam son of Nebat, an Ephraimite of Zeredah, the son of a widow whose name was Zeruah, was in Solomon's service; he raised his hand against the king. 27 The circumstances under which he raised his hand against the king were as follows: Solomon built the Millo and repaired the breach of the city of his father, David. 28 This Jeroboam was an able man, and when Solomon saw that the young man was a capable worker, he appointed him over all the forced labor of the House of Joseph.

29 During that time Jeroboam went out of Jerusalem and the prophet Ahijah of Shiloh met him on the way. He had put on a new robe; and when the two were alone in the open country, 30 Ahijah took hold of the new robe he was wearing and tore it into twelve pieces. 31 "Take ten pieces," he said to Jeroboam. "For thus said the LORD, the God of Israel: I am about to tear the kingdom out of Solomon's hands, and I will give you ten tribes. 32 But one tribe shall remain his—for the sake of My servant David and for the sake of Jerusalem, the city that I have chosen out of all the tribes of Israel. 33 For they have forsaken Me; they have worshiped Ashtoreth the goddess of the Phoenicians, Chemosh the god of Moab, and Milcom the god of the Ammonites; they have not walked in My ways, or done what is pleasing to Me, or [kept] My laws and rules, as his father David did. 34 However, I will not take the entire kingdom away from him, but will keep him as ruler as long as he lives for the sake of My servant David whom I chose, and who kept My commandments and My laws. 35 But I will take the kingship out of the hands of his son and give it to you—the ten tribes. 36 To his son I will give one tribe, so that there may be a lamp for My servant David forever before Me in Jerusalem—the city where I have chosen to establish My name. 37 But you have been chosen by Me; reign[b] wherever you wish, and you shall be

23–25: *Rezon*, a victim of David's victories over the Arameans, eventually wrested Damascus from Israelite control (cf. 2 Sam. 8.6). He may have threatened Israel with the very chariots that had been sold to him by Solomon. **26–40:** According to the author, Ahijah's message fomented Jeroboam's action. Jeroboam's defiance of Solomon on behalf of northern tribes—no details are provided and several words seem to be missing in the Heb text—had the support of a prophet. The full measure of Jeroboam's popularity is indicated in 12.1–6. **36:** The image of a *lamp* became a special metaphor for David and for the continuity of his line in the language of the author and like-minded people (2 Sam. 21.17; Ps. 132.17).

a Heb. "him."   b I.e., *establish your residence.*

king over Israel. ³⁸ If you heed all that I command you, and walk in My ways, and do what is right in My sight, keeping My laws and commandments as My servant David did, then I will be with you and I will build for you a lasting dynasty as I did for David. I hereby give Israel to you; ³⁹ and I will chastise David's descendants for that [sin], though not forever."

⁴⁰ Solomon sought to put Jeroboam to death, but Jeroboam promptly fled to King Shishak of Egypt; and he remained in Egypt till the death of Solomon.

⁴¹ The other events of Solomon's reign, and all his actions and his wisdom, are recorded in the book of the Annals of Solomon. ⁴² The length of Solomon's reign in Jerusalem, over all Israel, was forty years. ⁴³ Solomon slept with his fathers and was buried in the city of his father David; and his son Rehoboam succeeded him as king.

12 Rehoboam went to Shechem, for all Israel had come to Shechem to acclaim him as king. ² Jeroboam son of Nebat learned of it while he was still in Egypt; for Jeroboam had fled from King Solomon, ᵃ and had settled in Egypt. ᵃ ³ They sent for him; and Jeroboam and all the assembly of Israel came and spoke to Rehoboam as follows: ⁴ "Your father made our yoke heavy. Now lighten the harsh labor and the heavy yoke which your father laid on us, and we will serve you." ⁵ He answered them, "Go away for three days and then come back to me." So the people went away.

⁶ King Rehoboam took counsel with the elders who had served his father Solomon during his lifetime. He said, "What answer do you advise [me] to give to this people?" ⁷ They answered him, "If you will be a servant to those people today and serve them, and if you respond to them with kind words, they will be your servants always." ⁸ But he ignored the advice that the elders gave him, and took counsel with the young men who had grown up with him and were serving him. ⁹ "What," he asked, "do you advise that we reply to the people who said to me, 'Lighten the yoke that your father placed upon us'?" ¹⁰ And the young men who had grown up with him answered, "Speak thus to the people who said to you, 'Your father made our yoke heavy, now you make it lighter for us.' Say to them, 'My little finger is thicker than my father's loins. ¹¹ My father imposed a heavy yoke on you, and I will add to your yoke; my father flogged you with whips, but I will flog you with scorpions.'"

40: *Shishak* (Egyptian Shoshenq) was pharaoh 945–924 BCE. His relationship with Jeroboam bore fruit after the death of Solomon. **41–42:** In citing the sources of his information about Solomon and indicating that he has excerpted only part of the information from them, the author suggests the veracity of the descriptions which he has evaluated theologically. **41:** *The book of the Annals of Solomon* is presented as an actual document available to the author and to his readers. It is unknown aside from this reference to it. Whether or not it actually existed, the reference—like a footnote in a scholarly composition—indicates a reliance on written documents as a source of authority.

12.1–14.18: The secession of northern tribes from the united kingdom and the creation of the Northern Kingdom of Israel. 12.1–17: The negotiation at Shechem. Although prophets, acting on instructions from God, might anoint individuals as kings, the authority of any persons so anointed had to be publicly acclaimed by those over whom they ruled, as in the case of Saul (1 Sam. 11.14–15), David over Judah (2 Sam. 2.4, 7), David over all the tribes (2 Sam. 5.1–5), and Solomon (1 Kings 1.39–40). The northern tribes were ready to acclaim Rehoboam as their king, but only if he agreed to certain general conditions. The text has a clear polemical slant, and makes Rehoboam look foolish, thereby justifying the establishment of the Northern Kingdom. **1:** *Shechem,* the major city directly north of Jerusalem on the north-south highway, lay near the border of the two largest and most powerful northern tribes, Ephraim and Manasseh. *All Israel:* The meaning of this phrase changes from 11.42, where it means the entire kingdom, north (Israel) and south (Judah), to 12.16, where it means the north only. **2–3:** *Jeroboam* (11.26–40), summoned to Shechem from Egypt by a group of tribal leaders (*the assembly of Israel*), takes part in

---

a-a 2 Chron. 10.2 reads "So Jeroboam returned from Egypt."

¹²Jeroboam and all the people came to Rehoboam on the third day, since the king had told them: "Come back on the third day." ¹³The king answered the people harshly, ignoring the advice that the elders had given him. ¹⁴He spoke to them in accordance with the advice of the young men, and said, "My father made your yoke heavy, but I will add to your yoke; my father flogged you with whips, but I will flog you with scorpions." ¹⁵(The king did not listen to the people; for the LORD had brought it about in order to fulfill the promise that the LORD had made through Ahijah the Shilonite to Jeroboam son of Nebat.) ¹⁶When all Israel saw that the king had not listened to them, the people answered the king:

the negotiation. **11:** *Scorpions,* may refer to a particular thorny plant or to some type of whip. **15:** The author's theological comment on the illogical turn of events. All that transpired was a fulfillment of what God told Solomon (11.11) and what Ahijah told Jeroboam (11.31–36). **16:** Northerners take up the rallying cry of an earlier anti-David rebel, Sheba son of Bichri, whose rebellion had threatened to split the kingdom (2 Sam. 20.1).

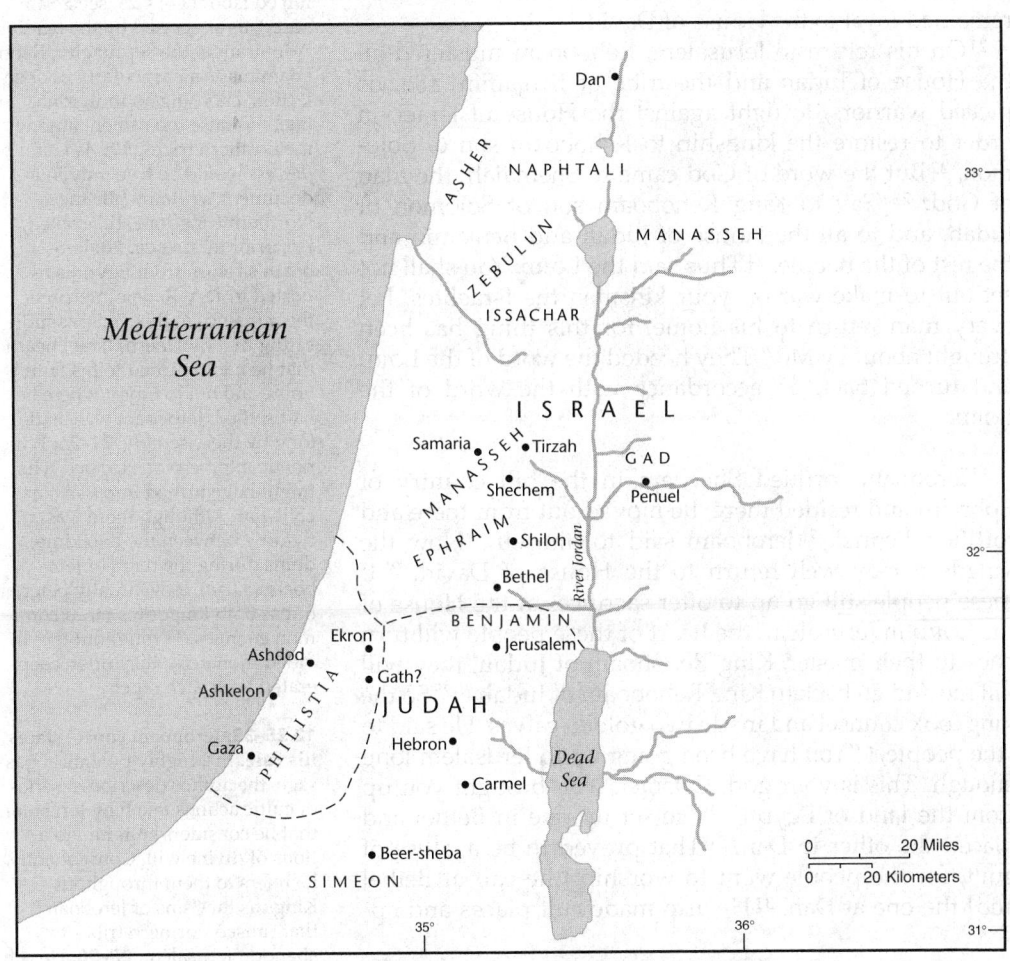

The divided monarchy. The dashed line shows the approximate boundaries between Israel, Judah, and Philistia.

"We have no portion in David,
No share in Jesse's son!
To your tents, O Israel!
Now look to your own House, O David."

So the Israelites returned to their homes.[a] [17] But Rehoboam continued to reign over the Israelites who lived in the towns of Judah.

[18] King Rehoboam sent Adoram,[b] who was in charge of the forced labor, but all Israel pelted him to death with stones. Thereupon King Rehoboam hurriedly mounted his chariot and fled to Jerusalem. [19] Thus Israel revolted against the House of David, as is still the case.

[20] When all Israel heard that Jeroboam had returned, they sent messengers and summoned him to the assembly and made him king over all Israel. Only the tribe of Judah remained loyal to the House of David.

[21] On his return to Jerusalem, Rehoboam mustered all the House of Judah and the tribe of Benjamin, 180,000 picked warriors, to fight against the House of Israel, in order to restore the kingship to Rehoboam son of Solomon. [22] But the word of God came to Shemaiah, the man of God: [23] "Say to King Rehoboam son of Solomon of Judah, and to all the House of Judah and Benjamin and the rest of the people: [24] Thus said the LORD: You shall not set out to make war on your kinsmen the Israelites. Let every man return to his home, for this thing has been brought about by Me." They heeded the word of the LORD and turned back, in accordance with the word of the LORD.

[25] Jeroboam fortified Shechem in the hill country of Ephraim and resided there; he moved out from there and fortified Penuel. [26] Jeroboam said to himself, "Now the kingdom may well return to the House of David. [27] If these people still go up to offer sacrifices at the House of the LORD in Jerusalem, the heart of these people will turn back to their master, King Rehoboam of Judah; they will kill me and go back to King Rehoboam of Judah." [28] So the king took counsel and made two golden calves. He said to [c]the people,[c] "You have been going up to Jerusalem long enough. This is your god, O Israel, who brought you up from the land of Egypt!" [29] He set up one in Bethel and placed the other in Dan. [30] That proved to be a cause of guilt, for the people went to worship [the calf at Bethel and] the one at Dan. [31] He also made cult places and ap-

17: Benjaminite clans living within view of Jerusalem may have cast their lot with Judah (v. 21); those farther north may have joined the northern confederation. *Judah,* here, refers not to the tribe but to the kingdom, dominated by the tribe, that also included Simeon, to the south of Judah.

12.18–24: Israel's rebellion and the truce. 18: Noting that the text does not clarify to where or for what *Adoram* was sent, Josephus suggests that *Rehoboam* sent him to apologize on the king's behalf. If this individual is identical to Adoniram, who was in charge of the forced labor (4.6; 5.28; see 2 Sam. 20.24), as suggested by the reading Adoniram in the Septuagint, Rehoboam made a particularly poor selection, choosing an individual likely to raise resentment among the northern tribes. **19:** *As is still the case* would be true only in a document written while the Northern Kingdom still existed, i.e., prior to 722 BCE. **20:** Jeroboam's return from Egypt is reported in 12.3. Radak interprets the reference in this verse as indicating that (northern) Israel heard that he had returned to his family home and not to Egypt where he had settled. Jeroboam was made king by the assembly. **21–24:** Prophetic intervention stopped what might have turned into a major civil war. Although there was fighting between the two kingdoms during the reign of Jeroboam (14.30), it eventually petered out as both kingdoms faced common enemies. Throughout the divided monarchy, they often cooperated with each other.

12.25–33: Jeroboam consolidates his rule. In a highly polemical passage, the author describes a series of cultic actions taken by Jeroboam that he considers spiteful violations of divine will. Consequently, he refers to them throughout Kings as the "sins of Jeroboam" that caused northern tribes to abandon Jerusalem. **28–30:** He set up images, one at *Dan,* the northernmost border city, and one at

---

a Lit. "tents."
b Elsewhere called Adoniram; cf. 2 Sam. 20.24 and note.   c-c Heb. "them."

pointed priests from the ranks of the people who were not of Levite descent.

32 He stationed at Bethel the priests of the shrines that he had appointed to sacrifice to the calves that he had made. And Jeroboam established a festival on the fifteenth day of the eighth month; in imitation of the festival in Judah, he established one at Bethel, and he ascended the altar [there]. 33 On the fifteenth day of the eighth month—the month in which he had contrived of his own mind to establish a festival for the Israelites—Jeroboam ascended the altar that he had made in Bethel.

13 As he ascended the altar to present an offering, 1 a man of God arrived at Bethel from Judah at the command of the LORD. While Jeroboam was standing on the altar[a] to present the offering, the man of God, at the command of the LORD, cried out against the altar: 2 "O altar, altar! Thus said the LORD: A son shall be born to the House of David, Josiah by name; and he shall slaughter upon you the priests of the shrines who bring offerings upon you. And human bones shall be burned upon you." 3 He gave a portent on that day, saying, "Here is the portent that the LORD has decreed: This altar shall break apart, and the ashes on it shall be spilled." 4 When the king heard what the man of God had proclaimed against the altar in Bethel, Jeroboam stretched out his arm above the altar and cried, "Seize him!" But the arm that he stretched out against him became rigid, and he could not draw it back. 5 The altar broke apart and its ashes were spilled—the very portent that the man of God had announced at the LORD's command. 6 Then the king spoke up and said to the man of God, "Please entreat the LORD your God and pray for me that I may be able to draw back my arm." The man of God entreated the LORD and the king was able to draw his arm back; it became as it was before.

7 The king said to the man of God, "Come with me to my house and have some refreshment; and I shall give you a gift." 8 But the man of God replied to the king, "Even if you give me half your wealth, I will not go in with you, nor will I eat bread or drink water in this place; 9 for so I was commanded by the word of the LORD: You shall eat no bread and drink no water, nor shall you go back by the road by which you came." 10 So he left by another road and did not go back by the road on which he had come to Bethel.

11 There was an old prophet living in Bethel; and his sons[b] came and told him all the things that the man of

Bethel, the southernmost main center of his kingdom. *Calves*, most likely small images of bulls such as have been found in excavations, were held to be in violation of Deut. 5.8–9. The story of Jeroboam's golden calves shares much in common with the episode of fashioning the single golden calf in the wilderness in Exod. ch 32. For example, the phrase "These are your gods, O Israel, who brought you out of the land of Egypt!" is also found though only one calf was made by Aaron (Exod. 32.4 *b-b*, which translates the Heb accurately). **31:** The shrines are held to be in violation of Deut. 12.13–14. **32–33:** Jeroboam celebrated Tabernacles, which was to be celebrated on the fifteenth day of the seventh month (Lev. 23.34), *on the fifteenth day of the eighth month* as determined in Jerusalem, but which was probably what he determined to be the seventh month (cf. 8.2). He may have intercalated a month to align calendared agricultural festivals with the actual harvest patterns of northern tribes, particularly those in Galilee. Tannaitic traditions from the Second Temple period indicate that the year could be intercalated under certain circumstances because of late grain or fruit harvests (*b. Sanh.* 11a–12b). As Solomon had apparently done (9.25), Jeroboam as king officiated on the altar.

13.1–33: Two prophetic stories connected to Bethel. 1–10: A prophecy against the Bethel altar which is part of a larger miracle story. Specific mention of *Josiah* connects this to the fulfillment narrative associated with that king in 2 Kings 23.15–16. Proof of the validity of long-range prediction is a short-range prediction in v. 3 fulfilled in v. 5. The story cannot have achieved its current form until after the reforms of Josiah, ca. 620 BCE. Like the following story, this narrative emphasizes the importance of divine obedience. **11–32:** A prophetic story in which a Bethel *prophet* deceptively tests the authenticity of the *man of God* and validates his long-term

a *I.e., at the top of the steps or ramp.*   b *Heb. "son."*

God had done that day in Bethel [and] the words that he had spoken to the king. When they told it to their father, [12] their father said to them, "Which road did he leave by?" [a]His sons had seen[a] the road taken by the man of God who had come from Judah. [13] "Saddle the ass for me," he said to his sons. They saddled the ass for him, and he mounted it [14] and rode after the man of God. He came upon him sitting under a terebinth and said to him, "Are you the man of God who came from Judah?" "Yes, I am," he answered. [15] "Come home with me," he said, "and have something to eat." [16] He replied, "I may not go back with you and enter your home; and I may not eat bread or drink water in this place; [17] the order I received by the word of the LORD was: You shall not eat bread or drink water there; nor shall you return by the road on which you came." [18] "I am a prophet, too," said the other, "and an angel said to me by command of the LORD: Bring him back with you to your house, that he may eat bread and drink water." He was lying to him. [19] So he went back with him, and he ate bread and drank water in his house.

[20] While they were sitting at the table, the word of the LORD came to the prophet who had brought him back. [21] He cried out to the man of God who had come from Judah: "Thus said the LORD: Because you have flouted the word of the LORD and have not observed what the LORD your God commanded you, [22] but have gone back and eaten bread and drunk water in the place of which He said to you, 'Do not eat bread or drink water [there],' your corpse shall not come to the grave of your fathers." [23] After he had eaten bread and had drunk, he saddled the ass for him—for the prophet whom he had brought back. [24] He set out, and a lion came upon him on the road and killed him. His corpse lay on the road, with the ass standing beside it, and the lion also standing beside the corpse. [25] Some men who passed by saw the corpse lying on the road and the lion standing beside the corpse; they went and told it in the town where the old prophet lived. [26] And when the prophet who had brought him back from the road heard it, he said, "That is the man of God who flouted the LORD's command; the LORD gave him over to the lion, which mauled him and killed him in accordance with the word that the LORD had spoken to him." [27] He said to his sons, "Saddle the ass for me," and they did so. [28] He set out and found the corpse lying on the road, with the ass and the lion standing beside the corpse; the lion

prediction. The prophet's prediction that the man of God would not be buried in a family tomb (vv. 21–22) is fulfilled in vv. 29–30.

---

a-a Septuagint reads "And his sons showed."

had not eaten the corpse nor had it mauled the ass. 29 The prophet lifted up the corpse of the man of God, laid it on the ass, and brought it back; ⁻ᵃit was brought⁻ᵃ to the town of the old prophet for lamentation and burial. 30 He laid the corpse in his own burial place; and they lamented over it, "Alas, my brother!" 31 After burying him, he said to his sons, "When I die, bury me in the grave where the man of God lies buried; lay my bones beside his. 32 For what he announced by the word of the LORD against the altar in Bethel, and against all the cult places in the towns of Samaria, shall surely come true."

33 Even after this incident, Jeroboam did not turn back from his evil way, but kept on appointing priests for the shrines from the ranks of the people. He ordained as priests of the shrines any who so desired. 34 Thereby the House of Jeroboam incurred guilt—to their utter annihilation from the face of the earth.

14 At that time, Abijah, a son of Jeroboam, fell sick. 2 Jeroboam said to his wife, "Go and disguise yourself, so that you will not be recognized as Jeroboam's wife, and go to Shiloh. The prophet Ahijah lives there, the one who predicted that I would be king over this people. 3 Take with you ten loaves, some wafers, and a jug of honey, and go to him; he will tell you what will happen to the boy." 4 Jeroboam's wife did so; she left and went to Shiloh and came to the house of Ahijah. Now Ahijah could not see, for his eyes had become sightless with age; 5 but the LORD had said to Ahijah, "Jeroboam's wife is coming to inquire of you concerning her son, who is sick. Speak to her thus and thus. When she arrives, she will be in disguise."

6 Ahijah heard the sound of her feet as she came through the door, and he said, "Come in, wife of Jeroboam. Why are you disguised? I have a harsh message for you. 7 Go tell Jeroboam: Thus said the LORD, the God of Israel: I raised you up from among the people and made you a ruler over My people Israel; 8 I tore away the kingdom from the House of David and gave it to you. But you have not been like My servant David, who kept My commandments and followed Me with all his heart, doing only what was right in My sight. 9 You have acted worse than all those who preceded you; you have gone and made for yourself other gods and molten images to vex Me; and Me you have cast behind your back. 10 Therefore I will bring disaster upon the House of Jeroboam and will

33: *This incident* refers to the healing event and its aftermath narrated above in vv. 6–10. The story of vv. 11–32 interrupts the flow between vv. 10 and 33, and may have been inserted by a later editor.

14.1–18: A second tale about the prophet Ahijah and Jeroboam inculcating the lesson that the divine retribution is worked out through natural and man-made disasters, and emphasizing the extraordinary power of the prophet. **3:** *Loaves . . . wafers . . . honey,* as a gift (1 Sam. 9.7–8). The *wafers* (Heb "nikudim," cf. Josh 9.5, "crumbly") were perhaps a kind of biscuit or hardtack, meant to last longer than regular bread. **4:** *Could not see . . . sightless,* so his identification of Jeroboam's wife is due only to God's revelation. **7–11:** A prophetic speech serving as a preamble to a prediction. Ahijah alludes to 11.37–38 where conditions which Jeroboam did not meet were set out. **10–11:** A medium-range prediction against Jeroboam's dynasty is fulfilled in 15.29.

a-a Lit. "it came."

cut off from Jeroboam every male, [a-]bond and free,[-a] in Israel. I will sweep away the House of Jeroboam utterly, as dung is swept away. [11] Anyone belonging to Jeroboam who dies in the town shall be devoured by dogs; and anyone who dies in the open country shall be eaten by the birds of the air; for the LORD has spoken. [12] As for you, go back home; as soon as you set foot in the town, the child will die. [13] And all Israel shall lament over him and bury him; he alone of Jeroboam's family shall be brought to burial, for in him alone of the House of Jeroboam has some devotion been found to the LORD, the God of Israel. [14] Moreover, the LORD will raise up a king over Israel who will destroy the House of Jeroboam, [b-]this day and even now.[-b]

[15] "The LORD will strike Israel until it sways like a reed in water. He will uproot Israel from this good land that He gave to their fathers, and will scatter them beyond the Euphrates, because they have provoked the LORD by the sacred posts that they have made for themselves. [16] He will forsake Israel because of the sins that Jeroboam committed and led Israel to commit."

[17] Jeroboam's wife got up and left, and she went to Tirzah. As soon as she stepped over the threshold of her house, the child died. [18] They buried him and all Israel lamented over him, in accordance with the word that the LORD had spoken through His servant the prophet Ahijah.

[19] The other events of Jeroboam's reign, how he fought and how he ruled, are recorded in the Annals of the Kings of Israel. [20] Jeroboam reigned twenty-two years; then he slept with his fathers, and his son Nadab succeeded him as king.

[21] Meanwhile, Rehoboam son of Solomon had become king in Judah. Rehoboam was forty-one years old when he became king, and he reigned seventeen years in Jerusalem—the city the LORD had chosen out of all the tribes of Israel to establish His name there. His mother's name was Naamah the Ammonitess. [22] Judah did what was displeasing to the LORD, and angered Him more than their fathers had done by the sins that they committed. [23] They too built for themselves shrines, pillars, and sacred posts on every high hill and under every leafy tree; [24] there were also male prostitutes in the land. [Judah] imitated all the abhorrent practices of the nations that the LORD had dispossessed before the Israelites.

a-a Meaning of Heb. uncertain; possibly "kinsman and friend," cf. 16.11.
b-b Meaning of Heb. uncertain.

12–13: A short-range prediction that Jeroboam's son Abijah will die is fulfilled in 14.17–18. These verses originally continued v. 6 in the narrative. **15:** A long-range prediction that Israel will be destroyed and its people scattered across the Euphrates is fulfilled in 2 Kings 17.5–6. *Sacred posts,* Heb "asherim," were symbols of the goddess Asherah. In northern Canaanite myths she was the wife of El, but in southern Canaanite traditions she was associated with Baal. Heb inscriptions from the 8th and 7th centuries BCE discovered at Khirbet el-Kom near Lachish and at Kuntillet Ajrud in Sinai provide extrabiblical proof that some people in Judah associated her with the God of Israel.

14.19–20: A concluding summary used throughout Kings. Jeroboam's reign included other administrative and military accomplishments that the author knows about from the *Annals of the Kings of Israel.* Nearly twenty-two years' worth of royal activites are not mentioned here; he cited only what was of interest to him for his purpose.

14.21–31: Rehoboam's reign in Jerusalem, like all accounts in Kings, is presented only in terms of what is essential to the author. **21:** A formula introduces each Judean king: name, age at beginning of reign, years of reign, name of mother, and an evaluation of the reign. These data are followed by some salient facts and sometimes by expansive stories. **22–28:** The author first presents a specific summary of what was wrong in the ritual behavior of Judah (vv. 22–24) followed by events that in context are understood as an expression of divine displeasure. **24:** *Male prostitutes* (Heb "kedeshim"), more likely foreign specialists, perhaps poets and musicians, who assisted at rites the author does not approve of. Asa deported them (15.12). **25–26:** *Shishak* raided the ancient Egyptian province of Canaan, leaving a record of 156 captured

25 In the fifth year of King Rehoboam, King Shishak of Egypt marched against Jerusalem 26 and carried off the treasures of the House of the LORD and the treasures of the royal palace. He carried off everything; he even carried off all the golden shields that Solomon had made. 27 King Rehoboam had bronze shields made instead, and he entrusted them to the officers of the guard[a] who guarded the entrance to the royal palace. 28 Whenever the king went into the House of the LORD, the guards would carry them and then bring them back to the armory of the guards.

29 The other events of Rehoboam's reign, and all his actions, are recorded in the Annals of the Kings of Judah. 30 There was continual war between Rehoboam and Jeroboam. 31 Rehoboam slept with his fathers and was buried with his fathers in the City of David; his mother's name was Naamah the Ammonitess. His son Abijam succeeded him as king.

15 In the eighteenth year of King Jeroboam son of Nebat, Abijam became king over Judah. 2 He reigned three years in Jerusalem; his mother's name was [b-]Maacah daughter of Abishalom.[-b] 3 He continued in all the sins that his father before him had committed; he was not wholehearted with the LORD his God, like his father David. 4 Yet, for the sake of David, the LORD his God gave him a lamp in Jerusalem, by raising up his descendant after him and by preserving Jerusalem. 5 For David had done what was pleasing to the LORD and never turned throughout his life from all that He had commanded him, except in the matter of Uriah the Hittite. 6 There was war between Abijam[c] and Jeroboam all the days of his life. 7 The other events of Abijam's reign and all his actions are recorded in the Annals of the Kings of Judah; there was war between Abijam and Jeroboam. 8 Abijam slept with his fathers; he was buried in the City of David, and his son Asa succeeded him as king.

9 In the twentieth year of King Jeroboam of Israel, Asa became king over Judah. 10 He reigned forty-one years in Jerusalem; his mother's name was Maacah daughter of Abishalom. 11 Asa did what was pleasing to the LORD, as his father David had done. 12 He expelled the male prostitutes from the land, and he removed all the idols that his ancestors had made. 13 He also deposed his mother Maacah from the rank of queen mother, because she had made

a Lit. "runners."

b-b 2 Chron. 13.2 reads "Micaiah daughter of Uriel of Gibeah"; cf. v. 10 below, where Maacah, daughter of Abishalom, appears as mother of Asa.

c So several mss.; most mss. and the editions read "Rehoboam."

cities on the wall of a temple in Karnak. Most cities listed were in Israel, the kingdom of Shishak's former protégé, Jeroboam. Abravanel suggested in the early 16th century that perhaps Jeroboam invited Shishak to attack Jerusalem on his behalf. Although the text seems to imply that Shishak took the plunder by force, it is more likely that Rehoboam despoiled the Temple and palace of all the treasure introduced by Solomon in order to pay ransom to save Jerusalem. This spoil may also have been a bribe to Shishak to finance raids in Israel. Fragments of an inscription with Shishak's name were excavated in Megiddo. **26:** This payment to Shishak despoiled most of the treasure that Solomon had invested in the Temple. Although later generations were able to replace some of the golden decorations of the Temple, later descriptions of the Temple do not refer to its gold plating (2 Kings 14.14; 18.16). **29, 31:** A standard concluding summary for kings of Judah. Cf. the information about Solomon (11.41–43) and Asa (15.23–24).

15.1–8: The short, undistinguished reign of Abijam son of Rehoboam. 4: *A lamp*, cf. 11.36. It is used here in the sense of continuity of the line (Jer. 25.10). **6:** Since border skirmishing continued into the reign of Abijam's son Asa (15.16), the reading adopted in NJPS on the basis of Hebrew and Greek manuscripts is preferable to the textual tradition preserved in the MT.

15.9–24: Presentation of the reign of Asa follows the regular pattern of formulaic introductory (vv. 9–11) and concluding (vv. 23–24) materials between which selected stories are provided. **12–13:** What earned Asa the author's praise was his abolition of idols, of some wooden object dedicated to Asherah, and what he considered illegitimate places of worship. *Male prostitutes*, see 14.24 n. **13:** The *queen mother* (Heb "gevirah") had some official *ᵃ*an abominable thing*ᵃ* for [the goddess] Asherah. Asa cut down her abominable thing and burnt it in the Wadi Kidron. ¹⁴The shrines, indeed, were not abolished; however, Asa was wholehearted with the LORD his God all his life. ¹⁵He brought into the House of the LORD all the consecrated things of his father and *ᵇ*his own consecrated things*ᵇ*—silver, gold, and utensils.

¹⁶There was war between Asa and King Baasha of Israel all their days. ¹⁷King Baasha of Israel advanced against Judah, and he fortified Ramah to prevent anyone belonging to King Asa from going out or coming in. ¹⁸So Asa took all the silver and gold that remained in the treasuries of the House of the LORD as well as the treasuries of the royal palace, and he entrusted them to his officials. King Asa sent them to King Ben-hadad son of Tabrimmon son of Hezion of Aram, who resided in Damascus, with this message: ¹⁹"There is a pact between you and me, and between your father and my father. I herewith send you a gift of silver and gold: Go and break your pact with King Baasha of Israel, so that he may withdraw from me." ²⁰Ben-hadad responded to King Asa's request; he sent his army commanders against the towns of Israel and captured Ijon, Dan, Abel-beth-maacah, and all Chinneroth, as well as all the land of Naphtali. ²¹When Baasha heard about it, he stopped fortifying Ramah and remained in Tirzah.

²²Then King Asa mustered all Judah, with no exemptions; and they carried away the stones and timber with which Baasha had fortified Ramah. With these King Asa fortified Geba of Benjamin, and Mizpah.

²³All the other events of Asa's reign, and all his exploits, and all his actions, and the towns that he fortified, are recorded in the Annals of the Kings of Judah. However, in his old age he suffered from a foot ailment. ²⁴Asa slept with his fathers and was buried with his fathers in the city of his father David. His son Jehoshaphat succeeded him as king.

²⁵Nadab son of Jeroboam had become king over Israel in the second year of King Asa of Judah, and he reigned over Israel for two years. ²⁶He did what was displeasing to the LORD; he continued in the ways of his father, in the sins which he caused Israel to commit. ²⁷Then Baasha son of Ahijah, of the House of Issachar, conspired against him; and Baasha struck him down at Gibbethon of the Philistines, while Nadab and all Israel were laying siege to Gib-

status and prerogatives; consequently she was accorded respect (2.19, 2 Kings 10.13; Jer. 13.18). Other women mentioned in this role played dominant roles in Israelite history: Jezebel (2 Kings 9.22) and Athaliah (2 Kings 11.1). Asa stripped his mother of her status and prerogatives. **14:** Despite the existence of the Temple, the shrines remained popular places of worship. **17:** *Ramah,* a short distance north of Jerusalem, controlled traffic into Jerusalem from the north and from the coast via northwest Benjaminite territories. **20:** Asa's bribe to the Arameans cost the Northern Kingdom most of eastern Galilee and all upper Galilee. The tribes of Dan and Naphtali fell under the political domination of Damascus. **22:** Exploiting Israel's weakness while Baasha was rushing to protect his northern borders, Asa literally moved his own northern border past Ramah, about 3.5 km (2 mi) deeper into Benjaminite territory, by fortifying Geba and Mizpah, two villages set on the hill abutting and controlling the main north-south approach to Jerusalem. Excavations at Tel en-Nasbeh, ancient Mizpah, uncovered traces of a rapidly constructed wall that was later replaced by a strongly bonded one.

15.25–32: Nadab's reign and Baasha's usurpation. The author considers *Nadab* of Israel irredeemably unworthy because he followed the way of Jeroboam (vv. 26, 30). The extirpation of Jeroboam's family is interpreted as fulfillment of a prophecy and hence a sign of divine providence. Baasha's usurpation, though not backed by a prophet like Ahijah, is considered divinely sanctioned.

---

a-a Exact meaning of Heb. uncertain.
b-b So kethib and 2 Chron. 15.18.

bethon. 28 Baasha killed him in the third year of King Asa of Judah and became king in his stead. 29 As soon as he became king, he struck down all the House of Jeroboam; he did not spare a single soul belonging to Jeroboam until he destroyed it—in accordance with the word that the LORD had spoken through His servant, the prophet Ahijah the Shilonite—30 because of the sins which Jeroboam committed and which he caused Israel to commit thereby vexing the LORD, the God of Israel.

31 The other events of Nadab's reign and all his actions are recorded in the Annals of the Kings of Israel.

32 There was war between Asa and King Baasha of Israel all their days. 33 In the third year of King Asa of Judah, Baasha son of Ahijah became king in Tirzah over all Israel—for twenty-four years. 34 He did what was displeasing to the LORD; he followed the ways of Jeroboam and the sins which he caused Israel to commit.

16 The word of the LORD came to Jehu son of Hanani against Baasha: 2 "Because I lifted you up from the dust and made you a ruler over My people Israel, but you followed the way of Jeroboam and caused My people Israel to sin, vexing Me with their sins—3 I am going to sweep away Baasha and his house. I will make your house like the House of Jeroboam son of Nebat. 4 Anyone belonging to Baasha who dies in the town shall be devoured by dogs, and anyone belonging to him who dies in the open country shall be devoured by the birds of the sky."

5 The other events of Baasha's reign and his actions and his exploits are recorded in the Annals of the Kings of Israel. 6 Baasha slept with his fathers and was buried in Tirzah. His son Elah succeeded him as king.

7 But the word of the LORD had come through the prophet Jehu son of Hanani against Baasha and against his house, that it would fare like the House of Jeroboam, ᵃ‑which he himself had struck down,‑ᵃ because of all the evil he did which was displeasing to the LORD, vexing him with his deeds.

8 In the twenty-sixth year of King Asa of Judah, Elah son of Baasha became king over Israel, at Tirzah—for two years. 9 His officer Zimri, commander of half the chariotry, committed treason against him while he was at Tirzah drinking himself drunk in the house of Arza, who was in charge of the palace at Tirzah. 10 Zimri entered, struck him down, and killed him; he succeeded him as king in the

15.33–16.7: Baasha's reign is treated sparsely, significant events having been provided in the sketch of Asa's career (15.17–21). The fact that Baasha continued the way of Jeroboam led to his denunciation by a prophet, *Jehu son of Hanani*. **4:** *Devoured . . . dogs . . . birds*, the bodies will not receive proper, respectful burial but will be carrion instead. **7:** This verse, paraphrasing vv. 3–4, lacks adequate connection to its context. Rashi, perhaps noting the mention of Elah's ascension in v. 6 and the absence of a formulaic condemnation of his reign after v. 8, explains that this verse actually refers to a repetition of Jehu's prophecy during the reign of Elah, already doomed by his father's policies.

16.8–22: The reign of Elah, the usurpation of Zimri, and the struggle between Tibni and Omri. 8–14: The author relates nothing about Elah's brief reign other than the circumstances under which Zimri assassinated him, usurped authority, and murdered his family.

a-a *Syntax of Heb. unclear.*

twenty-seventh year of King Asa of Judah. ¹¹ No sooner had he become king and ascended the throne than he struck down all the House of Baasha; he did not leave a single male of his, nor any kinsman or friend. ¹² Thus Zimri destroyed all the House of Baasha, in accordance with the word that the LORD had spoken through the prophet Jehu—¹³ because of the sinful acts which Baasha and his son Elah committed, and which they caused Israel to commit, vexing the LORD, the God of Israel, with their false gods. ¹⁴ The other events of Elah's reign and all his actions are recorded in the Annals of the Kings of Israel.

¹⁵ During the twenty-seventh year of King Asa of Judah, Zimri reigned in Tirzah for seven days. At the time, the troops were encamped at Gibbethon of the Philistines. ¹⁶ When the troops who were encamped there learned that Zimri had committed treason and had struck down the king, that very day, in the camp, all Israel acclaimed the army commander Omri king over Israel. ¹⁷ Omri and all Israel then withdrew from Gibbethon and laid siege to Tirzah. ¹⁸ When Zimri saw that the town was taken, he went into the citadel of the royal palace and burned down the royal palace over himself. And so he died—¹⁹ because of the sins which he committed and caused Israel to commit, doing what was displeasing to the LORD and following the ways of Jeroboam. ²⁰ The other events of Zimri's reign, and the treason which he committed, are recorded in the Annals of the Kings of Israel.

²¹ Then the people of Israel split into two factions: a part of the people followed Tibni son of Ginath to make him king, and the other part followed Omri. ²² Those who followed Omri proved stronger than those who followed Tibni son of Ginath; Tibni died and Omri became king.

²³ In the thirty-first year of King Asa of Judah, Omri became king over Israel—for twelve years. He reigned in Tirzah six years. ²⁴ Then he bought the hill of Samaria from Shemer for two talents of silver; he built [a town] on the hill and named the town which he built Samaria, after Shemer, the owner of the hill.

²⁵ Omri did what was displeasing to the LORD; he was worse than all who preceded him. ²⁶ He followed all the ways of Jeroboam son of Nebat and the sins which he committed and caused Israel to commit, vexing the LORD, the God of Israel, with their futilities. ²⁷ The other events of Omri's reign, [and] his actions, and the exploits he performed, are recorded in the Annals of the Kings of Israel. ²⁸ Omri slept with his fathers and was buried in Samaria; and his son Ahab succeeded him as king.

15–18: Zimri lacked any popular support, even from the chariot troops under his command. Omri, acclaimed king by his army (*all Israel*) while at the Philistine front, withdrew to *Tirzah* in the heart of Israel and captured it. *Zimri,* the assassin, committed suicide. **19:** The author appends a standard condemnation to his summary of Zimri's seven-day reign. So far as he is concerned, had Zimri reversed some of Jeroboam's cultic policies, he would have been lauded. **21–22:** These verses continue the narrative from v. 18. Despite the army's acclamation of Omri as king, the chronological notices suggest that the northern tribes were divided for almost four years (cf. vv. 15, 23) about who should be elected king: Omri or Tibni (possibly another military figure). Tibni's death resolved the matter. The author makes no evaluative comment about Tibni because he was never acknowledged officially as king.

16.23–28: The reign of Omri. Aside from formulary types of information, the single event reported for Omri is the construction of a new capital city, *Samaria.* According to an inscription left by Mesha, king of Moab in the mid-9th century (cf. 2 Kings 3.4), Omri was a powerful king, who conquered and colonized northern Moab. He achieved a level of renown for his *exploits* such that after his dynasty had been supplanted, an Assyrian inscription called Israel "the house of Omri." He established a dynasty that maintained itself through the reigns of three descendants.

16.29–22.40: Stories about the reign of Ahab include a large collection of stories about the charismatic prophet Elijah, who was intimately involved in the religious and political life of the kingdom. **16.29–34:** This section introduces the reign of Ahab in typical formulaic fashion. The concluding formulae are found in 22.39–40. The intervening narratives serve to support the author's extremely

²⁹ Ahab son of Omri became king over Israel in the thirty-eighth year of King Asa of Judah, and Ahab son of Omri reigned over Israel in Samaria for twenty-two years. ³⁰ Ahab son of Omri did what was displeasing to the LORD, more than all who preceded him. ³¹ Not content to follow the sins of Jeroboam son of Nebat, he took as wife Jezebel daughter of King Ethbaal of the Phoenicians, and he went and served Baal and worshiped him. ³² He erected an altar to Baal in the temple of Baal which he built in Samaria. ³³ Ahab also made a sacred post. Ahab did more to vex the LORD, the God of Israel, than all the kings of Israel who preceded him.

³⁴ During his reign, Hiel the Bethelite fortified Jericho. He laid its foundations at the cost of Abiram his first-born, and set its gates in place at the cost of Segub his youngest, in accordance with the words that the LORD had spoken through Joshua son of Nun.ᵃ

17 Elijah the Tishbite, an inhabitant of Gilead, said to Ahab, "As the LORD lives, the God of Israel whom I serve, there will be no dew or rain except at my bidding."

² The word of the LORD came to him: ³ "Leave this place; turn eastward and go into hiding by the Wadi Cherith, which is east of the Jordan. ⁴ You will drink from the wadi, and I have commanded the ravens to feed you there." ⁵ He proceeded to do as the LORD had bidden: he went, and he

a Cf. Josh. 6.26.

negative evaluation of Ahab's reign. **31:** *Jezebel daughter of King Ethbaal of the Phoenicians* (lit. "Sidonians"): Jezebel's name consists of two components, "'iy + zebel," which in Phoenician, the language of Tyre and Sidon, mean "where is glory/dominion." Compare Ichabod, Heb "'iy + kabod," meaning "where is honor/glory" (1 Sam. 4.21). In Ugaritic mythology, "zebul" is a title of Baal, god of rain and sweet water. Ethbaal's name means "with Baal." His title "king of the Sidonians" indicates that he was king of both Sidon and Tyre. Hiram in the time of David and Solomon held the same authority but used a different title (5.15). Following a common biblical topos, in this passage and elsewhere in the Ahab stories, the wife is blamed for leading the husband astray. **32–33:** In addition to wor-

shipping Baal, Ahab constructed a temple for him in Samaria with a special altar, and he also established an "'asherah," a *sacred post*, the symbol of the goddess Asherah, somewhere in the city, but not in the Baal temple itself (cf. 2 Kings 13.6). **33:** *Vex the LORD* (Heb "lehakh'is," expressing causality). The author, not believing that anybody could take idolatry seriously, explained that Ahab continued doing such things out of spite in order to anger God. **34:** Tragic events in the life of a certain *Hiel* from Bethel are presented as the actualization of Joshua's curse (Josh. 6.26). Ralbag interprets the placement of this verse as indicating that although Ahab should have understood what happened to Hiel as a warning of what might happen to him, he persisted in his ways.

17.1–19.21: Elijah stories occupy a significant place in the author's composition about the Northern Kingdom. The author, who uses a prediction-fulfillment pattern as a leitmotif in Kings, held prophets in high regard and had access to stores of prophetic tales. Some of these presented Elijah as being in contact and conflict with Ahab and Jezebel over religious matters. A zealous champion of God, a radical monotheist, Elijah, whose name means "my God is Yahu (the LORD)," fought for his cause fearlessly and at such personal risk that even Ahab held him in regard. The four major stories about him (17.1–18.46; 19.1–21; 21.1–29; 2 Kings 2.2–2.12) and similar prophets (20.1–43; 22.1–40) are presented because their heroes taught what the author believed and they acted in ways he thought appropriate. These stories, which do not assume the centrality of worship of God in Jerusalem (see esp. ch 18), comprise a source which became incorporated into Kings. Ch 17 seems to begin in the middle of the Elijah story, suggesting that not all of this source was used.

**17.1–18.46: The drought.
17.1:** Elijah predicts a drought. The mention of dew and rain challenges Ahab's notion that Baal, celebrated as god of fresh water, is responsible for them. Subsequent events suggest that the drought, limited to only Israelite territory and persisting for a long while, came to be seen as unnatural. At a theological level, the author presents this story because Elijah's prediction resonates with Deut. 11.13–17. **2–24:** Miracle stories about Elijah illustrate that God protected and provided for his sustenance and that he in turn provided sustenance for others. They also show that God responded to his prayers. **2:** *Wadi Cherith* in Transjordan may have been in Israelite territory but outside of Ahab's jurisdiction. Later, when the severity of the drought dried up local water, God directed Elijah to Zarephath in Phoenician territory (vv. 7–8).

stayed by the Wadi Cherith, which is east of the Jordan.
⁶ The ravens brought him bread and meat every morning
and every evening, and he drank from the wadi.

⁷ After some time the wadi dried up, because there was
no rain in the land. ⁸ And the word of the LORD came to
him: ⁹ "Go at once to Zarephath of Sidon, and stay there; I
have designated a widow there to feed you." ¹⁰ So he went
at once to Zarephath. When he came to the entrance of the
town, a widow was there gathering wood. He called out
to her, "Please bring me a little water in your pitcher, and
let me drink." ¹¹ As she went to fetch it, he called out to
her, "Please bring along a piece of bread for me." ¹² "As

10: *A widow:* The story presupposes that there was some external
sign that differentiated widows,
who were typically poor, from
other women, perhaps some item
of dress (Gen. 38.14). The widow
remains nameless in the two stories about her that follow because
the point of the stories is to celebrate the power of the named
prophet. Rashi, noting the similarity between Elijah's request for
water and that of Abraham's servant in Gen. 24.12–20, suggests
that like the servant, Elijah had

Places associated with the Elijah narratives. The dashed line shows the approximate boundaries
between Israel, Judah, and Philistia.

the LORD your God lives," she replied, "I have nothing baked, nothing but a handful of flour in a jar and a little oil in a jug. I am just gathering a couple of sticks, so that I can go home and prepare it for me and my son; we shall eat it and then we shall die." 13 "Don't be afraid," said Elijah to her. "Go and do as you have said; but first make me a small cake from what you have there, and bring it out to me; then make some for yourself and your son. 14 For thus said the LORD, the God of Israel: The jar of flour shall not give out and the jug of oil shall not fail until the day that the LORD sends rain upon the ground." 15 She went and did as Elijah had spoken, and she and he and her household had food for a long time. 16 The jar of flour did not give out, nor did the jug of oil fail, just as the LORD had spoken through Elijah.

17 After a while, the son of the mistress of the house fell sick, and his illness grew worse, until he had no breath left in him. 18 She said to Elijah, "What harm have I done you, O man of God, that you should come here to recall my sin and cause the death of my son?" 19 "Give me the boy," he said to her; and taking him from her arms, he carried him to the upper chamber where he was staying, and laid him down on his own bed. 20 He cried out to the LORD and said, "O LORD my God, will You bring calamity upon this widow whose guest I am, and let her son die?" 21 Then he stretched out over the child three times, and cried out to the LORD, saying, "O LORD my God, let this child's life return to his body!" 22 The LORD heard Elijah's plea; the child's life returned to his body, and he revived. 23 Elijah picked up the child and brought him down from the upper room into the main room, and gave him to his mother. "See," said Elijah, "your son is alive." 24 And the woman answered Elijah, "Now I know that you are a man of God and that the word of the LORD is truly in your mouth."

18 Much later, in the third year,ᵃ the word of the LORD came to Elijah: "Go, appear before Ahab; then I will send rain upon the earth." 2 Thereupon Elijah set out to appear before Ahab.

The famine was severe in Samaria. 3 Ahab had summoned Obadiah, the steward of the palace. (Obadiah revered the LORD greatly. 4 When Jezebel was killing off the prophets of the LORD, Obadiah had taken a hundred prophets and hidden them, fifty to a cave, and provided them with food and drink.) 5 And Ahab had said to Oba-

proposed a test to determine if this particular widow was the one designated by God. **14–16:** Elijah's prediction that the jars would have an unfailing supply of flour and oil (staple foodstuffs) is fulfilled immediately. **21:** Elijah attempted what is sometimes described as the first recorded case of artificial respiration on the child, who was critically ill but not dead; then he prayed on the child's behalf. A healing procedure in some Mesopotamian incantations against demons instructs the healer to superimpose his body over that of the patient, head to head, hand to hand, foot to foot. **24:** His success as a wonderworker is what convinced the widow that he was indeed a prophet. In Israel, the power to intercede with God was considered a prophetic gift (cf. Gen. 20.7). Elijah is here called *a man of God*, a term which in these narratives often emphasizes the prophet's superhuman powers. **18.4:** The author's parenthetical remark provides important information for this and subsequent narratives: (1) Elijah was not the only prophet in Israel during this time. (2) *Jezebel* had been persecuting and *killing off* prophets, most likely holding them culpable for the drought. (3) *Obadiah* was part of a coterie of devout people who followed, supported, and protected prophets like Elijah (cf. vv. 12–13).

---

a I.e., of the drought; see 17.1.

diah, "Go through the land, to all the springs of water and to all the wadis. Perhaps we shall find some grass to keep horses and mules alive, so that we are not left without beasts."

⁶They divided the country between them to explore it, Ahab going alone in one direction and Obadiah going alone in another direction. ⁷Obadiah was on the road, when Elijah suddenly confronted him. [Obadiah] recognized him and flung himself on his face, saying, "Is that you, my lord Elijah?" ⁸"Yes, it is I," he answered. "Go tell your lord: Elijah is here!" ⁹But he said, "What wrong have I done, that you should hand your servant over to Ahab to be killed? ¹⁰As the LORD your God lives, there is no nation or kingdom to which my lord has not sent to look for you; and when they said, 'He is not here,' he made that kingdom or nation swear that you could not be found. ¹¹And now you say, 'Go tell your lord: Elijah is here!' ¹²When I leave you, the spirit of the LORD will carry you off I don't know where; and when I come and tell Ahab and he does not find you, he will kill me. Yet your servant has revered the LORD from my youth. ¹³My lord has surely been told what I did when Jezebel was killing the prophets of the LORD, how I hid a hundred of the prophets of the LORD, fifty men to a cave, and provided them with food and drink. ¹⁴And now you say, 'Go tell your lord: Elijah is here.' Why, he will kill me!"

¹⁵Elijah replied, "As the LORD of Hosts lives, whom I serve, I will appear before him this very day."

¹⁶Obadiah went to find Ahab, and informed him; and Ahab went to meet Elijah. ¹⁷When Ahab caught sight of Elijah, Ahab said to him, "Is that you, you troubler of Israel?" ¹⁸He retorted, "It is not I who have brought trouble on Israel, but you and your father's House, by forsaking the commandments of the LORD and going after the Baalim. ¹⁹Now summon all Israel to join me at Mount Carmel, together with the four hundred and fifty prophets of Baal and the four hundred prophets of Asherah, ᵃ⁻who eat at Jezebel's table."⁻ᵃ

²⁰Ahab sent orders to all the Israelites and gathered the prophets at Mount Carmel. ²¹Elijah approached all the people and said, "How long will you keep hopping ᵇ⁻between two opinions?⁻ᵇ If the LORD is God, follow Him; and if Baal, follow him!" But the people answered him not a word. ²²Then Elijah said to the people, "I am the only prophet of the LORD left, while the prophets of Baal are

12: *The spirit of the LORD will carry you off:* One of the supernatural abilities that was attributed to Elijah as a man of God was the ability to travel large distances suddenly. **19–46:** The contest between Elijah and the Baal prophets on Mount Carmel pits the Israelite, in the presence of *all Israel,* against *four hundred and fifty prophets of Baal* and *four hundred prophets of Asherah* (18.19–20). **19:** *Mount Carmel,* at the south end of modern Haifa, is at the seaward end of a range that rises to 530 m (1,600 ft). **21:** Elijah's rhetorical question indicates that Israelites supported both Baal and God. (In 19.18, the author provides a statistic indicating this clearly.) In polytheistic pluralism, this was a valid position. Elijah, however, a radical monotheist, was intolerant of the "both . . . and" situation; he recasts Israelite options into an "either . . . or" choice for which they will have to bear consequences. **22–25:** Since Elijah seems to have determined the nature of the contest, he proposes that the Baal prophets select whichever *bull* they wish, perhaps to eliminate any suspicion of fraud.

a-a *I.e., who are maintained by Jezebel.*   b-b *Lit. "on the two boughs."*

four hundred and fifty men. ²³ Let two young bulls be given to us. Let them choose one bull, cut it up, and lay it on the wood, but let them not apply fire; I will prepare the other bull, and lay it on the wood, and will not apply fire. ²⁴ You will then invoke your god by name, and I will invoke the LORD by name; ªand let us agree:ª the god who responds with fire, that one is God." And all the people answered, "Very good!"

²⁵ Elijah said to the prophets of Baal, "Choose one bull and prepare it first, for you are the majority; invoke your god by name, but apply no fire." ²⁶ They took the bull that was given them; they prepared it, and invoked Baal by name from morning until noon, shouting, "O Baal, answer us!" But there was no sound, and none who responded; so they performed a hopping dance about the altar that had been set up. ²⁷ When noon came, Elijah mocked them, saying, "Shout louder! After all, he is a god. ᵇBut he may be in conversation, he may be detained, or he may be on a journey,ᵇ or perhaps he is asleep and will wake up." ²⁸ So they shouted louder, and gashed themselves with knives and spears, according to their practice, until the blood streamed over them. ²⁹ When noon passed, they ᶜkept ravingᶜ until the hour of presenting the meal offering. Still there was no sound, and none who responded or heeded.

³⁰ Then Elijah said to all the people, "Come closer to me"; and all the people came closer to him. He repaired the damaged altar of the LORD. ³¹ Then Elijah took twelve stones, corresponding to the number of the tribes of the sons of Jacob—to whom the word of the LORD had come: "Israel shall be your name"ᵈ—³² and with the stones he built an altar in the name of the LORD. Around the altar he made a trench large enough for two *seahs* of seed.ᵉ ³³ He laid out the wood, and he cut up the bull and laid it on the wood. ³⁴ And he said, "Fill four jars with water and pour it over the burnt offering and the wood." Then he said, "Do it a second time"; and they did it a second time. "Do it a third time," he said; and they did it a third time. ³⁵ The water ran down around the altar, and even the trench was filled with water.

³⁶ When it was time to present the meal offering, the prophet Elijah came forward and said, "O LORD, God of

27: The sarcastic comments, ostensibly directed to the Baal prophets, are intended for the ears of the audience. **32–35:** In dousing the ground around and under the altar, and drenching the sacrifice with water, the substance associated with Baal, Elijah indicates that even though Baal failed to ignite his own sacrifice he might be powerful enough to stop God. God's power is also heightened, as God ignites the soaking wet altar and sacrifice.

a-a Lit. "and it shall be."
b-b Meaning of Heb. uncertain.
c-c Others "prophesied"; see Num. 11.25–26.
d See Gen. 35.10.
e I.e., of an area which would require two seahs of seed if sown. Cf. Lev. 27.16; Isa. 5.10.

Abraham, Isaac, and Israel! Let it be known today that You are God in Israel and that I am Your servant, and that I have done all these things at Your bidding. ³⁷ Answer me, O LORD, answer me, that this people may know that You, O LORD, are God; ᵃ-for You have turned their hearts backward."-ᵃ

³⁸ Then fire from the LORD descended and consumed the burnt offering, the wood, the stones, and the earth; and it licked up the water that was in the trench. ³⁹ When they saw this, all the people flung themselves on their faces and cried out: "The LORD alone is God, The LORD alone is God!"

⁴⁰ Then Elijah said to them, "Seize the prophets of Baal, let not a single one of them get away." They seized them, and Elijah took them down to the Wadi Kishon and slaughtered them there.

⁴¹ Elijah said to Ahab, "Go up, eat and drink, for there is a rumbling of [approaching] rain," ⁴² and Ahab went up to eat and drink. Elijah meanwhile climbed to the top of Mount Carmel, crouched on the ground, and put his face between his knees. ⁴³ And he said to his servant, "Go up and look toward the Sea." He went up and looked and reported, "There is nothing." Seven times [Elijah] said, "Go back," ⁴⁴ and the seventh time, [the servant] reported, "A cloud as small as a man's hand is rising in the west." Then [Elijah] said, "Go say to Ahab, 'Hitch up [your chariot] and go down before the rain stops you.'" ⁴⁵ Meanwhile the sky grew black with clouds; there was wind, and a heavy downpour fell; Ahab mounted his chariot and drove off to Jezreel. ⁴⁶ The hand of the LORD had come upon Elijah. ᵇ-He tied up his skirts-ᵇ and ran in front of Ahab all the way to Jezreel.

19 When Ahab told Jezebel all that Elijah had done and how he had put all the prophetsᶜ to the sword, ² Jezebel sent a messenger to Elijah, saying, ᵈ-"Thus and more may the gods do-ᵈ if by this time tomorrow I have not made you like one of them."

³ Frightened,ᵉ he fled at once for his life. He came to Beer-sheba, which is in Judah, and left his servant there; ⁴ he himself went a day's journey into the wilderness. He came to a broom bush and sat down under it, and prayed

38: When the divine *fire* consumed everything, including the *water*, the message was clear. **39–40:** This cry indicates that they opted for God and monotheism. The same words are found elsewhere in the Bible (e.g., Deut. 4.35, 39), and were later used as the culminating confession of faith at the conclusion of Yom Kippur. Ahab, present through all this (v. 41; 19.1), says and does nothing. The author presents no information about the prophets of Asherah. **42–43:** Although the narrative is opaque, it appears that Elijah's posture is somehow responsible for bringing the cloud and the following rain. It is usually assumed that he was praying, but the fetal position is not known to have been adopted for prayer, and no word for prayer appears in the narrative. **46:** The strength and stamina for Elijah's long run came by virtue of the *hand of the LORD*. Since running before the royal chariot was both an honor and a way of honoring the king (1 Sam. 8.11; 1 Kings 1.5), Elijah's motivation for doing so may have been to show respect to Ahab who he thought had been won over to radical monotheism. Elijah did not enter Jezreel.

19.1–18: Elijah's flight from Jezebel into Judah, and the revelation at Mt. Horeb. **2:** Jezebel acts imperiously, warning Elijah of her plan to avenge the deaths of her countrymen. **3:** *Frightened,* he flees south, across Judah and into the wilderness beyond. **4–7:** Again, though Elijah is hiding far from food sources, his needs are provided for (cf. 17.6). The theme of a prophet's wishing for death out of a sense of isolation and failure in v. 4 are mimicked by the request and circumstances of Jonah in Jonah 4.3; that of being provisioned in the wilderness in vv. 5–6 parallels the story of Hagar in Gen. 21.14–19. **8:** *Horeb,* meaning "dry place," is the name preferred by Deuteronomy for the mountain designated Sinai in Exodus, Leviticus, and Numbers. Information in this verse contributes nothing toward determining its location.

---

a-a *Meaning of Heb. uncertain.*

b-b *Lit. "He bound up his loins."*

c *Of Baal; see 18.40.*

d-d *A formula of imprecation. Many Heb. mss. and Septuagint add "to me."*

e *So many Heb. mss. and Septuagint; most mss., and the editions, read "And he saw, and."*

that he might die. "Enough!" he cried. "Now, O Lord, take my life, for I am no better than my fathers."

5 He lay down and fell asleep under a broom bush. Suddenly an angel touched him and said to him, "Arise and eat." 6 He looked about; and there, beside his head, was a cake baked on hot stones and a jar of water! He ate and drank, and lay down again. 7 The angel of the Lord came a second time and touched him and said, "Arise and eat, or the journey will be too much for you." 8 He arose and ate and drank; and with the strength from that meal he walked forty days and forty nights as far as the mountain of God at Horeb. 9 There he went into a cave, and there he spent the night.

Then the word of the Lord came to him. He said to him, "Why are you here, Elijah?" 10 He replied, "I am moved by zeal for the Lord, the God of Hosts, for the Israelites have forsaken Your covenant, torn down Your altars, and put Your prophets to the sword. I alone am left, and they are out to take my life." 11 "Come out," He called, "and stand on the mountain before the Lord."

And lo, the Lord passed by. There was a great and mighty wind, splitting mountains and shattering rocks by the power of the Lord; but the Lord was not in the wind. After the wind—an earthquake; but the Lord was not in the earthquake. 12 After the earthquake—fire; but the Lord was not in the fire. And after the fire—a soft murmuring sound.[a] 13 When Elijah heard it, he wrapped his mantle about his face and went out and stood at the entrance of the cave. Then a voice addressed him: "Why are you here, Elijah?" 14 He answered, "I am moved by zeal for the Lord, the God of Hosts; for the Israelites have forsaken Your covenant, torn down Your altars, and have put Your prophets to the sword. I alone am left, and they are out to take my life."

15 The Lord said to him, "Go back by the way you came, [and] on to the wilderness of Damascus. When you get there, anoint Hazael as king of Aram. 16 Also anoint Jehu son of Nimshi as king of Israel, and anoint Elisha son of Shaphat of Abel-meholah to succeed you as prophet. 17 Whoever escapes the sword of Hazael shall be slain by Jehu, and whoever escapes the sword of Jehu shall be slain by Elisha. 18 I will leave in Israel only seven thousand—every knee that has not knelt to Baal and every mouth that has not kissed him."

19 He set out from there and came upon Elisha son of Shaphat as he was plowing. There were twelve yoke of

Since an unencumbered person used to walking can cover 15–25 miles a day, depending on the terrain, and Elijah is said to have traveled 40 days, the mountain could be 600–1,000 miles in any direction except north from some point south of Beer-sheba. Cf. Deut. 1.1–2. The forty days may suggest Moses, who spent forty days and nights atop Sinai (Exod. 24.18). In both cases, forty may be understood as a formulaic number, not to be taken literally. **9–14:** The combination of a cave and the divine revelation to the dispirited Elijah at Horeb/Sinai parallels thematically the cleft in the rock where God sheltered the overwhelmed Moses when He passed before him (Exod. 33.13–23), and helps to establish Elijah as a new Moses or a prophet like Moses (Deut. 18.15, 18). Elijah repeats in v. 14, after the revelation, what he said in v. 9, but the words ring less urgently. The revelation demonstrated that Elijah was not alone and restored a sense of proportion. **15–17:** Malbim suggests that each person to be anointed was in response to one of Elijah's complaints: Hazael would punish those who broke down the altars, Jehu would punish those responsible for killing prophets, and Elisha would be a prophet with and after him. No other prophet is recorded to have designated his own prophetic replacement, though here too there may be some echo of Moses choosing Joshua as a replacement in his own lifetime (Num. 27.15–23).

19.19–21: The choice of Elisha. Reassured, Elijah first attends to his third assigned task, appointing Elisha. (The account does not mention completing the first two tasks.) Elijah's call to Elisha consists of the apparently casual but symbolically rich act of throwing his mantle over him and walking on without a word.

---

a Others "a still, small voice."

oxen ahead of him, and he was with the twelfth. Elijah came over to him and threw his mantle over him. [20] He left the oxen and ran after Elijah, saying: "Let me kiss my father and mother good-by, and I will follow you." And he answered him, "Go back. What have I done to you?"[a] [21] He turned back from him and took the yoke of oxen and slaughtered them; he boiled [b]their meat[b] with the gear[c] of the oxen and gave it to the people, and they ate. Then he arose and followed Elijah and became his attendant.

20 King Ben-hadad of Aram gathered his whole army; thirty-two kings accompanied him with horses and chariots. He advanced against Samaria, laid siege to it, and attacked it. [2] And he sent messengers to Ahab inside the city [3] to say to him, "Thus said Ben-hadad: Your silver and gold are mine, and your beautiful wives and children are mine." [4] The king of Israel replied, "As you say, my lord king: I and all I have are yours." [5] Then the messengers came again and said, "Thus said Ben-hadad: When I sent you the order to give me your silver and gold, and your wives and children, [6] I meant that tomorrow at this time I will send my servants to you and they will search your house and the houses of your courtiers and seize everything you[d] prize and take it away."

[7] Then the king of Israel summoned all the elders of the land, and he said, "See for yourselves how that man is bent on evil! For when he demanded my wives and my children, my silver and my gold, I did not refuse him." [8] All the elders and all the people said, "Do not obey and do not submit!" [9] So he said to Ben-hadad's messengers, "Tell my lord the king: All that you first demanded of your servant I shall do, but this thing I cannot do." The messengers went and reported this to him. [10] Thereupon Ben-hadad sent him this message: [e]"May the gods do thus to me and even more,[e] if the dust of Samaria will provide even a handful for each of the men who follow me!"

[11] The king of Israel replied, "Tell him: Let not him who girds on his sword boast like him who ungirds it!"

[12] On hearing this reply—while he and the other kings were drinking together at Succoth—he[f] commanded his followers, "Advance!" And they advanced against the city. [13] Then a certain prophet went up to King Ahab of Israel and said, "Thus said the LORD: Do you see that great host? I will deliver it into your hands today, and you shall

20: The meaning of Elijah's response to Elisha's reasonable request is unclear. Perhaps it means that should he turn back from Elijah, the symbolic act will have lost its significance.

20.1–22.40: Narratives of the life and times of Ahab in which the king is the prime focus of attention and Elijah as well as other prophets appear in significant roles.

20.1–43: Ahab's war with Ben-hadad of Aram originally concerned the city of Samaria alone. Ben-hadad's aggression may have been precipitated after Ahab's closing of Aramean bazaars in the city, an international trade concession granted by Omri to Ben-hadad's father (v. 34). Although his whole army may have been mustered (v. 1), he first threatened the city with a small force, not anticipating a hostile response (vv. 15–20). The anonymous prophet who is the protagonist of the story has many thematic similarities to Elijah and to the nameless prophets earlier in the book. **2–4:** *Ben-hadad* demands payment from Ahab alone and Ahab accedes. **5–9:** Hearing Ahab's quick, docile response, Ben-hadad changes the terms and demands the right to loot property from Ahab's courtiers. Ahab, lacking any right to give away what is not his, consults with *the elders of the land,* who instruct him not to comply with the demand. **13:** An anonymous prophet counsels Ahab on military tactics. The reappearance of the figure bearing messages to Ahab throughout this story (vv. 28, 41) turns the historical narrative into a theological story about how an ungrateful Ahab turned a divinely orchestrated victory—the second battle—into a business opportunity.

---

a I.e., I am not stopping you.   b-b Lit. "them, the flesh."
c I.e., using it as firewood; cf. 2 Sam. 24.22.   d Several ancient versions read "they."
e-e See note at 19.2.   f I.e., Ben-hadad.

know that I am the LORD." ¹⁴"Through whom?" asked Ahab. He answered, "Thus said the LORD: Through the aides of the provincial governors." He asked, "Who shall begin the battle?" And he answered, "You."

¹⁵So he mustered the aides of the provincial governors, 232 strong, and then he mustered all the troops—all the Israelites—7,000 strong. ¹⁶They marched out at noon, while Ben-hadad was drinking himself drunk at Succoth together with the thirty-two kings allied with him. ¹⁷The aides of the provincial governors rushed out first. Ben-hadad sent [scouts], who told him, "Some men have come out from Samaria." ¹⁸He said, "If they have come out to surrender, take them alive; and if they have come out for battle, take them alive anyhow." ¹⁹But the others—the aides of the provincial governors, with the army behind them—had already rushed out of the city, ²⁰and each of them struck down his opponent. The Arameans fled, and Israel pursued them; but King Ben-hadad of Aram escaped on a horse with other horsemen. ²¹The king of Israel came out and attacked the horses and chariots, and inflicted a great defeat on the Arameans. ²²Then the prophet approached the king of Israel and said to him, "Go, keep up your efforts, and consider well what you must do; for the king of Aram will attack you at the turn of the year."

²³Now the ministers of the king of Aram said to him, "Their God is a God of mountains; that is why they got the better of us. But if we fight them in the plain, we will surely get the better of them. ²⁴Do this: Remove all the kings from their posts and appoint governors in their place. ²⁵Then muster for yourself an army equal to the army you lost, horse for horse and chariot for chariot. And let us fight them in the plain, and we will surely get the better of them." He took their advice and acted accordingly.

²⁶At the turn of the year, Ben-hadad mustered the Arameans and advanced on Aphek to fight Israel. ²⁷Now the Israelites had been mustered and provisioned, and they went out against them; but when the Israelites encamped against them, they looked like two flocks*ᵃ* of goats, while the Arameans covered the land. ²⁸Then the man of God approached and spoke to the king of Israel, "Thus said the LORD: Because the Arameans have said, 'The LORD is a God of mountains, but He is not a God of lowlands,' I will deliver that great host into your hands; and you shall know that I am the LORD."

²⁹For seven days they were encamped opposite each other. On the seventh day, the battle was joined and the Is-

14: *Aides* (Heb "na'ar"), youths who functioned as fighters (cf. Gen 14.24, where it is translated "servants"; 2 Sam 2.14, where it is translated "young men"). The prophet counsels him to initiate an attack using the aides as shock troops.

a Meaning of Heb. uncertain.

raelites struck down 100,000 Aramean foot soldiers in one day. ³⁰ The survivors fled to Aphek, inside the town, and the wall fell on the 27,000 survivors.

Ben-hadad also fled and took refuge inside the town, in an inner chamber. ³¹ His ministers said to him, "We have heard that the kings of the House of Israel are magnanimous kings. Let us put sackcloth on our loins and ropes on our heads, and surrender to the king of Israel; perhaps he will spare your life." ³²So they girded sackcloth on their loins and wound ropes around their heads, and came to the king of Israel and said, "Your servant Ben-hadad says, 'I beg you, spare my life.' " He replied, "Is he still alive? He is my brother." ³³ The men divined his meaning and quickly ᵃcaught the word from him,ᵃ saying, "Yes, Ben-hadad is your brother." "Go, bring him," he said. Ben-hadad came out to him, and he invited him into his chariot. ³⁴ Ben-hadad said to him, "I will give back the towns that my father took from your father, and you may set up bazaars for yourself in Damascus as my father did in Samaria." "And I, for my part," [said Ahab,] "will let you go home under these terms." So he made a treaty with him and dismissed him.

³⁵ A certain man, a disciple of the prophets, said to another, at the word of the Lord, "Strike me"; but the man refused to strike him. ³⁶ He said to him, "Because you have not obeyed the Lord, a lion will strike you dead as soon as you leave me." And when he left, a lion came upon him and killed him. ³⁷ Then he met another man and said, "Come, strike me." So the man struck him and wounded him. ³⁸ Then the prophet, disguised by a cloth over his eyes, went and waited for the king by the road. ³⁹ As the king passed by, he cried out to the king and said, "Your servant went out into the thick of the battle. Suddenly a man came over and brought a man to me, saying, 'Guard this man! If he is missing, it will be your life for his, or you will have to pay a talent of silver.' ⁴⁰ While your servant was busy here and there, [the man] got away." The king of Israel responded, "You have your verdict; you pronounced it yourself." ⁴¹ Quickly he removed the cloth from his eyes, and the king recognized him as one of the prophets. ⁴² He said to him, "Thus said the Lord: Because you have set free the man whom I doomed, your life shall be forfeit for his life and your people for his people." ⁴³ Dispirited and sullen, the king left for home and came to Samaria.

31–34: Ben-hadad capitulates totally to Ahab. Following his servants' advice, he humbled himself and referred to himself as Ahab's *servant.* Ahab, however, refers to him by the term *brother,* signaling that he regards the defeated Aramean as an equal partner and inviting him into his chariot where terms for Ben-hadad's freedom must have been discussed. Ahab is given cities lost by his father to the Arameans and market concessions in Damascus. Although victorious in the battle of Aphek, Ahab's negotiating position was weak. Since the days of Baasha, Arameans had retained control of northern Israelite tribal territories in upper Galilee and the eastern part of lower Galilee (cf. 15.20). 35–42: Ahab had no right to spare those whom he had not defeated. According to the oracle of v. 28, God, not Ahab, defeated Ben-hadad. Consequently, Ben-hadad fell into the category of one doomed (v. 42), i.e., dedicated by God to destruction (see 1 Sam. ch 15). The prophet's use of a parable to get the king to pronounce judgment on himself is similar to Nathan's ploy in the case of Uriah and David (2 Sam. 12.1–12).

a-a Meaning of Heb. uncertain.

21 [The following events] occurred sometime after-ward: Naboth the Jezreelite owned a vineyard in Jezreel, adjoining the palace of King Ahab of Samaria. [2] Ahab said to Naboth, "Give me your vineyard, so that I may have it as a vegetable garden, since it is right next to my palace. I will give you a better vineyard in exchange; or, if you prefer, I will pay you the price in money." [3] But Naboth replied, "The LORD forbid that I should give up to you what I have inherited from my fathers!" [4] Ahab went home dispirited and sullen because of the answer that Na-both the Jezreelite had given him: "I will not give up to you what I have inherited from my fathers!" He lay down on his bed and turned away his face, and he would not eat. [5] His wife Jezebel came to him and asked him, "Why are you so dispirited that you won't eat?" [6] So he told her, "I spoke to Naboth the Jezreelite and proposed to him, 'Sell me your vineyard for money, or if you prefer, I'll give you another vineyard in exchange'; but he answered, 'I will not give my vineyard to you.' " [7] His wife Jezebel said to him, "Now is the time to show yourself king over Is-rael. Rise and eat something, and be cheerful; I will get the vineyard of Naboth the Jezreelite for you."

[8] So she wrote letters in Ahab's name and sealed them with his seal, and sent the letters to the elders and the no-bles who lived in the same town with Naboth. [9] In the letters she wrote as follows: "Proclaim a fast and seat Naboth at the front of the assembly. [10] And seat two scoundrels opposite him, and let them testify against him: 'You have reviled God and king!' Then take him out and stone him to death."

[11] His townsmen—the elders and nobles who lived in his town—did as Jezebel had instructed them, just as was written in the letters she had sent them: [12] They pro-claimed a fast and seated Naboth at the front of the as-sembly. [13] Then the two scoundrels came and sat down opposite him; and the scoundrels testified against Naboth publicly as follows: "Naboth has reviled God and king." Then they took him outside the town and stoned him to death. [14] Word was sent to Jezebel: "Naboth has been stoned to death." [15] As soon as Jezebel heard that Naboth had been stoned to death, she said to Ahab, "Go and take possession of the vineyard which Naboth the Jezreelite re-fused to sell you for money; for Naboth is no longer alive, he is dead." [16] When Ahab heard that Naboth was dead, Ahab set out for the vineyard of Naboth the Jezreelite to take possession of it.

[17] Then the word of the LORD came to Elijah the Tishbite: [18] "Go down and confront King Ahab of Israel who [re-

21.1–29: Naboth's vineyard. This story reintroduces Elijah into the narrative. In contrast to the pre-ceding story, in which Ahab prof-ited by not putting to death one who had been doomed by God, here he profits by passively allow-ing corrupt courts acting in the name of God and king to execute an innocent person. **1–3:** Ahab's request to purchase or trade for Naboth's *vineyard* next to his *palace* was neither unreasonable nor ille-gal (Lev. 25.29–30), but Naboth may have refused because he did not wish to sell his inherited land (v. 3). **8–13:** Here too, Jezebel is blamed (16.31). In relating how Jezebel corrupted the legal system using two corroborating witnesses (cf. Deut. 17.6; 19.15), the pro-phetic story reveals that Israel did have a legal system with defined laws and procedures, some of which are found in the Torah. The crime of which Naboth is accused, and its prescribed punishment, is only partially known from the Torah (Lev. 24.15–16). No Torah legislation explicitly criminalizes cursing the king (but see Exod. 22.27).

sides] in Samaria. He is now in Naboth's vineyard; he has gone down there to take possession of it. ¹⁹Say to him, 'Thus said the LORD: Would you murder and take possession? Thus said the LORD: In the very place where the dogs lapped up Naboth's blood, the dogs will lap up your blood too.' "

²⁰Ahab said to Elijah, "So you have found me, my enemy?" "Yes, I have found you," he replied. "Because you have committed yourself to doing what is evil in the sight of the LORD, ²¹I will bring disaster upon you. I will make a clean sweep of you, I will cut off from Israel every male belonging to Ahab,ᵃbond and free.ᵃ ²²And I will make your house like the House of Jeroboam son of Nebat and like the House of Baasha son of Ahijah, because of the provocation you have caused by leading Israel to sin. ²³And the LORD has also spoken concerning Jezebel: 'The dogs shall devour Jezebel in the fieldᵇ of Jezreel. ²⁴All of Ahab's line who die in the town shall be devoured by dogs, and all who die in the open country shall be devoured by the birds of the sky.' "

(²⁵Indeed, there never was anyone like Ahab, who committed himself to doing what was displeasing to the LORD, at the instigation of his wife Jezebel. ²⁶He acted most abominably, straying after the fetishes just like the Amorites, whom the LORD had dispossessed before the Israelites.)

²⁷When Ahab heard these words, he rent his clothes and put sackcloth on his body. He fasted and lay in sackcloth and walked about subdued. ²⁸Then the word of the LORD came to Elijah the Tishbite: ²⁹"Have you seen how Ahab has humbled himself before Me? Because he has humbled himself before Me, I will not bring the disaster in his lifetime; I will bring the disaster upon his house in his son's time."

22 ᶜThere was a lull ofᶜ three years, with no war between Aram and Israel. ²In the third year, King Jehoshaphat of Judah came to visit the king of Israel. ³The king of Israel said to his courtiers, "You know that Ramoth-gilead belongs to us, and yet we do nothing to recover it from the hands of the king of Aram." ⁴And he said to Jehoshaphat, "Will you come with me to battle at Ramoth-gilead?" Jehoshaphat answered the king of Israel, "I will do what you do; my troops shall be your troops,

19-24: Elijah's denunciation of Ahab flows into a doom-laden series of predictions: *dogs will lap up Ahab's blood* (fulfilled in 22.38); dogs will *devour Jezebel* (fulfilled in 2 Kings 9.33–36); Ahab's dynasty will be destroyed (cf. 20.42; fulfilled in 2 Kings 10.11, 17). **24:** *Devoured . . . dogs . . . birds,* see 16.4 n. **25-26:** The author's comment about Ahab is not anchored in the context of the Naboth story. It addresses Ahab's idolatrous behavior and attributes part of it, at least, to the instigation of his foreign wife. The author used the same device, intended to ameliorate but not forgive the offensive activities, in commenting on Solomon (11.4–5). **27-28:** In view of Ahab's sincere contrition, God tells Elijah—who does not tell Ahab— that the destruction of his dynasty, announced to Ahab in vv. 21–22, will not occur in his lifetime. This qualification of the earlier pronouncement allows the author to maintain congruency between a prediction that was part of an early prophetic story and recorded events. It highlights the power of repentance while emphasizing that misdeeds must at some point be punished.

22.1-40: The battle for Ramoth-gilead. This ch resumes the historical narrative about the Aramean wars from ch 20. Ahab's final war against the Arameans was conducted as a joint undertaking with Jehoshaphat of Judah, with whom he was linked through the marriage of their children (2 Kings 8.18). Possibly their common interest was in weakening the Arameans so that Israel could reassert its authority in Galilee and north Transjordan while Judah could strengthen its influence in Edom and other parts of southern Transjordan. **1:** According to Assyrian sources, Ahab joined a coalition of thirteen kings against Shalmaneser III of Assyria, who planned to conquer territories west of the Euphrates. Shalmaneser's Monolith Inscription, which covers his early western campaigns, notes that Ahab's contribution of 2,000 chari-

a-a *See note at 14.10.*

b *So nine Heb. mss. and the parallel 2 Kings 9.36, as well as Targum and other ancient versions. Most texts read here "rampart."*

c-c *Lit. "They remained."*

my horses shall be your horses." [5] But Jehoshaphat said further to the king of Israel, "Please, first inquire of the LORD."

[6] So the king of Israel gathered the prophets, about four hundred men, and asked them, "Shall I march upon Ramoth-gilead for battle, or shall I not?" "March," they said, "and the Lord will deliver [it] into Your Majesty's hands." [7] Then Jehoshaphat asked, "Isn't there another prophet of the LORD here through whom we can inquire?" [8] And the king of Israel answered Jehoshaphat, "There is one more man through whom we can inquire of the LORD; but I hate him, because he never prophesies anything good for me, but only misfortune—Micaiah son of Imlah." But King Jehoshaphat said, "Don't say that, Your Majesty." [9] So the king of Israel summoned an officer and said, "Bring Micaiah son of Imlah at once."

[10] The king of Israel and King Jehoshaphat of Judah were seated on their thrones, arrayed in their robes, on the threshing floor at the entrance of the gate of Samaria; and all the prophets were prophesying before them. [11] Zedekiah son of Chenaanah had provided himself with iron horns; and he said, "Thus said the LORD: With these you shall gore the Arameans till you make an end of them." [12] And all the other prophets were prophesying similarly, "March upon Ramoth-gilead and triumph! The LORD will deliver it into Your Majesty's hands."

[13] The messenger who had gone to summon Micaiah said to him: "Look, the words of the prophets are with one accord favorable to the king. Let your word be like that of the rest of them; speak a favorable word." [14] "As the LORD lives," Micaiah answered, "I will speak only what the LORD tells me." [15] When he came before the king, the king said to him, "Micaiah, shall we march upon Ramoth-gilead for battle, or shall we not?" He answered him, "March and triumph! The LORD will deliver [it] into Your Majesty's hands." [16] The king said to him, "How many times must I adjure you to tell me nothing but the truth in the name of the LORD?" [17] Then he said, "I saw all Israel scattered over the hills like sheep without a shepherd; and the LORD said, 'These have no master; let everyone return to his home in safety.' " [18] "Didn't I tell you," said the king of Israel to Jehoshaphat, "that he would not prophesy good fortune for me, but only misfortune?" [19] But [Micaiah] said, "I call upon you to hear the word of the LORD! I saw the LORD seated upon His throne, with all the host of heaven standing in attendance to the right and to the left of Him. [20] The LORD asked, 'Who will entice Ahab so that he will march and fall at Ramoth-gilead?' Then one said

ots and 10,000 infantrymen comprised the largest single contingent. At the Battle of Qarqar, near the Orontes River, in 853 BCE, the coalition successfully halted Assyria's advance into western Asia. The author of Kings makes no mention of Ahab's crucial role or of his success at Qarqar. Since the Arameans faced a continual threat from Assyria to their northeast, Ahab may have thought that circumstances afforded him a unique opportunity to reassert his authority easily in territories to which he had claim. **3:** *Ramoth-gilead* in Transjordan had been a central city in one of Solomon's prefectures (4.13), a Levitical city (Josh. 21.36), and a city of refuge (Deut. 4.43; Josh. 20.8). **5–28:** The prophetic consultation. **5–6:** Despite the impression left by the Elijah stories that most of the prophets had been killed in Jezebel's pogrom, in this prophetic story the king of Israel—whose name has been suppressed to keep the focus on the prophets and good king Jehoshaphat—had no problem arranging a consultation with 400 prophets. **13:** Micaiah, who has clashed with the king of Israel, most likely Ahab, in the past (v. 8), is coached to deliver a favorable oracle. **19–23:** A similar scene of the divine retinue is found in Job chs 1–2. Micaiah does not doubt the integrity of the prophets who predicted victory. He explains that they uttered what God wanted the king to hear, a lie intended to lead Ahab to his downfall. Thus, these are true prophets espousing falsehoods so that Ahab will be punished according to God's will. Divine *spirit* ("ruaḥ") is frequently associated with prophecy.

thus and another said thus, 21 until a certain spirit came forward and stood before the LORD and said, 'I will entice him.' 'How?' the LORD asked him. 22 And he replied, 'I will go out and be a lying spirit in the mouth of all his prophets.' Then He said, 'You will entice and you will prevail. Go out and do it.' 23 So the LORD has put a lying spirit in the mouth of all these prophets of yours; for the LORD has decreed disaster upon you."

24 Thereupon Zedekiah son of Chenaanah stepped up and struck Micaiah on the cheek, and demanded, "Which way did the spirit of the LORD pass from me to speak with you?" 25 And Micaiah replied, "You'll find out on the day when you try to hide in the innermost room." 26 Then the king of Israel said, "Take Micaiah and turn him over to Amon, the city's governor, and to Prince Joash, 27 and say, 'The king's orders are: Put this fellow in prison, and let his fare be scant bread and scant water until I come home safe.' " 28 To which Micaiah retorted, "If you ever come home safe, the LORD has not spoken through me." ª-He said further, "Listen, all you peoples!"-ª

29 So the king of Israel and King Jehoshaphat of Judah marched upon Ramoth-gilead. 30 The king of Israel said to Jehoshaphat, ᵇ-"Disguise yourself and go-ᵇ into the battle; but you, wear your robes." So the king of Israel went into the battle disguised. 31 Now the king of Aram had instructed his thirty-two chariot officers: "Don't attack anyone, small or great, except the king of Israel." 32 So when the chariot officers saw Jehoshaphat, whom they took for the king of Israel, they turned upon him to attack him, and Jehoshaphat cried out. 33 And when the chariot officers became aware that he was not the king of Israel, they turned back from pursuing him. 34 Then a man drew his bow at random and he hit the king of Israel between ᶜ-the plates of-ᶜ the armor; and he said to his charioteer, "Turn ᵈ-the horses-ᵈ around and get me ᵉ-behind the lines;-ᵉ I'm wounded." 35 The battle ᶜ-raged all day long,-ᶜ and the king remained propped up in the chariot facing Aram; the blood from the wound ran down into the hollow of the chariot, and at dusk he died. 36 As the sun was going down, a shout went through the army: "Every man to his own town! Every man to his own district."

29: Jehoshaphat joins Ahab. On the one hand, 400 prophets had predicted success; on the other, nothing Micaiah said threatened him personally. 34: Ahab was killed by a random arrow, not by the Aramean charioteers searching to kill him. The author includes this piece of information to demonstrate the role of Providence in the fall of an arrow. 39: A standard concluding summary to the reigns of Israelite kings. *Ivory palace*, one with a room containing rich ivory inlays, such as were found in wood panels and furniture excavated at Samaria (cf. Amos 3.15; 6.4).

22.41–51: The reign of Jehoshaphat is presented briefly, omitting details of the Aramean campaign, while inserting a small list of other events into the standard formulary. Chronicles contains an extensive account of Jehoshaphat's judicial initiatives (2 Chron. ch 19), but the historicity of this account is debated. 44: There was no abatement in the popular practice of sacrificing and offering incense at the shrines. It continued even though the Temple was a well-established institution. The author mentions this as a blemish on the record but not as a fault of the king, who did not promote the open shrines. 45: *Submitted* (Heb "yashlem") is better translated "made peace" or "caused peace." Rashi thinks that it was necessary for the author to mention it because his father Asa had been at war with Baasha, king of Israel. Radak opines that the author intended this to be understood as a second blemish on Jehoshaphat's record, coming, as it does, after the first. 47: *Male prostitutes*, see 14.24 n. 48–51: Mention is made of Judah's control over Edom because *Ezion-geber*, from which Jehoshaphat had planned to launch his *Tarshish ships*, was an Edomite port (9.26). Apparently the Red Sea trade had stopped sometime after the death of Solomon.

a-a *Perhaps a notation suggesting that Micaiah was identical with Micah, whose prophecies begin, "Listen, all you peoples," Mic. 1.2.*

b-b *Targum and Septuagint read, "I will disguise myself and go."*

c-c *Meaning of Heb. uncertain.*

d-d *Lit. "your hand," because horses are guided by a pull on the appropriate rein; cf. 2 Kings 9.23.*

e-e *Lit. "outside the camp."*

³⁷ So the king died ^{a-}and was brought^{-a} to Samaria. They buried the king in Samaria, ³⁸ and they flushed out the chariot at the pool of Samaria. Thus the dogs lapped up his blood and the whores bathed [in it], in accordance with the word that the LORD had spoken.^b

³⁹ The other events of Ahab's reign, and all his actions— the ivory palace that he built and all the towns that he fortified—are all recorded in the Annals of the Kings of Israel. ⁴⁰ Ahab slept with his fathers, and his son Ahaziah succeeded him as king.

⁴¹ Jehoshaphat son of Asa had become king of Judah in the fourth year of King Ahab of Israel. ⁴² Jehoshaphat was thirty-five years old when he became king, and he reigned in Jerusalem for twenty-five years. His mother's name was Azubah daughter of Shilhi. ⁴³ He followed closely the course of his father Asa and did not deviate from it, doing what was pleasing to the LORD. ⁴⁴ However, the shrines did not cease to function; the people still sacrificed and offered at the shrines. ⁴⁵ And further, Jehoshaphat submitted to the king of Israel. ⁴⁶ As for the other events of Jehoshaphat's reign and the valor he displayed in battle, they are recorded in the Annals of the Kings of Judah. (⁴⁷ He also stamped out the remaining male prostitutes who had survived in the land from the time of his father Asa.)

⁴⁸ There was no king in Edom; ^{c-}a viceroy acted as king. ⁴⁹ Jehoshaphat^{-c} constructed Tarshish^d ships to sail to Ophir for gold. But he did not sail because the ships were wrecked at Ezion-geber. ⁵⁰ Then Ahaziah son of Ahab proposed to Jehoshaphat, "Let my servants sail on the ships with your servants"; but Jehoshaphat would not agree. ⁵¹ Jehoshaphat slept with his fathers and was buried with his fathers in the city of his father David, and his son Jehoram succeeded him as king.

⁵² [Meanwhile,] Ahaziah son of Ahab had become king of Israel, in Samaria, in the seventeenth year of King Jehoshaphat of Judah; he reigned over Israel two years. ⁵³ He did what was displeasing to the LORD, following in the footsteps of his father and his mother, and in those of Jeroboam son of Nebat who had caused Israel to sin. ⁵⁴ He worshiped Baal and bowed down to him; he vexed the LORD, the God of Israel, just as his father had done.

22.52–54: Ahaziah's reign.
Though Ahaziah is ostensibly credited with a two-year reign, the chronological information likely means that he reigned for several months in two different calendar years. Radak notes that v. 52 states that he ascended the throne in Jehoshaphat's seventeenth year while 2 Kings 3.1 indicates that Jehoram, Ahaziah's brother, came to power in Jehoshaphat's eighteenth year. Despite this, the author evaluates his reign negatively not only because he followed in the footsteps of Jeroboam, but also because he adopted the practices of his own parents, Ahab and Jezebel, serving and worshipping Baal. His story continues in 2 Kings 1.

---

a-a Lit. "he came."
b Cf. 21.19.
c-c Emendation yields "the viceroy of King Jehoshaphat."
d See note at 10.22.

מלכים ב

2 Kings

FIRST AND SECOND KINGS were originally one book. For information about 2 Kings, see the introduction preceding 1 Kings.

1 After Ahab's death, Moab rebelled against Israel. ² Ahaziah fell through the lattice in his upper chamber at Samaria and was injured. So he sent messengers, whom he instructed: "Go inquire of Baal-zebub, the god of Ekron, whether I shall recover from this injury." ³ But an angel of the LORD said to Elijah the Tishbite, "Go and confront the messengers of the king of Samaria and say to them, 'Is there no God in Israel that you go to inquire of Baal-zebub, the god of Ekron? ⁴ Assuredly, thus said the LORD: You shall not ᵃrise from the bed you are lying on,⁻ᵃ but you shall die.' " And Elijah went.

⁵ The messengers returned to Ahaziah;ᵇ and he asked, "Why have you come back?" ⁶ They answered him, "A man came toward us and said to us, 'Go back to the king who sent you, and say to him: Thus said the LORD: Is there no God in Israel that you must send to inquire of Baal-zebub, the god of Ekron? Assuredly, you shall not rise from the bed you are lying on, but shall die.' " ⁷ "What sort of man was it," he asked them, "who came toward you and said these things to you?" ⁸ "A hairy man," they replied, "with a leather belt tied around his waist." "That's Elijah the Tishbite!" he said.

⁹ Then he sent to him a captain of fifty with his fifty men. He climbed up to him, and found him sitting at the top of a hill. "Man of God," he said to him, "by order of the king, come down!" ¹⁰ Elijah replied to the captain of the fifty, "If I am a man of God, let fire come down from

1.1–2.12: The final cycle of Elijah stories. 1.1: Moab's rebellion after Ahab's death in the reign of Jehoram (see 3.4–5). It is mentioned here because Ahaziah died, Jehoram came to power, and Moab rebelled in the same calendar year (see 1 Kings 22.52).

1.2–18: The death of Ahaziah. Ahaziah, after being critically injured in Samaria, solicits a prognosis from *Baal-zebub, the god of Ekron*. This evolves into a confrontation with Elijah like the one between Elijah and Ahab (1 Kings 18.16–18). **2:** The *lattice* was probably a window covering made of thin strips of wood or reeds in a loose net in order to let in light and air while still providing some privacy; there were no glass windows in this period. *Baal-zebub,* "Lord of the flies," a god worshipped at Ekron, may have been known as a healer. This form of the name, however, may be the author's purposeful corruption of a likely original "Baal-zevul," "Lord of glory/dominion/majesty," understood as a reference to Baal. The word meaning "prince/glory," "zevul," is found as a personal name in Judg. 9.30 and is part of the name of Ahaziah's mother, Jezebel. In the New Testament, Jesus denies that he casts out demons, i.e., heals, in the

a-a Lit. *"descend from the bed you have mounted."*
b Heb. *"him."*

heaven and consume you with your fifty men!" And fire came down from heaven and consumed him and his fifty men. ¹¹ The king then sent to him another captain with his fifty men; and he ᵃaddressed himᵃ as follows: "Man of God, by order of the king, come down at once!" ¹² But Elijah answered him, "If I am a man of God, let fire come down from heaven and consume you with your fifty men!" And fire of God came down from heaven and consumed him and his fifty men. ¹³ Then he sent a third captain of fifty with his fifty men. The third captain of fifty climbed to the top, knelt before Elijah, and implored him, saying, "Oh, man of God, please have regard for my life and the lives of these fifty servants of yours! ¹⁴ Already fire has come from heaven and consumed the first two captains of fifty and their men;ᵇ I beg you, have regard for my life!"

¹⁵ Then the angel of the LORD said to Elijah, "Go down with him, do not be afraid of him." So he rose and went down with him to the king. ¹⁶ He said to him, "Because you sent messengers to inquire of Baal-zebub the god of Ekron—as if there were no God in Israel whose word you could seek—assuredly, you shall not rise from the bed which you are lying on; but you shall die."

¹⁷ And [Ahaziah] died, according to the word of the LORD that Elijah had spoken. Jehoramᶜ succeeded him as king, in the second year of King Jehoram son of Jehoshaphat of Judah, for he had no son. ¹⁸ The other events of Ahaziah's reign [and] his actions are recorded in the Annals of the Kings of Israel.

2 When the LORD was about to take Elijah up to heaven in a whirlwind, Elijah and Elisha had set out from Gilgal. ² Elijah said to Elisha, "Stay here, for the LORD has sent me on to Bethel." "As the LORD lives and as you live," said Elisha, "I will not leave you." So they went down to Bethel. ³ Disciples of the prophets at Bethel came out to

a-a Emendation yields "went up and said to him," cf. v. 9.
b Lit. "fifties."   c Brother of Ahaziah.

name of Baal-zevul (see Matt. 12.24–27). The reason that the author or later scribe may have changed the name is because in Solomon's prayer, the Temple is called a "house of zevul" ("A stately House") (1 Kings 8.13). *Ekron*, the northernmost city of the Philistine pentapolis, about 37 km (22 mi) east of Jerusalem, may

have been under Judah's control at this time. Excavations at the site indicate that its material culture mixed Aegean with local elements. **8:** The identifying physical characteristic of Elijah was most likely his hair. The leather belt around his garment may have been atypical, but was not a rare accoutrement. Ahaziah recognized him

not only by the physical description but also through the indictment in the message. **9–15:** The first two groups are destroyed miraculously because their captains failed to respect the *man of God* commanding him imperiously in the name of the king. The third captain humbled himself and made no request. In this story, Elijah does not pray for a miraculous fire; it comes, as if at his bidding. The Heb text is built around the pun between *man of God, "'ish 'elohim,"* and *fire of God, "'esh 'elohim."* **9–10:** The *captain* ordered that he *come down.* Elijah had punishing *fire come down* instead. **17:** The fulfillment statement here indicates that the author did not connect Ahaziah's death automatically to his critically injured condition. Had Ahaziah sought forgiveness and healing from the God of Israel, he would not have died. At one and the same time, physical and metaphysical laws of causation were operating in nature. Ahaziah was the third generation of the Omri dynasty. The notice that, in the absence of a son, rule passed to a brother, indicates that in the Northern Kingdom at this time kings were acclaimed according to the customs governing the inheritance of property.

2.1–12: Stories about the death of Elijah show the smooth transition of authority from one prophet to another, and with it, responsibility for groups of disciples living in different communities. Introductory v. 1 mentions the *whirlwind,* which appears in v. 11. **1:** Elijah did not die. See also the notation about Enoch in Gen 5.24. His heavenly assumption became the stuff of many legends in Judaism and traditions about him in prophetic circles. These legends, which suggest that Elijah periodically returns to the earth, and is especially associated with the arrival of the Messiah, already have a late biblical precedent (Mal. 3.23–24). **3:** The *disciples of the prophets* were radical monotheists following the teachings of prophets like Elijah, but were not necessarily prophets

Elisha and said to him, "Do you know that the LORD will take your master *away from you*[a] today?" He replied, "I know it, too; be silent."

⁴ Then Elijah said to him, "Elisha, stay here, for the LORD has sent me on to Jericho." "As the LORD lives and as you live," said Elisha, "I will not leave you." So they went on to Jericho. ⁵ The disciples of the prophets who were at Jericho came over to Elisha and said to him, "Do you know that the LORD will take your master *away from you*[a] today?" He replied, "I know it, too; be silent."

⁶ Elijah said to him, "Stay here, for the LORD has sent me on to the Jordan." "As the LORD lives and as you live, I will not leave you," he said, and the two of them went on. ⁷ Fifty men of the disciples of the prophets followed and stood by at a distance from them as the two of them stopped at the Jordan. ⁸ Thereupon Elijah took his mantle and, rolling it up, he struck the water; it divided to the right and left, so that the two of them crossed over on dry land. ⁹ As they were crossing, Elijah said to Elisha, "Tell me, what can I do for you before I am taken from you?" Elisha answered, "Let a *double portion*[b] of your spirit pass on to me." ¹⁰ "You have asked a difficult thing," he said. "If you see me as I am being taken from you, this will be granted to you; if not, it will not." ¹¹ As they kept on walking and talking, a fiery chariot with fiery horses suddenly appeared and separated one from the other; and Elijah went up to heaven in a whirlwind. ¹² Elisha saw it, and he cried out, "Oh, father, father! Israel's chariots and horsemen!" When he could no longer see him, he grasped his garments and rent them in two.

¹³ He picked up Elijah's mantle, which had dropped from him; and he went back and stood on the bank of the Jordan. ¹⁴ Taking the mantle which had dropped from Elijah, he struck the water and said, "Where is the LORD, the God of Elijah?" As he too struck the water, it parted to the

a-a Lit. "from your head."   b-b Lit. "two-thirds"; cf. Zech. 13.8.

name of his father) points out that, according to Deut. 21.17, the eldest son inherits a portion twice that of other brothers dividing their father's property. Elisha, therefore, is not asking for twice the spirit of Elijah, but for the larger amount due the eldest. (For the division of the spirit, cf. Num 11.17, 24–26.) Several rabbinic sources, however, understand double as literal, and suggest that Elijah performed eight miracles, and Elisha sixteen. Many of the miracles performed by Elijah and Elisha are similar, indicating that they shared the same *spirit* (see 1 Kings 22.19–33 n.). **12:** In addition to indicating a biological relationship, *father* indicates a tutorial one: "instructor, counselor, teacher, leader" (Gen. 45.8; Judg. 17.10; Jer. 31.9). *Israel's chariots and horsemen:* The same title, possibly an epithet of Elijah as Israel's defender, is addressed to Elisha when he is about to die in 13.14. In the case of Elisha, it may have been based on the incident recorded in 6.17–18. No similar story is recorded about Elijah.

2.13–13.20: The Elisha stories are presented in cycles and interspersed between historical and prophetic narratives, citations from chronicles, and remarks of the author. In contrast to the four major Elijah stories and the story of his death, there are fifteen Elisha stories of varying length. Though many of their activities are similar, Elisha is generally much more sympathetic to the Israelite king than his mentor, Elijah.

2.13–25: The first cycle of stories indicates how Elisha demonstrated that he was a prophet like Elijah and his spiritual heir. **13–14:** Elisha tests himself to determine if he inherited spirit from Elijah. Using his teacher's *mantle* he smites the water, invokes the *God of Elijah*, and smites the water again. The Jordan splits and he crosses on dry land towards Jericho. **15:** The *disciples of the prophets at Jericho* see and declare him heir of Elijah's spirit. He received more than the double portion that he requested (v. 9).

themselves. Many joined to live together in small communities. Somehow the groups at Bethel and Jericho (v. 5) knew that *the LORD* was about to *take* Elijah. They do not use words indicating death. **4:** In view of 1 Kings 16.34 and Josh. 6.26, the author must have understood that *Jericho* was not a cursed city after its rebuilding. Excavations at Tel es-Sultan, identified with Jericho of the biblical period, have discovered only sparse

finds from the 9th through 7th centuries BCE. **8:** Elijah uses his mantle to perform a miracle at the Jordan similar to Moses' parting of the waters (Exod. 14.21–22). Crossing the Jordan east of Jericho indicates that the place of Elijah's assumption was near Mt. Nebo, where Moses had died (Deut. 34.1–6). Thus, in his death, as in earlier texts, Elijah is patterned after Moses. **9:** *A double portion,* see translators' note b-b. Radak (in the right and to the left, and Elisha crossed over. ¹⁵ When the disciples of the prophets at Jericho saw him from a distance, they exclaimed, "The spirit of Elijah has settled on Elisha!" And they went to meet him and bowed low before him to the ground.

¹⁶ They said to him, "Your servants have fifty able men with them. Let them go and look for your master; perhaps the spirit of the Lᴏʀᴅ has carried him off and cast him upon some mountain or into some valley." "Do not send them," he replied. ¹⁷ But they kept pressing him for a long time, until he said, "Send them." So they sent out fifty

Places associated with the Elisha narratives. The dashed line shows the approximate boundaries between Israel, Judah, and Philistia.

men, who searched for three days but did not find him. [18] They came back to him while he was still in Jericho; and he said to them, "I told you not to go."

[19] The men of the town said to Elisha, "Look, the town is a pleasant place to live in, as my lord can see; but the water is bad and the land causes bereavement." [20] He responded, "Bring me a new dish and put salt in it." They brought it to him; [21] he went to the spring and threw salt into it. And he said, "Thus said the LORD: I heal this water; no longer shall death and bereavement come from it!" [22] The water has remained wholesome to this day, in accordance with the word spoken by Elisha.

[23] From there he went up to Bethel. As he was going up the road, some little boys came out of the town and jeered at him, saying, "Go away, baldhead! Go away, baldhead!" [24] He turned around and looked at them and cursed them in the name of the LORD. Thereupon, two she-bears came out of the woods and mangled forty-two of the children. [25] He went on from there to Mount Carmel, and from there he returned to Samaria.

3 Jehoram son of Ahab became king of Israel in Samaria in the eighteenth year of King Jehoshaphat of Judah; and he reigned twelve years. [2] He did what was displeasing to the LORD, yet not like his father and mother, for he removed the pillars of Baal that his father had made. [3] However, he clung to the sins which Jeroboam son of Nebat caused Israel to commit; he did not depart from them.

[4] Now King Mesha of Moab was a sheep breeder; and he used to pay as tribute to the king of Israel ᵃ-a hundred thousand lambs and the wool of a hundred thousand rams.-ᵃ [5] But when Ahab died, the king of Moab rebelled against the king of Israel. [6] So King Jehoram promptly set out from Samaria and mustered all Israel. [7] At the same time, he sent this message to King Jehoshaphat of Judah: "The king of Moab has rebelled against me; will you come with me to make war on Moab?" He replied, "I will go. I will do what you do: my troops shall be your troops, my horses shall be your horses." [8] And he asked, "Which route shall we take?" [Jehoram] replied, "The road through the wilderness of Edom."

[9] So the king of Israel, the king of Judah, and the king of Edom set out, and they marched for seven days until they

19–22: A magical "healing" story in which Elisha does and says things that, in combination, produce the desired result. All is done on his own authority, with no prayer for healing. Cf. 1.5–14. A long tradition points to Ein es-Sultan in contemporary Jericho as Elisha's spring. In its present form, the story is etiological, explaining the origin of the freshwater spring in Jericho that makes the whole region agriculturally rich. **23:** In calling Elisha *baldhead,* the boys seem to be mocking him; they may actually, however, be insulting him as a prophet by comparing him derogatorily to Elijah, who was hairy (1.8). Local tradition places the site of this story near the town of Deir Dibwan, "Lair of the two bears," about 1.5 km (1 mile) east of Bethel. **24:** Here, as in vv. 19–22, Elisha does and says something to produce the desired result. First he turns and looks at the boys, then curses them *in the name of the LORD.* He does not pray that they be punished, although he himself calls down the punishment. The bears did not kill and eat. The large carnage is mentioned as an indication that their behavior was not natural. This story, like the Elijah story in 1.9–16, emphasizes that the man of God must be treated with proper respect.

3.1–27: The Moabite war and Elisha's prophecy initiate the complex of Elisha stories in which the author mixed prophetic tales with archival materials.

3.1–3: Introduction to the reign of Jehoram son of Ahab. The author notes to the king's credit his removal of the pillars of Baal made by his father. This is the first notice that such pillars had been constructed. See also 10.26.

3.4–27: The rebellion of Mesha. The Mesha stele, found in 1868, provides a summary of this king's various achievements arranged in a rough chronological order. It notes the occupation of Moab in the days of Omri and his son, i.e.,

---

a-a Or "the wool of 100,000 lambs and of 100,000 rams."

rounded [the tip of the Dead Sea]; and there was no water left for the army or for the animals that were with them. ¹⁰ "Alas!" cried the king of Israel. "The Lord has brought these three kings together only to deliver them into the hands of Moab." ¹¹ But Jehoshaphat said, "Isn't there a prophet of the Lord here, through whom we may inquire of the Lord?" One of the courtiers of the king of Israel spoke up and said, "Elisha son of Shaphat, who ª‑poured water on the hands of‑ª Elijah, is here." ¹² "The word of the Lord is with him," said Jehoshaphat. So the king of Israel and Jehoshaphat and the king of Edom went down to him. ¹³ Elisha said to the king of Israel, "What have you to do with me? Go to your father's prophets or your mother's prophets." But the king of Israel said, "Don't [say that], for the Lord has brought these three kings together only to deliver them into the hands of Moab." ¹⁴ "As the Lord of Hosts lives, whom I serve," Elisha answered, "were it not that I respect King Jehoshaphat of Judah, I wouldn't look at you or notice you. ¹⁵ Now then, get me a musician."

As the musician played, the hand of the Lord came upon him, ¹⁶ and he said, "Thus said the Lord: This wadi shall be full of pools. ¹⁷ For thus said the Lord: You shall see no wind, you shall see no rain, and yet the wadi shall be filled with water; and you and your cattle and your pack animals shall drink. ¹⁸ And this is but a slight thing in the sight of the Lord, for He will also deliver Moab into your hands. ¹⁹ You shall conquer every fortified town and every splendid city; you shall fell every good tree and stop up all wells of water; and every fertile field you shall ruin with stones." ²⁰ And in the morning, when it was time to present the meal offering, water suddenly came from the direction of Edom and the land was covered by the water.

²¹ Meanwhile, all the Moabites had heard that the kings were advancing to make war on them; ᵇ‑every man old enough to bear arms‑ᵇ rallied, and they stationed themselves at the border. ²² Next morning, when they rose, the sun was shining over the water, and from the distance the water appeared to the Moabites as red as blood. ²³ "That's blood!" they said. "The kings must have fought among themselves and killed each other. Now to the spoil, Moab!"

²⁴ They entered the Israelite camp, and the Israelites arose and attacked the Moabites, who fled before them.

a-a I.e., personally attended.
b-b Lit. "from all those old enough to gird on a sword."

Ahab. It indicates that Mesha undertook actions against Israelites in occupied northern Moab before the death of Ahab. It may have been only after the death of Ahab that Mesha withheld tribute (1.1; 3.5), slaughtered people from the tribe of Gad in the city of Ataroth (noted on the stele), and moved aggressively north of the Arnon river. **7:** *King Jehoshaphat's* interest in assisting Jehoram may have been to discourage Judah's vassal, Edom, from seeking its own independence (cf. 1 Kings 22.48). In addition to national interests, Jehoshaphat had married his son Joram to Ahab's daughter (2 Kings 8.18). **8:** Jehoram's strategy was to march through Judah around the southern edge of the Dead Sea and approach Moab from the south. All of Mesha's activities, and presumably the majority of his forces, were north of the Arnon, but the core of his kingdom was south of the river up to the Edomite border. **9–10:** The success of Jehoram's strategy was dependent on an adequate supply of local water. The inadequate supply leads him to think that it is part of a divine plan against his coalition. **11–14:** Jehoshaphat, who wished to consult *a prophet* (cf. 1 Kings 22.7), knows of Elisha by reputation. Elisha, impolite and rude to the king of Israel (vv. 13–14), responds to the request for an oracle only because Jehoshaphat is also endangered by what may occur. **15:** The *musician* helps produce the atmosphere conducive for a divine visitation (cf. 1 Sam 10.5–6). **16:** The *pools* (Heb "gevim") are natural sinkholes and fissures in the limestone floor of the wadis that retain large amounts of water after a runoff (cf. Jer. 14.3). **22:** In the morning, the reflection of red sandstone mountains off the pooled waters is interpreted by the Moabites as *blood.* **24–25:** The three armies pursue Moabites north from the border, destroying fields, stopping wells, and uprooting fruit trees in fulfillment of Elisha's prediction (v. 19). The Moabites take shelter in *Kirhareseth,* identified with modern el-Kerak, a site on a high hill with *a*They advanced, constantly attacking*-a* the Moabites, 25 and they destroyed the towns. Every man threw a stone into each fertile field, so that it was covered over; and they stopped up every spring and felled every fruit tree. *b*Only the walls of*-b* Kir-hareseth were left, and then the slingers surrounded it and attacked it. 26 Seeing that the battle was going against him, the king of Moab led an attempt of seven hundred swordsmen to break a way through to the king of Edom;*c* but they failed. 27 So he took his first-born son, who was to succeed him as king, and offered him up on the wall as a burnt offering. A great wrath came upon Israel, so they withdrew from him and went back to [their own] land.

4 A certain woman, the wife of one of the disciples of the prophets, cried out to Elisha: "Your servant my husband is dead, and you know how your servant revered the LORD. And now a creditor is coming to seize my two children as slaves." 2 Elisha said to her, "What can I do for you? Tell me, what have you in the house?" She replied, "Your maidservant has nothing at all in the house, except a jug of oil." 3 "Go," he said, "and borrow vessels outside, from all your neighbors, empty vessels, as many as you can. 4 Then go in and shut the door behind you and your children, and pour [oil] into all those vessels, removing each one as it is filled."

5 She went away and shut the door behind her and her children. They kept bringing [vessels] to her and she kept pouring. 6 When the vessels were full, she said to her son, "Bring me another vessel." He answered her, "There are no more vessels"; and the oil stopped. 7 She came and told the man of God, and he said, "Go sell the oil and pay your debt, and you and your children can live on the rest."

8 One day Elisha visited Shunem. A wealthy woman lived there, and she urged him to have a meal; and whenever he passed by, he would stop there for a meal. 9 Once she said to her husband, "I am sure it is a holy man of God

---

a-a Meaning of Heb. uncertain.
b-b Lit. "Until the stones in"; meaning of Heb. uncertain.
c Emendation yields "Aram."

---

deep gorges around its salient. **27:** Mesha sacrifices his first-born son in an extreme, powerful act. Perhaps Mesha interpreted his losses as punishment for some offense that angered his national deity Chemosh, an offense that could be atoned for through the offering of his son (cf. Mic. 6.7). Although interpreters are unsure what the author meant by *a great wrath came upon Israel*, it sug-

gests that Mesha achieved his objective, and the human sacrifice was efficacious. The coalition abandoned the field and returned home.

4.1–6.23: The second cycle of Elisha stories. Perhaps the author inserts them at this point because Elisha was mentioned in the context of the Moabite campaign. The motifs of inadequate provisions and death recur in this cycle of stories, but the main theme is Elisha as a healer.

4.1–7: The miraculous provision of oil. A prophetic story whose central miracle parallels that of Elijah in 1 Kings 17.14–16. This story is atypical of the simple miracle stories in that it provides extraneous details about why the woman had some claim to Elisha's help. The story lacks any mention of prayer or divine presence. The sense of wonderment is thereby focused completely on the only named person in the narrative, Elisha. This story in particular shows signs of remnants of Israelite Hebrew, suggesting that many of these prophetic stories were composed in the north, and later incorporated into the Judean Book of Kings. **1:** The woman does not complain about social injustice but about her financial straits. *Seize my two children as slaves:* This was a long-established legal norm; see Exod. 21.2–11; Lev. 25.39–55; Deut. 15.12–15; Neh. 5.1–5. **2:** The fact that the seizure of the children is legal explains why Elisha's first reaction to her statement and implied request for help was to inquire what he could do.

4.8–37: The birth and revivification of the Shunammite's son. The narrative combines prediction and miracle stories in a tale whose chronology spans five to ten years. It is suffused with sufficient background to understand what motivates the actions of all main characters. The expression "one day" introduces each major part of the narrative: In v. 8 it introduces the

who comes this way regularly. [10] Let us make a small
[a]enclosed upper chamber[-a] and place a bed, a table, a
chair, and a lampstand there for him, so that he can stop
there whenever he comes to us." [11] One day he came there;
he retired to the upper chamber and lay down there. [12] He
said to his servant Gehazi, "Call that Shunammite
woman." He called her, and she stood before him. [13] He
said to him, "Tell her, 'You have gone to all this trouble for
us. What can we do for you? Can we speak in your behalf
to the king or to the army commander?' " She replied, "I
live among my own people." [14] "What then can be done
for her?" he asked. "The fact is," said Gehazi, "she has no
son, and her husband is old." [15] "Call her," he said. He
called her, and she stood in the doorway. [16] And Elisha
said, "At this season next year, you will be embracing a
son." She replied, "Please, my lord, man of God, do not
delude your maidservant."

[17] The woman conceived and bore a son at the same season the following year, as Elisha had assured her. [18] The
child grew up. One day, he went out to his father among
the reapers. [19] [Suddenly] he cried to his father, "Oh, my
head, my head!" He said to a servant, "Carry him to his
mother." [20] He picked him up and brought him to his
mother. And the child sat on her lap until noon; and he
died. [21] She took him up and laid him on the bed of the
man of God, and left him and closed the door. [22] Then she
called to her husband: "Please, send me one of the servants and one of the she-asses, so I can hurry to the man
of God and back." [23] But he said, "Why are you going to
him today? It is neither new moon nor sabbath." She answered, [b-]"It's all right."[-b]

[24] She had the ass saddled, and said to her servant, "Urge
[the beast] on;[c] see that I don't slow down unless I tell you."
[25] She went on until she came to the man of God on Mount
Carmel. When the man of God saw her from afar, he said to
his servant Gehazi, "There is that Shunammite woman.
[26] Go, hurry toward her and ask her, 'How are you? How is
your husband? How is the child?' " "We are well," she
replied. [27] But when she came up to the man of God on the
mountain, she clasped his feet. Gehazi stepped forward to
push her away; but the man of God said, "Let her alone, for
she is in bitter distress; and the Lord has hidden it from me
and has not told me." [28] Then she said, "Did I ask my lord
for a son? Didn't I say: 'Don't mislead me'?"

main characters in the house of the
Shunammite; in v. 11 the promise/
prediction of the child; in v. 18, the
story of the death and revivification of the child. **9:** Elisha traveled
a regular circuit, possibly visiting
groups of disciples of the prophets
(cf. Samuel in 1 Sam. 7.15–17).
12–16: Elisha begins by speaking
to the *woman* indirectly, through
Gehazi, but ends by addressing her
directly (see also vv. 26–28, 36).
20–22: The narrator informs readers that the child *died*; the Shunammite, however, may not have perceived that he was dead, only very
ill. She did not tell her husband
that the child was dead but proceeded to rush to the person who
she believed could heal her child.
23: Her husband's question assumes that when the Shunammite
visited Elisha it was typically
for the celebration of either a
new month or a Sabbath.

---

a-a Or "upper wall-chamber"; lit. "an upper chamber of wall(s)."

b-b Heb. Shalom.

c The servant runs behind the donkey and urges it on with a stick.

29 He said to Gehazi, ª-"Tie up your skirts,·ª take my staff in your hand, and go. If you meet anyone, do not greet him; and if anyone greets you, do not answer him. And place my staff on the face of the boy." 30 But the boy's mother said, "As the LORD lives and as you live, I will not leave you!" So he arose and followed her.

31 Gehazi had gone on before them and had placed the staff on the boy's face; but there was no sound or response. He turned back to meet him and told him, "The boy has not awakened." 32 Elisha came into the house, and there was the boy, laid out dead on his couch. 33 He went in, shut the door behind the two of them, and prayed to the LORD. 34 Then he mounted [the bed] and placed himself over the child. He put his mouth on its mouth, his eyes on its eyes, and his hands on its hands, as he bent over it. And the body of the child became warm. 35 He stepped down, walked once up and down the room, then mounted and bent over him. Thereupon, the boy sneezed seven times, and the boy opened his eyes. 36 [Elisha] called Gehazi and said, "Call the Shunammite woman," and he called her. When she came to him, he said, "Pick up your son." 37 She came and fell at his feet and bowed low to the ground; then she picked up her son and left.

38 Elisha returned to Gilgal. There was a famine in the land, and the disciples of the prophets were sitting before him. He said to his servant, "Set the large pot [on the fire] and cook a stew for the disciples of the prophets." 39 So one of them went out into the fields to gather sprouts. He came across a wild vine and picked from it wild gourds, as many as his garment would hold. Then he came back and sliced them into the pot of stew, for they did not know [what they were]; 40 and they served it for the men to eat. While they were still eating of the stew, they began to cry out: "O man of God, there is death in the pot!"ᵇ And they could not eat it. 41 "Fetch some flour," [Elisha] said. He threw it into the pot and said, "Serve it to the people and let them eat." And there was no longer anything harmful in the pot.

42 A man came from Baal-shalishah and he brought the man of God some bread of the first reaping—twenty loaves of barley bread, and some fresh grain ᶜ-in his sack.·ᶜ And [Elisha] said, "Give it to the people and let them eat." 43 His attendant replied, "How can I set this before a hun-

29–32: Gehazi was dispatched to perform a healing using Elisha's staff. Elisha thought that his presence was not actually needed for a healing to occur (cf. 4.5–6). Elisha's initial plan, executed by Gehazi, failed. Malbim suggests that from Gehazi's remark to Elisha in v. 31, it appears that Elisha misdiagnosed the problem on the basis of the Shunammite's information; God had not revealed anything of the matter to him (v. 27). The child was truly dead. **34–35:** The revivification performed here by Elisha is similar to what is described with fewer details about Elijah in 1 Kings 17.21–22.

4.38–41: Elisha neutralizes a poison. 39: *Sprouts:* Radak's opinion that Heb "'orot" refers to herbs, on the basis of Isa. 26.19, is reflected in the translation. Others suggest that it refers to Eruca sativa, a radish-like plant whose bitter leaves are edible. *Wild gourds* (Heb "pakuʿot"): Citrullus colocynthis, a melon-like plant, contains seeds in which there is a poisonous substance.

4.42–44: Elisha feeds a multitude.

a-a Lit. "Gird your loins"; cf. 1 Kings 18.46.
b The wild gourds cause severe cramps.
c-c Or "on the stalk"; perhaps connected with Ugaritic bṣql.

dred men?" But he said, "Give it to the people and let them eat. For thus said the LORD: They shall eat and have some left over." ⁴⁴So he set it before them; and when they had eaten, they had some left over, as the LORD had said.

5 Naaman, commander of the army of the king of Aram, was important to his lord and high in his favor, for through him the LORD had granted victory to Aram. But the man, though a great warrior, was a leper.ᵃ ²Once, when the Arameans were out raiding, they carried off a young girl from the land of Israel, and she became an attendant to Naaman's wife. ³She said to her mistress, "I wish Master could come before the prophet in Samaria; he would cure him of his leprosy." ⁴[Naaman] went and told his lord just what the girl from the land of Israel had said. ⁵And the king of Aram said, "Go to the king of Israel, and I will send along a letter."

He set out, taking with him ten talents of silver, six thousand shekels of gold, and ten changes of clothing. ⁶He brought the letter to the king of Israel. It read: "Now, when this letter reaches you, know that I have sent my courtier Naaman to you, that you may cure him of his leprosy." ⁷When the king of Israel read the letter, he rent his clothes and cried, "Am I God, to deal death or give life, that this fellow writes to me to cure a man of leprosy? Just see for yourselves that he is seeking a pretext against me!"

⁸When Elisha, the man of God, heard that the king of Israel had rent his clothes, he sent a message to the king: "Why have you rent your clothes? Let him come to me, and he will learn that there is a prophet in Israel."

⁹So Naaman came with his horses and chariots and halted at the door of Elisha's house. ¹⁰Elisha sent a messenger to say to him, "Go and bathe seven times in the Jordan, and your flesh shall be restored and you shall be clean." ¹¹But Naaman was angered and walked away. "I thought," he said, "he would surely come out to me, and would stand and invoke the LORD his God by name, and would wave his hand toward the spot, and cure the affected part. ¹²Are not the Amanah and the Pharpar, the rivers of Damascus, better than all the waters of Israel? I could bathe in them and be clean!" And he stalked off in a rage.

¹³But his servants came forward and spoke to him. "Sir,"ᵇ they said, "if the prophet told you to do something difficult, would you not do it? How much more when he has only said to you, 'Bathe and be clean.' " ¹⁴So he went down and immersed himself in the Jordan seven times, as

5.1–27: The healing of Naaman the leper. The story of Naaman the Aramean leper is a complex legend. Since only a few main characters are presented by name, the anonymity of the kings of Aram and Israel makes it impossible to attribute the story to a particular period in the life of Elisha. One motif of the story is that people of higher social status are dependent on people of lower status: Naaman on counsel from his wife reporting information from an Israelite slave girl (vv. 2–3); the king of Aram on the king of Israel, and the latter on Elisha (vv. 5–8); Naaman on the advice of his own servants and Elisha (vv. 13–15). **1:** The leprosy of Naaman was some sort of dermatological problem (see annotations on Lev. ch 13) that did not disfigure him or disqualify him from military office or entering temples in his homeland (see v. 18). **7–8:** In this story, the king of Israel is unaware of Elisha's healing powers although a little girl captured by the Arameans is (vv. 2–3). **10:** Elisha's prescription does not involve divine guidance or prayer.

a Cf. note on Lev. 13.3.   b Lit. "[My] father."

the man of God had bidden; and his flesh became like a little boy's, and he was clean. ¹⁵ Returning with his entire retinue to the man of God, he stood before him and exclaimed, "Now I know that there is no God in the whole world except in Israel! So please accept a gift from your servant." ¹⁶ But he replied, "As the LORD lives, whom I serve, I will not accept anything." He pressed him to accept, but he refused. ¹⁷ And Naaman said, "Then at least let your servant be given two mule-loads of earth; for your servant will never again offer up burnt offering or sacrifice to any god, except the LORD. ¹⁸ But may the LORD pardon your servant for this: When my master enters the temple of Rimmon to bow low in worship there, and he is leaning on my arm so that I must bow low in the temple of Rimmon—when I bow low in the temple of Rimmon, may the LORD pardon your servant in this." ¹⁹ And he said to him, "Go in peace."

When he had gone some distance from him, ²⁰ Gehazi, the attendant of Elisha the man of God, thought: "My master ᵃ‐has let that Aramean Naaman off without accepting what he brought!‐ᵃ As the LORD lives, I will run after him and get something from him." ²¹ So Gehazi hurried after Naaman. When Naaman saw someone running after him, he alighted from his chariot to meet him and said, "Is all well?" ²² "All is well," he replied. "My master has sent me to say: Two youths, disciples of the prophets, have just come to me from the hill country of Ephraim. Please give them a talent of silver and two changes of clothing." ²³ Naaman said, "Please take two talents." He urged him, and he wrapped the two talents of silver in two bags and gave them, along with two changes of clothes, to two of his servants, who carried them ahead of him. ²⁴ When [Gehazi] arrived at the citadel, he took [the things] from them and deposited them in the house. Then he dismissed the men and they went their way.

²⁵ He entered and stood before his master; and Elisha said to him, "Where have you been, Gehazi?" He replied, "Your servant has not gone anywhere." ²⁶ Then [Elisha] said to him, "Did not my spiritᵇ go along when a man got down from his chariot to meet you? Is this a time to take money in order to buy clothing and olive groves and vineyards, sheep and oxen, and male and female slaves? ²⁷ Surely, the leprosy of Naaman shall cling to you and to your descendants forever." And as [Gehazi] left his presence, he was snow-white with leprosy.

---

a-a Lit. "has prevented that Aramean Naaman from having what he brought accepted."
b Lit. "heart."

15–17: Naaman's experience convinces him of the radical monotheism of Elisha and of the author, but he concludes that though God is universal, He may be worshipped only on the soil of His chosen land. A main point of this story, then, is the sanctity of the land of Israel. **18:** *Rimmon*, an alternative name for the Aramean storm-god, Hadad (Zech. 12.11). **26:** Elisha had clairvoyant abilities. **27:** Gehazi's solicitation had made Elisha appear to be a fee-for-service healer, reducing the miraculous cure to a matter of arcane knowledge. Gehazi's leprosy demonstrated its divine nature.

6 The disciples of the prophets said to Elisha, "See, the place where we live under your direction is too cramped for us. ² Let us go to the Jordan, and let us each get a log there and build quarters there for ourselves to live in." "Do so," he replied. ³ Then one of them said, "Will you please come along with your servants?" "Yes, I will come," he said; ⁴ and he accompanied them. So they went to the Jordan and cut timber. ⁵ As one of them was felling a trunk, the iron ax head fell into the water. And he cried aloud, "Alas, master, it was a borrowed one!" ⁶ "Where did it fall?" asked the man of God. He showed him the spot; and he cut off a stick and threw it in, and he made the ax head float. ⁷ "Pick it up," he said; so he reached out and took it.

⁸ While the king of Aram was waging war against Israel, he took counsel with his officers and said, ᵃ⁻"I will encamp⁻ᵃ in such and such a place." ⁹ But the man of God sent word to the king of Israel, "Take care not to pass through that place, for the Arameans are encamped there." ¹⁰ So the king of Israel sent word to the place of which the man of God had told him. ᵇ⁻Time and again⁻ᵇ he alerted ᶜ⁻such a place⁻ᶜ and took precautions there. ¹¹ Greatly agitated about this matter, the king of Aram summoned his officers and said to them, "Tell me! Who of us is on the side of the king of Israel?" ¹² "No one, my lord king," said one of the officers. "Elisha, that prophet in Israel, tells the king of Israel the very words you speak in your bedroom." ¹³ "Go find out where he is," he said, "so that I can have him seized." It was reported to him that [Elisha] was in Dothan; ¹⁴ so he sent horses and chariots there and a strong force. They arrived at night and encircled the town.

¹⁵ When the attendant of the man of God rose early and went outside, he saw a force, with horses and chariots, surrounding the town. "Alas, master, what shall we do?" his servant asked him. ¹⁶ "Have no fear," he replied. "There are more on our side than on theirs." ¹⁷ Then Elisha prayed: "Lᴏʀᴅ, open his eyes and let him see." And the Lᴏʀᴅ opened the servant's eyes and he saw the hills all around Elisha covered with horses and chariots of fire. ¹⁸ [The Arameans] came down against him, and Elisha prayed to the Lᴏʀᴅ: "Please strike this people with a blinding light." And He struck them with a blinding light, as Elisha had asked.

¹⁹ Elisha said to them, "This is not the road, and that is not the town; follow me, and I will lead you to the man you want." And he led them to Samaria. ²⁰ When they en

6.1–7: Elisha makes an ax head float. 1: *Disciples of the prophets:* Elisha much more than Elijah is associated with a prophetic company. *Place where we live:* This seems to imply a regular community *under* Elisha's *direction.* **2:** Trees, and therefore *a log,* would be more readily found near the *Jordan.*

6.8–23: The Aramean raiders are foiled. A prophetic story celebrating how the clairvoyant Elisha, whose skill is known within court circles of the Arameans, captured a contingent of the Aramean army and delivered it to the king of Israel. The names of the Aramean and Israelite kings are not provided in this story either (cf. 5.1–27). This story concludes the second cycle (see 4.1). **8–13:** The story is set in a period when Aramean troops regularly made incursions deep into Israel, south of the Jezreel Valley, and were even able to attack the city of Dothan. The details, however, are insufficient to place them into a specific chronological setting. **17–18:** Elisha prays twice, once that his servant will see that his master is surrounded and protected by an invisible force and once that the Arameans will be blinded by light so that they cannot see. When Elisha requires miraculous intervention for himself, he prays for it.

a-a *Meaning of Heb. uncertain.*   b-b *Lit. "not once or twice."*   c-c *Heb. "it."*

tered Samaria, Elisha said, "O LORD, open the eyes of these men so that they may see." The LORD opened their eyes and they saw that they were inside Samaria. [21] When the king of Israel saw them, he said to Elisha, "Father, shall I strike them down?" [22] "No, do not," he replied. "Did you take them captive with your sword and bow that you would strike them down? Rather, set food and drink before them, and let them eat and drink and return to their master." [23] So he prepared a lavish feast for them and, after they had eaten and drunk, he let them go, and they returned to their master. And the Aramean bands stopped invading the land of Israel.

[24] Sometime later, King Ben-hadad of Aram mustered his entire army and marched upon Samaria and besieged it. [25] There was a great famine in Samaria, and the siege continued until a donkey's head sold for eighty [shekels] of silver and a quarter of a *kab* of ᵃdoves' dungᵃ for five shekels. [26] Once, when the king of Israel was walking on the city wall, a woman cried out to him: "Help me, Your Majesty!" [27] "Don't [ask me]," he replied. "Let the LORD help you! Where could I get help for you, from the threshing floor or from the winepress? [28] But what troubles you?" the king asked her. The woman answered, "That woman said to me, 'Give up your son and we will eat him today; and tomorrow we'll eat my son.' [29] So we cooked my son and we ate him. The next day I said to her, 'Give up your son and let's eat him'; but she hid her son." [30] When the king heard what the woman said, he rent his clothes; and as he walked along the wall, the people could see that he was wearing sackcloth underneath.

[31] He said, "Thus and more may God do to me if the head of Elisha son of Shaphat remains on ᵇhis shouldersᵇ today." [32] Now Elisha was sitting at home and the elders were sitting with him. The king had sent ahead one of his men; but before the messenger arrived, [Elisha] said to the elders, "Do you see—that murderer has sent someone to cut off my head! Watch when the messenger comes, and shut the door and hold the door fast against him. No doubt the sound of his master's footsteps will follow."

[33] While he was still talking to them, the messengerᶜ came to him and said, "This calamity is from the LORD. **7** What more can I hope for from the LORD?" [1] And Elisha replied, "Hear the word of the LORD. Thus said the LORD: This time tomorrow, a *seah* of choice flour shall sell

6.24–7.20: The siege of Samaria. 6.24: This introduction, contradicting v. 23, indicates these stories have not been combined in historical order. This siege story may have originally followed the story of the Moabite campaign (3.27). Ralbag's comment on v. 23 suggests how the author may have interpreted the two verses in a non-contradictory manner. Ralbag interprets vv. 23–24 as meaning that the Arameans stopped sending in contingents of soldiers and amassed a single army that besieged Samaria. **25:** Even the least desirable of foods are sold for a high price. **28:** The motif of cannibalism is associated with sieges also in Deut. 28.53–57; Ezek. 5.10; Lam. 2.20; 4.10. **30:** The king had been wearing sackcloth beneath his normal clothing as a sign of mourning or contrition. **31:** This oath against Elisha indicates that somehow the king held the prophet responsible for the siege. Rashi, Radak, and Joseph Kara suggest that it was because the king thought that Elisha could request relief from God. Ralbag, however, assumes that Elisha provided fair warning of the siege and starvation, just as Elijah had of the drought in 1 Kings 17.1, and that the king thought that it had gone on long enough. **6.33–7.1:** The king had a revolutionary change of heart. His messengers, in his name, acknowledge that God is the source of the calamity, and Elisha rewards the confession with a prediction that the famine would end the next day. **7.2:** The cynical aide next to the king challenges Elisha. In response Elisha predicts his death, a prediction fulfilled in vv. 17–20. **5–7:** These verses are a parenthetical explanation of how it happened that the lepers found the Aramean camp empty. **6:** Only Arameans encamped around Samaria heard sounds of the chariots and army. Cf. 6.16–17 that describe the invisible chariots protecting Elisha and 2 Sam. 5.24 that refers to the sounds of an invisible army of God.

a-a *Apparently a popular term for "carob pods," as in Akkadian.*
b-b *Lit. "him."*   c *Emendation yields "king."*

for a shekel at the gate of Samaria, and two *seahs* of barley
for a shekel." ²The aide on whose arm the king was leaning spoke up and said to the man of God, "Even if the
LORD were to make windows in the sky, could this come
to pass?" And he retorted, "You shall see it with your own
eyes, but you shall not eat of it."

³There were four men, lepers, outside the gate. They
said to one another, "Why should we sit here waiting for
death? ⁴If we decide to go into the town, what with the
famine in the town, we shall die there; and if we just sit
here, still we die. Come, let us desert to the Aramean
camp. If they let us live, we shall live; and if they put us to
death, we shall but die."
⁵They set out at twilight for the Aramean camp; but
when they came to the edge of the Aramean camp, there
was no one there. ⁶For the Lord had caused the Aramean
camp to hear a sound of chariots, a sound of horses—the
din of a huge army. They said to one another, "The king of
Israel must have hired the kings of the Hittites and the
kings of Mizraim[a] to attack us!" ⁷And they fled headlong
in the twilight, abandoning their tents and horses and
asses—the [entire] camp just as it was—as they fled for
their lives.
⁸When those lepers came to the edge of the camp, they
went into one of the tents and ate and drank; then they
carried off silver and gold and clothing from there and
buried it. They came back and went into another tent, and
they carried off what was there and buried it. ⁹Then they
said to one another, "We are not doing right. This is a day
of good news, and we are keeping silent! If we wait until
the light of morning, we shall incur guilt. Come, let us go
and inform the king's palace." ¹⁰They went and called out
to the gatekeepers of the city and told them, "We have
been to the Aramean camp. There is not a soul there, nor
any human sound; but the horses are tethered and the
asses are tethered and the tents are undisturbed."
¹¹The gatekeepers called out, and the news was passed
on into the king's palace. ¹²The king rose in the night and
said to his courtiers, "I will tell you what the Arameans
have done to us. They know that we are starving, so they
have gone out of camp and hidden in the fields, thinking:
When they come out of the town, we will take them alive
and get into the town." ¹³But one of the courtiers spoke
up, "Let a few[b] of the remaining horses that are still here

a Cf. 1 Kings 10.28 and note d there.
b Lit. "five."

be taken—ᵃthey are like those that are left here of the whole multitude of Israel, out of the whole multitude of Israel that have perished ᵃ—and let us send and find out."

¹⁴They took two teamsᵃ of horses and the king sent them after the Aramean army, saying, "Go and find out." ¹⁵They followed them as far as the Jordan, and found the entire road full of clothing and gear which the Arameans had thrown away in their haste; and the messengers returned and told the king. ¹⁶The people then went out and plundered the Aramean camp. So a *seah* of choice flour sold for a shekel, and two *seahs* of barley for a shekel—as the LORD had spoken.

¹⁷Now the king had put the aide on whose arm he leaned in charge of the gate; and he was trampled to death in the gate by the people—just as the man of God had spoken, as he had spoken when the king came down to him. ¹⁸For when the man of God said to the king, "This time tomorrow two *seahs* of barley shall sell at the gate of Samaria for a shekel, and a *seah* of choice flour for a shekel," ¹⁹the aide answered the man of God and said, "Even if the LORD made windows in the sky, could this come to pass?" And he retorted, "You shall see it with your own eyes, but you shall not eat of it." ²⁰That is exactly what happened to him: The people trampled him to death in the gate.

8 Elisha had said to the woman whose son he revived, "Leave immediately with your family and go sojourn ᵇsomewhere else;ᵇ for the LORD has decreed a seven-year famine upon the land, and it has already begun." ²The woman had done as the man of God had spoken; she left with her family and sojourned in the land of the Philistines for seven years. ³At the end of the seven years, the woman returned from the land of the Philistines and went to the king to complain about her house and farm. ⁴Now the king was talking to Gehazi, the servant of the man of God, and he said, "Tell me all the wonderful things that Elisha has done." ⁵While he was telling the king how [Elisha] had revived a dead person, in came the woman whose son he had revived, complaining to the king about her house and farm. "My lord king," said Gehazi, "this is the woman and this is her son whom Elisha revived." ⁶The king questioned the woman, and she told him [the story]; so the king assigned a eunuch to her and instructed him: "Restore all her property, and all the revenue from her farm from the time she left the country until now."

8.1–6: A story about Gehazi telling Elisha stories to the king of Israel. The brief tale most likely describes something that occurred after the death of Elisha: (1) the king asks to be told such stories (v. 4) and (2) the woman whose son had been revivified petitions the king on her own, indicating that her husband is dead and that Elisha, who could act on her behalf, is not available (4.13). **1:** The *seven-year famine* may have been a period prior to and during the siege of Samaria narrated in the preceding section.

---

a-a Meaning of Heb. uncertain.   *b-b Lit. "wherever you may sojourn."*

7 Elisha arrived in Damascus at a time when King Ben-hadad of Aram was ill. *The king* was told, "The man of God is on his way here," 8 and he said to Hazael, "Take a gift with you and go meet the man of God, and through him inquire of the LORD: Will I recover from this illness?" 9 Hazael went to meet him, taking with him as a gift forty camel-loads of all the bounty of Damascus. He came and stood before him and said, "Your son, King Ben-hadad of Aram, has sent me to you to ask: Will I recover from this illness?" 10 Elisha said to him, "Go and say to him, 'You will recover.' However, the LORD has revealed to me that he will die." 11 The man of God *kept his face expressionless* for a long time; and then he wept. 12 "Why does my lord weep?" asked Hazael. "Because I know," he replied, "what harm you will do to the Israelite people: you will set their fortresses on fire, put their young men to the sword, dash their little ones in pieces, and rip open their pregnant women." 13 "But how," asked Hazael, "can your servant, who is a mere dog, perform such a mighty deed?" Elisha replied, "The LORD has shown me a vision of you as king of Aram." 14 He left Elisha and returned to his master, who asked him, "What did Elisha say to you?" He replied, "He told me that you would recover." 15 The next day, [Hazael] took *a piece of netting,* dipped it in water, and spread it over his face. So [Ben-hadad] died, and Hazael succeeded him as king.

16 In the fifth year of King Joram[c] son of Ahab of Israel—Jehoshaphat had been king of Judah—Joram son of King Jehoshaphat of Judah became king. 17 He was thirty-two years old when he became king, and he reigned in Jerusalem eight years. 18 He followed the practices of the kings of Israel—whatever the House of Ahab did, for he had married a daughter[d] of Ahab—and he did what was displeasing to the LORD. 19 However, the LORD refrained from destroying Judah, for the sake of His servant David, in accordance with His promise to maintain a lamp for his descendants for all time. 20 During his reign, the Edomites rebelled against Judah's rule and set up a king of their own. 21 Joram crossed over to Zair with all his chariotry. *He arose by night and attacked the Edomites, who were surrounding him and the chariot commanders; but* his troops fled to their homes. 22 Thus Edom fell away from

8.7–15: The prophecy to Hazael, delivered by Elisha, was originally a task assigned to Elijah (1 Kings 19.15–17). **7–9:** Elisha's reputation as a prognosticator was well known among the Arameans, and Hazael addresses him in the name of Ben-hadad with great respect. Ben-hadad's inquiry of Elisha has no religious implications. As a simple consultation with an acknowledged expert, it was similar to Ahaziah's of Baal-zebub (2 Kings 1.2). **10–13:** Elisha does not lie, but instructs Hazael to do so. He proceeds to inform Hazael that God has foreordained his rise and even his victories over Israel. **15:** According to what may be gleaned from inscriptions of the Assyrian king Shalmaneser III, Hazael usurped the throne in Damascus after 845 but before 841 BCE.

8.16–24: The reign of Joram (Jehoram), king of Judah, paralleled that of his brother-in-law Joram, king of Israel. The author's negative evaluation of his reign cites behaviors modeled after Ahab's dynasty and attributes them directly to the king's wife. **22:** The growing strength of *Edom* can be discerned by comparing the terminology in this v. with 1 Kings 22.48, where Edomites were controlled through an acting king, and 3.9, where an independent king who was nonetheless a vassal of Judah reigned. The independence of Edom signaled Judah's final loss of control over the central Negev and all trade through it. The rebellion of *Libnah,* a Levitical city on the western fringe of Judah's territory (Josh. 10.29; 21.13), lacks an adequate explanation.

a-a *Brought up from v. 8 for clarity.*
b-b *Meaning of Heb. uncertain.*
c *Throughout this chapter, the name Joram is sometimes written Jehoram.*
d *Emendation yields "sister"; cf. v. 26.*

Judah, as is still the case. Libnah likewise fell away at that time.

²³ The other events of Joram's reign, and all his actions, are recorded in the Annals of the Kings of Judah. ²⁴ Joram slept with his fathers and was buried with his fathers in the City of David; his son Ahaziah succeeded him as king.

²⁵ In the twelfth year of King Joram son of Ahab of Israel, Ahaziah son of Joram became king of Judah. ²⁶ Ahaziah was twenty-two years old when he became king, and he reigned in Jerusalem one year; his mother's name was Athaliah daughter of King Omri of Israel. ²⁷ He walked in the ways of the House of Ahab and did what was displeasing to the LORD, like the House of Ahab, for he was related by marriage to the House of Ahab. ²⁸ He marched with Joram son of Ahab to battle against King Hazael of Aram at Ramoth-gilead, but the Arameans wounded Joram. ²⁹ King Joram retired to Jezreel to recover from the wounds which the Arameans had inflicted upon him at Ramah, when he fought against King Hazael of Aram. And King Ahaziah son of Joram of Judah went down to Jezreel to visit Joram son of Ahab while he was ill.

9 Then the prophet Elisha summoned one of the disciples of the prophets and said to him, "Tie up your skirts,ᵃ and take along this flask of oil, and go to Ramoth-gilead. ² When you arrive there, go and see Jehu son of Jehoshaphat son of Nimshi; get him to leave his comrades, and take him into an inner room. ³ Then take the flask of oil and pour some on his head, and say, 'Thus said the LORD: I anoint you king over Israel.' Then open the door and flee without delay."

⁴ The young man, the servant of the prophet, went to Ramoth-gilead. ⁵ When he arrived, the army commanders were sitting together. He said, "Commander, I have a message for you." "For which one of us?" Jehu asked. He answered, "For you, commander." ⁶ So [Jehu] arose and went inside; and [the disciple] poured the oil on his head, and said to him, "Thus said the LORD, the God of Israel: I anoint you king over the people of the LORD, over Israel. ⁷ You shall strike down the House of Ahab your master; thus will I avenge on Jezebel the blood of My servants the prophets, and the blood of the other servants of the LORD. ⁸ The whole House of Ahab shall perish, and I will cut off every male belonging to Ahab, ᵇ⁻bond and freeᵇ in Israel. ⁹ I will make the House of Ahab like the House of Jeroboam son of

8.25–29: The short reign of Ahaziah of Judah (not his dead uncle, Ahaziah of Israel) is linked to the fortunes of his living uncle Joram king of Israel. Ahaziah involved Judah in Israel's battle against the Arameans at Ramoth-gilead in Transjordan. His death and burial are noted without the usual formulae in the middle of the account of Jehu's revolt (9.27–29). **26:** In v. 18, Athaliah is referred to as the daughter of Ahab, which would make her Omri's granddaughter. It is possible that the Omrides fashioned all royal descendants as "sons/daughters of Omri," making Omri into something like what David was for the Southern Kingdom. Jehu, who killed off the Omrides, was identified as "son of Omri" on the Black Obelisk of Shalmaneser III. See also Solomon's wife, "the daughter of Pharaoh" in 1 Kings 3.1.

9.1–14a: The anointing of Jehu was the last unfinished task of Elijah left for Elisha to carry out (1 Kings 19.15–16). He dispatches one of the disciples of the prophets to carry it out. **3–4:** Elisha gives specific instructions about what the messenger is to do and say, but in fulfilling the instructions, the messenger deviates considerably from his charge (vv. 6–10). A rationale for doing so is provided in v. 4 which when translated literally yields: "And he went, the young man, the young man, the prophet, to Ramoth-gilead." Usually interpreted or explained by both classical and contemporary commentators as "the servant/ young man of the prophet," the text indicates that he was a prophet in his own right. Furthermore, Jehu's comment (v. 11) indicates that he was a well-known figure and that people were familiar with his pet concerns. **6:** The anointing is a private affair, as was that of Saul (1 Sam. 10.1). **7–9:** The charge to Jehu is delivered as an oracle of God, not a repetition of something that Elisha said. The prophecy contains an instruction that Jehu become the agent through which the prophecies of

---

ᵃ See note at 4.29.   ᵇ⁻ᵇ See note at 1 Kings 14.10.

Nebat, and like the House of Baasha son of Ahijah. [10] The dogs shall devour Jezebel in the field of Jezreel, with none to bury her." Then he opened the door and fled.

[11] Jehu went out to the other officers of his master, and they asked him, "Is all well? What did that madman come to you for?" He said to them, "You know the man and his ranting!" [12] "You're lying," they said. "Tell us [the truth]." Then he replied, "Thus and thus he said: Thus said the Lord: I anoint you king over Israel!" [13] Quickly each man took his cloak and placed it under him,[a] on [b]the top step.[b] They sounded the horn and proclaimed, "Jehu is king!" [14] Thus Jehu son of Jehoshaphat son of Nimshi conspired against Joram.

Joram and all Israel had been defending Ramoth-gilead against King Hazael of Aram, [15] but King Joram had gone back to Jezreel to recover from the wounds which the Arameans had inflicted on him in his battle with King Hazael of Aram.

Jehu said, "If such is your wish, allow no one to slip out of the town to go and report this in Jezreel." [16] Then Jehu mounted his chariot and drove to Jezreel; for Joram was lying ill there, and King Ahaziah of Judah had gone down to visit Joram. [17] The lookout was stationed on the tower in Jezreel, and he saw the troop of Jehu as he approached. He called out, "I see a troop!" Joram said, "Dispatch a horseman to meet them and let him ask: Is all well?" [18] The horseman went to meet him, and he said, "The king inquires: Is all well?" Jehu replied, "What concern of yours is it whether all is well? Fall in behind me." The lookout reported: "The messenger has reached them, but has not turned back." [19] So he sent out a second horseman. He came to them and said, "Thus says the king: Is all well?" Jehu answered, "What concern of yours is it whether all is well? Fall in behind me." [20] And the lookout reported, "The messenger has reached them, but has not turned back. And it looks like the driving of Jehu son of Nimshi, who drives wildly."

[21] Joram ordered, "Hitch up [the chariot]!" They hitched up his chariot; and King Joram of Israel and King Ahaziah

a I.e., Jehu.   b-b Meaning of Heb. uncertain.

Jehu repeated everything exactly (see 5.4 where the same Heb expression is translated "just what"). **13:** Other officers acclaim Jehu king, and make noise, typical parts of the coronation ritual (see 1 Kings 1.39–40).

9.14b–15a: An interpolation. Excavations at Jezreel indicate that it was primarily a fortified administrative center with remains of what may have been a large palace. Two fragments of a victory stele in the Aramaic language found in the excavations of Dan attest to Aramean control of the area in the 9th century as well as to Aramean victories over Israel and success in battle against someone from the Davidic dynasty. One fragment mentions two kings, one whose name ended "-rm" and another whose name ended "-yhw." Historians speculate that these are Jehoram and Ahazyahuw. The only king successful against both Israel and Judah whose respective kings' names match the letters on the fragment was Hazael.

9.15b–37: The battle with Joram of Israel and the death of Jezebel. 15b: This verse appears to pick up from 14a. The interpolation may have been inserted in order to explain why the news of Jehu's anointing as king should not be reported *in Jezreel*. **17–20:** The image created by the author is of a large force moving slowly, even ominously, toward Jezreel. *Jehu* apparently *drives* his chariot *wildly*, perhaps in a zig-zag in front of the advancing troop. The rate of advance is so slow two different riders are sent out to them and Joram and Ahaziah in their chariots go out to them before they enter Jezreel. The events in this chapter, as well as the rise of Hazael in Damascus, are dated to 842 BCE on the basis of correlations between biblical chronological notations, the Mesha stele, references to Ahab, Jehu, Hazael, and Joash in Assyrian inscriptions, and Aramaic inscriptions mentioning Hazael and Ben-hadad. **17:** *Well,* Heb "shalom," is repeated like a disso-

Elijah in 1 Kings 21.21–23 are fulfilled. V. 7 also indicates that Jezebel had not only persecuted *prophets* of God, but other *servants of the Lord* as well (see 1 Kings 18.4, 22). Years later, long after the period of the persecutions, there were most likely many descendants of those who had suffered under her hand willing to take revenge. **12:** *Thus and thus,* a conventional expression indicating that of Judah went out, each in his own chariot, to meet Jehu. They met him at the field of Naboth the Jezreelite. ²²When Joram saw Jehu, he asked, "Is all well, Jehu?" But Jehu replied, "How can all be well as long as your mother Jezebel carries on her countless harlotries and sorceries?" ²³Thereupon Joram turned his horses^a around and fled, crying out to Ahaziah, "Treason, Ahaziah!" ²⁴But Jehu drew his bow and hit Joram between the shoulders,^b so that the arrow pierced his heart; and he collapsed in his chariot.

²⁵Jehu thereupon ordered his officer Bidkar, "Pick him up and throw him into the field of Naboth the Jezreelite. Remember how you and I were riding side by side behind his father Ahab, when the LORD made this pronouncement about him: ²⁶'I swear, I have taken note of the blood of Naboth and the blood of his sons yesterday—declares the LORD. And I will requite you in this plot—declares the LORD.' So pick him up and throw him unto the plot in accordance with the word of the LORD."

²⁷On seeing this, King Ahaziah of Judah fled along the road to Beth-haggan. Jehu pursued him and said, "Shoot him down too!" [And they shot him] in his chariot at the ascent of Gur, which is near Ibleam. He fled to Megiddo and died there. ²⁸His servants conveyed him in a chariot to Jerusalem, and they buried him in his grave with his fathers, in the City of David. (²⁹Ahaziah had become king over Judah in the eleventh year of Joram son of Ahab.)

³⁰Jehu went on to Jezreel. When Jezebel heard of it, she painted her eyes with kohl and dressed her hair, and she looked out of the window. ³¹As Jehu entered the gate, she called out, "Is all well, Zimri, murderer of your master?"^c ³²He looked up toward the window and said, "Who is on my side, who?" And two or three eunuchs leaned out toward him. ³³"Throw her down," he said. They threw her down; and her blood spattered on the wall and on the horses, and they trampled her.

³⁴Then he went inside and ate and drank. And he said, "Attend to that cursed woman and bury her, for she was a king's daughter." ³⁵So they went to bury her; but all they found of her were the skull, the feet, and the hands. ³⁶They came back and reported to him; and he said, "It is just as the LORD spoke through His servant Elijah the Tishbite: The dogs shall devour the flesh of Jezebel in the field of Jezreel; ³⁷and the carcass of Jezebel shall be like dung on the ground, in the field of Jezreel, so that none will be able to say: 'This was Jezebel.'"

nant note throughout the scenes of the revolt as death is plotted and executed in vv. 18, 19, 22, 30. **28:** Although it is mentioned here, Ahaziah's body could only have been removed to Jerusalem later, after the revolt was over. **30–31:** Jezebel is portrayed as a proud, cold, noble woman. After hearing of the death of her son and son-in-law, she neither mourns nor tries to flee while Jehu and part of the troop are elsewhere. She pretties herself for a final scene and addresses a perfect barb to Jehu when he enters the palace grounds. **30:** *Kohl:* If the same as Arabic "kuhl," it is a sulphide of antimony, ground into powder, mixed with oil and applied to the eyelashes, an ancient mascara. *Zimri,* the assassin of Elah son of Baasha (1 Kings 16.8–14). Zimri eliminated all of the descendants of Baasha, as Baasha had eliminated all of the descendants of Jeroboam (1 Kings 15.27–30). Jehu has eliminated the house of Omri, but if he follows in the footsteps of Zimri his reign will be short (1 Kings 16.15).

---

a Lit. "hands"; see note at 1 Kings 22.34.   b Lit. "arms."   c See 1 Kings 16.8–10.

10 Ahab had seventy descendants in Samaria. Jehu wrote letters and sent them to Samaria, to the elders and officials of Jezreel[a] and to the guardians of [the children] of Ahab, as follows: 2 "Now, when this letter reaches you—since your master's sons are with you and you also have chariots and horses, and a fortified city and weapons—3 select the best and the most suitable of your master's sons and set him on his father's throne, and fight for your master's house." 4 But they were overcome by fear, for they thought, "If the two kings could not stand up to him, how can we?" 5 The steward of the palace and the governor of the city and the elders and the guardians sent this message to Jehu: "We are your subjects, and we shall do whatever you tell us to. We shall not proclaim anyone king; do whatever you like."

6 He wrote them a second time: "If you are on my side and are ready to obey me, take the heads of the attendants of your master's sons and come[b] to me in Jezreel tomorrow at this time." Now the princes, seventy in number, were with the notables of the town, who were rearing them. 7 But when the letter reached them, they took the princes and slaughtered all seventy of them; they put their heads in baskets and sent them to him in Jezreel. 8 A messenger came and reported to him: "They have brought the heads of the princes." He said, "Pile them up in two heaps at the entrance of the gate before morning." 9 In the morning he went out and stood there; and he said to all the people, "Are you blameless?[c] True, I conspired against my master and killed him; but who struck down all of these? 10 Know, then, that nothing that the LORD has spoken concerning the House of Ahab shall remain unfulfilled, for the LORD has done what he announced through His servant Elijah." 11 And Jehu struck down all that were left of the House of Ahab in Jezreel—and all his notables, intimates, and priests—till he left him no survivor.

12 He then set out for Samaria. On the way, when he was at Beth-eked of the shepherds, 13 Jehu came upon the kinsmen of King Ahaziah of Judah. "Who are you?" he asked. They replied, "We are the kinsmen of Ahaziah, and we have come to pay our respects to the sons of the king and the sons of the queen mother." 14 "Take them alive!" he said. They took them alive and then slaughtered them at the pit of Beth-eked, forty-two of them; he did not spare a single one.

15 He went on from there, and he met Jehonadab son of

10.1–17: The purge of the house of Ahab. 2–5: These verses illustrate that even after the many internal revolutions, the right to proclaim someone king remained vested with certain groups of people or their representatives. Jehu's message affirms the right even as his threat subverts it. **8–9:** Besides being a potent threat, the heads of Ahab's sons arrayed at the entrance of Jezreel proved silently that there was no Ahabite around whom anti-Jehu forces might rally. Jehu used them at Jezreel to argue that he was supported by the people of Samaria, the capital city constructed by Omri, Ahab's father. **11:** The killing extends to include those whose position and authority were based on their association with the royal house. The *priests* in this group may have served at the open shrines or the worship of Baal, or they may have been minor bureaucrats. Priests appear in the lists of royal officials in 2 Sam. 8.18; 20.26; 1 Kings 4.5, and as impoverished appointees (1 Sam. 2.36). These killings go beyond the prophetic charge to Jehu. **12–14:** Jehu extends the purge to a group of men from Judah claiming kinship with the (dead) Ahaziah. However related to Ahaziah, they were also connected to Athaliah, his mother, and through her to Ahab's family. **15–16:** Jehonadab, son of Rechab, founded a small traditionalist group within his clan that adopted a way of life similar to that of the Israelites before their settlement in the land. Rechabites abstained from wine, did not engage in any form of agriculture, and lived in tents (Jer 35.6–10). Jehu's invitation that Jehonadab join him to see his *zeal for the LORD* indicates that the Rechabites were also among the radical monotheists. The presence of Jehonadab in Jehu's chariots would have helped rally like-minded people to his support. Their combined *zeal for the LORD* is viewed positively as a continuation of the radical monotheism of Elijah (1 Kings 19.10, 14).

a   Emendation yields "of the city."
b   Targum and Septuagint read "and bring them."   c   Or "You are blameless."

Rechab coming toward him. He greeted him and said to him, "Are you as wholehearted with me as I am with you?" "I am," Jehonadab replied. "If so," [said Jehu,] "give me your hand." He gave him his hand and [Jehu] helped him into the chariot. 16 "Come with me," he said, "and see my zeal for the LORD." And he was taken along in the chariot. 17 Arriving in Samaria, [Jehu] struck down all the survivors of [the House of] Ahab in Samaria, until he wiped it out, fulfilling the word that the LORD had spoken to Elijah.

18 Jehu assembled all the people and said to them, "Ahab served Baal little; Jehu shall serve him much! 19 Therefore, summon to me all the prophets of Baal, all his worshipers, and all his priests: let no one fail to come, for I am going to hold a great sacrifice for Baal. Whoever fails to come shall forfeit his life." Jehu was acting with guile in order to exterminate the worshipers of Baal. 20 Jehu gave orders to convoke a solemn assembly for Baal, and one was proclaimed. 21 Jehu sent word throughout Israel, and all the worshipers of Baal came, not a single one remained behind. They came into the temple of Baal, and the temple of Baal was filled from end to end. 22 He said to the man in charge of the wardrobe,ᵃ "Bring out the vestments for all the worshipers of Baal"; and he brought vestments out for them. 23 Then Jehu and Jehonadab son of Rechab came into the temple of Baal, and they said to the worshipers of Baal, "Search and make sure that there are no worshipers of the LORD among you, but only worshipers of Baal." 24 So they went in to offer sacrifices and burnt offerings. But Jehu had stationed eighty of his men outside and had said, "Whoever permits the escape of a single one of the men I commit to your charge shall forfeit life for life."

25 When Jehu had finished presenting the burnt offering, he said to the guards and to the officers, "Come in and strike them down; let no man get away!" The guards and the officers struck them down with the sword and left them lying where they were; then they proceeded to the interiorᵇ of the temple of Baal. 26 They brought out the pillarsᶜ of the temple of Baal and burned them. 27 They destroyed the pillarᵈ of Baal, and they tore down the temple of Baal and turned it into latrines, as is still the case. 28 Thus Jehu eradicated the Baal from Israel. 29 However, Jehu did not turn away from the sinful objects by which Jeroboam son of Nebat had caused Israel to sin, namely, the golden calves at Bethel and at Dan.

10.18–28: The purge of Baalists from Israel. 18: It is unclear why Baalists believed Jehu's proclamation, and why they didn't become suspicious later when Jehonadab appeared with Jehu in the temple (v. 23). The narrative considers it sufficient that he promised to worship Baal more than Ahab. **22:** Some special item of clothing kept in the Temple was apparently necessary for the proper worship of Baal.

10.29–36: The rest of Jehu's reign. 29: Jehu's commitments did not go so far as to eliminate the institutions established by Jeroboam. No matter what the historical Jehu may have thought, the author considered this sinful.

a Meaning of Heb. uncertain.   b Lit. "city."
c Emendation yields "sacred posts"; cf. Deut. 12.3.   d Emendation yields "altar."

30 The LORD said to Jehu, "Because you have acted well and done what was pleasing to Me, having carried out all that I desired upon the House of Ahab, four generations of your descendants shall occupy the throne of Israel." 31 But Jehu was not careful to follow the Teaching of the LORD, the God of Israel, with all his heart; he did not turn away from the sins that Jeroboam had caused Israel to commit.

32 In those days the LORD began to reduce Israel; and Hazael harassed them throughout the territory of Israel 33 east of the Jordan, all the land of Gilead—the Gadites, the Reubenites, and the Manassites—from Aroer, by the Wadi Arnon, up to Gilead and Bashan.

34 The other events of Jehu's reign, and all his actions, and all his exploits, are recorded in the Annals of the Kings of Israel. 35 Jehu slept with his fathers and he was buried in Samaria; he was succeeded as king by his son Jehoahaz. 36 Jehu reigned over Israel for twenty-eight years in Samaria.

11 When Athaliah, the mother of Ahaziah, learned that her son was dead, she promptly killed off all who were of royal stock. 2 But Jehosheba, daughter of King Joram and sister of Ahaziah, secretly took Ahaziah's son Joash away from among the princes who were being slain, and [put]ᵃ him and his nurse in a bedroom. And theyᵇ kept him hidden from Athaliah so that he was not put to death. 3 He stayed with her for six years, hidden in the House of the LORD,ᶜ while Athaliah reigned over the land.

4 In the seventh year, Jehoiada sent for the chiefs of the hundreds of the Caritesᵈ and of the guards, and had them come to him in the House of the LORD. He made a pact with them, exacting an oath from them in the House of the LORD, and he showed them the king's son. 5 He instructed them: "This is what you must do: One-third of those who are on duty for the week ᵉshall maintain guardᵉ over the royal palace; 6 another third shall be [stationed] at the ᶠSur Gate;ᶠ and the other third shall be at the gate behind ᵍthe guards; you shall keep guard over the House on every side.ᵍ 7 The two divisions of yours who are off duty this

11.1–20: Athaliah's interregnum (842–836 BCE). **1–3:** Athaliah, with influence and power as queen mother, exploited the death of her son to have all males of royal stock killed, then assumed power. The author did not provide her with the usual opening or closing summary since he does not view her as a legitimate ruler. Jehosheba, who saved Joash's life, was spared since she could not claim the throne. According to the parallel account in 2 Chron. 22.11 she was the wife of Jehoiada the priest. **2:** *Joash* (cf. also 12.19, 20; 13.1) is also called Jehoash (12.1, 5). The difference in the form of the name is due to peculiarities in regional pronunciations of Heb during the biblical period. Both forms are found in Kings because the author tended to write names as he found them in his sources. Joash was the son of Ahaziah by a wife from Beer-sheba (12.2).

a Cf. 2 Chron. 22.11.   b 2 Chron. 22.11 reads "she."

c Jehosheba was the wife of the high priest Jehoiada; cf. 2 Chron. 22.11.

d Perhaps the Cherethites (cf. 2 Sam. 20.23) or the Carians. They were members of the king's bodyguard.

e-e Heb. "and who keep guard."

f-f 2 Chron. 23.5 reads "Foundation Gate."

g-g Meaning of Heb. uncertain.

week shall keep guard over the House of the LORD for the protection of the king. [8] You shall surround the king on every side, every man with his weapons at the ready; and whoever breaks through the ranks shall be killed. Stay close to the king in his comings and goings."

[9] The chiefs of hundreds did just as Jehoiada ordered: Each took his men—those who were on duty that week and those who were off duty that week—and they presented themselves to Jehoiada the priest. [10] The priest gave the chiefs of hundreds King David's spears[a] and quivers that were kept in the House of the LORD. [11] The guards, each with his weapons at the ready, stationed themselves—from the south end of the House to the north end of the House, at the altar and the House—to guard the king on every side. [12] [Jehoiada] then brought out the king's son, and placed upon him the crown and the insignia.[b] They anointed him and proclaimed him king; they clapped their hands and shouted, "Long live the king!"

[13] When Athaliah heard the shouting of the guards [and] the people, she came out to the people in the House of the LORD. [14] She looked about and saw the king standing by the pillar, as was the custom, the chiefs with their trumpets beside the king, and all the people of the land rejoicing and blowing trumpets. Athaliah rent her garments and cried out, "Treason, treason!" [15] Then the priest Jehoiada gave the command to the army officers, the chiefs of hundreds, and said to them, "Take her out c-between the ranks-c and, if anyone follows her, put him to the sword." For the priest thought: "Let her not be put to death in the House of the LORD." [16] They cleared a passageway for her and she entered the royal palace through the horses' entrance: there she was put to death.

[17] And Jehoiada solemnized the covenant between the LORD, on the one hand, and the king and the people, on the other—as well as between the king and the people—that they should be the people of the LORD. [18] Thereupon all the people of the land went to the temple of Baal. They tore it down and smashed its altars and images to bits, and they slew Mattan, the priest of Baal, in front of the altars. [Jehoiada] the priest then placed guards over the House of the LORD. [19] He took the chiefs of hundreds, the Carites,[d] the guards, and all the people of the land, and they escorted the king from the House of the LORD into

12: *Insignia* (Heb "'edut") may refer to an identifying object, such as the armband of Saul (2 Sam. 1.10), that marked its wearer as king; these are seen on royal reliefs of Mesopotamian kings. Most medieval and modern commentators interpret the word as "testimony/covenant/teaching" and understand that a document spelling out royal rights and obligations is intended by the word. **14:** The *pillar* may have been one of the two on the porch before the Temple that may have been symbolic of dynastic succession (1 Kings 7.15–22). The *people of the land* is often a technical term in Jeremiah and Ezekiel, prophetic books from the end of the monarchic period, and in 2 Kings and 2 Chronicles, historical books dealing with the late monarchy. It refers to an informal coalition of powerbrokers from important clans in Judah concerned with preserving the Davidic dynasty on the throne in Jerusalem (cf. 21.24; 25.19). The significance of their presence at the secret convocation was clear to Athaliah, who cried out *"Treason!"* **17:** After the anointing and public acclamation Jehoiada formalized two covenants. The first, a three-party covenant between the LORD, the people, and the king; the second, between the people and the king. The word "'edut" in v. 12 may refer to these. **18:** The *temple of Baal* in Jerusalem, mentioned here for the first time, may have been established by Athaliah during the interregnum, or earlier. This passage interrupts the natural flow from v. 17 to 19.

---

a 2 Chron. 23.9 adds "and shields."   *b Meaning of Heb. uncertain.*
c-c Meaning of Heb. uncertain.   *d Perhaps the Cherethites (cf. 2 Sam. 20.23) or the Carians. They were members of the king's bodyguard.*

the royal palace by the gate of the guards. And he ascended the royal throne. ²⁰ All the people of the land rejoiced, and the city was quiet. As for Athaliah, she had been put to the sword in the royal palace.

12 Jehoash was seven years old when he became king. ² Jehoash began his reign in the seventh year of Jehu, and he reigned in Jerusalem forty years. His mother's name was Zibiah of Beer-sheba. ³ All his days Jehoash did what was pleasing to the LORD, as the priest Jehoiada instructed him. ⁴ The shrines, however, were not removed; the people continued to sacrifice and offer at the shrines.

⁵ Jehoash said to the priests, "All the money, current money, brought into the House of the LORD as sacred donations—ᵃany money a man may pay as the money equivalent of persons,ᵃ or any other money that a man may be minded to bring to the House of the LORD—⁶ let the priests receive it, each from his benefactor; they, in turn, shall make repairs on the House, wherever damage may be found."

⁷ But in the twenty-third year of King Jehoash, [it was found that] the priests had not made the repairs on the House. ⁸ So King Jehoash summoned the priest Jehoiada and the other priests and said to them, "Why have you not kept the House in repair? Now do not accept money from your benefactors any more, but have it donated for the repair of the House." ⁹ The priests agreed that they would neither accept money from the people nor make repairs on the House.

¹⁰ And the priest Jehoiada took a chest and bored a hole in its lid. He placed it at the right side of the altar as one entered the House of the LORD, and the priestly guards of the threshold deposited there all the money that was brought into the House of the LORD. ¹¹ Whenever they saw that there was much money in the chest, the royal scribe and the high priest would come up and put the money accumulated in the House of the LORD into bags, and they would count it. ¹² Then they would deliver the money ᵇthat was weighed outᵇ to the overseers of the work, who were in charge of the House of the LORD. These, in turn, used to pay the carpenters and the laborers who worked on the House of the LORD, ¹³ and the masons and the stonecutters. They also paid for wood and for quarried stone with which to make the repairs on the House of the LORD, and for every other expenditure that

12.1–22: The reign of Jehoash/Joash began in 836–835 BCE. Both forms of the name are used by the author. **1:** The 40-year reign attributed to him includes the interregnum years of Athaliah, who officially had no reign. Counting his reign as beginning at the death of his father (842), he reigned until 802, though he may have reigned for a few more years. In Judah, at this time, the regnal year was counted from the seventh month, Tishri. **5:** Over 140 years had passed since Solomon had completed the Temple, and no major repairs had been undertaken. Jehoash, as royal patron of the Temple, not the priests, launches the project. *Sacred donations* were funds donated to the Temple for use by the clergy (Num. 18.19). These most likely included obligatory offerings of the half-shekel and freewill offerings made in a spirit of generosity. Joash orders that they be collected by the priests, be applied for repairs, and that the priests undertake the repairs themselves. **10–16:** A new system devised by Jehoash removes the priests from all responsibility and labor. Sacred donations are deposited directly into a coffer, counted by two officials, and distributed to special contractors for labor and materials. None of the funds can be used to enhance the Temple treasure and no accounting is demanded from the contractors. Funds deriving from the purification (NJPS sin) and guilt offerings could not be used for Temple repair, but remained priestly income. Income associated with positive feelings and spontaneous acts of kindness went into Temple repair; that associated with negative feelings born out of a sense of obligation or guilt went to the priests.

---

a-a *See Lev. 27.2–8.*   b-b *Meaning of Heb. uncertain.*

had to be made in repairing the House. [14] However, no silver bowls and no snuffers, basins, or trumpets—no vessels of gold or silver—were made at the House of the LORD from the money brought into the House of the LORD; [15] this was given only to the overseers of the work for the repair of the House of the LORD. [16] No check was kept on the men to whom the money was delivered to pay the workers; for they dealt honestly.

[17] Money brought ᵃas a guilt offering or as a sin offering-ᵃ was not deposited in the House of the LORD; it went to the priests.

[18] At that time, King Hazael of Aram came up and attacked Gath and captured it; and Hazael proceeded to march on Jerusalem. [19] Thereupon King Joash of Judah took all the objects that had been consecrated by his fathers, Kings Jehoshaphat, Jehoram, and Ahaziah of Judah, and by himself, and all the gold that there was in the treasuries of the Temple of the LORD and in the royal palace, and he sent them to King Hazael of Aram, who then turned back from his march on Jerusalem.

[20] The other events of Joash's reign, and all his actions, are recorded in the Annals of the Kings of Judah. [21] His courtiers formed a conspiracy against Joash and assassinated him at Beth-millo ᵇthat leads down to Silla.-ᵇ [22] The courtiers who assassinated him were Jozacar son of Shimeath and Jehozabad son of Shomer. He died and was buried with his fathers in the City of David; and his son Amaziah succeeded him as king.

13 In the twenty-third year of King Joash son of Ahaziah of Judah, Jehoahaz son of Jehu became king over Israel in Samaria—for seventeen years. [2] He did what was displeasing to the LORD. He persisted in the sins which Jeroboam son of Nebat had caused Israel to commit; he did not depart from them. [3] The LORD was angry with Israel and He repeatedly delivered them into the hands of King Hazael of Aram and into the hands of Benhadad son of Hazael. [4] But Jehoahaz pleaded with the LORD; and the LORD listened to him, for He saw the suffering that the king of Aram inflicted upon Israel. [5] So the LORD granted Israel a deliverer, and they gained their freedom from Aram; and Israel dwelt in its homes as before. [6] However, they did not depart from the sins which the House of Jeroboam had caused Israel to commit; they persisted in them. Even the sacred post stood in Samaria.

18–19: Hazael's threat to Jerusalem forced Joash to raid the Temple treasury. This provides the background for the author's notation in v. 14 that donated funds were not used for Temple vessels. People donating to the Temple were not obligated to restore treasure withdrawn by the king. Hazael could only have penetrated Judah so deeply because he was in control of Transjordan up to the Jabbok (modern Nahr es-Zerqa) and traversed parts of the kingdom of Israel without fear (see 13.3–7). **21:** The reasons for Joash's assassination are not given. The act was most likely not directed against his family or against the monarchy, but against him directly, perhaps because of his dismal handling of Hazael's incursions deep into the territory of Judah. The two men who killed him did not flee (14.5–6) and apparently had no interest in usurping the authority of the Davidic king.

13.1–9: The reign of Jehoahaz. The structure of this section has close parallels to that of the book of Judges, where Israel sins, a foreign nation punishes them, and God sends a savior to help them. Here, however, the additional element of divine prayer to God (v. 4), largely absent in Judges, is added.

a-a See Lev. 5.15.   b-b Meaning of Heb. uncertain.

⁷ᵃIn fact, Jehoahaz was left with a force of only fifty horsemen, ten chariots, and ten thousand foot soldiers; for the king of Aram had decimated them and trampled them like the dust under his feet.

⁸ The other events of Jehoahaz's reign, and all his actions and his exploits, are recorded in the Annals of the Kings of Israel. ⁹ Jehoahaz slept with his fathers and he was buried in Samaria; his son Joash succeeded him as king.

¹⁰ In the thirty-seventh year of King Joash of Judah, Jehoash son of Jehoahaz became king of Israel in Samaria—for sixteen years. ¹¹ He did what was displeasing to the LORD; he did not depart from any of the sins which Jeroboam son of Nebat had caused Israel to commit; he persisted in them.

¹² The other events of Joash's reign, and all his actions, and his exploits in his war with King Amaziah of Judah, are recorded in the Annals of the Kings of Israel. ¹³ Joash slept with his fathers and Jeroboam occupied his throne; Joash was buried in Samaria with the kings of Israel.

¹⁴ Elisha had been stricken with the illness of which he was to die, and King Joash of Israel went down to see him. He wept over him and cried, "Father, father! ᵇIsrael's chariots and horsemen!"ᵇ ¹⁵ Elisha said to him, "Get a bow and arrows"; and he brought him a bow and arrows. ¹⁶ Then he said to the king of Israel, "Grasp the bow!" And when he had grasped it, Elisha put his hands over the king's hands. ¹⁷ "Open the window toward the east," he said; and he opened it. Elisha said, "Shoot!" and he shot. Then he said, "An arrow of victory for the LORD! An arrow of victory over Aram! You shall rout Aram completely at Aphek." ¹⁸ He said, "Now pick up the arrows." And he picked them up. "Strike the ground!" he said to the king of Israel; and he struck three times and stopped. ¹⁹ The man of God was angry with him and said to him, ᶜ"If only you had struckᶜ five or six times! Then you would have annihilated Aram; as it is, you shall defeat Aram only three times."

²⁰ Elisha died and he was buried. Now bands of Moabites used to invade the land ᵈat the coming of every year.ᵈ ²¹ Once a man was being buried, when the people caught sight of such a band; so they threw the corpseᵉ into Elisha's

13.10–13: The reign of Joash/Jehoash of Israel. The highly stereotypical nature of this account of a king who reigned for sixteen years emphasizes that the historian of Kings only included information that fit his theological and ideological interests.

13.14–21: The death of Elisha.
14: *Israel's chariots and horsemen:* Elisha used this title at the assumption of Elijah (2.12).
17–18: Although both the shooting of the arrows and the hitting of the ground are presented as symbolic prophecies, a closer examination indicates that to be true only of the shooting. According to the prophetic story, Joash's decision on how many times to hit the ground actually determined the future and constituted an act of imitative magic. Elisha could only watch and interpret the significance of Joash's act. **20–21:** The prophetic story of Elisha's final miracle does not refer to something that happened when he was being buried in the ground or in an open grave. Elisha was most likely laid out in a typical Israelite burial cave on a stone bench where his body decomposed. Sometime later, under duress of circumstances, people in the midst of burying a man tossed his body unceremoniously into Elisha's cave where it touched that of Elisha. Elisha's power as a man of God lay not only in his prophetic abilities, but also in his person. Just as his inanimate staff could heal by contact (4.29), so could his bones.

a This verse would read well after v. 3.
b-b On Elisha as defender of Israel, see chapters 6–8.
c-c Lit. "to strike."
d-d Meaning of Heb. uncertain; emendation yields "year by year."
e Heb. "the man."

grave and ᵃmade off.ᵃ When the [dead] man came in contact with Elisha's bones, he came to life and stood up.

²²King Hazael of Aram had oppressed the Israelites throughout the reign of Jehoahaz. ²³But the Lᴏʀᴅ was gracious and merciful to them, and He turned back to them for the sake of His covenant with Abraham, Isaac, and Jacob. He refrained from destroying them, and He still did not cast them out from His presence. ²⁴When King Hazael of Aram died, his son Ben-hadad succeeded him as king; ²⁵and then Jehoash son of Jehoahaz recovered from Ben-hadad son of Hazael the towns which had been taken from his father Jehoahaz in war. Three times Joash defeated him, and he recovered the towns of Israel.

14 In the second year of King Joash son of Joahaz of Israel, Amaziah son of King Joash of Judah became king. ²He was twenty-five years old when he became king, and he reigned twenty-nine years in Jerusalem; his mother's name was Jehoaddan of Jerusalem. ³He did what was pleasing to the Lᴏʀᴅ, but not like his ancestor David; he did just as his father Joash had done. ⁴However, the shrines were not removed; the people continued to sacrifice and make offerings at the shrines. ⁵Once he had the kingdom firmly in his grasp, he put to death the courtiers who had assassinated his father the king. ⁶But he did not put to death the children of the assassins, in accordance with what is written in the Book of the Teaching of Moses, where the Lᴏʀᴅ commanded, "Parents shall not be put to death for children, nor children be put to death for parents; a person shall be put to death only for his own crime."ᵇ

⁷He defeated ten thousand Edomites in the Valley of Salt, and he captured Sela in battle and renamed it Joktheel, as is still the case. ⁸Then Amaziah sent envoys to King Jehoash son of Jehoahaz son of Jehu of Israel, with this message: "Come, let us confrontᶜ each other." ⁹King Jehoash of Israel sent back this message to King Amaziah of Judah: "The thistle in Lebanon sent this message to the cedar in Lebanon, 'Give your daughter to my son in marriage.' But a wild beast in Lebanon went by and trampled down the thistle. ¹⁰Because you have defeated Edom, you have become arrogant. Stay home and enjoy your glory, rather than provoke disaster and fall, dragging Judah down with you."

¹¹But Amaziah paid no heed; so King Jehoash of Israel

13.22–25: Victory over Aram. 25: Joash of Israel's minor successes against *Ben-hadad* were possible because Assyrian victory over the Arameans weakened them and drew forces away from Aram's southern front with Israel to the north. Joash is mentioned on a stele of the Assyrian king Adad-nirari as one who paid him tribute. The author has a narrower theo-historical perspective, and does not attribute the Israelite victories to these international events.

14.1–22: The reign of Amaziah son of Joash in Judah overlapped that of Joash son of Jehoahaz of Israel. **5–6:** Amaziah restricted his revenge to his father's assassins alone. The author explains that he did so in accordance with a law cited from Deut. 24.16 identified as coming from *the Book of the Teaching* ("torah") *of Moses*. This is a rare case in the Deuteronomistic History where a Torah law (not surprisingly from Deuteronomy), is explicitly cited. Even though it is listed as the first order of his business, avenging his father could not have been the first act of his reign. Since his father had left Judah weak and vulnerable to Aramean attack, the kingdom could not have been *firmly in his grasp* until that threat disappeared thanks to the Assyrians and Joash of Israel. **7–8:** His defeat of the *Edomites in the Valley of Salt* indicates that he was successful in limiting or eliminating their presence in the central Negev. There is a consensus that the sites mentioned are in or near the northern Arava. He did not, however, reestablish control of Edom. **11:** That Joash/Jehoash of Israel met his army at *Beth-shemesh,* by the foothills east of Jerusalem, indicates just how weak and unprepared Amaziah was for battle. **13:** The *Ephraim Gate* through which people went toward the territory of Ephraim was in the north wall of the city. Joash broke the wall here because Jerusalem, surrounded by gorges on its east, south, and west, is most vulnerable from the north. According to 2 Chron. 26.9, the breach

a-a *Heb. "he made off."*　　b *Deut. 24.16.*　　c *I.e., in battle.*

advanced, and he and King Amaziah of Judah confronted each other at Beth-shemesh in Judah. ¹²The Judites were routed by Israel, and they all fled to their homes. ¹³King Jehoash of Israel captured King Amaziah son of Jehoash son of Ahaziah of Judah at Beth-shemesh. He marched on Jerusalem, and he made a breach of four hundred cubits in the wall of Jerusalem, from ª the Ephraim Gate to the Corner Gate. ¹⁴He carried off all the gold and silver and all the vessels that there were in the House of the LORD and in the treasuries of the royal palace, as well as hostages; and he returned to Samaria.

¹⁵The other events of Jehoash's reign, and all his actions and exploits, and his war with King Amaziah of Judah, are recorded in the Annals of the Kings of Israel. ¹⁶Jehoash slept with his fathers, and was buried in Samaria with the kings of Israel; his son Jeroboam succeeded him as king.

¹⁷King Amaziah son of Joash of Judah lived fifteen years after the death of King Jehoash son of Jehoahaz of Israel. ¹⁸The other events of Amaziah's reign are recorded in the Annals of the Kings of Judah. ¹⁹A conspiracy was formed against him in Jerusalem and he fled to Lachish; but they sent men after him to Lachish, and they killed him there. ²⁰They brought back his body on horses, and he was buried with his fathers in Jerusalem, in the City of David.

²¹Then all the people of Judah took Azariah, who was sixteen years old, and proclaimed him king to succeed his father Amaziah. ²²It was he who rebuilt Elath and restored it to Judah, after King [Amaziah] slept with his fathers.

²³In the fifteenth year of King Amaziah son of Joash of Judah, King Jeroboam son of Joash of Israel became king in Samaria—for forty-one years. ²⁴He did what was displeasing to the LORD; he did not depart from all the sins that Jeroboam son of Nebat had caused Israel to commit. ²⁵It was he who restored the territory of Israel from Lebo-hamath to the sea of the Arabah, in accordance with the promise that the LORD, the God of Israel, had made through His servant, the prophet Jonah son of Amittai from Gath-hepher. ²⁶For the LORD saw the very bitter plight of Israel, with neither ᵇbond nor free-ᵇ left, and with none to help Israel. ²⁷And the LORD resolved not to blot out the name of Israel from under heaven; and he delivered them through Jeroboam son of Joash.

²⁸The other events of Jeroboam's reign, and all his actions and exploits, how he fought and recovered Damascus and Hamath ᶜfor Judah in Israel,ᶜ are recorded in the

was repaired by Amaziah's son. **17:** If Amaziah reigned 29 years (v. 2), and if he reigned 15 years after the death of Joash/Jehoash of Israel, then their reigns must have overlapped 14 years, not 2 as stated in v. 1. Furthermore, the conspiracy described in vv. 19–20 could not then have taken place immediately after the despoiling of Jerusalem. **21–22:** The *people of Judah*, perhaps the same group as the "people of the land" (11.14), placed Azariah on the throne. (Azariah is also referred to as Uzziah; see 15.13, 30, 32, 34. Both names combine a word meaning "strength" with a short form of the LORD's name, *-iah*. This is the same form as in "hallelujah," "hallelu + iah" meaning "praise + the LORD.") Some of Azariah's accomplishments are listed here.

14.23–28: The reign of Jeroboam II (788–747 BCE) was a long and prosperous one. The author of Kings indicates that, despite doing what displeased the LORD, in the course of his long reign he attained control in the north and in Transjordan of territories lost to the Arameans beginning in the days of Solomon. A somewhat one-sided view of the prosperity and self-confidence that characterized his reign is found in Amos. **25:** The author describes Jeroboam II's military accomplishments as fulfillment of God's promises through a prophet, Jonah son of Amittai. Jeroboam was able to extend Israel's borders deep into the territories once controlled by Arameans and into their kingdoms (v. 28) because the Assyrians had seriously weakened them. This connection between Israel and Assyria helped set the scene for someone in the 5th century to cast Jeroboam II's prophet as the protagonist in the book of Jonah. **26–27:** The author, who apparently knew the content of Jonah's proclamations in the days of Jeroboam II, suggests that sinful kingdom of the north was saved because of God's grace, rather than the people's repentance.

---

a Heb. "at."   *b-b* See note at 1 Kings 14.10.   *c-c* Emendation yields "for Israel."

Annals of the Kings of Israel. ²⁹Jeroboam slept with his fathers, the kings of Israel, and his son Zechariah succeeded him as king.

15 In the twenty-seventh year of King Jeroboam of Israel, Azariah son of King Amaziah of Judah became king. ²He was sixteen years old when he became king, and he reigned fifty-two years in Jerusalem; his mother's name was Jecoliah of Jerusalem. ³He did what was pleasing to the LORD, just as his father Amaziah had done. ⁴However, the shrines were not removed; the people continued to sacrifice and make offerings at the shrines. ⁵The LORD struck the king with a plague, and he was a leper until the day of his death; he lived ᵃin isolated quarters,ᵃ while Jotham, the king's son, was in charge of the palace and governed the people of the land.

⁶The other events of Azariah's reign, and all his actions, are recorded in the Annals of the Kings of Judah. ⁷Azariah slept with his fathers, and he was buried with his fathers in the City of David; his son Jotham succeeded him as king.

⁸In the thirty-eighth year of King Azariah of Judah, Zechariah son of Jeroboam became king over Israel in Samaria—for six months. ⁹He did what was displeasing to the LORD, as his fathers had done; he did not depart from the sins which Jeroboam son of Nebat had caused Israel to commit. ¹⁰Shallum son of Jabesh conspired against him and struck him down ᵇbefore the peopleᵇ and killed him, and succeeded him as king. ¹¹The other events of Zechariah's reign are recorded in the Annals of the Kings of Israel. ¹²This was in accord with the word that the LORD had spoken to Jehu: "Four generations of your descendants shall occupy the throne of Israel." And so it came about.ᶜ

¹³Shallum son of Jabesh became king in the thirty-ninth year of King Uzziah of Judah, and he reigned in Samaria one month. ¹⁴Then Menahem son of Gadi set out from Tirzah and came to Samaria; he attacked Shallum son of Jabesh in Samaria and killed him, and he succeeded him as king. ¹⁵The other events of Shallum's reign, and the conspiracy that he formed, are recorded in the Annals of the Kings of Israel.

¹⁶At that time, ᵃ[marching] from Tirzah,ᵃ Menahem

---

a-a *Meaning of Heb. uncertain.*
b-b *Some Septuagint mss. read "at Ibleam."*   c *Cf. 10.30.*

15.1–7: The reign of Azariah (Uzziah). Of all that transpired during Azariah's long reign, the author cares to mention only that he became a leper. By juxtaposing this fact to his notice that Azariah did nothing about the open shrines, the author may be implying that the leprosy was a punishment. (2 Chron. 26.16–21 provides a different and more explicit explanation for his punishment.) Azariah led successful campaigns against Philistia and established control of areas up to the Egyptian border, collected tribute from the Transjordanian Ammonites (and most likely reestablished influence in Edom; see 14.22), fortified Jerusalem, built towers and excavated cisterns in the wilderness, and undertook varied agricultural projects that increased royal wealth (2 Chron. 26.3–15). His sphere of influence in the south was similar to that of Solomon in his day. **1:** Radak, Ralbag, and modern commentators point out that based on this verse and 14.2, 17, 23, the synchronisms between the reigns of kings in Judah and Israel and the years of reign for each king do not work out. The numbers can be reconciled if it is assumed— the Tanakh does not say so explicitly—that Azariah became co-regent with his father at the age of 16 and these years were accounted to both his and his father's credit. **5:** Azariah's particular type of leprosy disqualified him from performing royal duties, so he was retired. (Naaman's leprosy did not disqualify him; cf. 5.1–2.) While he remained king in name, his son Jotham became a co-regent and king in fact. Both Azariah and Jotham were credited with the same years of reign. **7:** An inscribed Aramaic marble plaque from the Second Temple period, now in the Israel Museum, reads: "Here were brought the bones of Uzziah, King of Judah. Don't open." The wording suggests that although buried in the City of David, he was buried separately from other kings—perhaps because of the leprosy—whose bones were not reburied during the Sec-subdued Tiphsah and all who were in it, and its territory; and because it did not surrender, he massacred [its people] and ripped open all its pregnant women.

17 In the thirty-ninth year of King Azariah of Judah, Menahem son of Gadi became king over Israel in Samaria—for ten years. 18 He did what was displeasing to the LORD; throughout his days he did not depart from the sins which Jeroboam son of Nebat had caused Israel to commit. 19 King Pul of Assyria invaded the land, and Menahem gave Pul a thousand talents of silver that he might support him and strengthen his hold on the kingdom. 20 Menahem exacted the money from Israel: every man of means had to pay fifty shekels of silver for the king of Assyria. The king of Assyria withdrew and did not remain in the land. 21 The other events of Menahem's reign, and all his actions, are recorded in the Annals of the Kings of Israel. 22 Menahem slept with his fathers, and his son Pekahiah succeeded him as king.

23 In the fiftieth year of King Azariah of Judah, Pekahiah son of Menahem became king over Israel in Samaria—for two years. 24 He did what was displeasing to the LORD; he did not depart from the sins which Jeroboam son of Nebat had caused Israel to commit. 25 His aide, Pekah son of Remaliah, conspired against him and struck him down in the royal palace in Samaria; with him were fifty Gileadites, a-with men from Argob and Arieh;-a and he killed him and succeeded him as king.

26 The other events of Pekahiah's reign, and all his actions, are recorded in the Annals of the Kings of Israel.

27 In the fifty-second year of King Azariah of Judah, Pekah son of Remaliah became king over Israel and Samaria—for twenty years. 28 He did what was displeasing to the LORD; he did not depart from the sins which Jeroboam son of Nebat had caused Israel to commit. 29 In the days of King Pekah of Israel, King Tiglath-pileser of Assyria came and captured Ijon, Abel-beth-maacah, Janoah, Kedesh, Hazor—Gilead, Galilee, the entire region of Naphtali; and he deported b-the inhabitants-b to Assyria.

30 Hoshea son of Elah conspired against Pekah son of Remaliah, attacked him, and killed him. He succeeded him as king in the twentieth year of Jotham son of Uzziah. 31 The other events of Pekah's reign, and all his actions, are recorded in the Annals of the Kings of Israel.

a-a Meaning of Heb. uncertain.
b-b Heb. "them."

ond Temple period. There is no knowledge about where the plaque was originally found.

15.8–12: The reign of Zechariah. Zechariah of Israel was the fourth and final ruler of the Jehu dynasty in accordance with the prophecy of 10.30. He was assassinated by *Shallum son of Jabesh. Jabesh* most likely refers to the city of Jabesh in Transjordanian Gilead.

15.13: The reign of Shallum.

15.14–22: Menahem son of Gadi, most likely from the Transjordanian tribe of Gad, assassinated Shallum. **16:** *Tiphsah* was the northernmost city under Solomon's control near the Euphrates (1 Kings 5.4). The location of the city makes it unlikely that Menahem attacked it while engaged in an activity near Tirzah. His brutal reprisal against the people of Tiphsah was not unique (cf. 8.12; Hos. 14.1; Amos 1.13). The incident reported may be connected to the invasion of the Assyrians reported in v. 19. **19:** *Pul* is the Assyrian nickname of King Tiglath-pileser III of Assyria, mentioned by his longer name in v. 29. See 1 Chron. 5.26. Menahem paid tribute for Pul's support in helping him gain control over the kingdom. The tribute is mentioned in the annals of Tiglath-pileser from 738 BCE. The Assyrian may have entered territories claimed by Israel in northern Syria, but not the heartland. In retreating south, Israel effectively gave up control over the Aramean kingdoms.

15.23–26: The reign of Pekahiah. Menahem's son, Pekahiah, is assassinated by *Pekah,* supported by Transjordanian *Gileadites. Argob* in the Bashan was adjacent to Gilead (Deut. 3.4, 14–15). The catalyst may have been the breakaway of Arameans from Israelite control and a sense among Transjordanian Israelites that the monarch, safe in Samaria, had abandoned them.

15.27–31: The reign of Pekah. **29:** In his campaigns of 733–32 BCE, *Tiglath-pileser* conquered the same

³² In the second year of King Pekah son of Remaliah of Israel, Jotham son of King Uzziah of Judah became king. ³³ He was twenty-five years old when he became king, and he reigned sixteen years in Jerusalem; his mother's name was Jerusha daughter of Zadok. ³⁴ He did what was pleasing to the LORD, just as his father Uzziah had done. ³⁵ However, the shrines were not removed; the people continued to sacrifice and make offerings at the shrines. It was he who built the Upper Gate of the House of the LORD. ³⁶ The other events of Jotham's reign, and all his actions, are recorded in the Annals of the Kings of Judah. ³⁷ In those days, the LORD began to incite King Rezin of Aram and Pekah son of Remaliah against Judah. ³⁸ Jotham

block of territories taken by Arameans from Israel in the days of Baasha (1 Kings 15.20) along with Transjordanian Gilead. His annals mention that he took 13,520 people to Assyria. This marks the beginning of the Diaspora of the ten northern tribes.

15.32–38: The reign of Jotham. Little is told about the reign of Jotham in Judah. 2 Chron. 27.1–6 suggests that he maintained the borders of his father's kingdom, extending its control and influence into Ammonite territory. **37:** *Rezin*

Assyria and Israel and Judah in the book of Kings

slept with his fathers, and he was buried with his fathers in the city of his ancestor David; his son Ahaz succeeded him as king.

16 In the seventeenth year of Pekah son of Remaliah, Ahaz son of King Jotham of Judah became king. ² Ahaz was twenty years old when he became king, and he reigned sixteen years in Jerusalem. He did not do what was pleasing to the LORD his God, as his ancestor David had done, ³ but followed the ways of the kings of Israel. He even consigned his son to the fire, in the abhorrent fashion of the nations which the LORD had dispossessed before the Israelites. ⁴ He sacrificed and made offerings at the shrines, on the hills, and under every leafy tree.

⁵ Then King Rezin of Aram and King Pekah son of Remaliah of Israel advanced on Jerusalem for battle. They besieged Ahaz, but could not overcome [him]. ⁶ At that time King Rezin of Aram recovered Elath for Aram;ᵃ he drove out the Judites from Elath, and Edomites came to Elath and settled there, as is still the case.

⁷ Ahaz sent messengers to King Tiglath-pileser of Assyria to say, "I am your servant and your son; come and deliver me from the hands of the king of Aram and from the hands of the king of Israel, who are attacking me." ⁸ Ahaz took the gold and silver that were on hand in the House of the LORD and in the treasuries of the royal palace and sent them as a gift to the king of Assyria. ⁹ The king of Assyria responded to his request; the king of Assyria marched against Damascus and captured it. He deported ᵇ⁻its inhabitants⁻ᵇ to Kir and put Rezin to death.

¹⁰ When King Ahaz went to Damascus to greet King Tiglath-pileser of Assyria, he saw the altar in Damascus. King Ahaz sent the priest Uriah a sketch of the altar and a detailed plan of its construction. ¹¹ The priest Uriah did just as King Ahaz had instructed him from Damascus; the priest Uriah built the altar before King Ahaz returned from Damascus. ¹² When the king returned from Damascus, and when the king saw the altar, the king drew near the altar, ascended it, ¹³ and offered his burnt offering and meal offering; he poured his libation, and he dashed the blood of his offering of well-being against the altar. ¹⁴ As for the bronze altar which had been before the LORD, he moved it from its place in front of the Temple, ᶜ⁻between the [new] altar and the House of the LORD,⁻ᶜ and placed it

and *Pekah* formed a coalition against Jotham, planning to force him into an anti-Assyrian coalition.

16.1–20: The reign of Ahaz. Although the author does not evaluate Ahaz highly, his narrative indicates that Ahaz was an astute politician. **3:** *Consigned his son to the fire:* Although usually taken to mean that he sacrificed his son (cf. 3.27), the regular words of sacrifice are not used. It may mean that he had his son undergo some sort of fire ritual, perhaps a ritual singeing. **5–9:** The plan of *Rezin* and *Pekah* (15.37) gave rise to a brief Syro-Ephraimitic war (cf. Isa. chs 7–8) in 733–732 BCE. According to Isa. 7.6, they planned to replace Ahaz with a ruler willing to join their coalition. *Ahaz,* learning from the statecraft of Asa (1 Kings 15.18) and Menahem (2 Kings 15.19), bribed the enemy of his enemies to rescue him. **7:** *Your servant and your son:* In the diplomatic context of the ancient Near East, these phrases indicated Ahaz's friendly and voluntary submission to the authority of Tiglath-pileser III. **9:** The Assyrians responded by eliminating the threat from *Damascus. Kir,* location not known, but according to Amos 9.7, it was the original home of the Arameans. **10–16:** The Damascene type of *altar* introduced by Ahaz into the Jerusalem Temple was acceptable to the author. Ahaz, as Davidic patron of the Jerusalem Temple, could initiate these changes, to which *Uriah* the priest agreed. The altar that Ezek. 43.13–17 describes and prescribes for a future temple may be a copy of the Ahaz altar that Ezekiel saw in his youth.

a *Emendation yields "Edom."*
b-b *Heb. "it."*
c-c *Meaning of Heb. uncertain.*

on the north side of the [new] altar. ¹⁵ And King Ahaz commanded the priest Uriah: "On the great* altar you shall offer the morning burnt offering and the evening meal offering and the king's burnt offering and his meal offering, with the burnt offerings of all the people of the land, their meal offerings and their libations. And against it you shall dash the blood of all the burnt offerings and all the blood of the sacrifices. And I will decide* about the bronze altar."* ¹⁶ Uriah did just as King Ahaz commanded.

¹⁷ King Ahaz cut off the insets—the laver stands—and removed the lavers from them. He also removed the tank from the bronze oxen that supported it and set it on a stone pavement—¹⁸ on account of the king of Assyria.* He also extended to the House of the LORD *the sabbath passage that had been built in the palace and the king's outer entrance.*

¹⁹ The other events of Ahaz's reign, and his actions, are recorded in the Annals of the Kings of Judah. ²⁰ Ahaz slept with his fathers and was buried with his fathers in the City of David; his son Hezekiah succeeded him as king.

17 In the twelfth year of King Ahaz of Judah, Hoshea son of Elah became king over Israel in Samaria— for nine years. ² He did what was displeasing to the LORD, though not as much as the kings of Israel who preceded him. ³ King Shalmaneser marched against him, and Hoshea became his vassal and paid him tribute. ⁴ But the king of Assyria caught Hoshea in an act of treachery: he had sent envoys to King So of Egypt, and he had not paid the tribute to the king of Assyria, as in previous years. And the king of Assyria arrested him and put him in prison. ⁵ Then the king of Assyria marched against the whole land; he came to Samaria and besieged it for three years. ⁶ In the ninth year of Hoshea, the king of Assyria captured Samaria. He deported the Israelites to Assyria and settled them in Halah, at the [River] Habor, at the River Gozan, and in the towns of Media.

⁷ This happened because the Israelites sinned against the LORD their God, who had freed them from the land of Egypt, from the hand of Pharaoh king of Egypt. They worshiped other gods ⁸ and followed the customs of the nations which the LORD had dispossessed before the Israelites and the customs which the kings of Israel had prac-

a I.e., the new one.   b Meaning of Heb. uncertain
c I.e., the old one, cf. v. 14.
d I.e., because of the metal given him in tribute.
e-e Meaning of Heb. uncertain.

17–18: The removal of the various Temple furnishings was perhaps necessitated in order to meet the required payments to *Assyria.*

17.1–23: The end of the Northern Kingdom and the major exile of northern tribes. This ch appears confusing because the author (or a later editor) spliced together several documents in bringing this part of the history to a stirring finish and in driving home some didactic points. **1–3:** *Hoshea* (see 15.30), whose territorially reduced kingdom no longer included Galilee and Transjordan, submitted to Tiglath-pileser's son, *Shalmaneser* V. **4:** There was no pharaoh named *So.* Some historians consider it an Egyptian word for a high officer of the king; others consider *So* a reference to the delta city Sais whose kings of the 24th dynasty in the 720s were not friends of Assyria. In any case, the *king of Assyria* believed that *Hoshea . . . had sent envoys* to Egypt in order to enlist Egyptian aid in throwing off Assyrian domination. **6:** Cuneiform documents attribute the conquest of *Samaria* to both Shalmaneser V and Sargon II. Possibly, Shalmaneser died just before the capitulation of the city. The author of Kings, however, knows only Shalmaneser (see 18.9–12). Assyrian policy called for dispersing hostile populations throughout its empire. Israelites from Samaria were sent to *Gozan* on the Upper *Habor* river, to *Halah,* beyond the Tigris northeast of ancient Nineveh (see 15.29), and to towns on the Persian plateau. Large Jewish communities, descendants of these exiles, lived continuously in these or adjacent regions of Syria, Iraq, and Iran until the end of the 20th century. **7–23:** These verses summarize explicitly the philosophy of sin, covenant violation, and retribution by which the author evaluated all the kings of Israel. Nobody but Israel was responsible for the major calamities that befell the kingdom. This philosophical justification, however, differs from the typical remarks scattered throughout the book in that it holds the ticed. ⁹ The Israelites committedᵃ against the LORD their God acts which were not right: They built for themselves shrines in all their settlements, from watchtowers to fortified cities; ¹⁰ they set up pillars and sacred posts for themselves on every lofty hill and under every leafy tree; ¹¹ and they offered sacrifices there, at all the shrines, like the nations whom the LORD had driven into exile before them. They committed wicked acts to vex the LORD, ¹² and they worshiped fetishes concerning which the LORD had said to them, "You must not do this thing."

¹³ The LORD warned Israel and Judah by every prophet [and] every seer, saying: "Turn back from your wicked ways, and observe My commandments and My laws, according to all the Teaching that I commanded your fathers and that I transmitted to you through My servants the prophets." ¹⁴ But they did not obey; they stiffened their necks, like their fathers who did not have faith in the LORD their God; ¹⁵ they spurned His laws and the covenant that He had made with their fathers, and the warnings He had given them. They went after delusion and were deluded; [they imitated] the nations that were about them, which the LORD had forbidden them to emulate. ¹⁶ They rejected all the commandments of the LORD their God; they made molten idols for themselves—two calves—and they made a sacred post and they bowed down to all the host of heaven, and they worshiped Baal. ¹⁷ They consigned their sons and daughters to the fire; they practiced augury and divination, and gave themselves over to what was displeasing to the LORD and vexed Him. ¹⁸ The LORD was incensed at Israel and He banished them from His presence; none was left but the tribe of Judah alone.

¹⁹ Nor did Judah keep the commandments of the LORD their God; they followed the customs that Israel had practiced. ²⁰ So the LORD spurned all the offspring of Israel, and He afflicted them and delivered them into the hands of plunderers, and finally He cast them out from His presence.

²¹ For Israel broke away from the House of David, and they made Jeroboam son of Nebat king. Jeroboam caused Israel to stray from the LORD and to commit great sin, ²² and the Israelites persisted in all the sins which Jeroboam had committed; they did not depart from them. ²³ In the end, the LORD removed Israel from His presence, as He had warned them through all His servants the prophets. So the Israelites were deported from their land to Assyria, as is still the case.

people—considered as a collective body—culpable, along with rulers, for the consequences of their choice of religious practices. **7–18:** One explanation for the destruction of Israel is that under the influence of Canaanites and despite warnings, the people—not their rulers—persisted in doing wrong. The author does not agree with this view, regularly condemning the kings for following the ways of Jeroboam son of Nebat. **16:** The worship instituted in Bethel was illegitimate in the eyes of the Deuteronomistic historian, and is perceived as a continuation of earlier idolatrous practice. **19–20:** A comment indicating that the contents of vv. 7–18 were applicable also to Judah. **21–23:** A second explanation sketches a brief history of the Northern Kingdom, emphasizing its ignominious beginning and its deserved end. This is in harmony with the running comments and evaluations of the author, and assigns responsibility to Jeroboam's religious policies that were maintained by subsequent rulers.

a *Meaning of Heb. uncertain.*

24 The king of Assyria brought [people] from Babylon, Cuthah, Avva, Hamath, and Sephar-vaim, and he settled them in the towns of Samaria in place of the Israelites; they took possession of Samaria and dwelt in its towns. 25 When they first settled there, they did not worship the LORD; so the LORD sent lions against them which killed some of them. 26 They said to the king of Assyria: "The nations which you deported and resettled in the towns of Samaria do not know the rules of the God of the land; therefore He has let lions loose against them which are killing them—for they do not know the rules of the God of the land."

27 The king of Assyria gave an order: "Send there one of the priests whom you have deported; let him[a] go and dwell there, and let him teach them the practices of the God of the land." 28 So one of the priests whom they had exiled from Samaria came and settled in Bethel; he taught them how to worship the LORD. 29 However, each nation continued to make its own gods and to set them up in the cult places which had been made by the people of Samaria; each nation [set them up] in the towns in which it lived. 30 The Babylonians made Succoth-benoth, and the men of Cuth made Nergal, and the men of Hamath made Ashima, 31 and the Avvites made Nibhaz and Tartak; and the Sepharvites burned their children [as offerings] to Adrammelech and Anamelech, the gods of Sepharvaim. 32 They worshiped the LORD, but they also appointed from their own ranks priests of the shrines, who officiated for them in the cult places. 33 They worshiped the LORD, while serving their own gods according to the practices of the nations from which they had been deported. 34 To this day, they follow their former practices. They do not worship the LORD [properly]. They do not follow the laws and practices, the Teaching and Instruction that the LORD enjoined upon the descendants of Jacob—who was given the name Israel—35 with whom He made a covenant and whom He commanded: "You shall worship no other gods; you shall not bow down to them nor serve them nor sacrifice to them. 36 You must worship only the LORD your God, who brought you out of the land of Egypt with great might and with an outstretched arm: to Him alone shall you bow down and to Him alone shall you sacrifice. 37 You shall observe faithfully, all your days, the laws and the practices; the Teaching and Instruction that I[b] wrote down for you; do not worship other gods. 38 Do not forget the covenant that I made with you; do not worship

17.24–41: The practices of the people who were settled in Samaria. 24: This verse was originally part of the document used by the author for vv. 1–6. The emptied cities of *Samaria* were settled by people exiled there from northern Syria and from southern Mesopotamia. **25–33:** The new immigrants brought with them their own religions, which they tried to accommodate with local practices in order to appease *the God of the land*. In v. 41, which originally continued this section, the author notes that they never got it quite right and that the hybrid religious practices that they evolved persisted. **34–40:** Ralbag correctly suggests that these verses address the behavior of Israelites who had been left in the land; even the experience of exile did not chasten them to return to God. In either case, they most likely originally continued v. 23.

a Heb. "them."   b Heb. "He."

other gods. ³⁹Worship only the Lord your God, and He will save you from the hands of all your enemies." ⁴⁰But they did not obey; they continued their former practices. ⁴¹Those nations worshiped the Lord, but they also served their idols. To this day their children and their children's children do as their ancestors did.

18 In the third year of King Hoshea son of Elah of Israel, Hezekiah son of King Ahaz of Judah became king. ²He was twenty-five years old when he became king, and he reigned in Jerusalem twenty-nine years; his mother's name was Abi^a daughter of Zechariah. ³He did what was pleasing to the Lord, just as his father David had done. ⁴He abolished the shrines and smashed the pillars and cut down the sacred post. He also broke into pieces the bronze serpent that Moses had made, for until that time the Israelites had been offering sacrifices to it; it was called Nehushtan. ⁵He trusted only in the Lord the God of Israel; there was none like him among all the kings of Judah after him, nor among those before him. ⁶He clung to the Lord; he did not turn away from following Him, but kept the commandments that the Lord had given to Moses. ⁷And the Lord was always with him; he was successful wherever he turned. He rebelled against the king of Assyria and would not serve him. ⁸He overran Philistia as far as Gaza and its border areas, from watchtower to fortified town.

⁹In the fourth year of King Hezekiah, which was the seventh year of King Hoshea son of Elah of Israel, King Shalmaneser of Assyria marched against Samaria and besieged it, ¹⁰and he^b captured it at the end of three years. In the sixth year of Hezekiah, which was the ninth year of King Hoshea of Israel, Samaria was captured; ¹¹and the king of Assyria deported the Israelites to Assyria. He ^{c-}settled them in^{-c} Halah, along the Habor [and] the River Gozan, and in the towns of Media. ¹²[This happened] because they did not obey the Lord their God; they transgressed His covenant—all that Moses the servant of the

a 2 Chron. 29.1 reads "Abijah."

b So some mss. and ancient versions; most mss. and editions read "they."

c-c Lit. "led them to."

18.1–20.21: The reign of Hezekiah. The author dedicates three chapters to selected events from the reign of Hezekiah. He allots as much attention to this king as he did to the house of Ahab, and

highlights Isaiah in these narratives as he did Elijah in the earlier ones. Hezekiah is important to the author because he demonstrated that the high standard expected of a king could be and was indeed

met. V. 5, which contradicts 23.25, might suggest that an edition of the history originally ended with Hezekiah; this might explain why this section is so long and laudatory. The various sources used by the author to describe Hezekiah's reign are arranged only in a rough chronological order, and the author's thematic interests override the chronology, creating some confusion. 2 Kings 18.9–20.19 is paralleled with variations in 2 Chron. ch 29 and Isa. ch 36–39.

18.1–8: Hezekiah's reforms.
3: *What was pleasing . . . as . . . David:* Hezekiah is the first king evaluated so positively by the author. The phrase *his father David* is applied also to Asa (1 Kings 15.11) and Josiah (22.2, where NJPS properly renders "father" by "ancestor"). **4:** Elimination of the open *shrines* concentrated worship in Jerusalem (see v. 22). The author describes *Nehushtan*, a form of the word for *serpent*, as an ancient relic associated with the miraculous healings in the wilderness (Num. 21.8–9) held sacred by Israelites. Noting that the Heb actually says "he called it" (and not *it was called*), Rashi suggests that Hezekiah, the active subject of the sentence, labeled it "bronze serpent-thing," "nehushtan" in Heb, as a pejorative. **7–8:** Hezekiah planned to revolt against Assyrian control early in his reign, but waited until the opportunity was ripe. The campaign in *Philistia* was intended to bring all coastal cities into an anti-Assyrian coalition. Similarly, his fortification and enhancements around the Gihon spring, the main source of Jerusalem's water, were intended to help the city survive an extended siege (20.20). 2 Chron. 32 provides additional information about his preparation of storage facilities, weapons, and fortifications.

18.9–12: The Assyrian invasion of the Northern Kingdom. Cf. 17.1–6. The author abridges information given earlier so as to drive home the lesson learned from history in v. 12.

LORD had commanded. They did not obey and they did not fulfill it.

13 In the fourteenth year of King Hezekiah, King Sennacherib of Assyria marched against all the fortified towns of Judah and seized them. 14 King Hezekiah sent this message to the king of Assyria at Lachish: "I have done wrong; withdraw from me; and I shall bear whatever you impose on me." So the king of Assyria imposed upon King Hezekiah of Judah a payment of three hundred talents of silver and thirty talents of gold. 15 Hezekiah gave him all the silver that was on hand in the House of the LORD and in the treasuries of the palace. 16 At that time Hezekiah cut down the doors and the doorposts^a of the Temple of the LORD, which King Hezekiah had overlaid [with gold], and gave them to the king of Assyria.

17 But the king of Assyria sent ^b the Tartan, the Rabsaris, and the Rabshakeh^-b from Lachish with a large force to

a Meaning of Heb. uncertain.
b-b Assyrian titles.

18.13–37: Assyria threatens Judah. 13–16: A brief straightforward description of what happened in Jerusalem. The author may have cited it from a chronicle. *Sennacherib's* armies swept through *Judah* in 701 BCE, wreaking great havoc. The author focuses only on what happened at Jerusalem and hints that *Hezekiah* precipitated the Assyrian response (v. 14). Sennacherib's own accounts mention that he conquered 46 strong cities and forts, that he captured over 200,000 people, that he made "Hezekiah a prisoner in Jerusalem, like a bird in a cage," and that Hezekiah paid him a large tribute, including his daughters, palace women, and male and female singers. **14:** Assyrian headquarters were located near *Lachish*, about 45 km (30 mi)

Places associated with Sennacherib's invasion of Judah

King Hezekiah in Jerusalem. They marched up to Jerusalem; and when they arrived, they took up a position near the conduit of the Upper Pool, by the road of the Fuller's Field. [18] They summoned the king; and Eliakim son of Hilkiah, who was in charge of the palace, Shebna the scribe, and Joah son of Asaph the recorder went out to them.

[19] The Rabshakeh said to them, "You tell Hezekiah: Thus said the Great King, the King of Assyria: What makes you so confident? [20] You must think that mere talk is counsel and valor for war! Look, on whom are you relying, that you have rebelled against me? [21] You rely, of all things, on Egypt, that splintered reed of a staff, which enters and punctures the palm of anyone who leans on it! That's what Pharaoh king of Egypt is like to all who rely on him. [22] And if you tell me that you are relying on the LORD your God, He is the very one whose shrines and altars Hezekiah did away with, telling Judah and Jerusalem, 'You must worship only at this altar in Jerusalem.' [23] Come now, make this wager with my master, the king of Assyria: I'll give you two thousand horses if you can produce riders to mount them. [24] So how could you refuse anything even to the deputy of one of my master's lesser servants, relying on Egypt for chariots and horsemen? [25] And do you think I have marched against this land to destroy it without the LORD? The LORD Himself told me: Go up against that land and destroy it."

[26] Eliakim son of Hilkiah, Shebna, and Joah replied to the Rabshakeh, "Please, speak to your servants in Aramaic, for we understand it; do not speak to us in Judean in the hearing of the people on the wall." [27] But the Rabshakeh answered them, "Was it to your master and to you that my master sent me to speak those words? It was precisely to the men who are sitting on the wall—who will have to eat their dung and drink their urine with you." [28] And the Rabshakeh stood and called out in a loud voice in Judean: "Hear the words of the Great King, the King of Assyria. [29] Thus said the king: Don't let Hezekiah deceive

long between the narrative of vv. 13 and 14 above. The three Assyrian titles mean roughly "field marshal," "chief officer" (lit. "chief eunuch"), and "chief administrator" (lit. "chief butler"). The *Rabshakeh* was a highly placed Assyrian official. He was obviously well informed about Hezekiah's political alliances (v. 21), religious activities (v. 22), able to speak "Judean" (v. 26), and knowledgeable about Israelite religion (v. 25). His speech, although formally directed to the leaders, was intended for the ears of the common folk so that they would pressure their king to give in to Assyria. **19:** *The Great King, the King of Assyria* are actual titles found in the Assyrian annals. **21–25:** Judah's political ally will not save her. Judah's God will not save her either, for Judah has not, says the Rabshakeh, served God properly. The Rabshakeh speaks of Hezekiah's reforms as an affront to God, in his attempt to arouse opposition to Hezekiah's policy of opposing Assyria. **26:** *Aramaic* was the diplomatic language in the southwestern parts of the Assyrian empire. Assyrian reliefs depict two scribes recording events, one in cuneiform and one in Aramaic. *Judean* refers to the local dialect of Hebrew. Hebrew remained a spoken language, albeit in different dialectal forms, along with Aramaic until the 3rd century CE. Then it evolved into a liturgical language and a language of learned discourse and writing, like Classical Arabic and Latin. After 1,600 years, Hebrew was conscientiously revived as a mother tongue during the 19th and 20th centuries CE among Jews living in Israel. Aramaic remained an important language in the Middle East until displaced by Arabic in the 7th to 8th centuries CE. Aramaic remains a liturgical language in some Eastern tradition churches. At the end of the 20th century, it was spoken by elders in a few Lebanese villages and as a "Jewish" language in Israel by Jews from Kurdistan, but is no longer a mother tongue. **27:** *Eat . . . dung . . . urine*, a threat of famine brought about by a

southwest of Jerusalem. Wall reliefs from Sennacherib's palace in Nineveh, now in the British Museum, illustrate the siege and fall of Lachish in great detail. These suggest what Hezekiah wished to avoid in Jerusalem. **17:** This is the beginning of the expansive narratives that conclude at 19.37. They feature prophetic stories about Isaiah concerning the events treated

tersely in vv. 13–16; they incorporate legends, and are likely written after the events they describe to show how the God of Israel protected his city, Jerusalem, from the Assyrians. This theme of the inviolability of Jerusalem plays a major role in the work of the prophet Isaiah. Chronologically, the speeches presented in vv. 17–35, along with some story material in ch 19, be-you, for he will not be able to deliver you from my[a] hands. [30] Don't let Hezekiah make you rely on the LORD, saying: The LORD will surely save us: this city will not fall into the hands of the king of Assyria. [31] Don't listen to Hezekiah. For thus said the king of Assyria: Make your peace with me and come out to me,[b] so that you may all eat from your vines and your fig trees and drink water from your cisterns, [32] until I come and take you away to a land like your own, a land of grain [fields] and vineyards, of bread and wine, of olive oil and honey, so that you may live and not die. Don't listen to Hezekiah, who misleads you by saying, 'The LORD will save us.' [33] Did any of the gods of other nations save his land from the king of Assyria? [34] Where were the gods of Hamath and Arpad? Where were the gods of Sepharvaim, Hena, and Ivvah? [And] did they[c] save Samaria from me? [35] Which among all the gods of [those] countries saved their countries from me, that the LORD should save Jerusalem from me?" [36] But the people were silent and did not say a word in reply; for the king's order was: "Do not answer him." [37] And so Eliakim son of Hilkiah, who was in charge of the palace, Shebna the scribe, and Joah son of Asaph the recorder came to Hezekiah with their clothes rent, and they reported to him what the Rabshakeh had said.

19 When King Hezekiah heard this, he rent his clothes, and covered himself with sackcloth, and went into the House of the LORD. [2] He also sent Eliakim, who was in charge of the palace, Shebna the scribe, and the senior priests, covered with sackcloth, to the prophet Isaiah son of Amoz. [3] They said to him, "Thus said Hezekiah: This day is a day of distress, of chastisement, and of disgrace. [d] The babes have reached the birthstool, but the strength to give birth is lacking.[d] [4] Perhaps the LORD your God will take note of all the words of the Rabshakeh, whom his master the king of Assyria has sent to blaspheme the living God, and will mete out judgment for the words that the LORD your God has heard—if you will offer up prayer for the surviving remnant."

[5] When King Hezekiah's ministers came to Isaiah, [6] Isaiah said to them, "Tell your master as follows: Thus said the LORD: Do not be frightened by the words of blasphemy against Me that you have heard from the minions

siege. **31–32:** As an inducement to surrender, the Rabshakeh offers peace and resettlement in some land of exile described as a wonderful place. **34:** *Hamath . . . Ivvah,* cities that the Assyrians had previously conquered.

19.1–37: Hezekiah consults Isaiah. 1–4: Hezekiah goes directly to the Temple and also sends messengers to Isaiah, attempting to stimulate him to action by emphasizing the words of the Rabshakeh against *the LORD your God.*

---

a *So several mss. and ancient versions; most mss. and editions read "his."*
b *I.e., to my representative the Rabshakeh.*
c *I.e., the gods of Samaria.*
d-d *I.e., the situation is desperate and we are at a loss.*

of the king of Assyria. [7] I will delude[a] him; he will hear a rumor and return to his land, and I will make him fall by the sword in his land."

[8] The Rabshakeh, meanwhile, heard that [the king] had left Lachish; he turned back and found the king of Assyria attacking Libnah. [9] But [the king of Assyria] learned that King Tirhakah of Nubia had come out to fight him; so he again sent messengers to Hezekiah, saying, [10] "Tell this to King Hezekiah of Judah: Do not let your God, on whom you are relying, mislead you into thinking that Jerusalem will not be delivered into the hands of the king of Assyria. [11] You yourself have heard what the kings of Assyria have done to all the lands, how they have annihilated them; and can you escape? [12] Were the nations that my predecessors[b] destroyed—Gozan, Haran, Rezeph, and the Beth-edenites in Telassar—saved by their gods? [13] Where is the king of Hamath? And the king of Arpad? And the kings of Lair, Sepharvaim, Hena, and Ivvah?"

[14] Hezekiah took the letter from the messengers and read it. Hezekiah then went up to the House of the LORD and spread it out before the LORD. [15] And Hezekiah prayed to the LORD and said, "O LORD of Hosts, Enthroned on the Cherubim! You alone are God of all the kingdoms of the earth. You made the heavens and the earth. [16] O LORD, incline Your ear and hear; open Your eyes and see. Hear the words that Sennacherib has sent to blaspheme the living God! [17] True, O LORD, the kings of Assyria have annihilated the nations and their lands, [18] and have committed their gods to the flames and have destroyed them; for they are not gods, but man's handiwork of wood and stone. [19] But now, O LORD our God, deliver us from his hands, and let all the kingdoms of the earth know that You alone, O LORD, are God."

[20] Then Isaiah son of Amoz sent this message to Hezekiah: "Thus said the LORD, the God of Israel: I have heard the prayer you have offered to Me concerning King Sennacherib of Assyria. [21] This is the word that the LORD has spoken concerning him:

> "Fair Maiden Zion despises you,
> She mocks at you;
> Fair Jerusalem shakes
> Her head at you.
> 22 Whom have you blasphemed and reviled?
> Against whom made loud your voice

7: Isaiah's prophecy that the king of Assyria would hear a rumor, return to Assyria and be killed there are reported fulfilled in vv. 36–37. **9:** *King Tirhakah* was the last pharaoh of the twenty-fifth (Ethiopian) dynasty. Although he reigned 690–664 BCE, he was active militarily or had armies led in his name years before. He was not a king in 701 when Sennacherib besieged Jerusalem, but was known to have been one when the author wrote. **10–19:** A delegation from Sennacherib, now at Libnah north of Lachish, arrived with essentially the same message as that delivered by the Rabshakeh. **20–28:** These verses are not present in the book of Isaiah, but similar anti-Assyrian passages occur in Isa. 10.12–19; 14.24–27.

a Lit. "put a spirit in."
b Lit. "fathers."

And haughtily raised your eyes?
Against the Holy One of Israel!

23 Through your envoys you have blasphemed my
    Lord.
Because you thought,
'Thanks to my vast chariotry,
It is I who have climbed the highest mountains,
To the remotest parts of the Lebanon,
And have cut down its loftiest cedars,
Its choicest cypresses,
And have reached its ªremotest lodge,ª
ᵇIts densest forest.ᵇ

24 It is I who have drawnᶜ and drunk the waters of
    strangers;
I have dried up with the soles of my feet
All the streams of Egypt.'

25 Have you not heard? Of old
I planned that very thing,
I designed it long ago,
And now have fulfilled it.
And it has come to pass,
Laying waste fortified towns
In desolate heaps.

26 Their inhabitants are helpless,
Dismayed and shamed.
They were but grass of the field
And green herbage,
Grass of the roofs that is blasted
Before the ᵈstanding grain.ᵈ

27 I know your stayings
And your goings and comings,
And how you have raged against Me.

28 Because you have raged against Me,
And your tumult has reached My ears,
I will place My hook in your nose
And My bit between your jaws;
And I will make you go back by the road
By which you came.

29 "And this is the sign for you:ᵉ This year you eat what
grows of itself, and the next year what springs from that;
and in the third year, sow and reap, and plant vineyards
and eat their fruit. ³⁰ And the survivors of the House of

a-a *Isa. 37.24 reads "highest peak."*
b-b *Lit. "Its farmland forest"; exact meaning of Heb. uncertain.*
c *Or "dug"; meaning of Heb. uncertain.*
d-d *Emendation yields "east wind"; see note at Isa. 37.27.*
e *I.e., Hezekiah.*

29: It will take two years for life to return to normal after the invasion and siege. **32–34:** Known prophecies about the protected status of Jerusalem, combined with the fact that Sennacherib withdrew his forces, gave rise to a sense that the city was inviolable (Isa. 33.20; Zech. 12.8; Ps. 46.5–8).

Judah that have escaped shall regenerate its stock below
and produce boughs above.

31   For a remnant shall come forth from Jerusalem,
          Survivors from Mount Zion.
          The zeal of the LORD of Hosts
          Shall bring this to pass.

32 Assuredly, thus said the LORD concerning the king of
Assyria:

          He shall not enter this city:
          He shall not shoot an arrow at it,
          Or advance upon it with a shield,
          Or pile up a siege mound against it.
33   He shall go back
          By the way he came;
          He shall not enter this city
                              —declares the LORD.
34   I will protect and save this city for My sake,
          And for the sake of My servant David."

35 That night an angel of the LORD went out and struck
down one hundred and eighty-five thousand in the Assyrian camp, and the following morning they were all dead
corpses.

36 So King Sennacherib of Assyria broke camp and retreated, and stayed in Nineveh. 37 While he was worshiping in the temple of his god Nisroch, his sons Adrammelech and Sarezer struck him down with the sword. They
fled to the land of Ararat, and his son Esarhaddon succeeded him as king.

20 In those days Hezekiah fell dangerously ill. The
prophet Isaiah son of Amoz came and said to him,
"Thus said the LORD: Set your affairs in order, for you are
going to die; you will not get well." 2 Thereupon Hezekiah
turned his face to the wall and prayed to the LORD. He
said, 3 "Please, O LORD, remember how I have walked before You sincerely and wholeheartedly, and have done
what is pleasing to You." And Hezekiah wept profusely.

4 Before Isaiah had gone out of the middle court, the
word of the LORD came to him: 5 "Go back and say to Hezekiah, the ruler of My people: Thus said the LORD, the
God of your father David: I have heard your prayer, I
have seen your tears. I am going to heal you; on the third
day you shall go up to the House of the LORD. 6 And I will
add fifteen years to your life. I will also rescue you and
this city from the hands of the king of Assyria. I will protect this city for My sake and for the sake of My servant

35: There is no tradition of such a
plague other than here and in Isa.
37.36. **36:** This verse may have
originally followed 18.16, concluding a short summary of the siege
of 701, or after the prediction of
this event in 19.7. In its present
context, the verse leaves the impression that events occurring
over many decades actually took
place in a short while in fulfillment
of the prophecy of 19.7. Sennacherib did hear a rumor (about Tirhakah [v. 9]) and did return to
his land (from which he ventured
forth in the following years many
times on campaigns, primarily
against Babylonia), and died by
the sword in 681 BCE. **37:** We
now know from Assyrian sources
that Sennacherib was killed by
Arad-Ninlil, rather than his sons
Adrammelech and Sarezer; Sennacherib was, however, as stated
in the Bible, *succeeded* by *his son
Esarhaddon.*

**20.1–12: The story of Hezekiah's
illness** is loosely connected to its
context, and is out of chronological
order. Ralbag argues that it is not
connected to the Sennacherib
story. On the basis of v. 6 (= 19.34),
with its reference to an Assyrian
threat, he proposes that it addresses new threats by Esarhaddon, Sennacherib's son. Merodach-
baladan—reading the name
correctly as in Isa. 39.1—however,
was an anti-Assyrian ruler who
usurped the throne of Babylonia
twice: the first time, for eleven
years after the death of Shalmaneser V in 721 BCE and the second,
for nine months in 703 after the
death of Sargon II. The time of his
envoys' visit in v. 12, then, most
likely coincided with his planning
to revolt against Assyria in the
east, around 705, while Hezekiah
was making his own preparations
to revolt in the west. **4:** Contrition
accompanied by prayer can effect
a change in God's decision.

David."—⁷Then Isaiah said, "Get a cake of figs." And they got one, and they applied it to the rash, and he recovered.—⁸Hezekiah asked Isaiah, "What is the sign that the LORD will heal me and that I shall go up to the House of the LORD on the third day?" ⁹Isaiah replied, "This is the sign for you from the LORD that the LORD will do the thing that He has promised: Shallᵃ the shadow advance ten steps or recede ten steps?" ¹⁰Hezekiah said, "It is easy for the shadow to lengthen ten steps, but not for the shadow to recede ten steps." ¹¹So the prophet Isaiah called to the LORD, and He made the shadow which had descended on the dialᵇ of Ahaz recede ten steps.

¹²At that time, King Berodach-ᶜbaladan son of Baladan of Babylon sent [envoys with] a letter and a gift to Hezekiah, for he had heard about Hezekiah's illness. ¹³ᵈHezekiah heard about themᵈ and he showed them all his treasurehouse—the silver, the gold, the spices, and the fragrant oil—and his armory, and everything that was to be found in his storehouses. There was nothing in his palace or in all his realm that Hezekiah did not show them. ¹⁴Then the prophet Isaiah came to King Hezekiah. "What," he demanded of him, "did those men say to you? Where have they come to you from?" "They have come," Hezekiah replied, "from a far country, from Babylon." ¹⁵Next he asked, "What have they seen in your palace?" And Hezekiah replied, "They have seen everything that is in my palace. There was nothing in my storehouses that I did not show them."

¹⁶Then Isaiah said to Hezekiah, "Hear the word of the LORD: ¹⁷A time is coming when everything in your palace which your ancestors have stored up to this day will be carried off to Babylon; nothing will remain behind, said the LORD. ¹⁸And some of your sons, your own issue, whom you will have fathered, will be taken to serve as eunuchs in the palace of the king of Babylon." ¹⁹Hezekiah declared to Isaiah, "The word of the LORD that you have spoken is good." For he thought, "It means that ᵉsafety is assured forᵉ my time."

²⁰The other events of Hezekiah's reign, and all his exploits, and how he made the pool and the conduit and brought the water into the city, are recorded in the Annals of the Kings of Judah. ²¹Hezekiah slept with his fathers, and his son Manasseh succeeded him as king.

7: The *cake of figs* was applied as a poultice. The same medication is prescribed for horses in a text from Ugarit. **9–11:** The *sign* itself is unclear, but likely refers to *the shadow* of the sun*dial* moving in an unnatural direction.

20.13–21: The prediction of Babylonian conquest and the end of Hezekiah's reign. 19: *The word of the LORD . . . is good* expresses a fatalistic acceptance of what will be in the light of some acknowledged misconduct (cf. 1 Sam. 3.18; 2 Sam. 15.26). **20:** In 1880, the Siloam Tunnel inscription commemorating the completion of the tunneling project was found on the tunnel's wall. This tunnel conveyed water from outside Jerusalem into the city, assuring a water supply even in the time of siege.

---

a Cf. Targum.

b Heb. "steps." A model of a dial with steps has been discovered in Egypt.

c Several mss. and the parallel Isa. 39.1 read "Merodach."

d-d Isa. 39.2 reads "Hezekiah was pleased by their coming."

e-e Lit. "there shall be safety and faithfulness in."

21 Manasseh was twelve years old when he became king, and he reigned fifty-five years in Jerusalem; his mother's name was Hephzibah. ² He did what was displeasing to the LORD, following the abhorrent practices of the nations that the LORD had dispossessed before the Israelites. ³ He rebuilt the shrines that his father Hezekiah had destroyed; he erected altars for Baal and made a sacred post, as King Ahab of Israel had done. He bowed down to all the host of heaven and worshiped them, ⁴ and he built altars for them in the House of the LORD, of which the LORD had said, "I will establish My name in Jerusalem." ⁵ He built altars for all the hosts of heaven in the two courts of the House of the LORD. ⁶ He consigned his son to the fire; he practiced soothsaying and divination, and consulted ghosts and familiar spirits; he did much that was displeasing to the LORD, to vex Him. ⁷ The sculptured image of Asherah that he made he placed in the House concerning which the LORD had said to David and to his son Solomon, "In this House and in Jerusalem, which I chose out of all the tribes of Israel, I will establish My name forever. ⁸ And I will not again cause the feet of Israel to wander from the land that I gave to their fathers, if they will but faithfully observe all that I have commanded them—all the Teachings with which My servant Moses charged them." ⁹ But they did not obey, and Manasseh led them astray to do greater evil than the nations that the LORD had destroyed before the Israelites. ¹⁰ Therefore the LORD spoke through His servants the prophets: ¹¹ "Because King Manasseh of Judah has done these abhorrent things—he has outdone in wickedness all that the Amorites did before his time—and because he led Judah to sin with his fetishes, ¹² assuredly, thus said the LORD, the God of Israel: I am going to bring such a disaster on Jerusalem and Judah that both ears of everyone who hears about it will tingle. ¹³ I will ᵃ⁻apply to Jerusalem the measuring line of Samaria and the weights of the House of Ahab;⁻ᵃ I will wipe Jerusalem clean as one wipes a dish and turns it upside down. ¹⁴ And I will cast off the remnant of My own people and deliver them into the hands of their enemies. They shall be plunder and prey to all their enemies ¹⁵ because they have done what is displeasing to Me and have been vexing Me from the day that their fathers came out of Egypt to this day."

¹⁶ Moreover, Manasseh put so many innocent persons to death that he filled Jerusalem [with blood] from end to end—besides the sin he committed in causing Judah to do what was displeasing to the LORD.

---

a-a I.e., I will bring the same fate upon it.

21.1–18: Manasseh's long and peaceful reign (698–642 BCE) overlapped those of the three most powerful Assyrian kings: Sennacherib, Esarhaddon, and Ashurbanipal. These absolutely controlled Mesopotamia and, after Esarhaddon defeated Tirhakah in 671, Egypt and everything in between. Manasseh is mentioned as a loyal vassal in Assyrian inscriptions; this explains his peaceful reign. **3–9:** A list of all that Manasseh did wrong (v. 17). According to the author, Manasseh's reign was the worst period of apostasy in Israelite history. Not only did he sin, but he caused others to sin and he introduced illegal cults into the Temple itself. From the author's perspective, Manasseh undid everything that Hezekiah and Asa had achieved and then pressed beyond them to do wrong out of spite (v. 6). The destruction of Jerusalem is blamed on the heinous acts of Manasseh; this author, in contrast to the Chronicler, seems undisturbed that this destruction did not take place during the reign of Manasseh, who benefited from a long reign. **4:** *Establish My name in Jerusalem:* The quotation here and in v. 7 is from God's speech to Solomon in 1 Kings 9.3; cf. also 1 Kings 8.16. **8–15:** An insertion into the description of Manasseh's culpable acts. These vv. focus attention on the culpability of the king as one who causes others to sin. The emphasis on what the people of Israel did wrong reflects an exilic perspective. **10–15:** According to the author, these vv. are a collage of prophetic pronouncements, but he did not identify any prophet by name. None of the statements are found in any of the canonical prophetic books. They may have been added by the second author. **11:** *Amorites,* a term referring to pre-Israelite inhabitants of the land who could only be expelled after the measure of their iniquity reached a certain limit (Gen. 15.16 and cf. the imagery in Lev. 18.24–28). **16:** This v. concludes the inventory of Manasseh's wrongs from v. 7. Additional information about Manasseh's

17 The other events of Manasseh's reign, and all his actions, and the sins he committed, are recorded in the Annals of the Kings of Judah. 18 Manasseh slept with his fathers and was buried in the garden of his palace, in the garden of Uzza; and his son Amon succeeded him as king.

19 Amon was twenty-two years old when he became king, and he reigned two years in Jerusalem; his mother's name was Meshullemeth daughter of Haruz of Jotbah. 20 He did what was displeasing to the LORD, as his father Manasseh had done. 21 He walked in all the ways of his father, worshiping the fetishes which his father had worshiped and bowing down to them. 22 He forsook the LORD, the God of his fathers, and did not follow the way of the LORD.

23 Amon's courtiers conspired against him; and they killed the king in his palace. 24 But the people of the land put to death all who had conspired against King Amon, and the people of the land made his son Josiah king in his stead. 25 The other events of Amon's reign [and] his actions are recorded in the Annals of the Kings of Judah. 26 He was buried in his tomb in the garden of Uzza; and his son Josiah succeeded him as king.

22 Josiah was eight years old when he became king, and he reigned thirty-one years in Jerusalem. His mother's name was Jedidah daughter of Adaiah of Bozkath. 2 He did what was pleasing to the LORD and he followed all the ways of his ancestor David; he did not deviate to the right or to the left.

3 In the eighteenth year of King Josiah, the king sent the scribe Shaphan son of Azaliah son of Meshullam to the House of the LORD, saying, 4 "Go to the high priest Hilkiah and let him weigh*a* the silver that has been deposited in the House of the LORD, which the guards of the threshold have collected from the people. 5 And let it be delivered to the overseers of the work who are in charge at the House of the LORD, that they in turn may pay it out to the workmen that are in the House of the LORD, for the repair of the House: 6 to the carpenters, the laborers, and the masons, and for the purchase of wood and quarried stones for re-

---

a Meaning of Heb. uncertain. Emendation yields "melt down," cf. v. 9.

21.19–26: The reign of Amon.
The author indicates that Amon's short reign (641–640 BCE) did not differ from that of his father with regard to religious policies. **23:** The reason for the conspiracy is not mentioned. If political, he may have been killed by an anti-Assyrian group; if religious, by an anti-polytheistic group. **24:** The *people of the land* again stepped into the breech and guaranteed the continuity of the Davidic dynasty; cf. 11.14.

22.1–23.30: The reign of Josiah.
In the author's evaluation, Josiah (640–609 BCE) was the most outstanding of all the kings who ruled Judah, with no qualification. His personal piety and righteous zealousness were almost sufficient to avert the disaster which the most heinous of sinners, Manasseh, had sealed for Judah.

22.1–20: The discovery of a scroll.
The author's narrative about the discovery of a book in the Temple and the prophetic authentication of its contents is an artfully constructed narrative that emphasizes characteristics in Josiah's personality that the author wished to present to his readers. Unlike the staid narratives in Kings about individuals who lived after Solomon, this contains details in the manner of narratives in Samuel and withholds information to create slight tensions in order to achieve its objective: admiration for Josiah. Most, but not all, modern scholars consider this account to be largely historical, reflecting the "(re)discovery" of Deuteronomy in this period. **3:** Josiah was 26 years old in 622 BCE when he instituted a project for the refurbishing of the Temple, approximately 90 years after that of Jehoash (cf. 12.1–7). **4–7:** Josiah's instructions for the administration of the project and his instructions that contractors and suppliers are to be trusted are similar to those of Jehoash in 12.11–16. **4:** Instructions to collect silver for the refurbishing must have been given much earlier. Josiah's order here assumes that

---

religious activities may be inferred from the author's description of Josiah's activities in ch 23. **18:** Manasseh was not buried *with his fathers* in the City of David as were the kings of Judah before him

but in the garden of Uzza located on the grounds of his palace. Possibly the traditional cave tombs of the Davidic kings were filled and new ones were excavated elsewhere in the city.

pairing the House. [7] However, no check is to be kept on them for the silver that is delivered to them, for they deal honestly."

[8] Then the high priest Hilkiah said to the scribe Shaphan, "I have found a scroll of the Teaching in the House of the LORD." And Hilkiah gave the scroll to Shaphan, who read it. [9] The scribe Shaphan then went to the king and reported to the king: "Your servants have melted down the silver that was deposited in the House, and they have delivered it to the overseers of the work who are in charge at the House of the LORD." [10] The scribe Shaphan also told the king, "The high priest Hilkiah has given me a scroll"; and Shaphan read it to the king.

[11] When the king heard the words of the scroll of the Teaching, he rent his clothes. [12] And the king gave orders to the priest Hilkiah, and to Ahikam son of Shaphan, Achbor son of Michaiah, the scribe Shaphan, and Asaiah the king's minister: [13] "Go, inquire of the LORD on my behalf, and on behalf of the people, and on behalf of all Judah, concerning the words of this scroll that has been found. For great indeed must be the wrath of the LORD that has been kindled against us, because our fathers did not obey the words of this scroll to do all that has been prescribed for us."

[14] So the priest Hilkiah, and Ahikam, Achbor, Shaphan, and Asaiah went to the prophetess Huldah—the wife of Shallum son of Tikvah son of Harhas, the keeper of the wardrobe—who was living in Jerusalem in the Mishneh,[a] and they spoke to her. [15] She responded: "Thus said the LORD, the God of Israel: Say to the man who sent you to me: [16] Thus said the LORD: I am going to bring disaster upon this place and its inhabitants, in accordance with all the words of the scroll which the king of Judah has read. [17] Because they have forsaken Me and have made offerings to other gods and vexed Me with all their deeds, My wrath is kindled against this place and it shall not be quenched. [18] But say this to the king of Judah, who sent you to inquire of the LORD: Thus said the LORD, the God of Israel: As for the words which you have heard—[19] because your heart was softened and you humbled yourself before the LORD when you heard what I decreed against this place and its inhabitants—that it will become a desolation and a curse—and because you rent your clothes and wept before Me, I for My part have listened—declares the LORD. [20] Assuredly, I will gather you to your fathers and you will be laid in your tomb in peace. Your eyes shall not

what has been deposited suffices to complete the project. **8:** The *scroll of the Teaching* is referred to simply as *a scroll* in v. 10, but in 23.2 as "the covenant scroll" and in 2 Chron. 34.14 as "a scroll of the LORD's teaching given by Moses." *Scroll,* Heb "sefer," indicates that it was a longish document; *Teaching,* Heb "torah," that it contained instruction; "covenant," Heb "berit," that it contained a contract/agreement. Hilkiah's description suggests that what is novel about the find is that *the Teaching*—marked by the definite article as something already known— was found written in a scroll. The contents of this *scroll* and Josiah's and the people's reaction to it suggest that it was some form of the book of Deuteronomy. Most medieval Jewish exegetes posit variously that it was unique because either Ahaz or Manasseh had burnt all known scrolls, or—considering the notation in Chronicles—because it was the scroll written by Moses himself (Deut. 31.24–26). Abravanel, however, observing the author's description of Josiah's reaction in v. 11, cites a rabbinic tradition that the scroll was found open to the threat of exile directed against the people and the king in Deut. 28.36. **11:** Josiah's reaction to the contents of the scroll is described as a conventional response to hearing bad news (Gen. 37.34; 2 Sam. 1.11; 3.31; 2 Kings 5.7; 19.1). **13:** The message indicates that the scroll taught behaviors which Josiah knows had not been followed and spelled out dire consequences which he knew were about to befall him and his kingdom. **14:** *Huldah,* one of four named women prophets in the Tanakh; the others are Miriam (Exod. 15.20), Deborah (Judg. 4.4), and Noadiah (Neh. 6.14). Huldah lived in the *Mishneh* (cf. Zeph. 1.10), an area of the Old City of Jerusalem now covered by the Jewish and Armenian quarters. **16:** Although addressing only the punishments listed in the scroll, Huldah's pronouncement also authenticated the divine source of its teachings. **19–20:** Josiah's remorse postpones

a *A quarter in Jerusalem; cf. Zeph. 1.10.*

see all the disaster which I will bring upon this place." So they brought back the reply to the king.

23 At the king's summons, all the elders of Judah and Jerusalem assembled before him. ² The king went up to the House of the LORD, together with all the men of Judah and all the inhabitants of Jerusalem, and the priests and prophets—all the people, young and old. And he read to them the entire text of the covenant scroll which had been found in the House of the LORD. ³ The king stood ᵃ⁻by the pillar⁻ᵃ and solemnized the covenant before the LORD: that they would follow the LORD and observe His commandments, His injunctions, and His laws with all their heart and soul; that they would fulfill all the terms of this covenant as inscribed upon the scroll. And all the people ᵇ⁻entered into⁻ᵇ the covenant.

⁴ Then the king ordered the high priest Hilkiah, the priests of the second rank, and the guards of the threshold to bring out of the Temple of the LORD all the objects made for Baal and Asherahᶜ and all the host of heaven. He burned them outside Jerusalem in the fieldsᵈ of Kidron, and he removed the ashes to Bethel. ⁵ He suppressed the idolatrous priests whom the kings of Judah had appointed ᵉ⁻to make offerings⁻ᵉ at the shrines in the towns of Judah and in the environs of Jerusalem, and those who made offerings to Baal, to the sun and moon and constellations— all the host of heaven. ⁶ He brought out the [image of] Asherah from the House of the LORD to the Kidron Valley outside Jerusalem, and burned it in the Kidron Valley; he beat it to dust and scattered its dust over the burial ground of the common people. ⁷ He tore down the cubicles of the male prostitutes in the House of the LORD, at the place where the women wove coveringsᵈ for Asherah.

⁸ He brought all the priests from the towns of Judah [to Jerusalem] and defiled the shrines where the priests had been making offerings—from Geba to Beer-sheba. He also demolished the shrines of the gates, which were at the en-

a-a Or "on a platform," cf. Targum.

b-b Cf. Targum.

c For this goddess, cf. 1 Kings 18.19; ordinarily asherah is rendered "sacred post," e.g., 2 Kings 17.16.

d Meaning of Heb. uncertain.   e-e Lit. "and he offered."

see the destruction of the Temple implied by the words *your eyes shall not see all the disaster.*

23.1–25: The reforms of Josiah were instituted in response to Huldah's authentication of the scroll. Initially he mediated a covenant between the people and God and then instituted a course of action to fulfill the conditions of the agreement. **3:** His stand *by the pillar* may have been a symbol of dynastic authority; cf. 11.14. Josiah's role as mediator of the covenant is similar to that of Jehoiada in the days of Jehoash of Judah (11.17), Joshua at Shechem (Josh. 24.14–25), and particularly Moses at Sinai. Idioms in this verse echo those in Deuteronomy: *follow the LORD* (Deut. 13.5); *observe His commandments, His injunctions, and His laws* (Deut. 4.45 and 40 other verses); *all their heart and soul* (Deut. 4.29; 6.5); *entered into a covenant* (Deut. 29.11). Cf. 1 Kings 8.22–53. **4–7:** Josiah's purification of the Temple and elimination of shrines outside of Jerusalem illuminate the drastic changes that Manasseh introduced into Judah during his long reign. **4:** *Baal, Asherah,* and the *host of heaven* form a polytheistic triad worshipped in Judah in the days of Ahaz and Manasseh (17.16; 21.3 [NJPS translates Asherah by "sacred post"]). Manasseh must have instituted their worship in the Temple itself. See v. 6. Josiah acts in accord with Deut. 12.2. **5:** *Idolatrous priests* (Heb "kemarim") may refer to foreign-born specialists. Although their activities were discontinued, no action was taken against them. No mention is made of what was done to the native-born priests who served in the Temple. **8:** *Shrines* outside of Jerusalem where God was worshipped were defiled, restricting all worship to Jerusalem in accord with Deut. 12.4–7. *Geba to Beer-sheba:* These cities designated the northern and southern borders of his kingdom. *Shrines of the gates* have been excavated at Dan, Tirzah, and Geshur (an Aramean city near the northeast shore of the Sea of Galilee). They con-

the inevitable punishment until after his death. Compare the similar response to the contrite prayers of Ahab (1 Kings 21.27–29) and Hezekiah (2 Kings 20.2–6). Josiah died in battle in 609 BCE (cf.

23.29–30). Huldah's prophecy is mostly fulfilled by the events reported in 25.9–11, 18–21. Rashi and Radak, followed by others, consider the phrase *in peace* applied to Josiah fulfilled in that he did not trance of the gate of Joshua, the city prefect—ᵃ which were on a person's left [upon entering] the city gate.⁻ᵃ ⁹ᵇ⁻The priests of the shrines, however, did not ascend the altar of the LORD in Jerusalem, but they ate unleavened bread along with their kinsmen.⁻ᵇ ¹⁰ He also defiled Topheth, which is in the Valley of Ben-hinnom, so that no one might consign his son or daughter to the fire of Molech. ¹¹ He did away with the horses that the kings of Judah had dedicated to the sun, ᶜat the entrance⁻ᶜ of the House of the LORD, near the chamber of the eunuch Nathan-melech, which was in the precincts.ᵃ He burned the chariots of the sun. ¹² And the king tore down the altars made by the kings of Judah on the roof by the upper chamber of Ahaz, and the altars made by Manasseh in the two courts of the House of the LORD. He ᵈremoved them quickly from there⁻ᵈ and scattered their rubble in the Kidron Valley. ¹³ The king also defiled the shrines facing Jerusalem, to the south of the ᵉ⁻Mount of the Destroyer,⁻ᵉ which King Solomon of Israel had built for Ashtoreth, the abomination of the Sidonians, for Chemosh, the abomination of Moab, and for Milcom, the detestable thing of the Ammonites.ᶠ ¹⁴ He shattered their pillars and cut down their sacred posts and covered their sites with human bones.

¹⁵ As for the altar in Bethel [and] the shrine made by Jeroboam son of Nebat who caused Israel to sin—that altar, too, and the shrine as well, he tore down. He burned down the shrine and beat it to dust, and he burned the sacred post.

¹⁶ Josiah turned and saw the graves that were there on the hill; and he had the bones taken out of the graves and burned on the altar. Thus he defiled it, in fulfillment of the word of the LORD foretold by the man of God who foretold these happenings. ¹⁷ He asked, "What is the marker I see there?" And the men of the town replied, "That is the grave of the man of God who came from Judah and foretold these things that you have done to the altar of Bethel."ᵍ ¹⁸ "Let him be," he said, "let no one disturb his bones." So they left his bones undisturbed together with the bones of the prophetʰ who came from Samaria.ⁱ

sisted of a small area in which one or more standing stones were set up. **9:** The priests brought in from the open shrines were denied the right to serve at the altar in Jerusalem, in contrast to the teaching of Deut. 18.6–7. This denial was legitimated about 50 years later by Ezekiel (Ezek. 44.10–14). With this exception, all the other parts of this reform, with their emphasis on cultic purity and centralization in Jerusalem, closely mirror Deuteronomy. **13:** Josiah even eliminates monuments attesting the apostasy of Solomon (see 1 Kings 11.1–13). Neither Asa nor Hezekiah, both considered good kings by the author, had done so. **15–18:** Josiah eliminates structures attesting to the great tragedy of the sundering of Solomon's kingdom at the shrine developed by Jeroboam (1 Kings 12.29). The author relates his activities to the story of an anonymous prophet at Bethel (1 Kings 13.1–2). Josiah's presence in Bethel, north of his political border, indicates that he extended his authority into the former territory of Israel that Assyria had turned into a province, and that Assyrian authority in territories of the former Northern Kingdom had declined considerably. After 629 BCE Assyria's heartland was threatened by a newly powerful Babylonia from the south and by Medes descending from the Persian plateau from the northeast. Some therefore suggest that Josiah's reforms were both political and religious in nature.

---

a-a Meaning of Heb. uncertain.

b-b This verse may be understood in connection with vv. 21–23.

c-c Heb. "from entering."

d-d Heb. "ran from there." Emendation yields "smashed them there."

e-e Heb. har ha-mashḥith: a derogatory play on har ha-mishḥah ("Mount of Ointment"); Mishnah Middoth 2.4.   f Cf. 1 Kings 11.5, 7.

g Cf. 1 Kings 13.2–3.   h See 1 Kings 13.31–32 and note i below.

i The prophet lived in Bethel, which, in Josiah's time, was part of the Assyrian province of Samaria.

¹⁹ Josiah also abolished all the cult places in the towns of Samaria, which the kings of Israel had built, vexing [the LORD]. He dealt with them just as he had done to Bethel: ²⁰ He slew on the altars all the priests of the shrines who were there, and he burned human bones on them. Then he returned to Jerusalem.

²¹ The king commanded all the people, "Offer the passover sacrifice to the LORD your God as prescribed in this scroll of the covenant." ²² Now the passover sacrifice had not been offered in that manner in the days of the chieftains who ruled Israel, or during the days of the kings of Israel and the kings of Judah. ²³ Only in the eighteenth year of King Josiah was such a passover sacrifice offered in that manner to the LORD in Jerusalem. ²⁴ Josiah also did away with ^athe necromancers and the mediums,^{-a} the idols and the fetishes—all the detestable things that were to be seen in the land of Judah and Jerusalem. Thus he fulfilled the terms of the Teaching recorded in the scroll that the priest Hilkiah had found in the House of the LORD. ²⁵ There was no king like him before who turned back to the LORD with all his heart and soul and might, in full accord with the Teaching of Moses; nor did any like him arise after him.

²⁶ However, the LORD did not turn away from His awesome wrath which had blazed up against Judah because of all the things Manasseh did to vex Him. ²⁷ The LORD said, "I will also banish Judah from My presence as I banished Israel; and I will reject the city of Jerusalem which I chose and the House where I said My name would abide."

²⁸ The other events of Josiah's reign, and all his actions, are recorded in the Annals of the Kings of Judah. ²⁹ In his days, Pharaoh Neco, king of Egypt, marched against the king of Assyria^b to the River Euphrates; King Josiah marched toward him, but when he confronted him at Megiddo, [Pharaoh Neco] slew him. ³⁰ His servants conveyed

a-a Lit. "the ghosts and the familiar spirits."
b I.e., the Chaldean Empire; cf. Isa. 52.4 and note.

19–20: Josiah's drive north reaches the towns of Samaria where Assyrians had settled exiles from Syria and Babylonia (17.24). The author's silence about the campaigns themselves indicates that they were successful and that he considered them legitimate. Josiah was acting like a Davidic monarch prior to the formation of the breakaway northern confederacy. **20:** Priests who served at northern shrines are killed, unlike those who served at southern ones (cf. vv. 8–9). The northern priests may have been descendants of the non-Levitical priests appointed by Jeroboam I (1 Kings 12.31). **21–23:** The celebration of Passover in Jerusalem exclusively in accord with the prescription of Deut. 16.5 as understood by the author is possible only because no legitimate clergy and no purified shrine exist anywhere between the cities of Samaria and Beer-sheba except at Jerusalem. **22:** The author may mean that the last such Passover was celebrated in the days before the chieftains/judges, since Judg. 2.7 depicts that period as beginning a time when God was not worshipped properly. Radak considers the point of the author's comment to be that not since the time of the chieftains, among whom he includes Samuel, had the tribes been so dedicated to the LORD (1 Sam. 7.2), rid themselves of idolatrous practices, and served the LORD (1 Sam. 7.4). The Passover celebration of Hezekiah described in 2 Chron. 30.12–27 was not attended by all tribes (2 Chron. 30.10). **24:** This continues the list of Josiah's campaign against illegitimate personnel and activities from v. 20. *Necromancers . . . mediums,* see Deut. 18.9–14, which formulates compactly legislation found also in Lev. 19.26, 31; 20.27.

23.26–27: The inevitability of the end. This remark qualifies the high praise lavished on Josiah in the author's evaluation of v. 25. All of his accomplishments were of no avail to his kingdom. A later writer, someone other than the author, focuses the reader's attention back to Huldah's declaration (22.17–20) about the inevitability of Judah's end and introduces the twilight of Judah's history. Proper punishment for Manasseh's sins may be delayed (see Exod. 20.5 n.), but not postponed.

23.28–30: The death of Josiah. **29:** It is uncertain why *Josiah* confronted *Neco* at *Megiddo.* Nineveh had fallen in 612 BCE to Babylonia, but Assyrians were still fighting in northwest Assyria. Some historians speculate on the basis of 2 Chron. 35.20–24 and a cuneiform document, the Babylonian Chronicle, that Neco was actually moving north to support Assyrian forces against Babylonia and that Josiah acted as part of a Babylonian strategy that would have helped him his body in a chariot from Megiddo to Jerusalem, and they buried him in his tomb. Then the people of the land took Jehoahaz; they anointed him and made him king in place of his father.

³¹ Jehoahaz was twenty-three years old when he became king, and he reigned three months in Jerusalem; his mother's name was Hamutal daughter of Jeremiah of Libnah. ³² He did what was displeasing to the LORD, just as his fathers had done. ³³ Pharaoh Neco imprisoned him in Riblah in the region of Hamath, to keep him from reigning in Jerusalem. And he imposed on the land an indemnity of one hundred talents of silver and a talent of gold. ³⁴ Then Pharaoh Neco appointed Eliakim son of Josiah king in place of his father Josiah, changing his name to Jehoiakim. He took Jehoahaz and ᵃbrought himᵃ to Egypt, where he died. ³⁵ Jehoiakim gave Pharaoh the silver and the gold, and he made an assessment on the land to pay the money demanded by Pharaoh. He exacted from the people of the land the silver and gold to be paid Pharaoh Neco, according to each man's assessment.

³⁶ Jehoiakim was twenty-five years old when he became king, and he reigned eleven years in Jerusalem; his mother's name was Zebudah daughter of Pedaiah of Rumah. ³⁷ He did what was displeasing to the LORD, just as his ancestors had done.

24 In his days, King Nebuchadnezzar of Babylon came up, and Jehoiakim became his vassal for three years. Then he turned and rebelled against him. ² The LORD let loose against him the raiding bands of the Chaldeans, Arameans, Moabites, and Ammonites; He let them loose against Judah to destroy it, in accordance with the word that the LORD had spoken through His servants the prophets. ³ All this befell Judah at the command of the LORD, who banished [them] from His presence because of all the sins that Manasseh had committed, ⁴ and also because of the

a-a So 2 Chron. 36.4; Heb. here "he came."

maintain control over his enlarged kingdom. For the author, this death made no sense and remained unexplained. A later generation told the story in a way that provided some theological justification for Josiah's death: He was interfering with a divinely ordained plan (2 Chron. 35.20–27). **30:** The *people of the land* again assure a smooth transition to a legiti-

mate descendant in a period of uncertainty. Cf. 11.14; 14.21–22; 21.24. They decide, however, to skip Josiah's oldest son in favor of a brother at least two years younger (compare the ages at accession in vv. 31, 36).

23.31–33: The brief reign of Jehoahaz son of Josiah. Jeremiah refers to him by the name of Shallum

(Jer. 22.11), so Jehoahaz must be a throne name. **33:** Jehoahaz traveled to *Riblah* in northern Syria, most likely to submit formally to Neco as a vassal. Neco arrested him, had him taken to Egypt as a royal hostage, and imposed tribute on Judah. Jehoahaz and the people of the land may have been too closely identified with Josiah's expansionist ambitions for Neco's comfort.

23.34–24.7: Jehoiakim's reign and the collapse of Judah. Jehoiakim's foreign policy assumed that Egypt could be the instrument through which Judah might regain its former glory. **23.34–35:** *Eliakim* was placed on the throne by *Neco*, not the people of the land, and provided by the Egyptian with the throne name *Jehoiakim*. Cf. also 24.17. Eliakim fulfilled his fiscal obligation to Neco, delivering the tribute. **24.1:** According to the Babylonian Chronicle, Babylonians under Nebuchadnezzar defeated Neco's Egyptian forces in Syria in 605 BCE (cf. Jer. 46.1–2). Nebuchadnezzar's first move against Jerusalem would have happened around the same time (cf. Dan. 1.1), and Jehoiakim became a vassal of Babylonia around 604/3. **2:** Events encouraging rebellion may have developed in 601 after Nebuchadnezzar, unable to conquer Egypt in earlier campaigns, was subsequently forced by local conditions to remain in Babylonia in 600. Jer. 26.22 indicates that Jehoiakim colluded with Egypt and, expecting Egyptian support, may have rebelled. The author's mention that the attacks of *Chaldeans, Arameans, Moabites,* and *Ammonites* came in fulfillment of words *spoken through his servants the prophets* is problematic. No such predictions are extant. **3–7:** The author interprets the political reduction of Judah as the consequence of people reading political maps incompetently as well as the result of God's will after Manasseh's sins.

blood of the innocent that he shed. For he filled Jerusalem with the blood of the innocent, and the LORD would not forgive.

⁵ The other events of Jehoiakim's reign, and all of his actions, are recorded in the Annals of the Kings of Judah. ⁶ Jehoiakim slept with his fathers, and his son Jehoiachin succeeded him as king. ⁷ The king of Egypt did not venture out of his country again, for the king of Babylon had seized all the land that had belonged to the king of Egypt, from the Wadi of Egypt to the River Euphrates.

⁸ Jehoiachin was eighteen years old when he became king, and he reigned three months in Jerusalem; his mother's name was Nehushta daughter of Elnathan of Jerusalem. ⁹ He did what was displeasing to the LORD, just as his father had done. ¹⁰ At that time, the troops*a* of King Nebuchadnezzar of Babylon marched against Jerusalem, and the city came under siege. ¹¹ King Nebuchadnezzar of Babylon advanced against the city while his troops were besieging it. ¹² Thereupon King Jehoiachin of Judah, along with his mother, and his courtiers, commanders, and officers, surrendered to the king of Babylon. The king of Babylon took him captive in the eighth year of his reign. ¹³ He

a Heb. "servants."

5: *Annals of the Kings of Judah:* This last reference to this source in Kings raises the question of what sources were used by the author for descriptions of the final years of Judah. **7:** The author notes that the Babylonians controlled the area that had once comprised the Davidic-Solomonic empire.

24.8–17: Jehoiachin assumed the throne as the Babylonians were positioning themselves to destroy Jerusalem, all that was effectively left of Judah. His surrender in 597 BCE saved the city and led to the first exile from Judah. (The Babylonian Chronicle refers to it as the city of Judah.) **12–16:** The objective of the exile was to demilitarize, not punish, Judah by removing the court, high officials, administrators, military officials, and professional soldiers, as well as craftsmen who could manufacture new arms. Unlike the Assyrians, who dispersed populations, the Babylonians allowed them to resettle in exile as organic commu-

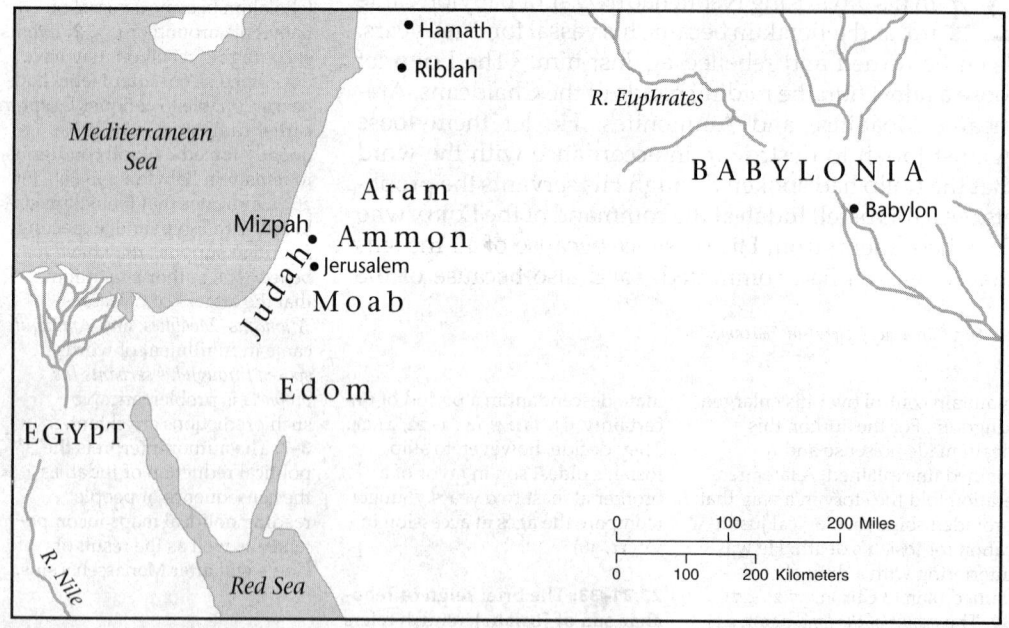

Babylonia and Judah ca. 600 BCE

carried off *a-from Jerusalem-a* all the treasures of the House of the Lᴏʀᴅ and the treasures of the royal palace; he stripped off all the golden decorations in the Temple of the Lᴏʀᴅ—which King Solomon of Israel had made—as the Lᴏʀᴅ had warned. ¹⁴ He exiled all of Jerusalem: all the commanders and all the warriors—ten thousand exiles— as well as all the craftsmen and smiths; only the poorest people in the land were left. ¹⁵ He deported Jehoiachin to Babylon; and the king's wives and officers and the notables of the land were brought as exiles from Jerusalem to Babylon. ¹⁶ All the able men, to the number of seven thousand—all of them warriors, trained for battle—and a thousand craftsmen and smiths were brought to Babylon as exiles by the king of Babylon. ¹⁷ And the king of Babylon appointed Mattaniah, Jehoiachin's*b* uncle, king in his place, changing his name to Zedekiah.

¹⁸ *c*Zedekiah was twenty-one years old when he became king, and he reigned eleven years in Jerusalem; his mother's name was Hamutal daughter of Jeremiah of Libnah. ¹⁹ He did what was displeasing to the Lᴏʀᴅ, just as Jehoiakim had done. ²⁰ Indeed, Jerusalem and Judah *d-*were a cause of anger for the Lᴏʀᴅ, so that*-d* He cast them out of His presence.

25 Zedekiah rebelled against the king of Babylon. ¹ And in the ninth year of his*e* reign, on the tenth day of the tenth month, Nebuchadnezzar moved against Jerusalem with his whole army. He besieged it; and they built towers against it all around. ² The city continued in a state of siege until the eleventh year of King Zedekiah. ³ By the ninth day [of the fourth month]*f* the famine had become acute in the city; there was no food left for the common people.

⁴ Then [the wall of] the city was breached. All the soldiers [left the city] by night through the gate between the double walls, which is near the king's garden—the Chaldeans were all around the city; and [the king] set out for the Arabah.*g* ⁵ But the Chaldean troops pursued the king, and they overtook him in the steppes of Jericho as his entire force left him and scattered. ⁶ They captured the king and brought him before the king of Babylon at Riblah; and they put him on trial. ⁷ They slaughtered Zedekiah's sons before his eyes; then Zedekiah's eyes were put out. He was chained in bronze fetters and he was brought to Babylon.

nities. The extent of the exile is probably exaggerated here; had all of these people been exiled, Judea could not have had the manpower to rebel against the Babylonians again a decade later. **17:** Mattaniah, provided with a throne name by Nebuchadnezzar, was the full brother of Jehoahaz (23.31) and the third son of Josiah to rule Judah.

24.18–25.21: The reign of Zedekiah (597–586 ʙᴄᴇ) and destruction of the Temple. Much of this material is paralleled in Jer. 39.1–4, Jer. ch 52, and 2 Chron. ch 36. The writer's interest in this king concerns his international politics, not his religious policies. **24.19–20:** The writer again provides a negative assessment and comment, preparing readers for the inevitable (cf. 24.3–7). Zedekiah's acts are likened to those of his half-brother Jehoiakim (23.36). The writer skips over the first nine years of the reign to what interests him. On the basis of remarks in Jeremiah and Ezekiel, it is apparent that Zedekiah joined a coalition that included coastal Phoenicians and Transjordanian kingdoms in planning a revolt. Nebuchadnezzar managed to abort it, but then, in 589/8, set out to punish Zedekiah. V. 20, though unclear, is a refrain, echoing v. 3. **25.1–3:** The siege of Jerusalem lasted 17 months. Ultimately, starvation led to the fall of the city. Jer. 34.7 indicates that a few other cities that might have supported Jerusalem were also besieged. **3–4:** The walls of the city, most likely in the northwest, were breached on the *ninth* of the month of Tamuz, *the fourth month* (v. 4 and see Jer. 39.2–4; 52.6). Jewish tradition observes the seventeenth of Tamuz as a fast day marking the breaching of the walls. The difference between the day of the breach and the fast is explained by claiming that it was only on the seventeenth that the Babylonians exploited the breach to enter the city. Events narrated in vv. 4–5 occupied them during the intervening days. The fast of the fourth month was known as an old observance

a-a Heb. "from there." b Heb. "his."
c For the rest of this book cf. Jer. 39 and 52. d-d Meaning of Heb. uncertain.
e I.e., Zedekiah's. f Cf. Jer. 52.6. g Hoping to escape across the Jordan.

8 On the seventh day of the fifth month—that was the nineteenth year of King Nebuchadnezzar of Babylon—Nebuzaradan, the chief of the guards, an officer of the king of Babylon, came to Jerusalem. 9 He burned the House of the LORD, the king's palace, and all the houses of Jerusalem; he burned down ªthe house of every notable person.·ª 10 The entire Chaldean force that was with the chief of the guard tore down the walls of Jerusalem on every side. 11 The remnant of the people that was left in the city, the defectors who had gone over to the king of Babylon—and the remnant of the population—were taken into exile by Nebuzaradan, the chief of the guards. 12 But some of the poorest in the land were left by the chief of the guards, to be vinedressers and field hands.

13 The Chaldeans broke up the bronze columns of the House of the LORD, the stands, and the bronze tank that was in the House of the LORD; and they carried the bronze away to Babylon. 14 They also took all the pails, scrapers, snuffers, ladles, and all the other bronze vessels used in the service. 15 The chief of the guards took whatever was of gold and whatever was of silver: firepans and sprinkling bowls. 16 The two columns, the one tank, and the stands that Solomon provided for the House of the LORD—all these objects contained bronze beyond weighing. 17 The one column was eighteen cubits high. It had a bronze capital above it; the height of the capital was three cubits, and there was a meshwork [decorated] with pomegranates about the capital, all made of bronze. And the like was true of the other column with its meshwork.

18 The chief of the guards also took Seraiah, the chief priest, Zephaniah, the deputy priest, and the three guardians of the threshold. 19 And from the city he took a eunuch who was in command of the soldiers; five royal privy councillors who were present in the city; the scribe of the army commander, who was in charge of mustering the people of the land; and sixty of the common people who were inside the city. 20 Nebuzaradan, the chief of the guards, took them and brought them to the king of Babylon at Riblah. 21 The king of Babylon had them struck down and put to death at Riblah, in the region of Hamath.

a-a Meaning of Heb. uncertain.

two generations after the Temple's destruction (Zech. 7.3; 8.19). **9:** Babylonians only gained access to the old part of Jerusalem where the Temple stood in the fifth month, the month of Av, 586 BCE. The Temple, palaces, and a large part of the city were set ablaze on the seventh day of the month, corresponding to August 16, 586. According to Jer. 52.12, they were burnt on the tenth of Av. In the talmudic tractate *Ta'anit* that deals with fasts, the dates were reconciled by explaining that on the seventh, the Babylonians gained access to the Temple, but they only set it afire late on the ninth, just before nightfall, and it burned through the tenth. Jewish tradition and contemporary practice maintains the ninth of Av as a 25-hour fast day commemorating the destruction of both the First Temple by the Babylonians and the Second Temple by the Romans. The fast itself was established early and is mentioned by Zechariah, a prophet who spoke about 60 years after the destruction, referring to the "fast of the fifth month" (Zech. 7.3; 8.19). **11–12:** A second group was taken into exile (see 24.12–16). This one consisted of Jerusalemites who had not fled, people who had defected to the Babylonians during the course of the siege, and a third group not clearly identifiable. Archeological evidence, however, as well as evidence from Ezra, which depicts significant antagonism between the Judeans who were exiled and those who remained behind in Judah, suggests that the exiles were not as extensive as these verses suggest. **18–21:** All official perpetrators of the ill-conceived revolt and resistance were executed.

25.22–26: The first appendix. The last administrative overseer of the people of Judah in the land was *Gedaliah*. His grandfather had been a high official in Josiah's cabinet (22.3), while his father had been in Josiah's court (22.12) and Jehoiakim's and had supported Jeremiah in counseling nonresistance to the Babylonians (Jer. 26.24). This was the same counsel he provided refugee bands of fighters and their leaders (v. 24). The writer of this appendix simply reported events without commenting on their meaning. **23:** *Mizpah*, the contemporary Tel en-Nasbeh, north of Jerusalem on the north-south highway, became the new administra-

Thus Judah was exiled from its land. 22 King Nebuchadnezzar of Babylon put Gedaliah son of Ahikam son of Shaphan in charge of the people whom he left in the land of Judah. 23 When the officers of the troops and their men heard that the king of Babylon had put Gedaliah in charge, they came to Gedaliah at Mizpah with Ishmael son of Nethaniah, Johanan son of Kareah, Seraiah son of Tanhumeth the Netophathite, and Jaazaniah son of the Maachite, together with their men. 24 Gedaliah reassured[a] them and their men, saying, "Do not be afraid [b]of the servants of the Chaldeans.[b] Stay in the land and serve the king of Babylon, and it will go well with you."

25 In the seventh month, Ishmael son of Nethaniah son of Elishama, who was of royal descent, came with ten men, and they struck down Gedaliah and he died; [they also killed] the Judeans and the Chaldeans who were present with him at Mizpah. 26 And all the people, young and old, and the officers of the troops set out and went to Egypt because they were afraid of the Chaldeans.

27 In the thirty-seventh year of the exile of King Jehoiachin of Judah, on the twenty-seventh day of the twelfth month, King Evil-merodach of Babylon, in the year he became king, [c]took note of[c] King Jehoiachin of Judah and released him from prison. 28 He spoke kindly to him, and gave him a throne above those of other kings who were with him in Babylon. 29 His prison garments were removed, and [Jehoiachin] received regular rations by his favor for the rest of his life. 30 A regular allotment of food was given him at the instance of the king—an allotment for each day—all the days of his life.

tive center (see 1 Kings 15.22). This is, ironically, the home territory of the House of Saul. The end of the monarchy is located near its beginning. **25:** The reasons for his assassination are not given in Kings. They were irrelevant to the work of the author. Jer. 40.13–41.18 makes clear that the assassin, Ishmael, was sent by Baalis, king of Ammon. Ishmael, of royal descent and dissatisfied over the Babylonian appointment of a non-Davidic ruler, may have formed a pact with Baalis, who was still fighting the Babylonians, that would have helped him to achieve rule over whatever remained of Judah. *The seventh month* is Tishri. The death of Gedaliah came to be seen as the final blow and the end of the commonwealth. It is marked by Jewish tradition as a fast on the day following Rosh Ha-Shanah (New Year). It is most likely the "fast of the seventh month" referred to in Zech. 7.5; 8.19.

25.27–30: The second appendix. *Jehoiachin,* son of Josiah, safe in exile since 597 BCE, was elevated in status by *Evil-merodach,* the son of Nebuchadnezzar who reigned 562–560 BCE. **28:** *Spoke kindly:* The Heb translates a technical expression in Babylonian that means to "reach an agreement, conclude a negotiation." The narrative refers to a legal grant recognizing a change in status that had far-reaching implications for Jehoiachin and the exiles. **30:** Lack of any death notice may suggest that this final note was appended before the death of Jehoiachin. The book appears to end with a glimmer of hope for the continuation of the Davidic dynasty. The detail is reported matter-of-factly, without comment. The author, perhaps living too close to the event itself, had no way of determining what significance, if any, it had.

a Lit. "took an oath to them."
b-b Jer. 40.9 reads "to serve the Chaldeans."
c-c Lit. "raised the head of."

ישעיה

Isaiah

ISAIAH IS PERHAPS THE BEST-LOVED of the prophetic books. It is cited more than any other prophetic text in rabbinic literature, and more haftarot are taken from Isaiah than from any other prophetic book. (Haftarot are the prophetic readings chanted in synagogue on the Sabbath, holidays, and fast days.) In Ashkenazic practice outside the land of Israel, nineteen haftarot are from Isaiah (twenty, if one follows Reform practice by assigning Isaiah 60.1–22 as the haftarah for Yom Ha-ʿatzmaʾut [Israeli Independence Day] in the Diaspora); by contrast, only nine are from Jeremiah and ten from Ezekiel. Second place goes to the books of Kings, which contributes sixteen haftarot. Isaiah is a major source of prooftexts for some of Judaism's main tenets, such as messianism, the centrality of Jerusalem, and economic and social justice. Not only rabbinic Judaism but also Christianity and Western culture have emphasized the book of Isaiah. First-time readers of Isaiah are often surprised to find that a well-known expression, a famous quotation, or even a favorite song comes from or is based on Isaiah. See, for example, 2.2–4; 6.3; 9.1; 9.5; 11.6–9; 12.3; 22.13; 32.17; 35.10; 40.1; 40.3; 52.2; 53.1–13; 56.7; 60.1; 62.5; 62.6; 66.10. (Some of these verses will be more familiar to people who attend synagogue, some to people who attend Sabbath meals, some to people who attend performances of Handel's *Messiah*.)

Most of the texts in this book are poetry, often of a highly complex and elusive sort. It is sometimes not clear where a particular prophecy begins and ends, and, especially in the first half of the book, one can sometimes debate whether a passage intends to comfort or castigate the nation. In many cases, verb forms are ambiguous, and we cannot be sure whether the passage predicts crucial events that will take place in the future or meditates on events that have already come to pass. As a result of all this, one cannot read quickly through Isaiah the way one might read a biblical book that tells a story, or even a book whose poems or sermons are demarcated in a fairly clear manner (such as the book of Psalms or Jeremiah). A reader will need to read slowly, and as a rule it will be necessary to read a text several times before one can even begin to understand it. It will probably not be helpful to read the whole book from beginning to end the way one reads, say, a novel. Rather, it is best to approach the book as a collection of texts or an anthology, in which each passage demands careful attention, thinking, rereading, and contemplation. Keeping in mind the historical setting of each prophecy will also aid the reader greatly.

The book of Isaiah is one of the most complex prophetic books. It contains at least two distinct sections, dating from two entirely different eras. Chs 1–39 are, in large part, the product of a prophet who lived in Jerusalem during the 8th century BCE. As early as the Middle Ages, however, the great rabbinic commentator Abraham Ibn Ezra recognized that chs 40 and following reflect another setting altogether, which he identified as the Babylonian exile of the 6th century. Similarly, Shadal (Samuel David Luzzato, a rabbinic exegete who lived during the 19th century) maintained that chs 40–66 were addressed to the Judean exiles in Babylonia and were not published until some time after 586 BCE (though Shadal still claimed that the 8th-century Isaiah had written them). All modern scholars share a perspective similar to Ibn Ezra's and believe that chs 40–66 (and also 34–35) were composed during and after the Babylonian exile in the 6th century. It will be necessary to address chs 1–39 and 40–66 separately in the introductory comments below.

Isaiah 1–39

THE PROPHET ISAIAH, the son of Amoz, lived in Jerusalem during the last half of the 8th century BCE. His prophecies are deeply rooted in his time and place, and many of them address current events of his day. Unfortunately, only rarely does he tell us what these events are (his audience, of course, would have known immediately, since they were living through them as well). As a result, scholars frequently need to reconstruct the political or historical settings of his prophecies. It will be helpful to review some major events of Isaiah's time, since these serve as the backdrop to his prophecies. During the 8th century, the Assyrian empire (located in what we know today as northern Iraq and southeastern Turkey) began to grow in power and influence. It put more and more pressure on the small kingdoms along the eastern coast of the Mediterranean Sea, including Judah and Israel. These countries sometimes accepted Assyria as their overlord, paying the Assyrian king tribute and relying on him for defense. At other times, these nations attempted to revolt against Assyria, often relying on Egypt as an ally. Usually, these revolts ended disastrously. In fact, the Northern Kingdom of Israel was destroyed by the Assyrians after one such revolt in 722 BCE, and much of its population was deported. For Isaiah, the rise of Assyria presented a pressing religious question: To what extent should the Judeans attempt to confront their enemies using the usual military and diplomatic means (which entailed entering into alliances with other nations), and to what extent should the Judeans stay free of alliances and rely solely on God to protect them? Unlike most of his contemporaries, Isaiah strongly preferred the latter option. A second major trend in Isaiah's day was the growth of large estates owned by aristocrats and the consequent impoverishment of the peasantry. Isaiah, like his contemporaries Micah and Amos, spoke out strongly against the accumulation of great wealth and the haughtiness of the rich.

Several main themes emerge from Isaiah's prophecies. Isaiah believed that Jerusalem, the holy city, would never fall to Judah's enemies. He emphasized social and economic justice. He referred repeatedly to the remnant of Israel, who would survive an enormous catastrophe that God would send to punish the nation for its lack of faith and hypocrisy.

This remnant would serve as the kernel from which a purified Israel would be renewed. (By definition, Jerusalem would be part of the remnant, since it would never fall.) He anticipated the dawn of a new era in which all nations would recognize the one true God. Each nation would be satisfied with its own land and would not covet other lands. Consequently empires—and warfare—would exist no more. During this new era the Judean king, a descendant of David, would rule all Israel in perfect justice. (From this set of ideas, later Judaism would construct the idea of the Messiah and the messianic era, though Isaiah never calls him Messiah.) Common to all these ideas is Isaiah's stress that only God can be great; all other haughty things (whether rich people, large empires, or high mountains) would be reduced to their proper place at the end of days. All sin, for Isaiah, stems from the failure to recognize that God alone can be exalted. Isaiah's prophecies are remarkable for their fairly consistent lack of oracles of vengeance against Judah's enemies. Assyria and Egypt would be punished in the future for their haughtiness and idolatry, but not for their treatment of Israel and Judah. After all, it was God who sent them to attack Israel and Judah in the first place. Once they had been taken to account for their haughtiness, they would be restored and live in peace, recognizing the one true God. Thus their fate, for worse and then for better, is identical to that of Israel.

Many modern scholars believe that large sections of Isaiah chs 1–33 were written by additional prophets and scribes who lived later than the historical Isaiah—that is, later than the 8th century. Others, including many leading Jewish biblical critics, attribute most or all of these chs to Isaiah himself. The annotations treat this material as largely dating to the 8th century, with a few possible exceptions (in particular, chs 13, 24–27, and 30.18–26). Chs 34–35 belong to the same time period as chs 40–66. Chs 36–39 narrate certain events in which Isaiah played an important role. They were not written by Isaiah but are taken, in a modified form, from the book of Kings.

Isaiah chs 1–39 contains the following subsections: Ch 1: Introductory prophecy, covering Isaiah's main themes. Chs 2–12: Prophecies concerning Judah and Jerusalem. Chs 13–23: Prophecies concerning many nations, including Judah but focusing on foreign peoples. Chs 24–27: Prophecies concerning the end of days, in an apocalyptic style. Chs 28–33: Prophecies concerning the end of days. Chs 34–35: Redemption for Judah. Chs 36–39: Narratives concerning the Assyrian invasion of Judah in 701 BCE and Isaiah's role in the events of that time. The book does not follow a chronological order; the same event is often treated in many different chs at a wide remove from one another.

Isaiah 40–66

THESE CHS, ALONG WITH CHS 34–35, were composed at the end of the Babylonian exile and during the early postexilic period. Because the name of this prophet is unknown, scholars refer to him (or perhaps her; women served as prophets in ancient Israel, as the examples of Miriam [Exod. 15.20], Deborah [Judg. 4.4–10; 5.1], and Huldah [2 Kings 22.14] show) as Deutero-Isaiah or Second Isaiah. This prophet lived in Babylonia a generation after the Babylonian empire destroyed the Judean state and sent much of its population

into exile. Deutero-Isaiah promised the Judean exiles that the Persians would allow them
to return to their homeland and to rebuild their Temple there. Deutero-Isaiah anticipated
the victory of the Persian king, Cyrus, over the Babylonian empire. From ch 49 on, the
prophet seems to be living in the land of Israel; it is likely that Deutero-Isaiah moved
there as soon as the Persians allowed Judean exiles to do so after Cyrus took control of
Babylonia. Many scholars believe that chs 56–66 or (more likely) 54–66 were written by yet
another prophet, or perhaps a group of prophets, whom they call Trito-Isaiah or Third
Isaiah. According to these scholars, Trito-Isaiah was a disciple of Deutero-Isaiah, and in
many respects these prophecies resemble those in chs 40–53. These prophecies are set in
the land of Israel shortly after the end of the exile, and they often display a sense of disappointment or frustration with the realities of the restoration, rather than the exuberant
hope that marks the prophecies in chs 40–53. It is impossible to be sure whether chs 54–66
were written by Deutero-Isaiah, a disciple, or a group of disciples, but it seems clear that
chs 34–35 and 40–66 as a whole are a single literary unit: They share many features of
poetic style and theological outlook. Because we can analyze them as a block, it will be
simplest to refer to their anonymous author or authors as Deutero-Isaiah.

   Chs 34–35 and 40–66 are first and foremost persuasive in character. Addressed to a despondent exilic and postexilic audience who have experienced a catastrophe, they attempt
to convince the Judeans that the God of Israel is still powerful and still loyal to the people
Israel. Deutero-Isaiah (that is, the author or authors of chs 34–35 and 40–66) proclaims in
an especially insistent manner that only one God exists; this deity alone created the world
and brings redemption. Alone among biblical texts, the author refers to God using not
only masculine metaphors but feminine ones as well (see 42.13–14; 45.10; 49.14–15; 66.13).
Deutero-Isaiah is an allusive poet: In every single chapter of this work, save ch 34, the
prophet borrows vocabulary from earlier biblical texts and reworks it in a very intricate
manner, using complex and delightful wordplays, repeating similar-sounding words, or
employing alliteration. (This feature, of course, is lost in translation.) Like Isaiah, Deutero-
Isaiah looks forward to the dawn of a new era, but one no longer senses any expectation
that a descendant of King David (or any other human being, for that matter) will reign as
king in the rebuilt Jerusalem. Rather, God alone will rule over all creation in that day.
Thus Deutero-Isaiah believes in a messianic era, but not in a personal Messiah. Initially,
Deutero-Isaiah predicted that the return to Zion at the time of the Persian king Cyrus
would usher in the renewal of the Judean commonwealth, the era of peace among all
nations, and the end of paganism the world over. In fact, the restoration did not have
these far-reaching effects: Judah became not an independent kingdom directly ruled by
God but a poor and insignificant province of Persia; relatively few exiles availed themselves of the opportunity to return to Zion; and the world as a whole remained unchanged. Still, Deutero-Isaiah continued to predict in chs 49 and following that a larger-
scale ingathering of exiles would occur and that the new world order would eventually
materialize.

   These chs contain the following subsections: Chs 40–48: Prophecies delivered to the exiles in Babylonia, predicting the restoration of Zion and the downfall of Babylon; the tone of these is excited and hopeful. Chs 49–57: Prophecies concerning Zion and the renewal of the community there. Their tone remains hopeful, but some disappointment becomes evident. Chs 58–66 and 34–35: Further prophecies concerning the coming of a new age, expressed with a greater sense of frustration at the failure of the earlier prophecies to materialize but with enduring hope in the older predictions (see, e.g., chs 60–62), and also with a notable emphasis on the distinction between faithful Judeans and impious or corrupt ones.

It is not clear to us when, or why, the prophecies of Deutero-Isaiah were combined with those of Isaiah son of Amoz. The strong emphasis in both literary corpora on God's universal kingship, the messianic era, and the future exaltation of Zion may have suggested that these texts belonged together. Already at the beginning of the 2nd century BCE, the Jewish sage Ben Sirach (whose writings are preserved in the Apocryphya, but not in the Jewish Bible) knew a version of the book of Isaiah that combined both blocks of material (see Sirach [Ecclesiasticus] 48.20, 24–25). The great scroll of Isaiah from the Dead Sea Scrolls (dating to the late 2nd century BCE) also contains the entire book of Isaiah as we know it today.   [BENJAMIN D. SOMMER]

1 The prophecies of Isaiah son of Amoz, who prophesied concerning Judah and Jerusalem in the reigns of Uzziah, Jotham, Ahaz, and Hezekiah, kings of Judah.

2   Hear, O heavens, and give ear, O earth,
     For the Lord has spoken:
     "I reared children and brought them up—
     And they have rebelled against Me!
3   An ox knows its owner,
     An ass its master's crib:
     Israel does not know,
     My people takes no thought."

4   Ah, sinful nation!
     People laden with iniquity!
     Brood of evildoers!
     Depraved children!
     They have forsaken the Lord,
     Spurned the Holy One of Israel,
     Turned their backs [on Him].

5   Why do you seek further beatings,
     That you continue to offend?
     Every head is ailing,
     And every heart is sick.
6   From head to foot

1.1: Superscription. Like most prophetic books, this one begins with a title written by an editor indicating the author and the time during which the author works; cf. Jer. 1.1–3, Hos. 1.1, Amos 1.1, Mic. 1.1. Isaiah prophesied between about 740 and 700 BCE.

1.2–31: A poem of indictment and hope. Some view this ch as a single speech that is especially comprehensive in subject matter and biting in tone. Alternatively, it may be a summary of the contents of the book as a whole, written specifically to be an introduction, probably to chs 1–33, but perhaps to the final form of the book (cf. 1.28–31 with 66.24). Much of this chapter (vv. 1–27) is read as the haftarah, or prophetic reading, on the Sabbath preceding Tish'ah be'av, which commemorates the destruction of the Temple. This section is thus seen as offering theological justification for that event.

1.2–20: The indictment: complaint, threats, call for repentance. This section is framed by the words, "For the Lord has spoken," which appear in vv. 2 and

No spot is sound:
All bruises, and welts,
And festering sores—
Not pressed out, not bound up,
Not softened with oil.

7 Your land is a waste,
Your cities burnt down;
Before your eyes, the yield of your soil
Is consumed by strangers—
A wasteland a-as overthrown by strangers!-a

8 Fair^b Zion is left
Like a booth in a vineyard,
Like a hut in a cucumber field,
Like a city beleaguered.

9 Had not the LORD of Hosts
Left us some survivors,
We should be like Sodom,
Another Gomorrah.

10 Hear the word of the LORD,
You chieftains of Sodom;
Give ear to our God's instruction,
You folk of Gomorrah!

11 "What need have I of all your sacrifices?"
Says the LORD.
"I am sated with burnt offerings of rams,
And suet of fatlings,
And blood of bulls;
And I have no delight
In lambs and he-goats.

12 That you come to appear before Me—
Who asked that ^c of you?
Trample My courts 13 no more;
Bringing oblations is futile,-c
Incense is offensive to Me.
New moon and sabbath,
Proclaiming of solemnities,
d-Assemblies with iniquity,-d
I cannot abide.

14 Your new moons and fixed seasons
Fill Me with loathing;
They are become a burden to Me,
I cannot endure them.

15 And when you lift up your hands,

---

a-a Emendation yields "like Sodom overthrown."   b Lit. "Daughter."
c-c Others "To trample My courts? / ¹³Bring no more vain oblations."
d-d Septuagint "Fast and assembly"; cf. Joel 1.14.

(with a slight variation) 20. Such framing devices often indicate the extent of a literary unit in biblical literature. **2–4:** The poem consists of a legal complaint concerning covenant violation by the Israelites, who are depicted as ungrateful and also less intelligent than farm animals. In ancient Israelite thinking, heaven and earth serve as witnesses to the covenant between God and Israel (see Deut. 4.26; 32.1); hence God calls on them to hear the charges against Israel. **5–9:** A metaphorical description of Israel's punishment (vv. 5–6) leads to a more specific description (vv. 7–8): Judah will be invaded and Jerusalem put under siege (indeed, Assyrians devastated Judah and surrounded Jerusalem in 701; see introductory annotations to chs 36–37 and to ch 29). The phrasing in v. 7 borrows quite precisely from the rhetoric of the Assyrian kings who invaded Judah, which is known from Akkadian documents. **8–9: Zion's inviolability.** Here this topic, which will play a large role in chs 1–39, is introduced: Though Judah will be devastated and Jerusalem (also known as Zion) threatened, the city will never fall, according to Isaiah. The same idea also appears in several of the Psalms (e.g., 46, 48, 87). Jeremiah, who lived in a later period, objected to this idea (see, e.g., Jer. 7.1–20). Later biblical and Jewish writers respond in various ways to the failure of Isaiah's prophecies regarding Jerusalem's eternal status. **10–20: Rite and right.** The sacrifices and prayers offered by Isaiah's contemporaries are useless because they are not accompanied by ethical action. This is a frequent prophetic theme; see esp. Amos 5.21–25; Isa. 58.1–9. **10–15:** God's attitude toward ritual. According to the translation of vv. 12–13 above, God rejects sacrifice altogether; but according to the alternative in the translators' note, God rejects only the vain rituals of unethical people. Both renderings are linguistically defensible; rabbinic commentators prefer the latter (cf. Prov. 21.27). **10:** *Sodom . . . Gomorrah:* Isaiah

I will turn My eyes away from you;
Though you pray at length,
I will not listen.
Your hands are stained with crime—
16   Wash yourselves clean;
Put your evil doings
Away from My sight.
Cease to do evil;
17   Learn to do good.
Devote yourselves to justice;
ᵃ⁻Aid the wronged.⁻ᵃ
Uphold the rights of the orphan;
Defend the cause of the widow.

18   "Come, ᵃ⁻let us reach an understanding,"⁻ᵃ
                                 —says the LORD.
"Be your sins like crimson,
They can turn snow-white;
Be they red as dyed wool,
They can become like fleece."
19   If, then, you agree and give heed,
You will eat the good things of the earth;
20   But if you refuse and disobey,
ᵇ⁻You will be devoured [by] the sword.⁻ᵇ—
For it was the LORD who spoke.

21   Alas, she has become a harlot,
The faithful city
That was filled with justice,
Where righteousness dwelt—
But now murderers.
22   Yourᶜ silver has turned to dross;
ᵃ⁻Your wine is cut with water.⁻ᵃ
23   Your rulers are rogues
And cronies of thieves,
Every one avid for presents
And greedy for gifts;
They do not judge the case of the orphan,
And the widow's cause never reaches them.

24   Assuredly, this is the declaration
Of the Sovereign, the LORD of Hosts,
The Mighty One of Israel:
"Ah, I will get satisfaction from My foes;
I will wreak vengeance on My enemies!

compares Jerusalem's inhabitants to those of the most notorious and sinful Canaanite cities, which were completely destroyed, according to biblical tradition. See Gen. ch 19. **15:** *Lift up your hands:* People lifted their hands when praying in ancient Israel; cf. Exod. 9.29, 33; 1 Kings 8.38, 54. **16–20:** The unit does not confine itself to complaint but ends with an invitation to repentance and ethical action. Calls to repentance are rare in Isaiah, especially compared with the work of other prophets; they never appear from ch 6 through 31.6.

1.21–27: Lament and hope. Like the last unit, this unit is defined by a framing device involving repeated vocabulary. In both vv. 21 and 26–27 we hear *faithful city, righteousness* and the root "sh-p-t," meaning *justice* (Heb "mishpat") in v. 21 and both *magistrates* (better, "judges," Heb "shofetayikh") and *justice* in 26–27. **21–25:** In the ancient Near East, laments for a city typically mourn a destruction that has already occurred, but this lament mourns the city's sinfulness, which will lead to a disaster in the future. **26–27:** Having been punished, Zion will again know justice and faithfulness. A new name is given to the reformed Jerusalem; cf. 62.2–4; Ezek. 48.35.

a-a *Meaning of Heb. uncertain.*
b-b *Or "you will be fed the sword."*   c *I.e., Jerusalem's.*

25   I will turn My hand against you,
    And smelt out your dross ᵃ-as with lye,-ᵃ
    And remove all your slag:
26   I will restore your magistrates as of old,
    And your counselors as of yore.
    After that you shall be called
    City of Righteousness, Faithful City."

27ᵇ   Zion shall be saved in the judgment;
    Her repentant ones, in the retribution.ᶜ
28   But rebels and sinners shall all be crushed,
    And those who forsake the Lᴏʀᴅ shall perish.

29   Truly, youᵈ shall be shamed
    Because of the terebinths you desired,
    And you shall be confounded
    Because of the gardens you coveted.
30   For you shall be like a terebinth
    Wilted of leaf,
    And like a garden
    That has no water,
31   ᵉ-Stored wealth-ᵉ shall become as tow,
    And he who amassed it a spark;
    And the two shall burn together,
    With none to quench.

2 The word that Isaiah son of Amoz prophesied concerning Judah and Jerusalem.

2   In the days to come,
    The Mount of the Lᴏʀᴅ's House
    Shall stand firm above the mountains
    And tower above the hills;
    And all the nations
    Shall gaze on it with joy.
3   And the many peoples shall go and say:
    "Come,
    Let us go up to the Mount of the Lᴏʀᴅ,
    To the House of the God of Jacob;
    That He may instruct us in His ways,
    And that we may walk in His paths."
    For instruction shall come forthᶠ from Zion,
    The word of the Lᴏʀᴅ from Jerusalem.

a-a Emendation yields "in a crucible"; cf. 48.10.
b Others "Zion shall be saved by justice, / Her repentant ones by righteousness."
c For this meaning cf. 5.16; 10.22.   d Heb. "they."
e-e Connecting ḥason with ḥasan, "to store" (23.18), and ḥosen, "treasure" (33.6).
f I.e., oracles will be obtainable.

1.28–31: The fiery punishment. Are the sinners whose end is described contrasted with the reformed Zion described in the preceding vv., which will be spared their fate? Or are residents of the sinful city as a whole the subject of these vv.? The prophet leaves the answer unclear, perhaps intentionally; it will be given by the inhabitants of Jerusalem themselves; through their behavior, they will lead God to decide whom to punish.

2.1: Another superscription (cf. 1.1), whose presence suggests that the following texts (chs 2–4 or 2–5) were once an independent collection of Isaiah's prophecies. The present book may be built from discrete documents, often several chs long, which preserved Isaiah's speeches. These documents are not organized in chronological order, since the same event is often treated in more than one document.

2.2–4.6: The Jerusalem of the future and of the present. This long section begins (2.2–4) and ends (4.2–6) with a description of Jerusalem as it should and will be: a city of peace, equity, and divine presence. The long middle section (2.6–4.1) focuses on the sinfulness of the current inhabitants and their grim fate. Running throughout this section is imagery relating to height: All that is elevated is brought low, since the Lᴏʀᴅ alone deserves to be exalted. One modest hill is raised up in 2.2, and that hill is the location of the Lᴏʀᴅ's own Temple.

2.2–4: An eschatological poem. One of the most famous texts in the Bible, this poem is also found, with minor variations, in Mic. 4.1–4. **2–3:** *The Mount of the Lᴏʀᴅ's House* is the Temple Mount (which today is bordered on the west by the Western Wall). *Gaze*, alternatively, "flow towards." *Instruction*, alternatively, "law" (Heb "torah"). The term *Zion* in the Bible refers to the Temple Mount (and, by extension, more broadly

4　Thus He will judge among the nations
　　And arbitrate for the many peoples,
　　And they shall beat their swords into plowshares[a]
　　And their spears into pruning hooks:
　　Nation shall not take up
　　Sword against nation;
　　They shall never again know[b] war.

5　O House of Jacob!
　　Come, let us walk
　　By the light of the Lord.

6　For you have forsaken [the ways of] your people,
　　O House of Jacob!
　　[c]For they are full [of practices] from the East,
　　And of soothsaying like the Philistines;
　　They abound in customs[d] of the aliens.[c]

7　Their land is full of silver and gold,
　　There is no limit to their treasures;
　　Their land is full of horses,
　　There is no limit to their chariots.

8　And their land is full of idols;
　　They bow down to the work of their hands,
　　To what their own fingers have wrought.

9　But man shall be humbled,
　　And mortal brought low—
　　[e]Oh, do not forgive them![e]

10　Go deep into the rock,
　　Bury yourselves in the ground,
　　Before the terror of the Lord
　　And His dread majesty!

11　Man's haughty look shall be brought low,
　　And the pride of mortals shall be humbled.
　　None but the Lord shall be
　　Exalted in that day.

12　For the Lord of Hosts has ready a day
　　Against all that is proud and arrogant,
　　Against all that is lofty—so that it is brought low:

13　Against all the cedars of Lebanon,
　　Tall and stately,

to the whole city of Jerusalem). But its narrow sense does not refer to the hill currently called by that name, which is located immediately south of the present-day Armenian quarter, southwest of the biblical Mount Zion. **4:** The prophet does not imagine a future without borders or distinct nationalities. International conflicts will still occur, but nations will no longer resolve them through warfare. Instead, nations will submit to arbitration at Mount Zion. The Temple will become the headquarters of a divine Security Council with a membership of one and unsurpassed ability to ensure compliance.

2.5–22: The current situation and its results. This passage seems to be a warning regarding the future; alternatively, it may be an attempt to explain the reason for an event that has already occurred, namely the devastating earthquake during the reign of King Uzziah early in Isaiah's career (cf. Amos 1.1 and Zech. 14.5). The tense of the verbs in v. 17 is ambiguous; what NJPS renders as the future tense could, linguistically, be the past. **5–9:** Criticism of the nation's sins: magic; amassing extraordinary amounts of wealth; pursuing military power; and idolatry. All these vices embody inappropriate confidence in humanity's own powers. This confidence is not only mistaken, but offensive to God. **10–22:** The fate of the proud. Both in nature and in culture, the high will be brought low, the great will be humbled, and vanity will perish. **17:** A summary of this section and, arguably, of the message of Isaiah as a whole.

---

a More exactly, the iron points with which wooden plows were tipped.
b Cf. Judg. 3.2.
c-c Emendation yields "For they are full of divination / and have abundance of soothsaying, / Like Philistines / And like alien folk."
d Cf. Targum; lit. "children."
e-e Meaning of Heb. uncertain. Emendation yields "And their idols with them"; cf. vv. 17–21.

And all the oaks of Bashan;

14 Against all the high mountains
And all the lofty hills;

15 Against every soaring tower
And every mighty wall;

16 Against all the ᵃships of Tarshish⁻ᵃ
And all the gallant barks.

17 Then man's haughtiness shall be humbled
And the pride of man brought low.
None but the LORD shall be
Exalted in that day.

18 As for idols, they shall vanish completely.

19 And men shall enter caverns in the rock
And hollows in the ground—
Before the terror of the LORD
And His dread majesty,
When He comes forth to overawe the earth.

20 On that day, men shall fling away,
To the ᵇflying foxes⁻ᵇ and the bats,
The idols of silver
And the idols of gold
Which they made for worshiping.

21 And they shall enter the clefts in the rocks
And the crevices in the cliffs,
Before the terror of the LORD
And His dread majesty,
When He comes forth to overawe the earth.

22 Oh, cease to glorify man,
Who has only a breath in his nostrils!
For by what does he merit esteem?

3 For lo!
The Sovereign LORD of Hosts
Will remove from Jerusalem and from Judah
Prop and stay,
Every prop of food
And every prop of water:ᶜ

2 Soldier and warrior,
Magistrate and prophet,
Augur and elder;

3 Captain of fifty,
Magnate and counselor,
Skilled artisan and expert enchanter;ᵈ

3.1–4.1: Wealth and woe. 3.1–15: Unworthy leaders and a society in ruins. As in other passages, it is difficult to be sure whether the prophet predicts the future or describes the present. **1–7:** If this is a prediction, then the prophet announces that God will remove Judah's food and its leaders; in their place inexperienced and immature people will rule, and the nation will be desperate for the stability that legitimate authorities bring. If this is a description of the present, then he criticizes the current leadership, asserting that they are like children. **1:** *Will remove* might refer to an action God is already taking or one that God will take in the near future.

---

a-a *Probably a type of large ship.*   b-b *Exact meaning of Heb. uncertain.*
c *Emendation yields "clothing"; cf. v. 7; 4.1.*   d *Emendation yields "craftsman."*

4   And He^a will make boys their rulers,
      And babes shall govern them.

5   So the people shall oppress one another—
      Each oppressing his fellow:
      The young shall bully the old;
      And the despised [shall bully] the honored.

6   For should a man seize his brother,
      ^bIn whose father's house there is clothing:^b
      "Come, be a chief over us,
      And let this ruin^c be under your care,"

7   The other will thereupon protest,
      "I will not be a dresser of wounds,
      With no food or clothing in my own house.
      You shall not make me chief of a people!"

8   Ah, Jerusalem has stumbled,
      And Judah has fallen,
      Because by word and deed
      They insult the LORD,
      Defying His majestic glance.

9   Their partiality in judgment^d accuses them;
      They avow their sins like Sodom,
      They do not conceal them.
      Woe to them! For ill
      Have they served themselves.

10   (Hail^e the just man, for he shall fare well;
      He shall eat the fruit of his works.

11   Woe to the wicked man, for he shall fare ill;
      As his hands have dealt, so shall it be done
          to him.)

12   My people's rulers are babes,
      It is governed by women.^f
      O my people!
      Your leaders are misleaders;
      They have confused the course of your paths.

13   The LORD stands up to plead a cause,
      He rises to champion peoples.^g

14   The LORD will bring this charge
      Against the elders and officers of His people:

8–15: The reasons for the crisis: Judah's leaders are corrupt. Here again the theme of hubris appears; rather than depending on divinely ordained standards of equity, they give judgments that magnify their own positions and wealth.

---

a Heb. "I."
b-b Emendation yields "His father's son, saying . . ."
c Meaning of Heb. uncertain. Emendation yields "wound."
d So Targum; cf. Deut. 1.17; 16.19.
e Emendation yields "Happy is."
f Emendation yields "boys"; cf. v. 4 (and v. 5).
g Septuagint "His people"; cf. vv. 14, 15.

"It is you who have ravaged the vineyard;
That which was robbed from the poor is in your
    houses.
15   How dare you crush My people
And grind the faces of the poor?"
          —says my Lord GOD of Hosts.

16   The LORD said:
"Because the daughters of Zion
Are so vain
And walk with *heads thrown back,*-ᵃ
With roving eyes,
And with mincing gait,
Making a tinkling with their feet"—
17   My Lord will bareᵇ the pates
Of the daughters of Zion,
The LORD will uncover their heads.

18 In that day, my LORD will strip off the fineryᶜ of the an-
klets, the fillets, and the crescents; 19 of the eardrops, the
bracelets, and the veils; 20 the turbans, the armlets, and the
sashes; of the talismans and the amulets; 21 the signet rings
and the nose rings; 22 of the festive robes, the mantles, and
the shawls; the purses, 23 the lace gowns, and the linen
vests; and the kerchiefs and the capes.

24   And then—
Instead of perfume, there shall be rot;
And instead of an apron, a rope;
Instead of a diadem of beaten-work,
A shorn head;
Instead of a rich robe,
A girding of sackcloth;
ᵈ-A burn instead of beauty.-ᵈ

25   Herᵉ men shall fall by the sword,
Her fighting manhood in battle;
26   And her gates shall lament and mourn,
And ᶠ-she shall be emptied,-ᶠ
Shall sit on the ground.

3.16–4.1: The haughtiness of wealthy women, and their downfall. The vertical imagery is significant: Women who are metaphorically too high (i.e., too wealthy and too eager to display their wealth) will be brought low. While in vv. 1–15 the prophet starts with punishment and then describes the reason for it, in this passage he describes the ostentatious affluence first (vv. 16–23) and then the punishment (v. 24). **3.25–4.1: The punishment.** The two themes of 3.1–23—corrupt and unworthy male leaders and immoral women—combine in a description of a single punishment suitable to both. The men are killed, leaving the women bereaved and impoverished.

a-a Lit. "throats bent back."
b So Saadia. To bare a woman's head in public was an intolerable humiliation; cf. Mishnah
Baba Kamma 8.6.
c Many of the articles named in vv. 18–24 cannot be identified with certainty.
d-d The complete Isaiah scroll from Qumran, hereafter 1QIsᵃ, reads "For shame shall take
the place of beauty"; cf. note b.
e I.e., Zion's; cf. vv. 16, 17; Heb. "your."
f-f Meaning of Heb. uncertain. Emendation yields "her wall"; cf. Lam. 2.8.

4 In that day, seven women shall take hold of one man, saying,

> "We will eat our own food
> And wear our own clothes;
> Only let us be called by your name—
> Take away our disgrace!"

2[a] In that day,

> The radiance of the LORD
> Will lend beauty and glory,
> And the splendor of [b]the land[-b]
> [Will give] dignity and majesty,
> To the survivors of Israel.
> [3] And those who remain in Zion
> And are left in Jerusalem—
> All who are inscribed for life in Jerusalem—
> Shall be called holy.

4

> When my Lord has washed away
> The filth of [c]the daughters of Zion,[-c]
> And from Jerusalem's midst
> Has rinsed out her infamy—
> In a spirit of judgment
> And in a spirit of purging—

[5] the LORD will create[d] over the whole shrine and meeting place of Mount Zion cloud by day and smoke with a glow of flaming fire by night. Indeed, over [e]all the glory[-e] shall hang a canopy, [6] which shall serve as a pavilion for shade from heat by day and as a shelter for protection against drenching rain.

5 Let me sing for my beloved
A song of my lover about his vineyard.

> My beloved had a vineyard
> [f]On a fruitful hill.[-f]
2
> He broke the ground, cleared it of stones,
> And planted it with choice vines.
> He built a watchtower inside it,
> He even hewed a wine press in it;
> For he hoped it would yield grapes.
> Instead, it yielded wild grapes.

---

a For the interpretation of this verse, cf. 28.5. For "radiance," cf. Septuagint and the Syriac ṣemḥa, and for "splendor," cf. the meaning of peri in 10.12.

b-b Emendation yields "my Lord"; cf. the parallelism (in reverse order) in 3.17.

c-c Emendation yields "Daughter Zion," i.e., Zion personified; cf. 1.8 and note.

d Emendation yields "spread"; cf. Ps. 105.39.

e-e Emendation yields "His whole shrine."   f-f Meaning of Heb. uncertain.

4.2–6: Another eschatological poem: redemption in Zion. Very abruptly, the tone changes, and the prophet describes the outcome of the cleansing punishment. The passage closely resembles 2.2–4 in outlook, but it focuses on Israel and Zion rather than on the universal aspect of God's reign. **2:** *In that day:* Redemption will come at the same time as, or immediately after, the disaster that will threaten Zion. *Radiance . . . splendor,* lit. "branch . . . fruit." The former term alludes to the royal line, as indicated by its use elsewhere in the Bible (Jer. 23.5; 33.15; Zech. 3.8; 6.12) and also in Phoenician. Following this sense, the Targum translates it as "Messiah." Some rabbinic commentators interpret it as a reference to King Hezekiah, who reigned at the very end of the 8th century. In the latter interpretation the passage does not deal with the far-away future but with political conditions of the 8th century. **3:** If the passage is closely focused on the situation in the late 8th century, this v. may refer to refugees from northern Israel. They settled in Jerusalem to escape the Assyrians, who destroyed the Northern Kingdom in 722 BCE (translate: "those who survived are in Zion, those who remained, in Jerusalem"). **4–6:** *Cloud* and *smoke* with *fire* indicate the LORD's presence at the sanctuary; cf. Exod. 40.34–38; Num. 9.15–23; 1 Kings 8.20–12.

5.1–30: A poem of rebuke.
1–7. The song of the vineyard. A parable, in which God is the farmer and Israel the vineyard. At first, the identity of the characters is not evident, and only gradually does the audience realize that it is they themselves who are being rebuked. Nathan's parable and its explanation in 2 Sam. 12.1–12 are structured similarly. **8–24: A series of divine complaints,** each introduced by the word Ah (Heb "hoy"). The term may simply be a call for attention ("Hey!"), or it may be an exclamation of woe concerning a punishment that will soon take place

3   "Now, then,
       Dwellers of Jerusalem
       And men of Judah,
       You be the judges
       Between Me and My vineyard:
4   What more could have been done for My vineyard
       That I failed to do in it?
       Why, when I hoped it would yield grapes,
       Did it yield wild grapes?

5   "Now I am going to tell you
       What I will do to My vineyard:
       I will remove its hedge,
       That it may be ravaged;
       I will break down its wall,
       That it may be trampled.
6   And I will ᵃmake it a desolation;ᵃ
       It shall not be pruned or hoed,
       And it shall be overgrown with briers and thistles.
       And I will command the clouds
       To drop no rain on it."

7   For the vineyard of the Lᴏʀᴅ of Hosts
       Is the House of Israel,
       And the seedlings he lovingly tended
       Are the men of Judah.
       ᵇAnd He hoped for justice,
       But behold, injustice;
       For equity,
       But behold, iniquity!

8   Ah,
       Those who add house to house
       And join field to field,
       Till there is room for none but you
       To dwell in the land!
9   In my hearing [said] the Lᴏʀᴅ of Hosts:
       Surely, great houses
       Shall lie forlorn,
       Spacious and splendid ones
       Without occupants.
10   For ten acres of vineyard
       Shall yield just one *bath*,ᶜ

("Warning!"). **8–10:** The first complaint is directed against wealthy landowners who expand their own property at the expense of farmers of modest means. The eviction of peasants and the growth of massive estates was a major problem in the 8th century (cf. Amos ch 2; Mic. ch 2). In Israelite thought (as reflected in both prophetic literature and the Torah), land was ideally supposed to remain in the hands of a family in perpetuity, so that both tremendous wealth and penury would become unlikely. The Torah includes several laws to prevent poor or modest families from losing their land; see Lev. 25.8; Num. 27.1–11, 35; Deut. 27.17.

a-a *Meaning of Heb. uncertain.*
b *This sentence contains two word-plays: "And He hoped for* mishpaṭ, *And there is* mispaḥ *[exact meaning uncertain]; / For* ṣedaqah, *But there is* ṣeʿaqah *[lit. 'outcry']."*
c *I.e., of wine. The* bath *was the liquid equivalent of the* ephah; *and the* ḥomer *was ten* baths *or ephahs (Ezek. 45.11).*

And a field sown with a *homer* of seed
Shall yield a mere *ephah*.

11 Ah,
Those who chase liquor
From early in the morning,
And till late in the evening
Are inflamed by wine!

12 ^aWho, at their banquets,
Have^{-a} lyre and lute,
Timbrel, flute, and wine;
But who never give a thought
To the plan of the LORD,
And take no note
Of what He is designing.

13 Assuredly,
My people will suffer exile
For not giving heed,
Its multitude victims of hunger
And its masses parched with thirst.

14 Assuredly,
Sheol has opened wide its gullet
And parted its jaws in a measureless gape;
And down into it shall go,
That splendor and tumult,
That din and revelry.

15 Yea, man is bowed,
And mortal brought low;
Brought low is the pride of the haughty.

16 And the LORD of Hosts is exalted by judgment,
The Holy God proved holy by retribution.

17^b Then lambs shall graze
As in their meadows,
And strangers shall feed
On the ruins of the stout.

18 Ah,
Those who haul sin with cords of falsehood
And iniquity as with cart ropes!

19 Who say,^c
"Let Him speed, let Him hasten His purpose,
If we are to give thought;

11–17: The second complaint: parties instead of piety. Appropriately, the people whose appetite is insatiable will feed the insatiable appetite of *Sheol,* the underworld (v. 14). Sheol is not comparable to later Jewish and Christian notions of hell; all humans, not just evil ones, go to Sheol when they die. See further 14.9–11 n. and 26.19 n. **13:** *Suffer exile* may refer to the fate of northern Israelites in the late 8th century (especially if the verb is in fact a past tense, which is likely); or it may predict the fate of the southern Judeans, some of whom will be exiled even though Zion will not fall. **18–19:** The third complaint. The people in v. 19 are guilty in one of two ways. The sinners quoted speak sarcastically and do not believe that God will in fact fulfill His purpose (so according to the translators' note *c*). Or the v. quotes faithful Israelites who impatiently demand that God act immediately.

a-a *Emendation yields* "whose interests are" *(mish'ehem, from sha'ah* "to turn to," *17.7, 8; 31.1).*

b *Meaning of verse uncertain. Emendation yields* "The lambs shall graze / In the pasture of the fat [rams], / And the kids shall feed / On the ranges of the stout [bucks]." *The lambs and the kids are the poor and the rams and bucks are the rich oppressors (cf. Ezek. 34.17–22).*

c *By way of retort to v. 12.*

Let the plans of the Holy One of Israel
Be quickly fulfilled,
If we are to give heed."

20   Ah,
Those who call evil good
And good evil;
Who present darkness as light
And light as darkness;
Who present bitter as sweet
And sweet as bitter!

21   Ah,
Those who are so wise—
In their own opinion;
So clever—
In their own judgment!

22   Ah,
Those who are so doughty—
As drinkers of wine,
And so valiant—
As mixers of drink!

23   Who vindicate him who is in the wrong
In return for a bribe,
And withhold vindication
From him who is in the right.

24   Assuredly,
As straw is consumed by a tongue of fire
And hay ᵃ·shrivels as it burns,·ᵃ
Their stock shall become like rot,
And their buds shall blow away like dust.
For they have rejected the instruction of the LORD
     of Hosts,
Spurned the word of the Holy One of Israel.

25   That is why
The LORD's anger was roused
Against His people,
Why He stretched out His arm against it
And struck it,
So that the mountains quaked,ᵇ
And its corpses lay
Like refuse in the streets.
Yet his anger has not turned back,
And His arm is outstretched still.

20–21: Two brief complaints dealing with sophistry. **22–24:** The last complaint mixes the themes of vv. 8–10 and 11–17. Misplaced abilities are focused on fine tasting wine; officials pervert justice for money. **22:** *Doughty,* or "mighty, heroic" (Heb "gibor"). **25–30: The coming disaster.** God is portrayed as bludgeoning the nation, both through an earthquake that has already taken place (v. 25) and—in greater detail—a foreign invasion yet to come.

a-a *Emendation yields "is burned by flame"; cf. 33.11–12; 47.14.*
b *An allusion to the destructive earthquake in the reign of King Uzziah: Amos 1.1; Zech. 14.5; cf. Isa. 9.18a.*

26   He will raise an ensign to a nation[a] afar,
      Whistle to one at the end of the earth.
      There it comes with lightning speed!
27   In its ranks, none is weary or stumbles,
      They never sleep or slumber;
      The belts on their waists do not come loose,
      Nor do the thongs of their sandals break.
28   Their arrows are sharpened,
      And all their bows are drawn.
      Their horses' hoofs are like flint,
      Their chariot wheels like the whirlwind.
29   Their roaring is like a lion's,
      They roar like the great beasts;
      When they growl and seize a prey,
      They carry it off and none can recover it.

30 But in that day, a roaring shall resound over him like
that of the sea;[b] and then he shall look below and, behold,
      Distressing darkness, with light;
      Darkness, [c]in its lowering clouds.[c]

6 In the year that King Uzziah died, I beheld my Lord
seated on a high and lofty throne; and the skirts of His
robe filled the Temple. 2 Seraphs stood in attendance
on Him. Each of them had six wings: with two he covered
his face, with two he covered his legs, and with two he
would fly.

3   And one would call to the other,
      "Holy, holy, holy!
      The LORD of Hosts!
      His presence fills all the earth!"

4 The doorposts[d] would shake at the sound of the one
who called, and the House kept filling with smoke. 5 I
cried,
      "Woe is me; I am lost!
      For I am a man [e]of unclean lips[e]
      And I live among a people
      Of unclean lips;
      Yet my own eyes have beheld
      The King LORD of Hosts."

26: *Ensign:* God acts as commander of the foreign army, showing them the way to Israel. **30:** This seems to belong to the description of the punishment. Elsewhere in Isaiah, however, the portrayal of a devastating invasion suddenly switches to a report of the invaders' defeat (see 28.16 n.; 29.1–14 n.; 31.5 n.; 31.15–20 n.). If translators' note *b* is correct, this v. may have originally functioned this way. Some have suggested that this passage originally belonged after 10.1–4, with which it has much in common.

6.1–13: Prophetic commissioning. Many read this passage as a description of Isaiah's initiation into prophecy and hence view it as the earliest text of Isaiah's career. They note similarities between this text and others describing the inauguration of prophets (Exod. chs 3–4; Exod. ch 6; Jer. ch 1; Ezek. chs 1–3). According to others, it depicts the beginning of a new stage in Isaiah's career; he receives a new assignment that differs from earlier ones. These scholars point out that the ch does not appear at the beginning of the book. Further, the first five chs call on the Judeans to repent, but from this ch until the last prophecy of Isaiah son of Amoz, the prophet does not call on the Israelites to repent; 6.9–10 may account for this difference. **1–4: The vision of the divine court.** Isaiah sees God and the deity's retinue (see also 1 Kings 22.19–23; Job chs 1–2). This is one of many passages indicating that some biblical authors conceive of God as a physical being whom a few people can see (cf. Exod. 24.11; 33.11; Num. 12.8). On the divine court, cf. 2 Kings 22.19–23; Job chs 1–2. **3:** Along with a v. from Ezekiel's inaugural vision (3.12), this v. serves as the centerpiece of the "kedushah" prayer, in which worshippers praise God using angelic liturgy. The "kedushah" appears in the communal recitation of the "ʿamidah" (the main statutory prayer in Judaism), which requires a prayer quorum ("minyan") of ten. It is also found in

---

a Heb. "nations."

b I.e., the LORD will intervene and come to his aid. Cf. 29.6–7; 30.27. This verse may constitute a transition between chaps. 8 and 9.

c-c Meaning of Heb. uncertain.   d Meaning of Heb. uncertain.

e-e I.e., speaking impiety; cf. 9.16, and contrast "pure of speech [lit. 'lip']" in Zeph. 3.9.

6 Then one of the seraphs flew over to me with a live coal, which he had taken from the altar with a pair of tongs. 7 He touched it to my lips and declared,

> "Now that this has touched your lips,
> Your guilt shall depart
> And your sin be purged away."

8 Then I heard the voice of my Lord saying, "Whom shall I send? Who will go for us?" And I said, "Here am I; send me." 9 And He said, "Go, say to that people:

> 'Hear, indeed, but do not understand;
> See, indeed, but do not grasp.'

10
> Dull that people's mind,
> Stop its ears,
> And seal its eyes—
> Lest, seeing with its eyes
> And hearing with its ears,
> It also grasp with its mind,
> And repent and save[a] itself."

11 I asked, "How long, my Lord?" And He replied:

> "Till towns lie waste without inhabitants
> And houses without people,
> And the ground lies waste and desolate—

12
> For the LORD will banish the population—
> And deserted sites are many
> In the midst of the land.

13 "But while a tenth part yet remains in it, it shall repent. It shall be ravaged like the terebinth and the oak, of which stumps are left even when they are felled: its stump shall be a holy seed."

7 In the reign of Ahaz son of Jotham son of Uzziah, king of Judah, King Rezin of Aram and King Pekah son of Remaliah of Israel marched upon Jerusalem to attack it; but they were not able to attack it.

a Lit. "heal."

services for all mornings, Sabbath afternoons, and Saturday nights in sections that can be recited in private. **5–7: Isaiah's reaction and purification.** Isaiah fears that he will die, because he is not worthy to see God. A *seraph* or angelic being purifies him and reassures him that he is safe. **8–13: The commissioning: repentance is no longer an option.** Isaiah is told of his mission. **8–10:** Shockingly, the prophet is not supposed to help the people understand the danger to which their sinfulness exposes them. Cf. 29.9–12. God no longer desires repentance; rather, God wants to vent divine anger on the nation. Some rabbinic commentators, unable to imagine such an interpretation, argue that the imperative verbs must be taken as future-tense verbs. Hence God does not order Isaiah to cause the people to misunderstand; rather, God predicts that they will not achieve understanding in spite of Isaiah's speeches, because the people do not want to acknowledge the truth. **11–12:** The divine judgment will involve the exile of most of the nation. **13:** According to the NJPS translation (which reads against the cantillation, the signs in the Masoretic biblical text which serve as punctuation marks as well as musical notations), a small remnant will repent after the disaster; from this kernel the nation will be renewed. The renewal involves not exiles who return from afar but survivors who remain in the land. Thus Isaiah's notion of renewal differs from the vision of renewal in Ezekiel, Jeremiah, and Second Isaiah. Alternatively (and in accordance with the cantillation), the first half of the v. can be translated much more negatively: "And when a tenth are left, they will again be burned." In this rendering, the few survivors are subject to additional disaster. The second half is also obscure, but it seems to refer to the fact that renewed life can come out of the stump of terebinth and oak trees. Here the notion of the remnant that is saved from a devastating calamity does appear, however subtly.

7.1–8.23: Prophecies delivered during the Syro-Ephraimite crisis. These passages, and perhaps some of the passages following them, deal with a series of events known from both biblical texts (2 Kings ch 16; 2 Chron. ch 28) and ancient Assyrian records. In 735 BCE the leaders of the kingdom of Damascus in Syria (or *Aram*) and of the northern Israelite kingdom (also known as Ephraim) attempted to create a coalition of small states to oppose the Assyrian empire. King Ahaz of Judah did not join their conspiracy, and the Arameans (Syrians) and Israelites (Ephraimites) marched against Judah, intending to depose Ahaz and replace him with an ally of their own, the son of Tabeel (his first

2 Now, when it was reported to the House of David that Aram had allied itself with Ephraim, their hearts and the hearts of their people trembled as trees of the forest sway before a wind. 3 But the LORD said to Isaiah, "Go out with your son Shear-jashub*a* to meet Ahaz at the end of the conduit of the Upper Pool, by the road of the Fuller's Field. 4 And say to him: Be firm and be calm. Do not be afraid and do not lose heart on account of those two smoking stubs of firebrands, on account of the raging of Rezin and his Arameans and the son of Remaliah.*b* 5 Because the Arameans— with Ephraim and the son of Remaliah—have plotted against you, saying, 6 'We will march against Judah and invade and conquer it, and we will set up as king in it the son of Tabeel,'*b* 7 thus said my Lord GOD:

It shall not succeed,
It shall not come to pass.

8   For the chief city of Aram is Damascus,
       And the chief of Damascus is Rezin;

9   The chief city of Ephraim is Samaria,
       And the chief of Samaria is the son of Remaliah.*c*
       d-And in another sixty-five years,
       Ephraim shall be shattered as a people.-*d*
       If you will not believe, for you *e*-cannot be
          trusted-*e*. . . ."

10 The LORD spoke further to Ahaz: 11 "Ask for a sign from the LORD your God, anywhere down to Sheol or up to the sky." 12 But Ahaz replied, "I will not ask, and I will not test the LORD." 13 "Listen, House of David," [Isaiah] retorted, "is it not enough for you to treat men as helpless that you also treat my God as helpless?*f* 14 Assuredly, my Lord will give you a sign of His own accord! Look, the young woman is with child and about to give birth to a son. Let her name him Immanuel.*g* 15 (By the time he learns to reject the bad and choose the good, people will be feeding on curds and honey.) 16 For before the lad knows to reject the bad and choose the good, the ground whose two kings you dread shall be abandoned. 17 The LORD will cause to come upon you and your people and your ancestral house such days as never have come since

name is not given, probably to slight him). Ahaz appealed to the Assyrian king, Tiglath-Pileser, for help. The Arameans and Ephraimites did not succeed in their efforts; Damascus was conquered entirely in 732, while Israel lost considerable territory to Assyria. Judah was saved, but it became dependent on Assyria.

7.1–17: A narrative about Isaiah and King Ahaz. 1: A brief introduction sets the scene by paraphrasing 2 Kings 16.5. **2–9:** Isaiah is sent to reassure Ahaz that the Syro-Ephraimite threat will not succeed. Isaiah's commitment to the Davidic dynasty and his belief in the inviolability of Zion play a crucial role here (see 1.8–9 n.). **3:** The notion of the remnant that will return is expressed by the name Isaiah gave to his son. **8b (printed here at the end of 9):** An especially obscure verse. Why does Isaiah attempt to reassure Ahaz by referring to an event relatively far in the future? One might view the v. as an addition by a later scribe, but in fact Damascus fell to the Assyrians in 733, only three years after the Syro-Ephraimite crisis; a later scribe would not have inserted an inaccurate "prediction." **10–17:** Apparently Ahaz chooses to rely on the intervention of the Assyrian king (cf. 2 Kings 16.7–9) rather than on God. **14–17:** The Immanuel passage. Isaiah provides a *sign*, the point of which is either to clarify his message (cf. his sign in ch 20) or to verify it (cf. the sign in Judg. 6.17–23). It is not clear whether the *sign* is the woman's pregnancy, the child's birth, his name, or his diet; nor is it clear when the sign comes to pass—immediately (if the sign is his name), soon (birth), or several years into the future. Similarly ambiguities occur in the case of other biblical signs; cf. Exod. 3.12. **14:** *Young woman* (Heb "'almah"). The Septuagint translates as "virgin," leading ancient and medieval Christians to connect this verse with the New Testament figure of Mary. All modern scholars, however, agree that the Heb merely de-

---

a Meaning "[only] a remnant will turn back," i.e., repent; cf. 6.13; 10.21.

b To refer to a person only as "the son of—" is slighting; cf. note at 1 Sam. 10.11.

c The thought is continued by 8.8b–10; cf. 2 Chron. 13.8–12.

d-d Brought down from v. 8 for clarity.

e-e Others "surely, you shall not be established."

f By insisting on soliciting the aid of Assyria (see 2 Kings 16.7 ff.; cf. below, v. 20). "Treat as helpless" follows the translation of Saadia; cf. Gen. 19.11.

g Meaning "with us is God."

Ephraim turned away from Judah—that selfsame king of Assyria!ᵃ

18 "In that day, the Lᴏʀᴅ will whistle to the flies at the ends of the water channels of Egypt and to the bees in the land of Assyria; 19 and they shall all come and alight in the rugged wadis, and in the clefts of the rocks, and in all the thornbrakes, and in all the watering places.

20 "In that day, my Lord will cut away with the razor that is hired beyond the Euphrates—with the king of Assyriaᵇ—the hair of the head and ᶜthe hair of the legs,ᶜ and it shall clip off the beard as well. 21 And in that day, each man shall save alive a heifer of the herd and two animals of the flock. 22 (And he shall obtain so much milk that he shall eat curds.) Thus everyone who is left in the land shall feed on curds and honey.

23 "For in that day, every spot where there could stand a thousand vines worth a thousand shekels of silverᵈ shall become a wilderness of thornbush and thistle. 24 One will have to go there with bow and arrows,ᵉ for the country shall be all thornbushes and thistles. 25 But the perils of thornbush and thistle shall not spread to any of the hills that could only be tilled with a hoe;ᶠ and here cattle shall be let loose, and ᵍsheep and goatsᵍ shall tramp about."

8 The Lᴏʀᴅ said to me, "Get yourself a large sheet and write on it ʰin common scriptʰ 'For Maher-shalal-hash-baz';ⁱ 2 and call reliable witnesses, the priest Uriah and Zechariah son of Jeberechiah, to witness for Me." 3 I was intimate with the prophetess,ʲ and she conceived and bore a son; and the Lᴏʀᴅ said to me, "Name him Maher-shalal-hash-baz.ⁱ 4 For before the boy learns to call 'Father' and 'Mother,' the wealth of Damascus and the spoils of Samaria, ᵏand the delights of Rezin and of the son of Remaliah,ᵏ shall be carried off before the king of Assyria."

a Cf. note on v. 13.

b Who was hired by Ahaz; cf. notes on vv. 13 and 17.

c-c I.e., the pubic hair.

d I.e., all the best farm land, corresponding to the hairiest parts of the body; v. 20.

e Because of dangerous beasts.

f Marginal farm land, too rocky for the plow, corresponding to areas of the body with scant hair.

g-g See note at Exod. 12.3.

h-h Meaning of Heb. uncertain.

i I.e., "Pillage hastens, looting speeds," indicating that two cities are to be pillaged at an early date; see v. 4.

j I.e., Isaiah's wife.

k-k Brought up from v. 6 for clarity.

notes a young woman of marriageable age, whether married or unmarried, whether a virgin or not. **15–17:** The message the sign represents is two-fold: God is with Judah, both to protect it (v. 16) and to punish it (v. 17).

7.18–25: Predictions of disaster for Judah. Ahaz has refused to rely solely on God's promises of enduring kingship for David (cf. 2 Sam. 7.8–16; Ps. 89.20–37) and of Jerusalem's eternal safety (cf. Pss. 46; 48). Consequently (or perhaps as a result of support among Judeans for the attempt to enthrone the son of Tabeel and for the Syro-Ephraimite alliance?), God will use the Assyrians not to rescue Judah but to decimate it. The disaster will not be total, however. Isaiah makes no reference to Jerusalem's capitulation. Agriculture will be curtailed and wild animals will roam in what had been farmland, but those who survive (v. 22) will have food to eat. The reference to *curds and honey* (vv. 15, 22) is unclear: They are either delicacies the survivors are privileged to enjoy (so several rabbinic commentators) or meager provisions left after the punishment. The passage exemplifies the ambivalent tone of Isaiah's doctrine of the surviving remnant: One is not sure whether the description of this future is to be viewed negatively (since only a remnant endure) or positively (since they do in fact endure). The final v. may be a description of the poverty-stricken circumstances after the disaster or of agricultural—hence national—rebirth. In fact the Assyrian invasion Isaiah predicts did not occur during Ahaz's reign, but it did take place during the reign of his son, Hezekiah.

8.1–22: Further predictions concerning the Syro-Ephraimite crisis. In the oracles collected here, Isaiah refers to himself in the first person (unlike those in the previous ch, which refer to Isaiah in the third person). They consist of oracles dating from the beginning of the crisis through its aftermath.

⁵ Again the LORD spoke to me, thus:

⁶   "Because that people has spurned
     The gently flowing waters of Siloam"ᵃ—

⁷   Assuredly,
     My Lord will bring up against them
     The mighty, massive waters of the Euphrates,
     The king of Assyria and all his multitude.
     It shall rise above all its channels,
     And flow over all its beds,

⁸   And swirl through Judah like a flash flood
     Reaching up to the neck.ᵇ

     ᶜBut with us is God,
     Whose wings are spread
     As wide as your land is broad!

⁹   Band together, O peoples—you shall be broken!
     Listen to this, you remotest parts of the earth:
     Gird yourselves—you shall be broken;
     Gird yourselves—you shall be broken!

¹⁰   Hatch a plot—it shall be foiled;
     Agree on action—it shall not succeed.
     For with us is God!

¹¹ For this is what the LORD said to me, when He took
me by the handᵈ and charged me not to walk in the path
of that people:

¹²ᵉ   "You must not call conspiracyᶠ
     All that that people calls conspiracy,ᶠ
     Nor revere what it reveres,
     Nor hold it in awe.

¹³   None but the LORD of Hosts
     Shall you account holy;
     Give reverence to Him alone,
     Hold Him alone in awe.

¹⁴   He shall be ᵍfor a sanctuary,
     A stone ⁻ᵍ men strike against:
     A rock men stumble over
     For the two Houses of Israel,

---

a The conduit—and later the tunnel—of Siloam conveyed into Jerusalem the waters of
Gihon, which symbolize "the LORD of Hosts who dwells on Mount Zion" (v. 18). For the
nature of the rejection see note at 7.13.

b I.e., Judah shall be imperiled, but, in contrast to Aram and Ephraim (v. 4), not destroyed.

c See note c at 7.9.

d I.e., singled me out; cf. 41.9, 13; 42.6; 45.1; Jer. 31.32 [31].

e The Heb. forms here and in vv. 13 and 19 are plural to include the disciples (v. 16) and the
children (v. 18).

f Meaning of Heb. uncertain. Emendation yields "holy"; cf. v. 13.

g-g Emendation yields ". . . for His holy domain [cf. Ps. 114.2] / A stone . . ."

1–4: A sign concerning the imminent destruction of Judah's enemies. The thrust of Isaiah's argument, as in ch 7 (with which it is likely to be contemporaneous) is that Ahaz need not rely on Assyrian aid. **5–8:** Isaiah's reaction to Ahaz's lack of faith. Ahaz rejected the God of Zion (symbolized by the waters of the Siloam which flow from the Gihon spring immediately below the Temple Mount) and chose the Assyrians; therefore God will bring Assyrians (represented by the river Euphrates) to punish him. Alternatively, it is possible that v. 6b (printed in NJPS as part of v. 4) should be translated, "And because you rejoiced in Rezin and the son of Remaliah." In this case, these vv. are addressed not to Ahaz but to Judeans who conspire against him on behalf of the Arameans and Israelites; God will punish their infidelity to the Davidic monarch by sending the Assyrians. **7–8:** The comparison of the Assyrian king to a devastating flood appears in Assyrian documents. *Multitude* could be translated "glory," a term also used in Assyrian descriptions of their king's terrifying power. **8:** Isaiah expresses the doctrine of Zion's inviolability poetically: The Assyrians will decimate the land of Judah but not Judah's head, which is Jerusalem. **9–10:** Failure awaits the plotters. The identity of the plotters is enigmatic: Are they (1) the Arameans and Israelites who attack Judah, (2) Judeans who support them against King Ahaz, (3) King Ahaz, who creates a conspiracy with the Assyrians against the Arameans and Israelites, or (4) the Assyrians who plan to take over the land of their new Judean ally—or all of these? **11–15:** These vv. are linguistically and interpretively very difficult. They seem to reflect the fact that Isaiah's advice opposes all his contemporaries' perspectives: He advocates joining neither the anti-Assyrian coalition nor the Assyrians themselves. **16–18:** Another obscure passage, perhaps from the end of the crisis. Isaiah's predictions had not come true in the short run: The Assyr-

And a trap and a snare for those
Who dwell in Jerusalem.
15 The masses shall trip over these
And shall fall and be injured,
Shall be snared and be caught.
16 Bind up the message,
Seal the instruction with My disciples."

17 So I will wait for the LORD, who is hiding His face from the House of Jacob, and I will trust in Him. 18 Here stand I and the children the LORD has given me as signs and portents in Israel from the LORD of Hosts, who dwells on Mount Zion.

19 Now, should people say to you, "Inquire of the ghosts and familiar spirits that chirp and moan; for a people may inquire of its divine beings[a]—of the dead on behalf of the living—20 for instruction and message," surely, for one who speaks thus there shall be no dawn. 21 [b-]And he shall go about in it wretched and hungry; and when he is hungry, he shall rage and revolt against his king and his divine beings.[-b] He may turn his face upward 22 or he may look below, but behold,

Distress and darkness, [c-]with no daybreak;[-c]
Straitness and gloom, [c-]with no dawn.[-c]
23 For [d-]if there were to be[-d] any break of day for that [land] which is in straits, only the former [king] would have brought abasement to the land of Zebulun and the land of Naphtali—while the later one would have brought honor to the Way of the Sea, the other side of the Jordan, and Galilee of the Nations.[e]

9 [f]The people that walked in darkness
Have seen a brilliant light;
On those who dwelt in a land of gloom
Light has dawned.
2 You have magnified that nation,
Have given it great joy;
They have rejoiced before You
As they rejoice at reaping time,
As they exult
When dividing spoil.

a I.e., the shades of the dead; cf. 1 Sam. 28.13.
b-b This sentence would read well after v. 22.
c-c Meaning of Heb. uncertain.   d-d So 1QIs[a]; the others have "there is not."
e Meaning of verse uncertain. The rendering here assumes that "the former [king]" refers to Pekah (cf. 2 Kings 15.29) and "the later" to Hoshea (ibid. 30). For the construction lu . . . ka'eth, see Judg. 13–23.
f See note b at 5.30.

ians did not invade Judah in Ahaz's day, and Ahaz's policy of turning to them for protection seems to have worked. Nonetheless, the prophet insists that his words would prove valid; he has them written down, bound up, and placed with his disciples for safekeeping. Ultimately it would become clear that the LORD's prophet spoke truly. During the Assyrian invasion three decades later (in the reign of Ahaz's son, Hezekiah), Isaiah's perspective was vindicated, since the Assyrians devastated Judah but did not capture Jerusalem. **19–21:** A polemic against other forms of divination. It may date to the period of the Syro-Ephraimite crisis, but it could also fit many other periods. *Ghosts and familiar spirits* are the demigods and deified ancestors to whom some Judeans, following Canaanite and Mesopotamian religious models, turned for guidance. Cf. Lev. 20.27; Deut. 18.9–15; 1 Sam. ch 28.

8.23: An unusually obscure verse. The Assyrian king Tiglath-pileser seized lands belonging to the tribes of *Zebulun* and *Naphtali*, along with parts of *Galilee* and Transjordan, from the Israelite king Pekah son of Remaliah in the aftermath of the Syro-Ephraimite crisis.

9.1–6: The ideal Davidic king. Isaiah describes liberation from some form of adversity (perhaps the Assyrian conquests of Israelite territory described in the previous vv., or Syro-Ephraimite pressures on Judah). The verbs are in the past tense. Some interpreters view them as examples of the "prophetic past," which predicts future events using the past tense because they are as good as done. Thus it is not clear whether the Davidic king whose birth and rule are described (vv. 5–6) has already been born (if the verbs are a regular past tense) or will be born in the future (prophetic past). If the former, the v. probably refers to Ahaz's son Hezekiah, as many modern and rabbinic commenta-

3 For the yoke that they bore
And the stick on their back—
The rod of their taskmaster—
You have broken as on the day of Midian.[a]

4 Truly, all the boots put on [b]to stamp with[b]
And all the garments donned in infamy
Have been fed to the flames,
Devoured by fire.

5 For a child has been born to us,
A son has been given us.
And authority has settled on his shoulders.
He has been named
"The Mighty God is planning grace;[c]
The Eternal Father, a peaceable ruler"—

6 In token of abundant authority
And of peace without limit
Upon David's throne and kingdom,
That it may be firmly established
In justice and in equity
Now and evermore.
The zeal of the LORD of Hosts
Shall bring this to pass.

7 My Lord
[d]Let loose a word[d] against Jacob
And it fell upon Israel.

8 But all the people noted[e]—
Ephraim and the inhabitants of Samaria—
In arrogance and haughtiness:

9 "Bricks have fallen—
We'll rebuild with dressed stone;
Sycamores have been felled—
We'll grow cedars instead!"

10 So the LORD let [f]the enemies of Rezin[f]
Triumph over it
And stirred up its foes—

11 Aram from the east
And Philistia from the west—
Who devoured Israel
With greedy mouths.

tors believe (though other possibilities exist depending on the date of the passage). Most later readers (both Jewish and Christian) understood the passage to describe an ideal future ruler, i.e., the Messiah. **5:** *"The Mighty God . . . ruler"*: This long sentence is the throne name of the royal child. Semitic names often consist of sentences that describe God; thus the name Isaiah in Hebrew means "The LORD saves"; Hezekiah, "The LORD strengthens"; in Akkadian, the name of the Babylonian king Merodach-baladan (Isa. 39.1) means "the god Marduk has provided an heir." These names do not describe that person who holds them but the god whom the parents worship. Similarly, the name given to the child in this v. does not describe that child or attribute divinity to him, contrary to classical Christian readings of this messianic verse.

9.7–10.4: The fate of the Northern Kingdom, Israel. A repeated refrain in 9.11, 16, 21, and 10.4 structures this poem into four sections. The same refrain is found in 5.25, and scholars speculate that 5.25–30 may originally have been the poem's fifth and final section. The verbs here are in the past tense, but their significance is unclear. They may predict disasters to come (in which case the verbs exemplify "the prophetic past" described in 9.1–6 n.); alternatively they may review disasters that God already sent in an unsuccessful attempt to chasten the Northern Kingdom (in which case the prophet does not predict coming events but presents an interpretation of recent history). The verbs in 5.26–30 clearly have a future tense and represent a prediction of Assyrian invasion which ends the poem. The following remarks assume the verbs in the first four sections refer to the past and are interpretations of recent events, not predictions of upcoming ones. **7–11:** The first section may refer to the earthquake that shook Israel and Judah early in Isaiah's career; cf. Amos 1.1; Zech. 14.5.

a See Judg. 7–8.
b-b Meaning of Heb. uncertain; emendation yields "in wickedness"; cf. Targum.
c As in 25.1.
d-d Septuagint reads "Let loose pestilence"; cf. Amos 4.10. In vv. 7–20 Isaiah alludes to and builds upon Amos 4.10–12.
e 1QIs[a] reads "shouted."
f-f Emendation yields "its enemies."

Yet His anger has not turned back,
And His arm is outstretched still.

12–17: The second section refers to the chaos in the Northern Kingdom during the coups and massacres described in the mid-740s (see 2 Kings ch 15). **18–20:** The third section recalls the earthquake, political chaos, and Israel's anti-Judean policies during the Syro-Ephraimite crisis.

12 For the people has not turned back
To Him who struck it
And has not sought
The LORD of Hosts.

13 So the LORD will cut off from Israel
Head and tail,
Palm branch and reed,
In a single day.

14 Elders ᵃ and magnates ᵃ—
Such are the heads;
Prophets who give false instruction,
Such are the tails ᵇ

15 That people's leaders have been misleaders,
So they that are led have been confused.

16 That is why my Lord
Will not spare ᶜ their youths,
Nor show compassion
To their orphans and widows;
For all are ungodly and wicked,
And every mouth speaks impiety.

17 Already wickedness has blazed forth like a fire
Devouring thorn and thistle.
It has kindled the thickets of the wood,
ᵈ Which have turned into billowing smoke. ᵈ

ᵉ Yet His anger has not turned back,
And His arm is outstretched still. ᵉ

18 By the fury of the LORD of Hosts,
The earth was shaken. ᶠ
Next, the people became like devouring fire:
No man spared his countryman.

19 They snatched on the right, but remained hungry,
And consumed on the left without being sated.
Each devoured the flesh of his ᵍ own kindred ᵍ—

20 Manasseh Ephraim's, and Ephraim Manasseh's, ʰ
And both of them against Judah! ⁱ

---

a-a Emendation yields "who practice partiality."
b Emendation yields "palm branches"; the elders and the prophets are the leaders, the people are the led; cf. 3.1–2, 12.
c Cf. Arabic samuḥa. 1QIsᵃ reads yḥmw.   *d-d Meaning of Heb. uncertain.*
e-e Moved down from v. 16 for clarity.   *f Cf. note at 5.25.*
g-g Meaning of Heb. uncertain. Emendation yields "fellow"; cf. Targum.
h Alludes to the civil wars of 2 Kings 15.10, 14–16, 25.   *i Cf. 7.1–9.*

Yet His anger has not turned back,
And His arm is outstretched still.

10 Ha!
Those who write out evil writs
And compose iniquitous documents,

2 To subvert the cause of the poor,
To rob of their rights the needy of My people;
That widows may be their spoil,
And fatherless children their booty!

3 What will you do on the day of punishment,
When the calamity comes from afar?
To whom will you flee for help,
And how will you save your carcasses[a]

4 From collapsing under [fellow] prisoners,
From falling beneath the slain?

Yet His anger has not turned back,
And his arm is outstretched still.

5 Ha!
Assyria, rod of My anger,
[b-]In whose hand, as a staff, is My fury![-b]

6 I send him against an ungodly nation,
I charge him against a people that provokes Me,
To take its spoil and to seize its booty
And to make it a thing trampled
Like the mire of the streets.

7 But he has evil plans,
His mind harbors evil designs;
For he means to destroy,
To wipe out nations, not a few.

8 For he thinks,
"After all, [c-]I have kings as my captains![-c]

9 Was Calno any different from Carchemish?
Or Hamath from Arpad?
Or Samaria from Damascus?

10 [d-]Since I was able to seize
The insignificant kingdoms,
Whose images exceeded
Jerusalem's and Samaria's,[-d]

---

a *Meaning of Heb. uncertain; for "carcasses," compare the rendering of* kabod *in v. 16; 22.18.*

b-b *Emendation yields* "Who is a staff in the hand of my fury."

c-c *Emendation yields* "all the kingdoms fared alike!"

d-d *Emendation yields* "Since I was able to seize / those kingdoms and their images, / Why is Jerusalem better than Samaria?"

10.1–4: The fourth section. As he comes to the climax of his indictment against the Northern Kingdom, the prophet returns to the theme of the rich who mistreat the poor and pervert justice for their own gain; cf. 1.17; 3.8–15; 5.8–10; 32.7.

10.5–12.6: The earth is the LORD's: from Assyrian conquest through Assyrian collapse to universal peace. The idea of universal history guided by one God comes to the fore in this three-part composition, which describes a divine plan that affects not only Israel but all the world. This plan will manifest itself in three stages. Assyria will serve as God's agent to punish Israel. Assyria's self-promotion will then arouse God's anger, so that Assyria will be punished. Finally, the peaceful era will emerge, in which an ideal Davidic king will reign justly. Repeated images connect the three sections, and each section leads directly into the next. The poem moves between specific geopolitical concerns of the 8th century and timeless ideals.

Part I. 10.5–27: The Assyrian emperor: lord of lords or pawn of the LORD? This section hearkens back to the names of children earlier in the book: cf. v. 6 with 8.2–4; vv. 20–21 with 7.3 and 9.5. **5–6:** God uses the Assyrian king to punish Israel. **7–15:** The king arrogantly and ignorantly attributes his success to his own might. His boasting here recalls inscriptions of the Assyrian kings, with which Isaiah was familiar. Assyrian kings claimed to achieve their conquests with the aid of Ashur, the Assyrian high god, and other gods, but to Isaiah these were human creations, and thus the inscriptions glorified human inventions rather than the God whose bidding Assyrians unknowingly performed. **8:** *Captains* is a bilingual pun: Heb "sar" is cognate to the Akkadian word for king. Vassal kings did serve the Assyrian king as military commanders or captains. **12, 16–19:** The Assyrians' hubris (and not

11   Shall I not do to Jerusalem and her images
        What I did to Samaria and her idols?"

12 But when my Lord has carried out all his purpose on
Mount Zion and in Jerusalem, He[a] will punish the majestic pride and overbearing arrogance of the king of Assyria.
13 For he thought,
        "By the might of my hand have I wrought it,
        By my skill, for I am clever:
        I have erased the borders of peoples;
        I have plundered their treasures,
        And exiled their vast populations.[b]
14   I was able to seize, like a nest,
        The wealth of peoples;
        As one gathers abandoned eggs,
        So I gathered all the earth:
        Nothing so much as flapped a wing
        Or opened a mouth to peep."

15   Does an ax boast over him who hews with it,
        Or a saw magnify itself above him who wields it?
        As though the rod raised him who lifts it,
        As though the staff lifted the man![c]

16   Assuredly,
        The Sovereign LORD of Hosts will send
        A wasting away in its[d] fatness;
        And under its body[e] shall burn
        A burning like that of fire,
        [f]Destroying frame and flesh.
        It shall be like a sick man who pines away.[f]
17   The Light of Israel will be fire
        And its Holy One flame.
        It will burn and consume its thorns
        And its thistles in a single day,
18   And the mass of its scrub and its farm land.
19   What trees remain of its scrub
        Shall be so few that a boy may record them.

20   And in that day,
        The remnant of Israel
        And the escaped of the House of Jacob

their attack on Israel) lead to their
downfall. **19:** The remnant motif is
applied here to Assyria rather than
to Israel. God treats Assyria like
God treats Israel (here, negatively). The implication of this
phenomenon is fully spelled out
in 19.23–25. **20–27:** Although the
Assyrian defeat follows Israel's
downfall, it will lead to repentance
among those who survive.

---

a Heb. "I."

b According to vv. 6–7, Assyria was to plunder, but not to exile.

c Lit. "not-wood."

d Presumably Israel's. These verses would read well after 9.16.

e Cf. note at v. 3.

f-f Brought up from v. 18 for clarity.

Shall lean no more upon him that beats it,[a]
But shall lean sincerely
On the Lord, the Holy One of Israel.

21 Only a remnant shall return,
Only a remnant of Jacob,
To Mighty God.

22 Even if your people, O Israel,
Should be as the sands of the sea,
Only a remnant of it shall return.
Destruction is decreed;
Retribution comes like a flood!

23 For my Lord God of Hosts is carrying out
A decree of destruction upon all the land.

24 Assuredly, thus said my Lord God of Hosts: "O My people that dwells in Zion, have no fear of Assyria, who beats you with a rod and wields his staff over you as did the Egyptians. 25 For very soon My wrath will have spent itself, and [b-My anger that was bent on wasting them."-b] 26 The Lord of Hosts will brandish a scourge over him as when He beat Midian at the Rock of Oreb,[c] and will wield His staff as He did over the Egyptians by the sea.

27 And in that day,
His burden shall drop from your back,
[d-And his yoke from your neck;]
The yoke shall be destroyed because of fatness.

28 He advanced upon Aiath,
He proceeded to Migron,
At Michmas he deposited his baggage.

29 They made the crossing;
"Geba is to be our night quarters!"[-d]
Ramah was alarmed;
Gibeah of Saul took to flight.

30 "Give a shrill cry, O Bath-gallim!
Hearken, Laishah!
Take up the cry, Anathoth!"

31 Madmenah ran away;

26: The prophet alludes to earlier events in which God saved Israel from more powerful and numerous nations.

Part II. 10.28–34: Assyria's near-victory. Isaiah returned constantly to the theme of Jerusalem sorely threatened and suddenly saved. He predicted an event like the one described here for decades. It finally came true when Sennacherib invaded in 701. (In this passage, however, Isaiah predicts the invader will come from the north, but in fact Sennacherib approached Jerusalem from the southwest; see chs 36–39; 2 Kings chs 18–19; 2 Chron. ch 32.) The events that should follow the defeat of the arrogant empire (see the following ch) have still not come to fruition, even though Isaiah probably thought they would happen in his own lifetime. **28–32:** The invader's route. *He* refers to the leader of the army (probably Assyrian, perhaps Syro-Ephraimite) who comes toward Jerusalem from the north. The locations that are identifiable are all within a few miles of the Old City. *Anathoth* is directly across a wadi from today's French Hill neighborhood. *Nob* is probably Mount Scopus, overlooking the Old City. **33–34:** Just as the invader is about to achieve his goal, he is cut down. Cf. 29.1–8. The prophet uses the term *Lebanon trees* ironically: Assyrian kings boasted in inscriptions that they cut down these mighty cedars, but here Assyrians themselves become the ax's victim.

---

a I.e., upon Assyria (see v. 24). Ahaz's reliance on Assyria was interpreted by Isaiah as lack of faith in the Lord; see 7.13 with note.

b-b Presumably Assyria; meaning of Heb. uncertain. Emendation yields "My anger against the world shall cease."

c See Judg. 7.25.

d-d Emendation yields "And his yoke shall leave your neck. / He came up from Jeshimon / 28 By the ascent of Aiath, / He proceeded to Migron; / At Michmas he commanded his forces: / 29 'Make the crossing; / Geba is to be our night quarters!' " Jeshimon is the southeast corner of the Jordan Valley, Num. 21.20; 23.28; Aiath is elsewhere called Ai.

The dwellers of Gebim sought refuge.
32   This same day at Nob
He shall stand and wave his hand.[a]

O mount of Fair Zion!
O hill of Jerusalem!
33   Lo! The Sovereign LORD of Hosts
Will hew off the tree-crowns with an ax:
The tall ones shall be felled,
The lofty ones cut down:
34   The thickets of the forest shall be hacked away
with iron,
And the Lebanon trees shall fall [b]in their
majesty.[b]

11 But a shoot shall grow out of the stump of Jesse,
A twig shall sprout from his stock.
2   The spirit of the LORD shall alight upon him:
A spirit of wisdom and insight,
A spirit of counsel and valor,
A spirit of devotion and reverence for the LORD.
3   [c]He shall sense the truth[c] by his reverence for the
LORD:
He shall not judge by what his eyes behold,
Nor decide by what his ears perceive.
4   Thus he shall judge the poor with equity
And decide with justice for the lowly of the land.
He shall strike down a land[d] with the rod of his
mouth
And slay the wicked with the breath of his lips.
5   Justice shall be the girdle of his loins,
And faithfulness the girdle of his waist.
6   The wolf shall dwell with the lamb,
The leopard lie down with the kid;
[e]The calf, the beast of prey, and the fatling[e]
together,
With a little boy to herd them.
7   The cow and the bear shall graze,
Their young shall lie down together;
And the lion, like the ox, shall eat straw.
8   A babe shall play
Over a viper's hole,

Part III. 11.1–12.10. The ideal king in the peaceful future: The poem's final section is a messianic and eschatological prophecy comparable to 2.1–4 and 9.1–6. Once vain human striving for empire ends (section II), a perfect Davidic king will reign in Jerusalem, and all the world will enjoy peace and equity. **1–5:** The ideal age as manifested in jurisprudence. The king will be endowed with prophetic insight. **1:** *Jesse* was King David's father; the *shoot . . . out of the stump of Jesse* is a king from David's dynasty. The imagery of the previous section continues here, linking the second and third sections of the poem. Whereas the high trees representing Assyria's imperial haughtiness will be cut down to size (10.33–34), real strength will emerge from the lowest part—the *stock* (lit. "roots")—of the humble tree representing David's dynasty. Isaiah's insistence on humility and displeasure with human conceit determine the contrast between the images of trees in 11.1 and 10.33–34; cf. 2.2–4.6. If the translation *stump* is correct, then this passage may presume that the Davidic dynasty will (or has) come to an end; this reading would deviate significantly from Isaiah's notion that Davidic kings will reign eternally (cf. 2 Sam. 7.8–16; Ps. 89.20–37). But the Heb "geza'" refers not only to a *stump* of a tree that has been cut down but also to the trunk of a living tree. The latter translation does not presuppose the dynasty's downfall. **4:** The messianic age will not be perfect; some people will still be *poor*, others ruthless or *wicked*. The difference from the current age will lie, rather, in the king's response to these problems: He will always render accurate and fair judgments. Cf. 2.2–4, where conflicts among nations continue but are settled nonviolently. **6–9:** The ideal age as manifested in nature.

a I.e., the Assyrian king, arriving at Nob (close to Jerusalem), shall beckon his army
onward; cf. 13.2.
b-b Or "by the bronze," connecting Heb. 'addir with Akkadian urudu, "bronze."
c-c Lit. "His sensing [shall be]"; meaning of Heb. uncertain.
d Emendation yields "the ruthless."
e-e 1QIs[a] reads: "The calf and the beast of prey shall feed"; so too the Septuagint.

And an infant pass[a] his hand
Over an adder's den.
9   In all of [b]My sacred mount[-b]
Nothing evil or vile shall be done;
For the land shall be filled with devotion to the
    Lord
As water covers the sea.

10   In that day,
The stock of Jesse that has remained standing
Shall become a standard to peoples—
Nations shall seek his counsel
And his abode shall be honored.

11 In that day, my Lord will apply His hand again to re-deeming the other part[c] of His people from Assyria—as also from Egypt, Pathros, Nubia, Elam, Shinar, Hamath, and the coastlands.

12   He will hold up a signal to the nations
And assemble the banished of Israel,
And gather the dispersed of Judah
From the four corners of the earth.

13   Then Ephraim's envy shall cease
And Judah's harassment shall end;
Ephraim shall not envy Judah,
And Judah shall not harass Ephraim.
14   They shall pounce on the back of Philistia to the
    west,
And together plunder the peoples of the east;
Edom and Moab shall be subject to them
And the children of Ammon shall obey them.

15 The Lord will dry up the tongue of the Egyptian sea.—He will raise His hand over the Euphrates with the might[a] of His wind and break it into seven wadis, so that it can be trodden dry-shod. 16 Thus there shall be a high-way for the other part[c] of His people out of Assyria, such as there was for Israel when it left the land of Egypt.

12 In that day, you shall say:
"I give thanks to You, O Lord!
Although You were wroth with me,
Your wrath has turned back and You comfort me,
2   Behold the God who gives me triumph!

10–16: The ideal age as manifested in Israel's relationship to other nations. **10:** As in 2.2–4, nations come to Jerusalem to receive instructions. The Davidic king will act as the prophetic conduit through whom responses to the nations' inquiries will come. **11–16:** The in-gathering of exiles, which is compared to the exodus from Egypt. Some view this passage as dating to the Babylonian exile (which began in 597, long after Isaiah's death) or thereafter. Northern Isra-elites had already been exiled in Isaiah's lifetime, however, and Isaiah predicted that many Judeans outside Jerusalem would be exiled by the Assyrians. **11:** The list of nations is found in Assyrian texts much earlier than 597. Thus some see no reason to deny Isaiah's au-thorship of vv. 11–16. *The other part,* or "remnant." Elsewhere in Isaiah this term refers to Judeans who, having survived Assyrian in-vasion, remain in the land of Is-rael. Its use here to refer to exiles who return to the land of Israel is unique and may support the sug-gestion that these vv. are a later addition. **13:** *Ephraim* and *Judah* refer to the Northern and Southern Kingdoms, whose relationship reached a low point during the Syro-Ephraimite crisis (see 7.1–8.23 n.). **14:** This is one of the only verses in First Isaiah that an-ticipates the Israelites and Judeans taking vengeance on their ene-mies. It contradicts not only the prediction of a nonviolent messi-anic age earlier in this ch but the consistent rejection of national re-venge in Isaiah's prophecies. It may shed additional doubt on Isa-ianic authorship of vv. 11–16. **12.1–6:** A song of thanksgiving to be recited in the ideal age. Many of these phrases occur in other songs of thanksgiving, especially those associated with the exodus from Egypt. Cf. v. 2 with Exod. 15.2 and Ps. 118.14; cf. v. 4 with Ps. 105.1 and 148.13. Isaiah or a later editor may have capped this section with quotations from these and other well-known hymns.

a Meaning of Heb. uncertain.   b-b I.e., the Holy Land; cf. Exod. 15.17; Ps. 78.54.
c I.e., the part outside the Holy Land; lit. "the rest that will remain."

I am confident, unafraid;
For Yah the LORD is my strength and might,[a]
And He has been my deliverance."

3 Joyfully shall you draw water
From the fountains of triumph,
4 And you shall say on that day:
"Praise the LORD, proclaim His name.
Make His deeds known among the peoples;
Declare that His name is exalted.
5 Hymn the LORD,
For He has done gloriously;
Let this be made known
In all the world!
6 Oh, shout for joy,
You who dwell in Zion!
For great in your midst
Is the Holy One of Israel."

13 The "Babylon" Pronouncement, a prophecy of Isaiah son of Amoz.

2 "Raise a standard upon a bare hill,
Cry aloud to them;
Wave a hand, and let them enter
The gates of the nobles!
3 I have summoned My purified guests
To execute My wrath;
Behold, I have called My stalwarts,
My proudly exultant ones."[b]

4 Hark! a tumult on the mountains—
As of[c] a mighty force;
Hark! an uproar of kingdoms,
Nations assembling!
The LORD of Hosts is mustering
A host for war.
5 They come from a distant land,
From the end of the sky—
The LORD with the weapons of His wrath—
To ravage all the earth!

6 Howl!
For the day of the LORD is near;

Chs 13–23: Oracles concerning various nations. Most of the individual oracles within this section begin with the word "masa'," meaning "oracle" or "pronouncement" (others, "burden"). This section includes prophecies by Isaiah supplemented by later texts. Similar collections that draw together prophecies of many nations' downfall appear in other prophetic books, and are often called "oracles against the nations." See Jer. chs 46–51; Ezek. chs 25–32; Amos 1.3–2.6; Zeph. 2.4–15; and Obadiah.

13.1–22: An oracle concerning the destruction of Babylonia. This oracle assumes that Babylonia, rather than Assyria, is the world power. Hence it is addressed to an exilic audience in the mid-6th century, not to the 8th-century audience of Isaiah son of Amoz.

13.1: Superscription. The oracle, and hence chs 13–23 as a whole, begins with its own superscription; cf. the superscriptions in 1.1 and 2.1.

13.2–22: The oracle. 2–5: The gathering of the armies that will defeat Babylonia. **6–16:** The Day of the LORD. The upcoming defeat of the Babylonians will be a cosmic event, which Israel's prophets have long anticipated, involving the punishment of God's enemies. Cf., for example, Isa. chs 22 and 34; Ezek. chs 7 and 30; Joel chs 2–3; Amos 5.18–20; Zeph. ch 1. In this oracle, the enemy is Babylonia, while in other Day of the LORD texts Israel is punished.

a Others "song."
b The impending slaughter is spoken of as a sacrificial meal, for which the guests were notified to purify themselves ritually; cf. Zeph. 1.7.
c Meaning of Heb. uncertain.

It shall come like havoc from Shaddai.ᵃ

7 Therefore all hands shall grow limp,
And all men's hearts shall sink;

8 And, overcome by terror,
They shall be seized by pangs and throes,
Writhe like a woman in travail.
They shall gaze at each other in horror,
Their faces ᵇlivid with fright.ᵇ

9 Lo! The day of the Lᴏʀᴅ is coming
With pitiless fury and wrath,
To make the earth a desolation,
To wipe out the sinners upon it.

10 The stars and constellations of heaven
Shall not give off their light;
The sun shall be dark when it rises,
And the moon shall diffuse no glow.

11 "And I will requite to the world its evil,
And to the wicked their iniquity;
I will put an end to the pride of the arrogant
And humble the haughtiness of tyrants.

12 I will make people scarcer than fine gold,
And men than gold of Ophir."

13 Therefore ᶜshall heaven be shaken,ᶜ
And earth leap out of its place,
At the fury of the Lᴏʀᴅ of Hosts
On the day of His burning wrath.

14 Then like gazelles that are chased,
And like sheep that no man gathers,
Each man shall turn back to his people,
They shall flee every one to his land.

15 All who remain shall be pierced through,
All who ᵈare caughtᵈ
Shall fall by the sword.

16 And their babes shall be dashed to pieces in their
sight,
Their homes shall be plundered,
And their wives shall be raped.

17 "Behold,
I stir up the Medes against them,
Who do not value silver

17–22: The text becomes more specific, attributing the coming destruction of Babylonia to the *Medes* (v. 17), a people who lived east of Babylonia in today's Iran. The kingdom of the Medes was conquered by the Persian king Cyrus, who was hence known as king of the Persians and Medes. He conquered Babylon in 539 BCE, but contrary to what vv. 19–22 anticipate, he did not destroy the city. **19:** The *Chaldeans* were a tribe who became increasingly influential in Babylonia starting in the 8th century; consequently the Bible often uses the term Chaldean as a synonym for Babylonian.

a Traditionally rendered "the Almighty."

b-b Taking the root lhb as a variant of bhl: others "shall be faces of flame."

c-c Lit. "I will shake heaven."

d-d Meaning of Heb. uncertain; emendation yields "flee."

Or delight in gold.
18   Their bows shall shatter the young;
            They shall show no pity to infants,
            They shall not spare the children."

19   And Babylon, glory of kingdoms,
            Proud splendor of the Chaldeans,
            Shall become like Sodom and Gomorrah
            Overturned by God.
20   Nevermore shall it be settled
            Nor dwelt in through all the ages.
            No Arab shall pitch his tent there,
            No shepherds make flocks lie down there.
21   But beasts[a] shall lie down there,
            And the houses be filled with owls;[a]
            There shall ostriches make their home,
            And there shall satyrs dance.
22   And jackals[a] shall abide in its castles
            And dragons[a] in the palaces of pleasure.
            Her hour is close at hand;
            Her days will not be long.

a Meaning of Heb. uncertain.

Places mentioned in the oracles against the nations

14 But the LORD will pardon Jacob, and will again choose Israel, and will settle them on their own soil. And strangers shall join them and shall cleave to the House of Jacob. ²For peoples shall take them[a] and bring them to their homeland; and the House of Israel shall possess them[b] as slaves and handmaids on the soil of the LORD. They shall be captors of their captors and masters to their taskmasters.

³ And when the LORD has given you rest from your sorrow and trouble, and from the hard service that you were made to serve, ⁴ you shall recite this song of scorn over the king of Babylon:

> How is the taskmaster vanished,
> How is oppression[c] ended!
>
> 5 The LORD has broken the staff of the wicked,
> The rod of tyrants,
>
> 6 That smote peoples in wrath
> With stroke unceasing,
> That belabored nations in fury
> In relentless pursuit.
>
> 7 All the earth is calm, untroubled;
> Loudly it cheers.
>
> 8 Even pines rejoice at your fate,
> And cedars of Lebanon:
> "Now that you have lain down,
> None shall come up to fell us."
>
> 9 Sheol below was astir
> To greet your coming—
> Rousing for you the shades
> Of all earth's chieftains,
> Raising from their thrones
> All the kings of nations.
>
> 10 All speak up and say to you,
> "So you have been stricken as we were,
> You have become like us!
>
> 11 Your pomp is brought down to Sheol,
> And the strains of your lutes!
> Worms are to be your bed,
> Maggots your blanket!"
>
> 12 How are you fallen from heaven,
> O Shining One, son of Dawn![d]

---

a I.e., the House of Jacob.   b I.e., the peoples.

c Reading *marhebah* with 1QIs*ᵃ* (cf. Septuagint). The traditional reading *madhebah* is of unknown meaning.   d A character in some lost myth.

14.1–23: A mock lament concerning Israel's oppressor. The poem in vv. 4b–21 describes the ignominious death of an Assyrian monarch of Isaiah's time, probably Sargon II, who was killed in battle in 705. It was later reinterpreted as predicting the death of a Babylonian monarch. **1–4a:** This introduction to Isaiah's poem was added by an editor during the time of the Babylonian exile (597–539). **4a–23:** Each Heb line in this poem divides into two halves, the first with three main beats, the second with two. This meter, often called qinah (dirge) meter, is typical of dirges (such as 1.21–27 and the poems in the book of Lamentations); it also occurs, as here, in mock laments (another such mock lament is found in Isa. ch 47). **4b–8:** The whole world is relieved at the death of the Assyrian king, whose brutality was renowned. **8:** In their inscriptions Assyrian kings often boast of their expeditions to cut down *pines* and *cedars* in *Lebanon*. Here, as in 10.7–15 and 10.33–34, Isaiah turns the Assyrians' own rhetoric against them. **9–11:** The king arrives in *Sheol,* or the underworld, and his pretensions to power are mocked by the other kings there; he had ruled over kings, but now he is stuck beneath the earth just as they are. Many ancient Semites and pre-classical Greeks believed that the dead dwelt in unpleasant conditions underground; the fate of the dead there depended in large part on whether the corpse received a proper burial. Whether Isaiah shared this conception of a shadowy life after death or merely uses the well-known motif as a literary convention is unclear. On notions of life after death in the Tanakh and ancient Judaism, see 26.19 n. **12–15:** The king's vain aspirations to god-like status are mocked. Isaiah refers ironically to the king as *Shining One, son of Dawn,* applying to him the name of a character from ancient Canaanite myth. (The term *Shining One* is not known from Canaanite texts, but his father, *Dawn,* is described in Canaanite myth as a son of the high

How are you felled to earth,
O vanquisher of nations!

13 Once you thought in your heart,
"I will climb to the sky;
Higher than the stars of God
I will set my throne.
I will sit in the mount of assembly,[a]
On the summit of Zaphon:[b]

14 I will mount the back of a cloud—
I will match the Most High."

15 Instead, you are brought down to Sheol,
To [c]the bottom of the Pit.[c]

16 They who behold you stare;
They peer at you closely:
"Is this the man
Who shook the earth,
Who made realms tremble,

17 Who made the world like a waste
And wrecked its towns,
[d]Who never released his prisoners to their
    homes?"

18 All the kings of nations
Were laid, every one, in honor[d]
Each in his tomb;

19 While you were left lying unburied,
Like loathsome carrion,[e]
Like a trampled corpse
[In] the clothing of slain gashed by the sword
Who sink to the very stones of the Pit.

20 You shall not have a burial like them;
Because you destroyed [f]your country,
Murdered your people.[f]

Let the breed of evildoers
Nevermore be named!

21 Prepare a slaughtering block for his sons
Because of the guilt of their father.[g]
Let them not arise to possess the earth!
Then the world's face shall be covered with towns.

god El. The name closely recalls Phaethon son of Eos [or "radiant one" son of "Dawn"] in Greek mythology. Phaethon, a presumptuous young god, was thrown down to earth by Zeus.) This character seems to have attempted to join the head of the pantheon, whether this was El (who was known in Canaanite texts as *Most High*) or Baal (whose palace was located on the *summit of* Mount *Zaphon*); Isaiah seems to mix the characteristics of these two Canaanite deities in his allusion to the myth. Similar references to a Canaanite myth in which an overreaching god is expelled from heaven occur in Ezek. ch 28 and Ps. 82, and possibly in Gen. 6.1–4. Rabbinic commentators identify the term *Shining One* with the morning star (the planet Venus, which is sometimes visible on the horizon at dawn). Indeed, the mythological figure to whom this poem refers may have been associated with the morning star in ancient Canaanite myth. **16–21:** The fate of the king's body. Denied a proper burial, he is condemned to the most miserable fate in the underworld.

a I.e., the assembly of the gods in council.   b The abode of the gods; cf. Ps. 48.3.
c-c A region of the netherworld reserved for those who have not received decent burial; cf.
Ezek. 32.21 ff.
d-d Emendation yields "Who chained to his palace gate / All the kings of nations? / Yet
they were all laid in honor . . ." The practice of chaining captive chieftains to gates is attested in Mesopotamia.
e So several ancient versions; cf. postbiblical neṣel, "putrefying flesh or blood."
f-f Emendation yields ". . . countries, / Murdered peoples."   g Heb. "fathers."

²²I will rise up against them—declares the LORD of Hosts—and will wipe out from Babylon name and remnant, kith and kin—declares the LORD—²³and I will make it a home of bitterns,ᵃ pools of water. I will sweep it with a broom of extermination—declares the LORD of Hosts.

22–23: A later editor added these lines to the original poem by Isaiah to connect it to the hoped-for destruction of Babylon.

14.24–27: A short prophecy on the downfall of Assyria, which Isaiah predicts (wrongly, as it turned out) will occur in a climactic battle to take place in the land of Israel. Cf. the similar prophecies in 10.5–15.

14.28–32: A short oracle concerning the Philistines. The sad and surprising fate of the Philistines after the death of an Assyrian ruler is contrasted with the security Zion will enjoy.

24   The LORD of Hosts has sworn this oath:
      "As I have designed, so shall it happen;
      What I have planned, that shall come to pass:
25   To break Assyria in My land,
      To crush him on My mountain."ᵇ
      And his yoke shall drop off them,
      And his burden shall drop from theirᶜ backs.
26   That is the plan that is planned
      For all the earth;
      That is why an arm is poised
      Over all the nations.
27   For the LORD of Hosts has planned,
      Who then can foil it?
      It is His arm that is poised,
      And who can stay it?

²⁸This pronouncement was made in the year that King Ahaz died:
29   Rejoice not, all Philistia,
      Because the staff of him that beat you is broken.
      For from the stock of a snake there sprouts an asp,
      A flying seraphᵈ branches out from it.
30   ᵉThe first-born of the poor shall graze⁻ᵉ
      And the destitute lie down secure.
      ᶠI will kill your stock by famine,⁻ᶠ
      And it shall slay the very last of you.
31   Howl, O gate; cry out, O city;
      Quake, all Philistia!
      ᵍFor a stout one is coming from the north
      And there is no straggler in his ranks.⁻ᵍ

32   And what will he answer the messengers of any
          nation?

a Meaning of Heb. uncertain.
b Heb. "mountains"; for the designation of the entire land of Israel as the LORD's mountain, cf. 11.9.
c Heb. "his." The last two lines of this verse would read well after v. 26.
d Others "fiery serpent"; cf. Num. 21.6, 8.
e-e Emendation yields "The poor shall graze in his pasture." This line and the next would read well after v. 32.
f-f Emendation yields "It shall kill your offspring with its venom (zar'ekh berosho)."
g-g Meaning of Heb. uncertain; the rendering "stout one" is suggested by the Syriac 'ashshīn.

That Zion has been established by the LORD:
In it, the needy of His people shall find shelter.

15 The "Moab" Pronouncement.

Ah, in the night Ar was sacked,
Moab was ruined;
Ah, in the night Kir was sacked,
Moab was ruined.

2 He went up to the temple to weep,
Dibon[a] [went] to the outdoor shrines.
Over Nebo and Medeba
Moab is wailing;
On every head is baldness,
Every beard is shorn.

3 In its streets, they are girt with sackcloth;
On its roofs, in its squares,
Everyone is wailing,
Streaming with tears.

4 Heshbon and Elealeh cry out,
Their voice carries to Jahaz.
Therefore,
b-The shock troops of Moab shout,-b
His body is convulsed.

5 My heart cries out for Moab—
His fugitives flee down to Zoar,
To Eglath-shelishiyah.
For the ascent of Luhith
They ascend with weeping;
On the road to Horonaim
They raise a cry of anguish.

6 Ah, the waters of Nimrim
Are become a desolation;
The grass is sear,
The herbage is gone,
Vegetation is vanished.

7 Therefore,
The gains they have made, and their stores,
They carry to the Wadi of Willows.

8 Ah, the cry has compassed
The country of Moab:

15.1–16.14: An oracle concerning Moab, with an addendum. *Moab* was the land immediately east of the Dead Sea. The Moabites, according to Gen. 19.36–37, were descended from Abraham's nephew Lot and are thus related to the Israelites, but relations between the two nations were usually tense (see, e.g., Num. 22.1–6; Judg. ch 3; 2 Kings ch 3). **15.1–16.12: A prediction of Moab's imminent defeat.** The prediction is expressed in a lament: The author "mourns" over an event that will soon occur. (Alternatively, the poem may have been composed as a real lament after Moab was defeated by some invader.) **15.1–4:** The suffering of Moab. *Ar, Kir, Dibon, Nebo,* and *Medeba* are locations in Moab. **5–9:** More descriptions of the distress of the Moabites, who flee toward Edom, the land immediately south of Moab. *Zoar, Luhith, Horonaim,* and *Nimrim* are located in southwestern Moab, near the Edomite border. These vv. seem to trace the path of the Moabite refugees on their way to Edom.

---

a *Regarded as the principal city of Moab.*
b-b *Change of vocalization yields "The loins of Moab are trembling."*

All the way to Eglaim her wailing,
Even at Beer-elim her wailing!

9   Ah, the waters of Dimon are full of blood[a]
For I pour added [water] on Dimon;
I drench[b] it—for Moab's refugees—
With soil[c] for its remnant.

16 [d]Dispatch as messenger
The ruler of the land,
From Sela in the wilderness
To the mount of Fair Zion:

2   "Like fugitive birds,
Like nestlings driven away,
Moab's villagers linger
By the fords of the Arnon.

3   Give advice,
[e]Offer counsel.[e]
At high noon make
Your shadow like night:
Conceal the outcasts,
Betray not the fugitives.

4   Let [f]Moab's outcasts[f]
Find asylum in you;
Be a shelter for them
Against the despoiler."

For violence has vanished,
Rapine is ended,
And marauders have perished from this land.

5   And a throne shall be established in goodness
In the tent of David,
And on it shall sit in faithfulness
A ruler devoted to justice
And zealous for equity.[g]

6   "We have heard of Moab's pride—
Most haughty is he—
Of his pride and haughtiness and arrogance,
And of the iniquity in him."[h]

16.1–5: The Moabite refugees in Edom send a message to the Judean king, seeking haven or aid. *Sela* (which means "rock") is an Edomite city, perhaps the city now known as Petra (which is Greek for "rock"). **2:** This v. may belong after 15.9; it describes the Moabite refugees lingering at the river Arnon while they were still in Moab on their way to Edom. **6:** The Judeans respond to the Moabites' request. **16.13–14: A later addition;** apparently the event predicted in 15.1–16.12 did not come to pass, and Isaiah asserts that the expected defeat of Moab will in fact occur soon. It is possible that 15.1–16.12 were written before Isaiah's time, and that Isaiah reused the text, adding 16.13–14 to relate the older lament or prediction to his own time. Jer. ch 48 is based on 15.1–16.12; there this oracle is expanded and reworked.

---

a *Emendation yields "tears."*   b *Cf. 16.9.*
c *Emendation yields "tears"; cf. Ugaritic 'dm't.*
d *Meaning of vv. 1 and 2 uncertain.*
e-e *Meaning of Heb. uncertain.*
f-f *Heb. "my outcasts, Moab."*
g *14.32, above, would read well here.*
h *Baddaw is a suffixed form of the preposition* bede: *Nah. 2.13; Hab. 2.13; Job 39.25; with*
suffixes, Job 11.3, 41.4.

7 Ah, let Moab howl;
   Let all in Moab howl!
   For the raisin-cakes[a] of Kir-hareseth
   You shall moan most pitifully.
8 The vineyards of Heshbon are withered,
   And the vines of Sibmah;
   [b-]Their tendrils spread
   To Baale-goiim,[-b]
   And reached to Jazer,
   And strayed to the desert;
   Their shoots spread out
   And crossed the sea.

9 Therefore,
   As I weep for Jazer,
   So I weep for Sibmah's vines;
   O Heshbon and Elealeh,
   I drench you with my tears.
   [c-]Ended are the shouts
   Over your fig and grain harvests.[-c]
10 Rejoicing and gladness
   Are gone from the farm land;
   In the vineyards no shouting
   Or cheering is heard.
   No more does the treader
   Tread wine in the presses—
   The shouts [d-]have been silenced.[-d]

11 Therefore,
   Like a lyre my heart moans for Moab,
   And my very soul for Kir-heres.

12 And when it has become apparent that Moab has gained nothing in the outdoor shrine, he shall come to pray in his temple—but to no avail. 13 That is the word that the LORD spoke concerning Moab long ago. 14 And now the LORD has spoken: In three years, fixed like the years of a hired laborer, Moab's population, with all its huge multitude, shall shrink. Only a remnant shall be left, of no consequence.

7–11: The lament for the Moabites continues; here as in ch 15 the genuine sympathy of the Judean author (in contrast to the official Judean response in 16.6) is evident. *Heshbon, Jazer,* and *Elealah* are places in Moab; the other locations are not known, but they must lie within Moab as well. **12:** This line may be part of the lament that begins in 16.7; or it may be the writer's suggestion regarding the refuge the Moabites request: Allow them to enter Judah, but not to pray at the Temple in Jerusalem (translating: "When Moab appears at the high place, and they weary themselves [there], they will come to His Temple to pray, but they shall not be allowed"). **13–14:** The older text in 15.1–16.12 is applied to Isaiah's present situation: Moab will be destroyed within three years. *Long ago* means merely "in the past," whether recent or distant. It is even possible that Isaiah himself authored the older text, and that he subsequently composed this addendum when his original prophecy did not come to pass. Cf. 8.16–18, which seems to reflect Isaiah's reaction to the apparent failure of his predictions earlier in chs 7–8.

a Jer. 48.36 has "men."
b-b Meaning of Heb. uncertain.
c-c Jer. 48.32 reads "A ravager has come down / Upon your fig and grape harvests."
d-d Lit. "I have silenced."

17 The "Damascus" Pronouncement.

Behold,
Damascus shall cease to be a city;
It shall become a heap of ruins.

2   ᵃThe towns of Aroer shall be deserted;⁻ᵃ
They shall be a place for flocks
To lie down, with none disturbing.

3   Fortresses shall cease from Ephraim,ᵇ
And sovereignty from Damascus;
The remnant of Aram shall become
Like the mass of Israelites
                —declares the LORD of Hosts.

4   In that day,
The mass of Jacob shall dwindle,
And the fatness of his body become lean:

5   After being like the standing grain
Harvested by the reaper—
Who reaps ears by the armful—
He shall be like the ears that are gleaned
In the Valley of Rephaim.

6   Only gleanings shall be left of him,
As when one beats an olive tree:
Two berries or three on the topmost branch,
Four or five ᶜon the boughs of the crown⁻ᶜ
                —declares the LORD, the God of Israel.

⁷ In that day, men shall turn to their Maker, their eyes look to the Holy One of Israel; ⁸ they shall not turn to the altars that their own hands made, or look to the sacred posts and incense stands that their own fingers wrought.

⁹ In that day, their fortress cities shall be like the deserted sites which ᵈthe Horesh and the Amir⁻ᵈ abandoned because of the Israelites; and there shall be desolation.

10   Truly, you have forgotten the God who saves you
And have not remembered the Rock who shelters
        you;
That is why, though you plant a delightfulᵉ
        sapling,
What you sow proves a disappointing slip.

a-a Emendation yields (cf. Septuagint) "Its towns shall be deserted forevermore."
b Emendation yields "Aram."
c-c Lit. "on her boughs, the many-branched one."
d-d Septuagint reads "the Amorites and the Hivites."
e Emendation yields "true." So Vulgate (cf. Septuagint); cf. Jer. 2.21.

17.1–14: An oracle concerning Damascus and the Northern Kingdom. This ch addresses the Syro-Ephraimite crisis, which took place in 735 BCE. This crisis is described in 7.1–8.23, and the background provided concerning those chs above should be consulted when reading this ch as well. This ch concerns not only *Damascus* (capital of Syria or Aram) but also their allies, the northern Israelites or Ephraimites, and the Assyrian empire against whom the Arameans (or Syrians) and Ephraimites revolted. **1–6:** As in chs 7–8, the downfalls of Damascus and Ephraim are predicted. The instrument of their destruction, the Assyrian empire, is not specified here. **2:** Several cities called *Aroer* are known in the Bible, but none are located in Aram, which is the main focus of vv. 1–3. Hence the emendation mentioned in translators' note *b* seems likely. **7–8:** A reflection on the effect these events will have on humanity generally; as elsewhere (2.1–4; 19.19–25), Isaiah maintains that God's intervention in political events will lead to an era in which humans universally acknowledge the one God. The Heb word translated here as *men* is "ha-ʾadam," which refers to human beings generally, not necessarily limited to Israelites or males. **9:** A continuation of the prophecy in vv.1–6 concerning the downfall of Israel and Aram, which will be emptied of their populations. **10–11:** A rebuke specifically directed toward the Israelites, who ally with Arameans rather than depending on God. Interestingly, these vv. also could be directed against Ahaz, the Judean king at the time of the Syro-Ephraimite crisis: He, too, relied on human saviors (the Assyrians) rather than God. Cf. Isaiah's criticism of Ahaz in 8.5–8. **10:** *Delightful sapling*, alternatively, "gardens for Adonis" or "gardens for the Delightful One." Some believe that this v. describes gardens planted in honor of a Semitic deity of vegetation (variously known as Dumuzi, Tammuz, or Baal, and called Adonis by the Greeks). Semites be-

11 On the day that you plant, you see it grow;
     On the morning you sow, you see it bud—
     But the branches wither away
     On a day of sickness and mortal agony.

12 Ah, the roar of many peoples
     That roar as roars the sea,
     The rage of nations that rage
     As rage the mighty waters—
13 Nations raging like massive waters!
     But He shouts at them, and they flee far away,
     Driven like chaff before winds in the hills,
     And like tumbleweed before a gale.
14 At eventide, lo, terror!
     By morning, it is no more.
     Such is the lot of our despoilers,
     The portion of them that plunder us.

18

Ah,
     a-land in the deep shadow of wings,-a
     Beyond the rivers of Nubia!

2 Go, swift messengers,
     To a nation b-far and remote,
     To a people thrust forth and away-b—
     A nation of gibber and chatterc—
     Whose land is cut off by streams;
     d-Which sends out envoys by sea,
     In papyrus vessels upon the water!-d

3 [Say this:]
     "All you who live in the world
     And inhabit the earth,
     When a flag is raised in the hills, take note!
     When a ram's horn is blown, give heed!"
4 For thus the LORD said to me:
     "I rest calm and confidente in My habitation—
     Like a scorching heat upon sprouts,
     f-Like a rain-cloud in the heat of reaping time."-f

a-a Or "Most sheltered land"; cf., e.g., 30.2, 3; Ps. 36.8; 57.2; 61.5.

b-b Meaning of Heb. uncertain.

c Meaning of Heb. uncertain; cf. 28.10. Biblical writers often characterize distant nations by their unintelligible speech; cf. 33.19; Deut. 28.49; Jer. 5.15.

d-d Brought down from beginning of verse for clarity. The Hebrew verb for "sends" agrees in gender with "nation," not with "land."

e Cf. hibbit "to rely" (Job 6.19). The related noun mabbaṭ occurs with similar meaning in Isa. 20.5, 6.

f-f I.e., like a threat of disaster; cf. Eccl. 11.4.

lieved that this god, like the grass or flowers in the desert, springs to life each year during the rainy season and dies during the summer. The Israelites were both unfaithful and self-defeating in their reliance on this false deity. **12–14:** The terrifying arrival and sudden defeat of the enemy. These vv. may refer to the coming arrival of the Syro-Ephraimite forces in Jerusalem; they may also (or alternatively) be intended to predict the arrival of Assyrian forces there. Cf. 8.5–8; 29.1–8. The description matches the surprising withdrawal of Assyrian forces in 701 BCE, three decades after the Syro-Ephraimite crisis (see 10.28–34 n.). Isaiah may have issued the prediction as early as the Syro-Ephraimite crisis in 735, thinking (mistakenly) that the Assyrians would overrun Judah then, even though it did not come true until 701. The comparison of an invading army to raging waters appears frequently in Assyrian propaganda of Isaiah's day.

18.1–7: An oracle concerning the Ethiopians. The setting, background, and meaning of this passage are not clear. *Nubia* (Heb "Kush") is the area south of Egypt, sometimes referred to as Ethiopia. In the late 700s and early 600s Egypt was ruled by Ethiopian pharaohs. This ch probably refers to diplomatic and military moves in which these Ethiopian pharaohs play the central role. **1–3:** Judah sends messengers to the Ethiopians, responding to ambassadors who had been sent to Judah. The Ethiopian ruler of Egypt may have been encouraging a revolt against the Assyrians. **3–6:** Isaiah encourages the Judeans to send a negative response to the anti-Assyrian overtures: Judah is safe, since the LORD is *calm and confident in (His) habitation,* the Temple Mount in Jerusalem. This passage reflects on the Isaianic notion of the inviolability of Zion. Because the LORD is present in His Temple, Jerusalem will never fall, and therefore the Judeans need not depend on alliances with other nations for their safety. Cf. 1.8–9; 7.2–9; 8.8.

5 For before the harvest,[a] yet after the budding,
When the blossom has hardened into berries,
He will trim away the twigs with pruning hooks,
And lop off the trailing branches.[b]

6 They shall all be left
To the kites of the hills
And to the beasts of the earth;
The kites shall summer on them
And all the beasts of the earth shall winter on
them.

7 In that time,
Tribute shall be brought to the LORD of Hosts
[From] a people far and remote,
From a people thrust forth and away—
A nation of gibber and chatter,
Whose land is cut off by streams—
At the place where the name of the LORD of Hosts
abides,
At Mount Zion.

19 The "Egypt" Pronouncement.

Mounted on a swift cloud,
The LORD will come to Egypt;
Egypt's idols shall tremble before Him,
And the heart of the Egyptians shall sink within
them.

2 "I will incite Egyptian against Egyptian:
They shall war with each other,
Every man with his fellow,
City with city
And kingdom with kingdom.[c]

3 Egypt shall be drained of spirit,
And I will confound its plans;
So they will consult the idols and the shades
And the ghosts and the familiar spirits.

4 And I will place the Egyptians
At the mercy of a harsh master,
And a ruthless king shall rule them"
—declares the Sovereign, the LORD of Hosts.

5 Water shall fail from the seas,
Rivers dry up and be parched,

4–6: The imagery describes the defeat of what had seemed a strong and promising empire, probably the Assyrians. *Kites,* a bird of prey; a better translation might be "vultures" or "carrion eaters," since the birds will be devouring the corpses littering the hills. **7:** The defeat of the enemy will lead to worldwide recognition of the God of Mount Zion.

19.1–24: A universalist oracle concerning Egypt. Like other oracles concerning the nations, this ch begins by describing the troubles with which God will afflict Egypt. It continues, however, by viewing these troubles as identical to the troubles with which God afflicts Israel: They will lead the Egyptians to recognize the one true God. The ch ends with a remarkably universalist perspective. **1–18: Divine judgment against Egypt.** The first section of the ch is negative in tone and poetic in structure. **1–10:** These vv. describe the collapse of Egypt's gods (vv. 1, 3), political stability (vv. 2–4), physical environment (vv. 5–7), and economy (vv. 8–10). **4:** The divine punishment will involve a foreigner coming to rule over Egypt; this v. may refer to the Ethiopian dynasty that took control of Egypt in the late 8th century (which is described in the previous ch) or, more likely, to an Assyrian invasion (which is also described in the next ch). **5–6:** *The seas:* Heb is singular and refers to the Nile, which is wide enough to be called a sea during the flood season. In Egypt, agriculture, transportation, and hence life in general depended on the Nile and its canals.

a Emendation yields "vintage."   b A figure of speech for the defeated enemy.
c I.e., the various districts of Egypt, which in Isaiah's time were governed by hereditary
princes.

6 Channels turn foul as they ebb,
   And Egypt's canals run dry.
   Reed and rush shall decay,
7 ᵃ-And the Nile papyrus by the Nile-side-ᵃ
   And everything sown by the Nile
   Shall wither, blow away, and vanish.
8 The fishermen shall lament;
   All who cast lines in the Nile shall mourn,
   And those who spread nets on the water shall
      languish.
9 The flax workers, too, shall be dismayed,
   Both carders and weavers chagrined.ᵇ
10ᶜ Her foundations shall be crushed,
   And all who make dams shall be despondent.

11 Utter fools are the nobles of Tanis;
   The sagest of Pharaoh's advisers
   [Have made] absurd predictions.
   How can you say to Pharaoh,
   "I am a scion of sages,
   A scion of Kedemite kings"?ᵈ
12 Where, indeed, are your sages?
   Let them tell you, let them discover
   What the Lᴏʀᴅ of Hosts has planned against
      Egypt.
13 The nobles of Tanis have been fools,
   The nobles of Memphis deluded;
   Egypt has been led astray
   By the chiefs of her tribes.
14 The Lᴏʀᴅ has mixed within her
   A spirit of distortion,
   Which shall lead Egypt astray in all her
      undertakings
   As a vomiting drunkard goes astray;
15 Nothing shall be achieved in Egypt
   By either head or tail,
   Palm branch or reed.ᵉ

¹⁶ In that day, the Egyptians shall be like women, trembling and terrified because the Lᴏʀᴅ of Hosts will raise His hand against them. ¹⁷ And the land of Judah shall also be the dread of the Egyptians; they shall quake whenever anybody mentions it to them, because of what the Lᴏʀᴅ of

10–15: The Egyptians rely on their traditional wisdom. Consequently, they fail to understand the cause of their troubles, which come directly from the one God of Israel. *Tanis* and *Memphis* were leading cities in ancient Egypt. **16–17:** The Egyptians come to realize that the God of Israel is the source of their troubles, and hence also of their salvation. **18–25: Divine grace toward Egypt.** This section describes the outcome of the inducements to change with which God afflicted the Egyptians. The style of this section differs from the first one, moving from poetry of rebuke to a series of prose oracles that are positive in nature. **18–22:** These vv. describe how the Egyptians will accept the one God and become His servants, just as the Israelites are. Thus they link up with texts such as 2.1–4 and 11.10. These passages share a vision of a new world order: Ethnicities will remain distinct, but all nations will adopt monotheism and will worship the God of Israel. Some, however, believe these vv. were added by later scribes, and that they refer to Jewish communities in Egypt during the postexilic period, when several Jewish temples existed in Egyptian cities such as Elephantine and Leontopolis. Similarly, the Talmud (*b. Menaḥ.* 109b) understands this section to predict the founding of the Jewish temple in Leontopolis in the 160s BCE, rather than foretelling a temple in which Egyptians worship the Lᴏʀᴅ.

---

a-a Meaning of Heb. uncertain.   b Meaning of Heb. uncertain.

c Meaning of verse uncertain; emendation yields "Her drinkers shall be dejected, / And all her brewers despondent."

d Or "advisers." The wisdom of the Kedemites was proverbial; cf. 1 Kings 5.10.

e I.e., a man of either high or low station; cf. 9.13, 14.

Hosts is planning against them. ¹⁸ In that day, there shall be several*ᵃ* towns in the land of Egypt speaking the language of Canaan and swearing loyalty to the LORD of Hosts; one*ᵇ* shall be called Town of Heres.*ᶜ*

¹⁹ In that day, there shall be an altar to the LORD inside the land of Egypt and a pillar to the LORD at its border.*ᵈ* ²⁰ They shall serve as a symbol and reminder of the LORD of Hosts in the land of Egypt, so that when [the Egyptians] cry out to the LORD against oppressors, He will send them a savior and champion to deliver them. ²¹ For the LORD will make Himself known to the Egyptians, and the Egyptians shall acknowledge the LORD in that day, and they shall serve [Him] with sacrifice and oblation and shall make vows to the LORD and fulfill them. ²² The LORD will first afflict and then heal the Egyptians; when they turn back to the LORD, He will respond to their entreaties and heal them.

²³ In that day, there shall be a highway from Egypt to Assyria. The Assyrians shall join with the Egyptians and Egyptians with the Assyrians, and then the Egyptians together with the Assyrians shall serve [the LORD].

²⁴ In that day, Israel shall be a third partner with Egypt and Assyria as a blessing*ᵉ* on earth; ²⁵ for the LORD of Hosts will bless them, saying, "Blessed be My people Egypt, My handiwork Assyria, and My very own Israel."

20 It was the year that the Tartan*ᶠ* came to Ashdod—being sent by King Sargon of Assyria—and attacked Ashdod and took it. ² Previously,*ᵍ* the LORD had spoken to Isaiah son of Amoz, saying, "Go, untie the sackcloth from your loins and take your sandals off your feet," which he had done, going naked and barefoot. ³ And now the LORD said, "It is a sign and a portent for Egypt and Nubia. Just as My servant Isaiah has gone naked and barefoot for three years, ⁴ so shall the king of Assyria drive off the captives of Egypt and the exiles of Nubia, young and old, naked and barefoot and with bared buttocks—to the shame of Egypt! ⁵ And they shall be dismayed and chagrined because of Nubia their hope and Egypt their boast. ⁶ In that day, the dwellers of this coastland shall say, 'If this

---

a Lit. "five."   b Or "each one."
c Meaning uncertain. Many Heb. mss. read ḥeres, "sun," which may refer to Heliopolis, i.e., Sun City, in Egypt. Targum's "Beth Shemesh" (cf. Jer. 43.13) has the same meaning.
d As a symbol of the LORD's sovereignty over Egypt.
e I.e., a standard by which blessing is invoked; cf. Gen. 12.2 with note.
f An Assyrian title meaning "General"; cf. 2 Kings 18.17 and note.
g Lit. "At that time."

18: *The language of Canaan* was the language spoken by the Israelites; Hebrew, a term never found in Tanakh, is a Canaanite dialect. *Heres* in Heb means "destruction." **23–25:** The universal kingdom of God. Even the archenemies of the Israelites will recognize the one God. Consequently, two empires that perennially fought each other (Egypt and Assyria) and a small nation variously attacked by either one (Israel) will be at peace with each other. Some rabbinic commentators (Targum, Rashi) were troubled by v. 25, which puts Israel's enemies on an equal spiritual footing with Israel. They paraphrase as follows: "Blessed be My people Israel, who came out of Egypt and saw My handiwork, which I performed against Assyria." This far-reaching reinterpretation is rejected by other rabbinic authorities (such as Radak), who insist the v. carries the strong universal message it so clearly presents.

20.1–6: A prophetic sign concerning the Egyptians. In 713, the king of the coastal city-state of *Ashdod* organized a revolt against the Assyrian empire, to whom the various states along the Mediterranean, including Judah, were obliged to send tribute. Assyrian records tell us that Judah participated in the rebellion. The rebellious states seem to have appealed to the pharaoh ruling over Egypt (who came from *Nubia*, i.e., Ethiopia) for help at the early stages of the rebellion. In 711, the Assyrian king, *Sargon,* sent his chief-of-staff or *Tartan* to subdue Ashdod. Ashdod and two other cities were besieged, and the Assyrians imprisoned the king of Ashdod. According to this ch, Isaiah argued vigorously against relying on Egyptian help in 713–711, just as he had argued against relying on the Assyrians in 735 (see 7.1–8.23). Isaiah made his point by means of a symbolic action: He imitated the fate that would await the Egyptians (and most likely many Judeans as well) if the situation developed into a full-fledged war could happen to those we looked to, to whom we fled for help and rescue from the king of Assyria, how can we ourselves escape?' "

21 ᵃThe "Desert of the Sea" Pronouncement.⁻ᵃ

Like the gales
That race through the Negeb,
It comes from the desert,
The terrible land.

2   A harsh prophecy
Has been announced to me:
"The betrayer is ᵇ·betraying,
The ravager ravaging.⁻ᵇ
Advance, Elam!
Lay siege, Media!
ᶜI have put an end
To all her sighing."⁻ᶜ

3   Therefore my loins
Are seized with trembling;
I am gripped by pangs
Like a woman in travail,
Too anguished to hear,
Too frightened to see.

4   My mind is confused,
I shudder in panic.
My night of pleasure
He has turned to terror:

5   "Set the table!"
To "Let the watchman watch!"
"Eat and drink!"
To "Up, officers! Greaseᵈ the shields!"

6   For thus my Lord said to me:
"Go, set up a sentry;
Let him announce what he sees.

---

a-a *Emendation yields "The 'From the Desert' Pronouncement," agreeing with the phrase farther on in the verse.*
b-b *Emendation yields "betrayed . . . ravaged"; cf. 33.1.*
c-c *Emendation yields "Put an end to all her merrymaking!"*
d *Emendation yields "Grasp."*

21.1–10: An oracle concerning Babylonia. This oracle may date from Isaiah's day, during the reign of the Babylonian king, Merodach-baladan, at the end of the 8th century. At that time the relatively small kingdom of Babylonia attempted to defeat the larger Assyrian empire. This ultimately futile attempt was relevant to the Judeans, because the Babylonians endeavored to persuade the Judean king, Hezekiah, to join the anti-Assyrian coalition. See ch 39, and also 2 Kings ch 20. If this is the setting of the passage, Isaiah predicts defeat for the Babylonians, in spite of their attempt to create a unified front with the Judeans. Alternatively, this text may date to a century after Isaiah, to a time in which the Babylonians had in fact become the great power of the ancient Near East. In that case, an unnamed prophet predicts the downfall of the Babylonians. The language of this oracle is unusually obscure. **1:** *Desert of the Sea,* i.e., Babylon. The term may be a Heb translation of an Akkadian term used to refer to southern Mesopotamia, where Babylon was located. (Akkadian was the language of Babylonia and Assyria.) **2:** *Elam, Media:* These two nations were located to the north of Assyria. Elam joined Merodach-baladan's doomed campaign against Assyria. If this text dates from the 8th century (that is, the era of Isaiah son of Amoz), then this v. calls on Elam and Media to defend themselves from the coming Assyrian onslaught. Elam and Media eventually became part of the Persian empire, and some late biblical writers seem to equate Elam and Media with Persia. If this text dates from the 6th century (and is thus much later than Isaiah son of Amoz's prophecies), then these vv. call on Elam and Media to wage war against Babylonia. They thus anticipate the fall of Babylonia to the Persians in 539 BCE, and resemble the prophecies of Deutero-Isaiah (see introduction). **6–9:** A description of prophetic inspiration: The prophet is like the sentry in a watchtower,

against Assyria. Other prophets also used symbolic actions to get their points across; see, for example, Jer. 13.1–14; Ezek. 4.1–5.17. **6:** *Dwellers of this coastland* refers most likely to the Ashdodites, who instigated the revolt against As-syria; the Philistine city of Ashdod is located on the coast. Many rabbinic commentators suggest, however, that "coastland" refers to the whole land of Israel, including the hill country where the Judeans lived.

7   He will see mounted men,
     Horsemen in pairs—
     Riders on asses,
     Riders on camels—
     And he will listen closely,
     Most attentively."
8   And ᵃ[like] a lion heᵃ called out:
     ᵇ"On my Lord's lookoutᵇ I stand
     Ever by day,
     And at my post I watch
     Every night.
9   And there they come, mounted men—
     Horsemen in pairs!"
     Then he spoke up and said,
     "Fallen, fallen is Babylon,
     And all the images of her gods
     Have crashed to the ground!"
10   ᶜMy threshing, the product of my threshing floor:ᶜ
     What I have heard from the LORD of Hosts,
     The God of Israel—
     That I have told to you.

11   The "Dumah"ᵈ Pronouncement.

     A call comes to me from Seir:
     "Watchman, what of the night?
     Watchman, what of the night?"
12   The watchman replied,
     "Morning came, and so did night.
     If you would inquire, inquire.
     Come back again."

13   The "In the Steppe" Pronouncement.

     In the scrub, in the steppe, you will lodge,
     O caravans of the Dedanites!
14   Meet the thirsty with water,
     You who dwell in the land of Tema;
     Greet the fugitive with bread.
15   For they have fled before swords:
     Before the whetted sword,
     Before the bow that was drawn,
     Before the stress of war.

16 For thus my Lord has said to me: "In another year,
fixed like the years of a hired laborer, all the multitude of

who sees the invading armies before anyone else can.

**21.11–12: An oracle concerning
Edom or northern Arabia.** This oracle is as obscure as it is brief; it is
not even clear to whom it is addressed. *Dumah* may be a poetic,
short form of the word "Edom,"
which was a nation located southeast of Judah. *Seir* was another
name for Edom. Alternatively,
Dumah may refer to a city in northern Arabia. These two explanations are not necessarily exclusive,
since the Arabian city in question
is due east of Edom. Thus the oracle may address both the Edomites
and the Arab tribes with whom
they traded. Finally, *Dumah* may
be a noun meaning "silence"—
an apt title for this oracle, whose
meaning is not spoken clearly to
us. In all likelihood, the oracle predicts that Edom and/or the northern Arabs will be defeated in the
upcoming upheaval described in
the previous ten vv. **12:** This v.
may be taken to refer to a real
watchman, who is asked whether
his watch has passed peacefully;
or it may be metaphorical, referring to the night of oppression (of
the Edomites and/or the Arabs? or
of the Judeans?) at the hands of the
conquerors.

**21.13–17: An oracle concerning
Arabia.** Like the previous oracle,
these vv. probably describe the defeat of various tribes who were either allied with Babylonia against
Assyria (if the oracle dates to the
8th century) or who were allied
with the Babylonian empire that is
about to fall (if the oracle dates to
the 6th century). **13:** *In the Steppe:*
A more likely translation is "Arabia." *Dedanites,* a nomadic Arab
tribe of northern Arabia; they are
often mentioned in the Bible along
with the Edomites, with whom
they seem to have had extensive
trade relations. **14:** *Tema,* a city located south of Dumah in Arabia.
These vv. seem to assume that the
defeated Dedanites will flee south
to Tema, where they will have to
seek refuge. **16:** *Kedar,* a tribe of
nomads who traded with the

a-a 1QIsᵃ reads "The watcher."   b-b Or "On a lookout, my lord."
c-c Connection of Heb. uncertain.   d Name of a people; cf. Gen. 25.14.

Kedar shall vanish; ¹⁷ the remaining bows of Kedar's warriors shall be few in number; for the LORD, the God of Israel, has spoken.

22 The ^{a-}"Valley of Vision"^{-a} Pronouncement.

^bWhat can have happened to you
That you have gone, all of you, up on the roofs,
2   O you who were full of tumult,
     You clamorous town,
     You city so gay?
     Your slain are not the slain of the sword
     Nor the dead of battle.^c
3   Your officers have all departed,
     They fled far away;
     Your survivors were all taken captive,
     ^{a-}Taken captive without their bows.^{-a}
4   That is why I say, "Let me be,
     I will weep bitterly.
     Press not to comfort me
     For the ruin of ^{d-}my poor people."^{-d}

5   For my Lord GOD of Hosts had a day
     Of tumult and din and confusion—
     ^{e-}Kir raged in the Valley of Vision,
     And Shoa on the hill;^{-e}
6   While Elam bore the quiver
     In troops of mounted men,
     And Kir bared the shield—
7   And your choicest lowlands
     Were filled with chariots and horsemen:
     They stormed at Judah's^f gateway
8   And pressed beyond its screen.^g
     You gave thought on that day
     To the arms in the Forest House,^h
9   And you took note of the many breaches
     In the City of David.

a-a Meaning of Heb. uncertain.
b Vv. 1–3 describe a scene of mourning to take place in Jerusalem in the near future. In the ancient Near East, public weeping took place on the low flat roofs as well as in the streets and squares; cf. above, 15.3; Jer. 48.38.
c I.e., executed, instead of dying in battle.
d-d Lit. "the young woman, my people."
e-e Meaning of Heb. uncertain. On Kir see 2 Kings 16.9; Amos 1.5; 9.7; on Shoa see Ezek. 23.23.
f Brought up from 8a for clarity.
g Judah's gateway is the upper course of the Valley of Elah. The screen is the fortress Azekah, at the mouth of the gateway, which was captured by the Assyrians.
h See 1 Kings 7.2–5; 10.16–17.

Edomites and other settled peoples; they were located in the extreme north of the Arabian desert.

22.1–14: An oracle concerning Judah and Jerusalem. This oracle was written, in all likelihood, before the Assyrian invasion in 705–701 BCE. Hezekiah, king of Judah, joined a revolt against the Assyrian king, Sennacherib. Sennacherib's army devastated most of Judah and surrounded Jerusalem but did not conquer it. See 2 Kings 18.13–20.21; Isa. chs 36–39; 2 Chron. ch 32. (Some, however, believe that the ch relates to the events of 713, described in 20.1–6 n.) Isaiah seems to have disapproved of the actions taken to fortify Jerusalem (see 2 Kings 20.20; 2 Chron. 32.2–5), perhaps because they betrayed a lack of confidence in the LORD. Alternatively, this ch may have been written after the surprising deliverance of Jerusalem. In that case, the ch expresses Isaiah's disapproval of the tone of the celebrations, which fail to recognize the divine source of deliverance sufficiently. **1:** *The "Valley of Vision" Pronouncement:* The title is taken from the phrase in v. 5. Jerusalem (or perhaps one particular valley within the hilly city) is referred to as the valley of vision. **1–4:** Isaiah foresees a dramatic turnabout: The city that is festive as it prepares for siege will be surrounded by ruin. **5–7:** The coming calamity. On the theme of the "Day of the LORD," see also Isa. chs 13, 34; Ezek. ch 7; Joel chs 2–3; Amos 5.18–20; Zeph. ch 1. Amos 5.18–20 is especially comparable, since there, as here, the Judeans believe the day will be one of celebration, but it turns out to be one of calamity. **8–14:** The preparations for the upcoming battle, which fail to attend to God's role in salvation. **8:** *The Forest House,* the building housing the royal treasury and weaponry. See 1 Kings 7.2–6; 10.17. **9:** *Breaches,* gaps or weak spots in the wall surrounding the main sector of the city; cf. 2 Kings 32.5.

ᵃ⁻And you collected the water of the Lower Pool;⁻ᵃ ¹⁰ and you counted the houses of Jerusalem and pulled houses down to fortify the wall; ¹¹ and you constructed a basin between the two walls for the water of the old pool.

But you gave no thought to Him who planned it,
You took no note of Him who designed it long
before.

¹² My Lord GOD of Hosts summoned on that day
To weeping and lamenting,
To tonsuring and girding with sackcloth.

¹³ Instead, there was rejoicing and merriment,
Killing of cattle and slaughtering of sheep,
Eating of meat and drinking of wine:
"Eat and drink, for tomorrow we die!"

¹⁴ Then the LORD of Hosts revealed Himself to my
ears:
"This iniquity shall never be forgiven you
Until you die," said my Lord GOD of Hosts.

¹⁵ Thus said my Lord GOD of Hosts: Go in to see that steward, that Shebna, in charge of the palace:

¹⁶ What have you here, and whom have you here,
That you have hewn out a tomb for yourself
here?—
O you who have hewn yourᵇ tomb on high;
O you who have hollowed out for yourselfᵇ an
abode in the cliff!

¹⁷ The LORD is about to shake you
ᶜ⁻Severely, fellow,⁻ᶜ and then wrap you around
Himself.ᵈ

¹⁸ Indeed, He will wind you about Him ᵉ⁻as a
headdress, a turban.⁻ᵉ
Off to a broad land!
There shall you die, and there shall be the
ᶠ⁻chariots bearing your body,⁻ᶠ
O shame of your master's house!

¹⁹ For I will hurl you from your station
And you shall be torn down from your stand.

²⁰ And in that day, I will summon My servant Eliakim son of Hilkiah, ²¹ and I will invest him with your tunic, gird him with your sash, and deliver your authority into

a-a This clause would read well after the prose part of v. 11a.
b Heb. "his," "himself."
c-c Emendation yields "as a garment is shaken out."
d I.e., and walk off with you; cf. Jer. 43.12.
e-e Emendation yields "as a turban is wound about."
f-f Emendation yields "abode [cf. v. 16] of your body" [cf. 10.3, 16].

10–11: A reference to the water-works project also mentioned in 2 Kings 20.20. Hezekiah directed workers to build a tunnel (now known as the Siloam Tunnel) to bring water from a spring outside the walls of the city, on the slopes south of the Temple Mount, into a pool known as the Siloam Pool inside the city. The tunnel ensured Jerusalem a safe water supply in the event of a siege. Rediscovered in the 19th century, the tunnel is now accessible to tourists. An inscription found inside the tunnel is perhaps the most famous ancient Heb text outside the Bible; it describes how workmen dug the tunnel from two sides and met in the middle.

22.15–25: An oracle concerning a royal official. Unique among biblical oracles, this text condemns a particular non-royal individual: *Shebna,* who was the royal *steward, in charge of the palace.* These titles are known from other biblical texts and also from ancient Heb inscriptions; they probably denote an office comparable to that of Prime Minister. Isaiah calls for Shebna to be deposed and replaced by a man named *Eliakim son of Hilkiah* (v. 20). In Isa. 36.3; 37.2 and 2 Kings 18.18 Eliakim does in fact have the positions described here, and Shebna has apparently been assigned to a lower-ranking position. Isaiah presumes his audience knows the political background of the conflict at hand, leaving modern readers to speculate as to the reasons that Isaiah objected to Shebna's policies. **16:** A large tomb belonging to a royal official with Shebna's title has been excavated on the eastern edge of the valley of Kidron across from the City of David (in today's Silwan neighborhood), but the inscription in the tomb is damaged, and we do not know the official's name. Archeological evidence points to an 8th-century date for the tomb, suggesting the possibility that it is the tomb described here. If so, Isaiah's prediction that Shebna would never enjoy his magnificent tomb is either incorrect or merely rhetorical, for the

his hand; and he shall be a father to the inhabitants of Jerusalem and the men of Judah. ²² I will place the keys of
David's palace on his shoulders; and what he unlocks
none may shut, and what he locks none may open. ²³ He
shall be a seat of honor to his father'sª household. I will fix
him as a peg in a firm place, ²⁴ on which all the substance
of his father'sª household shall be hung: ᵇ⁻the sprouts and
the leaves⁻ᵇ—all the small vessels, from bowls to all sorts
of jars.

²⁵ᶜ In that day—declares the Lᴏʀᴅ of Hosts—the peg
fixed in a firm place shall give way: it shall be cut down
and shall fall, and the weight it supports shall be destroyed. For it is the Lᴏʀᴅ who has spoken.

23 The "Tyre" Pronouncement.

Howl, you ᵈ⁻ships of Tarshish!⁻ᵈ
For havoc has been wrought, not a house is left;
As they came from the land of Kittim,
This was revealed to them.

2   Moan, you coastland dwellers,
You traders of Sidon,
Once thronged by seafarers,

3   Over many waters
Yourᵉ revenue came:
From the trade of nations,
From the grain of Shihor,
The harvest of the Nile.

4   Be ashamed, O Sidon!
For the sea—this stronghold of the sea—declares,
ᶠ⁻"I am as one who has⁻ᶠ never labored,
Never given birth,

a Emendation yields "master's"; cf. v. 18 end.
b-b Meaning of Heb. uncertain.   c Apparently continues v. 19.
d-d See note at 2.16.   e Heb. "her."   f-f Lit. "I have."

owner of that tomb was in fact interred there. **23–24:** The metaphor
here depicts Eliakim as a tent peg,
ensuring a secure place for his
family (the *sprouts and the leaves*
and various *vessels* of the metaphor), just as vessels and other
objects in a tent would be hung
from a rope firmly anchored in
the ground. **25:** The *peg* of this v.
seems to refer back to Shebna. Alternatively, if it is the same peg referred to in v. 23, then Eliakim is

ultimately subject to the same criticism as the man he replaces.

**23.1–18: Oracles concerning the
Phoenicians.** This passage is a
mock lament for *Tyre*. It is not clear
whether the mock lament was
composed as historical reflection
after Tyre was attacked by the Assyrian army or as a prophecy beforehand. Throughout the 8th century, the Phoenician city of *Tyre*
(located in southern Lebanon) was

the capital of a city-state that extended from Acre to *Sidon* and also
included colonies elsewhere in the
Mediterranean, notably in Cyprus
(Heb "Kitim"). Tyre was renowned
for its mighty ships; Tyrians grew
wealthy from their role as traders
and merchants. Indeed the term
"Phoenician" or "Canaanite" became a synonym in Heb for "merchant"; see Prov. 31.24. Although
Tyre retained some independence
from the Assyrian empire, Tyre
was required to pay tribute to the
Assyrians from the middle of the
8th century. It joined the revolt
against Assyria in 705–701. In 701
the Assyrian king Sennacherib
defeated the Tyrians. Tyre's king
fled to Cyprus; Sidon and other
cities along the coast of Lebanon
were removed from Tyrian control;
and the Assyrians may have
gained some control over parts of
Cyprus. Isaiah regards this event
favorably, for Tyre, like all wealthy
and powerful nations, had grown
too great. On the central theme of
humility in Isaiah (relevant both
for individuals and for nations), cf.
2.5–22; 3.8–15; 10.5–27; 11.1–12.10.
Here as in these other passages,
Isaiah contrasts the impious self-
confidence of human beings with
the true grandeur that must be recognized as belonging to God
alone. Tyre was located on an island about one-half mile off the
coast of Lebanon, and it was never
actually conquered during the biblical period, even though its mainland territories were often overrun
and its leadership was at times
forced to capitulate. Thus it resembles Jerusalem in Isaiah's day:
Judah was sorely pressed by the
Assyrians (and the Arameans and
Ephraimites before them), but the
capital never fell. Isaiah may have
viewed Tyre as parallel to inviolable Zion and Tyre's experience as
especially instructive to the Judeans. **1–14: A lament over the
Tyrian empire. 1–5:** Phoenician
merchant ships, various Tyrian
colonies, and Tyre's allies and
trading partners learn that Tyre
has been subjected to an enemy.
1: *Tarshish* was a Tyrian trading
colony in the western Mediter-

Never raised youths
Or reared maidens!"
5 When the Egyptians heard it, they quailed
As when they heard about Tyre.

6 Pass on to Tarshish—
Howl, you coastland dwellers!
7 Was such your merry city
In former times, of yore?
Did her feet carry her off
To sojourn far away?
8 Who was it that planned this
For crown-wearing Tyre,
Whose merchants were nobles,
Whose traders the world honored?
9 The LORD of Hosts planned it—
To defile all glorious beauty,
To shame all the honored of the world.

10 ᵃ⁻Traverse your land like the Nile,
Fair Tarshish;⁻ᵃ
This is a harbor ᵇ no more.

11 The LORD poised His arm o'er the sea
And made kingdoms quake;
It was He decreed destruction
For Phoenicia's ᶜ strongholds,
12 And said,
"You shall be gay no more,
O plundered one, Fair Maiden Sidon.
Up, cross over to Kittim—
Even there you shall have no rest."

13ᵈ Behold the land of Chaldea—
This is the people that has ceased to be.
Assyria, which founded it for ships,
Which raised its watchtowers,
Erected its ramparts,
Has turned it into a ruin.

14 Howl, O ships of Tarshish,
For your stronghold is destroyed!

ranean, perhaps located in today's Spain. **6–10:** The Phoenicians are urged to flee to their colonies elsewhere in the Mediterranean, for God is bringing destruction on the Phoenician coastlands. **11–12:** But God's power extends over the seas as well, so that even in exile the Phoenicians will find no rest. Cf. the fate of Israelites and Judeans sent into exile by God in texts such as Deut. 28.64–68. **13:** A very obscure verse. Because it mentions the *Chaldeans,* who took control of Babylonia a century after Isaiah's day, it is most likely a later gloss, but its meaning is unclear. **14:** The conclusion to the lament marks the end of the literary unit by repeating the opening words, "Howl, you ships of Tarshish" from v. 1. Such framing devices often indicate the extent of a literary unit in biblical literature. **15–18: A prophecy of restoration.** After a period of subjugation, Tyre will be both religiously purified and politically restored. Its fate closely resembles that of Egypt and Assyria in 19.18–25, as well as that of Israel throughout the Bible. God treats the Phoenicians precisely as God treats the Israelites: They are severely punished, then saved. **15:** *Seventy years:* Cf. the length of Jerusalem's punishment in Jer. 25.11; 29.10.

a-a Meaning of Heb. uncertain. Emendation yields "Pass on to the land of Kittim, / You ships of Tarshish."

b Meaning of Heb. uncertain; taking mezah as a by-form of maḥoz: cf. Ps. 107.30.

c Heb. "Canaan's."

d Meaning of verse uncertain. Emendation yields "The land of Kittim itself—/ Which the Sidonian people founded, / Whose watchtowers they raised, / Whose citadels they erected—/ Exists no more; / Assyria has turned it into a ruin."

15 In that day, Tyre shall remain forgotten for seventy years, equaling the lifetime of one king. After a lapse of seventy years, it shall go with Tyre as with the harlot in the ditty:

16   Take a lyre, go about the town,
    Harlot long forgotten;
    Sweetly play, make much music,
    To bring you back to mind.

17 For after a lapse of seventy years, the LORD will take note of Tyre, and she shall resume her ^{a-}"fee-taking" and "play the harlot"^{-a} with all the kingdoms of the world, on the face of the earth. 18 But her profits and "hire" shall be consecrated to the LORD. They shall not be treasured or stored; rather shall her profits go to those who abide before the LORD, that they may eat their fill and clothe themselves elegantly.

24

Behold,
The LORD will strip the earth bare,
    And lay it waste,
    And twist its surface,
    And scatter its inhabitants.
2   Layman and priest shall fare alike,
    Slave and master,
    Handmaid and mistress,
    Buyer and seller,
    Lender and borrower,
    Creditor and debtor.
3   The earth shall be bare, bare;
    It shall be plundered, plundered;
    For it is the LORD who spoke this word.

4   The earth is withered, sear;
    The world languishes, it is sear;
    ^{b-}The most exalted people of the earth^{-b} languish.
5   For the earth was defiled
    Under its inhabitants;
    Because they transgressed teachings,
    Violated laws,
    Broke the ancient covenant.^c
6   That is why a curse consumes the earth,
    And its inhabitants pay the penalty;

a-a I.e., "trading . . . trade."
b-b Change of vocalization yields "both sky and earth."
c I.e., the moral law, which is binding on all men (cf. Gen. 9.4–6).

Chs 24–27: Prophecies concerning the end of days. These chs form a distinct section within the book of Isaiah. They refer to no specific historical situation but are concerned instead with a future time in which the world will undergo sweeping devastation, after which redemption will come to survivors from all the nations. They describe humanity as deeply sinful in general terms, but, unlike other Isaianic passages, they do not specify what humanity's sins are, in contrast, for example, to chs 1–3. Like 2.1–4; 4.2–6; 11.1–12.10, they portray the ultimate and lasting divine judgment of the world, but they focus to a greater extent on the break between the end of the old age and the creation of the new world order. These chs share some features with later apocalyptic literature, which is best represented in the Tanakh by the book of Daniel. Consequently, many date chs 24–27 to the Persian or even the Hellenistic period. On the other hand, they also share many features with prophecies of Isaiah, such as the doctrine of the remnant and a thoroughgoing universalism. Whether these Isaianic features result from Isaiah's own authorship of these chs, and they should be considered protoapocalyptic, or from the influence of Isaiah's genuine writings on them cannot be determined, but most modern scholars opt for the latter explanation.

24.1–23: Cosmic chaos and divine judgment at the end of time. 1–3: A summary of the ch as a whole: In the coming destruction God will destroy the social and natural orders. **4–13:** The reason for the upheaval: Humanity is depraved. **4–5:** *The earth* could also be translated as "the land" (i.e., the land of Israel), in which case this section would refer to the Israelites and Judeans, not all humanity. In that case, *the ancient covenant* (or "everlasting commitment") refers to the laws given to Israel through Moses, especially the laws of the Sabbath and sacrifice (cf. Exod. 31.16; Lev. 24.8; Num. 18.19, where

That is why earth's dwellers have dwindled,
And but few men are left.

7 The new wine fails,
The vine languishes;
And all the merry-hearted sigh.

8 Stilled is the merriment of timbrels,
Ended the clamor of revelers,
Stilled the merriment of lyres.

9 They drink their wine without song;
Liquor tastes bitter to the drinker.

10 Towns are broken,ᵃ empty;
Every house is shut, none enters;

11 Even over wine, a cry goes up in the streets:
The sun has set on all joy,
The gladness of the earth is banished.

12 Desolation is left in the town
And the gate is battered to ruins.

13 For thus shall it be among the peoples
In the midst of the earth:
As when the olive tree is beaten out,
Like gleanings when the vintage is over.

14 These shall lift up their voices,
Exult in the majesty of the LORD.
They shall shout from the sea:

15 Therefore, honor the LORD with lights
In the coastlands of the sea—
The name of the LORD, the God of Israel.

16 From the end of the earth
We hear singing:
Glory to the righteous!
ᵇ⁻And I said:⁻ᵇ
ᶜ⁻I waste away! I waste away! Woe is me!
The faithless have acted faithlessly;
The faithless have broken faith!⁻ᶜ

17 ᵈ⁻Terror, and pit, and trap⁻ᵈ
Upon you who dwell on earth!

18 He who flees at the report of the terror
Shall fall into the pit;
And he who climbs out of the pit
Shall be caught in the trap.
For sluices are opened on high,
And earth's foundations tremble.

---

the same phrase appears in the Heb). But the reference to *the peoples* in v. 13 suggests that this ch is in fact concerned with all humanity and the whole earth, not just Israel and its land. **10:** *Towns*, lit. "the town" (singular). Various proposals regarding the identification of this town (e.g., Jerusalem) have been offered, but it probably refers not to a specific town but to towns as a collective. Hence the NJPS translation. This v. echoes 17.6 and broadens its meaning, the earlier v. referred to the punishment of Israel and this v. (more likely) to the punishment of all humanity. **14–16:** Some group (Judeans who have been saved? human beings generally?) begins to rejoice, thinking the destruction has ended. The prophet laments, however, realizing that the judgment will continue for some time. **16:** *I waste away:* Other commentators, especially rabbinic ones, understand the Heb to mean "I know a secret," i.e., the painful truth about the extent of the coming disaster. **17–23:** A vivid description of the inescapable terror that will overtake all creation. God will mete out punishments that affect not only the mighty among humanity but even nature itself.

---

a Emendation yields "left."   b-b Change of vocalization yields "They shall say."
c-c Meaning of Heb. uncertain. Emendation yields "Villain [Arabic razīl], foolish villain! /
The faithless who acted faithlessly / Have been betrayed in turn."
d-d Heb. paḥad wa-paḥath, wa-paḥ.

19 The earth is breaking, breaking;
   The earth is crumbling, crumbling.
   The earth is tottering, tottering;

20 The earth is swaying like a drunkard;
   It is rocking to and fro like a hut.
   Its iniquity shall weigh it down,
   And it shall fall, to rise no more.

21 In that day, the LORD will punish
   The host of heaven in heaven
   And the kings of the earth on earth.

22 They shall be gathered in a dungeon
   As captives are gathered;
   And shall be locked up in a prison.
   But after many days they shall be remembered.

23 Then the moon shall be ashamed,
   And the sun shall be abashed.
   For the LORD of Hosts will reign
   On Mount Zion and in Jerusalem,
   And the Presence will be revealed to His elders.

25 O LORD, You are my God;
   I will extol You, I will praise Your name.
   For You planned graciousness*a* of old,
   Counsels of steadfast faithfulness.

2 For You have turned a city into a stone heap,
   A walled town into a ruin,
   The citadel of strangers*b* into rubble,*c*
   Never to be rebuilt.

3 Therefore a fierce people must honor You,
   A city of cruel nations must fear You.

4 For You have been a refuge for the poor man,
   A shelter for the needy man in his distress—
   Shelter from rainstorm, shade from heat.
   When the fury of tyrants was like a winter*c*
         rainstorm,

5 The rage of strangers*b* like heat in the desert,
   You subdued the heat with the shade of clouds,
   The singing*d* of the tyrants was vanquished.

6 The LORD of Hosts will make on this mount*e*
   For all the peoples

21: *The host of heaven,* the stars above, or the angels, or both, since the stars were viewed by many ancient peoples as divinities. Cf. Jer. 33.22; 1 Kings 22.19; Neh. 9.6. Because the stars were worshipped by many peoples (including misguided Israelites), they too feel the brunt of God's anger.

25.1–12: The end of evil. This ch brings together two or three texts describing God's victory over evil and sorrow. **1–5:** A song of thanksgiving. These vv. seem to refer to some historical event in the past and to have a particular city in mind, though they give no indication whatsoever regarding the identity of the arrogant city that has been overthrown. In both respects this short song differs from most of chs 24–27. It is possible that these vv. originated as a song of triumph after the downfall of some major city such as the Assyrian capital and were later reused here as an example of the song that will be sung by the faithful remnant that endures after the end of days. **6–9:** The rejoicing of the faithful remnant and the end of sorrow in the future.

a See 9.5.   b Emendation yields "arrogant men."   c Meaning of Heb. uncertain.
d Meaning of Heb. uncertain. Emendation yields "rainstorm"; cf. 4d.
e I.e., the Holy Land, as in 11.9; 14.25; 57.13.

A banquet of ªrich viands,
A banquet of choice wines—
Of rich viands seasoned with marrow,
Of choice wines⁻ª well refined.

7 And He will destroy on this mountᵇ the
    shroud
That is drawn over the faces of all the
    peoples
And the covering that is spread
Over all the nations:

8 He will destroy deathᶜ forever.
My Lord GOD will wipe the tears away
From all faces
And will put an end to the reproach of ᵈHis
    peopleᵈ
Over all the earth—
For it is the LORD who has spoken.

9   In that day they shall say:
This is our God;
We trusted in Him, and He delivered us.
This is the LORD, in whom we trusted;
Let us rejoice and exult in His deliverance!

10 For the hand of the LORD shall descend
Upon this mount,ᵇ
And Moabᵉ shall be trampled under Him
As straw is threshed to bits at Madmenah.ᶠ

11 Then He will spread out His hands in their
    homeland,ᵍ
As a swimmer spreads his hands out to
    swim,
And He will humble their pride
Along with ʰthe emblems of their power.⁻ʰ

12 Yea, the secure fortification of theirⁱ walls
He will lay low and humble,
Will raze to the ground, to the very dust.

7: *Covering:* When the new cosmic order emerges, the illusions that befuddle the nations will disappear, and the survivors from all nations will enjoy access to true teachings, which emanate from the God of Zion. Cf. 2.1–4; 19.18–25; 23.15–18. **8:** *He will destroy death forever:* See 26.19 n. **10–12:** The destruction of Moab. These are the only vv. in chs 24–27 that refer to a specific nation, and they may have originally belonged in the oracles against the nations in chs 13–24. **10:** *Madmenah:* This may refer to a village in Moab; see Jer. 48.2 (where it is called Madmen). Alternatively, the word may be a noun meaning "muddy pit" or "manure pit," with a punning reference to the Moabite village.

a-a Meaning of Heb. uncertain.
b I.e., the Holy Land, as in 11.9; 14.25; 57.13.
c Perhaps an allusion to the mass killings committed by the Assyrians; cf. 10.7; 14.20.
d-d Emendation yields "peoples."
e Emendation yields "Assyria"; cf. 14.25.
f A village near Jerusalem; see 10.31. Emendation yields "As straw gets shredded in the threshing."
g Lit. "midst."
h-h Meaning of Heb. uncertain. Emendation yields "their citadels"; cf. the next verse.
i Heb. "your."

26

In that day, this song shall be sung
In the land of Judah:
Ours is a mighty city;
He makes victory our inner and outer wall.

2 Open the gates, and let
A righteous nation enter,
[A nation] that keeps faith.

3 The confident mind You guard in safety,
In safety because it trusts in You.

4 Trust in the LORD for ever and ever,
For in Yah the LORD you have an everlasting Rock.

5 For He has brought low those who dwelt high up,
Has humbled the secure city,
Humbled it to the ground,
Leveled it with the dust—

6 To be trampled underfoot,
By the feet of the needy,
By the soles of the poor.

7 The path is level for the righteous man;
O Just One, You make smooth the course of the
righteous.

8 For Your just ways, O LORD, we look to You;
We long for the name by which You are called.

9 At night I yearn for You with all my being,
I seek You with all ᵃthe spirit within me.ᵃ
For when Your judgments are wrought on earth,
The inhabitants of the world learn righteousness.

10 But when the scoundrel is spared, he learns not
righteousness;
In a place of integrity, he does wrong—
He ignores the majesty of the LORD.

11 O LORD!
They see not Your hand exalted.
Let them be shamed as they behold
Your zeal for Your people
And fire consuming Your adversaries.

12ᵇ O LORD!
May You appoint well-being for us,
Since You have also requited all our misdeeds.

13 O LORD our God!
Lords other than You possessed us,
But only Your name shall we utter.

a-a Emendation yields "my spirit in the morning."   b Meaning of verse uncertain.

26.1–21: A song of thanksgiving and supplication. This ch is highly varied: It begins with a song describing a future act of salvation, moves on to entreaties, and ends with a surprising prediction of triumph over death. 1–7: The thanksgiving song that will be sung in the future. This text resembles psalms of thanksgiving and praise in the book of Psalms, such as Pss. 117; 118. The song contrasts the security of a *mighty city* (v. 1), presumably Jerusalem, and the downfall of a *secure city* (v. 5; better, "exalted city"), which is not identified and is likely to be symbolic of oppressive nations generally. 8–10: A reflection on divine judgment, whose lessons the evil fail to accept. 11–19: A petition for salvation to the righteous and punishment to the wicked. These vv. move back and forth between confident expectations regarding the future and depressed reflections on the past or present plight of the nation. 11: The wicked have not yet been shown divine justice and thus do not respect God's power. 12–13: The Israelites confess their misdeeds, but they claim they have already suffered sufficiently for them.

14 They are dead, they can never live;
    Shades, they can never rise;
    Of a truth, You have dealt with them and wiped
        them out,
    Have put an end to all mention of them.

15a When You added to the nation, O LORD,
    When You added to the nation,
    Extending all the boundaries of the land,
    You were honored.

16 O LORD! In their distress, they sought You;
    Your chastisement reduced them
    To anguished[b] whispered prayer.

17 Like a woman with child
    Approaching childbirth,
    Writhing and screaming in her pangs,
    So are we become because of You, O LORD.

18 We were with child, we writhed—
    It is as though we had given birth to wind;
    We have won no victory on earth;
    The inhabitants of the world have not [c]come to
        life![c]

19 Oh, let Your dead revive!
    Let corpses[d] arise!
    Awake and shout for joy,
    You who dwell in the dust!—
    For Your dew is like the dew on fresh growth;
    You make the land of the shades [c]come to life.[c]

20 Go, my people, enter your chambers,
    And lock your doors behind you.
    Hide but a little moment,
    Until the indignation passes.

21 For lo!
    The LORD shall come forth from His place
    To punish the dwellers of the earth
    For their iniquity;
    And the earth shall disclose its bloodshed
    And shall no longer conceal its slain.

a Meaning of vv. 15–16 uncertain.
b Lit. "anguish"; taking ṣaqun as a noun formed like zadon and sason.
c-c Meaning of Heb. uncertain.   d Grammar of Heb. unclear.

19: Life after death? This v. and also 25.8 refer to God's triumph over death. Some understand these vv. as metaphors: They portray the surprising vindication of the downtrodden, who are figuratively compared to the dead. According to others, these vv. assert that at least some dead people will return to earth at the end of time, their bodies and spirits restored. Rabbinic Judaism emphasizes the belief in bodily resurrection for all humanity. Indeed, this belief is highlighted in the second paragraph of the "'Amidah" prayer, which is recited three times each day in traditional rabbinic liturgy and provides a succinct summary of the main points of rabbinic theology. The Tanakh, however, is much more circumspect regarding the possibility of life after death, avoiding discussions of the issue and in some passages apparently denying the possibility (Ps. 115.7; cf. Isa. 38.18–19). Some biblical passages refer to Sheol, where the spirits of the dead abide (e.g., Gen. 37.35; 42.38; Deut. 32.22; 1 Sam. 2.6; Ps. 88.4; Prov. 15.24), but they do not describe what happens to the spirits there or whether they can be regarded as truly alive. (An exception may be Isa. 14.9–11, 16–21, but that passage is more likely a poetic fantasy. See the comments on these vv.) In Ezek. ch 37 dry bones receive bodies and come back to life, but that text presents itself explicitly as a metaphor for national renewal (37.11): The Judeans, having "died" when they lost their land and kingdom, will "come back to life" as they return to their land to reestablish a commonwealth. Only in Daniel 12.2–3, 12 does the Tanakh unambiguously endorse the idea that humans will be given life after death. Belief in life after death became central to apocalyptic forms of Judaism (attested to in the book of Daniel and various postbiblical, pre-rabbinic documents). Those modern scholars who emphasize the apocalyptic elements in Isa. chs 24–27 understand 25.8 and 26.19 as a typical apocalyptic statement endorsing the notion of resurrection of the dead. Medieval Jewish philosophers and commentators point to this v. (not implausibly) as a biblical warrant for the rabbinic doctrine of life after death. Concerning this whole issue, see 66.24 n.

26.20–27.13: Additional descriptions of the future. The prayer in 26.1–19 has ended, and now the prophet addresses the people. As elsewhere in chs 24–27, the structure of this series of verses is often

27 In that day the LORD will punish,
With His great, cruel, mighty sword
Leviathan the Elusive[a] Serpent—
Leviathan the Twisting[a] Serpent;
He will slay the Dragon of the sea.[b]

2   In that day,
They shall sing of it:[c]
"Vineyard of Delight."[d]

3   I the LORD keep watch over it,
I water it every moment;
[e]That no harm may befall it,[e]
I watch it night and day.

4   There is no anger in Me:
[f]If one offers Me thorns and thistles,
I will march to battle against him,
And set all of them on fire.[f]

5   But if he holds fast to My refuge,
[f]He makes Me his friend;
He makes Me his friend.[f]

6   [In days] to come Jacob shall strike root,
Israel shall sprout and blossom,
And the face of the world
Shall be covered with fruit.

7   Was he beaten as his beater has been?
Did he suffer such slaughter as his slayers?

8   [g]Assailing them[g] with fury unchained,
His pitiless blast bore them off
On a day of gale.

9[h]   Assuredly, by this alone
Shall Jacob's sin be purged away;
This is the only price
For removing his guilt:
That he make all the altar-stones
Like shattered blocks of chalk—
With no sacred post left standing,

loose, and one notes abrupt changes of focus and tone. **26.20–21:** The faithful are instructed to wait patiently and safely until the divine wrath directed against the wicked finishes. **27.1:** Forces of chaos will finally be destroyed at the end of time. *Leviathan . . . Dragon:* All these terms occur in Canaanite mythology and elsewhere in the Bible (e.g., Pss. 74.13–15; 89.6–14; Job 26.5–13), where the sea-monsters are destroyed at the beginning of time, when the world is created. This text moves the event in which chaos is vanquished to the end of time, when the new world order emerges. **2–6: A song of the vineyard.** Israel is compared to a vineyard belonging to God, who will tend and protect it at the end of days. This text is based on 5.1–7, whose negative thrust it systematically reverses: The earlier text is a song of judgment against Israel, and this text is a song of restoration. **7–11: The purpose of punishment.** Israel's suffering and the reasons for it are described. The suffering purges Israel's sins. But those who refuse to repent (the text does not make clear whether this group consists of Jews, Gentiles, or both) will continue suffering.

a-a Meaning of Heb. uncertain.

b The monster which the Lord vanquished of old (cf. 51.9; Ps. 74.13–14) was the embodiment of chaos; here it stands for the forces of evil in the present world.

c Apparently the earth; cf. 26.21.

d So some mss. (cf. Amos 5.11); other mss. and the editions have "Wine."

e-e Meaning of Heb. uncertain; emendation yields "My eye is open upon it."

f-f Meaning of Heb. uncertain.

g-g Lit. "Striving with her"; meaning of verse uncertain.

h This verse would read well before v. 6; the thought of vv. 7–8, dealing with the punishment of Israel's enemies, is continued in vv. 10–11.

Nor any incense altar.
10 Thus fortified cities lie desolate,
Homesteads deserted, forsaken like a wilderness;
There calves graze, there they lie down
ᵃ‑And consume its boughs.
11 When its crown is withered, they break;⁻ᵃ
Women come and make fires with them.
For they are a people without understanding;
That is why
Their Maker will show them no mercy,
Their Creator will deny them grace.

¹² And in that day, the Lᴏʀᴅ will beat out [the peoples like grain] from the channel of the Euphrates to the Wadi of Egypt; and you shall be picked up one by one, O children of Israel!

¹³ And in that day, a great ram's horn shall be sounded; and the strayed who are in the land of Assyria and the expelled who are in the land of Egypt shall come and worship the Lᴏʀᴅ on the holy mount, in Jerusalem.

28 Ah, the proud crowns of the drunkards of Ephraim,
Whose glorious beauty is but wilted flowers
On the heads of men bloated ᵇ with rich food,
Who are overcome by wine!

2 Lo, my Lord has something strong and mighty,
Like a storm of hail,
A shower of pestilence.
Something like a storm of massive, torrential rainᶜ
Shall be hurled with force to the ground.
3 Trampled underfoot shall be
The proud crowns of the drunkards of Ephraim,
4 The wilted flowers—
On the heads of men bloated ᵇ with rich food—
That are his glorious beauty.
They shall be like an early fig
Before the fruit harvest;
Whoever sees it devours it
While it is still ᵈ‑in his hand.⁻ᵈ

⁵ In that day, the Lᴏʀᴅ of Hosts shall become a crown of beauty and a diadem of glory for the remnant of His peo-

---

a-a Meaning of Heb. uncertain. Emendation yields "Or like a terebinth whose boughs / Break when its crown is withered."
b Ge is contracted from ge'e; cf. Ibn Ezra.
c Lit. "water."
d-d Emendation yields "on the bough."

12–13: Two final prophecies. The end of days will bring terror for God's enemies, restoration for the exiled Israelites, and worship on the Temple Mount in Jerusalem.

28.1–29: Judgment against Samaria and against Jerusalem. The various sections of this ch share the theme of haughtiness, which is expressed in the rejection of divine counsel and leads to foolishness and drunkenness. God responds to this haughtiness by sending an enemy to punish Israel and Judah. **1–6: The downfall of Samaria.** These vv. are directed against *Ephraim,* or the northern Israelite kingdom, whose capital was located in Samaria. Thus they must date to some time before the final destruction of Samaria by the Assyrians in 722. The wealthy northerners are described as self-indulgent drunkards. Like all humans who are too proud, they will experience a brutal downfall. **1:** *On the heads of men . . . overcome by wine,* alternatively, this might be rendered: "Those above the fertile valley are overcome with wine." This sentence refers to the drunken inhabitants of the city of Samaria, which was located on a hill above a valley. **2:** *Something strong and mighty,* the Assyrians, who will come to punish the Northern Kingdom. **4:** *The wilted flowers—on the heads of men bloated with rich food:* This might be rendered, "The wilted flowers that are above the fertile valley"; the wilted flower refers to the ephemeral glory of Samaria. **5–6:** The fate of Samaria is contrasted to the fate of *the remnant of His people,* who will enjoy the glory that the northerners haughtily took as their own. Initially one may think that the favored groups described in these vv. consist of the Judeans in Jerusalem, which is the true place of divine manifestation, in contrast to Samaria. Jerusalem, too, however, will be subject to judgment, as the rest of the ch makes clear. **7–22: The judgment against Jerusalem.** Surprisingly, Jerusalem is not contrasted with Samaria but compared to it, for the fate of ple, [6]and a spirit of judgment for him who sits in judgment and of valor for those who repel attacks at the gate.

7   But these are also muddled by wine
     And dazed by liquor:
     Priest and prophet
     Are muddled by liquor;
     They are confused by wine,
     They are dazed by liquor;
     They are muddled in their visions,
     They stumble in judgment.
8   Yea, all tables are covered
     With vomit and filth,
     So that no space is left.

9   [a]"To whom would he give instruction?
     To whom expound a message?
     To those newly weaned from milk,
     Just taken away from the breast?
10   That same mutter upon mutter,
     Murmur upon murmur,
     Now here, now there!"

[11]Truly, as one who speaks to that people in a stammering jargon and an alien tongue [12]is he who declares to them, "This is the resting place, let the weary rest;[b] this is the place of repose." They refuse to listen. [13]To them the word of the LORD is:

     "Mutter upon mutter,
     Murmur upon murmur,
     Now here, now there."
     And so they will march,[c]
     But they shall fall backward,
     And be injured and snared and captured.

14   Hear now the word of the LORD,
     You men of mockery,
     [d-]Who govern that people[-d]
     In Jerusalem!
15   For you have said,
     "We have made a covenant with Death,
     Concluded a pact with Sheol.
     When the sweeping flood passes through,
     It shall not reach us;

drunken Samaria provides the model for the fate of drunken Jerusalem. **7:** *These are also muddled:* Not only those people (miles away in Samaria) but our people (here in Jerusalem) are guilty of drunken excess. It is not clear whether drunkenness here refers to the effects of liquor literally or the effects of the self-deluding policies with which the Judeans have become inebriated. **9–10:** In these vv. Isaiah summarizes the reaction of the priests and prophets in Jerusalem to his message. *He* in these vv., then, refers to Isaiah himself. **10:** *Murmur . . . now there:* The Heb consists of repetitive gibberish; Isaiah's audience disregards his poetic warnings as monotonous nonsense. **11–13:** Isaiah's response to those who mock him. **14–22:** The judgment oracle, directed especially against Jerusalem's leaders. **15:** Isaiah again summarizes his opponents, this time sarcastically putting into their mouths words that uncover the folly of their thinking: They believe that their *covenants* (their treaties with foreign powers such as Egypt or Assyria) will protect them. In fact, those covenants will be no more effective than an attempt to defy death, which inevitably comes to all humans.

---

a *This is the drunkards' reaction to Isaiah's reproof.*
b *I.e., do not embark on any political adventure at this time.*
c *I.e., embark on the political adventure.*
d-d *Or "composers of taunt-verses for that people."*

For we have made falsehood our refuge,
Taken shelter in treachery."

16   Assuredly,
Thus said the Lord GOD:
"Behold, I will found in Zion,
Stone by stone,
ᵃ A tower of precious cornerstones,⁻ᵃ
Exceedingly firm;
He who trusts need not fear.

17   But I will apply judgment as a measuring line
And retribution⁵ as weights;ᶜ
Hail shall sweep away the refuge of falsehood,
And flood-waters engulf your shelter.

18   Your covenant with Death shall be annulled,
Your pact with Sheol shall not endure;
When the sweeping flood passes through,
You shall be its victims.

19   It shall catch you
Every time it passes through;
It shall pass through every morning,
Every day and every night.
And it shall be sheer horror
To grasp the message."

20   The couch is too short for stretching out,
And the cover too narrow for curling up!

21   For the LORD will arise
As on the hill of Perazim,
He will rouse Himself
As in the vale of Gibeon,
To do His work—
Strange is His work!
And to perform His task—
Astounding is His task!ᵈ

22   Therefore, refrain from mockery,
Lest your bonds be tightened.
For I have heard a decree of destruction
From my Lord GOD of Hosts
Against all the land.

23   Give diligent ear to my words,
Attend carefully to what I say.

24   Does he who plows to sow

16: An oracle of promise suddenly changes the tone in the midst of the oracle of judgment. In spite of the harsh words against the Judeans, Isaiah reiterates the notion of Zion's inviolability (see 1.8–9 n.), which provides a measure of hope even in the midst of this prophecy of divine retribution. **20:** When the disaster comes, no rest will be possible for the weary nation. This line ironically comments on v. 12. **21:** *Perazim . . . vale of Gibeon,* an allusion to the victory God gave to David over the Philistines at two locations near Jerusalem; see 2 Sam. 5.20–25. This time, however, God's might will work against the Judeans. **23–29: A parable concerning God's plan in history.** The style and content of this complex passage resemble that of wisdom literature, particularly the book of Proverbs; like many texts in Proverbs and Job, this poem focuses on the depth of divine wisdom. (Wisdom influence has been suggested for Isaiah and a variety of non-wisdom texts.) When a farmer breaks up soil, overturns it, and levels it, his activities seem destructive but are in fact wise and ultimately life-giving. So too God has a purpose as He breaks up and levels nations. Further, God treats Israel and Judah in different ways, just as the farmer uses different techniques when planting and harvesting various types of grain. The fates of Israel and Judah seem similar, but Jerusalem will never suffer the degree of defeat meted out to Samaria.

---

a-a *Meaning of Heb. uncertain.*   b *As in 1.27; 5.16; 10.22.*
c *I.e., I will make judgment and retribution My plan of action; cf. 34.11; 2 Kings 21.13.*
d *Instead of giving victory, as at Baal-perazim and Gibeon (cf. 2 Sam. 5.19–25; 1 Chron. 14.9–16), He will inflict punishment.*

Plow all the time,
Breaking up and furrowing his land?
25 When he has smoothed its surface,
Does he not rather broadcast black cumin
And scatter cumin,
Or set wheat in a row,[a]
Barley in a strip,
And emmer in a patch?
26 For He teaches him the right manner,
His God instructs him.
27 So, too, black cumin is not threshed with a
threshing board,
Nor is the wheel of a threshing sledge rolled over
cumin;
But black cumin is beaten out with a stick
And cumin with a rod.
28 It is cereal that is crushed.[b]
For [c]even if[c] he threshes it thoroughly,
And the wheel of his sledge [d]and his horses
overwhelm it,[d]
He does not crush it.
29 That, too, is ordered by the LORD of Hosts;
His counsel is unfathomable,
His wisdom marvelous.

29 "Ah, Ariel,[e] Ariel,
City where David camped!
Add year to year,
Let festivals come in their cycles!
2 And I will harass Ariel,
And there shall be sorrow and sighing.
[d]She shall be to Me like Ariel.[d]
3 And I will camp against you [f]round about;[f]
I will lay siege to you [d]with a mound,[d]
And I will set up siegeworks against you.
4 And you shall speak from lower than the
ground,
Your speech shall be humbler than the sod;
Your speech shall sound like a ghost's from the
ground,
Your voice shall chirp from the sod.
5 And like fine dust shall be

29.1–24: Three poems on God's surprising treatment of Jerusalem. This ch contains brief poems that share several characteristics. Each suggests that Jerusalem deserves punishment, but each ultimately predicts salvation. **1–8: The first poem: Jerusalem surrounded, Jerusalem saved.** In this short poem, God first announces that He will bring an army to put David's city under siege. Just when disaster seems inevitable, however, the foreign army disappears. Similar predictions of destruction that leads not to defeat but to a sudden and surprising rescue appear often in Isaiah; cf. 3.25–5.6; 8.6–8; 8.22–9.1. The event described here closely resembles the sudden departure of the Assyrian army of Sennacherib during the reign of King Hezekiah in the year 701, which is narrated in chs 36–39; 2 Kings chs 18–19; 2 Chron. ch 32. The same event may form the basis for the prophecy in 22.1–14; see the comments on that passage. A crucial notion underlying this poem is the doctrine of the inviolability of Zion; see 1.8–9 n. **1:** *Ariel:* This poetic name for Jerusalem either means "hearth of God" (i.e., altar) or "lion of God."

a In some Near Eastern countries, wheat is actually planted rather than scattered.
b Emendation yields "threshed."
c-c Taking lo as equivalent to lu.
d-d Meaning of Heb. uncertain.
e A poetic name of Jerusalem; cf. 33.7.
f-f Meaning of Heb. uncertain. Septuagint reads "like David"; cf. v. 1.

The multitude of ᵃ‑your strangers;‑ᵃ
And like flying chaff,
The multitude of tyrants."

6 And suddenly, in an instant,
She shall be remembered of the LORD of Hosts
With roaring, and shaking, and deafening noise,
Storm, and tempest, and blaze of consuming fire.

7 Then, like a dream, a vision of the night,
Shall be the multitude of nations
That war upon Ariel,
And all her besiegers, and the siegeworks against
    her,
And those who harass her.

8 Like one who is hungry
And dreams he is eating,
But wakes to find himself empty;
And like one who is thirsty
And dreams he is drinking,
But wakes to find himself faint
And utterly parched—
So shall be all the multitude of nations
That war upon Mount Zion.

9 Act stupid and be stupefied!
Act blind and be blinded!
(They are drunk, but not from wine,
They stagger, but not from liquor.)

10 For the LORD has spread over you
A spirit of deep sleep,
And has shut your eyes, the prophets,
And covered your heads, the seers;

11 So that all prophecy has been to you
Like the words of a sealed document.

If it is handed to one who can read and he is asked to
read it, he will say, "I can't, because it is sealed"; 12 and if
the document is handed to one who cannot read and he is
asked to read it, he will say, "I can't read."

13 My Lord said:
Because that people has approached [Me] with its
    mouth
And honored Me with its lips,
But has kept its heart far from Me,
And its worship of Me has been

9–14: The second poem: A stubborn people, a surprising God. 9–12. The people fail to understand God's will, because God deliberately misleads them. Cf. 6.8–10. **13:** The Judeans' hypocritical and useless rituals. Cf. Hos. 7.14; 8.2; 10.1–2; Mic. 3.11; 6.6; Isa. 58.2. **14:** A surprising outcome is predicted, but not described. This may refer to either a punishment that goes beyond what even the wise can imagine in their worst nightmares or a sudden act of forgiveness, or both. **15–24: The third poem: Condemnation and redemption. 15–16:** The people's haughtiness: They presume to act as if God were unaware of their actions and to second-guess God's plans. **17–21:** Consequently, evildoers are punished, but the humble will be made glad. **18:** *Deaf . . . blind* may refer to the nation as a whole. In the previous poem (vv. 9–12) the people were deaf and blind because God removed their ability to perceive, but now God reverses His earlier action.

a-a Manuscript 1QIsᵃ reads "haughty men."

A commandment of men, learned by rote—
14 Truly, I shall further baffle that people
With bafflement upon bafflement;
And the wisdom of its wise shall fail,
And the prudence of its prudent shall vanish.

15 Ha! Those who would hide their plans
Deep from the LORD!
Who do their work in dark places
And say, "Who sees us, who takes note of us?"
16 ᵃHow perverse of you!
Should the potter be accounted as the clay?⁻ᵃ
Should what is made say of its Maker,
"He did not make me,"
And what is formed say of Him who formed it,
ᵇ⁻"He did not understand"?⁻ᵇ
17 Surely, in a little while,
Lebanon will be transformed into farm land,
And farm land accounted as mere brush.
18 In that day, the deaf shall hear even written words,
And the eyes of the blind shall see
Even in darkness and obscurity.
19 Then the humble shall have increasing joy through
the LORD,
And the neediest of men shall exult
In the Holy One of Israel.
20 For the tyrant shall be no more,
The scoffer shall cease to be;
And those diligent for evil shall be wiped out,
21 Who cause men to lose their lawsuits,
Laying a snare for the arbiter at the gate,
And wronging by falsehood
Him who was in the right.

22 Assuredly, thus said the LORD to the House of Jacob,
ᶜ⁻Who redeemed Abraham:⁻ᶜ

No more shall Jacob be shamed,
No longer his face grow pale.

23 For when he—that is, his children—behold what My
hands have wrought in his midst, they will hallow My
name.

a-a *Meaning of first line uncertain; emendation yields "Should the potter be accounted /
Like the jugs or like the clay?"*
b-b *Emendation yields "He did not fashion me."*
c-c *Emendation yields "Whose fathers He redeemed."*

Men will hallow the Holy One of Jacob
And stand in awe of the God of Israel.
24 And the confused shall acquire insight
And grumblers accept instruction.

30

Oh, disloyal sons!

—declares the LORD—

Making plans
Against My wishes,
Weaving schemes
Against My will,
Thereby piling
Guilt on guilt—
2 Who set out to go down to Egypt
Without asking Me,
To seek refuge with Pharaoh,
To seek shelter under the protection of Egypt.

3 The refuge with Pharaoh shall result in your
        shame;
The shelter under Egypt's protection, in your
        chagrin.
4 Though his officers are present in Zoan,*a*
And his messengers*b* reach as far as Hanes,
5 They all shall come to shame
Because of a people that does not avail them,
That is of no help or avail,
But [brings] only chagrin and disgrace.

6c-The "Beasts of the Negeb" Pronouncement.

Through a*-c* land of distress and hardship,
Of lion and roaring*d* king-beast,
Of viper and flying seraph,*e*
They convey their wealth on the backs of asses,
Their treasures on camels' humps,
To a people of no avail.
7 For the help of Egypt
Shall be vain and empty.
Truly, I call this,
f-"They are a threat that has ceased."*-f*

30.1–17: Reliance on humanity, disloyalty toward God. Several related poems address the Judeans' reliance on human helpers, which Isaiah sees as a lack of faith in God. Similar prophecies appear in chs 7–8. A similar idea is found in Ps. 118.6–9. 1–7: Oracles concerning Judah's diplomatic overtures toward Egypt. At some point, perhaps during the reign of Hezekiah (probably in either 714 or 701), the king of Judah sent an embassy to the Egyptians as a potential ally against Assyria. As the other major power of the era, the Egyptians were a natural counterweight to the Assyrian threat. Isaiah opposes this strategy. He insists that Judah take an independent path, neither capitulating to Assyria nor depending on Egyptian aid. 1–5: The first oracle, apparently composed when the overture to the Egyptians was being considered. 4: Zoan . . . Hanes, cities in northern and southern Egypt, respectively. 6–7: The second oracle, apparently composed after the ambassadors set out toward Egypt through the Negeb desert. 8–17: The rebellious nation. This poem also stresses that depending on humanity amounts to rejection of God. It is phrased in more general terms than the previous one, not mentioning Egypt specifically.

---

a Or "Tanis."
b Emendation yields "kings"; cf. 19.2 with note.
c-c Meaning of Heb. uncertain; emendation yields "Through the wasteland of the Negeb /
Through a . . ."
d Meaning of Heb. uncertain.
e See note on 14.29.
f-f Meaning of Heb. uncertain. Emendation yields "Disgrace and chagrin"; cf. v. 5.

8   Now,
     Go, write it down on a tablet
     And inscribe it in a record,
     That it may be with them for future days,
     A witness[a] forever.
9   For it is a rebellious people,
     Faithless children,
     Children who refused to heed
     The instruction of the LORD;
10   Who said to the seers,
     "Do not see,"
     To the prophets, "Do not prophesy truth to us;
     Speak to us falsehoods,
     Prophesy delusions.
11   Leave the way!
     Get off the path!
     Let us hear no more
     About the Holy One of Israel!"

12   Assuredly,
     Thus said the Holy One of Israel:
     Because you have rejected this word,
     And have put your trust and reliance
     In that which is fraudulent and tortuous—
13   Of a surety,
     This iniquity shall work on you
     Like a spreading breach that occurs in a lofty wall,
     Whose crash comes sudden and swift.
14   It is smashed as one smashes an earthen jug,
     Ruthlessly shattered
     So that no shard is left in its breakage
     To scoop coals from a brazier,
     Or ladle water from a puddle.

15   For thus said my Lord GOD,
     The Holy One of Israel,
     "You shall triumph by stillness and quiet;
     Your victory shall come about
     Through calm and confidence."
     But you refused.
16   "No," you declared.
     "We shall flee on steeds"—
     Therefore you shall flee!
     "We shall ride on swift mounts"—
     Therefore your pursuers shall prove swift!
17   One thousand before the shout of one—

8–11: Isaiah is commanded to write his prophecy down, so that when it proves correct, God will be on record as having warned the nation against the Egyptian alliance. That Isaiah is commanded to write this prophecy specifically suggests that he often delivered prophecies as speeches without writing them down. Cf. 8.16. **12–17:** Punishment will result from the people's refusal to rely exclusively on God.

a Understanding 'ad, with Targum, as a variant of 'ed.

You shall flee at the shout of five;
Till what is left of you
Is like a mast on a hilltop,
Like a pole upon a mountain.

18   Truly, the LORD is waiting to show you grace,
Truly, He will arise to pardon you.
For the LORD is a God of justice;
Happy are all who wait for Him.

¹⁹ Indeed, O people in Zion, dwellers of Jerusalem, you shall not have cause to weep. He will grant you His favor at the sound of your cry; He will respond as soon as He hears it. ²⁰ My Lord will provide for you meager bread and scant water. Then your Guide will no more ^{a-}be ignored,^{-a} but your eyes will watch your Guide; ²¹ and, whenever you deviate to the right or to the left, your ears will heed the command from behind you: "This is the road; follow it!" ²² And you will treat as unclean the silver overlay of your images and the golden plating of your idols. You will cast^b them away like a menstruous woman. "Out!" you will call to them.

²³ So rain shall be provided for the seed with which you sow the ground, and the bread that the ground brings forth shall be rich and fat. Your livestock, in that day, shall graze in broad pastures; ²⁴ as for the cattle and the asses that till the soil, they shall partake of salted fodder that has been winnowed with shovel and fan.

²⁵ And on every high mountain and on every lofty hill, there shall appear brooks and watercourses—on a day of heavy slaughter, when towers topple. ²⁶ And the light of the moon shall become like the light of the sun, and the light of the sun shall become sevenfold, like the light of the seven days, when the LORD binds up His people's wounds and heals the injuries it has suffered.

27   Behold the ^{c-}LORD Himself^{-c}
Comes from afar
In blazing wrath,
^{d-}With a heavy burden^{-d}—
His lips full of fury,
His tongue like devouring fire,
28   And his breath like a raging torrent
Reaching halfway up the neck—

30.18–33: God's justice and grace at the end of days. Two short passages of an eschatological nature. **18–26: Guidance and grace.** The first of the passages is similar in outlook and language to chs 24–27, and in all likelihood these vv., like those chs, were written in the postexilic era, several centuries after the life of Isaiah himself. The remarkable change in nature itself (v. 26) is typical of postexilic apocalyptic literature. See intro. to chs 24–27. These vv. are noteworthy for their lack of specific historical reference. They rely heavily on passages from the Torah, especially Deuteronomy. **18–21:** In the end of days, the nation will finally be fully receptive of divine teaching. Cf. Jer. 31.31–36, a postexilic text with a similar perspective. **22–26:** Idolatry will cease and nature will be gloriously transformed, to humanity's advantage. **27–33: The defeat of God's enemies at the end of days.** Like the preceding vv., this passage is concerned with the end of days. It has a specific historical setting, however, referring to *Assyria* in v. 31. Further, the literary styles of the passages differ markedly. **27–28:** God arrives on earth to punish the nations who oppressed

a-a *Meaning of Heb. uncertain.*
b *Change of vocalization yields "keep."*
c-c *Lit. "The name of the LORD."*
d-d *Presumably with a heavy load of punishment. Meaning of Heb. uncertain.*

To set a misguiding yoke[a] upon nations
And a misleading bridle upon the jaws of peoples,

29 For you, there shall be singing
As on a night when a festival is hallowed;
There shall be rejoicing as when they march
With flute, [b]with timbrels, and with lyres[b]
To the Rock of Israel on the Mount of the LORD.

30 For the LORD will make His majestic voice heard
And display the sweep of His arm
In raging wrath,
In a devouring blaze of fire,
In tempest, and rainstorm, and hailstones.

31 Truly, Assyria, who beats with the rod,
Shall be cowed by the voice of the LORD;

32 [c]And each time the appointed staff passes by,
The LORD will bring down [His arm] upon him
And will do battle with him as he waves it.[c]

33 The Topheth[d] has long been ready for him;
He too is destined for Melech[e]—
His firepit has been made both wide and deep,
With plenty of fire and firewood,
And with the breath of the LORD
Burning in it like a stream of sulfur.

31

Ha!
Those who go down to Egypt for help
And rely upon horses!
They have put their trust in abundance of chariots,
In vast numbers of riders,
And they have not turned to the Holy One of
    Israel,
They have not sought the LORD.

2 But He too is wise!
He has brought on misfortune,
And has not canceled His word.
So He shall rise against the house of evildoers,
And the allies[f] of the workers of iniquity.

3 For the Egyptians are man, not God,
And their horses are flesh, not spirit;
And when the LORD stretches out His arm,

Judah. **29:** But the Judeans will enjoy a festival of liberation, comparable to Passover. **30–33:** The downfall of Assyria. **33:** *Topheth . . . Melech,* see translators' notes *d, e.*

31.1–32.8: Rebuke, threat, and salvation. Like 30.1–17, this poem begins with a specific historical situation, the Judean strategy of relying on the Egyptians to counter Assyrian hegemony (see 30.1–17 n.). The poem moves on to broader issues, ending with a messianic passage concerning the end of days. **31.1–9: Human help, divine protection. 1–3:** The folly of relying on the Egyptians rather than God.

a *Interpreting* naphath *like Arabic* nāf; *meaning of line uncertain.*
b-b *Brought from v. 32 for clarity.*   c-c *Meaning of Heb. uncertain.*
d *A site near Jerusalem at which human beings were sacrificed by fire in periods of paganizing; see* 2 Kings 23.10.
e *Cf. Molech, Lev.* 18.21; 20.2–5.   f *Lit. "help."*

The helper shall trip
And the helped one shall fall,
And both shall perish together.

4 For thus the LORD has said to me:
As a lion—a great beast—
Growls over its prey
And, when the shepherds gather
In force against him,
Is not dismayed by their cries
Nor cowed by their noise—
So the LORD of Hosts will descend to make war
Against the mount and the hill of Zion.

⁵ Like the birds that fly, even so will the LORD of Hosts shield Jerusalem, shielding and saving, protecting and rescuing.

⁶ᵃ Return, O children of Israel,ᵃ to Him to whom they have been so shamefully false; ⁷ for in that day everyone will reject his idols of silver and idols of gold, which your hands have made for your guilt.

8 Then Assyria shall fall,
Not by the sword of man;
A sword not of humans shall devour him.
He shall shrivelᵇ before the sword,
And his young men ᶜpine away.ᶜ

9 His rock shall melt with terror,
And his officers shall ᵈcollapse from
weaknessᵈ—
Declares the LORD, who has a fire in Zion,
Who has an oven in Jerusalem.ᵉ

32 Behold, a king shall reign in righteousness,
And ministers shall govern with justice;

2 Every one of them shall be
Like a refuge from gales,
A shelter from rainstorms;
Like brooks of water in a desert,
Like the shade of a massive rock
In a languishing land.

3 Then the eyes of those who have sight shall not be
sealed,

4: As translated in the NJPS, this v. contains the oracle of judgment threat that concludes the divine complaint in vv. 1–3: It is God, not Assyria, who really threatens Jerusalem, and the Egyptians will be as useless to defend Zion against God as shepherds are against a lion. Some rabbinic commentators, however, read as follows: "So the LORD . . . will descend to make war at Mount Zion" (against the Assyrians who attack Zion). In that case, this v. marks the move from rebuke to consolation. **5:** God defends Zion, saving it suddenly. Cf. 29.1–8. *Protecting* (Heb "pasoaḥ"): The same verb describes God's protection of Israel in Egypt (Exod. 12.13, 23). The noun "pesah" (Passover) is from the same root, and originally meant "to protect," not "to pass over" (see Exod. 12.11 n.). **6–7:** This is the first passage in which Isaiah calls on the nation to repent since 6.9, where God ordered Isaiah not to engender penitence among the Judeans (see 6.9–10 n.). As the prophecies of Isaiah draw to their close (ch 33 or 34 is the last ch of the collection of Isaiah's own prophecies), this order in ch 6 seems to be rescinded. The reversal of 6.9–10 is made even more clear later in this poem, in 32.3–4. **8–9:** The fall of Assyria and salvation of Judah, which come due to God's intervention, not Egypt's. **32.1–8: The final salvation. 1–2:** The ideal ruler in the end of days. Cf. 9.1–6; 11.1–5. **3:** The nation was blind to God's message, initially because they refused to listen to it, and subsequently because God compounded their inability to hear; see 6.9–10. That fateful decision will be reversed in the end of days.

a-a *Emendation yields "Then the children of Israel shall return."*
b *From root* nss; *cf. 10.18; others "flee."*
c-c *From root* mss; *cf. 10.18; others "become tributary."*
d-d *Cf. note b; meaning of Heb. uncertain.*   e *Cf. 30.33.*

And the ears of those who have hearing shall
    listen;
4 And the minds of the thoughtless shall attend and
    note,
And the tongues of mumblers shall speak with
    fluent eloquence.
5 No more shall a villain be called noble,
Nor shall "gentleman" be said of a knave.
6 For the villain speaks villainy
And plots treachery;
To act impiously
And to preach disloyalty against the LORD;
To leave the hungry unsatisfied
And deprive the thirsty of drink.
7 As for the knave, his tools are knavish.
He forges plots
To destroy the poor with falsehoods
And the needy when they plead their cause.
8 But the noble has noble intentions
And is constant in noble acts.

9 You carefree women,
Attend, hear my words!
You confident ladies,
Give ear to my speech!
10 ⁻ᵃIn little more than a year,⁻ᵃ
You shall be troubled, O confident ones,
When the vintage is over
And no ingathering takes place.
11 Tremble, you carefree ones!
Quake, O confident ones!
Strip yourselves naked,
Put the cloth about your loins!
12 Lament ᵇ⁻upon the breasts,⁻ᵇ
For the pleasant fields,
For the spreading grapevines,
13 For my people's soil—
It shall be overgrown with briers and thistles—
Aye, and for all the houses of delight,
For the city of mirth.
14 For the castle shall be abandoned,
The noisy city forsaken;
Citadel and tower shall become
ᶜ⁻Bare places⁻ᶜ forever,
A stamping ground for wild asses,

4–8: True nobility of character will be the mark of the aristocracy of the future.

32.9–20: Another poem of rebuke followed by encouragement. 9–14: The corrupt women of Jerusalem and their downfall. 9–13: The women of Jerusalem are condemned. This passage is a counterpart to the condemnation of the (male) political leadership in Jerusalem in 30.1–17; 31.1–3. Cf. 3.16–26, a rebuke of wealthy women which immediately follows a rebuke of political leaders in 3.8–15. **12–14:** The downfall of Judah. **14:** *Citadel* (Heb "'ophel"), the neighborhood just south of the Temple Mount (today's Silwan neighborhood), which was the oldest section of the city. Uniquely in Isa. chs 1–33, this v. foresees the destruction of Jerusalem itself. It contradicts the doctrine of the inviolability of Zion, which is everywhere else central to Isaiah's beliefs. See 1.8–9 n.; 8.8 n.; 18.3–6 n.; 28.16 n.; 29.1–8 n.

a-a *Meaning of Heb. uncertain.*   b-b *Emendation yields "for the fields."*
c-c *Meaning of Heb. uncertain; emendation yields "Brushland, desert."*

A pasture for flocks[a]—

15 Till a spirit from on high is poured out on us,
And wilderness is transformed into farm land,
While farm land rates as mere brush.[b]

16 Then justice shall abide in the wilderness
And righteousness shall dwell on the farm land.

17 For the work of righteousness shall be peace,
And the effect of righteousness, calm and
     confidence forever.

18 Then my people shall dwell in peaceful homes,
In secure dwellings,
In untroubled places of rest.

19c And the brush shall sink and vanish,
Even as the city is laid low.

20 Happy shall you be who sow by all waters,
Who [d]send out cattle and asses to pasture.[d]

33 Ha, you ravager who are not ravaged,
You betrayer who have not been betrayed!
When you have done ravaging, you shall be
     ravaged;
When you have finished betraying, you shall be
     betrayed.

2 O LORD, be gracious to us!
It is to You we have looked;
[e]Be their arm[e] every morning,
Also our deliverance in time of stress.

3 At [Your] roaring, peoples have fled,
Before Your majesty nations have scattered;

4 And spoil[f] was gathered as locusts are gathered,
It[g] was amassed[h] as grasshoppers are amassed.[i]

5 The LORD is exalted,
He dwells on high!
[Of old] He filled Zion
With justice and righteousness.

6 Faithfulness to [j]Your charge[j] was [her] wealth,
Wisdom and devotion [her] triumph,
Reverence for the LORD—that was her[k] treasure.

---

a Emendation yields "onagers"; cf. Job 39.5.
b I.e., the transformed wilderness will surpass in fertility what is now used as farm land.
c Meaning of verse uncertain.
d-d Lit. "let loose the feet of cattle and asses"; cf. 7.25 end.
e-e Emendation yields "You have been our help."   f Heb. "your spoil."
g Meaning of Heb. uncertain. Emendation yields "booty"; cf. v. 23.
h Taking šqq as a cognate of qšš.   i Apparently for food; cf. Lev. 11.22.
j-j Meaning of Heb. uncertain.   k Heb. "his."

15–20: From destruction to renewal. Quite abruptly, the tone changes to one of salvation and comfort. Sudden and surprising changes of tone recur especially frequently in chs 28–33. **15:** Nature itself will be changed in the end of days, ending hunger and reducing toil. **17:** *The work of righteousness shall be peace,* alternatively: "The outcome of justice will be peace." This v. is the source of our contemporary saying, "If you want peace, work for justice."

33.1–24: A prayer and a prophecy. This ch includes sections that initially seem unrelated: Some vv. are spoken to God by the Judeans or by Isaiah on the Judeans' behalf, others are descriptions of a disaster, and some include prophecies of salvation. Many of the prayers in the book of Psalms are similarly diverse; see, e.g., Ps. 89. Thus this text is probably a prayer or psalm composed by Isaiah. **1:** *A denunciation of an enemy.* The enemy is not identified, perhaps because in Isaiah's historical context the enemy was obviously Assyria. On the theme of the destruction meted out to the destroyer, cf. chs 13–14. **2–9: The heart of the prayer: the petition.** The speakers call out for God's attention, make their request for divine intervention (v. 2), express their confidence in God's ability to save (vv. 3–6), and describe their current lamentable state (vv. 7–9). The combination of these four elements is very common in psalms; cf. Ps. 44.2, 24–27, 4–8, 10–17; Ps. 74.1, 2–3, 12–17, 4–9. **2:** *Arm,* or, "strength." **5:** *Zion . . . justice and righteousness:* This v. echoes 1.21, 27. Ch 33 may be the last ch of the original collection of Isaiah's prophecies (see intro.), and hence the reversal of a complaint from ch 1 may be intended to create a literary frame around the entire collection. **7:** *Arielites,* the inhabitants of Jerusalem; cf. 29.1, 2, 7–8. Alternative understandings of this term abound. According to many rabbinic texts, it refers to a class of angels, who are described here as weeping for Zion. (*Messengers* later in this v.

7   Hark! The Arielites[a] cry aloud;
     Shalom's[b] messengers weep bitterly.
8   Highways are desolate,
     Wayfarers have ceased.
     A covenant has been renounced,
     Cities[c] rejected
     [d-]Mortal man[-d] despised.
9   The land is wilted and withered;
     Lebanon disgraced and moldering,
     Sharon is become like a desert,
     And Bashan and Carmel are stripped bare.
10   "Now I will arise," says the LORD,
     "Now I will exalt Myself, now raise Myself high.
11   You shall conceive hay,
     Give birth to straw;
     My[e] breath will devour you like fire.
12   Peoples shall be burnings of lime,[f]
     Thorns cut down that are set on fire.
13   Hear, you who are far, what I have done;
     You who are near, note My might."

14   Sinners in Zion are frightened,
     The godless are seized with trembling:
     "Who of us can dwell with the devouring fire:
     Who of us can dwell with the never-dying blaze?"
15   He who walks in righteousness,
     Speaks uprightly,
     Spurns profit from fraudulent dealings,
     Waves away a bribe instead of grasping it,
     Stops his ears against listening to infamy,
     Shuts his eyes against looking at evil—
16   Such a one shall dwell in lofty security,
     With inaccessible cliffs for his stronghold,
     With his food supplied
     And his drink assured.

17   When your eyes behold [g-]a king in his beauty,[-g]
     When they contemplate the land round about,
18   Your throat[h] shall murmur in awe,
     "Where is one who could count? Where is one
        who could weigh?
     Where is one who could count [all these] towers?"
19   No more shall you see the barbarian folk,

could also be translated as "angels.") Other possibilities include "valiant men" and "the altar of the Temple." *Shalom's messengers,* see the translators' note *b.* Alternatively, "angels of peace," or, most likely, "messengers of peace," "peace envoys," perhaps referring to ambassadors sent by Hezekiah to the Assyrians at some point before the siege of Jerusalem in 701. (Concerning the events of 701, see 22.1–14 n. and chs 36–39 n.) Apparently, the diplomatic overture was rejected, and the Judeans reacted with dismay. This phrase is one of the sources for the wording of the hymn sung before dinner on Friday nights, "Shalom Aleikhem." **8:** *Covenant,* or, "treaty." The text may refer to an agreement between Judah and some other nation that has been discarded. **10–16: God's response to the prayer.** Responses to a prayer are sometimes found in the text of a psalm. **10–13:** God announces that God will take action. It is not initially clear, however, whether the doomed people are the sinful Judeans or their enemies. **14–16:** The effect of God's announcement. The ambiguity in the previous vv. is resolved: The doomed will include not only the enemies, but also sinners in Zion. On the question of who may dwell in Zion, cf. Ps. 24.3–10. **17–24: Conclusion: Zion at the end of days.** Cf. 2.1–4; 4.2–6; 9.1–6; 11.1–12.10. **17:** *King:* Scholars debate whether the passage refers to the future Davidic monarch (as in chs 9, 11, and 32.1–8) or to the LORD (as in v. 22 of this ch).

a *So a few manuscripts; cf. 29.1.*   b *I.e., Jerusalem's; cf. Salem (Heb.* Shalem*), Ps. 76.3.*
c *1QIs[a] reads "A pact."*   d-d *Emendation yields "an obligation."*
e *Heb. "your."*   f *Emendation yields "brambles"; cf. 32.13.*
g-g *Emendation yields "perfection of beauty"; cf. Ps. 50.2.*
h *As in 59.13 and elsewhere; others "heart."*

The people of speech too obscure to comprehend,
So stammering of tongue that they are not
      understood.

20 When you gaze upon Zion, our city of assembly,
Your eyes shall behold Jerusalem
As a secure homestead,
A tent not to be transported,
Whose pegs shall never be pulled up,
And none of whose ropes shall break.

21 For there the LORD in His greatness shall be for us
Like a region of rivers, of broad streams,
Where no floating vessels can sail
And no mighty craft can travel—
ᵃ·Theirᵇ ropes are slack,
They cannot steady the sockets of their masts,
They cannot spread a sail.·ᵃ

22 For the LORD shall be our ruler,
The LORD shall be our prince,
The LORD shall be our king:
He shall deliver us.

23 Then ᶜ·shall indeed much spoil be divided,·ᶜ
Even the lame shall seize booty.

24 And none who lives there shall say, "I am sick";
It shall be inhabited by folk whose sin has been
      forgiven.

34 Approach, O nations, and listen,
Give heed, O peoples!
Let the earth and those in it hear;
The world, and what it brings forth.

2 For the LORD is angry at all the nations,
Furious at all their host;
He has doomed them, consigned them to
      slaughter.

3 Their slain shall be left lying,
And the stench of their corpses shall mount;
And the hills shall be drenched with their blood,

4 ᵈ·All the host of heaven shall molder.·ᵈ
The heavens shall be rolled up like a scroll,
And all their host shall wither
Like a leaf withering on the vine,
Or shriveled fruit on a fig tree.

---

a-a Brought up from v. 23 for clarity. The passage means that the LORD will render Jerusalem as inaccessible to enemies as if it were surrounded by an impassable sea.

b Heb. "your."

c-c Meaning of Heb. uncertain; emendation yields "even a blind man shall divide much spoil."

d-d 1QIsᵃ reads "And the valleys shall be cleft, / And all the host of heaven shall wither."

20–24: The notion of the inviolability of Zion is repeated. This passage reverses but also echoes ch 1, which bitterly condemns Jerusalem's leaders yet describes the city's inviolability. These vv. form a fitting end to the prophecies of Isaiah son of Amoz.

Chs 34–35: Vengeance on Edom and the restoration of Israel. According to most modern scholars, these chs were written after the Babylonian exile, which ended in 538 BCE, probably by the same author responsible for chs 40–66 or 54–66. (On the authorship of Isa. chs 40–66 and 34–35, see intro.) Alternatively, these chs may have been written in the postexilic period as a bridge linking the prophecies of Isaiah in chs 1–33 with the exilic and postexilic prophecies in chs 40–66. **34.1–17: Judgment against the nations and against the Edomites in particular.** A disturbing ch, full of bitterness and anger, this text portrays the LORD as wreaking vengeance against the nations, apparently because they opposed Zion. It focuses in particular on Edom, a nation located southeast of Judah between the Dead Sea and the Gulf of Aqaba or Eilat. Relations between Edom and Judah during the preexilic period were often hostile (e.g, 2 Sam. 8.13–14). This hostility had deep roots: According to Genesis, the Edomites were descended from Esau, Jacob's brother and rival (see Gen. 25.20–34; 27.1–28.9; 33.1–20; Mal. 1.1–5). The Edomites were especially antagonistic towards the Judeans when the Babylonians conquered Judah at the end of the 6th century BCE, and Judean anger towards the Edomites was severe (see Ps. 137.7; Ezek. 25.12; 35.5–10; Obad. vv. 10–16). This ch predicts an utter disaster overcoming the Edomites in the strongest possible terms. This is ironic in light of later Jewish history, since the Edomites converted to Judaism en masse during the late 2nd century BCE, and were among the most zealous Jews during the conflict with Rome in the 1st century CE. Rabbinic literature understands Edom

5   For My sword shall *be drunk*[a] in the sky;
     Lo, it shall come down upon Edom,
     Upon the people I have doomed,
     To wreak judgment.
6   The LORD has a sword; it is sated with blood,
     It is gorged with fat—
     The blood of lambs and he-goats,
     The kidney fat of rams.
     For the LORD holds a sacrifice in Bozrah,
     A great slaughter in the land of Edom.
7   Wild oxen shall fall [b]with them,[b]
     Young bulls with mighty steers;
     And their land shall be drunk with blood,
     Their soil shall be saturated with fat.
8   For it is the LORD's day of retribution,
     The year of vindication for Zion's cause.
9   Its[c] streams shall be turned to pitch
     And its soil to sulfur.
     Its land shall become burning pitch,
10   Night and day it shall never go out;
     Its smoke shall rise for all time.
     Through the ages it shall lie in ruins;
     Through the aeons none shall traverse it.
11   [d]Jackdaws and owls[d] shall possess it;
     Great owls and ravens shall dwell there.
     He shall measure it with a line of chaos
     And with weights of emptiness.[e]
12   [d]It shall be called, "No kingdom is there,"[d]
     Its nobles and all its lords shall be nothing.
13   Thorns shall grow up in its palaces,
     Nettles and briers in its strongholds.
     It shall be a home of jackals,
     An abode of ostriches.
14[f] Wildcats shall meet hyenas,
     Goat-demons shall greet each other;
     There too the lilith[g] shall repose
     And find herself a resting place.
15   There the arrow-snake shall nest and lay eggs,
     And shall brood and hatch in its shade.
     There too the buzzards shall gather
     With one another.
16   Search and read it in the scroll of the LORD:
     Not one of these shall be absent,

in prophetic texts as a symbolic reference to the Roman empire and Christianity, rather than to the historical Edomites, who were in fact Jewish by the time rabbinic literature was composed. See, for example, Targum to v. 9. **1–4:** Judgment against the nations of the world. **5–8:** The slaughter of the Edomites. **9–17:** The everlasting destruction of Edom is depicted through two somewhat contradictory figures: In vv. 9–10, Edom becomes the site of an eternal fire (cf. 66.24); in vv. 11–17, Edom becomes a deserted wasteland, inhabited only by wild beasts. **14:** *Lilith:* In ancient Semitic folklore contemporaneous with the Bible (and also in rabbinic literature), this term referred to a group of female demons. They seduced and then killed single men, and they were especially dangerous to nursing mothers and infants. In later rabbinic and kabbalistic folklore, a character with this name was said to be the first wife of Adam. Their parting was not amicable; he later married Eve, and she embarked on a career killing young children. These legends about Adam and Lilith are postbiblical, however, and have no bearing on the term used here.

---

a-a 1QIs[a] reads "be seen"; cf. Targum.   b-b Emendation yields "with fatted calves."
c I.e., Edom's.   d-d Meaning of Heb. uncertain.
e I.e., He shall plan chaos and emptiness for it; cf. 28.17; Lam. 2.8.
f Most of the creatures in vv. 14–15 cannot be identified with certainty.
g A kind of demon.

Not one shall miss its fellow.
For His[a] mouth has spoken,
It is His spirit that has assembled them,

17 And it is He who apportioned it to them by lot,
Whose hand divided it for them with the line.
They shall possess it for all time,
They shall dwell there through the ages.

35

The arid desert shall be glad,
The wilderness shall rejoice
And shall blossom like a rose.[b]

2   It shall blossom abundantly,
It shall also exult and shout.
It shall receive the glory of Lebanon,
The splendor of Carmel and Sharon.
They shall behold the glory of the LORD,
The splendor of our God.

3   Strengthen the hands that are slack;
Make firm the tottering knees!

4   Say to the anxious of heart,
"Be strong, fear not;
Behold your God!
Requital is coming,
The recompense of God—
He Himself is coming to give you triumph."

5   Then the eyes of the blind shall be opened,
And the ears of the deaf shall be unstopped.

6   Then the lame shall leap like a deer,
And the tongue of the dumb shall shout aloud;
For waters shall burst forth in the desert,
Streams in the wilderness.

7   Torrid earth shall become a pool;
Parched land, fountains of water;
The home of jackals, a pasture;[c]
The abode [of ostriches],[d] reeds and rushes.

8   And a highway shall appear there,
Which shall be called the Sacred Way.
No one unclean shall pass along it,
But it shall be for them.[e]
[f]No traveler, not even fools, shall go astray.[f]

9   No lion shall be there,

35.1–10: The renewal of Israel and the return of the exiles. This ch is the converse of the previous one: In ch 34, a land inhabited by Judah's enemies becomes a desert; in ch 35, the desert is transformed so that Judean exiles in Babylonia can pass through it with ease on their journey to Zion. Normally, travelers from Babylonia to the land of Israel would move northwest along the Euphrates, then southwest through Syria, avoiding the route that went directly west through the impassable desert. But this prophecy insists that the exiles will be able to go directly and quickly through the desert, because the LORD will provide water and safety for them there. This passage borrows extensively from Jeremiah's prediction of the exiles' return in Jer. 31.7–9. It amplifies that prediction, while changing its historical referent from northern (Israelite) exiles in Assyria to southern (Judean) exiles in Babylonia. It also deliberately recalls the vocabulary of Isaiah 32.1–6. **6–10:** The return to Zion is portrayed as a new exodus, a major theme in Deutero-Isaiah: Like the Israelites fleeing slavery in Egypt, the returning exiles will receive water and protection in the desert as they go to the land of Israel. **8:** *No one unclean:* Since God would personally accompany the exiles (v. 4), they would have to be in a state of ritual purity.

---

a Heb. "My."   b Lit. "crocus."
c Meaning of Heb. uncertain; emendation yields "a marsh."   d Cf. 34.13.
e Emendation yields "for His people."   f-f Meaning of Heb. uncertain.

No ferocious beast shall set foot on it—
These shall not be found there.
But the redeemed shall walk it;
10   And the ransomed of the LORD shall return,
And come with shouting to Zion,
Crowned with joy everlasting.
They shall attain joy and gladness,
While sorrow and sighing flee.

36 ^aIn the fourteenth year of King Hezekiah, King Sennacherib of Assyria marched against all the fortified towns of Judah and seized them. ² From Lachish, the king of Assyria sent the Rabshakeh,^b with a large force, to King Hezekiah in Jerusalem. [The Rabshakeh] took up a position near the conduit of the Upper Pool, by the road of the Fuller's Field; ³ and Eliakim son of Hilkiah who was in

---

a Chaps. 36–39 occur also as 2 Kings 18.13–20.19, with a number of variants, some of which will be cited here in the footnotes.
b An Assyrian title; cf. "Tartan," 20.1.

Chs 36–39: Historical appendices to the prophecies of Isaiah son of Amoz. These chs closely resemble 2 Kings 18.13–20.19. It seems likely that they were originally part of 2 Kings, since they consist of historical narratives of the sort found throughout the books of Kings, rather than prophetic pronouncements of the sort found throughout the book of Isaiah. They were probably taken from 2 Kings and inserted into Isaiah (with several variations) because the prophet Isaiah plays an important role in these narratives. For detailed notes, see the relevant section in 2 Kings.

Chs 36–37: The invasion of Sennacherib in 701 BCE. The Assyrian king Sennacherib invaded the western edge of Asia to put down revolts there by his vassals, who were supported by the king of Egypt. This event serves as the backdrop of many prophecies of Isaiah, such as 1.5–9; 10.28–34; 22.1–14; 23.1–18; 29.1–24; 33.1–24, among others. The account here portrays the event as a disaster for Assyria and an impressive victory for Judah, as does 2 Chron. ch 32. The account in 2 Kings is largely identical, but it adds several vv. (2 Kings 18.14–16) which differ considerably, portraying the event as a partial Assyrian victory. **36.1–37.8: The arrival of Assyrian messengers and negotiations between them and the leadership of Judah. 1–3:** The arrival of the Assyrians. Assyrian records indicate that Assyrian troops vanquished forty-six Judean cities, but not Jerusalem. Isaiah had been predicting an invasion which would devastate Judah but spare Jerusalem since early in his career; cf. 1.5–9; 8.8; 29.1–24.

Places associated with Sennacherib's invasion of Judah

charge of the palace, Shebna the scribe, and Joah son of Asaph the recorder went out to him.

⁴ The Rabshakeh said to them, "You tell Hezekiah: Thus said the Great King, the king of Assyria: What makes you so confident? ⁵ I suppose*ᵃ* mere talk makes counsel and valor for war! Look, on whom are you relying, that you have rebelled against me? ⁶ You are relying on Egypt, that splintered reed of a staff, which enters and punctures the palm of anyone who leans on it. That's what Pharaoh king of Egypt is like to all who rely on him. ⁷ And if you tell me that you are relying on the LORD your God, He is the very one whose shrines and altars Hezekiah did away with, telling Judah and Jerusalem, 'You must worship only at this altar!' ⁸ Come now, make this wager with my master, the king of Assyria: I'll give you two thousand horses, if you can produce riders to mount them. ⁹ So how could you refuse anything, even to the deputy of one of my master's lesser servants, relying on Egypt for chariots and horsemen? ¹⁰ And do you think I have marched against this land to destroy it without the LORD? The LORD Himself told me: Go up against that land and destroy it."

¹¹ Eliakim, Shebna, and Joah replied to the Rabshakeh, "Please, speak to your servants in Aramaic, since we understand it; do not speak to us in Judean in the hearing of the people on the wall." ¹² But the Rabshakeh replied, "Was it to your master and to you that my master sent me to speak those words? It was precisely to the men who are sitting on the wall—who will have to eat their dung and drink their urine with you." ¹³ And the Rabshakeh stood and called out in a loud voice in Judean: ¹⁴ "Hear the words of the Great King, the king of Assyria! Thus said the king: Don't let Hezekiah deceive you, for he will not be able to save you. ¹⁵ Don't let Hezekiah make you rely on the LORD, saying, 'The LORD will surely save us; this city will not fall into the hands of Assyria!' ¹⁶ Don't listen to Hezekiah. For thus said the king of Assyria: Make your peace with me and come out to me,*ᵇ* so that you may all eat from your vines and your fig trees and drink water from your cisterns, ¹⁷ until I come and take you away to a land like your own, a land of bread and wine, of grain [fields] and vineyards. ¹⁸ Beware of letting Hezekiah mislead you by saying, 'The LORD will save us.' Did any of the gods of the other nations save his land from the king of Assyria? ¹⁹ Where were the gods of Hamath and Arpad? Where were the gods of Sepharvaim? And did

4–10: The Assyrian official's speech to the Judeans. The *Rabshakeh,* or Assyrian general, urges the Judeans to surrender. **6:** Isaiah disapproved of the Judean policy of relying on the Egyptians as a counterbalance against Assyria. See 30.1–11; 31.1–9. **7:** Hezekiah had centralized sacrificial worship in Jerusalem, closing many local temples and shrines throughout Judah. See 2 Kings 18.4–6; 2 Chron. 29.3–31.21. His actions were based on laws of centralization like those found in Deut. ch 12, but the Rabshakeh misinterprets them as blasphemous. **11–22:** The dialogue between the Assyrian official and the Judeans. **19–20:** Cf. the similar speech put into the mouth of the Assyrian king in 10.8–11.

---

a 2 Kings 18.20 "You must think."
b I.e., to my representative the Rabshakeh.

they^a save Samaria from me? ²⁰ Which among all the gods of those countries saved their countries from me, that the LORD should save Jerusalem from me?" ²¹ But they were silent and did not answer him with a single word; for the king's order was: "Do not answer him."

²² And so Eliakim son of Hilkiah who was in charge of the palace, Shebna the scribe, and Joah son of Asaph the recorder came to Hezekiah with their clothes rent, and they reported to him what the Rabshakeh had said.

37 When King Hezekiah heard this, he rent his clothes and covered himself with sackcloth and went into the House of the LORD. ² He also sent Eliakim, who was in charge of the palace, Shebna, the scribe, and the senior priests, covered with sackcloth, to the prophet Isaiah son of Amoz. ³ They said to him, "Thus said Hezekiah: This day is a day of distress, of chastisement, and of disgrace. ^{b-}The babes have reached the birthstool, but the strength to give birth is lacking.^{-b} ⁴ Perhaps the LORD your God will take note of the words of the Rabshakeh, whom his master the king of Assyria has sent to blaspheme the living God, and will mete out judgment for the words that the LORD your God has heard—if you will offer up prayer for the surviving remnant."

⁵ When King Hezekiah's ministers came to Isaiah, ⁶ Isaiah said to them, "Tell your master as follows: Thus said the LORD: Do not be frightened by the words of blasphemy against Me that you have heard from the minions of the king of Assyria. ⁷ I will delude^c him: He will hear a rumor and return to his land, and I will make him fall by the sword in his land."

⁸ The Rabshakeh, meanwhile, heard that [the King] had left Lachish; he turned back and found the king of Assyria attacking Libnah. ⁹ But [the king of Assyria] learned that King Tirhakah of Nubia had come out to fight him; and when he heard it, he sent messengers to Hezekiah, saying, ¹⁰ "Tell this to King Hezekiah of Judah: Do not let your God, on whom you are relying, mislead you into thinking that Jerusalem will not be delivered into the hands of the king of Assyria. ¹¹ You yourself have heard what the kings of Assyria have done to all the lands, how they have annihilated them; and can you escape? ¹² Were the nations that my predecessors^d destroyed—Gozan, Haran, Rezeph, and the Bethedenites in Telassar—saved by their gods?

37.1–7: The reaction of the Judeans. Hezekiah, the king of Judah, is dismayed. He seeks advice from Isaiah, who emphasizes that God has vowed to protect Jerusalem. **8:** The Assyrian general leaves. **37.9–36:** Assyrian messengers to the Judeans, and Judean reactions. The narrative sequence of vv. resembles that of the preceding ones, and they may present another version of the same events rather than a second series of negotiations between the Assyrians and Judeans. **9–13:** The Assyrians' message to the Judeans. Cf. 36.4–22. **11–13:** Cf. 36.11–22; 10.8–11.

a I.e., the gods of Samaria.
b-b I.e., the situation is desperate, and we are at a loss.
c Lit. "put a spirit in."   d Lit. "fathers."

¹³Where is the king of Hamath? and the king of Arpad? and the kings of Lair, Sepharvaim, Hena, and Ivvah?"

¹⁴Hezekiah received the letter from the messengers and read it. Hezekiah then went up to the House of the LORD and spread it out before the LORD. ¹⁵And Hezekiah prayed to the LORD: ¹⁶"O LORD of Hosts, enthroned on the Cherubim! You alone are God of all the kingdoms of the earth. You made the heavens and the earth. ¹⁷O LORD, incline Your ear and hear, open Your eye and see. Hear all the words that Sennacherib has sent to blaspheme the living God! ¹⁸True, O LORD, the kings of Assyria have annihilated all the nations^a and their lands ¹⁹and have committed their gods to the flames and have destroyed them; for they are not gods, but man's handwork of wood and stone. ²⁰But now, O LORD our God, deliver us from his hands, and let all the kingdoms of the earth know that You, O LORD, alone [are God]."^b

²¹Then Isaiah son of Amoz sent this message to Hezekiah: "Thus said the LORD, the God of Israel, to whom you have prayed, concerning King Sennacherib of Assyria— ²²this is the word that the LORD has spoken concerning him:

> Fair Maiden Zion despises you,
> She mocks at you;
> Fair Jerusalem shakes
> Her head at you.
> ²³ Whom have you blasphemed and reviled?
> Against whom made loud your voice
> And haughtily raised your eyes?
> Against the Holy One of Israel!
> ²⁴ Through your servants you have blasphemed my
> Lord.
> Because you thought,
> 'Thanks to my vast chariotry,
> It is I who have climbed the highest mountains,
> To the remotest parts of the Lebanon,
> And have cut down its loftiest cedars,
> Its choicest cypresses,
> And have reached its highest peak,
> ^cIts densest forest.^c
> ²⁵ It is I who have drawn^d
> And drunk water.

14–20: King Hezekiah's reaction is portrayed as more faithful and less lacking in confidence than it was in 37.1–7. 21–35: Isaiah's reaction. The poem attributed to Isaiah here resembles his prophecies throughout chs 1–33. Note especially the emphasis on Zion (v. 22), the criticism of haughtiness of the foreign empire (v. 23), the phrase *Holy One of Israel* (v. 23; cf., e.g., 1.4; 5.19; 10.20), the use of imagery taken from Assyrian propaganda (vv. 24–25; cf. 10.7–15; 10.33–24; 14.8; 17.12–14), the notion of the remnant of Judah from whom Israel will be renewed (vv. 31–32; cf. 6.13; 7.3) and especially the doctrine of the inviolability of Zion (vv. 33–35).

---

a So 2 Kings 19.17, and 13 mss. here; most mss. and editions read "lands."

b Supplied from 2 Kings 19.19.

c-c Lit. "Its farmland forest"; exact meaning of Heb. uncertain.

d Or "dug"; meaning of Heb. uncertain.

> I have dried up with the soles of my feet
> All the streams of Egypt.'

26 Have you not heard? Of old
> I planned that very thing,
> I designed it long ago,
> And now have fulfilled it.
> And it has come to pass,
> Laying fortified towns waste in desolate heaps.

27 Their inhabitants are helpless,
> Dismayed and shamed.
> They were but grass of the field
> And green herbage,
> Grass of the roofs ᵃ that is blasted
> Before the east wind.⁻ᵃ

28 I know your stayings
> And your goings and comings,
> And how you have raged against Me,

29 Because you have raged against Me,
> And your tumult has reached My ears,
> I will place My hook in your nose
> And My bit between your jaws;
> And I will make you go back by the road
> By which you came.

30 "And this is the sign for you:ᵇ This year you eat what grows of itself, and the next year what springs from that, and in the third year sow and reap and plant vineyards and eat their fruit. 31 And the survivors of the House of Judah that have escaped shall renew its trunk below and produce boughs above.

32 For a remnant shall come forth from Jerusalem,
> Survivors from Mount Zion.
> The zeal of the LORD of Hosts
> Shall bring this to pass.

33 "Assuredly, thus said the LORD concerning the king of Assyria:

> He shall not enter this city;
> He shall not shoot an arrow at it,
> Or advance upon it with a shield,
> Or pile up a siegemound against it.

34 He shall go back

---

a-a So ms. 1QIsᵃ; cf. 2 Kings 19.26. The usual reading in our passage means, literally, "and a field [?] before standing grain."
b I.e., Hezekiah.

By the way he came,
He shall not enter this city
                    —declares the LORD;

35   I will protect and save this city for My sake
        And for the sake of My servant David."

36 [That night]ᵃ an angel of the LORD went out and struck down one hundred and eighty-five thousand in the Assyrian camp, and the following morning they were all dead corpses. 37 So King Sennacherib of Assyria broke camp and retreated, and stayed in Nineveh. 38 While he was worshiping in the temple of his god Nisroch, he was struck down with the sword by his sons Adrammelech and Sarezer. They fled to the land of Ararat, and his son Esarhaddon succeeded him as king.

38 In those days Hezekiah fell dangerously ill. The prophet Isaiah son of Amoz came and said to him, "Thus said the LORD: Set your affairs in order, for you are going to die; you will not get well." 2 Thereupon Hezekiah turned his face to the wall and prayed to the LORD. 3 "Please, O LORD," he said, "remember how I have walked before You sincerely and wholeheartedly, and have done what is pleasing to You." And Hezekiah wept profusely.

4 Then the word of the LORD came to Isaiah: 5 "Go and tell Hezekiah: Thus said the LORD, the God of your father David: I have heard your prayer, I have seen your tears. I hereby add fifteen years to your life. 6 I will also rescue you and this city from the hands of the king of Assyria. I will protect this city. 7 And this is the sign for you from the LORD that the LORD will do the thing that He has promised: 8 I am going to make the shadow on the steps, which has descended on the dialᵇ of Ahaz because of the sun, recede ten steps." And the sun['s shadow] receded ten steps, the same steps as it had descended.

9 A poem by King Hezekiah of Judah when he recovered from the illness he had suffered:

10c   I had thought:
        I must depart in the middle of my days;
        I have been consigned to the gates of Sheol
        For the rest of my years.

36: The miraculous disappearance of the army that threatened Zion. Cf. 2 Chron. 32.21–23. In 2 Kings 18.14–16, the Assyrians leave only after having been offered tribute. 37–38: The withdrawal of the Assyrians and the death of Sennacherib. According to Assyrian records, Sennacherib was assassinated in 681 BCE, two decades after the events described here.

Chs 38–39: The illness of Hezekiah and the overtures of the Babylonian empire. The events described in chs 38–39 preceded the events described in chs 36–37 by at least ten years. Because chs 38–39 end with a prediction of the Babylonian exile, however, they were placed after chs 36–37, so that the prediction of the Babylonian exile would immediately precede ch 40, whose subject is the return from that exile. 38.1–8: Hezekiah's illness and prayer. 9–20: Hezekiah's psalm of thanksgiving. This text does not appear in the parallel version in 2 Kings 20. It is typical of psalms of thanksgiving found in the book of Psalms. Similar elements appear, for example, in the psalms of thanksgiving in Psalm 118 and in Jonah ch 2. 10–13: A description of the crisis that the speaker overcame. Cf. Ps. 118.5–7; 10–16; Jonah 2.4–7.

a Supplied from 2 Kings 19.35.
b Heb. "steps." A model of a dial with steps has been discovered in Egypt.
c Meaning of verse uncertain. in part.

11   I thought, I shall never see Yah,[a]
      Yah in the land of the living,
      Or ever behold men again
      Among those who inhabit the earth.
12   My dwelling is pulled up and removed from me
      Like a tent of shepherds;
      My life is rolled up like a web
      And cut from the thrum.

      [b-]Only from daybreak to nightfall
      Was I kept whole,
13   Then it was as though a lion
      Were breaking all my bones;
      I cried out until morning.
      (Only from daybreak to nightfall
      Was I kept whole.)[-b]
14   I piped like a swift or a swallow,
      I moaned like a dove,
      As my eyes, all worn, looked to heaven:
      "My Lord, I am in straits;
      Be my surety!"

15   What can I say? [b-]He promised me,[-b]
      And He it is who has wrought it.
      [b-]All my sleep had fled
      Because of the bitterness of my soul.
16   My Lord, for all that and despite it
      My life-breath is revived;[-b]
      You have restored me to health and revived me.
17   Truly, it was for my own good
      That I had such great bitterness:
      You saved my life
      From the pit of destruction,
      For You have cast behind Your back
      All my offenses.
18   For it is not Sheol that praises You,
      Not [the Land of] Death that extols You;
      Nor do they who descend into the Pit
      Hope for Your grace.
19   The living, only the living
      Can give thanks to You
      As I do this day;
      Fathers[c] relate to children
      Your acts of grace:
20   "[It has pleased] the LORD to deliver us,[c]

14: A reference to a lament or petition the speaker uttered during the crisis. Cf. Ps. 118.5; Jonah 2.3.
15–20: God's faithfulness: The speaker has been saved. Cf. Ps. 118.8–9; Jonah 2.7–8.

a I.e., visit His Temple. For "Yah" see 12.2; 26.4.
b-b Meaning of Heb. uncertain.   c Heb. singular.

That is why we offer up music[a]
All the days of our lives
At the House of the Lord."

²¹ When Isaiah said, "Let them take a cake of figs and apply it to the rash, and he will recover," ²² Hezekiah asked, "What will be the sign that I shall go up to the House of the Lord?"

39 At that time, Merodach-baladan son of Baladan, the king of Babylon, sent [envoys with] a letter and a gift to Hezekiah, for he had heard about his illness and recovery. ² Hezekiah was pleased by their coming, and he showed them his treasure house—the silver, the gold, the spices, and the fragrant oil—and all his armory, and everything that was to be found in his storehouses. There was nothing in his palace or in all his realm that Hezekiah did not show them. ³ Then the prophet Isaiah came to King Hezekiah. "What," he demanded of him, "did those men say to you? Where have they come to you from?" "They have come to me," replied Hezekiah, "from a far country, from Babylon." ⁴ Next he asked, "What have they seen in your palace?" And Hezekiah replied, "They have seen everything there is in my palace. There was nothing in my storehouses that I did not show them."

⁵ Then Isaiah said to Hezekiah, "Hear the word of the Lord of Hosts: ⁶ A time is coming when everything in your palace, which your ancestors have stored up to this day, will be carried off to Babylon; nothing will be left behind, said the Lord. ⁷ And some of your sons, your own issue, whom you will have fathered, will be taken to serve as eunuchs in the palace of the king of Babylon." ⁸ Hezekiah declared to Isaiah, "The word of the Lord that you have spoken is good." For he thought, "It means that [b]safety is assured for[b] my time."

40 Comfort, oh comfort My people,
Says your God.
²   Speak tenderly to Jerusalem,
And declare to her
That her term of service is over,
That her iniquity is expiated;
For she has received at the hand of the Lord
Double for all her sins.

---

a Neginothai *is a poetic form of* neginoth.
b-b Lit. *"there shall be safety and faithfulness in."*

21–22: The healing of Hezekiah. In 2 Kings 20.6–7, these vv. follow immediately on the prediction that God will add fifteen years to Hezekiah's life and protect him from the Assyrians in Isa. 38.5–6. Thus in 2 Kings ch 20, these vv. lead naturally into the sign oracle, which appears here in 38.7–8. **39.1–4: The ambassadors from Babylon.** *Merodach-baladan* was king of Babylonia in the 710s BCE. He attempted to lead a revolt against the Assyrians, and his messengers tried to entice Hezekiah to join the revolt. Ultimately, the revolt did not succeed; see the n. to ch 21. Here as in 21.1–10 Isaiah counsels against relying on the Babylonians. **5–8:** A prediction of the Babylonian exile. It is unlikely that this prophecy was in fact uttered by the historical Isaiah son of Amoz. Isaiah believed that Jerusalem would never fall, and he does not seem to have anticipated any break in the reign of Davidic kings, even though he predicted that Judah would be punished and the Davidic family sorely pressed. This prediction was probably attributed to Isaiah by the author of 2 Kings, and the whole passage was added to the book of Isaiah from Kings. It provides a link with the next section of the book of Isaiah, the prophecies of an anonymous prophet who lived in the Babylonian exile. See introduction.

Chs 40–48: The first prophecies of Deutero-Isaiah. On the authorship of chs 40–66, see intro. The first of the three sections within chs 40–66 was written by the anonymous exilic prophet in Babylonia, shortly before or immediately after the fall of Babylonia to the Persians led by Cyrus, but before Cyrus issued his decree allowing the Judean exiles to return to Zion (see Ezra 6.3–5; 2 Chron. 36.22–23). Chs 40–48 consist of several long speeches. In each, Deutero-Isaiah marshals evidence to show the depressed exiles that (1) God is genuinely powerful, and the Babylonian conquest does not indicate that God was defeated by some other alleged god or some other force; (2) God con-

3   A voice rings out:
       "Clear in the desert
       A road for the LORD!
       Level in the wilderness
       A highway for our God!
4   Let every valley be raised,
       Every hill and mount made low.
       Let the rugged ground become level
       And the ridges become a plain.
5   The Presence of the LORD shall appear,
       And all flesh, as one, shall behold—
       For the LORD Himself has spoken."

6   A voice rings out: "Proclaim!"
       ᵃ⁻Another asks,⁻ᵃ "What shall I proclaim?"
       "All flesh is grass,
       All its goodness like flowers of the field:

a-a 1QIsᵃ and Septuagint read "And I asked."

tinues to love the nation Israel, and the Babylonian conquest does not indicate that God has abandoned Israel; (3) God is reliable, and what God promises God does; and therefore (4) the exiles can be sure that they will soon return to their land. The prophet frequently seems to be responding to specific complaints, doubts, and expressions of hopelessness among the exiles. A few of these statements made by Deutero-Isaiah's listeners are cited explicitly (e.g., 40.27; 49.14; 50.1; 50.2). Each speech appearing in these chs moves through several types of reasoning to support these assertions; then the speech ends, and another one begins. It is often difficult (and, ultimately, unimportant) to delineate the precise beginning and end of each speech, since each one presents the same argument using the same types of evidence. This first section of Deutero-Isaiah's prophecies focuses on several themes that are absent in chs 49–66: They emphasize the uniqueness of the LORD, who is the only God; they identify the Persian king Cyrus as the individual through whom God brings salvation to Israel; and they compare "former things" that God had done with "new things" that

God is about to do. Since the major message of this prophet is reconciliation and comfort, eight sections from these chapters are read as the haftarah, or prophetic readings, in the summer, on the Sabbaths following Tishʿah beʾav, which commemorates the destruction of the Temple.

40.1–11: An introduction to the prophecies of Deutero-Isaiah. Vv. 1–11 introduce the main themes and motifs of the following chs: God comforts the nation, assures them that their term of punishment in the Babylonian exile has ended, and promises that they will soon return to Zion. This introductory passage echoes elements of the prophetic initiation scene (see n. to ch 6): God announces that God has a message that the prophet should convey to the nation Israel (vv. 1–5); the prophet objects and is reassured (vv. 6–9). This section also introduces a special feature of Deutero-Isaiah's work: This prophet frequently borrows and revises material from older biblical texts. This tendency to allude to earlier compositions is especially evident in these eleven vv., which use terms and images from ch 6;

28.1–2; Jer. 16.16–18; 31.15; Ezek. 21.2–12; Exod. 32.14–15; Lam. 1.2, 9, 16, 21. **1–2:** God's initial message of consolation. These initial two vv. summarize the main themes of chs 40–66 in their entirety. The verbs (*comfort, speak, declare*) are in the plural, indicating that God addresses not only Deutero-Isaiah but other messengers as well, probably angelic messengers in the heavenly court. As in ch 6 and 2 Kings ch 22, the prophet overhears and to some extent participates in the deliberations of God's angelic staff. **3–5:** God's highway. The *Presence* of God left the land of Israel along with the exiles (cf. Ezek. chs 8–11); now it will return with them (cf. Ezek. 43.1–5). On the motif of the *road* through the *desert*, see 35.1–10 n. (Chs 34 and 35 were written by Deutero-Isaiah.) *Double for all her sins:* The exiles may feel that they deserve punishment, and therefore salvation is remote. The prophet assures them that the punishment they have suffered is enough—indeed, more than enough—and there is no impediment to their salvation. Cf. Jer. 16.18 and Isa. 61.7. **6–8:** Objection and reassurance. A heavenly voice gives an order to issue a proclamation; another voice (probably that of the prophet, especially if the alternate version in translators' note a-a is correct) asks what should be proclaimed, and the first voice answers this question. According to the quotation marks added by the NJPS translation, the prophet's question is brief, and the answer takes up most of v. 6 and all of vv. 7–8. Thus the prophet must proclaim that humans are weak (and therefore the Babylonian conquerors will disappear), but God's strength is enduring. It is also possible, however, that the prophet's question continues all the way through the end of v. 7. In that case, these vv. are an objection to acting as conduit for the divine word: As a mere human, the prophet fears that he will be overcome by the powerful and destructive *breath of the LORD* (lit. "wind" or "Spirit" of the LORD, which is a

7   Grass withers, flowers fade
     When the breath of the Lord blows on them.
     Indeed, man is but grass:
8   Grass withers, flowers fade—
     But the word of our God is always fulfilled!"

9   Ascend a lofty mountain,
     O herald of joy to Zion;
     Raise your voice with power,
     O herald of joy to Jerusalem—
     Raise it, have no fear;
     Announce to the cities of Judah:
     Behold your God!
10   Behold, the Lord God comes in might,
     And His arm wins triumph for Him;
     See, His reward[a] is with Him,
     His recompense before Him.
11   Like a shepherd He pastures His flock:
     He gathers the lambs in His arms
     And carries them in His bosom;
     Gently He drives the mother sheep.

12   Who measured the waters with the hollow of His
                hand,
     And gauged the skies with a span,
     And meted earth's dust with a measure,[b]
     And weighed the mountains with a scale
     And the hills with a balance?
13   Who has plumbed the mind of the Lord,
     What man could tell Him His plan?
14   Whom did He consult, and who taught Him,
     Guided Him in the way of right?
     Who guided Him in knowledge
     And showed Him the path of wisdom?

15   The nations are but a drop in a bucket,
     Reckoned as dust on a balance;
     The very coastlands He lifts like motes.
16   Lebanon is not fuel enough,
     Nor its beasts enough for sacrifice.
17   All nations are as naught in His sight;
     He accounts them as less than nothing.

18   To whom, then, can you liken God,
     What form compare to Him?

technical term denoting the God-given capability to serve as a prophet). V. 8 contains the divine response: Even though the task of conveying God's words is frightening, it must be completed. **6:** *Goodness,* or, "loyalty, reliability." **9–11:** God's arrival in Jerusalem. Messengers are told to announce to Jerusalem that the Lord will soon arrive. Normally, a *herald* would inform a city that an army was arriving, but here God arrives as a gentle *shepherd,* not to destroy but to protect.

40.12–31: The incomparable God. In this speech, Deutero-Isaiah focuses on God's unique power. Because the Lord is the only true God and the creator of the world, the Lord will be able to defeat the Babylonians and restore Zion. Some Judeans probably believed that Babylonia's gods defeated their God, but the prophet insists that in fact no other being in the universe could do so. **12–17:** Divine grandeur. No entity in heaven or earth compares to God, and therefore none can prevent God from acting. **18–20:** A brief argument against idolatry: Certainly the God who created the world is mightier than the gods worshipped by most humans. Those gods, after all, are created, not creators.

a *The reward and recompense to the cities of Judah; cf. Jer. 31.14, 16.*
b Heb. shalish *"third," probably a third of an ephah.*

19   The idol? A woodworker shaped it,
And a smith overlaid it with gold,
-Forging links of silver.-a

20   As a gift, he chooses the mulberry[b]—
A wood that does not rot—
Then seeks a skillful woodworker
To make a firm idol,
That will not topple.

21   Do you not know?
Have you not heard?
Have you not been told
From the very first?
Have you not discerned
-How the earth was founded?-a

22   It is He who is enthroned above the vault of the
         earth,
So that its inhabitants seem as grasshoppers;
Who spread out the skies like gauze,
Stretched them out like a tent to dwell in.

23   He brings potentates to naught,
Makes rulers of the earth as nothing.

24   Hardly are they planted,
Hardly are they sown,
Hardly has their stem
Taken root in earth,
When He blows upon them and they dry up,
And the storm bears them off like straw.

25   To whom, then, can you liken Me,
To whom can I be compared?
                 —says the Holy One.

26   Lift high your eyes and see:
Who created these?
He who sends out their host by count,
Who calls them each by name:
Because of His great might and vast power,
Not one fails to appear.

27   Why do you say, O Jacob,
Why declare, O Israel,
"My way is hid from the Lord,
My cause is ignored by my God"?

28   Do you not know?

21–26: God's incomparable might as manifest in nature and in history. **27–31:** Deutero-Isaiah arrives at the point of the arguments marshalled in vv. 12–26. The Judean exiles have lamented that God no longer pays attention to them (v. 27). But God is still able to listen to them, for God never grows tired (vv. 28–31).

---

a-a *Meaning of Heb. uncertain.*

b *Heb. mesukkan; according to a Jewish tradition, preserved by Jerome, a kind of wood; a similar word denotes a kind of wood in Akkadian.*

Have you not heard?
The LORD is God from of old,
Creator of the earth from end to end,
He never grows faint or weary,
His wisdom cannot be fathomed.

29 He gives strength to the weary,
Fresh vigor to the spent.

30 Youths may grow faint and weary,
And young men stumble and fall;

31 But they who trust in the LORD shall renew their
    strength
As eagles grow new plumes:[a]
They shall run and not grow weary,
They shall march and not grow faint.

41 Stand silent before Me, coastlands,
And let nations [b]renew their strength.[b]
Let them approach to state their case;
Let us come forward together for argument.

2 Who has roused a victor[c] from the East,
Summoned him to His service?
Has delivered up nations to him,
And trodden sovereigns down?
Has rendered their[d] swords like dust,
Their[d] bows like wind-blown straw?

3 He pursues them, he goes on unscathed;
No shackle[e] is placed on his feet.

4 Who has wrought and achieved this?
He who announced the generations from the
    start—
I, the LORD, who was first
And will be with the last as well.

5 The coastlands look on in fear,
The ends of earth tremble.

They draw near and come;

6 Each one helps the other,
Saying to his fellow, "Take courage!"

7 The woodworker encourages the smith;
He who flattens with the hammer
[Encourages] him who pounds the anvil.
He says of the riveting, "It is good!"
And he fixes it with nails,
That it may not topple.

a Alluding to a popular belief that eagles regain their youth when they molt; cf. Ps. 103.5.
b-b Connection of Heb. uncertain.   c Lit. "victory."
d Heb. "his."   e 'rh has this meaning in Old Aramaic.

31: *Trust,* or, "wait with patience and hope."

41.1–42.17: The divine ruler and His servants. A lengthy speech that moves through several lines of reasoning to persuade the audience that God can and will redeem Israel. A theme uniting the whole passage is service to God: Cyrus acts as God's servant by defeating Babylonia (41.2, 25); Israel is God's servant and hence enjoys divine protection (41.8; 42.1). **41.1–7: A mock dialogue with the nations.** God calls on the nations to show whether they and their gods can match the true deity's power. Unable to respond, they are terrified. **1–4:** God asks whether any other nation or its gods has accomplished what the LORD has. **2:** *A victor from the East,* alternatively, "A righteous one from the east." This refers to Cyrus, king of the Persians, who lived east of Babylonia and achieved great victories over all the *nations* and *sovereigns* of the ancient Near East. The Targum takes this to refer to Abraham, the righteous man (see Gen. 15.6), whom God brought from Mesopotamia in the east to Canaan; in this case, it alludes to Abraham's military victory in Gen. ch 14. **4:** The LORD takes responsibility for Cyrus's (and perhaps also Abraham's) victories. The prophet refers especially to Cyrus's defeat of the Babylonian empire. This v. recalls earlier prophecies according to which the great Mesopotamian empire that defeated Judah would itself fall; see Isa. 10.5–27; 13.1–14.27; 21.1–10; Jer. 29.10; 30.11; Zeph. 2.15. Because the God of Israel correctly predicted the downfall of Babylonia in these prophetic passages, which were written years earlier, the God of Israel is clearly the true lord of history. **5–7:** The nations are unable to rely on their gods, who have not demonstrated such mastery over events as the God of Israel. Consequently, they are frightened, but rather than acknowledge the one true God, they foolishly rush to construct a new idol to save themselves.

8   But you, Israel, My servant,
     Jacob, whom I have chosen,
     Seed of Abraham My friend—
9   You whom I drew from the ends of the earth
     And called from its far corners,
     To whom I said: You are My servant;
     I chose you, I have not rejected you—
10   Fear not, for I am with you,
     Be not frightened, for I am your God;
     I strengthen you and I help you,
     I uphold you with My victorious right hand.
11   Shamed and chagrined shall be
     All who contend with you;
     They who strive with you
     Shall become as naught and shall perish.
12   You may seek, but shall not find
     Those who struggle with you;
     Less than nothing shall be
     The men who battle against you.
13   For I the LORD am your God,
     Who grasped your right hand,
     Who say to you: Have no fear;
     I will be your help.
14   Fear not, O worm Jacob,
     O ᵃmen ofᵃ Israel:
     I will help you

                     —declares the LORD—

     I your Redeemer, the Holy One of Israel.
15   I will make of you a threshing board,
     A new thresher, with many spikes;
     You shall thresh mountains to dust,
     And make hills like chaff.
16   You shall winnow them
     And the wind shall carry them off;
     The whirlwind shall scatter them.
     But you shall rejoice in the LORD,
     And glory in the Holy One of Israel.

17   The poor and the needy
     Seek water,ᵇ and there is none;
     Their tongue is parched with thirst.
     I the LORD will respond to them.
     I, the God of Israel, will not forsake them.
18   I will open up streams on the bare hills
     And fountains amid the valleys;

8–20: Encouragement to Israel, God's servant. The nations in vv. 5–7 are frightened, but the Israelites are told that they should fear no more. **8–16:** Israel's fortunes are reversed. The defeated nation will be able to defeat its enemies; the great nations that tormented Israel will lose power. **9:** *I have not rejected you:* a direct address to the exiles, who wonder whether the covenant between God and Israel came to an end with the destruction of the Temple in 586 BCE. **15:** Mighty nations are compared to mountains, which Israel will be able to destroy. On the theme of the haughty mountains and empires that will disappear at the end of days, cf. 2.10–22. **17–20:** Return from exile. The poor and thirsty nation will march through the desert, where God will fulfill all their needs. Here as in ch 35 Deutero-Isaiah compares the upcoming return to Zion with the exodus from Egypt, for God provided water and food for the Israelites as they traversed the Sinai desert to the land of Canaan.

---

a-a Emendation yields "maggot."
b I.e., on the homeward march through the desert.

I will turn the desert into ponds,
The arid land into springs of water.

19 I will plant cedars in the wilderness,
Acacias and myrtles and oleasters;
I will set cypresses in the desert,
Box trees and elms as well—

20 That men may see and know,
Consider and comprehend
That the LORD's hand has done this,
That the Holy One of Israel has wrought it.

21 Submit your case, says the LORD;
Offer your pleas, says the King of Jacob.

22 Let them approach[a] and tell us what will happen.
Tell us what has occurred,[b]
And we will take note of it;
Or announce to us what will occur,
That we may know the outcome.

23 Foretell what is yet to happen,
That we may know that you are gods!
Do anything, good or bad,
That we may be awed and see.[c]

24 Why, you are less than nothing,
Your effect is less than nullity;
One who chooses you is an abomination.

25 I have roused him from the north, and he has
come,
From the sunrise, one who invokes My name;
And he has trampled rulers like mud,
Like a potter treading clay.

26 Who foretold this from the start, that we may
note it;
From aforetime, that we might say, "He is right"?
Not one foretold, not one announced;
No one has heard your utterance!

27 [d]The things once predicted to Zion—
Behold, here they are![d]
And again I send a herald to Jerusalem.

28 But I look and there is not a man;
Not one of them can predict
Or can respond when I question him.

29 See, they are all nothingness,
Their works are nullity,
Their statues are naught and nil.

21–29: Another mock debate emphasizing God's sovereignty. As in vv. 1–4, the setting is a court-room or contest; God speaks, but the other side in the debate simply has nothing to say in its defense and remains silent. **21–23a:** The LORD argues against other gods and their believers, asking them to step forward and announce what great acts they have committed or what predictions they have successfully made. **23b:** God asks the other gods to do anything at all, so that at least their mere existence will be made clear. **24:** The inevitable conclusion: The other gods simply do not exist. **25–26:** The LORD, by contrast, has raised up Cyrus (*him from the north*—Persia is northeast of Babylonia) to defeat Babylonia, just as in the past the LORD brought the Mesopotamian rulers from the north to defeat Israel and Judah and predicted the downfall of Babylonia successfully. Cf. v. 4 in this ch. **27:** *The things once predicted to Zion* refers both to predictions of Zion's defeat (e.g., in prophecies throughout the book of Jeremiah) and also the predictions of Zion's renewal (e.g., Jer. chs 29–33). Because the former prophecies came true, one can be sure that the latter will come true as well—the LORD is reliable. **28–29:** *And there is not a man,* better: "and there is no one." God has asked other gods to come stake their claims to divinity, but none has come forward. This compels the conclusion that *they are all nothingness.* **29:** *See,* or, "Here is" (Heb "hen").

---

a Taking yaggishu intransitively; cf. hiqriv. Exod. 14.10.

b I.e., former prophecies by your gods which have been fulfilled.

c Change of vocalization yields "fear"; cf. v. 10.   d-d Meaning of Heb. uncertain.

42

This is My servant, whom I uphold,
My chosen one, in whom I delight.
I have put My spirit upon him,
He shall teach the true way to the nations.

2 He shall not cry out or shout aloud,
Or make his voice heard in the streets.

3 ᵃ·He shall not break even a bruised reed,
Or snuff out even a dim wick.·ᵃ
He shall bring forth the true way.

4 He shall not grow dim or be bruised
Till he has established the true way on earth;
And the coastlands shall await his teaching.

5 Thus said God the LORD,
Who created the heavens and stretched them out,
Who spread out the earth and what it brings forth,
Who gave breath to the people upon it
And life to those who walk thereon:

6 I the LORD, in My grace, have summoned you,
And I have grasped you by the hand.
I created you, and appointed you
A ᵇ·covenant people,·ᵇ ᶜ·a light of nations·ᶜ—

7 ᵈ·Opening eyes deprived of light,·ᵈ
Rescuing prisoners from confinement,
From the dungeon those who sit in darkness.

8 I am the LORD, that is My name;
I will not yield My glory to another,
Nor My renown to idols.

9 See, the things once predicted have come,
And now I foretell new things,
Announce to you ere they sprout up.

10 Sing to the LORD a new song,
His praise from the ends of the earth—
ᵉ·You who sail the sea and you creatures in it,
You coastlands·ᵉ and their inhabitants!

a-a Or "A bruised reed, he shall not be broken; / A dim wick, he shall not be snuffed out."
b-b Lit. "covenants of a people"; meaning of Heb. uncertain.
c-c See 49.6 and note.
d-d An idiom meaning "freeing the imprisoned"; cf. 61.1.
e-e Emendation yields "Let the sea roar and its creatures, / The coastlands . . ." Cf. Ps. 98.7.

42.1–9: God's servant. The identification of the servant in these vv. is hotly debated. Possibilities include Cyrus (according to Saadia Gaon), the prophet himself (so Ibn Ezra), the Messiah (so Targum and Radak), and the Israelite nation as a whole (so Septuagint and Rashi). See 52.13–53.12 n. The term "servant" in most other passages in chs 40–66 clearly refers to the nation Israel or to the faithful within Israel, and that is the most likely explanation here as well. This passage borrows vocabulary and ideas from both ch 11 and Jer.

31.31–36. Like those passages, this text looks forward to the ideal world of the future, in which justice will reign and the covenant between Israel and God will be observed perfectly. The servant in this passage is parallel to, though not identical with, the ideal Davidic king described in ch 11; promises made to the king there are transferred to the whole nation here. Cf. 55.3 n.; 60.1–22 n.; 65.25 n. **1–4:** God introduces the servant, whose gentle nature is emphasized. In these lines God addresses the nations of the world while pointing to the servant, the nation Israel. **1:** *This,* or, "Here is" (Heb "hen"). The term deliberately contrasts God's servant with the pagan gods and their worshippers introduced with the same term in the previous v. (see 41.29 n.). **4:** *Coastlands:* Even nations far away will know God as a result of God's treatment of Israel. This idea is further developed in v. 6. *His teaching,* or, "his law" (Heb "torah"). **5–7:** God addresses the servant directly and describes the reason that the servant has been chosen. **6:** *Created,* or "guarded." *A covenant people,* i.e., a nation that continues to exist by virtue of the covenant God formed with their ancestors long ago. In spite of their sins and in spite of the exile, the people Israel is assured of restoration because of the covenant. *A light of nations:* The nations of the world will witness God's faithfulness to the covenant when Israel is redeemed. Consequently, the people will be the tool through which God becomes known to all nations as mighty, just, and reliable. In this passage, the Israelites are a light to the nations by virtue of what happens to them, not because of what they do. **7:** *Opening . . . Rescuing:* The subject of the verbs may be either the people or God. **8–9: God's guarantee to the servant.** The servant is guaranteed salvation because his sponsor is the creator. **9:** *Things once predicted,* lit. "the former things." Cf. 41.4. **42.10–17: A concluding hymn.** The speech that began in 41.1 concludes with a song describing

11 Let the desert and its towns cry aloud,
   The villages where Kedar dwells;
   Let Sela's inhabitants shout,
   Call out from the peaks of the mountains.
12 Let them do honor to the LORD,
   And tell His glory in the coastlands.

13 The LORD goes forth like a warrior,
   Like a fighter He whips up His rage.
   He yells, He roars aloud,
   He charges upon His enemies.
14 "I have kept silent *far too long,*
   Kept still and restrained Myself;
   Now I will scream like a woman in labor,
   I will pant and I will gasp.
15 Hills and heights will I scorch,
   Cause all their green to wither;
   I will turn rivers into isles,*b*
   And dry the marshes up.
16 I will lead the blind
   By a road they did not know,
   And I will make them walk
   By paths they never knew.
   I will turn darkness before them to light,
   Rough places into level ground.
   These are the promises—
   I will keep them without fail.
17 Driven back and utterly shamed
   Shall be those who trust in an image,
   Those who say to idols,
   'You are our gods!' "

18 Listen, you who are deaf;
   You blind ones, look up and see!
19 Who is so blind as My servant,
   So deaf as the messenger I send?
   Who is so blind as the chosen*c* one,
   So blind as the servant of the LORD?
20 Seeing many things, *d he gives*d no heed;
   With ears open, he hears nothing.
21e The LORD desires His [servant's] vindication,
   That he may magnify and glorify [His]
      Teaching.

God's might and Israel's restoration. **10–12:** As in 42.1–4, the whole world witnesses God's saving power. **11:** *Kedar,* an area in the north of the Arabian desert, inhabited by nomads. *Sela,* an Edomite city, probably the city now known as Petra in the kingdom of Jordan. **13–17:** God goes to war on behalf of Israel. This passage deliberately mixes two types of images of God, as warrior fighting enemies and as mother giving birth, which are united by the extraordinary energy each involves. A bloody process ends with new creation.

42.18–44.5: God's loyalty, which is unshaken even by Israel's sins. This long speech comforts the exiles, assuring them that God is able and willing to redeem them, regardless of the sins they and their forebears committed. **42.18–43.8: The servant, who deserves punishment, will ultimately be redeemed. 18–21:** The nation Israel will serve God by becoming an object lesson for God's loyalty and ability to save (cf. 42.1–9 n.). Thus Israel is a *messenger;* through Israel's experiences, the world will come to know the one God. Israel is blind, however, and has not yet understood its own purpose in history. **21:** *His vindication:* This might refer to the vindication of the servant Israel or of God, or perhaps both; the former brings about the latter. *Teaching,* Heb "torah."

a-a Lit. "from of old."
b Emendation yields "desert."
c Meaning of Heb. uncertain.
d-d Heb. "you give."
e Meaning of verse uncertain; cf. 43.9–12.

22   Yet it is a people plundered and despoiled:
All of them are trapped in holes,
Imprisoned in dungeons.
They are given over to plunder, with none to
    rescue them;
To despoilment, with none to say "Give back!"

23   If only you would listen to this,
Attend and give heed from now on!

24   Who was it gave Jacob over to despoilment
And Israel to plunderers?
Surely, the Lord against whom they[a] sinned
In whose ways they would not walk
And whose Teaching they would not obey.

25   So He poured out wrath upon them,
His anger and the fury of war.
It blazed upon them all about, but they heeded
    not;
It burned among them, but they gave it no
    thought.

43 But now thus said the Lord—
Who created you, O Jacob,
Who formed you, O Israel:
Fear not, for I will redeem you;
I have singled you out by name,
You are Mine.

2   When you pass through water,
I will be with you;
Through streams,
They shall not overwhelm you.
When you walk through fire,
You shall not be scorched;
Through flame,
It shall not burn you.

3   For I the Lord am your God,
The Holy One of Israel, your Savior.
I give Egypt as a ransom for you,
Ethiopia and Saba in exchange for you.

4   Because you are precious to Me,
And honored, and I love you,
I give men in exchange for you
And peoples in your stead.

5   Fear not, for I am with you:
I will bring your folk from the East,
Will gather you out of the West;

22–25: The tone of these vv. seems bleak, but they in fact comfort the exiles. Deutero-Isaiah recalls Israel's sins (e.g., those described in 30.9–14, whose vocabulary is repeated here) in order to explain to the people why they are in their current state. They need not doubt the Lord's attention or power to save; the nation's plight is fully understandable and justifiable. Hence the exile gives no reason for despair. **43.1–7:** Just as the negative prophecies of the past were fulfilled, so too the people can have confidence that the new, positive ones will come true. **1–2:** Israel belongs to God, and therefore God will not abandon her, even though God punishes her. **3–4:** God will reward Cyrus with the conquest of far-off lands including *Egypt*, because his work allows the exiles to return home. In fact, Cyrus never conquered Egypt, but his son, Cambyses, did. **5–8:** The ingathering of the exiles, not only from Babylonia (which was *East* of the land of Israel) but from other areas as well. Some Judean refugees fled to Egypt and other areas after the Babylonian conquest; see Jer. chs 43–44.

a Heb. "we."

6 I will say to the North, "Give back!"
And to the South, "Do not withhold!
Bring My sons from afar,
And My daughters from the end of the earth—
7 All who are linked to My name,
Whom I have created,
Formed, and made for My glory—
8 Setting free that people,
Blind though it has eyes
And deaf though it has ears."

9 All the nations assemble as one,
The peoples gather.
Who among them declared this,
Foretold to us the things that have happened?
Let them produce their witnesses and be
vindicated,
That men, hearing them, may say, "It is true!"*

10 My witnesses are *you*
        —declares the LORD—
My servant, whom I have chosen.
To the end that you*b* may take thought,
And believe in Me,
And understand that I am He:
Before Me no god was formed,
And after Me none shall exist—
11 None but me, the LORD;
Beside Me, none can grant triumph.
12 I alone foretold the triumph
And I brought it to pass;
I announced it,
And no strange god was among you.
So you are My witnesses
        —declares the LORD—
And I am God.
13 Ever since day was, I am He;
None can deliver from My hand.
When I act, who can reverse it?

14 Thus said the LORD,
Your Redeemer, the Holy One of Israel:
For your sake *c-*I send to Babylon;
I will bring down all [her] bars,
And the Chaldeans shall raise their voice in
lamentation.*-c*

43.9–21: The arguments from prophecy and from history.
9–15: The fulfillment of prophecies concerning Babylonia. As in other speeches (41.4, 27; 42.9; 44.6–8, 24–26; 45.21; 46.10–11; 48.3), Deutero-Isaiah argues that one should believe in the God of Israel because God's predictions come true. Long ago the LORD foretold the downfall of the Mesopotamian empire that defeated Judah; see 10.5–27; 13.1–14.27; 21.1–10; Jer. 29.10; 30.11. Now that Babylonia has indeed fallen (or perhaps is about to fall), it is clear that the God of Israel alone rules time and space. **14:** *I send* Cyrus *to Babylon* to conquer it. *Chaldeans:* The Chaldeans were a leading tribe in Babylonia from the 7th century on, and the last kings of Babylonia stemmed from this group. As a result the term "Chaldean" became a synonym for Babylonian.

---

a *I.e., that the other nations' gods are real.*
b *Emendation yields "they."*   c-c *Meaning of Heb. uncertain.*

15 I am your Holy One, the Lord,
    Your King, the Creator of Israel.

16 Thus said the Lord,
    Who made a road through the sea
    And a path through mighty waters,
17 Who destroyed^a chariots and horses,
    And all the mighty host—
    They lay down to rise no more,
    They were extinguished, quenched like a wick:
18 Do not recall what happened of old,
    Or ponder what happened of yore!
19 I am about to do something new;
    Even now it shall come to pass,
    Suddenly you shall perceive it:
    I will make a road through the wilderness
    And rivers^b in the desert.
20 The wild beasts shall honor Me,
    Jackals and ostriches,
    For I provide water in the wilderness,
    Rivers in the desert,
    To give drink to My chosen people,
21 The people I formed for Myself
    That they might declare My praise.

22 But you have not worshiped Me, O Jacob,
    That you should be weary of Me, O Israel.
23 You have not brought Me your sheep for burnt
        offerings,
    Nor honored Me with your sacrifices.
    I have not burdened you with meal offerings,
    Nor wearied you about frankincense.
24 You have not bought Me fragrant reed with
        money,
    Nor sated Me with the fat of your sacrifices.
    Instead, you have burdened Me with your sins,
    You have wearied Me with your iniquities.
25 It is I, I who—for My own sake^c—
    Wipe your transgressions away
    And remember your sins no more.
26 Help me remember!
    Let us join in argument,
    Tell your version,
    That you may be vindicated.

16–21: Long ago God took Israel out of slavery and defeated the mighty Egyptians. The liberation from Babylonian exile will prove even more impressive than the exodus from Egypt. **16–17:** A reference to the parting of the Reed Sea and the defeat of Pharaoh's army there; see Exodus chs 14–15. **43.22–44.5: Israel's sin and redemption.** As in 42.22–25, God recalls the sins of the Israelites (especially of the exiles' ancestors), focusing on their failure to conduct proper sacrifices. The passage underscores the justice of their punishment and hence emphasizes that God is neither uncaring toward Israel nor too weak to save it. Once the punishment has been completed, there is no impediment to Israel's restoration. **22–24:** The passage is obscure. Deutero-Isaiah may maintain that the Israelites' sacrifices to the Lord were not accompanied by the proper intentions, and hence they really did not constitute worship of the Lord at all. (Cf. this prophet's criticism of the Israelites' fasts in 58.3–7; and see also other prophetic critiques of sacrifice as the Israelites practiced it, such as Isa. 1.11–13; Jer. 7.21–22; Amos 5.21–25.) Alternatively, the prophet may accuse them of neglecting the sacrificial cult and of worshipping other gods instead. Finally, this passage may simply take note of the fact that the exiles did not offer sacrifices, since they no longer had a legitimate Temple in which they could do so. **22:** *But you have not worshipped Me,* better: "It is not Me whom you have worshipped." The Heb emphasizes the word *Me*. **25:** The Israelites' failure or inability to offer proper sacrifices to the Lord is inconsequential; the Lord will redeem them not due to their righteousness but for the sake of God's own reputation. **43.26–44.5:** The Israelites' forebears were sinful, and hence they deserved punishment. But the punishment has run its course, and redemption is now called for.

a *Understanding* hoṣi, *here, as equivalent to Aramaic* sheṣi.
b 1QIs^a *reads* "paths"; *cf. v. 16.*
c *I.e., in order to put an end to the profanation of My holy name; cf. 48.9–11.*

27   Your earliest ancestor sinned,
     And your spokesmen transgressed against Me.
28   So I profaned ªthe holy princes;ª
     I abandoned Jacob to proscriptionᵇ
     And Israel to mockery.

44

But hear, now, O Jacob My servant,
Israel whom I have chosen!
2   Thus said the LORD, your Maker,
     Your Creator who has helped you since birth:
     Fear not, My servant Jacob,
     Jeshurunᶜ whom I have chosen,
3   Even as I pour water on thirsty soil,
     And rain upon dry ground,
     So will I pour My spirit on your offspring,
     My blessing upon your posterity.
4   And they shall sprout likeᵈ grass,
     Like willows by watercourses.
5   One shall say, "I am the LORD's,"
     Another shall use the name of "Jacob,"
     Another shall mark his arm "of the LORD"ᵉ
     And adopt the name of "Israel."

6   Thus said the LORD, the King of Israel,
     Their Redeemer, the LORD of Hosts:
     I am the first and I am the last,
     And there is no god but Me.
7ᶠ Who like Me can announce,
     Can foretell it—and match Me thereby?
     Even as I told the future to an ancient people,
     So let him foretell coming events to them.
8   Do not be frightened, do not be shaken!
     Have I not from of old predicted to you?
     I foretold, and you are My witnesses.
     Is there any god, then, but Me?
     "There is no other rock; I know none!"

9   The makers of idols
     All work to no purpose;
     And the things they treasure
     Can do no good,
     As they themselves can testify.

---

a-a *Emendation yields "My holy name"; see preceding note.*
b *Emendation yields "insult."*
c *A name for Israel; see note on Num. 23.10; cf. Deut. 32.15; 33.5, 26.*
d *Lit. "in among."*
e *It was customary to mark a slave with the owner's name.*
f *Meaning of verse uncertain.*

27: *Your earliest ancestor,* Jacob. *Spokesmen,* the priests and Levites; or, the kings of Israel and Judah and their advisers. **44.1:** See 43.1–2 n., which applies here as well. **3–4:** In the land of Israel, plants wither and remain brown for long periods until they are revived by rainfall. Israel in exile resembles these plants, which had looked dead but in fact were merely dormant. **5:** Possibly a reference to non-Jews who would adopt Jewish beliefs, practices, and ethnicity, which in fact did occur during the exilic and postexilic periods. This phenomenon is one of Deutero-Isaiah's particular concerns; see 56.3–6 n.; 56.7 n.

44.6–28: The persuasive power of monotheism and the folly of idolatry. This shorter speech focuses on the argument from prophecy and the ridiculous nature of idolatry. It gives particular emphasis to one of Deutero-Isaiah's main themes: the insistence that no other gods in fact exist. As with all of the speeches in chs 40–66, the main point is that the one true God can and will redeem Israel. The speech reaches its climax with the identification of the person through whom God brings redemption, the Persian king Cyrus. **6–8: The argument from prophecy.** The LORD is clearly unique, since only the LORD predicted so far in advance events that in fact came to be. Cf. 43.9–15. **9–20: A comic portrayal of an idolater.** The prophet mercilessly lampoons people who make their own gods to worship, implicitly contrasting them with people who worship the true God. The former worship their own creation; the latter, much more sensibly, worship their creator. Deutero-Isaiah to some extent misrepresents, or misunderstands, the actual nature of idolatry as practiced in the ancient Near East, however. Pagans did not believe that idols really were gods, but they believed that the presence of the god entered the idol as the result of complex rituals used to activate the idol after it had been made. **9–11:** The pointlessness of

They neither look nor think,
And so they shall be shamed.

10 Who would fashion a god
Or cast a statue
That can do no good?

11 Lo, all its adherents shall be shamed;
They are craftsmen, are merely human.
Let them all assemble and stand up!
They shall be cowed, and they shall be shamed.

12ᵃ The craftsman in iron, with his tools,
Works itᵇ over charcoal
And fashions it by hammering,
Working with the strength of his arm.
Should he go hungry, his strength would ebb;
Should he drink no water, he would grow faint.

13 The craftsman in wood measures with a line
And marks out a shape with a stylus;
He forms it with scraping tools,
Marking it out with a compass.
He gives it a human form,
The beauty of a man, to dwell in a shrine.

14 For his use he cuts down cedars;
He chooses plane trees and oaks.
He sets aside trees of the forest;
Or plants firs, and the rain makes them grow.

15 All this serves man for fuel:
He takes some to warm himself,
And he builds a fire and bakes bread.
He also makes a god of it and worships it,
Fashions an idol and bows down to it!

16 Part of it he burns in a fire:
On that part he roastsᶜ meat,
He eatsᶜ the roast and is sated;
He also warms himself and cries, "Ah,
I am warm! I can feelᵈ the heat!"

17 Of the rest he makes a god—his own carving!
He bows down to it, worships it;
He prays to it and cries,
"Save me, for you are my god!"

18 They have no wit or judgment:
Their eyes are besmeared, and they see not;
Their minds, and they cannot think.

idol-worship. **12–13:** This description of how idols are made shows detailed familiarity with this ancient Near Eastern industry. Some idols were made of metal (v. 12), some of wood (v. 13). **14–20:** The most biting, and humorous, section of the passage. For Deutero-Isaiah, the fact that the same piece of wood can be put to practical and idolatrous uses shows the idiocy of idolatry.

---

a The meaning of parts of vv. 12–13 is uncertain.   b I.e., the image he is making.
c Transposing the Heb. verbs for clarity.   d Lit. "see."

19 They do not give thought,
They lack the wit and judgment to say:
"Part of it I burned in a fire;
I also baked bread on the coals,
I roasted meat and ate it—
Should I make the rest an abhorrence?
Should I bow to a block of wood?"
20 He pursues ashes!ᵃ
A deluded mind has led him astray,
And he cannot save himself;
He never says to himself,
"The thing in my hand is a fraud!"
21 Remember these things, O Jacob
For you, O Israel, are My servant:
I fashioned you, you are My servant—
O Israel, never forget Me.ᵇ
22 I wipe away your sins like a cloud,
Your transgressions like mist—
Come back to Me, for I redeem you.

23 Shout, O heavens, for the LORD has acted;
Shout aloud, O depths of the earth!
Shout for joy, O mountains,
O forests with all your trees!
For the LORD has redeemed Jacob,
Has glorified Himself through Israel.

24 Thus said the LORD, your Redeemer,
Who formed you in the womb:
It is I, the LORD, who made everything,
Who alone stretched out the heavens
And unaidedᶜ spread out the earth;
25 Who annul the omens of diviners,
And make fools of the augurs;
Who turn sages back
And make nonsense of their knowledge;
26 But confirm the word of Myᵈ servant
And fulfill the prediction of Myᵈ messengers.
It is I who say of Jerusalem, "It shall be inhabited,"
And of the towns of Judah, "They shall be rebuilt;
And I will restore their ruined places."
27 [I,] who said to the deep, "Be dry;
I will dry up your floods,"

21–28: The result of rejecting idolatry. The recognition that idolatry is false leads to several practical conclusions. **21–22:** God formed Israel; in contrast pagans form their gods. Therefore Israel should serve, and trust, its God. Further it follows that God will forgive Israel. **23–28:** God tells the heaven to announce that God takes specific action to save Israel: God brings Cyrus, the Persian king who conquered Babylonia, to rebuild Jerusalem and its Temple. **24–26:** The monotheistic theme, with its argument from prophecy, is repeated; cf. vv. 6–8. God had earlier predicted the rebuilding of Jerusalem and the Temple in Jer. 30.18; 31.6–40; 33.10–18; Ezek. chs 40–48.

a Lit. "He shepherds ashes."
b Emendation yields "them," these things.
c Lit. "with none beside me," or (following many Heb. mss., kethib, and ancient versions)
"who was with me?"
d Heb. "His."

28 　　Am the same who says of Cyrus, "He is My
　　　　shepherd;[a]
　　　He shall fulfill all My purposes!
　　　He shall say of Jerusalem, 'She shall be rebuilt,'
　　　And to the Temple: 'You shall be founded again.' "

45 Thus said the LORD to Cyrus, His anointed one—
　　　Whose right hand [b]He has[b] grasped,
　　　Treading down nations before him,
　　　[c]Ungirding the loins of kings,[c]
　　　Opening doors before him
　　　And letting no gate stay shut:
2 　　I will march before you
　　　And level [d]the hills that loom up;[d]
　　　I will shatter doors of bronze
　　　And cut down iron bars.
3 　　I will give you treasures concealed in the dark
　　　And secret hoards—
　　　So that you may know that it is I the LORD,
　　　The God of Israel, who call you by name.
4 　　For the sake of My servant Jacob,
　　　Israel My chosen one,
　　　I call you by name,
　　　I hail you by title, though you have not known
　　　　Me.
5 　　I am the LORD and there is none else;
　　　Beside Me, there is no god.
　　　I engird you, though you have not known Me,
6 　　So that they may know, from east to west,
　　　That there is none but Me.
　　　I am the LORD and there is none else,
7 　　I form light and create darkness,
　　　I make weal and create woe—
　　　I the LORD do all these things.
8 　　Pour down, O skies, from above!
　　　Let the heavens rain down victory!
　　　Let the earth open up and triumph sprout,
　　　Yes, let vindication spring up:
　　　I the LORD have created it.

9 　　Shame on him who argues with his Maker,
　　　Though naught but a potsherd of earth!
　　　Shall the clay say to the potter, "What are you
　　　　doing?

45.1–25: The universal God. This speech focuses on the Persian king Cyrus as the tool through whom God brings salvation not only to Israel but to the whole world. After Cyrus allows the exiles to return to Jerusalem, peoples the world over will recognize the LORD's faithfulness to the covenant made with Israel, and consequently they will join Israel in worshipping the one true God. **1–8: An address to Cyrus, the liberator.** God speaks directly to Cyrus, who does not understand the true nature of his role. **1–3:** Cyrus's victories are summarized. **1:** *His anointed one,* Heb "mashiaḥ," often translated as "Messiah." It is striking that this term is used of Cyrus, and not of the ideal Davidic king, but according to Deutero-Isaiah, a Davidic king does not play a significant role in the expected restoration (see 55.3 n.). **4–8:** God did not give Cyrus these great victories for Cyrus's sake. Rather, the purpose of Cyrus's rise to power is twofold: to liberate Israel, and thus to spread the fame of the one true God of Israel throughout the world. **7:** This v. is quoted at the beginning of the morning service (immediately after the Barekhu or call to prayer), where the word *woe* (or "evil") is replaced with the euphemism, "everything." **9–13: Objection and response.** People (either the Judeans themselves or perhaps the nations of the world) are surprised by God's plan to bring salvation to the exiles by means of a Persian king. God rebukes them for their chutzpah in questioning the means through whom God chose to work. Cf. Isa. 10.15; 29.14–21.

a I.e., the king whom I have designated.　b-b Heb. "I have." Cf. note at 8.11.
c-c I.e., I made them helpless; one who wished to move freely belted his garment around the
waist; cf. "engird," v. 5.
d-d Meaning of Heb. uncertain.

ᵃ⁻Your work has no handles"?⁻ᵃ

10 Shame on him who asks his father, "What are you
begetting?"
Or a woman, "What are you bearing?"

11 Thus said the LORD,
Israel's Holy One and Maker:
ᵇ⁻Will you question Me⁻ᵇ on the destiny of My
children,
Will you instruct Me about the work of My hands?

12 It was I who made the earth
And created man upon it;
My own hands stretched out the heavens,
And I marshaled all their host.

13 It was I who roused himᶜ for victory
And who level all roads for him.
He shall rebuild My city
And let My exiled people go
Without price and without payment
—said the LORD of Hosts.

14 Thus said the LORD:
Egypt's wealth and Nubia's gains
And Sabaites, ᵈ⁻long of limb,⁻ᵈ
Shall pass over to you and be yours,
Pass over and follow you in fetters,
Bow low to you
And reverently address you:
"Only among you is God,
There is no other god at all!

15 You are indeed a God who concealed Himself,
O God of Israel, who bring victory!

16 Those who fabricate idols,
All are shamed and disgraced;
To a man, they slink away in disgrace.

17 But Israel has won through the LORD
Triumph everlasting.
You shall not be shamed or disgraced
In all the ages to come!"

18 For thus said the LORD,
The Creator of heaven who alone is God,
Who formed the earth and made it,
Who alone established it—

13: The exiles will not have to pay any price to Cyrus to gain their liberation. Rather (as the next v. makes clear) God will personally reward the Persian king. **14–17: Cyrus's reward.** God again addresses Cyrus (so Ibn Ezra), describing the vast territories he will receive for restoring Zion. Cf. 43.3. **14:** *Nubia* is the area south of Egypt, often referred to as Ethiopia in most Bible translations (it was probably closer to today's Sudan). *Sabaites* were residents of an area south of Egypt. *Only among you is God,* better, "Indeed, through you God [has worked]." Even far-off nations realize that the God who worked through Cyrus, the God of Israel, is the one true deity. Alternatively (and contrary to the quotation marks in NJPS), these words may be spoken by God to Cyrus, rather than by the African nations. **18–25: Universal recognition of the LORD.** The vv. again rely on the argument from prophecy, which Deutero-Isaiah uses to show the whole world that the LORD is the true master of history. The predictions made to earlier Israelite prophets were not secret, but were made public long ago.

---

a-a *Emendation yields "To its maker, 'You have no hands'?".*
b-b *Heb. imperative.*   c *I.e., Cyrus.*
d-d *Emendation yields "bearing tribute." For "tribute" cf. Ezra 4.20; 6.8; Neh. 5.4.*

He did not create it a waste,
But formed it for habitation:
I am the LORD, and there is none else.

19 I did not speak in secret,
At a site in a land of darkness;
I did not say to the stock of Jacob,
"Seek Me out in a wasteland"—
I the LORD, who foretell reliably,
Who announce what is true.

20 Come, gather together,
Draw nigh, you remnants of the nations!
No foreknowledge had they who carry their
        wooden images
And pray to a god who cannot give success.

21 Speak up, compare testimony—
Let them even take counsel together!
Who announced this aforetime,
Foretold it of old?
Was it not I the LORD?
Then there is no god beside Me,
No God exists beside Me
Who foretells truly and grants success.

22 Turn to Me and gain success,
All the ends of earth!
For I am God, and there is none else.

23 By Myself have I sworn,
From My mouth has issued truth,
A word that shall not turn back:
To Me every knee shall bend,
Every tongue swear loyalty.

24 ᵃThey shall say: "Only through the LORD
Can I find victory and might.ᵃ
When people ᵇtrust inᵇ Him,
All their adversaries are put to shame.

25 It is through the LORD that all the offspring of
        Israel
Have vindication and glory."

46 Belᶜ is bowed, Neboᶜ is cowering,
Their images are a burden for beasts and cattle;
The things youᵈ would carry [in procession]
Are now piled as a burden
On tired [beasts].

23: The nations of the world are invited to share in the worship of the true God and the benefits it brings. **25:** Israel's vindication leads other nations to worship the LORD as well. The mixture of nationalism and universalism here is noteworthy: A universalist outcome results from a particularist victory.

46.1–15: The gods of Babylonia vs. the God of Israel. This short speech contrasts the LORD, who is capable of mighty acts, and the gods of Babylonia, who are shown to be illusions. **1–4: The essential contrast between a God who carries His faithful and gods who must be carried by theirs. 1:** *Bel* is another name for Marduk, the chief deity of Babylon. His son, *Nebo* (Akkadian Nabû), became an increasingly important deity during the last century of Babylonian independence. *Carry [in procession]*: The Babylonians paraded the statues of their gods through the city on major holidays, such as the Akitu or New Year festival.

a-a Emendation yields "Only in the LORD / Are there victory and might for man."
b-b Lit. "come to"; for this idiom cf. Ps. 65.3; Job 6.20.
c Babylonian deities.   d Emendation yields "they."

2   They cowered, they bowed as well,
     They could not rescue the burden,ᵃ
     And they themselves went into captivity.

3   Listen to Me, O House of Jacob,
     All that are left of the House of Israel,
     Who have been carried since birth,
     Supported since leaving the womb:
4   Till you grow old, I will still be the same;
     When you turn gray, it is I who will carry;
     I was the Maker, and I will be the Bearer;
     And I will carry and rescue [you].

5   To whom can you compare Me
     Or declare Me similar?
     To whom can you liken Me,
     So that we seem comparable?
6   Those who squander gold from the purse
     And weigh out silver on the balance,ᵇ
     They hire a metal worker to make it into a god,
     To which they bow down and prostrate
              themselves.
7   They must carry it on their backs and transport it;
     When they put it down, it stands,
     It does not budge from its place.
     If they cry out to it, it does not answer;
     It cannot save them from their distress.
8   Keep this in mind, and ᶜstand firm!ᶜ
     Take this to heart, you sinners!
9   Bear in mind what happened of old;
     For I am God, and there is none else,
     I am divine, and there is none like Me.
10   I foretell the end from the beginning,
     And from the start, things that had not occurred.
     I say: My plan shall be fulfilled;
     I will do all I have purposed.
11   I summoned that swooping bird from the East;ᵈ
     From a distant land, the man for My purpose.
     I have spoken, so I will bring it to pass;
     I have designed it, so I will complete it.
12   Listen to Me, you ᵉstubborn of heart,ᵉ
     Who are far from victory:
13   I am bringing My victory close;

3–4: The maternal image of the LORD is significant here. Cf. 42.13–14; 45.10; 49.14–15; 66.13. **5–7: The folly of idolatry.** Cf. 40.18–20; 44.9–20; Ps. 115.4–8. **8–13: The former and latter things.** The listeners are urged to recall what God did in the past (specifically, God saved and made accurate predictions). These demonstrate the salvation that God will bring in the near future. The reliability of earlier prophets also demonstrates the trustworthiness of Deutero-Isaiah himself. **8:** *Sinners:* God addresses the exiles as rebellious because their forebears' misdeeds caused the exile, but perhaps also because many of them failed to believe in Deutero-Isaiah's message. **10–11:** The argument from prophecy.

a Emendation yields "him who carried [them]"; cf. Targum.
b Lit. "beam [of the balance]."
c-c Meaning of Heb. uncertain.
d I.e., Cyrus; cf. 41.2–3; 44.28–45.1.
e-e Septuagint reads, "who have lost heart."

It shall not be far,
And My triumph shall not be delayed.
I will grant triumph in Zion
To Israel, in whom I glory.

47 Get down, sit in the dust,
Fair Maiden Babylon;
Sit, dethroned, on the ground,
O Fair Chaldea;
Nevermore shall they call you
The tender and dainty one.

2 Grasp the handmill and grind meal.
Remove your veil,
Strip off your train, bare your leg,
Wade through the rivers.

3 Your nakedness shall be uncovered,
And your shame shall be exposed.
I will take vengeance,
^{a-}And let no man intercede.

4 Our Redeemer—LORD of Hosts is His name—
Is the Holy One of Israel.^{-a}

5 Sit silent; retire into darkness,
O Fair Chaldea;
Nevermore shall they call you
Mistress of Kingdoms.

6 I was angry at My people,
I defiled My heritage;
I put them into your hands,
But you showed them no mercy.
Even upon the aged you made
Your yoke exceedingly heavy.

7 You thought, "I shall always be
The mistress still."
You did not take these things to heart,
You gave no thought to the end of it.

8 And now hear this, O pampered one—
Who dwell in security,
Who think to yourself,
"I am, and there is none but me;
I shall not become a widow
Or know loss of children"—

9 These two things shall come upon you,
Suddenly, in one day:

47.1–15: A mock lament over Babylon, or Babylonia (the Heb term "bavel" is used for Babylon, the capital city, and for Babylonia, the country). This poem personifies Babylon as a haughty young woman of great wealth and prestige who has suddenly lost everything. It focuses on the surprising reversal of fortune meted out to the seemingly invincible empire that tormented the Judeans. Taunting songs directed against enemies appear several times in the Bible; see Isa. ch 14; Ezek. chs 27–28. **1–5: Babylon's reversal of fortune.** Once a princess, Babylon now must work as a lowly slavegirl. **1:** *Chaldea*, a synonym for Babylonia; see 43.14 n. **6–7: Babylonia's hubris.** Babylonia never was as strong and self-sufficient as she believed. Her victory resulted only from the LORD's decision to punish Judah. Babylonia took this commission too far, however, and now she must be punished as well. On the hubris of the foreign conqueror who unknowingly does God's work, cf. 10.5–15. **8–15: Babylon is sentenced.** God speaks directly to Babylon, informing her of her fate. **8:** The line spoken here by Babylon is a precise quotation of a line spoken by Nineveh, the capital of Assyria, in Zeph. 2.13. For Deutero-Isaiah, statements that earlier prophets made concerning Assyria should be understood as referring to the Babylonians, who inherited the Assyrians' empire and their role as Israel's oppressors.

---

a-a *Meaning of Heb. uncertain; emendation yields "And not be appeased, / Says our Redeemer, whose name is* LORD *of Hosts, / The Holy One of Israel."*

Loss of children and widowhood
Shall come upon you in full measure,
Despite your many enchantments
And all your countless spells.

10 You were secure in your wickedness;
You thought, "No one can see me."
It was your skill and your science
That led you astray.
And you thought to yourself,
"I am, and there is none but me."

11 Evil is coming upon you
Which you will not know how to ª-charm
    away;⁻ª
Disaster is falling upon you
Which you will not be able to appease;
Coming upon you suddenly
Is ruin of which you know nothing.

12 Stand up, with your spells and your many
    enchantments
On which you labored since youth!
Perhaps you'll be able to profit,
Perhaps you ᵇ-will find strength.⁻ᵇ

13 You are helpless, despite all your art.
Let them stand up and help you now,
The scannersͨ of heaven, the star-gazers,
Who announce, month by month,
Whatever will come upon you.

14 See, they are become like straw,
Fire consumes them;
They cannot save themselves
From the power of the flame;
This is no coal for warming oneself,
No fire to sit by!

15 This is what they have profited you—
The traders you dealt with since youth—
Each has wandered off his own way,
There is none to save you.

48 Listen to this, O House of Jacob,
Who bear the name Israel
And have issued from the waters͏ᵈ of Judah,
Who swear by the name of the LORD
And invoke the God of Israel—
Though not in truth and sincerity—

9–13: Deutero-Isaiah makes frequent reference to the famed magicians and soothsayers of Babylonia, whose skills turn out to be illusions.

48.1–22: Rebuke and consolation. The concluding speech in the first section of Deutero-Isaiah's prophecies (see chs 40–48 n.). It focuses attention on the sins that Israel had committed in the past. By reviewing the reasons Israel deserved punishment, the prophet explains why the exile had to occur and hence reassures the people that the LORD is neither weak nor fickle. The passage may also criticize the faithlessness of the Judean exiles in Babylonia, who were not as receptive to Deutero-Isaiah's message as they should have been. 1–16: The argument from prophecy. In previous passages (43.9–15; 44.6–8, 24–26; 45.18–25; 46.10–11) the prophet directed this argument (at least rhetorically) to foreigners or their gods; Deutero-Isaiah contrasted the illusion in which the Babylonians believed with the reliable LORD of the Israelites and thus rebuked the former. But here the rebuke is directed against the Israelites, who have prayed to idols and have failed to recognize their own God's power.

---

a-a Meaning of Heb. uncertain. Emendation yields "bribe."
b-b Taking 'araṣ as a variant of 'aṣar; cf. 2 Chron. 20.37.
c Meaning of Heb. uncertain.   d Emendation yields "loins."

2   For you[a] are called after [b]the Holy City[b]
     And you[a] do lean on the God of Israel,
     Whose name is LORD of Hosts:

3   Long ago, I foretold things that happened,
     From My mouth they issued, and I announced
          them;
     Suddenly I acted, and they came to pass.

4   Because I know how stubborn you are
     (Your neck is like an iron sinew
     And your forehead bronze),

5   Therefore I told you long beforehand,
     Announced things to you ere they happened—
     That you might not say, "My idol caused them,
     My carved and molten images ordained them."

6   You have [c]heard all this; look, must you not
          acknowledge it?[c]
     As of now, I announce to you new things,
     Well-guarded secrets you did not know.

7   Only now are they created, and not of old;
     [c]Before today[c] you had not heard them;
     You cannot say, "I knew them already."

8   You had never heard, you had never known,
     Your ears were not opened of old.

     Though I know that you are treacherous,
     That you were called a rebel from birth,
9   For the sake of My name I control My wrath;
     To My own glory, [c]I am patient[c] with you,
     And I will not destroy you.

10   See, I refine you, but not as silver;
     I test you in the furnace of affliction.

11   For My sake, My own sake, do I act—
     Lest [My name][d] be dishonored!
     I will not give My glory to another.

12   Listen to Me, O Jacob,
     Israel, whom I have called:
     I am He—I am the first,
     And I am the last as well.

13   My own hand founded the earth,
     My right hand spread out the skies.

     I call unto them, let them stand up.
14   Assemble, all of you, and listen!

9–11: In light of the people's sins, one may wonder why God wants to save them. The prophet answers this potential question: God will save the people for God's own sake, for the nation Israel is linked to God's reputation. Deutero-Isaiah lists several different reasons that the exiles are sure to be saved (see 40.1; 43.4), some of which contradict each other on a strictly literal level. The prophet's goal, however, is not to present a philosophical argument but to convince the exiles of their imminent return to Zion, using various lines of reasoning. These vv. utilize language from Jer. 9.6, and they confirm the accuracy of Jeremiah's predictions. **10:** *Refined,* alternatively, "purchased." *Not as silver,* better, "not for the silver." *Test,* or, "I choose."

a Heb. "they."   b-b Emendation yields "the holy people."
c-c Meaning of Heb. uncertain.
d These words are supplied in some ancient versions; cf. v. 9.

Who among you[a] foretold these things:
[b-]"He whom the Lord loves
Shall work His will against Babylon,
And, with His might, against Chaldea"?[-b]

15 I, I predicted, and I called him;
I have brought him and he shall succeed in his
　　mission.

16 Draw near to Me and hear this:
From the beginning, I did not speak in secret;
From the time anything existed, I was there.[c]

"And now the Lord God has sent me, [d-]endowed
　　with His spirit."[-d]

17 Thus said the Lord your Redeemer,
The Holy One of Israel:
I the Lord am your God,
Instructing you for your own benefit.
Guiding you in the way you should go.

18 If only you would heed My commands!
Then your prosperity would be like a river,
Your triumph like the waves of the sea.

19 Your offspring would be as many as the sand,
Their issue as many as its grains.[e]
Their name would never be cut off
Or obliterated from before Me.

20 Go forth from Babylon,
Flee from Chaldea!
Declare this with loud shouting,
Announce this,
Bring out the word to the ends of the earth!
Say:"The Lord has redeemed
His servant Jacob!"

21 They have known no thirst,
Though He led them through parched places;
He made water flow for them from the rock;
He cleaved the rock and water gushed forth.

22 There is no safety—said the Lord—for the wicked.

49 Listen, O coastlands, to me,
And give heed, O nations afar:
The Lord appointed me before I was born,
He named me while I was in my mother's womb.

a Heb. "them."　　b-b Meaning of Heb. uncertain.
c I.e., I foretold it through prophets.　　d-d Lit. "and His spirit."
e Meaning of Heb. uncertain.

14: A reference to Cyrus, the Persian king. *Chaldea*, a synonym for Babylonia; see 43.14 n. **17–19: An explanation for the exile.** Language used to described the exodus from Egypt in Ps. 81.6–17 is applied to the upcoming exodus from Babylonia. **20–22: Conclusion: The return to Zion is at hand.** Deutero-Isaiah calls on the exiles to leave Babylonia. The prophet took this exhortation seriously: From the beginning of the next ch on, Deutero-Isaiah seems no longer to be located in Babylonia but in Jerusalem. **22:** The same words appear—and make more sense—in 57.21, which marks the end of the second section within Deutero-Isaiah's prophecies. They have been copied here to indicate that this v. also marks the end of a section.

Chs 49–57: Prophecies of Zion. The second of the three sections within chs 40–66 seems to have been written in Jerusalem after the first wave of exiles returned there from Babylonia. Like chs 40–48, it consists of several long speeches, each of which attempts to convince the city of Jerusalem (usually referred to as Zion) or the returned exiles that their current wretched state will be transformed to a glorious one. Many of the arguments the prophet sets forth resemble those found in chs 40–48, but several characteristic themes of that first section no longer appear: Cyrus, Babylonia, the new exodus, and the theme of the former and latter things are never mentioned in chs 49–57. In their place one finds a stronger emphasis on Zion and the servant of the Lord, and one can sense disappointment at the reality of conditions in the restored Zion (cf. Ezra chs 1–3; Haggai; Zech. chs 1–8). This sense of disappointment leads the prophet to condemn the people for certain misdeeds toward the end of this section, in language somewhat harsher than the rebukes found in chs 40–48.

49.1–26: The role of the servant and encouragement for Zion. The

2 He made my mouth like a sharpened blade,
He hid me in the shadow of His hand,
And He made me like a polished arrow;
He concealed me in His quiver.

3 And He said to me, "You are My servant,
Israel in whom I glory."

4 I thought, "I have labored in vain,
I have spent my strength for empty breath."
But my case rested with the LORD,
My recompense was in the hands of my God.

5 And now the LORD has resolved—
He who formed me in the womb to be His
servant—
To bring back Jacob to Himself,
That Israel may be restored to Him.
And I have been honored in the sight of the LORD,
My God has been my strength.

6 For He has said:
"It is too little that you should be My servant
In that I raise up the tribes of Jacob
And restore the survivors of Israel:
I will also make you a light*a* of nations,
That My salvation may reach the ends of the
earth."

7 Thus said the LORD,
The Redeemer of Israel, his Holy One,
b-To the despised one,
To the abhorred nations,-*b*
To the slave of rulers:
Kings shall see and stand up;
Nobles, and they shall prostrate themselves—
To the honor of the LORD, who is faithful,
To the Holy One of Israel who chose you.

8 Thus said the LORD:
In an hour of favor I answer you,
And on a day of salvation I help you—
I created you and appointed you *c*a covenant
people-*c*—
Restoring the land,
Allotting anew the desolate holdings,

9 Saying to the prisoners, "Go free,"
To those who are in darkness, "Show yourselves."

first speech in this section divides into two parts, each of which comforts the people and assures them that Zion's full restoration is not far off. **1–13: The servant of the LORD and universal recognition of God.** The motif of God's servant or servants appeared briefly in chs 40–48, especially in 42.1–9. **1–6:** The servant speaks to the nations of the world as well as the Israelites. The identity of the servant has generated much debate. Most rabbinic commentators and some modern scholars argue that Deutero-Isaiah speaks here in the first person and that these vv. describe the prophet's own mission. Others argue that the whole nation Israel is the servant, and some suggest that an ideal Israel or a faithful subset of the nation is the servant. **5:** *To bring:* The subject of the Heb verb may be either God or the servant. **7–13:** The servant announces that all the world will recognize the one God when the whole Israelite nation returns to its land. At this early stage of Cyrus's reign, only a few Judean exiles took the opportunity to return to Zion. See Ezra chs 1–3. **8:** *A covenant people,* see 42.6 n.

a I.e., the agent of good fortune; cf. 42.1–4; 51.4–5.
b-b Meaning of Heb. uncertain. Emendation yields "Whose being is despised, / Whose body
is detested"; cf. 51.23.
c-c See note b-b at 42.6.

They shall pasture along the roads,
On every bare height shall be their pasture.
10 They shall not hunger or thirst,
Hot wind and sun shall not strike them;
For He who loves them will lead them,
He will guide them to springs of water.
11 I will make all My mountains a road,
And My highways shall be built up.
12 Look! These are coming from afar,
These from the north and the west,
And these from the land of Sinim.[a]
13 Shout, O heavens, and rejoice, O earth!
Break into shouting, O hills!
For the Lord has comforted His people,
And has taken back His afflicted ones in love.

14 Zion says,
"The Lord has forsaken me,
My Lord has forgotten me."
15 Can a woman forget her baby,
Or disown the child of her womb?
Though she might forget,
I never could forget you.
16 See, I have engraved you
On the palms of My hands,
Your walls are ever before Me.
17 Swiftly your children are coming;
Those who ravaged and ruined you shall leave
           you.
18 Look up all around you and see:
They are all assembled, are come to you!
As I live

                    —declares the Lord—

You shall don them all like jewels,
Deck yourself with them like a bride.
19 As for your ruins and desolate places
And your land laid waste—
You shall soon be crowded with settlers,
While destroyers stay far from you.
20 The children [b]you thought you had lost[b]
Shall yet say in your hearing,
"The place is too crowded for me;
Make room for me to settle."
21 And you will say to yourself,
"Who bore these for me
When I was bereaved and barren,

12: *Sinim,* Aswan, in southern Egypt, where a colony of Israelite soldiers lived during the Persian period and before. **14–26: Consolation for Zion.** Zion (i.e., Jerusalem) serves as a metaphor for the nation as a whole; the despair she feels (v. 14) is Israel's, and God speaks words of comfort to Israel through her. **14–23:** A dialogue between God and Zion, which is personified as a bereaved woman. Her "children"—the Judeans—have died or been sent into exile. Jerusalem's population fell after the Babylonians destroyed the city in 586 BCE, and it remained small even when the Persian king Cyrus allowed exiled Judeans to return there. **14–18:** These vv. recall, and reverse, God's complaint in Jer. 2.32. **19–20:** A recollection and reversal of the prophecy of doom in 6.10–12. **22–23:** The reversal of fortune for Zion and the Israelites. The text repeats the promises found in Isa. 11.10–12.3 and Pss. 2; 72. **24–26:** Israel's conqueror must give Israel back to God, and Israel's redemption brings knowledge of the one God to all humanity.

a 1QIs[a] reads "the Syenians"; cf. Ezek. 30.6.   b-b Lit. "of your bereavement."

Exiled and disdained[a]—
By whom, then, were these reared?
I was left all alone—
And where have these been?"

22 Thus said the Lord GOD:
I will raise My hand to nations
And lift up My ensign to peoples;
And they shall bring your sons in their bosoms,
And carry your daughters on their backs.

23 Kings shall tend your children,
Their queens shall serve you as nurses.
They shall bow to you, face to the ground,
And lick the dust of your feet.
And you shall know that I am the LORD—
Those who trust in Me shall not be shamed.

24 Can spoil be taken from a warrior,
Or captives retrieved from a victor?

25 Yet thus said the LORD:
Captives shall be taken from a warrior
And spoil shall be retrieved from a tyrant;
For *I* will contend with your adversaries,
And *I* will deliver your children.

26 I will make your oppressors eat their own flesh,
They shall be drunk with their own blood as with
    wine.
And all mankind shall know
That I the LORD am your Savior,
The Mighty One of Jacob, your Redeemer.

50 Thus said the LORD:
[b]Where is the bill of divorce
Of your mother whom I dismissed?
And which of My creditors was it
To whom I sold you off?
You were only sold off for your sins,
And your mother dismissed for your crimes.

2 Why, when I came, was no one there,
Why, when I called, would none respond?
Is my arm, then, too short to rescue,
Have I not the power to save?
With a mere rebuke I dry up the sea,
And turn rivers into desert.

50.1–51.8: A response to the nation's tribulations. God addresses the Israelites' despair at their plight. The previous section described Deutero-Isaiah's own prophetic mission (which is ultimately the mission of the whole nation) and proceeded to relay God's message to the city of Jerusalem. Similarly, this passage describes Deutero-Isaiah's mission (which is a model for all Israel) while relaying a divine message to the nation. **50.1–3: The relationship between God and Israel endures. 1:** The Israelites viewed themselves metaphorically as God's wife and also as God's children. If the former, they worry that God has divorced them and therefore cannot take them back (cf. Jer. 3.1; Deut. 24.1–4). If the latter, then God has sold them away (cf. Exod. 21.7–11; 2 Kings 4.1). But God insists that no divorce has taken place, and that the children remain God's own property. **2:** Behind God's frustrated words here may lie the failure of the exiles to accept the message of consolation. Only a small number of exiles took the opportunity to return to Zion after Cyrus (the Persian king who conquered Babylonia) allowed them to do so. *Dry up the sea,* an allusion to the splitting of the Reed Sea (see Exod. chs 14–15) and also to stories of divine combat at the time of the world's creation (see 51.9–11, Hab. 2.8–9; Pss. 74.13–15; 89.6–14; Job 26.5–13).

---

a *Meaning of Heb. uncertain.*

b *The mother (the country) has not been formally divorced, nor the children (the people) sold because of poverty. Therefore there is no obstacle to their restoration.*

Their fish stink from lack of water;
They lie dead ª·of thirst.·ª

3   I clothe the skies in blackness
And make their raiment sackcloth.

4   ᵇ·The Lord GOD gave me a skilled tongue,
To know how to speak timely words to the weary.·ᵇ
Morning by morning, He rouses,
He rouses my ear
To give heed like disciples.

5   The Lord GOD opened my ears,
And I did not disobey,
I did not run away.

6   I offered my back to the floggers,
And my cheeks to those who tore out my hair.
I did not hide my face
From insult and spittle.

7   But the Lord GOD will help me—
Therefore I feel no disgrace;
Therefore I have set my face like flint,
And I know I shall not be shamed.

8   My Vindicator is at hand—
Who dares contend with me?
Let us stand up together!ᶜ
Who would be my opponent?
Let him approach me!

9   Lo, the Lord GOD will help me—
Who can get a verdict against me?
They shall all wear out like a garment,
The moth shall consume them.

10   Who among you reveres the LORD
And heeds the voice of His servant?—
Though he walk in darkness
And have no light,
Let him trust in the name of the LORD
And rely upon his God.

11   But you are all kindlers of fire,
ᵈ·Girding on·ᵈ firebrands.
Walk by the blaze of your fire,
By the brands that you have lit!
This has come to you from My hand:
ᵇ·You shall lie down in pain.·ᵇ

4–11: The mission of the prophet and of the nation. As in 49.1–6, Deutero-Isaiah speaks in the first person. By doing so the prophet sets a model that the nation as a whole should follow, since the whole nation has a prophetic role to the world at large. **4–5:** The prophet is a disciple of older prophets, constantly borrowing their words and noting how their predictions proved true. **6–9:** Deutero-Isaiah, like all Israelites, suffered in the exile. But Deutero-Isaiah knows the punishment meted out to the exiles was just, accepts it, and awaits the vindication that surely follows. **10–11:** Israel's response: Some of Deutero-Isaiah's listeners will accept both divine punishment and divine reward, but others will continue to reject God's word, to their own detriment.

---

a-a *Change of vocalization yields "on the parched ground"; cf. 44.3.*

b-b *Meaning of Heb. uncertain.*

c *I.e., as opponents in court; cf. Num. 35.12.*

d-d *Emendation yields "Lighters of."*

51 Listen to Me, you who pursue justice,
You who seek the LORD:
Look to the rock you were hewn from,
To the quarry you were dug from.

2 Look back to Abraham your father
And to Sarah who brought you forth.
For he was only one when I called him,
But I blessed him and made him many.

3 Truly the LORD has comforted Zion,
Comforted all her ruins;
He has made her wilderness like Eden,
Her desert like the Garden of the LORD.
Gladness and joy shall abide there,
Thanksgiving and the sound of music.

4 Hearken to Me, [a]My people,[a]
And give ear to Me, O [a]My nation,[a]
For teaching shall go forth[b] from Me,
My way for the light of peoples.
In a moment I will bring it:

5 The triumph I grant is near,
The success I give has gone forth.
My arms shall [c]provide for[c] the peoples;
The coastlands shall trust in Me,
They shall look to My arm.

6 Raise your eyes to the heavens,
And look upon the earth beneath:
Though the heavens should melt away like smoke,
And the earth wear out like a garment,
And its inhabitants die out [d]as well,[d]
My victory shall stand forever,
My triumph shall remain unbroken.

7 Listen to Me, you who care for the right,
O people who lay My instruction to heart!
Fear not the insults of men,
And be not dismayed at their jeers;

8 For the moth shall eat them up like a garment,
The worm[e] shall eat them up like wool.
But My triumph shall endure forever,
My salvation through all the ages.

a-a Several mss. read "O peoples . . . O nations"; cf. end of this verse and v. 5.
b I.e., through My servant Israel; cf. 42.1–4; 49.6.
c-c Lit. "judge."
d-d Emendation yields "like gnats."
e Heb. sas, another word for "moth."

51.1–8: An exhortation to Israelites who despair. Four brief statements explain why the nation's
current state is not a cause for
hopelessness. Each statement
opens with an imperative verb addressed to the Israelites. 1–3: The
example of Abraham and Sarah:
they, like the current Israelites,
were few in number, yet God multiplied their descendants. 4–5: God
is the source of teaching, and thus
God can indeed save. 4: *Teaching*,
Heb "torah." Cf. Isa. 2.3. 6–7: Two
metaphors emphasize the enduring nature of the salvation that
God brings.

9 Awake, awake, clothe yourself with splendor.
O arm of the LORD!
Awake as in days of old,
As in former ages!
It was you that hacked Rahab[a] in pieces,
That pierced the Dragon.[a]

10 It was you that dried up the Sea,
The waters of the great deep;
That made the abysses of the Sea
A road the redeemed might walk.

11 So let the ransomed of the LORD return,
And come with shouting to Zion,
Crowned with joy everlasting.
Let them attain joy and gladness,
While sorrow and sighing flee.

12 I, I am He who comforts you!
What ails you that you fear
Man who must die,
Mortals who fare like grass?

13 You have forgotten the LORD your Maker,
Who stretched out the skies and made firm the
   earth!
And you live all day in constant dread
Because of the rage of an oppressor
Who is aiming to cut [you] down.
Yet of what account is the rage of an oppressor?

14b Quickly the crouching one is freed;
He is not cut down and slain,
And he shall not want for food.

15 For I the LORD your God—
Who stir up the sea into roaring waves,
Whose name is LORD of Hosts—

16 [c-Have put My words in your mouth
And sheltered you with My hand;-c]
I, who planted[d] the skies and made firm the earth,
Have said to Zion: You are My people!

17 Rouse, rouse yourself!
Arise, O Jerusalem,
You who from the LORD's hand
Have drunk the cup of His wrath,
You who have drained to the dregs
The bowl, the cup of reeling!

51.9–52.12: Lament and response. In the first part of this composition, the people pray for deliverance, bemoaning God's apparent abandonment of them. In the second part, God responds at length, assuring them that they have not been forgotten. **9–11: The people's entreaty.** These vv. contain the people's words to God. As in many psalms of lament, the people recall God's glorious victories in the past in an attempt to goad the LORD to action now. **9:** *Arm of the LORD,* a figure of speech referring to God's strength. **9–10:** *Rahab . . . Dragon . . . abysses of the Sea:* These refer to mythical beings whom God defeated to create the world; cf. 50.2 n. The people argue that the God who defeated the forces of evil at the beginning of time and who split the Reed Sea to liberate the Israelites from Egyptian bondage should use the same divine power to liberate Israel now. **51.12–52.6: God's positive response.** The divine answer echoes the language of the request; see esp. 51.17; 52.1, which echo 51.9. This section borrows vocabulary from several older prophecies: Jer. 4.20; 15.2–5; Isa. 29.9–10. Those passages predicted disaster for Zion and her people; now Deutero-Isaiah at once confirms the accuracy of the older predictions and reverses their message, telling Zion that the period of suffering is coming to an end. This passage also reverses the description of Zion's suffering found in Lam. 2.13–19. This highly allusive passage became the source for another highly allusive poem written 2,000 years later: "Lekha Dodi" (the hymn recited in Jewish liturgy at the outset of the Sabbath) borrows phrasing from these vv. **51.12–16:** God speaks to the nation Israel. Language that described the prophet Jeremiah in Jer. 1.9–10; 11.19–21 is applied to the nation as a whole here. **17–23:** God addresses Jerusalem. Zion, portrayed as a bereaved mother, gets her children back.

a Names of primeval monsters.
b Meaning of verse uncertain. Emendation yields (cf. Jer. 11.19; Job 14.7–9) "Quickly the tree buds anew; / It does not die though cut down, / And its sap does not fail."
c-c I.e., I have chosen you to be a prophet-nation; cf. 49.2; 59.21.
d Emendation yields "stretched out"; cf. Syriac version and v. 13.

18 She has none to guide her
Of all the sons she bore;
None takes her by the hand,
Of all the sons she reared.[a]

19 These two things have befallen you:
Wrack and ruin—who can console you?
Famine and sword—[b-]how shall I[-b] comfort you?

20 Your sons lie in a swoon
At the corner of every street—
Like an antelope caught in a net—
Drunk with the wrath of the LORD,
With the rebuke of your God.

21 Therefore,
Listen to this, unhappy one,
Who are drunk, but not with wine!

22 Thus said the LORD, your Lord,
Your God who champions His people:
Herewith I take from your hand
The cup of reeling,[c]
The bowl, the cup of My wrath;
You shall never drink it again.

23 I will put it in the hands of your tormentors,
Who have commanded you,
"Get down, that we may walk over you"—
So that you made your back like the ground,
Like a street for passersby.

52 Awake, awake, O Zion!
Clothe yourself in splendor;
Put on your robes of majesty,
Jerusalem, holy city!
For the uncircumcised and the unclean
Shall never enter you again.

2 Arise, shake off the dust,
Sit [on your throne], Jerusalem!
Loose the bonds from your neck,
O captive one, Fair Zion!

3 For thus said the LORD:
You were sold for no price,
And shall be redeemed without money.

4 For thus said the Lord GOD:
Of old, My people went down
To Egypt to sojourn there;

52.1–6: God speaks again to Zion, telling her that her nightmare is over. **2:** *Shake off the dust:* As a captive, the city sat in dirt, humiliated. **3:** God did not sell Judah to a creditor (cf. 50.1), and hence Judah still belongs to God. There is no impediment to Judah's redemption.

---

a *To guide a drunken parent home was a recognized filial duty in ancient Canaan and Egypt.*

b-b *Several ancient versions render "who can."*

c *A figure of speech for a dire fate; cf. Jer. 25.15 ff.*

But Assyria has robbed them,
Giving nothing in return.[a]

5   What therefore do I gain here?
                        —declares the LORD—
For My people has been carried off for nothing,
Their mockers howl
                        —declares the LORD—
And constantly, unceasingly,
My name is reviled.

6   Assuredly, My people shall learn My name,
Assuredly [they shall learn] on that day
That I, the One who promised,
Am now at hand.

7   How welcome on the mountain
Are the footsteps of the herald
Announcing happiness,
Heralding good fortune,
Announcing victory,
Telling Zion, "Your God is King!"

8   Hark!
Your watchmen raise their voices,
As one they shout for joy;
For every eye shall behold
The LORD's return to Zion.

9   Raise a shout together,
O ruins of Jerusalem!
For the LORD will comfort His people,
Will redeem Jerusalem.

10 The LORD will bare His holy arm
In the sight of all the nations,
And the very ends of earth shall see
The victory of our God.

11 Turn, turn away, touch naught unclean
As you depart from there;
Keep pure, as you go forth from there,
You who bear the vessels of the LORD![b]

12 For you will not depart in haste,
Nor will you leave in flight;
For the LORD is marching before you,
The God of Israel is your rear guard.

13 "Indeed, My servant shall prosper,
Be exalted and raised to great heights.

---

a *Whereas the Israelites themselves sought hospitality in Egypt, Assyria (i.e., the Chaldean
Empire) has exiled them by force.*
b *Cf. Ezra 1.7–8; 5.14–15.*

4: *Robbed them, giving nothing in return,* or, "oppressed them, gaining
nothing." The Assyrians acquired
no rights to Israel, who still belong
to the LORD. Emendation yields,
"oppressed them due to My
anger"; cf. 10.5. **5:** *Therefore,* rather,
"But now." The current exile in
Babylonia is contrasted with the
people's earlier exiles in Egypt and
in Assyria. *My name is reviled:*
God's own reputation is harmed
by the Babylonian exile, and for
this reason God is sure to liberate
the nation. **6:** *I . . . am now at hand,*
Heb "hineni." Elsewhere in the
Bible this word is used by human
beings responding to a divine call
(e.g., Gen. 22.1, 11; Exod. 3.4).
Only in Deutero-Isaiah does God
call "here I am" to humans (see
also 58.9; 65.1). **7–12: A concluding prophecy of restoration.**
God's response to the nation's
prayer ended in v. 6, and now the
prophet sums up the message: Redemption is at hand. **7–10:** God's
own Presence will return to Jerusalem; the prophet imagines that the
lookouts in Jerusalem's higher
buildings or fortifications will see
God's Presence as it comes toward
the city. Cf. 40.3–5 n. This passage
was composed after some Judeans
had already returned to Jerusalem
but before the full-fledged redemption that Deutero-Isaiah
anticipated had come to pass.
11–12: An exhortation to exiles
still in Babylonia to come to Jerusalem, bearing the Temple vessels
that the Babylonians had taken
from the Temple. Because they will
accompany the divine Presence in
Its journey, they must maintain ritual purity. **12:** The earlier exodus
from Egypt is contrasted with the
imminent exodus from Babylonia.
The former took place in haste and
confusion (see Exod. 12.11; Deut.
16.3), but the new exodus will be
more stately.

52.13–53.12: The servant. One of
the most difficult and contested
passages in the Bible, these fifteen
vv. have attracted an enormous
amount of attention from ancient,
medieval, and modern scholars. In
particular the identity of the ser-

14 Just as the many were appalled at him[a]—
   So marred was his appearance, unlike that of man,
   His form, beyond human semblance—

15 Just so he shall startle[b] many nations.
   Kings shall be silenced because of him,
   For they shall see what has not been told them,
   Shall behold what they never have heard."

53 "Who can believe what we have heard?
   Upon whom has [c]the arm of the LORD[c] been
       revealed?

2 For he has grown, by His favor, like a tree crown,
   Like a tree trunk out of arid ground.
   He had no form or beauty, that we should look
       at him:
   No charm, that we should find him pleasing.

3 He was despised, [d]shunned by men,[d]
   A man of suffering, familiar with disease.
   [e]As one who hid his face from us,[e]
   He was despised, we held him of no account.

4 Yet it was our sickness that he was bearing,
   Our suffering that he endured.
   We accounted him plagued,
   Smitten and afflicted by God;

5 But he was wounded because of our sins,
   Crushed because of our iniquities.
   He bore the chastisement that made us whole,
   And by his bruises we were healed.

6 We all went astray like sheep,
   Each going his own way;
   And the LORD visited upon him
   The guilt of all of us."

a Heb. "you."   b Meaning of Heb. uncertain.
c-c I.e., the vindication which the arm of the LORD effects.
d-d Meaning of Heb. uncertain.   e-e I.e., as a leper; cf. Lev. 13.45 ff.

Messiah is one of the hallmarks of Deutero-Isaiah's outlook (in contrast to that of First Isaiah). Because of marked similarities between the language describing the servant and Jeremiah's descriptions of himself (see Jer. 10.18–24; 11.19), Saadia Gaon argued that the text refers to Jeremiah, while the Talmud (b. Sot. 14a) records the opinion that it describes Moses. Both opinions have been echoed by modern scholars. On the other hand, equally impressive parallels between the servant and First Isaiah can be observed (see ch 6). Furthermore, many passages in Deutero-Isaiah view the prophet Jeremiah as a model for the nation as a whole without equating the nation and that prophet. Christians have argued that this passage in fact predicts the coming of Jesus. Medieval rabbinic commentators devoted considerable attention to refuting this interpretation. The passage is deeply allusive, drawing on the texts from Jeremiah and Isaiah noted above and also on Isa. 1.5–6; 2.12–14; 11.1–10; Ps 91.15–16. **52.12–15: God's first speech.** God describes the servant, who will ultimately, and surprisingly, achieve great things. **14:** *So marred . . . semblance*, rather, "His appearance was more disfigured than any man's, his form, more than any person's." **53.1–11a: The surprised observers' speech.** The identity of the speakers who express their shock at the career of the servant is unclear. Are they the kings and nations of the world (cf. 52.15)? If so, then the servant is probably the nation Israel, and the nations are stunned that such an insignificant and lowly group turns out to have been so important to the divine plan. (Cf. Deut. 7.7.) Alternatively, the speakers may be the Judeans themselves, in which case the servant is either a pious minority (the ideal Israel, in contrast to the mass of Judeans whose faith and behavior miss the mark God set for them) or some individual within the Israelite community. **4–6:** Either the servant suffered on behalf of the speakers (i.e., the guilty were not punished

vant is vigorously debated. Many argue that the servant symbolizes the entire Jewish people. The passage, then, describes the nation's unjust tribulations at the hands of the Babylonians (and later oppressors) as well as the nation's salvific role for the world at large. Others maintain that the passage describes a pious minority within the Jewish people; this minority suffers as a result of the sins committed by the nation at large. (Bolstering these interpretations is the

fact that the term "servant" in Deutero-Isaiah generally refers to the nation as a whole or an idealized representation of the nation; cf. 42.1–9 n.; 18–23 n.; 49.1–13 n.) Other scholars argue that the servant in this passage is a specific individual (cf. 50.4–11 n.). Targum and various midrashim identify the servant as the Messiah, but this suggestion is unlikely, since nowhere else does Deutero-Isaiah refer to the Messiah, and the absence of a belief in an individual

7 He was maltreated, yet he was submissive,
He did not open his mouth;
Like a sheep being led to slaughter,
Like a ewe, dumb before those who shear her,
He did not open his mouth.

8 By oppressive judgment he was taken away,
a-Who could describe his abode?-*a*
For he was cut off from the land of the living
Through the sin of my people, who deserved the
punishment.

9 And his grave was set among the wicked,
b-And with the rich, in his death-*b*—
Though he had done no injustice
And had spoken no falsehood.

10 But the LORD chose to crush him *a*-by disease,
That, if he made himself an offering for guilt,-*a*
He might see offspring*c* and have long life,
And that through him the LORD's purpose might
prosper.

11 Out of his anguish he shall see it;*d*
He shall enjoy it to the full through his devotion.*e*

"My righteous servant makes the many righteous,
It is their punishment that he bears;

12 Assuredly, I will give him the many as his portion,
He shall receive the multitude as his spoil.
For he exposed himself to death
And was numbered among the sinners,
Whereas he bore the guilt of the many
And made intercession for sinners."

54 Shout, O barren one,
You who bore no child!
Shout aloud for joy,
You who did not travail!
For the children of the wife forlorn
Shall outnumber those of the espoused
—said the LORD.

2 Enlarge the site of your tent,
f-Extend the size of your dwelling,-*f*
Do not stint!
Lengthen the ropes, and drive the pegs firm.

a-a Meaning of Heb. uncertain.
b-b Emendation yields "And his tomb with evildoers."
c Emendation yields "His arm," i.e., His vindication; cf. v. 1 with note.
d I.e., the arm of the LORD; see preceding note.
e For this sense of da'ath see 11.2, 9.
f-f Lit. "Let the cloths of your dwelling extend."

at all), or he suffered along with the guilty, even though he himself did not share in the guilt of his fellow Israelites. The former idea (i.e., the notion of vicarious suffering) would be unusual for the Bible; the latter idea (the idea of corporate guilt) is not. **8–9:** *Cut off from the land of the living . . . grave:* Scholars debate whether these lines describe the literal death of the servant or the severe straits he was in. Exaggerated descriptions of one's plight as equivalent to death are common in the Bible; see Pss. 18.5–6; 30.4; Jonah 2.2, 8. **10b–11a:** The servant is vindicated. Either he is saved from a fate like death, or he is actually described as being resurrected. In the latter case, his resurrection is probably a metaphor for the renewal of the nation at the end of the exile. Similarly, in Ezek. ch 37 Israel in exile is described as dead; the nation is brought back to life when the exile ends. **11b–12: God's concluding speech.** God describes the vindication of the servant, echoing and confirming the themes of the spectators' speech.

54.1–17: Zion, rebuilt and secure. As in several earlier speeches, the city of Jerusalem or Zion is portrayed as a woman; cf. 49.14–26; 50.1–3. She is childless (i.e., without inhabitants) and apparently forsaken by her husband (i.e., the LORD). This passage assures her, however, that God remains her husband and protector and that she will soon have abundant children. In other words, the exiles will soon return to Judah. The passage as a whole recalls Hos. ch 1, where similar metaphors convey the message that God will punish but not abandon Israel. Deutero-Isaiah at once confirms the accuracy of Hosea's prophecy of doom while repeating Hosea's assurance that the covenant between God and Israel will endure. **1–5: The prophet comforts Zion.** Due to the exile, Zion seemed empty and in ruins. Deutero-Isaiah assures Zion that not only will she have a tent to live in, she will need to enlarge it to accommodate her abundant

3 For you shall spread out to the right and the left;
   Your offspring shall dispossess nations[a]
   And shall people the desolate towns.

4 Fear not, you shall not be shamed;
   Do not cringe, you shall not be disgraced.
   For you shall forget
   The reproach of your youth,
   And remember no more
   The shame of your widowhood.

5 For He who made you will espouse you—
   His name is "Lord of Hosts."
   The Holy One of Israel will redeem you—
   He is called "God of all the Earth."

6 The Lord has called you back
   As a wife forlorn and forsaken.
   Can one cast off the wife of his youth?
                              —said your God.

7 For a little while I forsook you,
   But with vast love I will bring you back.

8 In slight anger, for a moment,
   I hid My face from you;
   But with kindness everlasting
   I will take you back in love
                  —said the Lord your Redeemer.

9 For this to Me is like the waters[b] of Noah:
   As I swore that the waters of Noah
   Nevermore would flood the earth,
   So I swear that I will not
   Be angry with you or rebuke you.

10 For the mountains may move
   And the hills be shaken,
   But my loyalty shall never move from you,
   Nor My covenant of friendship be shaken
   —said the Lord, who takes you back in love.

11 Unhappy, storm-tossed one, uncomforted!
   I will lay carbuncles[c] as your building stones
   And make your foundations of sapphires.

12 I will make your battlements of rubies,
   Your gates of precious stones,
   The whole encircling wall of gems.

offspring. The theme of Zion abundantly repopulated also appears in 49.17–21. This passage is based on Jer. 10.17–25, where the Judeans who are about to be exiled lament the loss of their children and the destruction of their tent (symbolizing the Temple), their city and kingdom, and their social structures generally. **6–10: God addresses Zion directly. 6–8:** God assures Zion that He has not divorced her (cf. 50.1–3). God's anger was brief and brought about a temporary separation; the reconciliation will last forever. **9–10:** God switches from a marital metaphor to a simile based on the story of Noah (Gen. chs 8–9). The former metaphor implied that the covenant between God and Israel is one of mutual obligation; the allusion to Noah recalls the notion of a covenant of grace, which God unilaterally grants to human beings. Deutero-Isaiah often moves back and forth between portrayals of Israel as God's spouse and God's child, hence insisting that both covenant models are valid; see 49.14–21; 50.1–3. **10:** On the steadfast nature of the covenant, see also Jer. 31.33–35, whose vocabulary and ideas Deutero-Isaiah borrows here. *Friendship,* or, "peace." **11–17: An eternal structure.** God promises that Zion will be rebuilt as a beautiful and enduring city, secure due to God's incomparable protection.

a I.e., the foreigners who had occupied regions from which Israelites had been exiled; cf. 2 Kings 17.24.

b Other Heb. mss. and the ancient versions read "days."

c Taking pukh as a byform of nophekh; so already Rashi.

13   And all your children shall be disciples of the
            Lord,
    And great shall be the happiness of your children;

14   You shall be established through righteousness.
    You shall be safe from oppression,
    And shall have no fear;
    From ruin, and it shall not come near you.

15[a]   Surely no harm can be done
    Without My consent:
    Whoever would harm you
    Shall fall because of you.

16   It is I who created the smith
    To fan the charcoal fire
    And produce the tools for his work;
    So it is I who create
    The instruments of havoc.

17   No weapon formed against you
    Shall succeed,
    And every tongue that contends with you at law
    You shall defeat.
    Such is the lot of the servants of the Lord,
    Such their triumph through Me
                 —declares the Lord.

55

Ho, all who are thirsty,
Come for water,
Even if you have no money;
Come, buy food and eat:
Buy food without money,
Wine and milk without cost.

2   Why do you spend money for what is not bread,
    Your earnings for what does not satisfy?
    Give heed to Me,
    And you shall eat choice food
    And enjoy the richest viands.

3   Incline your ear and come to Me;
    Hearken, and you shall be revived.
    And I will make with you an everlasting covenant,
    The enduring loyalty promised to David.

4   [b] As I made him a leader[c] of peoples,
    A prince and commander of peoples,

5   So you shall summon a nation you did not know,
    And a nation that did not know you
    Shall come running to you [b]—

a Meaning of verse uncertain.
b-b Cf. 2 Sam. 22.44–45 (Ps. 18.44–45).
c Cf. Targum; others "witness."

13: As in Jer. 31.33–35, the people in the restored community will learn God's teaching successfully, thus ensuring the eternal nature of the covenant. *All your children . . . your children,* alternatively: "All those who build you [O Zion] will be learned in the ways of the Lord, and great shall be the well-being of your inhabitants, endowed with understanding." The Heb letters "bnyk" appear twice in this verse, implying at once the idea of "children," "builders," and "those who understand," each of which fits the context of ch 54 (cf. *b. Ber.* 64a). Deutero-Isaiah frequently puns on various meanings of a single word.

55.1–13: An invitation to redemption. This passage differs from many earlier Deutero-Isaianic speeches because of its general nature. It contains few references to the exile or the trek through the desert to Judah, instead couching its description of the upcoming redemption in broad terms that are less anchored in a specific historical situation. The further one reads in chs 40–66, the more one finds a tendency away from concrete language that reflects the situation of the Babylonian exiles and toward phrasing that could apply to any historical era. Also noteworthy is the plea that people abandon sinful behavior, which is absent in the first division of Deutero-Isaiah's work (chs 40–48) but increasingly common in the second and third divisions (chs 49–57, 58–66). **1–5: God's invitation.** It is unclear whether these lines are addressed specifically to Judeans (which is implied by vv. 3–5, 12) or to any human being who wants to recognize the one God (so Ibn Ezra, Radak). *Water,* understood by rabbinic commentators as a metaphor for Torah. **3:** *The enduring loyalty promised to David:* In 2 Sam. 7.8–16 and Ps. 89.4, 20–37, God promised David that his descendants would rule Israel forever as an enduring royal dynasty. Here, Deutero-Isaiah extends that promise to the nation as a whole. The restored Judean commonwealth will have no

For the sake of the LORD your God,
The Holy One of Israel who has glorified you.

6   Seek the LORD while He can be found,
    Call to Him while He is near.
7   Let the wicked give up his ways,
    The sinful man his plans;
    Let him turn back to the LORD,
    And He will pardon him;
    To our God,
    For he freely forgives.
8   For My plans are not your plans,
    Nor are My ways[a] your ways[a]
                          —declares the LORD.
9   But as the heavens are high above the earth,
    So are My ways[a] high above your ways[a]
    And My plans above your plans.
10 For as the rain or snow drops from heaven
    And returns not there,
    But soaks the earth
    And makes it bring forth vegetation,
    Yielding [b]seed for sowing and bread for eating,[b]
11 So is the word that issues from My mouth:
    It does not come back to Me unfulfilled,
    But performs what I purpose,
    Achieves what I sent it to do.
12 Yea, you shall leave[c] in joy and be led home
              secure.
    Before you, mount and hill shall shout aloud,
    And all the trees of the field shall clap their hands.
13 Instead of the brier, a cypress shall rise;
    Instead of the nettle, a myrtle shall rise.
    These shall stand as a testimony to the LORD,
    As an everlasting sign that shall not perish.

56 Thus said the LORD:
    Observe what is right and do what is just;
    For soon My salvation shall come,
    And my deliverance be revealed.

2   Happy is the man who does this,
    The man who holds fast to it:
    Who keeps the sabbath and does not profane it,
    And stays his hand from doing any evil.

a *Emendation yields "words"; cf. v. 11 and 40.8.*
b-b *Lit. "seed for the sower and bread for the eater."*
c *I.e., leave the Babylonian exile.*

one human king, for all its members will have royal status. Thus Deutero-Isaiah transforms the older Davidic covenant by democratizing it. (Cf. Deutero-Isaiah's democratizing of the priesthood in 61.5–6 and n.) The prophet also saves the Davidic promise by means of this transformation, for the more natural reading of the Davidic promise in 2 Sam. ch 7 and Ps. 89 proved incorrect in light of the fall of the Davidic dynasty to the Babylonians in 586 BCE. On Deutero-Isaiah's attitude toward the monarchy, see also 42.1–9; 60.1–22; 65.25. **5:** Israel's royal status yields benefits for all humanity, who come to recognize, as a result of her redemption, the one true God. **6–7: A call to repentance. 8–11: The trustworthiness of God's words.** Deutero-Isaiah picks up the metaphor of water from v. 1 in a new way to emphasize a favorite theme: God's promises and the prophecies God issued through the prophets never fail to come true. Cf. 45.23. The metaphor is significant: God sends rain, which inevitably falls to the ground; then it is absorbed by soil and nourishes vegetation. Humans in turn harvest the vegetation and transform it into food. Similarly, God's word is sure to have a series of effects, the most important of which are indirect and involve human input. **12–13: The exodus from Babylonia.** The prophet again calls on the exiles to leave Babylonia. Cf. 48.20–23; 49.13; 52.11–12. The LORD's promise of glorious restoration will be fulfilled, but as the preceding vv. imply, the nature of their fulfillment may be indirect and will depend on human response to God's invitation. The prophet may be responding to the failure of most Judeans to move back to Zion after the Persian king Cyrus allowed them to do so in the 530s BCE.

56.1–8: Covenant and community. The prophet addresses the role that observance of the commandments plays in forming Judean identity. Not only does it bring happiness for Judeans (v. 2), but it

3 Let not the foreigner say,
Who has attached himself to the LORD,
"The LORD will keep me apart from His people";
And let not the eunuch say,
"I am a withered tree."

4 For thus said the LORD:
"As for the eunuchs who keep My sabbaths,
Who have chosen what I desire
And hold fast to My covenant—

5 I will give them, in My House
And within My walls,
A monument and a name
Better than sons or daughters.
I will give them an everlasting name
Which shall not perish.

6 As for the foreigners
Who attach themselves to the LORD,
To minister to Him,
And to love the name of the LORD,
To be His servants—
All who keep the sabbath and do not profane it,
And who hold fast to My covenant—

7 I will bring them to My sacred mount
And let them rejoice in My house of prayer.
Their burnt offerings and sacrifices
Shall be welcome on My altar;
For My House shall be called
A house of prayer for all peoples."

8 Thus declares the Lord GOD,
Who gathers the dispersed of Israel:
"I will gather still more to those already
          gathered."

9 All you wild beasts, come and devour,
All you beasts of the forest!

10 The[a] watchmen are blind, all of them,
They perceive nothing.
They are all dumb dogs

a Heb. "his."

topic that receives a great deal of attention in the books of Ezra and Nehemiah). Deutero-Isaiah assures the foreigners that through full observance of the covenant they can become like members of the Judean community. This passage shows the beginnings of the religious institution that later came to be called conversion, and rabbinic commentators understand the passage as referring to converts. The rhetoric in the books of Ezra and Nehemiah seems less welcoming to foreigners (see Ezra ch 9), but the policy reflected by those books is in fact identical to that advocated by this prophet: Outsiders become insiders if they embrace the covenant (see Ezra 6.21). **Eunuchs.** Some officials at the Babylonian court (including some exiled Judeans) were castrated. Judeans subject to this fate (and also perhaps foreigners attracted to monotheism) felt cut off from the Judean people in the sense that they would have no descendants; the nation in the future would not include their seed. Further, Lev. 21.16–23 disqualified eunuchs from priestly service; see also Deut. 23.2. Deutero-Isaiah reassures eunuchs that they nonetheless have an enduring future in the sacred community. **5:** *A monument and a name,* a memorial, lit. "a hand and a name" (Heb "yad vashem"). **7:** According to the Torah, foreigners' offerings are welcome at the Temple; see Num. 15.14–16; Lev. 22.18–25 (cf. 1 Kings 8.41–43). This text goes a step further, moving toward the institution of conversion. **8: Ingathering of exiles.** The first wave of exiles who returned to the land of Israel when the Persian king Cyrus allowed them to do so in the 530s was disappointingly small. The prophet looks forward to further, and more impressive, waves of "'aliyah."

56.9–57.21: Castigation and consolation. This section contains Deutero-Isaiah's harshest denunciation of the Judeans' behavior, and in many ways it resembles the rebukes found in First Isaiah, Jere-

allows foreigners to become members of the community as well (vv. 6–7). **1–2: The importance of observing the law.** The passage focuses in particular on the laws of the Sabbath. Cf. 58.13–14. **3–6: Foreigners and eunuchs.** The prophet responds to feelings of exclusion among these groups, emphasizing

that Torah observance renders them complete members of the community. **Foreigners.** During the period of the exile and the return to Zion, some foreigners became attracted to the monotheism of the Judeans. Further, non-Judeans mixed with the Judean population in the land of Israel (a

That cannot bark;
They lie sprawling,[a]
They love to drowse.

11 Moreover, the dogs are greedy;
They never know satiety.
[b-]As for the shepherds, they know not
What it is to give heed.[-b]
Everyone has turned his own way,
Every last one seeks his own advantage.

12 "Come, I'll get some wine;
Let us swill liquor.
And tomorrow will be just the same,
Or even much grander!"

57

The righteous man perishes,
And no one considers;
Pious men are taken away,
And no one gives thought
That because of evil
The righteous was taken away.

2 Yet he shall come to peace,
[c-]He shall have rest on his couch[-c]
Who walked straightforward.

3 But as for you, come closer,
You sons of a sorceress,
You offspring of an adulterer and a harlot![d]

4 With whom do you act so familiarly?
At whom do you open your mouth
And stick out your tongue?
Why, you are children of iniquity,
Offspring of treachery—

5 You who inflame[e] yourselves
Among the terebinths,
Under every verdant tree;
Who slaughter children in the wadis,
Among[f] the clefts of the rocks.

6 [g-]With such[h] are your share and portion,[-g]
They, they are your allotment;
To them you have poured out libations,
Presented offerings.
Should I relent in the face of this?

miah, and other preexilic prophets more than the bulk of the prophecies in chs 40–66. It ends, however, on a typically Deutero-Isaianic note, assuring the faithful among the Judean population that peace and salvation will eventually arrive. The description of the Judeans' sins focuses on Canaanite-influenced idolatry of the sort known from the preexilic era. Some suggest that idolatry became common in the period of the restoration as Judeans intermarried with the local population, a practice repeatedly condemned in the books of Ezra and Nehemiah. Others argue that this passage refers in fact to the sins of the exiles' ancestors and thus does not predict a new disaster but explains the reason for the exile that has already occurred. The whole passage is heavily allusive, borrowing vocabulary and literary motifs from 2.6–21; 6.1–10; 30.9–14; Jer. 2.23–25; 3.12–14; 6.13–14; 12.8–12. **56.9–57.2: Denunciation of Israel's corrupt leaders.** *Wild beasts* (v. 9)—i.e., foreign nations—are invited to devour Israel. Some argue that *dogs* (v. 10) and *shepherds* (v. 11) refer to false prophets, while others view them as political leaders. **57.3–13a: Idolatry.** A condemnation of pagan practices among the Judeans, whether past or present. Sexual imagery pervades this passage, not because the idolatrous worship involved lewd practices but because idolatry among Israelites is compared to adultery: The LORD is Israel's husband, and thus any worship of other gods by Israelites is an act of marital infidelity. **5–7:** Israelite pagan cult ceremonies are often depicted as taking place under leafy trees and on hilltops. Cf. 1 Kings 14.13; 2 Kings 17.10; Hos. 4.13; Jer. 2.20; 3.6–13; Ezek. 6.13.

---

a *Meaning of Heb. uncertain.*
b-b *Meaning of Heb. uncertain. Emendation yields "Neither do the shepherds ever know sufficiency (hon)." Cf.* hon *in Prov. 30.15, 16.*
c-c *Heb. "They shall have rest on their couches."*   d *Lit. "she acts the harlot."*
e *I.e., in some frenzied idolatrous rite.*   f *Heb. "under."*
g-g *Meaning of Heb. uncertain.*   h *The cult-trees referred to above in v. 5.*

7   On a high and lofty hill
    You have set your couch;
    There, too, you have gone up
    To perform sacrifices.
8   Behind the door and doorpost
    You have directed your thoughts;
    ^{a-}Abandoning Me, you have gone up
    On the couch you made so wide.
    You have made a covenant with them,^b
    You have loved bedding with them;^c
    You have chosen lust.^d
9   You have approached ^{-a} the king^e with oil,
    You have provided many perfumes.
    And you have sent your envoys afar,
    Even down to the netherworld.^f
10 Though wearied by much travel,
    You never said, "I give up!"
    You found gratification for your lust,
    And so you never cared.
11 ^{g-}Whom do you dread and fear,
    That you tell lies?^{-g}
    But you gave no thought to Me,
    You paid no heed.
    It is because I have stood idly by ^{h-}so long^{-h}
    That you have no fear of Me.
12 I hereby pronounce ⁱ⁻judgment upon your deeds:⁻ⁱ
    ^{j-}Your assorted [idols]^{-j} shall not avail you,
13 Shall not save you when you cry out.
    They shall all be borne off by the wind,
    Snatched away by a breeze.
    But those who trust in Me shall inherit the land
    And possess My sacred mount.
14 [The LORD] says:
    Build up, build up a highway!
    Clear a road!
    Remove all obstacles
    From the road of My people!
15 For thus said He who high aloft
    Forever dwells, whose name is holy:
    I dwell on high, in holiness;

13b–21: Salvation. Not all Judeans are guilty of these crimes, however, and God recognizes the Judeans' weaknesses and will help them overcome them. The faithful and the penitent will enjoy well-being, even as the inveterate sinners are punished. **14:** Cf. 40.3–5. **15:** The highest of all beings desires to dwell among the lowest. Deutero-Isaiah often portrays the LORD as voluntarily accepting human roles out of love for the people. Cf. 52.6; 58.9; 65.1. **19–21:** The prophet divides the nation into two groups: the true or faithful Israel for whom *it shall be well* (or, "there will be peace," Heb "shalom," v. 19), and the wicked, for whom *there is no safety* (or, "there will be no peace," v. 21). **19:** *The far and the near,* respectively, Israelites who remain in exile and those who already live in the land of Israel.

^{a-a} *Meaning of Heb. uncertain.*   ^b *The cult-trees referred to above in v. 5.*
^c *I.e., with the objects behind door and doorpost.*
^d *Like Ugaritic yd, from root ydd, "to love."*   ^e *Or "Molech."*
^f *I.e., you have brought tribute to alien cults as to a king.*
^{g-g} *Emendation yields "Them you dreaded and feared, / And so you gave them thought."*
^{h-h} *Emendation yields "and shut My eyes."*
ⁱ⁻ⁱ *Lit. "your retribution and your deeds."*
^{j-j} *Brought up from v. 13 for clarity.*

Yet with the contrite and the lowly in spirit—
Reviving the spirits of the lowly,
Reviving the hearts of the contrite.

16 For I will not always contend,
I will not be angry forever:
Nay, I [a-]who make spirits flag,[-a]
Also create the breath of life.

17 For their[b] sinful greed I was angry;
I struck them and turned away in My wrath.
[c-]Though stubborn, they follow the way of their
hearts,[-c]

18 I note how they fare and will heal them:
I will guide them and mete out solace to them,
And to the mourners among them [19]heartening,[d]
comforting[e] words:
It shall be well,
Well with the far and the near
—said the LORD—
And I will heal them.

20 But the wicked are like the troubled sea
Which cannot rest,
Whose waters toss up mire and mud.

21 There is no safety
—said my God—
For the wicked.

58 Cry with full throat, without restraint;
Raise your voice like a ram's horn!
Declare to My people their transgression,
To the House of Jacob their sin.

2 To be sure, they seek Me daily,
Eager to learn My ways.

---

a-a Meaning of Heb. uncertain.
b I.e., Israel's. Cf. "My people," v. 14.
c-c Meaning of Heb. uncertain. Emendation yields "When they have walked broken in the
contrition of their hearts."
d Lit. "the vigor of"; cf. Eccl. 12.1 and postbiblical bori.
e The Heb. nib is otherwise unknown; its meaning is inferred from that of nid (cf. the verb
nad "to condole") in the parallel expression in Job 16.5.

Chs 58–66: Further denunciations and promises. The third section of Deutero-Isaiah's prophetic collection. Chs 34–35 in all likelihood were originally part of this section as well. Like the second section (chs 49–57), these chs were composed in Jerusalem after the initial, somewhat disappointing, restoration had taken place in 538 BCE (see intro. to the book of Isaiah, section on chs 40–66). Several characteristics that begin to emerge in chs 49–57 become more pronounced here. The prophet rebukes the nation for moral and religious shortcomings. Further, Deutero-Isaiah responds to complaints regarding the full redemption's delay. The theme of the cleavage between faithful and unfaithful Judeans becomes a main focus of attention. On the other hand, several chs, especially 60–62 and parts of 65–66, recall the most exuberant prophecies of chs 40–48; these chs insist that the full redemption predicted in the earliest chs of Deutero-Isaiah's collection will indeed take place: All the exiles will return to the land of Israel, the nations of the world will join Israel in worshipping the one true God, and the Presence of God will journey back to Jerusalem, bringing great joy to the faithful within Israel and among the nations.

58.1–15: True piety and false piety. The prophet denounces the Judeans, focusing not on pagan practices (as in ch 57) but on apparently proper religious practices that the Judeans perform hypocritically. Lying behind the passage is an implied question: Why have the predictions of glorious restoration found in chs 40–48 not come true? Exiles had indeed returned to Jerusalem, but—contrary to what one expected from the opening chs of Deutero-Isaiah's work—the land remained under foreign control (the Persians having replaced the Babylonians as overlords), conditions were difficult, and God's presence was not manifest there. (On the difficulties facing the early postexilic community, see Ezra chs 4–6; Hag. chs 1–2; Zech. chs 1, 3.) Deutero-Isaiah maintains that it is now the people's sins that prevent the full-fledged restoration from taking place. **1–7: Fasting and justice.** The Judeans observe rituals such as fasting, but they do so only for their own benefit, not out of true devotion. Real humility toward God would engender a desire for justice toward the weak, compassion toward the downtrodden, and charity toward the poor. Then fasting would involve a willingness to give up one's own things rather than the hope to acquire salvation. These vv. borrow ideas and vocabulary from

Like a nation that does what is right,
That has not abandoned the laws of its God,
They ask Me for the right way,
They are eager for the nearness of God:

3 "Why, when we fasted, did You not see?
When we starved our bodies, did You pay no
    heed?"
Because on your fast day
You see to your business
And oppress all your laborers!

4 Because you fast in strife and contention,
And you strike with a wicked fist!
Your fasting today is not such
As to make your voice heard on high.

5 Is such the fast I desire,
A day for men to starve their bodies?
Is it bowing the head like a bulrush
And lying in sackcloth and ashes?
Do you call that a fast,
A day when the LORD is favorable?

6 No, this is the fast I desire:
To unlock fetters of wickedness,
And untie the cords of ᵃ·the yoke·ᵃ
To let the oppressed go free;
To break off every yoke.

7 It is to share your bread with the hungry,
And to take the wretched poor into your home;
When you see the naked, to clothe him,
And not to ignore your own kin.

8 Then shall your light burst through like the dawn
And your healing spring up quickly;
Your Vindicator shall march before you,
The Presence of the LORD shall be your rear guard.

9 Then, when you call, the LORD will answer;
When you cry, He will say: Here I am.
If you banish ᵃ·the yoke·ᵃ from your midst,
ᵇ·The menacing hand,·ᵇ and evil speech,

10 And you offer your compassionᶜ to the hungry
And satisfy the famished creature—
Then shall your light shine in darkness,
And your gloom shall be like noonday.

11 The LORD will guide you always;
He will slake your thirst in ᵈ·parched places·ᵈ

Mic. 3.6–12. **2:** *The right way,* alternatively, "victorious judgments." People pray for divine intervention in their quarrels against others; their prayers and fasts have selfish purposes, not sacred ones. **8–9a: The result of true righteousness.** Cf. 40.3; 52.12. Deutero-Isaiah repeats the earlier predictions that God's own Presence will return to Zion. Here, however, the prophecy is conditional: Only when the Judeans' behavior warrants divine presence will God arrive. **9a:** *Here I am,* Heb "hineni." See 52.6 n. **9b–12: Righteousness and restoration.** Although some exiles returned to Zion after the Persians defeated the Babylonians in 538, the land of Israel remained for the most part in ruins. The prophet attempts to explain why the rebuilding of the cities destroyed by the Babylonians has been delayed. **13–14: The Sabbath.** Deutero-Isaiah does not reject ritual in favor of ethical action but calls on the nation to attend to both, and focuses especially on the observance of the Sabbath. Cf. 56.6. These vv. borrow vocabulary from Deut. 32.9–13.

---

a-a *Change of vocalization yields "lawlessness"; cf.* muṭṭeh, *Ezek. 9.9.*
b-b *Lit. "Extending the finger."*
c *Some Heb. mss. and ancient versions read "bread."*   d-d *Meaning of Heb. uncertain.*

And give strength to your bones.
You shall be like a watered garden,
Like a spring whose waters do not fail.

12 Men from your midst shall rebuild ancient ruins,
You shall restore foundations laid long ago.
And you shall be called
"Repairer of fallen walls,
Restorer of lanes for habitation."

13 If you ᵃ‑refrain from trampling‑ᵃ the sabbath,
From pursuing your affairs on My holy day;
If you call the sabbath "delight,"
The Lᴏʀᴅ's holy day "honored";
And if you honor it and go not your ways
Nor look to your affairs, nor strike bargains—

14 Then you ᵇ‑can seek the favor of the Lᴏʀᴅ.‑ᵇ
I will set you astride the heights of the earth,
And let you enjoy the heritage of your father
     Jacob—
For the mouth of the Lᴏʀᴅ has spoken.

59 No, the Lᴏʀᴅ's arm is not too short to save,
Or His ear too dull to hear;

2 But your iniquities have been a barrier
Between you and your God,
Your sins have made Him turn His face away
And refuse to hear you.

3 For your hands are defiled with crimeᶜ
And your fingers with iniquity.
Your lips speak falsehood,
Your tongue utters treachery.

4 No one sues justly
Or pleads honestly;
They rely on emptiness and speak falsehood,
Conceiving wrong and begetting evil.

5 They hatch adder's eggs
And weave spider webs;
He who eats of those eggs will die,
And if one is crushed, it hatches out a viper.

6 Their webs will not serve as a garment,
What they make cannot serve as clothing;
Their deeds are deeds of mischief,
Their hands commit lawless acts,

7 Their feet run after evil,
They hasten to shed the blood of the innocent.

59.1–21: Rebuke, confession, and reconciliation. This ch presents a three-part dialogue. The prophet reprimands the nation; the nation, or at least the faithful among them, acknowledge their misdeeds; and then the prophet announces that God will bring justice and mercy to the people. God speaks directly to the faithful in the last v. This ch, like the previous one, attributes the delay of the redemption predicted in chs 40–48 to the people's sins. **1–8: Sin and its consequences. 1–2:** Here, as in 40.27; 49.14; 50.1–2, Deutero-Isaiah responds to specific complaints uttered by contemporaries. The Babylonians have been defeated, as Deutero-Isaiah and earlier prophets predicted, but the new age has failed to materialize: The exiles have not all returned to Zion, and the land remains mostly desolate. Consequently, some Judeans speculated that the Lᴏʀᴅ was not able to save them, or that God did not listen to their prayers. The prophet retorts that Israel's sins, not God's abilities, are the root of the problem. Earlier, Deutero-Isaiah seemed to think that sins were only a part of Israel's past, and that God would automatically treat the nation with grace after their punishment in Babylon (40.2; 43.25; 48.11), but now that an imperfect restoration has taken place, the prophet recognizes the continuing existence of sin and its unhappy consequences. **2:** *Your iniquities . . . Your sins:* The Heb word order emphasizes these nouns. Therefore, translate: "It is your *iniquities* that have been a barrier. . . . It is your *sins* that have made Him turn. . . ."

a-a Lit. "turn back your foot from."   b-b Cf. Ps. 37.4; Job 22.26–27; 27.10.
c Or "blood."

—901—

Their plans are plans of mischief,
Destructiveness and injury are on their roads.

8　They do not care for the way of integrity,
There is no justice on their paths.
They make their courses crooked,
No one who walks in them cares for integrity.

9　"That is why redress is far from us,
And vindication does not reach us.
We hope for light, and lo! there is darkness;
For a gleam, and we must walk in gloom.

10　We grope, like blind men along a wall;
Like those without eyes we grope.
We stumble at noon, as if in darkness;
ᵃAmong the sturdy, we areᵃ like the dead.

11　We all growl like bears
And moan like doves.
We hope for redress, and there is none;
For victory, and it is far from us.

12　For our many sins are before You,
Our guilt testifies against us.
We are aware of our sins,
And we know well our iniquities:

13　Rebellion, faithlessness to the LORD,
And turning away from our God,
Planning fraud and treachery,
Conceiving lies and uttering them with the
　　　throat.ᵇ

14　And so redress is turned back
And vindication stays afar,
Because honesty stumbles in the public square
And uprightness cannot enter.

15　Honesty has been lacking,
He who turns away from evil is despoiled."

The LORD saw and was displeased
That there was no redress.

16　He saw that there was no man,
He gazed long, but no one intervened.
Then His own arm won Him triumph,
His victorious right handᶜ supported Him.

17　He donned victory like a coat of mail,
With a helmet of triumph on His head;
He clothed Himself with garments of retribution,
Wrapped himself in zeal as in a robe.

9–15a: Confession. 9–11: The Judeans lament their fate. They thought that *vindication* (v. 9) was at hand, only to be disappointed. **11:** *Hope*, or, "anticipate." **12–15a:** The faithful confess their sins. Rather than distancing themselves from those responsible for the misdeeds, they acknowledge that they share culpability for their neighbors' sins. **15b–20: God's response.** God brings justice, which is good news for the faithful and dreadful news for everyone else. The phrasing here is often used of foreign nations in the Bible; here the guilty among Israel bear the brunt of divine wrath along with evildoers from other nations. **20:** *Those in Jacob who turn back from sin:* It is the penitent Israelites, not the whole nation, who will enjoy the salvation long predicted and thus far delayed. **21: The eternal covenant.** God speaks directly to the penitent. Cf. Jer. 31.31.

a-a Meaning of Heb. uncertain. Emendation yields "In the daytime . . ."
b Lit. "heart"; see note at 33.18 and frequently elsewhere.　　c Cf. Ps. 98.1–2.

18   a-According to their deserts,
       So shall He repay -ᵃ fury to His foes;
       He shall make requital to His enemies,
       Requital to the distant lands.
19   From the west, they shall revereᵇ the name of the
            LORD,
       And from the east, His Presence.
       For He shall come like a hemmed-in stream
       Which the wind of the LORD drives on;
20   He shall come as redeemer to Zion,
       To those in Jacob who turn back from sin
                                    —declares the LORD.

²¹ And this shall be My covenant with them, said the
LORD: My spiritᶜ which is upon you, and the words which
I have placed in your mouth, shall not be absent from
your mouth, nor from the mouth of your children, nor
from the mouth of your children's children—said the
LORD—from now on, for all time.ᵈ

60 Arise, shine, for your light has dawned;
       The Presence of the LORD has shone upon you!
2   Behold! Darkness shall cover the earth,
       And thick clouds the peoples;
       But upon you the LORD will shine,
       And His Presence be seen over you.
3   And nations shall walk by your light,
       Kings, by your shining radiance.

4   Raise your eyes and look about:
       They have all gathered and come to you.
       Your sons shall be brought from afar,
       Your daughters like babes on shoulders.
5   As you behold, you will glow;
       Your heart will throb and thrill—
       For the wealth of the seaᵉ shall pass on to you,
       The riches of nations shall flow to you.

a-a Meaning of Heb. uncertain.
b Or (with a number of mss. and editions) "see."
c I.e., the gift of prophecy; cf., e.g., 61.1.
d Israel is to be a prophet-nation; cf. 51.16.
e Emendation yields "coastlands."

Chs 60–62: Encouragement to Zion. This lengthy poem portrays Jerusalem (Zion) as a bereaved woman. In this respect it resembles many passages encountered in the previous section of Deutero-Isaiah's work, chs 49–57. Its enthusiasm and optimism recall the prophecies in chs 40–48, and like them it heralds the dawn of a new age. The restored Zion will be home for a righteous nation newly returned to its land and its God; universal recognition of the one God will lead all the nations to enrich Zion and her inhabitants. Unlike the prophecies in chs 40–48, however, this passage puts relatively little emphasis on the return from the exile and does not mention the fall of Babylonia. This section of the book was composed after the Persians under Cyrus defeated the Babylonians in 538 BCE. The restoration of Zion that followed proved in most ways disappointing (see chs 49–57 n.). Rather than giving up hope, the prophet repeats the earlier message, insisting that the LORD will become manifest to humanity and that Jerusalem will eventually achieve peace, security, wealth, and glory. The prophet focuses less on the return to Zion, since it has already begun. **60.1–22: Royal city, royal nation.** Throughout these vv., the prophet uses vocabulary and motifs associated with royalty in biblical and ancient Near Eastern literature. In particular, Deutero-Isaiah borrows royal vocabulary from texts that are concerned with the Davidic dynasty, including Isa. ch 11; Ps. 72. Here, however, the motifs are not applied to a Davidic king. Instead, they are transferred to the city of Zion and to the Israelite nation as a whole; the text makes no mention of the Davidic family. This prophet does not look forward to the arrival of a human Messiah to liberate the Israelites or a human king to govern them. Rather, God will rule the nation directly in the future, and the whole nation will enjoy royal status. Cf. 55.3 n. and also the democratization of the priesthood in 61.5–6. **60.1–3: Light shines in the darkness.** The prophet speaks to Zion, which literally becomes a light to the nations. Cf. 42.6; 49.6. **60.4–16: Zion and the nations.** Because the nations of the world will recognize and fear God, they will bring tribute to Zion. This passage deliberately echoes Isa. 2.1–4, but Deutero-Isaiah offers a different picture of what the nations will do: They will transport Judean exiles to Jerusalem and add to the city's

6   Dust clouds of camels shall cover you,
Dromedaries of Midian and Ephah.
They all shall come from Sheba;
They shall bear gold and frankincense,
And shall herald the glories of the LORD.

7   All the flocks of Kedar shall be assembled for you,
The rams of Nebaioth shall serve your needs;
They shall be welcome offerings on My altar,
And I will add glory to My glorious House.

8   Who are these that float like a cloud,
Like doves to their cotes?
9   ᵃˑBehold, the coastlands await me,ˑᵃ
With ᵇˑships of Tarshishˑᵇ in the lead,
To bring your sons from afar,
And theirᶜ silver and gold as well—
For the name of the LORD your God,
For the Holy One of Israel, who has glorified you.

10   Aliens shall rebuild your walls,
Their kings shall wait upon you—
For in anger I struck you down,
But in favor I take you back.

11   Your gates shall always stay open—
Day and night they shall never be shut—
To let in the wealth of the nations,
With their kings in procession.

12   For the nation or the kingdom
That does not serve you shall perish;
Such nations shall be destroyed.

13   The majesty of Lebanon shall come to you—
Cypress and pine and box—
To adorn the site of My Sanctuary,
To glorify the place where My feet rest.

14   Bowing before you, shall come
The children of those who tormented you;
Prostrate at the soles of your feet
Shall be all those who reviled you;
And you shall be called
"City of the LORD,
Zion of the Holy One of Israel."
15   Whereas you have been forsaken,
Rejected, with none passing through,

wealth. Isaiah's universalism gives way to a more national set of concerns. **6.** *Midian,* an area in the Sinai, inhabited by nomadic traders. *Ephah,* a Midianite tribe. *Sheba,* Yemen, the southwest corner of the Arabian peninsula, renowned for its wealth and exotic goods. **7:** *Kedar,* a tribe of nomadic traders located in the extreme north of the Arabian desert. *Nebaioth,* the Nabateans, an Arabian tribe located east of the Dead Sea. *Rams:* The Heb term could refer to animals or to political leaders. *They shall be welcome offerings:* If "rams" refers to animals, then translate, "They will go up willingly on My altar." If "rams" refers to leaders, then translate "They will offer acceptable offerings on My altar." The latter translation may suggest that foreigners will be able to serve in priestly roles in the Temple of the future. Cf. 54.7; 66.21. The issue is debated in the Babylonian Talmud (*b. A. Z.* 23b). **11:** Jerusalem will be secure and therefore the city gates will be kept open continuously. **13:** The rebuilt Temple, like the First Temple, will be constructed with wood from Lebanon; cf. 1 Kings 5.15–25. **14–16:** A reversal of fortune.

a-a *Emendation yields "The vessels of the coastlands are gathering."*
b-b *See note at 2.16.*   c *I.e., of the people of the coastlands.*

I will make you a pride everlasting,
A joy for age after age.

16 You shall suck the milk of the nations,
Suckle at royal breasts.[a]
And you shall know
That I the LORD am your Savior,
I, The Mighty One of Jacob, am your Redeemer.

17 Instead of copper I will bring gold,
Instead of iron I will bring silver;
Instead of wood, copper;
And instead of stone, iron.
And I will appoint Well-being as your
   government,
Prosperity as your officials.

18 The cry "Violence!"
Shall no more be heard in your land,
Nor "Wrack and ruin!"
Within your borders.
And you shall name your walls "Victory"
And your gates "Renown."

19 No longer shall you need the sun
For light by day,
Nor the shining of the moon
For radiance [by night[b]];
For the LORD shall be your light everlasting,
Your God shall be your glory.

20 Your sun shall set no more,
Your moon no more withdraw;
For the LORD shall be a light to you forever,
And your days of mourning shall be ended.

21 And your people, all of them righteous,
Shall possess the land for all time;
They are the shoot that I planted,
My handiwork in which I glory.

22 The smallest shall become a clan;
The least, a mighty nation.
I the LORD will speed it in due time.

61 The spirit of the Lord GOD is upon me,
Because the LORD has anointed me;
He has sent me as a herald of joy to the humble,
To bind up the wounded of heart,
To proclaim release to the captives,
Liberation to the imprisoned;

2 To proclaim a year of the LORD's favor

60.17–22: The city transformed. Jerusalem and its inhabitants will be secure and prosperous, and God's Presence will dwell in the city once again. **19–20:** According to biblical writers, the divine Presence consists of or is surrounded by an extraordinarily bright light (see Exod. 24.16–16; Isa. 4.5; Ezek. 1.26–28; 10.4; 43.2; Ps. 104.2). Because God's Presence will dwell on Zion, neither the sun nor the moon will be visible, much less necessary. **61.1–9: Jubilee for Jerusalem.** The identity of the speaker in these vv. is debated. It is possible that Zion speaks, but in the next passage, the speaker addresses Zion. Hence it is more likely that the speaker is the prophet. The text describes the prophet's divine inspiration and God-given mission. **1:** *Proclaim release:* The phrasing comes from Lev. 25.10, which discusses Israelite farmers who lost their land and were forced into indentured servitude. Leviticus rules that they may leave their servitude and regain their land every fifty years. Deutero-Isaiah applies this concept to the nation as a whole: In 586 it lost its land and was forced to live elsewhere. Fifty years later, its period of service ended when the Edict of Cyrus allowed them to leave Babylonia and to regain their ancestral land.

a Lit. "breasts of kings" or "breasts of kingdoms."
b So 1QIsᵃ, Septuagint, and Targum.

And a day of vindication by our God;
To comfort all who mourn—

3   ^{a-}To provide for^{-a} the mourners in Zion—
To give them a turban instead of ashes,
The festive ointment instead of mourning,
A garment of splendor instead of a drooping
       spirit.
They shall be called terebinths of victory,
Planted by the Lord for His glory.

4   And they shall build the ancient ruins,
Raise up the desolations of old,
And renew the ruined cities,
The desolations of many ages.

5   Strangers shall stand and pasture your flocks,
Aliens shall be your plowmen and vine-trimmers;

6   While you shall be called "Priests of the Lord,"
And termed "Servants of our God."
You shall enjoy the wealth of nations
And revel^b in their riches.

7   Because your shame was double—
^{c-}Men cried, "Disgrace is their portion"^{-c}—
Assuredly,
They shall have a double share in their land,
Joy shall be theirs for all time.

8   For I the Lord love justice,
I hate ^{d-}robbery with a burnt offering.^{-d}
I will pay them their wages faithfully,
And make a covenant with them for all time.

9   Their offspring shall be known among the nations,
Their descendants in the midst of the peoples.
All who see them shall recognize
That they are a stock the Lord has blessed.

10   I greatly rejoice in the Lord,
My whole being exults in my God.
For He has clothed me with garments of triumph,
Wrapped me in a robe of victory,
Like a bridegroom adorned with a turban,
Like a bride bedecked with her finery.

11   For as the earth brings forth her growth
And a garden makes the seed shoot up,
So the Lord God will make
Victory and renown shoot up
In the presence of all the nations.

5–6: The nations serve the Judeans (cf. 60.4–16), and the Judeans in turn serve the nations as priests. The priestly role that once belonged to the descendants of Aaron alone (i.e., the "Kohanim"; see Num. ch 18) is now extended to the whole nation. Cf. the idea of the democratization of the monarchy, discussed in 55.3 n.; 60.1–22 n. **61.10–62.7: Triumph for Zion.** The prophet speaks on behalf of the people. Royal motifs are applied to the prophet, to Zion, and thus to the whole nation; cf. Ps. 132.9–18. **61.10–62.2:** The nations witness the surprising vindication of Israel.

---

a-a Meaning of Heb. uncertain.   b Meaning of Heb. uncertain.
c-c Emendation yields "They inherited disgrace as their portion."
d-d Emendation yields "the robbing of wages."

62

For the sake of Zion I will not be silent,
For the sake of Jerusalem I will not be still,
Till her victory emerge resplendent
And her triumph like a flaming torch.

2 Nations shall see your victory,
And every king your majesty;
And you shall be called by a new name
Which the LORD Himself shall bestow.

3 You shall be a glorious crown
In the hand of the LORD,
And a royal diadem
In the palm of your God.

4 Nevermore shall you be called "Forsaken,"
Nor shall your land be called "Desolate";
But you shall be called "I delight in her,"
And your land "Espoused."
For the LORD takes delight in you,
And your land shall be espoused.

5 As a youth espouses a maiden,
ᵃ⁻Your sons⁻ᵃ shall espouse you;
And as a bridegroom rejoices over his bride,
So will your God rejoice over you.

6 Upon your walls, O Jerusalem,
I have set watchmen,
Who shall never be silent
By day or by night.
O you, the LORD's remembrancers,ᵇ
Take no rest

7 And give no rest to Him,
Until He establish Jerusalem
And make her renowned on earth.

8 The LORD has sworn by His right hand,
By His mighty arm:
Nevermore will I give your new grain
To your enemies for food,
Nor shall foreigners drink the new wine
For which you have labored.

9 But those who harvest it shall eat it
And give praise to the LORD;
And those who gather it shall drink it
In My sacred courts.

10 Pass through, pass through the gates!

62.2–6: The prophet addresses Jerusalem and informs her of the reversal of her sad plight. **6–7:** The postexilic setting is crucial for understanding these vv. The full redemption predicted for Zion has not yet arrived, even though some exiles have returned. Therefore the watchmen remind God that Jerusalem still awaits aid, for the city is not yet firmly established. **8–12: God addresses Zion.** Responding to the prophet's entreaties in vv. 6–7, God speaks directly to Zion. The LORD confirms the prophet's words, assuring the city that redemption will indeed come. **8–9:** Those who farm will enjoy the fruit of their own labor. Contrast Deut. 28.30–34.

a-a *Change of vocalization yields "He who rebuilds you."*
b *I.e., the watchmen just mentioned.*

Clear the road for the people;
Build up, build up the highway,
Remove the rocks!
Raise an ensign over the peoples!

11 See, the LORD has proclaimed
To the end of the earth:
Announce to Fair Zion,
Your Deliverer is coming!
See, his reward is with Him,
His recompense before Him.[a]

12 And they shall be called, "The Holy People,
The Redeemed of the LORD,"
And you shall be called, "Sought Out,
A City Not Forsaken."

63 Who is this coming from Edom,
In crimsoned garments from Bozrah—
Who is this, majestic in attire,
[b]Pressing forward[b] in His great might?
"It is I, who contend victoriously,
Powerful to [c]give triumph."[c]

2 Why is your clothing so red,
Your garments like his who treads grapes?[d]

3 "I trod out a vintage alone;
[e]Of the peoples[e] no man was with Me.
I trod them down in My anger,
Trampled them in My rage;
Their life-blood[f] bespattered My garments,
And all My clothing was stained.

4 For I had planned a day of vengeance,
And My year of redemption arrived.

5 Then I looked, but there was none to help;
I stared, but there was none to aid—
So My own arm wrought the triumph,
And [g]My own rage[g] was My aid.

6 I trampled peoples in My anger,
[h]I made them drunk with[h] My rage,
And I hurled their glory to the ground."

7 I will recount the kind acts of the LORD,
The praises of the LORD—

a See note at 40.10.   b-b Meaning of Heb. uncertain; emendation yields "striding."
c-c Change of vocalization yields "Who contest triumphantly"; cf. 19.20.
d Lit. "in a press."   e-e Emendation yields "Peoples, and . . ."
f Meaning of Heb. uncertain.
g-g Many mss. read weṣidqathi "My victorious [right hand]"; cf. 59.16.
h-h Many mss. and Targum read "I shattered them in"; cf. 14.25.

10: The road is for the use not only of Judeans who remain in exile but also for the divine Presence (v. 11). Cf. 40.3; 49.11. *Raise an ensign* or flag to guide the exiles back to the land of Israel.

63.1–6: The divine warrior. A short and disturbing passage concerning divine vengeance against God's enemies, symbolized especially by the Edomites. This passage is closely connected with ch 34, which also belongs to the Deutero-Isaianic collection; there, too, the prophet predicted a great slaughter in the land of Edom. On the Edomites and the background of this ch, see 34.1–17 n. **1:** God comes from the south, covered with the blood of enemies. A speaker (perhaps the prophet, perhaps the inhabitants or watchmen of Jerusalem) notices a figure approaching from the south and asks who it is; God replies in the second half of the v. *Edom* is the land southeast of Judah. *Botzrah* is a city in Edom. **2–6:** The speaker asks another question, and God gives a lengthier response.

63.7–64.11: A psalm of lament. A communal complaint, this text is spoken by the nation and addressed to God; it may also include lines spoken by God in response, which is a typical feature of a lament. The lament follows the pattern of similar prayers found in the book of Psalms. The presence of a psalm in prophetic literature is not unusual; see Isa. 33.1–9; Jonah ch 2. As is normal in laments, the description of the nation's current plight and the request for help are preceded by a review of God's mighty acts in the past. Deutero-Isaiah may have composed this prayer, or the prophet may have included (and perhaps modified) a psalm already in use. **63.7–14: God's mighty acts recalled.** Before outlining the complaint and the request for divine aid, the prayer calls God's kind deeds to mind. It is because God acted successfully and graciously in the past that the nation expects that God will intervene now. These

62

For all that the LORD has wrought for us,
The vast bounty to the House of Israel
That He bestowed upon them
According to His mercy and His great kindness.

8 He thought: Surely they are My people,
Children who will not play false.
ᵃSo He was their Deliverer.

9 In all their troubles He was troubled,
And the angel of His Presence delivered them.⁻ᵃ
In His love and pity
He Himself redeemed them,
Raised them, and exalted them
All the days of old.

10 But they rebelled, and grieved
His holy spirit;
Then He became their enemy,
And Himself made war against them.

11 Then theyᵇ remembered the ancient days,
ᶜHim, who pulled His people⁻ᶜ out [of the water]:
"Where is He who brought them up from the Sea
Along with the shepherdᵈ of His flock?
Where is He who put
In their midst His holy spirit,

12 Who made His glorious arm
March at the right hand of Moses,
Who divided the waters before them
To make Himself a name for all time,

13 Who led them through the deeps
So that they did not stumble—
As a horse in a desert,

14 Like a beast descending to the plain?"
'Twas the spirit of the LORD ᵉgave them rest;⁻ᵉ
Thus did You shepherd Your people
To win for Yourself a glorious name.

15 Look down from heaven and see,
From Your holy and glorious height!
Where is Your zeal, Your power?
Your yearning and Your love
Are being withheld from us!ᶠ

vv. at once bolster the Judeans' confidence and goad the LORD to live up to the divine reputation. **9:** As rendered in the NJPS, this v. reflects an important tendency of Deutero-Isaiah's theology: God participates in the suffering of the nation. Cf. 57.15. But many regard the translation in translators' note *a-a* as more accurate. **10:** Here again the prophet mentions God's pain. **11:** *They* (Heb "he") *remembered*: The subject of this verb is not clear: "He" may refer to God or to the nation as a collective. It is also possible to translate, "He who pulled his people out [of the water] remembered the ancient days," but even then it is not clear whether "He who pulled . . ." refers to God or to Moses. *Where is He who brought . . . :* The identity of the speaker here through v. 14a is not clear. One possibility is that the Judeans speak, wondering where their savior is (so most rabbinic commentators). Alternatively, God may ask these questions, as if saying, "Long ago I saved Israel—whatever became of that side of Me?" In that case, vv. 11b–14 mark the beginning of God's movement from wrath to grace. *Along with,* alternatively, "Specifically." *Shepherd of His flock:* The flock is the nation Israel; the shepherd is either Moses or God. (If the translation "shepherds" found in translators' note *d* is correct, then this word refers to Moses and Aaron and perhaps also to Miriam.) **63.15–64.11: Complaint and request for help.** Having expressed confidence in God's ability to save, the speaker now calls out for God's attention (63.15; 64.8), describes their current lamentable state (63.18–19a; 64.8–10), and requests divine intervention (63.19b–64.1; 64.8; 64.11). The combination of these four elements is very common in psalms of lament; see 33.2–9 n.

a-a Ancient versions read "So He was their Deliverer / ⁹In all their troubles. / No [so kethib] angel or messenger, / His own Presence delivered them." Cf. Deut. 4.37 and note.
b Heb. "he."
c-c Heb. moshe ʿammo, a play on the name Moshe (Moses).
d So many mss. and ancient versions; other texts "shepherds."
e-e Emendation yields "guided them."
f Heb. "me." Emendation yields "[Where are] Your yearning and Your love? / Let them not be restrained!"

16 Surely You are our Father:
    Though Abraham regard us not,
    And Israel recognize us not,
    You, O LORD, are our Father;
    From of old, Your name is "Our Redeemer."
17 Why, LORD, do You make us stray from Your ways,
    And turn our hearts away from revering You?
    Relent for the sake of Your servants,
    The tribes that are Your very own!
18 Our foes have trampled Your Sanctuary,
    Which Your holy people ᵃ‑possessed but a little
        while.ᵃ
19 We have become as a people You never ruled,
    To which Your name was never attached.

    If You would but tear open the heavens and come
        down,

64 So that mountains would quake before You—
    ᵇ‑As when fire kindles brushwood,
    And fire makes water boil—
    To make Your name known to Your adversaries
    So that nations will tremble at Your Presence,
2   When You did wonders we dared not hope for,
    You came down
    And mountains quaked before You.
3   Such things had never been heard or noted.
    No eye has seen [them], O God, but You,
    Who act for those who trust in You.ᶜ
4   Yet you have struck him who would gladly do
            justice,
    And remember You in Your ways.
    It is because You are angry that we have sinned;
    ᵈ‑We have been steeped in them from of old,
    And can we be saved?‑ᵈ
5   We have all become like an unclean thing,
    And all our virtues like a filthy rag.
    We are all withering like leaves,
    And our iniquities, like a wind, carry us off.
6   Yet no one invokes Your name,
    Rouses himself to cling to You.
    For You have hidden Your face from us,
    And ᵉ‑made us melt because of‑ᵉ our iniquities.
7   But now, O LORD, You are our Father;

63.16: *Israel:* Here this name refers
not to the nation as a whole but to
the patriarch Jacob; see Gen. 32.29;
35.9. **63.17, 64.4:** These vv. are remarkable and rather daring for
their assertion that God, too, must
accept some responsibility for the
Judeans' sins. Their continuing
hardships have worn away their
hope (so Radak). If the LORD
would intervene more quickly on
their behalf, they would have clear
reason to abandon their misdeeds
and adopt a firm belief in God's
authority. God's response to the
nation's sins has created a cycle:
Crime leads to punishment, punishment to disbelief, disbelief to
more crime. Some rabbinic commentators reject this interpretation, however, arguing that
only Israel is responsible for its
sins, and that these vv. do not
attribute responsibility to God.
63.18: As this v. indicates, the surrounding passage was written before the Temple was rebuilt in 516
(see also 64.9–10).

---

a-a Meaning of Heb. uncertain.   b Meaning of vv. 1–4 uncertain.
c Heb. "Him."
d-d Emendation yields "Because You have hidden Yourself we have offended." For the
thought cf. 63.17.
e-e Emendation yields "delivered us into the hands of . . ."

We are the clay, and You are the Potter,
We are all the work of Your hands.
8 Be not implacably angry, O LORD,
Do not remember iniquity forever.
Oh, look down to Your people, to us all!
9 Your holy cities have become a desert:
Zion has become a desert,
Jerusalem a desolation.
10 Our holy Temple, our pride,
Where our fathers praised You,
Has been consumed by fire:
And all that was dear to us is ruined.
11 At such things will You restrain Yourself, O LORD,
Will You stand idly by and let us suffer so heavily?

65 ᵃ˙I responded to˙ᵃ those who did not ask,
I was at hand to those who did not seek Me;
I said, "Here I am, here I am,"
To a nation that did not invoke My name.
2 I constantly spread out My hands
To a disloyal people,
Who walk the way that is not good,
Following their own designs;
3 The people who provoke My anger,
Who continually, to My very face,
Sacrifice in gardens and burn incense on tiles;
4 Who sit inside tombs
And pass the night in secret places;
Who eat the flesh of swine,
With broth of unclean things in their bowls;
5 Who say, "Keep your distance! Don't come closer!
ᵇ˙For I would render you consecrated."˙ᵇ
Such things make My anger rage,
Like fire blazing all day long.
6 See, this is recorded before Me;
I will not stand idly by, but will repay,
Deliver ᶜ˙their ᵈ sins˙ᶜ into their bosom,
7 And the sins of their fathers as well
—said the LORD—
For they made offerings upon the mountains
And affronted Me upon the hills.
I will count out their recompense in full,ᵉ

65.1–66.24: Blessing and doom. Earlier Deutero-Isaiah alluded to a distinction between faithful and sinful Judeans, intimating that the final act of salvation will benefit only the former; see 57.19–21, 59.1–21, and passages which contrast the ideal servant nation and the blind servant, such as 42.1–9, and 42.18–43.8. Here the prophet sharpens this distinction. The nation includes both those who patiently wait for the LORD's salvation and those who have taken up the worship of other deities in addition to or in place of the true God. The latter will suffer the sort of punishment often associated in the Bible with Assyrians, Babylonians, and Edomites. Conversely, the righteous from other nations will enjoy the privilege of worshipping at Zion. **65.1–16: The faithful and the apostates within Israel.** The opening vv. set up the contrast at the heart of this unit by describing the behavior and fate of each group. **1–2:** God responds to the nation, even though it includes sinners, and even though it may not seek God. **1:** This initial v. seems to respond directly to the last v. of the previous ch. *Here I am*, Heb "hineni"; see 52.6 n. **2:** *Spread out My hands:* Normally, humans pray to God by spreading out their hands (Exod. 9.29, 33; 1 Kings 8.22, 38; Isa. 1.15), but here, in an extraordinary gesture, the LORD stretches hands out to human beings. Cf. 52.6 n.; 57.15 n.; 63.9–10 n. **3–5:** A description of pagan practices adopted by some Israelites. **4:** *Who sit inside tombs:* Worship of deceased ancestors was common among Canaanites, and the Bible often warns Israelites against any such rite. See Lev. 19.31; 20.6, 27; Deut. 18.11. **6–7:** The punishment for these sins.

a-a Lit. "I let Myself be inquired of . . ."
b-b Taking qedashtikha as equivalent to qiddashtikha, cf. Ezek. 44.19; others "For I am holier than thou."
c-c Brought up from v. 7 for clarity.   d Heb. "your."
e Taking rishonah as equivalent to beroshah; cf. Lev. 5.24; Jer. 16.18. Meaning of Heb. uncertain.

Into their bosoms.

8   Thus said the LORD:
As, when new wine is present in the cluster,
One says, "Don't destroy it; there's good in it,"
So will I do for the sake of My servants,
And not destroy everything.

9   I will bring forth offspring from Jacob,
From Judah heirs to My mountains;
My chosen ones shall take possession,
My servants shall dwell thereon.

10   Sharon[a] shall become a pasture for flocks,
And the Valley of Achor a place for cattle to lie
        down,
For My people who seek Me.

11   But as for you who forsake the LORD,
Who ignore My holy mountain,
Who set a table for Luck[b]
And fill a mixing bowl for Destiny:[b]

12   I will destine you for the sword,
You will all kneel down, to be slaughtered—
Because, when I called, you did not answer,
When I spoke, you would not listen.
You did what I hold evil,
And chose what I do not want.

13   Assuredly, thus said the Lord GOD:
My servants shall eat, and you shall hunger;
My servants shall drink, and you shall thirst;
My servants shall rejoice, and you shall be
        shamed;

14   My servants shall shout in gladness,
And you shall cry out in anguish,
Howling in heartbreak.

15   You shall leave behind a name
By which My chosen ones shall curse:
"So may the Lord GOD slay you!"
But His servants shall be given a [c]different name.[c]

16   For whoever blesses himself in the land
Shall bless himself by the true God;
And whoever swears in the land
Shall swear by the true God.
The former troubles shall be forgotten,
Shall be hidden from My eyes.

8–10: The righteous remnant. Some Judeans reject the sins just described, and they will receive the promises of salvation. **10:** *Sharon,* the coastal plain from Jaffa to Haifa, a very fertile area marking the western extreme of the land of Israel. *Achor,* a valley near Jericho, a desolate area marking the land's eastern extreme. **11–16:** The prophet contrasts the fates of loyal and sinful Israelites.

a Emendation yields "Jeshimon," the bleak southeast corner of the Jordan Valley; cf. Num. 21.20; 23.8.
b Names of heathen deities.
c-c I.e., a name to be used in blessing.

17 For behold! I am creating
    A new heaven and a new earth;
    The former things shall not be remembered,
    They shall never come to mind.

18 Be glad, then, and rejoice forever
    In what I am creating.
    For I shall create Jerusalem as a joy,
    And her people as a delight;

19 And I will rejoice in Jerusalem
    And delight in her people.
    Never again shall be heard there
    The sounds of weeping and wailing.

20 No more shall there be an infant or graybeard
    Who does not live out his days.
    He who dies at a hundred years
    Shall be reckoned a youth,
    And he who fails to reach a hundred
    Shall be reckoned accursed.

21 They shall build houses and dwell in them,
    They shall plant vineyards and enjoy their fruit.

22 They shall not build for others to dwell in,
    Or plant for others to enjoy.
    For the days of My people shall be
    As long as the days of a tree,
    My chosen ones shall outlive[a]
    The work of their hands.

23 They shall not toil to no purpose;
    They shall not bear children [b]for terror,[-b]
    But they shall be a people blessed by the LORD,
    And their offspring shall remain with them.

24 Before they pray, I will answer;
    While they are still speaking, I will respond.

25 The wolf and the lamb shall graze together,
    And the lion shall eat straw like the ox,
    And the serpent's food shall be earth.
    In all My sacred mount[c]
    Nothing evil or vile shall be done
                    —said the LORD.

66 Thus said the LORD:
    The heaven is My throne
    And the earth is My footstool:
    Where could you build a house for Me,
    What place could serve as My abode?

17–25: The renewal of creation. This passage recalls the initial prophecies of Deutero-Isaiah in its exuberant tone and literary style, but the nature of the prediction goes beyond those found in chs 40–48: The world itself will be transformed in the new age that God brings. **20–23:** While the new age will be one of extraordinary longevity, these vv. do not predict eternal life or the resurrection of the dead, in contrast to rabbinic notions of the messianic era. **24:** In 51.9–11 and chs 63–64, the people wondered whether God listens to their prayers. God answers this question here: In the future, God will answer prayers before the people even utter them. **25:** This v. quotes two lines from 11.6–9. In that passage First Isaiah predicted a new era ushered in by an ideal Davidic king, but Deutero-Isaiah leaves the human king out of this re-prediction. Cf. 42.1–9 n.; 55.3 n.; 60.1–22 n. **66.1–4: Temple and sacrifice.** Deutero-Isaiah takes up an old prophetic theme. Although God commanded the nation to offer sacrifices, God does not need sacrifices. Neither generous attention to the Temple nor punctilious observance of cultic ritual grants Judeans license to sin. **1:** The Temple plays an important role in the prophet's thinking (see 44.28; 56.5–7; 64.10; 66.20). Nonetheless, the prophet recognizes that God hardly needs that particular building; the Temple exists for the sake of humanity, not for the benefit of God. Cf. 1 Kings 8.27.

a Lit. "wear out."
b-b Emendation yields "in vain."
c See note at 11.9.

2 All this was made by My hand,
   And thus it all came into being
                    —declares the LORD.
   Yet to such a one I look:
   To the poor and brokenhearted,
   Who is concerned about My word.

3a As for those who slaughter oxen and slay
            humans,
   Who sacrifice sheep and immolate[b] dogs,
   Who present as oblation the blood of swine,
   Who offer[c] incense and worship false gods—
   Just as they have chosen their ways
   And take pleasure in their abominations,

4 So will I choose to mock them,
   To bring on them the very thing they dread.
   For I called and none responded,
   I spoke and none paid heed.
   They did what I deem evil
   And chose what I do not want.

5 Hear the word of the LORD,
   You who are concerned about His word!
   Your kinsmen who hate you,
   Who spurn you because of Me,[d] are saying,
   "Let the LORD manifest His Presence,
   So that we may look upon your joy."
   But theirs shall be the shame.

6 Hark, tumult from the city,
   Thunder from the Temple!
   It is the thunder of the LORD
   As He deals retribution to His foes.

7 Before she labored, she was delivered;
   Before her pangs came, she bore a son.

8 Who ever heard the like?
   Who ever witnessed such events?
   Can a land pass through travail
   In a single day?
   Or is a nation born
   All at once?
   Yet Zion travailed
   And at once bore her children!

2: Cf. 57.15. **3:** This v. presents four lines in which a legitimate action is paired with an illegitimate one. The prophet condemns people who participate in legitimate or even sacred actions but also commit sins, whether by acting immorally toward other human beings or by practicing idolatrous rites in addition to worshipping the true God. The prophet fights not only outright apostasy but also pious hypocrisy. Cf. 1.10–20; 29.13; 58.1–14. **5–18a: Deliverance and destruction.** In highly emotional tones, the prophet lashes out against those disloyal to the LORD and predicts vindication for the faithful. This section passes abruptly from one subject to the other. **5–6:** The fate of the foes. **5:** *Your kinsmen . . . joy:* According to the NJPS, the enemies (who reject the LORD) mock the faithful, sarcastically saying, "*Let the* LORD *manifest His Presence. . . .*" Another translation, which more closely follows the Heb cantillation (see 6.13 n.), reads, "Your brothers who hate you and reject you say [self-righteously], 'For my sake the LORD will manifest His presence!' But we [the truly righteous] will see their joy discomfited." In this translation both groups, the prophet's and the enemies', regard themselves as followers of the LORD, but the other group will be unmasked as hypocritical when the LORD appears. **7–14:** Jerusalem consoled. As in previous passages, Jerusalem is portrayed as a bereaved woman (see 49.14–26; 50.1–3; 51.23; 54.1–17; chs 60–62). She will suddenly, without pain, bear children and become a bustling city, full of life.

a Vv. 3–4 refer to practitioners of idolatrous rites; cf. v. 17 and 57.5–8; 65.1–12.
b Lit. "break the necks of."
c Heb. mazkir refers to giving the "token portion" ('azkarah); cf. Lev. 2.2, etc.
d Lit. "My name."

9   Shall I who bring on labor not bring about
        birth?
                        —says the LORD.
    Shall I who cause birth shut the womb?
                        —said your God.

10   Rejoice with Jerusalem and be glad for her,
    All you who love her!
    Join in her jubilation,
    All you who mourned over her—

11   That you may suck from her breast
    Consolation to the full,
    That you may draw from her bosom^a
    Glory to your delight.

12   For thus said the LORD:
    I will extend to her
    Prosperity like a stream,
    The wealth of nations
    Like a wadi in flood;
    And you shall drink of it.
    You shall be carried on shoulders
    And dandled upon knees.

13   As a mother comforts her son
    So I will comfort you;
    You shall find comfort in Jerusalem.

14   You shall see and your heart shall rejoice,
    Your limbs shall flourish like grass.
    The power of the LORD shall be revealed
    In behalf of His servants;
    But He shall rage against His foes.

15   See, the LORD is coming with fire—
    His chariots are like a whirlwind—
    To vent His anger in fury,
    His rebuke in flaming fire.

16   For with fire will the LORD contend,
    With His sword, against all flesh;
    And many shall be the slain of the LORD.

¹⁷ Those who sanctify and purify themselves to enter the groves, ^bimitating one in the center,^{-b} eating the flesh of the swine, the reptile, and the mouse, shall one and all come to an end—declares the LORD. ¹⁸ᶜFor I [know] their deeds and purposes.

11: The Israelites, as Zion's children, take consolation from the city's breasts. **13:** The metaphor suddenly changes, and God is portrayed as the nation's mother. Cf. the feminine images of God in 42.13–14; 45.10; 49.14–15. **14b–18a:** Attention switches to the apostates within Israel, who will be punished rather than comforted. **17:** Another description of pagan rites among the Israelites. **18b–21:** Universal recognition of the LORD and the ingathering of exiles. All nations will come to know the one God and will travel to the Temple in Jerusalem. This passage repeats the prophecy of First Isaiah and Micah found in Isa. 2.1–4 and Mic. 4.1–4. Deutero-Isaiah adds that the nations of the world will bring exiled Israelites back to the land of Israel. **18:** *Behold My glory,* or "My Presence." This line repeats a prediction with which Deutero-Isaiah began this collection; see 40.5.

---

a *Cf. Akkadiam zīzu, Arabic zīzat, "udder."*
b-b *Meaning of Heb. uncertain.*
c *Exact construction of this verse uncertain; for the insertions in brackets, cf. Kimhi.*

[The time] has come to gather all the nations and tongues; they shall come and behold My glory. [19] I will set a sign among them, and send from them survivors to the nations: to Tarshish, Pul, and Lud—that draw the bow—to Tubal, Javan, and the distant coasts, that have never heard My fame nor beheld My glory. They shall declare My glory among these nations. [20] And out of all the nations, said the LORD, they shall bring all your brothers on horses, in chariots and drays, on mules and dromedaries, to Jerusalem My holy mountain as an offering to the LORD—just as the Israelites bring an offering in a pure vessel to the House of the LORD. [21] And from them likewise I will take some to be ᵃ·levitical priests,·ᵃ said the LORD.

22   For as the new heaven and the new earth
        Which I will make
        Shall endure by My will
                                —declares the LORD—
        So shall your seed and your name endure.
23   And new moon after new moon,
        And sabbath after sabbath,
        All flesh shall come to worship Me
                                —said the LORD.

24   They shall go out and gaze
        On the corpses of the men who rebelled against
            Me:
        Their worms shall not die,
        Nor their fire be quenched;
        They shall be a horror
        To all flesh.

        And new moon after new moon,
        And sabbath after sabbath,
        All flesh shall come to worship Me
                                —said the LORD.

a-a *Some Heb. mss. read "priests and Levites."*

19: *Set a sign among them,* i.e., God will perform a miracle that will convince them that the LORD is the only true God. *Survivors,* i.e., of the disaster described in v. 15. *Tarshish,* possibly an area west of Gibraltar in Spain. *Pul,* possibly a scribal error for "Put," an area in Libya. *Lud, Tubal,* areas in Asia minor (present-day Turkey). *Javan,* Greece. **21:** *From them likewise . . . :*

This v. allows two interpretations: (1) members of these other nations, having recognized the true God, will serve as priests in Jerusalem (a radical departure from Num. ch 18, which limits the priesthood to descendants of Moses' brother Aaron); or (2) some of the exiled Israelites whom the nations bring back to the land of Israel will serve as priests

alongside the priests who are already in Jerusalem. Cf. 61.5–6.
22–24: Reward and punishment. A final description of the fates awaiting those who accept the LORD and those who reject the LORD. The distinction between Judeans and non-Judeans is not mentioned here; the worshippers of the LORD in v. 23 include *all flesh,* not just Israelites; and *the men who rebelled* against God in v. 24 include Israelites, as the preceding two chs make clear. Thus the book ends on a highly universal note.
24: After worshipping (vv. 22–23), the righteous will pass by the Valley of Gei Hinnom, immediately south of the Temple Mount, and there they will see the burning corpses of those who rebelled against God. Many medieval rabbinic commentators take this v. as a reference to Gehinnom or hell, where sinners suffer punishment forever (or, according to Targum, until the righteous take pity on them and ask that the punishment cease). It is not clear, however, that Deutero-Isaiah imagines the sinners as remaining cognizant or in any sense alive; rather, the eternal fire burns but does not consume their corpses as a sign to those who pass by. Nonetheless, the later Jewish belief of punishment after death in a location called Gehinnom developed out of this v. On the idea of life after death in the Bible see 14.9–11 n.; 26.19 n.; Dan. 12.2 n. *And new moon . . . the LORD:* In Jewish practice, v. 23 is always printed again after v. 24, so that the book ends on a positive note. Cf. the end of Malachi, Ecclesiastes, and Lamentations. Because the *new moon* and the *sabbath* are mentioned together in v. 23, this chapter is read as the haftorah when Rosh Ḥodesh (the beginning of the month) occurs on a Sabbath.

יִרְמְיָה

Jeremiah

Character of the Work

THE BOOK OF JEREMIAH presents oracles attibuted to the prophet Jeremiah son of Hilkiah and narratives that depict the major events of his lifetime. Jeremiah lived during one of the most crucial and terrifying periods in the history of the Jewish people in biblical times: the destruction of Jerusalem and the Temple of Solomon, followed by the beginning of the Babylonian exile. Because he is one of the key witnesses to the last years of the kingdom of Judah, Jeremiah emerges as one of the major figures who grappled with the theological problems posed by the destruction of the nation, and who laid the foundations for the restoration of Jerusalem and the Temple in the years following the end of the exile. In the course of his struggles to understand the tragic events of his lifetime, he tells the reader more about himself than any other prophet, including his anguish and empathy at the suffering of his people, his outrage at God for forcing him to speak such terrible words of judgment against his own nation, and his firm belief that the people of Israel would return to their land and rebuild Jerusalem once the period of punishment was over.

The introduction to the book in 1.1–3 identifies Jeremiah as a priest from the city of Anathoth in the territory of the tribe of Benjamin. He is therefore a descendant of the priestly line of Eli, who presided as high priest in the sanctuary at Shiloh in the early years of Israel's history in the land (1 Sam. chs 1–4). Elide priests served as Israel's chief priests until the reign of King Solomon, who expelled Abiathar from Jerusalem to Anathoth in favor of Zadok, a high priest under David who founded the Zadokite priestly line in Jerusalem (1 Kings chs 1–2). The introduction further states that Jeremiah spoke from the thirteenth year of the reign of King Josiah son of Amon of Judah (627 BCE), through the reign of King Jehoiakim son of Josiah (608–598), and until the end of the eleventh year of King Zedekiah son of Josiah (597–586) when Jerusalem went into exile.

Thus, like Moses, who was of Levitical descent, Jeremiah is a priest and prophet who guided his people for forty years—often in the face of stiff opposition—but, unlike Moses who led the people from Egypt into the promised land, Jeremiah saw the exile of his people from that same promised land and lived out his own days in Egypt. He was a constant opponent of King Jehoiakim, an Egyptian sympathizer who led his nation into war against Babylonia, and of King Zedekiah, a Babylonian appointee who was unable to prevent a second war against Babylonia. Jeremiah claimed that Judah must submit to Babylonia or suffer the consequences, and he pointed to the destruction of his own ancestral sanctuary at Shiloh to make his point: The people must observe God's teaching *(torah)*, including its moral injunctions and its portrayal of Egypt as Israel's oppressor, rather than rely on the security symbolized by the existence of the Jerusalem Temple. He adhered to earlier traditions, especially Deuteronomy, which reflects a similar viewpoint concerning the necessity of observing *torah* and the consequences for failing to do so. Indeed, his oracles also frequently cite the earlier words of the prophet Isaiah son of Amoz, who spoke during the 8th century when Assyria threatened Israel, but Jeremiah apparently believed that Isaiah's words of judgment—and restoration—would not be realized until his own time, when the Babylonians would replace the Assyrians as God's agent of punishment. He was repeatedly imprisoned and castigated as a traitor for his views. When the Babylonians offered him a comfortable life in exile in recognition for his efforts, he refused it in order to remain with his people and begin the process of rebuilding even though the exile had just begun. Ultimately, Jeremiah fled to Egypt (ch 43), and he likely died there.

The Composition of Jeremiah

RABBINIC TRADITION MAINTAINS that Jeremiah wrote his own book as well as the books of Kings and Lamentations (*b. B. Bat.* 15a). The modern view is that, although the book of Jeremiah contains an extensive collection of the prophet's oracles, the present form of the book is not entirely the work of Jeremiah. The prophet's oracles appear in a narrative biographical framework in which other writers provide information about the prophet, the circumstances in which he spoke, and the major events of his life. Thus, the introduction in 1.1–3 provides basic information concerning Jeremiah's identity, home, and the years of his prophetic career; a series of prophetic word formulas ("the word which came to Jeremiah from the LORD" [7.1; 11.1; etc.]) introduce each of the major sections of the book. Jeremiah's oracles appear primarily in chs 2–25, 30–31, and 46–51, but they are interspersed with narratives, especially in chs 26–29, 32–45, and 52, that provide important information concerning the circumstances in which he spoke.

The book itself claims that the prophet's companion, the scribe Baruch ben Neriah, wrote several versions of Jeremiah's oracles (see esp. ch 36), and this may account for many of the narratives about the prophet. Furthermore, the literary style of the narratives and their overall perspective concerning the relationship between God and Israel correspond markedly to the narrative traditions of the books of Kings. Some modern scholars therefore maintain that Jeremiah and perhaps Baruch are associated with circles that composed the Deuteronomistic History (Deuteronomy, Joshua, Judges, Samuel, and Kings; see p. 453). Nevertheless, these observations do not account for the full compositional history of the book. Jeremiah appears in two versions: the Hebrew Masoretic Text that appears in all Jewish Bibles and that stands as the basis for the book in Protestant Christian circles, and the Greek Septuagint version that originally served as Scripture in the Roman

Catholic and Eastern Orthodox Christian traditions. Although the Greek version contains many of the same oracles and narratives as the Hebrew version, it is approximately one-eighth shorter and its content appears in a markedly different order; for instance, the oracles concerning the nations appear as chs 46–51 in the Hebrew version, but in the Greek version they appear as chs 25–31 with a different sequence of nations. Because the text of the Greek version corresponds with fragments of a Hebrew version of Jeremiah found among the Dead Sea Scrolls, many interpreters argue that the Greek version of the book represents an early edition of Jeremiah that was later expanded and rearranged to form the present Hebrew edition of the book. Other fragments of Jeremiah that correspond to the Hebrew Masoretic Text also appear among the Dead Sea Scrolls, indicating that the two versions of the book circulated among Jews for several centuries following the lifetime of the prophet. This of course points to the likelihood that writers other than Jeremiah or Baruch had a hand in the book's composition. The fact that 51.64 ends "Thus far the words of Jeremiah," but the book contains an additional chapter, is but one reflection of its complicated editorial history. Many modern scholars believe that an original Jeremianic core, largely poetic in nature, was supplemented by prose authors from the school of Deuteronomy, who re-edited the book and brought it more in line with Deuteronomic ideas and terminology. Though this theory has much to commend it, it is very difficult to disentangle the editorial layers of the book.

Guide to Reading

ALTHOUGH THE INTRODUCTION to the book indicates that Jeremiah spoke for a period of forty years from the reign of Josiah to the exile of Jerusalem, the order of the oracles and narratives in the book does not appear in a strictly chronological sequence. (This is not unusual; of the larger prophetic books, only Ezekiel is ordered chronologically.) There is some tendency to organize material topically in sections of the book (a collection of royal oracles begins in 21.11; a collection against false prophets begins in 23.9; the oracles against the nations are collected in chs 46–51). However, the main determinant of the sequence of materials is the concern to reflect upon the significance of the destruction of Jerusalem and the Babylonian exile. The book begins with the early oracles of Jeremiah and continues through the destruction of Jerusalem, but it frequently looks back into earlier periods to provide some perspectives on the later disaster as it proceeds through the prophet's career. Although Jeremiah clearly struggles with God over the nature of his prophetic role and message, the book attempts to defend God's righteousness by arguing that the people themselves brought punishment upon themselves by failing to observe God's *torah* and that God would act to restore Israel to Jerusalem once the punishment was over. Modern theology might justifiably raise questions about such premises, especially in the aftermath of the Holocaust, but the book of Jeremiah is the product of people who were adamant in their belief in God's righteousness and their adherence to Jewish tradition. Talmudic tradition claims that the book of Jeremiah is primarily a book of destruction (*b. B. Bat.* 14b), but it clearly points beyond the seventy years of punishment (ch 25) to a time when Jerusalem and the Temple would be rebuilt and the streets of Jerusalem filled with "the sound of mirth and gladness, the voice of bridegroom and bride, the voice of those who cry, 'Give thanks to the LORD of Hosts, for the LORD is good, for His kindness is everlasting!' " (33.11). In the end, the book of Jeremiah is the product of a debate within Jewish circles from the late monarchy and the exilic periods concerning the question of theodicy or the righteousness of God. Although fully aware of the theological problems posed by the destruction of the Temple and the exile of the Jewish people, the book affirms God's existence and righteousness as well as the future of the restored nation Israel on its land.

Summary of Contents

STRUCTURALLY, THE BOOK OF JEREMIAH can be presented as including seventeen sections. With the exception of the concluding narrative concerning the fall of Jerusalem, which appears to be a modified version of 2 Kings 24.18–25.30, each section begins with a form of the prophetic word formula, "the word which came to Jeremiah from the LORD."

[MARVIN A. SWEENEY]

1 The words of Jeremiah son of Hilkiah, one of the priests at Anathoth in the territory of Benjamin. ² The word of the Lord came to him in the days of King Josiah son of Amon of Judah, in the thirteenth year of his reign, ³ and throughout the days of King Jehoiakim son of Josiah of Judah, and until the end of the eleventh year of King Zedekiah son of Josiah of Judah, when Jerusalem went into exile in the fifth month.

⁴ The word of the Lord came to me:

5   Before I created you in the womb, I selected you;
       Before you were born, I consecrated you;
       I appointed you a prophet concerning the
              nations.

6   I replied:
       Ah, Lord God!
       I don't know how to speak,
       For I am still a boy.
7   And the Lord said to me:
       Do not say, "I am still a boy,"
       But go wherever I send you
       And speak whatever I command you.
8   Have no fear of them,
       For I am with you to deliver you
                            —declares the Lord.

1.1–6.30: Jeremiah's early oracles. The first major unit of the book contains the superscription or introduction to the book as a whole (1.1–3), Jeremiah's account of his commissioning as a prophet by God (1.4–10), his account of the two visions that confirmed his prophetic role and characterized his message (1.11–19), and a lengthy selection of oracles concerning Jerusalem, Judah, and Israel, most of which announced punishment in an effort to persuade them to return to God. Jer. 1.1–2.3 and 2.4–28; 3.4 (or 4.1–2) serve as the first two of the three haftarot of rebuke prior to the 9th of Av, which commemorates the destruction of the Temple. In addition, Sephardi synagogues read 1.1–2.3 as the haftarah for Shemot (Exod. 1.1–6.1) because of the parallels between the life of Moses and the life of Jeremiah; they are the two prophets who attempt to refuse the divine call.

1.1–3: The introduction to the book of Jeremiah. Prophetic books normally begin with a superscription that identifies the prophet and provides historical background (see Isa. 1.1; Ezek. 1.1–3). **1:** *Hilkiah* is one of the priests at *Anathoth*, which would make him a descendant of the Elide priest Abiathar. King Solomon expelled Abiathar from Jerusalem to Anathoth so that Zadok would serve as the sole high priest in Jerusalem (1 Kings 2.26–27; see also 1 Sam. chs 22–23; 2 Sam. 8.17; 1 Kings ch 1). Jeremiah is therefore descended from the high priest Eli of the Temple at Shiloh (1 Sam. chs 1–4). Rabbinic tradition maintains that Jeremiah is also the descendant of the proselyte Rahab from Jericho (see Josh. chs 2; 6) and Joshua (*Sifre Numbers* 78; *b. Meg.* 14b). *Anathoth* is often identified with the modern village Anata, about 5 km (3 mi) northeast of Jerusalem, although the biblical site is actually about a kilometer (half mile) to the southwest. Josh. 21.18 and 1 Chron. 6.60 identify it as a Levitical town in the territory of Benjamin. **2–3:** Jeremiah prophesied for forty years, from the *thirteenth year* of Josiah (627 BCE) until the *eleventh year* of Zedekiah (586) when the Temple was destroyed (see 2 Kings ch 25; Jer. ch 52). Rabbinic tradition compares Jeremiah to Moses, a prophet and Levitical priest who led Israel in the wilderness for forty years (*Pesik. Rab.* xiii. 112a).

1.4–10: The prophet's commission. Prophets often relate the way they were commissioned by God (see Exod. ch 3; Isa. ch 6; Ezek. chs 1–3). The accounts of commissioning share certain commonalities, such as the prophet being "sent" as a divine messenger. Yet each account is different, reflecting the particular role and personality of the individual prophet. The commissioning of Jeremiah is most similar to that of Moses in Exod. ch 3 in that he is reluctant to accept his commission and receives encouragement from God. **4:** Jeremiah employs a typical prophetic word formula to introduce statements by God (see 1 Sam. 15.10; 1 Kings 6.11; Jer. 7.1; 11.1; Ezek. 6.1; 7.1; Hos. 1.1; Joel 1.1; Mic. 1.1; Zeph. 1.1). The formula serves as an important marker for the literary subdivisions in prophetic books. **5:** Because the book of Jeremiah contains little material attributed to the reign of Josiah (see 3.6; cf. 22.11–17), some suppose that Jeremiah was commissioned as a prophet at his birth in the thirteenth year of Josiah, making him eighteen years old at Josiah's death in 609 BCE. **6–8:** Like Moses, Jeremiah contends that he is inadequate to the task of prophecy, but God overcomes his objections with the assurance, *I am with you*

⁹The LORD put out His hand and touched my mouth, and the LORD said to me: Herewith I put My words into your mouth.

10　See, I appoint you this day
　　Over nations and kingdoms:
　　To uproot and to pull down,
　　To destroy and to overthrow,
　　To build and to plant.

¹¹The word of the LORD came to me: What do you see, Jeremiah? I replied: I see a branch of an almond tree.ᵃ

12　The LORD said to me:
　　You have seen right,
　　For I am watchfulᵇ to bring My word to pass.

¹³And the word of the LORD came to me a second time: What do you see? I replied:
　　I see a steaming pot,
　　ᶜTipped away from the north.ᶜ
14　And the LORD said to me:
　　From the north shall disaster break loose
　　Upon all the inhabitants of the land!
15　For I am summoning all the peoples
　　Of the kingdoms of the north
　　　　　　　　—declares the LORD.
　　They shall come, and shall each set up a throne
　　Before the gates of Jerusalem,
　　Against its walls roundabout,
　　And against all the towns of Judah.
16　And I will argue My case against themᵈ
　　For all their wickedness:
　　They have forsaken Me
　　And sacrificed to other gods
　　And worshiped the works of their hands.

17　So you, gird up your loins,
　　Arise and speak to them
　　All that I command you.
　　Do not break down before them,
　　Lest I break you before them.
18　I make you this day
　　A fortified city,
　　And an iron pillar,
　　And bronze walls
　　Against the whole land—

a Heb. shaqed.　　b Heb. shoqed.
c-c Meaning of Heb. uncertain.　　d I.e., against Jerusalem and Judah.

(see Exod. 3.11–12; 4.10–17; cf. Isaiah's statement in Isa. 6.5–6). **9–10:** As with Isaiah, a divine touch of the mouth prepares Jeremiah for prophecy (cf. Isa. 6.6–7; Ezek. 3.1–3). The prophet's commission to speak includes four verbs of destruction and two of restoration to signify that in terms of the major themes of his message, destruction would predominate (cf. 12.14–17; 18.5–10; 24.6; 31.28, 40; 42.10; 45.4).

1.11–19: Two symbolic visions. Symbolic visions frequently accompany the commissioning of a prophet (see Exod. ch 3; Isa. ch 6; Ezek. chs 1–3) and illustrate aspects of the prophet's message (see 1 Kings ch 19; Ezek. chs 4–5; 8–11; 37; 40–48; Amos chs 7–9; Zech. 1.7–6.15). Jeremiah's visions are formulated like those of the chronologically earlier Amos 7.7–9; 8.1–14 and the later Zech. chs 4–5. **11–12:** A pun upon the word "shaked," *almond tree,* and "shoked," "watching." The almond tree is one of the first trees to blossom in the spring, signifying God's resolve to bring about the divine word concerning Jerusalem and Judah. A recently discovered ivory pomegranate blossom, believed to have come from the excavation of biblical Jerusalem, apparently was formed to fit on the end of a staff. The inscription on the pomegranate, "belonging to the Temple of the Lord, holy to the priests," indicates that it probably served as the cap for a priest's or Levite's staff in the Jerusalem Temple. The image also appears in Num. ch 17, where the sprouting of almond blossoms on Aaron's and the Levites' staffs marks them as the divinely chosen priests of Israel. It seems likely that Jeremiah's vision was based upon the image of a Levitical staff (cf. Zech. ch 11, in which the priest and prophet Zechariah employs a staff for a prophetic vision). **13–19:** Another pun: a steaming pot that is *tipped* and emptied *from the north* to portray the enemy that will bring judgment to Jerusalem *from the north.* Perhaps another Le-

Against Judah's kings and officers,
And against its priests and citizens.[a]

19 They will attack you,
But they shall not overcome you;
For I am with you—declares the LORD—to save
you.

2 The word of the LORD came to me, saying, [2]Go pro-
claim to Jerusalem: Thus said the LORD:
I accounted to your favor
The devotion of your youth,
Your love as a bride—
How you followed Me in the wilderness,
In a land not sown.

3 Israel was holy to the LORD,
The first fruits of His harvest.
All who ate of it were held guilty;
Disaster befell them   —declares the LORD.

4 Hear the word of the LORD, O House of Jacob,
Every clan of the House of Israel!

5 Thus said the LORD:
What wrong did your fathers find in Me
That they abandoned Me
And went after delusion and were deluded?

a Lit. "the people of the land."

vitical image: a pot used in the preparation of sacrificial meat (cf. 1 Sam. 2.12–17; Ezek. 24.1–14). Because biblical Jerusalem was protected by valleys to the east, south, and west, it was most vulnerable to attack from the north where the Temple stood. Since the Arabian desert makes an approach against the land of Israel from the east very difficult, ancient Mesopotamian invaders typically traveled through Aram (modern Syria) to attack Israel from the north. So the north would be the expected direction of attack for any enemy; in the early chs in Jeremiah, this enemy from the north is not yet identified, and takes on near-mythological connotations. The prophet's task is to condemn his own kings, officials, and people for wrongdoing, but God promises to stand by him (cf. 1.8) throughout the ordeal.

2.1–6.30: Jeremiah's summons to repentance directed to Jerusalem and Judah. An early speech by the prophet in which he attempts to persuade his audience to repent from their wrongdoing and worship of foreign gods so that they might return to God. Although these chs are clearly directed to Jerusalem and Judah in their present form (see 2.1–2; 4.3–6.30), many believe that the oracles in 2.2–4.2 were originally addressed by the prophet to the people of the former Northern Kingdom of Israel, destroyed by the Assyrians a century earlier (see 2 Kings ch 17). Jeremiah would have attempted to persuade them to accept the rule of King Josiah and the religious authority of the Jerusalem Temple, thereby reuniting all Israel as in the days of David and Solomon (see 2 Sam. chs 5–24; 1 Kings chs 1–11). The section was expanded

with an address to Jerusalem and Judah as well when it became apparent that King Josiah's death at the hands of the Egyptian Pharaoh Neco (2 Kings 23.28–30; 2 Chron. 35.20–27) signaled that Judah, like Israel before it, faced the very real possibility of invasion and exile.

2.1–3.5: God's divorce proceedings against Israel. The prophet begins with a lengthy speech that metaphorically portrays God's intention to "divorce" Israel. The use of the marriage metaphor was common among the prophets to portray the relationship between God and Israel (see Hos. chs 1–3; Isa. chs 40–55, esp. ch 54; Zeph. 3.14–20; Ezek. ch 16; 24.15–17). **2.1–3:** The prophet relates God's instructions to *Go proclaim to Jerusalem.* The reference to Jerusalem is missing in the Septuagint, which may reflect an earlier version of the book. Lacking this reference, the speech is directed to Israel, which is called to return to Zion or Jerusalem (3.14–4.2) in keeping with Josiah's attempts to reunite all Israel. God recalls the early period of the relationship with Israel in the wilderness as an ideal time, much like the northern Israelite prophet Hosea (Hos. 2.16–20). In contrast to the northern prophets Jeremiah and Hosea, the Zadokite priest and prophet Ezekiel and the wilderness traditions of the Torah depict the wilderness period as a time of Israel's rebellion against God. The use of priestly imagery is consistent with Jeremiah's identity as a priest. **2.4–3.5:** God's speech to Israel appears in the form of a courtroom statement in which a husband seeks a divorce from his wife. **2.4:** The "call to attention" formula typically introduces public presentations, such as songs, diplomatic statements, prophetic oracles, and instructional speeches (cf. Judg. 5.3; 2 Kings 18.28–29; Isa. 1.10; Ezek. 3.6; Hos. 4.1; Amos 3.1; Prov. 7.24). **5–11:** God claims to have been abandoned by the people, despite having led them out of Egypt and through the wilderness to the promised land. Biblical tradition maintains that proper moral

6 They never asked themselves, "Where is the LORD,
Who brought us up from the land of Egypt,
Who led us through the wilderness,
A land of deserts and pits,
A land of drought and darkness,
A land no man had traversed,
Where no human being had dwelt?"

7 I brought you to this country of farm land
To enjoy its fruit and its bounty;
But you came and defiled My land,
You made My possession abhorrent.

8 The priests never asked themselves, "Where is the
LORD?"
The guardians of the Teaching ignored Me;
The rulers[a] rebelled against Me,
And the prophets prophesied by Baal
And followed what can do no good.

9 Oh, I will go on accusing you
—declares the LORD—
And I will accuse your children's children!

10 Just cross over to the isles of the Kittim and look,
Send to Kedar and observe carefully;
See if aught like this has ever happened:

11 Has any nation changed its gods
Even though they are no-gods?
But My people has exchanged its glory
For what can do no good.

12 Be appalled, O heavens, at this;
Be horrified, utterly dazed!   —says the LORD.

13 For My people have done a twofold wrong:
They have forsaken Me, the Fount of living
waters,
And hewed them out cisterns, broken cisterns,
Which cannot even hold water.

14 Is Israel a bondman?
Is he a home-born slave?
Then why is he given over to plunder?

15 Lions have roared over him,
Have raised their cries.
They have made his land a waste,
His cities desolate, without inhabitants.

16 Those, too, in Noph and Tahpanhes[b]
[c]Will lay bare[c] your head.

behavior and ritual observance maintains the purity of the land of Israel, but immorality and apostasy defile it (see Leviticus; Ezek. ch 18; Hos. ch 4). **10:** The *isles of the Kittim* refers to the Greek islands or Cyprus, and *Kedar* refers to a confederation of Arab tribes in the north Arabian desert (see Gen. 25.13; Isa. 42.11; Jer. 49.28–29; Ezek. 27.21). The point is that even if you look far and wide, no comparable action has transpired. **12–28:** God's specific accusations against Israel include both political and religious charges, which are understood as connected: God is abandoned for Egypt. **14:** This type of rhetorical question is very typical of Jeremiah (so, e.g., in v. 31). **16:** *Noph* and *Tahpanhes* refer to the Egyptian cities of Memphis, the ancient capital of Egypt, and Tahpanhes, a northeastern Nile Delta city fortified by Pharaoh Psammetichus I (664–610 BCE). Psammetichus and his son Neco later allied with the Assyrians against Babylonia, and Neco killed King Josiah in 609, putting an end to Judah's attempts to gain independence from the Assyrians. God's speech likens Judah's submission to Egypt and Assyria as a return to Egyptian bondage and pagan gods (cf. Isa. 10.20–26).

a Lit. "shepherds"; cf. 3.15; 23.1 ff.
b Cities in Egypt. The Egyptians, like the Assyrians, will prove a disappointment; cf. v. 36.
c-c Meaning of Heb. uncertain.

17 See, ᵃ·that is the price you have paid
   For forsaking the LORD your God·ᵃ
   ᵇ·While He led you in the way.·ᵇ

18 What, then, is the good of your going to Egypt
   To drink the waters of the Nile?
   And what is the good of your going to Assyria
   To drink the waters of the Euphrates?

19 Let your misfortune reprove you,
   Let your afflictions rebuke you;
   Mark well how bad and bitter it is
   That you forsake the LORD your God,
   That awe for Me is not in you
               —declares the Lord GOD of Hosts.

20 For long ago youᶜ broke your yoke,
   Tore off your yoke-bands,
   And said, "I will not work!"ᵈ
   On every high hill and under every verdant tree,
   You recline as a whore.

21 I planted you with noble vines,
   All with choicest seed;
   Alas, I find you changed
   Into a base, an alien vine!

22 Though you wash with natron
   And use much lye,
   Your guilt is ingrained before Me
               —declares the Lord GOD.

23 How can you say, "I am not defiled,
   I have not gone after the Baalim"?
   Look at your deeds in the Valley,ᵉ
   Consider what you have done!
   Like a lustful she-camel,
   ᵇ·Restlessly running about,·ᵇ

24 Or like a wild ass used to the desert,
   Snuffing the wind in her eagerness,
   Whose passion none can restrain,
   None that seek her need grow weary—
   In her season, they'll find her!

25 Save your foot from going bare,
   And your throat from thirst.
   But you say, "It is no use.
   No, I love the strangers,ᶠ

23–24: Images of animals in heat symbolize Israel's eagerness to accept other gods in place of her "husband" the LORD. Throughout his lifetime, Jeremiah called for Judah to ally with Babylonia and to reject alliance with Egypt and Assyria (see chs 27–29).

a-a Lit. "that is what your forsaking the LORD your God is doing to you."
b-b Meaning of Heb. uncertain.
c For the form, cf. shaqqamti, Judg. 5.7; others "I."
d Following the kethib; qere "transgress."
e I.e., of Hinnom; cf. 7.31–32; 32.35.
f I.e., other gods.

And after them I must go."

26 Like a thief chagrined when he is caught,
So is the House of Israel chagrined—
They, their kings, their officers,
And their priests and prophets.

27 They said to wood, "You are my father,"
To stone, "You gave birth to me,"
While to Me they turned their backs
And not their faces.
But in their hour of calamity they cry,
"Arise and save us!"

28 And where are those gods
You made for yourself?
Let them arise and save you, if they can,
In your hour of calamity.
For your gods have become, O Judah,
As many as your towns!

29 Why do you call Me to account?
You have all rebelled against Me
—declares the LORD.

30 To no purpose did I smite your children;
They would not accept correction.
Your sword has devoured your prophets
Like a ravening lion.

31 ªO generation, behold ª the word of the LORD!
Have I been like a desert to Israel,
Or like a land of deep gloom?
Then why do My people say, "We have broken
     loose,
We will not come to You any more?"

32 Can a maiden forget her jewels,
A bride her adornments?
Yet My people have forgotten Me—
Days without number.

33 How skillfully you plan your way
To seek out love!
Why, you have even taught
The worst of women your ways.

34 Moreover, on your garments is found
The lifeblood of the innocent poor—
You did not catch them breaking in.ᵇ
ªYet, despite all these things,ª

35 You say, "I have been acquitted;
Surely, His anger has turned away from me."

2.29–3.5: God depicts Israel as an adulterous wife to confirm the grounds for a "divorce." Cf. Deut. 24.1–4, which forbids a man to remarry his divorced wife after she has married another man. Jeremiah, in contrast to most earlier prophets, demonstrates his familiarity with a range of Torah texts. This might reflect the gradual coming together of the Torah as a book in the late preexilic period and/or Jeremiah's knowledge of these traditions as a priest (see 18.18).

---

a-a Meaning of Heb. uncertain.
b In which case there might have been an excuse for killing them; cf. Exod. 22.1.

Lo, I will bring you to judgment
For saying, "I have not sinned."

36 How you cheapen yourself,
By changing your course!
You shall be put to shame through Egypt,
Just as you were put to shame through Assyria.
37 From this way, too, you will come out
^aWith your hands on your head;^a
For the LORD has rejected those you trust,
You will not prosper with them.

3 [The word of the LORD came to me] as follows: If a man divorces his wife, and she leaves him and marries another man, can he ever go back to her? Would not such a land be defiled?^b Now you have whored with many lovers: can you return to Me?—says the LORD.

2 Look up to the bare heights, and see:
Where have they not lain with you?
You waited for them on the roadside
Like a bandit^c in the wilderness.
And you defiled the land
With your whoring and your debauchery.
3 And when showers were withheld
And the late rains did not come,
You had the brazenness^d of a street woman,
You refused to be ashamed.
4 Just now you called to Me, "Father!
You are the Companion of my youth.
5 Does one hate^e for all time?
Does one rage^e forever?"
That is how you spoke;
You did wrong, and ^fhad your way.^f

6 The LORD said to me in the days of King Josiah: Have you seen what Rebel Israel did, going to every high mountain and under every leafy tree, and whoring there? 7 I thought: After she has done all these things, she will come back to Me. But she did not come back; and her sister, Faithless Judah, saw it. 8 I noted: Because Rebel Israel had committed adultery, I cast her off and handed her a bill of divorce; yet her sister, Faithless Judah, was not afraid—she too went and whored. 9 Indeed, the land was

3.6–10: Israel's and Judah's "adultery." Jeremiah relates God's earlier conversation with him about northern Israel and Judah during the days of King Josiah. He continues the metaphorical portrayal of Israel and Judah as God's wives. Whereas Israel left God to pursue other "lovers" or gods, Judah is insincere because she still claims to be God's "wife" despite her "adultery."

a-a A gesture of wild grief; cf. 2 Sam. 13.19.
b Cf. Deut. 24.1–4.   c Lit. "Arab."   d Lit. "forehead."
e Cf. Akkadian parallels nadāru and shamāru.   f-f Meaning of Heb. uncertain.

defiled by her casual immorality, as she committed adultery with stone and with wood.[a] 10 And after all that, her sister, Faithless Judah, did not return to Me wholeheartedly, but insincerely—declares the LORD.

11 And the LORD said to me: Rebel Israel has shown herself more in the right than Faithless Judah. 12 Go, make this proclamation toward the north, and say: Turn back, O Rebel Israel—declares the LORD. I will not look on you in anger, for I am compassionate—declares the LORD; I do not bear a grudge for all time. 13 Only recognize your sin; for you have transgressed against the LORD your God, and scattered your favors[b] among strangers under every leafy tree, and you have not heeded Me—declares the LORD.

14 Turn back, rebellious children—declares the LORD. Since I have espoused[c] you, I will take you, one from a town and two from a clan, and bring you to Zion. 15 And I will give you shepherds[d] after My own heart, who will pasture you with knowledge and skill.

16 And when you increase and are fertile in the land, in those days—declares the LORD—men shall no longer speak of the Ark of the Covenant of the LORD, nor shall it come to mind. They shall not mention it, or miss it, or make another. 17 At that time, they shall call Jerusalem "Throne of the LORD," and all nations shall assemble there, in the name of the LORD, at Jerusalem. They[e] shall no longer follow the willfulness of their evil hearts. 18 In those days, the House of Judah shall go with the House of Israel; they shall come together from the land of the north to the land I gave your fathers as a possession.

19 I had resolved to adopt you as My child, and I gave you a desirable land—the fairest heritage of all the nations; and I thought you would surely call Me "Father," and never cease to be loyal to Me. 20 Instead, you have broken faith with Me, as a woman breaks faith with a paramour, O House of Israel—declares the LORD.

21 Hark! On the bare heights is heard
The suppliant weeping of the people of Israel,
For they have gone a crooked way,
Ignoring the LORD their God.

22 Turn back, O rebellious children,
I will heal your afflictions!

3.11–6.30: God's appeal for the return of Israel and Judah. Notwithstanding the law of divorce in Deut. 24.1–4, God shows mercy by calling upon Israel and Judah to return (cf. Hos. chs 2–3; 14). **3.11–17:** Israel's experience of destruction, exile, and potential restoration to Zion or Jerusalem is a model for the experience of Judah. **12:** *Turn back* is a technical term meaning "to repent." In the Torah, it is first found in Deut. 4.30, and elsewhere in Deuteronomy. This thus represents one of the many connections between Deuteronomy and Jeremiah. **16:** The *Ark of the Covenant*, constructed in the wilderness at the time of the exodus to hold the tablets of the covenant (Exod. 25.10–22; 37.1–9; Deut. 10.1–5; cf. Num. 10.35–36), symbolized divine presence in Solomon's Temple (see 1 Kings 8.1–13; 2 Chron. 5.1–14). When the Temple was destroyed, no mention was made of the fate of the Ark (see 2 Kings ch 25; Jer. ch 52), suggesting that it had disappeared earlier. According to 2 Macc. 2.1–8, Jeremiah hid the Ark in a cave on Mt. Nebo or Pisgah in Moab, where Moses was buried (Deut. 32.49–52; 34.1–8). Rabbinic tradition maintains that Josiah hid the Ark so that it would not be taken to Babylon (*b. Yoma* 53b; *y. Shek.* 6:1; 49c). The ark that houses Torah scrolls in synagogues symbolizes the ancient Ark of the Covenant. **3.18–6.30:** God calls for Judah's repentance as well. **3.18–25:** The reunification of Israel and Judah was a major goal of Josiah's program of religious reform and national restoration. The return of all twelve tribes of Israel to the restored Jerusalem Temple is the foundation of Jewish thought concerning the days of the Messiah and the world to come (see Ezek. chs 40–48). The ingathering of all the exiles is likewise an important motif in modern Zionism.

a She deserted her God for idols of stone and wood.　　b Lit. "ways."
c Meaning of Heb. ba'alti uncertain; compare 31.32.
d Meaning of Heb. uncertain.　　e I.e., Israel and Judah.

"Here we are, we come to You,
For You, O Lord, are our God!
23 ᵃSurely, futility comes from the hills,
Confusion from the mountains.⁻ᵃ
Only through the Lord our God
Is there deliverance for Israel.
24 But the Shameful Thingᵇ has consumed
The possessions of our fathers ever since our
      youth—
Their flocks and herds,
Their sons and daughters.
25 Let us lie down in our shame,
Let our disgrace cover us;
For we have sinned against the Lord our God,
We and our fathers from our youth to this day,
And we have not heeded the Lord our God."

4 If you return, O Israel　—declares the Lord—
If you return to Me,
If you remove your abominations from My
      presence
And do not waver,
2 And ᶜswear, "As the Lord lives,"⁻ᶜ
In sincerity, justice, and righteousness—
Nations shall bless themselves by youᵈ
And praise themselves by you.ᵈ

³For thus said the Lord to the men of Judah and to Jerusalem:

Break up the untilled ground,
And do not sow among thorns.
4 Openᵉ your hearts to the Lord,
Remove the thickening about your hearts—
O men of Judah and inhabitants of Jerusalem—
Lest My wrath break forth like fire,
And burn, with none to quench it,
Because of your wicked acts.

5 Proclaim in Judah,
Announce in Jerusalem,
And say:
"Blow the horn in the land!"
Shout aloud and say:
"Assemble, and let us go

4.1–4: God's call for Judah's repentance is the primary goal of the larger text in chs 2–6. Vv. 1–2 conclude the haftarah reading of 2.4–28; 3.4; 4.1–2 for the parashah of Maseʿei (Num. 33.1–36.13), the second of the three haftarot of rebuke prior to the 9th of Av, to illustrate the principle that restoration will follow punishment. **4:** The imagery of circumcision (*Open,* lit. "circumcise," see translators' note *e*) symbolizes the rejuvenation of the covenant between God and Israel (see Gen. ch 17). **4.5–6.30:** *Evil from the north:* Although this passage is later read as a reference to the invasions of Judah by the Babylonians—who would have approached from the north in 597, 588 and 582 BCE (see 2 Kings chs 24–25; Jer. 41–43; 52)— some maintain that early in Jeremiah, the enemy from the north was thought to be the Scythians. According to the ancient Greek historian Herodotus (5th century BCE), the Scythians were a horseback-mounted people from the Caucasus (cf. 4.13; 6.22–23) who threatened Philistia and Judah in the 7th century BCE. **4.5–31:** The question of theodicy or divine righteousness in the face of evil.

a-a *I.e., the pagan rites celebrated on the hills are futile; exact force of Heb. uncertain.*
b *Heb. Bosheth, a contemptuous substitute for Baal.*
c-c *I.e., profess the worship of the Lord.*　d *Heb. "him."*
e *Lit. "circumcise"; cf. Deut. 10.16 and 30.6.*

Into the fortified cities!"

6   Set up a signpost: To Zion.
    Take refuge, do not delay!
    For I bring evil from the north,
    And great disaster.

7   The lion has come up from his thicket:
    The destroyer of nations has set out,
    Has departed from his place,
    To make your land a desolation;
    Your cities shall be ruined,
    Without inhabitants.

8   For this, put on sackcloth,
    Mourn and wail;
    For the blazing anger of the LORD
    Has not turned away from us.

9   And in that day   —declares the LORD—
    The mind of the king
    And the mind of the nobles shall fail,
    The priests shall be appalled,
    And the prophets shall stand aghast.

10a-And I said:-a Ah, Lord GOD! Surely You have deceived this people and Jerusalem, saying:
    It shall be well with you—
    Yet the sword threatens the very life!

11 At that time, it shall be said concerning this people
and Jerusalem:
    The conduct of b-My poor people-b is like searing
        wind
    From the bare heights of the desert—
    It will not serve to winnow or to fan.

12 A full blast from them comes against Me:
    Now I in turn will bring charges against
        them.

13 Lo, hec ascends like clouds,
    His chariots are like a whirlwind,
    His horses are swifter than eagles.
    Woe to us, we are ruined!

14 Wash your heart clean of wickedness,
    O Jerusalem, that you may be rescued.
    How long will you harbor within you
    Your evil designs?

9: The officials mentioned represent the secular and religious leaders of the late exilic period. **10:** Jeremiah suggests that God has deceived the people into thinking that all would be well (cf. Isa. 6.9–10).

a-a Septuagint reads "And they shall say."
b-b Lit. "the daughter that is My people"; so, frequently, in poetry.
c I.e., the invader of v. 7.

15   Hark, one proclaims from Dan
      And announces calamity from Mount Ephraim!
16   Tell the nations: Here they are!
      Announce concerning Jerusalem:
      Watchers^a are coming from a distant land,
      They raise their voices against the towns of Judah.
17   Like guards of fields, they surround her on every
            side.
      For she has rebelled against Me
                              —declares the LORD.

18   Your conduct and your acts
      Have brought this upon you;
      This is your bitter punishment;
      It pierces your very heart.

19   Oh, my suffering,^b my suffering!
      How I writhe!
      Oh, the walls of my heart!
      My heart moans within me,
      I cannot be silent;
      For ^cI hear^{-c} the blare of horns,
      Alarms of war.
20   Disaster overtakes disaster,
      For all the land has been ravaged.
      Suddenly my tents have been ravaged,
      In a moment, my tent cloths.
21   How long must I see standards
      And hear the blare of horns?

22   For My people are stupid,
      They give Me no heed;
      They are foolish children,
      They are not intelligent.
      They are clever at doing wrong,
      But unable to do right.

23   I look at the earth,
      It is unformed and void;
      At the skies,
      And their light is gone.
24   I look at the mountains,
      They are quaking;
      And all the hills are rocking.
25   I look: no man is left,

18: God contends that the suffering of the people is a punishment brought about by their own conduct. **19:** Jeremiah's clear pain at the suffering of his own people mirrors God's empathy at the suffering of the people, even if it is brought on by their own actions. These first-person laments by the prophet typify Jeremiah. **23–28:** The prophet draws upon Gen. 1.1–2.3 to argue that all creation suffers as a result of human wrongdoing. The suffering of God and all creation is addressed by proper human action throughout rabbinic literature and especially in Lurianic kabbalistic thought.

---

a I.e., the invader of v. 7.   b Lit. "entrails."
c-c Lit. "you, O my being, hear." Change of vocalization yields "I hear the blare of horns, /
My inner being, alarms of war."

And all the birds of the sky have fled.

26 I look: the farm land is desert,
And all its towns are in ruin—
Because of the LORD,
Because of His blazing anger.

27 (For thus said the LORD:
The whole land shall be desolate,
But I will not make an end of it.)

28 For this the earth mourns,
And skies are dark above—
Because I have spoken, I have planned,
And I will not relent or turn back from it.

29 At the shout of horseman and bowman
The whole city flees.
They enter the thickets,
They clamber up the rocks.
The whole city is deserted,
Not a man remains there.

30 And you, who are doomed to ruin,
What do you accomplish by wearing crimson,
By decking yourself in jewels of gold,
By enlarging your eyes with kohl?
You beautify yourself in vain:
Lovers despise you,
They seek your life!

31 I hear a voice as of one in travail,
Anguish as of a woman bearing her first child,
The voice of Fair Zion
Panting, stretching out her hands:
"Alas for me! I faint
Before the killers!"

5 Roam the streets of Jerusalem,
Search its squares,
Look about and take note:
You will not find a man,
There is none who acts justly,
Who seeks integrity—
That I should pardon her.

2 Even when they say, "As the LORD lives,"
They are sure to be swearing falsely.

3 O LORD, Your eyes look for integrity.
You have struck them, but they sensed no pain;
You have consumed them, but they would accept
    no discipline.
They made their faces harder than rock,
They refused to turn back.

5.1–31: In a series of oracles that share some similarities with the debate between God and Abraham over the destruction of Sodom and Gomorrah (Gen. ch 18), God attempts to persuade Jeremiah that the decision to punish Jerusalem is justified. **1–5:** God begins by challenging Jeremiah to find one righteous man in the city (cf. *Gen. Rab.* 49.13), but the prophet is unable to find anyone.

4   Then I thought: These are just poor folk;
      They act foolishly;
      For they do not know the way of the LORD,
      The rules of their God.
5   So I will go to the wealthy
      And speak with them:
      Surely they know the way of the LORD,
      The rules of their God.
      But they as well had broken the yoke,
      Had snapped the bonds.
6   Therefore,
      The lion of the forest strikes them down,
      The wolf of the desert ravages them.
      A leopard lies in wait by their towns;
      Whoever leaves them will be torn in pieces.
      For their transgressions are many,
      Their rebellious acts unnumbered.

7   Why should I forgive you?
      Your children have forsaken Me
      And sworn by no-gods.
      When I fed them their fill,
      They committed adultery
      And went trooping to the harlot's house.
8   They were ᵃ‑well-fed, lusty‑ᵃ stallions,
      Each neighing at another's wife.
9   Shall I not punish such deeds?
                                    —says the LORD—

      Shall I not bring retribution
      On a nation such as this?
10   Go up among her vinesᵇ and destroy;
      Lop off her trailing branches,
      For they are not of the LORD.
      (But do not make an end.)
11   For the House of Israel and the House of Judah
      Have betrayed Me   —declares the LORD.
12   They have been false to the LORD
      And said: "ᶜ‑It is not so!‑ᶜ
      No trouble shall come upon us,
      We shall not see sword or famine.
13   The prophets shall prove mere wind
      For the Word is not in them;
      Thus-and-thus shall be done to them!"

13: Jeremiah complains about false *prophets*. (The Heb uses the term "prophets," which the context shows to mean false prophets. In many cases like this in Jeremiah, the Greek Septuagint translates Hebrew "prophets" as "false prophets.") This is an important theme in Jeremiah (cf. ch 23), especially after the death of Josiah ended hopes for a Judean restoration that had been supported by prophetic tradition. Jeremiah challenges prophets who represent the older tradition of Isaiah that Jerusalem was inviolable, and would be delivered (see chs 27–28; cf. Isa. chs 5–12; 36–37; Zephaniah).

a-a *Meaning of Heb. uncertain.*
b *Lit. "rows."*
c-c *Or "Not He"; cf. Deut. 32.39; Isa. 43.13.*

14   Assuredly, thus said the LORD,
    The God of Hosts:
    Because they[a] said that,
    I am putting My words into your mouth as fire,
    And this people shall be firewood,
    Which it will consume.

15   Lo, I am bringing against you, O House of Israel,
    A nation from afar   —declares the LORD;
    It is an enduring nation,
    It is an ancient nation;
    A nation whose language you do not know—
    You will not understand what they say.

16   [b-]Their quivers[-b] are like a yawning grave—
    They are all mighty men.

17   They will devour your harvest and food,
    They will devour your sons and daughters,
    They will devour your flocks and herds,
    They will devour your vines and fig trees.
    They will batter down with the sword
    The fortified towns on which you rely.

18 But even in those days—declares the LORD—I will not make an end of you. 19 And when they[a] ask, "Because of what did the LORD our God do all these things?" you shall answer them, "Because you forsook Me and served alien gods on your own land, you will have to serve foreigners in a land not your own."

20   Proclaim this to the House of Jacob
    And announce it in Judah:

21   Hear this, O foolish people,
    Devoid of intelligence,
    That have eyes but can't see,
    That have ears but can't hear!

22   Should you not revere Me   —says the LORD—
    Should you not tremble before Me,
    Who set the sand as a boundary to the sea,
    As a limit for all time, not to be transgressed?
    Though its waves toss, they cannot prevail;
    Though they roar, they cannot pass it.

23   Yet this people has a wayward and defiant heart;
    They have turned aside and gone their way.

24   They have not said to themselves,
    "Let us revere the LORD our God,
    Who gives the rain,
    The early and late rain in season,

15–17: By pointing to *a nation from afar . . . whose language you do not know* that will devour the land, Jeremiah draws upon the prophecies of judgment from the Isaian tradition (e.g., Isa. 5.26–30) to argue that the time of punishment did not conclude with the Assyrian empire. **18–19:** Although God will not make a full end of the people, a new, unnamed enemy from the north will force the people to serve *alien gods* on their own land and *foreigners* in a land not their own.

a Heb. "you."   *b-b* Emendation yields "Whose mouths."

Who keeps for our benefit
The weeks appointed for harvest."

25 It is your iniquities that have diverted these
        things,
    Your sins that have withheld the bounty from you.

26 For among My people are found wicked men,
    ᵃ⁻Who lurk, like fowlers lying in wait;⁻ᵃ
    They set up a trap to catch men.

27 As a cage is full of birds,
    So their houses are full of guile;
    That is why they have grown so wealthy.

28 They have become fat and sleek;
    They ᵇ⁻pass beyond the bounds of wickedness,⁻ᵇ
    And they prosper.
    They will not judge the case of the orphan,
    Nor give a hearing to the plea of the needy.

29 Shall I not punish such deeds
                          —says the LORD—
    Shall I not bring retribution
    On a nation such as this?

30 An appalling, horrible thing
    Has happened in the land:

31 The prophets prophesy falsely,
    And the priests ᵃ⁻rule accordingly;⁻ᵃ
    And My people like it so.
    But what will you do at the end of it?

6   Flee for refuge, O people of Benjamin,
    Out of the midst of Jerusalem!
    Blow the horn in Tekoa,
    Set up a signal at Beth-haccerem!
    For evil is appearing from the north,
    And great disaster.

2   ᵃ⁻Fair Zion, the lovely and delicate,
    I will destroy.⁻ᵃ

3   Against her come shepherds with their flocks,
    They pitch tents all around her;
    Each grazes ᶜ⁻the sheep under his care.⁻ᶜ

4   ᵈ⁻Prepare for⁻ᵈ battle against her:
    "Up! we will attack at noon."
    "Alas for us! for day is declining,
    The shadows of evening grow long."

5   "Up! let us attack by night,
    And wreck her fortresses."

28: By charging that the people do not judge properly the cases of the poor and *the needy,* Jeremiah draws upon the traditions of social justice found both in the Torah (Exod. 22.21–26; Lev. 19.13–16; Deut. 14.27–29) and in the earlier prophets (Isa. 1.16–17; 3.13–15; Amos 2.6–7; 8.4–7). **6.1–30:** Having despaired of finding anyone righteous in the city, the prophet prepares for the coming punishment. **1:** He begins by calling upon the *people of Benjamin* to *flee.* The territory of the tribe of Benjamin lies immediately to the north of Jerusalem, the most likely approach for an enemy invasion (cf. Isa. 10.27–32; Hos. 5.8–9). According to Josh. 18.11–28, Jerusalem is included within the territory of Benjamin (cf. Judg. 1.21; contrast Josh. 16.63). Lighting of hilltop signal fires is to warn all Judah of the approaching enemy. *Tekoa* is the hometown of the prophet Amos (Amos 1.1), located in Judah, about 20 km (12 mi) south of Jerusalem and 10 km (6 mi) south of Bethlehem. The prophet is punning here, using the verb "tik'u" which plays on the place Tekoa. Puns are especially prevalent in Jeremiah. *Beth-haccerem* has been identified as either the village 'Ain Karim to the west of modern Jerusalem or more likely as Ramat Raḥel on the southern edges of the city. **3–15:** The enemy brings tents and sheep to prepare for a long siege and cuts down trees to prepare siegeworks for an assault (cf. Deut. 20.19–20, which forbids Israelite soldiers to cut down fruit trees to besiege a city).

---

a-a *Meaning of Heb. uncertain.*
b-b *Some ancient versions read "have transgressed My words for evil."*
c-c *Understanding yado as in Ps. 95.7.*   d-d *Lit. "Consecrate."*

6 For thus said the LORD of Hosts:
   Hew down her trees,
   And raise a siegemound against Jerusalem.
   ªShe is the city destined for punishment;ª
   Only fraud is found in her midst.
7 As a well flows with water,
   So she flows with wickedness.
   Lawlessness and rapine are heard in her;
   Before Me constantly are sickness and wounds.
8 Accept rebuke, O Jerusalem,
   Lest I come to loathe you,
   Lest I make you a desolation,
   An uninhabited land.

9 Thus said the LORD of Hosts:
   ᵇLet them gleanᵇ over and over, as a vine,
   The remnant of Israel.
   Pass your hand again,
   Like a vintager,
   Over its branches.

10ᶜ To whom shall I speak,
   Give warning that they may hear?
   Their ears are blocked
   And they cannot listen.
   See, the word of the LORD has become for them
   An object of scorn; they will have none of it.
11 But I am filled with the wrath of the LORD,
   I cannot hold it in.

   Pour it on the infant in the street,
   And on the company of youths gathered together!
   Yes, men and women alike shall be captured,
   Elders and those of advanced years.
12 Their houses shall pass to others,
   Fields and wives as well,
   For I will stretch out My arm
   Against the inhabitants of the country
                    —declares the LORD.
13 For from the smallest to the greatest,
   They are all greedy for gain;
   Priest and prophet alike,
   They all act falsely.
14 They offer healing offhand

11–15: Although the prophet warns of danger, not even the priests or prophets who are responsible for the people's welfare heed his warning; in fact, they inappropriately reassure the people.

---

a-a Emendation yields "She is the city of falseness."
b-b Emendation yields "Glean" (singular).
c The prophet speaks.

For the wounds of My people,
Saying, "All is well, all is well,"
When nothing is well.

15 They have acted shamefully;
They have done abhorrent things—
Yet they do not feel shame,
And they cannot be made to blush.
Assuredly, they shall fall among the falling,
They shall stumble at the time when I punish them
—said the LORD.

16 Thus said the LORD:
Stand by the roads and consider,
Inquire about ancient paths:
Which is the road to happiness?
Travel it, and find tranquillity for yourselves.
But they said, "We will not."

17 And I raised up watchmen[a] for you:
"Hearken to the sound of the horn!"
But they said, "We will not."

18 Hear well, O nations,
And know, [b]O community, what is in store for
them.[b]

19 Hear, O earth!
I am going to bring disaster upon this people,
The outcome of their own schemes;
For they would not hearken to My words,
And they rejected My Instruction.

20 What need have I of frankincense
That comes from Sheba,
Or fragrant cane from a distant land?
Your burnt offerings are not acceptable
And your sacrifices are not pleasing to Me.

21 Assuredly, thus said the LORD:
I shall put before this people stumbling blocks
Over which they shall stumble—
Fathers and children alike,
Neighbor and friend shall perish.

22 Thus said the LORD:
See, a people comes from the northland,
A great nation is roused
From the remotest parts of the earth.

23 They grasp the bow and javelin;
They are cruel, they show no mercy;
The sound of them is like the roaring sea.

16–21: Although the leaders could have chosen the *ancient paths* or "torah," they did not and therefore bring punishment upon themselves. 17: The *watchmen* are the prophets who were to guide the people. This image is developed in detail in Ezek. 3.17–21. 19: The prophet continues to draw upon the Isaian tradition; the statement that *they rejected My Instruction*, Heb "torah," echoes Isa. 5.24 (cf. Isa. 1.10). He charges that they were more concerned with their own wealth. 20: *Sheba*, identified with modern Yemen in southwest Arabia, was a well-known source for frankincense, other spices, gold, and precious stones (1 Kings ch 10; Isa. 60.6; Ezek. 27.25). Again, the prophet's statements concerning God's rejection of sacrifices recalls Isa. 1.10–17. 21: As in Isa. 8.14, God will place *stumbling blocks* before the people (cf. Isa. 3.8). 22–26: The description of the approaching northern enemy from the remotest parts of the earth with weapons in hand and roaring like the sea once again recalls the description of the Assyrians in Isa. 5.26–30.

a I.e., prophets.   *b-b Meaning of Heb. uncertain.*

They ride upon horses,
Accoutered like a man for battle,
Against you, O Fair Zion!

24 "We have heard the report of them,
Our hands fail;
Pain seizes us,
Agony like a woman in childbirth.
25 Do not go out into the country,
Do not walk the roads!
For the sword of the enemy is there,
Terror on every side."

26 ª⁻My poor people,⁻ª
Put on sackcloth
And strew dust on yourselves!
Mourn, as for an only child;
Wail bitterly,
For suddenly the destroyer
Is coming upon us.

27 I have made you an assayer of My people
—A refiner^b—
You are to note and assay their ways.
28 They are copper and iron:
They are all stubbornly defiant;
They ᶜ⁻deal basely⁻ᶜ
All of them act corruptly.
29 ᵈ⁻The bellows puff;
The lead is consumed by fire.⁻ᵈ
Yet the smelter smelts to no purpose—
The dross^b is not separated out.
30 They are called "rejected silver,"
For the Lᴏʀᴅ has rejected them.

7 The word which came to Jeremiah from the Lᴏʀᴅ:
² Stand at the gate of the House of the Lᴏʀᴅ, and there proclaim this word: Hear the word of the Lᴏʀᴅ, all you of Judah who enter these gates to worship the Lᴏʀᴅ!

a-a Lit. "Daughter that is My people"; so, frequently, in poetry. See 4.11 and note.
b Meaning of Heb. uncertain.   c-c See note at Lev. 19.16.
d-d Meaning of Heb. uncertain.

24: The image of a woman in childbirth also appears in Isa. 13.8; 26.17–18. **25:** The reference to *terror on every side* is characteristic of Jeremiah (20.3, 10; 46.5; 49.29). **27–30:** The portrayal of the enemy as *an assayer of My people—a refiner* who smelts and does not separate out *the dross* likewise draws on Isaiah's metaphorical portrayal of the purification of Jerusalem as a smelting process (Isa. 1.21–26). Throughout this passage, Jeremiah draws an analogy between the sit-

uation of his own time and that of the prophet Isaiah in an effort to warn the people of approaching danger and convince them to change their course of action. The way in which Jeremiah reuses Isaiah's oracles is behind the (chronologically impossible) suggestion that Isaiah was Jeremiah's teacher (*Lam. Rab.* 1.18).

7.1–10.25: Jeremiah's Temple sermon. A narrative account of the prophet's delivery of (a shortened version of) this sermon in the Temple and his subsequent trial for sedition appears in ch 26. The prophetic word formula introduces the entire section. According to 26.1, Jeremiah delivered this sermon at the beginning of King Jehoiakim's reign, which would have begun some three months after his father Josiah's death (609 ʙᴄᴇ) at the hands of the Egyptian Pharaoh Neco. Although the people of Judah placed Josiah's son, Jehoahaz, on the throne following his father's death, 2 Kings 23.28–37 reports that Neco deposed Jehoahaz and replaced him with his brother Jehoiakim, who would presumably be more receptive to Egyptian control. Jeremiah's sermon questions the protective role of the Temple in Jerusalem, the centerpiece of Josiah's program of religious reform and national restoration. It therefore seems likely that the prophet deemed Josiah's reform a failure and likened Judah to northern Israel in failing to observe divine Torah. In the prophet's view, Judah would suffer punishment like that of the Northern Kingdom of Israel unless it returned to the observance of Torah. Jer. 7.21–8.3; 9.22–23 constitutes the haftarah for the parashah of Tsav (Lev. 6.1–8.36), which outlines procedures for the presentation of sacrifices in the Temple as well as the ordination of priests. Jeremiah is understood as complementing the Torah reading by noting that ritual action alone is insufficient for assuring the divine Presence at the Temple, since he here speaks to the responsibility to observe both the moral and the rit-

3 Thus said the LORD of Hosts, the God of Israel: Mend your ways and your actions, and I will ᵃ‑let you dwell‑ᵃ in this place. 4 Don't put your trust in illusions and say, "The Temple of the LORD, the Temple of the LORD, the Temple of the LORD are these [buildings]." 5 No, if you really mend your ways and your actions; if you execute justice between one man and another; 6 if you do not oppress the stranger, the orphan, and the widow; if you do not shed the blood of the innocent in this place; if you do not follow other gods, to your own hurt— 7 then only will I ᵃ‑let you dwell‑ᵃ in this place, in the land that I gave to your fathers for all time. 8 See, you are relying on illusions that are of no avail. 9 Will you steal and murder and commit adultery and swear falsely, and sacrifice to Baal, and follow other gods whom you have not experienced,ᵇ 10 and then come and stand before Me in this House which bears My name and say, "We are safe"?—[Safe] to do all these abhorrent things! 11 Do you consider this House, which bears My name, to be a den of thieves? As for Me, I have been watching—declares the LORD.

12 Just go to My place at Shiloh, where I had established My name formerly, and see what I did to it because of the wickedness of My people Israel. 13 And now, because you do all these things—declares the LORD—and though I spoke to you persistently, you would not listen; and though I called to you, you would not respond— 14 therefore I will do to the House which bears My name, on which you rely, and to the place which I gave you and your fathers, just what I did to Shiloh. 15 And I will cast you out of My presence as I cast out your brothers, the whole brood of Ephraim.

16 As for you, do not pray for this people, do not raise a cry of prayer on their behalf, do not plead with Me; for I will not listen to you. 17 Don't you see what they are doing in the towns of Judah and in the streets of Jerusalem? 18 The children gather sticks, the fathers build the fire, and the mothers knead dough, to make cakes for the Queen of Heaven,ᶜ and they pour libations to other gods, to vex Me.

a-a Meaning of Heb. uncertain. Change of vocalization yields "dwell with you"; so Aquila and Vulgate.

b See note at Deut. 11.28.

c I.e., the mother goddess (Ishtar, Astarte) in whose honor these cakes were baked.

is not labeled a "sermon," its frequent references to and quotations of Torah texts might make this label appropriate here. This then forshadows the classical rabbinic sermon or "derashah" that was based on an exposition of biblical texts. **7.2:** Jeremiah must position himself where he can speak to the crowds as they enter the Temple grounds for worship. Prophets like Jeremiah sought as large an audience as they could, in order to influence public opinion. Moreover, in this instance the Temple location is especially meaningful, since the message is about the Temple. **3–11:** Jeremiah calls upon the people to mend their ways so that God will allow them to dwell in the land. The prophet does not simply announce punishment, but attempts to persuade the people to observe God's will. This presupposes the so-called "blessings and curses" that appear in Deut. chs 28–30 to encourage the people to observe Torah. Jeremiah clearly attacks the popular notion that the Temple alone will guarantee the security of the nation. Such an idea reflects God's eternal promise of a dynasty for King David in Jerusalem (2 Sam. ch 7) that is symbolized by the presence of God's Temple in the city (see 1 Kings ch 8). Jeremiah contends that moral action is also necessary, and he specifically cites part of the Decalogue (see Exod. ch 20; Deut. ch 5). **12–15:** Jeremiah notes that the Temple at *Shiloh* was destroyed long ago because the people failed to observe God's will, and the Jerusalem Temple could be destroyed for the same reason. It is unknown exactly when the Shiloh sanctuary was destroyed. **16–20:** God instructs Jeremiah not to plead for the people; they must take responsibility for their own actions. This remarkable request reflects the efficacy of prophetic prayer, a common theme of the Torah narratives in reference to Moses. **18:** *The Queen of Heaven* is most likely some form of the Mesopotamian goddess Ishtar, symbolized by the Morning Star or Venus, who represented both war

ual aspects of Torah. Jer. 8.13–9.23 serves as the haftarah for the morning service on the 9th of Av, because it expresses the prophet's grief at the coming loss of the Temple.

7.1–8.3: God's instructions to Jeremiah to preach the Temple sermon. This passage is formulated as God's instructions to Jeremiah to demonstrate the divine origin of his speech. Although this passage

19 Is it Me they are vexing?—says the LORD. It is rather themselves, to their own disgrace. 20 Assuredly, thus said the Lord GOD: My wrath and My fury will be poured out upon this place, on man and on beast, on the trees of the field and the fruit of the soil. It shall burn, with none to quench it.

21 Thus said the LORD of Hosts, the God of Israel: Add your burnt offerings to your other sacrifices and eat the meat! 22 For when I freed your fathers from the land of Egypt, I did not speak with them or command them concerning burnt offerings or sacrifice. 23 But this is what I commanded them: Do My bidding, that I may be your God and you may be My people; walk only in the way that I enjoin upon you, that it may go well with you. 24 Yet they did not listen or give ear; they followed their own counsels, the willfulness of their evil hearts. They have gone backward, not forward, 25 from the day your fathers left the land of Egypt until today. And though I kept sending all My servants, the prophets, to them[a] daily and persistently, 26 they would not listen to Me or give ear. They stiffened their necks, they acted worse than their fathers.

27 You shall say all these things to them, but they will not listen to you; you shall call to them, but they will not respond to you. 28 Then say to them: This is the nation that would not obey the LORD their God, that would not accept rebuke. Faithfulness has perished, vanished from their mouths.

29   Shear your locks and cast them away,
        Take up a lament on the heights,
        For the LORD has spurned and cast off
        The brood that provoked His wrath.

30 For the people of Judah have done what displeases Me—declares the LORD. They have set up their abominations in the House which is called by My name, and they have defiled it. 31 And they have built the shrines of Topheth in the Valley of Ben-hinnom to burn their sons and daughters in fire—which I never commanded, which never came to My mind. 32 Assuredly, a time is coming—declares the LORD— when men shall no longer speak of Topheth or the Valley of Ben-hinnom, but of the Valley of Slaughter; and they shall bury in Topheth until no room is left. 33 The carcasses

and fertility (see also Jer. 44.15–30). **7.21–8.3:** God recounts the people's stubbornness in the wilderness to show that they will not listen to Jeremiah. **7.29:** *Shear your locks:* Shaving the head is a sign of mourning (Lev. 21.5; Mic. 1.16; cf. Jer. 16.6). **31:** *Topheth* or *the Valley of Ben-hinnom* runs along the southwest borders of the biblical city of Jerusalem as it was expanded in the time of Hezekiah. It was an area known for tombs and the sacrifice of children to the pagan gods Baal and Molech (see Isa. 30.33; Jer. 19.6, 11–14; 2 Chron. 28.3; 33.6). King Josiah attempted to stop the practice (2 Kings 23.10), but it apparently continued after his death. The Heb expression, "gei' hinnom," "valley of Hinnom," underlies the terms "geihinnom" or "gehenna," which designates Hell in Jewish tradition (see *b. 'Eruv.* 19a; *b. Tamid* 32b). **32:** The phrase *Assuredly, a time is coming* is very common in the prophets for introducing either punishment or restoration. Often tradition understands this as referring to a time in the distant future, "the end of days," but passages such as this suggest that the reference is more typically to the near future.

a Heb. "you."

of this people shall be food for the birds of the sky and the beasts of the earth, with none to frighten them off. ³⁴ And I will silence in the towns of Judah and the streets of Jerusalem the sound of mirth and gladness, the voice of bridegroom and bride. For the whole land shall fall to ruin.

8 At that time—declares the LORD—the bones of the kings of Judah, of its officers, of the priests, of the prophets, and of the inhabitants of Jerusalem shall be taken out of their graves ² and exposed to the sun, the moon, and all the host of heaven which they loved and served and followed, to which they turned and bowed down. They shall not be gathered for reburial; they shall become dung upon the face of the earth. ³ And death shall be preferable to life for all that are left of this wicked folk, in all the other places to which I shall banish them—declares the LORD of Hosts.

4　　　Say to them: Thus said the LORD:
　　　When men fall, do they not get up again?
　　　If they turn aside, do they not turn back?
5　　　Why is this people—Jerusalem—rebellious
　　　With a persistent rebellion?
　　　They cling to deceit,
　　　They refuse to return.
6　　　I have listened and heard:
　　　They do not speak honestly.
　　　No one regrets his wickedness
　　　And says, "What have I done!"
　　　They all persist in their wayward course
　　　Like a steed dashing forward in the fray.
7　　　Even the stork in the sky knows her seasons,
　　　And the turtledove, swift, and crane
　　　Keep the time of their coming;
　　　But My people pay no heed
　　　To the law of the LORD.
8　　　How can you say, "We are wise,
　　　And we possess the Instruction of the LORD"?
　　　Assuredly, for naught has the pen labored,
　　　For naught the scribes!
9　　　The wise shall be put to shame,
　　　Shall be dismayed and caught;
　　　See, they reject the word of the LORD,
　　　So their wisdom amounts to nothing.

10　　Assuredly, I will give their wives to others,
　　　And their fields to dispossessors;

8.4–9.25: God's continued instruction and dialogue with Jeremiah. It is unlikely that this material was a part of Jeremiah's Temple sermon; it is probably placed here because it expresses similar concerns. **8.4–12:** God expresses frustration over the people's behavior. **7:** Even though animals, such as the *stork, turtledove, swift,* and *crane,* know their own times for proper action, God maintains that the people of Jerusalem do not. This observation (see Isa. 1.3) involves the traditions of wisdom literature, in which observation of the natural order of the world or the conduct of its creatures also serves as a source for the revelation of divine wisdom (see Prov. 8.22–36; 30.24–28; cf. Isa. 28.23–29). Indeed, wise men and women are mentioned frequently in the following unit, and much of the larger unit is addressed to this group. Biblical wisdom is typically equated with practical, rather than religious, knowledge, though in later Jewish tradition, wisdom is equated with Torah (see intro. to Proverbs).

For from the smallest to the greatest,
They are all greedy for gain;
Priest and prophet alike,
They all act falsely.
11   They offer healing offhand
For the wounds of My poor people,
Saying, "All is well, all is well,"
When nothing is well.
12   They have acted shamefully;
They have done abhorrent things—
Yet they do not feel shame,
They cannot be made to blush.
Assuredly, they shall fall among the falling,
They shall stumble at the time of their doom
                              —said the Lord.

13   *ᵃI will make an end of them*ᵃ
                              —declares the Lord:
No grapes left on the vine,
No figs on the fig tree,
The leaves all withered;
*ᵇWhatever I have given them is gone.*ᵇ
14   Why are we sitting by?
Let us gather into the fortified cities
And meet our doom there.
For the Lord our God has doomed us,
He has made us drink a bitter draft,
Because we sinned against the Lord.
15   We hoped for good fortune, but no happiness
            came;
For a time of relief—instead there is terror!
16   The snorting of their horses was heard from Dan;
At the loud neighing of their steeds
The whole land quaked.
They came and devoured the land and what was
            in it,
The towns and those who dwelt in them.

17   Lo, I will send serpents against you,
Adders that cannot be charmed,
And they shall bite you   —declares the Lord.

18   *ᵇWhen in grief I would seek comfort,*ᵇ
My heart is sick within me.

13–17: God informs Jeremiah of the decision to "gather" the people, translated here as *make an end of them*. See Zeph. 1.2 for a similar Heb phrase. The verb "ʾasaf," "to gather," is often employed for the gathering of a harvest (Exod. 23.20, 16; Lev. 23.39; Deut. 16.13). Compare the name for the festival of Sukkot, "Ḥag haʾasif," "the festival of the harvest" (lit. ingathering). Jeremiah takes the positive image of harvest and reverses it as a metaphor for the punishment of the people, who do not fully appreciate their obligations to God for what He has done for them (cf. Deut. 26.1–15). **18–23:** The prophet laments over the fate of his people. In this remarkable first-person passage (see 4.19 n.) the prophet imagines the people already in exile (v. 19) and creates a complex dialogue.

a-a Meaning of Heb. uncertain; change of vocalization yields "Their fruit harvest has been gathered in."
b-b Meaning of Heb. uncertain.

19a "Is not the LORD in Zion?
Is not her King within her?
Why then did they anger Me with their images,
With alien futilities?"

Hark! The outcry of my poor people
From the land far and wide:
20 "Harvest is past,
Summer is gone,
But we have not been saved."
21 Because my people is shattered I am shattered;
I am dejected, seized by desolation.
22 Is there no balm in Gilead?
Can no physician be found?
Why has healing not yet
Come to my poor people?
23 Oh, that my head were water,
My eyes a fount of tears!
Then would I weep day and night
For the slain of my poor people.

9 Oh, to be in the desert,
At an encampment for wayfarers!
Oh, to leave my people,
To go away from them—
For they are all adulterers,
A band of rogues.

2 They bend their tongues like bows;
They are valorous in the land
For treachery, not for honesty;
They advance from evil to evil.
And they do not heed Me
—declares the LORD.
3 Beware, every man of his friend!
Trust not even a brother!
For every brother takes advantage,
Every friend b-is base in his dealings.-b
4 One man cheats the other,
They will not speak truth;
They have trained their tongues to speak falsely;
c-They wear themselves out working iniquity.
5 You dwell in the midst of deceit.
In their deceit,-c they refuse to heed Me
—declares the LORD.

22: *Gilead* is the part of Israel located to the east of the Jordan River, south of Bashan (Golan Heights) and north of Moab. It was apparently a site where balm and other healing substances could be extracted from local plants (see Gen. 37.25). **9.1–10:** God expresses a desire to abandon Israel out in the desert, which recalls earlier traditions in which God proposed to destroy Israel in the wilderness and make a great people out of Moses (see Exod. chs 32–34; Num. ch 14). In both cases, Moses persuaded God to desist from destroying Israel. Instead, God determines to destroy Jerusalem and Judah (cf. Mic. 3.12). This unit begins with the same phrase "oh" (Heb "mi yiten") that concluded the previous unit. This type of editing, where units are combined based on common phrases ("catchwords"), is frequent in the prophets.

a Here God is speaking.   b-b See note at Lev. 19.16.
c-c Meaning of Heb. uncertain.

6   Assuredly, thus said the LORD of Hosts:
       Lo, I shall smelt and assay them—
       ᵃ·For what else can I do because of My poor
          people?·ᵃ
7   Their tongue is a sharpened arrow,
       They use their mouths to deceive.
       One speaks to his fellow in friendship,
       But lays an ambush for him in his heart.
8   Shall I not punish them for such deeds?
                              —says the LORD—
       Shall I not bring retribution
       On such a nation as this?

9   For the mountains I take up weeping and wailing,
       For the pastures in the wilderness, a dirge.
       They are laid waste; no man passes through,
       And no sound of cattle is heard.
       Birds of the sky and beasts as well
       Have fled and are gone.

10   I will turn Jerusalem into rubble,
       Into dens for jackals;
       And I will make the towns of Judah
       A desolation without inhabitants.

11   What man is so wise
       That he understands this?
       To whom has the LORD's mouth spoken,
       So that he can explain it:
       Why is the land in ruins,
       Laid waste like a wilderness,
       With none passing through?

¹²The LORD replied: Because they forsook the Teaching I had set before them. They did not obey Me and they did not follow it, ¹³but followed their own willful heart and followed the Baalim, as their fathers had taught them. ¹⁴Assuredly, thus said the LORD of Hosts, the God of Israel: I am going to feed that people wormwood and make them drink a bitter draft. ¹⁵I will scatter them among nations which they and their fathers never knew; and I will dispatch the sword after them until I have consumed them.

16   Thus said the LORD of Hosts:
       Listen!

11: Continuing the wisdom themes seen earlier in the larger unit, Jeremiah responds with perplexity over God's ways, much as Job responds to his own afflictions. **12–24:** This passage reiterates that the people are to be punished for their failure to observe Torah and their continued pursuit of foreign gods, such as Baal, the Canaanite god of rain and fertility. This explanation recalls the wilderness traditions in which Israel worshipped the golden calf (Exod. ch 32) or Baal-peor (Num. ch 25). Women were known for performing rituals of mourning in the ancient world, especially since Mesopotamian mythology depicted Ishtar's descent to the underworld to bring her dead lover Tammuz (or Baal in some traditions) back to life at springtime. The image of death climbing through the windows to kill babes and young men recalls Mot, the Canaanite god of death, as well as the tradition of the slaying of the firstborn in Egypt (Exod. chs 11–12).

a-a *Meaning of Heb. uncertain.*

Summon the dirge-singers, let them come;
Send for the skilled women, let them come.
17 Let them quickly start a wailing for us,
That our eyes may run with tears,
Our pupils flow with water.

18 For the sound of wailing
Is heard from Zion:
How we are despoiled!
How greatly we are shamed!
Ah, we must leave our land,
Abandon^a our dwellings!

19 Hear, O women, the word of the LORD,
Let your ears receive the word of His mouth,
And teach your daughters wailing,
And one another lamentation.
20 For death has climbed through our windows,
Has entered our fortresses,
To cut off babes from the streets,
Young men from the squares.

21 Speak thus—says the LORD:
The carcasses of men shall lie
Like dung upon the fields,
Like sheaves behind the reaper,
With none to pick them up.

22 Thus said the LORD:
Let not the wise man glory in his wisdom;
Let not the strong man glory in his strength;
Let not the rich man glory in his riches.
23 But only in this should one glory:
In his earnest devotion to Me.
For I the LORD act with kindness,
Justice, and equity in the world;
For in these I delight   —declares the LORD.

24 Lo, days are coming—declares the LORD—when I will take note of everyone ^bcircumcised in the foreskin:^{-b} 25 of Egypt, Judah, Edom, the Ammonites, Moab, and all the desert dwellers who have the hair of their temples clipped. For all these nations are uncircumcised, but all the House of Israel are ^cuncircumcised of heart.^{-c}

24: Israel, although physically circumcised, is "uncircumcised of heart"—they are not prepared to accept God's teachings (cf. Ezek. 44.7, 9). As in many prophetic texts, the emphasis is that physical ritual actions alone do not assure divine blessing.

a Lit. "They abandoned."
b-b Force of Heb. uncertain.
c-c I.e., their minds are blocked to God's commandments.

10

Hear the word which the LORD has spoken to you,
O House of Israel!

2   Thus said the LORD:
Do not learn to go the way of the nations,
And do not be dismayed by portents in the sky;
Let the nations be dismayed by them!

3   For ª the laws of the nations ª are delusions:
For it is the work of a craftsman's hands.
He cuts down a tree in the forest with an ax,

4   He adorns it with silver and gold,
He fastens it ᵇ with nails and hammer,
So that it does not totter.

5   They are like a scarecrow in a cucumber patch,
They cannot speak.
They have to be carried,
For they cannot walk.
Be not afraid of them, for they can do no harm;
Nor is it in them to do any good.

6   O LORD, there is none like You!
You are great and Your name is great in power.

7   Who would not revere You, O King of the nations?
For that is Your due,
Since among all the wise of the nations
And among all their royalty
There is none like You.

8   But they are both dull and foolish;
ᶜ[Their] doctrine is but delusion;ᶜ
It is a piece of wood,

9   Silver beaten flat, that is brought from Tarshish,
And gold from Uphaz,
The work of a craftsman and the goldsmith's
hands;
Their clothing is blue and purple,
All of them are the work of skilled men.

10 But the LORD is truly God:
He is a living God,
The everlasting King.
At His wrath, the earth quakes,
And nations cannot endure His rage.

11 ᵈThus shall you say to them: Let the gods, who did not make heaven and earth, perish from the earth and from under these heavens.

---

a-a *Emendation yields "the objects that the nations fear."*   b *Heb. "them."*
c-c *Meaning of Heb. uncertain.*   d *This verse is in Aramaic.*

10.1–25: God's concluding condemnation of the nations that oppress Israel. The prophet's account of the Temple sermon concludes with God's condemnation of those who oppress Israel. Although no texts from Isaiah ben Amoz are cited, this section reflects Isaian thinking in which nations are first brought by God to punish Israel and then condemned for their cruelty and failure to acknowledge God (cf. Isa. chs 5–12; 13–14). This section has many affinities with the exilic Second Isaiah (Isa. chs 40–55). **1–16:** Jeremiah conveys God's satirical assessment of the idols worshipped by the nations. The parallels with Second Isaiah's polemics against idols suggest that Second Isaiah may have drawn on the Jeremian tradition (see Isa. 40.18–20; 41.6–7; 44.9–20; cf. Ps. 115.3–8). **3–4:** Because idols are made by craftsmen from wood, *silver, gold, nails,* etc., they have no power to do either good or evil. As is typical in biblical rhetoric, the physical representations of the deities (idols) are intentionally confused, for polemical purposes, with the deities that they represent. **6:** The absolute incomparability of the LORD goes beyond the statement in the Song of the Sea (Exod. 15.11): "Who is like You, O LORD, among the celestials," reflecting a movement toward more radical monotheism by this period. **9:** The location of *Tarshish* is uncertain, though various biblical texts suggest that it was located somewhere in the Mediterranean, reachable by ship, and was far away from Israel (see 1 Kings 10.22; Isa. 23.1; Ezek. 27.25; Jonah 1.3). *Uphaz* is unknown (cf. Dan. 10.5). Some claim that the text should read Ophir, which was known as a source for gold (1 Kings 9.28). Royal garments were dyed *blue and purple,* and could be used to dress idols in antiquity. The condemnation of other gods appears also in Ps. 82 and Zeph. 2.11. **11:** This v. is the only one in Jeremiah written in Aramaic; this suggests that it is a later gloss. Aramaic was becoming the

12 He made the earth by His might,
Established the world by His wisdom,
And by His understanding stretched out the skies.

13 ᵃWhen He makes His voice heard,⁻ᵃ
There is a rumbling of water in the skies;
He makes vapors rise from the end of the earth,
He makes lightning for the rain,
And brings forth wind from His treasuries.

14 Every man is proved dull, without knowledge;
Every goldsmith is put to shame because of the
idol,
For his molten image is a deceit—
There is no breath in them.

15 They are delusion, a work of mockery;
In their hour of doom, they shall perish.

16 Not like these is the Portion of Jacob;
For it is He who formed all things,
And Israel is His very own tribe:
LORD of Hosts is His name.

17 Gather up your bundleᵇ from the ground,
You who dwell under siege!

18 For thus said the LORD: I will fling away the inhabitants of the land this time: I will harass them so that they
shall ᶜfeel it.⁻ᶜ

19 Woe unto me for my hurt,
My wound is severe!
I thought, "This is but a sickness
And I must bear it."

20 My tents are ravaged,
All my tent cords are broken.
My children have gone forth from me
And are no more;
No one is left to stretch out my tents
And hang my tent cloths.

21 For the shepherdsᵈ are dull
And did not seek the LORD;
Therefore they have not prospered
And all their flock is scattered.

22 Hark, a noise! It is coming,
A great commotion out of the north,
That the towns of Judah may be made a
desolation,
A haunt of jackals.

lingua franca of the Near Eastern world at this time, and the editor likely means to suggest that this verse may be quoted directly to non-Israelites, who would not understand Hebrew. The theme, God's role as creator, is a basic one in Second Isaiah (Isa. 40.12–31; 42.5) and in the Psalms (Ps. 29; 33; 104). **17–25:** The second portion of the ch focuses on the prophet's response to God's words. **20–21:** The portrayal of his ravaged tents, fleeing children, and scattered flocks contrasts with the portrayal of Mother Zion in Isa. ch 54, whose tents are stretched out to receive her returning children.

a-a Lit. "At the sound of His making."   b Meaning of Heb. uncertain.
c-c Emendation yields "have to leave."   d I.e., rulers; cf. note at 2.8.

23 I know, O Lord, that man's road is not his [to
choose],
That man, as he walks, cannot direct his own
steps.
24 Chastise me, O Lord, but in measure;
Not in Your wrath, lest You reduce me to naught.
25 Pour out Your wrath on the nations who have not
heeded You,
Upon the clans that have not invoked Your name.
For they have devoured Jacob,
Have devoured and consumed him,
And have laid desolate his homesteads.

11 The word which came to Jeremiah from the Lord:

2 "Hear the terms of this covenant, and recite them to
the men of Judah and the inhabitants of Jerusalem! 3 And
say to them, Thus said the Lord, the God of Israel: Cursed
be the man who will not obey the terms of this covenant,
4 which I enjoined upon your fathers when I freed them
from the land of Egypt, the iron crucible, saying, 'Obey
Me and observe them,[a] just as I command you, that you
may be My people and I may be your God'—5 in order to
fulfill the oath which I swore to your fathers, to give them
a land flowing with milk and honey, as is now the case."
And I responded, "Amen, Lord."

6 And the Lord said to me, "Proclaim all these things
through the towns of Judah and the streets of Jerusalem:
Hear the terms of this covenant, and perform them. 7 For I
have repeatedly and persistently warned your fathers
from[b] the time I brought them out of Egypt to this day,
saying: Obey My commands. 8 But they would not listen

a I.e., the terms of the covenant.   b Lit. "at."

23–25: The prophet concludes by
acknowledging God's sovereignty
and by asking for mercy and
justice. **25:** This v., which likely
reflects the destruction of Jerusalem, appears in Ps. 79.6–7 with
slightly different wording, and is
likely copied from the psalm to
this context. This reflects the nature of the growth of Jeremiah,
and of prophetic texts in general,
where the words of the original
author are often supplemented
for a variety of reasons by many
hands. After the Christian persecution of Jews in the medieval period, this v. has been recited dur-

ing the Passover Seder when
the door is opened to admit the
prophet Elijah. It expresses the
hope for ultimate divine justice in
the world.

**11.1–13.27: Jeremiah's lament
concerning Judah's broken covenant with God.** The prophetic
word formula in Jeremiah 11.1
marks the beginning of this unit,
which presents a dialogue between God and Jeremiah concerning Judah's breaking of its covenant. Whereas God instructs
Jeremiah to announce punishment
against Judah and to perform sym-

bolic actions to illustrate the
nation's guilt, Jeremiah laments
the situation and demands that
God act justly. **11.1–17:** Jeremiah
relates how God instructed him to
announce to the people of Jerusalem and Judah that they have broken the covenant made between
God and their ancestors. Many interpreters speculate that this text
may have been composed to call
upon the people of Jerusalem and
Judah to support Josiah's reform,
but that it was later reworked to
account for Judah's subjugation to
Egypt or Babylonia in the years
following Josiah's death or perhaps to explain the Babylonian
exile. The centrality of the notion
of "covenant" as well as much of
the terminology of this prose suggest clear affinities with Deuteronomy. **2:** *Hear* and *recite* are in the
plural because, according to traditional interpretation, this statement is addressed to the three
prophets active at this time. According to *Pesikta Rabbati,* the
prophetess Huldah (2 Kings
22.14–20; 2 Chron. 34.22–28), a relative of Jeremiah, spoke to the
women, while Jeremiah spoke to
the men on the streets (see v. 6).
Jeremiah's teacher, Zephaniah
(Zeph. 1.1), preached in the synagogue. **3–5:** The reference to the
curses that will overtake those
who do not obey the covenant recalls the curses directed against
those who disregard God's expectations in Deut. ch 27. God's statement, *that you may be My people and
I may be your God,* is a typical expression of the covenant relationship between God and Israel (Gen.
17.7–8; Exod. 6.7; Deut. 26.17–19;
29.12; Jer. 7.23; 31.1, 33). Jeremiah's
response, *Amen, Lord,* echoes
Israel's affirmation of the curses
in Deut. ch 27. *Amen,* from a root
meaning "true," is an exclamation
meaning "surely!" that signifies
the acceptance and endorsement of what has just been said.
6–8: God's instructions revert to
the singular as they are now addressed only to Jeremiah. *The terms*
(lit. "the words") *of this covenant*
refers to laws found in the "torah"
and the curses imposed if they are

or give ear; they all followed the willfulness of their evil hearts. So I have brought upon them all the terms[a] of this covenant, because they did not do what I commanded them to do."

9 The LORD said to me, "A conspiracy exists among the men of Judah and the inhabitants of Jerusalem. 10 They have returned to the iniquities of their fathers of old, who refused to heed My words. They, too, have followed other gods and served them. The House of Israel and the House of Judah have broken the covenant that I made with their fathers."

11 Assuredly, thus said the LORD: I am going to bring upon them disaster from which they will not be able to escape. Then they will cry out to me, but I will not listen to them. 12 And the townsmen[b] of Judah and the inhabitants of Jerusalem will go and cry out to the gods to which they sacrifice; but they will not be able to rescue them in their time of disaster. 13 For your gods have become as many as your towns, O Judah, and you have set up as many altars to Shame[c] as there are streets in Jerusalem—altars for sacrifice to Baal.

14 As for you, do not pray for this people, do not raise a cry of prayer on their behalf; for I will not listen when they call to Me on account of their disaster.

15   Why should My beloved be in My House,
      [d-]Who executes so many vile designs?
      The sacral flesh will pass away from you,
      For you exult while performing your evil deeds.[-d]
16   The LORD named you
      "Verdant olive tree,
      Fair, with choice fruit."
      But with a great roaring sound
      He has set it on fire,
      And its boughs are broken.[e]

17 The LORD of Hosts, who planted you, has decreed disaster for you, because of the evil wrought by the House of Israel and the House of Judah, who angered Me by sacrificing to Baal.

18   The LORD informed me, and I knew—
      Then You let me see their deeds.

a *I.e., the punishments prescribed for violation.*

b *Lit. "towns."*

c *See note at 3.24.*

d-d *Meaning of Heb. uncertain. Emendation yields "Who does such vile deeds? / Can your treacheries be canceled by sacral flesh / That you exult while performing your evil deeds?"*

e *Emendation yields "burned."*

---

not obeyed (Deut. chs 28–30). **9–13:** God's refusal to listen to the cries of the people presents theological problems, especially in light of the modern experience of the Shoah (Holocaust). The Talmud maintains that "the gates of tears are never shut" (*b. Ber.* 32b), but only for the truly penitent. The statement that *your gods have become as many as your towns, O Judah* appears also in Jer. 2.28. The word *Shame* (Heb "boshet") is sometimes substituted for Baal in proper names (e.g., Ish-bosheth, the son of Saul, in 2 Sam. 2.8, but Eshbaal in 1 Chron. 8.33). **14–17:** God refers to Judah as *My beloved*, which draws upon Isaiah's vineyard allegory (Isa. 5.1–7). Whereas Isaiah characterizes Israel and Judah as a vineyard, the passage in Jeremiah employs the image of an olive tree. Plant and flower imagery to depict lovers is typical (see Song 4.12–16; 6.1–3; 7.11–14; Hos. 14.6–9) and builds upon the portrayal of Israel as God's bride in 2.1–3. **14:** A variant of 7.16, reflecting the editorial compexity of the book.

11.18–23: Jeremiah's first lament. The first of the seven laments or complaints of Jeremiah (11.18–23; 12.1–6; 15.10–21; 17.14–18; 18.18–23; 20.7–13; 20.14–18), in which he complains to God concerning his own suffering for announcing divine judgment to the people. The language is typical of complaint language of the Psalms (e.g., Ps. 7) and Lamentations, but it nevertheless provides an intimate glimpse of the prophet's own feelings. These laments, sometimes called "confessions," typify Jeremiah, in whose book there is more biographical information than in those of all of the other prophets combined.

19 For I was like a docile lamb
Led to the slaughter;
I did not realize
That it was against me
They fashioned their plots:
"Let us destroy the tree with its fruit,ᵃ
Let us cut him off from the land of the living.
That his name be remembered no more!"

20 O Lord of Hosts, O just Judge,
Who test the thoughts and the mind,
Let me see Your retribution upon them,
For I lay my case before You.

²¹ Assuredly, thus said the Lord of Hosts concerning the men of Anathoth who seek your life and say, "You must not prophesy any more in the name of the Lord, or you will die by our hand"—²² Assuredly, thus said the Lord of Hosts: "I am going to deal with them: the young men shall die by the sword, their boys and girls shall die by famine. ²³ No remnant shall be left of them, for I will bring disaster on the men of Anathoth, the year of their doom."

12 You will win,ᵇ O Lord, if I make claim against You,
Yet I shall present charges against You:
Why does the way of the wicked prosper?
Why are the workers of treachery at ease?

2 You have planted them, and they have taken root,
They spread, they even bear fruit.
You are present in their mouths,
But far from their thoughts.

3 Yet You, Lord, have noted and observed me;
You have tested my heart, and found it with You.
Drive them out like sheep to the slaughter,
Prepare them for the day of slaying!

4 How long must the land languish,
And the grass of all the countryside dry up?
Must beasts and birds perish,
Because of the evil of its inhabitants,
Who say, "He will not look upon our future"?ᶜ

5ᵈ If you race with the foot-runners and they exhaust
you,
How then can you compete with horses?

19: Jeremiah portrays himself as a lamb led to slaughter, the victim of a conspiracy, a tree that is cut down. **20:** He pleads directly to God as though he were in a court of law to demand that God bring those who persecute him to justice. **21–23:** Although his oppressors demand that he no longer prophesy in the name of God, God as judge responds that his oppressors will die by the sword. Apparently, those who sought to kill Jeremiah are from his home town of Anathoth.

12.1–6: Jeremiah's second lament. The prophet employs legal language to charge that God has failed to do justice. **1:** Jeremiah's question, *Why does the way of the wicked prosper?*, is also voiced in Hab. 1.13 and Job 21.7 (cf. Ps. 70; Eccl. (5.7). **2:** The prophet employs a common biblical and Near Eastern metaphor of trees that grow and take root (see Ps. 1.3) to portray the wicked, in contrast to his own misfortune (see 11.16–17, 19). **5–6:** God's response suggests that even greater hardships are ahead, and that Jeremiah must prepare to meet them.

---

a Or "sap."   b Lit. "be in the right."   c Septuagint reads "ways."
d God here replies to Jeremiah's plea in vv. 1–3.

If you are ^{a-}secure only^{-a} in a tranquil land,
How will you fare in the jungle of the Jordan?
6   For even your kinsmen and your father's house,
Even they are treacherous toward you,
They cry after you as a mob.
Do not believe them
When they speak cordially to you.

7   I have abandoned My House,
I have deserted My possession,
I have given over My dearly beloved
Into the hands of her enemies.
8   My own people^b acted toward Me
Like a lion in the forest;
She raised her voice against Me—
Therefore I have rejected her.
9   ^{c-}My own people acts toward Me
Like a bird of prey [or] a hyena;
Let the birds of prey surround her!^{-c}
Go, gather all the wild beasts,
Bring them to devour!
10   Many shepherds have destroyed My vineyard,
Have trampled My field,
Have made My delightful field
A desolate wilderness.
11   ^{d-}They have^{-d} made her a desolation;
Desolate, she pours out grief to Me.
The whole land is laid desolate,
But no man gives it thought.
12   Spoilers have come
Upon all the bare heights of the wilderness.
For a sword of the LORD devours
From one end of the land to the other;
No flesh is safe.
13   They have sown wheat and reaped thorns,
They have endured pain to no avail.
Be shamed, then, by your harvest—
By the blazing wrath of the LORD!

14 Thus said the LORD: As for My wicked neighbors who encroach on the heritage that I gave to My people Israel— I am going to uproot them from their soil, and I will uproot the House of Judah out of the midst of them. 15 Then, after I have uprooted them, I will take them back into

12.7–17: God's lament over the destruction of Judah. God continues the dialogue with Jeremiah by offering a lament over the fate of Judah. *My house* refers to the Temple, and *My possession* to the nation of Judah. God continues to employ the metaphor of *My dearly beloved* for the people (cf. 11.15), which again draws on Isaiah's vineyard allegory (Isa. 5.1–7). God's vineyard is trampled in Isa. 5.5 (cf. Isa. 3.14) after God breaks down the protective hedges as a punishment. In the present context, God's own shepherds, i.e., the people of Jerusalem and Judah and their leaders, have trampled the vineyard themselves and left it exposed to those who would despoil it. **14–17:** A concluding oracle outlines God's plans to punish the nations that border Judah as well as Judah itself. The purpose is to provide them the opportunity to swear allegiance to God, though unlike Israel, they are not expected to follow the entire Torah.

a-a Some Septuagint mss. read "not secure."
b Lit. "possession"; the land as well as the people, as is clear in v. 14.
c-c Meaning of Heb. uncertain.
d-d Heb. "He has."

favor, and restore them each to his own inheritance and his own land. [16] And if they learn the ways of My people, to swear by My name—"As the LORD lives"—just as they once taught My people to swear by Baal, then they shall be ᵃbuilt up in the midst ofᵃ My people. [17] But if they do not give heed, I will tear out that nation, tear it out and destroy it—declares the LORD.

13 Thus the LORD said to me: "Go buy yourself a loincloth of linen, and put it around your loins, but do not dip it into water." [2] So I bought the loincloth in accordance with the LORD's command, and put it about my loins. [3] And the word of the LORD came to me a second time: [4] "Take the loincloth which you bought, which is about your loins, and go at once to Perathᵇ and cover it up there in a cleft of the rock." [5] I went and buried it at Perath, as the LORD had commanded me. [6] Then, after a long time, the LORD said to me, "Go at once to Perath and take there the loincloth which I commanded you to bury there." [7] So I went to Perath and dug up the loincloth from the place where I had buried it; and found the loincloth ruined; it was not good for anything.

[8] The word of the LORD came to me: [9] Thus said the LORD: Even so will I ruin the overweening pride of Judah and Jerusalem. [10] This wicked people who refuse to heed My bidding, who follow the willfulness of their own hearts, who follow other gods and serve them and worship them, shall become like that loincloth, which is not good for anything. [11] For as the loincloth clings close to the loins of a man, so I brought close to Me the whole House of Israel and the whole House of Judah—declares the LORD—that they might be My people, for fame, and praise, and splendor. But they would not obey.

[12] And speak this word to them: Thus said the LORD, the God of Israel: "Every jar should be filled with wine." And when they say to you, "Don't we know that every jar should be filled with wine?" [13] say to them, "Thus said the LORD: I am going to fill with drunkenness all the inhabitants of this land, and the kings who sit on the throne of

a-a Or "incorporated into."

b Or "the Euphrates"; cf. "Parah," Josh. 18.23.

13.1–27: Jeremiah's symbolic acts. Prophets in the ancient world sometimes performed symbolic actions to dramatize their messages. Zedekiah son of Chenaanah employed iron horns to demonstrate that Ahab and Jehoshaphat would defeat the Arameans (1 Kings ch 22). Isaiah walked about naked and barefoot to symbolize the Assyrian defeat of the Egyptians at Ashdod (Isa. ch 20). Ezekiel cut off his hair, burning one-third, cutting one-third with a sword, and scat-tering one-third to the wind to symbolize the fate of the people at the destruction of Jerusalem (Ezek. ch 5). The actions of these classical prophets differ fundamentally from the more "magical" type of actions of the earlier prophets such as Elijah and Elisha, though in some cases, including this chapter, it is unclear if the actions are merely symbolizing what will happen, or are helping to effect the future. **1–11:** Jeremiah relates God's instructions to buy a loincloth of linen. As an Elide priest, Jeremiah would dress entirely in linen, including any undergarments, as a symbol of Levitical purity and fitness to officiate in the Temple. In the priestly ordination ceremony, priests are washed and dressed in clean garments (Exod. 29.1–9; Lev. 8.1–9; cf. Zech. 3.1–5) as part of the procedure by which they are prepared for divine service at the Temple altar. **1:** Because God commands him to wear the loincloth without dipping it into water, it will of course become soiled to symbolize Jerusalem's and Judah's (and Jeremiah's) impurity. The priestly ordination also requires observance of God's commandments (Zech. 3.6–10), so that Jeremiah's impurity symbolizes the people's refusal to heed God's bidding. The closeness of the loincloth to Jeremiah also draws upon the marriage metaphor used to depict the relationship between God and the people. **4:** Placing the loincloth in a cleft of rock by the Perath, i.e., the Euphrates River in Mesopotamia, makes the loincloth filthy and symbolizes exile to Babylonia. Interpreters debate whether Jeremiah actually traveled to the Euphrates for this act or chose a location close to Jerusalem with a similar name. **12–14:** God instructs Jeremiah to perform a second symbolic act in which he will fill jars of wine. This apparently mundane action suggests that God will fill the leaders of the nation with wine so that they will become drunk and act without good judgment. The result will be disaster for the nation, symbolized by the jars of wine that will be smashed

David, and the priests and the prophets, and all the inhabitants of Jerusalem. ¹⁴ And I will smash them one against the other, parents and children alike—declares the LORD; no pity, compassion, or mercy will stop Me from destroying them."

15   Attend and give ear; be not haughty,
        For the LORD has spoken.
16   Give honor to the LORD your God
        Before He brings darkness,
        Before your feet stumble
        On the mountains in shadow—
        When you hope for light,
        And it is turned to darkness
        And becomes deep gloom.
17   For if you will not give heed,
        My inmost self must weep,
        Because of your arrogance;
        My eye must stream and flow
        With copious tears,
        Because the flock of the LORD
        Is taken captive.

18   Say to the king and the queen mother,
        "Sit in a lowly spot;
        For your diadems are abased,
        Your glorious crowns."
19   The cities of the Negeb are shut,
        There is no one to open them;
        ᵃJudah is exiled completely,
        All of it exiled.⁻ᵃ
20   Raise your eyes and behold
        Those who come from the north:
        Where are the sheep entrusted to you,
        The flock you took pride in?
21   ᵇWhat will you say when they appoint as your
                heads
        Those among you whom you trained to be tame?⁻ᵇ
        Shall not pangs seize you
        Like a woman in childbirth?
22   And when you ask yourself,
        "Why have these things befallen me?"
        It is because of your great iniquity
        That your skirts are lifted up,
        Your limbs exposed.

against each other and destroyed. **15–27:** The meaning of the symbolic actions is further clarified by the following oracles. **15–17:** The first takes up the images of *light* and *darkness* found in Isaiah's oracle concerning the darkness that will overtake the land prior to the emergence of the righteous Davidic monarch (Isa. 8.16–9.6). Isaiah had stated that he would wait for God who hides the divine face from Israel until the people walking in darkness see a great light (Isa. 8.17; 9.1). According to Jeremiah, the time of darkness and punishment has arrived in his own time. The prophet weeps because the time of the righteous Davidic monarch has not yet come. **18–22:** Instead, the king and queen mother are humbled, their crowns and diadems abased, and Judah is exiled or annexed by an alien people from the north. Notably, Isa. ch 28 points to the proud crowns worn by the drunkards of Ephraim. Jeremiah's symbolic actions pertaining to exile and drunkenness indicate that the judgment announced for Israel in Isa. ch 28 has now come upon Judah. **19:** A string of fortresses was built in the Negev desert in the southern part of Judah during the 7th century BCE, indicating that it had become a major Judean population and trade center. **21:** Jeremiah returns to the marriage metaphor and the symbol of the loincloth close to God, portraying Judah's pain like that of a woman in childbirth.

a-a I.e., most of Judah has been annexed by an alien people.
b-b Meaning of Heb. uncertain.

23 Can the Cushite change his skin,
   Or the leopard his spots?
   Just as much can you do good,
   Who are practiced in doing evil!

24 So I will scatter you^a like straw that flies
   Before the desert wind.

25 This shall be your lot,
   Your measured portion from Me
                    —declares the LORD.
   Because you forgot Me
   And trusted in falsehood,

26 I in turn will lift your skirts over your face
   And your shame shall be seen.

27 I behold your adulteries,
   Your lustful neighing,
   Your unbridled depravity, your vile acts
   On the hills of the countryside.
   Woe to you, O Jerusalem,
   Who will not be clean!
   How much longer shall it be?

14 The word of the LORD which came to Jeremiah concerning the droughts.

2 Judah is in mourning,
   Her settlements languish.
   Men are bowed to the ground,
   And the outcry of Jerusalem rises.

3 Their nobles sent their servants for water;
   They came to the cisterns, they found no
             water.
   They returned, their vessels empty.
   They are shamed and humiliated,
   They cover their heads.

4 ^{b-}Because of the ground there is dismay,^{-b}
   For there has been no rain on the earth.
   The plowmen are shamed,
   They cover their heads.

5 Even the hind in the field
   Forsakes her new-born fawn,
   Because there is no grass.

6 And the wild asses stand on the bare heights,
   Snuffing the air like jackals;
   Their eyes pine,
   Because there is no herbage.

23–27: By asking rhetorically whether *the Cushite* can *change his skin* or a *leopard his spots*, he suggests that Judah never changes. Judah, who lifted her skirts in wantonness, will have her skirts lifted in order to shame her.

14.1–17.27: The great drought and Judah's coming punishment. The prophetic word formula introduces a new section that begins with an oracle concerning drought in Judah. It continues by developing various nuances of suffering due to drought, such as the (false) prophets who claim no calamity is forthcoming, the coming plague, sword, famine, and captivity, Jeremiah's own celibacy, and the parched desert in which Judah will dwell.

14.1–22: The great drought. Judah apparently suffered a great drought that Jeremiah understood to symbolize divine judgment against the nation. Throughout the Bible, the LORD was portrayed as a God who controlled the cosmos and thus would bring rain to the people each year so that they would be able to grow crops and raise cattle to provide themselves with food (see, e.g., Deut. 11.13–17; 28.1–14; 1 Kings 17.1). In an ancient subsistence economy based upon agriculture, a drought frequently meant starvation for many (cf. 1 Kings chs 17–18). This was especially so in Israel, where rain was seasonal, falling in the fall and winter only. In later Judaism, various rites were performed to assure that rain would fall during the rainy season (*m. Sukkah* 4.9–10; cf. *b. Sukkah* 53a; *m. Ta'an.* 1.1–7). The oracle notes the fasting of the people, which begins in rabbinic tradition on the 17th of Marḥeshvan (typically in November) if no rain has fallen by then (*m. Ta'an.* 1.4–7).

a Heb. "them."
b-b Meaning of Heb. uncertain.

7   Though our iniquities testify against us,
    Act, O Lᴏʀᴅ, for the sake of Your name;
    Though our rebellions are many
    And we have sinned against You.
8   O Hope of Israel,
    Its deliverer in time of trouble,
    Why are You like a stranger in the land,
    Like a traveler who stops only for the night?
9   Why are You like a man who is stunned,
    Like a warrior who cannot give victory?
    Yet You are in our midst, O Lᴏʀᴅ,
    And Your name is attached to us—
    Do not forsake us!

10 Thus said the Lᴏʀᴅ concerning this people: "Truly, they love to stray, they have not restrained their feet; so the Lᴏʀᴅ has no pleasure in them. Now He will recall their iniquity and punish their sin."

11 And the Lᴏʀᴅ said to me, "Do not pray for the benefit of this people. 12 When they fast, I will not listen to their outcry; and when they present burnt offering and meal offering, I will not accept them. I will exterminate them by war, famine, and disease."

13 I said, "Ah, Lord Gᴏᴅ! The prophets are saying to them, 'You shall not see the sword, famine shall not come upon you, but I will give you unfailing security in this place.'"

14 The Lᴏʀᴅ replied: It is a lie that the prophets utter in My name. I have not sent them or commanded them. I have not spoken to them. A lying vision, an empty divination, the deceit of their own contriving—that is what they prophesy to you! 15 Assuredly, thus said the Lᴏʀᴅ concerning the prophets who prophesy in My name though I have not sent them, and who say, "Sword and famine shall not befall this land"; those very prophets shall perish by sword and famine. 16 And the people to whom they prophesy shall be left lying in the streets of Jerusalem because of the famine and the sword, with none to bury them—they, their wives, their sons, and their daughters. I will pour out upon them [the requital of] their wickedness.

17   And do you speak to them thus:
    Let my eyes run with tears,
    Day and night let them not cease,
    For ᵃ᠂my hapless people⁻ᵃ has suffered

11–12: These vv. suggest that prophetic prayer would be efficacious, but the ritual actions of the people are not effective unless they are accompanied by changed behaviors—a typical prophetic message. **13–22:** Jeremiah challenges the prophets who promise security to the people, just as he challenged the belief that the presence of the Temple in Jerusalem would protect the nation (7.1–8.3). Jeremiah frequently cites the prophet Isaiah, who represents the Davidic tradition (see esp. Isa. 7.1–17, esp. v. 9b) that promises God's protection of Zion (see Isa. chs 36–37). Many in Jeremiah's time would have read Isaiah's prophecies as signs of divine protection since the Assyrian oppressors had fallen. Jeremiah condemns such hopes as false prophecies (see chs 23; 27–28) as the time of punishment envisioned by Isaiah was about to be realized in Jeremiah's own time. Deut. 18.9–22 cautions against false prophets, i.e., prophets who speak in God's name but whose words do not come to pass. For Jeremiah, those who spoke of security for the nation, whether based on Isaiah or their own observations, were false prophets. The predicted death of these prophets (v. 15) follows the legislation of Deut. 18.20, and the story in Jer. 28.17. The book of Jeremiah as a whole suggests that Jeremiah was prophesying in an atmosphere where many prophets suggested that the Babylonians would not conquer Jerusalem and destroy the Temple. This explains the unpopularity of Jeremiah in his period.

a-a Lit. "the maiden daughter, My people."

A grievous injury, a very painful wound.

18 If I go out to the country—
Lo, the slain of the sword.
If I enter the city—
Lo, ᵃthose who are sick with ᵃ famine.
Both priest and prophet roamᵇ the land,
They know not where.

19 Have You, then, rejected Judah?
Have You spurned Zion?
Why have You smitten us
So that there is no cure?
Why do we hope for happiness,
But find no good;
For a time of healing,
And meet terror instead?

20 We acknowledge our wickedness, O LORD—
The iniquity of our fathers—
For we have sinned against You.

21 For Your name's sake, do not disown us;
Do not dishonor Your glorious throne.
Remember, do not annul Your covenant with us.

22 Can any of the false gods of the nations give rain?
Can the skies of themselves give showers?
Only You can, O LORD our God!
So we hope in You,
For only You made all these things.

15 The LORD said to me, "Even if Moses and Samuel were to ᶜintercede with Me,ᶜ I would not be won over to that people. Dismiss them from My presence, and let them go forth! ² And if they ask you, 'To what shall we go forth?' answer them, 'Thus said the LORD:

Those destined for the plague, to the plague;
Those destined for the sword, to the sword;
Those destined for famine, to famine;
Those destined for captivity, to captivity.

³ And I will appoint over them four kindsᵇ [of punishment]—declares the LORD—the sword to slay, the dogs to drag, the birds of the sky, and the beasts of the earth to devour and destroy. ⁴ I will make them a horror to all the kingdoms of the earth, on account of King Manasseh son of Hezekiah of Judah, and of what he did in Jerusalem.' "

5 But who will pity you, O Jerusalem,
Who will console you?

15.1–21: Jeremiah's lament over Jerusalem's inevitable punishment. The theme of Jerusalem's punishment continues, and Jeremiah laments his task and the city's fate. **1–9:** Jerusalem's punishment is inevitable; not even Moses and Samuel, the great earlier prophetic intercessors, could convince God to reverse the decision. **1:** The mention of *Moses and Samuel* indicates Jeremiah's Elide background, as Samuel was raised in the Shiloh sanctuary where Eli served as high priest (1 Sam. chs 1–4). Insofar as both figures were revered prophets, their mention here confirms God's resolve to punish the city. **2–3:** The four punishments—*plague, sword, famine,* and *captivity*—represent a comprehensive catalogue of punishments not unlike those mentioned in Ezek. ch 5. Even animals participate in the judgment. **4:** By making them *a horror* ("za'avah") *to all the kingdoms of the earth,* God cites the curses of Deut. 28.25. This v. follows the tradition of the book of Kings that King Manasseh of Judah was so evil that God decided to destroy Jerusalem because of him (2 Kings 21.1–18; 23.26–27; 24.3–4).

---

a-a Lit. "the sicknesses of." b Meaning of Heb. uncertain.
c-c Lit. "stand before Me," as Jeremiah is doing now; cf. 18.20.

Who will turn aside to inquire
About your welfare?

6 You cast Me off   —declares the LORD—
You go ever backward.
So I have stretched out My hand to destroy you;
I cannot relent.

7 I will scatter them as with a winnowing fork
Through the settlements of the earth.
I will bereave, I will destroy My people,
For they would not turn back from their ways.

8 Their widows shall be more numerous
Than the sands of the seas.
I will bring against them—
ᵃ⁻Young men and mothers together⁻ᵃ—
A destroyer at noonday.
I will bring down suddenly upon them
Alarmᵇ and terror.

9 She who bore seven is forlorn,
Utterly disconsolate;
Her sun has set while it is still day,
She is shamed and humiliated.
The remnant of them I will deliver to the sword,
To the power of their enemies
                              —declares the LORD.

10 Woe is me, my mother, that you ever bore me—
A man of conflict and strife with all the land!
I have not lent,
And I have not borrowed;
Yet everyone curses me.

11 The LORD said:
ᵃ⁻Surely, a mere remnant of you
Will I spare for a better fate!⁻ᵃ
By the enemy ᶜ⁻from the north⁻ᶜ
In a time of distress and a time of disaster,
Surely, I will have you struck down!

12 ᵈ⁻Can iron break iron and bronze?⁻ᵈ

13 ᵃ⁻I will hand over your wealth and your treasures
As a spoil, free of charge,
Because of all your sins throughout your territory.

14 And I will bring your enemies
By way of a land you have not known.⁻ᵃ
For a fire has flared in My wrath,
It blazes against you.

---

a-a *Meaning of Heb. uncertain.*   b *Meaning of Heb. uncertain.*
c-c *Moved up from v. 12 for clarity.*
d-d *Emendation yields "He shall shatter iron—iron and bronze!"*

6: The formula, *I have stretched out My hand to destroy you,* draws on the traditions of the Exodus plague tradition (Exod. 9.22, 23; 10.12, 13, 21, 22; etc.) and Isaiah (Isa. 5.25; 9.11, 16, 20; 10.4; 14.27). **8:** The statement that *their widows shall be more numerous than the sands of the seas* is an ironic reference to God's promise of many descendants to Abraham (Gen. 22.17) and Jacob (Gen. 32.13; cf. 1 Kings 4.20; Isa. 10.22; Hos. 2.1). The image of the forlorn mother who loses her sons draws upon Isa. 3.25–4.1. The theme is later developed in 2 Macc. ch 7 in relation to the martyrs of the Maccabean period. **10–21:** Jeremiah's third lament takes the form of the prophet's dialogue with God. Upon hearing God's decision, Jeremiah mourns his own birth, an idea expanded in a later text (20.14–18; cf. Job 3.11–19). **11–14:** God responds by claiming that a remnant will survive, a central prophetic idea that is especially prominent in Isaiah (cf. Isa. 4.2–6; 6.1–13; 7.1–9; 10.20–26; 37.30–32).

15 O Lord, you know—
Remember me and take thought of me,
Avenge me on those who persecute me;
Do not yield to Your patience,
ᵃDo not let me perish!ᵃ
Consider how I have borne insult
On Your account.

16 When Your words were offered, I devoured them;
Your word brought me the delight and joy
Of knowing that Your name is attached to me,
O Lord, God of Hosts.

17 I have not sat in the company of revelers
And made merry!
I have sat lonely because of Your hand upon me,
For You have filled me with gloom.

18 Why must my pain be endless,
My wound incurable,
Resistant to healing?
You have been to me like a spring that fails,
Like waters that cannot be relied on.

19 Assuredly, thus said the Lord:
If you turn back, I shall take you back
And you shall stand before Me;
If you produce what is noble
Out of the worthless,
You shall be My spokesman.
They shall come back to you,
Not you to them.

20 Against this people I will make you
As a fortified wall of bronze:
They will attack you,
But they shall not overcome you,
For I am with you to deliver and save you
—declares the Lord.

21 I will save you from the hands of the wicked
And rescue you from the clutches of the violent.

16 The word of the Lord came to me: ² You are not to marry and not to have sons and daughters in this place. ³ For thus said the Lord concerning any sons and daughters that may be born in this place, and concerning the mothers who bear them, and concerning the fathers who beget them in this land: ⁴ They shall die gruesome deaths. They shall not be lamented or buried; they shall be like dung on the surface of the ground. They

15–18: Jeremiah recounts his suffering and anguish to God as his own life becomes a model of Jerusalem's and Judah's suffering. He metaphorically devoured God's words just as Ezekiel would later eat the scroll with God's words to become a prophet (Ezek. 3.1–11). 19–21: God's response further draws the parallel in a measure-for-measure fashion between Jeremiah and Jerusalem/Judah, i.e., if he turns back (repents), God will take him back. V. 19 is somewhat unclear, but the phrase *I shall take you back And you shall stand before Me* seems to suggest that Jeremiah at some point was stripped of his prophetic status, perhaps because he protested too strongly against God, siding with the people. V. 20, which reflects the langauge of 1.18–19, may then be viewed as a recommissioning of Jeremiah as a prophet.

16.1–17.27: Jeremiah's celibacy as a model for Judah's punishment by drought. Jeremiah's failure to produce children serves as a model for Judah's inability to sustain life due to the drought that punishes the nation. **16.1–19:** God's instructions to Jeremiah not to marry or have children represents a reversal of the marriage motif that frequently portrays the relationship between God, the husband, and Israel, the bride (Hos. chs 1–3; Jer. ch 2; Zeph. 3.14–20; Isa. chs 49–54; Ezek. ch 16). According to rabbinic tradition, the command to "be fertile and increase, fill the earth and master it" (Gen. 1.28) is the first of the 613 commandments that all Jewish men are obliged to fulfill (*b. Mak.* 23b).

---

a-a Lit. "Do not take me away."

shall be consumed by the sword and by famine, and their corpses shall be food for the birds of the sky and the beasts of the earth.

5   For thus said the LORD:
        Do not enter a house of mourning,ᵃ
        Do not go to lament and to condole with them;
        For I have withdrawn My favor from that people
                        —declares the LORD—
        My kindness and compassion.
6   Great and small alike shall die in this land,
        They shall not be buried; men shall not lament
            them,
        Nor gash and tonsure themselves for them.
7   They shall not break breadᵇ for a mournerᶜ
        To comfort him for a bereavement,
        Nor offer one a cup of consolation
        For the loss of his father or mother.
8   Nor shall you enter a house of feasting,
        To sit down with them to eat and drink.

⁹ For thus said the LORD of Hosts, the God of Israel: I am going to banish from this place, in your days and before your eyes, the sound of mirth and gladness, the voice of bridegroom and bride.
¹⁰ And when you announce all these things to that people, and they ask you, "Why has the LORD decreed upon us all this fearful evil? What is the iniquity and what the sin that we have committed against the LORD our God?" ¹¹ say to them, "Because your fathers deserted Me—declares the LORD—and followed other gods and served them and worshiped them; they deserted Me and did not keep My Instruction. ¹² And you have acted worse than your fathers, every one of you following the willfulness of his evil heart and paying no heed to Me. ¹³ Therefore I will hurl you out of this land to a land that neither you nor your fathers have known, and there you will serve other gods, day and night; for I will show you no mercy."

¹⁴ Assuredly, a time is coming—declares the LORD—when it shall no more be said, "As the LORD lives who brought the Israelites out of the land of Egypt," ¹⁵ but rather, "As the LORD lives who brought the Israelites out of the northland, and out of all the lands to which He had banished them." For I will bring them back to their land, which I gave to their fathers.

5–8: God's refusal to allow mourning further reinforces the severity of the judgment; the notion seems to be that the calamity will be so extensive, there will be no opportunity for individual mourning. **5:** The reference to *a house of mourning* ("bet marzeaḥ") refers to Israel's adoption of a pagan ritual of mourning coupled with feasting and drinking on behalf of the dead (cf. Isa. ch 28, in which Isaiah satirizes such practice). According to Mesopotamian mythology, the world mourns and the rains stop when the god Tammuz dies at the end of the rainy season in the spring. The goddess Ishtar must travel to the underworld to bring him back to life and thus restore the rains and fertility to the world. Similar traditions are known for Dumuzi and Inanna (in Sumer) and Baal and Anath (in Canaan). The ritual is known from the Ugaritic texts, and was clearly part of broader Canaanite practices which Israel adopted, and to some extent adapted. **9:** *The sound of mirth and gladness, the voice of bridegroom and bride:* This phrase is unique to Jeremiah and serves as a refrain through the book (7.34; 25.10; 33.11). **10–15:** This passage, which concludes by stating that ultimately Israel will be restored just as God redeemed Israel from Egyptian bondage, is full of language that typifies Deuteronomy.

a Lit. "religious gathering."
b So a few mss. Most mss. and editions read "to them."   c Lit. "mourning."

16 Lo, I am sending for many fishermen
                    —declares the LORD—
      And they shall haul them out;
      And after that I will send for many hunters,
      And they shall hunt them
      Out of every mountain and out of every hill
      And out of the clefts of the rocks.
17 For My eyes are on all their ways,
      They are not hidden from My presence,
      Their iniquity is not concealed from My sight.
18 I will pay them in full*—
      Nay, doubly for their iniquity and their sins—
      Because they have defiled My land
      With the corpses of their abominations,*
      And have filled My own possession
      With their abhorrent things.
19 O LORD, my strength and my stronghold,
      My refuge in a day of trouble,
      To You nations shall come
      From the ends of the earth and say:
      Our fathers inherited utter delusions,
      Things that are futile and worthless.
20 Can a man make gods for himself?
      No-gods are they!
21 Assuredly, I will teach them,
      Once and for all I will teach them
      My power and My might.
      And they shall learn that My name is LORD.

17 The guilt of Judah is inscribed
      With a stylus of iron,
      Engraved with an adamant point
      On the tablet of their hearts,
      *And on the horns of their altars,
2   While their children remember*
      Their altars and sacred posts,
      By verdant trees,
      Upon lofty hills.
3   *Because of the sin of your shrines
      Throughout your borders,
      I will make your rampart a heap in the field,
      And all your treasures a spoil.*
4   *You will forfeit,* by your own act,

16: The *fishermen* who haul them out are presumably the nations who will do God's bidding (see Isa. chs 44–45; 66.18–24). This is a basic motif of Second Isaiah, who portrays the return from Babylonia as a second exodus (Isa. chs 40–48). **18:** Like Jeremiah, Isa. 40.2 notes that Jerusalem has paid double for her sins (cf. Exod. 22.6). **19:** Jeremiah responds by looking forward to the day when the nations will come to acknowledge God's sovereignty (Isa. 2.2–4; Mic. 4.1–5; Zech. 8.20–23). Jeremiah 16.19–17.14 is the haftarah for the parashah of Be-ḥukkotai (Lev. 26.3–27.34), which outlines both the blessings of observance of the covenant and the punishment of exile for disobedience. **16.20–17.11:** God responds with a polemic against the worship of idols (cf. Isa. 44.9–20). The initial rhetorical question asserts that humans cannot make gods for themselves, but God will teach the truth (Isa. 2.2–4; Mic. 4.1–5). **17.1:** The reference to *a stylus of iron, engraved with an adamant* [diamond] *point on the tablet of their hearts* is a metaphorical description of the indelible nature of Judah's wrongdoing. This image fits this section, which imagines Israel's sin as grave and its punishment as final, with no opportunity for repentance. In Jeremiah, this engraved sin will ultimately be replaced by divine instruction ("torah") written on the heart when the covenant is restored (see 31.31–34).

---

a See note to Isa. 65.7.   b I.e., their lifeless idols.
c-c Meaning of Heb. uncertain. Emendation yields "Surely the horns of their altars / Are as a memorial against them."
d-d Meaning of Heb. uncertain.
e-e Meaning of Heb. uncertain. Emendation yields "Your hand must let go."

The inheritance I have given you;
I will make you a slave to your enemies
In a land you have never known.
For you have kindled the flame of My wrath
Which shall burn for all time.

5 Thus said the LORD:
   Cursed is he who trusts in man,
   Who makes mere flesh his strength,
   And turns his thoughts from the LORD.
6 He shall be like a bush[a] in the desert,
   Which does not sense the coming of good:
   It is set in the scorched places of the wilderness,
   In a barren land without inhabitant.
7 Blessed is he who trusts in the LORD,
   Whose trust is the LORD alone.
8 He shall be like a tree planted by waters,
   Sending forth its roots by a stream:
   It does not sense the coming of heat,
   Its leaves are ever fresh;
   It has no care in a year of drought,
   It does not cease to yield fruit.

9 Most devious is the heart;
   It is perverse—who can fathom it?
10 I the LORD probe the heart,
   Search the mind—
   To repay every man according to his ways,
   With the proper fruit of his deeds.

11 b-Like a partridge hatching what she did not lay,-b
   So is one who amasses wealth by unjust means;
   In the middle of his life it will leave him,
   And in the end he will be proved a fool.

12 O Throne of Glory exalted from of old,
   Our Sacred Shrine!
13 O Hope of Israel! O LORD!
   All who forsake You shall be put to shame,
   Those in the land who turn from You[c]
   Shall be doomed[d] men,
   For they have forsaken the LORD,
   The Fount of living waters.

5–8: A person who relies on idols is like a bush in a parched land that knows nothing, but those who trust in God are like well-watered trees that produce fruit (see Ps. 1.3). The purpose of this metaphor is to point to worship of other gods as the cause of the drought. 11: Amassing wealth dishonestly is presented here as the consequence of idolatry. 12–18: Jeremiah praises God as Israel's hope and continues the metaphor of drought by comparing God to *a fountain of living waters* (see 2.13). The initial statement of his fourth lament in vv. 14–18, *Heal me, O Lord, and let me be healed*, is rewritten in the plural as "Heal us, O Lord, and let us be healed" in the daily "'Amidah" of the Prayer Book. Jeremiah appeals to God for support by pointing out how steadfastly he has resisted his enemies who challenge his prophecies.

a Or "tamarisk"; exact meaning of Heb. uncertain.
b-b Meaning of Heb. uncertain.
c Lit. "Me."
d Lit. "inscribed"; meaning of line uncertain.

14 Heal me, O Lord, and let me be healed;
   Save me, and let me be saved;
   For You are my glory.

15 See, they say to me:
   "Where is the prediction of the Lord?
   Let it come to pass!"

16 But I have not [a]evaded
   Being a shepherd in your service,[-a]
   Nor have I longed for the fatal day.
   You know the utterances of my lips,
   They were ever before You.

17 Do not be a cause of dismay to me;
   You are my refuge in a day of calamity.

18 Let my persecutors be shamed,
   And let not me be shamed;
   Let them be dismayed,
   And let not me be dismayed.
   Bring on them the day of disaster,
   And shatter them with double destruction.

19 Thus said the Lord to me: Go and stand in the People's Gate, by which the kings of Judah enter and by which they go forth, and in all the gates of Jerusalem, 20 and say to them: Hear the word of the Lord, O kings of Judah, and all Judah, and all the inhabitants of Jerusalem who enter by these gates! 21 Thus said the Lord: Guard yourselves for your own sake against carrying burdens[b] on the sabbath day, and bringing them through the gates of Jerusalem. 22 Nor shall you carry out burdens from your houses on the sabbath day, or do any work, but you shall hallow the sabbath day, as I commanded your fathers. (23 But they would not listen or turn their ear; they stiffened their necks and would not pay heed or accept discipline.) 24 If you obey Me—declares the Lord—and do not bring in burdens through the gates of this city on the sabbath day, but hallow the sabbath day and do no work on it, 25 then through the gates of this city shall enter kings who sit upon the throne of David, with their officers—riding on chariots and horses, they and their officers—and the men of Judah and the inhabitants of Jerusalem. And this city shall be inhabited for all time. 26 And people shall come from the towns of Judah and from the environs of Jerusalem, and from the land of Benjamin, and from the Shephelah, and from the hill country, and from the Negeb, bringing burnt offerings

19–27: God instructs Jeremiah to stand by the people's entrance to the Temple and announce that they should observe the Shabbat, i.e., the seventh day of rest and holy service to God which constitutes one of the fundamental signs of the covenant between God and Israel especially in the Priestly tradition (see Gen. 2.1–3; Exod. 20.8–11; 23.12; 31.12–17; 35.2–3; Lev. 23.3; Deut. 5.12–15). Although many modern interpreters consider this passage (and the emphasis on Shabbat) to be exilic or postexilic, Shabbat observance is mentioned in preexilic prophetic texts (Amos 8.5; Isa. 1.13). It is likely, however, that the Shabbat took on new significance in the exilic period, as holy space (the destroyed Temple) was replaced with holy time. 21: The emphasis on *carrying burdens* is somewhat surprising. Perhaps the reference is to doing work, which was prohibited (Amos 8.5). The Torah is very general, stating that "whoever does work on it" is punished (Exod. 31.14–15). In specifying what types of work are prohibited on the Sabbath, carrying, the focus of Jeremiah, is mentioned prominently in early rabbinic texts (e.g., *m. Shab.* 1.1–3; 6.1–10). 26: The passage describes people coming from places surrounding Jerusalem, including *Benjamin* to the north, the *Shephelah* (low-lying hill country) to the southwest, the *hill country* around Jerusalem itself, and the *Negeb* desert to the south. The "'olah," *burnt offerings,* the "zebaḥ (shelamim)," *sacrifices* (of well-being), "minḥah," *meal offerings,* and "levonah," *frankincense,* are discussed in detail in Lev. chs 1–3.

a-a Exact force of Heb. uncertain. Emendation yields "urged you to [bring] misfortune."
b Or "merchandise."

and sacrifices, meal offerings and frankincense, and bringing offerings of thanksgiving to the House of the LORD.
²⁷ But if you do not obey My command to hallow the sabbath day and to carry in no burdens through the gates of
Jerusalem on the sabbath day, then I will set fire to its
gates; it shall consume the fortresses of Jerusalem and it
shall not be extinguished.

18 The word which came to Jeremiah from the LORD:
² "Go down to the house of a potter, and there I will
impart My words to you." ³ So I went down to the house
of a potter, and found him working at the wheel. ⁴ ªAnd if
the vessel he was making was spoiled, as happens to clay
in the potter's hands,ª he would make it into another vessel, such as the potter saw fit to make.

⁵ Then the word of the LORD came to me: ⁶ O House of
Israel, can I not deal with you like this potter?—says the
LORD. Just like clay in the hands of the potter, so are you in
My hands, O House of Israel! ⁷ At one moment I may decree that a nation or a kingdom shall be uprooted and
pulled down and destroyed; ⁸ but if that nation against
which I made the decree turns back from its wickedness, I
change My mind concerning the punishment I planned to
bring on it. ⁹ At another moment I may decree that a nation or a kingdom shall be built and planted; ¹⁰ but if it
does what is displeasing to Me and does not obey Me,
then I change My mind concerning the good I planned to
bestow upon it.

¹¹ And now, say to the men of Judah and the inhabitants
of Jerusalem: Thus said the LORD: I am devisingᵇ disaster
for you and laying plans against you. Turn back, each of
you, from your wicked ways, and mend your ways and
your actions! ¹² But they will say, "It is no use. We will
keep on following our own plans; each of us will act in the
willfulness of his evil heart."

13   Assuredly, thus said the LORD:
      Inquire among the nations:
      Who has heard anything like this?
      Maiden Israel has done
      A most horrible thing.
14ᶜ   Does one forsake Lebanon snow
      From the mountainous rocks?
      Does one abandon cool water

a-a So some mss. and one early edition. Most mss. and editions read "And if the vessel that
he was making with clay in the potter's hands was spoiled."
b The same Hebrew word as is used above for "potter."
c Meaning of verse uncertain; cf. 2.13, 17.13.

18.1–20.18: The symbolic action of the potter and the jug. A new section that takes up Jeremiah's dialogue with God concerning the potter, the shattered jug, and the prophet's conflict with the priest Pashhur. Again, the prophet's experience prompts his lament to God.

18.1–23: Jeremiah's symbolic interpretation of the potter. 2: *Potter,* Heb "yotzer," is based on the verb "yatzar," "to form, fashion, create," and appears frequently in reference to God (Gen. 2.7, 8, 19; Isa. 43.1, 21; 44.21; 45.9, 11, 18; Ps 95.5; 104.26; etc.). **4:** God's statement draws an analogy with the work of the potter, i.e., if God makes a mistake in decreeing punishment, why cannot God reverse that decree if the nation repents? The opposite is also true, i.e., if God presumes that a nation is righteous and it then demonstrates an evil character, why should it not be punished? The analogy heightens the tremendous power of God vis-à-vis Israel: God is the master craftsman while Israel is the inanimate clay! This passage serves as the basis for a medieval liturgical poem ("piyyut") recited on the high holidays, which extends the metaphor to include the stone in the hand of the stoneworker, the ax in the hand of the smith, the tiller in the hand of the sailor, and other images. **7:** *Uprooted, pulled down, destroyed:* The same verbs are employed for punishment in Jeremiah's call narrative (1.10). **9:** *Be built, planted:* The same verbs express restoration in 1.10. **11–17:** God now turns to an announcement of the decision to punish Judah and Jerusalem despite a covenant relationship with the nation. In Heb, this picks up on the previous vv. (see v. 2 n.), since the word *devising,* "yotzer" (v. 11), is derived from the same root as "potter." **13–15:** Rhetorical questions and analogies typical of wisdom literature are used to make the case against *Maiden Israel,* i.e., God's metaphorical "wife." A series of accusations then follows in which God claims

Flowing from afar?

15 Yet My people have forgotten Me:
They sacrifice to a delusion:
They are made to stumble in their ways—
The ancient paths—
And to walk instead on byways,
On a road not built up.

16 So their land will become a desolation,
An object of hissing[a] for all time.
Every passerby will be appalled
And will shake his head.[a]

17 Like the east wind, I will scatter them
Before the enemy.
[b]I will look upon their back, not their face,[b]
In their day of disaster.

18 They said,[c] "Come let us devise a plot against Jeremiah—for instruction shall not fail from the priest, nor counsel from the wise, nor oracle from the prophet. Come, let us strike him with the tongue, and we shall no longer have to listen to all those words of his."

19 Listen to me, O LORD—
And take note of [d]what my enemies say![d]

20 Should good be repaid with evil?
Yet they have dug a pit for me.
Remember how I stood before You
To plead in their behalf,
To turn Your anger away from them!

21 Oh, give their children over to famine,
Mow them down by the sword.
Let their wives be bereaved
Of children and husbands,
Let their men be struck down by the plague,
And their young men be slain in battle by the
sword.

22 Let an outcry be heard from their houses
When You bring sudden marauders against them;
For they have dug a pit to trap me,
And laid snares for my feet.

23 O LORD, You know
All their plots to kill me.
Do not pardon their iniquity,

to have been abandoned by Israel. **17:** The *east wind* expresses God's power (e.g., at the Re[e]d Sea, Exod. 14.21; see also Exod. 10.13; Jonah 4.8; Ps. 48.8; Hos. 12.2; Isa. 27.8; Ps. 78.26). Called the "Sharav" in Heb or the "Hamsin" in Arabic, it is a dry desert wind that appears at the transitions from the dry to wet seasons and vice versa, often blowing a great deal of dust that blocks visibility and causes much damage. **18–23:** Jeremiah contends that his enemies are plotting against him. **19–23:** The prophet's fifth lament. He portrays himself as one who has stood up on behalf of God and consequently suffered at the hands of his (and God's) enemies. Whereas he once pleaded for divine mercy, he now asks for divine justice so that his enemies will suffer plagues much like the Egyptians at the time of the exodus.

---

a These actions were performed at the sight of ruin to ward off a like fate from the observer; cf. Lam. 2.15.

b-b Change of vocalization yields "I will show them [My] back and not [My] face."

c Cf. 20.10.

d-d Emendation yields "my case."

Do not blot out their guilt from Your presence.
Let them be made to stumble before You—
Act against them in Your hour of wrath!

19 Thus said the Lord: Go buy a jug of potter's ware. And [take] some of the elders of the people and the priests, ² and go out to the Valley of Ben-hinnom—ᵃ at the entrance of the Harsith Gate ᵃ—and proclaim there the words which I will speak to you.

³ Say: "Hear the word of the Lord, O kings of Judah and inhabitants of Jerusalem! Thus said the Lord of Hosts, the God of Israel: I am going to bring such disaster upon this place that the ears of all who hear about it will tingle. ⁴ For they and their fathers and the kings of Judah have forsaken Me, and have made this place alien [to Me]; they have sacrificed in it to other gods whom they have not experienced,ᵇ and they have filled this place with the blood of the innocent. ⁵ They have built shrines to Baal, to put their children to the fire as burnt offerings to Baal—which I never commanded, never decreed, and which never came to My mind. ⁶ Assuredly, a time is coming—declares the Lord—when this place shall no longer be called Topheth or Valley of Ben-hinnom, but Valley of Slaughter.

⁷ "And I will frustrateᶜ the plans of Judah and Jerusalem in this place. I will cause them to fall by the sword before their enemies, by the hand of those who seek their lives; and I will give their carcasses as food to the birds of the sky and the beasts of the earth. ⁸ And I will make this city an object of horror and hissing;ᵈ everyone who passes by it will be appalled and will hiss over all its wounds. ⁹ And I will cause them to eat the flesh of their sons and the flesh of their daughters, and they shall devour one another's flesh—because of the desperate straits to which they will be reduced by their enemies, who seek their life."

¹⁰ Then you shall smash the jug in the sight of the men who go with you, ¹¹ and say to them: "Thus said the Lord of Hosts: So will I smash this people and this city, as one smashes a potter's vessel, which can never be mended. And they shall bury in Topheth until no room is left for burying. ¹² That is what I will do to this place and its inhabitants—declares the Lord. I will make this city like Topheth: ¹³ the houses of Jerusalem and the houses of the kings of Judah shall be unclean, like that place Topheth— all the houses on the roofs of which offerings were made

19.1–15: The symbolic act of the broken jug. 2: The *Valley of Ben-hinnom,* see 7.31 n. The *Harsith Gate,* "Potsherd gate," is otherwise unknown. The Targum identifies it with the "Dung Gate" (Neh. 2.13; 3.13–14; 12.31), presumably because it refers to a place where refuse is thrown outside the city. The location of the Dung Gate in biblical times is unknown, but today it stands on the south side of the Old City of Jerusalem where it provides access to the Western Wall plaza and the Temple Mount. **3–6:** God's threat to bring disaster against Jerusalem resembles the threat to punish the city because of King Manasseh's actions (2 Kings 21.12). *Topheth,* see 7.31. *Valley of Slaughter:* Jeremiah's contemporary Zephaniah claimed that Jerusalem would become a place of slaughter on the day of the Lord because of the idolatry of its inhabitants (Zeph. 1.7). **7–9:** *I will frustrate,* lit. "I will empty" ("ubakoti"), draws upon the analogy between the jug ("bakbuk") and the people. The punishments rehearse the curses of Deut. chs 28–30. **10–13:** God instructs Jeremiah to smash the jug in front of the elders and priests who accompanied him as witnesses. His action symbolizes God's intention to *smash* or destroy the city of Jerusalem so that it becomes an unclean place of destruction like Topheth. **14–15:** Jeremiah returned to the Temple to announce his deed, so that it would be publicly known.

---

a-a Others "by way of the Potsherd Gate"; meaning of Heb. uncertain.

b See note at Deut. 11.28.

c Lit. "empty," Heb. u-baqqothi, a play on baqbuq, "jug" in v. 1.

d See note at 18.16.

to the whole host of heaven and libations were poured out to other gods."

14 When Jeremiah returned from Topheth, where the LORD had sent him to prophesy, he stood in the court of the House of the LORD and said to all the people: 15 "Thus said the LORD of Hosts, the God of Israel: I am going to bring upon this city and upon all its villages all the disaster which I have decreed against it, for they have stiffened their necks and refused to heed My words."

20 Pashhur son of Immer, the priest who was chief officer of the House of the LORD, heard Jeremiah prophesy these things. 2 Pashhur thereupon had Jeremiah flogged and put in the cell[a] at the Upper Benjamin Gate in the House of the LORD. 3 The next day, Pashhur released Jeremiah from the cell.

But Jeremiah said to him, "The LORD has named you not Pashhur, but Magor-missabib.[b] 4 For thus said the LORD: I am going to deliver you and all your friends over to terror: they will fall by the sword of their enemies while you look on. I will deliver all Judah into the hands of the king of Babylon; he will exile them to Babylon or put them to the sword. 5 And I will deliver all the wealth, all the riches, and all the prized possessions of this city, and I will also deliver all the treasures of the kings of Judah into the hands of their enemies: they shall seize them as plunder and carry them off to Babylon. 6 As for you, Pashhur, and all who live in your house, you shall go into captivity. You shall come to Babylon; there you shall die and there you shall be buried, and so shall all your friends to whom you prophesied falsely."

7   You enticed me, O LORD, and I was enticed;
    You overpowered me and You prevailed.
    I have become a constant laughingstock,
    Everyone jeers at me.

a *Meaning of Heb. uncertain.*   b *I.e., "Terror all around"; cf. v. 10.*

20.1–18: Jeremiah's persecution and further laments. A narrative concerning Jeremiah's persecution in the Temple introduces the prophet's final laments. The third-person narrative form contrasts with the first-person autobiographical accounts of the prophet's actions. It corresponds to the editorial framework of the book, particularly the prophetic word formulas that introduce each major section of the book, as well as to the narrative forms that appear throughout chs 26–45. **1–6:** *Pashhur son of Immer* is otherwise unknown. Curiously, his name is derived from an Egyptian term, "psh-hr," "portion of (the god) Horus," suggesting that Judah was open to Egyptian influence at this period; given its military alliances with Egypt, this is not surprising. Gedaliah son of Pashhur, who is part of a group in 38.1 that attempts to have Jeremiah put to death for sedition, may be this Pashhur's son. **2:** The *Upper Benjamin Gate in the House of the LORD* is likely not the same as the city gate called the Benjamin Gate (37.13; 38.7). Instead, it seems to be an entryway into the Temple complex. The name "Benjamin" suggests that both the city gate and the Temple gate were located on the north, since the territory of Benjamin is located immediately to the north of Jerusalem (Josh. 18.11–28, esp. 16; cf. Judg. 1.21; 1.8–10). Pashhur is himself a priest, apparently appointed to keep order at the Temple Mount. His flogging and imprisonment of Jeremiah illustrates the prophet's complaints that he is persecuted by enemies (cf. 18.18–23). **3–4:** He renames Pashhur as *Magor-missabib,* "terror all around" (see also 6.25; 46.5; 49.29; Ps. 31.14), to illustrate his prophecy that Pashhur and his *friends* (lit. "all who love you") will be killed by Judah's enemies. The prophecy that he and his house will go into exile resembles Isaiah's prophecy concerning the sons of Hezekiah (Isa. ch 39) and Amos's prophecy concerning Amaziah the high priest at Bethel (Amos 7.10–17). **6:** Although the narrative presents no statement by Pashhur, Jeremiah accuses him of prophesying falsely (cf. 14.14–16). **7–13:** Jeremiah's sixth lament. It is placed here associatively, because it uses the phrase "terror all around" (v. 10; see v. 3). **7:** The prophet employs strong language to characterize God's deceptive character. *Enticed:* Heb "patah," "to lure, entice," is employed in Exod. 22.16; Hos. 2.16 to describe a man's seduction of a woman, and in Judg. 14.15; 16.5 to describe a woman's seduction of a man. The following verbs, *You overpowered me and You prevailed,* suggest rape. Jeremiah continues to employ this metaphor when he describes the pain and humiliation caused him by the word of the LORD, i.e., al-

8 For every time I speak, I must cry out,
   Must shout, "Lawlessness and rapine!"
   For the word of the LORD causes me
   Constant disgrace and contempt.

9 I thought, "I will not mention Him,
   No more will I speak in His name"—
   But [His word] was like a raging fire in my
        heart,
   Shut up in my bones;
   I could not hold it in, I was helpless.

10 I heard the whispers of the crowd—
   Terror all around:
   "Inform! Let us inform against him!"
   All my [supposed] friends
   Are waiting for me to stumble:
   "Perhaps he can be entrapped,
   And we can prevail against him
   And take our vengeance on him."

11 But the LORD is with me like a mighty warrior;
   Therefore my persecutors shall stumble;
   They shall not prevail and shall not succeed.
   They shall be utterly shamed
   With a humiliation for all time,
   Which shall not be forgotten.

12 O LORD of Hosts, You who test the righteous,
   Who examine the heart and the mind,
   Let me see Your retribution upon them,
   For I lay my case before You.

13 Sing unto the LORD,
   Praise the LORD,
   For He has rescued the needy
   From the hands of evildoers!

14 Accursed be the day
   That I was born!
   Let not the day be blessed
   When my mother bore me!

15 Accursed be the man
   Who brought my father the news
   And said, "A boy
   Is born to you,"
   And gave him such joy!

16 Let that man[a] become like the cities
   Which the LORD overthrew without relenting!
   Let him hear shrieks in the morning
   And battle shouts at noontide—

though he does not want to be a prophet, he cannot resist God (cf. 1.6–8). **10:** The name that he applied to Pashhur, *Terror all around,* is now derisively applied to him by the watching crowd of people. Although his friends await his downfall, Jeremiah expresses his confidence that God will remain with him and that his enemies will eventually fall. **13:** The concluding statement, *sing unto the LORD, Praise the LORD,* recalls the formulaic language of the Song of the Sea (Exod. 15.21) and other psalms (Pss. 33.3; 68.5; 96.1; 98.1; cf. Isa. 42.10; Pss. 113.1; 135.1; 117.1; 148.1; 150.1). It is unclear why Jeremiah's mood shifts so suddenly here. **14–18:** Jeremiah's seventh and final lament. This passage is similar in content and vocabulary to Job ch 3, though the Jeremiah passage uses rather formulaic poetry, and Job ch 3 is far superior poetically, using much more vivid and less stereotypic imagery.

a Emendation yields "day."

17 Because he did not kill me before birth
So that my mother might be my grave,
And her womb big [with me] for all time.
18 Why did I ever issue from the womb,
To see misery and woe,
To spend all my days in shame!

21 The word which came to Jeremiah from the LORD, when King Zedekiah sent to him Pashhur son of Malchiah and the priest Zephaniah, son of Maaseiah, to say, 2 "Please inquire of the LORD on our behalf, for King Nebuchadrezzar of Babylon is attacking us. Perhaps the LORD will act for our sake in accordance with all His wonders, so that [Nebuchadrezzar] will withdraw from us."

3 Jeremiah answered them, "Thus shall you say to Zedekiah: 4 Thus said the LORD, the God of Israel: I am going to turn around the weapons in your hands with which you are battling outside the wall against those who are besieging you—the king of Babylon and the Chaldeans—and I will take them into the midst of this city; 5 and I Myself will battle against you with an outstretched mighty arm, with anger and rage and great wrath. 6 I will strike the inhabitants of this city, man and beast: they shall die by a terrible pestilence. 7 And then—declares the LORD—I will deliver King Zedekiah of Judah and his courtiers and the people—those in this city who survive the pestilence, the sword, and the famine—into the hands of King Nebuchadrezzar of Babylon, into the hands of their enemies, into the hands of those who seek their lives. He will put them to the sword without pity, without compassion, without mercy.

8 "And to this people you shall say: Thus said the LORD: I set before you the way of life and the way of death. 9 Whoever remains in this city shall die by the sword, by famine, and by pestilence; but whoever leaves and goes over to the Chaldeans who are besieging you shall live;

21.1–24.10: Jeremiah's oracles concerning the House of David and the prophets. The prophetic word formula introduces various oracles by the prophet concerning the leadership of Judah, including both the Davidic kings and the prophets. Although the beginning of the unit presupposes the Babylonian assault against Jerusalem that began in 588 BCE during the reign of King Zedekiah (see ch 52; 2 Kings ch 25), the prophet's oracles address the earlier reigns of Josiah, Jehoahaz, Jehoiakim, and Jehoiachin in an effort to point to divine judgment against Judah, due especially to the actions of its leaders, as the reason for the Babylonian assault.

21.1–14: Jeremiah's oracles to Zedekiah, the people of Judah, and the House of David at the time of the Babylonian assault. King Zedekiah ruled from 597 BCE until the destruction of Jerusalem by the Babylonians in 586 (2 Kings 24.18–25.21; 2 Chron. 36.11–21). He was a Davidic king, a younger son of King Josiah and the uncle of King Jehoiachin, whom the Babylonians placed on the throne and later deported from Jerusalem at the time of their first invasion of Judah in 597 BCE (2 Kings 24.1–17; 2 Chron. 36.5–10). **1:** *Pashhur son of Malchiah* is not the same person mentioned in ch 20, but a grandson of King Zedekiah (38.6). He was part of a group that later had Jeremiah imprisoned for treason (38.1–6). It is possible that this unit was attached here to follow closely the mention of Pashhur in the previous ch (20.1). The priest *Zephaniah son of Maaseiah* is not the prophet Zephaniah (Zeph. 1.1), but the deputy priest of the Temple (52.24). He was later criticized for not rebuking or imprisoning Jeremiah (29.24–32). Nebuchadnezzar put him to death together with other Judean officials at Riblah following the fall of Jerusalem (52.24–27). **2:** *King Nebuchadrezzar, son of Nabo-polassar,* the founder of the Neo-Babylonian empire, ruled Babylonia 605–562 BCE. His defeat of the Egyptians at Carchemish in 605 gave him control of Judah. He invaded Judah following revolts against his rule in the times of Jehoiakim (598), Zedekiah (588), and perhaps following the assassination of the Babylonian-appointed governor Gedaliah (582). (See 2 Kings chs 24–25; 2 Chron. ch 36; Jer. chs 41; 52.) *Nebuchadrezzar* is a dialectical form of Nebuchadnezzar, by which this king is more commonly known. **3–7:** Jeremiah's response to Pashhur's and Zephaniah's appeal to inquire of the LORD indicates that God supports the Babylonian invaders who are attacking Jerusalem. The declaration that Zedekiah would be delivered into the hands of the Babylonians would have been considered treason in ancient Judah (cf. Amos's condemnation of Jeroboam in Amos 7.10–17), since it contradicts the tradition of God's protection for Jerusalem and the House of David (see Pss. 2; 46; 47; 48; 110; 132; 2 Sam. ch 7). **8–10:** Jeremiah's urging the people ᵃhe shall at least gain his life.⁻ᵃ ¹⁰For I have set My face against this city for evil and not for good—declares the LORD. It shall be delivered into the hands of the king of Babylon, who will destroy it by fire."

¹¹To the House of the king of Judah: Hear the word of the LORD! ¹²O House of David, thus said the LORD:

> Render just verdicts
> Morning by morning;
> Rescue him who is robbed
> From him who defrauded him.
> Else My wrath will break forth like fire
> And burn, with none to quench it,
> Because of your wicked acts.

13

> I will deal with you, ᵇO inhabitants of the valley,
> O rock of the plain⁻ᵇ—declares the LORD—
> You who say, "Who can come down against us?
> Who can get into our lairs?"

14

> I will punish you according to your deeds
>   —declares the LORD.
> I will set fire to its forest;ᶜ
> It shall consume all that is around it.

22 Thus said the LORD: Go down to the palace of the king of Judah, where you shall utter this word. ²Say: "Hear the word of the LORD: O king of Judah, you who sit on the throne of David, and your courtiers and your subjects who enter these gates! ³Thus said the LORD: Do what is just and right; rescue from the defrauder him who is robbed; do not wrong the stranger, the fatherless, and the widow; commit no lawless act, and do not shed the blood of the innocent in this place. ⁴For if you fulfill this command, then through the gates of this palace shall enter kings of David's line who sit upon his throne, riding horse-drawn chariots, with their courtiers and their subjects. ⁵But if you do not heed these commands, I swear by Myself—declares the LORD—that this palace shall become a ruin."

⁶For thus said the LORD concerning the royal palace of Judah:

> You are as Gilead to Me,
> As the summit of Lebanon;
> But I will make you a desert,
> Uninhabited towns.

to go over to the Babylonians would likewise be considered an act of treason. He was later arrested for his statements (38.1–6). **11–14:** A second oracle calls upon the House of David to do justice for those who are robbed in accordance with the laws in Exod. 21.37–22.3. The king was responsible for justice in the land (2 Sam. 12.1–15; 1 Kings 3.16–28; Isa. 11.1–9; Ps. 72). Because of its failure to fill this role, Jeremiah condemns the dynasty despite God's promise that it would rule forever (2 Sam. ch 7; cf. 1 Kings 8.22–26; 9.4–5; Ps. 132). **14:** The *forest* refers to the royal palace, which was called the House of the Forest of Lebanon because it was built with Lebanese cedar (1 Kings 7.2–12; 10.17, 21; Isa. 22.8).

22.1–23.8: Further oracles concerning the kings of Judah. 22.1–9: The first oracle addresses the royal House of David in general without mentioning a specific king. It is thematically related to the previous oracle, focusing on the responsibility of the king to be just. **1–4:** The first part of the oracle takes up the themes of 21.11–14 by focusing on the king's responsibility to treat the disadvantaged people of the land justly. Jeremiah follows the view of 1 Kings 8.22–26; 9.4–5; Ps. 132 that the Davidic king will rule if he is righteous. Much like the covenant blessings and curses of Deut. chs 28–30, vv. 5–9 outline the consequences if the king is not righteous. **6:** *Gilead* is the territory of Israel east of the Jordan River from the wadi (river) Arnon in the south to the wadi Yarmuk in the north. Although it is now part of modern Jordan, it was the territory of the tribes of Gad and half of Manasseh in biblical times (Josh. 13.24–31). Gilead and Lebanon were both heavily forested areas in antiquity. The Assyrian and Babylonian kings frequently boasted of the trees from Lebanon for use in their own palaces and other projects.

---

a-a Lit. "he shall have his life as booty."

b-b Force of Heb. uncertain.

c Perhaps a reference to the royal palace; cf. 1 Kings 7.2.

7　　I will appoint destroyers against you,
　　　Each with his tools;
　　　They shall cut down your choicest cedars
　　　And make them fall into the fire.

8 And when many nations pass by this city and one man asks another, "Why did the LORD do thus to that great city?" 9 the reply will be, "Because they forsook the covenant with the LORD their God and bowed down to other gods and served them."

10　　Do not weep for the dead[a]
　　　And do not lament for him;
　　　Weep rather for [b]him who is leaving,[b]
　　　For he shall never come back
　　　To see the land of his birth!

11 For thus said the LORD concerning Shallum[b] son of King Josiah of Judah, who succeeded his father Josiah as king, but who has gone forth from this place: He shall never come back. 12 He shall die in the place to which he was exiled, and he shall not see this land again.

13　　Ha! he who builds his house with unfairness
　　　And his upper chambers with injustice,
　　　Who makes his fellow man work without pay
　　　And does not give him his wages,
14　　Who thinks: I will build me a vast palace
　　　With spacious upper chambers,
　　　Provided with windows,
　　　Paneled in cedar,
　　　Painted with vermilion!
15　　Do you think you are more a king
　　　Because you compete in cedar?
　　　Your father [c]ate and drank[c]

a I.e., Josiah; see 2 Kings 23.29–30.
b-b I.e., the king called by his throne name Jehoahaz in 2 Kings 23.31 ff., and by his private name Shallum here in v. 11 and in 1 Chron. 3.15.
c-c I.e., he was content with the simple necessities of life.

10–12: King Jehoahaz son of Josiah was deposed and exiled to Egypt by Pharaoh Neco three months after Neco killed his father Josiah at Megiddo (see 2 Kings 23.28–35; 2 Chron. 35.20–36.4). His mother was Hamutal daughter of Jeremiah of the city of Libnah, located along the border of Judah and Philistia in the Shephelah. Apparently, Jehoahaz supported Judah's alliance with Babylonia like his father Josiah. This would have been the reason for Neco's removal of Jehoahaz and his replacement with Jehoiakim, who favored alliance with Egypt against Babylonia. *Do not weep for the dead* refers to Josiah. Weep for *him who is leaving* refers to Jehoahaz, who died in exile in Egypt. Jehoahaz's personal name was *Shallum* (cf. 1 Chron.

3.5). The kings of Judah took throne names at their coronations. Thus, Solomon's personal name was Jedidiah (2 Sam. 12.25); Jehoiakim's name was Eliakim (2 Kings 23.34); Jehoiachin's name was Coniah (Jer. 22.24) or Jeconiah (Jer. 24.1); and Zedekiah's name was Mattaniah (2 Kings 24.17). **13–23:** Jeremiah's oracle concerning King Jehoiakim. Jehoiakim son of Josiah was placed on the throne by Pharaoh Neco of Egypt after he deposed and exiled Jehoahaz son of Josiah (2 Kings 23.36–24.7; 2 Chron. 36.5–8). His mother was Zebidah daughter of Pedaiah of the city of Rumah. Although Josh. 15.52 places Rumah in the territory of Judah, most interpreters follow the 1st-century CE Jewish historian Flavius Josephus, who identifies Rumah as the home of two Galileans who attacked the Tenth Roman Legion (*Jewish War* 3.7.21). It is sometimes identified with Abimelech's residence in Arumah (Judg. 9.41), although the exact location in Galilee is uncertain. Jehoiakim is clearly from the pro-Egyptian branch of the Davidic house in contrast to the pro-Babylonian positions of Jehoahaz, Zedekiah, and the family of Shaphan, who served as Josiah's scribe and adviser (2 Kings 22.3). Jeremiah's position is also pro-Babylonian (e.g., chs 27–29), and his supporters include various members of the Shaphan family (see 26.24; 29.3; 36.10; cf. 40.9; 41.1–2). The conflict between the pro-Egyptian Jehoiakim and the pro-Babylonian Jeremiah represents a larger conflict in Jerusalem over the future course of the nation. Although the Babylonians controlled Judah after 605 BCE, the pro-Egyptian elements were able to provoke the revolts against the Babylonians that ultimately led to the destruction of Jerusalem and the Babylonian exile. **13:** *Ha!* ("hoy") is best translated "Woe!" The exclamation frequently appears in prophetic oracles of judgment (e.g., Isa. 5.8–24; chs 28–33; Amos 5.18–20; Nah. 3.1; Hab. 2.6–20; 3.1). It is also employed to signal a warning of coming danger

And dispensed justice and equity—
Then all went well with him.

16 He upheld the rights of the poor and needy—
Then all was well.
ᵃThat is truly heeding Meᵃ
—declares the LORD.

17 But your eyes and your mind are only
On ill-gotten gains,
On shedding the blood of the innocent,
On committing fraud and violence.

18 Assuredly, thus said the LORD concerning Jehoiakim son of Josiah, king of Judah:
ᵇThey shall not mourn for him,
"Ah, brother! Ah, sister!"
They shall not mourn for him,
"Ah, lord! Ah, his majesty!"ᵇ

19 He shall have the burial of an ass,
Dragged out and left lying
Outside the gates of Jerusalem.

20ᶜ Climb Lebanon and cry out,
Raise your voice in Bashan,
Cry out from Abarim,
For all your lovers are crushed.

21 I spoke to you when you were prosperous;
You said, "I will not listen."
That was your way ever since your youth,
You would not heed Me.

22 All your shepherdsᵈ shall be devoured by the wind,
And your lovers shall go into captivity.
Then you shall be shamed and humiliated
Because of all your depravity.

23 You who dwell in Lebanon,
Nestled among the cedars,
ᵉHow much grace will you haveᵉ
When pains come upon you,
Travail as in childbirth!

24 As I live—declares the LORD—ᶠif you, O King Coniah, son of Jehoiakim, of Judah, wereᶠ a signet on my right

(Zech. 2.10) or an exclamation of mourning (22.18). Jeremiah's critique of Jehoiakim, like the earlier passages, accuses the king of failing to do justice on behalf of the people as his office requires. The charge that he *builds his house with unfairness* is a pun on the term "bayit," which refers to "house" or "dynasty," and may recall images of Solomon's self-indulgence in taking thirteen years to build his own palace (1 Kings 7.1) and only seven to build the Temple of God (1 Kings 6.37–38). Some have supposed that Jehoiakim refurbished the royal palace. Jeremiah contrasts Jehoiakim with his father Josiah who heeded God by upholding the rights of the people. The prophet calls for an ignominious death and burial for the king, which no doubt characterized the bitterness of his conflict with Jehoiakim (cf. Amos 7.10–17). The circumstances of Jehoiakim's death are not known, although he seems to have died during the first Babylonian invasion of Judah (2 Kings 24.6). **20–23:** Jeremiah employs feminine singular verbs to address Judah as a woman or bride of God in these vv., calling upon her to *cry out* over the loss of her *lovers* and *shepherds.* Kings in the ancient world are frequently portrayed as shepherds leading their flock (cf. Ezek. ch 34). **23:** The concluding reference to *you who dwell in Lebanon, / Nestled among the cedars* recalls the image of the royal palace or "House of the Cedars of Lebanon" (1 Kings 7.1), but the pains of childbirth are about to come upon the nation (cf. 30.6; Isa. 13.8). **24–30:** Jeremiah's oracle concerning Jehoiachin. Eighteen-year-old Jehoiachin son of Jehoiakim reigned for only three months during the Babylonian siege of Jerusalem before surrendering. Together with his mother and various officials of the kingdom, including the priest and prophet Ezekiel (Ezek. 1.1–3), he was exiled to Babylonia where he remained for the rest of his life (see 2 Kings 24.8–17; 25.27–30; 2 Chron. 36.9–10). **24:** *Coniah* is Jehoiachin. *A signet on my right hand* (cf. Hag.

a-a Or "That is the reward for heeding Me."

b-b They shall express neither sorrow at the loss of a relative nor grief at the death of a ruler.

c Israel is addressed.

d Change of vocalization yields "paramours."

e-e Septuagint reads "How you will groan."

f-f Heb. "If Coniah . . . were . . ."; Coniah (Jeconiah in 24.1) is identical with Jehoiachin, 2 Kings 24.8 ff.

hand, I would tear you off even from there. ²⁵ I will deliver you into the hands of those who seek your life, into the hands of those you dread, into the hands of King Nebuchadrezzar of Babylon and into the hands of the Chaldeans. ²⁶ I will hurl you and the mother who bore you into another land, where you were not born; there you shall both die. ²⁷ They shall not return to the land that they yearn to come back to.

²⁸ Is this man Coniah
A wretched broken pot,
A vessel no one wants?
Why are he and his offspring hurled out,
And cast away in a land they knew not?
²⁹ O land, land, land,
Hear the word of the Lord!
³⁰ Thus said the Lord:
Record this man as without succession,
One who shall never be found acceptable;
For no man of his offspring shall be accepted
To sit on the throne of David
And to rule again in Judah.

23 Ah, shepherds who let the flock of My pasture stray and scatter!—declares the Lord. ² Assuredly, thus said the Lord, the God of Israel, concerning the shepherds who should tend My people: It is you who let My flock scatter and go astray. You gave no thought to them, but I am going to give thought to you, for your wicked acts—declares the Lord. ³ And I Myself will gather the remnant of My flock from all the lands to which I have banished them, and I will bring them back to their pasture, where they shall be fertile and increase. ⁴ And I will appoint over them shepherds who will tend them; they shall no longer fear or be dismayed, and none of them shall be missing—declares the Lord.

⁵ See, a time is coming—declares the Lord—when I will raise up a true branch of David's line. He shall reign as king and shall prosper, and he shall do what is just and right in the land. ⁶ In his days Judah shall be delivered and Israel shall dwell secure. And this is the name by which he shall be called: "The Lord is our Vindicator."

⁷ Assuredly, a time is coming—declares the Lord— when it shall no more be said, "As the Lord lives, who brought the Israelites out of the land of Egypt," ⁸ but rather, "As the Lord lives, who brought out and led the offspring of the House of Israel from the northland and from all the lands to which I have banished them." And they shall dwell upon their own soil.

2.23) is a symbol of royal authority; this image, in which God wears the king as a signet ring, reflects the tremendous closeness between the Davidic king and God (see 2 Sam. 7.14; Ps. 110.1). **25:** *Chaldeans,* a name for the Neo-Babylonian empire of Nebuchadnezzar. **23.1–8:** Jeremiah's "woe" oracle (see 22.13) concerning the *shepherds,* or the kings of Judah who have allowed God's *flock* to go astray. "Shepherd" is a frequent title for kings in the ancient Near East; it is used, for example, of Hammurabi in his law collection or Code. Although the oracle begins with reference to judgment against Judah's leaders, it looks forward to the return of Judah's and Israel's exiles and the reestablishment of righteous Davidic rule in which both Israel and Judah will be reunited (cf. Isa. 11.1–16; Hos. 3.1–5). **3:** *They shall be fertile and increase* recalls the divine blessing of humankind at creation (Gen. 1.28). The restoration of Davidic rule over a reunited people was one of the goals of Josiah's reform. The image is developed especially in the works of Second Isaiah, who sees Israel's return from Babylonian exile as a second exodus (see Isa. chs 40–48). **6:** The name of the king, *the Lord is our Vindicator,* in Heb is a play on the name Zedekiah, and might suggest that the ideal future king will be named Yʜvʜ Tzidkenu, the same elements in the name Tzidkiyah (Zedekiah) in reverse order.

9 Concerning the prophets.

My heart is crushed within me,
All my bones are trembling;[a]
I have become like a drunken man,
Like one overcome by wine—
Because of the LORD and His holy word.
10 For the land is full of adulterers,
The land mourns because of [b]a curse;[b]
The pastures of the wilderness are dried up.
[c]For they run to do evil,
They strain to do wrong.[c]
11 For both prophet and priest are godless;
Even in My House I find their wickedness
              —declares the LORD.

12 Assuredly,
Their path shall become
Like slippery ground;
They shall be thrust into darkness
And there they shall fall;
For I will bring disaster upon them,
The year of their doom   —declares the LORD.
13 In the prophets of Samaria
I saw a repulsive thing:
They prophesied by Baal
And led My people Israel astray.
14 But what I see in the prophets of Jerusalem
Is something horrifying:
Adultery and false dealing.
They encourage evildoers,
So that no one turns back from his wickedness.
To Me they are all like Sodom,
And [all] its inhabitants like Gomorrah.

15 Assuredly, thus said the LORD of Hosts concerning the prophets:

I am going to make them eat wormwood
And drink a bitter draft;
For from the prophets of Jerusalem
Godlessness has gone forth to the whole land.

16 Thus said the LORD of Hosts:
Do not listen to the words of the prophets

23.9–40: Jeremiah's oracles concerning false prophets. Concern with false prophecy is an important theme in Jeremiah, as he is frequently in conflict with other prophets about the future course of the nation (see chs 20; 27–28; 29). Such conflicts among prophets' competing claims were common (see 1 Kings chs 13; 18; 22). Deut. 18.9–22 warns against following false prophets, but one may know a true or false prophet only by whether the prophet's words come true. Therefore, ancient Judeans would have to wait for the fulfillment—or the lack thereof—of the prophet's words. **9:** *Concerning the prophets* is a rare example of a title, indicating the topic of the group of oracles that follows. The charge that the false prophets are drunk is frequently employed by prophets to characterize their opponents (see Isa. 5.11–12, 22; Hab. 2.5; Zeph. 1.12–13). Jeremiah's words, however, seem to imply that he himself is as if drunk because of the falsity of the priests and prophets. **10:** The charge of adultery is also a frequent prophetic theme (Hos. chs 1–3; Ezek. ch 16) that builds upon Jeremiah's previous use of the marriage motif (2.1–3). **13–14:** The corruption of the prophets of Judah is as bad as or worse than the false prophecies of the prophets of *Samaria,* the capital of the former Northern Kingdom of Israel that was destroyed by the Assyrians in 722 BCE (see 2 Kings ch 17). Because of the false prophets, the people of Jerusalem have become as evil as those of Sodom and Gomorrah, the biblical image of excessive corruption (Gen. chs 18–19; Isa. 1.10; Jer. 20.16). **16–18:** Jeremiah demands that the people not listen to false prophets because they do not speak on behalf of the LORD. He claims to have *stood in the council of the LORD,* where he heard the divine word, proof that he is a true prophet (cf. 1 Kings 22.19–23; Isa. ch 6; cf. Ps. 82).

a *Meaning of Heb. uncertain.*
b-b *A few Heb. mss. and Septuagint read "these."*
c-c *Lit. "Their running is wickedness, / Their straining is iniquity."*

Who prophesy to you.
They are deluding you,
The prophecies they speak are from their own
　　minds,
Not from the mouth of the LORD.

17 They declare to men who despise Me:
The LORD has said:
"All shall be well with you";
And to all who follow their willful hearts they say:
"No evil shall befall you."

18 But he who has stood in the council of the LORD,
And seen, and heard His word—
He who has listened to His word must obey.[a]

19 [b]Lo, the storm of the LORD goes forth in fury,
A whirling storm,
It shall whirl down upon the heads of the wicked.

20 The anger of the LORD shall not turn back
Till it has fulfilled and completed His purposes.[b]
In the days to come
You shall clearly perceive it.

21 I did not send those prophets,
But they rushed in;
I did not speak to them,
Yet they prophesied.

22 If they have stood in My council,
Let them announce My words to My people
And make them turn back
From their evil ways and wicked acts.

23 Am I only a God near at hand
　　　　　　　　　　—says the LORD—
And not a God far away?

24 If a man enters a hiding place,
Do I not see him?　　　　—says the LORD.
For I fill both heaven and earth
　　　　　　　—declares the LORD.

25 I have heard what the prophets say, who prophesy falsely in My name: "I had a dream, I had a dream." 26[c]How long will there be[c] in the minds of the prophets who prophesy falsehood—the prophets of their own deceitful minds—27 the plan to make My people forget My name, by means of the dreams which they tell each other, just as their fathers forgot My name because of Baal? 28 Let

a Change of vocalization yields "announce it"; cf. vv. 22, 28.
b-b This section constitutes the word of God to which Jeremiah refers.
c-c Meaning of Heb. uncertain.

19–20: The use of storm imagery to portray God draws upon the theophanic tradition in which storm, clouds, lightning, etc., depict divine power (see Exod. ch 19; Job 38.1; 40.6; Hab. ch 3; Ps. 68). His contention that *the anger of the LORD shall not turn back* draws upon the Isaian tradition (see Isa. 5.25; 9.11, 16, 20; 10.4). Second Isaiah takes up the statement that God's anger will fulfill its purposes to point to the fulfillment of prophecy in the exilic period (Isa. 40.8; 55.11). **22:** Jeremiah challenges the false prophets to make the people repent, and contends that God will know what they have done because God sees all (cf. Amos 9.2–4). **25–40:** A speech by God which addresses the problem of false prophecy. **25–32:** Dreams were a standard means for receiving divine revelation, but these false prophets only claim to have dreamed; they speak whatever their own minds devise. **29:** *And like a hammer that shatters rock!* refers to the tremendous power and danger of biblical prophecy. In rabbinic tradition, however, this is a central phrase, suggesting that God's words may be interpreted in a wide variety of legitimate ways (*b. Sanh.* 34a). **31:** *Oracular utterances:* Heb "ne'um" is a technical expression for prophetic oracles, as in the expression *declares* ["ne'um"] *the LORD.* **33–40:** The second portion of the speech takes up the technical expression, "masa'," *burden* or "pronouncement." The English translation, *burden,* which can mean both a literal load that is carried and a metaphorical purport of one's message, embodies the ambiguities of the Heb term, which refers both to something that must be carried and to a type of prophetic oracle. In essence, a "masa'" is a prophetic responsibility that must be borne, although Jeremiah sometimes states that he does not want to do so (1.6–8; 20.8–9). When asked *"What is the burden of the LORD?"* Jeremiah is to respond that the burden is that you will be cast off ("natashta"), which employs the first verb from his initial the prophet who has a dream tell the dream; and let him who has received My word report My word faithfully! How can straw be compared to grain?—says the LORD. ²⁹ Behold, My word is like fire—declares the LORD—and like a hammer that shatters rock!

³⁰ Assuredly, I am going to deal with the prophets—declares the LORD—who steal My words from one another. ³¹ I am going to deal with the prophets—declares the LORD—who wagᵃ their tongues and make oracular utterances. ³² I am going to deal with those who prophesy lying dreams—declares the LORD—who relate them to lead My people astray with their reckless lies, when I did not send them or command them. They do this people no good—declares the LORD.

³³ And when this people—or a prophet or a priest—asks you, "What is the burdenᵇ of the LORD?" you shall answer them, ᶜ⁻"What is the burden?"⁻ᶜ I will cast you off"—declares the LORD.

³⁴ As for the prophet or priest or layman who shall say "the burden of the LORD," I will punish that person and his house. ³⁵ Thus you shall speak to each other, every one to his fellow, "What has the LORD answered?" or "What has the LORD spoken?" ³⁶ But do not mention "the burden of the LORD" any more. ᵈ⁻Does a man regard his own word as a "burden,"⁻ᵈ that you pervert the words of the living God, the LORD of Hosts, our God? ³⁷ Thus you shall speak to the prophet: "What did the LORD answer you?" or "What did the LORD speak?" ³⁸ But if you say "the burden of the LORD"—assuredly, thus said the LORD: Because you said this thing, "the burden of the LORD," whereas I sent word to you not to say "the burden of the LORD," ³⁹ I will utterly ᵉ⁻forget you⁻ᵉ and I will cast you away from My presence, together with the city that I gave to you and your fathers. ⁴⁰ And I will lay upon you a disgrace for all time, shame for all time, which shall never be forgotten.

24 The LORD showed me two baskets of figs, placed in front of the Temple of the LORD. This was after King Nebuchadrezzar of Babylon had exiled King Jeconiah son of Jehoiakim of Judah, and the officials of Judah, and the craftsmen and smiths, from Jerusalem, and had

prophetic commission ("lintosh," "to uproot") (1.10). Whereas the speech attempts to present Jeremiah as a true prophet, it argues that God will cast away those who falsely claim to speak a prophetic "masaʾ."

24.1–10: Jeremiah's vision of the good and the bad figs. Another symbolic action (see also 1.11–19; ch 19). This action takes place shortly after the exile of King Jehoiachin, when the Babylonians left his uncle Zedekiah in control of the country (2 Kings 24.8–25.30; 2 Chron. 36.9–21). The great rhetorical power of the chapter derives from its counterintuitive message: The good figs are the ones who were exiled! **1:** *Figs* were commonly offered at the Temple at Sukkot following the conclusion of the fruit harvest (see Deut. 26.1–15; Amos 8.1–3). *Jeconiah* is a shortened form of the name Jehoiachin.

---

a *Meaning of Heb. uncertain.*

b *I.e., pronouncement; cf. Isa. 13.1, 15.1, etc., where the word rendered "pronouncement" can also mean "burden."*

c-c *Septuagint and other versions read "You are the burden!"*

d-d *Meaning of Heb. uncertain.*   e-e *Some Heb. mss., Septuagint, and other versions read "lift you up," a word from the same root as "burden."*

brought them to Babylon. ²One basket contained very good figs, like first-ripened figs, and the other basket contained very bad figs, so bad that they could not be eaten.

³And the LORD said to me, "What do you see, Jeremiah?" I answered, "Figs—the good ones are very good, and the bad ones very bad, so bad that they cannot be eaten."

⁴Then the word of the LORD came to me:

⁵Thus said the LORD, the God of Israel: As with these good figs, so will I single out for good the Judean exiles whom I have driven out from this place to the land of the Chaldeans. ⁶I will look upon them favorably, and I will bring them back to this land; I will build them and not overthrow them; I will plant them and not uproot them. ⁷And I will give them the understanding to acknowledge Me, for I am the LORD. And they shall be My people and I will be their God, when they turn back to Me with all their heart.

⁸And like the bad figs, which are so bad that they cannot be eaten—thus said the Lord—so will I treat King Zedekiah of Judah and his officials and the remnant of Jerusalem that is left in this land, and those who are living in the land of Egypt: ⁹I will make them a horror—an evil—to all the kingdoms of the earth, a disgrace and a proverb, a byword and a curse^a in all the places to which I banish them. ¹⁰I will send the sword, famine, and pestilence against them until they are exterminated from the land that I gave to them and their fathers.

25 The word which came to Jeremiah concerning all the people of Judah, in the fourth year of King Jehoiakim son of Josiah of Judah, which was the first year of King Nebuchadrezzar of Babylon. ²This is what the prophet Jeremiah said to all the people of Judah and to all the inhabitants of Jerusalem:

³From the thirteenth year of King Josiah son of Amon of Judah, to this day—these twenty-three years—the word of the LORD has come to me. I have spoken to you persistently, but you would not listen. ⁴Moreover, the LORD constantly sent all his servants the prophets to you, but you

---

a I.e., a standard by which men curse; cf. Gen. 12.2 and note; Zech. 8.13.

2–10: By use of the contrasting images of a basket of *good figs* and a basket of *bad* or rotten *figs*, the symbolic act distinguishes the fate of those taken into Babylonian captivity with Jehoiachin and those left in the land under the rule of Zedekiah. **6:** The oracle concerning those exiled to Babylonia employs the verbs "banah,"

---

build, and "nata'," *plant*, to characterize the good that will befall them. The verbs "haras," *overthrow,* and "natash," *uproot,* apparently refer to the fate of those left behind. All four verbs appear in Jeremiah's initial call narrative (1.10). **7:** God promises to give the exiles *understanding to acknowledge Me,* lit. "a heart to know Me." This is further developed in 31.33–34. The mutual covenant formula, *they shall be My people and I will be their God,* expresses the restoration of the covenant relationship (7.23; 11.4; 30.22; 31.1, 33; 32.38). **8–10:** All those left in Judah with Zedekiah as well as those in Egypt will be destroyed. Ironically, Jeremiah was taken to Egypt after the fall of Jerusalem (ch 43).

25.1–29.32: Submission to Babylonia. The prophetic word formula introduces material in chs 25–29 which expresses the prophet's view that Judah must submit to Babylonia. The unit contains four major components: the oracle that Judah and the nations must accept Babylonia's rule as the will of God (ch 25); a narrative concerning the prophet's trial for delivering the Temple sermon (ch 26); Jeremiah's confrontation with the prophet Hananiah (chs 27–28); and Jeremiah's letter to the Babylonian exiles (ch 29).

25.1–38: Jeremiah's oracle calling upon Judah and the nations to submit to Babylonia. Both in terms of literary placement and message, this is the central chapter of Jeremiah. **1–14:** The punishment of Judah. **1:** *The fourth year of . . . Jehoiakim* and *the first year of . . . Nebuchadrezzar* is 605 BCE, the year that Nebuchadrezzar defeated Egypt at Carchemish and took control of Judah. **3–7:** *The thirteenth year of . . . Josiah,* 627 BCE, is the beginning of the prophet's career (1.1–3). According to 2 Chron. 34.3, Josiah began to purge Jerusalem and Judah of pagan religious practice in his twelfth year. The *twenty-three years* of the prophet's activity would extend from 627 to 605. In his view, the people failed to obwould not listen or incline your ears to hear ⁵when they said, "Turn back, every one, from your evil ways and your wicked acts, that you may remain throughout the ages on the soil which the LORD gave to you and your fathers. ⁶Do not follow other gods, to serve them and worship them. Do not vex Me with what your own hands have made,ᵃ and I will not bring disaster upon you." ⁷But you would not listen to Me—declares the LORD—but vexed Me with what your hands made, to your own hurt.

⁸Assuredly, thus said the LORD of Hosts: Because you would not listen to My words, ⁹I am going to send for all the peoples of the north—declares the LORD—and for My servant, King Nebuchadrezzar of Babylon, and bring them against this land and its inhabitants, and against all those nations roundabout. I will exterminate them and make them a desolation, an object of hissingᵇ—ruins for all time. ¹⁰And I will banish from them the sound of mirth and gladness, the voice of bridegroom and bride, and the sound of the mill and the light of the lamp. ¹¹This whole land shall be a desolate ruin.

And those nations shall serve the king of Babylon seventy years. ¹²When the seventy years are over, I will punish the king of Babylon and that nation and the land of the Chaldeans for their sins—declares the LORD—and I will make it a desolation for all time. ¹³And I will bring upon that land all that I have decreed against it, all that is recorded in this book—that which Jeremiah prophesied against all the nations. ¹⁴For they too shall be enslaved by many nations and great kings; and I will requite them according to their acts and according to their conduct.

¹⁵For thus said the LORD, the God of Israel, to me: "Take from My hand this cup of wine—of wrath—and make all the nations to whom I send you drink of it. ¹⁶Let them drink and retch and act crazy, because of the sword that I am sending among them."

¹⁷So I took the cup from the hand of the LORD and gave drink to all the nations to whom the LORD had sent me: ¹⁸Jerusalem and the towns of Judah, and its kings and officials, to make them a desolate ruin, an object of hissing and a curseᶜ—as is now the case; ¹⁹Pharaoh king of Egypt, his courtiers, his officials, and all his people; ²⁰all ᵈthe mixed peoples;⁻ᵈ all the kings of the land of Uz; all the kings of the land of the Philistines—Ashkelon, Gaza, Ekron, and what is left of Ashdod; ²¹Edom, Moab, and Ammon; ²²all the

serve Josiah's reforms from the outset. **5:** According to Jeremiah, a main function of prophecy is to cause the people to repent. This is about to change, and the prophet's new role will be more similar to that of (First) Isaiah, explaining the calamities and emphasizing that they derive from God. **9:** It is here that *the peoples of the north* are first identified as *Babylon*. This fits the historical background of the chapter (see v. 1 n.). **10:** The cessation of marriages is particularly pertinent in view of Jeremiah's decision not to marry (ch 16), but the continuation of the v. emphasizes that even much more basic, mundane activity will cease. **11:** The nations will serve Babylonia for the seventy years of Judah's punishment. The significance of the period is uncertain, though it likely reflects the human life span (Ps. 90.10). A period of seventy years of divine displeasure is also found in a Mesopotamian text. **12:** Like Assyria in the book of Isaiah (Isa. 10.5–34; 14.24–27), Babylonia will be punished after Judah's punishment is complete. **13:** V. 13a introduces the oracles against the nations in the Greek Septuagint version of the book of Jeremiah. **15–29:** For the metaphorical portrayal of punishment as drinking from a cup, see 49.12; 51.7; Pss. 11.6; 75.8; Isa. 51.17, 22; Lam. 4.21; Ezek. 23.31–34; Hab. 2.15–16. **18–26:** The nations listed were all part of the Persian empire following the end of the Babylonian exile. Many appear in Jeremiah's oracles concerning the nations: *Egypt* (46.2–28); *Uz*, the Arabian desert east of Israel (cf. Lam. 4.21), the home of Job (Job 1.1); *Edom, Moab, and Ammon*, in the Transjordan east of modern Israel (48.1–49.22); *Ashkelon . . . Ashdod*, the four cities of Philistia (ch 47); *Tyre* and *Sidon*, in Phoenicia (modern Lebanon); *Dedan*, a desert tribe located southeast of Edom (Gen. 25.3); *Tema*, a tribe from the Syrian desert (Gen. 25.15); *Buz*, a tribe descended from Nahor, Abraham's brother (Gen. 22.21); *Arabia*, the desert peoples (49.28–33); *Zimri*, unknown; *Elam* and *Media*, in

---

a I.e., idols.   *b* Cf. note at 18.16.   *c* Cf. note at 24.9.
d-d Meaning of Heb. uncertain.

kings of Tyre and all the kings of Sidon, and all the kings of the coastland across the sea; 23 Dedan, Tema, and Buz, and all those who have their hair clipped; 24 all the kings of Arabia, and all the kings of ᵃ the mixed peoples ᵃ who live in the desert; 25 all the kings of Zimri ᵇ and all the kings of Elam and all the kings of Media; 26 all the kings of the north, whether far from or close to each other—all the ᵃroyal lands which are on the earth. ᵃ And last of all, the king of Sheshach ᶜ shall drink.

27 Say to them: "Thus said the LORD of Hosts, the God of Israel: Drink and get drunk and vomit; fall and never rise again, because of the sword that I send among you." 28 And if they refuse to take the cup from your hand and drink, say to them, "Thus said the LORD of Hosts: You must drink! 29 If I am bringing the punishment first on the city that bears My name, do you expect to go unpunished? You will not go unpunished, for I am summoning the sword against all the inhabitants of the earth—declares the LORD of Hosts."

30 You are to prophesy all those things to them, and then say to them:

The LORD roars from on high,
He makes His voice heard from His holy dwelling;
He roars aloud over His [earthly] abode;
He utters shouts like the grape-treaders,
Against all the dwellers on earth.
31 Tumult has reached the ends of the earth,
For the LORD has a case against the nations,
He contends with all flesh.
He delivers the wicked to the sword
                              —declares the LORD.
32 Thus said the LORD of Hosts:
Disaster goes forth
From nation to nation;
A great storm is unleashed
From the remotest parts of earth.

33 In that day, the earth shall be strewn with the slain of the LORD from one end to the other. They shall not be mourned, or gathered and buried; they shall become dung upon the face of the earth.

34   Howl, you shepherds, and yell,
       Strew [dust] on yourselves, you lords of the flock!

modern Iran and Afghanistan (49.34–49). **26:** *Sheshach* is a coded reference to Babylonia. It employs a technique called "ᵃatbash," in which the last letter of the alphabet is substituted for the first, the penultimate letter for the second, and so forth. (Thus "b-b-l," "Babylonia" becomes "sh-sh-kh," *Sheshach*, because "shin" = "bet" and "kaf" = "lamed.") (Cf. 51.41.) Interpreters conjecture that it may have been unsafe to speak directly against Babylonia during the exile. **30–38:** God is portrayed as a lion roaring in judgment against the nations (cf. Amos 1.2).

---

a-a *Meaning of Heb. uncertain.*   b *Meaning of Heb. uncertain.*
c *A cipher for* Babel, *Babylon.*

For the day of your slaughter draws near.
^aI will break you in pieces,^a
And you shall fall like a precious vessel.

35 Flight shall fail the shepherds,
And escape, the lords of the flock.

36 Hark, the outcry of the shepherds,
And the howls of the lords of the flock!
For the LORD is ravaging their pasture.

37 The peaceful meadows shall be wiped out
By the fierce wrath of the LORD.

38 Like a lion, He has gone forth from His lair;
The land has become a desolation,
Because of the oppressive^b wrath,
Because of His fierce anger.

26 At the beginning of the reign of King Jehoiakim son of Josiah of Judah, this word came from the LORD:

2 "Thus said the LORD: Stand in the court of the House of the LORD, and speak to [the men of] all the towns of Judah, who are coming to worship in the House of the LORD, all the words which I command you to speak to them. Do not omit anything. 3 Perhaps they will listen and turn back, each from his evil way, that I may renounce the punishment I am planning to bring upon them for their wicked acts.

4 "Say to them: Thus said the LORD: If you do not obey Me, abiding by the Teaching that I have set before you, 5 heeding the words of My servants the prophets whom I have been sending to you persistently—but you have not heeded—6 then I will make this House like Shiloh, and I will make this city a curse^c for all the nations of earth."

7 The priests and prophets and all the people heard Jeremiah speaking these words in the House of the LORD. 8 And when Jeremiah finished speaking all that the LORD had commanded him to speak to all the people, the priests and the prophets and all the people seized him, shouting, "You shall die! 9 How dare you prophesy in the name of the LORD that this House shall become like Shiloh and this city be made desolate, without inhabitants?" And all the people crowded about Jeremiah in the House of the LORD.

10 When the officials of Judah heard about this, they went up from the king's palace to the House of the LORD and held a session at the entrance of the New Gate of ^dthe House of^d the LORD. 11 The priests and prophets said to

26.1–24: Jeremiah's trial for sedition. Jeremiah's trial for sedition as a result of his Temple sermon (7.1–8.3). **1:** The trial takes place *at the beginning of the reign of . . . Jehoiakim* in 608 BCE, four years prior to Jeremiah's oracle concerning the acceptance of Babylonian rule in ch 25. This explains why the prophet can still envision repentance (v. 3). **2–9:** God's instructions to Jeremiah to deliver the Temple sermon. The basic message of the speech emphasizes God's call for repentance on the part of the people in order to save the city. **6:** On *Shiloh,* see 7.12–15. **8:** The people react by calling for Jeremiah's death, the punishment for a false prophet (Deut. 18.20). *The priests* are upset because Jeremiah is threatening the Temple, their central institution and the basis of their livelihood, while *the prophets* feel that Jeremiah is an illegitimate competitor. **10–11:** Jeremiah's trial takes place at *the New Gate of the House of the LORD,* lit. "the new gate of the LORD." The location of the new gate is unknown.

---

a-a Meaning of Heb. uncertain.   *b Meaning of Heb. uncertain.*   *c Cf. note at 24.9.*
d-d So many mss. and ancient versions; other mss. and the editions omit these words.

the officials and to all the people, "This man deserves the death penalty, for he has prophesied against this city, as you yourselves have heard."

12 Jeremiah said to the officials and to all the people, "It was the LORD who sent me to prophesy against this House and this city all the words you heard. 13 Therefore mend your ways and your acts, and heed the LORD your God, that the LORD may renounce the punishment He has decreed for you. 14 As for me, I am in your hands: do to me what seems good and right to you. 15 But know that if you put me to death, you and this city and its inhabitants will be guilty of shedding the blood of an innocent man. For in truth the LORD has sent me to you, to speak all these words to you."

16 Then the officials and all the people said to the priests and prophets, "This man does not deserve the death penalty, for he spoke to us in the name of the LORD our God."

17 And some of the elders of the land arose and said to the entire assemblage of the people, 18 "Micah the Morashtite, who prophesied in the days of King Hezekiah of Judah, said to all the people of Judah: 'Thus said the LORD of Hosts:

Zion shall be plowed as a field,
Jerusalem shall become heaps of ruins
And the Temple Mount a shrine in the woods.'ᵃ

19 "Did King Hezekiah of Judah, and all Judah, put him to death? Did he not rather fear the LORD and implore the LORD, so that the LORD renounced the punishment He had decreed against them? We are about to do great injury to ourselves!"

20 There was also a man prophesying in the name of the LORD, Uriah son of Shemaiah from Kiriath-jearim, who prophesied against this city and this land the same things as Jeremiah. 21 King Jehoiakim and all his warriors and all the officials heard about his address, and the king wanted to put him to death. Uriah heard of this and fled in fear, and came to Egypt. 22 But King Jehoiakim sent men to Egypt, Elnathan son of Achbor and men with him to Egypt. 23 They took Uriah out of Egypt and brought him to King Jehoiakim, who had him put to the sword and his body thrown into the burial place of the common people. 24 However, Ahikam son of Shaphan protected Jeremiah, so that he was not handed over to the people for execution.

12–15: Jeremiah's defense is that he speaks as a true prophet of God. The priests and prophets calling for his death would therefore be false. **16–19:** *The officials* and *the people* defend Jeremiah by pointing to the prophecy of *Micah the Morashtite* (Mic. 1.1), who prophesied in the time of Hezekiah that Jerusalem would be destroyed. Micah's condemnation of Jerusalem appears in Mic. 3.12 with slightly different wording. They argue that because Hezekiah repented as a result of Micah's threat, the city was saved (cf. Isa. chs 36–37; 2 Kings chs 18–20, which portrays Isaiah's role in the deliverance of Jerusalem in Hezekiah's time). Jeremiah therefore should not be killed because he acts like Micah to save the city, and prophesying against Jerusalem should not be viewed as either false prophecy or treasonous. **20–23:** The priests and prophets call on the precedent of the prophet *Uriah son of Shemaiah* of the town of *Kiriath-jearim.* (He is not otherwise known.) Because Uriah was killed by King Jehoiakim for prophesying against Jerusalem, the priests and prophets claim that Jeremiah should also be killed. *Elnathan son of Achbor* is one of the officials who later attempt to persuade Jehoiakim against burning Jeremiah's scroll (36.12, 25). He also supported Josiah's reform (2 Kings 22.12). Some think he may be the maternal grandfather of Jehoiachin (2 Kings 24.8). **24:** Jeremiah is finally saved by *Ahikam son of Shaphan,* the son of Josiah's scribe. Both father and son supported Josiah's reform (2 Kings 22.3, 12). The Shaphan family were important allies of Jeremiah (29.3; 36.10; 40.9; 41.1–2).

ᵃ *Cf. Mic. 3.12.*

27 At the beginning of the reign of King Jehoiakim[a] son of Josiah of Judah, this word came to Jeremiah from the LORD:

2 Thus said the LORD to me: Make for yourself thongs and bars of a yoke, and put them on your neck. 3 b-And send them-[b] to the king of Edom, the king of Moab, the king of the Ammonites, the king of Tyre, and the king of Sidon, by envoys who have come to King Zedekiah of Judah in Jerusalem; 4 and give them this charge to their masters: Thus said the LORD of Hosts, the God of Israel: Say this to your masters:

5 "It is I who made the earth, and the men and beasts who are on the earth, by My great might and My out-stretched arm; and I give it to whomever I deem proper. 6 I herewith deliver all these lands to My servant, King Neb-uchadnezzar of Babylon; I even give him the wild beasts to serve him. 7 All nations shall serve him, his son and his grandson—until the turn of his own land comes, when many nations and great kings shall subjugate him. 8 The nation or kingdom that does not serve him—King Nebu-chadnezzar of Babylon—and does not put its neck under the yoke of the king of Babylon, that nation I will visit—declares the LORD—with sword, famine, and pestilence, until I have destroyed it by his hands. 9 As for you, give no heed to your prophets, augurs, dreamers,[c] diviners, and sorcerers, who say to you, 'Do not serve the king of Bab-ylon.' 10 For they prophesy falsely to you—with the result that you shall be banished from your land; I will drive you out and you shall perish. 11 But the nation that puts its neck under the yoke of the king of Babylon, and serves him, will be left by Me on its own soil—declares the LORD—to till it and dwell on it."

12 I also spoke to King Zedekiah of Judah in just the same way: "Put your necks under the yoke of the king of Babylon; serve him and his people, and live! 13 Otherwise you will die together with your people, by sword, famine, and pestilence, as the LORD has decreed against any na-tion that does not serve the king of Babylon. 14 Give no heed to the words of the prophets who say to you, 'Do not serve the king of Babylon,' for they prophesy falsely to you. 15 I have not sent them—declares the LORD—and they prophesy falsely in My name, with the result that I will drive you out and you shall perish, together with the prophets who prophesy to you."

27.1–28.17: Jeremiah's prophecy of Nebuchadnezzar's conquest and the confrontation with the prophet Hananiah son of Azzur. **27.2–4:** The *yoke* with *thongs and bars* (cf. 1 Kings 12.9–11; 22.11) symbolizes God's will that Judah submit to the rule of Babylonia (cf. ch 25). Zedekiah had apparently gathered the envoys of his neigh-bors to discuss the possibility of revolt against Babylonia. The con-ference would have taken place in the fourth year of Zedekiah (593 BCE), about five years before the revolt began. **5–11:** God's first statements are directed to the en-voys from Edom, Moab, Ammon, Tyre, and Sidon. The argument contends that God is creator of all the world, and has the authority to give the world to whomever He chooses. **6:** By designating Nebu-chadnezzar as *servant*, God indi-cates the divine will that all the nations submit to Babylonia. **9–10:** The reference to false proph-ecy is a key concern of the whole unit. **12–15:** God's statement to Zedekiah likewise demands that he submit to Babylonia. If he re-fuses, he will die with his people.

a Emendation yields "Zedekiah"; so a few mss. and Syriac; cf. vv. 3 and 12.
b-b Emendation yields "And send," i.e., a message.   c Lit. "dreams."

16 And to the priests and to all that people I said: "Thus said the LORD: Give no heed to the words of the prophets who prophesy to you, 'The vessels of the House of the LORD shall shortly be brought back from Babylon,' for they prophesy falsely to you. 17 Give them no heed. Serve the king of Babylon, and live! Otherwise this city shall become a ruin. 18 If they are really prophets and the word of the LORD is with them, let them intercede with the LORD of Hosts not to let the vessels remaining in the House of the LORD, in the royal palace of Judah, and in Jerusalem, go to Babylon!

19 "For thus said the LORD of Hosts concerning the columns, the tank,[a] the stands, and the rest of the vessels remaining in this city, 20 which King Nebuchadnezzar of Babylon did not take when he exiled King Jeconiah son of Jehoiakim of Judah, from Jerusalem to Babylon, with all the nobles of Judah and Jerusalem; 21 for thus said the LORD of Hosts, the God of Israel, concerning the vessels remaining in the House of the LORD, in the royal palace of Judah, and in Jerusalem: 22 They shall be brought to Babylon, and there they shall remain, until I take note of them—declares the LORD of Hosts—and bring them up and restore them to this place."

28 That year, early in the reign of King Zedekiah of Judah, in the fifth month of the fourth year, the prophet Hananiah son of Azzur, who was from Gibeon, spoke to me in the House of the LORD, in the presence of the priests and all the people. He said: 2 "Thus said the LORD of Hosts, the God of Israel: I hereby break the yoke of the king of Babylon. 3 In two years, I will restore to this place all the vessels of the House of the LORD which King Nebuchadnezzar of Babylon took from this place and brought to Babylon. 4 And I will bring back to this place King Jeconiah son of Jehoiakim of Judah, and all the Judean exiles who went to Babylon—declares the LORD. Yes, I will break the yoke of the king of Babylon."

5 Then the prophet Jeremiah answered the prophet Hananiah in the presence of the priests and of all the people who were standing in the House of the LORD. 6 The prophet Jeremiah said: "Amen! May the LORD do so! May the LORD fulfill what you have prophesied and bring back from Babylon to this place the vessels of the House of the LORD and all the exiles! 7 But just listen to this word which I address to you and to all the people: 8 The prophets who lived before you and me from ancient times prophesied

16–18: The statement to the priests and people expresses similar concerns with submission to Babylonia and false prophecy. 2 Kings 24.13 reports that Nebuchadnezzar carried away the treasures of the Temple when he took Jehoiachin into exile to Babylon. 19–22: God states that the remaining vessels of the Temple and royal palace will be taken if the people do not submit to Babylonia. The *columns* are named Jachin and Boaz, and flank the entrance to the great hall of the Temple (1 Kings 7.21–22). The *tank* is the "sea" or basin of water before Solomon's Temple that would have served to purify the priests for service at the Temple altar (1 Kings 7.23–26). The *stands* are the ten bronze laver stands inside the Temple (1 Kings 7.27–39). 2 Kings 25.13–17 reports that these and other items were broken up and taken to Babylon when Nebuchadnezzar destroyed Jerusalem. Ezra 1.7–8 describes the return of these vessels. 28.1: The *fifth month* is Av, and the *fourth year* of Zedekiah is 593 BCE. *Hananiah son of Azzur*, who is otherwise unknown, provides an example of the false prophecy that is of grave concern throughout the book of Jeremiah. 2–4: By breaking Jeremiah's yoke, Hananiah performs a symbolic act to illustrate his message that God would deliver Jerusalem and return King Jehoiachin *in two years*. His message of divine deliverance for the city and king is similar to that of Isaiah (Isa. 7.1–9.6). Rabbinic tradition maintains that Hananiah heard Jeremiah's prophecy that God would break the bow of Elam (49.35), and mistakenly concluded that God would break the yoke of Babylonia (b. Sanh. 89a). 5–9: Jeremiah's response expresses his wish that Hananiah's prophecy would indeed come true. 6: *Amen*, see 11.5 n. Jeremiah repeats in a modified form the principle of Deut. 18.9–22 that a prophecy may be recognized as true only when it comes to pass. 7–9: Jeremiah here advances the definition of true prophecy by accepting all prophecy of doom as true, ipso facto.

war, disaster, and pestilence against many lands and great kingdoms. [9] So if a prophet prophesies good fortune, then only when the word of the prophet comes true can it be known that the LORD really sent him."

[10] But the prophet Hananiah removed the bar from the neck of the prophet Jeremiah, and broke it; [11] and Hananiah said in the presence of all the people, "Thus said the LORD: So will I break the yoke of King Nebuchadnezzar of Babylon from off the necks of all the nations, in two years." And the prophet Jeremiah went on his way.

[12] After the prophet Hananiah had broken the bar from off the neck of the prophet Jeremiah, the word of the LORD came to Jeremiah: [13] "Go say to Hananiah: Thus said the LORD: You broke bars of wood, but ᵃyou shallᵃ make bars of iron instead. [14] For thus said the LORD of Hosts, the God of Israel: I have put an iron yoke upon the necks of all those nations, that they may serve King Nebuchadnezzar of Babylon—and serve him they shall! I have even given the wild beasts to him."

[15] And the prophet Jeremiah said to the prophet Hananiah, "Listen, Hananiah! The LORD did not send you, and you have given this people lying assurances. [16] Assuredly, thus said the LORD: I am going to banish you from off the earth. This year you shall die, for you have urged disloyalty to the LORD."

[17] And the prophet Hananiah died that year, in the seventh month.

29 This is the text of the letter which the prophet Jeremiah sent from Jerusalem to the priests, the prophets, the rest of the elders of the exile community, and to all the people whom Nebuchadnezzar had exiled from Jerusalem to Babylon—[2] after King Jeconiah, the queen mother, the eunuchs, the officials of Judah and Jerusalem, and the craftsmen and smiths had left Jerusalem. [3] [The letter was sent] through Elasah son of Shaphan and Gemariah son of Hilkiah, whom King Zedekiah of Judah had dispatched to Babylon, to King Nebuchadnezzar of Babylon.

[4] Thus said the LORD of Hosts, the God of Israel, to the whole community which I exiled from Jerusalem to Babylon: [5] Build houses and live in them, plant gardens and eat their fruit. [6] Take wives and beget sons and daughters; and take wives for your sons, and give your daughters to husbands, that they may bear sons and daughters. Multiply there, do not decrease. [7] And seek the welfare of the

The audience could not afford to wait to see if a prophecy of doom would come true. **10–11:** Hananiah breaks Jeremiah's yoke to symbolize that his own message of deliverance takes precedence over Jeremiah's message. The contest reaches a "tie" at this point; there is nothing more for Jeremiah to do, so he leaves. He returns when he receives a new oracle in v. 12. **12–17:** Jeremiah returns with an *iron yoke* to symbolize his message that submission to Babylonia is inevitable. The symbol is reinforced by Jeremiah's prediction that Hananiah will die (cf. Amos 7.10–17; Isa. chs 36–39). The *seventh month* is Tishri, two months later.

29.1–33: Jeremiah's letter to the exiles. Jeremiah's letter to those deported by Nebuchadnezzar to Babylon with Jehoiachin in 597 BCE (see 2 Kings 24.8–17; 2 Chron. 36.9–10). **2:** The *queen mother*, an important official in Judah, was Nehushta daughter of Elnathan of Jerusalem (2 Kings 24.8). **3:** *Elasah son of Shaphan* was the brother of Ahikam son of Shaphan (26.24) and the son of Josiah's scribe (2 Kings 22.3, 12). *Gemariah son of Hilkiah* may be the son of Josiah's high priest (2 Kings 22.4). **4–7:** Jeremiah's letter begins with God's instructions to accept life in Babylonia and to build lives and families there. The activites enumerated in vv. 5–6 are those of establishing a new home, indicating that for at least two generations Babylonia should be treated as home. **7:** The command to *seek the welfare of the city* and to *pray to the LORD in its behalf* anticipates the prayer for the government that appears as part of the Torah service for Shabbat and the festivals. The rhetoric of this verse is intended to shock—most people would have expected the words "*And seek the welfare of the city*" to refer to Jerusalem, not to Babylon.

a-a Septuagint reads "I will."

city to which I have exiled you and pray to the LORD in its behalf; for in its prosperity you shall prosper.

⁸ For thus said the LORD of Hosts, the God of Israel: Let not the prophets and diviners in your midst deceive you, and pay no heed to the dreams they*ᵃ* dream. ⁹ For they prophesy to you in My name falsely; I did not send them—declares the LORD.

¹⁰ For thus said the LORD: When Babylon's seventy years are over, I will take note of you, and I will fulfill to you My promise of favor—to bring you back to this place. ¹¹ For I am mindful of the plans I have made concerning you—declares the LORD—plans for your welfare, not for disaster, to give you a hopeful future. ¹² When you call Me, and come and pray to Me, I will give heed to you. ¹³ You will search for Me and find Me, if only you seek Me wholeheartedly. ¹⁴ I will be at hand for you—declares the LORD—and I will restore your fortunes. And I will gather you from all the nations and from all the places to which I have banished you—declares the LORD—and I will bring you back to the place from which I have exiled you.

¹⁵ But you say, "The LORD has raised up prophets for us in Babylon."*ᵇ*

¹⁶ Thus said the LORD concerning the king who sits on the throne of David, and concerning all the people who dwell in this city, your brothers who did not go out with you into exile—¹⁷ thus said the LORD of Hosts: I am going to let loose sword, famine, and pestilence against them and I will treat them as loathsome figs, so bad that they cannot be eaten.*ᶜ* ¹⁸ I will pursue them with the sword, with famine, and with pestilence; and I will make them a horror to all the kingdoms of the earth, a curse and an object of horror and hissing*ᵈ* and scorn among all the nations to which I shall banish them, ¹⁹ because they did not heed My words—declares the LORD—when I persistently sent to them My servants, the prophets, and they*ᵃ* did not heed—declares the LORD.

²⁰ But you, the whole exile community which I banished from Jerusalem to Babylon, hear the word of the LORD! ²¹ Thus said the LORD of Hosts, the God of Israel, concerning Ahab son of Kolaiah and Zedekiah son of Maaseiah, who prophesy falsely to you in My name: I am going to deliver them into the hands of King Nebuchadrezzar of Babylon, and he shall put them to death before your eyes. ²² And the whole community of Judah in Babylonia shall use a curse derived from their fate: "May God make you

8–9: The letter raises the issue of false prophets, a major theme of the preceding chs. **10–14:** Cf. 25.11 for the announcement that the nations would serve Babylonia for seventy years. **11:** God's promise of a *hopeful future* means lit. "future and hope" ("'aḥarit vetikvah"). **12:** God's promise to *heed* the people when they *call, come,* and *pray* to God, reverses the statement in Isa. 1.12–15 that God will not listen. Jeremiah again anticipates that Isaiah's scenario of judgment and restoration is to be realized in his own time (see also Isa. ch 11). **13:** A quotation of Deut. 4.29. **15:** Jeremiah cites the counter-argument that prophets in Babylon have apparently announced that God will overthrow Babylonia. **16–23:** Jeremiah portrays a scenario in which the king (Zedekiah) and the people left in the land of Judah will suffer further punishment from God at the hands of the Babylonians because they did not listen to the prophets. **21:** He then condemns the false prophets in Babylon, *Ahab son of Kolaiah and Zedekiah son of Maaseiah*. Both are otherwise unknown. The latter prophet may be the brother of Zephaniah son of Maaseiah, the deputy priest of the Temple (see vv. 24–28). Talmudic tradition maintains that both men were put to death for their attempt to commit adultery with Nebuchadnezzar's daughter, falsely claiming that God told them to do so (*b. Sanh.* 93a).

---

a Heb. "you."   *b* This verse is continued in vv. 20 ff.
c Cf. 24.1 ff.   *d* Cf. note at 18.16.

like Zedekiah and Ahab, whom the king of Babylon consigned to the flames!"—²³ because they did vile things in Israel, committing adultery with the wives of their fellows and speaking in My name false words which I had not commanded them. I am He who knows and bears witness—declares the LORD.

²⁴ Concerning Shemaiah the Nehelamite you[a] shall say: ²⁵ Thus said the LORD of Hosts, the God of Israel: Because you sent letters in your own name to all the people in Jerusalem, to Zephaniah son of Maaseiah and to the rest of the priests, as follows, ²⁶ "The LORD appointed you priest in place of the priest Jehoiada, [b]to exercise authority[b] in the House of the LORD over every madman who wants to play the prophet, to put him into the stocks[c] and into the pillory.[c] ²⁷ Now why have you not rebuked Jeremiah the Anathothite, who plays the prophet among you? ²⁸ For he has actually sent a message to us in Babylon to this effect: It will be a long time. Build houses and live in them, plant gardens and enjoy their fruit."—

²⁹ When the priest Zephaniah read this letter in the hearing of the prophet Jeremiah, ³⁰ the word of the LORD came to Jeremiah: ³¹ Send a message to the entire exile community: "Thus said the LORD concerning Shemaiah the Nehelamite: Because Shemaiah prophesied to you, though I did not send him, and made you false promises, ³² assuredly, thus said the LORD: I am going to punish Shemaiah the Nehelamite and his offspring. There shall be no man of his line dwelling among this people or seeing the good things I am going to do for My people—declares the LORD—for he has urged disloyalty toward the LORD."

30 The word which came to Jeremiah from the LORD: ² Thus said the LORD, the God of Israel: Write down in a scroll all the words that I have spoken to you. ³ For days are coming—declares the LORD—when I will restore

---

a I.e., Jeremiah.
b-b Lit. "that there might be officials."
c Meaning of Heb. uncertain.

24–28: *Shemaiah the Nehelamite* is apparently a prominent member of the exile who wrote to *Zephaniah son of Maaseiah* to demand that Jeremiah be rebuked. He is otherwise unknown. Zephaniah son of Maaseiah is the deputy priest of the Temple, who was later put to death after the fall of Jerusalem (52.24–26; cf. 21.1; 37.3). *Jehoiada*

was the high priest in Jerusalem who restored the seven-year-old Joash on the throne after the attempted coup of Athaliah (2 Kings ch 11). **29–32:** Jeremiah condemns Shemaiah as a false prophet who *has urged disloyalty,* a violation of Deut 13.6, and contends that he and his descendants will therefore never see the time of restoration.

30.1–31.40: **Jeremiah's book of consolation.** The poetic composition in chs 30–31 appears within the narrative material of the second half of the book; perhaps at an earlier stage it was the end of the book, following a tradition found in some prophetic books (Amos, Ezekiel), and continued in rabbinic tradition, that books should begin with rebuke and end with consolation. Because it looks forward to the return of Israel to the land, many interpreters maintain that it is an exilic or postexilic composition, but there is no reason to assume that all prophetic consolations were written after the restoration and falsely ascribed to prophets of rebuke. The emphasis on the return of Israel, Jacob, and Rachel to Jerusalem and Zion, however, suggests a plausible context of Josiah's efforts in the late 7th century to reunite northern Israel and Judah; these were later adapted to anticipate restoration after the exile. In its present position following chs 26–29, which focus on Babylonia as the instrument of divine action, chs 30–31 illustrate the prophet's message of consolation once the period of the exile concludes. Jer. 31.2–20 is the haftarah for the second day of Rosh Ha-Shanah. Its focus on the restoration of Rachel's lost children as a metaphor for the restoration of Israel corresponds to the deliverance of Isaac in the Torah portion (Gen. 22.1–24) and the continuance of creation and covenant for the coming year. **30.1–2:** The initial prophetic word formula introduces the passage, but the repeated appearances of the so-called prophetic messenger formula, "koh 'amar YHVH," *thus said the LORD,* marks the individual oracles which comprise the text. God's instruction to write these words *in a scroll* suggests that they may have once functioned as a separate "booklet." Their ultimate purpose will be to fully vindicate Jeremiah as a true prophet, whose words have been fulfilled (28.9). **3:** The initial oracle sets the theme for the whole, i.e., to restore and reunite Israel and Judah and re-the fortunes of My people Israel and Judah, said the LORD; and I will bring them back to the land that I gave their fathers, and they shall possess it. ⁴ And these are the words that the LORD spoke concerning Israel and Judah:

5 Thus said the LORD:
 We have heard cries of panic,
 Terror without relief.

6 Ask and see:
 Surely males do not bear young!
 Why then do I see every man
 With his hands on his loins
 Like a woman in labor?
 Why have all faces turned pale?

7 Ah, that day is awesome;
 There is none like it!
 It is a time of trouble for Jacob,
 But he shall be delivered from it.

⁸ In that day—declares the LORD of Hosts—I will break the yoke from off your neck and I will rip off your bonds. Strangers shall no longer make slaves of them; ⁹ instead, they shall serve the LORD their God and David, the king whom I will raise up for them.

10 But you,
 Have no fear, My servant Jacob
    —declares the LORD—
 Be not dismayed, O Israel!
 I will deliver you from far away,
 Your folk from their land of captivity.
 And Jacob shall again have calm
 And quiet with none to trouble him;

11 For I am with you to deliver you
    —declares the LORD.
 I will make an end of all the nations
 Among which I have dispersed you;
 But I will not make an end of you!
 I will not leave you unpunished,
 But will chastise you in measure.

12 For thus said the LORD:
 Your injury is incurable,
 Your wound severe;

13 ᵃNo one pleads for the healing of your sickness,ᵃ
 There is no remedy, no recovery for you.

14 All your lovers have forgotten you,

turn them to the land of Israel. The passage employs the formula, *for days are coming,* that appears at the beginning and end of these chs to point to the future (see 31.27, 31, 38). **4:** This v. introduces the following oracles. **5–11:** The oracle portrays a general scenario of panic and terror for the people, but promises that Jacob will be delivered. **7:** Although the name Jacob has come to designate all Israel and Judah, it is especially associated with the Northern Kingdom of Israel (see Gen. chs 25–35; Hosea). The portrayal of men suffering in pain as if they were women giving birth illustrates the cataclysmic nature of the nation's distress. **8:** The oracle alludes to the exodus tradition by promising that God will restore Israel from its oppressive slavery to other nations so that it might serve God and its Davidic king. **10–11:** The statements, *have no fear* and *I am with you to deliver you* are typical features of the prophetic oracle of reassurance in Israel (cf. Gen. 15.1; 2 Kings 6.16; Isa. 7.4–9; 10.24–37; 37.6–7; 40.9; 41.10) and Mesopotamia. The designation of Jacob as God's *servant* anticipates the so-called "servant songs" of Second Isaiah (Isa. 42.1–4; 49.1–6; 50.4–11; 52.13–53.12). The oracle indicates that Israel will be punished, but not destroyed, following the typical prophetic idea of a remnant. **12–17:** This oracle employs the metaphors of sickness and wounds to portray Israel's suffering, reversing the image of 8.21–22. As would be expected, a significant source for prophecies of consolation would be prophecies of destruction, which are overturned. Again, the image is crucial to Second Isaiah's servant songs (see Isa. 52.13–53.12). **14:** Radak claims that *all your lovers* refers to the nations to whom Israel appealed for aid.

a-a Meaning of Heb. uncertain.

They do not seek you out;
For I have struck you as an enemy strikes,
With cruel chastisement,
Because your iniquity was so great
And your sins so many.

15 Why cry out over your injury,
That your wound is incurable?
I did these things to you
Because your iniquity was so great
And your sins so many.

16 Assuredly,
All who wanted to devour you shall be devoured,
And every one of your foes shall go into
        captivity;
Those who despoiled you shall be despoiled,
And all who pillaged you I will give up to
        pillage.
17 But I will bring healing to you
And cure you of your wounds
                        —declares the LORD.

Though they called you "Outcast,
That Zion whom no one seeks out,"
18 Thus said the LORD:
I will restore the fortunes of Jacob's tents
And have compassion upon his dwellings.
The city shall be rebuilt on its mound,[a]
And the fortress in its proper place.
19 From them shall issue thanksgiving
And the sound of dancers.
I will multiply them,
And they shall not be few;
I will make them honored,
And they shall not be humbled.
20 His children shall be as of old,
And his community shall be established by My
        grace;
And I will deal with all his oppressors.
21 His chieftain shall be one of his own,
His ruler shall come from his midst;
I will bring him near, that he may approach Me
                —declares the LORD—
For who would otherwise dare approach Me?
22 You shall be My people,
And I will be your God.

30.18–31.1: The third oracle focuses on the rebuilding of the city of Jerusalem. 18: The initial statement, *I will restore the fortunes of Jacob's tents / And have compassion upon his dwellings,* may recall the blessing of Israel by the pagan prophet Balaam at the time of the wilderness wanderings, "How fair are your tents, O Jacob, Your dwellings, O Israel" (Num. 24.5). The *mound* ("tel") on which a city is built refers to the artificial hill of buried debris that accumulates as ancient cities are built, destroyed, and rebuilt on top of the remains of the old. 22: The covenant formula, *you shall be My people, and I will be your God,* marks the restoration of the relationship between God and Israel (see 7.23; 11.4; 31.33; 32.38).

a I.e., on the mound of ruins left after its previous destruction.

23 Lo, the storm of the LORD goes forth in fury,
    A raging tempest;
    It shall whirl down upon the head of the wicked.
24 The anger of the LORD shall not turn back
    Till it has fulfilled and completed His purposes.
    In the days to come
    You shall perceive it.

31 ᵃAt that time—declares the LORD—I will be God to
    all the clans of Israel, and they shall be My people.

2   Thus said the LORD:
    The people escaped from the sword,
    Found favor in the wilderness;
    When Israel was marching homeward
3   The LORD revealed Himself to meᵇ of old.
    Eternal love I conceived for you then;
    Therefore I continue My grace to you.
4   I will build you firmly again,
    O Maiden Israel!
    Again you shall take up your timbrels
    And go forth to the rhythm of the dancers.
5   Again you shall plant vineyards
    On the hills of Samaria;
    Men shall plant and live to enjoy them.
6   For the day is coming when watchmen
    Shall proclaim on the heights of Ephraim:
    Come, let us go up to Zion,
    To the LORD our God!

7   For thus said the LORD:
    Cry out in joy for Jacob,
    Shout at the crossroadsᶜ of the nations!
    Sing aloud in praise, and say:
    ᵈSave, O LORD, Your people,ᵈ
    The remnant of Israel.
8   I will bring them in from the northland,
    Gather them from the ends of the earth—
    The blind and the lame among them,
    Those with child and those in labor—
    In a vast throng they shall return here.
9   They shall come with weeping,
    And with compassionᵉ will I guide them.
    I will lead them to streams of water,

24: The statement that *the anger of the LORD shall not turn back/Till it has fulfilled and completed His purposes* recalls Isaiah's earlier prophecies (Isa. 5.25; 9.11, 16, 20; 10.4) and anticipates Second Isaiah (Isa. 40.8; 55.11). **31.2–6:** This oracle draws upon the wilderness traditions and the portrayal of Israel as God's bride (cf. ch 2; Hos. chs 1–3). It draws especially on the image of Miriam leading the women of Israel in dancing with timbrels at the Red Sea (Exod. 15.20–21). **5–6:** The references to *the hills of Samaria* and *Ephraim* (the central tribe of northern Israel) suggest that this oracle originally addressed the Northern Kingdom of Israel in a call to return to Zion or the Jerusalem Temple in the south. The phrase, *come, let us go up to Zion,* recalls Isa. 2.3, 5; Mic. 4.2 (cf. Zech. 8.21). **7–14:** This oracle continues to employ the imagery of the wilderness tradition to portray Israel's restoration and return to the land. **7:** The *remnant of Israel* appears as a characteristic theme in Isaiah to portray the decimated people of Israel who will form the basis of the restoration (Isa. 4.2–6; 6.12–13; 7.4–9; 10.20–26; 37.30–32). **8:** The reference to gathering Israel *from the northland* recalls both the exile of northern Israel to Mesopotamia, which requires travel to the north, and Jeremiah's warnings of an enemy from the north (chs 2–6).

---

a In some editions this verse is 30.25.
b Emendation yields "him."   c Lit. "head."
d-d Emendation yields "The LORD has saved His people."
e For this meaning, cf. Zech. 12.10.

By a level road where they will not stumble.
For I am ever a Father to Israel,
Ephraim is My first-born.

10 Hear the word of the LORD, O nations,
And tell it in the isles afar.
Say:
He who scattered Israel will gather them,
And will guard them as a shepherd his flock.
11 For the LORD will ransom Jacob,
Redeem him from one too strong for him.
12 They shall come and shout on the heights of
      Zion,
Radiant over the bounty of the LORD—
Over new grain and wine and oil,
And over sheep and cattle.
They shall fare like a watered garden,
They shall never languish again.
13 Then shall maidens dance gaily,
Young men and old alike.
I will turn their mourning to joy,
I will comfort them and cheer them in their grief.
14 I will give the priests their fill of fatness,
And My people shall enjoy My full bounty
                              —declares the LORD.

15 Thus said the LORD:
A cry is heard ᵃ·in Ramah·ᵃ—
Wailing, bitter weeping—
Rachel weeping for her children.
She refuses to be comforted
For her children, who are gone.
16 Thus said the LORD:
Restrain your voice from weeping,
Your eyes from shedding tears;
For there is a reward for your labor
                              —declares the LORD:
They shall return from the enemy's land.
17 And there is hope for your future
                              —declares the LORD:
Your children shall return to their country.

18 I can hear Ephraim lamenting:
You have chastised me, and I am chastised
Like a calf that has not been broken.
Receive me back, let me return,
For You, O LORD, are my God.

12: The portrayal of the land as *a watered garden* full of bounty contrasts with the arid wilderness and draws on traditions of God as creator and provider of rain and agricultural produce. **15:** The portrayal of Israel as *Rachel weeping* for her lost children draws upon the tragic tradition of Rachel, Jacob's beloved wife, who died while giving birth to Benjamin. Although Gen. 35.16–21 places her tomb on the road to Bethlehem, where the current structure stands, 1 Sam. 10.2 suggests that her tomb was on the road to *Ramah,* near modern Ramallah. The present text portrays Rachel weeping not for herself, but for her lost children who have gone into exile. According to 40.1, 4, the Babylonians assembled Judeans destined for exile to Babylon at Ramah. The portrayal of Rachel weeping and bereft of children is reversed in Isa. ch 54, which employs the metaphor of a mother whose children are restored. According to *Rab. Gen.* 82.10, Jacob deliberately buried Rachel by the road because he knew that his descendants would pass by as they went into exile. She would then weep and intercede for their return. **16–22:** This oracle provides an answer for Rachel's weeping by promising the return of her children. **18–19:** *Ephraim,* a son of Joseph and the main tribe of northern Israel, symbolizes the Northern Kingdom.

a-a Or "on a height."

19 Now that I have turned back, I am filled with
        remorse;
    Now that I am made aware, I strike my thigh.ᵃ
    I am ashamed and humiliated,
    For I bear the disgrace of my youth.

20 Truly, Ephraim is a dear son to Me,
    A child that is dandled!
    Whenever I have turnedᵇ against him,
    My thoughts would dwell on him still.
    That is why My heart yearns for him;
    I will receive him back in love
                    —declares the LORD.

21 Erect markers,
    Set up signposts;ᶜ
    Keep in mind the highway,
    The road that you traveled.
    Return, Maiden Israel!
    Return to these towns of yours!

22 How long will you waver,
    O rebellious daughter?
    (For the LORD has created something new on
        earth:
    A woman courtsᶜ a man.)

²³ Thus said the LORD of Hosts, the God of Israel: They
shall again say this in the land of Judah and in its towns,
when I restore their fortunes:
    "The LORD bless you,
    Abode of righteousness,
    O holy mountain!"

²⁴ Judah and all its towns alike shall be inhabited by the
farmers and ᵈ·such as move aboutᵈ with the flocks. ²⁵ For I
will give the thirsty abundant drink, and satisfy all who
languish.

²⁶ At this I awoke and looked about, and my sleepᵉ had
been pleasant to me.

²⁷ See, a time is coming—declares the LORD—when I
will sow the House of Israel and the House of Judah with
seed of men and seed of cattle; ²⁸ and just as I was watchful over them to uproot and to pull down, to overthrow
and to destroy and to bring disaster, so I will be watchful
over them to build and to plant—declares the LORD. ²⁹ In

20: The return of the previously exiled Northern Kingdom is envisioned. **21–22:** The image shifts to Israel, the bride who will return to God. The problematic phrase, *a woman courts a man,* lit. "a woman surrounds a man," apparently employs the imagery of gender reversal (cf. 30.6) to portray the highly unusual nature of the restoration. The Bible elsewhere presents brides who are brought to the man (Gen. 2.22; ch 24; 29.23). The statement provides a basis for the practice of a bride circling the groom seven times at a Jewish wedding. **23–34:** This oracle portrays the restoration of Israel to its land and cities as part of a new covenant with God. As in the consolation prophecy in Ezek. 48.35, a new name reflects the changed staus of the place. **26:** The prophet awakens from a deep sleep in which he has seen a vision much like that of Abraham (cf. Gen. 15.12–21), who also saw the future captivity and exodus of his people while making a covenant with God. **28:** The prophet's depiction of the future employs the verbs *uproot, pull down, overthrow, destroy, build,* and *plant* from his call narrative in 1.10 to portray both the punishment and the restoration of the people. **29:** He quotes the proverb, *Parents have eaten sour grapes and children's teeth are blunted* (v. 29) to illustrate his view that only the guilty should be punished for their own sins (cf. Ezek. 18.2–4, which employs the proverb to make the same point). Unlike Ezekiel, however, who sees this principle of every person being punished for his sin as operative already in his own time, for Jeremiah, it will only be true in the future ("*In those days*").

a I.e., as a gesture of self-reproach.   b Lit. "spoken."
c Meaning of Heb. uncertain.   d-d Lit. "they shall travel."
e I.e., the vision in the preceding verses.

—990—

those days, they shall no longer say, "Parents have eaten sour grapes and children's teeth are blunted."* 30 But every one shall die for his own sins: whosoever eats sour grapes, his teeth shall be blunted.

31 See, a time is coming—declares the LORD—when I will make a new covenant with the House of Israel and the House of Judah. 32 It will not be like the covenant I made with their fathers, when I took them by the hand to lead them out of the land of Egypt, a covenant which they broke, though I espoused* them—declares the LORD. 33 But such is the covenant I will make with the House of Israel after these days—declares the LORD: I will put My Teaching into their inmost being and inscribe it upon their hearts. Then I will be their God, and they shall be My people. 34 No longer will they need to teach one another and say to one another, "Heed the LORD"; for all of them, from the least of them to the greatest, shall heed Me—declares the LORD.

> For I will forgive their iniquities,
> And remember their sins no more.

35   Thus said the LORD,
     Who established the sun for light by day,
     The laws of moon and stars for light by night,
     Who stirs up the sea into roaring waves,
     Whose name is LORD of Hosts:
36   If these laws should ever be annulled by Me
                  —declares the LORD—
     Only then would the offspring of Israel cease
     To be a nation before Me for all time.

37 Thus said the LORD: If the heavens above could be measured, and the foundations of the earth below could be fathomed, only then would I reject all the offspring of Israel for all that they have done—declares the LORD.

38 See, a time is coming—declares the LORD—when the city shall be rebuilt for the LORD from the Tower of Hananel to the Corner Gate; 39 and the measuring line shall go straight out to the Gareb Hill, and then turn toward Goah. 40 And the entire Valley of the Corpses and Ashes, and all the fields as far as the Wadi Kidron, and the corner of the Horse Gate on the east, shall be holy to the LORD. They shall never again be uprooted or overthrown.

31: The *new covenant* has been interpreted by Christians as a prophecy of the new covenant through Jesus (New Testament means new covenant), but here it refers to the restoration of Israel after the Babylonian exile and the reconstruction of the Temple. According to this passage, it is not the content of the new covenant which will be different, but how it is learned. **33–34:** God places the *Teaching*, i.e., the Torah, in the *inmost being* or heart of the people so that the covenant cannot be broken again. This idea is developed in later Lurianic kabbalah, which maintains that all persons have a divine spark within. Since it is so inscribed, there will be no need for the Torah to be taught. **35–36:** This oracle draws upon God's role as creator to promise that Israel's covenant assures its existence as a nation for the duration of all creation. **37–40:** This oracle elaborates upon the preceding oracle. It portrays the rebuilding of Jerusalem. **38:** The *Tower of Hananel* was located on the north wall of the city near the northeast corner (Neh. 3.1; 12.39; Zech. 14.10). The *Corner Gate* was located on the northwest wall (2 Kings 14.13; 2 Chron. 25.23; 26.9). **39:** *Gareb Hill* and *Goah* are unknown. **40:** The *Valley of the Corpses and Ashes* would refer to the Valley of Ben-Hinnom on the southwest side of the city where child sacrifice was practiced (7.31–32; 19.2, 6; 32.35; 2 Kings 23.10). The *Wadi Kidron* defines the eastern border of the biblical city of Jerusalem. The *Horse Gate* is located on the southeast corner (Neh. 3.28). As the site of the Temple, the city is *holy to the LORD*, never to be destroyed again.

---

a Others "set on edge."
b Meaning of Heb. uncertain; compare 3.14.

32 The word which came to Jeremiah from the LORD in the tenth year of King Zedekiah of Judah, which was the eighteenth year of Nebuchadrezzar. ² At that time the army of the king of Babylon was besieging Jerusalem, and the prophet Jeremiah was confined in the prison compound attached to the palace of the king of Judah. ³ For King Zedekiah of Judah had confined him, saying, "How dare you prophesy: 'Thus said the LORD: I am delivering this city into the hands of the king of Babylon, and he shall capture it. ⁴ And King Zedekiah of Judah shall not escape from the Chaldeans; he shall be delivered into the hands of the king of Babylon, ᵃand he shall speak to him face to face and see him in person.ᵃ ⁵ And Zedekiah shall be brought to Babylon, there to remain until I take note of him—declares the LORD. When you wage war against the Chaldeans, you shall not be successful.' "

⁶ Jeremiah said: The word of the LORD came to me: ⁷ Hanamel, the son of your uncle Shallum, will come to you and say, "Buy my land in Anathoth, ᵇfor you are next in succession to redeem it by purchase."ᵇ ⁸ And just as the LORD had said, my cousin Hanamel came to me in the prison compound and said to me, "Please buy my land in Anathoth, in the territory of Benjamin; for the right of succession is yours, and you have the duty of redemption. Buy it." Then I knew that it was indeed the word of the LORD.

⁹ So I bought the land in Anathoth from my cousin Hanamel. I weighed out the money to him, seventeen shekels of silver. ¹⁰ I wrote a deed, sealed it, and had it witnessed; and I weighed out the silver on a balance. ¹¹ I took the deed of purchase, the sealed text and the open one ᶜaccording to rule and law,ᶜ ¹² and gave the deed to Baruch son of Neriah son of Mahseiah in the presence of my kinsman Hanamel, of the witnesses ᵈwho were namedᵈ in the deed, and all the Judeans who were sitting in the prison compound. ¹³ In their presence I charged Baruch as follows: ¹⁴ Thus said the

---

a-a Lit. "and his mouth shall speak with his mouth, and his eyes shall see his eyes."
b-b Lit. "for yours is the procedure of redemption by purchase."
c-c Force of Heb. uncertain.
d-d With many mss. and ancient versions; so ancient Near Eastern practice. Other mss. and the editions read "who wrote" (i.e., signed their names).

32.1–33.26: Jeremiah's symbolic actions and oracles concerning the restoration. The prophetic word formula in v. 1 introduces a new section in which Jeremiah's attempt to redeem his family's land in Anathoth becomes a metaphor for God's promise to restore Jerusalem, the house of David, and the Levitical priesthood once the punishment is over. It thus continues in prose form the poetry of the previous two chs.

32.1–44: Jeremiah's attempt to redeem family property in Anathoth. The *tenth year of King Zedekiah* would be 588 BCE when the Babylonian army invaded Judah a second time to put down the Judean revolt. Zedekiah imprisoned Jeremiah for treason because of his claims that God had given Jerusalem into the hands of Nebuchadnezzar. He was apparently arrested when he attempted to leave the city during a lull in the fighting to redeem family property in Anathoth (see 37.11–21). Jer. 32.6–27 is the haftarah for the parashah of Be-har (Lev. 25.1–26.2), which relates the laws concerning the redemption of property in sabbatical and jubilee years. **6–15:** Jeremiah relates God's instructions concerning the request of his cousin Hanamel to redeem the property of his father, Shallum (Jeremiah's uncle), in Anathoth. Although Jeremiah is imprisoned, he is able to complete the transaction. Lev. 25.25–28 indicates that a person might sell property to pay a debt, but family members had the first right to redeem the land. The details offered in these vv. add to the limited material we have from elsewhere to explain how property was transferred. **9:** The price of *seventeen shekels*, lit. "seven shekels and ten pieces of silver," could not have been very high since the annual Temple tax for an adult male was fifty shekels (Lev. 27.2) and the field of Ephron in Machpelah, where Abraham buried Sarah, was sold for 400 shekels (Gen. ch 23). The low price may be explained by the fact that the sale takes place during a siege. **12:** The sale is documented by Jeremiah's scribe, *Baruch son of Neriah son of Mahseiah.* The name Baruch son of Neriah appears on a clay bulla found inside a house in the city of Jerusalem that was destroyed during the Babylonian siege, and many believe that this bulla, which was originally used in ancient Israel to seal a document, belonged to the same individual. The role of Baruch in Jeremiah is greater than the role of a scribe in any other prophetic work

LORD of Hosts, the God of Israel: "Take these documents, this deed of purchase, the sealed text and the open one, and put them into an earthen jar, so that they may last a long time." [15] For thus said the LORD of Hosts, the God of Israel: "Houses, fields, and vineyards shall again be purchased in this land."

[16] But after I had given the deed to Baruch son of Neriah, I prayed to the LORD: [17] "Ah, Lord GOD! You made heaven and earth with Your great might and outstretched arm. Nothing is too wondrous for You! [18] You show kindness to the thousandth generation, but visit the guilt of the fathers upon their children after them. O great and mighty God whose name is LORD of Hosts, [19] wondrous in purpose and mighty in deed, whose eyes observe all the ways of men, so as to repay every man according to his ways, and with the proper fruit of his deeds! [20] You displayed signs and marvels in the land of Egypt ᵃwith lasting effect,ᵃ and won renown in Israel and among mankind to this very day. [21] You freed Your people Israel from the land of Egypt with signs and marvels, with a strong hand and an outstretched arm, and with great terror. [22] You gave them this land that You had sworn to their fathers to give them, a land flowing with milk and honey, [23] and they came and took possession of it. But they did not listen to You or follow Your Teaching; they did nothing of what You commanded them to do. Therefore you have caused all this misfortune to befall them. [24] Here are the siegemounds, raised against the city to storm it; and the city, because of sword and famine and pestilence, is at the mercy of the Chaldeans who are attacking it. What You threatened has come to pass—as You see. [25] Yet You, Lord GOD, said to me: Buy the land for money and call in witnesses—when the city is at the mercy of the Chaldeans!"

[26] Then the word of the LORD came to Jeremiah:
[27] "Behold I am the LORD, the God of all flesh. Is anything too wondrous for Me? [28] Assuredly, thus said the LORD: I am delivering this city into the hands of the Chaldeans and of King Nebuchadrezzar of Babylon, and he shall capture it. [29] And the Chaldeans who have been attacking this city shall come and set this city on fire and burn it down—with the houses on whose roofs they made offerings to Baal and poured out libations to other gods, so as to vex Me. [30] For the people of Israel and Judah have done nothing but evil in My sight since their youth; the

(see esp. ch 36), leading some to suggest that Jeremiah was illiterate. **15:** Jeremiah clearly understands his purchase to be a sign of his confidence in the future of Judah once the punishment is over. **16–25:** Jeremiah's prayer to God provides the basic outlines of God's relationship with Israel from the time of the exodus (cf. Deut. ch 26—as in that chapter, Sinai is not mentioned) and articulates his view that the Babylonian invasion and siege is a divinely ordained punishment for Israel's disobedience of God's *Teaching* (v. 23). The same Heb word, "torah," may refer to the Torah or to teaching(s) in general, and it is very difficult to know when it should be translated as Torah, namely the five books of Moses, more or less in the form they now exist, or a more amorphous set of teachings. **26–44:** God's answer to Jeremiah elaborates upon the prophet's attempt to explain the reasons for Judah's current plight, but it also points to future restoration once the punishment is over.

a-a Lit. "to this day."

people of Israel have done nothing but vex Me by their conduct—declares the LORD. [31] This city has aroused My anger and My wrath from the day it was built until this day; so that it must be removed from My sight [32] because of all the wickedness of the people of Israel and Judah who have so acted as to vex Me—they, their kings, their officials, their priests and prophets, and the men of Judah and the inhabitants of Jerusalem. [33] They turned their backs to Me, not their faces; though I have taught them persistently, they do not give heed or accept rebuke. [34] They placed their abominations in the House which bears My name and defiled it; [35] and they built the shrines of Baal which are in the Valley of Ben-hinnom, where they offered up their sons and daughters to Molech—when I had never commanded, or even thought [of commanding], that they should do such an abominable thing, and so bring guilt on Judah.

[36] But now, assuredly, thus said the LORD, the God of Israel, concerning this city of which you say, "It is being delivered into the hands of the king of Babylon through the sword, through famine, and through pestilence": [37] See, I will gather them from all the lands to which I have banished them in My anger and wrath, and in great rage; and I will bring them back to this place and let them dwell secure. [38] They shall be My people, and I will be their God. [39] I will give them a single heart and a single nature to revere Me for all time, and it shall be well with them and their children after them. [40] And I will make an everlasting covenant with them that I will not turn away from them and that I will treat them graciously; and I will put into their hearts reverence for Me, so that they do not turn away from Me. [41] I will delight in treating them graciously, and I will plant them in this land faithfully, with all My heart and soul.

[42] For thus said the LORD: As I have brought this terrible disaster upon this people, so I am going to bring upon them the vast good fortune which I have promised for them. [43] And fields shall again be purchased in this land of which you say, "It is a desolation, without man or beast; it is delivered into the hands of the Chaldeans." [44] Fields shall be purchased, and deeds written and sealed, and witnesses called in the land of Benjamin and in the environs of Jerusalem, and in the towns of Judah; the towns of the hill country, the towns of the Shephelah, and the towns of the Negeb. For I will restore their fortunes—declares the LORD.

40: God promises *an everlasting covenant* in which the people will look to God and God will ensure their security in the land. Everlasting covenants were made with Noah (Gen. 9.16; cf. Isa. 24.5 in which it is broken); Abraham (Gen. 17.7, 19); Israel (Exod. 31.16; Lev. 24.8, for the Shabbat); Phineas the priest (Num. 25.13); David (2 Sam. 23.5); Israel (Isa. 55.3, after the pattern of David); and Jerusalem (Ezek. 16.60). Obedience is placed *into their hearts,* as in 31.33. **44:** Jeremiah's hometown of Anathoth is located in the territory of *Benjamin.*

33

The word of the LORD came to Jeremiah a second time, while he was still confined in the prison compound, as follows:

2 Thus said the LORD who is planning it,
The LORD who is shaping it to bring it about,
Whose name is LORD:

3 Call to Me, and I will answer you,
And I will tell you wondrous things,
Secrets you have not known.

⁴ For thus said the LORD, the God of Israel, concerning the houses of this city and the palaces of the kings of Judah that were torn down ᵃ for [defense] against the siegemounds and against the sword, ⁵ and were filled by those who went to fight the Chaldeans,ᵃ—with the corpses of the men whom I struck down in My anger and rage, hiding My face from this city because of all their wickedness: ⁶ I am going to bring her relief and healing. I will heal them and reveal to them abundanceᵃ of true favor. ⁷ And I will restore the fortunes of Judah and Israel, and I will rebuild them as of old. ⁸ And I will purge them of all the sins which they committed against Me, and I will pardon all the sins which they committed against Me, by which they rebelled against Me. ⁹ And she shall gain through Me renown, joy, fame, and glory above all the nations on earth, when they hear of all the good fortune I provide for them.ᵇ They will thrill and quiver because of all the good fortune and all the prosperity that I provide for her.

¹⁰ Thus said the LORD: Again there shall be heard in this place, which you say is ruined, without man or beast— in the towns of Judah and the streets of Jerusalem that are desolate, without man, without inhabitants, without beast—¹¹ the sound of mirth and gladness, the voice of bridegroom and bride, the voice of those who cry, "Give thanks to the LORD of Hosts, for the LORD is good, for His kindness is everlasting!" as they bring thanksgiving offerings to the House of the LORD. For I will restore the fortunes of the land as of old—said the LORD.

¹² Thus said the LORD of Hosts: In this ruined place, without man and beast, and in all its towns, there shall again be a pasture for shepherds, where they can rest their flocks. ¹³ In the towns of the hill country, in the towns of the Shephelah, and in the towns of the Negeb, in the land of Benjamin and in the environs of Jerusalem and in the

33.1–26: Oracles concerning the restoration. A second set of oracles continues the focus on the coming restoration, but emphasizes that the House of David and the Levitical priesthood will also be a part of God's everlasting covenant with Israel. **2–9:** The divine oracle begins with a hymnic passage that relates God's role as creator. The interest in God's plans appears frequently in Isaiah as a means to explain disaster by asserting that God plans from the beginning to bring deliverance after a period of punishment (Isa. 10.13; 14.27; 28.23–29; 55.11). **3:** God's assurance of an *answer* when the people appeal reverses the statements of Isa. 1.15. **5–6:** God elaborates on this statement by claiming to bring *relief* for all the destruction that was visited upon the city and the palaces of the kings. Jeremiah's oracle here presupposes that God will no longer hide His face from Israel (contra Isa. 8.17). **10–11:** The celebration of weddings in the restored land is a reversal of earlier prophecies in 7.34; 16.9; 25.10. The refrain, *Give thanks to the LORD of Hosts, for the LORD is good, for His kindness is everlasting* (v. 11), appears in Pss. 106.1; 118.1; 136.1; Ezra 3.11, and in many contemporary liturgical settings. **12–18:** The restoration will also include farms and husbandry. **13:** The *Shephelah* refers to the low hills of southwestern Judah that border Philistia. The *Negeb* is the desert region to the south of the Judean hill country. *Benjamin* is the tribal territory to the north and east of Jerusalem.

a-a Meaning of Heb. uncertain.   b I.e., for Judah and Israel.

towns of Judah, sheep shall pass again under the hands of one who counts them—said the LORD. ¹⁴See, days are coming—declares the LORD—when I will fulfill the promise that I made concerning the House of Israel and the House of Judah. ¹⁵ In those days and at that time, I will raise up a true branch of David's line, and he shall do what is just and right in the land. ¹⁶ In those days Judah shall be delivered and Israel shall dwell secure. And this is what she shall be called: "The LORD is our Vindicator." ¹⁷ For thus said the LORD: There shall never be an end to men of David's line who sit upon the throne of the House of Israel. ¹⁸ Nor shall there ever be an end to the line of the levitical priests before Me, of those who present burnt offerings and turn the meal offering to smoke and perform sacrifices.

¹⁹ The word of the LORD came to Jeremiah: ²⁰ Thus said the LORD: If you could break My covenant with the day and My covenant with the night, so that day and night should not come at their proper time, ²¹ only then could My covenant with My servant David be broken—so that he would not have a descendant reigning upon his throne—or with My ministrants, the levitical priests. ²² Like the host of heaven which cannot be counted, and the sand of the sea which cannot be measured, so will I multiply the offspring of My servant David, and of the Levites who minister to Me.

²³ The word of the LORD came to Jeremiah: ²⁴ You see what this people said: "The two families which the LORD chose have now been rejected by Him." Thus they despise My people, ^aand regard them as no longer a nation.^{-a} ²⁵ Thus said the LORD: As surely as I have established My covenant with day and night—the laws of heaven and earth—²⁶ so I will never reject the offspring of Jacob and My servant David; I will never fail to take from his offspring rulers for the descendants of Abraham, Isaac, and Jacob. Indeed, I will restore their fortunes and take them back in love.

34 The word which came to Jeremiah from the LORD, when King Nebuchadrezzar of Babylon and all his army, and all the kingdoms of the earth and all the peoples under his sway, were waging war against Jerusalem and all its towns:

² Thus said the LORD, the God of Israel: Go speak to

a-a *Meaning of Heb. uncertain.*

15: The prophet states that the House of David will be included in the restoration, i.e., Davidic kingship will be restored as well. The reference to the *true branch of David's line* draws on Isa. 11.1–16, which portrays the righteous Davidic monarch as a branch ("tsemah") from the root of Jesse, language which is at home in the agriculturally centered world of ancient Israel, and is reused in the blessing of the "'Amidah" requesting the restoration of the Davidic monarchy. David was promised an eternal dynasty (2 Sam. ch 7) and eternal covenant (2 Sam. 23.5). Narratives concerning Solomon's prayer qualify the promise, however, by stating that the Davidic line will rule forever if it is righteous (1 Kings 8.22–26; 9.3–9; cf. Ps. 132.11–12). **16:** Note a simlar renaming in 31.23. **17:** Jeremiah's version of the Davidic promise reverts to the unconditioned model of 2 Sam. chs 7, 23. **18:** It adds an eternal promise to the Levitical priesthood, perhaps building on the priestly eternal covenant promised to Phineas son of Eleazar son of Aaron (Num. 25.13). The promise of a righteous Davidic branch was read as a reference to the priesthood in Zechariah, where the high priest and king seem to rule in tandem in the early postexilic period (Zech. 6.9–15; cf. 3.8). **19–22:** The covenant with David and the Levites is equated with the covenant that ensures the stability of the cosmos (Gen. 9.8–17; cf. Exod. 31.16–17; Ps. 89.20–38). **23–26:** This oracle is designed to counter arguments that God had abandoned the families of *Jacob* and *David.*

34.1–7: Jeremiah's oracle concerning King Zedekiah. 1: The initial v. sets the passage in the time of Nebuchadrezzar's siege of Jerusalem in 588 BCE. **5:** The promise of a *peaceful death* for Zedekiah resembles the oracle of the prophetess Huldah to Zedekiah's father Josiah (2 Kings 22.14–20; 2 Chron. 34.22–28) and contrasts markedly with Jeremiah's oracle for Jehoiakim (36.27–31; cf. 22.24–30). Jer.

King Zedekiah of Judah, and say to him: "Thus said the LORD: I am going to deliver this city into the hands of the king of Babylon, and he will destroy it by fire. ³ And you will not escape from him; you will be captured and handed over to him. ᵃ⁻And you will see the king of Babylon face to face and speak to him in person;⁻ᵃ and you will be brought to Babylon. ⁴ But hear the word of the LORD, O King Zedekiah of Judah! Thus said the LORD concerning you: You will not die by the sword. ⁵ You will die a peaceful death; and as incenseᵇ was burned for your ancestors, the earlier kings who preceded you, so they will burn incenseᵇ for you, and they will lament for you 'Ah, lord!' For I Myself have made the promise—declares the LORD."

⁶ The prophet Jeremiah spoke all these words to King Zedekiah of Judah in Jerusalem, ⁷ when the army of the king of Babylon was waging war against Jerusalem and against the remaining towns of Judah—against Lachish and Azekah, for they were the only fortified towns of Judah that were left.

⁸ The word which came to Jeremiah from the LORD after King Zedekiah had made a covenant with all the people in Jerusalem to proclaim a releaseᶜ among them—⁹ that everyone should set free his Hebrew slaves, both male and female, and that no one should keep his fellow Judean enslaved.

¹⁰ Everyone, officials and people, who had entered into the covenant agreed to set their male and female slaves free and not keep them enslaved any longer; they complied and let them go. ¹¹ But afterward they turned about and brought back the men and women they had set free, and forced them into slavery again. ¹² Then it was that the word of the LORD came to Jeremiah from the LORD:

¹³ Thus said the LORD, the God of Israel: I made a covenant with your fathers when I brought them out of the land of Egypt, the house of bondage, saying: ¹⁴ "In the seventh yearᵈ each of you must let go any fellow Hebrew ᵉ⁻who may be sold⁻ᵉ to you; when he has served you six years, you must set him free." But your fathers would not obey Me or give ear. ¹⁵ Lately you turned about and did what is proper in My sight, and each of you proclaimed a release to his countrymen; and you made a covenant ac-

52.7–11 (cf. 2 Kings 25.4–7) states that Zedekiah is in a Babylonian prison, having seen his sons slaughtered before his own eyes were put out, thus this is likely an unfulfilled prophecy of Jeremiah. It is quite remarkable that such prophecies were preserved. **7:** *Lachish and Azekah* were fortified Judean cities located respectively 60 km (35 mi) and 25 km (15 mi) southwest of Jerusalem in the Shephelah.

34.8–22: The oracle concerning slaves. This oracle attempts to provide justification for Zedekiah's punishment by accusing him of reneging on an agreement to release slaves during the siege of Jerusalem. **14:** According to the slave laws of Deut. 15.1–18; Exod. 21.1–11 (cf. Lev. 25.39–55), a person could become a slave to repay a debt. The laws specify six years as the period of time for such service. A man goes free in the seventh year, unless he formally and publicly declares his willingness to remain a slave forever (the laws for women differ between the two texts). According to Lev. ch 25, a "release" or "jubilee" is proclaimed every fiftieth year (seven weeks of years) so that property that was sold to pay a debt reverts to its original owner (the sale actually functions as a sort of loan in which the creditor gains use of the property for the specified period of time). This text in Jeremiah generally follows the law as it appears in Deut. ch 15, which is not surprising given the affinities of Jeremiah to Deuteronomy. The Deuteronomy text, however, seems to suggest that the slave is released at the beginning of the seventh year of service, while Jeremiah seems to understand this, perhaps based on the broader context of Deut. ch 15 (see esp. vv. 1–6), as meaning that all slaves are released at each sabbatical (seventh) year. **15–16:** Perhaps Zedekiah entered into an agreement to declare a release for all slaves in the city, so that they would be free to participate in Jerusalem's defense, and when the Babylonians lifted the siege of the

---

a-a For the idiom see note at 32.4.   b Lit. "burnings."   c Others "liberty."
d I.e., of servitude. Lit. "After a period of seven years"; cf. Deut. 14.28 and 15.1.
e-e Or "who sells himself."

cordingly before Me in the House which bears My name. [16] But now you have turned back and have profaned My name; each of you has brought back the men and women whom you had given their freedom, and forced them to be your slaves again.

[17] Assuredly, thus said the LORD: You would not obey Me and proclaim a release, each to his kinsman and country-man. Lo! I proclaim your release—declares the LORD—to the sword, to pestilence, and to famine; and I will make you a horror to all the kingdoms of the earth. [18] I will make the men who violated My covenant, who did not fulfill the terms of the covenant which they made before Me, [like] the calf which they cut in two so as to pass between the halves:[a] [19] The officers of Judah and Jerusalem, the officials, the priests, and all the people of the land who passed be-tween the halves of the calf [20] shall be handed over to their enemies, to those who seek to kill them. Their carcasses shall become food for the birds of the sky and the beasts of the earth. [21] I will hand over King Zedekiah of Judah and his officers to their enemies, who seek to kill them—to the army of the king of Babylon which has withdrawn from you. [22] I hereby give the command—declares the LORD—by which I will bring them back against this city. They shall attack it and capture it, and burn it down. I will make the towns of Judah a desolation, without inhabitant.

35 The word which came to Jeremiah from the LORD in the days of King Jehoiakim son of Josiah of Judah:

[2] Go to the house of the Rechabites and speak to them, and bring them to the House of the LORD, to one of the chambers, and give them wine to drink.

[3] So I took Jaazaniah son of Jeremiah son of Habazzi-niah, and his brothers, all his sons, and the whole house-hold of the Rechabites; [4] and I brought them to the House of the LORD, to the chamber of the sons of Hanan son of Igdaliah, the man of God, which is next to the chamber of the officials and above the chamber of Maaseiah son of Shallum, the guardian of the threshold. [5] I set bowls full of wine and cups before the men of the house of the Rech-abites, and said to them, "Have some wine."

[6] They replied, "We will not drink wine, for our ances-

a Cf. Gen. 15.9–10, 17–21.

halves of a slaughtered calf to make (lit. "cut") a covenant. The practice is attested in the Bible (Gen. 15.7–21) and in ancient Near East-ern treaties. The parties to an agreement pass between the two halves of slaughtered animals that represent what will happen to them if they violate the terms of the agreement. The practice func-tions as a formal ratification of an agreement. **21:** Because Zedekiah violated the covenant or agree-ment that he had made, Jeremiah contends that he is now subject to punishment at the hands of the Babylonians. Jer. 34.8–22; 33.35, 26 is the haftarah for the parashah of Mishpatim (Exod. 21.1–24.18), which contains the first collection of law from Sinai, beginning with the slave law.

35.1–39.18: The fall of Jerusalem. The prophetic word formula intro-duces a block of text that culmi-nates in the fall of Jerusalem to the Babylonian army in 586 BCE (ch 39). The preceding chs illus-trate why Jerusalem fell, beginning with the example of the Rechabites who were faithful to their own tra-dition (ch 35), King Jehoiakim's rejection of Jeremiah's oracles (ch 36), and the prophet's subse-quent imprisonment for treason during the siege of the city (chs 37–38).

35.1–19: The example of the Rechabites. The prophetic word formula places this narrative in the reign of Jehoiakim, in an effort to demonstrate that the reasons for Jerusalem's punishment go back at least to his reign. The Rechabites were an ancient religious group founded by Jonadab son of Rechab, who assisted Jehu in his successful revolt against the house of Omri in 842 BCE (2 Kings 10.15–28). Biblical tradition identi-fies the Rechabites as Kenites (1 Chron. 2.55), who would be descended from Moses' Kenite father-in-law, Jethro (Judg. 1.16; Exod. 3.1; 18.1), who in turn would be descended from Cain, after whom the Kenites are named (Gen. 4.1–16). **6–8:** Their prohibi-

city to fight a relief force sent by Egypt (see ch 37), Zedekiah and the creditors reneged, forcing those freed to return to their slave status. **17:** God invokes a type of measure for measure: The Judeans did not *release* slaves, so God will *release* destruction. Measure for measure is very common in the Bible, especially in prophetic pun-ishments. **18:** Jeremiah cites the practice of passing *between the* tor, Jonadab son of Rechab, commanded us: 'You shall never drink wine, either you or your children. [7] Nor shall you build houses or sow fields[a] or plant vineyards, nor shall you own such things; but you shall live in tents all your days, so that you may live long upon the land where you sojourn.' [8] And we have obeyed our ancestor Jonadab son of Rechab in all that he commanded us: we never drink wine, neither we nor our wives nor our sons and daughters. [9] Nor do we build houses to live in, and we do not own vineyards or fields for sowing; [10] but we live in tents. We have obeyed and done all that our ancestor Jonadab commanded us. [11] But when King Nebuchadrezzar of Babylon invaded the country, we said, 'Come, let us go into Jerusalem because of the army of the Chaldeans and the army of Aram.' And so we are living in Jerusalem."

[12] Then the word of the LORD came to Jeremiah:

[13] Thus said the LORD of Hosts, the God of Israel: Go say to the men of Judah and the inhabitants of Jerusalem: "You can learn a lesson [here] about obeying My commands—declares the LORD. [14] The commands of Jonadab son of Rechab have been fulfilled: he charged his children not to drink wine, and to this day they have not drunk, in obedience to the charge of their ancestor. But I spoke to you persistently, and you did not listen to Me. [15] I persistently sent you all My servants, the prophets, to say: 'Turn back, every one of you, from your wicked ways and mend your deeds; do not follow other gods or serve them. Then you may remain on the land that I gave to you and your fathers.' But you did not give ear or listen to Me. [16] The family of Jonadab son of Rechab have indeed fulfilled the charge which their ancestor gave them; but this people has not listened to Me. [17] Assuredly, thus said the LORD, the God of Hosts, the God of Israel: I am going to bring upon Judah and upon all the inhabitants of Jerusalem all the disaster with which I have threatened them; for I spoke to them, but they would not listen; I called to them, but they would not respond."

[18] And to the family of the Rechabites Jeremiah said: "Thus said the LORD of Hosts, the God of Israel: Because you have obeyed the charge of your ancestor Jonadab and kept all his commandments, and done all that he enjoined upon you, [19] assuredly, thus said the LORD of Hosts, the God of Israel: There shall never cease to be a man of the line of Jonadab son of Rechab standing before Me."

tion against drinking *wine* resembles a part of the Nazirite vow by which a person sanctifies him- or herself for divine service like a priest for the duration of the vow by refraining from wine, contact with the dead, and cutting the hair (Num. 6.1–21; cf. Judg. chs 13–16; 1 Sam. ch 1; *m. Naz.*; *b. Naz.*). **7:** The exact reasons for these prohibitions are unclear, though possibly the Rechabites are to live as a bedouin group after the manner of their ancestor Jethro, priest of Midian. **9:** They are neither Nazirites nor priests, although the concluding expression, *standing before Me* (v. 19), suggests a priestly role much like Jethro's. God instructs Jeremiah to use the Rechabites as an example of faithfulness to a religious tradition in order to emphasize the charges that Judah has not been faithful to its own tradition. **18–19:** Although punishment in Jeremiah is generally viewed as corporate, i.e., all Israel is to be punished for the sins of any of its members, these vv. exempt the extremely righteous Rechabites from the full fury of the impending disaster.

a Lit. "seed."

36

In the fourth year of King Jehoiakim son of Josiah of Judah, this word came to Jeremiah from the LORD:

[2] Get a scroll and write upon it all the words that I have spoken to you—concerning Israel and Judah and all the nations—from the time I first spoke to you in the days of Josiah to this day. [3] Perhaps when the House of Judah hear of all the disasters I intend to bring upon them, they will turn back from their wicked ways, and I will pardon their iniquity and their sin. [4] So Jeremiah called Baruch son of Neriah; and Baruch wrote down in the scroll, at Jeremiah's dictation, all the words which the LORD had spoken to him.

[5] Jeremiah instructed Baruch, "I am in hiding; I cannot go to the House of the LORD. [6] But you go and read aloud the words of the LORD from the scroll which you wrote at my dictation, to all the people in the House of the LORD on a fast day; thus you will also be reading them to all the Judeans who come in from the towns. [7] Perhaps their entreaty will be accepted by the LORD, if they turn back from their wicked ways. For great is the anger and wrath with which the LORD has threatened this people."

[8] Baruch son of Neriah did just as the prophet Jeremiah had instructed him, about reading the words of the LORD from the scroll in the House of the LORD. [9] In the ninth month of the fifth year of King Jehoiakim son of Josiah of Judah, all the people in Jerusalem and all the people coming from Judah proclaimed a fast before the LORD in Jerusalem. [10] It was then that Baruch—in the chamber of Gemariah son of Shaphan the scribe, in the upper court, near the new gateway of the House of the LORD—read the words of Jeremiah from the scroll to all the people in the House of the LORD.

[11] Micaiah son of Gemariah son of Shaphan heard all the words of the LORD [read] from the scroll, [12] and he went down to the king's palace, to the chamber of the scribe. There he found all the officials in session: Elishama the scribe, Delaiah son of Shemaiah, Elnathan son of Achbor, Gemariah son of Shaphan, Zedekiah son of Hananiah, and all the other officials. [13] And Micaiah told them all

the time . . . of Josiah to the present on a scroll. Many interpreters maintain that this would be an early edition of the book of Jeremiah, comprising elements from chs 1–20 or 1–25. The reference to the nations suggests that elements from the oracles concerning the nations in chs 46–51 would also have been included. The Septuagint version of Jeremiah, thought by many to be based on an earlier Hebrew edition of the book, places the oracles concerning the nations immediately after ch 25. **4–8:** Jeremiah instructs the scribe, *Baruch son of Neriah* (cf. 32.12), to prepare the scroll so that he might read it publicly. This suggests to some that Jeremiah was illiterate, unable to write his own scroll. **5:** Jeremiah is *in hiding* presumably because he is subject to arrest as a result of his support for Babylonia. **8:** Many interpreters maintain that Baruch is the final compiler of the book of Jeremiah and author of its narratives concerning the prophet's life. Several apocryphal and pseudepigraphical books are attributed to him (Baruch; 2–4 Baruch). His name appears on a clay bulla found in the excavations of the scribe's house in Jerusalem (see 32.12 n.). His brother Seraiah was also a royal official (51.59). **9–18:** Following his compliance with Jeremiah's instructions, Baruch is summoned by the royal scribes to read the scroll to them. **10:** *Gemariah son of Shaphan* is a son of Josiah's secretary (2 Kings 24.3) and brother of Ahikam son of Shaphan who interceded on the prophet's behalf at his sedition trial (26.24). The scroll would have been read to him first as a potential ally among the scribes. **11–12:** His son, *Micaiah son of Gemariah son of Shaphan,* reports the matter to the scribes in session at the royal *palace. Elishama* is otherwise unknown in the Bible, although his name appears in bullae from the scribe's house (see 32.12 n.). *Delaiah son of Shemaiah* is otherwise unknown. *Elnathan son of Achbor* would presumably be hostile to Jeremiah since he was sent to Egypt to fetch the prophet

36.1–32: Jehoiakim's burning of Jeremiah's scroll. This ch offers remarkably important evidence for the writing and re-editing of prophetic books. **1:** *The fourth year of . . . Jehoiakim* is 605 BCE, the year that the Babylonians defeated

Egypt at Carchemish and took control of Judah. The date suggests that this narrative coincides with Jeremiah's oracle that calls for a seventy-year period of Babylonian rule (25.1). **2–3:** God instructs Jeremiah to record his prophecies *from* that he had heard as Baruch read from the scroll in the hearing of the people.

¹⁴ Then all the officials sent Jehudi son of Nethaniah son of Shelemiah son of Cushi to say to Baruch, "Take that scroll from which you read to the people, and come along!" And Baruch took the scroll and came to them.

¹⁵ They said, ª-"Sit down and read it-ª to us." And Baruch read it to them. ¹⁶ When they heard all these words, they turned to each other in fear; and they said to Baruch, "We must report all this to the king."

¹⁷ And they questioned Baruch further, "Tell us how you wrote down all these words ᵇ-that he spoke."-ᵇ ¹⁸ He answered them, "He himself recited all those words to me, and I would write them down in the scroll in ink."

¹⁹ The officials said to Baruch, "Go into hiding, you and Jeremiah. Let no man know where you are!" ²⁰ And they went to the king in the court, after leaving the scroll in the chamber of the scribe Elishama. And they reported all these matters to the king.

²¹ The king sent Jehudi to get the scroll and he fetched it from the chamber of the scribe Elishama. Jehudi read it to the king and to all the officials who were in attendance on the king. ²² Since it was the ninth month, the king was sitting in the winter house, with a fire burning in the brazier before him. ²³ And every time Jehudi read three or four columns, [the king] would cut it up with a scribe's knife and throw it into the fire in the brazier, until the entire scroll was consumed by the fire in the brazier. ²⁴ Yet the king and all his courtiers who heard all these words showed no fear and did not tear their garments; ²⁵ moreover, Elnathan, Delaiah, and Gemariah begged the king not to burn the scroll, but he would not listen to them.

²⁶ The king ordered Jerahmeel, the king's son, and Seraiah son of Azriel, and Shelemiah son of Abdeel to arrest the scribe Baruch and the prophet Jeremiah. But the LORD hid them.

²⁷ The word of the LORD came to Jeremiah after the king had burned the scroll containing the words that Baruch had written at Jeremiah's dictation: ²⁸ Get yourself another scroll, and write upon it the same words that were in the first scroll that was burned by King Jehoiakim of Judah. ²⁹ And concerning King Jehoiakim of Judah you shall say: Thus said the LORD: You burned that scroll, say-

Uriah who was executed for sedition (26.25). He may also have been Jehoiachin's maternal grandfather (2 Kings 24.8). The name Achbor also appears on a bullae. *Zedekiah son of Hananiah* is otherwise unknown, although he could be the son of the prophet Hananiah (ch 28). **14:** *Jehudi son of Nethaniah son of Shelemiah son of Cushi* is otherwise unknown. **19–26:** The king's reaction is then described. The scene shows the bit-by-bit destruction of the scroll, vividly dramatizing how offensive its message was to the king and how intent he was on getting rid of it. **19:** Because the prophet's message is considered seditious, the scribes advise Baruch to *go into hiding* with Jeremiah. **22:** *The ninth month* is Kislev (November/December). The king's response upon hearing the scroll expresses his contempt for or fear of Jeremiah's message. **25:** Although *Elnathan, Delaiah, and Gemariah* intercede for Jeremiah and Baruch, Jehoiakim orders their arrest. **26:** *Jerahmeel, Seraiah son of Azriel,* and *Shelemiah son of Abdeel* are otherwise unknown. Versions of the names Jerahmeel, Seraiah, Azriel, and Abdeel appear among the bullae from Jerusalem. **27–32:** God's instructs Jeremiah to write *another scroll,* which many also see as an early edition of the book. The final words of the v., "and more of the like was added," clearly reflect the fact that the book went through subsequent editions.

---

a-a *Change of vocalization yields "Read it again"; cf. Targum and Septuagint.*
b-b *Force of Heb. uncertain.*

ing, "How dare you write in it that the king of Babylon will come and destroy this land and cause man and beast to cease from it?" [30] Assuredly, thus said the LORD concerning King Jehoiakim of Judah: He shall not have any of his line sitting on the throne of David; and his own corpse shall be left exposed to the heat by day and the cold by night. [31] And I will punish him and his offspring and his courtiers for their iniquity; I will bring on them and on the inhabitants of Jerusalem and on all the men of Judah all the disasters of which I have warned them—but they would not listen.

[32] So Jeremiah got another scroll and gave it to the scribe Baruch son of Neriah. And at Jeremiah's dictation, he wrote in it the whole text of the scroll that King Jehoiakim of Judah had burned; and more of the like was added.

37 Zedekiah son of Josiah became king instead of Coniah son of Jehoiakim, for King Nebuchadrezzar of Babylon set him up as king over the land of Judah. [2] Neither he nor his courtiers nor the people of the land gave heed to the words which the LORD spoke through the prophet Jeremiah.

[3] Yet King Zedekiah sent Jehucal son of Shelemiah and Zephaniah son of the priest Maaseiah to the prophet Jeremiah, to say, "Please pray on our behalf to the LORD our God." [4] (Jeremiah could still go in and out among the people, for they had not yet put him in prison. [5] The army of Pharaoh had set out from Egypt; and when the Chaldeans who were besieging Jerusalem heard the report, they raised the siege of Jerusalem.)

[6] Then the word of the LORD came to the prophet Jeremiah: [7] Thus said the LORD, the God of Israel: Thus shall you say to the king of Judah who sent you to Me to inquire of Me: "The army of Pharaoh, which set out to help you, will return to its own land, to Egypt. [8] And the Chaldeans will come back and attack this city and they will capture it and destroy it by fire." [9] Thus said the LORD: Do not delude yourselves into thinking, "The Chaldeans will go away from us." They will not. [10] Even if you defeated the whole army of the Chaldeans that are fighting against you, and only wounded men were left lying in their tents, they would get up and burn this city down!

[11] When the army of the Chaldeans raised the siege of Jerusalem on account of the army of Pharaoh, [12] Jeremiah was going to leave Jerusalem and go to the territory of

37.1–38.28: Jeremiah's imprisonment during the Babylonian siege. Having established Jehoiakim's unwillingness to listen to Jeremiah, the next two chs focus on Jeremiah's imprisonment during the Babylonian assault against Jerusalem. **1–2:** King *Zedekiah*, his officials, and the people refuse to listen to Jeremiah. *Coniah* is a shortened form of Jehoiachin. When the Babylonians deported him, they placed his uncle Mattaniah on the throne and renamed him Zedekiah (2 Kings 24.8–20). **3–5:** Although the Egyptians lost control of Judah when they were defeated by the Babylonians at Carchemesh in 605 BCE, Jehoiakim had been their ally. Under Pharaoh Hophra (also known as Apries; 589–570 BCE; cf. Jer. 44.30), they apparently sent a force to Judah in an attempt to lift the Babylonian siege of Jerusalem. The Egyptians were defeated and forced to withdraw. *Jehucal son of Shelemiah* is called Jucal in 38.1. *Zephaniah son of the priest Maaseiah* was the deputy priest of the Temple who was executed by the Babylonians (52.24). He had earlier read a letter from the exiles demanding that Jeremiah be rebuked (29.24–28). Jer. 21.1 reports that Zephaniah was sent earlier to seek an oracle of the prophet during the siege of Jerusalem (21.1). **6–10:** Jeremiah's response conveys two oracles. The first indicates that the Egyptians will be forced to withdraw and the *Chaldeans*, i.e., Babylonians, will return to resume the siege. The second indicates the inevitability of the Babylonian victory. **11–21:** Jeremiah attempts to leave the city during the lull in the Babylonian siege to redeem family property in Anathoth, located in the tribal territory of Benjamin (see also ch 32).

Benjamin a-to share in some property there-a among the people. 13 When he got to the Benjamin Gate, there was a guard officer there named Irijah son of Shelemiah son of Hananiah; and he arrested the prophet Jeremiah, saying, "You are defecting to the Chaldeans!" 14 Jeremiah answered, "That's a lie! I'm not defecting to the Chaldeans!" But Irijah would not listen to him; he arrested Jeremiah and brought him to the officials. 15 The officials were furious with Jeremiah; they beat him and put him into prison, in the house of the scribe Jonathan—for it had been made into a jail. 16 Thus Jeremiah came to the a-pit and the cells,-a and Jeremiah remained there a long time.

17 Then King Zedekiah sent for him, and the king questioned him secretly in his palace. He asked, "Is there any word from the LORD?" "There is!" Jeremiah answered, and he continued, "You will be delivered into the hands of the king of Babylon." 18 And Jeremiah said to King Zedekiah, "What wrong have I done to you, to your courtiers, and to this people, that you have put me in jail? 19 And where are those prophets of yours who prophesied to you that the king of Babylon would never move against you and against this land? 20 Now, please hear me, O lord king, and grant my plea: Don't send me back to the house of the scribe Jonathan b-to die there."-b

21 So King Zedekiah gave instructions to lodge Jeremiah in the prison compound and to supply him daily with a loaf of bread from the Bakers' Street—until all the bread in the city was gone. Jeremiah remained in the prison compound.

38 Shephatiah son of Mattan, Gedaliah son of Pashhur, Jucal son of Shelemiah, and Pashhur son of Malchiah heard what Jeremiah was saying to all the people: 2 "Thus said the LORD: Whoever remains in this city shall die by the sword, by famine, and by pestilence; but whoever surrenders to the Chaldeans shall live; c-he shall at least gain his life-c and shall live. 3 Thus said the LORD: This city shall be delivered into the hands of the king of Babylon's army, and he shall capture it."

4 Then the officials said to the king, "Let that man be put to death, for he disheartens d the soldiers, and all the people who are left in this city, by speaking such things to them. That man is not seeking the welfare of this people, but their harm!" 5 King Zedekiah replied, "He is in your hands; the king cannot oppose you in anything!"

13: He is charged with treason by *Irijah son of Shelemiah son of Hananiah*, apparently the grandson of the prophet Hananiah (ch 28). The *Benjamin Gate* would have been on the north side of the city where the territory of Benjamin was located. **14–16:** Although Jeremiah denied the charge, he was harshly imprisoned in *the house of the scribe Jonathan* in a *pit*, a cistern or tank in which water would collect during the rainy season. **17:** Despite his imprisonment, *Zedekiah* continues to ask him for prophetic oracles. In contrast to his brother Jehoiakim, Zedekiah was apparently a supporter of alliance with Babylonia, but his weak position as a regent appointed by the Babylonians in place of the legitimate king Jehoiachin prevented him from stopping the revolt. **21:** Zedekiah grants Jeremiah's request for mercy by placing him in *the prison compound* and giving him a daily loaf of bread. In a situation of siege, food supplies would eventually be exhausted. **38.1–2:** *Shephatiah son of Mattan* and *Gedaliah son of Pashhur* are otherwise unknown, although the latter may be the son of *Pashhur* who placed Jeremiah in stocks (21.1). *Jucal son of Shelemiah*, see 37.3. *Pashhur son of Malchiah*, see 21.1. **3–6:** Jeremiah is arrested for treason. *Malchiah* is Pashhur's father. His designation as *the king's son* indicates that he is a royal official (cf. Zeph. 1.8).

---

a-a *Meaning of Heb. uncertain.*   b-b *Lit. "and let me not die there."*
c-c *Lit. "he shall have his life as booty"; cf. 21.9.*   d *Lit. "weakens the hands of."*

⁶So they took Jeremiah and put him down in the pit of Malchiah, the king's son, which was in the prison compound; they let Jeremiah down by ropes. There was no water in the pit, only mud, and Jeremiah sank into the mud.

⁷Ebed-melech the Cushite, a eunuch who was in the king's palace, heard that they had put Jeremiah in the pit. The king was then sitting at the Benjamin Gate; ⁸so Ebed-melech left the king's palace, and spoke to the king: ⁹"O lord king, those men have acted wickedly in all they did to the prophet Jeremiah; they have put him down in the pit, to die there of hunger." For there was no more bread in the city.

¹⁰Then the king instructed Ebed-melech the Cushite, "Take with you thirty* men from here, and pull the prophet Jeremiah up from the pit before he dies." ¹¹So Ebed-melech took the men with him, and went to the king's palace, to ᵇa place belowᵇ the treasury. There they got worn cloths and rags, which they let down to Jeremiah in the pit by ropes. ¹²And Ebed-melech the Cushite called to Jeremiah, "Put the worn cloths and rags under your armpits, inside the ropes." Jeremiah did so, ¹³and they pulled Jeremiah up by the ropes and got him out of the pit. And Jeremiah remained in the prison compound.

¹⁴King Zedekiah sent for the prophet Jeremiah, and had him brought to him at the third entrance of the House of the LORD. And the king said to Jeremiah, "I want to ask you something; don't conceal anything from me."

¹⁵Jeremiah answered the king, "If I tell you, you'll surely kill me; and if I give you advice, you won't listen to me."

¹⁶Thereupon King Zedekiah secretly promised Jeremiah on oath: "As the LORD lives who has ᶜgiven us this life,ᶜ I will not put you to death or leave you in the hands of those men who seek your life."

¹⁷Then Jeremiah said to Zedekiah, "Thus said the LORD, the God of Hosts, the God of Israel: If you surrender to the officers of the king of Babylon, your life will be spared and this city will not be burned down. You and your household will live. ¹⁸But if you do not surrender to the officers of the king of Babylon, this city will be delivered into the hands of the Chaldeans, who will burn it down; and you will not escape from them."

7–13: *Ebed-melech:* The name means "servant of the king." He is called *the Cushite,* "Ethiopian." **14–28:** Zedekiah clearly lacks the power to protect Jeremiah fully, but he continues to consult him. Nevertheless, Jeremiah must conceal the topics of their conversation. **14:** The *third entrance* to the Temple is unknown, although Radak speculates that it was an entrance by which the people could go from the king's palace to the Temple. **17–18:** Jeremiah's advice to surrender to the Babylonians is consistent with his earlier position (chs 25–29). **22–23:** Jeremiah outlines the consequences of continued resistance; i.e., the men will be killed, the women taken by the Babylonians, and the city destroyed.

a One ms. reads "three."
b-b Emendation yields "the wardrobe of."
c-c Meaning of Heb. uncertain.

¹⁹King Zedekiah said to Jeremiah, "I am worried about the Judeans who have defected to the Chaldeans; that they [the Chaldeans] might hand me over to them to abuse me."

²⁰"They will not hand you over," Jeremiah replied. "Listen to the voice of the LORD, to what I tell you, that it may go well with you and your life be spared. ²¹For this is what the LORD has shown me if you refuse to surrender: ²²All the women who are left in the palace of the king of Judah shall be brought out to the officers of the king of Babylon; and they shall say:

The men who were your friends
Have seduced you and vanquished you.
Now that your feet are sunk in the mire,
They have turned their backs [on you].

²³They will bring out all your wives and children to the Chaldeans, and you yourself will not escape from them. You will be captured by the king of Babylon, and ᵃ˗this city shall be burned down."˗ᵃ

²⁴Zedekiah said to Jeremiah, "Don't let anyone know about this conversation, ᵇ˗or you will die.˗ᵇ ²⁵If the officials should hear that I have spoken with you, and they should come and say to you, 'Tell us what you said to the king; hide nothing from us, ᶜ˗or we'll kill you.˗ᶜ And what did the king say to you?' ²⁶say to them, 'I was presenting my petition to the king not to send me back to the house of Jonathan to die there.' "

²⁷All the officials did come to Jeremiah to question him; and he replied to them just as the king had instructed him. So they stopped questioning him, for the conversation had not been overheard. ²⁸Jeremiah remained in the prison compound until the day Jerusalem was captured.

When Jerusalem was captured . . .ᵈ

39 In the ninth year of King Zedekiah of Judah, in the tenth month, King Nebuchadrezzar of Babylon moved against Jerusalem with his whole army, and they laid siege to it. ²And in the eleventh year of Zedekiah, on the ninth day of the fourth month, the [walls of] the city were breached. ³All the officers of the king of Babylon entered, and took up quarters at the middle gate—Nergal-sarezer, Samgar-nebo, Sarsechim the Rab-saris,ᵉ Nergal-sarezer the Rab-mag,ᵉ and all the rest of the officers of the king of Babylon.

39.1–18: The fall of Jerusalem. The Babylonian capture and destruction of Jerusalem appears also in ch 52 and 2 Kings ch 25. (There are minor variations among these three sources.) It is related here to demonstrate that Jeremiah's words to Zedekiah came true, thereby affirming Jeremiah's status as a true prophet. **1–3:** Jer. 38.28b is the introduction to 39.1. The *ninth year of King Zedekiah* is 588 BCE. The *tenth month* is Tevet. The *eleventh year* is 586, and the *fourth month* is Tamuz. **3:** The Babylonian terms are a combination of names and titles that have also been read as Nergal-sarezer (Neriglissar) the Simmagir (known in Babylonian records as Nebuchadnezzar's son-in-law, who ruled Babylonia 560–556 BCE), Nebushazban (see v. 13) the chief court official (*Rab-saris*, "chief eunuch"), and Nergal-sarezer, the Rab-mag.

a-a So Targum and Septuagint and some mss. Most mss. and the editions read "you will burn down this city by fire."
b-b Lit. "that you may not die."   c-c Lit. "that we may not kill you."
d This clause would read well before 39.3.   e Titles of officers.

4 When King Zedekiah of Judah saw them, he and all the soldiers fled. They left the city at night, by way of the king's garden, through the gate between the double walls; and he set out toward the Arabah.ᵃ 5 But the Chaldean troops pursued them, and they overtook Zedekiah in the steppes of Jericho. They captured him and brought him before King Nebuchadrezzar of Babylon at Riblah in the region of Hamath; and he put him on trial. 6 The king of Babylon had Zedekiah's children slaughtered at Riblah before his eyes; the king of Babylon had all the nobles of Judah slaughtered. 7 Then the eyes of Zedekiah were put out and he was chained in bronze fetters, that he might be brought to Babylon.

8 The Chaldeans burned down the king's palace and the housesᵇ of the people by fire, and they tore down the walls of Jerusalem. 9 The remnant of the people that was left in the city, and the defectors who had gone over to him—the remnant of the people that was left—were exiled by Nebuzaradan, the chief of the guards, to Babylon. 10 But some of the poorest people who owned nothing were left in the land of Judah by Nebuzaradan, the chief of the guards, and he gave them vineyards and fields at that time.

a Hoping to escape across the Jordan.
b Taking Heb. singular as collective, with Kimhi.

4–7: The *Arabah* is the Jordan rift that extends south to the Gulf of Aqabah. *Riblah* is a city in the Beqaʻ Valley (modern Lebanon). *Hamath* (modern Hama in Syria) was a key city in ancient Aram. Rabbinic sources claim that Nebuchadnezzar did not come to Jerusalem for fear of suffering Sennacherib's fate (*b. Sanh.* 96b; *Lev. Rab.* 19.6; cf. Isa. 10.5–34; chs 36–37). For Zedekiah's blinding, see also Ezek. 12.13. **8–14:** Jerusalem falls. **9:** *Nebuzaradan,* the captain of the king's bodyguard, entered Jerusalem on the 10th of Av (52.12). **11–12:** Nebuchadnezzar apparently intended to protect Jeremiah as a Babylonian sympathizer. **14:** *Gedaliah son of Ahikam son of Shaphan* is the son of one of Jeremiah's key allies (26.24). The Shaphan family apparently supported alliance with Babylon. Gedaliah was appointed governor of Judah by the Babylonians, but was assassinated in an attempted revolt (chs 40–41). **15–18:** See 38.7–13 n. Even in the midst of the great national tragedy, individuals may be judged on their own mer-

Babylonia and Judah ca. 600 BCE

11 King Nebuchadrezzar of Babylon had given orders to Nebuzaradan, the chief of the guards, concerning Jeremiah: 12 "Take him and look after him; do him no harm, but grant whatever he asks of you." 13 So Nebuzaradan, the chief of the guards, and Nebushazban the Rab-saris, and Nergal-sarezer the Rab-mag, and all the commanders of the king of Babylon sent 14 and had Jeremiah brought from the prison compound. They committed him to the care of Gedaliah son of Ahikam son of Shaphan, *-that he might be left at liberty in a house.-* So he dwelt among the people.

15 The word of the LORD had come to Jeremiah while he was still confined in the prison compound: 16 Go and say to Ebed-melech the Ethiopian: "Thus said the LORD of Hosts, the God of Israel: I am going to fulfill My words concerning this city—for disaster, not for good—and they shall come true on that day in your presence. 17 But I will save you on that day—declares the LORD; you shall not be delivered into the hands of the men you dread. 18 I will rescue you, and you shall not fall by the sword. ᵇ-You shall escape with your life,-ᵇ because you trusted Me—declares the LORD."

40 The word that came to Jeremiah from the LORD, after Nebuzaradan, the chief of the guards, set him free at Ramah, to which he had taken him, chained in fetters, among those from Jerusalem and Judah who were being exiled to Babylon. 2 The chief of the guards took charge of Jeremiah, and he said to him, "The LORD your God threatened this place with this disaster; 3 and now the LORD has brought it about. He has acted as He threatened, because you sinned against the LORD and did not obey Him. That is why this has happened to you. 4 Now, I release you this day from the fetters which were on your hands. If you would like to go with me to Babylon, come, and I will look after you. And if you don't want to come with me to Babylon, you need not. See, the whole land is before you: go wherever seems good and right to you."—5ᵃ-But [Jeremiah] still did not turn back.-ᵃ—"Or go to Gedaliah son of Ahikam son of Shaphan, whom the king of Babylon has put in charge of the towns of Judah, and stay with him among the people, or go wherever you want to go."

its (see ch 35 as well, on the Rechabites). Trust in God is a major theme of some parts of the Deuteronomistic History, such as 2 Kings ch 18.

40.1–43.13: The assassination of Gedaliah and its consequences. A third attempt at revolt took place in 582 BCE with the assassination of Gedaliah son of Ahikam son of Shaphan, whom the Babylonians had appointed as governor of Judah. Although the revolt was quickly put down by Judeans, fear of the Babylonians was so great that the officers who survived the revolt fled to Egypt, taking Jeremiah and Baruch with them.

40.1–16: Gedaliah installed as governor of Judah. 1–5: *Nebuzaradan* offers Jeremiah the opportunity to live in Babylon under Babylonian protection. **1:** *Ramah* (near modern Ramallah) is an early Israelite city associated with the prophet Samuel (1 Sam. 9.1–10.16). **5:** Jeremiah's decision to remain in the land is consistent with the last two verbs employed in his prophetic commission, "to build" and "to plant."

a-a *Meaning of Heb. uncertain.*
b-b *See note at 38.2.*

The chief of the guards gave him an allowance of food, and dismissed him. [6] So Jeremiah came to Gedaliah son of Ahikam at Mizpah, and stayed with him among the people who were left in the land.

[7] The officers of the troops in the open country, and their men with them, heard that the king of Babylon had put Gedaliah son of Ahikam in charge of the region, and that he had put in his charge the men, women, and children—of the poorest in the land—those who had not been exiled to Babylon. [8] So they with their men came to Gedaliah at Mizpah—Ishmael son of Nethaniah; Johanan and Jonathan the sons of Kareah; Seraiah son of Tanhumeth; the sons of Ephai the Netophathite; and Jezaniah son of the Maacathite. [9] Gedaliah son of Ahikam son of Shaphan reassured[a] them and their men, saying, "Do not be afraid to serve the Chaldeans. Stay in the land and serve the king of Babylon, and it will go well with you. [10] I am going to stay in Mizpah to attend upon the Chaldeans who will come to us. But you may gather wine and figs[b] and oil and put them in your own vessels, and settle in the towns you have occupied."

[11] Likewise, all the Judeans who were in Moab, Ammon, and Edom, or who were in other lands, heard that the king of Babylon had let a remnant stay in Judah, and that he had put Gedaliah son of Ahikam son of Shaphan in charge of them. [12] All these Judeans returned from all the places to which they had scattered. They came to the land of Judah, to Gedaliah at Mizpah, and they gathered large quantities of wine and figs.[b]

[13] Johanan son of Kareah, and all the officers of the troops in the open country, came to Gedaliah at Mizpah [14] and said to him, "Do you know that King Baalis of Ammon has sent Ishmael son of Nethaniah to kill you?" But Gedaliah son of Ahikam would not believe them. [15] Johanan son of Kareah also said secretly to Gedaliah at Mizpah, "Let me go and strike down Ishmael son of Nethaniah before anyone knows about it; otherwise he will kill you, and all the Judeans who have gathered about you will be dispersed, and the remnant of Judah will perish!"

[16] But Gedaliah son of Ahikam answered Johanan son of Kareah, "Do not do such a thing: what you are saying about Ishmael is not true!"

6: The Babylonians installed *Gedaliah* as governor in *Mizpah* (cf. 2 Kings 25.22–26), located in Benjamin, about 13 km (8 mi) north of Jerusalem (probably Tel en-Nasbeh). According to *b. Gittin* 57a, Nebuzaradan's statements indicate that he converted to Judaism in remorse for the suffering he caused. **7–16:** A court forms around Gedaliah. **8:** *Ishmael son of Nethaniah* son of Elishama is identified as a member of the royal family in 41.1. His grandfather may have been Jehoiakim's scribe (36.12). *Johanan and Jonathan the sons of Kareah* are otherwise unknown. The name *Jezaniah son of the Maacathite* may employ an ethnic or place name in reference to his father (Maacah is a small state in the northern Golan; see Josh. 13.11, 13; 2 Sam. 10.6, 8; 1 Chron. 19.7). If so, he could be identified with Jezaniah son of Hoshaiah in Jer. 42.1. The use of the gentilic name could be an attempt to call the reader's attention to the succession narrative (2 Sam. chs 9–20) in which Maacah first opposed David, and then submitted to his rule (2 Sam. 10.19). The following narrative appears to contrast Ishmael's defeat in Benjaminite territory with David's victories in the same region. **13–16:** *Johanan* (v. 8) informed Gedaliah of Ishmael's intent to assassinate him, but the warning was rebuffed. The Ammonites apparently saw an opportunity to take control of Judah now that it was virtually powerless. **14:** *Ishmael* would likely cooperate with *Baalis* out of his own ambitions to claim the Davidic throne based on his own royal descent (cf. Rashi, Radak, Abravanel). The Ammonites did support David much earlier, during Absalom's revolt (see 2 Sam. 17.27–29). Perhaps this was another attempt to support the House of David, as Gedaliah was not of royal blood. *Baalis* is probably to be identified with "baʿalyashaʿ," whose name is found on a 6th-century Ammonite seal impression.

a Lit. "swore to."
b Lit. "summer fruit."

41 In the seventh month, Ishmael son of Nethaniah son of Elishama, who was of royal descent and one of the king's commanders, came with ten men to Gedaliah son of Ahikam at Mizpah; and they ate together there at Mizpah. ² Then Ishmael son of Nethaniah and the ten men who were with him arose and struck down Gedaliah son of Ahikam son of Shaphan with the sword and killed him, because the king of Babylon had put him in charge of the land. ³ Ishmael also killed all the Judeans who were with him—with Gedaliah in Mizpah—and the Chaldean soldiers who were stationed there.

⁴ The second day after Gedaliah was killed, when no one yet knew about it, ⁵ eighty men came from Shechem, Shiloh, and Samaria, their beards shaved, their garments torn, and their bodies gashed, carrying meal offerings and frankincense to present at the House of the LORD. ⁶ Ishmael son of Nethaniah went out from Mizpah to meet them, weeping as he walked. As he met them, he said to them, "Come to Gedaliah son of Ahikam." ⁷ When they came inside the town, Ishmael son of Nethaniah and the men who were with him slaughtered them [and threw their bodies] into a cistern.

⁸ But there were ten men among them who said to Ishmael, "Don't kill us! We have stores hidden in a field—wheat, barley, oil, and honey." So he stopped, and did not kill them along with their fellows.—⁹ The cistern into which Ishmael threw all the corpses of the men he had killed ᵃ·in the affair of Gedaliah was the one thatᵃ King Asa had constructed on account of King Baasha of Israel. That was the one which Ishmael son of Nethaniah filled with corpses.—¹⁰ Ishmael carried off all the rest of the people who were in Mizpah, including the daughters of the king—all the people left in Mizpah, over whom Nebuzaradan, the chief of the guards, had appointed Gedaliah son of Ahikam. Ishmael son of Nethaniah carried them off, and set out to cross over to the Ammonites.

¹¹ Johanan son of Kareah, and all the army officers with him, heard of all the crimes committed by Ishmael son of Nethaniah. ¹² They took all their men and went to fight against Ishmael son of Nethaniah; and they encountered him by the great pool in Gibeon. ¹³ When all the people held by Ishmael saw Johanan son of Kareah and all the army officers with him, they were glad; ¹⁴ all the people whom Ishmael had carried off from Mizpah turned back and went over to Johanan son of Kareah. ¹⁵ But Ishmael

---

a-a Septuagint reads "was a large cistern, which . . ."

41.1–18: The assassination of Gedaliah. 1: *The seventh month* is Tishri. The 3rd of Tishri is now observed as the Fast of Gedaliah, immediately following the two days of Rosh Ha-Shanah, and it is likely that this fast is "the fast of the seventh month" mentioned in Zech. 8.19. The assassination of Gedaliah was commemorated since it represented the end of even limited Judean autonomy in the land, and is the culmination of the events associated with the destruction of the Temple and the exile. **2–3:** *Because the king of Babylon . . . in charge of the land. . . . killed . . . the Chaldean soldiers:* It seems unlikely that Ishmael intended to revolt against Babylonia, but the killing of Babylonian soldiers together with Gedaliah indicates that perhaps the situation got out of control. **4–10:** Ishmael's subsequent actions appear to be unnecessarily brutal and desperate. **5:** *Shechem, Shiloh, and Samaria* are all cities in the territory of the former Northern Kingdom of Israel. The shaved beards, torn garments, and gashed bodies are clear signs of mourning for the destroyed Temple (see also Zech. 7.1–7). Although the Temple has been destroyed, non-animal sacrifices were still offered at the holy site of the Temple. The loyalty of these northern Israelite men to the Jerusalem Temple may indicate that Josiah's reforms and attempts to reunite Israel and Judah had been somewhat successful. **6–7:** Ishmael's killing of these men appears rash. He may have killed them in an attempt to keep the assassination of Gedaliah quiet, although his motives may have been pure robbery. **9:** King Asa's cistern is not mentioned elsewhere, although he did build up Geba and Mizpah (1 Kings 15.22; 2 Chron. 16.6). **10:** *The daughters of the king* would have been Ishmael's own relatives as members of the House of David. **11–18:** Gedaliah's followers fight back, but Ishmael escapes. **11–12:** *Johanan son of Kareah* defeated *Ishmael son of Nethaniah* at the pool of *Gibeon*, a key site in David's and Joab's defeat of a largely Benjaminite army led by son of Nethaniah escaped from Johanan with eight men, and went to the Ammonites.

16 Johanan son of Kareah and all the army officers with him took all the rest of the people whom ᵃ'he had rescued from Ishmael son of Nethaniah·ᵃ from Mizpah after he had murdered Gedaliah son of Ahikam—the men, soldiers, women, children, and eunuchs whom [Johanan] had brought back from Gibeon. 17 They set out, and they stopped at Geruthᵇ Chimham, near Bethlehem, on their way to go to Egypt 18 because of the Chaldeans. For they were afraid of them, because Ishmael son of Nethaniah had killed Gedaliah son of Ahikam, whom the king of Babylon had put in charge of the land.

42 Then all the army officers, with Johanan son of Kareah, Jezaniah son of Hoshaiah, and all the rest of the people, great and small, approached 2 the prophet Jeremiah and said, "Grant our plea, and pray for us to the LORD your God, for all this remnant! For we remain but a few out of many, as you can see. 3 Let the LORD your God tell us where we should go and what we should do."

4 The prophet Jeremiah answered them, "Agreed: I will pray to the LORD your God as you request, and I will tell you whatever response the LORD gives for you. I will withhold nothing from you."

5 Thereupon they said to Jeremiah, "Let the LORD be a true and faithful witness against us! We swear that we will do exactly as the LORD your God instructs us through you—6 Whether it is pleasant or unpleasant, we will obey the LORD our God to whom we send you, in order that it may go well with us when we obey the LORD our God."

7 After ten days, the word of the LORD came to Jeremiah. 8 He called Johanan son of Kareah and all the army officers, and the rest of the people, great and small, 9 and said to them, "Thus said the LORD, the God of Israel, to whom you sent me to present your supplication before Him: 10 If you remain in this land, I will build you and not overthrow, I will plant you and not uproot; for I regret the

a-a Emendation yields "Ishmael son of Nethaniah had carried off."
b Aquila reads "the sheepfolds of."

the experience of Ishmael with that of David to emphasize the House of David's (i.e., Ishmael's) opposition to God's will.

42.1–43.7: Jeremiah taken to Egypt. The narrative continues to emphasize the theme of Judean opposition to God's will by presenting the people's rejection of Jeremiah's oracle advising them to remain in the land of Judah as subjects of Babylonia. Whereas the previous episode reversed the theme of divine favor for David that was given in the so-called succession narrative (2 Sam. chs 9–20), these chs present the Judean return to Egypt as a reversal of the exodus narrative. **42.1–6:** Jeremiah complies with the request for guidance. **1:** *Johanan son of Kareah* is the leader of the Judean forces that defeated Ishmael. *Jezaniah son of Hoshaiah* may be the same man mentioned in 40.8, presuming that his father was earlier identified by an ethnic or place name. Azariah son of Hoshaiah (43.2) may be his brother. **5–6:** The narrative especially emphasizes the people's oath to do what God asks in order to highlight their disobedience in the following vv. **7–22:** Jeremiah gives the word. **7:** It is quite remarkable that God does not immediately answer the prophet. Abravanel therefore understands the *ten days* to be reckoned from the 1st of Tishri when Gedaliah was assassinated (41.1). Yom Kippur (the Day of Atonement) falls on the 10th of Tishri (Lev. 23.26–32; Num. 29.7–11). Jeremiah's oracle would therefore have come immediately following Yom Kippur (cf. Ezek. 40.1, which places Ezekiel's vision of the Temple on Yom Kippur). Such a reckoning of the date would emphasize the theme of the people's repentance, which of course does not take place in the following vv. However, there is no explicit indication that Yom Kippur was observed in this period. **10:** Jeremiah's oracle again repeats the basic verbs of his prophetic commission, *build . . . not overthrow . . . plant . . . not uproot* (1.10), to emphasize that the time for

Abner on behalf of Ish-bosheth, the son of Saul. David's victory was a key event in his rise to the throne of the Benjaminite Saul. It is ironic that Ishmael's defeat by forces loyal to Gedaliah takes place at the same location. **17:** *Ge-*ruth Chimham, "the dwelling place of Chimcham," recalls the name of the young man assigned by Barzillai the Gileadite to support David during Absalom's revolt (2 Sam. 19.31–40; cf. 17.27–29). Apparently, the narrative attempts to contrast punishment I have brought upon you. ¹¹ Do not be afraid of the king of Babylon, whom you fear; do not be afraid of him—declares the LORD—for I am with you to save you and to rescue you from his hands. ¹² I will dispose him to be merciful to you: he shall show you mercy and ᵃbring you back toᵃ your own land.

¹³ "But if you say, 'We will not stay in this land'—thus disobeying the LORD your God—¹⁴ if you say, 'No! We will go to the land of Egypt, so that we may not see war or hear the sound of the horn, and so that we may not hunger for bread; there we will stay,' ¹⁵ then hear the word of the LORD, O remnant of Judah! Thus said the LORD of Hosts, the God of Israel: If you turn your faces toward Egypt, and you go and sojourn there, ¹⁶ the sword that you fear shall overtake you there, in the land of Egypt, and the famine you worry over shall follow at your heels in Egypt too; and there you shall die. ¹⁷ All the men who turn their faces toward Egypt, in order to sojourn there, shall die by the sword, by famine, and by pestilence. They shall have no surviving remnant of the disaster that I will bring upon them. ¹⁸ For thus said the LORD of Hosts, the God of Israel: As My anger and wrath were poured out upon the inhabitants of Jerusalem, so will My wrath be poured out on you if you go to Egypt. You shall become ᵇan execration of woe, a curseᵇ and a mockery; and you shall never again see this place. ¹⁹ The LORD has spoken against you, O remnant of Judah! Do not go to Egypt! Know well, then—for I warn you this day ²⁰ that you were deceitful at heart when you sent me to the LORD your God, saying, 'Pray for us to the LORD our God; and whatever the LORD our God may say, just tell us and we will do it.' ²¹ I told you today, and you have not obeyed the LORD your God in respect to all that He sent me to tell you— ²² know well, then, that you shall die by the sword, by famine, and by pestilence in the place where you want to go and sojourn."

43 When Jeremiah had finished speaking all these words to all the people—all the words of the LORD their God, with which the LORD their God had sent him to them—² Azariah son of Hoshaiah and Johanan son of Kareah and all the arrogant men said to Jeremiah, "You are lying! The LORD our God did not send you to say, 'Don't go to Egypt and sojourn there'! ³ It is Baruch son of Neriah who is inciting you against us, so that we will be delivered

punishment is over and that the time for rebuilding is at hand. The oracle emphasizes God's own *regret* to emphasize divine empathy for the suffering of the people. **11:** An example of the reassurance oracle follows with its characteristic formulas, *do not be afraid* and *I am with you* (v. 11; cf. 1.8; Isa. 7.4–9; Gen. 15.1). **13–21:** Jeremiah's oracle clearly and unambiguously calls upon the people not to return to Egypt lest they suffer consequences. The "torah" of the king in Deut. 17.14–20 likewise emphasizes that the king is forbidden to return the people to Egypt. Such a position is consistent with that of Isaiah, whose oracles warned against alliance with Egypt (Isa. chs 18–20; 30–31). In Jeremiah's view, the time for the fulfillment of Isaiah's oracles had come. The oracle follows Isaiah in emphasizing that the people must remain in the land if the remnant of the people is to grow (Isa. 4.2–6; 10.20–26; 37.30–32). **43.1–7:** The guidance is rejected. **2:** *Azariah son of Hoshaiah* is probably the brother of Jezaniah son of Hoshaiah (42.1). The accusation that Jeremiah is lying is ironic given the emphasis on the problem of lying prophets in the book (23.9–40; chs 27–29).

---

a-a *Change of vocalization yields "let you dwell in."*
b-b *I.e., a standard by which men execrate and curse; cf. note at 24.9.*

into the hands of the Chaldeans to be killed or to be exiled to Babylon!"

⁴ So Johanan son of Kareah and all the army officers and the rest of the people did not obey the LORD's command to remain in the land of Judah. ⁵ Instead, Johanan son of Kareah and all the army officers took the entire remnant of Judah—those who had returned from all the countries to which they had been scattered and had sojourned in the land of Judah, ⁶ men, women, and children; and the daughters of the king and all the people whom Nebuzaradan the chief of the guards had left with Gedaliah son of Ahikam son of Shaphan, as well as the prophet Jeremiah and Baruch son of Neriah—⁷ and they went to Egypt. They did not obey the LORD.

They arrived at Tahpanhes, ⁸ and the word of the LORD came to Jeremiah in Tahpanhes: ⁹ Get yourself large stones, and embed them in mortar in the brick structure at the entrance to Pharaoh's palace in Tahpanhes, with some Judeans looking on. ¹⁰ And say to them: "Thus said the LORD of Hosts, the God of Israel: I am sending for My servant King Nebuchadrezzar of Babylon, and I*ᵃ* will set his throne over these stones which I have embedded. He will spread out his pavilion*ᵇ* over them. ¹¹ He will come and attack the land of Egypt, delivering

> Those destined for the plague, to the plague,
> Those destined for captivity, to captivity,
> And those destined for the sword, to the sword.

¹² And I*ᵃ* will set fire to the temples of the gods of Egypt; he will burn them down and carry them*ᶜ* off. He shall wrap himself up in the land of Egypt, as a shepherd wraps himself up in his garment. And he shall depart from there in safety. ¹³ He shall smash the obelisks of the Temple of the Sun which is in the land of Egypt, and he shall burn down the temples of the gods of Egypt.

44 The word which came to Jeremiah for all the Judeans living in the land of Egypt, living in Migdol, Tahpanhes, and Noph, and in the land of Pathros: ² Thus said the LORD of Hosts, the God of Israel: You

---

a Septuagint reads "he."　　b Meaning of Heb. uncertain.　　c I.e., the gods.

Nile Delta (Tel Deffeneh) that was intended to defend the Delta against foreign invasion. Thus, the book of Jeremiah as a whole fits the pattern of history developed in 2 Kings 17.14, that even after prophets were sent time and again to Israel, "they did not obey."

43.8–13: Jeremiah's oracle in Tahpanhes. This brief narrative concludes the account of Jeremiah's removal to Egypt. Jeremiah was likely just as welcome in Egypt as he was in Jerusalem. **9–11:** The prophet engages in a final symbolic action by setting up *stones . . . at the entrance to Pharaoh's palace* that would eventually support the throne of the Babylonian king when he came to conquer Egypt. Excavations at Tahpanhes have uncovered a wide pavement before the northern entrance to the fortress. **13:** *The obelisks of the Temple of the Sun* may refer to the city of On or Heliopolis, which was known for its obelisks and was a center for the worship of the sun god, Re. It is identified with Tel Hisn and Matariyeh, about seven miles northeast of Cairo. The city appears in Isa. 19.18 as one of five cities that will swear allegiance to God. Although the Babylonians never conquered Egypt, the Persian king Cambyses, who also ruled Babylonia, conquered Egypt in 525 BCE. This is another case (see 34.5) of a prophecy that is preserved although it was not fulfilled.

44.1–30: Jeremiah's oracle in Egypt. 1: *Migdol* was a city in northern Egypt, possibly identified with Tel el-Hier. For *Tahpanhes*, see 43.7, 8–13; 2.16. For *Noph*, identified with Memphis, see 2.16. *Pathros* is identified with Upper Egypt to the south of the Delta region (see also Isa. 11.11). Excavations on the island of Elephantine (Yeb), located in the Nile opposite Aswan in upper Egypt, demonstrate the existence of Persian-period (6th century BCE and later) Jewish settlements in Egypt that clearly originated in earlier times. The community was in communication

---

6: *The daughters of the king* had perhaps been recovered from Ishmael when he was defeated (cf. 41.10). The people take Jeremiah and Baruch with them to Egypt. Interpreters disagree as to whether they were forced to go or felt that duty required them to accompany their people. **7:** The text closes by noting the people's disobedience and their arrival in *Tahpanhes*, an Egyptian stronghold in the northeast have seen all the disaster that I brought on Jerusalem and on all the towns of Judah. They are a ruin today, and no one inhabits them, ³ on account of the wicked things they did to vex Me, going to make offerings in worship of other gods which they had not known—neither they nor you nor your fathers. ⁴ Yet I persistently sent to you all My servants the prophets, to say, "I beg you not to do this abominable thing which I hate." ⁵ But they would not listen or give ear, to turn back from their wickedness and not make offerings to other gods; ⁶ so My fierce anger was poured out, and it blazed against the towns of Judah and the streets of Jerusalem. And they became a desolate ruin, as they still are today.

⁷ And now, thus said the LORD, the God of Hosts, the God of Israel: Why are you doing such great harm to yourselves, so that every man and woman, child and infant of yours shall be cut off from the midst of Judah, and no remnant shall be left of you? ⁸ For you vex me by your deeds, making offering to other gods in the land of Egypt where you have come to sojourn, so that you shall be cut off and become a curse ͣ and a mockery among all the nations of earth. ⁹ Have you forgotten the wicked acts of your forefathers, of the kings of Judah and their ᵇ wives, and your own wicked acts and those of your wives, which were committed in the land of Judah and in the streets of Jerusalem? ¹⁰ No one has shown contrition to this day, and no one has shown reverence. You ͨ have not followed the Teaching and the laws that I set before you and before your fathers.

¹¹ Assuredly, thus said the LORD of Hosts, the God of Israel: I am going to set My face against you for punishment, to cut off all of Judah. ¹² I will take the remnant of Judah who turned their faces toward the land of Egypt, to go and sojourn there, and they shall be utterly consumed in the land of Egypt. They shall fall by the sword, they shall be consumed by famine; great and small alike shall die by the sword and by famine, and they shall become an execration ͣ and a desolation, a curse ͣ and a mockery. ¹³ I will punish those who live in the land of Egypt as I punished Jerusalem, with the sword, with famine, and with pestilence. ¹⁴ Of the remnant of Judah who came to sojourn here in the land of Egypt, no survivor or fugitive shall be left to return to the land of Judah. Though they all long to return and dwell there, none shall return except [a few] survivors.

with authorities in Jerusalem, although their religious practice was somewhat syncretistic. **2–14:** Jeremiah continues to accuse the people of disobeying God and worshipping other deities as a means to explain their current plight. Theologically, this passage is very similar to 2 Kings ch 17, which explains the earlier exile of the Northern Kingdom. **12:** In contrast to Isaiah, who saw the remnant of Israel as the basis for restoration, Jeremiah argues that the remnant of the people, as a result of their behavior, will die in Egypt. The prophet's condemnation especially emphasizes the theme of famine and rebellious acts of the people. This contrasts with the wilderness traditions of the Torah in order to emphasize the reversal of the exodus from Egypt. Whereas God answered the people's complaints about the lack of food by providing manna, water, and protection from enemies, etc. (Exod. chs 16–17; Num. ch 11), God would no longer provide such support in Egypt.

a See note at 24.9; 42.18.   b Heb. "his."   c Heb. "They."

15 Thereupon they answered Jeremiah—all the men who knew that their wives made offerings to other gods; all the women present, a large gathering; and all the people who lived in Pathros in the land of Egypt: 16 "We will not listen to you in the matter about which you spoke to us in the name of the LORD. 17 On the contrary, we will do *-everything that we have vowed-*—to make offerings to the Queen of Heaven and to pour libations to her, as we used to do,*b* we and our fathers, our kings and our officials, in the towns of Judah and the streets of Jerusalem. For then we had plenty to eat, we were well-off, and suffered no misfortune. 18 But ever since we stopped making offerings to the Queen of Heaven and pouring libations to her, we have lacked everything, and we have been consumed by the sword and by famine. 19 And when we make offerings to the Queen of Heaven and pour libations to her, is it without our husbands' approval that we have made cakes *c-in her likeness-c* and poured libations to her?"

20 Jeremiah replied to all the people, men and women— all the people who argued with him. He said, 21 "Indeed, the offerings you presented in the towns of Judah and the streets of Jerusalem—you, your fathers, your kings, your officials, and the people of the land—were remembered by the LORD and brought to mind! 22 When the LORD could no longer bear your evil practices and the abominations you committed, your land became a desolate ruin and a curse,*d* without inhabitant, as is still the case. 23 Because you burned incense and sinned against the LORD and did not obey the LORD, and because you did not follow His Teaching, His laws, and His exhortations, therefore this disaster has befallen you, as is still the case."

24 Jeremiah further said to all the people and to all the women: "Hear the word of the LORD, all Judeans in the land of Egypt! 25 Thus said the LORD of Hosts, the God of Israel: You and your wives have *e-confirmed by deed what you spoke in words:-e* 'We will fulfill the vows which we made, to burn incense to the Queen of Heaven and to pour libations to her.' So fulfill your vows; perform your vows!

26 "Yet hear the word of the LORD, all Judeans who dwell in the land of Egypt! Lo, I swear by My great name—said the LORD—that none of the men of Judah in all the land of Egypt shall ever again invoke My name, saying, 'As the Lord GOD lives!' 27 I will be watchful over

15–19: The people respond by insisting that they will continue their practices. The text suggests that women in particular were involved in this worship. Perhaps this is because women were more involved in "popular" religion, or because this text in particular is concerned with goddess worship. **17:** *The Queen of Heaven,* probably Ishtar, the Mesopotamian goddess of passion in war and love. Identified with the North Star or Venus, she represents stability in the world of creation. **18:** The people point out that disaster befell them when they discontinued worship of the goddess; the reference is most likely to Josiah's reforms, shortly after which Josiah was killed, and Judah became a vassal of Babylonia. **20–30:** Jeremiah retorts with a final condemnation of the Jewish community in Egypt. **27:** *I will be watchful* returns to the same verb used in the dedication in 1.12, implying that the doom declared by God is not over. **30:** *Pharaoh Hophra,* also known as Apries, ruled 589–570 BCE. He was assassinated by Amasis (570–526), a former court official who served as co-regent during the last three years of Hophra's reign.

---

a-a Lit. "everything that has gone forth from our mouth."   *b* Cf. 7.18.
c-c Meaning of Heb. uncertain.   *d* See note at 24.9; 42.18.
e-e Lit. "spoken with your mouth and fulfilled by your hands."

them to their hurt, not to their benefit; all the men of Judah in the land of Egypt shall be consumed by sword and by famine, until they cease to be. 28 Only the few who survive the sword shall return from the land of Egypt to the land of Judah. All the remnant of Judah who came to the land of Egypt to sojourn there shall learn whose word will be fulfilled—Mine or theirs!

29 "And this shall be the sign to you—declares the LORD—that I am going to deal with you in this place, so that you may know that My threats of punishment against you will be fulfilled: 30 Thus said the LORD: I will deliver Pharaoh Hophra, king of Egypt, into the hands of his enemies, those who seek his life, just as I delivered King Zedekiah of Judah into the hands of King Nebuchadrezzar of Babylon, his enemy who sought his life."

45 The word which the prophet Jeremiah spoke to Baruch son of Neriah, when he was writing these words in a scroll at Jeremiah's dictation, in the fourth year of King Jehoiakim son of Josiah of Judah:

2 Thus said the LORD, the God of Israel, concerning you, Baruch: 3 You say, "Woe is me! The LORD has added grief to my pain. I am worn out with groaning, and I have found no rest." 4 Thus shall you speak to him: "Thus said the LORD: I am going to overthrow what I have built, and uproot what I have planted—ᵃthis applies to the whole land.ᵃ 5 And do you expect great things for yourself? Don't expect them. For I am going to bring disaster upon all flesh—declares the LORD—but I will ᵇat least grant you your lifeᵇ in all the places where you may go."

46 The word of the LORD to the prophet Jeremiah concerning the nations.

---

a-a Meaning of Heb. uncertain.   b-b Cf. note at 21.9.

45.1–5: Jeremiah's oracle to Baruch. The prophetic word formula introduces this brief unit. The oracle is likely placed here to explain why Baruch suffers the punishment of having to go to Egypt with Jeremiah (43.6). It is one of the key texts, together with ch 36, that points to Baruch as the author of sections of or some form of the book of Jeremiah, particularly the narratives about the prophet. Radak cites an unknown midrashic source to interpret Baruch's expressions of pain as his statements of frustration that he was not granted the right to prophesy even though he wrote Jeremiah's oracles. **1:** It is dated to the *fourth year of . . . Jehoiakim* (605 BCE) when Baruch recorded Jeremiah's words on a scroll (ch 36). **3:** The prophet expresses his grief at having to warn Baruch at the outset of the difficult times that he will experience. **4:** The prophet's words reiterate the basic verbs of his prophetic commission to indicate that God will *overthrow* what is *built* and *uproot* what is *planted* (see

1.10). **5:** The reference to *great things* is unclear, though 43.3 indicates that Baruch may have been involved in various political machinations.

46.1–51.64: Jeremiah's oracles concerning the nations. An example of the prophetic word formula introduces the oracles concerning the nations, including Egypt (46.2–28), Philistia (47.1–7), Moab (48.1–47), the Ammonites (49.1–6), Edom (49.7–22), Damascus (49.23–27), Kedar and Hazor (49.28–33), Elam (49.34–39), and Babylonia (50.1–51.64). Similar collections of oracles concerning the nations appear in other prophetic books, including Isa. chs 13–23; Ezek. chs 25–32; Amos 1.2–2.16; Zeph. 2.4–15; Obadiah; and Nahum. The oracles concerning the nations do not address universally all the nations of the earth, but include nations selectively, e.g., Isa. chs 13–23 includes nations that were a part of the Persian empire, Ezek. chs 25–32 includes nations that were attacked by the Babylonians, and Amos 1.2–2.16 includes nations of the Syro-Israelite region that were incorporated into the Assyrian empire. Like Isa. chs 13–23, the oracles in Jer. chs 46–51 include nations that were conquered by the Persian empire beginning in 539 BCE in an effort to claim that God's judgment against Babylonia was carried out by the Persians. These oracles *concern the nations* (46.1) but are not addressed to the nations. They emphasize a point already made at the beginning of classical prophecy (Amos), that the God of Israel is a universal God who controls the destiny of all the nations of the world. In some cases, there are significant similarities between oracles against the nations recited by different prophets (see esp. Jer. 49.9–16; Obad. vv. 1–6), suggesting that prophets or editors of prophetic books borrowed these prophecies from one another. **46.1:** As in 21.11 and 33.9, prophetic oracles on the same topic are joined together and introduced with a thematic title, a method of

²Concerning Egypt, about the army of Pharaoh Neco, king of Egypt, which was at the river Euphrates near Carchemish, and which was defeated by King Nebuchadrezzar of Babylon, in the fourth year of King Jehoiakim son of Josiah of Judah.

3 Get ready buckler and shield,
  And move forward to battle!
4 Harness the horses;
  Mount, you horsemen!
  Fall in line, helmets on!
  Burnish the lances,
  Don your armor!
5 Why do I see them dismayed,

organization which is confined to Jeremiah.

46.2–28: The oracle concerning Egypt. Egypt was able to take control of Judah in 609 BCE following Pharaoh Neco's killing of King Josiah at Megiddo (2 Kings 23.28–37; 2 Chron. 35.20–36.4). Apparently, Josiah was attempting to stop the Egyptians from moving north to

Haran so that they might support the beleaguered Assyrian army against the Babylonians. Although Josiah died, Egypt was delayed long enough so that the Babylonians were able to destroy the Assyrians at Haran. The Egyptians were then left to face the Babylonians alone. Neco attempted to strengthen his position by removing Josiah's son Jehoahaz from the

Judean throne and replacing him with his pro-Egyptian brother Jehoiakim. Jeremiah was a constant critic of alliance with Egypt in keeping with his Elide priestly roots, which emphasized the exodus tradition and its portrayal of Egypt as Israel's enemy and his associations with the pro-Babylonian elements of the royal court, such as the family of Shaphan who served as Josiah's secretary. When the Egyptians were defeated at Carchemish in 605, the Babylonians took control of Judah. Subsequent revolts against Babylonia, prompted by pro-Egyptian elements in the monarchy, ultimately resulted in the destruction of Judah and Jerusalem and the Babylonian exile (586–539). **2–12:** Jeremiah's oracle concerning Egypt at the time of its defeat at Carchemish in 605. **2:** *Pharaoh Neco* ruled Egypt 610–595. He was the son of Psammetichus (664–610), the founder of the Twenty-sixth Saite Egyptian dynasty (664–525), which supported Assyria in its campaign to control Egypt and defeat the

Places mentioned in the oracles against the nations

Yielding ground?
Their fighters are crushed,
They flee in haste
And do not turn back—
Terror all around!   —declares the LORD.

6   a-The swift cannot get away,
        The warrior cannot escape.-a
        In the north, by the river Euphrates,
        They stagger and fall.

7   Who is this that rises like the Nile,
        Like streams whose waters surge?
8   It is Egypt that rises like the Nile,
        Like streams whose waters surge,
        That said, "I will rise,
        I will cover the earth,
        I will wipe out towns
        And those who dwell in them.
9   Advance, O horses,
        Dash madly, O chariots!
        Let the warriors go forth,
        Cush and Put, that grasp the shield,
        And the Ludim who grasp and draw the bow!"

10 But that day shall be for the Lord GOD of Hosts a day
when He exacts retribution from His foes. The sword shall
devour; it shall be sated and drunk with their blood. For
the Lord GOD of Hosts is preparing a sacrifice in the northland, by the river Euphrates.

11   Go up to Gilead and get balm,
        Fair Maiden Egypt.
        In vain do you seek many remedies,
        There is no healing for you.
12   Nations have heard your shame;
        The earth resounds with your screams.
        For warrior stumbles against warrior;
        The two fall down together.

13 The word which the LORD spoke to the prophet Jeremiah about the coming of King Nebuchadrezzar of Babylon to attack the land of Egypt:

14   Declare in Egypt, proclaim in Migdol,
        Proclaim in Noph and Tahpanhes!
        Say: Take your posts and stand ready,

Twenty-fifth Ethiopian dynasty.
Neco's defeat by the Babylonian
monarch *Nebuchadrezzar* at *Carchemish* in 605 forced Egypt to withdraw from Judah, and enabled
Babylonia to take control. Neco
was able to resist Nebuchadrezzar's attempted invasion of Egypt
in 601–600. The Saite dynasty
came to an end in 525 when the
Persians conquered Egypt. **5:** The
oracle employs Jeremiah's characteristic phrase, *terror all around,* to
describe the plight of the Egyptians (see 6.25; 20.3, 10; 49.29; Lam.
2.22; Ps. 31.14). **7:** The metaphor
of the rising waters of the *Nile*
portrays the Egyptian advance.
9: *Cush* is Ethiopia, and *Put* is
probably a region in Libya. The
Ludim are a north African people.
10: The Egyptian defeat is portrayed as a sacrifice (cf. Zeph. 1.7).
11: *Gilead* is located in the Transjordan, just south of the Golan (cf.
8.22). **13–28:** Jeremiah's oracle concerning Egypt at the time of Nebuchadnezzar's attempted invasion
in 601–600. This passage serves as
the haftarah for the parashah of
Bo' (Exod. 10.1–13.16), which relates the plagues of locusts, darkness, and the slaying of the first-
born at the time of the exodus
from Egypt. **14:** *Migdol,* see 44.1.
Noph, Memphis; see 2.16, 44.1.
Tahpanhes, see 2.16; 44.1. Memphis
was the ancient capital of Egypt;
Migdol and Tahpanhes were
defended cities in the Nile Delta
region.

a-a Lit. "Let not the swift get away, / Let not the warrior escape."

For the sword has devoured all around you!
15 Why are your stalwarts swept away?
They did not stand firm,
For the LORD thrust them down;
16 He made many stumble,
They fell over one another.

They said:
"Up! let us return to our people,
To the land of our birth,
Because of the deadly[a] sword."
17 There they called Pharaoh king of Egypt:
[b-]"Braggart who let the hour go by."[-b]

18 As I live—declares the King,
Whose name is LORD of Hosts—
[b-]As surely as Tabor is among the mountains
And Carmel is by the sea,
So shall this come to pass.[-b]
19 Equip yourself for exile,
Fair Egypt, you who dwell secure!
For Noph shall become a waste,
Desolate, without inhabitants.
20 Egypt is a handsome heifer—
A gadfly[c] from the north [d-]is coming, coming![-d]
21 The mercenaries, too, in her midst
Are like stall-fed calves;
They too shall turn tail,
Flee as one, and make no stand.
Their day of disaster is upon them,
The hour of their doom.
22 [b-]She shall rustle away like a snake[-b]
As they come marching in force;
They shall come against her with axes,
Like hewers of wood.
23 They shall cut down her forest
                              —declares the LORD—
Though it cannot be measured;
For they are more numerous than locusts,
And cannot be counted.
24 Fair Egypt shall be shamed,
Handed over to the people of the north.

25 The LORD of Hosts, the God of Israel, has said: I will
inflict punishment on Amon[e] of No and on Pharaoh—on

18: Mt. *Tabor* and the *Carmel* range flank the eastern and western borders of the Jezreel Valley in northern Israel. The oracle employs Jeremiah's earlier warnings of an enemy from the north against Egypt (cf. 1.14–19; chs 4–6). **25:** *Amon* is the Egyptian sun god whose temple was located in *No*, the Heb name for Thebes (cf. Nah. 3.8). The concluding reassurance oracles for Jacob also appear in 30.10–11.

___

a *Meaning of Heb. uncertain.*   b-b *Meaning of Heb. uncertain.*
c *Or "butcher"; meaning of Heb. uncertain.*   d-d *Many mss. read "will come upon her."*
e *Tutelary deity of the city No (Thebes); cf. Nah. 3.8.*

Egypt, her gods, and her kings—on Pharaoh and all who rely on him. [26] I will deliver them into the hands of those who seek to kill them, into the hands of King Nebuchad-rezzar of Babylon and into the hands of his subjects. But afterward she shall be inhabited again as in former days, declares the LORD.

27   But you,
        Have no fear, My servant Jacob,
        Be not dismayed, O Israel!
        I will deliver you from far away,
        Your folk from their land of captivity;
        And Jacob again shall have calm
        And quiet, with none to trouble him.
28   But you, have no fear,
        My servant Jacob   —declares the LORD—
        For I am with you.
        I will make an end of all the nations
        Among which I have banished you,
        But I will not make an end of you!
        I will not leave you unpunished,
        But I will chastise you in measure.

47 The word of the LORD that came to the prophet Jer-emiah concerning the Philistines, before Pharaoh conquered Gaza.

2   Thus said the LORD:
        See, waters are rising from the north,
        They shall become a raging torrent,
        They shall flood the land and its creatures,
        The towns and their inhabitants.
        Men shall cry out,
        All the inhabitants of the land shall howl,
3   At the clatter of the stamping hoofs of his stallions,
        At the noise of his chariots,
        The rumbling of their wheels,
        Fathers shall not look to their children
        Out of ᵃsheer helplessnessᵃ
4   Because of the day that is coming
        For ravaging all the Philistines,
        For cutting off every last ally
        Of Tyre and Sidon.
        For the LORD will ravage the Philistines,
        The remnant from the island of Caphtor.
5   Baldnessᵇ has come upon Gaza,

a-a Lit. "weakness of hands."
b Shaving the head and gashing the body were expressions of mourning; cf. Deut. 14.1.

47.1–7: Jeremiah's oracle concerning Philistia. The Philistines were descended from the so-called "Sea Peoples" who advanced by land and sea from the Greek islands through Asia Minor and the East-ern Mediterranean beginning in the 14th century BCE. They de-stroyed the ancient Hittite empire in Asia Minor, which has prompted some to identify them with Odysseus and his warriors in the Odyssey. They continued down the eastern Mediterranean coast, where they destroyed the city of Ugarit in Syria and attacked Egypt during the reign of Rameses III (1182–1152). Following their de-feat by Rameses III, some groups of the Sea Peoples settled along the Mediterranean coast of Canaan, where they merged with the local population to become the Philis-tines. The Philistine coalition in-cluded five major cities (a pentap-olis): Ashkelon, Ashdod, Ekron, Gaza, and Gath. Herodotus re-ports that Neco conquered Gaza, at the border of the desert on the way to Egypt, after his battle with Josiah at Megiddo (*History* 2.159). This view also appears in *Seder Olam* 26. Nebuchadnezzar's inva-sion of Philistia in 604 and his sub-sequent deportation of major ele-ments of the population brought an end to Philistia as a cohesive ethnic and national group. Al-though the Philistines play a major role in texts describing the early monarchy, especially in the story of Saul, they are hardly mentioned in texts from the divided monar-chy. Yet archeological finds and various texts confirm that they re-mained important and active through the period of Jeremiah. **2:** As in 46.7–8, the metaphor of rising waters depicts Egypt's advance against Philistia. The ref-erence to *the north* has puzzled in-terpreters for centuries, since Bab-ylonia is located to the north and Egypt to the south. Abravanel says that it must refer to Babylo-nia. **4:** The references to *Tyre* and *Sidon* in Phoenicia (modern Leba-non) suggest that they were allies of the Philistines, although such an alliance is not known at this time.

Ashkelon is destroyed.
O remnant of a-their valley,-a
How long will you b-gash yourself?-b

6   "O sword of the LORD,
When will you be quiet at last?
Withdraw into your sheath,
Rest and be still!"

7   How can it c be quiet
When the LORD has given it orders
Against Ashkelon and the seacoast,
Given it assignment there?

48 Concerning Moab. d

Thus said the LORD of Hosts, the God of Israel:
Alas, that Nebo should be ravaged,
Kiriathaim captured and shamed,
e-The stronghold-e shamed and dismayed!

2   Moab's glory is no more;
In Heshbon they have planned f evil against her:
"Come, let us make an end of her as a nation!"
You too, O Madmen, shall be silenced; g
The sword is following you.

3   Hark! an outcry from Horonaim,
Destruction and utter ruin!

4   Moab is broken;
h-Her young ones cry aloud;-h

5   They climb to Luhith
Weeping continually;
On the descent to Horonaim
A distressing cry of anguish is heard:

a-a Septuagint reads "the Anakites"; cf. Josh. 11.22.
b-b Shaving the head and gashing the body were expressions of mourning; cf. Deut. 14.1.
c Heb. "you."
d A number of parallels to this chapter occur in Isa. 15–16.
e-e Or "Misgab."
f Heb. ḥashebu, play on Heshbon.
g Heb. tiddommi, play on Madmen, the name of a town.
h-h Emendation yields "They cry aloud as far as Zoar"; cf. Isa. 15.5.

Caphtor is the island of Crete, which Amos 9.7 identifies as the original home of the Philistines.

48.1–47: Jeremiah's oracle concerning Moab. Ancient Moab was a nation situated east of the Dead Sea to the north of Edom and southwest of Ammon (and modern Amman) in what is now modern Jordan. The story about Moab's and Ammon's origin in Gen. 19.29–38 on the one hand reflects the political and familial closeness that Israel felt to these peoples, but also Israel's disdain toward them. Israel's relationship with Moab was generally tense. Traditions in Numbers and Deuteronomy report that Moab attempted to stop Israel from passing through its territory on the journey from Egypt to the land of Israel. The mid-9th century Moabite Stone (Mesha stele) reports that the Moabite King Mesha (cf. 2 Kings 3.4) conquered Israel's land in the Transjordan, including the territories of Reuben and Gad. The Moabites were allies of the Assyrians, but the Babylonians apparently destroyed Moab in the mid-6th century. Much of the material in Jeremiah's Moabite oracle is drawn from Isaiah's Moabite oracle in Isaiah chs 15–16, which would suggest that Jeremiah reused Isaiah's material in the belief that Isaiah's prophecies were being fulfilled in his own time. **1–10:** The initial oracle apparently describes Nebuchadnezzar's advance against Moab. Various phrases from the oracle appear in Isa. ch 15. **1:** *Nebo* is the name of the mountain from which Moses viewed the land of Israel prior to death and burial (Deut. ch 34). There was also a Moabite city by the same name (see Num. 32.3; Isa. 15.2) located at modern Khirbet Mekhayyet, 8 km (5 mi) southwest of Hesban. *Kiriathaim* (Num. 32.37; Josh. 13.19) is probably el-Qereiyat, 9 km (5.5 mi) northwest of Dibon. Hesbon was the capital of the Amorite king Sihon (Num. 21.26–30) and was later captured by Mesha. It is identified with modern Hesban. **2:** *Madmen* is a play on words drawn from Isa. 25.10b, which some render as "Moab shall be trodden down in his place, as straw is trodden down in a dung pit (madmenah)." It may also play on the name of the Moabite city Dimon (Isa. 15.9). **3–5:** The location of *Horonaim* is uncertain (see Isa. 15.5), although some identify it with el-Iraq, 9 miles east of the southeastern Dead Sea. *Luhith* is probably

6   Flee, save your lives!
        ª⁻And be like Aroer in the desert.⁻ª

7   Surely, because of your trust
        In your wealth and in your treasures,
        You too shall be captured.
        And Chemosh shall go forth to exile,
        Together with his priests and attendants.
8   The ravager shall come to every town;
        No town shall escape.
        The valley shall be devastated
        And the tableland laid waste
              —because the LORD has spoken.
9   Give ª⁻wings to Moab,
        For she must go hence.⁻ª
        Her towns shall become desolate,
        With no one living in them.

10 Cursed be he who is slack in doing the LORD's work!
Cursed be he who withholds his sword from blood!

11   Moab has been secure from his youth on—
        He is settled on his lees
        And has not been poured from vessel to vessel—
        He has never gone into exile.
        Therefore his fine flavor has remained
        And his bouquet is unspoiled.

12 But days are coming—declares the LORD—when I will send men against him to tip him over; they shall empty his vessels and smash his jars. 13 And Moab shall be shamed because of Chemosh, as the House of Israel were shamed because of Bethel, on whom they relied.

14   How can you say: We are warriors,
        Valiant men for war?
15   Moab is ravaged,
        His towns have been entered,
        His choice young men
        Have gone down to the slaughter
             —declares the King whose name is
                  LORD of Hosts.
16   The doom of Moab is coming close,
        His downfall is approaching swiftly.
17   Condole with him, all who live near him,
        All you who know him by name!

nearby (Isa. 15.5). **6:** *Aroer* is modern Ara'ir, located along the northern rim of the wadi Arnon where it defended ancient Moab's northern border. **7:** *Chemosh* is the chief god of Moab (1 Kings 11.7). **11–17:** The oracle employs the imagery of wine jars that have never been moved, thereby allowing the sediment *(lees)* to settle. Because of its cooperation with Assyria, Moab had never suffered exile, which apparently made it complacent in the Babylonian period. **12:** The coming destruction is portrayed as the smashing of wine jars. **13:** The prophet identifies adherence to Chemosh rather than God as the reason for their punishment, much as northern Israel had relied on King Jeroboam's temple at Beth El (see 1 Kings chs 12–13; 2 Kings ch 17), or perhaps the Semitic deity of the same name. The implications of this v.—that foreigners are punished for their pagan ways—is atypical of the oracles against the nations.

a-a *Meaning of Heb. uncertain.*

Say: "Alas, the strong rod is broken,
The lordly staff!"

18 　　Descend from glory
And sit in thirst,[a]
O inhabitant of Fair Dibon;
For the ravager of Moab has entered your town,
He has destroyed your fortresses.

19 　　Stand by the road and look out,
O inhabitant of Aroer.
Ask of him who is fleeing
And of her who is escaping:
Say, "What has happened?"

20 　　Moab is shamed and dismayed;
Howl and cry aloud!
Tell at the Arnon
That Moab is ravaged!

21 Judgment has come upon the tableland—upon Holon, Jahzah, and Mephaath; 22 upon Dibon, Nebo, and Beth-diblathaim; 23 upon Kiriathaim, Beth-gamul, and Beth-meon; 24 upon Kerioth and Bozrah—upon all the towns of the land of Moab, far and near.

25 　　The might of Moab has been cut down,
His strength is broken 　　　—declares the LORD.

26 　　Get him drunk
For he vaunted himself against the LORD.
Moab shall vomit till he is drained,
And he too shall be a laughingstock.

27 　　Wasn't Israel a laughingstock to you?
Was he ever caught among thieves,
That you should [b]shake your head[b]
Whenever you speak of him?

28 　　Desert the cities
And dwell in the crags,
O inhabitants of Moab!
Be like a dove that nests
In the sides of a pit.

29 　　We have heard of Moab's pride—
Most haughty is he—
Of his arrogance and pride,
His haughtiness and self-exaltation.

30 I know his insolence—declares the LORD—the wickedness that is in him,[c] the wickedness [d]he has[d] committed.

18–28: The prophet employs the imagery of a woman who has been raped to depict the suffering of Moab at the hands of the Babylonians. **18:** *Dibon* is modern Dhiban, located 22 km (13 mi) east of the Dead Sea and 5 km (3 mi) north of the Arnon along the ancient King's Highway, the major trade route through the Transjordan in antiquity (see Num. 21.21–31). **21:** The *tableland* refers to the central plateau north of the Arnon. The various cities located there are listed. **26:** The oracle builds on the imagery of the wine jars with the imagery of drunkenness. **29–39:** The prophet turns to a lament over the fall of Moab, identified by its characteristic 3/2 beat qinah ("lament") meter.

---

a *Meaning of Heb. uncertain.*　　b-b *I.e., in mockery.*
c *Cf. note at Isa. 16.6.*　　d-d *Heb. "they have."*

31   Therefore I will howl for Moab,
      I will cry out for all Moab,
      I[a] will moan for the men of Kir-heres.
32   With greater weeping than for Jazer
      I weep for you, O vine of Sibmah,
      Whose tendrils crossed the sea,
      Reached to the sea,[b] to Jazer.
      A ravager has come down
      Upon your fig and grape harvests.
33   Rejoicing and gladness
      Are gone from the farm land,
      From the country of Moab;
      I have put an end to wine in the presses,
      No one treads [the grapes] with shouting—
      [c]The shout is a shout no more.[c]
34   There is an outcry from Heshbon to Elealeh,
      They raise their voices as far as Jahaz,
      From Zoar to Horonaim and Eglath-shelishiah.
      The waters of Nimrim
      Shall also become desolation.
35   And I will make an end in Moab
                  —declares the LORD—
      Of those who offer at a shrine
      And burn incense to their god.
36   Therefore,
      My heart moans for Moab like a flute;
      Like a flute my heart moans
      For the men of Kir-heres—
      [c]Therefore,
      The gains they have made shall vanish[c]—
37   For every head is bald
      And every beard is shorn;
      On all hands there are gashes,
      And on the loins sackcloth.
38   On all the roofs of Moab,
      And in its squares
      There is naught but lamentation;
      For I have broken Moab
      Like a vessel no one wants
                  —declares the LORD.
39   How he is dismayed! Wail!
      How Moab has turned his back in shame!
      Moab shall be a laughingstock
      And a shock to all those near him.

31: *Kir-heres* is modern el-Kerak (Isa. 15.1), which was the ancient capital of Moab. **32:** The location of *Jazer* is uncertain, although it was probably a short distance west of Amman. *Sibmah* is probably modern Qurn el-Kibsh 8 km (5 mi) southwest of Hesban. **34:** *Elealeh* is modern el-Al 3 km (2 mi) northeast of Hesban. *Zoar* is one of the five cities of the plain associated with Sodom and Gomorrah (Gen. 14.1–12). It may be es-Safi, 8 km (5 mi) south of the Dead Sea. *Eglath-shelishiah* is unknown (see Isa. 15.5). **37:** *Bald . . . shorn . . . gashes . . . sackcloth:* All of these practices—shaving the head and beard, gashing oneself, wearing rough garmets—are expressions of mourning or grief.

a   Heb. "He."
b   Meaning of Heb. uncertain.
c-c Meaning of Heb. uncertain.

40 For thus said the LORD:
   See, he soars like an eagle
   And spreads out his wings against Moab!
41 Kerioth shall be captured
   And the strongholds shall be seized.
   In that day, the heart of Moab's warriors
   Shall be like the heart of a woman in travail.
42 And Moab shall be destroyed as a people,
   For he vaunted himself against the LORD.
43 ᵃTerror, and pit, and trap⁻ᵃ
   Upon you who dwell in Moab!
                              —declares the LORD.
44 He who flees from the terror
   Shall fall into the pit;
   And he who climbs out of the pit
   Shall be caught in the trap.
   For I will bring upon Moab
   The year of their doom   —declares the LORD.

45 In the shelter of Heshbon
   Fugitives halt exhausted;
   For fire went forth from Heshbon,
   Flame from the midstᵇ of Sihon,
   Consuming the brow of Moab,
   The pate of the people of Shaon.ᶜ
46 Woe to you, O Moab!
   The people of Chemosh are undone,
   For your sons are carried off into captivity,
   Your daughters into exile.

⁴⁷ But I will restore the fortunes of Moab in the days to
come—declares the LORD.

   Thus far is the judgment on Moab.

49 Concerning the Ammonites.

   Thus said the LORD:
   Has Israel no sons,
   Has he no heir?
   Then why has Milcomᵈ dispossessed Gad,
   And why have his people settled in Gad'sᵉ towns?
2 Assuredly, days are coming
                              —declares the LORD—
   When I will sound the alarm of war
   Against Rabbah of the Ammonites;

40–47: The metaphor of a woman in childbirth depicts Moab's pain (see Isa. 13.8). **42:** For Moab's vaunting itself against God, see Zeph. 2.8–10. **43–44:** Isa. 24.17–18 quotes vv. 43–44, but identifies the victims as the inhabitants of the land. **45–46:** A quotation, with variations, of Num. 21.28–29. Perhaps this quotation of a Torah text is used as a device to indicate that the unit is at an end; a final Torah quotation sometimes has this function in later rabbinic texts. **47:** The final v. promises restoration for Moab.

49.1–6: Jeremiah's oracle concerning the Ammonites. The Ammonites were closely connected geographically and in biblical narrative (see Gen. 19.29–38) to the Moabites, the subjects of the previous oracle. Ancient Ammon was centered around the city of Rabbath-Ammon, modern Amman. The Ammonites were sometimes foes and sometimes allies of Israel and Judah. The Ammonites supported Ishmael son of Nethaniah, a member of the Davidic family, in his revolt against Gedaliah (chs 41–42). Nebuchadnezzar's invasion put an end to the ancient Ammonite state (contrast v. 6). **1:** *Milcom* is the chief god of the Ammonites (1 Kings 11.5, 33). The Ammonites periodically encroached upon the bordering territory of *Gad* (Judg. 10.6–12.6; 2 Sam. 12.26–31). As noted, here and in v. 3 the Heb is vocalized as "malkam," "their king"—the consonants of "their king" and the deity "milkom" are identical. The correct reading Milkom is preserved in some of the early Bible translations, which transliterate the name; it is unclear if the Masoretic reading "their king" reflects a loss of knowledge that Milkom was the Ammonite high god, or reflects an intentional change aimed at denying the power or existence of this deity. **6:** The oracle concludes with a promise of restoration.

---

a-a *See note at Isa. 24.17.*   b *Emendation yields "house."*   c *Or "tumult."*
d *The name of the Ammonite deity; vocalized Malcam here and in v. 3.*   e *Heb. "his."*

It shall become a desolate mound,
And its villages shall be set on fire.
And Israel shall dispossess
Those who dispossessed him   —said the LORD.
3   Howl, O Heshbon, for Ai is ravaged!
Cry out, O daughters of Rabbah!
Gird on sackcloth, lament,
ᵃ⁻And run to and fro in the sheepfolds.⁻ᵃ
For Milcom shall go into exile,
Together with his priests and attendants.

4   ᵇ⁻Why do you glory in strength,
Your strength is drained,⁻ᵇ
O rebellious daughter,
You who relied on your treasures,
[Who said:] Who dares attack me?
5   I am bringing terror upon you
               —declares the Lord GOD of Hosts—
From all those around you.
Every one of you shall be driven ᶜ⁻in every
     direction,⁻ᶜ
And none shall gather in the fugitives.
   ⁶But afterward I will restore the fortunes of the Am-
monites—declares the LORD.

7   Concerning Edom.

Thus said the LORD of Hosts:
Is there no more wisdom in Teman?
Has counsel vanished from the prudent?
Has their wisdom gone stale?
8   Flee, turn away, sit down low,
O inhabitants of Dedan,
For I am bringing Esau's doom upon him,
The time when I deal with him.
9   ᵈ⁻If vintagers were to come upon you,
Would they leave no gleanings?
Even thieves in the night
Would destroy only for their needs!⁻ᵈ
10   But it is I who have bared Esau,
Have exposed his place of concealment;
He cannot hide.

49.7–22: Jeremiah's oracle concerning Edom. The Edomites were located to the southeast of the Dead Sea and east of the Arabah or Jordan rift that extends to the Gulf of Aqabah. Gen. chs 25–35 identifies the Edomites as the descendants of Jacob's brother Esau. The Bible bitterly recalls how the Edomites apparently joined in the Babylonian assault against Jerusalem (see Ps. 137.7; Lam. 4.21–22; Obad. 10–16). Following the destruction of Jerusalem, Edomites moved into the Negev region and established themselves in Hebron. They were known as the Idumeans in Hellenistic and Roman times. **7:** The location of *Teman* is unknown. *Edom* was in the east, an area associated with *wisdom* in the Bible (Job 1.3; Prov. 30.1; 31.1; cf. Isa. 2.6). **8:** *Dedan* is a trading center located in northwestern Arabia (see Gen. 10.6–7; 25.1–3; Ezek. 25.13). **9–10:** These vv. are similar to Obad. 5–6, which portrays Edom's punishment.

a-a Meaning of Heb. uncertain.
b-b Meaning of Heb. uncertain; for "strength" cf. Akkadian emuqu.
c-c Lit. "each man straight ahead."
d-d Obad. 1.5 reads: "If thieves were to come to you, / Marauders by night, / They would steal no more than they needed. / If vintagers came to you, / They would surely leave some gleanings."

> His offspring is ravaged,
> His kin and his neighbors—
> ªHe is no more.ª

11   "Leave your orphans with me,
> I will rear them;
> Let your widows rely on me!"

12 For thus said the LORD: If they who rightly should not drink of the cup must drink it, are you the one to go unpunished? You shall not go unpunished: you will have to drink! 13 For by Myself I swear—declares the LORD—Bozrah shall become a desolation, a mockery, a ruin, and a curse;ᵇ and all its towns shall be ruins for all time.

14   I have received tidings from the LORD,
> And an envoy is sent out among the nations:
> Assemble, and move against her,
> And rise up for war!
15   For I will make you least among nations,
> Most despised among men.
16   ᶜYour horrible nature,ᶜ
> Your arrogant heart has seduced you,
> You who dwell in clefts of the rock,
> Who occupy the height of the hill!
> Should you nest as high as the eagle,
> From there I will pull you down
>   —declares the LORD.

17 And Edom shall be a cause of appallment; whoever passes by will be appalled and will hissᵈ at all its wounds. 18 It shall be like the overthrow of Sodom and Gomorrah and their neighbors—said the LORD: no man shall live there, no human shall sojourn there. 19 It shall be as when a lion comes up out of the jungle of the Jordan against a secure pasture: in a moment ᵉI can harry him out of it and appoint over it anyone I choose.ᵉ Then who is like Me? Who can summon Me? Who is the shepherd that can stand up against Me? 20 Hear, then, the plan which the LORD has devised against Edom, and what He has purposed against the inhabitants of Teman:

> Surely the shepherd boys
> Shall drag them away;

13: *Bozrah* is the chief city and fortress of northern Edom, 13 km (8 mi) south of modern Tefileh. **14–16:** These vv. resemble Obad. 1–4, which describe Edom's arrogance. Bozrah was located on high ground where it was difficult to attack. **18:** *Sodom and Gomorrah* were located in what became Edomite territory, and therefore aid in depicting Edom's demise. The predicted complete destruction of Edom, in contrast to the restoration of Moab and Ammon, is likely motivated by the role they played in joining the Babylonians against Jerusalem. **22:** The imagery of the eagle apparently recalls Bozrah's location on the heights.

---

a-a Some Septuagint mss. read "And there is none to say."

b Cf. note at 24.9 and 42.18.

c-c Meaning of Heb. uncertain.

d Cf. note at 18.16.

e-e Emendation yields "he can harry them [i.e., the sheep] out of it; and what champion could one place in charge of them?"

Surely the pasture shall be
Aghast because of them.
21 At the sound of their downfall
The earth shall shake;
The sound of screaming
Shall be heard at the Sea of Reeds.
22 See, like an eagle he flies up,
He soars and spreads his wings against Bozrah;
And the heart of Edom's warriors in that day
Shall be like the heart of a woman in travail.

23 Concerning Damascus.

Hamath and Arpad are shamed,
For they have heard bad news.
They shake with anxiety,
Like^a the sea which cannot rest.
24 Damascus has grown weak,
She has turned around to flee;
Trembling has seized her,
Pain and anguish have taken hold of her,
Like a woman in childbirth.
25 ^bHow has the glorious city not been deserted,^b
The citadel of my joy!
26 Assuredly, her young men shall lie fallen in her
squares.
And all her warriors shall be stilled in that day
—declares the LORD of Hosts.
27 I will set fire to the wall of Damascus,
And it shall consume the fortresses of Ben-hadad.

28 Concerning Kedar and the kingdoms of Hazor,
which King Nebuchadrezzar of Babylon conquered.

Thus said the LORD:
Arise, march against Kedar,
And ravage the Kedemites!
29 They will take away their tents and their flocks,
Their tent cloths and all their gear;
They shall carry off their camels,
And shall proclaim against them:
Terror all around!
30 Flee, wander far,
Sit down low, O inhabitants of Hazor
—says the LORD.

49.23–27: Jeremiah's oracle concerning Damascus. Damascus was the ancient capital of Aram (modern Syria). It was destroyed in 734–732 BCE by the Assyrians, who later employed it as an administrative center. **23:** *Hamath* is modern Hama. *Arpad* was located 40 km (25 mi) north of Aleppo. Both were destroyed by the Assyrians (2 Kings 18.34; 19.13; Isa. 10.9; 36.19; 37.13). **27:** The concluding statement of the oracle is drawn from Amos 1.4. *Ben-hadad* is the name of several Aramean kings (1 Kings 15.18, 20; 2 Kings 13.24).

49.28–33: Jeremiah's oracles concerning Kedar and Hazor. 28: *Kedar* refers to a coalition of Arab tribes in the north Arabian desert that were descended from Ishmael (Gen. 25.13; 1 Chron. 1.29). *Hazor* is not the Israelite city (Josh. ch 11), but apparently refers to an unknown site associated with Arab tribes. Arab tribes frequently served with the Babylonians, especially in the 7th century when they were used to harass the Assyrians. Babylonian records note Nebuchadnezzar's campaigns against Arab tribes. **29:** The imagery of the v. emphasizes the nomadic nature of these groups. *Terror all around* appears frequently in Jeremiah (20.10, etc.).

a So a few mss. Most mss. and editions read "In."
b-b Emendation yields "How has the glorious city been deserted"; so Vulgate.

For King Nebuchadrezzar of Babylon
Has devised a plan against you
And formed a purpose against you:

31 Rise up, attack a tranquil nation
That dwells secure   —says the LORD—
That has no barred gates,
That dwells alone.

32 Their camels shall become booty,
And their abundant flocks a spoil;
And I will scatter to every quarter
Those who have their hair clipped;
And from every direction I will bring
Disaster upon them   —says the LORD.

33 Hazor shall become a lair of jackals,
A desolation for all time.
No man shall live there,
No human shall sojourn there.

³⁴ The word of the LORD that came to the prophet Jeremiah concerning Elam, at the beginning of the reign of King Zedekiah of Judah:

³⁵ Thus said the LORD of Hosts: I am going to break the bow of Elam, the mainstay of their strength. ³⁶ And I shall bring four winds against Elam from the four quarters of heaven, and scatter them to all those winds. There shall not be a nation to which the fugitives from Elam do not come. ³⁷ And I will break Elam before their enemies, before those who seek their lives; and I will bring disaster upon them, My flaming wrath—declares the LORD. And I will dispatch the sword after them until I have consumed them.

38 And I will set My throne in Elam,
And wipe out from there king and officials
—says the LORD.

³⁹ But in the days to come I will restore the fortunes of Elam—declares the LORD.

50 The word which the LORD spoke concerning Babylon, the land of the Chaldeans, through the prophet Jeremiah:

2 Declare among the nations, and proclaim;
Raise a standard, proclaim;
Hide nothing! Say:
Babylon is captured,
Bel*a* is shamed,

a Names of the city god of Babylon.

49.34–39: Jeremiah's oracles concerning Elam. Ancient Elam was located east of the Tigris River in Mesopotamia. Its capital was Shushan or Susa. The Assyrians sacked Susa in 646 BCE, and Elamite archers joined in Assyrian attacks against Judah (Isa. 21.2; 22.6). The Elamites were later controlled by Babylonia and Persia. The Persian monarch Darius established his winter palace in Susa. **36:** Dividing the world into *four* compass points is not an obvious, natural division, but is borrowed by Israel from Mesopotamia, where it seems to have first developed.

50.1–51.58: Jeremiah's oracle concerning Babylonia. Although Jeremiah consistently maintained that Judah must submit to Babylonia, he is hardly sympathetic to the Babylonians. Babylonian brutality in the destruction of Jerusalem and the Temple as well as the deportation of a major element of Judah's population would have prompted the prophet's condemnation. His views are much like those of Isaiah, who first argued that Assyria was the divinely appointed agent of Israel's punishment and then condemned the Assyrians for overstepping their bounds with their cruelty to Israel and blasphemy against God (Isa. chs 5–12; 13–14; 36–37). This oracle (or more likely, collection of oracles) is reserved for last, as a climax of the collection of oracles against the nations. Much of these two chs emphasizes that Babylonia will be destroyed through violence. In reality, however, Cyrus bloodlessly took over Babylon in 539 BCE, when the powerful priests of Marduk preferred him to the reigning Babylonian King Nabonidus (Nabu-naid). **50.2–7:** The image of the raised standard appears also in Isa. 11.10, 12 to signal the return of the exiles following the defeat of the Assyrian oppressor; here it signals Babylonia's downfall in keeping with Jeremiah's view that Isaiah's oracles are fulfilled in his own time. **2:** *Bel* ("master") is a name often given to Marduk (*Me-*

Merodach[a] is dismayed.
Her idols are shamed,
Her fetishes dismayed.

3 For a nation from the north has attacked her,
It will make her land a desolation.
No one shall dwell in it,
Both man and beast shall wander away.

⁴In those days and at that time—declares the LORD—the people of Israel together with the people of Judah shall come, and they shall weep as they go to seek the LORD their God. ⁵They shall inquire for Zion; in that direction their faces shall turn; [b-they shall come-b] and attach themselves to the LORD by a covenant for all time, which shall never be forgotten. ⁶My people were lost sheep: their shepherds led them astray, they drove them out to the mountains, they roamed from mount to hill, they forgot their own resting place. ⁷All who encountered them devoured them; and their foes said, "We shall not be held guilty, because they have sinned against the LORD, the true Pasture, the Hope of their fathers—the LORD."

8 Flee from Babylon,
Leave the land of the Chaldeans,
And be like he-goats that lead the flock!

9 For see, I am rousing and leading
An assemblage of great nations against Babylon
From the lands of the north.
They shall draw up their lines against her,
There she shall be captured.
Their arrows are like those of [c-a skilled warrior-c]
Who does not turn back without hitting the mark.

10 Chaldea shall be despoiled,
All her spoilers shall be sated
—declares the LORD.

11 For you rejoiced, you exulted,
You who plundered My possession;
You stamped like a heifer treading grain,
You neighed like steeds.

12 So your mother will be utterly shamed,
She who bore you will be disgraced.
Behold the end of the nations—
Wilderness, desert, and steppe!

13 Because of the LORD's wrath she shall not be
    inhabited;

rodach), the chief deity of Babylon. **3:** The *nation from the north* is a common motif in Jeremiah's oracles (see chs 4–6). Many see this as a reference to Persia, which conquered Babylonia in 539. Persia actually lies to the east of Babylonia. **4–5:** The portrayal of the people returning to seek God recalls Isa. 8.16–9.6; 11.1–16. It is unclear whether the image of the Northern Kingdom joining together with Judah, found in other contemporaneous prophecies (Ezek. 37.15–28), represents a reality, that the northern Israelites still maintained some ethnic identity after over a century in exile, or is idealistic. **6–7:** The metaphor of *shepherds* depicts Judah's leadership. **8–13:** The prophet's call to flee from Babylonia anticipates Second Isaiah's calls in Isa. 48.20–21. **8:** The *Chaldeans* were an influential tribe within Babylonia who gained a great deal of power, esp. beginning in the 8th century. Thus, Chaldeans may be used in the same sense as Babylonians. **9:** The portrayal of the enemy preparing to attack Babylonia likewise draws upon Isaiah's depiction of the Assyrians in Isa. 5.26–30. **10–13:** Jeremiah contends that Babylonia must be punished for cruelty just as Isaiah argued that Assyria will be punished for arrogance (Isa. 10.5–34; 14.24–27).

---

a Names of the city god of Babylon.   b-b Heb. "come ye."
c-c So many mss., editions, and versions; other mss. and editions read "a warrior who bereaves."

She shall be utterly desolate.
Whoever passes by Babylon will be appalled
And will hiss at all her wounds.

14　Range yourselves roundabout Babylon,
All you who draw the bow;
Shoot at her, don't spare arrows,
For she has sinned against the LORD.

15　Raise a shout against her all about!
ᵃShe has surrendered;ᵃ
Her bastions have fallen,
Her walls are thrown down—
This is the LORD's vengeance.
Take vengeance on her,
Do to her as she has done!

16　Make an end in Babylon of sowers,
And of wielders of the sickle at harvest time.
Because of the deadlyᵇ sword,
Each man shall turn back to his people,
They shall flee every one to his land.

17 Israel are scattered sheep, harried by lions. First the king of Assyria devoured them, and in the end King Nebuchadrezzar of Babylon crunched their bones. 18 Assuredly, thus said the LORD of Hosts, the God of Israel: I will deal with the king of Babylon and his land as I dealt with the king of Assyria. 19 And I will lead Israel back to his pasture, and he shall graze in Carmel and Bashan, and eat his fill in the hill country of Ephraim and in Gilead.

20　In those days and at that time
　　　　　　　　　—declares the LORD—
The iniquity of Israel shall be sought,
And there shall be none;
The sins of Judah,
And none shall be found;
For I will pardon those I allow to survive.

21　Advance against her—ᶜthe land of Merathaim ᶜ—
And against the inhabitants of Pekod;
Ruin and destroy after them to the last
　　　　　　　　　—says the LORD—
Do just as I have commanded you.

22　Hark! War in the land
And vast destruction!

14–16: The prophet exhorts the warriors who will attack Babylonia. Babylon ultimately surrendered peacefully to the Persian king Cyrus in 539. **17–19:** The image of Israel as *scattered sheep* appears also in Mic. 2.12–13; Ezek. ch 34. **19:** The *Carmel* is the mountain range that runs along the Mediterranean coast from Haifa to the south. The *Bashan* is now known as the Golan. *Ephraim* is the hill country of Israel that now comprises the northern part of the West Bank of Samaria (Shomron). *Gilead* is the Trans-Jordanian region to the south of the Golan in modern Jordan. All of these areas were a part of Israel in antiquity. **20–39:** The prophet announces Babylonia's punishment because of its harsh treatment of Israel and Judah. **21:** *Merathaim* is a pun that means "double rebellion," used here as a name for Babylonia. *Pekod* means "punishment," also used here as a name for Babylonia.

---

a-a Lit. "She has given her hand"; meaning of Heb. uncertain.
b Meaning of Heb. uncertain.　　c-c Meaning of Heb. uncertain.

23 How the hammer of the whole earth
    Has been hacked and shattered!
    How Babylon has become
    An appallment among the nations!
24 I set a snare for you, O Babylon,
    And you were trapped unawares;
    You were found and caught,
    Because you challenged the LORD.
25 The LORD has opened His armory
    And brought out the weapons of His wrath;
    For that is the task
    Of my Lord GOD of Hosts
    In the land of the Chaldeans.
26 Come against her ᵃfrom every quarter;ᵃ
    Break open her granaries,
    ᵃPile her up like heaps of grain,ᵃ
    And destroy her, let her have no remnant!
27 ᵇDestroy allᵇ her bulls,
    Let them go down to slaughter.
    Alas for them, their day is come,
    The hour of their doom!
28 Hark! fugitives are escaping
    From the land of Babylon,
    To tell in Zion of the vengeance of the LORD
          our God,
    Vengeance for His Temple.

29 Summon archers against Babylon,
    All who draw the bow!
    Encamp against her roundabout,
    Let none of her people escape.
    Pay her back for her actions,
    Do to her just what she has done;
    For she has acted insolently against the LORD,
    The Holy One of Israel.
30 Assuredly, her young men shall fall in her squares,
    And all her warriors shall perish in that day
          —declares the LORD.
31 I am going to deal with you, O Insolence
          —declares the Lord GOD of Hosts—
    For your day is come, the time when I doom you:
32 Insolence shall stumble and fall,
    With none to raise her up.
    I will set her cities on fire,
    And it shall consume everything around her.

24–32: Babylonia is accused of challenging God, destroying God's Temple, and insolence just as Assyria was charged with arrogance in threatening Jerusalem (Isa. 10.5–34; chs 36–37).

a-a Meaning of Heb. uncertain.
b-b Emendation yields "A sword against"; cf. vv. 35 ff.

33   Thus said the LORD of Hosts:
      The people of Israel are oppressed,
      And so too the people of Judah;
      All their captors held them,
      They refused to let them go.
34   Their Redeemer is mighty,
      His name is LORD of Hosts.
      He will champion their cause—
      So as to give rest to the earth,
      And unrest to the inhabitants of Babylon.

35   A sword against the Chaldeans
                    —declares the LORD—
      And against the inhabitants of Babylon,
      Against its officials and its wise men!
36   A sword against the diviners, that they be made
            fools of!
      A sword against the warriors, that they be
            dismayed!
37   A sword against its horses and chariots,
      And against all the motley crowd in its midst,
      That they become like women!
      A sword against its treasuries, that they be
            pillaged!
38   A drought^a against its waters, that they be
            dried up!
      For it is a land of idols;
      They are besotted by their ^{b-}dread images.^{-b}
39   Assuredly,
      ^{b-}Wildcats and hyenas^{-b} shall dwell [there],
      And ostriches shall dwell there;
      It shall never be settled again,
      Nor inhabited throughout the ages.

40 It shall be as when God overthrew Sodom and Gomorrah and their neighbors—declares the LORD; no man
shall live there, no human shall sojourn there.

41   Lo, a people comes from the northland;
      A great nation and many kings are roused
      From the remotest parts of the earth.
42   They grasp the bow and javelin,
      They are cruel, they show no mercy;
      The sound of them is like the roaring sea.
      They ride upon horses,

36–37: The announcement of a sword against Babylonia's *diviners, warriors, horses and chariots,* and *treasuries* appears to draw upon Isa. 2.6–21, which employs similar images in a call for judgment on the day of the LORD. **40–46:** *Sodom and Gomorrah* were destroyed by God because of their wickedness (Gen. chs 18–19). The prophets sometimes draw on the Sodom and Gomorrah tradition to portray the punishment of wicked nations (see 20.16; 23.14; cf. Isa. 1.10; 3.9; Amos 4.11; Zeph. 2.9). **41–43:** Jeremiah's portrayal of Babylonia's conqueror resembles Isaiah's depiction of Assyria in Isa. 5.26–30.

a Ḥoreb, *play on* ḥereb, *"sword" in preceding verses.*
b-b *Meaning of Heb. uncertain.*

Accoutered like a man for battle,
Against you, O Fair Babylon!
43 The king of Babylon has heard the report of them,
And his hands are weakened;
Anguish seizes him,
Pangs like a woman in childbirth.

44 It shall be as when a lion comes out of the jungle of
the Jordan against a secure pasture: in a moment ªI can
harry them out of it and appoint over it anyone I choose.ª
Then who is like Me? Who can summon Me? Who is the
shepherd that can stand up against Me? 45 Hear, then, the
plan that the LORD has devised against Babylon, and has
purposed against the land of Chaldea:
Surely the shepherd boys
Shall drag them away;
Surely the pasture shall be
Aghast because of them.
46 At the sound of Babylon's capture
The earth quakes,
And an outcry is heard among the nations.

51 Thus said the LORD:
See, I am rousing a destructive wind
Against Babylon and the inhabitants of Leb-
kamai.ᵇ
2 I will send strangersᶜ against Babylon, and they
shall winnow her.
And they shall strip her land bare;
They shall beset her on all sides
On the day of disaster.
3 Letᵈ the archer draw his bow,
And let him stand ready in his coat of mail!
Show no pity to her young men,
Wipe out all her host!
4 Let them fall slain in the land of Chaldea,
Pierced through in her streets.

5 For Israel and Judah were not bereftᵉ
Of their God the LORD of Hosts,
But their land was filled with guilt
Before the Holy One of Israel.

44–46: These vv. resemble the prophet's earlier statements concerning Edom in 49.19–21. 51.1–14: The impending downfall of Babylonia anticipates Persian and Median advances against Babylonia in 545 BCE. King Cyrus came to power by uniting Persia and Media under his rule. 1: The image of *a destructive wind* recalls the "Hamsin" or "Sharav," a dry desert wind much like the Santa Ana winds of southern California, that often causes great destruction at the transition of seasons in the spring and fall. *Leb-kamai,* lit. "the heart of those who rise against me," is another example of "'atbash," a cryptic reference to the "kasdim," "Chaldeans," the Heb word for the Neo-Babylonians (see 25.26). The passage specifically notes that God acts because of the Temple.

a-a See note at 49.19.
b A cipher for Kasdim, "Chaldea."
c Change of vocalization yields "winnowers."
d Some Heb. mss. and ancient versions read "Let not" here and in next line.
e Lit. "widowed."

6   Flee from the midst of Babylon
       And save your lives, each of you!
       Do not perish for her iniquity;
       For this is a time of vengeance for the LORD,
       He will deal retribution to her.

7   Babylon was a golden cup in the LORD's hand,
       It made the whole earth drunk;
       The nations drank of her wine—
       That is why the nations are mad.

8   Suddenly Babylon has fallen and is shattered;
       Howl over her!
       Get balm for her wounds:
       Perhaps she can be healed.

9   We tried to cure Babylon
       But she was incurable.
       Let us leave her and go,
       Each to his own land;
       For her punishment reaches to heaven,
       It is as high as the sky.

10   The LORD has proclaimed our vindication;
       Come, let us recount in Zion
       The deeds of the LORD our God.

11   Polish the arrows,
       Fill the quivers!
       The LORD has roused the spirit of the kings of
            Media,
       For His plan against Babylon is to destroy her.
       This is the vengeance of the LORD,
       Vengeance for His Temple.

12   Raise a standard against the walls of Babylon!
       Set up a blockade; station watchmen;
       Prepare those in ambush.
       For the LORD has both planned and
            performed
       What He decreed against the inhabitants of
            Babylon.

13   O you who dwell by great waters,
       With vast storehouses,
       Your time is come, ᵃthe hour of your end.ᵃ

14   The LORD of Hosts has sworn by Himself:
       I will fill you with men like a locust swarm,
       They will raise a shout against you.

a-a Meaning of Heb. uncertain.

15   He made the earth by His might,
      Established the world by His wisdom,
      And by His understanding stretched out the skies.

16   ᵃ⁻When He makes His voice heard,⁻ᵃ
      There is a rumbling of waters in the skies;
      He makes vapors rise from the end of the earth,
      He makes lightning for the rain,
      And brings forth wind from His treasuries.

17   Every man is proved dull, without knowledge;
      Every goldsmith is put to shame because of the
         idol,
      For his molten image is a deceit—
      There is no breath in them.

18   They are delusion, a work of mockery;
      In their hour of doom, they shall perish.

19   Not like these in the Portion of Jacob,
      For it is He who formed all things;
      And [Israel is] His very own tribe.
      Lᴏʀᴅ of Hosts is His name.

20   You are My war club, [My] weapons of battle;
      With you I clubbed nations,
      With you I destroyed kingdoms;

21   With you I clubbed horse and rider,
      With you I clubbed chariot and driver,

22   With you I clubbed man and woman,
      With you I clubbed graybeard and boy,
      With you I clubbed youth and maiden;

23   With you I clubbed shepherd and flock,
      With you I clubbed plowman and team,
      With you I clubbed governors and prefects.

24   But I will requite Babylon and all the inhabitants
         of Chaldea
      For all the wicked things they did to Zion before
         your eyes   —declares the Lᴏʀᴅ.

25   See, I will deal with you, O mountain of the
         destroyer   —declares the Lᴏʀᴅ—
      Destroyer of the whole earth!
      I will stretch out My hand against you
      And roll you down from the crags,
      And make you a burnt-out mountain.

26   They shall never take from you
      A cornerstone or foundation stone;
      You shall be a desolation for all time
                  —declares the Lᴏʀᴅ.

27   Raise a standard on earth,

15–19: The hymnic motifs of this passage extol God as creator. **20–26:** God states that Babylonia was the divinely chosen instrument of punishment, but Babylonia will be punished for its cruelty. **27–33:** God calls for the Medians to destroy Babylonia. **27:** *Ararat* refers to ancient Urartu, located in southeastern Turkey and northwest Iran. *Minni* refers to ancient Mannaya, located in northern Iraq. *Ashkenaz* probably refers to the Scythians, an Indo-European people who lived in the region of modern Armenia (cf. Gen. 10.3). Herodotus claims that they invaded Syria-Israel in the 7th century ʙᴄᴇ. The term now refers in modern Heb to Germany and Yiddish-speaking European Jews and their descendants.

a-a Lit. "At the sound of His making."

Sound a horn among the nations,
Appoint nations against her,
Assemble kingdoms against her—
Ararat, Minni, and Ashkenaz—
Designate a marshal against her,
Bring up horses like swarming^a locusts!

28 Appoint nations for war against her—
The kings of Media,
Her governors and all her prefects,
And all the lands they rule!

29 Then the earth quakes and writhes,
For the LORD's purpose is fulfilled against
        Babylon,
To make the land of Babylon
A waste without inhabitant.

30 The warriors of Babylon stop fighting,
They sit in the strongholds,
Their might is dried up,
They become women.
Her dwellings are set afire,
Her bars are broken.

31 Runner dashes to meet runner,
Messenger to meet messenger,
To report to the king of Babylon
That his city is captured, from end to end.

32 The fords are captured,
And the swamp thickets^a are consumed in fire;
And the fighting men are in panic.

33 For thus said the LORD of Hosts, the God of Israel:
Fair Babylon is like a threshing floor
Ready to be trodden;
In a little while her harvesttime will come.

34 "Nebuchadrezzar king of Babylon
Devoured me and discomfited me;
He swallowed me like a dragon,
He filled his belly with my dainties,
And set me down like an empty dish;
Then he ^b-rinsed me out.^-b

35 Let the violence done me and my kindred
Be upon Babylon,"
Says the inhabitant of Zion;
"And let my blood be upon the inhabitants of
        Chaldea,"
Says Jerusalem.

34–35: The *inhabitant of Zion* speaks to call for the punishment of *Nebuchadrezzar* and *Babylon* for oppression.

---

a *Meaning of Heb. uncertain.*   b-b *Meaning of Heb. uncertain.*

36 Assuredly, thus said the LORD:
I am going to uphold your cause
And take vengeance for you;
I will dry up her sea
And make her fountain run dry.

37 Babylon shall become rubble,
A den for jackals,
An object of horror and hissing,[a]
Without inhabitant.

38 Like lions, they roar together,
They growl like lion cubs.

39 [b]When they are heated, I will set out their drink
And get them drunk, that they may become
            hilarious[b]
And then sleep an endless sleep,
Never to awake   —declares the LORD.

40 I will bring them down like lambs for slaughter,
Like rams and he-goats.

41 How has Sheshach[c] been captured,
The praise of the whole earth been taken!
How has Babylon become
A horror to the nations!

42 The sea has risen over Babylon,
She is covered by its roaring waves.

43 Her towns are a desolation,
A land of desert and steppe,
A land no man lives in
And no human passes through.

44 And I will deal with Bel in Babylon,
And make him disgorge what he has swallowed,
And nations shall no more gaze on him with joy.
Even the wall of Babylon shall fall.

45 Depart from there, O My people,
Save your lives, each of you,
From the furious anger of the LORD.

46 Do not be downhearted or afraid
At the rumors heard in the land:
A rumor will come one year,
And another rumor the next year
Of violence in the land,
And of ruler against ruler.

47 Assuredly, days are coming,
When I will deal with Babylon's images;

36–44: God answers the inhabitant of Jerusalem, ensuring action against Babylonia. **41:** *Sheshach* is another example of "'atbash," a cryptic reference to Babylonia (see 25.26). **45–58:** The prophet calls upon Jews to escape from Babylonia, as it is now to be judged (cf. Isa. 48.20–21; contra Jer. ch 29).

a *See note at 18.16.*
b-b *Emendation yields "With poison [so Syriac] will I set out their drink / And get them drunk till they fall unconscious" (so ancient versions).*
c *See note at 25.26.*

Her whole land shall be shamed,
And all her slain shall fall in her midst.

48 Heavens and earth and all that is in them
Shall shout over Babylon;
For the ravagers shall come upon her from the
    north   —declares the LORD.

49 Yes, Babylon is to fall
[For] the slain of Israel,
As the slain of all the earth
Have fallen through Babylon.

50 You fugitives from the sword,
Go, don't delay!
Remember the LORD from afar,
And call Jerusalem to mind.

51 "We were shamed, we heard taunts;
Humiliation covered our faces,
When aliens entered
The sacred areas of the LORD's House."

52 Assuredly, days are coming
                —declares the LORD—
When I will deal with her images,
And throughout her land the dying shall groan.

53 Though Babylon should climb to the skies,
Though she fortify her strongholds up to heaven,
The ravagers would come against her from Me
                —declares the LORD.

54 Hark! an outcry from Babylon,
Great destruction from the land of the
    Chaldeans.

55 For the LORD is ravaging Babylon;
He will put an end to her great din,
Whose roar is like waves of mighty waters,
Whose tumultuous noise resounds.

56 For a ravager is coming upon Babylon,
Her warriors shall be captured, their bows shall be
    snapped.
For the LORD is a God of requital,
He deals retribution.

57 I will make her officials and wise men drunk,
Her governors and prefects and warriors;
And they shall sleep an endless sleep,
Never to awaken
                —declares the King whose name is
                    LORD of Hosts.

58 Thus said the LORD of Hosts:
Babylon's broad wall shall be knocked down,
And her high gates set afire.

48: This hymnic verse offers another example of measure for measure: Babylonia, the nation *from the north* (see 25.9 n.), will itself be punished *from the north.*

Peoples shall labor for naught,
And nations have wearied themselves for fire.

59 The instructions that the prophet Jeremiah gave to Seraiah son of Neriah son of Mahseiah, when the latter went with[a] King Zedekiah of Judah to Babylonia, in the fourth year of [Zedekiah's] reign. Seraiah was quartermaster.[b] 60 Jeremiah wrote down in one scroll all the disaster that would come upon Babylon, all these things that are written concerning Babylon. 61 And Jeremiah said to Seraiah, "When you get to Babylon, see that you read out all these words. 62 And say, 'O Lord, You Yourself have declared concerning this place that it shall be cut off, without inhabitant, man or beast; that it shall be a desolation for all time.' 63 And when you finish reading this scroll, tie a stone to it and hurl it into the Euphrates. 64 And say, 'Thus shall Babylon sink and never rise again, because of the disaster that I will bring upon it. And [nations] shall have wearied themselves [for fire].' "[c]

Thus far the words of Jeremiah.

52 [d]Zedekiah was twenty-one years old when he became king, and he reigned in Jerusalem for eleven years. His mother's name was Hamutal, daughter of Jeremiah of Libnah. 2 He did what was displeasing to the Lord, just as Jehoiakim had done. 3 Indeed, Jerusalem and Judah [e]were a cause of anger for the Lord, so that[e] He cast them out of His presence.

Zedekiah rebelled against the king of Babylon. 4 And in the ninth year of his[f] reign, on the tenth day of the tenth month, King Nebuchadrezzar moved against Jerusalem with his whole army. They besieged it and built towers against it all around. 5 The city continued in a state of siege until the eleventh year of King Zedekiah. 6 By the ninth

a Emendation yields "at the instance of."
b Meaning of Heb. uncertain.　　c Cf. v. 58, last line.
d For this chapter cf. chap. 39 above and 2 Kings 24–25.
e-e Meaning of Heb. uncertain.　　f I.e., Zedekiah's.

51.59–64: Jeremiah's instructions to Seraiah son of Neriah son of Mahseiah. 59: *Seraiah* is the brother of the scribe Baruch (see 32.12). His name appears on a clay bulla from ancient Jerusalem (see 32.11 n.). *The fourth year of [Zedekiah's] reign* would be 593 BCE. The reason for his journey to Babylon is not clear, although his title, "sar menuḥah," lit. "officer of rest" (translated as *quartermaster*), may actually read "sar minḥah," "officer of the tribute" (cf. *Tg. Jon.;* Rashi). This would suggest that he journeyed to Babylon to deliver Judah's annual tribute to the Babylonians. **62:** The prophet's words concerning the destruction of Babylonia appear to contradict his ad-

vice that the exiles accept Babylonian rule (ch 29), although they would point to Babylonia's punishment after its seventy-year rule is complete (cf. ch 25). **63:** The symbolic act of sinking the scroll in the Euphrates represents, or perhaps helps to bring about, Babylonia's downfall. Rabbinic sources suggest that Seraiah may be another name for Baruch, and employ this passage to justify the claim that Baruch is a prophet. The claim is disputed (see *Num. Rab.* 10.5; *b. Meg.* 14b–15a; *Num. Rab.* 8.9; *Midr. Ruth Rab.* 2.1; *Seder Olam* 20).

52.1–34: Narrative concerning the fall of Jerusalem. This ch largely duplicates 2 Kings 24.18–25.30, although it is slightly longer, and there are differences (see also ch 39). It appears here to illustrate the fulfillment of Jeremiah's prophecies that Judah would be punished if it did not submit to Babylonia (e.g., chs 25–29). The end of 51.64, *Thus far the words of Jeremiah,* clearly indicates that ch 52 was not an original part of the book, but was added as the book grew (cf. Ps. 72.20). The insertion of what might be termed "a historical narrative from Kings" that validates the earlier prophecies and legitimates the prophet may also be seen in Isa. chs 36–39. **1–3:** The initial regnal report gives personal details. Hamutal was also the mother of Jehoahaz, who was removed from the throne and deported to Egypt following Josiah's death in 609 BCE. Jehoiakim's mother was Zebudah daughter of Pedaiah of Rumah (2 Kings 23.36). **4–11:** The *ninth year of his reign* would be 589–588. The *tenth day of the tenth month* is the 10th of Tevet, which is observed as a fast day to mark the beginning of the siege (cf. Zech. 8.19). **5:** The *eleventh year of King Zedekiah* would be 587–586. **6:** The *ninth day of the fourth month* is the 9th of Tamuz. Although originally observed as a fast (Zech. 8.19), it was later replaced by the 17th day of Tamuz to commemorate the day that the Roman general Titus breached the walls of the day of the fourth month, the famine had become acute in the city; there was no food left for the common people.

⁷ Then [the wall of] the city was breached. All the soldiers fled; they left the city by night through the gate between the double walls, which is near the king's garden—the Chaldeans were all around the city—and they set out for the Arabah.ᵃ ⁸ But the Chaldean troops pursued the king, and they overtook Zedekiah in the steppes of Jericho, as his entire force left him and scattered. ⁹ They captured the king and brought him before the king of Babylon at Riblah, in the region of Hamath; and he put him on trial. ¹⁰ The king of Babylon had Zedekiah's sons slaughtered before his eyes; he also had all the officials of Judah slaughtered at Riblah. ¹¹ Then the eyes of Zedekiah were put out, and he was chained in bronze fetters. The king of Babylon brought him to Babylon and put him in prison, [where he remained] to the day of his death.

¹² On the tenth day of the fifth month—that was the nineteenth year of King Nebuchadrezzar, the king of Babylon—Nebuzaradan, the chief of the guards, came ᵇ⁻to represent⁻ᵇ the king of Babylon in Jerusalem. ¹³ He burned the House of the LORD, the king's palace, and all the houses of Jerusalem; he burned down the house of ᶜevery notable person.⁻ᶜ ¹⁴ The entire Chaldean force that was with the chief of the guards tore down all the walls of Jerusalem on every side. ¹⁵ The remnant of the people left in the city, the defectors who had gone over to the king of Babylon, and what remained of the craftsmenᵈ were taken into exile by Nebuzaradan, the chief of the guards. But some of the poorest elements of the population—¹⁶ some of the poorest in the land—were left by Nebuzaradan, the chief of the guards, to be vine-dressers and field hands.

¹⁷ The Chaldeans broke up the bronze columns of the House of the LORD, the stands, and the bronze tank that was in the House of the LORD; and they carried all the bronze away to Babylon. ¹⁸ They also took the pails, scrapers, snuffers, sprinkling bowls, ladles, and all the other bronze vessels used in the service. ¹⁹ The chief of the guards took whatever was of gold and whatever was of silver: basins, fire pans, sprinkling bowls, pails, lampstands, ladles, and jars. ²⁰ The two columns, the one tank and the twelve bronze oxen which supported it, and the stands, which King Solomon had provided for the House of the LORD—all these objects contained bronze beyond

Second Temple (see *b. Taʿan.* 28b). **7:** The *Arabah* is the dry Jordan rift that extends from the Jordan River and Dead Sea to the Gulf of Aqabah. **8:** *Jericho*, the major city in this region, is located west of the Jordan and 10 km (6 mi) north of the Dead Sea. **9–11:** *Hamath* is modern Hama in northern Syria. Nebuchadnezzar established his headquarters in *Riblah,* located in the Lebanese Beqaʿ Valley. Portions of vv. 10–11 are missing in 2 Kings 25.7. **12–16:** The *tenth day of the fifth month* is the 10th of Av, but 2 Kings 25.8 reads the *seventh day* or the 7th of Av. *B. Taʾanit* 29a reconciles these traditions by stating that Nebuzaradan entered the Temple on the 7th, set it on fire on the 9th, and it burned until the 10th. The 9th of Av (Tishʿah beʾav) is subsequently observed as the fast day. The Babylonians took skilled workers with them to Babylon, but left the poor and unskilled behind. **17–23:** A detailed list of the Temple vessels, furnishings, and fixtures that were taken by the Babylonians. See 1 Kings chs 6–7 for a detailed account of Solomon's construction and provision of the Temple. Some details do not appear in 2 Kings 25.13–17. **22:** The *pomegranates* were decorative, and may have symbolized the role of the Temple as the center of creation. **24–30:** The Babylonians deported a number of key officials and officers to Riblah, where they were executed before Nebuchadnezzar. **24:** *Seraiah the chief priest* is Seraiah son of Azariah (1 Chron. 5.40). Ezra is later identified as the son of Seraiah, which clearly must mean that he is a descendant of Seraiah (Ezra 7.1). *Zephaniah, the deputy priest,* cf. 21.1; 29.24; 37.3. **25:** Although this passage lists *seven royal privy councilors,* 2 Kings 25.19 lists only five. Rashi claims that two were of lesser importance. **28–30:** The passage enumerates the numbers of exiles for each of Nebuchadnezzar's three deportations: *the seventh year* (597 BCE) when Jehoiachin was deported; *the eighteenth year* (588) when Jerusalem was destroyed; *the twenty-third year* (582) when Gedaliah was as-

---

ᵃ *See note at 39.4.*   ᵇ⁻ᵇ *Lit. "he stood before."*   ᶜ⁻ᶜ *Meaning of Heb. uncertain.*
ᵈ *Apparently after the deportation of 2 Kings 24.14; meaning of Heb. uncertain.*

weighing. [21] As for the columns, each was eighteen cubits high and twelve cubits in circumference; it was hollow, and [the metal] was four fingers thick. [22] It had a bronze capital above it; the height of each capital was five cubits, and there was a meshwork [decorated] with pomegranates about the capital, all made of bronze; and so for the second column, also with pomegranates. [23] There were ninety-six pomegranates a-facing outward;-a all the pomegranates around the meshwork amounted to one hundred.

[24] The chief of the guards also took Seraiah the chief priest and Zephaniah, the deputy priest, and the three guardians of the threshold. [25] And from the city he took a eunuch who was in command of the soldiers; seven royal privy councilors, who were present in the city; the scribe of the army commander, who was in charge of mustering the people of the land; and sixty of the common people who were inside the city. [26] Nebuzaradan, the chief of the guards, took them and brought them to the king of Babylon at Riblah. [27] The king of Babylon had them struck down and put to death at Riblah, in the region of Hamath.

Thus Judah was exiled from its land. [28] This is the number of those whom Nebuchadrezzar exiled in the seventh year: 3,023 Judeans. [29] In the eighteenth year of Nebuchadrezzar, 832 persons [were exiled] from Jerusalem. [30] And in the twenty-third year of Nebuchadrezzar, Nebuzaradan, the chief of the guards, exiled 745 Judeans. The total amounted to 4,600 persons.

[31] In the thirty-seventh year of the exile of King Jehoiachin of Judah, on the twenty-fifth day of the twelfth month, King Evil-merodach of Babylon, in the year he became king, b-took note of-b King Jehoiachin of Judah and released him from prison. [32] He spoke kindly to him, and gave him a throne above those of other kings who were with him in Babylon. [33] He removed his prison garments and [Jehoiachin] ate regularly in his presence the rest of his life. [34] A regular allotment of food was given him by order of the king of Babylon, an allotment for each day, to the day of his death—all the days of his life.

sassinated (chs 41–42). 2 Kings 25.12 claims that the first deportation took place in Nebuchadnezzar's eighth year, but Radak states that the deportation began in the seventh and continued through the eighth. **28:** 2 Kings 25.14 claims that 10,000 Jews were deported at this time rather than 3,023. Rashi, following *Seder Olam,* reconciles the traditions by claiming that 10,000 refers to exiles from Israel and 3,023 refers to those from Judah. **29:** 2 Kings 25.8 states that the second deportation took place in the nineteenth, not the *eighteenth year* (cf. v. 12). Rashi and Radak indicate that the discrepancy follows from the earlier discrepancy concerning the first deportation. **31–34:** King Jehoiachin's release from prison. Many modern scholars view this concluding note as an attempt to end Jeremiah and Kings on an optimistic note, where the release of Jehoiachin is meant to foreshadow the broader return to Zion and reestablishment of the Davidic monarchy. **31:** The *twenty-fifth day of the twelfth month* is the 25th of Adar. 2 Kings 25.27 states that it was the twenty-seventh day. *Evil-merodach* is a Heb version of the name Amel-Marduk ("servant of Marduk"), the son of Nebuchadnezzar who ruled for only two years before he died (562–560).

a-a *Meaning of Heb. uncertain.*   b-b *Lit. "raised the head of."*

יחזקאל

Ezekiel

Character

THE BOOK OF EZEKIEL presents the words of Ezekiel son of Buzi, a prophet and a priest, and one of the Jerusalemites exiled to Babylonia with King Jehoiachin in 597 BCE by the Babylonian king Nebuchadnezzar (2 Kings 24.8–17). Like his older contemporary Jeremiah, Ezekiel lived through the time of the destruction of Jerusalem and the Temple in 586 and the early years of the Babylonian exile. He presents some of the most theologically challenging and dynamic material among the prophets of the Bible, and some of the most difficult and bizarre passages. His literary style is intricate, with striking imagery and extended metaphors. Many of his oracles are in prose, unlike the other classical prophets. Some of his visions border on the apocalyptic, and may be early examples of this type of literature. He wrestles with the problems posed by the tragedies of Jerusalem's destruction and the Babylonian exile: Why did God allow the Temple and Jerusalem to be destroyed? Why did God allow the people of Israel to be carried away into exile? What future is there for Israel?

The book of Ezekiel, like other biblical writings, attempts to justify the tragedy of the Babylonian exile by arguing that it was a divine punishment for the people's sin and by pointing to God's mercy in the future restoration. It contends that God intends to uphold the covenant with Israel for the sake of the sanctity of the divine name by restoring a remnant of the people to the land of Israel and placing a new Temple at its center. This new Temple is envisioned in detail at the end of the book. Indeed, the most famous chapter in Ezekiel (37), the prophecy concerning the valley of the dry bones, is part of that vision of restoration.

Ezekiel is both a priest and a prophet, and his writings are best understood as a combination of these aspects of his identity. As a priest of the House of Zadok (Zadok was appointed by Solomon as the high priest of the Jerusalem Temple [1 Kings 2.35]), he calls upon his own background to make his case. He often speaks in terms of purity and impurity, and alludes to the Priestly information in Leviticus. It is no accident that his book culminates with an extended description of the new Temple of the future restoration. Ezekiel also functions as a visionary prophet or oracle giver, much like Moses, who isolated himself to speak directly with God in the Tent of Meeting during the period of Israel's wandering in the wilderness (Exod. 33.7–11; 34.29–35; Num. 7.89). Ezekiel is keenly aware of his role as a prophet—as a watchman for Israel whose task is to warn of impending danger. His religious experiences are prophetic, as are his visions, symbolic actions, and oracles. They draw heavily upon Temple imagery and priestly practice, but they are couched in prophetic forms of discourse. His vision of the divine throne chariot or Presence of God in ch 1 appears to him in Babylonia, but it is based upon the features of the Ark of the Covenant that was housed in the Holy of Holies in the Jerusalem Temple. His portrayal of Jerusalem's destruction in ch 9 employs elements of priestly sacrifice at the altar, but it is the Temple itself that is destroyed. His vision of the new Temple in Jerusalem resembles the earlier wilderness tabernacle, Solomon's Temple, and the Second Temple, but it differs from all of them.

Composition

RABBINIC TRADITION MAINTAINS that the men of the great synagogue, a group of scholars that they believed lived in the early postexilic period, wrote Ezekiel (*b. B. Bat.* 15a). According to a rabbinic tradition, the book's status was questioned until R. Hananiah ben Hezekiah burned three hundred barrels of oil working nights in his upper chamber to resolve its contradictions with the Torah (*b. Shab.* 13b; *b. Ḥag.* 13a; *b. Menaḥ.* 45a). The Mishnah advises that ch 1 not be expounded before even one person unless he is a sage fully competent in Jewish tradition (*m. Ḥag.* 2.1), most likely because mystical traditions were associated with this text. Indeed, Ezekiel's visions of God later become the basis for the development of early Jewish mysticism in the rabbinic period and the later kabbalistic tradition.

Many modern scholars argue that Ezekiel is an edited book in which various elements, such as the prophecy concerning Gog of Magog (chs 38–39) or the vision of the new Temple (chs 40–48), are—in whole or in part—the products of writers other than Ezekiel, who form a "school of Ezekiel," namely a group deeply influenced by his writings who continued to write using his style and themes. Although a number of prophetic books—including Isaiah, Jeremiah, Hosea, and Amos—show clear signs of extensive later editing and composition, the case for Ezekiel is less compelling. The book is formulated largely as an autobiographical composition in which God instructs the prophet to speak or act out to Israelite exiles, much as God instructed Moses and Moses in turn instructed Israel. In a few cases there is evidence of later editorial work. For example, the clarification of the date of Ezekiel's first vision in 1.2–3 interrupts the prophet's autobiographical account with a third-person report of his name and other details. Additionally, the break in the chronological sequence beginning with the initial oracle concerning Egypt in 29.1 and the proliferation of date formulas for the other Egyptian oracles in 29.17; 30.20; 31.1; 32.1; and 32.17 suggest that the oracles concerning Egypt were an independent collection that was later incorporated into the present form of the book. Likewise, the reference to the twenty-seventh year in 29.17 disrupts the twenty-year chronological pattern that dominates the

rest of the book, and suggests to many that it was altered to account for the failure of Nebuchadnezzar to capture Tyre for some thirteen years (see 26.1). Otherwise, the formulation
of the book is well structured and relatively consistent, and appears to have been written
largely by the prophet himself.

Guide to Reading

RABBINIC TRADITION MAINTAINS that Ezekiel begins with judgment and ends in consolation (b. B. Bat. 14b). Modern scholars generally follow this view by arguing that the book
falls largely into three major parts: oracles of judgment against Jerusalem and Israel (chs
1–24); oracles of judgment against the nations (chs 25–32); oracles of restoration for Jerusalem and Israel at the center of the world (chs 33–48).

Although this accounts for the broad thematic patterns of the book, it appears to be organized according to a chronological scheme that is linked to the prophet's identity as a
Zadokite priest. The book begins with Ezekiel's inaugural vision of the divine throne
chariot in which he is commissioned by God to speak as a prophet to Israel (1.1–3.15). This
vision is dated to the fifth day of the fourth month in the thirtieth year, later specified as
the fifth year of the exile of King Jehoiachin, 5 Tamuz, 593 BCE. Apart from the reference to
the twenty-seventh year in 29.17 and the disruption of the chronological sequence in 29.1,
the book proceeds chronologically from the fifth year of Jehoiachin's exile to the twenty-
fifth year (40.1) with a series of major sections, each of which begins with its own date
formula. Each major section is further divided into oracle reports, each introduced with a
version of the prophetic word formula, "the word of the LORD came to me." The result is a
twenty-year sequence that begins with Ezekiel's visions by the Chebar canal in the Babylonian city of Tel Aviv, continues with oracles dated to the general period of the destruction of Jerusalem and the Temple, and culminates with his vision of the new Temple.
Insofar as the priests served in the Temple for twenty years, from the age of thirty to the
age of fifty (see Num. 4.23, 39; but note Num. 8.23–26, which specifies active service for
the Levites from the age of twenty-five to the age of fifty), it would appear that the book is
designed to portray Ezekiel's career in keeping with the period of active service for a
priest. This chronological ordering, where the progression of the oracles is connected to
the progress of the Babylonian destruction of Jerusalem, is unique among major prophetic
books, which are not otherwise organized chronologically. This ordering, however, com-
pensates for many of the other strange features of the book, and makes it relatively easy to
understand.

Summary of Contents

THE STRUCTURE OF THE BOOK includes thirteen major blocks, depicting his inaugural
vision in the fifth year of Jehoiachin's exile (593 BCE) and culminating with the vision of
the restored Temple in the twenty-fifth year (573).

[MARVIN A. SWEENEY]

1 In the thirtieth year,[a] on the fifth day of the fourth month, when I was in the community of exiles by the Chebar Canal, the heavens opened and I saw visions of God. [2] On the fifth day of the month—it was the fifth year of the exile of King Jehoiachin—[3] the word of the LORD came to the priest Ezekiel son of Buzi, by the Chebar Canal, in the land of the Chaldeans. And the hand of the LORD came upon him there.

a *We do not know the 30th of what.*

1.1–7.27: Introduction to the prophecy of Ezekiel: oracles concerning his inaugural vision. The first major section of the book begins with a date formula, which places the prophet's initial visions, symbolic actions, and oracles *in the thirtieth year, on the fifth day of the fourth month,* i.e., 5 Tamuz, 593 BCE (see 1.1–3 n.). The introduction includes a series of four narratives in 1.1–3.15; 3.16–5.17; 6.1–14; 7.1–27, each of which begins with a version of the formula *the word of the LORD came to me* (1.3; 3.16; 6.1; 7.1). These narrate his initial prophetic experiences in which God commissioned him to speak as a prophet. They include an account of his inaugural vision in 1.1–3.15, in which God commissions him to speak; his commission as a watchman in 3.16–5.17; his commission to prophesy against the hills of Israel in 6.1–14; and his commission to speak about the end of the land of Israel in 7.1–27. The date formula in 8.1 marks the beginning of the next major section of the book.

1.1–3.15: The inaugural vision and commissioning of Ezekiel. Ezekiel's first prophetic experience is stunningly graphic when compared to other inaugural visions of the prophets (that of Moses in Exod. ch 3 and of Isaiah in Isa. ch 6; cf. also 1 Kings 22.19–22). Ezekiel comes as close as possible to actually seeing God. He sees

God's throne, in technicolor detail, hears it move, and is literally swept away by the divine Presence. Ezek. 1.1–28; 3.12 serves as the haftarah reading for Exod. 19.1–20.23 (and Num. 28.26–31), read on the first day of Shav'uot (the Festival of Weeks) to commemorate the revelation of the Torah on Mt. Sinai. Rabbinic tradition refers to this narrative as "the episode of the chariot" because it employs the imagery of the Ark of the Covenant, referred to as God's chariot in 1 Chron. 28.18 (see also Pss. 68.18; 18.11), to depict the Presence of God. Because of the theologically sensitive nature of this material, the Mishnah requires that it be expounded only by a "sage that understands his own knowledge" (*m. Ḥag.* 2.1), i.e., by a sage with full competence in Jewish tradition. *M. Megillah* 4.10 states that the ch of the chariot should not be read at all, but R. Judah permits it. *T. Megillah* 4.34 also indicates that it could be read, but without the Aramaic Targum or translation that enabled many ancient Jewish congregations to understand the text. Ezekiel's vision of God's Presence later be-

⁴I looked, and lo, a stormy wind came sweeping out of the north—a huge cloud and flashing fire, surrounded by a radiance; and in the center of it, in the center of the fire, a gleam as of amber. ⁵In the center of it were also the figures of four creatures. And this was their appearance:

came the basis for a great deal of esoteric and mystical speculation concerning the nature of God and the hidden meanings of Scripture. Such works as 3 Enoch; the Heikhalot Rabbati ("the great palaces"); the Heikhalot Zutarti ("the lesser palaces"); Re'eyot Yeḥezkel ("the visions of Ezekiel"); and others depict attempts to ascend through the seven "palaces" or levels of heaven to behold the presence of God. Such works laid the foundation for the medieval kabbalistic and modern Hasidic traditions that continue to develop mystical notions concerning God, Scripture, and the world at large.

1.1–3: The introduction. Many prophetic books begin with a superscription that relates the identity, historical setting, and other relevant data about the prophet (Isa. 1.1; Jer. 1.1–3). Others begin with narrative statements by the editor of the book (Jonah 1.1; Zech. 1.1). Ezekiel is atypical in that it begins with a first-person autobiographical narrative, supplemented by an editor, that relates this information. **1:** The thirtieth year: The reference point of this is unclear. It may refer to the thirtieth year after the prophet's commission, the thirtieth year after Josiah's reform, the year of Jehoiachin's exile, or the date of the book's composition. The reference more likely refers to Ezekiel's age at the time of his commissioning. Ezekiel is a priest of the Zadokite line (1.3), and the age of Levitical priestly service begins at thirty (Num. 4.3; but Num. 8.23–25 states that it begins at twenty-five) and concludes at fifty. The dated oracles of the book extend from the fifth (1.2) to the twenty-fifth year of the exile (40.1), so that the book correlates Ezekiel's prophetic ora-

cles with the twenty years of active priestly service. The fifth day of the fourth month would be 5 Tamuz, the month in which the Babylonians later made the first breaches in the walls of Jerusalem (2 Kings 25.3–4; Jer. 52.6–7). The river Chebar is a canal known in Akkadian sources as "nar Kabari" that left the Euphrates River north of Babylon and continued for some 60 miles, passing through the city of Nippur and rejoining the Euphrates south of Warka or biblical Erech. **2:** The fifth year of the exile of King Jehoiachin, 593 BCE. Jehoiachin was exiled to Babylonia at the age of eighteen after only three months on the throne (2 Kings 24.8–17; cf. 2 Chron. 36.9–10). This v. is written by an editor, who apparently sought to relate the prophet's date to Jehoiachin's exile, a crucial and well-known event to his audience. **3:** The formula, the word of the LORD came to the priest Ezekiel, is based on the typical formula for introducing prophetic oracles (see 1 Sam. 15.10; 1 Kings 6.11; Jer. 1.4; Hos. 1.1). Other examples appear in Ezek. 3.16; 6.1; 7.1. According to the Mekhilta to Exod. 12.1, this statement employs an emphatic past tense verb to indicate that Ezekiel had already prophesied earlier in the land of Israel, since according to rabbinic tradition, the Shekhinah (divine presence) does not rest on a prophet outside of the land of Israel unless it has first rested upon the prophet in the land of Israel. The Mekhilta to Exod. 15.9 speculates that Ezek. 2.1 or 12.1 begin earlier prophecies received by Ezekiel while he was still in the land. Had he not been exiled, Ezekiel would probably have served as a Zadokite priest in the Temple. The land of the Chaldeans: Babylonia, so named after the Chaldeans, a tribe related to the Arameans that had become es-

pecially prominent in Babylonia by this time.

1.4–28a: The inaugural vision. The imagery of God's throne chariot (see 1 Chron. 28.15) is based on the Holy of Holies in the Temple where the Ark of the Covenant is kept under the cherubim (1 Kings ch 6; Exod. 25.10–22; 37.1–9). The Bible frequently refers to "the Ark of the Covenant of the LORD of Hosts enthroned on the Cherubim" (1 Sam. 4.4; 2 Sam. 6.2; 1 Chron. 13.6). Cherubim are composite creatures that combine features of different types of animals and human beings, e.g., the body of a lion or a bull, the wings of an eagle, and the head of a human being. Such creatures frequently appear in ancient Near Eastern art and architecture as the guardians of royal thrones, temples, and city gates and may have been well known to Ezekiel, who lived in Babylonia. Ezek. 10.1 later refers to the four creatures of this vision as cherubim. **4:** Wind, cloud, and fire appear frequently in texts that depict theophany or divine appearance in the world (Exod. ch 19; 1 Kings ch 19). The imagery of radiance reflects the gleaming gold with which the Ark and other Temple implements were overlaid (Exod. 25.10–22; 37.1–9). The exact meaning of the term "ḥashmal," translated here as a gleam as of amber, is uncertain. It may be derived from Akkadian or Egyptian terms for polished bronze. Talmudic tradition identifies it as a name for an angel or a combination of terms, such as "ḥayot" ("living creatures"), "'esh" ("fire"), or a combination of "ḥashot" ("silent") and "mimalelot" ("speaking"). The modern Heb "ḥashmal," "electricity," derives from this passage. **5:** The four creatures are the four cherubim that surround the Ark. Exod. 25.18–20; 37.7–9; 1 Kings 6.23–28; 1 Chron. 3.10–14 each mention only two cherubim, but this passage combines the totals. The combination is justified because the former texts mention two cherubim in relation to the Ark and the latter mention two

They had the figures of human beings. ⁶ However, each had four faces, and each of them had four wings; ⁷ the legs of each were [fused into] a single rigid leg, and the feet of each were like a single calf's hoof;ᵃ and their sparkleᵇ was like the luster of burnished bronze. ⁸ They had human hands below their wings. The four of them had their faces and their wings on their four sides. ⁹ Each one's wings touched those of the other. They did not turn when they moved; each could move in the direction of any of its faces.

¹⁰ Each of them had a human face [at the front]; each of the four had the face of a lion on the right; each of the four had the face of an ox on the left; and each of the four had the face of an eagle [at the back]. ¹¹ Such were their faces. As for their wings, they were separated: above, each had two touching those of the others, while the other two covered its body. ¹² And each could move in the direction of any of its faces; they went wherever the spirit impelled them to go, without turning when they moved.

¹³ Such then was the appearance of the creatures. With them was something that looked like burning coals of fire. This fire, suggestive of torches, kept moving about among the creatures; the fire had a radiance, and lightning issued from the fire. ¹⁴ᶜ Dashing to and fro [among] the creatures was something that looked like flares.ᶜ

¹⁵ As I gazed on the creatures, I saw one wheel on the ground next to each of the four-faced creatures. ¹⁶ As for the appearance and structure of the wheels, they gleamed like beryl. All four had the same form; the appearance and structure of each was as of two wheels cutting through each other. ¹⁷ And when they moved, each could move in the direction of any of its four quarters; they did not veer when they moved. ¹⁸ Their rims were tall and frightening, for the rims of all four were covered all over with eyes. ¹⁹ And when the creatures moved forward, the wheels moved at their sides; and when the creatures were borne above the earth, the wheels were borne too. ²⁰ Wherever the spirit impelled them to go, they went—wherever the spirit impelled them—and the wheels were borne alongside them; for the spirit of the creatures was in the wheels. ²¹ When those moved, these moved; and when those stood still, these stood still; and when those were borne above the earth, the wheels were borne alongside them— for the spirit of the creatures was in the wheels.

²² Above the heads of the creatures was a form: an expanse, with an awe-inspiring gleam as of crystal, was

cherubim as features of the Holy of Holies in the Temple. Ezekiel's total could be based upon his observation of the Ark in the Temple or his reading of earlier texts. The number four also presupposes the four horns of the Temple altar (Exod. 27.2; 38.2; Zech. 2.1–4), which represent the four "winds" or cardinal directions, indicating God's presence in the Temple at the center of creation. **7:** *Like:* The use of similes throughout this vision emphasizes that the prophet can only attempt to describe the divine Presence indirectly, as the limits of human understanding permit; the images are not to be understood as a literal representation of the divine Presence. This passage thus takes a middle position concerning the corporeality of God's representation; some texts describe God as having a human body (Exod. 24.10–11; Dan. 7.9), while others insist otherwise (Deut. 4.15). **10:** The four faces may represent the divine qualities of intelligence (*human*), royalty (*lion*), strength (*ox*), and mobility (*eagle*). **13–14:** The *burning coals of fire* presuppose the sacrificial altar of the Temple (Exod. 27.1–8; 38.1–7) or the incense altars (Exod. 30.1–10; 37.5–28). **15–21:** The *wheels* depict divine motion in all four directions. They are based on the image of the cart that carried the Ark of the Covenant from Philistia to Jerusalem (1 Sam. ch 6; 2 Sam. ch 6) and the rings that held the poles by which the Levites carried the Ark (Exod. 25.12– 15; 30.4–5). **16:** The *wheels cutting through each other* represent either a wheel with a hub or another attempt to depict wheels that could travel in any direction. **22:** *An expanse, with an awe-inspiring gleam as of crystal:* The priest Ezekiel is drawing on the Priestly Gen. 1.6–8, which uses the same term, "raki'a" (*expanse*, "firmament"), to depict the distinction between heaven and earth. The term "keraḥ" (*crystal*) also means "ice," which would draw upon the image of creation or manifestations of divine power as the congealing of waters (Gen. 1.8–9; Exod. 14.21–29; 15.8–9).

a I.e., cleft in front.   b Or "plumage."   c-c Meaning of Heb. uncertain.

spread out above their heads. ²³ Under the expanse, each had one pair of wings extended toward those of the others; and each had another pair covering its body. ²⁴ When they moved, I could hear the sound of their wings like the sound of mighty waters, like the sound of Shaddai,ª a tumult like the din of an army. When they stood still, they would let their wings droop. ²⁵ᵇ From above the expanse over their heads came a sound.·ᵇ When they stood still, they would let their wings droop.

²⁶ Above the expanse over their heads was the semblance of a throne, in appearance like sapphire; and on top, upon this semblance of a throne, there was the semblance of a human form. ²⁷ From what appeared as his loins up, I saw a gleam as of amber—ᵇ what looked like a fire encased in a frame;·ᵇ and from what appeared as his loins down, I saw what looked like fire. There was a radiance all about him. ²⁸ Like the appearance of the bow which shines in the clouds on a day of rain, such was the appearance of the surrounding radiance. That was the appearance of the semblance of the Presence of the LORD. When I beheld it, I flung myself down on my face. And I heard the voice of someone speaking.

2 And He said to me, "O mortal, stand up on your feet that I may speak to you." ² As He spoke to me, a spirit entered into me and set me upon my feet; and I heard what was being spoken to me. ³ He said to me, "O mortal, I am sending you to the people of Israel, that nation of rebels, who have rebelled against Me.—They as well as their fathers have defied Me to this very day; ⁴ for the sons are brazen of face and stubborn of heart. I send you to them, and you shall say to them: 'Thus said the Lord GOD'— ⁵ whether they listen or not, for they are a rebellious breed—that they may know that there was a prophet among them.

⁶ "And you, mortal, do not fear them and do not fear

Temple (1 Kings 8.54; Pss. 5.8; 99.5; 132.7; 138.2; 1 Chron. 16.29; 2 Chron. 20.5–18).

2.1–3.15: The commissioning of Ezekiel. For the commissioning of other prophets see Exod. ch 3; 1 Kings ch 22; Isa. ch 6; Jer. ch 1. **2.1–2:** God addresses Ezekiel as *mortal*, lit. "son of Adam" or "human," ninety-three times in the book. "Son of Adam" conveys Ezekiel's mortal status in contrast to God. *Midrash Tanḥuma, Zav* 13 understands the term disparagingly as it notes that unlike Isaiah's restrained account of God's revelation, Ezekiel relates everything that he saw. The *spirit* (lit. "wind") of the LORD, elsewhere associated with prophecy (see, e.g., 1 Kings 22.21–23), prepares Ezekiel to serve as a prophet (1 Sam. 10.6, 10; 1 Kings 18.12). **3–7:** The charge of Israel's rebellion against God is a constant theme throughout the prophets to justify Israel's suffering as an act of divine punishment. Habakkuk and Job question a theology in which those who suffer are presumed to have committed some sin, but they ultimately defend God's righteousness. Such charges of guilt for those who have suffered have been questioned by Jewish (and Christian) theologians in the aftermath of disasters such as the expulsion of the Jews from Spain in 1492 or the Shoah (Holocaust). **3:** The reference to *that nation of rebels* is actually plural ("those nations of rebels"), which rabbinic commentators generally understand as a reference to the tribes of Judah and Benjamin. **4:** The messenger formula, *Thus said the Lord GOD*, is a typical prophetic expression that indicates Ezekiel's role as God's representative (see Jer. 30.5, 12, 18; 31.2, 7, 15, 23, 35, 37; Amos 1.3, 6, 9, 11; 2.1). The formula ultimately derives from the practice of sending messengers for personal and business transactions or diplomatic purposes (Gen. 32.5; 45.9; 2 Kings 18.29; Isa. 36.14). **6:** *Do not fear*, a formula of encouragement, is said to Jeremiah in his dedication as

---

a Traditionally "the Almighty"; see Gen. 17.1.   *b-b Meaning of Heb. uncertain.*

24: *The sound of mighty waters* metaphorically portrays the vision as both auditory and visual. **26:** *Sapphire* (possibly lapis lazuli), see Exod. 24.10, which employs the imagery of blue sapphire or lapis to depict the pavement under God's feet, which humans see as the sky. **27:** *Gleam as of amber* and *fire* convey the power and incorporeality of the divine Presence. **28:** The rainbow symbolizes God's

covenant with creation (Gen. 9.8–17). *The Presence of the LORD*, a Priestly term for God's glory (Exod. 16.6–7; 40.34–38). *The voice of someone speaking:* Cf. 1 Kings 19.12, which portrays the divine Presence as "a still small voice" or "a soft murmuring sound." Ezekiel, in a sign of reverence and fear, lies prostrate before God just as one would lie prostrate before the Ark in the Holy of Holies of the their words, though thistles and thorns ᵃ-press against-ᵃ you, and you sit upon scorpions. Do not be afraid of their words and do not be dismayed by them, though they are a rebellious breed; ⁷ but speak My words to them, whether they listen or not, for they are rebellious.

⁸ "And you, mortal, heed what I say to you: Do not be rebellious like that rebellious breed. Open your mouth and eat what I am giving you." ⁹ As I looked, there was a hand stretched out to me, holding a written scroll. ¹⁰ He unrolled it before me, and it was inscribed on both the front and the back; on it were written lamentations, dirges, and woes.

3 He said to me, "Mortal, eat what is offered you; eat this scroll, and go speak to the House of Israel." ² So I opened my mouth, and He gave me this scroll to eat, ³ as He said to me, "Mortal, feed your stomach and fill your belly with this scroll that I give you." I ate it, and it tasted as sweet as honey to me.

⁴ Then He said to me, "Mortal, go to the House of Israel and repeat My very words to them. ⁵ For you are sent, not to a people of unintelligible speech and difficult language, but to the House of Israel—⁶ not to the many peoples of unintelligible speech and difficult language, whose talk you cannot understand. If I sent you to them, they would listen to you. ⁷ But the House of Israel will refuse to listen to you, for they refuse to listen to Me; for the whole House of Israel are brazen of forehead and stubborn of heart. ⁸ But I will make your face as hard as theirs, and your forehead as brazen as theirs. ⁹ I will make your forehead like adamant, harder than flint. Do not fear them, and do not be dismayed by them, though they are a rebellious breed."

¹⁰ Then He said to me: "Mortal, listen with your ears and receive into your mind all the words that I speak to you. ¹¹ Go to your people, the exile community, and speak to them. Say to them: Thus says the Lord GOD—whether they listen or not." ¹² Then a spirit carried me away, and behind me I heard a great roaring sound: ᵇ-"Blessed is the Presence of the LORD, in His place,"-ᵇ ¹³ with the sound of the wings of the creatures beating against one another, and the sound of the wheels beside them—a great roaring sound. ¹⁴ A spirit seized me and carried me away. I went in bitterness, in the fury of my spirit, while the hand of the LORD was strong upon me. ¹⁵ And I came to the exile community that dwelt in Tel Abib by the Chebar Canal, and I

well (1.8). **2.8–3.3:** Ezekiel eats the scroll to symbolize his internalizing the divine message. Symbolic actions using the prophet's mouth are an important part of other prophetic dedications (Isa. 6.6–7; Jer. 1.9). **3.3:** Although the scroll is inscribed with *lamentations, dirges, and woes* (2.10), Ezekiel states that it tasted *as sweet as honey* (Jer. 15.16). **3.4–11:** Ezekiel's mission is outlined. **6:** *Many peoples of unintelligible speech and difficult language,* see Isa. 33.19. Many peoples were conquered by the Assyrian and Babylonian empires, and the men were frequently required to serve in the conqueror's army. Such practice aids in explaining the many references throughout the Bible to the nations that threaten Jerusalem (Isa. 14.24–17; 17.12–14; Pss. 2; 46; 47; 48). God stresses that the message is for Israel, not the nations. **12–15:** The prophet relates his bitterness at being compelled to speak such a harsh message of judgment, yet he seems not to have the ambivalences concerning his prophetic role seen in Jeremiah. **12:** The statement, *Blessed is the Presence of the LORD, in His place*, appears as part of the "Kedushah" in the "ʿAmidah" prayer. The proposed emendation is almost certainly correct, and involves the confusion of a single letter with a very similar letter in the old Heb script. The emendation fits a main theme of the initial section of Ezekiel: divine abandonment reflected through the gradual departure of the divine spirit from the Temple (see esp. 11.23). **15:** *Tel Abib*, "hill of barley," likely derives from the Babylonian expression "til abubi," "hill of the flood"; the Tigris and Euphrates rivers make Babylonia prone to flooding in the spring. (The name was given to the new city of Tel Aviv in 1909 to symbolize the rebirth of the land of Israel.) As a result of this experience, Ezekiel sits stunned for seven days prior to speaking his oracles in the following passage. His seven days of silence may well relate to mourning practices (see esp. Job 2.13), or to the seven-day incubation period during the priestly or-

---

a-a Lit. "are with."
b-b Emendation yields "as the Presence of the LORD rose from where it stood."

remained where they dwelt. And for seven days I sat there stunned among them.

[16] After those seven days, the word of the LORD came to me: [17] "O mortal, I appoint you watchman for the House of Israel; and when you hear a word from My mouth, you must warn them for Me. [18] If I say to a wicked man, 'You shall die,' and you do not warn him—you do not speak to warn the wicked man of his wicked course in order to save his life—he, the wicked man, shall die for his iniquity, but I will require a reckoning for his blood from you. [19] But if you do warn the wicked man, and he does not turn back from his wickedness and his wicked course, he shall die for his iniquity, but you will have saved your own life. [20] Again, if a righteous man abandons his righteousness and does wrong, when I put a stumbling block before him, he shall die. He shall die for his sins; the righteous deeds that he did shall not be remembered; but because you did not warn him, I will require a reckoning for his blood from you. [21] If, however, you warn the righteous man not to sin, and he, the righteous, does not sin, he shall live because he took warning, and you will have saved your own life."

[22] Then the hand of the LORD came upon me there, and He said to me, "Arise, go out to the valley, and there I will speak with you." [23] I arose and went out to the valley, and there stood the Presence of the LORD, like the Presence that I had seen at the Chebar Canal; and I flung myself down on my face. [24] And a spirit entered into me and set me upon my feet. And He spoke to me, and said to me: "Go, shut yourself up in your house. [25] As for you, O mortal, cords have been placed upon you, and you have been bound with them, and you shall not go out among them.[a] [26] And I will make your tongue cleave to your palate, and you shall be dumb; you shall not be a reprover to them, for they are a rebellious breed. [27] But when I speak with

---

a I.e., the people.

---

dination ceremony (Lev. 8.33–35; Exod. 29.35–37). Ezekiel maintains priestly practice throughout the book, although he adapts his practice to account for his prophetic role and the changed circumstances of life outside of the Jerusalem Temple.

3.16–5.17: Initial commission as a watchman and related symbolic actions. This section presents oracles and symbolic actions that are concerned with the destruction of Jerusalem and fall of Judah. Although many scholars separate the accounts of Ezekiel's symbolic action in chs 4–5 from the accounts concerning his role as watchman (3.16–21) and his dumbness (3.22–27), these narratives provide an introduction to chs 4–5 by emphasizing Ezekiel's identity as a Zadokite priest. Chs 4–5 also continue the divine instruction speech that begins in

3.16–21, 3.22–27. **3.16–21:** God appoints Ezekiel as the *watchman for the House of Israel,* who is responsible for the lives and moral guidance of the people (Jer. 6.17; Hos. 9.8). This function corresponds to the fundamental responsibility of the priesthood to teach God's requirements to the people so that they will maintain their holy status (Lev. 10.10–11; Deut. 33.10; Ezek. 44.23; Hag. 2.20–23; 2 Chron. 15.3; cf. Exod. 24.12; 2 Kings 12.3). Like sentinels posted on city walls to watch for danger (2 Sam. 18.24; 2 Kings 9.14), gatekeepers are appointed from among the priests to guard the Temple (1 Chron. 9.17–27; 26.1–19). This watchman role is developed more fully in ch 33 and is consistent with the role of the prophet, who also watches and warns. The prophet's responsibility to warn the people concerning their wickedness is presented in four cases. If the prophet fails to warn the person, then he is responsible for the person's sin. If the person is warned, however, and fails to act righteously or abandons righteousness, then the person is responsible. These principles are further developed in rabbinic culture, where an individual is only fully culpable for a sin after being forewarned. **3.22–27:** The conditions of Ezekiel's mission: isolation and silence. The meaning of this silence is unclear, but may suggest that Ezekiel must be silent except when he is speaking the divine word. **24–25:** *Shut yourself up . . . you shall not go out:* Ezekiel's isolation resembles that of Moses, who spoke directly to God as an oracle diviner in the Tent of Meeting (Exod. 33.7–11; 34.35; Num. ch 11), and the high priest, who appears alone before God and the Ark at Yom Kippur or the Day of Atonement (Lev. ch 16). **26:** God prevents Ezekiel from carrying out his role as one who warns Israel. Like Balaam in Num. chs 22–24, he cannot speak except for what God tells him.

you, I will open your mouth, and you shall say to them, 'Thus says the Lord GOD!' He who listens will listen, and he who does not will not—for they are a rebellious breed."

4 "And you, O mortal, take a brick and put it in front of you, and incise on it a city, Jerusalem. ²Set up a siege against it, and build towers against it, and cast a mound against it; pitch camps against it, and bring up battering rams roundabout it. ³Then take an iron plate and place it as an iron wall between yourself and the city, and set your face against it. ᵃThus it shall be under siege, you shall besiege it. This shall be an omen for the House of Israel.

⁴ "Then lie on your left side, and let it bear the punishment of the House of Israel;ᵇ for as many days as you lie on it you shall bear their punishment. ⁵For I impose upon you three hundred and ninety days, corresponding to the number of the years of their punishment; and so you shall bear the punishment for the House of Israel. ⁶When you have completed these, you shall lie another forty days on your right side, and bear the punishment of the House of Judah.ᵇ I impose on you one day for each year.

⁷ "Then, with bared arm, set your face toward besieged Jerusalem and prophesy against it. ⁸Now I put cords upon you, so that you cannot turn from side to side until you complete your days of siege.

⁹ "Further, take wheat, barley, beans, lentils, millet, and emmer. Put them into one vessel and bake them into bread. Eat it as many days as you lie on your side: three hundred and ninety. ¹⁰The food that you eat shall be by weight, twenty shekels a day; this you shall eat in the space of a day. ¹¹And you shall drink water by measure; drink a sixth of a *hin* in the space of a day.

¹² "Eat it as a barleyᶜ cake; you shall bake it on human excrement before their eyes. ¹³So," said the LORD, "shall the people of Israel eat their bread, unclean, among the nations to which I will banish them." ¹⁴Then I said, "Ah,

---

a I.e., in hostility.
b Since left and right also denote north and south (e.g., 16.46), the left side represents Israel, the northern kingdom, and the right side Judah, the southern kingdom.
c Meaning of Heb. uncertain.

4.1–5.17: God instructs Ezekiel to perform symbolic actions. Prophets perform symbolic actions to dramatize their statements and enable them to take effect (Isa. ch 20; Jer. chs 13; 19). Such actions also support the fundamental role of the priests as the teachers of "torah" to the people (Lev. 10.10–11; Deut. 33.10). **4.1–8:** God instructs Ezekiel to build a model of Jerusalem under siege. The action draws upon the imagery of Jer. 1.18. **4–6:** The basis for calculating *three hundred and ninety* years for the sin of Israel and *forty* years for

the sin of Judah is not entirely certain. The Septuagint states that Ezekiel shall lie on his left side for one hundred fifty or one hundred ninety days for the sin of Israel and forty days for the sin of Judah. Ezekiel thus symbolically bears the punishment of the people in keeping with the role of the priests to bear the guilt of the sanctuary (Num. 18.1). Rashi follows *Seder Olam* 26 by stating that Israel sinned for three hundred ninety years from the time that Israel entered the land under Joshua until the destruction of the Northern Kingdom of Israel in the reign of King Hoshea Son of Elah. He also notes the calculations of R. Joseph, who states that Israel sinned in the period of the Judges for one hundred fifty-one years and in the period of the northern kings for two hundred thirty-nine years. The forty years of Judah's sin includes twenty-two years for King Manasseh son of Hezekiah (based on the statement in 2 Kings 21.3 that compares Manasseh to Ahab son of Omri, who ruled for twenty-two years), two years for Amon son of Manasseh, eleven years for Jehoiakim son of Josiah, and five years for Zedekiah son of Josiah (since Ezekiel received prophecy in the fifth year of his reign). Because Josiah was righteous, the years of his reign are not included. An alternative calculation is possible. If one counts backwards from the destruction of the Temple in 586 BCE, the total of four hundred thirty years points to the time of the establishment of the united monarchy of Israel under Saul in 1016 (the calculation of Saul's reign is problematic; see 1 Sam. 13.1). Three hundred ninety years forward from that date takes one to 627, the twelfth year of Josiah's reign, in which his reforms begin (2 Chron. 34.3; cf. 2 Kings 22.3). Josiah failed in his attempt to reunite Israel and Judah. The remaining forty years accounts for the time between the beginning of Josiah's reform and the destruction of Jerusalem in 586. **9–17:** God instructs Ezekiel to perform a second symbolic act that requires him to

Lord GOD, my person was never defiled; nor have I eaten anything that died of itself or was torn by beasts from my youth until now, nor has foul flesh entered my mouth." ¹⁵ He answered me, "See, I allow you cow's dung instead of human excrement; prepare your bread on that."

¹⁶ ᵃ And He said to me, "O mortal, I am going to break the staff of bread in Jerusalem, and they shall eat bread by weight, in anxiety, and drink water by measure, in horror, ¹⁷ so that, lacking bread and water, they shall stare at each

5 other, heartsick over their iniquity. ¹ And you, O mortal, take a sharp knife; use it as a barber's razor and pass it over your head and beard. Then take scales and divide the hair.ᵇ ² When the days of siege are completed, destroy a third part in fire in the city, take a third and strike it with the sword all around ᶜ the city,ᶜ and scatter a third to the wind and unsheatheᵈ a sword after them.

³ "Take also a few [hairs] from there and tie them up in your skirts. ⁴ And take some more of them and cast them into the fire, and burn them in the fire. From this a fire shall go out upon the whole House of Israel."

⁵ Thus said the Lord GOD: I set this Jerusalem in the midst of nations, with countries round about her. ⁶ But she rebelled against My rules and My laws, acting more wickedly than the nations and the countries round about her; sheᵉ rejected My rules and disobeyed My laws. ⁷ Assuredly, thus said the Lord GOD: Because you have outdone the nations that are round about you—you have not obeyed My laws or followed My rules, nor have you observed the rules of the nations round about you—⁸ assuredly, thus said the Lord GOD: I, in turn, am going to deal with you, and I will execute judgments in your midst in the sight of the nations. ⁹ On account of all your abominations, I will do among you what I have never done, and the like of which I will never do again.

¹⁰ Assuredly, parents shall eat their children in your midst, and children shall eat their parents. I will execute judgments against you, and I will scatter all your survivors in every direction.

¹¹ Assuredly, as I live—said the Lord GOD—because you defiled My Sanctuary with all your detestable things and all your abominations, I in turn will shear [you] awayᶠ and show no pity. I in turn will show no compassion: ¹² One-third of you shall die of pestilence or perish in your midst

eat impure food in an impure land. As a priest, Ezekiel would live in the holy precincts of the Temple and eat only food that had been properly offered by the people at the Temple and prepared in accordance with the dietary laws of the time (see Lev. chs 7; 10–11; Num. ch 18; Deut. ch 14). The coming disaster will result in the people lacking food, so that they and the priests will be compelled to violate their food restrictions, and will have to eat impure food when Jerusalem and the Temple are under seige and ultimately destroyed. Ezekiel mixes a variety of grains, including those not normally consumed in bread, to demonstrate that there is insufficient grain to make an entire loaf of bread. *Twenty shekels,* about 225 gm (10 ounces). *A sixth of a hin,* about six-tenths of a liter (two-thirds of a quart). In order to demonstrate the difficult and impure conditions of the coming siege, God commands Ezekiel to bake bread using human dung as fuel. When he protests that this is a severe breach of priestly purity, God allows him to use cow's dung, which was used as a fuel, especially when wood was not available. **16–17:** See Isa. 3.1. **5.1–4:** The *sharp knife* (alternatively, "sharp sword") or *barber's razor* (Isa. 7.20) symbolizes the weapons of the Babylonians. One third of the hair is burned to represent those who die when the city is burned; one third is struck with the sword to symbolize those killed around the city; and one third is scattered to symbolize those who escape only to be pursued by the Babylonians. Some of the hair is burned once again to symbolize the suffering of the people. **5–17:** God concludes the instruction speech to Ezekiel by summing up the significance of the punishment and impurity that Ezekiel's symbolic actions illustrate. Charging that Israel acts like the nations (see 1 Sam. 8.4–5) by defiling the Temple, God suggests that the people will be treated like the nations, and will suffer war and

a Resuming the thought of v. 11.   b Lit. "them."   c-c Heb. "it."
d Cf. v. 12; lit. "I will unsheathe."   e Heb. "they."
f Cf. Isa. 15.2 and Jer. 48.37; here an allusion to the symbolism in v. 1.

by famine, one-third shall fall by the sword around you, and I will scatter one-third in every direction and will unsheathe the sword after them. [13] I will vent all My anger and satisfy My fury upon them; and when I vent all My fury upon them, they shall know that I the LORD have spoken in My passion. [14] I will make you a ruin and a mockery among the nations roundabout you, in the sight of every passerby. [15] And when I execute judgment upon you in anger and rage and furious chastisement, you[a] shall be a mockery and a derision, a warning and a horror, to the nations roundabout you: I the LORD have spoken. [16] When I loose the deadly arrows of famine against those doomed to destruction, when I loose them against you to destroy you, I will heap more famine upon you and break your staff of bread. [17] I will let loose against you famine and wild beasts and they shall bereave you; pestilence and bloodshed shall sweep through you, and I will bring the sword upon you. I the LORD have spoken.

6 The word of the LORD came to me: [2] O mortal, turn your face toward the mountains of Israel and prophesy to them [3] and say: O mountains of Israel, hear the word of the Lord GOD. Thus said the Lord GOD to the mountains and the hills, to the streams and the valleys: See, I will bring a sword against you and destroy your shrines. [4] Your altars shall be wrecked and your incense stands smashed, and I will hurl down your slain in front of your fetishes. [5] I will cast the corpses of the people of Israel in front of their fetishes, and scatter your bones around your altars [6] in all your settlements. The towns shall be laid waste and the shrines shall be devastated. Thus your altars shall be laid waste and [b]-bear their punishment;[-b] your fetishes shall be smashed and annihilated, your incense stands cut down, and your handiwork wiped out; [7] and the slain shall fall in your midst. Then you shall know that I am the LORD. [8] Yet I will leave a remnant, in that some of you shall escape the sword among the nations and be scattered through the lands. [9] And those of you that escape will remember Me among the na-

a Heb. "she."   b-b Targum and other ancient versions read "shall be devastated."

exile, ultimately perishing by pestilence, famine, and sword. **14:** God's threat to make Israel *a ruin and a mockery among the nations roundabout you* and to unleash famine, wild animals, etc., against the people recalls threats made in the roughly contemporaneous Jer. 24.9–10 (see also Deut. 28.37; 1 Kings 9.7).

6.1–14: Oracle against the mountains of Israel. 1: The passage begins with the prophetic word for-

mula, *the word of the LORD came to me* (see 1.3; 3.16; 7.1). Ezekiel does not distinguish between Israel and Judah, but addresses the entire land and people of Israel arrayed around the Temple (Num. ch 2; Ezek. ch 48). The Holy of Holies serves as the sacred center of the Temple, the Jerusalem Temple as the sacred center of Israel, and Israel as sacred center of the world. **2:** *The mountains of Israel,* the biblical homeland of Israel in the hills of Samaria and Judah. The choice of mountains may reflect the invocation of *mountains* as witnesses elsewhere in the Bible (e.g., Deut. 32.1; Isa. 1.2). **3–7:** Ezekiel identifies the cause of punishment in the various altars and high places where the people worship, which compromise the sanctity of the land. An example of such a sanctuary was excavated at the site of 7th-century Arad, where a "matzevah" or cultic pillar was found in the Holy of Holies of the temple located there. Ezekiel holds that legitimate worship of God must take place only in the Jerusalem Temple (Deut. ch 12). In contrast to other prophets such as Amos and Isaiah, Ezekiel tends to emphasize the people's cultic infractions rather than moral sins. **5:** The scattering of dead corpses around the altars renders the land impure (Num. ch 19; see also Lev. 21.10–12). **7:** Ezekiel employs the so-called "proof saying," *then you shall know that I am the LORD,* throughout the book to identify God as the source of his prophetic words. The "proof saying" appears especially in the context of priestly instruction as a means to validate the particular teaching at hand (Exod. 20.2; Lev. 19.3, 4, etc.; see also Exod. 3.13–22; Deut. 5.6). It is extremely common in Ezekiel, appearing over fifty times, four times in this chapter alone (vv. 7, 10, 13, 14). **8–10:** Ezekiel relies on Isaiah's concept of a remnant of Israel (Isa. 4.2–6; 6.13; 10.20–23) to demonstrate that God's power to destroy and punish will leave only a portion of the people to be scattered among the tions where they have been taken captive, [a]how I was bro-kenhearted through[a] their faithless hearts which turned away from Me, and through their eyes which lusted after their fetishes. And they shall loathe themselves for all the evil they committed and for all their abominable deeds. [10] Then they shall realize it was not without cause that I the LORD resolved to bring this evil upon them.

[11] Thus said the Lord GOD: Strike your hands together and stamp your feet and cry: Aha! over all the vile abomi-nations of the House of Israel who shall fall by the sword, by famine, and by pestilence. [12] He who is far away shall die of pestilence, and he who is near shall fall by the sword, and he who survives and is protected shall die of famine. Thus I will spend My fury upon them. [13] And you shall know that I am the LORD, when your slain lie among the fetishes round about their altars, on every high hill, on all the mountaintops, under every green tree, and under every leafy oak—wherever they presented pleasing odors to all their fetishes.

[14] I will stretch out My hand against them, and lay the land waste and desolate in all their settlements, from the wilderness as far as Diblah;[b] then they shall know that I am the LORD.

7 The word of the LORD came to me: [2] You, O mortal, [say:] Thus said the Lord GOD to the land of Israel: Doom! Doom is coming upon the four corners of the land. [3] Now doom is upon you! I will let loose My anger against you and judge you according to your ways; I will requite you for all your abominations. [4] I will show you no pity and no compassion; but I will requite you for your ways and for the abominations in your midst. And you shall know that I am the LORD.

[5] Thus said the Lord GOD: [c]A singular disaster; a disas-ter[c] is coming. [6] Doom is coming! The hour of doom is coming! It stirs against you; there it comes! [7] [d]The cycle has come around for you, O inhabitants of the land; the time has come; the day is near. There is panic on the mountains, not joy.[d] [8] Very soon I will pour out My wrath

a-a Emendation yields "how I broke."

b A few Heb. mss. read "Riblah"; cf. 2 Kings 23.33; 25.6 ff.

c-c A number of mss. and editions, as well as Targum, read "Disaster after disaster."

d-d Meaning of Heb. uncertain.

nations. **11–14:** Ezekiel returns to the imagery of sword, pestilence, and famine (5.1–17) to tie his ora-cles against Israel to the fate of Je-rusalem. **13:** *Altars, on every high hill, on all the mountaintops, under every green tree, and under every leafy oak,* a common Deuteronomic formulaic description of pagan worship (Deut. 12.2; 1 Kings 14.23;

Jer. 2.20). **14:** The *wilderness* desig-nates the Negev desert in southern Judah. *Diblah:* Some manuscripts read *Riblah* (see translators' note *b;* Heb letters "resh" and "dalet" are similar and sometimes confused; see "Reuel" in Num. 2.14, but "Deuel" in Num. 1.14), apparently based on the reference to the Ara-mean city Riblah where Pharaoh Neco of Egypt imprisoned King Je-hoahaz son of Josiah after remov-ing him from the throne (2 Kings 23.33). It is also the place where the Babylonian king Nebuchad-nezzar camped during the de-struction of Jerusalem (2 Kings 25.6). Riblah is situated on the northern border of Israel (Num. 34.11).

7.1–27: Prophecy of doom. The passage begins with the prophetic word formula, *the word of the LORD came to me.* Ezekiel's three oracles draw upon the "Day of the LORD" traditions to announce the "doom" of Israel (Amos 5.18–20; 8.1–14; Isa. 2.6–22; ch 13). This passage is the culmination of the first major section of the book, presenting the "doom" of Israel as the outcome of God's initial revelation to Ezekiel in 1.1–3.15. Perhaps as the culmi-nating prophecy, it is more poetic in style than the previous chapters. The "Day of the LORD" motif ap-parently functioned originally as an announcement of God's de-fense of Israel, but various proph-ets reconfigured it as an announce-ment of God's punishment against Israel and Judah (see esp. Amos 5.18–20; Zeph. 1.7–18; 2.1–3). The motif could also express God's de-cision to punish the nations that carried out punishment against Is-rael (see Obadiah; Joel). **1–4:** The first oracle announces the doom of Israel. **2:** *Doom* is drawn from Amos's prophecy against Bethel (Amos 8.1–3), which includes the imagery of dead bodies scattered about the altar as in 6.1–7. The *four corners of the land* indicates the complete destruction of the land, and rehearses the four cardinal di-rections that underlie the symbol-ism of the four living creatures in ch 1 and the four horns of the Tem-upon you and spend My anger on you; I will judge you according to your ways, and I will requite you for all your abominations. 9 I will show you no pity and no compassion; but I will requite you for your ways, and for the abominations in your midst. And you shall know it was I the LORD who punished.

10 Here is the day! See, the ᵃ·cycle has come round; it has appeared. The rod has blossomed; arrogance has budded, 11 lawlessness has grown into a rod of wickedness. Nothing comes of them, nor of their abundance, nor of their wealth; nor is there preeminence among them.·ᵃ 12 The time has come, the day has arrived. Let not the buyer rejoice nor the seller mourn—for divine wrath shall overtake all her multitude. 13 For the seller shall not return to what he sold so long as they remain among the living. For the vision concerns all her multitude, it shall not be revoked. And because of his guilt, no man shall hold fast to his life.

14 They have sounded the horn, and all is prepared; but no one goes to battle, for My wrath is directed against all her multitude. 15 The sword is outside and pestilence and famine are inside; he who is in the open shall die by the sword, he who is in the town shall be devoured by famine and pestilence. 16 And if any survive, they shall take to the mountains; they shall be ᵇ·like doves of the valley, moaning together·ᵇ—every one for his iniquity. 17 All hands shall grow weak, and all knees shall turn to water. 18 They shall gird on sackcloth, and horror shall cover them; every face shall betray shame, and every head shall be made bald.

19 They shall throw their silver into the streets, and their gold shall be treated as something unclean. Their silver and gold shall not avail to save them in the day of the LORD's wrath—to satisfy their hunger or to fill their stomachs. Because they made them stumble into guilt—20 for out of their beautiful adornments, in which they took pride, they made their images and their detestable abominations—therefore I will make themᶜ an unclean thing to them. 21 I will give them as spoil to strangers, and as plunder to the wicked of the earth; and they shall defile them. 22 I will turn My face from them, and My treasures shall be defiled; ruffians shall invade it and defile it.

23 ᵃ·Forge the chain,·ᵃ for the land is full of bloody crimes, and the city is full of lawlessness. 24 I will bring in

ple altar (Exod. 27.1–2; 37.25; Zech. 2.1–4). **5–9:** Ezekiel again employs the statement *doom is coming*, but shifts his language to that of the "Day of the LORD" traditions. **10–27:** The third oracle elaborates upon the imagery of the land's destruction in the "Day of the LORD." **10–11:** The blossoming *rod* may recall Aaron's rod which designates Levi as the priestly tribe (Num. ch 17), but Jeremiah (also a priest) employs it as a sign of Judah's punishment (Jer. 1.11–12). The ivory pomegranate-shaped cap, recently acquired by the Israel Museum in Jerusalem, is believed to have once adorned the rod of a Temple priest. The reference to the budding *arrogance* indicates Ezekiel's view that the priestly rod is now employed for the punishment of Israel, just as Moses' rod punished Egypt (Exod. chs 7–11). **12–13:** Normal life will end. Radak maintains that the buyer is happy with a purchase whereas the seller mourns for that which is sold (see also *b. B. M.* 51a). The buyer may not rejoice because he will soon be exiled and therefore lose what he has bought. The seller may not mourn because he is going into exile and would have lost the property anyway. Normally, land that was sold to pay a debt would be returned to the original owner during the jubilee year (Lev. ch 25). **14–17:** Ezekiel again takes up the imagery of *sword, pestilence,* and *famine* (chs 5–6). **18–21:** See Isa. 2.6–21, which anticipates that people will throw away their silver and gold idols on the "Day of the LORD." **20:** *An unclean thing:* Heb "nidah," menstrual flow, considered ritually impure (Lev. 15.19–30; 18.19; 20.18), serves as a metaphor for the impurity of idols. See also Zeph. 1.18; Lam. 1.17. **22:** God will withdraw His protection from the people. *My treasures,* actually singular (Heb "tzafun"), lit. "hidden," is understood to refer to the Holy of Holies in the Temple, which shall be defiled when Jerusalem is taken. **23–27:** Ezekiel makes it clear that the leaders (vv. 26–27: *prophet, priest, elders, king, prince,*

a-a *Meaning of Heb. uncertain.*
b-b *Emendation yields "like moaning doves. All of them shall perish."*
c *I.e., their adornments.*

the worst of the nations to take possession of their houses; so shall I turn to naught the pride of the powerful, and their sanctuaries shall be defiled.

25 Horror[a] comes, and they shall seek safety, but there shall be none. 26 Calamity shall follow calamity, and rumor follow rumor. Then they shall seek vision from the prophet in vain; instruction shall perish from the priest, and counsel from the elders. 27 The king shall mourn, the prince shall clothe himself with desolation, and the hands of the people of the land shall tremble. I will treat them in accordance with their own ways and judge them according to their deserts. And they shall know that I am the LORD.

8 In the sixth year, on the fifth day of the sixth month, I was sitting at home, and the elders of Judah were sitting before me, and there the hand of the Lord GOD fell upon me. 2 As I looked, there was a figure that had the appearance of fire:[b] from what appeared as his loins down, [he was] fire; and from his loins up, his appearance was resplendent and had the color of amber. 3 He stretched out the form of a hand, and took me by the hair of my head. A spirit lifted me up between heaven and earth and brought me in visions of God to Jerusalem, to the entrance of the

a Meaning of Heb. uncertain.   b Septuagint "a man."

the people [others "the landed gentry"]) are responsible for the punishment because of their own actions. Because they did not act properly in the past, they will be unable to fulfill their roles at the time of disaster when the people will need them the most. The so-called "proof saying," *they shall know that I am the LORD,* brings the oracle to a close.

8.1–19.14: Oracles concerning the vision of God's departure from the Temple. The second major section of the book focuses on Ezekiel's vision of God's departure from the Jerusalem Temple and the following oracles that elaborate upon the significance of this event. The section begins with a date formula in 8.1, *in the sixth year, on the fifth day of the sixth month,* i.e., 5 Elul, 592 BCE, fourteen months after his inaugural vision. Following the initial presentation of his second vision in 8.1–11.13, a series

of fourteen oracle accounts follow in 11.14–25; 12.1–7; 12.8–16; 12.17–20; 12.21–25; 12.26–28; 13.1–23; 14.1–11; 14.12–23; 15.1–8; 16.1–63; 17.1–10; 17.11–24; 18.1–19.14. Whereas the vision account begins with the formula, *and there the hand of the Lord GOD fell upon me,* the oracle accounts each begin with a version of the typical prophetic formula, *and the word of the LORD came to me.* Many scholars group the prophet's vision of God's departure in chs 8–11 with the account of his inaugural vision in chs 1–7, but the presence of the date formulas and the prophetic formulas indicates an interest in setting out the prophet's vision, and then providing oracles that elaborate upon its significance or meaning. Overall, the oracles prompt the reader to consider the means by which Jerusalem will be purified later so that the restoration of Israel and God's Presence to Jerusalem may take place.

8.1–11.13: Vision of the destruction of Jerusalem. The account of Ezekiel's vision employs the imagery of priestly sacrifice to portray the destruction of Jerusalem and the departure of the divine Presence as an act that purges the city from impurity. The imagery draws upon the conceptualization of the purification (or sin) offering ("ḥaṭa't"; see Lev. 7.7–10; 4.1–5.13) and the guilt offering ("'asham"; see Lev. 7.1–6; 5.14–26), which both function as part of the process by which the priests purge the Temple by making atonement for the sins, particularly the ritual impurities, of the people (see also Num. 18.1; Lev. ch 16). Such atonement replaces the need to purge the community of persons who commit sins, but when the sanctity of the Temple is so thoroughly compromised, such sacrifices are hardly acceptable (see Hag. 1.1–11; 2.10–19). Instead, the people who have committed sins are to be purged themselves as part of the overall scenario for God's destruction of Jerusalem and the Temple. Accounts of such purges appear in Exod. chs 32–34, in which the Levites slaughtered those who worshipped the golden calf at Mt. Sinai; Num. ch 14, in which God decided to kill the wilderness generation because of their failure to accept God's promise of the land of Israel; Num. ch 16, in which Korah, Dathan, and Abiram were killed for compromising the sanctity of the people by making improper offerings; Josh. ch 7, in which Achan and his family were killed for having stolen from the sacred treasury of the people; 1 Kings ch 18, in which the four hundred fifty prophets of Baal and the four hundred prophets of Asherah were killed because of their idolatry; etc. Various narratives likewise recount the purging of the Temple in the time of Hezekiah (1 Kings 18.1–8; 2 Chron. chs 29–31); Josiah (2 Kings 23.1–25); and Judah the Maccabee (1 Macc. 4.36–51). Although Ezekiel functions as prophet in relating this vision, his prophetic role is heavily influenced by his priestly identity.

Penimith[a] Gate that faces north; that was the site of the in-furiating image that provokes fury. [4] And the Presence of the God of Israel appeared there, like the vision that I had seen in the valley.[b]

[5] And He said to me, "O mortal, turn your eyes north-ward." I turned my eyes northward, and there, [c]north of the gate of the altar, was[-c] that infuriating image on the ap-proach.[a] [6] And He said to me, "Mortal, do you see what they are doing, the terrible abominations that the House of Israel is practicing here, [d]to drive Me far[-d] from My Sanctuary? You shall yet see even greater abominations!"

[7] Then He brought me to the entrance of the court;[e] and I looked, and there was a hole in the wall. [8] He said to me, "Mortal, break through the wall"; so I broke through the wall and found an entrance. [9] And He said to me, "Enter and see the vile abominations that they are practicing here." [10] I entered and looked, and there all detestable forms of creeping things and beasts and all the fetishes of the House of Israel were depicted over the entire wall. [11] Before them stood seventy men, elders of the House of Israel, with Jaazaniah son of Shaphan standing in their midst. Everyone had a censer in his hand, and a thick cloud of incense smoke ascended. [12] Again He spoke to me, "O mortal, have you seen what the elders of the House of Israel are doing in the darkness, everyone in his image-covered chamber? For they say, 'The LORD does not

a Meaning of Heb. uncertain.   b See chap. 1 and 3.22–23.
c-c Meaning of Heb. uncertain; emendation yields "north of the gate was the altar of."
d-d Or "at a distance."   e I.e., the outer court of the Temple.

It is doubtful if all of the cultic in-fractions "observed" by Ezekiel were actually taking place contem-poraneously; it is more likely that he is being shown a set of infrac-tions that transpired over a long period of time which have cumu-latively caused the divine Presence to leave the Temple.

8.1–18: The impurity of the Tem-ple. 1: *In the sixth year, on the fifth day of the sixth month,* 5 'Elul, 592 BCE. The presence of *the elders* in Ezekiel's home indicates that the Jewish community in Babylonian exile was organized with recog-nized leadership and that Ezekiel's status in society was high (cf. 14.1). Many interpreters see this verse as evidence for the origins of the synagogue, but there is no evi-dence for the development of this institution for several centuries (see 11.16 n.). **2:** Ezekiel returns to the imagery of his inaugural vision to describe a human-like being. The Septuagint reads the expres-sion *a figure that had the appearance of fire* as "the appearance (or like-ness) of a man," apparently based upon the similarity of the Heb term "'esh" *(fire)* with "'ish" ("man"), although the consonantal Heb text does not support such a reading ("'sh" [fire], "'ysh" [man]). The language employed here, *fire* and *resplendent and had the color of amber,* describe a being that cannot be defined in earthly terms. The term "zohar" *(resplendent)* was later employed as the name of the well-known kabbalistic commen-tary on the Torah (see also Dan.

12.3). The exact meaning of the expression, *the entrance of the Penimith Gate that faces north,* is un-certain, although it may refer to a gate to the inner court of the Tem-ple on the north side. This would place the prophet at the entry of the most sacred areas of the Tem-ple. *The Presence of the God of Israel* indicates that the divine throne chariot from ch 1 has once again appeared. **5–6:** The *infuriating image* north of the altar indicates the presence of a pagan idol that would defile the holy Temple precincts. **7–13:** The portrayal of the prophet breaking or digging through the walls of the Temple suggests the later Babylonian at-tempts to breach the walls of Jeru-salem (2 Kings 25.1–4; Jeremiah 52.4–7). **10:** *Detestable forms . . . fetishes:* Such depictions were in di-rect disobedience to the command (Deut. 4.15–18) against images. In addition, *creeping things* are ritu-ally impure (see Lev. 20.25) and would defile the Temple. **11:** The *seventy men, elders of the house of Is-rael* and *Jaazaniah son of Shaphan* in-dicates that the highest leaders of the nation are involved in pagan worship inside the Temple. The in-stitution of Israel's seventy elders is well known in biblical tradition as the primary ruling body of the nation (Exod. 24.1; Num. 11.16) which later played a role in select-ing and advising kings (2 Sam. 5.3; cf. 1 Kings 12.6; 20.7). In postbibli-cal Judaism, the Sanhedrin was composed of seventy leaders. Shaphan played a major role in Josiah's reform (2 Kings ch 22); his sons Ahikam, Elasah, and Gema-riah, and grandson Micaiah sup-ported Jeremiah (Jer. chs 26; 29; 36). Although the text identifies Jaazniah as an apostate, his family's exemplary credentials as supporters of the Elide/Levitical priest Jeremiah suggest that Ezekiel's vision may reflect ten-sions between the Zadokite and Levitical priests, especially since the Levitical priests were associ-ated with sanctuaries outside of Je-rusalem that were deemed illegiti-mate (see 2 Kings 23.8–9). **12:** The claim that *the LORD has abandoned* see us; the Lord has abandoned the country.' " ¹³ And He said to me, "You shall see even more terrible abominations which they practice."

¹⁴ Next He brought me to the entrance of the north ᵃ·gate of the House of the Lord;ᵃ and there sat the women bewailing Tammuz.ᵇ ¹⁵ He said to me, "Have you seen, O mortal? You shall see even more terrible abominations than these."

¹⁶ Then He brought me into the inner court of the House of the Lord, and there, at the entrance to the Temple of the Lord, between the portico and the altar, were about twenty-five men, their backs to the Temple of the Lord and their faces to the east; they were bowing low to the sun in the east. ¹⁷ And He said to me, "Do you see, O mortal? Is it not enough for the House of Judah to practice the abominations that they have committed here, that they must fill the country with lawlessness and provoke Me still further and ᶜthrust the branch to their nostrils?ᶜ ¹⁸ I in turn will act with fury, I will show no pity or compassion; though they cry aloud to Me, I will not listen to them."

9 Then He called loudly in my hearing, saying, "Approach, you men in charge of the city, each bearing his weapons of destruction!" ² And six men entered by way of the upper gate that faces north, each with his club in his hand; and among them was another, clothed in linen, with a writing case at his waist. They came forward and stopped at the bronze altar. ³ Now the Presence of the God of Israel had moved from the cherub on which it had rested to the platformᵈ of the House. He called to the man clothed in linen with the writing case at his waist; ⁴ and

a-a I.e., the gate of the inner court.　　b A Babylonian god.
c-c Apparently meaning "goad Me to fury"; "their" is a euphemism for "My."
d The raised platform on which the Temple stood; cf. 47.1.

the country indicates the belief that God would no longer protect Jerusalem from Babylon. The quotation and refutation of a folk-saying by the prophet is characteristic of Ezekiel (see 11.2, 15; 18.2).
14–15: A pagan practice taking place at the Temple itself. Women weep for *Tammuz,* the Babylonian vegetation god who dies at the onset of the dry season and must be brought back to life to inaugurate the rains. According to Babylonian mythology, the goddess Ishtar descends to the underworld each year to return Tammuz to the world of the living for the six months of the rainy season. Mourning rituals by women for the dead Tammuz play a role in bringing the god back to life.
16–18: Ezekiel sees *twenty-five men* engaged in sun worship. The sun god Shamash was the Babylonian god of law and justice. They apparently turn their backs to the Temple to face the east where the sun rises. Traditional interpreters understand this as an expression of their rejection of God, since Jewish worshippers face the Temple and the Holy of Holies (see, as an earlier instance, Dan. 6.11). The meaning of the expression, *thrust the branch to their nostrils,* is unknown, although it is generally understood to refer to some noxious idolatrous practice. Radak follows the *Mekhilta* to Exod. 15.7 in maintaining that this statement is one of the eighteen "emendations of the scribes" that originally read, "thrust the branch to my (God's) nostrils." The various actions described in this narrative indicate that the Temple has been profaned, and must be purified to restore its sacred character.

9.1–11: The slaughter of Jerusalem. Ezekiel's depiction of the killing of the people of Jerusalem employs the imagery of sacrificial slaughter. It would also draw upon images of the Babylonian soldiers slaughtering the defenders of Jerusalem. **1:** The verb "karevu" *(approach)* frequently appears as a technical term that refers to the presentation of an offering to God (Exod. 29.4; 40.12; Lev. 3.6; 7.35; 8.6; Num. 8.9; 16.5). It may also refer to drawing near for battle (Exod. 14.20; Judg. 20.24). **2–3:** The *six men* come from the upper gate to the north with weapons in their hands to begin the slaughter. The Babylonian army would have entered Judah from the north (see Jer. 1.13–16). *The bronze altar* had been moved to the north by Ahaz to accommodate an Assyrian altar (2 Kings 16.14). The Talmud maintains that the bronze altar had been destroyed (*b. Shab.* 55a). *The man clothed in linen* wears the apparel of a priest who serves at the altar (Exod. 28.39; Lev. 6.10) and carries a *writing case* to record the sacrifices. Angels, who are generally understood as the heavenly counterparts to the priests, also dress in white linen (Dan. 10.5; 12.6). The living beings are now named cherubim. **4:** God commands that a *mark* (the ancient form of the Heb letter "tav," here translated *mark,* looks like an X) be placed on the foreheads of *the men who moan and* the LORD said to him, "Pass through the city, through Jerusalem, and put a mark on the foreheads of the men who moan and groan because of all the abominations that are committed in it." 5 To the others He said in my hearing, "Follow him through the city and strike; show no pity or compassion. 6 Kill off graybeard, youth and maiden, women and children; but do not touch any person who bears the mark. Begin here at My Sanctuary." So they began with the elders who were in front of the House. 7 And He said to them, "Defile the House and fill the courts with the slain. Then go forth." So they went forth and began to kill in the city. 8 When they were out killing, and I remained alone, I flung myself on my face and cried out, "Ah, Lord GOD! Are you going to annihilate all that is left of Israel, pouring out Your fury upon Jerusalem?" 9 He answered me, "The iniquity of the Houses of Judah and Israel is very very great, the land is full of crime and the city is full of corruption. For they say, 'The LORD has forsaken the land, and the LORD does not see.' 10 I, in turn, will show no pity or compassion; I will give them their deserts." 11 And then the man clothed in linen with the writing case at his waist brought back word, saying, "I have done as You commanded me."

10 I looked, and on the expanse over the heads of the cherubs, there was something like a sapphire stone; an appearance resembling a throne could be seen over them. 2 He spoke to the man clothed in linen and said, "Step inside the wheelwork, under the cherubs, and fill your hands with glowing coals from among the cherubs, and scatter them over the city." And he went in as I looked

he cites Rashi and *b. Shabbat* 55a who maintain that they were the men who kept Torah from "alef" to "tav," (first to last) indicating God's failure to keep a promise.

10.1–11.13: The LORD's departure from Jerusalem. God's throne chariot will return in 43.1–12 when the city is purified and the Temple reestablished. The departure of *the Presence* [Glory] *of the LORD* from the Temple contrasts with depictions of the manifestation of the divine Presence as fire and cloud in the wilderness Tabernacle (Exod. 40.34–38) and in Solomon's Temple (1 Kings 8.6–13; 2 Chron. 5.3–6.2). Once God has left, the city is open to foreign invasion and destruction. **10.1:** The *expanse over the heads of the cherubs* is associated with *sapphire.* The blue image of *sapphire* recalls the identification of the *expanse* as the sky or heavens in Gen. 1.6–8 and the pavement of sapphire (or lapis) under the feet of God seen by Moses, Aaron, Nadab, Abihu, and the seventy elders in Exod. 24.9–11. In later kabbalistic tradition, the term *sapphire* (Heb "sapir") is sometimes associated with the Heb term "sefirah" ("counting"), which in kabbalistic texts signify the "emanations" of God or divine qualities manifested in the world. The two terms, however, are not related etymologically. **2:** God commands the *man clothed in linen* to take *glowing coals from among the cherubs and scatter them over the city.* This act resembles Josiah's destruction of the Bethel altar in which he commanded that the altar be burned and ground to dust and that the bodies of the idolatrous priest be burned on the site to desecrate it (2 Kings 23.15–18). It also resembles the later purification of the Temple by Judah the Maccabee, who had to destroy the defiled altar in order to rededicate the Temple (1 Macc. 4.36–59). Insofar as Ezekiel envisions the restoration of the Temple at some time following its destruction (11.14–21; chs 40–48), the sacrificial imagery of this act also likens it to the purification and guilt offerings pre-

groan because of all the abominations to protect them from death. The mark presumably indicates someone who is to be spared. A mark on the doorpost protects the Israelites from God's plague against the Egyptians (Exod. 12.23), and a mark on the forehead of Cain is a sign of divine protection (Gen. 4.15). All who lack the mark are to die, defiling the sanctuary. But the meaning of this v. is not entirely certain as the ch subsequently depicts the slaughter of all Jerusalem's inhabitants except for Ezekiel (see 9.8–10). Interpreters therefore waver as to whether the mark indicates those who are guilty or innocent, and sometimes propose that God reneged by

slaughtering everyone without distinction. **8–9:** Ezekiel, as a prophet, attempts to intercede as Moses and other prophets did (Exod. 32.1–14; Num. ch 14), but God states that the people believe that God lacks power and therefore deserve the punishment. Unlike most prophets, who emphasize repentance, the theology of Ezekiel is that the peoples' sin is so great repentance at this point is impossible. (See similarly Jer. ch 25.) The purpose of Ezekiel's prophecies is thus to explain the disaster, not to try to avert it. Radak states that the executioners are to begin at the Temple with the seventy elders because they engaged in idolatry (Ezek. 8.11), but on. ³Now the cherubs were standing on the south side of the House when the man entered, and the cloud filled the inner court. ⁴But when the Presence of the LORD moved from the cherubs to the platformᵃ of the House, the House was filled with the cloud, and the court was filled with the radiance of the Presence of the LORD. ⁵The sound of the cherubs' wings could be heard as far as the outer court, like the voice of El Shaddaiᵇ when He speaks.

⁶When He commanded the man dressed in linen: "Take fire from among the cherubs within the wheelwork," he went in and stood beside a wheel. ⁷And a cherub stretched out his hand among the cherubs to the fire that was among the cherubs; he took some and put it into the hands of him who was clothed in linen, who took it and went out. ⁸The cherubs appeared to have the form of a man's hand under their wings.

⁹I could see that there were four wheels beside the cherubs, one wheel beside each of the cherubs; as for the appearance of the wheels, they gleamed like the beryl stone. ¹⁰In appearance, the four had the same form, as if there were two wheels cutting through each other. ¹¹And when they moved, each could move in the direction of any of its four quarters; they did not veer as they moved. The [cherubs] moved in the direction in which one of the heads faced, without turning as they moved. ¹²Their entire bodies—backs, hands, and wings—and the wheels, the wheels of the four of them, were covered all over with eyes. ¹³It was these wheels that I had heard called "the wheelwork."ᶜ ¹⁴Each one had four faces: One was a cherub's face, the second a human face, the third a lion's face, and the fourth an eagle's face.

¹⁵The cherubs ascended; those were the creatures that I had seen by the Chebar Canal. ¹⁶Whenever the cherubs went, the wheels went beside them; and when the cherubs lifted their wings to ascend from the earth, the wheels did not roll away from their side. ¹⁷When those stood still, these stood still; and when those ascended, these ascended with them, for the spirit of the creature was in them.

¹⁸Then the Presence of the LORD left the platformᵃ of the House and stopped above the cherubs. ¹⁹And I saw the cherubs lift their wings and rise from the earth, with the wheels beside them as they departed; and theyᵈ stopped at the entrance of the eastern gate of the House of the LORD, with the Presence of the God of Israel above them. ²⁰They were the same creatures that I had seen below the God of Israel at the Chebar Canal; so now I

sented in the Temple (Lev. chs 4–5; 7.1–10). Such sacrifices play a role in atoning for iniquity and impurity so that the offender can "return" as a member of the community. **4:** God's presence is signified by the *cloud* (Exod. 19.9; 1 Kings 8.10–11) and *radiance of the Presence of the LORD* as it moves about the Temple complex. **6–7:** Because of the sanctity of the throne chariot or ark, the man clothed in linen is unable to approach and a cherub hands him the fire (2 Sam. 6.6–11). **9–14:** Ezekiel's detailed description of the cherubim and the wheels differs from that in ch 1 in that one of their four faces is a cherub rather than an ox. **19:** *The Presence of the God of Israel* above *the entrance of the eastern gate of the House of the LORD* is the main or processional entrance to the Temple (Pss. 24.7–9; 118.19–20). **11.1–13:** Ezekiel continues to employ the image of sacrifice to prophesy judgment for the people. **1–4:** The *spirit* or "wind" transports Ezekiel to the east gate of the Temple where he sees twenty-five officials, apparently the same men who were worshipping the sun in 8.16. His earlier position in the inner court allowed him to see only their backs. Now that he is at the eastern gate, he can see their faces as they face the sun. **3:** Their statement, *there is no need now to build houses,* rejects Jeremiah's call to build and to plant (Jer. 1.10; 31.28). Their statement, *this [city] is the pot, and we are the meat,* indicates their belief that Jerusalem is to be sacrificed since sacrificial meat was cooked in pots (24.1–14; Jer. 1.13–19; 1 Sam. 2.12–17). Because they conclude that judgment is final, they have rejected God to worship the sun. **5–13:** God instructs Ezekiel to hold the twenty-five leaders responsible for the deaths of the people in Jerusalem. **7:** In stating that the dead will become *the meat* and the city *the pot,* God turns their statement against them and thereby continues the metaphorical portrayal of the destruction of Jerusalem with sacrificial imagery. Because the city of Jerusalem is to be purified by the

---

a See note at 47.1.　　b See note at Gen. 17.1.　　c See v. 2.　　d Lit. "it."

knew that they were cherubs.[a] 21 Each one had four faces and each had four wings, with the form of human hands under the wings. 22 As for the form of their faces, they were the very faces that I had seen by the Chebar Canal—their appearance and [b-]their features[-b]—and each could move in the direction of any of its faces.

11 Then a spirit lifted me up and brought me to the east gate of the House of the LORD, which faces eastward; and there, at the entrance of the gate, were twenty-five men, among whom I saw Jaazaniah son of Azzur and Pelatiah son of Benaiah, leaders of the people. 2 [The LORD] said to me, "O mortal, these are the men who plan iniquity and plot wickedness in this city, 3 who say: 'There is no need now to build houses; this [city] is the pot, and we are the meat.'[c] 4 I adjure you, prophesy against them; prophesy, O mortal!"

5 Thereupon the spirit of the LORD fell upon me, and He said to me, "Speak: Thus said the LORD: Such are your thoughts, O House of Israel; I know what comes into your mind. 6 Many have you slain in this city; you have filled its streets with corpses. 7 Assuredly, thus says the Lord GOD: The corpses that you have piled up in it are the meat for which it is the pot; but you shall be taken out of it. 8 You feared the sword, and the sword I will bring upon you—declares the Lord GOD. 9 I will take you out of it and deliver you into the hands of strangers, and I will execute judgments upon you. 10 You shall fall by the sword; I will punish you at the border of Israel. And you shall know that I am the LORD. 11 This [city] shall not be a pot for you, nor you the meat in it; I will punish you at the border of Israel. 12 Then you shall know that I am the LORD, whose laws you did not follow and whose rules you did not obey, acting instead according to the rules of the nations around you."

13 Now, as I prophesied, Pelatiah son of Benaiah dropped dead. I threw myself upon my face and cried out aloud, "Ah, Lord GOD! You are wiping out the remnant of Israel!"

14 Then the word of the LORD came to me: 15 "O mortal, [I will save] your brothers, your brothers, the men of your kindred,[d] all of that very House of Israel to whom the inhabitants of Jerusalem say, 'Keep far from the LORD; the land has been given as a heritage to us.' 16 Say then: Thus said the Lord GOD: I have indeed removed them far among the nations and have scattered them among the

process of sacrifice, they will be excluded from the pot. **10–11:** God alludes to their fear of foreign invaders, and again turns their fears against them by stating that they will die *at the border of Israel* (see 2 Kings 25.18–21; Jer. 52.24–27). **13:** The immediate death of *Pelatiah son of Benaiah* confirms Ezekiel's word and proves that he is a true prophet (see Amos 7.10–17; Isa. chs 36–37; Jer. chs 27–28).

11.14–21: Oracle concerning the restoration of Israel. The first of fourteen oracles associated with Ezekiel's vision of God's departure from Jerusalem anticipates the future restoration of Israel once the punishment is complete. It thereby attempts to point to divine mercy as the ultimate outcome of the process of judgment. **15:** The reference to *your brothers, the men of your kindred* can also be read as "your brothers, the men of your redemption." The Heb term "ge'ulatekha" has a background in the Priestly laws of redemption whereby a family member, "go'el," must redeem land sold to pay a debt in the jubilee year (Lev. 25.23–55; Ruth 2.20). Ezekiel apparently envisions that those exiled from the land of Israel will redeem the land following the destruction of those who defiled it. Ironically, those who remain in the land claim that the exiles (which would include Ezekiel) must keep far from God because they are no longer entitled to the land. **16:** God claims to be *a diminished sanctity:* God's presence in the world, rather than the Temple's presence in Jerusalem, insures their future. Jewish tradition reads into "mikdash me'at," "a little sanctuary," a reference to the origins of synagogues; based especially on the translation of *Targum Jonathan,* "and I have become for them synagogues, second to My Temple." Although the origins of synagogues are obscure, they can first be traced to the 3rd century BCE, and only emerged as the primary Jewish centers for study and worship following the destruction of the Second Temple by the Ro-

---

a *Because they had been called "cherubs" (cf. v. 2).*   b-b *Lit. "themselves."*
c *I.e., the exiles will not return.*   d *I.e., the exiles.*

countries, and I have become to them a diminished sanctity in the countries whither they have gone. ¹⁷ Yet say: Thus said the Lord GOD: I will gather you^a from the peoples and assemble you out of the countries where you have been scattered, and I will give you the Land of Israel. ¹⁸ And they shall return there, and do away with all its detestable things and all its abominations. ¹⁹ I will give them one heart and put a new spirit in them;^b I will remove the heart of stone from their bodies and give them a heart of flesh, ²⁰ that they may follow My laws and faithfully observe My rules. Then they shall be My people and I will be their God. ²¹ But as for them whose heart is set upon their detestable things and their abominations, I will repay them for their conduct—declares the Lord GOD."

²² Then the cherubs, with the wheels beside them, lifted their wings, while the Presence of the God of Israel rested above them. ²³ The Presence of the LORD ascended from the midst of the city and stood on the hill east of the city. ²⁴ A spirit carried me away and brought me in a vision by the spirit of God to the exile community in Chaldea. Then the vision that I had seen left me, ²⁵ and I told the exiles all the things that the LORD had shown me.

12 The word of the LORD came to me: ² O mortal, you dwell among the rebellious breed. They have eyes to see but see not, ears to hear but hear not; for they are a rebellious breed. ³ Therefore, mortal, get yourself gear for exile, and go into exile by day before their eyes. Go into exile from your home to another place before their very eyes; perhaps they will take note, even though they are a rebellious breed. ⁴ Carry out your gear as gear for exile by day before their very eyes; and go out again in the evening before their eyes, as one who goes out into exile. ⁵ Before their eyes, break through the wall and carry [the gear] out through it; ⁶ before their eyes, carry it on your shoulder. Take it out in the dark, and cover your face that you may not see the land; for I make you a portent to the House of Israel.

a I.e., the exiles.　　b Heb. "you."

will be their God, a formulation which characterizes the covenant between God and Israel/Judah (14.11; 36.28; 37.23; Jer. 7.23; 31.33; 32.38; Hos. 2.23; Zech. 8.8). Christianity understands this new covenant as a reference to the coming of Jesus (New Testament means "new covenant"). Judaism understands it as a continuation of the original covenant in which the people will renew their commitment to God. *Targum Jonathan* translates vv. 19–20, "and I will break the heart of wickedness, which is as strong as stone, from their flesh, and I shall give them a fearing heart before Me to perform My will."

11.22–24: The Presence of the LORD departs from the city. 23: Rabbinic tradition identifies *the hill east of the city* as the Mount of Olives, and claims that the divine Presence remained there for three and a half years hoping that Israel would repent (*Lam. Rab.* 25). **24:** Ezekiel is returned to *Chaldea* (Babylonia) to report to the exiles.

12.1–7: Symbolic action concerning the exile. God instructs Ezekiel to perform a symbolic act that depicts the exile of the House of Israel. Most interpreters maintain that Ezekiel's action is directed to his fellow exiles. **1:** Like the other oracles that follow Ezekiel's vision, the passage begins with the formula, *the word of the LORD came to me*. **2:** God calls Israel *the rebellious breed*, but adds *they have eyes to see but see not, ears to hear but hear not*, apparently in reference to Isa. 6.9–10. **3–6:** Ezekiel is to prepare his baggage, dig through the wall, and depart with his face covered so that all may see that the exile of Israel is taking place. Ironically, this action contrasts with Exod. 12.11, which instructs the people of Israel to eat the Passover sacrifice with "your loins girded, your sandals on your feet, and your staff in your hand." *Portent* frequently appears as a term for God's miracles at the time of the Exodus (Exod. 4.21; 7.3; Deut. 4.34; Ps. 78.43).

mans in 70 CE. **17:** God promises to gather the people from exile, to give them *the Land of Israel* so that they might purify it from abominations. **19:** The promise of *one heart* (some manuscripts read "a new heart") and *a new spirit in them* ("you") takes up a theme from Jeremiah (Jer. 32.39; see also Ezek. 18.31; 36.26) concerning a

new covenant in which God's "torah" is written upon their hearts (Jer. 31.33–34; see also Ezek. 16.59–63). These chs offer a radical solution to prevent Israel from sinning again and experiencing another exile: Free choice is replaced by a new *heart* which is pre-programmed for obedience. **20:** *They shall be My people, and I*

7 I did just as I was ordered: I took out my gear by day as gear for exile, and in the evening I broke through the wall ᵃwith my own hands.ᵃ In the darkness I carried [the gear] out on my shoulder, carrying it before their eyes.

8 In the morning, the word of the LORD came to me: 9 O mortal, did not the House of Israel, that rebellious breed, ask you, "What are you doing?" 10 Say to them: "Thus said the Lord GOD: This pronouncement concerns the prince in Jerusalem and all the House of Israel who are in it." 11 Say: "I am a portent for you: As I have done, so shall it be done to them; they shall go into exile, into captivity. 12 And the prince among them shall carry his gear on his shoulder as he goes out in the dark. Heᵇ shall break through the wall in order to carry [his gear] out through it; he shall cover his face, because he himself shall not see the land with his eyes." 13 I will spread My net over him, and he shall be caught in My snare. I will bring him to Babylon, the land of the Chaldeans, but he shall not see it;ᶜ and there he shall die. 14 And all those around him, his helpers and all his troops, I will scatter in every direction; and I will unsheathe the sword after them. 15 Then, when I have scattered them among the nations and dispersed them through the countries, they shall know that I am the LORD. 16 But I will spare a few of them from the sword, from famine, and from pestilence, that they may recount all their abominable deeds among the nations to which they come; and they shall know that I am the LORD!

17 The word of the LORD came to me: 18 O mortal, eat your bread in trembling and drink your water in fear and anxiety. 19 And say to the people of the land: Thus said the Lord GOD concerning the inhabitants of Jerusalem in the land of Israel: They shall eat their bread in anxiety and drink their water in desolation, because their land will be desolate of its multitudes on account of the lawlessness of all its inhabitants. 20 The inhabited towns shall be laid waste and the land shall become a desolation; then you shall know that I am the LORD.

21 The word of the LORD came to me: 22 O mortal, what is this proverb that you have in the land of Israel, that you

a-a Lit. "by hand."   b Heb. "They."   c Cf. 2 Kings 25.7.

12.8–16: Ezekiel's explanation for his symbolic action. God instructs Ezekiel to explain his action to satisfy the questions that it provokes. He relates the symbolic action to the exile of the Davidic king, which strikes at the foundation of Judean identity and the promise of God's protection of Jerusalem and the house of David (2 Sam. ch 7; Pss. 89; 132). **10:** He calls the action a *pronouncement*, a technical term for prophetic oracles that explain God's actions in the world (see Isa. 13.1; Hab. 1.1). **12–13:** Ezekiel's scenario of the prince's escape and capture reflects Zedekiah's capture near Jericho and blinding at Riblah prior to imprisonment in Babylon (2 Kings 25.1–7; Jer. 52.4–11). Rashi and Radak quote an unknown midrashic source indicating that Zedekiah tunneled out of Jerusalem to Jericho, but God caused a gazelle to run along the top of the tunnel pursued by Babylonian soldiers, who then captured him as he emerged. **16:** *But I will spare a few of them* reflects the tradition of a remnant that is common in prophetic literature. Yet the view of this remnant is bleak, in contrast to other prophetic passages (e.g., Isa. 6.13).

12.17–20: Symbolic action concerning eating and drinking. Eating meals in fear dramatizes the realities of exile. Again, eating and drinking in fear contrasts with the experience of the exodus, in which the Israelites carried their kneading bowls and hurriedly ate matzot (unleavened bread) as they escaped from Egypt to travel through the wilderness (Exod. 12.33–39; 13.1–8; cf. 12.11–15). The effectiveness of this symbolic action assumes that members of the exile community are regularly visting Ezekiel to observe his actions (see 8.1 n.).

12.21–25: Oracle concerning the fulfillment of prophecy. Ezekiel's oracle affirms the imminent fulfillment of God's visions and challenges those prophets and prophetesses who proclaim false messages of peace. Ezekiel responds to those who claim in essence that he is a false prophet, and that his visions will not be fulfilled (see 11.13 n.). **22:** *Proverb* here refers to a common saying among the people. *Vision* refers to both visual and auditory experience (see Isa. 2.1). Jeremiah also attacks false prophets (Jer. 23.9–40; chs 27–28; 29.20–28; cf. Deut. 18.15–22).

say, "The days grow many and every vision comes to naught?" 23 Assuredly, say to them, Thus said the Lord God: I will put an end to this proverb; it shall not be used in Israel any more. Speak rather to them: The days draw near, and the fulfillment of every vision. 24 For there shall no longer be any false vision or soothing divination in the House of Israel. 25 But whenever I the LORD speak what I speak, that word shall be fulfilled without any delay; in your days, O rebellious breed, I will fulfill every word I speak—declares the Lord God.

26 The word of the LORD came to me: 27 See, O mortal, the House of Israel says, "The vision that he sees is far ahead, and he prophesies for the distant future." 28 Assuredly, say to them: Thus said the Lord God: There shall be no more delay; whenever I speak a word, that word shall be fulfilled—declares the Lord God.

13 The word of the LORD came to me: 2 O mortal, prophesy against the prophets of Israel who prophesy; say to those who prophesy out of their own imagination: Hear the word of the LORD! 3 Thus said the Lord God: Woe to the degenerate prophets, who follow their own fancy, without having had a vision! 4 Your prophets, O Israel, have been like jackals among ruins. 5 You did not enter the breaches and repair the walls for the House of Israel, that they might stand up in battle in the day of the LORD. 6 They prophesied falsehood and lying divination; they said, "Declares the LORD," when the LORD did not send them, and then they waited for their word to be fulfilled. 7 It was false visions you prophesied and lying divination you uttered, saying, "Declares the LORD," when I had not spoken.

8 Assuredly, thus said the Lord God: Because you speak falsehood and prophesy lies, assuredly, I will deal with you—declares the Lord God. 9 My hand will be against the prophets who prophesy falsehood and utter lying divination. They shall not remain in the assembly of My people, they shall not be inscribed in the lists of the House of Israel, and they shall not come back to the land of Israel. Thus shall you know that I am the Lord God.

10 Inasmuch as they have misled My people, saying, "It is well," when nothing is well, daubing with plaster the flimsy wall which ᵃ·the people·ᵃ were building, 11 say to those daubers of plaster: It shall collapse; a driving rain shall descend—and you, O great hailstones, shall fall— and a hurricane wind shall rend it. 12 Then, when the wall

12.26–28: Oracle concerning the imminent fulfillment of Ezekiel's vision. Prophetic visions often do not have a clear time-period associated with them. In this context, Ezekiel responds to the charge that his visions will be fulfilled only in the distant future by stating that they are about to be realized.

13.1–23: Oracle concerning false prophets. Like Jeremiah, Ezekiel condemns prophets who announce well-being for the people of Israel (Jer. chs 27–28; cf. 23.9–40; 29.20–28). **2:** Ezekiel charges that they *prophesy out of their own imagination* rather than speaking the word of God. **4:** He compares them to *jackals* (lit. "foxes"), animals associated with ruins. Instead of helping to prevent the destruction, the prophets preside over it. **10:** God is against those prophets who announce *"It is well* [shalom]" *when nothing is well.* The expression may be translated, "saying, 'peace,' when there is no peace." Much like Hananiah in Jer. chs 27–28, such prophets of peace would have relied upon the Davidic tradition of God's promise of security for the monarchy and Jerusalem. Ezekiel compares these prophecies to *daubing with plaster* [a] *flimsy wall* that is destroyed by rain, hail, and wind. Walls made of sun-dried brick are frequently destroyed by heavy rain and wind. Heb "tafel" *(plaster)* also means "folly" (cf. Lam. 2.14), and may here function as a pun with "yipol/tipol" *(it shall collapse).* A somewhat similar metaphor appears in Amos's vision of the plumb line, in which God employs a plumb line to show him that the "wall" or Israel is about to fall (Amos 7.7–9).

a-a Heb. "it."

collapses, you will be asked, "What became of the plaster you daubed on?"

13 Assuredly, thus said the Lord GOD: In My fury I will let loose hurricane winds; in My anger a driving rain shall descend, and great hailstones in destructive fury. 14 I will throw down the wall that you daubed with plaster, and I will raze it to the ground so that its foundation is exposed; and when it falls, you shall perish in its midst; then you shall know that I am the LORD. 15 And when I have spent My fury upon the wall and upon those who daubed it with plaster, I will say to you: Gone is the wall and gone are its daubers, 16 the prophets of Israel who prophesy about Jerusalem and see a vision of well-being for her when there is no well-being—declares the Lord GOD.

17 And you, O mortal, set your face against the women of your people, who prophesy out of their own imagination. Prophesy against them 18 and say: Thus said the Lord GOD: Woe to those who sew pads[a] on all arm-joints and make bonnets[a] for the head of every person, in order to entrap! Can you hunt down lives among My people, while you preserve your own lives? 19 You have profaned [b-My name-b] among My people in return for handfuls of barley and morsels of bread; you have announced the death of persons who will not die and the survival of persons who will not live—lying to My people, who listen to your lies.

20 Assuredly, thus said the Lord GOD: I am going to deal with your pads,[a] [c-by which-c] you hunt down lives like birds, and I will tear them from your arms and free the persons whose lives you hunt down like birds. 21 I will tear off your bonnets[a] and rescue My people from your hands, and they shall no longer be prey in your hands; then you shall know that I am the LORD. 22 Because you saddened the heart of the innocent with lies, when I would not inflict suffering on him, and encouraged the wicked not to repent of his evil ways and so gain life— 23 assuredly, you shall no longer prophesy lies or practice divination! I will save My people from your hands, and you shall know that I am the LORD.

14 Certain elders of Israel came to me and sat down before me. 2 And the word of the LORD came to me: 3 O mortal, these men have turned their thoughts upon their fetishes and set their minds upon the sin through which they stumbled: Shall I respond to their inquiry?

a Meaning of Heb. uncertain.
b-b Heb. "Me." c-c Heb. "where."

17–23: Ezekiel then condemns the women who prophesy falsely and practice divination. Miriam (Exod. 15.20–21), Deborah (Judg. chs 4–5), the wife of Isaiah (Isa. 8.1–4), Huldah (2 Kings 22.14–20), and Noadiah (Neh. 6.14) demonstrate that female prophets appeared in both Israel and Judah. A careful analysis of the condemnation of these female prophets in contrast to their male counterparts reveals important assumptions about gender in ancient Israel. **18:** Ezekiel points to the divinatory side of their activities in which they employ wristbands and veils (see Moses' veil in Exod. 34.29–35), and indicates that they are paid for their services. The exact identity and function of these devices that the women use to aid them in prophecy are unclear. **19:** Prophecy is a profession in the ancient world for which payment is received (1 Sam. 9.7; but see Amos 7.10–17); Ezekiel's point is that they deliver life-and-death prophecies for negligible compensation. *Death of persons . . . survival of persons:* The false prophetesses and diviners apparently play a role in deciding capital cases in which a person's life is at stake. **20:** God will tear the bands from their hands and let the lives of such people go free *like birds.* Birds were frequently employed in divination in the ancient world (see Isa. 8.19).

14.1–11: Threats against false prophets and diviners. Here and in the following section, Ezekiel uses the form of case law, familiar from ancient Near Eastern and biblical law collections, to frame his address. As a priest, he would have been especially familiar with this type of law (see 7.26; 22.26; Jer. 18.18). Divination is prohibited in the Bible because it is associated with idolatry and apostasy (Deut. 13.2–6; Isa. 2.6–9). **1:** See 8.1 n. **3:** God states that the elders *have turned their thoughts upon their fetishes and set their minds upon the sin through which they stumbled,* apparently a reference to their consulting pagan diviners or a charge

4 Now speak to them and tell them: Thus said the Lord GOD: If anyone of the House of Israel turns his thoughts upon his fetishes and sets his mind upon the sin through which he stumbled, and yet comes to the prophet, I the LORD will respond to him ᵃ-as he comes with-ᵃ his multitude of fetishes. 5 Thus I will hold the House of Israel to account for their thoughts, because they have all been estranged from Me through their fetishes.

6 Now say to the House of Israel: Thus said the Lord GOD: Repent, and turn back from your fetishes and turn your minds away from all your abominations. 7 For if any man of the House of Israel, or of the strangers who dwell in Israel, breaks away from Me and turns his thoughts upon his fetishes and sets his mind upon the sins through which he stumbled, and then goes to the prophet to inquire of Me through him, I the LORD will respond to him directly. 8 I will set My face against that man and make him a sign and a byword, and I will cut him off from the midst of My people. Then you shall know that I am the LORD.

9 And if a prophet is seduced and does speak a word [to such a man], it was I the LORD who seduced that prophet; I will stretch out My hand against him and destroy him from among My people Israel. 10 Thus they shall bear their punishment: The punishment of the inquirer and the punishment of the prophet shall be the same, 11 so that the House of Israel may never again stray from Me and defile itself with all its transgressions. Then they shall be My people and I will be their God—declares the Lord GOD.

12 The word of the LORD came to me: 13 O mortal, if a land were to sin against Me and commit a trespass, and I stretched out My hand against it and broke its staff of bread, and sent famine against it and cut off man and beast from it, 14 even if these three men—Noah, Daniel, and Job—should be in it, they would by their righteousness save only themselves—declares the Lord GOD. 15 Or, if I were to send wild beasts to roam the land and they depopulated it, and it became a desolation with none passing through it because of the beasts, 16 as I live—declares the Lord GOD—those three men in it would save neither sons nor daughters; they alone would be saved, but the land would become a desolation. 17 Or, if I were to bring the sword upon that land and say, "Let a sword sweep through the land so that I may cut off from it man and beast," 18 if those three men should be in it, as I live—declares the Lord GOD—they would save neither sons nor daughters, but

that other Judean prophets are false. The coarse term for *fetishes*, lit. "dung balls," demonstrates Ezekiel's disdain for such persons and suggests that they are not worthy of an answer. **4:** In response to those who consult idols or false prophets, God states, *"I, the LORD, will respond to him."* **7:** The reference to *strangers who dwell in Israel* is generally understood as a reference to non-Israelites who joined the community, either in Babylonia or in the land of Israel (Exod. 12.19; Lev. 16.29; 17.8; 25.47; Num. 9.14; Deut. 1.16; 16.11; 26.11). **9:** Both the idolater and the prophet who *is seduced* into being his accomplice will be held accountable. God calls upon such persons to repent, but also claims deliberately to seduce or deceive the false prophets so that they will be destroyed. This recalls the case of Micaiah ben Imlah, who claims to have witnessed God's command to send a lying spirit to the prophets of Ahab (1 Kings ch 22). It also recalls God's commission to Isaiah to make sure that the people would not repent and be saved (Isa. ch 6). Jeremiah claims to have been seduced by God (Jer. 20.7). **11:** The covenant formula (see 11.14–21 n.), *they shall be My people and I will be their God*, conveys God's intention to convince the people to remain loyal. Formulae are often used to end oracles in Ezekiel.

14.12–23: Oracle concerning individual righteousness. Ezekiel claims that individual people are responsible for their own moral actions and that the wicked will not be saved because of the few among them who are righteous. Abraham (Gen. ch 18) argued with God to save Sodom if there could be found in it the minimum number of righteous people; Ezekiel argues that Jerusalem could not be saved even for the three most righteous. **13:** The form imitates the casuistic law collections, "if a man. . . ." **14:** *Noah, Daniel, and Job* were exemplary righteous persons who had the capacity to save others. Noah saved his family during

---

a-a *Emendation yields "directly, because of"; cf. v. 7.*

they alone would be saved. ¹⁹ Or, if I let loose a pestilence against that land, and poured out My fury upon it in blood, cutting off from it man and beast, ²⁰ should Noah, Daniel, and Job be in it, as I live—declares the Lord GOD—they would save neither son nor daughter; they would save themselves alone by their righteousness.

²¹ Assuredly, thus said the Lord GOD: How much less [should any escape] now that I have let loose against Jerusalem all four of My terrible punishments—the sword, famine, wild beasts, and pestilence—to cut off man and beast from it! ²² Yet there are survivors left of it, ^{a-}sons and daughters who are being brought out.^{-a} They are coming out to you; and when you see their ways and their deeds, you will be consoled for the disaster that I brought on Jerusalem, for all that I brought on it. ²³ You will be consoled through them, when you see their ways and their deeds and realize that not without cause did I do all that I did in it—declares the Lord GOD.

15 The word of the LORD came to me: ² O mortal, how is the wood of the grapevine better than the wood of any branch to be found among the trees of the forest? ³ Can wood be taken from it for use in any work? Can one take a peg from it to hang any vessel on? ⁴ Now suppose it was thrown into the fire as fuel and the fire consumed its two ends and its middle was charred—is it good for any use? ⁵ Even when it was whole it could not be used for anything; how much less when fire has consumed it and it is charred! Can it still be used for anything?

⁶ Assuredly, thus said the Lord GOD: Like the wood of the grapevine among the trees of the forest, which I have designated to be fuel for fire, so will I treat the inhabitants of Jerusalem. ⁷ I will set My face against them; they escaped from fire, but fire shall consume them. When I set my face against them, you shall know that I am the LORD. ⁸ I will make the land a desolation, because they committed trespass—declares the Lord GOD.

16 The word of the LORD came to me: ² O mortal, proclaim Jerusalem's abominations to her, ³ and say: Thus said the Lord GOD to Jerusalem: By origin and birth

---

a-a *Several ancient versions read "who are bringing out sons and daughters."*

(see 28.3). In a similar vein, Jeremiah argues that the wicked would suffer punishment even if Moses and Samuel were present (Jer. 15.1). The theme of this section, individual responsibility and retribution, is spelled out in greater detail in ch 18. **21–23:** The same punishments are applied to Jerusalem. Those who are righteous will survive to form the remnant of Israel.

15.1–8: The allegory of the useless vine. Ezekiel uses the genre of riddles, known in ancient Near Eastern wisdom literature, to compare the inhabitants of Jerusalem to the wood of a grapevine, which is entirely useless except for burning (see Judg. 9.7–21). The allegory may draw upon Isaiah's (Isa. 5.1–7) depiction of Israel as God's vineyard, which was planted with good grapes that went bad and was therefore destroyed, but it is not formulated with the poetic artistry of that ch. **3:** The wood of the vine cannot be used to make anything, since vine branches are twisted and weak. **4–5:** Even when burned, the charred ends are useless. **6–8:** Like useless vine branches, Jerusalem will be burned because of its trespasses.

16.1–63: The allegory of Jerusalem as God's adulterous wife. Prophets often employ the metaphor of marriage to portray the relationship between God, the husband, and Israel, the bride (Hos. chs 1–3; Jer. chs 2–3; Isa. chs 49–54; 66.7–14; 8.5–8; Zeph. 3.14–20). Rabbinic interpreters are very uncomfortable with the specific use of this imagery in this chapter because of its lewd portrayal of Jerusalem. R. Eliezer rules that it should not be read as a haftarah portion (*m. Meg.* 4.10). Maimonides read it as the haftarah for Shemot (Exod. 1.1–6.1), but it is no longer read as a haftarah for any text. Along with ch 23, which is similar, it has been the subject of much recent feminist interpretation. **1–5:** Ezekiel portrays Jerusalem as an unwanted baby who is abandoned to die. **3:** *Your*

---

the flood (Gen. chs 6–9), and Job saved his three friends who spoke wrongly about God (Job 42.7–9). Daniel probably refers not to the Daniel in the book of Daniel, but to Dan-El in the Canaanite legend of Aqhat, found among the Ugaritic tablets. The righteous Dan-El saves his son Aqhat from death. It is therefore striking that Dan-El in Ezekiel is spelled according to the Canaanite pattern you are from the land of the Canaanites—your father was an Amorite and your mother a Hittite. ⁴As for your birth, when you were born your navel cord was not cut, and you were not bathed in water to ᵃsmooth you;ᵃ you were not rubbed with salt, nor were you swaddled. ⁵No one pitied you enough to do any one of these things for you out of compassion for you; on the day you were born, you were left lying, rejected, in the open field. ⁶When I passed by you and saw you wallowing in your blood, I said to you: "Live in spite of your blood." ᵇYea, I said to you: "Live in spite of your blood."ᵇ ⁷I let you grow like the plants of the field; and you continued to grow up until you attained ᵃto womanhood,ᵃ until your breasts became firm and your hair sprouted.

You were still naked and bare ⁸when I passed by you [again] and saw that your time for love had arrived. ᶜSo I spread My robe over youᶜ and covered your nakedness, and I entered into a covenant with you by oath—declares the Lord Goᴅ; thus you became Mine. ⁹I bathed you in water, and washed the blood off you, and anointed you with oil. ¹⁰I clothed you with embroidered garments, and gave you sandals of ᵃdolphin leatherᵃ to wear, and wound fine linen about your head, and dressed you in silks. ¹¹I decked you out in finery and put bracelets on your arms and a chain around your neck. ¹²I put a ring in your nose, and earrings in your ears, and a splendid crown on your head. ¹³You adorned yourself with gold and silver, and your apparel was of fine linen, silk, and embroidery. Your food was choice flour, honey, and oil. You grew more and more beautiful, and became fit for royalty. ¹⁴Your beauty won you fame among the nations, for it was perfected through the splendor which I set upon you—declares the Lord Goᴅ.

¹⁵But confident in your beauty and fame, you played the harlot: you lavished your favors on every passerby; ᵃthey were his.ᵃ ¹⁶You even took some of your cloths and made yourself ᵃtapestried platformsᵃ and fornicated on them—ᵈnot in the future; not in time to come.ᵈ ¹⁷You took your beautiful things, made of the gold and silver that I had given you, and you made yourself phallic images and fornicated with them. ¹⁸You took your embroidered cloths to cover them; and you set My oil and My incense before them. ¹⁹The food that I had given you—the choice

father was an Amorite, and your mother a Hittite: The indigenous inhabitants of Canaan were idolaters, and Ezekiel is thus suggesting that Jerusalem has idolatrous antecedents and is therefore predisposed to sin. The Bible generally suggests that Israel's origins were elsewhere, and that they must be distinguished from the native Canaanites (see esp. Deut. 20.16–19). Some modern scholars, however, believe that this statement reflects the historical truth—that the people Israel originated in the land of Israel by differentiating itself from the native Canaanites. **4–5:** A catalogue of activities performed on the typical newborn. **6–7:** God wills the abandoned infant to live. She lives and grows to puberty. *Live in spite of your blood* may also be understood as "live because of your blood," and with this understanding these words are incorporated into the circumcision ceremony. **8:** Upon reaching puberty, she is ready for marriage. *I spread my robe over you and covered your nakedness* indicates God's marriage to the young woman; a similar metaphor expresses Boaz's marriage to Ruth (Ruth 3.9), and the rape of Israel by the Assyrians (Isa. 8.7–8). God is depicted in strikingly anthropomorphic terms (contrast ch 1). **9:** With her "marriage" to God comes Jerusalem's washing and anointing—that is, her purification and beautification. **10–13:** The description of fine clothing, jewelry, and food (see Isa. 3.18–23) demonstrates God's generosity to the unwanted Jerusalem, who is treated as a queen. **15–29:** God's charge that Jerusalem used the gifts to become a whore is a way to describe religious unfaithfulness. The metaphor then shifts to political and trade alliances with foreign nations. Israel allied itself with Egypt during the reigns of Solomon (1 Kings 3.1) and later Hoshea (2 Kings 17.4). Israel is depicted as a sexually overcharged ingrate. **29:** *Chaldea, that land of traders,* the Heb reads, "Chaldea, that land of Canaan." The term "Canaan"

a-a *Meaning of Heb. uncertain.*

b-b *This sentence is missing from some ancient versions and a few Heb. mss.*

c-c *An act symbolizing espousal; cf. note at Deut. 23.1, Ruth 3.9.*

d-d *See note at Exod. 25.4.*

flour, the oil, and the honey, which I had provided for you to eat—you set it before them for a pleasing odor.ᵃ And so it went—declares the Lord GOD. ²⁰ You even took the sons and daughters that you bore to Me and sacrificed them to those [images] as food—as if your harlotries were not enough, ²¹ you slaughtered My children and presented them as offerings to them! ²² In all your abominations and harlotries, you did not remember the days of your youth, when you were naked and bare, and lay wallowing in your blood.

²³ After all your wickedness (woe, woe to you!)— declares the Lord GOD—²⁴ you built yourself an eminence and made yourself a mound in every square. ²⁵ You built your mound at every crossroad; and you sullied your beauty and spread your legs to every passerby, and you multiplied your harlotries. ²⁶ You played the whore with your neighbors, the lustfulᵇ Egyptians—you multiplied your harlotries to anger Me. ²⁷ Now, I will stretch out My arm against you and withhold your maintenance; and I will surrender you to the will of your enemies, the Philistine women, who are shocked by your lewd behavior.

²⁸ In your insatiable lust you also played the whore with the Assyrians; you played the whore with them, but were still unsated. ²⁹ You multiplied your harlotries with Chaldea, that land of traders; yet even with this you were not satisfied.

³⁰ ᶜ How sick was your heart ᶜ—declares the Lord GOD—when you did all those things, the acts of a self-willed whore, ³¹ building your eminence at every crossroad and setting your mound in every square! Yet you were not like a prostitute, for you spurned fees; ³² [you were like] the adulterous wife who welcomes strangers instead of her husband. ³³ Gifts are made to all prostitutes, but you made gifts to all your lovers, and bribed them to come to you from every quarter for your harlotries. ³⁴ You were the opposite of other women: you solicited instead of being solicited; you paid fees instead of being paid fees. Thus you were just the opposite!

³⁵ Now, O harlot, hear the word of the LORD. ³⁶ Thus said the Lord GOD: Because of your brazen effrontery, offering your nakedness to your lovers for harlotry—ᵈ just like the blood of your children, which you gave to all your abominable fetishes:ᵈ—³⁷ I will assuredly assemble all the

sometimes signifies merchants or traders (Zeph. 1.11; Zech. 14.21; cf. Ezek. 17.4). Following Israel's destruction in 722 BCE, Assyria granted Philistia control of Israelite and Judean territory in the coastal plain. Israel made an alliance with Assyria during the reign of Menahem (2 Kings 15.17–22), and Judah turned to Assyria during the reign of Ahaz (2 Kings ch 16). Hezekiah established relations with Chaldea or Babylonia (2 Kings ch 20; Isaiah ch 39). **30–34:** Ezekiel charges that Jerusalem, contrary to the expectations of a prostitute, pays her lovers! Ahaz's "bribe" to Tiglathpileser (2 Kings 16.8) would be a case in point. When Nebuchadnezzar first conquered Jerusalem, he stripped the Temple of its wealth (2 Kings 24.10–17). **35–43:** God states that all of Jerusalem's lovers, the nations with whom she was allied, will come to punish her. Deut. 22.22–24 requires that an adulteress and her lover be stoned to death by the community, but here the paramours are destroying Jerusalem. As in many prophetic oracles, the punishment is introduced with the word *Now* ("lakhen").

a I.e., as a sacrifice; cf. Lev. 2.2.

b Lit. "big of phallus"; cf. 23.20.

c-c Change of vocalization yields "How furious I was with you"; lit. "How I was filled with your fury" (libbat, as in Akkadian and Old Aramaic).

d-d Construction of Heb. uncertain.

lovers to whom you gave your favors, along with everybody you accepted and everybody you rejected. I will assemble them against you from every quarter, and I will expose your nakedness to them, and they shall see all your nakedness. ³⁸ I will inflict upon you the punishment of women who commit adultery and murder, and I will direct bloody and impassioned fury against you. ³⁹ I will deliver you into their hands, and they shall tear down your eminence and level your mounds; and they shall strip you of your clothing and take away your dazzling jewels, leaving you naked and bare. ⁴⁰ Then they shall assemble a mob against you to pelt you with stones and pierce you with their swords. ⁴¹ They shall put your houses to the flames and execute punishment upon you in the sight of many women; thus I will put a stop to your harlotry, and you shall pay no more fees. ⁴² When I have satisfied My fury upon you and My rage has departed from you, then I will be tranquil; I will be angry no more.

⁴³ Because you did not remember the days of your youth, but infuriated Me with all those things, I ᵃ⁻will pay you back for your conduct⁻ᵃ—declares the Lord GOD.

Have you not committed depravity on top of all your other abominations? ⁴⁴ Why, everyone who uses proverbs applies to you the proverb "Like mother, like daughter." ⁴⁵ You are the daughter of your mother, who rejected her husband and children. And you are the sister of your sisters, who rejected their husbands and children; for you are daughters of a Hittite mother and an Amorite father. ⁴⁶ Your elder sister was Samaria, who lived with her daughters to the north of you; your younger sister was Sodom, who lived with her daughters to the south of you. ⁴⁷ Did you not walk in their ways and practice their abominations? Why, you were almostᵇ more corrupt than they in all your ways. ⁴⁸ As I live—declares the Lord GOD—your sister Sodom and her daughters did not do what you and your daughters did. ⁴⁹ Only this was the sin of your sister Sodom: arrogance! She and her daughters had plenty of bread and untroubled tranquillity; yet she did not support the poor and the needy. ⁵⁰ In their haughtiness, they committed abomination before Me; and so I removed them, as you saw.ᶜ ⁵¹ Nor did Samaria commit even half your sins. You committed more abominations than they, and by all the abominations that you committed you made your sisters look righteous. ⁵² Truly, you must bear the disgrace of

44–52: Charging that Jerusalem is like her mother *who rejected her husband and children,* God points to the sexual "abominations" of the nations who possessed the land before Israel (Lev. 18.24–30; 20.23; Gen. 15.16). **44:** Ezekiel again shows his familiarity with popular proverbs (see 8.12 n.). **46:** For shock value, God compares Jerusalem to *Samaria,* the *elder sister . . . to the north,* and *Sodom,* the *younger sister . . . to the south.* **47:** According to biblical tradition (2 Kings ch 17; Gen. chs 18–19), both cities were destroyed for their sins, but God states that Jerusalem's sins are even worse.

---

a-a *Construction of Heb. uncertain.*   b *Meaning of Heb. uncertain.*

c *Construed as second-person feminine; cf.* qere, *vv. 47 and 51; and see above vv. 13, 18, 22, 31, 43.*

serving as your sisters' advocate: Since you have sinned more abominably than they, they appear righteous in comparison. So be ashamed and bear your disgrace, because you have made your sisters look righteous.

53 I will restore their fortunes—the fortunes of Sodom and her daughters and the fortunes of Samaria and her daughters—and your fortunes along with theirs. 54 Thus you shall bear your disgrace and feel your disgrace for behaving in such a way that they could take comfort. 55 Then your sister Sodom and her daughters shall return to their former state, and Samaria and her daughters shall return to their former state, and you and your daughters shall return to your former state. 56 Was not your sister Sodom a byword in your mouth in the days of your pride, 57 before your own wickedness was exposed? So must you now bear the mockery of the daughters of Aram[a] and all her neighbors, the daughters of Philistia who jeer at you on every side. 58 You yourself must bear your depravity and your abominations—declares the LORD.

59 Truly, thus said the Lord GOD: I will deal with you as you have dealt, for you have spurned the pact and violated the covenant. 60 Nevertheless, I will remember the covenant I made with you in the days of your youth, and I will establish it with you as an everlasting covenant. 61 You shall remember your ways and feel ashamed, when you receive your older sisters and your younger sisters, and I give them to you as daughters, though they are not of your covenant. 62 I will establish My covenant with you, and you shall know that I am the LORD. 63 Thus you shall remember and feel shame, and you shall be too abashed to open your mouth again, when I have forgiven you for all that you did—declares the Lord GOD.

17 The word of the LORD came to me: 2 O mortal, propound a riddle and relate an allegory to the House of Israel. 3 Say: Thus said the Lord GOD: The great eagle with the great wings and the long pinions, [b-]with the full plumage and the brilliant colors,[-b] came to the Lebanon range and seized the top of the cedar. 4 He plucked off its

a Many Heb. mss. and editions read "Edom."
b-b This description suggests the golden eagle; the vulture, called by the same word in Heb. (nesher) has a bald head (Mic. 1.16) and dark feathers.

similar) and *Philistia*, Judah's surviving neighbors. **60–61:** The *everlasting covenant* with Jerusalem alludes to God's eternal protection for Jerusalem and the House of David (2 Sam. ch 7; Isa. 55.3). Many compare it to Jeremiah's new covenant (Jer. 31.31–34), but it is not "new"; God "remembers" the covenant, and calls upon Jerusalem to do the same. Jerusalem and not God is charged with violating the "eternal covenant," according to which Jerusalem is destroyed. Samaria and Sodom were sisters, but they will become Jerusalem's daughters, indicating Jerusalem's premier status. The remembrance of the covenant at the end of this unit may be patterned after Lev. 26.42, 45. **62:** *I will establish My covenant with you, and you shall know that I am the LORD* restates the covenant formula (Hos. 2.22). **63:** God's remembering (vv. 60–61) has as its ultimate goal making Israel *remember*.

17.1–24: The allegory of the eagles, the vine, and the cedar. The allegory describes Jehoiachin's exile to Babylon, the installation of Zedekiah as king, and Zedekiah's demise when he allied himself with Egypt and revolted against Babylonia (see 2 Kings chs 24–25; 2 Chron. ch 36; Jer. ch 52). **1–2:** God instructs Ezekiel to speak *a riddle* (i.e., a puzzle) and *an allegory* (elsewhere translated "proverb" [12.22], "theme" [Job 27.1] "byword" [Ps. 69.12]; the basic meaning is "likeness" or "comparison"). **3–10:** The allegory proceeds in three stages. **3–4:** The first describes an eagle, later identified as Nebuchadnezzar, who breaks off the *top* shoot of the *cedar* and carries it *to the land of traders* (lit. "to the land of Canaan"; cf. 16.29; Zeph. 1.11; Zech. 14.21) and *a city of merchants*. Lebanon was known for "the cedars of Lebanon" (Ps. 92.12), but a portion of the Davidic palace in Jerusalem, since it was built with cedar, is called the "House of the Forest of Lebanon" (1 Kings 7.2; Isa. 22.9). The "top shoot" therefore symbolizes the Davidic monarch, Jehoia-

53: God intends to *restore . . . the fortunes* of both Sodom and Samaria and their *daughters*, a reference to cities allied with each. In addition, God will restore Jerusalem. **54:** God intends to punish or cleanse Israel from sins so it will continue to experience the shame of its past actions. **57:** Jerusalem has become a mockery to *Aram* (some manuscripts read "Edom"; the letters "dalet" and "resh" are topmost bough and carried it off to the land of traders[a] and set it in a city of merchants. [5] He then took some of the seed of the land[b] and planted it in a fertile field; [c]he planted and set it like a willow[-c] beside abundant waters. [6] It grew and became a spreading vine of low stature; it became a vine, produced branches, and sent out boughs. [He had intended] that its twigs should turn to him, and that its roots should stay under him.

[7] But there was another great eagle with great wings and full plumage; and this vine now bent its roots in his direction and sent out its twigs toward him, that he might water it more than the bed where it was planted— [8] though it was planted in rich soil beside abundant water—so that it might grow branches and produce boughs and be a noble vine.

[9] Say: Thus said the Lord God: Will it thrive? Will he[d] not tear out its roots and rip off its crown, so that its entire foliage withers? It shall wither, despite any strong arm or mighty army [that may come] to remove it from its roots. [10] And suppose it is transplanted, will it thrive? When the east wind strikes it, it shall wither—wither upon the bed where it is growing.

[11] Then the word of the Lord came to me: [12] Say to the rebellious breed: Do you not know what these things mean? Say: The king of Babylon came to Jerusalem, and carried away its king and its officers and brought them back with him to Babylon. [13] He took one of the seed royal and made a covenant with him and imposed an oath on him, and he carried away the nobles of the land—[14] so that it might be a humble kingdom and not exalt itself, but keep his covenant and so endure.

[15] But [that prince] rebelled against him and sent his envoys to Egypt to get horses and a large army. Will he succeed? Will he who does such things escape? Shall he break a covenant and escape? [16] As I live—declares the Lord God—in the very homeland of the king who made him king, whose oath he flouted and whose covenant he broke—right there, in Babylon, he shall die. [17] Pharaoh will not fight at his side with a great army and with numerous troops in the war, when mounds are thrown up and siege towers erected to destroy many lives. [18] He flouted a pact and broke a covenant; he gave his promise and did all these things—he shall not escape. [19] Assuredly, thus said the Lord God: As I live, I will pay him back for flouting My pact and breaking My covenant. [20] I will spread My net

chin (Isa. 11.1); and the "land of trade" is Babylonia (Ezek. 16.29). **5–6:** The second stage describes the planting of seed that becomes a vine, which is identified as Zedekiah. **7–8:** The third stage describes the second *great eagle,* the Egyptian Pharaoh Psammetichus II, to whom Zedekiah turned for support in his revolt against Nebuchadnezzar (Jer. ch 27). **9–10:** The rhetorical questions portray the destruction of the vine. The first eagle, Nebuchadnezzar, will destroy the vine (Zedekiah). **11–21:** The allegory is explained; the realpolitik of the situation is detailed. **20:** God identifies with the Babylonian king by referring to Zedekiah's revolt against Babylonia as *the trespass which he committed against Me.* In 2 Chron. 36.13, Zedekiah is punished for not upholding his oath of vassaldom to Babylonia. **22–24:** God employs the allegory of *the cedar* to promise the restoration of the Davidic monarchy (Isa. 11.1–10; Jer. 23.5–6; 33.15). The cedar, the grandest of trees, will tower over all the other trees (nations), and all will see the power of God, who is responsible for the fall and rise of Judah. Radak maintains that these statements refer to Zerubbabel son of Shealtiel, the grandson of King Jehoiachin whom Haggai declared to be God's "signet ring" or regent (Hag. 2.20–23; see 1 Chron. 3.17–19, but note the problems in the genealogy), and who commenced the building of the Second Temple (Ezra ch 3). **24:** The ch is brought to a close by a modified, expanded version of formulae used throughout Ezekiel.

---

a Cf. 16.29.   b Emendation yields "cedar."
c-c Meaning of Heb. uncertain.   d I.e., the first eagle.

over him and he shall be caught in My snare; I will carry him to Babylon and enter with him into judgment there for the trespass which he committed against Me. [21] And all the fugitives[a] of all his battalions shall fall by the sword, and those who remain shall scatter in every direction; then you will know that I the LORD have spoken.

[22] Thus said the Lord GOD: Then I in turn will take and set [in the ground a slip] from the lofty top of the cedar; I will pluck a tender twig from the tip of its crown, and I will plant it on a tall, towering mountain. [23] I will plant it in Israel's lofty highlands, and it shall bring forth boughs and produce branches[b] and grow into a noble cedar. Every bird of every feather shall take shelter under it, shelter in the shade of its boughs. [24] Then shall all the trees of the field know that it is I the LORD who have abased the lofty tree and exalted the lowly tree, who have dried up the green tree and made the withered tree bud. I the LORD have spoken, and I will act.

18 The word of the LORD came to me: [2] What do you mean by quoting this proverb upon the soil of Israel, "Parents eat sour grapes and their children's teeth are blunted"?[c] [3] As I live—declares the Lord GOD—this proverb shall no longer be current among you in Israel. [4] Consider, all lives are Mine; the life of the parent and the life of the child are both Mine. The person who sins, only he shall die.

[5] Thus, if a man is righteous and does what is just and right: [6] If he has not eaten on the mountains[d] or raised his eyes to the fetishes of the House of Israel; if he has not defiled another man's wife or approached a menstruous woman; [7] if he has not wronged anyone; if he has returned the debtor's pledge to him and has taken nothing by robbery; if he has given bread to the hungry and clothed the naked; [8] if he has not lent at advance interest or exacted accrued interest;[e] if he has abstained from wrongdoing and executed true justice between man and man;

a Many mss. read "picked men."   b Others "fruit."   c Others "set on edge."
d I.e., in idolatry. Emendation yields "with the blood"; cf. 33.25; Lev. 17.10–11, 19.26.
e I.e., interest deducted in advance or interest added at the time of repayment; cf. Lev. 25.36.

18.1–19.14: Concerning the responsibility of the individual and the demise of the monarchy. The formula *the word of the LORD came to me* in 18.1 and its absence in 19.1 may indicate that chs 18 and 19 are to be read together. Ch 18 states the principle of individual moral responsibility. Ch 19 would therefore indicate that the House of David fell, not because of the sins of past kings (Josiah was righteous), but because of the sins of the kings (the sons and grandson of Josiah) during the current period leading up to the exile. 18.1–32: The prophet disputes the view that Israel's punishment is due to the sins of past generations. Instead, each individual is responsible for his or her own actions. Contrast the Decalogue (Exod. 20.5; Deut. 5.9), which indicates that God visits "the guilt of the parents upon the children, upon the third and upon the fourth generations of those who reject Me" (cf. Exod. 34.7). 2: The opposing view is quoted as a proverb, "*Parents eat sour grapes and their children's teeth are blunted.*" Jeremiah takes up the same proverb to argue for individual moral responsibility in the future (see Jer. 31.29–30), but for Ezekiel this principle of individual responsibility is already currently operative. It allows the individuals in exile to free themselves from the guilt that is ultimately responsible for the destruction of the Temple and Jerusalem. 5–23: Ezekiel describes four cases. 5–9: The first is a righteous man, whose actions are described largely in accordance with provisions from the Priestly Holiness Collection (Lev. chs 17–26). 6: *Eaten on the mountains,* eat meat without disposing of blood properly at the Temple (Lev. ch 17; 19.26; *Targum Jonathan* stipulates that this means "did not worship pagan deities by eating sacrifices of the dead"); *raised his eyes to the fetishes of the House of Israel,* improper worship of God (Exod. 20.4–6; Lev. 19.4); *defiled another man's wife,* adultery (Lev. 20.10; 19.20–22); *approached a menstruous woman,* had relations with a woman during her menstrual period (Lev. 15.19–24). 7: *Wronged anyone,* economic oppression is unholy (Lev. 19.13); *has returned the debtor's pledge to him and has taken nothing by robbery . . . has given bread to the hungry and clothed the naked,* a person's only cloak could be taken in pledge for a loan, but it had to be returned if the debtor needed it (Exod. 22.25–27). 8: *Has not lent at advance interest or exacted accrued interest* (Exod. 22.25; Lev. 25.35–38); *executed true justice be-*

⁹if he has followed My laws and kept My rules and acted honestly—he is righteous. Such a man shall live—declares the Lord GOD.

¹⁰Suppose, now, that he has begotten a son who is a ruffian, a shedder of blood, who ᵃdoes any of these things,⁻ᵃ ¹¹whereas he himself did none of these things. That is, [the son] has eaten on the mountains,ᵇ has defiled another man's wife, ¹²has wronged the poor and the needy, has taken by robbery, has not returned a pledge, has raised his eyes to the fetishes, has committed abomination, ¹³has lent at advance interest, or exacted accrued interest—shall he live? He shall not live! If he has committed any of these abominations, he shall die; he has forfeited his life.

¹⁴Now suppose that he, in turn, has begotten a son who has seen all the sins that his father committed, but has taken heed and has not imitated them: ¹⁵He has not eaten on the mountainsᵇ or raised his eyes to the fetishes of the House of Israel; he has not defiled another man's wife; ¹⁶he has not wronged anyone; he has not seized a pledge or taken anything by robbery; he has given his bread to the hungry and clothed the naked; ¹⁷he has ᶜrefrained from oppressing the poor;⁻ᶜ he has not exacted advance or accrued interest; he has obeyed My rules and followed My laws—he shall not die for the iniquity of his father, but shall live. ¹⁸To be sure, his father, because he practiced fraud, robbed his brother, and acted wickedly among his kin, did die for his iniquity; ¹⁹and now you ask, "Why has not the son shared the burden of his father's guilt?" But the son has done what is right and just, and has carefully kept all My laws: he shall live!

²⁰The person who sins, he alone shall die. A child shall not share the burden of a parent's guilt, nor shall a parent share the burden of a child's guilt; the righteousness of the righteous shall be accounted to him alone, and the wickedness of the wicked shall be accounted to him alone.

²¹Moreover, if the wicked one repents of all the sins that he committed and keeps all My laws and does what is just and right, he shall live; he shall not die. ²²None of the transgressions he committed shall be remembered against him; because of the righteousness he has practiced, he shall live. ²³Is it my desire that a wicked person shall die?—says the Lord GOD. It is rather that he shall turn back from his ways and live.

tween man and man, in a court of law (Lev. 19.15–19). **9:** The righteous person shall live. Note that Ezekiel's examples begin with issues between God and human beings and then turn to issues between humans, much like the Decalogue (Exod. ch 20; Deut. ch 5). **10–13:** If a righteous person's child sins, that child is responsible for his or her own sins and shall die. **14–18:** Conversely, if a sinner's child behaves righteously, that child shall be spared. **19–20:** Ezekiel's opponents contend in keeping with the statement in the Decalogue noted above that the son is guilty for the sins of the father, but Ezekiel explicitly polemicizes against the Decalogue, stating that only the person who commits sins shall be punished for them. **21–24:** A new principle enters the debate. Ezekiel contends that a wicked person who repents shall be saved, but a righteous person who sins shall be condemned. Even a person's own past actions do not determine his fate, if he changes his course of action. This concluding section of the ch in a sense takes the previous part metaphorically, understanding the father and children as the actions of single indviduals at different times of their lives.

---

a-a *Meaning of Heb. uncertain.*
b *I.e., in idolatry. Emendation yields "with the blood"; cf. 33.25; Lev. 17.10–11, 19.26.*
c-c *Lit. "turned his hand back from the poor." Emendation yields "abstained from wrong-doing"; cf. v. 8.*

24 So, too, if a righteous person turns away from his righteousness and does wrong, practicing the very abominations that the wicked person practiced, shall he live? None of the righteous deeds that he did shall be remembered; because of the treachery he has practiced and the sins he has committed—because of these, he shall die.

25 Yet you say, "The way of the Lord is unfair." Listen, O House of Israel: Is My way unfair? It is your ways that are unfair! 26 When a righteous person turns away from his righteousness and does wrong, he shall die for it; he shall die for the wrong he has done. 27 And if a wicked person turns back from the wickedness that he practiced and does what is just and right, such a person shall save his life. 28 Because he took heed and turned back from all the transgressions that he committed, he shall live; he shall not die.

29 Yet the House of Israel say, "The way of the Lord is unfair." Are My ways unfair, O House of Israel? It is your ways that are unfair! 30 Be assured, O House of Israel, I will judge each one of you according to his ways—declares the Lord God. Repent and turn back from your transgressions; let them not be a stumbling block of guilt for you. 31 Cast away all the transgressions by which you have offended, and get yourselves a new heart and a new spirit, that you may not die, O House of Israel. 32 For it is not My desire that anyone shall die—declares the Lord God. Repent, therefore, and live!

19 And you are to intone a dirge over the princes of Israel, 2 and say:

> What a lioness was your mother
> Among the lions!
> Crouching among the great beasts,
> She reared her cubs.
> 3 She raised up one of her cubs,
> He became a great beast;
> He learned to hunt prey—
> He devoured men.
> 4 Nations heeded [the call] against him;
> He was caught in their snare.
> They dragged him off with hooks
> To the land of Egypt.
> 5 When she saw herself frustrated,
> Her hope defeated,
> She took another of her cubs
> And set him up as a great beast.
> 6 He stalked among the lions,
> He was a great beast;

25–29: Ezekiel restates the preceding principle about repentance, to answer those living in Babylonia who think that all is lost and who might object, thinking that they are now being punished for sins of past generations **30–32:** *A new heart and a new spirit* (11.19; Jer. 31.31–34; 32.36–41): When considered in relation to the principle stated in the ten commandments above, Ezekiel's proposal is innovative. V. 32 has come to play a significant part in the high holiday liturgy, which under rabbinic influence is understood as a period of retrospection and personal repentence. **19.1–14:** Ezekiel illustrates his principle of individual moral responsibility with two allegories, concerning the demise of the Davidic monarch, styled as dirges or songs of mourning. **1:** *And you are to intone a dirge over the princes of Israel:* Heb poetry typically has three stressed syllables in each line. The lament, however, uses a three-stress line followed by a two-stress line. Poetry using the 3/2 stress pattern (called "qinah" or dirge meter) was recited at the death of an individual (e.g., 2 Sam. ch 1), but the prophets use it metaphorically to signal the demise of the people (Amos 5.1; Jer. 9.9). Ezekiel refers to the kings as "princes," thereby expressing the king's diminished status in relation to the priests (34.24; 45.7–8). **2–9:** The lion symbolizes the tribe of Judah and the royal House of David (Gen. 49.8–12). **2:** *A lioness was your mother* refers to Judah or all Israel. Note the identification of Israel or Jerusalem as the bride of God in Hos. chs 1–3; Zeph. 3.14–20; Jer. chs 2–3; Isa. chs 49–54; 66. **4:** The first cub who is brought *with hooks to the land of Egypt* is King Jehoahaz son of Josiah, who was exiled to Egypt by Pharaoh Neco after Josiah's death (2 Kings 23.31–34; 2 Chron. 36.1–4).

He learned to hunt prey—
He devoured men.

7   He ªravished their widows,ª
Laid waste their cities;
The land and all in it were appalled
At the sound of his roaring.

8   Nations from the countries roundabout
Arrayed themselves against him.
They spread their net over him,
He was caught in their snare.

9   With hooks he was put in a cage,
They carried him off to the king of Babylon
And confined him in a fortress,
So that never again should his roar be heard
On the hills of Israel.

10   Your mother was like a vine ᵇin your blood,ᵇ
Planted beside streams,
With luxuriant boughs and branches
Thanks to abundant waters.

11   And she had a mighty rodᶜ
Fit for a ruler's scepter.ᶜ
It towered highest ᵈamong the leafy trees,ᵈ
It was conspicuous by its height,
By the abundance of its boughs.

12   But plucked up in a fury,
She was hurled to the ground.
The east wind withered her branches,
They broke apart and dried up;
And her mighty rod was consumed by fire.

13   Now she is planted in the desert,
In ground that is arid and parched.

14   Fire has issued from her twig-laden branch
And has consumed her boughs,
She is left without a mighty rod,
A scepter to rule with.

This is a dirge, and it has become a [familiar] dirge.

20 In the seventh year, on the tenth day of the fifth month, certain elders of Israel came to inquire of the LORD, and sat down before me. ² And the word of the LORD came to me:

³ O mortal, speak to the elders of Israel and say to them:

---

a-a *Emendation yields "ravaged their castles."*
b-b *Meaning of Heb. uncertain; emendation yields "in a vineyard."*
c *Heb. plural.*
d-d *Meaning of Heb. uncertain.*

6: The second cub who *learned to hunt prey . . . devoured men* would be King Jehoiakim son of Josiah, whom Pharaoh Neco placed on the throne after exiling Jehoahaz. Jeremiah condemns Jehoiakim for his injustice (Jer. 21.11–22.19). **9:** *Carried him off to the king of Babylon and confined him in a fortress* refers to King Jehoiachin son of Jehoiakim, who was exiled to Babylon following Jehoiakim's failed revolt and death (2 Kings 24.8–17; 2 Chron. 36.9–10). **10–14:** This poem employs the imagery of the vine (see chs 15; 17; cf. Isa. 5.1–7). It is impossible to identify the poem's imagery with specific individuals or countries (see Isa. 10.5–11.16; 1.29–31; 6.13), though Radak identifies King Zedekiah son of Josiah, who is not referred to in the preceding vv., as the subject of the allegory. **12:** *The east wind withered her branches:* The "Sharav" or "Hamsin," a dry desert wind like the Santa Ana winds of southern California, is frequently employed as a symbol of God's power (Exod. 14.21; 15.8–10; Isa. 11.15). **13:** *Now she is planted in the desert:* Zedekiah was captured in the desert (wilderness) near Jericho, although he was exiled to Babylonia (2 Kings ch 25; Jer. ch 52).

20.1–23.49: Oracles concerning the punishment of Israel. The third major section of Ezekiel provides the basis for punishment against the entire land of Israel. This section begins with the introductory date formula, *In the seventh year, on the tenth day of the fifth month,* 10 Av, 591 BCE. Once again, the formula *and the word of the LORD* marks the various oracle reports that comprise this section, including 20.1–44; 21.1–5; 21.6–12; 21.13–22; 21.23–37; 22.1–16; 22.17–22; 22.23–31; 23.1–49. The sequence begins with an examination of Israel's past history in the wilderness, which provides a basis for returning the nation to the wilderness so that it might be purged. It continues with prophecies against the Negev desert, oracles concerning God's sword, and the

Thus said the Lord GOD: Have you come to inquire of Me? As I live, I will not respond to your inquiry—declares the Lord GOD.

⁴ ᵃ⁻Arraign, arraign them, O mortal!⁻ᵃ Declare to them the abhorrent deeds of their fathers. ⁵ Say to them: Thus said the Lord GOD:

On the day that I chose Israel, I ᵇ⁻gave My oath⁻ᵇ to the stock of the House of Jacob; when I made Myself known to them in the land of Egypt, I gave my oath to them. When I said, "I the LORD am your God," ⁶ that same day I swore to them to take them out of the land of Egypt into a land flowing with milk and honey, a land which I had sought out for them, the fairest of all lands.

⁷ I also said to them: Cast away, every one of you, the detestable things ᶜ⁻that you are drawn to,⁻ᶜ and do not defile yourselves with the fetishes of Egypt—I the LORD am your God. ⁸ But they defied Me and refused to listen to Me. They did not cast away the detestable things they were drawn to, nor did they give up the fetishes of Egypt. Then I resolved to pour out My fury upon them, to vent all My anger upon them there, in the land of Egypt. ⁹ But I acted for the sake of My name, that it might not be profaned in the sight of the nations among whom they were. For it was before their eyes that I had made Myself known to Israelᵈ to bring them out of the land of Egypt.

¹⁰ I brought them out of the land of Egypt and I led them into the wilderness. ¹¹ I gave them My laws and taught them My rules, by the pursuit of which a man shall live. ¹² Moreover, I gave them My sabbaths to serve as a sign between Me and them, that they might know that it is I the LORD who sanctify them. ¹³ But the House of Israel rebelled against Me in the wilderness; they did not follow My laws and they rejected My rules—by the pursuit of which a man shall live—and they grossly desecrated My sabbaths. Then I thought to pour out My fury upon them in the wilderness and to make an end of them; ¹⁴ but I acted for the sake of My name, that it might not be profaned in the sight of the nations before whose eyes I had

a-a Lit. "Will you arraign them, will you arraign, O mortal?"
b-b Lit. "raised My hand."   c-c Lit. "of his eyes."   d Lit. "them."

terms of Israel's rebellion, God's punishment, and divine compassion. Ezek. 20.12–20 serves as the haftarah for the parashah of Kedoshim (Lev. 19.1–20.27) in the Sephardi tradition. **1–2:** *The seventh year . . . tenth day . . . fifth month,* 10 Av, 591 BCE. According to Jer. 52.12, the Babylonians burned the Temple, the king's palace, and all the houses of Jerusalem (cf. 2 Kings 25.8, which states that was the seventh day), so that this oracle was delivered four years prior to the day when the Temple would be destroyed. **3–4:** *Inquire of* the LORD is a technical term for seeking a divine oracle. God refuses to answer *the elders,* and instead calls upon Ezekiel to judge them. Although God here states, *I will not respond to your inquiry,* God later states, *I will respond to the House of Israel* (36.37). **5–32:** God rehearses the history of Israel's rebellion during the exodus and wilderness periods (see Ps. 106). **5–6:** *I chose Israel,* God uses royal language (see 2 Sam. 6.21; 1 Kings 8.16) to prepare the reader for God's role as king (v. 33). *I the* LORD *am your God . . . I swore to them to take them out of the land of Egypt,* see also Exod. 20.2. **7–8:** Apostasy in Egypt; actually, immediately during and following the exodus (Exod. 14.10–12; Josh. 24.14; Ps. 106.7). **9:** *I acted for the sake of My name,* a key issue in Ezekiel (20.14, 22; 36.22; cf. Exod. 15.3; 32.12). **10–26:** Apostasy in the wilderness. See Exod. chs 32–34; Num. chs 14; 25. **11–12:** The Sabbath is the foundational sign of the covenant (Exod. 20.8–11; 31.12–17). Many scholars believe that the Sabbath became particularly significant in the exile, as holy time replaced the vacuum of holy space (the Temple); this might explain why the Sabbath plays such a significant role here. As in Exod. 31.13, 17 (in the Priestly tradition), it is viewed as a *sign,* namely a symbol acknowledging God as creator, following the Priestly creation story of Gen 1.1–2.4a. **13–17:** The rebellion of the first generation is the golden calf incident and the reaction to the report of the spies in

allegory of Oholah and Oholibah which outlines the sins of Samaria and Jerusalem. The date formula in 24.1 marks the beginning of the fourth major section of the book.

20.1–44: Ezekiel's assessment of Israel's past and future. Ezekiel's

overview of Israel's history in the wilderness calls for a new exodus, in which Israel will return to the wilderness so that it might be purged and restored to the land. This historical précis is very selective, and like that in Ps. 106 and Neh. ch 9, presents the past in led them out. [15] However, I swore[a] to them in the wilderness that I would not bring them into the land flowing with milk and honey, the fairest of all lands, which I had assigned [to them], [16] for they had rejected My rules, disobeyed My laws, and desecrated My sabbaths; their hearts followed after their fetishes. [17] But I had pity on them and did not destroy them; I did not make an end of them in the wilderness.

[18] I warned their children in the wilderness: Do not follow the practices of your fathers, do not keep their ways, and do not defile yourselves with their fetishes. [19] I the LORD am your God: Follow My laws and be careful to observe My rules. [20] And hallow My sabbaths, that they may be a sign between Me and you, that you may know that I the LORD am your God.

[21] But the children rebelled against Me: they did not follow My laws and did not faithfully observe My rules, by the pursuit of which man shall live; they profaned My sabbaths. Then I resolved to pour out My fury upon them, to vent all My anger upon them, in the wilderness. [22] But I held back My hand and acted for the sake of My name, that it might not be profaned in the sight of the nations before whose eyes I had led them out. [23] However, I swore[a] to them in the wilderness that I would scatter them among the nations and disperse them through the lands, [24] because they did not obey My rules, but rejected My laws, profaned My sabbaths, and looked with longing to the fetishes of their fathers. [25] Moreover, I gave them laws that were not good and rules by which they could not live: [26] When they set aside every first issue of the womb, I defiled them by their very gifts[b]—that I might render them desolate,[c] that they might know that I am the LORD.

[27] Now, O mortal, speak to the House of Israel and say to them: Thus said the Lord GOD: By this too your fathers affronted Me and committed trespass against Me: [28] When I brought them to the land that I had sworn[a] to give them, and they saw any high hill or any leafy tree, they slaughtered their sacrifices there and presented their offensive offerings there; there they produced their pleasing odors and poured out their libations. [29] Then I said to them, "What is this shrine which you visit?" (Therefore such [a shrine] is called bamah[d] to this day.)

[30] Now say to the House of Israel: Thus said the Lord GOD: If you defile yourselves as your fathers did and go astray after their detestable things, [31] and if to this very

which Moses persuaded God not to destroy the entire people (Exod. 33.12–33; Num. 14.13–25). **18–26:** Following Israel's rebellion at the report of the spies, God condemned the people to death in the wilderness (Num. 14.26–38). The rebellion of the second generation refers to acts of apostasy following the incident of the spies (e.g., Meribah, Num. ch 20; Baal Peor, Num. ch 25). Since the people disobeyed God's good laws, He gave them bad laws instead, exemplified by child sacrifice. Whether this is the way some Israelites intepreted Exod. 22.28; 34.19, and whether at an early point in Israelite religion sacrifice of the first-born was regularly practiced, is unclear. It seems, however, that some believed that God approved of child sacrifice (Deut. 12.29; Jer. 7.31; 19.5; 32.25). The notion that God misled the people so that He could then condemn them for it is found also in 14.9. **27–31:** Apostasy in the land of Israel.

---

a Lit. "raised My hand."　　b See v. 31.
c Emendation yields "guilty."　　d As if from ba "visit" and mah "what."

day you defile yourselves in the presentation of your gifts by making your children pass through the fire to all your fetishes, shall I respond to your inquiry, O House of Israel? As I live—declares the Lord GOD—I will not respond to you. ³² And what you have in mind shall never come to pass—when you say, "We will be like the nations, like the families of the lands, worshiping wood and stone." ³³ As I live—declares the Lord GOD—I will reign over you with a strong hand, and with an outstretched arm, and with overflowing fury. ³⁴ With a strong hand and an outstretched arm and overflowing fury I will bring you out from the peoples and gather you from the lands where you are scattered, ³⁵ and I will bring you into the wilderness of the peoples; and there I will enter into judgment with you face to face. ³⁶ As I entered into judgment with your fathers in the wilderness of the land of Egypt, so will I enter into judgment with you—declares the Lord GOD. ³⁷ I will make you pass under the shepherd's staff,ᵃ and I will bring you into the bondᵇ of the covenant. ³⁸ I will remove from you those who rebel and transgress against Me; I will take them out of the countries where they sojourn, but they shall not enter the land of Israel. Then you shall know that I am the LORD.

³⁹ As for you, O House of Israel, thus said the Lord GOD: Go, every one of you, and worship his fetishes and continue,ᵇ if you will not obey Me; but do not profane My holy name any more with your idolatrous gifts. ⁴⁰ For only on My holy mountain, on the lofty mount of Israel—declares the Lord GOD—there, in the land, the entire House of Israel, all of it, must worship Me. There I will accept them, and there I will take note of your contributions and the choicest offerings of all your sacred things. ⁴¹ When I bring you out from the peoples and gather you from the lands in which you are scattered, I will accept you as a pleasing odor; and I will be sanctified through you in the sight of the nations. ⁴² Then, when I have brought you to the land of Israel, to the country that I sworeᶜ to give to your fathers, you shall know that I am the LORD. ⁴³ There you will recall your ways and all the acts by which you defiled yourselves; and you will loathe yourselves for all the evils that you committed. ⁴⁴ Then, O House of Israel, you shall know that I am the LORD, when I deal with you for My name's sake—not in accordance with your evil ways and corrupt acts—declares the Lord GOD.

32: *We will be like the nations,* see Deut. 17.14; 1 Sam. 8.4–5 concerning the institution of kingship. **33–44:** God returns Israel to the wilderness to purge and to restore the nation. *A strong hand, and . . . an outstretched arm,* typically used of God liberating Israel from Egypt (e.g., Deut. 4.34), are here reversed, and used of God punishing Israel. **33:** *I will reign over you,* one of God's fundamental claims to kingship. **35:** *Wilderness of the peoples* associates Israel's exile among the nations with the wilderness tradition. **37:** *Pass under the shepherd's staff,* be counted like the sheep to determine the offering due to God (see Lev. 27.32). God uses this metaphor to portray the purge of Israel that will take place when the Temple is destroyed. A similar image is developed more extensively in ch 34. **40–44:** *My holy mountain,* the Jerusalem Temple where the people will present their offerings to God. As in the conclusion to ch 23, Ezekiel emphasizes that Israel's restoration is for God's sake only, and that Israel will fully understand its shame in the future.

a *I.e., to be counted; see Lev. 27.32.*

b *Meaning of Heb. uncertain.*

c *Lit. "raised My hand."*

21 The word of the LORD came to me: ²O mortal, set your face toward Teman,ᵃ and proclaim to Darom,ᵃ and prophesy against the brushland of the Negeb.ᵃ ³Say to the brushland of the Negeb: Hear the word of the LORD. Thus said the Lord GOD: I am going to kindle a fire in you, which shall devour every tree of yours, both green and withered. Its leaping flame shall not go out, and every face from south to north shall be scorched by it. ⁴Then all flesh shall recognize that I the LORD have kindled it; it shall not go out. ⁵And I said, "Ah, Lord GOD! They say of me: He is just a riddlemonger."

⁶Then the word of the LORD came to me: ⁷O mortal, set your face toward Jerusalem and proclaim against her sanctuaries and prophesy against the land of Israel. ⁸Say to the land of Israel: Thus said the LORD: I am going to deal with you! I will draw My sword from its sheath, and I will wipe out from you both the righteous and the wicked. ⁹In order to wipe out from you both the righteous and the wicked, My sword shall assuredly be unsheathed against all flesh from south to north; ¹⁰and all flesh shall know that I the LORD have drawn My sword from its sheath, not to be sheathed again.

¹¹And you, O mortal, sigh; with tottering limbs and bitter grief, sigh before their eyes. ¹²And when they ask you, "Why do you sigh?" answer, "Because of the tidings that have come." Every heart shall sink and all hands hang nerveless; every spirit shall grow faint and all knees turn to water because of the tidings that have come. It is approaching, it shall come to pass—declares the Lord GOD.

¹³The word of the LORD came to me: ¹⁴O mortal, prophesy and say: Thus said the Lord GOD: A sword! A sword has been whetted and polished. ¹⁵It has been whetted to wreak slaughter; ᵇ[therefore] it has been ground to a brilliant polish.ᵇ ᶜHow can we rejoice? My son, it scornsᶜ the rod and every stick. ¹⁶It has been given to be polished and then grasped in the hand; for this has the sword been whetted, for this polished—to be put into the hand of a slayer. ¹⁷Cry and wail, O mortal, for this shall befall My people, this shall befall all the chieftains of Israel: they shall be cast before the sword together with My people; oh, strike the thigh [in grief]. ¹⁸ᶜConsider: How shall it fail to happen, seeing that it even scorns the rod?ᶜ—says the Lord GOD.

¹⁹Further, O mortal, prophesy, striking hand against

21.1–5: A prophecy against the Negeb. The *Negeb* (Negev) is the desert region of southern Judah; here it is an allusion to Jerusalem. **2:** *Teman* designates the location of the Edomites (25.13), who are condemned for assisting Babylonia in Judah's destruction (25.12–14). Both *Teman* and *Darom* refer to the south. The repetition is for emphasis. **5:** *Riddlemonger*, Heb "memashal meshalim," "an allegorizer of allegories" (echoing 17.2).

21.6–12: The first oracle concerning God's sword. The three oracles concerning God's sword in 21.6–12; 21.13–22; and 21.23–27 may have accompanied a symbolic action involving a sword (see 5.1–4; 14.21). Ezekiel speaks toward the Jerusalem sanctuary as the holy center of the nation. **8:** God's threat to *wipe out from you both the righteous and the wicked* contradicts Ezekiel's concept of individual moral responsibility (ch 18), and instead conforms to the portrayal of slaughter in ch 9.

21.13–22: The second oracle concerning the sword. 15: *My son, it scorns the rod and every stick:* A rod might normally be used for discipline (Prov. 10.13; 22.15), but now a deadly instrument is required. **19:** The third strike of the sword is enigmatic, although the commentators understand it as a reference to Zedekiah's disaster, which was far greater than Jehoiakim's or Jehoiachin's.

---

a *Teman, Darom, Negeb are three terms for "the south." The allusion is to Jerusalem (v. 7), which was always approached from Babylon by way of the north.*

b-b *Lit. "it has been polished in order that it may have lightning."*

c-c *Meaning of Heb. uncertain.*

hand. Let the sword strike a second time and yet a third time; it is a sword for massacre, a sword for great carnage, that presses*a* upon them. ²⁰ Thus hearts shall lose courage and many shall fall. At all their gates I have appointed slaughter*a* by the sword. Ah! it is made to flash brilliantly, it is honed*a* for slaughter. ²¹ Be united,*b* go to the right, turn left; whither are you bound? ²² I, too, will strike hand against hand and will satisfy My fury upon you; I the LORD have spoken.

²³ The word of the LORD came to me: ²⁴ And you, O mortal, choose two roads on which the sword of the king of Babylon may advance, both issuing from the same country; and select a spot, select it where roads branch off to [two] cities. ²⁵ Choose a way for the sword to advance on Rabbah of the Ammonites or on fortified Jerusalem in Judah. ²⁶ For the king of Babylon has stood at the fork of the road, where two roads branch off, to perform divination: He has shaken arrows, consulted teraphim, and inspected the liver.*c* ²⁷ In his right hand came up the omen against Jerusalem—to set battering rams, to proclaim murder, to raise battle shouts, to set battering rams against the gates, to cast up mounds, to erect towers.

²⁸ *d*In their eyes, the oaths they had sworn to them were like empty divination; but this shall serve to recall their guilt, for which they shall be taken to task. ²⁹ Assuredly, thus said the Lord GOD: For causing your guilt to be recalled, your transgressions to be uncovered, and your sins to be revealed—all your misdeeds—because you have brought yourselves to [My] mind, you shall be taken to task.

³⁰ And to you, O dishonored wicked prince of Israel, whose day has come—the time set for your punishment—³¹ thus said the Lord GOD: Remove the turban and lift off the crown! This shall not remain as it is; exalt the low and abase the high. ³² Ruin, an utter ruin I will make it. *e-*It shall be no more*-e* until he comes to whom it rightfully belongs; and I will give it to him.

³³ Further, O mortal, prophesy and say: Thus said the Lord GOD concerning the Ammonites and their blasphemies: Proclaim: O sword! O sword unsheathed for slaughter, polished to the utmost, to a flashing brilliance! ³⁴ Because they have prophesied falsely about you and have

21.23–37: The third oracle concerning the sword. The sword of Babylonia. **23–28:** When the Babylonian king reaches a fork in the road, he employs divination to decide which route to take. His alternatives are Jerusalem and Rabbah (the modern city of Amman, Jordan), the capital of Ammon. Ammon is one of Judah's allies against Babylonia (Jer. 27.3). Jerusalem is a former ally of Babylonia (2 Kings 20.12–19; Isa. ch 39), but Judah's revolt justifies the protracted siege. **26:** *He has shaken arrows, consulted teraphim, and inspected the liver,* reflecting Ezekiel's familiarity with common techniques of divination. *Teraphim,* family gods (Gen. 31.19; Judg. 17.5; 18.17, 20). **30:** The *dishonored, wicked prince of Israel,* Zedekiah. **33–37:** The sword will be wielded against Ammon, but it will be destroyed in Babylonia where it was created.

---

a *Meaning of Heb. uncertain.*
b *Meaning of Heb. uncertain; Targum reads "Be whetted." Cf. vv. 14–16.*
c *I.e., of a sacrificed animal.*   d *The inhabitants of Jerusalem disregarded their oaths to the Babylonians; cf. 17.13 ff.*
e-e *Meaning of Heb. uncertain.*

divined deceitfully concerning you, you shall be wielded over the necks of the dishonored wicked ones, for their day has come, the time ᵃ⁻set for their punishment.⁻ᵃ

35 ᵇ⁻Return it to its sheath!⁻ᵇ In the place where you were created, in the land of your origin, I will judge you. 36 I will pour out My indignation upon you, I will blow upon you with the fire of My wrath; and I will deliver you into the hands of barbarians, craftsmen of destruction. 37 You shall be fuel for the fire, your blood shall sink into the earth, you shall not be remembered, for I the LORD have spoken.

22 The word of the LORD came to me: 2 Further, O mortal, ᶜ⁻arraign, arraign⁻ᶜ the city of bloodshed; declare to her all her abhorrent deeds! 3 Say: Thus said the Lord GOD: O city in whose midst blood is shed, so that your hour is approaching; within which fetishes are made, so that you have become unclean! 4 You stand guilty of the blood you have shed, defiled by the fetishes you have made. You have brought on your day; ᵈ⁻you have reached your year.⁻ᵈ Therefore I will make you the mockery of the nations and the scorn of all the lands. 5 Both the near and the far shall scorn you, O besmirched of name, O laden with iniquity!

6 Every one of the princes of Israel in your midst used his strength for the shedding of blood. 7 Fathers and mothers have been humiliated within you; strangers have been cheated in your midst; orphans and widows have been wronged within you. 8 You have despised My holy things and profaned My sabbaths.

9 Baseᵉ men in your midst were intent on shedding blood; in you they have eaten ᶠ⁻upon the mountains;⁻ᶠ and they have practiced depravity in your midst. 10 In you they have uncovered their fathers' nakedness;ᵍ in you they have ravished women during their impurity. 11 They have committed abhorrent acts with other men's wives; in their depravity they have defiled their own daughters-in-law; in you they have ravished their own sisters, daughters of their fathers. 12 They have taken bribes within you to shed blood. You have taken advance and accrued interest;ʰ you have defrauded your countrymen to your profit. You have forgotten Me—declares the Lord GOD.

22.1–16: Oracle concerning bloodshed in Jerusalem. Ezek. 22.1–19 in the Ashkenazi tradition or Ezek. 22.1–16 in the Sephardi tradition serve as the haftarah portion for the parashah of 'Aḥarei Mot (Lev. 16.1–18.30), which focuses on the atonement of guilt at Yom Kippur, the proper treatment of blood, and incestuous sexual relations. Ezek. 22.1–16 draws heavily on Isa. 1.2–31. Ezekiel's preoccupation with blood derives from his role as a priest, which requires the proper treatment of blood (Lev. ch 17). Rabbinic interpretation relates this oracle to Manasseh's shedding of innocent blood in Jerusalem (2 Kings 21.6). As in ch 18, the catalogue of crimes listed here derives especially from the Holiness Collection in Lev. chs 17–26. **2–6:** *Bloodshed* (Lev. 19.26; Gen. 9.1–7). **7:** Contempt for parents (Lev. 20.9; Exod. 21.17); extortion of the aliens, orphans, and widows (Lev. 19.33–34; Exod. 22.21–22; Deut. 14.29). **8:** *Despised . . . holy things . . . sabbaths* (Lev. 19.30). **9:** *Base men* employs a term commonly used for slander (Lev. 19.16). **10:** *Uncovered their father's nakedness* (Lev. 18.8; 20.11; Radak relates this to the Talmud's charge based on 2 Chron. 33.23 that King Ammon had relations with his mother [*b. Sanh.* 103b]); relations with menstruating women (Lev. 18.19). **11:** Incest (Lev. chs 18; 20). **12:** Bribery (Lev. 19.15; Deut. 16.19); interest on loans (Lev. 25.36–37); extortion of a neighbor (Lev. 19.15–18, 35–36).

---

a-a *Meaning of Heb. uncertain.*

b-b *Emendation yields "Return to your scabbard!" In this and the following verses, the prophet describes the future punishment of Babylon, still symbolized by the sword.*

c-c *Lit. "will you arraign, arraign."*   d-d *Some Babylonian mss. and ancient versions read "the time of your years has come."*   e *Meaning of Heb. uncertain.*

f-f *I.e., in idolatry. Emendation yields "with the blood"; cf. Lev. 19.26.*

g *I.e., have cohabited with a former wife of the father; cf. Lev. 18.7–8.*   h *Cf. note at 18.8.*

13 Lo, I will strike My hands over the ill-gotten gains that you have amassed, and over the bloodshed that has been committed in your midst. 14 Will your courage endure, will your hands remain firm in the days when I deal with you? I the LORD have spoken and I will act. 15 I will scatter you among the nations and disperse you through the lands; I will consume the uncleanness out of you. 16 You shall be dishonored in the sight of nations, and you shall know that I am the LORD.

17 The word of the LORD came to me: 18 O mortal, the House of Israel has become dross to Me; they are all copper, tin, iron, and lead. ᵃ But in a crucible, the dross shall turn into silver.ᵃ 19 Assuredly, thus said the Lord GOD: Because you have all become dross, I will gather you into Jerusalem. 20 As silver, copper, iron, lead, and tin are gathered into a crucible to blow the fire upon them, so as to melt them, so will I gather you in My fierce anger and cast you [into the fire] and melt you. 21 I will gather you and I will blow upon you the fire of My fury, and you shall be melted in it. 22 As silver is melted in a crucible, so shall you be melted in it. And you shall know that I the LORD have poured out My fury upon you.

23 The word of the LORD came to me: 24 O mortal, say to her: You are an uncleansed land, ᵃ not to be washed with rain ᵃ on the day of indignation. 25 ᵇ Her gang of prophets ᵇ are like roaring lions in her midst, rending prey. They devour human beings; they seize treasure and wealth; they have widowed many women in her midst. 26 Her priests have violated My Teaching: they have profaned what is sacred to Me, they have not distinguished between the sacred and the profane, they have not taught the difference between the unclean and the clean, and they have closed their eyes to My sabbaths. I am profaned in their midst. 27 Her officials are like wolves rending prey in her midst; they shed blood and destroy lives to win ill-gotten gain. 28 Her prophets, too, daub the wall for them with plaster:ᶜ They prophesy falsely and divine deceitfully for them; they say, "Thus said the Lord GOD," when the LORD has not spoken. 29 And the people of the land have practiced fraud and committed robbery; they have wronged the poor and needy, have defrauded the stranger without redress. 30 And I sought a man among them to repair the wall or to stand in the breach before Me in behalf of this

22.17–22: Oracle concerning the smelting of Jerusalem. Again, this oracle draws heavily upon Isa. 1.2–31, esp. Isa. 1.21–26, which employs the metaphor of metal smelting to portray the purification of Jerusalem. Just as precious metals are smelted to remove *dross*, Israel will be purified in fire to remove its sins and impurities.

22.23–31: Oracle condemning the leadership and people of Jerusalem. Again, the oracle draws upon the imagery of Isa. 1.2–31, which focuses on the wrongdoing of Jerusalem's leaders and the people at large. The emphasis is on the ritual impurity created through these actions; as in the Holiness Collection, Ezekiel believes that both cultic infractions and ethical violations create impurity. **25–29:** The prophet names all classes of people in Jerusalem, including *her . . . prophets, her priests, her officials,* and *the people of the land* (a technical term for the landed gentry).

a-a *Meaning of Heb. uncertain.*
b-b *Septuagint reads "Whose chieftains."*   c *Cf.* 13.10 *ff.*

land, that I might not destroy it; but I found none. ³¹ I have therefore poured out My indignation upon them; I will consume them with the fire of My fury. I will repay them for their conduct—declares the Lord GOD.

23 The word of the LORD came to me: ²O mortal, once there were two women, daughters of one mother. ³They played the whore in Egypt; they played the whore while still young. There their breasts were squeezed, and there their virgin nipples were handled. ⁴Their names were: the elder one, Oholah;ᵃ and her sister, Oholibah.ᵇ They became Mine, and they bore sons and daughters. As for their names, Oholah is Samaria, and Oholibah is Jerusalem.

⁵Oholah whored while she was Mine, and she lusted after her lovers, after the Assyrians, warriorsᶜ ⁶clothed in blue, governors and prefects, horsemen mounted on steeds—all of them handsome young fellows. ⁷She bestowed her favors upon them—upon all the pick of the Assyrians—and defiled herself with all their fetishes after which she lusted. ⁸She did not give up the whoring she had begun with the Egyptians; for they had lain with her in her youth, and they had handled her virgin nipples and had poured out their lust upon her. ⁹Therefore I delivered her into the hands of her lovers, into the hands of the Assyrians after whom she lusted. ¹⁰They exposed her nakedness; they seized her sons and daughters, and she herself was put to the sword. And because of the punishment inflicted upon her, she became a byword among women.

¹¹Her sister Oholibah saw this; yet her lusting was more depraved than her sister's, and her whoring more debased. ¹²She lusted after the Assyrians, governors and prefects, warriorsᶜ gorgeously clad, horsemen mounted on steeds—all of them handsome young fellows. ¹³And I saw how she had defiled herself. Both of them followed the same course, ¹⁴but she carried her harlotries further. For she saw men sculptured upon the walls, figures of Chaldeans drawn in vermilion, ¹⁵girded with belts round their waists, and with flowing turbans on their heads, all of them looking like officers—a picture of Babylonians whose native land was Chaldea. ¹⁶At the very sight of them she lusted after them, and she sent messengers for them to Chaldea. ¹⁷So the Babylonians came to her for lovemaking and defiled her with their whoring; and she defiled herself with them until she turned from them in disgust. ¹⁸She flaunted her harlotries and exposed her

23.1–49: Oholah and Oholibah. Presupposing the portrayal of Israel as God's wife (cf. Hos. chs 1–3; Jer. chs 2–3), Ezekiel employs the metaphor of harlotry to describe Samaria and Jerusalem. Here as elsewhere, adultery is equated with idolatry. The punishment for adultery is death, and so the adulterous cities are destroyed. This ch has much in common with ch 16. **3:** In contrast to modern sensibilities, Israel is being blamed for its own abuse. **4:** *Oholah*, "her tent," refers to Samaria. The name Oholah alludes to the presence of God, who dwells in a tent (according to the exodus and wilderness traditions; see 2 Sam. 7.6). *Oholibah*, "my tent is in her," refers to Jerusalem and the presence of the Temple (Rashi, Radak). **5–10:** Oholah's or Samaria's relations with the officers of Assyria presuppose its earlier alliance with Assyria under the Jehu dynasty, specifically, Menahem (2 Kings 15.17–22), and Hoshea (2 Kings 17.1–6). Ezekiel portrays this alliance as harlotry, and argues that it led to Israel's destruction (in 722 BCE). The reference to *the Assyrians, warriors,* deliberately employs the ambiguous Heb term "kerovim," lit. "those who draw near," for war, sacrifice, sex, etc. **11–21:** Ezekiel charges that *Oholibah,* Jerusalem, was even worse than her sister in pursuing both the Assyrians and the Chaldeans or Babylonians (see Jer. 3.6–10, 11). King Ahaz of Judah requested Assyrian assistance against Israel in the Syro-Ephraimitic War (2 Kings ch 16), and Hezekiah later made an alliance with Babylonia against Assyria (2 Kings 20.11–19; Isa. ch 39). The reference to relations with Egypt may recall Solomon's early alliance with Egypt (1 Kings 3.1) and Jehoiakim's support from Pharaoh Neco before he turned to Babylonia (2 Kings 23.31–24.7).

---

a I.e., "Tent."   *b I.e., "My Tent Is in Her."*   *c Meaning of Heb. uncertain.*

nakedness, and I turned from her in disgust, as I had turned disgusted from her sister. ¹⁹ But she whored still more, remembering how in her youth she had played the whore in the land of Egypt; ²⁰ she lusted for concubinage with them, whose members were like those of asses and whose organsᵃ were like those of stallions. ²¹ Thus you reverted to the wantonness of your youth, rememberingᵇ your youthful breasts, when the men of Egypt handled your nipples.

²² Assuredly, Oholibah, thus said the Lord GOD: I am going to rouse against you the lovers from whom you turned in disgust, and I will bring them upon you from all around—²³ the Babylonians and all the Chaldeans, [the people of] Pekod, Shoa, and Koa, and all the Assyrians with them, all of them handsome young fellows, governors and prefects, officers and warriors,ᵃ all of them riding on horseback. ²⁴ They shall attack you with fleetsᵃ of wheeled chariots and a host of troops; they shall set themselves against you on all sides with bucklers, shields, and helmets. And I will entrust your punishment to them, and they shall inflict their punishments on you. ²⁵ I will direct My passion against you, and they shall deal with you in fury: they shall cut off your nose and ears. The last of you shall fall by the sword; theyᶜ shall take away your sons and daughters, and your remnant shall be devoured by fire. ²⁶ They shall strip you of your clothing and take away your dazzling jewels. ²⁷ I will put an end to your wantonness and to your whoring in the land of Egypt, and you shall not long for them or remember Egypt any more.

²⁸ For thus said the Lord GOD: I am going to deliver you into the hands of those you hate, into the hands of those from whom you turned in disgust. ²⁹ They shall treat you with hate, and they shall take away all you have toiled for, and leave you naked and bare; your naked whoredom, wantonness, and harlotry will be exposed. ³⁰ These things shall be done to you for your harlotries with the nations, for defiling yourself with their fetishes. ³¹ You walked in your sister's path; therefore I will put her cup into your hand.

³² Thus said the Lord GOD:

> You shall drink of your sister's cup,
> So deep and wide;
> It shall cause derision and scorn,
> It holds so much.

22–35: As in ch 16, Ezekiel declares that Oholibah's "lovers," the Babylonians and their allies, will strip and conquer Jerusalem. **23:** *Pekod* (see Jer. 50.21), *Shoa*, and *Koa*, Aramean tribes allied with Babylonia. **32:** Drinking from the *sister's cup*, a common motif in Judean prophecy (Isa. 51.17, 22; Jer. 25.15–29; 51.7; Hab. 2.16). As in other contexts, the cup contains strong wine and ultimately poison.

---

a *Meaning of Heb. uncertain.*   b *Lit. "for the sake of."*
c *I.e., the former lovers, vv. 22 ff.*

33   You shall be filled with drunkenness and woe.
    The cup of desolation and horror,
    The cup of your sister Samaria—
34   You shall drink it and drain it,
    ᵃ⁻And gnaw its shards;⁻ᵃ
    And you shall tear your breasts.
For I have spoken—declares the Lord GOD.

35 Assuredly, thus said the Lord GOD: Because you have forgotten Me and cast Me behind your back, you in turn must suffer for your wanton whoring.

36 Then the LORD said to me: O mortal, arraignᵇ Oholah and Oholibah, and charge them with their abominations. 37 For they have committed adultery, and blood is on their hands; truly they have committed adultery with their fetishes, and have even offered to them as food the children they bore to Me. 38 At the same time they also did this to Me: they defiled My Sanctuary and profaned My sabbaths. 39 On the very day that they slaughtered their children to their fetishes, they entered My Sanctuary to desecrate it. That is what they did in My House.

40 Moreover, they sent for men to come from afar, [men] to whom a messenger was sent; and they came. For them, [Oholibah,] you bathed, painted your eyes, and donned your finery; 41 and you sat on a grand couch with a set table in front of it—and it was My incense and My oil you laid upon it. 42 And the noise of a carefree multitude was there, ᵃ⁻of numerous men brought drunk from the desert;⁻ᵃ and they put bracelets on their arms and splendid crowns upon their heads. 43 Then I said, ᵃ⁻"To destruction with adultery! Look, they are still going on with those same fornications of hers."⁻ᵃ 44 And they would go to her as one goes to a prostitute; that is how they went to Oholah and Oholibah, wanton women. 45 But righteous men shall punish them with the punishments for adultery and for bloodshed, for they are adulteresses and have blood on their hands.

46 For thus said the Lord GOD: Summon an assembly against them, and make them an object of horror and plunder. 47 Let the assembly pelt them with stones and cut them down with their swords; let them kill their sons and daughters, and burn down their homes. 48 I will put an end to wantonness in the land; and all the women shall take warning not to imitate your wantonness. 49 They shall punish you for your wantonness, and you shall suffer the penalty for your sinful idolatry. And you shall know that I am the Lord GOD.

38: *They defiled My Sanctuary and profaned My sabbaths,* see ch 8. **39:** *They slaughtered their children,* see 20.26. **40:** *Moreover, they sent for men to come from afar,* a reference to Judean attempts to find allies (cf. Jer. 27.3). **46–47:** The sisters' punishment reflects that of an adulterous woman (Lev. 20.10) or a person who profanes God (Lev. 20.2–5). **48:** The metaphorical nature of the image is forgotten, and is here literalized—real women are to learn proper sexual behavior from this metaphor. **49:** The prophecy is brought to a close, like so many others, with the stereotypical *And you shall know that I am the Lord GOD.*

a-a Meaning of Heb. uncertain.   b Lit. "will you arraign"; cf. 22.2.

24 In the ninth year, on the tenth day of the tenth month, the word of the LORD came to me: [2] O mortal, record this date, this exact day; for this very day the king of Babylon has laid siege to Jerusalem. [3] Further, speak in an allegory to the rebellious breed and say to them: Thus said the Lord GOD:

Put the caldron [on the fire], put it on,
And then pour water into it.

[4] Collect in it the pieces [of meat].
Every choice piece, thigh and shoulder;
Fill it with the best cuts[a]—

[5] Take the best of the flock.
Also pile the cuts[b] under it;
Get it boiling briskly,
And cook the cuts in it.

[6] Assuredly, thus said the Lord GOD:
Woe to the city of blood—
A caldron whose scum[c] is in it,
Whose scum has not been cleaned out!
Empty it piece by piece;
[d] No lot has fallen upon it.[d]

[7] For the blood she shed is still in her;
She set it upon a bare rock;
She did not pour it out on the ground
To cover it with earth.

[8] She[e] set her blood upon the bare rock,
So that it was not covered,
So that it may stir up [My] fury
To take vengeance.

[9] Assuredly, thus said the Lord GOD:
Woe to the city of blood!
I in turn will make a great blaze.

[10] Pile on the logs,
Kindle the fire,

---

a Lit. "limbs."   b Emendation yields "wood"; cf. v. 10.
c Or "rust."   d-d Meaning of Heb. uncertain.
e Heb. "I."

24.1–25.17: Symbolic actions concerning the destruction of Jerusalem and condemnation of neighboring nations. The introductory date formula marks Ezek. 24.1–25.17 as the fourth major section of the book. *The ninth year, on the tenth day of the tenth month* would be 10 Tevet, 589–588 BCE, which is identified as the day that the Babylonian king Nebuchadnezzar laid siege to Jerusalem (see also 2 Kings 25.1; Jer. 52.4; cf. Zech. 8.19). The day is marked as a public fast day in Judaism. The prophetic word formula introduces each of three oracle reports that comprise the section, including the allegory of the pot (24.1–14), the death of Ezekiel's wife (24.15–27), and the oracles against Israel's neighbors (25.1–27). Although most interpreters view ch 25 as the first ch of the oracles concerning the nations which comprise chs 25–32, the date formula and the prophetic word formula indicate a different understanding of the arrangement of these oracles. The first two oracles take up symbolic actions concerning the destruction of Jerusalem; the oracles against Israel's neighbors, including Ammon, Moab, Edom, and Philistia, condemn nations that assisted the Babylonians in their destruction of Jerusalem and Judah. A new date formula introduces the oracle against Tyre in 26.1.

24.1–14: The allegory of the pot. As a Temple priest, Ezekiel's duties include tending to pots used to cook sacrificial meat (1 Sam. 2.12–17). Like Jeremiah (a priest descended from Eli), he employs activities from his own life as symbolic actions to express God's words (see Jer. 1.13). **1–2:** *The ninth year . . . the tenth day . . . the tenth month,* 10 Tevet, 589–588 BCE, the day on which Nebuchadnezzar began the siege of Jerusalem (2 Kings 25.1; Jer. 52.4; cf. Zech. 8.19), observed as a public fast day in Judaism. **4:** *Thigh and shoulder:* The choice offerings (Num. 18.12), including the breast and thigh (Exod. 29.26–28; Lev. 7.28–36; 10.12–15; Num. 18.18; Gen. 32.32), are given to the priests. **6–8:** The imagery of the corroded bottom of the pot symbolizes the bloody crimes of Jerusalem. Blood must be covered when shed (Lev. 17.13–16; Gen. 9.1–7). **7:** Rabbinic interpretation relates this v. to the murder of Zechariah son of Jehoiada, the prophet and priest, during the reign of King Joash son of Ahaziah (2 Chron. 24.20–22). His blood had not been requited (2 Chron. 24.22), but lay seething on the pavement when Nebuchadnezzar's commander Nebuzaradan entered the Temple courts. Nebuzaradan therefore killed thousands of people in order to appease it (*b. Git.* 57b; *Pesik. Rav Kah.* 122a; *Lam. Rab.* 23). **9–14:** As a cauldron is cleansed by fire, Ezekiel calls for the "cleansing" of Jerusalem by fire.

Cook the meat through
And ᵃstew it completely,ᵃ
And let the bones be charred.

11 Let it stand empty on the coals,
Until it becomes so hot
That the copper glows.
Then its uncleanness shall melt away in it,
And its rust be consumed.

12 ᵇIt has frustrated all effort,
Its thick scum will not leave it—
Into the fire with its scum!ᵇ

13 For your vile impurity—because I sought to cleanse you of your impurity, but you would not be cleansed—you shall never be clean again until I have satisfied My fury upon you. 14 I the LORD have spoken: It shall come to pass and I will do it. I will not refrain or spare or relent. You shall be punished according to your ways and your deeds—declares the Lord GOD.

15 The word of the LORD came to me: 16 O mortal, I am about to take away the delight of your eyes from you

24.15–27: The death of Ezekiel's wife. The death of Ezekiel's wife symbolizes the destruction of Jerusalem, and in his treatment of it, Ezekiel makes it a radical symbolic action. The ch seems to suggest that regular rituals of mourning are insufficient for the cataclysmic destruction of the Temple. **15–18:** Ezekiel's action draws upon priestly sanctity to symbolize the inability of God and the people of Judah to mourn the loss of Jerusalem when in exile. Priests may not come into contact with the dead (Lev. 21.1–12), and the high priest may not mourn for the dead (Lev. 21.10–12; cf. 10.1–7). **16:** *The delight of your eyes:* The same term is used for the Temple in v. 21. **17:** Rabbinic tradition reads this v. as an instruction for proper mourning. A mourner does not wear tefillin or shoes; he wraps his head; and others serve him food (b. Mo'ed Kat. 15, 27b). **21:** *I am going to desecrate My Sanctuary:* Only the priests could enter the Holy of Holies. **23:** The people

a-a Emendation yields "Pour out the broth."   b-b Meaning of Heb. uncertain.

Places mentioned in the oracles against the nations

through pestilence; but you shall not lament or weep or let your tears flow. [17] Moan softly; observe no mourning for the dead: Put on your turban and put your sandals on your feet; do not cover over your upper lip, and do not eat the bread of comforters."[a]

[18] In the evening my wife died, and in the morning I did as I had been commanded. And when I spoke to the people that morning, [19] the people asked me, "Will you not tell us what these things portend for us, that you are acting so?" [20] I answered them, "The word of the LORD has come to me: [21] Tell the House of Israel: Thus said the Lord GOD: 'I am going to desecrate My Sanctuary, your pride and glory, the delight of your eyes and the desire of your heart; and the sons and daughters you have left behind shall fall by the sword. [24] [b]And Ezekiel shall become a portent for you: you shall do just as he has done, when it happens; and you shall know that I am the Lord GOD.' [22] Accordingly, you shall do as I have done: you shall not cover over your upper lips or eat the bread of comforters;[a] [23] and your turbans shall remain on your heads, and your sandals upon your feet. You shall not lament or weep, but you shall be heartsick because of your iniquities and shall moan to one another."[b]

[25] You, O mortal, take note: On the day that I take their stronghold from them, their pride and joy, the delight of their eyes and the longing of their hearts—their sons and daughters—[26] on that day a fugitive will come to you, to let you hear it with your own ears. [27] On that day your mouth shall be opened to the fugitive, and you shall speak and no longer be dumb. So you shall be a portent for them, and they shall know that I am the LORD.

25 The word of the LORD came to me: [2] O mortal, set your face toward the Ammonites and prophesy against them. [3] Say to the Ammonites: Hear the word of the Lord GOD! Thus said the Lord GOD: Because you cried

---

a Lit. "men."   b V. 24 moved up for clarity.

---

are to be fully dressed, with *turbans* and *sandals*, as they go into exile. See the portrayal of the Israelites at the time of the exodus and at the observance of Passover in the Jerusalem Temple (Exod. 12.11, 33–39; 13.18 ["armed" is sometimes understood as "girded"]). **25–27:** During the Temple service, the priests officiated in silence. When the Temple

is destroyed, Ezekiel will be able to speak again. The arrival of the *fugitive* is recorded in 33.21, in a ch immediately following the oracles concerning the nations (chs 25–32). The placement of these oracles here thus disrupts the flow of the book, but also heightens the tension, as the destruction of the Temple is imminent.

25.1–32.32: Oracles concerning the nations. Like other prophetic books (Isa. chs 13–23; Jer. chs 46–51), Ezekiel contains a section of oracles concerning foreign nations, which demonstrate that God is not merely a national God, concerned with His people and land, Israel, but expresses His power throughout the world. The nations included here, Ammon, Moab, Edom, Philistia, Tyre, and Egypt, would all be considered as targets of the Babylonian empire, although Egypt was never taken. Ezekiel, like Jeremiah, identifies the projected expansion of Babylonia as an act of God. In contrast to Jer. chs 50–51, however, Ezekiel does not prophesy against Babylonia. The appearance of the date formulas in 24.1; 26.1; 29.1; 29.17; 30.20; 31.1; 32.1; 32.17 mark the major segments within the larger structure of the book of Ezekiel.

25.1–17: Oracles condemning Israel's neighbors: Ammon, Moab, Edom, Philistia. The oracles against Ammon, Moab, Edom, and Philistia are grouped together with the oracle reports of the allegories concerning the pot (24.1–14) and the death of Ezekiel's wife (24.15–27). Insofar as the earlier oracles take up the destruction of Jerusalem, these oracles condemn those neighboring nations that are understood to have assisted Babylonia in carrying out the destruction. (There is no extrabiblical information concerning the participation of nations in the attack on Jerusalem.) The entire ch is formulated as an instruction speech in which God tells Ezekiel what to say. The prophetic messenger formula, *Thus said the Lord GOD*, introduces each oracle. Ammon, Moab, and Edom are mentioned in this order following their geographic location, from north to south. **1–7: Oracle concerning Ammon.** The Babylonians employed Ammonites against Judah (2 Kings 24.1–2). Later, the Ammonites joined Judah in an anti-Babylonian coalition (Jer. 27.3). Ammon was located east of the Jordan River. **3:** The Ammonites are condemned

"Aha!" over My Sanctuary when it was desecrated, and over the land of Israel when it was laid waste, and over the House of Judah when it went into exile—⁴assuredly, I will deliver you to the Kedemites as a possession. They shall set up their encampments among you and pitch their dwellings in your midst; they shall eat your produce and they shall drink your milk. ⁵I will make Rabbah a pasture for camels and Ammon a place for sheep to lie down. And you shall know that I am the LORD.

⁶For thus said the Lord GOD: Because you clapped your hands and stamped your feet and rejoiced over the land of Israel with such utter scorn—⁷assuredly, I will stretch out My hand against you and give you as booty to the nations; I will cut you off from among the peoples and wipe you out from among the countries and destroy you. And you shall know that I am the LORD.

⁸Thus said the Lord GOD: Because Moab ᵃand Seir⁻ᵃ said, "See, the House of Judah is like all other nations"— ⁹assuredly, I will lay bare the flank of Moab, all its towns to the last one—Beth-jeshimoth, Baal-meon, and Kiria-thaim, the glory of the country. ¹⁰I will deliver it, together with Ammon, to the Kedemites as their possession. Thus Ammon shall not be remembered among the nations, ¹¹and I will mete out punishments to Moab. And they shall know that I am the LORD.

¹²Thus said the Lord GOD: Because Edom acted vengefully against the House of Judah and incurred guilt by wreaking revenge upon it—¹³assuredly, thus said the Lord GOD: I will stretch out My hand against Edom and cut off from it man and beast, and I will lay it in ruins; from Tema to Dedan they shall fall by the sword. ¹⁴I will wreak My vengeance on Edom through My people Israel, and they shall take action against Edom in accordance with My blazing anger; and they shall know My vengeance—declares the Lord GOD.

¹⁵Thus said the Lord GOD: Because the Philistines, in their ancient hatred, acted vengefully, and with utter scorn sought revenge and destruction—¹⁶assuredly, thus said the Lord GOD: I will stretch out My hand against the Philistines and cut off the Cherethites and wipe out the last survivors of the seacoast. ¹⁷I will wreak frightful vengeance upon them by furious punishment; and when I inflict My vengeance upon them, they shall know that I am the LORD.

in part for mocking the destruction of the Jerusalem Temple. **4:** *The Kedemites,* "sons of the east," are nomadic Arab tribes from the northern Arabian desert who moved into Ammon and Moab following their destruction by Babylonia. **5:** *Rabbah,* the site of present day Amman, Jordan, was the capital of Ammon. Jeremiah indicates that the Ammonites instigated the assassination of the Judean governor Gedaliah following the destruction of Jerusalem (Jer. 40.14) and that they seized the territory of the tribe of Gad (cf. Zeph. 2.8). **8–11: Oracle concerning Moab.** Like Ammon, the Moabites assisted the Babylonians against Judah (2 Kings 24.1–2) and later joined the anti-Babylonian coalition (Jer. 27.3). Moab was located east of the southern portion of the Dead Sea. Cf. Zeph. 2.8. Both geographical proximity and familial relations (see Gen. 19.37–38) are responsible for Moab and Ammon being mentioned adjacently here, as they are so often in the Bible. **9:** *Beth-jeshimoth* is situated in southern Moab, northeast of the Dead Sea (Num. 33.49; Josh. 1.3; 13.20). *Baal-meon* is Beth-baal-meon, located a few miles inland from the Dead Sea (Josh. 13.17), and *Kiriathaim* is to its south (Num. 32.37; Josh. 13.19; Jer. 48.1, 23). **12–14: Oracle concerning Edom.** Edom symbolizes God's wrath, perhaps because of its role in the destruction of the Jerusalem Temple (Ps. 137.7; Lam. 4.21–22; Obadiah 1–14). It was located southeast of the Dead Sea, and sometimes encroached upon southern Judean territories. Edom's ancestor, Esau, was Jacob's twin brother (Gen. chs 25–35). *Tema to Dedan,* towns associated with Edom (Jer. 49.7–8). They are several hundred km southeast of Judah. **15–17: Oracle concerning Philistia.** The Philistine territory was occupied by Assyria in the 8th and 7th centuries BCE and turned into an industrial center for the production of olive oil. It is not clear what action the Philistines took against Judah in the 6th century. Philistia was located along

a-a Lacking in some Septuagint mss.

26 In the eleventh year, on the first of the month,[a] the word of the LORD came to me: [2] O mortal, because Tyre gloated over Jerusalem, "Aha! The gateway[b] of the peoples is broken, it has become mine; I shall be filled, now that it is laid in ruins"—[3] assuredly, thus said the Lord GOD:

> I am going to deal with you, O Tyre!
> I will hurl many nations against you,
> As the sea hurls its waves.
> [4] They shall destroy the walls of Tyre
> And demolish her towers;
> And I will scrape her soil off her
> And leave her a naked rock.
> [5] She shall be in the heart of the sea
> A place for drying[c] nets;
> For I have spoken it   —declares the Lord GOD.
> She shall become spoil for the nations,
> [6] And her daughter-towns in the country
> Shall be put to the sword.
> And they shall know that I am the LORD.

[7] For thus said the Lord GOD: I will bring from the north, against Tyre, King Nebuchadrezzar of Babylon, a king of kings, with horses, chariots, and horsemen—a great mass of troops.

> [8] Your daughter-towns in the country
> He shall put to the sword;
> He shall erect towers against you,
> And cast up mounds against you,
> And raise [a wall of] bucklers against you.
> [9] He shall turn the force of his battering rams
> Against your walls
> And smash your towers with his axes.[d]
> [10] From the cloud raised by his horses
> Dust shall cover you;
> From the clatter of horsemen
> And wheels and chariots,
> Your walls shall shake—
> When he enters your gates
> As men enter a breached city.
> [11] With the hoofs of his steeds
> He shall trample all your streets.
> He shall put your people to the sword,
> And your mighty pillars shall crash to the ground.
> [12] They shall plunder your wealth

---

a *The month is not indicated.*   b *Targum reads "trafficker"; cf. 27.3.*
c *Lit. "spreading out."*   d *Lit. "swords."*

the Mediterranean coast, west and south of the hill country of Judah. **16:** *Cherethites,* the Cretans, ancestors of the Philistines (Zeph. 2.5; cf. 2 Sam. 8.18; Amos 9.7).

26.1–28.19: Oracles concerning Tyre and its rulers. The initial date formula identifies the oracles concerning Tyre in 26.1–28.19 as the fifth major section of the book of Ezekiel. The prophetic word formula introduces the various segments of this section in 26.1–21; 27.1–36; 28.1–10; 28.11–19; 28.20–26. *The eleventh year, on the first of the month* is uncertain because the month is not recorded. The year would be 586 BCE, when the city of Jerusalem fell (2 Kings 25.2; Jer. 52.5). Tyre, the preeminent maritime power of the ancient world, joined Judah in revolt against Babylonia (Jer. 27.3). The Phoenician city of Tyre was an island until its conquest in 332 BCE by Alexander the Great, who built an earthen corridor through the water to assault the city by land. Shortly after his conquest of Jerusalem, Nebuchadrezzar laid siege to Tyre for thirteen years. Although he was not able to conquer the city, it finally submitted to him. The large number of oracles about Tyre reflects its economic significance at this time.

26.1–21: Four oracles concerning the destruction of Tyre. 1: *The eleventh year, on the first of the month,* 586 BCE, shortly after the fall of Jerusalem. **2–6:** Ezekiel's indictment and sentencing of Tyre presupposes that the city was a commercial rival to Judah. **2:** *The gateway of the peoples,* lit. "gateways," indicates Judah's role in controlling inland trade routes. **4:** *Naked rock,* "selaʿ" or *rock* in Heb, plays upon the Hebrew name "Tzor," *Tyre,* which is another term for *rock.* **6:** *Daughter-towns* designates nearby towns (suburbs) that were subsidiary to Tyre. **7–14:** Ezekiel's description presupposes the tactics and weapons of land warfare, which were useless against an island state. **7:** *Nebuchadrezzar,* the Akkadian (the lan-

And loot your merchandise.
They shall raze your walls
And tear down your splendid houses,
And they shall cast into the water
Your stones and timber and soil.

13 I will put an end to the murmur of your songs,
And the sound of your lyres shall be heard no
more.

14 I will make you a naked rock,
You shall be a place for drying[a] nets;
You shall never be rebuilt.
For I have spoken   —declares the Lord GOD.

15 Thus said the Lord GOD to Tyre: The coastlands shall quake at the sound of your downfall, when the wounded groan, when slaughter is rife within you. 16 All the rulers of the sea shall descend from their thrones; they shall remove their robes and strip off their embroidered garments. They shall clothe themselves with trembling, and shall sit on the ground; they shall tremble every moment, and they shall be aghast at you. 17 And they shall intone a dirge over you, and they shall say to you:

How you have perished, [b]you who were peopled[-b]
from the seas,
O renowned city!
Mighty on the sea were she and her inhabitants,
Who cast their terror on all [c]its inhabitants.[-c]

18 Now shall the coastlands tremble
On the day of your downfall,
And the coastlands by the sea
Be terrified at your end.

19 For thus said the Lord GOD: When I make you a ruined city, like cities empty of inhabitants; when I bring the deep over you, and its mighty waters cover you, 20 then I will bring you down, with those who go down to the Pit, to the people of old. I will install you in the netherworld, with those that go down to the Pit, like the ruins of old, so that you shall not be inhabited and shall not radiate[d] splendor in the land of the living. 21 I will make you a horror, and you shall cease to be; you shall be sought, but shall never be found again—declares the Lord GOD.

27 The word of the LORD came to me: 2 Now you, O mortal, intone a dirge over Tyre. 3 Say to Tyre:

---

guage of ancient Mesopotamia) name, Nabu-kudurri-utzur ("May Nebo [the name of a Babylonian god] protect my labor"), is frequently mispronounced in Heb as Nebuchadnezzar (Dan. 1.1). **16:** *Rulers of the sea,* an allusion to Tyre's trading partners and allies. **17:** *They shall intone a dirge over you,* see 19.1 n. **19–21:** Ezekiel employs mythological language to portray Tyre's fall. **19:** *I bring the deep over you* reverses the imagery of creation in which dry land emerges from the waters (Gen. ch 1). **20:** *Go down to the Pit,* descend into the underworld at death (see 32.17–22; Isa. 24.22; Pss. 63.9; 139.15). This was a characteristic motif of Babylonian mythology, in which the fertility god Tammuz had to be rescued from the underworld each year by the goddess Ishtar.

27.1–36: Lamentation over Tyre. The ch begins as a eulogy for the commercial beauty and prominence of Tyre, a vibrant center of trade, where people from distant and exotic lands came to exchange their wares. **3–9:** Ezekiel portrays Tyre as a well-built ship, which symbolizes the way in which Tyre achieved wealth through maritime trade.

---

a Lit. "spreading out."   b-b Septuagint reads "vanished."
c-c I.e., of the sea. Emendation yields "the dry land."
d Understanding nathatti as second-person singular feminine; cf. 16.50 and note. But meaning of Heb. uncertain.

O you who dwell at the gateway of the sea,
Who trade with the peoples on many coastlands:
Thus said the Lord GOD:
ªO Tyre, you boasted,
I am perfect in beauty.⁻ª

4   Your frontiers were on the high seas,
    Your builders perfected your beauty.
5   From cypress trees of Senir
    They fashioned your planks;
    They took a cedar from Lebanon
    To make a mast for you.
6   From oak trees of Bashan
    They made your oars;
    Of boxwood from the isles of Kittim,
    Inlaid with ivory,
    They made your decks.
7   Embroidered linen from Egypt
    Was the cloth
    That served you for sails;
    Of blue and purple from the coasts of Elishah
    Were your awnings.
8   The inhabitants of Sidon and Arvad
    Were your rowers;
    ᵇYour skilled men, O Tyre,⁻ᵇ were within you,
    They were your pilots.
9   Gebal's elders and craftsmen were within you,
    Making your repairs.

    All the ships of the sea, with their crews,
    Were ᶜin your harbor⁻ᶜ
    To traffic in your wares.
10 Men of Paras, Lud, and Put
    Were in your army,
    Your fighting men;
    They hung shields and helmets in your midst,
    They lent splendor to you.
11 Men of Arvad and Helech
    Manned your walls all around,
    And men of Gammad were stationed in your
        towers;
    They hung their quivers all about your walls;
    They perfected your beauty.
12 Tarshish traded with you because of your wealth of
all kinds of goods; they bartered silver, iron, tin, and lead

5: *Senir,* Mt. Hermon in northern Israel (Deut. 3.9). **6:** *Bashan,* the region east of the Sea of Galilee. The *isles of Kittim,* the Greek islands, although later usage includes the Romans. **7:** *Elishah,* Cyprus (cf. Gen. 10.4). **8:** *Sidon* is north of Tyre (Gen. 10.15). *Arvad,* Phoenicia (Gen. 10.18). *Zemar* (see translators' note *b-b*), "Tyre" in Heb. **9:** *Gebal,* Byblos (1 Kings 5.32), a major center of papyrus production in antiquity. **10–11:** Tyre's defenders include mercenary troops. **10:** *Paras,* Persia. *Lud,* Lydia. *Put,* Libya. **11:** *Helech* means "your army" in Heb. *Gammad* is uncertain, although *Targum Jonathan* identifies it with Cappodocia. **12–25a:** A prose section contains a catalogue of Tyre's extensive commercial relations. **12:** *Tarshish,* Tartessos in southern Spain.

a-a *Emendation yields:* "O Tyre, you are a ship / Perfect in beauty."
b-b *Emendation yields* "The skilled men of Zemar"; *cf. Gen. 10.18.*
c-c *Lit.* "in you."

for your wares. ¹³ Javan, Tubal, and Meshech—they were your merchants; they trafficked with you in human beings and copper utensils. ¹⁴ From Beth-togarmah they bartered horses, horsemen, and mules for your wares. ¹⁵ The people of Dedan were your merchants; many coastlands traded under your rule and rendered you tribute in ivory tusks and ebony. ¹⁶ Aram traded with you because of your wealth of merchandise, dealing with you in turquoise, purple stuff, embroidery, fine linen, coral, and agate.ª ¹⁷ Judah and the land of Israel were your merchants; they trafficked with you in wheat of ᵇMinnith and Pannag,ᵇ honey, oil, and balm. ¹⁸ Because of your wealth of merchandise, because of your great wealth, Damascus traded with you in Helbon wine and white wool. ¹⁹ ᶜVedan and Javan from Uzal traded for your wares; they trafficked with you in polished iron, cassia, and calamus. ²⁰ Dedan was your merchant in saddlecloths for riding.ᶜ ²¹ Arabia and all Kedar's chiefs were traders under your rule; they traded with you in lambs, rams, and goats. ²² The merchants of Sheba and Raamah were your merchants; they bartered for your wares all the finest spices, all kinds of precious stones, and gold. ²³ Haran, Canneh, and Eden, the merchants of Sheba, Assyria, and Chilmad traded with you. ²⁴ ᶜThese were your merchants in choice fabrics, embroidered cloaks of blue, and many-colored carpets tied up with cords and preserved with cedar—among your wares.ᶜ ²⁵ The ships of Tarshish were in the service of your trade.

ᵈSo you were full and richly laden
On the high seas.

²⁶ Your oarsmen brought you out
Into the mighty waters;
The tempest wrecked you
On the high seas.

²⁷ Your wealth, your wares, your merchandise,
Your sailors and your pilots,
The men who made your repairs,
Those who carried on your traffic,
And all the fighting men within you—
All the multitude within you—
Shall go down into the depths of the sea
On the day of your downfall.

²⁸ At the outcry of your pilots

13: *Javan,* Ionians or Greeks. *Tubal and Meshech,* Asia Minor (Gen. 10.2). **14:** *Beth-togarmah,* Armenia (Gen. 10.3). **15:** *Dedan,* an Arabian people south of Israel in central Arabia (Gen. 10.6–7; 25.1–3; Isa. 21.13; Jer. 25.23; 49.8). **16:** *Turquoise, purple stuff, embroidery:* Phoenicia was known for trade in purple dye derived from a shellfish. The names for the country, Phoenicia (Gk, "Phoinikos") and Canaan, both mean "purple." **17:** *Minnith,* in Ammonite territory (Judg. 11.33). *Pannag:* Radak considers this to be a place name, but the meaning is uncertain. **18:** *Helbon,* 22 km (13 mi) north of Damascus. **19:** *Vedan and Javan from Uzal:* Uzal is Sana in Yemen (Gen. 10.27). **20:** *Dedan,* in central Arabia. **21:** *Kedar,* in Arabia (Gen. 25.13). **22:** *Sheba,* in Arabia or Ethiopia (Gen. 10.7). *Raamah* is believed to be near the Persian Gulf. **23:** *Haran, Canneh, Eden,* cities in Syria (Gen. 12.4; 10.10; Isa. 10.9; 2 Kings 19.12; Isa. 37.12; Amos 1.5). *Assyria,* the ancient Assyrian empire in northern Iraq. *Chilmad,* Media. **25b–36:** The lament resumes with a description of Tyre as a ship sinking by *the tempest,* lit. "the east wind," a common symbol of God's power (Exod. 14.21). As the city-ship sinks into the sea, losing all her precious cargo, all those around her mourn and lament. Many of these laments are expressed in the qinah or dirge meter.

a *The exact identity of these stones is uncertain.*
b-b *Meaning of Heb. uncertain; cf. "Minnith," Judg. 11.33.*
c-c *Meaning of Heb. uncertain.*
d *Resuming the description of Tyre as a ship, as in vv. 3b–9a.*

The billows shall heave;
29 And all the oarsmen and mariners,
All the pilots of the sea,
Shall come down from their ships
And stand on the ground.
30 They shall raise their voices over you
And cry out bitterly;
They shall cast dust on their heads
And strew ashes on themselves.
31 On your account, they shall make
Bald patches on their heads,
And shall gird themselves with sackcloth.
They shall weep over you, brokenhearted,
With bitter lamenting;
32 They shall intone a dirge over you as they wail,
And lament for you thus:

Who was like Tyre when she was silenced
In the midst of the sea?
33 When your wares were unloaded from the seas,
You satisfied many peoples;
With your great wealth and merchandise
You enriched the kings of the earth.
34 But when you were wrecked on the seas,
In the deep waters sank your merchandise
And all the crew aboard you.
35 All the inhabitants of the coastlands
Are appalled over you;
Their kings are aghast,
Their faces contorted.[a]
36 The merchants among the peoples hissed[b] at you;
You have become a horror,
And have ceased to be forever.

28 The word of the LORD came to me: [2] O mortal, say
to the prince of Tyre: Thus said the Lord GOD:
Because you have been so haughty and have said, "I am
a god; I sit enthroned like a god in the heart of the seas,"
whereas you are not a god but a man, though you deemed
your mind equal to a god's[c]—
3   Yes, you are wiser than Daniel;
     In no hidden matter can anyone
     Compare to you.
4   By your shrewd understanding
     You have gained riches,

28.1–10: Oracle concerning the prince of Tyre. 2: Self-deification was a claim of some ancient Near Eastern rulers, but in this case, says Ezekiel, the prince has gone too far and is guilty of hubris. **3:** *Yes, you are wiser than Daniel:* Ezekiel apparently holds the Tyrian king in high regard and compares him to Daniel (Heb, Dan El), the wise ruler of Canaanite mythology who may stand behind the figure of Daniel in biblical tradition (see 14.12–20).

a *Meaning of Heb. uncertain.*
b *I.e., to ward off the calamity from the viewer; cf. Jer. 18.16, 49.17; Job 27.23; Lam. 2.15.*
c *This sentence is continued in v. 6; vv. 3–5 are parenthetical.*

And have amassed gold and silver
In your treasuries.

5   By your great shrewdness in trade
You have increased your wealth,
And you have grown haughty
Because of your wealth.

6 Assuredly, thus said the Lord GOD: Because you have deemed your mind equal to a god's,

7   I swear I will bring against you
Strangers, the most ruthless of nations.
They shall unsheathe their swords
Against your prized shrewdness,
And they shall strike down[a] your splendor.

8   They shall bring you down to the Pit;
In the heart of the sea you shall die
The death of the slain.

9   Will you still say, "I am a god"
Before your slayers,
When you are proved a man, not a god,
At the hands of those who strike you down?

10   By the hands of strangers you shall die
The death of the uncircumcised;[b]
For I have spoken   —declares the Lord GOD.

11 The word of the LORD came to me: 12 O mortal, intone a dirge over the king of Tyre and say to him: Thus said the Lord GOD:

You were the seal of perfection,
Full of wisdom and flawless in beauty.

13   You were in Eden, the garden of God;
Every precious stone was your adornment:
Carnelian, chrysolite, and amethyst;
Beryl, lapis lazuli, and jasper;
Sapphire, turquoise, and emerald;
And gold [c-]beautifully wrought for you,
Mined for you, prepared the day you were created.[-c]

14   [d-]I created you as a cherub
With outstretched shielding wings;[-d]
And you resided on God's holy mountain;
You walked among stones of fire.

15   You were blameless in your ways,
From the day you were created
Until wrongdoing was found in you.

5: Ezekiel charges that the king has overstepped his bounds. **8:** The mythological language of descent into the sea and the *Pit* reappears. **10:** *The uncircumcised:* While the Phoenicians (Tyrians) practiced circumcision, they are threatened with the death of the uncircumcised, thought to be worse than the death of the circumcised.

28.11–19: Dirge for the king of Tyre. While it was the "prince" who was condemned in vv. 1–10, here the lament is for the "king." This king is pictured as a quasi-mythical being in a bejeweled garden of Eden. References to the garden of Eden are quite rare outside of Genesis; it is mentioned in Joel 2.3, and several times in Ezekiel. The king boasts of his wisdom and beauty, qualities that Israelite kings as well were expected to have (e.g., 1 Sam. 16.18, of David). **12:** *Seal,* a sign of royal authority. **13–15:** Ezekiel employs the imagery of the garden of Eden story to describe the Tyrian king's downfall. **14:** He employs the imagery of the *cherub* to stress the Tyrian king's power and high position. The once-perfect creature is shown to have sinned and therefore was struck down. **16:** The prophet charges the king with corrupt trade practices.

---

a Meaning of Heb. uncertain.
b According to popular belief, those who die uncircumcised and those left unburied are relegated to the lower level of the netherworld; cf. 31.18; 32.19 ff.
c-c Meaning of Heb. uncertain. On the stones, see note at Exod. 28.17.
d-d Meaning of Heb. uncertain.

16   By your far-flung commerce
      You were filled with lawlessness
      And you sinned.
      So I have struck you down
      From the mountain of God,
      And I have destroyed you, O shielding cherub,
      From among the stones of fire.
17   You grew haughty because of your beauty,
      You debased your wisdom for the sake of your
          splendor;
      I have cast you to the ground,
      I have made you an object for kings to stare at.
18   By the greatness of your guilt,
      Through the dishonesty of your trading,
      You desecrated your sanctuaries.
      So I made a fire issue from you,
      And it has devoured you;
      I have reduced you to ashes on the ground,
      In the sight of all who behold you.
19   All who knew you among the peoples
      Are appalled at your doom.
      You have become a horror
      And have ceased to be, forever.

20 The word of the LORD came to me: 21 O mortal, set your face toward Sidon and prophesy against her. 22 Say: Thus said the Lord GOD:
      I am going to deal with you, O Sidon.
      I will gain glory in your midst;
      And they shall know that I am the LORD,
      When I wreak punishment upon her
      And show Myself holy through her.
23   I will let pestilence loose against her
      And bloodshed into her streets.
      And the slain shall fall in her midst
      When the sword comes upon her from all sides.
      And they shall know that I am the LORD.

24 Then shall the House of Israel no longer be afflicted with prickling briers and lacerating thorns from all the neighbors who despise them; and they shall know that I am the Lord GOD.

25 Thus said the Lord GOD: When I have gathered the House of Israel from the peoples among which they have been dispersed, and have shown Myself holy through them in the sight of the nations, they shall settle on their own soil, which I gave to My servant Jacob, 26 and they shall dwell on it in security. They shall build houses and plant vineyards, and shall dwell on it in security, when I

28.20–26: Oracle concerning Sidon. 21: *Sidon,* another Phoenician port city, 40 km (25 mi) north of Tyre. Sidon joined the revolt (Jer. 27.3) and probably fell to Nebuchadrezzar. **25–26:** Once the nations that treated Israel with contempt are destroyed, the exiles will return to the land of Israel sworn to Jacob (Gen. chs 28; 35) and rebuild their community; thus will they manifest God's holiness in the world. *And they shall know that I the* LORD *am their God,* the self-identification formula.

have meted out punishment to all those about them who despise them. And they shall know that I the LORD am their God.

29 In the tenth year, on the twelfth day of the tenth month, the word of the LORD came to me: ² O mortal, turn your face against Pharaoh king of Egypt, and prophesy against him and against all Egypt. ³ Speak these words:

> Thus said the Lord GOD:
> I am going to deal with you, O Pharaoh king of
>   Egypt,
> Mighty monster, sprawling in your[a] channels,
> Who said,
> My Nile is my own;
> I made it for myself.

4
> I will put hooks in your jaws,
> And make the fish of your channels
> Cling to your scales;
> I will haul you up from your channels,
> With all the fish of your channels
> Clinging to your scales.

5
> And I will fling you into the desert,
> With all the fish of your channels.
> You shall be left lying in the open,
> Ungathered and unburied:
> I have given you as food
> To the beasts of the earth
> And the birds of the sky.

6
> Then all the inhabitants of Egypt shall know
> That I am the LORD.
> Because you[b] were a staff of reed
> To the House of Israel:

7
> When they grasped you with the hand, you would
>   splinter,
> And wound all their shoulders,[c]
> And when they leaned on you, you would break,
> And make all their loins unsteady.[d]

a Lit. "its."
b Lit. "they."
c Septuagint and Syriac read "palms"; cf. 2 Kings 18.21; Isa. 36.6.
d Taking ʿamad as a byform of maʿad; cf. Syriac translation.

29.1–16: The first oracle concerning Egypt. The initial date formula marks 29.1–16 as the first of five sections concerned with oracles against Egypt and its rulers in 29.1–16; 29.17–30.19; 30.20–26; 31.1–18; 32.1–32 (+33.1–39.29). Because of its focus on the downfall of Egypt, 28.25–29.21 transcends these divisions to constitute the haftarah reading for the parashah of Va-'era' (Exod. 6.2–9.35), which relates the plagues against Egypt at the time of the exodus. Egypt played a major role in instigating the revolt against its enemy Babylonia. When Pharaoh Hophra attempted to relieve Jerusalem from the Babylonian siege in 588 BCE, he was repulsed (Jer. ch 37; 44.30; see also Jer. ch 32). **1:** Commentators note that the initial date formula, *in the tenth year, on the twelfth day of the tenth month*, 12 Tevet, 588–587 BCE, disrupts the chronological sequence of the book since it is perhaps some three months earlier than the date given in 26.1 for the oracles concerning Tyre. Radak states that the oracle concerning Tyre appears first because it was fulfilled first, i.e., whereas Tyre submitted to Nebuchadnezzar in 573 BCE after thirteen years of siege, Egypt was conquered by the Persian king Cambyses in 525. Although it is not clear in the English translation, this particular date formula lacks the verb "vayehi" ("and it came to pass") that appears in the other chronological formulae of the book (except 40.1). When considered in relation to the disruption of the book's chronological sequence, this suggests that the oracles concerning Egypt may have once circulated independently, and were combined here as a group. **2–7:** God instructs Ezekiel to address Pharaoh, probably Hophra (ruled 589–570) after his failed attempt to rescue Jerusalem. **3:** *Mighty monster*, lit. "the great dragon." Egypt is compared to a dragon in Isa. 11.15, which employs the imagery of the seven-headed Leviathan (Lothan) of Canaanite mythology, and in Isa. 30.7 to the sea dragon Rahab (see also Isa. 51.9–10; Job 9.13; 26.12–13; Ps. 89.9–10). The *Nile* river forms the natural "backbone" of Egypt and serves as the source of Egypt's life. **6:** *A staff of reed to the House of Israel* symbolizes an unreliable support (cf. Isa. 36.6 ‖ 2 Kings 18.21). **8–12:** Egypt's judgment results from Pharaoh's claim that the Nile is his and not God's (28.2). **10:** *From Migdol to Syene*, cities that define the northern and southern borders of Egypt. Syene is modern

⁸ Assuredly, thus said the Lord God: Lo, I will bring a sword against you, and will cut off man and beast from you, ⁹ so that the land of Egypt shall fall into desolation and ruin. And they shall know that I am the Lord—because he boasted, "The Nile is mine, and I made it." ¹⁰ Assuredly, I am going to deal with you and your channels, and I will reduce the land of Egypt to utter ruin and desolation, ^{a-}from Migdol to Syene, all the way to the border of Nubia.^{-a} ¹¹ No foot of man shall traverse it, and no foot of beast shall traverse it; and it shall remain uninhabited for forty years. ¹² For forty years I will make the land of Egypt the most desolate of desolate lands, and its cities shall be the most desolate of ruined cities. And I will scatter the Egyptians among the nations and disperse them throughout the countries.

¹³ Further, thus said the Lord God: After a period of forty years I will gather the Egyptians from the peoples among whom they were dispersed. ¹⁴ I will restore the fortunes of the Egyptians and bring them back to the land of their origin, the land of Pathros,^b and there they shall be a lowly kingdom. ¹⁵ It shall be the lowliest of all the kingdoms, and shall not lord it over the nations again. I will reduce the Egyptians,^c so that they shall have no dominion over the nations. ¹⁶ Never again shall they be the trust of the House of Israel, recalling its guilt in having turned to them. And they shall know that I am the Lord God.

¹⁷ In the twenty-seventh year, on the first day of the first month, the word of the Lord came to me: ¹⁸ O mortal, King Nebuchadrezzar of Babylon has made his army expend vast labor on Tyre; every head is rubbed bald and every shoulder scraped. But he and his army have had no return for the labor he expended on Tyre. ¹⁹ Assuredly, thus said the Lord God: I will give the land of Egypt to Nebuchadrezzar, king of Babylon. He shall carry off her wealth and take her spoil and seize her booty; and she shall be the recompense of his army. ²⁰ As the wage for which he labored, for what they did for Me, I give him the land of Egypt—declares the Lord God.

²¹ On that day I will ^{d-}endow the House of Israel with strength, and you shall be vindicated^{-d} among them. And they shall know that I am the Lord.

a-a I.e., the length of Egypt, from north to south. Syene is modern Aswan.
b I.e., southern Egypt.
c Heb. "them."
d-d Lit. "cause a horn to sprout for the House of Israel, and I will grant you opening of the mouth."

Aswan. **11:** *Forty years,* a common number for a complete and lengthy period of time (Num. 14.33; Judg. 3.31; 1 Kings 2.11). **13–16:** Egypt will be restored to its land as a minor kingdom. The prophet clearly has in mind Egypt's failure to aid Israel in its time of need. **14:** *Pathros,* Upper Egypt, the southern portion of the kingdom. In Egypt, "up" is south (upstream on the Nile) and "down" is north (downstream on the Nile). **16:** The oracle ends with the self-identification formula, but it is applied to Egypt rather than to Israel.

29.17–30.19: The second block of oracles concerning Egypt. The initial date formula marks 29.17–30.19 as the seventh major section of the book of Ezekiel. The prophetic word formula, *the word of the Lord came to me,* in 29.17 and 30.1 marks the two oracle reports that appear in this section. **29.17:** *The twenty-seventh year, on the first day of the first month,* 1 Nisan 571–570 BCE. This date falls outside of the twenty-year pattern evident in the other date formulae throughout the book (see 1.1–3 n.). *Seder Olam Rabbah* 26 maintains that this refers to the twenty-seventh year (578 BCE) of Nebuchadnezzar's reign when Egypt fell into his hands. Nebuchadrezzar reigned for forty-three years, 605–562, but he never conquered Egypt. Modern commentators maintain that this date was written at a later time, perhaps by Ezekiel himself in old age or by someone else, following the delayed fulfillment of the oracle concerning Tyre. The oracle may originally have been dated to the eleventh year (see 26.1; 30.20). **18:** Ezekiel refers to Nebuchadrezzar's failure to conquer Tyre as a basis for his campaign against Egypt. Following the conclusion of his siege against Tyre in 573 BCE, Nebuchadrezzar attacked Egypt in 668 but failed to conquer the land. Although Tyre submitted to him, the failure to conquer the city meant that his troops would receive little booty. **21:** *I will endow*

30

The word of the LORD came to me: [2] O mortal, prophesy and say: Thus said the Lord GOD:

Wail, alas for the day!
[3] For a day is near;
A day of the LORD is near.
It will be a day of cloud,
An hour of [invading] nations.
[4] A sword shall pierce Egypt,
And Nubia shall be seized with trembling,
When men fall slain in Egypt
And her wealth is seized
And her foundations are overthrown.

[5] Nubia, Put, and Lud, and all *the mixed populations,*-a and Cub, and the inhabitants of the allied countries shall fall by the sword with them.

[6] Thus said the LORD:
Those who support Egypt shall fall,
And her proud strength shall sink;
There they shall fall by the sword,
From Migdol to Syene
—declares the Lord GOD.

[7] They shall be the most desolate of desolate lands, and her cities shall be the most ruined of cities, [8] when I set fire to Egypt and all who help her are broken. Thus they shall know that I am the LORD.

[9] On that day, messengers shall set out at My bidding to strike terror into confident Nubia. And they shall be seized with trembling on Egypt's day [of doom]—for it is at hand.

[10] Thus said the Lord GOD: I will put an end to the wealth of Egypt through King Nebuchadrezzar of Babylon. [11] He, together with his troops, the most ruthless of the nations, shall be brought to ravage the land. And they shall unsheathe the sword against Egypt and fill the land with the slain.

[12] I will turn the channels into dry ground, and I will deliver the land into the hands of evil men. I will lay waste the land and everything in it by the hands of strangers. I the LORD have spoken.

[13] Thus said the Lord GOD: I will destroy the fetishes and make an end of the idols in Noph; and no longer shall there be a prince in the land of Egypt; and I will strike the land of Egypt with fear. [14] I will lay Pathros waste, I will set fire to Zoan, and I will execute judgment on No. [15] I

a-a *Meaning of Heb. uncertain.*

the House of Israel with strength, lit. "I will cause a horn to sprout for the house of Israel": the restoration of the Davidic monarchy in the aftermath of Egypt's collapse (see Isa. 11.1–16; Ps. 132.17). This phrase plays a prominent role in the daily "'Amidah" prayer concerning the restoration of Davidic kingship. **30.1–19:** This section contains four oracles (vv. 2–5, 6–9, 10–12, 13–19), each identified by the prophetic messenger formula, *thus said the Lord GOD.* **2–5:** God instructs Ezekiel to lament for Egypt and Ethiopia. Egypt was ruled by an Ethiopian dynasty during the late 7th and early 6th centuries BCE (see Isa. ch 20). The prophet employs the "Day of the LORD" motif (Amos 5.18–20; Joel chs 1–2; Isa. 2.6–21; chs 13; 34; Obadiah; Zeph. 1.2–18; 2.1–3) to express the overthrow of Egypt. **5:** *Put, and Lud,* see 27.10–11 n. *Cub* is unknown. **6–9:** This oracle resembles oracles in Isaiah. **6:** *Proud strength shall sink,* Isa. 2.6–21. **9:** *Messengers shall set out,* Isa. 18.1–2. **12:** *I will turn the channels into dry ground,* Isa. 19.1–15. **13–19:** Ezekiel cites Egyptian place names to demonstrate that destruction will encompass the entire land. **13:** *Noph* is Memphis, the early capital south of Cairo. **14:** *Pathros,* see 29.14. *Zoan,* also called Rameses, Tanis, and Avaris, the site where the Heb slaves worked in the Nile Delta (Ps. 78.12, 43; Exod. 1.11; Num. 13.22). *No* is Thebes, Egypt's capital throughout much of Israel's history (Nah. 3.8; Jer. 46.25). **15:** *Sin* is Pelusium, near Zoan in the northeastern Delta. **17:** *Aven* is "On" or Heliopolis, 10 km (6 mi) northeast of Cairo (Jer. 43.13). *Pi-beseth,* Bubastis in the eastern Delta. **18:** *Tehaphnehes,* by the north shore of the Gulf of Suez (Jer. 2.16; 43.7, 8–13). **19:** The *judgment* executed against Egypt recalls language of the exodus tradition (e.g., Exod. 6.6), suggesting that this event, the biblical paradigm for God's power, will be reenacted.

30.20–26: The first oracle concerning Pharaoh. The introductory date formula marks this as the will pour out my anger upon Sin, the stronghold of Egypt, and I will destroy the wealth of No. [16] I will set fire to Egypt; Sin shall writhe in anguish and No shall be torn apart; [a-]and Noph [shall face] adversaries in broad daylight.[-a] [17] The young men of Aven[b] and Pi-beseth shall fall by the sword, and those [towns] shall go into captivity. [18] In Tehaphnehes[c] daylight shall be withheld,[d] when I break there the power of Egypt, and there her proud strength comes to an end. [The city] itself shall be covered with cloud, and its daughter towns shall go into captivity.

19   Thus I will execute judgment on Egypt;
        And they shall know that I am the Lord.

[20] In the eleventh year, on the seventh day of the first month, the word of the Lord came to me: [21] O mortal, I have broken the arm of Pharaoh king of Egypt; it has not been bound up to be healed nor firmly bandaged to make it strong enough to grasp the sword. [22] Assuredly, thus said the Lord God: I am going to deal with Pharaoh king of Egypt. I will break his arms, both the sound one and the injured, and make the sword drop from his hand. [23] I will scatter the Egyptians among the nations and disperse them throughout the countries. [24] I will strengthen the arms of the king of Babylon and put My sword in his hand; and I will break the arms of Pharaoh, and he shall groan before him with the groans of one struck down. [25] I will make firm the arms of the king of Babylon, but the arms of Pharaoh shall fail. And they shall know that I am the Lord, when I put My sword into the hand of the king of Babylon, and he lifts it against the land of Egypt. [26] I will scatter the Egyptians among the nations and disperse them throughout the countries. Thus they shall know that I am the Lord.

31 In the eleventh year, on the first day of the third month, the word of the Lord came to me: [2] O mortal, say to Pharaoh king of Egypt and his hordes:

        Who was comparable to you in greatness?
3   Assyria was a cedar in Lebanon
        With beautiful branches and [e-]shady thickets,[-e]
        Of lofty stature,
        With its top among [f-]leafy trees.[-f]

eighth major section of the book. **20:** *In the eleventh year, on the seventh day of the first month,* 7 Nisan, 587–586 BCE. **21:** The broken arm of Pharaoh refers to Nebuchadrezzar's defeat of Hophra, who attempted to relieve Jerusalem in 588 (2 Kings 24.7; Jer. 37.5). **22–26:** The prophet anticipates an even more devastating defeat of Egypt, but this did not transpire.

31.1–18: The second oracle concerning Pharaoh. The introductory date formula identifies 31.1–18 as the ninth major section of the book of Ezekiel. The imagery of a fallen cedar of Lebanon portrays Pharaoh's downfall. The fall of Assyria forms the precedent and model for the fall of Egypt. Isa. 14.3–23 likewise portrays the downfall of the Babylonian king, and relates it to the downfall of Assyria (Isa. 14.24–27). Thematically, this oracle is similar to those against Tyre in chs 27 and 28. **1:** *In the eleventh year, on the first day of the third month,* 1 Sivan, 587–586 BCE, six days prior to the festival of Shavu'ot, and about two months prior to the destruction of the Temple. **2–9:** See Isaiah's portrayal of the Assyrian monarch as a tall tree that is to be felled (Isa. 10.5–34) and the tradition of the well-watered tree in the garden of Eden that plays a role in the downfall of Adam and Eve (Gen. chs 2–3).

---

a-a *Meaning of Heb. uncertain.*
b *Elsewhere called "On"; cf. Gen. 41.45, 50; 46.20.*
c *Elsewhere vocalized "Tahpanhes"; e.g., Jer. 2.16; 44.1.*
d *Some Heb. mss. and editions read "darkened."*
e-e *Meaning of Heb. uncertain.*   f-f *Septuagint reads "clouds."*

4
Waters nourished it,
The deep made it grow tall,
Washing with its streams
The place where it was planted,
Making its channels well up
ᵃ-To allᵃ the trees of the field.

5
Therefore it exceeded in stature
All the trees of the field;
Its branches multiplied and its boughs grew long
Because of the abundant water
That welled up for it.

6
In its branches nested
All the birds of the sky;
All the beasts of the field
Bore their young under its boughs,
And in its shadow lived
All the great nations.

7
It was beautiful in its height,
In the length of its branches,
Because its stock stood
By abundant waters.

8
Cedars in the garden of God
Could not compare with it;
Cypresses could not match its boughs,
And plane trees could not vie with its branches;
No tree in the garden of God
Was its peer in beauty.

9
I made it beautiful
In the profusion of its branches;
And all the trees of Eden envied it
In the garden of God.

10 Assuredly, thus said the Lord GOD: Because itᵇ towered high in stature, and thrust its top up among the ᶜ-leafy trees,-ᶜ and it was arrogant in its height, 11 I delivered it into the hands of the mightiest of nations. They treated it as befitted its wickedness. I banished it. 12 Strangers, the most ruthless of nations, cut it down and abandoned it; its branches fell on the mountains and in every valley; its boughs were splintered in every watercourse of the earth; and all the peoples of the earth departed from its shade and abandoned it. 13 Upon its fallen trunk all the birds of the sky nest, and all the beasts of the field lodge among its boughs—14 so that no trees by water should exalt themselves in stature or set their tops among the ᶜ-leafy trees,-ᶜ

10–14: Because of its height and arrogance, the tree is cut down (see Isa. 2.6–21; 10.5–34). 11: *The mightiest of nations,* lit. "the ram of the nations," Nebuchadrezzar. The Babylonians boasted of the trees they took from Lebanon. 14: *Pit,* the underworld (see Isa. 14.3–23). 15–18: *Sheol,* the Heb name for the underworld.

a-a *Meaning of Heb. uncertain; emendation yields "more than for all."*
b *Heb. "you."*   c-c *Septuagint reads "clouds."*

and that no well-watered tree may reach up to them in height. For they are all consigned to death, to the lowest part of the netherworld,[a] together with human beings who descend into the Pit.

15 Thus said the Lord GOD: On the day it went down to Sheol, I closed[b] the deep over it and covered it; I held back its streams, and the great waters were checked. I made Lebanon mourn deeply for it, and all the trees of the field languished on its account. 16 I made nations quake at the crash of its fall, when I cast it down to Sheol with those who descend into the Pit; and all the trees of Eden, the choicest and best of Lebanon, all that were well watered, were consoled in the lowest part of the netherworld. 17 They also descended with it into Sheol, to those slain by the sword, together with its supporters,[c] they who had lived under its shadow among the nations.

18 [Now you know] who is comparable to you in glory and greatness among the trees of Eden. And you too shall be brought down with the trees of Eden to the lowest part of the netherworld; you shall lie among the uncircumcised and those slain by the sword. Such shall be [the fate of] Pharaoh and all his hordes—declares the Lord GOD.

32 In the twelfth year, on the first day of the twelfth month, the word of the LORD came to me: 2 O mortal, intone a dirge over Pharaoh king of Egypt. Say to him:
> [d]O great beast among the nations,[d] you are
> doomed!
> You are like the dragon in the seas,
> Thrusting through their[e] streams,
> Stirring up the water with your feet
> And muddying their streams!
>
> 3 Thus said the Lord GOD:
> I will cast My net over you
> In an assembly of many peoples,
> And you shall be hauled up in My toils.
> 4 And I will fling you to the ground,
> Hurl you upon the open field.
> I will cause all the birds of the sky
> To settle upon you.
> I will cause the beasts of all the earth
> To batten on you.
> 5 I will cast your carcass upon the hills
> And fill the valleys with your [d]rotting flesh.[d]

32.1–16: Oracle concerning Pharaoh and Egypt. The introductory date formula identifies 32.1–16 as the tenth major section of the book. *In the twelfth year, on the first day of the twelfth month,* 1 Adar, 585 BCE, the year following the destruction of the Temple. The oracle is in the form of a dirge. **2–15:** The portrayal of Pharaoh's defeat by God draws upon the mythological traditions of God's defeat of the sea dragon Leviathan at creation (Isa. 11.15; 27.1; Pss. 74.12–17; 104.7–9; Job 38.8–11; see also Exod. ch 15). In addition, it evokes the crocodiles of the Nile; Pharaoh is a monster crocodile. The motif of oozing blood (v. 6) recalls the plague of blood (Exod. 7.19–24); the motif of darkness recalls the plague of darkness against Egypt (Exod. 10.21–29) and also the Day of the LORD traditions (Joel 2.1–2; 3.15; Zeph. 1.15).

a To which popular belief relegated those who died uncircumcised or by the sword; cf. v. 18.
b Cf. Aramaic 'abulla, "gate."   c Heb. "arm."
d-d Meaning of Heb. uncertain.   e Heb. "your."

6 I will drench the earth
   With your oozing blood upon the hills,
   And the watercourses shall be filled with your
      [gore].
7 When you are snuffed out,
   I will cover the sky
   And darken its stars;
   I will cover the sun with clouds
   And the moon shall not give its light.
8 All the lights that shine in the sky
   I will darken above you;
   And I will bring darkness upon your land
                     —declares the Lord GOD.
9 I will vex the hearts of many peoples
   When I bring your ᵃshattered remnants·ᵃ among
      the nations,
   To countries which you never knew.
10 I will strike many peoples with horror over your
      fate;
   And their kings shall be aghast over you,
   When I brandish My sword before them.
   They shall tremble continually,
   Each man for his own life,
   On the day of your downfall.
11 For thus said the Lord GOD:
   The sword of the king of Babylon shall come
      upon you.
12 I will cause your multitude to fall
   By the swords of warriors,
   All the most ruthless among the nations.
   They shall ravage the splendor of Egypt,
   And all her masses shall be wiped out.
13 I will make all her cattle vanish from beside
      abundant waters;
   The feet of man shall not muddy them any
      more,
   Nor shall the hoofs of cattle muddy them.
14 Then I will let their waters settle,
   And make their rivers flow like oil
                     —declares the Lord GOD:
15 When I lay the land of Egypt waste,
   When the land is emptied of [the life] that filled it,
   When I strike down all its inhabitants.
   And they shall know that I am the LORD.
16 This is a dirge, and it shall be intoned;
   The women of the nations shall intone it,

11: *The sword of the king of Babylon,*
Nebuchadrezzar. The nations
will witness God's victory (Exod.
15.13–18). **16:** Women served as
mourners in the ancient Near East
(see Jer. 9.17–18).

**32.17–33.20: Final oracle concern-
ing the nations and Ezekiel's role
as the watchman of Israel.** Although 32.17–32 is the last of the
oracles concerning Egypt—and the
nations in general—the presence
of the date formula in 32.17 and
the absence of a date formula until
33.21 indicates that 32.17–33.20
forms the eleventh major block of
material in the book of Ezekiel.
The prophetic word formula, *the
word of the LORD came to me*, identifies oracle reports of this block as
32.17–32 and 33.1–20. It is unlikely
that these oracles were originally
composed as a single block, but
the current arrangement combines
the motifs of the downfall of
Israel's enemies among the nations, beginning with Egypt, and
God's designation of Ezekiel as
Israel's watchman. Insofar as the
oracle defines his role in relation to
the repentance of Israel, this block
anticipates the emphasis on the
restoration of Israel that follows in
33.21–39.29. Such a combination of
motifs suggests a second exodus in
the aftermath of the Babylonian
destruction of Jerusalem (see also
Second Isaiah, Isa. chs 40–55, who
stresses the concept of a second exodus at the time of Babylonia's
submission to Cyrus of Persia).
This combination also helps to better anchor the oracles concerning
the nations in their current place.

a-a Septuagint reads "captives."

> They shall intone it over Egypt and all her
> multitude   —declares the Lord GOD.

17 In the twelfth year, on the fifteenth day of the month,[a] the word of the LORD came to me: 18 [b]O mortal, wail [the dirge]—along with the women of the mighty nations—over the masses of Egypt, accompanying their descent to the lowest part of the netherworld, among those who have gone down into the Pit. 19 [c]Whom do you surpass in beauty? Down with you, and be laid to rest with the uncircumcised! 20 They shall lie amid those slain by the sword,[-c] [b][amid those slain by] the sword [Egypt] has been dragged and left with all her masses.

21 From the depths of Sheol the mightiest of warriors speak to him and his allies; the uncircumcised, the slain by the sword, have gone down and lie [there]. 22 Assyria is there with all her company, their graves round about, all of them slain, fallen by the sword. 23 Their graves set in the farthest recesses of the Pit, all her company are round about her tomb, all of them slain, fallen by the sword—they who struck terror in the land of the living. 24 There too is Elam and all her masses round about her tomb, all of them slain, fallen by the sword—they who descended uncircumcised to the lowest part of the netherworld, who struck terror in the land of the living—now they bear their shame with those who have gone down to the Pit. 25 They made a bed for her among the slain, with all her masses; their graves are round about her. They are all uncircumcised, slain by the sword. Though their terror was once spread over the land of the living, they bear their shame with those who have gone into the Pit; they are placed among the slain. 26 Meshech and Tubal and all their masses are there; their graves are round about. They are all uncircumcised, pierced through by the sword—they who once struck terror in the land of the living. 27 And they do not lie with the fallen uncircumcised warriors, who went down to Sheol with their battle gear, who put their swords beneath their heads and their iniquities[d] upon their bones—for the terror of the warriors was upon the land of the living. 28 And you too shall be shattered amid the uncircumcised, and lie among those slain by the sword. 29 Edom is there, her kings and all her chieftains, who, for all their might, are laid among those who are slain by the sword; they too lie with the uncircumcised and with those who have gone down to the Pit. 30 All the

32.17–32: Oracle against Egypt and the nations. *In the twelfth year, on the fifteenth day of the month,* 15 Adar, 585 BCE. Although the month is not specified, it likely follows from the reference to the twelfth month in 32.1 (see translators' note *a* on v. 17). Ironically, this date would later mark Shushan Purim, the day following Purim in which the victory over Israel's enemies is celebrated in walled cities, such as Shushan (Susa), the capital of the Persian empire (Esth. 9.6–19). The association highlights the motif of coming restoration. **18:** God instructs Ezekiel to wail for Egypt as its people descend into the underworld. **19–32:** Egypt will join the nations that have been destroyed. **22:** *Assyria* was conquered by Babylonia and Media during the period 627–609, and was thus representative of a once great nation now totally destroyed. **24:** *Elam* was destroyed by the Assyrians in the mid-7th century BCE. **26:** *Meshech and Tubal,* two unidentified kingdoms in Asia Minor that perhaps were taken by Assyria. **29:** *Edom* was conquered by Babylonia.

---

a Presumably the twelfth month; cf. v. 1.   b Construction of these verses uncertain.
c-c Cf. 31.18 ff. and note a on 31.14.   d Emendation yields "shields."

princes of the north and all the Sidonians are there, who went down in disgrace with the slain, in spite of the terror that their might inspired; and they lie, uncircumcised, with those who are slain by the sword, and bear their shame with those who have gone down to the Pit.

31 These Pharaoh shall see, and he shall be consoled for all his masses, those of Pharaoh's men slain by the sword and all his army—declares the Lord God. 32 a-I strike terror into the land of the living; Pharaoh-a and all his masses are laid among the uncircumcised, along with those who were slain by the sword—said the Lord God.

33 The word of the Lord came to me: 2 O mortal, speak to your fellow countrymen and say to them: When I bring the sword against a country, the citizens of that country take one of their number and appoint him their watchman. 3 Suppose he sees the sword advancing against the country, and he blows the horn and warns the people. 4 If anybody hears the sound of the horn but ignores the warning, and the sword comes and dispatches him, his blood shall be on his own head. 5 Since he heard the sound of the horn but ignored the warning, his bloodguilt shall be upon himself; had he taken the warning, he would have saved his life. 6 But if the watchman sees the sword advancing and does not blow the horn, so that the people are not warned, and the sword comes and destroys one of them, that person was destroyed for his own sins; however, I will demand a reckoning for his blood from the watchman.

7 Now, O mortal, I have appointed you a watchman for the House of Israel; and whenever you hear a message from My mouth, you must transmit My warning to them. 8 When I say to the wicked, "Wicked man, you shall die," but you have not spoken to warn the wicked man against his way, he, that wicked man, shall die for his sins, but I will demand a reckoning for his blood from you. 9 But if you have warned the wicked man to turn back from his way, and he has not turned from his way, he shall die for his own sins, but you will have saved your life.

10 Now, O mortal, say to the House of Israel: This is what you have been saying: "Our transgressions and our sins weigh heavily upon us; we are sick at heart about them. How can we survive?" 11 Say to them: As I live—declares the Lord God—it is not My desire that the wicked shall die, but that the wicked turn from his [evil] ways and live. Turn back, turn back from your evil ways, that you may not die, O House of Israel!

30: *The princes of the north,* probably the Phoenicians, as indicated by the reference to the *Sidonians.*

33.1–20: Ezekiel's appointment as Israel's watchman. This is a transitional section in the book, bridging the oracles concerning the nations and the end of the book, mostly comprised of prophecies of consolation. This short section contains many echoes of earlier portions of Ezekiel. **1–9:** The role of a prophet is like that of a watchman who stands watch over a city; this picks up on the earlier use of the image (see 3.16–21). The watchman is not responsible for the fate of the people if he warns them, but he is fully responsible if he does not. The passage presupposes that the threat of death for the wicked can be reversed if they change their ways. **10–20:** This paraphrases many sections of 18.21–32. Ezekiel debates with those who believe that past righteousness can deliver someone who commits wrongdoing later in life and that past wrongdoing will still condemn those who have turned to righteousness.

---

a-a Emendation yields "because he struck terror in the land of the living, Pharaoh."

¹²Now, O mortal, say to your fellow countrymen: The righteousness of the righteous shall not save him when he transgresses, nor shall the wickedness of the wicked cause him to stumble when he turns back from his wickedness. The righteous shall not survive through ᵃhis righteousness⁻ᵃ when he sins. ¹³When I say of the righteous "He shall surely live," and, relying on his righteousness, he commits iniquity, none of his righteous deeds shall be remembered; but for the iniquity that he has committed he shall die. ¹⁴So, too, when I say to the wicked, "You shall die," and he turns back from his sinfulness and does what is just and right—¹⁵if the wicked man restores a pledge, makes good what he has taken by robbery, follows the laws of life,ᵇ and does not commit iniquity—he shall live, he shall not die. ¹⁶None of the sins that he committed shall be remembered against him; since he does what is just and right, he shall live.

¹⁷Your fellow countrymen say, "The way of the Lord is unfair." But it is their way that is unfair! ¹⁸When a righteous man turns away from his righteous deeds and commits iniquity, he shall die ᶜfor it.⁻ᶜ ¹⁹And when a wicked man turns back from his wickedness and does what is just and right, it is he who shall live by virtue of these things. ²⁰And will you say, "The way of the Lord is unfair"? I will judge each one of you according to his ways, O House of Israel!

²¹In the twelfth year of our exile, on the fifth day of the tenth month, a fugitive came to me from Jerusalem and reported, "The city has fallen." ²²Now the hand of the LORD had come upon me the evening before the fugitive arrived, and He opened my mouth before he came to me in the morning; thus my mouth was opened and I was no longer speechless.

²³The word of the LORD came to me: ²⁴O mortal, those who live in these ruins in the land of Israel argue, "Abraham was but one man, yet he was granted possession of the land. We are many; surely, the land has been given as a possession to us." ²⁵Therefore say to them: Thus said the Lord GOD: You eat with the blood, you raise your eyes to your fetishes, and you shed blood—yet you expect to possess the land! ²⁶You have relied on your sword, you have committed abominations, you have all defiled other men's wives—yet you expect to possess the land! ²⁷Thus shall you speak to them: Thus said the Lord

33.21–39.29: Oracles concerning the restoration of Israel. The introductory date formula and the absence of another date formula until 40.1 identify 33.21–39.29 as the twelfth major block of the book. Once the prophet is informed of the fall of Jerusalem (33.21–22), the book emphasizes restoration for Israel (33.21–39.29) and the Temple (chs 40–48). Following the notification of Jerusalem's fall, the prophetic word formulas identify six oracular reports in this block, including 33.23–33; 34.1–31; 35.1–36.15; 36.16–37.14; 37.15–28; 38.1–39.29, which take up various aspects and images of Israel's restoration. Many of the prophecies of restoration take images from the earlier prophecies of retribution and overturn them. **33.21–22:** *In the twelfth year of our exile, on the fifth day of the tenth month,* 5 Sivan, 585 BCE. The prophet first receives word of Jerusalem's fall some seven months after the event, at which time he is released from his speechlessness (3.26–27), as was predicted in 24.27. **23–29:** Ezekiel counters the claim that *those who live in these ruins,* desert nomads, will take control of the land. Ezekiel argues that they will be destroyed because they do not observe God's requirements for holy life in the land (see Lev. chs 17–18). For the crimes enumerated here, see ch 18. Following the failure of the Bar Kokhba revolt, Jewish legend states that R. Shimeon dwelt in a cave for twelve years teaching his son the secrets of heaven or Jewish mysticism (*b. Shab.* 33b). This would help to explain his association with *those who are in the strongholds and caves.* He is later portrayed as a primary figure in the "Zohar."

a-a Heb. "it."   b Cf. Lev. 18.5.
c-c Or "in spite of them," i.e., his righteous deeds.

GOD: As I live, those who are in the ruins shall fall by the sword, and those who are in the open I have allotted as food to the beasts, and those who are in the strongholds and caves shall die by pestilence. ²⁸I will make the land a desolate waste, and her proud glory shall cease; and the mountains of Israel shall be desolate, with none passing through. ²⁹And they shall know that I am the LORD, when I make the land a desolate waste on account of all the abominations which they have committed.

³⁰Note well, O mortal: your fellow countrymen who converse about you by the walls and in the doorways of their houses and say to each other and propose to one another, "Come and hear what word has issued from the LORD." ³¹They will come to you ᵃin crowds and sit before you in throngs⁻ᵃ and will hear your words, but they will not obey them. For ᵇthey produce nothing but lust with their mouths;⁻ᵇ and their hearts pursue nothing but gain. ³²To them you are just a singer of bawdy songs, who has a sweet voice and plays skillfully; they hear your words, but will not obey them. ³³But when itᶜ comes—and come it will—they shall know that a prophet has been among them.

34 The word of the LORD came to me: ²O mortal, prophesy against the shepherdsᵈ of Israel. Prophesy, and say to them:

To the shepherds: Thus said the Lord GOD: Ah, you shepherds of Israel, who have been tending yourselves! Is it not the flock that the shepherds ought to tend? ³You partake of the fat,ᵉ you clothe yourselves with the wool, and you slaughter the fatlings; but you do not tend the flock. ⁴You have not sustained the weak, healed the sick, or bandaged the injured; you have not brought back the strayed, or looked for the lost; but you have driven them with harsh rigor, ⁵and they have been scattered for want of anyone to tend them; scattered, they have become prey for every wild beast. ⁶My sheep stray through all the mountains and over every lofty hill; My flock is scattered all over the face of the earth, with none to take thought of them and none to seek them. ⁷Hear then, O shepherds, the word of the LORD! ⁸As I live—declares the Lord GOD: Because My flock has been a spoil—My flock has been a prey for all the wild beasts, for want of anyone to tend them since My shepherds have not taken thought of My flock,

29: In many ways, this v. summarizes the main point of Ezekiel: Contrary to what many people believed, the destruction of Jerusalem does not indicate that God is powerless and has abandoned the Israelites, but that He is powerfully and legitimately punishing them for their deeds. **30–33:** God charges that people come to hear Ezekiel, but will not do as he says. That attitude, however, will change with the destruction of the Temple, when Ezekiel is fully legitimated as a true prophet.

34.1–31: Oracle concerning Israel's leaders or "shepherds." Ezekiel contends that Israel's leaders have acted improperly and must be replaced. Yet ultimately this ch does not suggest the abolition of Davidic kingship, but a type of power-sharing between David and God. **1–10:** The image of the shepherd is commonly used to portray monarchs in biblical and ancient Near Eastern literature (e.g., David, 1 Sam. 16.11; ch 17; and much earlier, Hammurabi of Babylon). God charges that the "shepherds" have not taken care of the "flock" so that they are "scattered" or sent into exile. **2:** *Ah*, lit. "woe!"

a-a Meaning of Heb. uncertain. Lit. "as a people come, and sit before you as My people."
b-b Meaning of Heb. uncertain.   c I.e., the punishment predicted.   d I.e., rulers.
e Septuagint and Vulgate, reading the Hebrew consonants with different vowels, translate "milk."

for the shepherds tended themselves instead of tending the flock—⁹hear indeed, O shepherds, the word of the LORD: ¹⁰Thus said the Lord GOD: I am going to deal with the shepherds! I will demand a reckoning of them for My flock, and I will dismiss them from tending the flock. The shepherds shall not tend themselves any more; for I will rescue My flock from their mouths, and it shall not be their prey. ¹¹For thus said the Lord GOD: Here am I! I am going to take thought for My flock and I will seek them out. ¹²As a shepherd seeks out his flock when some [animals] in his flock have gotten separated, so I will seek out My flock, I will rescue them from all the places to which they were scattered on a day of cloud and gloom. ¹³I will take them out from the peoples and gather them from the countries, and I will bring them to their own land, and will pasture them on the mountains of Israel, by the watercourses and in all the settled portions of the land. ¹⁴I will feed them in good grazing land, and the lofty hills of Israel shall be their pasture. There, in the hills of Israel, they shall lie down in a good pasture and shall feed on rich grazing land. ¹⁵I Myself will graze My flock, and I Myself will let them lie down—declares the Lord GOD. ¹⁶I will look for the lost, and I will bring back the strayed; I will bandage the injured, and I will sustain the weak; and the fat and healthy ones I will destroy.ᵃ I will tend them rightly.

¹⁷And as for you, My flock, thus said the Lord GOD: I am going to judge between one animal and another.

To the rams and the bucks: ¹⁸Is it not enough for you to graze on choice grazing ground, but you must also trample with your feet what is left from your grazing? And is it not enough for you to drink ᵇ⁻clear water,⁻ᵇ but you must also muddy with your feet what is left? ¹⁹And must My flock graze on what your feet have trampled and drink what your feet have muddied? ²⁰Assuredly, thus said the Lord GOD to them: Here am I, I am going to decide between the stout animals and the lean. ²¹Because you pushed with flank and shoulder against the feeble ones and butted them with your horns until you scattered them abroad, ²²I will rescue My flock and they shall no longer be a spoil. I will decide between one animal and another.

²³Then I will appoint a single shepherd over them to tend them—My servant David. He shall tend them, he shall be a shepherd to them. ²⁴I the LORD will be their God, and My servant David shall be a ruler among them—I the LORD have spoken. ²⁵And I will grant them a

11–16: God acts as the ideal "shepherd" (Ps. 23) who will return the people who have been scattered. **12:** This verse is reused in the "unetaneh tokef" prayer of the high holidays, as part of the image of God's annual judgment of each Jew. **16:** *The fat and healthy ones I will destroy:* They will be destroyed because they neglected the people. Heb reads "'ashmid" (*I will destroy*), the Greek Septuagint reads "I will tend them rightly" (presumably based on Heb "'eshmor," ["resh" looks like "dalet" and the two are often confused]; see translators' note a). **17–22:** Ezekiel portrays the leaders as stronger sheep who trample the pasture and dirty the water that others must use, and who push the weaker aside. Thus, some of the flock must be destroyed. **23–31:** God's rule will be manifested in the establishment of a David as *ruler* ("nasi" rather than "melekh"). Though other biblical passages imagine a descendant of David as the ideal, future king (e.g., Isa. 11.1–10), this passage seems to envisage a return of David himself, the earlier, ideal king. **24:** It is possible that the title *ruler* ("nasi'" rather than "melekh") given here and in chs 40–48 to the king represents a diminution of royal power: He is a ruler, but not a full-fledged king. **25:** *A covenant of friendship,* the idyllic situation for those whom God will return to the land. Contrary to those who assert that "those who live in these ruins" will take over the land (33.23–29), Ezekiel maintains that God will protect the people of Israel.

---

a Several ancient versions read "guard."   *b-b Lit. "water that has settled."*

covenant of friendship. I will banish vicious beasts from their land, and they shall live secure in the wasteland, they shall even sleep in the woodland. 26 I will make ᵃ-these and the environs of My hill-ᵃ a blessing: I will send down the rain in its season, rains that bring blessing. 27 The trees of the field shall yield their fruit and the land shall yield its produce. [My people] shall continue secure on its own soil. They shall know that I am the LORD when I break the bars of their yoke and rescue them from those who enslave them. 28 They shall no longer be a spoil for the nations, and the beasts of the earth shall not devour them; they shall dwell secure and untroubled. 29 I shall establish for them ᵃ-a planting of renown;-ᵃ they shall no more be carried off by famine, and they shall not have to bear again the taunts of the nations.ᵇ 30 They shall know that I the LORD their God am with them and they, the House of Israel, are My people—declares the Lord GOD.

31 For you, My flock, flock that I tend, are men; and I am your God—declares the Lord GOD.

35 The word of the LORD came to me: 2 O mortal, set your face against Mount Seir and prophesy against it. 3 Say to it: Thus said the Lord GOD: I am going to deal with you, Mount Seir: I will stretch out My hand against you and make you an utter waste. 4 I will turn your towns into ruins, and you shall be a desolation; then you shall know that I am the LORD. 5 Because you harbored an ancient hatred and handed the people of Israel over to the sword in their time of calamity, the time set for their punishment—6 assuredly, as I live, declares the Lord GOD, ᵃ-I will doom you with blood; blood shall pursue you; I swear that, for your bloodthirsty hatred, blood shall pursue you.-ᵃ 7 I will make Mount Seir an utter waste, and I will keep all passersby away from it. 8 I will cover its mountains with the slain; men slain by the sword shall lie on your hills, in your valleys, and in all your watercourses. 9 I will make you a desolation for all time; your towns shall never be inhabited. And you shall know that I am the LORD.

10 Because you thought "The two nations and the two lands shall be mine and we shall possess them"—ᶜ-although the LORD was there-ᶜ—11 assuredly, as I live, declares the Lord GOD, I will act with the same anger and passion that you acted with in your hatred of them. And I will make Myself known through them when I judge you.

27–29: The references to *trees* and *beasts of the earth* together with the threat of enemies (see Lev. ch 26) recall God's role as creator of the natural world and protector in the human world. **31:** *For you, My flock, flock that I tend, are men; and I am your God,* a variation of the covenant formula (11.20; 14.11) that emphasizes that God will be Israel's ultimate shepherd-king.

35.1–36.15: Edom and Israel. Ezekiel delivers contrasting oracles to *Mount Seir*, which personifies Edom, concerning judgment against Edom (see Isa. ch 34; Jer. 49.7–22; Obadiah) and to the *mountains of Israel* concerning the restoration of Israel. The restoration here, as elsewhere in prophetic literature, envisions the restoration of both kingdoms, Israel and Judah. The oracles presuppose Edom's actions against Jerusalem at the time of the Babylonian assault (see Obadiah 11–14; Ps. 137.7–9). This may explain their placement here, rather than with the earlier collection of oracles concerning the nations. **35.1–15:** The prophecy concerning Edom begins with an initial oracle in vv. 3–4, followed by "proof sayings" in vv. 5–9, 10–13 that establish the grounds for punishment. **2:** *Mount Seir,* the mountain range extending south from the Dead Sea and east of the Arabah that was Edom's homeland (Gen. 36.8; Num. 24.18; cf. Gen. 33.16). **3–4:** The initial oracle calls for Edom's destruction. **5–9:** The first "proof saying" indicates that Edom played a role in Israel's destruction; it has Edom's desolation as its theme, and repeats this word several times. **5:** *Ancient hatred* likely alludes to the feud between Esau (= Edom) and Jacob or the long history of conflict between Israel and Edom (Num. 20.14–21). **10–13:** The second "proof saying." **10:** *The two nations and the two lands:* In addition to the conflict between Esau and Jacob, there is a tradition of God's self-revelation from Seir (Deut. 33.2; Judg. 5.4).

---

a-a *Meaning of Heb. uncertain.*　　　b *Cf. 36.30.*
c-c *Meaning of Heb. uncertain; emendation yields "and the LORD heard it."*

12 You shall know that I the LORD have heard all the taunts you uttered against the hills of Israel: "They have been laid waste; they have been given to us as prey." 13 And you spoke arrogantly against Me and ᵃmultiplied your wordsᵃ against Me: I have heard it.

14 Thus said the Lord GOD: When the whole earth rejoices, I will make you a desolation. 15 As you rejoiced when the heritage of the House of Israel was laid waste, so will I treat you: the hill country of Seir and the whole of Edom, all of it, shall be laid waste. And they shall know that I am the LORD.

36 And you, O mortal, prophesy to the mountains of Israel and say: O mountains of Israel, hear the word of the LORD:

2 Thus said the Lord GOD: Because the enemy gloated over you, "Aha! Those ancient heights have become our possession!" 3 therefore prophesy, and say: Thus said the Lord GOD: Just because ᵇthey eagerly lusted to see you become a possession of the other nations round about, so that you have become the butt of gossip in every language and of the jibes from every peopleᵇ—4 truly, you mountains of Israel, hear the word of the Lord GOD: Thus said the Lord GOD to the mountains and the hills, to the watercourses and the valleys, and to the desolate wastes and deserted cities which have become a prey and a laughingstock to the other nations round about:

5 Assuredly, thus said the Lord GOD: I have indeed spoken in My blazing wrath against the other nations and against all of Edom which, ᵇwith wholehearted glee and with contempt, have made My land a possession for themselves for pasture and for prey.ᵇ 6 Yes, prophesy about the land of Israel, and say to the mountains and the hills, to the watercourses and to the valleys, Thus said the Lord GOD: Behold, I declare in My blazing wrath: Because you have suffered the taunting of the nations, 7 thus said the Lord GOD: I hereby swear that the nations which surround you shall, in their turn, suffer disgrace. 8 But you, O mountains of Israel, shall yield your produce and bear your fruit for My people Israel, for their return is near. 9 For I will care for you: I will turn to you, and you shall be tilled and sown. 10 I will settle a large population on you, the whole House of Israel; the towns shall be resettled, and the ruined sites rebuilt. 11 I will multiply men and beasts upon you, and they shall increase and be fertile, and I will resettle you as you were formerly, and will

14–15: Edom disappeared following the 6th century as it was overrun by Arab nomads who later became known as the Nabateans.

36.1–15: The oracle concerning the restoration of the mountains of Israel is a deliberate contrast with that against Mount Seir. As a prophecy of consolation, it also reverses some of the imagery of the prophecy of retribution in ch 6. **2:** God begins by citing Edom's intentions to take control of Israel. **3–12:** The oracle presupposes the depopulation and desolation of the entire land, which must now be replenished. **3, 5:** *The other nations,* lit. "the remnant of the nations"; Edom elsewhere is a symbol for nations that threaten Israel (Isa. ch 34; 63.1–6). **11:** *They shall increase and be fertile,* see Gen. 1.22, 28; 9.7.

---

a-a *Emendation yields "and spoke arrogantly."*   b-b *Meaning of Heb. uncertain.*

make you more prosperous than you were at first. And you shall know that I am the Lord. [12] I will lead men—My people Israel—to you, and they shall possess you. You shall be their heritage, and you shall not again cause them to be bereaved.

[13] Thus said the Lord God: Because they say to you, "You are [a land] that devours men, you have been a bereaver of your nations,"[a] [14] assuredly, you shall devour men no more, you shall never again bereave your nations—declares the Lord God. [15] No more will I allow the jibes of the nations to be heard against you, no longer shall you suffer the taunting of the peoples; and never again shall you cause your nations to stumble[b]—declares the Lord God.

[16] The word of the Lord came to me: [17] O mortal, when the House of Israel dwelt on their own soil, they defiled it with their ways and their deeds; their ways were in My sight like the uncleanness of a menstruous woman. [18] So I poured out My wrath on them for the blood which they shed upon their land, and for the fetishes with which they defiled it. [19] I scattered them among the nations, and they were dispersed through the countries: I punished them in accordance with their ways and their deeds. [20] But when they came [c]to those nations,[c] they caused My holy name to be profaned,[d] in that it was said of them, "These are the people of the Lord, yet they had to leave His land." [21] Therefore I am concerned for My holy name, which the House of Israel have caused to be profaned among the nations to which they have come.

[22] Say to the House of Israel: Thus said the Lord God: Not for your sake will I act, O House of Israel, but for My holy name, which you have caused to be profaned among the nations to which you have come. [23] I will sanctify My great name which has been profaned among the nations—among whom you have caused it to be profaned. And the nations shall know that I am the Lord—declares the Lord God—when I manifest My holiness before their eyes through you. [24] I will take you from among the nations and gather you from all the countries, and I will bring you back to your own land. [25] I will sprinkle clean water upon you, and you shall be clean: I will cleanse you from all your uncleanness and from all your fetishes. [26] And I will give you a new heart and put a new spirit into you: I will

---

a I.e., Israel and Judah; cf. 37.15–22.

b Many mss. read "be bereaved"; cf. vv. 13–14.

c-c Lit. "the nations they came to."

d I.e., the exile of Israel was taken by the nations to be evidence of the Lord's weakness.

13–15: The prophet promises that the land will no longer be open to the accusation of devouring *the peoples*.

36.16–37.14: The purification and restoration of Israel. The prophetic word formula, *the word of the Lord came to me*, marks 36.16–37.14 as a unit, although many scholars see them as two separate oracles. Ezek. 36.16–38 speaks of the purification of the defiled people and their land, and 37.1–14 portrays the resuscitation of the dead bones, representing the coming back to life of Israel.

36.16–38: Sanctification of God's name. Ezek. 36.16–38 (Sephardi lectionary, 36.16–36) serves as the haftarah on Shabbat Parah, the third of the four special Shabbats preceding Passover (*m. Meg.* 3.4). Num. 19.1–22 discusses the laws of the red heifer, whose ashes are used for purification from corpse contamination, and the haftarah likewise takes up purification. **16–22:** The prophet initially employs the imagery of menstrual blood (see Lev. 15.19–30) to portray the impurity of the land. The impurity resulted from the *blood which they shed upon their land*, which is another metaphor for idolatrous practices (see Ps. 104.38). The exile of the people profanes God's name in that it may suggest to others that the Israelite God is weaker than other gods, and did not have the power to prevent their exile. **22–32:** In order to reclaim God's name, Israel must be restored. As the vv. make clear, this is done for God's sake, not because Israel is deserving. **25:** God intends to purify Israel with *clean water*, which is the standard procedure for purification in such cases (Lev. 15.7, 11–12, etc.; see also Lev. 14.5–6, 50–52; Num. 19.17). Women and men immerse themselves in running water for purification (Lev. 11.36). **26–27:** Once the land and people are cleansed, God will provide *a new heart* and *a new spirit* (11.19; 18.31; Jer. 31.31–34) that will prompt the people to live a holy remove the heart of stone from your body and give you a heart of flesh; 27 and I will put My spirit into you. Thus I will cause you to follow My laws and faithfully to observe My rules. 28 Then you shall dwell in the land which I gave to your fathers, and you shall be My people and I will be your God.

29 And when I have delivered you from all your uncleanness, I will summon the grain and make it abundant, and I will not bring famine upon you. 30 I will make the fruit of your trees and the crops of your fields abundant, so that you shall never again be humiliated before the nations because of famine. 31 Then you shall recall your evil ways and your base conduct, and you shall loathe yourselves for your iniquities and your abhorrent practices. 32 Not for your sake will I act—declares the Lord GOD— take good note! Be ashamed and humiliated because of your ways, O House of Israel!

33 Thus said the Lord GOD: When I have cleansed you of all your iniquities, I will people your settlements, and the ruined places shall be rebuilt; 34 and the desolate land, after lying waste in the sight of every passerby, shall again be tilled. 35 And men shall say, "That land, once desolate, has become like the garden of Eden; and the cities, once ruined, desolate, and ravaged, are now populated and fortified." 36 And the nations that are left around you shall know that I the LORD have rebuilt the ravaged places and replanted the desolate land. I the LORD have spoken and will act.

37 Thus said the Lord GOD: Moreover, in this I will respond to the House of Israel and act for their sake: I will multiply their people like sheep. 38 As Jerusalem is filled with sacrificial sheep during her festivals, so shall the ruined cities be filled with flocks of people. And they shall know that I am the LORD.

37 The hand of the LORD came upon me. He took me out by the spirit of the LORD and set me down in the valley. It was full of bones. 2 He led me all around them; there were very many of them spread over the valley, and they were very dry. 3 He said to me, "O mortal, can these bones live again?" I replied, "O Lord GOD, only You know." 4 And He said to me, "Prophesy over these bones and say to them: O dry bones, hear the word of the LORD! 5 Thus said the Lord GOD to these bones: I will cause breath to enter you and you shall live again. 6 I will lay sinews upon you, and cover you with flesh, and form skin over you. And I will put breath into you, and you shall live again. And you shall know that I am the LORD!"

life in accordance with God's commandments. **28:** The covenant formula signifies the restoration of Israel's relationship with God and the fertility of the land. **33–36:** Replenishing of the land to resemble *the garden of Eden* (Gen. chs 2–3) reveals God to the nations (Exod. 15.13–18). **37–38:** Along with the agricultural plenty comes the image of pastoral plenty, which is then related to the abundance of sacrificial sheep that fill Jerusalem during festivals, suggesting that these festivals will once again be celebrated in Jerusalem.

37.1–14: The valley of dry bones. Ezekiel's vision of the dry bones symbolizes the restoration of the people Israel. Ezekiel is speaking metaphorically in this vision; he was not envisioning an actual physical resurrection of the dead. But when, in postbiblical times, the doctrine of resurrection took hold, Ezekiel's vision was interpreted literally. Modern commentators assume that, if the vision has a basis in reality, it is based upon the prophet's observation of a battlefield filled with the bones of dead soldiers. When Shabbat falls during the intermediate days of Passover, 36.37–37.14 (Sephardi lectionary, 37.1–14) is read as the haftarah, most likely because the restoration envisaged here is interpreted as a second, liberating Passover-like experience or because of the rabbinic tradition that the second, ultimate liberation would transpire on Passover. **1–10:** God instructs him to prophesy. **1–2:** *Valley,* or "plain," the location of his initial visions (1.22–27). **5, 8, 9:** *Breath,* lit. "wind."

⁷I prophesied as I had been commanded. And while I was prophesying, suddenly there was a sound of rattling, and the bones came together, bone to matching bone. ⁸I looked, and there were sinews on them, and flesh had grown, and skin had formed over them; but there was no breath in them. ⁹Then He said to me, "Prophesy to the breath, prophesy, O mortal! Say to the breath: Thus said the Lord GOD: Come, O breath, from the four winds, and breathe into these slain, that they may live again." ¹⁰I prophesied as He commanded me. The breath entered them, and they came to life and stood up on their feet, a vast multitude.

¹¹And He said to me, "O mortal, these bones are the whole House of Israel. They say, 'Our bones are dried up, our hope is gone; we are doomed.' ¹²Prophesy, therefore, and say to them: Thus said the Lord GOD: I am going to open your graves and lift you out of the graves, O My people, and bring you to the land of Israel. ¹³You shall know, O My people, that I am the LORD, when I have opened your graves and lifted you out of your graves. ¹⁴I will put My breath into you and you shall live again, and I will set you upon your own soil. Then you shall know that I the LORD have spoken and have acted"—declares the LORD.

¹⁵The word of the LORD came to me: ¹⁶And you, O mortal, take a stick and write on it, "Of Judah and the Israelites associated with him"; and take another stick and write on it, "Of Joseph—the stick of Ephraim—and all the House of Israel associated with him." ¹⁷Bring them close to each other, so that they become one stick, joined together in your hand. ¹⁸And when any of your people ask you, "Won't you tell us what these actions of yours mean?" ¹⁹answer them, "Thus said the Lord GOD: I am going to take the stick of Joseph—which is in the hand of Ephraim—and of the tribes of Israel associated with him, and I will place the stick of Judah ᵃupon itᵃ and make them into one stick; they shall be joined in My hand." ²⁰You shall hold up before their eyes the sticks which you have inscribed, ²¹and you shall declare to them: Thus said the Lord GOD: I am going to take the Israelite people from among the nations they have gone to, and gather them from every quarter, and bring them to their own land. ²²I will make them a single nation in the land, on the hills of Israel, and one king shall be king of them all. Never again shall they be two nations, and never again shall they be

a-a Meaning of Heb. uncertain.

11–14: Traditional Jewish exegetes find here the idea of the resurrection of the dead before the day of judgment, a fundamental belief of rabbinic Judaism ascribed to Moses (*m. Sanh.* 10.1; *b. Sanh.* 90b; see also Isa. 26.19; Dan. 12.1–4). In its plain-sense meaning, the image symbolizes the restoration of Israel to its own land. **11:** As elsewhere, Ezekiel refutes a popular proverb (see 8.12 n).

37.15–28: The two sticks. Ezekiel's symbolic action represents the unification of Israel and Judah under the rule of a Davidic king. Isa. ch 11 also employs the image of a growing tree to symbolize the unification of Israel and Judah under a Davidic king. Ezek. 37.15–28 serves as the haftarah for the parashah of Va-yiggash (Gen. 44.18–47.17), in which Joseph reveals himself to his brothers, thereby reuniting the twelve sons of Jacob. This may be a highly idealized prophecy, since it is unlikely that significant remnants of the ten northern tribes survived until this period. **15–19:** On the use of a stick or staff to represent a tribe, see Num. 17.1–26. **16:** *Judah* is the Southern Kingdom, and *Joseph* is the father of *Ephraim*, the central tribe of the Northern Kingdom, Israel. *Stick*, lit. "tree" or "wood." **20–28:** Just as one gathers sticks for a fire (Isa. 27.11), God will gather the exiles to establish them as one nation, with David as their king, undoing the damage caused after the death of Solomon with the division of the monarchy. King David, however, is clearly subservient to God: He is God's servant (v. 24) and is called a prince (v. 25) rather than a full-fledged king. **26:** Ezekiel draws upon the tradition of permanent Davidic rule (2 Sam. ch 7; Pss. 89; 132), the eternal *covenant of friendship*, lit. "covenant of peace," granted to the priest Phineas the son of Eleazar and grandson of Aaron (Num. 25.10–13; see also Ezek. 34.25); and upon the role of the Temple as the center of both Israel and all credivided into two kingdoms. ²³ Nor shall they ever again defile themselves by their fetishes and their abhorrent things, and by their other transgressions. I will save them in all their settlements where they sinned, and I will cleanse them. Then they shall be My people, and I will be their God.

²⁴ My servant David shall be king over them; there shall be one shepherd for all of them. They shall follow My rules and faithfully obey My laws. ²⁵ Thus they shall remain in the land which I gave to My servant Jacob and in which your fathers dwelt; they and their children and their children's children shall dwell there forever, with My servant David as their prince for all time. ²⁶ I will make a covenant of friendship with them—it shall be an everlasting covenant with them—I will establish*ᵃ* them and multiply them, and I will place My Sanctuary among them forever. ²⁷ My Presence*ᵇ* shall rest over them; I will be their God and they shall be My people. ²⁸ And when My Sanctuary abides among them forever, the nations shall know that I the Lᴏʀᴅ do sanctify Israel.

38 The word of the Lᴏʀᴅ came to me: ² O mortal, turn your face toward Gog of the land of Magog, the chief prince of Meshech and Tubal. Prophesy against him ³ and say: Thus said the Lord Gᴏᴅ: Lo, I am coming to deal with you, O Gog, chief prince of Meshech and Tubal! ⁴ I will turn you around and put hooks in your jaws, and lead you out with all your army, horses, and horsemen, all of them clothed in splendor, a vast assembly, all of them with bucklers and shields, wielding swords. ⁵ Among them shall be Persia, Nubia, and Put, everyone with shield and helmet; ⁶ Gomer and all its cohorts, Beth-togarmah [in] the remotest parts of the north and all its cohorts—the many peoples with you.*ᶜ* ⁷ Be ready, prepare yourselves, you and all the battalions mustered about you, and hold yourself in reserve for them.*ᵈ* ⁸ After a long time you shall be summoned; in the distant future you shall march against the land [of a people] restored from the sword, gathered from the midst of many peoples—against the mountains of Israel, which have long lain desolate—[a people] liberated from the nations, and now all dwelling secure. ⁹ You shall advance, coming like a storm; you shall be like a cloud covering the earth, you and all your cohorts, and the many peoples with you.

¹⁰ Thus said the Lord Gᴏᴅ: On that day, a thought will

ation (Exod. ch 40; see also Gen. 2.1–3).

38.1–39.29: The Gog and Magog oracles. Ezekiel's oracles against Gog, ruler from the land of Magog, express an apocalyptic scenario of God's victory over the nations that threaten Israel. The original identity of *Gog* is uncertain, although some have identified him with Gyges, a 7th-century ruler of Lydia in Asia Minor. The land of *Magog* appears together with *Meshech, Tubal, Gomer* (Cimmerians in central Asia Minor), and *Togarmah* (cf. *Beth-togarmah,* in Armenia), apparently in reference to lands in Asia Minor and Greece. Gomer, Magog, Meshech, and Tubal were sons of Japheth (Gen. 10.2), who is associated with Europe and Asia beyond the Middle East. Ezekiel's oracles draw upon Isaiah's prophecies concerning the downfall of a Mesopotamian ruler (Isa. ch 14) and Jeremiah's prophecies concerning a "foe from the north" (Jer. chs 2–3). The original identity of Gog matters little as later interpreters have understood him to be a transnational symbol of evil, much like Edom and Egypt (e.g., Isa. ch 34; 63.1–6; Mal. 1.2–5; Exod. ch 15) or chaos monsters such as Leviathan or behemoth (Pss. 74; 104; Job chs 38–41). Ezek. 38.18–39.16 is the haftarah for the Intermediate Days of Sukkot when Exod. 33.12–34.26 and the relevant day's passage from Num. ch 29 are read as the Torah portion. Exod. 33.12–34.26 relates God's revelation to Moses and the restoration of the two tablets of the covenant after the golden calf incident, which corresponds to the focus on Israel's restoration in Ezek. 38.1–39.16. **38.1–9:** God's initial instructions to Ezekiel present Gog as the leader of a host of nations that threaten Israel, a well-known motif in the tradition about Zion as an invincible fortress (cf. Pss. 2; 46–48). **5:** *Persia, Nubia* (or Ethiopia), and *Put* (Libya) are distant lands from throughout the ancient Near Eastern world. **10–13:** God portrays Gog's intentions to plun-

---

a Meaning of Heb. uncertain.   *b Lit. "dwelling place."*
c I.e., with Gog.   *d Septuagint reads "Me."*

occur to you, and you will conceive a wicked design. [11] You will say, "I will invade a land of open towns, I will fall upon a tranquil people living secure, all of them living in unwalled towns and lacking bars and gates, [12] in order to take spoil and seize plunder"—to turn your hand against repopulated wastes, and against a people gathered from among nations, acquiring livestock and possessions, living at the center of the earth. [13] Sheba and Dedan, and the merchants and all the magnates of Tarshish will say to you, "Have you come to take spoil? Is it to seize plunder that you assembled your hordes—to carry off silver and gold, to make off with livestock and goods, to gather an immense booty?"

[14] Therefore prophesy, O mortal, and say to Gog: Thus said the Lord GOD: Surely, on that day, when My people Israel are living secure, you will ᵃtake note,⁻ᵃ [15] and you will come from your home in the farthest north, you and many peoples with you—all of them mounted on horses, a vast horde, a mighty army—[16] and you will advance upon My people Israel, like a cloud covering the earth. This shall happen on that distant day: I will bring you to My land, that the nations may know Me when, before their eyes, I manifest My holiness through you, O Gog!

[17] Thus said the Lord GOD: Why, you are the one I spoke of in ancient days through My servants, the prophets of Israel, who prophesied for years in those days that I would bring you against them!

[18] On that day, when Gog sets foot on the soil of Israel—declares the Lord GOD—My raging anger shall flare up. [19] For I have decreed in My indignation and in My blazing wrath: On that day, a terrible earthquake shall befall the land of Israel. [20] The fish of the sea, the birds of the sky, the beasts of the field, all creeping things that move on the ground, and every human being on earth shall quake before Me. Mountains shall be overthrown, cliffs shall topple, and every wall shall crumble to the ground. [21] ᵇI will then summon the sword against him throughout My mountains⁻ᵇ—declares the Lord GOD—and every man's sword shall be turned against his brother. [22] I will punish him with pestilence and with bloodshed; and I will pour torrential rain, hailstones, and sulfurous fire upon him and his hordes and the many peoples with him. [23] Thus will I manifest My greatness and My holiness, and make Myself known in the sight of many nations. And they shall know that I am the LORD.

der nations. **13:** *Sheba,* southern Arabia. *Dedan,* central Arabia, although some identify it as Rhodes. *Tarshish,* Tartessos in Spain. **14–16:** God portrays Gog's advance with a mighty army against Israel. **16:** *That distant day* (others "in the latter days") normally refers to the future, and many believe the expression to have eschatological meaning in contexts such as this one. *That the nations may know Me* draws upon earlier traditions (e.g., Exod. ch 15; Isa. 2.1–4; Mic. 4.1–5; Pss. 46–48) in which the nations recognize God's power and sovereignty. **17–23:** The Lord GOD portrays the defeat of Gog as a cosmic event that was announced by the prophets. This suggests that by the period of Ezekiel, a collection of prophetic works was available to be studied. **18:** *On that day* is a formula that appears throughout Isa. chs 1–39 (e.g., Isa. 4.2; 7.18, 20, 21, 23). **19–20:** The cosmic dimensions of the defeat appear in the quaking of the land, including *the fish of the sea, the birds of the sky, the beasts of the field, all creeping things,* and *every human being,* which alludes to the created order as described in the Priestly creation story of Gen. ch 1. **21–22:** Likewise, the defeat of Gog by the sword and natural elements, such as *torrential rain, hailstones,* and *sulfurous fire,* appeals to God's role as creator as well as to the tradition about the destruction of Sodom and Gomorrah (Gen. chs 18–19). This is logical in this context, which suggests the universal acknowledgment of God.

---

a-a Septuagint reads "rouse yourself."
b-b Meaning of Heb. uncertain.

39

And you, O mortal, prophesy against Gog and say: Thus said the Lord GOD: I am going to deal with you, O Gog, chief prince of Meshech and Tubal! [2] I will turn you around and ᵃdrive you on,ᵃ and I will take you from the far north and lead you toward the mountains of Israel. [3] I will strike your bow from your left hand and I will loosen the arrows from your right hand. [4] You shall fall on the mountains of Israel, you and all your battalions and the peoples who are with you; and I will give you as food to carrion birds of every sort and to the beasts of the field, [5] as you lie in the open field. For I have spoken—declares the Lord GOD. [6] And I will send a fire against Magog and against those who dwell secure in the coastlands. And they shall know that I am the LORD. [7] I will make My holy name known among My people Israel, and never again will I let My holy name be profaned. And the nations shall know that I the LORD am holy in Israel. [8] Ah! it has come, it has happened— declares the Lord GOD: this is that day that I decreed.

[9] Then the inhabitants of the cities of Israel will go out and make fires and feed them with the weapons—shields and bucklers, bows and arrows, clubs and spears; they shall use them as fuel for seven years. [10] They will not gather firewood in the fields or cut any in the forests, but will use the weapons as fuel for their fires. They will despoil those who despoiled them and plunder those who plundered them—declares the Lord GOD.

[11] On that day I will assign to Gog a burial site there in Israel—the Valley of the Travelers, east of the Sea. It shall block the path of travelers, for there Gog and all his multitude will be buried. It shall be called the Valley of Gog's Multitude. [12] The House of Israel shall spend seven months burying them, in order to cleanse the land; [13] all the people of the land shall bury them. ᵃThe day I manifest My glory shall bring renown to themᵃ—declares the Lord GOD. [14] And they shall appoint men to serve permanently, to traverse the land and bury any invaders who remain above ground, in order to cleanse it. The search shall go on for a period of seven months. [15] As those who traverse the country make their rounds, any one of them who sees a human bone shall erect a marker beside it, until the buriers have interred them in the Valley of Gog's Multitude. [16] ᵃThere shall also be a city named Multitude.ᵃ And thus the land shall be cleansed.

[17] And you, O mortal, say to every winged bird and to all the wild beasts: Thus said the Lord GOD: Assemble,

39.4–5: Unburied corpses on the mountains recall the imagery of the vision of dry bones (37.1–14), the death of the Babylonian king in the open (Isa. 14.3–23), and the defeat of Assyria on the mountains of Israel (Isa. 14.24–27). Lying unburied reflected serious shame in antiquity. **9:** The victory fires that burn for *seven years* throughout the land represent the vast amount of weaponry that could not defeat Israel, protected by its God. It also recalls the sabbatical (seven-year) agricultural and economic cycle (Lev. 25.1–7; Exod. 23.10–11 [cf. 21.1–6]; Deut. 15.1–18). **11:** The burial of Gog marks the final stage of the cleansing of the land of Israel prior to its restoration. *The Valley of the Travelers* or the "Valley of those who pass by" is apparently a word play on the Valley of Abarim east of the Dead Sea. Heb for "travelers, passers-by" is "haʿorim." *The Valley of Gog's Multitude* (Heb "geiʾ hamon gog"), a wordplay on the Valley of Hinnom, southwest of Jerusalem, which was known for idolatry, the burning of children, and dead bodies (2 Kings 23.10; Jer. 7.30–34). **12–13:** The seven months of burial purify the land so that God's *glory* or presence may appear. The length of time again emphasizes the vast number of people who were defeated by God. **16:** *A city named Multitude* (Heb "Hamonah"), see above, v. 11 n. **17–29:** The feast of the birds and wild animals recalls the covenant curses (e.g., Deut. 28.16–44) in which Israel is fed to the birds and animals, but they are now applied to Israel's enemies (Lev. 26.22; Deut. 28.26).

---

a-a Meaning of Heb. uncertain.

come and gather from all around for the sacrificial feast that I am preparing for you—a great sacrificial feast—upon the mountains of Israel, and eat flesh and drink blood. [18] You shall eat the flesh of warriors and drink the blood of the princes of the earth: rams, lambs, he-goats, and bulls—fatlings of Bashan all of them. [19] You shall eat fat to satiety and drink your fill of blood from the sacrificial feast that I have prepared for you. [20] And you shall sate yourselves at My table with horses, charioteers,[a] warriors, and all fighting men—declares the Lord GOD. [21] Thus will I manifest My glory among the nations, and all the nations shall see the judgment that I executed and the power that I wielded against them.

[22] From that time on, the House of Israel shall know that I the LORD am their God. [23] And the nations shall know that the House of Israel were exiled only for their iniquity, because they trespassed against Me, so that I hid My face from them and delivered them into the hands of their adversaries, and they all fell by the sword. [24] When I hid My face from them, I dealt with them according to their uncleanness and their transgressions.

[25] Assuredly, thus said the Lord GOD: I will now restore the fortunes of Jacob and take the whole House of Israel back in love; and I will be zealous for My holy name. [26] They will bear[b] their shame and all their trespasses that they committed against Me, when they dwell in their land secure and untroubled, [27] when I have brought them back from among the peoples and gathered them out of the lands of their enemies and have manifested My holiness through them in the sight of many nations. [28] They shall know that I the LORD am their God when, having exiled them among the nations, I gather them back into their land and leave none of them behind. [29] I will never again hide My face from them, for I will pour out My spirit upon the House of Israel—declares the Lord GOD.

40 In the twenty-fifth year of our exile,[c] the fourteenth year after the city had fallen, at the beginning of the year, the tenth day of the month—on that very day—the hand of the LORD came upon me, and He brought me

a Lit. "chariots"; Septuagint reads "riders."
b Change of diacritical point yields "forget."
c I.e., the exile of King Jehoiachin; see 1.2.

17: The *sacrificial feast* reverses the imagery of the banquet on Zion (Isa. 25.6–10). **18–21:** These actions enable God to display the divine glory to the nations. **23–24:** The image of God hiding His face, namely turning away from Israel and choosing not to help them, is common in the Bible (e.g., Deut. 31.17–18; Ps. 13.2), but is found only here in Ezekiel, and never in Priestly literature. **25:** *Restore the fortunes of Jacob* recalls God's promise to remember the covenant of Jacob (Lev. 26.40–45) if the people confess their iniquity.

40.1–48.35: The vision of the restored Temple in Jerusalem. The date formula identifies 40.1–48.35 as the thirteenth and culminating major section of the book of Ezekiel. *In the twenty-fifth year . . . at the beginning of the year, the tenth day of the month,* 10 Tishri, 573–572 BCE, Yom Kippur. Ezekiel's vision of the Temple builds upon God's earlier promises (37.24–38) to make a covenant of friendship (peace) with Israel and to place the sanctuary among them forever. This vision provides a literary and conceptual envelope for the book that complements the visions of God's departure and the Temple's destruction in chs 1–7; 9–11 with one of the Temple's restoration and God's return. Ezek. 40.1–43.12 relates instruction concerning the building of the Temple and the return of God's glory; 43.13–47.12 provides instruction concerning the associated structures and activities of the Temple complex; and 47.13–48.35 guides the reestablishment of the land and people of Israel around the Temple. The details of the Temple, its courts, furnishing, and laws and the technical terminology presented here differ in many respects from those for the wilderness Tabernacle (see esp. Exod. chs 25–30; 35–45), Solomon's Temple (1 Kings chs 6–7; 2 Chron. chs 3–4), and the Second Temple (*m. Mid.* 5). It is unclear if certain of these details reflect the Temple standing in Jerusalem when Ezekiel was exiled in 597, or if they are fanciful. Indeed, the differences in the portrayal of the Temple were, according to the Rabbis, a major discrepancy that Hananiah son of Hezekiah reconciled so that Ezekiel could be included in the biblical canon (*b. Shab.* 13b). Because of the discrepancies, Jewish tradition regards these chs as Ezekiel's vision of the Third Temple to be built in the days of the Messiah (*Seder Olam* 26; Rashi; Radak).

there. ²He brought me, in visions of God, to the Land of Israel, and He set me down on a very high mountain* on which there seemed to be the outline of a city **on the south.** ³He brought me over to it, and there, standing at the gate, was a man who shone like copper. In his hand were a cord of linen and a measuring rod. ⁴The man spoke to me: "Mortal, look closely and listen attentively and note well everything I am going to show you—for you have been brought here in order to be shown—and report everything you see to the House of Israel."

⁵Along the outside of the Temple [area] ran a wall on every side. The rod that the man held was six cubits long, plus one handbreadth for each cubit; and when he applied it to that structure, it measured one rod deep* and one rod high.

⁶He went up to the gate that faced eastward and mounted its steps. He measured the threshold of the gate; it was one rod deep*—*ᵈ*the one threshold was one rod deep.*ᵈ* ⁷Each recess was one rod wide and one rod deep, with [a partition of] 5 cubits between recesses; and the threshold of the gate, at the inner vestibule of the gate, was one rod deep. ⁸*ᵈ*For when he measured it at the inner vestibule of the gate, it was one rod [deep].*ᵈ* ⁹Next he measured the vestibule of the gate, and it measured 8 cubits and its supports 2 cubits; the vestibule of the gate was at its inner end. ¹⁰*ᵉ*On either side of this eastern gate there were three recesses, all three of the same size; of identical sizes were also the supports*ᶠ* on either side. ¹¹He measured the opening of the gate and found it 10 cubits wide, while the gate itself measured 13 cubits across.*ᵍ* ¹²At the fronts of the recesses on either side were *ᵈ*barriers of one cubit;*ᵈ* the recesses on either side were 6 cubits [deep]. ¹³Their openings faced each other directly across the gate passage, so that when he measured from rear*ʰ* of recess to rear*ʰ* of recess he obtained a width of 25 cubits.*ⁱ* ¹⁴*ᵈ*He made the vestibule*ʲ*— 60 cubits—and the gate next to the support on every side of the court.*ᵈ* ¹⁵And [the distance] from the front of the outer*ʰ*

---

a Cf. Isa. 2.1; Mic. 4.1.   b-b Septuagint reads "in the distance."

c In this description, the Hebrew word which ordinarily corresponds to English "width" sometimes designates a measurement from an opening or outer surface inward, and so corresponds to the English "depth"; and the word which ordinarily corresponds to English "length" designates the distance from side to side of a vestibule or a passage, and so corresponds to the English "width."

d-d Meaning of Heb. uncertain.   e This verse would read well before v. 7.

f In connection with recesses, the "supports" are partitions.

g The opening was perhaps narrowed by a stone on each side for receiving the hinge of a door-leaf.   h Meaning of Heb. uncertain.   i Since each of the recesses was 6 cubits deep (v. 7a) and the passage in the middle was 13 cubits wide (v. 11).

j Elim here is the same as elam in vv. 16, 21, 22, etc.

40.1–43.12: The Temple and the return of God's Presence. 40.1: The date is 10 Tishri, Yom Kippur, 573–572 BCE. Ezekiel's visions began at the age of thirty in the fifth year of the exile (1.1–3). After twenty years, Ezekiel would be ready to retire from priestly service at the age of fifty (Num. 4.3; 8.23–25). *The beginning of the year,* not the first day of the year but 10 Tishri or Yom Kippur (the Day of Atonement; Lev. 23.26–32; Num. 29.7–11). Yom Kippur is also the day when the high priest would enter the Holy of Holies and speak the name of God as part of the atonement on behalf of Israel (Lev. ch 16; *m. Yoma* 3.8; 4.2; 6.2; *m. Sot.* 7.6; *m. Tamid* 3.8; 7.2). **2:** Ezekiel is transported to Mt. Zion, the site of the Temple (see Isa. 2.1; Mic. 4.1). The city of Jerusalem is immediately to *the south.* **3:** Ezekiel's guide recalls the bronze-colored creatures that supported God's throne chariot (1.5–14; see also 8.2). The *cord of linen* and the *measuring rod* enable the guide to instruct Ezekiel in the dimensions of the Temple structures. **5–47:** The Temple walls, gates, and courtyards. **5:** *Six cubits long, plus one handbreadth for each cubit,* over 3 m (10 ft). Whereas the normal cubit is five handbreadths, the cubit used for the construction of the Temple is six handbreadths. The long cubit is about 518 mm or 20.68 in. **6–7:** The *gate that faced eastward* is the main gate of the Temple complex, which faces east toward the sun. It is built according to the basic pattern of the fortified Solomonic gates at Gezer, Hazor, and Megiddo, with an initial *threshold of the gate,* three recessed chambers on either side, and the *inner vestibule of the gate.* **9:** *Its supports,* projecting columns that may have served as a door jamb. Windows provide light for the recessed chambers and the vestibule. **14:** *And the gate next to the support on every side of the court:* There were five gates to the women's courtyard of the Second Temple, the two Huldah gates to the south, the Kiponos gate to the west, the Tadi gate to the north, gate to the front of the inner vestibule of the gate was 50 cubits. [16] The recesses—and their supports—had windows [a]with frames[a] on the interior of the gate complex on both sides, and the interiors of the vestibules also had windows on both sides; and the supports were adorned with palms.

[17] He took me into the outer court. There were chambers there, and there was a pavement laid out all around the court. There were 30 chambers on the pavement. [18] The pavements flanked the gates; the depth of the lower[b] pavements paralleled that of the gates. [19] Then he measured the width of [c]the lower[b] court, from in front of the inner gate to in front of the outer gate[c]—100 cubits.

[a]After the east [gate], the north [gate].[a] [20] Next he measured the gate of the outer court that faced north: its length and its width, [21] its three recesses on either side and its supports, as also its vestibule. It measured, like the first gate, 50 cubits in length and 25 cubits in width. [22] Its windows and [those of] its vestibule, as also its palm trees, corresponded to those of the gate that faced east. [From the outside] one had to climb 7 steps to reach it, and its vestibule was [d]ahead of them.[d] [23] Like the east gate, the north gate faced a gate leading into the inner forecourt; and when he measured the distance from gate to gate, it was 100 cubits.

[24] Then he took me to the south side. There was also a gate on the south side, and he got the same measurements as before for its supports and its vestibule. [25] Both it and its vestibule had windows like the aforementioned ones. It was 50 cubits long and 25 cubits wide. [26] Its staircase consisted of 7 steps; its vestibule was [d]ahead of them,[d] and its supports were decorated on both sides with palm trees. [27] The inner court likewise had a gate facing south; and on the south side, too, he measured a distance of 100 cubits from the [outer] gate to the [inner] gate.

[28] He now took me into the inner forecourt through its south gate. When he measured this south gate, it had the same measurements as the foregoing. [29] Its recesses, its supports, and its vestibule had the same measurements. Both it and its vestibule had windows on both sides; it was 50 cubits long and 25 cubits wide—[30][e]vestibules on both sides, 25 cubits long, 5 cubits wide.[e] [31] Its vestibule,

and the eastern gate (*m. Mid.* 1.3). **17–19:** The *30 chambers* that line the *outer court* (the "women's court"; *m. Mid.* 2.5) were used by the Levites for various activities (Jer. 35.2–4; Neh. 13.4–14). *The lower court* and *the inner gate* rearranges the nouns and adjectives so that they will agree in gender (see translators' note *c-c*). They likely refer to the "inner court" in Heb, and "the lower gate," that would allow entry. **20–27:** The gates for the outer court to the north and south are similar to the eastern gate. There is no western gate mentioned here as the Temple occupies the western side of the compound (contra *m. Mid.* 1.3, which mentions the western gate, but states that the northern gate was not used). Each of the three gates faces corresponding gates to the inner court. **28–37:** The south, east, and north gates to the *inner forecourt* (lit. "the inner court," or the "court of the Israelites"; *m. Mid.* 2.6) are similar to those for the outer court. The Second Temple had seven gates to this court (*m. Mid.* 1.4–5), three to the south (Kindling, Firstlings, and Water Gates); three to the north (Flame, Offering, and Chamber of the Hearth Gates), and one to the east (Nicanor Gate).

a-a *Meaning of Heb. uncertain.*

b *The outer court and its gates were 8 steps lower than the inner ones: v. 34.*

c-c *In this rendering, the adjectives "lower" and "inner" are construed, not with the nouns they stand next to in the Hebrew, but with those with which they agree in gender.*

d-d *Septuagint reads "at its inner end."*

e-e *Connection unclear; wanting in some Heb. mss. and versions.*

however, gave on the outer court.[a] Its supports were adorned on either side with palms, and its staircase consisted of 8 steps.

[32] Then he took me to the eastern side of the inner forecourt; and when he measured the gate there, he got the same measurements: [33] its recesses, supports, and vestibule had the above measurements. Both it and its vestibule had windows on both sides; it was 50 cubits long and 25 cubits wide, [34] and its vestibule gave on the outer court. Its supports were decorated on both sides with palm trees, and its staircase consisted of 8 steps.

[35] Then he took me to the north gate, and found its measurements to be identical, [36] with the same recesses, supports, vestibule, windows on both sides, and a length of 50 cubits and a width of 25 cubits. [37] Its supports[b] gave on the outer court; its supports were decorated on both sides with palm trees; and its staircase consisted of eight steps.

[38] A chamber opened into the gate;[c] there the burnt offering would be washed. [39] And inside the vestibule of the gate, there were two tables on each side, at which the burnt offering, the sin offering, and the guilt offering were to be slaughtered; [40] while outside—[d]as one goes up toward[d] the opening of the north gate—there were two tables on one side, and there were two tables on the other side of the gate's vestibule. [41] Thus there were four tables on either flank of the gate—eight tables in all—at which [the sacrifices] were to be slaughtered. [42] As for the four tables for the burnt offering[e]—they were of hewn stone, one and a half cubits long, one and a half cubits wide, and one cubit high—[f]on them were laid out the instruments with which burnt offerings and sacrifices were slaughtered.[f] [43] Shelves,[g] one handbreadth wide, were attached all around the inside; and the sacrificial flesh was [laid] on the tables.

[44] There were [h]chambers for singers[h] in the inner forecourt: [one] beside the north gate facing south, and one beside the east[i] gate facing north. [45] [The man] explained to me: "The chamber that faces south is for the priests who perform the duties of the Temple; [46] and the chamber that

38–43: Chambers were built by the vestibule of the gate to prepare sacrificial animals for the *burnt offering* (Lev. 1.3–17), the *sin* (or purification) *offering* (Lev. 4.1–5.13), and the *guilt offering* (Lev. 5.14–6.7). **44–47:** Chambers were placed by the sides of the north and east (Septuagint reads "south") for the priests who have charge of the Temple and the altar. The measurements of the inner court of the Second Temple differ from the 100 square cubit figure given here. *M. Middot* 2.6 states that they are 135 by 11 cubits.

---

a I.e., in the inner gates the vestibules were situated at their entrances, and so they were true vestibules, in contrast to the "inner vestibules" of the outer gates.

b Septuagint reads "vestibules"; cf. vv. 31, 34.

c Heb. "gates"; the reference is apparently to the north gate; cf. v. 40 and Lev. 1.11; 4.24; 7.2.   d-d Emendation yields "the vestibule at."

e See v. 39.   f-f This clause would read well after v. 43.

g Meaning of Heb. uncertain.   h-h Septuagint reads "two chambers."

i Septuagint reads "south."

faces north is for the priests who perform the duties of the altar—they are the descendants of Zadok, who alone of the descendants of Levi may approach the LORD to minister to Him."

⁴⁷ He then measured the forecourt: 100 cubits long and 100 cubits broad—foursquare. In front of the Temple stood the altar. ⁴⁸ He took me into the portico of the Temple and measured it. The jambs^a of the portico were 5 cubits deep on either side. The width of the gate-opening was ^b[14 cubits, and the flanking wall of the gate was]^b 3 cubits on either side. ⁴⁹ The portico was 20 cubits wide^c and 11^d cubits deep, and ^eit was by steps that it was reached.^e There were columns by the jambs on either side.

41 He then led me into the great hall. He measured the jambs, 6 cubits on either side; such was the depth^f of each jamb.^g ² The entrance was 10 cubits wide, and the flanking walls of the entrance were each 5 cubits wide. Next he measured the depth [of the hall], 40 cubits, and the width, 20 cubits. ³ And then he entered the inner room. He measured each jamb of the entrance, 2 cubits [deep]; the entrance itself, 6 cubits across; and the width of ^h[the flanking wall on either side of]^h the entrance, 7 cubits. ⁴ Then he measured the depth, 20 cubits; and the width at the inner end of the great hall was also 20 cubits. And he said to me, "This is the Holy of Holies."

⁵ Then he measured the wall of the Temple. [It was] 6 cubits [thick] on every side of the Temple, and the side-chamber measured 4 cubits [across].ⁱ ⁶ The side chambers were arranged one above the other, in 33 sections.^j All around, there were projections in the Temple wall to serve the side chambers as supports, so that [their] supports should not be the Temple wall itself. ⁷ The ^kwinding passage^k of the side chambers widened from story to story; ^land since the structure was furnished all over with winding passages from story to story, the structure itself became wider from story to story.^l It was by this means that

40.48–41.26: The Temple.
40.48–41.4: The Temple is constructed according to a three-room pattern, like that of Solomon's Temple (1 Kings ch 6) and other examples of temples and royal palaces from Canaan and elsewhere. The detail offered here may seem excessive, but is much less than the detail offered at the end of Exodus concerning the construction of the Tabernacle. This great concern with detail in both cases reflects the notion that God's house must be custom-built to its exact specification so God will enjoy dwelling there amidst Israel. **40.48:** The *portico* (Heb, "'ulam," 20 by 11 cubits [about 10 m by 6 m, 30 ft by 17 ft]) was an entry or reception room. **41.1:** The *great hall* (Heb, "heikhal," 40 by 20 cubits [about 20 m by 10 m, 60 ft by 30 ft]) was the main hall where the Temple furnishings are placed. **3:** The 2 cubit (1 m, 3 ft) measurement for the *entrance* conflicts with the 1 cubit (.5 m, 18 in) mentioned in *m. Middot* 4.7. **4:** The *Holy of Holies* (20 by 20 cubits [10 m by 10 m, 30 ft by 30 ft]) was God's throne room, which according to Kings housed the Ark of the Covenant in Solomon's Temple. After the Ark was removed, only a stone remained in the Second Temple (*m. Yoma* 5.2). Ezekiel does not enter the *Holy of Holies* as this is restricted to the high priest on Yom Kippur or the Day of Atonement (Lev. ch 16; *m. Yoma* 5.1). **5–11:** Three stories of chambers with thirty chambers each line the walls of the Temple. They have an independent support structure so that they are not supported by the Temple itself. **7:** A *winding passage*, perhaps a spiral staircase, provides access to the upper stories. The supports and stairways occupy more space on the lower stories so that each story is progressively larger.

a I.e., the edges of the flanking walls.   b-b Preserved in the Septuagint.

c See note on v. 5.   d Septuagint reads "12"; see note d on 41.13.

e-e Septuagint reads "it was reached by ten steps."   f See note on 40.5.

g This sense is demanded by the context; usually, ohel means "tent."

h-h Preserved in the Septuagint.

i I.e., on the ground level; cf. v. 7.

j Lit. "times." Emendation yields "in three sections of three tiers each," i.e., one section next to each of the two side walls of the Temple and one next to its rear wall; cf. v. 7.

k-k So Targum; cf. Mishnah Tamid 1.1.

l-l Exact meaning of Heb. uncertain, but for the general sense cf. 1 Kings 6.6a, 8b.

one ascended from the bottom story to the top one by way of the middle one.

8 I observed that the Temple was surrounded by a raised pavement—the foundations of the side chambers; its elevation was a rod's length, or 6 cubits. 9 The outer wall of the side chamber was 5 cubits thick, and that which served as a walk between the Temple's side chambers 10 and the chamber complexes[a] was 20 cubits wide all around the Temple. 11 Of entrances to the side chambers giving on the walk, there was one entrance on the north side and one entrance on the south side; and the space[b] of the walk was 5 cubits thick all around. 12 And the structure that fronted on the vacant space at the [Temple's] western end was 70 cubits deep;[c] the walls of the structure were 5 cubits thick on every side; and it was 90 cubits wide.[c]

13 He measured the [total] depth of the Temple, 100 cubits;[d] and the depth of the vacant space and of the structure, with its walls, also came to 100 cubits.[e] 14 The front side of the Temple, like the vacant space on the east, was 100 cubits wide.[f] 15 He also measured the width[c] of the structure facing the vacant space in the rear, inclusive of its ledges,[g] 100 cubits.

Both the great hall inside and the portico next to the court—16 [h]the thresholds[-h]—and the windows [i]with frames[-i] and the ledges[j] at the threshold, all over the three parts of each, were completely overlaid[k] with wood. There was wainscoting from the floor to the windows, including the window [frame]s 17 and extending above the openings, [i]both in the inner Temple and outside.[-i] And all over the wall, [i]both in the inner one and in the outer,[-i] ran a pattern.[k] 18 It consisted of cherubs and palm trees, with a palm tree between every two cherubs. Each cherub had two faces: 19 a human face turned toward the palm tree on one side

8: *Raised pavement,* the *foundations of the side chambers* (cf. "foundations of the earth"; Mic. 6.2; Isa. 24.18; Jer. 31.37; Ps. 82.5).
12–15a: The unidentified building is behind the Temple to the west.
15b–26: The interior decoration of the Temple. **18–19:** The *cherubs* and *palm trees* carved into the wainscoting or paneling of the interior walls represent images from the garden of Eden. Unlike the cherubim who bear the throne chariot, these have only two faces, a human and a young lion (see 1 Kings 6.29).

---

a See 42.1 ff.   b Emendation yields "parapet."   c See note on 40.5.

d Comprising the 5 cubits of 40.48, the 12 of 40.49 (see note there), the 6 of 41.1, the 40 of 41.2, the 2 of 41.3, the 20 of 41.4, the 6 of 41.5a, the 4 of 41.5b, and the 5 of 41.9.

e The structure was 70 cubits deep and its front and rear walls each 5 cubits thick (v. 12). The remaining 20 cubits are accounted for by the vacant space; cf. 42.1–2.

f To the inside width of 20 cubits (40.49; 41.2–4) must be added on each side: one Temple wall of 6 cubits equals 12; one side-chamber wall of 5 cubits equals 10; one side chamber's inner depth of 4 cubits equals 8; a walk's width of 20 cubits (40.9–10) equals 40; and a parapet's thickness of 5 cubits (v. 11) equals 10; totaling 100 cubits.

g Emendation yields "walls"; cf. v. 12.   h-h Septuagint reads "were paneled."

i-i Meaning of Heb. uncertain.

j Here perhaps designating the door frames, since it is these that (as required by the continuation of the verse) are situated at the threshold and consist of three parts (a lintel and two doorposts).   k Meaning of Heb. uncertain.

l-l Meaning perhaps the great hall and the vestibule; cf. v. 5.

and a lion's face turned toward the palm tree on the other side. This was repeated all over the Temple; 20 the cherubs and the palm trees were carved on[a] the wall from the floor to above the openings.

As regards the great hall, 21 the great hall had four door-posts; and before the Shrine was something resembling 22 a wooden altar 3 cubits high and 2 cubits long and having inner corners;[b] and its length[c] and its walls were of wood. And he said to me, "This is the table[d] that stands before the LORD." 23 The great hall had a double door, and the Shrine likewise had 24 a double door, and each door had two [e]swinging leaves:[e] two for the one door and two [e]such leaves[e] for the other. 25 Cherubs and palm trees were carved on these—on the doors of the hall—just as they were carved on the walls; and there was a lattice[f] of wood outside in front of the portico. 26 And there were windows [e]with frames[e] and palm trees on the flanking walls of the portico on either side [of the entrance] [e]and [on] the Temple's side chambers and [on] the lattices.[e]

42 He took me out, by way of the northern gate, into the outer court, and he led me [westward] up to a [g]complex of chambers[g] that ran parallel to the northern ends of the vacant space and the structure. 2 The width[h] of its façade—[i]its north side, the one from which it was en-tered[i]—was 100 cubits, and its depth[h] was 50 cubits. 3 At right angles to the 20 cubits[j] of the inner court and to the pavement of the outer court,[k] the complex rose ledge by ledge[l] in three tiers. 4 There was an areaway, 10 cubits wide and [m]a road of one cubit,[m] running along the inner-court side of the chamber complex, but its entrances were on its north side. 5 Here its upper chambers were cut back, because ledges took away from them as construction pro-ceeded backward from the bottom ones and then from the middle ones. 6 For they were arranged in three tiers, and they had no columns like those of the chambers in the courts.[n] That is why the rise proceeded by stages: from the

21–22: *Something resembling a wooden altar*, the table for the pres-entation of rows of "showbread" (Exod. 25.23–30; Lev. 24.5–9; 1 Kings 6.20–22). *The table that stands before the LORD*, i.e., the altar. Talmudic tradition cites this v. to argue that the table in the Jewish home may substitute for the altar (*b. Ber.* 55a). **42.1–14:** Chambers are built in three stories along the walls that define the outer and inner courts.

a Heb. "and."

b Apparently meaning that it had a rim around the top, like the table of Exod. 25.25; see the final note on the present verse.

c Septuagint reads "base."

d Serving to hold the bread of display; cf. Exod. 25.30; 40.22–23; 1 Kings 7.48.

e-e Meaning of Heb. uncertain.   f Meaning of Heb. uncertain.   g-g Heb. simply "chambers," and so elsewhere.   h See note c at 40.6.   i-i Lit. "the north entrance"; but cf. v. 4.   j I.e., the vacant space; cf. 41.13 with note e.   k Cf. 40.17.

l Because this part of the inner court was considerably higher than the outer; 40.28–31 and 41.8, 9b–10.

m-m Septuagint and Syriac read "and 100 cubits long"; cf. vv. 2–3.

n See vv. 8–9 referring to chambers along the west wall.

ground, from the bottom ones, and from the middle ones. [7] In the outer court, a wall 50 cubits long ran parallel to the chamber complex up to the chambers in the outer court;[a] [8] for the chambers in the outer court were themselves 50 cubits deep, thus completing 100 cubits alongside the edifice.[b] [9] Thus, at the foot of that complex of chambers ran a passage[c]—[d]of a width set by the wall in the outer court[-d]—which one entered from the east in order to gain access to them from the outer court.

[10] There was another chamber complex to the east[e] of the vacant space and the structure, [11] likewise with a passage in front—just like the complex on the north side, with which this one agreed in width[f] and depth[f] and in the exact layout of its exits and entrances. [12] Accordingly, the entrances to the chamber complex on the south side were approached from the east by the entrance at the head of [g]the corresponding passage along the matching wall.[-g]

[13] And he said to me, "The northern chambers and the southern chambers by the vacant space are the consecrated chambers in which the priests who have access to the LORD shall eat the most holy offerings. There they shall deposit the most holy offerings—the meal offerings, the sin offerings, and the guilt offerings, for the place is consecrated. [14] When the priests enter, they shall not proceed from the consecrated place to the outer court without first leaving here the vestments in which they minister; for the [vestments] are consecrated. Before proceeding to the area open to the people,[h] they shall put on other garments."

[15] When he had finished the measurements of the inner Temple [area], he led me out by way of the gate which faces east, and he measured off the entire area. [16] He measured the east side with the measuring rod, 500 [cubits]—in rods, by the measuring rod. He turned [17][and] measured the north side: 500 [cubits]—in rods, by the measuring rod. He turned [18][and] measured the south side: 500 [cubits]—in rods, by the measuring rod. [19] Then he turned to the west side [and] measured it: 500 cubits—in rods, by the measuring rod. [20] Thus he measured it on the four sides; it had a wall completely surrounding it, 500 [cubits] long [i]on each side,[-i] to separate the consecrated from the unconsecrated.

13–14: The priests use the chambers to store and eat "the grain offering" (Lev. 2.1–16), "the sin (or purification) offering" (Lev. 4.1–5.13), and "the guilt offering" (Lev. 5.14–6.7). The priests must leave their holy vestments in these chambers before entering the outer court. **15–20:** The Temple complex is 500 *rods* square. Based on Ezek. 40.5, a *rod* is 6 cubits so that the Temple complex is 3,000 cubits square (Rashi), or about 1,500 m (4,500 ft) on a side. This is an extremely large area, equivalent to about 500 acres or two-thirds the area of Central Park in New York. Based on Ezek. 45.2, Radak argues that it is 500 cubits square, but does not explain the term *rods*. (This interpretation, giving an area of about 250 m [750 ft] on a side, or about 14 acres, is the one followed in the NJPS.) The outer wall marks the separation between the holy Temple and the profane world.

---

a See vv. 8–9 referring to chambers along the west wall.

b Apparently meaning the chamber complex of v. 1.

c So kethib; qere "thing giving access."   d-d Brought up from v. 10 for clarity.

e Septuagint reads "south"; cf. v. 13.   f See note c at 40.6.

g-g Exact meaning of Heb. uncertain; the phrase apparently refers to vv. 7–8.

h Cf. 44.19 and note b.   i-i Lit. "and 500 wide."

43

Then he led me to a gate, the gate that faced east. ² And there, coming from the east with a roar like the roar of mighty waters, was the Presence of the God of Israel, and the earth was lit up by His Presence. ³ The vision was like the vision I had seen when I[a] came to destroy the city, the very same vision that I had seen by the Chebar Canal. Forthwith, I fell on my face.

⁴ The Presence of the LORD entered the Temple by the gate that faced eastward. ⁵ A spirit carried me into the inner court, and lo, the Presence of the LORD filled the Temple; ⁶ and I heard speech addressed to me from the Temple, though [the] man[b] was standing beside me. ⁷ It said to me:

O mortal, this is the place of My throne and the place for the soles of My feet, where I will dwell in the midst of the people Israel forever. The House of Israel and their kings must not again defile My holy name by their apostasy and by the corpses of their kings [c]at their death.[c] ⁸ When they placed their threshold next to My threshold and their doorposts next to My doorposts with only a wall between Me and them,[d] they would defile My holy name by the abominations that they committed, and I consumed them in My anger. ⁹ Therefore, let them put their apostasy and the corpses of their kings far from Me, and I will dwell among them forever.

¹⁰ [Now] you, O mortal, describe the Temple to the House of Israel,[e] and let them measure its design. But let them be ashamed of their iniquities: ¹¹ When they are ashamed of all they have done, make known to them the plan of the Temple and its layout, its exits and entrances—its entire plan, and all the laws and instructions pertaining to its entire plan. Write it down before their eyes, that they may faithfully follow its entire plan and all its laws. ¹² Such are the instructions for the Temple on top of the mountain: the entire area of its enclosure shall be most holy. Thus far the instructions for the Temple.

¹³ [f]And these are the dimensions of the altar, in cubits where each is a cubit and a handbreadth. The trench[g] shall be a cubit deep and a cubit wide, with a rim one span high

43.1–12: The divine Presence (chs 1; 8–11) returns to the Temple complex through the eastern gate from which it had earlier departed (10.19). **5:** Ezekiel recalls his inaugural vision, and reports that he is transported to the inner court where he sees *the Presence of the LORD* filling the Temple (Exod. 40.34–35; 1 Kings 8.10–13). **7:** God informs him that this will be *the place of My throne* (see 1 Chron. 28.2; Ps. 132.7; Isa. 60.13; Lam. 2.1). *The corpses of their kings* refers to burials of kings near the Temple, which defile it (1 Kings 2.10; 11.43; 2 Kings 21.18, 26). **10–12:** God instructs Ezekiel to teach the people the plan for the Temple.

43.13–47.12: The Temple complex and its activities. Instructions concerning structures associated with the Temple and regulations concerning Temple rituals and practice. **43.13–27:** The altar (Exod. 20.21–23) is a four-level stepped structure, like a Mesopotamian ziggurat (a type of pyramid). **13:** The *trench*, also rendered "base," lit. "bosom of the earth" (signifying the placement of the altar at the center of the earth), is 18 cubits (about 9 m, 27 ft) square.

---

a Six mss. and two ancient versions read "He."

b I.e., the guide of 40.3 ff.

c-c So with a number of Heb. mss. The usual vocalization yields "their shrines."

d The south wall of the First Temple enclosure was also the north wall of the royal enclosure; the two communicated by the Gate of the Guard (2 Kings 11.19). Thus Temple and palace could be regarded as a single dwelling ("tent") in the sense of Num. 19.14, and the death of a king in the palace would defile the Temple. Hence the zoning provisions of 45.2 ff.

e In accordance with the three preceding chapters; cf. 40.4.

f Some of the terms and details in vv. 13–17 are obscure.

g Lit. "bosom."

around its edge. And the height[a] shall be as follows: [14] From the trench in the ground to the lower ledge, which shall be a cubit wide: 2 cubits; from the [b-]lower ledge to the upper[-b] ledge, which shall likewise be a cubit wide: 4 cubits; [15] and the height of the altar hearth shall be 4 cubits, with 4 horns projecting upward from the hearth: 4 cubits. [16] Now the hearth shall be 12 cubits long and 12 broad, square, with 4 equal sides. [17] Hence, the [upper] base[c] shall be 14 cubits broad, with 4 equal sides. The surrounding rim shall be half a cubit [high],[d] and the surrounding trench shall measure one cubit. And the ramp[e] shall face east.

[18] Then he[f] said to me: O mortal, thus said the Lord GOD: These are the directions for the altar on the day it is erected, so that burnt offerings may be offered up on it and blood dashed against it. [19] You shall give to the levitical priests who are of the stock of Zadok, and so eligible to minister to Me—declares the Lord GOD—a young bull of the herd for a sin offering. [20] You shall take some of its blood and apply it to [g-]the four horns [of the altar],[-g] to the four corners of the base, and to the surrounding rim; thus you shall purge it and perform purification upon it. [21] Then you shall take the bull of sin offering and burn it in the [h-]designated area[-h] of the Temple, outside the Sanctuary.

[22] On the following day, you shall offer a goat without blemish as a sin offering; and the altar shall be purged [with it] just as it was purged with the bull. [23] When you have completed the ritual of purging, you shall offer a bull of the herd without blemish and a ram of the flock without blemish. [24] Offer them to the LORD; let the priests throw salt on them and offer them up as a burnt offering to the LORD. [25] Every day, for seven days, you shall present a goat of sin offering, as well as a bull of the herd and a ram of the flock; you[i] shall present unblemished ones. [26] Seven days they shall purge the altar and cleanse it; [j-]thus shall it be consecrated.[-j]

[27] And when these days are over, then from the eighth day onward the priests shall offer your burnt offerings and your offerings of well-being on the altar; and I will extend My favor to you—declares the Lord GOD.

14: The *lower ledge* is 16 cubits (about 8 m or 24 ft) square. The *upper ledge* is 14 cubits (about 7 m or 21 ft) square. **15:** The *hearth* (Heb "hahar'el," "mountain of God" or "God appeared"; compare Ariel of Isa. 29.1) with *4 horns*, see Exod. 27.2; 29.12; 1 Kings 1.50–51; Zech. 2.1–4. The height of the structure is 10 cubits (5 m or 15 ft). **17:** Its *ramp* faces the eastern gate. **18–26:** The seven-day consecration of the altar is performed at Sukkot (Tabernacles; 1 Kings 8.65–66; Ezra 3.1–7; but cf. Num. ch 7) and resembles the ordination of priests (Exod. 29.1–37; Lev. ch 8). **20:** The purification of the altar with blood is analogous to the sprinkling of blood on the priests at their ordination (Exod. 29.16), on the altar at Yom Kippur to make atonement for the people (Lev. 16.18–19), and on the people to seal the covenant (Exod. 24.1–8). In Priestly literature, blood is understood as a ritual detergent. **22–25:** The use of a *goat* as sin offering for the dedication of the Temple is an innovation. **24:** *Salt* is offered with grain offerings (Lev. 2.13; Num. 18.19). Ezek. 43.10–27 is the haftarah for the parashah of Tetsavveh (Exod. 27.20–30.10), which relates the consecration of the priests and the construction of the altar.

a Lit. "bulge."   b-b Lit. "lesser ledge to the greater."

c Heb. ʿazarah, which in v. 14 means "ledge." The altar consists of 3 blocks, each smaller than the one below it.

d Half a cubit is identical with the one span of v. 13.

e Leading up to the altar; cf. Exod. 20.23.

f I.e., the guide of 40.3 ff.   g-g Heb. "its four horns."

h-h Meaning of Heb. uncertain. Emendation yields "burning place"; cf. Lev. 6.2; Isa. 33.14; Ps. 102.4 (for the word), and Lev. 4.12; 6.4 (for the place).

i Heb. "they."   j-j Lit. "they shall fill its hands"; cf. note at Exod. 28.41.

44 Then he led me back to the outer gate of the Sanctuary that faced eastward; it was shut. [2] And the LORD said to me: This gate is to be kept shut and is not to be opened! No one shall enter by it because the LORD, the God of Israel, has entered by it; therefore it shall remain shut. [3] Only the prince may sit in it and eat bread before the LORD, since he is a prince; he shall enter by way of *ᵃ the vestibule of the gate,*ᵃ and shall depart by the same way.

[4] Then he led me, by way of the north gate, to the front of the Temple. I looked, and lo! the Presence of the LORD filled the Temple of the LORD; and I fell upon my face. [5] Then the LORD said to me: O mortal, mark well, look closely and listen carefully to everything that I tell you regarding all the laws of the Temple of the LORD and all the instructions regarding it. Note well who may enter the Temple and all who must be excluded from the Sanctuary. [6] And say to the rebellious House of Israel: Thus said the Lord GOD: Too long, O House of Israel, have you committed all your abominations, [7] admitting aliens, uncircumcised of spirit and uncircumcised of flesh, to be in My Sanctuary and profane My very Temple, when you offer up My food—the fat and the blood. Youᵇ have broken My covenant with all your abominations. [8] You have not discharged the duties concerning My sacred offerings, but have appointed them to discharge the duties of My Sanctuary for you.

[9] Thus said the Lord GOD: Let no alien, uncircumcised in spirit and flesh, enter My Sanctuary—no alien whatsoever among the people of Israel. [10] But the Levites who forsook Me when Israel went astray—straying from Me to follow their fetishes—shall suffer their punishment: [11] They shall be servitors in My Sanctuary, appointed over the Temple gates, and performing the chores of My Temple; they shall slaughter the burnt offerings and the sacrifices for the people. They shall attend on them and serve them. [12] Because they served the House of Israel in the presence of their fetishes and made them stumble into guilt, therefore—declares the Lord GOD—I have sworn concerning them that they shall suffer their punishment: [13] They shall not approach Me to serve Me as priests, to come near any of My sacred offerings, the most holy things. They shall bear their shame for the abominations that they committed. [14] I will make them watchmen of the Temple, to perform all its chores, everything that needs to be done in it.

44.1–46.24: Regulations concerning the Temple. **44.1–3:** The eastern gate remains closed because God enters the Temple through the eastern gate. The *prince* eats here. Following 37.25 he is no longer called "king." **4–14:** Those who have engaged in idolatry or abominations are to be excluded from the Temple. **9:** Foreigners shall not enter (Lev. 22.25; contrast Isa. 56.3–8). **10–14:** Deut. 18.6–8 allows Levites to serve at the altar, but they are disenfranchised here for idolatrous behavior and allowed to perform only secondary service. The passage may presuppose the judgment leveled against the house of Eli (1 Sam. ch 2) for inappropriate Levitical service at the high places mentioned throughout Kings.

a-a *This does not contradict v. 2 because the vestibule is at the inner end of the gate; cf. 40.9.*
b *Heb. "They."*

15 *a*·But the levitical priests descended from Zadok,·*a* who maintained the service of My Sanctuary when the people of Israel went astray from Me—they shall approach Me to minister to Me; they shall stand before Me to offer Me fat and blood—declares the Lord GOD. 16 They alone may enter My Sanctuary and they alone shall approach My table to minister to Me; and they shall keep My charge. 17 And when they enter the gates of the inner court, they shall wear linen vestments: they shall have nothing woolen upon them when they minister inside the gates of the inner court. 18 They shall have linen turbans on their heads and linen breeches on their loins; they shall not gird themselves with anything that causes sweat. 19 When they go out to the outer court—the outer court where the people are—they shall remove the vestments in which they minister and shall deposit them in the sacred chambers;*b* they shall put on other garments, lest they make the people consecrated*c* by [contact with] their vestments. 20 They shall neither shave their heads nor let their hair go untrimmed; they shall keep their hair trimmed. 21 No priest shall drink wine when he enters into the inner court. 22 They shall not marry widows*d* or divorced women; they may marry only virgins of the stock of the House of Israel, or widows who are widows of priests.

23 They shall declare to My people what is sacred and what is profane, and inform them what is clean and what is unclean. 24 In lawsuits, too, it is they who shall act as judges; they shall decide them in accordance with My rules. They shall preserve My teachings and My laws regarding all My fixed occasions; and they shall maintain the sanctity of My sabbaths.

25 [A priest] shall not defile himself by entering [a house] where there is a dead person. He shall defile himself only for father or mother, son or daughter, brother or unmarried sister. 26 After he has become clean, seven days shall be counted off for him; 27 and on the day that he reenters the inner court of the Sanctuary to minister in the Sanctuary, he shall present his sin offering—declares the Lord GOD.

28 This shall be their portion, for I am their portion; and no holding shall be given them in Israel, for I am their holding. 29 The meal offerings, sin offerings, and guilt offerings shall be consumed by them. Everything proscribed*e* in Israel shall be theirs. 30 All the choice first fruits

15–31: This passage serves as the haftarah for the parashah of 'Emor (Lev. 21.1–24.23), which relates regulations concerning the sanctity and roles of the priests. **15–16:** The Levites of the Zadokite line (1 Kings 2.26–27) shall enter the sanctuary and serve at the altar. **17–31:** They shall wear only linen (Exod. 28.39); they shall not wear holy garments outside of the inner court (Ezek. 42.14); they shall trim their hair, but not shave it (Lev. 21.5); they shall not drink wine in the inner court (Lev. 10.9); they shall marry only virgins or the widows of other priests (Lev. 21.7, 13–14); they shall instruct the people concerning holiness and purity (Lev. 10.10–11; Deut. 33.8–10; Hag. 2.10–13); they shall act as judges (Exod. 22.9; Deut. 17.8–9; 19.17; 21.1–5); they shall observe the festivals (Lev. ch 23; Num. chs 28–29; Deut. ch 16); they shall avoid contact with the dead and mourning, except for parents and siblings (Lev. 21.1–3; Num. ch 19); they shall receive no inheritance other than a share of the first fruits and offerings at the Temple (Num. ch 18; Lev. 27.28–29); and they shall not eat meat that was not properly slaughtered (Lev. 22.8).

---

a-a *By contrast with the Levite-priests whose demotion has just been announced.*
b *Cf. 42.13–14.*   c *Thereby rendering the people unfit for ordinary activity.*
d *I.e., of laymen.*   e *See Lev. 27.28.*

of every kind, and all the gifts of every kind—of all your contributions—shall go to the priests. You shall further give the first of the yield of your baking[a] to the priest, that a blessing may rest upon your home.

31 Priests shall not eat anything, whether bird or animal, that died or was torn by beasts.

45 When you allot the land as an inheritance, you shall set aside from the land, as a gift sacred to the LORD, an area[b] 25,000 [cubits] long and 10,000[c] wide: this shall be holy through its entire extent. 2 Of this, a square measuring a full 500 by 500 shall be reserved for the Sanctuary,[d] and 50 cubits for an open space all around it. 3 Of the aforesaid area, you shall measure off, as most holy and destined to include the Sanctuary, [a space] 25,000 long by 10,000 wide; 4 it is a sacred portion of the land; it shall provide space for houses for the priests, the ministrants of the Sanctuary who are qualified to minister to the LORD, as well as holy ground for the Sanctuary. 5 Another [space], 25,000 long by 10,000 wide, shall be the property of the Levites, the servants of the Temple—[e]twenty chambers.[e] 6 Alongside the sacred reserve, you shall set aside [a space] 25,000 long by 5,000 wide, as the property of the city; it shall belong to the whole House of Israel. 7 And to the prince shall belong, on both sides of the sacred reserve and the property of the city and alongside the sacred reserve and the property of the city, on the west extending westward and on the east extending eastward, a portion[b] corresponding to one of the [tribal] portions that extend from the western border to the eastern border 8 of the land.[f] That shall be his property in Israel; and My princes shall no more defraud My people, but shall leave the rest of the land to the several tribes of the House of Israel.

9 Thus said the Lord GOD: Enough, princes of Israel! Make an end of lawlessness and rapine, and do what is right and just! Put a stop to your evictions of My people— declares the Lord GOD. 10 Have honest balances, an honest ephah, and an honest bath.[g] 11 The ephah and the bath shall comprise the same volume, the bath a tenth of a homer and the ephah a tenth of a homer; their capacity shall be gauged by the homer. 12 And the shekel shall weigh 20 gerahs. [h]20 shekels, 25 shekels [and] 10 plus 5 shekels shall count with you as a mina.[h]

45.1–9: The size and distribution of the gift sacred to the LORD in the land for the use of the priests, the Levites, Israel, and the prince. 1: According to the Heb text, 10,000 [cubits] wide, the combined land area is 250,000,000 square cubits, slightly more than 13,000 acres. The priestly portion includes the area for the sanctuary. 5–6: The Levites' portion equals that of the priests, but the portion for the rest of Israel is half of that. 7–9: The portion of the prince is not included in the sacred reserve or city; he may not evict Israel. 10–12: Holiness in the Temple requires just, standardized measures (Lev. 19.35–36; Deut. 25.13–16; cf. Amos 8.5; Mic. 6.10–11; Prov. 11.1; 20.10). The homer equals 229.7 liters (6.524 bushels); the ephah is a dry measure that equals 22.9 liters (20.878 quarts); the bath is a liquid measure that equals 23 liters (6.073 gallons); the shekel is a measure of weight equivalent to 11.42 gm (176.29 grains); 50 shekels constitute a mina equivalent to 571.2 gm (20.148 ounces); if this passage refers to the Mesopotamian mina (see translators' note h-h), it is then equivalent to 685.44 gm (24.178 ounces).

---

a See Num. 15.20–21.   b Lit. "length."   c Septuagint reads 20,000; cf. vv. 3–5.

d Cf. 42.15 ff.   e-e Septuagint reads "for towns to dwell in."

f Cf. for all the foregoing 48.1 ff.

g The ephah is used for dry measure and the bath for liquid measure.

h-h The Mesopotamian mina of 60 shekels; but meaning of Heb. uncertain.

¹³ This is the contribution you shall make: One-sixth of an *ephah* from every *ḥomer* of wheat and one-sixth of an *ephah* from every *ḥomer* of barley, ¹⁴ while the due from the oil—ᵃ the oil being measured by the *bath*-ᵃ—shall be one-tenth of a *bath* from every *kor*.—As 10 *baths* make a *ḥomer*, so 10 *baths* make a *ḥomer*.ᵇ—¹⁵ And [the due] from the flock shall be one animal from every 200. [All these shall be contributed] from Israel's productsᶜ for meal offerings, burnt offerings, and offerings of well-being, to make expiation for them—declares the Lord GOD. ¹⁶ In this contribution, the entire population must join with the prince in Israel.

¹⁷ But the burnt offerings, the meal offerings, and the libations on festivals, new moons, sabbaths—all fixed occasions—of the House of Israel shall be the obligation of the prince; he shall provide the sin offerings, the meal offerings, the burnt offerings, and the offerings of well-being, to make expiation for the House of Israel.

¹⁸ Thus said the Lord GOD: On the first day of the first month, you shall take a bull of the herd without blemish, and you shall cleanse the Sanctuary. ¹⁹ The priest shall take some of the blood of the sin offering and apply it to the doorposts of the Temple, to the four corners of the ledgeᵃ of the altar, and to the doorposts of the gate of the inner court. ²⁰ You shall do the same ᵈ on the seventh day of the month-ᵈ to purge the Temple from uncleanness caused by unwitting or ignorant persons.

²¹ On the fourteenth day of the first month you shall have the passover sacrifice; and during a festival of seven days unleavened bread shall be eaten. ²² On that day, the prince shall provide a bull of sin offering on behalf of himself and of the entire population; ²³ and during the seven days of the festival, he shall provide daily—for seven days—seven bulls and seven rams, without blemish, for a burnt offering to the LORD, and one goat daily for a sin offering. ²⁴ He shall provide a meal offering of an *ephah*ᵉ for each bull and an *ephah* for each ram, with a *hin* of oil to every *ephah*. ²⁵ So, too, during the festival of the seventh month, for seven days from the fifteenth day on, he shall provide the same sin offerings, burnt offerings, meal offerings, and oil.

46 Thus said the Lord GOD: The gate of the inner court which faces east shall be closed on the six working days; it shall be opened on the sabbath day and it shall be opened on the day of the new moon. ² The prince shall

13–17: The people pay percentages of wheat (1.5 percent), barley (1.5 percent), oil (1 percent), sheep (.5 percent) as a tax for the *meal offerings* (Lev. ch 2), the *burnt offerings* (Lev. ch 1), and the *offerings of well-being* (Lev. ch 3). **16:** The people pay their tax to the prince. The prince in turn is obligated to provide the "sin offerings" (Lev. 4.1–5.13), the "meal offerings" (Lev. ch 2), the "burnt offerings" (Lev. ch 1), and the "offerings of well-being" (Lev. ch 3) on behalf of the people at all "festivals, new moons, sabbaths," and "fixed occasions" (appointed festivals). Ezek. 45.16–46.18 (Sephardi lectionary 45.18–46.15) serves as the haftarah for Shabbat Ha-Ḥodesh (the Shabbat prior to 1 Nisan or 1 Nisan if it is Shabbat). **18–25:** Observance of Passover and Sukkot (Tabernacles). R. Joshua (and Radak) maintain that Israel's redemption from exile will begin in Nisan (*b. Rosh Hash.*11a). **18–20:** The prescribed ritual is similar to that performed on the 10th of Tishri, Yom Kippur (Lev. ch 16). This would suggest that the Temple was purified twice annually, a custom not attested elsewhere. **19:** The blood of a *sin offering* purifies the Temple, altar, and inner court on the first day of the first month. The animal blood atones for an individual who has sinned inadvertently. Note the smearing of blood on the doorposts at the exodus (Exod. 12.21–28). **21–25:** Many regard this as a festival calendar, but it merely specifies the obligation of the prince to provide offerings for Passover (Exod. 23.15; Lev. 23.4–8; Deut. 16.1–8) and Sukkot (Exod. 23.16; Lev. 23.33–36; Deut. 16.13–15). **22:** There is no precedent for the offering of a *bull* on 14 Nisan. **23:** The offering of *seven bulls and seven rams* daily conflicts with Num. 28.19 (cf. *b. Menaḥ.* 45a). **46.1–18:** Regulations concerning offerings and property for the prince and the people. **1–8:** The eastern gate is opened on Sabbaths and new moons so that the prince may enter to present his offerings.

---

a-a Meaning of Heb. uncertain.
b The Vulgate reads "kor"; ḥomer and kor are synonyms. c Meaning of Heb. uncertain.
d-d Septuagint reads "in the seventh month." e Of choice flour.

enter by way of the vestibule outside the gate, and shall attend at the gatepost while the priests sacrifice his burnt offering and his offering of well-being; he shall then bow low at the threshold of the gate and depart. The gate, however, shall not be closed until evening. [3] The common people[a] shall worship before the LORD on sabbaths and new moons at the entrance of the same gate.

[4] The burnt offering which the prince presents to the LORD on the sabbath day shall consist of six lambs without blemish and one ram without blemish—[5] with a meal offering of an *ephah* for the ram, a meal offering of as much as he wishes for the lambs, and a *hin* of oil with every *ephah*. [6] And on the day of the new moon, it shall consist of a bull of the herd without blemish, and six lambs and a ram—they shall be without blemish. [7] And he shall provide a meal offering of an *ephah* for the bull, an *ephah* for the ram, and as much as he can afford for the lambs, with a *hin* of oil to every *ephah*.

[8] When the prince enters, he shall come in by way of the vestibule of the gate, and he shall go out the same way.

[9] But on the fixed occasions, when the common people come before the LORD, whoever enters by the north gate to bow low shall leave by the south gate; and whoever enters by the south gate shall leave by the north gate. They shall not go back through the gate by which they came in, but shall go out [b]by the opposite one.[b] [10] And as for the prince, he shall enter with them when they enter and leave when they leave.

[11] On festivals and fixed occasions, the meal offering shall be an *ephah* for each bull, an *ephah* for each ram, and as much as he wishes for the lambs, with a *hin* of oil for every *ephah*.

[12] The gate that faces east shall also be opened for the prince whenever he offers a freewill offering—be it burnt offering or offering of well-being—freely offered to the LORD, so that he may offer his burnt offering or his offering of well-being just as he does on the sabbath day. Then he shall leave, and the gate shall be closed after he leaves.

[13] Each day you shall offer a lamb of the first year without blemish, as a daily burnt offering to the LORD; you shall offer one every morning. [14] And every morning regularly you shall offer a meal offering with it: a sixth of an *ephah*, with a third of a *hin* of oil to moisten the choice flour, as a meal offering to the LORD—a law for all time.

2: The prince *shall attend at the gatepost* (see 2 Kings 11.14) and bow down at the *threshold of the gate*. **3:** The people bow down at the same gate entrance. **4:** The sacrifice of *six lambs* and *one ram* conflicts with Num. 28.9. See Num. 28.9–15 for Sabbath and new moon sacrifices. **9–10:** The people enter by the north and south gates, but exit by the opposite gates for efficient crowd management. **11–15:** The freewill and daily offerings of the prince are specified (Lev. 22.18–23, vow or freewill offering; Num. 28.3–8, daily offering).

___

a *I.e., those other than the priests, the Levites, and the prince; lit. "the people of the land."*
b-b *Lit. "straight before him."*

15 The lamb, the meal offering, and oil shall be presented every morning as a regular burnt offering.

16 Thus said the Lord GOD: If the prince makes a gift to any of his sons, it shall become the latter's inheritance; it shall pass on to his sons; it is their holding by inheritance. 17 But if he makes a gift from his inheritance to any of his subjects, it shall only belong to the latter until the year of release.[a] Then it shall revert to the prince; his inheritance must by all means pass on to his sons.

18 But the prince shall not take property away from any of the people and rob them of their holdings. Only out of his own holdings shall he endow his sons, in order that My people may not be dispossessed of their holdings.

19 Then he led me into the passage at the side of the gate to the sacred chambers of the priests, which face north, and there, at the rear of it, in the west, I saw a space. 20 He said to me, "This is the place where the priests shall boil the guilt offerings and the sin offerings, and where they shall bake the meal offerings, so as not to take them into the outer court and [b]make the people consecrated."[-b] 21 Then he led me into the outer court and led me past the four corners of the court; and in each corner of the court there was an enclosure. 22 These unroofed[c] enclosures, [each] 40 [cubits] long and 30 wide, were in the four corners of the court; the four corner enclosures had the same measurements. 23 [On the inside,] running round the four of them, there was a row of masonry, equipped with hearths under the rows all around. 24 He said to me, "These are the kitchens where the Temple servitors shall boil the sacrifices of the people."

47 He led me back to the entrance of the Temple, and I found that water was issuing from below the platform[d] of the Temple—eastward, since the Temple faced east—but the water was running out at the [e-]south of the altar,[-e] under the south wall of the Temple. 2 Then he led me out by way of the northern gate and led me around to the outside of the outer gate that faces in the direction of the east;[f] and I found that water was gushing from [under] the south wall. 3 As the man went on eastward

16–18: The prince may pass property on to his sons, but property passed to servants reverts to the prince at the jubilee year (Lev. 25.8–17). The prince may not pass property of the people to his own sons. **19–24:** Areas for the preparation of sacrifices for consumption by the priests are located in the northwestern area of the inner court. Kitchens for the people are located at the four corners of the outer court. **47.1–12:** Once the Temple is reestablished, water streams up from *below the platform of the Temple—eastward* to water the land of Israel. This indicates the role of the Temple as the center of creation (the garden of Eden, Gen. 2.10–14; Ps. 46.4). The course of the water reflects that of the Gihon spring (cf. the Edenic river, Gen. 2.10, 13), and emerges east of the City of David where its waters flow south into the Siloam pool (see 1 Kings 1.32–40; Isa. 7.3; 2 Chron. 32.4). The water flows into the Jordan Valley and eventually into the *Arabah* (the Jordan rift where the Dead Sea is located) to transform the waters of the Dead Sea into fresh water that supports fish and fruit trees (see Gen. 2.1–14).

a Cf. Lev. 25.10.   b-b See note c at 44.19.

c So Mishnah Middoth 2.5; emendation yields "small."

d See note at 9.3.

e-e Connection unclear. Emendation yields "southeast."

f The end of the verse explains why he could not have made the detour by way of the south gate. For the reasons why he could not have proceeded to his present position directly by way of the east gate, see 43.1–2; 44.1–2.

with a measuring line in his hand, he measured off a thousand cubits and led me across the water; the water was ankle deep. ⁴Then he measured off another thousand and led me across the water; the water was knee deep. He measured off a further thousand and led me across the water; the water was up to the waist. ⁵When he measured yet another thousand, it was a stream I could not cross; for the water had swollen into a stream that could not be crossed except by swimming. ⁶"Do you see, O mortal?" he said to me; and he led me back to the bank of the stream.

⁷As I came back, I saw trees in great profusion on both banks of the stream. ⁸"This water," he told me, "runs out to the eastern region, and flows into the Arabah; and when it comes into the sea, into ᵃthe sea of foul waters,ᵃ the water will become wholesome. ⁹Every living creature that swarms will be able to live wherever this stream goes; the fish will be very abundant once these waters have reached there. It will be wholesome, and everything will

a-a I.e., the Dead Sea.

Tribal territories in the restored Israel

live wherever this stream goes. [10] Fishermen shall stand beside it all the way from En-gedi to En-eglaim; it shall be a place for drying nets; and the fish will be of various kinds [and] most plentiful, like the fish of the Great Sea. [11] But its swamps and marshes shall not become wholesome; they will serve to [supply] salt. [12] All kinds of trees for food will grow up on both banks of the stream. Their leaves will not wither nor their fruit fail; they will yield new fruit every month, because the water for them flows from the Temple. Their fruit will serve for food and their leaves for healing."

[13] Thus said the Lord GOD: These shall be the boundaries of the land that you shall allot to the twelve tribes of Israel. Joseph shall receive two portions, [14] and you shall share the rest equally. As I swore to give it to your fathers, so shall this land fall to you as your heritage. [15] These are the boundaries of the land:

As the northern limit: From the Great Sea by way of Hethlon, Lebo-ªhamath,ª Zedad, [16] Berathah, Sibraim—which lies between the border of Damascus and the border of Hamath—[down to] Hazer-hatticon, which is on the border of Hauran. [17] Thus the boundary shall run from the Sea to ᵇHazar-enon,ᵇ to the north of the territory of Damascus, with the territory of Hamath to the north of it. That shall be the northern limit.

[18] As the eastern limit: A line between Hauran and Damascus, and between Gilead and the land of Israel: with the Jordan as a boundary, you shall measure down to the ᶜEastern Sea.ᶜ That shall be the eastern limit.

[19] The southern limit shall run: A line from Tamar to the waters of Meriboth-kadesh, along the Wadi [of Egypt and] the Great Sea. That is the southern limit.

[20] And as the western limit: The Great Sea shall be the boundary up to a point opposite Lebo-hamath. That shall be the western limit.

[21] This land you shall divide for yourselves among the tribes of Israel. [22] You shall allot it as a heritage for yourselves and for the strangers who reside among you, who have begotten children among you. You shall treat them as Israelite citizens; they shall receive allotments along with you among the tribes of Israel. [23] You shall give the stranger an allotment within the tribe where he resides—declares the Lord GOD.

47.13–48.35: The reestablishment of the land and people of Israel. The reconstruction of the Temple and the resulting renewal of creation provide the basis for the reestablishment of the land and people of Israel. **47.13–23:** The boundaries of the land are an idealized portrayal of the greatest extent of the Davidic kingdom and that of Jeroboam II (2 Sam. 8.5–12; 2 Kings 14.25; cf. Num. 34). **15–17:** The northern border runs from the Mediterranean east to *Hazar-enon,* between Hamath (modern Hama) to the north and Damascus to the south (Num. 34.7–9). **19:** The eastern border runs south through the Jordan Valley to *Tamar* just south of the Dead Sea (Num. 34.10–12). The southern border runs through the Negev to the *Wadi [of Egypt]* (modern Wadi el-Arish in the northeastern Sinai peninsula; see Num. 34.3–5) **20:** The western border runs along the Mediterranean coast (Num. 34.6). **22:** *The strangers who reside among you* (Heb "gerim," "sojourners") are those who joined the Jewish community during the exile. They live according to the same laws as Israelites (Lev. 19.34; Num. 15.29).

a-a *Brought up from v. 16 for clarity.*
b-b *Apparently identical with Hazer-hatticon in v. 16.*
c-c *I.e., the Dead Sea.*

48 These are the names of the tribes:
At the northern end, along the Hethlon road, [from] Lebo-hamath to Hazar-enan—which is the border of Damascus, with Hamath to the north—from the eastern border to the Sea: Dan—one [tribe].

² Adjoining the territory of Dan, from the eastern border to the western border: Asher—one.

³ Adjoining the territory of Asher, from the eastern border to the western border: Naphtali—one.

⁴ Adjoining the territory of Naphtali, from the eastern border to the western border: Manasseh—one.

⁵ Adjoining the territory of Manasseh, from the eastern border to the western border: Ephraim—one.

⁶ Adjoining the territory of Ephraim, from the eastern border to the western border: Reuben—one.

⁷ Adjoining the territory of Reuben, from the eastern border to the western border: Judah—one.

⁸ Adjoining the territory of Judah, from the eastern border to the western border, shall be the reserve that you set aside: 25,000 [cubits] in breadth and in length equal to one of the portions from the eastern border to the western border; the Sanctuary shall be in the middle of it. ⁹ The reserve that you set aside for the LORD shall be 25,000 long and 10,000ᵃ wide. ¹⁰ It shall be apportioned to the following: The sacred reserve for the priests shall measure 25,000 [cubits] on the north, ᵇ10,000 on the west, 10,000 on the east, and 25,000 on the south,·ᵇ with the LORD's Sanctuary in the middle of it. ¹¹ This consecrated area shall be for the priests of the line of Zadok, who kept My charge and did not go astray, as the Levites did when the people of Israel went astray. ¹² It shall be a special reserve for them out of the [total] reserve from the land, most holy, adjoining the territory of the Levites. ¹³ Alongside the territory of the priests, the Levites shall have [an area] 25,000 long by 10,000 wide; the total length shall be 25,000 and the breadth 10,000.ᶜ ¹⁴ None of it—the choicest of the land—may be sold, exchanged, or transferred; it is sacred to the LORD.

¹⁵ The remaining 5,000 in breadth by 25,000 shall be for common use—serving the city for dwellings and pasture. The city itself shall be in the middle of it; ¹⁶ and these shall be its measurements: On the north side 4,500 cubits, on the south side 4,500, on the east side 4,500, and on the

48.1–35: The tribes are assigned equal portions of land and are arrayed along the length of the land from north to south. 1–7: The northern tribes are listed from north to south as Dan, Asher, Naphtali, Manasseh, Ephraim, Reuben, Judah. 8–22: The *sacred reserve,* or Levitical allotment (45.1–9), is defined in detail. The priests are placed in the north, and the sanctuary is assigned to their portion; the Levites are placed to the south of the priests; and the portion reserved for Israel, which contains *the city* (Jerusalem), is to the south of the Levites. The portion allotted to the *prince* is on either side of the *sacred reserve.*

---

a *Emendation yields "25,000"; cf. 45.3–6.*
b-b *Lit. "10,000 in breadth on the west; 10,000 in breadth on the east; and 25,000 in length on the south."*
c *Septuagint reads "20,000"; cf. note a.*

west side 4,500. ¹⁷ The pasture shall extend 250 cubits to the north of the city, 250 to the south, 250 to the east, and 250 to the west. ¹⁸ As for the remaining 10,000 to the east and 10,000 to the west, adjoining the long side[a] of the sacred reserve, the produce of these areas adjoining the sacred reserve shall serve as food for the workers in the city; ¹⁹ the workers in the city from all the tribes of Israel shall cultivate it. ²⁰ The entire reserve, 25,000 square, you shall set aside as the sacred reserve plus the city property. ²¹ What remains on either side of the sacred reserve and the city property shall belong to the prince. The prince shall own [the land] from the border of the 25,000 [b] of the reserve [b] up to the eastern boundary, and from the border of the 25,000 on the west up to the western boundary, corresponding to the [tribal] portions. The sacred reserve, with the Temple Sanctuary in the middle of it ²² and the property of the Levites and the city property as well, shall be in the middle of the [area belonging] to the prince; [the rest of the land] between the territory of Judah and the territory of Benjamin shall belong to the prince.

²³ As for the remaining tribes:[c] From the eastern border to the western border: Benjamin—one.

²⁴ Adjoining the territory of Benjamin, from the eastern border to the western border: Simeon—one.

²⁵ Adjoining the territory of Simeon, from the eastern border to the western border: Issachar—one.

²⁶ Adjoining the territory of Issachar, from the eastern border to the western border: Zebulun—one.

²⁷ Adjoining the territory of Zebulun, from the eastern border to the western border: Gad—one.

²⁸ The other border of Gad shall be the southern boundary. This boundary shall run from Tamar to the waters of Meribath-kadesh, to the Wadi [of Egypt], and to the Great Sea.

²⁹ That is the land which you shall allot as a heritage to the tribes of Israel, and those are their portions—declares the Lord God.

³⁰ And these are the exits from the city: On its northern side, measuring 4,500 cubits, ³¹ the gates of the city shall be—three gates on the north—named for the tribes of Israel: the Reuben Gate: one; the Judah Gate: one; the Levi Gate: one. ³² On the eastern side, [measuring] 4,500 cubits—there shall be three gates: the Joseph Gate: one; the Benjamin Gate: one; and the Dan Gate: one. ³³ On the southern side, measuring 4,500 cubits, there shall be three

23–29: The southern tribes are listed from north to south as Benjamin, Simeon, Issachar, Zebulun, and Gad. **30–35:** There are three gates allotted to the tribes on each side of the square city. The northern gates include Reuben, Judah, and Levi; the eastern gates include Joseph, Benjamin, and Dan; the southern gates include Simeon, Issachar, and Zebulun; and the western gates include Gad, Asher, and Naphtali. The name of the city is *The Lord Is There* to signify the return of God's Presence (see Isa. 60.14; Jer. 23.6), reversing the divine abandonment that was the theme of the prophecies of retribution in the bulk of the book.

a *I.e., the south side.*   b-b *Emendation yields "on the east."*
c *The tribes not provided for in vv. 1–7, and lying south of the sacred gift.*

gates: the Simeon Gate: one; the Issachar Gate: one; and the Zebulun Gate: one. ³⁴ And on the western side, [measuring] 4,500 cubits—there shall be three gates: the Gad Gate: one; the Asher Gate: one; the Naphtali Gate: one.

³⁵ Its circumference [shall be] 18,000 [cubits]; and the name of the city from that day on shall be "The LORD Is There."

תרי עשר

The Twelve

THE TWELVE IS A COLLECTION of twelve prophetic books. A prophetic book is a biblical book that claims association with a prophetic personage of the past (e.g., Isaiah, Micah, Haggai) and presents itself as the LORD's word or communication. Thus all of these books claim to communicate authoritative knowledge about the LORD. Some of these prophetic books are explicitly set in a particular time period in Israel's past, somewhere between what we call the 8th and the 5th centuries BCE. According to the Talmud, "the Men of the Great Assembly [who they believed lived in the Persian period] wrote the Twelve" (*b. B. Bat.* 15a). Today, many modern scholars think that all or most of the prophetic books in the Twelve—at least in their present form—were either composed or edited after the fall of the monarchy (586 BCE) and probably during the Persian period (539–332). Many scholars argue also that forerunners (or earlier editions) of some of the present books may date to monarchic times, or that the scribes who composed or edited the prophetic books as we know them had access to textual sources and traditions from periods earlier than their own.

There were substantial differences between the monarchic and the postmonarchic periods. Judah was a relatively prosperous kingdom even during the late monarchic period (the last decades before the destruction of the Temple in 586). Jerusalem was at the time an important city whose population (about 25,000 people) was about a third of that of the kingdom as a whole (about 75,000). Postmonarchic Judah was much smaller and poorer. For instance, the population of Jerusalem in the second half of the Persian period (450–332) was likely around 1,500 inhabitants; the highest estimate in historical circles today is 4,500. Likewise, the province of Yehud (Persian Judah) after "the restoration" reached a population peak of probably only 17,000. An analysis of the material culture shows similar differences between late monarchic Judah and Yehud. The once independent Davidic kingdom has become a relatively small and peripheral province in a large empire. Moreover, the fall of Jerusalem and Judah in 586 had more than just political, demographic, and economic impact. From an insider's religious perspective, when the monarchic period came to a close, Jerusalem (= the LORD's city), the Temple (= the LORD's house), and the Davidic dynasty (= the LORD's chosen dynasty) all fell. There is no doubt that the events of 586 represent a watershed in the history of Judah and ancient Israel, and were understood as such by those who lived after these events. Postmonarchic Judahites tried to understand them in terms of divine justice and tried to understand themselves within a world in which their community, from their perspective the LORD's people, was so powerless compared to other nations and compared to the memory of monarchic Judah. These issues loomed large in the postmonarchic communities within which the prophetic books were written or reached their present form, and certainly were of great concern to the people for whom they were written. Reflections on these issues are abundant in many of the prophetic books, often taking one or the other of two forms: either condemnations of monarchic Judah for sins so great that they justified the LORD's destruction of Jerusalem, or messages of hope and restoration that reassured the postmonarchic community that their present situation was not the "end of the road" but only a minor stop in a journey that led to an ideal and glorious future for Israel—and at times, for the nations too.

Prophetic books were written texts meant to be read, or more properly, to be re-read and studied. Texts written to be read many times tend to show more than passing instances of ambiguity or multiple meanings. Such multiple meanings abound in the prophetic books, as the annotations will show. Traditional Jewish interpreters maintained that the prophetic books were given to Israel to call for its repentance and to provide guidance, that is, to affect, not merely to inform, their readers. We know that already in the late biblical period prophetic works were read, re-read, and studied in order to find such guidance.

There are fifteen prophetic books in the Bible: the collection called "the Twelve," plus Isaiah, Jeremiah, and Ezekiel. (Unlike Christian Bibles, the Jewish Bible does not include Daniel as one of the prophets, but rather treats it as one of the Kethuvim, or Writings.) Each of the fifteen prophetic books is associated with a single prophetic personage. In the Twelve, each book displays distinctive language and themes that set it apart from the other books. Thus the human speaker in each book has his own voice. There are no prophetic books associated with women prophets, although there were female prophets in ancient Israel (see, e.g., 2 Kings 2.14, Neh. 6.14). Even the divine speaker, God, is distinctive in each book, with a voice that is similar to (and at times blends with) that of the particular human speaker.

The lengths of the books in this collection range from one chapter to fourteen. Even the longest, however, is short compared to the lengths of the three major prophets, Isaiah, Jeremiah, and Ezekiel. Therefore, while each of the major prophets was most likely written on one scroll, the smaller books in the book of the Twelve were at some point collected and copied together on one scroll so no single prophetic work would be lost, since the total length of the Twelve approximates the length of one of the major prophetic books. Nevertheless, they have been read as separate books rather than as chapters of a single book. Rabbinic tradition also tends to treat each prophet separately rather than approaching the twelve as a group.

We do not know when the twelve prophetic books were first collected onto one scroll. The practice is probably implied in Sirach 49.10 (early second century BCE): "May the bones of the Twelve Prophets / send forth new life from where they lie, / for they comforted the people of Jacob / and delivered them with confident hope."

The oldest extant manuscript of the Twelve is among the Dead Sea Scrolls (4QXII[a]) and dates from the middle of the 2nd century BCE, therefore indicating that by that time these books were seen as a collection. Significantly, in this manuscript the book of Jonah follows that of Malachi. In fact, the individual and separate character of each book in the collection allowed the order in which the twelve books appear in the scroll to remain fluid for a relatively long period (as was also the case with the later collection called the Kethuvim/Writings; see pp. 1275–79). Eventually the Septuagint (LXX), the ancient Greek translation of the Hebrew Bible, and the Hebrew text tradition itself finalized the order of these books, though in slightly different ways. To be sure, once a collection of books is set in a particular order, the latter cannot but convey a certain meaning. For the book of the Twelve, it is clear that to some extent a chronological principle governs the present order in the Masoretic Text (and in the LXX). For instance, Hosea is the first because he was probably considered the first of four prophets who prophesied at one particular, early period, the others being Isaiah, Amos, and Micah (see *b. B. Bat.* 14a). The books of Haggai, Zechariah, and Malachi, who "came at the end of the prophets," close the collection. It is also clear that chronological concerns were not the only consideration. It seems that an emphatic focus on Jerusalem and Judah was either a main concern for those who ordered the books in the Masoretic tradition or was a background belief that became reflected in the way in which the order of the books was finalized in this tradition.

A significant clue for an understanding of these and the other three prophetic books within their historical setting stands at the conclusion of Hosea. The final verse, 14.10, may be translated as follows: "Those who are wise understand these things [i.e., the prophetic readings included in the book]; those who are discerning know them. For the ways of the LORD are right, and the upright walk in them, but transgressors stumble in them."

Beyond the evaluative, theological language used here, the passage reflects social reality. Since the prophetic books were written texts, only those able to read could approach them directly and thus the literate minority served as brokers of divine knowledge to the vast majority who could not read. These scholars studied the texts, and read and interpreted them to others. Since the texts were considered to communicate (authoritative) knowledge about the LORD, early interpretations of what they meant had to be consistent with what was known about the LORD from other sources. This put certain limitations on the kinds of interpretations that were acceptable. It is likely that the earliest extant summary of the book's message in Sirach 49.10 reflects a predominant way in which they were read in antiquity. The very basic message that they conveyed to their ancient readership is well summarized in that passage: "They [these Twelve Prophets] comforted the people of Jacob and delivered them with confident hope." This is quite remarkable, since divine punishment rather than consolation predominates in these books. (See also the specific introductions to the individual prophetic books.)

The last book of the Twelve and, accordingly the entire section of *Nevi'im*/Prophets in

the Tanakh concludes—whether by design or, more likely, fortuitously—with a passage
that includes a verse that may be translated as follows: "Remember the Torah of Moses,
my servant, which I commanded him at Horeb for all of Israel—its decrees and statutes"
(Mal. 3.22). Such a conclusion communicates a clear sense that this section is subordinate
in importance to the Torah of Moses. Maimonides in the *Mishneh Torah* quoted this verse
as a proof that prophets are not supposed to bring a new Torah, but to warn people not to
trespass the Torah. This position, of course, is central to traditional Judaism. Critical biblical scholarship, however, has seen the Torah and the prophets as separate corpora originating in the same time period, with differing sets of norms and beliefs.

This very end of the prophetic collection reads: "Lo, I will send the prophet Elijah to
you before the coming of the awesome, fearful day of the LORD" (Mal. 3.23–24). In other
words, it keeps a tension and balance between the activities of the scholars and of all Israel
in their present circumstances and their hopes for a most positive change in the future,
a change that was later understood in messianic terms (see the *Mishneh Torah* of Maimonides). Significantly, the entire Christian Old Testament concludes with Malachi
3.23–24 and calls as it were for the realization of that messianic time. The Tanakh,
however, moves from these verses directly to the Writings, to either Psalm 1, whose spirit
may be understood as consonant with Hosea 14.10 and Malachi 3.22 or in the Leningrad
Codex, for instance, to Chronicles, which recounts and reinterprets the history of Israel in
a way that is deeply informed by the Torah.   [EHUD BEN ZVI]

הושע

Hosea

AS ITS TITLE SAYS (1.1), the book of Hosea presents itself as the record of the LORD's word to a prophet from the past, Hosea. The book's main themes are Israel's abandoning of the LORD, the LORD's punishment of Israel for that abandonment, calls for Israel's repentance, and hope for an ideal future of reconciliation between the LORD and Israel.

Israel's abandoning of the LORD is expressed in terms of cultic, religious, social, sexual, and political offenses. Horrifying imagery, along with references to Israel's destruction in the land and its exile from it, as well as of the fall of the northern monarchy, express the theme of the LORD's punishment of Israel. To be sure, no prophetic book concerns itself only with condemnation and punishment. All of them convey hope for the future. Hosea does so in highly poetic language. Yet hope for the future, for a restoration of the ideal relation between the LORD and Israel, demands that Israel turn from its ways and return to the LORD, so the call for repentance is an important theme in the book.

It is precisely the element of hope—hope against a background of apparent hopelessness—that has led to the book's wide use in Jewish liturgy. Thus Hosea 14.2–10 is read in the afternoon service of Tishʿah beʾav (Sephardic and Yemenite traditions; others read Isa. 55.6–56.8) and on Shabbat Shuvah, the Sabbath between Rosh Ha-Shanah (the New Year) and Yom Kippur (the Day of Atonement). Hosea 2.1–22 is read as the haftarah for the parashah of Be-midbar (Num. 1.1–4.20). Hosea 2.21–22 are recited as part of the ritual for donning tefillin (phylacteries).

Like other prophetic books, Hosea often employs sexual and family metaphors to express the relationship between God and Israel. Within the metaphorical world of the book of Hosea, God takes the role of an angry husband who condemns, severely punishes, and publicly dishonors his unfaithful wife, who fails to recognize how good he had been to her. After his violent and shaming punishment is carried out, he will be willing to accept her back. The basic imagery present here is quite common in the society within which the prophetic books were written (see also Ezek. chs 16, 23), and in the ancient Near East as a whole. To be sure, the text was not written to glorify or justify family violence or violence against women in general, but rather to explain the reasons for the disasters that befell Israel, to persuade the readers to live their lives in a way consistent with the will of the LORD, and to give them hope for the future. Nevertheless, this imagery carries connotations that are very troublesome for many contemporary readers, and especially painful for those who cannot but associate their reading of the text with their, or their acquaintances', personal experiences (see chs 1–3, and particularly 2.3–15). The book is set in the last period of political strength of the Northern Kingdom of Israel—from our perspective, middle 8th century BCE—and the time of its destruction by Assyria in 722 (see 1.1 n.). While the threat of Assyrian invasion hovers in the background, the book focuses on the behavior of Israel, which it evaluates and condemns in very sharp terms. It is a period of apostasy, of social disintegration, of wrongful leadership, of failed alliances, in sum a period in which knowledge of (and reverence for) the LORD are lacking.

The setting of the book of Hosea is one of the earliest among the book of the Twelve, and this may be one of the reasons for its place at the beginning of the collection (for a traditional Jewish text on the matter, see *b. B. Bat.* 14b).

The book contains an introduction (1.1), and a very significant conclusion that provides a key for its interpretation (14.10; see intro. to The Twelve). The rest of the book consists of two main sections: 1.2–3.5, in which narrative and imageries of whoredom are prominent, and 4.1–14.9, which consists of a set of readings that report prophetic announcements associated with Hosea. An alternative subdivision of 1.2–14.9 is: (a) chs 1–3; (b) chs 4–11; and (c) chs 12–14.　　　　　　　　　　　　　　　　　　　　[EHUD BEN ZVI]

1 The word of the LORD that came to Hosea son of Beeri, in the reigns of Kings Uzziah, Jotham, Ahaz, and Hezekiah of Judah, and in the reign of King Jeroboam son of Joash of Israel.

2 When the LORD first spoke to Hosea, the LORD said to Hosea, "Go, get yourself ᵃa wife of whoredom and children of whoredom; for the land will stray ᵇ from following the LORD." ᵃ 3 So he went and married Gomer daughter of

a-a Force of Heb. uncertain.　　*b Lit. "whore away."*

1.1: Superscription. The verse characterizes the book as a particular instance of the LORD's word (that is, as a prophetic book), set in a particular time and associated with a prophetic character from the past, Hosea. Although the setting for the book is the Northern Kingdom of Israel, its intended readers are the Judeans who may constructively reflect upon the demise of the Northern Kingdom in 722 BCE. References to the kings of Judah precede, and are more elaborate than, the reference to the Is-

raelite king. Further, since *Jeroboam* (II) died during the reign of *Uzziah* (2 Kings 15.8), the temporal references do not match. From the Israelite perspective, the book is anchored in the last period of strength of the Northern Kingdom; from the Judahite perspective it is anchored in a period in which Israel moves from a political position of strength to the beginning of its demise in the days of *Hezekiah*. This double perspective is no mistake, but a rhetorical clue for the reading of the book.

1.2–3.5: Between "proper marriage" and "whoredom." A set of readings that develops a sharp contrast between Israel's reported abandonment of the LORD and the future reconciliation between the two. Punishment, however, is presented as a kind of bridge that leads from one situation to another. These passages are built around images of "whoredom" and "(proper) marriage." **2–8:** Was Hosea's marriage meant to be taken literally or as a figurative symbol of a prophetic message? Among traditional Jewish commentators, some opted for a literal reading (e.g., *b. Pes.* 87a; Rashi, Abravanel) while others maintained that the text is an account of a prophetic vision (Ibn Ezra, Radak, Maimonides). The Targum's understanding that these verses are figurative becomes clear in its rendition of 2.2–4: "The beginning of the word of the LORD with Hosea: The LORD said to Hosea: Go (and) speak a prophecy against the inhabitants of the idolatrous city, who continue to sin.

Diblaim. She conceived and bore him a son, [4] and the Lord instructed him, "Name him Jezreel; for, I will soon punish the House of Jehu[a] for the [b]bloody deeds at Jezreel[-b] and put an end to the monarchy of the House of Israel. [5] In that day, I will break the bow of Israel in the Valley of Jezreel."

[6] She conceived again and bore a daughter; and He said to him, "Name her Lo-ruhamah;[c] for I will no longer accept the House of Israel [d]or pardon them.[-d] ([7] But I will accept the House of Judah. And I will give them victory through the Lord their God; I will not give them victory with bow and sword and battle, by horses and riders.)"

[8] After weaning Lo-ruhamah, she conceived and bore a son. [9] Then He said, "Name him Lo-ammi;[e] for you[f] are not My people, and [g]I will not be your [God]."[-g]

2 [h]The number of the people of Israel shall be like that of the sands of the sea, which cannot be measured or

a Emendation yields "Israel"; cf. next note.

b-b See 1 Kings 21.1–24; 2 Kings 9.21–35. Emendation yields "the Baal days"; cf. 2.15.

c I.e., "Not-accepted"; cf. 2.3, 6, and 25.

d-d Meaning of Heb. uncertain; emendation yields "but will disown them"; cf. 9.15 and elsewhere.

e I.e., "Not-My-People."   f I.e., you and your fellow countrymen.

g-g Cf. 2.25.   h Vv. 1–3 anticipate the conclusion of the chapter.

For the inhabitants of the land surely go astray from the worship of the Lord. So he went and prophesied concerning them that, if they repented, they would be forgiven; but, if not, they would fall as the leaves of a fig-tree fall. But they continued to do wicked deeds. And the Lord said to him, 'Call their name "scattered ones" [pun on *Jezreel*, see below] for in a little while I will avenge the blood. . . .' " As for the text itself, the main concern (see the final clause of v. 2) is not the reported sexual sins and marital life of Gomer (or of the unnamed woman in ch 3), but rather what they symbolize. These descriptions point to the "harlotry of the land and its inhabitants," that is, the worship of gods other than the Lord. (The image of God married to Israel predominates in this reading, but occurs elsewhere, e.g., in the books of Jeremiah and Ezekiel.) Moreover, within their larger context in chs 1–3, or even 1–14, these references point toward the possibility

of repentance and return to the proper relation between the Lord and Israel (see 2.20–25 for one expression of that proper relation; 3.5 for another). The Targum (quoted above), although clearly departing from the literal meaning, captures the book's theological message. **2:** A more literal translation is "Go take for yourself a wife of whoredom and children of whoredom, for the land whores, whores away from following the Lord." The emphasis on the motif of "whoredom" and "committing whoredom" is clearly expressed by the quadruple repetition at the center of the verse. Around the center are the references to the woman and the land, i.e., to those who commit whoredom, and at the beginning of the verse, are the "wronged husbands," namely the Lord and Hosea. The imagery also suggests that the people of Israel are metaphorically the children of the land of Israel and of her husband (the Lord). According to the text even if the father clearly acknowl-

edges that the children are his, he can justifiably reject them because of the behavior of the mother (cf. 2.6). **4:** *Jezreel* is a plain in central Israel and a city on its perimeter. The allusion is likely to the events described in 1 Kings 21.1–24; 2 Kings 9.21–35, involving the murder of Naboth at the instance of Ahab and Jezebel in order to seize his property, and the consequent assassination of their son at the same location. The name *Jezreel* means "El/God sows," and has numerous positive connotations; still, "sowing" means "scattering seed." More important, ancient Heb poets played with the similarly sounding "zr'" (sow seed) and "zrh" (scatter)—see Ps. 106.27; Mal. 2.3, and the Targum (see above). *The House of Jehu* was the last stable dynasty of Israel (ca. 842–747 BCE). After the lengthy rule of Jeroboam II (ca. 788–747), his son Zechariah reigned only six months. He was murdered, and so were almost all the kings who followed him in rapid succession (2 Kings 15.8–25). The reference in this v. to the future punishment of the House of Jehu explains why only Jeroboam is mentioned among the kings of Israel in v. 1. **6–8:** *Lo-ruhamah* may also be translated "Unpitied" and *Lo-ammi* means "not my people" (see translators' note *e*); these are symbolic names that signify the rejection of Israel, but they carry a very suggestive potential for reversal; see 2.1–3. **7:** The mention of Judah reflects the Judahite readership of the book of Hosea in its final form.

2.1–25: Denunciations and promises. Condemnations and judgments are interspersed with announcements of future restoration and hope (e.g., Mic. 2.12–13). Readers are made aware of seeds and promises of hope and contemplate their eventual blooming even as they read the most difficult texts about their past sinful deeds. These deeds are "their" deeds, because they identify—at least in part—with the Israel of the book. **1:** A reversal of the name and fate given in 1.9. The language here counted; and instead of being told, "You are Not-My-People,"[a] they shall be called Children-of-the-Living-God. [2] The people of Judah and the people of Israel shall assemble together and appoint one head over them; and they shall rise from the ground[b]—for marvelous shall be [c]the day of Jezreel![c]

3   Oh, call[d] your brothers "My People,"
     And your sisters "Lovingly Accepted!"

4   Rebuke[d] your mother, rebuke her—
     For she is not My wife
     And I am not her husband—
     And let her put away her harlotry from her face
     And her adultery from between her breasts.

5   Else will I strip her naked
     And leave her as on the day she was born:
     And I will make her like a wilderness,
     Render her like desert land,
     And let her die of thirst.

6   I will also disown her children;
     For they are now a harlot's brood,

7   In that their mother has played the harlot,
     She that conceived them has acted shamelessly—
     Because she thought,
     "I will go after my lovers,
     Who supply my bread and my water,
     My wool and my linen,
     My oil and my drink."

8   Assuredly,
     I will hedge up her[e] roads with thorns
     And raise walls against her,
     And she shall not find her paths.

9   Pursue her lovers as she will,
     She shall not overtake them;
     And seek them as she may,
     She shall never find them.
     Then she will say,
     "I will go and return
     To my first husband,
     For then I fared better than now."

---

a See 1.9.

b Meaning, perhaps, "from their wretched condition," or "to ascendancy over the land."

c-c I.e., the day when the name Jezreel will convey a promise (2.23–25) instead of a threat (1.4–5).

d The LORD addresses Hosea and his fellow North Israelites; see 1.9. The mother is the nation; her children the individual North Israelites.

e Heb. "your." Vv. 8–9 would read well after v. 15.

and that present in the promises to the patriarchs (Gen. 22.17; 32.13) echo each other. **2–3:** The motif of a future reunification of (northern) Israel and Judah appears elsewhere in prophetic literature (cf. Ezek. 37.15–28), though it was never fulfilled. *Jezreel* (see 1.4 n.), a place of bloody deeds and divine punishment, here becomes a place of future redemption. Similarly, the names of the other two children will have their meaning reversed, turning separation from the LORD into future closeness to Him. **4:** *Rebuke,* or "remonstrate." The word carries a legal connotation of arguing against someone in a court of law, while at the same time it means "reprove" in the hope of correcting the behavior of someone (cf. Radak and Targum). This "someone" is metaphorically both the community of Israel and the land. *For she is not My wife* may be the legal language used in a declaration of divorce. **5:** As in Ezek. ch 16, the punishment for the reported sexual promiscuity is sexual shaming. The image of the woman then becomes the image of the land, punished by drying up, losing its fertility. **6:** The land/woman will lose her children, the population of the land. Disown (Heb "will not pity") is another play on the name Lo-ruhamah. (Cf. 1.2, 6.) **7:** *Lovers,* male providers whom she loved; a reference to rulers of other nations and particularly to their gods. **8:** Heb reads, "your roads . . ." (see translators' note *e*). The second person conveys direct face-to-face address meant to have an affective impact. **9–15:** The other male providers are no good. The wife (Israel) sought material benefits from other males, all the while ignorant of the fact that it was her husband (the LORD) who provided for her. But now her husband (the LORD) will remove His provisions, including food and clothing. Without the clothing, she (Israel) will be naked and shamed. Her joy will disappear and none of her lovers will be able to help her against her angry husband (the LORD).

10 And she did not consider this:
    It was I who bestowed on her
    The new grain and wine and oil;
    I who lavished silver on her
    And gold—which they used for Baal.

11 Assuredly,
    I will take back My new grain in its time
    And My new wine in its season,
    And I will snatch away My wool and My linen
    That serve to cover her nakedness.

12 Now will I uncover her shame
    In the very sight of her lovers,
    And none shall save her from Me.

13 And I will end all her rejoicing:
    Her festivals, new moons, and sabbaths—
    All her festive seasons.

14 I will lay waste her vines and her fig trees,
    Which she thinks are a fee
    She received from her lovers;
    I will turn them into brushwood,
    And beasts of the field shall devour them.

15 Thus will I punish her
    For the days of the Baalim,
    On which she brought them offerings;
    When, decked with earrings and jewels,
    She would go after her lovers,
    Forgetting Me   —declares the Lord.

16 Assuredly,
    I will speak coaxingly to her
    And lead her through the wilderness[a]
    And speak to her tenderly.

17 I will give her her vineyards from there,
    And the Valley of Achor[b] as a [c]plowland of hope.[c]
    There she shall respond as in the days of her
       youth,
    When she came up from the land of Egypt.

18 And in that day   —declares the Lord—
    You will call [Me] Ishi,[d]
    And no more will you call Me Baali.[d]

19 For I will remove the names of the Baalim from
       her mouth,
    And they shall nevermore be mentioned by name.

15: *Days of the Baalim*, festivals and other occasions in which offerings were sacrificed to different Baals (Baalim is the plural of the deity Baal). "Baal" means "lord" or "owner" and in the Bible often refers to a Phoenician or Canaanite god of the same name. The term was also used as a title for the Lord (see 2 Sam. 5.20; 1 Chron. 14.11), though the book of Hosea does not support that practice (2.18). "Baal" can also mean "husband" and, as a verb, "marry" or "take a woman as a sexual partner." Baals stand for the unidentified "lovers" mentioned before, and all the connotations that the term carries suit well the general atmosphere permeating the text. **16–25: Marital reconciliation.** The husband will bring the wife (Israel) back. The wife will be faithful forever, and the husband (the Lord) will provide, i.e., the fertility of the land will return. All of nature participates in the renewal of the marital covenant. **17:** *Valley of Achor*, see Josh. 7.24–26; 15.7; Isa. 65.10. The name may be translated as "Valley of Trouble." Significantly, this valley will be transformed into a "Door of Hope" (see translators' note c-c), Heb "Petach Tikwah," the name of a city in modern Israel. **18:** "You will call Me 'my Man' (or husband), and no more will you call Me 'my Baal' (or husband)." Although the two terms can both mean "husband," their connotations are very different. The text uses the wordplay to project an image of a future rejection of the cult of Baal (i.e., a Phoenician and Canaanite god) and Israel's acceptance of the Lord as her "Man."

a *I.e., her ravaged land (see vv. 5, 10–11, 14); so Ibn Ezra.*
b *A desolate region; cf. Isa. 65.10; see further Josh. 7.25–26.*
c-c *Connecting* pethaḥ *with* pittaḥ *"to plow" (see Isa. 28.24). Meaning of Heb. uncertain; others "door of hope."*
d *Both* Ishi *and* Baali *mean "my husband," but the latter also means "my Baal."*

²⁰In that day, I will make a covenant for them with the beasts of the field, the birds of the air, and the creeping things of the ground; I will also banish^a bow, sword, and war from the land. Thus I will let them lie down in safety.

²¹   And I will espouse you forever:
    I will espouse you ^{b-}with righteousness and
        justice,
    And with goodness and mercy,
²²   And I will espouse you with faithfulness;^{-b}
    Then you shall be devoted to the LORD.
²³   In that day,
    I will respond   —declares the LORD—
    I will respond to the sky,
    And it shall respond to the earth;
²⁴   And the earth shall respond
    With new grain and wine and oil,
    And they shall respond to Jezreel.^c
²⁵   I will sow her in the land as My own;
    And take Lo-ruhamah back in favor;
    And I will say to Lo-ammi, "You are My people,"
    And he will respond, "[You are] my God."

3 The LORD said to me further, "Go, ^{d-}befriend a woman who, while befriended by a companion, consorts with others, just as the LORD befriends the Israelites,^{-d} but they turn ^{e-}to other gods and love the cups of the grape."^{-e}

²Then I hired her for fifteen [shekels of] silver, a *ḥomer* of barley, and ^{f-}a *lethech* of barley;^{-f 3} and I stipulated with her, ^{g-}"In return,^{-g} you are to go a long time without either fornicating or marrying; even I [shall not cohabit] with you."

⁴For the Israelites shall go a long time without king and without officials, without sacrifice^h and without cult pillars, and without ephod and teraphim. ⁵ Afterward, the Israelites will turn back and will seek the LORD their God and David their king—and they will thrill over the LORD and over His bounty in the days to come.

21–22: These verses are well known from Jewish liturgy. They are usually translated more literally, "And I will betroth you [i.e., Israel] to Me for ever; I will betroth you to Me in righteousness and in justice, in kindness and in mercy. I will betroth you to Me in faithfulness; and you shall know the LORD." Traditional Jews say these verses when winding the straps of the tefillin [phylacteries] three times round the middle finger. **23–25:** These verses emphasize that the Israelites were wrong to assume that Baal was the fertility god—the LORD controls fertility. **3.1–5:** Another passage dealing with a marriage metaphor. **1:** An alternative translation would be: "Go again, love a woman who has a lover and is an adulteress. [This is just] as the love of LORD for the Children of Israel, who turn to other gods." Scholars disagree on whether it refers to Gomer (1.3) or to another woman. The text leaves her unnamed and by doing so leaves both options open. Clearly, though, Hosea's relationship to this woman symbolizes again God's relationship to Israel. **2:** A *ḥomer* is probably about 6.5 bushels (230 liters), and a *lethech* is half a homer. **5:** References to God and (human) kings are not rare in the Tanakh. Still it is important to note that the book in its final form tells its readers of a northern (Israelite) prophet who, even though the Israelite monarchy is at its political zenith, not only perceives that its end is near, but also that *the Israelites will turn back* to *David their king,* the dynasty of the Southern Kingdom. (See similarly the final version of the conclusion of Amos.)

a Lit. "break."
b-b As the bride-price which the bridegroom will pay, He will confer these qualities on her, so that she will never offend again.
c I.e., "God sows." The names of Hosea's children (1.3–8) are applied here to Israel.
d-d For "befriend," see Deut. 10.19. For God's befriending Israel, see Hos. 2.10.
e-e Meaning of Heb. uncertain; emendation yields " 'to other gods.' And so I befriended a woman of lust."
f-f Septuagint reads "a jar of wine."
g-g Lit. "for me."
h Emendation yields "altar."

4

Hear the word of the LORD,
O people of Israel!
For the LORD has a case
Against the inhabitants of this land,
Because there is no honesty and no goodness
And no obedience to God in the land.

2 [False] swearing, dishonesty, and murder,
And theft and adultery are rife;
Crime follows upon crime!

3 For that, the earth is withered:
Everything that dwells on it languishes—
Beasts of the field and birds of the sky—
Even the fish of the sea perish.

4 "Let no man rebuke, let no man protest!"
ª·For this your people has a grievance against
[you],
O priest!·ª

5 So you shall stumble by day,
And by night ᵇ·a prophet·ᵇ shall stumble as well,
And I will destroy your kindred.ᶜ

6 My people is destroyed because of [your]
disobedience!
Because you have rejected obedience,
I reject you as My priest;
Because you have spurned the teaching of your
God,
I, in turn, will spurn your children.

7 The more they increased, the more they sinned
against Me:
I will change their dignity to dishonor.

8 They feed on My people's sin offerings,
And so they desire its iniquity.

9 Therefore, the people shall fare like the priests:
I will punish it for its conduct,
I will requite it for its deeds.

10 Truly, they shall eat, but not be sated;
They shall swill,ᵈ but not be satisfied,
Because they have forsaken the LORD

a-a For failing to reprove; but meaning of Heb. uncertain.
b-b Emendation yields "your children"; cf. v. 6 end.
c Lit. "mother."   d For this meaning of hiznah cf. v. 18.

4.1–14.9: Reports of prophetic announcements associated with Hosea. The remainder of the book consists of a collection of prophetic speeches that accuse monarchic Israel and Judah of unfaithfulness, announce the judgment that will be passed on the people, but also foreshadow the hope of restoration and return. Most of this material (4.1–12.1; 12.7–14.9) deals with Israel; 12.3–7 focuses on Judah.

4.1–19: On Israel's corruption, rejection of divine teaching and worship, harlotry, and divine punishment. 1: *Hear the word of the LORD:* This phrase or variants of it conveys the legitimacy and importance of what follows. In addition, it often serves to mark the beginning of a new section (cf. 5.1). In the world of the book, people are supposed to hear "this word," but in the actual world the readers of the book are asked to read and study "the word of the LORD" and to convey it to those who cannot read it by themselves. **2:** The center of the Decalogue may be paraphrased here. **5:** The v. ends with "I will destroy your mother" (see translators' note c), which may refer to the mother of the priest (possibly all priests?), and the land (Gomer) as the mother of Israel; see the opening of v. 6. The former would point to the punishment of the mother for the sin of her children. The text carries both meanings, which are complementary. **6:** *Teaching* translates Heb "torah." Many later Jewish readers and commentators understood the term "torah" as "the Torah," i.e., a reference to the traditional Jewish Torah. This understanding of Torah is much later than the time of the composition of the book of Hosea, and for that matter, of the first five books of the Bible, which was later understood as the "written Torah." The association of *teaching* and priests here is quite common in prophetic literature (Jer. 18.18; Ezek. 7.26; 22.26; Zeph. 3.4; Hag. 2.11; Mal. 2.7). Within this context, "torah" or *teaching* points at the divine instructions that the priests were responsible for keeping and transmitting. **10:** The text imparts, at least by connotation, the following meaning: ". . . but not be sated; they shall play the whore, but not multiply." The image of sexual promiscuity is linked to the idea that since these sexual relations were illicit, they would "bear no fruit." (The text implies that the desired fruit of all sexual relations, even "illicit relations," is to have children.) **11:** A rendering of the first

To practice[a] 11 lechery.
Wine[b] and new wine destroy
The mind of 12 My people:
It consults its stick,[c]
Its rod[c] directs it!
A lecherous impulse has made them go wrong,
And they have strayed[d] from submission to
　　their God.

13　They sacrifice on the mountaintops
And offer on the hills,
Under oaks, poplars, and terebinths
Whose shade is so pleasant.
That is why their[e] daughters fornicate
And their daughters-in-law commit adultery!

14　I will not punish their daughters for fornicating
Nor their daughters-in-law for committing
　　adultery;
For they themselves [f]turn aside[f] with whores
And sacrifice with prostitutes,
And a people that is without sense[g] must stumble.

15　If you are a lecher, Israel—
Let not Judah incur guilt—
Do not come to Gilgal,[h]
Do not make pilgrimages to Beth-aven,[i]
And do not swear by the LORD![j]

16　Ah, Israel has balked
Like a stubborn cow;
Therefore,
The LORD will graze him
On the range, like a sheep.[k]

17[l]　Ephraim is addicted to images—
Let him be.

18　They drink to excess—
Their liquor turns against them.
They "love" beyond measure—
Disgrace is the "gift"

19　Which the wind [m]is bringing;[m]
They shall garner shame from their sacrifices.

word as "whoredom" instead of
lechery better reflects the emphatic
repetition of terms and the images
they evoke that characterizes the
Heb here, and that closely links it
to chs 1–3. **12:** The same holds true
for "spirit of whoredom" instead
of *lecherous impulse*. The conclusion
may also be translated more literally: "they have played the whore,
forsaking their God," again hammering away at the root for
"whore." **14:** Similarly, "I will not
punish your daughters when they
play the whore, nor your daughters-in-law when they commit
adultery; for the men themselves
go aside with whores, and sacrifice
with prostitutes." **15:** Bethel and
Gilgal were two main cultic centers
in the Northern Kingdom of Israel
(cf. Amos 4.4). *Beth-aven* (namely,
"House of Iniquity" or "Delusion";
see translators' note *h*) is a sarcastic way of referring to Bethel. See
also 12.12 ("if Gilgal is iniquity"—
NJPS, "as for Gilead, it is worthless") and cf. 9.15. **16:** *On the range*,
i.e., in a "broad pasture." The
image of God as a shepherd is a
common biblical and ancient Near
Eastern image. It is very open-
ended, and may refer to the munif-
icent care of the ideal shepherd
(Ps. 23), or the punishment of the
straying sheep by the harsh shepherd (Ezek. ch 34). **17:** *Ephraim:* An
alternative name for the Northern
Kingdom that is widely used in
the book of Hosea. The first king
and founder of the kingdom came
from Ephraim, and the territory
of Ephraim remained at the heart
of the kingdom until its very end.
18: The second half of the v. connotes, "they surely fornicate (or
commit acts of whoredom)."

---

a Cf. 12.7.　　b Emendation yields "New grain"; cf. 7.14; 9.1–2.
c I.e., its phallus, meaning "its lust."
d See note b at 1.2.　　e Heb. "your," here and through v. 14.
f-f Meaning of Heb. uncertain.　　g Cf. vv. 11–12.
h One who participates in the debaucheries of the open-air shrines is not fit to visit a temple building.　　i Lit. "House of Delusion," substituted for Bethel (cf. Amos 4.4).
j I.e., you are not fit to profess His religion; see Jer. 12.16.
k Instead of giving them fodder in return for their work; cf. Isa. 30.23–24.
l Meaning of vv. 17–19 uncertain in part.
m-m Lit. "has bound up in the corners of its garment"; see note at Mal. 3.20.

5 Hear this, O priests,
   Attend, O House[a] of Israel,
   And give ear, O royal house;
   For right conduct is your responsibility!
   But you have been a snare to Mizpah
   And a net spread out over Tabor;

2 [b]For when trappers dug deep pitfalls,
   I was the only reprover of them all.[b]

3 Yes, I have watched Ephraim,
   Israel has not escaped my notice:
   Behold, you have fornicated, O Ephraim;
   Israel has defiled himself!

4 Their habits do not let them
   Turn back to their God;
   Because of the lecherous impulse within them,
   They pay no heed to the Lord.

5 [c]Israel's pride shall be humbled before his very
         eyes,
   As Israel and Ephraim fall because of their sin
   (And Judah falls with them).

6 Then they will go with their sheep and cattle
   To seek the Lord, but they will not find Him.[c]

   [b]He has cast them off:[b]

7 [Because] they have broken faith with the Lord,
   Because [d]they have[d] begotten
   Alien children.
   Therefore, [b]the new moon
   Shall devour their portion.[b]

8 Sound a ram's horn in Gibeah,
   A trumpet in Ramah;
   Give the alarm in Beth-aven;[e]
   [f]After you,[f] Benjamin!

9 Ephraim is stricken with horror
   On a day of chastisement.

   Against the tribes[g] of Israel
   I proclaim certainties:

10 The officers of Judah have acted
   Like shifters of field boundaries;

5.1–15: Further denunciations of monarchic Israel and Judah and announcements of their punishment. 4: *Lecherous impulse,* see 4.12 n. **5:** References to Judah are not minor parenthetical remarks, but major markers of where the interest of the present book lies (see, among others, 1.7; 3.5; 4.15; 5.5, 10, 12, 14; 6.11; 12.3). **6:** This echoes a common prophetic motif: Sacrifices alone are not sufficient to assure divine presence (see esp. Isa. 1.10–17). **7:** *They have broken faith . . . children:* Another translation, "They have been unfaithful to the Lord, for they have brought bastards to birth." *The new moon shall devour their portion:* The second half of the verse probably means that a "new time [namely, a new period] will destroy them with their lands." **8–14:** Some scholars argue that the passage may reflect the circumstances of the Syro-Ephraimitic war in 734–733 BCE, when Israel (Ephraim) and Aram (Syria) were allied in trying to force Judah to join them in a revolt against Assyria, but this runs counter to the gist of the text, since at that time Israel stood against Assyria, rather than as her ally. **8:** The ram's horn (shofar) was used to call troops to war or to sound an alarm. *Beth-aven* (i.e., Bethel; see 4.15 n.), *Gibeah,* and *Ramah* are all close to each other in the territory of Benjamin. **10:** *Shifters of field boundaries:* Moving the boundary marker of a field, which was equivalent to stealing property, was a severe violation of proper behavior (see Deut. 19.14, 27.17; Prov. 22.28; admonitions against moving boundary markers occur elsewhere in the ancient Near East).

a Emendation yields "prophets."   b-b Meaning of Heb. uncertain.
c-c This passage would read well after 5.15; cf. 5.6 with 6.6.
d-d Emendation yields "He has."
e The three towns named, in the territory of Benjamin, are now being wrested from Israel
by Judah; see v. 10.
f-f Emendation yields "Stir up."
g I.e., the kingdoms of Judah and Israel (Ephraim).

On them I will pour out
My wrath like water.

11 Ephraim is defrauded,
Robbed of redress,
Because he has witlessly
Gone after futility.[a]

12 For it is I who am like rot to Ephraim,
Like decay to the House of Judah;[i]

13 Yet when Ephraim became aware of his
sickness,
Judah[b] of his sores,
Ephraim repaired to Assyria—
He sent envoys to a patron[c] king!
He will never be able to cure you,
Will not heal you of your sores.

14 No, I will be like a lion to Ephraim,
Like a great beast to the House of Judah;[b]
I, I will attack and stride away,
Carrying the prey that no one can rescue;

15 And I will return to My abode—
Till they realize their guilt.
In their distress, they will seek Me
And beg for My favor.

6 [d]"Come, let us turn back to the LORD:
He attacked, and He can heal us;
He wounded, and He can bind us up.

2 In two days He will make us whole again;
On the third day He will raise us up,
And we shall be whole by His favor.

3 Let us pursue obedience to the LORD,
And we shall become obedient.
His appearance is as sure as daybreak,
And He will come to us like rain,
Like latter rain that refreshes[e] the earth."

4 What can I do for you, Ephraim,
What can I do for you, Judah,[f]
When your goodness is like morning clouds,
Like dew so early gone?

15: The idea of *seeking God in their distress* is found in Deut. 4.29–30 as well. In general, there are many vocabulary links between Hosea and Deuteronomy. Some scholars attribute these links to the fact that Deuteronomy was originally a northern work, and thus shares the vocabulary of the northern Hosea. Others think the final form of Hosea was particularly influenced by Deuteronomy.

6.1–7.16: The LORD is reluctant to hear the people's appeal. Further condemnations of monarchic Israel and Judah. 6.1–3: The book quotes a human voice urging repentance, saying that just as God wounded, He will heal. The appearance of God is as assured as the daybreak, as refreshing as rain. **4:** The text here presents a divine response to the earlier speech. Here and in the following vv. the images of daybreak and rain are turned on their head as they apply to monarchic Israel. The LORD is probably presented here in the image of a father who laments his inability to help a wayward son: *what can I do for you?* or, as others read, "what can I do with you?" The implied answer is "nothing." *Morning clouds . . . dew,* both of which evaporate at the first warmth of day. Israel's good intentions do not last.

---

a Cf. Targum and Septuagint; but meaning of Heb. uncertain.

b Emendation yields "Israel."

c Compare the verb ryb in the sense of "to champion, uphold the cause of," in Isa. 1.17; 3.13; 19.20 end; 51.22.

d As anticipated at the end of chapter 5, Israel seeks the LORD's favor; His answer begins with v. 4.

e Taking yoreh as equivalent of yarweh.

f Emendation yields "Israel"; cf. "Ephraim . . . Israel" in v. 10.

5   That is why I have hewn down ᵃ·the prophets,·ᵃ
     Have slain them with the words of My mouth:
     ᵇ·And the day that dawned [brought on] your
          punishment.·ᵇ
6   For I desire goodness, not sacrifice;
     Obedience to God, rather than burnt offerings.
7ᶜ   But they, to a man, have transgressed the
          Covenant.
     This is where they have been false to Me:
8   Gilead is a city of evildoers,
     Tracked up with blood.
9   The gang of priests is
     Like the ambuscade of bandits
     Who murder on the road to Shechem,
     For they have encouragedᵈ depravity.
10   In ᵉ·the House of Israel·ᵉ I have seen
     A horrible thing;
     Ephraim has fornicated there,
     Israel has defiled himself.
11   ᶠ·(Even Judah has reaped a harvest of you!)·ᶠ

7   When I would restore My people's fortunes,
     ¹ When I would heal Israel,
     The guilt of Ephraim reveals itself
     And the wickedness of Samaria.
     For they have acted treacherously,
     With thieves breaking in
     And bands raiding outside.
2   And they do not consider
     That I remembered all their wickedness.
     Why, their misdeeds have been all around
          them,ᵍ
     They have been ever before Me.

3ʰ   In malice they make a king merry,
     And officials in treachery.
4   They ⁱ·commit adultery,·ⁱ all of them,
     Like an oven fired by a baker,
     Who desists from stoking only
     From the kneading of the dough to its
          leavening.
5   The day they made our king sick

6: Not a condemnation of sacrifice but rather a statement about the primacy of morality over sacrifices. Needless to say, sacrifices offered by those unworthy of bringing an offering to the deity are not efficacious (cf. 5.6; 8.13).
7.1: *Samaria*, the capital of the Northern Kingdom, and therefore another synonym for it (like *Ephraim*; see 4.17 n.). **5–6:** These verses are difficult. An alternative translation would be: "On the day of our king the officials/ became sick with the heat of wine;/ he stretched out his hand with mockers./ For they are kindled like an oven, their heart burns within them;/ all night their anger smolders;/ in the morning it blazes like a flaming fire" (NRSV).

a-a Emendation yields "your children"; cf. 9.13.
b-b Cf. v. 3; but meaning of Heb. uncertain.
c Meaning of vv. 7–11 unclear in part.
d Heb. "done"; cf. 5.1–3.   e-e Emendation yields "Beth-shean."
f-f Cf. 5.9–10; but meaning of clause uncertain.   g Emendation yields "Me."
h Vv. 3–6 would read well in the order 4, 6, 3, 5.   i-i Emendation yields "rage."

[And] officials with the poison of wine,
ᵃ·He gave his hand to traitors.·ᵃ

6   ᵇ·For they approach their ambush
With their hearts like an oven:·ᵇ
Through the night
Their bakerᶜ has slept;
In the morning, it flares up
Like a blazing fire.

7   They all get heated like an oven
And devour their rulers—
None of them calls to Me.
All their kings have fallen [by their hand].

8   ᵇ·Ephraim is among the peoples;
He is rotting away.
Ephraim is like a cake—
Incapable of turning.·ᵇ

9   Strangers have consumed his strength,
But he has taken no notice;
Also, moldᵈ is scattered over him,
But he has taken no notice.

10 Though Israel's pride has been humbled
Before his very eyes,
They have not turned back
To their God the LORD;
They have not sought Him
In spite of everything.

11 Instead, Ephraim has acted
Like a silly dove with no mind:
They have appealed to Egypt!
They have gone to Assyria!

12 When they go, I will spread
My net over them,
I will bring them down
Like birds of the sky;
ᵇ·I will chastise them
When I hear their bargaining.·ᵇ

13 Woe to them
For straying from Me;
Destruction to them
For rebelling against Me!
For I was their Redeemer;
Yet they have plotted treason against Me.

11: Relying on other nations is viewed as tantamount to rebelling against God, a view governing other biblical texts, especially Isaiah and Chronicles (e.g., Isa. 31.1; 2 Chron 16.7–9). *Egypt* and *Assyria* (cf. 11.5; 12.2) were the main powers of the period in which the book is set, and particularly toward the end of that period. They remained the two main powers until Babylonia replaced Assyria as the main northern power in the late 7th century BCE. Reliance on Egypt vs. Assyria (later Babylonia) is a common theme in prophetic literature. Historically, however, the debacle of the Northern Kingdom followed its disastrous alliance with Aram, the main regional power that opposed Assyria at the time. Egypt's intervention in these events was quite marginal. But references to the Aram vs. Assyria conflict that predominated in the time period noted in the superscription of the book (1.1) is found nowhere in Hosea.

---

a-a I.e., he trusted traitors; but meaning of verse uncertain.
b-b Meaning of Heb. uncertain.
c-c Emendation yields "rage."
d Like Akkadian shibu; others "gray hairs."

14a But they did not cry out to Me sincerely
   As they b-lay wailing.-b
   They debauch[c] over new grain and new wine,
   They are faithless[d] to Me.

15 I braced, I strengthened their arms,
   And they plot evil against Me!
16 They come back;
   They have been of no use,[e]
   Like a slack bow.
   Their officers shall fall by the sword,
   Because of the stammering[f] of their tongues.
   Such shall be [the results of] their jabbering[g]
   In the land of Egypt.

8 [Put] a ram's horn to your mouth—
   h-Like an eagle-h over the House of i-the LORD;-i
   Because they have transgressed My covenant
   And been faithless to My teaching.
2 Israel cries out to Me,
   "O my God, we are devoted to You."[j]

3 Israel rejects what is good;
   k-An enemy shall pursue him.-k
4 They have made kings,
   But not with My sanction;
   They have made officers,
   But not of My choice.
   Of their silver and gold
   They have made themselves images,
   To their own undoing.
5 l-He rejects-l your calf, Samaria!
   I am furious with them!
   Will they never be capable of m-purity?
6 For it was Israel's doing;-m
   It was only made by a joiner,
   It is not a god.
   No, the calf of Samaria shall be
   Reduced to splinters!

8.1–14: On Israel's unfaithfulness to the LORD. 1: Traditional Jewish interpreters associated the *eagle* with Nebuchadnezzar (cf. Ezek. 17) who destroyed the Temple in 586; this association implies an identification of the house of the LORD with the Temple in Jerusalem. *The House of the LORD:* The reference to the legitimate house of the LORD was most likely understood as pointing at the Temple in Jerusalem by the Judahite readership of the book of Hosea. For them, therefore, Israel in v. 3 must carry two meanings: Israel in the sense of the Northern Kingdom and Israel as the people in a covenantal relationship with the LORD, which includes both the Northern and Southern Kingdoms, as well as the intended readership of the book (later Jews). *My teaching* (Heb "torah") here and in 8.12 was later understood by many Jewish readers as "My Torah" (i.e., a reference to the traditional Jewish Torah). **4–6:** The mention of illegitimate *kings* may point to the rapid succession of kings in the last twenty-five years of the Northern Kingdom (see 1.4 n.), but in the light of 3.5 may well point to all northern kings, from Jeroboam I on, who from a Judahite perspective were illegitimate. The reference to the *images* (i.e., idols) and the *calf* (a young bull, usual representation of strength and fertility) seem to reinforce the latter interpretation (see 1 Kings 12.25–33).

---

a *This verse would read well after 8.2.*   b-b *I.e., in penitence; cf. Isa. 58.5.*

c *Cf. Aramaic gar/yegur "to commit adultery"; for the thought, cf. 4.11.*

d *Taking yasuru as equivalent to yasoru, from sarar; cf. 9.15 end.*

e *Meaning of Heb. uncertain.*   f *Cf. Arabic zaghūm and zughmūm "a stammerer."*

g *I.e., the negotiations conducted in the Egyptian language.*

h-h *Meaning of Heb. uncertain.*

i-i *Emendation yields "Israel."*   j *See note g at 7.14.*

k-k *Emendation yields "They pursue delusion."*   l-l *Emendation yields "I reject."*

m-m *Emendation yields "understanding, / That House of Israel?"*

7 They sow wind,
And they shall reap whirlwind—
Standing stalks devoid of ears
And yielding no flour.
If they do yield any,
Strangers shall devour it.

8 Israel is bewildered;[a]
They have now become among the nations
Like an unwanted vessel,

9 [Like] a lonely wild ass.
For they have gone up to Assyria,
[b]Ephraim has[b] courted friendship.

10 And while they are courting among the nations,
[c]There I will hold them fast;[c]
[d]And they shall begin to diminish in number
From the burden of king [and] officers.[d]

11 For Ephraim has multiplied altars—for guilt;
His altars have redounded to his guilt:

12 The many teachings I wrote for him
Have been treated as something alien.

13 [d]When they present sacrifices to Me,[d]
It is but flesh for them to eat:
The LORD has not accepted them.
Behold, He remembers their iniquity,
He will punish their sins:
Back to Egypt with them!

14 Israel has ignored his Maker
And built temples
(And Judah has fortified many cities).
So I will set fire to his cities,
And it shall consume their fortresses.

9 Rejoice not, O Israel,
As other peoples exult;
For you have strayed
Away from your God:
[e]You have loved a harlot's fee
By every threshing floor of new grain.

2 Threshing floor and winepress
Shall not join them,
And the new wine shall betray her.[e]

---

a A play on words: The Heb. root balaʿ, which means "bewildered" here (cf. Isa. 28.7), means "devour" in the preceding verse.

b-b Emendation yields "In Egypt they have."

c-c Cf. 9.6; but meaning of Heb. uncertain.   d-d Meaning of Heb. uncertain.

e-e Emendation and rearrangement yield: "You have loved fornication / By every threshing floor and press; / The new grain shall not join them, / And the new wine shall fail them."

8: The beginning of the verse may be translated as "Israel is devoured"; cf. the last line of the previous verse and translators' note a. **12:** Note that the "teaching" (singular in Heb) of the LORD is conceived as a written document, just as "the word of the LORD that came to Hosea" (1.1) is the book of Hosea, a written text too. See also 8.1 n. **13:** *Back to Egypt,* or more literally, "they shall go back to Egypt." Is this a reference to exile to Egypt or a reversal of the exodus? The text may have carried more than one meaning. Cf. Deut. 28.68, and see also 9.3. **14:** Judah's sin is not the setting up of multiple religious centers or the calf statues, as Israel had done; but Judah had also sinned, perhaps by not relying sufficiently on God to defend them (see 7.11 n.).

9.1–17: On the results of divine punishment. 1: *You have strayed away,* lit. "For you [male] have committed deeds of whoredom" (cf. 1.2; 2.7; 3.3; 4.10, 12, 13, 14, 15, 18; 5.3; and see previous notes). **1–2:** The *threshing floor* and the *winepress,* along with the references to joy, create an image of agricultural festivals (e.g., the harvest festival). The mention of the threshing floor under these circumstances (cf. Ruth ch 3) and the explicit reference to a harlot's fee and the statement "you committed deeds of whoredom" all contribute to the text's construction of an atmosphere of illicit sexual activity. In the book of Hosea these images are associated with the theme of Israel's abandoning the LORD. The precise metaphor here was already a matter of debate among traditional Jewish interpreters. Is the male worshipping other gods, as *other peoples* do, and so presented as abandoning the LORD, a husband figure, and therefore compared to a female prostitute (a common image in the book; cf. Radak)? Or is the male happy to receive his grain as a present from his gods—not the LORD, and therefore compared to a prostitute coming to pick up her fees (Rashi)? Or are these two readings comple-

3   They shall not be able to remain
       In the land of the LORD.
       But Ephraim shall return to Egypt
       And shall eat unclean food in Assyria.[a]

4   It shall be for them like the food of mourners,
       All who partake of which are defiled.
       They will offer no libations of wine to the LORD,
       And no sacrifices of theirs will be pleasing to Him;
       But their food will be only for their hunger,
       It shall not come into the House of the LORD.

5   What will you do about feast days,
       About the festivals of the LORD?

6   Behold, they have gone [b]from destruction[b]
       [With] the silver they treasure.
       Egypt shall [c]hold them fast,[c]
       Moph[d] shall receive them in burial.
       Weeds are their heirs;
       Prickly shrubs occupy their [old] homes.

7   The days of punishment have come
       For your heavy guilt;
       The days of requital have come—
       Let Israel know it!

       The prophet was distraught,
       The inspired man driven mad
       By constant harassment.

8   Ephraim watches for [e]my God.
       As for the prophet,[e]
       Fowlers' snares are on all his paths,
       Harassment in the House of his God.

9   They have been as grievously corrupt
       As in the days of Gibeah;[f]
       He will remember their iniquity,
       He will punish their sins.

10   I found Israel [as pleasing]
       As grapes in the wilderness;
       Your fathers seemed to Me
       [g]Like the first fig to ripen on a fig tree.[g]
       But when they came to Baal-peor,
       They turned aside to shamefulness;[h]

mentary rather than alternative? In any case, whereas the peoples may rejoice, Israel will have no reason for joy since the threshing floor and the winepress will not join them, i.e., they will not provide them with food or drink. Even the *new wine* will disappoint them. In sum, the text plays again with the motif of God as the provider, who ceases to provide for his sinful, whoring wife. Whereas Israel is first represented as a male (v. 1), the image shifts to a female character *(her)* when the theme of the provider who ceases to provide is fully developed (v. 2). For proposed emendations of the text see translators' note *e-e* on p. 1156.
6: *Moph,* Memphis, one of the most important cities in Egypt. **9:** *The days of Gibeah,* see Judg. chs 19–20; Hos. 10.9. **10:** Although there are idyllic elements in the depiction of Israel's past (cf. Jer. 2.2; 31.2), it is viewed as fundamentally problematic, as in Ps. 106. The idyllic elements serve here to enhance the negative description of Israel's past. *Baal Peor,* see Num. ch 25; Deut. 4.3–4. In the stories alluded to, sinful sexual behavior is associated with the two places.

---

a *The lands of the heathen and the food there are unclean; cf. Ezek. 4.13; Amos 7.17.*
b-b *Emendation yields "to Assyria."*   c-c *Cf. 8.10.*
d *Believed to be Memphis, elsewhere called Noph.*
e-e *Emendation yields "the prophet of my God."*
f *See Judg. 19–20.*
g-g *Emendation yields "like a ripe fig in a waterless waste"; cf. 13.5.*
h *Cf. Num. 25.1–3.*

ᵃThen they became as detested
As they had been loved.·ᵃ

11 From birth, from the womb, from conception
Ephraim's glory shall be
Like birds that fly away.ᵇ

12 Even if they rear their infants,
I will bereave them of men.
ᶜWoe to them indeed
When I turn away from them!·ᶜ

13 ᵃIt shall go with Ephraim
As I have seen it go with Tyre,
Which was planted in a meadow;·ᵃ
Ephraim too must bring out
His children to slayers.

14 Give them, O Lᴏʀᴅ—give them what?
Give them a womb that miscarries,
And shriveled breasts!

15 All their misfortune [began] at Gilgal,
For there I disowned them.ᵈ
For their evil deeds
I will drive them out of My House.
I will accept them no more;
ᵉAll their officials are·ᵉ disloyal.

16ᵇ Ephraimᶠ is stricken,
Their stock is withered;
They can produce no fruit.
Even if they do bear children,
I will slay their cherished offspring.

17 My God rejects them
Because they have not obeyed Him,
And they shall go wandering
Among the nations.

10 Israel is a ravaged vine
And its fruit is like it.
When his fruit was plentiful,
He made altars aplenty;
When his land was bountiful,
Cult pillars abounded.

11–12: Illicit sexual relations do not provide offspring (cf. 4.10 n.). **13:** *Tyre,* a major Phoenician city-port and an important regional power. The area under its control bordered on Israel. It was often, but not always, an ally of Israel. **15:** *My House,* see 8.1 n.

10.1–15: The vine and the heifer: Agricultural images show Israel's failure and consequent ruin.
1: *Cult pillars:* Pillars and altars were part of a cultic site (cf. Exod. 24.4–5). During the monarchic period pillars were also involved in the worship of the Lᴏʀᴅ. Several biblical texts command the destruction of altars and pillars used in the worship of gods other than the Lᴏʀᴅ (e.g., Exod. 34.13; Deut. 7.5; 12.3); others condemn the making and use of pillars in general (Lev. 26.1). **5:** *Priestlings,* a derogatory term for the priests of Samaria, who were condemned before (see ch 4). *Beth-aven,* see 4.15 n. **9:** *Gibeah:* See 9.9 n.

a-a Meaning of Heb. uncertain.
b V. 16 would read well after v. 11.
c-c Emendation yields: "Even if they wean their babes, / They shall be dismayed because of them."
d The specific allusion is uncertain.
e-e Emendation yields "They are all."
f Targum reads "Their crown," i.e., of a tree.

2   Now that his boughs^a are broken up,
He feels his guilt;
He himself pulls apart his altars,
Smashes his pillars.

3   Truly, now they say,
"We have no king;
For, since we do not fear the LORD,
What can a king do to us?"

4   So they conclude agreements and make covenants
With false oaths,
And justice ^{b-}degenerates into poison weeds,
Breaking out^{-b} on the furrows of the fields.

5   The inhabitants of Samaria fear
For the calf of Beth-aven;^c
Indeed, its people and priestlings,
^{d-}Whose joy it once was,^{-d}
Mourn over it for the glory
That is departed from it.

6   It too shall be brought to Assyria
As tribute to a patron^e king;
Ephraim shall be chagrined,
Israel shall be dismayed
Because of his plans.^f

7   Samaria's monarchy^g is vanishing
Like foam upon water,

8   Ruined shall be the shrines of [Beth-]aven,^c
That sin of Israel.
Thorns and thistles
Shall grow on their altars.
They shall call to the mountains, "Bury us!"
To the hills, "Fall on us!"

9   You have sinned more, O Israel,
Than in the days of Gibeah.^h
^{d-}There they stand [as] at Gibeah!
Shall they not be overtaken
By a war upon scoundrels

10   As peoples gather against them?^{-d}

When I chose [them], I broke them in,
Harnessing them for two furrows.

a Cf. 2 Sam. 18.14, where the word is rendered "thick growth."

b-b Cf. Amos 6.12; lit. "breaks out like poison weeds."

c See note i at 4.15.   d-d Meaning of Heb. uncertain.   e See note c at 5.13.

f Emendation yields "image," referring to the calf.

g The Heb. verb agrees with this word, not with "Samaria."   h See note at 9.9.

11 Ephraim became a trained heifer,
But preferred to thresh;
I ^aplaced a yoke
Upon her sleek neck.^{-a}
I will make Ephraim ^bdo advance plowing;^{-b}
Judah^c shall do [main] plowing!
Jacob shall do final plowing!

12 "Sow righteousness for yourselves;
Reap ^dthe fruits of^{-d} goodness;
Break for yourselves betimes fresh ground
Of seeking the Lord,
So that you may obtain ^ea teacher^{-e} of
righteousness."

13 You have plowed wickedness,
You have reaped iniquity—
[And] you shall eat the fruits of treachery—
Because you relied on your way,^f
On your host of warriors.

14 But the din of war shall arise in your own people,
And all your fortresses shall be ravaged
As Beth-arbel was ravaged by Shalman^g
On a day of battle,
When mothers and babes were dashed to death
together.

15 This ^his what Bethel has done to you^{-h}
For your horrible wickedness:
ⁱAt dawn⁻ⁱ shall Israel's monarchy
Utterly perish.

11 I fell in love with Israel
When he was still a child;
And I have called [him] My son
Ever since Egypt.

2^j Thus were they called,
But they went their own way;
They sacrifice to Baalim^k
And offer to carved images.

a-a Lit. "passed over the comeliness of its neck."
b-b Taking rkb in the sense of the Arabic krb.
c Emendation yields "Israel."
d-d Lit. "according to."
e-e Meaning of Heb. uncertain; Septuagint reads "the fruits."
f Septuagint reads "chariots."
g Perhaps identical with the Shallum of 2 Kings 15.10 ff.; cf. the atrocities of Shallum's rival, ibid., v. 16.
h-h Emendation yields "will I do to you, O House of Israel."
i-i Meaning, perhaps, "swiftly as the dawn"; cf. v. 7 above, "like foam upon water."
j Meaning of parts of vv. 2–7 uncertain.　　k Emendation yields "calves"; cf. 8.4–6; 13.2.

11–15: Instead of plowing correctly, Israel, the trained heifer, plows wickedness. **11:** *Ephraim . . . Judah . . . Jacob,* together, the totality of Israel. The three kinds of *plowing* suggest the initial breaking up of the ground, then plowing to cover the seed, then plowing (or "harrowing" [cf. NRSV]) to clear the ground for the next cycle. **12:** Cf. 8.7. The text is difficult, and can also be translated as: "Sow righteousness for yourselves; reap according to [divine] kindness; break up for yourselves fallow ground; for it is time to seek the Lord till He comes and teaches you righteousness" (or perhaps, "rains righteousness upon you" [cf. NRSV]). **14:** *Shalman* is probably a reference to Shalmanesser V, king of Assyria, who attacked and defeated Israel. The imagery regarding the fate of women and children is relatively common; see 2 Kings 8.12; Isa. 13.16; Nah. 3.10; Ps. 137.9; Hos. 14.1.

11.1–11: On consistent paternal love for a rebellious son. 1–4: The father-child relationship is used often in prophetic books as a metaphor for the relation between God and Israel. The child is often stubborn and rebellious and is chastised by the father, but the father nonetheless loves the child. As in the case of the husband-wife metaphor, many of today's readers may find the image of a father severely punishing his son troublesome, even if the father is presented as loving. The paternal metaphor, however, was commonly used in the ancient Near East to express the relation between ruler and ruled, sovereign and subject. It is not incongruous for prophets to mix metaphors, such as Israel as God's wife and as God's child.

3 I have pampered Ephraim,
   Taking them in My[a] arms;
   But they have ignored
   My healing care.
4 I drew them with human ties,
   With cords of love;
   But I seemed to them as one
   Who imposed a yoke on their jaws,
   Though I was offering them food.
5 No!
   They return to the land of Egypt,
   And Assyria is their king.
   Because they refuse to repent,
6 A sword shall descend upon their towns[b]
   And consume their limbs
   And devour [c][them] because of their designs.[c]
7 [d]For My people persists
   In its defection from Me;
   When it is summoned upward,
   It does not rise at all.[d]

8 How can I give you up, O Ephraim?
   How surrender you, O Israel?
   How can I make you like Admah,
   Render you like Zeboiim?[e]
   I have had a change of heart,
   All My tenderness is stirred.
9 I will not act on My wrath,
   Will not turn to destroy Ephraim.
   For I am God, not man,
   [d]The Holy One in your midst:
   I will not come in fury.[d]

10 The LORD will roar like a lion,
    And they shall march behind Him;
    When He roars, His children shall come
    Fluttering out of the west.
11 They shall flutter from Egypt like sparrows,
    From the land of Assyria like doves;
    And I will settle them in their homes
                    —declares the LORD.

8: *Admah* and *Zeboiim*, examples of cities that were utterly destroyed (see, among others, Deut. 29.22). **9:** God's change of heart and the decision not to obliterate Ephraim (cf. Jonah ch 3) are associated with the phrase "I am God, not a human being." The very same language is used to convey the opposite meaning in Num. 23.19.

a Heb. "his."
b Emendation yields "bodies," lit. "skins"; cf. Job 18.13.
c-c Emendation yields "their bones."
d-d Meaning of Heb. uncertain.
e Admah and Zeboiim were destroyed with neighboring Sodom and Gomorrah; cf. Gen. 10.19; 14.2, 8; Deut. 29.22.

12

Ephraim surrounds Me with deceit,
The House of Israel with guile.ᵃ
ᵇ⁻(But Judah stands firm with God
And is faithful to the Holy One.)⁻ᵇ

2   Ephraim tends the wind
     And pursues the gale;
     He is forever adding
     Illusion to calamity.ᶜ
     Now they make a covenant with Assyria,
     Now oil is carried to Egypt.ᵈ

3   The LORD once indicted Judah,ᵉ
     And punished Jacob for his conduct,
     Requited him for his deeds.
4   In the womb he tried to supplant his brother;
     Grown to manhood, he strove with a divine
          being,ᶠ
5   He strove with an angel and prevailed—
     The other had to weep and implore him.
     At Bethel [Jacob] would meet him,
     There to commune with him.ᵍ
6   Yet the LORD, the God of Hosts,
     Must be invoked as "LORD."ʰ
7   You must return to your God!
     Practice goodness and justice,
     And constantly trust in your God.

8   A trader who uses false balances,
     Who loves to overreach,
9   Ephraim thinks,
     "Ah, I have become rich;
     I have gotten power!
     ᵇ⁻All my gains do not amount
     To an offense which is real guilt."⁻ᵇ
10   I the LORD have been your God
     Ever since the land of Egypt.
     I will let you dwell in your tentsⁱ again
     As in the days of old,ʲ
11   When I spoke to the prophets;
     For I granted many visions,

Commentary

12.1–14.1: Further condemnation of Israel and its consequences.
12.3: Here Judah is singled out, rather than being the poetic parallel of Israel. **4–5:** See Gen. 25.26; 27.36; 32.23–33. Such recollections of ancestral traditions (see also v. 13) are relatively rare in prophetic discourse. **11:** The reference to the LORD speaking in *parables* to the prophets helps us to understand the way in which prophetic words were understood in antiquity. **13:** An allusion to Gen. ch 29, the story of Jacob's flight to Laban and his marriage to Leah and Rachel. Sections of Hosea that retell these ancestral stories are used as the haftarah for the corresponding portions of Genesis. **14:** The *prophet* is Moses, who is considered to be the greatest prophet (see, e.g., Deut. 34.10; Exod. 23.20; Num. 20.16).

---

a I.e., the deceit and guile they practice on each other (below vv. 8–9) is constantly noted by the LORD.

b-b Meaning of Heb. uncertain.   c Septuagint reads "futility."

d I.e., they foolishly depend on alliances instead of on the LORD; cf. 5.13; 7.10–11.

e Presumably the patriarch Judah. Emendation would yield "Israel"; cf. next note.

f Cf. Gen. 25.26 and 32.29.   g Heb. "us."

h I.e., one should not invoke any of the angelic hosts.

i I.e., securely; see 2 Kings 13.5.   j Lit. "fixed season."

ª⁻And spoke parables through the prophets.
12 As for Gilead, it is worthless;
And to no purpose⁻ª have they
Been sacrificing oxen in Gilgal:
The altars of these are also
Like stone heaps upon a plowed field.ᵇ

13 Then Jacob had to fleeᶜ to the land of Aram;
There Israel served for a wife,
For a wife he had to guard [sheep].
14 But when the Lord
Brought Israel up from Egypt,
It was through a prophet;ᵈ
Through a prophetᵈ they were guarded.
15ᵉ Ephraim gave bitter offense,
And his Lord cast his crimes upon him
And requited him for his mockery.

13

When Ephraim spoke piety,
He was exalted in Israel;
But he incurred guilt through Baal,ᶠ
And so he died.
2 And now they go on sinning;
They have made them molten images,
Idols, by their skill, from their silver,
Wholly the work of craftsmen.
ª⁻Yet for these they appoint men to sacrifice;⁻ª
They are wont to kiss calves!
3 Assuredly,
They shall be like morning clouds,
Like dew so early gone;
Like chaff whirled away from the threshing floor.
And like smoke from a lattice.
4 Only I the Lord have been your God
Ever since the land of Egypt;
You have never known a [true] God but Me,
You have never had a helper other than Me.
5 I looked after you in the desert,
In a thirsty land.
6 When they grazed, they were sated;
When they were sated, they grew haughty;
And so they forgot Me.
7 So I am become like a lion to them,
Like a leopard I lurk on the way;

13.2–4: As elsewhere in the Bible, the book is assuming that the calves are not alternate ways of depicting the Lord, as many northern Israelites likely believed, but represent foreign deities. **3:** *Morning clouds . . . dew,* see 6.4 n. *Chaff . . . smoke,* further images of evanescence. **7:** The image of the Lord as a *lion* is common in the prophetic books (cf. Amos 3.8). In Hosea it is clearly a double-edged image. It may point to restoration and hope (11.10–11) or horrifying punishment (5.14; 13.7–8). God is powerful to punish and to restore. A reader who understands the described punishment as a past event and sees the restoration as still standing in the future can find much solace in this imagery.

a-a Meaning of Heb. uncertain.
b I.e., the cults of Gilead and Gilgal are as worthless as that of Bethel.
c This is the punishment mentioned in 12.3.   d I.e., not through an angel.
e Meaning of 12.15–13.1 uncertain.   f I.e., Baal-peor; cf. 9.10.

8 Like a bear robbed of her young I attack them
And rip open the casing of their hearts;
ᵃI will devour them there like a lion,ᵃ
The beasts of the field shall mangle them.

9 ᵇYou are undone, O Israel!
You had no help but Me.ᵇ

10 Where now is your king?
Let him save you!
Where are the chieftains in all your towns
From whom you demanded:
"Give me a king and officers"?

11 I give you kings in my ire,
And take them away in My wrath.

12 Ephraim's guilt is bound up,
His sin is stored away.ᶜ

13 Pangs of childbirth assail him,
ᵇAnd the babe is not wise—
For this is no time to survive
At the birthstool of babes.ᵇ

14ᵈ From Sheol itself I will save them,
Redeem them from very Death.
Where, O Death, are your plagues?
Your pestilence where, O Sheol?
ᵉRevenge shall be far from My thoughts.ᵉ

15 For though he flourish among reeds,
A blast, a wind of the LORD,
Shall come blowing up from the wilderness;
His fountain shall be parched,
His spring dried up.
That [wind] shall plunder treasures,
Every lovely object.

14 Samaria must bear her guilt,
For she has defied her God.
They shall fall by the sword,
Their infants shall be dashed to death,
And their women with child ripped open.

2 Return, O Israel, to the LORD your God,
For you have fallen because of your sin.

3 Take words with you

a-a Emendation yields "There dogs shall devour them"; cf. Septuagint.
b-b Meaning of Heb. uncertain.   c I.e., for future retribution.
d This verse would read well before 14.5.
e-e Lit. "Satisfaction (for this meaning of nḥm see Deut. 32.36; Isa. 1.24) shall be hidden from My eyes."

10: The institution of human kingship is viewed negatively here, as a rejection of God's kingship, as in some of the narratives concerning the origins of the monarchy (see, e.g., 1 Sam. 10.17–19). **13:** *The babe is not wise . . . birthstool of babes,* a metaphor in which the son is partially compared to a woman in labor. The son will suffer the pains associated with childbirth. This child is so unwise that "at the right time he does not come to the birthstool," i.e., he resists birth, endangering himself and the one who gives birth and prolonging her (and here, his) pain. The birth here symbolizes the turning of the heart necessary for a new beginning. In other words, if Ephraim repents soon it will end its suffering and begin a new era of divine blessing, but Ephraim, a foolish son, does not do so. **14:** *Sheol,* the netherworld, the land of the dead. The LORD will save Israel even from Sheol, if Israel repents. **15:** *Though he flourish among reeds,* a double wordplay: Ephraim and "flourish" sound similar in Heb, but more importantly so do *reeds* or "marshes" and "brothers" (Rashi favors the first meaning, Radak, the second). *Reeds* might be an allusion to Egypt; "brothers," a reference to the place of Ephraim at the head of his brothers (the other northern tribes; cf. Gen. 48.19). *A blast, a wind,* Heb "an east wind." The east wind is a dry, scorching wind and is often associated with disaster and/or God's power (Exod. 14.21; Isa. 27.8; Jer. 18.17; cf. Gen. 41.6). If the reference to reeds is an allusion to Egypt, then this wind may be reminiscent of the east wind at the Reed Sea (Exod. 14.21; 15.8). **14.1:** Cf. 10.14. **2–9:** *Return, O Israel:* Because of the powerful call for repentance and hope it conveys and the high poetic languages it uses, 14.1–10 eventually became a "classical" text in Jewish tradition and liturgy. As mentioned in the intro., it is read on Shabbat Shuvah (the Shabbat that precedes Yom Kippur) and in the afternoon service of Tish'ah be'av (Sephardic and

And return to the LORD.
Say to Him:
ᵃ·"Forgive all guilt
And accept what is good;
Instead of bulls we will pay
[The offering of] our lips.·ᵃ

4   Assyria shall not save us,
No more will we ride on steeds;ᵇ
Nor ever again will we call
Our handiwork our god,
Since in You alone orphans find pity!"

5   I will heal their affliction,ᶜ
Generously will I take them back in love;
For My anger has turned away from them.ᵈ

6   I will be to Israel like dew;
He shall blossom like the lily,
He shall strike root like a ᵉ·Lebanon tree.·ᵉ

7   His boughs shall spread out far,
His beauty shall be like the olive tree's,
His fragrance like that of Lebanon.

8   They who sit in his shade shall be revived:
They shall bring to life new grain,
They shall blossom like the vine;
His scent shall be like the wine of Lebanon.ᶠ

9   Ephraim [shall say]:
"What more have I to do with idols?
When I respond and look to Him,
I become like a verdant cypress."
ᵃ·Your fruit is provided by Me.·ᵃ

10 He who is wise will consider these words,
He who is prudent will take note of them.
For the paths of the LORD are smooth;
The righteous can walk on them,
While sinners stumble on them.

Yemenite traditions). As in Deut. ch 30, once Israel returns, God returns to take them back. **4:** *Find pity* recalls "Lo-ruhamah" of 1.8 and its reversal in 2.3. The verse as a whole is a rejection by Israel of its past behavior, rejecting improper political alliances and foreign deities. **8:** Contrast with 9.1–2. **10:** The prophetic word should not merely be heard once, but must be carefully studied (see intro. to The Twelve).

---

a-a *Meaning of Heb. uncertain.*
b *I.e., we will no longer depend on an alliance with Egypt; cf. 2 Kings 18.24 (Isa. 36.9); Isa. 30.16.*
c *For this meaning of* meshubah *see Jer. 2.19; 3.22.*   d *Heb. "him."*
e-e *Emendation yields "poplar."*   f *Emendation yields "Helbon"; cf. Ezek. 27.18.*

יואל

Joel

THE BOOK OF JOEL is an unusual prophetic book. Although it contains readings in the form of oracles, announcements of judgment against the nations, and promises of an ideal future, it does not follow the usual structure of most prophetic books. The readers of the book of Joel are asked to imagine a terrifying plague of locusts and its horrifying impact on society and the natural environment created by the human society. Then the locusts become a mighty army sent by the LORD against Judah. As the text leads the readers to sense that human society and culture in Judah are at the brink of obliteration, it asks them to identify with a prophetic voice that calls on them to return to the LORD, to fast and lament. Then the book moves to Judah's salvation and to a range of passages dealing with the ideal future, in which the fate of the nations figures prominently.

Unlike other prophetic books (for instance, Hosea, Amos, Micah, Zechariah) the book is not set in a particular era of Israel's past. There is no temporal note in Joel 1.1 mentioning any particular king or any datable event. Although there are references to an invasion by an enemy, none is specified. The lack of references to specific events in Israel's past (locust plagues were not uncommon) and the overall imagery of the book encourage its readers to understand it against the background of Israel's past in general.

In the view of most scholars, the book of Joel dates to the Persian period (539–332 BCE), and most likely the period around 400–350. The reference to *Ionians* (Greek inhabitants from Ionia, a region in western Asia Minor, today's Turkey) in 4.6 is often mentioned among the grounds for this dating. More important, the book of Joel has an "anthological quality." In a relatively large number of cases, the book seems to be quoting, commenting on, or elaborating on other biblical, mainly prophetic, texts. This adds prestige to the human speaker of the book, who is depicted as a learned individual.

The book shows apocalyptic concerns. Some scholars think that it represents some form of transitional or hybrid work that stands between prophetic and apocalyptic texts; given its likely date of composition, this is quite possible. Certainly, the book conveys images and reassurances of "once and for all" actions of the LORD on behalf of Judah and Jerusalem, and against those who persecuted them. Moreover, it presents the message that this future is already known to those able to read the book of Joel (i.e., the scribes of Yehud) and to those to whom they may read the book (i.e., the vast majority of the people of Yehud who did not know how to read).

There are several possible ways to understand the structure of Joel. Each points to a particular but partial reading that emphasizes certain aspects of the book and de-emphasizes others. These partial readings inform each other, and all together create a much richer meaning. The following is one of these possible outlines:

1. Superscription (1.1).
2. A set of prophetic readings that concerns mostly divine judgment against Judah and its response (1.2–2.17).
3. A set of prophetic readings that concerns mostly divine forgiveness and future restoration for Judah along with judgment and calamity for its enemies (2.18–4.21).

Standard Christian translations divide the book into three chapters: 1.1–20 (as here); 2.1–32 (including the current text's 2.1–27, plus 3.1–5); and 3.1–21 (corresponding to the current text's 4.1–21). The division of biblical books into chapters dates to medieval times and originated within Christianity. The first rabbinic Bible (1517) shows the then popular division of the text of Joel in three chapters, but the second rabbinic Bible and all subsequent Hebrew Bibles, including the NJPS divide the book in four chapters.

Joel 2.15–27 is included in the haftarah for Shabbat Shuvah (the Shabbat that precedes Yom Kippur) in several Jewish traditions (e.g., Ashkenazi, Conservative) because of its theme of repentance, lamentation, divine forgiveness, and restoration. The theme is certainly appropriate for the 'Aseret Yemei Teshuvah ("Ten Days of Repentance" from Rosh Ha-Shanah to Yom Kippur). Note especially the conclusion of the reading, 2.27.

[EHUD BEN ZVI]

1 The word of the LORD that came to Joel son of Pethuel.

2   Listen to this, O elders,
        Give ear, all inhabitants of the land.
        Has the like of this happened in your days
        Or in the days of your fathers?
3   Tell your children about it,
        And let your children tell theirs,
        And their children the next generation!
4   What the cutter[a] has left, the locust has devoured;

a The Heb. terms translated "cutter, locust, grub, and hopper" are of uncertain meaning; they probably designate stages in the development of the locust.

1.1: Superscription. The superscription introduces the book and characterizes it as the LORD's word, a prophetic book. As mentioned above, Joel is not set in any particular period. Readers, beginning in ancient times, have suggested various settings. In Jewish tradition, Joel is associated with at least three different periods: (a) the days of Jehoram, the son of Ahab (b. Ta'an. 5a), (b) the time of Samuel (Joel is the son of Samuel, who eventually repented and turned into a prophet, according to Rashi and others), and (c) the time of Manasseh (*Seder Olam Rabbah*). Joel, like its inverted form Elijah, probably means "the LORD is God."

1.2–2.17: On divine judgment against Judah and its response. 1.2–3: A call to read the text. This call emphasizes the link between generations, and thus the everlasting truth and relevance of what follows. **1.4–2.17: On the plague of locusts and the corresponding communal cry (or lamentation) to the LORD. 4:** *Cutter . . . locust . . . grub . . . hopper:* There are many references to locusts in ancient Near Eastern texts. Some of these references associate the imagery of swarms of locusts with that of large invading armies or troops. The use of these four terms may

What the locust has left, the grub has devoured;
And what the grub has left, the hopper has
    devoured.
5 Wake up, you drunkards, and weep,
Wail, all you swillers of wine—
For the new wine that is ^{a-}denied you!^{-a}
6 For a nation has invaded my land,
Vast beyond counting,
With teeth like the teeth of a lion,
With the fangs of a lion's breed.
7 They have laid my vines waste
And splintered my fig trees:
They have stripped off their bark and thrown [it]
    away;
Their runners have turned white.

8 Lament—like a maiden girt with sackcloth
For the husband of her youth!
9 Offering and libation have ceased
From the House of the LORD;
The priests must mourn
Who minister to the LORD.
10 The country is ravaged,
The ground must mourn;
For the new grain is ravaged,
The new wine is dried up,
The new oil has failed.
11 Farmers are dismayed
And vine dressers wail
Over wheat and barley;
For the crops of the field are lost.
12 The vine has dried up,
The fig tree withers,
Pomegranate, palm, and apple—
All the trees of the field are sear.
And joy has dried up
Among men.

13 Gird yourselves and lament, O priests,
Wail, O ministers of the altar;
Come, spend the night in sackcloth,
O ministers of my God.
For offering and libation are withheld
From the House of your God.
14 Solemnize a fast,
Proclaim an assembly;

represent an attempt to convey a sense of completeness, rather than express a biological, detailed focus. Abravanel understands the text as metaphorical: The four kinds of locusts refer to four nations that will rule over Israel—Babylonia, Persia, Greece, and Rome. **7:** *Vines . . . fig trees:* a reversal of a traditional image of agrarian peace (cf. Mic. 4.4; Zech. 3.10). The speaker is presented as one who owns vines and fig trees. **8:** *Maiden,* Heb "betulah," means a young woman of marriageable age; here, a newly married woman. *Husband of her youth,* an emotive counterpart to the expression "wife of his youth" (cf. Prov. 1.5; Isa. 54.6; Mal. 2.14–15). The association of Judah in distress with a powerless, lamenting (young) woman is common in the Bible, and parallels exist in other ancient Near Eastern literature. Such imagery suggests, or creates an expectation for, a redemptive action by a caring (male) patron, who in this case would be the LORD. Usually such references to women point directly at or seem to suggest some negatively valued behavior on the part of the woman, here Judah, which within the world of the text justifies her present situation. The last part of the verse appears in a well-known poetic lament (qinah) recited on the 9th of Av, the traditional day of fasting and mourning for the destruction of the Temple. **9:** The text shifts from the young woman in one verse to an indirect reference to the LORD in the next, and to the (male) *priests* who are (partially) responsible for keeping an effective and positive interaction between the people and God. **12:** *Among men* (Heb "min-bnei 'adam"), "among the people." **13:** The priests and many others believed that the daily offerings were a prerequisite to divine beneficence; the plague would thus be viewed as an extreme disaster. **14:** *Fast . . . cry out:* Cf. 2.15. The actions are a typical response to an upcoming disaster (cf. Jonah 3.6–8). This verse serves in *b. Ta'an.* 12b to explain why one is not to

a-a Lit. "cut off from your mouth."

Gather the elders—all the inhabitants of the
    land—
In the House of the LORD your God,
And cry out to the LORD.

15   Alas for the day!
For the day of the LORD is near;
It shall come like havoc from Shaddai.^a

16   For food is cut off
Before our very eyes,
And joy and gladness
From the House of our God.

17   ^{b-}The seeds have shriveled
Under their clods.^{-b}
The granaries are desolate,
Barns are in ruins,
For the new grain has failed.

18   How the beasts groan!
The herds of cattle are bewildered
Because they have no pasture,
And the flocks of sheep are dazed.^c

19   To You, O LORD, I call.
For fire^d has consumed
The pastures in the wilderness,
And flame^d has devoured
All the trees of the countryside.

20   The very beasts of the field
Cry out to You;
For the watercourses are dried up,
And fire has consumed
The pastures in the wilderness.

2   Blow a horn in Zion,
Sound an alarm on My holy mount!
Let all dwellers on earth tremble,
For the day of the LORD has come!
It is close—

2   A day of darkness and gloom,
A day of densest cloud
Spread like soot over the hills.
A vast, enormous horde—
Nothing like it has ever happened,
And it shall never happen again
Through the years and ages.

work on a day of fast: because
such a day is to be treated as a day
of a solemn assembly.

1.15–20: The cry. 15: *Day of the
LORD* (cf. Isa. 13.6; Ezek. 30.2, 3;
Obad. 15; Zeph. 1.14–15, among
others), a relatively common term
in prophetic literature. It points to
a day in which the LORD dramatically alters the regular order of
things. In many places it refers to
an extraordinary day of judgment
for the wicked (e.g., Isa. 13.9), and
it is often associated with images
of darkness and cosmic upheaval
(e.g., 2.1–2; Amos 5.18–20; Zeph.
1.14–15). Here the images stress
the absence and lack of what is
necessary for life. **20:** If God is not
to pity the (sinful) people, He
should at least pity the blameless
animals (similarly Jonah 4.11).

**2.1–11: On the mighty army of
the LORD.** Military imagery is
pervasive in this section; in this
context, the army is a personification of the locusts (see Prov.
6.6–7); this is made explicit in
2.25. **1:** Cf. 1.15 and 2.15; Hos.
5.8. *Sound an alarm*, usually the
task of the guards on the wall.
2: Cf. Zeph. 1.14–15; Zech. 8.22.

---

a *Traditionally "the Almighty"; see Gen. 17.1.*   b-b *Meaning of Heb. uncertain.*
c *Meaning of Heb. uncertain.*   d *I.e., scorching heat.*

3   Their vanguard is a consuming fire,
     Their rear guard a devouring flame.
     Before them the land was like the Garden of Eden,
     Behind them, a desolate waste:
     Nothing has escaped them.

4   They have the appearance of horses,
     They gallop just like steeds.

5   With a clatter as of chariots
     They bound on the hilltops,
     With a noise like a blazing fire
     Consuming straw;
     Like an enormous horde
     Arrayed for battle.

6   Peoples tremble before them,
     All faces ªturn ashen.ª

7   They rush like warriors,
     They scale a wall like fighters.
     And each keeps to his own track.
     Their paths never cross;ᵇ

8   No one jostles another,
     Each keeps to his own course.
     ᶜAnd should they fall through a loophole,
     They do not get hurt.ᶜ

9   They rush up the wall,
     They dash about in the city;
     They climb into the houses,
     They enter like thieves
     By way of the windows.

10   Before them earth trembles,
     Heaven shakes,
     Sun and moon are darkened,
     And stars withdraw their brightness.

11   And the LORD roars aloud
     At the head of His army;
     For vast indeed is His host,
     Numberless are those that do His bidding.
     For great is the day of the LORD,
     Most terrible—who can endure it?

12   "Yet even now"—says the LORD—
     "Turn back to Me with all your hearts,
     And with fasting, weeping, and lamenting."

13   Rend your hearts
     Rather than your garments,
     And turn back to the LORD your God.
     For He is gracious and compassionate,

3: Cf. Isa. 51.3; Ezek. 36.35. **6:** Cf. Nah. 2.11.

2.12–17: On the need to turn back to the LORD, and for a communal lamentation. This must be done before the arrival of the Day of the LORD, which is near or close (1.15; 2.1), otherwise Israel too will be the victim of God's power. **13:** Cf. Exod. 34.6; Num. 14.18; Jonah 4.2; Nah. 1.3; Pss. 86.15; 103.8; 145.8; Neh. 9.17, 31; 2 Chron. 30.9. Some of these have a more complete list of God's attributes, which include intergenerational punishment. As in Jonah 4.2, this is lacking here. Also cf. m. 'Avot 2.13.

a-a Meaning of Heb. uncertain; cf. Nah. 2.11.   b Meaning of Heb. uncertain.
c-c Meaning of Heb. uncertain.

Slow to anger, abounding in kindness,
And renouncing punishment.

14 Who knows but He may turn and relent,
And leave a blessing behind
For meal offering and drink offering
To the Lord your God?[a]

15 Blow a horn in Zion,
Solemnize a fast,
Proclaim an assembly!

16 Gather the people,
Bid the congregation purify themselves.[b]
Bring together the old,
Gather the babes
And the sucklings at the breast;
Let the bridegroom come out of his chamber,
The bride from her canopied couch.

17 Between the portico and the altar,
Let the priests, the Lord's ministers, weep
And say:
"Oh, spare Your people, Lord!
Let not Your possession become a mockery,
To be taunted by nations!
Let not the peoples say,
'Where is their God?' "

18 Then the Lord was roused
On behalf of His land
And had compassion
Upon His people.

19 In response to His people
The Lord declared:
"I will grant you the new grain,
The new wine, and the new oil,
And you shall have them in abundance.
Nevermore will I let you be
A mockery among the nations.

20 I will drive the northerner[c] far from you,
I will thrust it into a parched and desolate land—
Its van to the Eastern Sea[d]
And its rear to the Western Sea;[e]
And the stench of it shall go up,
And the foul smell rise."
For [the Lord] shall work great deeds.

a When the locusts depart, there will again be yield enough for offerings; see 1.9.
b Cf. Exod. 19.10; Zeph. 1.7.
c I.e., the locusts. Emendation yields "My multitude"; cf. "nation" (1.6), "horde," "army,"
and "host" (2.2, 5, 11, and 25).   d The Dead Sea.   e The Mediterranean Sea.

14: Cf. Jonah 3.9. The verse implies uncertainty about divine response to human repentance; this idea was disturbing to many classical readers of the text, who filled it in to read "He [who] knows [that he has sins], he should return and repent" (so Targum and Rashi, but not Ibn Ezra). **15:** *Blow a horn:* The same phrase used to give the alarm of war in v. 1 is here used to call the people for a communal lamentation. The latter here, and elsewhere, includes calls to repentance and requires their repentance to be effective (cf. Jonah 3.5–10). **16:** The entire community must assemble. **17:** Cf. Ps. 79.10. Similar arguments are made in the Torah, e.g., Exod. 32.12. The emphasis is on God's concern for His image rather than Israel's guiltlessness.

2.18–4.21: Forgiveness and restoration for Judah, divine judgment against their enemies. 2.19: Cf. 1.10; Deut. 7.13; 11.14; 14.23; 33.28; Jer. 31.12; Hos. 2.10. **20:** *Parched and desolate:* The description of the land to which the *northerner* will be driven may be compared to that in Zeph. 2.13 (there "arid," Heb "parched"). The reference points on the surface to the locust, but also to a mighty invading army sent by the Lord, evoking the common imagery of a powerful and at times mythic enemy coming from the north (see, among others, Jer. 1.13–15; 4.6; Ezek. 38.6, 15; 39.2; cf. Isa. 5.26–30). The Targum reads: "I will remove the people who come from the north far from you, . . . for they have done much evil." The first portion of the quoted text points to the Targum's understanding of the "northerners" as referring to an enemy army. The second portion reflects one of the two possible understandings of the Heb text. The text does not specify the subject of the verb *work* or "do." The most likely subject is *the northerner,* in which case the Targum adds the obvious, that the northerner has done great evil, perhaps overstepped its bounds by inflicting too great a punishment (see Isa.

21 Fear not, O soil, rejoice and be glad;
    For the LORD has wrought great deeds.
22 Fear not, O beasts of the field,
    For the pastures in the wilderness
    Are clothed with grass.
    The trees have borne their fruit;
    Fig tree and vine
    Have yielded their strength.
23 O children of Zion, be glad,
    Rejoice in the LORD your God.
    For He has given you the early rain in [His]
        kindness,
    Now He makes the rain fall [as] formerly—
    The early rain and the late—
24 And threshing floors shall be piled with grain,
    And vats shall overflow with new wine and oil.

25 "I will repay you *for the years*⁻ᵃ
    Consumed by swarms and hoppers,
    By grubs and locusts,
    The great army I let loose against you.
26 And you shall eat your fill
    And praise the name of the LORD your God
    Who dealt so wondrously with you—
    My people shall be shamed no more.
27 And you shall know
    That I am in the midst of Israel:
    That I the LORD am your God
    And there is no other.
    And My people shall be shamed no more."

3 After that,
    I will pour out My spirit on all flesh;
    Your sons and daughters shall prophesy;
    Your old men shall dream dreams,
    And your young men shall see visions.
2 I will even pour out My spirit
    Upon male and female slaves in those days.

3 ᵇ⁻Before the great and terrible day of the LORD
        comes,⁻ᵇ

a-a *Emendation yields "double what was."*   b-b *Brought up from v. 4 for clarity.*

tion is based on a slight revocalization of the term for northerner and sets the verse in a different sphere. According to *b. Sukkah* 52a, the relevant section of the verse reads "but I will remove far off from you the hidden one" (i.e., instead of "northerner") and then it goes on and explains that this hidden one is "yetzer ha-ra'," that is, "the evil inclination" which is constantly hidden in the heart of humans. The verse is thus understood as stating that in an ideal future, God will drive this inclination away from humanity into a land barren and desolate. **21:** Cf. Ps. 126.3. **23:** *For He has given you the early rain in [His] kindness:* Other possibilities for the meaning of this sentence include: "For He has given you the early rain in its season"; "For He has given you the early rain for your vindication"; "For He has given you back your teacher in righteousness"; "For He has given you a teacher for righteousness"; "For He has given you a righteous teacher." The word translated "rain" ("moreh," the same as in Ps. 84.7) is usually "yoreh," and "moreh" can mean "teacher." If the word is understood as "teacher," then who is the teacher? The LORD? Furthermore, it is possible that this is another case of a main denoted meaning (probably "the early rain in its season") along with a connoted meaning ("teacher"). The Qumran community seems to have derived their conception of the teacher of righteousness, an early leader of the group, from this v. **27:** Cf. Isa. 45.5, 6, 18.

3.1–5: A glorious future for the faithful. Men and women, male and female slaves, all are included. **1:** Cf. Ezek. 39.29. Prophecy, *dreams*, and *visions* were the three recognized ways in which human beings received communications from God. God will once again reveal himself to people. **3–4:** *Before the great and terrible . . . comes*, in the Heb at the conclusion of v. 4. *Portents . . . blood . . . fire . . . pillars of smoke:* The language evokes the plagues preceding the exodus

10.5–11). But, particularly in the light of v. 21, it is possible to understand a secondary connoted meaning in this phrase, "the LORD has done great deeds," namely that God has restored the land's vegetation. This "turning point" verse in Joel carries two instances of multiple meanings conveyed by a careful choice of words or their omission at critical places in the text. A later, talmudic interpreta-

I will set portents in the sky and on earth:
Blood and fire and pillars of smoke;

4   The sun shall turn into darkness
     And the moon into blood.

⁵ But everyone who invokes the name of the LORD shall escape; for there shall be a remnant on Mount Zion and in Jerusalem, as the LORD promised. ᵃAnyone who invokes the LORD will be among the survivors.ᵃ

4 For lo! in those days
   And in that time,
   When I restore the fortunes
   Of Judah and Jerusalem,

2   I will gather all the nations
     And bring them down to the Valley of
        Jehoshaphat.ᵇ
     There I will contend with them
     Over My very own people, Israel,
     Which they scattered among the nations.
     For they divided My land among themselves

3   And cast lots over My people;
     And they bartered a boy for a whore,
     And sold a girl for wine, which they drank.

⁴ What is this you are doing to Me, O Tyre, Sidon, and all the districts of Philistia? Are you requiting Me for something I have done, or are you doing something for My benefit? Quick as a flash, I will pay you back; ⁵ for you have taken My gold and My silver, and have carried off My precious treasures to your palaces; ⁶ and you have sold the people of Judah and the people of Jerusalem to the Ionians, so that you have removed them far away from their homeland. ⁷ Behold, I will rouse them to leave the place you have sold them to, and I will pay you back: ⁸ I will deliver your sons and daughters into the hands of the people of Judah, and they will sell them into captivity to a distant nation—for the LORD has spoken.

9   Proclaim this among the nations:
     Prepare for battle!
     Arouse the warriors,
     Let all the fighters come and draw near!

10   Beat your plowsharesᶜ into swords,
     And your pruning hooks into spears.

(Exod. chs 7–11) and the presence of the LORD during the exodus (Exod. 13.21). For this reason the expression "I will set portents in the sky and on the earth; blood, fire and pillars of smoke" is included in the Passover Haggadah. **5:** For the first section of the v., cf. Obad. 17. The conclusion of the v. is often translated "and among survivors whom the LORD calls."

4.1–21: Judgment and calamity for the nations; restoration for Israel. The text reflects the motif of the enemy gathering massive forces against Jerusalem but being finally destroyed. Cf. Ezek. chs 32, 38, 39; Zech. ch 14. Towards the end, the ch presents a view of the restoration of Israel in terms of agricultural plenty and peace. **1:** Cf. Jer. 33.15; 50.4, 20. As is typical, the time period when this will transpire is not specified. **2:** Cf. Isa. 66.18; Zech. 14.2. Here and in v. 12 there is wordplay on the name of the valley, based on whether the meaning of the Heb word is "contend" or "judge" (see translators' notes *b* on p. 1173 and *b* on p. 1174). **3:** Note the relation between the two "sale prices." **6:** *Ionians:* See intro. to Joel. **8:** The nations are punished measure for measure, a typical prophetic punishment. **10:** A reversal of the well-known image of Isa. 2.4 and Mic. 4.3.

a-a *Meaning of Heb. uncertain.*

b *Here understood as "The LORD contends"; contrast v. 12.*

c *See note at Isa. 2.4.*

Let even the weakling say, "I am strong."

11 *Rouse yourselves* and come,
    All you nations;
    Come together
    From roundabout.
    There *bring down*
    Your warriors, O LORD!

12 Let the nations rouse themselves and march up
    To the Valley of Jehoshaphat;[b]
    For there I will sit in judgment
    Over all the nations roundabout.

13 Swing the sickle,
    For the crop is ripe;
    Come and tread,
    For the winepress is full,
    The vats are overflowing!
    For great is their wickedness.

14 Multitudes upon multitudes
    In the Valley of Decision!
    For the day of the LORD is at hand
    In the Valley of Decision.

15 Sun and moon are darkened,
    And stars withdraw their brightness.

16 And the LORD will roar from Zion,
    And shout aloud from Jerusalem,
    So that heaven and earth tremble.
    But the LORD will be a shelter to His people,
    A refuge to the children of Israel.

17 And you shall know that I the LORD your
          God
    Dwell in Zion, My holy mount.
    And Jerusalem shall be holy;
    Nevermore shall strangers pass through it.

18 And in that day,
    The mountains shall drip with wine,
    The hills shall flow with milk,
    And all the watercourses of Judah shall flow
          with water;
    A spring shall issue from the House of the
          LORD
    And shall water the Wadi of the Acacias.

19 Egypt shall be a desolation,
    And Edom a desolate waste,

16: See Amos 1.2. The book of Amos follows Joel in the Masoretic order of the prophetic books within the Twelve, though not in that of the Septuagint (LXX). It is possible that, among other considerations, the presence of a phrase at the ending of Joel and the beginning of Amos influenced the position of Joel in the Masoretic order of the Twelve. **17:** Cf. Ezek. 39.28 and passim; also cf. Joel 2.27. Other prophetic texts suggest that the Temple would be open to certain foreigners (Isa. 56.6–7). **18:** Cf. Amos 9.13. **19:** Edom is elsewhere condemned for joining in with the Babylonians at the destruction of the First Temple (see Obad. 10–11). There is a tradition of late antiquity and medieval Jewish interpretation that associated Edom first with the Roman empire and later with Christendom. **21:** The first section of this v. may be understood as (a) "I will avenge their blood, yet unavenged," (b) "I will avenge their blood, and I will not clear the guilty," or (c) "though I cleanse their blood(shed), I will not cleanse." The final words of the book are a fitting conclusion given the centrality of Zion, which is mentioned seven times in this short book.

---

a-a Meaning of Heb. uncertain.

b Here understood as "The LORD judges"; contrast v. 2.

> Because of the outrage to the people of
>   Judah,
> In whose land they shed the blood of the
>   innocent.

20 But Judah shall be inhabited forever,
   And Jerusalem throughout the ages.

21 Thus ᵃ⁻I will treat as innocent their blood
   Which I have not treated as innocent;⁻ᵃ
   And the LORD shall dwell in Zion.

---

a-a *Emendation yields "their unavenged blood shall be avenged."*

עמוס

Amos

THE FIRST VERSE OF THE BOOK sets the text in the days of Uzziah, king of Judah, and Jeroboam, king of Israel—from our perspective, the 8th century BCE. The book is set in the monarchic period, in a world in which the sanctuary at Bethel served as a central cultic place of the Northern Kingdom. Some scholars propose that the book of Amos was written (wholly or in the main) in the 8th century; others that it is the result of a lengthy process of redaction that spanned centuries; still others focus on the present text of Amos and date it to the postmonarchic period, since it implies the fall of the monarchy (9.11–15).

Even a cursory reading of the book shows that it deals mainly with the malady of Israel, its condemnation, and the future restoration and glory of Israel within a friendly, renewed physical world. When it condemns Israel, it repeatedly stresses social and political ills. (Contrast Hosea, which largely concerns religious ills.) As expected in a prophetic book meant to be read again and again, and meditated upon—as all prophetic books are—these social and political ills are described in relatively general terms. Thus, the critique becomes applicable to different historical and social circumstances. It is thus not surprising that a substantial number of readers in the 20th century considered either the book or the prophet it describes an inspiring source for their endeavors in social reform. For instance, Labor parties in the first decades of the State of Israel and its leaders (e.g., David Ben Gurion) considered Amos a source of inspiration. Currently, some advocates of "liberation theology" in Latin America see the book as a source of support for their theological and social positions.

The book also makes an unequivocal but somewhat implicit claim about the absolute primacy of Jerusalem/Zion, linked to a strong condemnation of the sanctuary of Bethel. The theme of repentance is important in the book, and so is the distinctive relation between the LORD and Israel along with its limitations; for example, not only that the LORD executes judgment against Israel like all other nations (2.6–3.2), but also explicitly states, "To Me, O Israelites, you are just like the Ethiopians" (9.7) and yet says "You [Israel] alone have I singled out of all the families of the earth" (3.2). The book also restates the common prophetic position about the primacy of morality over sacrifices.

The basic structure of the book is unambiguous. It includes a superscription or title that serves as an introduction (1.1), a clear motto that communicates one of the most significant messages of the book (1.2), and a series of prophetic readings of which the last two encapsulate much of the book: The LORD announces a severe, future punishment for the condemned nation, then an ideal and plentiful future to follow the deserved punishment (9.7–15). The series of prophetic readings begins with announcements of judgment against the nations, including Judah and Israel (1.3–2.16) and continues with reports of prophetic speeches and visions of the fate of Israel, along with a biographical vignette in 7.10–17.

Amos 2.6–3.8 is read as the haftarah for the parashah of Va-yeshev (Gen. 37.1–40.23), and in the Ashkenazi tradition 9.7–15 as the haftarah for the parashah of ʾAḥarei Mot (Lev. 16.1–18.30).

[EHUD BEN ZVI]

1 The words of Amos, a sheepbreeder from Tekoa, who prophesied concerning Israel in the reigns of Kings Uzziah of Judah and Jeroboam son of Joash of Israel, two years before the earthquake.[a]

2 He proclaimed:

> The LORD roars from Zion,
> Shouts aloud from Jerusalem;
> And the pastures of the shepherds shall languish,
> And the summit of Carmel shall wither.

3   Thus said the LORD:
> For three transgressions of Damascus,
> For four, I will not revoke it:[b]
> Because they threshed Gilead
> With threshing boards of iron.

a See Zech. 14.5.   b I.e., the decree of punishment.

1.1: Superscription. The superscription introduces the book and characterizes it as a prophetic book. It associates the book with *Amos*, sets its world in the monarchic period, specifically in the days of Uzziah and Jeroboam of the 8th century BCE, and provides additional information about Amos. The v. tells the readers that Amos was a herdsman, a sheep and cattle breeder (see also 7.14). As such, Amos was a relatively wealthy man (cf. Mesha, 2 Kings 3.4). He was not a poor shepherd, as is at times erroneously claimed. He was from Tekoa, a Judahite town about 8 km (5 mi) south of Bethlehem. He *prophesied concerning Israel*: The meaning is ambiguous; it certainly

points to the Northern Kingdom to the exclusion of Judah, but particularly from the perspective of a postmonarchic readership, it points to "the LORD's people" (e.g., 9.14) who stand in a covenantal relationship with the LORD, and as such to both the former kingdoms, northern and southern, as well as to the much later intended readership of the book. The temporal reference is *two years before the earthquake* (cf. Zech. 14.5) enhances the verisimilitude, that is, the quality of appearing to be true or real, of the temporal frame and the reliability of the authorial voice in the book, since the imagery in 9.1–6 may be understood as earthquake imagery. Further, since earth-

quakes were seen as acts of God, it suggests an additional divine validation of the message of the book.

1.2: Motto and theophany. The book is unique in opening with a motto, a short, general thematic statement that is meant to (re)focus how the book should be understood. Its general imagery follows that of many theophanic reports. It is common in these reports to depict a manifestation of the deity's power as leading to an upheaval in the natural world. Further, the LORD is likened to a lion (cf. Hos. 5.14; 11.10; 13.7), a relatively common motif in the ancient Near East. But one detail in the text is of utmost importance: The lion *roars from Zion.* The Jerusalem-centric message is abundantly clear, and the book presents itself as a work that conveys the message of that roaring lion from Zion, namely Jerusalem. *Carmel* is a fertile, mountainous area in the Northern Kingdom (southeast of modern Haifa), but the Heb word "carmel" refers also to farmland (cf. Isa. 32.15) or an orchard (and particularly to a vineyard). The general character of *the pastures of the shepherd* supports and plays on the broader meaning. The geographical reference is not meant to restrict the horizon of the text to particular region of the Northern Kingdom.

1.3–2.16: Reports of announcements of judgment against the nations. The unit is kept together not only by its unifying theme, but

4   I will send down[a] fire upon the palace of Hazael,
    And it shall devour the fortresses of Ben-hadad.[b]

5   I will break the gate bars of Damascus,
    And wipe out the inhabitants from the Vale of
        Aven
    And the sceptered ruler of Beth-eden;
    And the people of Aram shall be exiled to Kir
                —said the LORD.

6   Thus said the LORD:
    For three transgressions of Gaza,
    For four, I will not revoke it:
    Because they exiled[c] an entire population,
    Which they delivered to Edom.[d]

a Cf. Lam. 1.13.   b Cf. 2 Kings 13.22–25.
c I.e., they cooperated in the annexation of Israelite territory; cf. Jer. 13.19 with note.
d Emendation yields "Aram"; cf. Isa. 9.11.

also by a careful balance between repetition and differentiation among the different subunits. Nations other than Israel and Judah are condemned for transgressions against other nations; Judah for the rejection of God's teaching and Israel for actions against God's teaching. (The nations mentioned here are neighbors of Israel/Judah. Assyria, for instance, is not mentioned.) Rhetorically, the readers are sucked into this passage, eagerly anticipating the punishment of their neighbors, until the prophecy is turned against them as well. While Judah and Israel are condemned for covenant infractions, their neighbors are condemned for violating basic norms of decency. **1.3:** The "it" in *I will not revoke it* is anticipatory, i.e., it points to the following decree of punishment. **4–5:** *Hazael* and *Benhadad* are the names of two kings of Aram Damascus (see 2 Kings 8.7–15; 13.22–25). The territory of the kingdom of Aram Damascus (or simply Aram, as often in the Bible) partially overlaps that of Syria today. *Vale of Aven* and *Betheden:* Although Beth-eden points to an area near the Euphrates River, the wordplay is clear; the first name means "valley of disaster, nothingness" (or valley of delusion; cf. 5.5), the second "house of bliss." Within the book of Amos, *Kir* is the place of origin for the Arameans (see 9.7). Its whereabouts are unknown, but 2 Kings 16.9 reports that the Assyrians deported the Arameans to Kir, after they put an end to the kingdom of Aram. **6:** *Gaza* here represents all the Philistine cities. Three others are men-

Places mentioned in the oracles against the nations

7   I will send down fire upon the wall of Gaza,
     And it shall devour its fortresses;
8   And I will wipe out the inhabitants of Ashdod
     And the sceptered ruler of Ashkelon;
     And I will turn My hand against Ekron,
     And the Philistines shall perish to the last man
                         —said the Lord GOD.

9   Thus said the LORD:
     For three transgressions of Tyre,
     For four, I will not revoke it:
     Because they handed over
     An entire population to Edom,ᵃ
     Ignoring the covenant of brotherhood.ᵇ
10   I will send down fire upon the wall of Tyre,
     And it shall devour its fortresses.

11   Thus said the LORD:
     For three transgressions of Edom,
     For four, I will not revoke it:
     Because he pursued his brother with the sword
     And repressed all pity,
     Because his anger raged unceasing
     And his fury stormedᶜ unchecked.
12   I will send down fire upon Teman,
     And it shall devour the fortresses of Bozrah.

13   Thus said the LORD:
     For three transgressions of the Ammonites,
     For four, I will not revoke it:
     Because they ripped open the pregnant women of
         Gilead
     In order to enlarge their own territory.
14   I will set fire to the wall of Rabbah,
     And it shall devour its fortresses,
     Amid shouting on a day of battle,
     On a day of violent tempest.
15   Their king and his officers shall go
     Into exile together   —said the LORD.

2 Thus said the LORD:
     For three transgressions of Moab,
     For four, I will not revoke it:
     Because he burned the bones
     Of the king of Edom to lime.

tioned by name, *Ashdod, Ashkelon,* and *Ekron.* The same four cities are mentioned in the same order in Zeph. 2.4. **9:** *Tyre,* situated in Lebanon of today, along with Sidon, two of the most important Phoenician cities for many centuries. **11:** Cf. Obad. 10–14. Edom was situated in the area south of the Dead Sea. The last lines of the v. translated, "and destroyed his womenfolk, because his anger raged unceasing and he kept his wrath forever." **12:** *Teman* and *Bozrah* are elsewhere situated in Edomite territory (cf. Isa. 34.6; 63.1; Jer. 49.7; Obad. 9). **13–14:** *Gilead* was a region north of Ammon. It was a disputed area that changed hands several times in the monarchic period. From the perspective of the Bible it was Israelite territory, though not always under Israelite control. *Rabbah,* the capital of Ammon, is situated within the area of today's Amman. On the imagery, cf. 2 Kings 8.12; Isa. 13.16; Hos. 10.14; 14.1; Nah. 3.10; Ps. 137.9. **2.1–2:** The kingdom of *Moab* was east of the Dead Sea, within the territory of present-day Jordan. Ruth, for instance, was a Moabite woman (see book of Ruth).

a *Emendation yields "Aram."*   b *Cf. 1 Kings 5.26; 9.12–13.*
c *Cf. Akkadian* shamaru *and Jer. 3.5.*

2   I will send down fire upon Moab,
And it shall devour the fortresses of Kerioth.
And Moab shall die in tumult,
Amid shouting and the blare of horns;

3   I will wipe out the ruler from within her
And slay all her officials along with him
                    —said the LORD.

4   Thus said the LORD:
For three transgressions of Judah,
For four, I will not revoke it:
Because they have spurned the Teaching of the
    LORD
And have not observed His laws;
They are beguiled by the delusions
After which their fathers walked.

5   I will send down fire upon Judah,
And it shall devour the fortresses of Jerusalem.

6   Thus said the LORD:
For three transgressions of Israel,
For four, I will not revoke it:
Because they have sold for silver
Those whose cause was just,
And the needy for a pair of sandals.

7   [Ah,] you ᵃ who trample the heads of the poor
Into the dust of the ground,
And make the humble walk a twisted course!ᐧᵃ
Father and son go to the same girl,
And thereby profane My holy name.

8   They recline by every altar
On garments taken in pledge,
And drink in the House of their God
Wine bought with fines they imposed.

9   Yet I
Destroyed the Amorite before them,
Whose stature was like the cedar's
And who was stout as the oak,
Destroying his boughs above
And his trunk below!

10   And I
Brought you up from the land of Egypt
And led you through the wilderness forty years,
To possess the land of the Amorite!

11   And I raised up prophets from among your sons

a-a *Understanding* sho'afim *as equivalent to* shafim. *Emendation yields: "Who crush on the ground / The heads of the poor, / And push off the road / The humble of the land"; cf. Job 24.4.*

4: Many Jewish readers understood *the Teaching* [Heb "torah"] *of the* LORD as a reference to the Torah (see Hos. 4.6 n.). The same holds true for, among others, Hos. 8.1, 12. For the pair "teaching" (Torah, "torah") and "decrees" or "statutes" ("ḥukim") see, for instance, Deut. 17.19; Isa. 24.5; Mal. 3.22; Ezra 7.10; Neh. 9.13; 2 Chron. 19.10; 33.8; and cf. Exod. 18.16, 20; Lev. 26.46; Deut. 4.8. **6–16:** Who is Israel here? Does Israel mean only the Northern Kingdom? On the surface, the answer seems positive; for Israel is set as a nation other than Judah, see vv. 5–6. V. 10, however, which refers to the exodus, suggests a broad understanding of Israel. The text plays with the ambiguity of the term Israel and allows and even encourages the readership of the book—which lives in the post-monarchic period (that is, the Jews, the "remnant of Judah")— to identify with the Israel of the book; they are their ancestors and their fate is important to them. The main transgressions are of a social nature and involve the oppression of the powerless. Sexual and cultic behaviors are also explicitly mentioned. **6:** This begins the haftarah (prophetic reading) for the Torah portion concerned with the sale of Joseph, most likely reflecting an interpretive tradition that Joseph was the *just* person sold *for* [the price of] *a pair of sandals.* **8:** *On garments taken in pledge,* cf. Deut. 4.17; Job 22.6; 24.3–4, 9 and contrast this element and the entire description of the sinners here with the one of the pious son in Ezek. 18.15–17. **9–11:** The summary of the LORD's dealings with Israel is meant to contrast the faithfulness of the patron of Israel (i.e., the LORD) with the long history of unfaithfulness of the patron's client (i.e., Israel). The readers of the book know that such a pattern of behavior calls for the punishment of the client (Israel) and provides just grounds for punishment of the latter. But is the LORD going to revoke the status of Israel? The answer of the book of Amos is a clear no.

And nazirites from among your young men.
Is that not so, O people of Israel?
                                        —says the LORD.

12   But you made the nazirites drink wine
      And ordered the prophets not to prophesy.

13   a-Ah, I will slow your movements
      As a wagon is slowed
      When it is full of cut grain.-a

14   Flight shall fail the swift,
      The strong shall find no strength,
      And the warrior shall not save his life.

15   The bowman shall not hold his ground,
      And the fleet-footed shall not escape,
      Nor the horseman save his life.

16   Even the most stouthearted warrior
      Shall run away unarmed b that day
                                        —declares the LORD.

3   Hear this word, O people of Israel,
         That the LORD has spoken concerning you,
         Concerning the whole family that I brought up
               from the land of Egypt:

2   You alone have I singled out
         Of all the families of the earth—
         That is why I will call you to account
         For all your iniquities.

3   Can two walk together
         Without having met?

---

a-a *Meaning of verse uncertain; alternatively: "I will slow your movements / As a thresh-*
ing sledge (cf. Isa. 28.27–28) is slowed / When clogged by cut grain."
b *Lit. "naked."*

12: *Nazirites drink wine:* The
Nazirite vow forbade the consumption of wine or any derivation of grapes (Num. 6.3; Judg.
13.7). **14–16:** The description of the
warrior men points at an upside-
down order caused by divine intervention. It parallels the one
caused by human intervention
(i.e., prophets who do not talk,
Nazirites who drink). The term
translated as *unarmed* means lit.
"naked" (see translators' note *b*).

**3.1–6.14 Three readings about
judgment.** The readers are presented with a set of three units,
each beginning with the phrase

Hear this word. Thus the phrase
serves also to mark the book into
subunits, just as the phrase ending
the previous chapter, *declares the
LORD,* typically expresses the end
of a subunit. Each of these units
shows internal subdivisions that
are marked at times by the repetition of another phrase, such as
"Assuredly" (or "therefore") units
(5.13, 16) and "Ah" (or "Woe")
units (see 5.18; 6.1). In ancient
times there were no paragraph
markers, but the repetition of an
important word, particularly at the
beginning of a section, served approximately the same purpose. But
ancient writers and readers often

weakened the boundaries between
literary subunits. For instance,
they created links that cut across
different units within the book
(e.g., there is a fourth "Hear" unit
in 8.4–14, which is linked to the
surrounding text in the book and
to these three units at the same
time). Moreover, particularly in
prophetic books, texts were written to allow multiple ways of subdividing them. In these cases, each
of these different subdividings
points to a particular, but partial
reading. These partial readings inform each other, and all together
create a meaning much richer than
any of them separately. In the
world of the book, people are supposed to hear "this word," but in
the actual world the readers of the
book are asked to read and study
"this word" and to read it to those
who cannot read by themselves.
Each of these units (3.1–15; 4.1–13;
5.1–6.14) deals with judgment (see
below), and each of them is presented as a reliable report of "this
word," that is, of a "prophetic
word" (Heb "davar") from the
monarchic past. But they do not
repeat themselves. Far from it,
each of them addresses the matter
in a different way, and all together
provide the reader with a multifaceted image of Israel and of its impending judgment.

**3.1–15: First report of a prophetic
word in the monarchic period
announcing judgment against
Israel. 1:** *The whole family:* This inclusive reference to Israel allows
and encourages the identification
of the readership with Israel,
though, as expected, vv. 9, 12 point
to Israel as the Northern Kingdom.
The text shifts its references to the
LORD from the third to the first
person, and accordingly human
and divine speech become interwoven and their respective limits
blurred. This is common in prophetic books. **2:** The LORD states
that this unique relationship carries obligations, and punishment
will result if the obligations are not
fulfilled (see 1.9–11 n.). **3–8:** A series of rhetorical questions, invoking cause-and-effect situations,

4   Does a lion roar in the forest
     When he has no prey?
     Does a great beast let out a cry from its den
     Without having made a capture?
5   Does a bird drop on the ground—in a trap—
     With no snare there?
     Does a trap spring up from the ground
     Unless it has caught something?
6   When a ram's horn is sounded in a town,
     Do the people not take alarm?
     Can misfortune come to a town
     If the LORD has not caused it?
7   Indeed, my Lord GOD does nothing
     Without having revealed His purpose
     To His servants the prophets.
8   A lion has roared,
     Who can but fear?
     My Lord GOD has spoken,
     Who can but prophesy?
9   Proclaim in the fortresses of Ashdod[a]
     And in the fortresses of the land of Egypt!
     Say:
     Gather on the hill[b] of Samaria
     And witness the great outrages within her
     And the oppression in her midst.
10   They are incapable of doing right
                           —declares the LORD;
     They store up lawlessness and rapine
     In their fortresses.
11   Assuredly,
     Thus said my Lord GOD:
     An enemy, all about the land!
     He shall strip you of your splendor,
     And your fortresses shall be plundered.
12   Thus said the LORD:
     As a shepherd rescues from the lion's jaws
     Two shank bones or the tip of an ear,
     So shall the Israelites escape
     Who dwell in Samaria—
     With the leg[c] of a bed or the head[c] of a couch.

13   Hear [this], and warn the House of Jacob
     —says my Lord GOD, the God of Hosts—
14   That when I punish Israel for its transgressions,
     I will wreak judgment on the altar[d] of Bethel,

serves didactic purposes. The questions lead up to the implicit question: How is it that the prophet warns of the impending doom to be caused by God, but the people do not pay any attention? **12:** The lion imagery emerges again (cf. 1.2; 3.4, 8), this time with sarcasm. Just as two bones or the tip of an ear are useless remnants of an attack, so the small material remains of the Northern Kingdom will be useless, serving only as tokens and reminders of what had been before. Yet, following a theme that would be developed later in this book, and is developed in other prophetic books, there would be some kind of remnant. **14:** *Bethel*, a city and one of the main centers of worship in the Northern Kingdom. It plays an important role in the book of Amos; see 4.4; 5.5; 7.10, and is important in numerous biblical traditions (e.g., Gen. 12.8; Judg. 21.2; 1 Kings 12.29; Hos. 10.15; 12.5).

a Septuagint reads "Assyria."   b Heb. plural; but cf. 4.1; 6.1.
c Meaning of Heb. uncertain.   d Heb. plural, but cf. "altar" in next line.

And the horns of the altar shall be cut off
And shall fall to the ground.

15 I will wreck the winter palace
Together with the summer palace;
The ivory palaces shall be demolished,
And the great houses shall be destroyed
————declares the LORD.

4 Hear this word, you cows of Bashan
On the hill of Samaria—
Who defraud the poor,
Who rob the needy;
Who say to your[a] husbands,
"Bring, and let's carouse!"

2 My Lord GOD swears by His holiness:
Behold, days are coming upon you
[b-]When you will be carried off in baskets,
And, to the last one, in fish baskets,

3 And taken out [of the city]—
Each one through a breach straight ahead—
And flung on the refuse heap[-b]
————declares the LORD.

4 Come to Bethel and transgress;
To Gilgal, and transgress even more:
Present your sacrifices the next morning
And your tithes on the third day;

5 And burn a thank offering of leavened bread;[c]
And proclaim freewill offerings loudly.
For you love that sort of thing, O Israelites
————declares my Lord GOD.

6 I, on My part, have given you
Cleanness of teeth in all your towns,
And lack of food in all your settlements.
Yet you did not turn back to Me
————declares the LORD.

7 I therefore withheld the rain from you
Three months before harvesttime:
I would make it rain on one town
And not on another;
One field would be rained upon
While another on which it did not rain
Would wither.

8 So two or three towns would wander
To a single town to drink water,
But their thirst would not be slaked.

15: *Winter palace . . . summer palace,* perhaps a reference to the wealthy who can afford two houses, but also a merism, i.e., a reference to extremes (e.g., "young and old") to convey totality ("all your houses"). *Ivory palaces,* ornamented with, not made of, ivory. Since ivory was costly, this is an extravagantly luxurious house. Pieces of well-crafted ivory inlay have been excavated from Samaria.

4.1–13: Second report of a prophetic word in the monarchic period announcing judgment against Israel. Israel is here given many warnings and chances; the phrase *Yet you did not turn back to Me—declares the LORD* repeats as a litany, justifying the punishment of Israel, but also emphasizing that repenting or returning is efficacious. **1:** *Cows of Bashan,* "well-fed, plump cows," in this context, elite women. According to the text these women oppressed the poor and encouraged their husbands to do so for their benefit. Although today it is clearly offensive to call a woman "a plump cow," it is uncertain if this was the case at the time of the composition of the book. **2–3:** The precise meaning of the verses is uncertain, but they surely point to deportation. The identity of the enemy that will exile the people is not mentioned, nor is it anywhere in the book, though exile is announced repeatedly (e.g., 5.5, 27; 6.7; 7.11, 17; cf. 9.4). **4–5:** The sarcasm is striking. **4:** *Gilgal,* a main center of worship in the Northern Kingdom (cf. Josh. 4.20–22; Hos. 4.15; 9.15; 12.2). **6:** *Cleanness of teeth,* a euphemism for famine. Since there will be nothing to eat, the teeth will be

---

a Heb. "their."   b-b Meaning of Heb. uncertain.
c Cf. Lev. 7.12–14; where, however, the bread is not to be burned.

Yet you did not turn back to Me
        —declares the LORD.

9 I scourged you with blight and mildew;
Repeatedly[a] your gardens and vineyards,
Your fig trees and olive trees
Were devoured by locusts.
Yet you did not turn back to Me
        —declares the LORD.

10 I sent against you pestilence
In the manner of Egypt;[b]
I slew your young men with the sword,
Together with your captured horses,
And I made the stench of your armies
Rise in your very nostrils.
Yet you did not turn back to Me
        —declares the LORD.

11 I have wrought destruction among you
As when God destroyed Sodom and Gomorrah;
You have become like a brand plucked from
    burning.
Yet you have not turned back to Me
        —declares the LORD.

12 Assuredly,
[c]Because I am doing that to you,[c]
Even so will I act toward you, O Israel—
Prepare to meet your God, O Israel!

13 Behold,
He who formed the mountains,
And created the wind,
And has told man what His wish[a] is,
Who turns blackness[d] into daybreak,
And treads upon the high places of the earth—
His name is the LORD, the God of Hosts.

5 Hear this word which I intone
As a dirge over you, O House of Israel:
2 Fallen, not to rise again,
Is Maiden Israel;
Abandoned on her soil
With none to lift her up.
3 For thus said my Lord GOD
About the House of Israel:

very clean. **10:** *In the manner of Egypt*, an allusion to the plagues (Exod. chs 7–12). **11–12:** The list of ever-increasing calamities seems to reach its peak with the reference to *Sodom and Gomorrah*, which were traditional, conventional examples of cities destroyed because of immorality, but there is even more. V. 12 may be translated, "Therefore, thus I am about to do to you (sing.), O Israel: because this is what I will do to you—Prepare to meet your God, O Israel." The exact punishment, narrated to Israel in the second-person singular, in contrast to the previous second-person plurals, is meant to increase its affective appeal, though the exact punishment is left to the reader's imagination.

5.1–6.14: Third report of a prophetic word in the monarchic period announcing judgment against Israel. This section concludes with two expanded "Ah" (or "Woe") units (see 5.18–27; 6.1–14). **1–2:** Amos uses the funeral qinah or dirge (used to lament the death of individuals) metaphorically to show that the nation is "dead." **3:** Again, the idea of a remnant (see 3.12 n.).

---

a Meaning of Heb. uncertain.
b Alluding to the plagues at the time of the Exodus.
c-c Emendation yields "Because you are acting thus toward Me."
d Cf. Joel 2.2. Emendation yields "darkness"; cf. 5.8.

The town that marches out a thousand strong
Shall have a hundred left,
And the one that marches out a hundred strong
Shall have but ten left.

4 Thus said the LORD
To the House of Israel:
Seek Me, and you will live.

5 Do not seek Bethel,
Nor go to Gilgal,
Nor cross over^a to Beer-sheba;
For Gilgal shall go into exile,
And Bethel shall become a delusion.

6 Seek the LORD, and you will live,
^{b-}Else He will rush like fire upon^{-b} the House of
      Joseph
And consume Bethel^c with none to quench it.

7 [Ah,] you who turn justice into wormwood
And hurl righteousness to the ground!
[Seek the LORD,]

8 Who made the Pleiades and Orion,
Who turns deep darkness into dawn
And darkens day into night,
Who summons the waters of the sea
And pours them out upon the earth—
His name is the LORD!

9 ^{b-}It is He who hurls destruction upon strongholds,
So that ruin comes upon fortresses!^{-b}

10 They hate the arbiter in the gate,
And detest him whose plea is just.

11 Assuredly,
Because you ^{b-}impose a tax^{-b} on the poor
And exact from him a levy of grain,
You have built houses of hewn stone,
But you shall not live in them;
You have planted delightful vineyards,
But shall not drink their wine.

12 For I have noted how many are your crimes,
And how countless your sins—
You enemies of the righteous,
You takers of bribes,
You who subvert in the gate
The cause of the needy!

4–6: The emphasis must be on seeking God, which cannot be accomplished by seeking out the traditional sites where He is worshipped. **5:** The Heb is punning: *For Gilgal shall go into exile* ("galoh yigleh"). **6:** *House of Joseph,* the Northern Kingdom. **7:** *Wormwood,* an aromatic plant that yields a bitter extract and tastes bitter (cf. Deut. 29.7; Jer. 9.14; 23.15; Prov. 5.4; Lam. 3.15, 19). Justice is supposed to be sweet, but they turn it bitter and by doing so they embitter the life of the poor; cf. 6.12. **8:** Allusions to creation are often invoked to show God's power. **11:** The image of building houses and establishing vines but being denied the ability to enjoy them points to the futility of human activities in the face of divine judgment (cf. Deut. 28.39; Mic. 6.15; Zeph. 1.13). Later (9.4) the image is turned around to exemplify the bliss that results from human activity under divine blessing. **12:** *In the gate,* where justice was dispensed (cf. Deut. 16.18; 17.8; Zech. 8.10, among others). Again, the infractions are ethical rather than cultic.

a I.e., into Judah; cf. 1 Kings 19.3.
b-b Meaning of Heb. uncertain.
c Septuagint reads "the House of Israel."

13 Assuredly,
    At such a time the prudent man keeps silent,
    For it is an evil time.

14 Seek good and not evil,
    That you may live,
    And that the Lord, the God of Hosts,
    May truly be with you,
    As you think.
15 Hate evil and love good,
    And establish justice in the gate;
    Perhaps the Lord, the God of Hosts,
    Will be gracious to the remnant of Joseph.

16 Assuredly,
    Thus said the Lord,
    My Lord, the God of Hosts:
    In every square there shall be lamenting,
    In every street cries of "Ah, woe!"
    And the farm hand shall be
    Called to mourn,
    And those skilled in wailing
    To lament;
17 For there shall be lamenting
    In every vineyard, too,
    When I pass through your midst
                              —said the Lord.

18 Ah, you who wish
    For the day of the Lord!
    Why should you want
    The day of the Lord?
    It shall be darkness, not light!—
19 As if a man should run from a lion
    And be attacked by a bear;
    Or if he got indoors,
    Should lean his hand on the wall
    And be bitten by a snake!
20 Surely the day of the Lord shall be
    Not light, but darkness,
    Blackest night without a glimmer.

21 I loathe, I spurn your festivals,
    I am not appeased by your solemn assemblies.
22 If you offer Me burnt offerings—or your meal
        offerings—
    I will not accept them;
    I will pay no heed

14–15: This picks up on the theme of seeking, developed in vv. 4–6. The emphasis on ethical behavior here and in similar verses (e.g., Mic. 6.8) contributed much to an understanding of the prophets as bearers of ethical monotheism. These vv. are much cherished for this reason in modern liberal streams in Judaism. Within its ancient context, the v. claims that a sharp turn toward ethical behavior may influence God to revoke the divine decree against Israel. Still, whereas repentance is necessary for the annulment of the decree, the book claims that repentance by itself is not sufficient. God decides whether to revoke or not. On this understanding of ethical monotheism, see also 5.21–25. **18–20:** On *the day of the Lord* here and elsewhere see Joel 1.15 n. As the context suggests, the popular understanding of this Day was a day in which Israel would be saved through God's great power, while the prophetic suggestion is that God will use His power against His enemies, here Israel. If this v. is authentic to the prophet Amos, it is the earliest reference to the Day of the Lord. **21–25:** The text does not state that sacrifices—or any other cultic rituals—are wrong per se, but rather that those brought by people who behave in a manner offensive to God are unacceptable to God. From the perspective of the intended readers of the book, the time in the wilderness is comparable to the time between the destruction of the First and the building of the Second Temple, since there was no Temple at either time.

To your gifts of fatlings.
23   Spare Me the sound of your hymns,
      And let Me not hear the music of your lutes.
24   But let justice well up like water,
      Righteousness like an unfailing stream.
25   Did you offer sacrifice and oblation to Me
      Those forty years in the wilderness,
      O House of Israel?

26a   And you shall carry off your "king"—
      Sikkuth[b] and Kiyyun,[b]
      The images you have made for yourselves
      Of your astral deity—
27   As I drive you into exile beyond Damascus
                  —Said the Lord,
          whose name is God of Hosts.[c]

6   Ah, you who are at ease in Zion[d]
      And confident on the hill of Samaria,
      You notables of the leading nation
      On whom the House of Israel [e]pin their hopes:[e]
2   Cross over to Calneh and see,
      Go from there to Great Hamath,
      And go down to Gath of the Philistines:
      Are [you] better than those kingdoms,
      [f]Or is their territory larger than yours?[f]
3   [g]Yet you ward off [the thought of] a day of woe
      And convene a session of lawlessness.[g]
4   They lie on ivory beds,
      Lolling on their couches,
      Feasting on lambs from the flock
      And on calves from the stalls.
5   [g]They hum snatches of song
      To the tune of the lute—
      They account themselves musicians[g] like David.
6   They drink [straight] from the wine bowls
      And anoint themselves with the choicest oils—
      But they are not concerned about the ruin of
          Joseph.
7   Assuredly, right soon

25: This contradicts the Priestly tradition reflected in the Torah, which suggests that offerings were a crucial part of the wilderness experience. **26:** The passage has a strong satiric tone. Their *"king"*— *Shikutz,* is a Mesopotamian, astral deity. *Kiyyun* refers to Saturn, *your astral deity.* The god Sikkuth is mentioned here because of the aural pun created by his name and "shikutz" (detestable things). The people are satirically depicted carrying their images as in a (ritual) procession, but they walk into exile! **6.2:** *Calneh . . . Great Hamath . . . Gath,* cities and territories that were conquered by the Assyrians. The author or authors and the intended readers of the book were either unaware or thought it irrelevant that these cities and territories were actually conquered years after the period in which the book is set (see 1.1). **5:** The tradition of David as the archetypal musician is reflected in later Jewish tradition, which attributes the entire book of Psalms to him.

---

a *Vv. 26–27 would read well after 6.14.*
b *Two Akkadian names applied to Saturn, here deliberately pointed with the vowels of Heb.*
shiqquṣ, *"detestable thing."*
c *I.e., who is Lord of all the astral bodies.*
d *Emendation yields "Joseph," cf. v. 6, and 5.6, 15, where "Joseph" denotes the northern*
kingdom.   e-e *Taking ba' l- as synonymous with ba' 'ad; see Isa. 45.24 and note b-b.*
f-f *Emendation yields "Or is your territory larger than theirs?"*
g-g *Meaning of Heb. uncertain.*

They shall head the column of exiles;
They shall loll no more at festive meals.

8   My Lord GOD swears by Himself:
       I loathe ᵃthe Pride of Jacob,⁻ᵃ
       And I detest his fortresses.
       I will declare forfeit city and inhabitants alike
                —declares the LORD, the God of Hosts.
⁹If ten people are left in one house, they shall die.
¹⁰ᵇ⁻And if someone's kinsman—who is to burn incense for
him—comes to carry the remains out of a house,⁻ᵇ and he
calls to the one at the rear of the house, "Are there any
alive besides you?" he will answer, "No, none." And he
will say, "Hush!"—so that no one may utter the name of
the LORD.
¹¹   For the LORD will command,
       And the great house shall be smashed to bits,
       And the little house to splinters.

12   Can horses gallop on a rock?
       ᶜCan it be plowed with oxen?⁻ᶜ
       Yet you have turned justice into poison weed
       And the fruit of righteousness to wormwood.
13   [Ah,] those who are so happy about Lo-dabar,ᵈ
       Who exult, "By our might
       We have captured Karnaim"!ᵈ
14   But I, O House of Israel,
       Will raise up a nation against you
                —declares the LORD, the God of Hosts—
       Who will harass you from Lebo-Hamath
       To the Wadi Arabah.

7 This is what my Lord GOD showed me: He was creating [a plague of] locusts at the time when the late-
sown crops were beginning to sprout—ᵉthe late-sown
crops after the king's reaping.⁻ᵉ ²When it had finished devouring the herbage in the land, I said, "O Lord GOD, pray
forgive. How will Jacob survive? He is so small." ³The
LORD relented concerning this. "It shall not come to pass,"
said the LORD.

8: The reference to *the Pride of Jacob* points to the arrogance of the people. It also ridicules one of the most positive self-descriptions of Israel (see Ps. 47.5). Note the strong contrast between the text there and this v. Ironically, in 8.7, God swears by this pride which He here condemns. **13:** The reference to *Lo-dabar* points to a city east of the Jordan (and so does *Karnaim*). At the same time, it conveys a pun on the basic meaning of "lo-davar," that is, "not a thing," nothing. Similarly, Karnaim suggests to the readers a pun on "keren," horn, a symbol of strength. Wordplays are common in prophetic books.

7.1–9: Three reports of prophetic visions of judgment. These are the first three of five reports about prophetic visions (7.1–3; 4–6, 7–9; 8.1–3; 9.1–6). The series leads up to the vision of the destruction in 9.1–6. In the first two of the present three cases, the LORD relents. **1–3:** Judgment by locusts (cf. Joel).

a-a A poetic designation of the northern kingdom.
b-b Meaning of Heb. uncertain.
c-c Meaning of Heb. uncertain; emendation yields "Can one plow the sea with oxen?"
d Two towns east of the Jordan recovered for Israel by Jeroboam II (see 2 Kings 14.25). For
Lo-dabar, cf. 2 Sam. 9.4, 5; 17.27; for Karnaim, cf. Gen. 14.5.
e-e Meaning of Heb. uncertain. The king's reaping of fodder apparently occurred near the
end of the rainy season, and whatever the locust destroyed after that could not be replaced
for another year.

4 This is what the Lord GOD showed me: Lo, my Lord GOD was summoning a-to contend by-a fire which consumed the Great Deep and was consuming the fields. 5 I said, "Oh, Lord GOD, refrain! How will Jacob survive? He is so small." 6 The LORD relented concerning this. "That shall not come to pass, either," said my Lord GOD.

7 This is what He showed me: He was standing on a wall b-checked with a plumb line-b and He was holding a plumb line.c 8 And the LORD asked me, "What do you see, Amos?" "A plumb line,"c I replied. And my Lord declared, "I am going to apply a plumb linec to My people Israel; I will pardon them no more. 9 The shrines of Isaac shall be laid waste, and the sanctuaries of Israel reduced to ruins; and I will turn upon the House of Jeroboam with the sword."

10 Amaziah, the priest of Bethel, sent this message to King Jeroboam of Israel: "Amos is conspiring against you within the House of Israel. The country cannot endure the things he is saying. 11 For Amos has said, 'Jeroboam shall die by the sword, and Israel shall be exiled from its soil.'"

12 Amaziah also said to Amos, "Seer, off with you to the land of Judah! d-Earn your living-d there, and do your prophesying there. 13 But don't ever prophesy again at Bethel; for it is a king's sanctuary and a royal palace." 14 Amos answered Amaziah: "I am not a prophet,e and I am not a prophet's disciple. I am a cattle breederf and a tender of sycamore figs. 15 But the LORD took me away from following the flock, and the LORD said to me, 'Go, prophesy to My people Israel.' 16 And so, hear the word of the LORD. You say I must not prophesy about the House of Israel or preach about the House of Isaac; 17 but this, I swear, is what the LORD said: Your wife shall g-play the harlot-g in the town, your sons and daughters shall fall by the sword, and your land shall be divided up with a measuring line. And you yourself shall die on unclean soil;h for Israel shall be exiled from its soil."

8 This is what my Lord GOD showed me: There was a basket of figs.i 2 He said, "What do you see, Amos?" "A basket of figs," I replied. And the LORD said to me:

4–6: Judgment by fire. **7–9:** The House of Jeroboam refers to Jeroboam II or better, the "House of Jehu," the last stable dynasty of the Northern Kingdom. The term refers also—at least by connotation—to the Northern Kingdom as a whole.

7.10–17: Narrative about Amos and the priest Amaziah. In some cases the term "Israel" here points only to the Northern Kingdom, but in others it may evoke a more inclusive idea of Israel to the post-monarchic readers of the book and accordingly allow them to identify with that Israel. Although this section disrupts the narrative of "This is what my Lord GOD showed me," it is placed here, where it is contextually appropriate, immediately following the oracle against Jeroboam in v. 9. **11:** Amos's prophecy was considered treasonous because it would demoralize the people. **12:** The prophet is a Judahite, and so Amaziah sends him back to Judah. **14:** Amos maintains that he is not a professional prophet, who may be hired for his services (see 1 Sam. 9.7) and thus "bought"; rather, God took him away from his job to perform a particular task (cf. 2 Sam. 7.8). This being so, he has no alternative but to prophesy. Amos's reply enhances the authority associated with his message.

8.1–3: Fourth report of a prophetic vision of judgment: the basket of summer fruit. Figs, lit. "summer basket" or "basket of summer fruit," plays on the words "kayitz" and "the end" ("ketz"). V. 2 may be translated "The end has come upon My people Israel."

a-a Emendation yields "flaming."
b-b Or "destined for the pickax"; meaning of Heb. uncertain.
c Or "pickax"; meaning of Heb. uncertain.
d-d Lit. "eat bread." e I.e., by profession.
f Meaning of Heb. uncertain; emendation yields "sheep breeder"; cf. the next verse and 1.1.
g-g Emendation yields "be ravished"; cf. Lam. 5.11. h Cf. Hos. 9.3 and note.
i Heb. qayiṣ, lit. "summer fruit."

"The [a]hour of doom[a] has come for My people Israel; I will not pardon them again. [3] And the singing women of the palace shall howl on that day—declares my Lord GOD:

> So many corpses
> Left lying everywhere!
> Hush!"

[4] Listen to this, you [b]who devour the needy, annihilating the poor of the land,[b] [5] saying, "If only the new moon were over, so that we could sell grain; the sabbath, so that we could offer wheat for sale, [c]using an *ephah* that is too small, and a shekel that is too big,[c] tilting a dishonest scale, [6] and selling grain refuse as grain! We will buy the poor for silver, the needy for a pair of sandals." [7] The LORD swears by[d] the Pride of Jacob: "I will never forget any of their doings."

[8]
> Shall not the earth shake for this
> And all that dwell on it mourn?
> Shall it not all rise like the Nile
> And surge and subside like the Nile of Egypt?

[9]
> And in that day   —declares my Lord GOD—
> I will make the sun set at noon,
> I will darken the earth on a sunny day.

[10]
> I will turn your festivals into mourning
> And all your songs into dirges;
> I will put sackcloth on all loins
> And tonsures on every head.
> I will make it[e] mourn as for an only child,
> All[f] of it as on a bitter day.

[11] A time is coming—declares my Lord GOD—when I will send a famine upon the land: not a hunger for bread or a thirst for water, but for hearing the words of the LORD. [12] Men shall wander from [g]sea to sea[g] and from north to east to seek the word of the LORD, but they shall not find it.

[13] In that day, the beautiful maidens and the young men shall faint with thirst—

[14]
> Those who swear by the guilt of Samaria,
> Saying, "As your god lives, Dan,"[h]

---

a-a Heb. qeṣ.

b-b Emendation yields "who on every new moon devour the needy, and on every sabbath the humble of the land"; cf. v. 5.

c-c Giving short measures of grain, but using oversize weights for the silver received in payment.

d Or "concerning"; cf. 6.8 with note.   e I.e., the earth; cf. vv. 8 and 9d.

f Lit. "the end."   g-g Emendation yields "south to west."   h See 1 Kings 12.28–29.

8.4–14: Report of a prophetic word in the monarchic period. Another "Hear" unit (cf. 3.1–6.14). **4–5:** *New moon,* the beginning of a month, traditionally observed as a holiday. The text clearly implies that days of religious observance (Shabbath, new moon) are supposed to be kept, though observance of the new moon by ceasing from work is nowhere recorded in Torah legislation. The book of Amos is certainly not against cultic observance. The problem here is that people are eager for the holiday to be over so they can get on with making money through dishonest means. The text associates lack of reverence for these religious observances and dishonest trade (see Lev. 19.35–37); cf. Amos 5.21–25 n. *Ephah . . . small . . . shekel . . . big:* The measure with which the corrupt merchants sell grain is smaller than it should be, allowing them to sell less than an ephah (a unit of dry measure of perhaps 23 liters) for the full price; on the other hand, the weight with which they buy grain is larger than it should be, allowing them to get more for the shekel (about 11.4 gm) than they should. **9:** A solar eclipse is a portent of doom and a reversal of the natural order. Compare the description of the Day of the LORD in 5.18–20. **10:** The idea of reversal continues. The festivals, which the people do not respect, will be turned into times of *mourning.* **11–14:** Famine, which is one of the ways God punishes the people's sins, and which often accompanies destruction, is here used metaphorically. **11–12:** The people will be hungry and thirsty for God's word. Rabbinic sources understand this text as pointing to a time in which the Torah (*the words of the LORD*) will be forgotten: "Our Rabbis taught: When our Masters entered the vineyard at Yabneh, they said, The Torah is destined to be forgotten in Israel, as it is said, Behold, the days come, saith the LORD God, that I will send a famine in the land . . ." *b. Shab.* 138b [Soncino ET]; and see also *t.* *'Ed.* 1.1).

And "As the way to Beer-sheba lives"[a]—
They shall fall to rise no more.

9 I saw my LORD standing by the altar, and He said:
[b]Strike the capitals so that the thresholds quake, and
make an end of the first of them all.[b] And I will slay the
last of them with the sword; not one of them shall escape,
and not one of them shall survive.

2   If they burrow down to Sheol,
    From there My hand shall take them;
    And if they ascend to heaven,
    From there I will bring them down.

3   If they hide on the top of Carmel,
    There I will search them out and seize them;
    And if they conceal themselves from My sight
    At the bottom of the sea,
    There I will command
    The serpent to bite them.

4   And if they go into captivity
    Before their enemies,
    There I will command
    The sword to slay them.
    I will fix My eye on them for evil
    And not for good.

5   It is my Lord the GOD of Hosts
    At whose touch the earth trembles
    And all who dwell on it mourn,
    And all of it swells like the Nile
    And subsides like the Nile of Egypt;

6   Who built His chambers in heaven
    And founded His vault on the earth,
    Who summons the waters of the sea
    And pours them over the land—
    His name is the LORD.

7   To Me, O Israelites, you are
    Just like the Ethiopians   —declares the LORD.
    True, I brought Israel up
    From the land of Egypt,
    But also the Philistines from Caphtor
    And the Arameans from Kir.

8   Behold, the Lord GOD has His eye
    Upon the sinful kingdom:
    I will wipe it off
    The face of the earth!

9.1–6: Fifth report of a prophetic vision of judgment: the LORD at the altar. Which altar? The text carefully avoids an explicit reference to the altar at Bethel, which would have constrained the intended readers of the book. **2:** *Sheol,* the place of the dead. The nadir of the earth; the opposite of heaven. **3:** *Carmel,* a peak in northern Israel. Here it serves as both a reference to the highest point on earth that an Israelite may think of reaching and as a symbol of the highest point on earth in cosmic terms (cf. 1.2); the opposite of the bottom of the sea. *Serpent,* here a mythical sea-creature. **5–6:** Theophanic (cf. 1.2) and creation imagery is used to emphasize God's power. Such descriptions, called doxologies (praises of God) are interspersed throughout Amos, and characterize this prophetic book.

9.7–10: The final account of judgment provides also a glimmer of hope. 7: Israel is not granted special privileges by the LORD, even if God took them out of Egypt. **8–9:** The severe condemnation and punishment of Israel in the past (from the viewpoint of the readership) shifts now to a promise of restoration and ideal conditions for Israel in the future.

---

a See 5.5 with note.   *b-b Meaning of Heb. uncertain.*

But, I will not wholly wipe out
The House of Jacob   —declares the LORD.
9   For I will give the order
And shake the House of Israel—
Through all the nations—
As one shakes [sand] in a sieve,[a]
And not a pebble falls to the ground.
10   All the sinners of My people
Shall perish by the sword,
Who boast,
"Never shall the evil
Overtake us or come near us."

11   In that day,
I will set up again the fallen booth of David:
I will mend its breaches and set up its ruins anew.
I will build it firm as in the days of old,
12   [b-]So that they shall possess the rest of Edom
And all the nations once attached to My name[-b].
                         —declares the LORD
                         who will bring this to pass.
13   A time is coming   —declares the LORD—
When the plowman shall meet the reaper,[c]
And the treader of grapes
Him who holds the [bag of] seed;
When the mountains shall drip wine
And all the hills shall wave [with grain].

14   I will restore My people Israel.
They shall rebuild ruined cities and inhabit them;
They shall plant vineyards and drink their wine;
They shall till gardens and eat their fruits.
15   And I will plant them upon their soil,
Nevermore to be uprooted
From the soil I have given them
                         —said the LORD your God.

9.11–15: Hope: restoration and an ideal future are promised.
11: Rabbinic sources understood the reference to setting up the *fallen booth of David* as pointing to the messianic era (e.g., *b. Sanh.* 96b–97a). Some Jewish medieval commentators understood the booth as a reference to the Temple, but the majority to the Davidic kingdom. Most modern scholars associate the image of the fallen booth of David with the fall of monarchic Judah and the exile. Ibn Ezra associates the verse with Hezekiah's successful stand against Sennacherib (see 2 Kings 18.13–19.37; Isa. 36.1–37.38; 2 Chron. 32.1–23). (The majority of contemporary historians agree that Hezekiah was not successful against Sennacherib, either militarily or politically [see 2 Kings chs 18–20]. But the image of Hezekiah's success had already in biblical times become central to the way Israel understood its past.) As for the particular reference to Edom, see Obadiah and n. there. **13:** Cf. Lev. 26.5. The produce will be so abundant that the harvesting will continue through the time for planting new seeds. **15:** The book concludes with a highly optimistic, unconditional promise: *Nevermore* will the disaster foretold, which actually transpired to the post-monarchic community, be repeated.

a A coarse sieve used for cleansing grain of straw and stones, or sand of pebbles and shells.
b-b I.e., the House of David shall reestablish its authority over the nations that were ruled by David.
c Cf. Lev. 26.5.

עבדיה

Obadiah

OBADIAH IS THE SHORTEST BOOK in the Bible, containing only 291 Heb words. Nonetheless, like all prophetic books, it is meant to be read, read again, and studied. The book's main topic is the destruction of Jerusalem in 586 BCE, and the putative actions of Edom against Judah at the time. The Edomites, the central characters of the book, were regarded as kin to the Israelites, since they were supposedly descended from Esau, Jacob's brother (see Gen. 25.30; 36.8; Num. 20.14; Deut. 2.4, 8, passim). In Obadiah, Edom serves both as a reference to the nation of that name that was considered to be Israel's brother—a motif explicitly mentioned in Obadiah 10—and also to the nations in general. Subsequently, Jews identified Edom with Rome and later with Christendom. For them, the book of Obadiah referred at least in part to the events associated with the destruction of the Second Temple (cf. Radak), or to future events associated with the coming of the messianic era (e.g., Abravanel). Of course, ancient and medieval Christian readers were convinced that they were (the true) Israel, not Edom (cf. Rom. 9.6–13).

According to the book, the Edomites did not behave as brothers to the people of Judah in their worst hour but rather joined the enemy forces (cf. Ps. 137.7; Lam. 4.21–22). The book of Obadiah presents therefore a major confrontation between the LORD and Edom (and the nations it represents) that is in sharp contrast to God's relation with Judah/Israel, which will enjoy an eventual utopian future that will be consistent with God's kingdom on earth.

Some scholars differentiate between an original book of Obadiah and the present book, which they view as an expansion around an earlier core. Others emphasize the coherence of the text as it stands. The present book was composed in the postmonarchic period, as the references to the fall of Jerusalem, the exile, and the exilic community in Sardis (a city in modern Turkey that was the capital of the ancient kingdom of Lydia) demonstrate.

There are clear similarities between Obadiah 1–7 and Jer. 49.7–22 (or more precisely Jer. 49.7a, 14–16, 9–10). According to some, the author of the book of Obadiah borrowed from Jeremiah; according to others the opposite happened. More likely, however, the author of both texts borrowed from a common text whose full length and precise wording are unrecoverable.

The book of Obadiah is read as the haftarah for the parashah of Va-yishlaḥ (Gen. 32.4–

36.43) in the Sephardic and Yemenite traditions; the Ashkenazic traditions read Hos. 11.7–12.12 instead of, or in addition to, Obadiah. Gen. chs 32–33 tells of the meeting between Jacob and Esau after Jacob's sojourn with Laban.

The book begins with an introduction (v. 1), then moves to a set of passages each of which deals with Edom's condemnation and judgment (vv. 2–4, 5–7, 8–15). By the end it becomes clear that Edom also stands for all the nations other than Israel. The theme of the judgment of the nations, and of Edom as a paradigm for the nations, is intertwined with that of Zion's glorious future in vv. 15b–18. The book concludes (vv. 19–21) with an image of an ideal future in which Israel is restored and the dominion is the LORD's (v. 21).

[EHUD BEN ZVI]

1 The prophecy of Obadiah.

We have received tidings from the LORD,
And an envoy has been sent out among the
      nations:
"Up! Let us rise up against her for battle."

Thus said my Lord GOD concerning Edom:
2   I will make you least among nations,
    You shall be most despised.
3   Your arrogant heart has seduced you,
    You who dwell in clefts of the rock,
    In your lofty abode.
    You think in your heart,
    "Who can pull me down to earth?"
4   Should you nest as high as the eagle,
    Should your eyrie be lodged 'mong the stars,
    Even from there I will pull you down
                —declares the LORD.

5   If thieves were to come to you,
    Marauders by night,

Edom." More importantly, the four lines of the translation that follow the title of the book (1a) are rearranged. The Heb text places "Thus said the LORD God concerning Edom" before *We have received tidings from the LORD*. Those who favor rearrangement of the text adopted in NJPS maintain that it makes more contextual sense to have *thus said . . .* just before v. 2. But others claim that the presence of the expression at the beginning of the book points to an important theological claim, namely that the entire prophetic book—including words uttered by God but also by a human prophetic speaker—is to be considered the LORD's word, and as such shares divine origin and authority.

2–4: First condemnation of Edom: its foolishness and self-deluding reliance on its own terrain. These vv. use well-known rhetorical techniques to characterize Edom as foolish while it claims to be wise. They represent Edom as one who inanely claims that the LORD is unable to reach it because of its mountainous territory, and at the same time considers scaling into the celestial realm. This type of characterization of the "enemy" is common in the ancient Near East. Edom was associated with wisdom in the Bible (v. 8; Jer. 49.7). **3:** *Rock* (Heb "sela'") is a pun on the name "Sela," one of the important cities of Edom (perhaps near the ancient city of Petra).

1: Introduction to the book.
1a: NJPS follows the Targum and translates the title of the book as *The prophecy of Obadiah*. This translation is preferable to the usual, more etymological "The vision of Obadiah" (e.g., NRSV), because visual elements do not figure prominently in the book (the same holds true for Isa. 1.1). The title, however, should be not understood as meaning that the ensuing text contains only a report of God's words to Obadiah. God is surely not the

only speaker in the book. It is unusual to introduce a biblical character by one name only, without a patronymic or name of a father (contrast Isa. 1.1; Jer. 1.1; Hos. 1.1; etc.). The lack of a more precise reference to Obadiah allowed the readers of the book to wonder whether the Obadiah of this book was the same Obadiah who figures prominently in 1 Kings ch 18. **1b:** *Thus said my Lord GOD concerning Edom:* The Heb reads, "Thus said the LORD God concerning

They would steal no more than they needed.
If vintagers came to you,
They would surely leave some gleanings.
How utterly you are destroyed!

6 How thoroughly rifled is Esau,
How ransacked his hoards!

7 All your allies turned you back
At the frontier;
Your own confederates
Have duped and overcome you;
[Those who ate] your bread
Have planted snares under you.

He is bereft of understanding.

8 In that day   —declares the LORD—
I will make the wise vanish from Edom,
Understanding from Esau's mount.

9 Your warriors shall lose heart, O Teman,
And not a man on Esau's mount
Shall survive the slaughter.

10 For the outrage to your brother Jacob,
Disgrace shall engulf you,
And you shall perish forever.

11 On that day when you stood aloof,
When aliens carried off his goods,
When foreigners entered his gates
And cast lots for Jerusalem,
You were as one of them.

12 ᵃHow could youᵃ gaze with glee
On your brother that day,
On his day of calamity!
How could you gloat
Over the people of Judah
On that day of ruin!
How could you loudly jeer
On a day of anguish!

13 How could you enter the gate of My people
On its day of disaster,
Gaze in glee with the others
On its misfortune
On its day of disaster,
And lay hands on its wealth
On its day of disaster!

14 How could you stand at the passesᵇ

a-a Lit. "Do not," and so through v. 14.   *b Meaning of Heb. uncertain.*

5–7: Second condemnation of Edom: its foolishness and self-deluding reliance on human allies. These verses represent Edom as one who inanely trusts unreliable allies, who will turn against it and utterly destroy it. The section leads up to the obvious conclusion: *He [Edom] is bereft of understanding.* This type of characterization of the "enemy" is also common in the ancient Near East. **5:** *Vintagers* (Heb "botzrim") clearly evokes the name of another main Edomite city, "Botzrah" (Bozrah). **7:** Another possible, and perhaps more likely, understanding of the first part of the v. is: "All your allies have deceived you, they have driven you to the border" (e.g., NRSV). In any case, it is clear that the trusted allies of Edom contributed to its downfall. Eating bread together was a sign of close relationship.

8–15: Judgment over Edom: the two days of destruction. Edom and the nations (other than Israel). The last passage in the set focuses on the actions of Edom against his brother *on the day* of Jerusalem's destruction and directly relates it to the future day of Edom's destruction (notice the repetition of "on the day"). The motto of this section is to a large extent *as you did so shall it be done to you* (v. 15, and contrast with Prov. 24.29). But as the unit concludes, the object of the divine wrath shifts from Edom to *all nations* (that is, nations other than Israel), suggesting to the readers that Edom also functions as a symbol for all the nations. Edom's actions, behavior, and future judgment are not an aberration, but rather paradigmatic for those of the nations. **8:** *In that day,* Heb "on that day," just as all other "on . . . day" in this unit. **9:** *Teman,* a grandson of Esau (Edom, Gen. 36.11), here, as often in prophetic literature, a synonym for Edom (e.g., Jer. 49.7, 20; Ezek. 25.13). The name itself means "South." Edom was south of Judah. **10:** *Your brother Jacob,* i.e., Israel. Jacob and Esau were brothers (Gen. 25.20–34).

To cut down its fugitives!
How could you betray those who fled
On that day of anguish!

15 As you did, so shall it be done to you;
Your conduct shall be requited.

Yea, against all nations
The day of the LORD is at hand.

16 That same cup that you[a] drank on My Holy
   Mount
Shall all nations drink evermore,[b]
Drink till their speech grows thick,
And they become as though they had never
   been.

17 But on Zion's mount a remnant shall survive,
And it shall be holy.[c]
The House of Jacob shall dispossess
Those who dispossessed them.

18 The House of Jacob shall be fire,
And the House of Joseph flame,
And the House of Esau shall be straw;
They shall burn it and devour it,
And no survivor shall be left of the House of Esau
                    —for the LORD has spoken.

19[d]Thus they shall possess the Negeb and Mount Esau
as well, the Shephelah and Philistia. They shall possess
the Ephraimite country and the district of Samaria,[e] and
Benjamin[f] along with Gilead. 20 And that exiled force of
Israelites [shall possess] what belongs to the Phoenicians

a I.e., the Israelites.
b Emendation yields "at My hand," cf. Isa. 51.17; Jer. 25.15; Ps. 75.9.
c I.e., inviolate; cf. Jer. 2.3.
d Meaning of parts of vv. 19–21 uncertain.
e After the exile of the northern tribes, the city and district of Samaria were occupied
mainly by non-Israelites.
f Emendation yields "the land of the Ammonites."

15b–18: On salvation for post-monarchic Israel/Zion and judgment over Edom/the nations.
15b: This line is shared by the previous unit and this one. Sharing of expressions or lines between two neighboring units within a literary text is not uncommon. This feature brings the two units together, makes the book more cohesive, and contributes to the flow of the reading. **16–17:** The text creates both a temporal differentiation be-tween Israel that already drank the cup (see Jer. 25.15–29), and the nations that shall drink it, and a spatial one between holy Mt. Zion and the rest of the world. **17:** The Heb clearly states that it is *Zion's mount* that *shall be holy*, not the *remnant.* **18:** *And no survivor shall be left of the House of Esau:* This claim has later been understood as pointing to the world to come and to the place of "those whose evil deeds are like to those of Esau"

rather than specifically to Romans (or non-Jews in general). See *b. A. Z.* 10b.

19–21: The concluding note of the book: a particular image of, and a divine promise for, the ideal future. As the translators' note in NJPS suggests, the text is some-what difficult. V. 19 is probably better understood as follows: "Those of the Negev (South) will and should inherit/possess [the whole of] Mt. Esau (the mountain of Esau); those of the Shephelah will and should inherit/possess the [whole of (the land of) the] Philistines; they (i.e., those of the Shephelah) will and should in-herit/possess [all of] the land/highland of Ephraim and [all of] the land/highland of Samaria; and the Benjaminites, [all of the Gil-ead]"; cf. the Targum. A number of alternative readings and under-standings of v. 20 have been ad-vanced. Among them, "The exiles (/exilic community) of this terri-tory who are (/consist of) the Isra-elites who are among the Canaan-ites (i.e., Phoenicians) will and should inherit/possess [what be-longs to the Canaanites/Phoeni-cians] as far as Zarephath, while the Jerusalemite exiles (/exilic community) who are in Sepharad will and should inherit/possess the towns of the Negev/South." Although all agree that the text communicates that Israel will re-possess the land, the question at stake is which social and geo-graphical structure is envisioned for that Israel. There is much more agreement concerning v. 21, but see below. *Sepharad* was identified in the Targum as Spain. (It is more likely to be Sardis, a main city in Asia Minor.) The equation Sepha-rad = Spain, however, became a cornerstone in Jewish self-identification for centuries. The Jews of Spain and their descen-dants are called, and call them-selves, Sepharadim (or Sefaradim). Some scholars would prefer to translate "saviors" instead of *liber-ators* and "to judge" rather than *to wreak judgment on Mount Esau.* The conclusion of the book originally as far as Zarephath,ª while the Jerusalemite exile community of Sepharadᵇ shall possess the towns of the Negeb. ²¹ For ᶜliberators shall march upᵉ on Mount Zion to wreak judgment on Mount Esau; and dominion shall be the LORD's.

evoked the language associated with the time of the Judges, who are sometimes called deliverers or liberators (see, e.g., Judg. 3.9). In later Jewish tradition, some understood the text as pointing to a messianic time. Such an understanding raises questions about the identity of the mentioned saviors (see Radak on Mic. 5.4; Ibn Ezra; Abravanel). The final sentence may be translated as "the kingdom will be the LORD's" or even better, "the kingship (i.e., the office of the king) will be the LORD's." In other words, at that time the LORD will be manifest (in Israel and in the entire world) as the king. In this case, Obadiah, like Deutero-Isaiah, is imagining an ideal future in which a Davidic messiah plays no role.

a A town in southern Phoenicia; see 1 Kings 17.9.
b Probably Asia Minor, called Saparda in Persian cuneiform inscriptions.
c-c Several ancient versions read, "they [the exiles from Jerusalem named in the preceding verse] shall march up victorious."

יונה

Jonah

THE BOOK OF JONAH was included in "the Twelve," among the other prophetic books, because it was accepted as a prophetic book. Yet it is unlike all the other prophetic books in many and diverse ways. For one thing, the book of Jonah is a narrative, whereas the others are not, though they may include some narrative sections. Prophetic books tend to allocate a large share of their text to reports of divine announcements (or "oracles") and of prophetic addresses to a public other than the LORD or the prophet alone. This is clearly not the case in Jonah. Further, none of the other eleven prophets rebels against God and takes practical steps to preempt the fulfillment of the explicit divine will as communicated to the prophet. The motif of Jonah's active opposition to the LORD's command and will, and accordingly his reluctance to show honor and reverence to his Master, is overtly emphasized in the text through contrast with the inhabitants of Nineveh and with other non-Israelites. Despite the typically negative view of Assyria in the Bible, the book characterizes the entire population of Nineveh (the capital of Assyria), including its elite, the sailors, and even all creation, as clearly responsive to the LORD. Finally, according to this book, this extremely atypical prophet is the most successful in the Bible (see the annotations).

The book itself has been characterized in different ways, among them: as a satire, a story that presents an implicit ideal by means of an exaggerated portrait of its opposite; as a parable, which makes its theological, spiritual, or moral point implicitly through narrative; and as didactic fiction, perhaps a narrative philosophical tractate. It is perhaps better to understand it as a meta-prophetic book, that is, a book that probes the role of the prophet, and as a book that is to be studied as the LORD's word or teaching (see below). As such it uses humor and elements of satire and parody and it carries a strong didactic message.

Some have argued that the principal theme of the book of Jonah concerns the power of repentance; others that its main focus and message contrast a doctrine of retributive justice to one of divine grace. Still others maintain that the main issue in Jonah is a conflict between God's universalist approach and Jonah's nationalistic tendencies. Another group of scholars is convinced that the focus of the book is the contrast or conflict between an understanding of God as constrained by particular rules known to human beings and another that stresses the radical independence of such a being. All of these and similar approaches to the book have failed to command overwhelming assent for the simple reason that the book cannot be reduced to one main theme.

At one level, the basic narrative is quite simple, but at another, it shows much sophistication and polyvalence (that is, multiple meanings). For instance, in the basic story Nineveh is saved from destruction because, as the LORD states, "Should not I care about Nineveh, that great city, in which there are more than a hundred and twenty thousand persons who do not yet know their right hand from their left, and many beasts as well!" (4.11). But if so, what are the readers of the book supposed to make of the well-known fact in their time that historical Nineveh had long been totally destroyed and never rebuilt? Surely, they thought, such destruction must have been a manifestation of God's will. But if so, are some of God's words, as recorded in the prophetic books, valid at one time but not another, even if God's explicit argument seems universal? Are prophetic words contingent on a set of particular historical circumstances and therefore of no absolute value and general scope? Is it possible to distinguish between the contingent and the noncontingent words, and if so how? Or are all of them contingent? The book raises many other issues concerning the role of prophets, the question of if and when prophecies will be fulfilled, and the limitations of human knowledge based on reading Scripture. It bears noting that Jonah is described as one who knows Scripture well; nevertheless, his understanding of the role of prophecy and of God's will is presented as defective.

Although there is some debate on the matter, the usual date for the composition of Jonah is the Persian period. No critical scholar today advocates the historicity of the prophet and his fantastic misadventures.

The book is read in the afternoon service of Yom Kippur, the Day of Atonement (see *b. Meg.* 31a) because of the theme of repentance. On that day Jews are supposed to identify with the Ninevites and their plea (certainly not with Jonah; and cf. already *m. Ta'an.* 2.1; on the completeness and truthfulness of the Ninevites' repentance see, for instance, *b. Ta'an.* 16a, cf. Rambam, *Mishneh Torah, b. Ta'an.* 4.2; the Jerusalem Talmud, however, shows other voices, e.g., R. Yohanan in *y. Ta'an.* 9a; perek b, halakhah a).

The basic structure of the book of Jonah is clear and quite symmetrical. There are two divine calls to Jonah, both worded in a similar manner. In the first case, Jonah disobeys the divine command; in the second, he obeys (cf. 1.1–3 and 3.1–3). In both cases he interacts with non-Israelites who show fear of the LORD, and in both he stands in sharp contrast to them (cf. 1.4–15 and 3.5–10). Both interactions lead Jonah to address the LORD in distress (2.2–10 and 4.1–3). The main difference is that in the concluding case, the LORD responds in words and enters into a didactic dialogue with Jonah (4.4–11).   [EHUD BEN ZVI]

1 The word of the LORD came to Jonah[a] son of Amittai: ²Go at once to Nineveh, that great city, and proclaim judgment upon it; for their wickedness has come before Me.

³Jonah, however, started out to flee to Tarshish from the LORD's service. He went down to Joppa and found a ship going to Tarshish. He paid the fare and went aboard to sail with the others to Tarshish, away from the service of the LORD.

⁴But the LORD cast a mighty wind upon the sea, and such a great tempest came upon the sea that the ship was in danger of breaking up. ⁵In their fright, the sailors cried out, each to his own god; and they flung the ship's cargo overboard to make it lighter for them. Jonah, meanwhile, had gone down into the hold of the vessel where he lay down and fell asleep. ⁶The captain went over to him and cried out, "How can you be sleeping so soundly! Up, call upon your god! Perhaps the god will be kind to us and we will not perish."

⁷The men said to one another, "Let us cast lots and find out on whose account this misfortune has come upon us." They cast lots and the lot fell on Jonah. ⁸They said to him, "Tell us, you who have brought this misfortune upon us, what is your business? Where have you come from? What is your country, and of what people are you?" ⁹"I am a Hebrew," he replied. "I worship the LORD, the God of Heaven, who made both sea and land." ¹⁰The men were greatly terrified, and they asked him, "What have you done?" And when the men learned that he was fleeing from the service of the LORD—for so he told them—¹¹they said to him, "What must we do to you to make the sea calm around us?" For the sea was growing more and more

a Mentioned in 2 Kings 14.25.

1.1–16: Jonah's first call from God and his response. Contrast between Jonah and the sailors. **1:** The opening of the book, *the word of the LORD came to Jonah,* is a common one for a prophetic narrative that is embedded in a book, but it does not occur elsewhere as the opening of a book, so from the start, Jonah is different. This opening suggests to the readers that the book begins, as it were, "in the middle," and that much of the background of the story is not told in the book. It is up to them to fill the gap. *Jonah son of Amittai:* The name of the prophet is identical with that of a prophet mentioned in 2 Kings 14.25, who prophesied in the days of Jeroboam II, king of Israel. It seems possible and even likely that the text here serves to encourage its readers to identify the two, or at least to fill the mentioned gap with their knowledge about the prophet in Kings, who is depicted as one who prophesied territorial conquests for Israel. **2:** *Nineveh* was the capital of Assyria, the conqueror of Samaria in 722 BCE; it was itself destroyed by the Babylonians and their allies in 612. Numerous prophetic texts characterize the Assyrians as extremely cruel and savage. Although this unflattering characterization pervaded much of biblical literature, the book of Jonah, which calls them Ninevites, never Assyrians, describes them as sinners who fully repented. The choice of words for this (first) call of Jonah reverberates in the second divine call (3.1–2). **3:** *To flee to Tarshish,* from the perspective of the readers a faraway place (cf. Isa. 66.19) in the opposite direction from Nineveh. Tarshish may have been in the Tarsus region on the southern coast of Turkey, but many other places have been suggested including Tartessus in Spain. *Joppa* was just outside Israelite territory, on the Mediterranean at the northern border of Philistia. Its modern name is Jaffa/Yafo (near Tel Aviv in modern Israel), and it is still a port. Jonah found a ship "coming from Tarshish" rather than *going to Tarshish,* as usually translated. Many scholars accept the translation *he paid the fare* but there is good reason to prefer "he paid its hire" (that is, he hired the ship and its sailors; cf. already *b. Ned.* 38a). In other words, he was "lucky" to find a ship just coming to port and hastened so much that he hired everyone so as to leave for the sea, on the spot. **3:** Jonah first *went down* to the port, and then *went aboard* (lit. "down to") the ship. **5:** Once in the ship he went *down into the hold of the vessel.* Eventually he will go down into the deep of the sea. Jonah *fell asleep,* but his was a "deep sleep," perhaps akin to a trance. **7:** *Cast lots,* a way to determine the divine will. **9:** Jonah speaks to the sailors in terms they can relate to. He tells them he is a Hebrew, a term sometimes used when speaking to non-Israelites, and he identifies God as the creator of the sea and land, putting the sea first, since that is the important element to the sailors. **10–16:** The sailors' reverence for and fear of the LORD is explicitly emphasized by the expanded repetition of v. 10 in v. 16, and by the stormy. [12] He answered, "Heave me overboard, and the sea will calm down for you; for I know that this terrible storm came upon you on my account." [13] Nevertheless, the men rowed hard to regain the shore, but they could not, for the sea was growing more and more stormy about them. [14] Then they cried out to the LORD: "Oh, please, LORD, do not let us perish on account of this man's life. Do not hold us guilty of killing an innocent person! For You, O LORD, by Your will, have brought this about." [15] And they heaved Jonah overboard, and the sea stopped raging.

[16] The men feared the LORD greatly; they offered a sacrifice to the LORD and they made vows.

2 The LORD provided a huge fish to swallow Jonah; and Jonah remained in the fish's belly three days and three nights. [2] Jonah prayed to the LORD his God from the belly of the fish. [3] He said:

> In my trouble I called to the LORD,
> And He answered me;
> From the belly of Sheol I cried out,
> And You heard my voice.

4
> You cast me into the depths,
> Into the heart of the sea,
> The floods engulfed me;
> All Your breakers and billows
> Swept over me.

5
> I thought I was driven away
> Out of Your sight:
> Would I ever gaze again
> Upon Your holy Temple?

6
> The waters closed in over me,
> The deep engulfed me.
> Weeds twined around my head.

7
> I sank to the base of the mountains;
> The bars of the earth closed upon me
>   forever.
> Yet You brought my life up from the pit,
> O LORD my God!

8
> When my life was ebbing away,
> I called the LORD to mind;

sponsible for the death of the prophet. To be sure, God knows that their action will not lead to Jonah's death, but rather serves as a necessary step for the completion of Jonah's mission and of God's overall intention. But the sailors do not know that. As for Jonah, he probably thought that death was the best available way out of his mission. Had he died, he would have successfully escaped from God's call. Of course, the readers know that God will not let this happen. As soon as Jonah is thrown overboard, they expect a divine action aimed at saving Jonah from death. Their expectations are fulfilled.

2.1–11: Jonah in the big fish. The fish (never called a whale) rescues Jonah from the sea. Most of this section of the book consists of Jonah's prayer. **3–10:** The prayer of Jonah is a pastiche of different verses taken from Psalms (see v. 3 and cf. Pss. 18.7; 30.3; 118.5; 120.1; 130.1, 2; v. 4 and cf. Ps. 42.8; v. 5 and cf. Ps. 31.23; v. 6 and cf. Pss. 18.5–6 and 69.2; v. 7 and cf. Pss. 30.4 and 71.20; v. 8a and cf. Pss. 142.4 and 143.4; v. 8b and cf. Pss. 5.8; 18.7 and 88.3; v. 9 and cf. Ps. 31.7; v. 10a and cf. Pss. 42.5; 50.14, 23 and 66.13; v. 10b and cf. Ps. 3.9). Jonah is thereby presented as a person well versed in the language of Psalms and able to compose a sophisticated prayer on their basis (cf. David or Solomon as described in Chronicles). In contrast to the rest of the book, which is a prose narrative, the text here is poetry. The verbs translated here in the past tense are probably better translated in the present. They point to events that are either happening or will happen (thus, "In my trouble I call to the LORD" rather than *In my trouble I called to the* LORD). **3:** *Sheol,* the Pit or the netherworld. It is the utter bottom of the world (in this case the depths of the sea) and also the land of the dead. **5:** *Would I ever gaze again* reflects a minor emendation, and may be understood as "Nevertheless I shall gaze again" (cf. Targum).

description of their actions. They seem convinced that the storm was due to Jonah's presence, but they are more than reluctant to "murder" a prophet even if he is a fugitive servant of the LORD. In

fact, the LORD has to force them to heave Jonah overboard, a point that is emphasized and embellished in *Midrash Tanḥuma* and *Pirkei Rabbi Eliezer.* Even then they are afraid of being held re-

And my prayer came before You,
Into Your holy Temple.
9 They who cling to empty folly
Forsake their own welfare,[a]
10 But I, with loud thanksgiving,
Will sacrifice to You;
What I have vowed I will perform.
Deliverance is the LORD's!

[11] The LORD commanded the fish, and it spewed Jonah out upon dry land.

3 The word of the LORD came to Jonah a second time: [2] "Go at once to Nineveh, that great city, and proclaim to it what I tell you." [3] Jonah went at once to Nineveh in accordance with the LORD's command.

Nineveh was [b-]an enormously large city[-b] a three days' walk across. [4] Jonah started out and made his way into the city the distance of one day's walk, and proclaimed: "Forty days more, and Nineveh shall be overthrown!"

[5] The people of Nineveh believed God. They proclaimed a fast, and great and small alike put on sackcloth. [6] When the news reached the king of Nineveh, he rose from his throne, took off his robe, put on sackcloth, and sat in ashes. [7] And he had the word cried through Nineveh: "By decree of the king and his nobles: No man or beast—of flock or herd—shall taste anything! They shall not graze, and they shall not drink water! [8] They shall be covered with sackcloth—man and beast—and shall cry mightily to God. Let everyone turn back from his evil ways and from the injustice of which he is guilty. [9] Who knows but that God may turn and relent? He may turn back from His wrath, so that we do not perish."

[10] God saw what they did, how they were turning back

a Meaning of Heb. uncertain.
b-b Lit. "a large city of God."

9: The final line of the verse conveys more than one meaning. *Forsake their own welfare,* "forsake their (true) loyalty," "forsake their bounty" are all possible understandings. Further, since *empty folly* can be understood as a reference to idols, and since *cling to* connotes worshipping, then the final line may be understood also as "forsake their idols," as some medieval Jewish commentators interpreted it.

3.1–10: Jonah's second call and the repentance of the Ninevites. 1–2: Jonah's call to prophesy from ch 1 is replayed, but this time Jonah accepts his commission. **3:** *An enormously large city,* another case of double meaning. The text also means "a large city that belongs to God" (cf. translators' note b-b). According to NJPS, and many scholars, the text states that the city was a three-day walk across, an impossibly large distance for an

ancient city. The text may be stating that the city was at a distance of three days' walk from Jonah's place. **4:** What Jonah means and what he is saying are not exactly the same. Jonah means to say, "Forty days more, and Nineveh is undone" but the readers notice that he is actually saying, "Forty days more, and Nineveh is overturned." Jonah chooses language that is reminiscent of God's destruction of Sodom and Gomorrah in Gen. ch 19. But the careful readers of the book notice the irony of the situation: Jonah's words potentially carry two, opposite meanings: (a) "Nineveh is undone," and (b) "Nineveh turns over (i.e., reforms itself)." One feature of his proclamation is unambiguous: Jonah's proclamation is extremely short and includes no call to repentance, unlike many other prophetic proclamations. **5–9:** Still it is the most effective, since the entire city immediately turns from its ways and repents. (Sackcloth, ashes, and fasting are typical signs of repentance.) Jonah does not wish to be a prophetic voice calling for repentance, and does not ask for the divine judgment to be turned into mercy (contrast Abraham in the case of Sodom and Gomorrah, Gen. 18.16–32), but he is still the most successful prophet in the Bible who achieves both in an unparalleled, complete, and immediate way—even the animals repent! The message is that the success of the prophet is not dependent on his attributes or rhetorical power, but on the will of God. And yet, there is a second reading. Jonah's message "Nineveh is undone" was fulfilled in history, as the readers of the book know well. If so, Jonah's understanding of his prophecy was fulfilled too. The problem was then that Jonah erred by believing that his prophecy must be fulfilled in his own days. The latter may well be an important message for readers of prophetic books in the Persian period. Prophetic words, especially those concerning the ideal status of the restored Israel, will be fulfilled, from their evil ways. And God renounced the punishment He had planned to bring upon them, and did not carry it out.

4 This displeased Jonah greatly, and he was grieved. ²He prayed to the LORD, saying, "O LORD! Isn't this just what I said when I was still in my own country? That is why I fled beforehand to Tarshish. For I know that You are a compassionate and gracious God, slow to anger, abounding in kindness, renouncing punishment. ³Please, LORD, take my life, for I would rather die than live." ⁴The LORD replied, "Are you that deeply grieved?"

⁵Now Jonah had left the city and found a place east of the city. He made a booth there and sat under it in the shade, until he should see what happened to the city. ⁶The LORD God provided a ricinus plant,ᵃ which grew up over Jonah, to provide shade for his head and save him from discomfort. Jonah was very happy about the plant. ⁷But the next day at dawn God provided a worm, which attacked the plant so that it withered. ⁸And when the sun rose, God provided a sultryᵇ east wind; the sun beat down on Jonah's head, and he became faint. He begged for death, saying, "I would rather die than live." ⁹Then God said to Jonah, "Are you so deeply grieved about the plant?" "Yes," he replied, "so deeply that I want to die."

a Meaning of Heb. uncertain; others "gourd."
b Meaning of Heb. uncertain.

but even prophets do not know when.

4.1–11: Jonah and the LORD discuss the matter. Jonah is upset, but why? Because his proclamation did not come true, from his perspective (see Deut. 18.21–22). He associates this lack of fulfillment with God's attributes (in v. 3 he is using Joel 2.13; Pss. 86.15; 103.8; 145.8 as key interpretative texts for Exod. 34.6–7 and Num. 14.18), and by doing so he is raising a theological confrontation between himself and God. One has to infer that Jonah thought that God should behave according to the paradigm advanced in another set of biblical texts (see Num. 23.19, 1 Sam. 15.29), but he was sure that God's behavior would not follow this paradigm. So God was in the wrong, from his perspective. Some

Jewish and non-Jewish interpreters have supported a different understanding. According to them, Jonah was upset that God relented from punishment only because those who were to be punished were not Israelites. A variant of this interpretation posits that the issue was not that they were not Israelites per se, but that they were Ninevites, i.e., the same people who will later oppress Israel and Judah. Those for whom Jonah is a stern chauvinist text—and there are still some contemporaneous readers who think so—tend to maintain that the book was a theological attack against those who may identify with this jingoist Jonah and his positions. The problem with this approach is that Jonah never says that he wants the Ninevites destroyed because they are not Israelites. Furthermore,

there is not even a hint of the tension between Israel and the nations in the book of Jonah. **6–8:** This scene may be based on Elijah in 1 Kings 19.4. If so, Jonah is being parodied as an anti-Elijah figure. **6:** *The LORD God provided:* The repetition of this language links the fish (2.1), the plant here, the successful *worm* in v. 7, and the extremely scorching *wind* in v. 8. All of them are provided or appointed by God. *Ricinus plant* (see translators' note a): Scholars have tried to identify the type of plant, but there is no general agreement. More important, the particular plant described here belongs to the realm of the fantastic that is provided only by God, just as was the "great fish" in whose belly a man can be accommodated. This plant suddenly grows to provide shade over Jonah's head and just as suddenly it withers. **7:** The east wind is a dry, scorching wind and is often associated with disaster and/or God's power (Exod. 14.21; Isa. 27.8; Jer. 18.17; cf. Gen. 41.6). **10:** There is an additional underlying dissymmetry in the comparison advanced in 4.6–11 that makes Jonah's position even more difficult. God cared about the fate of God's creation, but Jonah did not really care for the plant, but rather for himself, for the shade that the plant provided him. **11:** Midrash Yonah adds the following: "At this moment he (Jonah) fell upon his face and said: Guide Your world by the attribute of mercy, as it is written: 'To the LORD our God belong mercy and forgiveness . . .' [Dan. 9.9]." The biblical book of Jonah, however, does not end with Jonah's acceptance of God's position. It rather leaves the question open, asking the reader to fill the gap. Some modern readers who imagine Jonah as a prophet who knew too well what Assyria will do (later) to Israel think that Jonah remained unconvinced, and praise him for that, in the light of holocaust theology. Many other readers point out that the future actions of Assyria are not mentioned in the text at all, and are introduced into the text by the readers themselves.

10 Then the Lord said: "You cared about the plant, which you did not work for and which you did not grow, which appeared overnight and perished overnight. 11 And should not I care about Nineveh, that great city, in which there are more than a hundred and twenty thousand persons who do not yet know their right hand from their left, and many beasts as well!"ᵃ

The translation "yet" in *who do not yet know* is an interpretation of the verse rather than a reflection of any necessity of the Heb. It is not present in most English translations.

---

a Infants and beasts are not held responsible for their actions.

מיכה

Micah

THE FIRST VERSE OF THE BOOK sets the text in the days of Kings Jotham, Ahaz, and Hezekiah of Judah—in modern chronology the latter half of the 8th and the early years of the 7th century BCE (1.1), approximately the same chronological setting as for Isaiah 1–39. The book is associated in 1.1 with the figure of the prophet Micah, who is characterized as a Morashtite prophet, from a town in Judah. (The same characterization appears in the reference to Mic. 3.12 in Jer. 26.18.) The intended readers of the book were, however, Jerusalemites.

Many scholars attribute much, but not all of the book of Micah either to the historical prophet or to someone close to the time mentioned in 1.1. Other scholars note that the text includes, among other references, an explicit reference to the Babylonian exile (4.10), and therefore they date it to the postmonarchic period (cf. 7.11–13), at least in its final form.

The book begins with an introduction or superscription and then moves to sets of prophecies. The first one (1.2–2.13) concerns mostly divine judgment, exile, and social ethics, but—as expected—also provides hope for the future (2.5, 12–13). The second one (3.1–12) explains the fall of Jerusalem in terms of wrongful leadership. The third one (4.1–5.14) raises diverse images of a utopian future and touches on aspects of the relations between Israel and the nations at that time. The book concludes with a didactic prophecy (6.1–8), another explanation for the judgment that fell upon monarchic Jerusalem (6.9–16), an expression of trust in the LORD in spite of and as a response to social disintegration (7.1–7), and finally a confirmation of the LORD's distinct relationship with Zion and Judah (7.7–20) that leads to an upbeat conclusion of the entire book (7.18–20).

Micah 5.6–6.8 is the haftarah (prophetic reading) for the parashah of Balak (Num. 22.2–25.9), since 6.5 explicitly mentions Balak and Balaam. Micah 7.18–20 has been incorporated into the supplication that follows the reading of the story of Abraham's sacrifice (Gen. 22.1–19) in the morning service. The reference to "hurl" (Heb "tashlikh") in v. 19 has been associated with tashlikh (a ritual on the first day of Rosh Ha-Shanah symbolizing a desire to get rid of sins, to "hurl them away," and be forgiven by God). In the Sepharadic and Yemenite traditions, Micah 7.18–20 is read after Hosea 14.2–10 on Shabbat Shuvah (the Shabbat preceding Yom Kippur), following Jonah in the Minḥah service of Yom Kippur, and also in the Minḥah service of Tish'ah be'av (commemorating the destruction of the Temple). Conservative Judaism reads Hosea 14.2–10; Micah 7.18–20; Joel 2.15–27 on Shabbat Shuvah.

[EHUD BEN ZVI]

1 The word of the LORD that came to Micah the Morashtite, who prophesied concerning Samaria and Jerusalem in the reigns of Kings Jotham, Ahaz, and Hezekiah of Judah.

2   Listen, all you peoples,
        Give heed, O earth, and all it holds;
        And let my Lord GOD be your accuser—
        My Lord from His holy abode.

3   For lo! the LORD
        Is coming forth from His dwelling-place,
        He will come down and stride
        Upon the heights of the earth.

4   The mountains shall melt under Him
        And the valleys burst open—
        Like wax before fire,
        Like water cascading down a slope.

5   All this is for the transgression of Jacob,
        And for the sins of the House of Israel.
        What is the transgression of Jacob
        But Samaria,
        And what the shrines[a] of Judah
        But Jerusalem?

6   So I will turn Samaria
        Into a ruin in open country,
        Into ground for planting vineyards;
        For I will tumble her stones into the valley
        And lay her foundations bare.

7   All her sculptured images shall be smashed,
        And all her harlot's wealth be burned,
        And I will make a waste heap of all her idols,
        For they were amassed from fees for harlotry,
        And they shall become harlots' fees again.

a Emendation yields "sins."

1.1: Superscription. The verse characterizes the book as a particular instance of the LORD's word (that is, as a prophetic book), sets it in a particular time, and associates it with a prophetic character from the past, Micah (see introduction). The word of the LORD concerned both Samaria and Jerusalem, the capitals of the Northern and Southern Kingdoms respectively. But most of this "word" (i.e., the book of Micah) deals with the fate of Jerusalem and Judah. In this book references to Samaria serve only to preface and sharpen the message concerning Judah.

1.2–2.13: A set of readings about divine judgment, exile, social ethics, and divine hope. The set consists of four main sections: 1.2–16; 2.1–5; 2.6–11; 2.12–13.

1.2–16: About divine judgment and exile. The punishment moves from Israel to Judah, a reflection of the exile of Israel which was followed by that of Judah. **2:** On literary units in prophetic books that begin with "hear" or *listen* (Heb "shim'u") see Amos 3.1–6.14 n. *Listen, all you peoples:* The Heb is more emphatic: "Hear, O peoples, all of them." *My Lord GOD:* Heb "Adonai YHVH" vocalized (MT) as "Adonai Elohim" as in Amos 1.8, Obad. 1, and many other places. In most instances where YHVH appears in the Heb, it is vocalized "Adonai." Where it appears alongside "Adonai," as here, this is not possible, so YHVH is vocalized "Elohim," and the translation indicates this by printing "GOD." Although *be your accuser* is a possible reading—it is based on an interpretation of the phrase as "be a witness against you"—so is "be a witness among you." The text encourages this ambiguity. **3, 5:** A wordplay: *Heights* is echoed in *shrines* (same word in the Heb). The latter could also be translated "high places." **7:** *Harlot's wealth (or hire) . . . idols . . . harlotry:* The metaphorical association of sinful worship with prostitution is common in the prophetic books; see esp. Hos. chs 1–3. Many readers today raise the question of the problematic ways in which this metaphorical association may have colored the way in which gender roles are viewed in society (e.g., "the worshipper" is male and he is at risk of going astray because of enticing females whose job is to snare him). See

8 Because of this I will lament and wail;
I will go stripped and naked!
I will lament as sadly as the jackals,
As mournfully as the ostriches.

9 For her[a] wound is incurable,
It has reached Judah,
It has spread to the gate of my people,
To Jerusalem.

10[b] Tell it not in Gath,
Refrain from weeping;[c]
In Beth-leaphrah,
Strew dust[d] over your [head].

11 Pass on, inhabitants of Shaphir!
Did not the inhabitants of Zaanan
Have to go forth naked in shame?
There is lamentation in Beth-ezel—
It will withdraw its support from you.

12 Though the inhabitants of Maroth
Hoped for good,
Yet disaster from the LORD descended
Upon the gate of Jerusalem.

13 Hitch the steeds to the chariot,
Inhabitant of Lachish!
It is the beginning
Of Fair Zion's guilt;
Israel's transgressions
Can be traced to you!

14 Truly, you must give a farewell gift
To Moresheth-gath.
[e-]The houses of Achzib are[-e]
To the kings of Israel
Like a spring that fails.

a I.e., the nation's.

b Meaning of much of vv. 10–13 uncertain. They may refer to the transfer of part of western Judah to Philistine rule by Sennacherib of Assyria in the year 701 B.C.E.

c So that enemies may not gloat; cf. 2 Sam. 1.20.

d Heb. 'aphar, a play on Beth-leaphrah; vv. 10–15 contain several similar puns.

e-e Emendation yields "Fair Achzib is."

notes on the book of Hosea.
8: *I will lament:* The speaker in v. 7 is the LORD, as it is in v. 9, but most readers think that here it must be a human character, most likely the prophet (see Radak, Ibn Ezra). The Targum has "they" instead of "I" and represents an understanding of the speaker as the people of Israel. The subject of these actions in the Heb is, however, ambiguous. The image of the LORD lamenting and grieving, and even metaphorically going *stripped and naked* because of the fate of His people, may have been unthinkable to the Targum and medieval commentators, but not necessarily so to biblical writers, who stressed the divine pathos (e.g., Isa. 63.10; Hos. 11.8–9), a point often emphasized by the American rabbi and philosopher, Abraham Joshua Heschel. **10–16:** In some places it is difficult to understand the Heb. All agree however that the most salient feature of this text is its concentration of wordplays on the names of towns, each of which substantially contribute to the meaning of the unit. (Note that towns and their inhabitants are represented by female imagery.) English renderings of some of these wordplays and the connoted message they communicate would be as follows: **10:** "In Dust-house I will roll myself in dust." **11:** "Pass on your way, girl of Pretty-town, in shameful nakedness." **12:** "The girl of Bitterness-town aches for good, yet evil has come down from the LORD to the gate of Jerusalem." **14:** "The houses of Deception-ville shall be a deception to the kings of Israel." Whereas in all these instances the name of the town is constructed as an omen about its future, no such claim is made for Jerusalem. Jerusalem stands in a category of its own, no nomen-omen for it. Some scholars maintain that the list may reflect the results of military campaigns in the area either in 734–732, 722, 712, or for the most part, 701 BCE, i.e., the victorious campaign against Judah by Sennacherib, the Assyrian king. The text itself does not ask its readers to identify the disaster described in these vv. with any particular military campaign. The name Sennacherib does not occur anywhere, the disaster is not particularly associated with the name of any Judahite king, nor is the world of the text directly associated with chronological information (contrast Isa. 7.1; 20.1; Jer. 32.1; 46.1–2; Hag. 1.1). These features are not the result of chance. The book of Micah does not set any of its literary units in a narrowly marked historical period. The result is a literary work that may be read in general terms because it downplays particular historical situa-

15 A dispossessor will I bring to you
  Who dwell in Mareshah;
  At Adullam the glory
  Of Israel shall set.

16 ªShear off your hair and make yourself bald
  For the children you once delighted in;
  Make yourself as bald as a vulture,
  For they have been banished from you.

2 Ah, those who plan iniquity
  And design evil on their beds;
  When morning dawns, they do it,
  For they have the power.

2 They covet fields, and seize them;
  Houses, and take them away.
  They defraud men of their homes,
  And people of their land.

³ Assuredly, thus said the LORD: I am planning such a misfortune against this clan that you will not be able to free your necks from it. You will not be able to walk erect; it will be such a time of disaster.

4 In that day,
  One shall recite a poem about you,
  And utter a bitter lament,
  And shall say:
  ᵇ⁻"My people's portion changes hands;
  How it slips away from me!
  Our field is allotted to a rebel.ᶜ
  We are utterly ravaged."⁻ᵇ

5 Truly, none of you
  Shall cast a lot cordᵈ
  In the assembly of the LORD!

6 "Stop preaching!" they preach.
  "That's no way to preach;
  ᵇ⁻Shame shall not overtake [us].

7 Is the House of Jacob condemned?⁻ᵇ
  Is the LORD's patience short?
  Is such His practice?"

  To be sure, My words are friendly
  To those who walk in rectitude;
8 But ᵉ⁻an enemy arises against⁻ᵉ My people.

a A common rite of mourning; cf. Jer. 7.29.
b-b Meaning of Heb. uncertain.
c Emendation yields "ravager."
d On a piece of land, thus acquiring title to it; cf. Josh. 18.6 and Ps. 16.6.
e-e Meaning of Heb. uncertain; emendation yields "you arise as enemies against."

tions. **15:** The text is equivocal: *Dispossessor* may also be understood as (rightful) inheritor; *the glory* (or honor) *of Israel* may refer to Israel's wealth, might, or army, or to the LORD; the name of the town *Adullam* evokes a possible association with Heb "ʿolam," "forever." **16:** *For they have been banished from you* may be translated also as "for they have gone from you into exile." The readers of the book who were aware of the exile to Babylonia (see 4.10, and intro.) identified such exile with the Babylonian exile.

2.1–5: On social ethics, divine judgment, and hope. 1–3: Another wordplay with a strong message. Elite people within society *design* (or, "work") *evil*; the LORD plans (Heb) "evil" (*misfortune*) against them. Moreover, members of this group are able to do so because *they have the power*; the LORD certainly has the power to carry "evil" (*misfortune*), and God's might is infinitely superior to that of these people (cf. Prov. 22.23; 17.5). **5:** The descendants of the transgressors will not be part of the assembly of the LORD. This verse suggests a transgenerational aspect in the divine punishment.

2.6–11: On social ethics, divine character, mistaken positions, and judgment. 7: The speaker is the LORD. Thus the first three lines point at the LORD's representation of the theological thought of the evildoers described above. Given their actions, the LORD will not refrain from acting against them. **8:** It is possible to understand the v. as stating, "but yesterday My people rose as an enemy (i.e., of the LORD)." If so, the text maintains that the evildoers, despite their deeds, remain Jacob, the LORD's people. To be sure, these evildoers attack and dispossess Israelites too—who, of course, are also God's people (cf. v. 9). The continued reference to the evildoers in the second person following this phrase stresses the affective element of the condemnation. Several scholars have advanced pro-

You strip the mantle [a-]with the cloak[-a]
Off such as pass unsuspecting,
[b-]Who are turned away from war.[-b]

9   You drive the women of My people away
From their pleasant homes;
You deprive their infants
Of My glory forever.

10   Up and depart!
This is no resting place
[b-]Because of [your] defilement.
Terrible destruction shall befall.[-b]

11   If a man were to go about uttering
Windy, baseless falsehoods:
"I'll preach to you in favor of wine and liquor"—
He would be a preacher [acceptable] to that
    people.

12[c] I will assemble Jacob, all of you;
I will bring together the remnant of Israel;
I will make them all like sheep [d-]of Bozrah,[-d]
Like a flock inside its pen[e]—
They will be noisy with people.

13   One who makes a breach
Goes before them;
They enlarge it to a gate
And leave by it.
Their king marches before them,
The LORD at their head.

3   I said:
Listen, you rulers of Jacob,
You chiefs of the House of Israel!
For you ought to know what is right,

2[f]   But you hate good and love evil.

3   You have devoured My people's flesh;
You have flayed the skin off them,

a-a Meaning of Heb. uncertain; emendation yields "off peaceful folk."
b-b Meaning of Heb. uncertain.
c Vv. 12–13 may be an example of such "acceptable" preaching.
d-d Emendation yields "in a fold [Arabic sīrah]."   e Meaning of Heb. uncertain.
f Syntax of vv. 2–3 uncertain.

posals for emending this line to mean, "But you rise against my people as an enemy."

2.12–13: A promise of hope following judgment. The set of readings has dealt mainly with judgment; they end with a reassuring statement of hope. These vv. interweave the related images of shepherd and king. The image of God as shepherd, however, is ambiguous in the Bible: The shepherd may lead his flock gently (Ps. 23), or may punish those who are out of step (Ezek. ch 34). Most interpreters (including the Targum) understand these vv. as an announcement of future well-being, of Jacob's return from exile. A minority considers them as one of punishment (e.g., Radak who thinks that the king referred to is Zedekiah). Ibn Ezra (and a few modern scholars) relate these vv. to the false prophets (cf. translators' note c). According to *Pesikta de Rav Kahana* 24.14, the reference in v. 13 to "their king" is a reference to the Shekhinah (a Jewish concept that might be translated as "the divine presence"), and the entire v. points at the return of the exiles of Israel. **12:** *Sheep* ("flock") *of Bozrah:* Wordplays and multiple, complementary meanings; the Heb carries two basic meanings: "flock in a fenced place," and *sheep of Bozrah* (an Edomite city; see Amos 1.12). *Sheep of Bozrah,* evoking the quality or quantity of the flock, connotes a sense of plenty. "Flock in a fenced place" completes the metaphor of the good shepherd (the LORD) who leads the flock to safety. **13:** It is unclear if a human king is meant, or whether the LORD here is the King.

3.1–12: The failures of leadership that led to the fall of Jerusalem. The destruction of Jerusalem is explained as due to the failures of its leaders. The high value attached to the loss of Jerusalem demands a highly negative description of the leadership (cf. *b. Yoma* 9b). The structure of the unit is ABA: The rulers and chiefs are condemned in the first and third sections (A: 1–4, 9–12), and the prophets in the middle section (B: 5–8). The issue of wrong, "hopeful" theology is also revisited (3.11; cf. 2.6–7). **2–3:** The translation reflects some rearrangement of the Heb, but this does not affect the main picture: the incredible violence perpetrated by the rulers of Jacob against Jacob, or in the theological term advanced in the book, "My people."

And their flesh off their bones.
ᵃ⁻And after tearing their skins off them,
And their flesh off their bones,⁻ᵃ
And breaking their bones to bits,
You have cut it up ᵇ⁻as into⁻ᵇ a pot,
Like meat in a caldron.

4   Someday they shall cry out to the LORD,
But He will not answer them;
At that time He will hide His face from them,
In accordance with the wrongs they have done.

5   Thus said the LORD to the prophets
Who lead My people astray,
Who cry "Peace!"
When they have something to chew,
But launch a war on him
Who fails to fill their mouths:

6   Assuredly,
It shall be night for you
So that you cannot prophesy,
And it shall be dark for you
So that you cannot divine;
The sun shall set on the prophets,
And the day shall be darkened for them.

7   The seers shall be shamed
And the diviners confounded;
They shall cover their upper lips,ᶜ
Because no response comes from God.

8   But I,
I am filled with strength by the spirit of the LORD,
And with judgment and courage,
To declare to Jacob his transgressions
And to Israel his sin.

9   Hear this, you rulers of the House of Jacob,
You chiefs of the House of Israel,
Who detest justice
And make crooked all that is straight,

10   Who build Zion with crime,
Jerusalem with iniquity!

11   Her rulers judge for gifts,
Her priests give rulings for a fee,
And her prophets divine for pay;
Yet they rely upon the LORD, saying,

---

a-a *Brought down from v. 2 for clarity.*
b-b *Meaning of Heb. uncertain; Septuagint and Syriac read "like flesh in."*
c *As a sign of mourning; cf. Ezek. 24.17, 22; Lev. 13.45.*

4: The Targum understands *He will hide His face from them* as "He will remove His Shekhinah from them." On the concept of the LORD's hiding the divine face, see Deut. 31.17. The concept, common in biblical texts, was developed later in Judaism and served to bridge the tension between divine goodness and acute suffering. **5:** *When they have something to chew,* or more literally, "when they have something to bite with their teeth." The point is not so much that prophets received gifts from their "clients." This behavior seems to have been widely accepted (see 1 Sam. 9.8; 1 Kings 14.3; 2 Kings 4.42; 8.8–9; Amos 7.12), and the prophets needed their bread too. Rather, these prophets shaped or announced their prophecies to please their clients, so as to increase the gifts they received from them. By doing so they perverted their office (and the LORD's trust) for material gain. The precise choice of words in the Heb implies additional powerful connotations. The choice of expression "bite with their teeth" allows not only the wordplay between teeth and *mouths,* but also a description of the behavior of the prophets that evokes the animal behavior of other leaders (v. 3). The verb "nashakh," "to bite," has a sound reminiscent to that of "naḥash," "snake." The same verb "nashakh" means in other contexts "to charge interest" and carries negative connotations (cf. Hab. 2.7; Deut. 23.20). To some extent, the text suggests that they are like beastly creditors or snakes that bite the flesh of Israel with their teeth (cf. v. 3). **8:** The beginning of the v. offers an emphatic contrast between the true and the false prophet. Heb has no term for a false prophet; thus, in v. 5 they are called "nevi'im," the same term that would be used of true prophets. In many such cases, the ancient Septuagint translation clarifies the meaning of the text by inserting the word "false" ("pseudo"). **12:** Cf. Jer. 26.18. This is a rare instance of a quotation of prophetic character by another prophetic

"The LORD is in our midst;
No calamity shall overtake us."
12 Assuredly, because of you
Zion shall be plowed as a field,
And Jerusalem shall become heaps of ruins,
And the Temple Mount
A shrine in the woods.

4 ªIn the days to come,
The Mount of the LORD's House shall stand
Firm above the mountains;
And it shall tower above the hills.
The peoples shall gaze on it with joy,
2 And the many nations shall go and shall say:
"Come,
Let us go up to the Mount of the LORD,
To the House of the God of Jacob;
That He may instruct us in His ways,
And that we may walk in His paths."
For instruction shall come forthᵇ from Zion,
The word of the LORD from Jerusalem.
3 Thus He will judge among the many peoples,
And arbitrate for the multitude of nations,
However distant;
And they shall beat their swords into plowsharesᶜ
And their spears into pruning hooks.
Nation shall not take up
Sword against nation;
They shall never again knowᵈ war;
4 But every man shall sit
Under his grapevine or fig tree
With no one to disturb him.
For it was the LORD of Hosts who spoke.
5 Though all the peoples walk
Each in the names of its gods,
We will walk
In the name of the LORD our God
Forever and ever.

a For vv. 1–3 cf. Isa. 2.2–4.   b I.e., oracles will be obtainable.

c More exactly, the iron points with which wooden plows were tipped.   d Cf. Judg. 3.2.

character in a different book, and it indicates that prophetic books were studied in antiquity. Some scholars slightly emend the last phrase of this v. so as to read, "the Temple mountain shall belong to the wild animals." The motif of wild animals taking control of de-stroyed cities is relatively common in ancient Near Eastern literature, including the Bible.

4.1–5.14: A series of texts about the future. This section consists of six different subunits (4.1–5; 4.6–8; 4.8–5.1; 5.1–5; 5.6–8; 5.9–15). Each of these literary subunits presents a portrait of a future. These images of the future are widely different from one another, allowing each one to inform and balance the other. One of the most significant differences among these images of an ideal future concerns the fate of the nations other than Israel. Are they going to flow to Jerusalem to learn divine teachings coming from Jerusalem and its religious elite (4.2), or are they going to be crushed (5.14)? Despite these sig-nificant differences, this section should be viewed as a collection of oracles of consolation. **4.1–5:** In this portrait of the future, Jerusa-lem and the Temple Mount are the center of the world. Vv. 1–3 are nearly identical with Isa. 2.2–4; the exact literary relationship be-tween these two units is debated. **2:** *Instruction,* Heb "torah." The text clearly associates "torah" with "the word of the LORD." In Jewish liturgy this portion of the verse, *For instruction shall come forth from Zion,/ The word of the LORD from Je-rusalem,* is read when the Torah scroll is taken out of the Ark to be read. **3:** *He will judge:* The one who will judge is the LORD. Some me-dieval commentators, however, identified the judge with the Mes-siah (Ibn Ezra, Radak) and thus re-formulated to some extent the image of the ideal period. In its biblical context, however, this pas-sage depicts a messianic age with-out a personal messiah. *They shall beat their swords into plowshares . . . they shall never again know* [others translate, "train for"] *war* is one of the most popular, condensed de-scriptions of an ideal future. (Con-trast it with Joel 4.10.) **5:** This v. has been considered "narrowly particularistic" or "nationalistic" (as opposed to "universalistic") and has certainly been read in such a fashion (cf. Targum, Rashi, *Exod. Rab.* 15.15). In its context in Micah, however, the v. rejects the "imperial" model of everyone be-coming Israel. Instead, it supports the concept that non-Israelites may accept the word of the LORD from Jerusalem and still maintain their non-Israelite identity and

6 In that day　　　　　　—declares the LORD—
I will assemble the lame [sheep]
And will gather the outcast
And those I have treated harshly;

7 And I will turn the lame into a remnant
And the expelled[a] into a populous nation.
And the LORD will reign over them on Mount Zion
Now and for evermore.

8 And you, O Migdal-eder,[b]
[c]Outpost of Fair Zion,
It shall come to you:[c]
The former monarchy shall return—
The kingship of [d]Fair Jerusalem.[d]

9 Now why do you utter such cries?
Is there no king in you,
Have your advisors perished,
That you have been seized by writhing
Like a woman in travail?

10 Writhe and scream,[e] Fair Zion,
Like a woman in travail!
For now you must leave the city
And dwell in the country—
And you will reach Babylon.
There you shall be saved,
There the LORD will redeem you
From the hands of your foes.

11 Indeed, many nations
Have assembled against you
Who think, "Let our eye
[c]Obscenely gaze[c] on Zion."

12 But they do not know
The design of the LORD,
They do not divine His intent:
He has gathered them
Like cut grain to the threshing floor.

13 Up and thresh, Fair Zion!
For I will give you horns of iron
And provide you with hoofs of bronze,
And you will crush the many peoples.
You[f] will devote their riches to the LORD,
Their wealth to the Lord of all the earth.

worship (cf. the sailors in Jonah ch 1). **8:** *Migdal-eder,* "tower of the flock," reinforces the previous image of Israel as "flock" whose shepherd is the LORD. *Outpost of Fair Zion* may be translated as "Ophel (or stronghold) of the daughter of Zion." **10:** The explicit reference to the Babylonian exile of Judah shows the authorship's awareness of both the historical event and its importance for post-monarchic Israel. The actual writer cannot be identified with Micah, because the latter lived—according to the book—more than a century before the destruction of Jerusalem and the exile to Babylonia. Quite remarkably, this v. views the Babylonian exile as a positive experience, and along with other vv. helps to explain why those who returned to Yehud (Judah) after the exile felt superior to those who remained behind, a major theme of Ezra-Nehemiah.

---

a *Meaning of Heb. uncertain; emendation yields "weaklings"; cf. Ezek. 34.4.*
b *Apparently near Bethlehem; see Gen. 35.19–21.*　　c-c *Meaning of Heb. uncertain.*
d-d *Emendation yields "the House of Israel"; cf. 5.1–2.*　　e *Meaning of Heb. uncertain.*
f *Heb. -ti serves here as the ending of the second-person singular feminine; cf. Judg. 5.7 and note; Jer. 2.20; etc.*

14　Now you gash yourself ᵃ·in grief.·ᵃ
They have laid siege to us;
They strike the ruler of Israel
On the cheek with a staff.

5　And you, O Bethlehem of Ephrath,ᵇ
Least among the clans of Judah,
From you one shall come forth
To rule Israel for Me—
One whose origin is from of old,
From ancient times.

2　ᵃ·Truly, He will leave them [helpless]
Until she who is to bear has borne;ᶜ
Then the rest of his countrymen
Shall return to the children of Israel.·ᵃ

3　He shall stand and shepherd
By the might of the Lord,
By the power of the name
Of the Lord his God,
And they shall dwell [secure].
For lo, he shall wax great
To the ends of the earth;

4　And that shall afford safety.
Should Assyria invade our land
And tread upon our fortresses,ᵈ
We will set up over itᵉ seven shepherds,
Eight princes of men,

5　Who will shepherd Assyria's land with swords,
The land of Nimrod ᶠ·in its gates.·ᶠ
Thus he will deliver [us]
From Assyria, should it invade our land,
And should it trample our country.

6　The remnant of Jacob shall be,
In the midst of the many peoples,
Like dew from the Lord,
Like droplets on grass—
Which do not look to any man
Nor place their hope in mortals.

7　The remnant of Jacob
Shall be among the nations,
In the midst of the many peoples,

5.1: The reference is to David, from *Bethlehem* in *Judah*. **2:** *Until she who is to bear has borne:* Traditional Jewish interpretations of this v. tend to focus on comparisons between the birth pangs of a woman and the hardship of Israel prior to the coming of the Messiah. See the following text: "Rab said: The son of David will not come until the [Roman] power enfolds Israel for nine months, as it is written, Therefore will he give them up, until the time that she which travaileth hath brought forth: then the remnant of his brethren shall return unto the children of Israel. 'Ulla said: Let him [The Messiah] come, but let me not see him. Rabbah said likewise: Let him come, but let me not see him . . . Abaye enquired of Rabbah: 'What is your reason [for not wishing to see him]? Shall we say, because of the birth pangs [preceding the advent] of the Messiah?' But it has been taught, R. Eleazar's disciples asked him: 'What must a man do to be spared the pangs of the Messiah?' [He answered,] 'Let him engage in study and benevolence; and you Master do both.' " (*b. Sanh.* 98b [Soncino ET]). **5:** *The land of Nimrod,* Assyria (cf. Gen. 10.8–12). *Nimrod* is chosen because might was associated with him (Gen. 10.8), but this image is turned against him.

a-a　*Meaning of Heb. uncertain.*
b　*The clan to which the Bethlehemites belonged; see 1 Sam. 17.12; Ruth 1.2; 4.11.*
c　*I.e., a ruler, shepherd (v. 3), to deliver Israel from the Assyrians (vv. 4–5).*
d　*Septuagint and Syriac read "soil"; cf. v. 5.*　　e　*I.e., Assyria.*
f-f　*Emendation yields "with drawn blades"; cf. Ps. 37.14; 55.22.*

Like a lion among beasts of the wild,
Like a fierce lion among flocks of sheep,
Which tramples wherever it goes
And rends, with none to deliver.

8 Your hand shall prevail over your foes,
And all your enemies shall be cut down!

9 In that day　　　　　　　—declares the LORD—
I will destroy the horses in your midst
And wreck your chariots.

10 I will destroy the cities of your land
And demolish all your fortresses.

11 I will destroy the sorcery you practice,
And you shall have no more soothsayers.

12 I will destroy your idols
And the sacred pillars in your midst;
And no more shall you bow down
To the work of your hands.

13 I will tear down the sacred posts in your midst
And destroy your cities.ᵃ

14 In anger and wrath
Will I wreak retribution
On the nationsᵇ that have not obeyed.

6 Hear what the LORD is saying:
Come, present [My] case before the mountains,
And let the hills hear you pleading.

2 Hear, you mountains, the case of the LORD—
ᶜYou firmᶜ foundations of the earth!
For the LORD has a case against His people,
He has a suit against Israel.

3 "My people!
What wrong have I done you?
What hardship have I caused you?
Testify against Me.

4 In fact,
I brought you up from the land of Egypt,
I redeemed you from the house of bondage,
And I sent before you
Moses, Aaron, and Miriam.

5 "My people,
Remember what Balak king of Moab
Plotted against you,

9–14: A divine purge of Israel and the nations that serves to emphasize the importance of obedience to the LORD. Note the rhetorically powerful repetitions of "you/your" and "I will" that serve to stress the main point of the text, namely the relation between the LORD and Israel in the future envisioned in these vv., as the destruction of sinful elements of Judah is transformed at the last moment to *retribution on the nations.*

6.1–8: A didactic section about divinely ordained behavior. The text advances the legal metaphor of a lawsuit so as to address the relationship between God and Israel. Of course, this is not a usual lawsuit. Mountains, hills, and the very foundations of the earth are summoned. The Heb of vv. 1–2 abounds in multiple (possible) meanings, but the message of vv. 3–5 is unequivocal: Israel had no reason to abandon God, for God has done no wrong, but rather many *gracious acts* for Israel. The acts explicitly mentioned relate to the exodus from Egypt, the period of wandering in the desert, including the Balak-Balaam story (see Num. chs 22–24), and the crossing of the Jordan (see Josh. chs 3–4). **4:** Miriam here plays a role equal to her brothers, in contrast to the Torah narrative.

a Emendation yields "idols."　　　　b Emendation yields "arrogant."
c-c Emendation yields "Give ear, you."

And how Balaam son of Beor
Responded to him.
[Recall your passage]
From Shittim to Gilgal[a]—
And you will recognize
The gracious acts of the LORD."

6   With what shall I approach the LORD,
      Do homage to God on high?
      Shall I approach Him with burnt offerings,
      With calves a year old?
7   Would the LORD be pleased with thousands of
            rams,
      With myriads of streams of oil?
      Shall I give my first-born for my transgression,
      The fruit of my body for my sins?

8   "He has told you, O man, what is good,
      And what the LORD requires of you:
      Only to do justice
      And to love goodness,
      And [b-]to walk modestly with your God;[-b]
9   [c-]Then will your name achieve wisdom."[-c]

      Hark! The LORD
      Summons the city:
      [d-]Hear, O scepter;
      For who can direct her [10]but you?[-d]
      Will I overlook,[e] in the wicked man's house,
      The granaries of wickedness
      And the accursed short *ephah?*[f]
11   Shall he[g] be acquitted despite wicked
            balances
      And a bag of fraudulent weights?—
12[h] Whose rich men are full of lawlessness,
      And whose inhabitants speak treachery,
      With tongues of deceit in their mouths.

13   I, in turn, have beaten you sore,
      Have stunned [you] for your sins:

a I.e., the crossing of the Jordan; see Josh. 3.1, 14–4.19.
b-b Or "It is prudent to serve your God."
c-c Emendation yields "And it is worthwhile to revere His name."
d-d Meaning of Heb. uncertain.
e Taking ish as from nashah "to forget"; cf. Deut. 32.18.
f Cf. Amos 8.4–5.
g Heb. "I"; change of vocalization yields "Will I acquit him."
h This verse would read well after "city" in v. 9.

6–8: The text here should not be interpreted as a rejection of Temple offerings; rather it expresses the common biblical and ancient Near Eastern concept of the primacy of morality over sacrifices (e.g., 1 Sam. 15.22; Prov. 21.3). **7:** This v. seems to assume that human sacrifice, at least in extreme circumstances, was thought to have been acceptable and efficacious (see Gen. ch 22; 2 Kings 3.27). **8:** This didactic saying is one of the most influential and often quoted sayings in prophetic literature. It was considered as a possible compendium of all the Mitzvot. "R. Simlai when preaching said: Six hundred and thirteen precepts were communicated to Moses, three hundred and sixty-five negative precepts . . . Micah came and reduced them to three [principles], as it is written, He has told you, O human, what is good, and what the LORD requires of you: only to do justice, and to love goodness, and to walk humbly with your God. 'To do justice,' this concerns justice; 'and to love goodness,' this concerns "gemilut hasadim" (acts of kindness); 'and to walk humbly with your God,' this concerns walking in funeral and bridal processions" (*b. Mak.* 23b–24a; cf. *b. Sukkah* 49b and Radak). *To walk modestly with your God* (cf. Targum) is usually translated as "to walk humbly with your God," but its original meaning is likely to be "to walk wisely with your God" (and cf. v. 9).

6.9–16: Another explanation for the fall of Jerusalem. 9: The text is difficult and some emendations have been suggested. The rendition of this v. reflects an emendation of the MT. The latter may be translated as: "The voice of the LORD cries out to the city— it is sound wisdom to fear Your name—'Hear, O tribe and city assembly!' " If so, the expression within dashes serves as a comment made by the narrator that is easily understood by the readership of the book.

14 You have been eating without getting your fill,
   ^aAnd there is a gnawing at your vitals;
   You have been conceiving without bearing
        young,^a
   And what you bore I would deliver to the sword.
15 You have been sowing, but have nothing to reap;
   You have trod olives, but have no oil for rubbing,
   And grapes^b but have no wine to drink.
16 Yet ^cyou have kept^c the laws of Omri,
   And all the practices of the House of Ahab,
   And have followed what they devised.
   Therefore I will make you an object of horror
   And ^dher inhabitants^d an object of hissing;^e
   And you shall bear the mockery of peoples.^f

7 Woe is me!^g
   I am become like leavings of a fig harvest,
   Like gleanings when the vintage is over,
   There is not a cluster to eat,
   Not a ripe fig I could desire.
2 The pious are vanished from the land,
   None upright are left among men;
   All lie in wait to commit crimes,
   One traps the other in his net.
3 ^aThey are eager to do evil:
   The magistrate makes demands,
   And the judge [judges] for a fee;
   The rich man makes his crooked plea,
   And they grant it.^a
4 The best of them is like a prickly shrub;
   The [most] upright, worse than a barrier of thorns.
   ^aOn the day you waited for,^a your doom has
        come—
   Now their confusion shall come to pass.
5 Trust no friend,
   Rely on no intimate;
   Be guarded in speech
   With her who lies in your bosom.
6 For son spurns father,
   Daughter rises up against mother,
   Daughter-in-law against mother-in-law—
   A man's own household
   Are his enemies.

16: *Omri . . . Ahab*, the most notorious kings of the dynasty of Omri/Ahab. The text reflects the common characterization of the House of Ahab as the primary example of a sinful royal house of northern Israel; see 2 Kings 8.18; 21.3, 13; 2 Chron. 21.13; 22.4; 1 Kings 16.23–22.40; 2 Kings chs 10–28. Likewise, 2 Kings 17.19, 22, and other texts condemn Judah for following the ways of Israel.

7.1–7: A text about trust in the LORD despite and in response to social disintegration. The book teaches the readers that the response to social disintegration must be trust in the LORD (see v. 7 to which the text leads up). **6:** The situation envisioned here is reversed in the eschatological image of Mal. 3.24. **7:** *Yet I will look to the LORD* may be translated "As for me, I will look to the LORD." The "me" is, of course, the pious speaker in the text with whom the readers are supposed to identify.

---

a-a *Meaning of Heb. uncertain.*   b *Lit. "new wine."*
c-c *Heb. "is kept."*   d-d *I.e., those of the city of v. 9, apparently Samaria.*
e *See note at Jer. 18.16.*   f *Heb. "My people."*
g *The speaker is feminine (cf. 'elohayikh, v. 10), probably Samaria personified; cf. note d-d at 6.16.*

7   Yet I will look to the LORD,
    I will wait for the God who saves me,
    My God will hear me.

8   Do not rejoice over me,
    O my enemy![a]
    Though I have fallen, I rise again;
    Though I sit in darkness, the LORD is my light.

9   I must bear the anger of the LORD,
    Since I have sinned against Him,
    Until He champions my cause
    And upholds my claim.
    He will let me out into the light;
    I will enjoy vindication by Him.

10 When my enemy[a] sees it,
    She shall be covered with shame,
    She who taunts me with "Where is He,
    The LORD your God?"
    My eyes shall behold her [downfall];
    Lo, she shall be for trampling
    Like mud in the streets.

11 A day for mending your walls[b]—
    That is a far-off day.

12 This is rather a day when to you
    [Tramplers] will come streaming
    From Assyria and the towns of Egypt—
    From [every land from] Egypt to the Euphrates,
    From sea to sea and from mountain to mountain—

13 And your[c] land shall become a desolation—
    Because of those who dwell in it—
    As the fruit of their misdeeds.

14 Oh, shepherd Your people with Your staff,
    Your very own flock.
    May they who dwell isolated
    [d]In a woodland surrounded by farmland[-d]
    Graze[e] Bashan and Gilead
    As in olden days.

15 [f]I will show him[-f] wondrous deeds
    As in the days when You sallied forth from the
        land of Egypt.

7.8–20: A concluding note of hope. A confirmation that the relationship between the LORD and Judah and Jerusalem is maintained, that the LORD forgives and Israel will be restored. **14:** *Bashan and Gilead*, fertile lands in Transjordan. **15:** As elsewhere in prophetic literature, particularly in Deutero-Isaiah (Isa. chs 40ff.), the exodus is paradigmatic for restoration and salvation.

a Heb. feminine, apparently referring to Damascus.
b To keep out tramplers (end of preceding verse); cf. Isa. 5.5; Ps. 80.13–14.
c Heb. "the."
d-d I.e., the land west of the Jordan, which is represented as far less fertile than adjacent regions.
e Emendation yields "possess."
f-f Emendation yields "Show us."

16 Let nations behold and be ashamed
Despite all their might;
Let them put hand to mouth;
Let their ears be deafened!

17 Let them lick dust like snakes,
Like crawling things on the ground!
*Let them come trembling out of their
strongholds*
To the LORD our God;
Let them fear and dread You!

18 Who is a God like You,
Forgiving iniquity
And remitting transgression;
Who has not maintained His wrath forever
Against the remnant of His own people,
Because He loves graciousness!

19 He will take us back in love;
He will cover up our iniquities,
You will hurl all our *b* sins
Into the depths of the sea.

20 You will keep faith with Jacob,
Loyalty to Abraham,
As You promised on oath to our fathers
In days gone by.

18–20: These vv. provide an up-beat, extremely hopeful conclusion of the book. Such conclusions are expected in prophetic books (see intro. to The Twelve). Because of their assurance of God's forgive-ness, these vv. are used in the liturgy for Rosh Ha-Shanah and Yom Kippur (see intro. to Micah).

a-a *Meaning of Heb. uncertain.*   b *Heb. "their."*

נחום

Nahum

THE DOUBLE TITLE OF THE BOOK of Nahum (1.1) points to its main characteristics. It is a written prophetic book associated with Nahum. It is also, in the main, a pronouncement against Nineveh. From the readers' viewpoint Nineveh was both a historical city, the capital of the Assyrian empire, and a symbol of a sinful, overbearing, exceedingly oppressive political structure which was totally destroyed and never rebuilt. From the perspective of a readership well aware of the fall of Nineveh, such a fall from the pinnacle of glory and might becomes a paradigmatic example of the fate of worldly, powerful oppressors and, above all, of the even greater power of the LORD who brings them down. As such, the book served as a message of hope and trust in the LORD to those who saw themselves as oppressed by their own "Nineveh."

The text does not set the book in any particular period in monarchic Judah. From the perspective of the intended readership, the only restriction was that Nahum must have lived before the destruction of the city, because prophetic characters in a prophetic book are supposed to prophesy about what will be, not what has already happened. The date of the composition of the book is another matter. Some scholars argue that the vivid description of the destruction of Nineveh (612 BCE) indicates that the author of the book must have written it (or a portion of it) soon after the events; others disagree. The reference to the conquest and sack of the Egyptian capital of Thebes (No-amon) as a past event in 3.8 indicates that the book was composed later than this event (663). The question of how much later remains open. *Seder Olam Rabbah* and other Jewish traditional sources claim that Nahum prophesied in the days of Manasseh, that is, sometime in the first half of the 7th century BCE.

The book as it stands may be subdivided in different ways. One possibility is that there are three main sections or readings. After the superscription (1.1), the first section (1.2–14) deals mainly with the LORD's character and responses to opponents (symbolized by Assyria) and to Israel's plight. The second section (2.1–14) first links the actions of the LORD to Judah's joy, restoration, and freedom from oppressive scoundrels and marauders (vv. 1–3). The reference to the end of the latter flows into a vivid description of the fall of Nineveh (2.4–14). The last passage (3.1–19) dwells on Nineveh's hubris—which is understood as a challenge to the LORD—and the fall of the city. Indirectly, it deals again with the matter of God's character and attributes. Other divisions of the text are possible; for instance, a hymn of theophany (ch 1) is followed by a taunt song against Nineveh (chs 2–3). Another possibility: 1.2–11 "The LORD is mighty and avenges evil"; 1.12–2.14 "The judgment of Nineveh"; 3.1–9 " 'Ah, Nineveh.' " Or possibly 1.2–2.11 "A prophetic challenge to opponents of the LORD"; 2.12–3.19, "A challenge to Nineveh's hubris." As in many other prophetic books this multiplicity of possible outlines contributes to the ability of the community to read, re-read, and continually study the prophetic book, and to emphasize one aspect of the book in one reading and another in a different reading. All in all, this multiplicity creates a situation in which different readings based on particular outlines inform and balance each other and all together communicate a meaning much richer than any of them separately.

[EHUD BEN ZVI]

1 A pronouncement on Nineveh: The Book of the Prophecy of Nahum the Elkoshite.

2 The LORD is a passionate, avenging God;
The LORD is vengeful and fierce in wrath.
The LORD takes vengeance on His enemies,
He rages against His foes.

3 The LORD is slow to anger and of great
    forbearance,
But the LORD does not remit all punishment.
He travels in whirlwind and storm,
And clouds are the dust on His feet.

4 He rebukes the sea and dries it up,
And He makes all rivers fail;
Bashan and Carmel languish,
And the blossoms[a] of Lebanon wither.

5 The mountains quake because of Him,
And the hills melt.
The earth heaves[b] before Him,
The world and all that dwell therein.

6 Who can stand before His wrath?
Who can resist His fury?
His anger pours out like fire,
And rocks are shattered because of Him.

7 The LORD is good to [those who hope in Him],
A haven on a day of distress;
He is mindful of those who seek refuge in Him.

8 And with a sweeping flood
He makes an end of [c]her place,[c]
And chases His enemies into darkness.

a Lit. "bud."   b Meaning of Heb. uncertain.
c-c Meaning of Heb. uncertain; emendation yields "those who oppose Him."

1.1: Superscription. As mentioned in the introduction, this is an unusual double title, thereby emphasizing the central theme of the book, the fall of Nineveh. *Elkoshite:* There is no known location that may correspond to this town. Some scholars doubt that the reference is to a town at all and others (cf. Targum) have suggested that the writer may have invented it as a wordplay (Heb "God is harsh"; cf. Isa. 19.4).

1.2–14: The LORD responds to Assyria and to Israel's plight. There are remnants of an acrostic in these vv., but this has been disrupted through the transmission of the passage, and can no longer be reconstructed. These initial vv. are extremely traditional, quoting common themes and phrases. **2–3:** These vv. offer an interpretation and elaboration of Exod. 34.6–7 (cf. Num. 14.18; Jonah 4.2; Ps. 145.8); also cf. Josh. 24.19; Jer. 3.5, 12. **4:** *The sea,* often considered a mythological place of chaos (cf. Isa. 27.1). *Dries it up,* as during the exodus (Exod. 14.21; Ps. 106.9). **5:** For similar theophanic imagery, see Mic. 1.5; Isa. 13.13; Jer. 4.24; 2 Sam. 22.8 ‖ Ps 18.8, among many others. **7:** As the community reads about the LORD's power and the ridiculousness of any attempt to withstand God's fury, this v. serves to reassure them that not all need be afraid of such fury and power. **8:** If *her place* is correct, it

9 Why will you plot against the Lord?
He wreaks utter destruction:
No adversary[a] opposes Him twice!

10 [b-]For like men besotted with drink,
They are burned up like tangled thorns,
Like straw that is thoroughly dried.[-b]

11c The base plotter
Who designed evil against the Lord
Has left you.

12 Thus said the Lord:
[b-]"Even as they[d] were full and many,
Even so are they over and gone;
As surely as I afflicted you,
I will afflict you no more."[-b]

13 And now
I will break off his yoke bar from you
And burst your cords apart.

14 The Lord has commanded concerning him:[e]
[b-]No posterity shall continue your name.[-b]
I will do away with
The carved and graven images
In the temples of your gods;
I will make your grave
[b-]Accord with your worthlessness.[-b]

2 Behold on the hills
The footsteps of a herald
Announcing good fortune!
"Celebrate your festivals, O Judah,
Fulfill your vows.
Never again shall scoundrels invade you,
They have totally vanished."

2f A shatterer has come up against you.
Man the guard posts,
Watch the road;
Steady your loins,
Brace all your strength!

3 For the Lord has restored [g-]the Pride[h] of Jacob
As well as the Pride[h] of Israel,[-g]

refers to Nineveh. The same consonantal text may be read "His opposition" (see translators' note c–c on p. 1220). **11:** The verse may be translated as follows: "From you has come forth a plotter of evil against the Lord, a lawless counselor." This counselor is identified as an Assyrian king, or as an "archetypal Assyrian king," and in the Jewish tradition in particular, as Sennacherib (see 2 Kings 18.13–19.37). Readers would associate the figure of this counselor with that of the leader of whatever group they are opposing.

2.1–14: The two poles: Judah's joy and peace and the conquest and destruction of Nineveh.
1: Cf. Isa. 52.7. **3:** The pride of Jacob as well as the pride of Israel; or "the pride of Jacob, yea, the pride of Israel." Here Jacob and Israel are likely to be synonyms that stand for all Israel or, given that the passage as a whole focuses on Judah, on Judah as its legitimate representative.

---

a Cf. Ugaritic ṣrt.   b–b Meaning of Heb. uncertain.
c Vv. 11–14 would read well after 2.1.   d I.e., the days of your affliction.
e Heb. "you."   f This verse would read well after v. 3.
g–g "Jacob" refers to the northern kingdom (cf. Amos 6.8; 8.7); Israel refers to the southern kingdom, regarded as the remnant of Israel after the fall of the northern kingdom (cf. Mic. 1.13–15).
h Emendation yields "vine."

Though marauders have laid them waste
And ravaged their branches.

4   His warriors' shields are painted red,
     And the soldiers are clothed in crimson;
     The chariots are like flaming torches,[a]
     On the day they are made ready.
     [b]The [arrows of] cypress wood are poisoned,[b]
5   The chariots dash about frenzied in the fields,
     They rush through the meadows.
     They appear like torches,
     They race like streaks of lightning.
6   [c]He commands his burly men;
     They stumble as they advance,
     They hasten up to her wall,
     Where [d]wheeled shelters[d] are set up.[c]
7   [e]The floodgates are opened,
     And the palace is deluged.[e]
8   [f]And Huzzab is exiled and carried away,[f]
     While her handmaidens [g]escort [her][g]
     As with the voices of doves,
     Beating their breasts.
9   Nineveh has been like a [placid] pool of water
     [c]From earliest times;[c]
     Now they flee.
     "Stop! Stop!"—
     But none can turn them back.
10   "Plunder silver! Plunder gold!"
     There is no limit to the treasure;
     It is a hoard of all precious objects.

11   Desolation, devastation, and destruction!
     Spirits sink,
     Knees buckle,
     All loins tremble,
     All faces [h]turn ashen.[h]
12   What has become of that lions' den,
     That pasture[i] of great beasts,
     Where lion and lion's breed walked,

4–10: A narrative account of the destruction of Nineveh begins with siege and defense and concludes with the plunder of the city, and the confused and terrified response of those who survived. The precise wording of the narrative sets a tempo that conveys a sense of the intensity, chaos, and confusion of the battle scene; much of this is lost in translation. **4:** *His warriors' shields*, the shields of those attacking Nineveh. Note that the beginning of the narrative has no clear antecedent. **6:** The v. may be translated: "He calls (or assigns) his mighty men (or commanders); they stumble as they go; they hurry to her wall [Nineveh's wall], and the siege shelters [to protect the troops from the weaponry of the besieged] are set up." The language of the v. stresses the speed of the actions. **7:** The floodgates refer to the gates of the canals and dams. This is both a reflection on the physical environment of Nineveh and a metaphorical reference to the conquering flood of the enemy. The fall of the palace is the beginning of the end of Nineveh. **8:** The reference to *Huzzab* is unclear. Given the reference to her maidservants, one may assume that the v. contains a reference to an Assyrian woman of high status, either metaphorically or not. The Targum, Rashi, and other medieval interpreters understood the term as "queen." **11:** The English reflects the striking alliteration of the Heb: "bukah umevukah umevulakah." **12:** The language resembles a lament. This sharpens the message by heightening the irony and prepares the reader for the next passage (3.1–19). The repetition of *lion* may play on the common motif of lions in Assyrian palace reliefs; here the lion imagery is ironically turned against the Assyrians.

a Understanding peladoth *as equivalent to* lappidoth.
b-b *Meaning of Heb. uncertain. Emendation yields* "The horsemen charge"; *cf. 3.3.*
c-c *Meaning of Heb. uncertain.*
d-d *To protect the crews that swung the battering rams.*
e-e *I.e., the walls are breached and the palace is overrun.*
f-f *Meaning of Heb. uncertain. Emendation yields* "And its mistress is led out and exiled."
g-g *Emendation yields* "moan."
h-h *Meaning of Heb. uncertain; cf. note at Joel 2.6.*
i *Emendation yields* "cave."

And lion's cub—with none to disturb them?

13 [Where is] the lion that tore victims for his cubs
And strangled for his lionesses,
And filled his lairs with prey
And his dens with mangled flesh?

14 I am going to deal with you
——declares the LORD of Hosts:
I will burn down ᵃher chariots in smoke,ᵃ
And the sword shall devour your great beasts;
I will stamp out your killings from the earth,
And the sound of your messengersᵇ
Shall be heard no more.

3 Ah, city of crime,
Utterly treacherous,
Full of violence,
Where killing never stops!

2 Crack of whip
And rattle of wheel,
Galloping steed
And bounding chariot!

3 Charging horsemen,
Flashing swords,
And glittering spears!
Hosts of slain
And heaps of corpses,
Dead bodies without number—
They stumble over bodies.

4 Because of the countless harlotries of the harlot,
The winsome mistress of sorcery,
Who ensnaredᶜ nations with her harlotries
And peoples with her sorcery,

5 I am going to deal with you
——declares the LORD of Hosts.
I will lift up your skirts over your face
And display your nakedness to the nations
And your shame to kingdoms.

6 I will throw loathsome things over you
And disfigure you
And make a spectacle of you.

7 All who see you will recoil from you
And will say,
"Nineveh has been ravaged!"
Who will console her?

3.1–19: On Nineveh's pride and its fall. The passage begins *Ah* (v. 1) and concludes with the clapping of hands (v. 19), from an ironic imitation of a lament to universal joy. The entire section explains the fall of the city in terms of its behavior. **1:** This is an instance of the typical "Ah" (Heb "hoy") formula. Usually "ah" is followed by a noun phrase (or a participle) that not only identifies for whom the exclamation is due, but also explains their fate in terms of just punishment (e.g., Zeph. 3.1). *City of crime* (more lit. "city of blood[shed]") follows this pattern. The NJPS translation of the v. is not fully literal. **4–7:** On the general imagery, cf. Lam. ch 1. **4:** The association of a female metaphor for the city with the negative, female imagery of *harlotries* and *sorcery* is obvious. Such metaphors were common in the societies in which biblical texts were written and first read, though problematic to many readers today.

a-a *Emendation yields "your thicket in fire."*   b *Emendation yields "devouring."*
c *Meaning of Heb. uncertain.*

Where shall I look for
Anyone to comfort you?

8 Were you any better than No-amon,[a]
Which sat by the Nile,
Surrounded by water—
Its rampart a river,[b]
Its wall [c]consisting of sea?[c]

9 Populous Nubia
And teeming Egypt,
Put and the Libyans—
They were her[d] helpers.

10 Yet even she was exiled,
She went into captivity.
Her babes, too, were dashed in pieces
At every street corner.
Lots were cast for her honored men,
And all her nobles were bound in chains.

11 You too shall be drunk
And utterly overcome;[e]
You too shall seek
A refuge from the enemy.

12 All your forts are fig trees
With[f] ripe fruit;
If shaken they will fall
Into the mouths of devourers.

13 Truly, the troops within you are women;
The gates of your land have opened themselves
To your enemies;
Fire has consumed your gate bars.

14 Draw water for the siege,
Strengthen your forts;
Tread the clay,
Trample the mud,
Grasp the brick mold!

15 There fire will devour you,
The sword will put an end to you;
It will devour you like the grub.
[g]Multiply like grubs,
Multiply like locusts![g]

16 You had more traders
Than the sky has stars—

8: *No-amon,* Thebes, the Egyptian capital, one of the most impressive and wealthy cities of the ancient Near East. It was conquered by Assyria in the days of Ashurbanipal (663 BCE). The main enemy of the Assyrians was an Ethiopian dynasty that ruled over Egypt. The pun on words and historical background is clear. **10:** On the image of smashed babies, cf. 2 Kings 8.12; Isa. 13.16; Hos. 10.14; 14.1; Ps. 137.9. **11:** The *you* (fem.) refers back to Nineveh. The metaphor is one of a drunken woman; see v. 12. **13:** The language of the text reflects a worldview in which women are seen as weak and defenseless. The relevant section of the verse may be understood not only as *the troops within you are women* but also as "Behold! Your people: women in your midst!" Cf. Isa. 19.16; Jer. 30.57; 51.30. **15, 17:** The text plays on two common associations of the locust, with troops and with being a multitude (cf. Joel). Some translations have "locust" or "chewing locust" instead of *grub* in v. 15. The point is that the locust (enemy) will devour Assyria whereas its multitude (locust) of troops, merchants, scribes, and the like will not be able to save Assyria. The word translated *marshals* may also be translated "scribes." **19:** On clapping hands for joy, cf. Ps. 47.2. Everyone has suffered because of Assyria and now rejoices in its permanent fall.

---

a *Amon was the tutelary deity of No (Thebes; cf. Jer. 46.25), which the Assyrians had sacked in 663 B.C.E.*
b *Heb. "sea."*   c-c *Change of vocalization yields "water."*
d *Heb. "your."*   e *Meaning of Heb. uncertain.*
f *Emendation yields "Your troops are"; cf. next verse.*   g-g *Meaning of Heb. uncertain.*

The grubs cast their skins and fly away.

17 Your guards were like locusts,
Your marshals like piles of hoppers
Which settle on the stone fences
On a chilly day;
When the sun comes out, they fly away,
And where they are nobody knows.

18 Your shepherds are slumbering,
O king of Assyria;
Your sheepmasters are ᵃ‑lying inert;ᵃ
Your people are scatteredᵇ over the hills,
And there is none to gather them.

19 There is no healingᶜ for your injury;
Your wound is grievous.
All who hear the news about you
Clap their hands over you.
For who has not suffered
From your constant malice?

a-a Lit. "dwelling"; emendation yields "asleep."
b Meaning of Heb. uncertain.
c Heb. kehah, a variant of gehah; see Prov. 17.22.

חבקוק
Habakkuk

THE BOOK OF HABAKKUK consists of a report of a dialogue between the prophet and the LORD (chs 1–2) and a prayer or psalm (ch 3). It is most significant that a book that contains mainly human speech is considered to be "the (prophetic) pronouncement that Habakkuk, the prophet, saw (i.e., perceived in a revelation/vision)." In other words, the written report of the words of a prophet to God becomes a revelation or divinely originated vision. (The same process may have led to the consideration of the book of Psalms, for instance, as Scripture.)

From the perspective of the intended readers, it would be absurd for the text to maintain that a true prophet of the LORD prophesied about events that have already happened; therefore, the text presents Habakkuk's vision as preceding the fall of Babylon. Needless to say, nothing about the date of composition of the book or a historical Habakkuk can be learned from this observation. The most that can be said is that the book presumes the situation that began with the rise of Babylonian power around 612 BCE, and therefore is not earlier than that date. The text assumes a readership (and authorship) that was aware that Babylonia was the main power in the area at some point. For readerships that were also aware of the fall of the Babylonian (or Chaldean) empire—as any Persian period readership would be—the book is not so much about why justice does not emerge, but is rather about living under injustice. How do readers relate the known attributes of the LORD to an international system in which the dominant imperial power "slays nations without pity," or "seizes homes not their own" and which surely does not place its trust in the LORD? How is a pious person supposed to deal with this situation? From the perspective of such readers the fact that Babylonia has already fallen makes a prominent contribution to the persuasive power of the book and its message.

As mentioned above, following the superscription, the book contains a report of a dialogue between the prophet and the LORD. It is possible to divide this dialogue into four parts: (a) Habakkuk's first complaint (1.2–4), (b) The LORD's response (1.5–11), (c) Habakkuk's second complaint (1.12–17), and (d) Habakkuk's report of the LORD's response (ch 2). The book concludes with the prayer or psalm of Habakkuk (ch 3). This section has its own title or subtitle (see 3.1) and contains a short, human petition to God to manifest God's power (3.2), a lengthy report about an appearance of the LORD in the world (a theophany) (vv. 3–15), and above all concludes with an expression of human confidence in the LORD (vv. 16–19).

Many scholars maintain that some sections of the text (especially the prayer) existed prior to the book. The book as it stands, however, presents all three chapters as "the (prophetic) pronouncement that Habakkuk, the prophet, saw (i.e., perceived in a revelation/vision)."

A long commentary on the first two chapters of Habakkuk has been preserved among the Dead Sea Scrolls. This commentary, called by scholars *Pesher Habakkuk,* understands this prophetic work as being actualized in its author's own day, centuries after Habakkuk was written. Specifically, it identifies Habakkuk's Chaldeans, a name for the Babylonians, with the Kittim, almost certainly the Romans. This offers clear proof of how prophetic works were read and studied within a Jewish group that lived in the late Maccabean period as works that contain information about the life of their community of readers rather than arcane reports of past historical periods.   [EHUD BEN ZVI]

1 The pronouncement made by the prophet Habakkuk.

2   How long, O LORD, shall I cry out
        And You not listen,
        Shall I shout to You, "Violence!"
        And You not save?
3   Why do You make me see iniquity
        ª-[Why] do You look-ª upon wrong?—
        Raiding and violence are before me,
        Strife continues and contention ᵇ-goes on.-ᵇ
4   That is why decision fails
        And justice never emerges;
        For the villain hedges in the just man—
        Therefore judgment emerges deformed.

5   "Look among the nations,
        Observe well and be utterly astounded;
        For a work is being wrought in your days
        Which you would not believe if it were told.
6   For lo, I am raising up the Chaldeans,
        That fierce, impetuous nation,

a-a *Targum and Syriac "So that I look."*   b-b *Meaning of Heb. uncertain.*

1.1: Superscription. A more literal translation of the verse would be "the (prophetic) pronouncement that Habakkuk, the prophet, saw (i.e., perceived in a revelation/vision)." Some scholars consider this title to refer only to chs 1 and 2, because ch 3 has its own title. It is more likely, however, that 3.1 served as a subtitle, whereas 1.1 performs the usual role of title and introduction to the entire book.

1.2–2.20: A dialogue between Habakkuk and the LORD. 1.2–4: This is the beginning of the dialogue between the LORD and a prophetic voice (Habakkuk). The human speaker initiates the dialogue with a series of pointed, rhetorical questions. The issue at stake is not simply theodicy but the very order and possibility of existence of the world (see below). Nothing in the text directly anchors the questions to a particular historical situation. The speaker implicitly identifies himself with the righteous, but not much about them is told. The text is written in general terms so readers may identify with the speaker and the speaker's questions. **4:** *That is why decision fails,* probably better, "therefore torah slacks." The word "torah" here points to the divine teaching that maintains the order of the world, and that was later understood by traditional Jewish commentators as "the Torah." **5–11:** These verses present the divine response to the human complaint. On the surface, it seems incongruous, since it announces that the LORD gives victory to the Babylonians, who are described by the same divine voice in the most terrifying terms. So not only will the wicked prosper and have dominion, but even the righteous in Judah will continue to suffer at the hands of a dread and fierce, wicked power. The divine response, in fact, strengthens

Who cross the earth's wide spaces
To seize homes not their own.

7   They are terrible, dreadful;
ᵃThey make their own laws and rules.ᵃ

8   Their horses are swifter than leopards,
Fleeter than wolves of the steppe.ᵇ
Their steeds gallop—ᶜtheir steedsᶜ
Come flying from afar.
Like vultures rushing toward food,

9   They all come, bent on rapine.
The thrustᵈ of their van is forward,
And they amass captives like sand.

10   Kings they hold in derision,
And princes are a joke to them;
They laugh at every fortress,
They pile up earth and capture it.

11   ᵉThen they pass on like the wind,
They transgress and incur guilt,
For they ascribe their might to their god."ᵉ

12   You, O LORD, are from everlasting;
My holy God, Youᶠ never die.
O LORD, You have made them a subject of
    contention;
O Rock, You have made them a cause for
    complaint.

13   You whose eyes are too pure to look upon evil,
Who cannot countenance wrongdoing,
Why do You countenance treachery,
And stand by idle
While the one in the wrong devours
The one in the right?

14   You have made mankind like the fish of the sea,
Like creeping things ᵍthat have no ruler.ᵍ

15   He has fished them all up with a line,
Pulled them up in his trawl,
And gathered them in his net.
That is why he rejoices and is glad.

16   That is why he sacrifices to his trawl
And makes offerings to his net;
For through them his portionʰ is rich

rather than weakens the case advanced in the human complaint. **7:** *They make their own laws and rules,* they take upon themselves a role that is the LORD's (see translators' note *a-a*). Still, despite their arrogance, the LORD raises them up. **11:** There is an ongoing debate on how to translate this v. Although several substantially different proposals have been advanced, the general gist of the text is clear: The Babylonians do not think that their power is established and maintained by the LORD. **12–17:** The reaction of the prophetic voice to such a reply is—as one may expect—a second complaint, one that takes into account the divine response and the aggravating circumstances that it describes. **12:** The Heb actually says something akin to "we shall not die" or "let us not die." There is a tradition that the original text read, "You [i.e., the LORD] never die," and that scribes changed it because of its embarrassing content. (These emendations are called "Tiqqunei Soferim.") There is a considerable debate on how to evaluate this tradition concerning v. 12, and accordingly, about the wording of the original text of the v. It seems more likely that the v. read, "let us not die" or the like. **13:** The meaning of the last two lines in the v. is something like "[why do you] remain silent when the wicked swallow those more righteous than they?" The question is not why one who is absolutely righteous would suffer, but why the hierarchy of people in the spectrum of righteousness-wickedness runs opposite to that of power in the "real world." **14:** This is a reversal of people's role as described in Gen. 1.26, 28.

a-a *Lit. "Their law and majesty proceed from themselves."*
b *Understanding ʿereb as synonymous with ʿarabah; cf. Jer. 5.6.*
c-c *The Qumran Habakkuk commentary (hereafter 1QpHab) reads "and spread [wings]."*
d *Meaning of Heb. uncertain.*   e-e *Meaning of Heb. uncertain.*
f *Heb. "we," a change made by a pious scribe.*
g-g *1QpHab "[for him] to rule over"; cf. Gen. 1.28; Ps. 8.7–9.*
h *Emendation yields "bread"; cf. Gen. 49.20.*

And his nourishment fat.

17 Shall he then keep ᵃ‑emptying his trawl,‑ᵃ
And slaying nations without pity?

2 I will stand on my watch,
Take up my station at theᵇ post,
And wait to see what He will say to me,
What Heᶜ will reply to my complaint.

2 The LORD answered me and said:
Write the prophecy down,
Inscribe it clearly on tablets,
So that it can be read easily.

3 For ᵈ‑there is yet a prophecy‑ᵈ for a set term,
A truthful witness for a time that will come.
Even if it tarries, wait for it still;
For it will surely come, without delay:

4 ᵉ‑Lo, his spirit within him is puffed up, not
        upright,
But‑ᵉ the righteous man is rewarded with life
For his fidelity.

5 How much less then shall the defiantᶠ go
        unpunished,
The treacherous, arrogant man
Who has made his maw as wide as Sheol,
Who is as insatiable as Death,
Who has harvested all the nations
And gathered in all the peoples!

6 Surely all these shall pronounce a satire against
        him,
A pointed epigram concerning him.
They shall say:
Ah, you who pile up what is not yours—
How much longer?—
And make ever heavier your load of indebtedness!

7 Right suddenly will your creditorsᵍ arise,

a-a 1QpHab "drawing his sword."   b 1QpHab reads "my."
c Taking 'ashib as equivalent to yashib.
d-d Emendation yields "the prophecy is a witness."
e-e Meaning of Heb. uncertain. Emendation yields "Lo, there is a reward for the upright—
/ the life breath within him—/ And . . ."
f Connecting hyyn (1QpHab hwn) with the root hwn, Deut. 1.41; for the thought cf.
Prov. 11.31. Meaning of rest of line uncertain.   g Lit. "usurers."

2.1–20: At this point, the reader waits to see how the LORD will respond. The response comes in the form of the speaker's report of a revelation. **3:** This verse is associated in Jewish tradition with the coming of the Messiah and is reflected in the language of the twelfth principle of the thirteen principles of faith of Maimonides.

4: *But the righteous man is rewarded with life for his fidelity,* often translated "the righteous one lives (or shall live) by his faith" or "the righteous one shall live through (or is sustained by) his faith." According to one of the Rabbis in *b. Mak.* 23b, this saying encapsulates all the commandments. The saying also had an important influence in Christianity, and in particular in the doctrine of justification through faith (see Rom. 1.17; Gal. 3.11; Heb. 10.38–39). In its original context the saying is clearly interwoven with the first part of the v. The saying there focuses on a person whose life is swollen and crooked. Then the v. moves to the opposite pole, a pious person who keeps his or her trust in the LORD under the dire circumstances described in the book, i.e., when the righteous are asked to wait while those who do not deserve worldly power wield it over them. The text does not identify such persons with any particular characters, thereby facilitating different identifications and accordingly, diverse readings of the text. Given the general focus in the book on Babylonia and its wickedness, readers may have understood the negative character in the first line as pointing at the king of Babylonia, as an archetypal representative of both the Babylonian empire and any proud people who rely on their own power. **5:** *Sheol,* the Pit or the netherworld, where all people descend upon death, it is the utter bottom of the world. Human attributes are associated with Sheol here. It has a "maw" and, of course, the "maw of Sheol" is surely insatiable, like that of Death (see also Isa. 5.14, cf. Ps. 141.7). **6a:** *A pointed epigram concerning him. They shall say: . . . ,* or "Shall not all these take up a parable about him and a metaphor, and riddles regarding him? One will say: . . ." **6b–20:** What this "one" will say is presented as a series of five *Ah* or "woe" passages marked by the formula, *Ah, you* (vv. 6, 9, 12, 15, 19). The enemy is now denounced as a spoiler, greedy, unjust, lawless, and idolatrous. (On

And those who remind[a] you will awake,

And you will be despoiled by them.

8   Because you plundered many nations,

All surviving peoples shall plunder you—

For crimes against men and wrongs against lands,

Against cities and all their inhabitants.

9   Ah, you who have acquired gains

To the detriment of your own house,

[b]Who have destroyed many peoples[b]

In order to set your nest on high

To escape disaster!

10 You have plotted shame for your own house,

And guilt for yourself;

11 For a stone shall cry out from the wall,

And a rafter shall answer it from the woodwork.

12 Ah, you who have built a town with crime,

And established a city with infamy,

13 So that peoples have had to toil for the fire,[c]

And nations to weary themselves for naught!

[d]Behold, it is from the LORD of Hosts:

14 [e]For the earth shall be filled

With awe for the glory of the LORD

As water covers the sea.[e]

15 Ah, you who make others drink to intoxication

[f]As you pour out[f] your wrath,

In order to gaze upon their nakedness![g]

16 You shall be sated with shame

Rather than glory:

Drink in your turn and stagger![h]

The cup in the right hand of the LORD

Shall come around to you,

And [i]disgrace to[i] your glory.

17 [j]For the lawlessness against Lebanon shall cover

you,

The destruction of beasts shall overwhelm you[j]—

For crimes against men and wrongs against

lands,

Against cities and all their inhabitants.

the structure of these *Ah* oracles, see Nah. 3.1 n.). **14:** This is nearly identical with the second half of Isa. 11.9. A more literal translation would be, "for the earth shall be filled with the knowledge of the glory of the LORD, as water covers the sea." In other words, just as there is no place in the sea without water, there will be no place on the earth that will not be filled with the knowledge of the glory of the LORD. Some traditional commentators have suggested that the text is elliptic and means ". . . shall be filled *by the will* to know the glory." The Targum seems to assume that people cannot really know the glory of the LORD, so it translates and reinterprets the text to mean, ". . . to know the fear of the LORD." **20:** When the LORD is present in the Temple, silence is required (cf. Zeph. 1.7; Zech. 2.17). Some scholars argue that the sacrificial service was conducted in silence.

a Lit. "shake"; the same verb means "to call to mind" in Samaritan Aramaic.

b-b Brought up from v. 10 for clarity.   c I.e., without profit.

d Connection with the next four lines uncertain; they might read better after v. 20.

e-e Cf. Isa. 11.9.

f-f Meaning of Heb. uncertain. Emendation yields "from the bowl of."

g Cf. Gen. 9.21–22.   h Emendation yields "uncover yourself"; cf. Lam. 4.21.

i-i Or "vomit of disgrace upon."   j-j Meaning of Heb. uncertain.

18ª   What has the carved image availed,
        That he who fashioned it has carved it
        For an image and a false oracle—
        That he who fashioned his product has trusted
            in it,
        Making dumb idols?

19   Ah, you who say, "Wake up" to wood,
        "Awaken," to inert stone!
        Can that give an oracle?
        Why, it is encased in gold and silver,
        But there is no breath inside it.

20   But the LORD in His holy Abode—
        Be silent before Him all the earth!

3 A prayer of the prophet Habakkuk. In the mode of
  Shigionoth.ᵇ

2   O LORD! I have learned of Your renown;
        I am awed, O LORD, by Your deeds.
        Renew them in these years,
        Oh, make them known in these years!
        Though angry, may You remember compassion.

3   God is coming from Teman,
        The Holy One from Mount Paran.   Selah.ᶜ
        His majesty covers the skies,
        His splendor fills the earth:

4   ᵈ·It is a brilliant light
        Which gives off rays on every side—
        And therein His glory is enveloped.·ᵈ

5   Pestilence marches before Him,
        And plague comes forth at His heels.

6   When He stands, He makes the earth shake;ᵉ
        When He glances, He makes nations tremble.
        The age-old mountains are shattered,
        The primeval hills sink low.

7   ᵈ·His are the ancient routes:
        As a scene of havoc I beholdᵈ·

a This verse would read well after v. 19.

b Meaning uncertain; perhaps "psalms of supplication"; cf. Ps. 7.1.

c A musical direction of uncertain meaning.   d-d Meaning of Heb. uncertain.

e Cf. Targum and Septuagint.

3.1–19: The psalm of Habakkuk.
The prayer/psalm contains a title
(v. 1), a petition to God to manifest
His power (v. 2), a lengthy report
about a theophany (vv. 3–15), an
expression of confidence by the
human speaker (vv. 16–19), and
musical instructions (v. 19). There
are several instructions for performance in ch 3. They include three
occurrences of Selah (vv. 3, 9, 13)
and the concluding phrase (v. 19);

these are otherwise only attested
in the book of Psalms, and for this
reason many consider this to be a
psalm that became part of Habakkuk. It is abundantly clear that ch
3 asks its intended readers to envision it not only as a prophetic
reading, but also as a composition
to be performed. At points, the
language of this ch is difficult, and
perhaps archaic. **1:** The exact
meaning of Shigionoth is unclear,
but it has something to do with a
musical aspect of the performance
of the psalm (cf. Ps. 7.1; Radak).
According to a certain traditional
Jewish interpretation, this phrase
is not a musicological note, but
should be translated, ". . . for erroneous speech/utterances." This
reading reflects a particular understanding of the claims made by the
human speaker in these dialogues
(contrast with Job 42.8). The Targum reflects a different interpretation of the title of the prayer: "The
prayer which Habakkuk the
prophet prayed when it was revealed to him concerning the extension of time which he gives to
the wicked, that if they return to
the law with a perfect heart they
shall be forgiven and all their sins
. . . shall be as sins of ignorance."
3–15: The theophanic description
serves to emphasize the awesome
power of God and to reassure the
readers that the LORD will vanquish their enemies, in judgment.
Mythological references (vv. 5, 8),
images of shaking in the natural
and human world (vv. 6–7, 10),
and of destruction of enemies (vv.
12–15) are common in theophanic
reports. **3:** In this theophany, the
LORD is coming from the south:
Both Teman and Mount Paran (v. 3)
are in the south from a Judahite
perspective (cf. Deut. 33.2; Judg.
5.4). **5:** Pestilence, some translate
"plague" or "Plague" since it is
personified. The personification
contributes to the mythological atmosphere of this passage. The Targum identifies "Plague" with the
angel of death. Plague, some translate "Fever" (Heb "reshef"), a
West-Semitic mythological figure.
7: Cushan . . . Midian, two tent-
dwellers, "nomadic" groups south,

The tents of Cushan;
Shaken are the pavilions
Of the land of Midian!

8 Are You wroth, O LORD, with Neharim?
Is Your anger against Neharim,
Your rage against Yam[a]—
That You are driving Your steeds,
Your victorious chariot?

9 All bared and ready is Your bow.
[b-]Sworn are the rods of the word.[-b]   Selah.
You make the earth burst into streams,

10 The mountains rock at the sight of You,
A torrent of rain comes down;
Loud roars the deep,
[b-]The sky returns the echo.[-b]

11 Sun [and] moon stand still on high
As Your arrows fly in brightness,
Your flashing spear in brilliance.

12 You tread the earth in rage,
You trample nations in fury.

13 You have come forth to deliver Your people,
To deliver Your anointed.[c]
[d-]You will smash the roof of the villain's house,
Raze it from foundation to top.   Selah.

14 You will crack [his] skull with Your[e] bludgeon;
Blown away shall be his warriors,
Whose delight is to crush me suddenly,
To devour a poor man in an ambush.[-d]

15 [f-]You will make Your steeds tread the sea,
Stirring the mighty waters.

16 I heard and my bowels quaked,
My lips quivered at the sound;
Rot entered into my bone,

or southeast, of Judah. As mentioned above, the LORD is presented as coming from the south in this theophany (see v. 3). **8:** *Neharim,* or "River" or "Floods" or "rivers." *Neharim* is another West-Semitic mythological figure (cf. Reshef in v. 6) and so is *Yam,* "Sea" or "sea." See translators' note *a.* **16–19:** The text here advances the normative position that the readers of the book should take to heart, namely that despite all worldly circumstances (v. 17), the righteous rejoice and exult in a God that delivers them, who is their strength (v. 19).

---

a Neharim (lit. "Floods") and Yam (lit. "Sea") were marine monsters vanquished by the LORD in hoary antiquity. On Yam see Ps. 74.13; Job 7.12. A being called both Yam and Nahar figures in early Canaanite literature.

b-b Meaning of Heb. uncertain.   c I.e., the king of Judah.

d-d Emendation yields: You will strike the heads of men of evil, / Smash the pates of Your adversaries. Selah. / You will crack their skulls with Your bludgeon; / Dispersed, blown like chaff shall be they / Who lie in wait to swallow the innocent, / To devour the poor in an ambush.

e Heb. "His."

f-f Or: 15You will make Your steeds tread the sea, / Stirring the mighty waters, / 16That I may have rest on a day of distress, / When a people come up to attack us. / But this report made my bowels quake, / These tidings made my lips quiver; / Rot entered into my bone, / I trembled where I stood: / 17That the fig tree does not bud, / And no yield is on the vine; / The olive crop has failed, / And the fields produce no grain; / The sheep have vanished from the fold, / And no cattle are in the pen.

I trembled where I stood.
Yet I wait calmly for the day of distress,
For a people to come to attack us.

17 Though the fig tree does not bud
And no yield is on the vine,
Though the olive crop has failed
And the fields produce no grain,
Though sheep have vanished from the fold
And no cattle are in the pen,-ᶠ

18 Yet will I rejoice in the LORD,
Exult in the God who delivers me.

19 My Lord GOD is my strength:
He makes my feet like the deer's
And lets me stride upon the heights.

ᵃFor the leader; with instrumental music.⁻ᵃ

---

a-a *Meaning of Heb. uncertain.*

צפניה

Zephaniah

THE BOOK OF ZEPHANIAH claims to be a particular instance of the LORD's word, namely that associated with Zephaniah, the son of Cushi (see 1.1 and n.). The book is set in the time of Josiah (late 7th century BCE), the last great king of Judah according to the books of Kings and Chronicles. Judah as described in Zephaniah is quite an ungodly place, however. This is to be expected: Prophetic books that include divine announcements of judgment and destruction against Judah tend for obvious reasons to describe the social and religious situation in monarchic Judah in harsh, negative terms.

Some scholars attempted to harmonize the godly image of Josianic times in the historical books and its negative characterization here by assigning the circumstances described in the book to a time when Josiah was still a minor and consequently did not actually rule over the land, or to a time after his death. But this is not the claim of the book of Zephaniah. To be sure, the king is not explicitly criticized when all the leadership of Judah is condemned, but the same can be said of other prophetic books (e.g., Micah) and it is difficult to reach historical conclusions on this basis. Some scholars associate the oracles against the nations in chapter 2 with a presumed plan for territorial expansion that was advanced by King Josiah, but either never materialized or did so to only a very small extent, but this is speculative.

Many scholars attribute much of the book of Zephaniah to the monarchic period, but they agree that some portion of the book dates to the postmonarchic period. It is worth stressing that the division of the text of the book between words that go back to Zephaniah or monarchic times and words that come from a later time is nowhere made in the book. Moreover, the usual association between supposedly earlier sections and increased authoritative status (and supposedly later and less authoritative status) is contrary to the basic claim of the book, namely that it is in its entirety the LORD's word, all equal in value.

The book uses wordplay and potential or actual ambiguities that channel the attention of the readers and contribute to the possibility of multiple readings. These features are typical in prophetic books because they facilitate the continuous reading and study of these texts.

The book begins like most prophetic books with an introduction or superscription and then moves to sets of prophetic pronouncements. The book announces severe judgment against Judah and nations other than Israel, and, as do all other prophetic books, Zephaniah includes reports of prophecies of hope. Even the announcements of doom against Judah serve, in part, to emphasize hope from the perspective of the postmonarchic readers of the book of Zephaniah, because for them the fact that the announcements of doom were fulfilled in the past, as written, reassured them that those of hope will also be fulfilled in the future.

There are several possible ways to outline the book of Zephaniah, each pointing to a particular but partial reading that emphasizes certain aspects of the book and de-emphasizes others. These partial readings inform each other, and all together create a meaning much richer than any of them separately. This is a common situation in prophetic books. The following is one of these possible outlines:

1. Announcement of doom (1.2–9)
2. Description of doom (1.10–18)
3. The last chance to repent (2.1–4)
4. Against the nations and their gods (2.5–15)
5. Against the overbearing city (3.1–13)
6. Joy to Jerusalem (3.14–20)

[EHUD BEN ZVI]

1 The word of the LORD that came to Zephaniah son of Cushi son of Gedaliah son of Amariah son of Hezekiah, during the reign of King Josiah son of Amon of Judah.

2   I will sweep everything away
       From the face of the earth
                                   —declares the LORD.
3   I will sweep away man and beast;
       I will sweep away the birds of the sky
       And the fish of the sea.
       ª·I will make the wicked stumble,·ª
       And I will destroy mankind
       From the face of the earth
                                   —declares the LORD.

4   I will stretch out My arm against Judah
       And against all who dwell in Jerusalem;
       And I will wipe out from this place
       Every vestige of Baal,
       And the name of the priestlings[b] along with the
             priests;

a-a *Meaning of Heb. uncertain.*
b *Heb.* kemarim, *a term used only of priests of heathen gods.*

1.1: Superscription. *Cushi,* in principle, may also mean "Cushite" (i.e., Ethiopian). Because of the context in which it appears, however, it can only be a personal name. The last of the ancestors mentioned in the list is Hezekiah. Some interpreters maintained that this Hezekiah was the famous king of Judah (Ibn Ezra, but contrast with Radak). Again, such a claim is not advanced in the text. (The Sages understood the list as pointing at Zephaniah as a righteous man who is himself a son of a righteous man; see *b. Meg.* 15a.) On the reference to the reign of Josiah, see introduction.

1.2–9: Announcement of doom. 2–3: The translation suggests a universal scenario of destruction. The Heb is more ambiguous. It can certainly be understood in such a way, but also as pointing to the total destruction of a particular area. **3:** *I will make the wicked stumble* reflects an emendation of the Masoretic Text. The latter may be translated as "[I will sweep away] the stumbling blocks along with

5   And those who bow down on the roofs
        To the host of heaven;
        And those who bow down and swear to the Lord
        But also swear by Malcam;[a]
6   And those who have forsaken the Lord,
        And those who have not sought the Lord
        And have not turned to Him.

7   Be silent before my Lord God,
        For the day of the Lord is approaching;
        For the Lord has prepared a [b-]sacrificial feast,[-b]
        Has bidden His guests purify themselves.
8   And on the day of the Lord's sacrifice
        I will punish the officials
        And the king's sons,[c]
        [d-]And all who don a foreign vestment.
9   I will also punish on that day
        Everyone who steps over the threshold,[-d]
        Who fill their master's[e] palace
        With lawlessness and fraud.
10   In that day there shall be
                            —declares the Lord—
        A loud outcry from the Fish Gate,
        And howling from the Mishneh,[f]
        And a sound of great anguish from the hills.
11   The dwellers of the Machtesh[g] howl;
        For all the tradesmen have perished,
        All who weigh silver are wiped out.

12   At that time,
        I will search Jerusalem with lamps;

a Apparently identical with "Milcom the abomination of the Ammonites"; cf. 1 Kings 11.5.
b-b I.e., a slaughter of sinners.
c Apparently brothers of King Amon, who exercised influence during the minority of King Josiah (2 Kings 22.1).
d-d Apparently references to two customs of heathen worship; cf. 2 Kings 10.22 and 1 Sam. 5.5.
e I.e., King Josiah's.   f A quarter of Jerusalem; cf. 2 Kings 22.14.
g Another quarter of Jerusalem.

the wicked" or "[I will sweep away] the stumbling blocks of the wicked" or "[I will sweep away] what makes the wicked stumble." The text does not identify these stumbling blocks, but readers throughout generations filled this information gap, and by doing so they expressed their worldview and particular circumstances. For instance, many associated them with the animals previously mentioned in the text. But if so, why do the animals make people stumble? According to Gen. Rabbah, because they provide abundance, and abundance may lead to sin. According to many others, because they may lead to idolatrous worship (b. A. Z. 55a). 5: Malcam, or "their king." Medieval Jewish interpretation tends to follow the Targum and to associate "their king" with "false deities" (Rashi, Radak), a rendering supported by the poetic parallelism of the v. Similarly, some modern interpreters see here Milcom, the head of the pantheon of Ammon (1 Kings 11.5; 33; 2 Kings 23.13); or Molech, a deity to whom children were sacrificed or passed through fire (see Lev. 18.21; 20.2; 2 Kings 23.10; cf. 1 Kings 11.7). Other modern scholars maintain that "their king" means just "their king" (cf. Exod. 22.27; 1 Kings 21.10; Isa. 8.21). It has also been suggested that "their king" points to the Lord, wrongly worshipped. 7: The last two lines in the v. can be translated as "the Lord has prepared a sacrifice; he has consecrated those he has invited." This translation communicates better the double entendre of the Heb. Are the guests consecrated so they can take part in the sacrificial meal? Or, are they consecrated because they are about to be slaughtered for the meal? Are they going to be at the meal, or be the "meal"? The Heb is likely intentionally ambiguous. 8: King's sons refers to the royal family in general, and perhaps even to royal officers; in other words, to the elite of the kingdom, which was understood as the "king's house(hold)" over which the king rules as a "father." 9: There are two main interpretations to everyone who steps over the threshold. According to the first, this is a reference to an imitation of the ways of idolaters in general or Philistines (see 1 Sam. 5.4–5) in particular (e.g., Targum, and most of recent scholarship); according to the second it points to social injustice, oppression, and thievery (e.g., Radak; Ibn Ezra). The reference to their master's palace is ambiguous: It may refer to the Temple of the Lord or to the palace of the king, or to both.

1.10–18: Description of doom. 10: The Mishneh or "Second Quarter" probably refers to the Upper City of Jerusalem, the Western Hill, where the upper social strata of Jerusalem dwelled. 12: It is God

And I will punish the men
Who rest untroubled on their lees,
Who say to themselves,
"The Lord will do nothing, good or bad."

13 Their wealth shall be plundered
And their homes laid waste.
They shall build houses and not dwell in them,
Plant vineyards and not drink their wine.

14 The great day of the Lord is approaching,
Approaching most swiftly.
ᵃ·Hark, the day of the Lord!
It is bitter:
There a warrior shrieks!·ᵃ

15 That day shall be a day of wrath,
A day of trouble and distress,
A day of calamity and desolation,
A day of darkness and deep gloom,
A day of densest clouds,

16 A day of horn blasts and alarms—
Against the fortified towns
And the lofty corner towers.

17 I will bring distress on the people,
And they shall walk like blind men,
Because they sinned against the Lord;
Their blood shall be spilled like dust,
And their fatᵇ like dung.

18 Moreover, their silver and gold
Shall not avail to save them.
On the day of the Lord's wrath,
In the fire of His passion,
The whole land shall be consumed;
For He will make a terrible end
Of all who dwell in the land.

2 Gather together, gather,
ᶜO nation without shame,
2 Before the day the decree is born—
The day flies by like chaffᶜ—
Before the fierce anger
Of the Lord overtakes you,
Before the day of anger
Of the Lord overtakes you.
3 Seek the Lord,

---

who will be searching Jerusalem with lamps. The Targum, and some later interpreters, reinterpreted the v. to avoid the anthropomorphism that this image involves. **13:** The text sounds as a reverberation of the curse in Deut. 28.30, and it points to the futility of human actions contrary to divine will. **14–18:** The traditional prophetic Day of the Lord imagery is employed to reflect the great disaster (see Joel 1.15 n.).

2.1–4: The last chance to repent. 1: The Heb term translated as *without shame* may be understood as "not desiring [God]" or as "not desired [by God]." The context indicates that this nation is (Josianic) Judah.

---

a-a Emendation yields: "The day of the Lord is faster than a runner, / Fleeter than a warrior"; cf. Ps. 19.6.
b Or "marrow"; meaning of Heb. uncertain.
c-c Meaning of Heb. uncertain. Emendation yields: "O straw [Aramaic gel] not gathered in, / Before you are driven like flying chaff"; cf. Ps. 35.5.

All you humble of the land
Who have fulfilled His law;
Seek righteousness,
Seek humility.
Perhaps you will find shelter
On the day of the LORD's anger.

4   Indeed, Gaza shall be deserted
And Ashkelon desolate;
Ashdod's people shall be expelled in broad
    daylight,
And Ekron shall be uprooted.

5   Ah, nation of Cherethites
Who inhabit the seacoast!
There is a word of the LORD against you,
O Canaan,ᵃ land of the Philistines:
I will lay you waste
Without inhabitants.

6   The seacoast Cherothᵇ shall become
An abode for shepherds and folds for flocks,

7   And shall be a portion for the remnant of the
    House of Judah;
On these [pastures] they shall graze [their flocks],
They shall ᶜlie downᶜ at eventide
In the houses of Ashkelon.
For the LORD their God will take note of them
And restore their fortunes.

8   I have heard the insults of Moab
And the jeers of the Ammonites,
Who have insulted My people
And gloated over their country.

9   Assuredly, as I live
                    —declares the LORD of Hosts,
                        the God of Israel—
Moab shall become like Sodom
And the Ammonites like Gomorrah:
Clumpsᵇ of weeds and patchesᵇ of salt,
And desolation evermore.
The remnant of My people shall plunder them,
The remainder of My nation shall possess them.

10 That is what they'll get for their haughtiness,
For insulting and jeering
At the people of the LORD of Hosts.

4: English translations are unable to convey the puns on the terms Gaza and Ekron that feature prominently in the Heb text. Something like "Powertown shall be powdered" or "Gaza shall be ghastful," and "Rootville—or perhaps Uprootville—will be uprooted" may suggest the force of the pun to English readers. The towns mentioned, including *Ashkelon* and *Ashdod*, were Philistine cities.

2.5–15: Against the nations and their gods. Such oracles against the nations are typical of prophetic books, which emphasize that God is universal in His control. **5:** *Nation of Cherethites*, people of Crete (an island in the eastern Mediterranean Sea). The *Cherethites* are associated with Philistines in Ezek. 25.16. Another wordplay: The main three letters of *Cherethites* in Heb connote a sense of "cut off" (cf. v. 6).

---

a Or "Phoenicia," of which Philistia is regarded as an extension southward.
b Meaning of Heb. uncertain.
c-c Change of vocalization yields "rest [them]"; cf. Song of Songs 1.7.

11 The LORD will show Himself terrible against
      them,
   Causing all the gods on earth to shrivel;[a]
   And all the coastlands of the nations
   Shall bow down to Him—
   Every man in his own home.

12 You Cushites too—
   [b]They shall be slain by My sword.[b]

13 And He will stretch out His arm against the north
   And destroy Assyria;
   He will make Nineveh a desolation,
   Arid as the desert.

14 In it flocks shall lie down,

a Meaning of Heb. uncertain.
b-b Emendation yields "shall be slain by the sword of the LORD."

11: The v. may be translated "The LORD is awesome against them, for He shrivels [or weakens] all the gods of the earth." The text does not claim that the *gods on earth* do not exist (cf. Exod. 15.11), or that the LORD will or has destroyed them (cf. Ps 82.6–7). It claims, rather, that the LORD is superior to them and that this superiority will be manifested so that people from far away countries ("all the islands/coastlands of the nations") will bow down to the LORD, each in his or her place. This v. stands in the midst of an announcement of judgment against the nations. It is a central text and a theologically driven explanatory note on this type of announcement. It maintains that the purpose of the LORD is not to destroy nation after nation—as might be suggested by a plain reading of a sequence of announcements against nations—but to bring these nations to bow to the LORD (cf. Zeph. 3.9). The contents, and often the language, of this v. are reminiscent of those in many Psalms (e.g., Pss. 29.1; 82.2, 6; 95.3; 96.4–10; 97.6–9). **14–15:** The language points to the image of a wilderness retaking a place of culture and city (cf. 2.6–7). The characterization of Nineveh in v. 15 is almost identical to that of Babylon in Isa. 47.8. The message is not so much that the historical Ninevites or Babylonians actually thought that way and thus deserve punishment—other reasons could have been adduced—but rather that such proud thinking is fully unacceptable and those who indulge in it will be punished by an active God who

Places mentioned in the oracles against the nations

Every ᵃspecies of beast,
While jackdaws and owls roost on its capitals,
The great owl hoots in the window,
And the raven [croaks] on the threshold.
For he has stripped its cedarwork bare.ᵃ

15 Is this the gay city
That dwelt secure,
That thought in her heart,
"I am, and there is none but me"?
Alas, she is become a waste,
A lair of wild beasts!
Everyone who passes by her
Hisses and gestures with his hand.ᵇ

3 Ah, sullied, polluted,
Overbearingᶜ city!
2 She has been disobedient,
Has learned no lesson;
She has not trusted in the LORD,
Has not drawn near to her God.
3 The officials within her
Are roaring lions;
Her judges are wolves ᵃof the steppe,
They leave no bone until morning.ᵃ
4 Her prophets are reckless,
Faithless fellows;
Her priests profane what is holy,
They give perverse rulings.
5 But the LORD in her midst is righteous,
He does no wrong;
He issues judgment every morning,
As unfailing as the light.

The wrongdoer knows no shame!
6 I wiped out nations:
Their corner towers are desolate;
I turned their thoroughfares into ruins,
With none passing by;
Their towns lie waste without people,
Without inhabitants.
7 And I thought that sheᵈ would fear Me,
Would learn a lesson,
And that the punishment I brought on themᵉ

can bring good (or blessing) but also evil (or judgment); cf. 1.12.

3.1–13: Against the overbearing city. 1–2: The Heb exudes ambiguity. It is uncertain whether the city is Nineveh or Jerusalem. *Sullied* can be understood as "revered or feared"; *polluted* as "redeemed"; and *overbearing* (or "oppressing") as "the dove city" (i.e., a powerless city). In this particular case the ambiguities are unequivocally resolved within the context of the text. V. 2 clarifies that the city is not powerless and redeemed, but polluted and oppressing. The descriptions of wrongdoing in the following vv. show that the city is Jerusalem. This type of ambiguity shows the artistry of the book's composition and also points to the use of ambiguity as a rhetorical device to capture the readers' attention, and then lead them to a central issue: the identity and main characteristics of the city. It is the polluted, sinful, late monarchic (Josianic) Jerusalem. **3–4:** Compare the language with Ezek. 22.25, 27, 26 and for similar descriptions cf. Mic. 3.1–7.

a-a Meaning of Heb. uncertain.
b To ward off a like fate from himself; cf. Jer. 18.16 and note.
c Meaning of Heb. uncertain. Emendation yields "harlot"; cf. Isa. 1.21.
d Heb. "you."   e Heb. "her."

Would not be ᵃ·lost on her.·ᵃ
Instead, all the more eagerly
They have practiced corruption in all their
            deeds.

8   But wait for Me—says the LORD—
    For the day when I arise as an accuser;ᵇ
    When I decide to gather nations,
    To bring kingdoms together,
    To pour out My indignation on them,
    All My blazing anger.
    Indeed, by the fire of My passion
    All the earth shall be consumed.

9   For then I will make the peoples pure of speech,
    So that they all invoke the LORD by name
    And serve Him with one accord.ᶜ

10 From beyond the rivers of Cush, My suppliantsᵈ
    Shall bring offerings to Me in Fair Puzai.ᵉ

11 In that day,
    You will no longer be shamed for all the deeds
    By which you have defied Me.
    For then I will remove
    The proud and exultant within you,
    And you will be haughty no more
    On My sacred mount.ᶠ

12 But I will leave within you
    A poor, humble folk,
    And they shall find refuge
    In the name of the LORD.

13 The remnant of Israel
    Shall do no wrong
    And speak no falsehood;
    A deceitful tongue
    Shall not be in their mouths.
    Only such as these shall graze and lie down,
    With none to trouble them.

14 Shout for joy, Fair Zion,
    Cry aloud, O Israel!
    Rejoice and be glad with all your heart,
    Fair Jerusalem!

15 The LORD has annulled the judgment against you,

10: There are three main understandings of this difficult v. They are represented by the following translations: (a) "from beyond the rivers of Cush (i.e., from far, far away) my suppliants, Fair scattered (i.e., Israel in exile), shall bring my offering"; (b) "from beyond the rivers of Cush (i.e., from far, far away) my suppliants, Fair Puzai (i.e., a faraway nation), shall bring my offering"; and (c) "from beyond the rivers of Cush (i.e., from far, far away) my suppliants, Fair scattered (i.e., Israel in exile), they (i.e., the nations) shall bring as my offering" (cf. Isa. 66.20). The text plays again with ambiguity, and this time one that is not resolved by its context. **13:** The remnant is a central prophetic idea (see Isa. 6.13 n.).

3.14–20: Joy to Jerusalem. 15: As in some other prophetic texts, here God is king (Sovereign), obviating the need for an ideal human king

a-a Lit. "cut off [from] her vision."
b Understanding ʿad as equivalent to ʿed, with Septuagint and Syriac.
c Lit. "back," i.e., like beasts of burden.
d Meaning of Heb. uncertain.
e Emendation yields "Zion." For the thought, cf. Isa. 18.1, 7.
f I.e., in My holy land; cf. Isa. 11.9; 57.13; 65.25.

He has swept away your foes.
Israel's Sovereign the LORD is within you;
You need fear misfortune no more.

16 In that day,
This shall be said to Jerusalem:
Have no fear, O Zion;
Let not your hands droop!

17 Your God the LORD is in your midst,
A warrior who brings triumph.
He will rejoice over you and be glad,
He will shout over you with jubilation.
He will ᵃsoothe with His love

18 Those long disconsolate.⁻ᵃ
I will take away from you ᵇthe woe
Over which you endured mockery.⁻ᵇ

19 At that time I will make [an end]
Of all who afflicted you.
And I will rescue the lame [sheep]
And gather the strayed;
And I will exchange their disgrace
For fame and renown in all the earth.

20 At that time I will gather you,
And at [that] time I will bring you [home];
For I will make you renowned and famous
Among all the peoples on earth,
When I restore your fortunes
Before theirᶜ very eyes   —said the LORD.

(a "messiah"). **18:** The Heb is extremely difficult. Tentative, and at times quite divergent translations have been proposed. One possibility is: "Those who are afflicted because they are deprived of the festivals, I [i.e., the LORD] have gathered, they were from you, (they were) a sign on her, (they were) a (source of) mockery." **20:** The book concludes with a strong announcement of hope for the readership of the book; such positive conclusions typify biblical books. The fortunes of Israel/Judah will be restored, and this restoration includes the gathering of the exiles (on this point, cf. Amos 9.14–15—though in Amos the image of restoration is agrarian). Because of its tone this v. has been included in Jewish liturgy.

---

a-a *Meaning of Heb. uncertain. Emendation yields "renew His love / As in the days of old."*

b-b *Meaning of Heb. uncertain.*   c *Heb. "your."*

חגי

Haggai

THE REBELLION OF JUDAH against the Babylonian empire led to the fall of Jerusalem (586 BCE), the destruction of the Temple, a severe decrease in population due to death and deportation, and the end of monarchy in Judah. The Babylonian empire fell at the hands of a Persian dynasty (the Achaemenid dynasty) in 539. As a result, the Babylonian province of Judah became the Persian or Achaemenid province of Yehud. According to 2 Chronicles 36.22–23, the Persian conqueror of Babylon, Cyrus II (reigned 559–530) issued a proclamation in his first year after the conquest of Babylon (538) that stated, "The Lord, God of Heaven, has given me all the kingdoms of the earth and He has commanded me to build Him a Temple in Jerusalem, which is in Judah. Whoever is among you of his entire people, may the Lord be with him, and let him go up [to Jerusalem, to build the Temple]" (cf. Ezra 1.1–4). The book of Haggai is set about eighteen years later, in the second year of the Persian king Darius I, that is, 520 BCE, and clearly implies that the Temple was still not rebuilt at that time. The book contains reports of theologically based exhortations to undertake the work of reconstruction and discusses the central role of the Temple in the life of the community. (Historians agree that the construction of the Jerusalem Temple was encouraged or even mandated by the Persian imperial center.)

The book of Haggai consists of four narrative reports about four particular divine communications and their circumstances. These communications are set in a precise historical timeframe: namely, the second year of Darius (520), and specifically, the first day of the sixth month, the twenty-first day of the seventh month, and the twenty-fourth day of the ninth month (this last date has two reports). Such specific dating, beyond what is found in other prophetic books (except for the beginning of the following book, Zechariah), creates an important temporal framework within the narrative, and, in addition, strengthens the rhetorical claim for the reliability of the account.

The four reports are integrated into a close literary unit. They are kept together by the figure of Haggai, with whom they are explicitly and repeatedly associated, by their common introduction, structure, and even choice of words. Each of the reports provides a kind of snapshot, and all together they address the restoration of the Temple, Judah, and Jerusalem in the Persian period. The main focus of the book as a whole is the Temple, or to be more precise, the necessary character, centrality, and legitimacy of the Second Temple.

The book of Haggai, in its present form, must have been written later than the last date mentioned in the text (24th of Kislev, 520 BCE), at some point within the Persian period. The matters mentioned above, however, remained central in the discourse of Judah throughout the Persian and Hellenistic period, and thereafter. Questions of leadership in the Second Temple polity are also addressed in this book.

In Jewish tradition, Haggai, Zechariah, and Malachi are the last prophets; after them, prophecy ceased. According to tradition, they were among the members of the "Great Assembly," a group that was the precursor of the Sanhedrin, and after their death, the Holy Spirit departed from Israel, though "bat kol" (lit. the "daughter of the voice," or echo) remained available to Israel (see *b. Yoma* 9b; *b. Sot.* 48b; *b. Sanh.* 11a). This "echo" of the voice of God is sometimes available to the Rabbis in their deliberations about legal interpretation (halakhah), but it is not on the same level as prophecy, and the "echo" cannot overrule legal decisions arrived at by the established methods (*b. B. M.* 59b). As the final representatives of the prophetic tradition, Haggai, Zechariah, and Malachi represent the link in the transmission of the oral Torah between prophets and sages. Certain sages in the Talmud mention rulings and sayings by Haggai, or Haggai, Zechariah, and Malachi (e.g., *b. Yebam.* 16a; *b. Kid.* 43a; *b. Ḥul.* 137b). Further, according to talmudic traditions, not only the books included in the Twelve were written by the members of the Great Assembly (*b. B. Bat.* 15a) but the Targum of the prophets was written under the guidance of these three prophets (*b. Meg.* 3a). The Haggai of the biblical book of Haggai, however, is not characterized in these terms.

[EHUD BEN ZVI]

1 In the second year of King Darius, on the first day of the sixth month, this word of the LORD came through the prophet Haggai to Zerubbabel son of Shealtiel, the governor of Judah, and to Joshua son of Jehozadak, the high priest:

2 Thus said the LORD of Hosts: These people say, *ᵃ*"The time has not yet come*ᵃ* for rebuilding the House of the LORD."

a-a Lit. "It is not time for the coming of the time."

1.1–15a: A report of a divine announcement or exhortation and the people's response to it. This is the first report. It includes an introduction of the divine announcement (v. 1), the divine announcement itself (vv. 2–11), and a report of the reception of the announcement (vv. 12–15a). **1:** The beginning of the book serves as an introduction to the entire book. It deals with the *word of the LORD* that is associated with a particular prophet of the past, namely *Haggai. In the* *second year of King Darius, on the first day of the sixth month:* The year is 520 BCE, and the day is the 1st of 'Elul (= 29 August, 520 BCE). This date refers to the first divine message reported in the book. The month is the last before the seventh month—i.e., Tishri—with all its appointed festivals and sacred occasions (see Lev. ch 23, esp. vv. 23–36; Num. ch 29), the month associated with the building and dedication of the first Temple (see 1 Kings ch 8). This date may have connoted a sense of a new beginning to the readers. The second year of Darius, 520, is the one in which he consolidated his control over the empire, after a difficult civil war. This year is mentioned as the time of the renewed beginning of the building of the Second Temple in Ezra 4.24; according to Ezra 6.15, the house was completed in the sixth year of Darius. The second year of Darius is also associated with divine messages reported in the book of Zechariah. The divine message here is not directed to all the people, but to the two leaders, *Zerubbabel, son of Shealtiel, the governor of Judah* and the high priest, *Joshua.* Thus the book already conveys and legitimates a model of dual leadership. (This was the model of local government of Yehud during the Persian period. It replaced that of the monarchic period that came to an end when the Babylonian king Nebuchadnezzar abolished the

³ And the word of the LORD through the prophet Haggai continued:

⁴ Is it a time for you to dwell in your paneled houses, while this House is lying in ruins? ⁵ Now thus said the LORD of Hosts: Consider how you have been faring! ⁶ You have sowed much and brought in little; you eat without being satisfied; you drink without getting your fill; you clothe yourselves, but no one gets warm; and he who earns anything earns it for a leaky purse.

⁷ᵃThus said the LORD of Hosts: Consider how you have fared: ⁸ Go up to the hills and get timber, and rebuild the House; then I will look on it with favor and I will ᵇ⁻be glorified⁻ᵇ—said the LORD.

⁹ You have been expecting much and getting little; and when you brought it home, I would blow on it!ᶜ Because of what?—says the LORD of Hosts. Because of My House which lies in ruins, while you all hurry to your own houses! ¹⁰ That is why the skies above you have withheld [their] moisture and the earth has withheld its yield, ¹¹ and I have summoned fierce heat upon the land—upon the hills, upon the new grain and wine and oil, upon all that the ground produces, upon man and beast, and upon all the fruits of labor.

¹² Zerubbabel son of Shealtiel and the high priest Joshua son of Jehozadak and all the rest of the people gave heed to the summons of the LORD their God and to the words of the prophet Haggai, when the LORD their God sent him; the people feared the LORD. ¹³ And Haggai, the LORD's messenger, fulfilling the LORD's mission, spoke to the people, "I am with you—declares the LORD."

¹⁴ Then the LORD roused the spirit of Zerubbabel son of Shealtiel, the governor of Judah, and the spirit of the high

a Vv. 7–8 would read well after v. 11.
b-b Emendation yields "glorify it"; see 2.7–9.
c Meaning, perhaps, cast a curse on.

kingdom of Judah, and in turn it was replaced by one in which the high priest became the local ruler by the early Hellenistic period.) The divine message reported here concerns building the Temple. Building temples is the prerogative and obligation of kings. The construction of a major temple had to be approved and supported by the king. The book recognizes that the king at the time was Darius (see Hag. 1.1, 15; 2.10). Still, the text does not relate the construction of the Temple to Darius, or to any Persian king for that matter (contrast Ezra 1.2; 5.13; 6.14 and see the tone of Ezra ch 6). In Haggai, the dual leadership of a *high priest* and a *governor* fulfills the expected role of a king. The claim in the text that the LORD encouraged

them to build the Temple conveys necessary legitimacy to their leadership and their role as temple builders, as well as to the fruit of their work, the Second Temple. Conversely, the building of the Temple certainly conferred some kingly imagery on the two leaders. Still, the text here unequivocally refers to one as the high priest (see also 1.12, 14; 2.2, 4) and the other as the governor (see also 1.14; 2.2, 21). On the role of the personage Zerubbabel, see also Ezra chs 3–4; Zech. ch 4 and following notes. Some Jewish traditions claimed that the Darius mentioned here is the son of Esther and Ahasuerus (see Rashi; Ibn Ezra; cf. *Lev. Rab.* 13.4). From a historical perspective, this claim is certainly impossible, but the value of this interpretation does not rest in its historicity, but rather in the way it expresses beliefs and worldviews and responds to questions that the reading of the text may raise. Here this interpretation directly links the ruler who allowed and encouraged the building of the Temple with the Jewish people in general, and in particular their heroine, Esther (cf. Tamar, Ruth, Hannah). **2:** The text implies that the people thought that there was a correct, prescribed time for rebuilding the Temple, and that such a time had not yet come (cf. 2 Chron. 36.20–23; Ezra 1.1–2). In the ancient Near East, temples were not supposed to be built by anyone except royal figures (see above), and they were not supposed to be built at any random time, but at the time favored by the gods. The people's attitude is facilitated by the success they felt in Babylonia, where God's presence was not expressed through the building of a temple. **4–10:** The basic message is that the presence of the Temple is a necessary condition for the prosperity of the land and the people. Of course, the Temple, to be effective, must be a proper one from a divine perspective. The passages that follow in the book deal with that matter. **13:** Cf. 2.5; Isa. 40.10; 43.5. **14:** Cf. 2 Chron. 36.22; Hag 1.2 n.

priest Joshua son of Jehozadak, and the spirit of all the rest of the people: They came and set to work on the House of the LORD of Hosts, their God, 15on the twenty-fourth day of the sixth month. In the second year of King 2 Darius, 1on the twenty-first day of the seventh month, the word of the LORD came through the prophet Haggai:

2Speak to Zerubbabel son of Shealtiel, the governor of Judah, and to the high priest Joshua son of Jehozadak, and to the rest of the people: 3Who is there left among you who saw this House in its former splendor? How does it look to you now? It must seem like nothing to you. 4But be strong, O Zerubbabel—says the LORD—be strong, O high priest Joshua son of Jehozadak; be strong, all you people of the land—says the LORD—and act! For I am with you—says the LORD of Hosts. 5So I promised you when you came out of Egypt, and My spirit is still in your midst. Fear not!

6For thus said the LORD of Hosts: In just a little while longer I will shake the heavens and the earth, the sea and the dry land; 7I will shake all the nations. And the precious things of all the nations shall come [here], and I will fill this House with glory, said the LORD of Hosts. 8Silver is Mine and gold is Mine—says the LORD of Hosts. 9The glory of this latter House shall be greater than that of the former one, said the LORD of Hosts; and in this place I will grant prosperity—declares the LORD of Hosts.

10On the twenty-fourth day of the ninth [month], in the second year of Darius, the word of the LORD came to the prophet Haggai:
11Thus said the LORD of Hosts: Seek a ruling from the

Can this temple be appropriate? May they expect such a temple to be pleasing to the LORD, even if it has not received the type of legitimating sign seen at the completion of the first Temple (1 Kings 8.10–11)? Would the LORD be with them in such a case? The report serves to allay these concerns of both the people described in the book and, above all, the readers for whom the book was written, since the incongruity characterized their days too. Further, according to the book, it was the LORD who answered these questions and legitimized the readership's Temple. Still the text recognizes the incongruity and maintains that in the future it will be rectified. At that time the wealth of the world would flow to the house of the LORD of all (vv. 7–8). Here the text assumes common, ancient Near Eastern concepts, namely that the wealth of a dominion should flow to the house of the ruler of the dominion, and that the manifestation of the glory of a king relates to the wealth flowing to him from the different nations and places under his dominion. **6:** This v. is quite remarkable within the prophetic worldview. Usually consolation is predicted for some vague future time, rather than *In just a little while longer.* **8:** The expression *silver is Mine and gold is Mine* was taken by the Rabbis as teaching that gaining silver or gold is not an appropriate goal for mortals. Instead they stressed that Torah and good deeds are such goals. See *m. 'Avot* 6.9. **9:** The LXX adds at the end of the v. a sentence that may be translated as "and peace of soul as a possession for all who build, to erect this temple."

15: According to the text, the two leaders and the people set to work on the Temple on the 24th of 'Elul, just before the beginning of the seventh month. In a relatively unusual case, the v. includes both the final sentence of the first report and the introduction of the second one (*In the second . . .*).

1.15b–2.9: A report of a divine announcement: The new Temple will be an appropriate "house of the LORD." The divine message here is addressed to both the two leaders and all the people. It is set on the 21st of Tishri, about a month since the leaders and the

people took action, and in the last day of a festival, Sukkot. The text does not address the potential significance of this time of the year for the narrative, but leaves it for the book's readers to discern. The divine message reported here does not deal with the construction of the Temple per se, but with the question of whether the new Temple is an appropriate Temple for the LORD. The underlying issue is the plain incongruity between the expected glory of the house of a king who is sovereign over all and the absolute lack of splendor of a relatively small temple of a minor, poor province (cf. Ezra 3.12–13).

2.10–19: Report of divine announcement: The Temple will be effective and the LORD will secure blessings on the people. The divine communication is set three months later than the day in which the two leaders and the people set to build the Temple (1.15). It seems to imply that some cultic facility, including an altar, has already been used and that it has its own priests, as follows: ¹²If a man is carrying sacrificial flesh in a fold of his garment, and with that fold touches bread, stew, wine, oil, or any other food, will the latter become holy? In reply, the priests said, "No." ¹³Haggai went on, "If someone defiled by a corpse touches any of these, will it be defiled?" And the priests responded, "Yes."

¹⁴Thereupon Haggai said: That is how this people and that is how this nation looks to Me—declares the LORD—and so, too, the work of their hands: Whatever they offer there is defiled. ¹⁵And now take thought, from this day backward:ᵃ As long as no stone had been laid on another in the House of the LORD, ¹⁶if one came to a heap of twenty measures,ᵇ it would yield only ten; and if one came to a wine vat to skim off fifty measures, the press would yield only twenty. ¹⁷I struck you—all the works of your hands—with blight and mildew and hail, but ᶜyou did not returnᶜ to Me—declares the LORD. ¹⁸Take note, from this day forward—from the twenty-fourth day of the ninth month, from the day when the foundation was laid for the LORD's Temple—take note ¹⁹while the seed is still in the granary, and the vine, fig tree, pomegranate, and olive tree have not yet borne fruit. For from this day on I will send blessings.

²⁰And the word of the LORD came to Haggai a second time on the twenty-fourth day of the month: ²¹Speak to Zerubbabel the governor of Judah: I am going to shake the heavens and the earth. ²²And I will overturn the thrones

a Or "forward."
b I.e., of grain.
c-c Lit. "there was not with you to Me"; cf. Amos 4.9.

from the others. It focuses on a future event, carries some apocalyptic tones, and a large geographical horizon. Moreover, it does not directly relate to the matter of building a legitimate, efficacious temple, or turning material lack into prosperity. The readers are invited, however, to associate the divine communication reported here with the preceding one because the text assigns them to the same date (*a second time*, v. 20). As mentioned above, since the two leaders of the project were involved in a kind of kingly role—i.e., the building of the Temple—one may expect the development of some form of royal imagery in their characterization in the texts of the community (cf. Zech. chs 3–4; see also 1 Chron. 3.19), though not an overtly explicit one. **21–22:** The language of these vv. is as vivid as it is open-ended. If they point to the fall of the Persian empire, then they remained unfulfilled as far as the Persian period is concerned. If they refer to the revolts in the first two years of Darius, then the date associated with the message reflects a lack of awareness or interest in the precise chronology of the events. In any case, unlike other sections of the book of Haggai, the text here is very general (e.g., no nation, ruler, or particular time is mentioned), and accordingly it encourages multiple readings.

personnel. The text emphasizes again that an effective Temple is a precondition for the prosperity of people and land (cf. 1.2–11). Lack of defilement is an obvious precondition for an effective Temple, and for the divine presence. But it is a difficult precondition. To be sure, purity requires—within the discourse of the period—an appropriate cultic facility, which suggests that the people and their produce are impure in its absence. If the latter are impure, then they cannot come or be brought to a sacred place, lest they defile it. This logic leads to a breakdown of any hope of a new, untarnished beginning. This portion of the book of Haggai informs the readers that the LORD can overcome these cir-

cumstances and accordingly, a new beginning and the establishment of an effective cultic facility become a possible and actual reality (v. 19). This divine communication concerning the possibility of purification and of a new Temple that overcomes earlier defilement is dated to the 24th of Kislev (cf. the later festival of Hanukkah, which begins on 25 Kislev). **11:** Purity and the avoidance of the defilement of the cultic facility is possible only if there are priests who know how to differentiate between holy and defiled, and teach and rule accordingly (cf. Lev. 10.10–11).

2.20–23: The coming of the ideal age. The last report is different of kingdoms and destroy the might of the kingdoms of the nations. I will overturn chariots and their drivers. Horses and their riders shall fall, each by the sword of his fellow. [23] On that day—declares the LORD of Hosts—I will take you, O My servant Zerubbabel son of Shealtiel—declares the LORD—and make you as a signet;[a] for I have chosen you—declares the LORD of Hosts.

23: The characterization of the present governor of Judah as a personage who will become *a signet* of the LORD at some point in the future evokes the royal imagery of Jer. 22.24 (see Maimonides, *Mishneh Torah, Sefer ha-Mada* 7.7; cf. Ezek. 28.12), suggesting that earlier prophetic books were studied in the Persian period, but it is overtly open-ended. Just as a signet represents the power of an earthly king, the signet here may represent the power of the divine King. But one may interpret the metaphor as playing on the idea that a person never leaves his (or her) signet. Similarly, the language *I have chosen you* (cf. 1 Chron. 28.6) or *My servant* may evoke Davidic, royal connotations, but not necessarily so (e.g., Num. 17.20; Isa. 44.1; Job 1.8; 2.3; 42.8). (Significantly, in Chronicles—but nowhere else in the Bible—Zerubbabel is explicitly associated with the Davidic line.) Had the language been more unequivocal, readers would have seen the concluding statement not only as unfulfilled, but unfulfillable after the death of Zerubbabel. Conversely, the fact that the Temple was built may have led the readers to accept that at least in some sense Zerubbabel actually served as a "signet of the LORD," even if he was not crowned king of Judah.

a *I.e., bring you close to Me; contrast Jer. 22.24–30.*

זכריה

Zechariah

THE BOOK OF ZECHARIAH is set in the same period as the book of Haggai: the early years of Darius I (reigned 522–486 BCE). The book of Ezra associates Haggai and Zechariah (Ezra 5.1; 6.14) and the building of the Temple; rabbinic sources associate these two prophets with Malachi, and so they create the triad of last prophets (see introductions to Haggai and Malachi).

The book of Zechariah deals with issues similar to those in the book of Haggai: the restoration of the community in the Persian period. Like Haggai, it legitimizes the rebuilding of the Temple and the dual leadership under which it was built. It emphasizes repentance and exhorts the community directly addressed within the book, and above all, that of the readership to behave in accordance with the divine will, so as to avoid the fate of their ancestors (see, e.g., 1.2–6; 7.8–13; 8.13–17).

The book also addresses the dissonance between the actual status and power of the community and the Temple and what they should be according to the theological beliefs of the readership. This dissonance is solved in a way that conveys hope and reaffirms the beliefs of the community about its own place in the divine economy. The text communicates divine, unequivocal assertions about an ideal future in which the remnant of Israel will grow and prosper, Jerusalem will take its proper place, the Temple will become the focal point of worship for the entire world, and the kingship of the LORD will be recognized by all nations.

The book as a whole shows a strong orientation toward the future, particularly the ideal future. Not only does it communicate promises of a future glory for Zion, but it also provides some scenarios that would lead to its realization. These scenarios directly address the question of the relations between Zion (and Judah) and the nations in the future, ideal world. They also involve direct action by the LORD, much conflict and stern divine judgment. The book brings to the readers vivid images of the nations' final attack against Jerusalem and a cosmic upheaval that leads to the creation of a new landscape for Jerusalem and for the land as a whole (ch 14). The book has certain eschatological and even apocalyptic overtones.

Although there are clear temporal and thematic links between Zechariah and Haggai, the two books, as they stand today, are markedly different in style, structure, and tone. Zechariah opens with a superscription (1.1) that along with the following passage (1.2–6) serves as an introduction to the book as a whole. The rest of the book consists of a series of prophetic texts about divine communications associated with Zechariah. At the heart of the first set of texts (1.7–8.23) are eight visions mediated by an angelic figure (see 1.7–6.15) that have no parallel in Haggai, even if the issues they address are similar to those in Haggai. The next sets, 9.1–11.17 and 12.1–14.21, are obviously different from Haggai. Chapter 9 opens with "a pronouncement," separating the chs that follow from those that precede.

Many scholars have argued that the book of Zechariah originally included only chs 1–8, and that only at a later stage were chs 9–14 attached to them. According to this position, the first eight chs were written before the rest—chs 9–14 are usually dated to either the late Persian or the Hellenistic period—and each part was written by a different author. This may well be the case, but the book of Zechariah in its present form does not ask its readers to approach it with this information in mind. To the contrary, the book associates all its texts with the prophet Zechariah mentioned in 1.1.

Many ancient readers found in Zechariah numerous references to messianic times. As expected, some early Christian readers understood them in christological terms (see, for instance, Mark 14.27 and Zech. 13.7; Matt. 27.9 and Zech. 11.12–13; John 19.37 and Zech. 12.10; John 12.15 and Zech. 9.9). Rabbinic Judaism interpreted many of these texts in relation to a messianic time still to come (e.g., Zech. 3.8; 6.12 in the Targum; in relation to Zech. 6.12 see *Num. Rab.* 18.21; for Zech. 9.9 see *Gen. Rab.* 56.2, 98.9; and for Zech. 12.10 as pointing to the Messiah from the House of Joseph, see *b. Sukkah* 52a).

Some vv. of Zechariah have been included in Jewish liturgy. The best-known example is 14.9, which concludes the *'Aleinu* prayer. Zechariah 14.1–21 is the haftarah for the first day of Sukkot since that festival is mentioned there; Zechariah 2.14–4.7 for the first shabbat of Hanukkah and for the parashah of Be-ha'alotekha (Num. 8.1–12.16), since the lampstand ("menorah") plays a central role in this passage. [EHUD BEN ZVI]

1 In the eighth month of the second year of Darius, this word of the LORD came to the prophet Zechariah son of Berechiah son of Iddo:[a] 2 The LORD was very angry with your fathers. 3 Say to them further:

Thus said the LORD of Hosts: Turn back to me—says the LORD of Hosts—and I will turn back to you—said the LORD of Hosts. 4 Do not be like your fathers! For when the earlier prophets called to them, "Thus said the LORD of Hosts: Come, turn back from your evil ways and your evil deeds, they did not obey or give heed to Me—declares the LORD. 5 Where are your fathers now? And did the proph-

1.1–6: Superscription, introduction, and call to repentance. The text assumes that the words of the earlier prophets are available and are being studied. **1:** The month is Marḥeshvan, in fall 520 BCE. This divine communication is set slightly later than those reported in Hag. 1.1, 15; 2.1, but slightly earlier than those in Hag. 2.10, 20. This temporal note suggests to the readers of the book that they are supposed to read 1.2–6 in the light of the texts in Haggai and vice versa. **6:** *He purposed* may also be understood as "He considered

a A clause like "Say to the people" is here understood; cf. 7.5.

ets live forever? 6 But the warnings and the decrees with which I charged My servants the prophets overtook your fathers—did they not?—and in the end they had to admit, 'The LORD has dealt with us according to our ways and our deeds, just as He purposed.' "

7 On the twenty-fourth day of the eleventh month of the second year of Darius—the month of Shebat—this word of the LORD came to the prophet Zechariah son of Berechiah son of Iddo:

8 In the night, I had a vision. I saw a man, mounted on a bay horse, standing a-among the myrtles-a in the Deep, and behind him were bay,b sorrel,c and white horses. 9 I asked, "What are those, my lord?" And the angel who talked with me answered, "I will let you know what they are." 10 Then the man who was standing a-among the myrtles-a spoke up and said, "These were sent out by the LORD to roam the earth."

11 And in fact, they reported to the angel of the LORD who was standing a-among the myrtles,-a "We have roamed the earth, and have found all the earth dwelling in tranquility."d 12 Thereupon the angel of the LORD exclaimed, "O LORD of Hosts! How long will You withhold pardon from Jerusalem and the towns of Judah, which You placed under a curse seventy years ago?"

13 The LORD replied with kind, comforting words to the angel who talked with me.
14 Then the angel who talked with me said to me: "Proclaim! Thus said the LORD of Hosts: I am very jealous for Jerusalem—for Zion—15 and I am very angry with those nations that are at ease; for I was only angry a little, but they overdid the punishment. 16 Assuredly, thus said the LORD: I graciously return to Jerusalem. My House shall be built in her—declares the LORD of Hosts—the measuring line is being applied to Jerusalem. 17 Proclaim further: Thus said the LORD of Hosts: My towns shall yet overflow with bounty. For the LORD will again comfort Zion; He will choose Jerusalem again."

---

a-a Septuagint reads "between the mountains"; cf. 6.1. In 6.1 ff. four teams of horses leave the LORD's abode to roam the four quarters of the earth; in 1.8 ff. they are about to reenter His abode after such a reconnaissance.
b Septuagint adds "dappled"; cf. 6.3.
c Meaning of Heb. uncertain. Emendation yields "black"; cf. 6.2.
d Upheavals at the start of Darius' reign had encouraged hopes of an early restoration of the Davidic dynasty (cf. Hag. 2.21 ff.). Now these hopes were dashed.

[doing]," thereby conveying a conditional element from the outset in God's plans: If the (monarchic period) Israelites had heard their prophets, the punishment would not have come.

1.7–6.15: Reports of eight visions. The visions are described in graphic, and highly symbolic, detail, as are most apocalyptic visions. The "tour" by an angelic being is also typical of apocalypse, as is the use of specific numbers. Unlike most later apocalyptic visions, however, the mediating angel is here anonymous.

1.7–17: The first vision: the horsemen. 7: Within the world of the present book, this date seems to apply to 1.7–6.15, i.e., the entire series of eight visions. The date is just two months after the divine communications in Hag. 2.10, 20. Given the closeness of the dates, and the similarity of the basic themes and of the formula itself, it seems that the readers of the book are supposed to read these two texts as informing each other; see also Ezra 5.1; 6.14. **9:** The term *angel* here and elsewhere in the book (e.g., vv. 11, 12, 4.1, 5.10) may be translated as "messenger," in the sense of a divine messenger. Is this messenger the same *man* mentioned in these verses, as Ibn Ezra and others think? Or, are these two beings, one a "man" and the other a "messenger"? The text itself leaves the question open. **11:** *Tranquility* carries here a negative connotation, because it is associated with a status quo in which Judah and Jerusalem have not been restored. The implicit connotation is that their (full) restoration necessitates much turmoil and probably judgment against the nations (see v. 15 and cf. ch 14). Some scholars associate this tranquility with the imperial peace achieved by Darius I in his second year, though the point is not made in the text. Darius plays no active role whatsoever in the book of Zechariah. **12:** *Seventy years* is a clear reference to Jer. 25.11 (cf. 29.10), another clear indication that pro-

2 I looked up, and I saw four horns.[a] [2]I asked the angel who talked with me, "What are those?" "Those," he replied, "are the horns that tossed Judah, Israel, and Jerusalem."[a] [3]Then the LORD showed me four smiths. [4]"What are they coming to do?" I asked. He replied: "Those are the horns that tossed Judah, so that no man could raise his head; and these men have come [b]to throw them into a panic,[-b] to [c]hew down[-c] the horns of the nations that raise a horn against the land of Judah, to toss it."

[5]I looked up, and I saw a man holding a measuring line. [6]"Where are you going?" I asked. "To measure Jerusalem," he replied, "to see how long and wide it is to be." [7]But the angel who talked with me came forward, and another angel came forward to meet him. [8]The former said to him, "Run to that young man and tell him:

"Jerusalem shall be peopled as a city without walls, so many shall be the men and cattle it contains. [9]And I Myself—declares the LORD—will be a wall of fire all around it, and I will be a glory inside it.

[10]"Away, away! Flee from the land of the north—says the LORD—though I swept you [there] like the four winds of heaven—declares the LORD."

[11]Away, escape, O Zion, you who dwell in Fair Babylon! [12]For thus said the LORD of Hosts—He [d]who sent me after glory[-d]—concerning the nations that have taken you as spoil: "Whoever touches you touches the pupil of [e]his own[-e] eye. [13]For I will lift My hand against them, and they shall be spoil for those they enslaved."—Then you shall know that I was sent by the LORD of Hosts.

[14]Shout for joy, Fair Zion! For lo, I come; and I will dwell in your midst—declares the LORD. [15]In that day many nations will attach themselves to the LORD and become His[f] people, and He[g] will dwell in your midst. Then you will know that I was sent to you by the LORD of Hosts.

[16]The LORD will [h]take Judah to Himself as His portion[-h] in the Holy Land, and He will choose Jerusalem once more.

[17]   Be silent, all flesh, before the LORD!
   For He is roused from His holy habitation.

---

a The four horns correspond to the four winds of v. 10.
b-b Meaning of Heb. uncertain; emendation yields "to sharpen ax heads."
c-c Meaning of Heb. uncertain.
d-d Emendation yields "whose Presence sent me."
e-e According to ancient Jewish tradition, a scribal change for "My."
f Heb. "My."   g Heb. "I."
h-h Emendation yields "allot to Judah its portion"; cf. Num. 34.17.

phetic works were being studied at this period. That text also plays a crucial role in Dan. ch 9.

2.1–4: The second vision: the four horns. 2–3: *Horns* are symbols of power. Here they represent politico-military agents, nations. The number *four* connotes a sense of totality, because it points to the four points of the compass (a concept also attested in Mesopotamian literature); see also 2.10.

2.5–9: The third vision: the man with the measuring line. 5–6: Questions of the type "who are those?" (1.9; 2.2) are omitted now. The prophet is described as getting more and more acquainted with his (and God's) visionary world. Ezek. 48.15–20 describes the size of ideal Jerusalem also in terms of length and width (see also Ezek. 45.1–6). **7–9:** There is no need to measure Jerusalem, for it will be or grow without any material limit, such as the one created by a city wall. Of course, a city without walls might evoke the image of a defenseless city, but the LORD will be its wall.

2.10–17: The establishment of ideal Zion, from the departure from Babylonia to an ideal future. 10: *Away, away! Flee from the land of the north . . . four winds of heaven:* The return from Zion is given some cataclysmic dimensions. The text does not say "return" or the like, but *Away, away! Flee* as if from a disaster about to happen. There is also the explicit comparison with the *four winds,* and Babylonia is referred to as *the land of the north,* a place often imagined as a source of chaos or chaotic forces (cf. Isa. 14.31; Jer. 1.14–15; 4.6; 10.22). **12:** The v. may be translated "For thus said the LORD of Hosts (after [the/His] glory sent me) concerning. . . ." According to *Mekhilta,* (Shirata 6.10), the original text read, "the pupil of My own eye," and was changed by the soferim (scribes) so as to avoid the obvious anthropomorphism. **15:** The Heb reads "and become My people, and I will dwell in your midst."

3 He further showed me Joshua, the high priest, standing before the angel of the LORD, and the Accuser[a]
standing at his right to accuse him. [2] But [the angel of] the
LORD said to the Accuser, "The LORD rebuke you, O Accuser; may the LORD who has chosen Jerusalem rebuke
you! For this is a brand plucked from the fire."[b] [3] Now
Joshua was clothed in filthy garments when he stood
before the angel. [4] The latter spoke up and said to his
attendants, "Take the filthy garments off him!" And he
said to him, "See, I have removed your guilt from you,
and you shall be clothed in [priestly] robes." [5] Then he[c]
gave the order, "Let a pure[d] diadem be placed on his
head." And they placed the pure diadem on his head and
clothed him in [priestly] garments,[e] as the angel of the
LORD stood by.

[6] And the angel of the LORD charged Joshua as follows:
[7] "Thus said the LORD of Hosts: If you walk in My paths
and keep My charge, you in turn will rule My House and
guard My courts, and I will permit you to move about
among these attendants. [8] Hearken well, O High Priest
Joshua, you and your fellow priests sitting before you! For
those men are a sign that I am going to bring My servant
the Branch.[f] [9] For mark well this stone which I place before
Joshua, a single stone with seven eyes.[g] I will execute its
engraving—declares the LORD of Hosts—and I will remove that country's guilt in a single day. [10] In that day—
declares the LORD of Hosts—you will be inviting each
other to the shade of vines and fig trees."

4 The angel who talked with me came back and woke
me as a man is wakened from sleep. [2] He said to me,
"What do you see?" And I answered, "I see a lampstand
all of gold, with a bowl above it. The lamps on it are seven
in number, and the [h]lamps above it have[h] seven pipes;
[3] and by it are two olive trees, one on the right of the bowl
and one on its left." [4] I, in turn, asked the angel who talked
with me, "What do those things mean, my lord?" [5] "Do

a Others "Satan."
b Joshua's father (Hag. 1.1; 1 Chron. 5.40–41) was exiled and his grandfather executed
(2 Kings 25.18–21) by the Babylonians, but Joshua returned.
c Heb. "I."
d I.e., ritually pure.
e Joshua has now been rendered fit to associate with the heavenly beings (v. 7); cf. Isa.
6.6–8.
f I.e., the future king of David's line. See 6.12; Jer. 23.5–6; 33.15–16; cf. Isa. 11.1.
g Meaning of Heb. uncertain. The stone apparently symbolizes the God-given power of the
future Davidic ruler; see below 4.6–7.
h-h Emendation yields "bowl above it has."

The shift to direct divine speech
might have conveyed some emphasis on the part of the LORD.
Note that the unique relation between Zion and the LORD is not diminished, but to the contrary
re-emphasized by the vision of
many nations becoming God's
people.

**3.1–10: The fourth vision: the
high priest Joshua is purified.
1:** NJPS correctly translates the
Heb "ha-satan," as the *Accuser* instead of the common, but erroneous, "Satan." (On the development of this notion in the Persian
period, see Job 1.6 n.) **5:** *Then he
gave the order:* The Heb reads,
"Then I gave the order." See
translators' note c. **8:** *The Branch*
(or "the Sprout") has been understood in terms of a Davidic, most
often messianic figure based on
Jer. 23.5–6; 33.15–16 (cf. Isa. 11.1—
again, earlier prophetic material is
being studied and interpreted).
According to 6.12–13, the Sprout
will build the Temple and assume
majesty. Many medieval Jewish
commentators (e.g., Rashi, Ibn
Ezra) and many modern scholars
maintain that the reference to the
Branch was meant to be understood as pointing to Zerubbabel
(see 4.8, and the reference to his
partner in the leadership, the high
priest Joshua in 6.11), whose name
means "the seed of Babylon."
Even if there is a lionization of
Zerubbabel (see 4.6–7), the book of
Zechariah does not explicitly state
that he is the expected Sprout.
Moreover, it is unlikely that the
readership of the book as a
whole—as opposed to that of readers of any possible source embedded somehow in the book—would
have understood references to a
messianic king (cf. Jer. 23.5–6;
33.15–16) as being actually fulfilled
in the person of Zerubbabel or by
the time he built the Temple.

**4.1–14: The fifth vision: the
lampstand and the olive trees.
2:** *Lampstand,* Heb "menorah."

you not know what those things mean?" asked the angel who talked with me; and I said, "No, my lord." [6] Then he explained to me as follows:[a]

"This is the word of the LORD to Zerubbabel:[b] Not by might, nor by power, but by My spirit[c]—said the LORD of Hosts. [7] Whoever you are, O great mountain in the path of Zerubbabel, turn into level ground! For he shall produce that excellent stone; it shall be greeted with shouts of 'Beautiful! Beautiful!' "

[8] And the word of the LORD came to me: [9] "Zerubbabel's hands have founded this House and Zerubbabel's hands shall complete it. Then you shall know that it was the LORD of Hosts who sent me to you. [10] Does anyone scorn a day of small beginnings? When they see [d]the stone of distinction[d] in the hand of Zerubbabel, they shall rejoice.

"Those seven are the eyes of the LORD, ranging over the whole earth."

[11] "And what," I asked him, "are those two olive trees, one on the right and one on the left of the lampstand?" [12] And I further asked him, "What are the two tops[e] of the olive trees that feed their gold[f] through those two golden tubes?"[g] [13] He asked me, "Don't you know what they are?" And I replied, "No, my lord." [14] Then he explained, "They are the two [h]anointed dignitaries[h] who attend the Lord of all the earth."

5 I looked up again, and I saw a flying scroll. [2] "What do you see?" he asked. And I replied, "A flying scroll, twenty cubits long and ten cubits wide." [3] "That," he explained to me, "is the curse which goes out over the whole land. [i]For everyone who has stolen, as is forbidden on one side [of the scroll], has gone unpunished; and everyone who has sworn [falsely], as is forbidden on the other side of it, has gone unpunished.[i] [4] [But] I have sent it forth—declares the LORD of Hosts—and [the curse] shall enter the house of the thief and the house of the one who swears falsely by My name, and it shall lodge inside their

---

a The explanation is given in the last sentence of v. 10.

b A grandson of King Jehoiachin (1 Chron. 3.17–19) and the secular head of the repatriated community (Hag. 1.1; etc.).

c I.e., Zerubbabel will succeed by means of spiritual gifts conferred upon him by the LORD; cf. Isa. 11.2.ff.

d-d Meaning of Heb. uncertain; others "plummet."

e Meaning of Heb. uncertain; literally "ears" (as of grain).

f Emendation yields "oil"; cf. v. 14.

g Or "funnels"; through them the oil runs from the olive trees into the bowl of vv. 2 and 3.

h-h I.e., the high priest and the king (cf. 3.8–9 with note); lit. "sons of oil."

i-i Meaning of Heb. uncertain.

6–7: See 3.8 n. **6:** This v. has often played a significant role within Judaism, which has felt small and powerless, yet comforted by its reliance on God. It is inscribed on the front of the Synagogue of Cologne reconstructed after World War II. **10:** The expression *the stone of distinction* may be translated as "the stone of the plumb" or "the plummet." The text implies and criticizes a sentiment akin to the one expressed in Hag. 2.3. *Those seven are the eyes of the LORD,* probably the answer to the question in v. 4 regarding the meaning of the seven lamps of the lampstand. Cf. 3.9. **14:** The two *anointed dignitaries,* lit. "sons of oil." The term is different from the one translated as "anointed" in Lev. 4.3; 1 Sam. 2.10, 35; 26.9; Ps. 2.2, and passim. The two "sons of oil" represent Joshua, the high priest, and Zerubbabel, the nonpriestly ruler who shares some royal responsibilities. It is not by chance that the text coins a unique expression rather than using a very common one. Most likely, the point is to avoid depicting Zerubbabel as a significant royal or messianic figure. Unlike the situation in the book of Haggai, Zerubbabel is not called "governor" in Zechariah, but neither is he called "king," nor is it stated explicitly anywhere in the book that he is from David, nor can we assume that he was anointed. The openness of the text in this matter is remarkable, and hardly unintentional. (The high priest was presumably anointed—see Num. 3.3, 25—but his anointing did not carry any kingly attributes.)

5.1–4: The sixth vision: the flying scroll. 2: The *scroll* stands for the contents of the written text it contains—i.e., the curse against wrongdoers—and for the implementation of the curse. In other words, the curse (i.e., the written scroll) curses, or carries out the curse. *Twenty cubits . . . ten cubits:* approx. 10 m by 5 m (30 ft by 15 ft), the size of the portico of the Great Hall of Solomon's Temple (1 Kings 6.3). *Over the whole land* houses and shall consume them to the last timber and stone."

⁵ Then the angel who talked with me came forward and said, "Now look up and note this other object that is approaching." ⁶ I asked, "What is it?" And he said, "This tub*ᵃ* that is approaching—this," said he, "is their eye*ᵇ* in all the land." ⁷ And behold, a disk of lead was lifted, revealing a woman seated inside the tub. ⁸ "That," he said, "is Wickedness"; and, thrusting her down into the tub, he pressed the leaden weight into its mouth.

⁹ I looked up again and saw two women come soaring with the wind in their wings—they had wings like those of a stork—and carry off the tub between earth and sky. ¹⁰ "Where are they taking the tub?" I asked the angel who talked with me. ¹¹ And he answered, "To build a shrine for it in the land of Shinar;*ᶜ* [a stand] shall be erected for it, and it shall be set down there upon the stand."

6 I looked up again, and I saw: Four chariots were coming out from between the two mountains; the mountains were of copper. ² The horses of the first chariot were bay, the horses of the second chariot were black; ³ the horses of the third chariot were white, and the horses of the fourth chariot were spotted—dappled. ⁴ And I spoke up and asked the angel who talked with me: "What are those, my lord?" ⁵ In reply, the angel said to me, "Those are the four winds of heaven coming out after presenting themselves to the Lord of all the earth. ⁶ The one with the black horses is going out to the region of the north; the white ones *ᵈ*have gone out*ᵈ* to *ᵉ*what is to the west of them;*ᵉ* the spotted ones *ᵈ*have gone out*ᵈ* to the region of the south; ⁷ and *ᶠ*the dappled ones have gone out . . . "*ᶠ* They were ready to start out and range the earth, and he gave them the order, "Start out and range the earth!" And they ranged the earth. ⁸ Then he alerted me, and said to me, "Take good note! Those that went out to the region of the north have *ᵍ*done my pleasure*ᵍ* in the region of the north."*ʰ*

... *who has stolen ... who has sworn [falsely]: Over the whole land* is a possible translation, but so is "over the whole earth" as the same Heb phrase has been translated in 1.11; 4.14; 6.5; 14.9 (but not in 14.10, and with good reason there). The flying scroll or curse creates an ideal society in which there will be no social transgressors such as those mentioned above. If one reads "over the whole earth," this society is not restricted to Judah or Jerusalem, but will cover the entire world (cf. 14.9).

5.5–11: The seventh vision: the woman in the tub. 6: The *tub* (Heb "ephah") suggests a container of that capacity, 23 liters (21 quarts), dimensions too small for what is inside it. **8:** *Wickedness* is represented by a female figure, and her mouth is to be shut with the *leaden weight*. Further, female figures take Wickedness to the *land of Shinar*, namely Babylonia. The text reflects (and contributes to shape) gendered constructions.

6.1–8: The eighth vision: the four chariots. The *horses, winds,* etc., symbolize all directions and therefore cover the earth. It is unknown if the further details (e.g., the colors of the horses) are symbolic, or are given merely to add vividness to the description.

a Heb. ephah, *a measure of capacity.*
b *Septuagint and Syriac read "guilt."*
c *I.e., Babylonia; cf. Gen. 10.10; 11.2, 9.*
d-d *Change of vocalization yields "will go out."*
e-e *Cf.* 'aḥor, *"west," Isa. 9.11. Emendation yields "the region of the west."*
f-f *Emendation yields "the bay ones will go out to the region of the east."*
g-g *Cf. postbiblical* naḥath ruaḥ, *"gratification." Emendation yields, "done the* Lord*'s pleasure."*
h *I.e., Babylonia, whose communication with Judah was via North Mesopotamia and Syria; cf. 2.10–11.*

9 The word of the LORD came to me: 10 Receive from[a] the exiled community—from Heldai, Tobijah, and Jedaiah, who have come from Babylon—and you, in turn, proceed the same day to the house of Josiah son of Zephaniah. 11 Take silver and gold and make crowns. Place [one] on the head of High Priest Joshua son of Jehozadak, 12 and say to him, "Thus said the LORD of Hosts: Behold, a man called the Branch[b] shall branch out from the place where he is, and he shall build the Temple of the LORD. 13 He shall build the Temple of the LORD and shall assume majesty, and he shall sit on his throne and rule. And there shall also be a priest [c]seated on his throne,[c] and harmonious understanding shall prevail between them."

14 The crowns shall remain in the Temple of the LORD as a memorial to Helem,[d] Tobijah, Jedaiah, and Hen[e] son of Zephaniah. 15 Men from far away shall come and take part in the building of the Temple of the LORD, and you shall know that I have been sent to you by the LORD of Hosts— if only you will obey the LORD your God!

7 In the fourth year of King Darius, on the fourth day of the ninth month, Kislev, the word of the LORD came to Zechariah—2 when Bethel-sharezer [f]and Regem-melech and his men sent[f] to entreat the favor of the LORD, 3 [and] to address this inquiry to the priests of the House of the LORD and to the prophets: "Shall I weep and practice abstinence in the fifth month,[g] as I have been doing all these years?"

4 Thereupon the word of the LORD of Hosts came to me: 5 Say to all the people of the land and to the priests: When you fasted and lamented in the fifth and seventh months all these seventy years, did you fast for my benefit? 6 And when you eat and drink, who but you does the eating, and who but you does the drinking? 7 Look, this is the message that the LORD proclaimed through the earlier prophets, when Jerusalem and the towns about her were peopled and tranquil, when the Negeb and the Shephelah were peopled.

8 And the word of the LORD to Zechariah continued: 9 Thus said the LORD of Hosts: Execute true justice; deal loyally and compassionately with one another. 10 Do not

6.9–15: The coronation of the high priest. 11–12: One would expect that the king would be crowned, but only the high priest Joshua is. Ibn Ezra, Radak, Rashi, and others consider Zerubbabel to be the Branch, and the person for whom the other crown was meant. The Targum, however, reflects a different understanding: "And you shall take silver and gold and make a large crown and set it upon the head of Joshua, son of Jehozadak, the high priest. And you shall speak to him, saying, 'Thus speaks the LORD of hosts, saying, behold, the man whose name is Anointed will be revealed and he shall be raised up, and shall build the temple of the LORD.'" Significantly, it is likely that the text read "crown" in vv. 11 and 14 (see NRSV) rather than *crowns*. If this is the case, then there was only one crown in the world of the book, and it was Joshua's. 14: In the ideal future, both the Branch and the priest will sit, each on his own throne. 15: The concluding words *if only you will obey* are an almost exact quotation of Deut. 28.1 and may allude to that ch, on the assumption that at this point in history, Deuteronomy was well known.

7.1–14: A passage about fasting and true obedience. 2–3: The fifth month is the month of Av. The events described in 2 Kings 25.8–12 are the reason for the weeping and abstinence. V. 2 may also be translated: "When the people of Bethel had sent Sharezer and Regem-melech and his (or their) men, to entreat. . . ." If this is the case, the text emphasizes that the people from Bethel, the place of the ancient sanctuary of northern Israel, recognize now the authority of Jerusalem and ask its priests and prophets for instructions. 5: The fifth month is Av and the seventh month is Tishri. The reference is to the commemoration of destruction of the First Temple. No dates of the month are given. Rabbinic literature and subsequent Jewish practice commemorate the destruction on 9 Av. The mention

a Emendation yields "the gift of."

b See note at 3.8.

c-c Septuagint reads "on his right side."

d The Syriac version reads "Heldai"; cf. v. 10.

e In v. 10, "Josiah."

f-f Emendation yields "sent Regem-melech and his men."

g Because of the destruction of the Temple and Jerusalem; cf. 2 Kings 25.8 ff.

defraud the widow, the orphan, the stranger, and the poor; and do not plot evil against one another.—11 But they refused to pay heed. They presented a balky back and turned a deaf ear. 12 They hardened their hearts like adamant against heeding the instruction and admonition that the LORD of Hosts sent to them by His spirit through the earlier prophets; and a terrible wrath issued from the LORD of Hosts. 13 Even as He called and they would not listen, "So," said the LORD of Hosts, "let them call and I will not listen." 14 I dispersed them among all those nations which they had not known, and the land was left behind them desolate, without any who came and went. They caused a delightful land to be turned into a desolation.

8 The word of the LORD of Hosts came [to me]: 2 Thus said the LORD of Hosts: I am very jealous for Zion, I am fiercely jealous for her. 3 Thus said the LORD: I have returned to Zion, and I will dwell in Jerusalem. Jerusalem will be called the City of Faithfulness, and the mount of the LORD of Hosts the Holy Mount.

4 Thus said the LORD of Hosts: There shall yet be old men and women in the squares of Jerusalem, each with staff in hand because of their great age. 5 And the squares of the city shall be crowded with boys and girls playing in the squares. 6 Thus said the LORD of Hosts: Though it will seem impossible to the remnant of this people in those days, shall it also be impossible to Me?—declares the LORD of Hosts. 7 Thus said the LORD of Hosts: I will rescue My people from the lands of the east and from the lands of the west, 8 and I will bring them home to dwell in Jerusalem. They shall be My people, and I will be their God—in truth and sincerity.

9 Thus said the LORD of Hosts: Take courage, you who now hear these words which the prophets spoke when the foundations were laid for the rebuilding of the Temple, the House of the LORD of Hosts.

10 aFor before that time, the earnings of men were nil, and profits from beasts were nothing. It was not safe to go about one's business on account of enemies; and I set all men against one another. 11 But now I will not treat the remnant of this people as before—declares the LORD of Hosts—12 but what it sows shall prosper: The vine shall produce its fruit, the ground shall produce its yield, and the skies shall provide their moisture. I will bestow all these things upon the remnant of this people. 13 And just

of the seventh month could be an early reference to the Fast of Gedaliah (2 Kings 25.25; Jer. 41.1–3; the Fast of Gedaliah on 3 Tishri marks the end of the independence of Judah, and is still observed as a fast day). **10:** The offenses include plotting evil in one's heart, not just the actual commission of evil against another.

8.1–23: A set of divine announcements of hope dealing with an ideal future for Jerusalem and Judah. 3: The ideal Jerusalem is also renamed in Isa. 1.26; 62.2; Ezek. 48.35. **4:** According to a well-known story in *b. Mak.* 24b, the certainty that this announcement will be fulfilled was the reason of R. Akiva's joy at the sight of painful markers of the Roman destruction of Jerusalem. He thought that just as the announced judgment was fulfilled, so will be the announced future glory of the city. **13:** Cf. Gen. 12.12.

a Cf. Hag. 1.6.

as you were a curse[a] among the nations, O House of Judah and House of Israel, so, when I vindicate you, you shall become a blessing.[a] Have no fear; take courage!

[14] For thus said the Lord of Hosts: Just as I planned to afflict you and did not relent when your fathers provoked Me to anger—said the Lord of Hosts—[15] so, at this time, I have turned and planned to do good to Jerusalem and to the House of Judah. Have no fear! [16] These are the things you are to do: Speak the truth to one another, render true and perfect justice in your gates. [17] And do not contrive evil against one another, and do not love perjury, because all those are things that I hate—declares the Lord.

[18] And the word of the Lord of Hosts came to me, saying, [19] Thus said the Lord of Hosts: The fast of the fourth month, the fast of the fifth month, the fast of the seventh month, and the fast of the tenth month[b] shall become occasions for joy and gladness, happy festivals for the House of Judah; but you must love honesty and integrity.

[20] Thus said the Lord of Hosts: Peoples and the inhabitants of many cities shall yet come—[21] the inhabitants of one shall go to the other and say, "Let us go and entreat the favor of the Lord, let us seek the Lord of Hosts; I will go, too." [22] The many peoples and the multitude of nations shall come to seek the Lord of Hosts in Jerusalem and to entreat the favor of the Lord. [23] Thus said the Lord of Hosts: In those days, ten men from nations of every tongue will take hold—they will take hold of every Jew by a corner of his cloak and say, "Let us go with you, for we have heard that God is with you."

9 A pronouncement: The word of the Lord.

He will reside in the land of Hadrach and
　　Damascus;
For all men's eyes will turn to the Lord—
Like all the tribes of Israel—
[2]　Including Hamath, which borders on it,[c]
And Tyre and Sidon, though they are very wise.
[3]　Tyre has built herself a fortress;
She has amassed silver like dust,
And gold like the mud in the streets.
[4]　But my Lord will impoverish her;

14: See 1.6 n. **16–17:** Cf. 8.9–11.
19: This divine announcement returns to the question asked at the beginning of ch 7, but incorporates the intervening material, noting that only when the ideal restoration is completed will these fast days be transformed. It served as a basis for the traditional Jewish belief that present days of fast and lamentation will become days of joy in the messianic era; see, e.g., Maimonides, *Mishneh Torah, Taʿan.* 5.19.

9.1–11.17: A divine pronouncement: another word of the Lord associated with Zechariah. See also 12.1. This section of the book of Zechariah has its own introduction (9.1a) that characterizes the entire text as a divine pronouncement (Heb "massaʾ"; the precise meaning of the term in Heb is a matter of debate). A set of announcements of judgment against the nations and of a glorious restoration for Jerusalem and Judah follows the introduction. The section contains numerous descriptions of an ideal future, but also of the period that leads up to such an ideal future (see 11.4–17). The issue of leadership, good and bad, figures prominently in 9.1–11.17. **9.1:** The *land of Hadrach* is in Aram (today, Syria), north of Damascus. The v. may be translated also as, "the word of the Lord is against Hadrach and its resting place, Damascus, for to the Lord belongs the spring of humanity/humankind [that is, all humanity], as do all the tribes of Israel." **2:** *Hamath,* an important city and kingdom in the territory of today's Syria. *Tyre and Sidon,* two of the most important eastern Mediterranean city ports and capital cities of two Phoenician kingdoms. The cities are located in today's Lebanon.

---

a I.e., a standard by which men curse or bless; cf. Gen. 12.2 and note.
b Commemorating, respectively, the events of 2 Kings 25.3 ff. (Jer. 52.6 ff.); 2 Kings 25.8 ff. (Jer. 52.12 ff.); 2 Kings 25.25 ff. (Jer. 41); 2 Kings 25.1 ff. (Jer. 52.4).
c I.e., on the land of Hadrach and Damascus.

He will defeat her forces at sea,
And she herself shall be consumed by fire.

5   Ashkelon shall see it and be frightened,
       Gaza shall tremble violently,
       And Ekron, at the collapse of her hopes.
       Kingship shall vanish from Gaza,
       Ashkelon shall be without inhabitants,

6   And ᵃa mongrel peopleᵃ shall settle in Ashdod.
       I will uproot the grandeur of Philistia.

7   But I will clean out the blood from its mouth,
       And the detestable things from between its teeth.
       Its survivors, too, shall belong to our God:
       They shall become like a clan in Judah,
       And Ekron shall be like the Jebusites.

8   And I will encamp in My House ᵇagainst armies,ᵇ
       Against any that come and go,
       And no oppressor shall ever overrun them again;
       For I have now taken note ᶜwith My own eyes.ᶜ

9   Rejoice greatly, Fair Zion;
       Raise a shout, Fair Jerusalem!
       Lo, your king is coming to you.
       He is victorious, triumphant,
       Yet humble, riding on an ass,
       On a donkey foaled by a she-ass.

10   Heᵈ shall banish chariots from Ephraim
       And horses from Jerusalem;
       The warrior's bow shall be banished.
       He shall call on the nations to surrender,ᵉ
       And his rule shall extend from sea to sea
       And from ocean to land's end.

11ᶠ   You, for your part, have releasedᵍ
       Your prisoners from the dry pit,ʰ
       For the sake of the blood of your covenant,

12   [Saying], "Return to Bizzaron,ⁱ

5–6: *Ashkelon . . . Gaza . . . Ekron . . . Ashdod*, Philistine cities. **7:** *Jebusites*, former inhabitants of Jerusalem (cf. Judg. 19.10; 2 Sam. 5.6, 8; 24.16, 18; 1 Kings 9.20; 1 Chron. 11.4). **9:** This image of the ideal future king (Messiah) has been very influential in Jewish tradition, and has influenced the depiction of Jesus in the Gospels (see introduction). **10:** The Heb has "I shall banish/cut off." See 2.15 n. Cf. the conclusion of this verse with Ps. 72.8. The phrase is often translated in English by "his dominion" rather than "his rule." The phrase inspired the Canadian "Fathers of the Confederation" to give the new country its official title, Dominion of Canada. **11:** An alternative translation of the v. reads, "As for you [fem.] also, because of the blood of My covenant with you, I will set your [fem.] prisoners free from the waterless pit/dungeon." The feminine "you" is most likely "Fair Zion" (see v. 9). **12:** *Bizzaron* may mean "Fortress" or "a fortress."

---

a-a *Heb.* mamzer; *cf. note at Deut. 23.3.*

b-b *Change of vocalization yields "as a garrison."*

c-c *Emendation yields "of their suffering"; cf. 1 Sam. 1.11.*

d *Heb. "I."*   e *Cf. Deut. 20.10–12 and note.*

f *Exact meaning and connection of vv. 11–12 uncertain.*

g *Taking* shillaḥti *as a second-person singular feminine form, with Septuagint; cf. Judg. 5.7 with note.*

h *I.e., a pit that serves as a dungeon rather than a cistern (both are called* bor *in Heb.).*

i *Perhaps a nickname ("fortress") for Samaria (Heb.* Shomeron).

You prisoners of hope."
In return [I] announce this day:
I will repay you double.

13 For I have drawn Judah taut,
And applied [My hand] to Ephraim as to a bow,
And I will arouse your sons, O Zion,
Against your sons, O Javan,
And make you like a warrior's sword.

14 And the LORD will manifest Himself to them,[a]
And His arrows shall flash like lightning;
My Lord GOD shall sound the ram's horn
And advance in a stormy tempest.[b]

15 The LORD of Hosts will protect them:
[c][His] slingstones shall devour and conquer;
They shall [d]drink, shall rage as with[-d] wine,
And be filled [with it] like a dashing bowl,
Like the corners of an altar.

16 The LORD their God shall prosper them
On that day;
[He shall pasture] His people like sheep.
[They shall be] like crown jewels glittering on His
    soil.

17 How lovely, how beautiful they shall be,
Producing young men like new grain,
Young women like new wine!

10 Ask the LORD for rain
In the [e-]season of late rain.[-e]
It is the LORD who causes storms;[f]
And He will provide rainstorms [g-]for them,
Grass in the fields for everyone.[-g]

2 For the teraphim[h] spoke delusion,
The augurs predicted falsely;
And dreamers speak lies
And console with illusions.
That is why My people have strayed[f] like a flock,
They suffer[f] for lack of a shepherd.

14: Another possible translation of the v. is, "and advance in the storm-winds of the south." 17: There are a number of alternative translations of this verse: (a) "For what goodness and beauty are His! Grain shall make the young men flourish, and new wine the young women" (NRSV); (b) "For what is His goodness and His beauty? Grain that makes the young men flourish, and new wine that makes the young women flourish." In any case, the cultural association of grain with males and new wine with females is noteworthy. 10.2: For *teraphim* see, among others, Gen. 31.19; Judg. 17.5; 1 Sam. 15.23; Ezek. 21.26. Here it points to images that were consulted for the purpose of divination. False prophets continued into the Persian period (Neh. 6.14). 3: There were *shepherds* (cf. v. 2), but they failed. These failed, oppressive leaders are also characterized as rams (cf. Jer. 50.8; Ezek. 39.18).

---

a I.e., Judah.

b Lit. "tempests of wind"; for teman in the sense of wind, cf. Job 9.9; 39.26.

c The meaning of much of the rest of the chapter is uncertain.

d-d Some Septuagint mss. read "drink blood like."

e-e Septuagint reads "in its season / The early rain and the late." Cf. Deut. 11.14.

f Meaning of Heb. uncertain.

g-g Emendation yields "[producing] food for men, / Grass in the fields for cattle." Cf. Deut. 11.14–15.

h Idols consulted for oracles; cf. 1 Sam. 15.23; Ezek. 21.26.

3   My anger is roused against the shepherds,
       And I will punish the he-goats.ª

       For the Lord of Hosts has taken thought
       In behalf of His flock, the House of Judah;
       He will make them like majestic chargers in
              battle.
4   From them shall come ᵇ⁻cornerstones,
       From them tent pegs,⁻ᵇ
       From them bows of combat,
       And every captain shall also arise from them.
5   And together they shall be like warriors in battle,
       Tramping in the dirt of the streets;
       They shall fight, for the Lord shall be with them,
       And they shall put horsemen to shame.
6   I will give victory to the House of Judah,
       And triumph to the House of Joseph.
       I will restore them, for I have pardoned them,
       And they shall be as though I had never disowned
              them;
       For I the Lord am their God,
       And I will answer their prayers.
7   ᶜEphraim shall be like a warrior,
       And theyᶜ shall exult as with wine;
       Their children shall see it and rejoice,
       They shall exult in the Lord.
8   I will whistle to them and gather them,
       For I will redeem them;
       They shall increase ᵈ⁻and continue increasing.⁻ᵈ
9   For though I sowed them among the nations,
       In the distant places they shall remember Me,
       They shall escape with their children and shall
              return.
10   I will bring them back from the land of Egypt
       And gather them from Assyria;
       And I will bring them to the lands of Gilead and
              Lebanon,
       And even they shall not suffice for them.
11   ᵈ⁻A hemmed-in force shall pass over the sea
       And shall stir up waves in the sea;⁻ᵈ
       And all the deeps of the Nile shall dry up.
       Down shall come the pride of Assyria,
       And the scepter of Egypt shall pass away.

a I.e., oppressive leaders; cf. Ezek. 34.17 ff.
b-b Emendation yields "shields and bucklers."
c-c Emendation yields "And when Ephraim is victorious, / They . . ."
d-d Meaning of Heb. uncertain.

12 But I will make them[a] mighty through the Lord,
And they shall [b]march proudly[b] in His name
—declares the Lord.

11 Throw open your gates, O Lebanon,
And let fire consume your cedars!
2 Howl, cypresses, for cedars have fallen!
How the mighty are ravaged!
Howl, you oaks of Bashan,
For the stately forest is laid low!
3 Hark, the wailing of the shepherds,
For their [c]rich pastures[c] are ravaged;
Hark, the roaring of the great beasts,
For the jungle of the Jordan is ravaged.

4 Thus said my God the Lord: Tend the sheep meant for slaughter, 5 whose buyers will slaughter them with impunity, whose seller will say, "Praised be the Lord! I'll get rich," and whose shepherd will not pity them. 6 For I will pity the inhabitants of the land no more—declares the Lord—but I will place every man at the mercy of every other man and at the mercy of his king; they shall break the country to bits, and I will not rescue it from their hands.

7 So I tended the sheep meant for slaughter, [d]for those poor men of the sheep.[d] I got two staffs, one of which I named Favor and the other Unity, and I proceeded to tend the sheep. 8 But I lost [e]the three shepherds[e] in one month; then my patience with them was at an end, and they in turn were disgusted with me. 9 So I declared, "I am not going to tend you; let the one that is to die die and the one that is to get lost get lost; and let the rest devour each other's flesh!"

10 Taking my staff Favor, I cleft it in two, so as to annul the covenant I had made with all the peoples;[f] 11 and when it was annulled that day, [g]the same poor men of the sheep[g] who watched[h] me realized that it was a message from the Lord. 12 Then I said to them, "If you are satisfied, pay me my wages; if not, don't." So they weighed out my wages, thirty shekels of silver—13 [c]the noble sum that I was worth in their estimation.[c] The Lord said to me, "De-

11.1–17: The readers of this literary subunit learn much about the worthless shepherds and their fate. Building upon common ancient Near Eastern and biblical imagery, these shepherds are political leaders, but significantly their identity is never revealed, nor even hinted at, so as to allow and even encourage multiple interpretations. 13: See introduction.

a I.e., Judah and Ephraim.
b-b Meaning of Heb. uncertain. Emendation yields "have glory"; cf. Isa. 45.25.
c-c Meaning of Heb. uncertain.
d-d Emendation yields "for the sheep dealers"; cf. the word rendered "trader" in 14.21.
e-e Emendation yields "a third of the flock."
f Perhaps alluding to the prediction of 14.1–3.
g-g Emendation yields "the sheep dealers."   h Emendation yields "hired."

posit it in the treasury."[a] And I took the thirty shekels and deposited it in the treasury in the House of the LORD. [14] Then I cleft in two my second staff, Unity, in order to annul the brotherhood between Judah and Israel.[b]

[15] The LORD said to me further: Get yourself the gear of a foolish shepherd. [16] For I am going to raise up in the land a shepherd who will neither miss the lost [sheep], nor seek the strayed,[a] nor heal the injured, nor sustain the frail,[a] but will feast on the flesh of the fat ones and [c]tear off their hoofs.[-c]

17   Oh, the worthless shepherd
            Who abandons the flock!
            Let a sword descend upon his arm
            And upon his right eye!
            His arm shall shrivel up;
            His right eye shall go blind.

12 A pronouncement: The word of the LORD concerning Israel.

            The utterance of the LORD,
            Who stretched out the skies
            And made firm the earth,
            And created man's breath within him:

[2] Behold, I will make Jerusalem a bowl of reeling for the peoples all around. Judah shall be caught up in the siege upon Jerusalem, [3] when all the nations of the earth gather against her. In that day, I will make Jerusalem a stone for all the peoples to lift; all who lift it shall injure themselves. [4] In that day—declares the LORD—I will strike every horse with panic and its rider with madness. But I will [d]watch over the House of Judah while I strike every horse of[-d] the peoples with blindness. [5] And the clans of Judah will say to themselves, [e]"The dwellers of Jerusalem are a task set for us by[-e] their God, the LORD of Hosts." [6] In that day, I will make the clans of Judah like a flaming brazier among sticks and like a flaming torch among sheaves. They shall devour all the besieging peoples right and left; and Jerusalem shall continue on its site, in Jerusalem.[f]

[7] The LORD will give victory to the tents of Judah first, so that the glory of the House of David and the glory of the

12.1–14.21: Another divine pronouncement associated with Zechariah: The word of the LORD concerning Israel. This section is set apart from the preceding one (9.1–11.17) by the presence of an unmistakable, composite subtitle that serves as an introduction to the unit in 12.1 (see 9.1). The repetition of the opening expression *in that day* provides much cohesion and structure to this literary unit within the book. The section as a whole is meant to bridge the gap between the actual world of the authorship and readership of the book and an expected future in which the kingship of the LORD over all the earth will be clearly manifested and acknowledged by all. Thus the unit reports a divine communication about the process that will lead to that future and about that future itself. Following earlier prophetic traditions, this process involves political and military turmoil, as well as astronomic or cosmic disturbances and the transformation of the landscape of Jerusalem. **12.1:** The v. reaffirms the authority and legitimacy of the following text three times: (prophetic) *pronouncement, the word of the LORD,* and *the utterance of the LORD.* This v. asks the readers to interpret the ensuing text (12.2–14.21) as a divine pronouncement concerning Israel, even if the nations play a major role in it. **2:** *Bowl of reeling:* The metaphor of a divinely induced, incapacitating drunkenness under judgment occurs elsewhere in the prophets. The classical examples are Jer. 25.15–29 and Isa. 51.17–23. In the present text, however, the nations, rather than Jerusalem, are incapacitated.

---

a *Meaning of Heb. uncertain.*   b *Two mss. of the Septuagint have "Jerusalem"; cf.* 12.2–3; 14.14.   c-c *Meaning of Heb. uncertain.*
d-d *Emendation yields "open the eyes of Judah while I strike all."*
e-e *Emendation yields "We will save the dwellers of Jerusalem with the help of."*
f *Emendation yields "safety."*

inhabitants of Jerusalem may not be too great for Judah. [8] In that day, the LORD will shield the inhabitants of Jerusalem; and the feeblest of them shall be in that day like David, and the House of David like a divine being—like an angel of the LORD—at their head.

[9] In that day I will [a]all but annihilate[-a] all the nations that came up against Jerusalem. [10] But I will fill the House of David and the inhabitants of Jerusalem with a spirit of pity and compassion; and they shall lament[b] to Me about those who are slain, wailing over them as over a favorite son and showing bitter grief as over a first-born. [11] In that day, the wailing in Jerusalem shall be as great as the wailing at Hadad-rimmon in the plain of Megiddon.[c] [12] The land shall wail, each family by itself: The family of the House of David by themselves, and their womenfolk by themselves; the family of the House of Nathan by themselves, and their womenfolk by themselves; [13] the family of the House of Levi by themselves, and their women-folk by themselves; the family of the Shimeites by themselves, and their womenfolk by themselves; [14] and all the other families, every family by itself, with their womenfolk by themselves.[d]

13 In that day a fountain shall be open to the House of David and the inhabitants of Jerusalem for purging and cleansing.

[2] In that day, too—declares the LORD of Hosts—I will erase the very names of the idols from the land; they shall not be uttered any more. And I will also make the "prophets" and the [e]unclean spirit[-e] vanish from the land. [3] If anyone "prophesies" thereafter, his own father and mother, who brought him into the world, will say to him, "You shall die, for you have lied in the name of the LORD"; and his own father and mother, who brought him into the world, will put him to death when he "prophesies." [4] In that day, every "prophet" will be ashamed of the "visions" [he had] when he "prophesied." In order to deceive, he[f] will not wear a hairy mantle;[g] [5] and he will declare, "I am not a 'prophet'; [h]I am a tiller of the soil;[-h] you see, [i]I was plied with the red stuff[-i] from my youth on."

10: An alternative and more common type of translation, which is at home in christological interpretation, is represented by "And I will pour out a spirit of compassion and supplication on the house of David and the inhabitants of Jerusalem, so that, when they look on the one whom they have pierced, they shall mourn for him, as one mourns for an only child, and weep bitterly over him, as one weeps over a firstborn" (NRSV). The Heb is ambiguous, because it may refer to a person or a group whom they have pierced. Although the identity of the pierced one/ones is unclear, if the text is read as the continuation of v. 9—as the structure of the section set by the *in that day* openings suggests—it is more likely that it points to an individual or group from within the nations. For an understanding of the verse as pointing to the Messiah from the House of Joseph, see *b. Sukkah* 52a. Radak reads the text differently; for him it describes such a salvation that if even one person of Israel were killed in the battle, they will be astonished. **13.2–6: Away with the prophets.** Although the removal of the idols is mentioned, the obvious emphasis is on the removal of the prophets. It is likely that a particular group or type of prophets is meant. **4:** The *hairy mantle* is an allusion to Elijah (see 2 Kings 1.8). **5:** The language seems to allude to Amos 7.14, but with a most significant shift that results in a possible association with Cain (see Gen. 4.2). **6:** Possibly a reference to ecstatic prophecy.

---

a-a *For the idiom cf. Gen. 43.30; it is also attested in postbiblical Hebrew.*

b *Meaning of Heb. uncertain.*   c *Usually "Megiddo."*

d *In this way, apparently, they will prevail upon the LORD to spare the remnant of the besieging nations; cf. v. 10.*

e-e *To which abnormal human behavior was attributed.*

f *Heb. "They."*   g *In imitation of Elijah; cf. 2 Kings 1.8.*

h-h *I.e., I was addicted to wine like Noah, the tiller of the soil (cf. Gen. 9.20–21), hence my hallucinations and ravings; cf. Prov. 23.33.*

i-i *Connecting 'adam with 'adom "red" (cf. Prov. 23.31); but meaning of Heb. uncertain.*

⁶ And if he is asked, "What are those ᵃsores on your back?"·ᵃ he will reply, "From being beaten in the homes of my friends."ᵇ

7ᶜ   O sword!
     Rouse yourself against My shepherd,
     The man ᵈ·in charge of My flock·ᵈ
                          —says the LORD of Hosts.
     Strike down the shepherd
     And let the flock scatter;
     And I will also turn My hand
     Against all the shepherd boys.
8   Throughout the land   —declares the LORD—
     Two-thirds shall perish, shall die,
     And one-third of it shall survive.
9   That third I will put into the fire,
     And I will smelt them as one smelts silver
     And test them as one tests gold.
     They will invoke Me by name,
     And I will respond to them.
     I will declare, "You are My people,"
     And they will declare,
     "The LORD is our God!"

14 Lo, a day of the LORD is coming when yourᵉ spoil shall be divided in your very midst! ² For I will gather all the nations to Jerusalem for war: The city shall be captured, the houses plundered, and the women violated; and a part of the city shall go into exile. But the rest of the population shall not be uprooted from the city. ³ Then the LORD will come forth and make war on those nations as He is wont to make war on a day of battle. ⁴ On that day, He will set His feet on the Mount of Olives, near Jerusalem on the east; and the Mount of Olives shall split across from east to west, and one part of the Mount shall shift to the north and the other to the south, a huge gorge. ⁵ᶠ And the Valley in the Hills shall be stopped up, for the Valley of the Hills shall reach only to Azal; it shall be stopped up as it was stopped up as a result of the earthquake in the days of King Uzziah of Judah.—And

14.1–21: Earth-shaking events lead to the establishment of Jerusalem as the center of the world and the place from which the LORD reigns over all. **4–5:** *Mount of Olives,* a mount east of, and in the vicinity of, Jerusalem. *Valley in the Hills,* perhaps, "valley in/between the hills." The Heb word for "hill" is often translated "mount" or "mountain." *And the Valley . . . shall be stopped up:* Heb reads "you shall flee by the valley of My hills/mountains" (i.e., the new valley created by the LORD). *Azal,* an unknown location in the area. Some scholars assume that the original text read "'etzel," i.e., "side" and, accordingly, that the text read: "the valley between the hills reached to each side (of the now split Mount of Olives)."

a-a Lit. "sores between your arms"; cf. 2 Kings 9.24. Sores are sometimes symptoms of hysteria.
b Presumably for making drunken scenes; cf. Prov. 23.35.
c Vv. 7–9 would read well after 11.17.   d-d Meaning of Heb. uncertain.
e Jerusalem is addressed.
f Vocalizing [we] nistam with Targum, Septuagint, and an old Heb. ms. Other mss. and printed editions read, "You [pl.] shall flee [to] the Valley in the Hills, for the Valley of the Hills shall reach up to Azal. You shall flee as you fled because of the earthquake . . ."

the Lord my God, with all the holy beings, will come to you.

⁶ªIn that day, there shall be neither sunlight nor cold moonlight, ⁷but there shall be a continuous day—only the Lord knows when—of neither day nor night, and there shall be light at eventide.

⁸In that day, fresh water shall flow from Jerusalem, part of it to the Eastern Sea*ᵇ* and part to the Western Sea,*ᶜ* throughout the summer and winter.

⁹And the Lord shall be king over all the earth; in that day there shall be one Lord with one name.*ᵈ*

¹⁰Then the whole country shall become like the Arabah,*ᵉ* *ᶠ*from Geba to Rimmon south of Jerusalem.*ᶠ* The latter, however, shall perch high up where it is, and *ᵍ*shall be inhabited*ᵍ* from the Gate of Benjamin to the site of the Old Gate, down to the Corner Gate, and from the Tower of Hananel to the king's winepresses. ¹¹Never again shall destruction be decreed, and Jerusalem shall dwell secure.

¹²As for those peoples that warred against Jerusalem, the Lord will smite them with this plague: Their flesh shall rot away while they stand on their feet; their eyes shall rot away in their sockets; and their tongues shall rot away in their mouths.

¹³In that day, a great panic from the Lord shall fall upon them, and everyone shall snatch at the hand of another, and everyone shall raise his hand against everyone else's hand. ¹⁴Judah shall join the fighting in Jerusalem, and the wealth of all the nations roundabout—vast quantities of gold, silver, and clothing—shall be gathered in.

¹⁵The same plague shall strike the horses, the mules, the camels, and the asses; the plague shall affect all the animals in those camps.

¹⁶All who survive of all those nations that came up against Jerusalem shall make a pilgrimage year by year to bow low to the King Lord of Hosts and to observe the Feast of Booths. ¹⁷Any of the earth's communities that does not make the pilgrimage to Jerusalem to bow low to the King Lord of Hosts shall receive no rain. ¹⁸However, if the community of Egypt does not make this pilgrimage, it shall not be visited by the same affliction with which the

9: See introduction. The verse evokes the language of Deut. 6.4, the beginning of what became the Shema prayer in later Judaism, and, given its context, it most likely means that in that day all humanity will acknowledge and worship the Lord alone and invoke the Lord's name alone. (Contrast with the different vision in Mic. 4.5.) **10:** *Like the Arabah* means as low and plain as the Jordan Valley. *From Geba to Rimmon south of Jerusalem* refers to the territory of Judah. Jerusalem will be higher than its surroundings; cf. Mic. 4.1; Isa. 2.2. The expression it *shall be inhabited,* placed in our translation in v. 10 for clarity, stands in v. 11 in the Heb. V. 11 then reads, "And it [Jerusalem] shall be inhabited, for never again shall destruction be decreed, Jerusalem shall dwell secure." **16–17:** The *Feast of Booths,* Sukkot, stands at the beginning of the rainy season and is the time for petitioning rain from the Lord (see Rashi). As in other biblical calendars, Sukkot rather than Rosh Ha-Shanah (the New Year) or Yom Kippur (the Day of Atonement) is the central festival. **18:** Egypt's agriculture was not dependent on rain, but on the Nile. **21:** Holiness will be so pervasive that every mundane household object will be holy, and therefore there will be no need for merchants to sell ritually pure vessels.

---

a *Meaning of verse uncertain; cf. Job 21.26.*

b *I.e., the Dead Sea; cf. Joel 2.20.*

c *I.e., the Mediterranean Sea; cf. Joel 2.20.*

d *I.e., the Lord alone shall be worshiped and shall be invoked by His true name.*

e *I.e., shall be depressed like the Jordan Valley.*

f-f *I.e., from the northern border of the Kingdom of Judah (1 Kings 15.22; 2 Kings 23.8) to the southern border (Josh. 15.32; 19.7).*

g-g *Brought up from v. 11 for clarity.*

Lord will strike the other nations that do not come up to
observe the Feast of Booths.[a] [19] Such shall be the punishment of Egypt and of all other nations that do not come up
to observe the Feast of Booths.

[20] In that day, even the bells on the horses shall be inscribed "Holy to the Lord." The metal pots in the House
of the Lord shall be like the basins before the altar; [21] indeed, every metal pot in Jerusalem and in Judah shall be
holy to the Lord of Hosts. And all those who sacrifice
shall come and take of these to boil [their sacrificial meat]
in; in that day there shall be no more traders[b] in the House
of the Lord of Hosts.

a Because Egypt is not dependent on rain, it will suffer some other punishment, presumably that described in v. 12.
b To sell ritually pure vessels.

Malachi

THE BOOK OF MALACHI is set in a period when the Second Temple was rebuilt and sacrificial worship was resumed. It was composed in the Persian period, and is addressed originally to the inhabitants of the Persian province of Yehud (Judah). Because of the reference to intermarriage (2.11), some modern scholars assume that it belongs to a time closely preceding that of Ezra's actions on the matter (cf. *b. Meg.* 15a).

Some scholars have argued that the book was composed to provide an appropriate closing to the book of the Twelve, or that its conclusion (3.22–24, or a portion thereof) was written as a conclusion to the Twelve rather than to Malachi, or that substantial portions of the book were originally associated with some form of the book of Zechariah. None of these proposals is compelling.

Since Malachi means "my messenger," it has been thought from the earliest times that it was not the name of the prophet, but an appellation, perhaps based on 3.1, "Behold, I am sending My messenger to clear the way before Me." The Septuagint, the ancient Greek translation (ca. 3rd century BCE) does not read "Malachi" as a personal name, but translates it as "His messenger." There is a tradition in the Targum that Malachi is Ezra; a similar tradition is brought to bear in *b. Meg.* 15a; an alternate tradition of R. Naḥman claims that Malachi was Mordecai. Still the Rabbis of the classical period (and later Ibn Ezra, Radak, and Maimonides) maintained that Malachi is the name of the prophet. Haggai, Zechariah, and Malachi are all understood by the Rabbis as the last of the prophets, and the Talmud mentions rulings and sayings by this prophet that seem to characterize him as an early sage, in addition to his being a prophet (see intro. to Haggai). Despite these traditions, it is likely that Malachi should be understood as a personal name.

The readers of the book of Malachi are asked to look at some pitfalls in everyday life and in the cult at the Temple, and particularly at how they affect the relationship between the LORD and Israel, resulting in a lack of prosperity. Issues concerning proper offerings, marriage practices, and tithes are especially prominent in the book.

Messages of cultic reform and proper worship are deeply interwoven with the conviction of the coming of a future day in which the LORD will trample all evildoers. Such optimism about an ideal future is typical in prophetic works. Further, the book asks its readers to identify proper behavior in these and all matters with following the Torah (or Teaching) of Moses. As a whole, the book is aimed at persuading its readership to follow the Torah of Moses, or at strengthening their resolve to continue to do so. This message must be understood within the book's historical setting, soon after the canonization of the Torah. Thus, the book presents a prophetic voice that ultimately asserts the superiority of Torah over prophecy.

The use of a disputation format in much of the book contributes rhetorically to that purpose, for it allows the arguments of evildoers to be heard, in order to be countered and neutralized. Further, it allows the readers some limited form of self-identification with the actions of the evildoers, and as such serves as a call for them to examine themselves and repent.

The book uses imagery that refers to the structure of ancient patriarchal family groups. The Lord, as the main power figure, is imagined as a father, and at times (given the tone of the book) as an infuriated patriarchal figure. To be sure, this figure loves Israel/Judah, but within this world, the loved one should fulfill its role and obligations as the father figure envisages them. This type of metaphor is common in its historical setting, but it is difficult for many contemporary readers because our understanding of family life differs significantly from the one presumed in the book. Certainly modern readers who have had a damaging experience of an overbearing patriarch find the message of such texts difficult to accept (cf. the book of Hosea). Other aspects of the imagery of the book of Malachi, and particularly its ending, have brought much hope and comfort. In fact, the reference to Elijah in 3.23–24 was often understood as an affirmation of hope for a final liberation, one even greater than the exodus from Egypt, for after Israel's first liberation it eventually becomes enslaved, but it will not after the one promised in Malachi (see *Pesiq. Rab.* 4.3). Similarly the language of 3.4 is repeated often in traditional Jewish liturgy as an expression of hope about the restoration of appropriate worship in a future, third Temple.

Malachi 1.1–2.7 is read as the haftarah for the parashah of Toledot (Gen. 25.19–28.9), since these share the themes of Jacob and Esau, and Malachi 3.4–24 as that of Shabbat Ha-Gadol, the Sabbath preceding Passover, most likely because of the association of Elijah and the forthcoming messianic liberation, which is traditionally connected to Passover. (In the Yemenite tradition Mal. 1.1–3.4 is read with the parashah of Toledot.)   [EHUD BEN ZVI]

---

1 A pronouncement: The word of the Lord to Israel through Malachi.

²I have shown you love, said the Lord. But you ask, "How have You shown us love?" After all—declares the

1.1: Superscription. The book has a double title, *a* (prophetic) *pronouncement* and *the word of the Lord*. It is important to note that *the word* is *to Israel*, meaning here Israel as a people with a particular relation to the Lord (see, e.g., 2.16), a particular history, and a particular obligation to follow the Torah of Moses (cf. 3.22) and to worship in Jerusalem. This conception of Israel is especially associated with the Persian period Yehud (or Judah), and it assumes a partial overlap between the concepts of "Israel" and "Judah" (a more geographico-political term). Thus references to Judah in 2.11 and 3.4 are identical with Israel in 1.1. The ancient readers of the book in ancient Yehud most likely identified themselves with both Judah and Israel.

Lord—Esau is Jacob's brother; yet I have accepted Jacob ³and have rejected Esau. I have made his hills a desolation, his territory ᵃa home for beasts·ᵃ of the desert. ⁴If Edom thinks, "Though crushed, we can build the ruins again," thus said the Lord of Hosts: They may build, but I will tear down. And so they shall be known as the region of wickedness, the people damned forever of the Lord. ⁵Your eyes shall behold it, and you shall declare, "Great is the Lord beyond the borders of Israel!"

⁶A son should honor his father, and a slaveᵇ his master. Now if I am a father, where is the honor due Me? And if I am a master, where is the reverence due Me?—said the Lord of Hosts to you, O priests who scorn My name. But you ask, "How have we scorned Your name?" ⁷You offer defiled food on My altar. But you ask, "How have we defiled You?"ᶜ By saying, "The table of the Lord can be treated with scorn." ⁸When you present a blind animal for sacrifice—it doesn't matter! When you present a lame or sick one—it doesn't matter! Just offer it to your governor: Will he accept you? Will he show you favor?—said the Lord of Hosts. ⁹And now implore the favor of God! Will He be gracious to us? This is what you have done—will He accept any of you?

The Lord of Hosts has said: ¹⁰If only you would lock My doors, and not kindle fire on My altar to no purpose! I take no pleasure in you—said the Lord of Hosts—and I will accept no offering from you. ¹¹For from where the sun rises to where it sets, My name is honored among the nations, and everywhere incense and pure oblation are offered to My name; for My name is honored among the nations—said the Lord of Hosts. ¹²But you profane it when you say, "The table of the Lord is defiled and the meat,ᵈ the food, can be treated with scorn." ¹³You say, "Oh, what a bother!" And so you degradeᵈ it—said the Lord of Hosts—and you bring the stolen, the lame, and the sick; and you offer such as an oblation. Will I accept it from you?—said the Lord.

¹⁴A curse on the cheat who has an [unblemished] male in his flock, but for his vow sacrifices a blemished animal to the Lord! For I am a great King—said the Lord of Hosts—and My name is revered among the nations.

---

a-a Meaning of Heb. uncertain.
b Septuagint and Targum add "should reverence"; cf. next part of verse.
c Septuagint "it."
d Meaning of Heb. uncertain.

1.2–5: The Lord loves Jacob. This section is meant to persuade or remind the readers of the Lord's special relationship with them. This is shown in the divine preference of Jacob over Esau. Esau stands both for Edom and for all the other nations. The contrast between the fates of the siblings (Esau/Edom and Jacob/Israel) is a central motif in the book of Obadiah. (On the later identifications of Esau/Edom, see notes on Obadiah.) In the book of Malachi, however, the issue is not central; rather it is used for rhetorical purposes within an argument developed against a particular group in Israel. The central point is that Israel is beloved, even if certain of its members are acting improperly.

1.6–14: Improper cultic practices at the Temple. 8: The logic of the argument is that if an animal cannot be offered to a provincial governor without risking punishment, it is certainly not a suitable offering for the King of Kings (cf. vv. 13–14). From the Lord's perspective, the fact that these offerings are still brought demonstrates the priests' disrespect for, and lack of fear of, the Lord, as proven by the validity of the previous statement of the Lord, *O priests who scorn My name* (v. 6). There are numerous references in the Bible to the belief that blemished animals were not acceptable for sacrifice (e.g., Exod. 12.5; 29.1; Lev. 1.3, 10; 3.1; 22.22, passim). **10:** The first sentence may be translated as, "Oh, that someone among you would shut the temple doors, so that you would not kindle fire on my altar in vain" (NRSV). The Lord prefers no sacrifices at all, and even the closing of the Temple, over the improper situation described in these vv. **14:** [*Unblemished*] *male:* Blemished animals, which were not fit for sacrifice (cf. Lev. 1.3), were offered even by those who had unblemished animals. The main opposition in the text is not between female and male offerings, but between blemished and unblemished male animals. In Israel, as in other agrarian societies, the most

2 And now, O priests, this charge is for you: ²Unless you obey and unless you lay it to heart, and do honor to My name—said the LORD of Hosts—I will send a curse and turn your blessings into curses. (Indeed, I have turned them into curses, because you do not lay it to heart.) ³I will ᵃput your seed under a ban,ᵃ and I will strew dung upon your faces, the dung of your festal sacrifices, and you shall be carried out to its [heap].

⁴Know, then, that I have sent this charge to you that My covenant with Levi may endure—said the LORD of Hosts. ⁵I had with him a covenant of life and well-being, which I gave to him, and of reverence, which he showed Me. For he stood in awe of My name.

6ᵇ   Proper rulings were in his mouth,
       And nothing perverse was on his lips;
       He served Me with complete loyalty
       And held the many back from iniquity.
7   ᶜFor the lips of a priest guard knowledge,
       And men seek rulings from his mouth;ᶜ
       For he is a messenger of the LORD of Hosts.

⁸But you have turned away from that course: You have made the many stumble through your rulings;ᵈ you have corrupted the covenant of the Levites—said the LORD of Hosts. ⁹And I, in turn, have made you despicable and vile in the eyes of all the people, because you disregard My ways and show partiality in your rulings.

¹⁰Have we not all one Father? Did not one God create us? Why do we break faith with one another, profaning the covenant of our ancestors? ¹¹Judah has broken faith; abhorrent things have been done in Israel and in Jerusalem. For Judah has profaned what is holy to the LORD— what He desires—and espoused daughters of alien gods.

a-a Meaning of Heb. uncertain.
b See Hag. 2.10–13; cf. Lev. 10.8–11, Deut. 33.8, 10.
c-c Or: For the lips of a priest are observed; / Knowledge and ruling are sought from his mouth.
d By ruling falsely that an act was licit or an object ritually pure.

there cannot be proper worship, with all the consequences that this might entail. **4:** Cf. 2.8; Neh. 13.29. **9:** *Show partiality in your rulings* seems to point to the priests' acceptance of unacceptable offerings brought by powerful members of society (e.g., Radak; cf. Prov. 18.5). Notice also the reference back to 1.8. (The Heb idiom translated as *show . . . favor* in 1.8 is the same as *show partiality* here.) The point of the verse is that the priests' privileged status is conditional and can be overturned.

2.10–16: On marriage. The improper behavior of (male) Israel. This passage condemns male Judah because of intermarriage and because they "acted treacherously" against their Judahite wives. It concludes with another reported speech of the LORD (v. 6) supporting the message conveyed by the preceding vv. Scholars have debated whether the language of intermarriage should be taken literally or symbolically, as a reference to idolatry. The majority of scholars support the first alternative, but the text may have more than one level of meaning. **10–11:** *Have we not all one Father? Did not one God create us?* These words have been used numerous times to point to the unity (or, brotherhood or siblinghood) of all humanity (see *b. Taʿan.* 18a) and to advance ethical claims about the treatment of different groups on that basis. Within Malachi, however, these expressions carry a different meaning. Because *we* equals Israel, which in turn was identified with Persian Yehud (see intro.), they refer to inner Israelite responsibilities to "keep faith" with one another and to honor the covenant of their fathers. If this understanding of the text is accepted, then the term *Father* has two meanings: (a) the LORD as father of Israel; and (b) the patriarchs of Israel, and esp. Jacob (e.g., Ibn Ezra). The first meaning relates this verse to other sections in Malachi in which the LORD is characterized as father. The second meaning emphasizes the border between Israel and the

common sacrifice was that of a male animal. Female sacrifices were rarer and more expensive, since each female is potentially a separate breeding animal, but any number of males can be sacrificed as long as one is kept to impregnate the females.

2.1–9: The improper behavior of the priest. The readers overhear,

as it were, the LORD's speech to the priests as reported in these vv. The speech reminds the readers of the importance of the rulings/torah/teachings of the priests (cf. Hag. 2.10–13), and of their role as "the LORD's messengers" (see v. 7 and notice the pun on the name Malachi, "My messenger"). To be sure, unless the priests perform their duty as the LORD expects them to,

12 May the LORD leave to him who does this ᵃno descendants-ᵃ dwelling in the tents of Jacob and presenting offerings to the LORD of Hosts. 13 And this you do ᵇas well:-ᵇ You cover the altar of the LORD with tears, weeping, and moaning, so that He refuses to regard the oblation any more and to accept ᶜwhat you offer.-ᶜ 14 But you ask, "Because of what?" Because the LORD is a witness between you and the wife of your youth with whom you have broken faith, though she is your partner and covenanted spouse. 15 Did not the One make [all,] ᵃso that all remaining life-breath is His? And what does that One seek but godly folk? So be careful of your life-breath,-ᵃ and let no one break faith with the wife of his youth. 16 For I detest divorce—said the LORD, the God of Israel—ᵃand covering oneself with lawlessness as with a garment-ᵃ—said the LORD of Hosts. So be careful of your life-breath and do not act treacherously.

17 You have wearied the LORD with your talk. But you ask, "By what have we wearied [Him]?" By saying, "All who do evil are good in the sight of the LORD, and in them He delights," or else, "Where is the God of justice?"

a-a Meaning of Heb. uncertain.
b-b Lit. "a second time"; Septuagint reads "which I detest"; cf. v. 16.
c-c Lit. "from your hand."

nations, which is an important issue in the unit, and directly links the reference to the ancestral fathers at the conclusion of the v. (and perhaps even alludes to the reference to Jacob and Esau in 1.2–3). (The use of the capital "F" for *Father*, indicating the deity, is a translation choice that is not present in the Heb, which cannot make a distinction between common and proper nouns.) There is an alternative tradition of reading these expressions within their context in the book of Malachi. Within this tradition *Have we not all one Father? Did not one God create us?* actually points at the unity of humanity, but it is said by the (sinful) Judahites to justify their actions. To them, the prophetic voice in the text answers, *Judah has broken faith.* (It is also possible to understand *father* as referring to Adam.) The expression translated *break faith with one another* may also be translated "act treacherously, a man to

his brother." If the latter translation is followed, then v. 11 should be translated, "Judah has acted treacherously." The text clearly conveys to the readers that marrying daughters of alien gods (i.e., foreign women) is tantamount to profaning what is holy to the LORD and committing abominations; Judah acting treacherously is the equivalent of a Judahite man breaking faith with his brothers. Thus, within the book intermarriage is presented here not only as a husband-wife affair, but as a brother-brother affair, and a son-patriarch affair (since the latter's covenant is breached), and a matter between Israel and the LORD, with grave cultic and covenantal implications (see vv. 12–13). The precise language chosen to describe the women, namely not as "foreign women" but rather as *daughters of alien gods*, is rhetorically significant. **13–16:** Judahite men failed on another account.

They "have acted treacherously" against (or *broken faith* with) their Judahite wives whom they married in their *youth*. Their actions not only caused great pain to these women, but also involved covenant breaking, and as such they carried grave cultic implications: The LORD rejected the offerings of those Judahites and of Judah. The sentence translated *I detest* [or "hate"] *divorce—said the LORD, the God of Israel* has attracted much attention in the last decades. The Heb is difficult. Moreover, a text of the v. in a Dead Sea Scrolls manuscript may be translated "But if you hate [your wife] divorce [her]!" (4Q12ᵃ). Significantly, this is also the way in which the Targum, the Vulgate, and (likely) the LXX understood the v. (cf. *b. Git.* 8ob). This reading is consistent with the liberal attitude toward divorce of the House of Hillel and R. Akiva (*m. Git.* 9.10); cf. Deut. 24.1–2; Sir. 25.26. Even if the MT version of the v. represents the original text, it is indisputable that different interpretations and versions of it already existed in ancient times. Controversies about its meaning are also well attested in medieval times.

2.17–3.21: The coming day: judgment for the doers of evil and a "sun of righteousness" for those who revere the LORD's name. Although there is some debate about the scope of the different units included in these vv., it is clear that they address issues such as theodicy, a response to those who claim that the LORD is either unjust or unable to provide justice in this world, strong affirmations of a great day of judgment to come, a reference to a long history of Israel turning away from the LORD, and calls for repentance. As a whole, the emphasis on the future, and the general tone of hope, sets ch 3 apart from the previous chs in Malachi. Mal. 3.6–12, however, is closely related to 1.2–5. **2.17:** Despite the present division according to chs, the v. is to be read as directly linked to the following vv. The scribal tradition of

3 Behold, I am sending My messenger to clear the way before Me, and the Lord whom you seek shall come to His Temple suddenly. As for the angel of the covenant[a] that you desire, he is already coming. [2] But who can endure the day of his coming, and who can hold out when he appears? For he is like a smelter's fire and like fuller's lye. [3] He shall act[b] like a smelter and purger of silver; and he shall purify the descendants of Levi and refine them like gold and silver, so that they shall present offerings in righteousness. [4] Then the offerings of Judah and Jerusalem shall be pleasing to the Lord as in the days of yore and in the years of old. [5] But [first] I will step forward to contend against you, and I will act as a relentless accuser against those who have no fear of Me: Who practice sorcery, who commit adultery, who swear falsely, who cheat laborers of their hire, and who subvert [the cause of] the widow, orphan, and stranger, said the Lord of Hosts.

[6] [c]For I am the Lord—I have not changed; and you are the children of Jacob—you have not ceased to be. [7] From the very days of your fathers you have turned away from My laws and have not observed them. Turn back to Me, and I will turn back to you—said the Lord of Hosts. But you ask, "How shall we turn back?" [8] Ought man to defraud[d] God? Yet you are defrauding Me. And you ask, "How have we been defrauding You?" In tithe and contribution.[e] [9] You are suffering under a curse, yet you go on defrauding Me—the whole nation of you. [10] Bring the full tithe into the storehouse,[f] and let there be food in My House, and thus put Me to the test—said the Lord of Hosts. I will surely open the floodgates of the sky for you and pour down blessings on you; [11] and I will banish the locusts[g] from you, so that they will not destroy the yield of your soil; and your vines in the field shall no longer miscarry—said the Lord of Hosts. [12] And all the nations shall account you happy, for you shall be the most desired of lands—said the Lord of Hosts.

[13] You have spoken hard words against Me—said the Lord. But you ask, "What have we been saying among ourselves against You?" [14] You have said, "It is useless to

the MT has a break after 2.16 reflected in the paragraph division in NJPS. **3.1–2:** Cf. Isa. 40.3. Much of the discussion on the "messianic" tone of Malachi centers on 3.23 and this v. The identity of the messenger in 3.1 has been highly debated. Is *My messenger* (Heb "malakhi") Malachi? Or is there at least a pun on the name of the prophet? Is the messenger the *angel of the covenant,* a zealous, powerful enforcer of the covenant who is *like a smelter's fire and like fuller's lye* (i.e., a purifying, caustic treatment)? Is he Elijah (see v. 23)? Or is Elijah the *angel of the covenant?* Does the text indicate an expectation of a priestly Messiah? There is a very long history of interpretation on this v., with multiple meanings already in antiquity. The New Testament merges this v. with Isa. 40.3 and identifies the expected messenger as John the Baptist (Matt. 11.10; Mark 1.2; Luke 7.27). **4:** See introduction. **8–9:** The repeated use of terms translated as *defraud* and the like (Heb "kaba‘") is a pun on the name Jacob ("Ya‘akob") and its negative connotations (cf. Gen. 27.36; Jer. 9.3; Hos. 12.4) See translators' note d. **10:** Cf. Neh. 13.10–11; Dan. 1.2.

---

a Apparently the messenger of the previous sentence is regarded as Israel's tutelary angel.

b Lit. "sit."

c Vv. 6–12 resume the thought of 1.2–5.

d Heb. qaba‘, a play on the name of Jacob (v. 6); cf. Gen. 27.36.

e I.e., the contributions to the priests from the new grain, oil, and wine; see Num. 18.12.

f I.e., the public storehouse; see Neh. 13.10–13.

g Lit. "devourer."

serve God. What have we gained by keeping His charge and walking in abject awe of the LORD of Hosts? [15] And so, we account the arrogant happy: they have indeed done evil and endured; they have indeed dared God and escaped." [16] In this vein have those who revere the LORD been talking to one another. The LORD has heard and noted it, and a scroll of remembrance has been written at His behest concerning those who revere the LORD and esteem His name. [17] And on the day that I am preparing, said the LORD of Hosts, they shall be My treasured possession; I will be tender toward them as a man is tender toward a son who ministers to him. [18] And you shall come to see the difference between the righteous and the wicked, between him who has served God and him who has not served Him.

[19] For lo! That day is at hand, burning like an oven. All the arrogant and all the doers of evil shall be straw, and the day that is coming—said the LORD of Hosts—shall burn them to ashes and leave of them neither stock nor boughs. [20] But for you who revere My name a sun of victory shall rise *to bring healing.*[a] You shall go forth and stamp like stall-fed calves, [21] and you shall trample the wicked to a pulp, for they shall be dust beneath your feet on the day that I am preparing—said the LORD of Hosts.

[22] Be mindful of the Teaching of My servant Moses, whom I charged at Horeb with laws and rules for all Israel.

[23] Lo, I will send the prophet Elijah to you before the coming of the awesome, fearful day of the LORD. [24] He shall reconcile parents with children and children with their parents, so that, when I come, I do not strike the whole land with utter destruction.

Lo, I will send the prophet Elijah to you before the coming of the awesome, fearful day of the LORD.

16: This *scroll of remembrance* is found elsewhere in the Bible (e.g., Exod. 32.32); it is a Mesopotamian concept which becomes especially developed in the idea of the book of life associated with the Jewish high holiday liturgy. **19–24:** In most English translations these vv. appear as Mal. 4.1–6. **20:** *A sun of victory,* lit. and in most translations, "a sun of righteousness." *To bring healing,* lit. and in most translations, "with healing in its wings." The background of the imagery is mythological. The rising of "a sun of righteousness" is a metaphor for the dawn of a new "day," i.e., era of history. **22–24:** At its conclusion, Malachi asserts the dominance of Mosaic Torah over the prophetic tradition. See intro. to Malachi and intro. to The Twelve. **23:** There is a long tradition of interpretation of this v. expanding on the role of Elijah, the herald of the messianic era; see, e.g., *b. Sanh.* 118a; *b. 'Eruv.* 43b. Since Elijah did not die, but ascended to heaven (2 Kings 2.11), he can return. The *awesome, fearful day of the LORD* is associated with the "travails of the messiah" in *b. Sanh.* 118a. It is traditional in Jewish liturgy to repeat this v. after 3.24 so as to conclude the public reading on a strong, hopeful note, rather than the threat of the final phrase of v. 24. This liturgical reading is represented in NJPS by the repetition of the text of v. 23 in a smaller font. (The same holds true for the conclusion of Isaiah, Lamentations, and Ecclesiastes.) **24:** The connection between intergenerational reconciliation and Elijah is enigmatic.

---

a-a Lit. "with healing in the folds of its garments"; others "with healing in its wings."

כתובים

KETHUVIM

Terminology and Content

THE VAGUE TERM KETHUVIM, "WRITINGS," reflects the variety of material collected in this canonical division, ranging from historical works (e.g., Chronicles), prayers (Psalms), wisdom works (e.g., Job), and apocalyptic prophecy (the second half of Daniel). It is likely that the various books now in this section entered the canon for quite different reasons: Psalms was used for prayers, the Song of Songs was probably first canonized as an ancient erotic poem used in wedding ceremonies, while the books of Job, Proverbs, and Ecclesiastes may have been placed together in the canon because all three belong to a category of writing known as wisdom literature. Most likely the books now in Kethuvim came together and were viewed as authoritative and ultimately canonized toward the end of the Second Temple period, after the canonical section Nevi'im was closed, and thus the books now comprising Kethuvim were assembled together, despite their differences, into a single group. The wide variety of the ordering of these books found in manuscripts and canonical lists also reflects the fact that Kethuvim was canonized later than Torah, which has a fixed order, and Nevi'im, where there is only slight variation in the order of the books.

An early order, where the books are largely arranged in what the Rabbis understood to be their chronological sequence (from Ruth to Chronicles), is found in the Babylonian Talmud (b. B. Bat.15a). No surviving manuscripts, however, have this order. Most sources divide Kethuvim into three parts; however, unlike "the former prophets" and "the latter prophets," no names are extant for each part.

The first section is composed of the three large books Psalms, Proverbs, and Job, either in that order, or in the order Psalms, Job, and Proverbs. Psalms is always the first book, suggesting that in some early sources (e.g., Luke 24.44 and the Dead Sea Scrolls) Psalms may be the title for the entire collection of Kethuvim.

These three large books are typically followed by five smaller books called *ḥamesh megillot*, "the five scrolls." These books were likely copied together (much like the prophetic collection the Twelve) so that individual short scrolls would not get lost. Many orders exist for these books. The NJPS translation follows one common order, which arranges these books in the order in which they are read in the liturgical year: Song of Songs (Passover in the early spring), Ruth (Shavuot in the late spring), Lamentations (the fast of the ninth of Av in the summer), Ecclesiastes (Sukkot in the fall), and Esther (Purim in the late winter). Another common manuscript order arranges these books according to their attributed dates of authorship: Ruth (period of judges), Song of Songs (by Solomon as a youth), Ecclesiastes (by Solomon when he was old and jaded), Lamentations (by Jeremiah after the destruction of the Temple), and Esther (by Mordecai, during the Persian period).

The last collection is of three historical texts: Daniel (which also contains apocalyptic prophecy), Ezra-Nehemiah, which narrates the history of the early postexilic period, and Chronicles, which very selectively retells history from Adam through the Cyrus declaration of 538 BCE. This is the order found in the NJPS translation, which follows some manuscripts and most printed editions. It is a strange order, since Ezra-Nehemiah is a logical continuation of Chronicles, quite literally beginning where Chronicles ends, with the Cyrus declaration. It is thus not surprising that most manuscripts have Ezra-Nehemiah as the final book of the Bible.

Finally, it is noteworthy that Chronicles and Ezra-Nehemiah are each viewed by Jewish tradition as a single book. Like Samuel and Kings (see "Nevi'im," p. 451), only under the influence of the Septuagint did some manuscripts and early printed versions of the Bible divide these books into two.

Authorship

THESE BOOKS COME FROM widely diverse time periods. Many show clear linguistic signs of being postexilic; for example, there is clear late Aramaic influence on Ecclesiastes, and Greek influence on Daniel (see the introductions to these books). In fact, historical references in Daniel would place its composition in the 2nd century BCE. Lamentations is clearly from the exilic period (586–538) or very shortly thereafter. Many attributed Ruth to the preexilic period, but it is increasingly being seen nowadays as a postexilic work. Psalms is a collection, containing some psalms which are considered among the earliest of biblical literature (e.g., Ps. 68), and others that are dated on the basis of language or content to the exilic or postexilic periods (Pss. 135; 145). Rabbinic literature attributes many of the works now found in Kethuvim to traditional figures; thus Jeremiah is considered the author of Lamentations, and Solomon is considered the author of Ecclesiastes. In the case of Song of Songs, an attribution of Solomonic authorship was even secondarily added as the first verse of the composition. These attributions, however, are not historically accurate; rather, they reflect a late biblical and early rabbinic desire to enhance these books by connecting them to figures who are central in tradition. Linguistic and other internal evidence, which is investigated in the introductions to each of the books in Kethuvim, is a more reliable way of dating these books.

Wisdom Literature

ACCORDING TO MOST BIBLICAL SCHOLARS, the three books Job, Proverbs, and Ecclesiastes should be viewed together as wisdom literature. "Wisdom literature" describes works that do not focus on the nation Israel, on its great formative historical memories, such as the exodus and conquest, on the Temple and Jerusalem, or on covenant as the central theological notion binding together God, the people Israel, and the land of Israel. Wisdom books are thus in some ways a departure from the concerns of other biblical books. They share, rather, as their focus, reflection on universal human concerns, especially the understanding of individual experiences and the maintenance of ordered relationships that lead both to success on the human plane and to divine approval.

In more recent scholarship, the concept of "wisdom" has been criticized as too elastic and amorphous. Indeed, the three wisdom books in this collection are remarkably different from one another and do not form a clear unit: Proverbs, in contrast to Job, suggests that the righteous are rewarded and do not suffer, while Ecclesiastes, in contrast to both Job and Proverbs, is deeply skeptical of the utility of wisdom. In addition, "wisdom" is a modern category, deriving from the beginning of the twentieth century, and thus Job, Proverbs, and Ecclesiastes were not originally grouped together on generic grounds. They nevertheless share a thematic interdependence. Proverbs provides a normative version of a type of ancient Near Eastern thought that looked for pattern and repetition in nature and in the moral life. In this tradition, the regular recurrence of natural phenomena could provide an analogy to guide human beings in their social interactions:

> Charcoal for embers and wood for a fire
> And a contentious man for kindling strife. (26.21)

The inevitability of the natural occurrence is mirrored in the inevitability of the social one. This kind of thinking then was extended to moral behavior, with the argument that good behavior, like good farming practice, will be rewarded:

> He who tends a fig tree will enjoy its fruit,
> And he who cares for his master will be honored. (27.18)

Job and Ecclesiastes relate to this normative tradition in different ways. Job denies the inevitability of rewards for living an upright life and decisively refutes the idea that human suffering is always deserved. Ecclesiastes treats the idea of inevitability in a still different way, emphasizing the great power of God that may be seen through the natural repetitions of seasons, tasks, and occupations. Human attempts to circumvent this power, or even to understand it fully, are futile. The themes found in these wisdom texts are found in other biblical texts as well, suggesting that the wisdom school did not have a narrow sphere of influence. Additionally, the themes of the wisdom tradition are continued (with significant changes, as wisdom and Torah become identified) in later postbiblical Jewish works, such as the Apocryphal book of the Wisdom of (Ben) Sirach, which is also known as Ecclesiasticus.

The Historical Books in Kethuvim

MANY OF THE BOOKS IN KETHUVIM (Ruth, Esther, Chronicles, Ezra-Nehemiah, Daniel chs 1–6) may be understood as historical books in the sense that they narrate a past. Much like the historical texts now found in the Former Prophets (see p. 453), however, those found in

Kethuvim are not historical in our sense, that is, they are not narratives giving an accurate systematic account that conforms to what really happened.

This is particularly true of the book of Chronicles, which is a retelling with significant variations of the books of Genesis through Kings. It is unclear if its author had access to a significant number of external sources not found in our canonical Bibles, but in any case, a close examination of the book illustrates the remarkable way in which its author deals with sources, rewriting them to fit a particular notion of "historical probability," namely, what really should have happened based on notions of how the world worked. For example, in the book of Kings, which does not have a clear retribution theory (a theory concerning punishment and reward), the Judean King Manasseh (698/687–642 BCE) is depicted as the most evil king of Judah, who is ultimately responsible for the destruction of the Temple in 586 (2 Kings ch 21). The same source, however, indicates that Manasseh reigned for fifty-five years.

This "contradiction" between the behavior of Manasseh and his long reign did not bother the Deuteronomist, who did not believe that each individual king needed to be punished or rewarded for his behavior. The Chronicler, however, did believe in this type of retribution theology, and the Deuteronomist's depiction of Manasseh in Kings was clearly very troublesome. For this reason, the Chronicler rewrote the life of Manasseh, adding 2 Chronicles 33.10–13: "The LORD spoke to Manasseh and his people, but they would not pay heed, so the LORD brought against them the officers of the army of the king of Assyria, who took Manasseh captive in manacles, bound him in fetters, and led him off to Babylon. In his distress, he entreated the LORD his God and humbled himself greatly before the God of his fathers. He prayed to Him, and He granted his prayer, heard his plea, and returned him to Jerusalem to his kingdom. Then Manasseh knew that the LORD alone was God." Thus, Manasseh fits the paradigms that the author of Chronicles believed to be true: All people need to be warned before they are punished; repentance is extremely efficacious; and individuals may only succeed if their behavior is meritorious. These external beliefs forced a revision of the source's account so that Manasseh's life could be properly illustrative. Other examples of this type of revisionism are found throughout Chronicles, and are discussed in the introduction to that book (pp. 1712–1717).

Scholars have found similarities between Chronicles and Ezra-Nehemiah and have posited that these works belong to a single large history composed by the Chronicler, which parallels the Deuteronomistic History. A closer look at Chronicles and Ezra-Nehemiah, however, shows that they differ from each other in outlook and vocabulary, and that the general similarities between them are best attributed to the common time in which they were written, most likely the fourth century BCE. Like Chronicles, a strong ideological bias may be detected in Ezra-Nehemiah, and even though it purports to be written close to the events it describes, it must be used with great care by the contemporary historian of ancient Israel.

Ruth and Esther, both now found among the five scrolls, and Daniel are different in genre from Chronicles or Ezra-Nehemiah. They are fictional stories set in historical backgrounds, serving ideological and perhaps esthetic purposes. Clearly artistic from a literary point of view, these books are not simply entertainment: They narrate a past (sometimes a fanciful past) in order to convey lessons relevant to the community. Ruth, a deceptively simple pastoral tale, promotes the principles of *ḥesed*, "loyalty," and of family continuity, elevating it to the national level with the genealogy of David. Esther, a comic farce that uses drinking parties as a major plot device, provides an etiology or origin for the festival of Purim and shows that, despite dire threats to their security, Diaspora Jews can triumph and succeed. Daniel chs 1–6, like Esther, models success in a foreign court and, unlike Esther, stresses that Jews should be faithful to their religious beliefs and practices in the Diaspora. The particular characteristics of these three very different books may be found in the introductions to each book (pp. 1578–79, 1623–25, and 1640–42).

Kethuvim as a Collection

THE OBSERVATIONS ABOVE SHOW THAT KETHUVIM is the most diverse collection of the three canonical divisions. Even though various texts may be grouped together, e.g., as wisdom literature or as historical texts, the individual works that comprise these categories (e.g., Job and Proverbs) have little in common. Kethuvim has no central theme or idea, in the way that the Torah (or Hexateuch) might have the land promise and its fulfillment as its center, or the Prophets as a whole might illustrate the significance of heeding the mediated divine word. In fact, with the exception of Psalms and the five scrolls, which have significant liturgical uses, Kethuvim has not received much attention within Jewish tradition.

This lack of attention is quite unfortunate, for these books are among the most interesting biblical books, and also among the most significant for understanding the Bible as a whole and for following the development from biblical Israel to rabbinic Judaism. Since this collection contains some of the latest books in the Bible (Chronicles, Ezra-Nehemiah, Daniel, Ecclesiastes), it shows us how classical biblical ideas evolved and changed in the late biblical period, as they began to develop into notions that would be much more familiar to readers of Jewish texts beginning with the Hellenistic period (Apocrypha, Pseudepigrapha, and Dead Sea Scrolls) and continuing in early rabbinic literature.

[MARC ZVI BRETTLER]

תהלים

Psalms

THE BOOK OF PSALMS IS THE FIRST BOOK of Kethuvim, or Writings—probably because of its size and significance and also perhaps because it was the first book in Kethuvim to become authoritative. A text from the Dead Sea Scrolls, MMT[d] (4Q397: 14–21; C.9–10), speaks of "the books of Moses and the books of the Prophets and David," thus indicating its status. (For "David" as a locution for Psalms, see below.)

Psalms is a collection, actually a collection of collections, of poetic prayers. (Prose prayers are also found throughout the Bible, but they are ad hoc, private prayers of individuals.) The origin of most of these poetic prayers is lost in obscurity, but they were preserved because they were likely used liturgically in ancient Israel, certainly in the Second Temple and in some cases perhaps in the First Temple. The Hebrew name of the book, *Tehilim*, "songs of praise," is found often in rabbinic literature and is also attested in one of the Dead Sea Scrolls, in a Psalms scroll (11QPs[a], lines 4–5) which says that David wrote 3,600 *tehilim* plus other compositions (see below for David as the author of Psalms). The English title "Psalms" derives from the Greek *psalmos*, a translation of Hebrew *mizmor*, "a song with the accompaniment of a stringed instrument."

There are 150 chapters or psalms in the Masoretic Text of the Hebrew Bible; some chapters may contain two separate psalms (possibly Pss. 19 and 40), while in other cases, one composition has been split into two chapters (e.g., Pss. 9–10 and 42–43). The book crystallized in several different forms in different communities: The LXX contains an additional psalm at the end of the book, and the Syriac Peshitta Bible translation contains five additional psalms. Several of these, as well as some previously unknown compositions, have been found in the Qumran Psalm scroll (11QPs[a]), suggesting that the collection and arrangement of psalms in the early Psalter was fluid, within certain parameters, with no fixed order nor even a set list of compositions to be included.

The book of Psalms is subdivided into five "Books": I, chapters 1–41 (most of the "Psalms of David" are in this collection); II, 42–72 (containing some psalms of Korah and Asaph); III, 73–89 (almost exclusively the psalms of Korah and Asaph); IV, 90–106 (mostly untitled psalms); V, 107–150 (mostly liturgical psalms for pilgrimages to the Temple and for festivals). The division into books is marked by the insertion of doxologies, short hymnic praises of God, at the end of each book. The doxologies to Books I–IV all begin with the words "Blessed is the LORD." The last psalm, Ps. 150, serves as the concluding doxology for Book V and for the book of Psalms as a whole (just as Psalm 1 may be viewed as an introduction to the entire book). The division into five books of psalms is designed to parallel the five books of the Torah. As the Rabbis put it: "Moses gave the five books of the Torah to Israel and David gave the five books of Psalms to Israel" (*Midrash Shoḥer Tov*, 1.2). This arrangement into five books is artificial and relatively late, and reflects the development from Psalms as a liturgical collection to a Torah-like book to be studied. Strong evidence for the existence of separate collections is: (1) the end of one collection, Ps. 72.20, is clearly marked by the words "End of the prayers of David son of Jesse"; and (2) some psalms were included in two different collections, as is seen by the fact that Pss. 14 and 53 are nearly identical, as are Ps. 18 and 2 Sam. ch 22; Ps. 70 is comprised of Ps. 40.14–18. The first three books seem to have been in place before the last two were added, judging from the fact that 28 out of 33 untitled psalms are found in Books IV and V, and that the differences between the Dead Sea Psalms text and the Masoretic Text occur mostly in Books IV and V. Within the present collections are smaller collections, for example, the Songs of Ascents (the ascent of pilgrims to the Temple Mount; Pss. 120–134), so named from their opening words. Modern scholars speak of the Elohist psalter, Pss. 42–83, in which God is typically referred to as Elohim rather than as LORD (YHVH). Some scholars see clusters of psalms that begin or end with "hallelujah" as subcollections (Pss. 105–106; 111–113; 115–117; 146–150). Other collections have been isolated as well. It remains unclear, however, if the psalms within each collection, and the collections themselves, were arranged according to any overarching principle. It is clear, though, that Psalms, even at 150 chapters, is not the single definitive collection of ancient Israel's psalms, since similar poems are also found outside of the Psalter (e.g., 1 Sam. 2.1–10; 2 Sam. 23.1–7; Jonah ch 3; Hab. ch 3).

An ancient and pervasive tradition, going back to the Bible itself, attributes the authorship of Psalms to David. David is "the favorite of the songs of Israel" (2 Sam. 23.1), the one who soothed Saul with music (1 Sam. 16.17–23), the classic example of a musician (Amos 6.5), and the founder of Temple singing (2 Chron. 23.18). Deriving from and reinforcing this tradition are the many psalm superscriptions or titles that contain "a psalm of David." Other superscriptions link a psalm with a specific event in the life of David (Pss. 3; 18; 34; 51; 56). These superscriptions are not original to these psalms, but reflect early interpretive additions that derive from the notion of David as author of the psalms. Early extrabiblical sources show that ancient Jewish and Christian tradition also assumed that David wrote all or most of Psalms. As mentioned above, a Psalms scroll from the Dead Sea Scrolls attributes 3,600 psalms to David (a tradition on the analogy of the Bible's attribution of 3,000 proverbs and 1,005 songs to Solomon in 1 Kings 5.12). Additionally, Davidic superscriptions occur in that scroll in Pss. 104 and 123, although they are lacking in the Masoretic Text. Along the same lines, the author of Acts, the first century CE New Testament book, assigns Ps. 2 to David (Acts 4.25), even though the psalm itself has no such ascription. This evidence suggests that there was widespread acceptance of the Davidic authorship of the entire Psalter, a tradition that is echoed in rabbinic literature and has continued until modern times in both Jewish and Christian circles. Davidic authorship, however, on the basis of lingustic and contextual evidence, is not accepted as historical fact by modern scholars, but is viewed as a way the ancients linked biblical writings with the appropriate inspired well-known biblical figure, thereby confirming the divine inspiration and the authority of those writings (as is the case in the ascription of Proverbs to Solomon, Lamentations to Jeremiah, and so forth). Not all psalms are specifically attributed to David; some are attributed to the sons of Korah (Ps. 42), to Asaph (Ps. 50), to Ethan the Ezrahite (Ps. 89), to Heman the Ezrahite (Ps. 88), to Solomon (Ps. 72), and to Moses (Ps. 90)—and others bear no ascription at all.

Dating the psalms is notoriously difficult, partly because they contain few explicit references to specific historical events or personages (as noted above, the superscriptions are not useful in this regard). While many modern scholars believe that at least some, perhaps even many of the psalms are from the preexilic period (before 586 BCE), none can be dated on linguistic grounds to the tenth century BCE, the period of David. There is little consensus on the dating of preexilic psalms, or even on which psalms are preexilic. Linguistic analysis can, in general, differentiate between preexilic and postexilic Hebrew, but the analysis is not always refined enough to be definitive. For one thing, poetry is often archaizing, so the presence of older-sounding phrases does not, in itself, prove an early date. Moreover, the hints to specific events that scholars find in the psalms often have more than one possible reference. Dating of psalms is subject to trends in biblical scholarship: At one time many psalms were thought to have originated in the Maccabean era (2nd century BCE), then in the preexilic period, and now more are being seen as products of the exilic or postexilic period. Some psalms clearly date from exilic or postexilic times, as we know from their references to events or their linguistic usages (e.g., Pss. 137; 145). It is also likely that some psalms have an ancient core that was reshaped after the exile into a new psalm. The bane of historical critics may be the virtue of the book of Psalms: The absence of specific historical references results in the poems' being seen as timeless, appropriate to many recurring occasions in the life of the individual or the community.

Many of the psalms have superscriptions containing information other than a personal name. Their terms are not well understood, but some are thought to be musical directions or instruments; for example: *sheminith* (Ps. 12); *ayyeleth ha-shahar* (Ps. 22); *maskil* (Ps. 32). The *menatzeah* or "leader" often referred to is presumably a choir-leader or chief musician. It is likely that the psalms were sung or recited to musical accompaniment. Psalm 150 indicates that music was a form of praise to God, and terms for praise include "sing . . . a new song" (96.1; 98.1; 149.1), "chant hymns" (147.1), and "sing joyously" (95.1). Unfortunately, the acoustic dimension has been lost, but it must have been an important component of the performance of psalms.

While no psalm is exactly identical with another and many show considerable creativity, all the psalms have similar style, vocabulary, and forms of expression. They share these features with other ancient Near Eastern prayers as well; Israel's borrowing from its neighbors included forms of religious expression. Like all biblical poetry, the psalms make much use of repetition, parallelism, and imagery (see essay on "Biblical Poetry," pp. 2097–2104). They also have recourse to many of the same themes found elsewhere in the Bible, for these themes were central to the corporate identity of Israel. Included are the themes of creation (which shows God's supreme power over everything in the world); the promise to Abraham of land and progeny (especially important after the exile); the exodus (the foundational experience in the formation of the people of Israel and their covenant with God); the exile (the key event in the formation of Jewish identity after 586 BCE); the Davidic monarchy (symbol of the continuity of Judah); the centrality of Jerusalem, Zion, and the Temple. (Striking in its absence is the giving of the Decalogue or Torah at Sinai.) In addition, psalms borrow mythological motifs found at Ugarit and elsewhere in the ancient Near East that were known in ancient Israel, such as God the warrior defeating Israel's enemies, the conquest of the primeval waters (the forces of chaos), and God as king enthroned amid a heavenly court. Not surprisingly, the psalms draw heavily on the religious concepts of ancient Israel; for modern scholars they are a window into the religious experience that the Bible chose to preserve (see essay on the "Religion of the Bible," pp. 2021–40).

Based on the literary structure or "form" of each psalm, modern form-critical scholars have been concerned to assign to each psalm a genre and a specific social setting (the German term *Sitz im Leben* is often used) in the religious practice of ancient Israel. This is often conjectural, based on interpreting hints contained in the psalms (see, e.g., Ps. 67.7–8 n.). It is surprising that the psalms contain so few hints (but see 118.27 n.). Like dates, and for much the same reasons, genre labels must be assigned tentatively. Most psalms fall into three general categories (sometimes a psalm partakes of more than one category): hymns of praise; complaints or pleas for help (sometimes called laments); and thanksgiving psalms. Other subcategories, like wisdom psalms (see Ps. 1), royal psalms (see Ps. 2), or Zion psalms, have also been discerned. Several do not address God at all, and can only with great difficulty be classified as prayers. Psalms may be written in the first-person singular, called a psalm of the individual, or in the first-person plural, communal psalms. The speaking voice should not be understood as a sign of authorship, but rather as a literary persona through whom the psalm is conveyed. In fact, psalms often move from an individual speaker to communal speaker; and all psalms, by their inclusion in the Psalter, are property of the community. As is the case in later prayer, a psalm may be recited privately by an individual or publicly by an individual or by a group.

Psalms also occupies a prominent place in Jewish liturgy; some entire psalms are recited as part of the regular service or on special occasions, and many individual verses or passages have found their way into later prayers (see list in "The Bible in the Liturgy," pp. 1937–48). Additional psalms are recited publicly or privately at times of joy or danger. Some individuals or groups take upon themselves the recitation of all the psalms on a weekly basis.

Praise is the quintessential nature of psalms, and hymns of praise are the most common type of psalm in the Psalter. In the words of Ps. 92.2: "It is good to praise the LORD, to sing hymns to Your name, O Most High." Most psalms are, in one way or another, aimed at praising God—for His power and beneficence, for His creation of the world, and for His past acts of deliverance to Israel. Often the praise comes after the psalmist has prayed for help from sickness or enemies (the typical subject of complaints) and his prayer has been answered. As part of his complaint, he promises to praise God when he has been delivered from trouble. Thanksgiving for God's help or beneficence is another form of praise. According to the outlook of Psalms, the main religious function of human beings is to offer praise to God, to proclaim His greatness throughout the world. Thus, the psalms enjoin others to praise God, and they envision a world in which everyone and everything will praise God. This implies a relationship between God and humans, another important dimension of Psalms. God is called upon to hear prayers and to respond; this is one of His attributes. Worst of all is when He "hides His face" and refuses to pay attention to the psalmist, because this puts into question the efficacy of prayer. If there is one primary underlying assumption of the book of Psalms, it is the potential efficacy of prayer.

[ADELE BERLIN AND MARC ZVI BRETTLER]

BOOK ONE

1 Happy is the man who has not followed the
    counsel of the wicked,
  or taken the path of sinners,
  or joined the company of the insolent;

2 rather, the teaching of the Lord is his delight,
  and he studies[a] that teaching day and night.

3 He is like a tree planted beside streams of water,
  which yields its fruit in season,
  whose foliage never fades,
  and whatever [b]it produces thrives.[b]

4 Not so the wicked;
  rather, they are like chaff that wind blows away.

a Or "recites"; lit. "utters."   b-b Or "he does prospers."

Ps. 1: This psalm serves as an introduction to the Psalter, as is suggested by its lack of a superscription or introduction mentioning David unlike most psalms in Book I. It depicts a straightforward system of personal retribution that stands behind many psalms (see also Ezek. ch 18), and it contains a reference to "torah" (v. 2), translated as "teaching," but perhaps understood as Torah ("Teaching"), the five books of Moses. By placing a reference to Torah at the be-

ginning of this canonical section, the centrality of the first part of the canon, the Torah, is reinforced (see similarly Josh. 1.7–8). The mention of Torah here may also be connected to the fact that the Psalter is divided into five books (see introduction to Psalms), and thus study of the Psalter may also be intended. Many scholars consider Ps. 1 to be a wisdom psalm, based on the contrast between the righteous and the wicked as seen in Proverbs, Job, and Ecclesiastes (see

the discussion of "wisdom literature" in "Kethuvim," pp. 1276–77). Ps. 1, however, does not share extensive terminology with these books, and scholars are beginning to question the usefulness of the designation "wisdom psalms." **1–3:** Standard biblical imagery (e.g., Jer. 17.9 for a tree image and Josh. 1.8 for reciting "torah" day and night) is used to develop the picture of the ideal righteous individual. This individual is first described through what he does not do (v. 1), then through what he does (v. 2), and then via a simile. *Followed . . . taken . . . joined . . .* does not fully capture the imagery of location and movement in the Heb "walk, stand, sit." **2:** *Day and night* is figurative for "always," though the Dead Sea Scroll community took it literally, suggesting that "[I]n the place in which the Ten assemble there should not be missing a man to interpret the law day and night, always relieving each other" (1QS 6.6–7, as translated in Florentino García Martínez and Eibert J.C. Tigchelaar, *The Dead Sea Scrolls Study Edition* [Leiden: Brill, 1997], vol. 1, p. 83). This psalm is unusual in its stress on Torah study rather than observance based on Torah study (see Josh. 1.7–8); it

5 Therefore the wicked will not survive judgment,
       nor will sinners, in the assembly of the
          righteous.
6 For the LORD cherishes the way of the righteous,
       but the way of the wicked is doomed.

2 Why do nations assemble,
       and peoples plot*a* vain things;
2   kings of the earth take their stand,
       and regents intrigue together
       against the LORD and against His anointed?
3 "Let us break the cords of their yoke,
       shake off their ropes from us!"
4 He who is enthroned in heaven laughs;
       the Lord mocks at them.
5 Then He speaks to them in anger,
       terrifying them in His rage,
6 "But I have installed My king
       on Zion, My holy mountain!"
7 Let me tell of the decree:
       the LORD said to me,
       b-"You are My son,
       I have fathered you this day."*-b*

---

a Lit. "utter."   b-b Compare 2 Sam. 7.14, and Ps. 89.27 ff.

---

thus approaches the rabbinic ideal of "torah lishmah," Torah study for its own sake, as an end in itself. **3:** *And whatever it produces thrives* is ambiguous, referring either to the *tree* or the righteous individual. **4–5:** The depiction of the wicked is much shorter, and in the plural, whereas the righteous person was spoken of in the singular. In contrast to the deeply rooted tree, the wicked are insubstantial *chaff,* the light outside husk of grain that flies away during winnowing. **5:** *Judgment* refers to a court case. Medieval Jewish interpretation traditionally understands this judgment as the afterworld (e.g., Ibn Ezra and Radak), but interest in the afterworld is largely a postbiblical development (see Dan. 12.2 n.). **6:** The final v. sums up the fate of both the *righteous* of vv. 1–3 and *the wicked* of vv. 4–5. Most biblical verses may be divided into two halves of relatively equal size (see "Biblical Poetry," pp. 2097–2104). Here, the second

half is substantially shorter than the first, mimicking the structure of vv. 4–5 in contrast to vv. 1–3, again emphasizing the insubstantial nature of the wicked.

Ps. 2: Some traditions see this as a continuation of Ps 1. (A variant in the New Testament quotes from this psalm, calling it "the first," and the Talmud in *b. Ber.* 9b–10a notes that Pss. 1–2 are a single psalm, enclosed by the inclusio "happy" [1.1 and 2.12]). There are several vocabulary links between these psalms, but the differences in style, tone, and theme outweigh these similarities, suggesting that the medieval tradition, which sees them as separate psalms, is correct. Most modern scholars classify this psalm as a royal psalm, and connect it to other psalms concerning kings. (One possible list of royal psalms: Pss. 2; 18; 20; 21; 45; 72; 89; 101; 110; 132; 144.) None of these mentions a specific king by name, and

their origin and uses remain obscure. The context in which this psalm might be recited is also obscure, though it is significant to note that a divine (perhaps prophetic) oracle is quoted (vv. 6–9), and that the nations are spoken to as if they are present (vv. 10–12). Like Ps. 1, it lacks a superscription; Ps. 2 may not have originally been at the beginning of the Psalter, but perhaps was inserted toward the beginning to emphasize the royal nature (connected with King David) of the Psalter. **1–2:** The attack depicted is extreme and hyperbolic. **2:** Since anointing was the major performative ritual of kingship (e.g., 1 Sam. 10.1), *His anointed* may refer to the king. The same term "mashiah" is used in postbiblical literature (but never in the Bible) to refer to the ideal future Davidic king, and is the origin of the term "Messiah." The relationship between God and king is very close; the attack *against the* LORD is equated with that *against His anointed,* suggesting that the (Davidic) king was viewed by some as God's earthly representative. (See also the striking filial language in v. 7 and Ps. 45.) This idea is picked up in many depictions of the ideal future Davidic king, called Messiah in postbiblical texts. **3:** Similar animal yoke imagery is found later in rabbinic expressions: "the yoke of the commandments," "the yoke of the Torah," and "the yoke of the kingdom of heaven." **4:** The Bible contains various conceptions of where God resides. 1 Kings 8.32 similarly argues that God dwells *in heaven;* for two different conceptions see 1 Kings 8.13 and 27. **6:** *Zion,* a synonym for Jerusalem, is typically depicted as *holy* (e.g., Isa. 52.1; Ps. 20.3); Zion and Davidic kingship are often connected in the Bible. God is here envisaged as present both in heaven (v. 4) and in Jerusalem (see 1 Kings 8.13), perhaps (hyperbolically) where this mountain and heaven meet. **7:** Adoption language expresses the close kinship between God and the king, and is common in the ancient Near East. Some biblical passages may sug-

8   Ask it of Me,
         and I will make the nations your domain;
         your estate, the limits of the earth.
9   You can smash them with an iron mace,
         shatter them like potter's ware."

10   So now, O kings, be prudent;
         accept discipline, you rulers of the earth!
11   Serve the LORD in awe;
         ᵃtremble with fright,ᐧᵃ
12   ᵇpay homage in good faith,ᐧᵇ
         lest He be angered, and your way be doomed
         in the mere flash of His anger.
         Happy are all who take refuge in Him.

3 A psalm of David when he fled from his son Absalom.

2   O LORD, my foes are so many!
         Many are those who attack me;
3   many say of me,
         "There is no deliverance for him through God."
         *Selah.*ᶜ
4   But You, O LORD, are a shield about me,
         my glory, He who holds my head high.
5   I cry aloud to the LORD,
         and He answers me from His holy mountain.
         Selah.
6   I lie down and sleep and wake again,
         for the LORD sustains me.
7   I have no fear of the myriad forces
         arrayed against me on every side.

a-a *Meaning of Heb. uncertain; others "rejoice with trembling."*
b-b *Meaning of Heb. uncertain.*   c *A liturgical direction of uncertain meaning.*

ual asks God for help. **1:** Several psalms have introductions which connect their content to the life of David as depicted in Samuel (e.g., Pss. 18; 51); the superscription here refers to events narrated in 2 Sam. 15–19. These historical superscriptions reflect a type of inner-biblical interpretation (see "Inner-biblical Interpretation," pp. 1829–35, and "Midrash," pp. 1863–75) in which individual psalms are connected to the life of David. The Heb and Gk (Septuagint) texts show significant variation in these superscriptions, indicating that they are a late, secondary element. The phrase *of David* may mean written by David, or in the style of David (cf. a Miltonic Ode); already in early postbiblical tradition, the former was assumed, in support of other traditions that see David as the author of Psalms (see introduction). The word *psalm,* translating Heb "mizmor," is a borrowing from Gk. Both words mean a song sung to the accompaniment of a stringed instrument (see esp. 33.2; 92.4; 144.9). **2–3:** A description of the psalmist's numerous troubles; this is highlighted by the threefold repetition of *many.* **3:** *Selah* is most likely a musicological term, of uncertain meaning and etymology, typically appearing at major disjunctures in a psalm. The Septuagint translates it as "an interlude," while another ancient Gk translation, the early Church father Jerome, and some medievals render it as "always." Radak understands it as "with a raised voice," from the Heb root "s-l-l," "to raise." Some modern scholars view it as an abbreviation, though it is not known to what extent abbreviations were used in ancient Israel. *Selah* is found only in the Psalter and in the psalm in Hab. ch 3. **4–7:** The contrast between the many enemies and the single God, more powerful than the lot of them. **5:** It is unclear exactly how God *answers me from His holy mountain,* in other words whether the psalmist saw or heard some clear sign or oracle of God's attention. **6–7:** The confidence motif is central to many such

gest that some groups in ancient Israel viewed the king as divine; see 45.7 n. The *son* language here has played a significant role in medieval Jewish-Christian polemic (e.g., the final comment of Radak on this psalm). The *decree* cited may be 2 Sam. 7.14, where God says to David concerning his heir: "I will be a father to him, and he shall be a son to Me." **10–12:** In a rhetorical flourish, God is depicted as speaking directly to the foreign monarchs. A similar depiction of the centrality of God and Zion for all nations is also found in Isa. 2.2–4, but is there in an eschatolog-

ical setting. **12:** As noted, the translation *in good faith* is uncertain. The Heb word "bar" can also mean "son," especially in Aramaic, and this has sometimes been connected to the divinely adopted son ("ben") in v. 7.

Ps. 3: This may have originally been the first psalm (see introductory notes to Pss. 1 and 2); it is the first of many psalms with a superscription or title mentioning David. It also reflects a typical genre of psalms, the individual petition (also called the lament of the individual), in which an individ-

8   Rise, O LORD!
     Deliver me, O my God!
     For You slap all my enemies in the face;[a]
        You break the teeth of the wicked.
9   Deliverance is the LORD's;
        Your blessing be upon Your people!   *Selah.*

4 [b-]For the leader; with instrumental music.[-b]
     A psalm of David.

2   Answer me when I call,
        O God, my vindicator!
     You freed me from distress;
        have mercy on me and hear my prayer.
3   You men, how long will my glory be mocked,
        will you love illusions,
        have recourse to frauds?   *Selah.*
4   Know that the LORD singles out the faithful for
        Himself;
        the LORD hears when I call to Him.
5   So tremble, and sin no more;
        ponder it on your bed, and sigh.[c]
6   Offer sacrifices in righteousness
        and trust in the LORD.

7   Many say, "O for good days!"
     [d-]Bestow Your favor on us,[-d] O LORD.
8   You put joy into my heart
        when their grain and wine show increase.
9   Safe and sound, I lie down and sleep,
        [e-]for You alone, O LORD, keep me secure.[-e]

a Lit. "cheek."
b-b Meaning of Heb. uncertain.
c Others "be still."
d-d Lit. "Lift up the light of Your countenance upon us"; cf. Num. 6.25 f.
e-e Or "for You, O LORD, keep me alone and secure."

psalms. The psalmist may have received some type of sign or oracle of divine support (see v. 5 n.), or perhaps the recitation of the psalm itself put him into a confident mood. (See also 6.9–11 n.) **8–9:** These vv. have an odd mixture of tenses and moods not fully conveyed in the English: God is commanded to act, but the defeat of the enemies is depicted in the past. This may reflect the certainty

of the psalmist that his petition has been heeded. Such mixing of tenses is frequent at the conclusion of individual petitions. **9:** The psalm concludes by moving from the individual to the community, *upon Your people.*

Ps. 4: This is an unusual individual petition: it is unclear what the petitioner's problem might be; it highlights the psalmist's confi-

dence in God more than his troubles; and it focuses more on others than on the psalmist. Radak, followed by some early modern commentators, connects this psalm to the previous one and understands "them" as those allied with Absalom and his rebellion against David. More likely, v. 6, *Offer sacrifices in righteousness,* suggests a Temple setting. **1:** The meaning of the two terms translated as *leader* and *instrumental music* is uncertain; it was already lost in antiquity, as reflected in the divergent renditions found in the ancient biblical translations. **2:** The Heb, followed in this translation, reflects an imperative, a past, and two imperatives, suggesting that based on a past experience of salvation, the psalmist, again in straits, wants to be saved again; other ancient translations reflect different tenses. **3–7:** The psalmist's adversaries are addressed; they are called *men* (v. 3) and *many* (v. 7). **4:** *Faithful* translates "hasid." In most psalms "hasid" is likely a generic term for the righteous individual, though in some Second Temple writings, it may refer to a specific group of Jews (see 2 Maccabees 14.6, where the Greek "asidaioi" refers to the followers of Judah the Maccabee). **6:** The Heb tolerates both *sacrifices in righteousness* (Ibn Ezra, Radak) and *sacrifices* of *righteousness* (Rashi). If the former is meant, it may be connected to Isa. 1.10–17, which stresses that sacrifices are not automatically efficacious, while the latter idea may be connected to Ps. 51.19, "True sacrifice to God is a contrite spirit." In either case, the word *righteousness* ("tzedek") recalls God's title in v. 2 as *my vindicator,* lit. "of my righteousness" ("tzidki")—a righteous deity must be offered righteous offerings. **7:** *Bestow Your favor on us* is lit. "lift up for us the light of your face." As in the priestly blessing in Num. 6.25, the striking anthropomorphism of God's shining face refers to divine blessing. **9:** Anxiety causes sleeplessness (6.7–8), while full confidence in God allows for untroubled *sleep,* even in distress, as in 3.6.

5 ^aFor the leader; on *neḥiloth.*^{-a} A psalm of David.

2 Give ear to my speech, O LORD;
   consider my utterance.

3 Heed the sound of my cry,
   my king and God,
   for I pray to You.

4 Hear my voice, O LORD, at daybreak;
   at daybreak I plead before You, and wait.

5 For You are not a God who desires wickedness;
   evil cannot abide with You;

6 wanton men cannot endure in Your sight.
You detest all evildoers;

7 You doom those who speak lies;
   murderous, deceitful men the LORD abhors.

8 But I, through Your abundant love, enter Your
   house;
   I bow down in awe at Your holy temple.

9 O LORD, ^blead me along Your righteous [path]^{-b}
   because of my watchful foes;
   make Your way straight before me.

10 For there is no sincerity on their lips;^c
   their heart is [filled with] malice;
   their throat is an open grave;
   their tongue slippery.

11 Condemn them, O God;
   let them fall by their own devices;
   cast them out for their many crimes,
   for they defy You.

12 But let all who take refuge in You rejoice,
   ever jubilant as You shelter them;
   and let those who love Your name exult in
   You.

13 For You surely bless the righteous man, O LORD,
   encompassing him with favor like a shield.

a-a Meaning of Heb. uncertain.
b-b Or "as You are righteous, lead me."
c Lit. "mouth."

Ps. 5: Petitions to God have a similar structure to petitions to a human: The one petitioned is invoked; a petition explaining the need, typically in the imperative, is offered; and (a) motivation(s) for why this petition should be heard is/are outlined. Here, God is invoked as *O LORD* (v. 2) with the imperatives *Give ear, consider, Heed,* and *Hear* (vv. 2–4). The psalmist's need in this case is vague; this allows the psalm to be reused in a wide variety of situations. Several reasons are given for why God should heed the petition: God despises evildoers (vv. 5–7), *because of my watchful foes* (vv. 9–11), and because rectification of the situation will encourage the already faithful (vv. 12–13). The poetic diction of the psalm is quite standard, often using parallelism (see "Biblical Poetry," pp. 2097–2104), as in v. 2: *Give ear* || *consider* and *my speech* || *my utterance.* **3:** The psalmist's view of God is highly personal, as *my king and* (my) *God.* The image of God as king is frequent in the psalms, esp. in Pss. 93–100; here it expresses God's interest in His subjects and His ability to help them. In the words of Radak: "I am crying out to you just as one cries out to a king." **4:** This verse may reflect a ritual performed at *daybreak,* or *daybreak* as the expected time of divine deliverance (see 46.6). **6–8:** These vv. express the idea that sinners were not welcome at the Jerusalem Temple (see intro. to Ps. 15). **6:** The *evildoers* ("poʿalei ʾaven") are often mentioned in Psalms, always in the plural, and may represent a particular group of maleficent individuals. **8:** It is uncertain if this is a description of the individual worshipping in Jerusalem, as in this translation, or if it should be read as a wish, ". . . may I enter . . . may I bow," in which case the psalmist's enemies are preventing him from going to Jerusalem. *Love* here translates "ḥesed," a frequent attribute of God in the Bible. "Ḥesed," a common biblical term, describes the relationship between individuals or groups, and between God and human beings, especially Israel. It expresses both an attitude and actions devolving from that attitude; English "loyalty" best approximates its sense, which combines obligation and kindness or favor. When used of God toward Israel, it may be related to the covenant, and it expresses God's faithfulness, goodness, and graciousness. **12–13:** As in 3.9, the conclusion moves from the individual to the community. **13:** Since the theme of the psalm is divine protection from enemies, it concludes with the simile of God as *a shield.*

6 ^aFor the leader; with instrumental music on the *sheminith.*^{-a} A psalm of David.

2   O LORD, do not punish me in anger,
        do not chastise me in fury.

3   Have mercy on me, O LORD, for I languish;
        heal me, O LORD, for my bones shake with
        terror.

4   My whole being is stricken with terror,
        while You, LORD—O, how long!

5   O LORD, turn! Rescue me!
    Deliver me as befits Your faithfulness.

6   For there is no praise of You among the dead;
        in Sheol, who can acclaim You?

7   I am weary with groaning;
        every night I drench my bed,
        I melt my couch in tears.

8   My eyes are wasted by vexation,
        worn out because of all my foes.

9   Away from me, all you evildoers,
        for the LORD heeds the sound of my weeping.

10   The LORD heeds my plea,
        the LORD accepts my prayer.

11   All my enemies will be frustrated and stricken
        with terror;
        they will turn back in an instant, frustrated.

7 ^a*Shiggaion* of David,^{-a} which he sang to the LORD, concerning Cush, a Benjaminite.

2   O LORD, my God, in You I seek refuge;
        deliver me from all my pursuers and save me,

a-a Meaning of Heb. uncertain.

Ps. 6: This psalm has entered the Jewish liturgy as the daily prayer for supplication ("taḥanun"), recited every weekday morning. It is the paradigmatic individual petition (see intro. to Ps. 5), opening with a divine invocation (v. 2, *O LORD*), followed by imperatives describing the petitioner's condition and problems (vv. 2–3), and offering a set of motivations for divine intervention: God's "ḥesed" (see 5.8 n.), and the fact that if God kills the petitioner, He will no longer hear his praise (v. 6). The psalm is tightly structured, in balanced verses. It uses repetition very effectively, as seen in "b-h-l" in vv. 3 (*shake with terror*), 4 (*stricken with terror*), and 11 (*stricken with terror*). The Heb expresses the turn in fortunes through an anagram: God's turning ("shuv" v. 5) is transposed into the enemies' becoming frustrated ("bush" v. 11); these are combined at the psalm's conclusion "yashuvu yevoshu," *they will turn back . . . frustrated.* The psalmist is ill (v. 3), scared (v. 4), and is being persecuted by enemies (v. 11). This allows the psalm to be used on multiple occasions. **1:** The

sheminith is most likely a type of musical instrument, perhaps with eight strings (from Heb "shemoneh"). **2–4:** The plea, *O, how long,* found in other psalms as well (e.g., 74.10; 80.5), is part of the Near Eastern prayer tradition; see, for example, a Mesopotamian prayer to the goddess Ishtar, which includes: "How long, O my Lady, will you be angered so that your face is turned away? How long, O my Lady, will you be infuriated so that your spirit is enraged?" (modified translation from *ANET*, p. 385). **2:** Like other psalms of this type, this psalm contains no confession of guilt. **4–5:** The elliptical *O, how long!* is connected to the following *turn;* the psalmist is saying, How long will You neglect me, hiding Your face from me (see introduction; Deut. 31.18)? On God's *faithfulness* ("ḥesed"), see 5.8. **6:** Biblical Israel knew of no afterlife with reward and punishment—everyone, irrespective of behavior or social status, descended to "She'ol," the dark underworld, and lived a quasi-life there. *Among the dead* may also be translated "in the place of death," paralleling "She'ol." **9–11:** The Heb tenses are better reflected by rendering: "Away . . . has heard . . . has heeded . . . will be frustrated." The back-and-forth movement may express the psalmist's religious conviction that God will hear his prayer, and thus he simultaneously expresses hope and certainty. Alternately, a ritual was performed (perhaps by a cultic prophet) through which the psalmist understood that God will come to his help; perhaps this is reflected in Lam. 3.57, "You have ever drawn nigh when I called You; You have said, 'Do not fear!'" A similar ritual may also be reflected in Ps. 12.6, where God is quoted in the middle of the psalm.

Ps. 7: This psalm is a petition of the individual like the previous one; the two are very different, however, in structure and tone, illustrating the flexibility of the

3 lest, like a lion, they tear me apart,
   rending in pieces, and no one save me.

4 O Lord, my God, if I have done such things,
   if my hands bear the guilt of wrongdoing,

5 if I have dealt evil to my ally—
   a-I who rescued my foe without reward-a—

6 then let the enemy pursue and overtake me;
   let him trample my life to the ground,
   and lay my body in the dust.   Selah.

7 Rise, O Lord, in Your anger;
   assert Yourself b-against the fury of my foes;-b
   bestir Yourself on my behalf;
   You have ordained judgment.

8 c-Let the assembly of peoples gather about You,
   with You enthroned above, on high.-c

9 The Lord judges the peoples;
   vindicate me, O Lord,
   for the righteousness and blamelessness that are
   mine.

10 Let the evil of the wicked come to an end,
   but establish the righteous;
   he who probes the mind and conscience[d] is God
   the righteous.

11 e-I look to God to shield me;-e
   the deliverer of the upright.

12 God vindicates the righteous;
   God f-pronounces doom-f each day.

13 g-If one does not turn back, but whets his sword,
   bends his bow and aims it,

14 then against himself he readies deadly weapons,
   and makes his arrows sharp.-g

15 See, he hatches evil, conceives mischief,
   and gives birth to fraud.

16 He has dug a pit and deepened it,
   and will fall into the trap he made.

17 His mischief will recoil upon his own head;
   his lawlessness will come down upon his skull.

18 I will praise the Lord for His righteousness,
   and sing a hymn to the name of the Lord Most
   High.

a-a Meaning of Heb. uncertain; others "or stripped my foe clean."
b-b Or "in Your fury against my foes."   c-c Meaning of Heb. uncertain.
d Lit. "kidneys."   e-e Cf. Ibn Ezra and Kimhi; lit. "My Shield is upon God."
f-f Others "has indignation."
g-g Meaning of vv. 13–14 uncertain; an alternate rendering, with God as the main subject,
is: ¹³If one does not turn back, He whets His sword, / bends His bow and aims it; / ¹⁴deadly
weapons He prepares for him, / and makes His arrows sharp.

genre. Ps. 7, unlike 6, contains a protestation of innocence (vv. 4–6), emphasizes God's role as a warrior (see v. 7 n.), and concludes with the wisdom idea that evil will befall the one who initiates it (vv. 13–17). **1:** In contrast to other superscriptions that refer to events mentioned in Samuel, the reference to *Cush* is puzzling; no such name occurs in Samuel. Rabbinic interpreters (e.g., Targum, but rejected by Ibn Ezra) took *Cush* as a reference to "Saul, son of Kish." The superscription may refer to a story about David that was not incorporated into Samuel. **4–6:** This short section, concluded by *Selah* (see 3.3 n.), is a protestation of innocence in the form of a self-imprecation. A much longer self-imprecation is found in Job ch 31; in Pss. 17 and 26 the psalmists likewise insist that they are punished unfairly by God. **7:** In the previous psalm, the individual feels that God is unjustly using his *anger* against him; our psalmist wants God to use his *anger* justly against his enemies. The demand to *rise* (Heb "kumah") may recall God's role as warrior, as in Num. 10.35, "Advance (or rise: Heb "kumah"), O Lord! May Your enemies be scattered, And may Your foes flee before You!" *Bestir Yourself* (Heb "'urah") is more literally "awake." Some psalms imagine God as sleeping, as in 44.24, "Rouse Yourself (Heb "'urah"); why do You sleep, O Lord? Awaken, do not reject us forever!" while 121.4 states categorically: "See, the guardian of Israel neither slumbers nor sleeps!" **9–10:** Through the punishment of the *wicked*, the psalmist is *vindicated*. **11:** As in 5.13, God is a shield, protecting the supplicant from his enemies. **15–17:** A similar notion predominates in wisdom texts, e.g., Prov. 26.27: "He who digs a pit will fall in it, And whoever rolls a stone, it will roll back on him." **18:** A common motif in petitions is that if the plea is heeded, the psalmist will utter praise and thanksgiving to God. *Most High* (Heb "'elyon") is an ancient Canaanite divine epithet

8

^{a-}For the leader; on the *gittith.*^{-a} A psalm of David.

2   O LORD, our Lord,
        How majestic is Your name throughout the
          earth,
        ^{b-}You who have covered the heavens with Your
          splendor!^{-b}
3   ^{a-}From the mouths of infants and sucklings
        You have founded strength on account of Your
          foes,
        to put an end to enemy and avenger.^{-a}
4   When I behold Your heavens, the work of Your
          fingers,
        the moon and stars that You set in place,
5   what is man that You have been mindful
          of him,
        mortal man that You have taken note of him,
6   that You have made him little less than divine,^c
        and adorned him with glory and majesty;
7   You have made him master over Your
          handiwork,
        laying the world at his feet,
8   sheep and oxen, all of them,
        and wild beasts, too;
9   the birds of the heavens, the fish of the sea,
        whatever travels the paths of the seas.
10   O LORD, our Lord, how majestic is Your name
        throughout the earth!

9

^{d-}For the leader; *'almuth labben.*^{-d} A psalm of David.

2   I will praise You, LORD, with all my heart;
        I will tell all Your wonders.

---

a-a *Meaning of Heb. uncertain.*
b-b *Meaning of Heb. uncertain; or "You whose splendor is celebrated all over the heavens!"*
c *Or "the angels."*
d-d *Meaning of Heb. uncertain; some mss. and ancient versions,* 'al muth labben, *as though "over the death of the son."*

2: The parallelism highlights the complete extent of God's power (*name*) and splendor, on *the earth* and in *the heavens.* 3: Though somewhat obscure, this seems to emphasize that even very young children recognize God's majesty. The *enemy and avenger* likely refer to sea-monsters, whom God subdued while creating the world. Though this is not mentioned in Genesis, fragments of a creation story known from Ugarit, where God subdues the sea, are found throughout the Bible and in rabbinic literature (see 74.12–17; Job 26.12; Isa. 51.9 n.). 4: The finery of God's creation is not handiwork, but *the work of Your fingers.* As noted by Ibn Ezra and Radak, the sun is lacking; according to some medieval and modern scholars, this is because the psalm was recited at night. 6–9: As in Gen. 1.26–30, humans are very highly regarded (contrast Job 17.17–18 and ch 26). "'Elohim" is properly translated as *divine*; this explains why people are *adorned . . . with glory and majesty,* typically divine qualities. Thus, the tradition that "'elohim" should be rendered here as angels (Septuagint, Targum, Radak) is incorrect, and is the result of the discomfort of depicting humans as too God-like—a discomfort surely not shared by this psalmist.

Ps. 9: As v. 2 suggests (*I will praise You,* LORD, *with all my heart*), this is a psalm of thanksgiving. Various pieces of evidence taken together suggest, however, that Ps. 9 does not stand by itself; rather 9–10 were originally a single psalm. The Septuagint treats them as a single psalm. Ps. 10 is the only psalm between Pss. 3 and 32 lacking a superscription, a sign that it is the second half of Ps. 9. Finally, the beginning and ending of an acrostic is preserved in the combined Pss. 9–10 (the first two letters are found in 9.2, 4, while the last two are found in 10.15, 17; fuller acrostics occur in Pss. 25; 34; 37; 111; 112; 119; 145; and Lam. chs 1–4). **1:** This superscription is especially difficult, and many medievals struggle

used for the deities Baal and El; it was taken over by Israel, and used of God.

Ps. 8: Five consecutive individual petitions (Pss. 3–7) are followed by a hymn, a psalm singing God's praises. This psalm is pure praise, without any request, and like other hymns from the Bible and the ancient Near East expresses the religious moment when the individual stands before the deity and appreciates the greatness and power of the divine. Like Pss. 19 and 104, its hymnic focus is on creation, a motif that shows God's power over the entire world. This psalm is tightly structured, framed by the inclusio (vv. 2, 10): "O LORD, our Lord, How majestic is Your name throughout the earth."

3   I will rejoice and exult in You,
         singing a hymn to Your name, O Most High.

4   When my enemies retreat,
         they stumble to their doom at Your presence.

5   For You uphold my right and claim,
         enthroned as righteous judge.

6   You blast the nations;
         You destroy the wicked;
         You blot out their name forever.

7   ᵃ⁻The enemy is no more—
         ruins everlasting;
         You have torn down their cities;
         their very names are lost.⁻ᵃ

8   But the LORD abides forever;
         He has set up His throne for judgment;

9   it is He who judges the world with
             righteousness,
         rules the peoples with equity.

10   The LORD is a haven for the oppressed,
         a haven in times of trouble.

11   Those who know Your name trust You,
         for You do not abandon those who turn to You,
             O LORD.

12   Sing a hymn to the LORD, ᵇ⁻who reigns in Zion;⁻ᵇ
         declare His deeds among the peoples.

13   ᶜ⁻For He does not ignore the cry of the afflicted;
         He who requites bloodshed is mindful of
             them.⁻ᶜ

14   Have mercy on me, O LORD;
         see my affliction at the hands of my foes,
         You who lift me from the gates of death,

15   so that in the gates of ᵈ⁻Fair Zion⁻ᵈ
         I might tell all Your praise,
         I might exult in Your deliverance.

16   The nations sink in the pit they have made;
         their own foot is caught in the net they have
             hidden.

17   The LORD has made Himself known:
         He works judgment;
         the wicked man is snared by his own devices.
         *Higgaion.*ᵉ   *Selah.*

18   Let the wicked beᶠ in Sheol,
         all the nations who ignore God!

to understand the possible historical context of "over the death of
the son," if that is the correct translation (see translators' note).
2–3: Each of the four lines opens
with "alef," the first letter of the
Heb alphabet, anchoring the
acrostic. **3:** On *Most High,* see 7.8.
4–7: The finality of the vanquishing of the enemy *(forever, no more,
everlasting, are lost)* is hyperbolic,
since the enemies reappear in vv.
20–21. **5:** The main image is God
enthroned as king; like the ancient
Israelite king, He is judge and
warrior, but He carries out these
roles with greater power and
equity than human monarchs.
8–9: Parts of these vv., with slight
variants, are found elsewhere (v. 8:
Pss. 29.10; 102.13; Lam. 5.19; v. 9:
Pss. 96.13; 98.9); such repetitions
offer some hints about the composition of the psalms, as
authors reused traditional phrases.
8: *Abides* is better rendered "is
enthroned," continuing the
main theme of God's kingship.
10–13: As in many other places in
the Bible, Psalms shows great concern for *the oppressed, afflicted,* and
poor. **12–15:** The call to others to
praise God and the explicit mention of *the gates of Fair Zion* suggest
that psalms such as this were recited publicly, though not always
at the Temple. **12:** God reigns in
Zion, enthroned in the Temple (see
Exod. 25.21–22). **14:** Images such
as *lift me from the gates of death* or
"You brought me up from Sheol"
(30.4) are always metaphorical in
the Bible, which by and large lacks
a concept of personal resurrection;
similar phrases are used in Akkadian literature to express salvation
from severe illness or danger.
16: See 7.15–17. **17:** *Higgaion* is
probably a musical notation, related to the Heb root "h-g-h"
meaning to utter (quietly) or recite.
18: A polite way of saying
"may *the wicked* die" (see 6.6 n.).
19–21: Beginning with an acknowledgment that God is not *always* or immediately fair in doling
out retribution, the psalmist calls
upon God to *rise,* namely to immediately show Himself as a warrior
(see 7.7 n. and Ps. 13). The psalm-

---

a-a Meaning of Heb. uncertain.   *b-b Or "O You who dwell in Zion."*
c-c Order of Hebrew clauses inverted for clarity.   *d-d Lit. "the Daughter of Zion."*
e Meaning of Heb. uncertain.   *f Others "return to."*

19 Not always shall the needy be ignored,
    nor the hope of the afflicted forever lost.

20 Rise, O LORD!
    Let not men have power;
    let the nations be judged in Your presence.

21 ᵃStrike fear into them,⁻ᵃ O LORD;
    let the nations know they are only men.
                                            Selah.

10 Why, O LORD, do You stand aloof,
    heedless in times of trouble?

2 The wicked in his arrogance hounds the lowly—
    ᵇ⁻may they be caught in the schemes they
        devise!⁻ᵇ

3 ᵃ⁻The wicked crows about his unbridled lusts;
    the grasping man reviles and scorns the LORD.

4 The wicked, arrogant as he is,
    in all his scheming [thinks],⁻ᵃ
    "He does not call to account;
    ᶜGod does not care."⁻ᶜ

5 His ways prosper at all times;
    Your judgments are far beyond him;
    he snorts at all his foes.

6 He thinks, "I shall not be shaken,
    through all time never be in trouble."

7 His mouth is full of oaths, deceit, and fraud;
    mischief and evil are under his tongue.

8 He lurks in outlying places;
    from a covert he slays the innocent;
    his eyes spy out the hapless.

9 He waits in a covert like a lion in his lair;
    waits to seize the lowly;
    he seizes the lowly as he pulls his net shut;

10 he stoops, he crouches,
    ᵃ⁻and the hapless fall prey to his might.⁻ᵃ

11 He thinks, "God is not mindful,
    He hides His face, He never looks."

12 Rise, O LORD!
    ᵈ⁻Strike at him,⁻ᵈ O God!
    Do not forget the lowly.

13 Why should the wicked man scorn God,
    thinking You do not call to account?

14 You do look!
    You take note of mischief and vexation!
    ᵃ⁻To requite is in Your power.⁻ᵃ

ist's claim that God should do this for His own sake, for the sake of His reputation (rather than for the psalmist or for Israel), is a major theme of Ezekiel (e.g., 5.13; 20.9). **20:** The conception of humanity here is in stark contrast to the previous psalm (see vv. 6–9), a striking reminder of the number of different religious moods encompassed in the Psalter.

Ps. 10: A continuation of the previous psalm (see Ps. 9 n.). The calls to God to act (vv. 1, 12, 15) continue 9.20–21. In fact, both 9.20 and 10.12 begin *Rise, O LORD!*, further suggesting the unity of these two psalms. **1:** The psalmist continues, wanting to know why God hides His face (see v. 11 and 6.4–5 n.). **2:** Continuing a previous theme, the persecution of *the lowly* (see also vv. 9, 10, 14, 18). **3–5:** These vv. are unusually obscure. The acrostic of Pss. 9–10 is not apparent here, suggesting that the vv. are corrupt. **4:** The translation of Heb "There is no God" as *God does not care* is based on the assumption that atheism did not exist in antiquity (see also 14.1). People could, however, believe in a deity who created the world, but then absented himself from running it. **7:** Here and elsewhere in Psalms there is tremendous concern for what is in the mouth of the wicked person. Some modern scholars therefore believe that the evildoers of the Psalms are evil magicians, casting spells upon the hapless. **8–9:** The emphasis is on *covert* places; the wicked are not seen in their activities and cannot be punished by human courts, so the psalmist needs to call on God (Radak to v. 1). **11–12:** The Heb root "sh-k-ḥ" joins these two vv. together: the wicked believes that God has forgotten (translated *God is not mindful*), but the psalmist tells God *Do not forget the lowly*.

a-a *Meaning of Heb. uncertain.*
b-b *Or "they (i.e., the lowly) are caught by the schemes they devised."*
c-c *Lit. "There is no God."*   d-d *Lit. "Lift Your hand."*

To You the hapless can entrust himself;
    You have ever been the orphan's help.

15 O break the power of the wicked and evil man,
    so that when You ª⁻look for⁻ª his wickedness
    You will find it no more.

16 The LORD is king for ever and ever;
    the nations will perish from His land.

17 You will listen to the entreaty of the lowly,
    O LORD,
    You will make their hearts firm;
    You will incline Your ear

18 to champion the orphan and the
    downtrodden,
    ᵇ⁻that men who are of the earth tyrannize no
    more.⁻ᵇ

11 For the leader. Of David.

In the LORD I take refuge;
    how can you say to me,
    "Take to ᶜ⁻the hills like a bird!⁻ᶜ

2 For see, the wicked bend the bow,
    they set their arrow on the string
    to shoot from the shadows at the upright.

3 ᵈ⁻When the foundations are destroyed,
    what can the righteous man do?"⁻ᵈ

4 The LORD is in His holy palace;
    the LORD—His throne is in heaven;
    His eyes behold, His gaze searches mankind.

5 The LORD seeks out the righteous man,
    but loathes the wicked one who loves
    injustice.

6 He will rain down upon the wicked blazing coals
    and sulfur;
    a scorching wind shall be ᵉ⁻their lot.⁻ᵉ

7 For the LORD is righteous;
    He loves righteous deeds;
    the upright shall behold His face.

16: The image of God as king (and thus judge and warrior) that stands behind these two psalms is made explicit here. *The LORD is king for ever and ever* recalls the earlier (9.6), "You blot out their name forever." **17:** The Heb ends with a past tense, "you have heeded," expressing a pattern of confidence seen at the conclusion of many psalms (see 3.6–7 n.); the translation *You will listen,* which sees the tense as less significant, follows Radak.

Ps. 11: Though this psalm contains standard motifs of the Psalter, it is odd structurally. It invokes divine punishment (vv. 4–7), but God is referred to in the third person, not the second person that typifies other petitions. Perhaps the psalmist is speaking from the Temple to his friends, rejecting their advice that he flee from the persecution of the evildoers (see comments below). **1–3:** Though *taking refuge* in God is frequently used metaphorically in the Psalms, it is literal in 61.5, "O that I might dwell in Your tent forever, take refuge under Your protecting wings," and perhaps here. The psalmist is thus seeking refuge at the Temple (see 1 Kings 1.50 n.) and rejecting his friends' advice. **4–5:** Many medieval and modern commentators understand *Holy palace* and *heaven* as synonymous. More likely, the point of the psalmist is that (paradoxically) God is located both in the Jerusalem Temple (*His holy palace*), where He can offer protection, and *in heaven,* from where *His eyes behold* and *seek out* and punish evildoers. **6:** These are supernatural punishments, like that of Sodom (Gen. 19.24). **7:** *The LORD is righteous* in the sense of being fair in retribution: this is emphasized through the word-repetition *For the LORD is righteous; He loves righteous deeds. Behold His face:* This may refer to being in God's presence or to seeing a manifestation of God at the Temple, yet another hint that this psalmist is praying at the Temple, and wants to remain there. Other biblical texts suggest that the worshipper

---

a-a A play on darash, which in vv. 4 and 13 means "to call to account."

b-b Meaning of Heb. uncertain.

c-c Meaning of Heb. uncertain; lit. "your hill, bird!"

d-d Or "For the foundations are destroyed; what has the Righteous One done?" Or "If the foundations are destroyed, what has the righteous man accomplished?"

e-e Lit. "the portion of their cup."

12
For the leader; on the *sheminith*. A psalm of David.

2 Help, O Lord!
For the faithful are no more;
   the loyal have vanished from among men.

3 Men speak lies to one another;
   their speech is smooth;
   they talk with duplicity.

4 May the Lord cut off all flattering lips,
   every tongue that speaks arrogance.

5 They say, "By our tongues we shall prevail;
   with lips such as ours, who can be our master?"

6 "Because of the groans of the plundered poor and
   needy,
   I will now act," says the Lord.
   a-"I will give help," He affirms to him.-a

7 The words of the Lord are pure words,
   silver purged in an earthen crucible,
   refined sevenfold.

8 You, O Lord, will keep them,
   guarding each a-from this age-a evermore.

9 On every side the wicked roam
   a-when baseness is exalted among men.-a

13
For the leader. A psalm of David.

2 How long, O Lord; will You ignore me forever?
How long will You hide Your face from me?

3 How long will I have cares on my mind,
   grief in my heart all day?
How long will my enemy have the upper hand?

4 Look at me, answer me, O Lord, my God!
Restore the luster to my eyes,
   lest I sleep the sleep of death;

5 lest my enemy say, "I have overcome him,"
   my foes exult when I totter.

a-a Meaning of Heb. uncertain.

could *behold* the *face* of God at a temple (see Exod. 33.11; but contrast 33.17–23).

Ps. 12: This psalm has an unusual structure: after the superscription (v. 1) it contains a standard petition (vv. 2–5), but this is followed by the divine response (v. 6) and the psalmist's answer (vv. 7–9). It is difficult to understand how this

psalm was used liturgically—perhaps since the divine response is positive, a supplicant might recite it as a way of "assuring" a positive hearing. The main theme has to do with words—the false and arrogant words of the wicked against the righteous, and God's pure words. **2:** *Faithful* translates "ḥasid"; see 4.4 n. This v. compactly contains the three crucial

parts of the petition: the invocation (*O Lord*), the plea in the imperative (*Help*), and the motivation (*for the faithful . . .*). **3–5:** The emphasis here is only on the danger of the word, which may reflect slander, a false oath, or magic (see 10.7 n.); no physical harm is described. **6:** The divine speech reflects care for the underclasses (see 9.10–13 n.). **7:** *Sevenfold* is a typologically large number (see Ibn Ezra and Radak). **8–9:** Unfortunately, the psalm's conclusion is likely corrupt and defies precise translation, though the general sense of God preserving the faithful from the evildoers is clear.

Ps. 13: In this poignant individual petition, the petitioner feels abandoned, as in the more famous 22.2: "My God, my God, why have You abandoned me?" The typical elements for the petition are all found: the invocation, *O Lord* (v. 2), the petition, which here takes up most of the psalm (vv. 2–4a), and a short, double motivation, *lest I sleep the sleep of death; lest my enemy . . .* (vv. 4b–5). A typical expression of divine confidence concludes the psalm (v. 6). **2–3:** The four-fold repetition of *How long* forms a refrain, emphasizing the psalmist's long-standing sense of abandonment. The paradoxical *How long . . . will You ignore* (lit. "forget") *me forever?* heightens the petitioner's pain. On God hiding His face, see 6.4–5 n. In Torah and prophetic contexts, God's hidden face is typically a result of punishment; in many psalms, including this one, the psalmist suggests that this hiddenness is instead the result of divine neglect. **4:** If God *looks,* he is no longer hiding his face (see Ibn Ezra and Radak). *Restore the luster to my eyes* refers to strength (see 1 Sam. 14.27). *The sleep of death* represents the ultimate and permanent separation between God and humans, for in death one cannot praise God (Ps. 6.6). **5:** This v. contains a classic illustration of the notion that in biblical poetry the second half heightens the first (see "Biblical Poetry," pp. 2097–2104), as we

6 But I trust in Your faithfulness,
  my heart will exult in Your deliverance.
I will sing to the LORD,
  for He has been good to me.

14 ᵃFor the leader. Of David.

The benighted man thinks,
  ᵇ⁻"God does not care."⁻ᵇ
Man's deeds are corrupt and loathsome;
  no one does good.
2 The LORD looks down from heaven on mankind
  to find a man of understanding,
  a man mindful of God.
3 All have turned bad,
  altogether foul;
  there is none who does good,
  not even one.
4 Are they so witless, all those evildoers,
  who devour my people as they devour food,
  and do not invoke the LORD?
5 There they will be seized with fright,
  for God is present in the circle of the righteous.
6 You may set at naught the counsel of the lowly,
  but the LORD is his refuge.

7 O that the deliverance of Israel might come from
    Zion!
When the LORD restores the fortunes of His
    people,
  Jacob will exult, Israel will rejoice.

a Cf. Ps. 53.
b-b Lit. "There is no God"; cf. Ps. 10.4.

move from *enemy* (singular) to *foes* (plural). **6:** As in other petitions, the tenses are confusing (see 3.8–9 n.; 6.9–11), and a more literal rendering would be: "But I trust in your faithfulness ('ḥesed,' see 5.8 n.), may my heart exult in Your deliverance. May I sing to the LORD because He has been good to me."

Ps. 14: This is an atypical psalm—it is not addressed to God, instead referring to Him in the third person; for this reason, some modern scholars view it as a psalm of instruction. Ps. 53, from the Elohistic Psalter (see introduction, p. 1281) is a variant of this psalm; the variations both small (e.g., 14.3 *All have turned bad* ["hkl sr"]; 53.4 "Everyone is dross" ["klw sg"]) and large (e.g., 14.5b–6: *for God is present in the circle of the righteous. You may set at naught the counsel of the lowly, but the LORD is his refuge;* 53.6 "There they will be seized with fright—never was there such a fright—for God has scattered the bones of your besiegers; you have put them to shame, for God has rejected them") offer important data about the transmission of psalms

in antiquity. The medievals viewed both as Davidic compositions. Rashi, for example, viewed Ps. 14 as David's words concerning the destruction of the First Temple (586 BCE), while Ps. 53, which is so similar, is about the destruction of the Second Temple (70 CE). Radak much more prosaically suggests in his intro. to Ps. 53: "and now he [David] repeated himself here in slightly different words." **1:** Heb "naval," *benighted*, is a very strong term that can carry moral overtones; see esp. 2 Sam. 13.13, in relation to Amnon's rape of his half-sister Tamar. On *God does not care*, see 10.4. The claim of this *benighted* individual would invalidate two of the basic assumptions of Psalms: the ability of God to hear prayers, and the ability of God to punish the human wrongs that various psalmists lament. **2:** On God in *heaven*, see 2.6 n. Being *mindful of God* ("doresh 'et 'elohim") may also be understood as praying to God (see esp. Ps. 77.3); note the prayer language in v. 4, *invoke the LORD.* **6:** The wicked are spoken to in the second person (*You*), rather than in the third person as earlier in the psalm (e.g., v. 5 *they*). Such changes in person are frequent in biblical poetry (e.g., Isa. 1.2–9). **7:** Many modern scholars see this final v. as secondary, since it does not fit the theme or tone of the psalm. (In antiquity, it was easiest to make additions at the end of a composition.) The phrase *restores the fortunes* is ambiguous in the Bible; it may refer to personal restoration (see esp. Job 42.10), or more specifically to the return from the Babylonian exile (see esp. Ps. 126.4). The latter sense explains why many medievals (e.g., Rashi, Radak) view the psalm as a Davidic prophecy concerning the Babylonian exile. Many other individual petitions conclude with general verses about the community (e.g., 3.9).

15

A psalm of David.

LORD, who may sojourn in Your tent,
  who may dwell on Your holy mountain?

2 He who lives without blame,
  who does what is right,
  and in his heart acknowledges the truth;

3 *a*-whose tongue is not given to evil;-*a*
  who has never done harm to his fellow,
  or borne reproach for [his acts toward] his
    neighbor;

4 for whom a contemptible man is abhorrent,
  but who honors those who fear the LORD;
  who stands by his oath even to his hurt;

5 who has never lent money at interest,
  or accepted a bribe against the innocent.
The man who acts thus shall never be shaken.

16

A *michtam*[b] of David.

Protect me, O God, for I seek refuge in You.

2 I say to the LORD,
  "You are my Lord, *c*-my benefactor;
  there is none above You."-*c*

3 *d*-As to the holy and mighty ones that are in the
    land,
  my whole desire concerning them is that

4 those who espouse another [god]
  may have many sorrows!-*d*
I will have no part of their bloody libations;
  their names will not pass my lips.

5 The LORD is my allotted share and portion;[e]
  You control my fate.

a-a *Meaning of Heb. uncertain; or "who has no slander upon his tongue."*
b *Meaning of Heb. uncertain.*   c-c *Others "I have no good but in You."*
d-d *Meaning of Heb. uncertain; "holy and mighty ones" taken as epithets for divine beings; cf. qedoshim in Ps. 89.6, 8, and 'addirim in 1 Sam. 4.8.*
e *Lit. "cup."*

Ps. 15: Perhaps like the previous psalm, this may be considered a psalm of instruction, teaching the listener to become an individual who *shall never be shaken* (v. 5). In Jewish ritual, the psalm is often used as a type of eulogy, expressing the ideal human qualities that assure the deceased a place in the afterlife (see Radak to v. 5: "Even at his death he *shall never be shaken,* since his soul will rest in the place of glory"); this is, however, a post-biblical notion. Most modern scholars take v. 1 literally, and suggest that the psalm functioned as an entrance liturgy for the Temple, where *who may sojourn in Your tent, who may dwell on Your holy mountain?* functions as the beginning of a dialogue between the priest and the worshipper who wishes to enter the Temple precincts. Such liturgies are suggested by Egyptian and Mesopotamian texts, and may also stand behind Ps. 24.3–4: "Who may ascend the mountain of the LORD? Who may stand in His holy place?—He who has clean hands and a pure heart, who has not taken a false oath by My life or sworn deceitfully." The psalm, like much prophetic literature, emphasizes general moral, rather than cultic, characteristics. As in the Decalogue and later medieval lists of precepts, these are listed in groupings of positive and negative qualities. The qualities listed in this psalm are included among epitomes of the commandments (e.g., Isaiah 33.14–16; Micah 6.8) listed in *b. Makkot* 24a. **1:** *Tent* may refer to a temple or sanctuary (see 1 Kings 2.28). **2:** The list begins with very general positive qualities *(He who lives without blame, who does what is right),* followed by a more specific positive quality *(and in his heart acknowledges the truth),* which is to be connected to the following v. **3–4:** Three qualities, all expressed as negatives, balanced by three positive qualities. **5:** Two negative qualities conclude the list. To *be shaken* or to totter is the opposite of the ideal of stability. It is uncertain how this conclusion connects to the opening "who may sojourn in Your tent, who may dwell on Your holy mountain?"

Ps. 16: The structure of this psalm is anomalous in that while it opens as a typical personal petition, the rest of the psalm expresses the psalmist's confidence in God; perhaps this serves as an extended motivation for why his petition should be heard. **1:** The obscure term *michtam* is found only here and in a cluster of Psalms (56–60); the Septuagint translates it as "a stele or pillar inscription." **2:** Alternately, this may be understood as the individual praying citing his earlier prayer, "I have said *to the* LORD . . ." **3–4:** These are among the most obscure verses in the Psalter. **5–6:** With the exception of *portion* (lit. "cup"), it is striking

6 Delightful country has fallen to my lot;
   lovely indeed is my estate.
7 I bless the LORD who has guided me;
   my conscience[a] admonishes me at night.
8 I am ever mindful of the LORD's presence;
   He is at my right hand; I shall never be shaken.
9 So my heart rejoices,
   my whole being exults,
   and my body rests secure.
10 For You will not abandon me to Sheol,
   or let Your faithful one see the Pit.
11 You will teach me the path of life.
   In Your presence is perfect joy;
   delights are ever in Your right hand.

17 A prayer of David.

Hear, O LORD, what is just;
   heed my cry, give ear to my prayer,
   uttered without guile.
2 My vindication will come from You;
   Your eyes will behold what is right.
3 You have visited me at night, probed my mind,
   You have tested me and found nothing amiss;
   [b-]I determined that my mouth should not
   transgress.
4 As for man's dealings,
   in accord with the command of Your lips,[-b]
   I have kept in view the fate[c] of the lawless.
5 My feet have held to Your paths;
   my legs have not given way.

6 I call on You;
   You will answer me, God;
   turn Your ear to me,
   hear what I say.
7 Display Your faithfulness in wondrous deeds,
   You who deliver with Your right hand
   those who seek refuge from assailants.
8 Guard me like the apple of Your eye;
   hide me in the shadow of Your wings

a Lit. "kidneys."   b-b Meaning of Heb. uncertain.   c Cf. Prov. 1.19; lit. "paths."

being, "kevodi," might also be a play on "kevedi," my liver); this is matched (v. 11) by God's face (translated here as _presence_) and _right hand._ **8:** The phrase _I am ever mindful of the LORD's presence_ was frequently used for meditation within the kabbalistic tradition; as a result, it is often inscribed on the Ark or at the front of the synagogue. **10:** On _Sheol,_ see 6.6 n.; on _faithful_ ("ḥasid"), see 4.4 n. **11:** The tense of the first word allows for both the translation _You will teach me,_ followed here (so Rashi), as well as "May you teach me," as a prayer or request (so Radak). The right hand is more powerful, as in 118.16, "The right hand of the LORD is exalted! The right hand of the LORD is triumphant!" As elsewhere in the Bible (see esp. Exod. 24.10–11), God is often depicted anthropomorphically.

Ps. 17: This individual petition is similar to Ps. 7, which is also characterized by a protestation of innocence (see esp. 7.4–6). The word "tzedek," _just,_ is used in the first and last v., framing the psalm, and offering a summary of sorts: a just God may not let the just suffer. **1:** _Prayer_ ("tefilah") is the most general, all-encompassing word for a prayer (see 72.20), though etymologically it refers to an intercessory prayer. The poetry of the verse is very striking: after demanding three times, through typical biblical poetic diction, that God hear, the pattern is broken by introducing the next sub-theme of the petitioner's innocence: _uttered without guile._ Biblical poetry thus combines patterns and broken patterns. **2–5:** The protestation of innocence. **2:** The psalmist's acknowledgment of God's role as judge is a subtle demand that he be adjudicated fairly. **6–12:** The second section of the psalm is introduced by another call for divine justice; this section emphasizes the enemies and their evil activities. **7:** On God's faithfulness ("ḥesed"), see 5.8 n. **8:** _The apple of Your eye_ is the pupil. The second half of the v. uses a stereotypical image of God as a protective bird (36.8; 57.2;

and unusual that all the nouns used of God refer to the land and land allocation (_allotted share and portion, Delightful country, my estate_). **7–11:** The conclusion of the

psalm is unified through references to body parts. The psalmist speaks of his kidneys (the seat of his _conscience_), right hand, heart, and body (lit. "flesh"; _my whole_

9 from the wicked who despoil me,
 ᵃmy mortal enemies whoˑᵃ encircle me.

10 ᵇˑTheir hearts are closed to pity;ᵇ
 they mouth arrogance;

11 now they hem in our feet on every side;
 they set their eyes roaming over the land.

12 He is like a lion eager for prey,
 a king of beasts lying in wait.

13 Rise, O Lᴏʀᴅ! Go forth to meet him.
 Bring him down;
 rescue me from the wicked with Your sword,

14 ᵇˑfrom men, O Lᴏʀᴅ, with Your hand,
 from men whose share in life is fleeting.
 But as to Your treasured ones,
 fill their bellies.ˑᵇ
 Their sons too shall be satisfied,
 and have something to leave over for their
 young.

15 Then I, justified, will behold Your face;
 awake, I am filled with the vision of You.

18 ᶜFor the leader. Of David, the servant of the Lᴏʀᴅ,
who addressed the words of this song to the Lᴏʀᴅ
after the Lᴏʀᴅ had saved him from the hands of all his enemies and from the clutches of Saul.

2 He said:
 ᵈˑI adore you, O Lᴏʀᴅ, my strength,ˑᵈ

a-a *Or "from my enemies who avidly."*   b-b *Meaning of Heb. uncertain.*
c *This poem occurs again at 2 Sam. 22, with a number of variations, some of which are
cited in the following notes.*   d-d *Not in 2 Sam. 22.2.*

63.8). **11:** The psalmist suddenly speaks in the plural (*our feet);* this and similar cases have led some scholars to suggest that the "I" of the individual petitions may be the king or some other significant individual who speaks on behalf of the entire community. **12:** Lions roamed the countryside of ancient Israel, and are mentioned frequently in the Bible. They were symbols of great power; this is why a standard scene of the Assyrian royal reliefs depicts the king killing a lion. Compare David's statement in 1 Sam. 17.34–35. **13–16:** This final section is also introduced by a set of imperatives. **13:** *Rise* is again being used in a

military sense (see Ibn Ezra, "to show your strength," and 7.7 n.), carefully playing against the enemies who are brought *down.* **15:** This v. is better taken as expressing a wish or desire ("may I behold . . . ; may I be filled . . ."), perhaps a wish to see God at the Temple (see 11.7 n.), or even expressing a type of mystical yearning to see God, as in the vision in Ezek. ch 1. Many medieval interpreters (e.g., Rashi, Radak) understand this as a reference to seeing God in heaven after death, but as noted (see 6.6 n.), the conception of a heavenly afterworld is absent from the Bible.

Ps. 18: Linguistic and stylistic evidence suggest that this may be one of the oldest psalms in the Psalter, dating most likely from the tenth century ʙᴄᴇ. It is also one of the longest psalms, and its flow is not entirely clear. It is nearly identical to 2 Sam. ch 22, which, based on linguistic evidence, is older than the psalm, though it is unclear if Ps. 18 was copied from 2 Sam. 22, or if they were both copied from a common source. As in Ps. 14, which is parallel to Ps. 53, the many types of differences are illustrative of the process of textual transmission. A major difference is the extra v. found in the psalm but not in Samuel (v. 2). Sometimes synonyms or near synonyms are used (e.g., Ps. 18.5 *ropes of Death;* 2 Sam. 22.5, "breakers of Death"); a singular in place of a plural (e.g., *lightning* in v. 15 is singular in 2 Sam. 22 ["brk"] and plural in Ps. 18 ["brkym"]); word order may vary (e.g., Ps. 18.50 *among the nations,* Lᴏʀᴅ; 2 Sam. 22.50, "Lᴏʀᴅ, among the nations"); and graphically similar letters are confused (e.g., Ps. 18.11 "vydᵓ," *gliding,* vs. 2 Sam. 22.11 "vyrᵓ," "He was seen"). Some medievals understood the variants in Ps. 18 as reflecting David's divinely inspired reworking of his earlier composition as he revised it for inclusion in the Psalter (see esp. Abravanel to 2 Sam. ch 22), while others paid less attention to the variants, believing that they reflect the same meaning (Radak at Ps. 18.1). **1:** David's troubles are described in 1 Sam. ch 18–2 Sam. ch 20. As elsewhere in the Psalter, this superscription is secondary, reflecting an attempt to understand the psalms biographically (see 3.1 n.); the superscription here, however, is unique in its reference to a broad set of events, rather than to a particular event—this long and general psalm has been assigned to a long period of general troubles. *The servant of the Lᴏʀᴅ* is lacking in the parallel in Samuel; for similar phrases concerning David, see, e.g., 2 Sam. 7.8; 1 Kings 8.66; Jer. 33.26; Pss. 4; 21; 89. **2:** Lacking in 2 Sam. 22.

3　　O Lᴏʀᴅ, my crag, my fortress, my rescuer,
　　　　my God, my rock in whom I seek refuge,
　　　　my shield, my ᵃ‑mighty champion,‑ᵃ my haven.
4　　　ᵇ‑All praise! I called on the Lᴏʀᴅ‑ᵇ
　　　　and was delivered from my enemies.
5　　Ropesᶜ of Death encompassed me;
　　　　torrents of Belialᵈ terrified me;
6　　　ropes of Sheol encircled me;
　　　　snares of Death confronted me.
7　　In my distress I called on the Lᴏʀᴅ,
　　　　cried out to my God;
　　　　in His temple He heard my voice;
　　　　my cry to Him reached His ears.
8　　Then the earth rocked and quaked;
　　　　the foundations of the mountains shook,
　　　　rocked by His indignation;
9　　　smoke went up from His nostrils,
　　　　from His mouth came devouring fire;
　　　　live coals blazed forth from Him.
10　　He bent the sky and came down,
　　　　thick cloud beneath His feet.
11　　He mounted a cherub and flew,
　　　　gliding on the wings of the wind.
12　　He made darkness His screen;
　　　　dark thunderheads, dense clouds of the sky
　　　　were His pavilion round about Him.
13　　Out of the brilliance before Him,
　　　　hail and fiery coals ᵉ‑pierced His clouds.‑ᵉ
14　　Then the Lᴏʀᴅ thundered from heaven,
　　　　the Most High gave forth His voice—
　　　　ᶠ‑hail and fiery coals.‑ᶠ
15　　He let fly His shafts and scattered them;
　　　　He discharged lightning and routed them.
16　　The ocean bed was exposed;
　　　　the foundations of the world were laid bare
　　　　by Your mighty roaring, O Lᴏʀᴅ,
　　　　at the blast of the breath of Your nostrils.
17　　He reached down from on high, He took me;
　　　　He drew me out of the mighty waters;
18　　He saved me from my fierce enemy,
　　　　from foes too strong for me.
19　　They confronted me on the day of my calamity,
　　　　but the Lᴏʀᴅ was my support.

3: Slightly shorter than the parallel in Samuel, a list of divine attributes connected to God's strength, highlighting the theme of the psalm, God the warrior. The Samuel parallel is the longest such list of divine qualities in the Bible. **5–7:** Highly mythological underworld imagery is used to express the psalmist's former dire straits. Given that God descends (v. 10), the psalmist's *cry* is likely ascending to God's heavenly *temple* (see Isa. 6.1–4). **8–16:** A description of a divine theophany. These descriptions often emphasize God as a thunderstorm deity, and likely borrowed similar, earlier descriptions of the Canaanite deity, Baal. **11:** *A cherub* is a winged composite figure, combining various human and animal elements. **15:** *His shafts* represent both arrows thrust against the enemies, as well as *lightning* mentioned later in the v. **16:** The description of the theophany in Hab. ch 3 likewise emphasizes the fear of the primordial waters. **17–20:** A single deity saves a single individual against many enemies because of that person's righteousness. **18:** Mighty waters are associated with chaos that was vanquished by God in some biblical creation stories (see 8.3 n.).

a-a Lit. "horn of rescue."　　b-b Construction of Heb. uncertain.
c 2 Sam. 22.5, "breakers."
d I.e., the netherworld, like "Death" and "Sheol."
e-e 2 Sam. 22.13, "blazed."　　f-f Not in 2 Sam. 22.14.

20 He brought me out to freedom;
    He rescued me because He was pleased
      with me.

21 The Lord rewarded me according to my merit;
    He requited the cleanness of my hands;
22   for I have kept to the ways of the Lord,
      and have not been guilty before my God;
23   for I am mindful of all His rules;
    I have not disregarded His laws.
24 I have been blameless toward Him,
    and have guarded myself against sinning;
25   and the Lord has requited me according to my
      merit,
    the cleanness of my hands in His sight.

26 With the loyal, You deal loyally;
    with the blameless man, blamelessly.
27 With the pure, You act purely,
    and with the perverse, You are wily.
28 It is You who deliver lowly folk,
    but haughty eyes You humble.
29 It is You who light my lamp;
    the Lord, my God, lights up my darkness.
30 With You, I can rush a barrier;[a]
    with my God I can scale a wall;
31   the way of God is perfect;
    the word of the Lord is pure;
    He is a shield to all who seek refuge in Him.
32 Truly, who is a god except the Lord,
    who is a rock but our God?—
33   the God who girded me with might,
    who made my way perfect;
34   who made my legs like a deer's,
    and let me stand firm on the[b] heights;
35   who trained my hands for battle;
    my arms can bend a bow of bronze.
36 You have given me the shield of Your protection;
    Your right hand has sustained me,
    Your care[c] has made me great.
37 You have let me stride on freely;
    my feet have not slipped.
38 I pursued my enemies and overtook them;
    I did not turn back till I destroyed them.

21–25: Vv. 21 and 25 are almost identical, framing the intervening protestation of innocence. **26–31:** These vv. show particular affinity to wisdom texts; see esp. v. 31 and Prov. 30.5, "Every word of God is pure, / A shield to those who take refuge in Him." **26–27:** God works in a fair, measure-for-measure manner. **32:** Vv. declaiming the absolute exclusivity of God are typically found in later biblical literature (cf. Exod. 15.11 n. and Isa. 44.6). **33–49:** It is God who helps the psalmist totally and completely annihilate the enemy. **34:** An image of swiftness and stability.

a *Cf. note to 2 Sam. 22.30; or "troop."*
b *Taking* bamothai *as a poetic form of* bamoth; *cf. Hab. 3.19; others "my."*
c *Meaning of Heb. uncertain; others "condescension."*

39 I struck them down,
   and they could rise no more;
   they lay fallen at my feet.

40 You have girded me with strength for battle,
   brought my adversaries low before me,

41 made my enemies turn tail before me;
   I wiped out my foes.

42 They cried out, but there was none to deliver;
   [cried] to the Lord, but He did not answer
   them.

43 I ground them fine as windswept dust;
   I trod them flat as dirt of the streets.

44 You have rescued me from the strife of people;
   You have set me at the head of nations;
   peoples I knew not must serve me.

45 At the mere report of me they are submissive;
   foreign peoples cower before me;

46 foreign peoples lose courage,
   a-and come trembling out of their strongholds.-a

47 The Lord lives! Blessed is my rock!
   Exalted be God, my deliverer,

48 the God who has vindicated me
   and made peoples subject to me,

49 who rescued me from my enemies,
   who raised me clear of my adversaries,
   saved me from lawless men.

50 For this I sing Your praise among the nations,
      Lord,
   and hymn Your name:

51 b-He accords great victories-b to His king,
   keeps faith with His anointed,
   with David and his offspring forever.

19 For the leader. A psalm of David.

2 The heavens declare the glory of God,
   the sky proclaims His handiwork.

3 Day to day makes utterance,
   night to night speaks out.

a-a *Meaning of Heb. uncertain.*   b-b *2 Sam. 22.51, "Tower of victory."*

47: *The Lord lives!* A similar statement about the Canaanite deity Baal is found in the Ugaritic epics. When used in biblical literature, "living" with respect to God often carries the connotation of power. **40:** Bringing *adversaries* low may be a literal reference to stepping on the necks of enemies (see v. 39, "they lay fallen at [lit. 'under'] my feet"). **49:** As the psalm moves to a close, it returns to the word *rescue*, found also in v. 3. **50:** *Singing God's praise* is a

major theme of the Psalter, appearing in over sixty vv. **51:** *Anointed*, Heb "mashiaḥ"; see 2.2 n. The final v. suggests that this psalm was recited by or on behalf of a Davidic king.

Ps. 19: This psalm is recited as part of the preliminary morning service on Saturday and at festivals. It divides neatly into three sections: Vv. 2–7 are a hymn, focusing on creation, specifically on the sun; vv. 8–11 are a hymn focusing on torah; and vv. 12–15, which are connected to the immediately preceding section (see v. 12, *them*), are a petition to be saved from sin, and for prayers to be heard. Many scholars believe that either two psalms have been combined (vv. 2–7 and 8–15), or that a later psalmist who composed vv. 8–15 incorporated the earlier vv. 2–7, which have a different topic, style, and poetic structure. Vv. 8–15, but not 2–7, show significant connections to wisdom ideas and vocabulary (see below). The difference between vv. 2–7 and 8–15 was realized already by the medieval Jewish interpreters, who suggested various ways that creation, the sun, and torah may be connected. The discovery of ancient Near Eastern texts, where justice is often part of the sun god's realm (so, e.g., Shamash, the Mesopotamian sun god), has offered a new way of understanding the psalm as a unity. Some modern scholars have understood the poem as a whole as focused on God's revelation in heaven and on the earth (Radak is similar), while others have noted that torah is associated with light (e.g., Prov. 6.23), allowing the two sections to function together. **2–7:** The absence of God's personal name ("Yhvh"; Lord in NJPS) here suggests to some that this section may have been adapted from a non-Israelite hymn praising the sun. **2–4:** The cosmos praises God; the creation testifies to God's greatness. It is unclear if the *sound* is metaphorical, or if some Israelites believed in the music of the spheres, an idea later associated

4   There is no utterance,
        there are no words,
        ᵃwhose sound goes unheard.ᐟᵃ
5   Their voiceᵇ carries throughout the earth,
        their words to the end of the world.
    He placed in themᶜ a tent for the sun,
6   who is like a groom coming forth from the
            chamber,
        like a hero, eager to run his course.
7   His rising-place is at one end of heaven,
        and his circuit reaches the other;
        nothing escapes his heat.

8   The teaching of the LORD is perfect,
        renewing life;
        the decrees of the LORD are enduring,
        making the simple wise;
9   The precepts of the LORD are just,
        rejoicing the heart;
        the instruction of the LORD is lucid,
        making the eyes light up.
10 The fear of the LORD is pure,
        abiding forever;
        the judgments of the LORD are true,
        righteous altogether,
11   more desirable than gold,
        than much fine gold;
        sweeter than honey,
        than drippings of the comb.
12 Your servant pays them heed;
        in obeying them there is much reward.
13 Who can be aware of errors?
    Clear me of unperceived guilt,
14   and from ᵈwillful sinsᐟᵈ keep Your servant;
        let them not dominate me;
        then shall I be blameless
        and clear of grave offense.
15 May the words of my mouth
        and the prayer of my heartᵉ
        be acceptable to You,
        O LORD, my rock and my redeemer.

with Pythagoras. An Ugaritic epic speaks of "Speech of tree and whisper of stone, converse of heaven with earth" (*ANET*, p. 136). An alternative rendering of v. 4, "their sound is not heard," means that the celestial bodies "speak" soundlessly; they convey their message simply by their being. **5–7:** The sun was typically associated with a major deity in the ancient Near East. Cylinder seals with winged sundisks have been found in Israel, and 2 Kings 23.11 and other sources offer evidence for solar worship in ancient Israel. **6–7:** The sun, shining and eager, traverses the sky. **8–11:** This section is suffused with wisdom terminology, including *simple, wise, fear of the LORD,* and wisdom or torah being compared to *gold* (of great value, and in this case, also the color of the sun). The highly stylized, repetitive form of vv. 8–10 is very striking, though in Heb, v. 10 is slightly different in structure from the previous vv.; v. 11 concludes this section by breaking the structure altogether. Heb "torah" is here translated as *instruction,* on the assumption that this psalm was written before the Torah was canonized; traditional Jewish interpretation, which assumes that this is a Davidic composition from the period after a Mosaic Torah, understands "torah" as the Torah. **13:** In Heb, *unperceived guilt* ("nistarot") plays with v. 7, "escapes" ("nistar"), lending additional unity to the psalm. (See similarly v. 9, "light up," which as Rashi points out [v. 8], connects back to the sun.) **15:** This v. is reused as part of the conclusion of the "'Amidah," the main daily prayer. In its original context, it is unclear if *the words of my mouth and the prayer of my heart* refer to the immediately preceding vv., asking forgiveness from sins, or if this entire psalm served as an introduction to a larger liturgical complex.

a-a *With Septuagint, Symmachus, and Vulgate; or "their sound is not heard."*
b *Cf. Septuagint, Symmachus, and Vulgate; Arabic* qawwah, *"to shout."*
c *Viz., the heavens.*
d-d *Or "arrogant men"; cf. Ps. 119.51.*
e *For* leb *as a source of speech, see note to Eccl. 5.1.*

20 For the leader. A psalm of David.

2 May the LORD answer you in time of trouble,
the name of Jacob's God keep you safe.

3 May He send you help from the sanctuary,
and sustain you from Zion.

4 May He receive the tokens[a] of all your meal
offerings,
and approve[b] your burnt offerings. *Selah.*

5 May He grant you your desire,
and fulfill your every plan.

6 May we shout for joy in your victory,
arrayed by standards in the name of our God.
May the LORD fulfill your every wish.

7 Now I know that the LORD will give victory to His
anointed,
will answer him from His heavenly sanctuary
with the mighty victories of His right arm.

8 They [call] on chariots, they [call] on horses,
but we call on the name of the LORD our God.

9 They collapse and lie fallen,
but we rally and gather strength.

10 ᶜO LORD, grant victory!
May the King answer us when we call.ᶜ

21 For the leader. A psalm of David.

2 O LORD, the king rejoices in Your strength;
how greatly he exults in Your victory!

3 You have granted him the desire of his heart,
have not denied the request of his lips. *Selah.*

4 You have proffered him blessings of good things,
have set upon his head a crown of fine gold.

5 He asked You for life; You granted it;
a long life, everlasting.

6 Great is his glory through Your victory;
You have endowed him with splendor and
majesty.

7 You have made him blessed forever,
gladdened him with the joy of Your presence.

8 For the king trusts in the LORD;
Through the faithfulness of the Most High
he will not be shaken.

---

a *Reference to azkara, "token portion" of meal offering; Lev. 2.2, 9, 16, etc.*
b *Meaning of Heb. uncertain.*
c-c *Or in the light of v. 7, "O LORD, grant victory to the king; may He answer us when we call."*

Ps. 20: This is a prayer for the king before battle. A very close parallel to this psalm from Papyrus Amherst 63 was published in 1983. That version, however, was written in Aramaic in Demotic script (late Egyptian characters) and opens: "May Horus [an Egyptian deity]/the master answer us in our straits; send your messenger from the temple of Arash" (translation from Ziony Zevit, *The Religions of Ancient Israel: A Synthesis of Parallactic Approaches* [London: Continuum, 2001], p. 669). Initially, it was thought that this Aramaic text was a paganized version of the biblical psalm, but more recently it has been suggested that both the Aramaic Egyptian text and Ps. 20 derive from a common non-Israelite poem, most likely to Baal (see intro. to Ps. 29). Ps. 20 is now recited toward the conclusion of the morning weekday service. **2:** The reference to "His anointed" in v. 7 makes it clear that the *you* is the king. *The name of Jacob's God* is an odd circumlocution of LORD, perhaps used so that both verse-halves would be of approximately the same size. **3:** God is envisioned as enthroned in the *sanctuary* in *Zion.* **4:** This may reflect a ritual of sacrificing before going to battle (1 Sam. 7.9–10). **7:** *Now I know* may reflect a positive answer to a ritual; see Ps 6.9–11 n.; 1 Sam. 30.8; 28.6. **8:** The strength of divine presence over military might is a central biblical theme. **10:** As noted, it is unclear where this v. should be divided. This translation (following the Targum) takes the king to be the divine *King,* God. The Septuagint read it as: "O LORD grant victory to the king; answer us when we call"; this is the origin of the expression, "God save the king!" The psalm begins as it ends, with a request for an *answer.*

Ps. 21: A blessing for the king, who will lead his nation to victory. A companion hymn to Ps. 20 sharing vocabulary and theme (cf. 20.5 and 21.3; 20.7c and 21.9b). Vv. 1–7 rejoice in God's beneficence to the king; vv. 8–13 express trust that God will grant victory. **3:** *Selah,* see

9   Your hand is equal to all Your enemies;
         Your right hand overpowers Your foes.

10   You set them ablaze like a furnace
         [a-]when You show Your presence.[-a]
     The LORD in anger destroys them;
         fire consumes them.

11   You wipe their offspring from the earth,
         their issue from among men.

12   For they schemed against You;
         they laid plans,
         but could not succeed.

13   [b-]For You make them turn back[-b]
         by Your bows aimed at their face.

14   Be exalted, O LORD, through Your strength;
         we will sing and chant the praises of Your
             mighty deeds.

22   For the leader; on [b-]ayyeleth ha-shaḥar.[-b]
     A psalm of David.

2   My God, my God,
         why have You abandoned me;
         why so far from delivering me
         and from my anguished roaring?

3   My God,
         I cry by day—You answer not;
         by night, and have no respite.

4   [c-]But You are the Holy One,
         enthroned,
         the Praise of Israel.[-c]

5   In You our fathers trusted;
         they trusted, and You rescued them.

6   To You they cried out
         and they escaped;
         in You they trusted
         and were not disappointed.

a-a Or "at the time of Your anger."
b-b Meaning of Heb. uncertain.
c-c Or "But You are holy, enthroned upon the praises of Israel."

3.3 n. **5:** A past request for the long life of the king was granted (1 Kings 3.14; Ps. 61.6). **6:** *Glory . . . splendor and majesty,* the nimbus of light surrounding gods and kings (Ps. 8.6). Through the victory that God grants, the king is enhanced. **8:** This abundant royal blessing is here predicated on royal obedience. **10:** For the fiery wrath of God, see Isa. 29.6; 66.15–16. The image of God's blazing fury burning up the enemy is common, and may reflect the reality of war in which cities were set ablaze. **11:** See Ps. 37.38. **12:** The plots against Israel are plots against God; cf. Ps. 83.5–6. **14:** God's strength frames the psalm (see v. 2) and is the source of the king's strength.

Ps. 22: The psalm opens with a plea from a person in dire straits, apparently a serious illness. His prayers having been answered, he brings the offerings he vowed and gives public acclaim to God as he promised. God is praised for His care of all people, and all people, now and in the future, should praise God. The structure of the psalm is complex and not obvious. A refrainlike repetition occurs in vv. 2, 12, and 20, suggesting one way the psalm might be subdivided. NJPS has made four subdivisions based on the contents, but they do not correlate with the refrain-like lines. Another possibility is to see two main parts: vv. 2–22, the petition in time of trouble, and 23–31, the vow to praise God. The first of these sections is framed by *You answer not* (v. 3) and "answer me" (v. 22; NJPS main translation: *rescue me*). The second is framed by *will I proclaim* (v. 23) and *shall be proclaimed* (v. 31). Jewish tradition interprets this psalm as a lament by David over the future exile (Rashi), more specifically the threat against the Jews by Haman in the book of Esther (various Rabbis). For that reason there is a custom to read it on Purim (Sephardic custom reads it on the Fast of Esther and on Purim). **1:** *Ayyeleth ha-shaḥar* (perhaps "Deer of the Dawn"; see translators' note *b-b*), a musical term, which may indicate the melody to which the words were sung. **2–12:** Why does God, who cared for the ancestors (vv. 5–6) and the psalmist (vv. 10–11) in the past, not do so now? **2:** Divine abandonment is a major theme of the Psalter; see Ps. 10.1. The first part of this v. occurs in the New Testament, uttered by Jesus when he is being crucified (Matt. 27.46; Mark 15.34). **4:** *Praise of Israel:* Cf. Exod. 15.11. According to the alternate translation, prayers form the throne upon which God sits—a

7   But I am a worm, less than human;
         scorned by men, despised by people.
8   All who see me mock me;
         ᵃthey curl their lips,ᵃ
         they shake their heads.
9   "Let him commit himself to the Lᴏʀᴅ;
         let Him rescue him,
         let Him save him,
         for He is pleased with him."
10   You ᵇdrew meᵇ from the womb,
         made me secure at my mother's breast.
11   I became Your charge at birth;
         from my mother's womb You have been my
             God.
12   Do not be far from me,
         for trouble is near,
         and there is none to help.
13   Many bulls surround me,
         mighty ones of Bashan encircle me.
14   They open their mouths at me
         like tearing, roaring lions.
15   ᶜMy life ebbs away:ᶜ
         all my bones are disjointed;
         my heart is like wax,
         melting within me;
16   my vigor dries up like a shard;
         my tongue cleaves to my palate;
         You commit me to the dust of death.
17   Dogs surround me;
         a pack of evil ones closes in on me,
         ᵈlike lions [they maul] my hands and feet.ᵈ
18   I take the count of all my bones
         while they look on and gloat.
19   They divide my clothes among themselves,
         casting lots for my garments.

20   But You, O Lᴏʀᴅ, be not far off;
         my strength, hasten to my aid.
21   Save my life from the sword,
         my precious lifeᵉ from the clutches of a dog.
22   Deliver me from a lion's mouth;
         from the horns of wild oxen rescueᶠ me.
23   Then will I proclaim Your fame to my brethren,
         praise You in the congregation.

lovely metaphor stressing the importance of prayer. **7–8:** The psalmist feels less than human. He is scorned by those who think that God will not help him. *Curl their lips:* gestures of derision. **9:** The scorners open their mouths to mock and to devour (v. 14). **10–12:** The psalmist hopes that God who was with him since conception will not abandon him now. **13–22:** The psalmist's opponents as animal predators (Ps. 17.12). The mixing of metaphors and similes of various types is common in Psalms. **13:** *Bashan,* a region in northern Transjordan famous for its fat, strong cattle, which are here predators. **15–19:** A graphic description of mortal illness. The psalmist feels his body stop working and disintegrate. He sees himself die, his body so dried up that it turns to dust. The scorners are like dogs (and lions, according to NJPS) hunting prey (cf. v. 14). They gloat at his death and are eager to take his possessions. **20–23:** At his lowest point, the psalmist calls on God to save him from what has just been described. **23–24:** See Ps. 35.18–19. **24–31:** The psalmist's recovery is a sign of God's power and mercy, an example for all, and an occasion for praise. With his reintegration into the community, all Israel is invited to join him in praise. **24:** *You who fear the* Lᴏʀᴅ: Yʜᴠʜ-fearers is a term that occurs elsewhere in Psalms; sometimes it is a general designation for those who worship the God of Israel and at other times it seems to be a group within Israel—proselytes, according to some scholars. Here it is the former. **28:** On praise of God by the nations, see Pss. 47.10; 67.3–5; 86.9; 117.1. **30:** The healthy and the sick should praise God. *Those at death's door:* Heb "those who go down to dust," usually a reference to the dead or the almost dead. If the reference is to the dead, it would contradict the belief that the dead do not praise God (Ps. 6.6); but it is perhaps a poetic way to reinforce the idea of the surrounding vv. that everyone, in every time and every place, should

a-a Lit. "they open wide with a lip."   b-b Meaning of Heb. uncertain.
c-c Lit. "I am poured out like water."
d-d With Rashi; cf. Isa. 38.13.   e Lit. "only one."   f Lit. "answer."

24 You who fear the LORD, praise Him!
All you offspring of Jacob, honor Him!
Be in dread of Him, all you offspring of Israel!

25 For He did not scorn, He did not spurn
the plea[a] of the lowly;
He did not hide His face from him;
when he cried out to Him, He listened.

26 [b-]Because of You I offer praise[-b] in the great
congregation;
I pay my vows in the presence of His
worshipers.

27 Let the lowly eat and be satisfied;
let all who seek the LORD praise Him.
Always be of good cheer!

28 Let all the ends of the earth pay heed and turn to
the LORD,
and the peoples of all nations prostrate
themselves before You;

29 for kingship is the LORD'S
and He rules the nations.

30 [c-]All those in full vigor shall eat and prostrate
themselves;
all those at death's door, whose spirits flag,
shall bend the knee before Him.[-c]

31 Offspring shall serve Him;
the Lord's fame shall be proclaimed to the
generation to come;
they shall tell of His beneficence to people
yet to be born,
for He has acted.

23 A psalm of David.

The LORD is my shepherd;
I lack nothing.

2 He makes me lie down in green pastures;
He leads me to [d-]water in places of repose;[-d]

3 He renews my life;
He guides me in right paths
as befits His name.

4 Though I walk through [e-]a valley of deepest
darkness,[-e]

praise God. **31:** God's power to cure will be proclaimed to future generations.

Ps. 23: God, the divine shepherd-king, leads his people to nourishment and safety (vv. 1–4), keeping them alive and protecting them. In vv. 5–6 the psalmist is hosted by God and hopes to remain in His presence all his life. Some scholars now interpret the psalm as an exilic or postexilic portrait of a new exodus, from the exile to the return in the land of Israel (cf. Isa. 40.3–5; 49.8–13; Ps. 78.43–55— the exodus is a common exilic trope for the return). This interpretation helps to see the psalm's two parts as a unity: God guides the people through the difficult journey from Babylonia and then hosts them at His own table, the rebuilt Temple. **1–4:** The shepherd-sheep metaphor for God and Israel (see also Ps. 95.7). The shepherd leads the sheep to pasture, to water, and through difficult terrain. *Shepherd* is a frequent biblical and ancient Near Eastern metaphor for royalty (Isa. 40.11; Ezek. 34; Ps. 80). This is the case with David (and Moses); the Babylonian king Hammurabi is called "the shepherd" (*ANET*, p. 164). **2:** The alternate reading "still waters" (translators' note *d-d*) means that the waters are not turbulent and hence are easy to drink from. **3:** See Ps. 31.4. **4:** The shepherd's *rod* and *staff*, implements that prod and guide the sheep, provide the comfort that comes from divine guidance.

a Or "plight."   b-b Lit. "From You is my praise."
c-c Meaning of Heb. uncertain; others "All the fat ones of the earth shall eat and worship; /
All they that go down to the dust shall kneel before Him, / Even he that cannot keep his soul
alive."
d-d Others "still waters."
e-e Others "the valley of the shadow of death."

I fear no harm, for You are with me;
Your rod and Your staff—they comfort me.

5 You spread a table for me in full view of my
    enemies;
You anoint my head with oil;
    my drink is abundant.

6 Only goodness and steadfast love shall pursue me
    all the days of my life,
and I shall dwell in the house of the LORD
    for many long years.

24

Of David. A psalm.

The earth is the LORD's and all that it holds,
    the world and its inhabitants.

2 For He founded it upon the ocean,
    set it on the nether-streams.

3 Who may ascend the mountain of the LORD?
Who may stand in His holy place?—

4 He who has clean hands and a pure heart,
    who has not taken a false oath by My[a] life
    or sworn deceitfully.

5 He shall carry away a blessing from the LORD,
    a just reward from God, his deliverer.

6 Such is the circle[b] of those who turn to Him,
    Jacob, who seek Your presence.   *Selah.*

7 O gates, lift up your heads!
Up high, you everlasting doors,
    so the King of glory may come in!

8 Who is the King of glory?—
    the LORD, mighty and valiant,
    the LORD, valiant in battle.

9 O gates, lift up your heads!
Lift them up, you everlasting doors,
    so the King of glory may come in!

---

a Ancient versions and some mss. read "His."
b Lit. "generation."

5–6: The shepherd metaphor is replaced by a banquet metaphor: God's luxurious care of the psalmist. **5:** God hosts with luxury. A set or spread table (cf. Ezek. 23.41; Prov. 9.2) and oil on the head (cf. Eccl. 9.8; Ps. 92.11) are signs of luxury. Oil was placed on the heads of guests at banquets. Ps. 78.19 speaks of the preparation of *a table* in the wilderness for the first exodus generation. This lends support for seeing our psalm as a reference to the (second) exodus. **6:** *Goodness and steadfast love,* covenant blessings, rather than curse, *pursue* the psalmist (Deut. 28.3, 15, 45). **6:** *The house of the LORD:* The Temple (Ps. 27.4). The psalmist hopes to be in God's presence at the Temple (have access to God) throughout his long life. If this is an exilic psalm, it implies the return to the land of Israel. *For many long years:* lit. "for length of days." This refers to one's natural life (to live a long life was a blessing), but it has traditionally been understood as referring to the next life (after death), and hence this psalm is customarily recited at funerals or on occasions commemorating the dead.

Ps. 24: A liturgy on entering the sanctuary. A hymn celebrating God, creator and victor, with an "entrance liturgy" (vv. 3–6; Pss. 5; 15). After an introduction celebrating God as the creator, the psalm has two parts; in the first (vv. 3–6), pilgrims enter the Temple, and in the second (vv. 7–10), the Ark enters. The two are separated by "Selah." Each part has rhetorical questions and their answers; perhaps they were recited antiphonally. The psalm is used in Jewish liturgy on festivals, when the Torah is returned to the Ark. **1–2:** God tamed the primeval waters and founded the earth upon them (Ps. 136.6); He is therefore to be acknowledged as the supreme sovereign of the world. The Temple is a microcosm of the world (cf. Gen. 2.1–3; Exod. 39.32, 42–43) and thus God's act of creation forms an appropriate introduction to this Temple liturgy. **3–6:** The requirements for participation in Temple worship are predominantly moral, signifying obedience to God; see Ps. 15.2–5. **3:** *The mountain of the LORD:* The Temple mount, with an echo of Mt. Sinai. **6:** *Jacob:* Israel, the congregation present at the ceremony. *Selah* (also v. 10), see Ps. 3.3 n. **7–10:** God, as it were, enters the Temple. The Temple gates open for the Ark, symbolizing God's presence, to enter. The gates "lift up their heads," a metaphoric expression for joyously welcoming God, pictured as a victorious king returning home to his palace.

10 Who is the King of glory?—
the LORD of hosts,
He is the King of glory! *Selah.*

25 Of David.

א O LORD, I set my hope on You;
2 ב my God, in You I trust;
may I not be disappointed,
may my enemies not exult over me.
3 ג O let none who look to You be disappointed;
let the faithless be disappointed, empty-handed.
4 ד Let me know Your paths, O LORD;
teach me Your ways;
5 הו guide me in Your true way and teach me,
for You are God, my deliverer;
it is You I look to at all times.
6 ז O LORD, be mindful of Your compassion
and Your faithfulness;
they are old as time.
7 ח Be not mindful of my youthful sins and
transgressions;
in keeping with Your faithfulness consider what
is in my favor,
as befits Your goodness, O LORD.
8 ט Good and upright is the LORD;
therefore He shows sinners the way.
9 י He guides the lowly in the right path,
and teaches the lowly His way.
10 כ All the LORD's paths are steadfast love
for those who keep the decrees of His covenant.
11 ל As befits Your name, O LORD,
pardon my iniquity though it be great.
12 מ Whoever fears the LORD,
he shall be shown what path to choose.
13 נ He shall live a happy life,
and his children shall inherit the land.
14 ס The counsel[a] of the LORD is for those who fear
Him;
to them He makes known His covenant.
15 ע My eyes are ever toward the LORD,
for He will loose my feet from the net.
16 פ Turn to me, have mercy on me,
for I am alone and afflicted.
17 צ [b]My deep distress[b] increases;
deliver me from my straits.

10: *The* LORD *of hosts,* a relatively infrequent divine epithet in Psalms, emphasizes God's role in leading the heavenly hosts in battle, and is associated with the Ark, which could precede Israel in battle (see 1 Sam. ch 4). A plausible setting for the psalm might be the return from battle of the Ark, a symbol of (v. 8) "the LORD, mighty and valiant, the LORD, valiant in battle."

Ps. 25: An individual's petition in acrostic form: the first line begins with the first letter of the Hebrew alphabet, the first word of the second line with the second letter of the alphabet, and so on to the final letter (see Pss. 9–10 n.). Two letters are missing and two are doubled, likely reflecting changes that the psalm has undergone in its transmission. The psalm is made up of alternating petitions and expressions of trust. It resembles wisdom literature in its concern with learning and finding the right path, but has the religious concerns of Psalms in its hope for forgiveness and for deliverance from distress. **1:** *Set my hope on You,* lit. "lift my soul to You" (cf. 86.4; 143.8), i.e., "turn to You for protection." **2–3:** The plea for the "shaming" of one's enemies is frequent in complaints (6.11; 35.4, 26; 40.15–16). **4–5:** Prayer for (moral) guidance, with a wisdom cast; cf. vv. 8–10, 12. **6–7:** Prayer for divine mercy and forgiveness of sins. A key word is "z-k-r," "remember," translated as *be mindful* and *consider.* God should remember that He is merciful and not remember (take into account) the psalmist's sins. *Youthful sins:* Since God's mercy dates from the beginning of time, the psalmist mentions sins that date from the beginning of his life. **11:** The request for forgiveness of sins closes the first half of the psalm; *name* here means essence. *Pardon my iniquity* echoes Moses' words in Exod. 34.9. **12–13:** Those who fear the LORD and their children shall be blessed (Ps. 37.28–29). Possession of *the land* is a major theme of Ps. 37. **17:** *Increases,* Heb "broadens," the

a Or "secret."   *b-b Lit. "The distress of my heart."*

18 ר Look at my affliction and suffering,
and forgive all my sins.

19 See how numerous my enemies are,
and how unjustly they hate me!

20 ש Protect me and save me;
let me not be disappointed,
for I have sought refuge in You.

21 ת May integrity and uprightness watch over me,
for I look to You.

22 O God, redeem Israel
from all its distress.

26 Of David.

Vindicate me, O Lord,
for I have walked without blame;
I have trusted in the Lord;
I have not faltered.

2 Probe me, O Lord, and try me,
test my ᵃ-heart and mind;-ᵃ

3 ᵇ-for my eyes are on Your steadfast love;
I have set my course by it.-ᵇ

4 I do not consort with scoundrels,
or mix with hypocrites;

5 I detest the company of evil men,
and do not consort with the wicked;

6 I wash my hands in innocence,
and walk around Your altar, O Lord,

7 raising my voice in thanksgiving,
and telling all Your wonders.

8 O Lord, I love Your temple abode,
the dwelling-place of Your glory.

9 Do not sweep me away with sinners,
or [snuff out] my life with murderers,

10 who have schemes at their fingertips,
and hands full of bribes.

11 But I walk without blame;
redeem me, have mercy on me!

12 My feet are on level ground.
In assemblies I will bless the Lord.

27 Of David.

The Lord is my light and my help;
whom should I fear?

a-a Lit. "kidneys and heart."
b-b Or "I am aware of Your faithfulness, and always walk in Your true [path]."

opposite of *distress* and *straits,*
with their meaning of narrowness.
19: Here as elsewhere, *enemies*
need not be literal but stands for
trouble in general. **21:** *Integrity and
uprightness,* characteristics of Job
(1.1), here personified as protecting guardians. **22:** As in many
psalms, the end of a prayer of an
individual becomes a prayer for
the community. A v. beginning
with the letter "pe" follows the
acrostic (see also Ps. 34.23). It has
been suggested that this arrangement makes the first letter "alef,"
the middle letter "lamed," and the
last letter "pe"—spelling the word
"to learn, teach" and thereby emphasizing the instructional nature
of the psalm.

Ps. 26: A prayer for divine justice.
The bulk of the psalm is a protestation of innocence, where the
psalmist insists that he has conducted his life as God requires and
therefore should not be punished
like the wicked. His plea is based
on the assumption that the righteous are rewarded and the
wicked punished, yet in his case
this expectation seems not yet to
have been fulfilled. Like Ps. 25,
this psalm uses some language of
wisdom literature. **1–3:** The psalmist prays that God adjudicate him
and find him righteous (7.9;
17.2–5). **4–5:** The psalmist's protestation of innocence and his nonassociation with the wicked is similar to 1.1–2. **6–8:** The mention of
the *altar* and *temple* suggests to
some that the psalmist is a priest,
but he may be an ordinary person
who delights in coming to the
Temple. Clean hands (literally or
metaphorically) are required for
entrance to the Temple (Ps. 24.4).
8: *Glory,* the light streaming from
the deity (36.10; 63.3). **9–10:** If the
psalmist is swept away with the
evildoers, he will not be able to
come to the Temple, which he
loves (v. 8). **11–12:** *I walk without
blame* forms an inclusio, with a
change of tense, with v. 1; the
psalmist was blameless in the past
and continues to be. *My feet are on
level ground,* Heb "my foot stands
on level ground" recalls the walk-

The Lord is the stronghold of my life,
    whom should I dread?
2   When evil men assail me
    [a-]to devour my flesh[-a]—
    it is they, my foes and my enemies,
    who stumble and fall.
3   Should an army besiege me,
    my heart would have no fear;
    should war beset me,
    still would I be confident.

4   One thing I ask of the Lord,
    only that do I seek:
    to live in the house of the Lord
    all the days of my life,
    to gaze upon the beauty of the Lord,
    [b-]to frequent[-b] His temple.
5   He will shelter me in His pavilion
    on an evil day,
    grant me the protection of His tent,
    raise me high upon a rock.
6   Now is my head high
    over my enemies roundabout;
    I sacrifice in His tent with shouts of joy,
    singing and chanting a hymn to the Lord.

7   Hear, O Lord, when I cry aloud;
    have mercy on me, answer me.
8   [b-]In Your behalf[-b] my heart says:
    "Seek My face!"
    O Lord, I seek Your face.
9   Do not hide Your face from me;
    do not thrust aside Your servant in anger;
    You have ever been my help.
    Do not forsake me, do not abandon me,
    O God, my deliverer.
10   Though my father and mother abandon me,
    the Lord will take me in.
11   Show me Your way, O Lord,
    and lead me on a level path
    because of my watchful foes.
12   Do not subject me to the will of my foes,
    for false witnesses and unjust accusers
    have appeared against me.
13   Had I not the assurance
    that I would enjoy the goodness of the Lord
    in the land of the living . . .

ing in vv. 1, 3. Heb *without blame* and *level ground* echoes the words "tam" and "yashar," "to have integrity and be upright," the desired traits of the righteous person (cf. 25.21).

Ps. 27: A psalm of trust; the psalmist has no fear of enemies in the protective refuge of the Temple. This psalm is recited from 1 'Elul (in the late summer) through Hoshanah Rabbah in the early fall, the period of seeking forgiveness from God surrounding Rosh Ha-Shanah and Yom Kippur. **1:** *My light*, see 36.10; Mic. 7.8; Job 33.30. As in other psalms, various metaphors, here *light* and *stronghold*, are combined to reflect different aspects of God's great power. **2:** *Devour my flesh*, an idiom for harmful, malicious speech (cf. English "backbite"; see translators' note *a-a*); it can also refer to enemies as predators. **4–6:** The Temple as a place of refuge, where the psalmist can experience God's presence. The same theme occurs in Ps. 26.6–8. For another connection between these two psalms cf. 27.11 and 26.12. **4:** *Live in the house of the Lord*, the psalmist hopes to visit the Temple on pilgrimages throughout his life (23.6; 84.5). **5:** *Pavilion* (Heb "sukkah") and *tent* are terms for the Temple (cf. 76.3; 15.1; 61.5). **7–13:** The psalmist seeks God, worried that God will abandon him (see 6.4–5 n.). **10:** Even if his parents abandon him, through death or otherwise, the psalmist will have a divine "parent" who will protect and instruct him. The motif of the god as a parent of the king is familiar from Mesopotamian hymns and elsewhere in biblical literature, where God is the superlative parent (see esp. Isa. 49.15). **12:** The foes are lying witnesses testifying against the psalmist. **13:** *The land of the living*, as opposed to the land of the dead, where there is no access to God; a metaphor for the Temple.

a-a *Or "to slander me"; cf. Dan. 3.8; 6.25.*   b-b *Meaning of Heb. uncertain.*

14 Look to the LORD;
  be strong and of good courage!
  O look to the LORD!

28 Of David.

  O LORD, I call to You;
  my rock, do not disregard me,
  for if You hold aloof from me,
  I shall be like those gone down into the Pit.

2 Listen to my plea for mercy
  when I cry out to You,
  when I lift my hands
  toward Your inner sanctuary.

3 Do not ᵃcount meᵃ with the wicked and
    evildoers
  who profess goodwill toward their fellows
  while malice is in their heart.

4 Pay them according to their deeds,
  their malicious acts;
  according to their handiwork pay them,
  give them their deserts.

5 For they do not consider the LORD's deeds,
  the work of His hands.
  May He tear them down,
  never to rebuild them!

6 Blessed is the LORD,
  for He listens to my plea for mercy.

7 The LORD is my strength and my shield;
  my heart trusts in Him.
  I was helped,ᵇ and my heart exulted,
  so I will glorify Him with my song.

8 The LORD is ᶜtheir strength;ᶜ
  He is a stronghold for the deliverance of His
    anointed.

9 Deliver and bless Your very own people;
  tend them and sustain them forever.

a-a Or "drag me off"; Meaning of Heb. uncertain.

b Or "strengthened."

c-c Septuagint, Saadia, and others render, and some mss. read, 'oz le'ammo, "the strength of His people."

14: Possibly a response to the psalmist's prayer, this sums up the psalm's message.

Ps. 28: A plea for deliverance from enemies; perhaps a royal psalm (cf. vv. 8–9). God is described in terms of military strength: a *rock, strength, shield, stronghold.* In vv. 1–5 the psalmist prays for God's response, arguing that he should not be grouped with the wicked, whom God correctly distances from Himself, punishing them with death. Vv. 6–9 follow God's response; the psalmist praises Him and encourages others to do likewise. V. 9 moves from the personal to the national, praying for God's ongoing protection of Israel. **1:** *Disregard,* lit. "be deaf" to my call. *The Pit,* a synonym for Sheol, the abode of the dead. One cut off from God is like the dead, who were permanently cut off from God. **2:** To *lift* one's *hands* was the typical position of biblical prayer (see, e.g., 1 Kings 8.22; cf. Ps. 44.21 n.). **3:** The deceitful, untrustworthy speech of the wicked is commonplace (Ps. 27.12), but if this is a royal psalm, as some think (cf. vv. 8–9), it may refer to conspiracy against the king. **4:** Prayer for measure-for-measure retribution (Ps. 94.2). **6–7:** The characteristic move from complaint and petition to praise, with expressions of trust. **8–9:** The mention of *His anointed* (a Davidic king) and the prayer for the people (cf. 3.9) suggest that the speaker is a king.

Ps. 29: A hymn celebrating God's awesome power over nature. Cf. Pss. 46–48; 96–99. God is portrayed as a storm, an earthquake—a theme associated with theophany (cf. *b. Zevaḥ.* 116a where a link is made with the giving of the Torah at Sinai). More commonly, the psalm is considered a prayer for rain. According to the Talmud, *b. Sukkah* 55a, the psalm was recited in the Temple on the first of the intermediate days of Sukkot; LXX associates it with the end of Sukkot ("Shemini 'Atzeret"), the time for the prayer for rain; *b. Rosh Hash.* 32a and *b. Meg.* 17b link it with the paragraph about rain in the "Shemoneh 'Esrei" prayer. A number of themes and linguistic usages that are also found in Ugaritic literature, as well as the mention of northern locations (Lebanon and Sirion, v. 6), have led modern scholars to see this psalm as an adaptation of a Ugaritic hymn to Baal (or to Hadad, the storm-god). Others see the psalm as part of a more generally shared ancient Near Eastern tradition rather than as a direct borrowing. Either way,

29

A psalm of David.

Ascribe to the LORD, O divine beings,
　　ascribe to the LORD glory and strength.

2　Ascribe to the LORD the glory of His name;
　　bow down to the LORD, majestic in holiness.

3　The voice of the LORD is over the waters;
　　the God of glory thunders,
　　the LORD, over the mighty waters.

4　The voice of the LORD is power;
　　the voice of the LORD is majesty;

5　the voice of the LORD breaks cedars;
　　the LORD shatters the cedars of Lebanon.

6　^{a-}He makes Lebanon skip like a calf,^{-a}
　　Sirion, like a young wild ox.

7　The voice of the LORD kindles flames of fire;

8　the voice of the LORD convulses the wilderness;
　　the LORD convulses the wilderness of Kadesh;

9　the voice of the LORD causes hinds to calve,
　　^{b-}and strips forests bare;^{-b}
　　while in His temple all say "Glory!"

10　The LORD sat enthroned at the Flood;
　　the LORD sits enthroned, king forever.

11　May the LORD grant strength to His people;
　　may the LORD bestow on His people wellbeing.

30

A psalm of David. A song for the dedication of the House.^c

2　I extol You, O LORD,
　　for You have lifted me up,

a-a Lit. "He makes them skip like a calf, Lebanon and Sirion, etc."
b-b Or "brings ewes to early birth."
c I.e., the Temple.

the basic theme is built on the "combat-myth," known in Ugarit and Mesopotamia and reflected in other biblical passages, in which the hero-god defeats the forces of chaos and is then acclaimed by the other gods as their leader. The psalm shares with Ps. 24 the themes of God's triumph over the forces of chaos (primeval waters) and God enthroned as king in His Temple. Ps. 29 is used liturgically on the Sabbath when the Torah is returned to the Ark. **1–2:** Cf. 96.7–9; 1 Chron. 16.28–30. **1:** *Divine beings,* lit. "sons of God," or "sons of gods," subordinate deities in the heavenly assembly. In Israelite thought these divine beings are part of God's retinue, his heavenly court (Exod. 15.11; Pss. 82.1; 89.6–8; Job chs 1–2). Probably because of its pagan overtones, Ps. 96.7 substitutes "families of the peoples" for this term. *Glory and strength,* cf. Ps. 63.3. *Glory,* Heb "kavod," may refer to the divine radiance, the visual manifestation of God. **2:** *Majestic in holiness,* "be-hadrat kodesh," an odd phrase but

cf. 110.3, "behadrei kodesh." LXX and Peshitta (Syriac) render "in His holy court." Cf. *b. Ber.* 30b. **3–9:** *The voice of the LORD* (claps of thunder), signifying God's power over the natural world, occurs seven times in these vv. **3:** The LORD battles the *mighty waters,* the primeval forces of chaos (cf. 24.2). **5:** The *cedars of Lebanon* were famous for their height and strength. **6–8:** Earthquake is a traditional accompaniment of a theophany or divine manifestation (18.8; 114.7). **6:** *Sirion,* Mount Hermon (see Deut. 3.9), at the southern border of *Lebanon.* For mountains skipping, see also 114.4. **8:** *The wilderness of Kadesh,* in western Syria; or, the wilderness of Zin at Qadesh, to the south of Israel, where the Israelites encamped during their wanderings (Num. 20.1; 33.36). **9:** Reading with translators' note b-b makes a closer parallelism. An alternate emendation of *causes hinds ("ʾayalot") to calve* yields "causes ʾelot' (oak trees) to tremble." *In His temple,* praise from the subordinate deities in the heavenly temple. **10:** The LORD's enthronement as king at *the Flood* (see Ps. 93) may be a double entendre, signifying that God defeated the waters (forces of chaos) and that He reigned since the time of the flood, and will reign forever. **11:** A prayer that God, supremely powerful and enthroned forever, will grant well-being to Israel.

Ps. 30: The superscription reinterprets the hymn, perhaps originally a thanksgiving hymn upon recovering from illness, as a prayer about the sickness of the community—i.e., national calamity—and its recovery, the restoration from exile and the rebuilding of the Temple (in 515 BCE; cf. Ezra 6.15–18). An older view sees the occasion as the rededication of the Temple in 164 BCE, following the victory of Judah Maccabee (cf. 1 Macc. 4.36–59). Following tractate *Soferim,* this psalm is read on Hanukkah. It is also part of the introductory liturgy for the daily, Sabbath, and festival morning service. **1:** The translation inverts the and not let my enemies rejoice over me.

3   O LORD, my God,
        I cried out to You,
        and You healed me.

4   O LORD, You brought me up from Sheol,
        preserved me from going down into the Pit.

5   O you faithful of the LORD, sing to Him,
        and praise His holy name.

6   For He is angry but a moment,
        and when He is pleased there is life.
    *One may lie down weeping at nightfall;*ᵃ
        but at dawn there are shouts of joy.

7   When I was untroubled,
        I thought, "I shall never be shaken,"

8   for You, O LORD, when You were pleased,
        made [me]ᵇ firm as a mighty mountain.
    When You hid Your face,
        I was terrified.

9   I called to You, O LORD;
        to my LORD I made appeal,

10 "What is to be gained from my death,ᶜ
        from my descent into the Pit?
    Can dust praise You?
    Can it declare Your faithfulness?

11 Hear, O LORD, and have mercy on me;
        O LORD, be my help!"

12 You turned my lament into dancing,
        you undid my sackcloth and girded me
            with joy,

13 that [my] whole being might sing hymns
            to You endlessly;
        O LORD my God, I will praise You forever.

31

For the leader. A psalm of David.

2   I seek refuge in You, O LORD;
        may I never be disappointed;
        as You are righteous, rescue me.

3   Incline Your ear to me;
        be quick to save me;
        be a rock, a stronghold for me,

words, which in Heb are "A psalm, a song of dedication of the House; of David." The mention of David in connection with the dedication of the Temple is anachronistic, since it occurred under Solomon (1 Kings 8; 2 Chron. 5–7); see Ps. 3.1 n. For that reason, some scholars think that the "house" is David's royal residence (2 Sam. 5.11; 7.1–2). **2:** *Lifted me up,* lit. "drew me up" (like water from a well); it complements the idea of being raised from the Pit (v. 4). **4:** God brought the psalmist back from a near-death state, from imminent death; he did not let the psalmist actually die. Here, as in Mesopotamian literature, the image of being brought up from death (*Sheol* and *the Pit;* 28.1 n.) reflects recovery from serious illness, and not resurrection from death. **5–6:** The ritual of thanksgiving in the Temple, involving family and friends celebrating the psalmist's reintegration into the community. God is angry only momentarily (cf. Isa. 54.7–8); His (normal) favor is life-sustaining. An alternative meaning: God is angry for but a moment; His favor lasts a lifetime. **7:** The psalmist was apparently in God's favor for a long time, as evidenced by his good health; he expected to remain so indefinitely. He was terrified when God *hid* His *face,* was no longer accessible. **9–11:** The psalmist quotes his earlier appeal for divine help. **10:** *Dust,* the dead, who have returned to dust. On the inability of the dead to praise God, see 6.5–6; 88.4–6, 11–13; 115.7; 118.17; Isa. 38.18–19. For this reason, argues the psalmist, God should keep him alive; so he can continue to fulfill the main purpose of human life— praising God (cf. v. 13). **12:** God replaces the psalmist's *lament* (mourning) with *dancing,* and his sackcloth with a festal robe, signifying that God has brought him back from near-death into God's presence. *Dancing* is a form of praising God (149.3; 150.4).

Ps. 31: An anthological psalm, drawing on vv. from other psalms and Jeremiah, it calls on God for

a-a *Or "Weeping may linger for the night."*
b *Following Saadia, R. Isaiah of Trani; cf. Ibn Ezra.*
c *Lit. "blood."*

a citadel, for my deliverance.

4   For You are my rock and my fortress;
     You lead me and guide me as befits Your
       name.

5   You free me from the net laid for me,
     for You are my stronghold.

6   Into Your hand I entrust my spirit;
     You redeem me, O Lord, faithful God.

7   I detest those who rely on empty folly,
     but I trust in the Lord.

8   Let me exult and rejoice in Your faithfulness
     when You notice my affliction,
     are mindful of my deep distress,

9   and do not hand me over to my enemy,
     but ᵃ·grant me relief.·ᵃ

10   Have mercy on me, O Lord,
     for I am in distress;
     my eyes are wasted by vexation,
     ᵇ·my substance and body too.·ᵇ

11   My life is spent in sorrow,
     my years in groaning;
     my strength fails because of my iniquity,
     my limbs waste away.

12   Because of all my foes
     I am the particular butt of my neighbors,
     a horror to my friends;
     those who see me on the street avoid me.

13   I am put out of mind like the dead;
     I am like an object given up for lost.

14   I hear the whisperings of many,
     intrigueᶜ on every side,
     as they scheme together against me,
     plotting to take my life.

15   But I trust in You, O Lord;
     I say, "You are my God!"

16   My fate is in Your hand;
     save me from the hand of my enemies and
       pursuers.

17   Show favor to Your servant;
     as You are faithful, deliver me.

18   O Lord, let me not be disappointed when I call You;
     let the wicked be disappointed;
     let them be silenced in Sheol;

help and affirms the psalmist's trust in God. **1–5:** God is a refuge, described in terms connoting physical strength and protection (*rock, stronghold, citadel, fortress*). **1–3:** Cf. 71.1–3. **5:** The *net* is a military weapon used to capture prisoners. **6:** The language of commercial borrowing and lending. The psalmist entrusts to God his *spirit,* the animating force that keeps him alive (this is not the "body" and "soul" dichotomy), as one would give a valuable object as a pledge. He is sure that his pledge will be redeemed, returned to him and not forfeited. God will return his life to him, because He is a *faithful God,* He keeps faith with those who trust in Him. **7:** *Empty folly* is the opposite of the *faithful God* (v. 6). **9:** The psalmist is not entrapped in an enemy's *net* (v. 5), but finds a "broad place" in the care of God (25.15). **10–11:** Physical wasting away, perhaps by illness or perhaps a metaphor for the psalmist's distress. Because of illness the psalmist is shunned by all (38.12; 88.9). Cf. 6.3, 8 for similar phraseology. **12–13:** The scorn or shame felt by the petitioner is a major theme of Psalms (e.g., 22.7), and of the Bible as a whole (e.g., Job 19.19; Jer. 23.40), reflecting the fact that ancient Israel was a shame culture. **13:** Cf. Eccl. 9.5. **14:** Cf. Jer. 20.10. **15:** In the preceding vv., the psalmist was the object of other people's thoughts or actions. Now he is the grammatical subject, expressing his own beliefs. The opening words, *But I,* contrast the psalmist's trust in God with his troubled condition. **17:** See Ps. 4.7. **18–21:** Counterpoised to Sheol, the abode of the silent dead, is the Temple, residence of the living God. The psalmist prays that the wicked will *be silenced in Sheol,* while he, like all Godfearers, will be granted *the protection of Your presence* and will be sheltered *in Your pavilion* (the Temple). **18:** Let the wicked suffer the fate that the psalmist almost suffered. The sin of the wicked is their arrogant speech against the righteous; cf. v. 21.

a-a Lit. "make my feet stand in a broad place."
b-b Meaning of Heb. uncertain.   c Others "terror."

19　　　　let lying lips be stilled
　　　　　　that speak haughtily against the righteous
　　　　　　with arrogance and contempt.

20　　　　How abundant is the good
　　　　　　that You have in store for those who fear
　　　　　　　　You,
　　　　　　that You do in the full view of men
　　　　　　for those who take refuge in You.

21　　　　You grant them the protection of Your presence
　　　　　　ᵃ⁻against scheming men;⁻ᵃ
　　　　　　You shelter them in Your pavilion
　　　　　　from contentious tongues.

22　　　　Blessed is the LORD,
　　　　　　for He has been wondrously faithful to me,
　　　　　　a veritable bastion.

23　　　　Alarmed, I had thought,
　　　　　　"I am thrust out of Your sight";
　　　　　　yet You listened to my plea for mercy
　　　　　　when I cried out to You.

24　　　　So love the LORD, all you faithful;
　　　　　　the LORD guards the loyal,
　　　　　　and more than requites
　　　　　　him who acts arrogantly.

25　　　　Be strong and of good courage,
　　　　　　all you who wait for the LORD.

32　Of David. ᵃ⁻A *maskil*.⁻ᵃ

　　　　　Happy is he whose transgression is forgiven,
　　　　　　whose sin is covered over.

2　　　　Happy the man whom the LORD does not hold
　　　　　　guilty,
　　　　　　and in whose spirit there is no deceit.

3　　　　As long as I said nothing,
　　　　　　my limbs wasted away
　　　　　　from my anguished roaring all day long.

4　　　　For night and day
　　　　　　Your hand lay heavy on me;
　　　　　　my vigor waned
　　　　　　as in the summer drought.　　　　　　*Selah.*

5　　　　Then I acknowledged my sin to You;
　　　　　　I did not cover up my guilt;
　　　　　　I resolved, "I will confess my transgressions to
　　　　　　　　the LORD,"
　　　　　　and You forgave the guilt of my sin.　　*Selah.*

21: Cf. Ps. 76.3. **22:** *A veritable bastion:* According to this reading, God is a bastion; cf. v. 3. Heb reads "in the besieged city," which might mean "while the psalmist felt himself under siege." **23:** *Thrust out of Your sight,* separated from the presence of God in the Temple (2 Chron. 26.21; Hos. 9.15; Jonah 2.5). Like v. 15, this v. begins in Heb with "but I," this time contrasting the "before" and the "after." **24–25:** A ritual of public thanksgiving with the psalmist's community (30.12–13). The psalmist's experience validates the principle of trusting in God and encourages others to do so.

Ps. 32: The happiness of the sinner who is forgiven. The psalm has some affinity to wisdom texts (vv. 1–2, 8–9; cf. Ps. 1). The term *maskil,* of unknown meaning, resonates with "'askilkha," "let me enlighten you" (v. 8). **1:** *Forgiven . . . covered over,* divine passives; it is God who forgives sin and covers it (i.e., puts it out of sight). **3–5:** The psalmist's silence (not confessing his sin) brought on illness; acknowledgment of sin brought healing and forgiveness. **4:** *Selah* (also vv. 5, 7), see Ps. 3.3 n. **7:** *You preserve me from distress* in Heb is a soundplay, "mitzar" and "titzreni." **8–9:** A teacher's instruction, promising guidance for life. *Senseless horse . . . ,* cf. Prov. 26.3. **10–11:** The varying fates of the wicked and the upright (1.6). Sickness and pain are punishment for sin. *Favor,* Heb "ḥesed," God's faithful care (cf. 5.8 n.). The psalm ends on a high note of joyful praise (see 97.12), leading into the next psalm.

a-a Meaning of Heb. uncertain.

6   Therefore let every faithful man pray to You
     ᵃ⁻upon discovering [his sin],⁻ᵃ
     that the rushing mighty waters
     not overtake him.

7   You are my shelter;
     You preserve me from distress;
     You surround me with the joyous shouts of
      deliverance.   *Selah.*

8   Let me enlighten you
     and show you which way to go;
     let me offer counsel; my eye is on you.

9   Be not like a senseless horse or mule
     ᵇ⁻whose movement must be curbed by bit and
      bridle;⁻ᵇ
     ᶜ⁻far be it from you!⁻ᶜ

10   Many are the torments of the wicked,
     but he who trusts in the Lᴏʀᴅ
     shall be surrounded with favor.

11   Rejoice in the Lᴏʀᴅ and exult, O you righteous;
     shout for joy, all upright men!

33

Sing forth, O you righteous, to the Lᴏʀᴅ;
     it is fit that the upright acclaim Him.

2   Praise the Lᴏʀᴅ with the lyre;
     with the ten-stringed harp sing to Him;

3   sing Him a new song;
     play sweetly with shouts of joy.

4   For the word of the Lᴏʀᴅ is right;
     His every deed is faithful.

5   He loves what is right and just;
     the earth is full of the Lᴏʀᴅ's faithful care.

6   By the word of the Lᴏʀᴅ the heavens were made,
     by the breath of His mouth, all their host.

7   He heaps up the ocean waters like a mound,
     stores the deep in vaults.

8   Let all the earth fear the Lᴏʀᴅ;
     let all the inhabitants of the world dread Him.

9   For He spoke, and it was;
     He commanded, and it endured.

10   The Lᴏʀᴅ frustrates the plans of nations,
     brings to naught the designs of peoples.

11   What the Lᴏʀᴅ plans endures forever,
     what He designs, for ages on end.

Ps. 33: Praise of God's faithful care and the joy of trusting in God. The creator of the world maintains control of it; in contrast to Him, all human power pales in significance. Pss. 33 and 34 have been incorporated into the introductory prayers to the morning service on Sabbath and festivals. **1–3:** For music as a form of worship, see 81.2–4; 92.2–4; 150.3–5. **4–6:** The world that God created by his *word*, which is right, is full of God's faithful care. The world is, as a result of how it was created, a place of rightness, justice, and "ḥesed." **6–9:** As in Gen. ch 1, creation is by the divine word: the making of the "heavens," the confinement of the chaotic *waters*, and the peopling of the earth (Gen. 1.6–10). **7:** Cf. Exod. 15.8 where the water of the Sea of Reeds is piled in a heap. **8–11:** All inhabitants of the world must be in awe of the creator. Human plans can easily come to naught, but God's plans are eternal.

a-a *Meaning of Heb. uncertain; others "in a time when You may be found."*
b-b *Meaning of Heb. uncertain.*
c-c *Meaning of Heb. uncertain; for this rendering cf. Ibn Ezra.*

12 Happy the nation whose God is the LORD,
      the people He has chosen to be His own.
13 The LORD looks down from heaven;
      He sees all mankind.
14 From His dwelling-place He gazes
      on all the inhabitants of the earth—
15 He who fashions the hearts of them all,
      who discerns all their doings.

16 Kings are not delivered by a large force;
      warriors are not saved by great strength;
17 horses are a false hope for deliverance;
      for all their great power they provide no
      escape.
18 Truly the eye of the LORD is on those who fear
      Him,
      who wait for His faithful care
19 to save them from death,
      to sustain them in famine.
20 We set our hope on the LORD,
      He is our help and shield;
21 in Him our hearts rejoice,
      for in His holy name we trust.
22 May we enjoy, O LORD, Your faithful care,
      as we have put our hope in You.

34 Of David, ᵃwhen he feigned madness in the pres-
      ence of Abimelech, who turned him out, and he
left.ᵃ

2 א I bless the LORD at all times;
        praise of Him is ever in my mouth.
3 ב I glory in the LORD;
        let the lowly hear it and rejoice.
4 ג Exalt the LORD with me;
        let us extol His name together.
5 ד I turned to the LORD, and He answered me;
        He saved me from all my terrors.
6 ה Men look to Him and are radiant;
   ו   let their faces not be downcast.
7 ז Here was a lowly man who called,
        and the LORD listened,
        and delivered him from all his troubles.
8 ח The angel of the LORD camps around those who
          fear Him
        and rescues them.

12: Israel's special relationship with God. 13–14: Cf. Deut. 26.15; 1 Kings 8.30, 39; Pss. 14.2; 53.3; 102.20; 113.4–6; Lam. 3.50. 16–17: Armies and military equipment, however strong, are no match for God's power. *Horses* pulled war-chariots. 19: *Death* and *famine* were common results of war and siege. 20: *Shield* is an apt image in a military context. 22: The psalm ends with the hope of God's continued care and protection, for which the psalm has been praising Him.

Ps. 34: Praise of God for deliverance from trouble. An acrostic psalm (see Pss. 9–10 n.) with the letter "vav" missing. As in Ps. 25, an additional verse, beginning with the letter "pe," follows the acrostic. The psalm can be divided into two sections, vv. 2–11 and 12–22; the second half in particular has wisdom affinities. Frequent reference is made to parts of the body: *mouth, tongue, lips, eyes, ears, face, bones;* and to actions associated with them: seeing, hearing, tasting, shouting. 1: See 1 Sam. 21.12–15, where the king, who is here called *Abimelech,* is referred to as Achish; see also Ps. 3. 3: *The lowly,* those completely dependent on God. 6: *Radiant,* the external manifestation of happiness, a bright, smiling face. 8: Protection by a guardian angel, a member of the heavenly court or a manifestation of God (Gen. 24.4; 48.16; Ps. 35.5–6).

a-a Cf. 1 Sam. 21.14 ff.

9 ט Taste and see how good the LORD is;
    happy the man who takes refuge in Him!

10 י Fear the LORD, you His consecrated ones,
    for those who fear Him lack nothing.

11 כ Lions have been reduced to starvation,
    but those who turn to the LORD shall not lack
      any good.

12 ל Come, my sons, listen to me;
    I will teach you what it is to fear the LORD.

13 מ Who is the man who is eager for life,
    who desires years of good fortune?

14 נ Guard your tongue from evil,
    your lips from deceitful speech.

15 ס Shun evil and do good,
    seek amity[a] and pursue it.

16 ע The eyes of the LORD are on the righteous,
    His ears attentive to their cry.

17 פ The face of the LORD is set against evildoers,
    to erase their names from the earth.

18 צ They[b] cry out, and the LORD hears,
    and saves them from all their troubles.

19 ק The LORD is close to the brokenhearted;
    those crushed in spirit He delivers.

20 ר Though the misfortunes of the righteous be
      many,
    the LORD will save him from them all,

21 ש Keeping all his bones intact,
    not one of them being broken.

22 ת One misfortune is the deathblow of the wicked;
    the foes of the righteous shall be ruined.

23 The LORD redeems the life of His servants;
    all who take refuge in Him shall not be ruined.

35 Of David.

    O LORD, strive with my adversaries,
      give battle to my foes,
2   take up shield and buckler,
    and come to my defense;
3   ready the spear and javelin
    against my pursuers;
    tell me, "I am your deliverance."
4   Let those who seek my life
    be frustrated and put to shame;
    let those who plan to harm me
    fall back in disgrace.

10–11: Predatory carnivores (the proud and arrogant) suffer want, while the humble are sustained by God. **12–15:** A sage's address to students, teaching fear of the LORD (Job 28.28; Prov. 1.7). In order to achieve a good life, one should guard one's tongue, etc. Questions and riddles were among the ancient pedagogic techniques. **16–18:** The LORD's benevolent gaze on the righteous, and His angry face, glaring at evildoers. If we follow the order of the alphabet found in Lam. 2, 3, and 4, and read v. 17 after v. 18, the verses flow more smoothly. **19:** *Brokenhearted . . . crushed in spirit*, the depressed and despondent who call on God. **20–23:** The varying fates of *the righteous* and *the wicked*. **20:** An admission that the righteous do encounter misfortune but that it is temporary; God will remove it. **23:** This v. stands outside the acrostic and provides a happy ending for the psalm. See 25.22 n.

Ps. 35: The speaking persona is a military leader, possibly the king, who prays for deliverance from his enemies. In vv. 1–10 the enemies are portrayed as foreign countries with armies; in vv. 11–16 they are false witnesses and treacherous friends, that is, allies who proved untrustworthy. **1–3:** Prayer that God, the Divine Warrior, arm Himself for battle against the psalmist's foes. **4–6:** Traditional invective against enemies; punishment by God's angelic forces (40.15–16).

---

a Or "integrity."   b Viz., the righteous of v. 16.

5   Let them be as chaff in the wind,
        the LORD's angel driving them on.
6   Let their path be dark and slippery,
        with the LORD's angel in pursuit.
7   For without cause they hid a net to trap me;
        without cause they dug a pit[a] for me.
8   Let disaster overtake them unawares;
        let the net they hid catch them;
        let them fall into it when disaster [strikes].
9   Then shall I exult in the LORD,
        rejoice in His deliverance.
10 All my bones shall say,
        "LORD, who is like You?
    You save the poor from one stronger than he,
        the poor and needy from his despoiler."

11 Malicious witnesses appear
        who question me about things I do not
            know.
12 They repay me evil for good,
        [seeking] my bereavement.
13 Yet, when they were ill,
        my dress was sackcloth,
        I kept a fast—
        [b]may what I prayed for happen to me![b]
14 I walked about as though it were my friend or my
            brother;
        I was bowed with gloom, like one mourning for
            his mother.
15 But when I stumble, they gleefully gather;
        wretches gather against me,
        I know not why;
        [c]they tear at me without end.
16 With impious, mocking grimace[c]
        they gnash their teeth at me.

17   O Lord, how long will You look on?
    Rescue me [c]from their attacks,[c]
        my precious life, from the lions,
18   that I may praise You in a great congregation,
        acclaim You in a mighty throng.
19 Let not my treacherous enemies rejoice over me,
        or those who hate me without reason wink their
            eyes.

5: As in the previous psalm (v. 7), the focus moves to *the LORD's angel,* a manifestation of God. This commonality may explain the adjacent placement of these two psalms. *Chaff* is easily blown away (Ps. 1.4; Isa. 17.13). **7–8:** By the law of talion or equivalent retribution (see 3.8), *net* and *pit* entrap those who used them to ensnare others. **8:** *Disaster,* Heb "sho'ah," the term now used for the Holocaust. *Unawares:* Just as the enemy plotted to catch the psalmist without warning, so their measure-for-measure punishment will come without warning. **10:** *All my bones,* my whole being. **13–18:** The king is betrayed by those he prayed for (former allies). **13:** Typical mourning practices. **19–21:** The language of conspiracy. **22–25:** Appeal to God to intervene; the psalmist assumes that God has *seen* (v. 22), but for unknown reasons, has not acted. **27–28:** In place of the enemies' damaging speech (vv. 11–12, 20–21), the psalmist's tongue tells of the LORD's victory.

---

a Transferred from first clause for clarity.
b-b Meaning of Heb. uncertain; lit. "my prayer returns upon my bosom."
c-c Meaning of Heb. uncertain.

20 For they do not offer amity,
  but devise fraudulent schemes against harmless
    folk.

21 They open wide their mouths at me,
  saying, "Aha, aha, we have seen it!"

22 You have seen it, O Lord;
  do not hold aloof!
 O Lord, be not far from me!

23 Wake, rouse Yourself for my cause,
  for my claim, O my God and my Lord!

24 Take up my cause, O Lord my God, as You are
    beneficent,
  and let them not rejoice over me.

25 Let them not think,
  "Aha, just what we wished!"
 Let them not say,
  "We have destroyed him!"

26 May those who rejoice at my misfortune
  be frustrated and utterly disgraced;
 may those who vaunt themselves over me
  be clad in frustration and shame.

27 May those who desire my vindication
  sing forth joyously;
 may they always say,
  "Extolled be the Lord
  who desires the well-being of His servant,"

28 while my tongue shall recite Your beneficent
    acts,
  Your praises all day long.

36 For the leader. Of the servant of the Lord, of David.

2 *a-I know-a* what Transgression says to the wicked;
  he has no sense of the dread of God,

3 *b-because its speech is seductive to him
  till his iniquity be found out and he be hated.-b*

4 His words are evil and deceitful;
  he will not consider doing good.

5 In bed he plots mischief;
  he is set on a path of no good,
  he does not reject evil.

6 O Lord, Your faithfulness reaches to heaven;
  Your steadfastness to the sky;

7 Your beneficence is like the high mountains;

Ps. 36: Rejoicing in the Temple, protected from evildoers. The poem consists of instruction about the wicked (vv. 2–5), a hymn lauding the Temple (vv. 6–10), and a prayer for God's care of the righteous and the fall of the wicked (vv. 11–13). **1:** *Servant of the Lord,* 18.1. **2:** Personified transgression speaks in oracular form (as prophets do). To the wicked, this voice is authoritative. The Rabbis identified it with the evil inclination. **2–5:** The wicked have no dread of God, nothing to motivate them to desist from evil thoughts and speech, which occupy them privately *(in bed)* and publicly *(on a path)*. **6–11:** Contrasted with the wicked are those who seek God in his Temple. **6–7:** Though He is worshipped at the Temple, God's beneficent justice is of cosmic proportion, reaching everywhere. **7–9:** These vv. are recited when donning the tallit (prayer shawl).

a-a Lit. "In my heart is."   b-b Meaning of Heb. uncertain.

Your justice like the great deep;
        man and beast You deliver, O Lord.

8   How precious is Your faithful care, O God!
        Mankind shelters in the shadow of Your wings.

9   They feast on the rich fare of Your house;
        You let them drink at Your refreshing stream.

10 With You is the fountain of life;
        by Your light do we see light.

11 Bestow Your faithful care on those devoted to You,
        and Your beneficence on upright men.

12 Let not the foot of the arrogant tread on me,
        or the hand of the wicked drive me away.

13 There lie the evildoers, fallen,
        thrust down, unable to rise.

37 Of David.

א   Do not be vexed by evil men;
        do not be incensed by wrongdoers;

2   for they soon wither like grass,
        like verdure fade away.

3   ב Trust in the Lord and do good,
        abide in the land and remain loyal.

4   Seek the favor of the Lord,
        and He will grant you the desires of your heart.

5   ג Leave all[a] to the Lord;
        trust in Him; He will do it.

6   He will cause your vindication to shine forth like
            the light,
        the justice of your case, like the noonday sun.

7   ד Be patient and wait for the Lord,
        do not be vexed by the prospering man
        who carries out his schemes.

8   ה Give up anger, abandon fury,
        do not be vexed;
        it can only do harm.

9   For evil men will be cut off,
        but those who look to the Lord—
        they shall inherit the land.

10 ו A little longer and there will be no wicked man;
        you will look at where he was—
        he will be gone.

11 But the lowly shall inherit the land,
        and delight in abundant well-being.

12 ז The wicked man schemes against the righteous,
        and gnashes his teeth at him.

a Lit. "your way."

8–10: The Temple protects and its sacrificial meals provide *rich fare,* the meat and fat eaten by the sacrificer. *Refreshing stream,* the river of life-giving water that goes out from the Temple; cf. Ezek. 47.1–2; Joel 4.18; Zech. 14.8; Ps. 46.5. Heb for "refreshing" is "'adanekha," forming a nexus with the rivers of Eden (Gen. 2.10); Eden is also known as the Garden of God. These waters are the *fountain* (source) *of life. Light* signifies life. **12–13:** The psalmist hopes to be safe from the wicked, *arrogant* in that they do not recognize a higher power. The wicked will be made permanently powerless. **13:** *There,* at Mt. Zion, where the wicked cannot come. Alternatively, it may mean the underworld (cf. Job 3.17) or be an adverb of time ("then").

Ps. 37: An acrostic psalm (see Pss. 9–10 n.; 25 n.) whose themes, structure, and vocabulary are characteristic of Proverbs. "Wisdom" is mentioned explicitly in v. 30, and thus the psalm should be considered a wisdom psalm, written by someone who was part of the wisdom movement or heavily influenced by it. It expresses the certainty that ultimately the righteous will succeed and will inherit the land, and the wicked will fail. Inheriting the land is a major theme, repeated six times. The authors of the Dead Sea Scrolls wrote a "pesher" (a type of commentary) on this psalm in which they apply it to their own situation (4Q171 = 4QpPs[a]). They see "Ephraim" and "Manasseh" (their code words for Pharisees and Sadducees) as the wicked and themselves as the people who will, in the future, inherit the land. **1–2:** *Do not be vexed* by the apparent success of *evil men:* Repeated in vv. 7–8; see Prov. 23.17–18; 24.1, 19–20. **2:** *Like grass,* the evanescence of the wicked (90.5–6; 102.5, 12; 103.15; Job 8.12–13), especially apt in the context of "the land"; cf. vv. 20, 35. **3:** The first occurrence of the refrainlike promise of possessing the land (vv. 9, 11, 22, 29, 34). **9–10:** *Cut off,* separated from the land (cf. vv. 28, 38; Prov. 2.21–22).

13   The Lord laughs at him,
      for He knows that his day will come.

14 ח The wicked draw their swords, bend their bows,
      to bring down the lowly and needy,
      to slaughter ^aupright men.^{-a}

15   Their swords shall pierce their own hearts,
      and their bows shall be broken.

16 ט Better the little that the righteous man has
      than the great abundance of the wicked.

17   For the arms of the wicked shall be broken,
      but the Lord is the support of the righteous.

18 י The Lord is concerned for the need^b of the
        blameless;
      their portion lasts forever;

19   they shall not come to grief in bad times;
      in famine, they shall eat their fill.

20 כ But the wicked shall perish,
      and the enemies of the Lord shall be consumed,
      like meadow grass^c consumed in smoke.

21 ל The wicked man borrows and does not repay;
      the righteous is generous and keeps giving.

22   Those blessed by Him shall inherit the land,
      but those cursed by Him shall be cut off.

23 מ The steps of a man are made firm by the Lord,
      when He delights in his way.

24   Though he stumbles, he does not fall down,
      for the Lord gives him support.

25 נ I have been young and am now old,
      but I have never seen a righteous man
        abandoned,
      or his children seeking bread.

26   He is always generous, and lends,
      and his children are held blessed.

27 ס Shun evil and do good,
      and you shall abide forever.

28   For the Lord loves what is right,
      He does not abandon His faithful ones.
    They are preserved forever,
      while the children of the wicked will be cut off.

29   The righteous shall inherit the land,
      and abide forever in it.

30 פ The mouth of the righteous utters wisdom,
      and his tongue speaks what is right.

31   The teaching of his God is in his heart;
      his feet do not slip.

13: God's derisive laughter at the pretensions of the wicked (2.4; 59.9). **14–15:** The weapons of the wicked "backfire" and are broken, as are their arms (v. 17). **16:** *Better . . . than,* characteristic wording of wisdom literature (e.g., Prov. 15.16–17). **18–20:** The varying fates of the righteous and the wicked. **27:** See v. 3; Ps. 34.15; Prov. 13.19.

---

a-a Lit. "those whose way is upright."   b Lit. "days."
c Meaning of Heb. uncertain.

32 צ The wicked watches for the righteous,
        seeking to put him to death;
33   the LORD will not abandon him to his
            power;
        He will not let him be condemned in
            judgment.
34 ק Look to the LORD and keep to His way,
        and He will raise you high that you may inherit
            the land;
        when the wicked are cut off, you shall see it.
35 ר I saw a wicked man, powerful,
        well-rooted like a robust native tree.
36   Suddenly he vanished and was gone;
        I sought him, but he was not to be found.
37 ש Mark the blameless, note the upright,
        for there is a future for the man of integrity.
38   But transgressors shall be utterly destroyed,
        the future of the wicked shall be cut off.
39 ת The deliverance of the righteous comes from the
            LORD,
        their stronghold in time of trouble.
40   The LORD helps them and rescues them,
        rescues them from the wicked and delivers
            them,
        for they seek refuge in Him.

38 A psalm of David. *Lehazkir.*[a]

2   O LORD, do not punish me in wrath;
        do not chastise me in fury.
3   For Your arrows have struck me;
        Your blows have fallen upon me.
4   There is no soundness in my flesh because of Your
            rage,
        no wholeness in my bones because of my sin.
5   For my iniquities have [b]overwhelmed me;[b]
        they are like a heavy burden, more than I can
            bear.
6   My wounds stink and fester
        because of my folly.
7   I am all bent and bowed;
        I walk about in gloom all day long.
8   For my sinews are full of fever;
        there is no soundness in my flesh.
9   I am all benumbed and crushed;
        I roar because of the turmoil in my mind.

35–38: The varying fates of the children of the righteous (v. 25) and of the transgressors; this type of contrast also typifies wisdom literature. Wisdom literature often employs empirical observation, as in vv. 25 and 35 "to see." This word occurs eighteen times in Ecclesiastes.

Ps. 38: A sinner prays for healing, a sign that his sins are forgiven. The psalm contains an extensive description of physical illness and mental anguish (see Pss. 6; 13; 22; 31). The list of ailments—which includes the entire body racked with pain, festering wounds, inability to stand erect, fever, dull eyes, lack of strength—sounds like a catalogue of all possible maladies, suggesting that the illness is metaphoric; they are manifestations (perhaps physical) of sin. Burdened by his sins, the psalmist is in mental and physical anguish. Understood thus, the psalm is more a prayer for forgiveness (see esp. v. 19) than a prayer for healing. **2:** Sickness was thought to be the punishment for sin. Cf. 6.2; the similarity suggests that either some psalmists copied from each other, or that psalmists used various stock phrases or verses. **3:** The punishing illness is described as arrows sent by God (Job 6.4; 16.12–13). **4–6:** Sin as the cause of the psalmist's malady (Isa. 1.5–6). Most psalms of complaint lack confes-

a Meaning of Heb. uncertain.   _b-b Lit. "passed over my head."_

10 O Lord, You are aware of all my entreaties;
   my groaning is not hidden from You.

11 My mind reels;
   my strength fails me;
   my eyes too have lost their luster.

12 My friends and companions stand back from my
      affliction;
   my kinsmen stand far off.

13 Those who seek my life lay traps;
   those who wish me harm speak malice;
   they utter deceit all the time.

14 But I am like a deaf man, unhearing,
   like a dumb man who cannot speak up;

15 I am like one who does not hear,
   who has no retort on his lips.

16 But I wait for You, O Lord;
   You will answer, O Lord, my God.

17 For I fear they will rejoice over me;
   when my foot gives way they will vaunt
      themselves against me.

18 For I am on the verge of collapse;
   my pain is always with me.

19 I acknowledge my iniquity;
   I am fearful over my sin;   •

20 for my mortal enemies are numerous;
   my treacherous foes are many.

21 Those who repay evil for good
   harass me for pursuing good.

22 Do not abandon me, O Lord;
   my God, be not far from me;

23 hasten to my aid,
   O Lord, my deliverance.

39 For the leader; for *Jeduthun*. A psalm of David.

2 I resolved I would watch my step
   lest I offend by my speech;
   I would keep my mouth muzzled
   while the wicked man was in my presence.

3 I was dumb, silent;
   I was very[a] still
   while my pain was intense.

4 My mind was in a rage,
   my thoughts were all aflame;
   I spoke out:

sions. **12–13:** Friends and family distance themselves from the psalmist, showing indifference (see 31.9–13 n.), while enemies speak against him. **14–18:** The psalmist cannot or will not respond to his foes, pretending that he does not hear them. He prefers to wait for God's response, without which the psalmist will die. He worries that if his death occurs, his foes will rejoice, a common theme of Psalms (e.g., 13.5). As a sinner, the psalmist has no way to withstand evildoers by himself. **14:** *Deaf*, i.e., ignorant of the plotting of his foes in v. 13. **19:** Confession of sin (32.5). **22–23:** Like the opening, highly stereotypical language; see 22.12, 20; 40.14.

Ps. 39: A meditation on the brevity of human life (cf. Pss. 90; 102), with the hope that the short time the psalmist has to live will be spent in God's favor. This psalm has some commonality with Ps. 38 (admission that suffering is the result of sin, being "dumb"), but it does not emphasize physical suffering. It also shares major themes with Eccl.: the idea of the brevity of life, expressed by the term "hevel," "a breath," (see the refrain in vv. 6 and 12), a questioning of the purpose of life, and the conclusion that people should use their time in the service of God. **1:** *Jeduthun* was a famous Temple musician; see 1 Chron. 16.42; 25.6; Pss. 62; 77. **2–5:** Avoidance of sins of speech is a common concern of Psalms. Here, speech would challenge God or express anger at His actions against the psalmist, so the psalmist keeps silent as long as he can (cf. v. 10); but at last he speaks out, asking God how long he has to live, that is, how long he must bear his suffering. (Cf. Job, who

---

a Cf. use of ṭwb in Hos. 10.1; Jonah 4.4.

5 Tell me, O LORD, what my term is,
what is the measure of my days;
I would know how fleeting my life is.

6 You have made my life just handbreadths long;
its span is as nothing in Your sight;
^ano man endures any longer than a breath.^{-a}

Selah.

7 Man walks about as a mere shadow;
mere futility is his hustle and bustle,
amassing and not knowing who will gather in.

8 What, then, can I count on, O Lord?
In You my hope lies.

9 Deliver me from all my transgressions;
make me not the butt of the benighted.

10 I am dumb, I do not speak up,
for it is Your doing.

11 Take away Your plague from me;
I perish from Your blows.

12 You chastise a man in punishment for his sin,
consuming like a moth what he treasures.
No man is more than a breath. *Selah.*

13 Hear my prayer, O LORD;
give ear to my cry;
do not disregard my tears;
for like all my forebears
I am an alien, resident with You.

14 Look away from me, ^athat I may recover,^{-a}
before I pass away and am gone.

40 For the leader. A psalm of David.

2 I put my hope in the LORD;
He inclined toward me,
and heeded my cry.

3 He lifted me out of the miry pit,
the slimy clay,
and set my feet on a rock,
steadied my legs.

4 He put a new song into my mouth,
a hymn to our God.
May many see it and stand in awe,
and trust in the LORD.

5 Happy is the man who makes the LORD his trust,
who turns not to the arrogant or to followers of
falsehood.

a-a *Meaning of Heb. uncertain.*

does not hesitate to challenge God.) **6:** *Selah* (also v. 11), see 3.3 n. **7:** For the theme of one's wealth left for others, see 49.17–18; Eccl. 2.18–19. **8:** Given that life is short and unpredictable, the only durable hope is faith in God, which the psalmist professes. This faith should lead God to forgive his sins and remove his punishment. **12:** Here and in v. 7 the suffering seems to be financial loss rather than illness. **13:** *An alien, resident*, a resident alien, a legal term (see Lev. 25.23; 1 Chron. 29.15) used metaphorically to mean that the psalmist resides only temporarily and conditionally with God. **14:** *Look away from me,* stop punishing me. *Am gone,* there is no thought of an afterlife in Psalms.

Ps. 40: The psalmist seeks a public and permanent venue for praising God, to acknowledge God's past favors and in anticipation of the current favor now requested. This balance between anticipatory praise and a request for deliverance is not unusual (cf. Ps. 22), but here the emphasis is on praise rather than on complaint about misfortune. This psalm is perhaps a combination of two psalms, the second of which (vv. 14–18) is preserved as Ps. 70. (NJPS makes the break after v. 12.) Alternatively, the psalm was one composition and Ps. 70 has lost the first part. **3:** *Pit . . . slimy clay,* synonyms for the abode of the dead; as in 30.4, death is used to refer to grave illness. The terra firma image of *a rock* contrasts with the slippery and sinking image of *slimy clay.* **4:** *A new song,* cf. Ps. 33.3. **5:** Ps. 34.9; Prov. 16.20. **6:** *Cannot be set out before you,* or, "cannot be compared to you." **7–9:** Difficult to interpret. A general statement about sacrifice is illustrated by listing several main types: *sacrifice,* a nonspecific term for animal offerings; *meal offering,* a

6   *a-You, O LORD my God, have done many things;
         the wonders You have devised for us
         cannot be set out before You;-a
         I would rehearse the tale of them,
         but they are more than can be told.
7   b-You gave me to understand that-b
         You do not desire sacrifice and meal offering;
         You do not ask for burnt offering and sin
         offering.
8   Then I said,
         b-"See, I will bring a scroll recounting what befell
         me."-b
9   To do what pleases You, my God, is my desire;
         Your teaching is in my inmost parts.
10   I proclaimed [Your] righteousness in a great
         congregation;
         see, I did not withhold my words;
         O LORD, You must know it.
11   I did not keep Your beneficence to myself;
         I declared Your faithful deliverance;
         I did not fail to speak of Your steadfast love in a
         great congregation.
12   O LORD, You will not withhold from me Your
         compassion;
         Your steadfast love will protect me always.

13   For misfortunes without number envelop me;
         my iniquities have caught up with me;
         I cannot see;
         they are more than the hairs of my head;
         c-I am at my wits' end.-c
14d O favor me, LORD, and save me;
         O LORD, hasten to my aid.
15   Let those who seek to destroy my life
         be frustrated and disgraced;
         let those who wish me harm
         fall back in shame.
16   Let those who say "Aha! Aha!" over me
         be desolate because of their frustration.
17   But let all who seek You be glad and rejoice in You;
         let those who are eager for Your deliverance
         always say, "Extolled be the LORD!"
18   But I am poor and needy;
         may the Lord devise [deliverance] for me.

grain offering accompanying animal sacrifice; *burnt offering,* in which the entire sacrifice is consumed by fire; *sin offering,* a purification offering. This is not a critique of the sacrificial system, but rather a notice that sacrifice is not required in this instance and does not satisfy the psalmist's desire *to do what pleases . . . God.* God is pleased if people follow his *teaching,* his torah, written in a scroll (cf. Deut. 31.26). Doing what pleases God is preferable to sacrifice (1 Sam. 15.22; Jer. 7.21–23; Mic. 6.6–7). For the idea that a psalm or prayer may please God more than a sacrifice or may take the place of (unavailable) sacrifice, cf. Pss. 69.30–32; 141.2. **8:** This v. is a crux. NJPS interprets a scroll as the psalmist's hymn or a record of his experience. Other interpretations are: the Torah (Jer. 31.31–34); or the book of life, which appears elsewhere in the Bible (e.g., Exod. 32.32; Pss. 69.29; 139.16; Dan. 12.1)—this idea is further developed in later Judaism, especially in the Rosh Ha-Shanah liturgy; or, if the psalmist is a king, the law of the king (Deut. 17.14–20). *Recounting what befell me* translates Heb "katuv ʿalay," "written on/about me." According to this translation, the psalmist brings a written, and therefore permanent, account of his experience in place of a sacrifice—a very literary touch by a man of words. Others understand "written of me" to mean "prescribed to me," that is, the Torah is prescribed to the psalmist. **10:** *Great congregation,* the psalmist's community, participants in the thanksgiving ceremony (cf. Pss. 22.26; 35.18). Praise is only meaningful if it is public. **13:** God's deeds are too numerous to recount (v. 6) and the psalmist's misfortunes are too many to list. **15–17:** The psalmist prays that the enemy be repulsed and shamed, and that those who seek God join the psalmist in praise, a typical trope in Psalms. **18:** The righteous are often called *poor and needy* (cf. Ps. 86.1). *Do not delay,* lit. "do not be late," as though only a short time remains.

---

a-a Or "You, O LORD my God, have done many things—/ the wonders You have devised
for us; / none can equal You."   b-b Meaning of Heb. uncertain.
c-c Or "my courage fails me."   d With vv. 14–18, cf. Ps. 70.

You are my help and my rescuer;
my God, do not delay.

41
For the leader. A psalm of David.

2   Happy is he who is thoughtful of the wretched;
    in bad times may the LORD keep him from
        harm.

3   May the LORD guard him and preserve him;
    and may he be thought happy in the land.
    Do not subject him to the will of his enemies.

4   The LORD will sustain him on his sickbed;
        ᵃ⁻You shall wholly transform his bed of
            suffering.⁻ᵃ

5   I said, "O LORD, have mercy on me,
    heal me, for I have sinned against You."

6   My enemies speak evilly of me,
    "When will he die and his name perish?"

7   If one comes to visit, he speaks falsely;
    his mind stores up evil thoughts;
    once outside, he speaks them.

8   All my enemies whisper together against me,
    imagining the worst for me.

9   "Something baneful has settled in him;
    he'll not rise from his bed again."

10 My ally in whom I trusted,
    even he who shares my bread,
        ᵃ⁻has been utterly false to me.⁻ᵃ

11 But You, O LORD, have mercy on me;
    let me rise again and repay them.

12 Then shall I know that You are pleased with me:
    when my enemy cannot shout in triumph
        over me.

13 You will support me because of my integrity,
    and let me abide in Your presence forever.

14 Blessed is the LORD, God of Israel,
    from eternity to eternity.
    Amen and Amen.

BOOK TWO

42
For the leader. A *maskil* of the Korahites.

2   Like a hind crying for water,ᵇ
    my soul cries for You, O God;

---

a-a *Meaning of Heb. uncertain.*   b *Lit. "watercourses."*

Ps. 41: A prayer for healing, with similarities to Pss. 38 and 39. **2–4:** God's protection of the ill. **5–9:** The psalmist contrasts what he says to what the enemies have said. **5:** The petitioner believes that sin is the cause of the illness (39.12). **6–9:** The psalmist's enemies are guilty of insincere and damaging speech (38.13). *Whisper together* suggests a curse or spell against the sick person, quoted in v. 9. **10:** Cf. 35.11–16. **11:** *Let me rise,* "raise me up," in contrast to the words of the enemies: "he'll not rise . . ." **12–13:** In the context of a plea for healing, these vv. may suggest that, once prevented by his illness from coming to the Temple (cf. 2 Chron. 26.21), the psalmist is confident that he will be healed and readmitted to God's presence. **13:** *Integrity* and being in God's *presence forever* are found elsewhere at the close of a psalm (e.g., 23; 26). **14:** The doxology or blessing that closes Book I of the Psalter is not originally part of the psalm, but reflects the editing of the psalter into five books. Similar doxologies are found at the end of the other book divisions (72.19; 89.53; 106.48).

Ps. 42: Pss. 42–43 are a single psalm, as indicated by their shared refrain (42.6, 12; 43.5), and common theme of the desire to come to the Temple despite enemy persecution (42.3; 43.3–4; cf. Pss. 9–10, also thought to have been one psalm). Ps. 42 begins a collection called the Elohistic Psalter. Comprised of Pss. 42–83, this section much prefers the Heb "'elohim," "God" (sometimes translated "god") to LORD (Hebrew "YHVH"), in sharp contrast to the rest of the Psalter. Phrases like (Ps. 43.4) "O God, my God" are awkward in Heb, and may reflect a revision of the more common and expected, "O LORD, my God" (e.g., Jonah 2.7). Likewise, the use of "God" throughout Ps. 82 is confusing, and is likely secondary (see 82.1 n.). Scholars suggest that most of the references to God in this grouping are secondary, and were originally LORD ("YHVH"); these

3   my soul thirsts for God, the living God;
          O when will I come to appear before God!

4   My tears have been my food day and night;
          I am ever taunted with, "Where is your God?"

5   When I think of this, I pour out my soul:
          how I ᵃ⁻walked with the crowd, moved with
              them,⁻ᵃ
          the festive throng, to the House of God
          with joyous shouts of praise.

6   Why so downcast, my soul,
          why disquieted within me?
     Have hope in God;
          I will yet praise Him
          ᵇ⁻for His saving presence.⁻ᵇ

7   O my God, my soul is downcast;
          therefore I think of You
          in this land of Jordan and Hermon,
          in Mount Mizar,

8   where deep calls to deep
          in the roar of ᵃ⁻Your cataracts;⁻ᵃ
          all Your breakers and billows have swept
              over me.

9   By day may the LORD vouchsafe His faithful
              care,
          so that at night a song to Him may be with me,
          a prayer to the God of my life.

10   I say to God, my rock,
          "Why have You forgotten me,
          why must I walk in gloom,
          oppressed by my enemy?"

11   ᵃ⁻Crushing my bones,⁻ᵃ
          my foes revile me,
          taunting me always with, "Where is your
              God?"

a-a Meaning of Heb. uncertain.
b-b Several ancient versions and Heb. mss. connect the first word in v. 7 with the end of 6,
reading yeshuʿot panai weʾElohai, "my ever-present help, my God," as in vv. 12 and Ps.
43.5.

were changed by an editor who preferred to call the deity "ʾelohim," God. A parallel phenomenon is the use of "elohim" in the E source in the Torah. Ps. 42 also introduces the collection of Korahite psalms. These are found in Pss. 42(–43); 44–49; 84–85; 87–88, in other words in two collections, one in the Elohistic Psalter (42–49), one outside it (84–88). The separation of this collection in two sections of Psalms is one of many indications of the complexity of the editing of the Psalter. As indicated by 2 Chron. 20.19, "Levites of the sons of Kohath and of the sons of Korah got up to extol the LORD God of Israel at the top of their voices," the Korahites had a special role in Temple singing. (Contrast the negative depiction of the Korahites in Num. ch 16.) There are some common phrases in the collection (e.g., Pss. 42.3 and 84.3, "the living God"; 42.3 and 84.8, "appear[ing] before God"), but attempts at finding strong thematic similarities between them are not compelling. Similarly unconvincing are attempts to read the Korahite collection as a whole, especially as stages of a ritual. **1:** On *maskil*, see 32.1 n.; a disproportionate number of psalms with this word appear in the Elohistic Psalter. **2–3:** The imagery is very striking (see also 63.2). God is the basic nourishment for the psalmist. **3:** On *the living God*, see 18.47 n. Some ancient biblical translations render *to appear before God* as "to see God"; the consonantal Heb text allows this translation. This may reflect an idea that God could actually be seen at a temple, manifest through an image (see 11.7 n.). Zion plays a disproportionately significant role in the Korah psalms; see esp. Ps. 48. **4:** Instead of divine nourishment, the psalmist's food and drink is his tears. The taunt of the enemies is that his God is powerless to relieve his current predicament. **5–6:** This psalm is remarkable for the inner dialogues it relates. *Soul* reflects the inner being; the Bible does not partake in the (Greek) notion of a bipartite being, comprised of body and soul. **6:** A refrain (see also v. 12 and 43.6). God's *saving presence* refers back to seeing God in v. 3 (the word "face" [Heb "panim"] is used in both verses). **7:** The northern geographical locations (Mount Mizar is probably near Hermon) mentioned suggest that the psalmist is distant from Jerusalem; some have suggested that this psalm, and perhaps all of the Korahite psalms, are northern in origin. **8:** A mythological reference, perhaps also alluding to the sources of the Jordan River in northern Israel. **9:** *The God of my life* refers back to v. 3; this psalm has an unusual number of refrains and cross-references. **10–11:** *Foes* are finally revealed to be the main topic

12 Why so downcast, my soul,
        why disquieted within me?
    Have hope in God;
        I will yet praise Him,
        my ever-present help, my God.

43 ^aVindicate me, O God,
        champion my cause
        against faithless people;
        rescue me from the treacherous, dishonest
            man.
2   For You are my God, my stronghold;
        why have You rejected me?
    Why must I walk in gloom,
        oppressed by the enemy?
3   Send forth Your light and Your truth;
        they will lead me;
        they will bring me to Your holy mountain,
        to Your dwelling-place,
4   that I may come to the altar of God,
        God, my delight, my joy;
        that I may praise You with the lyre,
        O God, my God.
5   Why so downcast, my soul,
        why disquieted within me?
    Have hope in God;
        I will yet praise Him,
        my ever-present help, my God.

44 For the leader. Of the Korahites. A *maskil*.

2   We have heard, O God,
        our fathers have told us
        the deeds You performed in their time,
        in days of old.
3   With Your hand You planted them,
        displacing nations;
        You brought misfortune on peoples,
        and drove them out.
4   It was not by their sword that they took the land,
        their arm did not give them victory,
        but Your right hand, Your arm, and Your
            goodwill,
        for You favored them.
5   You are my king, O God;
        decree victories for Jacob!

of this petition. *Taunting me always with, "Where is your God?"* serves as a refrain with v. 4. **12:** See v. 6 n.

Ps. 43: Pss. 42–43 form a single unit (see above). It is unclear when and how they became separated; perhaps the fact that Ps. 42 nostalgically focuses on the past, while Ps. 43 is more concerned with the future, promoted this division. In addition, Ps. 43 opens with the common initial elements of an individual petition (e.g., 5.2–3). **1–2:** These reflect the typical features of a petition: invocation (*O God*), petition in the imperative or related forms (*vindicate, champion, rescue*), and motivation (*For You . . .*) **3–4:** The main theme, the desire to visit the Temple, is reiterated (see 42.3 n.). *Dwelling-place* is the plural of the word used to express "Tabernacle" ("mishkan") in Priestly literature. It is not entirely clear how God's *light and . . . truth* will save the psalmist from his enemies. Ibn Ezra and Radak note that the *light* is a countermeasure to the gloom, lit. darkness, that the psalmist felt in v. 2. **5:** A concluding refrain; see 42.6 n.

Ps. 44: This is a community petition; it begins with a hymn about God's past deliverance (vv. 2–9), followed by a complaint about the current situation (vv. 10–17). A protestation of innocence (vv. 18–23) and the petition itself (vv. 24–27) conclude the psalm. **2:** On parents teaching children, see, e.g., Deut. 6.20–25. **3:** On planting as a metaphor for possessing the land of Israel, see Exod. 15.17. **4:** Even Rahab the foreign prostitute acknowledges that it is through divine help that Israel succeeds militarily (Josh. 2.9–11). **5:** In the ancient Near Eastern world, the king led his people in battle; thus God's role as warrior is part of His role as *king*.

a A continuation of Ps. 42.

6   Through You we gore our foes;
            by Your name we trample our adversaries;
7   I do not trust in my bow;
            it is not my sword that gives me victory;
8   You give us victory over our foes;
            You thwart those who hate us.
9   In God we glory at all times,
            and praise Your name unceasingly.   *Selah.*

10   Yet You have rejected and disgraced us;
            You do not go with our armies.
11   You make us retreat before our foe;
            our enemies plunder us at will.
12   You let them devour us like sheep;
            You disperse us among the nations.
13   You sell Your people for no fortune,
            You set no high price on them.
14   You make us the butt of our neighbors,
            the scorn and derision of those around us.
15   You make us a byword among the nations,
            a laughingstock[a] among the peoples.
16   I am always aware of my disgrace;
            I am wholly covered with shame
17   at the sound of taunting revilers,
            in the presence of the vengeful foe.

18   All this has come upon us,
            yet we have not forgotten You,
            or been false to Your covenant.
19   Our hearts have not gone astray,
            nor have our feet swerved from Your path,
20   though You cast us, crushed, to where the
            [b-]sea monster[-b] is,
            and covered us over with deepest darkness.
21   If we forgot the name of our God
            and spread forth our hands to a foreign god,
22   God would surely search it out,
            for He knows the secrets of the heart.
23   It is for Your sake that we are slain all day long,
            that we are regarded as sheep to be slaughtered.

24   Rouse Yourself; why do You sleep, O Lord?
            Awaken, do not reject us forever!
25   Why do You hide Your face,
            ignoring our affliction and distress?

9: This is a typical case where *Selah* appears at a main division of a psalm (see 3.3 n.), in this case, demarcating the hymn from the complaint. **10:** *You do not go with our armies* may be a play on God's role as LORD of hosts, who is supposed to lead his heavenly hosts or armies in Israel's defense. **12:** The sheep metaphor illustrates dispersal of the defeated troops in battle; cf. 1 Kings 22.17: "I saw all Israel scattered over the hills like sheep without a shepherd." **18:** *Covenant*s are mutual obligations; the psalmist is saying that even though God has broken His side, the community continues to maintain its obligations. **20:** For this myth, see 8.1 n. **21–22:** See the similar self-imprecation at 7.4–6. *Spread forth our hands* refers to praying; this was the typical prayer position in the ancient Near East, and a stele from Hazor shows two upraised hands, representing the supplicant. On God knowing people's secret thoughts, see Jer. 17.10. **24–27:** This section contains the typical elements of a petition: the invocation (*O LORD*), imperatives (*rouse, awaken, arise, help*), and a motivation (*as befits Your faithfulness*). This motivation goes beyond the ideas expressed in vv. 21–23, suggesting that even if the people are culpable, they must be forgiven. **24:** On God sleeping, see 7.7 n. **25:** On God hiding His face, see 6.4–5 n.

a *Lit. "a wagging of the head."*
b-b *Heb.* tannim = tannin, *as in Ezek. 29.3 and 32.2.*

26 We lie prostrate in the dust;
  our body clings to the ground.
27 Arise and help us,
  redeem us, as befits Your faithfulness.

45 For the leader; *ᵃon shoshannim.ᵃ* Of the Korahites.
A *maskil.* A love song.

2 My heart is astir with gracious words;
  I speak my poem to a king;
  my tongue is the pen of an expert scribe.

3 You are fairer than all men;
  your speech is endowed with grace;
  rightly has God given you an eternal blessing.
4 Gird your sword upon your thigh, O hero,
  in your splendor and glory;
5 ᵃin your glory, win success;
  ride on in the cause of truth and meekness and
    right;
  and let your right hand lead you to awesome
    deeds.ᵃ
6 Your arrows, sharpened,
  ᵇ[pierce] the breast of the king's enemies;
  peoples fall at your feet.ᵇ
7 Your ᶜdivine throneᶜ is everlasting;
  your royal scepter is a scepter of equity.
8 You love righteousness and hate wickedness;
  rightly has God, your God, chosen to anoint
    you
  with oil of gladness over all your peers.
9 All your robes [are fragrant] with
  myrrh and aloes and cassia;

a-a *Meaning of Heb. uncertain.*
b-b *Order of Heb. clauses inverted for clarity.*   c-c *Cf. 1 Chron. 29.23.*

26: These represent military subjugation (see Josh. 10.24). **27:** *Arise* may have military connotations; see 7.7 n. On God's *faithfulness,* see 5.8 n.

Ps. 45: A unique psalm, commemorating a royal wedding. It mentions the name of neither king nor queen, and thus could be reused for other royal weddings. Scholars have speculated on the psalm's original setting. Ahab is a leading contender since he married Jeze-

bel, a Phoenician princess (see v. 13), and built a palace inlaid with ivory (see v. 9 and 1 Kings 22.39); some have even suggested the verb (v. 8) *You love* ("ᵃahavta") is a play on the name Ahab. Medievals read the psalm about David (Ibn Ezra, first opinion) or about the Messiah (Ibn Ezra, second opinion, Radak). In the Christian community, this was typically read Christologically, and Radak concludes his commentary with a long polemic against this reading. Al-

though the psalm is singular as a royal wedding psalm, it shares the following motifs with Ps. 72, another royal psalm: the king's might, his justice, and a conclusion that all nations shall praise him. **1:** A unique superscription with many attributes. *Shoshannim* (lilies?) predominate in the Song of Songs, and are seen as erotic (e.g., Song 5.13); this connects to the attribute *A love song.* **2:** This too is unique—no other psalm has this type of introduction, speaking to an audience classifying the following psalm (*my poem to a king*). **3:** Beauty was a royal attribute (see 1 Sam. 9.2 of Saul and 1 Sam. 16.12 of David); Egyptian kings are also described as very handsome. **4–6:** Israelite kings led their nation in battle and were expected to be warriors; here the king is depicted as an ideal, successful warrior. **4:** *Splendor and glory* are elsewhere divine attributes (e.g., 104.1); this raises the possibility that the king is here viewed as divine (see v. 7 n.). **7–8:** Justice was an important royal quality; see esp. 1 Kings 3.4–14 (of Solomon) and the description of the ideal future king in Isa. 11.3–5. **7:** This may also be translated "Your throne, O God ("ᵃelohim"), is everlasting" (so LXX), where the king is referred to as God. If this is taken literally, this psalm would be unique in the entire Bible in explicitly depicting the king as divine (see v. 4 and v. 18 n.), a notion that existed at times in other ancient Near Eastern cultures but is otherwise absent in biblical thought. Other modern scholars render the v. as "Your throne is like God's throne" (so already Ibn Ezra) or "Your throne is supreme." The Targum and Saadia add the words "will establish," reading "God will establish your throne," while Rashi understands "ᵃelohim" as judges (see Exod. 21.6, translators' note). These medieval and modern translations, including NJPS (*Your divine throne*), make this v. fit other texts, which do not view the biblical king as divine. **8:** *Anointing* is the central ritual of kingship (see 2.2 n.). **9–10:** A description of the pomp and cere-

from ivoried palaces
lutes entertain you.

10 Royal princesses are your favorites;
the consort stands at your right hand,
decked in gold of Ophir.

11 Take heed, lass, and note,
incline your ear:
forget your people and your father's house,

12 and let the king be aroused by your beauty;
since he is your lord, bow to him.

13 O Tyrian lass,
the wealthiest people will court your favor with
gifts,

14 ª⁻goods of all sorts.

The royal princess,
her dress embroidered with golden
mountings,

15 is led inside to the king;·ª
maidens in her train, her companions,
are presented to you.

16 They are led in with joy and gladness;
they enter the palace of the king.

17 Your sons will succeed your ancestors;
you will appoint them princes throughout the
land.

18 I commemorate your fame for all generations,
so peoples will praise you forever and ever.

46 For the leader. Of the Korahites; ª⁻on *alamoth.*·ª
A song.

2 God is our refuge and stronghold,
a help in trouble, very near.

3 Therefore we are not afraid
though the earth reels,
though mountains topple into the sea—

4 its waters rage and foam;
in its swell mountains quake.   *Selah.*

5 There is a river whose streams gladden God's
city,
the holy dwelling-place of the Most High.

a-a Meaning of Heb. uncertain.

mony of the wedding. **10:** The psalmist avoids the usual word for queen, choosing *consort* ("shegal"), a rare loanword from Akkadian. **11–12:** In the ancient Near East, wives were subservient to their husbands, and abandoned the practices and religion of their birth family for those of their husbands; even queens must do so. **13:** Others assume that a Tyrian woman from Phoenicia was part of the wedding party, though not necessarily the bride. **14–17:** A continuation of the description of the wedding ceremony. **14:** The Heb is difficult; in classical Jewish sources, the first part of the v. is connected to notions of female modesty, and is understood as suggesting that a woman's place is in her house rather than in public (e.g., *b. Yebam.* 67a and *b. Git.* 12a). **18:** A remarkable conclusion, where the king is praised in language typically reserved for God; the royal Ps. 72.17 offers a similar conclusion.

Ps. 46: This psalm expresses the community's confidence in God. It is unclear when and by whom such psalms were recited; perhaps they are to be connected to the demand of Ps. 62.9: "Trust in Him at all times, O people; pour out your hearts before Him; God is our refuge. *Selah.*" Some modern commentators connect it to the deliverance of Jerusalem from Sennacherib in 701 (see 1 Kings chs 18–20), but there is nothing specific in the psalm to support this. Like Ps. 48, another Korahite psalm, its focus is on Jerusalem. **1:** The meaning of *alamoth* is uncertain, though some connect it to the same word meaning "maidens." **2:** Similar imagery is in 18.3. **3–4:** Mythological language going back to Canaanite traditions (see 8.3 n.). Before these myths were recovered, the psalm was often connected to the eschatological battles (so Rashi and Radak). **5:** As in 104.6–13, the waters of chaos are domesticated. This description might be imaginative, since the Gihon Spring, the main water source of Jerusalem, is too small to fit the depiction of the

6 God is in its midst, it will not be toppled;
    by daybreak God will come to its aid.
7 Nations rage, kingdoms topple;
    at the sound of His thunder the earth dissolves.
8 The LORD of hosts is with us;
    the God of Jacob is our haven.   *Selah.*

9 Come and see what the LORD has done,
    how He has wrought desolation on the earth.
10 He puts a stop to wars throughout the earth,
    breaking the bow, snapping the spear,
    consigning wagons to the flames.
11 "Desist! Realize that I am God!
    I dominate the nations;
    I dominate the earth."
12 The LORD of hosts is with us;
    the God of Jacob is our haven.   *Selah.*

47 For the leader. Of the Korahites. A psalm.

2 All you peoples, clap your hands,
    raise a joyous shout for God.
3 For the LORD Most High is awesome,
    great king over all the earth;
4 He subjects peoples to us,
    sets nations at our feet.
5 He chose our heritage for us,
    the pride of Jacob whom He loved.   *Selah.*

6 God ascends midst acclamation;
    the LORD, to the blasts of the horn.
7 Sing, O sing to God;
    sing, O sing to our king;

v.; others suggest that this psalm was originally northern (see the Korahite psalm 42.8 n.). In the Korahite 87.2, however, *God's city* clearly refers to Jerusalem. **6:** As in Ps. 2.6, God is envisioned as dwelling in Jerusalem. *Daybreak,* when dangerous night ends, is traditionally seen as an auspicious time, a time when deliverance comes. **7:** The *kingdoms topple,* matching the defeat of chaos ("mountains topple") in v. 3. **8:** *LORD of hosts,* associated with God as warrior (see 24.10 n.), is infrequent in Psalms, but is used here as contextually appropriate.

10: God is so great a warrior that He can end all war (see Isa. 2.4 ‖ Mic. 4.3). **11:** Most likely, some cultic official spoke this v. in God's name; in content and style (note the imperatives) it matches v. 9. **12:** A refrain (see Ps. 42.6 n.) with v. 8.

Ps. 47: Pss. 47; 93; 96–99 are called kingship psalms because they all explicitly refer to God as king. Ps. 47, in the Korahite collection, shares many elements with the other kingship psalms; it is uncertain if they all functioned together in a ritual commemorating God's

kingship or enthronement. If such a ritual existed in the biblical period, it may have been associated with the new year (postbiblical Rosh Ha-Shanah, early biblical Sukkot; see Exod. 23.16 n.), which in the rabbinic period has the kingship of God as one of its major themes. (See also introduction to Ps. 93.) This understanding of the psalm developed in the early twentieth century, when an attempt was made to understand the ritual background of each psalm; most traditional Jewish interpreters understood the psalm eschatologically (see esp. Radak to v. 9, who connects the theme of universal acknowledgment of God to Zech. 14.9). In the Middle Ages, Ps. 47 began to be recited on Rosh Ha-Shanah before the blowing of the shofar (ram's horn), most likely under the influence of v. 6. **2:** It is unclear how the nations are being invoked; v. 10 seems to suggest that their representatives were actually present. The theme is thus God's universal kingship. This psalm may then be seen as an actualization of the immediately preceding Ps. 46.11, "Desist! Realize that I am God! I dominate the nations; I dominate the earth." Such close connections between adjacent psalms are unusual. Great noise and *a joyous shout* are part of the typical human coronation ritual (e.g., 1 Kings 1.39–40), here projected onto God. This suggests that this psalm may be viewed as an enthronement psalm, and that through a set of rituals, God was (re)enthroned annually. **3:** The epithet *great king,* a popular epithet of Mesopotamian kings, is used of no Israelite king, perhaps because it was reserved for God as King. **4:** *The pride of Jacob* seems to be a nickname of Israel or Jerusalem. **6:** *Ascends* ("'alah") refers back to God as "Most High" (v. 3, "'elyon"; the Heb root is the same). It most likely refers to God ascending the royal throne. **7–8:** *Sing* is repeated five times; perhaps the human king had a group of singers who entertained him. Angelic singing, or at least chanting to God as king, is described in Isa.

8 for God is king over all the earth;
   sing a hymn.[a]
9 God reigns over the nations;
   God is seated on His holy throne.
10 The great of the peoples are gathered together,
   the retinue of Abraham's God;
   for the guardians of the earth belong to God;
   He is greatly exalted.

48 A song. A psalm of the Korahites.

2 The LORD is great and much acclaimed
   in the city of our God,
   His holy mountain—
3 fair-crested, joy of all the earth,
   Mount Zion, summit of Zaphon,[b]
   city of the great king.
4 Through its citadels, God has made Himself
   known as a haven.
5 See, the kings joined forces;
   they advanced together.
6 At the mere sight of it they were stunned,
   they were terrified, they panicked;
7 they were seized there with a trembling,
   like a woman in the throes of labor,
8 as the Tarshish fleet was wrecked
   in an easterly gale.[c]
9 The likes of what we heard we have now
   witnessed
   in the city of the LORD of hosts,
   in the city of our God—
   may God preserve it forever!   *Selah.*

10 In Your temple, God,
   we meditate upon Your faithful care.

a Heb. maskil, *a musical term of uncertain meaning.*
b *A term for the divine abode.*
c *See 1 Kings 22.49.*

6.1–5. The structure of these vv., an imperative followed by *for,* mirrors vv. 2–3. **8:** *God is* (or "has become") *king* mirrors the human enthronement declaration; see, e.g., "Absalom has become king" (2 Sam. 15.10). *God is seated on His holy throne* describes God's re-enthronement. In contrast to the human throne, only God's is *holy.*

This throne may be in His heavenly or His earthly palace (see Ps. 2.4, 6 n.). **10:** Most likely this reflects a wish rather than a reality; it is difficult to believe that at any time *the great of the peoples* gathered to acknowledge the universal sovereignty of God. The final word, *exalted* ("na'aleh"), reflects the theme of the psalm, and picks up

on the usage of the root "'-l-h" in vv. 3 and 6 (see v. 6 n.).

Ps. 48: This is a communal hymn with strong thematic connections to the previous two psalms: it too focuses on Jerusalem as God's city, and is primarily concerned with a conflict between Israel and the nations, where God ultimately saves Israel. It reworks certain old myths (see v. 3 n.), but historicizes them. It most likely reflects an ideal rather than a real battle; this explains why several medievals read this eschatologically (see, e.g., Rashi and Radak). It also, however, contains hints of a ritual (see vv. 13–14 n.), suggesting the psalm as a whole reflects a ritualized commemoration of a divine victory. **2:** His *holy mountain,* a reference to Mount Zion (which is actually more like a hill), mirrors the previous psalm's "holy throne" (47.9). **3:** The centrality of Jerusalem is likewise expressed in the eschatological Isa. 23.2–3, but in this psalm, it is imagined as happening in the present. *Zaphon* refers to the mountain where Baal resided according to the Ugaritic myths (see, e.g., *ANET,* p. 136, "my mount Godly Zaphon"). Some believe that this psalm therefore originally referred to a northern city (see 42.8 and 46.6 n.); more likely, this is a remarkable reuse of old mythological material, where the Israelite God has absorbed qualities of Baal (see Ps. 29 n.), including even his place of residence! In this context, it is likely that the *great king* is God (see 47.3), rather than the Davidic king. **8:** The identification of Tarshish is uncertain; biblical texts suggest that it is a faraway place in the western Mediterranean, reachable by boat (see esp. Jonah 1.3). Thus, the Tarshish fleet represents well-built boats, capable of long journeys. **9:** It is God's physical presence in Jerusalem (see Ps. 2.3 n.) that makes Jerusalem inviolable. The beginning of Ezekiel describes the divine presence leaving the Temple, which allows the city's conquest (Ezek. 10.18; 11.23). **10:** God's *faithful care* ("ḥesed"; see 5.8 n.) is localized in the Temple,

11 The praise of You, God, like Your name,
　　reaches to the ends of the earth;
　　Your right hand is filled with beneficence.
12 Let Mount Zion rejoice!
　Let the towns*a* of Judah exult,
　　because of Your judgments.

13 Walk around Zion,
　　circle it;
　　count its towers,
14 　take note of its ramparts;
　　*b-*go through*-b* its citadels,
　　that you may recount it to a future age.
15 For God—He is our God forever;
　　He will lead us *b-*evermore.*-b*

49 For the leader. Of the Korahites. A psalm.

2 　Hear this, all you peoples;
　　give ear, all inhabitants of the world,
3 　men of all estates,
　　rich and poor alike.
4 My mouth utters wisdom,
　　my speech*c* is full of insight.
5 I will turn my attention to a theme,
　　set forth my lesson to the music of a lyre.

6 　In time of trouble, why should I fear
　　the encompassing evil of those who would
　　　supplant me—
7 　men who trust in their riches,
　　who glory in their great wealth?
8 　*d-*Ah, it*-d* cannot redeem a man,
　　or pay his ransom to God;
9 　the price of life is too high;
　　and so one ceases to be, forever.
10 Shall he live eternally,
　　and never see the grave?

a Or "women." b-b Meaning of Heb. uncertain.

c Lit. "utterance of my heart"; on leb, cf. Ps. 19.15.　　d-d Or "A brother."

ers; the Heb reads "over death" ("*'al mavet*"). Most likely, this is a corruption of the word "*'alamot*" used in the superscription to Ps. 46; it probably was misplaced from the beginning of Ps. 49 to the end of Ps. 48.

Ps. 49: This is an unusual and difficult psalm. Unlike most psalms, it is addressed to the (human) community, and not to God. It also is very difficult textually; for example, it is unclear if the refrain in vv. 13 and 21 differs intentionally or as a result of error. In vocabulary (see v. 4 n.) and in theme the psalm, especially its first few vv., shares much with wisdom literature; most scholars therefore consider it a wisdom psalm. It is highly didactic, teaching that the wealthy should not be envied, a common theme of parts of Proverbs (e.g., 28.6) and Ecclesiastes (e.g., 10.6). **2:** As elsewhere in the Korahite psalms, foreigners are the imagined audience (see 47.10 n.). **4–5:** These vv. are full of wisdom terms (*wisdom, insight, theme, lesson*), but these are integrated into the psalm through the mention of *the music of a lyre*, a psalm formula. **6–13:** The wealthy cannot take their wealth with them to Sheol, the biblical underworld. Proverbs often has a more positive, pragmatic attitude toward wealth (e.g., 14.20; 18.11); the attitude here more closely resembles Ecclesiastes (e.g., 2.1–11; 5.9, 12–13; 6.1–6). **8–9:** In certain cases, according to various texts, a *ransom* might be taken by a human to *redeem* a person from a capital offense (see Exod. 21.30; Prov. 6.35), but even the great wealth of the rich cannot be used by them to attain eternal

where God resides. **11:** Names express essence in ancient Israel (see 1 Sam. 25.25). **12:** *Mount Zion* rejoices at God's *judgments* of retribution against the assembled enemies. Either *Mount Zion* is personified (see Isa. 35.1), or the word "inhabitants of" is elided or assumed (Radak raises both options). **13–14:** A ritual of circumambulating the city walls stands behind this description; see Neh. 12.27–43. **15:** *Evermore* follows the tradition of the Septuagint, Menachem ben Saruq (quoted in Rashi), Ibn Ezra, Radak, and oth-

11   For one sees that the wise die,
            that the foolish and ignorant both perish,
            leaving their wealth to others.
12   Their grave[a] is their eternal home,
            the dwelling-place for all generations
            of those once famous on earth.
13   Man does not abide in honor;
            he is like the beasts that perish.

14   Such is the fate of those who are self-confident,
            [b]the end of those pleased with their own talk.[-b]
                                                            Selah.

15   Sheeplike they head for Sheol,
            with Death as their shepherd.
        The upright shall rule over them at daybreak,
            [b]and their form shall waste away in Sheol
            till its nobility be gone.[-b]
16   But God will redeem my life from the clutches of
            Sheol,
            for He will take me.   Selah.

17   Do not be afraid when a man becomes rich,
            when his household goods increase;
18   for when he dies he can take none of it along;
            his goods cannot follow him down.
19   Though he congratulates himself in his lifetime
            —[b]"They must admit that you did well by
            yourself"[-b]—
20   yet he must join the company of his ancestors,
            who will never see daylight again.
21   Man does not understand honor;
            he is like the beasts that perish.

50 A psalm of Asaph.

        [c]God, the LORD God[-c] spoke
            and summoned the world from east to west.

a Taken with ancient versions and medieval commentators as the equivalent of qibram.
b-b Meaning of Heb. uncertain.   c-c Heb. 'El 'Elohim YHWH.

life from God. **13:** See Eccl. 3.19, "For in respect of the fate of man and the fate of beast, they have one and the same fate: as the one dies so dies the other, and both have the same lifebreath; man has no superiority over beast, since both amount to nothing."

14: It is unclear if this refers to the wealthy, or if a new subject is being (briefly) introduced. **15:** Textually very difficult. It is possible that Death ("Mot") here recollects the Canaanite deity of the same name, known from Ugarit. **16:** It is uncertain if the

psalmist wishes to be saved (temporarily) from death (Ps 30.4 n.), or if he desires to be like Enoch or Elijah who do not die (Gen. 5.24; 2 Kings 2.11), or if this psalm partakes of the notion of personal resurrection, expressed clearly only in Dan. 12.2. The medieval period knew a much more developed notion of heaven and hell, and the v. is thus traditionally understood in reference to the afterworldly reward of the righteous. **20:** Sheol, underground, is a dark place (88.13; Job 17.13). **21:** A refrain; see v. 13.

Ps. 50: This is the first psalm of an Asaphite collection; it is distant from the other eleven Asaphite psalms, found in Pss. 73–83. The "sons (or guild) of Asaphites" were Levites who served as Temple singers in the Second Temple (Neh. 7.44), though in 1 Chron. 16.7 the connection between Asaph and Temple music is traced back to Davidic times. 2 Chron. 29.30 refers to "Asaph the seer," suggesting that for some, the liturgical poetry produced by this clan was understood to be divinely inspired. More than other psalms, several of the Asaphite psalms have prophetic echos, refer to past historical events, and reflect northern Israel (see esp. Pss. 80; 81). The collection also often characterizes the relation between God and Israel as that between a shepherd and his flock, and it has an unusually large number of allusions to the Song of the Sea (Exod. ch 15). Ps. 50 is not addressed to God, but is an admonition from God. As such, it shares much with prophetic oracles, and it is unclear if this is modeled after such oracles, or reflects a prophetic utterance within a ritual context (a cultic prophet). After an introduction (vv. 1–6), the main admonition is addressed to the community (vv. 7–15), a special admonition is addressed to the wicked (vv. 16–21), and a general conclusion is offered (vv. 22–23). **1–6:** God appears in a theophany, preceded by *fire* (so, e.g., 18.8; 97.3) and *storm* (see esp. Job 38.1; 40.6). As *judge* indicting

2   From Zion, perfect in beauty,
      God appeared

3   —let our God come and not fail to act!
    Devouring fire preceded Him;
      it stormed around Him fiercely.

4   He summoned the heavens above,
      and the earth, for the trial of His people.

5   "Bring in My devotees,
      who made a covenant with Me over sacrifice!"

6   Then the heavens proclaimed His righteousness,
      for He is a God who judges.   *Selah.*

7   "Pay heed, My people, and I will speak,
      O Israel, and I will arraign you.
    I am God, your God.

8   I censure you not for your sacrifices,
      and your burnt offerings, made to Me daily;

9   I claim no bull from your estate,
      no he-goats from your pens.

10   For Mine is every animal of the forest,
      the beasts on ᵃ a thousand mountains.ᵃ

11   I know every bird of the mountains,
      the creatures of the field are subject to Me.

12   Were I hungry, I would not tell you,
      for Mine is the world and all it holds.

13   Do I eat the flesh of bulls,
      or drink the blood of he-goats?

14   Sacrifice a thank offering to God,
      and pay your vows to the Most High.

15   Call upon Me in time of trouble;
      I will rescue you, and you shall honor Me."

16   And to the wicked, God said:
      "Who are you to recite My laws,
      and mouth the terms of My covenant,

17   seeing that you spurn My discipline,
      and brush My words aside?

18   When you see a thief, you fall in with him,
      and throw in your lot with adulterers;

19   you devote your mouth to evil,
      and yoke your tongue to deceit;

20   you are busy maligning your brother,
      defaming the son of your mother.

21   If I failed to act when you did these things,
      you would fancy that I was like you;
      so I censure you and confront you with charges.

a-a *Meaning of Heb. uncertain.*

His people in a "riv" (covenantal lawsuit), He calls upon *heavens above, and the earth* as witnesses (so, e.g., Isa. 1.2). **2:** On *Zion*, Jerusalem, as beautiful, see Ps. 48.3. **5:** Perhaps the heaven and earth (so, e.g., Rashi), or other divine beings are addressed. On *devotees*, translated elsewhere as "faithful ones" (Heb "ḥasid"), see 4.4 n. **7–15:** Like the prophetic texts in Isa. 1.10–17 and Micah 6.6–8, these vv. polemicize against the Priestly notion that sacrifices by themselves are efficacious. The psalm does not object to sacrifices per se (see esp. vv. 14, 23), but insists that (1) they must be understood symbolically, rather than as food for the deity (contrast, e.g., Lev. 1.13), and (2) they are not sufficient, but must be accompanied by other activities (vv. 14–15, 22–23). A more negative attitude toward sacrifices is reflected in the following psalm (51.18–21). **7:** *I am God, your God* may recall the opening of the Decalogue (Exod. 20.2; Deut. 5.6); see v. 18 n. The substitution of "'elohim" for the Tetragrammaton, Yʜᴠʜ, is especially noticeable. **10–12:** Of God as owner of all, see Deut. 10.14. In style and content, the psalm is similar to Deuteronomy. **13–14:** The *thank offering* is partially eaten by the person who brings it, usually as a result of a *vow* (see Lev. 7.12–15; 2 Sam. 15.7). **16–17:** The wicked is accused of hypocrisy. **18:** Citing part of the Decalogue (Exod. 20.13; Deut. 5.17). **19–20:** For the prohibition against slander, see, e.g., Lev. 19.16. **22–23:** The conclusion is chiastic, mentioning first the wicked (vv. 16–21), and then returning to the righteous (vv. 7–15).

Ps. 51: An individual complaint expressing an extreme sense of guilt. Although written in good classical Heb, internal evidence suggests that this psalm may be exilic or early postexilic (see vv. 5, 9, 11, 12, 20–21 n.). **2:** See 2 Sam. ch 12, where Nathan rebukes David for two grave offences: committing adultery with Bathsheba, and having her husband, Uriah, murdered. Given the

22   Mark this, you who are unmindful of God,
          lest I tear you apart and no one save you.

23   He who sacrifices a thank offering honors Me,
          ᵃ·and to him who improves his way·ᵃ
        I will show the salvation of God."

51   For the leader. A psalm of David, ²when Nathan
      the prophet came to him after he had come to Bath-
sheba.ᵇ

3   Have mercy upon me, O God,
          as befits Your faithfulness;
        in keeping with Your abundant compassion,
          blot out my transgressions.
4   Wash me thoroughly of my iniquity,
          and purify me of my sin;
5   for I recognize my transgressions,
          and am ever conscious of my sin.
6   Against You alone have I sinned,
          and done what is evil in Your sight;
        so You are just in Your sentence,
          and right in Your judgment.
7   Indeed I was born with iniquity;
          with sin my mother conceived me.
8   ᵃ·Indeed You desire truth about that which is
          hidden;
        teach me wisdom about secret things.·ᵃ

9   Purge me with hyssop till I am pure;
          wash me till I am whiter than snow.
10   Let me hear tidings of joy and gladness;
          let the bones You have crushed exult.
11   Hide Your face from my sins;
          blot out all my iniquities.
12   Fashion a pure heart for me, O God;
          create in me a steadfast spirit.
13   Do not cast me out of Your presence,
          or take Your holy spirit away from me.
14   Let me again rejoice in Your help;
          let a vigorous spirit sustain me.
15   I will teach transgressors Your ways,
          that sinners may return to You.

16   Save me from bloodguilt,
          O God, God, my deliverer,
        that I may sing forth Your beneficence.

tremendous guilt expressed in the psalm, and the specific request to be saved "from bloodguilt" (v. 16), it is understandable that tradition would explicitly connect this psalm to those events. **3–4:** The complaint in a nutshell, containing four imperatives (*Have mercy; blot out; purify; Wash me thoroughly,* lit. "be thorough; wash me"), an invocation (*O God*), and the motivations (*as befits Your faithfulness; in keeping with Your abundant compassion*). God is asked to act according to His faithfulness, "ḥesed"; see 5.8 n. **5:** Confessions are not typical of psalms, but are frequently mentioned in late biblical literature (see Dan. 9.4; Ezra 10.1; Neh. 9.2; 2 Chron. 30.22). **7:** So extreme are the psalmist's guilt feelings that he sees himself as sinful even before birth; in other words, he is, by nature, a sinful being. The idea of the inherent sinfulness of humans is rarely expressed in the Bible, except for Gen. 8.21: "the devisings of man's mind are evil from his youth" (see also Job 25.4). Christianity developed the notion of original sin. **9:** God, rather than the impure individual, uses the hyssop for the purification ritual (contrast Num. 19.6, 18), perhaps because the Temple is not standing and the Temple-bound purification ritual cannot be performed. **11:** In a remarkable reversal of the standard idiom, the psalmist asks God to *hide* His *face*—not from the supplicant (see 6.4–5 n.), but from *sins.* Unlike 2 Sam. ch 12, the supplicant does not request that the sin and punishment be transferred (see 2 Sam. 12.13 n.), but rather that it be blotted *out,* an idea found in the exilic Deutero-Isaiah (Isa. 43.25; 44.22). **12:** See similarly the exilic Ezek. 36.26. **13–14:** A poetic request not to be killed by God. **15–16:** The motivation for that request. *Bloodguilt* has severe consequences for the individual and the community (see Ezek. 9.9).

a-a *Meaning of Heb. uncertain.*   b *Cf. 2 Sam. 12.*

17 O Lord, open my lips,
    and let my mouth declare Your praise.
18 You do not want me to bring sacrifices;
    You do not desire burnt offerings;
19 True sacrifice to God is a contrite spirit;
    God, You will not despise
    a contrite and crushed heart.

20 May it please You to make Zion prosper;
    rebuild the walls of Jerusalem.
21 Then You will want sacrifices offered in
        righteousness,
    burnt and whole offerings;
    then bulls will be offered on Your altar.

52 For the leader. A *maskil* of David, ²when Doeg
the Edomite came and informed Saul, telling him,
"David came to Ahimelech's house." ᵃ

3 Why do you boast of your evil, brave fellow?
    God's faithfulness ᵇ never ceases. ᵇ
4 Your tongue devises mischief,
    like a sharpened razor that works treacherously.
5 You prefer evil to good,
    the lie, to speaking truthfully.   *Selah.*
6 You love all pernicious words,
    treacherous speech.
7 So God will tear you down for good,
    will break you and pluck you from your tent,
    and root you out of the land of the living.
                                                Selah.
8 The righteous, seeing it, will be awestruck;
    they will jibe at him, saying,
9 "Here was a fellow who did not make God his
        refuge,
    but trusted in his great wealth,
    relied upon his mischief."

10 But I am like a thriving olive tree in God's house;
    I trust in the faithfulness of God forever and
        ever.
11 I praise You forever, for You have acted;
    ᶜ I declare that Your name is good ᶜ
    in the presence of Your faithful ones.

17–19: Prayer is more effective than sacrifices; this stands in stark contrast to the Priestly tradition, which emphasizes the efficacy of sacrifices, largely ignoring prayer. The content of v. 17 has made it appropriate for the introduction to the standard statutory prayer (the "ʿAmidah"). **20–21:** The psalm's conclusion suggests that the acceptability of prayer instead of sacrifices is due to a catastrophe, which has made access to the Temple impossible. Many modern scholars see these vv. as an addition, an opinion already cited in Ibn Ezra in the name of "one of the Spanish scholars."

Ps. 52: An atypical psalm, addressed not to God, but to a particular "brave fellow" (v. 3). **2:** Given the tendency to identify psalms with events in David's life as recorded in Samuel, it is logical to equate the treacherous brave fellow of the psalm with *Doeg the Edomite* (see 1 Sam. 22.9–11). **3–5:** The emphasis is on damaging speech (see 10.7 n.). **7:** This sets up two contrasts with v. 10: the wicked will be removed from his *tent,* while the righteous will live "in God's house"; and the wicked will be *rooted out,* while the righteous psalmist is "like a thriving olive tree." **8:** The Heb is punning: the *righteous see* ("veyir'u") and are *awestruck* ("veyira'u"). **10–11:** The psalmist will express God's *faithfulness* ("ḥesed") *in the presence of . . . faithful ones* ("ḥasid"). **10:** Olive trees were of great significance for the oil they produced, which was used in the Temple. It is uncertain if the psalmist is a religious official in the Temple *(God's house),* or is a lay Israelite who wants to enjoy God's proximity at the Temple (see Ps. 23.6 n.).

a Cf. 1 Sam. 22.9 ff.
b-b Lit. "is all the day."
c-c Meaning of Heb. uncertain; others "I will wait for Your name for it is good."

53

^aFor the leader; on *mahalath.*^b A *maskil* of David.

2   The benighted man thinks,
        ^{c-}"God does not care."^{-c}
    Man's wrongdoing is corrupt and loathsome;
        no one does good.
3   God looks down from heaven on mankind
        to find a man of understanding,
        a man mindful of God.
4   Everyone is dross,
        altogether foul;
        there is none who does good,
        not even one.
5   Are they so witless, those evildoers,
        who devour my people as they devour food,
        and do not invoke God?
6   There they will be seized with fright
        —^{d-}never was there such a fright—
        for God has scattered the bones of your
            besiegers;
        you have put them to shame,^{-d}
        for God has rejected them.

7   O that the deliverance of Israel might come from
            Zion!
    When God restores the fortunes of His people,
        Jacob will exult, Israel will rejoice.

54

For the leader; with instrumental music. A *maskil* of David, ²when the Ziphites came and told Saul, "Know, David is in hiding among us."^e

3   O God, deliver me by Your name;
        by Your power vindicate me.
4   O God, hear my prayer;
        give ear to the words of my mouth.
5   For strangers have risen against me,
        and ruthless men seek my life;
        they are unmindful of God.   *Selah.*

6   See, God is my helper;
        the Lord is my support.
7   He will repay the evil of my watchful foes;
        by Your faithfulness, destroy them!

Ps. 53: This is the Elohistic Psalter's (see introduction to Ps. 42) version of Ps. 14; see annotations there.

Ps. 54: A typical individual petition. It is stylistically simplistic, with standard parallelisms. **2:** The psalm is secondarily connected to 1 Sam. 23.15–20; this is thematically appropriate, though not compelling. **3–5:** The petition, with an invocation (*O God*), four imperatives expressing the urgent request of the supplicant, and a motivation (*For strangers . . .*). **3:** On God's *name*, see 48.11 n. **6–9:** As in other such prayers, the tense and tone change, reflecting the psalmist's certainty of salvation (see Ps. 6.9–11 n.).

a Cf. Ps. 14.   b Meaning of Heb. unknown.
c-c Lit. "There is no God"; cf. Ps. 10.4.   d-d Meaning of Heb. uncertain.
e Cf. 1 Sam. 23.19.

8 Then I will offer You a freewill sacrifice;
    I will praise Your name, LORD, for it is good,
9   for it has saved me from my foes,
    and let me gaze triumphant upon my enemies.

55 For the leader; with instrumental music.
    A *maskil* of David.

2 Give ear, O God, to my prayer;
    do not ignore my plea;
3   pay heed to me and answer me.
I am tossed about, complaining and moaning
4   at the clamor of the enemy,
    because of the oppression of the wicked;
    for they bring evil upon me
    and furiously harass me.
5 My heart is convulsed within me;
    terrors of death assail me.
6 Fear and trembling invade me;
    I am clothed with horror.
7 I said,
    "O that I had the wings of a dove!
    I would fly away and find rest;
8   surely, I would flee far off;
    I would lodge in the wilderness;   *selah*
9   I would soon find me a refuge
    from the sweeping wind,
    from the tempest."

10 O Lord, confound their speech, confuse it!
For I see lawlessness and strife in the city;
11   day and night they make their rounds on its
        walls;
    evil and mischief are inside it.
12 Malice is within it;
    fraud and deceit never leave its square.

13   It is not an enemy who reviles me
    —I could bear that;
    it is not my foe who vaunts himself against me
    —I could hide from him;
14   but it is you, my equal,
    my companion, my friend;
15   sweet was our fellowship;
    we walked together in God's house.
16 Let Him incite death against them;
    may they go down alive into Sheol!
For where they dwell,
    there evil is.

8: For the details of the freewill sacrifice, see Lev. 22.18–25; Num. 15.1–16.

Ps. 55: Although an individual petition like the previous psalm (cf. esp. 55.2 and 54.4), this psalm is as innovative as the previous one is standard. The structure of Ps. 55 is unusually complex; the psalmist's complaint, for example, is found in three different sections (vv. 4–9, 11–12, 21–22), and the vocabulary of the psalm is unique and quite difficult. **5–9:** The description of the psalmist's troubles is unusually long and flowery, and functions to motivate God to heed his petition. **10–12:** These vv. emphasize both the geographical and chronological (*day and night*) ubiquity of the *evil*. **10:** On improper speech as a psalmist's problem, see 10.7 n. **13–16:** As in Job, the great tragedy is that friends have turned into enemies. **16:** The phrase to go *down alive into Sheol,* also used in Num. 16.33, expresses sudden death.

17 As for me, I call to God;
   the Lord will deliver me.

18 Evening, morning, and noon,
   I complain and moan,
   and He hears my voice.

19 He redeems me unharmed
   from the battle against me;
   ᵃit is as though many are on my side.⁻ᵃ

20 God who has reigned from the first,
   who will have no successor,
   hears and humbles those who have no fear
      of God.   *Selah.*

21 He*ᵇ* harmed his ally,
   he broke his pact;

22 his talk was smoother than butter,
   yet his mind was on war;
   his words were more soothing than oil,
   yet they were drawn swords.

23 Cast your burden on the Lord and He will sustain
      you;
   He will never let the righteous man collapse.

24 For You, O God, will bring them down to the
      nethermost Pit—
   those murderous, treacherous men;
   they shall not live out half their days;
   but I trust in You.

56 For the leader; ᵃon *yonath elem rehokim.*⁻ᵃ Of David. A
   michtam; when the Philistines seized him in Gath.

2 Have mercy on me, O God,
   for men persecute me;
   all day long my adversary oppresses me.

3 My watchful foes persecute me all day long;
   many are my adversaries, O Exalted One.

4 When I am afraid, I trust in You,

5 in God, whose word I praise,
   in God I trust;
   I am not afraid;
   what can mortals*ᶜ* do to me?

6 All day long ᵃthey cause me grief in my affairs,⁻ᵃ
   they plan only evil against me.

7 They plot, they lie in ambush;
   they watch my every move, hoping for my
      death.

17: It is unclear if this and the following vv. express certainty of deliverance, as in other such prayers, or if instead of *the Lord will deliver me,* we should translate "may the Lord deliver me." **18:** This v. suggests that the liturgical day began at or after sunset, as in postbiblical Jewish practice. Prayer three times daily may be suggested here; this was normative in rabbinic times, and is already expressed in a late biblical text, Dan. 6.10. **21–24:** As in vv. 13–16, the enemy is referred to in both the singular and the plural. **24:** The psalm concludes with a return to the theme of v. 16.

Ps. 56: This individual petition emphasizes the great confidence or trust of the psalmist. In expressing his trust in God rather than humans, it shares certain phrases with Pss. 116–118 (see vv. 5, 14 n.). **1:** An extremely long, multilayered and complex superscription. On *michtam,* found in Pss. 56–60 and 16, see 16.1 n. A time *when the Philistines seized him* [David] *in Gath* is never recorded in Samuel; it might be inferred from 1 Sam. 21.11–16, or the superscription may reflect another story about David that was not preserved in the canonical Samuel (see introduction to Ps. 7). **2:** The psalm proper begins with the typical imperative (*Have mercy on me*), invocation (*O God*), and motivation (*for . . .*). **4–5:** The repetition of *I trust* highlights the psalm's theme. **5:** Cf. 118.6, "The Lord is on my side, I have no fear;

a-a *Meaning of Heb. uncertain.*   b *I.e., the friend of v. 14.*   c *Lit. "flesh."*

8   Cast them out for their evil;
       subdue peoples in Your anger, O God.

9   ᵃ⁻You keep count of my wanderings;
       put my tears into Your flask,
       into Your record.⁻ᵃ

10   Then my enemies will retreat when I call on You;
       this I know, that God is for me.

11   In God, whose word I praise,
       in the LORD, whose word I praise,

12   in God I trust;
       I am not afraid;
       what can man do to me?

13   I must pay my vows to You, O God;
       I will render thank offerings to You.

14   For You have saved me from death,
       my foot from stumbling,
       that I may walk before God in the light of life.

57 For the leader; ᵃal tashḥeth.ᵃ Of David. A *michtam*; when he fled from Saul into a cave.

2   Have mercy on me, O God, have mercy on me,
       for I seek refuge in You,
       I seek refuge in the shadow of Your wings,
       until danger passes.

3   I call to God Most High,
       to God who is good to me.

4   He will reach down from heaven and deliver me:
       God will send down His steadfast love;
       my persecutor reviles.   *Selah.*

5   As for me, I lie down among man-eating lions
       whose teeth are spears and arrows,
       whose tongue is a sharp sword.

a-a Meaning of Heb. uncertain.

---

what can man do to me?" **9:** God's *record* may refer to divine ledgers, where He keeps track of human activities (see Exod. 32.32 and Mal. 3.16). These are well known from earlier Mesopotamia, and later rabbinic tradition, especially concerning the ledger books that are open and written on Rosh Ha-Shanah. The Heb has a wordplay on *my wanderings,* "nodi," and *Your flask,* "no'dekha." Additionally, the root "s-p-r" is repeated in

You keep count and *into Your record.* **11:** This v., unusual in its repetition of two identical words in a parallelism, forms a quasi-refrain with v. 5. **12:** The refrain continues; see v. 5. **13:** See 50.14. **14:** Cf. 116.8–9: "You have delivered me from death, my eyes from tears, my feet from stumbling. I shall walk before the LORD in the lands of the living." As is common in these petitions, the certainty of hearing is presented in the past

tense, reflecting the supplicant's certainty of a positive divine answer.

Ps. 57: The psalmist's confidence in God's salvation is less prominent in this personal petition, which instead is full of urgent cries for divine help, including the refrain (vv. 6, 12), *Exalt Yourself over the heavens, O God, let Your glory be over all the earth!* **1:** An unusually long, multi-part superscription, likely reflecting various layers of composition. *Al tashḥeth* means "do not destroy." It may be the incipit (first words) of a different song to whose melody this psalm was recited; alternately, Pss. 57; 58; 59; 75, all of which contain *al tashḥeth,* served together in a ritual petitionary context. (These four psalms, like the Asaph or the Korah psalms [see introductions to Pss. 42; 50], likely were once a mini-collection that was broken up in the process of editing of Psalms.) *When he fled from Saul into a cave,* probably the latest element in this superscription, reflecting the application of Psalms to the biography of David, may refer to events in 1 Sam. chs 24 or 26. This cannot be the original context of the psalm, which does not fit these chs precisely: In Samuel, David's main protagonist is Saul alone, while this psalm mentions many enemies. However, the Heb of v. 5 mentions a spear in the singular (translated here generically as "spears"); this may have reminded a creative editor, drawing on his traditions, of the story in 1 Sam. ch 26, which highlights the role of Saul's spear, taken by David while Saul slept "a deep sleep from the LORD" (v. 12; on the "spear" see vv. 7, 8, 11, 12, 16, 22). **2:** The exact repetition of *Have mercy on me* (see also Ps. 123.3), rather than use of a synonym, is unusual, but may reflect the psalmist's desperation (see Radak), though exact verbal repetition characterizes this psalm in general. *The shadow of Your wings* is a standard Psalms image, of God as a large protective bird (17.8; 36.8; 63.8). **3:** On *Most High* ("ᵉelyon"), see 7.18 n. **4:** On God in

6   Exalt Yourself over the heavens, O God,
       let Your glory be over all the earth!

7   They prepared a net for my feet ᵃto ensnare me;ᵃ
       they dug a pit for me,
       but they fell into it.   *Selah.*

8ᵇ My heart is firm, O God;
       my heart is firm;
       I will sing, I will chant a hymn.

9   Awake, O my soul!
       Awake, O harp and lyre!
       I will wake the dawn.

10 I will praise You among the peoples, O Lord;
       I will sing a hymn to You among the nations;

11 for Your faithfulness is as high as heaven;
       Your steadfastness reaches to the sky.

12 Exalt Yourself over the heavens, O God,
       let Your glory be over all the earth!

58

For the leader; *al tashḥeth.* Of David. A *michtam.*

2   ᶜO mighty ones,ᶜ do you really decree what is
       just?
     Do you judge mankind with equity?

3   In your minds you devise wrongdoing in the land;
       ᶜwith your hands you deal out lawlessness.ᶜ

4   The wicked are defiant from birth;
       the liars go astray from the womb.

5   Their venom is like that of a snake,
       a deaf viper that stops its ears

6   so as not to hear the voice of charmers
       or the expert mutterer of spells.

7   O God, smash their teeth in their mouth;
       shatter the fangs of lions, O LORD;

8   let them melt, let them vanish like water;
       let Him aim His arrows that they be cut down;

9   ᶜlike a snail that melts away as it moves;ᶜ
       like a woman's stillbirth, may they never see
       the sun!

10 Before ᶜthe thorns grow into a bramble,
       may He whirl them away alive in fury.ᶜ

11 The righteous man will rejoice when he sees
       revenge;
     he will bathe his feet in the blood of the wicked.

a-a *Cf. Mishnaic Heb.* kefifah, *a wicker basket used in fishing.*
b *With vv. 8–12, cf. Ps. 108.2–6.*   c-c *Meaning of Heb. uncertain.*

heaven, see 2.4 n. The Heb for *God will send down His steadfast love,* lit. "His faithfulness and His steadfastness," may retain echoes of God controlling minor deities who serve His will. **6:** The psalmist wants God, though residing in *the heavens* (see v. 4), to be manifest on *the earth.* God is exalted and His *glory* is expressed by granting victory to the supplicant. **7:** A fulfillment of Prov. 26.27, "He who digs a pit will fall in it." Nets appear in a surprising number of psalms (9; 10; 25; 31; 35; 37; 57; 140); this may simply reflect the realities of ancient Israelite trapping techniques, although others suggest that this refers to magical practices. **8–10:** The psalmist is implying that he should be saved so that God will continue to hear his praises; see more explicitly 30.13. **8:** The first half of the v. is a protestation of innocence, justifying divine intervention. **10:** On the presence of nations, see Ps. 47. **11:** A recasting of v. 4, returning to *heaven, faithfulness,* and *steadfastness.*

Ps. 58: The language of the psalm is very difficult, and it is likely that it has been imperfectly preserved. Though it does not begin with an address to God, and initially looks like a psalm of instruction (see Ps. 14), the second half of the psalm, including the long curse of the wicked (vv. 7–10), makes it clear that it is a petition, although it does not follow the typical form of that genre. The psalm is unusually rich in animal imagery. **2:** Many scholars suggest that "ʾelem" (*mighty ones*) refers to minor deities, and that this psalm, like Ps. 82, originally referred to the demotion of these deities due to their malfeasance. **7–10:** This may be a seven-fold curse, with seven functioning as a magical number. Petitions of the individual are characterized by imperatives, typically asking God to save the petitioners (e.g., 57.2 "have mercy on me"); here these are transformed with requests to punish the wicked. **11–12:** Like v. 11, Isa. 63.1–6 similarly revels in bloody gore. But the

12   Men will say,
            "There is, then, a reward for the righteous;
              there is, indeed, divine justice on earth."

59 For the leader; *al tashḥeth.* Of David. A *michtam;*
       when Saul sent men to watch his house in order to
put him to death.[a]

2   Save me from my enemies, O my God;
              secure me against my assailants.
3   Save me from evildoers;
              deliver me from murderers.
4   For see, they lie in wait for me;
              fierce men plot against me
              for no offense of mine,
              for no transgression, O LORD;
5   for no guilt of mine
              do they rush to array themselves against me.
            Look, rouse Yourself on my behalf!
6   You, O LORD God of hosts,
              God of Israel,
              bestir Yourself to bring all nations to account;
              have no mercy on any treacherous villain.
                                              Selah.

7   They come each evening growling like dogs,
              roaming the city.
8   They rave with their mouths,
              [b-sharp words-b] are on their lips;
              [they think,] "Who hears?"
9   But You, O LORD, laugh at them;
              You mock all the nations.

10   O my[c] strength, I wait for You;
              for God is my haven.
11   My faithful God will come to aid me;
              God will let me gloat over my watchful foes.
12   Do not kill them lest my people be unmindful;
              with Your power make wanderers of them;
              bring them low, O our shield, the Lord,
13   because of their sinful mouths,
              the words on their lips.
            Let them be trapped by their pride,
              and by the imprecations and lies they utter.
14   In Your fury put an end to them;
              put an end to them that they be no more;

point is not pure *revenge*, but high-lighting the power of *divine justice*, thereby encouraging others to be righteous. **12:** *Divine justice* trans-lates the anomalous "Gods who judge" ("ᵉelohim shoftim"), per-haps a textual error.

Ps. 59: This individual petition has clearly grown over time, as it is quite diffuse in content and style; it suggests, for example, that the supplicant is hounded by both personal (vv. 2–4) and national (v. 6) enemies. As noted by Ibn Ezra and Radak, the psalm incor-porates a significant number of words from the root "ᶜ-z-z," "strong, fierce": this helps to unify it. **1:** *To watch his house in order to put him to death* is a near quotation of 1 Sam. 19.11, where Saul sent men to kill David, but David's wife Michal saved him. The con-tent of the psalm, where the indi-vidual is surrounded and is wor-ried about being killed (v. 3), suggests this context; it is also pos-sible that the Heb for "fierce men" (v. 4 "ᶜazim") suggested the house-hold idol covered with goat's hair (1 Sam. 19.13, "ᶜizim") that Michal used to impersonate David, fool-ing Saul's men. **3:** On *evildoers,* see Ps. 5.6 n. **4–5:** A protestation of in-nocence; see 7.4–6 n. **5:** On *rouse Yourself* (Heb "ᶜurah"), see 7.7 n. **6:** *Hosts* refers to God's role as leader of divine armies; see 46.8 n. **7:** This serves as a refrain with v. 15; the reference is to packs of wild *dogs* (see Ps. 22.17). **9:** Cf. 2.4. **12–14:** Usually the petitioner re-quests the death of his persecutors (see esp. the immediately preced-ing 58.11); for punishment as vehi-cle for education, see Exod. 9.16.

a Cf. 1 Sam. 19.11.   b-b Lit. "swords."   c With several mss.; cf. v. 18; lit. "His."

that it may be known to the ends of the earth
that God does rule over Jacob.   *Selah.*

15 They come each evening growling like dogs,
    roaming the city.
16 They wander in search of food;
    and whine if they are not satisfied.
17 But I will sing of Your strength,
    extol each morning Your faithfulness;
    for You have been my haven,
    a refuge in time of trouble.

18   O my strength, to You I sing hymns;
    for God is my haven, my faithful God.

60 For the leader; on ª-*shushan eduth.*-ª A *michtam* of
David (to be taught), 2 when he fought with Aram-
Naharaim and Aram-Zobah, and Joab returned and de-
feated Edom—[an army] of twelve thousand men—in the
Valley of Salt.ᵇ

3   O God, You have rejected us,
    You have made a breach in us;
    You have been angry;
    restore us!
4   You have made the land quake;
    You have torn it open.
    Mend its fissures,
    for it is collapsing.
5   You have made Your people suffer hardship;
    ᶜ-You have given us wine that makes us reel.-ᶜ
6   ª-Give those who fear You because of Your truth
    a banner for rallying.-ª   *Selah.*
7ᵈ That those whom You love might be rescued,
    deliver with Your right hand and answer me.

8   God promised ᵉ-in His sanctuaryᵉ
    that I would exultingly divide up Shechem,
    and measure the Valley of Sukkoth;

a-a *Meaning of Heb. uncertain.*   b *Cf. 2 Sam. 8; 1 Chron. 18.*
c-c *Or "You have sated Your people with a bitter draft."*
d *Cf. Ps. 108.7–14.*   e-e *Or "by His holiness."*

17–18: As in 57.8–10, the psalmist
wants to be kept alive in order to
praise God. **17:** Perhaps morning
was a standard time of prayer; alternately, the supplicant prayed
after surviving the difficulties of
the night. **18:** This is an expanded
reworking of v. 10. *My haven*
("misgav") returns to the opening of the psalm, "secure me"
("tesagveni"); on God as *faithful*,
see 5.8 n.

Ps. 60: This communal petition is
unusual in mentioning specific
geographical locations (vv. 8–10).
1: In the superscription, *on shushan
eduth* and *to be taught* are unique
and obscure. **2:** David's wars
against Aram (Syria) are narrated
in 2 Sam. 8.3–8; 10.6–18; it is likely
that the editor who added this superscription was referring to ch 8,
which opens with references to
the Philistines and Moabites (see
Ps. 60.10). The second half of the
v. is based on 2 Sam. 8.13, "David
gained fame when he returned
from defeating Edom in the Valley
of Salt, 18,000 in all." The number
of casualties has changed in transmission, as has the city-state; in
Heb, Edom ("ʾdm") and Aram
("ʾrm") are nearly identical, and in
many cases the letters "dalet" and
"resh" are confused due to their
similarity in both the old and new
Heb script. (Traditional attempts
at reconciling these different accounts, as in Radak, are forced.)
Although these historical superscriptions are not to be taken literally for dating the psalms, the content of the psalm suggests the
Northern Kingdom did not exist
as a separate entity, which would
date the psalm to the period either
before the development, or after
the destruction, of the Northern
Kingdom. **3:** Divine anger leads to
divine abandonment. Punishment
as a result of divine anger is a
common ancient Near Eastern
idea; the Moabite Mesha Inscription describes Moab's military
losses "because Chemosh [the Moabite national god] was angry at
his land" (*ANET*, p. 320), using the
same root for "angry" as this v.
5: On the poison cup of God, see
esp. Jer. 25.15–29. **7:** The motivation for God to act. *Answer me* may
reflect a call for a divine oracle,
which is delivered in the following
vv. **8–10:** In contrast to the surrounding vv., these are formed as
tricola, vv. with three sections, instead of the typical two (bicola).
8: From *His sanctuary*, the Temple,
God provides a positive answer
(so Ibn Ezra, Radak), perhaps
through a cultic prophet. *Shechem*
and *Sukkoth* are two cities in cen-

9 Gilead and Manasseh would be mine,
Ephraim my chief stronghold,
Judah my scepter;

10 Moab would be my washbasin;
on Edom I would cast my shoe;
acclaim me, O Philistia!

11 Would that I were brought to the bastion!
Would that I were led to Edom!

12 But You have rejected us, O God;
God, You do not march with our armies.

13 Grant us Your aid against the foe,
for the help of man is worthless.

14 With God we shall triumph;
He will trample our foes.

61

For the leader; with instrumental music. Of David.

2 Hear my cry, O God,
heed my prayer.

3 From the end of the earth I call to You;
when my heart is faint,
You lead me to a rock that is high above me.

4 For You have been my refuge,
a tower of strength against the enemy.

5 O that I might dwell in Your tent forever,
take refuge under Your protecting wings.
                                              Selah.

6 O God, You have heard my vows;
grant the request[a] of those who fear Your name.

7 Add days to the days of the king;
may his years extend through generations;

8 may he dwell in God's presence forever;
appoint[b] steadfast love to guard him.

9 So I will sing hymns to Your name forever,
as I fulfill my vows day after day.

62

For the leader; on *Jeduthun.* A psalm of David.

2 Truly my soul waits quietly for God;
my deliverance comes from Him.

3 Truly He is my rock and deliverance,
my haven; I shall never be shaken.

tral Israel, to the west and east of the Jordan. **9:** *Gilead* is treated as a tribe, as in the early Song of Deborah (Judg. 5.17). *Judah my scepter* recalls the enigmatic blessing of Jacob (Gen. 49.10), "The scepter shall not depart from Judah, Nor the ruler's staff from between his feet." **10:** *Casting a shoe* may reflect ownership (Ruth 4.7). **11:** Perhaps the human response to the divine oracle. **12:** The psalmist is suggesting that God is not fulfilling His role as Lord of hosts (see 44.10 n.). **13–14:** As often in historiographical and prophetic literature (e.g., Zech. 4.6), a single God is more effective than any number of human fighters.

Ps. 61: The beginning of the psalm is a personal petition (vv. 2–5), while the second half (vv. 6–9) is a prayer for the king; "Selah" divides the psalm in half (see 3.3 n.). It is unclear if two separate psalms have been combined, or if, as in Mesopotamia, an individual might incorporate a royal prayer into a petition. **2–5:** The supplicant is hyperbolically at *the end of the earth,* distant from the Temple (*Your tent;* so Ibn Ezra and Radak; see 15.1 n.), where he wants to reside under divine protection (see 57.2 n.). This petition includes the typical elements: imperatives (*Hear . . . heed*), an invocation (*O God*), and a motivation (*For you . . .*). **6–9:** This second unit is framed by the mention of the *vow.* **7–8:** Similar hyperbolic language about the king is reflected in Pss. 21.5; 72.5, and reflects notions of the king being (close to) divine (see 45.7 n.). **9:** Ps. 30.13 concludes in a similar fashion.

Ps. 62: This is an oblique form of an individual petition. It lacks that genre's usual pattern of invocation, imperatives, and motivation, but instead indirectly notes expected deliverance from God (vv. 2–3) and highlights God's great power. Except for the last v., it is addressed to the community rather than to God. The Heb is unique in its sixfold repetition of

---

a Taking the noun yršt *as an alternate form of* 'ršt; *cf. Ps. 21.3.*
b *Meaning of Heb. uncertain.*

4 How long will all of you attack[a] a man,
    to crush[a] him, as though he were
    a leaning wall, a tottering fence?
5 They lay plans to topple him from his rank;
    they delight in falsehood;
    they bless with their mouths,
    while inwardly they curse.   *Selah.*

6 Truly, wait quietly for God, O my soul,
    for my hope comes from Him.
7 He is my rock and deliverance,
    my haven; I shall not be shaken.
8 I rely on God, my deliverance and glory,
    my rock of strength;
    in God is my refuge.
9 Trust in Him at all times, O people;
    pour out your hearts before Him;
    God is our refuge.   *Selah.*

10 Men are mere breath;
    mortals, illusion;
    placed on a scale all together,
    they weigh even less than a breath.
11 Do not trust in violence,
    or put false hopes in robbery;
    if force bears fruit pay it no mind.
12 One thing God has spoken;
    two things have I heard:
    that might belongs to God,
13   and faithfulness is Yours, O Lord,
    to reward each man according to his deeds.

63 A psalm of David, when he was in the Wilderness of Judah.

2 God, You are my God;
    I search for You,
    my soul thirsts for You,
    my body yearns for You,
    as a parched and thirsty land that has no water.
3 I shall behold You in the sanctuary,
    and see Your might and glory,

---

a *Meaning of Heb. uncertain.*

"'akh," "truly" (vv. 2, 3, 5, 6, 7, 10; NJPS does not translate all of them), expressing the petitioner's great certainty. **1:** On *Jeduthun,* see 39.1. **2–3:** The repetition of *deliver-ance* and the surrounding imagery suggest persecution by enemies. **5:** As in other contexts, this persecution is connected to false speech (see 10.7 n.). **6:** A slight variant

of v. 2, functioning as a refrain. **7:** Nearly identical to v. 3. **9:** The psalmist moves from his personal trust, exhorting the listeners to do the same: God moves from being "my refuge" to becoming *our refuge.* **10:** This may reflect the weighing of people's deeds or hearts, well attested in ancient Egypt, especially in illustrations accompanying the Book of the Dead. **12:** Numbers are paralleled by X || X+1; this explains why *one* is paralleled by *two.* Thus, God has spoken, perhaps via an oracle answering the psalmist, one thing only: *that might belongs to God.* This is a direct answer to the psalmist's indirect request for deliverance (see vv. 2–3). This parallelism is one of the classic texts expounded in rabbinic culture to mean that God's word is multivalent and needs to be interpreted in a variety of special ways (see, e.g., *b. Sanh.* 34a). It is also used to explain why the Decalogue versions in Exod. ch 20 and Deut. ch 5 differ: God spoke once, but people heard two different utterances (*Mek., In the Month,* section 7 and parallels, cited by Rashi). **13:** This is the psalmist's response to the divine oracle; on divine *faithfulness* ("ḥesed"), see 5.8 n. It functions as an oblique request that he will be *reward*ed *according to his deeds,* in other words, saved from the enemies.

Ps. 63: This psalm defies classification; it is characterized by a deep spiritual, almost mystical sense. In theme and vocabulary Pss. 42–43; 73; 84 are similar. **1:** The superscription is likely based on the "parched and thirsty land" described in v. 2. David was in the wilderness on various occasions when fleeing from Saul and Absalom. **2:** Ps. 42 opens with a similar image. **3:** This derives from the idea of seeing the cult statue at a temple; see 11.7 n. It is easy to imagine that such a statue could artistically express God's *might and glory,* especially since *glory* may represent the glow so easy to depict in a metal image.

4   Truly Your faithfulness is better than life;
        my lips declare Your praise.
5   I bless You all my life;
        I lift up my hands, invoking Your name.
6   I am sated as with a ᵃrich feast,ᵃ
        I sing praises with joyful lips
7   when I call You to mind upon my bed,
        when I think of You in the watches of the
            night;
8   for You are my help,
        and in the shadow of Your wings
            I shout for joy.
9   My soul is attached to You;
        Your right hand supports me.

10 May those who seek to destroy my life
        enter the depths of the earth.
11 May they be gutted by the sword;
        may they be prey to jackals.
12 But the king shall rejoice in God;
        all who swear by Him shall exult,
        when the mouth of liars is stopped.

64 For the leader. A psalm of David.

2   Hear my voice, O God, when I plead;
        guard my life from the enemy's terror.
3   Hide me from a band of evil men,
        from a crowd of evildoers,
4   who whet their tongues like swords;
        they aim their arrows—cruel words—
5   to shoot from hiding at the blameless man;
        they shoot him suddenly and without fear.
6   ᵇThey arm themselves with an evil word;
        when they speak, it is to conceal traps;ᵇ
        they think, "Who will see them?"
7ᶜ Let the wrongdoings ᵈthey have concealed,ᵈ
        each one inside him, his secret thoughts,
        be wholly exposed.
8   God shall shoot them with arrows;
        they shall be struck down suddenly.
9   Their tongue shall be their downfall;
        all who see them shall recoil in horror;

4: *Faithfulness* reflects "ḥesed"; see 5.8 n. **5:** On lifting up *hands* as the ancient prayer position, see 44.21–22 n. **6:** This v. conceptually joins prayer and sacrifice (see the translators' note "suet and fat"), as in Pss. 50 and 51. **7:** Night is a typical time for reflection and meditation (4.5; 16.7; 119.55). Nighttime was divided into three or four *watches.* **8:** See 57.2 n. **9:** The Heb for *attached* ("davkah") is very intense, showing close proximity and longing. **10–11:** Such requests typify individual petitions. **12:** Compare the ending of Ps. 61. It is uncertain if the people are swearing by God (this translation) or by the king (see, e.g., 1 Sam. 17.55), or possibly by both (see, e.g., 2 Sam. 15.21).

Ps. 64: A prayer for deliverance from evildoers, whose words are the means of their wickedness. Military metaphors make the wicked into enemies and their speech into weapons of war: *swords, arrows, traps,* and ambushes. **4:** For the metaphor of *tongues* as *swords* (damaging speech), cf. Pss. 57.5; 59.8. **6:** *"Who will see them?,"* the confidence of the evildoers that their activity goes unnoticed (Pss. 10.11; 59.8). **7:** The *secret thoughts* may be a reference to sorcery (see 10.7 n.); or it may simply be plotting in one's mind. **8:** Just as the wicked shoot arrows at others, so will God shoot arrows at them (Ibn Ezra). Cf. Pss. 7.13–14; 38.3. The enemies are described at length while God's action is instantaneous. **9–11:** Vengeance is not the motive; rather the defeat of the wicked causes *all men* (human beings) to *stand in awe* and *proclaim the work of God,* and causes the *upright* to *exult.*

a-a *Lit. "suet and fat."*
b-b *Meaning of Heb. uncertain.*
c *Meaning of verse uncertain.*
d-d *Reading* ṭamnu *with some mss. (cf. Minḥat Shai) and Rashi; most printed editions* ṭamnu, *traditionally rendered "they have accomplished."*

10   all men shall stand in awe;
      they shall proclaim the work of God
      and His deed which they perceived.

11   The righteous shall rejoice in the LORD,
      and take refuge in Him;
      all the upright shall exult.

65 For the leader. A psalm of David. A song.

2   Praise befits You in Zion, O God;
         vows are paid to You;
3   all mankind[a] comes to You,
         You who hear prayer.
4   When all manner of sins overwhelm me,
         it is You who forgive our iniquities.
5   Happy is the man You choose and bring near
         to dwell in Your courts;
         may we be sated with the blessings of Your
            house,
         Your holy temple.

6   Answer us with victory through awesome deeds,
         O God, our deliverer,
         in whom all the ends of the earth
         and the distant seas
         put their trust;
7   who by His power fixed the mountains firmly,
         who is girded with might,
8   who stills the raging seas,
         the raging waves,
         and tumultuous peoples.
9   Those who live at the ends of the earth are awed
            by Your signs;
         You make the lands of sunrise and sunset shout
            for joy.
10   You take care of the earth and irrigate it;
         You enrich it greatly,
         with the channel of God full of water;
         You provide grain for men;
         for so do You prepare it.
11   Saturating its furrows,
         leveling its ridges,
         You soften it with showers,
         You bless its growth.
12   You crown the year with Your bounty;
         fatness is distilled in Your paths;

a Lit. "flesh."

Ps. 65: The beginning of the psalm celebrates God and the Temple, the place where vows are paid (vv. 2–5). The psalmist is thankful for the privilege of entering the Temple—i.e., coming into God's presence—in order to pay his vow (present an offering). The payment is made possible by the bounteous harvest that God has provided. The vow may have been to bring a special offering for a good harvest. The body of the psalm praises God for His power over the sources of water and His beneficence in providing water for irrigation. It is possible that this psalm was sung during Sukkot, the Feast of Tabernacles, which marks the end of the summer harvest and the beginning of the rainy season. In postbiblical times it featured prayers for rain for the coming rainy season. **2:** *Zion*, sometimes a synonym for Jerusalem or, as here, the site of the Temple. On the paying of vows at the Temple, see Ps. 66.13. **3:** The translation reverses the clauses in this v. *All mankind* gives a more universal flavor to the psalm, as does v. 9, "Those who live at the ends of the earth." Zech. 14.17 envisions survivors of all nations making a pilgrimage to Jerusalem on Sukkot. **4:** Divine forgiveness of sin is the precondition for winter rains and an abundant harvest (Deut. 11.13–17). **5:** *The blessings of Your house* may refer to general prosperity, or specifically to the rain that God will send. Alternatively, it may refer to the sacrificial meal at the Temple. **6–10:** The hope for adequate rainfall is couched in descriptions of God as the supreme power of the world, especially over the cosmic water: *seas, waves,* and water *channel. Awesome deeds*, God's acts of creation by His victory over the forces of primeval chaos (*the . . . seas*; Pss. 29; 93), and His provision of rain. **10:** *The channel of God*, the conduit that brings rain to the earth (Job 38.25–26), perhaps associated with the Temple (see Ps. 36.9). **11–14:** The potentially destructive cosmic water forces are tamed by God and become the gentle rain and run-off that irrigates the earth,

13   the pasturelands distill it;
          the hills are girded with joy.
14   The meadows are clothed with flocks,
          the valleys mantled with grain;
          they raise a shout, they break into song.

66   For the leader. A song. A psalm.

      Raise a shout for God, all the earth;
2   sing the glory of His name,
          make glorious His praise.
3   Say to God,
          "How awesome are Your deeds,
          Your enemies cower before Your great
              strength;
4   all the earth bows to You,
          and sings hymns to You;
          all sing hymns to Your name."   *Selah.*

5   Come and see the works of God,
          who is held in awe by men for His acts.
6   He turned the sea into dry land;
          they crossed the river on foot;
          we therefore rejoice in Him.
7   He rules forever in His might;
          His eyes scan the nations;
          let the rebellious not assert themselves.
                                                      Selah.

8   O peoples, bless our God,
          celebrate His praises;
9   who has granted us life,
          and has not let our feet slip.

10   You have tried us, O God,
          refining us, as one refines silver.
11   You have caught us in a net,
          ª caught us in trammels.ª
12   You have let men ride over us;
          we have endured fire and water,
          and You have brought us through to prosperity.

13   I enter Your house with burnt offerings,
          I pay my vows to You,
14   [vows] that my lips pronounced,
          that my mouth uttered in my distress.

providing vegetation and flocks
with their nourishment. All the
creatures who are thus nourished
join humankind in the praise of
the beneficent God (Pss. 69.35;
96.11–12; 98.7–8). The picture of
the harvest sounds eschatological;
cf. Joel 4.18; Amos 9.13.

Ps. 66: The theme of this psalm is
not obvious; some themes echo
those in the previous psalm (victory through God's awesome
deeds, universal blessing of God,
bringing offerings to the Temple).
It is unclear at times whether the
psalmist is speaking of events in
the past or the present. The psalm
begins and ends with praise, surrounding passages of communal
and individual thanksgiving. The
date of the psalm is unknown and
its context is quite general. It may
be interpreted as praise to God for
the return from exile and the rebuilding of the Temple. All peoples of the world witnessed this
event, which redounds to God's
praise. **1:** This v. is formulaic; cf.
98.4; 100.1. **2–4:** Universal acclamation for God for His deliverance of Israel (Josh. 2.9–11).
4: *Selah* (also vv. 7, 15), see Ps. 3.3
n. This term may divide sections
of the psalm. **5–7:** The world is invited to consider God's acts, which
are epitomized by His splitting of
the sea during the exodus and the
drying up of the Jordan when the
Israelites entered the promised
land (Exod. 14.21–22; Josh. 4.23).
The parallelism between sea and
Jordan in Ps. 114.3–5 suggests that
river refers to the Jordan. The exo-
dus-conquest theme may hint at
the theme of the return from exile
and re-entrance to Judah (the exodus was a common symbol for the
return in postexilic times, especially in Second Isaiah). **8–9:** All
peoples should praise Israel's God,
who has not let His people perish.
10–12: A recent event in which Israel has been threatened but delivered from harm parallels the exodus. This may be a reference to
the exile, expressed in terms of the
exodus from Egypt, the arduous
trek through the wilderness (*fire*),
and the crossing of the Jordan

_____
a-a Lit. "put a trammel on our loins."

15 I offer up fatlings to You,
   with the odor of burning rams;
   I sacrifice bulls and he-goats.   *Selah.*

16 Come and hear, all God-fearing men,
   as I tell what He did for me.
17 I called aloud to Him,
   glorification on my tongue.
18 Had I an evil thought in my mind,
   the Lord would not have listened.
19 But God did listen;
   He paid heed to my prayer.
20 Blessed is God who has not turned away my
        prayer,
   or His faithful care from me.

67 For the leader; with instrumental music.
   A psalm. A song.

2 May God be gracious to us and bless us;
   may He show us favor,   *selah*
3   that Your way be known on earth,
   Your deliverance among all nations.

4 Peoples will praise You, O God;
   all peoples will praise You.
5 Nations will exult and shout for joy,
   for You rule the peoples with equity,
   You guide the nations of the earth.   *Selah.*
6 The peoples will praise You, O God;
   all peoples will praise You.

7 May the earth yield its produce;
   may God, our God, bless us.
8 May God bless us,
   and be revered to the ends of the earth.

68 ªFor the leader. Of David. A psalm. A song.

2 God will arise,
   His enemies shall be scattered,
   His foes shall flee before Him.
3 Disperse them as smoke is dispersed;

a *The coherence of this psalm and the meaning of many of its passages are uncertain.*

God-fearers that God hears people's prayers. **20:** Final benediction (2 Sam. 7.15). On *faithful care* ("ḥesed"), see 5.8 n.

Ps. 67: A prayer that good harvests continue, with a refrain in vv. 4, 6. It bears some resemblance to Ps. 65 and continues the theme of blessing found in the conclusion of Ps. 66. All three psalms speak of the universal acknowledgment of God. **2:** An echo of the Aaronic (priestly) blessing (Num. 6.24–26; Ps. 4.6). *Show . . . favor,* lit. "make His face shine." The shining face of God is the visible expression of His benevolence; the opposite is God's hiding His face. *Selah* (also vv. 4, 7), see Ps. 3.3 n. **5:** See Pss. 96.10–13; 98.7–9. **7–8:** *May God . . . bless us,* with copious winter rain (Lev. 26.4; Deut. 11.17; Ezek. 34.27). The hymn may be associated with the fall festival of Sukkot (Tabernacles). **8:** The conclusion, like the entire psalm, balances particularistic *(us)* and universal *(ends of the earth)* concerns.

Ps. 68: A hymn describing God's victory over His foes and His choice of Jerusalem as the place of His dominion. It draws on an ancient tradition, found also in the very old poem in Judg. ch 5, about the southern origins (Sinai) of Israel's God. It invokes themes from the exodus and the conquest. Because the psalm appears disjointed, some scholars see it as a combination of numerous psalms or a list of their opening lines. Its vocabulary includes fifteen words found nowhere else in the Bible, plus other rare words, adding to the difficulty of interpreting it. Indeed, much of it remains obscure, and many consider it to be the most difficult psalm in the Psalter. **2:** Num. 10.35 is similar, suggesting that the psalm was perhaps associated with the Ark. The Ark was taken out to battle at the head of the troops (1 Sam. ch 4). **3:** God will make the enemies (= the wicked) disappear in such a way that they will no longer exist; like smoke or melted wax, they will have no substance. For another

(water); cf. Isa. 43.2. **10:** The refining process is arduous but purifies that which is refined. **13–15:** Abundant thanksgiving sacrifices in the Temple. The

psalmist can now deliver the sacrifices he vowed to bring if God would rescue him from his distress (cf. Ps. 65.2). **16–20:** The psalmist's experience serves as proof to all

as wax melts at fire,
so the wicked shall perish before God.

4 But the righteous shall rejoice;
they shall exult in the presence of God;
they shall be exceedingly joyful.

5 Sing to God, chant hymns to His name;
extol Him who rides the clouds;
the LORD is His name.
Exult in His presence—

6 the father of orphans, the champion of widows,
God, in His holy habitation.

7 God restores the lonely to their homes,
sets free the imprisoned, safe and sound,
while the rebellious must live in a parched land.

8 O God, when You went at the head of Your army,
when You marched through the desert,
selah

9 the earth trembled, the sky rained because of
God,
yon Sinai, because of God, the God of Israel.

10 You released a bountiful rain, O God;
when Your own land languished, You sustained
it.

11 Your tribe dwells there;
O God, in Your goodness You provide for the
needy.

12 The Lord gives a command;
the women who bring the news are a great
host:

13 "The kings and their armies are in headlong
flight;
housewives are sharing in the spoils;

14 even for those of you who lie among the
sheepfolds
there are wings of a dove sheathed in silver,
its pinions in fine gold."

15 When Shaddai scattered the kings,
it seemed like a snowstorm in Zalmon.

16 O majestic mountain, Mount Bashan;
O jagged mountain, Mount Bashan;

17 why so hostile, O jagged mountains,
toward the mountain God desired as His
dwelling?
The LORD shall abide there forever.

smoke metaphor in connection with the wicked, see Ps. 37.20. **4:** Joy is equated, in a ritual sense, with being in God's presence. The enemies cannot be in God's presence. **5:** *Who rides the clouds,* God's stormcloud chariot (v. 34; Ps. 65.12). The image and language are found in Ugaritic writings. **7:** *Restores the lonely to their homes,* a difficult phrase, perhaps better translated "he sets individuals (who are not part of a family) in households"; cf. Ps. 113.7–9. It is parallel to the rest of the v., which is concerned with assigning befitting living-places to prisoners and to rebellious people. If this psalm is exilic, or the v. is a late addition, *the imprisoned* may refer to the captives of the exile (cf. Ps. 69.34), who will be returned home. **8–9:** An allusion, with changes, to Judg. 5.4–5. A reference to the exodus. **8:** *Selah* (also vv. 20, 33), see Ps. 3.3 n. **9:** One of the few references to *Sinai* outside of the Torah; it is not, however, explicitly connected here to the giving of the Torah. **10–11:** The mention of rain in the allusion provokes further description of God's bountiful rain, by which He cares for His people. This is a major theme of the three previous psalms. **11:** *Needy,* not simply the underprivileged mentioned in vv. 6–7 but all the people. The community often calls itself "needy" ("'ani," or a synonym; cf. Ps. 18.28; 74.21). **12–15:** God *gives a command* for war; women announce the good *news* of God's victory (Exod. 15.20; 1 Sam. 18.6–7). **13:** *Sharing in the spoils,* Judg. 5.30. **14:** *Among the sheepfolds,* Judg. 5.16. *Wings of a dove . . . ,* presumably some treasure found among the spoil. **15:** The specific incident referred to cannot be identified. *Zalmon* may be the same mountain mentioned in Judg. 9.48. Another possibility is Zalmonah, in the south (Num. 33.41–42). **16–24:** God's move from Mount Sinai (v. 9) to Mount Zion, God's choice for his royal residence (Isa. 2.3). Mount Bashan looks upon this move with hostility. **16:** *Bashan,* a region in northern Transjordan. The specific

18 God's chariots are myriads upon myriads,
        thousands upon thousands;
        the Lord is among them as in Sinai in holiness.

19 You went up to the heights, having taken
            captives,
        having received tribute of men,
        even of those who rebel
        against the LORD God's abiding there.

20 Blessed is the Lord.
    Day by day He supports us,
        God, our deliverance.   *Selah.*

21 God is for us a God of deliverance;
        GOD the Lord provides an escape from death.

22 God will smash the heads of His enemies,
        the hairy crown of him who walks about in his
            guilt.

23 The Lord said, "I will retrieve from Bashan,
        I will retrieve from the depths of the sea;

24   that your feet may wade through blood;
        that the tongue of your dogs may have its
            portion of your enemies."

25 Men see Your processions, O God,
        the processions of my God, my king,
        into the sanctuary.

26 First come singers, then musicians,
        amidst maidens playing timbrels.

27 In assemblies bless God,
        the LORD, O you who are from the fountain of
            Israel.

28 There is little Benjamin who rules them,
        the princes of Judah who command them,
        the princes of Zebulun and Naphtali.

29 Your God has ordained strength for you,
        the strength, O God,
        which You displayed for us

30   from Your temple above Jerusalem.
    The kings bring You tribute.

31 Blast the beast of the marsh,
        the herd of bulls among the peoples, the
            calves,
        till they come cringing with pieces of silver.
    Scatter the peoples who delight in wars!

32 Tribute-bearers shall come from Egypt;
        Cush shall hasten its gifts to God.

mountain referred to is unknown.
16–17: *Mountain . . . His dwelling,*
cf. Exod. 15.17; Ps. 132.13–14.
18: Cf. Deut. 33.2. **24:** *Feet . . .
blood,* see 58.11. *Dogs,* for dogs lap-
ping up the blood of the dead, cf.
1 Kings 21.19; 22.38. **25–28:** Processions into the Temple (Ps. 24.7–10).
28: Cf. Judg. 5.14–18. *Little Benjamin who rules them* sounds like
a reference to King Saul, who
was from the tribe of Benjamin.
29–36: International praise for
God and tribute from all the
kings of the world—a theme
of the three previous psalms,
and a scene not unlike that pictured in Isa. 2.2–4 and Mic. 4.1–3,
where Mt. Zion is the religious
center of the world. Cf. Zeph.
3.9–10. **32:** *Cush,* Ethiopia.

33 O kingdoms of the earth,
sing to God;
chant hymns to the Lord, *selah*
34 to Him who rides the ancient highest
heavens,
who thunders forth with His mighty voice.
35 Ascribe might to God,
whose majesty is over Israel,
whose might is in the skies.
36 You are awesome, O God, in Your holy places;
it is the God of Israel who gives might and
power to the people.
Blessed is God.

69 For the leader. On *shoshannim*.ª Of David.

2 Deliver me, O God,
for the waters have reached my neck;
3 I am sinking into the slimy deep
and find no foothold;
I have come into the watery depths;
the flood sweeps me away.
4 I am weary with calling;
my throat is dry;
my eyes fail
while I wait for God.
5 More numerous than the hairs of my head
are those who hate me without reason;
many are those who would destroy me,
my treacherous enemies.
Must I restore what I have not stolen?
6 God, You know my folly;
my guilty deeds are not hidden from You.
7 Let those who look to You,
O Lord, GOD of hosts,
not be disappointed on my account;
let those who seek You,
O God of Israel,
not be shamed because of me.
8 It is for Your sake that I have been reviled,
that shame covers my face;
9 I am a stranger to my brothers,
an alien to my kin.
10 My zeal for Your house has been my undoing;
the reproaches of those who revile You have
fallen upon me.

33–36: Cf. 29.1–3, 11. God's power at the end of the psalm forms an inclusio with its beginning.

Ps. 69: An individual complains that he is drowning, figuratively, from the hatred of his enemies: members of his own society and even his family. He calls to God for help, trusting that God will accept his prayer with favor. While this seems like a very general prayer by an individual hoping for the return to Zion and the rebuilding of Judah (v. 36), it is best interpreted as a petition by a person lamenting the destruction of the Temple—one of the "mourners for Zion" (v. 10). The psalmist's troubles stem from his public mourning for the lost Temple, acts for which his friends and family taunt him (vv. 10–13). The idea of exile and mourning is suggested at numerous points in the psalm. **1:** *Shoshannim*, "lilies," perhaps a melody or a musical instrument; see Ps. 45.1. **2–3:** The drowning metaphor is well developed (cf. Ps. 130.1). We can see the speaker sinking further and further into the water until he is swept away. **5–6:** The friends' hatred for the psalmist takes the form of false accusations, which the psalmist denies. But he does not claim to be perfect; God knows his errors. **7–13:** The psalmist is criticized by his society for what he considers his pious devotion, especially in regard to Jerusalem. **9:** For similar language see Ps. 38.12; Job 19.13–15. **10:** *My zeal for Your house:* Like the mourners for Zion in Isa. 61.2–3 and Zech. 7.3, the psalmist mourns for the destroyed Temple by weeping (that is, crying out in lament), fasting, and wearing sackcloth. This behavior causes everyone to revile him.

---

a *Meaning of Heb. uncertain.*

11 When I wept and fasted,
    I was reviled for it.
12 I made sackcloth my garment;
    I became a byword among them.
13 Those who sit in the gate talk about me;
    I am the taunt of drunkards.

14 As for me, may my prayer come to You, O LORD,
    at a favorable moment;
    O God, in Your abundant faithfulness,
    answer me with Your sure deliverance.
15 Rescue me from the mire;
    let me not sink;
    let me be rescued from my enemies,
    and from the watery depths.
16 Let the floodwaters not sweep me away;
    let the deep not swallow me;
    let the mouth of the Pit not close over me.
17 Answer me, O LORD,
    according to Your great steadfastness;
    in accordance with Your abundant mercy
    turn to me;
18 do not hide Your face from Your servant,
    for I am in distress;
    answer me quickly.
19 Come near to me and redeem me;
    free me from my enemies.

20 You know my reproach,
    my shame, my disgrace;
    You are aware of all my foes.
21 Reproach breaks my heart,
    I am in despair;[a]
    I hope for consolation, but there is none,
    for comforters, but find none.
22 They give me gall for food,
    vinegar to quench my thirst.
23 May their table be a trap for them,
    a snare for their allies.
24 May their eyes grow dim so that they cannot
    see;
    may their loins collapse continually.
25 Pour out Your wrath on them;
    may Your blazing anger overtake them;
26 may their encampments be desolate;
    may their tents stand empty.

13: *Those who sit in the gate:* The gate was the main public meeting-place, where business and legal transactions took place. Those who sit in the gate are the leading officials of the city. At the other end of the spectrum of those who congregate publicly are the *drunkards*. **14:** *At a favorable moment,* at a time when God is most disposed to accept his prayer. Human beings do not know when these times are. **16:** *The Pit:* The usual word for the Pit is "bor," "cistern," and it symbolizes the grave, or death (cf. Pss. 28.1; 30.4; 88.5; 143.7), although the similar-sounding "be'er," "well," as here, can be used in the same sense (Ps. 55.24). The use of "be'er" in the context of the other water imagery is apt, for a cistern may be full or empty but a well always contains water. The picture of a person in a well or cistern brings to mind Joseph, who was held in a dry cistern (Gen. 37.24), and Jeremiah, who was in a muddy one (Jer. 38.6). A cistern or well is, then, a place of imprisonment. Cf. Lam. 3.53–54, which can be interpreted as an individual imprisoned in a full cistern with its lid being closed, and Lam. 3.55, a call to be saved from the Pit. See also Ps. 40.3. Exilic literature often uses prison (real or metaphoric) as a symbol of exile, and this v.— and indeed all the drowning imagery—symbolizes the exile in which the psalmist feels himself to be. **17–19:** The psalmist prays that God will not *hide* His *face* (be inattentive to the psalmist's prayers). *Answer me* occurs in vv. 17 and 18, harking back to v. 14.

a Meaning of Heb. uncertain.

27 For they persecute those You have struck;
      they talk about the pain of those You have
      felled.
28 Add that to their guilt;
      let them have no share of Your beneficence;
29 may they be erased from the book of life,
      and not be inscribed with the righteous.

30 But I am lowly and in pain;
      Your help, O God, keeps me safe.
31 I will extol God's name with song,
      and exalt Him with praise.
32 That will please the LORD more than oxen,
      than bulls with horns and hooves.
33 The lowly will see and rejoice;
      you who are mindful of God, take heart!
34 For the LORD listens to the needy,
      and does not spurn His captives.
35 Heaven and earth shall extol Him,
      the seas, and all that moves in them.
36 For God will deliver Zion
      and rebuild the cities of Judah;
      they shall live there and inherit it;
37 the offspring of His servants shall possess it;
      those who cherish His name shall dwell there.

70 For the leader. Of David. *Lehazkir.*[a]

2[b] Hasten, O God, to save me;
      O LORD, to aid me!
3   Let those who seek my life
      be frustrated and disgraced;
      let those who wish me harm,
      fall back in shame.
4   Let those who say, "Aha! Aha!"
      turn back because of their frustration.

5   But let all who seek You be glad and rejoice in You;
      let those who are eager for Your deliverance
         always say,
      "Extolled be God!"
6   But I am poor and needy;
      O God, hasten to me!
    You are my help and my rescuer;
      O LORD, do not delay.

a *Meaning of Heb. uncertain.*
b *Cf. Ps. 40.14–18.*

27: *Those You have struck* and *those You have felled* refer to the punishment of exile. The psalmist's friends make light of his sense of being in exile. **29:** *The book of life* in which God inscribes the righteous; see 56.9 n. **32:** The animal sacrifices could not take place without the Temple; prayer was the substitute for sacrifice until the Temple could be rebuilt (cf. Pss. 51.17–19; 141.2). **34:** *Captives*, Heb "'asirim," is another reference to the exiles (as in Pss. 79.11; 102.21; 107.10, 14). **36:** The psalmist derives comfort and the strength to persist in his mourning from his firm belief that God will rebuild the Temple, Jerusalem, and the country of Judah, and will return the exiles to it. They will not only live in Judah, but will *inherit it*, possess ownership that can be bequeathed as an inheritance to their children. *Offspring of His servants* are the descendants of those the Bible calls God's servants. Psalms applies this designation to Abraham (Ps. 105.6, 42), Jacob (Ps. 136.22), Moses (Ps. 105.26), and David (Ps. 78.70). The psalmist is underlining the continuity between the returnees from exile who *cherish His name* and their ancient ancestors.

Ps. 70: This psalm expresses a great sense of urgency in calling on God to save the speaker from those who threaten his life. It contrasts the disgrace that will come to the psalmist's opponents with the joy of those who trust in God. The psalm repeats with minor variations Ps. 40.14–18. "The LORD" in Ps. 40.14, 17 is here *God* (vv. 2, 5), typical of the Elohist psalms. The translation inverts the order of the phrases in vv. 1–5. **3–4:** The public shaming (shame is the opposite of honor) of the psalmist's opponents will prove God's power to protect His faithful ones. *Aha! Aha!* expresses derisive joy; cf. 35.21; 40.16. **6:** *Poor and needy*, typical language of the psalmist and his community. The poor have no protector in society; the psalmist is figuratively poor in that he has no protector and calls on God to protect him.

71

I seek refuge in You, O LORD;
   may I never be disappointed.

2 As You are beneficent, save me and rescue me;
   incline Your ear to me and deliver me.

3 Be a sheltering rock for me to which I may always
      repair;
   decree my deliverance,
   for You are my rock and my fortress.

4 My God, rescue me from the hand of the wicked,
   from the grasp of the unjust and the lawless.

5 For You are my hope,
   O Lord GOD,
   my trust from my youth.

6 While yet unborn, I depended on You;
   in the womb of my mother, You were my
      support;[a]
   I sing Your praises always.

7 I have become an example for many,
   since You are my mighty refuge.

8 My mouth is full of praise to You,
   glorifying You all day long.

9 Do not cast me off in old age;
   when my strength fails, do not forsake me!

10 For my enemies talk against me;
   those who wait for me are of one mind,

11 saying, "God has forsaken him;
   chase him and catch him,
   for no one will save him!"

12 O God, be not far from me;
   my God, hasten to my aid!

13 Let my accusers perish in frustration;
   let those who seek my ruin be clothed in
      reproach and disgrace!

14 As for me, I will hope always,
   and add to the many praises of You.

15 My mouth tells of Your beneficence,
   of Your deliverance all day long,
   though I know not how to tell it.

16 I come with praise of Your mighty acts, O Lord
      GOD;
   I celebrate Your beneficence, Yours alone.

17 You have let me experience it, God, from my
      youth;
   until now I have proclaimed Your wondrous
      deeds,

Ps. 71: An individual, now aged and infirm (vv. 9, 18), who has been faithful to God all his life, even while in the womb (v. 6), prays that God not forsake him as he reaches the end of his life. Central is the idea that the purpose of human life is to offer praise to God, and that if one dies, that praise will cease. If praise for God is to continue (that is, if God is to be known throughout the world), God must keep people alive and in good health. The psalm has a number of refrainlike repetitions (vv. 9, 18; 8, 15, 24). The thematic similarity to Ps. 70 and the lack of superscription in Ps. 71 have led some to suggest that these two psalms were once one psalm. **3:** *Sheltering rock,* "tzur ma'on," perhaps suggests the Temple (see 76.3), where the psalmist may be praying for healing. **5–9:** Divine care for the psalmist, from birth to old age (Ps. 22.10–11). The psalmist has always depended on God and has not yet been disappointed. **7:** *Example,* in a positive sense, that others see how God protects the psalmist. **9:** Perhaps implied is that the psalmist wishes not to be abandoned even when he no longer has the strength to serve God. **10–11:** When others see that God does not protect the psalmist, they take advantage of him. **12:** See Ps. 22.2, 12, 20. **14–16:** The psalmist looks forward to praising God, most likely in the Temple.

---

a *Meaning of Heb. uncertain.*

18 and even in hoary old age do not forsake me,
        God,
    until I proclaim Your strength to the next
        generation,
    Your mighty acts, to all who are to come,

19 Your beneficence, high as the heavens, O God,
    You who have done great things;
    O God, who is Your peer!

20 You who have made me undergo many troubles
        and misfortunes
    will revive me again,
    and raise me up from the depths of the earth.

21 You will grant me much greatness,
    You will turn and comfort me.

22 Then I will acclaim You to the music of the lyre
    for Your faithfulness, O my God;
    I will sing a hymn to You with a harp,
    O Holy One of Israel.

23 My lips shall be jubilant, as I sing a hymn to You,
    my whole being, which You have redeemed.

24 All day long my tongue shall recite Your
        beneficent acts,
    how those who sought my ruin were frustrated
        and disgraced.

72 Of Solomon.

O God, endow the king with Your judgments,
    the king's son with Your righteousness;
2   that he may judge Your people rightly,
    Your lowly ones, justly.

3 Let the mountains produce well-being for the
        people,
    the hills, the reward of justice.

4 Let him champion the lowly among the people,
    deliver the needy folk,
    and crush those who wrong them.

5 Let them fear You as long as the sun shines,
    while the moon lasts, generations on end.

6 Let him be like rain that falls on a mown field,
    like a downpour of rain on the ground,

7   that the righteous may flourish in his time,
    and well-being abound, till the moon is no
        more.

8 Let him rule from sea to sea,
    from the river to the ends of the earth.

9 Let desert-dwellers kneel before him,
    and his enemies lick the dust.

18: The psalmist does not have many years of life left to praise God; he wants to perpetuate the praise of God beyond his own lifetime. **20:** *Depths of the earth*, Sheol, the abode of the dead, where there is no praising God (Ps. 6.6). The psalmist prays that God will *revive* him (cure his malady). **22:** When his illness is cured, the psalmist will perform a thanksgiving ritual in the Temple (Pss. 50.14; 56.13–14).

Ps. 72: A prayer for the success of the king, perhaps a coronation ode. Only Pss. 72 and 127 are headed by *Of Solomon*. Ps. 72 is probably ascribed to Solomon because it emphasizes qualities and events for which he was known: judicial wisdom (1 Kings 3.16–28), the great extent of the kingdom and the gifts and tribute he collected (1 Kings 5.1–3), including from Tarshish (cf. 1 Kings 10.22), and from Sheba (cf. 1 Kings 10.10); he is also the first king who may be called (v. 1) "the king's son." **1–2:** The king's responsibility to uphold and administer justice (2 Sam. 8.15; Jer. 22.15–16), with divine assistance. *The king's son*, the dynastic successor, a reference to the Davidic covenant. Rashi attributes this psalm to David, who prayed it on behalf of his son Solomon when David foresaw that Solomon would ask God for wisdom. **3–4:** Moral order (justice for the poor and oppressed) in the world brings about cosmic order (fertility and bounty). **5:** Let the wrongdoers fear the king's punishment; or, let the people fear, that is, respect, the king. **6:** A good king ensures the prosperity of his people. **8:** The extent of the king's dominion *from sea to sea*, from the Mediterranean Sea to the Persian Gulf, and from *the river*, the Euphrates (1 Kings 5.4). This is hyperbolic court style; or, alternatively, the language is mythic, signifying that the king reigns over the entire universe (cf. Ps. 89.26; Zech. 9.10). **10–11:** Homage to the Israelite monarch by distant kings (1 Kings 4.21); a reflection of the king's great power. *Tarshish*,

10 Let kings of Tarshish and the islands pay tribute,
  kings of Sheba and Seba offer gifts.
11 Let all kings bow to him,
  and all nations serve him.

12 For he saves the needy who cry out,
  the lowly who have no helper.
13 He cares about the poor and the needy;
  He brings the needy deliverance.
14 He redeems them from fraud and lawlessness;
  ᵃ·the shedding of their blood weighs heavily
    upon him.·ᵃ

15 So let him live, and receive gold of Sheba;
  let prayers for him be said always,
  blessings on him invoked at all times.
16 ᵇ·Let abundant grain be in the land, to the tops of
    the mountains;
  let his crops thrive like the forest of Lebanon;
  and let men sprout up in towns like country
    grass.
17 May his name be eternal;
  while the sun lasts, may his name endure;·ᵇ
  let men invoke his blessedness upon
    themselves;
  let all nations count him happy.

18 Blessed is the LORD God, God of Israel,
  who alone does wondrous things;
19 Blessed is His glorious name forever;
  His glory fills the whole world.
  Amen and Amen.

20 End of the prayers of David son of Jesse.

BOOK THREE

73 A psalm of Asaph.

  God is truly good to Israel,
    to those whose heart is pure.
2   As for me, my feet had almost strayed,
    my steps were nearly led off course,
3   for I envied the wanton;
    I saw the wicked at ease.

the city of Tarsus on the southern coast of Turkey, or Tartessus in southern Spain; see 1 Kings 10.22. *The islands*, the islands of the eastern Aegean Sea. *Sheba*, in southwestern Arabia; cf. 1 Kings 10.1. *Seba*, probably also southwestern Arabia, or perhaps Ethiopia; cf. Isa. 43.3. **16:** Extremely difficult; it apparently deals with agricultural bounty, as in v. 3. **17:** The king's *name* means both his fame (1 Kings 3.14) and his progeny. *All nations . . . happy*, the promises to the ancestors (Gen. 12.3) fulfilled in the Davidic realm and dynasty. **18–19:** Not a part of the psalm, but the concluding doxology of Book II of the Psalter (see 41.14; 89.53; 106.48). **20:** Important evidence for the gradual editing of the psalter; contrast the "Davidic" psalms found later, e.g., 86; 101; 103.

Ps. 73: The psalm invokes typical wisdom themes (as in Prov. and Eccl.) about God's justice in the world and His punishment of evil. The psalmist, seeing how wicked people prosper and how they have no fear of punishment, almost abandoned his belief that God rewards the good and punishes the evil. But a visit to the Temple, with its aura of being in God's presence, caused the psalmist to reconsider. His faith was strengthened and he renews his praise of God. **1:** This psalm begins a collection attributed to *Asaph* (Pss. 73–83), a Levite who established a guild of Temple singers (1 Chron. ch 25); see also Ps. 50 n. **1–3:** The psalmist affirms

a-a Or *"their life is precious in his sight."*
b-b *Meaning of some Heb. phrases in these verses uncertain.*

4 Death has no pangs for them;
  their body is healthy.
5 They have no part in the travail of men;
  they are not afflicted like the rest of mankind.
6 So pride adorns their necks,
  lawlessness enwraps them as a mantle.
7 ᵃFat shuts out their eyes;
  their fancies are extravagant.·ᵃ
8 They scoff and plan evil;
  from their eminence they plan wrongdoing.
9 They set their mouths against heaven,
  and their tongues range over the earth.
10 ᵃSo they pound His people again and again,
  until they are drained of their very last tear.·ᵃ
11 Then they say, "How could God know?
  Is there knowledge with the Most High?"
12 Such are the wicked;
  ever tranquil, they amass wealth.

13 It was for nothing that I kept my heart pure
  and washed my hands in innocence,
14 seeing that I have been constantly afflicted,
  that each morning brings new punishments.
15 Had I decided to say these things,
  I should have been false to the circle of Your
  disciples.
16 So I applied myself to understand this,
  but it seemed a hopeless task
17 till I entered God's sanctuary
  and reflected on their fate.

18 You surround them with flattery;
  You make them fall through blandishments.
19 How suddenly are they ruined,
  wholly swept away by terrors.
20 ᵃWhen You are aroused You despise their image,
  as one does a dream after waking, O Lord.·ᵃ

21 My mind was stripped of its reason,
  ᵇmy feelings were numbed.·ᵇ
22 I was a dolt, without knowledge;
  I was brutish toward You.

23 Yet I was always with You,
  You held my right hand;

God's goodness to the upright, although he came close to rejecting this idea when he saw the good fortune of the wicked. **4–10:** The prosperity and contentment of the wicked. The wicked are successful, arrogant, materialistic, and they doubt God's power. **4–5:** Illness and early death were thought to be punishments for sin, yet the wicked do not suffer these things nor do they worry about suffering them. They seem to have it easy in life. **11:** See Pss. 10.11; 64.6; 94.7. There was no atheism in ancient times, only the notion that God lacked knowledge and power. **13–15:** The psalmist found no benefit in his righteousness. He hesitated to utter his doubts publicly, and sought to understand his observations. **16–17:** Reason alone could not solve the psalmist's dilemma or quiet his doubts; a religious experience in *God's sanctuary* provided him with an answer. *Sanctuary* is plural in Heb, perhaps referring to the Temple, or, alternatively, to assembly-places of the wise. **18–20:** The wicked may look successful but ruin will come upon them suddenly (cf. Ps. 37; Job 4.8–9). **21–22:** The psalmist apologizes for his earlier doubts. **23–24:** God has helped the psalmist in the past, and he looks forward to similar help now.

a-a Meaning of Heb. uncertain.
b-b Lit. "I was pierced through in my kidneys."

24 You guided me by Your counsel
      ᵃ·and led me toward honor.·ᵃ
25 Whom else have I in heaven?
      And having You, I want no one on earth.
26 My body and mind fail;
      but God is the stayᵇ of my mind, my portion
      forever.
27 Those who keep far from You perish;
      You annihilate all who are untrue to You.
28 As for me, nearness to God is good;
      I have made the Lord GOD my refuge,
      that I may recount all Your works.

74 A *maskil* of Asaph.

    Why, O God, do You forever reject us,
      do You fume in anger at the flock that You tend?
2   Remember the community You made Yours long
        ago,
      Your very own tribe that You redeemed,
      Mount Zion, where You dwell.
3   ᶜ·Bestir Yourself·ᶜ because of the ᵈ·perpetual
        tumult,·ᵈ
      all the outrages of the enemy in the sanctuary.
4   Your foes roar inside Your meeting-place;
      they take their signs for true signs.
5   ᵈ·It is like men wielding axes
      against a gnarled tree;
6   with hatchet and pike
      they hacked away at its carved work.·ᵈ
7   They made Your sanctuary go up in flames;
      they brought low in dishonor the dwelling-place
        of Your presence.
8   They resolved, "Let us destroy them altogether!"
      They burned all God's tabernacles in the land.
9   No signs appear for us;
      there is no longer any prophet;
      no one among us knows for how long.

10 Till when, O God, will the foe blaspheme,
      will the enemy forever revile Your name?
11 Why do You hold back Your hand, Your right
        hand?
      ᵈ·Draw it out of Your bosom!·ᵈ

25: God is his only help, in heaven or on earth. Having God, he has no need of another source of help. **26:** *My portion,* see Ps. 16.5. **27:** *Untrue* in Heb is "zoneh," the same word for "to prostitute oneself"; prostitution or infidelity was the common term for idolatry. **28:** The psalmist favors *nearness to God,* as opposed to *those who keep far from You* (v. 27).

Ps. 74: An exilic lament for the destruction of Jerusalem. The psalmist calls upon God to end the exile. God, the creator of the world and the vanquisher of the mythic forces of chaos, is called upon to vanquish the Babylonians, who are identified with the forces of chaos. Vv. 3–18 resemble Lamentations in the way they make the destruction of Jerusalem vivid. **1:** *Asaph,* see Ps. 73 n. **1–2:** Experiencing disaster and exile, the psalmist recalls the early history of the relationship between God and Israel. This special relationship, the fact that God chose Judah and dwelled on Zion, are the reasons that He should restore Judah and Zion (cf. also v. 20). *The flock that You tend,* in the exodus (Exod. 15.13, 16–17). *The community You made Yours,* through the covenant at Sinai. *Your very own tribe,* Judah, the tribe in which Jerusalem was located. **5:** For the Babylonians coming as woodcutters with *axes,* see Jer. 46.22–23. **9–10:** There is no reliable prophet to tell them how long the exile will last (see Amos 8.11). **11:** A plea to God to take action against the enemy.

a-a *Meaning of Heb. uncertain; others "And afterward receive me with glory."*
b *Lit. "rock."*   c-c *Lit. "Lift up Your feet."*
d-d *Meaning of Heb. uncertain.*

12 O God, my King from of old,
　　who brings deliverance throughout the land;
13 it was You who drove back the sea with Your
　　　might,
　　who smashed the heads of the monsters in the
　　　waters;
14 it was You who crushed the heads of Leviathan,
　　who left him as food for ᵃ‑the denizens of the
　　　desert;‑ᵃ
15 it was You who released springs and torrents,
　　who made mighty rivers run dry;
16 the day is Yours, the night also;
　　it was You who set in place the orb of the sun;
17 You fixed all the boundaries of the earth;
　　summer and winter—You made them.

18 Be mindful of how the enemy blasphemes the
　　　LORD,
　　how base people revile Your name.
19 Do not deliver Your dove to the wild beast;
　　do not ignore forever the band of Your lowly
　　　ones.
20 Look to the covenant!
　　For the dark places of the land are full of the
　　　haunts of lawlessness.
21 Let not the downtrodden turn away disappointed;
　　let the poor and needy praise Your name.
22 Rise, O God, champion Your cause;
　　be mindful that You are blasphemed by base
　　　men all day long.
23 Do not ignore the shouts of Your foes,
　　the din of Your adversaries that ascends all the
　　　time.

75 For the leader; al tashḥeth.
　　A psalm of Asaph, a song.

2 We praise You, O God;
　　we praise You;
　　Your presence is near;
　　men tell of Your wondrous deeds.

3 "At the time I choose,
　　I will give judgment equitably.
4 Earth and all its inhabitants dissolve;
　　it is I who keep its pillars firm.　　　　Selah.

a-a Or "seafaring men"; meaning of Heb. uncertain.

12–17: The classic example of God's power is the creation of the world, here retold in a mythological way (different from Gen. chs 1–3) so as to emphasize God's might over the forces of chaos. A God as powerful as this can certainly defeat the Babylonians. Cf. also Ps. 89.9–14. **14:** *Leviathan,* the forces of chaos represented as a sea-monster (Job 3.8; 26.12–13; 41.1; Isa. 27.1), also mentioned in the myths from Ugarit. **16–17:** Just as God fixed the spatial boundaries of the world, confining the waters and making them flow where he wanted, so he fixed temporal boundaries, creating day and night, and the seasons. **19:** *Your dove,* sacrificial animal of the poor (e.g., Lev. 5.7); here a metaphor for those slaughtered by Babylonia like sacrificed animals (Isa. 34.6–7). **20:** Despite the destruction and exile, God's covenant with Israel is still in force. The covenant implies that God must protect Israel. **23:** Here the *foes* and *adversaries* are both the Babylonians and the forces of chaos (vv. 12–17). The Babylonians are made to look as dangerous as the forces of chaos, which God must destroy so that the world will continue to exist as God created it.

Ps. 75: Praise for God, who renders justice. The wicked should not be arrogant because God will judge them as they deserve. **1:** *Al tashḥeth,* perhaps "do not destroy"; see Ps. 57.1. *Asaph,* see Ps. 73.1 n. **2:** *Your presence,* Heb "Your name." God is accessible. **3–5:** The psalmist is quoting God in these vv. **3:** *At the time,* the time God sets for judging. Humans do not know when God will render judgment but they should rest assured that the time will come. God's justice is equitable. **4:** Just as the earth has "pillars" to keep it firm, so justice keeps society firm. *Pillars,* see 1 Sam. 2.8. *Selah,* see Ps. 3.3 n. If God's words continue in the next v., this does not seem to be the place for subdividing the psalm. Ibn Ezra suggests that v. 5 begins the words of the psalmist.

5   To wanton men I say, 'Do not be wanton!'
     to the wicked, 'Do not lift up your horns!' "

6   Do not lift your horns up high
     ᵃ·in vainglorious bluster.ᵃ

7   For what lifts a man comes not from the east
     or the west or the wilderness;ᵇ

8   for God it is who gives judgment;
     He brings down one man, He lifts up
     another.

9   There is a cup in the LORD's hand
     with foaming wine fully mixed;
     from this He pours;
     all the wicked of the earth drink,
     draining it to the very dregs.

10   As for me, I will declare forever,
     I will sing a hymn to the God of Jacob.

11   "All the horns of the wicked I will cut;
     but the horns of the righteous shall be lifted
     up."

76 For the leader; with instrumental music.
A psalm of Asaph, a song.

2   God has made Himself known in Judah,
     His name is great in Israel;

3   Salem became His abode;
     Zion, His den.

4   There He broke the fiery arrows of the bow,
     the shield and the sword of war.   *Selah.*

5   You were resplendent,
     glorious, on the mountains of prey.

6   The stout-hearted were despoiled;
     they were in a stupor;
     the bravest of men could not lift a hand.

---

a-a Lit. "with arrogant neck you speak."
b Reading *midbār* with many mss.

5: *Lift up your horns,* an idiom meaning to be victorious. The wicked lift their horns in arrogance, as if they have won, but ultimately their horns will be cut (they will be deprived of power) and the horns of the righteous will be lifted up in victory over evil (v. 11 and cf. Ibn Ezra on v. 11).

7: *Wilderness:* The v. is difficult. If the word "harim" is read, it may mean "mountains," signifying the north (the opposite of "wilderness," referring to the south), or it may be a verb, "to raise up." **9:** The *cup* (of the LORD's wrath in Isa. 51.17; Jer. 25.15) signifies punishment.

Ps. 76: A hymn praising God, the victorious warrior, who resides in Jerusalem. Attempts have been made to identify the specific battle that may have occasioned the psalm, but there is no consensus. An ancient tradition, reflected in the LXX, rabbinic midrashim, and Rashi, connects it with the defeat of Sennacherib (2 Kings 19.35). Others interpret the battle as eschatological. In either case, as elsewhere in the Bible, God is depicted as the divine warrior. The two aspects of God highlighted here are His strength as a warrior and as a judge—these are the attributes of successful kings; God is envisioned as the supreme king, known to Israel and Judah at the beginning of the psalm and acknowledged by all the kings of the earth at the end. The text is not well preserved and consequently interpreting it is difficult. **1:** *Asaph,* see Ps. 73.1 n. **2:** *Judah . . . Israel:* If *Israel* is the Northern Kingdom, this would date the psalm to the time of the divided monarchy. Alternatively, "Israel" may be a general designation that is used to parallel Judah. **3:** *Salem,* variant name for Jerusalem (Gen. 14.18). *His abode . . . His den:* Heb "sukkah" and "maʿon" have two sets of associations, God's protective pavilion (the Temple or the sky) and a lion's den. For "sukkah" as the Temple, cf. Pss. 27.5; 31.21; cf. Exod. 40.3; for a lion's den, Ps. 10.9. For "maʿon" as the Temple, cf. Ps. 26.8; for a den, Amos 3.4; Nah. 2.12; Song 4.8. "Maʿon" and "sukkah" are used in parallelism for a lion's den in Job 38.39–40. God as a lion is an image of fearsome strength. Jer. 25.30 also invokes this association: God roars from his holy "maʿon." It may explain Amos 1.2 as well. **4:** *There,* Some commentators see this as referring to David's conquest of Jerusalem. For the breaking of the (enemies') weapons, see Ps. 46.10. *Selah* (also v. 10), see Ps. 3.3 n. **5:** *Mountains of prey,* A strange phrase, variously interpreted as "mountains of booty," "mountains rich with game," or, with an emendation,

7 At Your blast, O God of Jacob,
    horse and chariot lay stunned.

8 O You! You are awesome!
Who can withstand You
    when You are enraged?

9 In heaven You pronounced sentence;
    the earth was numbed with fright

10 as God rose to execute judgment,
    to deliver all the lowly of the earth.　　*Selah.*

11 ᵃ·The fiercest of men shall acknowledge You,
    when You gird on the last bit of fury.·ᵃ

12 Make vows and pay them to the Lᴏʀᴅ your God;
    ᵃ·all who are around Him shall bring tribute to
    the Awesome One.·ᵃ

13 He curbs the spirit of princes,
    inspires awe in the kings of the earth.

77 For the leader; on *Jeduthun.* Of Asaph. A psalm.

2 I cry aloud to God;
    I cry to God that He may give ear to me.

3 In my time of distress I turn to the Lord,
    ᵃ·with my hand [uplifted];
    [my eyes] flow all night without respite;·ᵃ
    I will not be comforted.

4 I call God to mind, I moan,
    I complain, my spirit fails.　　*Selah.*

5 You have held my eyelids open;
    I am overwrought, I cannot speak.

6 My thoughts turn to days of old,
    to years long past.

7 I recall at night their jibes at me;
    I commune with myself;
    my spirit inquires,

8 "Will the Lord reject forever
    and never again show favor?

9 Has His faithfulness disappeared forever?
Will His promise be unfulfilled for all time?

10 Has God forgotten how to pity?
Has He in anger stifled His compassion?"　　*Selah.*

11 And I said, ᵃ·"It is my fault
    that the right hand of the Most High has
    changed."·ᵃ

"everlasting mountains." If taken as *mountains of prey* it connects with the image of God as a lion (v. 3); for *prey* associated with a "maᶜon" of a lion, cf. Amos 3.4; Nah. 2.13; Job 38.40. **7:** *At your blast* ("roar"), God's war-cry. **9–10:** As in Ps. 75, God is a powerful judge. When God pronounces and executes his judgment, the world is terrified. **11:** Very difficult; *the fiercest of men* may be Israel's enemies. Some read "ᵓedom" (Edom, a kingdom south of Judah) instead of "ᵓadam," "men," and "ḥamat" (Hamath, a kingdom to the north) instead of *fury,* Heb "ḥemot." **12:** Tribute is brought to God by the kings of the earth (Ps. 72.10–11), showing that God is recognized by all as the supreme king.

Ps. 77: An individual calls upon God in his time of trouble, connecting his personal plight to the nation's past, specifically to the exodus, the paradigm for the return from the exile; like Rashi, we may see this psalm as lamenting the exile and hoping for a new exodus. The God of the exodus is known for His faithfulness and mercy, yet now God seems to have lost these characteristics. "Has God changed?" wonders the psalmist. "How long will he ignore me?" The psalm climaxes in a paean of praise in which the exodus, specifically the splitting of the sea, is couched in terms of the victory over chaos at the time of the creation. The implication is that the return from exile will not only be a new exodus, but also a new creation. **1:** *Jeduthun,* see Ps. 39.1. *Asaph,* see Ps. 73.1 n. **2–4:** Initial appeal for divine help (Ps. 142.2–4). **3:** *Night* is the time when pain and trouble seem most unbearable; cf. Ps. 6.7; Lam. 1.2. Rashi equates *night* with the exile. **4:** *I call . . . to mind . . . moan . . . complain:* These verbs connote uttering aloud. *Selah* (also vv. 10, 16), see Ps. 3.3 n. **5–7:** The speaker, who cannot sleep at night, ponders the past and his present situation. **5:** *Eyelids open,* watchful, as in night vigils (Rashi). **6:** *Days of old,*

---

a-a *Meaning of Heb. uncertain.*

12 I recall the deeds of the LORD;
    yes, I recall Your wonders of old;

13 I recount all Your works;
    I speak of Your acts.

14 O God, Your ways are holiness;
    what god is as great as God?

15 You are the God who works wonders;
    You have manifested Your strength among the
        peoples.

16 By Your arm You redeemed Your people,
    the children of Jacob and Joseph.   *Selah.*

17 The waters saw You, O God,
    the waters saw You and were convulsed;
    the very deep quaked as well.

18 Clouds streamed water;
    the heavens rumbled;
    Your arrows flew about;

19 Your thunder rumbled like wheels;
    lightning lit up the world;
    the earth quaked and trembled.

20 Your way was through the sea,
    Your path, through the mighty waters;
    Your tracks could not be seen.

21 You led Your people like a flock
    in the care of Moses and Aaron.

78 A *maskil* of Asaph.

    Give ear, my people, to my teaching,
        turn your ear to what I say.

2   I will expound a theme,
        hold forth on the lessons of the past,

enemy, as in: "He let fly His shafts and scattered them; He discharged lightning and routed them" (Ps. 18.15). *Your thunder rumbled like wheels:* On the noise of chariot wheels, see Jer. 47.3; Ezek. 26.10. The mention of wheels may recall the chariots of the pursuing Egyptians (cf. Exod. 14.9, 23–25), the topic of this section.

Ps. 78: This is the second-longest psalm, after Ps. 119. It defies categorization; its opening is very wisdom-like, while much of the rest is a historical precis consisting of a reinterpretation of earlier biblical traditions. In the latter sense it is similar to Pss. 105 and 106, with which it is often compared. Perhaps it may be considered a didactic historical psalm in that it uses a narrative about the past to teach about the present. It is addressed to the public (v. 1 "Give ear, my people") rather than to God. Its introduction suggests that its purpose is to encourage the listeners to be obedient, in contrast to previous generations (vv. 6–7). The psalm concludes, however, with a justification for the destruction of the Northern Kingdom (722 BCE), and praise for Davidic kingship centered in the chosen city of Zion. Thus, like many psalms, this one may have gone through a process of revision; in any case, it needs to be dated in its final form after the fall of the Northern Kingdom in 722, if not to exilic times. The narrative as recounted in the psalm differs from that found in the Torah. This is in part because of the specific focus of the psalm, which might explain why certain events are omitted and others are told in a particular fashion. It is based on non-Priestly narrative traditions (especially the source J) as well as traditions which were ultimately not canonized. Traditional Jewish interpretation, however, assumes that this psalm follows the authoritative Torah, and therefore expends much effort in reconciling these texts. **1–2:** These vv. show affinities to wisdom literature, and to Deuteronomy, which itself is influenced by wisdom tra-

the time of the exodus, the paradigmatic act of divine liberation (vv. 20–21). **7:** *Recall . . . commune:* These are the same verbs, "z-k-r" and "s-y-ḥ," that occur in v. 4: *call . . . to mind* and *complain.* **8–10:** God, who is known for His faithfulness, for keeping His promise, and for His mercy (cf. Exod. 34.6), is not manifesting these qualities. The psalmist wonders if God's nature has changed. **12–21:** The psalmist recalls ("z-k-r") the classic demonstration of God's power on behalf of Israel, the exodus and the splitting of the sea, which is likened to the mythical victory over the forces of chaos. **12:** Just as

he voiced his complaint in vv. 4 and 7, the psalmist voices praise for God here. **16:** *Jacob and Joseph,* the ancestors immediately preceding the exodus, from whom Israel descended. Some see in *Joseph* a reference to the Northern Kingdom; perhaps an earlier version of the psalm derived from the North. **17–21:** The sea of the exodus is identified with the *waters* of chaos, defeated by God (Isa. 51.9–10; cf. Pss. 18.8–16; 114.3–6). **18–19:** Language of theophany; God appeared on Sinai amidst thunder and lightning. *Your arrows* are flashes of lightning and also the weapons God uses against the

3   things we have heard and known,
      that our fathers have told us.
4   We will not withhold them from their children,
      telling the coming generation
      the praises of the LORD and His might,
      and the wonders He performed.
5   He established a decree in Jacob,
      ordained a teaching in Israel,
      charging our fathers
      to make them known to their children,
6   that a future generation might know
      —children yet to be born—
      and in turn tell their children
7   that they might put their confidence in God,
      and not forget God's great deeds,
      but observe His commandments,
8   and not be like their fathers,
      a wayward and defiant generation,
      a generation whose heart was inconstant,
      whose spirit was not true to God.

9   Like the Ephraimite bowmen
      who played false in the day of battle,
10 they did not keep God's covenant,
      they refused to follow His instruction;
11 they forgot His deeds
      and the wonders that He showed them.
12 He performed marvels in the sight of their fathers,
      in the land of Egypt, the plain of Zoan.
13 He split the sea and took them through it;
      He made the waters stand like a wall.
14 He led them with a cloud by day,
      and throughout the night by the light of fire.
15 He split rocks in the wilderness
      and gave them drink as if from the great deep.
16 He brought forth streams from a rock
      and made them flow down like a river.

17 But they went on sinning against Him,
      defying the Most High in the parched land.
18 To test God was in their mind
      when they demanded food for themselves.
19 They spoke against God, saying,
      "Can God spread a feast in the wilderness?
20 True, He struck the rock and waters flowed,
      streams gushed forth;
      but can He provide bread?
   Can He supply His people with meat?"

ditions. **4:** Traditions that reflect on *the praises of the LORD and His might, and the wonders* are emphasized. **5–7:** Context suggests that *decree* and *teaching* refer to the following narrative, which is to be told generation to generation. This is not, however, the usual meaning of the terms, and the pair "covenant" and "instruction," used in v. 10, likewise suggests legal matters. V. 7 might bridge these notions of law and history, by suggesting that recalling God's great acts for Israel leads to observance of the law (see also vv. 10–11). **9:** This is very unclear; much traditional Jewish interpretation (so, e.g., Rashi, Radak) connects it to an abortive first exodus organized by the Ephraimites. **11:** In contrast to *wonders, deeds* is not an important term of the exodus tradition. **12:** *Zoan,* in the Nile Delta, is not mentioned in association with the exodus tradition in the Torah. **13:** *Like a wall* quotes Exod. 15.8, suggesting that the Song of the Sea was among this psalmist's sources. **14:** See Exodus 13.21 (J). **15–31:** These traditions are similar to Exod. chs 17 (water from the rock) and 16 (manna and birds; see also Num. 11), but their order is reversed. **17:** Similar notices (e.g., vv. 21, 32) create a type of refrain, emphasizing the main point: Israel's sinfulness. **19–20:** Comparable sentiments are attributed to Moses in Num. 11.21–22.

21 The LORD heard and He raged;
  fire broke out against Jacob,
  anger flared up at Israel,
22 because they did not put their trust in God,
  did not rely on His deliverance.
23 So He commanded the skies above,
  He opened the doors of heaven
24 and rained manna upon them for food,
  giving them heavenly grain.
25 Each man ate a hero's meal;
  He sent them provision in plenty.
26 He set the east wind moving in heaven,
  and drove the south wind by His might.
27 He rained meat on them like dust,
  winged birds like the sands of the sea,
28 making them come down inside His camp,
  around His dwelling-place.
29 They ate till they were sated;
  He gave them what they craved.
30 They had not yet wearied of what they craved,
  the food was still in their mouths
31 when God's anger flared up at them.
  He slew their sturdiest,
  struck down the youth of Israel.
32 Nonetheless, they went on sinning
  and had no faith in His wonders.
33 He made their days end in futility,
  their years in sudden death.
34 When He struck[a] them, they turned to Him
  and sought God once again.
35 They remembered that God was their rock,
  God Most High, their Redeemer.
36 Yet they deceived Him with their speech,
  lied to Him with their words;
37 their hearts were inconstant toward Him;
  they were untrue to His covenant.
38 But He, being merciful, forgave iniquity
  and would not destroy;
  He restrained His wrath time and again
  and did not give full vent to His fury;
39 for He remembered that they were but flesh,
  a passing breath that does not return.

40 How often did they defy Him in the
      wilderness,
  did they grieve Him in the wasteland!

25: Exod. 16.17–18, in contrast, emphasizes the moderate, though sufficient quantity of manna. Many scholars understand *hero's meal* as food of the angels, and so does ancient interpretation. 27–31: See Num. 11 (J), though the psalmist nowhere calls the meat quail. 38: This v., an important theological explanation for divine mercy, is reused in several later Jewish penitential contexts. 39: Clearly this author, as is typical of the biblical period, does not believe in resurrection. 41: Num. 14.22, which states that the people "have tried Me these many times and have disobeyed Me," has a similar understanding of the wilderness period.

a Lit. "killed."

41 Again and again they tested God,
vexed[a] the Holy One of Israel.
42 They did not remember His strength,
or the day He redeemed them from the foe;
43 how He displayed His signs in Egypt,
His wonders in the plain of Zoan.
44 He turned their rivers into blood;
He made their waters undrinkable.
45 He inflicted upon them swarms of insects to
devour them,
frogs to destroy them.
46 He gave their crops over to grubs,
their produce to locusts.
47 He killed their vines with hail,
their sycamores [b]with frost.[b]
48 He gave their beasts over to hail,
their cattle to lightning bolts.
49 He inflicted His burning anger upon them,
wrath, indignation, trouble,
a band of deadly messengers.
50 He cleared a path for His anger;
He did not stop short of slaying them,
but gave them over to pestilence.
51 He struck every first-born in Egypt,
the first fruits of their vigor in the tents of Ham.
52 He set His people moving like sheep,
drove them like a flock in the wilderness.
53 He led them in safety; they were unafraid;
as for their enemies, the sea covered them.
54 He brought them to His holy realm,[c]
the mountain His right hand had acquired.
55 He expelled nations before them,
[d]settled the tribes of Israel in their tents,
allotting them their portion by the line.[d]

56 Yet they defiantly tested God Most High,
and did not observe His decrees.
57 They fell away, disloyal like their fathers;
they played false like a treacherous bow.
58 They vexed Him with their high places;
they incensed Him with their idols.
59 God heard it and was enraged;
He utterly rejected Israel.
60 He forsook the tabernacle of Shiloh,
the tent He had set among men.

42–43: The terms *redeemed* from Egypt and *signs* and *wonders* are characteristic of Deuteronomy (e.g., 7.8, 19). **44–51:** Rather than ten plagues, as in Exodus, seven plagues are described: blood (44), swarms of frogs (45), locusts (46), hail affecting agriculture (47), hail affecting livestock (48), pestilence (50), and death of the first-born (51). The missing plagues from the perspective of the Torah include darkness (contrast Ps. 105.28, where it is the first plague), and lice, which is only mentioned in the Priestly source. **45:** The Heb is simply *swarms* ("'arov"), and here refers to *swarms* of frogs. In Exod. 9.16–28, "'arov" is a free-standing plague of either swarms of insects or animals. **49:** This v. is an interlude, describing no plague in particular; it plays a major role in a midrash quoted in the Passover Haggadah, where it serves to multiply the number of plagues. For Radak, it alludes to the plagues mentioned in Exodus but not explicit in this psalm, so that Psalms may be reconciled with Exodus. **50:** The expression *gave them over to pestilence* may suggest the pestilence was viewed as a minor deity (see also "a band of deadly messengers" in the previous v.). **52–53:** The wanderings in the desert, alluded to earlier in the psalm, are glossed over here. **54:** Another echo of the Song of the Sea (Exod. 15.17). **55:** A remarkably concise summary of Joshua. **56–64:** The destruction of Shiloh because of the idolatry of the Northern tribes. **58:** This v. is suffused with the terminology of Deuteronomy and related books. **60:** The destruction of Shiloh, the central site in the period of Samuel, is never narrated in Samuel, and is assumed to have been accomplished by the Philistines.

a Or "set a limit to."   b-b Meaning of Heb. uncertain.
c Or "hill" with Septuagint and Saadia.   d-d Inverted for clarity.

61 He let His might[a] go into captivity,
    His glory into the hands of the foe.
62 He gave His people over to the sword;
    He was enraged at His very own.
63 Fire consumed their young men,
    and their maidens [b]remained unwed.[b]
64 Their priests fell by the sword,
    and their widows could not weep.

65 The Lord awoke as from sleep,
    like a warrior [c]shaking off[c] wine.
66 He beat back His foes,
    dealing them lasting disgrace.
67 He rejected the clan of Joseph;
    He did not choose the tribe of Ephraim.
68 He did choose the tribe of Judah,
    Mount Zion, which He loved.
69 He built His Sanctuary like the heavens,
    like the earth that He established forever.
70 He chose David, His servant,
    and took him from the sheepfolds.
71 He brought him from minding the nursing ewes
    to tend His people Jacob, Israel, His very own.
72 He tended them with blameless heart;
    with skillful hands he led them.

79 A psalm of Asaph.

O God, heathens have entered Your domain,
    defiled Your holy temple,
    and turned Jerusalem into ruins.
2 They have left Your servants' corpses
    as food for the fowl of heaven,
    and the flesh of Your faithful for the wild beasts.
3 Their blood was shed like water around
        Jerusalem,
    with none to bury them.
4 We have become the butt of our neighbors,
    the scorn and derision of those around us.

a I.e., the Ark; cf. Ps. 132.8.
b-b Lit. "had no nuptial song."
c-c Meaning of Heb. uncertain.

64: They did *not weep* due to the huge magnitude of the catastrophe. **65:** On God awaking, see 7.7 n. **67:** *The clan of Joseph* and *the tribe of Ephraim* refer to the Northern Kingdom as a whole: it is named after its most significant groups. **68–72:** The choosing of Jerusalem as a royal city and of David as the first king are here tightly linked in what modern scholars call "the Royal Zion theology"; the order of these events here is the opposite of that narrated in Samuel, where first David, and then Jerusalem, was chosen. **70–72:** This partakes in the common ancient Near Eastern image of the king as the shepherd of his people. **72:** The depiction of David is highly idealized, more like Chronicles than Samuel.

Ps. 79: An exilic lament for the destruction of Jerusalem and the Temple, like Ps. 74 and Lamentations. The psalm sees the destruction as an affront to God rather than to the people of Judah, and calls upon God to redress the heinous act for the sake of His name (v. 9). The psalm draws on a common stock of phrases and motifs of lament. This psalm is recited at the Western Wall on Friday evenings and on the 9th of Av. **1:** *Asaph,* see Ps. 73.1 n. *Heathens,* Heb "goyim," is used in a neutral sense of other nations; here it refers to Babylonia and its allies (Ps. 137.7–8). *Your domain,* God's "naḥalah," the land of Israel, or in this case, Judah. *Ruins* ("'iyim") is a rare word, possibly alluding to the well-known prophecy of Mic. 3.12 (see Jer. 26.18), "Jerusalem shall become heaps of ruins ("'iyim")." **2–3:** To be left unburied and exposed to scavengers is in the ancient Near East a terrible disgrace (Josh. 10.27; 2 Kings 9.25–26). For variations on this image, see Ezek. 32.4–6; Zeph. 1.17. When sacrifices were brought to the Temple, or when meat was eaten, the blood was to be poured out like water (Deut. 12.24, 27), so there is an ironic element here, in that Judah was a sacrifice whose blood was poured out. In addition, blood defiles, as does a corpse. So the heathens have defiled Jerusalem not only by the simple act of entering God's holy precinct (which according to some views was off-limits to them; see Lam. 1.10), but further by contaminating it with blood and corpses. Concerning *Your faithful,* see Ps. 4.4 n. **4:** Ps. 44.14. The scorn heaped upon the defeated Judah is a conventional motif.

5   How long, O LORD, will You be angry forever,
      will Your indignation blaze like fire?
6   Pour out Your fury on the nations that do not
      know You,
      upon the kingdoms that do not invoke Your
      name,
7   for they have devoured Jacob
      and desolated his home.
8   Do not hold our former iniquities against us;
      let Your compassion come swiftly toward us,
      for we have sunk very low.
9   Help us, O God, our deliverer,
      for the sake of the glory of Your name.
      Save us and forgive our sin,
      for the sake of Your name.
10   Let the nations not say, "Where is their God?"
      Before our eyes let it be known among the nations
      that You avenge the spilled blood of Your
      servants.
11   Let the groans of the prisoners reach You;
      reprieve those condemned to death,
      as befits Your great strength.
12   Pay back our neighbors sevenfold
      for the abuse they have flung at You, O Lord.
13   Then we, Your people,
      the flock You shepherd,
      shall glorify You forever;
      for all time we shall tell Your praises.

80 For the leader; on *shoshannim, eduth.*
Of Asaph. A psalm.

2   Give ear, O shepherd of Israel
      who leads Joseph like a flock!
      Appear, You who are enthroned on the cherubim,

ish the enemy for the destruction, which is an affront to God (also v. 12). **11:** *Prisoners,* exiles. *Those condemned to death:* Being denied access to the Temple is like death, for one cannot praise God (cf. Ps. 137.4). When the restoration has taken place, the people will be able to praise God (v. 13). Cf. Ps. 142.8. **12:** The psalmist appeals for *sevenfold* retribution on Babylonia's allies. Many laments end with a plea for retribution against the enemy; this is not to be taken as simple revenge, but as a way of expressing the hope for the return of the right world order, where evil has no place and all acknowledge God. *Pay back . . . sevenfold,* a stereotypical number that may evoke the vengeance of Cain (Gen. 4.15). Like Cain, Israel was banished from its land/soil and from God's presence. *For the abuse they have flung at You:* An attack on God's Temple and His people is an affront to God, as in v. 1. **13:** Like Pss. 77 and 78, Ps. 79 ends with the image of the divine shepherd; Ps. 80 begins with the same image, thereby joining together this cluster of Asaphite psalms.

Ps. 80: Its references to the Northern Kingdom suggest that this may originally have been a lament for the fall of the Northern Kingdom (722 BCE), but its placement after Ps. 79, with which it shares phraseology, indicates that the psalm was reworked and in its present form serves as a lament for the destruction of Judah. In addition to the mention of the northern tribes (Joseph, Ephraim, Manasseh, Benjamin), there are echoes of the reign of Saul (cf. vv. 5, 18). A refrain occurs in vv. 4, 8, 20. **1:** *Shoshannim* ("lilies"), see Ps. 45.1.; cf. Ps. 60.1. *Asaph,* see Ps. 73.1 n. **2:** *Shepherd of Israel:* Pastoral imagery is found in other Asaph psalms (74.1; 78.52; 79.13). Cf. Gen. 48.14–15; 49.24. *Appear* (lit. "shine"), theophany (divine manifestation) language (Ps. 50.2; 94.1). **2–3:** *Israel . . . Joseph . . . Ephraim, Benjamin, and Manasseh,* the Northern Kingdom. More specifically, the sons of Rachel (Joseph and

5: Cf. Ps. 89.47. The question about the duration of divine wrath, which seems endless, is typical of laments (Ps. 74.9–10). **6–7:** Jer. 25.10. These vv. were added to the end of the Passover Haggadah during the Middle Ages, reacting to Jewish persecution; they are part of the hope for the redemption of Israel. **8–9:** One of the few laments that contains an admission of Israel's sins. *Former iniquities* may mean the earlier (pre-exilic) iniquities of the speakers that, according to the Deutero-

nomic idea assumed here, led to the destruction. Another interpretation is "iniquities of former generations," which would refer to the idea of intergenerational punishment (see Exod. 34.7). The emphasis, however, is not on Israel's guilt, but on God's future actions. **10:** Incremental movement from the admission of sins and the hope that they will not be held against the community (v. 8), to a plea that God forgive the sins (v. 9), to the idea that God avenge *the spilled blood of Your servants,* that is, pun-

3   at the head of Ephraim, Benjamin, and
        Manasseh!
    Rouse Your might and come to our help!
4   Restore us, O God;
       show Your favor that we may be delivered.

5   O Lord, God of hosts,
       how long will You be wrathful
       toward the prayers of Your people?
6   You have fed them tears as their daily bread,
       made them drink great measures of tears.
7   You set us at strife with our neighbors;
       our enemies mock us at will.
8   O God of hosts, restore us;
       show Your favor that we may be delivered.

9   You plucked up a vine from Egypt;
       You expelled nations and planted it.
10   You cleared a place for it;
       it took deep root and filled the land.
11   The mountains were covered by its shade,
       mighty cedars by its boughs.
12   Its branches reached the sea,
       its shoots, the river.
13   Why did You breach its wall
       so that every passerby plucks its fruit,
14   wild boars gnaw at it,
       and creatures of the field feed on it?

15   O God of hosts, turn again,
       look down from heaven and see;
       take note of that vine,
16   the stock planted by Your right hand,
       the stem[a] you have taken as Your own.
17   For it is burned by fire and cut down,
       perishing before Your angry blast.
18   Grant Your help[b] to the man at Your right hand,
       the one You have taken as Your own.
19   We will not turn away from You;
       preserve our life that we may invoke Your
         name.
20   O Lord, God of hosts, restore us;
       show Your favor that we may be delivered.

Benjamin), and grandsons (Joseph's sons: Ephraim and Manasseh). The tribes of Ephraim, Manasseh, and Benjamin were encamped under one banner according to the list in Num. 2.18–24. Benjamin's tribal territory lay just south of Ephraim. Benjamin joined Judah when the kingdom was divided; this psalm may predate that event, or may be an idealized retrojection to the time before the monarchy. Alternatively, *Benjamin* may symbolize the Southern Kingdom, making this a prayer for all Israel. **4:** *Show Your favor* (Heb "light up your face"), expressing God's benevolence; see Num. 6.24–26; Pss. 4.7; 67.2. **5:** These epithets of God along with *enthroned on the cherubim* (v. 2) suggest God's presence in the Ark that went out to battle (1 Sam. 4.4; 2 Sam. 6.2). *Be wrathful toward the prayers:* Reject the prayers, prevent them from reaching you. Cf. Lam. 3.44. **6:** See Pss. 42.4; 102.10. **9–17:** The pastoral imagery shifts to an agricultural metaphor in which Israel is a *vine* (cf. Isa. 5.1–7; Jer. 2.21; Ezek. 17.1–10), plucked from Egypt and planted in the Promised Land where it took root and flourished. But then God in His anger allowed its protecting wall to be breached, and the vine was destroyed by human and animal forces. **12:** *The river,* the Euphrates. **17:** See Ps. 74.5–7. **18:** *The man at Your right hand,* a reference to the king (Ps. 110.1). If the psalm dates from, or is a retrojection to, the early monarchy, this may refer to Saul, a Benjaminite (1 Sam. 9.1). *The one You have taken as Your own,* a reference to the Davidic dynasty. The psalmist's main concern is not the north but Judah, threatened with defeat in the eighth century by the Assyrians and subsequently conquered by the Babylonians in 586 BCE.

a Lit. "son."   *b* Lit. "hand."

81

For the leader; on the *gittith*. Of Asaph.

2 Sing joyously to God, our strength;
   raise a shout for the God of Jacob.

3 Take up the song,
   sound the timbrel,
   the melodious lyre and harp.

4 Blow the horn on the new moon,
   on the full moon for our feast day.

5 For it is a law for Israel,
   a ruling of the God of Jacob;

6 He imposed it as a decree upon Joseph
   when ᵃ·he went forth from·ᵃ the land of Egypt;
   I heard a language that I knew not.

7 I relieved his shoulder of the burden,
   his hands were freed from the basket.

8 In distress you called and I rescued you;
   I answered you from the ᵇ·secret place of
       thunder·ᵇ
   I tested you at the waters of Meribah.   *Selah.*

9 Hear, My people, and I will admonish you;
   Israel, if you would but listen to Me!

10 You shall have no foreign god,
    you shall not bow to an alien god.

11 I the LORD am your God
    who brought you out of the land of Egypt;
    open your mouth wide and I will fill it.

12 But My people would not listen to Me,
    Israel would not obey Me.

13 So I let them go after their willful heart
    that they might follow their own devices.

14 If only My people would listen to Me,
    if Israel would follow My paths,

15 then would I subdue their enemies at once,
    strike their foes again and again.

a-a Or "He went forth against."   b-b Meaning of Heb. uncertain.

Ps. 81: A call to praise God with music; perhaps a hymn for the festivals (v. 4). God speaks in the first person in vv. 7–16, 17b, reviewing the exodus and wandering, with emphasis on Israel's disobedience. If Israel is obedient, God will subdue its enemies and grant agricultural abundance. This psalm shares themes with Ps. 95 but reflects a strong interest in the Northern Kingdom, as do Pss. 78 and 80. This psalm is recited in the morning service on Thursdays. **1:** *The gittith,* see Ps. 8.1. *Asaph,* see Ps. 73.1 n. **2:** *The God of Jacob,* repeated in v. 5; this epithet, along with "Israel" (vv. 5, 9, 12, 14) and "Joseph" (v. 6; a term for the Northern Kingdom) indicate northern provenance (seven uses in all). **4:** *New moon,* observed as a holiday in ancient Israel; here likely refers to the New Year, announced with loud blasts (Lev. 23.23–25; Num. 29.1). *Full moon,* when Passover and Sukkot begin. *Our feast day,* likely the festival of Sukkot (Lev. 23.33–34), also called "the feast," "he-ḥag" (1 Kings 8.2; Neh. 8.14; and in rabbinic literature). Rabbinic interpretation takes the second part of the v. as referring to Rosh Ha-Shanah, the New Year. This is based on a different understanding of "keseh": instead of *full moon* it is interpreted as "new moon," the time when the moon is covered (from Heb "k-s-h"). The "new moon" that is a "feast day" is Rosh Ha-Shanah. The practice of reciting this v. to introduce the daytime kiddush (blessing over wine) on Rosh Ha-Shanah derives from this rabbinic interpretation. **6:** *A language that I knew not,* the language of Egypt; cf. Ps. 114.1. **7:** Deliverance from slavery and oppression in Egypt (Exod. 6.6–7). The *basket* is the workbasket that symbolizes subjugated people (often captives of war). **8:** *Meribah,* the place where Israel tested God (Exod. 17.7; Num. 20.13; Ps. 95.8–9), but here seen as a test of Israel (as in Deut. 33.8, where God tested the Levites); it epitomizes Israel's rebellion. *Selah,* see Ps. 3.3 n. **10–11:** An allusion to the beginning of the Decalogue (Exod. 20.1–2; Deut. 5.6). It is cited in reverse order *(You shall have no foreign God . . . I the* LORD *am your God).* (Some scholars see this type of reversal as indicating a quotation—the ancient equivalent of quotation marks.) Instead of "other gods" as in the commandment, the psalm has "foreign . . . alien gods." *Foreign god,* see Deut. 32.12, where the reference is presumably to Egyptian gods. Cf. Ps. 44.21 where Babylonian gods are meant. The reference here is to Canaanite gods. **11:** God fills the mouths of the people with food (v. 17). **12–13:** The infidelity of the wilderness generation (Ps. 78.17, 40), a warning to the psalmist's contemporaries. **14–17:** Is-

16 Those who hate the LORD shall cower before Him;
their doom shall be eternal.
17 He fed them[a] the finest wheat;
I sated you with honey from the rock.

82 A psalm of Asaph.

God stands in the divine assembly;
among the divine beings He pronounces
judgment.
2 How long will you judge perversely,
showing favor to the wicked?   *Selah.*
3 Judge the wretched and the orphan,
vindicate the lowly and the poor,
4 rescue the wretched and the needy;
save them from the hand of the wicked.

5 They neither know nor understand,
they go about in darkness;
all the foundations of the earth totter.
6 I had taken you for divine beings,
sons of the Most High, all of you;
7 but you shall die as men do,
fall like any prince.

8 Arise, O God, judge the earth,
for all the nations are Your possession.

---

a Lit. "him," i.e., Israel.

rael's obedience would mean victory over foes and agricultural bounty. **17:** The v. switches abruptly from third person to first person. *Finest wheat,* see Deut. 32.14; Ps. 147.14. *Honey from the rock,* see Deut. 32.13.

Ps. 82: A vision of a heavenly court scene where God condemns those who judge unfairly. The psalm plays on the word "'elo-him," which means "God" as well as "divine beings." The notion that other divine beings exist is found elsewhere in the Bible (see v. 1 n.). In later biblical thought these beings serve as ministering angels to God and are never equal to God (cf. Ps. 89.5–8). An earlier view is reflected, and then rejected, in this psalm, according to which the divine beings each represent one na-

tion, serving as that nation's protector, a remnant of the idea that the world was populated by many gods, each assigned to a different nation (cf. Deut. 4.19 and 32.8, according to LXX and the Dead Sea Scrolls). This psalm forcefully rejects the idea of other gods; God deprives them of their divinity and He alone has dominion over all nations. In content and language, the psalm resembles prophetic criticisms of the oppression of the poor, including the denial of access to the judicial system and the disadvantages faced by the poor in obtaining just verdicts. Through the scenario of the heavenly tribunal, the psalm speaks to the issue of a just society, without which the world cannot exist. It also speaks to the universality of God, the supreme judge over all

nations. **1:** *Asaph,* see Ps. 73.1 n. *God,* "'elohim," as is the preference in Pss. 42–83, rather than the Tetragrammaton (YHVH); this substitution creates some confusion in the Heb. *Stands,* rises to render a verdict. Cf. Isa. 3.13–14. *Divine assembly,* Heb "the assembly of El." El was the head of the Ugaritic pantheon. Perhaps originally a separate deity in early Israelite religion, the name "El" became synonymous with YHVH. *Divine beings,* the celestial council. Cf. Isa. ch 6; 1 Kings ch 22; Job 1.6. Some commentators prefer to interpret this use of "'elohim" as human judges, but this is less likely. **2:** *Selah,* see Ps. 3.3 n. **3:** Let the cases of the poor be heard and, when they bring a case against the rich, make it possible for them to win it if they are in the right. Cf. Isa. 1.23. **5:** Without justice the world is in danger of collapse (Jer. 4.23–26). Justice is a cornerstone of the cosmos. **6:** *Sons of the Most High,* members of God's heavenly court. "Elyon" is an ancient Canaanite epithet, here applied to God (7.18 n.). **7:** Divine beings are immortal but humans are subject to death. Unjust divine beings are unmasked as not being divine. The gods of the other nations are not real gods. **8:** God alone is the true judge; He does not pervert justice. Cf. Isa. 3.13–14; Ps. 76.9. He is therefore called upon to judge the world, including the nations thought to belong to other gods or divine beings, which here are shown to be God's possessions. God's justice is universal.

83

A song, a psalm of Asaph.

2 O God, do not be silent;
　　do not hold aloof;
　　do not be quiet, O God!
3 For Your enemies rage,
　　Your foes ᵃ‑assert themselves.‑ᵃ
4 They plot craftily against Your people,
　　take counsel against Your treasured ones.
5 They say, "Let us wipe them out as a
　　　nation;
　　Israel's name will be mentioned no
　　　more."
6 Unanimous in their counsel
　　they have made an alliance against You—
7 the clans of Edom and the Ishmaelites,
　　Moab and the Hagrites,
8 Gebal, Ammon, and Amalek,
　　Philistia with the inhabitants of Tyre;
9 Assyria too joins forces with them;
　　they give support to the sons of Lot.　　Selah.

10 Deal with them as You did with Midian,
　　with Sisera, with Jabin,
　　at the brook Kishon—
11 who were destroyed at En-dor,
　　who became dung for the field.
12 Treat their great men like Oreb and Zeeb,
　　all their princes like Zebah and Zalmunna,
13 who said, "Let us take the meadows of
　　　God as our possession."
14 O my God, make them like thistledown,
　　like stubble driven by the wind.
15 As a fire burns a forest,
　　as flames scorch the hills,
16 pursue them with Your tempest,
　　terrify them with Your storm.
17 Cover ᵇ their faces with shame
　　so that they seek Your name, O Lord.
18 May they be frustrated and terrified,
　　disgraced and doomed forever.
19 May they know
　　that Your name, Yours alone, is the
　　　Lord,
　　supreme over all the earth.

a-a Lit. "lift up the head."
b Lit. "Fill."

Ps. 83: A plea to be saved from all the enemies surrounding Israel. Since psalms rarely contain historical information, it is doubtful that an actual military campaign provoked this psalm, and the list of hostile nations is better understood as a composite of all the traditional enemies encircling Israel. The list begins with countries to the east and south of Israel, and moves to the west and north, returning in v. 9 to the sons of Lot, Moab, and Edom (previously mentioned in v. 7). Vv. 10–13 allude to the defeat of enemies in the book of Judges, viewed as an idealized period of divine intervention, hoping that the current enemies will suffer the same fate. **1:** *Asaph*, see Ps. 73.1 n. **2–5:** The silence of God is contrasted with the *rage* and speech of the enemies against Israel and its God. **3:** Israel's enemies are, according to this psalmist, by definition *Your* (God's) *enemies.* Cf. vv. 5–6. **5–6:** The threat against Israel is a threat against God. If Israel's name is no longer mentioned, God's name will be forgotten. Cf. v. 19. **7–9:** Enemies of Israel. *Hagrites,* descendants of Hagar; a tribe of pastoralists in northern Transjordan (1 Chron. 5.10, 18–22). *Gebal,* later Byblos, north of Beirut on the coast of Lebanon. Alternatively, a place near Edom. *The sons of Lot,* Moab and Edom (Gen. 19.36–38). *Selah,* see Ps. 3.3 n. **10–13:** See Judg. chs 4–8. **11:** *En-dor* is not mentioned in Judges. **14–16:** See Isa. 17.13–14. *Thistledown* and *stubble* are easily burnt up. **15–16:** Combining fire imagery and tempest imagery, the picture that emerges is of enemies being burnt up as if in a forest fire by God's powerful windstorm that will fan the flames into a huge conflagration. **17–19:** The confounding of the enemies' plans will cause them to recognize God's name and His supremacy over the earth. As in Ps. 82, the theme of Ps. 83 is God's supremacy over all nations. Cf. Pss. 47.2; 97.9.

84

For the leader; on the *gittith*. Of the Korahites. A psalm.

2   How lovely is Your dwelling-place,
       O Lord of hosts,

3   I long, I yearn for the courts of the Lord;
       my body and soul shout for joy to the living
         God.

4   Even the sparrow has found a home,
       and the swallow a nest for herself
       in which to set her young,
       near Your altar, O Lord of hosts,
       my king and my God.

5   Happy are those who dwell in Your house;
       they forever praise You.   *Selah.*

6   Happy is the man who finds refuge in You,
       whose mind is on the [pilgrim] highways.

7   They pass through the Valley of Baca,
       ᵃregarding it as a place of springs,
       as if the early rain had covered it with
         blessing.ᵃ

8   They go from ᵇrampart to rampart,ᵇ
       appearing before God in Zion.

9   O Lord, God of hosts,
       hear my prayer;
       give ear, O God of Jacob.   *Selah.*

10   O God, behold our shield,
       look upon the face of Your anointed.

11   Better one day in Your courts than a thousand
       [anywhere else];
       I would rather stand at the threshold of God's
         house
       than dwell in the tents of the wicked.

12   For the Lord God is sunᶜ and shield;
       the Lord bestows grace and glory;
       He does not withhold His bounty from those
         who live without blame.

13   O Lord of hosts,
       happy is the man who trusts in You.

85

For the leader. Of the Korahites. A psalm.

2   O Lord, You ᵈwill favorᵈ Your land,
       restoreᵉ Jacob's fortune;

Ps. 84: A celebration of the pilgrimage to the Temple. The psalmist yearns to be in God's presence and rehearses every step of the way to Jerusalem. It is one of the psalms that glorify Zion (see also Pss. 46; 48; 76; 87; 122). **1:** *Gittith,* see Ps. 8.1. *Korahites,* see Ps. 42.1. **2:** *Lovely,* Heb "yedidot," is not just "beautiful" but "beloved." There is almost a mystical quality in the intensity of the psalmist's desire (with his entire being, v. 3) to be in God's presence. **3:** *The courts,* the outer parts of the Temple complex. **4:** The movement progresses from the courts to the altar, near which birds find a home, much as the psalmist wishes to find a home near God. **5:** *Selah* (also v. 9), see Ps. 3.3. **6:** *Happy,* in a fortunate state; cf. vv. 6, 13. **7:** *Valley of Baca* is an unknown place on the way to the Temple. Some interpret this as the valley of Rephaim, where the baca trees grow (2 Sam. 5.22–24). The *early rain* falls in the land of Israel at the beginning of winter. This reference suggests that the pilgrimage is for the festival of Sukkot, just before the start of the rainy season, when prayers for rain are offered. **9:** *God of Hosts* is a substitute for "Lord of Hosts" (cf. v. 4). **10:** *Shield* and *anointed* refer to the king, whom God is asked to look upon with favor. **11:** The psalmist prefers to stand at God's threshold, merely setting his foot at the entrance and not fully entering the Temple, rather than to dwell, to reside fully, in the tents of the wicked (Heb "tents of wickedness"). **12:** *His bounty,* rain; cf. v. 7.

Ps. 85: An exilic or postexilic psalm, praying for the restoration of Israel to its land. The land is mentioned in vv. 2, 10, 13. Depending on how the tense of the verbs in vv. 1–4 is interpreted, the Jews have already returned, or the return is in the future. If the former, the plea is for an additional favor of restoration, perhaps because of the problems encountered by the returnees. The hope is for a moral and prosperous society.

---

a-a *Meaning of Heb. uncertain.*
b-b *Others "strength to strength."*   c *Or "bulwark," with Targum; cf. Isa. 54.12.*
d-d *Or "have favored."*   e *Or "have restored."*

3   You ᵃwill forgiveᵃ Your people's iniquity,
       pardonᵇ all their sins;   *selah*

4   You ᶜwill withdrawᶜ all Your anger,
       turnᵈ away from Your rage.

5   Turn again, O God, our helper,
       revoke Your displeasure with us.

6   Will You be angry with us forever,
       prolong Your wrath for all generations?

7   Surely You will revive us again,
       so that Your people may rejoice in You.

8   Show us, O Lᴏʀᴅ, Your faithfulness;
       grant us Your deliverance.

9   Let me hear what God, the Lᴏʀᴅ, will speak;
       He will promise well-being to His people, His
          faithful ones;
       may they not turn to folly.

10   His help is very near those who fear Him,
       to make His glory dwell in our land.

11   Faithfulness and truth meet;
       justice and well-being kiss.

12   Truth springs up from the earth;
       justice looks down from heaven.

13   The Lᴏʀᴅ also bestows His bounty;
       our land yields its produce.

14   Justice goes before Him
       as He sets out on His way.

86 A prayer of David.

     Incline Your ear, O Lᴏʀᴅ,
       answer me,
       for I am poor and needy.

2   Preserve my life, for I am steadfast;
       O You, my God,
       deliver Your servant who trusts in You.

3   Have mercy on me, O Lord,
       for I call to You all day long;

4   bring joy to Your servant's life,
       for on You, Lord, I set my hope.

5   For You, Lord, are good and forgiving,
       abounding in steadfast love to all who call on
          You.

6   Give ear, O Lᴏʀᴅ, to my prayer;
       heed my plea for mercy.

1: *Korahites,* see Ps. 42 n. **2:** *Restore Jacob's fortune,* a common phrase for the return from exile (Jer. 30.3, 18; Amos 9.14). **3–7:** Forgiveness of Israel's sin is necessary for the restoration. **3:** *Selah,* see Ps. 3.3 n. **7:** If the nation returns and the Temple is rebuilt, the people may *rejoice in* God, that is, be in His presence and in His favor. **8:** God's *faithfulness* ("ḥesed"—see Ps. 5.8 n.) to his covenant with Israel remains constant despite the exile, and is invoked here. **13:** *Bounty,* rain (Lev. 26.1–6; Deut. 28.12; Ps. 67.6).

Ps. 86: An individual calls on God's help. The "I" and "You" of the psalm is strongly felt. The psalm is anthological, reusing language and motifs occurring elsewhere in the Bible. **1:** *A prayer,* cf. Pss. 90; 102. *Poor and needy* are common terms for the psalmist and his community. While these terms may refer to a low socioeconomic status, it is just as likely that they function as literary tropes to signify the absence of protection that the psalmist feels. **5:** The first of two references (also v. 15) to Exod. 34.6–7. This v. is part of the High Holy Day liturgy. As in Jonah 4.2, only the "forgiveness" aspects of the divine attributes are cited in this psalm. **8:** Divine incomparability is an expression of Israel's monotheism (Pss. 40.6 [see note a-a]; 71.19; cf. Exod. 15.11). **9:** God created all the nations although they do not yet recognize

a-a Or "have forgiven."   *b Or "have pardoned."*
c-c Or "have withdrawn."   *d Or "have turned."*

7   In my time of trouble I call You,
         for You will answer me.

8   There is none like You among the gods, O Lord,
         and there are no deeds like Yours.
9   All the nations You have made
         will come to bow down before You, O Lord,
         and they will pay honor to Your name.
10   For You are great and perform wonders;
         You alone are God.
11   Teach me Your way, O LORD;
         I will walk in Your truth;
         let my heart be undivided in reverence for Your
             name.
12   I will praise You, O Lord, my God, with all my
             heart
         and pay honor to Your name forever.
13   For Your steadfast love toward me is great;
         You have saved me from the depths of Sheol.

14   O God, arrogant men have risen against me;
         a band of ruthless men seek my life;
         they are not mindful of You.
15   But You, O Lord, are a God
         compassionate and merciful,
         slow to anger, abounding in steadfast love and
             faithfulness.
16   Turn to me and have mercy on me;
         grant Your strength to Your servant
         and deliver the son of Your maidservant.
17   Show me a sign of Your favor,
         that my enemies may see and be frustrated
         because You, O LORD, have given me aid and
             comfort.

87   ^{a1-2}Of the Korahites. A psalm. A song.

         ^{b-}The LORD loves the gates of Zion,
             His foundation on the holy mountains,^{-b}
             more than all the dwellings of Jacob.
3   Glorious things are spoken of you,
             O city of God.   Selah.
4   I mention Rahab^c and Babylon among those who
             acknowledge Me;

a The meaning of many passages in this psalm is uncertain.
b-b Order of lines inverted for clarity.
c A primeval monster; here, a poetic term for Egypt; cf. Isa. 30.7.

that; but soon they will. See Ps. 22.28. **13:** *Sheol*, the abode of the dead. **14:** See Ps. 54.5. **16:** *Turn to me and have mercy on me*, a paraphrase of the middle of the priestly blessing (Num. 6.25). *Son of Your maidservant*, parallel to *Your servant* but expressing even more humility. **17:** *Show me a sign:* Give me an indication that You will help me; or, when You help me, that will be a sign to my enemies of Your power.

Ps. 87: A hymn celebrating Zion as God's specially chosen city, the center of the world, to which all nations will come (cf. Isa. 2.2–4). The psalm is structured around "(in) you/her" ("bakh, bah") = Zion and "there" ("sham") = the other nations. The nations are thereby contrasted with Zion and at the same time drawn into her orbit. There are numerous textual difficulties. **1–2:** *Korahites*, see Ps. 42 n. *All the dwellings of Jacob*, the places in Israel that were considered holy sites before the Temple, like Shiloh. Another interpretation: the northern temples (Bethel, Dan) that God rejected in favor of Zion (Ps. 78.67–69). **3:** *Selah* (also v. 6), see Ps. 3.3 n. **4–6:** The LORD records the names of those from the Gentiles who have adopted Judaism; they are now part of God's people (Isa. 44.5). **4:** *Rahab*, a mythical monster, here designates

Philistia, and Tyre, and Cush—each was born
there.

5 Indeed, it shall be said of Zion,
"Every man was born there."
^aHe, the Most High, will preserve it.^a

6 The LORD will inscribe in the register of peoples
that each was born there.   *Selah.*

7 Singers and dancers alike [will say]:
"All my roots^b are in You."

88 A song. A psalm of the Korahites. For the leader;
^con *maḥalath leannoth.*^c A *maskil* of Heman the Ezra-
hite.

2 O LORD, God of my deliverance,
^dwhen I cry out in the night^d before You,

3 let my prayer reach You;
incline Your ear to my cry.

4 For I am sated with misfortune;
I am at the brink of Sheol.

5 I am numbered with those who go down to the
Pit;
I am a helpless man

6 abandoned^e among the dead,
like bodies lying in the grave
of whom You are mindful no more,
and who are cut off from Your care.

7 You have put me at the bottom of the Pit,
in the darkest places, in the depths.

8 Your fury lies heavy upon me;
You afflict me with all Your breakers.   *Selah.*

9 You make my companions shun me;
You make me abhorrent to them;
I am shut in and do not go out.

10 My eyes pine away from affliction;
I call to You, O LORD, each day;
I stretch out my hands to You.

11 Do You work wonders for the dead?
Do the shades rise to praise You?   *Selah.*

12 Is Your faithful care recounted in the grave,
Your constancy in the place of perdition?

13 Are Your wonders made known in the
netherworld,^f
Your beneficent deeds in the land of oblivion?

---

a-a Or "He will preserve it supreme."   b Lit. "sources."
c-c Meaning of Heb. uncertain.   d-d Or "by day I cry out [and] by night."
e Lit. "released."   f Lit. "darkness."

Egypt; see Isa. 30.7. Egypt and
Babylonia were the great world
powers after the fall of Assyria in
612 BCE. *Philistia . . . Tyre . . . Cush,*
smaller countries to the west,
north, and south of Judah. Cush is
Ethiopia or Nubia. **5–7:** Everyone
will recognize Zion as the primary
place in the world, the source of all
nations; all peoples will think of
themselves as citizens of Zion.
7: *Roots* (Heb "sources"; see note b)
perhaps springs of water, the
source of life. See Pss. 36.8; 46.4;
Ezek. 47.1–12.

Ps. 88: A desperate complaint by a
person mortally ill; perhaps to be
interpreted as symbolizing the national catastrophe, the destruction
and exile (Sheol may represent the
exile), which could potentially
sever the connection between Israel and God. Prolonged thoughts
of death dominate, with many
synonyms for the place of the
dead: *Sheol, Pit, grave, depths, place
of perdition,* darkness (the netherworld), *land of oblivion.* In the
realm of the dead, humankind is
cut off from God and completely
forgotten; the sense of isolation
and finality is overwhelming. The
psalm ends without hope or resolution; there is no expectation that
God will cure the psalmist and
no promise to praise God upon recovery. **1:** *Korahites,* see Ps. 42 n.
Maḥalath leannoth, probably a
melody. The term "maḥalath" may
be related to the word "maḥalah,"
"illness," making this a sad
melody or a melody for the sick
(cf. Ps. 53.1). Alternatively, it may
derive from "ḥalil," "flute."
Heman, a famous Temple musician
(1 Chron. 25.5–6), mentioned only
here in the Psalter. **4–6:** The psalmist is on the brink of *Sheol,* the
abode of the dead, separated from
and forgotten by God. **5:** *Helpless
man,* a man lacking the vigor to
live. **6:** *Abandoned,* or "released,
freed." Cf. Job 3.19. The dead are
released from the socioeconomic
hierarchy of the living. According
to traditional Jewish interpretation, the dead are free of their obligation to God. **7–8:** The psalmist's
troubles come from God. **8:** *Break-*

14 As for me, I cry out to You, O Lᴏʀᴅ;
      each morning my prayer greets You.

15 Why, O Lᴏʀᴅ, do You reject me,
      do You hide Your face from me?

16 From my youth I have been afflicted
      and near death;
      I suffer Your terrors ᵃ⁻wherever I turn.⁻ᵃ

17 Your fury overwhelms me;
      Your terrors destroy me.

18 They swirl about me like water all day long;
      they encircle me on every side.

19 You have put friend and neighbor far from me
      and my companions out of my sight.ᵇ

89 A *maskil* of Ethan the Ezrahite.

2   I will sing of the Lᴏʀᴅ's steadfast love forever;
      to all generations I will proclaim Your
         faithfulness with my mouth.

3   I declare, "Your steadfast love is confirmed
         forever;
      there in the heavens You establish Your
         faithfulness."

4   "I have made a covenant with My chosen one;
      I have sworn to My servant David:

5   I will establish your offspring forever,
      I will confirm your throne for all generations."
                                                Selah.

6   Your wonders, O Lᴏʀᴅ, are praised by the
         heavens,
      Your faithfulness, too, in the assembly of holy
         beings.

7   For who in the skies can equal the Lᴏʀᴅ,
      can compare with the Lᴏʀᴅ among the divine
         beings,

a-a Following Saadia; meaning of Heb. uncertain.   b Lit. "into darkness."

ers, death (2 Sam. 22.5; Pss. 42.8; 69.2–3). *Selah* (also v. 11), see Ps. 3.3 n. **9:** His illness made him a recluse, abandoned by friends. See v. 19; 31.12–14; Job 19.13; 30.10. **11:** The psalmist feels himself already dead and therefore expects no wonders from God. **12–13:** God does not take care of the dead (v. 11) and the dead cannot praise God (Pss. 6.6; 30.10). All links between God and humans are sev-

ered at death. **12:** *Place of perdition,* Heb "'abadon," "destruction, loss," another name for the abode of the dead. **14–19:** A replay of previous thoughts at a higher pitch. **14:** *As for me:* In contrast to the dead, the psalmist still can and does call out to God. *Morning* is the time God is expected to answer prayers (cf. Ps. 90.14). **16–17:** His troubles are not recent; his entire life has been one of mis-

ery, a victim of God's *fury* (cf. v. 8); there is no admission that his own sin caused this punishment. **18:** *Like water,* cf. *breakers,* v. 8. **19:** The psalmist is shunned by his community (v. 9). Another interpretation of *my companions out of sight* is "my companions are (those of) darkness," i.e., the other residents of Sheol.

Ps. 89: An exilic or postexilic psalm praying for the restoration of the Davidic dynasty, that is, for the end of the exile and the restoration of the Jews to their land as an independent people, as they were before the exile. In the first part, God is proclaimed king (vv. 2–19); He then proclaims David and his dynasty king (vv. 20–38); the psalm ends with a lament for the loss of the Davidic dynasty and the hope for its return (vv. 39–52). The psalm consists largely of a poetic reinterpretation of the promise to David in 2 Sam. 7.11–17. But whereas 2 Sam. ch 7 is concerned with the building of the Temple and the establishment of the dynastic succession, Ps. 89 omits references to the Temple and focuses on the permanence of Davidic kingship. This is a striking departure from most exilic psalms, which are more concerned with the Temple than with the dynasty. Keywords connecting these chs include *steadfast love, faithfulness, forever, covenant, throne.* **1:** *Ethan,* a Temple musician (1 Chron. 15.17, 19), mentioned only here in Psalms. **2–5:** The psalmist's praise of God's *steadfast love* and *faithfulness,* his choice of *David* and his establishment of the Davidic dynasty, which is eternal and unconditional (cf. 2 Sam. 7.15–16; contrast Ps. 132.12). The faithfulness with which the dynastic promise was made is the main theme of the psalm. At the end (v. 50), the psalmist will remind God of it. **4:** Cf. Ps. 132.11–12. **5:** The wording of the covenant. *Selah* (also vv. 38, 46, 49), see Ps. 3.3 n. **6–9:** The heavenly council, in whose presence God announces his decree, praises the incomparable and awesome God; cf.

8 a God greatly dreaded in the council of holy
beings,
held in awe by all around Him?

9 O LORD, God of hosts,
who is mighty like You, O LORD?
Your faithfulness surrounds You;

10 You rule the swelling of the sea;
when its waves surge, You still them.

11 You crushed Rahab; he was like a corpse;
with Your powerful arm You scattered Your
enemies.

12 The heaven is Yours,
the earth too;
the world and all it holds—
You established them.

13 North and south—
You created them;
Tabor and Hermon sing forth Your name.

14 Yours is an arm endowed with might;
Your hand is strong;
Your right hand, exalted.

15 Righteousness and justice are the base of Your
throne;
steadfast love and faithfulness stand before You.

16 Happy is the people who know the joyful shout;
O LORD, they walk in the light of Your presence.

17 They rejoice in Your name all day long;
they are exalted through Your righteousness.

18 For You are their strength in which they glory;
our horn is exalted through Your favor.

19 Truly our shield is of the LORD,
our king, of the Holy One of Israel.

20 Then[a] You spoke to Your faithful ones in a vision
and said, "I have conferred power upon a
warrior;
I have exalted one chosen out of the people.

21 I have found David, My servant;
anointed him with My sacred oil.

22 My hand shall be constantly with him,
and My arm shall strengthen him.

23 No enemy shall [b]oppress him,[b]
no vile man afflict him.

24 I will crush his adversaries before him;
I will strike down those who hate him.

Pss. 29.1; 82.1; Exod. 15.11; Jer. 23.18, 21–22. **8:** *Holy beings,* cf. Job 5.1. **10–14:** Having defeated the mythical chaotic waters, God is the victorious creator of the universe, over which He has dominion (see Ps. 74.12–17). **11:** *Rahab,* a name for the primeval chaos monster; Job 26.12; Isa. 51.9. **13:** *Tabor and Hermon,* two prominent mountains; Tabor is south of the Sea of Galilee (Ps. 68; Hos. 5.1) and Hermon is to the north, in Syria (Pss. 42.6; 133.3). The mountains, like the heavenly court, sing praise to God. **15:** God's reign is founded upon the principles of *righteousness* and *justice;* He is heralded by *steadfast love* and *faithfulness.* These abstract principles are personified as parts of God's heavenly installation and His servants. Mesopotamian tradition also associates justice and righteousness ("kittu" and "mesharu") as attributes and as metaphorical guardians of gods and kings. The emphasis on the moral attributes of God's rule stresses that God does not break His promise; cf. vv. 34–35. **16–19:** Like the cosmos, the people will also proclaim loudly that God is king. The psalm here moves from the cosmic to the national. **16:** *Joyful shout,* Heb "teru'ah" is also a blast of the ram's horn, proclaiming God king. Vv. 16–18 are part of the Rosh Ha-Shanah liturgy, before the blowing of the shofar. **18–19:** *Horn,* a metaphor for *strength* (also v. 25). *Horn* and *shield,* the king protects his people and leads them to victory. Depending on the interpretation, v. 19 is the climax of the expression of the kingship of God, or it is a transition to the idea of David as king. The first interpretation takes the Heb letter "lamed"—rendered as *of* in *of the* LORD and *of the Holy One*—to be an emphatic particle: "our shield is indeed the LORD . . . our king is indeed the Holy One." The second interpretation yields "our shield belongs to the LORD, our king to the Holy One" (so NRSV). **20–38:** The covenant with David and his descendants ("David" represents the Davidic dynasty), which will be eternal

---

a Referring to vv. 4–5; cf. 2 Sam. 7.1–17.   b-b Meaning of Heb. uncertain.

25   My faithfulness and steadfast love shall be with
        him;
        his horn shall be exalted through My name.
26   I will set his hand upon the sea,
        his right hand upon the rivers.
27   He shall say to Me,
        'You are my father, my God, the rock of my
        deliverance.'
28   I will appoint him first-born,
        highest of the kings of the earth.
29   I will maintain My steadfast love for him
        always;
        My covenant with him shall endure.
30   I will establish his line forever,
        his throne, as long as the heavens last.
31   If his sons forsake My Teaching
        and do not live by My rules;
32   if they violate My laws,
        and do not observe My commands,
33   I will punish their transgression with the rod,
        their iniquity with plagues.
34   But I will not take away My steadfast love from
        him;
        I will not betray My faithfulness.
35   I will not violate My covenant,
        or change what I have uttered.
36   I have sworn by My holiness, once and for all;
        I will not be false to David.
37   His line shall continue forever,
        his throne, as the sun before Me,
38   as the moon, established forever,
        an enduring witness in the sky."   *Selah.*

39   Yet You have rejected, spurned,
        and become enraged at Your anointed.
40   You have repudiated the covenant with Your
        servant;
        You have dragged his dignity in the dust.
41   You have breached all his defenses,
        shattered his strongholds.
42   All who pass by plunder him;
        he has become the butt of his neighbors.
43   You have exalted the right hand of his
        adversaries,
        and made all his enemies rejoice.
44   You have turned back the blade of his
        sword,
        and have not sustained him in battle.

(vv. 29–30, 36–38) even in the face of human sin (vv. 31–35). This is a poetic reformulation of 2 Sam. 7.11–17, which like that text assumes an eternal, unbreakable Davidic covenant; contrast Ps. 132.11–12; 1 Kings 9.4–9. **20:** *In a vision,* through a prophet. Cf. 2 Sam. 7.17. **26:** The powers associated with God in vv. 10–11 are here bestowed upon David. **27–28:** A widespread ancient Near Eastern tradition sees the king as the adopted son of a god who ordained that he should rule (Ps. 2.7; 2 Sam. 7.14). This king, however, is also the *first-born,* specially privileged. **28–30:** The promise of a dynasty. **31–38:** If the Davidic kings sin, they will be punished, but the dynasty will never come to an end. It will endure as long as the *sun* and the *moon* endure. These celestial bodies are *an enduring witness* testifying to God's promise. **39–52:** The destruction of Jerusalem and the end of the Davidic dynasty is seen as a betrayal of God's promise, a repudiation of His covenant. These vv. echo many terms in vv. 2–38; at the same time, they share thoughts and language with Lamentations. **39:** *Anointed,* the Davidic king (v. 21). The king symbolizes the kingship or the people in the following vv. **40:** *Dragged his dignity in the dust,* lit. "desecrated his crown [by making it fall] to the ground," signifying the besmirching of the kingship.

45   You have brought ᵃ his splendor ᵃ to an end
     and have hurled his throne to the ground.
46   You have cut short the days of his youth;
     You have covered him with shame.   *Selah.*
47   How long, O Lᴏʀᴅ; will You forever hide Your
     face,
     will Your fury blaze like fire?
48   O remember ᵃ how short my life is; ᵃ
     why should You have created every man in
     vain?
49   What man can live and not see death,
     can save himself from the clutches of Sheol?
     Selah.
50   O Lord, where is Your steadfast love of old
     which You swore to David in Your faithfulness?
51   Remember, O Lord, the abuse flung at Your
     servants
     ᵃ that I have borne in my bosom [from] many
     peoples, ᵃ
52   how Your enemies, O Lᴏʀᴅ, have flung abuse,
     abuse at Your anointed at every step.

53   Blessed is the Lᴏʀᴅ forever;
     Amen and Amen.

BOOK FOUR

90
A prayer of Moses, the man of God.

   O Lord, You have been our refuge in every
     generation.
2   Before the mountains came into being,
     before You brought forth the earth and the
     world,
     from eternity to eternity You are God.

3   You return man to dust; ᵇ
     You decreed, "Return you mortals!"
4   ᵃ For in Your sight a thousand years
     are like yesterday that has passed,
     like a watch of the night.
5   You engulf men in sleep; ᵃ
     at daybreak they are like grass that renews
     itself;
6   at daybreak it flourishes anew;
     by dusk it withers and dries up.

46: The kingship or nation has been cut off in its prime. This is not necessarily a reference to the age of a particular king. **49:** *Sheol,* the abode of the dead and a metaphor for the exile. **53:** A doxology closing Book III of the Psalter (cf. Pss. 41.14; 72.18–19; 106.48).

Ps. 90: Human mortality and God's eternity. Words for time figure prominently: *years, day, watch of the night, span of our life, daybreak.* They are used to contrast God's eternity and human beings' transience and fragility. Human life is perceived as, by its nature, difficult and sorrowful. The psalmist prays that, with God's help, life will be satisfying and joyful. This psalm and Ps. 91 are recited in the introductory prayers of the morning service on Shabbat and festivals. **1–2:** God is eternal; He was a refuge even before there was a physical habitat. The language of birth, rather than the language of creating, is used of the world; God gave birth to the world. **1:** This psalm alone is associated with Moses, perhaps because, on one hand, he died prematurely, before entering the land, and on the other hand, he lived until 120, the ideal life span, with eyes undimmed and vigor unabated (Deut. 34.7). *The man of God,* the prophet. **3:** *To dust,* see Gen. 2.7; 3.19. **4:** Human time is in a different scale from divine time. *A watch of the night,* less than one day. The night was divided into three or four watches of three to four hours each, depending on the time of year. **5:** *Grass* grows and withers quickly (Ps. 102.25–28; Isa. 40.6–8).

a-a Meaning of Heb. uncertain.   *b Or "contrition."*

7 So we are consumed by Your anger,
   terror-struck by Your fury.

8 You have set our iniquities before You,
   our hidden sins in the light of Your face.

9 All our days pass away in Your wrath;
   we spend our years like a sigh.

10 The span of our life is seventy years,
   or, given the strength, eighty years;
   but the *a*-best of them*-a* are trouble and sorrow.
   They pass by speedily, and we *b*-are in darkness.*-b*

11 Who can know Your furious anger?
   Your wrath matches the fear of You.

12 Teach us to count our days rightly,
   that we may obtain a wise heart.

13 Turn, O LORD!
   How long?
   Show mercy to Your servants.

14 Satisfy us at daybreak with Your steadfast love
   that we may sing for joy all our days.

15 Give us joy for as long as You have afflicted us,
   for the years we have suffered misfortune.

16 Let Your deeds be seen by Your servants,
   Your glory by their children.

17 May the favor of the Lord, our God, be upon us;
   let the work of our hands prosper,
   O prosper the work of our hands!

91 O you who dwell in the shelter of the Most High
   and abide in the protection of Shaddai—

2 I say of the LORD, my refuge and stronghold,
   my God in whom I trust,

3 that He will save you from the fowler's trap,
   from the destructive plague.

4 He will cover you with His pinions;
   you will find refuge under His wings;
   His fidelity is an encircling shield.

5 You need not fear the terror by night,
   or the arrow that flies by day,

---

a-a Meaning of Heb. uncertain.   *b-b* Or "fly away."

8–10: Human lives are brief and troubled. Trouble was thought to result from sin, which God, in his anger, punished. Gen. chs 2–3 explains human mortality as a result of disobeying God. **10:** *Seventy years:* Seventy (like seven) represents completion and perfection. Most people in ancient times did not reach this age, but some did. The ideal life span of 120 years (Gen. 6.3) is not realistic; a life span of 70 is. **13–17:** Darkness ends and daybreak comes; sorrow is mitigated by joy. **13:** *Turn . . . Show mercy:* God is called upon to repent, or relent—to stop bringing punishment; and to be comforted—not to be angry any longer. The words are similar to Moses' plea after the golden calf incident (Exod. 32.12)—another reason that the psalm is called the prayer of Moses. **14:** *Daybreak:* Morning is the time of renewal, the time that God answers prayers (Pss. 30.6; 46.6; 143.8). **15:** The psalmist prays for parity between days of joy and days of affliction. **16–17:** The limited "immortality" of human beings is in their children and their achievements, *the work of our hands.* The psalmist prays that his own generation and his children's will be able to rejoice in God's deeds and that their own deeds will prosper.

Ps. 91: God protects from all harm those who trust Him. The many terms for protection, shelter, refuge, and the like emphasize the theme. A speaker in the first person addresses an audience, encouraging them to trust God so no harm will befall them (vv. 1–13); God responds (vv. 14–16), reinforcing the speaker's words. According to some commentators, *the shelter of the Most High* (v. 1) is the Temple, and the psalm was part of the liturgy for entering or departing from the Temple. It is not clear how metaphorical the language is or whether it reflects popular religion and superstition; whether the dangers are from demons or from the ordinary dangers of plague, war, and wild animals. **1–2:** *Shelter . . . protection . . . refuge and strong-hold:* For the Temple as a place of protection see Pss. 27.5; 31.21. *Most High* ("*'elyon*") and *Shaddai* are old epithets for God, borrowed from the Canaanites, who applied them to the head of their pantheon. **4:** *Wings* may be a metaphor for divine protection, the outspread wings of a bird (Pss. 17.8; 36.8), or may refer to the wings of the cherubim on either side of the Ark (Exod. 25.17–22). **5–6:** God protects at all times: night and day, *darkness* (when there is no light), and *noon* (the brightest light). *Terror by night,* perhaps an attack by de-

6 the plague that stalks in the darkness,
  or the scourge that ravages at noon.
7 A thousand may fall at your left side,
  ten thousand at your right,
  but it shall not reach you.
8 You will see it with your eyes,
  you will witness the punishment of the wicked.
9 Because you took the Lord—my refuge,
  the Most High—as your haven,
10 no harm will befall you,
  no disease touch your tent.
11 For He will order His angels
  to guard you wherever you go.
12 They will carry you in their hands
  lest you hurt your foot on a stone.
13 You will tread on cubs and vipers;
  you will trample lions and asps.

14 "Because he is devoted to Me I will deliver him;
  I will keep him safe, for he knows My name.
15 When he calls on Me, I will answer him;
  I will be with him in distress;
  I will rescue him and make him honored;
16 I will let him live to a ripe old age,
  and show him My salvation."

92 A psalm. A song; for the sabbath day.

2 It is good to praise the Lord,
  to sing hymns to Your name, O Most High,
3 To proclaim Your steadfast love at daybreak,
  Your faithfulness each night
4 With a ten-stringed harp,
  with voice and lyre together.
5 You have gladdened me by Your deeds, O Lord;
  I shout for joy at Your handiwork.
6 How great are Your works, O Lord,
  how very subtle*a* Your designs!
7 A brutish man cannot know,
  a fool cannot understand this:

a Or "profound."

reassuring him of God's protection. **16:** *A ripe old age,* length of days is a sign of God's favor, and is especially welcome after Ps. 90, which dwells on the shortness of human life.

Ps. 92: A hymn praising God; to be recited on the Sabbath, according to the superscription. According to early rabbinic tradition, particular psalms were recited each day of the week by the Levites at the Temple (*m. Tamid* 7.4 and parallels; see list in "The Bible in the Liturgy," pp. 1947–48), but the Bible indicates a psalm only for the "sabbath day." The psalm contains seven uses of the Tetragrammaton (Yhvh), suggesting a link with the seventh day of creation (see *b. Ber.* 4.3 and parallels). It is uncertain when the psalm became connected with the Sabbath and when in the Sabbath liturgy in the Temple it was recited. Rabbinic and much medieval tradition understand the psalm eschatologically (*b. Rosh Hash.* 31a; Rashi). **1:** An unusual superscription, with no ascription of authorship; midrashic tradition suggests that Adam recited it (*Shoher Tov* to Ps. 92). **2:** A simple but profound religious expression; in contrast to many individual petitions, which contain specific requests from God, here it is simply *good to praise the Lord.* The *praise* may be related to the frequent liturgical formula: "Praise the Lord for He is good; His steadfast love is eternal" (see 106.1 n.) On *Most High,* see 7.18 n. **3:** It is uncertain if this refers to two specific times (*daybreak, night*) at which God was praised in the Temple service, or is a merism for "always." **4:** The characteristics of a "mizmor" or psalm: a melody sung to the accompaniment of a stringed instrument (see 3.1 n.). **5:** On *handiwork* referring to creation, see 8.4 n. **6:** On *works* as the objects of creation, see 104.24. **8–9:** A strong contrast between the temporary flourishing of the wicked and God's permanence. **8:** A variant on the imagery of Ps. 1: here the wicked may prosper, but only for a short time.

monic forces (Song 3.8). *Plague* and *scourge* may also be demons. **7–9:** Even if all those who do not have God's protection fall (and the numbers are exaggerated), the one who trusts in God will be safe. **8:** *The wicked,* those who lack trust in God. **11–12:** The psalmist's "guardian angels" (Exod. 23.20; Pss. 34.8; 103.20); perhaps the protectors against the demonic forces mentioned in vv. 5–6. **14–16:** God, speaking in the first person, responds to the psalmist,

8   though the wicked sprout like grass,
     though all evildoers blossom,
     it is only that they may be destroyed forever.

9   But You are exalted, O LORD, for all time.

10   Surely, Your enemies, O LORD,
     surely, Your enemies perish;
     all evildoers are scattered.

11   You raise my horn high like that of a wild ox;
     I am soaked in freshening oil.

12   I shall see the defeat of my watchful foes,
     hear of the downfall of the wicked who
       beset me.

13   The righteous bloom like a date-palm;
     they thrive like a cedar in Lebanon;

14   planted in the house of the LORD,
     they flourish in the courts of our God.

15   In old age they still produce fruit;
     they are full of sap and freshness,

16   attesting that the LORD is upright,
     my rock, in whom there is no wrong.

93 The LORD is king,
     He is robed in grandeur;
     the LORD is robed,
     He is girded with strength.
     The world stands firm;
     it cannot be shaken.

2   Your throne stands firm from of old;
     from eternity You have existed.

3   The ocean sounds, O LORD,
     the ocean sounds its thunder,
     the ocean sounds its pounding.

4   Above the thunder of the mighty waters,
     more majestic than the breakers of the sea
     is the LORD, majestic on high.

imagery (cf. v. 8). **13:** *Cedars of Lebanon* were known for strength; they were used in constructing the Temple, and thus offer a subtle segue into the following v. **14:** For the desire to remain in the Temple, proximate to God, see 23.6; 27.5. **16:** *Attesting,* lit. "to proclaim," forming a frame with v. 3.

Ps. 93: This enthronement psalm (see introduction to Ps. 47) narrates God's ascent to the throne after defeating the powers of chaos, represented in vv. 3–4 as the ocean. It is an Israelite adoption and transformation of the Canaanite myth about Baal's kingship (see 92.10). In classical rabbinic (see *b. Rosh Hash.* 31a) and later liturgical tradition, it is recited on Friday nights. Like the previous psalm, it concerns creation, and thus is connected to the Sabbath, which commemorates the completion of creation; a superscription in the LXX also connects it to the Sabbath. The kingship psalms grouped together (93–99) may have been seen as a subcollection in antiquity; none has a Davidic superscription. **1:** Heb may be translated as *The LORD is king* or "The LORD has become king"; context favors the latter, though in other psalms, which lack this psalm's explicit mythological background, the former may be preferable. (This translation difference determines whether these should be called enthronement psalms, those commemorating God's ascent to the throne, or kingship psalms that celebrate His ongoing role as king.) This v. narrates God's creation after defeating His mythological enemies. *Robed,* an image of an enthronement ceremony; God becomes king. God enrobed in His creation is an image known also from 104.1–2, where God's enthronement is by means of His creation. **2:** From the time of creation (in mythological terms, from the time of the defeat of the mythological enemies) God's *throne stands firm.* **3–4:** God successfully vanquishes the rebellious oceans.

9: This v. is also an introduction to the following, since according to the Canaanite mythological tradition that Israel shared (see v. 10 n.), the high God ascended as king *for all time* only after his enemies had been vanquished. **10:** A reuse and revision of the material known from the Baal epic, where Baal defeats the rebellious Sea, a myth that is reflected in much of the Bible (see 8.3 n.): "Now your

enemy, O Baal, Now your enemy will you smite; Now will you cut off your adversaries" (*ANET*, p. 131, slightly modified). Here God's enemies are not mythological creatures but human evildoers (cf. v. 8). **11:** Symbols of victory; see 75.5 n. Others translate this and the following v. in the past tense, and view the psalm as having elements of thanksgiving. **13–15:** The psalmist again uses agricultural

5   Your decrees are indeed enduring;
        holiness befits Your house,
        O Lord, for all times.

94 God of retribution, Lord,
        God of retribution, appear!
2   Rise up, judge of the earth,
        give the arrogant their deserts!
3   How long shall the wicked, O Lord,
        how long shall the wicked exult,
4   shall they utter insolent speech,
        shall all evildoers vaunt themselves?
5   They crush Your people, O Lord,
        they afflict Your very own;
6   they kill the widow and the stranger;
        they murder the fatherless,
7   thinking, "The Lord does not see it,
        the God of Jacob does not pay heed."

8   Take heed, you most brutish people;
        fools, when will you get wisdom?
9   Shall He who implants the ear not hear,
        He who forms the eye not see?
10   Shall He who disciplines nations not punish,
        He who instructs men in knowledge?
11   The Lord knows the designs of men to be futile.

12   Happy is the man whom You discipline, O Lord,
        the man You instruct in Your teaching,
13   to give him tranquillity in times of misfortune,
        until a pit be dug for the wicked.
14   For the Lord will not forsake His people;
        He will not abandon His very own.
15   Judgment shall again accord with justice
        and all the upright shall rally to it.

16   Who will take my part against evil men?
        Who will stand up for me against wrongdoers?
17   Were not the Lord my help,
        I should soon dwell in silence.

5: This defeat has theological implications for the validity of the Temple (*Your house*) as the place of worship and for the validity of God's *decrees*.

Ps. 94: This psalm, a request for the destruction of evildoers, does not explicitly deal with God's kingship like the surrounding Pss. 93–99. The image of God as judge may, however, be subsumed under God's kingship (see esp. 96.13; 99.4), and it is possible that v. 20, which mentions a (human) throne, draws a contrast with the divine throne. There are additional thematic and lexical similarities to the surrounding psalms. The psalm has several affinities to wisdom literature, including interest in educating the fool (v. 8; see also vv. 11–12 n.). The destruction of the wicked is a major theme of prophetic eschatology, and thus Radak, citing Mal. 3.19, understands this psalm as a request for the arrival of the eschaton. **1:** *Retribution* (Heb "nekamot"), some translate "vengeance," fostering a picture of a vengeful "Old Testament" deity (versus a loving God of the New Testament). Though "n-k-m" may have this sense elsewhere in the Bible, in this psalm fair retribution and not vengeance is being sought. Verbal repetition characterizes the opening (*God of retribution;* v. 3 "how long") and the closing (v. 23, "annihilate") of the psalm. **2:** *Rise up* may reflect human institutions, where the judge may have stood up to offer his verdict (cf. 82.1 n.). **3–6:** The focus here is on internal rather than external enemies; it is impossible to determine whether a specific group is meant. **6:** *Widow, stranger, fatherless* are the defenseless in society; Deut. commands their protection (e.g., 10.18; 14.29). **7:** Similar quotations are in 10.11 and 73.11. Heb uses the root "'-m-r" to indicate both verbal and internal speech (thought); the translation could be *thinking* or "saying"; v. 11 suggests the former. **11:** Although couched as a general statement, the v. refers to the wicked fools; perhaps a wisdom epigram is quoted here ("hevel," *futile,* is a characteristic term in Ecclesiastes, a wisdom text). **12:** This v. shares the wisdom notion (see esp. Prov. 3.11–12; Job 5.17) that divine chastisement is beneficial. "Torah" likely here reflects general *teaching,* as in much wisdom literature (e.g., Prov. 1.8), though traditional Jewish commentary understands it as Torah on the assumption that the Mosaic Torah was canonical for David, the author of Psalms. **16:** A protestation of innocence; the psalmist is opposed by the *wrongdoers* or evil

18 When I think my foot has given way,
  Your faithfulness, O LORD, supports me.
19 When I am filled with cares,
  Your assurance soothes my soul.

20 Shall the seat of injustice be Your partner,
  that frames mischief by statute?
21 They band together to do away with the righteous;
  they condemn the innocent to death.
22 But the LORD is my haven;
  my God is my sheltering rock.
23 He will make their evil recoil upon them,
  annihilate them through their own wickedness;
  the LORD our God will annihilate them.

95 Come, let us sing joyously to the LORD,
  raise a shout for our rock and deliverer;
2 let us come into His presence with praise;
  let us raise a shout for Him in song!
3 For the LORD is a great God,
  the great king of all divine beings.
4 In His hand are the depths of the earth;
  the peaks of the mountains are His.
5 His is the sea, He made it;
  and the land, which His hands fashioned.

6 Come, let us bow down and kneel,
  bend the knee before the LORD our maker,
7 for He is our God,
  and we are the people He tends, the flock in His
    care.
  O, if you would but heed His charge this day:
8 Do not be stubborn as at Meribah,
  as on the day of Massah, in the wilderness,
9 when your fathers put Me to the test,
  tried Me, though they had seen My deeds.
10 Forty years I was provoked by that generation;
  I thought, "They are a senseless people;
  they would not know My ways."
11 Concerning them I swore in anger,
  "They shall never come to My resting-place!"

men ("po'alei 'aven"; see 5.6 n.) of v. 4. **18:** On God's "ḥesed," see 5.8 n. **22:** Compare the extensive fortress language applied to God in 18.13. **23:** As frequently occurs, especially at the end of personal petitions, the tenses are unclear;

the first verb is in the past ("he has"), while *annihilate* is in the future.

Ps. 95: A kingship psalm (see v. 3, *the great king*), which, after an introductory call to worship

(vv. 1–3), focuses on God as creator of the world (vv. 4–5) and creator of Israel (vv. 6–7). Just as human kings were responsible for major building projects, God as king has created the world and Israel. Like Ps. 81, to which it is thematically similar, it concludes with a rebuke (vv. 8–11; cf. 81.9–17). The psalm can also be understood as having two calls to worship (vv. 1–2, 6), each followed by the impetus for that call, introduced by "ki," *for*; a similar structure is found in the early Song of the Sea recited by Miriam in Exod. 15.21, "Sing to the LORD, for ("ki") He has triumphed gloriously." This psalm (and those that follow through Ps. 99) is recited during the Friday night service. **1–2:** The *shout* is modeled after the acclaim for the new king at his enthronement (see 47.2 n.; 98.4, 6). **1:** *Rock* connects to the conclusion of the previous psalm (94.22). **3:** God is incomparable. As in Exod. 15.11 and elsewhere, the existence of other, less powerful deities is acknowledged; they serve to show God's superiority even over other divine beings. Medieval interpreters understand the divine beings as "angels" (Ibn Ezra, Radak). **7:** The image of God as shepherd is part of royal imagery; see 23.1–4 n. **8–11:** This is a rare case where divine speech, perhaps spoken through a religious official, is quoted in psalms. The tradition offered stands in stark contrast with other traditions that see the wilderness period as ideal (esp. Jer. 2.2). The traditions about *Meribah* and *Massah* are in Exod. 17.17 and Deut. 33.8 (cf. Num. 20.1–13 about Meribah alone). This psalm connects the forty years of wandering to rebellion at these sites, in contrast to Num. 14.33–34; 32.13, which connect the forty years to the sin of the spies (but see Deut. 8.2; Josh. 5.6). These vv. function as an admonition, telling the people what to do if they want to remain in God's favor as His *people*. **9:** Like Exod. 17.2, this v. explains the etymology of Massah by the root "n-s-h," to *put to the test*. **11:** *Resting-place* refers to the land of Israel (Deut. 12.9).

96
ᵃSing to the LORD a new song,
　　sing to the LORD, all the earth.
2　Sing to the LORD, bless His name,
　　proclaim His victory day after day.
3　Tell of His glory among the nations,
　　His wondrous deeds, among all peoples.
4　For the LORD is great and much acclaimed,
　　He is held in awe by all divine beings.
5　All the gods of the peoples are mere idols,
　　but the LORD made the heavens.
6　Glory and majesty are before Him;
　　strength and splendor are in His temple.

7　Ascribe to the LORD, O families of the peoples,
　　ascribe to the LORD glory and strength.
8　Ascribe to the LORD the glory of His name,
　　bring tribute and enter His courts.
9　Bow down to the LORD majestic in holiness;
　　tremble in His presence, all the earth!
10　Declare among the nations, "The LORD is king!"
　　the world stands firm; it cannot be shaken;
　　He judges the peoples with equity.
11　Let the heavens rejoice and the earth exult;
　　let the sea and all within it thunder,
12　the fields and everything in them exult;
　　then shall all the trees of the forest shout for joy
13　at the presence of the LORD, for He is coming,
　　for He is coming to rule the earth;
　　He will rule the world justly,
　　and its peoples in faithfulness.

97
The LORD is king!
Let the earth exult,
　　the many islands rejoice!

a Cf. 1 Chron. 16.23–33.

Ps. 96: This kingship psalm is similar in structure to the previous one, also containing two calls to worship, beginning in vv. 1 and 7. Like Ps. 95, it emphasizes God as creator; like Ps. 94, it emphasizes God as judge. It is, however, more universal in outlook, demanding that all nations acknowledge God (vv. 1, 7); perhaps there is a progression or intensification as we move through the kingship psalms. A variant of this psalm appears in 1 Chron. 16.23–33, where it is combined with different psalms (see annotations there), and is used in connection with the installation of the Ark in Jerusalem. A similar tradition is related in the LXX superscription to Ps. 96: "when the house was being rebuilt after the captivity"; these pieces of evidence suggest a role for the psalm in the Second Temple. The psalm (and several other kingship psalms) shares significant elements with Deutero-Isaiah (see 4.5 n.); the psalm may be exilic or

later. **1–3:** It is unclear what song is meant—perhaps the psalm as a whole, or perhaps part of v. 10, "The LORD is king!" The rhetorical presence of other *nations* (see 47.10 n.) shows that God's glory is worldwide. **4–5:** God is depicted as more incomparable than in 95.3. The depiction of other deities as mere idols is a major theme of Deutero-Isaiah (e.g., Isa. 40.18–20). **6:** *Glory and majesty* (as well as *strength*) are typically royal attributes (21.6; 45.4), here shared by God as King. These qualities are localized with God at *His temple.* **7–8:** A reworked citation of Ps. 29.1–2; there the "divine beings" offer the praise that here is to be offered by the *families of the peoples.* Ascribing *to the LORD* and bringing *tribute* (offerings) to *His courts* (at the Temple) may be a single action, or two coordinated actions of song and sacrifice. **10:** The formula to be recited *among the nations* may either end with *king*, or may extend until the end of the v. In contrast to 93.1, this and the following psalms do not imagine a (re)enthronement of God, so the phrase "YHVH malakh" is best translated in these psalms as *The LORD is king!* **11–13:** Here the entire natural world plays the role of the populace at the coronation, rejoicing loudly (see 47.2 n.). **13:** The verb "ba'" may be translated as *is coming* or "has come." The phrase is repeated, following a usage in Semitic poetry; Radak plausibly notes: "the second *[is coming]* explains the first, and the doubling functions to strengthen [the rhetoric]." The end of the v. returns to the theme of justice, a central royal task, paraphrasing the end of v. 10. Human kings did not always mete out justice fairly, so these psalms express a desire for an ideal, divine royal judge.

Ps. 97: Thematically, this is similar to the previous two kingship psalms, emphasizing God's justice and power (though not His role as creator). Structurally it is quite different; it contains no call to worship, and rather than beginning with imperatives, it concludes

2 Dense clouds are around Him,
 righteousness and justice are the base of His
  throne.
3 Fire is His vanguard,
 burning His foes on every side.
4 His lightnings light up the world;
 the earth is convulsed at the sight;
5 mountains melt like wax at the LORD's
  presence,
 at the presence of the Lord of all the earth.
6 The heavens proclaim His righteousness
 and all peoples see His glory.
7 All who worship images,
 who vaunt their idols,
  are dismayed;
 all divine beings bow down to Him.
8 Zion, hearing it, rejoices,
 the towns[a] of Judah exult,
  because of Your judgments, O LORD.
9 For You, LORD, are supreme over all the earth;
 You are exalted high above all divine beings.

10 O you who love the LORD, hate evil!
 He guards the lives of His loyal ones,
  saving them from the hand of the wicked.
11 Light is sown for the righteous,
 radiance[b] for the upright.
12 O you righteous, rejoice in the LORD
 and acclaim His holy name!

98 A psalm.

 Sing to the LORD a new song,
  for He has worked wonders;
 His right hand, His holy arm,
  has won Him victory.
2 The LORD has manifested His victory,
 has displayed His triumph in the sight of the
  nations.

_____
a Or "women."   b Others "joy."

with them. It builds upon the earlier kingship psalms, moving the declaration *The LORD is king!* to the psalm's beginning. As in other kingship psalms, a utopian world is depicted; this motivates Radak to say: "many similar psalms were written to strengthen the hearts of people who despaired of redemption due to the length of the exile." **1:** See 96.11–13. *Islands* are far-off places. **2–5:** God appears as powerful in a theophany (see introduction to Ps. 29). **6:** Both the natural and human world react. **7:** This degrades the other deities even more than 96.4–5, showing progression in these psalms. **8:** God's *judgments*, either against other nations, or in the sense of divine justice (see v. 2, "righteousness and justice are the base of His throne") are the cause for rejoicing. **9:** Ps. 47.3, another kingship psalm, is similar. **10–12:** A concluding call to the righteous. Calls seem to be part of this genre, though here the call itself is different from the surrounding psalms. **10:** On *loyal ones* ("ḥasid"), see 12.2 n. **11–12:** Heb "simḥah," the opening word of the second line, is a pun, meaning both *radiance* and joy. *And acclaim His holy name,* namely praise Him, may be a stock psalm phrase; see 30.5. The psalm concludes with a call to *rejoice,* echoing joy, a major theme of the psalm. It thus asserts that joy rather than fear is the proper reaction to God's great power—at least for those who are righteous.

Ps. 98: This kingship psalm highlights the military victory of God. It is closely related to Ps. 96: Both open with the same formula, *Sing to the LORD a new song,* and the conclusion of this psalm is a variant of the conclusion of 96. Both emphasize the role of nature in praising God, and both mention God's kingship in the middle rather than at the beginning. In fact, Ps. 98 can be seen as an actualized version of Ps. 96. Ps. 96.3 commands: "Tell of His glory among the nations, His wondrous deeds, among all peoples," and 98.3 claims (in the past): "all the ends of the earth beheld the victory of our God." **1:** The short superscription, *A psalm,* is unique in Psalms; the LXX introduces all of the kingship psalms with "A psalm of David." This psalm collapses the typically longer summons to worship and motivation (introduced by "ki," *for*) into a single v.; see introductory note to Ps. 95. Like many of the other kingship psalms, this too shows affinities to Deutero-Isaiah; compare vv. 1–2 with Isa. 52.10: "The LORD will bare His holy arm / In the sight of all the nations, / And the very ends of earth

3   He was mindful of His steadfast love and
       faithfulness toward the house of Israel;
       all the ends of the earth beheld the victory of
         our God.

4   Raise a shout to the LORD, all the earth,
       break into joyous songs of praise!

5   Sing praise to the LORD with the lyre,
       with the lyre and melodious song.

6   With trumpets and the blast of the horn
       raise a shout before the LORD, the King.

7   Let the sea and all within it thunder,
       the world and its inhabitants;

8   let the rivers clap their hands,
       the mountains sing joyously together

9   at the presence of the LORD,
       for He is coming to rule the earth;
       He will rule the world justly,
       and its peoples with equity.

99

   a-The LORD, enthroned on cherubim, is king,
       peoples tremble, the earth quakes.-*a*

2   The LORD is great in Zion,
       and exalted above all peoples.

3   They praise Your name as great and awesome;
       He is holy!

4   *b*-Mighty king-*b* who loves justice,
       it was You who established equity,
       You who worked righteous judgment in Jacob.

5   Exalt the LORD our God
       and bow down to His footstool;
       He is holy!

6   Moses and Aaron among His priests,
       Samuel, among those who call on His name—
       when they called to the LORD,
       He answered them.

a-a Clauses transposed for clarity.   *b-b Meaning of Heb. uncertain.*

7–8: See 96.11–12. These vv. possibly allude to the myth concerning the rebellion of the waters (see Ps. 93), in which case they suggest that the *sea* and *rivers* have been totally subdued, and are now paying homage to God. Thus, this v. may not merely be a personification of the sea (so Rashi, Radak), but may contain a recollection of the Sea as a deity. **8:** Another strong connection to Deutero-Isaiah; see Isa. 55.12: "Yea, you shall leave in joy and be led home secure. / Before you, mount and hill shall shout aloud, / And all the trees of the field shall clap their hands." **9:** A variant of 96.13.

Ps. 99: The final kingship psalm. Much of vv. 1–4 is similar to the previous kingship psalms, while vv. 5–9, framed by a refrain and focused on prophetic intercession and divine response, are unique. **1:** Quaking of people and nature accompanies theophanies (Exod. 19.16, 18). *Enthroned on cherubim* refers to God's presence in the Temple, where the Ark serves as His throne (see 1 Sam. 4.4 n.). This kingship psalm, more than the others, focuses on God's presence in the Jerusalem Temple (vv. 5, 9) in Zion (v. 2). **2:** God is exalted over *all peoples*, rather than greater than other gods, as in 95.3; 96.4; 97.9, though some LXX manuscripts here read "gods, divine beings" rather than *peoples*. **3:** *Great* and *awesome* are also paired in the kingship psalms 47.3 and 96.4. *He is holy!* may be the actual words of praise; see Isa. 6.3, where the seraphs declare: "Holy, holy, holy! The LORD of Hosts! His presence fills all the earth!" **4:** Similar themes and vocabulary are used in 97.2 and 98.9. **5:** The typical call to worship. Several LXX manuscripts suggest that "ki," "for" has been lost before *He is holy* (see the parallel in v. 9); this would fit the typical pattern (see introduction to Ps. 95). The *footstool* is the Ark (see 1 Chron. 28.2); the phrase is only known in exilic and later literature (Isa. 66.1; Lam. 2.1). **6:** In contrast to the Priestly tradition, Moses is viewed as a priest. The singling

shall see / The victory of our God." **3:** *Steadfast love* and *faithfulness* are often connected to covenant obligations. **4–8:** These mirror the noisy acclaim of the new king (see 47.2 n.), a common motif in the kingship psalms. **6:** The mention of the *horn* ("shofar") is especially significant given 1 Kings 1.39, concerning the coronation of Solomon: "They sounded the horn ("shofar") and all the people shouted, 'Long live King Solomon!' " This and other affinities to the coronation ritual may suggest that these psalms celebrate the (re)enthronement of God, perhaps during an annual ritual. The central significance of the shofar or ram's horn in the Rosh Ha-Shanah (New Year) celebration may be a remnant of this biblical ritual.

7 He spoke to them in a pillar of cloud;
   they obeyed His decrees,
   the law He gave them.
8 O Lord our God, You answered them;
   You were a forgiving God for them,
   but You exacted retribution for their misdeeds.

9 Exalt the Lord our God,
   and bow toward His holy hill,
   for the Lord our God is holy.

100 A psalm *for praise.*

Raise a shout for the Lord, all the earth;
2   worship the Lord in gladness;
     come into His presence with shouts of joy.
3 Acknowledge that the Lord is God;
   He made us and *we are His,*
   His people, the flock He tends.
4 Enter His gates with praise,
   His courts with acclamation.
   Praise Him!
   Bless His name!
5 For the Lord is good;
   His steadfast love is eternal;
   His faithfulness is for all generations.

101 Of David. A psalm.

I will sing of faithfulness and justice;
I will chant a hymn to You, O Lord.

a-a Traditionally "for the thanksgiving offering."
b-b So qere; kethib and some ancient versions "not we ourselves."

out of Samuel as an intercessor is somewhat surprising, though he sometimes has that role in Samuel (e.g., 1 Sam. 19.5, 9). Priests and prophets, but no king is mentioned; perhaps this highlights the incomparable nature of God's kingship. **8:** This v. is puzzling; it seems to telescope, with some changes, the traditions preserved elsewhere in the Bible. Moses and Samuel also appear together as intercessors in Jer. 15.1. God does not appear in *a pillar of cloud* to Samuel. *Decrees* in reference to Samuel may mean laws pertaining to the monarchy (1 Sam. 8.9,

11; 10.25). This v. seems to be an oblique request for a divine answer for the psalmist. It is one of many biblical reuses of the divine attributes of Exod. 34.6–7; specifically *You were a forgiving God for them* reflects "forgiving iniquity, transgression, and sin," while *but You exacted retribution for their misdeeds* reworks "yet He does not remit all punishment." **9:** Although the phrase *holy hill* is found in Psalms (e.g., 15.1), it predominates in Deutero-Isaiah (e.g., 56.7), offering a final connection between that prophet and the kingship psalms.

Ps. 100: This psalm is formally distinct from the kingship psalm collection (93–99): it nowhere mentions the kingship of God, and unlike 93–99, it has a typical superscription. Nevertheless, as noted below, it shares many themes and words with these psalms. The reference in v. 3 recalls the royal shepherd image. It even has the same structure as Pss. 95–97: a call to worship followed by a reason introduced by "ki," *for*. The many similarities between Ps. 100 and the previous ones suggest that Ps. 100 serves as an anthology or summary for the collection. It may also be understood as a general call to worship, and may have functioned as an introduction to larger liturgical works; it serves a similar role now when recited in the daily morning service. It is universalistic like Deutero-Isaiah in the sense that *all the earth* is expected to *acknowledge that the Lord is God.* **1:** It is uncertain if "todah" should be translated *for praise,* specifying the genre of the psalm (see Radak), or if it refers to the thanksgiving offering (so Rashi; see 50.13–14 n.), suggesting a liturgy to be recited in conjunction with the sacrifice. On shouting, see 47.2 n., and 95.1–2; 98.4, 6. **2:** On *gladness,* see 97.11; contrast 2.11: "Serve the Lord in awe; tremble with fright." **3:** The Lord (Yhvh) as sole or most powerful God is emphasized in Pss. 96–98. On *the flock,* see 95.7. **4:** This type of call to worship typifies 95–99; on *courts* see 96.8. *With praise* may also be rendered "with a thanksgiving offering." **5:** On the formula *For the Lord is good; His steadfast love is eternal,* see 106.1 n. For *steadfast love* and *faithfulness,* see 98.3.

Ps. 101: While any individual could have recited this psalm, the speaker sounds like a ruler (see esp. v. 8) and therefore many scholars consider it a royal psalm, perhaps sung at a coronation. Cf. Pss. 2 and 110. In the first part (vv. 1–4), the speaker promises to conduct himself with honesty and uprightness; compare this declaration with the instructions for a

2   I will study the way of the blameless;
         when shall I attain it?
     I will live without blame within my house.
3   I will not set before my eyes anything base;
         I hate crooked dealing;
         I will have none of it.
4   Perverse thoughts will be far from me;
         I will know nothing of evil.
5   He who slanders his friend in secret I will destroy;
         I cannot endure the haughty and proud man.
6   My eyes are on the trusty men of the land,
         to have them at my side.
     He who follows the way of the blameless
         shall be in my service.
7   He who deals deceitfully
         shall not live in my house;
     he who speaks untruth
         shall not stand before my eyes.
8   Each morning I will destroy
         all the wicked of the land,
     to rid the city of the Lord
         of all evildoers.

102   A prayer of the lowly man when he is faint and
      pours forth his plea before the Lord.

2   O Lord, hear my prayer;
         let my cry come before You.
3   Do not hide Your face from me
         in my time of trouble;
         turn Your ear to me;
     when I cry, answer me speedily.
4   For my days have vanished like smoke
         and my bones are charred like a hearth.
5   My body is stricken and withered like grass;
         ᵃ-too wasted-ᵃ to eat my food;
6   on account of my vehement groaning
         my bones ᵇ-show through my skin.-ᵇ
7   I am like a great owl in the wilderness,
         an owl among the ruins.
8   I lie awake; I am like
         a lone bird upon a roof.
9   All day long my enemies revile me;
         my deriders use my name to curse.
10   For I have eaten ashes like bread
         and mixed my drink with tears,

a-a Others "I forget."   b-b Lit. "cling to my flesh."

king in Deut. 17.18–20 and the farewell speech of Samuel in 1 Sam. 12.2–5. In the second part (vv. 5–8) the speaker might be addressing his courtiers, explaining how he will ensure that his royal court will meet the highest moral standards. **1:** *Faithfulness and justice,* a reference to God's loyalty to the Davidic monarchy. Cf. 89.2–5. This v. is interpreted in Jewish traditional sources (Targum, Rashi) to mean that whether God acts with favor ("ḥesed") or with justice ("mishpat"), the psalmist will always praise him. **2:** *My house* may be "my palace" (also v. 7), another hint that this is a royal psalm. **3–5:** The king's protestation of innocence (18.22–24); for nonassociation with evildoers, see 1.1; 26.4–5. **8:** *Each morning:* Morning is the time that justice is rendered (Jer. 21.12) and the time that deliverance is expected (46.6; Isa. 37.36; Lam. 3.23). *The city of the Lord,* Jerusalem (Targum), the capital of the Davidic dynasty.

Ps. 102: A psalm lamenting the destruction of Jerusalem and praying for its restoration. Rabbinic tradition (*m. Taʿan.* 2.3) assigns this psalm to fast days. A prayer for personal restoration (vv. 2–12, 24–29) frames the prayer for the rebuilding of Zion (Jerusalem) after the exile (vv. 13–23). **1:** The *lowly man* of the superscription is one of the exiles. **3:** God's hiding His face ("hester panim"; see 6.4–5 n.) became a theological concept in later Jewish thought. It represents God's withdrawal of His presence from the world. **4–8:** The psalmist describes his trouble as a physical illness; he is stricken with pain and weakness. **7–8:** The bird similes suggest loneliness and shrieks of pain which are calls for help. The birds mentioned are unclean birds (Lev. 11.17–18) and are therefore perceived negatively. They inhabit ruins (Zeph. 2.14). **9:** Taunting from enemies is a common usage in the psalms and need not be taken literally. The psalmist feels socially isolated as well as physically ill. **10:** These actions indicate mourning and lamenting;

11 because of Your wrath and Your fury;
      for You have cast me far away.
12 My days are like a lengthening shadow;
      I wither like grass.

13 But You, O LORD, are enthroned forever;
      Your fame endures throughout the ages.
14 You will surely arise and take pity on Zion,
      for it is time to be gracious to her;
      the appointed time has come.
15 Your servants take delight in its stones,
      and cherish its dust.
16 The nations will fear the name of the LORD,
      all the kings of the earth, Your glory.
17 For the LORD has built Zion;
      He has appeared in all His glory.
18 He has turned to the prayer ᵃ·of the destitute·ᵃ
      and has not spurned their prayer.
19 May this be written down for a coming
        generation,
      that people yet to be created may praise the
        LORD.
20 For He looks down from His holy height;
      the LORD beholds the earth from heaven
21 to hear the groans of the prisoner,
      to release those condemned to death;
22 that the fame of the LORD may be recounted in
        Zion,
      His praises in Jerusalem,
23 when the nations gather together,
      the kingdoms, to serve the LORD.

24 He drained my strength in mid-course,
      He shortened my days.
25 I say, "O my God, do not take me away
      in the midst of my days,
      You whose years go on for generations on end.
26 Of old You established the earth;
      the heavens are the work of Your hands.
27 They shall perish, but You shall endure;
      they shall all wear out like a garment;
      You change them like clothing and they pass
        away.
28 But You are the same, and Your years never end.
29 May the children of Your servants dwell securely
      and their offspring endure in Your presence."

cf. 42.4; 80.6. **12–13:** The transitory nature of humankind (*grass;* cf. Isa. 40.6) contrasted with the eternity of God (see Ps. 90.1–6). See also vv. 24–28. **12:** The psalmist feels he is nearing the end of his life. Cf. v. 24. **13:** Cf. Lam. 5.19: "But You, O LORD, are enthroned forever, Your throne endures through the ages." **14–17:** The psalmist prays that God will rebuild Zion and that the divine glory will again appear there (Ezek. 43.1–5); foreign kings will come to acknowledge God's supremacy (Isa. 60.1–3; Jer. 30.18). **14:** *The appointed time* may be unspecified or the psalmist may have known of a specific prophecy, like Jeremiah's prophecy (Jer. 25.11–12; 29.10–14) that Babylonia would be overthrown in seventy years. **20–21:** God hears the groaning of the exiles (79.11), as he looks down from heaven (11.4–5; 14.2). **22–23:** The reinstitution of Temple worship will lead to the further glorification of God. All peoples will gather there to serve God, an idea similar to Isa. 2.2–3; Micah 4.1–2. **24–25:** The psalmist prays that he not suffer premature death (55.23; 89.45). Perhaps the psalmist is expressing regret that he will not live to see the restoration, but in v. 29 he hopes that his children will. **26:** Job 38.4; Ps. 104.5; Prov. 8.29; Isa. 48.13. **27–29:** The permanence of God is contrasted with the most permanent objects in the world, heaven and earth, usually thought of as existing forever (Eccl. 1.4). God created them and God will let them perish, but God will continue to exist for eternity, beyond all measure of time. The permanence of God gives hope that He will, at some time in the future, restore Israel. **28:** This v. is part of the liturgy for Rosh Ha-Shanah and Yom Kippur. **29:** There is hope of restoration for a future generation. To endure in God's presence is the opposite of God's hiding His face.

a-a *Meaning of Heb. uncertain.*

103 Of David.

Bless the LORD, O my soul,
all my being, His holy name.

2 Bless the LORD, O my soul
and do not forget all His bounties.

3 He forgives all your sins,
heals all your diseases.

4 He redeems your life from the Pit,
surrounds you with steadfast love and mercy.

5 He satisfies you with good things in ᵃ the prime of
life, ⁻ᵃ
so that your youth is renewed like the eagle's.

6 The LORD executes righteous acts
and judgments for all who are wronged.

7 He made known His ways to Moses,
His deeds to the children of Israel.

8 The LORD is compassionate and gracious,
slow to anger, abounding in steadfast love.

9 He will not contend forever,
or nurse His anger for all time.

10 He has not dealt with us according to our sins,
nor has He requited us according to our
iniquities.

11 For as the heavens are high above the earth,
so great is His steadfast love toward those who
fear Him.

12 As east is far from west,
so far has He removed our sins from us.

13 As a father has compassion for his children,
so the LORD has compassion for those who fear
Him.

14 For He knows how we are formed;
He is mindful that we are dust.

15 Man, his days are like those of grass;
he blooms like a flower of the field;

16 a wind passes by and it is no more,
its own place no longer knows it.

17 But the LORD's steadfast love is for all eternity
toward those who fear Him,
and His beneficence is for the children's
children

18 of those who keep His covenant
and remember to observe His precepts.

Ps. 103: A hymn of praise for God's nature (divine attributes) and for His acts on behalf of Israel; it contains quotations from and allusions to Exodus and Isaiah. **1–2:** A double self-invitation to praise God. *Bless the LORD, O my soul* was likely a stock introduction to a psalm (104.1). *Soul* means one's being. There is as yet no concept of the soul as distinct from the body. **3–4:** Among God's blessings are the forgiveness of sin and the healing of mortal illness (32.1–5), which might have been thought of as punishment for sin. **3:** *He forgives all your sins,* see Exod. 34.7. **4:** *The Pit,* a poetic term for Sheol, the abode of the dead. **7–8:** See Exod. 33.13; 34.6. **9–13:** Interpreting or elaborating on the meaning and current application of Exod. 34.6, quoted in v. 8. **9:** Cf. Isa. 57.16. **11:** Cf. Isa. 55.9. **13:** The relationship between God and his worshippers is here portrayed as that between a father and a son (cf. Mal. 3.16–17). The compassionate father also figures in Jer. 31.20. **14–17:** The creaturely and ephemeral status of humanity (Gen. 2.7; Ps. 90.3–6), and the permanence of God's covenant with those who fear Him. **15–16:** Cf. Isa. 40.6–8. **19–22:** God is lauded by His heavenly council, and by all He has created (cf. Ps. 148); thus human praise of God mimics angelic praise, a significant theme of later Jewish prayer. The psalm ends as it began, forming an inclusio.

a-a Meaning of Heb. uncertain.

19   The Lord has established His throne in heaven,
     and His sovereign rule is over all.

20   Bless the Lord, O His angels,
     mighty creatures who do His bidding,
     ever obedient to His bidding;
21   bless the Lord, all His hosts,
     His servants who do His will;
22   bless the Lord, all His works,
     through the length and breadth of His realm;
     bless the Lord, O my soul.

104

Bless the Lord, O my soul;
     O Lord, my God, You are very great;
     You are clothed in glory and majesty,
2   wrapped in a robe of light;
     You spread the heavens like a tent cloth.
3   He sets the rafters of His lofts in the waters,
     makes the clouds His chariot,
     moves on the wings of the wind.
4   He makes the winds His messengers,
     fiery flames His servants.
5   He established the earth on its foundations,
     so that it shall never totter.
6   You made the deep cover it as a garment;
     the waters stood above the mountains.
7   They fled at Your blast,
     rushed away at the sound of Your thunder,
8   —mountains rising, valleys sinking—
     to the place You established for them.
9   You set bounds they must not pass
     so that they never again cover the earth.

10   You make springs gush forth in torrents;
     they make their way between the hills,
11   giving drink to all the wild beasts;
     the wild asses slake their thirst.
12   The birds of the sky dwell beside them
     and sing among the foliage.
13   You water the mountains from Your*a* lofts;
     the earth is sated from the fruit of Your work.
14   You make the grass grow for the cattle,
     and herbage for man's labor
     that he may get food out of the earth—
15   wine that cheers the hearts of men
     *b-*oil that makes the face shine,*-b*
     and bread that sustains man's life.

a Lit. "His."   *b-b Lit. "to make the face shine from oil."*

Ps. 104: In praise of the creator of a perfect world. The creation, an ecological harmony in which all are provided for, is an ideal world in which evil has no place. Structured on Gen. ch 1, but incorporating other creation traditions, the description is more poetic. It resembles both the divine catalogue of creation in Job chs 38–39 (which is more exotic and less idyllic) and the Egyptian "Hymn to Aten" (*ANET* 369–71), from which some scholars think it was adapted. This hymn is recited on the new moon. **1–4:** God is clothed in the glory of His creation; He is housed in it; He is transported by it. **2:** The creation of light and of the firmament. *Spread the heavens,* Job 9.8; Isa. 40.22; 42.5; Zech. 12.2. **3:** *Moves on . . . the wind,* Pss. 18.11; 68.5. **4:** See 148.8: "fire and hail, snow and smoke, storm wind that executes His command." **5:** See 102.26. **6–9:** God created the primordial waters (which Gen. says were there at the beginning of creation), and then separated them from the dry land. God's blast put the chaotic waters to flight (29.3; Jer 5.22). In their flight they ran up and down the mountains (v. 8), which had been submerged before (v. 6). Never again will the waters of chaos cover the earth. These vv. incorporate recollections of the Canaanite mythological tradition attested at Ugarit and also found elsewhere in the Bible (cf. Job 38.8–10; Prov. 8.29). **10–18:** The emergence of the ordered, habitable world, where God provides water and food to all his creatures. **10–11:** Instead of the waters of chaos, God made springs that meander among the hills so that animals would have drink. **12:** Near the springs the birds live. **13–15:** The mention of the sky leads to the mention of rain, which waters the vegetation and enables herding and agricultural production. **13:** See 36.9; 65.10. **14:** Cf. 147.9. *Get food out of the earth:* The blessing over bread before meals uses this wording to bless God for bringing bread out of the earth. Here it is humans, through God's planning, who get food from the earth. **15:** The three main crops of

16 The trees of the LORD drink their fill,
　　the cedars of Lebanon, His own planting,
17 where birds make their nests;
　　the stork has her home in the junipers.
18 The high mountains are for wild goats;
　　the crags are a refuge for rock-badgers.

19 He made the moon to mark the seasons;
　　the sun knows when to set.
20 You bring on darkness and it is night,
　　when all the beasts of the forests stir.
21 The lions roar for prey,
　　seeking their food from God.
22 When the sun rises, they come home
　　and couch in their dens.
23 Man then goes out to his work,
　　to his labor until the evening.

24 How many are the things You have made, O LORD;
　　You have made them all with wisdom;
　　the earth is full of Your creations.
25 There is the sea, vast and wide,
　　with its creatures beyond number,
　　living things, small and great.
26 There go the ships,
　　and Leviathan that You formed to sport with.
27 All of them look to You
　　to give them their food when it is due.
28 Give it to them, they gather it up;
　　open Your hand, they are well satisfied;
29 hide Your face, they are terrified;
　　take away their breath, they perish
　　and turn again into dust;
30 send back Your breath, they are created,
　　and You renew the face of the earth.

31 May the glory of the LORD endure forever;
　　may the LORD rejoice in His works!
32 He looks at the earth and it trembles;
　　He touches the mountains and they smoke.
33 I will sing to the LORD as long as I live;
　　all my life I will chant hymns to my God.
34 May my prayer be pleasing to Him;
　　I will rejoice in the LORD.
35 May sinners disappear from the earth,
　　and the wicked be no more.
　　Bless the LORD, O my soul.
　　Hallelujah.

the agricultural year: grain (for *bread*, May-June), grapes (for *wine*, August-September), and olives (for *oil*, October). Wine is associated with pleasure and oil with luxury (oil was a cosmetic). **16–18:** The trees, also nourished by the water God provides, were created for birds to live in; mountains and caves were made to be homes for wild animals. **19–23:** The creation of the celestial bodies (Gen. 1.14–18) sets in motion the diurnal cycle. Each creature has its place in this cycle. Predators seek their food at night, and people labor during the day. **19:** Although the (full) moon marks the seasons—actually the celebration of the seasonal festivals (Sukkot and Passover)—it is better to render *to mark the seasons* as "to mark the set times," that is, the time for day and night. Cf. Gen. 1.16. **21:** Job 38.39. **24–26:** Both the land and the sea are marvels of God's creation. **26:** Manmade ships are seen as part of God's creations in the sea. They are accompanied by the *Leviathan,* elsewhere the great marine chaos monster (74.14; Job ch 41). In Ugaritic literature, Leviathan (Lotan) was also a "beloved" of the deity El, a plaything, and that idea may be reflected here. Another quite different interpretation, not mythological, understands "Leviathan" in its literal sense of "the escort"—the dolphins or large fish often found near ships. **27–30:** God maintains His providential care of the world. According to Gen. 2.7 (cf. Ps. 103.14), God formed the human from dust and breathed life into him, but here God's breath animates all living things and without it they return to dust. **29:** *Hide Your face,* see 102.3. **31–32:** The creation is a theophany, accompanied by convulsions of the earth (114.7) and the mountains surrounded with smoke (144.5). **35:** There is no place in this harmonious creation for sinners. As in the previous psalm, this concludes as it began. *Hallelujah,* "Praise the LORD." These words occur at the end and sometimes at the beginning of a number of psalms from this point on (see 105; 106; 111–113;

105

Praise the LORD;
call on His name;
   proclaim His deeds among the peoples.

2 Sing praises to Him;
   speak of all His wondrous acts.

3 Exult in His holy name;
   let all who seek the LORD rejoice.

4 Turn to the LORD, to His might;[a]
   seek His presence constantly.

5 Remember the wonders He has done,
   His portents and the judgments He has
     pronounced,

6 O offspring of Abraham, His servant,
   O descendants of Jacob, His chosen ones.

7 He is the LORD our God;
   His judgments are throughout the earth.

8 He is ever mindful of His covenant,
   the promise He gave for a thousand generations,

9 that He made with Abraham,
   swore to Isaac,

10 and confirmed in a decree for Jacob,
   for Israel, as an eternal covenant,

11 saying, "To you I will give the land of Canaan
   as your allotted heritage."

12 They were then few in number,
   a mere handful, sojourning there,

13 wandering from nation to nation,
   from one kingdom to another.

14 He allowed no one to oppress them;
   He reproved kings on their account,

15 "Do not touch My anointed ones;
   do not harm My prophets."

16 He called down a famine on the land,
   destroyed every staff of bread.

a I.e., the Ark; cf. Ps. 78.61; 132.8.

115–117; 135; 146–150); these may have been part of one or more subcollections.

Ps. 105: Like 78, 106, 135, and 136, this psalm invokes selected authoritative Torah traditions along with exegetical comments on them in praise of God. The main theme is God's covenant with Abraham to give him the promised land.

This covenant, a popular theme in postexilic times (e.g., Isa. 41.8; 51.2; 63.16; Neh. 9.7), was eternal and unconditional, and therefore still in effect (v. 8) despite the exile and the fact that Jews both in and outside the land of Israel lived under Persian rule. It provides encouragement and assurance to the postexilic audience (most likely those who had returned to the land of Israel) that they are entitled to the land of Israel by divine right. Vv. 1–15 are quoted in 1 Chron. 16.8–22. **1:** God's deeds and wondrous acts are those recorded in the Torah, which the psalm goes on to recite and reinterpret. The psalmist knew some form of the Torah traditions, which had already become authoritative. **4:** *Seek His presence*, in the Temple. **5:** *Portents* recalls the wonders in Egypt and *judgments He has pronounced* recalls the giving of the law at Sinai (Exod. 21.1). **6:** The audience is addressed as the offspring (seed) of Abraham, thereby making them the fulfillment of God's promise to give Abraham many offspring (Gen. 15.3–6). *Descendants of Jacob* (lit. "children of Jacob") again emphasizes the continuity between the patriarchs and the audience. *His chosen ones*, the present generation is just as "chosen" as the forefathers. **9–11:** The covenant with Abraham was reiterated for Isaac and Jacob (Gen. 15; 17.7–8; 28.13–14). The wording of v. 11 is similar to Gen. 17.8, with the addition of "your allotted heritage" from Deut. 32.9, further strengthening the bond between Israel and its land. **12–15:** The story of the ancestors before they possessed the land highlights their wanderings in and out of Canaan, making them "exiles" just like the audience. The use of allusions and phrases associated with exile strengthen this theme that the patriarchs experienced exile like the contemporary audience. **12:** The wording alludes to Deut. 4.27; 28.62, and most closely to Deut. 26.5. In all these cases "few in number" is associated with being in exile. **14–15:** Cf. Gen. 20, where God *reproved* King Abimelech, and where Abraham is called a *prophet*. Cf. also Gen. 12.10–20; 26.1–2. *Anointed ones*, a synonym for "prophets," who were sometimes anointed (1 Kings 19.16; Isa. 61.1). Cf. Damascus Document 2.12; 6.1 (a Dead Sea Scroll text). **16–22:** The *Joseph* story (Gen. 37–50) retold with interpretive additions, ending with Joseph as a wisdom teacher (Gen. 41.39). **16:** *Staff of*

17 He sent ahead of them a man,
    Joseph, sold into slavery.

18 His feet were subjected to fetters;
    an iron collar was put on his neck.

19 Until his prediction came true
    the decree of the LORD purged him.

20 The king sent to have him freed;
    the ruler of nations released him.

21 He made him the lord of his household,
    empowered him over all his possessions,

22 to discipline his princes at will,
    to teach his elders wisdom.

23 Then Israel came to Egypt;
    Jacob sojourned in the land of Ham.

24 He made His people very fruitful,
    more numerous than their foes.

25 ᵃHe changed their heart⁻ᵃ to hate His people,
    to plot against His servants.

26 He sent His servant Moses,
    and Aaron, whom He had chosen.

27 They performed His signs among them,
    His wonders, against the land of Ham.

28 He sent darkness; it was very dark;
    ᵇdid they not defy His word?⁻ᵇ

29 He turned their waters into blood
    and killed their fish.

30 Their land teemed with frogs,
    even the rooms of their king.

31 Swarms of insects came at His command,
    lice, throughout their country.

32 He gave them hail for rain,
    and flaming fire in their land.

33 He struck their vines and fig trees,
    broke down the trees of their country.

34 Locusts came at His command,
    grasshoppers without number.

35 They devoured every green thing in the land;
    they consumed the produce of the soil.

36 He struck down every first-born in the land,
    the first fruit of their vigor.

37 He led Israelᶜ out with silver and gold;
    none among their tribes faltered.

38 Egypt rejoiced when they left,
    for dread of Israelᶜ had fallen upon them.

a-a Or "Their heart changed."   b-b Meaning of Heb. uncertain.
c Lit. "them."

bread, a phrase used in connection with the famine that results from enemy sieges (Lev. 26.26; Ezek. 4.16; 5.16; 14.13), forming another link between the forefathers' experience and that of the exiles. **18:** This treatment is not recounted in Genesis; it is an exegetical addition making Joseph into a prisoner of war, like the deportees after the destruction. **23–38:** The exodus story. Its telling emphasizes the destruction of the land of Egypt, showing God's power over that land. The exodus is a common metaphor for the return from captivity. **23–25:** Israel in *Egypt,* oppressed yet fruitful (Exod. ch 1). *Ham,* Egypt; see 78.51. **26–36:** The plagues (Exod. chs 7–12). The number and order of plagues differs from the Exodus account (see Ps. 78.43–51). **30:** *Their king,* Heb "kings" (plural), reflecting an ancient tradition that also appears in Wisdom of Solomon 10.16 and Sirach 45.3. **33:** *Vines and fig trees,* an exegetical comment elaborating on the hail plague. Cf. 78.47 for a similar elaboration. **37:** Exod. 12.33–36. *None among their tribes,* an interpretation of Exod. 6.26 and 12.51, where God took out the Israelites "troop by troop." This interpretation is found in Josephus (*Ant.* 14.6) and in traditional Jewish commentaries. **37:** Exegetical additions justify the taking of the gold and silver; this episode has a long history of interpretation, going back at least to this psalm. **39–44:** The wandering in the wilderness and the coming to the promised land. **39:** The pillar of cloud that led the Israelites (Exod. 13.21) takes on a protective function (Exod. 14.19) and is easily conflated with the cloud of the theophany that protects the people from direct contact with the divine (which would be fatal); cf. Exod. 33.1–10; Lev. 16.2; Num. 14.14. Isa. 4.5–6 applies the image to Mt. Zion. **40:** The provision of Israel with food (Exod. 16.1–17.7). No mention is made of the people's complaints (Exod. ch 16 and Num. ch 11); the point is that God takes care of Israel's needs. **44:** An inclusio returns

39 He spread a cloud for a cover,
   and fire to light up the night.
40 They asked and He brought them quail,
   and satisfied them with food from heaven.
41 He opened a rock so that water gushed forth;
   it flowed as a stream in the parched land.
42 Mindful of His sacred promise
   to His servant Abraham,
43 He led His people out in gladness,
   His chosen ones with joyous song.
44 He gave them the lands of nations;
   they inherited the wealth of peoples,
45 that they might keep His laws
   and observe His teachings.
   Hallelujah.

106

Hallelujah.
   Praise the LORD for He is good;
   His steadfast love is eternal.
2 Who can tell the mighty acts of the LORD,
   proclaim all His praises?

3 Happy are those who act justly,
   who do right at all times.
4 Be mindful of me, O LORD, when You favor Your
       people;
   take note of me when You deliver them,
5 that I may enjoy the prosperity of Your chosen
       ones,
   share the joy of Your nation,
   glory in Your very own people.

6 We have sinned like our forefathers;
   we have gone astray, done evil.
7 Our forefathers in Egypt did not perceive Your
       wonders;
   they did not remember Your abundant love,
   but rebelled at the sea, at the Sea of Reeds.
8 Yet He saved them, as befits His name,
   to make known His might.
9 He sent His blast against the Sea of Reeds;
   it became dry;
   He led them through the deep as through a
       wilderness.
10 He delivered them from the foe,
   redeemed them from the enemy.
11 Water covered their adversaries;
   not one of them was left.

to the promise to Abraham.
45: The community is enjoined to obey the Torah traditions, the same traditions that the psalmist has utilized and reinterpreted to give the community encouragement.

Ps. 106: This postexilic psalm presents a history of Israel's sins that culminates in idolatrous practices that polluted the land of Israel and led to the destruction and exile. The catalogue of sins shows how forbearing and forgiving God has been throughout the past, and, by implication, how forgiving He will continue to be, since He maintains His covenant and is merciful (vv. 43–45). The past history of God and Israel is the model for the future. The exile of 586 BCE, says the psalmist, is no different from earlier punishments, after which God took Israel back into His favor. The psalm is both a praise to God and a request to be gathered from among the nations, that is, returned from exile. Like Ps. 105, this psalm invokes Torah traditions along with interpretive comments. It adopts the Deuteronomic view that the exile was caused by Israel's sins. **1:** *Praise the LORD for He is good; His steadfast love is eternal* was a ritual exclamation in the exilic period; see 107.1; 118.1, 29; 136.1; 1 Chron. 16.41; 2 Chron. 7.6. **4–5:** The psalmist wishes to be included in the national favor that God will grant. **6:** The present generation joins itself to past generations of sinners, implicitly suggesting that it should be forgiven, as they were. Cf. Lam. 5.7. **8–12:** God's rescue of Israel at the sea and Israel's initial obedience (Exod. 14.26–15.19).

12	Then they believed His promise,
	and sang His praises.
13	But they soon forgot His deeds;
	they would not wait to learn His plan.
14	They were seized with craving in the wilderness,
	and put God to the test in the wasteland.
15	He gave them what they asked for,
	then made them waste away.
16	There was envy of Moses in the camp,
	and of Aaron, the holy one of the LORD.
17	The earth opened up and swallowed Dathan,
	closed over the party of Abiram.
18	A fire blazed among their party,
	a flame that consumed the wicked.
19	They made a calf at Horeb
	and bowed down to a molten image.
20	They exchanged their glory
	for the image of a bull that feeds on grass.
21	They forgot God who saved them,
	who performed great deeds in Egypt,
22	wondrous deeds in the land of Ham,
	awesome deeds at the Sea of Reeds.
23	He would have destroyed them
	had not Moses His chosen one
	confronted Him in the breach
	to avert His destructive wrath.
24	They rejected the desirable land,
	and put no faith in His promise.
25	They grumbled in their tents
	and disobeyed the LORD.
26	So He raised His hand in oath
	to make them fall in the wilderness,
27	to disperse[a] their offspring among the nations
	and scatter them through the lands.
28	They attached themselves to Baal Peor,
	ate sacrifices offered to the dead.
29	They provoked anger by their deeds,
	and a plague broke out among them.
30	Phinehas stepped forth and intervened,
	and the plague ceased.
31	It was reckoned to his merit
	for all generations, to eternity.
32	They provoked wrath at the waters of Meribah
	and Moses suffered on their account,
33	because they rebelled against Him
	and he spoke rashly.

13–33: Rebellion in the wilderness. **14–15:** The feeding of Israel and their testing of God (Exod. 16–17; Num. ch 11). **15:** *Then made them waste away,* see Num. 11.33. **16–18:** The rebellion of Dathan and Abiram (Num. 16). **19–20:** The making of the golden calf (Exod. 32.1–10). **19:** *Horeb,* an alternate name for Sinai favored by Deuteronomy. **20:** *Their glory,* God. *That feeds on grass,* an interpretive comment belittling the molten calf. **22:** *Ham,* Egypt; see 78.51. **23:** The intercession of Moses (Exod. 32.11–14). **24–27:** The Israelites' wish to return to Egypt rather than to enter Canaan, God's anger at them, and Moses' plea on their behalf (Num. 14.1–35). **28–31:** The worship of Baal of Peor and the episode of the Midianite woman (Num. 25.1–9). **28:** *Ate sacrifices offered to the dead,* the sacrifices of foreign gods (Ibn Ezra). Some modern scholars associate Canaanite worship with worship of the dead—the "marzeaḥ" feast. **30–31:** Num. 25.6–9. The Zadokite priests, who ministered during the Judean monarchy, traced themselves to Phinehas (1 Chron. 5.30–41). **32–33:** *The waters of Meribah,* Num. 20.2–13 (cf. Exod. 17.1–7). **34–36:** Because they left the holy war (extermination of their enemies) incomplete, the Israelites learned their practices (Deut. 20.18), and the land was polluted with idolatry.

a Cf. Targum, Kimhi.

34 They did not destroy the nations
as the Lord had commanded them,
35 but mingled with the nations
and learned their ways.
36 They worshiped their idols,
which became a snare for them.
37 Their own sons and daughters
they sacrificed to demons.
38 They shed innocent blood,
the blood of their sons and daughters,
whom they sacrificed to the idols of Canaan;
so the land was polluted with bloodguilt.
39 Thus they became defiled by their acts,
debauched through their deeds.
40 The Lord was angry with His people
and He abhorred His inheritance.
41 He handed them over to the nations;
their foes ruled them.
42 Their enemies oppressed them
and they were subject to their power.
43 He saved them time and again,
but they were deliberately rebellious,
and so they were brought low by their
iniquity.
44 When He saw that they were in distress,
when He heard their cry,
45 He was mindful of His covenant
and in His great faithfulness relented.
46 He made all their captors kindly disposed toward
them.

47 Deliver us, O Lord our God,
and gather us from among the nations,
to acclaim Your holy name,
to glory in Your praise.

48 Blessed is the Lord, God of Israel,
From eternity to eternity.
Let all the people say, "Amen."
Hallelujah.

BOOK FIVE

107 "Praise the Lord, for He is good;
His steadfast love is eternal!"
2 Thus let the redeemed of the Lord say,
those He redeemed from adversity,
3 whom He gathered in from the lands,

37–39: The passing of children through fire as a form of sacrifice to foreign gods is often condemned in the Bible (Deut. 12.31; 2 Kings 16.3; 21.6; Jer. 19.5; Ezek. 20.31; 23.37). **37:** No mention is made here of passing the children through fire; rather, the pagan practice is called sacrificing *to demons*—a later interpretation of a practice that was no longer current (and which remains incompletely understood by modern scholars). **40–42:** The destruction and exile resulted from the people's accumulated sins of idolatry, which God could no longer leave unpunished. **44–47:** As God saved the people in the past, the exiles ask for a new act of deliverance, the regathering of the people from their captivity (v. 27; 1 Chron. 16.35–36). **48:** The doxology ending Book IV of the Psalter (cf. 41.14; 72.18–19; 89.53). *Amen*, an affirmation of the words just spoken.

Ps. 107: The division between Books IV and V of the Psalter is late and improperly placed: Ps. 107, with its allusions to earlier traditions, belongs with Pss. 103–107. Furthermore, the opening of Ps. 107, *"Praise the Lord, for He is good; His steadfast love is eternal!"* connects it to Pss. 105 and 106; the connection is even more striking if the word "Hallelujah" is restored at the beginning of the psalm, following the LXX. The last v. clarifies the psalm's purpose: *The wise man will take note of these things; he will consider the steadfast love of the Lord,* namely that these beneficent events reflect God's *steadfast love* or "ḥesed" (see 5.8 n.). The psalm may be divided

from east and west,
from the north and from the sea.

4 Some lost their way in the wilderness,
in the wasteland;
they found no settled place.

5 Hungry and thirsty,
their spirit failed.

6 In their adversity they cried to the LORD,
and He rescued them from their troubles.

7 He showed them a direct way
to reach a settled place.

8 Let them praise the LORD for His steadfast love,
His wondrous deeds for mankind;

9 for He has satisfied the thirsty,
filled the hungry with all good things.

10 Some lived in deepest darkness,
bound in cruel irons,

11 because they defied the word of God,
spurned the counsel of the Most High.

12 He humbled their hearts through suffering;
they stumbled with no one to help.

13 In their adversity they cried to the LORD,
and He rescued them from their troubles.

14 He brought them out of deepest darkness,
broke their bonds asunder.

15 Let them praise the LORD for His steadfast love,
His wondrous deeds for mankind,

16 For He shattered gates of bronze,
He broke their iron bars.

17 There were fools who suffered for their sinful way,
and for their iniquities.

18 All food was loathsome to them;
they reached the gates of death.

19 In their adversity they cried to the LORD
and He saved them from their troubles.

20 He gave an order and healed them;
He delivered them from the pits.[a]

21 Let them praise the LORD for His steadfast love,
His wondrous deeds for mankind.

22 Let them offer thanksgiving sacrifices,
and tell His deeds in joyful song.

23 Others go down to the sea in ships,
ply their trade in the mighty waters;

into two large units: vv. 1–32 and 33–43; several scholars believe that two originally separate psalms have been combined. In contrast to the latter unit, the former, after an introduction (vv. 1–3), is divided into stanzas (vv. 4–9; 10–16; 17–22; 23–32), each of which has the double refrain *In their adversity they cried to the LORD, / and He rescued them from their troubles* (vv. 6, 13, 19, 28) and *Let them praise the LORD for His steadfast love, / His wondrous deeds for mankind* (vv. 8, 15, 21, 31), followed in each stanza by a single, concluding v. This section shares many motifs with Job. The psalm shows some signs of late biblical Heb, and vv. 1–2 are likely influenced by Isa. 62.12 and 43.5; it is thus a postexilic psalm. The Rabbis used this psalm as the basis for requiring a special blessing thanking God from those who survived the desert, those released from prison, seafarers, and those who were seriously ill (*b. Ber.* 54b). **1–2:** Compare the opening of Ps. 118. **2–3:** A reference to the return from the Babylonian exile. **4–9:** Deliverance in the wilderness, symbolizing the difficulties of the exile and the return. The theme of God's care in the wilderness became particularly important in the early postexilic period as the return from Babylonia was viewed by Deutero-Isaiah as a second exodus (see Isa. 43.16–21 n.). The Targum through its additions (v. 4, "He [David, author of Psalms] is prophesying concerning His nation Israel"; cf. v. 10, "concerning Zedekiah . . .") makes it clear that this psalm is to be read in reference to specific events in Israel's past. **10–16:** V. 10 is a reference to the exile; v. 14 to a release from exile. **17–22:** Two general descriptions of those who are being punished for misdeeds; they too will be forgiven. **21–26, 40:** Each of these vv. begins with an inverted Heb letter "nun," adapted from a sign used in Greek manuscript editing, to indicate that lines are isolated or separated from the surrounding material (the same indication occurs at Num. 10.35–36), but their use here is enigmatic.

a *Viz., of death.*

24   they have seen the works of the Lᴏʀᴅ
        and His wonders in the deep.
25   By His word He raised a storm wind
        that made the waves surge.
26   Mounting up to the heaven,
        plunging down to the depths,
        disgorging in their misery,
27   they reeled and staggered like a drunken man,
        all their skill to no avail.
28   In their adversity they cried to the Lᴏʀᴅ,
        and He saved them from their troubles.
29   He reduced the storm to a whisper;
        the waves were stilled.
30   They rejoiced when all was quiet,
        and He brought them to the port they desired.
31   Let them praise the Lᴏʀᴅ for His steadfast love,
        His wondrous deeds for mankind.
32   Let them exalt Him in the congregation of the
        people,
        acclaim Him in the assembly of the elders.

33   He turns the rivers into a wilderness,
        springs of water into thirsty land,
34   fruitful land into a salt marsh,
        because of the wickedness of its inhabitants.
35   He turns the wilderness into pools,
        parched land into springs of water.
36   There He settles the hungry;
        they build a place to settle in.
37   They sow fields and plant vineyards
        that yield a fruitful harvest.
38   He blesses them and they increase greatly;
        and He does not let their cattle decrease,
39   after they had been few and crushed
        by oppression, misery, and sorrow.
40   He pours contempt on great men
        and makes them lose their way in trackless
        deserts;
41   but the needy He secures from suffering,
        and increases their families like flocks.

42   The upright see it and rejoice;
        the mouth of all wrongdoers is stopped.
43   The wise man will take note of these things;
        he will consider the steadfast love of the Lᴏʀᴅ.

23–32: This stanza, longer than the others, deals with the dangers of sailing (see Jonah chs 1–2). **32:** This clarifies that "praise" must be public; although the Temple is a natural site for this, an *assembly of the elders* is not elsewhere associated with the Temple. **33–36:** These vv., concerning the return to Israel, hark back to vv. 4–9, and show close affinities to Deutero-Isaiah. **37–39:** Blessings in the land. **40–42:** A qualifier, using typical psalmic language, noting that only the *needy* and *upright* prosper. **43:** In several places, the *steadfast love of the Lᴏʀᴅ* seems to be a technical term for the past beneficent acts of God in history (89.2; Isa. 63.7).

108 A song. A psalm of David.

2a My heart is firm, O God;
 I will sing and chant a hymn with all my soul.

3 Awake, O harp and lyre!
 I will wake the dawn.

4 I will praise You among the peoples, O Lord,
 sing a hymn to You among the nations;

5 for Your faithfulness is higher than the heavens;
 Your steadfastness reaches to the sky.

6 Exalt Yourself over the heavens, O God;
 let Your glory be over all the earth!

7b That those whom You love may be rescued,
 deliver with Your right hand and answer me.

8 God promised ᶜin His sanctuaryᶜ
 that I would exultingly divide up Shechem,
 and measure the Valley of Sukkoth;

9 Gilead and Manasseh would be mine,
 Ephraim my chief stronghold,
 Judah my scepter;

10 Moab would be my washbasin;
 on Edom I would cast my shoe;
 I would raise a shout over Philistia.

11 Would that I were brought to the bastion!
 Would that I were led to Edom!

12 But You have rejected us, O God;
 God, You do not march with our armies.

13 Grant us Your aid against the foe,
 for the help of man is worthless.

14 With God we shall triumph;
 He will trample our foes.

109 For the leader. Of David. A psalm.

O God of my praise,
 do not keep aloof,

2 for the wicked and the deceitful
 open their mouth against me;
 they speak to me with lying tongue.

3 They encircle me with words of hate;
 they attack me without cause.

4 They answer my love with accusation
 ᵈ·and I must stand judgment.·ᵈ

---

a With vv. 2–6, cf. Ps. 57.8–12.   b With vv. 7–14, cf. Ps. 60.7–14.
c-c Or "by His holiness."
d-d Or "but I am all prayer"; meaning of Heb. uncertain, but see v. 7.

Ps. 108: After a unique superscription, vv. 2–6 duplicate 57.8–12 and vv. 7–14 duplicate 60.7–14. As in other cases (see Ps. 13, intro.), there are slight variations in these duplicates, suggesting that there was some flexibility in the transmission of passages. It is not clear why these two passages should be joined in this fashion, but it is noteworthy that v. 7, the first v. from the second passage, serves as a logical continuation of v. 6; v. 6 is a request, and in its new home, v. 7 offers the motivation or justification for that request. The result of the join fits the structure of communal petitions. The reuse of sections from one passage to create a new passage was accepted practice in the ancient world (see Isa. 2.2–4 n.). For medieval commentators, the problem of repeated passages was more severe. Radak, for example glosses: "and he [David] repeated it here, and we do not know why." On specific vv., see the notes to Pss. 57 and 60.

Ps. 109: This individual petition has the expected structure: it opens with an invocation (*O God of my praise*), followed by a petition in the imperative (*Do not keep aloof*), and it contains a variety of motivations, reasons why this petition should be answered (esp. vv. 30–31). In other ways, however, it is unusual: the wording of the invocation is unique, and the center of the psalm, vv. 6–19, is a long vituperative curse of the enemies. The psalm, particularly this section, resembles the Mesopotamian "namburbi," lit. "untying," a type of prayer intended to undo a magical spell. It is thus noteworthy that vv. 2–4 emphasize the harmful words of the enemy (see 10.7 n.). **1:** The invocation, *O God of my praise,* here functions as a motivation, alluding to the psalm's conclusion (vv. 30–31): God must save the supplicant so He will continue to be praised (see 6.6). *Do not keep aloof,* lit. "do not be silent," fitting the psalm's context of evil words. **2–5:** The complaint focuses on the evil words rather than the actions of the enemies; for this reason,

5 They repay me with evil for good,
    with hatred for my love.

6 Appoint a wicked man over him;
    may an accuser stand at his right side;
7   may he be tried and convicted;
    may he be judged and found guilty.
8 May his days be few;
    may another take over ᵃ his position.ᵃ
9 May his children be orphans,
    his wife a widow.
10 May his children wander from their hovels,
    begging in search of [bread].
11 May his creditor seize all his possessions;
    may strangers plunder his wealth.
12 May no one show him mercy;
    may none pity his orphans;
13   may his posterity be cut off;
    may their names be blotted out in the next
    generation.
14 May God be ever mindful of his father's iniquity,
    and may the sin of his mother not be blotted out.
15 May the Lord be aware of them always
    and cause their names to be cut off from the
    earth,
16   because he was not minded to act kindly,
    and hounded to death the poor and needy man,
    one crushed in spirit.
17 He loved to curse—may a curse come upon him!
    He would not bless—may blessing be far from
    him!
18 May he be clothed in a curse like a garment,
    may it enter his body like water,
    his bones like oil.
19 Let it be like the cloak he wraps around him,
    like the belt he always wears.
20 May the Lord thus repay my accusers,
    all those who speak evil against me.

21 Now You, O God, my Lord,
    act on my behalf as befits Your name.
    Good and faithful as You are, save me.
22 For I am poor and needy,
    and my heart is pierced within me.
23 I fade away like a lengthening shadow;
    I am shaken off like locusts.

many scholars posit that here and elsewhere the enemies are magicians. **6–20:** Although other psalms have short and powerful curses (see esp. 139.9), this is by far the longest curse in the Psalter. Some scholars understand this to be the curse of the enemy, and understand v. 20 as a declarative statement, rather than a wish: "This is the action of my accusers." The curses themselves are rather typical of the Bible and the ancient Near East. **14:** An allusion to intergenerational punishment; see Exod. 34.7 and 2 Sam. 12.13–14. **16:** Concern for the *poor and needy man* is a major concern of the Psalter. **21–29:** This section, marked off from what precedes by *Now You, O God,* highlights the reasons that God should respond positively. The psalmist does not claim to be innocent (contrast, e.g., Pss. 7; 17), but offers a wide variety of arguments meant to motivate God. These are all found elsewhere in Psalms and in other biblical literature: God should act for the sake of his *name* (v. 21; see 23.3 n.), for his "ḥesed" (vv. 21, 26; see 5.8 n.), because of the supplicant's lowly status (v. 22; see also v. 16) and pain (vv. 23–24), and so that the enemies will appreciate God's power (v. 27; see, e.g., 1 Sam. 17.46; 2 Kings 19.19; Isa. 41.20).

a-a *Meaning of Heb. uncertain.*

24 My knees give way from fasting;
    my flesh is lean, has lost its fat.
25 I am the object of their scorn;
    when they see me, they shake their head.
26 Help me, O LORD, my God;
    save me in accord with Your faithfulness,
27 that men may know that it is Your hand,
    that You, O LORD, have done it.
28 Let them curse, but You bless;
    let them rise up, but come to grief,
    while Your servant rejoices.
29 My accusers shall be clothed in shame,
    wrapped in their disgrace as in a robe.

30 My mouth shall sing much praise to the LORD;
    I will acclaim Him in the midst of a throng,
31 because He stands at the right hand of the
    needy,
    to save him from those who would condemn
    him.

110 Of David. A psalm.

The LORD said to my lord,
    "Sit at My right hand
    while I make your enemies your footstool."

2 The LORD will stretch forth from Zion your mighty
    scepter;
    hold sway over your enemies!
3 ⁻ᵃYour people come forward willingly on your day
    of battle.
    In majestic holiness, from the womb,
    from the dawn, yours was the dew of youth.⁻ᵃ

4 The LORD has sworn and will not relent,
    "You are a priest forever, ᵇ⁻a rightful king by My
    decree."⁻ᵇ

a-a *Meaning of Heb. uncertain.*
b-b *Or "after the manner of Melchizedek."*

28: Curses are not self-effectuating, but are affected by God, who can subvert them (see Deut. 23.6). **30–31:** A final reason why God should save this *needy* person: so He will be praised. This type of argument concludes the individual petitions 7.18 and 52.11 as well.

Ps. 110: A royal psalm (see Ps. 2 intro.). It is quite difficult because v. 3 is totally obscure, and the psalm changes speakers often. In Christian interpretation, it is understood as a reference to Jesus, as a messianic and sometimes eschatological psalm; Radak polemi-

cizes against this view. **1:** Here, God is speaking to the king, called *my lord;* perhaps these are the words spoken by a prophet. The king is very proximate to God, in a position of privilege, imagined as being on His right in the divine council. The second-in-command was seated to the right of the king in the ancient Near East. Such images are rare in Psalms, but see 45.7 n. If the king trods on the back of his *enemies* (see Josh. 10.24), they poetically become his *footstool.* **2:** In contrast to v. 1, God is spoken of in the third person. The Zion tradition (see Isa. 2.1–4; 60.1–22) and royal tradition are here connected. While vv. 1–2 express the great power of the king, they also emphasize that it comes from God. **3:** Though extremely obscure and likely corrupt, this verse, like 2.7, may refer to the king as the child of God. Some find in *the dawn,* Heb "shaḥar," a reference to the deity Shaḥar known from Ugarit and elsewhere, also the morning star (thus *dawn*). **4:** A second divine quotation, mirroring v. 1; this, however, is likely a citation of an old oracle; note 1 Sam. 15.11, where God repents that he made Saul king. David and Solomon often perform priestly roles (e.g., 2 Sam. 6.14; 1 Kings 8), and 2 Sam. 8.18 concludes: "David's sons were priests." The translation of the second half of the v. (see translators' note) depends on whether "malki-tzedek" is understood as two common nouns (*a rightful king*) or a personal name (Melchizedek). If the latter is correct, this is likely an allusion to Gen. 14.18: "And King Melchizedek of Salem [most likely an abbreviated form of Jerusalem] brought out bread and wine; he was a priest of God Most High." (This verse influences some classical rabbis [*b. Ned.* 32b], followed by Rashi, to interpret this psalm in relation to Abraham.) Melchizedek, having the double role of priest and king at Jerusalem, is seen as offering precedent for the similar roles of Davidic kings. Melchizedek played a significant role in a Dead Sea Scroll and in early Jewish and

5 The Lord is at your right hand.
　　He crushes kings in the day of His anger.

6 He works judgment upon the nations,
　　heaping up bodies,
　　crushing heads far and wide.

7 He drinks from the stream on his way;
　　therefore he holds his head high.

111

Hallelujah.
א I praise the Lord with all my heart
ב 　in the assembled congregation of the upright.
2 ג The works of the Lord are great,
ד 　　ᵃwithin reach of all who desire them.ᵃ
3 ה His deeds are splendid and glorious;
ו 　　His beneficence is everlasting;
4 ז 　He has won renown for His wonders.
ח The Lord is gracious and compassionate;
5 ט 　He gives food to those who fear Him;
י 　He is ever mindful of His covenant.
6 כ He revealed to His people His powerful works,
ל 　in giving them the heritage of nations.
7 מ His handiwork is truth and justice;
נ 　all His precepts are enduring,
8 ס 　well-founded for all eternity,
ע 　wrought of truth and equity.
9 פ He sent redemption to His people;
צ 　He ordained His covenant for all time;
ק 　His name is holy and awesome.
10 ר The beginningᵇ of wisdom is the fear of the Lord;
ש 　all who practice it gain sound understanding.
ת Praise of Him is everlasting.

112

Hallelujah.
א Happy is the man who fears the Lord,
ב 　who is ardently devoted to His commandments.

---

a-a Meaning of Heb. uncertain.
b Or "chief part."

Christian literature, and it is likely that a variety of stories no longer preserved in the Bible circulated about him in the biblical period. **5:** *The Lord is at your right hand,* a reversal of places with v. 1. Here the idea is that God stands ready to assist the king, or, more specifically, is the king's weapon (the right hand held the weapon); cf. 16.8; 18.36; 109.31. **7:** Perhaps this reflects part of the coronation ritual, held near the Gihon Spring (1 Kings 1.38–40); alternately, it refers to the king and army drinking water from faraway streams, a practice often mentioned in Mesopotamian royal inscriptions. In the words of Ibn Ezra: "The enemies were so afraid of them because when they went along the roads they would drink from their streams, and they were powerless to stop them." Holding one's *head high* is a symbol of triumph, the opposite of being a footstool (v. 1).

Ps. 111: This is the first of two acrostic psalms introduced by "Hallelujah," comprised of short lines that often quote traditional expressions (see some examples below), and containing wisdom ideas. They are somewhat disjointed, and look like very successful answers to the following (possibly student) exercise: Compose a logical, complete acrostic of short lines using traditional statements. Perhaps the simple style suggests that these were didactic poems for children. Stylistically, the two are so similar that they have been characterized as "twins." Yet, the two psalms are of different genres and have different foci. In the words of Rashi (to 111.1): "The first tells of the praise of God [i.e., it is a hymn], while the second tells of the praise of the righteous individual." V. 2 suggests that Ps. 111 was a hymn recited publicly, *in the assembled congregation of the upright.* **1:** Cf. Ps. 9.2: "I will praise You, Lord, with all my heart." **3:** *Splendid and glorious* are a frequent pair concerning God (e.g., 96.6). *His beneficence is everlasting* is a refrain joining Pss. 111–112 (see 112.3, 9). **4:** *Gracious and compassionate* are a common pair of divine epithets; see Exod. 34.6 (in the opposite order). The word order here is common in late texts (e.g., Neh. 9.17). **5:** Such an eternal *covenant* (see also v. 9) typifies Priestly thinking (see Gen. 17.7) and is found elsewhere in Psalms (105.8, 10). **9:** *Holy and awesome* are found in the opposite order in 99.3. **10:** See Prov. 1.7: "The fear of the Lord is the beginning of knowledge"; this line serves as a bridge to the following psalm, which focuses on the righteous individual. *Sound understanding* ("sekhel tov"), a wisdom phrase, is in the Heb of Prov. 3.4 and 13.15.

Ps. 112: A didactic poem, actually more of a catalogue, about the righteous man; see the intro. to

2 ג His descendants will be mighty in the land,
   ד   a blessed generation of upright men.
3 ה Wealth and riches are in his house,
   ו   and his beneficence lasts forever.
4 ז ᵃ A light shines ᵃ for the upright in the darkness;
   ח   he is gracious, compassionate, and beneficent.
5 ט All goes well with the man who lends generously,
   י   who conducts his affairs with equity.
6 כ He shall never be shaken;
   ל   the beneficent man will be remembered forever.
7 מ He is not afraid of evil tidings;
   נ   his heart is firm, he trusts in the Lord.
8 ס His heart is resolute, he is unafraid;
   ע   in the end he will see the fall of his foes.
9 פ He gives freely to the poor;
   צ   his beneficence lasts forever;
   ק   his horn is exalted in honor.
10 ר The wicked man shall see it and be vexed;
   ש   he shall gnash his teeth; his courage shall fail.
   ת The desire of the wicked shall come to nothing.

113

Hallelujah.
   O servants of the Lord, give praise;
      praise the name of the Lord.
2 Let the name of the Lord be blessed
      now and forever.
3 From east to west
      the name of the Lord is praised.
4 The Lord is exalted above all nations;
      His glory is above the heavens.

a-a Or "He shines as a light."

Ps. 111. The poem's subject, the "tzadik," the "righteous" or *beneficent man,* appears at the center of the poem in v. 6. **1:** Compare the opening of Ps. 1, and esp. 128.1, "Happy are all who fear the Lord." The fear of the Lord is a major wisdom theme in Proverbs; see Prov. 1.7. **2–4:** These vv. outline the recompense of the righteous man. **3:** *Wealth* is a major concern of wisdom literature. *And his beneficence lasts forever* (see also v. 6) ties this together with Ps. 111 (see v. 3); this refrain equates God's and the righteous man's *beneficence.* **4:** On *he is gracious, compassionate,* see 111.4. **5:** Lending generously is a major theme of wisdom literature.

6: Compare the conclusion of the catalogue of qualities of the individual who may enter the Temple precincts in 15.5: "The man who acts thus shall never be shaken." **7:** *His heart is firm,* see 57.8 and 108.2. **10:** Like Ps. 1, the depiction of the righteous gains force through comparison with *the wicked,* though here even less attention is given to the wicked than in Ps. 1. This v. in particular is based on other sources; see 37.12, "The wicked man schemes against the righteous, and gnashes his teeth at him" and Prov. 10.28, "But the hope of the wicked is doomed" (the Heb of these vv. differs by one letter only). Radak's paraphrase

clarifies this v.: "When the wicked sees the honor accorded to the righteous, he will be vexed from jealousy . . . and if he had the power to kill him, he would."

Pss. 113–118 are known in Jewish liturgy as the Egyptian Hallel, or just Hallel (praise), named for the reference to the exodus from Egypt in Ps. 114.1. The Egyptian Hallel is recited in the synagogue at the end of the morning service on the three pilgrimage festivals (Passover, Shavuot, Sukkot), and on Hanukkah, and it has been incorporated into the Passover Seder. In many synagogues it is also recited on Yom Haʿatzmaʾut, Israel Independence Day. Beginning with the second day of Passover, and on Rosh Ḥodesh (the new moon) the Half Hallel, omitting the first parts of Pss. 115 and 116, is recited. These psalms lack superscriptions and most, but not all, begin or end with *Hallelujah,* "Praise the Lord" (cf. also Pss. 111–112), but it is not certain that these were an ancient collection prior to the compilation of the Psalter. While praise for God is the dominant theme, other themes or genres of psalms are represented.

Ps. 113: Praise for God, who is exalted above all in the cosmos, should extend throughout the world because God is everywhere in the world. The psalm is pure praise; there is no hint of petition. It was perhaps recited antiphonally, at least in part. V. 1 calls on the worshippers to praise God; v. 2 may contain their response. Various word repetitions form a kind of echo throughout the psalm: *praise* (vv. 1, 3), *name of the Lord* (vv. 1, 2, 3), *heaven* (vv. 4, 6), *enthroned/sets* ("lashevet," v. 5; "lehoshiv," v. 8; "moshivi," v. 9), *exalted/lifts up* ("ram," "yarim"). **1:** *Servants,* worshippers. The idea of worshipping is serving God, as a servant serves a master. **2–3:** Praise for God at all times and in all places. **3:** *From east to west* (Heb "from sun's rising to setting"), globally. **4–6:** God is above the cosmos, above the sky, and

5 Who is like the LORD our God,
who, enthroned on high,
6 sees what is below,
in heaven and on earth?
7 He raises the poor from the dust,
lifts up the needy from the refuse heap
8 to set them with the great,
with the great men of His people.
9 He sets the childless woman among her household
as a happy mother of children.
Hallelujah.

114 When Israel went forth from Egypt,
the house of Jacob from a people of strange
speech,
2 Judah became His ᵃ·holy one,·ᵃ
Israel, His dominion.
3 The sea saw them and fled,
Jordan ran backward,
4 mountains skipped like rams,
hills like sheep.
5 What alarmed you, O sea, that you fled,
Jordan, that you ran backward,
6 mountains, that you skipped like rams,
hills, like sheep?
7 Tremble, O earth, at the presence of the Lord,
at the presence of the God of Jacob,
8 who turned the rock into a pool of water,
the flinty rock into a fountain.

115 Not to us, O LORD, not to us
but to Your name bring glory
for the sake of Your love and Your faithfulness.
2 Let the nations not say,
"Where, now, is their God?"

a-a Or "sanctuary."

looks down to see it. Cf. v. 6 and Ps. 18.10. **7–9:** The extremes on the vertical axis are brought together as God, the highest being imaginable, raises up the lowest human beings. Vv. 7–8 echo 1 Sam. 2.8 and v. 9 bears a resemblance to 1 Sam. 2.5. **7:** *Poor* and *needy* are terms often used of the psalmist's group, i.e., righteous Israelites, although in this instance the description may suggest the more literal meaning of those with low social status. *The refuse heap* is where the homeless live; cf. Lam. 4.5. **9:** Like the poor, a woman without children had no social standing.

Ps. 114: The exodus and its aftermath is celebrated not only as the liberation of Israel, but as an event through which all of nature came to see the power of God. The exodus is a cosmic theophany that alters the course of nature. The poem is structured on events in-volving water: the splitting of the sea, the crossing of the Jordan, and the supplying of water in the wilderness. **1–2:** In v. 1, *Israel* is the entire nation; *the house of Jacob;* in v. 2, *Judah* and *Israel* refer to the Southern and Northern Kingdoms. **1:** *Strange speech,* ancient peoples were categorized not by race but by language; cf. Gen. 10. Foreign-ness is conveyed in similar, but not identical, terms in Deut. 28.49; Isa. 33.19; Jer. 5.15. **2:** *His holy one . . . His dominion:* The parallelism breaks up a single thought and distributes it over two lines; the meaning is that Judah and Israel are His holy dominion. Cf. Exod. 19.6; Jer. 2.3. **3–6:** The passage through the sea (Exod. 14.29) is paralleled by the crossing of the Jordan (Josh. 3.14–17), the begin-ning and end of the exodus. These waters are personified and their splitting is imagined as their flight from the awe of God. The *moun-tains* and *hills* remind one of Mount Sinai (so Radak), but here the the-ophany takes on cosmic propor-tions. Compare the sea fleeing in terror from God (104.7), and the theophanous quaking of the earth (68.9; Judg. 5.4–5). **8:** Water in the desert (Exod. 17.6; Num. 20.11). On the cosmic level, God has power over all the material of the earth and can alter it as He wishes.

Ps. 115: The power of God is con-trasted with the impotence of idols. Pss. 114–115 are written as one psalm in the LXX, the Aleppo Codex and the Leningrad Codex, and in R. Saadia Gaon's transla-tion. Understood as one unit, Ps. 114 speaks of God's past acts of deliverance and Ps. 115 asks for God's help in the present. **1:** God is not asked to do favors for Israel on account of their merit, but in order to glorify His name; a typical thought in Psalms. **1:** God's *love* ("ḥesed") and *faithfulness* to Israel are often connected in Psalms and elsewhere; they bring Him glory. *Let the nations not say,* Heb is phrased as a rhetorical question: "Why should the nations say." *Where, now, is their God?* While Is-rael glorifies the divine name, the

3　when our God is in heaven
　　and all that He wills He accomplishes.
4ᵃ　Their idols are silver and gold,
　　the work of men's hands.
5　They have mouths, but cannot speak,
　　eyes, but cannot see;
6　they have ears, but cannot hear,
　　noses, but cannot smell;
7　they have hands, but cannot touch,
　　feet, but cannot walk;
　　they can make no sound in their throats.
8　Those who fashion them,
　　all who trust in them,
　　shall become like them.
9　O Israel, trust in the LORD!
　　He is their help and shield.
10　O house of Aaron, trust in the LORD!
　　He is their help and shield.
11　O you who fear the LORD, trust in the LORD!
　　He is their help and shield.

12　The LORD is mindful of us.
　　He will bless us;
　　He will bless the house of Israel;
　　He will bless the house of Aaron;
13　He will bless those who fear the LORD,
　　small and great alike.

14　May the LORD increase your numbers,
　　yours and your children's also.
15　May you be blessed by the LORD,
　　Maker of heaven and earth.
16　The heavens belong to the LORD,
　　but the earth He gave over to man.
17　The dead cannot praise the LORD,
　　nor any who go down into silence.
18　But we will bless the LORD
　　now and forever.
　　Hallelujah.

116

ᵇ⁻I love the LORD
　　for He hears⁻ᵇ my voice, my pleas;
2　for He turns His ear to me
　　whenever I call.
3　The bonds of death encompassed me;
　　the torments of Sheol overtook me.

---

a *With vv. 4–11, cf. Ps. 135.15–20.*
b-b *Heb. transposed for clarity; others "I would love that the LORD hear," etc.*

nations question God's effective presence (42.4; Ezek. 36.22–32). **3–7:** The existence of Israel's God is contrasted with the gods of the nations. Israel's God dwells in the heavens (that is, He is real but invisible), while the nations' gods are not real at all but are visible as impotent representations. **4:** *Silver and gold,* elsewhere idols are called "wood and stone." The idol-worshippers adorned their idols with precious metals, making them into a valuable commodity; this is ironic mockery since the idols are worthless. *The work of men's hands,* the idols are no different from other objects of human manufacture; there is nothing divine about them. **5–7:** Unlike the God of Israel, who has no physical representation but can act in the world, the idols have physical features but cannot act. **8–9:** Those who make and worship idols will be as powerless as their idols (Deut. 4.28; 2 Kings 17.15); cf. Ps. 135.15–18. By contrast, Israel believes in the true God who has the power to help them. **10:** *House of Aaron,* the priestly leaders of the postexilic community. **11:** *You who fear the LORD,* non-Jews who attached themselves to the Jewish community (cf. Ezra 6.21; Neh. 10.28; Rashi: "proselytes"). Some modern scholars think the LORD-fearers here refer to special champions of YHVH over all other gods; others suggest they were a subset of the priests (cf. 135.19–20). **14:** A blessing of prosperity and progeny. **15:** *Maker of heaven and earth,* the idols are made by people; God made the world. **16–17:** The cosmos is envisioned as having three levels: heaven is the abode of God, earth is the domain God assigned to human beings, and Sheol, below the earth, is the realm of the dead. Those who *go down into silence* are the dead, for in Sheol one cannot praise God. By implication, those who do not praise God, that is, the idolatrous nations, are like the dead. Israel, ever alive, continues its vocal praise of God (cf. 30.13).

Ps. 116: Thanksgiving for healing. A thanksgiving psalm of antholog-

4 I came upon trouble and sorrow
and I invoked the name of the LORD,
"O LORD, save my life!"

5 The LORD is gracious and beneficent;
our God is compassionate.

6 The LORD protects the simple;
I was brought low and He saved me.

7 Be at rest, once again, O my soul,
for the LORD has been good to you.

8 You[a] have delivered me from death,
my eyes from tears,
my feet from stumbling.

9 I shall walk before the LORD
in the lands of the living.

10 [b-]I trust [in the LORD];
out of great suffering I spoke[-b]

11 and said rashly,
"All men are false."

12 How can I repay the LORD
for all His bounties to me?

13 I raise the cup of deliverance
and invoke the name of the LORD.

14 I will pay my vows to the LORD
in the presence of all His people.

15 The death of His faithful ones
is grievous in the LORD's sight.

16 O LORD,
I am Your servant,
Your servant, the son of Your maidservant;
You have undone the cords that bound me.

17 I will sacrifice a thank offering to You
and invoke the name of the LORD.

18 I will pay my vows to the LORD
in the presence of all His people,

19 in the courts of the house of the LORD,
in the midst of[c] Jerusalem.
Hallelujah.

117

Praise the LORD, all you nations;
extol Him, all you peoples,

2 for great is His steadfast love toward us;
the faithfulness of the LORD endures forever.
Hallelujah.

ical character, quoting from other psalms (e.g., 18.2–7; 56.13–14). **1–4:** God has answered the psalmist's cry for help in the past, and now he calls on God's help again. **3:** *Sheol*, the abode of the dead. A common symbol for dire sickness or trouble. **5:** An echo of God's attributes in Exod. 34.6. **6–7:** Expressions of trust, characteristic of laments and thanksgivings. **8–9:** To remain alive is to have the opportunity to be in God's presence; the dead are cut off from God. See 56.14. **12–14:** The psalmist vows a public thanksgiving offering if God will help him. **13:** *Cup of deliverance*, a libation celebrating the psalmist's deliverance. This may be taken literally, as referring to the libation accompanying the thanksgiving offering, or metaphorically, as a kind of "toast" to God invoking His name to publicize His great deeds. Just as the psalmist invoked God's name when asking for His help (v. 4), he invokes His name when offering thanks. **14:** The vow made in time of trouble was not fulfilled earlier but can now be paid (cf. Jonah 2.10). The psalmist cannot truly repay God *for all His bounties* (v. 12); the thank offering (v. 17) is a token of this payment. **15:** *Grievous*, Heb "yakar," "precious," is difficult but is traditionally interpreted as here. As Radak says, "Their blood is precious in his sight" (72.14). God does not wish His adherents to die; therefore, the psalmist is reassured that God will keep him alive. **16:** *Servant . . . maidservant*, an epithet of extreme humility; see 86.16. *Cords that bound me*, perhaps a reference to an illness; or a general description of being constricted, being in trouble. Cf. *bonds of death* (v. 3). **17–19:** The *thank offering* will be offered in the Temple in Jerusalem.

Ps. 117: The shortest hymn in the Psalter, calling on all the nations to praise God (Pss. 67; 100). **2:** God's *steadfast love* and *faithfulness* (the same terms as in 115.1) to Israel are divine attributes—what gives God His special identity in the world—and are worthy of univer-

---

a I.e., God.   b-b Meaning of Heb. uncertain.   c Others "of you."

118

Praise the LORD, for He is good,
His steadfast love is eternal.

2 Let Israel declare,
"His steadfast love is eternal."

3 Let the house of Aaron declare,
"His steadfast love is eternal."

4 Let those who fear the LORD declare,
"His steadfast love is eternal."

5 In distress I called on the LORD;
the LORD answered me and brought me relief.

6 The LORD is on my side,
I have no fear;
what can man do to me?

7 With the LORD on my side as my helper,
I will see the downfall of my foes.

8 It is better to take refuge in the LORD
than to trust in mortals;

9 it is better to take refuge in the LORD
than to trust in the great.

10 All nations have beset me;
by the name of the LORD I will surely ᵃcut them
down.⁻ᵃ

11 They beset me, they surround me;
by the name of the LORD I will surely cut them
down.

12 They have beset me like bees;
they shall be extinguished like burning thorns;
by the name of the LORD I will surely cut them
down.

13 Youᵇ pressed me hard,
I nearly fell;
but the LORD helped me.

14 The LORD is my strength and might;ᶜ
He has become my deliverance.

15 The tents of the victoriousᵈ resound with joyous
shouts of deliverance,
"The right hand of the LORD is triumphant!

16 The right hand of the LORD is exalted!
The right hand of the LORD is triumphant!"

17 I shall not die but live
and proclaim the works of the LORD.

---

a-a *Meaning of* ʾamilam *in this and the following two verses uncertain.*
b *I.e., the enemy.*   c *Others "song."*   d *Or "righteous."*

sal praise. God is not expected to work on behalf of other nations, but only on behalf of Israel. This, in turn, demonstrates to the other nations God's fidelity to His people, and for that they will praise Him. *For great . . . toward us:* Heb "gavar ʿalenu," "prevailed over us" in the sense that God's faithfulness to Israel is manifest in His heroic acts ("gevurah"), which usually refers to His saving Israel from its enemies. There is a certain irony in universal praise deriving from God's particularistic acts. Radak, who sees this psalm as applying to the future, at the time of the coming of the messiah, explains that the other nations will feel compelled to praise God when He frees Israel from their control, in recognition of God's fidelity to Israel throughout the long period of the Diaspora.

Ps. 118: The mention of the nations and the battle imagery (vv. 10–16) suggest that this is a victory song, possibly reformulated to celebrate the return from exile and the rebuilding of the Temple. The psalm gives the impression that it was recited in a ceremony upon entering the Temple. It is anthological (like Pss. 116 and 135) with numerous allusions to other texts; v. 1 is quoted in 1 Chron. 16.34. **1–4:** Praise from Israel, the Aaronic priesthood, and the LORD-fearers (possibly proselytes); see 115.9–11. **5:** *Distress,* lit. a narrow, constricted space; correspondingly, a "relief," Heb "a broad space," connotes deliverance, release (4.2; 18.20). **6–8:** No human can harm the psalmist as long as God is on his side; conversely, no human is as reliable as God. **6:** See 56.5, 12. **8–9:** See 146.3. **10–13:** The attack of the nations, cf. v. 7; the one praying is perhaps a kingly persona, or the psalmist on behalf of the nation. **11–12:** Perhaps a siege image. Military imagery recurs in v. 15, *tents of the victorious.* The enemy swarms around the psalmist like bees, numerous and about to attack. Note the involvement of sound in the buzzing bees and the crackling thorns.

18   The Lord punished me severely,
         but did not hand me over to death.

19   Open the gates of victory[a] for me
         that I may enter them and praise the Lord.

20   This is the gateway to the Lord—
         the victorious[b] shall enter through it.

21   I praise You, for You have answered me,
         and have become my deliverance.

22   The stone that the builders rejected
         has become the chief cornerstone.

23   This is the Lord's doing;
         it is marvelous in our sight.

24   This is the day that the Lord has made—
         let us exult and rejoice on it.

25   O Lord, deliver us!
     O Lord, let us prosper!

26   May he who enters be blessed in the name of the
         Lord;
     we bless you from the House of the Lord.

27   The Lord is God;
         He has given us light;
         [c]bind the festal offering to the horns of the altar
         with cords.[c]

28   You are my God and I will praise You;
         You are my God and I will extol You.

29   Praise the Lord for He is good,
         His steadfast love is eternal.

119   א Happy are those whose way is blameless,
            who follow the teaching of the Lord.
  2   Happy are those who observe His decrees,
            who turn to Him wholeheartedly.

---

a Or "righteousness."   *b Or "righteous."*   *c-c Meaning of Heb. uncertain.*

12: Thorns are easily consumed by fire. **14–16:** See Exod. 15.2, 6; Isa. 12.2. **16:** *The right hand* with which God defends Israel against the enemy. **19–20:** An allusion to entrance rituals whereby the righteous gain admittance to the Temple (Pss. 15; 24.3–6). **22:** A metaphor of reversal of expectations (cf. 113.7–9); once rejected, Israel is now the keystone. The architectural imagery links with *gates* and

gateway in vv. 19–20. **23–28:** A thanksgiving ritual in the Temple amid the psalmist's friends and family (*us . . . we* in vv. 23–26). The shift to first-person plural suggests that vv. 23–27 may have been recited by all those assembled. Certainly vv. 25–26 sound like public proclamations. **27:** *Bind the festal . . . ,* likely the instructions for a ritual accompanying the sacrifice that entered the text of the

psalm. **29:** This v. forms a frame or inclusio with v. 1. The second part of the v., or perhaps the entire v., was recited by the congregation. Cf. 136.1.

Ps. 119: This is the longest Psalm, indeed the longest ch in the Bible. It is comprised of an eight-fold alphabetic acrostic. Comparable to it is an Akkadian text, the "Babylonian Theodicy," an eleven-fold acrostic of 297 lines, not alphabetic—Akkadian had no alphabet—but spelling out the author's name and occupation. Many earlier critical scholars considered this psalm monotonous and devalued its emphasis on "law." More recently, the skill of the poet in composing this tour de force has been appreciated. For example, there are eight main words used for "torah" (their English translations include: *word, law, commandment, rules, decree, precepts, teaching*), corresponding to the eight-fold acrostic; approximately 176 of these synonyms are found in the 176 vv. of the psalm (noted as early as Ibn Ezra and Radak). Why the author chose eight, rather than a more common number like seven, is unknown. It is difficult to know exactly how to translate "torah" and its synonyms in this psalm. The psalm is postexilic (even Ibn Ezra hints that it is non-Davidic in authorship), and certainly may know a canonized Torah; on the other hand, it is closely connected to wisdom texts, where "torah" often means the teaching of the wise (see, e.g., Prov. 28.7, "An intelligent son heeds instruction ['torah']"). Neither of these understandings of "torah" quite fits: the origin of torah in the psalm is clearly with God, yet it does not come from Sinai, and Moses as intermediary is never mentioned.

The psalm is often seen as anthological, i.e., quoting earlier verses (see Pss. 111–112), especially from Jeremiah, Isaiah, Proverbs, and Job. In echoing Torah texts and ideas, it is much closer to Deuteronomy than to the Priestly tradition, yet certain core ideas of

3 They have done no wrong,
   but have followed His ways.
4 You have commanded that Your precepts
   be kept diligently.
5 Would that my ways were firm
   in keeping Your laws;
6 then I would not be ashamed
   when I regard all Your commandments.
7 I will praise You with a sincere heart
   as I learn Your just rules.
8 I will keep Your laws;
   do not utterly forsake me.

9 ב How can a young man keep his way pure?—
   by holding to Your word.
10 I have turned to You with all my heart;
   do not let me stray from Your commandments.
11 In my heart I treasure Your promise;
   therefore I do not sin against You.
12 Blessed are You, O Lord;
   train me in Your laws.
13 With my lips I rehearse
   all the rules You proclaimed.
14 I rejoice over the way of Your decrees
   as over all riches.
15 I study Your precepts;
   I regard Your ways;
16 I take delight in Your laws;
   I will not neglect Your word.

17 ג Deal kindly with Your servant,
   that I may live to keep Your word.
18 Open my eyes, that I may perceive
   the wonders of Your teaching.
19 I am only a sojourner in the land;
   do not hide Your commandments from me.
20 My soul is consumed with longing
   for Your rules at all times.
21 You blast the accursed insolent ones
   who stray from Your commandments.
22 Take away from me taunt and abuse,
   because I observe Your decrees.

Deuteronomy—the centrality of Moses, the Torah as a book, and covenant—are lacking. It also shows certain affinities to the nonbiblical wisdom book of Ben Sirach.

The psalmist's depiction of "torah" is unique and verges on the mystical. He *clings* ("d-b-k") to it—a very strong term, often with sexual connotations (see, e.g., Gen. 2.24; 34.3, and compare the later

Jewish conception of "devekut," "clinging" to God). What is most remarkable is that a close relationship to Torah replaces a close relationship with God, and that in general, "torah" as a manifestation of the deity supplants God. For example, the "torah" rather than God is the source of life (vv. 50, 93). In Ps. 18.29 and its parallel in 2 Sam. 22.29, God is the psalmist's "light" ("ner"), but in v. 105, "Your word is a lamp to my feet, a light for my path." God's "deliverance" is not understood as coming from divine intervention to save the psalmist, but from God's words (v. 123): "My eyes pine away for Your deliverance, for Your righteous words" (author's translation). Other examples of this transformation from God to "torah" are noted below. V. 135 captures the psalm's unique and innovative understanding of Torah. Like the priestly blessing (Num. 6.25), it is interested in having God shine His face, but this is expressed not through God's shining face, but through Torah (v. 135): "Show favor to Your servant [lit. "shine Your Face upon Your servant"], and teach me Your laws."
   The celebration of "torah" ends with a final stanza in which the psalmist petitions to be granted understanding of the very "torah" that he has been extolling throughout the poem. Though they predominate at the end, petitionary elements are interspersed throughout the psalm (vv. 8, 10, 17, etc.). **1:** *Happy are*, common in Psalms, is sometimes used to open a psalm (e.g., 1; 41; 112). It declares the blameless to be in a fortunate state. **8:** The plea *do not . . . forsake me* typifies individual petitions (27.9; 38.22; 71.9, 18). **12:** The formula *Blessed are You, O Lord*, a postexilic phrase (see 1 Chron. 29.10), is later expanded with "our God, king of the universe" to become the standard rabbinic blessing formula. **14:** Comparison of wisdom or "torah" to riches typifies wisdom literature (cf. v. 72). **19:** In contrast to the conventional request that God not hide His face (see Ps. 10.1 n.), the psalmist requests *do*

23   Though princes meet and speak against me,
     Your servant studies Your laws.
24   For Your decrees are my delight,
     my intimate companions.

25 ד My soul clings to the dust;
     revive me in accordance with Your word.
26   I have declared my way, and You have answered
     me;
     train me in Your laws.
27   Make me understand the way of Your precepts,
     that I may study Your wondrous acts.
28   I am racked with grief;
     sustain me in accordance with Your word.
29   Remove all false ways from me;
     favor me with Your teaching.
30   I have chosen the way of faithfulness;
     I have set Your rules before me.
31   I cling to Your decrees;
     O Lord, do not put me to shame.
32   I eagerly pursue Your commandments,
     for You broaden my understanding.

33 ה Teach me, O Lord, the way of Your laws;
     I will observe them ªto the utmost.ª
34   Give me understanding, that I may observe Your
     teaching
     and keep it wholeheartedly.
35   Lead me in the path of Your commandments,
     for that is my concern.
36   Turn my heart to Your decrees
     and not to love of gain.
37   Avert my eyes from seeing falsehood;
     by Your ways preserve me.
38   Fulfill Your promise to Your servant,
     which is for those who worship You.
39   Remove the taunt that I dread,
     for Your rules are good.
40   See, I have longed for Your precepts;
     by Your righteousness preserve me.

41 ו May Your steadfast love reach me, O Lord,
     Your deliverance, as You have promised.
42   I shall have an answer for those who taunt me,
     for I have put my trust in Your word.
43   Do not utterly take the truth away from my
     mouth,

not hide Your commandments from me. **30:** Compare *I have set Your rules before me* ("shiviti") with the more typical "I am ever mindful ("shiviti") of the Lord's presence" (16.8). **33:** *Teach me, O Lord, the way of Your laws* is a revision of 27.11 and 86.11: "Show me Your way, O Lord." Once again, God is replaced by His laws. **39:** God's *rules,* rather than God, are *good.*

a-a *Meaning of Heb. uncertain.*

for I have put my hope in Your rules.

44 I will always obey Your teaching,
forever and ever.

45 I will walk about at ease,
for I have turned to Your precepts.

46 I will speak of Your decrees,
and not be ashamed in the presence of kings.

47 I will delight in Your commandments,
which I love.

48 I reach out for Your commandments, which I love;
I study Your laws.

49 ז Remember Your word to Your servant
through which You have given me hope.

50 This is my comfort in my affliction,
that Your promise has preserved me.

51 Though the arrogant have cruelly mocked me,
I have not swerved from Your teaching.

52 I remember Your rules of old, O Lord,
and find comfort in them.

53 I am seized with rage
because of the wicked who forsake Your
teaching.

54 Your laws are ᵃa source of strength to meᵃ
wherever I may dwell.

55 I remember Your name at night, O Lord,
and obey Your teaching.

56 This has been my lot,
for I have observed Your precepts.

57 ח The Lord is my portion;
I have resolved to keep Your words.

58 I have implored You with all my heart;
have mercy on me, in accordance with Your
promise.

59 I have considered my ways,
and have turned back to Your decrees.

60 I have hurried and not delayed
to keep Your commandments.

61 Though the bonds of the wicked are coiled round
me,
I have not neglected Your teaching.

62 I arise at midnight to praise You
for Your just rules.

63 I am a companion to all who fear You,
to those who keep Your precepts.

48: Lit. "I will stretch out my palms," an allusion to the prayer position of outstretched arms to God (see 44.21–22 n.), but here God has been replaced by *commandments*. **52**: Again, rules replace God; compare 77.4: "I call God to mind (z-k-r)." **62**: The mystical custom of offering special prayers at midnight ("tikun ḥatzot") derives from this v.

a-a Or "songs for me."

64 Your steadfast love, O Lᴏʀᴅ, fills the earth;
      teach me Your laws.

65 ט You have treated Your servant well,
      according to Your word, O Lᴏʀᴅ.
66 Teach me good sense and knowledge,
      for I have put my trust in Your commandments.
67 Before I was humbled I went astray,
      but now I keep Your word.
68 You are good and beneficent;
      teach me Your laws.
69 Though the arrogant have accused me falsely,
      I observe Your precepts wholeheartedly.
70 Their minds are thick like fat;
      as for me, Your teaching is my delight.
71 It was good for me that I was humbled,
      so that I might learn Your laws.
72 I prefer the teaching You proclaimed
      to thousands of gold and silver pieces.

73 י Your hands made me and fashioned me;
      give me understanding that I may learn Your
         commandments.
74 Those who fear You will see me and rejoice,
      for I have put my hope in Your word.
75 I know, O Lᴏʀᴅ, that Your rulings are just;
      rightly have You humbled me.
76 May Your steadfast love comfort me
      in accordance with Your promise to Your
         servant.
77 May Your mercy reach me, that I might live,
      for Your teaching is my delight.
78 Let the insolent be dismayed, for they have
         wronged me without cause;
      I will study Your precepts.
79 May those who fear You,
      those who know Your decrees,
         turn again to me.
80 May I wholeheartedly follow Your laws
      so that I do not come to grief.

81 כ I long for Your deliverance;
      I hope for Your word.
82 My eyes pine away for Your promise;
      I say, "When will You comfort me?"
83 Though I have become like a water-skin dried in
         smoke,
      I have not neglected Your laws.

68: God's goodness and benefi-cence are not expressed through His compassion, as elsewhere (e.g., 145.9), but through *teaching* of *laws.* **72:** Comparison to *gold and silver* typify wisdom literature (e.g., Prov. 22.1). The order "silver and gold" is more common in ear-lier biblical books, while *gold and silver* is often found in later texts (compare 2 Sam. 8.10 and 1 Chron. 18.10). **75:** The emphasis is on *just rulings,* rather than on a just God. **81:** Hoping or longing ("y-ḥ-l") for God's *word* (see also vv. 43, 81, 114, 147) rather than for God (e.g., 31.25; 38.16) typifies the psalmist's attitude.

84 How long has Your servant to live?
        when will You bring my persecutors to
            judgment?
85 The insolent have dug pits for me,
        flouting Your teaching.
86 All Your commandments are enduring;
        I am persecuted without cause; help me!
87 Though they almost wiped me off the earth,
        I did not abandon Your precepts.
88 As befits Your steadfast love, preserve me,
        so that I may keep the decree You proclaimed.

89 ל The LORD exists forever;
        Your word stands firm in heaven.
90 Your faithfulness is for all generations;
        You have established the earth, and it stands.
91 They stand this day to [carry out] Your rulings,
        for all are Your servants.
92 Were not Your teaching my delight
        I would have perished in my affliction.
93 I will never neglect Your precepts,
        for You have preserved my life through them.
94 I am Yours; save me!
        For I have turned to Your precepts.
95 The wicked hope to destroy me,
        but I ponder Your decrees.
96 I have seen that all things have their limit,
        but Your commandment is broad beyond
            measure.

97 מ O how I love Your teaching!
        It is my study all day long.
98 Your commandments make me wiser than my
            enemies;
        they always stand by me.
99 I have gained more insight than all my teachers,
        for Your decrees are my study.
100 I have gained more understanding than my
            elders,
        for I observe Your precepts.
101 I have avoided every evil way
        so that I may keep Your word.
102 I have not departed from Your rules,
        for You have instructed me.
103 How pleasing is Your word to my palate,
        sweeter than honey.
104 I ponder Your precepts;
        therefore I hate every false way.

84–88: Typical themes concerning *persecutors* from the individual petition are mixed with praise for the "torah." **94:** This expresses the essence of the psalm's theology: Devotion to God is expressed by following his *precepts*. **97:** The Deuteronomic ideal of loving God (e.g., Deut. 6.5) is replaced by loving His *teaching*. **99–100:** He is wisest since, unlike his teachers, only divine teaching, as opposed to secular wisdom, is his guide.

105 ‫נ‬ Your word is a lamp to my feet,
       a light for my path.
106   I have firmly sworn
       to keep Your just rules.
107   I am very much afflicted;
       O LORD, preserve me in accordance with Your
       word.
108   Accept, O LORD, my freewill offerings;
       teach me Your rules.
109   Though my life is always in danger,
       I do not neglect Your teaching.
110   Though the wicked have set a trap for me,
       I have not strayed from Your precepts.
111   Your decrees are my eternal heritage;
       they are my heart's delight.
112   I am resolved to follow Your laws
       ^ato the utmost^{-a} forever.

113 ‫ס‬ I hate men of divided heart,
       but I love Your teaching.
114   You are my protection and my shield;
       I hope for Your word.
115   Keep away from me, you evildoers,
       that I may observe the commandments of my
       God.
116   Support me as You promised, so that I may live;
       do not thwart my expectation.
117   Sustain me that I may be saved,
       and I will always muse upon Your laws.
118   You reject all who stray from Your laws,
       for they are false and deceitful.
119   You do away with the wicked as if they were dross;
       rightly do I love Your decrees.
120   My flesh creeps from fear of You;
       I am in awe of Your rulings.

121 ‫ע‬ I have done what is just and right;
       do not abandon me to those who would wrong
       me.
122   Guarantee Your servant's well-being;
       do not let the arrogant wrong me.
123   My eyes pine away for Your deliverance,
       for Your promise of victory.
124   Deal with Your servant as befits Your steadfast
       love;
       teach me Your laws.

110: *Traps* are mentioned else-where in personal petitions (e.g., 140.6). **117:** In contrast to those who bless God always (34.2), or al-ways hope for Him (71.14), this psalmist *will always muse upon Your laws.*

a-a *Meaning of Heb. uncertain.*

—1421—

125 I am Your servant;
        give me understanding,
        that I might know Your decrees.
126 It is a time to act for the LORD,
        for they have violated Your teaching.
127 Rightly do I love Your commandments
        more than gold, even fine gold.
128 Truly ^aby all [Your] precepts I walk straight;^{-a}
        I hate every false way.

129 פ Your decrees are wondrous;
        rightly do I observe them.
130 ^{b-}The words You inscribed give^{-b} light,
        and grant understanding to the simple.
131 I open my mouth wide, I pant,
        longing for Your commandments.
132 Turn to me and be gracious to me,
        as is Your rule with those who love Your
        name.
133 Make my feet firm through Your promise;
        do not let iniquity dominate me.
134 Redeem me from being wronged by man,
        that I may keep Your precepts.
135 Show favor to Your servant,
        and teach me Your laws.
136 My eyes shed streams of water
        because men do not obey Your teaching.

137 צ You are righteous, O LORD;
        Your rulings are just.
138 You have ordained righteous decrees;
        they are firmly enduring.
139 I am consumed with rage
        over my foes' neglect of Your words.
140 Your word is exceedingly pure,
        and Your servant loves it.
141 Though I am belittled and despised,
        I have not neglected Your precepts.
142 Your righteousness is eternal;
        Your teaching is true.
143 Though anguish and distress come upon me,
        Your commandments are my delight.
144 Your righteous decrees are eternal;
        give me understanding, that I might live.

126: In postbiblical legal literature, this v. is decontextualized and translated as "When it is time to act for the LORD, you may abrogate the Torah," in other words in extremis, one may violate a precept to preserve the Torah as a whole. **136:** The same image is used about the destruction in 586 (Lam. 3.48): "My eyes shed streams of water / Over the ruin of my poor people." "Torah" is thus equated with Temple, monarchy, and the land of Israel, all of which were lost in 586. **141:** It is doubtful that this can be taken literally, suggesting that the psalmist is young, as some have suggested.

a-a Or "I declare all [Your] precepts to be just."
b-b With Targum; or "The exposition of Your words gives"; meaning of Heb. uncertain.

145 ק I call with all my heart;
    answer me, O Lord,
    that I may observe Your laws.

146 I call upon You; save me,
    that I may keep Your decrees.

147 I rise before dawn and cry for help;
    I hope for Your word.

148 My eyes greet each watch of the night,
    as I meditate on Your promise.

149 Hear my voice as befits Your steadfast love;
    O Lord, preserve me, as is Your rule.

150 Those who pursue intrigue draw near;
    they are far from Your teaching.

151 You, O Lord, are near,
    and all Your commandments are true.

152 I know from Your decrees of old
    that You have established them forever.

153 ר See my affliction and rescue me,
    for I have not neglected Your teaching.

154 Champion my cause and redeem me;
    preserve me according to Your promise.

155 Deliverance is far from the wicked,
    for they have not turned to Your laws.

156 Your mercies are great, O Lord;
    as is Your rule, preserve me.

157 Many are my persecutors and foes;
    I have not swerved from Your decrees.

158 I have seen traitors and loathed[a] them,
    because they did not keep Your word in mind.

159 See that I have loved Your precepts;
    O Lord, preserve me, as befits Your steadfast
    love.

160 Truth is the essence of Your word;
    Your just rules are eternal.

161 ש Princes have persecuted me without reason;
    my heart thrills at Your word.

162 I rejoice over Your promise
    as one who obtains great spoil.

163 I hate and abhor falsehood;
    I love Your teaching.

164 I praise You seven times each day
    for Your just rules.

165 Those who love Your teaching enjoy well-being;
    they encounter no adversity.

146: Contrast other individual petitions that plea for deliverance so *that* the supplicant may praise God (e.g., 57.10). **153:** Typical psalmic language; see 9.14; 25.18. **161–169:** At least by late medieval times, the twenty-first letter of the alphabet was pronounced in two ways, distinguished by a dot over the left or right side of that letter ("sin" and "shin," pronounced "s" and "sh"). These two sounds are mixed in these vv., as in the biblical period this difference was not marked. **163, 167:** As in v. 97, and elsewhere in this psalm, *love* of "torah" replaces love of God.

a Or "have contended with."

166 I hope for Your deliverance, O LORD;
　　I observe Your commandments.
167 I obey Your decrees
　　and love them greatly.
168 I obey Your precepts and decrees;
　　all my ways are before You.

169 ת May my plea reach You, O LORD;
　　grant me understanding according to Your
　　　word.
170 May my petition come before You;
　　save me in accordance with Your promise.
171 My lips shall pour forth praise,
　　for You teach me Your laws.
172 My tongue shall declare Your promise,
　　for all Your commandments are just.
173 Lend Your hand to help me,
　　for I have chosen Your precepts.
174 I have longed for Your deliverance, O LORD;
　　Your teaching is my delight.
175 Let me live, that I may praise You;
　　may Your rules be my help;
176 I have strayed like a lost sheep;
　　search for Your servant,
　　for I have not neglected Your commandments.

120 A song of ascents.[a]

　In my distress I called to the LORD
　　and He answered me.
2 O LORD, save me from treacherous lips,
　　from a deceitful tongue!
3 What can you profit,
　　what can you gain,
　　O deceitful tongue?
4 A warrior's sharp arrows,
　　with hot coals of broom-wood.

a *A term of uncertain meaning.*

169–176: As noted, elements of the personal petition predominate here. **175:** Consistent with the psalm's focus, the psalmist wishes that God's *rules* rather than God will be his *help.* **176:** It is God's *commandments,* the embodiment of "torah," that must not be *neglected* or forgotten (sh-k-ḥ); contrast 44.18: "yet we have not forgotten (sh-k-ḥ) You."

Ps. 120: Pss. 120–134 all begin "A song of [or 'for'] ascents," forming the clearest collection of psalms in the Psalter; while other collections do exist, they are not found in a single block (see introductions to Pss. 42 and 50 on the Asaphite and Korahite psalms), but are identified by common ascription. It is likely that these fifteen psalms were already a unit when they were incorporated into the Psalter, though it is uncertain what this superscription means and what function the collection served. The word "ma'alah," typically translated "ascent," may refer to a step (see, e.g., Ezekiel 40.26). Early rabbinic tradition thus connects these fifteen psalms to the fifteen steps of the Temple, according to Ezek. 40.26, 31, where the Levites sang (*m. Mid.* 2.5; *b. Sukkah* 51b). "Ma'alah" is also used to express the "journey up from Babylon" in Ezra 7.9, and thus some modern scholars connect these psalms to the return from exile. Others see them as pilgrimage psalms (so Radak); the first-century allegorist Philo understood them as expressing the ascent of the individual to God, while some scholars see "ma'alah" as referring to some technical poetic aspect of these psalms. No single interpretation is compelling. These psalms comprise a variety of genres, and were written over a long period of time; some, but not all, show clear linguistic or other signs of being postexilic (see esp. 126). Certain phrases such as "May it be well with Israel!" are found in this collection only (125.5; 128.6), and the Songs of Ascents share certain linguistic and stylistic oddities, reinforcing the notion that there is some sort of unity to this collection. Nevertheless, the opinion of some scholars that they comprise a complex ritual is not compelling. In addition, with the exception of Ps. 132, they are all relatively short (3–9 vv.). Ps. 120, the first of the collection, is an individual petition. It is characterized by repetitions of the same phrase in contiguous vv. ("deceitful tongue" in 2, 3; "dwell/dwelt" in 5, 6; "peace" in 6, 7), a frequent stylistic aspect of this collection. **1:** A unique introduction to the individual petition, saying at the beginning that it was effective. **2–4:** Two of the typical elements of the petition are the invocation (*O LORD*), and the petition itself in the imperative (*save me*). As in many other psalms, the emphasis is on the danger of speech, here ex-

5 Woe is me, that I live with Meshech,
　　that I dwell among the clans of Kedar.
6 Too long have I dwelt with those who hate peace.
7 I am all peace;
　　but when I speak,
　　they are for war.

121 A song for ascents.

I turn my eyes to the mountains;
　　from where will my help come?
2 My help comes from the LORD,
　　maker of heaven and earth.
3 He will not let your foot give way;
　　your guardian will not slumber;
4 See, the guardian of Israel
　　neither slumbers nor sleeps!
5 The LORD is your guardian,
　　the LORD is your protection
　　at your right hand.
6 By day the sun will not strike you,
　　nor the moon by night.
7 The LORD will guard you from all harm;
　　He will guard your life.
8 The LORD will guard your going and coming
　　now and forever.

pressed through the strong metaphors of v. 4 (see 10.7 n.). The typical motivation—why God should hear this petition—is absent here. **5:** This is very enigmatic, since *Meshech* is near the Caspian Sea, while the *clans of Kedar* are in the Arabian Peninsula; either one of these names should be emended so that the locations are proximate, or the psalmist has intentionally chosen two faraway places to express the notion of distance. For scholars who read the Songs of Ascents as a group, it is this initial distance (see also Ps. 121) that is crucial, since the psalms express overcoming this distance, concluding with praying at the Temple. **6–7:** The residents of Meshech and Kedar are stereotyped as barbaric warmongers.

Ps. 121: This psalm expresses great confidence in God as a guardian; the root "sh-m-r," "to guard," appears six times. In many contemporary Jewish communities, it is recited at times of trouble as a way of offering comfort and assurance. As in the previous psalm, words are often repeated in adjacent vv. (vv. 1–2, "my help"; vv. 3–4, "slumber"; vv. 7–8, "guard"). **1:** Uniquely, the opening is *A song for ascents* rather than "to ascents." It is unclear why the psalmist is looking to the mountains; some have suggested that this is a polemic against deities on the mountains (see esp. Ezek. 18.6), or this expresses the pilgrim as he moves toward Jerusalem in the Judean hills; more likely "it is the custom of anyone in straits to lift his eyes to see if help will come to repel the enemy" (Ibn Ezra). **2:** This psalm is remarkable for recounting the psalmist's inner dialogue. The psalmist answers himself confidently either "through prophecy or expressing hope" (Ibn

Ezra). The epithet *maker of heaven and earth* is found three times in the Songs of Ascents (here, 124.8; 134.3), and twice outside them (115.5; 146.6). It is likely that this epithet became popular in postexilic times (see 2 Chron. 2.11). In this context, raising the eyes to the mountains, as if to appreciate the heaven and the earth, takes on additional meaning. **3–4:** This is polemicizing against the notion often expressed in psalms that God does sleep; see, e.g., 44.24, "Rouse Yourself; why do You sleep, O LORD? Awaken, do not reject us forever!" (see 7.7 n.). **5:** *Protection* ("tzel") refers to shade or refuge from the hot sun (see v. 6); note the biblical personal name (e.g., Exod. 31.2) Bezalel, "in the protection of God." *Right hand* expresses proximity (cf. 110.5). **6:** It is unclear how *the moon by night* might afflict a person: the notion of being moonstruck is postbiblical. Most likely this half verse is a type of filler, resulting from the use of parallelism, where *by night* formally parallels *by day,* and *moon* parallels *sun.* **8:** *Going and coming* means daily work (Deut. 31.2; 2 Kings 11.8). If this is a pilgrimage song, it may refer more specifically to setting out on the journey to the Temple and returning home. The psalm concludes with a temporal reference; as a whole, then, the psalm says that God guards the individual at all times everywhere. The expression *now and forever* is found disproportionately in the Songs of Ascents (here; 125.2; 131.3, and outside them in the Psalter only in 115.8).

122

A song of ascents. Of David.

I rejoiced when they said to me,
"We are going to the House of the LORD."

2 Our feet stood inside your gates, O Jerusalem,

3   Jerusalem built up, a city knit together,

4   to which tribes would make pilgrimage,
      the tribes of the LORD,
      —as was enjoined upon Israel—
      to praise the name of the LORD.

5 There the thrones of judgment stood,
   thrones of the house of David.

6 Pray for the well-being of Jerusalem;
   "May those who love you be at peace.

7 May there be well-being within your ramparts,
   peace in your citadels."

8 For the sake of my kin and friends,
   I pray for your well-being;

9   for the sake of the house of the LORD our God,
   I seek your good.

123

A song of ascents.

To You, enthroned in heaven,
   I turn my eyes.

2 As the eyes of slaves follow their master's hand,
   as the eyes of a slave-girl follow the hand of her
   mistress,

Ps. 122: This psalm is a pilgrim's ode to Jerusalem. This is the only Song of Ascents that clearly describes the ritual of ascending to Jerusalem. Various linguistic clues (e.g., the spelling of David, "dvyd" with a "yod" rather than "dvd" in v. 5) as well as its nostalgic attitude toward the preexilic past (v. 5, "there") suggest that the psalm is postexilic. The psalm is full of echoes of the sounds in the name "Yerushalayim," "Jerusalem"—the letter "resh" (corresponding to "r") is overrepresented, along with the word "shalom" (peace) and "sham" (there), esp. in vv. 4–8. Jerusalem is thus etymologized as the city of peace. **1:** Like Pss. 124, 131, and 133, *A song of ascents* is augmented with *Of David*, though as noted above, Davidic authorship is most unlikely. Radak glosses; "This psalm quotes the exiles, who in their great desire to build the Temple remembered Israel's pilgrimages, and spoke about their ancestors at the time that the Temple was standing." The psalm is probably even later, since Jerusalem is depicted as built up (v. 3), and this was likely only accomplished by Nehemiah in the mid-fifth century. *We are going to the House of the LORD* is likely formulaic; cf. Isa. 2.3, "Come, Let us go up to the Mount of the LORD." **1–2:** The psalmist moves from the singular to the plural (v. 1, *I*, to v. 2, *our*); in both vv., it is unclear who is addressed. **4:** The period of the united monarchy, when various tribes made pilgrimages, is recalled with nostalgia. The first half of the v. alliteratively recalls Jerusalem (Heb "Yerushalayim"): "*she-sham 'alu shevatim shivtei yah*." The end of the v., where *the name of*

the LORD rather than God Himself is praised, follows the norms of Deuteronomy (see Deut. 12.5 n.). **5:** Administration of justice was a significant function of the king, as highlighted in the stories about Solomon as a just king (1 Kings 3.16–28) and prophecies such as Jer. 21.12, "O House of David, thus said the LORD: Render just verdicts Morning by morning." **6:** The alliteration of the first four words is striking: "sha'alu shelom Yerushalayim yishlayu." The v. is a reversal of Jer. 29.7, "And seek the welfare of the city to which I have exiled you," insisting that one must pray for Babylon, not for Jerusalem. **7:** *Well-being* ("shalom") and *peace* ("shalvah") both play on the name Jerusalem, "Yerushalayim." **8:** The psalmist identifies himself with his community (see v. 2). **9:** The climax refers to the Temple, *the house of the LORD our God,* which makes Jerusalem so significant; this forms an inclusio with v. 1.

Ps. 123: An expression of dependence on God (vv. 1–2) serves as an introduction to a communal petition. An individual perspective (v. 1) quickly shifts to the plural (vv. 2–4), as in Ps. 122. Like Pss. 120 and 121, adjacent vv. use the same words (vv. 1–2, "eyes"; vv. 2–3, "favor"; vv. 3–4, "contempt, enough"). **1:** On God *in heaven,* see 2.4 n. **2:** A tricolon, i.e., a v. divided into three rather than two parallel segments. The imagery expresses the dependence of both men and women on God. **3:** A typical communal petition, with an imperative request (*Show us favor*), an invocation (*O LORD*), and a motivation ([For] *we have . . .*). **4:** *The complacent* may be the upper classes who abuse the lower classes, as in Amos 6.1.

Ps. 124: The beginning of this psalm, expressing the congregation's confidence in God, contains repetition of lines, like many of the other Songs of Ascents. **1:** Alternately, this may be understood as "May Israel now declare [or, 'sing'] the song that begins with

so our eyes are toward the LORD our God,
  awaiting His favor.
3 Show us favor, O LORD,
  show us favor!
We have had more than enough of contempt.
4 Long enough have we endured
  the scorn of the complacent,
  the contempt of the haughty.

124 A song of ascents. Of David.

Were it not for the LORD, who was on our side,
  let Israel now declare,
2   were it not for the LORD, who was on our side
  when men assailed us,
3   they would have swallowed us alive
  in their burning rage against us;
4   the waters would have carried us off,
  the torrent would have swept over us;
5   over us would have swept
  the seething waters.
6 Blessed is the LORD, who did not let us
  be ripped apart by their teeth.
7 We are like a bird escaped from the fowler's trap;
  the trap broke and we escaped.
8 Our help is the name of the LORD,
  maker of heaven and earth.

125 A song of ascents.

Those who trust in the LORD
  are like Mount Zion
  that cannot be moved,
  enduring forever.
2 Jerusalem, hills enfold it,
  and the LORD enfolds His people
  now and forever.
3   ᵃ⁻The scepter of the wicked shall never rest
  upon the land allotted to the righteous,
  that the righteous not set their hand to
    wrongdoing.⁻ᵃ
4 Do good, O LORD, to the good,
  to the upright in heart.
5   ᵃ⁻But those who in their crookedness act corruptly,⁻ᵃ
  let the LORD make them go the way of evildoers.
May it be well with Israel!

a-a *Meaning of Heb. uncertain.*

the words 'Were it not for the LORD, who was on our side' "—namely the song that begins in v. 2. In ancient Semitic cultures, compositions were typically known by their first words, so, e.g., what we call The Epic of Gilgamesh was known as He who Saw Everything. The same is now true for the books of the Torah, whose Heb names are the opening words of each. **2:** The referents are vague (*men*, Heb "'adam," "human beings"), so the psalm could be applied to many new situations. **3–7:** The mixture of images—*swallowing, waters, teeth,* and *traps*—is odd to modern sensibilities, but biblical poems often use a variety of intersecting images to strengthen their point. **8:** This is similar to 121.2, "My help comes from the LORD, maker of heaven and earth," with a change from singular to plural and a slight difference in "help is the name" and "help comes from the LORD."

Ps. 125: This psalm, about the exalted status of "those who trust in the LORD" (v. 1), is difficult; it does not cohere and does not flow well (see, e.g., the change of perspective about God from second to third person between vv. 4–5). **1:** Trusting *in the LORD* is a significant biblical theme in many genres; it implies action and is not merely an abstract notion. On *Mount Zion*, see Ps. 48. The stability of Jerusalem, and by extension *those who trust in the LORD*, is expressed through the doubling of *cannot be moved, enduring forever.* **2:** The order of the nouns in vv. 1–2 (*LORD, Zion, Jerusalem, LORD*) is reversed as the same point is emphasized: the stability of Jerusalem and Israel. *Forever* repeats v. 1. **3:** The Heb here is difficult. **4:** Only God can determine who is *upright in heart.* **5:** *The way of evildoers* is destruction, as in 1.4; the ultimate result of their annihilation is the end of the conflict between those who are good and those who are evil; thus the concluding expression, which became popular in postexilic times: "Peace/well-being over Israel." This expression is found in

126 A song of ascents.

When the LORD restores the fortunes of Zion
—ᵃwe see it as in a dream ᵃ—

2 our mouths shall be filled with laughter,
       our tongues, with songs of joy.
   Then shall they say among the nations,
       "The LORD has done great things for them!"

3 The LORD will do great things for us
       and we shall rejoice.

4 Restore our fortunes, O LORD,
       like watercourses in the Negeb.

5 They who sow in tears
       shall reap with songs of joy.

6 Though he goes along weeping,
       carrying the seed-bag,
   he shall come back with songs of joy,
       carrying his sheaves.

127 A song of ascents. Of Solomon.

Unless the LORD builds the house,
   its builders labor in vain on it;
unless the LORD watches over the city,
   the watchman keeps vigil in vain.

2 In vain do you rise early
       and stay up late,
   you who toil for the bread you eat;
       ᵇHe provides as much for His loved ones while
       they sleep.ᵇ

3 Sons are the provisionᶜ of the LORD;
       the fruit of the womb, His reward.

a-a Lit. "we are veritable dreamers."
b-b Meaning of Heb. uncertain.   c Lit. "heritage."

the famous Byzantine (sixth- to seventh-century CE) synagogue at Jericho, where it is incorporated into a mosaic below a menorah (candelabrum) flanked by a shofar (ram's horn) and a lulav (palm frond).

Ps. 126: Two problems make this psalm difficult to interpret: it is unclear how to reconcile vv. 1–3, which speak in the past, and vv. 4–6, which speak of hopes for the future; and it is uncertain how v. 1, *restores the fortunes*, should be understood. This psalm is recited before grace after meals on Sabbath and festivals. **1:** *Restores the fortunes* may be a specific reference to the return from Babylonian exile (so, e.g., Rashi), or may be a general term for improvement of one's lot (see 14.7 n.). Perhaps the *dream*-like nature of this vision explains how this restoration is both realized (vv. 1–3) and hoped for (vv. 4–6). **2–3:** These vv. are framed by *laughter* and *rejoicing*, with *the LORD* doing *great things* doubled in the middle. That expression is otherwise only found in Joel (2.20, 21), which has other affinities to this psalm (see v. 1 and Joel 4.1). **4:** V. 1 is recapitulated, but as an imperative. *Negeb watercourses* or wadis (seasonal streams) fill suddenly and completely after winter storms. **5–6:** Perhaps ritual *weeping* is alluded to, which was meant to bring about rainfall through sympathetic magic. As here, agricultural imagery is entwined with and represents the restoration of the people to their land in Amos 9.11–15.

Ps. 127: This psalm is didactic, teaching that God is the source of all. It divides into two parts: vv. 1–2, with the focus on "house" and "city," and vv. 3–5, with the focus on sons. The two are connected, however, since "house" may be a metaphor for family (see esp. 2 Sam. 7.11), and the "quiver" of v. 5 is likely a metaphor for the "house" that is filled with "arrows," namely "sons" (Radak). Like Pss. 128 and 131, the images are familial. **1–2:** The attribution *of Solomon* is due to the understanding of the *house* as the Temple, but more likely the psalm is addressed to Israelites in general, and "house" and "city" have no specific referent (cf. 128.5–6 n.). Many medievals (including Rashi, Ibn Ezra, and Radak) assume that this is a Davidic psalm, recited about *(of)* Solomon. The second half of v. 2 is hopelessly difficult and probably poorly preserved, yet as a whole, these vv. express an idea especially common in wisdom texts, that God ultimately controls all (e.g., Prov. 21.31: "The horse is readied for the day of battle, But victory comes from the LORD"). **3–5:** The view is very military and masculine. The term "gever" *(man)* in v. 5 is clearly male. The importance of a large family is a major theme of the ancestral narratives in Genesis. By using phrases such as "the LORD opened her womb" or "the LORD remembered her"

4 Like arrows in the hand of a warrior
  are sons born to a man in his youth.
5 Happy is the man who fills his quiver with them;
  they shall not be put to shame
  when they contend with the enemy in the gate.

128 A song of ascents.

Happy are all who fear the LORD,
  who follow His ways.
2 You shall enjoy the fruit of your labors;
  you shall be happy and you shall prosper.
3 Your wife shall be like a fruitful vine within your
  house;
  your sons, like olive saplings around your table.
4 So shall the man who fears the LORD be blessed.

5 May the LORD bless you from Zion;
  may you share the prosperity of Jerusalem
  all the days of your life,
6 and live to see your children's children.
May all be well with Israel!

129 A song of ascents.

Since my youth they have often assailed me,
  let Israel now declare,
2 since my youth they have often assailed me,
  but they have never overcome me.
3 Plowmen plowed across my back;
  they made long furrows.
4 The LORD, the righteous one,
  has snapped the cords of the wicked.

5 Let all who hate Zion
  fall back in disgrace.
6 Let them be like grass on roofs
  that fades before it can be pulled up,

house. (See Radak: "Even in her house she should be modest . . . she should be in the corner of the house so that only her husband and household will see her.")
4: A summary v. **5–6:** These vv. extend the original blessing to all *Israel,* and note that this blessing comes from God's dwelling-place, *Zion.* The psalmist may here be using traditional formulae; on *May the LORD bless you from Zion,* see 134.3 (and possibly 135.21); on *May all be well with Israel!,* see 125.5. *Children's children* signifies a blessing of long life and great progeny—the ideal in ancient Israel. Given average life expectancy, living to see grandchildren was a special blessing; seeing great-grandchildren was an exceptional blessing (see Job 42.16). With this psalm in its present position, after Ps. 127, it is easy to understand how "city" in 127.1 came to be understood as Jerusalem.

Ps. 129: This psalm has two parts: vv. 1–4 tell of the psalmist's past persecution by enemies, and his deliverance by God, and vv. 5–8 are an imprecation against "all who hate Zion" (v. 5). It is uncertain how the two parts fit together; perhaps the psalmist's past salvation gives power to this imprecation. **1–2:** The enemies are referred to by the pronoun *they;* not until v. 4 does *the wicked* appear. As usual, the referents are vague, allowing the psalm to apply to a wide variety of situations. **1:** See 124.1; this v. may also be translated "May Israel now declare [or, 'sing'] the song that begins with the words 'Since my youth they have often assailed me.'" **3:** A unique and graphic biblical metaphor, sharing the agricultural world of the previous psalm and several other Songs of Ascents. **4:** A new metaphor is introduced with *cords;* such mixing of metaphors is common in biblical poetry (see 124.3–7 n.) **5:** *Zion* is disproportionately mentioned in the Songs of Ascents (125.1; 126.1; 128.5; 129.5; 132.13; 133.3; 134.3). **6–7:** The image, again taken from the agricultural world (see v. 3),

(see esp. Gen. 30.22), those narratives emphasize the same point as these vv.: These (male) children are God's gift.

Ps. 128: This is thematically similar to the previous psalm, emphasizing that God is the source of blessing to those who "fear the LORD." **1:** The structure of this v. makes it clear that *fearing the LORD* is not an abstract attitude, but in-

volves *following His ways.* Although it seems to be addressed to *all,* vv. 3–4 make it clear that the addressees are male. **2:** Contrast Gen. 3.19, "By the sweat of your brow / Shall you get bread to eat." **3:** Lit. "Your wife shall be like a fruitful vine in the depths/corner/innermost parts of your house," perhaps a reference to the kitchen, typically located in the back corner of the ancient Israelite

7　　that affords no handful for the reaper,
　　　no armful for the gatherer of sheaves,
8　　no exchange with passersby:
　　　"The blessing of the LORD be upon you."
　　"We bless you by the name of the LORD."

130　A song of ascents.

　　Out of the depths I call You, O LORD.
2　　O Lord, listen to my cry;
　　　let Your ears be attentive
　　　to my plea for mercy.
3　　If You keep account of sins, O LORD,
　　　Lord, who will survive?
4　　Yours is the power to forgive
　　　so that You may be held in awe.

5　　I look to the LORD;
　　　I look to Him;
　　　I await His word.
6　　I am more eager for the Lord
　　　than watchmen for the morning,
　　　watchmen for the morning.

7　　O Israel, wait for the LORD;
　　　for with the LORD is steadfast love
　　　and great power to redeem.
8　　It is He who will redeem Israel from all their
　　　iniquities.

131　A song of ascents. Of David.

　　O LORD, my heart is not proud
　　　nor my look haughty;
　　　I do not aspire to great things
　　　or to what is beyond me;
2　　ᵃbut I have taught myself to be contented
　　　like a weaned child with its mother;
　　　like a weaned child am I in my mind.ᵃ

a-a Meaning of Heb. uncertain.

is of the insubstantial grass that grows on roofs that are covered with a small coating of soil.
8: This is a continuation of the image of the preceding v., since blessings were part of the reaping process (see Ruth 2.4, cited by Radak). It is uncertain whether *The blessing of the LORD be upon you.*

We bless you by the name of the LORD is a single blessing, or a blessing and its response, as in Ruth 2.4: "He greeted the reapers, 'The LORD be with you!' And they responded, 'The LORD bless you!' " Like Pss. 128 and 134, this Song of Ascents also ends with a blessing.

Ps. 130: The main part of the psalm is a personal petition (vv. 1–6); this is followed by an address to the wider community (vv. 7–8), which builds upon this petition, explaining why it is good to petition God. This address mirrors the vocabulary and expressions of vv. 1–6. It is thus possible that an editor, the author of vv. 7–8, has taken up and expanded an older psalm. **1:** *Depths*, elsewhere in Psalms only in 69.3, 15; perhaps here a reference to the underworld, of being in a state near death (see Jonah 2.3–7). **2:** A stereotypical v. in personal petitions; see, e.g., 86.6: "Give ear, O LORD, to my prayer; heed my plea for mercy." **3–4:** The theological notion expressed is that God must forgive since all people sin (see Job ch 7), and forgiveness rather than punishment causes people to hold God *in awe.* No ritual is necessary for this forgiveness, and the sin is completely erased as in Jer. 50.20, "The iniquity of Israel shall be sought, / And there shall be none; / The sins of Judah, / And none shall be found; / For I will pardon all I allow to survive." **5:** Perhaps the psalmist is awaiting an oracle of deliverance (see 3.5–7 n.). **6:** The psalmist waits expectantly for God's deliverance, which elsewhere comes in the morning (56.6). **7:** On steadfast love ("ḥesed"), see 5.8 n. **8:** Sinners or their descendants normally need to be punished (see Exod. 34.7), but here God *redeems*, that is, forgives, so no one is punished. As in many psalms, the personal becomes the communal.

Ps. 131: Like the previous psalm, this too starts in the singular (vv. 1–2) and moves to concerns about the community (v. 3); in fact, the last vv. of these two psalms share the phrase, "O Israel, wait for the LORD." **1:** An initial protestation of innocence (see Pss. 7; 17; 26). The psalmist claims to be "lowly," an ideal in Psalms (e.g., 10.17). As such, he does not *aspire to great things*, or *what is beyond*; these are, as Radak notes, "divine concerns" (e.g., Pss. 86.10; 136.4; Job 5.9). **2:** Once weaned, the child can no

3   O Israel, wait for the L<small>ORD</small>
        now and forever.

132

A song of ascents.

    O L<small>ORD</small>, remember in David's favor
        his extreme self-denial,

2   how he swore to the L<small>ORD</small>,
        vowed to the Mighty One of Jacob,

3   "I will not enter my house,
        nor will I mount my bed,

4   I will not give sleep to my eyes,
        or slumber to my eyelids[a]

5   until I find a place for the L<small>ORD</small>,
        an abode for the Mighty One of Jacob."

6   We heard it was in Ephrath;
        we came upon it in the region of Jaar.[b]

7   Let us enter His abode,
        bow at His footstool.

8   Advance, O L<small>ORD</small>, to Your resting-place,
        You and Your mighty Ark!

9   Your priests are clothed in triumph;
        Your loyal ones sing for joy.

10   For the sake of Your servant David
        do not reject Your anointed one.

11   The L<small>ORD</small> swore to David
        a firm oath that He will not renounce,
        "One of your own issue I will set upon your
            throne.

12   If your sons keep My covenant
        and My decrees that I teach them,
        then their sons also,
        to the end of time,
        shall sit upon your throne."

13   For the L<small>ORD</small> has chosen Zion;
        He has desired it for His seat.

14   "This is my resting-place for all time;
        here I will dwell, for I desire it.

15   I will amply bless its store of food,

---

a Lit. "eyes."   b Cf. 1 Sam. 7.1–2; 1 Chron. 13.5–6.

---

longer depend on its mother for its milk. Only here in Psalms is God viewed as a mother, though this image is found elsewhere in the Bible (e.g., Isa. 49.14–16). **3:** See 130.7; 121.8; 125.2.

Ps. 132: Like several other Songs of Ascents, this psalm emphasizes the significance of Zion, but in other ways it differs from this group: it is significantly longer, and stylistically unlike all the oth-ers. Its focus is on various promises made by and to David, and thus exhibits the same reciprocity seen in 134. It may recreate a ritual involving the Ark; according to 2 Chron. 6.41–42, vv. similar to 132.8–9 were used in connection with Solomon's dedication of the Temple. It is impossible, however, to reconstruct this ritual. Like Psalm 89, it does not exactly agree with the book of Samuel as it rein-terprets earlier traditions about David. **1–2:** This self-denial is not found in Samuel, nor is David's desire to build a Temple expressed as an oath there. *The Mighty One of Jacob* is an old divine epithet, used only here and in v. 5 in the Psalter (e.g., Gen. 49.24). **3–5:** An exagger-ated poetic rendition of 2 Sam. 7.2: "Here I am dwelling in a house of cedar, while the Ark of the L<small>ORD</small> abides in a tent!" **6:** The referent of *it* (feminine in Heb) is uncertain, though it likely refers to traditions about the Ark (masculine!) wan-dering; it is unclear if these agree exactly with Samuel. **7:** On *abode* ("mishkanot") and *footstool,* see 43.3–4 and 99.5 n. **8–9:** See 2 Chron. 6.41–42 (no parallel in 1 Kings ch 8); as noted by Radak, "there are slight changes between these verses, but they have the same meaning"; these vv. appear to have been used somehow in an ancient ritual. *Advance* (lit. "Arise," "kumah"), is often used to rouse God into battle—note *Your mighty Ark* (see 7.7 n.). **10:** On David as God's *servant,* see 18.1 n.; on *anointed one,* see 2.2 n. **11:** The di-vine oath is a response of David's oath (v. 2), creating symmetry in the psalm. In 2 Sam. ch 7, "oath" is not used: the promise is called "words" and "prophecy" (2 Sam. 7.17). *One of your own issue* is a po-etic restatement of 2 Sam. 7.12. **12:** In 2 Sam. ch 7 and related liter-ature (see esp. Ps. 89), the promise is of an eternal ("'olam") dynasty; here, as in 1 Kings 9.4–9, the prom-ise is conditional (see annotations to 1 Kings ch 9 and intro. to that book). **13:** *For* connects the choos-ing of David and of Zion (see 78.68–72 n.). **14:** *Resting-place:* See v. 8, of the *Ark,* God's throne or

give its needy their fill of bread.
16 I will clothe its priests in victory,
   its loyal ones shall sing for joy.
17 There I will make a horn sprout for David;
   I have prepared a lamp for My anointed one.
18 I will clothe his enemies in disgrace,
   while on him his crown shall sparkle."

133 A song of ascents. Of David.

How good and how pleasant it is
   that brothers dwell together.
2 It is like fine oil on the head
   running down onto the beard,
   the beard of Aaron,
   that comes down over the collar of his robe;
3 like the dew of Hermon
   that falls upon the mountains of Zion.
There the LORD ordained blessing,
   everlasting life.

134 A song of ascents.

Now bless the LORD,
   all you servants of the LORD
   who stand nightly
   in the house of the LORD.
2 Lift your hands toward the sanctuary
   and bless the LORD.
3 May the LORD,
   maker of heaven and earth,
   bless you from Zion.

the Northern and Southern Kingdoms (see Ezek. 37.15–28). **2–3:** It is uncertain if the *oil* and *dew* are being compared to the dwelling together, as this translation suggests, or if they are only being compared to each other (Like fine oil . . . is the dew of Hermon). On the oil used for anointing Aaron, see Exod. 30.22–33; the depiction of the overflowing, effulgent nature of this anointing is lacking in the Torah. Mount *Hermon*, on the northern tip of Israel, was very high, and therefore received much *dew*. This is the only reference to mountains (plural!) of Zion—perhaps the hills surrounding Jerusalem are meant, though the Dead Sea Psalms scroll reads the more usual "mountain." *Zion* might here be associated with Mount *Hermon*, as one of the northern mountains, as in 48.3 (see n. there). *Blessing* refers to fertility, as in Lev. 25.21; the word *blessing* anticipates the theme of the following psalm. *Everlasting life* is hyperbolic; the Dead Sea Psalms scroll instead concludes this psalm; "There the LORD ordained blessing forever; May all be well with Israel" (see Pss. 125.5; 128.6).

Ps. 134: This psalm, the last of the Songs of Ascents, is about blessing: the people's blessing of God (vv. 1–2) and God's blessing of the people (v. 3). The root "b-r-k," "to bless," occurs in every v. **1:** This v. shows clear affinities to the contiguous 135.2. *Servants of the LORD* may refer to those present in the Temple (see 135.1–2 n.), or they may be a special group of Temple functionaries. The Heb for *stand* also has a technical sense of "minister," which may be its sense here. It is uncertain what activity is performed *nightly*, other than guard duty by the Levites (1 Chron. 9.23–27). **2:** Lifting of *hands* typically accompanies prayer (see 44.21–22 n.), though here it may indicate blessing, as in Lev. 9.22. Since God rather than the people is being blessed, the hands are lifted in the direction of the sanctuary. **3:** These are formulae from elsewhere in this collection: see

footstool. **15:** The *needy* are a frequent concern of Psalms. **16:** On *loyal ones* ("ḥasid"), see 4.4 n. **17:** *Horn* often expresses military victory. In 2 Sam. 21.17, David is called "the lamp of Israel." **18:** *Shame* is the gravest punishment; ancient Israel was a shame-oriented society. This image reverses v. 16, "I will clothe its priests in victory" (Radak). The *crown* is a symbol of royalty (2 Sam. 1.10; 2 Kings 11.12).

Ps. 133: A short psalm, difficult to interpret; its precise point is uncertain, since the meaning of its images, and their connection, are de-

bated. Its focus on Zion, however, is common in the Songs of Ascents. Like several other of these poems, phrases in one line are repeated in the next (vv. 1–2 "tov," *good, fine*; vv. 2–3 "y-r-d," *running down, comes down, falls*). The images used combine to produce a picture of great blessing in Zion. This psalm, together with the previous one, mentions rituals concerning the king and high priest, who shared power in the post-exilic period (see Zech. 6.13). **1:** While often taken to refer to brotherly harmony in a general sense, the v. is better understood as a hope for the reunification of

135

Hallelujah.
Praise the name of the LORD;
give praise, you servants of the LORD
2 who stand in the house of the LORD,
in the courts of the house of our God.
3 Praise the LORD, for the LORD is good;
sing hymns to His name, for it is pleasant.
4 For the LORD has chosen Jacob for Himself,
Israel, as His treasured possession.

5 For I know that the LORD is great,
that our Lord is greater than all gods.
6 Whatever the LORD desires He does
in heaven and earth,
in the seas and all the depths.
7 He makes clouds rise from the end of the earth;
He makes lightning for the rain;
He releases the wind from His vaults.
8 He struck down the first-born of Egypt,
man and beast alike;
9 He sent signs and portents against[a] Egypt,
against Pharaoh and all his servants;
10 He struck down many nations
and slew numerous kings—
11 Sihon, king of the Amorites,
Og, king of Bashan,
and all the royalty of Canaan—
12 and gave their lands as a heritage,
as a heritage to His people Israel.

13 O LORD, Your name endures forever,
Your fame, O LORD, through all generations;
14 for the LORD will champion His people,
and obtain satisfaction for His servants.

15[b] The idols of the nations are silver and gold,
the work of men's hands.
16 They have mouths, but cannot speak;
they have eyes, but cannot see;
17 they have ears, but cannot hear,
nor is there breath in their mouths.
18 Those who fashion them,
all who trust in them,
shall become like them.

19 O house of Israel, bless the LORD;
O house of Aaron, bless the LORD;

128.5; 121.2; 124.8. Their juxtaposition emphasizes that a universal God is centered at Zion. The collection's conclusion emphasizes Zion, a major theme of the Songs of Ascents, and also shows close connections with the conclusion of the following psalm (135.21). Perhaps an editor placed together psalms that shared certain similarities, or phrases moved from one psalm to an adjacent one, making the Psalter into a more coherent book.

Ps. 135: The greatness of God—as demonstrated by His creation of the world, freeing His people from Egypt, and leading them safely to the promised land—is contrasted with the impotent gods of other nations. This psalm resembles others that review the traditions found in the Torah in order to show God's power (Pss. 78; 105; 106; 136). Here the traditions are more abbreviated. The psalm is an anthology of several other psalms and reworks some Torah traditions. This psalm appears in the liturgy for the introductory morning service for Sabbath and festivals. **1–2:** *Servants of the LORD* are all those who show allegiance to Him. The psalm is directed to those who have come to the Temple (cf. 113.1 and 134.1). **3:** Cf. 136.3. **4:** All gods have their peoples and Israel is the LORD's special people (cf. Deut. 32.8–9). **5:** Israel's God is superior to all other gods (cf. Exod. 18.11; Ps. 96.4–5). **6:** As elsewhere in the Bible (cf. 115.16–17), the cosmos is perceived as having three strata: the sky, the earth, and the water below the earth. **7:** Either a poetic rendering of the first stages of creation or a portrait of God's power over the natural world. **8–12:** A shortened version of 136.10–22. **8:** The poet skips to the last plague against Egypt, the one that finally convinced Pharaoh to let the Israelites leave. **11:** *Sihon* and *Og* were the first Canaanite kings defeated by Israel (Num. 21.21–35). **13:** A reuse of Exod. 3.15. **15–18:** Similar to 115.4–8 (with the omission of 115.7). **19–20:** Cf. 115.11 (omitting "house of Levi").

a Others "against you."   b With vv. 15–20, cf. Ps. 115.4–11.

20　O house of Levi, bless the LORD;
　　you who fear the LORD, bless the LORD.
21　Blessed is the LORD from Zion,
　　He who dwells in Jerusalem.
　　Hallelujah.

136

　　Praise the LORD; for He is good,
　　His steadfast love is eternal.
2　Praise the God of gods,
　　His steadfast love is eternal.
3　Praise the Lord of lords,
　　His steadfast love is eternal;
4　Who alone works great marvels,
　　His steadfast love is eternal;
5　Who made the heavens with wisdom,
　　His steadfast love is eternal;
6　Who spread the earth over the water,
　　His steadfast love is eternal;
7　Who made the great lights,
　　His steadfast love is eternal;
8　the sun to dominate the day,
　　His steadfast love is eternal;
9　the moon and the stars to dominate the
　　　night,
　　His steadfast love is eternal;
10　Who struck Egypt through their first-born,
　　His steadfast love is eternal;
11　and brought Israel out of their midst,
　　His steadfast love is eternal;
12　with a strong hand and outstretched arm,
　　His steadfast love is eternal;
13　Who split apart the Sea of Reeds,
　　His steadfast love is eternal;
14　and made Israel pass through it,
　　His steadfast love is eternal;
15　Who hurled Pharaoh and his army into the
　　　Sea of Reeds,
　　His steadfast love is eternal;
16　Who led His people through the wilderness,
　　His steadfast love is eternal;
17　Who struck down great kings,
　　His steadfast love is eternal;
18　and slew mighty kings—
　　His steadfast love is eternal;
19　Sihon, king of the Amorites,
　　His steadfast love is eternal;
20　Og, king of Bashan—
　　His steadfast love is eternal;

Ps. 136: This psalm is known in Jewish liturgy as the Great Hallel and has been incorporated into the Passover Seder. Like 135, it is part of the introductory prayers to the morning service on Sabbath and festivals. The psalm is probably written to be chanted responsively, with the assembly chanting the refrain after each line. *His steadfast love,* Heb "ḥesed" means a favor done out of loyalty (see 5.8 n.). God's "ḥesed" to Israel is eternal. The word "ki," left untranslated in NJPS, does not here mean "because" but rather "indeed"; thus the meaning is "Indeed his steadfast love is eternal." The psalm recounts in chronological order the many acts of "ḥesed" that God did for Israel in the past, and the refrain confirms that these acts of "ḥesed" will continue. Like 78, 105, 106, and 135, this psalm utilizes Torah traditions for its recitation of the mighty acts of God that constitute praise of God. The division of heaven and earth and the creation of the celestial bodies (vv. 5–9) is followed by the tenth plague against the Egyptians (cf. 135.8), the exodus from Egypt, the splitting of the Reed Sea, and the travels in the wilderness (vv. 10–20). The recitation of past marvels concludes with the acquisition of the promised land (vv. 21–22). Since God *took note of us in our degradation* and *rescued us from our enemies* in the past (vv. 23–24), there is assurance that He will do so again. These vv. bespeak the exilic condition, the probable time of this psalm's composition. The psalm ends on a note of the universality of God's care. **2–3:** *God of gods . . . Lord of lords,* an allusion to Deut. 10.17. This is a superlative form, like "Song of Songs." **4:** Any notion of the presence of other gods in vv. 2–3 is banished by the fact that God *alone* works great marvels. **6:** Compare Gen. 1.6 where the firmament separates the waters above it from the waters below it, and Gen. 1.9 where the waters below the firmament are gathered together so as to expose the dry land. The psalm has a more mythological conception,

21 and gave their land as a heritage,
His steadfast love is eternal;

22 a heritage to His servant Israel,
His steadfast love is eternal;

23 Who took note of us in our degradation,
His steadfast love is eternal;

24 and rescued us from our enemies,
His steadfast love is eternal;

25 Who gives food to all flesh,
His steadfast love is eternal.

26 Praise the God of heaven,
His steadfast love is eternal.

137 By the rivers of Babylon,
there we sat,
sat and wept,
as we thought of Zion.

2 There on the poplars
we hung up our lyres,

3 for our captors asked us there for songs,
our tormentors,[a] for amusement,
"Sing us one of the songs of Zion."

4 How can we sing a song of the LORD
on alien soil?

5 If I forget you, O Jerusalem,
let my right hand wither;[b]

6 let my tongue stick to my palate
if I cease to think of you,
if I do not keep Jerusalem in memory
even at my happiest hour.

7 Remember, O LORD, against the Edomites
the day of Jerusalem's fall;
how they cried, "Strip her, strip her
to her very foundations!"

a Meaning of Heb. uncertain.   b Others "forget its cunning."

like that in 24.2, in which the earth
is set upon the waters (forces of
chaos), which are thereby immobi-
lized. The word for "spreads" is
"roka'," the same root as "rakia',"
"firmament," in Gen. ch 1. **12:** *A
strong hand and outstretched arm:* cf.
Deut. 4.34; 5.15; 7.19. **19:** Cf. Num.
21.21–35 and Ps. 135.11. **23–25:** A
recapitulation of the exodus
theme: God took note of the people (Exod. 2.24), rescued them
(Exod. chs 14–15), and fed them

bread from heaven (Exod. 16.4,
15). **26:** The phrase *God of heaven*
is unique, and comports with an
exilic date, when God was not
imagined as localized at the
Temple.

Ps. 137: A lament for Jerusalem, in
its final form from the postexilic
era; the Babylonian captivity (vv.
1, 2, 4, 8) is *there* (v. 1 n.). The main
theme is remembering Zion. This
psalm is often recited on the 9th of

Av, the day that commemorates
the destruction of the Temple, and
before the grace after meals on
weekdays. **1:** *Rivers of Babylon:*
Babylonia was known for its network of irrigation canals, in contrast to Israel where the seasonal
rainfall provided irrigation. *There
we sat:* "There" indicates that the
speaker is now somewhere else;
not in Babylonia but (most likely)
in the land of Israel. *There,* along
with *alien soil* (v. 4), stresses the
otherness of the place of exile.
2–4: The Babylonian captors demand musical entertainment but
the captives, who can only cry,
hang up their instruments and refuse to make music. They cannot
express joy as long as they are in
exile. Joy, which is synonymous
with being in God's presence, is no
longer possible when the Temple
is destroyed. Exile is equated with
descent into the world of the dead;
like the dead, the exiles are unable
to praise God (30.10; 88.11–13).
2: The poplars, or willows, grow
along the canals. **3–4:** *Songs of
Zion,* some scholars identify Zion
songs as specific types of hymns
about the Temple (46; 48) or as the
pilgrimage psalms (84; 120–134).
More likely, the Babylonians are
asking for any native Judean song.
The psalmist equates them with *a
song of the LORD,* that is, any song
sung in the Temple, and therefore
they can no longer be sung.
5–6: An oath never to forget Jerusalem. This is a central idea in Jewish tradition, enshrined in the
liturgy, in the practice of leaving
an interior wall facing Jerusalem
undecorated or with a "mizraḥ"
(plaque indicating the east), and
in the breaking of the glass at the
conclusion of the wedding ceremony (which symbolizes, according to one explanation, placing the
memory of the destruction of Jerusalem above one's greatest joy, that
of being wed). *Right hand wither,* or
become useless, paralyzed. *My
tongue stick to my palate,* be unable
to utter a sound (Ezek. 3.26; Lam.
4.4). The paralysis of the *right hand*
and *tongue* make it impossible to
play the lyre and to sing (Radak).
7: Just as Israel must remember Je-

8 Fair Babylon, you predator,[a]
     a blessing on him who repays you in kind
       what you have inflicted on us;
9   a blessing on him who seizes your babies
       and dashes them against the rocks!

138 Of David.

   I praise You with all my heart,
     sing a hymn to You before the divine beings;
2 I bow toward Your holy temple
     and praise Your name for Your steadfast love
       and faithfulness,
     because You have exalted [b-]Your name, Your
       word, above all.[-b]
3 When I called, You answered me,
     [b-]You inspired me with courage.[-b]
4 All the kings of the earth shall praise You, O Lord,
     for they have heard the words You spoke.
5 They shall sing of the ways of the Lord,
     "Great is the majesty of the Lord!"
6 High though the Lord is, He sees the lowly;
     lofty, He perceives from afar.
7 Though I walk among enemies,
     You preserve me in the face of my foes;
     You extend Your hand;
     with Your right hand You deliver me.
8 The Lord will settle accounts for me.
   O Lord, Your steadfast love is eternal;
     do not forsake the work of Your hands.

139 For the leader. Of David. A psalm.

   O Lord, You have examined me and know me.
2 When I sit down or stand up You know it;
     You discern my thoughts from afar.
3 [b-]You observe[-b] my walking and reclining,
     and are familiar with all my ways.
4 There is not a word on my tongue
     but that You, O Lord, know it well.
5 You hedge me before and behind;
     You lay Your hand upon me.
6 It is beyond my knowledge;
     it is a mystery; I cannot fathom it.
7 Where can I escape from Your spirit?
   Where can I flee from Your presence?

rusalem, God must remember who destroyed it. The Edomites, who joined Babylonia in the attack on Jerusalem (Obad. 11–14) are cursed. **8–9:** Thoughts of retribution are commonly found in laments (5.11; 35.4–8; 69.23–28; 79.10; Lam. 1.21–22; 3.64–66; 4.21–22). On dashing babies against rocks, see 2 Kings 8.12; Isa. 13.16; Hos. 14.1; Nah. 3.10. *Against the rocks,* Heb "ha-selaʿ," "the Rock" (possibly Petra), the fortress-city of Edom and also an epithet for Edom (2 Kings 14.7). The gist of this pun is that the rock-fortress protecting Edom will become the vehicle for Edom's punishment.

Ps. 138: This is the first of a collection of hymns (138–145) that concludes the Psalter. Petitions characterize the Psalter's opening, and many see an intentional movement from petitions to hymns as part of the structure that the editor tried to convey. The book of Psalms would then reflect a movement from lament to praise. The psalmist praises God, certain that God protects individuals and will not fail to protect the psalmist. **1:** *Before the divine beings,* the divine council (82.1; 89.7–8; 95.3). **2:** In Deuteronomic theology, the name of the Lord resides in the Temple (Deut. 12.11). The Temple is the place where humans come into ritual contact with God, but God is not contained within the Temple. **4–5:** Human kings praise God because they have seen how God protects those who call upon Him (cf. 67.4–6; 126.2). **7–8:** See 23.4. *The work of Your hands,* creation and deliverance (*Your hand . . . Your right hand* in v. 7).

Ps. 139: God knows all that can be known; He is present in all places; no one can escape His reach. These attributes of God (vv. 1–18) become the basis for the psalmist's plea for God to destroy his enemies, who are also God's enemies (vv. 19–24). The text is difficult in vv. 3, 11, 16, and 20. **1–18:** An exquisitely detailed and poetic description of divine omniscience.

a *With Targum; others "who are to be destroyed."*   b-b *Meaning of Heb. uncertain.*

8   If I ascend to heaven, You are there;
         if I descend to Sheol, You are there too.
9   If I take wing with the dawn
         to come to rest on the western horizon,
10   even there Your hand will be guiding me,
         Your right hand will be holding me fast.
11   If I say, "Surely darkness ᵃ⁻will conceal me,
         night will provide me with cover," ⁻ᵃ
12   darkness is not dark for You;
         night is as light as day;
         darkness and light are the same.
13   It was You who created my conscience;ᵇ
         You fashioned me in my mother's womb.
14   I praise You,
         for I am awesomely, wondrously made;
         Your work is wonderful;
         I know it very well.
15   My frame was not concealed from You
         when I was shaped in a hidden place,
         knit together in the recesses of the earth.
16   Your eyes saw my unformed limbs;
         they were all recorded in Your book;
         in due time they were formed,
         ᶜ⁻to the very last one of them.⁻ᶜ
17   How weighty Your thoughts seem to me, O God,
         how great their number!
18   I count them—they exceed the grains of sand;
         I end—but am still with You.

19   O God, if You would only slay the wicked—
         you murderers, away from me!—
20   ᶜ⁻who invoke You for intrigue,
         Your enemies who swear by You falsely.⁻ᶜ
21   O Lᴏʀᴅ, You know I hate those who hate You,
         and loathe Your adversaries.
22   I feel a perfect hatred toward them;
         I count them my enemies.

23   Examine me, O God, and know my mind;
         probe me and know my thoughts.
24   See if I have vexatious ways,
         and guide me in ways everlasting.

2: *Sit down . . . stand up,* an expression comprising the whole of one's life and activity (Deut. 6.7). 5: The *hand* of the Lᴏʀᴅ is an expression for divine control and assistance (v. 10). 8: *Sheol,* the abode of the dead, below the ground; here it is the nadir of the earth. Unlike other usages of Sheol, to signify being cut off from God, here the psalmist says, perhaps in a rhetorical overstatement, that one cannot escape from God even in Sheol. 9: V. 8 gives the vertical axis, from apex to nadir; v. 9 gives the horizontal axis, from east to west. 11–12: *Darkness,* where humans can hide from each other, is no hiding place from God. 13–16: The mysteriously wonderful process of gestation. God saw the psalmist even in the womb (cf. Jer. 1.5). 16: *Recorded in Your book:* According to Rashi, this is the book containing a list of all people ever to be born, which God showed to Adam. According to Ibn Ezra, it is the blueprint according to which the person is formed. No such book is mentioned in Genesis, though a common rabbinic tradition imagines that the Torah served as the divine blueprint during creation. 17–18: God's thoughts are unfathomable (cf. Isa. 55.8–9). 21–22: The psalmist shows his solidarity with God by declaring hatred for God's enemies. 23–24: A return to the theme of knowledge: An all-knowing God surely knows the psalmist's righteousness.

a-a *Cf. Rashi, Ibn Ezra; meaning of Heb. uncertain.*
b *Lit. "kidneys."*
c-c *Meaning of Heb. uncertain.*

140
For the leader. A psalm of David.

2 Rescue me, O Lord, from evil men;
    save me from the lawless,

3 whose minds are full of evil schemes,
    who plot war every day.

4 They sharpen their tongues like serpents;
    spiders' poison is on their lips.   *Selah.*

5 O Lord, keep me out of the clutches of the wicked;
    save me from lawless men
    who scheme to ªmake me fall.⁻ª

6 Arrogant men laid traps with ropes for me;
    they spread out a net along the way;
    they set snares for me.   *Selah.*

7 I said to the Lord: You are my God;
    give ear, O Lord, to my pleas for mercy.

8 O God, my Lord, the strength of my deliverance,
    You protected my head on the day of battle.ᵇ

9 O Lord, do not grant the desires of the wicked;
    do not let their plan succeed,
    ᶜelse they be exalted.   *Selah.*

10 May the heads of those who beset me
    be covered with the mischief of their lips.⁻ᶜ

11 may coals of fire drop down upon them,
    and they be cast into pits, never to rise again.

12 Let slanderers have no place in the land;
    let the evil of the lawless man drive him into
    corrals.

13 I know that the Lord will champion
    the cause of the poor, the right of the needy.

14 Righteous men shall surely praise Your name;
    the upright shall dwell in Your presence.

141
A psalm of David.

I call You, O Lord, hasten to me;
    give ear to my cry when I call You.

2 Take my prayer as an offering of incense,
    my upraised hands as an evening sacrifice.

3 O Lord, set a guard over my mouth,
    a watch at the door of my lips;

4 let my mind not turn to an evil thing,
    to practice deeds of wickedness

Ps. 140: A prayer for deliverance from enemies. **4:** Sins of speech of the psalmist's foes (v. 12). For the metaphor of *tongues* and *poison* used of damaging speech, see 57.5; 58.5–7. *Selah* (also vv. 6, 9), see 3.3 n. **5–6:** The psalmist is hunted down by his foes; the metaphors come from the realm of warfare. **10–12:** The evildoers will suffer retribution equal to their deeds ("lex talionis"): They will be overcome by their own venomous words (v. 3) and will be hunted and entrapped (v. 4–5). **13–14:** The psalmist's assurance of divine justice. For *poor* and *needy*, see 86.1 n.

Ps. 141: A prayer requesting that prayer be efficacious. The psalm asks for deliverance from enemies in a way that emphasizes the importance of words and speaking. The text of vv. 5–7 is difficult. **2:** Prayer is seen metaphorically as sacrifice, with the hope that the prayer will rise up to God and be accepted just like incense and offerings. This does not mean that the psalmist sees prayer as a replacement for sacrifice, as was the case in post-Temple rabbinic times and afterwards, though it may suggest that prayer accompanied the evening incense offering. **3–4:** The psalmist wants God to prevent him from wrongful speech and from association with the wicked (1.1; 26.4). The ideas in these vv. are similar to those in Proverbs, where there is also concern with proper speech, with avoiding evildoers, and with the contrast between the righteous and the wicked. **7:** A graphic picture of *Sheol*, the abode of the dead. **9–10:** Retribution. As in the previous psalm, planning to entrap the psalmist, the evildoers are themselves entrapped (35.7–8; 140.5), an idea especially common in wisdom literature.

a-a Lit. *"push my feet."*   b Lit. *"arms."*   c-c *Meaning of Heb. uncertain.*

with men who are evildoers;
let me not feast on their dainties.

5a Let the righteous man strike me in loyalty,
let him reprove me;
let my head not refuse such choice oil.
My prayers are still against their[b] evil deeds.

6 May their judges slip on the rock,
but let my words be heard, for they are sweet.

7 As when the earth is cleft and broken up
our bones are scattered at the mouth of Sheol.

8 My eyes are fixed upon You, O GOD my Lord;
I seek refuge in You, do not put me in jeopardy.

9 Keep me from the trap laid for me,
and from the snares of evildoers.

10 Let the wicked fall into their nets
while I alone come through.

142

A *maskil* of David, while he was in the cave.[c]
A prayer.

2 I cry aloud to the LORD;
I appeal to the LORD loudly for mercy.

3 I pour out my complaint before Him;
I lay my trouble before Him

4 when my spirit fails within me.
You know my course;
they have laid a trap in the path I walk.

5 Look at my right and see—
I have no friend;
there is nowhere I can flee,
no one cares about me.

6 So I cry to You, O LORD;
I say, "You are my refuge,
all I have in the land of the living."

7 Listen to my cry, for I have been brought very
low;
save me from my pursuers,
for they are too strong for me.

8 Free me from prison,
that I may praise Your name.
The righteous [d-]shall glory in me[-d]
for Your gracious dealings with me.

Ps. 142: 1: For a similar superscription see 57.1. The incident referred to is in 1 Sam. 24.3–4, when David was fleeing from Saul. These superscriptions are the ancient editor's interpretations of the context in which the psalm was to be read. Some modern commentators see *the cave* as a reference to prison (see v. 8) and attribute the psalm to a person confined in a prison. **4:** See 140.6; 141.9–10. **8:** *Prison,* a metaphor for Sheol, the abode of the dead, where praising God is not possible (30.4–5; 115.17–18).

a *Meaning of vv. 5–7 uncertain.*
b *I.e., the evildoers of v. 4.*
c *Cf. 1 Sam. 24.3–4.*
d-d *Meaning of Heb. uncertain.*

143 A psalm of David.

O Lord, hear my prayer;
  give ear to my plea, as You are faithful;
  answer me, as You are beneficent.

2 Do not enter into judgment with Your servant,
  for before You no creature is in the right.

3 My foe hounded me;
  he crushed me to the ground;
  he made me dwell in darkness
  like those long dead.

4 My spirit failed within me;
  my mind was numbed with horror.

5 Then I thought of the days of old;
  I rehearsed all Your deeds,
  recounted the work of Your hands.

6 I stretched out my hands to You,
  longing for You like thirsty earth.   Selah.

7 Answer me quickly, O Lord;
  my spirit can endure no more.
  Do not hide Your face from me,
  or I shall become like those who descend into
    the Pit.

8 Let me learn of Your faithfulness by daybreak,
  for in You I trust;
  let me know the road I must take,
  for on You I have set my hope.

9 Save me from my foes, O Lord;
  ᵃ‑to You I look for cover.‑ᵃ

10 Teach me to do Your will,
  for You are my God.
  Let Your gracious spirit lead me
  on level ground.

11 · For the sake of Your name, O Lord, preserve me;
  as You are beneficent, free me from distress.

12 As You are faithful, put an end to my foes;
  destroy all my mortal enemies,
  for I am Your servant.

144 Of David.

Blessed is the Lord, my rock,
  who trains my hands for battle,
  my fingers for warfare;

a-a Meaning of Heb. uncertain.

Ps. 143: This psalm contrasts the dead, who have no access to God, with the living, who do. The psalmist pleads to remain among the living. "Enemies" and "illness" are typical threats to the psalmist's well-being. There are thematic and verbal connections with the previous psalm; see especially v. 4. **2:** *For before You no creature is in the right* is an idea also expressed by Job's friends (Job 4.17–21). **3:** *Darkness,* the realm of the dead. *Long dead,* better "eternally dead." The idea is that the dead can never live again. **5–6:** In his darkest days, the psalmist remembers God's past deeds. In a move that is the opposite of being dead, he stretches out his hand in prayer, seeking access to God. See 63.2; 77.12–13. **6:** *Selah,* see 3.3 n. **7:** *Hide Your face,* see 102.1. *The Pit,* a poetic term for Sheol, the abode of the dead. **8:** *Daybreak,* in contrast to the darkness of death, morning brings a response from God. See 101.8 n. **10:** *Your gracious spirit,* an expression for divine power, contrasted with the weakness of the psalmist (vv. 4, 7). **11:** A common theme in Psalms is that God should preserve the life of the psalmist not because the psalmist is worthy but so that others may see God's power and beneficence and so that the psalmist can offer praise. *For the sake of Your name,* so that the psalmist can praise God, which he cannot do if he dies (see e.g., 6.6). **11:** *You are beneficent,* God's beneficence, "tzedakah," frames the psalm and contrasts with the fact that "no human is in the right" ("yitzdak").

Ps. 144: A royal psalm, perhaps recited on the eve of battle by a king who lived after David and who looks to him and other Judean kings as precedents of kings who were saved from danger by God (v. 10). The psalm is anthological, containing language found in a number of other psalms, esp. 18 and 143. It concludes with a prayer for blessings on the people (vv. 12–15). **1–2:** The king as warrior (18.2–3). God is portrayed in military terms as a strong sheltering

2   my faithful one, my fortress,
           my haven and my deliverer,
           my shield, in whom I take shelter,
           who makes peoples^a subject to me.

3   O Lord, what is man that You should care about
           him,
           mortal man, that You should think of him?
4   Man is like a breath;
           his days are like a passing shadow.
5   O Lord, bend Your sky and come down;
           touch the mountains and they will smoke.
6   Make lightning flash and scatter them;
           shoot Your arrows and rout them.
7   Reach Your hand down from on high;
           rescue me, save me from the mighty waters,
           from the hands of foreigners,
8   whose mouths speak lies,
           and whose oaths^b are false.

9   O God, I will sing You a new song,
           sing a hymn to You with a ten-stringed harp,
10   to You who give victory to kings,
           who rescue His servant David from the deadly
           sword.
11   Rescue me, save me from the hands of
           foreigners,
           whose mouths speak lies,
           and whose oaths^b are false.

12c   For our sons are like saplings,
           well-tended in their youth;
           our daughters are like cornerstones
           trimmed to give shape to a palace.
13   Our storehouses are full,
           supplying produce of all kinds;
           our flocks number thousands,
           even myriads, in our fields;
14   our cattle are well cared for.
       There is no breaching and no sortie,
           and no wailing in our streets.

15   Happy the people who have it so;
           happy the people whose God is the Lord.

---

a So Targum, Saadia; others "my people."
b With Rashi; lit. "right hand."
c The meaning of several phrases in vv. 12–14 is uncertain.

fortress. **3:** See 8.5; Job 7.7, 17. **4–7:** Humans are transient and weak; God is an all-powerful cosmic force (39.6, 7; 109.23). **3:** The language resembles 8.5, but the emphasis is different. Here humans are helpless without God. **7:** *Mighty waters,* of the cosmos. *Foreigners,* the human foes, perhaps the Babylonians (if this is an exilic psalm) or the non-Judeans living in Judah at the time of the return (if the psalm is postexilic). **10:** *David* is paralleled with *kings,* suggesting that *David* represents the Davidic dynasty. **12–14:** The picture is of a well-structured society, youthful and vigorous, with abundance of food and wealth. This is the psalm's wish for the people.

145 A song of praise. Of David.

א I will extol You, my God and king,
   and bless Your name forever and ever.

2 ב Every day will I bless You
   and praise Your name forever and ever.

3 ג Great is the LORD and much acclaimed;
   His greatness cannot be fathomed.

4 ד One generation shall laud Your works to another
   and declare Your mighty acts.

5 ה The glorious majesty of Your splendor
   ᵃand Your wondrous acts⁻ᵃ will I recite.

6 ו Men shall talk of the might of Your awesome deeds,
   and I will recount Your greatness.

7 ז They shall celebrate Your abundant goodness,
   and sing joyously of Your beneficence.

8 ח The LORD is gracious and compassionate,
   slow to anger and abounding in kindness.

9 ט The LORD is good to all,
   and His mercy is upon all His works.

10 י All Your works shall praise You, O LORD,
   and Your faithful ones shall bless You.

11 כ They shall talk of the majesty of Your kingship,
   and speak of Your might,

12 ל to make His mighty acts known among men
   and the majestic glory of His kingship.

13 מ Your kingship is an eternal kingship;
   Your dominion is for all generations.

14 ס The LORD supports all who stumble,
   and makes all who are bent stand straight.

15 ע The eyes of all look to You expectantly,
   and You give them their food when it is due.

16 פ You give it openhandedly,
   feeding every creature to its heart's content.

17 צ The LORD is beneficent in all His ways
   and faithful in all His works.

18 ק The LORD is near to all who call Him,
   to all who call Him with sincerity.

19 ר He fulfills the wishes of those who fear Him;
   He hears their cry and delivers them.

20 ש The LORD watches over all who love Him,
   but all the wicked He will destroy.

21 ת My mouth shall utter the praise of the LORD,
   and all creaturesᵇ shall bless His holy name
      forever and ever.

Pss. 145–150: The Daily Hallel, recited every day in the preliminary morning service.

Ps. 145: An alphabetic acrostic (see Pss. 9–10), with the "nun" (between vv. 13 and 14) omitted (it is supplied, most likely secondarily, in the LXX, the Peshitta, and the Qumran Psalter). The psalm focuses on praise for the kingship of God. This psalm is recited in the three daily prayer services (cf. *b. Ber.* 4b). **1–2:** Eternal blessing of the divine name recurs in v. 21. **3:** See 147.5. **4:** God is known through His acts, and proclaiming them is a form of praise. **5:** See 77.13; 105.2; 119.27. **8:** The creed of Exod. 34.6 (Ps. 86.5). **10:** The things that God has created will offer praise to Him (cf. v. 21 and Ps. 148); or, by their very existence they serve as praise of Him. **14–16:** As the ideal king, God sustains the oppressed and starving (104.27–28; 146.7–8). **18–19:** True prayer is efficacious. **20:** Many psalms end with the destruction of the wicked (cf. 1; 146.9). **21:** An inclusio joins the praise of the first-person speaker (vv. 1–2) with that of *all creatures*, all human beings.

a-a A Qumran Pss. scroll reads: "they will speak of, and Your wonders."
b Lit. "flesh."

146

Hallelujah.
Praise the LORD, O my soul!

2 I will praise the LORD all my life,
sing hymns to my God while I exist.

3 Put not your trust in the great,
in mortal man who cannot save.

4 His breath departs;
he returns to the dust;
on that day his plans come to nothing.

5 Happy is he who has the God of Jacob for his help,
whose hope is in the LORD his God,

6 maker of heaven and earth,
the sea and all that is in them;
who keeps faith forever;

7 who secures justice for those who are wronged,
gives food to the hungry.
The LORD sets prisoners free;

8 The LORD restores sight to the blind;
the LORD makes those who are bent stand
straight;
the LORD loves the righteous;

9 The LORD watches over the stranger;
He gives courage to the orphan and widow,
but makes the path of the wicked tortuous.

10 The LORD shall reign forever,
your God, O Zion, for all generations.
Hallelujah.

147

Hallelujah.
It is good to chant hymns to our God;
it is pleasant to sing glorious praise.

2 The LORD rebuilds Jerusalem;
He gathers in the exiles of Israel.

3 He heals their broken hearts,
and binds up their wounds.

4 He reckoned the number of the stars;
to each He gave its name.

5 Great is our Lord and full of power;
His wisdom is beyond reckoning.

6 The LORD gives courage to the lowly,
and brings the wicked down to the dust.

7 Sing to the LORD a song of praise,
chant a hymn with a lyre to our God,

Ps. 146: Pss. 146–150 form the concluding doxology of the Psalter. Ps. 146 praises God as creator (v. 6) and redeemer (vv. 7–9). Its style is anthological; many of the thoughts and phrases appear elsewhere in the Psalter. **1:** *Praise the LORD, O my soul,* cf. "Bless the LORD, O my soul" (103.1). **3–4:** *Mortal man,* even a prince *(the great),* cannot be relied upon because his life is limited, but God reigns forever (v. 10). **4:** An allusion to the second creation story (Gen. 3.19; Ps. 104.29). **6–8:** God relieves oppression and hunger. **7:** *Sets prisoners free,* as a reference to the exiles, cf. Isa. 49.9. **9:** *Stranger . . . orphan and widow,* those in society who lack human family protectors. See Deut. 24.17; 27.19; Ps. 94.6; Jer. 7.5–6; Zech. 7.10. **10:** The eternal kingship of God. The conclusion recalls and supplements Exod. 15.18. *Zion,* Jerusalem.

Ps. 147: A postexilic psalm in which praise for God the creator alternates with praise for God the redeemer of Israel, who restored the exiles and rebuilt Jerusalem. The restoration is like the creation in that it shows God's great power over the world, and for it God is worthy of praise. Implicit logic leads to the conclusion that, just as God continues to care for the natural world, so He will not cease to care for Israel. **3:** God heals those broken in spirit and in body, that is, the exiles. *Broken hearts,* those who are contrite or penitent (51.19). **4:** That God remembers each and every one of the stars is proof of His power and wisdom (cf. Isa. 40.26). Just as God pays attention to all the stars, so does He attend to all His people.

8 who covers the heavens with clouds,
  provides rain for the earth,
  makes mountains put forth grass;
9 who gives the beasts their food,
  to the raven's brood what they cry for.
10 He does not prize the strength of horses,
  nor value the fleetness[a] of men;
11 but the LORD values those who fear Him,
  those who depend on His faithful care.

12 O Jerusalem, glorify the LORD;
  praise your God, O Zion!
13 For He made the bars of your gates strong,
  and blessed your children within you.
14 He endows your realm with well-being,
  and satisfies you with choice wheat.

15 He sends forth His word to the earth;
  His command runs swiftly.
16 He lays down snow like fleece,
  scatters frost like ashes.
17 He tosses down hail like crumbs—
  who can endure His icy cold?
18 He issues a command—it melts them;
  He breathes—the waters flow.
19 He issued His commands to Jacob,
  His statutes and rules to Israel.
20 He did not do so for any other nation;
  of such rules they know nothing.
  Hallelujah.

148
Hallelujah.
  Praise the LORD from the heavens;
  praise Him on high.
2 Praise Him, all His angels,
  praise Him, all His hosts.
3 Praise Him, sun and moon,
  praise Him, all bright stars.
4 Praise Him, highest heavens,
  and you waters that are above the heavens.
5 Let them praise the name of the LORD,
  for it was He who commanded that they be
    created.
6 He made them endure forever,
  establishing an order that shall never
    change.

a Lit. "thighs."

8–9: God created an ecologically harmonious world in which creatures are cared for (cf. 104.10–16); the psalm stresses God's ongoing care for His creatures. 10–11: Those who survive are not necessarily the swiftest or most powerful, but those who *fear* the LORD (see esp. Prov. 21.31). *Fear* of the LORD, i.e., respect for God that leads to following His ways, is a major principle in wisdom teachings. 12: Jerusalem is personified as a mother praising God (cf. Lam. ch 1 where she is personified as a widow, mourning and lamenting). 13–14: *The bars of your gates*, protection against enemies. God brings to Jerusalem security and prosperity. 15–18: God's commands are always carried out. He creates the ice and hail through His command, and then orders them to melt. The terms *word* and *command* occur four times in these vv. God's *command* to nature in v. 15 becomes *His commands to Jacob, His statutes and rules to Israel* in v. 19. Just as the world is operated by God's command, so Israel should conduct itself by God's commandments, which are a special gift to Israel.

Ps. 148: God is praised for His creation by all that He created, from celestial beings to all the world's rulers and people, including the animate and inanimate (mountains, trees). Praise emanates from the sky and its creations (vv. 1–6) and from the earth (including the sea) and its creations (vv. 7–12), for God's splendor is over earth and sky (v. 13). The psalm echoes part of the story of creation in Gen. ch 1 but includes exotic meteorological phenomena (cf. Job ch 38). 2: The word translated as "angel" is "mal'akh," "messenger." This may refer to the idea that God is surrounded by an entourage of angels or divine beings (8.6; Job 1.6), or that the celestial bodies are God's messengers (cf. 104.4). 4: For *wa-*

7 Praise the LORD, O you who are on earth,
all sea monsters and ocean depths,
8 fire and hail, snow and smoke,
storm wind that executes His command,
9 all mountains and hills,
all fruit trees and cedars,
10 all wild and tamed beasts,
creeping things and winged birds,
11 all kings and peoples of the earth,
all princes of the earth and its judges,
12 youths and maidens alike,
old and young together.
13 Let them praise the name of the LORD,
for His name, His alone, is sublime;
His splendor covers heaven and earth.
14 He has exalted the horn of His people
for the glory of all His faithful ones,
Israel, the people close to Him.
Hallelujah.

149 Hallelujah.
Sing to the LORD a new song,
His praises in the congregation of the faithful.
2 Let Israel rejoice in its maker;
let the children of Zion exult in their king.
3 Let them praise His name in dance;
with timbrel and lyre let them chant His praises.
4 For the LORD delights in His people;
He adorns the lowly with victory.
5 Let the faithful exult in glory;
let them shout for joy upon their couches,
6 with paeans to God in their throats
and two-edged swords in their hands,
7 to impose retribution upon the nations,
punishment upon the peoples,
8 binding their kings with shackles,
their nobles with chains of iron,
9 executing the doom decreed against them.
This is the glory of all His faithful.
Hallelujah.

150 Hallelujah.
Praise God in His sanctuary;

hail and *snow,* cf. Job 38.22–30. For *wind* and *fire* as God's messengers, cf. 104.4. **9:** *Cedars* are the stateliest of trees and were used in the construction of the Temple. **13–14:** These vv. are included in the liturgy for returning the Torah to the Ark since the Torah may be seen as representing God. They proclaim that God alone is sublime and that He raises *the horn,* the power, of His people Israel. God's *name* is His essence. The entire world is to praise God for the victory He has given to His people. Cf. 117.2.

Ps. 149: An exilic or postexilic psalm, depending on whether the event envisioned has already taken place or is yet to come. The event is God's deliverance of His people from exile and their restoration to Judah. The psalm envisions a reversal whereby Israel is the victor and its enemies the vanquished. The threefold repetition of *the faithful* ("ḥasid," vv. 1, 5, 9; see 4.4 n.) emphasizes loyalty to God. **1:** *A new song,* in the eschatological future. Cf. Isa. 42.10; Pss. 96.1; 144.9. **2:** *Their king,* God. Judah is no longer independent and therefore has no human king. **3:** Cf. 150.3–5; Exod. 15.20; 2 Sam. 6.5. **5:** *Upon their couches,* at night in private (Ibn Ezra). Some emend to "their clans." **7:** The idea of retribution against those who harmed Israel is common (Lam. 3.34–66; 4.22). It signifies that God maintains power over the enemy and that His relationship with Israel is still in force. **8:** The treatment received by prisoners of war. The kings who were victorious over Israel are, in turn, defeated and taken captive. **9:** God has already decreed the fate of the enemy.

Ps. 150: Resounding praise for God. The command to *praise,* "hallelu," occurs in every v. This psalm concludes the section and the book of Psalms as a whole, capturing the essence of the book. Instead of closing with a doxological v., the book closes with an entire ch that serves as a doxology. **1:** *His sanctu-*

ters that are above the heavens, cf. Gen. 1.7. **6–7:** A reference to the mythological destruction of the sea-monster (cf. 74.13–14; Isa. 51.9–10), suppressed and neutral-ized, as it is in Gen. 1.21, to which this is an allusion. For *ocean depths,* that is, "creatures of the deep," cf. Isa. 42.10. **6:** For God's setting lim-its to the water, cf. Jer. 5.22. **8:** For

praise Him in the sky, His stronghold.
2   Praise Him for His mighty acts;
          praise Him for[a] His exceeding greatness.
3   Praise Him with blasts of the horn;
          praise Him with harp and lyre.
4   Praise Him with timbrel and dance;
          praise Him with lute and pipe.
5   Praise Him with resounding cymbals;
          praise Him with loud-clashing cymbals.
6   Let all that breathes praise the LORD.
          Hallelujah.

ary, lit. "His holy (place)," which may mean the Temple—where formal or ritual praise took place and where psalms were sung—or, as the following line suggests, the heavens. *The sky, His stronghold,* the site of praise is enlarged to include the whole world. God does not dwell in the Temple; He dwells in the sky (Isa. 66.1), so heaven is His Temple. For similar thought and language see 11.4: "The LORD is in His holy palace; the LORD—His throne is in heaven." *His stronghold,* Heb "ʿuzo" sometimes refers to the Ark (78.61; 105.4; 132.8) or is an attribute of God or His Temple (29.2; 63.3; 96.6). **2:** *His mighty acts,* all the great deeds He did for His people. Praising God for His deeds is not a reward for God but a tribute to His nature. God is known by His deeds. Another way to understand this phrase is "Praise Him 'with' (the recitation of) His mighty acts." The preposition "b-" before *His mighty acts* is the same preposition as before *with harp* (v. 3) and the other musical instruments, and may be construed as the means by which God is to be praised: with words of His deeds and with music. **3–5:** A symphony of praise. Psalms were accompanied by music played on various instruments: stringed, wind, and percussion. **6:** *All that breathes,* all creatures in the world. Universal praise for God is a common theme (e.g., 145.21). Here, it climactically concludes the psalm and the Psalter as a whole.

a Or "as befits."

Proverbs

Setting and Major Themes

THE BOOK OF PROVERBS opens a window to a realm of ancient Israelite experience little seen elsewhere in the Bible: everyday life. Proverbs guides individuals (not the nation) in how to do what is wise in their day-to-day lives. It teaches the attitudes and courses of actions that are right, just, and pious, and the ways of behavior that facilitate and strengthen personal relationships, the forms of communication and commerce that make the life of the community congenial and secure, and the types of prudence and industry that help one achieve financial security.

The English title of the book, Proverbs, is a misnomer, since the book contains more than proverbs. The Hebrew word *mashal*, of which *mishlei*, proverbs, is a form of the plural, can also mean a comparison. The book, however, contains a variety of genres beyond the short proverb and comparison, incorporating a diversity of material that reflects on daily life.

Proverbs is a paean to the power of the human mind. Its authors are convinced that everyone who attends to the wisdom of the past and employs his powers of rational thinking has the ability to know what to do and what to avoid. These powers and the knowledge that goes with them are called wisdom. Wisdom—Heb *ḥokhmah*—is the great virtue that, for Proverbs, entails all others. No divine revelation is necessary, for God gave humanity the faculty of wisdom, and people need only listen to her call (ch 8). Thus, there is a certain tension between Proverbs and Torah books, which insist on the significance of revealed law.

Authorship

THE BOOK OF PROVERBS, HEBREW *mishlei* (for *Mishlei Shlomo*, "Proverbs of Solomon"), is one of three biblical books ascribed to Solomon. According to tradition, he wrote the love lyrics of the Song of Songs when he was young, the wisdom of Proverbs in his midlife, and the disillusioned complaints of Ecclesiastes when he was old (*Song Rab.* §10). Some sections of the book are ascribed to other sages (24.23; 30.1–14; 31.1–9; and probably 22.17—see the note to that verse). In fact, actual Solomonic authorship of any part of the book is doubtful. Neither the language nor the content fits Solomon's time. Proverbs is a collective work, holding the wisdom of mostly anonymous wise men (and women, who could make up sayings as well as men; see 31.1) from many walks of life and different periods.

Wisdom Literature

THE WISDOM TEXTS IN THE BIBLE are Proverbs, Job, and Ecclesiastes, which need to be read within the framework of an international Near Eastern wisdom tradition (see intro. to Kethuvim, pp. 1276–77). Proverbs and the postbiblical book of Sirach belong to the genre of didactic wisdom. They offer instructions and observations directing the reader in the formation of ethical character and in leading a successful and happy life. Ecclesiastes, in spite of its sometimes unorthodox ideas, belongs in this group. Books very similar in character and content were written in Egypt and Mesopotamia, starting in the late third millennium BCE and extending to the Hellenistic period, as late as the third century BCE.

Egyptian wisdom books in particular are close in form and content to Proverbs. Most important is the *Instruction of Amenemope* (probably dating from the 13th or 12th century), which is the source of much of Proverbs 22.17–23.11 (see 22.17–23.11 n.). Foreign wisdom books provide the intellectual context of Proverbs and clarify its ideas and goals. In the annotations, reference will be made primarily to the translations of Egyptian wisdom in Miriam Lichtheim's *Ancient Egyptian Literature (AEL)*, vols. 1–3 (Berkeley: University of California).

Proverbs in Jewish Thought

THE HEBREW WORD *TORAH* MEANS "instruction." In Proverbs, this *torah* is human wisdom, the wise man's teachings. Likewise *ḥokhmah* ("wisdom") is human wisdom. Later Jewish sages would understand *torah* as the Torah of Moses and equate "wisdom" with this Torah. All that is said about "torah" and "wisdom" in Proverbs was understood in this way. For example, Proverbs 8.22 was read to mean that Torah was created before the rest of the world, and 3.17–18, which refer to wisdom, became incorporated in the Torah service in the synagogue.

Proverbs is widely quoted in the midrash and in subsequent homiletic literature, such as medieval sermons. It was a foundational text of the Musar movement, a pietistic movement among European Jews in the 18th to 19th centuries.

Reading Proverbs

THE BOOK IS BEST READ WITH ATTENTION to the different genres it contains. Collection I, chs 1–9, is made up of fifteen relatively long, carefully structured and interrelated poems. Collection VI, chs 30 and 31, holds four relatively long poems. Collection I should be read as a unit, and each of the four poems in Collection VI should be read as a unit. Very different are the four middle collections, in chs 10–29. These are composed of short sayings, mostly of two lines, though there are occasionally epigrams of several lines, such as 24.30–34. There is no overall organization, and few literary units extend beyond the single-verse couplet. Often, however, one saying continues the general theme of the preceding one or repeats its key terms, thus producing proverb strings. Here it does not matter much in what order they are read. One way of reading them is sequentially, with an attempt to grasp the ideas that unite them all. Another valid approach is to dip into them at random, reading a few at a time and thinking about the ones with striking ideas, metaphors, or imagery.

Finally, it should be remembered that Proverbs is an anthology, and the sayings in it should be judged individually. Not all sayings will speak to every reader, but everyone should find many sayings and poems that pack insight and good sense into brief and memorable forms.

Major Units of the Book and Their Titles

I	1.1–9.18	"The proverbs of Solomon son of David, king of Israel" (1.1)
II	10.1–22.16	"The proverbs of Solomon" (10.1)
III	22.17–24.22	"Words of the Sages" (22.17, emended)
IV	24.23–34	"These also are by the sages" (24.23)
V	25.1–29.27	"These too are proverbs of Solomon, which the men of King Hezekiah of Judah copied" (25.1)
VI	30.1–31.31	Appendices
a	30.1–14	"The words of Agur"
b	30.15–33	Numerical epigrams
c	31.1–9	"The words of Lemuel"
d	31.10–31	The Woman of Strength

[MICHAEL V. FOX]

1 The proverbs of Solomon son of David, king of Israel:

2 For learning wisdom and discipline;
   For understanding words of discernment;
3 For acquiring the discipline for success,
   Righteousness, justice, and equity;
4 For endowing the simple with shrewdness,
   The young with knowledge and foresight.

1.1–9.18: Collection I. Though chs 1–9 serve as an introduction to the book, the section was probably written later as a guide to interpreting the old sayings in chs 10–29. After the prologue (1.1–7), there are two distinct series of poems, the ten "Lectures" (I–X) and the five "Interludes" (A–E). The Lectures are formulated as father-to-son instruction, and each develops a single topic in a three-part structure: (1) A Call to Attention, in which the speaker exhorts his son to hear his wisdom and remember it, because thus he will receive great rewards; e.g., 1.8–9. (2) A Lesson, which is the main body of the teaching; e.g., 1.10–18. (3) A Conclusion, which is a statement of the general principle underlying the Lesson; e.g., 1.19. Sometimes the conclusion is missing. Of the five Interludes, C is a collection of four epigrams that stands apart from the rest of the unit, while A, B, D, and E are interpretive additions in praise of wisdom, which portray wisdom as a nearly divine woman who represents a power transcending the individual teachings (see 1.20–33 n.).

1.1–7: The prologue, added at a late stage in the book's growth, explains the use of the book and commends it to readers. **1: The title** ascribes the book to King Solomon, the archetypal wise man. See 1 Kings 3.4–28; 5.10–14. On the historical veracity of this inscription, see intro. **2–6: The statement of purpose** defines the twofold purpose of the book: to inculcate the basic virtues of wisdom

5   —The wise man, hearing them, will gain more
      wisdom;
    The discerning man will learn to be adroit;

6   For understanding proverb and epigram,
    The words of the wise and their riddles.

7   The fear of the LORD is the beginning[a] of
      knowledge;
    Fools despise wisdom and discipline.

8   My son, heed the discipline of your father,
    And do not forsake the instruction of your mother;
9   For they are a graceful wreath upon your head,
    A necklace about your throat.

10   My son, if sinners entice you, do not yield;
11   If they say, "Come with us,
    Let us set an ambush to shed blood,
    Let us lie in wait for the innocent
    (Without cause!)
12   Like Sheol, let us swallow them alive;
    Whole, like those who go down into the Pit.
13   We shall obtain every precious treasure;
    We shall fill our homes with loot.
14   Throw in your lot with us;
    We shall all have a common purse."
15   My son, do not set out with them;
    Keep your feet from their path.
16   For their feet run to evil;
    They hurry to shed blood.
17   In the eyes of every winged creature
    The outspread net means nothing.
18   But they lie in ambush for their own blood;
    They lie in wait for their own lives.
19   Such is the fate of all who pursue unjust gain;
    It takes the life of its possessor.

a Or "best part."

and ethical behavior in the young, and to enable the mature wise man to increase his wisdom and hone his skills in interpreting literary wisdom. In both cases, the assumed audience is male. **7:** *Fear of the* LORD is the ground for wisdom to grow in; it is essentially conscience. In its most basic form, in the untutored child, it is unreflective fear of consequences. As wisdom develops, fear of God becomes a cognitive awareness of what God wants and does, and this type of fear is equivalent to knowledge of the LORD (2.5). Fear of God is effective in keeping one from evil even in secret deeds and even in spheres of behavior where the law does not apply. *Beginning of knowledge:* The commentators debated whether "re'shit" (here translated "beginning") means first in time or first in quality, that is, the best part. The variant of this verse in 9.10 uses a word that definitely means "beginning."

1.8–19: Lecture I: Avoid gangs. In vv. 8–9, the father, who speaks throughout the Lectures in chs 1–9, identifies the instruction he is about to deliver as both his own and his wife's (similarly 6.20), even though the specific words are his. Elsewhere in wisdom literature there is occasional allusion to mothers as teachers. For example, the Egyptian Duachety concludes his instruction with the words, "Praise God for your father and your mother, who set you on the way of life!" (*AEL* 2.191). Also, 31.1–9 is spoken by a woman. **10–14:** *My son,* many scholars understand the "son" to be a student in a school and "father" to be a schoolteacher, but there is no evidence for this. Egyptian instructions are consistently presented as a father's words to his actual son, and the mention of the mother in 1.8; 4.3; 6.20 points to a family context, at least as the fictional setting of wisdom instruction. The texts could secondarily be used in schools, as they were in Egypt. In the following annotations, "pupil" means the youth to whom the teaching is directed, without presumption of a school setting. *Come with us,* the invitation a gang of thugs might use to entice a young man to join them in plotting a murderous mugging. They have grandiose notions of their power. They think that they are as powerful as *Sheol,* the netherworld. They hold out promises of comradeship and a share of the wealth. **15–18:** Even a bird has enough sense to avoid a trap laid out in plain sight, but the criminals are too stupid for that. *They hurry to shed blood,* not realizing that it is *their own.* **19:** Conclusion: Evildoers destroy themselves by means of the evil that they themselves create. Cf. 5.21–23.

1.20–33: Interlude A: Lady Wisdom chastises the foolish. In Interludes A, D, and E, wisdom is described as if she were a woman.

20 Wisdom[a] cries aloud in the streets,
Raises her voice in the squares.
21 At the head of the busy streets she calls;
At the entrance of the gates, in the city, she
speaks out:
22 "How long will you simple ones love
simplicity,
You scoffers be eager to scoff,
You dullards hate knowledge?
23 You are indifferent to my rebuke;
I will now speak my mind to you,
And let you know my thoughts.
24 Since you refused me when I called,
And paid no heed when I extended my
hand,
25 You spurned all my advice,
And would not hear my rebuke,
26 I will laugh at your calamity,
And mock when terror comes upon you,
27 When terror comes like a disaster,
And calamity arrives like a whirlwind,
When trouble and distress come upon you.
28 Then they shall call me but I will not answer;
They shall seek me but not find me.
29 Because they hated knowledge,
And did not choose fear of the Lord;
30 They refused my advice,
And disdained all my rebukes,
31 They shall eat the fruit of their ways,
And have their fill of their own counsels.
32 The tranquillity of the simple will kill them,
And the complacency of dullards will destroy
them.
33 But he who listens to me will dwell in safety,
Untroubled by the terror of misfortune."

2 My son, if you accept my words
And treasure up my commandments;
2 If you make your ear attentive to wisdom
And your mind open to discernment;
3 If you call to understanding
And cry aloud to discernment,
4 If you seek it as you do silver
And search for it as for treasures,
5 Then you will understand the fear of the Lord
And attain knowledge of God.

a In Proverbs, wisdom is personified as a woman.

(In Heb, the word for wisdom, "ḥokhmah," is a feminine abstract noun.) Such personification is briefly suggested in 2.3; 3.13–20; 4.8–9; 7.4. There are various theories to account for the origins of the wisdom personification. Some commentators believe that it derives from a goddess, such as a Canaanite wisdom goddess (though no such deity is known) or the Egyptian Ma'at, goddess of truth and justice, or the Egyptian Isis, goddess of wisdom. Lady Wisdom does bear some similarities to ancient Near Eastern goddesses, but in Proverbs she is a literary figure created as a vivid and memorable way of speaking about human wisdom. **20–21:** Wisdom is by no means secret or esoteric. She is public, frequenting the busiest parts of the town (*the gates* of a city were the location of much public and private business) and calling to all to accept her. Cf. 8.1.

1.22–30: Wisdom castigates fools. They spurned her warning, in other words, ignored the teachings and warnings of their elders. In return, Wisdom will scorn the fools when they most need her, when they find themselves in trouble and are in desperate need of clear and effective thinking. **31–33:** The punishment threatened here, as so often in Proverbs, is the natural consequence of the evil action.

2.1–22: Lecture II: The path to wisdom. The entirety of ch 2 is a single Lecture. The extended Call to Attention (vv. 1–11) says that if you (the pupil) attend to my (the father's) words and seek for wisdom diligently, you will, with God's help, gain true wisdom and piety. The Lesson says that wisdom will protect you from the wicked man (vv. 12–15) and the wicked woman (vv. 16–20). The Conclusion (vv. 21–22) recapitulates the two paths that people must choose between. **5:** *The fear of the Lord* is both the starting point of wisdom (1.7; 9.10) and its goal. The wise man attains a deeper, cognitive conscience, and this is linked to *knowledge of God*. This is

6　For the LORD grants wisdom;
　　Knowledge and discernment are by His
　　　　decree.
7　He reserves ability for the upright
　　And is a shield for those who live blamelessly,
8　Guarding the paths of justice,
　　Protecting the way of those loyal to Him.
9　You will then understand what is right, just,
　　And equitable—every good course.
10　For wisdom will enter your mind
　　And knowledge will delight you.
11　Foresight will protect you,
　　And discernment will guard you.
12　It will save you from the way of evil men,
　　From men who speak duplicity,
13　Who leave the paths of rectitude
　　To follow the ways of darkness,
14　Who rejoice in doing evil
　　And exult in the duplicity of evil men,
15　Men whose paths are crooked
　　And who are devious in their course.
16　It will save you from the forbidden[a] woman,
　　From the alien woman whose talk is smooth,
17　Who forsakes the companion of her youth
　　And disregards the covenant of her God.
18　Her house sinks down to Death,
　　And her course leads to the shades.
19　All who go to her cannot return
　　And find again the paths of life.

20　So follow the way of the good
　　And keep to the paths of the just.
21　For the upright will inhabit the earth,
　　The blameless will remain in it.
22　While the wicked will vanish from the land
　　And the treacherous will be rooted out of it.

a Lit. "strange."

not theological knowledge, but rather a constant awareness of God's will. **6:** God is the ultimate source of the faculty of wisdom, though not the specific words. **12–15:** One grave danger facing a youth is *evil men*. These men are inherently corrupt and crooked. Their values are perverted, so that they do not merely do evil as a means, they positively *rejoice* in it. **16–20:** The second danger is the wicked woman, the sexually predatory female, lit. "the strange woman." Warnings against the "strange woman" appear in 2.16–22; 5.1–23; 6.20–35; 7.1–27, and more briefly in 22.14; 23.27. She is in some ways contrasted with Dame Wisdom and she provides the traits for the personification of Lady Folly in 9.13–18. The "strange woman" has been interpreted in various ways, including: (1) a symbol of folly and wicked counsels; (2) a figure for heresy, in medieval Jewish interpretation, and particularly Christianity; (3) foreign wisdom, such as Greek philosophy; (4) a foreign love goddess (Aphrodite-Ishtar); (5) a devotee of the love goddess; (6) a prostitute; (7) the "Other," the repository or symbol of lust, chaos, and evil; (8) a human adulteress, another man's wife. The last is most likely. **16:** "Strange" (see translators' note *a*) means an outsider, in this case, one who does not belong in the context of a particular marriage. *Alien* has the same meaning. The strange woman in Proverbs is married to another man (see 2.17; 6.26, 29, 34; 7.19; possibly 5.10 as well). The strange woman's allure lies less in her looks (mentioned only in 6.25) than in her words (5.3; 6.24; 7.5, 21; cf. 22.14). Her speech is *smooth*, lit. "slippery"—flattering, tricky, and ingratiating. Ch 7 is an extended demonstration of her verbal powers. **17:** The *covenant of her God* is often understood (esp. by traditional Jewish commentators) as the covenant at Sinai, whose law forbids adultery, but this is unlikely in wisdom contexts. It probably means the covenant of marriage, which is made before God. See Mal. 2.14 and Hos. 2.18–22. **18:** Going to the strange woman's house puts one on the slopes to the underworld; the equation between the foreign woman and death is a common theme of these poems. **21–22:** Many traditional Jewish interpreters understood *earth* ("'eretz") to refer to eternal life, a postbiblical notion. Others explained it as the land of Israel. More likely, *earth* is this world. The righteous will *inhabit* it insofar as they will be blessed with a long life, while the wicked will die prematurely.

3.1–12: Lecture III: The wisdom of piety. The Lesson (vv. 5–12), composed of distinct sayings, teaches humility, faith in God, fulfillment of cultic duties, and submission to divine chastisement. Unusually for Proverbs, it does not insist on the importance of wis-

3 My son, do not forget my teaching,
But let your mind retain my commandments;

2 For they will bestow on you length of days,
Years of life and well-being.

3 Let fidelity and steadfastness not leave you;
Bind them about your throat,
Write them on the tablet of your mind,

4 And you will find favor and approbation
In the eyes of God and man.

5 Trust in the Lord with all your heart,
And do not rely on your own understanding.

6 In all your ways acknowledge Him,
And He will make your paths smooth.

7 Do not be wise in your own eyes;
Fear the Lord and shun evil.

8 It will be a cure for your body,[a]
A tonic for your bones.

9 Honor the Lord with your wealth,
With the best of all your income,

10 And your barns will be filled with grain,
Your vats will burst with new wine.

11 Do not reject the discipline of the Lord, my
son;
Do not abhor His rebuke.

12 For whom the Lord loves, He rebukes,
As a father the son whom he favors.

13 Happy is the man who finds wisdom,
The man who attains understanding.

14 Her value in trade is better than silver,
Her yield, greater than gold.

15 She is more precious than rubies;
All of your goods cannot equal her.

16 In her right hand is length of days,
In her left, riches and honor.

17 Her ways are pleasant ways,
And all her paths, peaceful.

18 She is a tree of life to those who grasp her,
And whoever holds on to her is happy.

19 The Lord founded the earth by wisdom;
He established the heavens by understanding;

20 By His knowledge the depths burst apart,
And the skies distilled dew.

21 My son, do not lose sight of them;
Hold on to resourcefulness and foresight.

dom, nor does it equate wisdom and religious virtues. **3:** Wear the teachings close to your body so that you will always have them with you (1.9; 4.9; 6.21 n.). *Write them on the tablet of your mind* ("heart"), hold them permanently in memory. **9:** *Honor the* Lord by bringing sacrificial donations to the Temple. **11–12:** Sometimes suffering can be interpreted as divine discipline, a warning intended to spare one greater punishments. On the basis of vv. 11–12 and Ps. 94.12, the Talmud develops the concept of "afflictions of love" (*b. Ber.* 8a, etc.).

3.13–20: Interlude B: In praise of wisdom. 14–15: Wisdom is precious beyond price. **16:** In the background of this passage may be the Egyptian practice of depicting gods holding the symbols of their powers and blessings (particularly "life" and "prosperity"). **17–18:** These verses are recited in the Torah service, when the Torah is returned to the Ark. The subject of the sentences is wisdom, which is consistently understood in Jewish interpretation to designate Torah. **18:** The *tree of life* was a widespread ancient Near Eastern mythological symbol, which is especially popular in Mesopotamian palace reliefs. It represented a divine source of well-being and life, sometimes meaning eternal life. In Proverbs, the symbol has lost its mythological connections and is simply a metaphor for a source of life and health. Based on the present verse, the Rabbis identified the *tree of life* with Torah. **19–20:** The highest praise of wisdom is that God Himself possesses it, used it in creating the world, and continues to use it. The welling up of springs and the descent of dew belong to both original creation and ongoing providence.

3.21–35: Lecture IV: The wisdom of honesty. The Lesson, vv. 27–31, comprises five admonitions, all beginning with *do not*. The general theme of the Lecture is the importance of honesty in social relations. **21:** *Them:* "My words" may have

---

a Lit. *"navel."*

22 They will give life to your spirit
And grace to your throat.

23 Then you will go your way safely
And not injure your feet.

24 When you lie down you will be unafraid;
You will lie down and your sleep will be sweet.

25 You will not fear sudden terror
Or the disaster that comes upon the wicked,

26 For the LORD will be your trust;
He will keep your feet from being caught.

27 Do not withhold good from one who deserves it
When you have the power to do it [for him].

28 Do not say to your fellow, "Come back again;
I'll give it to you tomorrow," when you have it
with you.

29 Do not devise harm against your fellow
Who lives trustfully with you.

30 Do not quarrel with a man for no cause,
When he has done you no harm.

31 Do not envy a lawless man,
Or choose any of his ways;

32 For the devious man is an abomination to the
LORD,
But He is intimate with the straightforward.

33 The curse of the LORD is on the house of the
wicked,
But He blesses the abode of the righteous.

34 At scoffers He scoffs,
But to the lowly He shows grace.

35 The wise shall obtain honor,
But dullards get disgrace as their portion.

4 Sons, heed the discipline of a father;
Listen and learn discernment,

2 For I give you good instruction;
Do not forsake my teaching.

3 Once I was a son to my father,
The tender darling of my mother.

4 He instructed me and said to me,
"Let your mind hold on to my words;
Keep my commandments and you will live.

5 Acquire wisdom, acquire discernment;
Do not forget and do not swerve from my
words.

6 Do not forsake her and she will guard you;
Love her and she will protect you.

once stood in the Heb, or perhaps there was once a couplet like 4.20a before this verse. **22:** *Grace to your throat* suggests the necklace metaphor, used in 1.9 and 3.3b. **24:** God will protect you when you sleep (Ps 4.9) and spare you nightmares (such as Job suffered; see Job 7.14). **25:** Cf. 1.27. **28:** When someone comes to claim something rightly his—a loan, for example, or property left in your safekeeping—do not dawdle in restoring it to him. **29:** It is especially unethical to scheme to injure someone who trusts you. **30:** You may not quarrel for no cause. Sometimes, however, a quarrel is justifiable and unavoidable; see 25.9. **31:** Do not envy or imitate a prospering sinner, because his downfall is inevitable. This is the message of Pss. 37 and 73 as well. **32:** *Abomination* refers to something that causes disgust. In Proverbs, it is used particularly with reference to falsity in thought and words. It is most often used with regard to sins which are not easily detected or which are not formally illegal. **33–35:** The Conclusion consists of three aphorisms contrasting the consequences of wisdom and folly.

4.1–9: Lecture V: Loving wisdom, hating evil. 1–4: The speaker recounts how he received instruction from his own father and quotes his teaching (vv. 4bc–9). The message is: get wisdom. **6:** It is not enough to obey wisdom. One must *love* it, just as one must love God (Deut. 6.5, etc.). **7:** The first step in attaining wisdom is to *acquire* (absorb) the teachings of wisdom, to hear and assimilate them, even before one can properly understand and apply them.

7 The beginning[a] of wisdom is—acquire wisdom;
   With all your acquisitions, acquire discernment.
8 Hug her to you and she will exalt you;
   She will bring you honor if you embrace her.
9 She will adorn your head with a graceful wreath;
   Crown you with a glorious diadem."

10 My son, heed and take in my words,
   And you will have many years of life.
11 I instruct you in the way of wisdom;
   I guide you in straight courses.
12 You will walk without breaking stride;
   When you run, you will not stumble.
13 Hold fast to discipline; do not let go;
   Keep it; it is your life.
14 Do not enter on the path of the wicked;
   Do not walk on the way of evil men.
15 Avoid it; do not pass through it;
   Turn away from it; pass it by.
16 For they cannot sleep unless they have done evil;
   Unless they make someone fall they are robbed of
       sleep.
17 They eat the bread of wickedness
   And drink the wine of lawlessness.
18 The path of the righteous is like radiant sunlight,
   Ever brightening until noon.
19 The way of the wicked is all darkness;
   They do not know what will make them
       stumble.

20 My son, listen to my speech;
   Incline your ear to my words.
21 Do not lose sight of them;
   Keep them in your mind.
22 They are life to him who finds them,
   Healing for his whole body.
23 More than all that you guard, guard your mind,
   For it is the source of life.
24 Put crooked speech away from you;
   Keep devious talk far from you.
25 Let your eyes look forward,
   Your gaze be straight ahead.
26 Survey the course you take,
   And all your ways will prosper.
27 Do not swerve to the right or the left;
   Keep your feet from evil.

4.10–19: Lecture VI: The two paths. One who chooses the right course of behavior will naturally find himself going in the right direction and will prosper and be safe. One must avoid the twisted and murky path of the wicked, for the wicked live in turmoil and anxiety. **13:** *Discipline,* Heb "musar," is one way wisdom is conveyed. It generally implies physical chastisement of some sort. Even this kind of teaching must be embraced passionately. **17:** The values of the wicked are twisted. They live on *wickedness* and *lawlessness*; see 2.12–15.

4.20–27: Lecture VII: The straight path. Whereas Lecture VI spoke of the two paths of life, good and evil, this one pictures a single path, which is a person's mode of behavior, for better or worse. One must walk straight, for evil and dangers lurk on either side, and look straight ahead, because temptations beckon all around. In biblical literature, "straight" is a common metaphor for correct behavior.

a Or "best part."

5

My son, listen to my wisdom;
Incline your ear to my insight,

2 That you may have foresight,
While your lips hold fast to knowledge.

3 For the lips of a forbidden[a] woman drip honey;
Her mouth is smoother than oil;

4 But in the end she is as bitter as wormwood,
Sharp as a two-edged sword.

5 Her feet go down to Death;
Her steps take hold of Sheol.

6 She does not chart a path of life;
Her course meanders for lack of knowledge.

7 So now, sons, pay heed to me,
And do not swerve from the words of my mouth.

8 Keep yourself far away from her;
Do not come near the doorway of her house

9 Lest you give up your vigor to others,
Your years to a ruthless one;

10 Lest strangers eat their fill of your strength,
And your toil be for the house of another;

11 And in the end you roar,
When your flesh and body are consumed,

12 And say,
"O how I hated discipline,
And heartily spurned rebuke.

13 I did not pay heed to my teachers,
Or incline my ear to my instructors.

14 Soon I was in dire trouble
Amidst the assembled congregation."

15 Drink water from your own cistern,
Running water from your own well.

16 Your springs will gush forth
In streams in the public squares.

17 They will be yours alone,
Others having no part with you.

18 Let your fountain be blessed;
Find joy in the wife of your youth—

19 A loving doe, a graceful mountain goat.
Let her breasts satisfy you at all times;
Be infatuated with love of her always.

a Lit. "strange."

5.1–23: Lecture VIII: Stick to your own wife. This is the first of three Lectures on the "strange woman" (5.1–23; 6.20–35; 7.1–27). See 2.16–20 n. The adulteress is deadly (vv. 3–6), and every man must keep away from her, or he will pay a severe price (vv. 7–14). Instead, a man should take his sexual pleasures with his own wife (vv. 15–20). God sees everything and sin is inevitably punished (6.21–23). **3–6:** The strange woman's words are sweet and seductive (2.16), but they leave a bitter aftertaste, and her dulcet speech turns out to be deadly. **9–10:** *Vigor* and *strength* may refer to the adulterer's property, which he will waste on the woman, or to his sexual potency (see 31.3), which he will *give up* in the sense that the son he begets will be reckoned as belonging to the cheated husband, who will benefit from the adulterer's "labor." The *ruthless one* is the enraged husband (see vv. 34–35). The *others* may be his family. **11–14:** The fornicator will be forced to publicly confess his folly. V. 11 seems to refer to venereal disease. *The assembled congregation* may be a judicial tribunal, or more likely, the community. Public shaming is a powerful means of social control, especially in Proverbs. **15–19:** This is the only passage in the Bible that explicitly celebrates the pleasures of marital sex. Your wife alone (the father tells his son) is yours, and she is more attractive than anyone else. The author is seeking to dissuade young men from following a fierce and anarchic urge and so depicts the delights of sanctioned sex as no less intense than those of "stolen waters" (9.17). The metaphors in vv. 15–18 speak of a man's wife as his well, a source of refreshment that slakes (sexual) thirst. Compare the "well" and "drinking" metaphors in 7.18; 9.17, and Song of Songs 4.12, 15. V. 16 may be a deliberate riddle. As translated here, it seems to promise a reward—many progeny—for sexual fidelity. **17–18:** Enjoy erotic pleasures with your wife alone. Then her "fountain"—i.e., her womb—will be fruitful (vv. 16–17). **19:** The *doe* connotes grace, tenderness, and affection in the Song of Songs. *Loving* (Heb "'ahavim") has strong sexual connotations. *Breasts* (Heb "dadim") should probably be vocalized "dodim," "lovemaking," as in 7.18, yielding better parallelism with *love*; but there may be a play on the two words. **20:** *Infatuated* (Heb "tishgeh"), lit. "go astray," a negative value judgment. Rather than going astray with a forbidden woman, the

20 Why be infatuated, my son, with a forbidden^a
        woman?
    Why clasp the bosom of an alien woman?
21 For a man's ways are before the eyes of God;
    He surveys his entire course.
22 The wicked man will be trapped in his iniquities;
    He will be caught up in the ropes of his sin.
23 He will die for lack of discipline,
    Infatuated by his great folly.

6   My son, if you have stood surety for your fellow,
    Given your hand for another,^b
2   You have been trapped by the words of your
        mouth,
    Snared by the words of your mouth.
3   Do this, then, my son, to extricate yourself,
    For you have come into the power of your fellow:
    Go grovel—and badger your fellow;
4   Give your eyes no sleep,
    Your pupils no slumber.
5   Save yourself like a deer out of the hand [of a
        hunter],
    Like a bird out of the hand of a fowler.

6   Lazybones, go to the ant;
    Study its ways and learn.
7   Without leaders, officers, or rulers,
8   It lays up its stores during the summer,
    Gathers in its food at the harvest.
9   How long will you lie there, lazybones;
    When will you wake from your sleep?
10 A bit more sleep, a bit more slumber,
    A bit more hugging yourself in bed,
11 And poverty will come ^ccalling upon you,^{-c}
    And want, like a man with a shield.

12 A scoundrel, an evil man
    Lives by crooked speech,
13 Winking his eyes,
    Shuffling his feet,
    Pointing his finger.

a Lit. "strange."   b Or "a stranger."   c-c Meaning of Heb. uncertain.

young man should "lose himself" in his wife's love.

6.1–19: Interlude C: Four Epigrams on folly and evil. This four-part passage does not follow the structure of the Lectures and differs in subject matter. It was probably added later. Epigrams i and ii (vv. 1–5 and 6–11) concern folly, and iii and iv (vv. 12–15 and 16–19) concern evil. Notice the humorous and facetious tone of the first two Epigrams.

6.1–5: Epigram i. Do not go surety for another's loan. If you have done so, do your best to get released from your promise. (20.16 tells what happens to one who gets himself into this mess.) Rather than putting up his own property as collateral, a borrower could have the loan underwritten by someone else, whose possessions would then be liable to seizure. Going surety is always risky, but doing so for a stranger (which one might do for a fee) is tantamount to loss; see 27.13. See also 11.15; 17.18; 22.26–27. The tone and practical main message of this epigram differs significantly from the emphasis on helping the poor found in some Torah texts (e.g., Deut. 15.9).

6.6–11: Epigram ii: Sloth and industry. Cf. 24.30–34. In vv. 6–8, the ant is held up as a model of industry and self-motivation. (Cf. 30.25.) In vv. 9–11, the lazy man is rebuked in humorous tones. **11:** Better, "and penury will come upon you like a vagabond, and poverty like a man of arms." In this vivid trope, a poor man is used as a metaphor for poverty. We should picture the vagabond not as an indigent begging for alms, but as a potentially dangerous armed wanderer.

6.12–15: Epigram iii: The good-for-nothing. The scoundrel's speech is crooked and dishonest. He betrays his nature by certain body gestures. The enumeration of the outward signs of villainy implies a warning to avoid people thus marked. The passage draws together phrases and ideas from 16.27–30, 24.22b, and 29.1b. **13:** *Winking* (more precisely, squinting) the eye was considered a symptom of secretive, hostile thoughts; see Ps 35.19. *Shuffling* the feet was probably considered symptomatic of an unquiet soul. *Pointing his finger* seems to be a sign of derision (Isa. 58.9).

14 Duplicity is in his heart;
    He plots evil all the time;
    He incites quarrels.
15 Therefore calamity will come upon him without
        warning;
    Suddenly he will be broken beyond repair.

16 Six things the LORD hates;
    Seven are an abomination to Him:
17 A haughty bearing,
    A lying tongue,
    Hands that shed innocent blood,
18 A mind that hatches evil plots,
    Feet quick to run to evil,
19 A false witness testifying lies,
    And one who incites brothers to quarrel.

20 My son, keep your father's commandment;
    Do not forsake your mother's teaching.
21 Tie them over your heart always;
    Bind them around your throat.
22 When you walk it will lead you;
    When you lie down it will watch over you;
    And when you are awake it will talk with you.
23 For the commandment is a lamp,
    The teaching is a light,
    And the way to life is the rebuke that disciplines.
24 It will keep you from an evil woman,
    From the smooth tongue of a forbidden^a woman.
25 Do not lust for her beauty
    Or let her captivate you with her eyes.
26 The last loaf of bread will go for a harlot;
    A married woman will snare a person of honor.
27 Can a man rake embers into his bosom
    Without burning his clothes?
28 Can a man walk on live coals
    Without scorching his feet?
29 It is the same with one who sleeps with his
        fellow's wife;
    None who touches her will go unpunished.
30 A thief is not held in contempt
    For stealing to appease his hunger;
31 Yet if caught he must pay sevenfold;
    He must give up all he owns.
32 He who commits adultery is devoid of sense;
    Only one who would destroy himself does such a
        thing.

a Lit. "alien."

6.16–19: Epigram iv: What God loathes. Seven abominable things are described. Like Epigram iii, Epigram iv makes the incitement of quarrels the ultimate offense. The use of ascending numbers ("six and seven" or "three and four") for listing items serves a didactic and rhetorical purpose. See 30.15–31 n. and Amos 1.3, 6, 9, 11, 13; 2.1, 4, 6.

6.20–35: Lecture IX: Adultery kills. Even though an adulterer might think that his is the most secretive of sins, he cannot evade punishment. The speaker argues the point in a logical fashion, using analogies to other kinds of self-inflicted harm. The message is blunt and memorable: Keep away from another man's wife or he'll kill you. **20:** *Mother,* see 1.8–19 n. **21:** *Bind* the teachings (figuratively) like a pendant on a cord about your neck, so that they will rest over your heart. These are metaphors for keeping a valuable object close to oneself always, and they stress the beauty and worth of the teachings. Cf. 3.3; Exod. 28.29; and Song 8.6. Possibly the pendant originally was a protective amulet. **22–23:** The relationship between these two verses is clearer when they are read in reverse order. **23:** The *commandment* ("mitzvah") and the *teaching* ("torah") are here the parental teachings, or perhaps wisdom teachings generally. In the traditional Jewish reading, they are God's commandments and his Torah. **24:** The *forbidden woman's* first means of seduction is speech; see 2.16; 5.3–6. **25–33:** The punishment for adultery is inherent in the crime. It comes naturally, without any direct intervention by God or a court. **26:** Better, "For a harlot costs but a loaf of bread, but a married woman hunts for a precious life." Harlotry costs money (29.3); adultery kills. **27–29:** As surely as burning coals will scorch the clothes of the man who holds them or the feet of one who walks on them, so too will the man who fools with the fire of adultery inevitably suffer his punishment.

33 He will meet with disease and disgrace;
His reproach will never be expunged.

34 The fury of the husband will be passionate;
He will show no pity on his day of vengeance.

35 He will not have regard for any ransom;
He will refuse your bribe, however great.

7 My son, heed my words;
And store up my commandments with you.

2 Keep my commandments and live,
My teaching, as the apple of your eye.

3 Bind them on your fingers;
Write them on the tablet of your mind.

4 Say to Wisdom, "You are my sister,"
And call Understanding a kinswoman.

5 She will guard you from a forbidden[a] woman;
From an alien woman whose talk is smooth.

6 From the window of my house,
Through my lattice, I looked out

7 And saw among the simple,
Noticed among the youths,
A lad devoid of sense.

8 He was crossing the street near her corner,
Walking toward her house

9 In the dusk of evening,
In the dark hours of night.

10 A woman comes toward him
b-Dressed like a harlot, with set purpose.-b

11 She is bustling and restive;
She is never at home.

12 Now in the street, now in the square,
She lurks at every corner.

13 She lays hold of him and kisses him;
Brazenly she says to him,

14 "I had to make a sacrifice of well-being;
Today I fulfilled my vows.

a Lit. "strange."
b-b Meaning of Heb. uncertain.

30–33: If even he who steals out of necessity, and therefore deserves some public sympathy, is forced to pay heavy penalties when caught, how much more will an adulterer, who lacks any excuse for his crime, be severely punished. Unlike the thief, he will not be able to buy his way out of trouble (v. 35).

"Sevenfold" in the present verse may be a way of saying "greatly," though some LXX manuscript readings at 2 Sam. 12.6 suggest that sevenfold compensation for theft was known in ancient Israel. The maximum compensation stipulated in the Torah is fivefold, for an animal that is stolen and killed

(Exod. 21.37). The adulterer will suffer "wounds" (not *disease*), namely those inflicted on him by the enraged husband. No such punishment by the husband is known in Torah legislation. **34–35: The conclusion.** Sometimes, the payment of *ransom*—monetary gifts and compensation—can appease the wronged party (21.14; Exod. 21.30), but not in the case of adultery.

7.1–27: Lecture X: Beware the seductress. On the *forbidden* or "strange" woman, see 2.16–20 n. In this lecture, the speaker tells how he once witnessed a woman approaching a young man in the dark street and luring him to her house for a night of sex. Her words were silky, brazen, and lewd, and the dupe followed after her like an animal going to slaughter. **3:** These are metaphors for memory, though traditionally Jews have given the reminders concrete form in the practice of tefilin. **4:** *My sister*, some commentators say that "sister" is a term of (erotic) affection, as in the Song of Songs. But "sister" and "kinswoman" may just connote intimacy. **6:** *Window . . . lattice:* The window was enclosed with a lattice or trelliswork, through which one could peer without being seen. **10:** *Dressed like a harlot:* Harlots may have worn a heavy veil (Gen. 38.14). The strange woman is dressed as if she were a harlot, perhaps to conceal her identity, but she does not offer herself for money. *With set purpose,* better, "with hidden intent," lit. "with guarded heart." **11–13:** Rather like the scoundrel with his nervous gesticulations (6.13), this woman is afflicted by a constant disquiet. She *lurks* or "lies in ambush" at *every corner,* like a beast of prey—or the muggers in 1.11. Then she pounces. **14:** The woman explains why she has meat available for a fine meal. Meat was very costly and was eaten mostly on special occasions, as when bringing a sacrifice to the Temple (most of the meat would be kept by the worshipper, the rest given to the

15 Therefore I have come out to you,
Seeking you, and have found you.

16 I have decked my couch with covers
Of dyed Egyptian linen;

17 I have sprinkled my bed
With myrrh, aloes, and cinnamon.

18 Let us drink our fill of love till morning;
Let us delight in amorous embrace.

19 For the man of the house is away;
He is off on a distant journey.

20 He took his bag of money with him
And will return only at mid-month."

21 She sways him with her eloquence,
Turns him aside with her smooth talk.

22 Thoughtlessly he follows her,
Like an ox going to the slaughter,
ª·Like a fool to the stocks for punishment·ª—

23 Until the arrow pierces his liver.
He is like a bird rushing into a trap,
Not knowing his life is at stake.

24 Now, sons, listen to me;
Pay attention to my words;

25 Let your mind not wander down her ways;
Do not stray onto her paths.

26 For many are those she has struck dead,
And numerous are her victims.

27 Her house is a highway to Sheol
Leading down to Death's inner chambers.

8 It is Wisdom calling,
Understanding raising her voice.

2 She takes her stand at the topmost heights,
By the wayside, at the crossroads,

3 Near the gates at the city entrance;
At the entryways, she shouts,

4 "O men, I call to you;
My cry is to all mankind.

5 O simple ones, learn shrewdness;
O dullards, instruct your minds.

6 Listen, for I speak noble things;
Uprightness comes from my lips;

7 My mouth utters truth;
Wickedness is abhorrent to my lips.

8 All my words are just,
None of them perverse or crooked;

priest) or when repaying vows.
15: This seems to be a parodic reversal of the woman in the Song of Songs (3.1–4), who goes forth at night in search of her beloved, finds him, and embraces him.
16–18: These verses share much language with the Song of Songs (see esp. 4.14). In them, the sexual innuendo becomes clear, then explicit. **19–20:** She reassures the boy that her husband is away. Since the scene takes place in the deep darkness, when the moon has waned (v. 9), the full moon (*mid-month*) is two weeks off. **22–23:** The teacher does not have to witness the results. He knows what this must be: death. **22:** By a minor emendation the end of the verse reads, "like a stag bounding to bonds." **23:** This verse makes better sense if we place the third line at the beginning of the verse. Its sexual imagery is transparent. **24–27:** The speaker warns all young men (*sons*) to avoid the path to the strange woman's house, for it is really the way to death.

8.1–36: Interlude D: Wisdom's self-praise. Whereas the strange woman of ch 7 is to be shunned, (personified) wisdom is to be pursued and embraced. The structure of this well-designed chapter is as follows: I. Introduction: the setting and call (1–3); II. Call to Attention (4–11); III. Wisdom's present state (12–21); IV. Wisdom's past (22–31); V. Call to Attention renewed (32–36). Wisdom is personified as a woman of nearly divine stature; see 1.20–33 n. There may be subtle erotic connotations (e.g., vv. 17, 35) that suggest the power of Wisdom's attractiveness. Wisdom calls to human beings, praises herself, promises rewards to her devotees, and tells mankind to listen to her, that is to say, to the wisdom in this book and wherever it may be found. **1–5:** Wisdom calls for attention. In naturalistic terms, this is the voice of reason, heard in wisdom teachings and in the individual mind. Wisdom calls to people in the most prominent public places, including the city gates, where many of the city's

a-a Meaning of Heb. uncertain.

9 All are straightforward to the intelligent man,
  And right to those who have attained knowledge.
10 Accept my discipline rather than silver,
  Knowledge rather than choice gold.
11 For wisdom is better than rubies;
  No goods can equal her.

12 "I, Wisdom, live with Prudence;
  I attain knowledge and foresight.
13 To fear the LORD is to hate evil;
  I hate pride, arrogance, the evil way,
  And duplicity in speech.
14 Mine are counsel and resourcefulness;
  I am understanding; courage is mine.
15 Through me kings reign
  And rulers decree just laws;
16 Through me princes rule,
  Great men and all the ᵃ·righteous judges.·ᵃ
17 Those who love me I love,
  And those who seek me will find me.
18 Riches and honor belong to me,
  Enduring wealth and success.
19 My fruit is better than gold, fine gold,
  And my produce better than choice silver.
20 I walk on the way of righteousness,
  On the paths of justice.
21 I endow those who love me with substance;
  I will fill their treasuries.

22 "The LORD created me at the beginning of His
    course
  As the first of His works of old.
23 In the distant past I was fashioned,
  At the beginning, at the origin of earth.
24 There was still no deep when I was brought forth,
  No springs rich in water;
25 Before [the foundation of] the mountains were
    sunk,
  Before the hills I was born.
26 He had not yet made earth and fields,
  Or the world's first clumps of clay.

a-a *According to some Heb. mss. and printed editions, "judges of the earth."*

commercial and legal transactions take place. Wisdom is international, offering her teachings to *all mankind*. She is even available to the simple and dullards, if they would just listen to her. **6–9:** Just as the father in the Lectures extols the wisdom he is teaching, so does Lady Wisdom praise her own teachings. **10–11:** Cf. 3.14–15 and 16.16. **12–14:** *Prudence . . . knowledge and foresight*, better, "cunning

. . . knowledge of shrewdness." The virtues in question are practical savvy and good sense. These useful faculties come with wisdom, as do *resourcefulness* and *courage*. **15–16:** Insofar as rulers govern justly, they do so through wisdom. **17:** To gain wisdom, one must *love* it, eagerly desiring to grasp its message. Without this love, even superficial learning is unlikely, and knowledge cannot be translated into action. Later, this was interpreted as love of Torah study, a principle inculcated in the postexilic Ps 119. **18–21:** Wisdom promises material rewards, but she also emphasizes that she is superior to gold and silver (as in 3.14–15) and that she bestows wealth only in honest ways. **22–26:** Wisdom recounts her creation and her presence during the creation of the world. She was the very first of God's creations. An important Jewish interpretation, starting with *Gen. Rab.* 1.2, 5 and found in the Rashi to Gen 1.1, uses Prov. ch 8 to argue that the Torah (identified with wisdom) was created before the world and was used by God in creating it. **22:** *Created me:* Since ancient times, interpreters have disputed whether the verb "kanah" means "created" or "acquired." The latter allows for the possibility that wisdom existed from eternity and was coeval with God. Some Christian groups preferred this, since they identified wisdom with the Logos, which was in turn identified with the Christ. It is, however, clear from v. 23 that wisdom is a created being. In fact, "kanah" refers to acquisition by any means, including creation, as here. **24:** According to Gen. 1.2, the *deep* (the primordial sea) existed before creation began. Wisdom insists that she preceded in existence even this most primordial of entities. *I was brought forth:* This word is usually used of birth. The background metaphor of divine parenthood is reinforced by v. 30. **25:** The mountains were thought to rest on foundations or on pillars set (miraculously, see Job 38.6) in the abyss or the underworld.

27 I was there when He set the heavens into place;
   When He fixed the horizon upon the deep;

28 When He made the heavens above firm,
   And the fountains of the deep gushed forth;

29 When He assigned the sea its limits,
   So that its waters never transgress His command;
   When He fixed the foundations of the earth,

30 I was with Him as a confidant,
   A source of delight every day,
   Rejoicing before Him at all times,

31 Rejoicing in His inhabited world,
   Finding delight with mankind.

32 Now, sons, listen to me;
   Happy are they who keep my ways.

33 Heed discipline and become wise;
   Do not spurn it.

34 Happy is the man who listens to me,
   Coming early to my gates each day,
   Waiting outside my doors.

35 For he who finds me finds life
   And obtains favor from the LORD.

36 But he who misses me destroys himself;
   All who hate me love death."

9 Wisdom has built her house,
   She has hewn her seven pillars.

2 She has prepared the feast,
   Mixed the wine,
   And also set the table.

3 She has sent out her maids to announce
   On the heights of the town,

His ward, like a child He was caring for. This fits the context best. Nowhere does the chapter imply that Lady Wisdom helped God create the earth. On the contrary, vv. 30–31 emphasize that she played while God worked. Wisdom's playing before God represents the "play" of the wise, which is study. Cf. Ps. 119.92. **31:** Just as God gets pleasure from wisdom, so does she delight in humankind. **32–36:** Having established her unparalleled credentials, Lady Wisdom speaks as a mature lady and addresses her "sons." Fortunate is he who obeys wisdom and eagerly goes to her house, which is any place where wisdom is taught. **35–36:** The vital importance of loving wisdom. The finding of wisdom recalls the finding of a beloved woman; cf. 18.22. V. 36 states the principle that the evildoer is harmed by the evil he creates; cf. 1.19. Those who hate wisdom are not just stupid, they are depraved. Their values are twisted. They may not realize it, but the things they love are really deadly.

9.1–18: Interlude E: Two banquets. This poem elaborates the motif of Wisdom's invitation to her house (8.34) into a figure of two contrary invitations: Lady Wisdom's (vv. 1–6, 11) and Lady Folly's (vv. 13–18). Life offers two "feasts": one is rich yet prudent, the other is enticing but poisonous. Vv. 7–10 and v. 12 do not fit in either vignette and are probably later insertions. It is best to first read the chapter without them, then to consider them separately. **1–6, 11:** Lady Wisdom builds a house (v. 1), prepares a feast (v. 2), and issues an open invitation (vv. 3–5). She then explains the meaning of her invitation (v. 6) and reinforces her exhortation (v. 11). **1:** Some consider wisdom's *house* to be a mythological allusion, but this identification is uncertain. *Seven* connotes completeness or expansiveness. **2–3:** Like a noble woman, Wisdom prepares a rich banquet and sends out her maids to invite guests.

27–31: Wisdom declares that she was present when God produced the inhabited world. **27:** The *horizon* is pictured as a circle engraved at the join of heaven and earth, as appears to be the case when one is at sea. **28:** *Heavens*, actually, "clouds." The paradox of God "firming up" the clouds (so that they stay in the sky) heightens the miraculousness of His deed. **29:** In several creation traditions found outside of Genesis, the sea is ever trying to break forth and flood the earth, but God set its boundary (Ps 104.9), namely the beach (Jer. 5.22), which may also be imagined as a barred door (Job 38.8, 10). These mythological conceptions have Ca-

naanite antecedents. **30:** This is one of the most disputed verses in the Bible and has weighty theological implications. The word translated *confidant* is "ʾamon." There are three basic ways of interpreting this word: (1) "Artisan" (which is elsewhere "ʾoman"). This translation implies that wisdom aided God in creation. In a similar vein, a midrash likens wisdom (equated with Torah) to a tool God used in creation, as an architect looks at a blueprint when constructing a palace (*Gen. Rab.* 1.2). (2) "Constant(ly), faithful(ly)"; "confidant." (3) "Ward" or "nursling" (or as a verb, "growing up"). Wisdom was with God as

4   "Let the simple enter here";
     To those devoid of sense she says,
5   "Come, eat my food
     And drink the wine that I have mixed;
6   Give up simpleness and live,
     Walk in the way of understanding."

7   To correct a scoffer,
     ᵃOr rebuke a wicked man for his blemish,
     Is to call down abuse on oneself.ᵃ
8   Do not rebuke a scoffer, for he will hate you;
     Reprove a wise man, and he will love you.
9   Instruct a wise man, and he will grow wiser;
     Teach a righteous man, and he will gain in
          learning.
10   The beginning of wisdom is fear of the LORD,
     And knowledge of the Holy One is understanding.
11   For through me your days will increase,
     And years be added to your life.
12   If you are wise, you are wise for yourself;
     If you are a scoffer, you bear it alone.
13   The stupid woman bustles about;
     She is simple and knows nothing.
14   She sits in the doorway of her house,
     Or on a chair at the heights of the town,
15   Calling to all the wayfarers
     Who go about their own affairs,
16   "Let the simple enter here";
     And to those devoid of sense she says,
17   "Stolen waters are sweet,
     And bread eaten furtively is tasty."
18   He does not know that the shades are there,
     That her guests are in the depths of Sheol.

10   The proverbs of Solomon:

     A wise son brings joy to his father;
     A dull son is his mother's sorrow.

a-a Clauses transposed for clarity.

4–6: Wisdom is the sustenance of the soul. (Cf. Deut. 8.3.) Wisdom's wine is *mixed*, probably with fragrant spices. **7–10:** Someone has inserted these verses in a cautionary reaction to Wisdom's invitation to the simple. The insert says that there are some people who are constitutionally unable to learn wisdom. Wisdom requires the right attitude, namely the fear of God. See 1.7. **11:** The continuation of v. 6. **12:** This seems to be an addition identifying the recipient of wisdom's benefits. Wisdom profits its holder while impudence and arrogance hurt their possessor alone. **13–18:** Lady Folly's "feast." **13:** The *stupid woman*, lit. "woman of folly." In this chapter, where the

"woman of folly" is contrasted with personified Lady Wisdom, the "woman of folly" is best understood as a personification as well. *Bustles about* is better translated "is boisterous" (cf. her human counterpart, 7.11a), for unlike Lady Wisdom, Folly does not put effort into the feast. She just sits at her door or in a public place calling out to passers-by. The underlying picture may reflect the deportment of a prostitute. **16:** Folly mimics Wisdom's call, but to opposite effect. **17:** Lady Folly is telling the truth. The wise recognize in her invitation an unintended warning to beware of her. The foolish hear it as an inducement to enjoy the forbidden, titillating sweets of illegitimate pleasures. Waters can allude to sexual pleasures, as in 5.15–20, but the statement applies to other pleasures as well. **18:** The nitwits who take Folly's bait are blithely unaware that they are about to enter the domain of death, the netherworld, where the *shades* (ghosts) reside. Like the previous two units, death of the fool ends the passage, effecting closure (7.26–27; 7.36).

10.1–22.16: Collection II. This collection holds mostly antithetical poetic couplets, in which the second line restates basically the same idea in reversed terms (e.g., *wise son . . . joy* is echoed by *dull son . . . sorrow*). Although they are mostly similar stylistically, they reflect a wide variety of situations and attitudes. They differ from many popular proverbs embedded in other biblical books, which do not have the same poetic structure (e.g., 1 Sam. 24.14, "Wicked deeds come from wicked men"). The proverbs in 10.1–15.33 typically contrast two character types: the wise and the foolish, or the righteous and the wicked. These pairs should not be identified, as they typically are in postbiblical literature; the wise are versed in applying secular wisdom, while being righteous is a religious value. As a whole, the proverbs create a paradigm of the wise and the righteous person, on

2 Ill-gotten wealth is of no avail,
  But righteousness saves from death.
3 The LORD will not let the righteous go hungry,
  But He denies the wicked what they crave.
4 Negligent hands cause poverty,
  But diligent hands enrich.
5 He who lays in stores during the summer is a
    capable son,
  But he who sleeps during the harvest is an
    incompetent.
6 Blessings light upon the head of the righteous,
  But lawlessness covers the mouth of the wicked.
7 The name of the righteous is invoked in blessing,
  But the fame of the wicked rots.
8 He whose heart is wise accepts commands,
  But he whose speech is foolish comes to grief.
9 He who lives blamelessly lives safely,
  But he who walks a crooked path will be found
    out.
10 He who winks his eye causes sorrow;
   He whose speech is foolish comes to grief.
11 The mouth of the righteous is a fountain of life,
   But lawlessness covers the mouth of the wicked.
12 Hatred stirs up strife,
   But love covers up all faults.
13 Wisdom is to be found on the lips of the intelligent,
   But a rod is ready for the back of the senseless.
14 The wise store up knowledge;
   The mouth of the fool is an imminent ruin.
15 The wealth of a rich man is his fortress;
   The poverty of the poor is his ruin.
16 The labor of the righteous man makes for life;
   The produce of the wicked man makes for want.
17 He who follows discipline shows the way to life,
   But he who ignores reproof leads astray.
18 He who conceals hatred has lying lips,
   While he who speaks forth slander is a dullard.
19 Where there is much talking, there is no lack of
     transgressing,
   But he who curbs his tongue^a shows sense.
20 The tongue of a righteous man is choice silver,
   But the mind of the wicked is of little worth.
21 The lips of the righteous sustain many,
   But fools die for lack of sense.
22 It is the blessing of the LORD that enriches,
   And no toil can increase it.

a Lit. "lips."

which the pupil (and reader) can model his own actions. Like proverbs in any language, the proverbs that follow are extremely terse and dense, and often ambiguous, and their full meaning cannot be explicated in translation.

10.1–12.15: Contrasts between the wise and the foolish, the upright and the wicked. Several proverbs speak about a son's merits or faults in terms of the effect they have on his parents. The same message is addressed to the son in 27.11a. Cf. 15.20; 17.21, 25; 19.13; 23.24–25; 28.7. **10.2:** The _ill-gotten wealth_ or "treasures of wickedness" are riches gained by wicked means. _Saves from death_ does not suggest immortality but rather (as comparison with 11.4 shows) protection in the day of general disaster. In such circumstances, wealth will not help. **3:** This proverb is not a statement of fact but a declaration of faith in a principle: Eventually people will receive the material rewards due them. Cf. Ps. 37.25. **4:** The Sages believed that negligence causes poverty and diligence brings wealth. They did not, however, interpret poverty as a sign of negligence or wealth as a sign of diligence, since these conditions can have other causes as well. **5:** The word translated _incompetent_ means, more precisely, "disappointing [one]" or "disgraceful [one]." This proverb is concerned with the effects of diligence and laziness on one's parents. Cf. 10.1. **6:** As translated here, the second line means that the evildoer's own lawlessness, which he covers up, destroys him. **7:** For examples of these two fates, see Gen. 48.20; Jer. 29.22. **9:** _Lives,_ lit. "walks." There are two ways of walking through life: straight and honestly, or crookedly and deviously. **10:** See 6.13 and 16.30. **12:** Love can and should cover up others' offenses against oneself, but not one's own offenses. **13:** The _rod_ here is probably the intelligent man's verbal rebukes. **15:** This is a blunt observation of social realities (contrast v. 2). But by stating the misery of the desti-

23 As mischief is sport for the dullard,
So is wisdom for the man of understanding.

24 What the wicked man plots overtakes him;
What the righteous desire is granted.

25 When the storm passes the wicked man is gone,
But the righteous is an everlasting foundation.

26 Like vinegar to the teeth,
Like smoke to the eyes,
Is a lazy man to those who send him on a
mission.

27 The fear of the LORD prolongs life,
While the years of the wicked will be shortened.

28 The righteous can look forward to joy,
But the hope of the wicked is doomed.

29 The way of the LORD is a stronghold for the
blameless,
But a ruin for evildoers.

30 The righteous will never be shaken;
The wicked will not inhabit the earth.

31 The mouth of the righteous produces wisdom,
But the treacherous tongue shall be cut off.

32 The lips of the righteous know what is pleasing;
The mouth of the wicked [knows] duplicity.

11 False scales are an abomination to the LORD;
An honest[a] weight pleases Him.

2 When arrogance appears, disgrace follows,
But wisdom is with those who are unassuming.

3 The integrity of the upright guides them;
The deviousness of the treacherous leads them to
ruin.

4 Wealth is of no avail on the day of wrath,
But righteousness saves from death.

5 The righteousness of the blameless man smooths
his way,
But the wicked man is felled by his wickedness.

6 The righteousness of the upright saves them,
But the treacherous are trapped by their malice.

7 At death the hopes of a wicked man are doomed,
And the ambition of evil men comes to nothing.

8 The righteous man is rescued from trouble
And the wicked man takes his place.

9 The impious man destroys his neighbor through
speech,
But through their knowledge the righteous are
rescued.

tute the observation teaches a moral lesson, stated explicitly elsewhere: the need of the poor for special protection. Cf. 14.20–21, 31; 19.17; 22.22–23; 23.10–11; 28.27. **18–21:** Wise speech and foolish speech. **22:** This proverb reminds a person to give credit for his successes to God, not to his own talents. It also teaches that, although diligence and energetic work are prized, excessive straining for wealth is useless. **23:** The fool enjoys causing trouble. The sensible man gets his pleasure from wisdom. Wisdom is a source of delight to God Himself (8.30). **24:** Cf. 1.27. **26:** Messengers—meaning anyone who is sent out on a task for someone else—were crucial in the ancient world. Communication at a distance, including business and diplomatic dealings, required sending messengers on one's behalf. See also 13.17; 22.21; 25.13; 26.6. **28:** Cf. 10.24. **29:** God's *way*—His characteristic behavior—has a two-pronged effect, protecting the innocent and ruining evildoers (cf. Hos. 14.10). **30:** See 2.21–22. **11.1:** By nicking off a bit of the balance stone when measuring grain, a merchant could inflate the payment he was receiving, and by using a heavier stone when measuring the silver, he could make the payment seem less than it was really worth. The stability of commerce depends on reliable weights. God demands them (20.10). In fact, He is the source of the standards of weights and measures (16.11). Cf. Lev. 19.36; Deut. 25.15; Amos 8.5; Mic. 6.11; Amenemope §§16, 17 (*AEL* 2.156–57). **2:** Cf. 13.10; 16.6, 18; 29.23. **4:** Cf. 10.2 and Ezek. 7.19a. **7:** *Ambition of evil men,* rather, "expectation of (procreative) strength." The threat implied in this proverb, then, is the loss of family continuity and the sort of permanence this was thought to provide. **8:** This returns to the theme of vv. 4–6. The traditional Jewish commentators often adduce Haman (Esth. 7.10; 9.24–25) as a satisfying instance of this doctrine.

a Lit. "whole."

10 When the righteous prosper the city exults;
    When the wicked perish there are shouts of joy.

11 A city is built up by the blessing of the upright,
    But it is torn down by the speech of the wicked.

12 He who speaks contemptuously of his fellowman
        is devoid of sense;
    A prudent man keeps his peace.

13 A base fellow gives away secrets,
    But a trustworthy soul keeps a confidence.

14 For want of strategy an army falls,
    But victory comes with much planning.

15 Harm awaits him who stands surety for another;[a]
    He who spurns pledging shall be secure.

16 A graceful woman obtains honor;
    Ruthless men obtain wealth.

17 A kindly man benefits himself;
    A cruel man makes trouble for himself.

18 The wicked man earns illusory wages,
    But he who sows righteousness has a true
        reward.

19 Righteousness is a prop of life,
    But to pursue evil leads to death.

20 Men of crooked mind are an abomination to the
        Lord,
    But those whose way is blameless please Him.

21 Assuredly,[b] the evil man will not escape,
    But the offspring of the righteous will be safe.

22 Like a gold ring in the snout of a pig
    Is a beautiful woman bereft of sense.

23 What the righteous desire can only be good;
    What the wicked hope for [stirs] wrath.

24 One man gives generously and ends with more;
    Another stints on doing the right thing and incurs
        a loss.

25 A generous person enjoys prosperity;
    He who satisfies others shall himself be sated.

26 He who withholds grain earns the curses of the
        people,
    But blessings are on the head of the one who
        dispenses it.

27 He who earnestly seeks what is good pursues
        what is pleasing;
    He who is bent on evil, upon him it shall come.

28 He who trusts in his wealth shall fall,
    But the righteous shall flourish like foliage.

10–12: The effect people have on their fellow citizens, particularly by their speech. **14:** Cf. 20.18. These appreciative assessments of the value of advisers and planners must come from one of their number. **15:** See 6.1–5 n.; 20.16 n. **16:** We should probably emend *ruthless* ("ʿaritzim") to "diligent" ("ḥarutzim"), following the ancient Greek translation. **20:** See 3.32. **22:** Like an elegant ornament, beauty—fine in itself—becomes ludicrous when attached to a foolish woman. This may be applied to anything which is externally attractive but intrinsically of low value. **24:** Literally: "There is one who scatters yet gets more, and one who saves out of honesty yet ends up in need." The point of this paradox is that we should not admire the rich or despise the poor, because sometimes deeds and efforts do not produce the expected reward. The NJPS translation reflects a traditional moralizing interpretation, which understood the first line to refer to a man who gives charity *(Midr. Prov.)*. **26:** One who withholds grain in time of famine (as Joseph did, Gen. 47.13–26) in order to keep its price high will be despised by his countrymen. **27:** A summary of vv. 24a, 25–26. **28:** Cf. 10.2 and 11.4.

a Or "a stranger."
b Lit. "Hand to hand"; meaning of Heb. uncertain.

29   He who makes trouble for his household shall
          inherit the wind;
      A fool is a slave to the wise-hearted.

30   The fruit of the righteous is a tree of life;
      A wise man captivates people.

31   If the righteous on earth get their deserts,
      How much more the wicked man and the
          sinner.

12 He who loves discipline loves knowledge;
      He who spurns reproof is a brutish man.

2   A good man earns the favor of the LORD,
      A man of intrigues, His condemnation.

3   A man cannot be established in wickedness,
      But the root of the righteous will not be shaken
          loose.

4   A capable wife is a crown for her husband,
      But an incompetent one is like rot in his bones.

5   The purposes of the righteous are justice,
      The schemes of the wicked are deceit.

6   The words of the wicked are a deadly ambush,
      But the speech of the upright saves them.

7   Overturn the wicked and they are gone,
      But the house of the righteous will endure.

8   A man is commended according to his
          intelligence;
      A twisted mind is held up to contempt.

9   Better to be lightly esteemed and have a servant
      Than to put on airs and have no food.

10   A righteous man knows the needs of his beast,
      But the compassion of the wicked is cruelty.

11   He who tills his land shall have food in plenty,
      But he who pursues vanities is devoid of sense.

12   ªThe wicked covet the catch of evil men;
      The root of the righteous yields [fruit].ª

13   Sinful speech is a trap for the evil man,
      But the righteous escapes from trouble.

14   A man gets his fill of good from the fruit of his
          speech;
      One is repaid in kind for one's deeds.

15   The way of a fool is right in his own eyes;
      But the wise man accepts advice.

16   A fool's vexation is known at once,
      But a clever man conceals his humiliation.

17   He who testifies faithfully tells the truth,
      But a false witness, deceit.

29: A trouble-making son will inherit nothing. The family slave will do better than him; cf. 17.2. **12.1:** Sometimes even the wise require reproof, but they, unlike the fools, know enough to appreciate it. **4:** The capable woman is praised at length in 31.10–31. **6:** The scenario in 1.8–19 illustrates this verse. **7:** When disaster strikes, the wicked are the first to disappear; cf. 10.25a. **9:** In some circumstances, material debasement is worse than lack of prestige. **10:** The Bible shows concern for animals. See also Exod. 22.29; 23.19; 34.26; Lev. 22.27, 28; Deut. 14.21; 22.6; 25.4. **11:** Cf. 28.19. **15:** It is wise to take counsel (v. 15b). The fool is too smug to do so (v. 15a).

12.16–23: Proverbs on speech, advocating restraint, honesty, and gentleness.

a-a Meaning of Heb. uncertain.

18 There is blunt talk like sword-thrusts,
  But the speech of the wise is healing.
19 Truthful speech abides forever,
  A lying tongue for but a moment.
20 Deceit is in the minds of those who plot evil;
  For those who plan good there is joy.
21 No harm befalls the righteous,
  But the wicked have their fill of misfortune.
22 Lying speech is an abomination to the LORD,
  But those who act faithfully please Him.
23 A clever man conceals what he knows,
  But the mind of a dullard cries out folly.
24 The hand of the diligent wields authority;
  The negligent are held in subjection.
25 If there is anxiety in a man's mind let him quash it,
  And turn it into joy with a good word.
26 A righteous man a-gives his friend direction,-a
  But the way of the wicked leads astray.
27 A negligent man never has game to roast;
  a-A diligent man has precious wealth.-a
28 The road of righteousness leads to life;
  By way of its path there is no death.

13 A wise son—it is through the discipline of his
  father;
  A scoffer—he never heard reproof.
2 A man enjoys good from the fruit of his speech;
  But out of the throat of the treacherous comes
  lawlessness.
3 He who guards his tongue[b] preserves his life;
  He who opens wide his lips, it is his ruin.
4 A lazy man craves, but has nothing;
  The diligent shall feast on rich fare.
5 A righteous man hates lies;
  The wicked man is vile and disgraceful.
6 Righteousness protects him whose way is
  blameless;
  Wickedness subverts the sinner.
7 One man pretends to be rich and has nothing;
  Another professes to be poor and has much
  wealth.
8 Riches are ransom for a man's life,
  The poor never heard a reproof.
9 The light of the righteous is radiant;
  The lamp of the wicked is extinguished.

18: Though truth, even when critical, is essential (v. 22), it should be cushioned by being expressed in gentle terms (15.1). **21:** An assertion about how things usually work, not an absolute statement.

12.24–16.9: More contrasts.
12.24: Cf. 17.2. **25–26:** Obscure. **27:** The deceitful man may cheat and "hunt" others, but he will get no benefit from his gains. **28:** The second line was traditionally understood as affirming immortality. But the Heb is obscure, and even if this translation is correct, it could imply the avoidance of a premature death. **13.2–3:** *Speech*, lit. "mouth." *Throat*, Heb "nefesh," also means "person" or "emotion." Cf. 12.14a and 18.20a. **7:** This insight into human character derides phonies and indirectly warns the reader to avoid pretensions. **8:** Contrary to 11.4, people sometimes can save themselves by money. A "ransom" is money paid to get out of trouble. V. 8b is puzzling. **9:** *Light* or *lamp* are metaphors for life itself but also for the quality of life; cf. Job 18.5–6. Darkness is misery.

a-a Meaning of Heb. uncertain.
b Lit. "mouth."

10   *Arrogance yields nothing but strife;* *
      Wisdom belongs to those who seek advice.
11   Wealth may dwindle to less than nothing,
      But he who gathers little by little increases it.
12   Hope deferred sickens the heart,
      But desire realized is a tree of life.
13   He who disdains a precept will be injured thereby;
      He who respects a command will be rewarded.
14   The instruction of a wise man is a fountain of life,
      Enabling one to avoid deadly snares.
15   Good sense wins favor;
      The way of treacherous men is unchanging.*
16   Every clever man acts knowledgeably,
      But a dullard exposes his stupidity.
17   Harm befalls a wicked messenger;
      A faithful courier brings healing.
18   Poverty and humiliation are for him who spurns
            discipline;
      But he who takes reproof to heart gets honor.
19   Desire realized is sweet to the soul;
      To turn away from evil is abhorrent to the stupid.
20   He who keeps company with the wise becomes
            wise,
      But he who consorts with dullards comes to
            grief.
21   Misfortune pursues sinners,
      But the righteous are well rewarded.
22   A good man has what to bequeath to his
            grandchildren,
      For the wealth of sinners is stored up for the
            righteous.
23   The tillage of the poor yields much food;
      But substance is swept away for lack of
            moderation.
24   He who spares the rod hates his son,
      But he who loves him disciplines him early.
25   The righteous man eats to his heart's content,
      But the belly of the wicked is empty.

14   The wisest of women builds her house,
      But folly tears it down with its own hands.
2   He who maintains his integrity fears the LORD;
      A man of devious ways scorns Him.
3   In the mouth of a fool is a rod of haughtiness,
      But the lips of the wise protect them.
4   If there are no oxen the crib is clean,

11: It is a mistake to try to get rich too quickly; see 10.22; 20.21; 28.20, 22. **12:** The tree of life represents a source of health and vitality (see 3.18). **13–14:** *Precept* (lit. "word") and *command* refer to the teachings of the wise. These save lives by steering people away from deadly temptations. **17:** See 10.26 n. **23:** *Moderation,* rather, "justice" (Heb "mishpat"). A poor man's plot of land can supply his needs, but this is lost when injustice is rife. **24:** A paradox: a harshness inspired by love, a leniency motivated by hatred. A lax parent is treating his son as if he hated him. See also 23.13–14; 29.17. **25:** Cf. 10.3; 13.2, 4, 12, 19. Corporal punishment was common in the pre-modern world. **14.1:** *Folly,* a foolish woman. **3:** The speech of *the wise* can protect them against the pain caused by haughty, arrogant words. Cf. 12.6. **4:** *Clean,* that is, empty of produce. It is a good idea to invest in farming "equipment."

a-a Meaning of Heb. uncertain.   b Or "harsh."

But a rich harvest comes through the strength of
    the ox.

5 An honest witness will not lie;
    A false witness testifies lies.

6 A scoffer seeks wisdom in vain,
    But knowledge comes easily to the intelligent
    man.

7 Keep your distance from a dullard,
    For you will not learn wise speech.

8 It is the wisdom of a clever man to understand his
    course;
    But the stupidity of the dullard is delusion.

9 Reparations mediate between fools,
    Between the upright, good will.

10 The heart alone knows its bitterness,
    And no outsider can share in its joy.

11 The house of the wicked will be demolished,
    But the tent of the upright will flourish.

12 A road may seem right to a man,
    But in the end it is a road to death.

13 The heart may ache even in laughter,
    And joy may end in grief.

14 An unprincipled man reaps the fruits of his ways;
    ᵃ-A good man, of his deeds.-ᵃ

15 A simple person believes anything;
    A clever man ponders his course.

16 A wise man is diffident and shuns evil,
    But a dullard rushes in confidently.

17 An impatient man commits folly;
    A man of intrigues will be hated.

18 Folly is the lot of the simple,
    But clever men ᵇ-glory in knowledge.-ᵇ

19 Evil men are brought low before the good,
    So are the wicked at the gates of the righteous.

20 A pauper is despised even by his peers,
    But a rich man has many friends.

21 He who despises his fellow is wrong;
    He who shows pity for the lowly is happy.

22 Surely those who plan evil go astray,
    While those who plan good earn steadfast love.

23 From all toil there is some gain,
    But idle chatter is pure loss.

24 The ornament of the wise is their wealth;
    The stupidity of dullards is stupidity.

25 A truthful witness saves lives;
    He who testifies lies [spreads] deceit.

6: A scoffer might desire wisdom in the sense of learning or cunning, but he does not have the ability to acquire it. Only one with the right mind-set can do so. **9:** Better: "Fools scorn a guilt offering, but the upright find acceptance." Fools lack the humility to admit their guilt and to bring an offering to expiate it. **10:** No one can truly understand what another is feeling. This is restated in v. 13a. **16–17:** Exercise caution and avoid impulsiveness; similarly v. 29. **20–21:** V. 21 seems to respond to the rather cynical observation of v. 20.

a-a Taking ʿal as from ʾll; cf. Hos. 12.3.   b-b Meaning of Heb. uncertain.

26 Fear of the Lord is a stronghold,
   A refuge for a man's children.
27 Fear of the Lord is a fountain of life,
   Enabling one to avoid deadly snares.
28 A numerous people is the glory of a king;
   Without a nation a ruler is ruined.
29 Patience results in much understanding;
   Impatience gets folly as its portion.
30 A calm disposition gives bodily health;
   Passion is rot to the bones.
31 He who withholds what is due to the poor affronts
       his Maker;
   He who shows pity for the needy honors Him.
32 The wicked man is felled by his own evil;
   The righteous man finds security in his death.
33 Wisdom rests quietly in the mind of a prudent man,
   But among dullards it makes itself known.
34 Righteousness exalts a nation;
   Sin is a reproach to any people.
35 The king favors a capable servant;
   He rages at an incompetent one.

15 A gentle response allays wrath;
   A harsh word provokes anger.
2 The tongue of the wise produces much
       knowledge,
   But the mouth of dullards pours out folly.
3 The eyes of the Lord are everywhere,
   Observing the bad and the good.
4 A healing tongue is a tree of life,
   But a devious one makes for a broken spirit.
5 A fool spurns the discipline of his father,
   But one who heeds reproof becomes clever.
6 In the house of the righteous there is much
       treasure,
   But in the harvest of the wicked there is trouble.
7 The lips of the wise disseminate knowledge;
   Not so the minds of dullards.
8 The sacrifice of the wicked is an abomination to
       the Lord,
   But the prayer of the upright pleases Him.
9 The way of the wicked is an abomination to the
       Lord,
   But He loves him who pursues righteousness.
10 Discipline seems bad to him who forsakes the way;
   He who spurns reproof will die.
11 Sheol and Abaddon lie exposed to the Lord,
   How much more the minds of men!

26: A man's righteousness benefits his children as well; cf. 20.6. **27:** For a contrasting notion, see 13.14, "The instruction of a wise man *is a fountain of life, enabling one to avoid deadly snares.*" The difference between these two proverbs highlights the way that the book has ultimately combined largely secular ("the instruction of a wise man") and religious notions ("Fear of the Lord"). **30:** *Passion*, rather, "jealousy." **31:** The poor too are God's handiwork (22.2). As such they are worthy of respect, and mistreating them is an affront to their creator. **32:** In the second line, we should probably read "be-tumo," "in his innocence," for "be-moto," *in his death.* **33:** The wise man's wisdom is evident even when he is in a crowd of fools. **15.3:** This verse attributes "geographical omniscience" to God, namely that He sees everything everywhere, but does not suggest that God is omniscient in the sense that He knows the future. **4:** *A healing tongue,* see 15.1. *Tree of life,* see 3.18. A *devious* tongue disheartens others. Dishonesty is depressing. **5:** The humility to accept chastisement is crucial to learning. See 1.7; 5.12; 6.23; 8.33. **6:** The righteous get rich. The wicked too might get rich, but their prosperity will be tainted by strife and worry; see 10.24. **8:** Sacrifices and prayers must be accompanied by ethical behavior; see, e.g., 21.3; 1 Sam. 15.22b; Isa. 1.10–17; 29.12; Amos 5.21–25; Mic. 6.6–8. **11:** God sees everything, even hidden thoughts; see v. 3. *Abaddon,* lit. "place of destruction," a term found only in wisdom literature (e.g., Job 26.6; 31.12; Ps. 88.12 [translated "place of perdition"]); see also 27.20. Synonymous with Sheol, it is the realm of the dead.

12 The scoffer dislikes being reproved;
   He will not resort to the wise.

13 A joyful heart makes a cheerful face;
   A sad heart makes a despondent mood.

14 The mind of a prudent man seeks knowledge;
   The mouth of the dullard pursues folly.

15 All the days of a poor man are wretched,
   But contentment is a feast without end.

16 Better a little with fear of the LORD
   Than great wealth with confusion.

17 Better a meal of vegetables where there is love
   Than a fattened ox where there is hate.

18 A hot-tempered man provokes a quarrel;
   A patient man calms strife.

19 The way of a lazy man is like a hedge of thorns,
   But the path of the upright is paved.

20 A wise son makes his father happy;
   A fool of a man humiliates his mother.

21 Folly is joy to one devoid of sense;
   A prudent man walks a straight path.

22 Plans are foiled for want of counsel,
   But they succeed through many advisers.

23 A ready response is a joy to a man,
   And how good is a word rightly timed!

24 For an intelligent man the path of life leads upward,
   In order to avoid Sheol below.

25 The LORD will tear down the house of the proud,
   But He will establish the homestead of the widow.

26 Evil thoughts are an abomination to the LORD,
   But pleasant words are pure.

27 He who pursues ill-gotten gain makes trouble for
      his household;
   He who spurns gifts will live long.

28 The heart[a] of the righteous man rehearses his
      answer,
   But the mouth of the wicked blurts out evil things.

29 The LORD is far from the wicked,
   But He hears the prayer of the righteous.

30 What brightens the eye gladdens the heart;
   Good news puts fat on the bones.

31 He whose ear heeds the discipline of life
   Lodges among the wise.

32 He who spurns discipline hates himself;
   He who heeds reproof gains understanding.

33 The fear of the LORD is the discipline of wisdom;
   Humility precedes honor.

a For *leb* as a source of speech, see note to Eccl. 5.1.

13: One's emotions are visible on his face and in his demeanor (*mood*, lit. "spirit"). 15: To be sure, the days of a poor man are (objectively) wretched—that is a fact of life—but if he has inner happiness, he enjoys, as it were, an unending feast. This is confirmed by the next verse. 16–17: This pair of sayings probably derives from the Egyptian sage Amenemope, who said, "Better is poverty in the hand of the god than wealth in the storehouse. Better is bread with a happy heart than wealth with vexation" (§6; *AEL* 2.152). 20: See 10.1. 21: The perverse values of the fool; see 9.7–8. 22: This saying shows an appreciation of collective, cooperative wisdom; see 24.6. 23: *A word rightly timed* (lit. "a word in its time"), which meets the needs of the particular situation, is satisfying to both speaker and listener. 24: See 2.18–19; 7.27; 15.19. 25: *Homestead*, lit. "boundary." God will protect the widow's property from encroachments by the greedy. At the same time, it is forbidden to attempt such encroachments (22.28; 23.10). A widow without grown sons had a precarious legal status in ancient Israel because only adult males had independent access to the courts. 30: *What brightens the eye*, lit. "brightness of eye," an event or report that makes one happy. *Fat* or "moist" bones were identified with health. 31–33: The importance of being receptive to correction; see 3.11–12.

16.1: Though one may plan what he wants to say, God determines what will actually come out; cf. v. 9. These verses highlight divine omnipotence rather than divine omniscience. 2: *Motives*, lit. "hearts," that is, thoughts. One may smugly imagine that all his deeds are pure (14.12), but God sees deeper. Cf. 21.2; 1 Sam. 16.7. 3: Once one has done his work and applied his wisdom to his practical affairs, he should leave the outcome to God and trust that the results will be appropriate. 4: We would expect a proverb to say that God made the *evil day* (that is, a time of troubles) for the

16

A man may arrange his thoughts,
But what he says depends on the LORD.

2 All the ways of a man seem right to him,
But the LORD probes motives.

3 Entrust your affairs to the LORD,
And your plans will succeed.

4 The LORD made everything for a purpose,
Even the wicked for an evil day.

5 Every haughty person is an abomination to the
LORD;
Assuredly,[a] he will not go unpunished.

6 Iniquity is expiated by loyalty and faithfulness,
And evil is avoided through fear of the LORD.

7 When the LORD is pleased with a man's conduct,
He may turn even his enemies into allies.

8 Better a little with righteousness
Than a large income with injustice.

9 A man may plot out his course,
But it is the LORD who directs his steps.

10 There is magic on the lips of the king;
He cannot err in judgment.

11 Honest scales and balances are the LORD's;
All the weights in the bag are His work.

12 Wicked deeds are an abomination to kings,
For the throne is established by righteousness.

13 Truthful speech wins the favor of kings;
They love those who speak honestly.

14 The king's wrath is a messenger of death,
But a wise man can appease it.

15 The king's smile means life;
His favor is like a rain cloud in spring.

16 How much better to acquire wisdom than gold;
To acquire understanding is preferable to silver.

17 The highway of the upright avoids evil;
He who would preserve his life watches his
way.

18 Pride goes before ruin,
Arrogance, before failure.

19 Better to be humble and among the lowly
Than to share spoils with the proud.

20 He who is adept in a matter will attain success;
Happy is he who trusts in the LORD.

21 The wise-hearted is called discerning;
One whose speech is pleasing gains wisdom.

purpose of punishing the wicked. This verse turns things around and says that God made the evil man so that the *evil day* will have someone to punish. **7:** God protects a righteous man by encompassing him in a sphere of peace. **8:** Cf. 15.16. **9:** Whatever a man's plans, it is God who determines the outcome. See v. 1.

16.10–15: The king's powers and responsibilities. Sayings that declare the king's powers and righteousness hold a mirror up to the monarch and set forth an ideal for him to emulate. On the king's power, see 19.12; 20.2; 24.21. On his righteousness, see 20.8, 26, 28; 22.11; 29.4, 14. Though Proverbs holds kings and rulers in highest esteem, it does not assume that they are inevitably righteous (see 28.15). The concern with royal matters is a very significant theme in some Egyptian wisdom books, which often focus on training royal officials, but it is highlighted less in Proverbs. **10b:** Rather: "No one can defy his command." **11:** See 11.1. **12:** This proverb seems meant for the attention of a king or prince. **14–15:** These proverbs speak to someone, such as a royal scribe, who might find himself close enough to the king to dread his wrath or benefit from his favor. Cf. Eccl. 8.1–5; 10.4.

16.16–17.28: Further maxims.
16.16: See 8.10. **17–20:** Pride versus trust in God. **18:** *Goes before* means "precedes." An arrogant overconfidence in one's abilities to control his fate prepares the way for disaster. **21–24:** Wise and gracious behavior is also effective. **21:** *Gains wisdom,* or "increases learning," i.e., teaches others effectively.

---

a Lit. "Hand to hand"; meaning of Heb. uncertain.

22 Good sense is a fountain of life to those who have
    it,
And folly is the punishment of fools.

23 The mind of the wise man makes his speech
    effective
And increases the wisdom on his lips.

24 Pleasant words are like a honeycomb,
Sweet to the palate and a cure for the body.

25 A road may seem right to a man,
But in the end it is a road to death.

26 The appetite of a laborer labors for him,
Because his hunger[a] [b-]forces him on.[-b]

27 A scoundrel plots[c] evil;
What is on his lips is like a scorching fire.

28 A shifty man stirs up strife,
And a querulous one alienates his friend.

29 A lawless man misleads his friend,
Making him take the wrong way.

30 He closes his eyes while meditating deception;
He purses his lips while deciding upon evil.

31 Gray hair is a crown of glory;
It is attained by the way of righteousness.

32 Better to be forbearing than mighty,
To have self-control than to conquer a city.

33 Lots are cast into the lap;
The decision depends on the LORD.

17 Better a dry crust with peace
Than a house full of feasting with strife.

2 A capable servant will dominate an incompetent
    son
And share the inheritance with the brothers.

3 For silver—the crucible;
For gold—the furnace,
And the LORD tests the mind.

4 An evildoer listens to mischievous talk;
A liar gives ear to malicious words.

5 He who mocks the poor affronts his Maker;
He who rejoices over another's misfortune will not
    go unpunished.

6 Grandchildren are the crown of their elders,
And the glory of children is their parents.

7 Lofty words are not fitting for a villain;
Much less lying words for a great man.

25: People can be deluded about the quality of their own behavior. See 16.2. **26:** *Hunger,* lit. "mouth." Cf. Eccl. 6.7. **27–30:** Three types of evildoers and their harmful speech. **27:** The word translated *plots* is "koreh," lit. "digs," or "mines." The metaphor is of a smelting furnace, which is hot and dangerous. **29–30:** Compare the body language of the scoundrel in 6.13. His intentions are supposedly readable in his facial expression. **31:** Righteousness is supposed to be the path to a long life. Hence old age is an indicator of virtue, though not an absolute one. **33:** The casting of lots was a widespread means of divination in the ancient world. In one form, names, or "yes" and "no," would be written on stones, which were shaken till one fell out. This was thought to indicate what God wanted. Some suggest that the priestly Urim and Thummim (see Exod. 28.30) were lots, and the answering of yes-no questions by God in texts like Judg. 20.28 likely reflects the casting of lots. **17.1:** *A house full of feasting with strife,* lit. "a house full of sacrifices of strife." When people took an animal to the Temple as a sacrifice, they brought most of the meat back home for feasting. Better a crust of bread than a luxurious banquet at which there is quarreling. See 15.16–17 n. **2:** *Servant* is more precisely rendered "slave," since such a person was owned by his master or at least indentured to him. A capable slave could rise to a position of responsibility in a large household, in spite of his legal inferiority. **3:** A furnace *tests* or assays and purifies ore by heating it until the pure silver or gold melts and rises, where it can be separated from the heavier dross. The analogy, then, implies more than God's just looking into the heart. It implies a painful test to prove the purity of the sufferer's faithfulness. Prov. 3.12 expresses a similar idea. **4:** Liars and slanderers not only speak lies and slanders, they like to hear them. **5:** See 14.31 n. **6:** One generation can take pride in another. **7:** *Lofty:* better, "exces-

---

a Lit. "mouth."   b-b Meaning of Heb. uncertain.   c Meaning of Heb. uncertain.

8   A bribe seems like a charm to him who uses it;
He succeeds at every turn.

9   He who seeks love overlooks faults,
But he who harps on a matter alienates his
friend.

10   A rebuke works on an intelligent man
More than one hundred blows on a fool.

11   An evil man seeks only to rebel;
A ruthless messenger will be sent against him.

12   Sooner meet a bereaved she-bear
Than a fool with his nonsense.

13   Evil will never depart from the house
Of him who repays good with evil.

14   To start a quarrel is to open a sluice;
Before a dispute ᵃflares up,ᵃ drop it.

15   To acquit the guilty and convict the innocent—
Both are an abomination to the LORD.

16   What good is money in the hand of a fool
To purchase wisdom, when he has no mind?

17   A friend is devoted at all times;
A brother is born to share adversity.

18   Devoid of sense is he who gives his hand
To stand surety for his fellow.

19   He who loves transgression loves strife;
He who builds a high threshold invites broken
bones.

20   Man of crooked mind comes to no good,
And he who speaks duplicity falls into trouble.

21   One begets a dullard to one's own grief;
The father of a villain has no joy.

22   A joyful heart makes for ᵇgood health;ᵇ
Despondency dries up the bones.

23   The wicked man draws a bribe out of his bosom
To pervert the course of justice.

24   Wisdom lies before the intelligent man;
The eyes of the dullard range to the ends of the
earth.

25   A stupid son is vexation for his father
And a heartache for the woman who bore him.

26   To punish the innocent is surely not right,
Or to flog the great for their uprightness.

27   A knowledgeable man is sparing with his words;
A man of understanding is reticent.

28   Even a fool, if he keeps silent, is deemed wise;
Intelligent, if he seals his lips.

sive." **8:** This seems to praise bribes, but it probably describes a course of behavior that seems valuable but is really destructive (14.12; 16.2). **9:** That is, faults or offenses of others toward oneself. **10:** This proverb counterbalances the preceding by reminding us of the importance of a rebuke. See 19.11. **11:** The "ruthless messenger" may be an angel, called "messenger" ("malʾakh") in Heb. **12:** Fools are not only a nuisance, they are dangerous. **16:** The fool might think he can buy wisdom—whose prestige and practical advantages he might covet—but he lacks the wits (or the attitude) to receive it. **18:** On the dangers of guaranteeing another's loan, see 6.1–5 n. **19:** Perhaps building a tall portal (not "threshold") to one's house is a metaphor for displaying arrogance. **21:** See 10.1 n. **22:** See 15.30. **23:** The Heb probably refers to the wicked man's taking a *bribe*. What is condemned is not gift giving (see 18.16) but its misuse. **24:** Wisdom is near at hand, and the intelligent person sees it. The dullard, in contrast, looks for wisdom (which he might value in the form of practical cleverness) everywhere except right in front of him. **25:** See 10.1. **26:** The second line is better translated: "Or to strike the noble man for his honesty," i.e., for speaking frankly. "Noble" can refer to a generous character. **27–28:** The value of reserve in speech. *Reticent,* actually, "cool of spirit." The wise man (in Egyptian wisdom too) is "cool," retaining his repose and controlling his mouth even under provocation.

a-a *Meaning of Heb. uncertain.*
b-b *Or "a cheerful face"; meaning of Heb. uncertain.*

18

¹ ªHe who isolates himself pursues his desires;
He disdains all competence.⁻ª

² The fool does not desire understanding,
But only to air his thoughts.

³ Comes the wicked man comes derision,
And with the rogue, contempt.

⁴ The words a man speaks are deep waters,
A flowing stream, a fountain of wisdom.

⁵ It is not right to be partial to the guilty
And subvert the innocent in judgment.

⁶ The words of a fool lead to strife;
His speech invites blows.

⁷ The fool's speech is his ruin;
His words are a trap for him.

⁸ The words of a querulous man are bruising;ᵇ
They penetrate one's inmost parts.

⁹ One who is slack in his work
Is a brother to a vandal.

¹⁰ The name of the LORD is a tower of strength
To which the righteous man runs and is safe.

¹¹ The wealth of a rich man is his fortress;
ªIn his fancy⁻ª it is a protective wall.

¹² Before ruin a man's heart is proud;
Humility goes before honor.

¹³ To answer a man before hearing him out
Is foolish and disgraceful.

¹⁴ A man's spirit can sustain him through illness;
But low spirits—who can bear them?

¹⁵ The mind of an intelligent man acquires
knowledge;
The ears of the wise seek out knowledge.

¹⁶ A man's gift eases his way
And gives him access to the great.

¹⁷ The first to plead his case seems right
Till the other party examines him.

¹⁸ The lot puts an end to strife
And separates those locked in dispute.

¹⁹ A brother offended is more formidable than a
stronghold;
Such strife is like the bars of a fortress.

²⁰ A man's belly is filled by the fruit of his mouth;
He will be filled by the produce of his lips.

²¹ Death and life are in the power of the tongue;
Those who love it will eat its fruit.

²² He who finds a wife has found happiness
And has won the favor of the LORD.

18.1–8: Maxims on speech and its potentials. 1: Obscure. **4:** Human speech has the potential to be a deep fount of wisdom. **5–8:** The fool's speech incites strife and thus harms both himself and others.

18.9–22.16: Further maxims. 18.9: An idler causes damage not only to himself but also to those who work with him and depend on his contribution to the enterprise. **10–11:** The juxtaposition of these two antithetical proverbs may contrast real (v. 10) and delusive (v. 11) fortresses. **12:** Pride leads to destructive overconfidence, whereas humility precedes and opens the way to wisdom and prudence. **14:** One's frame of mind has powerful psychosomatic effects. **15:** One who is truly wise continues to seek for knowledge beyond what he already has. **16:** This proverb just gives practical advice. While bribes to subvert justice are condemned (17.23; Deut. 10.17; 16.19), other sorts of gifts and payments (to gain access to an official, for example) are acceptable (Prov. 18.16; 21.14). **17:** A cautionary message to judges and officials: do not jump to conclusions, but wait until all the facts are before you. **18:** See 16.33 n. **20–21:** One bears the effects of his own words. **22:** Marriage is a blessing. There may be exceptions (e.g., 19.13; 21.9, 19), but this is the rule.

---

a-a *Meaning of Heb. uncertain.*   b *Meaning of Heb. uncertain.*

23 The poor man speaks beseechingly;
   The rich man's answer is harsh.
24 There are companions to keep one company,
   And there is a friend more devoted than a
        brother.

19 Better a poor man who lives blamelessly
   Than one who speaks perversely and is a
        dullard.
2 A person without knowledge is surely not good;
   He who moves hurriedly blunders.
3 A man's folly subverts his way,
   And his heart rages against the LORD.
4 Wealth makes many friends,
   But a poor man loses his last friend.
5 A false witness will not go unpunished;
   He who testifies lies will not escape.
6 Many court the favor of a great man,
   And all are the friends of a dispenser of gifts.
7 All the brothers of a poor man despise him;
   How much more is he shunned by his friends!
   ᵃ⁻He who pursues words—they are of no avail.⁻ᵃ
8 He who acquires wisdom is his own best friend;
   He preserves understanding and attains
        happiness.
9 A false witness will not go unpunished;
   He who testifies falsely is doomed.
10 Luxury is not fitting for a dullard,
   Much less that a servant rule over princes.
11 A man shows intelligence by his forebearance;
   It is his glory when he overlooks an offense.
12 The rage of a king is like the roar of a lion;
   His favor is like dew upon the grass.
13 A stupid son is a calamity to his father;
   The nagging of a wife is like the endless dripping
        of water.
14 Property and riches are bequeathed by fathers,
   But an efficient wife comes from the LORD.
15 Laziness induces sleep,
   And a negligent person will go hungry.
16 He who has regard for his life pays regard to
        commandments;
   He who is heedless of his ways will die.
17 He who is generous to the poor makes a loan to
        the LORD;
   He will repay him his due.

23: This is the way things are, not the way they should be. **24:** Two levels of friendship.

19.3: People blame God for troubles they bring on themselves. **4, 6–7:** Further observations on social realities, which are not always fair. A line seems to be missing before 7c, which is not balanced. **8:** *Wisdom*, lit. "heart." "Acquiring a heart"—gaining the right mindset—is a prerequisite to gaining wisdom. **10:** The Sages had a conservative view of society. While they demanded fair and compassionate treatment of the lower classes, they assumed that the structure of society as they knew it was fundamentally the right one. Hence it was thought unseemly for a *servant* (more precisely "slave") to *rule over princes* (see 30.21–22). **11:** This refers to overlooking an offense against oneself (cf. 10.12). **12:** An expression of awe at the power of the king; see 16.14–15; cf. 20.2. **13:** This proverb does not condemn all women any more than it condemns all sons. Like the entirety of Proverbs, however, it does evaluate relationships from the standpoint of the adult male. There is no comparable criticism about a vexatious husband, except in a general way in 11.29. **14:** Counterbalancing v. 13, this proverb declares the value of a (good) wife. Cf. 31.10–31. *Efficient*: better, "intelligent" or "insightful."

a-a *Meaning of Heb. uncertain.*

18   Discipline your son while there is still hope,
      And^a do not ^bset your heart on his destruction.^{-b}
19   A hot-tempered man incurs punishment;
      ^cIf you try to save him you will only make it
            worse.^{-c}
20   Listen to advice and accept discipline
      In order that you may be wise in the end.
21   Many designs are in a man's mind,
      But it is the LORD's plan that is accomplished.
22   ^cGreed is a reproach to a man;^{-c}
      Better be poor than a liar.
23   He who fears the LORD earns life;
      ^cHe shall abide in contentment,^{-c}
      Free from misfortune.
24   The lazy man buries his hand in the bowl;
      He will not even bring it to his mouth.
25   Beat the scoffer and the simple will become clever;
      Reprove an intelligent man and he gains
            knowledge.
26   A son who causes shame and disgrace
      Plunders his father, puts his mother to flight.
27   My son, cease to stray from words of knowledge
      And receive discipline.
28   A malicious witness scoffs at justice,
      And the speech of the wicked conceals mischief.
29   Punishments are in store for scoffers
      And blows for the backs of dullards.

20   Wine is a scoffer, strong drink a roisterer;
      He who is muddled by them will not grow wise.
2   The terror of a king is like the roar of a lion;
      He who provokes his anger risks his life.
3   It is honorable for a man to desist from strife,
      But every fool ^cbecomes embroiled.^{-c}
4   In winter the lazy man does not plow;
      At harvesttime he seeks, and finds nothing.
5   The designs in a man's mind are deep waters,
      But a man of understanding can draw them out.
6   He calls many a man his loyal friend,
      But who can find a faithful man?
7   The righteous man lives blamelessly;
      Happy are his children who come after him.
8   The king seated on the throne of judgment
      Can winnow out all evil by his glance.

18: See 13.24 n. 24: A humorous picture of extreme sloth. 25: A "simple" or uneducated boy may take warning from seeing the scoffer beaten. (The scoffer himself is probably hopeless.) But verbal rebukes are enough to straighten out an intelligent person. 28: *Conceals*, better, "gobbles up." *Mischief* (or "iniquity") is the wicked person's "food." See 4.17. 29: Implicit threats like these suggest that the intended audience of the collection (but not necessarily of the individual proverbs) is a boy, a son or pupil. 20.1: *Wine* and *strong drink* (more likely, "beer") are personified, as if they were drunken men. 3: Conflicts often revolve on questions of "honor," but the true honor belongs to him who refrains from strife. 5: *Deep*, concealed and hard to discover. *Draw . . . out* or "draw up," as one draws water. 6: *He*, indefinite: "a man." 8: The royal ideal.

a Or "But."
b-b Or "pay attention to his moaning."
c-c Meaning of Heb. uncertain.

9 Who can say, "I have cleansed my heart,
   I am purged of my sin"?
10 False weights and false measures,
   Both are an abomination to the LORD.
11 A child may be dissembling in his behavior
   Even though his actions are blameless and proper.
12 The ear that hears, the eye that sees—
   The LORD made them both.
13 Do not love sleep lest you be impoverished;
   Keep your eyes open and you will have plenty of
      food.
14 "Bad, bad," says the buyer,
   But having moved off, he congratulates himself.
15 Gold is plentiful, jewels abundant,
   But wise speech is a precious object.
16 Seize his garment, for he stood surety for another;[a]
   Take it as a pledge, [for he stood surety] for an
      unfamiliar woman.
17 Bread gained by fraud may be tasty to a man,
   But later his mouth will be filled with gravel.
18 Plans laid in council will succeed;
   Wage war with stratagems.
19 He who gives away secrets is a base fellow;
   Do not take up with a garrulous man.
20 One who reviles his father or mother,
   Light will fail him when darkness comes.
21 An estate acquired in haste at the outset
   Will not be blessed in the end.
22 Do not say, "I will requite evil";
   Put your hope in the LORD and He will deliver
      you.
23 False weights are an abomination to the LORD;
   Dishonest scales are not right.
24 A man's steps are decided by the LORD;
   What does a man know about his own way?
25 It is a snare for a man [b-]to pledge a sacred gift
      rashly[-b]
   And to give thought to his vows only after they
      have been made.
26 A wise king winnows out the wicked,
   And turns the wheel upon them.
27 The lifebreath of man is the lamp of the LORD
   Revealing all his inmost parts.
28 Faithfulness and loyalty protect the king;
   He maintains his throne by faithfulness.

a Or "a stranger."
b-b Meaning of Heb. uncertain.

9: No human is free of inner sins. This may respond to the perhaps too reverent view of the king in v. 8. **10:** See 11.1 and cf. Deut. 25.13. An ephah was the most common dry measure, about 23 liters (21 qts). **11:** An observation of human nature. **12:** God gave humans these faculties, which are the sources of wisdom, so He certainly wants them used. **14:** Dissembling is common both in the market and in life in general. **16:** These are the words the lender might say when a man guaranteed the loan of a stranger, who then defaulted. See 6.1–5. The "garment" is a large cloak that one could wear in the cold and wrap himself in at night. Its importance is shown by the fact that Torah (Exod. 22.25–26; Deut. 24.12–13) requires that a garment given in pledge be returned each evening so its owner could use it. **17:** Stolen pleasures have a special—and deceptive—tang; see 9.17b. **18:** Better, "Plans made with counsel." Plans made in group deliberation are more effective. See 11.14; 24.6. **20:** *Light will fail* may imply that such a man will leave no children of his own when he dies. **21:** See 10.22. **24:** Expressions of humility such as this saying counterbalance the confident assumption, expressed in numerous proverbs, that humans can determine the course of their lives by choosing the right path. The notion of divine inscrutability informs other ancient Near Eastern wisdom literature as well, and may be a main theme of the LORD's speeches in Job chs 38–41. **25:** Vows were taken very seriously; see Lev. 27.28–29; Eccl. 5.3–5. The Rabbis discouraged the making of vows but also developed legal means for releasing people from precipitous vows. One formula for this is retained in the Kol Nidre ("All vows," an early medieval prayer on the eve of Yom Kippur for the nullification of vows). **26:** *Winnows:* Wheat was thrown in the air so that the wind would blow away the useless chaff and leave the good grain. A heavy wheel was rolled over grain to crack the husk. **27:** The breath that

29 The glory of youths is their strength;
The majesty of old men is their gray hair.

30 Bruises and wounds are repayment[a] for evil,
Striking at one's inmost parts.

21 Like channeled water is the mind of the king in
the Lord's hand;
He directs it to whatever He wishes.

2 All the ways of a man seem right to him,
But the Lord probes the mind.

3 To do what is right and just
Is more desired by the Lord than sacrifice.

4 Haughty looks, a proud heart—
The tillage of the wicked is sinful.

5 The plans of the diligent make only for gain;
All rash haste makes only for loss.

6 Treasures acquired by a lying tongue
[b]Are like driven vapor, heading for extinction.[b]

7 The violence of the wicked sweeps them away,
For they refuse to act justly.

8 The way of a man may be tortuous and strange,
Though his actions are blameless and proper.

9 Dwelling in the corner of a roof is better
Than a contentious wife in a [b]spacious house.[b]

10 The desire of the wicked is set upon evil;
His fellowman finds no favor in his eyes.

11 When a scoffer is punished, the simple man is
edified;
When a wise man is taught, he gains insight.

12 The Righteous One observes the house of the
wicked man;
He subverts the wicked to their ruin.

13 Who stops his ears at the cry of the wretched,
He too will call and not be answered.

14 A gift in secret subdues anger,
A present in private, fierce rage.

15 Justice done is a joy to the righteous,
To evildoers, ruination.

16 A man who strays from the path of prudence
Will rest in the company of ghosts.

17 He who loves pleasure comes to want;
He who loves wine and oil does not grow rich.

18 The wicked are the ransom of the righteous;
The traitor comes in place of the upright.

19 It is better to live in the desert
Than with a contentious, vexatious wife.

gives man life illuminates the depths of the human soul. The concept behind this is not clear. **29:** This expresses appreciation for the glories of both youth and old age, the sign of which is *gray hair.* Old age was something to take pride in, for it implied (in the Sages' view) both a successful life and the wisdom of years. **21.1:** The king's intentions are under God's control and thus express his will. *Channeled water* is used in irrigation and is productive. This proverb expresses great esteem for kingship. See 16.10–15 n. **2:** God perceives a human's subconscious intentions, possibly finding (and judging) unworthy attitudes that even their possessor is unaware of. **3:** Cf. 15.8; contrast 21.27. **4:** *The tillage* of the wicked—what they produce—is "sin" (rather than *sinful*). **5:** Cf. 19.2; 28.20. **6:** Wealth acquired dishonestly is both ephemeral and deadly. *Heading for extinction* should be emended to "deadly snares." **8:** Strange and even circuitous behavior is not always immoral. **11:** *He* in the second line is probably the *simple man* (actually "simple one," probably meaning a boy). The simple, callow boy can learn by observing how others are "taught," each in his own way; cf. 19.25. **13:** If one ignores the suffering of others, God will ignore his cry when he gets into trouble. **14:** *Present,* more precisely, "bribe." Gifts or bribes were acceptable, even recommended, if the intention was good; see 18.16 n. Gifts might be used to placate an angry official or a man who considered himself wronged. **17:** *Pleasure* refers to feasting. One who loves sybaritic pleasures too much will squander his time and his money. **18:** The underlying notion is that when God is angry (at a nation, for example), His anger is assuaged by the punishment of the wicked. They take the place of the upright, who might otherwise have suffered in the general catastrophe. Cf. 11.8. **19:** See 19.13. **22:** The power of wisdom in war; see 16.32; 24.6; contrast 21.31. **23:** The importance

a Meaning of Heb. uncertain.   b-b Meaning of Heb. uncertain.

20 Precious treasure and oil are in the house of the
        wise man,
    And a fool of a man will run through them.
21 He who strives to do good and kind deeds
    Attains life, success, and honor.
22 One wise man prevailed over a city of warriors
    And brought down its mighty stronghold.
23 He who guards his mouth and tongue
    Guards himself from trouble.
24 The proud, insolent man, scoffer is his name,
    Acts in a frenzy of insolence.
25 The craving of a lazy man kills him,
    For his hands refuse to work.
26 All day long he is seized with craving
    While the righteous man gives without stint.
27 The sacrifice of the wicked man is an
        abomination,
    The more so as he offers it in depravity.
28 A false witness is doomed,
    But one who really heard will testify with
        success.
29 The wicked man is brazen-faced;
    The upright man discerns his course.
30 No wisdom, no prudence, and no counsel
    Can prevail against the LORD.
31 The horse is readied for the day of battle,
    But victory comes from the LORD.

22 Repute is preferable to great wealth,
    Grace is better than silver and gold.
2 Rich man and poor man meet;
    The LORD made them both.
3 The shrewd man saw trouble and took cover;
    The simple kept going and paid the penalty.
4 The effect of humility is fear of the LORD,
    Wealth, honor, and life.
5 Thorns and snares are in the path of the crooked;
    He who values his life will keep far from them.
6 Train a lad in the way he ought to go;
    He will not swerve from it even in old age.
7 The rich rule the poor,
    And the borrower is a slave to the lender.
8 He who sows injustice shall reap misfortune;
    His rod of wrath shall fail.
9 The generous man is blessed,
    For he gives of his bread to the poor.
10 Expel the scoffer and contention departs,
    Quarrel and contumely cease.

of controlling one's speech, to avoid blurting out offensive or stupid things; see 4.23. **25–26:** These sayings are linked by the word *craving,* but they are independent thoughts. The lazy man is wracked with his appetites, but he refuses to work to satisfy them. In contrast to a greedy man, the righteous man is generous. **27:** See 15.8. **30–31:** No intellectual skills are effective if they are used contrary to God's will. *Prudence,* better, "understanding." **22.1:** *Grace,* "good favor," the favor or esteem which others have for oneself. **2:** When rich and poor come together, their differences are accentuated, and the sage does not blur them (v. 7). But they are both God's handiwork, and the rich man should keep this in mind. **7:** A warning against borrowing money. **8:** *Rod,* a flail used in threshing grain. The power of the unjust man's anger will prove ineffective. **10:** The *scoffer,* arrogant and contemptuous of others (21.24), provokes quarrels wherever he goes.

11 A pure-hearted friend,
His speech is gracious;
He has the king for his companion.

12 The eyes of the LORD watch the wise man;
He subverts the words of the treacherous.

13 The lazy man says, "There's a lion in the street;
I shall be killed *if I step outside."*-a

14 The mouth of a forbidden*b* woman is a deep pit;
He who is doomed by the LORD falls into it.

15 If folly settles in the heart of a lad,
The rod of discipline will remove it.

16 To profit by withholding what is due to the poor
Is like making gifts to the rich—pure loss.

17 Incline your ear and listen to the words of the
sages;
Pay attention to my wisdom.

18 It is good that you store them inside you,
And that all of them be constantly on your lips,

19 That you may put your trust in the LORD.
I let you know today—yes, you—

20 Indeed, I wrote down for you *a threefold lore,*-c
Wise counsel,

21 To let you know truly reliable words,
That you may give a faithful reply to him who
sent you.

22 Do not rob the wretched because he is wretched;
Do not crush the poor man in the gate;

23 For the LORD will take up their cause
And despoil those who despoil them of life.

24 Do not associate with an irascible man,
Or go about with one who is hot-tempered,

---

a-a Lit. "in the square." *b Lit. "strange."* *c-c Meaning of Heb. uncertain.*

11: The king wants honest, gracious men for his intimates. This proverb seems to be directed to someone who spends his time in the royal court. **12:** *The wise man,* rather, "knowledge." God protects authentic knowledge and gives it success, whereas He foils the deceits of the treacherous. **13:** The lazy man finds the silliest excuses to beg off work; cf. 26.13. **14:** The strange woman (see 2.16) works her seduction above all by her slippery speech. Falling into her trap is so deadly it must be reckoned a sign of divine anger. **16:** Better,

"There is one who oppresses the poor, yet makes him (the poor man) profit, and there is one who gives to a rich man, yet he (the rich man) ends up lacking." This is a paradox like 13.7a, and shows that humans do not always know and control the effects of their actions.

22.17–24.22: Collection III. These are mostly admonitions ("Do not . . ."), and in contrast to the previous collection, are often longer than a single two-part verse. Many are particularly relevant to a young man looking forward to his career. They emphasize the inner virtues of humility, compassion, and serenity. Three sections (A–C) are discernible.

22.17–23.11: Collection III, section A. Since 1923 it has been recognized that 22.17–23.11 is based on the Egyptian "Instruction of Amenemope." Though there may be centuries of reworking from the time the Egyptian book was translated into the Canaanite predecessor of Hebrew, the relationship is close, and the sayings in this unit follow the order of the parallel sayings in Amenemope. In the following, the parallel passages in Amenemope are indicated by chapter number (§) and can be found for example in *AEL* 2.146–63. **22.17:** We should read, "The words of the sages. Incline your ear and listen, pay attention to my words." By this reading, this unit too has a title, "Words of the Sages." Cf. 24.23. **17b–21:** The prologue. This is similar to the prologue of Amenemope (*AEL* 2.148) and a sentence from its conclusion, §30. It also resembles the Calls to Attention in Proverbs 1–9. **20:** *A threefold lore,* Heb "shalishim" means "officers," which was traditionally construed to mean "excellent things." But at the end of his book, Amenemope tells his son, "Look to these thirty chapters. They inform; they educate" (*AEL* 2.162). This suggests that we change the vowels of the Heb word to read "sheloshim," "thirty." There is disagreement, however, on identifying thirty proverbs in the present form of section A. **21:** Amenemope's prologue promises to teach the reader "To reply to one who sends a message." Proper "replies" are a topic of special concern in Egyptian wisdom—though not in Prov. 22.17–23.11, in spite of the present verse. **22–23:** The wretched man's wretchedness is a reason *not* to cheat him. The city gate was where disputes and legal cases were adjudicated. The poor may lack a human protector, but they have a divine one. **24:** Cf. Amenemope §9. **26–27:** See 6.1–5 n. *Bed* is a

25 Lest you learn his ways
And find yourself ensnared.

26 Do not be one of those who give their hand,
Who stand surety for debts,

27 Lest your bed be taken from under you
When you have no money to pay.

28 Do not remove the ancient boundary stone
That your ancestors set up.

29 See a man skilled at his work—
He shall attend upon kings;
He shall not attend upon ªobscure men.ª

23 When you sit down to dine with a ruler,
Consider well who is before you.

2 Thrust a knife into your gullet
If you have a large appetite.

3 Do not crave for his dainties,
For they are counterfeit food.

4 Do not toil to gain wealth;
Have the sense to desist.

5 You see it, then it is gone;
It grows wings and flies away,
Like an eagle, heavenward.

6 Do not eat of a stingy man's food;
Do not crave for his dainties;

7 He is like one keeping accounts;
"Eat and drink," he says to you,
But he does not really mean it.

8 The morsel you eat you will vomit;
You will waste your courteous words.

9 Do not speak to a dullard,
For he will disdain your sensible words.

10 Do not remove ancient boundary stones;
Do not encroach upon the field of orphans,

11 For they have a mighty Kinsman,
And He will surely take up their cause with you.

12 Apply your mind to discipline
And your ears to wise sayings.

13 Do not withhold discipline from a child;
If you beat him with a rod he will not die.

14 Beat him with a rod
And you will save him from the grave.

blanket or garment a person would roll up in. Though a debtor had some legal protection in this regard (see 20.16 n.), a guarantor did not. **28:** Moving a boundary stone between your land and your neighbor's was a grave offense, because it was easily done and hard to detect. See 23.10; Deut. 19.14; Amenemope §6. **29–30:** This unit aims to train young men who would likely become officials, and, if very successful, might even land a job in the royal court. Cf. Amenemope §30. **23.1–3:** Proper comportment at a ruler's table: When dining with a ruler, control your appetite. A *ruler* may be any superior. Egyptian writings give similar instructions and show that formal dinners headed by a superior official had a role in professional life (cf. Amenemope §23). The official showed whom he favored among his underlings by giving them different size portions (see Gen. 43.34). **1:** *Consider well,* that is, look at the portion you receive and not what others get. *Thrust a knife into your gullet,* control your appetite at all costs. His dainties are *counterfeit food* in the sense that if you fill up on them, you may find the result dissatisfying. **4–5:** An extension of the principle of vv. 1–3: Do not be greedy. If you strain for wealth, it disappears. Cf. 28.20; Amenemope §7. **6–8:** Dinner with a stingy man is an occasion of hypocrisy on all sides and is nauseating. **9:** Some people just cannot learn; see 9.7–10. **10–11:** See 22.28. *Kinsman,* rather, "redeemer," one who will punish the transgressor. The redeemer was originally a kinsman who could sue on behalf of the widow and orphan in the "gate"; see 22.22–23.

23.12–35: Collection III, section B. Advice addressed to a son in an affectionate tone, emphasizing the joy parents get from wise and upright children and the misery they suffer from foolish ones. **13–14:** Corporal punishment can save a child from sins that will lead to his death; see 13.24.

a-a *Meaning of Heb. uncertain.*

15 My son, if your mind gets wisdom,
My mind, too, will be gladdened.

16 I shall rejoice with all my heart*
When your lips speak right things.

17 Do not envy sinners in your heart,
But only God-fearing men, at all times,

18 For then you will have a future,
And your hope will never fail.

19 Listen, my son, and get wisdom;
Lead your mind in a [proper] path.

20 Do not be of those who guzzle wine,
Or glut themselves on meat;

21 For guzzlers and gluttons will be impoverished,
And drowsing will clothe you in tatters.

22 Listen to your father who begot you;
Do not disdain your mother when she is old.

23 Buy truth and never sell it,
And wisdom, discipline, and understanding.

24 The father of a righteous man will exult;
He who begets a wise son will rejoice in him.

25 Your father and mother will rejoice;
She who bore you will exult.

26 Give your mind to me, my son;
Let your eyes watch my ways.

27 A harlot is a deep pit;
A forbidden*b* woman is a narrow well.

28 She too lies in wait as if for prey,
And destroys the unfaithful among men.

29 Who cries, "Woe!" who, "Alas!";
Who has quarrels, who complaints;
Who has wounds without cause;
Who has bleary eyes?

30 Those whom wine keeps till the small hours,
Those who gather to drain the cups.

31 Do not ogle that red wine
As it lends its color to the cup,
As it flows on smoothly;

32 In the end, it bites like a snake;
It spits like a basilisk.

33 Your eyes will see strange sights;
Your heart*c* will speak distorted things.

34 You will be like one lying in bed on high seas,
Like one lying *d-*on top of the rigging.*-d*

17–18: Admire the God-fearing.
20–21: A life of dissolution and indulgence will lead to poverty.
22: Cf. 30.17. **27–28:** Avoid harlots. There is a pun here: A woman's sexuality is a *pit* and a *well*. With the wrong woman, these are pitfalls (22.14). The sexuality of a man's own wife, however, is a blessed, joyous, productive well (5.15–18). **29–35:** A humorous and caustic portrayal of the drunkard. He acts like a fool, staggers around in inebriation, and has a horrible hangover. But he starts again the next day.

a Lit. "kidneys."   *b Lit. "alien."*
c See note to 15.28.   *d-d Meaning of Heb. uncertain.*

35 "They struck me, but I felt no hurt;
    They beat me, but I was unaware;
    As often as I wake,
    I go after it again."

24 Do not envy evil men;
    Do not desire to be with them;
2   For their hearts[a] talk violence,
    And their lips speak mischief.

3   A house is built by wisdom,
    And is established by understanding;
4   By knowledge are its rooms filled
    With all precious and beautiful things.

5   A wise man is strength;
    A knowledgeable man exerts power;
6   For by stratagems you wage war,
    And victory comes with much planning.

7   Wisdom is too lofty for a fool;
    He does not open his mouth in the gate.
8   He who lays plans to do harm
    Is called by men a schemer.
9   The schemes of folly are sin,
    And a scoffer is an abomination to men.

10 If you showed yourself slack in time of trouble,
    Wanting in power,
11 If you refrained from rescuing those taken off to
        death,
    Those condemned to slaughter—
12 If you say, "We knew nothing of it,"
    Surely He who fathoms hearts will discern [the
        truth],
    He who watches over your life will know it,
    And He will pay each man as he deserves.
13 My son, eat honey, for it is good;
    Let its sweet drops be on your palate.
14 Know: such is wisdom for your soul;
    If you attain it, there is a future;
    Your hope will not be cut off.

15 Wicked man! Do not lurk by the home of the
        righteous man;
    Do no violence to his dwelling.

24.1–22: Collection III, section C. Maxims mostly praising wisdom and condemning the schemes of the wicked. **1–2:** Of the various dangers that evil people present, Proverbs emphasizes their bad influence on those who consort with them rather than the harm they inflict directly. **3–6:** True prosperity (vv. 3–4) and strength (vv. 5–6) comes from wisdom, not from nefarious schemes and crude exercise of power. **7:** The fool *does not*—or rather, "cannot"—*open his mouth* insofar as no one will pay attention to him. *Gate*, see 1.20–21 n. **8–9:** Like folly, scheming is held in contempt. **10–12:** The obligation to fight injustice: It is not enough to refrain from committing injustices; you must actively try to prevent them. *Rescuing* may refer to standing up for an unjustly accused defendant in a capital case. **13–14:** Learning wisdom is not just a matter of hard work and harsh discipline. If pursued with love, learning is a joy. Ps. 119.103 uses similar language about Torah. **15:** *Wicked man* looks like a pointless addition.

a See note to 15.28.

16 Seven times the righteous man falls and gets
        up,
    While the wicked are tripped by one misfortune.

17 If your enemy falls, do not exult;
    If he trips, let your heart not rejoice,
18 Lest the LORD see it and be displeased,
    And avert His wrath from him.

19 Do not be vexed by evildoers;
    Do not be incensed by the wicked;
20 For there is no future for the evil man;
    The lamp of the wicked goes out.

21 Fear the LORD, my son, and the king,
    And do not mix with dissenters,
22 For disaster comes from them suddenly;
    The doom both decree who can foreknow?

23 These also are by the sages:

    It is not right to be partial in judgment.
24 He who says to the guilty, "You are innocent,"
    Shall be cursed by peoples,
    Damned by nations;
25 But it shall go well with them who decide justly;
    Blessings of good things will light upon them.

26 Giving a straightforward reply
    Is like giving a kiss.
27 Put your external affairs in order,
    Get ready what you have in the field,
    Then build yourself a home.
28 Do not be a witness against your fellow without
        good cause;
    Would you mislead with your speech?
29 Do not say, "I will do to him what he did to me;
    I will pay the man what he deserves."

30 I passed by the field of a lazy man,
    By the vineyard of a man lacking sense.
31 It was all overgrown with thorns;
    Its surface was covered with chickweed,
    And its stone fence lay in ruins.
32 I observed and took it to heart;
    I saw it and learned a lesson.
33 A bit more sleep, a bit more slumber,
    A bit more hugging yourself in bed,

16: The righteous have a "future" (v. 14b) because they can recover from misfortune, but wickedness is a dead-end road (vv. 19–20). **17–19:** God resents it when you gloat at another's suffering, even if deserved, and might punish you by failing to punish him. Cf. 25.21–22; contrast 11.10b. **21:** The striking parallelism between *the LORD* and *the king* suggests that the Sages held kingship in awe and believed in the fundamental rightness of the social order as they knew it. See 16.10–15 n.

24.23–34: Collection IV. This short collection is ascribed to anonymous sages. **23–24, 28:** Honesty in judgment. **25–26:** *Them who decide justly,* or, "those who give reproof." Honest words, like kisses, are an expression of love (v. 26) and one who reproves others, though ostensibly harsh, will receive praise and good wishes in the end. **27:** Lay the right groundwork for your home, and for major projects generally. **29:** Do not seek revenge on your own; rather rely on God to execute justice (see 24.12b). **30–34:** A little narrative illustrating the consequences of sloth. The sage passed by the field of the lazy man and saw it had gone wild. He draws a lesson by applying a proverb, vv. 33–34, which is found also in 6.10–11 (see 6.11 n.).

34 And poverty will come [a]·calling upon you,[·a]
And want, like a man with a shield.

25 These too are proverbs of Solomon, which the men of King Hezekiah of Judah copied:

2 It is the glory of God to conceal a matter,
And the glory of a king to plumb a matter.

3 Like the heavens in their height, like the earth in
its depth,
Is the mind of kings—unfathomable.

4 The dross having been separated from the silver,
A vessel emerged for the smith.

5 Remove the wicked from the king's presence,
And his throne will be established in justice.

6 Do not exalt yourself in the king's presence;
Do not stand in the place of nobles.

7 For it is better to be told, "Step up here,"
Than to be degraded in the presence of the great.

Do not let what your eyes have seen
8 Be vented rashly in a quarrel;
Think[b] of what it will effect in the end,
When your fellow puts you to shame.

9 Defend your right against your fellow,
But do not give away the secrets of another,

10 Lest he who hears it reproach you,
And your bad repute never end.

11 Like golden apples in silver showpieces[c]
Is a phrase well turned.

12 Like a ring of gold, a golden ornament,
Is a wise man's reproof in a receptive ear.

13 Like the coldness of snow at harvesttime
Is a trusty messenger to those who send him;
He lifts his master's spirits.

14 Like clouds, wind—but no rain—
Is one who boasts of gifts not given.

15 Through forbearance a ruler may be won over;
A gentle tongue can break bones.

16 If you find honey, eat only what you need,
Lest, surfeiting yourself, you throw it up.

a-a Meaning of Heb. uncertain.   b Lit. "Lest."   c Meaning of Heb. uncertain.

25.1–29.27: Collection V. Characteristic of this collection is the frequency of proverbial comparisons in which an image (e.g., "Like clouds, wind—but no rain—" in v. 14a) is followed by the phenomenon being described (e.g., "one who boasts of gifts not given," v. 14b). **25.1:** *Copied,* better, "transmitted" or "collected." This shows that the royal court in Israel, as elsewhere in the ancient Near East, was one place where traditional wisdom was collected and put in writing. Hezekiah reigned from 715 to 687 BCE. *These too* of this superscription refers back to the superscription of the book in 1.1. **2–7:** Kings and their courts. These proverbs seem to be directed at a scribe or future scribe who might work in the royal court but would not necessarily be of noble rank (v. 6). The proverbs speak of kings and their vast wisdom with reverence, even sycophancy. See 16.10–15 n. **2:** It redounds to God's glory to create mysteries in the world and to the king's to investigate mysteries—not necessarily the same ones. The king would investigate matters when sitting in judgment. **3:** The king's wisdom is vast and his intentions cannot be fully understood. **4–5:** Just as removing dross from silver leaves pure silver, which can be made into a fine vessel, so does removing the wicked from the royal court allow the king's reign to be founded firmly on righteousness. **6–7b:** This proverb instructs a young man who might become a royal scribe or official to remember his rank and not to put himself forward. **7c–10:** This maxim, whose text and meaning is uncertain, apparently warns against blurting out something you know about someone else when you are in an argument with him. Preserve his secrets even when you are angry with him. If you violate his confidence, your own reputation will be harmed. **11–15:** Four comparisons concerning speech. **11–12:** Eloquent words—even reprimands—are like precious, well-crafted works of art. **13:** The *harvesttime* in question is probably the wheat harvest in May-June, at which time it can be quite hot. It is refreshing to have a reliable messenger. **15:** *Won over,* more precisely, "beguiled" or "tempted." Subtle, gentle speech has real power, even over the mighty. The second line is a paradox. **16–17:** Do not overdo good things. If you wear out your welcome,

17 Visit your neighbor sparingly,
　　Lest he have his surfeit of you and loathe you.
18 Like a club, a sword, a sharpened arrow,
　　Is a man who testifies falsely against his fellow.
19 Like a loose tooth and an unsteady leg,
　　Is a treacherous support in time of trouble.
20 Disrobing on a chilly day,
　　Like vinegar on natron,
　　Is one who sings songs to a sorrowful soul.

21 If your enemy is hungry, give him bread to eat;
　　If he is thirsty, give him water to drink.
22 You will be heaping live coals on his head,
　　And the LORD will reward you.

23 A north wind produces rain,
　　And whispered words, a glowering face.
24 Dwelling in the corner of a roof is better
　　Than a contentious woman in *ᵃ*a spacious house.*ᵃ*
25 Like cold water to a parched throat
　　Is good news from a distant land.
26 Like a muddied spring, a ruined fountain,
　　Is a righteous man fallen before a wicked one.
27 It is not good to eat much honey,
　　*ᵃ*Nor is it honorable to search for honor.*ᵃ*
28 Like an open city without walls
　　Is a man whose temper is uncurbed.

26

Like snow in summer and rain at harvesttime,
So honor is not fitting for a dullard.
2 As a sparrow must flit and a swallow fly,
　　So a gratuitous curse must backfire.*ᵇ*
3 A whip for a horse and a bridle for a donkey,
　　And a rod for the back of dullards.
4 Do not answer a dullard in accord with his folly,
　　Else you will become like him.
5 Answer a dullard in accord with his folly,
　　Else he will think himself wise.
6 He who sends a message by a dullard
　　Will wear out legs and *ᶜ*must put up with*ᶜ*
　　　　lawlessness.
7 As legs hang limp on a cripple,
　　So is a proverb in the mouth of dullards.
8 Like a pebble in a sling,
　　So is paying honor to a dullard.

a-a Meaning of Heb. uncertain.
b Kethib, "fail."　　c-c Lit. "drink."

you will be like honey that your neighbor gorges on and throws up. **18–20:** Four comparisons describing hurtful behaviors. **20:** The text of this verse is in doubt, and the first line might be a mistake. As it stands, the proverb offers two images: undressing in the cold and pouring acid on a base. To these are compared the effect that cheerful music has on a melancholy person. The first action causes a chill, the second causes fizzing and hissing, which may suggest irritation and incompatibility. Without the first analogy (which many scholars excise), "vinegar on natron" might imply neutralization of the sorrow. **21–22:** Rather than seeking vengeance, treat a vulnerable enemy kindly. Then he will be ashamed and God will reward your kindness. Amenemope (§2) advises that when the wicked man is in trouble, "Fill his belly with bread of your own, that he be sated and weep." **23:** Enigmatic. **24:** V. 24 = 21.9. Proverbs is a collection of collections, so it is not surprising to see a proverb repeated in different sections. **25–26:** Comparisons to "good" and "bad" water. In Heb these verses (and v. 28) lack the word *like*, and are striking metaphors rather than similes. The defeat of a righteous person is a scandal, fouling the quality of a society. **28:** Like a city wall, self-control holds in the temper (lit. "spirit" or "wind") and also protects its owner. An angry man's wall is breached and he is vulnerable. **26.1:** *Honor,* better, "prestige." **2:** Better, "So a gratuitous [that is, undeserved] insult will not arrive." It will not reach and hurt the person it is sent against.

26.3–12: Sayings on the dullard. The *dullard* (Heb "kesil") is not merely a man of low intelligence. He is the kind of fool who is obtuse because of smug overconfidence. See, e.g., 1.32b. **4–5:** Two contradictory proverbs. The second one seems like a rejoinder to the more standard message of the first. If you answer the fool in kind

9   As a thorn comes to the hand of a drunkard,
    So a proverb to the mouth of a dullard.

10 ^{a-}A master can produce anything,^{-a}
    But he who hires a dullard is as one who hires
        transients.^a

11 As a dog returns to his vomit,
    So a dullard repeats his folly.

12 If you see a man who thinks himself wise,
    There is more hope for a dullard than for him.

13 A lazy man says,
    "There's a cub on the road, a lion in the squares."

14 The door turns on its hinge,
    And the lazy man on his bed.

15 The lazy man buries his hand in the bowl;
    He will not even bring it to his mouth.

16 The lazy man thinks himself wiser
    Than seven men who give good advice.

17 A passerby who gets embroiled in someone else's
        quarrel
    Is like one who seizes a dog by its ears.

18 Like a madman^a scattering deadly firebrands,
        arrows,

19 Is one who cheats his fellow and says, "I was only
        joking."

20 For lack of wood a fire goes out,
    And without a querulous man contention is
        stilled.

21 Charcoal for embers and wood for a fire
    And a contentious man for kindling strife.

22 The words of a querulous man are bruising;^b
    They penetrate one's inmost parts.

23 Base silver laid over earthenware
    Are ardent lips with an evil mind.

24 An enemy dissembles with his speech,
    Inwardly he harbors deceit.

25 Though he be fair-spoken do not trust him,
    For seven abominations are in his mind.

26 His hatred may be concealed by dissimulation,
    But his evil will be exposed to public view.

27 He who digs a pit will fall in it,
    And whoever rolls a stone, it will roll back on him.

(that is, in a crude and harsh fashion), you will resemble him, but if you do not, he will think that he has impressed or confounded you. Some interpreters think that this juxtaposition suggests the paradoxical difficulties of being wise. **6:** Better, "cuts off his own legs and drinks poison." **7, 9:** The *dullard* is a verbal cripple. To be effective, a proverb must be spoken at the right time (15.23) and in the right fashion (25.11). **8, 10:** Obscure. **11:** A deliberately disgusting characterization of the way some people repeat stupid behavior. Dogs for some reason often lick up their vomit, giving the impression they like it. **12:** As bad as the dullard is, far worse is the man who thinks he is wise (but is not), for he has no hope of improving.

26.13–29.27: Further maxims.
26.13–16: Humorous characterizations of the sluggard. **14:** See 22.13. **15:** See 19.24. **16:** The sluggard, like the dullard (v. 12) is smug and conceited. **17–22:** The dangers of strife. **20, 22:** *Querulous man*, or "slanderer." **23–28:** The hypocrite hides his hatred and hostile schemes under a cheap sheen of unctuous words. V. 27 states the principle that the schemer is preparing his own punishment.

28 A lying tongue hates ᵃthose crushed by it;⁻ᵃ
  Smooth speech throws one down.

27 Do not boast of tomorrow,
  For you do not know what the day will bring.
2 Let the mouth of another praise you, not yours,
  The lips of a stranger, not your own.
3 A stone has weight, sand is heavy,
  But a fool's vexation outweighs them both.
4 There is the cruelty of fury, the overflowing of
    anger,
  But who can withstand jealousy?
5 Open reproof is better than concealed love.
6 Wounds by a loved one are long lasting;
  The kisses of an enemy are profuse.
7 A sated person disdains honey,
  But to a hungry man anything bitter seems sweet.
8 Like a sparrow wandering from its nest
  Is a man who wanders from his home.
9 Oil and incense gladden the heart,
  And the sweetness of a friend is better than one's
    own counsel.
10 Do not desert your friend and your father's friend;
  Do not enter your brother's house in your time of
    misfortune;
  A close neighbor is better than a distant brother.
11 Get wisdom, my son, and gladden my heart,
  That I may have what to answer those who taunt
    me.
12 The shrewd man saw trouble and took cover;
  The simple kept going and paid the penalty.
13 Seize his garment, for he stood surety for another;ᵇ
  Take it as a pledge, [for he stood surety] for an
    unfamiliar woman.
14 He who greets his fellow loudly early in the
    morning
  Shall have it reckoned to him as a curse.
15 An endless dripping on a rainy day
  And a contentious wife are alike;
16 As soon repress her as repress the wind,
  Or declare one's right hand to be oil.
17 As iron sharpens iron
  So a man sharpens the witᶜ of his friend.
18 He who tends a fig tree will enjoy its fruit,
  And he who cares for his master will be honored.

27.1: Do not praise yourself for future achievements. **5:** Friendship often takes the form of forthright reproof of faults. **6:** *Long lasting,* or "trustworthy." The *wounds* are verbal, as in v. 5, and they are intended to be beneficial. In contrast, an enemy feigns friendship, but this, of course, means nothing. **8:** The wanderer and the bird are imagined as hapless and lonely. **9:** The word translated *sweetness* may mean "counsel." It is more satisfying to discuss something with another person than to deliberate on it alone. **10:** Three one-line sayings on friends and relations. Together they say that friends can be a better support than relatives in a time of difficulty and should be held precious. **11:** When one is being taunted, if his son is smart, he can brag about him. The background circumstances are unclear. **12:** See 22.3. **13:** See 20.16. **14:** People tend to be irritated by loud cheeriness too early in the morning. **15–16:** A nagging wife is like a drizzle—irritating and unrelenting. See 19.13 n. **17:** If this translation of the difficult verse is correct, it means that good conversation sharpens the wits. **18:** This should be read as a comparison.

a-a Meaning of Heb. uncertain.
b Or "a stranger."　　c Lit. "face."

19   As face answers to face in water,
  So does one man's heart to another.
20   Sheol and Abaddon cannot be satisfied,
  Nor can the eyes of man be satisfied.
21   For silver—the crucible, for gold—the furnace,
  And a man is tested by his praise.
22   Even if you pound the fool in a mortar
  With a pestle along with grain,
  His folly will not leave him.

23   Mind well the looks of your flock;
  Pay attention to your herds;
24   For property does not last forever,
  Or a crown for all generations.
25   Grass vanishes, new grass appears,
  And the herbage of the hills is gathered in.
26   The lambs will provide you with clothing,
  The he-goats, the price of a field.
27   The goats' milk will suffice for your food,
  The food of your household,
  And the maintenance of your maids.

28 The wicked flee though no one gives chase,
  But the righteous are as confident as a lion.
2   When there is rebellion in the land, many are its
   rulers;
  a-But with a man who has understanding and
   knowledge, stability will last.-a
3   A poor man who withholds what is due to the
   wretched
  Is like a destructive rain that leaves no food.
4   Those who forsake instruction praise the
   wicked,
  But those who heed instruction fight them.
5   Evil men cannot discern judgment,
  But those who seek the Lord discern all things.
6   Better is a poor man who lives blamelessly
  Than a rich man whose ways are crooked.
7   An intelligent son heeds instruction,
  But he who keeps company with gluttons
   disgraces his father.
8   He who increases his wealth by loans at discount
   or interest
  Amasses it for one who is generous to the poor.
9   He who turns a deaf ear to instruction—
  His prayer is an abomination.

19: *Answers* is not in the Heb. The saying is obscure. **20:** The human eye (desire) is insatiable; see Eccl. 1.8. *Abaddon*, see 15.11 n. **21:** *By his praise*, perhaps read "his praisers." To see what a man is really like, consider what sort of person praises him; see 28.4. **23–27:** An epigram on the advantages of animal husbandry as a livelihood. (*Property* and *a crown* in v. 24 refer to other kinds of wealth and power.) Grass (unlike, say, silver) renews itself and feeds the flocks, whose yield provides for many needs. **28.1:** The wicked live in constant fear (1.26–27; 10.24), knowing that punishment is approaching but being ignorant of when it will arrive. The righteous enjoy a sense of security; see 1.33; 3.23–26. **2:** *Rebellion* (or "crime") brings anarchy, and with it an oppressive multiplicity of *rulers*. The second line is obscure. **4–5:** These proverbs emphasize the bond between the intellectual power of wisdom and the quality of one's values. *All things* means all things relevant to wisdom teachings. He who seeks God finds wisdom; see 2.4–5. **7:** A variant of 29.3. The *gluttons* are probably guilty of generally licentious and dissolute behavior. **8:** Profit-taking on a loan to a distressed Israelite is forbidden in Exod. 22.24; Lev. 25.36; Deut. 23.20. Such loans are to be given interest free, as an act of charity. **9:** If one does not listen to *instruction* ("torah"), God will not listen to him. It is possible that "torah" here, unlike most occurrences in Proverbs (where it usually means parental instructions), means God's Torah. See also 29.18.

a-a Meaning of Heb. uncertain.

10 He who misleads the upright into an evil course
Will fall into his own pit,
But the blameless will prosper.

11 A rich man is clever in his own eyes,
But a perceptive poor man can see through him.

12 When the righteous exult there is great glory,
But when the wicked rise up men make
  themselves scarce.

13 He who covers up his faults will not succeed;
He who confesses and gives them up will find
  mercy.

14 Happy is the man who is anxious always,
But he who hardens his heart falls into
  misfortune.

15 A roaring lion and a prowling bear
Is a wicked man ruling a helpless people.

16 A prince who lacks understanding is very
  oppressive;
He who spurns ill-gotten gains will live long.

17 A man oppressed by bloodguilt will flee to a pit;
Let none give him support.

18 He who lives blamelessly will be delivered,
But he who is crooked in his ways will fall all at
  once.

19 He who tills his land will have food in plenty,
But he who pursues vanities will have poverty in
  plenty.

20 A dependable man will receive many blessings,
But one in a hurry to get rich will not go
  unpunished.

21 To be partial is not right;
A man may do wrong for a piece of bread.

22 A miserly man runs after wealth;
He does not realize that loss will overtake it.

23 He who reproves a man will in the end
Find more favor than he who flatters him.

24 He who robs his father and mother and says, "It is
  no offense,"
Is a companion to vandals.

25 A greedy man provokes quarrels,
But he who trusts the LORD shall enjoy prosperity.

26 He who trusts his own instinct is a dullard,
But he who lives by wisdom shall escape.

27 He who gives to the poor will not be in want,
But he who shuts his eyes will be roundly
  cursed.

28 When the wicked rise up, men go into hiding,
But when they perish the righteous increase.

10: If one leads someone onto a bad path, he himself will fall. **12:** *Men make themselves scarce*, lit. "a man is sought for." "A man" ("ʾadam") can mean a worthy man. Compare the use of "ʾadam" in Eccl. 7.28. People seek for a worthy man but (it may be implied) cannot find one. **14:** Here, *is anxious* (lit. "fears") means fearing one's own sins and being willing to repent of them. **17:** Text and sense very uncertain. **19:** See 12.11. **20:** See 23.4. **21:** Perhaps: Although partiality in judgment is not right, not even toward a poor man (Exod. 23.3), a judge should remember that a man may commit a crime for bread (6.30–31) and show some mercy. **23:** Cf. 27.5–6. **24:** One might convince himself that exploiting his parents' wealth is no crime, since he will be inheriting it eventually. Such a one is no better than an ordinary thug. **26:** *Instinct*, rather, "heart," meaning one's own mind, even if untutored and callow. One must rely on a mind infused with the principles and attitudes taught by wisdom. **28:** Cf. v. 12. When the wicked come to power, people hunker down and try to make themselves inconspicuous. When these rulers perish, the moral level of the society rises. See 29.2.

29

One oft reproved may become stiffnecked,
But he will be suddenly broken beyond repair.

2 When the righteous become great the people
rejoice,
But when the wicked dominate the people groan.

3 A man who loves wisdom brings joy to his father,
But he who keeps company with harlots will lose
his wealth.

4 By justice a king sustains the land,
But a fraudulent man tears it down.

5 A man who flatters his fellow
Spreads a net for his feet.

6 An evil man's offenses are a trap for himself,
But the righteous sing out joyously.

7 A righteous man is concerned with the cause of
the wretched;
A wicked man cannot understand such concern.

8 Scoffers inflame a city,
But the wise allay anger.

9 When a wise man enters into litigation with a fool
There is ranting and ridicule, but no satisfaction.

10 Bloodthirsty men detest the blameless,
But the upright seek them out.

11 A dullard vents all his rage,
But a wise man calms it down.

12 A ruler who listens to lies,
All his ministers will be wicked.

13 A poor man and a fraudulent man meet;
The Lord gives luster to the eyes of both.

14 A king who judges the wretched honestly,
His throne will be established forever.

15 Rod and reproof produce wisdom,
But a lad out of control is a disgrace to his mother.

16 When the wicked increase, offenses increase,
But the righteous will see their downfall.

17 Discipline your son and he will give you peace;
He will gratify you with dainties.

18 For lack of vision a people lose restraint,
But happy is he who heeds instruction.

19 A slave cannot be disciplined by words;
Though he may comprehend, he does not
respond.

20 If you see a man hasty in speech,
There is more hope for a fool than for him.

21 A slave pampered from youth
a-Will come to a bad end.-a

29.3: A variant of 28.7. One who goes to whores will *lose his wealth* because he wastes his money on them (cf. 31.3) or because his father will diminish his inheritance. **5:** Flattery or "slippery speech" is the device by which the strange woman too lays her trap (2.16; 7.5). **7:** Rather, "A righteous man knows the just claim of the wretched"—what is theirs by right. The wicked man is ignorant of this. **8–13:** Proverbs on deceit and anger. **9:** Translation uncertain. Apparently: It is a mistake to enter into litigation (or just "argue") with fools. Nothing will be resolved. Cf. 26.5. **10:** *Seek them out,* lit. "seek his life." This elsewhere means to try to kill someone, but here the sense may be reversed: They seek his life in order to protect it. **11:** *Rage,* lit. "wind." He lets forth a storm, which the wise man can pacify. Contrast v. 9. **12:** Corruption starts at the top of the regime and inevitably spreads downwards. **13:** *Fraudulent man,* meaning uncertain; possibly "contentious man." God "gives their eyes light" (rather than *luster*) means that he gives life to all. **14–21:** Proverbs on discipline and anarchy, both domestic and social. **14:** Cf. 20.28; 25.5. **17:** Raise your son strictly and he will take care of you when you are old. **18:** *Vision* means prophecy, which was a source of discipline and reproof for Israelite society. *Instruction* is "torah," which in Proverbs usually means parental instruction. Here it possibly refers to God's Torah (see also 28.9). **19, 21:** Since a *slave* was deprived of material interests of his own, it was assumed that he had to be treated like a child and beaten into submission. Pampering would spoil him. According to Exod. 21.20–21, 26–27, a male or female slave could be beaten at will though not killed or permanently injured.

---

a-a *Meaning of Heb. uncertain.*

22 An angry man provokes a quarrel;
   A hot-tempered man commits many offenses.

23 A man's pride will humiliate him,
   But a humble man will obtain honor.

24 He who shares with a thief is his own enemy;
   He hears the imprecation and does not tell.[a]

25 A man's fears become a trap for him,
   But he who trusts in the Lord shall be
     safeguarded.

26 Many seek audience with a ruler,
   But it is from the Lord that a man gets justice.

27 The unjust man is an abomination to the
     righteous,
   And he whose way is straight is an abomination to
     the wicked.

30 The words of Agur son of Jakeh, [man of] Massa;
   The speech of the man to Ithiel, to Ithiel and Ucal:

2 I am brutish, less than a man;
   I lack common sense.

3 I have not learned wisdom,
   Nor do I possess knowledge of the Holy One.

4 Who has ascended heaven and come down?
   Who has gathered up the wind in the hollow of his
     hand?
   Who has wrapped the waters in his garment?
   Who has established all the extremities of the
     earth?
   What is his name or his son's name, if you know
     it?

5 Every word of God is pure,
   A shield to those who take refuge in Him.

a Cf. Lev. 5.1.

24: Upon the discovery of a crime, a proclamation was issued requiring everyone who knew about it to come forward and testify; see Lev. 5.1. *Tell* (as in Leviticus) means "testify." The proclamation was accompanied by an *imprecation*, a conditional curse that would fall on whoever had information and failed to come forward. **25:** *A man's fears* may mean "what he fears." These, in the case of the evildoer, will be precisely the punishment he suffers (10.24). Alternatively, this may mean that exces-

sive fears can impel anyone to rash steps. **27:** Values, right and perverse. See 28.4.

30.1–31.31: Collection VI. Appendices. The book ends with a number of miscellaneous poems and epigrams. In style and sometimes in content they are quite different from the earlier chapters and from each other.

30.1–6: Agur. This mysterious poem is ascribed to an otherwise unknown, apparently foreign,

sage. Its message is the overriding importance of piety, which it does not require wisdom to possess. The poem seems like a cautionary response to the rest of the book of Proverbs, which makes wisdom a value of the highest order. Such is the poem's difficulty that other commentators read it as an expression of skepticism or as a claim to a superhuman or mystical knowledge superior to human wisdom. **1:** The text and meaning of the title of this poem, after the word *Jakeh,* are very uncertain. It is usually thought that Agur was a Massaite, a member of the North Arabian tribe of Massa. 1 Kings 5.10 shows that the Israelites had respect for the wisdom of "the sons of the East," of which this passage might preserve an example. The ascription to a foreign sage may be a fiction, however, intended to show that even a foreigner can see the plain truth that pious obedience to God's word supersedes all human wisdom. Agur calls his *speech* a "ne'um," which actually means "oracle," a communication from God. Compare the way the foreign prophet Balaam introduces his oracle ("ne'um") in Num. 24.3–4. Perhaps Ithiel and Ucal are Agur's sons. These words can, however, also be read as a sentence: "I am weary, God, and perishing." **2–3:** Agur declares that he has not learned wisdom, meaning the lore and learning of the ancients. *Common sense,* better, "human knowledge." Agur disavows even ordinary human wisdom. In v. 3b, NJPS continues the negative from 3a, but it is not in the text. We should translate, "but I do possess knowledge of the Holy One." Similarly, the seer Balaam claimed to have "knowledge of the Most High" (Num. 24.15–19). Knowledge of God (see 2.5; 9.10) is awareness of His will and ways. **4:** These provocative questions may be answered in different ways: (1) God, and He alone, has done these things. As in Job chs 38–41, human wisdom consists in recognizing God's infinite and incomparable powers. (2) No one—no human, that is—has done them.

6   Do not add to His words,
     Lest He indict you and you be proved a liar.

7   Two things I ask of you; do not deny them to me
         before I die:
8   Keep lies and false words far from me;
     Give me neither poverty nor riches,
     But provide me with my daily bread,
9   Lest, being sated, I renounce, saying,
     "Who is the LORD?"
     Or, being impoverished, I take to theft
     And profane[a] the name of my God.
10   Do not inform on a slave to his master,
     Lest he curse you and you incur guilt.

11   There is a breed of men that brings a curse on its
         fathers
     And brings no blessing to its mothers,
12   A breed that thinks itself pure,
     Though it is not washed of its filth;
13   A breed so haughty of bearing, so supercilious;
14   A breed whose teeth are swords,
     Whose jaws are knives,
     Ready to devour the poor of the land,
     The needy among men.

15   The leech has two daughters, "Give!" and
         "Give!"
     Three things are insatiable;
     Four never say, "Enough!":
16   Sheol, a barren womb,
     Earth that cannot get enough water,
     And fire which never says, "Enough!"

17   The eye that mocks a father
     And disdains the homage due a mother—
     The ravens of the brook will gouge it out,
     Young eagles will devour it.

a Meaning of Heb. uncertain.

might profane the name of the LORD by using it in a false vow of innocence. **10:** An isolated admonition placed between the two poems. *Incur guilt,* or "be punished."

30.11–14: Four breeds of men, each with its own type of corruption. The word translated *breed,* Heb "dor," usually means "generation," and that may be applicable here. There is a notion that certain generations, such as the generation of the flood (Gen. 6.5–12) and the generation of the Tower of Babel (Gen. 11.1–9), are characterized by a certain failing. The failings in the present passage are contempt of parents (v. 11), self-righteousness (v. 12), arrogance (v. 13), and rapaciousness (v. 14). Perhaps this list, and some of those that follow, were answers to riddles whose questions are no longer preserved.

30.15–31: Numerical sayings, which associate things sharing a certain feature. When two numbers are mentioned in parallel, the second number is usually what is really meant. Sometimes the numbered items are followed by a supernumerary item which represents the extreme or surprising case. Numerical sayings are common in the Bible (e.g., Amos chs 1–2, Prov. 6.16–19) and other Canaanite literature. **15a:** The *leech* is a bloodsucker. Her *daughters* are like her, greedy and demanding. The message: Watch out. Your children will be like you. The image can be extended to other greedy things. A midrash in the Talmud (*b. A. Z.* 17a) says that the daughters are heresy and government.

30.15b–16: Four insatiable things. *Sheol,* the underworld, the realm of the dead (see 27.20). *A barren womb,* a barren woman, who yearns endlessly for a child. The *earth* always needs more rain. *Fire* always "needs"—can consume—more fuel. **17:** An isolated saying excoriating the person who treats his parents with contempt.

Either way, the point is that God is infinitely powerful and wise and man lowly and limited. Human intellect, therefore, must bow before God's word. **5:** This statement is found also in Ps. 18.31 (= 2 Sam. 22.31). **6:** This is said of the Torah in Deut. 4.2 (similarly Deut. 13.1).

30.7–10: Agur's prayer. This is the only prayer in Proverbs. **8–9:** Agur asks, first, to be kept from lies and, second, to be given possessions in moderation. Excess wealth may make one overconfident, and poverty too can corrupt. *Profane,* lit. "grab." If arrested, a thief

18   Three things are beyond me;
     Four I cannot fathom:
19   How an eagle makes its way over the sky;
     How a snake makes its way over a rock;
     How a ship makes its way through the high seas;
     How a man has his way with a maiden.
20   Such is the way of an adulteress:
     She eats, wipes her mouth,
     And says, "I have done no wrong."

21   The earth shudders at three things,
     At four which it cannot bear:
22   A slave who becomes king;
     A scoundrel sated with food;
23   A loathsome woman who gets married;
     A slave-girl who supplants her mistress.

24   Four are among the tiniest on earth,
     Yet they are the wisest of the wise:
25   Ants are a folk without power,
     Yet they prepare food for themselves in summer;
26   The badger is a folk without strength,
     Yet it makes its home in the rock;
27   The locusts have no king,
     Yet they all march forth in formation;
28   You can catch the lizard[a] in your hand,
     Yet it is found in royal palaces.

29   There are three that are stately of stride,
     Four that carry themselves well:
30   The lion is mightiest among the beasts,
     And recoils before none;
31   [b-]The greyhound, the he-goat,
     The king whom none dares resist.[-b]

a Or "spider."   b-b Meaning of Heb. uncertain.

30.18–19: Four amazing "ways." The word translated *how* is literally "the way of." The wonder of the "ways" or movement of the eagle, the snake, and the ship may lie in the fact that they do not leave traces or that they are smooth and graceful. As for the way of *a man* with *a maiden*, love is a mystery, but just how it is mysterious is left to the imagination.

30.20: The additional wonder. This verse seems mechanically tacked on and inappropriate, but it might be intended as a shocking climax. The four "ways" are mysterious and graceful and leave no trace. The *way*—that is, behavior—of the adulteress too is amazing: She is unbelievably smug. She thinks she can wipe her sin away as if wiping the crumbs off her face.

30.21–23: Four things the earth cannot bear, so unnatural are they. (1) *A slave who becomes king* violates the social hierarchy, which the sages of Proverbs assumed was the right and natural order. (See 19.10b.) *Becomes king,* lit. "rules," with the sense dominates, controls. Perhaps this line implies that one should not let his slave become the master of his household (as Potiphar did to Joseph, though to good effect; Gen. 39.4). (2) A *scoundrel*—a disobedient slave or son, perhaps—should not be indulged, but should be punished by deprivation (cf. 19.10). (3) A *loathsome woman,* lit. "hated woman," has (the author presumes) done something deserving of disgust and is unworthy of marriage. Perhaps the point is that one should not force his son to marry a woman he dislikes. The word for "hated" seems to mean "unloved" or "dispreferred" in Gen. 29.30–31 and Deut. 21.15–17. (4) A *slave-girl* should be kept in her place and not *supplant* or, more precisely, "disinherit" *her mistress.* This would happen if a man favored his concubine and made her children his heirs. A well-to-do Egyptian, Djefai-hapi, boasts, "I did not let a slave woman be valued above her mistress" (M. Lichtheim, *Maat in Egyptian Autobiographies and Related Studies* [1992], p. 38). The four items may thus have messages for a head of a household.

30.24–28: Four small (or "weak") but clever creatures. *Ants* work without a leader (6.6–8). *Badgers*—meaning rock badgers—are clever enough to live in fortress-like cliffs. *Locusts,* also leaderless, move like an army. The *lizard* can slip into the greatest of houses. All these exemplify the superiority of wisdom over size and strength.

30.29–31: Four animals who move in a majestic fashion. *Greyhound,* better "cock." The real point of the epigram lies in the fourth item: the king's incomparability.

30.32–33: Avoid strife. If you are *arrogant* or scheming, at least keep your mouth shut. Just as squeezing (or "churning") *milk* or a *nose*

32   If you have been scandalously arrogant,
      If you have been a schemer,
      Then clap your hand to your mouth.

33   As milk under pressure produces butter,
      And a nose under pressure produces blood,
      So patience under pressure produces strife.

31 The words of Lemuel, king of Massa, with which his mother admonished him:

2   No, my son!
     No, O son of my womb!
     No, O son of my vows!

3   Do not give your strength to women,
     Your vigor,[a] [b-]to those who destroy kings.[-b]

4   Wine is not for kings, O Lemuel;
     Not for kings to drink,
     Nor any strong drink for princes,

5   Lest they drink and forget what has been
       ordained,
     And infringe on the rights of the poor.

6   Give strong drink to the hapless
     And wine to the embittered.

7   Let them drink and forget their poverty,
     And put their troubles out of mind.

8   Speak up for the dumb,
     For the rights of all the unfortunate.

9   Speak up, judge righteously,
     Champion the poor and the needy.

10 א   What a rare find is a capable wife!
       Her worth is far beyond that of rubies.

11 ב   Her husband puts his confidence in her,
       And lacks no good thing.

---

a Lit. "ways."   *b-b Meaning of Heb. uncertain.*

---

produces *butter* or *blood*, so does squeezing someone's *patience* produce conflict. There is a wordplay in v. 33: Heb "'af," *nose*, also means "anger" in certain idioms and Heb "'apayim," *patience*, also means "nose."

31.1–9: Lemuel's mother. Like Agur (30.1), Lemuel is from the North Arabian nation of Massa. The present passage has several Aramaisms and probably is foreign in origin. Though the passage

is called "words of Lemuel," meaning a teaching he would repeat, it was composed by his mother. See 1.8–19 n. This unit and the next (31.10–31) share the theme of a wise mother. The passage is an instruction for a king, showing a fine sense of social responsibility. In the first part, vv. 3–7, Lemuel's mother first admonishes her son to avoid dissipating his strength on wine and women, for wine may make him forget his duties to the poor and women waste his

strength. Rather, one should give strong drink or wine to the poor, to let them drown their troubles in alcohol. This advice is unparalleled. The warning about women is countered by the book's concluding poem in vv. 10–31. In the second part (vv. 8–9), Lemuel's mother exhorts him to give justice to the needy.

31.10–31: The woman of strength. So far, the book of Proverbs has been devoted to inculcating the ideal of a wise man. It now concludes with a poem describing a wise woman, praising her energy, her economic talents, and her personal virtues. This is not one specific woman but an ideal, a paragon of female virtues. These virtues are essentially shared by the ideal man described elsewhere. She is a proud and splendid woman, mistress of a prosperous manor. Contrary to a common notion of woman's status in the ancient world, this woman has considerable independence in interacting with outsiders and conducting business, even in acquiring real estate. This allows her husband to spend his time sitting in the city gates, presumably conducting civic business and serving as a judge. Some commentators have interpreted the passage as an allegory, with the wise woman representing wisdom itself. But this woman has a husband and children and is very much a human being, though an ideal one. The poem is traditionally recited by Jewish men to their wives on Sabbath evening, before the Kiddush (the sanctification of the Sabbath over wine). It is also often recited at funerals of women. The poem is an acrostic, with each line beginning with a letter of the Hebrew alphabet in sequence. **10:** *What a rare find*, lit. "who can find," as in 20.6. This is an exclamation of value, not of rarity. Cf. 18.22; 19.14. *Capable wife*, Heb "'eshet ḥayil," is commonly translated "woman of valor." "Woman of strength" would be a better translation. Heb "ḥayil" refers to strength of all sorts, whether in

12 ג She is good to him, never bad,
All the days of her life.

13 ד She looks for wool and flax,
And sets her hand to them with a will.

14 ה She is like a merchant fleet,
Bringing her food from afar.

15 ו She rises while it is still night,
And supplies provisions for her household,
The daily fare of her maids.

16 ז She sets her mind on an estate and acquires it;
She plants a vineyard by her own labors.

17 ח She girds herself with strength,
ᵃ⁻And performs her tasks with vigor.⁻ᵃ

18 ט She sees ᵇ that her business thrives;
Her lamp never goes out at night.

19 י She sets her hand to the distaff;
Her fingers work the spindle.

20 כ She gives generously to the poor;
Her hands are stretched out to the needy.

21 ל She is not worried for her household because of
snow,
For her whole household is dressed in crimson.

22 מ She makes covers for herself;
Her clothing is linen and purple.

23 נ Her husband is prominent in the gates,
As he sits among the elders of the land.

24 ס She makes cloth and sells it,
And offers a girdle to the merchant.

25 ע She is clothed with strength and splendor;
She looks to the future cheerfully.

26 פ Her mouth is full of wisdom,
Her tongue with kindly teaching.

27 צ She oversees the activities of her household
And never eats the bread of idleness.

28 ק Her children declare her happy;
Her husband praises her,

29 ר "Many women have done well,
But you surpass them all."

30 ש Grace is deceptive,
Beauty is illusory;
It is for her fear of the LORD
That a woman is to be praised.

31 ת Extol her for the fruit of her hand,
And let her works praise her in the gates.

physical or military prowess, in social influence, in wealth, or in personal ethical and intellectual powers, as here. Beneath all this woman's virtues and talents lies a deep and solid strength of character. **19:** *Distaff* and *spindle*, implements used in hand spinning of flax or wool. Providing cloth for a household would require incessant spinning. **30:** *Fear of the* LORD: This is the culminating virtue of the woman of strength, just as it is wisdom's starting point (1.7; 9.10) and high point (2.5).

---

a-a Lit. "And exerts her arms."   b Lit. "tastes."

Job

Character

THE BOOK OF JOB TAKES THE FORM of a symposium, a dramatic dialogue or debate between a man who, though righteous, has been subjected to extreme suffering, and his friends, whose speeches alternate with Job's responses. It then culminates with speeches from the LORD. Readers through the centuries have debated the book's genre. Although it has characters and speeches it is not a drama, and though it engages in argument it is not a philosophical treatise. Some scholars have suggested a fruitful analogy from the classical Greek and Roman literary tradition: the "philosophical diatribe," a type of classical writing in which a particular viewpoint is presented as if it is being argued in a speech. In some diatribes—many of which take the form of attacks on vice—a second voice, present mainly in order to be refuted, expresses an opposing view to that of the main speaker. Although Job is not a work from this classical tradition, the dialogue between Job and his friends, and subsequently between Job and the LORD, serves to express particular viewpoints with an immediacy and passion similar to that of a diatribe, qualities that a more straightforward essay would lack. The multiple characters express variations of the same viewpoints in heightened, poetic language; but the formal, cyclical nature of the dialogue is interrupted at several points, and the speeches of the LORD raise the argument to a new level entirely, and then close off all further conversation without directly answering any of the deep and painful questions that have been raised along the way. Job is a wisdom book (see intro. to Kethuvim, pp. 1276–77), and such dialogues characterize ancient Near Eastern wisdom literature, especially that from Mesopotamia.

The Argument

THE BOOK OF JOB AS WE HAVE IT makes three main points, which are interrelated. The first, most obvious point is that human suffering is not necessarily deserved; that is, though in some cases we may bring our own suffering about by, for instance, neglecting our health or engaging in risky behavior—or, from a religious perspective, by our sin or immorality—the real problem with suffering comes with the many cases in which someone's pain, sorrow, or distress are clearly unrelated to anything they have done or failed to do. This point is the one that Job argues most forcibly against his friends. Those friends, who are concerned to safeguard the goodness of the LORD (seen as the cause of all things, good or bad), argue the contrary view: that if a person suffers, the suffering must somehow be deserved. This leads to the second point. The claim that all suffering is deserved will inevitably persuade those who hold that view to falsify either the character of the sufferer or the character of the LORD. Thus, Job's friends argue that Job is a sinner, deserving of his punishment, while Job claims that the LORD has acted unfairly and is indifferent to human suffering. The third point, however, is the most theologically difficult and gives the book its sense of profundity and at the same time its inconclusive conclusion: There is no way of understanding the meaning of suffering. That is, in the LORD's argument, the reasons for suffering—if there are any—are simply beyond human comprehension.

Difficulties in Interpreting Job

JOB IS THE MOST DIFFICULT BOOK of the Bible to interpret, not only because of its elaborate arguments, especially in the LORD's speeches in the final chapters, but also because of its highly poetic language, which is particularly ambiguous and contains a large number of unusual or unique words (*hapax legomena*, "things said once," that is, words not appearing elsewhere in the Bible). Thus, any translation of the book must be tentative, as translators or commentators have often understood the same verse or phrase in diametrically opposite ways. The translators' notes in the text call attention to some, but by no means all, of these difficulties.

There are also larger structural issues which confound the interpreter, most significantly the relationship of the various parts of the book. A prose prologue (1.1–3.1) and prose epilogue (42.7–17), which share a similar style and theme, frame a series of poetic speeches by Job, his friends, and the LORD. How should the prose and poetry, neither of which is complete in and of itself, be read as a whole, especially since they are so different in tone, and to some extent, in content? In addition, the speeches themselves seem to contain compositions added at different times, and a pattern present at the beginning seems to be abandoned by the end. Job 3.2–31.40 presents a conversation between Job and three friends, Eliphaz, Bildad, and Zophar. At first, this conversation follows a cyclical pattern: After an introductory lament from Job (3.2–26), Eliphaz speaks, Job replies, Bildad speaks, Job replies, Zophar speaks, Job replies, and the cycle begins again. Two full cycles (4.1–14.22; 15.1–21.34) are given; in the third cycle (22.1–31.40), the first two friends speak as before, but Zophar does not, and Job's final speech (26.1–31.40) is much longer; it also contains passages that seem to contradict Job's arguments from previous speeches. At 32.2 a new character, Elihu, enters and speaks uninterruptedly (though with several breaks) from 32.6 to 37.24. At 38.1 the LORD speaks, replying not to Elihu but to Job, who has not spoken since 31.40.

The peculiarities of this arrangement have led scholars to propose various theories for the book's composition. Most of these theories suppose that the book took shape over a longer period of time, rather than being composed more or less sequentially in one short period, and that the author (or possibly another writer or writers) returned to it to add further materials. It is also possible that speeches originally written for one character were, probably accidentally, assigned to another. Some scholars find Zophar's missing third speech in 27.7–23, and some have proposed that at least part of ch 28 may be from another composition entirely. In any event, it is clear that in the view of many scholars, the text of Job has undergone considerable upheaval in the course of its transmission, and parts of it have become misplaced. Though there is no direct manuscript evidence of this for Job, evidence from the Dead Sea Scroll versions of other books suggests that biblical books grew over time, and that different recensions (versions or editions) of the same book could circulate in ancient Israel. (See the intro. to Jeremiah and the essay "The Bible in the Dead Sea Scrolls," pp. 1920–28.) Unfortunately, however, the problems with the structure and growth of Job are so trenchant that there is no scholarly consensus concerning the stages of development of the book.

For the purposes of the annotations here, we presuppose the following. The "dream vision," 4.12–21, originally followed 3.26, the end of Job's first speech (see 4.12–21 n.). Chs 22–31, generally designated "the third cycle," can be understood in the following way: We do not presuppose that the body of material contained in these chs, like the material in chs 4–14 and 15–21, originally consisted of six speeches presented by Eliphaz, Job, Bildad, Job, Zophar, Job. The most obvious deviation from this scheme is the absence from chs 22–31 of a speech attributed to Zophar. Samuel ben Nissim Masnuth (12th century) and S. R. Driver (a British biblical scholar of the 19th and early 20th centuries) both suggested that the absence of a speech by Zophar was part of the author's design. By not providing a third speech for Zophar, the author sought to show that the friends had exhausted their arguments. Most modern scholars, however, try to reconstruct a lost speech of Zophar from parts of ch 27. But to do so is to ignore the editors' designation of Job 27.1–29.1 as a separate block of text introduced by the peculiar formula, "Job again took up his theme and said," repeated at 27.1 and 29.1. If this is a separate block of material, we must assume either that the absence of Zophar's third speech is intentional or that the speech was lost and no remnants of it are to be found in the extant book. By a process of dislocation such a speech disappeared while 27.1–29.1 found its way into the book in between the end of the second cycle at 26.14 and Job's soliloquy found in 29.2–31.40. A similar process of dislocation has taken place in ch 25 where v. 1 attributes vv. 2–6 to Bildad while the ideas expressed can only be the words of Job (see 4.12–21 n.). Finally, 26.5–14 should be seen as Bildad's speech, which expresses ideas characteristic of Job's friends and uncharacteristic of Job.

Thus, if we combine the observation that 25.2–6 is a speech of Job with the observation that 26.5–14 belongs to a speech of Bildad, we have successfully accounted for: 25.1, which attributes a speech to Bildad; 26.1, which attributes a speech to Job; 25.2–6, which belongs after 26.1; and 26.5–14, which belongs after 25.1. What of 26.2–4? A crucial observation is that Job always addresses his friends in the second-person plural and that they always address him in the second-person singular. On the basis of this observation, 26.2–4, which is in the second person singular, must be seen as a verbal attack upon Job made on behalf of his three friends by one of them. Since 25.2–6 should be assigned to Job and 26.5–14 should be assigned to Bildad, and since 26.2–4 must also be assigned to one of Job's friends, it follows that the most reasonable solution to the problem of the attributions in chs 25–26 is simply to interchange 26.1 and 25.1 so as to attribute 25.2–6 to Job and 26.2–14 to Bildad. Thus the so-called third cycle consists of Eliphaz's speech (ch 22); Job's reply (chs 23–24); Bildad's reply (25.1 + 26.2–14); Job's reply (26.1 + 25.2–6), possibly originally followed by Zophar's speech and Job's reply (both missing); and Job's soliloquy (29.2–31.40). This scheme requires only that the names Job and Bildad be interchanged in 25.1 and 26.1, and that the order of these chapters be reversed. This solution avoids both tampering with the integrity of 27.1–29.1, and creating an exception to the author's rhetorical convention by which Job always addresses the friends in the second-person plural while the friends always address Job in the second-person singular. Attribution of 4.12–21 to Job and the restoration of 25.2–6 to Job and thereby to its proper place (immediately after 26.1) at the end of the symposium results in the appearance of the almost identical utterances in 4.17–21 and 25.2–6 as an inclusio or envelope, which encloses the debate between Job and his three friends. Thus the thesis presented in the "dream vision"—that neither angels nor mortals can expect to be acquitted by the heavenly tribunal by virtue of their behavior—is the framework for the debate between Job and his friends. Typical of this debate are 5.1 and 15.2–13, where Eliphaz ridicules Job's relying upon what he heard from a "holy being," and 6.10, where Job finds consolation in his not having hidden the words of that same holy being (see the annotations at these points).

Date of Composition and Authorship

THE BABYLONIAN TALMUD, *b. Bava Batra* 15a, shows that on the basis of linguistic criteria and historical allusions there is hardly a period of biblical literature to which the book of Job does not have affinities. Because of the abundance of allusions to the exilic and postexilic Isaiah chs 40–66 and the use of the Hebrew *ha-satan*, "the Adversary," in a manner very similar to that in which the term is employed in the postexilic Zechariah ch 3, it is generally agreed that the book of Job was composed sometime during the period from the mid-6th century to the mid-4th century, the Persian (Achaemenid) period (539–332 BCE). Nevertheless, there are significant affinities between the language of Job and earlier biblical literature, suggesting that its author was archaizing in his presentation of this story from long, long ago (see below, "Setting"). As with the authors of most biblical books, the author of Job is anonymous and unknown.

History of Composition

SOME INTERPRETERS HAVE PROPOSED that four or more distinct and sometimes overlapping compositions can be discerned within Job as it stands. The common theme of these different books is the apparently undeserved suffering of a legendary hero, Job. The first composition is the prose narrative of Job's beginning in 1.1–3.1. The second is the Book of

Job the Patient, who loses his material posessions, his children, and his health and who is urged on by his wife and his friends to blaspheme God and thereby to confirm the Adversary's accusation that if Job were made to suffer, he would indeed commit blasphemy. This second book consists of 1.1–2.13; chs 27–28 (in which Job, speaking to his wife and friends, refuses to blaspheme God, insists that in the long run the wicked are punished and the virtuous are rewarded, and contends that true wisdom is the cultivation of those very virtues for which he has been lauded in 1.1, 8 and 2.3, namely fearing God and shunning evil); and 42.7–17. The third book—chs 1–31, 38–42—is the highly profound Book of Job the Impatient, in which the rather banal story of how the LORD, egged on by Satan, tested Job and found him worthy (i.e., 1.1–3.1 and 42.7–14) serves as the narrative framework for a debate between Job and his friends as to whether justice prevails in this world. In the end, in this book, God vindicates Job in his contention that indeed innocent people suffer and guilty people prosper, and He orders Job's friends to apologize. The fourth book is the Book of Job the Impatient with the addition of the three speeches of Elihu the Intruder (chs 32–37). The purpose of these additions is debated: They are particularly problematic because on the one hand Elihu is presented as a bumbler, while on the other hand his arguments closely mirror those of the LORD in the following chapters. Some scholars, as mentioned above, see in ch 28, the Hymn to Wisdom, a separate, fifth composition unrelated either to the narrative framework or the poetic symposium; some even suggest that it was incorporated into the book of Job by mistake because pages containing it were found among the writings composed by the author of the symposium.

Setting

THE SETTING EVOKES THE PATRIARCHAL PERIOD, when great biblical heroes like Abraham were the nomadic herders of large flocks of cattle, sheep, and goats. Sacrifices were offered up in a family setting without any elaborate temples or officiating priesthood. The location is Uz (1.1); this is a poetic name for Edom (Lam. 4.21). Transjordan, of which Edom is the southernmost part, is often referred to in the Bible and other ancient Near Eastern texts as Kedem, translated in 1.3 as "the East," and Kedemites were known for their wisdom (1 Kings 5.10). It is not surprising, therefore, that an author would choose to set the traditional story of Job in Edom, a region within Kedem, the legendary home of wisdom.

The Book of Job the Patient

BECAUSE THE TWO SPEECHES IN 27.2–28.28 are set apart from the rest of the book by the distinct formula at 27.1 and 29.1, "Job again took up his theme and said," and because the theology of these chapters is less radical than the theology of the rest of the material attributed to Job, some scholars have concluded that 27.2–28.28 belongs to a composition distinct from the symposium in 3.1–26.4. In this speech Job refuses to blaspheme God (27.2–6), and he affirms that in the end justice prevails (27.7–23). Then in 28.28, echoing Psalm 111.10 and Proverbs 1.7; 9.10, Job states that true wisdom consists of Job's own twin virtues, fearing the LORD and shunning evil (cf. Job 1.1, 8; 2.3). This speech therefore would originally have served as a response to Eliphaz, Bildad, and Zophar who, like Job's wife in 2.9, urged Job to respond to his suffering by cursing God and dying. In this reading the speech of Job in chs 27–28 was followed originally by a divine promise (which has been lost) to reward his steadfastness; this was followed, in turn, by 42.7–17 (the current prose epilogue), in which Job is rewarded for what he has said in chs 27–28 and the friends are castigated for having encouraged Job to blaspheme God. The other solutions to the dilemma of chs 27–28 involve reassigning most of 27.7–23 to Zophar (thereby completing the third cycle) and treating ch 28 as an independent Hymn to Wisdom composed by the author of the book of Job. For reasons explained above, this commentary does not adopt that view. The rather banal message of this reconstructed "Job the Patient"—the heart of which, 27.7–23, echoes almost verbatim the view of Eliphaz, Bildad, and Zophar that wicked people ultimately come to a bad end (see 4.8; 8.13; 11.20; 15.17–35; 18.5–21; 20.5–29)—is that indeed Job, despite both his unbearable ordeal and the intense urging of his friends, did not blaspheme God.

The Book of Job the Impatient

FAR MORE PROFOUND IS THE CANONICAL BOOK of Job, which has literally relegated "Job the Patient" to a sort of appendix and replaced this speech with what is universally acknowledged to be the most profound part of the book of Job. This largest and most important part of the book of Job is a symposium carried on by Job and his three friends—Eliphaz, Bildad, and Zophar—in 3.2–26.14. This symposium in poetic form is joined to the prose tale in which God wins His wager with the Adversary by the account, also in prose (2.11–13) of Job's three friends paying a combination condolence call and hospital visit to Job upon hearing of the calamities that befell him. It is pointed out in 2.13 that the three friends remained silent for seven days and seven nights until it was Job who broke the silence with his soliloquy in 3.3–26 in which, bereft of his children and himself afflicted with a debilitating illness, he wishes that he had never been born or even conceived and prays that he might at least die. This speech upsets Job's friends, who begin to suggest to him that Job brought his suffering upon himself (so Eliphaz in 4.7; so also Zophar 11.14) and that Job's children died as punishment for their own sins (Bildad in 8.4)—exactly the opposite of what we were told in chs 1–2. Throughout the condolence call turned into symposium, Job continually argues that his suffering is undeserved. The friends become progressively more hostile in their accusations, suggesting that his suffering is deserved. In addition, he repeatedly challenges God to put an end to his undeserved suffering (ch 7; 9.25–10.22; 13.17–14.22; 16.18–17.16; ch 23; 26.5–14). The symposium carried on between Job and his friends is launched by Eliphaz's response to Job's lament in ch 3, and the symposium (chs 4–26) is followed by Job's soliloquy (chs 29–31), the last ch of which is Job's oath proclaiming his innocence. When in the epilogue of the canonical book of Job God says to Job's three friends, "You have not spoken the truth about Me as did My servant Job" (42.8), God is in effect agreeing with Job's contention, among others, "He destroys the blameless and the guilty" (9.22). The LORD's lengthy discourse on the power of the mythical monster Leviathan in 40.25–41.26 (see esp. 41.2: "There is no one so fierce as to rouse him; Who then can stand up to Me [who made him]?") echoes and vindicates Job's own observation in Job 9.13:

> God does not restrain His anger;
> Under Him Rahab's helpers sink down.
> How then can I answer Him,
> Or choose my arguments against Him?

One of the ideas that sets the poem of Job apart from the Book of Job the Patient and from other ancient Near Eastern poems about righteous sufferers is the book's detailed pronouncement by the LORD that people who behave as badly as Job's friends need to apologize to both Job and to the LORD and to be retrained by an expert in the field, Job himself (ch 29).

[MAYER GRUBER]

1 There was a man in the land of Uz named Job. That man was blameless and upright; he feared God and shunned evil. ² Seven sons and three daughters were born to him; ³ his possessions were seven thousand sheep, three thousand camels, five hundred yoke of oxen and five hundred she-asses, and a very large household. That man was wealthier than anyone in the East.

⁴ It was the custom of his sons to hold feasts, each on his set day in his own home. They would invite their three sisters to eat and drink with them. ⁵ When a round of feast

1.1–3.1: The prologue. The LORD points out to the Adversary that Job is the most virtuous person on earth, but the Adversary suggests that Job's virtue is a function of his material success, arguing that if Job were to suffer he would cease to be a man who fears God and would "blaspheme You [God] to Your face" (1.11). God thereupon empowers the Adversary, a kind of heavenly prosecutor, to afflict Job with undeserved suffering in order to test by experiment the LORD's thesis that Job's virtue is unconditional. The verdict of the prologue is that, contrary to the Adversary's expectations, Job responds to the loss of all his material goods and the death by natural disaster of his seven sons and three daughters by praising God and refusing to blaspheme (1.21–22). When the Adversary

challenges the LORD to perform an additional experiment to see if physically afflicting Job himself might cause Job to commit blasphemy, the LORD again agrees (2.6). Once again, even though Job's wife attempts to goad Job into blasphemy (2.9), "Job said nothing sinful," and he thereby vindicates God in His argument with the Adversary. The prologue constitutes a drama of five scenes, alternating between heaven and earth, as follows: Scene One (1.1–5): Job's way of life and his good fortune; Scene Two (1.6–12): the first dialogue between the LORD and the Adversary about Job; Scene Three (1.13–22): Job in the first phase of his trial; Scene Four (2.1–6): the second dialogue between the LORD and the Adversary about Job; Scene Five (2.7–3.1): Job in the second phase

of his trial. **1.1:** *Uz,* or Edom, in the East, was a traditional source of wisdom (see intro.). *Job,* the hero of the book, bears the name given to a virtuous person of hoary antiquity mentioned by Ezekiel (Ezek. 14.12–20), who, along with Noah and Daniel, is a paradigm of righteousness. *Blameless . . . upright . . . feared God . . . shunned evil:* These characteristics underline Job's goodness, indeed, his perfection, and his subsequent actions (vv. 4–5) will demonstrate this perfection. *Fear* of God (or fear of the LORD) is the major principle in wisdom literature (Prov. 1.7; Eccl. 12.13) and signifies obedience to God's will. Even a non-Israelite like Job can be God-fearing. The reason for Job's fear of God will soon be questioned by the Adversary. A Talmudic tradition (*b. B. Bat.* 15b) considers Job to have been more virtuous than Abraham because only the fear of God is ascribed to Abraham and Job's other virtues are not. **2:** The numbers three and seven are special numbers in the Bible, and here they indicate that Job's family was the perfect size. So, too, his possessions are great, a sign that God has blessed him for his virtue. Many of the numbers used in the prologue are stereotypical, and help to create a fairytale-like atmosphere in the book. **5:** *Blasphemed God in their* days was over, Job would send word to them to sanctify themselves, and, rising early in the morning, he would make burnt offerings, one for each of them; for Job thought, "Perhaps my children have sinned and blasphemed God in their thoughts." This is what Job always used to do.

⁶One day the divine beings presented themselves before the LORD, ᵃand the Adversary⁻ᵃ came along with them. ⁷The LORD said to the Adversary, "Where have you been?" The Adversary answered the LORD, "I have been roaming all over the earth." ⁸The LORD said to the Adversary, "Have you noticed My servant Job? There is no one like him on earth, a blameless and upright man who fears God and shuns evil!" ⁹The Adversary answered the LORD, "Does Job not have good reason to fear God? ¹⁰Why, it is You who have fenced him round, him and his household and all that he has. You have blessed his efforts so that his possessions spread out in the land. ¹¹But lay Your hand upon all that he has and he will surely blaspheme You to Your face." ¹²The LORD replied to the Adversary, "See, all that he has is in your power; only do not lay a hand on him." The Adversary departed from the presence of the LORD.

¹³One day, as his sons and daughters were eating and drinking wine in the house of their eldest brother, ¹⁴a messenger came to Job and said, "The oxen were plowing and the she-asses were grazing alongside them ¹⁵when Sabeans attacked them and carried them off, and put the boys to the sword; I alone have escaped to tell you." ¹⁶This one was still speaking when another came and said, "God's fire fell from heaven, took hold of the sheep and the boys, and burned them up; I alone have escaped to tell you." ¹⁷This one was still speaking when another came and said, "A Chaldean formation of three columns made a raid on the camels and carried them off and put the boys to the sword; I alone have escaped to tell you." ¹⁸This one was still speaking when another came and said, "Your sons and daughters were eating and drinking

a-a Heb. ha-satan.

iah son of Imlah in 1 Kings 22.19–23, by the prophet Isaiah in Isa. ch 6, and in Ps. 82 and Dan. 7.9–10. The members of the heavenly court, here and in Ps. 82 called *divine beings* (here lit. "sons of the gods"; in Ps. 82.2 lit. "gods") are called in 1 Kings ch 22 "the heavenly host"; in Job 4.18 they are called "servants" and "angels"; in 15.15 they are called "holy ones" and "the heavens," while in 25.5 they are identified with the moon and stars, who, with the sun, are called "the whole heavenly host" in Deut. 4.19. Typically, these divine beings, though they have great power, may not act independently of God. *The Adversary,* or "the Accuser," Heb "hasatan," is one of the divine beings. He functions as a kind of prosecuting attorney, and should not be confused with the character of Satan as it developed in the late biblical (see 1 Chron. 21.1) and especially the postbiblical period, that is, the source of evil and rebellion against God. (Heb "ha-" is the definite article, which cannot precede a proper noun, "Satan.") Later, the idea of Satan developed into the devil, but these associations were not present at the time of our story. **8:** The LORD repeats the four attributes by which the narrator characterized Job in v. 1, thereby confirming them. **9:** *Does Job not have good reason to fear God?* Some scholars hold that this issue—whether Job's piety is disinterested—is the center around which the legend revolves, and that the ultimate answer of the book is that such disinterested piety is possible. **13–19:** The first test is the removal of all Job's possessions, including his children, by sudden catastrophes that alternate between acts of war and acts of nature. The phrase *"I alone have escaped to tell you"* serves as a refrain, highlighting the increasing horror of these escalating catastrophes. **15:** *Sabeans,* nomads from Arabia; it is the same place as in "Queen of Sheba." **17:** *Chaldean:* The term usually refers to Neo-Babylonians, from southern Mesopotamia, but here it may mean

thoughts: The plot turns on what Job will say out loud, whether, when deprived of his good life, he will curse God (v. 11). Here, virtuous Job shows his extreme piety by worrying whether his children, in a moment of levity, may have thought unseemly thoughts about God. The Heb throughout the prologue euphemistically uses the root "b-r-k," lit. "bless," to indicate "blaspheme." **6:** *The divine beings presented themselves before the LORD:* Similar meetings of the LORD enthroned on His heavenly throne and all the heavenly host standing before Him on either side are reported by the prophet Mica-wine in the house of their eldest brother ¹⁹when suddenly a mighty wind came from the wilderness. It struck the four corners of the house so that it collapsed upon the young people and they died; I alone have escaped to tell you."

²⁰Then Job arose, tore his robe, cut off his hair, and threw himself on the ground and worshiped. ²¹He said, "Naked came I out of my mother's womb, and naked shall I return there; the LORD has given, and the LORD has taken away; blessed be the name of the LORD."

²²For all that, Job did not sin nor did he cast reproach on God.

2 One day the divine beings presented themselves before the LORD. The Adversary came along with them to present himself before the LORD. ²The LORD said to the Adversary, "Where have you been?" The Adversary answered the LORD, "I have been roaming all over the earth." ³The LORD said to the Adversary, "Have you noticed My servant Job? There is no one like him on earth, a blameless and upright man who fears God and shuns evil. He still keeps his integrity; so you have incited Me against him to destroy him for no good reason." ⁴The Adversary answered the LORD, ᵃ-"Skin for skin⁻ᵃ—all that a man has he will give up for his life. ⁵But lay a hand on his bones and his flesh, and he will surely blaspheme You to Your face." ⁶So the LORD said to the Adversary, "See, he is in your power; only spare his life." ⁷The Adversary departed from the presence of the LORD and inflicted a severe inflammation on Job from the sole of his foot to the crown of his head. ⁸He took a potsherd to scratch himself as he sat in ashes. ⁹His wife said to him, "You still keep your integrity! Blaspheme God and die!" ¹⁰But he said to her, "You talk as any shameless woman might talk! Should we accept only good from God and not accept evil?" For all that, Job said nothing sinful.

¹¹When Job's three friends heard about all these calamities that had befallen him, each came from his home—

---

a-a *Apparently a proverb whose meaning is uncertain.*

semi-nomadic marauders. **19:** In the fourth catastrophe, the *four corners* collapse, just as there are *three columns* in the third catastrophe (v. 17). This, along with the notice that the enemies are coming from all different parts of the globe, highlights the fairytale-like ambiance of the narrative. **21:** *The LORD has given . . . :* This phrase is often recited at Jewish burial services. Job blesses the LORD rather than blaspheming. This verse contains a unique biblical reference to mother earth (*naked shall I return there*). **2.9:** *His wife:* This is the first

of three references (see 19.17; 31.10) to Job's wife, who remains nameless. Second Temple Jewish literature and later Jewish, Christian, and Muslim exegetical literature tend to identify unknown and unnamed persons, often with known and named persons. In the apocryphal *Testament of Job*, Job's wife is named Sitis, probably from "sitos," Gk for "food" or "bread," reflecting a tradition that Job's wife supported him from her work during the time that his illness made it impossible for him to work. In 1st-century CE Pseudo-Philo (*L.A.B.*), and in *Gen. Rab.* Job's wife was Dinah, the daughter of Jacob and Leah (see Gen. 30.21; ch 34). Thus, several later Jewish traditions develop and improve the image of Job's wife. However, both the Church Father Augustine and the Jewish sage Rabbi Abba b. Kahana (*Gen. Rab.* 19.12) compare Job and his wife to Adam and Eve, noting that both men were urged by their wives to transgress and that Job, unlike Adam, withstood the test. **10:** *Shameless woman*, Heb "nevalot," plural of "nevalah," translated "outrage" at Gen. 34.7 and "shameful thing" in Deut. 22.21, is a very strong term, referring in both of those texts to extramarital sex. Drawing on this connotation, the medieval Job Targum here translates "women who engage in premarital sex." Many modern translations prefer "foolish," however, without sexual connotations, though this may be too weak. **10:** It is difficult to know how closely we should read the phrase *said nothing sinful*; might it imply, in contrast to 1.22, *Job did not sin*, that at this point, he harbored sinful thoughts, as suggested by one talmudic sage (*b. B. Bat.* 16a)? **11:** *Eliphaz* and *Zophar* bear names associated with the Transjordanian peoples called Kedemites. Kedem was a traditional source of wisdom (see intro.). *Temanite*, Teman was a grandson of Esau, ancestor of the Edomites (Gen. 36.11). *Shuhite*, Shuah was a son of Abraham by Keturah (Gen. 25.1–2), and probably also stands for the Edomites.

Eliphaz the Temanite, Bildad the Shuhite, and Zophar the Naamathite. They met together to go and console and comfort him. 12 When they saw him from a distance, they could not recognize him, and they broke into loud weeping; each one tore his robe and threw dust into the air onto his head. 13 They sat with him on the ground seven days and seven nights. None spoke a word to him for they saw how very great was his suffering.

3 aAfterward, Job began to speak and cursed the day of his birth. 2 Job spoke up and said:

3   Perish the day on which I was born,
     And the night it was announced,
     "A male has been conceived!"
4   May that day be darkness;
     May God above have no concern for it;
     May light not shine on it;
5   May darkness and deep gloom reclaim it;
     May a pall lie over it;
     May b what blackens-b the day terrify it.
6   May obscurity carry off that night;
     May it not be counted among the days of the year;
     May it not appear in any of its months;
7   May that night be desolate;
     May no sound of joy be heard in it;
8   May those who cast spells upon the day c damn it,
     Those prepared to disable Leviathan;
9   May its twilight stars remain dark;
     May it hope for light and have none;
     May it not see the glimmerings of the dawn—
10   Because it did not block my mother's womb,
     And hide trouble from my eyes.

11   Why did I not die at birth,
     Expire as I came forth from the womb?
12   Why were there knees to receive me,
     Or breasts for me to suck?
13   For now would I be lying in repose, asleep and at
          rest,
14   With the world's kings and counselors who
          rebuild ruins for themselves,

a There are many difficulties in the poetry of Job, making the interpretation of words, verses, and even chapters uncertain. The rubric "Meaning of Heb. uncertain" in this book indicates only some of the extreme instances.
b-b Meaning of Heb. uncertain.
c Or "sea," taking Heb. yom as equivalent of yam; compare the combination of sea with Leviathan in Ps. 74.13, 14 and with Dragon in Job 7.12; cf. also Isa. 27.1.

Zophar the Naamathite is probably from Sabean (Arabian) territory (see 1.15 n.). To console, Heb "lanud," "to nod," short for "to nod their heads" (Jer. 18.16), a nonverbal expression of empathy. Unfortunately, Job's friends forgot their empathy; see 21.2. 13: Sitting on the ground for seven days resembles the Jewish mourning practice of "sitting shiv'ah" (sitting for seven [days]). See Gen. 50.10 n.

3.1–26: Job's lament. In similar language to that in which Job curses his very being, the prophet Jeremiah (20.14–18), regretting that the LORD convinced him to accept the thankless job of prophet, curses the day on which he was born. This is a masterful chapter, playing on the light and day, darkness and night, and particularly on the two definitions of day: the twenty-four hour period, and daylight. 1: We expect the verse to be continued "and cursed God," but Job only curses the day of his birth. 2: Job spoke up and said: According to b. Mo'ed Kat. 28b, this clause inspires Judaism's guidelines concerning the comforting of mourners (see Shulhan Arukh, Yoreh Deah 376.1), according to which, "The persons paying a condolence call should not open their mouths until the mourner first opens his or her mouth." 3–10: Job curses the day he was born, wishing that the day itself had never existed and that it could have been erased from the calendar. 8: Cast spells . . . Leviathan, perhaps sorcerers who curse the cosmos. Leviathan is a mythical sea-monster who played a role in the mythology of Ugarit (in modern Syria), and was known in the Bible as well as in creation stories (e.g., Isa. 27.1; Ps. 74.14), though he does not appear in the canonical story at the beginning of Genesis. 11–23: Job wishes he had died at birth or as a newborn, or had been stillborn. He views death as a release from suffering. Life, on the other hand, brings with it suffering and misery. 13–15: In his miserable state, Job depicts death in an

15 Or with nobles who possess gold and who fill
        their houses with silver.
16 Or why was I not like a buried stillbirth,
        Like babies who never saw the light?
17 There the wicked cease from troubling;
        There rest those whose strength is spent.
18 Prisoners are wholly at ease;
        They do not hear the taskmaster's voice.
19 Small and great alike are there,
        And the slave is free of his master.

20 Why does He give light to the sufferer
        And life to the bitter in spirit;
21 To those who wait for death but it does not
        come,
        Who search for it more than for treasure,
22 Who rejoice to exultation,
        And are glad to reach the grave;
23 To the man who has lost his way,
        Whom God has hedged about?

24 My groaning serves as my bread;
        My roaring pours forth as water.
25 For what I feared has overtaken me;
        What I dreaded has come upon me.
26 I had no repose, no quiet, no rest,
        And trouble came.

4 Then Eliphaz the Temanite said in reply:

2   If one ventures a word with you, will it be too
        much?
        But who can hold back his words?
3   See, you have encouraged many;
        You have strengthened failing hands.
4   Your words have kept him who stumbled from
        falling;
        You have braced knees that gave way.
5   But now that it overtakes you, it is too much;
        It reaches you, and you are unnerved.
6   Is not your piety your confidence,
        Your integrity your hope?
7   Think now, what innocent man ever perished?
        Where have the upright been destroyed?
8   As I have seen, those who plow evil
        And sow mischief reap them.
9   They perish by a blast from God,
        Are gone at the breath of His nostrils.

idealized fashion. **21:** In traditional wisdom literature, wisdom, not death, is compared to treasure (Prov. 2.4). **23:** *Whom God has hedged about* uses the same root as 1.10, "Why, it is You who have fenced him round," creating cohesion between the different parts of the book.

4.1–5.27: Eliphaz opens the debate. Though each friend is named in his speeches and speaks several times, it is difficult to attribute particular characteristics or personalities to each; they seem to serve generically as advocates of traditional wisdom perspectives and foils to Job's position. **2:** *If one ventures a word with you, will it be too much? But who can hold back his words?* Eliphaz begins tentatively, asking permission before beginning to speak and apologizing that he can no longer keep silent but needs to express his own feelings in response to Job's speech. By the third cycle of argument, in chs 22–26, Eliphaz (ch 22) becomes at best sarcastic, at worst convinced that the virtuous tragic hero of the book of Job is guilty of merciless greed at the expense of the poor, the widow, and the fatherless. **3–5:** *See, you have encouraged many . . . But now that it overtakes you, it is too much:* Eliphaz observes that in the past, Job has helped others in their time of trouble but now he, himself is in need of help. Job confirms (29.12–17) that he has, in fact, successfully provided moral and monetary support to persons in need as well as free legal services to the indigent. Eliphaz at this point accuses Job only of encouraging others to believe that there is no straightfoward system of retribution, and thus indirectly encouraging them to sin, but he is not yet directly accusing Job of sinning. **6–7:** *Is not your piety your confidence, your integrity your hope? Think now, what innocent man ever perished?* Eliphaz spouts the conventional wisdom that good people prosper and do not suffer. This, of course, is exactly the wisdom that Job challenges. *Integrity,* the same word used of Job in 1.1;

10 The lion may roar, the cub may howl,
    But the teeth of the king of beasts ᵃ·are broken.·ᵃ
11 The lion perishes for lack of prey,
    And its whelps are scattered.

12 A word came to me in stealth;
    My ear caught a whisper of it.
13 In thought-filled visions of the night,
    When deep sleep falls on men,
14 Fear and trembling came upon me,
    Causing all my bones to quake with fright.
15 A wind passed by me,
    Making the hair of my flesh bristle.
16 It halted; its appearance was strange to me;
    A form loomed before my eyes;
    I heard a murmur, a voice,
17 "Can mortals be acquitted by God?
    Can man be cleared by his Maker?
18 If He cannot trust His own servants,
    And casts reproachᵇ on His angels,
19 How much less those who dwell in houses of clay,
    Whose origin is dust,
    Who are crushed like the moth,

a-a Meaning of Heb. uncertain.   b Meaning of Heb. uncertain.

2.3, 9. **10–11:** Eliphaz chooses a *lion* since one might think that the lion provides a counterexample to the claims of the traditional system of retribution, but Eliphaz claims that ultimately the lion fares poorly.

4.12–21: The dream vision. The dream vision, or revelation, is conventionally assigned, in accord with the chapter heading at 4.1, to Eliphaz. Some scholars, however, argue that it belongs after 3.26 as the conclusion of Job's lament; this may be reflected in the poetry of the early great Paytan (liturgical poet) from the land of Israel, Eliezer ha-Qallir, who ascribes this section to Job, and may have had a text in which 4.12–21 followed 3.26, forming the end of Job's lament. If it is reassigned to Job—on the grounds that it is an interruption in its current location, that it expresses Job's fear that, right or wrong, human beings cannot prevail in argument against God, and

that it fits better at the end of ch 3—then subsequent references to it in 9.2 (from Job); 15.12–16 (where Eliphaz addresses Job); and 25.4–6 (attributed to Bildad) support Job's argument that mortals cannot be *acquitted by God.* **14:** *Fear and trembling came upon me:* This translation reflects the insight of Rashbam (c. 1085–1174) that here as in Exod. 1.10 the Heb verb "kara'" with final "alef," typically "to read," corresponds in meaning to "karah," "happened," with final "heh." This phrase is reflected in the liturgical poem *Unetaneh Tokef* recited at Rosh Ha-Shanah and on Yom Kippur. There it is stated, "The angels are dismayed; they experience fear and trembling." In fact, that entire liturgical poem is full of reverberations of this passage. **16:** *I heard a murmur, a voice,* lit. "A murmur and a voice I heard." This clause also is reflected in *Unetaneh Tokef:* "The sound of a still small voice [cf. 1 Kings 19.12: 'a soft murmuring sound'] will be

heard." **17:** *Can mortals be acquitted by God? Can man be cleared by his Maker?* These two clauses constitute a double rhetorical question, whose structure was described by Rashi in his commentary on Jeremiah (at Jer. 14.22). In such a question the first clause is introduced by the interrogative particle "ha-" while the second, synonymous clause is introduced by the interrogative particle "'im." The ancient and authentic Jewish interpretation of the two-part question as a plea for mercy, altogether appropriate in the mouth of Job and totally inappropriate in the mouth of Eliphaz, is reflected in a medieval Italian penitential prayer "seliḥah." *Mortals,* better, "a human"; Heb "'enosh" is singular. *By God . . . by his Maker,* better, "before God . . . before his Maker." The two rhetorical questions refer to one's day in court, standing literally "before" the heavenly tribunal. A similar notion is found in 25.4. **18:** *If He cannot trust . . . His angels,* cf. 15.15: "He puts no trust in His holy ones; the heavens are not guiltless in His sight." Both the parallelism here and in 15.15 make it clear that the *servants* are the personified heavenly host, which includes the personified sky, sun, moon, and stars; cf. 25.5: "Even the moon is not bright, And the stars are not pure in His sight." Given the role of the heavenly Adversary in chs 1–2, there is a certain justice to this claim. These ideas—that even God's servants and messengers (Heb "mal'akh" and Gk "angelos" both mean "messenger") are to be arraigned in judgment and that even the members of the heavenly host must throw themselves upon the mercy of the court—are taken over by the liturgical poem *Unetaneh Tokef* and used as Israel's collective defense in the face of the unjustified suffering of both individuals and collective Israel. In light of the clear influence these passages from Job have had on *Unetaneh Tokef,* it should be clear that the interpretation of this passage as a defense of Job that is mocked by Eliphaz in 5.1 represents not only an interpre-

20 Shattered between daybreak and evening,
    Perishing forever, unnoticed.
21 Their cord is pulled up
    And they die, and not with wisdom."

5 Call now! Will anyone answer you?
    To whom among the holy beings will you turn?
2 Vexation kills the fool;
    Passion slays the simpleton.
3 I myself saw a fool who had struck roots;
    Impulsively, I cursed his home:
4 May his children be far from success;
    May they be oppressed in the gate with none to
        deliver them;
5 May the hungry devour his harvest,
    ᵃCarrying it off in baskets;
    May the thirsty swallow their wealth.ᵃ
6 Evil does not grow out of the soil,
    Nor does mischief spring from the ground;
7 For man is born to [do] mischief,
    Just as sparks fly upward.

8 But I would resort to God;
    I would lay my case before God,
9 Who performs great deeds which cannot be
        fathomed,
    Wondrous things without number;
10 Who gives rain to the earth,
    And sends water over the fields;
11 Who raises the lowly up high,
    So that the dejected are secure in victory;
12 Who thwarts the designs of the crafty,
    So that their hands cannot gain success;
13 Who traps the clever in their own wiles;
    The plans of the crafty go awry.
14 By day they encounter darkness,
    At noon they grope as in the night.
15 But He saves the needy from the sword of their
        mouth,
    From the clutches of the strong.
16 So there is hope for the wretched;
    The mouth of wrongdoing is stopped.

17 See how happy is the man whom God reproves;
    Do not reject the discipline of the Almighty.
18 He injures, but He binds up;
    He wounds, but His hands heal.

a-a Meaning of Heb. uncertain.

tation which makes the very best sense of the book of Job but also one with strong roots in the Judaism of the common liturgy. **19–21:** References to the frailness and transience of human habitation and human life. *Whose origin is dust* probably means "whose foundations are in dust"—i.e., the foundations of the houses just mentioned. It is often interpreted using the metaphor of a person as a house, to mean that the origin or basic component of humans is dust, as in the story of the garden of Eden (Gen. chs 2–3). *Their cord is pulled up*, perhaps referring to a tent cord, i.e., their home; or perhaps their wealth.

5.1–27: Continuation of Eliphaz's speech. 1: *To whom . . . will you turn?* As in 15.13 Eliphaz ridicules Job's reliance upon the dream vision (see 4.12–21 n.). Job (6.10; 9.2ff.) finds consolation in what he learned from that vision. *Holy beings*, Heb "kedoshim," lit. "holy ones," here a reference to the heavenly court (4.18), continuing the image of the previous chapter. See 6.10 n. **7:** This begins to develop one of the friends' main claims, that humans are fundamentally sinful, and thus Job must have sinned. This misunderstands Job's complaint: He does not claim to be perfect, but does claim that his behavior has not merited the extreme punishment he seems to be receiving. **8:** Here Eliphaz introduces a significant theme of the book: God's great power. For the friends, God's power implies His fairness, as seen in v. 15, *But He saves the needy from the sword of their mouth.* Job believes that God often uses His power in a negative or abusive fashion (see esp. 12.7–25). God's power is the major theme of the speeches from the whirlwind as well (chs 38–41), but they do not clearly resolve whether Job or his friends are correct. **17:** Suffering, says Eliphaz, should be welcomed because it is God's way of disciplining a person; as in Prov. 3.12, it is proof of divine love. **18–26:** A parallel assurance is given in

19 He will deliver you from six troubles;
   In seven no harm will reach you:

20 In famine He will redeem you from death,
   In war, from the sword.

21 You will be sheltered from the scourging tongue;
   You will have no fear when violence comes.

22 You will laugh at violence and starvation,
   And have no fear of wild beasts.

23 For you will have a pact with the rocks in the field,
   And the beasts of the field will be your allies.

24 You will know that all is well in your tent;
   When you visit your wife*a* you will never fail.

25 You will see that your offspring are many,
   Your descendants like the grass of the earth.

26 You will come to the grave *b-*in ripe old age,*-b*
   As shocks of grain are taken away in their season.

27 See, we have inquired into this and it is so;
   Hear it and accept it.

6 Then Job said in reply:

2 If my anguish were weighed,
   My full calamity laid on the scales,

3 It would be heavier than the sand of the sea;
   That is why I spoke recklessly.*c*

4 For the arrows of the Almighty are in me;
   My spirit absorbs their poison;
   God's terrors are arrayed against me.

5 Does a wild ass bray when he has grass?
   Does a bull bellow over his fodder?

6 Can what is tasteless be eaten without salt?
   Does *b-*mallow juice*-b* have any flavor?

7 I refuse to touch them;
   They are like food when I am sick.

8 Would that my request were granted,
   That God gave me what I wished for;

9 Would that God consented to crush me,
   Loosed His hand and cut me off.

10 Then this would be my consolation,
   *b-*As I writhed in unsparing*-b* pains:
   That I did not *d-*suppress my words against the
      Holy One.*-d*

11 What strength have I, that I should endure?
   How long have I to live, that I should be patient?

---

a Lit. "home."   b-b Meaning of Heb. uncertain.   c Meaning of Heb. uncertain.
d-d Meaning of Heb. uncertain; others "deny the words of the Holy One."

Ps. 91. **22:** *Laugh at violence and starvation:* Eliphaz's overconfidence that the merit of the righteous will protect them must have seemed insensitive to Job and to the reader. Eliphaz and his two friends, Bildad and Zophar, show little empathy with Job; similarly, Zophar in 8.22; see also 12.4 n., and contrast Job's confession of innocence of this very sin of gloating over the misfortunes of one's enemies in 31.29. Prov. 17.5; 24.17 condemn this sin and warn that God will punish those who commit it. **27:** This verse, like much of the book, shares a major tenet of wisdom literature, that human inquiry rather than revelation is a sufficient source for understanding the world and how it functions.

6.1–7.21: Job responds to Eliphaz.

6.1–30: Job addresses the friends. 6.2–7, 11–13: Eliphaz has suggested both that Job brought his suffering upon himself (4.7–9; 5.2–16) and that, alternatively, Job should look upon his sufferings as God's way of disciplining him in preparation for his reward (5.17–26). Job makes an emotional response to Eliphaz's rational explanations, expressing once again the reasons for his anguish and hoping that God will end his misery by granting him death (see ch 3). **3:** *Recklessly:* The translation's uncertainty (note *c*) is because Heb "laʿu" is only attested twice, here and in Obad. 1.16, where NJPS translates "their speech grows thick," referring to the slurred speech of drunkards. Job thus more likely refers to slurred speech. Job apologizes for rambling on, when in fact his friends should be apologizing for insulting him (4.2–9) and suggesting that someone else's calamity is a laughing matter (5.22). **5–6:** Rhetorical questions are typical of wisdom literature (see v. 12; Prov. 6.27–28). **9:** Job again asks to be killed, so his suffering may be relieved. **10:** *Suppress,* Heb "kiḥed" always means "conceal, suppress, withhold" as it does also in 15.18. There Eliphaz proudly asserts that

12 Is my strength the strength of rock?
Is my flesh bronze?

13 Truly, I cannot help myself;
I have been deprived of resourcefulness.

14 ᵃ⁻A friend owes loyalty to one who fails,
Though he forsakes the fear of the Almighty;⁻ᵃ

15 My comrades are fickle, like a wadi,
Like a bed on which streams once ran.

16 ᵃ⁻They are dark with ice;
Snow obscures them;⁻ᵃ

17 But when they thaw, they vanish;
In the heat, they disappear where they are.

18 Their course twists and turns;
They run into the desert and perish.

19 Caravans from Tema look to them;
Processions from Sheba count on them.

20 They are disappointed in their hopes;
When they reach the place, they stand aghast.

21 So you are as nothing:ᵇ
At the sight of misfortune, you take fright.

22 Did I say to you, "I need your gift;
Pay a bribe for me out of your wealth;

23 Deliver me from the clutches of my enemy;
Redeem me from violent men"?

24 Teach me; I shall be silent;
Tell me where I am wrong.

25 ᵃ⁻How trenchant honest words are;⁻ᵃ
But what sort of reproof comes from you?

26 Do you devise words of reproof,
But count a hopeless man's words as wind?

27 You would even cast lots over an orphan,
Or barter away your friend.

28 Now be so good as to face me;
I will not lie to your face.

29 Relent! Let there not be injustice;
Relent! I am still in the right.

30 Is injustice on my tongue?
Can my palate not discern evil?

---

a-a *Meaning of Heb. uncertain.*
b *Following* kethib, *with Targum; meaning of Heb. uncertain.*

The Holy One (translators' note d-d): better, "a holy being"; since the Heb text here does not employ the definite article, Job here reaffirms his reliance on what he learned in the vision (4.17–21), and Eliphaz has in 5.1 ridiculed Job precisely for his reliance on a holy being. On the other hand, it is Eliphaz who says: "But I would resort to God" (5.8); "I will declare that which wise men have transmitted from their fathers, and have not withheld" (15.17–18). Additionally, in 15.15 in Eliphaz's attribution of the dream vision to Job (which Eliphaz ridicules in 15.12–13) the expression "His holy ones" refers to the same heavenly host called "His own servants ‖ His angels" in 4.18 and "the moon and stars" in 25.5. *Consolation:* Just as the readers learn from chs 1–2 that Job is not to blame for his suffering, so also does Job in 4.12–21. His friends, relying upon what they learned from their teachers and from their own limited experience (see 15.7–18), will not know this until the Lord Himself tells them in 42.7–8. In the meantime Job must deal not only with debilitating illness, the death of his children, and the loss of his worldly goods, but also with the cognitive dissonance created by the fact that his three friends keep telling him that, contrary to what he has been told in his dream and what his instincts and experience tell him, he brought all his troubles on himself. It is Job's knowledge gained from on high, which his friends do not yet understand, that is his consolation in the face of his friends' total lack of sympathy. **14–30:** Job rebukes his friends for their lack of loyalty and support in his time of need. **15:** *Wadi,* a seasonal stream that may be dangerously overflowing in winter and dry in summer. **19:** *Tema, Sheba,* areas in northern and southwestern Arabia, respectively. **24:** This foreshadows the Lord's answer in 38.2–3. **30:** Though this two-chapter speech seems like a disjointed set of speeches, food imagery ties much of it together: 6.5–7, 30; 7.4 ("sated"), 19 ("spittle").

he and his friends rely on the wisdom they learned from their forebears, which they have not withheld. Here Job, true to character, asserts that he relies on what he learned from a divine being in a vision of the night (4.12–21; 9.2–3; 15.13–16; 25.4–6). For "kihed" meaning "conceal," see also 20.12; 27.11. *The words of* (translators' note d-d): This reflects the vowel points in the traditional Heb text, while the rendering *my words* requires changing the vocalization.

7 Truly man has a term of service on earth;
His days are like those of a hireling—

2 Like a slave who longs for [evening's] shadows,
Like a hireling who waits for his wage.

3 So have I been allotted months of futility;
Nights of misery have been apportioned to me.

4 When I lie down, I think,
"When shall I rise?"
Night ᵃ-drags on,-ᵃ
And I am sated with tossings till morning twilight.

5 My flesh is covered with maggots and clods of
earth;
My skin is broken and festering.

6 My days fly faster than a weaver's shuttle,
And come to their end ᵇ-without hope.-ᵇ

7 Consider that my life is but wind;
I shall never see happiness again.

8 The eye that gazes on me will not see me;
Your eye will seek me, but I shall be gone.

9 As a cloud fades away,
So whoever goes down to Sheol does not come up;

10 He returns no more to his home;
His place does not know him.

11 On my part, I will not speak with restraint;
I will give voice to the anguish of my spirit;
I will complain in the bitterness of my soul.

12 Am I the sea or the Dragon,ᶜ
That You have set a watch over me?

13 When I think, "My bed will comfort me,
My couch will share my sorrow,"

14 You frighten me with dreams,
And terrify me with visions,

15 Till I prefer strangulation,
Death, to my wasted frame.

16 I am sick of it.
I shall not live forever;
Let me be, for my days are a breath.

17 What is man, that You make much of him,
That You fix Your attention upon him?

18 You inspect him every morning,
Examine him every minute.

19 Will You not look away from me for a while,
Let me be, till I swallow my spittle?

7.1–14: Job continues. Formally, this is a continuation of Job's response to Eliphaz, but the tone changes, becoming more philosophical, and Job directs his words to God. Job sees all life, not only his own, as a struggle. He then says how hopeless is his suffering. Job's vision of people as God's slaves contradicts the typical image of human free choice found in much of the canon, but fits the view of the wisdom book Koheleth (Ecclesiastes), which stresses that God controls everything. **2:** *[Evening's] shadows . . . wage:* Laborers were paid daily, at evening, so that they could buy food (Lev. 19.13, Deut. 24.15). **5:** Job's point is that he is in a state of living death, and would prefer actual death. **9:** *Sheol* is the underworld, where everyone goes after death. Only in postbiblical thought did a differentiated idea of heaven and hell develop. **12:** *Sea . . . Dragon:* As in 3.8, the author is building upon Canaanite mythology, best known from the myths discovered at Ugarit, where the sea (actually the deity Yam) and Dragon rebelled against the high god Baal. Job is asking God rhetorically if he is to be presumed extremely guilty like the sea or Dragon, for only that could explain his severe punishment. **17–18:** These vv. are a parody of Ps. 8.5–10, which magnifies the role of humanity in creation. In the psalm God's unceasing concern with humans renders Him praiseworthy, but for Job God's unceasing concern is like the unnerving meddling of an overprotective parent. He yearns for a release from God's attention. As elsewhere, Job is admitting that he is not perfect, but insisting that he must be judged fairly. **19:** *Till I swallow my spittle,* i.e., for an instant. This seemingly indelicate expression is one of many expressions in ancient Semitic languages describing the very briefest interval one can imagine as the time requisite for a bodily reflex, such as "the twinkling of an eye." **21:** *Why do you not pardon my transgression and forgive my iniquity?* In 6.29–30; 9.17–21; 13.23; 23.4–12;

a-a *Meaning of Heb. uncertain.*   b-b *Or "when the thread runs out."*
c *See note at 3.8.*

20 If I have sinned, what have I done to You,
Watcher of men?
Why make of me Your target,
And a burden to myself?

21 Why do You not pardon my transgression
And forgive my iniquity?
For soon I shall lie down in the dust;
When You seek me, I shall be gone.

8 Bildad the Shuhite said in reply:

2 How long will you speak such things?
Your utterances are a mighty wind!

3 Will God pervert the right?
Will the Almighty pervert justice?

4 If your sons sinned against Him,
He dispatched them for their transgression.

5 But if you seek God
And supplicate the Almighty,

6 If you are blameless and upright,
He will protect you,
And grant well-being to your righteous home.

7 Though your beginning be small,
In the end you will grow very great.

8 Ask the generation past,
Study what their fathers have searched out—

9 For we are of yesterday and know nothing;
Our days on earth are a shadow—

10 Surely they will teach you and tell you,
Speaking out of their understanding.

11 Can papyrus thrive without marsh?
Can rushes grow without water?

12 While still tender, not yet plucked,
They would wither before any other grass.

13 Such is the fate of all who forget God;
The hope of the impious man comes to naught—

14 Whose confidence is a-thread of gossamer,-a
Whose trust is a spider's web.

15 He leans on his house—it will not stand;
He seizes hold of it, but it will not hold.

16 He stays fresh even in the sun;
His shoots spring up in his garden;

17 a-His roots are twined around a heap,
They take hold of a house of stones.-a

18 When he is uprooted from his place,
It denies him, [saying,]

24.25; 31.3 (see there) Job insists that he is innocent; here, as also in 13.26; 14.16–17, he admits some measure of guilt; otherwise he could not ask God to pardon and forgive. This admission of less than total innocence on an absolute scale, however (apart from Job's being the most virtuous person on earth relative to other humans according to 1.1, 8; 2.3), is in consonance with the message of the dream vision which Job affirms in 6.10; 9.2 (see also 4.12–21; 15.13–16; 25.2–6; 5.1). *When You seek me:* As in Psalms, the assumption is that God needs people; as in Ps. 6.6, Job is reminding God that if Job is killed, he will no longer be able to praise Him.

8.1–22: Bildad's first speech.
2: *How long will you speak such things?* Job has already needlessly apologized in 6.3 for his rambling utterance (ch 3), which was itself a perfectly reasonable response. Instead of comforting Job, Bildad insults him for having expressed his feelings. In 11.2–3 Zophar will do the same thing. Eliphaz will follow suit in 15.1. Bildad insists that God acts justly and if one is suffering, it must be because he has sinned. Nevertheless, Bildad urges Job to seek God's mercy and forgiveness. It is God, after all, who sustains the world. **8–12:** The source of knowledge is experiential. Former generations are the source of wisdom and without a link to them, people cannot succeed. **11:** Rhetorical questions are again used to develop a point (see 6.5–6 n.). **13–19:** The impious man may look prosperous, but his "growth" is in a ruined place and if uprooted, he has no future.

a-a Meaning of Heb. uncertain.

"I never saw you."

19 Such is his happy lot;
And from the earth others will grow.

20 Surely God does not despise the blameless;
He gives no support to evildoers.

21 He will yet fill your mouth with laughter,
And your lips with shouts of joy.

22 Your enemies will be clothed in disgrace;
The tent of the wicked will vanish.

9 Job said in reply:

2 Indeed I know that it is so:
Man cannot win a suit against God.

3 If he insisted on a trial with Him,
He would not answer one charge in a thousand.

4 Wise of heart and mighty in power—
Who ever challenged Him and came out whole?—

5 Him who moves mountains without their
knowing it,
Who overturns them in His anger;

6 Who shakes the earth from its place,
Till its pillars quake;

7 Who commands the sun not to shine;
Who seals up the stars;

8 Who by Himself spread out the heavens,
And trod on the back of the sea;

9 Who made the Bear[a] and Orion,
Pleiades, and the chambers of the south wind;

10 Who performs great deeds which cannot be
fathomed,
And wondrous things without number.

11 He passes me by—I do not see Him;
He goes by me, but I do not perceive Him.

12 He snatches away—who can stop Him?
Who can say to Him, "What are You doing?"

13 God does not restrain His anger;
Under Him Rahab's[b] helpers sink down.

14 How then can I answer Him,
Or choose my arguments against Him?

15 Though I were in the right, I could not speak out,
But I would plead for mercy with my judge.

16 If I summoned Him and He responded,
I do not believe He would lend me His ear.

17 For He crushes me [c]for a hair;[c]
He wounds me much for no cause.

---

a Meaning of Heb. uncertain.   b A primeval monster.
c-c With Targum and Peshitta; or "with a storm."

9.1–10.22: Job responds to Bildad. 9.2: *Indeed I know that it is so:* As suggested by the colon at the end of 9.2a, the following clause, 2b, *Man cannot win a suit against God,* is a paraphrase of the main thesis of the dream vision (4.12–21) set forth there in the form of a double rhetorical question, "Can mortals be acquitted by God? Can man be cleared by his Maker?" (4.17). In fact, it would be better to translate the Heb as a question: "Can man win a (law)-suit before God?" Since Job shares Abraham's view that ultimately "the Judge of all the earth will deal justly" (cf. Gen. 18.25), Job would like to take God to court and sue Him for treating him unjustly. Job explains in this passage, however, that he has decided not to do so because the dream vision has taught him that there is no point in taking God to court. Forensic, or law-court, imagery typifies this speech, and much of the rest of the book. Job feels, correctly, that he is facing an insurmountable problem: God is both the prosecutor and the judge, and thus Job's case cannot possibly be adjudicated fairly. In addition, Job has no parity with God as judge. **5–10:** Job returns to the central theme of God's power, again implying that God abuses that power. **8a:** *Who by Himself spread out the heavens,* an expression borrowed from Isa. chs 40–66, where it occurs five times: see Isa. 40.22; 42.5; 44.24; 45.12; 51.13. This description of God is best known from the Adoration or "Aleynu" recited at the end of every synagogue worship service. Ironically, while Job here invokes God's mastery over the forces of nature as an argument why God should not be afraid to meet Job in court, the LORD, in chs 38–39, invokes His mastery over the forces of nature as an argument why Job, who has no such mastery, is incapable of understanding how the universe is governed. Equally ironically, in 40.3–5, Job concurs and apologizes. **8b:** *And trod on the back of the sea:* In the mythological texts recovered from Late Bronze Age Ugarit, frequent reference is

18 He does not let me catch my breath,
But sates me with bitterness.

19 If a trial of strength—He is the strong one;
If a trial in court—who will summon Him for me?

20 Though I were innocent,
My mouth would condemn me;
Though I were blameless, He would prove me
crooked.

21 I am blameless—I am distraught;
I am sick of life.

22 It is all one; therefore I say,
"He destroys the blameless and the guilty."

23 When suddenly a scourge brings death,
He mocks as the innocent fail.

24 The earth is handed over to the wicked one;
He covers the eyes of its judges.
If it is not He, then who?

25 My days fly swifter than a runner;
They flee without seeing happiness;

26 They pass like reed-boats,
Like an eagle swooping onto its prey.

27 If I say, "I will forget my complaint;
Abandon my sorrow *a* and be diverted,"

28 I remain in dread of all my suffering;
I know that You will not acquit me.

29 It will be I who am in the wrong;
Why then should I waste effort?

30 If I washed with soap,
Cleansed my hands with lye,

31 You would dip me in muck
Till my clothes would abhor me.

32 He is not a man, like me, that I can answer Him,
That we can go to law together.

33 No arbiter is between us
To lay his hand on us both.

34 If He would only take His rod away from me
And not let His terror frighten me,

35 Then I would speak out without fear of Him;
For I know myself not to be so.

10 I am disgusted with life;
I will give rein to my complaint,
Speak in the bitterness of my soul.

2 I say to God, "Do not condemn me;
Let me know what You charge me with.

a Lit. "face."

made to the rivalry among the deities responsible for the sky, the sea, and the summer drought for hegemony over the world. In the Israelite version of this myth, reflected in the Bible—including Gen. 1.21, and esp. in Isaiah (27.1), Psalms (74.13–14), Proverbs (8.29), and Job—a personified, deified sea is no longer a competitor of the storm deity Baal but rather a creature fashioned by God. (In rabbinic literature he becomes the divinely appointed heavenly prince in charge of the sea just as 'Af-Beri [see 37.11] is the divinely appointed prince in charge of rain, and Canaanite Mot, death personified [cf. Ps. 49.15b], becomes the divinely appointed "angel of death.") Like men and women, personified sea (referred to also by the proper names of Leviathan [serpent] and Rahab [blusterer; see 9.13]) has the audacity to rebel against the LORD. It is God's subduing of personified sea, who has attempted, like men and women, to rival and challenge God, that is referred to here. *Trod on the back* refers to the gesture of a victor over the vanquished. **10:** *Who performs great deeds . . . :* This v. is quoted verbatim in the benediction "True and Faithful" in the Evening Service every day of the year. **12b:** *Who can say to Him, "What are You doing?"* In the present context Job anticipates what he will be told by the LORD in chs 38–41: Humankind is too insignificant to understand an explanation of how God rules the cosmos even if such an explanation were to be forthcoming. **17:** The alternative reading in translators' note *c-c, with a storm* (or tempest), foreshadows the divine revelation in chs 38–41. **22–24:** A basic assumption of Job, like other biblical books, is that God is omnipotent. Thus, given his personal experience, Job can insist, *If it is not He, then who?* **25–35:** This section of the speech returns to the theme of vv. 2–3, the fundamental unfairness of a case brought by God against Job, a human. **10.2:** *I say to God, "Do not condemn me":* This introduces the speech (vv. 2b–22) that Job would

3 Does it benefit You to defraud,
To despise the toil of Your hands,
While smiling on the counsel of the wicked?

4 Do You have the eyes of flesh?
Is Your vision that of mere men?

5 Are Your days the days of a mortal,
Are Your years the years of a man,

6 That You seek my iniquity
And search out my sin?

7 You know that I am not guilty,
And that there is none to deliver from Your hand.

8 "Your hands shaped and fashioned me,
Then destroyed every part of me.

9 Consider that You fashioned me like clay;
Will You then turn me back into dust?

10 You poured me out like milk,
Congealed me like cheese;

11 You clothed me with skin and flesh
And wove me of bones and sinews;

12 You bestowed on me life and care;
Your providence watched over my spirit.

13 Yet these things You hid in Your heart;
I know that You had this in mind:

14 To watch me when I sinned
And not clear me of my iniquity;

15 Should I be guilty—the worse for me!
And even when innocent, I cannot lift my head;
So sated am I with shame,
And drenched in my misery.

16 ᵃ·It is something to be proud of·ᵃ to hunt me like a
    lion,
To ᵇ·show Yourself wondrous through·ᵇ me time
    and again!

17 You keep sending fresh witnesses against me,
Letting Your vexation with me grow.
ᵃ·I serve my term and am my own replacement.·ᵃ

18 "Why did You let me come out of the womb?
Better had I expired before any eye saw me,

19 Had I been as though I never was,
Had I been carried from the womb to the grave.

20 My days are few, so desist!
Leave me alone, let me be diverted a while

21 Before I depart—never to return—
For the land of deepest gloom;

like to address to God if indeed
Job should be granted a day in
court. **4–6:** Job's sarcastic accusation here is among the most powerful in the book, demanding that
God act like God, and not like a
human being. **8–12:** These vv.
show some similarity to the creation stories in Gen. chs 2–3, but
do not convey exactly the same
picture. **17:** This section ends with
a final forensic image: The witnesses may refer to the variety of
punishments sent against Job
which are seen as testifying to this
guilt. **18–22:** *Why did You let me
come out of the womb?* Job returns to
the image of ch 3. **19b:** *Had I been
carried from the womb to the grave:*
Job repeats the wish he expressed
in 3.11–12. **21–22:** A description of
Sheol, the abode of the dead; cf.
3.17–19; his mention of *darkness* returns us to another central image
of ch 3.

---

a-a *Meaning of Heb. uncertain.*   b-b *Or "make sport of"; cf. Pal. Aram. 'afli.*

22 A land whose light is darkness,
    All gloom and disarray,
    Whose light is like darkness."

11 Then Zophar the Naamathite said in reply:

2   Is a multitude of words unanswerable?
    Must a loquacious person be right?
3   Your prattle may silence men;
    You may mock without being rebuked,
4   And say, "My doctrine is pure,
    And I have been innocent in Your sight."
5   But would that God might speak,
    And talk to you Himself.
6   He would tell you the secrets of wisdom,
    ⁻ᵃFor there are many sides to sagacity;
    And know that God has overlooked for you some
        of your iniquity.⁻ᵃ

7   Would you discover the mystery of God?
    Would you discover the limit of the Almighty?
8   Higher than heaven—what can you do?
    Deeper than Sheol—what can you know?
9   Its measure is longer than the earth
    And broader than the sea.
10 ᵃ⁻Should He pass by, or confine,
    Or call an assembly, who can stop Him?⁻ᵃ
11 For He knows deceitful men;
    When He sees iniquity, does He not discern it?
12 ᵃ⁻A hollow man will get understanding,
    When a wild ass is born a man.⁻ᵃ

13 But if you direct your mind,
    And spread forth your hands toward Him—
14 If there is iniquity with you, remove it,
    And do not let injustice reside in your tent—
15 Then, free of blemish, you will hold your head
        high,
    And, ᵇ⁻when in straits,⁻ᵇ be unafraid.
16 You will then put your misery out of mind,
    Consider it as water that has flowed past.
17 ᵃ⁻Life will be brighter than noon;⁻ᵃ
    You will shine, you will be like the morning.
18 You will be secure, for there is hope,
    ᵃ⁻And, entrenched,⁻ᵃ you will rest secure;

**11.1–20: Zophar's first speech.
2–3:** *Is a multitude of words unanswerable?* Like Bildad in 8.2, Zophar here, in the house of a man bereft of his children (1.18–19) and infested with maggots (7.5), has the colossal nerve to tell Job, the master of the house, that he talks too much! Just because a person talks a lot, says Zophar, does not mean that he is right. **7–11:** Can Job, or any person, really understand God? And should God's actions be limited to those that human beings find rational or just? Here, like the other friends, Zophar suggests that God's great power (vv. 7–10) shows that He is a fair judge, who punishes iniquity only (v. 11). **12:** This is a proverb. Wisdom writings typically quote proverbs, integrating them into their own compositions (see, e.g., the "better" proverbs integrated in Eccl. [Koheleth] ch 7). Zophar is using this proverb to suggest that Job is *a hollow man,* and that he will never get understanding. **17:** A response to the darkness imagery used at the end of Job's previous speech.

a-a Meaning of Heb. uncertain.
b-b Heb. muṣaq; other Heb. editions muṣṣaq, "you will be firm."

19 You will lie down undisturbed;
   The great will court your favor.
20 But the eyes of the wicked pine away;
   Escape is cut off from them;
   They have only their last breath to look forward
       to.

12 Then Job said in reply:

2 Indeed, you are the [voice of] the people,
   And wisdom will die with you.
3 But I, like you, have a mind,
   And am not less than you.
   Who does not know such things?
4 I have become a laughingstock to my friend—
   "One who calls to God and is answered,
   Blamelessly innocent"—a laughingstock.
5   *In the thought of the complacent there is
           contempt for calamity;
   It is ready for those whose foot slips.*
6 Robbers live untroubled in their tents,
   And those who provoke God are secure,
   Those whom God's hands have produced.

7 But ask the beasts, and they will teach you;
   The birds of the sky, they will tell you,
8 Or speak to the earth, it will teach you;
   The fish of the sea, they will inform you.
9 Who among all these does not know
   That the hand of the LORD has done this?
10 In His hand is every living soul
   And the breath of all mankind.
11 Truly, the ear tests arguments
   As the palate tastes foods.
12 Is wisdom in the aged
   And understanding in the long-lived?
13 With Him are wisdom and courage;
   His are counsel and understanding.

a-a Meaning of Heb. uncertain.

12.1–14.22: Job responds to Zophar. 12.2–3: *Indeed, you are the [voice of] the people, and wisdom will die with you:* Better, rhetorically: "Are you really the whole people, and will wisdom die with you?" The authority invoked by Job's three friends is wisdom tradition (we might say "common knowledge"), which wise people teach as the lesson of the past and which older sages can confirm from life experience. Consequently, Eliphaz appealed both to his own experience, what "I have seen" (4.8 and 5.3) and what "we have inquired" (5.27). Eliphaz will refer again in 15.17–18 to both of his sources of authority: his own life experience, and the teachings of the Sages.

Like Eliphaz, Bildad in 8.8–10 also invokes the teachings of the wise, as does Zophar in 20.4. **3:** *Who does not know such things?* lit., "Who does not have like these?" Rashbam suggests that Job refers to the friends' previous arguments. Some contemporary scholars construe "these" as referring to Job's parody in vv. 4–6 of the friends' arguments (especially Eliphaz in 5.19–24). **4–6:** Following this reading, we may understand these vv. as follows: "He laughs at mischance and disaster, just calls to God and is answered—the blameless good man laughs. He scorns misfortune, is tranquil in time of calamity, firm in time of foot-slipping. Tents are unharmed despite marauders, there is security despite those who provoke God, for him whom God shelters with His hand." Job here refers to Eliphaz's assertion in 5.22 and Bildad's similar assertion in 8.21 that a virtuous person should simply laugh at the disasters which befall other persons. See 5.22 n. and 31.29 n. **5:** *Contempt for calamity:* In *Tosefta Sotah* 3.12 this is taken as an apt description of the people of Sodom who refused to take seriously the warning of impending disaster conveyed by God's messengers (cf. Gen. 19.4). **7–8:** Understanding these vv. as Job's parodic quotation of the friends, note that in other parts of the text, Job consistently addresses the friends in the second-person plural and they consistently address him in the second-person singular. Here, however, *you* is singular, indicating that Job is quoting the friends, not speaking to them. Alternatively this may be Job's counterargument to his friends: They claim that they have the wisdom of generations, but Job suggests that he possesses greater wisdom, based on the less biased, all-seeing animals. **9:** *Who among all these does not know:* Here, as in 3, Job refers critically to his friends' assertions. **13–25:** Again, Job returns to a central theme, the power of God, asserting very clearly that God is extremely powerful, but abuses His power and uses it for

14 Whatever He tears down cannot be rebuilt;
   Whomever He imprisons cannot be set free.

15 When He holds back the waters, they dry up;
   When He lets them loose, they tear up the land.

16 With Him are strength and resourcefulness;
   Erring and causing to err are from Him.

17 He makes counselors go about naked[a]
   And causes judges to go mad.

18 He undoes the belts of kings,
   And fastens loincloths on them.

19 He makes priests go about naked,[a]
   And leads temple-servants[b] astray.

20 He deprives trusty men of speech,
   And takes away the reason of elders.

21 He pours disgrace upon great men,
   And loosens the belt of the mighty.

22 He draws mysteries out of the darkness,
   And brings obscurities to light.

23 He exalts nations, then destroys them;
   He expands nations, then leads them away.

24 He deranges the leaders of the people,
   And makes them wander in a trackless waste.

25 They grope without light in the darkness;
   He makes them wander as if drunk.

13 My eye has seen all this;
   My ear has heard and understood it.

2 What you know, I know also;
   I am not less than you.

3 Indeed, I would speak to the Almighty;
   I insist on arguing with God.

4 But you invent lies;
   All of you are quacks.

5 If you would only keep quiet
   It would be considered wisdom on your part.

6 Hear now my arguments,
   Listen to my pleading.

7 Will you speak unjustly on God's behalf?
   Will you speak deceitfully for Him?

8 Will you be partial toward Him?
   Will you plead God's cause?

9 Will it go well when He examines you?
   Will you fool Him as one fools men?

10 He will surely reprove you
   If in ᶜyour heartᶜ you are partial toward Him.

destructive purposes. **13:** Job returns to the forensic imagery of ch 9. **13.4–6:** Job's plea that his friends listen is logical, given that when each friend replies to Job, he is not actually replying to what Job had just said, and sometimes the friends even put false statements into Job's mouth (e.g., 22.13). **5:** This reflects a common wisdom notion, seen in Prov. 17.28: "Even a fool, if he keeps silent, is deemed wise; / Intelligent, if he seals his lips." **9–10:** Job is ultimately proven correct in 42.7.

a A sign of madness.

b Cf. Ugaritic ytnm, a class of temple servants; others "the mighty."

c-c Lit. "secret."

11 His threat will terrify you,
   And His fear will seize you.
12 Your briefs are empty[a] platitudes;
   Your responses are unsubstantial.[b]
13 Keep quiet; I will have my say,
   Come what may upon me.
14 How long! I will take my flesh in my teeth;
   I will take my life in my hands.
15 [c]He may well slay me; I may have no hope;[c]
   Yet I will argue my case before Him.
16 In this too is my salvation:
   That no impious man can come into His presence.

17 Listen closely to my words;
   Give ear to my discourse.
18 See now, I have prepared a case;
   I know that I will win it.
19 For who is it that would challenge me?
   I should then keep silent and expire.
20 But two things do not do to me,
   So that I need not hide from You:
21 Remove Your hand from me,
   And let not Your terror frighten me.
22 Then summon me and I will respond,
   Or I will speak and You reply to me.
23 How many are my iniquities and sins?
   Advise me of my transgression and sin.
24 Why do You hide Your face,
   And treat me like an enemy?
25 Will You harass a driven leaf,
   Will You pursue dried-up straw,
26 That You decree for me bitter things
   And make me [d]answer for[d] the iniquities of my
       youth,
27 That You put my feet in the stocks
   And watch all my ways,
   [e]Hemming in my footsteps?[e]
28 Man wastes away like a rotten thing,
   Like a garment eaten by moths.

14 Man born of woman is short-lived and sated with
       trouble.
2 He blossoms like a flower and withers;
   He vanishes like a shadow and does not endure.

27: Job returns to the theme of 7.12–21, that God watches people too closely; this is further developed at the beginning of the following chapter. **14.1:** *Man born of woman,* Gen. 1.27, "God created the "ʾadam" ("human"). . . . He created them male and female" proves that in biblical Heb "ʾadam," here translated *man,* refers to both every individual human of either sex and to humankind collectively. This understanding is reflected in ancient rabbinic exegesis (see, e.g., *Sifra* at Lev. 1.2). *Born of woman* (Heb "yelud ʾishah") is peculiar to Job (found only twice more in the entire Bible, in Job 15.14; 25.4). It signifies the mortality of human beings. Some commentators read this as a reference to the impurity of childbirth. **2:** The image of a flower will be picked up and developed in v. 7.

a Lit. "ashen."   b Lit. "clayey."
c-c So with kethib; others with qere "Though He slay me, yet will I trust in Him."
d-d Lit. "inherit."   e-e Meaning of Heb. uncertain.

3   Do You fix Your gaze on such a one?
     Will You go to law with me?

4   ᵃ·Who can produce a clean thing out of an unclean
        one? No one!·ᵃ

5   His days are determined;
     You know the number of his months;
     You have set him limits that he cannot pass.

6   Turn away from him, that he may be at ease
     Until, like a hireling, he finishes out his day.

7   There is hope for a tree;
     If it is cut down it will renew itself;
     Its shoots will not cease.

8   If its roots are old in the earth,
     And its stump dies in the ground,

9   At the scent of water it will bud
     And produce branches like a sapling.

10   But mortals languish and die;
     Man expires; where is he?

11   The waters of the sea fail,
     And the river dries up and is parched.

12   So man lies down never to rise;
     He will awake only when the heavens are no more,
     Only then be aroused from his sleep.

13   O that You would hide me in Sheol,
     Conceal me until Your anger passes,
     Set me a fixed time to attend to me.

14   If a man dies, can he live again?
     All the time of my service I wait
     Until my replacement comes.

15   You would call and I would answer You;
     You would set Your heart on Your handiwork.

16   Then You would not count my steps,
     Or keep watch over my sin.

17   My transgression would be sealed up in a pouch;
     You would coat over my iniquity.

18   Mountains collapse and crumble;
     Rocks are dislodged from their place.

19   Water wears away stone;
     Torrents wash away earth;
     So you destroy man's hope,

20   You overpower him forever and he perishes;
     You alter his visage and dispatch him.

21   His sons attain honor and he does not know it;
     They are humbled and he is not aware of it.

6: The hireling image builds on the opening of ch 7. **7–12:** Job is full of ironies. Picking up on the image of the withering flower of v. 2, Job insists that trees are better off than people, since they renew themselves, while human death cannot be reversed. **13–14:** *O that you would hide me in Sheol. . . . If a man dies, can he live again?* The notion of an afterlife, the resurrection of the dead, or a world to come where people are rewarded or punished for their deeds in this world, had not yet developed at the time that Job was written. He thus has, in general, no recourse to these ideas or beliefs in his argument, although there may be the seeds of this idea in v. 14. **18–22:** God's power again is invoked by Job, and cast in a negative light.

a-a Meaning of Heb. uncertain.

22   He feels only the pain of his flesh,
      And his spirit mourns in him.

15 Eliphaz the Temanite said in reply:

2   Does a wise man answer with windy opinions,
      And fill his belly with the east wind?
3   Should he argue with useless talk,
      With words that are of no worth?
4   You subvert piety
      And restrain prayer to God.
5   Your sinfulness dictates your speech,
      So you choose crafty language.
6   Your own mouth condemns you—not I;
      Your lips testify against you.

7   Were you the first man born?
      Were you created before the hills?
8   Have you listened in on the council of God?
      Have you sole possession of wisdom?
9   What do you know that we do not know,
      Or understand that we do not?
10   Among us are gray-haired old men,
      Older by far than your father.
11   Are God's consolations not enough for you,
      And His gentle words to you?
12   How your heart has carried you away,
      How your eyes *have failed*ᵃ you,
13   That you could vent your anger on God,
      And let such words out of your mouth!
14   What is man that he can be cleared of guilt,
      One born of woman, that he be in the right?
15   He puts no trust in His holy ones;
      The heavens are not guiltless in His sight;
16   What then of one loathsome and foul,
      Man, who drinks wrongdoing like water!

17   I will hold forth; listen to me;
      What I have seen, I will declare—
18   That which wise men have transmitted from their
          fathers,

a-a *Meaning of Heb. uncertain.*

15.1–35: Eliphaz's second speech.
Following the wisdom tradition,
this speech begins with a large
number of rhetorical questions.
2–3: These rhetorical questions, to
which the answer is no, are meant
to undermine Job's claim in 12.2–6,
11–12; 13.1–5 that he is wise (i.e.,
an embodiment of education in the
truth) and that his three friends are
foolish (i.e., uneducated, miseducated, or possibly ineducable).
3: *Useless talk:* Echoing Bildad in
8.2ff. and Zophar in 11.2–3, Eliphaz begins his speech by insulting Job for talking too much.
4: *And restrain prayer to God,* better,
"And did you remove conversa-
tion [that took place] before
God?"—referring back to the
dream vision recorded in 4.12–21
(see annotations there) and referred to again most positively by
Job in 9.2 (see there). **8:** *Have you
listened in on the council of God?* Another mocking reference to Job's
report of the dream vision (see
above at v. 4 and see 4.12–21; 9.2);
for the mocking by the friends of
Job's account of his dream vision,
see 5.1, and see Job's deriving consolation in 6.10 from his having
told of his dream vision. **10:** The
wisdom accumulated by elders is
a major theme in biblical and ancient Near Eastern wisdom literature. **11:** *God's consolations,* better,
with Gersonides (1288–1344),
"*these* consolations," i.e., the consolations offered by Eliphaz, Bildad, and Zophar. The Heb particle
"*el*" here, as in Gen. 19.8, 25; 26.3,
4; Lev. 18.27, etc., is a biform of the
common demonstrative adjective
"*eleh*," "these," and it should not
be confused with its homonym,
the generic term for God or a
god. NJPS here follows Rashi
(1040–1105). **11b:** *And His gentle
words to you?* better, "For there is
with you (i.e., you know) some
word that reached you with
stealth," following Ibn Ezra
(1089–1164) and Gersonides.
13: *Vent your anger on God,* better,
"blow your wind at these men."
This also follows Gersonides' interpretation (see v. 11a n. above).
13: *Out of your mouth!* Since Eliphaz now mockingly quotes Job's
account of his dream vision, the
exclamation mark should be replaced by a colon, and vv. 14–16
should be placed within quotation
marks as they are an almost verbatim quotation of 4.12–21 (see also
9.2; 25.4–6). **14:** *What is man that
can be cleared of guilt?* Heb "mah-
'enosh ki-yizkeh," which inspires
the alphabetical "piyyut" (liturgical poem) "'Enosh Ma-Yizkeh,"
"How can man be clear," by Meshullam b. Kalonymos of Rome, in
the Morning Service for Yom Kip-

And have not withheld,

19 To whom alone the land was given,
No stranger passing among them:

20 The wicked man writhes in torment all his days;
Few years are reserved for the ruthless.

21 Frightening sounds fill his ears;
When he is at ease a robber falls upon him.

22 He is never sure he will come back from the dark;
A sword stares him in the face.

23 He wanders about for bread—where is it?
He knows that the day of darkness has been
readied for him.

24 Troubles terrify him, anxiety overpowers him,
Like a king ᵃˉexpecting a siege.ˉᵃ

25 For he has raised his arm against God
And played the hero against the Almighty.

26 He runs at Him defiantlyᵇ
ᵃˉWith his thickly bossed shield.

27 His face is covered with fat
And his loins with blubber.ˉᵃ

28 He dwells in cities doomed to ruin,
In houses that shall not be lived in,
That are destined to become heaps of rubble.

29 He will not be rich;
His wealth will not endure;
ᵃˉHis produce shall not bend to the earth.ˉᵃ

30 He will never get away from the darkness;
Flames will sear his shoots;
ᵃˉHe will pass away by the breath of His mouth.

31 He will not be trusted;
He will be misled by falsehood,
And falsehood will be his recompense.ˉᵃ

32 He will wither before his time,
His boughs never having flourished.

33 He will drop his unripe grapes like a vine;
He will shed his blossoms like an olive tree.

34 For the company of the impious is desolate;
Fire consumes the tents of the briber;

35 For they have conceived mischief, given birth to
evil,
And their womb has produced deceit.

16

Job said in reply:

2 I have often heard such things;
You are all mischievous comforters.

pur. Both Job and his friends agree that people are worthless (see Bildad in 8.17–21). They disagree, however, concerning the implications of this premise: For the friends, it means that people are fundamentally sinners, while for Job it suggests that God needs to give people more leeway in judging them. **14b:** *Born of woman,* see above n. at 14.1, and below at 25.4. **15:** *He puts no trust in His holy ones,* see 4.18 n. *The heavens are not guiltless in His sight:* This clause appears in its entirety as the ninth clause in the "piyyut" (liturgical poem) " ʾEnosh ʾEikh Yitzdak," "How can man be proved innocent before his Creator?" in the Additional (Musaf) Service for Yom Kippur. Composed by the most important of the medieval "payyetanim" (liturgical poets), Eleazar ha-Qallir, who lived in the land of Israel during the 7th century CE, this poem is clearly inspired by an ancient Jewish interpretation of Job 15.14–16 and its parallel passages (4.12–21; 9.2; 25.4–6) as a plea for mercy appropriate in the mouth of Job and consequently in the mouth of downtrodden Israel (i.e., the Jewish people) and thoroughly inappropriate in the mouth of Eliphaz except as a quotation of Job's plea for mercy. This plea is here based upon the reasoning that if personified heavens (said to be pure in Exod. 24.10) are not pure in God's sight, how much the more are human beings impure; hence collective Israel, following Job's example, throws himself on the mercy of the divine court. See also the paraphrase of Job 15.15 in the most famous "piyyut," recited on both the New Year and the Day of Atonement, *Unetaneh Tokef:* "Indeed, even they [the heavenly host] will not be pure in Your eyes during the judicial process." **20–35:** This is one of the longest descriptions by one of Job's friends of the fate of the wicked; it is developed with great detail and certainty.

16.1–17.16: Job's reply to Eliphaz's second speech. Job begins by criticizing his friends'

---

a-a Meaning of Heb. uncertain.   *b Lit. "with neck."*

3 Have windy words no limit?
   What afflicts you that you speak on?
4 I would also talk like you
   If you were in my place;
   I would barrage you with words,
   I would wag my head over you.
5 I would encourage you with words,[a]
   My moving lips would bring relief.
6 If I speak, my pain will not be relieved,
   And if I do not—what have I lost?
7 Now He has truly worn me out;
   You have destroyed my whole community.
8 You have shriveled me;
   My gauntness serves as a witness,
   And testifies against me.
9 In His anger He tears and persecutes me;
   He gnashes His teeth at me;
   My foe stabs me with his eyes.
10 They open wide their mouths at me;
   Reviling me, they strike my cheeks;
   They inflame themselves against me.
11 God hands me over to an evil man,
   Thrusts me into the clutches of the wicked.
12 I had been untroubled, and He broke me in pieces;
   He took me by the scruff and shattered me;
   He set me up as His target;
13 His bowmen surrounded me;
   He pierced my kidneys; He showed no mercy;
   He spilled my bile onto the ground.
14 He breached me, breach after breach;
   He rushed at me like a warrior.
15 I sewed sackcloth over my skin;
   I [b-buried my glory-b] in the dust.
16 My face is red with weeping;
   Darkness covers my eyes
17 [c-For no injustice on my part
   And for the purity of my prayer!-c]

18 Earth, do not cover my blood;
   Let there be no resting place for my outcry!
19 Surely now my witness is in heaven;
   He who can testify for me is on high.
20 O my advocates, my fellows,
   Before God my eyes shed tears;

words, but soon the focus shifts from the friends to God, who is spoken of in the third person and also addressed in the second person. God has become Job's foe, ruining his life, in ways that are described, perhaps metaphorically, as physical attacks on parts of Job's body. Job feels social rejection as well as physical ailments (a common complaint in ancient Near Eastern, including biblical, lament literature). In 16.18–17.1 Job returns to the idea that he has no recourse against God and that all he can do is wait for death. He seems to have lost all hope. **16.3:** This echoes Eliphaz in 15.2–3; the friends accuse Job of being a windbag and vice versa. This theme will also play a major role in the first speech of Elihu, in 32.18–19. **9:** *My foe* in this context is likely God, a very strong accusation, representing the tremendous alienation that Job is feeling. **18:** *Earth, do not cover my blood:* Job does not want his suffering to be forgotten or unrequited. The idea behind this phrase is the belief that the blood of the innocent cries out from the ground, as in the case of Abel (Gen. 4.10; see also Ezek. 24.7–8). In a ritual context, Lev. 17.13 states that if an animal or bird is hunted down, its blood must be poured out and covered with earth in order for it to be permitted as food. More recently, this verse has become associated with the Holocaust; it appears, for example, in an inscription in Warsaw marking the site where Jews were transported to Treblinka. **19:** In this reference to heaven, Job may also be recalling the ancient tradition that heaven and earth may serve as unbiased witnesses (see Deut. 32.1).

---

a Lit. "my mouth."
b-b Lit. "made my horn enter into."
c-c Or "Though I did no injustice, / And my prayer was pure."

21 Let Him arbitrate between a man and God
   As between a man and his fellow.
22 For a few more years will pass,
   And I shall go the way of no return.

17 My spirit is crushed, my days run out;
   The graveyard waits for me.

2 Surely mocking men keep me company,
   And with their provocations I close my eyes.
3 Come now, stand surety for me!
   Who will give his hand on my behalf?
4 You have hidden understanding from their minds;
   Therefore You must not exalt [them].
5 He informs on his friends for a share [of their
        property],
   And his children's eyes pine away.

6 He made me a byword among people;
   I have become like Tophet[a] of old.
7 My eyes fail from vexation;
   All shapes seem to me like shadows.
8 The upright are amazed at this;
   The pure are aroused against the impious.
9 The righteous man holds to his way;
   He whose hands are clean grows stronger.
10 But all of you, come back now;
   I shall not find a wise man among you.
11 My days are done, my tendons severed,
   The strings of my heart.
12 They say that night is day,
   That light is here—in the face of darkness.
13 If I must look forward to Sheol as my home,
   And make my bed in the dark place,
14 Say to the Pit, "You are my father,"
   To the maggots, "Mother," "Sister"—
15 Where, then, is my hope?
   Who can see hope for me?
16 Will it descend to Sheol?
   Shall we go down together to the dust?

18 Then Bildad the Shuhite said in reply:

2 How long? Put an end to talk!
   Consider, and then we shall speak.
3 Why are we thought of as brutes,
   Regarded by you as stupid?

a *That consumed children; cf. Jer. 7.31.*

17.10–14: After explicitly raising the issue of wisdom in v. 10, Job reworks a well-known wisdom notion that wisdom would be your relative in a perverse fashion in v.14.

18.1–21: Bildad's second speech. As before, this speech opens with words about making speeches. Bildad rejects Job's characterization of the friends as stupid, suggesting instead that Job makes himself too important, takes his suffering too seriously. He repeats his former views about the fate of the wicked. This is longer and more metaphor-

4 You who tear yourself to pieces in anger—
Will ᵃearth's order be disrupted ᵃ for your sake?
Will rocks be dislodged from their place?

5 Indeed, the light of the wicked fails;
The flame of his fire does not shine.

6 The light in his tent darkens;
His lamp fails him.

7 His iniquitous strides are hobbled;
His schemes overthrow him.

8 He is led by his feet into the net;
He walks onto the toils.

9 The trap seizes his heel;
The noose tightens on him.

10 The rope for him lies hidden on the ground;
His snare, on the path.

11 Terrors assault him on all sides
And send his feet flying.

12 His progeny hunger;
Disaster awaits his wife.ᵇ

13 The tendons under his skin are consumed;
Death's first-born consumes his tendons.

14 He is torn from the safety of his tent;
Terror marches him to the king.ᶜ

15 It lodges in his desolate tent;
Sulfur is strewn upon his home.

16 His roots below dry up,
And above, his branches wither.

17 All mention of him vanishes from the earth;
He has no name abroad.

18 He is thrust from light to darkness,
Driven from the world.

19 He has no seed or breed among his people,
No survivor where he once lived.

20 Generations to come will be appalled at his fate,
As the previous ones are seized with horror.

21 "These were the haunts of the wicked;
Here was the place of him who knew not God."

19 Job said in reply:

2 How long will you grieve my spirit,
And crush me with words?

3 ᵈTime and againᵈ you humiliate me,
And are not ashamed to abuse me.

4 If indeed I have erred,
My error remains with me.

ical than the similar description of Eliphaz at the end of ch 15. **13–14:** *Death's first-born . . . Terror . . . to the king:* These may be mythological references; the deity Mot ("Death") is well-attested in Ugaritic mythology. V. 14 ends with "le-melekh balahot," apparently an epithet, better translated as "to King-of-Terrors."

19.1–29: **Job's reply to Bildad's second speech.** Job complains again about the treatment he receives from his friends and from God. He then describes his feelings of alienation from his family, servants, and friends (vv. 13–20). The chapter concludes with a cry for pity, and a wish that his state be recorded for posterity, so that in the future he will be vindicated.

a-a Lit. "the earth be abandoned."   b Lit. "rib" (cf. Gen. 2.22); or "stumbling."
c Viz., of the netherworld.   d-d Lit. "Ten times."

5   Though you are overbearing toward me,
    Reproaching me with my disgrace,

6   Yet know that God has wronged me;
    He has thrown up siege works around me.

7   I cry, "Violence!" but am not answered;
    I shout, but can get no justice.

8   He has barred my way; I cannot pass;
    He has laid darkness upon my path.

9   He has stripped me of my glory,
    Removed the crown from my head.

10 He tears down every part of me; I perish;
    He uproots my hope like a tree.

11 He kindles His anger against me;
    He regards me as one of His foes.

12 His troops advance together;
    They build their road toward me
    And encamp around my tent.

13 He alienated my kin from me;
    My acquaintances disown me.

14 My relatives are gone;
    My friends have forgotten me.

15 My dependents and maidservants regard me as a
            stranger;
    I am an outsider to them.

16 I summon my servant but he does not respond;
    I must myself entreat him.

17 My odor is repulsive to my wife;
    I am loathsome to my children.

18 Even youngsters disdain me;
    When I rise, they speak against me.

19 All my bosom friends detest me;
    Those I love have turned against me.

20 My bones stick to my skin and flesh;
    I escape with the skin of my teeth.

21 Pity me, pity me! You are my friends;
    For the hand of God has struck me!

22 Why do you pursue me like God,
    a-Maligning me insatiably?-a

23 O that my words were written down;
    Would they were inscribed in a record,

24 Incised on a rock forever
    With iron stylus and lead!

25 But I know that my Vindicator lives;
    In the end He will testify on earth—

26 This, after my skin will have been peeled off.

8–13: The repetition of "he" and "me" serves as a powerful accusation against God. **17:** *My odor is repulsive to my wife:* This is the second of three references to Job's wife (see 2.10; 31.10). **17b:** *I am loathsome to my children:* This verse would seem to demonstrate the independence of the poetic symposium from the prose framework, according to which by the time Eliphaz, Bildad, and Zophar came to visit Job, the latter's seven sons and three daughters had all perished. Inconsistencies in details such as these between prose narrative frameworks and poems set within such narrative frameworks are found elsewhere (Exod. chs 14–15; Judg. chs 4–5; Jonah). **23–24:** Job is so certain of his innocence that he wants his case to be inscribed on a monumental stele, rather than the more temporary parchment or papyrus used in biblical antiquity. **25:** *But I know that my Vindicator lives:* The word for *Vindicator* is "go'el," "redeemer," the legal term for the person in the family responsible for avenging the murder of other members (Num. 35.19; Deut. 19.6). While the term "go'el" is sometimes applied to God, who is the "redeemer" of Israel, Job is not speaking about God but rather about a future kinsman who will vindicate him, who will take revenge on God for what God has done to Job.

a-a Lit. "You are not satisfied with my flesh."

27	But I would behold God while still in my flesh,
	I myself, not another, would behold Him;
	Would see with my own eyes:
	My heart*a* pines within me.
28	You say, "How do we persecute him?
	The root of the matter is in him."*b*
29	Be in fear of the sword,
	For [your] fury is iniquity worthy of the sword;
	Know there is a judgment!

20 Zophar the Naamathite said in reply:

2   In truth, my thoughts urge me to answer
    (It is because of my feelings
3   When I hear reproof that insults me);
    A spirit out of my understanding makes me reply:
4   Do you not know this, that from time immemorial,
    Since man was set on earth,
5   The joy of the wicked has been brief,
    The happiness of the impious, fleeting?
6   Though he grows as high as the sky,
    His head reaching the clouds,
7   He perishes forever, like his dung;
    Those who saw him will say, "Where is he?"
8   He flies away like a dream and cannot be found;
    He is banished like a night vision.
9   Eyes that glimpsed him do so no more;
    They cannot see him in his place any longer.
10 His sons ingratiate themselves with the poor;
    His own hands must give back his wealth.
11 His bones, still full of vigor,
    Lie down in the dust with him.
12 Though evil is sweet to his taste,
    And he conceals it under his tongue;
13 Though he saves it, does not let it go,
    Holds it inside his mouth,
14 His food in his bowels turns
    Into asps' venom within him.
15 The riches he swallows he vomits;
    God empties it out of his stomach.
16 He sucks the poison of asps;
    The tongue of the viper kills him.
17 Let him not enjoy the streams,
    The rivers of honey, the brooks of cream.
18 He will give back the goods unswallowed;
    The value of the riches, undigested.

20.1–29: Zophar's second speech. As if all of Job's previous words meant nothing, Zophar speaks about the fate of the wicked. The dominant image calls upon the digestive system (vv. 12–18). Zophar allows for the possibility that the wicked may triumph, but only briefly (contrast Ps. 1). Though not stated directly, the implication of the speech is that Job, who is suffering all of the punishments of the wicked, must therefore be wicked.

---

a Lit. "kidneys."   *b* With many mss. and versions; printed editions, "me."

19 Because he crushed and tortured the poor,
   He will not build up the house he took by
      force.
20 He will not see his children tranquil;
   He will not preserve one of his dear ones.ª
21 With no survivor to enjoy it,
   His fortune will not prosper.
22 When he has all he wants, trouble will come;
   Misfortunes of all kinds will batter him.
23 Let that fill his belly;
   Let Him loose His burning anger at him,
   And rain down His weapons upon him.
24 Fleeing from iron arrows,
   He is shot through from a bow of bronze.
25 Brandished and run through his body,
   The blade, through his gall,
   Strikes terror into him.
26 Utter darkness waits for his treasured ones;
   A fire fanned by no man will consume him;
   Who survives in his tent will be crushed.
27 Heaven will expose his iniquity;
   Earth will rise up against him.
28 His household will be cast forth by a flood,
   Spilled out on the day of His wrath.
29 This is the wicked man's portion from God,
   The lot God has ordained for him.

21 Job said in reply:

2 Listen well to what I say,
   And let that be your consolation.
3 Bear with me while I speak,
   And after I have spoken, you may mock.
4 Is my complaint directed toward a man?
   Why should I not lose my patience?
5 Look at me and be appalled,
   And clap your hand to your mouth.
6 When I think of it I am terrified;
   My body is seized with shuddering.

7 Why do the wicked live on,
   Prosper and grow wealthy?
8 Their children are with them always,
   And they see their children's children.
9 Their homes are secure, without fear;
   They do not feel the rod of God.

a For this meaning of beṭen and ḥamud, cf. Hos. 9.16.

21.1–34: Job's reply to Zophar's second speech. In this last speech in the second cycle, Job insists that, contrary to what his friends have been saying, the wicked do prosper. **2–3:** *Listen well . . . be your consolation:* Job suggests that the way the friends can bring him consolation, which was their intent (2.11), is to listen to him, instead of berating him. **7–34:** Job complains that the wicked prosper and that the success of the wicked demonstrates that justice does not prevail. In the same vein, Jeremiah asks in 12.1, "Why does the way of the wicked prosper? Why are the workers of treachery at ease?" Commenting on vv. 9–14, the Tosefta, which many view as the oldest commentary on the Mishnah (220 CE, at *Sotah* 3.6), sees in Job's graphic description of the material success of the wicked an account of the prosperity of the generation that perished in the flood described in Gen. ch 7. Tosefta Sotah thereby neutralizes the scriptural evidence, which contradicts the assertion of *Mishnah Sotah* 1.7 = *Tosefta Sotah* 3.1 that everyone is rewarded or punished in direct proportion to that person's positive or negative behavior. Moreover, *Tosefta Sotah* 3.7 contends that "the bounty with which God favored them [the people who perished in the flood] led to the following: 'They say to God "Leave us alone . . ." ' " (Job 21.14a); "[the declaration] 'What is Shaddai that we should serve Him?' " (21.15a), which means, according to Tosefta: "They said, 'Do we need Him [God] for anything except a few drops of rain? Look, we have rivers and wells which are more than enough for us in the summer and in the rainy season.' " Tosefta understands that the vivid description of the prosperity of the wicked in Job 21.8–17, 30–33 seriously undermines the Mishnah's and Tosefta's assertion that ultimately justice prevails. Tosefta's interpretive strategy to defuse the power of Job's account of the prosperity of the wicked is to treat that depiction not as it certainly appears in its biblical context, as a

10 Their bull breeds and does not fail;
    Their cow calves and never miscarries;
11 They let their infants run loose like sheep,
    And their children skip about.
12 They sing to the music of timbrel and lute,
    And revel to the tune of the pipe;
13 They spend their days in happiness,
    And go down to Sheol in peace.
14 They say to God, "Leave us alone,
    We do not want to learn Your ways;
15 What is Shaddai that we should serve Him?
    What will we gain by praying to Him?"
16 Their happiness is not their own doing.
    (The thoughts of the wicked are beyond me!)
17 How seldom does the lamp of the wicked fail,
    Does the calamity they deserve befall them,
    Does He apportion [their] lot in anger!
18 Let them become like straw in the wind,
    Like chaff carried off by a storm.
19 [You say,] "God is reserving his punishment for
        his sons";
    Let it be paid back to him that he may feel it,
20 Let his eyes see his ruin,
    And let him drink the wrath of Shaddai!
21 For what does he care about the fate of his family,
    When his number of months runs out?
22 Can God be instructed in knowledge,
    He who judges from such heights?
23 One man dies in robust health,
    All tranquil and untroubled;
24 His pails are full of milk;
    The marrow of his bones is juicy.
25 Another dies embittered,
    Never having tasted happiness.
26 They both lie in the dust
    And are covered with worms.

27 Oh, I know your thoughts,
    And the tactics you will devise against me.
28 You will say, "Where is the house of the great
        man—
    And where the tent in which the wicked dwelled?"
29 You must have consulted the wayfarers;
    You cannot deny their evidence.
30 For the evil man is spared on the day of calamity,
    On the day when wrath is led forth.
31 Who will upbraid him to his face?
    Who will requite him for what he has done?

depiction of the human situation in all times and places, but rather as a description of one historical event, which occurred at one time in the very remote past and which culminated in the happy ending in which the virtuous few—Noah and his family—survived while the wicked majority perished. **19:** *[You say,]:* The brackets indicate that the translators believe that Job here quotes the view of Bildad in 18.12, 19 and of Zophar in 20.20–21, according to which Job's innocent children died as recompense for Job's guilt; for another view see Zophar at 8.4. Zophar need not be consistent. It is not a debate between philosophers that is portrayed here, but rather a random discussion between a suffering individual and his highly educated friends. **20:** *Drink the wrath,* better, "drink the poison," referring to capital punishment by means of a cup of poison such as was administered to Socrates. **29:** Again it is experience which is the ultimate arbiter in wisdom literature. What makes the book of Job so striking is that both Job and his friends view the same world in such diametrically opposed ways. Only an outside event, such as a divine revelation, can settle this debate, and this is precisely what happens in chs 38–42.

32 He is brought to the grave,
While a watch is kept at his tomb.
33 The clods of the wadi are sweet to him,
Everyone follows behind him,
Innumerable are those who precede him.
34 Why then do you offer me empty consolation?
Of your replies only the perfidy remains.

22

Eliphaz the Temanite said in reply:

2 Can a man be of use to God,
A wise man benefit Him?
3 Does Shaddai gain if you are righteous?
Does He profit if your conduct is blameless?
4 Is it because of your piety that He arraigns you,
And enters into judgment with you?
5 You know that your wickedness is great,
And that your iniquities have no limit.
6 You exact pledges from your fellows without
reason,
And leave them naked, stripped of their clothes;
7 You do not give the thirsty water to drink;
You deny bread to the hungry.
8 The land belongs to the strong;
The privileged occupy it.
9 You have sent away widows empty-handed;
The strength of the fatherless is broken.
10 Therefore snares are all around you,
And sudden terrors frighten you,
11 Or darkness, so you cannot see;
A flood of waters covers you.

12 God is in the heavenly heights;
See the highest stars, how lofty!
13 You say, "What can God know?
Can He govern through the dense cloud?
14 The clouds screen Him so He cannot see
As He moves about the circuit of heaven."
15 Have you observed the immemorial path
That evil men have trodden;

. . . *occupy it,* better, "The man of violence owns the earth, and the man who is an object of favoritism is enthroned therein." The ancient Dead Sea Scroll Aramaic translation of Job recovered from Qumran Cave 11 anticipated modern scholarship in understanding this verse as Eliphaz's quoting Job's viewpoint as expressed in 9.24; 15.19. (One of the many problems of interpreting Job is that, like other wisdom texts, it quotes sayings in order to refute them, but there is no equivalent of quotation marks in ancient Heb.) Some scholars suggest that originally 22.8 was after 22.14. **10:** Eliphaz here repeats what he stated in 4.7–9 and what Bildad stated in 8.4 concerning the death of Job's children: "They had it coming to them." **11–14:** Holding that Eliphaz is serious in his allegations in 22.5–9, some modern interpreters, inspired by Rashi and Ibn Ezra, see in 22.11–14 an explanation of Job's disregard of the poor and the weak: "You thought, God is above the stars and therefore cannot judge men." Since in the end Job's friends are made to apologize to Job for blaming him for his own suffering, and since in v. 13a Eliphaz explicitly says, "You say . . . ," it is possible to see in vv. 12, 13b–14, and 8 a speech that Eliphaz puts into Job's mouth so that he can rebut it in vv. 15–30. Of course, Job has said no such thing. This is another indication that there is no true dialogue here, and Job's accusations that his "friends" are not listening to him are true. **15–30:** Eliphaz repeats what he stated in 5.17–27; 15.17–35; what Bildad stated in 8.13–22; 18.5–21; and what Zophar stated in 11.13–20; 20.4–29: that in the long run justice will prevail, and that Job, if he is indeed essentially innocent, will be vindicated and prosper if he will desist from whatever misdemeanors he has committed. **15–18:** Here Eliphaz addresses Job, echoing Job's allegations in 21.14–16. As elsewhere, the truth may be learned from observation of how the world works.

22.1–30: Eliphaz's third and final speech. 2–4: Eliphaz refers here to Job's begging in 10.2; 13.23 that God tell him just where he has gone wrong so as to deserve the loss of children, wealth, and health, and insists that God is unbiased. **5–7, 9:** Eliphaz here provides the kind of bill of particulars that Job had requested in 10.2; 13.23. These follow naturally from his immediately preceding comments: If God is unbiased and punishes only the wicked, and Job is being punished, then he must be very wicked. In his final speech, Eliphaz has moved far from his initial position in 4.3–6. **8:** *The land*

16   How they were shriveled up before their time
And their foundation poured out like a river?

17   They said to God, "Leave us alone;
What can Shaddai do about it?"

18   But it was He who filled their houses with good
       things.
(The thoughts of the wicked are beyond me!)

19   The righteous, seeing it,ᵃ rejoiced;
The innocent laughed with scorn.

20   Surely their substance was destroyed,
And their remnant consumed by fire.

21   Be close to Him and wholehearted;
Good things will come to you thereby.

22   Accept instruction from His mouth;
Lay up His words in your heart.

23   If you return to Shaddai you will be restored,
If you banish iniquity from your tent;

24   If you regard treasure as dirt,
Ophir-gold as stones of the wadi,

25   And Shaddai be your treasure
And precious silver for you,

26   When you seek the favor of Shaddai,
And lift up your face to God,

27   You will pray to Him, and He will listen to you,
And you will pay your vows.

28   You will decree and it will be fulfilled,
And light will shine upon your affairs.

29   When others sink low, you will say it is pride;
For He saves the humble.

30   He will deliver the guilty;
He will be delivered through the cleanness of your
       hands.

23

Job said in reply:

2   Today again my complaint is bitter;
ᵇ⁻My strength is spent⁻ᵇ on account of my groaning.

3   Would that I knew how to reach Him,
How to get to His dwelling-place.

4   I would set out my case before Him
And fill my mouth with arguments.

5   I would learn what answers He had for me
And know how He would reply to me.

6   Would He contend with me overbearingly?
Surely He would not accuse me!

23.1–24.25: Job's reply to Eliphaz's third speech. In this speech Job does not even address Eliphaz. He complains about God (23.2–17); he accuses God of not intervening to prevent injustice (24.1–12); and he provides numerous examples of the material success of the unjust, and he wishes that God would punish the wicked. He concludes his speech emphatically with 24.25: *"Surely no one can confute."* **23.2–10:** The theme is again forensic. Job is insisting that God is hiding. This picks up on a major theological theme of the Bible, especially in Psalms, that God sometimes hides His face from individuals, allowing them to be punished unjustly (e.g., Job 13.24; Ps. 13.2).

a Referring to v. 16.   b-b Lit. "My hand is heavy."

7 There the upright would be cleared by Him,
And I would escape forever from my judge.

8 But if I go East—He is not there;
West—I still do not perceive Him;

9 North—since He is concealed, I do not behold
Him;
South—He is hidden, and I cannot see Him.

10 But He knows the way I take;
Would He assay me, I should emerge pure as gold.

11 I have followed in His tracks,
Kept His way without swerving,

12 I have not deviated from what His lips
commanded;
I have treasured His words more than my daily
bread.

13 He is one; who can dissuade Him?
Whatever He desires, He does.

14 For He will bring my term to an end,
But He has many more such at His disposal.

15 Therefore I am terrified at His presence;
When I consider, I dread Him.

16 God has made me fainthearted;
Shaddai has terrified me.

17 Yet I am not cut off by the darkness;
He has concealed the thick gloom from me.

24 Why are times for judgment not reserved by
Shaddai?
Even those close to Him cannot foresee His
actions.[a]

2 People remove boundary-stones;
They carry off flocks and pasture them;

3 They lead away the donkeys of the fatherless,
And seize the widow's bull as a pledge;

4 They chase the needy off the roads;
All the poor of the land are forced into hiding.

5 Like the wild asses of the wilderness,
They go about their tasks, seeking food;
The wilderness provides each with food for his
lads;

6 They harvest fodder in the field,
And glean the late grapes in the vineyards of the
wicked.

7 They pass the night naked for lack of clothing,
They have no covering against the cold;

24.2–12: All of the sins mentioned by Job are general in nature, and express universal moral expectations of all people, not just Israelites. Similar expectations are found in ancient Near Eastern wisdom literature, and in passages such as Amos 1.3–2.3, which contain oracles of condemnation against nations other than Israel. **2:** *People remove boundary-stones,* i.e., they expropriate other people's real estate; see Deut. 19.14; 27.17; Prov. 23.10.

a Lit. "days."

8 They are drenched by the mountain rains,
And huddle against the rock for lack of shelter.

9a They snatch the fatherless infant from the breast,
And seize the child of the poor as a pledge.

10 They go about naked for lack of clothing,
And, hungry, carry sheaves;

11 Between rows [of olive trees] they make oil,
And, thirsty, they tread the winepresses.

12 Men groan in the city;
The souls of the dying cry out;
Yet God does not regard it as a reproach.

13 They are rebels against the light;
They are strangers to its ways,
And do not stay in its path.

14 The murderer arises b-in the evening-b
To kill the poor and needy,
And at night he acts the thief.

15 The eyes of the adulterer watch for twilight,
Thinking, "No one will glimpse me then."
He masks his face.

16 In the dark they break into houses;
By day they shut themselves in;
They do not know the light.

17 For all of them morning is darkness;
It is then that they discern the terror of darkness.

18c May they be flotsam on the face of the water;
May their portion in the land be cursed;
May none turn aside by way of their vineyards.

19 May drought and heat snatch away their snow
waters,
And Sheol, those who have sinned.

20 May the womb forget him;
May he be sweet to the worms;
May he be no longer remembered;
May wrongdoers be broken like a tree.

21 May he consort with a barren woman who bears
no child,
Leave his widow deprived of good.

22 Though he has the strength to seize bulls,
May he live with no assurance of survival.

23 Yet [God] gives him the security on which he
relies,
And keeps watch over his affairs.

---

a This verse belongs to the description of the wicked in vv. 2–4a.
b-b Cf. Mishnaic Heb. 'or, Aramaic 'orta, "evening"; others "with the light."
c From here to the end of the chapter the translation is largely conjectural.

9b: *And seize the child of the poor as a pledge:* For children enslaved because they were collateral on their parents' debts, see 2 Kings 4.1. **15–25:** Here as in 21.7–34 Job complains that the wicked prosper and that the success of the unjust demonstrates that justice does not prevail in the world, but he goes beyond what he stated before by showing that injustice is compounded by the fact that the success of the wicked is achieved at the expense of orphans (vv. 3, 9), widows (v. 3), and the poor (vv. 5–8, 14). Such undeserved suffering of those on the lowest rungs of the socioeconomic ladder proves that justice does not prevail in the world. Using the third person, he condemns all unjust individuals, preparing the way for the stronger (first-person) self-imprecation in ch 31. **15:** *The eyes of the adulterer watch for twilight, / Thinking, "No one will glimpse me then." / He masks his face.* Tosefta Sotah 3.5 comments as follows: "She did it [i.e., committed adultery] in secret [Heb "beseter"] as it is stated in Scripture, 'The eyes of the adulterer watch for twilight, Thinking . . . ,' and she does not know that He who is enthroned in the Secret Place [a form of "beseter" inspired by this v.] of the world has set [His] face against her (cf. Jer. 44.11; Ezek. 15.7) in accord with what is stated in Scripture (Job 24.15), 'He puts [away] the face mask,' which teaches that God removes what is hidden into the open, as it is said in Scripture (Prov. 26.26), 'His hatred may be concealed [by dissimulation, but his evil will be exposed to public view].' " NJPS concurs with Tosefta in understanding Heb "seter" as mask. Where NJPS interprets literally "he puts [on] face mask," Tosefta gives the verb "yasim," "put," the unlikely meaning of "put off, remove." Moreover, while NJPS construes *adulterer* in the first half of the verse as the subject of the verb "puts" and correctly understands the verse as one more item in a catalogue of injustices that populate the world, Tosefta seeks here, (see 21.7–34 n.) to defuse Scripture's

24   Exalted for a while, let them be gone;
      Be brought low, and shrivel like mallows,
      And wither like the heads of grain.

25   Surely no one can confute me,
      Or prove that I am wrong.

25 Bildad the Shuhite said in reply:

2   Dominion and dread are His;
      He imposes peace in His heights.
3   Can His troops be numbered?
      On whom does His light not shine?
4   How can man be in the right before God?
      How can one born of woman be cleared of guilt?
5   Even the moon is not bright,
      And the stars are not pure in His sight.
6   How much less man, a worm,
      The son-of-man, a maggot.

26 Then Job said in reply:

2   You would help without having the strength;
      You would deliver with arms that have no power.
3   Without having the wisdom, you offer advice
      And freely give your counsel.
4   To whom have you addressed words?
      Whose breath issued from you?

5   The shades tremble
      Beneath the waters and their denizens.
6   Sheol is naked before Him;
      Abaddon has no cover.

vivid portrayal of human injustice and to read into the biblical text God's dispensing of justice.

25.1–6: Continuation of Job's speech. Although ascribed to Bildad, these vv. should be assigned to Job (see intro.). **2b:** *He imposes peace in His heights:* This half verse is found as the first clause of the final line of long versions of kaddish, and is also recited silently at the end of the "Shemoneh 'Esrei" (Eighteen Benedictions). The reference here is to God controlling His heavenly council (see chs 1–2). **4:** *Born of woman,* for this expres-

sion, which is unique to the book of Job, see 14.1 n.; 15.14 n.

26.1–14: Bildad's reply. Here Bildad, to whom we have restored vv. 2–4 (because, as we noted, Job always addresses the friends in the plural and they always address him in the singular; see intro.), repeats with slight variations the rhetorical questions addressed to Job by Eliphaz in 4.3–4. There, as here, the import of these questions is the friends' inability to understand why Job cannot apply his wisdom to his own case. Were he able to do so, he would not upset

his visitors by his expressions of a death wish for himself and his conclusion that his own unjust suffering proves that injustice ultimately prevails in the conduct of the cosmos. **2:** *You would help without having the strength,* better, "Did you help persons without strength?"; cf. the assertions in 4.3b–4: "You have strengthened failing hands. / Your words have kept him who stumbled from falling; / You have braced knees that gave way." Cf. also Job's own recollection of better days gone by when he was literally "eyes to the blind, feet to the lame . . . father to the needy . . . one who consoles mourners" (29.12–25). **3:** *Without having the wisdom,* better, "Did you offer advice to persons lacking wisdom and give counsel to the multitude?" See comments on v. 2 above; cf. 29.21–22. **4:** *To whom have you addressed words?* In light of the clear parallels between 26.2–3 and both 4.3–4 and 29.12–25, it should be obvious that in 26.4 Bildad attempts to remind Job of what Job himself declares about his former success as both a listening ear and a person who says the right thing at the right time in the right place in 29.21–25. *Whose breath issued from you?* In light of the questions posed to Job in vv. 2–4a and the affirmative answers later provided to those questions by Job in 29.12–25, v. 4b must refer to the renewed lease on life that Job, by means of his listening ear and empathetic discourse, provided others. Here as in 4.3–4 the friends scold Job for not doctoring himself as he had doctored others. **5–14:** Like Elihu in 37.2–24 and like the LORD in ch 38 and anticipated by Job himself in 9.4–13, so also Bildad here argues that the majesty of God's power should preclude Job from challenging God to account for Job's allegedly undeserved suffering. As the friends have argued before, the implication of God's great power is His fair justice. **5:** *The shades,* Heb "refa'im," refers to the dead who abide in Sheol. The same word is found also in Isa. 14.9; 26.14, 19; Ps. 88.11; Prov. 2.18; 9.18;

7 He it is who stretched out Zaphon^a over chaos,
Who suspended earth over emptiness.

8 He wrapped up the waters in His clouds;
Yet no cloud burst under their weight.

9 ^{b-}He shuts off the view of His throne,
Spreading His cloud over it.^{-b}

10 He drew a boundary on the surface of the waters,
At the extreme where light and darkness meet.

11 The pillars of heaven tremble,
Astounded at His blast.

12 By His power He stilled the sea;
By His skill He struck down Rahab.

13 By His wind the heavens were calmed;
His hand pierced the ^{c-}Elusive Serpent.^{-c}

14 These are but glimpses of His rule,
The mere whisper that we perceive of Him;
Who can absorb the thunder of His mighty deeds?

27 Job again took up his theme and said:

2 By God who has deprived me of justice!
By Shaddai who has embittered my life!

3 As long as there is life in me,
And God's breath is in my nostrils,

4 My lips will speak no wrong,
Nor my tongue utter deceit.

5 Far be it from me to say you are right;
Until I die I will maintain my integrity.

a Used for heaven; cf. Isa. 14.13; Ps. 48.3.
b-b Meaning of Heb. uncertain.   c-c Cf. Isa. 27.1.

21.16; and the same term refers to the dead in their repose on two Phoenician sarcophagi from Sidon, belonging to 6th-century BCE Tabnit and 5th-century BCE Eshmunazor II, respectively, and on a 1st-century CE Neo-Punic inscription. **7:** *Stretched out Zaphon,* cf. 9.8, "spread out the heavens" and the parallels cited there. **9:** *He shuts off the view of His throne, / Spreading His cloud over it,* cf. Ps. 97.2: "Dense clouds are around Him . . . His throne." **10:** *He drew a boundary on the surface of the waters:* Here, as in Gen. 1.1–3; Ps. 104.6–9; Prov. 8.27, creation is described as God's making order out of an already existing chaos, which consisted of a watery abyss. *At the extreme where light and darkness meet:* According to Gen. 1.2–3 the first act of creation was God's commanding the light into existence alongside the preexisting darkness. Isa. 45.7, on the other hand, asserts that the LORD is the creator of both light and darkness. The NJPS translation of 26.10 follows Ibn Ezra and suggests that the boundary between earth and preexisting water was made at the point where preexisting light and preexisting darkness met. **12:** *Rahab,* the personified sea. Here, as in 9.13, the creation of the cosmos is pictured as the victory of God over the sea. This epithet is found in Job only at 9.13 and here; it appears also in Isa. 30.7; 51.9; Pss. 87.4; 89.11. **13:** *Elusive Serpent,* Heb "naḥash bariaḥ," translating "bariaḥ" as an

Aramaic form of Heb "boreaḥ," "fleeing." The same word is translated "bar" (i.e., a straight rod or support) in Exod. 26.26–29 and elsewhere. The Baal Epic from Late Bronze Age Ugarit says, "You will destroy Lotan [= Heb Leviathan] the straight [b-r-ḥ] serpent / the twisted serpent with seven heads"; and Isa. 27.1, a parallel, reads, "Leviathan the 'bariaḥ' serpent / Leviathan the twisting serpent." Consequently, it may be preferable to translate "bariaḥ" both here and in Isa. 27.1 as "straight."

27.1–28.28: The continuation of Job's speech. Conventional modern biblical scholarship treats ch 27 as a collection of leftover verses from which to reconstruct the speech of Zophar and Job's reply to that speech, and ch 28 as possibly a separate composition that was erroneously included in an early copy of Job. For reasons given in the introduction, a different approach is taken here. When interpreting the book as a complete work it is possible to see in these chapters Job's long reply to the suggestion on the part of his wife (2.9) and friends in the Book of Job the Patient (see intro.) that Job blaspheme God. (*Integrity* in 27.5 is the same word, "tam," translated "blameless" in 1.1 and 2.3.) In so doing, of course, Job would have enabled the Adversary rather than God to win the wager described in 1.6–12; 2.2–8.

27.1–23: Job's speech continues. 2–6: Notwithstanding his loss of property, children, and health, and the friends' urging him to blaspheme God, he is swearing an oath by God not to blaspheme God. **2:** *By God,* i.e., "I swear." Having been urged by his wife to blaspheme God, Job refuses to do so (2.9–10). **4:** *My lips will speak no wrong,* the content of the oath referred to in v. 2. Consequently, each clause begins with "'im," which means "no, nor" in the context of an oath. Here we see the dramatization of what the narrator asserted in 2.10: "Job said nothing

6   I persist in my righteousness and will not yield;
     a-I shall be free of reproach-a as long as I live.

7   May my enemy be as the wicked;
     My assailant, as the wrongdoer.

8   For what hope has the impious man when he is
       cut down,
     When God takes away his life?

9   Will God hear his cry
     When trouble comes upon him,

10   When he seeks the favor of Shaddai,
     Calls upon God at all times?

11   I will teach you what is in God's power,
     And what is with Shaddai I will not conceal.

12   All of you have seen it,
     So why talk nonsense?

13   This is the evil man's portion from God,
     The lot that the ruthless receive from Shaddai:

14   Should he have many sons—they are marked for
       the sword;
     His descendants will never have their fill of bread;

15   Those who survive him will be buried in a plague,
     And their widows will not weep;

16   Should he pile up silver like dust,
     Lay up clothing like dirt—

17   He may lay it up, but the righteous will wear it,
     And the innocent will share the silver.

18   The house he built is like a bird's nest,
     Like the booth a watchman makes.

19   He lies down, a rich man, with [his wealth]
       intact;
     When he opens his eyes it is gone.

20   Terror overtakes him like a flood;
     A storm wind makes off with him by night.

21   The east wind carries him far away, and he is
       gone;
     It sweeps him from his place.

22   Then it hurls itself at him without mercy;
     He tries to escape from its force.

23   It claps its hands at him,
     And whistles at him from its place.

28 There is a mine for silver,
     And a place where gold is refined.
2   Iron is taken out of the earth,
     And copper smelted from rock.

a-a Meaning of Heb. uncertain.

sinful." **5:** *To say you are right:* The plural *you* here may be addressed to Job's three friends, who, in a now lost version of the narrative framework, joined with Job's wife in urging him to curse God. **6:** *I shall be free of reproach,* lit. "my heart will not blaspheme." Contrary to Rava in *b. Bava Batra* 16a, and going beyond what the narrator states in 2.10, and also beyond what Job himself imputed to his children in 1.5, Job declares unequivocally that he has blasphemed God neither aloud nor in his thoughts. **7–23:** Job expresses the conviction that it is not wise to blaspheme God because, in the end, virtuous people are rewarded, and wicked people are punished. In this Job the Patient agrees with what in the Book of Job the Impatient Eliphaz states in 4.7–11, Zophar in 8.3–22, and Bildad in 11.13–20. **15:** *Their widows will not weep* because they will not be sad. One of the common beliefs reflected in the books of Job and Koheleth (Ecclesiastes) is that virtuous people deserve elaborate funerals and that the wicked ought to be punished by not being mourned (Eccl. 8.10–14; 9.1–6); see 21.30–33.

28.1–28: Hymn of Wisdom or more of Job the Patient. According to many modern scholars, ch 28 is a hymn in praise of wisdom. In fact, this chapter does not praise wisdom. Wisdom is claimed by both Job and his friends as their possession. It is attributed to both King Solomon on the one hand and the Kedemites and Egyptians on the other (1 Kings 5.10), and it is claimed by both Nebuchadnezzar's learned advisers and Daniel in Daniel ch 2. The point of ch 28 is not that wisdom is to be praised but that wisdom is very difficult to acquire. Here, as in Ps. 111.10 and Prov. 1.7; 9.10, are praises of the twin virtues of fearing the LORD and shunning evil, virtues that merit the LORD's bestowing upon Joseph, Solomon, Job, and Daniel knowledge which enables them to surpass what all the other "wise people" in the world attempt to

3 He sets bounds for darkness;
To every limit man probes,
To rocks in deepest darkness.

4 ᵃ·They open up a shaft far from where men live,
[In places] forgotten by wayfarers,
Destitute of men, far removed.·ᵃ

5 Earth, out of which food grows,
Is changed below as if into fire.

6 Its rocks are a source of sapphires;
It contains gold dust too.

7 No bird of prey knows the path to it;
The falcon's eye has not gazed upon it.

8 The proud beasts have not reached it;
The lion has not crossed it.

9 Man sets his hand against the flinty rock
And overturns mountains by the roots.

10 He carves out channels through rock;
His eyes behold every precious thing.

11 He dams up the sources of the streams
So that hidden things may be brought to
    light.

12 But where can wisdom be found;
Where is the source of understanding?

13 No man can set a value on it;
It cannot be found in the land of the living.

14 The deep says, "It is not in me";
The sea says, "I do not have it."

15 It cannot be bartered for gold;
Silver cannot be paid out as its price.

16 The finest gold of Ophir cannot be weighed
    against it,
Nor precious onyx, nor sapphire.

17 Gold or glass cannot match its value,
Nor vessels of fine gold be exchanged for it.

18 Coral and crystal cannot be mentioned with it;
A pouch of wisdom is better than rubies.

19 Topaz from Nubia cannot match its value;
Pure gold cannot be weighed against it.

20 But whence does wisdom come?
Where is the source of understanding?

21 It is hidden from the eyes of all living,
Concealed from the fowl of heaven.

22 Abaddon and Death say,
"We have only a report of it."

achieve on the basis of their education and life experience. As in parts of Proverbs, fear of the LORD is presented as superior to this elusive wisdom. **1–11:** An extended image of the inaccessibility of ores and gems sets the scene for the question posed in v. 12. Gold, the most precious metal, must be extracted at great effort from the earth, where it is hidden away. Vv. 4–5 are an especially vivid description of the opening of a mine. The world under the ground is very different from the world above ground. **12–19:** Wisdom is more precious than gold and precious gems. Where can it be found? **19:** *Nubia* (Heb "Kush"), or Ethiopia. **20–28:** Unlike gold or precious gems, wisdom cannot be found in the physical world, even in far-off, exotic places. Even Death does not know where it resides. Only God, who created the world and knows the source of all things, knows where wisdom is. He gives it to those who fear the LORD and shun evil. Fear of the LORD is the sine qua non for attaining wisdom; and fearing God and shunning evil are the attributes of Job.

a-a *Meaning of Heb. uncertain.*

23 God understands the way to it;
  He knows its source;
24 For He sees to the ends of the earth,
  Observes all that is beneath the heavens.
25 When He fixed the weight of the winds,
  Set the measure of the waters;
26 When He made a rule for the rain
  And a course for the thunderstorms,
27 Then He saw it and gauged it;
  He measured it and probed it.
28 He said to man,
  "See! Fear of the Lord is wisdom;
  To shun evil is understanding."

29 Job again took up his theme and said:

2 O that I were as in months gone by,
  In the days when God watched over me,
3 When His lamp shone over my head,
  When I walked in the dark by its light,
4 When I was in my prime,
  When God's company graced my tent,
5 When Shaddai was still with me,
  When my lads surrounded me,
6 When my feet were bathed in cream,
  And rocks poured out streams of oil for me.
7 When I passed through the city gates
  To take my seat in the square,
8 Young men saw me and hid,
  Elders rose and stood;
9 Nobles held back their words;
  They clapped their hands to their mouths.
10 The voices of princes were hushed;
  Their tongues stuck to their palates.
11 The ear that heard me acclaimed me;
  The eye that saw, commended me.
12 For I saved the poor man who cried out,
  The orphan who had none to help him.
13 I received the blessing of the lost;
  I gladdened the heart of the widow.
14 I clothed myself in righteousness and it robed me;
  Justice was my cloak and turban.
15 I was eyes to the blind
  And feet to the lame.
16 I was a father to the needy,
  And I looked into the case of the stranger.
17 I broke the jaws of the wrongdoer,
  And I wrested prey from his teeth.

29.1–31.40: Job's soliloquy. These chapters form a logical progression: Job recalls the good old days (ch 29), laments his current physical and social afflictions (ch 30), and offers a powerful self-imprecation, insisting on his innocence (ch 31). Toward the end of his soliliquy, he returns to the forensic imagery (31.35–37) that typifies many of his arguments earlier in the book. **29.2–4:** *O that I were . . . when I was in my prime:* Job prefers the memory of his former state to his present situation. In earlier times, when God blessed him and made him successful, he was an honored member of society, respected and heeded by all, who helped those in need. **3:** *Lamp . . . light,* cf. Ps. 119.105; 139.12. **7:** *Gates . . . square,* the centers of legal transactions and business activity. Those who sat here were the decision-makers of society.

18 I thought I would end my days with my family,ᵃ
    And ᵇ⁻be as long-lived as the phoenix,⁻ᵇ
19 My roots reaching water,
    And dew lying on my branches;
20 My vigor refreshed,
    My bow ever new in my hand.
21 Men would listen to me expectantly,
    And wait for my counsel.
22 After I spoke they had nothing to say;
    My words were as drops [of dew] upon them.
23 They waited for me as for rain,
    For the late rain, their mouths open wide.
24 When I smiled at them, they would not believe it;
    They never expectedᶜ a sign of my favor.
25 I decided their course and presided over them;
    I lived like a king among his troops,
    Like one who consoles mourners.

30 But now those younger than I deride me,
    [Men] whose fathers I would have disdained to
            put among my sheep dogs.
2   Of what use to me is the strength of their
            hands?
    All their vigorᵈ is gone.
3   Wasted from want and starvation,
    They flee to a parched land,
    To the gloom of desolate wasteland.
4   They pluck saltwort and wormwood;
    The roots of broom are their food.
5   Driven out ᵉ⁻from society,⁻ᵉ
    They are cried at like a thief.
6   They live in the gullies of wadis,
    In holes in the ground, and in rocks,
7   Braying among the bushes,
    Huddling among the nettles,
8   Scoundrels, nobodies,
    Stricken from the earth.

9   Now I am the butt of their gibes;
    I have become a byword to them.
10 They abhor me; they keep their distance from me;
    They do not withhold spittle from my face.
11 Because Godᶠ has disarmedᵍ and humbled me,
    They have thrown off restraint in my presence.

20: A reference to physical or sexual vigor. **25:** *Like one who consoles mourners:* High social status is afforded the person who succeeds in consoling mourners in their bereavement. Given the failure of Job's friends to condole with him properly, Job's words are all the more poignant. **30.1:** *But now those younger than I deride me:* Those with less wisdom than Job now think they are wiser and no longer respect him. Job feels like an outcast; he has lost his position in society because of his suffering. **2–8:** The elderly and the infirm are banished so as not to be seen. **10–14:** Young people taunt and even physically abuse the elderly and the infirm.

a Lit. "nest."   b-b Others "multiply days like sand."
c Taking yappilun as from pll; cf. Gen. 48.11.   d Meaning of Heb. uncertain.
e-e Meaning of Heb. uncertain.   f Lit. "He."   g Lit. "loosened my [bow] string."

12   Mere striplings assail me at my right hand:
      They put me to flight;
      They build their roads for my ruin.
13   They tear up my path;
      They promote my fall,
      Although it does them no good.
14   They come as through a wide breach;
      They roll in ᵃ·like raging billows.·ᵃ
15   Terror tumbles upon me;
      It sweeps away my honor like the wind;
      My dignityᵇ vanishes like a cloud.
16   So now my life runs out;
      Days of misery have taken hold of me.
17   By night my bones feel gnawed;
      My sinews never rest.
18   ᵃ·With great effort I change clothing;
      The neck of my tunic fits my waist.·ᵃ
19   He regarded me as clay,
      I have become like dust and ashes.

20   I cry out to You, but You do not answer me;
      I wait, but You do [not] consider me.
21   You have become cruel to me;
      With Your powerful hand You harass me.
22   You lift me up and mount me on the wind;
      You make my courage melt.
23   I know You will bring me to death,
      The house assigned for all the living.
24   ᵃ·Surely He would not strike at a ruin
      If, in calamity, one cried out to Him.·ᵃ
25   Did I not weep for the unfortunate?
      Did I not grieve for the needy?
26   I looked forward to good fortune, but evil came;
      I hoped for light, but darkness came.
27   My bowels are in turmoil without respite;
      Days of misery confront me.
28   I walk about in sunless gloom;
      I rise in the assembly and cry out.
29   I have become a brother to jackals,
      A companion to ostriches.
30   My skin, blackened, is peeling off me;
      My bones are charred by the heat.
31   So my lyre is given over to mourning,
      My pipe, to accompany weepers.

a-a *Meaning of Heb. uncertain.*
b *Heb.* yeshuʿathi *taken as related to* shoaʿ, "*noble.*"

31

1 I have covenanted with my eyes
Not to gaze on a maiden.
2 What fate is decreed by God above?
What lot, by Shaddai in the heights?
3 Calamity is surely for the iniquitous;
Misfortune, for the worker of mischief.
4 Surely He observes my ways,
Takes account of my every step.

5 Have I walked with worthless men,
Or my feet hurried to deceit?
6 Let Him weigh me on the scale of righteousness;
Let God ascertain my integrity.
7 If my feet have strayed from their course,
My heart followed after my eyes,
And a stain sullied my hands,
8 May I sow, but another reap,
May the growth of my field be uprooted!
9 If my heart was ravished by the wife of my
neighbor,
And I lay in wait at his door,
10 May my wife grind for another,
May others kneel over her!
11 For that would have been debauchery,
A criminal offense,
12 A fire burning down to Abaddon,
Consuming the roots of all my increase.

31.1–40: Job's confession of innocence. This summation by the defense before both the Lord and Job's three friends most certainly constitutes Job's last word in his trial (see 32.1). Eliphaz accused Job of failing to provide for the needs of the impoverished (22.7) and of adding to the suffering of widows and orphans (22.9). Here (vv. 16–19) Job responds with a plea of innocence to these and other charges that have been mentioned or implied in the course of the condolence call turned into symposium (chs 4–26). With this plea Job rests his case. Many scholars have compared Job's confession of innocence with the negative confession in the Egyptian Book of the Dead from the Egyptian New Kingdom (1555–1085 BCE). In the latter text the deceased declares—before Osiris, the divine ruler of the

realm of the dead (who himself had overcome death), and forty-two judges—the deceased person's innocence of thirty-six offenses, including both murder and shortcomings with respect to religious rites. Job ch 31 has three especially significant rhetorical features: First, a list of 14 (i.e., 7 × 2) sins from which Job claims innocence, similar to the listing of 14 capital offenses punishable by stoning to death in *m. Sanh.* 7.4; to the 14 ages of humans in *m. 'Avot* 5.21; and to the 14 qualities induced by the study of Torah according to 'Avot 6.7. Second, twenty instances of the particle "'im" in three distinct meanings: (1) "if" in the protasis (conditional clause) of an ordinary conditional sentence (31.19); (2) "if" in the protasis describing a crime where the apodosis (concluding clause) de-

scribes the penalty (vv. 7–8; 9–10; 21–22; 38–40); (3) the interrogative particle introducing a rhetorical question which calls for a negative reply (vv. 5, 13, 16, 19, 24, 25, 26, 33). Third, virtual quotations of Job's thought processes in vv. 2–4 and 14–15 [Robert Gordis, *The Book of Job* (New York, 1978), pp. 543–545]. The self-imprecation (curse) of this chapter would have been seen as very serious in antiquity, and not as a mere rhetorical statement. Many of the consequences suggested for offences reflect the biblical principle of measure-for-measure, which is further developed in the rabbinic period (see esp. vv. 9–10 and 21–22; note, e.g., Exod. 22.20–23). **1:** *Not to gaze on a maiden:* Heb "betulah," "maiden," like its Akkadian masculine and feminine cognates, can designate a young, unmarried person of marriageable age. In some contexts (e.g., Deut. 22.13–21) it means specifically "virgin." The exact reference of this verse is obscure and many scholars relocate it to later in the chapter. **3:** *Calamity is surely for the iniquitous:* Here, as in 6.29–30; 9.17, 21; 13.23; 23.4–12; 24.25, Job protests that he is totally innocent and that his suffering is totally undeserved. Contrast 7.21; 13.26; 14.16–17, and see the discussion at 7.21. Job wavers between admitting that he is, like all persons, guilty of some misdemeanors, for which he would like to be forgiven, and asserting his total innocence. **5–6:** An affirmation that Job has not cheated in business; for the prohibition see Lev. 19.35–36; Deut. 25.13–16. **7–8:** An affirmation that Job has not expropriated material goods belonging to others; for the relevant prohibitions in the Torah see Lev. 5.20–26; 19.11–13. **9–12:** Committing adultery with another man's wife is an offense against that man's property in ancient Near Eastern law. In "measure-for-measure" penalties, or the law of talion, found in the Bible and the ancient Near East, if a man injures or mistreats a member of another man's family, the comparable member of the criminal's family is

13   Did I ever brush aside the case of my servants,
       man or maid,
  When they made a complaint against me?

14   What then should I do when God arises;
  When He calls me to account, what should I
       answer Him?

15   Did not He who made me in my mother's belly
       make him?
  Did not One form us both in the womb?

16   Did I deny the poor their needs,
  Or let aᵃ widow pine away,

17   By eating my food alone,
  The fatherless not eating of it also?

18   Why, from my youth he grew up with me as
       though I were his father;
  Since I left my mother's womb I was herᵇ guide.

19   I never saw an unclad wretch,
  A needy man without clothing,

20   Whose loins did not bless me
  As he warmed himself with the shearings of my
       sheep.

21   If I raised my hand against the fatherless,
  Looking to my supporters in the gate,

22   May my arm drop off my shoulder;
  My forearm break off ᶜat the elbow.ᶜ

23   For I am in dread of God-sent calamity;
  I cannot bear His threat.

24   Did I put my reliance on gold,
  Or regard fine gold as my bulwark?

25   Did I rejoice in my great wealth,
  In having attained plenty?

26   If ever I saw the light shining,
  The moon on its course in full glory,

27   And I secretly succumbed,

---

a Lit. "the eyes of a."   b Viz., the widow's.
c-c Lit. "from its shaft," i.e., the humerus.

similarly injured or mistreated. There is, however, no biblical law stating that an adulterer's wife may be sexually used by the man whose own wife engaged in the adulterous relationship. Job is merely speaking rhetorically here, to show how innocent of wrongdoing he is. He invokes the principle of talion against himself in the following vv. as well, for the same reason. **13–14:** The rhetorical question requiring a negative answer is tantamount to asserting that Job has granted his slaves the full protection of the law; see Exod. 21.20–21, 26–27; Deut. 23.16–17. Likewise, he expects that God will treat His servant, i.e., Job, just as fairly. **14–15:** Here (as in vv. 2–4, 11–12) is a virtual quotation of Job's thoughts which led to his virtuous behavior described in v. 13. **15:** *One,* a possible name of God; see also Zech. 14.9. **16–19:** Job claims for himself innocence of the principal offenses ascribed to the people of Sodom in Ezek. 16.49. **16a:** Here Job denies ever having failed to provide for the needs of the impoverished. If so, Eliphaz in 22.7 is either mistaken or sarcastic. Alternatively, Job could be lying. In that case, God would not have praised his virtue in 1.8; 2.3 and again defended him in 42.7 against the insults hurled upon him by his friends. The virtue to which Job confesses here is commanded in Lev. 19.9–10; 23.22; Deut. 14.22–29; 15.8. **16b:** *Or let a widow pine away:* Heb "ʾalmanah," commonly translated "widow," actually means a once-married woman who has no means of financial support and who is thus in need of special legal protection. *Pine away,* better, "cry her eyes out." The Heb "kilah ʿeinei" refers to causing someone's eyes to empty, as it were, by profuse crying. It is taken for granted here as also in 22.9 that Job, as an extremely affluent person, would have been expected by the social norms of the Late Bronze Age and Iron Age Levant (see, e.g., Isa. 1.17) to provide legal and financial aid to the underprivileged, including the " ʾalmanah." His failure to do so would be a crime. **17:** Contrast Eliphaz's assertion in 22.9b. **19:** Contrast Eliphaz's assertion in 22.6. **21:** *Raised my hand,* i.e., engaged in physical violence. *In the gate,* here (as in Deut. 21.19; 22.15, 24; Ruth ch 4) the public place of one's community, which was located just inside any of the gates of the city walls. It was here that judges tried cases and issued legal decisions, and this is where the verdicts of the court were carried out. Consequently, the extended meaning is "in the process of litigation." **26:** *The light:* As pointed out by Rashi and Ibn Ezra, this refers to the sun; hence *the moon* is in the following clause. **27:** *And I secretly succumbed* to worship of the sun and moon. Deut. 4.19 prohibits worship of the sun and moon only to Israelites. Job, however, like Adam, Noah, Jethro, Rahab, and Ruth, is portrayed in Scripture and in rabbinic literature as a non-Israelite who is faithful to

And my hand touched my mouth in a kiss,

28 That, too, would have been a criminal offense,
For I would have denied God above.

29 Did I rejoice over my enemy's misfortune?
Did I thrill because evil befell him?

30 I never let my mouth[a] sin
By wishing his death in a curse.

31 (Indeed, the men of my clan said,
"We would consume his flesh insatiably!")

32 No sojourner spent the night in the open;
I opened my doors to the road.

33 Did I hide my transgressions like Adam,
Bury my wrongdoing in my bosom,

34 That I should [now] fear the great multitude,
And am shattered by the contempt of families,
So that I keep silent and do not step outdoors?

35 O that I had someone to give me a hearing;
O that Shaddai would reply to my writ,
Or my accuser draw up a true bill!

36 I would carry it on my shoulder;
Tie it around me for a wreath.

37 I would give him an account of my steps,
Offer it as to a commander.

38 If my land cries out against me,
Its furrows weep together;

39 If I have eaten its produce without payment,
And made its [rightful] owners despair,

40 May nettles grow there instead of wheat;
Instead of barley, stinkweed!

The words of Job are at an end.

32 These three men ceased replying to Job, for he considered himself right. [2] Then Elihu son of Barachel the Buzite, of the family of Ram, was angry—angry at Job because he thought himself right against God. [3] He was angry as well at his three friends, because they found no reply, but merely condemned Job. [4] Elihu waited out Job's speech, for they were all older than he. [5] But when Elihu saw that the three men had nothing to reply, he was angry.

a Lit. "palate."

the LORD. This verse is thus anomalous within this chapter, which otherwise notes infractions of customs shared by both Israelites and non-Israelites. *My hand . . . in a kiss,* blowing a kiss into one or both palms, a gesture of worship frequently illustrated pictorially on cylinder seals from ancient Mesopotamia. **33:** A rare reference outside of Genesis to the Garden story. **35–37:** This interrupts the flow of the chapter, but returns to a main theme of the book. **36:** As elsewhere, Job is using a wisdom image with a twist: It is wisdom that is typically worn as adornment or jewelry (see, e.g., Prov. 3.22).

32.1: The end of the debate with the three friends. Just as in ch 31 Job presents a veritable summation for the defense, so here the friends rest their case because they have exhausted every available argument. As Rashbam puts it: "For indeed in his own perception he was innocent, and he continually said that the Holy One Blessed be He had perverted judgment in his case. His three friends responded to him many times until they found no answer with which to respond to him."

Chs 32–37: Elihu the intruder. After apologizing for even opening his mouth in 32.6–22, Elihu addresses four speeches to Job in chs 32–33; 34; 35; 36–37. Most scholars regard the speeches of Elihu as a later addition by a different author, for the following reasons: Elihu is not mentioned in the narrative sections in chs 2 and 42; neither Job nor God replies to him; he speaks in a Hebrew that differs from both the prose and the poetry of other parts of the book; and he seems to add nothing to what has been said before. This last argument, at least, is weakened by the fact that many of the speeches of the others also do not advance the argument in any way, yet they are not regarded as interpolations of a later redactor. In distinction to the others, however, Elihu is an excellent listener, the only speaker in the entire book who quotes other people's ideas verbatim. For example, in 33.9 and 34.5 he quotes Job's protestation of innocence in 16.17. In 33.11 he quotes Job's statement in 13.27; in 33.12–13 he responds to what Job said in 9.3–4; in 34.3 he quotes what Job had said in 12.11. If, in the end, Elihu contributes anything of substance

⁶ Then Elihu son of Barachel the Buzite said in reply:

I have but few years, while you are old;
Therefore I was too awestruck and fearful
To hold forth among you.

7   I thought, "Let age speak;
Let advanced years declare wise things."

8   But truly it is the spirit in men,
The breath of Shaddai, that gives them
    understanding.

9   It is not the aged who are wise,
The elders, who understand how to judge.

10   Therefore I say, "Listen to me;
I too would hold forth."

11   Here I have waited out your speeches,
I have given ear to your insights,
While you probed the issues;

12   But as I attended to you,
I saw that none of you could argue with Job,
Or offer replies to his statements.

13   I fear you will say, "We have found the wise
    course;
God will defeat him, not man."

14   He did not set out his case against me,
Nor shall I use your reasons to reply to him.

15   They have been broken and can no longer reply;
Words fail them.

16   I have waited till they stopped speaking,
Till they ended and no longer replied.

17   Now I also would have my say;
I too would like to hold forth,

18   For I am full of words;
The wind in my belly presses me.

19   My belly is like wine not yet opened,
Like jugs of new wine ready to burst.

20   Let me speak, then, and get relief;
Let me open my lips and reply.

21   I would not show regard for any man,
Or temper my speech for anyone's sake;

22   For I do not know how to temper my speech—
My Maker would soon carry me off!

33 But now, Job, listen to my words,
Give ear to all that I say.

2   Now I open my lips;
My tongue forms words in my mouth.

3   My words bespeak the uprightness of my heart;
My lips utter insight honestly.

to the book, it is his elaboration (in 33.16–30; 36.16) upon a thesis presented earlier by Eliphaz in 5.17–26. According to this thesis, suffering is a divine gift comparable to parents disciplining their children. Such discipline enables people to correct their behavior and thereby to secure and not to lose their just reward. It is difficult to know how to evaluate Elihu's remarks. On the one hand, what he says is closely parallel to the following speeches by the LORD. On the other, he presents himself as a windbag (32.18–20) and is exceedingly pompous. This dichotomy may even be evident in his genealogy (v. 2): He is a Buzite, which may be etymologized as "contemptible," but of the family of Ram, "elevated." "Elihu," a variant form of Elijah ("Eliyahu"), means "my God [is] the LORD."

32.2–6: Elihu is introduced. 4: Respect for elders is a key point of general and Israelite wisdom literature, as of other biblical literature (e.g., Lev. 19.32). **6:** *Said in reply,* see 38.1 n.

32.6–33.33: Elihu's first speech. Elihu has held back because he is younger, and therefore presumably less wise, than the other friends. But he finds the words of the friends unsatisfying, and offers his own answers to Job. He rejects Job's characterization of God as unjust or capricious, suggesting that suffering is God's way of warning people, and that God will bring back the sufferer from the brink of death. A similar notion that chastisements reflect God's love is found in Prov. 3.11–12 (see n. there). This idea took root and was expanded greatly in the rabbinic tradition, where it is called "yisurin shel ʾahavah," "chastisement of love." **32.19:** The image is that of fermenting wine, producing much gas, an image which may easily be seen as mocking Elihu.

4   The spirit of God formed me;
     The breath of Shaddai sustains me.
5   If you can, answer me;
     Argue against me, take your stand.
6   You and I are the same before God;
     I too was nipped from clay.
7   You are not overwhelmed by fear of me;
     My pressure does not weigh heavily on you.

8   Indeed, you have stated in my hearing,
     I heard the words spoken,
9   "I am guiltless, free from transgression;
     I am innocent, without iniquity.
10   But He finds reasons to oppose me,
     Considers me His enemy.
11   He puts my feet in stocks,
     Watches all my ways."

12   In this you are not right;
     I will answer you: God is greater than any man.
13   Why do you complain against Him
     That He does not reply to any of man's charges?
14   For God speaks ᵃtime and againᵃ—
     Though man does not perceive it—
15   In a dream, a night vision,
     When deep sleep falls on men,
     While they slumber on their beds.
16   Then He opens men's understanding,
     And by disciplining them leaves His signature
17   To turn man away from an action,
     To suppress pride in man.
18   He spares him from the Pit,
     His person, from perishing by the sword.
19   He is reproved by pains on his bed,
     And the trembling in his bones is constant.
20   He detests food;
     Fine food [is repulsive] to him.
21   His flesh wastes away till it cannot be seen,
     And his bones are rubbed away till they are
          invisible.
22   He comes close to the Pit,
     His life [verges] on death.
23   If he has a representative,
     One advocate against a thousand
     To declare the man's uprightness,
24   Then He has mercy on him and decrees,

33.15–16: This idea as well, that dreams play a significant role in warning people of their deviant behavior, was not stressed by the friends. **23:** *A representative . . . One advocate:* It is not clear if this refers to a supernatural intercessor, or a human friend who serves as an intercessor.

a-a Lit. "once . . . twice."

"Redeem him from descending to the Pit,
For I have obtained his ransom;
25   Let his flesh be healthier*a* than in his youth;
Let him return to his younger days."
26   He prays to God and is accepted by Him;
He enters His presence with shouts of joy,
For He requites a man for his righteousness.
27   He*b* declares*a* to men,
"I have sinned; I have perverted what was right;
But I was not paid back for it."
28   He redeemed *c*him from passing into the Pit;
He*c* will enjoy the light.
29   Truly, God does all these things
Two or three times to a man,
30   To bring him back from the Pit,
That he may bask in the light of life.

31   Pay heed, Job, and hear me;
Be still, and I will speak;
32   If you have what to say, answer me;
Speak, for I am eager to vindicate you.
33   But if not, you listen to me;
Be still, and I will teach you wisdom.

34

Elihu said in reply:

2   Listen, O wise men, to my words;
You who have knowledge, give ear to me.
3   For the ear tests arguments
As the palate tastes food.
4   Let us decide for ourselves what is just;
Let us know among ourselves what is good.
5   For Job has said, "I am right;
God has deprived me of justice.
6   I declare the judgment against me false;
My arrow-wound is deadly, though I am free from
transgression."
7   What man is like Job,
Who drinks mockery like water;
8   Who makes common cause with evildoers,
And goes with wicked men?
9   For he says, "Man gains nothing
When he is in God's favor."

10   Therefore, men of understanding, listen to me;
Wickedness be far from God,

34.1–37: Elihu's second speech.
Elihu strongly insists that God is
not unjust, directly countering
many of Job's earlier claims. He
says nothing new, however, but repeats various arguments made by
the friends. According to many
scholars, this makes Elihu look
foolish, for he had claimed that he
was patiently waiting to hear out
the friends before he presented his
new arguments (32.3–5). **1:** *Elihu
said in reply:* Since no one has addressed Elihu, it is likely that here,
as in 3.1, the poet has employed
the verb root "*-n-y*" in the sense
"declaim" rather than the homonym "*-n-y*" meaning "reply"; also
in 35.1.

---

a Meaning of Heb. uncertain.   *b I.e., the contrite man.*
c-c Or with kethib, "me . . . I."

Wrongdoing, from Shaddai!

11 For He pays a man according to his actions,
And provides for him according to his conduct;

12 For God surely does not act wickedly;
Shaddai does not pervert justice.

13 Who placed the earth in His charge?
Who ordered the entire world?

14 If He but intends it,
He can call back His spirit and breath;

15 All flesh would at once expire,
And mankind return to dust.

16 If you would understand, listen to this;
Give ear to what I say.

17 Would one who hates justice govern?
Would you condemn the Just Mighty One?

18 Would you call a king a scoundrel,
Great men, wicked?

19 He is not partial to princes;
The noble are not preferred to the wretched;
For all of them are the work of His hands.

20 Some die suddenly in the middle of the night;
People are in turmoil and pass on;
Even great men are removed—not by human
hands.

21 For His eyes are upon a man's ways;
He observes his every step.

22 Neither darkness nor gloom offers
A hiding-place for evildoers.

23 He has no set time for man
To appear before God in judgment.

24 He shatters mighty men without number
And sets others in their place.

25 Truly, He knows their deeds;
Night is over, and they are crushed.

26 He strikes them down with the wicked
Where people can see,

27 Because they have been disloyal to Him
And have not understood any of His ways;

28 Thus He lets the cry of the poor come before Him;
He listens to the cry of the needy.

29 When He is silent, who will condemn?
If He hides His face, who will see Him,
Be it nation or man?

30 The impious man rule no more,
Nor do those who ensnare the people.

31 Has he said to God,
"I will bear [my punishment] and offend no more.

32   What I cannot see You teach me.
        If I have done iniquity, I shall not do so again"?

33   Should He requite as you see fit?
        But you have despised [Him]!
        You must decide, not I;
        Speak what you know.

34   Men of understanding say to me,
        Wise men who hear me,

35   "Job does not speak with knowledge;
        His words lack understanding."

36   Would that Job were tried to the limit
        For answers which befit sinful men.

37   He adds to his sin;
        He increases his transgression among us;
        He multiplies his statements against God.

35   Elihu said in reply:

2   Do you think it just
        To say, "I am right against God"?

3   If you ask how it benefits you,
        "What have I gained from not sinning?"

4   I shall give you a reply,
        You, along with your friends.

5   Behold the heavens and see;
        Look at the skies high above you.

6   If you sin, what do you do to Him?
        If your transgressions are many,
        How do you affect Him?

7   If you are righteous,
        What do you give Him;
        What does He receive from your hand?

8   Your wickedness affects men like yourself;
        Your righteousness, mortals.

9   Because of contention the oppressed cry out;
        They shout because of the power of the great.

10   But none says, "Where is my God, my Maker,
        Who gives strength in the night;

11   Who gives us more knowledge than the beasts of
              the earth,
        Makes us wiser than the birds of the sky?"

12   Then they cry out, but He does not respond
        Because of the arrogance of evil men.

13   Surely it is false that God does not listen,
        That Shaddai does not take note of it.

14   Though you say, "You do not take note of it,"
        The case is before Him;

35.1–15: Elihu's third speech.
God surely sees everything
that transpires on earth. If He
seems indifferent, that is because
His response is not immediate.
1: See 34.1 n. 2–8: Like the
friends, Elihu argues that
God is an impartial judge.

So wait for Him.

15 ᵃ·But since now it does not seem so,
He vents his anger;
He does not realize that it may be long drawn out.·ᵃ

16 Hence Job mouths empty words,
And piles up words without knowledge.

36 Then Elihu spoke once more.

2 Wait a little and let me hold forth;
There is still more to say for God.

3 I will make my opinions widely known;
I will justify my Maker.

4 In truth, my words are not false;
A man of sound opinions is before you.

5 See, God is mighty; He is not contemptuous;
He is mighty in strength and mind.

6 He does not let the wicked live;
He grants justice to the lowly.

7 He does not withdraw His eyes from the
righteous;
With kings on thrones
He seats them forever, and they are exalted.

8 If they are bound in shackles
And caught in trammels of affliction,

9 He declares to them what they have done,
And that their transgressions are excessive;

10 He opens their understanding by discipline,
And orders them back from mischief.

11 If they will serve obediently,
They shall spend their days in happiness,
Their years in delight.

12 But if they are not obedient,
They shall perish by the sword,
Die for lack of understanding.

13 But the impious in heart become enraged;
They do not cry for help when He afflicts them.

14 They die in their youth;
[Expire] among the depraved.

15 He rescues the lowly from their affliction,
And opens their understanding through distress.

16 Indeed, He draws you away from the brink of
distress
To a broad place where there is no constraint;
Your table is laid out with rich food.

16: Unlike Eliphaz in 22.5–7, Elihu does not explicitly state that Job has acted wickedly, but stresses instead Job's ignorance (see 34.35).

36.1–37.24: Elihu's fourth and last speech. Elihu glorifies God, describing, in a manner that anticipates God's speech in chs 38–39, God's supremacy over the natural world. This foreshadowing of the LORD's speeches helps to integrate Elihu into the book, but also presents a serious interpretive problem: If Elihu's claims are wrong, how are we to view the LORD's claims in the following chapters, which are prefigured by Elihu, and even by Elihu's name, which as noted above means "My God is the LORD"? **36.1:** *Then Elihu spoke once more,* better: "Elihu continued speaking." **5–6:** This introduction is the key to Elihu's claim, mirroring what the friends had earlier claimed: God is powerful and just. The rest of the speech notes God's great power as witness to God's justice.

a-a Meaning of Heb. uncertain.

17   You are obsessed with the case of the wicked man,
          But the justice of the case will be upheld.

18   Let anger at his affluence not mislead you;
          Let much bribery not turn you aside.

19   ᵃ·Will your limitless wealth avail you,·ᵃ
          All your powerful efforts?

20   Do not long for the night
          When peoples vanish where they are.

21   Beware! Do not turn to mischief;
          Because of that you have been tried by affliction.

22   See, God is beyond reach in His power;
          Who governs like Him?

23   Who ever reproached Him for His conduct?
          Who ever said, "You have done wrong"?

24   Remember, then, to magnify His work,
          Of which men have sung,

25   Which all men have beheld,
          Men have seen, from a distance.

26   See, God is greater than we can know;
          The number of His years cannot be counted.

27   He forms the droplets of water,
          Which cluster into rain, from His mist.

28   The skies rain;
          They pour down on all mankind.

29   Can one, indeed, contemplate the expanse of
              clouds,
          The thunderings from His pavilion?

30   See, He spreads His lightning over it;
          It fills the bed of the sea.

31   By these things He controls peoples;
          He gives food in abundance.

32   Lightning fills His hands;
          He orders it to hit the mark.

33   Its noise tells of Him.
          ᵃ·The kindling of anger against iniquity.·ᵃ

37   Because of this, too, my heart quakes,
          And leaps from its place.

2   Just listen to the noise of His rumbling,
          To the sound that comes out of His mouth.

3   He lets it loose beneath the entire heavens—
          His lightning, to the ends of the earth.

4   After it, He lets out a roar;
          He thunders in His majestic voice.
          No one can find a trace of it by the time His voice
              is heard.

a-a Meaning of Heb. uncertain.

5   God thunders marvelously with His voice;
    He works wonders that we cannot understand.

6   He commands the snow, "Fall to the ground!"
    And the downpour of rain, His mighty downpour
        of rain,

7   Is as a sign on every man's hand,
    That all men may know His doings.

8   Then the beast enters its lair,
    And remains in its den.

9   The storm wind comes from its chamber,
    And the cold from the constellations.

10 By the breath of God ice is formed,
    And the expanse of water becomes solid.

11 He also loads the clouds with moisture
    And scatters His lightning-clouds.

12 ᵃ·He keeps turning events by His stratagems,·ᵃ
    That they might accomplish all that He commands
        them
    Throughout the inhabited earth,

13 Causing each of them to happen to His land,
    Whether as a scourge or as a blessing.

14 Give ear to this, Job;
    Stop to consider the marvels of God.

15 Do you know what charge God lays upon them
    When His lightning-clouds shine?

16 Do you know the marvels worked upon the
        expanse of clouds
    By Him whose understanding is perfect,

17 ᵃ·Why your clothes become hot·ᵃ
    When the land is becalmed by the south wind?

18 Can you help him stretch out the heavens,
    Firm as a mirror of cast metal?

19 Inform us, then, what we may say to Him;
    We cannot argue because [we are in] darkness.

20 Is anything conveyed to Him when I speak?
    Can a man say anything when he is confused?

21 Now, then, one cannot see the sun,
    Though it be bright in the heavens,
    Until the wind comes and clears them [of clouds].

22 By the north wind the golden rays emerge;
    The splendor about God is awesome.

23 Shaddai—we cannot attain to Him;
    He is great in power and justice
    And abundant in righteousness; He does not
        torment.

37.11: *Also . . . with moisture:* This translation construes Heb "'af-beri" as a combination of the common coordinate conjunction "'af," "also," the common prefix "be-," "with," and the otherwise unattested "ri," "moisture," derived from the common Heb root "r-v-y," "saturate, be abundant" (see, e.g., Ps. 23.5: "my drink is abundant ['revayah']"; Jer. 31.25: "I will give the thirsty abundant drink ['hirveyti']." Ancient rabbinic tradition concerning the expression is reflected in the first of the series of liturgical poems ("piyyutim") sung by the cantor wearing a white robe before the open Ark in the synagogue on the festival of "Shemini ʿAtzeret" (also called the Eighth Day of Solemn Assembly because it immediately follows the seven days of Sukkot or Tabernacles). In these poems, composed by Eliezer ha-Qallir (7th century CE), God is asked to grant abundant rain in the land of Israel, whose agriculture and drinking water relies on the seasonal rain that, if it arrives at all, begins in October and ends in May. The poem, called "'Af-Beri" from its opening phrase, is incorporated into the first of the seven benedictions of the Additional Service on "Shemini ʿAtzeret." In that poem Af-Beri is said to be "the name given to the heavenly angel in charge of rain." *He . . . loads:* This translation reflects an assumption that the abstract sense (attested in rabbinic Heb), "encumber, burden, trouble," is a later development from an earlier concrete sense "burden, load." In context, the rain is one of God's many gifts that demonstrate divine interest and intervention, which Job has questioned (see, e.g., vv. 9–10). **18:** Like Gen. 1.6–7, this verse envisions the sky as a metal plate, hammered thin, that separates the water above from the water below. **23:** Just as he opened this final speech with his thesis (see n. on 36.5–6), he concludes with a summary, *He is great in power and justice.*

---

a-a Meaning of Heb. uncertain.

24 Therefore, men are in awe of Him
    Whom none of the wise can perceive.

38 Then the LORD replied to Job out of the tempest
    and said:

2   Who is this who darkens counsel,
    Speaking without knowledge?
3   Gird your loins like a man;
    I will ask and you will inform Me.

4   Where were you when I laid the earth's
        foundations?
    Speak if you have understanding.
5   Do you know who fixed its dimensions
    Or who measured it with a line?
6   Onto what were its bases sunk?
    Who set its cornerstone
7   When the morning stars sang together
    And all the divine beings shouted for joy?

8   Who closed the sea behind doors
    When it gushed forth out of the womb,
9   When I clothed it in clouds,
    Swaddled it in dense clouds,
10 When I made breakers My limit for it,
    And set up its bar and doors,
11 And said, "You may come so far and no farther;
    Here your surging waves will stop"?

12 Have you ever commanded the day to break,
    Assigned the dawn its place,
13 So that it seizes the corners of the earth
    And shakes the wicked out of it?
14 It changes like clay under the seal
    Till [its hues] are fixed like those of a garment.
15 Their light is withheld from the wicked,
    And the upraised arm is broken.

38.1–41.26: The speeches of the LORD.

38.1–39.30: The LORD's first speech. In a series of rhetorical questions that contrast the power and wisdom of God with that of Job, the speech argues that, since Job was not present at the creation (v. 4), and has no notion of how such matters as the sun's rising occur (v. 12), let alone how many other natural phenomena happen, he has no right to demand explanations. (Such rhetorical questions have typified the book as wisdom literature, and the cumulative effect of them here is very powerful.) God will not give Job a straight answer to his demand for a hearing (6.8–13; 7.11–21; 9.2–20, 25–35; ch 10; 13.17–14.22). If the reader is looking for God to explain why bad things happen to good people and how justice reigns in the cosmos, neither God nor the book of Job as a whole provides an answer. If the message of the book is construed as a question of virtue—whether a person should be righteous even in the face of apparent injustice—then no answer would be expected, nor would it be appropriate. If the book poses the question of why the righteous suffer, then the conclusion may be that we cannot know the ways of God, and that to insist that God act in a certain way is to limit God's great power and knowledge. The effect of God's speech is to put Job in his place, to awe him with God's might. Other interpretations have been offered for this speech. Some suggest that God does answer Job by His appearance; the revelation itself is a sufficient answer. Others suggest that if Job is arguing that God is powerful and unjust, and the friends are arguing that God is powerful and just, the LORD's speeches "resolve" this debate by insisting only that God is powerful. Still others take such statements as 38.12–13, "Have you ever commanded the day to break, / Assigned the dawn its place, / So that it seizes the corners of the earth / And shakes the wicked out of it?" not as rhetorical questions, but as God conceding His weakness, and asking Job if he could do any better in running the world fairly. Unfortunately, it is difficult to decide between these (and still other) interpretive possibilites, especially because the speeches are indirect and ambiguous, and Job's answers to the LORD's speeches, which might help us understand what God is saying, are also somewhat ambiguous. Perhaps this is best, given the nature of the issues that the book is grappling with. **38.1:** *Replied to Job,* lit. "answered Job," with Job marked by the definite accusative particle "'et" as direct object of the verb. Comparison of this expression here and in 40.1 and 40.6 and in many other places

16 Have you penetrated to the sources of the sea,
    Or walked in the recesses of the deep?
17 Have the gates of death been disclosed to you?
    Have you seen the gates of deep darkness?
18 Have you surveyed the expanses of the earth?
    If you know of these—tell Me.

19 Which path leads to where light dwells,
    And where is the place of darkness,
20 That you may take it to its domain
    And know the way to its home?
21 Surely you know, for you were born then,
    And the number of your years is many!

22 Have you penetrated the vaults of snow,
    Seen the vaults of hail,
23 Which I have put aside for a time of adversity,
    For a day of war and battle?
24 By what path is the west wind*a* dispersed,
    The east wind scattered over the earth?
25 Who cut a channel for the torrents
    And a path for the thunderstorms,
26 To rain down on uninhabited land,
    On the wilderness where no man is,
27 To saturate the desolate wasteland,
    And make the crop of grass sprout forth?
28 Does the rain have a father?
    Who begot the dewdrops?
29 From whose belly came forth the ice?
    Who gave birth to the frost of heaven?
30 Water congeals like stone,
    And the surface of the deep compacts.

31 Can you tie cords to Pleiades
    Or undo the reins of Orion?
32 Can you lead out Mazzaroth*b* in its season,
    Conduct the Bear with her sons?
33 Do you know the laws of heaven
    Or impose its authority on earth?

34 Can you send up an order to the clouds
    For an abundance of water to cover you?
35 Can you dispatch the lightning on a mission
    And have it answer you, "I am ready"?
36 Who put wisdom in the hidden parts?
    Who gave understanding to the mind?*c*

in Job may support the view (similarly Rashi) against NJPS that in all of those cases the verbal root "'-n-y" means "declaim" and corresponds to Arabic "gh-n-y."
36: *The rooster:* This interpretation (in translators' note c) is reflected in the ancient benediction with which the prayer leader begins every morning service of the synagogue: "Praised are You, O Lord our God, King of the universe, who gave understanding to the rooster to distinguish between day and night." The source of this benediction is *b. Berakhot* 60b, which states that this benediction should be recited each morning upon hearing the crowing of the rooster.

a *As Aramaic* 'urya.   b *Evidently a constellation.*
c *Or* "rooster"; *meaning of Heb. uncertain.*

37 Who is wise enough to give an account of the
     heavens?
    Who can tilt the bottles of the sky,
38 Whereupon the earth melts into a mass,
    And its clods stick together.

39 Can you hunt prey for the lion,
    And satisfy the appetite of the king of beasts?
40 They crouch in their dens,
    Lie in ambush in their lairs.
41 Who provides food for the raven
    When his young cry out to God
    And wander about without food?

39 Do you know the season when the mountain
     goats give birth?
    Can you mark the time when the hinds calve?
2 Can you count the months they must complete?
    Do you know the season they give birth,
3 When they couch to bring forth their offspring,
    To deliver their young?
4 Their young are healthy; they grow up in the
     open;
    They leave and return no more.

5 Who sets the wild ass free?
    Who loosens the bonds of the onager,
6 Whose home I have made the wilderness,
    The salt land his dwelling-place?
7 He scoffs at the tumult of the city,
    Does not hear the shouts of the driver.
8 He roams the hills for his pasture;
    He searches for any green thing.

9 Would the wild ox agree to serve you?
    Would he spend the night at your crib?
10 Can you hold the wild ox by ropes to the
     furrow?
    Would he plow up the valleys behind you?
11 Would you rely on his great strength
    And leave your toil to him?
12 Would you trust him to bring in the seed
    And gather it in from your threshing floor?

13 The wing of the ostrich beats joyously;
    Are her pinions and plumage like the stork's?
14 She leaves her eggs on the ground,
    Letting them warm in the dirt,

39.13–18: The ostrich provides an example of the problems of interpreting this speech as a whole. For some, it points to God's great power: Only He understands why such a foolish creature exists. For others, it hints at the imperfections in God's creation. (See similarly the end of the chapter: "His young gulp blood; / Where the slain are, there is he.")

15 Forgetting they may be crushed underfoot,
   Or trampled by a wild beast.
16 Her young are cruelly abandoned as if they were
       not hers;
   Her labor is in vain for lack of concern.
17 For God deprived her of wisdom,
   Gave her no share of understanding,
18 Else she would soar on high,
   Scoffing at the horse and its rider.

19 Do you give the horse his strength?
   Do you clothe his neck with a mane?
20 Do you make him quiver like locusts,
   His majestic snorting [spreading] terror?
21 He[a] paws with force, he runs with vigor,
   Charging into battle.
22 He scoffs at fear; he cannot be frightened;
   He does not recoil from the sword.
23 A quiverful of arrows whizzes by him,
   And the flashing spear and the javelin.
24 Trembling with excitement, he swallows[b] the land;
   He does not turn aside at the blast of the trumpet.
25 As the trumpet sounds, he says, "Aha!"
   From afar he smells the battle,
   The roaring and shouting of the officers.

26 Is it by your wisdom that the hawk grows pinions,
   Spreads his wings to the south?
27 Does the eagle soar at your command,
   Building his nest high,
28 Dwelling in the rock,
   Lodging upon the fastness of a jutting rock?
29 From there he spies out his food;
   From afar his eyes see it.
30 His young gulp blood;
   Where the slain are, there is he.

40

The LORD said in reply to Job.

2 [c]Shall one who should be disciplined complain
       against Shaddai?[c]
   He who arraigns God must respond.

3 Job said in reply to the LORD:

4 See, I am of small worth; what can I answer You?
   I clap my hand to my mouth.

19: While all the other examples are taken from the exotic or mysterious, the image of the horse is closer to human life. Yet the image is one of magnificent power.

40.3–5: The first reply of Job. It is very difficult to understand the tone with which this is said: Is Job defiant, frightened, or sincere? Yet in v. 2 the LORD insisted that Job must *respond*, but Job insists in v. 5 that he *will not reply* (the Heb uses the same word as *respond*). Thus, the LORD must offer another speech, beginning in v. 6.

---

a Lit. "They..."   b Or "digs up."   c-c Meaning of Heb. uncertain.

5   I have spoken once, and will not reply;
     Twice, and will do so no more.

6   Then the LORD replied to Job out of the tempest
     and said:

7   Gird your loins like a man;
     I will ask, and you will inform Me.

8   Would you impugn My justice?
     Would you condemn Me that you may be right?

9   Have you an arm like God's?
     Can you thunder with a voice like His?

10   Deck yourself now with grandeur and eminence;
     Clothe yourself in glory and majesty.

11   Scatter wide your raging anger;
     See every proud man and bring him low.

12   See every proud man and humble him,
     And bring them down where they stand.

13   Bury them all in the earth;
     Hide their faces in obscurity.

14   Then even I would praise you
     For the triumph your right hand won you.

15   Take now behemoth, whom I made as I did you;
     He eats grass, like the cattle.

16   His strength is in his loins,
     His might in the muscles of his belly.

17   a-He makes his tail stand up-a like a cedar;
     The sinews of his thighs are knit together.

18   His bones are like tubes of bronze,
     His limbs like iron rods.

19   He is the first of God's works;
     Only his Maker can draw the sword against him.

20   The mountains yield him produce,
     Where all the beasts of the field play.

21   He lies down beneath the lotuses,
     In the cover of the swamp reeds.

22   The lotuses embower him with shade;
     The willows of the brook surround him.

23   He can restrain the river from its rushing;
     He is confident the stream[b] will gush at his
       command.

24   Can he be taken by his eyes?
     Can his nose be pierced by hooks?

25   Can you draw out Leviathan by a fishhook?
     Can you press down his tongue by a rope?

a-a Meaning of Heb. uncertain.   b Lit. "Jordan."

40.6–41.26: The LORD's second speech. 40.7: This is identical with 38.3, from the first speech, suggesting that the two speeches will be thematically similar. **11–14:** Most readers understand these verses sarcastically, as a challenge to Job to try to be as just as God, while some read these as an admission of divine imperfection. **15–24, 25–32:** *Behemoth . . . Leviathan:* Many scholars interpret *behemoth* as designating a mythologized hippopotamus (see Isa. 30.6), and *leviathan* as a mythologized crocodile. Heb "tanin," "Dragon," appears as a synonym of Rahab (on which see Job 9.13; 26.12), the personified sea in Isa. 51.9 and in Job 7.12. The same term, however, designates the crocodile in Ezek. 29.3; 32.2. Since in Ugaritic poetry the corresponding "tnn" appears as a poetic synonym of "ltn," i.e., Leviathan (see 26.13 n.), it follows that Leviathan here could refer to the crocodile rather than to the personified sea, which rebels against but is ultimately subdued by the LORD, in an ancient Israelite myth to which Job and other biblical books frequently refer. Since Isa. 27.1 intimates that there may have been two Leviathans (see also Gen. 1.21: "the great sea monsters") and that Leviathan is yet to be killed, while Ps. 74.14 hints that God has already smashed the heads of Leviathan, *b. Bava Batra* 74b concludes that originally there were two Leviathans, one of each sex, who might have procreated and taken over the cosmos. Therefore God castrated the male and killed the female and preserved her in salt to be served up at the great eschatological feast to which all the righteous will be invited and at which a principal food item will be Leviathan. It was but one more step to note that behemoth, which is paired with Leviathan only in Job 40.15–32, must represent another principal food item to be served up at the eschatologial banquet, namely a choice kind of beef (also called "shor ha-bar," i.e., "wild bull"). A further leap of the Jewish imagination led to the realization that the menu of the escha-

26   Can you put a ring through his nose,
     Or pierce his jaw with a barb?
27   Will he plead with you at length?
     Will he speak soft words to you?
28   Will he make an agreement with you
     To be taken as your lifelong slave?
29   Will you play with him like a bird,
     And tie him down for your girls?
30   ᵃ-Shall traders traffic in him?-ᵃ
     Will he be divided up among merchants?
31   Can you fill his skin with darts
     Or his head with fish-spears?
32   Lay a hand on him,
     And you will never think of battle again.

41 See, any hope [of capturing] him must be
         disappointed;
     One is prostrated by the very sight of him.
2   There is no one so fierce as to rouse him;
     Who then can stand up to Me?
3   Whoever confronts Me I will requite,
     For everything under the heavens is Mine.
4   ᵃ-I will not be silent concerning him
     Or the praise of his martial exploits.-ᵃ
5   Who can uncover his outer garment?
     Who can penetrate the folds of his jowls?
6   Who can pry open the doors of his face?
     His bared teeth strike terror.
7   His protective scales are his pride,
     Locked with a binding seal.
8   One scale touches the other;
     Not even a breath can enter between them.
9   Each clings to each;
     They are interlocked so they cannot be parted.
10   His sneezings flash lightning,
     And his eyes are like the glimmerings of dawn.
11   Firebrands stream from his mouth;
     Fiery sparks escape.
12   Out of his nostrils comes smoke
     As from a steaming, boiling cauldron.
13   His breath ignites coals;
     Flames blaze from his mouth.
14   Strength resides in his neck;
     Power leaps before him.
15   The layers of his flesh stick together;
     He is as though cast hard; he does not totter.

tological banquet, which certainly could not have provided only fish, and which included both Leviathan conceived of as fish and behemoth conceived of as beef, must also include some kind of fowl. This last menu item was provided by the enigmatic Ziz, translated as "creatures [of the field]" by NJPS at Pss. 50.11; 80.14. Job anticipated in 9.13 the argument that the LORD's power over the mythical sea-monsters proves that God is indeed in charge of the universe and that cosmic anarchy cannot explain Job's unjust suffering.

a-a Meaning of Heb. uncertain.

16 His heart is cast hard as a stone,
    Hard as the nether millstone.
17 Divine beings are in dread as he rears up;
    As he crashes down, they cringe.
18 No sword that overtakes him can prevail,
    Nor spear, nor missile, nor lance.
19 He regards iron as straw,
    Bronze, as rotted wood.
20 No arrow can put him to flight;
    Slingstones turn into stubble for him.
21 Clubs[a] are regarded as stubble;
    He scoffs at the quivering javelin.
22 His underpart is jagged shards;
    It spreads a threshing-sledge on the mud.
23 He makes the depths seethe like a cauldron;
    He makes the sea [boil] like an ointment-pot.
24 His wake is a luminous path;
    He makes the deep seem white-haired.
25 There is no one on land who can dominate him,
    Made as he is without fear.
26 He sees all that is haughty;
    He is king over all proud beasts.

42 Job said in reply to the LORD:

2   I know that You can do everything,
    That nothing you propose is impossible for You.
3   Who is this who obscures counsel without
        knowledge?
    Indeed, I spoke without understanding
    Of things beyond me, which I did not know.
4   Hear now, and I will speak;
    I will ask, and You will inform me.
5   I had heard You with my ears,
    But now I see You with my eyes;
6   Therefore, I recant and relent,
    Being but dust and ashes.

7 After the LORD had spoken these words to Job, the LORD said to Eliphaz the Temanite, "I am incensed at you and your two friends, for you have not spoken the truth about Me as did My servant Job. 8 Now take seven bulls and seven rams and go to My servant Job and sacrifice a burnt offering for yourselves. And let Job, My servant, pray for you; for to him I will show favor and not treat you vilely, since you have not spoken the truth about Me

a Meaning of Heb. uncertain.

42.1–6: Job's recantation. 3–4: It is likely that the first half of v. 3 and all of v. 4 are quotations of God by Job, to which Job is responding. **5:** Job suggests that before he had only indirect knowledge of God, but now he has direct knowledge. One of his desires was for his accuser, God, to appear, and God has now done this. Job, however, ignores the fact that God has not directly answered his questions. **6:** As Job's final comment, this verse would seem to be key to understanding the book as a whole. The Heb of the text, unlike the rest of Job, is not difficult, but is very ambiguous. The verb translated as *recant* more typically means "despise," and neither verb in the first half has the expected direct object—what does Job recant/despise or relent? As translated, the second half reflects Job's basic creaturehood, the fact that unlike God, he is a mere mortal, *dust and ashes.* The preposition that opens this section is more naturally translated "on," however, and thus this phrase may be a prosaic notice that Job feels this way while he is mourning on a dust-heap (see 2.8). Thus, the highly ambiguous poetry concludes with this seemingly simple but ambiguous verse. Whatever it means, the LORD seems to be satisfied that Job has responded adequately (see 40.5), so the poetic section of the work is concluded.

42.7–17: Prose epilogue. 8: *Seven bulls and seven rams . . . a burnt offering:* According to Lev. 1.3–17 a burnt offering can be a male from the herd, a male from the flock, of sheep or of goats, or a turtledove or a pigeon. A ram, on the other hand, is presented as a guilt offering (see Lev. 5.15–26). A bull, according to Lev. 4.1–21, is appropriate for the sin or purification offering of either "the anointed priest" or "the whole community of Israel." Job's friends repeatedly offended God by intimating that Job somehow brought his suffering upon himself. They describe themselves and are described by Job as communal leaders. It is altoas did My servant Job." [9] Eliphaz the Temanite and Bildad the Shuhite and Zophar the Naamathite went and did as the LORD had told them, and the LORD showed favor to Job. [10] The LORD restored Job's fortunes when he prayed on behalf of his friends, and the LORD gave Job twice what he had before.

[11] All his brothers and sisters and all his former friends came to him and had a meal with him in his house. They consoled and comforted him for all the misfortune that the LORD had brought upon him. Each gave him one *kesitah*[a] and each one gold ring. [12] Thus the LORD blessed the latter years of Job's life more than the former. He had fourteen thousand sheep, six thousand camels, one thousand yoke of oxen, and one thousand she-asses. [13] He also had seven sons and three daughters. [14] The first he named Jemimah, the second Keziah, and the third Keren-happuch. [15] Nowhere in the land were women as beautiful as Job's daughters to be found. Their father gave them estates together with their brothers. [16] Afterward, Job lived one hundred and forty years to see four generations of sons and grandsons. [17] So Job died old and contented.

gether appropriate that they should be asked to present, in addition to an unspecified number of burnt offerings, the sin offering appropriate either to "the anointed priest" or "the whole community." Each of the seven rams would be equally appropriate as expiation for sacrilege (Lev. 5.15; cf. Job 42.7): "when a person, without knowing it, sins in regard to any of the LORD's commandments about things not to be done, and then realizes his guilt" (Lev. 5.17) or "when a person sins and commits a trespass [i.e., sacrilege] against the LORD by dealing deceitfully with his fellow" (Lev. 5.21). The author of the book of Job knew the Torah, and therefore knew quite well that both seven bulls and seven rams have nothing to do with what is commonly called a burnt offering. Job must *pray for* the friends, showing the empathy that they had not shown, and leaving his cocoon of self-interest and self-pity. **11:** The *kesitah* is mentioned only in Gen. 33.19 and Josh. 24.32, texts describing the ancestral period. The author uses it here (rather than the much more common shekel) to help set this story in hoary antiquity. **14:** *Jemimah,* usually explained by Arabic "yumayma," "little dove." *Keziah,* usually explained as the aromatic plant cassia mentioned in Ps. 45.9. *Keren-happuch,* "a flask of blue eyeshadow," mentioned also in Jer. 4.30. The ending of the book should not be construed as a reward for Job, but simply as the end of the test begun in ch 1 and Job's restoration to his status quo ante. **16:** Living to a ripe old age and having many progeny is the ideal of the blessed person in the Bible. Job's life span of 140 years is twice the ideal life span of seventy years (see Ps. 90.10). **17:** The ending is formulaic, much like "and they lived happily ever after."

a A unit of unknown value.

חמש מגלות

The Five Megillot (Scrolls)

IN PRINTED EDITIONS OF THE TANAKH, the three initial large books of Kethuvim, Psalms, Proverbs, and Job (sometimes ordered Psalms, Job, Proverbs), are followed by five smaller books. In this translation, they appear in the order of the Songs of Songs, Ruth, Lamentations, Ecclesiastes, and Esther. In the Middle Ages, these were called *ḥamesh megillot*, the five scrolls.

These books are counted as individual books and were not always perceived as a single unit. In the Septuagint, Ruth, which opens "In the days that the judges ruled," appears after Judges, and Lamentations is placed after Jeremiah since an ancient tradition ascribes the authorship of Lamentations to Jeremiah. The Babylonian Talmud as well does not know of the *ḥamesh megillot*; it suggests (*b. B. Bat.* 14b) that the order of the beginning of the Kethuvim is: Ruth, Psalms, Job, Proverbs, Ecclesiastes, Song of Songs, Lamentations. A small number of medieval Hebrew manuscripts follow this tradition, as well as other orders that do not place these five books together.

The order in the NJPS Tanakh translation is a common one, found in numerous manuscripts. The books are arranged in the order in which they are read liturgically in the annual cycle, beginning with the spring new year (see Exod. 12.2): Song of Songs is read on Passover (April), Ruth on Shavuot (May–June), Lamentations on the ninth of Av (July–August), Ecclesiastes on Sukkot (September–October), and Esther on Purim (March). Another common order, found in the best early manuscripts (Aleppo Codex, the first complete Masoretic manuscript [10th century], and Leningrad Codex B19A, the earliest extant complete manuscript [11th century]; see essay "Masoretic Bible," pp. 2077–84), have a different order. These manuscripts place the *megillot* in chronological order according to theories of traditional authorship: Ruth (Samuel), Song of Songs (Solomon in his youth), Ecclesiastes (Solomon in his old age), Lamentations (Jeremiah), and Esther (Mordecai, after the Babylonian exile). Many other orders exist. The grouping of the five books together reflects their common liturgical use, and perhaps a desire to have another pentad, to parallel the five books in the Torah and the five books within the book of Psalms. [ADELE BERLIN AND MARC ZVI BRETTLER]

שיר השירים

The Song of Songs

THE SONG OF SONGS is the Tanakh's only extensive discourse on human, erotic love. The book consists of a series of poems in which the speech of two lovers is interspersed with occasional comments by other voices. Throughout the poems, the lovers describe themselves and each other, and their feelings of love, desire, and longing. While the book has no narrative plot, the relationship between the lovers is marked by cycles of absence and presence. Poems which celebrate the presence of a lover alternate with poems of longing and poems of invitation. While both lovers speak within the text, the woman is the more active and articulate character. Her experiences, feelings, and perceptions are the central content of the poem. This suggests to some that a woman may have authored (parts of) the Song.

The Song is characterized by a wide range of poetic techniques. The poets draw from the language of the natural, domestic, and urban spheres. They use techniques of wordplay, pun and soundplay, repetition, simile, metaphor, and double entendre to highlight the relationship between the two lovers. One of the most striking literary features of the Song is the oscillation among the different spheres and modes. The poetic voices shift repeatedly from praise to adjuration, from playfulness to violence, and from third-person to second-person address, creating dynamic movement. The poetic techniques, many of which have parallels in Egyptian and Mesopotamian love poetry, provide an apt vehicle and a literary mirror for the lushness, exuberance, and movement of the relationship which they describe.

The compositional history and origin of the Song of Songs remain matters of debate. Most commentators agree that the book is a collection of poetic units which are linked by theme, language, and style. There are disagreements, however, over the extent of each unit and the degree of coherence of the collection. Some scholars insist that the poem is the work of a single author who might have relied on earlier sources or traditions. Others insist that the canonical text is the product of a redactor who edited together preexistent poems and poetic fragments.

The date of composition of the Song is also unclear. With the exception of the few references to King Solomon, there is no mention of known historical figures or events. Nor do the references to human behavior correlate to the attitudes or situations of a particular historical period. In addition, the book contains both archaic language and relatively late words, which makes it difficult to establish a date on linguistic grounds. Contemporary scholarly consensus hypothesizes that the poem probably has its roots in early folk and literary traditions but was composed or redacted in the 4th or 3rd century BCE.

The original genre and function of the text have also been the subject of much research and debate. Over the past century, three major theories have been adduced. The first is that the Song is the script of a drama which told the story of a love affair. This theory was quite popular in the 19th century, but has since been abandoned. The second theory holds that the Song evolved from a Mesopotamian liturgical context which described the sacred marriage of a god and goddess. This theory is based on perceived similarities between the Song and ancient Mesopotamian sacred marriage texts. Like the dramatic theory, this theory has become less popular in recent years, but it remains possible that some of the images of the poem originate in liturgical or mythological traditions. The third, most satisfactory theory maintains that the text is a collection of poems about human love, some of which may have originally been used in wedding celebrations.

The Song's positive focus on human, erotic love, its silence regarding the central theological and historical themes of the rest of the biblical text, and the centrality of its female character, make it unique within the biblical canon. Some scholars have argued that already by the time of its inclusion in the canon, the Song was understood not only as human love poetry but also, and perhaps primarily, as a description of the love relationship between God and Israel. This theory rests partly on the use of the human love relationship as a metaphor for the God-Israel relationship in the prophetic literature (e.g., Isa. 54.4–8; Jer. 2.1–2; Ezek. chs 16, 23; Hos. chs 1–3). While it is possible that the allegorical understanding of the poem was already current at the time of the book's canonization, it is also possible that the poems were introduced into the canon because, as secular love songs, they occupied an important place in the culture of ancient Israel in biblical and Second Temple times. Once the book became part of the canon, the tendency to interpret it allegorically increased.

Song of Songs in Jewish Tradition

WHILE THE BOOK'S ORIGIN remains obscure, the history of interpretation of the Song in Jewish tradition is well documented. From as early as the 2nd century CE, it has been understood in both human and divine terms. In rabbinic tradition, the Song narrates the words which God and Israel spoke to each other at the Red Sea, at Sinai, or in the Tent of Meeting. The descriptions of the male lover are understood as allegorical descriptions of God while the descriptions of the female lover are understood as divine praise of Israel. The statements of desire and love are read as expressions of love and intimacy between God and Israel. The Targum to the Song employs a similar strategy of expounding the Song as a historical allegory; it interprets the Song as a description of Israel's ongoing history of redemption by God. The allegorical interpretation plays a particularly important role in early Jewish mysticism. In medieval mystical texts, the theme of love remains constant but the identification of the protagonists changes. The lovers are sometimes identified as God and Israel, and sometimes interpreted as God and the individual soul or, alternatively, as the male and female aspects of the divine. The Song of Songs also plays a role in the Jewish liturgical tradition. It is recited at Passover and, in some communities, is recited or sung as part of the *kabbalat shabbat* (welcoming the Sabbath) service on Friday night.

While there has been a constant tradition of theological interpretation of the Song within Judaism, there has also been a tradition of secular, humanistic interpretation. The Talmud (*b. Sanh.* 101a) testifies to the singing of the Song in the secular settings of feasts and drinking halls, though it polemicizes against this use. In addition, words and images from the Song of Songs have figured prominently in Jewish marriage art, music, and liturgy since at least the Middle Ages. The Song was also a popular biblical text for the early Zionist movement. Its lush descriptions of the natural world and the flora and fauna of the land of Israel gave voice to the early Zionist love for the land.

Although the Song of Songs was not written by a single author as a narrative whole, the various poetic devices—including verbatim repetitions, recurring genres, and thematic echoes—encourage it to be read as an unfolding story. Much of the book's richness and meaning is communicated through its poetic structures and techniques, its choice of language and use of imagery, and the relationship between different poetic units. The poet uses partial or exact repetition in different ways to communicate patterns and changes in the lovers' relationship. Throughout the poem, motifs such as spices, vineyards and gardens, gazelles and doves, hiding and seeking, king and mother, communicate details about the lovers' relationship and the variety and scope of their feelings for one another.

[ELSIE STERN]

1 The Song of Songs, by[a] Solomon.

2   [b]Oh, give me of the kisses of your mouth,[b]
      For your love is more delightful than wine.
3   Your ointments yield a sweet fragrance,
      Your name is like finest[c] oil—
      Therefore do maidens love you.
4   Draw me after you, let us run!
      [d]The king has brought me to his chambers.[d]

a *Or "concerning."*   b-b *Heb. "Let him give me of the kisses of his mouth!"*
c *Meaning of Heb. uncertain.*
d-d *Emendation yields "Bring me, O king, to your chambers."*

1.1: Title. Internal evidence suggests that this v. is secondary, and does not represent an ancient tradition of authorship. *Song of Songs* is a superlative phrase meaning "the greatest or preeminent song." *By Solomon,* or "about Solomon."

According to Jewish tradition, Solomon authored the books of Proverbs, Ecclesiastes, and Song of Songs. These attributions are based on Song 1.1 and Eccl. 1.1. Also, biblical tradition describes Solomon as the author of Proverbs

and the Song, an expert in flora and fauna (1 Kings 5.9–14), and a lover of many women (1 Kings 11.1). In both the Targum and the midrash, the name "Shlomo" (Solomon) is interpreted as a reference to God. According to this interpretation, the Song is a description of the love between God and Israel. Modern scholars do not accept the idea of Solomonic authorship.

1.2–4: The woman expresses her desire for her lover. 2: *Wine:* The repeated references to wine (2.4, 7; 4.10; 5.1; 7.10; 8.2) may suggest an original context in wedding feasts or other celebrations where wine was drunk. Alternatively, wine is used poetically as a symbol of sensuous pleasure. *Finest oil,* or, "oil poured out"; the lover's excellent reputation is widespread. **4:** *The*

Let us delight and rejoice in your love,
Savoring it more than wine—
^{a-}Like new wine^{-a} they love you!

5   I am dark, but comely,
O daughters of Jerusalem—
Like the tents of Kedar,
Like the pavilions of Solomon.

6   Don't stare at me because I am swarthy,
Because the sun has gazed upon me.
My mother's sons quarreled with me,
They made me guard the vineyards;
My own vineyard I did not guard.

7   Tell me, you whom I love so well;
Where do you pasture your sheep?
Where do you rest them at noon?
Let me not be ^{b-}as one who strays^{-b}
Beside the flocks of your fellows.

8   If you do not know, O fairest of women,
Go follow the tracks of the sheep,
And graze your kids^c
By the tents of the shepherds.

9   I have likened you, my darling,
To a mare in Pharaoh's chariots:

10   Your cheeks are comely with plaited wreaths,
Your neck with strings of jewels.

11   We will add wreaths of gold
To your spangles of silver.

12   While the king was on his couch,
My nard gave forth its fragrance.

13   My beloved to me is a bag of myrrh
Lodged between my breasts.

14   My beloved to me is a spray of henna blooms
From the vineyards of En-gedi.

15   Ah, you are fair, my darling,
Ah, you are fair,
With your dove-like eyes!

16   And you, my beloved, are handsome,
Beautiful indeed!
Our couch is in a bower;

17   Cedars are the beams of our house,
Cypresses the rafters.

king: References to a king and to King Solomon (1.12; 3.9, 11; 6.8–9; 7.6) support interpretations of the Song as a royal wedding song or cultic song. In rabbinic interpretations, references to the king are understood as references to God, and the royal chambers refer to the Temple. In most modern readings, the references to the king are complimentary references to the male lover.

1.5–6: The woman describes herself. 5: *Dark, but comely,* or "dark and comely." In 5.10, fair skin is a sign of masculine beauty. Here, the woman's darkness may be either an asset or a liability, and is the likely result of her work outdoors, described in the following vv. *Kedar,* northern Assyrian nomadic tribe. Kedar means "dark." **6:** *Vineyard:* In the Song, the vineyard often represents both a physical place and the woman's own sexuality (1.14; 2.15; 7.13; 8.12).

1.7–17: Dialogue between the lovers. 9: *I have likened . . . :* Throughout the Song, the lovers use comparison to praise one another's beauty and charm. *Mare in Pharaoh's chariots,* either an image of adorned majesty (the horses were decorated with ornaments) or a reference to an ancient battle strategy in which a mare was let loose among cavalry to distract the stallions. **12–14:** The physical closeness of the lovers— their scent—is described. *Nard . . . myrrh . . . henna,* precious spices used in perfumes. Nard and myrrh were exotic imports while henna was indigenous to biblical Israel. **14:** *En-gedi,* a fertile oasis in the Judean wilderness. Given that wine grapes did not grow there, this too is a likely allusion to the woman's own sexuality.

---

a-a *Understanding* mesharim *as related to* tirosh; *cf. Aramaic* merath.
b-b *Meaning of Heb. uncertain.*   c *As a pretext for coming.*

2 I am a rose[a] of Sharon,
A lily of the valleys.

2 Like a lily among thorns,
So is my darling among the maidens.

3 Like an apple tree among trees of the forest,
So is my beloved among the youths.
I delight to sit in his shade,
And his fruit is sweet to my mouth.

4 He brought me to the banquet room
[b-]And his banner of love was over me.[-b]

5 "Sustain me with raisin cakes,
Refresh me with apples,
For I am faint with love."

6 His left hand was under my head,
His right arm embraced me.

7 I adjure you, O maidens of Jerusalem,
By gazelles or by hinds of the field:
Do not wake or rouse
Love until it please!

8 Hark! My beloved!
There he comes,
Leaping over mountains,
Bounding over hills.

9 My beloved is like a gazelle
Or like a young stag.
There he stands behind our wall,
Gazing through the window,
Peering through the lattice.

10 My beloved spoke thus to me,
"Arise, my darling;
My fair one, come away!

11 For now the winter is past,
The rains are over and gone.

12 The blossoms have appeared in the land,
The time of pruning[c] has come;
The song of the turtledove
Is heard in our land.

13 The green figs form on the fig tree,
The vines in blossom give off fragrance.
Arise, my darling;
My fair one, come away!

14 "O my dove, in the cranny of the rocks,
Hidden by the cliff,

2.1–3: The lovers praise one another for their uniqueness. 1: *Sharon,* fertile plain in northern Israel. **3:** *Apple tree:* The precise type of fruit is unknown (apples are not indigenous to Israel); perhaps quince or apricot.

2.4–7: The woman reminisces about her lover. 7: *I adjure you . . . :* This recurring refrain (3.5; 5.8; 8.4), whose exact meaning is ambiguous, is addressed to the woman's female companions. *By gazelles . . . :* In Heb, the names of these animals function as wordplays on the name of God (e.g., *gazelles,* "tzeva'ot," also means "hosts," as in "LORD of hosts"), which would be expected in such an adjuration; they also underscore the earthy quality of the oath and resonate with the use of these animals as symbols of love and beauty throughout the Song.

2.8–17: The woman's wish for the couple to run away together, to be alone in nature in the springtime. This passage is full of flora and fauna. **10–13:** *Arise, my darling . . . arise, my darling:* The repetition of the phrase sets these vv. apart as a separate unit. While many biblical texts are concerned with the land of Israel and its fertility, this is one of the few that celebrate the beauty of the land of Israel. **14:** *O my dove:* The dove, a symbol of purity, gentleness, and fidelity, is a frequent epithet for the woman in the Song (cf. 2.15; 5.2; 6.9). **15:** *Catch us . . . :* The relationship of this fragment to the surrounding vv. is unclear. It may be either a fragment of a separate poem or proverb or the woman's response to the man's request in 2.14. **16:** *My beloved is mine:* This declaration of mutual love appears frequently in wedding liturgies, music, and art. **17:** This v. is mirrored in the conclusion of the Song.

a Lit. *"crocus." b-b Meaning of Heb. uncertain. c Or "singing."*

Let me see your face,
Let me hear your voice;
For your voice is sweet
And your face is comely."

15 Catch us the foxes,
The little foxes
That ruin the vineyards—
For our vineyard is in blossom.

16 My beloved is mine
And I am his
Who browses among the lilies.

17 When the day *a-blows gently-a*
And the shadows flee,*b*
Set out, my beloved,
Swift as a gazelle
Or a young stag,
For the hills of spices!*c*

3 Upon my couch at night*d*
I sought the one I love—
I sought, but found him not.

2 "I must rise and roam the town,
Through the streets and through the squares;
I must seek the one I love."
I sought but found him not.

3 *e-*I met the watchmen*-e*
Who patrol the town.
"Have you seen the one I love?"

4 Scarcely had I passed them
When I found the one I love.
I held him fast, I would not let him go
Till I brought him to my mother's house,
To the chamber of her who conceived me

5 I adjure you, O maidens of Jerusalem,
By gazelles or by hinds of the field:
Do not wake or rouse
Love until it please!

6 Who is she that comes up from the desert
Like columns of smoke,
In clouds of myrrh and frankincense,
Of all the powders of the merchant?

7 There is Solomon's couch,
Encircled by sixty warriors

3.1–6: The woman searches for her lover. This passage may be interpreted as a dream scene, although it is sufficiently ambiguous to allow other interpretations as well. The dreamlike quality of the episode, found here and at the beginning of ch 5, is one of the many poetic techniques employed in the Song. **2:** *I sought, but found him not:* The desperate tone here contrasts with the playful, hide-and-go-seek mode of the previous ch. **4:** *My mother's house:* Motherhood is a central image in the Song (cf. 3.4, 11; 6.9; 8.1, 5). Here, the mother represents security and support for the lovers.

3.6–11: Vision of royal wedding procession. This section consists of two parallel descriptions. The first (vv. 6–8) employs the language of war and has an undertone of violence; the second (vv. 9–11) employs the language of royalty and romance. **6:** *Who is she,* or, what is this? The feminine form of the pronoun (she) probably refers to Solomon's couch.

---

a-a Emendation yields "declines"; cf. Jer. 6.4.
b Septuagint reads "lengthen"; cf. Jer. 6.4.
c Heb. bather of uncertain meaning; 8.14 reads besamim, "spices."
d I.e., in a dream.   e-e Lit. "The watchmen met me."

Of the warriors of Israel,
8 All of them trained[a] in warfare,
Skilled in battle,
Each with sword on thigh
Because of terror by night.

9 King Solomon made him a palanquin
Of wood from Lebanon.
10 He made its posts of silver,
Its back[b] of gold,
Its seat of purple wool.
Within, it was decked with [c]love
By the maidens of Jerusalem.[c]
11 O maidens of Zion, go forth
And gaze upon King Solomon
Wearing the crown that his mother
Gave him on his wedding day,
On his day of bliss.

4 Ah, you are fair, my darling,
Ah, you are fair.
Your eyes are like doves
Behind your veil.
Your hair is like a flock of goats
Streaming down Mount Gilead.
2 Your teeth are like a flock of ewes[d]
Climbing up from the washing pool;
All of them bear twins,
And not one loses her young.
3 Your lips are like a crimson thread,
Your mouth is lovely.
Your brow behind your veil
[Gleams] like a pomegranate split open.
4 Your neck is like the Tower of David,
Built [e]to hold weapons,[e]
Hung with a thousand shields—
All the quivers of warriors.
5 Your breasts are like two fawns,
Twins of a gazelle,
Browsing among the lilies.
6[f] When the day blows gently
And the shadows flee,

a Cf. Akkadian aḥāzu, "to learn."
b Meaning of Heb. uncertain.
c-c Emendation yields "ebony, / O maidens of Jerusalem!"
d Cf. 6.6; exact nuance of qeṣuboth uncertain, perhaps "shorn ones."
e-e Apparently a poetic figure for jewelry; meaning of Heb. uncertain.
f See notes at 2.17.

9–11: *Solomon made . . . :* These vv. may be among the oldest parts of the Song. *Palanquin,* a covered chair that was set on poles and carried on the shoulders of four men. **10:** *Silver . . . gold . . . purple wool,* symbols of wealth and royalty. They were also used in the construction of the Tabernacle (Exod. ch 26). Consequently, the rabbinic commentators interpreted these vv. in reference to the Tabernacle. **11:** *Wearing the crown:* Grooms wore crowns in the Second Temple period. After the destruction of the Second Temple, the practice was abolished as a sign of mourning. *On his wedding day:* Rabbinic interpreters understood this as a reference to the giving of Torah at Mt. Sinai. The idea that God and Israel were married at Sinai appears in *Song of Songs Rabbah,* other midrashic texts, and liturgical texts from the rabbinic and medieval periods.

4.1–16: The man praises his lover's beauty and charms. The beginning of this unit corresponds to a genre called the "wasf." In this genre, which is known from Arabic poetry and ancient Egyptian love poetry, each part of the body is compared to a different object with which it shares one trait. As a result, the comparisons are often surprising and whimsical. In this wasf, the objects of comparison are drawn primarily from the pastoral and natural spheres. **1:** The woman's wavy hair flows down her back. *Behind your veil:* In biblical times, women wore veils in public. *Mount Gilead,* rich pastureland in the Transjordan region. **2:** *A flock of ewes . . . her young,* an extended simile for the whiteness and evenness of the woman's teeth. The similarity in sound between the Heb words "shekulam" (all of them) and "shakulah" (loses her young) reinforces the notion of symmetry on the level of sound. **3:** *Pomegranate,* common symbol in the Song for color and taste. Here, either a reference to the color or shape of her brow or of the play of light and dark between her skin and her veil. **4:** *Tower of David:* This

I will betake me to the mount of myrrh,
To the hill of frankincense.
7   Every part of you is fair, my darling,
There is no blemish in you
8   From Lebanon come with me;
From Lebanon, my bride, with me!
Trip down from Amana's peak,
From the peak of Senir[a] and Hermon,
From the dens of lions,
From the hills[b] of leopards.

9   You have captured my heart,
My own,[c] my bride,
You have captured my heart
With one [glance] of your eyes,
With one coil of your necklace.
10 How sweet is your love,
My own, my bride!
How much more delightful your love than wine,
Your ointments more fragrant
Than any spice!
11 Sweetness drops
From your lips, O bride;
Honey and milk
Are under your tongue;
And the scent of your robes
Is like the scent of Lebanon.

12 A garden locked
Is my own, my bride,
A fountain locked,
A sealed-up spring.
13 Your limbs are an orchard of pomegranates
And of all luscious fruits,
Of henna and of nard—
14 Nard and saffron,
Fragrant reed and cinnamon,
With all aromatic woods,
Myrrh and aloes—
All the choice perfumes.
15 [d][You are] a garden spring,
A well of fresh water,[d]
A rill of Lebanon.

structure is not mentioned elsewhere in the Bible, and is not identical with the tower of the same name in modern Jerusalem. The image is that of a long neck adorned with necklaces. **6:** *The mount of myrrh* and *the hill of frankincense* most likely refer to the woman's breasts. **8:** *Lebanon, Amana, Senir, Hermon,* mountains in the north of Israel. In the midrash, this v. is used as a prooftext for the idea that God goes into exile with Israel and will return to the land of Israel with the people. **9:** *My own,* lit. "my sister." Brother and sister are also used as terms of endearment in Egyptian love poetry. They symbolize closeness here, and are not to be taken literally. See 8.1. **10:** *How much more delightful . . . :* The man's praise echoes the woman's in 1.2. **11:** *Sweetness drops:* The Heb words "nofet titofnah" form an onomatopoetic phrase which mimics the sound of dripping liquid. *Honey and milk,* symbols of agricultural plenty. "Land of milk and honey" is a frequent epithet for the land of Israel (e.g., Exod. 3.8). **12–16:** The garden represents the woman's sexuality, which is inaccessible in v. 12 and into which she invites her lover in v. 16.

a *Cf. Deut. 3.9.*
b *Emendation yields "lairs"; cf. Nah. 2.13.*
c *Lit. "sister"; and so frequently below.*
d-d *Emendation yields "The spring in my garden / Is a well of fresh water."*

16 Awake, O north wind,
Come, O south wind!
Blow upon my garden,
That its perfume may spread.
Let my beloved come to his garden
And enjoy its luscious fruits!

5 I have come to my garden,
My own, my bride;
I have plucked my myrrh and spice,
Eaten my honey and honeycomb,
Drunk my wine and my milk.

Eat, lovers, and drink:
Drink deep of love!

2*a* I was asleep,
But my heart was wakeful.
Hark, my beloved knocks!
"Let me in, my own,
My darling, my faultless dove!
For my head is drenched with dew,
My locks with the damp of night."

3 I had taken off my robe—
Was I to don it again?
I had bathed my feet—
Was I to soil them again?

4 My beloved *b-*took his hand off the latch,*-b*
And my heart was stirred *c-*for him.*-c*

5 I rose to let in my beloved;
My hands dripped myrrh—
My fingers, flowing myrrh—
Upon the handles of the bolt.

6 I opened the door for my beloved,
But my beloved had turned and gone.
I was faint *d-*because of what he said.*-d*
I sought, but found him not;
I called, but he did not answer.

7 I met the watchmen*e*
Who patrol the town;
They struck me, they bruised me.
The guards of the walls
Stripped me of my mantle.

5.1: The man responds. The string of four first-person (*I*) verbs followed by direct objects with possessive suffixes communicates a sense of completion and possession. *Eat, lovers, and drink:* Either an exhortation to the lovers by an unidentified speaker or an exhortation by the man to his companions.

5.2–7: Second nighttime episode. This unit echoes the dreamlike sequence in 3.1–4. Here, however, the ending is dark and violent, suggesting unfulfilled desire. The unit's imagery is replete with sexual innuendo, where the house may represent the woman's body. **5–6:** *I rose . . . I opened:* The repetition of the personal pronoun *I* ("'ani") lends emphasis to the woman's actions. **6–7:** *I sought . . . him . . . my mantle:* The repetition of the word "found" and the symmetrical structure of v. 7 lend coherence to this ironic episode in which the watchmen, who are supposed to protect the city, perpetrate an act of unexplained, and seemingly unmotivated, violence.

a *In vv. 2–8 the maiden relates a dream.*
b-b *Meaning of Heb. uncertain.*
c-c *Many manuscripts and editions read "within me" ('alai).*
d-d *Change of vocalization yields "because of him."*
e *See note at 3.3.*

8   I adjure you, O maidens of Jerusalem!
     If you meet my beloved, tell him this:
     That I am faint with love.

9   How is your beloved better than another,[a]
     O fairest of women?
     How is your beloved better than another[a]
     That you adjure us so?

10   My beloved is clear-skinned and ruddy,
     Preeminent among ten thousand.
11   His head is finest gold,
     His locks are curled
     And black as a raven.
12   His eyes are like doves
     By watercourses,
     Bathed in milk,
     [b]Set by a brimming pool.[b]
13   His cheeks are like beds of spices,
     [c]Banks of[c] perfume
     His lips are like lilies;
     They drip flowing myrrh.
14   His hands are rods of gold,
     Studded with beryl;
     His belly a tablet of ivory,
     Adorned with sapphires.
15   His legs are like marble pillars
     Set in sockets of fine gold.
     He is majestic as Lebanon,
     Stately as the cedars.
16   His mouth is delicious
     And all of him is delightful.
     Such is my beloved,
     Such is my darling,
     O maidens of Jerusalem!

6   "Whither has your beloved gone,
     O fairest of women?
     Whither has your beloved turned?
     Let us seek him with you."
2   My beloved has gone down to his garden,
     To the beds of spices,
     To browse in the gardens
     And to pick lilies.

8: *I adjure you,* variation of 2.7; 5.8; 8.4. **9:** *How is your beloved,* either a request for identifying information or a question regarding the reasons for the woman's intense love.

5.10–16: The woman praises the man's beauty. This unit corresponds to the wasf in 4.1–7 and is the only extended description of the male body in the Song. The imagery is drawn from the realms of animals, plants, and precious materials, and is more static than the wasfs of the woman.

6.1–3: Dialogue between the woman and the daughters of Jerusalem. *My beloved has gone down to his garden,* description of a sexual encounter (cf. 5.2). *I am my beloved's,* see 5.6 n.

a Or "What sort of beloved is your beloved?"
b-b Meaning of Heb. uncertain.
c-c Septuagint vocalizes as participle, "producing."

3   I am my beloved's
    And my beloved is mine;
    He browses among the lilies.

4   You are beautiful, my darling, as Tirzah,
    Comely as Jerusalem,
    ᵃ⁻Awesome as bannered hosts.⁻ᵃ
5   Turn your eyes away from me,
    For they overwhelm me!
    Your hair is like a flock of goats
    Streaming down from Gilead.
6   Your teeth like a flock of ewes
    Climbing up from the washing pool;
    All of them bear twins,
    And not one loses her young.
7   Your brow behind your veil
    [Gleams] like a pomegranate split open.
8   There are sixty queens,
    And eighty concubines,
    And damsels without number.
9   Only one is my dove,
    My perfect one,
    The only one of her mother,
    The delight of her who bore her.
    Maidens see and acclaim her;
    Queens and concubines, and praise her.

10 Who is she that shines through like the
        dawn,
    Beautiful as the moon,
    Radiant as the sun
    ᵃ⁻Awesome as bannered hosts?⁻ᵃ

11 I went down to the nut grove
    To see the budding of the vale;
    To see if the vines had blossomed,
    If the pomegranates were in bloom.
12 ᵃ⁻Before I knew it,
    My desire set me
    Mid the chariots of Ammi-nadib.⁻ᵃ

7   Turn back, turn back,
    O maid of Shulem!
    Turn back, turn back,
    That we may gaze upon you.
    "Why will you gaze at the Shulammite

6.4–9: The man describes his lover. 4: *Tirzah,* capital of the Northern Kingdom of Israel in the late 10th and early 9th centuries BCE. *Jerusalem:* To Jerusalem is ascribed legendary and mythic beauty in both the Bible (e.g., Ps. 48.3; Lam. 2.16) and later Jewish texts. *Awesome as bannered hosts,* or visions. This v. introduces a series of vivid visual images. **5–7:** *Your hair . . . split open,* cf. 4.1b–3. **8:** *There are sixty queens . . . :* The man's praise echoes the woman's praise in 2.2–3; 5.10. *Mother,* see 3.4 n. **10:** *Beautiful . . . sun:* The terms for sun and moon here are highly poetic and refer to the whiteness of the moon and the heat of the sun.

6.11–12: Episode fragment. Again a seeming escape to the world of nature, the site of lovemaking. The meaning of v. 12 eludes scholars.

7.1: Address to the woman by a group of men. *Maid of Shulem:* Shulem as a place name is unattested elsewhere in the Bible. It may be a variation of Shunem, a shortened form of Jerusalem, or a derivation from the root "shalem" which refers to Solomon or to the woman's wholeness and perfection. *In the Mahanaim dance:* A variant version means "as the Mahanaim dance." The woman says: Don't look at me as you would look at a dance.

7.2–7: Description of the woman. While other wasfs describe the body from top down, this wasf, of the woman dancing, begins at the woman's feet and moves up. Artisanal images dominate. **2:** *Daughter of nobles:* "Bat-nadiv" echoes the enigmatic phrase in 6.12. **3:** *Heap of wheat,* a reference either to the shape and color of her belly or to its fertility. **5:** *Tower of ivory,* cf. 4.4. *Heshbon,* city in ancient Moab. *Bath-rabbim:* The location is unattested elsewhere in the Bible. *Nose:* This comparison has troubled commentators. Some have suggested "face" instead of "nose" and read the simile as a symbol of stateliness. **6:** *Crimson wool,*

a-a Meaning of Heb. uncertain.

In[a] the Mahanaim dance?"

2 How lovely are your feet in sandals,
   O daughter of nobles!
   Your rounded thighs are like jewels,
   The work of a master's hand.

3 Your navel is like a round goblet—
   Let mixed wine not be lacking!—
   Your belly like a heap of wheat
   Hedged about with lilies.

4 Your breasts are like two fawns,
   Twins of a gazelle.

5 Your neck is like a tower of ivory,
   Your eyes like pools in Heshbon
   By the gate of Bath-rabbim,
   Your nose like the Lebanon tower
   That faces toward Damascus.

6 The head upon you is like [b]crimson wool,[b]
   The locks of your head are like purple—
   [c]A king is held captive in the tresses.[c]

7 How fair you are, how beautiful!
   O Love, with all its rapture!

8 Your stately form is like the palm,
   Your breasts are like clusters.

9 I say: Let me climb the palm,
   Let me take hold of its branches;
   Let your breasts be like clusters of grapes,
   Your breath like the fragrance of apples,

10 And your mouth like choicest wine.
   "Let it flow to my beloved as new wine[d]
   [c]Gliding over the lips of sleepers."[c]

11 I am my beloved's,
   And his desire is for me.

12 Come, my beloved,
   Let us go into the open;
   Let us lodge [e]among the henna shrubs.[e]

13 Let us go early to the vineyards;
   Let us see if the vine has flowered,
   If its blossoms have opened,
   If the pomegranates are in bloom.
   There I will give my love to you.

or, "like the Carmel mountain range," another image of stateliness. **8–10:** The wasf serves as a kind of sexual foreplay that the lover wishes to consummate.

7.11–14: The woman speaks to her lover. Again, nature is the setting for love. **11:** *I am my beloved's . . . ,* explicitly erotic variation on the mutual declaration of love (cf. 5.6; 6.3). **12:** *Come, my beloved:* This v. is the opening line of the song, "lekha dodi," which was incorporated by kabbalists in early modern times into the Sabbath eve liturgy. **13:** *Vineyards,* see 1.6 n.

a With many manuscripts and editions; others read "like." Meaning of entire line uncertain.

b-b So Ibn Janah and Ibn Ezra, taking karmel as a by-form of karmil: cf. 2 Chron. 2.6, 13; 3.14.

c-c Meaning of Heb. uncertain.

d See note at 1.4 end.

e-e Or "in the villages."

14 The mandrakes yield their fragrance,
   At our doors are all choice fruits;
   Both freshly picked and long-stored
   Have I kept, my beloved, for you.

8 If only it could be as with a brother,
   As if you had nursed at my mother's breast:
   Then I could kiss you
   When I met you in the street,
   And no one would despise me.

2 I would lead you, I would bring you
   To the house of my mother,
   Of her who taught[a] me—
   I would let you drink of the spiced wine,
   Of my pomegranate juice.

3 His left hand was under my head,
   His right hand caressed me.

4 I adjure you, O maidens of Jerusalem:
   Do not wake or rouse
   Love until it please!

5 Who is she that comes up from the desert,
   Leaning upon her beloved?

   Under the apple tree I roused you;
   It was there your mother conceived you,
   There she who bore you conceived you.

6 Let me be a seal upon your heart,
   Like the seal upon your hand.[b]
   For love is fierce as death,
   Passion is mighty as Sheol;
   Its darts are darts of fire,
   A blazing flame.

7 Vast floods cannot quench love,
   Nor rivers drown it.
   If a man offered all his wealth for love,
   He would be laughed to scorn.

8 "We have a little sister,
   Whose breasts are not yet formed.
   What shall we do for our sister
   When she is spoken for?

9 If she be a wall,
   We will build upon it a silver battlement;

14: *Mandrakes*, aphrodisiac and fertility plant (cf. Gen. 30.14–15). *At our doors . . . for you*, cf. 1.6 in which the woman states that she has not kept her vineyard.

8.1–6: The woman speaks of her love and desire. 1: The woman longs for closeness with her lover and an openly affectionate relationship. **2:** *House of my mother*, see 3.4 n. **4:** *I adjure you*, see 2.7 n. **5:** *Who is she . . . :* This fragment seems unconnected to the surrounding vv. It echoes 3.6a and 6.10. *Apple tree*, see 2.3 n.

8.6–7: Testimony to the power of love. These vv. are unique in the poem because they deal with love in the abstract. In addition, the cosmic, mythic language contrasts with the bucolic, pastoral, and artisanal images that dominate the rest of the poem. **6:** *Seal upon your heart*, sign of intimate connection and identity. Seals of semiprecious metals or stones were worn around the neck and were used to prove identity, as we use a signature. See Gen. 38.18. *Sheol*, land of the dead. The connection between love and death is particularly evocative. **7:** *If a man*: This v. returns to the humanistic language which is more typical of the poem.

8.8–10: Dialogue between the woman and her brothers. 8–9: Scholars disagree over the relationship between wall and door here. Some read the two terms as synonyms. In this case, the brothers vow to protect her inviolability. Others read them as opposites. If the woman is inaccessible like a wall, her brothers will reward her. If she is open like a door, they will board her up.

---

a *Emendation yields "bore"; cf. 6.9; 8.5.*   b *Lit. "arm."*

If she be a door,
We will panel it in cedar."

10 I am a wall,
My breasts are like towers.
So I became in his eyes
As one who finds favor.

11 Solomon had a vineyard
In Baal-hamon.
He had to post guards in the vineyard:
A man would give for its fruit
A thousand pieces of silver.

12 I have my very own vineyard:
You may have the thousand, O Solomon,
And the guards of the fruit two hundred!

13 O you who linger in the garden,[a]
A lover[a] is listening;
Let me hear your voice.

14 "Hurry, my beloved,
Swift as a gazelle or a young stag,
To the hills of spices!"

8.11–12: The woman compares herself to Solomon's vineyard. *I have my very own vineyard,* cf. 1.6. Solomon's vineyard had many keepers, but this vineyard (the beloved) is kept by and for one person only.

8.13–14: The woman's final invitation to her lover. The final vv. of the poem return to the imagery of the garden, spices, and gazelles. Yet following a fundamental ambiguity of the Song, it is unclear if the woman is here suggesting that she will flee with her lover, or is telling him to flee from her. In line with this ambiguity, the hills of spices may refer to a place outside, or to the woman herself (see 4.6 n.).

a *Heb. plural. Meaning of verse uncertain.*

רות

Ruth

THIS BEAUTIFUL SHORT STORY revolves around the relationship between Naomi, a woman from Bethlehem, in Judah, and her Moabite daughter-in-law, Ruth. Naomi, her husband, and their two sons have come to Moab to escape from famine in Bethlehem. The first chapter recounts, in short order, the death of Naomi's husband, the marriage of her sons to Moabite women, the sons' deaths ten years later, and Naomi's decision to return to Bethlehem. One daughter-in-law, Orpah, returns to her Moabite family. The other, Ruth, declares allegiance to Naomi and to the God of Israel and returns with Naomi. Despite Ruth's company, Naomi is embittered at her many losses. In the course of the coming weeks, however, these losses are all reversed. In the second chapter, Ruth gleans in the field of Naomi's kinsman, Boaz, and acquires enough grain to sustain Naomi and herself for some time. In the third chapter, Naomi devises a plan for Ruth's future security: Ruth will pay a nighttime visit to the threshing floor where Boaz has been winnowing the barley harvest, and will thereby elicit a promise of marriage. The plan is successful and culminates, in chapter four, in the marriage of Ruth and Boaz and the birth of their child, Obed. The book ends with a genealogy which traces the line of Obed back to Perez, the child of Judah and Tamar (Gen. ch 38), and forward to King David.

The simplicity of the story belies the literary craft of the book. Its central theme is the movement from emptiness to fulfillment. This theme is expressed on two planes, the agricultural and the personal. The agricultural sequence anticipates the personal sequence by one step all along the way. The famine precedes Naomi's bereavement, whereas the renewed harvest during which Ruth gleans in Boaz's fields anticipates the abundance that awaits Naomi herself with Obed's birth. The fidelity and love between Naomi and Ruth is the most positive portrayal of women's relationships in biblical literature. The centrality of women is also emphasized by the references in Ruth 4.11–12 to other prominent biblical women, namely, Leah and Rachel, the two wives of Jacob, and Tamar, whose son by Judah, who himself is Jacob's son, is an ancestor of Boaz, and therefore of Obed and David as well.

The story portrays Ruth, Naomi, and Boaz as models of *ḥesed,* that is, of loyalty and commitment that go beyond the bounds of law or duty. *Ḥesed* is exemplified in the fidelity of Ruth to Naomi, the loving concern of Naomi for Ruth, and the kindness of Boaz to both women. Related to the motif of *ḥesed* is the role of God. God is mentioned numerous times by the three main characters, but the actions of the story are never explicitly mentioned as deriving from God. Rather, God remains in the shadows, implying that divine activity lies behind the reversal of the deprivations that have afflicted Naomi and the nation as a whole.

The authorship of the book is unknown and its date is difficult to establish. Many scholars propose a date between 950 and 700 BCE, that is, between the time of David and the Assyrian conquest of the Northern Kingdom of Israel. Others suggest a date during the period of the Babylonian exile or in the early period of the return (586–500 BCE). In the latter case, the book may be read as promising that those who return from exile will be blessed, just as Naomi was when she returned from Moab to Bethlehem. A story recounting the lineage of David might also have had special meaning at a time after the Davidic monarchy had come to an end. If the story is dated to the early exilic period, its positive depiction of Ruth the Moabite may be polemical, emphasizing, in contrast to Ezra-Nehemiah, that foreigners may be integrated into the Jewish community.

In the Jewish Scriptures, Ruth is included among the five "megillot" (scrolls) in the third division, namely, the "writings" (Kethuvim). Because the book is read in the synagogue on Shavuot, the Feast of Weeks, it usually appears second among the megillot, after Song of Songs, which is read at Passover, though other sequences for these five books are found in manuscripts. The association with Shavuot is appropriate. The events told in Ruth span a period somewhat equivalent to that of Passover to Shavuot, that is, a seven-week period from the beginning of the barley harvest to the end of the wheat harvest. Furthermore, King David, the culmination of the genealogy in Ruth 4.18–22, was traditionally thought to have been born and to have died on Shavuot. Finally, Shavuot has been identified since the 2nd or 3rd centuries of the Common Era as the time of the giving of the Torah to Moses on Mount Sinai (cf. Exod. chs 19–20). This element of the feast is related to the prevalent rabbinic theme of Ruth as the ideal convert to Judaism who takes the Torah upon herself just as the Israelites did at Mount Sinai.

In non-Jewish versions and translations of the Bible, Ruth is placed between Judges and the books of Samuel, following the order of the Septuagint. This placement acknowledges the fact that the book is set in the period of the judges (1.1) and ends with a genealogy of David (4.18–22). It therefore provides a link between the chaotic period when Israel was ruled by judges and the stories that lead up to the establishment of the monarchy, which reaches its highest point in the reign of David.   [ADELE REINHARTZ]

1 In the days when the chieftains[a] ruled, there was a famine in the land; and a man of Bethlehem in Judah, with his wife and two sons, went to reside in the country

1.1–22: From Moab to Bethlehem.
1.1–5: Naomi and her family in Moab. 1: The judges (*chieftains*) were tribal leaders of Israel in the period before the monarchy. Several biblical texts reflect tension

---

a I.e., the leaders who arose in the period before the monarchy; others "judges."

of Moab. 2 The man's name was Elimelech, his wife's name was Naomi, and his two sons were named Mahlon and Chilion—Ephrathites of Bethlehem in Judah. They came to the country of Moab and remained there.

3 Elimelech, Naomi's husband, died; and she was left with her two sons. 4 They married Moabite women, one named Orpah and the other Ruth, and they lived there about ten years. 5 Then those two—Mahlon and Chilion—also died; so the woman was left without her two sons and without her husband.

6 She started out with her daughters-in-law to return from the country of Moab; for in the country of Moab she had heard that the LORD had taken note of His people and given them food. 7 Accompanied by her two daughters-in-law, she left the place where she had been living; and they set out on the road back to the land of Judah.

8 But Naomi said to her two daughters-in-law, "Turn back, each of you to her mother's house. May the LORD deal kindly with you, as you have dealt with the dead and with me! 9 May the LORD grant that each of you find security in the house of a husband!" And she kissed them farewell. They broke into weeping 10 and said to her, "No, we will return with you to your people."

11 But Naomi replied, "Turn back, my daughters! Why should you go with me? Have I any more sons in my body who might be husbands for you? 12 Turn back, my daughters, for I am too old to be married. Even if I thought there was hope for me, even if I were married tonight and I also bore sons, 13 should you wait for them to grow up? Should you on their account debar yourselves from marriage? Oh no, my daughters! My lot is far more bitter than yours, for the hand of the LORD has struck out against me."

14 They broke into weeping again, and Orpah kissed her mother-in-law farewell. But Ruth clung to her. 15 So she said, "See, your sister-in-law has returned to her people and her gods. Go follow your sister-in-law." 16 But Ruth replied, "Do not urge me to leave you, to turn back and not follow you. For wherever you go, I will go; wherever you lodge, I will lodge; your people shall be my people, and your God my God. 17 Where you die, I will die, and

"consumptive"; *Orpah* is interpreted as "back of the neck"; *Ruth* may be "friend" or "companion"; *Naomi* is "pleasant"; and *Boaz* (2.1) is "in him is strength." These traits describe, to some degree, the role or the fate of the character within the story. Combined with the pun in v. 1, the symbolic nature of these names suggests that Ruth should not be read as a historical text.

1.6–18: Naomi plans her return to Bethlehem. 6: Naomi attributes relief from the famine to God. This is one of several hints of a divine hand guiding the events in the story. **8:** The term *mother's house* occurs elsewhere (Gen. 24.28; Song 3.4; 8.2). Childless widows are normally portrayed as returning to their fathers' homes (Gen. 38.11; Lev. 22.13). The unusual formulation is appropriate because Naomi is asking the young women to return to their mothers rather than remaining with their mother-in-law. **11:** According to Deut. 25.5–10, a childless widow is bound to marry her dead husband's brother. This is referred to as levirate law (from Latin "levir," "brother-in-law"). The first son of a levirate marriage will legally be the dead man's son for purposes of inheritance. Even were Naomi to give birth to more sons, they would not be obligated by levirate law to marry the widows, because they would not have had the same father as did the dead men. **12:** *Ruth Rabbah* points out that Naomi urges her daughters-in-law to turn back three times (vv. 8, 11, 12). This number corresponds to the number of times that potential converts should be strongly discouraged. Those who persist, however, should be educated and accepted as sincere converts. **14:** *Ruth clung to her:* Ruth's attachment to Naomi is reminiscent of Gen. 2.24, which refers to the "clinging" of husband to wife. The connotation here is not sexual, but rather signifies Ruth's unswerving devotion to Naomi. **16–17:** This moving plea is among the best-known lines of the book. It expresses Ruth's devotion and loy-

between the Israelites and the Moabites, who lived east of the Dead Sea (see Num. 21.29–30; Deut. 23.4; Jer. 48.1–9). This tension, however, is not apparent in the book of Ruth (cf. 1 Sam. 22.3–4). *Bethlehem* means "house of bread"; this v. thus contains a pun of a *famine* in

"the house of bread." **2:** *Ephrathites:* Ephrathah (see 4.11) is another name for Bethlehem. **3–5:** The names of Naomi and her family members may have symbolic significance. *Elimelech* literally means "my God is king"; *Mahlon* means "sickness"; *Chilion* may mean there I will be buried. [a-]Thus and more may the LORD do to me[-a] if anything but death parts me from you." 18 When [Naomi] saw how determined she was to go with her, she ceased to argue with her; 19 and the two went on until they reached Bethlehem.

When they arrived in Bethlehem, the whole city buzzed with excitement over them. The women said, "Can this be Naomi?" 20 "Do not call me Naomi,[b]" she replied. "Call me Mara,[c] for Shaddai[d] has made my lot very bitter. 21 I went away full, and the LORD has brought me back empty. How can you call me Naomi, when the LORD has [e-]dealt harshly with[-e] me, when Shaddai has brought misfortune upon me!"

22 Thus Naomi returned from the country of Moab; she returned with her daughter-in-law Ruth the Moabite. They arrived in Bethlehem at the beginning of the barley harvest.

2 Now Naomi had a kinsman on her husband's side, a man of substance, of the family of Elimelech, whose name was Boaz.

2 Ruth the Moabite said to Naomi, "I would like to go to the fields and glean among the ears of grain, behind someone who may show me kindness." "Yes, daughter, go," she replied; 3 and off she went. She came and gleaned in a field, behind the reapers; and, as luck would have it, it was the piece of land belonging to Boaz, who was of Elimelech's family.

4 Presently Boaz arrived from Bethlehem. He greeted the reapers, "The LORD be with you!" And they responded, "The LORD bless you!" 5 Boaz said to the servant who was in charge of the reapers, "Whose girl is that?" 6 The servant in charge of the reapers replied, "She is a Moabite girl who came back with Naomi from the country of Moab. 7 She said, 'Please let me glean and gather among the sheaves behind the reapers.' She has been on her feet ever since she came this morning. [f-]She has rested but little in the hut."[-f]

a-a A formula of imprecation.
b I.e., "Pleasantness."
c I.e., "Bitterness."
d Usually rendered "the Almighty."
e-e Others "testified against."
f-f Meaning of Heb. uncertain.

scores the seriousness of her declaration. It has been interpreted to mean "only death will part us" or "not even death will part us."

1.19–23: Naomi and Ruth arrive in Bethlehem. 20–21: *Shaddai,* a divine epithet, perhaps used here as an archaism; in Job, where it is frequent (5.17ff.), it is translated "the Almighty" (see translators' note d). **22:** *The beginning of the barley harvest* is associated in Lev. 23.10 with the Passover festival, in the spring.

2.1–23: The field. 2.1–7: Ruth's plan. 1: *Boaz,* see 1.3–5 n. **2:** According to biblical law, the poor were permitted to walk behind the harvesters and gather the grain that they left behind (Lev. 19.9; 23.22; Deut. 24.19). Ruth's remark is puzzling in that she apparently plans to work *among the ears* themselves, that is, in the area that has not yet been harvested. This differs from what was permitted in extant biblical law, but some laws differed in different times and places in the biblical period. The fact that Naomi calls Ruth *daughter* suggests that Ruth's love, devotion, and sense of responsibility is now reciprocated by Naomi. **3:** *Luck:* By coincidence—or perhaps divine providence—the field in which Ruth hopes to glean is that belonging to Boaz. Ruth is apparently unaware of the connection between Boaz and Naomi. **7:** *Among the sheaves:* Ruth's request exceeds biblical law. Here the text suggests that Ruth will glean in the area of harvested grain. Some interpreters suggest that her request was a ploy to meet the owner of the field, since special permission to glean among the sheaves is granted in 2.15. *She has rested . . . hut:* The literal translation is "this is her sitting the house a little." Some commentators emend the text by omitting "the house," in conformity with the Septuagint. The overall sense is clear, however. The servant is commenting on Ruth's stamina and perseverance, perhaps with some admiration.

alty to Naomi. *Ruth Rabbah* and Rashi view Ruth's passionate declaration of allegiance as the point at which Naomi instructs Ruth in a formal process of conversion. The story, however, contains no reference to formal conversion, since that institution did not come into existence until rabbinic times. *Thus . . . do to me:* Ruth's oath under-

⁸ Boaz said to Ruth, ᵃ⁻"Listen to me, daughter.⁻ᵃ Don't go to glean in another field. Don't go elsewhere, but stay here close to my girls. ⁹ Keep your eyes on the field they are reaping, and follow them. I have ordered the men not to molest you. And when you are thirsty, go to the jars and drink some of [the water] that the men have drawn."

¹⁰ She prostrated herself with her face to the ground, and said to him, "Why are you so kind as to single me out, when I am a foreigner?"

¹¹ Boaz said in reply, "I have been told of all that you did for your mother-in-law after the death of your husband, how you left your father and mother and the land of your birth and came to a people you had not known before. ¹² May the LORD reward your deeds. May you have a full recompense from the LORD, the God of Israel, under whose wings you have sought refuge!"

¹³ She answered, "You are most kind, my lord, to comfort me and to speak gently to your maidservant—though I am not so much as one of your maidservants."

¹⁴ At mealtime, Boaz said to her, "Come over here and partake of the meal, and dip your morsel in the vinegar." So she sat down beside the reapers. He handed her roasted grain, and she ate her fill and had some left over.

¹⁵ When she got up again to glean, Boaz gave orders to his workers, "You are not only to let her glean among the sheaves, without interference, ¹⁶ but you must also pull some [stalks] out of the heaps and leave them for her to glean, and not scold her."

¹⁷ She gleaned in the field until evening. Then she beat out what she had gleaned—it was about an *'ephah* of barley—¹⁸ and carried it back with her to the town. When her mother-in-law saw what she had gleaned, and when she also took out and gave her what she had left over after eating her fill, ¹⁹ her mother-in-law asked her, "Where did you glean today? Where did you work? Blessed be he who took such generous notice of you!" So she told her mother-in-law whom she had worked with, saying, "The name of the man with whom I worked today is Boaz."

²⁰ Naomi said to her daughter-in-law, "Blessed be he of the LORD, who has not failed in His kindness to the living or to the dead! For," Naomi explained to her daughter-in-law, "the man is related to us; he is one of our redeeming kinsmen."ᵇ ²¹ Ruth the Moabite said, "He even told me, 'Stay close by my workers until all my harvest is fin-

2.8–16: Ruth meets Boaz in the field where she is gleaning.
8: Like Naomi, Boaz refers to Ruth as *daughter*. This form of address conveys his warm attitude toward her, and also stresses the generational difference between them. **12:** This v. summarizes the message of the book: Whoever seeks shelter with the God of Israel will be rewarded. Rabbinic interpreters understand this phrase as a reference to Ruth's conversion. **14:** *Vinegar*, actually a refreshing drink of sour wine and oil. Boaz's generosity, in providing drink and *roasted grain*, foreshadows the important role he will come to play in providing for both Ruth and Naomi.

2.17–23: Ruth reports back to Naomi. 17: An *'ephah* is approximately two-thirds of a bushel, a substantial amount for one day of gleaning. **20:** By identifying Boaz as *one of our redeeming kinsmen*, Naomi suggests his potential role in providing for Ruth and herself, since a "go'el" (redeeming kinsman: see translators' note *b*) had a special obligation to the family.

---

a-a Lit. "Have you not heard, daughter?"
b Cf. Lev. 25.25 and note and Deut. 25.5–6. The fact that Boaz was a kinsman of Ruth's dead husband opened up the possibility of providing an heir for the latter.

ished.' " ²²And Naomi answered her daughter-in-law Ruth, "It is best, daughter, that you go out with his girls, and not be annoyed in some other field." ²³So she stayed close to the maidservants of Boaz, and gleaned until the barley harvest and the wheat harvest were finished. Then she stayed at home with her mother-in-law.

³ Naomi, her mother-in-law, said to her, "Daughter, I must seek a home for you, where you may be happy. ²Now there is our kinsman Boaz, whose girls you were close to. He will be winnowing barley on the threshing floor tonight. ³So bathe, anoint yourself, dress up, and go down to the threshing floor. But do not disclose yourself to the man until he has finished eating and drinking. ⁴When he lies down, note the place where he lies down, and go over and uncover his feet and lie down. He will tell you what you are to do." ⁵She replied, "I will do everything you tell me."

⁶She went down to the threshing floor and did just as her mother-in-law had instructed her. ⁷Boaz ate and drank, and in a cheerful mood went to lie down beside the grainpile. Then she went over stealthily and uncovered his feet and lay down. ⁸In the middle of the night, the man gave a start and pulled back—there was a woman lying at his feet!

⁹"Who are you?" he asked. And she replied, "I am your handmaid Ruth. ^{a-}Spread your robe over your hand-maid,^{-a} for you are a redeeming kinsman."

¹⁰He exclaimed, "Be blessed of the LORD, daughter! Your latest deed of loyalty is greater than the first, in that you have not turned to younger men, whether poor or rich.^b ¹¹And now, daughter, have no fear. I will do in your behalf whatever you ask, for all the ^{c-}elders of my town^{-c}

---

a-a A formal act of espousal; cf. Ezek. 16.8.

b I.e., she sought out a kinsman of her dead husband; see note at 2.20 above. Her first act of loyalty had been to return with Naomi.

c-c Lit. "gate of my people."

3.1–18: The threshing floor.
3.1–6: Naomi's plan. 2: The *threshing floor* is an elevated open space where the kernels of grain were separated from the chaff (winnowed). *Winnowing* was done in the evening when strong breezes would carry the chaff away. **3:** Rashi, following *b. Shabbat* 113b, comments that Ruth reversed the order of preparation that Naomi had proposed. First

she went down to the threshing floor and then beautified herself, lest passers-by believe her to be a harlot. According to Rashi, following *y. Pe'ah* 8.7, Ruth's preparations related directly to her conversion. In washing herself, Ruth purified herself from her earlier idolatry; in anointing herself, she took upon herself the commandments; in dressing, she put on Sabbath garments, that is, full obser-

vance of the Sabbath. **4:** The crucial aspect of Naomi's instructions to Ruth, to *uncover* Boaz's *feet* and *lie down*, is also the most ambiguous. Naomi may simply mean that Ruth should uncover a place at Boaz's feet and lie down. The word *feet*, however, may also be a euphemism for sexual organs (see Isa. 7.20). In this case, Naomi may have a bolder and less respectable act in mind. Similarly, the verb *lie down*, which appears eight times in this chapter, may be a euphemism for sexual intercourse. The frequent use of the verb "to know" also contributes to the sexual innuendo. Most commentators agree that sexual intercourse did not actually take place, though several suggest that after awakening from a drunken stupor after a long day's work (3.7), Boaz was unsure whether or not he had intercourse with Ruth. The language conveys the sexual tension that must have been present.

3.7–13: Ruth meets Boaz at the threshing floor after he has winnowed. 9: Rather than wait for Boaz's instruction, as Naomi had proposed, Ruth takes the initiative. She asks him to *spread* his *robe* ("kanaf") over her, because he is a *redeeming kinsman*. In doing so, she echoes his own words in 2.12, in which he describes her as seeking shelter under God's wing (also "kanaf"). Ruth's words are also a marriage proposal (see translators' note *a-a*). In referring to Boaz as a *redeeming kinsman*, Ruth links the concepts of redemption and levirate marriage that are not otherwise connected in the Bible. The situation is not precisely that of levirate marriage, however. Had Boaz in fact been the brother of Ruth's dead husband, Mahlon, he would have been obligated by law to marry Ruth. No elaborate pretense would have been required. This might suggest that the legislation of Deut. 25.5–10 was not normative at this period. **10:** Boaz may be suggesting that Ruth's proposal of marriage is an even more daring and comprehensive attempt to provide for Naomi's well-know what a fine woman you are. [12] But while it is true I am a redeeming kinsman, there is another redeemer closer than I. [13] Stay for the night. Then in the morning, if he will act as a redeemer, good! let him redeem. But if he does not want to act as redeemer for you, I will do so myself, as the LORD lives! Lie down until morning."

[14] So she lay at his feet until dawn. She rose before one person could distinguish another, for he thought, "Let it not be known that the woman came to the threshing floor." [15] And he said, "Hold out the shawl you are wearing." She held it while he measured out six measures of barley, and he put it on her back.

When she[a] got back to the town, [16] she came to her mother-in-law, who asked, "How is it with you, daughter?" She told her all that the man had done for her; [17] and she added, "He gave me these six measures of barley, saying to me, 'Do not go back to your mother-in-law empty-handed.'" [18] And Naomi said, "Stay here, daughter, till you learn how the matter turns out. For the man will not rest, but will settle the matter today."

4 Meanwhile, Boaz had gone to the gate and sat down there. And now the redeemer whom Boaz had mentioned passed by. He called, "Come over and sit down here, So-and-so!" And he came over and sat down. [2] Then [Boaz] took ten elders of the town and said, "Be seated here"; and they sat down.

[3] He said to the redeemer, "Naomi, now returned from the country of Moab, must sell the piece of land which belonged to our kinsman Elimelech. [4] I thought I should disclose the matter to you and say: Acquire it in the presence of those seated here and in the presence of the elders of my people. If you are willing to redeem it, redeem! But if you[b] will not redeem, tell me, that I may know. For there is no one to redeem but you, and I come after you." "I am willing to redeem it," he replied. [5] Boaz continued, "When you acquire the property from Naomi [c]and from Ruth the Moabite, you must also acquire the wife of the deceased,[-c]

a So in many Heb. mss; most mss. read "he."

b So many Heb. mss., Septuagint, and Targum; most mss. read "he."

c-c Emendation yields "you must also acquire Ruth the Moabite, the wife of the deceased"; cf. v. 10.

her symbolizes the "seed" that he will later provide in order for their child to be conceived. Noting that *six measures of barley* is far too much for a single person to carry, the Rabbis suggested symbolic interpretations. Rashi, following *Ruth Rabbah* and various talmudic traditions, claimed that the text literally meant "six grains of barley," as a portent that their future son would be blessed with six blessings: the spirit of wisdom and discernment, counsel and might, the spirit of knowledge, and the fear of the LORD (see Isa. 11.2). *Ruth Rabbah* suggests that the six grains of barley refer to six righteous descendants: David, Hezekiah, Josiah, Hananiah, Mishael, and Azariah. **16:** Naomi's question means, "How do things stand with you, my daughter?" It echoes that of Boaz in v. 9 and thereby links the two older people, though they do not encounter one another directly. **17:** Here, as in 2.21, the words that Ruth reports to Naomi are not part of Boaz's original words to Ruth. Ruth may be fabricating or embroidering in order to emphasize that Boaz's care for Ruth extended to his concern for Naomi.

4.1–22: The gate. 4.1–12: Boaz "acquires" Ruth. 1: *The gate* was the commercial and judicial center of the town, where legal, business, and political transactions were conducted. Here Boaz encounters "Ploni 'Almoni," the unnamed *redeemer* (3.12). Although Boaz must have known the name of the kinsman, the narrative does not report it. According to Rashi, following *Ruth Rabbah,* and many contemporary commentators, the anonymity expresses the narrator's disapproval of the man's behavior. **2:** *Ten* as the number of a quorum (Heb "minyan") is derived by some from this verse (*b. Ketub.* 7b). **3–4:** Certain textual difficulties in vv. 3–5 make it difficult to reconstruct exactly the legal background of these proceedings. It is only here that we learn of Elimelech's land, which needs to be redeemed in order to provide for Naomi and Ruth. On redemption

being than was her gleaning in the field. Ruth's decision to link her life with him is clearly flattering, particularly because she could have had her choice of young men.

3.14–18: Ruth reports back to Naomi. 15: Here, as at the end of ch 2, Ruth is provided with a large amount of grain to bring home to Naomi. The grain that Boaz gives so as to perpetuate the name of the deceased upon his estate." 6 The redeemer replied, "Then I cannot redeem it for myself, lest I impair my own estate.ᵃ You take over my right of redemption, for I am unable to exercise it."

7 Now this was formerly done in Israel in cases of redemption or exchange: to validate any transaction, one man would take off his sandal and hand it to the other. Such was the practiceᵇ in Israel. 8 So when the redeemer said to Boaz, "Acquire for yourself," he drew off his sandal. 9 And Boaz said to the elders and to the rest of the people, "You are witnesses today that I am acquiring from Naomi all that belonged to Elimelech and all that belonged to Chilion and Mahlon. 10 I am also acquiring Ruth the Moabite, the wife of Mahlon, as my wife, so as to perpetuate the name of the deceased upon his estate, that the name of the deceased may not disappear from among his kinsmen and from the gate of his home town. You are witnesses today."

11 All the people at the gate and the elders answered, "We are. May the Lᴏʀᴅ make the woman who is coming into your house like Rachel and Leah, both of whom built up the House of Israel! Prosper in Ephrathahᶜ and perpetuate your name in Bethlehem! 12 And may your house be like the house of Perez whom Tamar bore to Judah— through the offspring which the Lᴏʀᴅ will give you by this young woman."

13 So Boaz married Ruth; she became his wife, and he cohabited with her. The Lᴏʀᴅ let her conceive, and she bore a son. 14 And the women said to Naomi, "Blessed be the Lᴏʀᴅ, who has not withheld a redeemer from you today! May his name be perpetuated in Israel! 15 He will renew your life and sustain your old age; for he is born of your daughter-in-law, who loves you and is better to you than seven sons."

16 Naomi took the child and held it to her bosom. She became its foster mother, 17 and the women neighbors gave him a name, saying, "A son is born to Naomi!" They

of the land. Nevertheless, it is clear that within this story, the link that is articulated by Ruth on the threshing floor is accepted as a fundamental premise by the other characters as well as by the narrator. **8:** The *sandal* represents the conveying of goods or rights from one party to another. In Heb it is not clear whether it was the redeemer who gave his sandal to Boaz or the other way around. *Ruth Rabbah* opts for the latter, on the principle that it is the purchaser who gives the pledge. Modern interpreters generally prefer the former. In their view, the act symbolizes the fact that "Ploni ʾAlmoni" relinquishes the obligation and the privilege of redeeming the land and marrying Ruth.

4.13–17: The birth of Obed.
15: Though Ruth has disappeared from the story, she is acknowledged and given her due by the women who speak to Naomi after the birth of Boaz and Ruth's son. **16:** It is unlikely that Naomi has become the child's wet-nurse or adoptive parent. The child symbolizes the complete reversal of Naomi's ill-fortune, her restoration to fullness, and the continuation of her family. It is possible that the association of the child with Naomi rather than Ruth is meant to remove the taint of foreign birth from the child.

---

a *I.e., by expending capital for property which will go to the son legally regarded as Mahlon's; see Deut. 25.5–6.*
b *Understanding Heb.* teʿudah *in the sense of the Arabic* ʿādah *and Syriac* ʿyādā. Cf. Ibn Ezra.
c *Ephrathah is another name applied to Bethlehem; cf. 1.2; Gen. 35.16, 19; 48.7; Mic. 5.1.*

---

of land, see Lev. 25.24–34, 47–55; Jer. 32.7–15. **5:** Boaz implies that the acquisition of Ruth as wife is necessarily tied to the redemption of land. According to biblical law, levirate marriage pertains only to the brother of the dead husband (Deut. 25.5–10). For this reason, neither Boaz nor the other kinsman is legally bound to marry Ruth. Nor does biblical law link levirate marriage with redemption named him Obed; he was the father of Jesse, father of David.

¹⁸ This is the line of Perez: Perez begot Hezron, ¹⁹ Hezron begot Ram, Ram begot Ammi-nadab, ²⁰ Amminadab begot Nahshon, Nahshon begot Salmon,ᵃ ²¹ Salmon begot Boaz, Boaz begot Obed, ²² Obed begot Jesse, and Jesse begot David.

4.18–22: Generations from Perez to David. Obed's genealogy is traced through Boaz, and not through Mahlon as it would be in the case of levirate marriage. The genealogy draws a direct line between *Perez* (son of Tamar) through *Obed* (son of Ruth) to *David*. In this way the theme of family continuity and divine favor through Ruth is extended to embrace national continuity and divine favor through David. The genealogy also helps to frame the book, which opens with Bethlehem, the home of David, and concludes with the genealogy of David.

Lamentations

LAMENTATIONS, CALLED *'ekhah* ("alas") in Hebrew, after its initial word, commemorates the destruction of the First Temple in 586 BCE. The Talmud refers to the book as *Kinot*, "Elegies," or "Lamentations." The book is a collection of five laments, in moving poetry, reflecting on the suffering and dislocation that resulted from the destruction of Jerusalem and the Temple and the exile that followed. It is the Bible's primary literature of destruction and became the paradigm for later Jewish literature of destruction. Lamentations is a form of mourning for a destruction that was to become a linchpin in Jewish history and Jewish religious thought. More than that, Lamentations eternalizes the destruction, thereby helping to make it a central event in the Jewish memory. In summarizing rabbinic interpretation of Lamentations in *Lamentations Rabbah*, Shaye J. D. Cohen wrote (in *Prooftexts* 2 [1982]:20) that Lamentations is "the eternal lament for all Jewish catastrophes, past, present, and future."

The five chapters are five separate poems, each with a distinctive tone and theme. All of the poems accept the standard biblical theology that the disaster is God's punishment for Israel's sins. In fact, the Babylonians are never mentioned by name. It is God who is responsible for the destruction. Nowhere is there any doubt about the power of God, and it is this power, and also His mercy, that the poets call on for help in their present plight. But the end of Judah's suffering seems far away for most of the book. The emphasis is on the grief and suffering of the present.

The book is among the most difficult in the canon. It is highly poetic, using rare words and unusual grammatical structures, and the thematic logic of the ordering of the verses is often tenuous. Abrupt changes in speaking voices mark shifts in perspectives, so that we hear various aspects of the siege and destruction of Jerusalem as well as diverse responses to the catastrophe. We see Jerusalem, the lonely and shamed city, grieving for her lost inhabitants. Feminine imagery is especially prominent, and especially effective, in reference to Jerusalem in ch 1, pictured as a shameful and then shamed woman, abandoned by her lovers (her supposed allies), emptied of all she holds dear, mocked by passers-by, and lacking comfort. In ch 2 we find ourselves looking at the siege of the city and all the horror of starvation and disease that accompanied it. We can imagine ourselves among the deportees being led into exile, or among the survivors who remained in Judah under Babylonian occupation. Complex imagery abounds, and it is not easy to understand all of it, but it is clear that the imagery contributes to the vividness of the portrayal and the emotional impact it has on the reader.

While Lamentations is surely the Bible's lament par excellence, there are other poems of lament in Psalms, both individual and communal laments, that may have served as generic forerunners to the book. Another forerunner may be the funeral dirge, a eulogy used to lament the death of individuals (like David's lament over Saul and Jonathan in 2 Sam. 1). Looking beyond the Bible, we find in ancient Mesopotamia, centuries before 586 BCE, laments for destroyed cities (e.g., "Lamentation over the Destruction of Ur," "Lamentation over the Destruction of Sumer and Ur," "Nippur Lament"). Exactly if and how these other types of laments influenced the authors of Lamentations is unclear. No literary genre arises in a vacuum; but Lamentations surpasses by far, both in its poetic sophistication and in its effect on its readers, any of its forerunners.

Poetic Structure

THE POETRY OF CHS 1–4 is marked by lines broken into two parts, the first possessing three accentual units and the second, two. Karl Budde, a Hebraist at the end of the 19th century, wrote (in *Das hebräische Klaglied*, 1882) that the second part of the line "seems, as it were, to die away . . . and a plaintive, melancholy cadence is thus produced." This "meter" has, therefore, been called qinah ("elegiac") meter.

The first four chapters are structured as alphabetic acrostics, with each verse beginning with a letter of the Hebrew alphabet, in sequence. Ch 3 is a triple acrostic. (The sequence in chs 2–4 reverses the order of the letters "pe" and "'ayin"; this reflects an alternative order of the alphabet found on inscriptions from Izbet Sartah and Kuntillet Ajrud.) Alphabetic acrostics occur elsewhere in the Bible: for instance, Ps. 119 and Prov. 31.10–31. The use of all the letters of the alphabet may imply fullness of expression—everything from A to Z—thereby symbolizing the completeness of the devastation being described and also of the mourning being expressed. The alphabetic order might also serve as an aid to memory, prompting the recall of successive lines. Acrostics of different types were used elsewhere in the ancient world; in Mesopotamia, for example, several poems spell out their author's name through acrostics. In Hebrew liturgical poetry *(piyyutim)* there is much use of both alphabet acrostics and name acrostics.

The verses in chs 1 and 2 are relatively long, with three "poetic lines" in each. Ch 3 is composed of short verses, three for each letter of the alphabet, with each verse falling into two parts. Ch 4 returns to the use of longer verses, but with two "lines" in each instead of three. Ch 5, although not an acrostic, has twenty-two single-line stanzas. (Twenty-two is the number of letters in the alphabet, so the last poem has the same number of verses as chs 1, 2, and 4.) Parallelism, the outstanding characteristic of biblical poetry, is found throughout the book, but is most obvious in ch 5.

Date and Authorship

ANCIENT TRADITION, REFLECTED IN THE TALMUD, the Septuagint, and the Vulgate, ascribes authorship of the book to Jeremiah, the leading prophet at the time of the destruction, whose book bears a resemblance to the language of Lamentations. Modern scholars do not accept the notion of Jeremian authorship (as they do not accept the ancient ascription of other biblical books to biblical figures). They ascribe each chapter to a different, anonymous author, whose identity is impossible to ascertain. The poems were probably written shortly after 586 BCE and collected together shortly thereafter, probably by 520 BCE when the postexilic community began to rebuild the Temple.

Place in the Bible and in Jewish Liturgy

IN MASORETIC MANUSCRIPTS and in Jewish Bibles, Lamentations is found among the Five Megillot, all of which are recited publicly on specific occasions during the year. The recitation of Lamentations takes place on Tishʿah beʾav, the 9th of Av (in July or August), which commemorates the destruction of the First Temple in 586 BCE and the Second Temple in 70 CE, and around which the commemoration of other Jewish destructions and catastrophes have coalesced. Tishʿah beʾav is a day of public mourning and fasting. As part of the rites of mourning, the reader and congregation sit on the floor or low benches when Lamentations is recited, during the evening and morning services of Tishʿah beʾav. Other, later poems of lament are customarily added afterwards.   [DANIEL GROSSBERG]

1ª א Alas!
       Lonely sits the city
       Once great with people!
       She that was great among nations
       Is become like a widow;
       The princess among states
       Is become a thrall.

2   ב Bitterly she weeps in the night,
       Her cheek wet with tears.
       There is none to comfort her
       Of all her friends.
       All her allies have betrayed her;
       They have become her foes.

3   ג Judah has gone into exile
       Because of misery and harsh oppression;
       When she settled among the nations,
       She found no rest;
       All her pursuers overtook her

1.1–22: Jerusalem in mourning, with no one to comfort her. First the poet and then the city lament the destruction of Jerusalem. The chapter may be divided into two parts, vv. 1–11 and 12–22, corresponding to the two speaking voices. There is an interlocking design that binds the two parts together: 1.22, 21, 20, 19, 18, and 12 echo 1.1, 2, 3, 4, 5, and 11, respectively.

1.1–11: The poet's lament. The city is described as a woman, widowed, abandoned, and shamed. **1.1:** *Alas!* This mournful cry is characteristic of the Hebrew elegy and also opens chs 2 and 4 (cf. Isa. 1.21; 2.1; 4.1). It suggests a contrast between a former glorious state and the current state of misery. The image of the widow evokes loneliness and bereavement, and also vulnerability. **2:** *Bitterly she weeps:* "To weep"

a *Chaps. 1–4 are alphabetical acrostics, i.e., the verses begin with the successive letters of the Heb. alphabet. Chap. 3 is a triple acrostic. In chaps. 2–4 the letter* pe *precedes the* ʿayin.

ᵃIn the narrow places.ᵃ

4 ד Zion's roads are in mourning,
      Empty of festival pilgrims;
      All her gates are deserted.
      Her priests sigh,
      Her maidens are unhappy—
      She is utterly disconsolate!

5 ה Her enemies are now the masters,
      Her foes are at ease,
      Because the LORD has afflicted her
      For her many transgressions;
      Her infants have gone into captivity
      Before the enemy.

6 ו Gone from Fair Zion are all
      That were her glory;
      Her leaders were like stags
      That found no pasture;
      They could only walk feebly
      Before the pursuer.

7 ז All the precious things she had
      In the days of old
      Jerusalem recalled
      In her days of woe and sorrow,
      When her people fell by enemy hands
      With none to help her;
      When enemies looked on and gloated
      Over her downfall.

8 ח Jerusalem has greatly sinned,
      Therefore she is become a mockery.
      All who admired her despise her,
      For they have seen her disgraced;
      And she can only sigh
      And shrink back.

9 ט Her uncleanness clings to her skirts.
      She gave no thought to her future;
      She has sunk appallingly,
      With none to comfort her.—
      See, O LORD, my misery;
      How the enemy jeers!

10 י The foe has laid hands
      On everything dear to her.
      She has seen her Sanctuary
      Invaded by nations
      Which You have denied admission
      Into Your community.

means to cry out, to utter sounds of sadness. Heb "bakhoh tivkeh," "weeping she weeps": a common grammatical construction indicating intensity. The Talmud explains the double occurrence of the verbal root, as referring to the destruction of both Temples (b. Sanh. 104.2). *Friends,* her political allies, who should have aided and comforted her. The term also points to Judah's idolatry, her pursuit of "friends" other than her "husband," God. **3:** *Misery and harsh oppression* recall the enslavement in Egypt (Gen. 15.13; Exod. 1.11; Deut. 26.6). Judah's exile to Babylonia is like a second Egyptian enslavement. The verse makes more sense if translated "after misery" rather than "because of misery." *No rest,* no resting place, no place to dwell secure. **4:** The once-busy thoroughfares are empty of pilgrims to the Temple, for the Temple is destroyed and the people are gone. (The idea that Judah was totally depopulated is a rhetorical exaggeration—many Judeans were not exiled and remained behind.) **5:** *Her many transgressions,* first of several admissions (1.8, 9, 14, 18, 20) that the sins of Israel brought on the destruction. **6:** *Fair Zion,* lit. "Daughter of Zion," the designation of the personified city that appears most frequently throughout Lamentations and the Prophets (e.g., 2.1, 4, 8, 10, 13, 18; 4.22; Isa. 1.8; 52.2; Jer. 4.31; Mic. 4.8). **8:** *A mockery,* or, alternatively, she has been banished. *Her disgraced,* lit. "her nakedness," meaning her shame. **9:** *Her uncleanness;* The metaphor of ritual impurity (Lev. 15.16–24) is used to indicate Fair Zion's moral impurity. Zion has "exposed herself" immodestly and is sexually immoral. Sexual immorality is, in turn, a metaphor for idolatry, the sin which caused the exile. *See, O LORD, my misery:* Personified Zion's words (1.12), introduced into the poet's lament, integrate the two parts of ch 1. **10:** The Temple has been violated as a woman is sexually violated. **11:** A second interjection of personified Zion's words into the

<hr>

a-a Meaning of Heb. uncertain.

11 כ   All her inhabitants sigh
         As they search for bread;
         They have bartered their treasures for food,
         To keep themselves alive.—
         See, O LORD, and behold,
         ᵃ·How abject·ᵃ I have become!

12 ל   ᵇ·May it never befall you,·ᵇ
         All who pass along the road—
         Look about and see:
         Is there any agony like mine,
         Which was dealt out to me
         When the LORD afflicted me
         On His day of wrath?

13 מ   From above He sent a fire
         Down into my bones.
         He spread a net for my feet,
         He hurled me backward;
         He has left me forlorn,
         In constant misery.

14c נ   The yoke of my offenses is bound fast,
         Lashed tight by His hand;
         Imposed upon my neck,
         It saps my strength;
         The Lord has delivered me into the hands
         Of those I cannot withstand.

15 ס   The Lord in my midst has rejected
         All my heroes;
         He has proclaimed a set time against me
         To crush my young men.
         As in a press the Lord has trodden
         Fair Maiden Judah.

16 ע   For these things do I weep,
         My eyes flow with tears:
         Far from me is any comforter
         Who might revive my spirit;
         My children are forlorn,
         For the foe has prevailed.

17 פ   Zion spreads out her hands,
         She has no one to comfort her;
         The LORD has summoned against Jacob
         His enemies all about him;
         Jerusalem has become among them
         A thing unclean.

poet's lament. *See, O LORD, and behold, how abject I have become:* A cry to God for compassion ends the first half of the ch (see 1.12).

1.12–22: Personified Zion's lament. The pain of Jerusalem and the harsh treatment she has suffered. 12: Jerusalem calls out for sympathy to passers-by as she called out to God in the previous verse. *His day of wrath:* God's destruction is often depicted as transpiring in a single day, as in the Day of the LORD (e.g., Isa. 13.13; Joel 2.1; Amos 5.18; Obad. 15). **13:** The imagery of war—fire and nets to capture prisoners—is invoked to describe God's actions against Judah. **14:** The yoke of submission is constructed from Judah's sins; i.e., it is the sins that led to this situation. **15:** The blood of Judah is squeezed out of her like wine in a winepress. **16:** *Comforter:* The lack of a comforter is mentioned in vv. 2, 9, 16, 17, 21 and is a major theme in the ch. With no comforter, Jerusalem's mourning cannot be completed. **17:** *A thing unclean,* lit. a menstruating woman, who is ritually impure. Again, ritual impurity serves as a metaphor for the moral impurity of adultery/idolatry.

a-a Or (ironically) "What a glutton"; cf. Prov. 23.20–21.
b-b Meaning of Heb. uncertain.
c Meaning of parts of vv. 14 and 15 uncertain.

18 צ   The LORD is in the right,
    For I have disobeyed Him.
    Hear, all you peoples,
    And behold my agony:
    My maidens and my youths
    Have gone into captivity!

19 ק   I cried out to my friends,
    But they played me false.
    My priests and my elders
    Have perished in the city
    As they searched for food
    To keep themselves alive.

20 ר   See, O LORD, the distress I am in!
    My heart is in anguish,
    a·I know how wrong I was·*a*
    To disobey.
    Outside the sword deals death;
    Indoors, the plague.

21 ש   When they heard how I was sighing,
    There was none to comfort me;
    All my foes heard of my plight and exulted.
    For it is Your doing:
    b·You have brought on the day that You
        threatened.
    Oh, let them become like me!·*b*

22 ת   Let all their wrongdoing come before You,
    And deal with them
    As You have dealt with me
    For all my transgressions.
    For my sighs are many,
    And my heart is sick.

2 א   Alas!
    The Lord in His wrath
    Has shamed*c* Fair Zion,
    Has cast down from heaven to earth
    The majesty of Israel.
    He did not remember His Footstool*d*
    On His day of wrath.

2 ב   The Lord has laid waste without pity
    All the habitations of Jacob;
    He has razed in His anger
    Fair Judah's strongholds.
    He has brought low in dishonor

18: *The LORD is in the right,* an admission of Judah's guilt and a confirmation of the justice of God. **20:** *I know how wrong I was to disobey:* An alternate translation is "How very bitter I am." **22:** The enemy is no more righteous than Judah, and deserves a punishment like hers. *Are many,* Heb "rabot," recalls "great [with]" Heb "rabati" (twice in 1.1). They frame the ch and contrast the former "rabati" ("great with people" and "great among nations") to the latter "rabot" (*my sighs are many*).

2.1–22: The second lament. In contrast to the previous ch, where the tone is one of despair and mourning, the tone of this ch is angry. God is depicted throughout as an angry enemy who destroyed the physical structures of Jerusalem with violent force. The ch has an interlocking design with 2.22, 21, 20, 13 and 12 echoing 2.1, 2, 3, 10, and 11, respectively.

2.1–9: The details of how God destroyed Judah. 1: *Alas!* See 1.1 n., cf. 4.1. *The Lord in His wrath has shamed Fair Zion:* God has made His holy Temple into an abomination. "Abomination" is elsewhere linked with idolatry, to be shunned by Israel. *The majesty of Israel,* epithet for the Temple. *His Footstool,* a designation for the Temple (Ps. 132.7). *Day of wrath,* with echoes in vv. 21 and 22, frames and characterizes ch 2. (See 1.12 and note.) **3:** *All the might of Israel,* lit. "Horn of Israel," a common metaphor for power and pride (e.g., Jer. 48.25; Ps. 75.11). *His right hand,* a symbol of divine power (e.g., Exod. 15.6, 12), is here used to prevent the protection of Judah. **4:** *The Tent,* the places where Judeans live, or, the Temple (Ps. 27.5). **6:** *His Booth* here signifies the Temple (Ps. 27.5). *Like a garden:* The phrase is grammatically difficult and makes better sense if rendered "as in a garden," meaning that God has destroyed the Temple ("His Booth") as easily as if it were a hut ("booth," a temporary structure used during harvest time) in a garden. *Has ended in*

---

a-a Lit. "My heart has turned over within me"; cf. Exod. 14.5; Hos. 11.8.
b-b Emendation yields "Oh, bring on them what befell me, / And let them become like me!"
c Meaning of Heb. uncertain.   *d* I.e., the Temple.

The kingdom and its leaders.

3 ג In blazing anger He has cut down
All the might of Israel;
He has withdrawn His right hand
In the presence of the foe;
He has ravaged Jacob like flaming fire,
Consuming on all sides.

4 ד He bent His bow like an enemy,
Poised His right hand like a foe;
He slew all who delighted the eye.
He poured out His wrath like fire
In the Tent of Fair Zion.

5 ה The Lord has acted like a foe,
He has laid waste Israel,
Laid waste all her citadels,
Destroyed her strongholds.
He has increased within Fair Judah
Mourning and moaning.

6 ו He has stripped His Booth[a] like a garden,
He has destroyed His Tabernacle;[b]
The LORD has ended in Zion
Festival and sabbath;
In His raging anger He has spurned
King and priest.

7 ז The Lord has rejected His altar,
Disdained His Sanctuary.
He has handed over to the foe
The walls of its citadels;
They raised a shout in the House of the
LORD
As on a festival day.

8 ח The LORD resolved to destroy
The wall of Fair Zion;
[c]He measured with a line,[c] refrained not
From bringing destruction.
He has made wall and rampart to mourn,
Together they languish.

9 ט Her gates have sunk into the ground,
He has smashed her bars to bits;
Her king and her leaders are [d]in exile,[d]
Instruction[e] is no more;
Her prophets, too, receive
No vision from the LORD.

10 י Silent sit on the ground

Zion / Festival and sabbath: God has cast into oblivion the Temple sacrifices on those days. **7:** *They raised a shout . . . as on a festival day:* The joyous sounds of Temple worship, now silenced, have been replaced by the enemies' exultant crowing. **8:** *Measured with a line* is the normal procedure for erecting a building, but here God is measuring how to destroy it (cf. Amos 7.7–9).

2.10–19: The survivors bewail their suffering. 10: Each action is a sign of mourning (see Ezek. 27.30; Job 2.12–13). Some current Jewish mourning practices reflect these ancient practices. Mention of *elders* and *maidens* is an example of a merism, a literary device whereby two opposites are used to express totality: The two and all in between mourn.

---

a I.e., the Temple.   b Lit. "(Tent of) Meeting."
c-c I.e., He made His plans.   d-d Lit. "among the nations."
e Heb. torah, here priestly instruction; cf. Jer. 18.18; Hag. 2.11; Mal. 2.6.

The elders of Fair Zion;
They have strewn dust on their heads
And girded themselves with sackcloth;
The maidens of Jerusalem have bowed
Their heads to the ground.

11 כ My eyes are spent with tears,
My heart is in tumult,
ᵃMy being melts away⁻ᵃ
Over the ruin of ᵇmy poor people,⁻ᵇ
As babes and sucklings languish
In the squares of the city.

12 ל They keep asking their mothers,
"Where is bread and wine?"
As they languish like battle-wounded
In the squares of the town,
As their life runs out
In their mothers' bosoms.

13 מ What can I ᶜtake as witness⁻ᶜ or liken
To you, O Fair Jerusalem?
What can I match with you to console you,
O Fair Maiden Zion?
For your ruin is vast as the sea:
Who can heal you?

14 נ Your seers prophesied to you
Delusion and folly.
They did not expose your iniquity
So as to restore your fortunes,
But prophesied to you oracles
Of delusion and deception.

15 ס All who pass your way
Clap their hands at you;
They hiss and wag their head
At Fair Jerusalem:ᵈ
"Is this the city that was called
Perfect in Beauty,
Joy of All the Earth?"

16 פ All your enemies
Jeer at you;
They hiss and gnash their teeth,
And cry: "We've ruined her!
Ah, this is the day we hoped for;
ᵉWe have lived to see it!"⁻ᵉ

13: *Vast as the sea*, simile expressing infinite size (see Isa. 48.18; Ps. 104.25; Job 11.9). **14:** Denunciation of false prophets. *Oracles of delusion and deception*, see Jer. 14.13–16; 23.25–27. **15:** Complaint about enemies. *Clap their hands . . . hiss . . . wag their head*, gestures of shock or derision. **16:** In this acrostic, and in the following two chs, the letter "pe" precedes the "ʿayin," reflecting an alternative order of the alphabet, attested in inscriptions from Izbet Sartah and Kuntillet Ajrud. **17:** *Has carried out the decree*, to punish sinners (1 Kings 9.6–9). **18–19:** A call to Zion (according to the emendation). The "wall" is personified as a supplicant to God on behalf of the city.

a-a Lit. "My liver spills on the ground."

b-b Lit. "the daughter of my people"; so elsewhere in poetry.

c-c Emendation yields "compare."

d These gestures were intended to ward off the calamity from the viewer; cf., e.g., Jer. 18.16 and note; Job 27.23.

e-e Lit. "We have attained, we have seen."

17 ע   The Lord has done what He purposed,
       Has carried out the decree
       That He ordained long ago;
       He has torn down without pity.
       He has let the foe rejoice over you,
       Has exalted the might of your enemies.

18 צ   ᵃ-Their heart cried out-ᵃ to the Lord.
       O wall of Fair Zion,
       Shed tears like a torrent
       Day and night!
       Give yourself no respite,
       Your eyes no rest.

19 ק   Arise, cry out in the night
       At the beginning of the watches,
       Pour out your heart like water
       In the presence of the Lord!
       Lift up your hands to Him
       For the life of your infants,
       Who faint for hunger
       At every street corner.

20 ר   See, O Lord, and behold,
       To whom You have done this!
       Alas, women eat their own fruit,
       Their new-bornᵇ babes!
       Alas, priest and prophet are slain
       In the Sanctuary of the Lord!

21 ש   Prostrate in the streets lie
       Both young and old.
       My maidens and youths
       Are fallen by the sword;
       You slew them on Your day of wrath,
       You slaughtered without pity.

22 ת   You summoned, as on a festival,
       My neighbors from roundabout.
       On the day of the wrath of the Lord,
       None survived or escaped;
       Those whom I boreᵇ and reared
       My foe has consumed.

3 א   I am the man ᶜ-who has known affliction
      Under-ᶜ the rod of His wrath;
  2   Me He drove on and on
      In unrelieved darkness;

2.20–22: Direct address to the Lord; lament becomes prayer. **20:** *See, O Lord, and behold,* a call to God for divine compassion. *Eat . . . babes* (cf. 4.10), a stark reversal of the norm during the siege (2 Kings 6.28) and a punishment for violation of the covenant (Deut. 23.53–57). Cannibalism is a motif often associated with literary descriptions of sieges. **21:** *You slew . . . You slaughtered:* Israel's prayer may include accusations against God alongside supplication for divine mercy and admission of guilt. **22:** *Day of wrath,* see 2.1 and n.; 2.22.

3.1–66: Individual and collective laments. Theological reflection is mixed with lament; hope alternates with despair. The identification of the individual has perplexed scholars for centuries. Some have identified the first-person speaker as a historical individual, but it seems better to take him (he is definitely male) as the counterpart of the female city of ch 1 or as the voice of a survivor going into exile. He is a Job-like figure, crying out to God in his suffering, trying to provoke a response from God. In contrast to the rest of Lamentations, it is likely that this chapter was originally written for a different purpose, and only secondarily was connected to the destruction of the Temple and the exile.

3.1–20: The lament of an individual. 1: *I am the man:* The male voice may represent a survivor, perhaps one going into exile. He may also be thought of as the collective voice of the people. (Later in the ch, the "I" merges with the "we.") *Rod of His wrath,* the shepherd's crook used for divine punishment (e.g., 2 Sam. 7.14; Ps. 89.33). The following verses continue the image of the shepherd, but instead of protecting his flock and leading them to water and good pastures (as in Ps. 23), this shepherd leads his flock into danger, which seems to symbolize the exile. **2–17a:** The Lord is the implied subject of the actions; the poet is the object; a

a-a *Emendation yields "Cry aloud."*
b *The root has this meaning in Arabic; others "dandled."*
c-c *Emendation yields "whom the Lord has shepherded with."*

3 On none but me He brings down His hand
   Again and again, without cease.

4 ב He has worn away my flesh and skin;
   He has shattered my bones.

5 All around me He has built
   Misery[a] and hardship;

6 He has made me dwell in darkness,
   Like those long dead.

7 ג He has walled me in and I cannot break out;
   He has weighed me down with chains.

8 And when I cry and plead,
   He shuts out my prayer;

9 He has walled in my ways with hewn blocks,
   He has made my paths a maze.

10 ד He is a lurking bear to me,
    A lion in hiding;

11 [b]He has forced me off my way[b] and mangled me,
    He has left me numb.

12 He has bent His bow and made me
    The target of His arrows:

13 ה He has shot into my vitals
    The shafts of His quiver.

14 I have become a laughingstock to all people,
    The butt of their gibes all day long.

15 He has filled me with bitterness,
    Sated me with wormwood.

16 ו He has broken my teeth on gravel,
    Has ground me into the dust.

17 My life was bereft of peace,
    I forgot what happiness was.

18 I thought my strength and hope
    Had perished before the LORD.

19 ז To recall my distress and my misery
    Was wormwood and poison;

20 Whenever I thought of them,
    I was bowed low.

21 But this do I call to mind,
    Therefore I have hope:

22 ח The kindness of the LORD has not ended,
    His mercies are not spent.

23 They are renewed every morning—
    Ample is Your grace!

a Taking rosh *as equivalent to* resh.
b-b *Meaning of Heb. uncertain.*

scathing condemnation of God the abusive shepherd (cf. 2.2–8 and Job's laments). **2:** *Me He drove*, with the shepherd's rod. *On and on in unrelieved darkness*, to a death-like state (Job 10.21–22; Lam. 3.6). Reversal of care and security usually associated with shepherd imagery (Ps. 23.1–4; 77.21; 78.52–53). *Darkness*, and not light, a reversal of the positive image of deliverance from darkness as symbol of redemption (Isa. 42.16; 49.9). "Darkness" also connotes imprisonment, anticipating 3.6–7. **8:** *He shuts out my prayer*, lamenting theological distress as well as physical calamities (see 3.44). This is consistent with the Psalms' emphasis on God's ability to "forget" the worshipper or to hide his face (e.g., Ps. 13.2). **10:** *Bear . . . lion*, the LORD, depicted just before as a shepherd, turns into fearsome beasts (cf. Isa. 38.13; Hos. 13.8), from whom the shepherd is supposed to protect the flock. **12–13:** The LORD shoots disaster and affliction from His bow (Deut. 32.23–24; Ps. 38.2–3; Job 16.12–13). **15:** *Filled me . . . sated me with wormwood:* Drinking bitter liquid is a common symbol of suffering (cf. 4.21; 3.19; Jer. 9.14; Job 9.18). **16:** *He has broken my teeth on gravel:* The midrash explains this literally in *Lam. Rab.* 3:16, suggesting that on their way into exile, Israelites kneaded dough on the ground, picking up grit along with the dough. The custom of dipping hard-boiled eggs or bread into ashes at the meal preceding the Fast of Tish'ah be'av derives from this midrash. **18:** *I thought my strength and hope had perished before the LORD*, a shift to the subjective reactions of the poet to punishments and the first mention of the LORD in this ch. **19:** *Wormwood and poison*, see 3.15.

3.21–24: Expression of faith and hope. 21: *I call to mind . . . I have hope:* The reasons for hope are explained in the following verses. **22–23:** *Kindness . . . mercies*, with *grace* (or "faithfulness" in 3.23) constitute three of the Thirteen Attributes of God (Heb "shelosh 'esreh midot," Exod. 34.6–7). The

24   "The LORD is my portion," I say with full
          heart;
      Therefore will I hope in Him.

25 ט   The LORD is good to those who trust in Him,
      To the one who seeks Him;

26   It is good to wait patiently
      Till rescue comes from the LORD.

27   It is good for a man, when young,
      To bear a yoke;

28 י   Let him sit alone and be patient,
      When He has laid it upon him.

29   Let him put his mouth to the dust—
      There may yet be hope.

30   Let him offer his cheek to the smiter;
      Let him be surfeited with mockery.

31 כ   For the Lord does not
      Reject forever,

32   But first afflicts, then pardons
      In His abundant kindness.

33   For He does not willfully bring grief
      Or affliction to man,

34 ל   Crushing under His feet
      All the prisoners of the earth.

35   To deny a man his rights
      In the presence of the Most High,

36   To wrong a man in his cause—
      This the Lord does not choose.

37 מ   Whose decree was ever fulfilled,
      Unless the Lord willed it?

38   Is it not at the word of the Most High,
      That weal and woe befall?

39   Of what shall a living man complain?
      Each one of his own sins!

40 נ   Let us search and examine our ways,
      And turn back to the LORD;

41   Let us lift up our hearts with[a] our hands
      To God in heaven:

42   We have transgressed and rebelled,
      And You have not forgiven.

a Lit. "to"; emendation yields "rather than"; cf. Joel 2.13.

thank You, everliving King, who has mercifully restored my soul within me; ample is Your grace." In *Lam. Rab.* 3:16, the midrash interprets, "Because You renew us every morning, we know that ample is Your grace to redeem us." **24:** The word *hope* appears in both v. 21 and v. 24, framing and featuring bracketed verses.

3.25–39: Pious wisdom on human suffering. 25–27: *Good,* Heb "tob," first word of each of three verses, suggests a benefit to trustful waiting, hoping (Pss. 27.14; 40.5; Prov. 20.22), and resigned suffering. **28:** *Let him sit alone,* cf. 1.1. *It,* His chastisement. **29:** *Let him put his mouth to the dust,* accepting God's discipline submissively. **30:** *Let him offer his cheek . . . be surfeited with mockery,* suffering abasement with resignation. **33:** Rationale for accepting suffering with patient trust. Divine punishment is of limited duration; the LORD is ultimately compassionate; and the chastisement is not arbitrary. **32:** *Pardons, kindness,* Heb terms are the same as "kindness" and "mercies" in v. 22. **33:** *Willfully,* capriciously, lit. "from His heart." God afflicts only in response to human misconduct. **34–39:** A restatement of standard biblical retribution theology: All is according to the divine will; suffering is the divine punishment for sin, to be accepted willingly. **39:** *Each one,* Heb "gever," "man." With "gever," "man" in v. 1 it defines the poetic unit spoken by the individual (vv. 1–39).

3.40–47: Communal lament. 40: *Let us,* an appeal for introspection and repentance in the first-person plural. **41:** *Our hearts with* (or "rather than") *our hands* stresses sincerity, not mere outward gesture (cf. Joel 2.13). **42:** *We have transgressed and rebelled,* confession of sin in first-person plural using multiple terms for sin. The Yom Kippur Confession of Sin ("viduy") exhibits the same form and is preceded by recitation of the Thirteen Attributes of God (see 3.22–23 n.). *And You,* better "but

Thirteen Attributes are often cited in biblical texts; they are also recited on festivals and fast days, and in penitential prayers during the High Holy Day period. Similar praise of God's goodness appears in promises to David (Ps. 89).

23: *They are renewed every morning—Ample is Your grace!* It is only through God's grace that the poet wakes up every morning from sleep, a mini-death. This verse is the basis for the Jewish prayer recited upon waking from sleep, "I

43 ס   You have clothed Yourself in anger and pursued us,
       You have slain without pity.
44   You have screened Yourself off with a cloud,
       That no prayer may pass through.
45   You have made us filth and refuse
       In the midst of the peoples.
46 פ   All our enemies loudly
       Rail against us.
47   Panic and pitfall are our lot,
       Death and destruction.
48   My eyes shed streams of water
       Over the ruin of my poor[a] people.

49 ע   My eyes shall flow without cease,
       Without respite,
50   [b]Until the LORD looks down
       And beholds from heaven.
51   My eyes have brought me grief[-b]
       Over all the maidens of my city.
52 צ   My foes have snared me like a bird,
       Without any cause.
53   They have ended my life in a pit
       And cast stones at me.
54   Waters flowed over my head;
       I said: I am lost!

55 ק   I have called on Your name, O LORD,
       From the depths of the Pit.
56   Hear my plea;
       Do not shut Your ear
       To my groan, to my cry!
57   You have ever drawn nigh when I called You;
       You have said, "Do not fear!"
58 ר   You championed my cause, O Lord,
       You have redeemed my life.
59   You have seen, O LORD, the wrong done me;
       Oh, vindicate my right!
60   You have seen all their malice,
       All their designs against me;
61 ש   You have heard, O LORD, their taunts,
       All their designs against me,
62   The mouthings and pratings of my adversaries
       Against me all day long.
63   See how, at their ease or at work,
       I am the butt of their gibes.

You," although the Heb has no conjunction. This introduces a shift back to accusation. *You have not for-given:* The expected result of repentance and confession did not occur. **43–45:** More charges of divine abandonment. **47:** *Panic and pitfall,* a proverbial expression (Isa. 24.17–18; Jer. 48.43–44); NJPS imitates the alliteration of Heb "paḥad wapaḥat" and also of *Death and destruction,* (Heb "hashet vehashaver").

3.49–63: Return to lament of the individual. 53: *Pit,* a cistern for collecting water; it also stands for the grave, the realm of the dead. **54:** *Waters flowed over my head,* metaphor for desperation (cf. Jonah 2.6–7; 2 Sam. 22.5–6 = Ps. 18.5–6). *I am lost!,* dead, cut off from God (Isa. 53. 8; Ps. 88.6). **56:** Many verbs translated as imperatives in vv. 56–66 are in the past tense. This change in tense, found in several psalms as well (e.g., Ps. 6.10) may reflect a wish, or a newfound confidence in the worshipper, perhaps after hearing an oracle that God has heard the prayer. **57–61:** *Drawn nigh, I called, have said, championed, have redeemed,* etc.: These verbs are in the perfect tense, which usually refers to past actions, but some interpreters understand them as futures or imperatives. The meaning would be "draw nigh when I call," "Champion my cause," and the like. This is a plea by the poet to God for future action. **59–61:** Complaint about the enemy anticipates an appeal for retribution (vv. 64–66).

---

a Lit. *"the daughter of my"; so frequently in poetry.*
b-b Emendation yields: *⁵⁰"Until the LORD looks down from heaven / And beholds ⁵¹my af-fliction. / The LORD has brought me grief."*

64 ת Give them, O Lᴏʀᴅ, their deserts
According to their deeds.

65 Give them anguish*a* of heart;
Your curse be upon them!

66 Oh, pursue them in wrath and destroy them
From under the heavens of the Lᴏʀᴅ!

4 א Alas!
The gold is dulled,*a*
Debased the finest gold!
The sacred*b* gems are spilled
At every street corner.

2 ב The precious children of Zion;
Once valued as gold—
Alas, they are accounted as earthen pots,
Work of a potter's hands!

3 ג Even jackals offer the breast
And suckle their young;
But my poor people has turned cruel,
Like ostriches of the desert.

4 ד The tongue of the suckling cleaves
To its palate for thirst.
Little children beg for bread;
None gives them a morsel.

5 ה Those who feasted on dainties
Lie famished in the streets;
Those who were reared in purple
Have embraced refuse heaps.

6 ו The guilt*c* of my poor*d* people
Exceeded the iniquity*c* of Sodom,
Which was overthrown in a moment,
Without a hand striking it.

7 ז Her elect were purer than snow,
Whiter than milk;
Their limbs were ruddier than coral,
Their bodies*a* were like sapphire.

8 ח Now their faces are blacker than soot,
They are not recognized in the streets;
Their skin has shriveled on their bones,
It has become dry as wood.

9 ט Better off were the slain of the sword
Than those slain by famine,
*e*Who pined away, [as though] wounded,
For lack of*e* the fruits of the field.

10 י With their own hands, tenderhearted women

3.64–66: Closing call for retribution against enemies. 64: *Give them . . . their deserts,* calls for retribution, which will reestablish God's justice in the world (cf. 1.21–22; Ps. 3.8). **66:** *Pursue them in wrath* appears in the Haggadah for Passover among a collection of verses ("shefokh ḥamatkha," "Pour out Thy wrath") whose theme is petition for vengeance on the nations oppressing Israel (see Ps. 79.6 n.).

4.1–22: Description of the siege of Jerusalem and the suffering and degradation of its inhabitants, ending in threats against Edom and blessings for Israel.

4.1–10: Contrasts between former grandeur and wretched present. 1: *Alas!* See 1.1 and n.; 2.1. **1–2:** *Gold* and *gems,* metaphors for people who, though precious, are now treated as worthless, throwaway objects (potsherds). **3:** *Even jackals:* Israel compares unfavorably even with the vilest animals (Isa. 1.3; Jer. ch 8). *Ostriches,* known proverbially for neglect of their young (Job 39.13–18). **4:** Infants are so weak they cannot cry or suck. Children are starving. **6:** *Sodom,* infamous for its wickedness (Gen. 19.1–11; Deut. 32.32; Isa. 1.10; 3.9; Jer. 23.14; Ezek. 16.46–56) and sudden and total destruction (Deut. 29.22; Isa. 1.9; 13.19; Jer. 49.18; 50.40; Amos 4.11; Zeph. 2.9). Jerusalem's slow agony is worse than Sodom's quick punishment. **9:** A quick death in battle would be preferable to slow starvation. **10:** *Have cooked,* see 2.20 n.

---

a Meaning of Heb. uncertain.　　*b Emendation yields "precious."*
c I.e., punishment.　　*d See note at 3.48.*　　*e-e Meaning of Heb. uncertain.*

Have cooked their children;
Such became their fare,
In the disaster of my poor[a] people.

11 כ The LORD vented all His fury,
Poured out His blazing wrath;
He kindled a fire in Zion
Which consumed its foundations.

12 ל The kings of the earth did not believe,
Nor any of the inhabitants of the world,
That foe or adversary could enter
The gates of Jerusalem.

13 מ It was for the sins of her prophets,
The iniquities of her priests,
Who had shed in her midst
The blood of the just.

14 נ They wandered blindly through the streets,
Defiled with blood,
So that no one was able
To touch their garments.

15 ס "Away! Unclean!" people shouted at them,
"Away! Away! Touch not!"
So they wandered and wandered again;
For the nations had resolved:
"They shall stay here no longer."

16 פ [b]The LORD's countenance has turned away from
    them,
He will look on them no more.
They showed no regard for priests,
No favor to elders.

17 ע Even now our eyes pine away
In vain for deliverance.
As we waited, still we wait
For a nation that cannot help.

18 צ Our steps were checked,
We could not walk [c]in our squares.[c]
Our doom is near, our days are done—
Alas, our doom has come!

19 ק Our pursuers were swifter
Than the eagles in the sky;
They chased us in the mountains,
Lay in wait for us in the wilderness.

20 ר The breath of our life, the LORD's anointed,
Was captured in their traps—
He in whose shade we had thought
To live among the nations.

4.11–16: Misery is divine chastisement. 11: *Fire,* symbol of divine wrath (e.g., 2.3; Deut. 32.22; Isa. 10.17; Jer. 17.27); also actual fire that burned down the city. **12:** Even foreign kings are shocked that God would let an enemy conquer His people. Faith in Jerusalem's inviolability, a theme of Isa.1–39 (see also Pss. 46.5; 48.3–8), a Judean thought here projected on foreigners, is recognized as myth. **13:** *Prophets . . . priests,* religious leaders singled out for blame (cf. 2.14). **14–15:** The formerly respected are now scorned and shunned as lepers (cf. Lev. 13.45–46). **16:** *LORD's countenance,* the sign of divine favor (Lev. 6.26–27), is averted from Israel. *Priests,* faithful priests, in contrast to the priests of v. 13.

4.17–22: Communal lament. The "we" uttered by the city reemerges. **17:** *A nation,* Egypt (see Jer. 37.5–10), to which Judah had looked in vain for relief. **20:** *The LORD's anointed,* breath of our life, divinely ordained kings (1 Sam. 24.7, 11; 2 Sam. 1.14, 16). The reference may be to King Zedekiah. The kings were also of no avail, and now the kingdom has lost its independence. **21:** *Rejoice and exult,* ironic charge to the enemy to exult as long as she can, for soon she, too, will suffer divine punishment. *Edom,* singled out for a curse (cf. Ezek. ch 35; Obad. 11; Ps. 137.8). "Fair" Edom parallels "Fair" Zion; the two will exchange places in terms of misery. *The cup,* of God's wrath (cf. 3.15; Jer. 25.15–29; 49.12; 51.7; Hab. 2.15–16). **22:** *Your iniquity,* i.e., punishment for your iniquity. *Is expiated,* lit. "is complete," and therefore the exile will end. Consolation of Israel (cf. Isa. 40.2) contrasted to imprecation against Edom.

---

a See note at 3.48.   b Meaning of line uncertain.   c-c Or "With long strides."

21 ש   Rejoice and exult, Fair Edom,
Who dwell in the land of Uz!
To you, too, the cup shall pass,
You shall get drunk and expose your nakedness.

22 ת   Your iniquity, Fair Zion, is expiated;
He will exile you no longer.
Your iniquity, Fair Edom, He will note;
He will uncover your sins.

5   Remember, O LORD, what has befallen us;
Behold, and see our disgrace!

2   Our heritage has passed to aliens,
Our homes to strangers.

3   We have become orphans, fatherless;
Our mothers are like widows.

4   We must pay to drink our own water,
Obtain our own kindling at a price.

5   We are hotly[a] pursued;
Exhausted, we are given no rest.

6   We hold out a hand to Egypt;
To Assyria, for our fill of bread.

7   Our fathers sinned and are no more;
And we must bear their guilt.

8   Slaves are ruling over us,
With none to rescue us from them.

9   We get our bread at the peril of our lives,
Because of the [b]sword of the wilderness.[b]

10   Our skin glows like an oven,
With the fever of famine.

11   They[c] have ravished women in Zion,
Maidens in the towns of Judah.

12   Princes have been hanged by them;[c]
No respect has been shown to elders.

13   Young men must carry millstones,
And youths stagger under loads of wood.

14   The old men are gone from the gate,
The young men from their music.

15   Gone is the joy of our hearts;
Our dancing is turned into mourning.

16   The crown has fallen from our head;
Woe to us that we have sinned!

17   Because of this our hearts are sick,
Because of these our eyes are dimmed:

5.1–22: Communal lament and prayer for restoration.

5.1: Appeal to God to take note. *Remember, O LORD, . . . Behold, and see* echoes 1.9, 11, 20; 3.59–60. Petition to God to take heed is complemented by a final petition to God to take action (v. 21).

5.2–18: Communal recounting of suffering. The main institutions of Judean society have been broken down. Families lack a head of household, family inheritances are lost, the elite of society have lost their status, economic deprivation is widespread, as is violence and lawlessness. **2:** *Heritage,* the land passed on by inheritance from one member of a family to the next; also the land God gave to Israel (Deut. 4.38; 25.19; 26.1). **6:** *Egypt . . . Assyria,* the two dominant powers of the ancient Near East in an earlier time, used figuratively for "east and west" i.e, "anyone, anywhere." **7:** *Our fathers sinned . . . we must bear their guilt,* better, "bear their punishment" (see Exod. 20.5; 34.7). With v. 16, the recognition that rebelliousness against God is the cause for catastrophe and that Israel has a long history of rebelling against God. **13:** *Carry millstones:* Grinding, usually the work of women, slaves, and prisoners (Exod. 11.5; Judg. 16.21; Isa. 47.2), is now forced upon the young men. Carrying wood is also among the most menial of labors. **14:** *Old men* administered justice at the city gates (Deut. 22.15; 25.7; Ruth 4.1–2, 11). **16:** *We have sinned,* admission of guilt (cf. 3.42 and n. 5.7). **17:** *Because of this* refers back to vv. 2–16 as well as forward to v. 18.

a Lit. "on our neck"; meaning of Heb. uncertain.
b-b Or "heat (cf. Deut. 28.22) of the wilderness"; meaning of Heb. uncertain.
c I.e., the slaves of v. 8.

18   Because of Mount Zion, which lies desolate;
      Jackals prowl over it.

19   But You, O LORD, are enthroned forever,
      Your throne endures through the ages.
20   Why have You forgotten us utterly,
      Forsaken us for all time?
21   Take us back, O LORD, to Yourself,
      And let us come back;
      Renew our days as of old!
22   For truly, You have rejected us,
      Bitterly raged against us.

          Take us back, O LORD, to Yourself,
          And let us come back;
          Renew our days as of old!

18: *Jackals prowl,* a conventional sign of desolation (Isa. 13.22; 34.13; Zeph. 2.14–15; and in ancient Near Eastern curses).

5.19–21: Praise of the LORD and appeal for restoration of divine favor. 19: *Enthroned:* God remains king even though His earthly throne, the Temple, has been destroyed. This faith in divine sovereignty (Pss. 44.5–6; 74.12) is the basis for the question and prayer that follow. **20:** *Why:* Questioning of God is a frequent element of prayer (Pss. 22.1; 44.24–25; 89.47). **21:** *Take us back . . . Renew our days,* imperatives echoing those in v. 1 frame the description of Zion's anguish and suggest it is only the LORD who can alleviate the disaster. *Take us back,* a fitting close to the book, a call for return (cf. Jer. 31.18). *Days as of old,* i.e., days evoked in 1.1 when Jerusalem was "great with people," "great among nations," and "princess among states."

5.22: Final dire pronouncement. *For truly, You have rejected us* emphasizes the urgency in the preceding call for remembrance and divine mercy. The call for God that echoes throughout the book remains unanswered. *Take us back . . . as of old:* In order not to conclude on a dire note, it is the Jewish custom at any public reading of Lamentations to repeat the last positive phrase (v. 21). Similar repetitions of the penultimate verse apply to the final chapters of Isaiah, Malachi, and Ecclesiastes.

קהלת

Ecclesiastes

AS LITERATURE, ECCLESIASTES BELONGS, along with Proverbs, Job, and some other sections of the Bible, in the category of wisdom. Wisdom texts reflect on the nature of the world and the God who created and controls it, and on the place of humans in this divine creation. These observations are usually presented as the work of one or more sages, who arrive at the observations by exercising wisdom—a faculty based on their own experience and that of other sages before them, and sometimes also on divine revelation. But whether from experience or revelation, the wisdom is regularly understood to have God as its ultimate source. In the case of Ecclesiastes, the wisdom is presented as experiential. The sage who comes to it through his experiences, one might even say experiments, is designated in Hebrew as Koheleth, and so supplies the Hebrew title for the book. Christian tradition generally uses, for book and sage, Ecclesiastes, "the one who assembled," which is the Greek rendering of Koheleth found in the Septuagint (see 1.1 n.).

The twelve chs of Koheleth cover a miscellany of topics: the cycles of the natural order; the amassing of wealth in property and other forms; the opposing forces that govern life; friendship, particularly as an antidote to life's wearying uncertainties; the virtues and difficulties of human authority; the nature of folly and the possibilities and limitations of wisdom; the enjoyment of one's toil; the terrors of old age. Behind these topics, it appears, are certain fundamental themes. The first is expressed by the term "futility" (hevel) (1.2 n.). For Koheleth, this is foremost the inability of humans to make sense of the world around them—to see a coherent pattern, a plan to their lives and to nature, in the sense of a movement toward lasting goals, a line of development or progress. Koheleth, it appears, does not deny that there may be coherent patterns of activity for each human, animal, and other phenomenon, and he uses the word ma'aseh ("deed, work, action" from '-s-h, "do, make") for these (ch 8), indicating also that they seem folded into the larger ma'aseh of God. But the human ability to discern what these are is frustrated, he argues, again and again; most significantly, the traditional doctrine of reward and punishment for the good and the wicked does not appear to work, at least in this life. In this regard, Koheleth is arguing against the position evident in the book of Deuteronomy or the bulk of Proverbs.

The one thing that is clear for Koheleth is death. It is the final point in each one's *ma'aseh,* the one immutable event in life that every human, animal, and other organism must succumb to; it cuts across all categories of morality and class. If there is any survival beyond death, either physically or in terms of memory and influence, humans cannot know this, and so cannot rely on it. What is left to humans, then, as Koheleth sees it—though he does raise an occasional doubt (e.g., 6.1–12 n.)—is principally to enjoy their toil while they are alive. This "portion" *(ḥelek)* (2.21) is granted to them by God as part of their activity. Individual rewards and punishments, however, have no enduring significance because they are canceled out by death and cannot be passed on to future generations. The capacity to discern all of this—to understand what can be known and what cannot—is for Koheleth the task of wisdom. Wisdom, therefore, is most effective when it is used to clarify its own limits. In so doing, wisdom need not deny—nor does Koheleth deny—that God is in control and has a coherent pattern of activity that will bring every creature to account. Accordingly, it makes sense not to tempt the anger of God, say, by making rash prayer at the sanctuary or rash vows (4.17–5.5). This affirmation of God's authority and judgment is, indeed, what rabbinic interpreters have emphasized as the central element in Koheleth, and while some modern critics have assigned the vv. that express it to later, or-thodox editor(s) of the book, it comports well with the limits on human wisdom, a central theme of the original author.

These topics and themes are not developed in a systematic exposition from the begin-ning to the end of the book; rather, a number of them, like futility and enjoyment of toil, are revisited, several times. These recurrences often involve new perspectives that build on, even contradict, what has come before (e.g., ch 8; 9.1–12; ch 10). At times, therefore, the recurrences and contradictions can be confusing, and in any case they make reading Ko-heleth no easy task.

But there are occasional indications of structure in the book. Thus, a frame surrounds most of the book, as 1.2 is essentially repeated in 12.8; the assertion in these two vv. that everything is futility should then reflect what the author regards as the fundamental theme of all the intervening material. Within the frame are various smaller units defined by formal markers, balance in the placement of vv., or a certain connectedness in the flow of narrative. The catalogue of polarities in 3.1–8 is the most obvious example, with the op-posites arranged as syntactic parallels. (Other examples are considered in the annotations below.) These structures create a loose coherence. This is reinforced by the repetition of certain nouns for key concepts, like "futility" *(hevel)* and "portion" *(ḥelek),* and of certain verbs, like "set my mind" *(natati et-libi,* 1.13) and "probe" *(tur,* 1.13), which represent a technical terminology assembled to describe Koheleth's intellectual search. Put together, then, the recurrences of themes and terminology testify to the leisurely, self-conscious, ru-minative process in which Koheleth is engaged, meandering through, around, and back to his favorite issues, considering them first from one angle, then from another.

If the Koheleth of the book is depicted throughout as a sage, he is also, in the first two chs, described as a king, more specifically, as recognized from the earliest Bible transla-tions (e.g., Septuagint, Targum), as Solomon son of David. To be sure, the name Solomon is nowhere used in the book; conversely, Koheleth does not occur elsewhere in the Bible. Yet the genealogy and descriptions given of Koheleth in his book (1.1, 12, 16; 2.7, 9) make the identification with Solomon clear. The Solomonic depiction is consistent with the depiction of Koheleth as sage, given the clear biblical tradition of Solomon as wise man (1 Kings ch 3; 5.9–14), and indeed, the larger ancient Near Eastern association of kingship and wisdom. Classical rabbinic tradition generally accepted that Koheleth was really Solomon, and thus that the book originated from the Solomonic period, but internal evidence points to a much later date of origin. Thus, the book's two Persian words, *pardes* ("grove," 2.5) and *pitgam* ("sentence," 8.11) indicate that in its present form it does not date from before the postexilic period (latter 6th century BCE on) and the emergence of the Achaemenid Persian empire that ruled Judah and most of the ancient Near East. This date comports with the variety of late grammatical features of Koheleth's Hebrew. At the other chronological end, Koheleth cannot be later than the first half of the 2nd century BCE, the date of a fragment of Koheleth found among the Dead Sea Scrolls and of the apocryphal work, the Wisdom of Solomon—and, perhaps, also of Sirach—which implicitly refers to Koheleth. Within these chronological limits, scholars continue to debate whether Koheleth belongs in the Achaemenid Persian period (late 6th to end of 4th centuries BCE) or to the following early Hellenistic period, perhaps during the 3rd century BCE. In either instance, the several positive references to political hierarchy, wealth in land, and money *(kesef)* all mark the author of Koheleth as probably of the landed gentry.

Although Koheleth belongs in content and language with Proverbs and Job as a wisdom book, in post-talmudic Jewish tradition, sometime between the 8th and 10th centuries CE, it came to be classified as one of the five megillot (scrolls), alongside Ruth, Esther, Song of Songs, and Lamentations, each of them to be read on a religious festival of the year. Koheleth is read on Sukkot, celebrating the completion originally of the fall harvest and later also of the yearly cycle of reading the Torah. This celebration of work completed, expressed both as joy and as a mood of reflection on memory and time past, resonates with themes in Koheleth, and so may have established the connection between the book and the festival.

Despite the firm place Koheleth has in the biblical canon, rabbinic tradition is ambivalent about the book. The evidence is rather laconic and concerns, in particular, the debates of the 1st century BCE through the early 2nd century CE, dealing also with certain other controversial biblical books like Ezekiel and the Song of Songs. Two features of Koheleth, and in varying fashion of these other books, appear to have provoked discussion: that they exhibit contradictions, in the case of Koheleth, self-contradictions; and that they offer unorthodox views that do not comport with the mainstream of Jewish thinking about God and Torah in the Bible. The result was, as various rabbinic Sages argued—others disagreeing—that Koheleth and these other books did not reflect divine inspiration, or in the ancient terminology, "did not make the hands impure" and deserved to "be removed from use and stored away" (e.g., *b. Shab.* 30b; *m. 'Ed.* 5.3; *b. Meg.* 7a). These rabbinic discussions are all post facto, after Koheleth and the other books had already been included in the biblical canon. While they may contain, therefore, some memory of earlier debates about inclusion in the canon, they more likely reflect an ongoing challenge of how to correlate the ideas and formulations of Koheleth and the other books with the rest of the biblical canon. In this regard, they are matched by the actual efforts of many classical Jewish commentators on Koheleth to make this correlation, by taming various troublesome sections of the book (see, e.g., 3.9–12 n.; 6.1–12 n.; ch 7) and by asserting that the statements in the epilogue, which appear orthodox, represent, indeed, the basic sense of the book. In the latter effort, the commentators may not be far wrong (12.9–14 n.).

[PETER MACHINIST]

1 The words of Koheleth[a] son of David, king in Jerusalem.

2   Utter futility!—said Koheleth—
     Utter futility! All is futile!

3   What real value is there for a man
     In all the gains[b] he makes beneath the sun?

4   One generation goes, another comes,
     But the earth remains the same forever.

5   The sun rises, and the sun sets—
     And glides[c] back to where it rises.

6   Southward blowing,
     Turning northward,
     Ever turning blows the wind;
     On its rounds the wind returns.

7   All streams flow into the sea,
     Yet the sea is never full;
     To the place [from] which they flow
     The streams flow back again.[d]

a Probably "the Assembler," i.e., of hearers or of sayings; cf. 12.9–11.
b So Rashbam. Heb. 'amal usually has this sense in Ecclesiastes; cf. Ps. 105.44.
c So Targum; cf. Bereshith Rabbah on Gen. 1.17.
d According to popular belief, through tunnels; so Targum and Rashi.

1.1: Introductory caption. As in some other biblical wisdom texts (e.g., Prov. 30.1), this introduction identifies the sage responsible for the reflections and sayings that follow. Koheleth is a sobriquet for this sage, who is described here as if he were Solomon. Koheleth, of feminine grammatical gender, may be used of males (cf. similar words that are so used, e.g., in Ezra 2.55, 57 ‖ Nehemiah 7.57, 59). Koheleth is derived from the root "k-h-l,"

"to assemble"; thus the Gk translation "Ecclesiastes," "the one of the assembly." But whether Koheleth may be understood as "the one who has assembled wisdom" (e.g., Rashi), or "assembled conflicting opinions and decided on the correct ones" (*Metzudat Zion*), or "assembled the people around to speak or preach wisdom to them" (cf. 12.9, as well as the Septuagint, *Eccl. Rab.*, and much modern scholarship)—no one of these or

other opinions about the name has established itself decisively.

1.2: The theme. *Futility* here translates Heb "hevel," the most frequent technical term in Koheleth (38 occurrences). From its literal meaning, "air, breath," the word has acquired the sense of something fleeting, without substance (cf. its occurrence as the name "Abel," Gen. ch 4), or even unreliable. In Koheleth, the literal meaning "air/breath" has not fully disappeared, since "hevel" is often paired with the phrase "pursuit of wind" (e.g., 2.26). The acquired sense, however, is what dominates, and it concerns actions and work that do not last, or appear to lead to no lasting goal, or cannot be explained in any rational, i.e., human, way. Within Jewish commentary, one emphasis applies *futility* to actions of humans for themselves alone, since actions can last and be worthwhile only if they are involved with Torah and labor for God.

1.3–11: Round and around. This section provides the first illustration of what Koheleth means by "futility." Vv. 4–8 give several examples of the ceaselessly circular, or oscillating movement that for him governs all activity in the world: the passage of generations, the cycle of the sun, the flow of the water. There is, in short, no linear, goal-oriented activity, and the result is that the world never changes. Vv. 3 and 9–11 draw out the implications of these examples

8   All such things are wearisome:
     No man can ever state them;
     The eye never has enough of seeing,
     Nor the ear enough of hearing.
9   Only that shall happen
     Which has happened,
     Only that occur
     Which has occurred;
     There is nothing new
     Beneath the sun!

10 Sometimes there is a phenomenon of which they say, "Look, this one is new!"—it occurred long since, in ages that went by before us. 11 The earlier ones are not remembered; so too those that will occur later ᵃwill no more be remembered thanᵃ those that will occur at the very end.

12 I, Koheleth, was king in Jerusalem over Israel. 13 I set my mind to study and to probe with wisdom all that happens under the sun.—An unhappy business, that, which God gave men to be concerned with! 14 I observed all the happenings beneath the sun, and I found that all is futile and pursuitᵇ of wind:
15   A twisted thing that cannot be made straight,
      A lack that cannot be made good.

16 I said to myself: "Here I have grown richer and wiser than any that ruled before me over Jerusalem, and my mind has zealously absorbed wisdom and learning." 17 And so I set my mind to appraise wisdom and to appraise madness and folly. And I learned—that this too was pursuit of wind:
18   For as wisdom grows, vexation grows;
      To increase learning is to increase heartache.

2 I said to myself, "Come, I will treat you to merriment. Taste mirth!" That too, I found, was futile.
2   Of revelry I said, "It's mad!"
     Of merriment, "What good is that?"

3 I ventured to tempt my flesh with wine, and to grasp folly, while letting my mind direct with wisdom, to the

---

a-a Lit. "will not be remembered like . . ." For 'im meaning "like," cf. 2.16; 7.11; Job 9.26.
b Lit. "tending," from root ra'ah, "to shepherd."

---

to affirm that nothing new occurs, and so there is nothing one can show for his toil, nothing to learn (to "remember," v. 11) and to build on. **9:** Put another way, as the sun cycles, so there is *nothing new beneath the sun*. Some classical Jewish commentators argue, following on v. 2, that the problem under discussion here is a wrong-headed focus on daily human or natural activities at the expense of the spiritual. Rashi, in particular, elaborates on this in a midrashic play on the phrase *nothing new beneath the sun*—a phrase that is unique to Koheleth in the Bible, although with antecedents and parallels both in the ancient Near East (e.g., Mari and Phoenicia) and in the Greek world. In Rashi's interpretation, the phrase contrasts futile daily activity done "in place of the Sun (= Light = Torah)," i.e., in contrast to the spiritual activity of Torah study and living.

1.12–18: Koheleth sets his task. Koheleth introduces himself here in the first person, drawing upon a style used in ancient Near Eastern royal inscriptions. Through the persona of Solomon, he aims to establish his preeminent ability to investigate wisdom, over against folly and madness. Yet, anticipating the fuller discussion that comes later, Koheleth admits that the investigation yields no satisfying outcome, only pain and vexation from the futility of explaining and correcting the crooked. Various traditional commentaries (e.g., Rashi) sought to reconcile this image of Koheleth with the successful Solomon of 1 Kings by positing that Koheleth/Solomon is here looking back from the end of his life, after the excesses of his material and religious policies (cf. 1 Kings ch 11) had gone far to undermine his achievements. Alternatively, the Targum saw this pessimism as a prophecy of Solomon forecasting the collapse of his kingdom by division after his death.

2.1–26: Experiments with wisdom and their results. Having set his task to discover what, if anything, wisdom can yield, Koheleth now turns to find the answer. Vv. 1–2, serving as a bridge to the preceding vv., introduce, with a note of pessimism, the task at hand. They do so by proposing, as a point of argument, that life appears to furnish no enjoyment. Vv. 3–11 and 12–16 describe two experiments Koheleth undertakes to test this proposition. **3–11:** The first is in end that I might learn which of the two was better for men to practice in their few days of life under heaven. [4] I multiplied my possessions. I built myself houses and I planted vineyards. [5] I laid out gardens and groves, in which I planted every kind of fruit tree. [6] I constructed pools of water, enough to irrigate a forest shooting up with trees. [7] I bought male and female slaves, and I acquired stewards. I also acquired more cattle, both herds and flocks, than all who were before me in Jerusalem. [8] I further amassed silver and gold and treasures of kings and provinces; and I got myself male and female singers, as well as the luxuries of commoners—coffers[a] and coffers of them. [9] Thus, I gained more wealth than anyone before me in Jerusalem. In addition, my wisdom remained with me: [10] I withheld from my eyes nothing they asked for, and denied myself no enjoyment; rather, I got enjoyment out of[b] all my wealth. And that was all I got out of my wealth.

[11] Then my thoughts turned to all the fortune my hands had built up, to the wealth I had acquired and won—and oh, it was all futile and pursuit of wind; there was no real value under the sun! [12] [c]For what will the man be like who will succeed [d]the one who is ruling[d] over what was built up long ago?

My thoughts also turned to appraising wisdom and madness and folly. [13] I found that

> Wisdom is superior to folly
> As light is superior to darkness;
[14] A wise man has his eyes in his head,
> Whereas a fool walks in darkness.

But I also realized that the same fate awaits them both. [15] So I reflected: "The fate of the fool is also destined for me; to what advantage, then, have I been wise?" And I came to the conclusion that that too was futile, [16] because the wise man, just like[e] the fool, is not remembered forever; for, as the succeeding days roll by, both are forgotten. Alas, the wise man dies, just like[e] the fool!

[17] And so I loathed life. For I was distressed by all that goes on under the sun, because everything is futile and pursuit of wind.

[18] So, too, I loathed all the wealth that I was gaining under the sun. For I shall leave it to the man who will succeed me—[19] and who knows whether he will be wise or

acquiring material property and other wealth—the regular mark of royal power and success (cf. Solomon in 1 Kings chs 4–10). **5:** Among such wealth is the building of *gardens;* though this is not otherwise attested for Solomon, it is familiar from other monarchs in the ancient Near East and beyond. **10:** His wealth gives him momentary pleasure as his "portion" ("ḥelek") from his labor (for this key term, see also 2.11; 3.22; 5.17, 18; 9.6, 9. NJPS freely translates here: *And that was all I got out of my wealth*). **11–12:** But the wealth has no lasting value for him and will fall to an unknown successor. **12–16:** The second experiment is in determining if there is an advantage to *wisdom* over *folly.* Like the first experiment with wealth, it does not, in Koheleth's view, finally succeed. **13–14:** For in a similar way to wealth, wisdom may at first confer the advantage of "finding/observing" ("ra'ah")—perhaps of understanding the limits of one's situation—but in the end it is negated by the fact that wise and fool alike have the same *fate* ("mikreh," yet another important word: lit. "happening"; see also 3.19–20; 9.2, 3, 11). **16:** *Fate* here means death, which wipes out the advantage of the wise over the fool, since both are equally forgotten.

2.17–23: The negative conclusions reached in vv. 1–16 are here elaborated.

2.24–26: A solution. Koheleth now offers a way to deal with the negative outcome of his experiments. Returning especially to the question of enjoyment, he reshapes the argument by proposing—and this is the interpretation of various classical Jewish commentators (e.g., *Eccl. Rab.,* Rashi)—that it is God's plan that one should at least enjoy the work while one does it, and by implication not worry about what will come afterward. For, Koheleth affirms, that kind of enjoyment is an outgrowth of the wisdom and knowledge that together are God's

---

a *The Heb.* shiddah *occurs only here in the Bible; in the Mishnah it designates a kind of chest.*

b *Septuagint and a few Heb. manuscripts have "(in exchange) for"; cf. 2.24; 3.13, 22; 5.17.*

c *The order of the two sentences in this verse is reversed in the translation for clarity.*

d-d *Change of vocalization yields "me, and who is to rule"; cf. vv. 18–19.*

e *See note on 1.11.*

foolish?—and he will control all the wealth that I gained by toil and wisdom under the sun. That too is futile. [20] And so I came to view with despair all the gains I had made under the sun. [21] For sometimes a person whose fortune was made with wisdom, knowledge, and skill must hand it on to be the portion of somebody who did not toil for it. That too is futile, and a grave evil. [22] For what does a man get for all the toiling and worrying he does under the sun? [23] All his days his thoughts are grief and heartache, and even at night his mind has no respite. That too is futile!

[24] There is nothing worthwhile for a man but to eat and drink and afford himself enjoyment with his means. And even that, I noted, comes from God. [25] For who eats and who enjoys but myself?[a] [26] To the man, namely, who pleases Him He has given [b]the wisdom and shrewdness to enjoy himself;[b] and to him who displeases, He has given the urge to gather and amass—only for handing on to one who is pleasing to God. That too is futile and pursuit of wind.

3 A season is set for everything, a time for every experience under heaven:[c]

2   A time for [d]being born[d] and a time for dying,
    A time for planting and a time for uprooting the planted;
3   A time for [e]slaying and a time for healing,[e]
    A time for tearing down and a time for building up;
4   A time for weeping and a time for laughing,
    A time for wailing and a time for dancing;
5   A time for throwing stones and a time for gathering stones,
    A time for embracing and a time for shunning embraces;
6   A time for seeking and a time for losing,
    A time for keeping and a time for discarding;
7   A time for ripping and a time for sewing,
    A time for silence and a time for speaking;
8   A time for loving and a time for hating;
    A time for war and a time for peace.

[9] What value, then, can the man of affairs get from what he earns? [10] I have observed the business that God gave

gift to one He finds pleasing. The one who displeases God, on the other hand, suffers the fate depicted in the experiments above, namely, that God makes him focus simply on accumulating wealth, only then to see it handed over to another who pleases God.

3.1–8: The catalogue of polarities. Koheleth's interest in life's polarities, found often in the book (e.g., 4.13–14), is most strikingly expressed in this poem. The poem moves across various kinds of human activity, arranged in pairs that are either constructive-destructive or the reverse. Rabbinic commentary often, but not always, tried to go beyond the contextual meaning of the pairs, which refers to universal human activities, to something more specific, concerning biblical history or the proper behavior of Israel as mandated by God. **5:** For example, the contextual meaning of *throwing* or *gathering stones*, though debated, would appear to lie somewhere among meanings like demolishing or constructing a building, sexual profligacy versus restraint, and destroying the fertility of a field by throwing stones on it or promoting its fertility by gathering and removing them. For *Eccl. Rab.* (followed by Rashi), however, the gathering of stones indicates the end of Jewish exile and the ingathering to Israel.

3.9–22: Reflections on the catalogue. 9: The first comment questions whether there is for one's labor any *value*, "advantage" or "profit" ("yitron," another favorite word of Koheleth and unique to him in the Bible: see 1.3; 2.11, 13; 5.8, 15; 7.12; 10.10, 11; it is often used negatively as here). The questioning in this instance must arise out of the constructive and destructive actions just catalogued: They suggest life is an endless circle of such actions, canceling or balancing each other out, and thus, once more, leading toward no goal, no "advantage." **10–15:** This cannot, however, be understood to deny God's control of everything,

a *Some mss. and ancient versions read* mimmennu, *"by His doing."*
b-b *Lit. "wisdom and knowledge and enjoyment."*
c *I.e., all human experiences are preordained by God; see v. 11.*
d-d *Lit. "giving birth."*
e-e *Emendation yields "wrecking . . . repairing"; cf. 1 Kings 18.30.*

man to be concerned with: [11] He brings everything to pass precisely at its time; He also puts eternity in their mind,[a] but without man ever guessing, from first to last, all the things that God brings to pass. [12] Thus I realized that the only worthwhile thing there is for them is to enjoy themselves and do what is good[b] in their lifetime; [13] also, that whenever a man does eat and drink and get enjoyment out of all his wealth, it is a gift of God.

[14] I realized, too, that whatever God has brought to pass will recur evermore:

Nothing can be added to it
And nothing taken from it—

and God has brought to pass that men revere Him.
[15c] What is occurring occurred long since,

And what is to occur occurred long since:

and God seeks the pursued. [16] And, indeed, I have observed under the sun:

Alongside justice there is wickedness,
Alongside righteousness there is wickedness.

[17] I mused: "God will doom both righteous and wicked, for [d]there is[d] a time for every experience and for every happening." [18c] So I decided, as regards men, to dissociate them [from] the divine beings and to face the fact that they are beasts.[e] [19] For in respect of the fate of man and the fate of beast, they have one and the same fate: as the one dies so dies the other, and both have the same lifebreath; man has no superiority over beast, since both amount to nothing. [20] Both go to the same place; both came from dust and both return to dust. [21] Who knows if a man's lifebreath does rise upward and if a beast's breath does sink down into the earth?

[22] I saw that there is nothing better for man than to enjoy his possessions, since that is his portion. For who can enable him to see what will happen afterward?

4 I further observed[f] all the oppression that goes on under the sun: the tears of the oppressed, with none to comfort them; and the power of their oppressors—with none to comfort them. [2] Then I accounted those who died long since more fortunate than those who are still living; [3] and happier than either are those who have not yet come into being and have never witnessed the miseries that go on under the sun.

a I.e., He preoccupies man with the attempt to discover the times of future events; cf. 8.17.
b I.e., what the author has already concluded (2.24) is good.
c Meaning of parts of verse uncertain.
d-d Shift of a diacritical point yields "He has set."
e Contrast Ps. 8.5–6.　　f Cf. 3.16.

which these vv. then affirm, echoing and extending 2.24–26. **11:** One part of this control is the fact that God puts *eternity* into human minds, i.e., gives humans a sense that divine activity determines events beyond what they can see and understand, and so defines for them the limits of their reason. **12:** By compensation, God allows humans, in another part of His control, to *enjoy* if not the "advantage" of their labor, then their labor while they are doing it. **16–22:** God's control is further explored. Here it is applied to two new pairs of opposites, not mentioned in the earlier catalogue. **16–17:** The first is *wickedness* versus *justice*, both of which God allows to occur, each in its own time and season. **18–22:** The second pair is animals versus humans. **19–21:** Here Koheleth questions the difference that evidently others in his community were asserting: that humans have an afterlife above (in heaven) and *beasts* only one below (in the netherworld). All Koheleth can see, however, is the same *fate* of the *dust* of death for both. He does not deny that there may be something more, and some rabbinic Sages, trying to harmonize Koheleth with their own beliefs, reinterpret all these lines to make Koheleth finally affirm a human afterlife with God. **22:** Yet, once again, Koheleth says, the best thing is for humans to focus on enjoying what they have—here the familiar term, their "portion"— now in their lifetimes.

4.1–16: Futility and human relationships. This ch explores several kinds of human interactions and their consequences. There are five sections, vv. 1–3, 4–6, 7–8, 9–12, and 13–16. The clause of self-reference, "I have observed/ noted" (1, 4, 7, 15), and of comparisons in the form "better than" (3, 6, 8, 9, 13) bind these together. Of these five sections, four describe negative interactions, only one positive. **1–3:** The first negative is oppressor overwhelming oppressed, a constant occurrence that makes death, or even not

⁴I have also noted that all labor and skillful enterprise come from men's envy of each other—another futility and pursuit of wind!

5
   [True,]
   The fool folds his hands together[a]
   And has to eat his own flesh.
6
   [But no less truly,]
   Better is a handful of gratification
   Than two fistfuls of labor which is pursuit of
      wind.

⁷And I have noted this further futility under the sun: ⁸the case of the man who is alone, with no companion, who has neither son nor brother; yet he amasses wealth without limit, and his eye is never sated with riches. For whom, now, [b-]is he amassing it while denying himself[-b] enjoyment? That too is a futility and an unhappy business.

⁹[c-]Two are better off than one, in that they have greater [d-]benefit from[-d] their earnings. ¹⁰For should they fall, one can raise the other; but woe betide him who is alone and falls with no companion to raise him! ¹¹Further, when two lie together they are warm; but how can he who is alone get warm? ¹²Also, if one attacks, two can stand up to him. A threefold cord is not readily broken!

¹³Better a poor but wise youth than an old but foolish king who no longer has the sense to heed warnings. ¹⁴For the former can emerge from a dungeon to become king; while the latter, even if born to kingship, can become a pauper.[e] ¹⁵[However,] I reflected about [f-]all the living who walk under the sun with[-f] that youthful successor who steps into his place. ¹⁶Unnumbered are the multitudes of all those who preceded them;[g] and later generations will not acclaim him either.[h] For that[i] too is futile and pursuit of wind.

¹⁷[j-]Be not overeager to go[-j] to the House of God: more acceptable is obedience than the offering of fools, for they know nothing [but] to do wrong.

---

a I.e., does not work; cf. Prov. 6.10; 24.33.

b-b Lit. "am I amassing . . . myself."

c 4.9–5.8 consists of a series of observations, each of which is introduced by some slight association with what precedes. The theme of 4.4–8 is not resumed until 5.9.

d-d Emendation yields "hope for"; cf. 2.20.

e Taking rash as a verb; cf. Ps. 34.11.

f-f I.e., "the contemporaries of."

g And so never heard of the gifted youth.

h For despite his wisdom, he too will be forgotten; cf. 2.16.

i I.e., the advantage of wisdom over folly.

j-j Lit. "Guard your foot when it [or, you] would go."

being born, better options (cf. 6.3 and Job ch 3, but, for the opposite view, Eccl. 9.4–6). **4–6:** The second negative is *envy* leading to futile labor. **7–8:** A person alone, and the futility, thus, of having no one to whom to bequeath the fruits of his labor, constitutes the third negative. **9–12:** The one positive interaction comes in contrast to the person alone, and it celebrates the advantages and rewards of companionship. **12:** The strength of such a relationship is compared to that of a *threefold* (three-ply) *cord,* an image that appears to go back to Sumerian literature of the late 3rd millennium BCE. Rabbinic commentary, however, took this cord to imply the advantages and greater strength of three persons functioning as companions, particularly in the matter of living and transmitting Torah, as against the two with which the section otherwise deals. **13–16:** The fourth and final negative interaction: a *poor,* though *wise youth* who succeeds where an *old, foolish king* fails, but whose achievement does not last because it was never known by the many generations before him and will be forgotten by those coming after (cf. 2.16).

4.17–5.6: Responding properly to God. This unit contains a set of warnings against various kinds of behavior that might at first seem acceptable to God and humans, but when carried to extremes, become objectionable and even dangerous, as they could provoke God's anger. **4.17:** The unit begins here, since 4.16 serves as a conclusion to the preceding discussion (cf. 2.26). It mentions first false sacrifice, which, as rabbinic commentary recognized, tries to cover up for sinful acts (cf., e.g., Amos 5.21–24).

5 Keep your mouth from being rash, and let not your throat[a] be quick to bring forth speech before God. For God is in heaven and you are on earth; that is why your words should be few. [2] Just as dreams come with much brooding, so does foolish utterance come with much speech. [3] When you make a vow to God, do not delay to fulfill it. For He has no pleasure in fools; what you vow, fulfill. [4] It is better not to vow at all than to vow and not fulfill. [5] Don't let your mouth bring you into disfavor, and don't plead before the messenger[b] that it was an error, [c-]but fear God;[-c] else God may be angered by your talk and destroy your possessions. [6] [d]For much dreaming leads to futility and to superfluous talk.

[7] If you see in a province oppression of the poor and suppression of right and justice, don't wonder at the fact; for one high official is protected by a higher one, and both of them by still higher ones. [8] Thus the greatest advantage in all the land is his: he controls a field that is cultivated.[e]

[9] A lover of money never has his fill of money, nor a lover of wealth his fill of income. That too is futile. [10] As his substance increases, so do those who consume it; what, then, does the success of its owner amount to but feasting his eyes? [11] A worker's[f] sleep is sweet, whether he has much or little to eat; but the rich man's abundance doesn't let him sleep.

[12] Here is a grave evil I have observed under the sun: riches hoarded by their owner to his misfortune, [13] in that those riches are lost in some unlucky venture; and if he begets a son, he has nothing in hand.

[14] [g-]Another grave evil is this: He must depart just as he came.[-g] As he came out of his mother's womb, so must he depart at last, naked as he came. He can take nothing of his wealth to carry with him. [15] So what is the good of his toiling for the wind? [16] Besides, all his days [h-]he eats in darkness,[-h] with much vexation and grief and anger.

[17] Only this, I have found, is a real good: that one should

a Heb. *leb*, lit. "heart," sometimes designates the organ of speech; cf. Isa. 33.18; 59.13; Ps. 19.15; 49.4; Job. 8.10.

b Some ancient versions read "God."

c-c Moved up from v. 6 for clarity.

d Meaning of verse uncertain. Emendation yields "Much brooding results in dreams; and much talk in futilities"; cf. v. 2.

e I.e., the high official profits from the labor of others; but meaning of verse uncertain.

f Some ancient versions have "slave's."

g-g Moved up from v. 15 for clarity.

h-h Septuagint reads "are [spent] in darkness and mourning."

5.1–2: Uncontrolled speech is a common motif in biblical and other ancient Near Eastern wisdom, where it is often juxtaposed to the virtue of silence; Rashbam here understands it as excessively long prayer. **3–5:** Making rash vows that cannot, or are not intended to, be paid (cf. Deut. 23.22–24; Prov. 20.25; Sir. 18.21). **2, 6:** The reference to *dreams* may stand as a negative image for anything ephemeral and unstable (e.g., Job 20.8 and ancient Egyptian literature). Alternately, the reference may be to the widespread Near Eastern, including biblical, appeal to dreams as a form of divine communication, here warning against undue reliance on them because they could be vague and misleading (cf. dreams of false prophets in Deut. 13.2, 4, 6; Jer. 23.25, 27, 28, 32; 27.9; 29.8; Zech. 10.2).

5.7–8: The virtues of authority. 7: The hierarchy of authority outlined here may well be modeled on the actual system of Koheleth's time, whether that be Achaemenid or early Hellenistic (see introduction). The system serves justice, it appears, because the possible failures of the lower ranks of officials are watched over and corrected by the higher ranks, as in the Egyptian wisdom story, "The Tale of the Eloquent Peasant." If the higher ranks here ultimately include God—though this is not specified—then the v. would connect with the preceding 4.17–5.6, where failures of human behavior are answerable to God. **8:** This v. is difficult, though it seems to describe, as classical rabbinic tradition already saw, the value and "advantage/profit" that agriculture brings. More precisely, the emphasis may not be on owning land, which is criticized in 2.1–11, but on the enjoyment and value of toiling on the land, as in 5.11, 17–18 (and also 2.24; 3.22; 8.15).

5.9–20: The problem of wealth and the solution. 9–16: The main focus, the futility of accumulating wealth, stands in deliberate con-eat and drink and get pleasure with all the gains he makes under the sun, during the numbered days of life that God has given him; for that is his portion. [18] Also, whenever a man is given riches and property by God, and is also permitted by Him to enjoy them and to take his portion and get pleasure for his gains—that is a gift of God. [19] For [such a man] will not brood much over the days of his life,[a] because God keeps him busy enjoying himself.

6 There is an evil I have observed under the sun, and a grave one it is for man: [2] that God sometimes grants a man riches, property, and wealth, so that he does not want for anything his appetite may crave, but God does not permit him to enjoy it; instead, a stranger will enjoy it. That is futility and a grievous ill. [3] Even if a man should beget a hundred children and live many years—no matter how many the days of his years may come to, if his gullet is not sated through his wealth, I say: The stillbirth, though it was not even accorded a burial,[b] is more fortunate than he. [4] Though it comes into futility and departs into darkness, and its very name is covered with darkness, [5] though it has never seen or experienced the sun, it is better off than he—[6] yes, even if the other lived a thousand years twice over but never had his fill of enjoyment! For are not both of them bound for the same place? [7c] All of man's earning is for the sake of his mouth, [d] yet his gullet is not sated. [8] What advantage then has the wise man over the fool, what advantage has the pauper who knows how to get on in life?[-d] [9e] Is the feasting of the eyes more important than the pursuit of desire? That, too, is futility and pursuit of wind.

[10] Whatever happens, it was designated long ago and it was known that it would happen; as for man, he cannot contend with what is stronger than he. [11] Often, much talk means much futility. How does it benefit a man? [12] Who

a The thought of which is depressing; see v. 16.

b Stillbirths were cast into pits or hidden in the ground in no recognizable graves; cf. v. 4 end.

c Cf. Prov. 16.26.

d-d Meaning of Heb. uncertain; emendation yields "And if the gullet is not sated, [8] what advantage has the wise man over the fool, he who knows how to get on in life over the pauper?"

e Meaning of first half of verse uncertain.

trast with 5.8, on the value of toil. Some of the earlier reasons for the futility (chs 2, 4) are here resumed. **9:** Added is the particular problem of accumulating *money* (5.9; lit. "silver" ["kesef"]), which once ac-

quired leaves one insatiable for more. **11, 17–20:** The contrasting situation, namely, the value of toil, is here reintroduced. As elsewhere in Koheleth (2.24–25; 3.12–13; 8.15; 9.7, 9; cf. 3.22; 11.8), it is God who

is said to preside over the whole matter. But now the focus is on God's grant of the power to enjoy wealth and goods and the toil presumably associated with them, without worry about where it will lead or how much is to be accumulated. Some medieval commentators (e.g., Rashi and Sforno) added that God's gift of enjoyment is for those who earn it by meritorious deeds, and who would enjoy the blessing of their deeds not only on earth, but finally in the afterlife (cf. 3.9–22 n.).

6.1–12: Again wealth, toil, and the meaning of life. 1–6: The first unit continues the focus on the futility of accumulating wealth (5.12–16; 2.18–19; some of its language echoes that in 5.17–20). But here Koheleth adds a sharper and more negative twist to these earlier occurrences, noting that God can deny people the power to enjoy wealth. Indeed, He can give that wealth to a stranger, i.e., someone outside the kin group of the owner, who could thus alienate the wealth from the group. **3b–5:** The sharpness of this first unit reaches its climax. Recalling the image of the unborn in 4.3, Koheleth here substitutes for it the uglier image of the stillborn, who is said to be more fortunate in his briefly earned rest than the living possessor of wealth who long accumulates it but is not allowed to enjoy it. The pessimism that all of this manifests is deepened in the remaining two units of the ch. **7–9:** The second unit questions whether a human being can ever find satisfaction in toil, and so whether it makes any difference to be wise, foolish, or poor. **10–12:** The third unit, going further, returns to the earlier theme of time's circularity and the lack of anything new (e.g., 1.9–10). It draws out of this circularity the conclusion, also found earlier (5.2, 6; 2.11–13), that human efforts are futile, in the light of God's strength in power and argument, to determine what sense life has or will lead to. Later interpreters (e.g., the Targum) sought to allevican possibly know what is best for a man to do in life—the few days of his fleeting life? For[a] who can tell him what the future holds for him under the sun?

7 [b]A good name is better than fragrant oil, and the day of death than the day of birth.[c]

2 It is better to go to a house of mourning than to a house of feasting; for that is the end of every man, and a living one should take it to heart.

3 Vexation is better than revelry;[d] for though the face be sad, the heart may be glad. 4 Wise men are drawn to a house of mourning, and fools to a house of merrymaking.

5 It is better to listen to a wise man's reproof than to listen to the praise of fools. 6 For the levity[e] of the fool is like the crackling of nettles under a kettle. [f]But that too is illusory; 7 for cheating[g] may rob the wise man of reason and destroy the prudence of the cautious.[h]

8   The end of a matter is better than the beginning of it.

     Better a patient spirit than a haughty spirit.

9 Don't let your spirit be quickly vexed, for vexation abides in the breasts of fools.

10 Don't say, "How has it happened that former times were better than these?" For it is not wise of you to ask that question.

11 Wisdom is as good as a patrimony, and even better, for those who behold the sun. 12 For to be in the shelter of wisdom is to be also in the shelter of money,[i] and the advantage of intelligence is that wisdom preserves the life of him who possesses it.

13 [j]Consider God's doing! Who can straighten what He has twisted? 14 So in a time of good fortune enjoy the good fortune; and in a time of misfortune, reflect: The one no less than the other was God's doing; consequently, man may find no fault with Him.[k]

---

a Lit. "according to the shadow that"; cf. Qumran Aramaic betel and Syriac meṭṭol; and see 8.13.

b The author now offers a number of practical maxims, which, however, he concludes (vv. 23–24) are of limited value.

c Until a man dies, there is always danger that he may forfeit his good name.

d For empty revelry precludes real happiness; cf. 2.2.

e Emendation yields "praise" (shbḥ).

f This section, to end of verse 7, is apparently a continuation of the thought in vv. 11–12 and 19.

g Emendation yields "riches."

h Lit. "caution"; cf. postbiblical mathun, "cautious."

i Emendation yields "For the possessor of wisdom becomes a possessor of money."

j Vv. 13–14 continue the thought of v. 10.

k So Rashi; cf. the same thought in Job 1.22; 2.10.

ate this section's pessimism by supposing that the vv. teach that human meaning can come by devotion not to material pursuits, but to spiritual, such as study of Torah, and by understanding that the final reward is to be sought in the afterlife (cf. 3.9–22 n.).

7.1–29: Proverbial sayings and the problem of wisdom. The pessimism of ch 6 is here examined further. **1–10:** The ch begins with a section of proverbs, the largest part of which, as in 4.3, 6, 9, 18, is arranged in a series of "better than" comparisons concerning wisdom and folly. Wisdom here, in line with 4.2 (cf. 4.3; 6.3–6), is what recognizes that the only certain thing in life is its end, death; fools, on the contrary, focus on life and its illusory pleasures of laughter and feasting. **10:** It is also unwise to spend time longing for the better days that are now past, if indeed they were better. **7:** Yet even wisdom is not always reliable, because of the capacity of wise men to be corrupted. **11–29:** These reflections are enlarged in the next two sections, vv. 11–14, 15–29. On the one hand, in vv. 11–12, 19, 26, the power of wisdom and the punishment of the sinner are affirmed. Yet questions about the human practice of wisdom resurface and are elaborated. **20:** Thus, in an echo of v. 7, righteous humans, who are equated with the wise (cf. v. 16), are said not to be immune from sin. **21–22:** Warnings are also given against (excessive) reliance on the opinions of others. **15:** Further, reward and punishment are observed not always to work as they should for righteous and wicked people. **16–18:** This leads Koheleth to recommend that a person avoid being too righteous and wise, and too wicked and foolish. Exactly what is meant here is not clear, although the advice recalls the Greek philosophical adage (e.g., Theognis, Aristotle) to do "nothing overmuch." **14:** Perhaps the point is more intellectual than practical: Do not act as if you know with certainty what is right and wicked; human beings do not

15 In my own brief span of life, I have seen both these things: sometimes a good man perishes in spite of his goodness, and sometimes a wicked one endures in spite of his wickedness. 16 So don't overdo goodness and don't act the wise man to excess, or you may be dumfounded. 17 Don't overdo wickedness and don't be a fool, or you may die before your time. 18 It is best that you grasp the one without letting go of the other, for one who fears God will do his duty[a] by both.

19 Wisdom is more of a stronghold to a wise man than [b]ten magnates[-b] that a city may contain.

20 [c]For there is not one good man on earth who does what is best[d] and doesn't err.

21 Finally, don't pay attention to everything that is said, so that you may not hear your slave reviling you; 22 for well you remember[e] the many times that you yourself have reviled others.

23 All this I tested with wisdom. I thought I could fathom it,[d] but it eludes me. 24 [The secret of] what happens is elusive and deep, deep down; who can discover it? 25 I put my mind to studying, exploring, and seeking wisdom and the reason of things, and to studying wickedness, stupidity, madness, and folly. 26 Now, I find woman more bitter than death; she is all traps, her hands are fetters and her heart is snares. He who is pleasing to God escapes her, and he who is displeasing is caught by her. 27 See, this is what I found, said Koheleth, item by item in my search for the reason of things. 28 As for what I sought further but did not find, I found only one human being in a thousand, and the one I found among so many was never a woman. 29 But, see, this I did find: God made men plain, but they have engaged in too much reasoning.

8 [f]Who is like the wise man,[-f] and who knows the meaning of the adage:
   "A man's wisdom lights up his face,
      So that his deep discontent[g] is dissembled"?

a Cf. postbiblical yaṣa yede.
b-b Emendation yields "the riches of the magnates"; cf. Prov. 18.11.
c Apparently continuing the thought of v. 16.
d Refers back to 6.12.
e Lit. "your heart knows"; the same idiom occurs again in 8.5.
f-f Some ancient versions read "Who here is wise."
g Lit. "face"; cf. 1 Sam. 1.18; Job 9.27.

balanced behavior, which Koheleth connects with the fear of God (v. 18). **26:** To underscore the point, the author introduces the image, known in other Near Eastern wisdom, both biblical (e.g., Prov. 2.16–19; 7.5–27) and nonbiblical (Egyptian and Mesopotamian), of the woman who waits to entrap the unwary and the sinner, that is, the one not favored by God. (For a more positive image of women, see 9.9.) **29:** But wisdom's limits and moderation, Koheleth concedes, are something humans generally will not recognize and accept, tempted as they are to use their own "rational devices" (*too much reasoning*) to reach for certain truth. The difficult and troubling character of Koheleth's thoughts in this ch was, once more, recognized by the classical rabbinic interpreters, even as they sought to clarify and tame it. So the apparent pessimism of wisdom's focus on the end, not the beginning, of life (see vv. 1–4) was understood positively by the medieval philosopher Joseph Albo, among others: Death is to be celebrated because only then can a human being know and have realized his intellectual and spiritual potential. Similarly, for the pessimism of v. 14. This states that a human being cannot make sense of his life and of what will come after him (lit. "will not find anything after him"), given that he has to endure, evidently in a way difficult to predict, both fortune and misfortune, which God has created. In Rashi's view, however, followed by NJPS, v. 14 refers to God's creating good and evil, and the reward and punishment that go respectively with each; a human being cannot and should not find any fault with Him (i.e., God, not a human being) about unjust punishment.

8.1–17: Wisdom and its limits, again. The ch is framed by two statements about wisdom. **1:** The first appears to be positive, affirming the power of wisdom to make sense of things (translating the end of 1a as "who knows the meaning of a thing?") and so to produce

have that wisdom; only God does, who is the source of both good ("tov," *good fortune*) and evil ("ra'," *misfortune*). **18–28:** At the most, then, human wisdom teaches the limits of what that wisdom can know (vv. 23–24, 27–28), and, therefore, the need for moderate,

[2] I do! "Obey the king's orders—and [a-]don't rush[-a] into uttering an oath by God."[b] [3c-]Leave his presence; do not tarry[-c] in a dangerous situation, for he can do anything he pleases; [4] inasmuch as a king's command is authoritative, and none can say to him, "What are you doing?" [5] One who obeys orders will not suffer from the dangerous situation.

A wise man, however, will bear in mind[d] that there is a time of doom.[e] [6] For there is a time for every experience, including the doom; for a man's calamity[f] overwhelms him. [7] Indeed, he does not know what is to happen; even when it is on the point of happening, who can tell him? [8] No man has authority over the lifebreath—to hold back the lifebreath;[g] there is no authority over the day of death. There is no mustering out from that war; wickedness[h] is powerless to save its owner.

[9] All these things I observed; I noted all that went on under the sun, while men still had authority over men to treat them unjustly. [10] And then I saw scoundrels [i-]coming from the Holy Site and being brought to burial,[-i] while such as had acted righteously were forgotten in the city.

And here is another frustration: [11] the fact that the sentence imposed for evil deeds is not executed swiftly, which is why men are emboldened to do evil—[12] the fact that a sinner may do evil a hundred times and his [punishment] still be delayed. For although I am aware that "It will be well with those who revere God since they revere Him, [13] and it will not be well with the scoundrel, and he will not live long, because[j] he does not revere God"—[14] here is a frustration that occurs in the world: sometimes an upright man is requited according to the conduct of the scoundrel; and sometimes the scoundrel is requited according to the conduct of the upright. I say all that is frustration.

[15] I therefore praised enjoyment. For the only good a man can have under the sun is to eat and drink and enjoy

a-a Moved up from v. 3 for English word order.

b The answer to the inquiry about the implications of the proverb in v. 1 is given in the form of another proverb, of which only the first half is relevant and is enlarged upon.

c-c Or "Give ground before him; do not resist."

d The same idiom as in 7.22.

e Lit. "time and doom"; cf. the synonymous "time of misfortune," lit. "time and misfortune," 9.11.

f Still another term for death; cf. "the time of calamity" for "the hour of death," 9.12.

g From leaving the body when the time comes; see 12.7; cf. Ps. 104.29; 146.4.

h Emendation yields "riches."

i-i Meaning uncertain; emendation yields "approaching [to minister]. They would come and profane the Holy Site."

j See note on 6.12.

contentment. **16–17:** This contradicts the final vv., in which Koheleth argues yet again (7.14, 23–24, 27–28; 6.12; 3.11, 22) that his investigation of the nature of wisdom reveals wisdom's limits—its inability to find out the ultimate goal and meaning of the "activity" ("maʿaseh"; for this characteristic word of Koheleth, see also 3.11; 8.14, 17; 9.10; 11.5) of God and the world. This contradiction is not easy to resolve. One possibility is that v. 1 begins its affirmation of wisdom in a question form, suggesting uncertainty that would then be confirmed by the final vv. (16–17). Alternatively, this unit may reflect Koheleth's slow, ruminative approach, as he tries to figure out what value wisdom may have, changing his mind along the way. This would comport well with the vv. in between the two wisdom statements. **2–9:** Thus, *command* or "power" (v. 4: "shilton") is first something positive and effective: the property of the king, who must be obeyed because with it he is irresistible and because his commands are even like oaths to God (vv. 2–4). **8:** But, as Koheleth then observes (see Rashi, Rashbam, and others), no person, royal or otherwise, is "powerful" enough ("shalit," "shilton"), to hold on to his "lifebreath" ("ruaḥ," the animating force) on the day of his death and to do battle, that is, with death. **9:** Indeed, finally, a person can use his "power/authority" ("shalat") to do another harm. This progressive qualification of human "power," from royal authority commanding obedience to the evil ability to cause harm, leads to a second theme in which Koheleth also plays with different views. **9–14:** The theme is the treatment of the good and wicked. On this theme Koheleth goes beyond what he has said earlier (e.g., 7.15) to express directly the tension between his personal conviction, following traditional wisdom, that the good are rewarded and the wicked punished (vv. 12–13), and his observation that in reality this does not always work out (vv. 10, 14). The himself. That much can accompany him, in exchange for his wealth, through the days of life that God has granted him under the sun.

16 For I have set my mind to learn wisdom and to observe the business that goes on in the world—even to the extent of going without sleep day and night—17 and I have observed all that God brings to pass. Indeed, man cannot guess the events that occur under the sun. For man tries strenuously, but fails to guess them; and even if a sage should think to discover them he would not be able to guess them.

9 For all this I noted, and I ascertained[a] all this: that the actions of even the righteous and the wise are determined by God. [b]Even love! Even hate! Man knows none of these in advance—2 none![b] For the same fate is in store for all: for the righteous, and for the wicked; for the good and pure,[c] and for the impure; for him who sacrifices, and for him who does not;[d] for him who is pleasing,[e] and for him who is displeasing; and for him who swears, and for him who shuns oaths.[f] 3 That is the sad thing about all that goes on under the sun: that the same fate is in store for all. (Not only that, but men's hearts are full of sadness, and their minds of madness, while they live; and then—to the dead!) 4 For he who is [g]reckoned among[g] the living has something to look forward to—even a live dog is better than a dead lion—5 since the living know they will die. But the dead know nothing; they have no more recompense,[h] for even the memory of them has died. 6 Their loves, their hates, their jealousies have long since perished; and they have no more share till the end of time in all that goes on under the sun.

7 Go, eat your bread in gladness, and drink your wine in joy; for your action was long ago approved by God.[i] 8 Let your clothes always be freshly washed, and your head never lack ointment. 9 Enjoy happiness with a woman you love all the fleeting days of life that have been granted to you under the sun—all your fleeting days. For that alone is what you can get out of life and out of the means you ac-

conclusion to this dilemma is Koheleth's favorite: It is all "hevel"—beyond human comprehension (cf. 1.2; etc.). **15:** The consequent recommendation is likewise familiar (cf., e.g., 2.24–25): to enjoy the toil that one does while one is alive and doing it. **16–17:** This conclusion and recommendation, then, are reinforced by the assertion that human wisdom cannot make any sense of the divine "activity" of the world.

9.1–12: Death is the final equalizer. Like ch 8, these vv. are also framed by two statements (vv. 1–6, 10b–12). In this instance the theme is death as the final end, or *fate* ("mikreh") for all humans, regardless of behavior, power, or ability. While this theme and language are familiar (2.13–16; 3.19–21), they have here some new emphases. **1:** All righteous and wise people and their deeds are under God's control, but whether the deeds turn out to involve love or hate, humans cannot know beforehand. **4:** Contrary to 4.2–3; 7.11, being alive is better than being dead, because (vv. 5–6, 10b) in Sheol, the netherworld, the place where all dead reside, no labor, reward, emotion, or thought is possible. **7–10a:** These vv. offer a practical response to the situation just described, namely, to enjoy life while you live it (cf. 2.24–25; 8.15). Yet in this advice, again, are new motifs. **8:** One of them connects enjoyment with symbols of purity, a white garment and the head anointed with oil. Some rabbinic sages (e.g., *b. Shab.* 143b; Ibn Paquda) understood this to mean that one's behavior in life should always be morally exemplary and spiritually elevated: ready at any time for death and God's judgment, and avoiding the excesses that would stain one's character as they would stain a white garment. **9:** The other motif states that enjoyment should include having a wife to love—a sentiment that appears to differ from the negative image of women in 7.26, 28.

a *Meaning of verb uncertain; construction as in Hos. 12.3; Ezra 3.12.*

b-b *Emendation yields "Even love, even hate, no man can know in advance. All* 2*are insignificant."*

c *I.e., those who observe the laws of ritual purity.*

d *Cf. 4.17.*   e *I.e., to God; cf. 2.26; 7.26.*

f *Cf. 8.2.*   g-g *Lit. "joined to all."*

h *Emendation yields "hope."*   i *Cf. 2.24–25; 3.13; 5.18.*

quire under the sun. ¹⁰ Whatever it is in your power to do, do with all your might. For there is no action, no reasoning, no learning, no wisdom in Sheol, where you are going.

11   I have further observed under the sun that
        The race is not won by the swift,
        Nor the battle by the valiant;
        Nor is bread won by the wise,
        Nor wealth by the intelligent,
        Nor favor by the learned.

For the time of mischance* comes to all.ᵇ ¹² And a man cannot even know his time. As fishes are enmeshed in a fatal net, and as birds are trapped in a snare, so men are caught at the time of calamity,ᵃ when it comes upon them without warning.

¹³ This thing too I observed under the sun about wisdom, and it affected me profoundly. ¹⁴ There was a little city, with few men in it; and to it came a great king, who invested it and built mighty siege works against it. ¹⁵ Present in the city was a poor wise man ᶜwho might have saved ᶜ it with his wisdom, but nobody thought of that poor man. ¹⁶ So I observed: Wisdom is better than valor; but

        A poor man's wisdom is scorned,
        And his words are not heeded.

¹⁷ᵈWords spoken softly by wise men are heeded ᵉsooner than those shouted by a lord in folly.ᵉ

¹⁸ Wisdom is more valuable than ᶠweapons of war,ᶠ but a single error destroys much of value.

10 Dead flies turn the perfumer's ointment fetid and putrid;ᵍ so a little folly outweighs massive wisdom.

² A wise man's mind tends toward the right hand, a fool's toward the left.ʰ ³ A fool's mind is also wanting when he travels, and he lets everybody know he is a fool.

⁴ If the wrath of a lord flares up against you, don't give up your post;ⁱ for ʲwhen wrath abates, grave offenses are pardoned.ʲ

⁵ Here is an evil I have seen under the sun as great as an

---

a Euphemism for death.

b I.e., the insignificant duration of life renders all successes illusory; cf. 4.15–16.

c-c Others "who saved."

d Verses 9.17–10.19 constitute a group of loosely connected aphorisms.

e-e Lit. "than the scream of a lord in [the manner of] the fools."

f-f Emendation yields "everything precious."

g Meaning of Heb. uncertain.

h I.e., a wise man's mind brings him good luck; a fool's brings him bad luck.

i Emendation yields "hope."

j-j Lit. "abatement (2 Chron. 36.16) remits grave offenses." For hinniaḥ, "to remit," cf. Abodah Zarah 13a; cf. hanaḥah, "remission of taxes," Esth. 2.18.

9.13–18: Again the problematic of wisdom. The challenge posed by deciding how to live in the face of death brings Koheleth back to the theme of wisdom and its limits. First in a parable (vv. 14–16) recalling 4.13 (cf. also 7.19), and then in a final statement (vv. 17–18), the author asserts the potential value of wisdom over royal authority and military prowess, and yet admits the vulnerability of that wisdom, of its effectiveness, to human neglect and sin. **15:** Some traditional commentators (e.g., Rashi, Ibn Ezra) sought to mitigate the expression of vulnerability by proposing that *nobody thought of that poor man* does not refer to the time after he had saved the city, when people forgot his achievement, but to the time before, when his true wisdom was not yet known.

10.1–20: Maxims on wisdom and folly. The miscellany of maxims in this ch, a number of them expressed as oppositions between wisdom and folly, picks up several themes adumbrated earlier, but, again, with some new images. Thus, v. 1 links with the preceding 9.13–18 to describe how wisdom can be undone by just a little folly, but compares this now to flies that spoil fragrant oil. **4, 5–7, 16–17, 20:** In turn, the recognition of, respect for, even fear of social and political hierarchy, and the rulers at its top, which was evident in 5.7–8; 8.2–5, reappears here. **5–7:** But this recognition is formulated in a new image for Koheleth, though one well known elsewhere in the Bible (e.g., Prov. 30.21–23) and in other ancient Near Eastern traditions, esp. Egyptian and Mesopotamian, namely, the reversal of hierarchy as a sign of chaos and destruction and of the triumph of folly. This last point suggests that Koheleth in this ch has not given up on the rightness and power of wisdom. **8–11:** Accordingly, Koheleth gives us a series of maxims appealing to the honored convention of wisdom born of experience to show that there are rules in the world which dictate that certain actions, here described error committed by a ruler: ⁶Folly was placed on lofty heights, while rich men sat in low estate. ⁷I have seen slaves on horseback, and nobles walking on the ground like slaves.

⁸He who digs a pit will fall into it; he who breaches a stone fence will be bitten by a snake. ⁹He who quarries stones will ᵃbe hurt by them; he who splits wood will be harmed by⁻ᵃ it. ¹⁰ᵇIf the ax has become dull and he has not whetted the edge, he must exert more strength. Thus the advantage of a skill [depends on the exercise of] prudence. ¹¹If the snake bites because no spell was uttered, no advantage is gained by the trained charmer.

¹²A wise man's talk brings him favor, but a fool's lips are his undoing. ¹³His talk begins as silliness and ends as disastrous madness. ¹⁴Yet the fool talks and talks!

ᶜA man cannot know what will happen; who can tell him what the future holds?

¹⁵ᵈA fool's exertions tire him out, for he doesn't know how to get to a town.

¹⁶Alas for you, O land whose king is a lackey and whose ministers dine in the morning! ¹⁷Happy are you, O land whose king is a master and whose ministers dine at the proper time—with restraint, not with guzzling!

¹⁸   Through slothfulness the ceiling sags,
       Through lazy hands the house caves in.

¹⁹Theyᵉ make a banquet for revelry; wine makes life merry, and money answers every need.

²⁰   Don't revile a king even among your intimates.ᶠ
       Don't revile a rich man even in your bedchamber;
       For a bird of the air may carry the utterance,
       And a winged creature may report the word.

11 Send your bread forth upon the waters; for after many days you will find it. ²Distribute portions to seven or even to eight, for you cannot know what misfortune may occur on earth.

³If the clouds are filled, they will pour down rain on the

a-a *Emendation yields "profit . . . shall make use of."*
b *Meaning of verse uncertain.*
c *The thought of this sentence is resumed at v. 20.*
d *This verse continues the thought of v. 3.*
e *I.e., the ministers of v. 16.*   f *Others "thoughts"; meaning of Heb. uncertain.*

7.16–18). What follows, then, is a statement that no one can know what the future will bring (e.g., 3.22; 6.12). This statement might be taken to undermine the confidence Koheleth has been showing in the present ch in the value of wisdom, unless one returns to the view that wisdom is above all the faculty of knowing clearly what one cannot know. On the other hand, various Jewish commentators (e.g., Yosef Ibn Yachya, Moshe Alshich) note that this statement about ignorance of the future follows directly on the rebuke of the fool's prattling, and is then itself followed (v. 15) by another rebuke of the fool's wearisome behavior. So connected, the statement becomes an example of the fool's prattling—and, consequently, an implied criticism of Koheleth's earlier affirmation of the view it expresses. **16–18:** While these vv. take for granted the necessity of kingship, they sharply distinguish between wise and foolish rulers (cf. 4.13–14), between those who govern with propriety and restraint and those who endanger the community by acting as a simple, untested "young man" ("naʿar"; cf. its parallel with "simple-minded" in Prov. 1.4) and carousing lazily at all hours.

11.1–10: Seize the day, for the future is dark and uncertain. Three sections take up this theme, vv. 1–6, 7–8, 9–10. **1–6:** The initial advice, about casting bread and giving a portion, was understood by rabbinic Sages (e.g., *Eccl. Rab.*) to mean to act generously to others, because it may be repaid you, and even in a time of your own misfortune. The misfortune here, however, is probably the general uncertainty Koheleth has elsewhere expressed about the course of life, such that one should not be cowed by this uncertainty into avoiding a charitable deed. **2:** The sequence seven-eight is a conventional expression, in biblical and Canaanite literature, for a significant quantity. **3:** The following observations appear to move away from uncertainty as they describe

as largely negative, will inevitably bring their negative consequences. **12–14:** This is extended to an observation about speech, specifically about the contrast between a wise man's presumably measured speech and the favor it brings him, over against the fool's uncontrolled prattling and its disastrous results—all of this recalling earlier admonitions about the fool and the avoidance of excess (5.6; 6.11;

earth; and [a]if a tree falls to the south or to the north, the tree will stay where it falls.[-a] [4] If one watches the wind, he will never sow; and if one observes the clouds, he will never reap. [5] Just as you do not know how the lifebreath passes into[b] the limbs within the womb of the pregnant woman, so you cannot foresee the actions of God, who causes all things to happen. [6] Sow your seed in the morning, and don't hold back your hand in the evening, since you don't know which is going to succeed, the one or the other, or if both are equally good.

[7] How sweet is the light, what a delight for the eyes to behold the sun! [8] Even if a man lives many years, let him enjoy himself in all of them, remembering how many the days of darkness are going to be. The only future is nothingness!

[9] O youth, enjoy yourself while you are young! Let your heart lead you to enjoyment in the days of your youth. Follow the desires of your heart and the glances of your eyes—but know well that God will call you to account for all such things—[10] and banish care from your mind, and pluck sorrow out of your flesh! For youth and black hair are fleeting.

12 So appreciate your vigor[c] in the days of your youth, before those days of sorrow come and those years arrive of which you will say, "I have no pleasure in them"; [2] before sun and light and moon and stars grow dark, and the clouds come back again after the rain:

a-a *Emendation yields, "if a thunderbolt (lit. arrow, cf., e.g., 2 Sam. 22.15) falls . . . where the thunderbolt falls, only there will it strike."*

b *So many mss. and Targum; most mss. read "like."*

c *Cf. postbiblical* bori; *others "Remember thy Creator."*

inevitable cause-and-effect actions in the natural world. Yet uncertainty can be detected here indirectly in the matter of timing—a matter that Koheleth has already discussed explicitly several times, especially in 3.1–11. The point seems to be that even if humans know that clouds bring rain and trees fall, they cannot predict when these actions will occur. **4–5:** Thus, anyone who wastes too much time calculating the occurrence of meteorological phenomena will not get on with the basic activities of planting and reaping.

What humans do not know about nature, then, is confirmed by what they do not know about their own birth, and all of this only underscores that they do not understand the essential *actions* ("ma'aseh") of God, who is behind all of these and everything else. **6:** Summing up the whole matter, Koheleth returns to the earlier agricultural theme and asserts that faced with uncertainty about the future, it is better to sow and till than to do nothing, because at least then there is a chance of success. **7–8:** These vv. look at the "seize the day"

theme by contrasting the pleasure of living, expressed as the sweet goodness of experiencing the *light* of *the sun* (cf. 6.6; 7.11), with the coming days of darkness and the *nothingness* ("hevel") they bring—the days here referring to death and the pains of old age that immediately precede it (cf. 12.1–2; 6.3–4). Given the darkness that is to come, Koheleth again emphasizes that humans must enjoy life while they have it. **9–10:** This enjoyment is something best suited to the *young*, and so Koheleth advises them not to lose that opportunity, since youth is something *fleeting* ("hevel," echoing the "hevel" of v. 8, but in another of its senses). The observation that the way a young person behaves will eventually be judged by God has been regarded by some modern interpreters as an orthodox addition to the original text of Koheleth, since it presumably clashes with the uncertainty about knowing God that Koheleth otherwise expresses. But Koheleth's hope in the possibility of divine judgment was already stated in 3.17, where it seems natural to the context, and so it could be here.

12.1–8: The terrors of old age. A contrast with the previous unit about the pleasures of youth is made explicit in v. 1, *the days of your youth* and *those days of sorrow*. That vv. 1–8 is the last unit in the book attributed to Koheleth is signaled by the final v., 8; this is a virtual repetition of 1.2, which, following the introductory rubric, opens the book. To be sure, 1.2 gives the phrase *Utter futility* twice, while here, in the main Masoretic texts, it is given only once; it does, however, appear twice in some other Heb manuscripts and the ancient Syriac version. The virtual identity of 1.2 and 12.8 forms, thus, an inclusio and gives the book closure by symmetry; this is confirmed by the fact that the following vv., 9–14, function as an epilogue. That Koheleth's book ends, therefore, on the dark note of old age is no accident; rather, it reaffirms the transitory nature of

3   When the guards of the house[a] become shaky,
       And the men of valor[b] are bent,
       And the maids that grind,[c] grown few, are idle,
       And the ladies that peer through the windows[d]
         grow dim,

4   And the doors to the street[e] are shut—
       With the noise of the hand mill growing fainter,
       And the song of the bird [f]·growing feebler,·[f]
       And all the strains of music dying down;[g]

5   When one is afraid of heights
       And there is terror on the road.—
       For the almond tree may blossom,
       [h]·The grasshopper be burdened,·[h]
       And the caper bush may bud again;[i]
       But man sets out for his eternal abode,
       With mourners all around in the street.—

6   Before the silver cord snaps
       And the golden bowl crashes,
       The jar is shattered at the spring,
       And the jug[j] is smashed at the cistern.[k]

7   And the dust returns to the ground
       As it was,
       And the lifebreath returns to God
       Who bestowed it.

8   Utter futility—said Koheleth—
       All is futile!

[9] A further word: Because Koheleth was a sage, he continued to instruct the people. He listened to and tested the

a *I.e., the arms.*   b *I.e., the legs.*   c *I.e., the teeth.*   d *I.e., the eyes.*
e *I.e., the ears.*   f-f *Exact meaning of Heb. uncertain.*   g *Cf. 2 Sam. 19.36.*
h-h *Emendation yields "The squill (postbiblical Heb. ḥaṣab) resume its burden," i.e., its blossom-stalk and its leaves.*
i *These plants, after seeming dead for part of the year, revive, unlike man; cf. Job 14.7–10.*
j *So in Punic; others "wheel."*   k *Poetic figure for the end of life.*

life, with no certainty of continuity or afterward, that has been stated throughout (e.g., 2.18–21; 5.12–16; 9.5–6). In the present instance we have a graphic picture of the decrepitude of old age in a variety of images. **2:** The first is that of darkness and light, last discussed in 11.7–8. Here it is elaborated and intensified such that the darkness (of old age) envelops the light (of vigorous life), whether that light comes during the day (of the sun) or the night (the moon and the stars) (cf., e.g., Isa. 13.10; Ezek.

32.7–8). **3–4a:** This darkness, in turn, is connected with the weakening of basic human vocations: house managers, men of wealth or warriors, grinders of flour, sequestered women who have to look through windows; and of basic human activities: doors opening on the bustling business of the street-market, and grinding. **4b–5a:** All of these are finally linked up with nature—birds, almond trees, grasshoppers—and their decline or expressions of fear at the approaching darkness. What

these images denote has been debated. Classical rabbinic thought (see, e.g., *Eccl. Rab.*, Targum, Rashi) has suggested an allegory wherein the words for managers, men of wealth, etc. denote different parts of the human body, here thus in rapid deterioration. An alternative suggestion is that the images pertain to an estate of a wealthy landowner—echoing Koheleth's experiment in ch 2—which here is in serious decline. **5b–7:** Whatever the precise solution, the imagery clearly points to human death, given the references to funeral mourning, to the breaking of a pitcher used to raise water from a well (so Ibn Ezra; cf. Zech. 4.2–3), and to the return of each human body to dust, so echoing 3.20 and Gen. 3.19. **7:** Significantly, each human *lifebreath* ("ruaḥ"; cf. 11.5) will return to God who gave it, thus suggesting a difference from what is expressed in 3.19–21 and Gen. 3.19.

12.9–14: Editorial reflections. Interpreters, whether traditional Jewish or modern critical, generally agree that these final vv. constitute an epilogue, after the conclusion of the book of Koheleth proper. Many traditional Jewish interpreters assume that Koheleth/Solomon is still speaking here, but some (e.g., Rashbam) suppose that it is an editorial addition, a common opinion of modern critics. The formal indications of the separation of these vv. from the core of the book are twofold: the framework, noted above, that encloses 1.2–12.8; and the shift here to third-person discussion of Koheleth from the first-person remarks by him within 1.2–12.8. Since this third-person discussion echoes the introductory rubric of 1.1, the two together provide a second, larger framework around the one within 1.2–12.8. A third formal marker breaks vv. 9–14 into two parts, reflecting perhaps two separate editorial additions: 9–11 and 12–14, for each begins with the phrase *A further word.* **9–11:** These vv. identify Koheleth as a sage and describe his characteristic activity soundness[a] of many maxims. [10] Koheleth sought to discover useful sayings and recorded[b] genuinely truthful sayings. [11] The sayings of the wise are like goads, like nails fixed [c]in prodding sticks.[c] [d]They were given by one Shepherd.[d]

[12] A further word: [e]Against them,[e] my son, be warned! The making of many books is without limit And much study[f] is a wearying of the flesh. [13] The sum of the matter, when all is said and done: Revere God and observe His commandments! For this applies to all mankind: [14] that God will call every creature to account for [g]everything unknown,[g] be it good or bad.

The sum of the matter, when all is said and done: Revere God and observe His commandments! For this applies to all mankind.

a A noun, like dibber (Jer. 5.13), which occurs in such postbiblical phrases as shanim kethiq(qe)nan, "normal years" (lit. "years according to their propriety").

b Wekhathub is equivalent to wekhathob, an infinitive employed as in Esth. 9.16 and elsewhere.

c-c Meaning of Heb. uncertain. Others "are those that are composed in collections."

d-d Meaning of Heb. uncertain. Emendation yields "They are accounted as a sharp ox goad" (post-biblical mardea').

e-e Emendation yields "Slow, there!" Cf. Arabic mah and mah mah; so also mah (meh) in Prov. 31.2.

f Meaning of Heb. uncertain.

g-g Emendation yields "all their conduct."

of teaching by means of wise sayings, emphasizing the careful construction of the sayings (v. 9c) and their provocative impact, like the goads and pricks of a shepherd (v. 11) to control the animals under his supervision. **11:** Traditional interpretation identifies the *Shepherd* with Moses (e.g., Targum, *Eccl. Rab.*, Rashi). **12–14:** These vv. assert that with Koheleth's sayings collected, it is not desirable to add anything more (cf. Deut. 4.2; 13.1). Further, this second part strives to sum up Koheleth's teaching with the instruction (v. 13b) to fear (*revere*) God and to keep His commandments, a common trope in wisdom literature (cf. Prov. 1.7; Job 1.1; 28.28). **14:** The reason for this instruction is that God will bring every action, even if kept hidden up to this point, into judgment, whether for good or for ill. Significantly, when read in Jewish liturgy,

v. 13 and its instruction to fear and to keep is repeated after v. 14. This prevents the book from ending on a negative note (see the similar practice in Isaiah, Malachi, and Lamentations); it also has the effect of highlighting v. 13 as central to the meaning of the book. Some modern critics, on the other hand, have understood this instruction to fear and to keep as the work of a later orthodox editor, who wished to tone down, if not to reshape, what he regarded as the radical challenge of Koheleth to the tradition of God's covenantal demands with their assurance of a strict reward-and-punishment justice. It is true that the instruction here to keep God's commandments does not appear as such elsewhere in Koheleth (but cf. 8.5, where, however, the reference is to the command of a human king), but the other clause, to fear God, is

found (3.14; 5.6; 7.18; 8.12–13), as is the statement about God's judgment (3.17, cf. 3.15; 11.9). Thus, this concluding instruction may in fact be congruent with the views in the rest of the book. The point would be, in sum, that just because human rational inquiry leads nowhere, in terms of demonstrating a system of reward and punishment or lasting achievements, it does not invalidate the power and sovereignty of God nor disprove the possibility that in some way He does call everyone and everything to account.

Esther

IN JEWISH TRADITION, THE BOOK OF ESTHER, *megillat 'ester,* "the scroll of Esther," is inextricably bound up with the holiday of Purim. The book provides the raison d'etre for Purim; it supplies the etiology (story of its origin) for the holiday, authorizes its annual observance, and models how it is to be celebrated. Purim, the only biblical festival not mentioned in the Torah, needed a reason and an authorization. It gets its reason in the pseudohistorical tale of how the Jews were saved from their archenemy, and it gets its authorization in the letter of Mordecai (and Esther) that this book includes. The book of Esther is the centerpiece of the observance of Purim; it is traditionally read publicly in the synagogue on Purim eve and the following morning, accompanied by the noisy blotting out of Haman's name by children and adults, many of them dressed in funny costumes. Purim is a carnivalesque holiday, replete with mock reenactments of the Esther story, partying and excessive drinking, carnivals and masquerades, and a general sense of frivolity uncharacteristic of Jewish festivals. The Talmud (*b. Meg.* 7b) encourages one to get so drunk that one cannot distinguish between "Cursed be Haman" and "Blessed be Mordecai." Like Purim, the book is full of boisterous merrymaking—a comic farce for a carnivalesque holiday. The book sets the tone for the holiday, "days of feasting and merrymaking" (9.22). It also initiates the other customs of the holiday: sending (food) gifts to friends and neighbors and presents to the poor (9.22).

Esther is best read as a comedy. Rabbinic midrashim seem to have intuited this, and they add to the fun by their preposterous embellishments of the story and its characters, extending in the most unsubtle ways the farce or burlesque inherent in the book, with its bawdiness and slap-stick humor. The voyeurism of ch 1—drunken nobles hoping to ogle the queen—is made more explicit in the midrash (e.g., *Esth. Rab.*) on 1.11 that says that Vashti was bidden to appear "wearing a royal diadem" and nothing else, that is, naked. Ch 2, with its inside view of the harem, where the girls apply their cosmetics for a year in preparation for a night in the king's bed, is no less sexually suggestive. The lavishness of the Persian court and the ten drinking banquets in the story add to the aura of comic excess. The misunderstandings between Ahasuerus and Haman in chs 6 and 7, the climax of the plot, produce belly laughs. All of these attributes are characteristic of low comedy.

The story's plot is structured on improbabilities, exaggerations, misunderstandings, and reversals. Esther keeps her identity hidden although her relationship to Mordecai the Jew was known; an insignificant Jewish minority kills 75,000 of its enemies; Haman erects a seven-story stake for impaling his enemy. The characters are caricatures. Ahasuerus is a buffoon, never sure quite what to do, completely at the mercy of his ministers and servants, giving away his power without a thought. Haman is an erratic egomaniac, with wild mood swings, concerned only for his own honor and his enemy's disgrace. Even the heroes, Mordecai and Esther, seem one-dimensional and unrealistic. In fact, nothing about the events of the story is realistic, and therefore attempts to read history from it are misguided. The setting of the Persian court is authentic, but the events are fictional. There was no known Jewish queen of Persia. Moreover, the Persian empire was tolerant of its ethnic minorities and is an unlikely place for an edict to eradicate the Jewish population.

The story draws on conventional themes of ancient storytelling known from the Bible and from extrabiblical sources from the Persian period (especially Greek sources): a rivalry between courtiers (this one focusing on honor and shame), a woman who uses her charm to save her people, an ancient ethnic feud, hidden identities, and the triumph of the forces of good over the forces of evil. The portrayal of the Persian court is equally conventional, if at times made into a burlesque. Like the many Greek stories about Persia (in Herodotus and other contemporary works), Esther features royal luxury bordering on decadence, concern for protocol and legalities, wine parties, and the renowned communication system. Esther is, then, in tune with contemporary literary works about Persia. At the same time, it draws on biblical traditions, most significantly those about Saul and Agag, king of the Amalekites, who are reincarnated, as it were, in Mordecai and Haman. The stories of Joseph and Daniel also resemble Esther in that they feature Jewish courtiers in foreign courts. (The stories in Daniel chs 1–6 are roughly contemporary with Esther.) Finally, Esther echoes the book of Kings in its mention of royal annals, and some scholars have found other similar phraseology in the two books.

Noticeably absent is any mention of God or of religious observance (prayer, Jewish dietary restrictions, traditional modesty, and endogamous marriage). The Rabbis were troubled by Esther's marriage to a non-Jew, and solved the problem by explaining that she remained completely passive in the king's bed or that she never actually consummated the marriage. They also provide her with kosher food, although the Bible is silent about her diet (unlike Daniel, who became a vegetarian so as to maintain the Jewish dietary laws; see Dan. ch 1). Mordecai and the Jews mourn and fast, but do not pray—a most striking omission (Daniel also prays). In its omission of God and religion, the Hebrew text is highly unusual, so much so that in the Greek version of Esther there are prayers, the name of God occurs, and Esther desists from eating forbidden food and drinking forbidden wine. (There are other major differences in the Greek Esther as well, especially its tone.) It is not clear whether these religious items were part of the original story and then removed, or added to an original story that lacked them. The best explanation for their absence, especially the absence of God's name, is that, given that the story is so comic, at times bordering on lewd, such reticence about things religious is preferable, lest religion be debauched.

The book does have a serious side, and an important function as a Diaspora story, a story written about and for (and perhaps by) Jews of the Diaspora. As such, it promotes Jewish identity, solidarity within the Jewish community, and a strong connection with Jewish (biblical) tradition. It is more centered on the Diaspora than most Jewish works of its time; it does not refer to the land of Israel (other than the mention of the exile of Jehoiachin) or to the Temple. It addresses the inherent problems of a minority people, their vulnerability to political forces and government edicts, their lack of autonomy, and their dependence on royal favor and on the sagacity of their own leaders. More specifically, Haman's false claim about the Jews is a prototype of anti-Semitism, which must have been familiar enough to resonate with the book's original audience. In the end, though, the message is positive: Good triumphs and evil is eradicated; the threat of Jewish annihilation is averted and the Jewish community is assured of continuity and prosperity. It is no wonder that Haman became the symbol of later enemies of the Jews, and that "minor Purims" were celebrated in medieval and early modern times in communities where great danger was averted. The psychological release that is embodied in a carnivalesque holiday like Purim and in the book of Esther lends itself to similar celebrations of the communal triumph over danger. The book succeeds in putting a serious message in a comic form.

The book was probably written sometime between 400 and 300 BCE, toward the end of the Persian period. It apparently adapted an earlier tale about Mordecai, Esther, and Haman and shaped it into an etiology of Purim, a holiday whose origin is lost in obscurity. The story appears in rather different form in the Greek version of Esther (LXX), where it has six major additions not found in the Masoretic version plus a number of other significant differences throughout the story. The Greek version is less comic and more melodramatic, and in its present form it reflects Hellenistic concerns (Jewish ritual observance, including circumcision) not found in the surviving Hebrew version. An ancient body of midrashic interpretation attaches to Esther, found in the Talmud (*b. Meg.* 10b–17a), in Josephus's paraphrase (*Antiquity of the Jews*, Book 11, ch 6), in the two Targumim (Aramaic renderings) to Esther, and in several midrashic collections. There is no consensus on the date of the book's canonization, partly because there is no consensus on the date of the canonization of the Kethuvim. Some scholars put it as early as the mid-2nd century BCE; others date it to the 1st century CE. Interestingly, Esther is the only biblical book of which no remnant has been found at Qumran; apparently the Dead Sea community did not preserve this book (although they seem to have had stories of the same genre), perhaps because they did not observe Purim, which according to their 364-day calendar would always fall on the Sabbath, creating a conflict of observance (according to the Jewish calendar now in use, Purim can never fall on the Sabbath).   [ADELE BERLIN]

1 It happened in the days of Ahasuerus—that Ahasuerus who reigned over a hundred and twenty-seven provinces from India to Ethiopia. [2] In those days, when King Ahasuerus occupied the royal throne in the fortress[a] Shushan, [3] in the third year of his reign, he gave a banquet for all the officials and courtiers—the administration of Persia and Media, the nobles and the governors of the provinces in his service. [4] For no fewer than a hundred and eighty days he displayed the vast riches of his kingdom and the splendid glory of his majesty. [5] At the end of this period, the king gave a banquet for seven days in the court of the king's palace garden for all the people who lived in the fortress Shushan, high and low alike. [6] [b][There were hangings of] white cotton and blue wool, caught up by cords of fine linen and purple wool to silver rods and alabaster columns; and there were couches of gold and silver on a pavement of marble, alabaster, mother-of-pearl, and mosaics. [7] Royal wine was served in abundance, as befits a king, in golden beakers, beakers of varied design. [8] And the rule for the drinking was, "No restrictions!" For the king had given orders to every palace steward to comply with each man's wishes. [9] In addition, Queen Vashti gave a banquet for women, in the royal palace of King Ahasuerus.

[10] On the seventh day, when the king was merry with wine, he ordered Mehuman, Bizzetha, Harbona, Bigtha, Abagtha, Zethar, and Carcas, the seven eunuchs in atten-

---

a I.e., the fortified city.   b Meaning of part of this verse uncertain.

1.1–22: Wine and women. This ch is a prologue to the main story, setting the scene and the tone: luxury, bureaucracy, and bawdiness—all to excess. The Persian court is decadently lavish and mired in protocol. King Ahasuerus is all-powerful and totally inept. The dismissal of Vashti paves the way for Esther's entrance. **1–8: Wine: partytime in Persia.** We enter the opulent Persian court, filled from ceiling to floor with expensive and exotic furnishings, exquisite drinking-vessels, and then the wine, the cause of all that is to follow. **1:** *Ahasuerus,* usually identified with Xerxes I (reigned 486–465 BCE), although the Septuagint and the Peshitta read Artaxerxes. But this Ahasuerus is a fictional character, a comic figurehead concerned with the trappings of

power but exercising little of his own. *From India to Ethiopia:* The extent of his sovereignty shows how powerful he was. The Persian empire stretched from "Hi(n)dush"—the area in the Indus valley, in the modern province of Sind in southern Pakistan—to "Nubia," south of Egypt, and is described in these terms in Persian documents. *A hundred and twenty-seven provinces:* This is one of several large numbers that add to the tone of exaggeration. **2:** *The fortress Shushan:* Susa, one of the four Persian capitals (besides Ecbatana [Hamadan], Babylon, and Persepolis), was the main administrative capital and the king's winter residence. The *fortress* refers to the acropolis, the seat of the government, and *Shushan* or

"the city of Shushan" refers to the lower city. **3–5:** The king displays his wealth. This scene parodies the Persian institution of the "King's Table," an occasion for the bringing of tribute from the provinces and the bestowing of gifts from the king to high officials. Persian palaces at Persepolis and Susa had large assembly halls (Persian, "apadana," Heb, "bitan") separate from the palace. **7:** Persian parties were famous for their wine-drinking. Herodotus (*Histories* 1.133) notes that the Persians decided important issues when they were drunk and reconsidered when they were sober, and vice versa. Ahasuerus will not have a chance to reconsider (cf. 2.1–2). **8:** *The rule for the drinking was, "No restrictions!":* The usual drinking practice was not followed. The best explanation is that the wine normally reserved "by royal law" for the exclusive use of the king was served to the guests. The phrase is then better translated "As for drinking according to the rule, no one enforced it." Many commentaries, however, take the phrase as a reference to the amount of wine: Each man could drink as much or as little as he liked.

1.9–22: Women: the Vashti incident. 9: It was considered indecent for wives of the Persian nobility to attend male drinking parties; the only female attendees were dancing girls. Therefore the queen hosted a separate party for the women. **10:** The tongue-twisting names of the servants are Persian-sounding, but probably fake. The names in v. 14 mirror this list (Mehuman/Memucan, and so forth). **11:** Just as the king has displayed his wealth, so he wishes to display his queen. Just as the royal wine is not reserved exclusively for the king, so the king's wife is not kept for his eyes alone. *A royal diadem,* a mark of belonging to the royal household. **12:** Vashti tries to protect her own honor and her drunken husband's, but must disobey a royal command to do so. **13:** Ever concerned with the dance on King Ahasuerus, [11] to bring Queen Vashti before the king wearing a royal diadem, to display her beauty to the peoples and the officials; for she was a beautiful woman. [12] But Queen Vashti refused to come at the king's command conveyed by the eunuchs. The king was greatly incensed, and his fury burned within him.

[13] Then the king consulted the sages learned in procedure.[a] (For it was the royal practice [to turn] to all who were versed in law and precedent. [14] His closest advisers were Carshena, Shethar, Admatha, Tarshish, Meres, Marsena, and Memucan, the seven ministers of Persia and Media who had access to the royal presence and occupied the first place in the kingdom.) [15] "What," [he asked,] "shall be done, according to law, to Queen Vashti for failing to obey the command of King Ahasuerus conveyed by the eunuchs?"

[16] Thereupon Memucan declared in the presence of the king and the ministers: "Queen Vashti has committed an offense not only against Your Majesty but also against all the officials and against all the peoples in all the provinces of King Ahasuerus. [17] For the queen's behavior will make all wives despise their husbands, as they reflect that King Ahasuerus himself ordered Queen Vashti to be brought before him, but she would not come. [18] This very day the ladies of Persia and Media, who have heard of the queen's behavior, will cite it to all Your Majesty's officials, and there will be no end of scorn and provocation!

[19] "If it please Your Majesty, let a royal edict be issued by you, and let it be written into the laws of Persia and Media, so that it cannot be abrogated, that Vashti shall never enter the presence of King Ahasuerus. And let Your Majesty bestow her royal state upon another who is more worthy than she. [20] Then will the judgment executed by Your Majesty resound throughout your realm, vast though it is; and all wives will treat their husbands with respect, high and low alike."

[21] The proposal was approved by the king and the ministers, and the king did as Memucan proposed. [22] Dispatches were sent to all the provinces of the king, to every province in its own script and to every nation in its own language, that every man should wield authority in his home and speak the language of his own people.

2 Some time afterward, when the anger of King Ahasuerus subsided, he thought of Vashti and what she had done and what had been decreed against her. [2] The king's

a Lit. "the times."

proper way of doing things, the king consults *sages learned in procedure,* the legal experts, or better, the experts in protocol. *Law,* Heb "dat," from the Persian "data," occurs nineteen times in the book, with meanings ranging from "law" to "custom" to "practice." In later Heb, it means "religion"; there is no biblical word for "religion." **16–22:** A domestic incident becomes a national crisis. The danger Memucan sees in Vashti's refusal is preposterous, as is his solution. His attempt to preserve the king's honor makes the king look even sillier and more vulnerable. **19:** Vashti refused to appear, and now she may never appear again. *Cannot be abrogated,* generally understood to mean that a law cannot be revoked, but the expression more likely means "may not be broken" or "to which there is no exception." (Cf. 8.5, 8.) Memucan may have said this out of concern that the king himself will want to make an exception and take Vashti back. **22:** *Dispatches were sent:* The Persians were noted for their excellent communications network. See also 3.12–13; 8.9–14, where the dispatches become progressively more urgent. *To every province in its own script and to every nation* [or "people"] *in its own language:* This would ensure that the edict could be understood by all in the multiethnic empire. The usual practice was for communications to be promulgated in Aramaic, the common language of the empire, and to be translated locally. *That every man should wield authority in his home:* This is not the wording of the edict but the reason for its publication. Cf. 3.14; 8.13; and perhaps 9.21. *Speak the language of his own people,* a difficult phrase, perhaps meaning that the dispatches were sent in vernacular languages so that every husband could readily understand the message and report the contents to his wife.

2.1–18: Mordecai enters the story and Esther enters the harem. 2: The advisers suggest a replacement for Vashti before Ahasuerus can decide to take her back.

servants who attended him said, "Let beautiful young virgins be sought out for Your Majesty. ³ Let Your Majesty appoint officers in every province of your realm to assemble all the beautiful young virgins at the fortress Shushan, in the harem under the supervision of Hege, the king's eunuch, guardian of the women. Let them be provided with their cosmetics. ⁴ And let the maiden who pleases Your Majesty be queen instead of Vashti." The proposal pleased the king, and he acted upon it.

⁵ In the fortress Shushan lived a Jew by the name of Mordecai, son of Jair son of Shimei son of Kish, a Benjaminite. ⁶ [Kish] had been exiled from Jerusalem in the group that was carried into exile along with King Jeconiah of Judah, which had been driven into exile by King Nebuchadnezzar of Babylon.—⁷ He was foster father to Hadassah—that is, Esther—his uncle's daughter, for she had neither father nor mother. The maiden was shapely and beautiful; and when her father and mother died, Mordecai adopted her as his own daughter.

⁸ When the king's order and edict was proclaimed, and when many girls were assembled in the fortress Shushan under the supervision of Hegai,ᵃ Esther too was taken into the king's palace under the supervision of Hegai, guardian of the women. ⁹ The girl pleased him and won his favor, and he hastened to furnish her with her cosmetics and her rations, as well as with the seven maids who were her due from the king's palace; and he treated her and her maids with special kindness in the harem. ¹⁰ Esther did not reveal her people or her kindred, for Mordecai had told her not to reveal it. ¹¹ Every single day Mordecai would walk about in front of the court of the harem, to learn how Esther was faring and what was happening to her.

¹² When each girl's turn came to go to King Ahasuerus at the end of the twelve months' treatment prescribed for women (for that was the period spent on beautifying them: six months with oil of myrrh and six months with perfumes and women's cosmetics, ¹³ and it was after that that the girl would go to the king), whatever she asked for would be given her to take with her from the harem to the king's palace. ¹⁴ She would go in the evening and leave in the morning for a second harem in charge of Shaashgaz, the king's eunuch, guardian of the concubines. She would not go again to the king unless the king wanted her, when she would be summoned by name. ¹⁵ When the turn came for Esther daughter of Abihail—the uncle of Mordecai,

4: A beauty contest is hardly the way real queens of Persia were chosen. In fact, Persian queens had to be from the Persian nobility. 5–7: Mordecai is a prominent upper-class Jew of the Babylonian exile, with an obliquely expressed link to King Saul. 5: *A Jew by the name of Mordecai:* "Yehudi" does not refer to a member of the tribe of Judah (Mordecai was from the tribe of Benjamin), but to a Jew from the kingdom of Judah (where all the Babylonian exiles were from); this is the beginning of the usage of "Jew" in the sense that we now know it. "Mordecai" was a common personal name in the Persian period (cf. Neh. 7.7); "Marduka" was its Babylonian form. It is not a direct reference to the Babylonian god Marduk (just as Esther is not a reference to the goddess Ishtar). *Shimei:* According to rabbinic interpretation, this is Shimei son of Gera, the member of Saul's clan who supported him against David (2 Sam. 16.5–8); this book, in contrast to Samuel, reflects favorably on Saul and his household and on the tribe of Benjamin. 6: *[Kish],* better, "he." The reference is most likely to Mordecai, who, like Daniel, was exiled from Jerusalem—a sign of authentic Jewish pedigree in the Diaspora. Because this would make Mordecai incredibly old (115 years), traditional Jewish exegesis prefers to understand Kish as the person exiled. 7: Esther is introduced indirectly, through the introduction of Mordecai; her patronymic is not given until v. 15. "Hadassah" means "myrtle." "Esther" is probably derived from the Persian name for "star." It was not uncommon for Diaspora Jews to have both a Heb and a vernacular name, as did Daniel and his friends, and Judah Maccabee. If Mordecai had a Heb name, it is not mentioned. 10: It stretches credibility to imagine that Esther could keep her ethnic identity a secret, but it is vital to the plot. 12: *Oil of myrrh:* Myrrh is associated with love-making (Song 1.13; Prov. 7.17). The excess continues, along with the bureaucracy.

a Identical with Hege in v. 3.

who had adopted her as his own daughter—to go to the king, she did not ask for anything but what Hegai, the king's eunuch, guardian of the women, advised. Yet Esther won the admiration of all who saw her.

[16] Esther was taken to King Ahasuerus, in his royal palace, in the tenth month, which is the month of Tebeth, in the seventh year of his reign. [17] The king loved Esther more than all the other women, and she won his grace and favor more than all the virgins. So he set a royal diadem on her head and made her queen instead of Vashti. [18] The king gave a great banquet for all his officials and courtiers, "the banquet of Esther." He proclaimed a remission of taxes[a] for the provinces and distributed gifts as befits a king.

[19b] When the virgins were assembled a second time, Mordecai sat in the palace gate. [20] But Esther still did not reveal her kindred or her people, as Mordecai had instructed her; for Esther obeyed Mordecai's bidding, as she had done when she was under his tutelage.

[21] At that time, when Mordecai was sitting in the palace gate, Bigthan and Teresh, two of the king's eunuchs who guarded the threshold, became angry, and plotted to do away with King Ahasuerus. [22] Mordecai learned of it and told it to Queen Esther, and Esther reported it to the king in Mordecai's name. [23] The matter was investigated and found to be so, and the two were impaled on stakes. This was recorded in the book of annals at the instance of the king.

3 Some time afterward, King Ahasuerus promoted Haman son of Hammedatha the Agagite; he advanced him and seated him higher than any of his fellow officials. [2] All the king's courtiers in the palace gate knelt and bowed low to Haman, for such was the king's order con-

a Or "an amnesty."   b Meaning of verse uncertain.

not rewarded; the lack of reward will be remembered in 6.2. A rabbinic principle is derived from this verse: "A person who quotes something in the name of the one who said it brings about the redemption of the world" (*m. ʾAvot* 6.6). **23:** *Impaled on stakes:* Impalement was not the method of execution but a way of disgracing a person through the public display of his corpse. (Cf. Gen. 40.19; Deut. 21.22; Josh. 8.29; 10.26; 1 Sam. 31.10.) Herodotus (*Histories* 3.125; 7.238; cf. 9.79) also mentions the impalement of corpses as a sign of great disgrace. This is the first impalement in the story and foreshadows Haman's plot to impale Mordecai.

3.1–15: Haman plots to kill the Jews. The main plot, the rivalry between the two courtiers, begins here. The personal rivalry between Haman and Mordecai quickly takes on national implications. **1:** *Promoted Haman:* Mordecai's good deed in saving the king's life goes unrewarded while Haman is promoted for no apparent reason. *The Agagite,* a descendant of Agag, the Amalekite king responsible for Saul's loss of the kingship (1 Sam. 15.8). The ancient enmity between Israel and Amalek informs the relationship between Haman and Mordecai. The Amalekite connection is reinforced in the synagogue lectionary cycle by the reading, on the Sabbath preceding Purim, of the passage in Deut. 25.17–19 ("Remember what Amalek did to you . . . you shall blot out the memory of Amalek") and the haftarah from 1 Sam. ch 15 (containing the story of Saul and Agag). On Purim itself the Torah reading is Exod. 17.8–16, the battle between Israel and Amalek. Both Targumim to Esther extend Haman's genealogy back to Esau, echoing Gen. 36.12, thereby extending the rivalry between Mordecai and Haman even further back to Esau and Jacob. **2:** *Would not kneel or bow low:* Mordecai's refusal is not based on religious principles, for biblical Jews or Israelites may bow to superiors (Gen. 23.7; 43.28; Exod. 18.7; 1 Kings

14: *Second harem:* Perhaps there was a second harem, but more likely the women return to the same harem, this time to be looked after by *Shaashgaz.* **16:** *The tenth month, which is the month of Tebeth:* In Zechariah, Ezra, Nehemiah, and Esther a double system of naming months is used: the ordinal number of the more ancient Israelite calendar and the month name, adopted from the Babylonian calendar via Aramaic. **17:** *Women . . . virgins,* all the women who have already come and all the virgins

yet to come. *A royal diadem,* perhaps the same diadem that Vashti was bidden to appear with in 1.11. **19:** This v. is difficult, and may be a scribal error. **21–23:** Mordecai uncovers a plot against the king. **21:** *In the palace gate,* "the king's gate." More than a physical location, this is Mordecai's official position at court. Mordecai is a member of the king's secret police. **22:** Mordecai's job is to ferret out plots against the king. *In Mordecai's name:* Mordecai's loyalty to the king is demonstrated but he is cerning him; but Mordecai would not kneel or bow low. [3] Then the king's courtiers who were in the palace gate said to Mordecai, "Why do you disobey the king's order?" [4] When they spoke to him day after day and he would not listen to them, they told Haman, in order to see whether Mordecai's resolve would prevail; for he had explained to them that he was a Jew.[a] [5] When Haman saw that Mordecai would not kneel or bow low to him, Haman was filled with rage. [6] But he disdained to lay hands on Mordecai alone; having been told who Mordecai's people were, Haman plotted to do away with all the Jews, Mordecai's people, throughout the kingdom of Ahasuerus.

[7] In the first month, that is, the month of Nisan, in the twelfth year of King Ahasuerus, *pur*—which means "the lot"—was cast before Haman concerning every day and every month, [until it fell on] the twelfth month, that is, the month of Adar. [8] Haman then said to King Ahasuerus, "There is a certain people, scattered and dispersed among the other peoples in all the provinces of your realm, whose laws are different from those of any other people and who do not obey the king's laws; and it is not in Your Majesty's interest to tolerate them. [9] If it please Your Majesty, let an edict be drawn for their destruction, and I will pay ten thousand talents of silver to the stewards for deposit in the royal treasury." [10] Thereupon the king removed his signet ring from his hand and gave it to Haman son of Hammedatha the Agagite, the foe of the Jews. [11] And the king said, "The money and the people are yours to do with as you see fit."

[12] On the thirteenth day of the first month, the king's scribes were summoned and a decree was issued, as Haman directed, to the king's satraps, to the governors of every province, and to the officials of every people, to every province in its own script and to every people in its own language. The orders were issued in the name of King Ahasuerus and sealed with the king's signet. [13] Accordingly, written instructions were dispatched by couriers to all the king's provinces to destroy, massacre, and exterminate all the Jews, young and old, children and women, on a single day, on the thirteenth day of the twelfth month—that is, the month of Adar—and to plunder their possessions. [14] The text of the document was to the effect that a law should be proclaimed in every single province; it was to be publicly displayed to all the peoples, so that they might be ready for that day.

1.23), but on ethnic grounds so as not to give honor to an enemy of Israel. Rabbinic interpretation recasts the refusal in terms of a religious prohibition, saying that Haman was wearing an image of an idol on his chest and that in bowing to him Mordecai would be bowing to an idol. Another rabbinic explanation (also found in the LXX and at home in the Hellenistic and Roman periods) is that it was improper to bow to anyone but God. **5:** *Filled with rage:* The mercurial mood-swings of Haman begin. Haman is a glutton for honor, as will become more evident in ch 6. **6:** *Mordecai's people:* Haman is motivated by both personal and ethnic reasons. **7:** *Pur,* from Akkadian; the practice of casting lots by means of a small stone die is known from ancient Mesopotamia. Similar techniques were used in Israel and Greece. The propitious month is Adar but no date is given until v. 13. **8:** Haman's accusation against the Jews contains the essence of what was later to grow into the classic anti-Semitic argument that the Jews are xenophobic and misanthropic. Haman is implying (falsely) that the Jews do not acknowledge the sovereignty of the king, and are therefore guilty of treason. The irony is that Mordecai demonstrated his loyalty to the king at the end of ch 2. *It is not in Your Majesty's interest:* Heb "shoveh" may also mean "profit," that is, there is no profit for the king in letting the Jews live. **9:** Haman offers an inducement to the king in the form of revenue for the royal treasury. Perhaps it is to offset any loss of taxes that might have been paid by the Jews, or perhaps simply a bribe. *Ten thousand talents of silver,* estimated to be 333 tons or 302 metric tons of silver—an enormous amount, close to the total sum of the annual tribute of the entire Persian empire. Another exaggerated number in a story full of exaggerations. **10:** *Signet ring,* the authority to sign and seal a royal edict. **12:** *Its own script . . . its own language,* see 1.22. **13:** *To plunder their possessions,*

---

a I.e., that as a Jew he could not bow to a descendant of Agag, the Amalekite king; see 1 Sam. 15, and cf. Exod. 17.14–16; Deut. 25.17–19.

15 The couriers went out posthaste on the royal mission, and the decree was proclaimed in the fortress Shushan. The king and Haman sat down to feast, but the city of Shushan was dumbfounded.

4 When Mordecai learned all that had happened, Mordecai tore his clothes and put on sackcloth and ashes. He went through the city, crying out loudly and bitterly, 2 until he came in front of the palace gate; for one could not enter the palace gate wearing sackcloth.—3 Also, in every province that the king's command and decree reached, there was great mourning among the Jews, with fasting, weeping, and wailing, and everybody lay in sackcloth and ashes.—4 When Esther's maidens and eunuchs came and informed her, the queen was greatly agitated. She sent clothing for Mordecai to wear, so that he might take off his sackcloth; but he refused. 5 Thereupon Esther summoned Hathach, one of the eunuchs whom the king had appointed to serve her, and sent him to Mordecai to learn the why and wherefore of it all. 6 Hathach went out to Mordecai in the city square in front of the palace gate; 7 and Mordecai told him all that had happened to him, and all about the money that Haman had offered to pay into the royal treasury for the destruction of the Jews. 8 He also gave him the written text of the law that had been proclaimed in Shushan for their destruction. [He bade him] show it to Esther and inform her, and charge her to go to the king and to appeal to him and to plead with him for her people. 9 When Hathach came and delivered Mordecai's message to Esther, 10 Esther told Hathach to take back to Mordecai the following reply: 11 "All the king's courtiers and the people of the king's provinces know that if any person, man or woman, enters the king's presence in the inner court without having been summoned, there is but one law for him—that he be put to death. Only if the king extends the golden scepter to him may he live. Now I have not been summoned to visit the king for the last thirty days."

12 When Mordecai was told what Esther had said, 13 Mordecai had this message delivered to Esther: "Do not imagine that you, of all the Jews, will escape with your life by being in the king's palace. 14 On the contrary, if you keep silent in this crisis, relief and deliverance will come to the Jews from another quarter, while you and your father's house will perish. And who knows, perhaps you have attained to royal position for just such a crisis." 15 Then Esther sent back this answer to Mordecai: 16 "Go, assemble all the Jews who live in Shushan, and fast in my

cf. 8.11; see 9.10 n. **15:** *The couriers went out posthaste,* cf. 8.14. *Sat down to feast,* more partying, as if nothing out of the ordinary had happened, in contrast with the reaction of the city and of the Jews in 4.1. *The city of Shushan was dumbfounded:* The decree is shocking to normal people. The counterpart is in 8.15.

4.1–17: Mordecai and Esther plan to save their people. Mourning replaces partying, at least among the Jews. God's presence is most strongly felt in this ch, although His absence from the text is maintained. **1:** Typical signs of grief (Jonah 3.6; Neh. 9.1), which also serve here as a public protest. **4:** The harem, formerly a place of indulgence, is now a place of constriction for Esther. She cannot leave it and Mordecai cannot enter it. *So that he might take off his sackcloth:* This would mean he could enter the palace precinct, as in 2.11. **8:** The book's emphasis on written texts is felt even here. **11:** Esther takes the initiative, hinting at the strategy she will use to carry out Mordecai's instructions. *Man or woman,* even a woman of whom the king may be enamored. Esther has no special privilege in this regard. *Enters the king's presence in the inner court:* Mordecai said nothing about going to the *inner court;* this is Esther's idea. There were other ways to communicate with the king, as we know from 2.2. Esther is not refusing to plead for the Jews. Rather, she is outlining a daring plan to do so. **14:** *From another quarter:* In Jewish tradition "mi-makom ʾaḥer" is interpreted as a reference to God, who is called "Ha-makom," i.e., "Omnipresent," in rabbinic writings. This is as close as the author can get to hinting at divine intervention in a book where God's name is studiously avoided. *You and your father's house will perish:* Mordecai is all that is left of Esther's father's house. The point is to personalize the danger to Esther (cf. Amos 7.17). **16–17:** Esther now gives the orders and Mordecai carries them out; a reversal behalf; do not eat or drink for three days, night or day. I and my maidens will observe the same fast. Then I shall go to the king, though it is contrary to the law; and if I am to perish, I shall perish!" ¹⁷ So Mordecai went about [the city] and did just as Esther had commanded him.

5 On the third day, Esther put on royal apparel and stood in the inner court of the king's palace, facing the king's palace, while the king was sitting on his royal throne in the throne room facing the entrance of the palace. ² As soon as the king saw Queen Esther standing in the court, she won his favor. The king extended to Esther the golden scepter which he had in his hand, and Esther approached and touched the tip of the scepter. ³ "What troubles you, Queen Esther?" the king asked her. "And what is your request? Even to half the kingdom, it shall be granted you." ⁴ "If it please Your Majesty," Esther replied, "let Your Majesty and Haman come today to the feast that I have prepared for him." ⁵ The king commanded, "Tell Haman to hurry and do Esther's bidding." So the king and Haman came to the feast that Esther had prepared.

⁶ At the wine feast, the king asked Esther, "What is your wish? It shall be granted you. And what is your request? Even to half the kingdom, it shall be fulfilled." ⁷ "My wish," replied Esther, "my request—⁸ if Your Majesty will do me the favor, if it please Your Majesty to grant my wish and accede to my request—let Your Majesty and Haman come to the feast which I will prepare for them; and tomorrow I will do Your Majesty's bidding."

⁹ That day Haman went out happy and lighthearted. But when Haman saw Mordecai in the palace gate, and Mordecai did not rise or even stir on his account, Haman was filled with rage at him. ¹⁰ Nevertheless, Haman controlled himself and went home. He sent for his friends and his wife Zeresh, ¹¹ and Haman told them about his great wealth and his many sons, and all about how the king had promoted him and advanced him above the officials and the king's courtiers. ¹² "What is more," said Haman, "Queen Esther gave a feast, and besides the king she did not have anyone but me. And tomorrow too I am invited by her along with the king. ¹³ Yet all this means nothing to me every time I see that Jew Mordecai sitting in the palace gate." ¹⁴ Then his wife Zeresh and all his friends said to him, "Let a stake be put up, fifty cubits high, and in the morning ask the king to have Mordecai impaled on it. Then you can go gaily with the king to the feast." The proposal pleased Haman, and he had the stake put up.

from 2.10, 20. **16:** *Do not eat or drink for three days*, an unrealistically long fast. The post-talmudic Fast of Esther lasts from sunrise until sundown on 'Adar 13, not the date given here. *If I am to perish, I shall perish:* Mordecai says she will perish if she doesn't go to the king (v. 14); here Esther is resigned to the possibility of perishing if she does go to the king.

5.1–8: Esther's audience with the king. Esther carries out the first part of her strategy. The happy mood returns and the partying resumes. **1:** *Put on royal apparel*, dressed in her official garb as queen, for a formal audience with the king. *Inner court*, the area where it was forbidden to come unsummoned (4.11). **3:** *Even to half the kingdom*, an idiom for a large gift, cf. "half your household" (1 Kings 13.8). **4:** Esther's language is very formal but she deflects the king's magnanimous offer and instead invites him to a banquet. **7–8:** On the verge of stating her request, Esther interrupts herself with another invitation—the result is comic. **8:** *I will prepare for them,* cf. v. 4: "I have prepared for him." Now the party is as much for Haman as for the king—a clever rhetorical move to make Haman think he was the center of attention. And so he will be. The pronouns change to fit the audience. In v. 4, only the king was present; now both the king and Haman are present. Cf. the words of Potiphar's wife in Gen. 39.14, 17. **9–14:** Haman's mood-swings. Seeing Mordecai spoils all the fun. **9:** *Did not rise or even stir:* Worse than not bowing (3.2), here Mordecai makes no motion at all to acknowledge Haman. **11:** *His great wealth and his many sons*, signs of success (cf. Job 1.1–3). Haman will lose both (8.1; 9.6–10). **12:** The invitation to dine privately with the king and queen is the most recent and highest in a string of honors. **13:** *That Jew Mordecai:* The person and his people continue to irritate Haman. *Sitting in the palace gate:* The very presence of Mordecai is enough to upset Haman. More-

6 That night, sleep deserted the king, and he ordered the book of records, the annals, to be brought; and it was read to the king. ²There it was found written that Mordecai had denounced Bigthana and Teresh, two of the king's eunuchs who guarded the threshold, who had plotted to do away with King Ahasuerus. ³"What honor or advancement has been conferred on Mordecai for this?" the king inquired. "Nothing at all has been done for him," replied the king's servants who were in attendance on him. ⁴"Who is in the court?" the king asked. For Haman had just entered the outer court of the royal palace, to speak to the king about having Mordecai impaled on the stake he had prepared for him. ⁵"It is Haman standing in the court," the king's servants answered him. "Let him enter," said the king. ⁶Haman entered, and the king asked him, "What should be done for a man whom the king desires to honor?" Haman said to himself, "Whom would the king desire to honor more than me?" ⁷So Haman said to the king, "For the man whom the king desires to honor, ⁸let royal garb which the king has worn be brought, and a horse on which the king has ridden and on whose head a royal diadem has been set; ⁹and let the attire and the horse be put in the charge of one of the king's noble courtiers. And let the man whom the king desires to honor be attired and paraded on the horse through the city square, while they proclaim before him: This is what is done for the man whom the king desires to honor!" ¹⁰"Quick, then!" said the king to Haman. "Get the garb and the horse, as you have said, and do this to Mordecai the Jew, who sits in the king's gate. Omit nothing of all you have proposed." ¹¹So Haman took the garb and the horse and arrayed Mordecai and paraded him through the city square; and he proclaimed before him: This is what is done for the man whom the king desires to honor!

The king speaks first, as is proper, and Haman never gets a chance to state why he came. **8:** The ceremony that Haman designs goes beyond the conventional ways of honoring those favored by the king. It is calculated to make Haman appear to be the king. *Royal garb which the king has worn,* clothing actually worn by the king. According to Gk sources (Plutarch, *Artaxerxes* 5), this is tantamount to asking for the kingship. *A horse on which the king has ridden and on whose head a royal diadem has been set,* the king's own horse, marked as such by a special diadem on its head. Another sign that Haman wants to replace the king. Cf. 1 Kings 1.32–49. The nexus between the throne and the horse (a portable throne, as it were) can be seen in *m. Sanh.* 2.5, which forbids one to ride on the king's horse, to sit on his throne, or to use his scepter. The only sign of a grab for the throne that is missing is taking the king's wife, and that is what Ahasuerus accuses Haman of in 7.8. **9:** *One of the king's noble courtiers:* The king will choose the noblest, Haman himself. *Be paraded:* The Heb means "be mounted" or "be placed to ride." The honoree should be mounted on a *horse in the city square,* visible to all. If this is where Mordecai was stationed in 4.6, then Haman would be publicly honored right in front of Mordecai. **10:** *Mordecai the Jew, who sits in the king's gate:* Ahasuerus's description of Mordecai includes exactly those characteristics that antagonize Haman. Haman hates the Jews, and gets upset every time he sees Mordecai sitting in the king's gate (5.9, 13). **11:** The last time Mordecai was in the city square (4.6) he was dressed in mourning garb. What a reversal! Some midrashim embellish the scene, adding to Haman's subservience and dishonor, by imagining the preparations to include Haman's washing of Mordecai, since he was still covered in the ashes of mourning (and even having to wash the bath house), dressing him, and lowering himself so that Mordecai could step upon his neck

over, Mordecai is *sitting;* he did not rise or stir (v. 9). **14:** Haman does not himself come up with the idea of impaling Mordecai, but quickly accepts it. *Fifty cubits high:* About seventy-five feet, as tall as a seven-story building. Not even Persian palaces were that tall; this is another exaggerated number. *Impaled on it,* the ultimate form of disgrace. See 2.23.

6.1–11: Haman designs a ceremony to honor himself, but must honor Mordecai instead. A comic misunderstanding makes this ch

one of the funniest in the book. **1:** *That night,* the same night that Haman erected a stake for Mordecai. *The book of records,* cf. 2.23. **2:** *Mordecai had denounced:* The plot had been reported in Mordecai's name (2.22). **4:** *Haman had just entered the outer court:* One could enter the outer court without a royal summons, but not the inner court (4.11). Haman had come to obtain approval to dishonor (impale) Mordecai. **6:** The comic misunderstanding begins: Mordecai is on the king's mind and on Haman's, but for opposite reasons.

12 Then Mordecai returned to the king's gate, while Haman hurried home, his head covered in mourning. 13 There Haman told his wife Zeresh and all his friends everything that had befallen him. His advisers and his wife Zeresh said to him, "If Mordecai, before whom you have begun to fall, is of Jewish stock, you will not overcome him; you will fall before him to your ruin."

14 While they were still speaking with him, the king's eunuchs arrived and hurriedly brought Haman to the banquet which Esther had prepared.

7 So the king and Haman came to feast with Queen Esther. 2 On the second day, the king again asked Esther at the wine feast, "What is your wish, Queen Esther? It shall be granted you. And what is your request? Even to half the kingdom, it shall be fulfilled." 3 Queen Esther replied: "If Your Majesty will do me the favor, and if it pleases Your Majesty, let my life be granted me as my wish, and my people as my request. 4 For we have been sold, my people and I, to be destroyed, massacred, and exterminated. Had we only been sold as bondmen and bondwomen, I would have kept silent; for ᵃthe adversaryᵃ is not worthy of the king's trouble."

5 Thereupon King Ahasuerus demanded of Queen Esther, "Who is he and where is he who dared to do this?" 6 "The adversary and enemy," replied Esther, "is this evil Haman!" And Haman cringed in terror before the king and the queen. 7 The king, in his fury, left the wine feast for the palace garden, while Haman remained to plead with Queen Esther for his life; for he saw that the king had resolved to destroy him. 8 When the king returned from the palace garden to the banquet room, Haman was lying prostrate on the couch on which Esther reclined. "Does he

a-a Emendation yields "a trifle" (ḥiṣṣar), lit. "little finger."

in order to mount the horse. **12–14:** Haman is crestfallen. *His head covered in mourning,* ashamed and dejected. A covered head is a sign of mourning, despair, or humiliation (2 Sam. 15.30; Jer. 14.3). The reversal between Haman and Mordecai is complete; Mordecai has gone from mourning to splendor, and Haman has gone from splendor to mourning. His wife and friends understand that he is doomed, but the final step in Haman's fall remains for the next ch.

7.1–10: The villain is unmasked and dispatched. As in the preceding ch, a comic misunderstanding is the centerpiece. The rivalry between Mordecai and Haman will come to a permanent end, and the evil Haman will be dispatched. But it remains for the following ch for the plot against the Jews to be successfully countered. **3:** Esther's words are heavy with formal language. She builds her case on her personal relationship to the king (cf. 8.5). *My life . . . my people:* Esther equates her life (self) with her

people, but does not name them as the Jews. **4:** *We have been sold,* perhaps a hint of Haman's attempted bribe, which Esther learned about from Mordecai in 4.7; or, perhaps, the sense is "handed over, betrayed" as in Judg. 2.14; 3.8. *To be destroyed, massacred, and exterminated:* The same three terms are used in Haman's edict in 3.13. *Had we only been sold as bondmen and bondwomen:* The hypothetical threat of slavery is ironic, part of the rhetorical buildup. But Esther may be subtly recasting Haman's offer of money as a treasonous act against the king. An entire people could become enslaved only if another political entity conquered them. The implication is that Haman was taking over the king's loyal subjects—an act of treason, trivial compared with the real danger. How ironic, for in 3.8 Haman had framed the Jews as traitors. *Not worthy of the king's trouble:* Heb "nezek" means "trouble, annoyance" (cf. Akkadian "niziqtu" and "nizqu"). There is, however, a tradition of interpreting "nezek" in its mishnaic Heb sense of "damage." **5:** *Who is he and where is he:* The culprit is sitting right there. An alternative rendering, "which one is he" (cf. Jonah 1.8; Eccl. 2.3; 11.6; *m. 'Avot* 4.1), conveys Ahasuerus's sputtering in confusion. **6:** *The adversary and enemy,* not only an enemy of the Jews, but of the queen, and hence of the king. **7:** *The king, in his fury, left:* Instead of verbal reactions to Esther's accusation there are physical movements, as if a chain reaction pantomime is being enacted: Haman cringes, Ahasuerus rises, Haman stands, the king returns, and Haman falls. *Haman remained:* "'amad" means "to stand, to take up a position." Haman had been reclining on his couch, as one did at ancient banquets, and now he stands to approach Esther to plead for his life. **8:** *Lying prostrate,* lit."to fall," the gesture of a supplicant, as in 8.3 (cf. 1 Sam. 25.24). In the mode of a comic farce, Ahasuerus misinterprets Haman's pose, casting the supplicant as a seducer. *To ravish the queen in my own palace,* mean," cried the king, "to ravish the queen in my own palace?" No sooner did these words leave the king's lips than Haman's face *was covered.*[-a] [9] Then Harbonah, one of the eunuchs in attendance on the king, said, "What is more, a stake is standing at Haman's house, fifty cubits high, which Haman made for Mordecai—the man whose words saved the king." "Impale him on it!" the king ordered. [10] So they impaled Haman on the stake which he had put up for Mordecai, and the king's fury abated.

8 That very day King Ahasuerus gave the property of Haman, the enemy of the Jews, to Queen Esther. Mordecai presented himself to the king, for Esther had revealed how he was related to her. [2] The king slipped off his ring, which he had taken back from Haman, and gave it to Mordecai; and Esther put Mordecai in charge of Haman's property.

[3] Esther spoke to the king again, falling at his feet and weeping, and beseeching him to avert the evil plotted by Haman the Agagite against the Jews. [4] The king extended the golden scepter to Esther, and Esther arose and stood before the king. [5] "If it please Your Majesty," she said, "and if I have won your favor and the proposal seems right to Your Majesty, and if I am pleasing to you—let dispatches be written countermanding those which were written by Haman son of Hammedatha the Agagite, embodying his plot to annihilate the Jews throughout the king's provinces. [6] For how can I bear to see the disaster which will befall my people! And how can I bear to see the destruction of my kindred!"

[7] Then King Ahasuerus said to Queen Esther and Mordecai the Jew, "I have given Haman's property to Esther, and he has been impaled on the stake for scheming against the Jews. [8] And you may further write with regard to the Jews as you see fit. [Write it] in the king's name and seal it with the king's signet, for an edict that has been written in the king's name and sealed with the king's signet may not be revoked."

[9] So the king's scribes were summoned at that time, on the twenty-third day of the third month, that is, the month of Sivan; and letters were written, at Mordecai's dictation, to the Jews and to the satraps, the governors and the officials of the one hundred and twenty-seven provinces from India to Ethiopia: to every province in its own script and to every people in its own language, and to the Jews in their own script and language. [10] He had them written in

the pretext to punish Haman, for Haman's real wrong, plotting to kill the Jews, had the king's official endorsement. An attempt to take a king's wife or concubine has the political connotation of attempting to take the kingship (see Ibn Ezra; 2 Sam. 3.7; 16.21–22; 1 Kings 2.15–17, 22; Gen. 35.22; Plutarch, *Artaxerxes* 26.2). *Haman's face was covered:* The meaning is unclear; perhaps it signals that Haman was condemned to death or perhaps even put to death. Alternatively, emend to "ashamed, downcast," (cf. Ps. 34.6). **9:** Another touch of irony and reversal: The stake prepared by Haman for Mordecai will conveniently be used for Haman himself. Once again, a switch from the dishonor of Mordecai to the dishonor of Haman. **10:** *The king's fury abated:* As in 2.1, a replacement will be needed for the person dispatched when the king was angry.

8.1–17: Haman's edict is countermanded. Esther will again step forward to save her people. **1–2:** The reversal between Haman and Mordecai (and Esther) is complete. **3–14:** Haman is gone but his decree remains in force. Esther has it revoked. The scene replays parts of chs 3 and 5. **3:** *Beseeching,* cf. 4.8. Esther is now fulfilling Mordecai's instructions. **7:** The king has done his part; now it is up to Esther and Mordecai to do the rest. **8:** A new law is written to offset the old law. *May not be revoked:* Here the meaning is that the law truly may not be revoked (unlike at 1.19, see n.). A legal system in which this principle obtains is unwieldy, to say the least. This is another example of the lighthearted mocking of Persian culture, part of the comic farce. **9:** *To the Jews in their own script and language:* The message affects the Jews in particular.

the name of King Ahasuerus and sealed with the king's signet. Letters were dispatched by mounted couriers, riding steeds ᵃused in the king's service, bred of the royal stud,⁻ᵃ 11 to this effect: The king has permitted the Jews of every city to assemble and fight for their lives; if any people or province attacks them, they may destroy, massacre, and exterminate its armed force together with women and children, and plunder their possessions—12 on a single day in all the provinces of King Ahasuerus, namely, on the thirteenth day of the twelfth month, that is, the month of Adar. 13 The text of the document was to be issued as a law in every single province: it was to be publicly displayed to all the peoples, so that the Jews should be ready for that day to avenge themselves on their enemies. 14 The couriers, mounted on royal steeds, went out in urgent haste at the king's command; and the decree was proclaimed in the fortress Shushan.

15 Mordecai left the king's presence in royal robes of blue and white, with a magnificent crown of gold and a mantle of fine linen and purple wool. And the city of Shushan rang with joyous cries. 16 The Jews enjoyed light and gladness, happiness and honor. 17 And in every province and in every city, when the king's command and decree arrived, there was gladness and joy among the Jews, a feast and a holiday. And many of the people of the land professed to be Jews, for the fear of the Jews had fallen upon them.

9 And so, on the thirteenth day of the twelfth month— that is, the month of Adar—when the king's command and decree were to be executed, the very day on which the enemies of the Jews had expected to get them in their power, the opposite happened, and the Jews got their enemies in their power. 2 Throughout the provinces of King Ahasuerus, the Jews mustered in their cities to attack those who sought their hurt; and no one could withstand them, for the fear of them had fallen upon all the peoples. 3 Indeed, all the officials of the provinces—the satraps, the governors, and the king's stewards—showed deference to the Jews, because the fear of Mordecai had fallen upon them. 4 For Mordecai was now powerful in the royal palace, and his fame was spreading through all the provinces; the man Mordecai was growing ever more powerful. 5 So the Jews struck at their enemies with the sword, slaying and destroying; they wreaked their will upon their enemies.

a-a Meaning of Heb. uncertain.

10: *Steeds used in the king's service, bred of the royal stud:* Horses specially bred for speed were used in the Persian postal system. 11: *To assemble and fight for their lives:* Permission is given for defensive measures. *Destroy, massacre, and exterminate its armed force together with women and children:* The original edict in 3.13 contained similar wording, and so does its reversal. *Together with women and children:* Although distasteful to the modern reader, this was normal in the ancient world. *Plunder their possessions,* as in Haman's edict (3.13), but see 9.10, 15, 16. 13: *Avenge themselves* signifies justified retaliation. 14: *Urgent haste,* even more urgently than in 3.15. 15–17: Mordecai emerges triumphant and the Jews rejoice. 15: *Royal robes of blue and white:* Mordecai's outfit reminds us of Joseph and Daniel, two other successful Jewish courtiers (Gen. 41.42; Dan. 5.7, 29). The colorful textiles also recall the tapestries in 1.6. *The city of Shushan rang with joyous cries,* a reversal of 3.15. 16: This v. is recited (with the addition "so may it befall us") in the "havdalah" service, marking the conclusion of the Sabbath. 17: *Holiday,* "Yom tov," "good day"; also in 9.19, 22. Esther is the only place in the Bible where "yom tov" is used in its later sense of a set festival. *People of the land,* non-Jews. *Professed to be Jews,* or, identified with the Jews. There was not yet a process of formal conversion.

9.1–19: The Jews triumph over their enemies. The events of the story are connected with the institution of the festival of Purim; the ch provides the reason for the holiday and instructions for its celebration. The gleeful violence that permeates this ch is part of the carnivalesque character of the book, and should not be taken seriously; this is an "orgy," not a massacre. 2: *To attack those who sought their hurt,* in self-defense, not revenge. 3: The enemy masses were deterred by fear of the Jewish masses, and the officials were deterred by fear of an official.

⁶ In the fortress Shushan the Jews killed a total of five hundred men. ⁷ They also killed[a]

> Parshandatha,
> Dalphon,
> Aspatha,
⁸ Poratha,
> Adalia,
> Aridatha,
⁹ Parmashta,
> Arisai,
> Aridai,
> and Vaizatha,

¹⁰ the ten sons of Haman son of Hammedatha, the foe of the Jews. But they did not lay hands on the spoil. ¹¹ When the number of those slain in the fortress Shushan was reported on that same day to the king, ¹² the king said to Queen Esther, "In the fortress Shushan alone the Jews have killed a total of five hundred men, as well as the ten sons of Haman. What then must they have done in the provinces of the realm! What is your wish now? It shall be granted you. And what else is your request? It shall be fulfilled." ¹³ "If it please Your Majesty," Esther replied, "let the Jews in Shushan be permitted to act tomorrow also as they did today; and let Haman's ten sons be impaled on the stake." ¹⁴ The king ordered that this should be done, and the decree was proclaimed in Shushan. Haman's ten sons were impaled: ¹⁵ and the Jews in Shushan mustered again on the fourteenth day of Adar and slew three hundred men in Shushan. But they did not lay hands on the spoil.

¹⁶ The rest of the Jews, those in the king's provinces, likewise mustered and fought for their lives. They disposed of their enemies, killing seventy-five thousand of their foes; but they did not lay hands on the spoil. ¹⁷ That was on the thirteenth day of the month of Adar; and they rested on the fourteenth day and made it a day of feasting and merrymaking. (¹⁸ But the Jews in Shushan mustered on both the thirteenth and fourteenth days, and so rested on the fifteenth, and made it a day of feasting and merrymaking.) ¹⁹ That is why village Jews, who live in unwalled towns, observe the fourteenth day of the month of Adar and make it a day of merrymaking and feasting, and as a holiday and an occasion for sending gifts to one another.

²⁰ Mordecai recorded these events. And he sent dispatches to all the Jews throughout the provinces of King Ahasuerus, near and far, ²¹ charging them to observe the

7–10: The list of foreign-sounding names is amusing, like the names in 1.10, 14; and the tradition of reading them all out in one breath when the megillah is read publicly on Purim (b. Meg. 16b) adds to the amusement. The killing of Haman's sons is one more way that Haman's glory is diminished. It also brings his line to an end; no future threat to the Jews will come from him. Amalek is at last wiped out. **10:** *They did not lay hands on the spoil:* Taking spoil, a normal practice in warfare, was permitted in Haman's decree and in Mordecai's counterdecree. The notice that the Jews did not take spoil (also vv. 15, 16) reinforces the connection with 1 Sam. ch 15, where Saul took the Amalekite spoil, contrary to God's command. The Jews of Persia, led by Mordecai, apparently a descendant of Saul, "correct" Saul's error, permitting the descendants of Saul to triumph at last over the descendants of Agag. **16:** Seventy-five thousand is another exaggerated number. These battles are not to be taken literally; they are the mock battles of carnivalesque literature. **18–19:** There is some confusion about where Adar 14 was observed and where Adar 15 was observed. According to rabbinic tradition, Jews in all cities that had been walled since the time of Joshua (according to the Rabbis, e.g., Jerusalem) are to celebrate Purim on Adar 15—Shushan Purim—and Jews elsewhere were to celebrate on Adar 14. Thus, following rabbinic tradition, Purim is celebrated on Adar 15 in Jerusalem. **20–28:** The festival is established in perpetuity. **20:** *Mordecai recorded these events:* Rashi takes the book of Esther to be Mordecai's record of events; modern interpreters take it to be vv. 24–25. **21:** *To observe the fourteenth and fifteenth days of Adar,* whichever day was appropriate to the location of the celebrant.

---

a *Moved up from v. 10 for greater clarity.*

fourteenth and fifteenth days of Adar, every year—²²the same days on which the Jews enjoyed relief from their foes and the same month which had been transformed for them from one of grief and mourning to one of festive joy. They were to observe them as days of feasting and merry-making, and as an occasion for sending gifts to one another and presents to the poor. ²³ The Jews accordingly assumed as an obligation that which they had begun to practice and which Mordecai prescribed for them.

²⁴ For Haman son of Hammedatha the Agagite, the foe of all the Jews, had plotted to destroy the Jews, and had cast *pur*—that is, the lot—with intent to crush and exterminate them. ²⁵ But when [Esther] came before the king, he commanded: ᵃ"With the promulgation of this decree,⁻ᵃ let the evil plot, which he devised against the Jews, recoil on his own head!" So they impaled him and his sons on the stake. ²⁶ For that reason these days were named Purim, after *pur*.

In view, then, of all the instructions in the said letter and of what they had experienced in that matter and what had befallen them, ²⁷ the Jews undertook and irrevocably obligated themselves and their descendants, and all who might join them, to observe these two days in the manner prescribed and at the proper time each year. ²⁸ Consequently, these days are recalled and observed in every generation: by every family, every province, and every city. And these days of Purim shall never cease among the Jews, and the memory of them shall never perish among their descendants.

²⁹ ᵇThen Queen Esther daughter of Abihail wrote a second letter of Purim for the purpose of confirming with full authority the aforementioned one of Mordecai the Jew. ³⁰ Dispatches were sent to all the Jews in the hundred and twenty-seven provinces of the realm of Ahasuerus with an ordinance of "equity and honesty:"ᶜ ³¹ These days of Purim shall be observed at their proper time, as Mordecai the Jew—and now Queen Esther—has obligated them to do, and just as they have assumed for themselves and their descendants the obligation of the fasts with their lamentations.ᵈ

22: *Feasting and merrymaking . . . sending gifts . . . presents to the poor:* These elements, along with the recitation of the scroll of Esther, constitute the halakhic requirements for the celebration of the festival. **24–26:** A summary of the story, emphasizing the etiology of the festival's name, *pur* and Purim, and the defeat of Haman, with credit to the king. **26:** *Purim:* Our earliest reference outside of Esther calls it "The Day of Mordecai" (2 Macc. 15.36). **28:** The festival is to be celebrated by Jews in all places for all time. **29–32:** The second Purim letter, further confirming the festival. The writer is either Esther, or Esther along with Mordecai. **31:** Just as the Jews took upon themselves new fast days not mentioned in the Torah (Zech. 8.19), so will they now take upon themselves the celebration of a new festival, likewise not in the Torah. This first non-Torah festival needed to be authorized.

a-a *Meaning of Heb. uncertain.*

b *Force of vv. 29–31 uncertain in part. Verse 29 reads literally, "Then Queen Esther, daughter of Abihail, and Mordecai the Jew, wrote with full authority to confirm this second letter of Purim."*

c *I.e., of new holidays, the instituting of which is linked to love of equity and honesty in Zech. 8.19.*

d *The Jews had long been observing fast days in commemoration of national calamities; see Zech. 7.5; 8.19.*

32 And Esther's ordinance validating these observances of Purim was recorded in a scroll.

10 King Ahasuerus imposed tribute on the mainland and the islands. 2 All his mighty and powerful acts, and a full account of the greatness to which the king advanced Mordecai, are recorded in the Annals of the Kings of Media and Persia. 3 For Mordecai the Jew ranked next to King Ahasuerus and was highly regarded by the Jews and popular with the multitude of his brethren; he sought the good of his people and interceded for the welfare of all his kindred.

10.1–3: The accomplishments of the great king Ahasuerus and his Jewish courtier, Mordecai. 1: *Tribute:* Levying tribute signifies having sovereignty over the area. *The mainland and the islands,* a merism for the entire inhabited world (cf. Isa. 42.4, 10). Now Ahasuerus's control extends beyond the 127 provinces of 1.1. **2:** *Are recorded in the Annals of the Kings of Media and Persia,* presumably the same annals mentioned in 6.1. This imitates the summary statements in the book of Kings (e.g., 1 Kings 14.19, 29; 15.31), lending a pseudo-historical tone to the story and official authority to the recounting of it. **3:** In a story where honor is paramount, Mordecai has achieved the highest honor possible. At the end, it is Mordecai rather than Esther who is in the spotlight; he is a model of Jewish success in the Diaspora. The ending assures the reader that the Jewish community is secure.

דניאל

Daniel

THE BOOK OF DANIEL, probably written in its final version in 164 BCE, is probably the latest composition of the Hebrew Bible. Its narrative, however, is set much earlier, during the reigns of the powerful kings of Babylonia, Media, and Persia in the 6th century BCE. The figure of Daniel, known from the *Aqhat Epic* found at Ugarit and mentioned in Ezekiel 14.14; 28.3 as a wise and righteous hero of the past, becomes here a new model of Jewish faithfulness to God. A member of the exile community in Babylonia, he soon rises to become an important Jewish courtier. The anonymous author thus uses the period of exile as a setting to address the challenging issues of Jews living under foreign kings.

Problems Encountered in Interpreting Daniel

THE BOOK PRESENTS to the reader a number of difficulties that render it a challenging yet fascinating text. First, it can be divided into two equal halves of different genres and different origins. Chs 1–6 are composed of six "court legends" that utilize third-person narration to recount the adventures of Jewish heroes in the highest court in the land (cf. the Joseph story in Gen. chs 37–50; Esther). The legends reflect an entertaining, humorous, even satirical side. Chs 7–12 are made up of four apocalyptic visions, told in the first person, that are revelations of the events that lead to the cataclysmic end and transformation of history. The two halves of the book appear to arise at different times in Israel's history. Chs 1–6, probably originally oral, circulated most likely in the 4th to 2nd centuries BCE, when they were collected into a cycle of Daniel legends. Chs 7–12 are most likely written compositions, datable to the last year of the Maccabean revolt (164 BCE). In editing chs 1–12 together, the author of the visions made the whole into an apocalyptic book. (Apocalypses often mix different genres.) Despite their separate origins, several themes hold the two halves of the book of Daniel together: God's sovereignty over history and foreign monarchs, the special wisdom and insight of the one devoted to God, and the ideal of heroic obedience, even to the point of death. Daniel is the only apocalypse in the Hebrew Bible; Ezekiel has some apocalyptic elements but is still within the genre of prophetic books. Jewish apocalypses were written earlier than Daniel (parts of *1 Enoch, Jubilees*), and after Daniel (other parts of *1 Enoch, 4 Ezra* [2 Esdras chs 3–14], and in the New Testament, Revelation), but these were not incorporated into the Hebrew Bible.

Another peculiar characteristic of Daniel is its use of two languages: 1.1–2.4a and 8.1–12.13 are in Heb, while 2.4b–7.28 are in Aramaic. (This does not correspond to the division by genre noted above.) Scholars have proposed two explanations for this: Either two languages were used in the original work, a combination that was retained in the multilingual world of the land of Israel in the 2nd century BCE; or the whole work was originally composed in one language, and one part was later translated into the other language. In this latter theory, Aramaic, the common international language of the ancient Near East at that time, is usually suggested as the original language of the whole. Neither explanation has met with complete scholarly agreement, but the most likely reconstruction is that chs 2–6 and separately, ch 7, were written in Aramaic, and chs 8–12, at a date slightly later than ch 7, in Hebrew. Ch 1 may have been written in Hebrew, or translated from Aramaic into Hebrew as a more appropriate language for the introduction.

Historical and Political Context of Daniel

THE MAJOR EMPIRES of the ancient Near East figure prominently in the book of Daniel. The narrative begins during the Neo-Babylonian empire. It was Nebuchadnezzar (also called Nebuchadrezzar), king of the Babylonians, who conquered Jerusalem and destroyed the first Temple in 586 BCE, inaugurating the period of the exile (2 Kings chs 24–25; Jeremiah). Contemporary with the Babylonian empire in the west was the empire of the Medes in the east. Cyrus of Persia arose in the mid-6th century BCE and conquered first the Medes and then the Babylonians in 539. In Judea the Medes and Persians were sometimes perceived as a joint kingdom, and at other times as following one after the other.

The Persian kings—the first four being Cyrus, Cambyses, Darius, and Xerxes—ruled the Jews more benevolently than the Babylonians. The first, Cyrus, encouraged the Judeans to return from their exile in 538, and allowed them to rebuild their Temple, which was constructed in 520–515 BCE. This state of affairs—limited autonomy under Persian rule—continued until the rise of Alexander the Great (356–323), the brilliant Macedonian-Greek king who defeated the Persians to found a new empire. Alexander conquered the land of Israel in 333. He died young, however, and his vast empire split into several Greek-ruled kingdoms, the most important of which for the book of Daniel were the Seleucid, centered in Syria and Babylonia, and the Ptolemaic in Egypt. Judea lay at the intersection between the two empires, and the influences of these empires over Jerusalem ebbed and flowed; Jews were often split in their allegiances to one or the other. After gaining control of Judea at the beginning of the 2nd century BCE, the Seleucid kings suffered reversals, and their king Antiochus IV Epiphanes turned his attention to the control of the Jerusalem Temple and the gold that was stored there. This is the background of the events indirectly described in the visions of chs 7–12.

Because of the detailed nature of apocalyptic timetables, the dating of at least the last chs of Daniel can be established precisely. Scholars consider the predictions in this book, as in other apocalypses, to be prophecies after the fact, purportedly written down centuries earlier and kept secret in order to give credence to other predictions about the end of history. The recounting of history, then, though symbolic, can be matched quite easily with the history of the ancient Near East in the Greek period. The predictions are detailed and accurate until the end of the Maccabean revolt in 164. At that point, however, they veer dramatically from what we know of the actions of the Seleucid king (see annotations to ch 11), and scholars assume that the author lived and wrote at the precise time when the predictions become inaccurate.

The scribal visionaries who produced Daniel were strongly opposed to Antiochus IV Epiphanes (whose name meant "god manifest"), yet they were probably not closely aligned with the Maccabees. The group is probably to be identified with those who are "knowledgeable" in 11.33, 12.3. (The same word in its verbal form, "to give understanding," is used at 9.22.) Their instruction includes the knowledge of future events that is contained in the visions, and their role is one of guardian to the "many."

Daniel in Jewish Tradition

THE BOOK OF DANIEL has been evaluated differently in Jewish and Christian tradition. Daniel was evidently considered a prophet at Qumran and elsewhere in early Judaism (Josephus, *Antiquities* 10.266–68), but because prefigurations of Christ and Christian resurrection were seen in Daniel by the early church, the rabbinic tradition hesitated to embrace the visions of Daniel. The Rabbis denied that Daniel was predicting events after the Maccabean revolt, and especially not the end of time, and assigned him a role as seer, not prophet (*b. Meg.* 3a, *b. Sanh.* 94a). Jewish tradition was also sometimes critical of what appeared to be a positive relationship between Daniel and Nebuchadnezzar. The different status of Daniel in Judaism and Christianity is thus reflected in the position of the book in the two canons. In the Christian Old Testament Daniel is placed with the major prophets, Isaiah, Jeremiah, and Ezekiel, while in the Jewish Scriptures it is placed with the Kethuvim, or Writings. Although the book of Daniel has not held central importance in Jewish tradition, it has had an influence on Jewish liturgy—probably because of its late date, when proto-liturgy was being formed—and it is significant in revealing a great deal about the social and theological world of Jews at the end of the biblical era. [LAWRENCE M. WILLS]

1 In the third year of the reign of King Jehoiakim of Judah, King Nebuchadnezzar of Babylon came to Jerusalem and laid siege to it. ² The Lord delivered King Jehoiakim of Judah into his power, together with some of the vessels of the House of God, and he brought them to the land of Shinar to the house of his god; he deposited the vessels in the treasury of his god. ³ Then the king ordered Ashpenaz, his chief officer, to bring some Israelites of royal descent and of the nobility—⁴ youths without blemish, handsome, proficient in all wisdom, knowledgeable and intelligent, and capable of serving in the royal palace—and teach them the writings and the language of

1.1–6.29: Collection of court legends. Chs 1–6 probably circulated as independent stories before being collected and edited together (see introduction). Chs 2, 4, and 5 demonstrate that Daniel is superior to the king's other courtiers, while chs 3 and 6 dramatically depict the persecution and vindication of the Jewish protagonists at the hands of the other courtiers. Ch 1 serves as an introduction to this collection. The positive resolution of the narrative in chs 1–6 and the sometimes humor-the Chaldeans. [5] The king allotted daily rations to them from the king's food and from the wine he drank. They were to be educated for three years, [a]at the end of which they[-a] were to enter the king's service.

[6] Among them were the Judahites Daniel, Hananiah, Mishael, and Azariah. [7] The chief officer gave them new names; he named Daniel Belteshazzar, Hananiah Shadrach, Mishael Meshach, and Azariah Abed-nego. [8] Daniel resolved not to defile himself with the king's food or the wine he drank, so he sought permission of the chief officer not to defile himself, [9] and God disposed the chief officer to be kind and compassionate toward Daniel. [10] The chief officer said to Daniel, "I fear that my lord the king, who allotted food and drink to you, will notice that you look out of sorts, unlike the other youths of your age—and you will put my life[b] in jeopardy with the king." [11] Daniel replied to the guard whom the chief officer had put in charge of Daniel, Hananiah, Mishael and Azariah, [12] "Please test your servants for ten days, giving us legumes to eat and water to drink. [13] Then compare our appearance with that of the youths who eat of the king's food, and do with your servants as you see fit." [14] He agreed to this plan of theirs, and tested them for ten days. [15] When the ten days were over, they looked better and healthier than all the youths who were eating of the king's food. [16] So the guard kept on removing their food, and the wine they were supposed to drink, and gave them legumes. [17] God made all four of these young men intelligent and proficient in all writings and wisdom, and Daniel had understanding of visions and dreams of all kinds.[18] When the time the king had set for their presentation had come, the chief officer presented them to Nebuchadnezzar.[19] The king spoke with them, and of them all none was equal to Daniel, Hananiah, Mishael and Azariah; so these entered the king's service. [20] Whenever the king put a question to them requiring wisdom and understanding, he found them to be ten times better than all the magicians and exorcists throughout his realm. [21] Daniel was there until the first year of King Cyrus.

a-a Or "and some of them."
b Lit. "head."

ous tone indicate that the tension did not result from the national crisis of the Maccabean revolt, but rather from the more general conflict of loyalties that existed for Jews living in the Diaspora in the centuries preceding that.

1.1–21: Daniel and his three companions are introduced and tested. This chapter introduces the main Jewish characters—Daniel and his three friends—as well as Nebuchadnezzar and also the Temple vessels, which will figure

in ch 5. In addition, though God's great power is emphasized, it is power that is exercised at a distance and through intermediaries, a theme that will be developed in terms of God's role in the court of the great foreign kings in chs 1–6 and in world history in chs 7–12. **1–2:** The fall of Judah and the beginnings of exile are introduced quickly. To establish the pedigree of the hero, the book of Daniel does not dwell here on Nebuchadnezzar as the archvillain of ancient Jewish history, or on the exile as tragedy. *The Lord* still controls human events, even the successes of foreign kings over Judah. The dating of events is not accurate: The third year of *King Jehoiakim* was 606 BCE, but *Nebuchadnezzar* captured Jerusalem in 597 BCE. *Vessels*, Ezra 1.7–8. *Shinar*, Babylonia. **3:** The "history" of the exile quickly turns to the fortunes of the four Jewish protagonists at the court of Nebuchadnezzar. They are heroic and aristocratic in bearing. Compare the treatment of the fallen king Jehoiachin in 2 Kings 25.27–30, Jer. 52.31–34. **4:** *Chaldeans:* A name for a region and language of Babylonia, it was also associated with the wisdom and learning of Eastern courtiers. In some passages in Daniel it refers to the ethnic group, in others it means courtiers. *The language of the Chaldeans* was Akkadian. **5:** The training of courtiers in languages, court protocol, and international relations was common in the ancient world. **7–8:** *Belteshazzar,* see 4.5 n. Prominent Jews sometimes took Babylonian names, and at Gen. 41.45 Joseph is given an Egyptian name. Although Daniel and his friends refuse *the king's food,* presumably because it violated the food laws in Lev. ch 11 and Deut. ch 14, there appears to be no objection to receiving Babylonian court names. The names *Shadrach, Meshach,* and *Abed-nego* have not been satisfactorily explained. This v. also offers the only biblical indication of the later rabbinic law that Jews should not drink pagan wine. **8:** In the Diaspora there arose a stronger

2 In the second year of the reign of Nebuchadnezzar, Nebuchadnezzar had a dream; his spirit was agitated, [a]yet he was overcome by[a] sleep. [2]The king ordered the magicians, exorcists, sorcerers, and Chaldeans to be summoned in order to tell the king what he had dreamed. They came and stood before the king, [3]and the king said to them, "I have had a dream and I am full of anxiety to know what I have dreamed." [4]The Chaldeans spoke to the king in Aramaic, "O king, live forever! Relate the dream to your servants, and we will tell its meaning." [5]The king said in reply to the Chaldeans, "I hereby decree: If you will not make the dream and its meaning known to me, you shall be torn limb from limb and your houses confiscated.[b] [6]But if you tell the dream and its meaning, you shall receive from me gifts, presents, and great honor; therefore, tell me the dream and its meaning." [7]Once again they answered, "Let the king relate the dream to his servants, and we will tell its meaning." [8]The king said in reply, "It is clear to me that you are playing for time, since you see that I have decreed [9]that if you do not make the dream known to me, there is but one verdict for you. You have conspired to tell me something false and fraudulent until circumstances change; so relate the dream to me, and I will then know that you can tell its meaning." [10]The Chaldeans said in reply to the king, "There is no one on earth who can [c]satisfy the king's demand,[c] for great king or ruler—none has ever asked such a thing of any magician, exorcist, or Chaldean. [11]The thing asked by the king is difficult; there is no one who can tell it to the king except the gods whose abode is not among mortals."[d] [12]Whereupon the king flew into a violent rage, and gave an order to do away with all the wise men of Babylon.

[13]The decree condemning the wise men to death was issued. Daniel and his companions were about to be put to death [14]when Daniel remonstrated with Arioch, the captain of the royal guard who had set out to put the wise men of Babylon to death. [15]He spoke up and said to Arioch, the royal officer, "Why is the decree of the king so urgent?" Thereupon Arioch informed Daniel of the matter. [16]So Daniel went to ask the king for time, that he might tell the meaning to the king. [17]Then Daniel went to his house and informed his companions, Hananiah, Mishael, and Azariah, of the matter,[18]that they might implore the God of Heaven for help regarding this mystery, so that

emphasis on dietary laws as a way of living a pious life without (or away from) the Temple, reflected here and in many works in the Apocrypha (Tobit 1.10–11; Judith 10.5; 1 Macc. 1.62–63, 2 Macc. 5.27).

2.1–49: Daniel is able to interpret the king's dream. 1: *Second year* is inconsistent with 1.1–4. **2:** Lists of court officers—and other items as well—occur often in chs 1–6. The humorous tone of the pretentiousness of the list is meant to contrast with the understated power of Daniel's abilities. Unlike 1.4, *Chaldeans* here means courtiers, since the king would have been a Chaldean as well. **4:** With the words *O king,* the text switches from Heb to Aramaic. The interpretation of royal dreams was common in the ancient Near East (cf. ch 4; Gen. ch 41), but a twist is introduced when the king demands that the courtiers tell him the content of his dream as well as its interpretation. The king's threat indicates the high stakes and potential danger to the life of the courtier (cf. 2.12). Although there are many records of dream interpretation from the ancient Near East, there is no record of a courtier recounting the content of someone else's dream. The courtiers raise an objection on these grounds, setting the stage for Daniel, with the help of God (v. 30), to do what no ordinary human being could do. As in the other chs, Daniel serves as a vehicle for expressing God's great power. **13–23:** It is possible that these vv. were added to tie the chs together; the mention of the three friends connects this episode with chs 1 and 3, and the prayer is similar to those in chs 3, 4, and 6; see also Neh. 9.5; 1 Sam. ch 2, Prov. ch 8. Cf. 5.11–12 n. **18:** *Mystery,* a Persian word, generally used in Jewish apocalypticism to mean the special, restricted knowledge of the heavens and what is to happen in the future. Daniel's wisdom and knowledge provides another connection between chs 1–6 and 7–12: He is capable of receiving extraordinary revelations from God.

---

a-a *Meaning of Heb. uncertain; others "and he could not."*
b *Meaning uncertain; or "turned into ruins."*
c-c *Lit. "tell the king's matter."*   d *Lit. "flesh."*

Daniel and his colleagues would not be put to death together with the other wise men of Babylon.

20: The central words of the
later Jewish kaddish prayer are
based on the beginning of this v.

¹⁹ The mystery was revealed to Daniel in a night vision;
then Daniel blessed the God of Heaven. ²⁰ Daniel spoke
up and said:

> "Let the name of God be blessed forever and ever,
> For wisdom and power are His.

21   He changes times and seasons,
> Removes kings and installs kings;
> He gives the wise their wisdom
> And knowledge to those who know.

22   He reveals deep and hidden things,
> Knows what is in the darkness,
> And light dwells with Him.

23   I acknowledge and praise You,
> O God of my fathers,
> You who have given me wisdom and power,
> For now You have let me know what we asked of
>   You;
> You have let us know what concerns the king."

²⁴ Thereupon Daniel went to Arioch, whom the king
had appointed to do away with the wise men of Babylon;
he came and said to him as follows, "Do not do away with
the wise men of Babylon; bring me to the king and I will
tell the king the meaning!" ²⁵ So Arioch rushed Daniel into
the king's presence and said to him, "I have found among
the exiles of Judah a man who can make the meaning
known to the king!" ²⁶ The king said in reply to Daniel
(who was called Belteshazzar), "Can you really make
known to me the dream that I saw and its meaning?"
²⁷ Daniel answered the king and said, "The mystery about
which the king has inquired—wise men, exorcists, magicians, and diviners cannot tell to the king. ²⁸ But there is a
God in heaven who reveals mysteries, and He has made
known to King Nebuchadnezzar what is to be at the end
of days. This is your dream and the vision that entered
your mind in bed: ²⁹ O king, the thoughts that came to
your mind in your bed are about future events; He who
reveals mysteries has let you know what is to happen.
³⁰ Not because my wisdom is greater than that of other
creatures has this mystery been revealed to me, but in
order that the meaning should be made known to the
king, and that you may know the thoughts of your mind.

³¹ "O king, as you looked on, there appeared a great
statue. This statue, which was huge and its brightness surpassing, stood before you, and its appearance was awesome. ³² The head of that statue was of fine gold; its breast
and arms were of silver; its belly and thighs, of bronze; ³³ its

legs were of iron, and its feet part iron and part clay. ³⁴ As you looked on, a stone was hewn out, not by hands, and struck the statue on its feet of iron and clay and crushed them. ³⁵ All at once, the iron, clay, bronze, silver, and gold were crushed, and became like chaff of the threshing floors of summer; a wind carried them off until no trace of them was left. But the stone that struck the statue became a great mountain and filled the whole earth.

³⁶ "Such was the dream, and we will now tell the king its meaning. ³⁷ You, O king—king of kings, to whom the God of Heaven has given kingdom, power, might, and glory; ³⁸ into whose hands He has given men, wild beasts, and the fowl of heaven, wherever they may dwell; and to whom He has given dominion over them all—you are the head of gold. ³⁹ But another kingdom will arise after you, inferior to yours; then yet a third kingdom, of bronze, which will rule over the whole earth. ⁴⁰ But the fourth kingdom will be as strong as iron; just as iron crushes and shatters everything—and like iron that smashes—so will it crush and smash all these. ⁴¹ You saw the feet and the toes, part potter's clay and part iron; that means it will be a divided kingdom; it will have only some of the stability of iron, inasmuch as you saw iron mixed with common clay. ⁴² And the toes were part iron and part clay; that [means] the kingdom will be in part strong and in part brittle. ⁴³ You saw iron mixed with common clay; that means: ᵃthey shall intermingle with the offspring of men,⁻ᵃ but shall not hold together, just as iron does not mix with clay. ⁴⁴ And in the time of those kings, the God of Heaven will establish a kingdom that shall never be destroyed, a kingdom that shall not be transferred to another people. It will crush and wipe out all these kingdoms, but shall itself last forever—⁴⁵ just as you saw how a stone was hewn from the mountain, not by hands, and crushed the iron, bronze, clay, silver, and gold. The great God has made known to the king what will happen in the future. The dream is sure and its interpretation reliable."

⁴⁶ Then King Nebuchadnezzar prostrated himself and paid homage to Daniel and ordered that a meal offering and pleasing offerings be made to him. ⁴⁷ The king said in reply to Daniel, "Truly your God must be the God of gods and Lord of kings and the revealer of mysteries to have enabled you to reveal this mystery." ⁴⁸ The king then elevated Daniel and gave him very many gifts, and made him governor of the whole province of Babylon and chief prefect of all the wise men of Babylon. ⁴⁹ At Daniel's re-

31–45: Portentous dreams of the fate of kingdoms were common in the ancient world; cf. Herodotus, *Histories* 1.108, 7.19. Here, however, the author uses an older prediction of four world kingdoms—understood as Babylonia, Media, Persia, and Greece—and emphasizes their decreasing value. They are followed by a mixed kingdom of *iron* and *clay*, which signifies the divided Greek kingdom and the Ptolemaic and Seleucid kings who ruled in the eastern Mediterranean. Although Daniel predicts the demise of the Babylonian kingdom and its ultimate replacement by the *kingdom* of the *God of Heaven*, Nebuchadnezzar nevertheless reveres Daniel for his insight. **46:** *Prostrated . . . paid homage* implies that the king worshipped Daniel, but Jewish interpreters assumed that Daniel declined the reverence (*Gen. Rab.* 96.5). The Rabbis were often quite critical of Daniel, however, for enjoying such a positive relationship with the tyrant who destroyed the first Temple (see 4.16–24 n.). The original narratives in chs 1–6 were probably oriented toward entertainment at the expense of the pagan kings.

ᵃ⁻ᵃ *Meaning uncertain.*

quest, the king appointed Shadrach, Meshach, and Abed-nego to administer the province of Babylon; while Daniel himself was at the king's court.

3 King Nebuchadnezzar made a statue of gold sixty cubits high and six cubits broad. He set it up in the plain of Dura in the province of Babylon. [2] King Nebuchadnezzar then sent word to gather the satraps, prefects, governors, counselors, treasurers, judges, officers, and all the provincial officials to attend the dedication of the statue that King Nebuchadnezzar had set up. [3] So the satraps, prefects, governors, counselors, treasurers, judges, officers, and all the provincial officials assembled for the dedication of the statue that King Nebuchadnezzar had set up, and stood before the statue that Nebuchadnezzar had set up. [4] The herald proclaimed in a loud voice, "You are commanded, O peoples and nations of every language, [5] when you hear the sound of the horn, pipe, zither, lyre, psaltery, bagpipe, and all other types of instruments, to fall down and worship the statue of gold that King Nebuchadnezzar has set up. [6] Whoever will not fall down and worship shall at once be thrown into a burning fiery furnace." [7] And so, as soon as all the peoples heard the sound of the horn, pipe, zither, lyre, psaltery, and all other types of instruments, all peoples and nations of every language fell down and worshiped the statue of gold that King Nebuchadnezzar had set up.

[8] Seizing the occasion, certain Chaldeans came forward to slander the Jews. [9] They spoke up and said to King Nebuchadnezzar, "O king, live forever! [10] You, O king, gave an order that everyone who hears the horn, pipe, zither, lyre, psaltery, bagpipe, and all types of instruments must fall down and worship the golden statue, [11] and whoever does not fall down and worship shall be thrown into a burning fiery furnace. [12] There are certain Jews whom you appointed to administer the province of Babylon, Shadrach, Meshach, and Abed-nego; those men pay no heed to you, O king; they do not serve your god or worship the statue of gold that you have set up."

[13] Then Nebuchadnezzar, in raging fury, ordered Shadrach, Meshach, and Abed-nego to be brought; so those men were brought before the king. [14] Nebuchadnezzar spoke to them and said, "Is it true, Shadrach, Meshach, and Abed-nego, that you do not serve my god or worship the statue of gold that I have set up? [15] Now if you are ready to fall down and worship the statue that I have made when you hear the sound of the horn, pipe, zither, lyre, psaltery, and bagpipe, and all other types of instru-

3.1–33: Daniel's three companions are tested in the fiery furnace. Daniel himself is not mentioned in ch 3. The story about the three young men may have circulated as an independent oral legend and later been incorporated into the tradition of Daniel narratives because of thematic similarities. The religious intolerance depicted in the ch is very atypical of the ancient Near Eastern world. Although the king's demand that Jews worship a statue has parallels to the events of the Maccabean revolt, the parallels are not close, and this section of Daniel is likely pre-Maccabean. It is unclear whether this story is based on a real event or is created to illustrate the power of God. **1:** *Statue of gold:* Herodotus 1.183 mentions a giant figure made of gold in the temple of Bel in Babylon. **2:** In this ch, lists, which are characteristic of Daniel, are used particularly often, perhaps for satirical effect. Even the names of the protagonists in their Babylonian form, "Shadrach, Meshach, and Abed-nego," are repeated often. The comic effect of the lists is even more marked if the narrative is read aloud, as it was probably originally recounted. The pomp and organization of officials, including the title *satrap*, seem to be more indicative of Persian administration, when the story may have been composed, rather than the Neo-Babylonian empire when the story is set. Ch 6 indicates that the editor of the collection is familiar with Persian administration. **8:** The threat from other courtiers, who are presumably jealous, is emphasized here and at 6.1–5; cf. also Esth. ch 3.

ments, [well and good]; but if you will not worship, you shall at once be thrown into a burning fiery furnace, and what god is there that can save you from my power?" [16] Shadrach, Meshach, and Abed-nego said in reply to the king, "O Nebuchadnezzar, we have no need to answer you in this matter, [17] for if so it must be, our God whom we serve is able to save us from the burning fiery furnace, and He will save us from your power, O king. [18] But even if He does not, be it known to you, O king, that we will not serve your god or worship the statue of gold that you have set up."

[19] Nebuchadnezzar was so filled with rage at Shadrach, Meshach, and Abed-nego that his visage was distorted, and he gave an order to heat up the furnace to seven times its usual heat. [20] He commanded some of the strongest men of his army to bind Shadrach, Meshach, and Abed-nego, and to throw them into the burning fiery furnace. [21] So these men, in their shirts, trousers, hats, and other garments, were bound and thrown into the burning fiery furnace. [22] Because the king's order was urgent, and the furnace was heated to excess, a tongue of flame killed the men who carried up Shadrach, Meshach, and Abed-nego. [23] But those three men, Shadrach, Meshach, and Abed-nego, dropped, bound, into the burning fiery furnace.

[24] Then King Nebuchadnezzar was astonished and, rising in haste, addressed his companions, saying, "Did we not throw three men, bound, into the fire?" They spoke in reply, "Surely, O king." [25] He answered, "But I see four men walking about unbound and unharmed in the fire and the fourth looks like a divine being." [26] Nebuchadnezzar then approached the hatch of the burning fiery furnace and called, "Shadrach, Meshach, Abed-nego, servants of the Most High God, come out!" So Shadrach, Meshach, and Abed-nego came out of the fire. [27] The satraps, the prefects, the governors, and the royal companions gathered around to look at those men, on whose bodies the fire had had no effect, the hair of whose heads had not been singed, whose shirts looked no different, to whom not even the odor of fire clung. [28] Nebuchadnezzar spoke up and said, "Blessed be the God of Shadrach, Meshach, and Abed-nego, who sent His angel to save His servants who, trusting in Him, flouted the king's decree at the risk of their lives rather than serve or worship any god but their own God. [29] I hereby give an order that [anyone of] any people or nation of whatever language who blasphemes the God of Shadrach, Meshach, and Abed-nego shall be torn limb from limb, and his house confiscated, for there is no other God who is able to save in this way."

15: *What god is there?* Without realizing it, the king invokes the God who does have the power to save the three Jews, unlike the many gods whom the king worships. **19:** The bluster of the king is emphasized, perhaps also for comic effect. **25:** *The fourth looks like a divine being,* an angel. Angels become particularly important in this period; cf. 7.13–14 n.; 8.15–16 n. **31–33:** The first doxology (praise of God) of the pagan kings; cf. 4.31–34; 6.27–28. The theme of all the doxologies is that God's kingship is superior to any earthly kingship. The implausibility of the Babylonian king Nebuchadnezzar blessing the God of Israel and making a decree of protection argues for a humorous interpretation of this ch. These vv. are sometimes taken as the introduction to ch 4 rather than concluding ch 3.

30 Thereupon the king promoted Shadrach, Meshach, and Abed-nego in the province of Babylon.

31 "King Nebuchadnezzar to all people and nations of every language that inhabit the whole earth: May your well-being abound! 32 The signs and wonders that the Most High God has worked for me I am pleased to relate. 33 How great are His signs; how mighty His wonders! His kingdom is an everlasting kingdom, and His dominion endures throughout the generations."

4 I, Nebuchadnezzar, was living serenely in my house, flourishing in my palace. 2 I had a dream that frightened me, and my thoughts in bed and the vision of my mind alarmed me. 3 I gave an order to bring all the wise men of Babylon before me to let me know the meaning of the dream. 4 The magicians, exorcists, Chaldeans, and diviners came, and I related the dream to them, but they could not make its meaning known to me. 5 Finally, Daniel, called Belteshazzar after the name of my god, in whom the spirit of the holy gods was, came to me, and I related the dream to him, [saying], 6 "Belteshazzar, chief magician, in whom I know the spirit of the holy gods to be, and whom no mystery baffles, tell me the meaning of my dream vision that I have seen. 7 In the visions of my mind in bed

> I saw a tree of great height in the midst of the earth;
>
> 8 The tree grew and became mighty;
> Its top reached heaven,
> And it was visible to the ends of the earth.
>
> 9 Its foliage was beautiful
> And its fruit abundant;
> There was food for all in it.
> Beneath it the beasts of the field found shade,
> And the birds of the sky dwelt on its branches;
> All creatures fed on it.

10 In the vision of my mind in bed, I looked and saw a holy Watcher coming down from heaven. 11 He called loudly and said:

> 'Hew down the tree, lop off its branches,
> Strip off its foliage, scatter its fruit.
> Let the beasts of the field flee from beneath it
> And the birds from its branches,
>
> 12 But leave the stump with its roots in the ground.
> In fetters of iron and bronze
> In the grass of the field,
> Let him be drenched with the dew of heaven,
> And share earth's verdure with the beasts.

4.1–34: Daniel predicts Nebuchadnezzar's madness. 1: *I, Nebuchadnezzar:* The narrative begins in the first person, recounted by Nebuchadnezzar himself, which is typical of Neo-Babylonian royal inscriptions and of royal letters. Nebuchadnezzar was never absent from office for any extended period, but the king's temporary absence here likely suggests that the model for this story is not Nebuchadnezzar but Nabonidus, the last Babylonian king (556–539 BCE). He spent ten years at Teima, in the Arabian peninsula, allowing his son Belshazzar to reign as viceroy in his stead (see ch 5). The "Prayer of Nabonidus" (4Q242) from Qumran presents Nabonidus's first-person account of being cured by an unnamed Jewish seer after an affliction of seven years. **5:** *Belteshazzar . . . the name of my god,* see 1.7 n. Although the author understandably assumes that the name is related to the Babylonian god Bel, it actually means "protect his life" or perhaps "protects the prince's life," and is not based on the god Bel. **6:** *Mystery,* see 2.18 n. **7:** The "world-tree" is often used in the ancient Near East as a symbol of a great empire; cf. Ezek. 17.1–10; 31.3–14; Herodotus 1.108; 7.19. **10:** *Watcher,* an angelic figure, common in Jewish apocalyptic literature (*Jubilees* 4.15), who executes God's justice. In some texts watchers are fallen angels (1 *Enoch* chs 10–16).

13 Let his mind be altered from that of a man,
   And let him be given the mind of a beast,
   And let seven seasons pass over him.

14 This sentence is decreed by the Watchers;
   This verdict is commanded by the Holy Ones
   So that all creatures may know
   That the Most High is sovereign over the realm of
      man,
   And He gives it to whom He wishes
   And He may set over it even the lowest of men.'

15 "I, King Nebuchadnezzar, had this dream; now you, Belteshazzar, tell me its meaning, since all the wise men of my kingdom are not able to make its meaning known to me, but you are able, for the spirit of the holy gods is in you."

16 Then Daniel, called Belteshazzar, was perplexed for a while, and alarmed by his thoughts. The king addressed him, "Let the dream and its meaning not alarm you." Belteshazzar replied, "My lord, would that the dream were for your enemy and its meaning for your foe! 17 The tree that you saw grow and become mighty, whose top reached heaven, which was visible throughout the earth, 18 whose foliage was beautiful, whose fruit was so abundant that there was food for all in it, beneath which the beasts of the field dwelt, and in whose branches the birds of the sky lodged—19 it is you, O king, you who have grown and become mighty, whose greatness has grown to reach heaven, and whose dominion is to the end of the earth. 20 The holy Watcher whom the king saw descend from heaven and say,

   Hew down the tree and destroy it,
   But leave the stump with its roots in the ground.
   In fetters of iron and bronze
   In the grass of the field,
   Let him be drenched with the dew of heaven,
   And share the lot of the beasts of the field
   Until seven seasons pass over him—

21 this is its meaning, O king; it is the decree of the Most High which has overtaken my lord the king. 22 You will be driven away from men and have your habitation with the beasts of the field. You will be fed grass like cattle, and be drenched with the dew of heaven; seven seasons will pass over you until you come to know that the Most High is sovereign over the realm of man, and He gives it to whom He wishes. 23 And the meaning of the command to leave the stump of the tree with its roots is that the kingdom will remain yours from the time you come to know that Heaven is sovereign. 24 Therefore, O king, may my advice

16–24: The story slips into third-person narration with Daniel's role, but returns to first-person narration at v. 31. Daniel urges the king to reform his practices (v. 24), but in light of Nebuchadnezzar's conquest of Judah and the destruction of the Temple, his repentance could not have been seriously maintained. Daniel's concern for Nebuchadnezzar did not always meet with approval in rabbinic tradition (*b. B. Bat.* 4a); some rabbis, however, assumed that "my lord" (v. 16) must refer to God and the "enemy" must be Nebuchadnezzar himself. The point of these episodes, though told whimsically, seems to be that even Nebuchadnezzar could be forced to recognize the sovereignty of the one true God (cf. the book of Jonah). **28:** *Voice,* cf. Daniel 5. **31–34:** Cf. 3.32–33; 6.27–28.

be acceptable to you: Redeem your sins by beneficence and your iniquities by generosity to the poor; then your serenity may be extended."

25 All this befell King Nebuchadnezzar. 26 Twelve months later, as he was walking on the roof of the royal palace at Babylon, 27 the king exclaimed, "There is great Babylon, which I have built by my vast power to be a royal residence for the glory of my majesty!" 28 The words were still on the king's lips, when a voice fell from heaven, "It has been decreed for you, O King Nebuchadnezzar: The kingdom has passed out of your hands. 29 You are being driven away from men, and your habitation is to be with the beasts of the field. You are to be fed grass like cattle, and seven seasons will pass over you until you come to know that the Most High is sovereign over the realm of man and He gives it to whom He wishes." 30 There and then the sentence was carried out upon Nebuchadnezzar. He was driven away from men, he ate grass like cattle, and his body was drenched with the dew of heaven until his hair grew like eagle's [feathers] and his nails like [the talons of] birds.

31 "When the time had passed, I, Nebuchadnezzar, lifted my eyes to heaven, and my reason was restored to me. I blessed the Most High, and praised and glorified the Ever-Living One,

> Whose dominion is an everlasting dominion
> And whose kingdom endures throughout the
>   generations.

32   All the inhabitants of the earth are of no account.
> He does as He wishes with the host of heaven,
> And with the inhabitants of the earth.
> There is none to stay His hand
> Or say to Him, 'What have You done?'

33 There and then my reason was restored to me, and my majesty and splendor were restored to me for the glory of my kingdom. My companions and nobles sought me out, and I was reestablished over my kingdom, and added greatness was given me. 34 So now I, Nebuchadnezzar, praise, exalt, and glorify the King of Heaven, all of whose works are just and whose ways are right, and who is able to humble those who behave arrogantly."

5 King Belshazzar gave a great banquet for his thousand nobles, and in the presence of the thousand he drank wine. 2 Under the influence of the wine, Belshazzar ordered the gold and silver vessels that his father Nebuchadnezzar had taken out of the temple at Jerusalem to be brought so that the king and his nobles, his consorts, and

5.1–29: Daniel interprets the writing on the wall. 1–2: *Belshazzar* was the son of Nabonidus. He was never king, and only reigned as viceroy during his father's absence. *Great banquet:* Babylonian and Persian royal feasts were notorious for their excess; cf. Esth. ch 1. It is the sacrilege of drinking from the Temple vessels, however, especially by the *concubines*, that is most emphasized. According to rabbinic tradition (*b. Meg.* 11b–12a), Belshazzar was celebrating because he thought that the prediction of the demise of the Babylonian kingdom after seventy years (Jer. 25.11; cf. Dan. ch 9) had been proven wrong. He had miscalculated, however, by one year. *Vessels,* see 1.2.

his concubines could drink from them. ³ The golden vessels that had been taken out of the sanctuary of the House of God in Jerusalem were then brought, and the king, his nobles, his consorts, and his concubines drank from them. ⁴ They drank wine and praised the gods of gold and silver, bronze, iron, wood, and stone. ⁵ Just then, the fingers of a human hand appeared and wrote on the plaster of the wall of the king's palace opposite the lampstand, so that the king could see the hand as it wrote. ⁶ The king's face darkened, and his thoughts alarmed him; the joints of his loins were loosened and his knees knocked together. ⁷ The king called loudly for the exorcists, Chaldeans, and diviners to be brought. The king addressed the wise men of Babylon, "Whoever can read this writing and tell me its meaning shall be clothed in purple and wear a golden chain on his neck, and shall rule as ᵃ⁻one of threeᵃ in the kingdom."

⁸ Then all the king's wise men came, but they could not read the writing or make known its meaning to the king. ⁹ King Belshazzar grew exceedingly alarmed and his face darkened, and his nobles were dismayed. ¹⁰ Because of the state of the king and his nobles, the queen came to the banquet hall. The queen spoke up and said, "O king, live forever! Let your thoughts not alarm you or your face darken. ¹¹ There is a man in your kingdom who has the spirit of the holy gods in him; in your father's time, illumination, understanding, and wisdom like that of the gods were to be found in him, and your father, King Nebuchadnezzar, appointed him chief of the magicians, exorcists, Chaldeans, and diviners. ¹² Seeing that there is to be found in Daniel (whom the king called Belteshazzar) extraordinary spirit, knowledge, and understanding to interpret dreams, to explain riddles and solve problems, let Daniel now be called to tell the meaning [of the writing]."

¹³ Daniel was then brought before the king. The king addressed Daniel, "You are Daniel, one of the exiles of Judah whom my father, the king, brought from Judah. ¹⁴ I have heard about you that you have the spirit of the gods in you, and that illumination, knowledge, and extraordinary wisdom are to be found in you. ¹⁵ Now the wise men and exorcists have been brought before me to read this writing and to make known its meaning to me. But they could not tell what it meant. ¹⁶ I have heard about you, that you can give interpretations and solve problems. Now if you can read the writing and make known its meaning to me, you shall be clothed in purple and wear a golden chain on your neck and rule as one of three in the kingdom."

4: *Gods of gold and silver:* A common feature of Judaism at this time was the "parody of idols," usually focusing on their material origin and their inability to respond to prayer; cf. 5.23; Isa. 44.9–20; Ps. 115.4–8; in the Apocrypha, Wisdom of Solomon 13.1–15.17; Bel and the Dragon; and at Qumran, the "Prayer of Nabonidus." 5: *The fingers of a human hand:* Compare the finger of God that brings the plagues in Exod. 8.19, or writes the ten commandments in Exod. 31.18. 10: *Queen,* probably the queen-mother, the wife of Nebuchadnezzar. 11–12: Daniel's wisdom is spelled out by the queen-mother. Evidently she alone remembers his service to Nebuchadnezzar and his extraordinary abilities. This is one of the few places in chs 1–6 that connects the individual stories, and it is likely a redactional addition to make the book more coherent. See 2.13–23 n. 23: Because of the sacrilege of the Temple vessels, the sins of Belshazzar are more pointedly *against the Lord of Heaven* than was the case with Nebuchadnezzar. 25–28: The words are interpreted on two levels. They are weights: Mᴇɴᴇ in Aramaic is a mina (a little more than half a kilogram, about 20 ounces); ᴛᴇᴋᴇʟ is a shekel (11 grams or less than half an ounce); and ᴜᴘʜᴀʀsɪɴ (a dual form of "peres") is two half-minas. They also sound like verbs: Mᴇɴᴇ sounds like the verb "to number," ᴛᴇᴋᴇʟ "to weigh," and ᴜᴘʜᴀʀsɪɴ "to divide." The last is also similar to the word "Persians." It is possible that the words originally referred only to the decreasing "weight" or importance of particular Babylonian monarchs, and the dynasty was thereby condemned. A more explicit level of prophetic condemnation was then added in terms of the verbal meanings.

a-a Cf. Dan. 6.3; or "third in rank."

17 Then Daniel said in reply to the king, "You may keep your gifts for yourself, and give your presents to others. But I will read the writing for the king, and make its meaning known to him. 18 O king, the Most High God bestowed kingship, grandeur, glory, and majesty upon your father Nebuchadnezzar. 19 And because of the grandeur that He bestowed upon him, all the peoples and nations of every language trembled in fear of him. He put to death whom he wished, and whom he wished he let live; he raised high whom he wished and whom he wished he brought low. 20 But when he grew haughty and willfully presumptuous, he was deposed from his royal throne and his glory was removed from him. 21 He was driven away from men, and his mind made like that of a beast, and his habitation was with wild asses. He was fed grass like cattle, and his body was drenched with the dew of heaven until he came to know that the Most High God is sovereign over the realm of man, and sets over it whom He wishes. 22 But you, Belshazzar his son, did not humble yourself although you knew all this. 23 You exalted yourself against the Lord of Heaven, and had the vessels of His temple brought to you. You and your nobles, your consorts, and your concubines drank wine from them and praised the gods of silver and gold, bronze and iron, wood and stone, which do not see, hear, or understand; but the God who controls your lifebreath and every move you make—Him you did not glorify! 24 He therefore made the hand appear, and caused the writing to be inscribed. 25 This is the writing that is inscribed: MENE MENE TEKEL UPHARSIN. 26 And this is its meaning: MENE—God has numbered[a] [the days of] your kingdom and brought it to an end; 27 TEKEL—[b]you have been weighed[b] in the balance and found wanting; 28 PERES—your kingdom [c]has been divided[c] and given to the Medes and the Persians." 29 Then, at Belshazzar's command, they clothed Daniel in purple, placed a golden chain on his neck, and proclaimed that he should rule as one of three in the kingdom.

30 That very night, Belshazzar, the Chaldean king, was 6 killed, and Darius the Mede received the kingdom, being about sixty-two years old. 2 It pleased Darius to appoint over the kingdom one hundred and twenty satraps to be in charge of the whole kingdom; 3 over them were three ministers, one of them Daniel, to whom these satraps reported, in order that the king not be troubled. 4 This man Daniel surpassed the other ministers and satraps by virtue of his extraordinary spirit, and the king

5.30–6.29: Daniel in the lions' den. 5.30–6.1: These vv. were likely added to provide a smooth transition between the separate stories in chs 5 and 6. **1:** *Darius the Mede* is unhistorical. Darius was a famous Persian king (522–486 BCE) responsible for organizing his empire into provinces headed by "satraps" or governors. According to Herodotus, *Histories* 3.89, Darius established twenty satrapies; contrast the exaggerated tradition of Esth. 1.1. The four-empires schema requires that Media be represented in chs 2 and 7, and it is possible that a story originally involving Darius of Persia has been altered to fit this schema. The events of 5.30 are likewise ahistorical. **3:** In the stories of court conflict, an initial balance among the courtiers is disturbed when one of them is promoted above the others; cf. 2.49 (in reference to ch 3); Esth. 3.1.

a Aramaic mena.   b-b Aramaic tekilta.   c-c Aramaic perisat.

considered setting him over the whole kingdom. [5] The ministers and satraps looked for some fault in Daniel's conduct in matters of state, but they could find neither fault nor corruption, inasmuch as he was trustworthy, and no negligence or corruption was to be found in him. [6] Those men then said, "We are not going to find any fault with this Daniel, unless we find something against him in connection with the laws of his God." [7] Then these ministers and satraps came thronging in to the king and said to him, "O King Darius, live forever! [8] All the ministers of the kingdom, the prefects, satraps, companions, and governors are in agreement that a royal ban should be issued under sanction of an oath that whoever shall address a petition to any god or man, besides you, O king, during the next thirty days shall be thrown into a lions' den. [9] So issue the ban, O king, and put it in writing so that it be unalterable as a law of the Medes and Persians that may not be abrogated." [10] Thereupon King Darius put the ban in writing.

[11] When Daniel learned that it had been put in writing, he went to his house, in whose upper chamber he had had windows made facing Jerusalem, and three times a day he knelt down, prayed, and made confession to his God, as he had always done. [12] Then those men came thronging in and found Daniel petitioning his God in supplication. [13] They then approached the king and reminded him of the royal ban: "Did you not put in writing a ban that whoever addresses a petition to any god or man besides you, O king, during the next thirty days, shall be thrown into a lions' den?" The king said in reply, "The order stands firm, as a law of the Medes and Persians that may not be abrogated." [14] Thereupon they said to the king, "Daniel, one of the exiles of Judah, pays no heed to you, O king, or to the ban that you put in writing; three times a day he offers his petitions [to his God]." [15] Upon hearing that, the king was very disturbed, and he set his heart upon saving Daniel, and until the sun set made every effort to rescue him. [16] Then those men came thronging in to the king and said to the king, "Know, O king, that it is a law of the Medes and Persians that any ban that the king issues under sanction of oath is unalterable." [17] By the king's order, Daniel was then brought and thrown into the lions' den. The king spoke to Daniel and said, "Your God, whom you serve so regularly, will deliver you." [18] A rock was brought and placed over the mouth of the den; the king sealed it with his signet and with the signet of his nobles, so that nothing might be altered concerning Daniel.

[19] The king then went to his palace and spent the night fasting; no diversions were brought to him, and his sleep

8: The interdict is historically implausible. No king of this period who claimed divine status forbade the worship of other gods. Darius the Persian was supportive of local religions, including that of the Jews. The exclusive worship of one god was a Jewish view, and this exclusive notion is projected onto an Eastern divine monarch. The narrative thus reflects Jewish tensions about remaining monotheistic in a mixed Diaspora culture. **9:** Some ancient authors believed that the law of the Persian king, once enacted, could not be altered (Esth. 1.19; 8.8; Diodorus Siculus 17.30). This is likely only a popular tradition, however, and is emphasized for dramatic effect (cf. 6.14–17). **11:** Praying *three times a day* became a common Jewish practice by the mishnaic period, though it has earlier precedents (Ps. 55.18; Judith 9.1). Likewise, the Mishnah legislates praying toward Jerusalem (*m. Ber.* 4.5).

fled from him. [20] Then, at the first light of dawn, the king arose and rushed to the lions' den. [21] As he approached the den, he cried to Daniel in a mournful voice; the king said to Daniel, "Daniel, servant of the living God, was the God whom you served so regularly able to deliver you from the lions?" [22] Daniel then talked with the king, "O king, live forever! [23] My God sent His angel, who shut the mouths of the lions so that they did not injure me, inasmuch as I was found innocent by Him, nor have I, O king, done you any injury." [24] The king was very glad, and ordered Daniel to be brought up out of the den. Daniel was brought up out of the den, and no injury was found on him, for he had trusted in his God. [25] Then, by order of the king, those men who had slandered Daniel were brought and, together with their children and wives, were thrown into the lions' den. They had hardly reached the bottom of the den when the lions overpowered them and crushed all their bones.

[26] Then King Darius wrote to all peoples and nations of every language that inhabit the earth, "May your well-being abound! [27] I have hereby given an order that throughout my royal domain men must tremble in fear before the God of Daniel, for He is the living God who endures forever; His kingdom is indestructible, and His dominion is to the end of time; [28] He delivers and saves, and performs signs and wonders in heaven and on earth, for He delivered Daniel from the power of the lions." [29] Thus Daniel prospered during the reign of Darius and during the reign of Cyrus the Persian.

7 In the first year of King Belshazzar of Babylon, Daniel saw a dream and a vision of his mind in bed; afterward he wrote down the dream. Beginning the account, [2] Daniel related the following:

"In my vision at night, I saw the four winds of heaven stirring up the great sea. [3] Four mighty beasts different from each other emerged from the sea. [4] The first was like a lion but had eagles' wings. As I looked on, its wings were plucked off, and it was lifted off the ground and set on its feet like a man and given the mind of a man. [5] Then I saw a second, different beast, which was like a bear but raised on one side, and with three fangs in its mouth among its teeth; it was told, 'Arise, eat much meat!' [6] After that, as I looked on, there was another one, like a leopard, and it had on its back four wings like those of a bird; the beast had four heads, and dominion was given to it. [7] After that, as I looked on in the night vision, there was a fourth beast—fearsome, dreadful, and very powerful,

25: The importance of family identity in the ancient Near East could result in family members receiving the punishment of the male heads; cf. Num. 16.25–33; 2 Sam. 21.1–9; Esth. 9.13–14; but in contrast to this, Jer. 31.28–29; Ezek. ch 18. **26–28:** A concluding doxology similar to 3.28, 32–33; 4.31–34. The story is told for dramatic effect. It is unlikely that Darius would invoke Daniel's God, although this has been the theme of chs 1–6, as it was in "Prayer of Nabonidus" from Qumran and Bel and the Dragon from the Apocrypha. Keeping lions in an underground den is unknown; this and the sealing of the stone with the king's ring heighten the drama. **29:** *Cyrus the Persian* was the first Persian king (559–530 BCE). He was followed by Cambyses, Darius, and Xerxes; see 9.1.

7.1–12.13: Daniel's apocalyptic visions. This is the second half of the book; see the introduction on the difference in genre, date, and political situation of chs 7–12, and the difference in language between chs 7 and 8–12.

7.1–28: Vision of the four beasts. Ch 7, in Aramaic, may have been composed before chs 8–12. Like ch 2, it involves a dream interpretation and a four-kingdom schema, and like chs 2–6 it is in Aramaic. The depiction of the end of time in apocalyptic visions is often similar to biblical depictions of the beginning of time, that is, creation. The sea and monsters here are paralleled in many stories of creation (Gen. ch 1; Job 26.12–13; Pss. 33.6–7; 74.12–14; Isa. 27.1). **1:** *First year of King Belshazzar,* 553 BCE. The author of ch 7, like the author of ch 5, incorrectly thinks of Belshazzar as king. **2–3:** *Four winds . . . four mighty beasts:* The tumult of all four winds blowing at once and the violence of the sea portend threatening events. The recurrence of the number four evokes the four kingdoms of ch 2, and ch 7 will develop a four-kingdom schema further. **4–8:** The animals are like the mythological figures of ancient with great iron teeth—that devoured and crushed, and stamped the remains with its feet. It was different from all the other beasts which had gone before it; and it had ten horns. [8] While I was gazing upon these horns, a new little horn sprouted up among them; three of the older horns were uprooted to make room for it. There were eyes in this horn like those of a man, and a mouth that spoke arrogantly. [9] As I looked on,

> Thrones were set in place,
> And the Ancient of Days took His seat.
> His garment was like white snow,
> And the hair of His head was like lamb's[a] wool.
> His throne was tongues of flame;
> Its wheels were blazing fire.
> 10 A river of fire streamed forth before Him;
> Thousands upon thousands served Him;
> Myriads upon myriads attended Him;
> The court sat and the books were opened.

[11] I looked on. Then, because of the arrogant words that the horn spoke, the beast was killed as I looked on; its body was destroyed and it was consigned to the flames. [12] The dominion of the other beasts was taken away, but an extension of life was given to them for a time and season. [13] As I looked on, in the night vision,

> One like a human being
> Came with the clouds of heaven;
> He reached the Ancient of Days
> And was presented to Him.
> 14 Dominion, glory, and kingship were given to him;
> All peoples and nations of every language must
>   serve him.
> His dominion is an everlasting dominion that shall
>   not pass away,
> And his kingship, one that shall not be destroyed.

[15] As for me, Daniel, my spirit was disturbed within me and the vision of my mind alarmed me. [16] I approached one of the attendants and asked him the true meaning of all this. He gave me this interpretation of the matter: [17] 'These great beasts, four in number [mean] four kingdoms[b] will arise out of the earth; [18] then holy ones of the Most High will receive the kingdom, and will possess the kingdom forever—forever and ever.' [19] Then I wanted to ascertain the true meaning of the fourth beast, which was different from them all, very fearsome, with teeth of iron, claws of bronze, that devoured and crushed, and stamped the remains; [20] and of the ten horns on its head; and of the

Near Eastern art, but are also ferocious predators known to Israelite imagery, e.g., Hos. 13.7–8. (On the empires symbolized here, see the introduction.) The winged *lion* represents the Babylonian kingdom, the ravenous *bear* the Medes, the winged *leopard* the Persians, and the last *beast* the Greek empire of Alexander the Great, with the *ten horns* representing the Seleucid successors of Alexander in the Near East. The last beast is the most fearsome and chaotic, and the last horn represents the Seleucid Antiochus IV Epiphanes, who killed some of his rivals. The human transformation of the first beast may be an allusion to ch 4. The general cast of this scene is also like Ezek. ch 1, with its composite creatures and symbolic weight. **9–14:** The chaos and destructive power of the beasts is followed by an even more awesome judgment scene. The model for the judgment scene is the ancient Near Eastern council of gods in heaven, often utilized in the Bible to depict God's council (Ps. 82.1; Job ch 1). The *throne* formed from *tongues of flame* echoes Isa. ch 6; Ezek. 1.25–28. **9:** *Ancient of Days:* God is described in corporeal terms in the way that El is pictured in Canaanite myth, with the warrior-god Baal coming before him after slaying the sea-monster. It is significant, however, that combat is not mentioned here in Daniel, only judgment. As in Gen. ch 1, God has absolute sovereignty over the world, and does not need to establish authority through conflict. Cf. the role of angels in 10.20–21. **11:** The arrogance of the last horn is now seen as provocation for the most severe punishment. In ch 5 it was the arrogance and sacrilege of the latecomer Belshazzar, not the destructive history of Nebuchadnezzar, that provoked the strongest condemnation. **13–14:** *Human being,* lit. "son of man," which in the Bible is idiomatic for human being (Dan. 8.17; Ezek. 2.1; Job 25.6). Here, however, the celestial being is *like* a human being, i.e., has a human countenance. For the author it

a Or "clean." b Lit. "kings."

new one that sprouted, to make room for which three fell—the horn that had eyes, and a mouth that spoke arrogantly, and which was more conspicuous than its fellows. 21 (I looked on as that horn made war with the holy ones and overcame them, 22 until the Ancient of Days came and judgment was rendered in favor of the holy ones of the Most High, for the time had come, and the holy ones took possession of the kingdom.) 23 This is what he said: 'The fourth beast [means]—there will be a fourth kingdom upon the earth which will be different from all the kingdoms; it will devour the whole earth, tread it down, and crush it. 24 And the ten horns [mean]—from that kingdom, ten kings will arise, and after them another will arise. He will be different from the former ones, and will bring low three kings. 25 He will speak words against the Most High, and will harass the holy ones of the Most High. He will think of changing times and laws, and they will be delivered into his power for a ª time, times, and half a time. ª 26 Then the court will sit and his dominion will be taken away, to be destroyed and abolished for all time. 27 The kingship and dominion and grandeur belonging to all the kingdoms under Heaven will be given to the people of the holy ones of the Most High. Their kingdom shall be an everlasting kingdom, and all dominions shall serve and obey them.' " 28 Here the account ends.

I, Daniel, was very alarmed by my thoughts, and my face darkened; and I could not put the matter out of my mind.

8 In the third year of the reign of King Belshazzar, a vision appeared to me, to me, Daniel, after the one that had appeared to me earlier. 2 I saw in the vision—at the time I saw it I was in the fortress of Shushan, in the province of Elam—I saw in the vision that I was beside the Ulai River. 3 I looked and saw a ram standing between me and the river; he had two horns; the horns were high, with one higher than the other, and the higher sprouting last. 4 I saw the ram butting westward, northward, and southward. No beast could withstand him, and there was none to deliver from his power. He did as he pleased and grew

a-a I.e., a year, two years, and a half a year.

arguing either that the predictions had all been fulfilled in the past (*b. Sanh.* 97b), or that Daniel's predictions did not include the end of time (*Gen. Rab.* 98.2). Later in Jewish tradition the messianic interpretation faded and the *one like a human being* was seen as representing Israel (Ibn Ezra, Rashi). **14:** *Dominion . . . peoples and nations:* The tone and the words used here and in 7.27 tie this ch to the doxologies of chs 1–6 (see 3.31–33 n.). **16:** In chs 2 and 4 Daniel's extraordinary spiritual insights, bestowed by God, allowed him to interpret the dreams successfully, but the apocalyptic genre typically included a divine interpreter; cf. 8.15–16; 9.21–23; chs 10–12; Zech chs 1–6. *Interpretation:* The word used here ("peshar") is the Aramaic form of the word used later at Qumran for a type of biblical interpretation. (It is translated as "meaning" at 4.13; 5.15, 26.) **18:** *Holy ones of the Most High:* Some scholars see here a reference to the pious Jews of Daniel's circle, called "knowledgeable" in ch 12, but others argue, noting v. 27 and using the analogy of texts from Qumran, that *the holy ones* are the angelic host.

8.1–27: Vision of the ram and the he-goat. With the beginning of ch 8, the language changes from Aramaic back to Heb, and continues in Heb to the end. The symbolic visions of chs 8–12 are less poetic, more detailed, and more focused on recent events from the author's perspective. **1:** *Third year . . . Belshazzar,* see 7.1. **2:** *Shushan,* Susa, the winter capital of the Persian empire. *Ulai River:* Daniel twice has visions by a river (cf. 10.4), as does Ezekiel (Ezekiel 1.1). Rivers create a natural boundary, and in the ancient world boundaries and crossroads were considered ideal locations for communication with the divine. **3–14:** *Ram . . . he-goat:* The traditional four-kingdom schema is abandoned here in favor of one that is less compelling but better symbolizes the recent past from the author's perspective. The two-horned ram represents the Medes and Persians, and the

most likely represents a heavenly figure who will exercise judgment, perhaps Michael (see 10.13 n.). Christian tradition, especially in the Gospels, saw this as a prediction of Jesus as a heavenly "son of man." A messianic use of this title is also found in postbiblical Jewish literature (*1 Enoch* 46.1; 48.10; *4 Ezra* [2 Esdras] ch 13; *b. Sanh.* 98a). Some Rabbis rejected the future messianic interpretation by great. ⁵As I looked on, a he-goat came from the west, passing over the entire earth without touching the ground. The goat had a conspicuous horn on its forehead. ⁶He came up to the two-horned ram that I had seen standing between me and the river and charged at him with furious force. ⁷I saw him reach the ram and rage at him; he struck the ram and broke its two horns, and the ram was powerless to withstand him. He threw him to the ground and trampled him, and there was none to deliver the ram from his power. ⁸Then the he-goat grew very great, but at the peak of his power his big horn was broken. In its place, four conspicuous horns sprouted toward the four winds of heaven. ⁹From one of them emerged a small horn, which extended itself greatly toward the south, toward the east, and toward the beautiful land. ¹⁰It grew as high as the host of heaven and it hurled some stars of the [heavenly] host to the ground and trampled them. ¹¹It vaunted itself against the very chief of the host; on its account the regular offering was suspended, and His holy place was abandoned. ¹²ᵃ⁻An army was arrayed iniquitously against the regular offering;⁻ᵃ it hurled truth to the ground and prospered in what it did.

¹³Then I heard a holy being speaking, and another holy being said to whoever it was who was speaking, "How long will [what was seen in] the vision last—ᵃ⁻the regular offering be forsaken because of transgression; the sanctuary be surrendered and the [heavenly] host be trampled?"⁻ᵃ ¹⁴He answered me,ᵇ "For twenty-three hundred evenings and mornings; then the sanctuary shall be cleansed." ¹⁵While I, Daniel, was seeing the vision, and trying to understand it, there appeared before me one who looked like a man. ¹⁶I heard a human voice from the middle of Ulai calling out, "Gabriel, make that man understand the vision." ¹⁷He came near to where I was standing, and as he came I was terrified, and fell prostrate. He said to me, "Understand, O man, that the vision refers to the time of the end." ¹⁸When he spoke with me, I was overcome by a deep sleep as I lay prostrate on the ground. Then he touched me and made me stand up, ¹⁹and said, "I am going to inform you of what will happen when wrath is at an end, for [it refers] to the time appointed for the end.

²⁰"The two-horned ram that you saw [signifies] the kings of Media and Persia; ²¹and the buck, the he-goat—the king of Greece; and the large horn on his forehead, that is the first king. ²²One was broken and four came in

he-goat represents Alexander the Great, who died *at the peak of his power*. The *four conspicuous horns* represent the four kingdoms that succeeded Alexander, one of which was the Seleucid, over which Antiochus IV Epiphanes came to rule. This vision thus overlaps to a large extent with ch 7. **9:** *Beautiful land*, Judea. **11:** *Regular offering . . . abandoned:* Antiochus IV suppressed the practice of Judaism and turned the Temple into a pagan worship site (1 Macc. 1.54–61; 2 Macc. 4.11–6.11). **14:** *Twenty-three hundred evenings and mornings*, i.e., 1,150 days, about the same as the three and a half years of 7.25; 9.27; 12.7. **15–16:** *One who looked like a man:* An expression different from 7.13–14 is used here, which is a play on the name of *Gabriel*. Angels appear in the Bible, but only in Daniel and postbiblical texts do they have names; see also 12.1. **17–19:** Here and elsewhere (e.g., 8.26–27) a number of literary devices are used, typical of apocalypses, that increase the sense of awe, secrecy, and mystery, even though the events predicted seem very clear. The command to "keep the vision a secret" (v. 26) emphasizes that it was supposedly received by Daniel centuries earlier, but was not known until now at the *time of the end* when it finds its realization.

---

a-a Meaning of Heb. uncertain.   *b Several ancient versions "him."*

its stead—that [means]: four kingdoms will arise out of a nation, but without its power. 23 When their kingdoms are at an end, when the measure of transgression[a] has been filled, then a king will arise, impudent and versed in intrigue. 24 He will have great strength, but not through his own strength. He will be extraordinarily destructive; he will prosper in what he does, and destroy the mighty and the people of holy ones. 25 By his cunning, he will use deceit successfully. He will make great plans, will destroy many, taking them unawares, and will rise up against the chief of chiefs, but will be broken, not by [human] hands. 26 What was said in the vision about evenings and mornings is true. Now you keep the vision a secret, for it pertains to far-off days." 27 So I, Daniel, was stricken,[b] and languished many days. Then I arose and attended to the king's business, but I was dismayed by the vision and no one could explain it.

9 In the first year of Darius son of Ahasuerus, of Median descent, who was made king over the kingdom of the Chaldeans—2 in the first year of his reign, I, Daniel, consulted the books concerning the number of years that, according to the word of the LORD that had come to Jeremiah the prophet, were to be the term of Jerusalem's desolation—seventy years. 3 I turned my face to the Lord God, devoting myself to prayer and supplication, in fasting, in sackcloth and ashes. 4 I prayed to the LORD my God, making confession thus: "O Lord, great and awesome God, who stays faithful to His covenant with those who love Him and keep His commandments! 5 We have sinned; we have gone astray; we have acted wickedly; we have been rebellious and have deviated from Your commandments and Your rules, 6 and have not obeyed Your servants the prophets who spoke in Your name to our kings, our officers, our fathers, and all the people of the land. 7 With You, O Lord, is the right, and the shame is on us to this very day, on the men of Judah and the inhabitants of Jerusalem, all Israel, near and far, in all the lands where You have banished them, for the trespass they committed against You. 8 The shame, O LORD, is on us, on our kings, our officers, and our fathers, because we have sinned against You. 9 To the Lord our God belong mercy and forgiveness, for we rebelled against Him, 10 and did not obey the LORD our God by following His teachings that He set before us through His servants the prophets. 11 All Israel has violated Your teaching and gone astray,

9.1–27: Daniel reinterprets Jeremiah's prophecy of seventy years. 1: *Darius . . . Ahasuerus:* On Darius, see 6.1 n. Ahasuerus is Xerxes, like Darius a Persian and not a Mede, and was the son, not father, of Darius. *Of Median descent,* possibly an effort to harmonize the fact that Ahasuerus and Darius were Persian with the statement in 6.1 that Darius was a Mede. **2:** The author grapples with the prophetic prediction in Jer. 25.11–12 that Babylon would fall after *seventy years.* This is one of the few explicit references in a biblical book to another biblical book; it does not necessarily reflect the canonization of the Prophets, but suggests that like the Torah, certain prophetic texts were studied intensively at this time. **3:** *Fasting, sackcloth,* and *ashes* were aspects of ritual mourning in the Bible, but were also signs of penitence as well as preparation for fervent prayer and for visions (*4 Ezra* [*2 Esdras*] 5.13; 9.24). The rise of penitential theology in postbiblical Judaism suggests that, although Daniel's prayer is a response to particular historical events, it also reflects in Judaism a new personal, penitential religious life that is taken up in various ways by the Qumran sectarians, Pharisees, and Christians. This can also be found in some strands of rabbinic tradition (*b. Taʿan.* 11b–12a), but there is also found in the Talmud a tendency to rein in excessive penitential asceticism (*b. Taʿan.* 11a; *b. B. Bat.* 60b). **5:** Later Jewish confessions share this structure of listing words for various prohibited activities in the first-person plural.

---

a Lit. "transgressors."   b Meaning of Heb. uncertain.

disobeying You; so the curse and the oath written in the Teaching of Moses, the servant of God, have been poured down upon us, for we have sinned against Him. ¹²He carried out the threat that He made against us, and against our rulers who ruled us, to bring upon us great misfortune; under the whole heaven there has never been done the like of what was done to Jerusalem. ¹³All that calamity, just as is written in the Teaching of Moses, came upon us, yet we did not supplicate the LORD our God, did not repent of our iniquity or become wise through Your truth. ¹⁴Hence the LORD was intent upon bringing calamity upon us, for the LORD our God is in the right in all that He has done, but we have not obeyed Him.

¹⁵"Now, O Lord our God—You who brought Your people out of the land of Egypt with a mighty hand, winning fame for Yourself to this very day—we have sinned, we have acted wickedly. ¹⁶O Lord, as befits Your abundant benevolence, let Your wrathful fury turn back from Your city Jerusalem, Your holy mountain; for because of our sins and the iniquities of our fathers, Jerusalem and Your people have become a mockery among all who are around us.

¹⁷"O our God, hear now the prayer of Your servant and his plea, and show Your favor to Your desolate sanctuary, for the Lord's sake. ¹⁸Incline Your ear, O my God, and hear; open Your eyes and see our desolation and the city to which Your name is attached. Not because of any merit of ours do we lay our plea before You but because of Your abundant mercies. ¹⁹O Lord, hear! O Lord, forgive! O Lord, listen, and act without delay for Your own sake, O my God; for Your name is attached to Your city and Your people!"

²⁰While I was speaking, praying, and confessing my sin and the sin of my people Israel, and laying my supplication before the LORD my God on behalf of the holy mountain of my God—²¹while I was uttering my prayer, the man Gabriel, whom I had previously seen in the vision, was sent forth in flight and reached me about the time of the evening offering. ²²He made me understand by speaking to me and saying, "Daniel, I have just come forth to give you understanding. ²³A word went forth as you began your plea, and I have come to tell it, for you are precious; so mark the word and understand the vision.

²⁴"Seventy weeks[a] have been decreed for your people and your holy city until the measure of transgression is filled and that of sin complete, until iniquity is expiated, and eternal righteousness ushered in; and prophetic vision

15–19: The penitential prayer and confession of Israel's sins expresses Deuteronomistic theology, i.e., a view expressed often in the books from Deuteronomy through 2 Kings: Israel has sinned, and if it repents, God will act graciously once more. 24: *Seventy weeks* [of years], that is, 490 years, the true prediction of Jeremiah according to this interpretation (see v. 2 and n.). This interpretation is based on reading a single word in Jer. 25.11–12 in two different ways, as "shavʿuim" (weeks) and "shivʿim" (seventy). Such close textual study and revocalization of texts for interpretive purposes would characterize later rabbinic interpretation. *Holy of Holies anointed,* finally accomplished by Judas Maccabee in 164 BCE (1 Macc. 4.26–59), shortly after the final editing of Daniel. 25–26: *Anointed leader . . . anointed one:* The word *anointed* in vv. 25 and 26 is the Heb "mashiaḥ" (Messiah); thus these vv. have given rise to much Christian speculation. In the context of the other historical references, however, the *anointed leader* probably refers to either Zerubbabel or the high priest Joshua (Ezra 3.2; Hag. ch 1; Zech. 6.9–15), while the *anointed one* is most likely the high priest Onias III, killed in 171 BCE (2 Macc. 4.30–34). The prince is Antiochus IV Epiphanes. 27: *Half a week,* the three and a half years of the Maccabean revolt that had transpired to that time. See 7.25 n.; cf. 8.14. *Appalling abomination,* probably new altar stones placed upon the altar in the Temple, upon which pagan sacrifices were offered (1 Macc. 1.54; 2 Macc. 6.5).

a *Viz., of years.*

ratified,[a] and the Holy of Holies anointed. [25] You must know and understand: From the issuance of the word to restore and rebuild Jerusalem until the [time of the] anointed leader is seven weeks; and for sixty-two weeks it will be rebuilt, square and moat, but in a time of distress. [26] And after those sixty-two weeks, the anointed one will disappear and vanish.[b] The army of a leader who is to come will destroy the city and the sanctuary, but its end will come through a flood. Desolation is decreed until the end of war. [27] During one week he will make a firm covenant with many. For half a week he will put a stop to the sacrifice and the meal offering. At the [c]corner [of the altar][c] will be an appalling abomination until the decreed destruction will be poured down upon the appalling thing."

10 In the third year of King Cyrus of Persia, an oracle was revealed to Daniel, who was called Belteshazzar. That oracle was true, [c]but it was a great task to understand the prophecy; understanding came to him through the vision.[c]

[2] At that time, I, Daniel, kept three full weeks of mourning. [3] I ate no tasty food, nor did any meat or wine enter my mouth. I did not anoint myself until the three weeks were over. [4] It was on the twenty-fourth day of the first month, when I was on the bank of the great river—the Tigris—[5] that I looked and saw a man dressed in linen, his loins girt in [d]fine gold.[d] [6] His body was like beryl, his face had the appearance of lightning, his eyes were like flaming torches, his arms and legs had the color of burnished bronze, and the sound of his speech was like the noise of a multitude.

[7] I, Daniel, alone saw the vision; the men who were with me did not see the vision, yet they were seized with a great terror and fled into hiding. [8] So I was left alone to see this great vision. I was drained of strength, my vigor was destroyed, and I could not summon up strength. [9] I heard him speaking; and when I heard him speaking, overcome by a deep sleep, I lay prostrate on the ground. [10] Then a hand touched me, and shook me onto my hands and knees. [11] He said to me, "O Daniel, precious man, mark what I say to you and stand up, for I have been sent to you." After he said this to me, I stood up, trembling. [12] He then said to me, "Have no fear, Daniel, for from the first day that you set your mind to get understanding, practicing abstinence before your God, your prayer was heard,

10.1–12.13: Vision of the last days. Chs 10–12 constitute one extended vision that is much more detailed and focused on events contemporary with the author.

10.1–21: Daniel is strengthened by a heavenly being. 1: *Third year . . . Cyrus,* 536 BCE. **2–3:** Daniel's preparation is common for fervent prayer or visions (see 9.3 n.); here, however, it is particularly lengthy and detailed. **4:** *Bank . . . river,* see 8.2 n. **5–6:** The appearance of the man is described like other divine beings (Ezek. 1.4–14; 9.2–3).

incubation

---

a Lit. "sealed."   b Meaning of Heb. uncertain.
c-c Meaning of Heb. uncertain.   d-d Or "gold of Uphaz."

and I have come because of your prayer. [13] However, the prince of the Persian kingdom opposed me for twenty-one days; now Michael, a prince of the first rank, has come to my aid, after I was detained there with the kings of Persia. [14] So I have come to make you understand what is to befall your people in the days to come, for there is yet a vision for those days."

[15] While he was saying these things to me, I looked down and kept silent. [16] Then one who looked like a man touched my lips, and I opened my mouth and spoke, saying to him who stood before me, "My lord, because of the vision, I have been seized with pangs and cannot summon strength. [17] How can this servant of my lord speak with my lord, seeing that my strength has failed and no spirit is left in me?" [18] He who looked like a man touched me again, and strengthened me. [19] He said, "Have no fear, precious man, all will be well with you; be strong, be strong!" As he spoke with me, I was strengthened, and said, "Speak on, my lord, for you have strengthened me!" [20] Then he said, "Do you know why I have come to you? Now I must go back to fight the prince of Persia. When I go off, the prince of Greece will come in. [21] a-No one is helping me against them except your prince, Michael. However, I will tell you what is recorded in the book of truth.-a

11 "In the first year of Darius the Mede, I took my stand to strengthen and fortify him. [2] And now I will tell you the truth: Persia will have three more kings, and the fourth will be wealthier than them all; by the power he obtains through his wealth, he will stir everyone up against the kingdom of Greece. [3] Then a warrior king will appear who will have an extensive dominion and do as he pleases. [4] But after his appearance, his kingdom will be broken up and scattered to the four winds of heaven, but not for any of his posterity, nor with dominion like that which he had; for his kingdom will be uprooted and belong to others beside these.

[5] "The king of the south will grow powerful; however, one of his officers will overpower him and rule, having an extensive dominion. [6] After some years, an alliance will be made, and the daughter of the king of the south will come to the king of the north to effect the agreement, but she will not maintain her strength, nor will his strength endure. She will be surrendered together with those who escorted her and the one who begot her and helped her during those times. [7] A shoot from her stock will appear in his place, will come against the army and enter the fortress of

a-a Order of clauses inverted for clarity.

13: *Prince of the Persian kingdom,* the guardian angel of Persia. *Michael* was a warrior angel, found in later Jewish and Christian literature (*1 Enoch* 9.1; Qumran *War Scroll* 9.15–16; Rev. 12.7). See also 8.15–16 n. **20:** *Prince of Greece,* the guardian angel of the Seleucid empire. The guardian angels of Israel battle those of Persia and Greece in turn. The battle of the heavenly forces is also found at Qumran.

11.1–45: The heavenly being reveals future events. A detailed description follows representing events in the conflicted relations between the Seleucid empire of Syria and Babylonia and the Ptolemaic empire of Egypt. The symbolic aspect of the vision is less compelling than ch 7 or even ch 8; it also sometimes bogs down in historical correspondences. Apocalyptic writings, as well as some of those from Qumran (the Dead Sea Scrolls), typically refer to historical figures indirectly (as if in code), rather than by name. Daniel follows this practice. As the visions progress, and relate to the time of the author rather than to earlier times, they become more detailed. Thus, the detail allows a precise dating of the final composition and editing of Daniel. **1:** *First year of Darius the Mede,* see 9.1 n. **2–4:** It is unclear what Persian kings are intended; the *fourth* may be the last Persian king, Darius III (336–331). The *warrior king* is Alexander the Great, whose kingdom was broken up after his death, and ruled by various successor kingdoms. **5:** *The king of the south,* Ptolemy I Soter (323–285), who established the Ptolemaic kingdom in Egypt; one of his officers is Seleucus I, who founded the Seleucid kingdom in Babylonia. **6:** An *alliance* based on marriage was effected between the Ptolemies and the Seleucids. The *daughter* of Ptolemy II and others were murdered. **7–8:** Her brother, Ptolemy III (246–221), a *shoot from her stock,* retaliated. **9:** Seleucus II, the *king of the north* (v. 7), invaded Egypt, *the realm of the king of the south,* but returned north. **10–13:** The *sons of* the king of the north; he will fight and overpower them. [8] He will also take their gods with their molten images and their precious vessels of silver and gold back to Egypt as booty. For some years he will leave the king of the north alone, [9] who will [later] invade the realm of the king of the south, but will go back to his land.

[10] "His sons will wage war, collecting a multitude of great armies; he will advance and sweep through as a flood, and will again wage war as far as his stronghold. [11] Then the king of the south, in a rage, will go out to do battle with him, with the king of the north. He will muster a great multitude, but the multitude will be delivered into his [foe's] power. [12] But when the multitude is carried off, he will grow arrogant; he will cause myriads to perish, but will not prevail. [13] Then the king of the north will again muster a multitude even greater than the first. After a time, a matter of years, he will advance with a great army and much baggage. [14] In those times, many will resist the king of the south, and the lawless sons of your people will assert themselves to confirm the vision, but they will fail. [15] The king of the north will advance and throw up siege ramps and capture a fortress city, and the forces of the south will not hold out; even the elite of his army will be powerless to resist. [16] His opponent will do as he pleases, for none will hold out against him; he will install himself in the beautiful land with destruction within his reach. [17] He will set his mind upon invading the strongholds throughout his [foe's] kingdom, but in order to destroy it he will effect an agreement with him and give him a daughter in marriage; he will not succeed at it and it will not come about. [18] He will turn to the coastlands and capture many; but a consul will put an end to his insults, nay pay him back for his insults. [19] He will head back to the strongholds of his own land, but will stumble, and fall, and vanish. [20] His place will be taken by one who will dispatch an officer to exact tribute for royal glory, but he will be broken in a few days, not by wrath or by war. [21] His place will be taken by a contemptible man, on whom royal majesty was not conferred; he will come in unawares and seize the kingdom through trickery. [22] The forces of the flood will be overwhelmed by him and will be broken, and so too the covenant leader. [23] And, from the time an alliance is made with him, he will practice deceit; and he will rise to power with a small band. [24] He will invade the richest of provinces unawares, and will do what his father and forefathers never did, lavishing on them[a] spoil, booty,

Seleucus II grew in strength and attacked Egypt. One of them, Antiochus III the Great (223–187), finally defeated Ptolemy V. There were Jews sympathetic to both sides (2 Macc. chs 3–4). **14:** The *lawless sons of your people* probably refers to the Seleucid sympathizers. **15–16:** The Battle of Paneas in 200 BCE gave Antiochus III control of the *beautiful land,* Judea. **17:** Another *marriage* is arranged to normalize relations, but it did not achieve its end. **18–19:** Antiochus III turns his attentions elsewhere but is unsuccessful and ultimately dies. **20:** Seleucus IV Philopator, who succeeded Antiochus III, sent Heliodorus to rob the Jerusalem Temple treasury. According to 2 Macc. ch 3, this attempt was unsuccessful because Heliodorus was chastised by a divine apparition, i.e., *not by wrath or by war.* **21–22:** Antiochus IV Epiphanes (175–164) succeeds Seleucus IV. Under his rule the *covenant leader,* the high priest Onias III, was murdered (see 9.26). **24:** Antiochus IV was notoriously lavish with sacrifices.

a I.e., his followers.

and wealth; he will have designs upon strongholds, but only for a time.

25 "He will muster his strength and courage against the king of the south with a great army. The king of the south will wage war with a very great and powerful army but will not stand fast, for they will devise plans against him. 26 Those who eat of his food will ruin him. His army will be overwhelmed, and many will fall slain. 27 The minds of both kings will be bent on evil; while sitting at the table together, they will lie to each other, but to no avail, for there is yet an appointed term. 28 He will return to his land with great wealth, his mind set against the holy covenant. Having done his pleasure, he will return to his land. 29 At the appointed time, he will again invade the south, but the second time will not be like the first. 30 Ships from Kittim will come against him. He will be checked, and will turn back, raging against the holy covenant. Having done his pleasure, he will then attend to those who forsake the holy covenant. 31 Forces will be levied by him; they will desecrate the temple, the fortress; they will abolish the regular offering and set up the appalling abomination. 32 He will flatter with smooth words those who act wickedly toward the covenant, but the people devoted to their God will stand firm. 33 The knowledgeable among the people will make the many understand; and for a while they shall fall by sword and flame, suffer captivity and spoliation. 34 In defeat, they will receive a little help, and many will join them insincerely. 35 Some of the knowledgeable will fall, that they may be refined and purged and whitened until the time of the end, for an interval still remains until the appointed time.

36 "The king will do as he pleases; he will exalt and magnify himself above every god, and he will speak awful things against the God of gods. He will prosper until wrath is spent, and what has been decreed is accomplished. 37 He will not have regard for the god of his ancestors or for the one dear to women; he will not have regard for any god, but will magnify himself above all. 38 He will honor the god of fortresses on his stand; he will honor with gold and silver, with precious stones and costly things, a god that his ancestors never knew. 39 He will deal with fortified strongholds with the help of an alien god. He will heap honor on those who acknowledge him, and will make them master over many; he will distribute land for a price. 40 At the time of the end, the king of the south will lock horns with him, but the king of the north will attack him with chariots and riders and many ships. He will invade lands, sweeping through them like a flood; 41 he

25–27: Antiochus IV again defeats Egypt. 28: In the midst of his constant campaigns, Antiochus IV had designs once again on the gold in the Jerusalem Temple (1 Macc. ch 1). 29–31: When Antiochus IV invades Egypt once more, he is opposed by ships from *Kittim*, or Rome, now a Mediterranean power. Jewish sympathizers, along with Antiochus's appointed high priest, will forsake the covenant and introduce new sacrifices, including the *apalling abomination*. 32–35: Some faithful Jews resist, and those who are *knowledgeable* will instruct the *many* (cf. 12.3). On the identity of the knowledgeable, see the introduction. Many will, for the first time in Jewish history, suffer martyrdom (1 Macc. 1.63), namely death due to their religious beliefs. The *little help* they receive perhaps indicates the lack of an effective alliance between the militant Maccabees and Daniel's circle (cf. 1 Macc. 2.29–38). 36–39: The author depicts the arrogance of Antiochus IV as conflict in the divine council (cf. Isa. 14.12–21; Ezek. 28.1–10). The offense of Antiochus IV is not only against the God of gods, but also against his own ancestral god and the *one dear to women*, the Mesopotamian god Tammuz (Ezek. 8.14). It has been thought that Antiochus elevated the cult of Zeus Olympios above all other gods, but ancient authors saw him as active in the worship of many deities and divine heroes. To the author of Daniel, however, the installation of Zeus Olympios in the sanctuary was *alien* both to Jews and to the Seleucid dynasty, which had previously favored Apollo as a patron deity. 40–45: From this point, the predictions do not correspond to events as known from other sources, and scholars agree that the author must have been writing at the time of the events described in the preceding vv. (see introduction). What is described is a cataclysmic battle of the major powers that would mark the end of the present age (cf. Ezek. 38–39), but the campaigns predicted here did not occur. This helps to date will invade the beautiful land, too, and many will fall, but these will escape his clutches: Edom, Moab, and the chief part of the Ammonites. ⁴²He will lay his hands on lands; not even the land of Egypt will escape. ⁴³He will gain control over treasures of gold and silver and over all the precious things of Egypt, and the Libyans and Cushites will follow at his heel. ⁴⁴But reports from east and north will alarm him, and he will march forth in a great fury to destroy and annihilate many. ⁴⁵He will pitch his royal pavilion between the sea and the beautiful holy mountain, and he will meet his doom with no one to help him.

12 "At that time, the great prince, Michael, who stands beside the sons of your people, will appear. It will be a time of trouble, the like of which has never been since the nation came into being. At that time, your people will be rescued, all who are found inscribed in the book. ²Many of those that sleep in the dust of the earth will awake, some to eternal life, others to reproaches, to everlasting abhorrence. ³And the knowledgeable will be radiant like the bright expanse of sky, and those who lead the many to righteousness will be like the stars forever and ever.

⁴"But you, Daniel, keep the words secret, and seal the book until the time of the end. Many will range far and wide and knowledge will increase."

⁵Then I, Daniel, looked and saw two others standing, one on one bank of the river, the other on the other bank of the river. ⁶One said to the man clothed in linen, who was above the water of the river, "How long until the end of these awful things?" ⁷Then I heard the man dressed in linen, who was above the water of the river, swear by the Ever-Living One as he lifted his right hand and his left hand to heaven: "For a ᵃtime, times, and half a time;ᵃ and when the breaking of the power of the holy people comes to an end, then shall all these things be fulfilled."

⁸I heard and did not understand, so I said, "My lord, what will be the outcome of these things?" ⁹He said, "Go, Daniel, for these words are secret and sealed to the time of the end. ¹⁰Many will be purified and purged and refined; the wicked will act wickedly and none of the wicked will understand; but the knowledgeable will understand. (¹¹From the time the regular offering is abolished, and an appalling abomination is set up—it will be a thousand two hundred and ninety days. ¹²Happy the one who waits and reaches one thousand three hundred and thirty-five days.) ¹³But you, go on to the end; you shall rest, and arise to your destiny at the end of the days."

Daniel to the middle of the persecutions of Antiochus IV.

12.1–13: Vision of the end. 1: A judgment scene similar to ch 7. *Michael,* see 8.15–16 n.; 10.13 n. *Book:* The book of life, prominent in the Jewish liturgy of the high holidays, is borrowed from Mesopotamia and is found in the Bible (Exod. 32.32–33; Isa. 4.3). Here it is more eschatological, i.e., oriented toward the end of time, and may have inscribed only a small subset of the people Israel, as it does in other Jewish apocalyptic texts. **2–3:** *Many . . . will awake,* i.e., not all; presumably *some* who deserve *eternal life, others* who deserve *everlasting abhorrence.* The doctrine of resurrection and judgment probably came about during the persecutions of Antiochus IV as a means to effect justice at a time when pious people, the *knowledgeable,* were being martyred. Unlike Ezekiel's vision of dry bones (Ezek. ch 37), the resurrection here is not a metaphor for the rebirth of Israel, but individual resurrection for judgment. Whether bodily resurrection or some form of spiritual resurrection is intended is not stated. This is the only certain biblical reference to this doctrine, a doctrine that became central in Christian theology and remained a strong current in Judaism as well. It was a tenet of belief for the Pharisees, and Maimonides, centuries later, included it among his thirteen principles of Jewish faith. **4:** See 8.26 n. **7:** See 7.25 n. **11–12:** Other time predictions are added, pushing the expected end slightly later than those that have come before. It is possible that the failure of the end to come prompted two successive adjustments.

a-a See note at 7.25.

עזרא

Ezra

EZRA-NEHEMIAH, WHICH BEGINS where Chronicles ends, is written as a continuation of Chronicles. It contains historical traditions, records significant liturgical developments in the newly reconstituted Second Temple community, and preserves important geneaolgical lists of returnees, priests, Levites, and other leadership and Temple personnel. In presenting this material concerning the early postexilic period, Ezra-Nehemiah emphasizes repeatedly their continuity with the Israelite preexilic past. Ezra explicitly appropriates Mosaic authority as he is represented as regiving the Torah in a kind of repetition of the Sinai event. Indeed, Ezra and Nehemiah insist that their legal innovations are already part of Mosaic Torah, i.e., that they are accurate applications of Mosaic Torah and have authoritative Mosaic status. Furthermore, the narrative of Ezra-Nehemiah repeatedly invokes and identifies with the "conquest" of the land of Israel during the time of Joshua as a way of authorizing the returnees' appropriation of Judah and their insistence on rebuilding the Temple and the wall of Jerusalem. The narrative of Ezra-Nehemiah thus represents the self-understanding of the reconstituted Second Temple community as fulfilling the Abrahamic covenant of promised land, a land which, in their textual memory, had been violently torn from them by the Babylonian king Nebuchadnezzar. Ezra-Nehemiah also repeatedly invokes the prophetic traditions of promise for return after the exile. They see themselves as part of the divine fulfillment of earlier prophecies for return and hope uttered by Isaiah, Jeremiah, and others. This identification was meant, in part, to encourage the returnees to identify with and revere their past textual history and overcome the profound disappointment that must have overwhelmed the exiles in Babylonia.

During the reign of Cyrus II (559–530 BCE), the king issued a proclamation encouraging nations to establish their own temples in their indigenous lands. At this time Sheshbazzar was the appointed governor (or leader) of Judah, now a province in the Persian empire, known as Yehud. As a result of Cyrus's decree of 538, known in different forms in Ezra 1.1–4 (see 2 Chron. 36.22–23) and Ezra 6.1–5, some Judean exiles returned to Israel. Returnees began to reconstruct the Jerusalem Temple and resettle in Judah and surrounding environs. During the reign of Cambyses (530–522), Zerubbabel was governor of Judah and the rebuilding of the Jerusalem Temple continued. During the reign of Darius I (522–486) Haggai and Zechariah prophesied in Jerusalem, and the Jerusalem Temple was rebuilt and

dedicated in 516. The rebuilding of the Jerusalem wall and surrounding areas continued
under Xerxes I (486–465) and Artaxerxes I Longimanus (465–424). Ezra arrived in Jerusalem in 458. Nehemiah, governor of Judah, was sent to Jerusalem to rebuild the city in 445
and served under both Artaxerxes I and Darius II (423–405), who, following the general
Persian policy of religious tolerance, continued to support Judah during his reign.

Date and Composition of Ezra-Nehemiah

MOST SCHOLARS DATE THE PRESENT VERSION of Ezra-Nehemiah to the 4th century BCE.
Ezra-Nehemiah describes events that occurred, for the most part, in the 5th century BCE,
but there are a number of references to later events and important figures. For instance,
the Persian king Darius II (423–405) is mentioned in Nehemiah 12.22; this is the latest king
mentioned and would support the claim that the traditions were compiled and completed
by the early 4th century, and not later. Other significant details that would be expected in
a late-4th-century or later composition are totally lacking.

Some scholars have suggested that Ezra-Nehemiah is produced by the same author(s)
and editor(s) responsible for producing Chronicles, and thus Chronicles-Ezra-Nehemiah
should be understood to form a single literary work. This proposal stems from the following arguments: The three share major themes; the conclusion of 2 Chronicles (36.22–23)
overlaps with the introduction of Ezra (1.1–3); and 1 Esdras (in the Septuagint) combines
parts of all three works. This thesis was first articulated in 1832 by the German-Jewish
scholar Leopold Zunz and has since received wide support from other scholars. More recently scholars have challenged this theory on the basis of significantly different theological assumptions and differences in use of language in Ezra-Nehemiah and Chronicles; this
newer position, which does not assign the same authorship to these works, is now widely
accepted.

There is significant ancient debate surrounding the question of the unity of Ezra-
Nehemiah. In rabbinic tradition Ezra-Nehemiah was recognized as a single work authored
by Ezra (b. B. Bat. 15 a). Ezra-Nehemiah is considered a single unified work in early
Hebrew biblical manuscripts, in the Greek version of the Bible (the Septuagint), and in
later Jewish traditions.

The first formal division of Ezra-Nehemiah into two separate works appears in the 3rd
century CE, among Christians, in the work of the early church father, Origen. This division
is also reflected in Jerome's extremely influential Latin translation, the Vulgate, which was
completed in the 4th century CE. The division of the book into Ezra and Nehemiah among
Jews appears in the first printed editions of the Heb text in the 15th century CE. However,
in spite of this borrowed division, Masoretic tradition reflects that the end of the book is at
the conclusion of Nehemiah. Titles for Ezra-Nehemiah differ in the various translations.
Ezra is titled 2 Esdras in the Septuagint and 1 Esdras in the Vulgate. Nehemiah is titled
3 Esdras in the Septuagint and 2 Esdras in the Vulgate.

The Septuagint and Vulgate also preserve books related to the Ezra-Nehemiah narrative. The Apocryphal work called 1 Esdras in the Septuagint (3 Esdras in the Vulgate;

1 Esdras in modern Bibles) preserves a translation of 2 Chronicles 35–36; Ezra 1–10; Nehemiah 8.1–13; and a major addition that is lacking in the Hebrew version in 1 Esdras 3.1–5.6. Another related book is called "the Apocalypse of Ezra" or *4 Ezra* in the Vulgate and 2 Esdras in modern Bibles. These related versions preserve interpretations and alternate versions of the Ezra-Nehemiah narrative and are very important for acquiring a more complete understanding of this period and the development of Judaism.

Although Ezra-Nehemiah is presented as a single unified work in the Masoretic tradition, recent scholarship has debated its unity, suggesting that Ezra and Nehemiah are separate works, each drawn from various sources. The significant linguistic differences between Ezra and Nehemiah suggest that they were not written by the same author. The inclusion of overlapping but inconsistent genealogical lists also suggests that these two works were originally two independent texts. Finally, the entire book of Ezra focuses on the restoration of the Temple, establishing a community in Jerusalem, and the implementation of the Mosaic law. Nehemiah, on the other hand, focuses on resettlement of the returnees, rebuilding the Jerusalem wall, and insuring the economic stability of the people and of the Temple staff (the priests and Levites). These thematic differences further suggest that Ezra and Nehemiah were originally composed as two independent works.

Underlying Ezra-Nehemiah are earlier sources that were incorporated and then reworked into a largely coherent narrative. In fact, Ezra-Nehemiah, like other works of this period, is fond of quoting official documents. The authenticity of these documents, however, and their historical accuracy are debated by modern scholars. Below is a list of the likely sources that have been woven together to form the current book:

- Cyrus's decree: Ezra 1.2–4 (Heb); Ezra 6.3–5 (Aramaic); Ezra 5.13–15 (paraphrase of the decree)
- List of returnees: Ezra 2.1–67, thought to be taken from Neh. 7.6–68, which is a combination of lists of different returns in the early Persian period
- Rehum's letter to Artaxerxes and Artaxerxes' reply: Ezra 4.7–22
- Tattenai's letter to Darius and Darius's reply: Ezra 5.6–17; 6.6–12
- Artaxerxes justifies the return and rebuilding: Ezra 7.12–26
- List of families who journeyed to Jerusalem: Ezra 8.1–14
- List of families who intermarried: Ezra 10.18–43
- Ezra's confession: Ezra 9.6–15
- Nehemiah's memoir: Neh. 1.1–7; 9.1–2; 12.27–43; 13.3, 31
- Authentic part of the Ezra narrative: Neh. 7.72b–9.5
- Confession: Neh. 9.6–37
- Temple archives material: Neh. 9.38–10.39
- Wall dedication: Neh. 12.27–33
- Purification of the Jerusalem community: Neh. 12.44–13.3

Ezra and Nehemiah are unique among biblical books in that they also include a genre identified as memoirs. These include both first-person and third-person narratives concerning Ezra and Nehemiah. The first-person narratives are typically considered to be authentic autobiographical accounts of Ezra and Nehemiah. The third-person parts of the memoirs are attributed to the editors of the final version of Ezra-Nehemiah. The Ezra memoir is thought to consist of parts of Ezra and Nehemiah and should be ordered in the following manner: Ezra 7–8; Nehemiah 8; Ezra 9–10; Nehemiah 9. Nehemiah's memoir is thought to consist of Nehemiah 1.1–7.72a (although some scholars have excluded 3.1–32 and 5.14–19 from the Nehemiah memoir); 11.1–2; 12.31–43; 13.4–31.

Guide to Reading Ezra-Nehemiah

THE NARRATIVE OF EZRA-NEHEMIAH begins with a lengthy account of the returnees' arrival in Jerusalem and the rebuilding of the Jerusalem Temple (Ezra 1–6). The memoirs of Ezra and Nehemiah follow. Ezra's memoir consists of Ezra 7–10 and Nehemiah 8–10. Chs 7 and 8 of Ezra contain reports of the initial difficulties Ezra confronted when he first began to build and the repeated appeal he made to Cyrus's initial decree. In addition, an elaborate account is presented of the legal crises that the returnees faced in light of the widespread practice of intermarriage. Finally, in ch 10 of Ezra, Ezra resolves the legal crisis and completes the rebuilding of the Temple. The conclusion of the Ezra memoir is preserved in the text of Nehemiah (7.27–10.40). Here Ezra conducts a public reading of the law, holds a celebration of the festival of the Booths, a delayed Yom Kippur, and finally presents a covenant that is signed by the leaders of the community with the entire community present.

The Nehemiah memoir (Neh. 1.1–7.72) begins by focusing on a different project of restoration, namely the challenge of rebuilding the wall around Jerusalem. Nehemiah was determined to rebuild the wall, despite extensive harassment from the local peoples. The final section of the book (11.1–13.31) recounts a number of political and religious measures taken by Nehemiah in order to ensure the economic and religious preservation of the returnees and of the Temple personnel.

Importance for Judaism

THE IMPORTANCE OF EZRA for the creation and formation of what came to be known as rabbinic Judaism cannot be overestimated. According to the Bible, Ezra was the one who brought the Torah to the returning exiles, read and interpreted it publicly, and oversaw the people's solemn recommitment to its teachings (Neh. chs 8–10). Thus Ezra is like a second Moses. The Rabbis imply this by stating: "Ezra was sufficiently worthy that the Torah could have been given through him if Moses had not preceded him" (*t. Sanh.* 4.4). A number of ordinances called the ten *takanot* (regulations) are attributed to Ezra, although they are nowhere mentioned in the text of Ezra-Nehemiah. In addition, he is celebrated for other important accomplishments: He is said to be involved in the writing of the book of Psalms (*Song Rab.* 4.19), and he had the Torah restored to its "original Mosaic" Assyrian characters, thereby leaving the old Hebrew characters for the Samaritans (e.g., *b. Sanh.* 21b). These legal innovations, along with other notable accomplishments, reflect the way

Ezra is received and embraced by rabbinic Judaism. Ezra is both an authoritative scribe and priest, as well as a kind of proto-Rabbi who also has the authority of a prophet. His legal innovations are not seen as such, but are depicted as proper interpretation of eternally binding Mosaic law (see Ezra 7.10; Neh. 8.1). This principle is at the heart of rabbinic interpretation, and his authenticity is never called into question within rabbinic Judaism.

Summary of Contents

[HINDY NAJMAN]

1 In the first year of King Cyrus of Persia, when the word of the LORD spoken by Jeremiah was fulfilled,[a] the LORD roused the spirit of King Cyrus of Persia to issue a proclamation throughout his realm by word of mouth and in writing as follows: ² "Thus said King Cyrus of Persia: The LORD God of Heaven has given me all the kingdoms of the earth and has charged me with building Him a house in Jerusalem, which is in Judah. ³ Anyone of you of all His people—may his God be with him, and let him go up to Jerusalem that is in Judah and build the House of the LORD God of Israel, the God that is in Jerusalem; ⁴ and all who stay behind, wherever he may be living, let the people of his place assist him with silver, gold, goods, and livestock, besides the freewill offering to the House of God that is in Jerusalem." ⁵ So the chiefs of the clans of Judah and Benjamin, and the priests and Levites, all whose spirit had been roused by God, got ready to go up to build the House of the LORD that is in Jerusalem. ⁶ All their neighbors supported them with silver vessels, with gold, with goods, with livestock, and with precious objects, besides what had been given as a freewill offering. ⁷ King Cyrus of Persia released the ves-

a Cf. Jer. 29.10.

1.1–4: Jeremiah's prophecy is fulfilled through the decree of King Cyrus of Persia. This introductory section, until the words "let him go up," also appears as 2 Chron. 36.22–23. **1:** *In the first year of King Cyrus of Persia:* Although Cyrus became king of Persia in 559 BCE, the v. refers to Cyrus's first year as the ruler of Babylonia, 539–538. Cyrus granted the nations under his control the right to worship their own gods and build their temples. This decree typifies the tolerant religious policy of the Persians. *When the word of the LORD spoken by Jeremiah was fulfilled:* Throughout the book of Jeremiah the people of Judah are instructed to accept as a divine decree Babylonian rule and exile from their land. In some of the Jeremianic prophecies Nebuchadnezzar is even identified as the servant of God. However, Jeremiah also prophesies that there will eventually be a return to Judah in which the people of Judah will rebuild the Temple (e.g., Jer. 29.4–10; 31.27–34; 32.36–44). In the Second Temple period Cyrus's decree was interpreted as the fulfillment of Jeremiah's prophecy; it is possible that this was seen as a specific fulfillment of Jer. ch 25, a widely cited ch in other books, that suggested that Babylonia would dominate the world for seventy years. The

LORD roused the spirit of King Cyrus of Persia: The intimate relationship between the LORD and Cyrus is emphasized in Isa. 44.28, where the LORD says, "He is my shepherd; He shall fulfill all My purposes!" Josephus (*Ant.* 11.1.2) suggests that Cyrus knew this passage from Isaiah. Cyrus is also referred to as the anointed one of the LORD in Isa. 45.1. In rabbinic traditions Cyrus is praised as a sage for his decree of 538 which permitted the rebuilding of the Jerusalem Temple. Cyrus is also held up as a model in Gk writings of the Persian period. **3–4:** The narrative of Ezra understands Cyrus's decree to rebuild the Temple to require all of the Jewish exiles to support the rebuilding of the Temple, but not necessarily to return to Judah. It appears from Ezra-Nehemiah that many exiles were reluctant to give up the lives they had established for themselves in Babylonia and to return to Judah where their sustenance and future seemed less certain. *The God that is in Jerusalem:* This follows the typical ancient Near Eastern pattern in which gods are viewed as national deities, localized at their capitals. In rabbinic traditions Cyrus's wisdom is said to be limited because he appears to confine to Jerusalem the power of the God of Israel and thereby to deny God's dominion over the world (*Esth. Rab.* proem 6 and 1.5).

1.5–11: The exiles return to Judah with the original Temple vessels. 5–6: Whoever shares Cyrus's divine inspiration returns. Those who choose to remain in exile, although they support the rebuilding project financially, are implicitly reproached. **7–11:** Cyrus's return of the Temple vessels is also sels of the LORD's house which Nebuchadnezzar had taken away from Jerusalem and had put in the house of his god. [8] These King Cyrus of Persia released through the office of Mithredath the treasurer, who gave an inventory of them to Sheshbazzar the prince of Judah. [9] This is the inventory: 30 gold basins, 1,000 silver basins, 29 knives, [10] 30 gold bowls, 410 silver [a]double bowls,[a] 1,000 other vessels; [11] in all, 5,400 gold and silver vessels. Sheshbazzar brought all these back when the exiles came back from Babylon to Jerusalem.

2 [b]These are the people of the province who came up from among the captive exiles whom King Nebuchadnezzar of Babylon had carried into exile to Babylon, who returned to Jerusalem and Judah, each to his own city, [2] who came with Zerubbabel, Jeshua, Nehemiah, Seraiah, Reelaiah, Mordecai, Bilshan, Mispar, Bigvai, Rehum, Baanah:

The list of the men of the people of Israel: [3] the sons of Parosh—2,172; [4] the sons of Shephatiah—372; [5] the sons of Arah—775; [6] the sons of Pahath-moab: the sons of Jeshua and Joab—2,812; [7] the sons of Elam—1,254; [8] the sons of Zattu—945; [9] the sons of Zaccai—760; [10] the sons of Bani—642; [11] the sons of Bebai—623; [12] the sons of Azgad—1,222; [13] the sons of Adonikam—666; [14] the sons of Bigvai—2,056; [15] the sons of Adin—454; [16] the sons of Ater: Hezekiah—98; [17] the sons of Bezai—323; [18] the sons of Jorah—112; [19] the sons of Hashum—223; [20] the sons of Gibbar—95; [21] the sons of Bethlehem—123; [22] the sons of Netophah—56; [23] the sons of Anathoth—128; [24] the sons of Azmaveth—42; [25] the sons of Kiriath-arim: Chephirah and Beeroth—743; [26] the sons of Ramah and Geba—621; [27] the men

a-a Meaning of Heb. uncertain.
b This chapter appears as Neh. 7.6–73 with variations in the names and numbers.

reported in Ezra 5.14; 6.5. A corroborating account of Nebuchadnezzar's removal of the Temple vessels appears in 2 Chron. 36.10, 18. The removal is also reported in 2 Kings 24.13, but there it also notes that Nebuchadnezzar "stripped off" the gold from all of the Temple vessels. This is not mentioned in Ezra, which has as a major theme the continuity between the Second Temple and the preexilic past.

2.1–70: List of exiles who return to Jerusalem and Judah (= Neh.

7.6–72). Neh. 7.5 titles this list "the genealogical register of those who were the first to come up." Although both lists purport to record the same group of returnees, they exhibit significant differences. Scholars suggest that both lists were in fact compiled later than the first wave of return, on the basis of either censuses or tax registers. The present place of the lists thus exaggerates the extent of response to Cyrus's decree. The Rabbis ask why Ezra did not return to Jerusalem immediately following Cyrus's decree in 538 BCE, and

suggest that Ezra delayed his return because he was deeply immersed in the study of Torah under the tutelage of Jeremiah's scribe, Baruch son of Neriah. Thus, according to the Rabbis, Ezra was correct to delay his return in order to better prepare himself in the area of Torah study, which takes precedence even over the rebuilding of the Temple (b. Meg. 16b; Song Rab. 5.5). This tradition reflects a general tendency in classical rabbinic thought to privilege Torah study over Temple service and worship, and to find virtue in situations that may raise questions. **2:** The genealogical record is prefaced by a list of prominent returnees. It is unclear whether these leaders returned together. Zerubbabel is governor of the province of Judah during the reign of Darius I. Intimately involved in the rebuilding of the Temple, Zerubbabel is mentioned in the narratives of Haggai and Zechariah as the person who will finish the work of rebuilding the Temple. Yet he vanishes from the scene and is never heard of again. There is some speculation that he was removed by the Persians because he was perceived to be too powerful, especially since he was a descendant of the Davidic king Jehoiachin. In some rabbinic traditions, Zerubbabel becomes an Elijah-like figure who will explain the unanswered questions of Torah study in the time to come. Other rabbinic traditions identify him as one of the men of the great assembly, a group of sages imagined by the later Rabbis to have functioned as a judicial body in this period and who served as an important link in the transmission of the Torah from biblical to rabbinic times. Zerubbabel is also said to have succeeded Daniel in the service of Darius I and is said, like Daniel, to be an interpreter of secrets, signs, and dreams. In another tradition he is said to be identical with Nehemiah (b. Sanh. 38a). Jeshua is the head of a prominent priestly family who returns from exile with Zerubbabel. He is credited with reinstituting the ritual functions of the of Michmas—122; [28] the men of Beth-el and Ai—223; [29] the men of Nebo—52; [30] the sons of Magbish—156; [31] the sons of the other Elam—1,254; [32] the sons of Harim—320; [33] the sons of Lod, Hadid, and Ono—725; [34] the sons of Jericho—345; [35] the sons of Senaah—3,630.

[36] The priests: the sons of Jedaiah: the house of Jeshua—973; [37] the sons of Immer—1,052; [38] the sons of Pashhur—1,247; [39] the sons of Harim—1,017.

[40] The Levites: the sons of Jeshua and Kadmiel: the sons of Hodaviah—74.

[41] The singers: the sons of Asaph—128.

[42] The gatekeepers: the sons of Shallum, the sons of Ater, the sons of Talmon, the sons of Akkub, the sons of Hatita, the sons of Shobai, all told—139.

[43] The temple servants: the sons of Ziha, the sons of Hasupha, the sons of Tabbaoth, [44] the sons of Keros, the sons of Siaha, the sons of Padon, [45] the sons of Lebanah, the sons of Hagabah, the sons of Akkub, [46] the sons of Hagab, the sons of Salmai, the sons of Hanan, [47] the sons of Giddel, the sons of Gahar, the sons of Reaiah, [48] the sons of Rezin, the sons of Nekoda, the sons of Gazzam, [49] the sons of Uzza, the sons of Paseah, the sons of Besai, [50] the sons of Asnah, the sons of Meunim, the sons of Nephusim, [51] the sons of Bakbuk, the sons of Hakupha, the sons of Harhur, [52] the sons of Bazluth, the sons of Mehida, the sons of Harsha, [53] the sons of Barkos, the sons of Sisera, the sons of Temah, [54] the sons of Neziah, the sons of Hatipha.

[55] The sons of Solomon's servants: the sons of Sotai, the sons of Hassophereth, the sons of Peruda, [56] the sons of Jaalah, the sons of Darkon, the sons of Giddel, [57] the sons of Shephatiah, the sons of Hattil, the sons of Pochereth-hazzebaim, the sons of Ami.

[58] The total of temple servants and the sons of Solomon's servants—392.

[59] The following were those who came up from Tel-melah, Tel-harsha, Cherub, Addan, and Immer—they were unable to tell whether their father's house and descent were Israelite: [60] the sons of Delaiah, the sons of Tobiah, the sons of Nekoda—652.

[61] Of the sons of the priests, the sons of Habaiah, the sons of Hakkoz, the sons of Barzillai who had married a daughter of Barzillai and had taken his[a] name—[62] these searched for their genealogical records, but they could not be found, so they were disqualified for the priesthood. [63] The Tirshatha[b] ordered them not to eat of the most holy things until a priest with Urim and Thummim should appear.

a Lit. "their."   b A Persian title.

priesthood and with rebuilding the altar. According to 1 Chron. 5.41, Jeshua is the descendant of Jozadak, the last high priest, who was exiled by Nebuchadnezzar to Babylonia. Thus, Jeshua's genealogical connection to the preexilic priesthood authorizes him to re-establish the rituals of the priestly practices. In Haggai and Zechariah, but not in Ezra-Nehemiah, he is called "high priest." *Mordecai* is named after the Babylonian god, Marduk. Some rabbinic sources suggest that this is the same Mordecai mentioned in the book of Esther and that he returned to Judah with the exiles mentioned in ch 2, though this is unlikely. *Bigvai* is the governor of the province of Judah 410–407 BCE, is also listed as the leader of a prominent family in Neh. 7.19, and is connected to the covenant in Neh. 10.17. **41:** *Asaph:* The Asaphites are a group of musicians from the tribe of Levi. Pss. 50 and 73–83 are attributed to Asaph, and the Asaphites are also mentioned in 1 Chron. 6.24; 16.5–7, 37; 25.2, 9; 2 Chron. 5.12. **62:** The search for accurate and convincing genealogical connection is a theme throughout Ezra-Nehemiah, reflecting the growing concern for preserving hierarchy and lineage that persisted throughout the exilic and postexilic periods. On the disqualification of questionable priests from the eating of "terumah" (sacred gifts belonging to the priests), see *b. Ketub.* 24b; *b. Kid.* 69b. **63:** *Tirshata* is an Old Persian term meaning "revered," often taken to mean governor in rabbinic traditions. 1 Esdras 5.40 and later rabbinic tradition understand *Tirshatha* to be referring to Nehemiah in his role as governor (see Rashi's commentary to *b. Ketub.* 24b in a discussion of Ezra 2.62). *Urim and Thummim* were used to divine the opinion of God and were consulted on a variety of matters. See, e.g., Exod. 28.30; Lev. 8.8; Num. 27.21; Deut. 33.8; 1 Sam. 28.6. Rabbinic tradition does not understand Ezra 2.63 to suggest actual postexilic use of the Urim and Thummim. It is unclear why this

64 The sum of the entire community was 42,360, 65 not counting their male and female servants, those being 7,337; they also had 200 male and female singers. 66 Their horses—736; their mules—245; 67 their camels—435; their asses—6,720.

68 Some of the chiefs of the clans, on arriving at the House of the LORD in Jerusalem, gave a freewill offering to erect the House of God on its site. 69 In accord with their means, they donated to the treasury of the work: gold— 6,100 drachmas, silver—5,000 minas, and priestly robes— 100.

70 The priests, the Levites and some of the people, and the singers, gatekeepers, and the temple servants took up residence in their towns and all Israel in their towns.

3 When the seventh month arrived—the Israelites being settled in their towns—the entire people assembled as one man in Jerusalem. 2 Then Jeshua son of Jozadak and his brother priests, and Zerubbabel son of Shealtiel and his brothers set to and built the altar of the God of Israel to offer burnt offerings upon it as is written in the Teaching of Moses, the man of God. 3 They set up the altar on its site because they were in fear of the peoples of the land, and they offered burnt offerings on it to the LORD, burnt offerings each morning and evening. 4 Then they celebrated the festival of Tabernacles as is written, with its daily burnt offerings in the proper quantities, on each day as is prescribed for it, 5 followed by the regular burnt offering and the offerings for the new moons and for all the sacred fixed times of the LORD, and whatever freewill offerings were made to the LORD. 6 From the first day of the seventh

bazzar because both are credited with building the Second Temple. However, it seems most likely that Sheshbazzar initiated the rebuilding and that Zerubbabel completed it. **2:** The combination of Jeshua, the priest, and Zerubbabel, a governor of Davidic descent, establishes an authoritative link to preexilic times, though in preexilic texts such close cooperation between the Davidic king and the Aaronide (high) priest is rarely recorded. There is no king because Judah remained under Persian sovereignty. *Teaching:* The returnees understand themselves to live in accordance with the very same law and Temple ritual that governed the preexilic community in Judah. The exact nature of this Teaching or Torah is unclear from the texts in Ezra-Nehemiah, though it seems likely to be very similar to the current form of the Torah. **3:** *They set up the altar:* In later midrashic traditions, the Rabbis point out that the altar was prioritized, not only in Ezra, but also when the Israelites first entered the land in Josh. 8.31 (*Midr. Hagadol,* Yitro [Exod.] 20.21). Ezra-Nehemiah repeatedly alludes to Joshua's conquest in order to authorize the returnees' claim to the land. *Because they were in fear of the peoples:* The returnees are intimidated by the hostile behavior of the local peoples, and are offering sacrifice to God in order to appeal for divine protection. This conflict between the returnees and the local people, many of whom were likely Judeans who were not exiled to Babylonia, is a major theme of the book. 1 Esdras 5.50, in contrast, mentions that some of the local peoples joined Ezra in the rededication. **4:** See Num. 29.12–32 for a detailed description of the prescribed sacrifices. **7:** Note the echoes of Solomon's practices: 1 Kings 5.15–32; 2 Chron. 2.2–4.22.

3.8–9: Reappointing priests and Levites to conduct the service in the house of God. 8: *Age of twenty:* This age limit also appears in the divisions of the Levites in 1 Chron. 23.24, 27.

system of lot setting was not reestablished in this period, though the Rabbis suggest that the Urim and Thummim are akin to prophecy and are thus considered to have become unusable once prophecy ceased, after the latter prophets (Haggai, Zechariah, and Malachi), or perhaps even after the former prophets (*b. Sot.* 48a). Although Ezra lived after the time of prophecy, he is nevertheless said by the Rabbis to have been worthy of receiving divine inspiration "ruaḥ hakodesh," the holy spirit (*t. Sot.* 13.3). Nevertheless, in rabbinic interpretation, even Ezra could not resolve genealogical questions about all those who claimed to be priests.

3.1–7: Resuming Temple ritual and sacrifice on Sukkot (festival of Booths). The returnees are preparing to celebrate the festival of Booths in Tishri, the seventh month. According to 2 Chron. 7.8, the dedication of Solomon's Temple took place during the festival of Tabernacles. Ezra deliberately invokes preexilic Temple practice in order to authorize the second Temple as an authentic restoration of the first Temple. **1:** The building begins under the governorship of Sheshbazzar (1.8–14; 5.14–16). After an interruption, the building resumes under the governorship of Zerubbabel and the priestly instruction of Jeshua. Some scholars identify Zerubbabel with Shesh-month they began to make burnt offerings to the Lord, though the foundation of the Temple of the Lord had not been laid. [7] They paid the hewers and craftsmen with money, and the Sidonians and Tyrians with food, drink, and oil to bring cedarwood from Lebanon by sea to Joppa, in accord with the authorization granted them by King Cyrus of Persia.

[8] In the second year after their arrival at the House of God, at Jerusalem, in the second month, Zerubbabel son of Shealtiel and Jeshua son of Jozadak, and the rest of their brother priests and Levites, and all who had come from the captivity to Jerusalem, as their first step appointed Levites from the age of twenty and upward to supervise the work of the House of the Lord. [9] Jeshua, his sons and brothers, Kadmiel and his sons, [a]the sons of Judah,[a] together were appointed in charge of those who did the work in the House of God; also the sons of Henadad, their sons and brother Levites.

[10] When the builders had laid the foundation of the Temple of the Lord, priests in their vestments with trumpets, and Levites sons of Asaph with cymbals were stationed to give praise to the Lord, as King David of Israel had ordained. [11] They sang songs extolling and praising the Lord, [b]"For He is good, His steadfast love for Israel is eternal."[b] All the people raised a great shout extolling the Lord because the foundation of the House of the Lord had been laid. [12] Many of the priests and Levites and the chiefs of the clans, the old men who had seen the first house, wept loudly at the sight of the founding of this house. Many others shouted joyously at the top of their voices. [13] The people could not distinguish the shouts of joy from the people's weeping, for the people raised a great shout, the sound of which could be heard from afar.

4 When the adversaries of Judah and Benjamin heard that the returned exiles were building a temple to the Lord God of Israel, [2] they approached Zerubbabel and the chiefs of the clans and said to them, "Let us build with you, since we too worship your God, having offered sacrifices to Him since the time of King Esarhaddon of Assyria, who brought us here." [3] Zerubbabel, Jeshua, and the rest of the chiefs of the clans of Israel answered them, "It is not for you and us to build a House to our God, but we alone will build it to the Lord God of Israel, in accord with the charge that the king, King Cyrus of Persia, laid upon us." [4] Thereupon the people of the land undermined the re-

a-a I.e., Hodaviah of 2.40.   b-b Cf. Pss. 106.1; 136.

3.10–13: Laying the foundations for the Temple and the dedication. 10: *As King David of Israel had ordained:* David's authority with respect to Temple sacrifice and practice is also invoked, e.g., in 1 Chron. 6.31; 15.1–24; 16.4–42; 25.1; 2 Chron. 29.25, 30; 35.4; Neh. 12.45. **11:** *They sang songs extolling and praising the Lord, "For He is good, His steadfast love . . . is eternal":* This phrase, found in several psalms (106.1; 107.1; 118.1, 29; 136.1) became particularly prominent in Second Temple liturgy (see 1 Chron. 16.34; 2 Chron. 5.13; 7.3). **12–13:** Although continuity with preexilic practices is emphasized, the loss of the First Temple and its glory is still mourned. Compare the returnees' response to the dedication of the walls in Neh. 12.43. Josephus emphasizes the irrevocable loss of the First Temple by interpreting the v. to mean that the sound of the elders and priests wailing was louder than the sound of joy and trumpets (*Ant.* 11.4.2). Similarly, the Rabbis interpret these vv. to suggest that the majority of the returnees could recall the First Temple and its glory.

4.1–5: Building is interrupted during the reign of Cyrus. 1: *Adversaries of Judah and Benjamin:* The adversaries are presumably the same peoples of the land who are harassing and intimidating the returnees. See 3.3. **2:** *King Esarhaddon of Assyria* (681–669 BCE): This seems to reflect the resettlement of people from elsewhere in the Assyrian empire by Esarhaddon, after the exile of the Northern Kingdom of Israel to the Assyrian empire in 722, when Shalmaneser V was king. In subsequent Assyrian campaigns, foreign nations were resettled in northern Israel by Esarhaddon and later by Osnappar (see 4.10 n.). Cf. 2 Kings 17.6, 24–44. **3:** *In accord with the charge that the king, King Cyrus of Persia:* The returnees use the decree of Cyrus in their struggle to preserve control over the rebuilding of the Temple and the wall, over the ritual practices, and over solve of the people of Judah, and made them afraid to build. [5] They bribed ministers in order to thwart their plans all the years of King Cyrus of Persia and until the reign of King Darius of Persia.

[6] And in the reign of Ahasuerus, at the start of his reign, they drew up an accusation against the inhabitants of Judah and Jerusalem.

[7] And in the time of Artaxerxes, Bishlam, Mithredath, Tabeel, and the rest of their colleagues wrote to King Artaxerxes of Persia, a letter written in Aramaic and translated.[a]

Aramaic:[b] [8] Rehum the commissioner and Shimshai the scribe wrote a letter concerning Jerusalem to King Artaxerxes as follows: ([9c] Then Rehum the commissioner and Shimshai the scribe, and the rest of their colleagues, the judges, officials, officers, and overseers, the men of Erech, and of Babylon, and of Susa—that is the Elamites—[10] and other peoples whom the great and glorious Osnappar deported and settled in the city of Samaria and the rest of the province Beyond the River [wrote]—and now [11] this is the text of the letter which they sent to him:)—"To King Artaxerxes [from] your servants, men of the province Beyond the River. And now [12] be it known to the king that the Jews who came up from you to us have reached Jerusalem and are rebuilding that rebellious and wicked city; they are completing the walls and repairing the foundation. [13] Now be it known to the king that if this city is rebuilt and the walls completed, they will not pay tribute, poll-tax, or land-tax, and in the end it will harm the kingdom. [14] Now since we eat the salt of the palace, and it is not right that we should see the king dishonored, we have written to advise the king [of this] [15] so that you may search the records of your fathers and find in the records and know that this city is a rebellious city, harmful to kings and states. Sedition has been rife in it from early times; on that account this city was destroyed. [16] We advise the king that if this city is rebuilt and its walls are completed, you will no longer have any portion in the province Beyond the River."

[17] The king sent back the following message: "To Rehum the commissioner and Shimshai the scribe, and the rest of their colleagues, who dwell in Samaria and in the rest of the province of Beyond the River, greetings.

the genealogical purity of the reconstituted community in Judah. Josephus explains that only the returnees, namely the Jews, were permitted to participate in the rebuilding of the Temple, while the local peoples were told that they were permitted to worship at the Temple once it was completed (*Ant.* 11.4.3). Rabbinic interpretations justify the exclusion of the local peoples by claiming either that they were not descendants of Israel but Cutheans (*Pirqe R. El.* 38), or that they were idol worshippers (*b. 'Arak.* 5b) and therefore prohibited from involvement in the rebuilding and rededication of the Temple.

4.6–24: Opposition to building during the reigns of Xerxes and Artaxerxes. The narrative shifts forward in time, giving a more extensive account of the complaints raised by local peoples against the recent returnees. The letter recorded here is dated to the period after Darius I (522–486 BCE), prior to Ezra's mission. The section in 4.8–6.18, incorporating several official Aramaic documents, is in Aramaic, the lingua franca of this period. **6:** *In the reign of Ahasuerus:* This is apparently Xerxes (486–465), who ruled over Persia after Darius I. Rabbinic interpretations identify Artaxerxes with the Persian king in the book of Esther. **10:** The name *Osnappar* does not occur in the Assyrian chronicles, and is most likely a corruption of the name of the Assyrian king, Assurbanipal (669–627), who immediately succeeded Esarhaddon (681–669). *Beyond the River:* This large Persian province was west of the Euphrates River and extended as far as Egypt (including Judah). **11:** *King Artaxerxes:* This is Artaxerxes I Longimanus (Long Hand), who ruled 465–424. **14:** *We eat the salt of the palace,* an expression signifying the common interests of loyal allies. Apparently an oath was taken and solemnized through participation in a common meal. **15:** *Search the records of your fathers:* The book relies heavily on official documents. Arta-

---

a Cf. below v. 18 and note d.

b A note indicating that what follows is in the Aramaic language.

c Vv. 9–11 amplify v. 8.

18 Now the letter that you wrote me has been read to me in translation.[a] 19 At my order a search has been made, and it has been found that this city has from earliest times risen against kings, and that rebellion and sedition have been rife in it. 20 Powerful kings have ruled over Jerusalem and exercised authority over the whole province of Beyond the River, and tribute, poll-tax, and land-tax were paid to them. 21 Now issue an order to stop these men; this city is not to be rebuilt until I so order. 22 Take care not to be lax in this matter or there will be much damage and harm to the kingdom."

23 When the text of the letter of King Artaxerxes was read before Rehum and Shimshai the scribe and their colleagues, they hurried to Jerusalem, to the Jews, and stopped them by main force. 24 At that time, work on the House of God in Jerusalem stopped and remained in abeyance until the second year of the reign of King Darius of Persia.

5 Then the prophets, Haggai the prophet and Zechariah son of Iddo, prophesied to the Jews in Judah and Jerusalem, [b]inspired by the God of Israel.[b] 2 Thereupon Zerubbabel son of Shealtiel and Jeshua son of Jozadak began rebuilding the House of God in Jerusalem, with the full support of the prophets of God. 3 At once Tattenai, governor of the province of Beyond the River, Shethar-bozenai, and their colleagues descended upon them and said this to them, "Who issued orders to you to rebuild this house and complete its furnishing?" 4 Then we[c] said to them, "What are the names of the men who are engaged in the building?" 5 But God watched over the elders of the Jews and they were not stopped while a report went to Darius and a letter was sent back in reply to it.

6 This is the text of the letter that Tattenai, governor of the province of Beyond the River, and Shethar-bozenai and his colleagues, the officials of Beyond the River, sent to King Darius. 7 They sent a message to him and this is what was written in it: "To King Darius, greetings, and so forth. 8 Be it known to the king, that we went to the province of Judah,

a I.e., from Aramaic to Persian.
b-b Lit. "with the name of the God of Israel upon them."
c The officials of v. 3; cf. v. 10. Greek and Syriac read "they."

Yehud will rebel, trying to assert its independence, and others will follow suit. **17–22:** In rabbinic traditions both Darius I and Artaxerxes are identified with Cyrus (see 6.14 n.). Cyrus is therefore regarded as retracting the permission to rebuild the Temple which he had previously granted, hence losing his wisdom and becoming a fool (Eccl. Rab. 10.1). **23:** Stopped them by main force: Neh. 1.3 suggests that the objectors not only prevented further rebuilding, but also destroyed what had already been built. **24:** The second year of the reign of King Darius of Persia: Here Ezra-Nehemiah resumes the narrative of 4.5, returning to the resumption of building in the time of Darius.

5.1–2: Under Darius's reign the rebuilding of the Temple resumes and is completed. 2: With the full support of the prophets of God: The rebuilding of the Temple by Zerubbabel and Jeshua is connected to the divine prophecy received by Haggai and Zechariah, which is preserved in the books by those names.

5.3–17: Tattenai writes to Darius and questions the authenticity of the returnees' claim. 3: Tattenai: During the reign of Darius, Tattenai is the governor of the province Beyond the River. As is clear from 6.13, Tattenai adheres to the ruling of Darius and does not interfere with the rebuilding of the Jerusalem Temple. Shethar-bozenai: This name always appears just after Tattenai. Some scholars suggest that this is an official title of Tattenai; others suggest that it was the name of Tattenai's official scribe. **6:** King Darius: Darius I ruled the Persian empire 522–486 BCE. He is highly regarded for extending Cyrus's generous policy toward non-Persian peoples. **8–11:** The great king of v. 11 is Solomon. God of heaven and earth, a very universalistic expression, appropriate when identifying God to non-Judeans. The narrative of Ezra recalls the building of the first, pre-exilic Temple in order to authorize

xerxes (465–424) is asked to consult the Babylonian and Assyrian chronicles for records of the rebellions and eventual exiles of both the Northern Kingdom of Israel and the Southern Kingdom of

Judah. He is asked, in particular, for records of the Judean rebellions against Babylonia and Nebuchadnezzar's eventual destruction of Jerusalem. **16:** This is the crux of their argument: The province of to the house of the great God. It is being rebuilt of hewn stone, and wood is being laid in the walls. The work is being done with dispatch and is going well. [9]Thereupon we directed this question to these elders, 'Who issued orders to you to rebuild this house and to complete its furnishings?' [10]We also asked their names so that we could write down the names of their leaders for your information. [11]This is what they answered us: 'We are the servants of the God of heaven and earth; we are rebuilding the house that was originally built many years ago; a great king of Israel built it and completed it. [12]But because our fathers angered the God of Heaven, He handed them over to Nebuchadnezzar the Chaldean, king of Babylon, who demolished this house and exiled the people to Babylon. [13]But in the first year of King Cyrus of Babylon, King Cyrus issued an order to rebuild this House of God. [14]Also the silver and gold vessels of the House of God that Nebuchadnezzar had taken away from the temple in Jerusalem and brought to the temple in Babylon—King Cyrus released them from the temple in Babylon to be given to the one called Sheshbazzar whom he had appointed governor. [15]He said to him, "Take these vessels, go, deposit them in the temple in Jerusalem, and let the House of God be rebuilt on its original site." [16]That same Sheshbazzar then came and laid the foundations for the House of God in Jerusalem; and ever since then it has been under construction, but is not yet finished.' [17]And now, if it please the king, let the royal archives there in Babylon be searched to see whether indeed an order had been issued by King Cyrus to rebuild this House of God in Jerusalem. May the king convey to us his pleasure in this matter."

6 Thereupon, at the order of King Darius, they searched the archives where the treasures were stored in Babylon. [2]But it was in the citadel of Ecbatana, in the province of Media, that a scroll was found in which the following was written: "Memorandum: [3]In the first year of King Cyrus, King Cyrus issued an order concerning the House of God in Jerusalem: 'Let the house be rebuilt, a place for offering sacrifices, with a base built up high. Let it be sixty cubits high and sixty cubits wide, [4]with a course of unused timber for each three courses of hewn stone. The expenses shall be paid by the palace. [5]And the gold and silver vessels of the House of God which Nebuchadnezzar had taken away from the temple in Jerusalem and transported to Babylon shall be returned, and let each go back to the temple in Jerusalem where it belongs; you shall deposit it in the House of God.'

and justify the building of the Second Temple. **14:** *Sheshbazzar* is the first governor of Judah under Cyrus. His appointment began at the time of Cyrus's decree in 538. See 3.1 n. 1 Esdras 6.18 inserts Zerubbabel in this v. as having received gifts along with Sheshbazzar.

6.1–5: Locating Cyrus's decree in the citadel of Ecbatana.
2: *Citadel of Ecbatana,* an important center for the Persian empire. Perhaps the phrase refers to the general area of Ecbatana (modern Hamadan) rather than a location within Ecbatana. The citadel of Ecbatana was a summer palace in the eastern part of the Persian empire. Although mentioned nowhere else in the Bible, Ecbatana is mentioned in three apocryphal traditions: 2 Macc. 9.3; Judith 1.1, 2, 14; and many times in Tobit. **4:** *The expenses shall be paid by the palace:* In contrast, according to the Heb version in Ezra ch 1, the Temple is paid for by the Judean exiles, not by the Persian government. This is one of several discrepancies, sometimes irreconcilable, in Ezra-Nehemiah. These may reflect conflicting accounts or records.

6 "Now[a] you, Tattenai, governor of the province of Beyond the River, Shethar-bozenai and colleagues, the officials of the province of Beyond the River, stay away from that place. [7] Allow the work of this House of God to go on; let the governor of the Jews and the elders of the Jews rebuild this House of God on its site. [8] And I hereby issue an order concerning what you must do to help these elders of the Jews rebuild this House of God: the expenses are to be paid to these men with dispatch out of the resources of the king, derived from the taxes of the province of Beyond the River, so that the work not be stopped. [9] They are to be given daily, without fail, whatever they need of young bulls, rams, or lambs as burnt offerings for the God of Heaven, and wheat, salt, wine, and oil, at the order of the priests in Jerusalem, [10] so that they may offer pleasing sacrifices to the God of Heaven and pray for the life of the king and his sons. [11] I also issue an order that whoever alters this decree shall have a beam removed from his house, and he shall be impaled on it and his house confiscated.[b] [12] And may the God who established His name there cause the downfall of any king or nation that undertakes to alter or damage that House of God in Jerusalem. I, Darius, have issued the decree; let it be carried out with dispatch."

[13] Then Tattenai, governor of the province of Beyond the River, Shethar-bozenai, and their colleagues carried out with dispatch what King Darius had written. [14] So the elders of the Jews progressed in the building, urged on by the prophesying of Haggai the prophet and Zechariah son of Iddo, and they brought the building to completion under the aegis of the God of Israel and by the order of Cyrus and Darius and King Artaxerxes of Persia. [15] The house was finished on the third of the month of Adar in the sixth year of the reign of King Darius. [16] The Israelites, the priests, and the Levites, and all the other exiles celebrated the dedication of the House of God with joy. [17] And they sacrificed for the dedication of this House of God one hundred bulls, two hundred rams, four hundred lambs, and twelve goats as a purification offering for all of Israel, according to the number of the tribes of Israel. [18] They appointed the priests in their courses and the Levites in their divisions for the service of God in Jerusalem, according to the prescription in the Book of Moses.

[19c] The returned exiles celebrated the Passover on the fourteenth day of the first month, [20] for the priests and Le-

6.6–12: Response of Darius. Darius's reply to Tattenai seems not to reflect an actual historical event, but rather to be an elaboration of Cyrus's decree of 538 BCE.

6.13–18: Completion of the Temple and its dedication. 14: *By the order of Cyrus and Darius and King Artaxerxes of Persia:* Rabbinic interpretations suggest that these three names refer to the very same king of Persia. This leads to a significant misrepresentation of Persian chronology in rabbinic traditions (*Seder Olam R.* 30; *b. Rosh Hash.* 3b). **15:** *The house was finished on the third of the month of Adar:* 1 Esdras 7.5 and Josephus *Ant.* 11.4.7 mention the 23rd of Adar as the day of completion. **18:** *They appointed the priests in their courses and the Levites in their divisions for the service of God in Jerusalem, according to the prescription in the Book of Moses:* The courses of priests and divisions of Levites are not mentioned in any preexilic or exilic tradition, suggesting that this is an attempt to legitimate a later institution by false connect to the Torah. In 2 Chron. 35.4–5 the organization of the priests is also said to be preexilic, but is attributed to David and Solomon, not to Moses.

6.19–22: Celebration of the festival of Passover. The text returns to Heb from 6.19 through 7.11. In Josh. 5.10 the Israelites were able to offer the Passover sacrifice following their circumcision. Here too, purification is followed by the Passover sacrifice. Priestly texts in particular, which became particularly authoritative in this period, suggest the importance of eating the Passover offering in a state of ritual purity (Num. 9.6–13).

a This introduces the text of the reply of Darius that doubtless contained the preceding narrative (vv. 1–5) as a preliminary.

b Meaning uncertain; or "turned into ruins."   c Hebrew resumes here.

vites had purified themselves to a man; they were all pure. They slaughtered the passover offering for all the returned exiles, and for their brother priests and for themselves. ²¹ The children of Israel who had returned from the exile, together with all who joined them in separating themselves from the uncleanliness of the nations of the lands to worship the LORD God of Israel, ate of it. ²² They joyfully celebrated the Feast of Unleavened Bread for seven days, for the LORD had given them cause for joy by inclining the heart of the Assyrian king toward them so as to give them support in the work of the House of God, the God of Israel.

7 After these events, during the reign of King Artaxerxes of Persia, Ezra son of Seraiah son of Azariah son of Hilkiah ² son of Shallum son of Zadok son of Ahitub ³ son of Amariah son of Azariah son of Meraioth ⁴ son of Zerahiah son of Uzzi son of Bukki ⁵ son of Abishua son of Phinehas son of Eleazar son of Aaron the chief priest—⁶ that Ezra came up from Babylon, a scribe expert in the Teaching of Moses which the LORD God of Israel had given, whose request the king had granted in its entirety, thanks to the benevolence of the LORD toward him.

(⁷ Some of the Israelites, the priests and Levites, the singers, the gatekeepers, and the temple servants set out for Jerusalem in the seventh year of King Artaxerxes, ⁸ arriving in Jerusalem in the fifth month in the seventh year of the king.) ⁹ On the first day of the first month the journey up from Babylon was started, and on the first day of the fifth month he arrived in Jerusalem, thanks to the benevolent care of his God for him. ¹⁰ For Ezra had dedicated himself to study the Teaching of the LORD so as to observe it, and to teach laws and rules to Israel.

¹¹ The following is the text of the letter which King Artaxerxes gave Ezra the priest-scribe, a scholar in matters

which destroyed the Southern Kingdom (586), and the Persian empire which now fulfills the divine promise of restoration.

7.1–10: Ezra joins the Jerusalem returnees. The introduction to Ezra's mission illustrates what was considered necessary to preserve and perpetuate the newly reconstituted Jerusalem community. The information that is included is intended to demonstrate that Ezra possessed the required authority and sufficient preparation for the job. First, Ezra is included in the Aaronide line of priests and is therefore a priest with the highest pedigree, authorized to conduct Temple sacrifice and ritual, perhaps even a high priest himself. (It is odd, however, that Ezra is never included in any of the high priestly lineages.) Second, Ezra is a scribe who is an *expert in the Teaching of Moses*. He therefore provides an authoritative link to the returnees' preexilic past. Third, Ezra is said to have *dedicated himself to study the Teaching of the LORD*. Thus, Ezra is prepared for the task of interpreting, explaining, and applying the ancient law to a new context in which Israel is ruled, not by a Davidic monarch, but by a Persian king. Finally, Ezra is said to be in the favor of the LORD (v. 6) and of God (v. 9). Ezra continues to be celebrated in later Jewish traditions, and is often compared to Ezekiel and Moses. See, for example, *t. Sanh.* 4.4: "Ezra was sufficiently worthy that the Torah could have been given through him if Moses had not preceded him." **1–5:** Ezra's lineage establishes authentic priestly credentials. The Rabbis write that if Aaron had been living during the time of Ezra, he would have been considered inferior to Ezra (*Eccl. Rab.* 1.4). **6:** Ezra will assume the position of instructor of the people in the *Teaching of Moses;* thus it is very important to establish his reliability as a scribe and knowledge of the text itself (see v. 10) early in Ezra's memoir (Ezra chs 7–10). *Came up:* Rabbinic interpretation makes an analogy between Moses

21: On the Passover celebration, cf. Exod. 12.16–51; Lev. 23.4–8; Num. 28.16–25; Deut. 16.1–8. As in some of these texts, the practice here reflects a one-day Passover celebration, followed by a seven-day "Matzot" (unleavened bread) festival (see esp. Lev. 23.5–8). **22:** *They joyfully celebrated the Feast of Unleavened Bread:* Compare this to 2 Chron. 30.21, describing Hezekiah's Passover, and 2 Chron. 35.17, describing Josiah's Passover—the continuity between First and Second Temple practice is

again emphasized. *The LORD had given them cause for joy by inclining the heart of the Assyrian king toward them:* Just as Cyrus is said in Ezra 1.1 to be inspired by the LORD, so is Darius's decree said to be under divine influence. Josephus refers to the "Persian king," not to the *Assyrian king,* in his retelling of the Ezra narrative (*Ant.* 11.4.8). Perhaps the reference to Assyria here alludes to the continuity between the Assyrian empire which destroyed the Northern Kingdom (722 BCE), the Babylonian empire concerning the commandments of the LORD and His laws to Israel:

12 a"Artaxerxes king of kings, to Ezra the priest, scholar in the law of the God of heaven, b-and so forth.-b And now, 13 I hereby issue an order that anyone in my kingdom who is of the people of Israel and its priests and Levites who feels impelled to go to Jerusalem may go with you. 14 For you are commissioned by the king and his seven advisers to regulate Judah and Jerusalem according to the law of your God, which is in your care, 15 and to bring the freewill offering of silver and gold, which the king and his advisers made to the God of Israel, whose dwelling is in Jerusalem, 16 and whatever silver and gold that you find throughout the province of Babylon, together with the freewill offerings that the people and the priests will give for the House of their God, which is in Jerusalem. 17 You shall, therefore, with dispatch acquire with this money bulls, rams, and lambs, with their meal offerings and libations, and offer them on the altar of the House of your God in Jerusalem. 18 And whatever you wish to do with the leftover silver and gold, you and your kinsmen may do, in accord with the will of your God. 19 The vessels for the service of the House of your God that are given to you, deliver to God in Jerusalem, 20 and any other needs of the House of your God that it falls to you to supply, do so from the royal treasury. 21 I, King Artaxerxes, for my part, hereby issue an order to all the treasurers in the province of Beyond the River that whatever request Ezra the priest, scholar in the law of the God of Heaven, makes of you is to be fulfilled with dispatch 22 up to the sum of one hundred talents of silver, one hundred *kor* of wheat, one hundred *bath* of wine, one hundred *bath* of oil, and salt without limit. 23 Whatever is by order of the God of Heaven must be carried out diligently for the House of the God of Heaven, else wrath will come upon the king and his sons. 24 We further advise you that it is not permissible to impose tribute, poll tax, or land tax on any priest, Levite, singer, gatekeeper, temple servant, or other servant of this House of God. 25 And you, Ezra, by the divine wisdom you possess, appoint magistrates and judges to judge all the people in the province of Beyond the River who know the laws of your God, and to teach those who do not know them. 26 Let anyone who does not obey the law of your God and the law of the king be punished with dispatch, whether by death, corporal punishment, confiscation of possessions, or imprisonment."

and Ezra and states that just as Moses went up to Sinai to receive the Torah, so too Ezra went up to Jerusalem to receive the Torah (*b. Sanh.* 21b). *A scribe expert in the Teaching of Moses:* Some rabbinic traditions attribute the special markings over selected words in the Bible to the hand of Ezra, who, as the expert scribe, was privy to secret interpretive traditions concerning Mosaic Torah (*Num. Rab.* 3.13). **7-8:** The seventh year of Artaxerxes I Longimanus is 458 BCE. **9:** Ezra is perhaps alluding to the exodus from Egypt, which also occurred in the first month of the year. If so, as in Deutero-Isaiah (e.g., Isa. 52.12), the return of the Babylonian exiles is implicitly connected to the Israelites' original journey to the promised land after their enslavement and years of wandering in the desert. In addition, the celebration of the first and subsequent Passovers also occurred in the first month (Exod. 12.2; Num. 33.3). **10:** The language in this passage is highly influenced by Deuteronomy; cf., e.g., Deut. 4.14. Ezra is here envisioned as a lawgiver like Moses, who will provide the people with the law along with its "correct" interpretation. According to the Rabbis, Ezra restored the Torah to the Assyrian script (the Hebrew letters in their current form, not their older, paleo-Heb form) in which it was originally given to Moses (*b. Sanh.* 21b).

7.11-26: Artaxerxes' letter commissioning Ezra's mission. 12-26: The narrative at this point is written in Aramaic and purports to preserve the correspondence between the Persian kings and their officials in Judah. **26:** *The law of the king,* imperial law of Persia, which all Persian subjects must obey. The Persian legal system permitted the observance of both local law (here called "the law of your God") and imperial law.

---

a Aramaic resumes here through v. 26.   b-b Meaning uncertain.

27 [a]Blessed is the LORD God of our fathers, who put it into the mind of the king to glorify the House of the LORD in Jerusalem, 28 and who inclined the king and his counselors and the king's military officers to be favorably disposed toward me. For my part, thanks to the care of the LORD for me, I summoned up courage and assembled leading men in Israel to go with me.

8 These are the chiefs of the clans and the register of the genealogy of those who came up with me from Babylon in the reign of King Artaxerxes: 2 Of the sons of Phinehas, Gershom; of the sons of Ithamar, Daniel; of the sons of David, Hattush. 3 Of the sons of Shecaniah: of the sons of Parosh, Zechariah; through him the genealogy of 150 males was registered. 4 Eliehoenai son of Zerahiah, of the sons of Pahath-moab, and with him 200 males. 5 Of the sons of Shecaniah son of Jahaziel; and with him 300 males. 6 And of the sons of Adin, Ebed son of Jonathan; and with him 50 males. 7 And of the sons of Elam, Jeshaiah son of Athaliah; and with him 70 males. 8 And of the sons of Shephatiah, Zebadiah son of Michael; and with him 80 males. 9 Of the sons of Joab, Obadiah son of Jehiel; and with him 218 males. 10 And of the sons of Shelomith, the son of Josiphiah; and with him 160 males. 11 And of the sons of Bebai, Zechariah son of Bebai; and with him 28 males. 12 And of the sons of Azgad, Johanan son of Hakkatan; and with him 110 males. 13 And of the sons of Adonikam, who were the last; and these are their names: Eliphelet, Jeiel, and Shemaiah; and with them 60 males. 14 And of the sons of Bigvai, Uthai and Zaccur; and with them 70 males.

15 These I assembled by the river that enters Ahava, and we encamped there for three days. I reviewed the people and the priests, but I did not find any Levites there. 16 I sent for Eliezer, Ariel, Shemaiah, Elnathan, Jarib, Elnathan, Nathan, Zechariah, and Meshullam, the leading men, and also for Joiarib and Elnathan, the instructors, 17 and I gave them an order for Iddo, the leader at the place [called] Casiphia. I gave them a message to convey to Iddo [and] his brother, temple-servants at the place [called] Casiphia, that they should bring us attendants for the House of our God. 18 Thanks to the benevolent care of our God for us, they brought us a capable man of the family of Mahli son of Levi son of Israel, and Sherebiah and his sons and brothers, 18 in all, 19 and Hashabiah, and with him Jeshaiah of the family of Merari, his brothers

a Hebrew resumes here.

7.27–28: Ezra's prayer. 28: Ezra regards the gathering of some of Israel's leaders to return to Israel as partial fulfillment of the prophecies of Isaiah and Jeremiah.

8.1–14: Returnees who accompanied Ezra on his mission to Jerusalem. Josephus maintains that the ten tribes (apart from Judah and Benjamin) are still living beyond the Euphrates and did not return with Ezra (*Ant.* 11.5.2). While by this time, these tribes had assimilated due to the Assyrian policy of forced population exchanges, the tradition of their continued existence is found in, for instance, Tobit. **2:** Emphasis is placed on genealogical connections to the priesthood and to the Davidic line. These links are necessary if the preexilic and exilic Israelite prophecies of return are to be fulfilled. (See, e.g., Ezek. 37.24–28.) Moreover, authentic genealogies provide the returnees with the authority to oversee Temple ritual and to legislate to the people.

8.15–20: Ezra's examination and instruction of those who accompanied him. Ezra must check the genealogical links of those who accompany him, because of the importance of authentic lineage. These examinations also prepare the reader for the long discussion concerning the intermarriage crisis in chs 9 and 10. The crisis in finding Levites may be because they had a subsidiary role to the priests in the Temple service, and preferred to remain in Babylonia, without these Temple responsibilities. **15:** *These I assembled:* The narrative resumes here from 7.28. To emphasize this resumption, Ezra uses the very same verb, "to assemble," used at the conclusion of the prayer in 7.28. *Ahava:* The precise location of this river (or, perhaps, town) is not known. It may have been one of Babylonia's waterways, and it appears to be located on the route of Ezra's return to Judah. 1 Esdras 8.41 and 61 mention the river "Thares" instead of the river *Ahava*. **17:** *Casiphia:* This place-name occurs only and their sons, 20 in all; [20] and of the temple servants whom David and the officers had appointed for the service of the Levites—220 temple servants, all of them listed by name. [21] I proclaimed a fast there by the Ahava River to afflict ourselves before our God to beseech Him for a smooth journey for us and for our children and for all our possessions; [22] for I was ashamed to ask the king for soldiers and horsemen to protect us against any enemy on the way, since we had told the king, "The benevolent care of our God is for all who seek Him, while His fierce anger is against all who forsake Him." [23] So we fasted and besought our God for this, and He responded to our plea. [24] Then I selected twelve of the chiefs of the priests, namely Sherebiah and Hashabiah with ten of their brothers, [25] and I weighed out to them the silver, the gold, and the vessels, the contribution to the House of our God which the king, his counselors and officers, and all Israel who were present had made. [26] I entrusted to their safekeeping the weight of six hundred and fifty talents of silver, one hundred silver vessels of one talent each, one hundred talents of gold; [27] also, twenty gold bowls worth one thousand *darics* and two vessels of good, shining bronze, as precious as gold. [28] I said to them, "You are consecrated to the LORD, and the vessels are consecrated, and the silver and gold are a freewill offering to the LORD God of your fathers. [29] Guard them diligently until such time as you weigh them out in the presence of the officers of the priests and the Levites and the officers of the clans of Israel in Jerusalem in the chambers of the House of the LORD." [30] So the priests and the Levites received the cargo of silver and gold and vessels by weight, to bring them to Jerusalem to the House of our God. [31] We set out for Jerusalem from the Ahava River on the twelfth of the first month. We enjoyed the care of our God, who saved us from enemy ambush on the journey.

[32] We arrived in Jerusalem and stayed there three days. [33] On the fourth day the silver, gold, and vessels were

preexilic Davidic and priestly authority.

8.21–23: Ezra proclaims a fast. Though he is designated by the king, Ezra, a religious functionary, is fearful; contrast Nehemiah, appointed as governor, in Neh. 2.7–9. **21:** *I proclaimed a fast:* In the Second Temple period, fasting becomes a particularly important rite, and is generally accompanied by prayer and confession (see Zech. 7.1–7; 8.18–19; Esth. 4.15–16; Dan. 9.3–4; Neh. 9.1). *A smooth journey:* The phrase "derekh yesharah" appears in a number of exilic texts prophesying the return to Judah (see, e.g., Jer. 31.9; Isaiah 40.3).

8.24–30: Ezra appoints the priests and entrusts them with the Temple vessels. 28: *"You are consecrated to the* LORD, *and the vessels are consecrated":* Here the Heb word "kadosh" signifies separation, distinction, and chosenness. The assertion that *you are consecrated to the* LORD recalls assertions of the consecrated status of the people throughout the Priestly narratives in the Torah. At the same time, the assertion that *the vessels are consecrated* serves as a warning that with consecrated status comes the responsibility to care for the Temple vessels and to ensure that they are not removed from their sacred place.

8.31–36: Ezra and returnees travel to Jerusalem. 32: The arrival occurred on the first day of the fifth month, Av, according to 7.8–9. Since, according to 2 Kings 25.8, it was in the fifth month that the first Temple was destroyed (see also Zech. 7.3), the occurrence of the return in Av may be therapeutic. This is also a solemn time for the returnees as they recall the lost glories of their past (cf. 3.12). In later Jewish traditions, the 9th of Av is the day when the Jewish community mourns the destruction of both the First and Second Temples. *And stayed there three days:* In Gen. Rab. 56.1, the Rabbis connect Ezra's third day to the

here. Since Ezra calls it *the place,* an expression used for places of Jewish worship in, e.g., Gen. 28.17; Deut. 12.5; 1 Kings 8.29, it may have been a religious center for Babylonians. Some scholars suggest that "Casiphia" may be related to "kesef," the Heb word for silver, and that the place may have been associated with silver production. **18–19:** *Mahli son of*

Levi: Mahli was one of Merari's children (Num. 3.20). *Sherebiah, Hashabiah, Jeshaiah* are all from the line of Merari, one of the three sons of Levi (Num. 3.14, 20), to whom was assigned the responsibility for carrying the Tabernacle and related objects (Num. 4.29–33). **20:** *David and the officers had appointed for the service of the Levites:* Ezra's mission will reinstitute weighed out in the House of our God into the keeping of Meremoth son of Uriah the priest, with whom was Eleazar son of Phinehas. Jozabad son of Jeshua, and Noadiah son of Binnui, the Levites, were with them. [34] Everything accorded as to number and weight, the entire cargo being recorded at that time.

[35] The returning exiles who arrived from captivity made burnt offerings to the God of Israel: twelve bulls for all Israel, ninety-six rams, seventy-seven lambs and twelve he-goats as a purification offering, all this a burnt offering to the LORD. [36] They handed the royal orders to the king's satraps and the governors of the province of Beyond the River who gave support to the people and the House of God.

9 When this was over, the officers approached me, saying, "The people of Israel and the priests and Levites have not separated themselves from the peoples of the land whose abhorrent practices are like those of the Canaanites, the Hittites, the Perizzites, the Jebusites, the Ammonites, the Moabites, the Egyptians, and the Amorites. [2] They have taken their daughters as wives for themselves and for their sons, so that the holy seed has become intermingled with the peoples of the land; and it is the officers and prefects who have taken the lead in this trespass."

[3] When I heard this, I rent my garment and robe, I tore hair out of my head and beard, and I sat desolate. [4] Around me gathered all who were concerned over the words of the God of Israel because of the returning exiles' trespass, while I sat desolate until the evening offering. [5] At the time of the evening offering I ended my self-affliction; still in my torn garment and robe, I got down on my knees and spread out my hands to the LORD my God, [6] and said, "O my God, I am too ashamed and mortified to lift my face to You, O my God, for our iniquities [a-]are overwhelming[-a] and our guilt has grown high as heaven. [7] From the time of our fathers to this very day we have been deep in guilt. Because of our iniquities, we, our

a-a Lit. "are numerous above the head."

third day of Abraham's final trial at the binding of Isaac, on which Abraham received divine revelation. Cf. Exod. 19.16. Three days, used frequently in the Bible, may simply signify a short time. **35:** The Rabbis are puzzled by the fact that the returnees, who were considered to have sinned willfully, were permitted to offer sacrifices. This is said to be a legal exception to the rule that would ordinarily allow only those who had sinned inadvertently to offer a sacrifice of atonement (*b. Hor.; b. Tem.* 15b).

9.1–2: Intermarriage crisis. According to rabbinic tradition (e.g., *Num. Rab.* 19.3; *Eccl. Rab.* 7.23, section 4) and many modern scholars, the prohibition of intermarriage is rooted in Deut. 7.3: "Do not give your daughters to their sons or take their daughters for your sons." However, Ezra insists on two points that are not explicit in any earlier text. First, intermarriage with any non-Israelite people is prohibited, not only intermarriage with the Canaanite nations referred to in Deuteronomy (see also Deut. 20.16–18). Second, if one has intermarried, one must divorce one's foreign wife and expel any children resulting from the prohibited marriage. When Ezra says that the prohibition—including the aforementioned two points—is from the Teaching ("torah") and the commandment of our God (10.3), he seems to presuppose that Mosaic authority should be ascribed not only to the law explicitly stated in Deut. 7.3, but also to its interpretation or elaboration. This is similar to 1 Kings 11.1–2, an exilic text which suggests that Solomon's marriage to various foreign wives is a violation of Torah law. In *b. Meg.* 15a, Ezra is identified with the prophet Malachi because of the reference to a prohibition against intermarriage in Mal. 2.11. **1:** 1 Esdras 8.69 mentions the Edomites but does not mention the Ammonites or the Amorites. **2:** *It is the officers and prefects who have taken the lead in this trespass:* For a list of the transgressors, see the conclusion of Ezra (10.18–44). Even the priest, Jeshua, is included in the list of offenders (10.18). Though other biblical texts prohibit intermarriage to varying extents, nowhere else is it described in such highly charged theological language: *the holy seed has become intermingled with the peoples of the land.* This may be a reference to Isa. 6.13, which suggests that the exile will purify "the holy seed," making them unsuitable for mixture with anyone else, likely including those of Judean descent who did not experience the purifying power of the exile.

kings, and our priests have been handed over to foreign kings, to the sword, to captivity, to pillage, and to humiliation, as is now the case.

8 "But now, for a short while, there has been a reprieve from the LORD our God, who has granted us a surviving remnant and given us a stake in His holy place; our God has restored the luster to our eyes and furnished us with a little sustenance in our bondage. 9 For bondsmen we are, though even in our bondage God has not forsaken us, but has disposed the king of Persia favorably toward us, to furnish us with sustenance and to raise again the House of our God, repairing its ruins and giving us a hold[a] in Judah and Jerusalem.

10 "Now, what can we say in the face of this, O our God, for we have forsaken Your commandments, 11 which You gave us through Your servants the prophets when You said, 'The land that you are about to possess is a land unclean through the uncleanness of the peoples of the land, through their abhorrent practices with which they, in their impurity, have filled it from one end to the other. 12 Now then, do not give your daughters in marriage to their sons or let their daughters marry your sons; do nothing for their well-being or advantage, then you will be strong and enjoy the bounty of the land and bequeath it to your children forever.' 13 After all that has happened to us because of our evil deeds and our deep guilt—though You, our God, have been forbearing, [punishing us] less than our iniquity [deserves] in that You have granted us such a remnant as this—14 shall we once again violate Your commandments by intermarrying with these peoples who follow such abhorrent practices? Will You not rage against us till we are destroyed without remnant or survivor? 15 O LORD, God of Israel, You are benevolent,[b] for we have survived as a remnant, as is now the case. We stand before You in all our guilt, for we cannot face You on this account."

10 While Ezra was praying and making confession, weeping and prostrating himself before the House of God, a very great crowd of Israelites gathered about him, men, women, and children; the people were weeping bitterly. 2 Then Shecaniah son of Jehiel of the family of Elam spoke up and said to Ezra, "We have trespassed against our God by bringing into our homes foreign women from the peoples of the land; [c]but there is still hope for Israel despite this.[c] 3 Now then, let us make a

9.3–15: Ezra's public repentance and prayer. 3: Ezra's behavior is similar to that of earlier Jewish leaders who tried to avert a national disaster. For example, Josiah tears his clothing upon hearing the reading of the discovered Torah scroll (2 Kings 22.11); Mordecai and Esther fast and engage in mourning practices (Esth. 4.1–3, 16); and Jehoshaphat proclaims a fast and prays for deliverance from Israel's enemies (2 Chron. 20.1–13). Josephus states that Ezra and the returnees were concerned that God would punish them as He did in the past and therefore they fast and repent (*Ant.* 11.5.3). **5:** Ezra takes the typical position of the praying individual in the Bible (see, e.g., 1 Kings 8.22, 38). **6–7:** Cf. Daniel's prayer (Dan. 9.4–19), where the exiles' responsibility for the destruction of Jerusalem and the Temple is fully accepted. In Ezra's view, if the crisis of intermarriage is not averted, the returnees will risk losing Jerusalem, Judah, and the right to practice Temple ritual. These confessions of communal guilt typify postexilic liturgy. **12:** The concern for intermarriage in terms of both genders is unusual in the Bible; most texts emphasize the danger of foreign wives rather than husbands.

10.1–4: Community repents and empowers Ezra to act on their behalf. See 9.1–2 n. **2:** Shecaniah speaks in the first person plural. For this reason, he is listed in rabbinic traditions as one of several exemplary leaders who take responsibility for the sins of the community and are thereby able to take the lead in resolving a problem (*b. Sanh.* 11a). **3:** The decision to expel all foreign wives and the children who were born to them is understood in rabbinic traditions to be the basis for the laws concerning matrilineal descent as a defining marker of Jewish identity (*Gen. Rab.* 7.2); biblical narratives suggest the priority of patrilineal descent in matters of genealogy and inheritance.

---

a Lit. "fence."   b Or "in the right."   c-c Or "Is there . . . ?"

covenant with our God to expel all these women and those who have been born to them, in accordance with the bidding of the Lord and of all who are concerned over the commandment of our God, and let the Teaching be obeyed. [4] Take action, for the responsibility is yours and we are with you. Act with resolve!"

[5] So Ezra at once put the officers of the priests and the Levites and all Israel under oath to act accordingly, and they took the oath. [6] Then Ezra rose from his place in front of the House of God and went into the chamber of Jehohanan son of Eliashib; there, he ate no bread and drank no water, for he was in mourning over the trespass of those who had returned from exile. [7] Then a proclamation was issued in Judah and Jerusalem that all who had returned from the exile should assemble in Jerusalem, [8] and that anyone who did not come in three days would, by decision of the officers and elders, have his property confiscated and himself excluded from the congregation of the returning exiles.

[9] All the men of Judah and Benjamin assembled in Jerusalem in three days; it was the ninth month, the twentieth of the month. All the people sat in the square of the House of God, trembling on account of the event and because of the rains. [10] Then Ezra the priest got up and said to them, "You have trespassed by bringing home foreign women, thus aggravating the guilt of Israel. [11] So now, make confession to the LORD, God of your fathers, and do His will, and separate yourselves from the peoples of the land and from the foreign women."

[12] The entire congregation responded in a loud voice, "We must surely do just as you say. [13] However, many people are involved, and it is the rainy season; it is not possible to remain out in the open, nor is this the work of a day or two, because we have transgressed extensively in this matter. [14] Let our officers remain on behalf of the entire congregation, and all our townspeople who have brought home foreign women shall appear before them at scheduled times, together with the elders and judges of each town, in order to avert the burning anger of our God from us on this account." [15] Only Jonathan son of Asahel and Jahzeiah son of Tikvah remained for this purpose, assisted by Meshullam and Shabbethai, the Levites. [16] The returning exiles did so. Ezra the priest and the men who were the chiefs of the ancestral clans—all listed by name—sequestered themselves on the first day of the tenth month to study the matter. [17] By the first day of the first month they were done with all the men who had brought home foreign women. [18] Among the priestly fam-

10.6–11: Ezra takes legal action to resolve the intermarriage crisis. Ezra requires the leadership of the returning community to take an oath to act in accordance with the law. Perhaps this is necessary in light of the charges that are made against the community leaders in 9.2. **6:** The sin is seen as so extreme that, like Moses after the construction of the golden calf, Ezra fasts completely (see Exod. 34.28; Deut. 9.18). **8:** The Rabbis take this v. as a legal precedent for their power to expropriate when it is beneficial for the community (*b. Git.* 36b).

10.12–14: Community accepts Ezra's legal action. This section of the narrative is deeply influenced by numerous Torah narratives involving the Israelites' willingness to accept the authority of Moses and to agree to obey particular laws.

10.15–44: Determining which returnees intermarried. Though this list would seem to be an odd conclusion to a biblical book, it is quite suitable for the middle of the larger book Ezra-Nehemiah, especially since the theme of intermarriage will return in Nehemiah. **15:** Jonathan son of Asahel, who is mentioned first, is said by the Rabbis to have carried out the work with a special zeal (*Exod. Rab.* 50.5). **16:** *To study the matter:* This apparently refers to the study of existing legal traditions and to the interpretation emerging from that study. The v. recalls Ezra's priestly lineage (7.1–5), perhaps to authorize Ezra as an interpreter. He has already been authorized by being described as a scribe (chs 7, 6, 11), as one who is well versed in biblical interpretation (7.10), and as a priest whose known lineage qualifies him to participate in Temple rituals. See 7.1–10 n. **18:** Jeshua's intermarriage implicates even the priestly leadership in the intermarriage crisis. In 1 Esdras 9.19 only the descendants of Jeshua are said to have foreign wives, not Jeshua himself. **44:** *Who had borne children,* cf. 1 Esdras 9.36.

ilies who were found to have brought foreign women were Jeshua son of Jozadak and his brothers Maaseiah, Eliezer, Jarib, and Gedaliah. [19] They gave their word[a] to expel their wives and, acknowledging their guilt, offered a ram from the flock to expiate it. [20] Of the sons of Immer: Hanani and Zebadiah; [21] of the sons of Harim: Maaseiah, Elijah, Shemaiah, Jehiel, and Uzziah; [22] of the sons of Pashhur: Elioenai, Maaseiah, Ishmael, Nethanel, Jozabad, and Elasah; [23] of the Levites: Jozabad, Shimei, Kelaiah who is Kelita, Pethahiah, Judah, and Eliezer. [24] Of the singers: Eliashib. Of the gatekeepers: Shallum, Telem, and Uri. [25] Of the Israelites: of the sons of Parosh: Ramiah, Izziah, Malchijah, Mijamin, Eleazar, Malchijah, and Benaiah; [26] of the sons of Elam: Mattaniah, Zechariah, Jehiel, Abdi, Jeremoth, and Elijah; [27] of the sons of Zattu: Elioenai, Eliashib, Mattaniah, Jeremoth, Zabad, and Aziza; [28] of the sons of Bebai: Jehohanan, Hananiah, Zabbai, and Athlai; [29] of the sons of Bani: Meshullam, Malluch, Adaiah, Jashub, Sheal, and Ramoth; [30] of the sons of Pahath-moab: Adna, Chelal, Benaiah, Maaseiah, Mattaniah, Bezalel, Binnui, and Manasseh; [31] of the sons of Harim: Eliezer, Isshijah, Malchijah, Shemaiah, and Shimeon; [32] also Benjamin, Malluch, and Shemariah; [33] of the sons of Hashum: Mattenai, Mattattah, Zabad, Eliphelet, Jeremai, Manasseh, and Shimei; [34] of the sons of Bani: Maadai, Amram, and Uel; [35] also Benaiah, Bedeiah, Cheluhu, [36] Vaniah, Meremoth, Eliashib, [37] Mattaniah, Mattenai, Jaasai, [38] Bani, Binnui, Shimei, [39] Shelemiah, Nathan, Adaiah, [40] Machnadebai, Shashai, Sharai, [41] Azarel, Shelemiah, Shemariah, [42] Shallum, Amariah, and Joseph; [43] of the sons of Nebo: Jeiel, Mattithiah, Zabad, Zebina, Jaddai, Joel, and Benaiah.

[44] All these had married foreign women, among whom were some women [b-]who had borne children.[-b]

a Lit. "hand."   b-b Meaning of Heb. uncertain.

Nehemiah

FOR INTRODUCTION TO NEHEMIAH, see introduction to Ezra.

Summary of Contents

[HINDY NAJMAN]

1 The narrative of Nehemiah son of Hacaliah: In the month of Kislev of the twentieth year,[a] when I was in the fortress of Shushan, [2] Hanani, one of my brothers, together with some men of Judah, arrived, and I asked them about the Jews, the remnant who had survived the captivity, and about Jerusalem. [3] They replied, "The survivors who have survived the captivity there in the province are in dire trouble and disgrace; Jerusalem's wall is full of breaches, and its gates have been destroyed by fire."

[4] When I heard that, I sat and wept, and was in mourning for days, fasting and praying to the God of Heaven. [5] I said, "O LORD, God of Heaven, great and awesome God, who stays faithful to His covenant with those who love Him and keep His commandments! [6] Let Your ear be attentive and Your eyes open to receive the prayer of Your servant that I am praying to You now, day and night, on behalf of the Israelites, Your servants, confessing the sins that we Israelites have committed against You, sins that I and my father's house have committed. [7] We have offended You by not keeping the commandments, the laws, and the rules that You gave to Your servant Moses. [8] Be mindful of the promise You gave to Your servant Moses: 'If you are unfaithful, I will scatter you among the peo-

a I.e., of King Artaxerxes; cf. 2.1.

1.1–3: News of Jerusalem in crisis. Although both the Masoretic tradition and the Septuagint present Ezra-Nehemiah as a single work, the transition from the conclusion of Ezra to the opening section of Nehemiah is awkward. **1:** "Nehemiah" means "the LORD is compassionate." Most date this to 445 BCE (the twentieth year of Artaxerxes I), shortly after some kind of attack on the returnees reflected in the narrative of v. 3. **3:** *Jerusalem's wall is full of breaches, and its gates have been destroyed by fire:* The language recalls the destruction and burning of Jerusalem under the direction of Nebuzara-

dan, the chief of the guards under Nebuchadnezzar some 140 years earlier. Nehemiah expresses an urgent need to prevent what threatens to be a second destruction of the Jerusalem Temple. Cf. 2 Kings 25.8–12.

1.4–11a: Prayer of Nehemiah. 4: Nehemiah's behavior accords with mourning and supplication practices that are characteristic of exilic and Second Temple narratives. Cf. Ezra 9.3–15, where Ezra participates in mourning rituals, fasts, confesses his sins, and then offers an elaborate prayer to the LORD. Similarly, in Dan. 9.3ff., Daniel prays while fasting and wearing sackcloth and ashes, then confesses and offers an elaborate prayer to the LORD. **5:** Petionary prayers typically start with an invocation, often just "LORD" or "God." The unusually long invocation of this v. is meant to remind God of both His power and His obligation to redress the situation. **6:** Nehemiah employs the formula used by priests in the confession on Yom Kippur when he says: *Confessing the sins that we Israelites have committed against You, sins that I and my father's house have committed.* See Lev. ch 16 and *m. Yoma* 6.2. **7–11:** By recalling the history of Israel, Nehemiah reminds God of the promises made to Israel and also of God's own compassion at times when the Israelites strayed from their course. Much of this passage is a paraphrase of sections of Deuteronomy, though concepples; [9] but if you turn back to Me, faithfully keep My commandments, even if your dispersed are at the ends of the earth,[a] I will gather them from there and bring them to the place where I have chosen to establish My name.' [10] For they are Your servants and Your people whom You redeemed by Your great power and Your mighty hand. [11] O Lord! Let Your ear be attentive to the prayer of Your servant, and to the prayer of Your servants who desire to hold Your name in awe. Grant Your servant success today, and dispose that man to be compassionate toward him!"

I was the king's cupbearer at the time.

2 In the month of Nisan, in the twentieth year of King Artaxerxes, wine was set before him; I took the wine and gave it to the king—I had never been out of sorts in his presence. [2] The king said to me, "How is it that you look bad, though you are not ill? It must be bad thoughts." I was very frightened, [3] but I answered the king, "May the king live forever! How should I not look bad when the city of the graveyard of my ancestors lies in ruins, and its gates have been consumed by fire?" [4] The king said to me, "What is your request?" With a prayer to the God of Heaven, [5] I answered the king, "If it please the king, and if your servant has found favor with you, send me to Judah, to the city of my ancestors' graves, to rebuild it." [6] With the consort seated at his side, the king said to me, "How long will you be gone and when will you return?" So it was agreeable to the king to send me, and I gave him a date. [7] Then I said to the king, "If it please the king, let me have letters to the governors of the province of Beyond the River, directing them to grant me passage until I reach Judah; [8] likewise, a letter to Asaph, the keeper of the King's Park, directing him to give me timber for roofing the gatehouses of the temple fortress and the city walls and for the house I shall occupy." The king gave me these, thanks to my God's benevolent care for me. [9] When I came to the governors of the province of Beyond the River I gave them the king's letters. The king also sent army officers and cavalry with me.

[10] When Sanballat the Horonite and Tobiah the Ammonite servant heard, it displeased them greatly that someone had come, intent on improving the condition of the Israelites.

[11] I arrived in Jerusalem. After I was there three days [12] I got up at night, I and a few men with me, and telling no one what my God had put into my mind to do for Jerusa-

tions from Priestly literature, such as Israel being *unfaithful* (v. 8) are mixed in, suggesting that the author was working from a complete Torah similar to our own.

1.11b–2.9: Nehemiah's request to return to Jerusalem is granted. 6: Nehemiah either demonstrates quick thinking or he has planned this response in advance. Josephus seems to prefer the first option, reporting this event as occurring on the same day on which Nehemiah is informed of Jerusalem's present situation. **1.11b:** As the cupbearer, Nehemiah occupies a significant and trusted position in the palace of Artaxerxes. **2.8:** This v. is adduced as proof that it is permissible to accept a gift for the Temple from an idol worshipper only if the gift is from the government (b. *ʿArak.* 6a).

2.10: Report of opposition to Nehemiah's arrival in Judah. *Sanballat the Horonite* is mentioned in documents from Elephantine in Egypt as the governor of Samaria. This verse is anticipatory; a major theme of Nehemiah is the opposition of these people to his restoration of Jerusalem.

2.11–16: Nehemiah secretly assesses the damage to Jerusalem. The secret nighttime evaluation of the walls begins and ends at the Valley Gate.

---

a Lit. "sky."

lem, and taking no other beast than the one on which I was riding, [13] I went out by the Valley Gate, at night, toward the Jackals' Spring and the Dung Gate; and I surveyed the walls of Jerusalem that were breached, and its gates, consumed by fire. [14] I proceeded to the Fountain Gate and to the King's Pool, where there was no room for the beast under me to continue. [15] So I went up the wadi by night, surveying the wall, and, entering again by the Valley Gate, I returned. [16] The prefects knew nothing of where I had gone or what I had done, since I had not yet divulged it to the Jews—the priests, the nobles, the prefects, or the rest of the officials.

[17] Then I said to them, "You see the bad state we are in—Jerusalem lying in ruins and its gates destroyed by fire. Come, let us rebuild the wall of Jerusalem and suffer no more disgrace." [18] I told them of my God's benevolent care for me, also of the things that the king had said to me, and they said, "Let us start building!" They were encouraged by [His] benevolence.

[19] When Sanballat the Horonite and Tobiah the Ammonite servant and Geshem the Arab heard, they mocked us and held us in contempt and said, "What is this that you are doing? Are you rebelling against the king?" [20] I said to them in reply, "The God of Heaven will grant us success, and we, His servants, will start building. But you have no share or claim or stake[a] in Jerusalem!"

3 Then Eliashib the high priest and his fellow priests set to and rebuilt the Sheep Gate; they consecrated it and set up its doors, consecrating it as far as the Hundred's Tower, as far as the Tower of Hananel. [2] Next to him, the men of Jericho built. Next to them,[b] Zaccur son of Imri. [3] The sons of Hassenaah rebuilt the Fish Gate; they roofed it and set up its doors, locks, and bars. [4] Next to them, Meremoth son of Uriah son of Hakkoz repaired; and next to him,[c] Meshullam son of Berechiah son of Meshezabel. Next to him,[c] Zadok son of Baana repaired. [5] Next to him,[c] the Tekoites repaired, though their nobles would not [d]take upon their shoulders[d] the work of their lord. [6] Joiada son of Paseah and Meshullam son of Besodeiah repaired the Jeshanah Gate; they roofed it and set up its doors, locks, and bars. [7] Next to them, Melatiah the Gibeonite and Jadon the Meronothite repaired, [with] the men of Gibeon and Mizpah, [e]under the jurisdiction[e] of the governor of the province of Beyond the River. [8] Next to them,[b] Uzziel son of

2.17–18: Nehemiah charges his attendants to assist him in rebuilding Jerusalem. 17: *Suffer no more disgrace:* The term "disgrace" is used elsewhere to characterize the destruction of the Temple and the exile. See Isa. 4.1–3; 22.18; 25.6–8; Jer. 23.39–40; 24.8–10; 25.8–11; Lam. 5.1; Ezek. 16.52–58; 22.1–5; Dan. 9.16.

2.19–20: Confrontation between Nehemiah and local leaders: Sanballat, Tobiah, and Geshem. 19: *Geshem* or "Gashmu" (6.6) may be a king of Kedar, since a recovered bowl from the Persian period is inscribed: "Cain son of Gashmu king of Kedar." The Kedarites are referred to in Gen. 25.13; Ps. 120.5; Isa. 21.16–17; 42.11; 60.7; Jer. 2.10; 49.28–30; Ezek. 27.21; 1 Chron. 1.29; Song 1.5. They likely originated in the Arabian peninsula. By the middle of the 5th century BCE, they may have been a significant presence in the land of Israel. **20:** The success of the small community due to divine support becomes an increasingly prominent theme in postexilic literature, especially in Chronicles.

3.1–38: Nehemiah and returnees repair the wall. 1: The high priest Eliashib was the grandson of the priest Jeshua. He is mentioned elsewhere in Nehemiah (12.10, 22; 13.4). **1–5:** The northern section with eight work assignments. **6–13:** The western section with ten work assignments.

---

a Lit. "record."   b Lit. "him."   c Lit. "them."   d-d Lit. "bring their neck into."
e-e Lit. "of the throne"; meaning of Heb. uncertain.

Harhaiah, [of the] smiths, repaired. Next to him, Hananiah, of[a] the perfumers. They restored Jerusalem as far as the Broad Wall. [9] Next to them, Rephaiah son of Hur, chief of half the district of Jerusalem, repaired. [10] Next to him,[b] Jedaiah son of Harumaph repaired in front of his house. Next to him, Hattush son of Hashabneiah repaired. [11] Malchijah son of Harim and Hasshub son of Pahath-moab repaired a second stretch, including the Tower of Ovens. [12] Next to them,[c] Shallum son of Hallohesh,[d] chief of half the district of Jerusalem, repaired—he and his daughters. [13] Hanun and the inhabitants of Zanoah repaired the Valley Gate; they rebuilt it and set up its doors, locks, and bars. And [they also repaired] a thousand cubits of wall to the Dung Gate. [14] Malchijah son of Rechab, chief of the district of Beth-haccerem, repaired the Dung Gate; he rebuilt it and set up its doors, locks, and bars. [15] Shallun son of Colhozeh, chief of the district of Mizpah, repaired the Fountain Gate; he rebuilt it and covered it, and set up its doors, locks, and bars, as well as the wall of the irrigation[e] pool of the King's Garden as far as the steps going down from the City of David. [16] After him, Nehemiah son of Azbuk, chief of half the district of Beth-zur, repaired, from in front of the graves of David as far as the artificial pool, and as far as the House of the Warriors. [17] After him, the Levites repaired: Rehum son of Bani. Next to him, Hashabiah, chief of half the district of Keilah, repaired for his district. [18] After him, their brothers repaired: Bavvai son of Henadad, chief of half the district of Keilah. [19] Next to him, Ezer son of Jeshua, the chief of Mizpah, repaired a second stretch, from in front of the ascent to the armory [at] the angle [of the wall]. [20] After him, Baruch son of Zaccai zealously repaired a second stretch, from the angle to the entrance to the house of Eliashib, the high priest. [21] After him, Meremoth son of Uriah son of Hakkoz repaired a second stretch, from the entrance to Eliashib's house to the end of Eliashib's house. [22] After him, the priests, inhabitants of the plain, repaired. [23] After them,[c] Benjamin and Hasshub repaired in front of their houses. After them,[c] Azariah son of Maaseiah son of Ananiah repaired beside his house. [24] After him, Binnui son of Henadad repaired a second stretch, from the house of Azariah to the angle, to the corner. [25] Palal son of Uzai— from in front of the angle and the tower that juts out of the house of the king, the upper [tower] of the prison compound. After him, Pedaiah son of Parosh. ([26] The temple

14–15: The southern section with two work assignments. **16–32:** The eastern section with twenty-one work assignments. **33–35:** Sanballat and Tobiah discourage the building. Cf. Ezra 4.4. **36–37:** Nehemiah offers a lament over the destruction. **38:** Completion of the wall.

4.1–6: Repeated opposition by local people. 3: Nehemiah's response is both religious and pragmatic. **4:** The people appear very disheartened in their lament.

---

a Lit. "son of," i.e., member of the guild of.
b Lit. "them." c Lit. "him." d I.e., the charmer.
e Following Kimhi; cf. Mishnaic Heb. bet hashelaḥin, *irrigated field*.

servants were living on the Ophel, as far as a point in front of the Water Gate in the east, and the jutting tower.) 27 After him, the Tekoites repaired a second stretch, from in front of the great jutting tower to the wall of the Ophel. 28 Above the Horse Gate, the priests repaired, each in front of his house. 29 After them,ᵃ Zadok son of Immer repaired in front of his house. After him, Shemaiah son of Shechaniah, keeper of the East Gate, repaired. 30 After him, Hananiah son of Shelemiah and Hanun, the sixth son of Zalaph, repaired a second stretch. After them,ᵃ Meshullam son of Berechiah repaired in front of his chamber. 31 After him, Malchijah of the smiths repaired as far as the house of the temple servants and the merchants, [from] in front of the Muster Gate to the corner loft. 32 And between the corner loft to the Sheep Gate the smiths and the merchants repaired.

33 When Sanballat heard that we were rebuilding the wall, it angered him, and he was extremely vexed. He mocked the Jews, 34 saying in the presence of his brothers and the Samarian force, "What are the miserable Jews doing? Will they restore, offer sacrifice, and finish one day? Can they revive those stones out of the dust heaps, burned as they are?" 35 Tobiah the Ammonite, alongside him, said, "That stone wall they are building—if a fox climbed it he would breach it!"

36 Hear, our God, how we have become a mockery, and return their taunts upon their heads! Let them be taken as spoil to a land of captivity! 37 Do not cover up their iniquity or let their sin be blotted out before You, for they hurled provocations at the builders.

38 We rebuilt the wall till it was continuous all around to half its height; for the people's heart was in the work.

4 When Sanballat and Tobiah, and the Arabs, the Ammonites, and the Ashdodites heard that healing had come to the walls of Jerusalem, that the breached parts had begun to be filled, it angered them very much, 2 and they all conspired together to come and fight against Jerusalem and to throw it into confusion. 3 Because of them we prayed to our God, and set up a watch over themᵇ day and night.

4 Judah was saying,
"The strength of the basket-carrier has failed,
And there is so much rubble;
We are not able ourselves
To rebuild the wall."

_____

a Lit. "him."   b I.e., the workers on the walls.

5 And our foes were saying, "Before they know or see it, we shall be in among them and kill them, and put a stop to the work." 6 When the Jews living near them[a] would arrive, they would tell us [b]time and again[-b] [c]". . . from all the places where . . . you shall come back to us . . ."[-c] 7 I stationed, on the lower levels of the place, behind the walls, on the bare rock—I stationed the people by families with their swords, their lances, and their bows. 8 Then I decided to exhort the nobles, the prefects, and the rest of the people, "Do not be afraid of them! Think of the great and awesome Lord, and fight for your brothers, your sons and daughters, your wives and homes!"

9 When our enemies learned that it had become known to us, since God had thus frustrated their plan, we could all return to the wall, each to his work. 10 From that day on, half my servants did work and half held lances and shields, bows and armor. And the officers stood behind the whole house of Judah 11 who were rebuilding the wall. The basket-carriers were burdened, doing work with one hand while the other held a weapon. 12 As for the builders, each had his sword girded at his side as he was building. The trumpeter stood beside me. 13 I said to the nobles, the prefects, and the rest of the people, "There is much work and it is spread out; we are scattered over the wall, far from one another. 14 When you hear a trumpet call, gather yourselves to me at that place; our God will fight for us!" 15 And so we worked on, while half were holding lances, from the break of day until the stars appeared.

16 I further said to the people at that time, "Let every man with his servant lodge in Jerusalem, that we may use the night to stand guard and the day to work." 17 Nor did I, my brothers, my servants, or the guards following me ever take off our clothes, [d][or] each his weapon, even at the water.[-d]

5 There was a great outcry by the common folk and their wives against their brother Jews. 2 Some said, "Our sons and daughters are numerous; we must get grain to eat in order that we may live!" 3 Others said, "We must pawn our fields, our vineyards, and our homes to get grain to stave off hunger." 4 Yet others said, "We have borrowed money against our fields and vineyards to pay the king's tax. 5 Now [e]we are as good as[-e] our brothers, and

4.7–17: Nehemiah empowers the returnees. Nehemiah calls upon God as a divine warrior; thus Nehemiah's subjects seem to be participating in a religious war for the future of the returnees and their families. **8:** Just a little over a century prior to Nehemiah, Jeremiah was exhorting the people to build homes in Babylonia and plant gardens there (Jer. 29.5, 28). Now, Nehemiah tells the people to fight for their recovered land and for their right to live in their land. **15:** *From the break of day until the stars appeared:* This v. offers one definition of daytime; the Rabbis use it to argue that one can fulfill the commandment of reciting the evening Shema (Deut. 6.4) only once the stars appear (*b. Ber.* 2b). In addition, this v. is used to define the beginning of night for purposes of purification (*b. Meg.* 20b).

5.1–5: Economic crisis among the returnees. The claim is that the creditors are seizing property that the returnees pledged when they needed to take loans. This is forbidden in the case of the poor (see Exod. 22.24–26). In earlier periods, such concerns fell under the purview of the prophets such as Amos, but prophecy as an institution was weakened in the postexilic period, so Nehemiah takes control of the situation. **1:** *Outcry* refers to a legal challenge as in Gen. 18.20–21; Job 34.28. **5:** *Daughters to slavery—some of our daughters are already subjected:* According to Exod. 21.7–11, an enslaved female loses the possibility of liberation if she is taken as a wife by her master, excluding maltreatment by her new master.

5.6–13: Nehemiah resolves the economic crisis. Nehemiah uses this occasion to declare a jubilee. See Lev. 25.1–55; Deut. 15.1–18. Due to his great power, Nehemiah is heeded (contrast Jer. 34.8–22), the community is stabilized, and work on the walls is resumed. Both civic and religious leaders seem to have been involved in these crimes, according to 6.7, 12.

a *I.e., the foes.*   b-b *Lit. "ten times."*
c-c *Heb. seems to be abbreviated; a possible restoration of the sentence, with the missing elements enclosed in brackets, is: [of their evil plan; and we would say to them,] "From all the places where [you get such information] you shall come back to us [and convey it]."*
d-d *Meaning of Heb. uncertain.*   e-e *Lit. "our flesh is as good as the flesh of."*

our children as good as theirs; yet here we are subjecting our sons and daughters to slavery—some of our daughters are already subjected—and we are powerless, while our fields and vineyards belong to others."

6 It angered me very much to hear their outcry and these complaints. 7 After pondering the matter carefully, I censured the nobles and the prefects, saying, "Are you pressing claims on loans made to your brothers?" Then I raised a large crowd against them 8 and said to them, "We have done our best to buy back our Jewish brothers who were sold to the nations; will you now sell your brothers so that they must be sold [back] to us?" They kept silent, for they found nothing to answer. 9 So I continued, "What you are doing is not right. You ought to act in a God-fearing way so as not to give our enemies, the nations, room to reproach us. 10 I, my brothers, and my servants also have claims of money and grain against them; let us now abandon those claims! 11 Give back at once their fields, their vineyards, their olive trees, and their homes, and [abandon] the claims for the hundred pieces of silver, the grain, the wine, and the oil that you have been pressing against them!" 12 They replied, "We shall give them back, and not demand anything of them; we shall do just as you say." Summoning the priests, I put them under oath to keep this promise. 13 I also shook out the bosom of my garment and said, "So may God shake free of his household and property any man who fails to keep this promise; may he be thus shaken out and stripped." All the assembled answered, "Amen," and praised the LORD.

The people kept this promise.

14 Furthermore, from the day I was commissioned to be governor in the land of Judah—from the twentieth year of King Artaxerxes until his thirty-second year, twelve years in all—neither I nor my brothers ever ate of the governor's food allowance. 15 The former governors who preceded me laid heavy burdens on the people, and took from them for bread and wine more than[a] forty shekels of silver. Their servants also tyrannized over the people. But I, out of the fear of God, did not do so. 16 I also supported the work on this wall; we did not buy any land, and all my servants were gathered there at the work. 17 Although there were at my table, between Jews and prefects, one hundred and fifty men in all, beside those who came to us from surrounding nations; 18 and although what was prepared for each day came to one ox, six select sheep, and fowl, all prepared for me, and at ten-day intervals all sorts

5.14–19: Nehemiah does not make use of the governor's food allowance. Nehemiah leads by example even to the point of refusing what is legally his allotment. **14:** *Twelve years in all:* Nehemiah served two terms as governor, according to 13.6. The first one lasts twelve years, while the second is not specified.

---

a Lit. "after"; meaning of Heb. uncertain.

of wine in abundance—yet I did not resort to the governor's food allowance, for the [king's] service lay heavily on the people. ⁱ⁹O my God, remember to my credit all that I have done for this people!

6 When word reached Sanballat, Tobiah, Geshem the Arab, and the rest of our enemies that I had rebuilt the wall and not a breach remained in it—though at that time I had not yet set up doors in the gateways—²Sanballat and Geshem sent a message to me, saying, "Come, let us get together in Kephirim in the Ono valley"; they planned to do me harm. ³I sent them messengers, saying, "I am engaged in a great work and cannot come down, for the work will stop if I leave it in order to come down to you." ⁴They sent me the same message four times, and I gave them the same answer. ⁵Sanballat sent me the same message a fifth time by his servant, who had an open letter with him. ⁶Its text was: "Word has reached the nations, and Geshemᵃ too says that you and the Jews are planning to rebel—for which reason you are building the wall—and that you are to be their king. ᵇ⁻Such is the word.⁻ᵇ ⁷You have also set up prophets in Jerusalem to proclaim about you, 'There is a king in Judah!' Word of these things will surely reach the king; so come, let us confer together."

⁸I sent back a message to him, saying, "None of these things you mention has occurred; they are figments of your imagination"—⁹for they all wished to intimidate us, thinking, "They will desist from the work, and it will not get done." Now strengthen my hands!

¹⁰Then I visited Shemaiah son of Delaiah son of Mehetabel when he was housebound, and he said,

> "Let us meet in the House of God, inside the sanctuary,
> And let us shut the doors of the sanctuary, for they are coming to kill you,
> By night they are coming to kill you."

¹¹I replied, "Will a man like me take flight? Besides, who such as I can go into the sanctuary and live? I will not go in." ¹²Then I realized that it was not God who sent him, but that he uttered that prophecy about me—Tobiah and Sanballat having hired him—¹³because he was a hireling, that I might be intimidated and act thus and commit a sin, and so provide them a scandal with which to reproach me.

¹⁴"O my God, remember against Tobiah and Sanballat

19: *Remember to my credit:* Similar prayers are found in 13.14, 23, 31. In the Bible, they typify Nehemiah, though similar requests are common in a variety of ancient Near Eastern prayers.

6.1–13: Opposition tries to distract and harm Nehemiah. 5–9: In a second attempt to stop the rebuilding, an unsealed—i.e., publicly accessible—letter accuses Nehemiah and his supporters of rebelling against Artaxerxes. Nehemiah is clear and direct in his rejection of these false claims: *They are figments of your imagination.* **6–7:** The accusation is that Judah wants to become independent of Persia, with its own king, anointed by a prophet, as was the case before 586 BCE. There is no evidence to suggest that this ever was the intention of the returnees. **10–13:** In the final attempt to distract Nehemiah, a false prophet is hired to lure him into a situation that would brand him as a transgressor of Temple law. Nehemiah uncovers the plot and escapes in time.

6.14: Nehemiah prays to God for protection. While Nehemiah has Persian authority to control the political situation in Jerusalem, he must rely completely on God to handle external conflict. Noadiah is one of a few named female prophets; others are Miriam (Exod. 15.20), Deborah (Judg. 4.4), and Huldah (2 Kings 22.14).

---

a Heb. Gashmu.   *b-b Meaning of Heb. uncertain.*

these deeds of theirs,[a] and against Noadiah the prophetess, and against the other prophets that they wished to intimidate me!"

15 The wall was finished on the twenty-fifth of Elul, after fifty-two days. 16 When all our enemies heard it, all the nations round about us were intimidated, and fell very low in their own estimation; they realized that this work had been accomplished by the help of our God.

17 Also in those days, the nobles of Judah kept up a brisk correspondence with Tobiah, and Tobiah with them. 18 Many in Judah were his confederates, for he was a son-in-law of Shecaniah son of Arah, and his son Jehohanan had married the daughter of Meshullam son of Berechiah. 19 They would also speak well of him to me, and would divulge my affairs to him. Tobiah sent letters to intimidate me.

7 When the wall was rebuilt and I had set up the doors, tasks were assigned to the gatekeepers, the singers, and the Levites. 2 I put Hanani my brother and Hananiah, the captain of the fortress, in charge of Jerusalem, for he was a more trustworthy and God-fearing man than most. 3 I said to them, "The gates of Jerusalem are not to be opened until the heat of the day,[b] and [c]before you leave your posts[c] let the doors be closed and barred. And assign the inhabitants of Jerusalem to watches, each man to his watch, and each in front of his own house."

4 The city was broad and large, the people in it were few, and houses were not yet built. 5 My God put it into my mind to assemble the nobles, the prefects, and the people, in order to register them by families. I found the genealogical register of those who were the first to come up, and there I found written:

6[d] These are the people of the province who came up from among the captive exiles that Nebuchadnezzar, king of Babylon, had deported, and who returned to Jerusalem and to Judah, each to his own city, 7 who came with Zerubbabel, Jeshua, Nehemiah, Azariah, Raamiah, Nahamani, Mordecai, Bilshan, Mispereth, Bigvai, Nehum, Baanah.

The number of the men of the people of Israel: 8 the sons of Parosh—2,172; 9 the sons of Shephatiah—372; 10 the sons of Arah—652; 11 the sons of Pahath-moab: the sons of Jeshua and Joab—2,818; 12 the sons of Elam—1,254; 13 the sons of Zattu—845; 14 the sons of Zaccai—760; 15 the sons of Binnui—648; 16 the sons of Bebai—628; 17 the sons of

6.15–16: The rebuilding of the wall is complete. *Fifty-two days:* This incredibly short time indicates the blessing and protection of God over the work. Cf. Ezra 6.14–15.

6.17–19: Tobiah tries to intimidate Nehemiah. While most of the surrounding peoples are said to desist from opposition because they recognize that the work on the wall was the work of God, Tobiah is still trying to harass and intimidate Nehemiah. Tobiah is to be contrasted with the two men Nehemiah places in charge of Jerusalem because they are "God fearing" (7.2). Some scholars suggest that Tobiah's attempted intimidation may in fact have occurred prior to the completion of the wall.

7.1–3: Nehemiah appoints gatekeepers, singers, and Levites to protect the gates and the doors. 1: *Hanani my brother:* This is the same individual who brought word about the condition of Jerusalem in 1.2. *And Hananiah:* Some scholars suggest that, since the verb is singular, only one person known by two similar names (Hanani and Hananiah) is intended, not two people. *Tasks were assigned:* The service of these Temple personnel as protectors may have a precedent in the protection of Jehoash recorded in 2 Kings ch 11. The Levites are also charged with this duty in Neh. 13.22.

7.4–72a: The genealogical register. 4–5: Nehemiah assembles the people and discovers a genealogical register. **6–72a:** See Ezra 2.1–70 n. According to the Rabbis, the genealogical list in Ezra reflects the initial return from Babylonia, and the list in Nehemiah reflects a return that is linked to the dedication of the Temple. According to b. Meg. 16b, Nehemiah's return occurs twenty-four years after the initial return of Ezra.

a Lit. "his."   b Lit. "sun."   c-c Lit. "while they are still standing."
d Vv. 6–43 appear as Ezra 2 with variations in the names and numbers.

Azgad—2,322; [18] the sons of Adonikam—667; [19] the sons of Bigvai—2,067; [20] the sons of Adin—655; [21] the sons of Ater: Hezekiah—98; [22] the sons of Hashum—328; [23] the sons of Bezai—324; [24] the sons of Hariph—112; [25] the sons of Gibeon—95; [26] the men of Bethlehem and Netophah—188; [27] the men of Anathoth—128; [28] the men of Beth-azmaveth—42; [29] the men of Kiriath-jearim, Chephirah, and Beeroth—743; [30] the men of Ramah and Geba—621; [31] the men of Michmas—122; [32] the men of Bethel and Ai—123; [33] the men of the other Nebo—52; [34] the sons of the other Elam—1,254; [35] the sons of Harim—320; [36] the sons of Jericho—345; [37] the sons of Lod, Hadid, and Ono—721; [38] the sons of Senaah—3,930.

[39] The priests: the sons of Jedaiah: the house of Jeshua—973; [40] the sons of Immer—1,052; [41] the sons of Pashhur—1,247; [42] the sons of Harim—1,017.

[43] The Levites: the sons of Jeshua: Kadmiel, the sons of Hodeiah—74.

[44] The singers: the sons of Asaph—148.

[45] The gatekeepers: the sons of Shallum, the sons of Ater, the sons of Talmon, the sons of Akkub, the sons of Hatita, the sons of Shobai—138.

[46] The temple servants: the sons of Ziha, the sons of Hasupha, the sons of Tabbaoth, [47] the sons of Keros, the sons of Siah, the sons of Padon, [48] the sons of Lebanah, the sons of Hagabah, the sons of Shalmai, [49] the sons of Hanan, the sons of Giddel, the sons of Gahar, [50] the sons of Reaiah, the sons of Rezin, the sons of Nekoda, [51] the sons of Gazzam, the sons of Uzza, the sons of Paseah, [52] the sons of Besai, the sons of Meunim, the sons of Nephishesim, [53] the sons of Bakbuk, the sons of Hakupha, the sons of Harhur, [54] the sons of Bazlith, the sons of Mehida, the sons of Harsha, [55] the sons of Barkos, the sons of Sisera, the sons of Temah, [56] the sons of Neziah, the sons of Hatipha.

[57] The sons of Solomon's servants: the sons of Sotai, the sons of Sophereth, the sons of Perida, [58] the sons of Jala, the sons of Darkon, the sons of Giddel, [59] the sons of Shephatiah, the sons of Hattil, the sons of Pochereth-hazzebaim, the sons of Amon.

[60] The total of temple servants and the sons of Solomon's servants—392.

[61] The following were those who came up from Tel-melah, Tel-harsha, Cherub, Addon, and Immer—they were unable to tell whether their father's house and de-

scent were Israelite: [62] the sons of Delaiah, the sons of To-biah, the sons of Nekoda—642.

[63] Of the priests: the sons of Habaiah, the sons of Hak-koz, the sons of Barzillai who had married a daughter of Barzillai the Gileadite and had taken his[a] name—[64] these searched for their genealogical records, but they could not be found, so they were disqualified for the priesthood. [65] The Tirshatha[b] ordered them not to eat of the most holy things until a priest with Urim and Thummim should appear.

[66] The sum of the entire community was 42,360, [67] not counting their male and female servants, these being 7,337; they also had 245 male and female singers. [68][c][Their horses—736, their mules—245,][c] camels—435, asses—6,720.

[69] Some of the heads of the clans made donations for the work. The Tirshatha donated to the treasury: gold—1,000 drachmas, basins—50, priestly robes—530.

[70] Some of the heads of the clans donated to the work treasury: gold—20,000 drachmas, and silver—2,200 minas.

[71] The rest of the people donated: gold—20,000 drach-mas, silver—2,000, and priestly robes—67.

[72] The priests, the Levites, the gatekeepers, the singers, some of the people, the temple servants, and all Israel took up residence in their towns.

8 When the seventh month arrived—the Israelites being [settled] in their towns—[1] the entire people assembled as one man in the square before the Water Gate, and they asked Ezra the scribe to bring the scroll of the Teaching of Moses with which the LORD had charged Israel. [2] On the first day of the seventh month, Ezra the priest brought the Teaching before the congregation, men and women and all who could listen with understanding. [3] He read from it, facing the square before the Water Gate, from the first light until midday, to the men and the women and those who could understand; the ears of all the people were given to the scroll of the Teaching.

[4] Ezra the scribe stood upon a wooden tower made for the purpose, and beside him stood Mattithiah, Shema, Anaiah, Uriah, Hilkiah, and Maaseiah at his right, and at his left Pedaiah, Mishael, Malchijah, Hashum, Hashbad-danah, Zechariah, Meshullam. [5] Ezra opened the scroll in the sight of all the people, for he was above all the people; as he opened it, all the people stood up. [6] Ezra blessed the

7.72b–8.8: Ezra reads from the Mosaic Torah ("torat moshe"). Cf. the narrative of the discovered Torah scroll during the reign of Josiah, king of Judah, in 2 Kings chs 22–23 (esp. 23.1–3). This narra-tive's use of exactly the same time description as Ezra 3.1 may indi-cate that the passage about the dedication of the altar and the pas-sage about the reading of the Torah of Moses are to be read to-gether. **8.1:** *Water Gate,* on the east side of Jerusalem and directly op-posite the Temple. **2:** *On the first day of the seventh month,* later known as Rosh Ha-Shanah, the New Year festival (see also Lev. 23.23–25; Num. 29.1–6). The com-munity here includes women, as in Deut. 1.12; contrast Exod. 19.14–15. **4:** Elevated upon a wooden platform, Ezra reenacts the Sinai event and the people, like their an-cestors, publicly accept the law. Whereas at Sinai Moses records what God reveals, Ezra now reads what Moses has written. Cf. the earlier, preexilic, public reading of the Torah of Moses in Josh. 8.30–35. Rabbinic traditions state that the wooden platform upon which Ezra stood was the Temple Mount (e.g., *t. Sot.,* 7.13; *b. Yoma* 69b; *b. Sot.* 40b–41a). The Rabbis state that the six people called to read pub-licly from the Torah scroll on the Day of Atonement represent the six people who stand at Ezra's left and the six people who stand at Ezra's right during the public reading of the Torah. (The Rabbis take Meshulam as another name for Zechariah, so there are six, not seven people [see *b. Meg.* 23a]). **5:** *All the people stood up:* The Rab-bis use this v. to illustrate correct conduct during the public reading of a Torah scroll. The people's standing is understood to reflect complete silence. A contemporary reflection of this v. is seen in syna-gogue worship: When the Torah scroll is raised, the congregation rises. **6:** *Ezra blessed the* LORD, *the great God:* The Rabbis explain that the phrase *the great God* refers to Ezra's use of the Tetragramma-ton, the four-letter name of God (YHVH) (*b. Yoma* 69b). By the rab-

---

a Lit. "their."   b A Persian title.
c-c These words are missing in some mss. and editions; but cf. Ezra 2.66.

Lord, the great God, and all the people answered, "Amen, Amen," with hands upraised. Then they bowed their heads and prostrated themselves before the Lord with their faces to the ground. [7]Jeshua, Bani, Sherebiah, Jamin, Akkub, Shabbethai, Hodiah, Maaseiah, Kelita, Azariah, Jozabad, Hanan, Pelaiah, and the Levites explained the Teaching to the people, while the people stood in their places. [8]They read from the scroll of the Teaching of God, translating it and giving the sense; so they understood the reading.

[9]Nehemiah the Tirshatha, Ezra the priest and scribe, and the Levites who were explaining to the people said to all the people, "This day is holy to the Lord your God: you must not mourn or weep," for all the people were weeping as they listened to the words of the Teaching. [10]He further said to them, "Go, eat choice foods and drink sweet drinks and send portions to whoever has nothing prepared, for the day is holy to our Lord. Do not be sad, for your rejoicing in the Lord is the source of your strength." [11]The Levites were quieting the people, saying, "Hush, for the day is holy; do not be sad." [12]Then all the people went to eat and drink and send portions and make great merriment, for they understood the things they were told.

[13]On the second day, the heads of the clans of all the people and the priests and Levites gathered to Ezra the scribe to study the words of the Teaching. [14]They found written in the Teaching that the Lord had commanded Moses that the Israelites must dwell in booths during the festival of the seventh month, [15]and that they must announce and proclaim throughout all their towns and Jerusalem as follows, "Go out to the mountains and bring leafy branches of olive trees, pine[a] trees, myrtles, palms and [other] leafy[a] trees to make booths, as it is written." [16]So the people went out and brought them, and made themselves booths on their roofs, in their courtyards, in the courtyards of the House of God, in the square of the Water Gate and in the square of the Ephraim Gate. [17]The whole community that returned from the captivity made booths and dwelt in the booths—the Israelites had not done so from the days of Joshua[b] son of Nun to that day—and there was very great rejoicing. [18]He read from the scroll of the Teaching of God each day, from the first to the last day. They celebrated the festival seven days, and there was a solemn gathering on the eighth, as prescribed.

a Meaning of Heb. uncertain.
b Heb. Jeshua.

binic period pronouncing this name had become taboo, and it begins to fall out of use in postexilic texts. **8:** The exact meaning of each of these words is uncertain, though together they reflect the idea that the Torah text cannot simply be read and understood in a straightforward way, an idea that is particularly prominent within rabbinic culture. *Translating it:* Rabbinic interpretation understands the Heb "meforash" to refer to the Targum, the Aramaic translation of the verse, which was recited in public along with the verse. Unable to understand the Heb text, the returnees required both Aramaic translation and interpretation (*b. Meg.* 3a; *b. Ned.* 37b; *Gen. Rab.* 36.8).

8.9–12: The people celebrate the first of Tishri, a holy and joyful festival. Cf. the response following the laying of the foundations of the Temple in Ezra 3.10–13. Nehemiah's attitude is that this reenacted revelation must be characterized by joy, not mourning, as in 2 Kings 22.11, or fear, as in the Sinai revelation (Exod. ch 19).

8.13–18: Ezra and the people celebrate the festival of Sukkot (the feast of Booths). Compare Solomon's celebration of Sukkot in 2 Chron. 7.8–10. **14:** See Exod. 23.16; 34.22; Lev. 23.33–43; Num. 29.1–38. **15:** These four species (*olive trees, pine trees, myrtles, palms and [other] leafy trees*) differ from the four species (palm, myrtle, willow, etrog) understood from later tradition based on Lev. 23.40 (see 2 Macc. 10.7; Josephus *Ant.* 3.10.4; *m. Sukkah* 4.1–7; *Lev. Rab.* 30.15; *b. Sukkah* 12a and 38a, where the Rabbis attempt to resolve this inconsistency). Most remarkable, rabbinic tradition suggests that these four species should be taken in hand, while here, perhaps based on the contiguity of Lev. 23.40, 42, they are used for constructing the booths. **18:** Cf. Lev. 23.33–36; Num. 29.35 regarding the festival of Sukkot, particularly the *solemn gathering* on the eighth day; this is lacking in Deut. 16.15; 1 Kings 8.66.

9 On the twenty-fourth day of this month, the Israelites assembled, fasting, in sackcloth, and with earth upon them. [2] Those of the stock of Israel separated themselves from all foreigners, and stood and confessed their sins and the iniquities of their fathers. [3] Standing in their places, they read from the scroll of the Teaching of the LORD their God for one-fourth of the day, and for another fourth they confessed and prostrated themselves before the LORD their God. [4] On the raised platform of the Levites stood Jeshua and Bani, Kadmiel, Shebaniah, Bunni, Sherebiah, Bani, and Chenani, and cried in a loud voice to the LORD their God. [5] The Levites Jeshua, Kadmiel, Bani, Hashabniah, Sherebiah, Hodiah, and Pethahiah said, "Rise, bless the LORD your God who is from eternity to eternity: 'May Your glorious name be blessed, exalted though it is above every blessing and praise!'

[6] "You alone are the LORD. You made the heavens, the highest[a] heavens, and all their host, the earth and everything upon it, the seas and everything in them. You keep them all alive, and the host of heaven prostrate themselves before You. [7] You are the LORD God, who chose Abram, who brought him out of Ur of the Chaldeans and changed his name to Abraham. [8] Finding his heart true to You, You made a covenant with him to give the land of the Canaanite, the Hittite, the Amorite, the Perizzite, the Jebusite, and the Girgashite—to give it to his descendants. And You kept Your word, for You are righteous. [9] You took note of our fathers' affliction in Egypt, and heard their cry at the Sea of Reeds. [10] You performed signs and wonders against Pharaoh, all his servants, and all the people of his land, for You knew that they acted presumptuously to-

---

a Lit. "the heavens of the."

9.1–5: People fast and confess their sins. 1: This passage suggests that a festival similar to Yom Kippur is observed on the 24th day of Tishri, after the celebration of Sukkot, not on the 10th of Tishri as reflected in other biblical texts (Lev. 16.29; 23.27–28; 25.9; Num. 29.7) and later rabbinic traditions. **2:** *Separated themselves from all foreigners:* This may refer to a crisis similar to the one recorded in Ezra chs 9–10; Neh. 10.31; 12.23–31. **3:** This passage is cited in rabbinic literature as an example of how one should divide one's day between study and prayer. One should divide the period from midday until the evening into two parts. In the first part, one should study the weekly portion of the Torah and the haftarah. In the second part, one should confess one's sins to God (*b. Meg.* 30b; *b. Ta'an.* 12b). **4:** *And cried in a loud voice to the LORD their God:* The Rabbis understand the people's cry as a confession for idolatrous practices that are said to have caused the destruction of the sanctuary, the burning of the temple, the murder of the righteous, and the Babylonian exile (*b. Sanh.* 64a; *b. Yoma* 69b). **5:** Introduction to the confession. Cf. Dan. 2.20–23. The Rabbis comment that Neh. 9.5 reflects

the fact that in the Temple liturgy the people did not respond to blessings with "Amen," but rather gave praise to God following each blessing (*b. Ber.* 63a; *b. Sot.* 40b; and the more extensive discussion of Temple liturgy in *b. Ta'an.* 16b).

9.6–37: Communal confession. Cf. Nehemiah's prayer to Joshua's recounting of Israelite history in Josh. ch 24. Like all historical retellings, it is remarkably selective in what it narrates. For example, for the ancestral period, only Abraham is mentioned. This prayer is incorporated into the daily morning prayer in Jewish liturgy. **6:** The prayer begins with a declaration of God as creator. This relies mainly on the Priestly account of creation in Gen. 1.1–2.4. *The highest heavens, and all their host* is found elsewhere, though these are not Priestly terms (see, e.g., Deut. 10.14; 1 Kings 8.27; 2 Chron. 6.18). The author of this prayer is thus combining concepts from originally separate sources that have become integrated in the Torah. R. Oshaia uses this verse as a proof that the "Shekhinah" (divine presence) is in every place (*b. B. Bat.* 25a). **7–8:** The prayer alludes to the following events: Abraham was brought out of Ur (Gen. ch 12), God changed Abram's name to Abraham (Gen. ch 17); Abraham's heart was found to be faithful (Gen. ch 22); God made a covenant with Abram to give him and his descendants the land of the surrounding peoples (Gen. ch 15). As in later retellings of biblical events, the order of events may be rearranged. **9–12:** The prayer continues with the retelling of the miraculous exodus from Egypt. The relatively extensive space given to the exodus reflects its general importance in biblical tradition and its special significance for those who have undergone an "exodus" of their own. **9:** Here, the prayer alludes to God's speech to Moses at the burning bush in Exod. 3.7 and later in the exodus narrative, Exod. 14.10. **10:** The language in Nehemiah ward them. You made a name for Yourself that endures to this day. ¹¹ You split the sea before them; they passed through the sea on dry land, but You threw their pursuers into the depths, like a stone into the raging waters.

¹² "You led them by day with a pillar of cloud, and by night with a pillar of fire, to give them light in the way they were to go. ¹³ You came down on Mount Sinai and spoke to them from heaven; You gave them right rules and true teachings, good laws and commandments. ¹⁴ You made known to them Your holy sabbath, and You ordained for them laws, commandments and Teaching, through Moses Your servant. ¹⁵ You gave them bread from heaven when they were hungry, and produced water from a rock when they were thirsty. You told them to go and possess the land that You swore to give them. ¹⁶ But they—our fathers—acted presumptuously; they stiffened their necks and did not obey Your commandments. ¹⁷ Refusing to obey, unmindful of Your wonders that You did for them, they stiffened their necks, and in their defiance resolved to return to their slavery. But You, being a forgiving God, gracious and compassionate, long-suffering and abounding in faithfulness, did not abandon them. ¹⁸ Even though they made themselves a molten calf and said, 'This is your God who brought you out of Egypt,' thus committing great impieties, ¹⁹ You, in Your abundant compassion, did not abandon them in the wilderness. The pillar of cloud did not depart from them to lead them on the way by day, nor the pillar of fire by night to give them light in the way they were to go. ²⁰ You endowed them with Your good spirit to instruct them. You did not withhold Your manna from their mouth; You gave them water when they were thirsty. ²¹ Forty years You sustained them in the wilderness so that they lacked nothing; their clothes did not wear out, and their feet did not swell.

²² "You gave them kingdoms and peoples, and ᵃ⁻allotted them territory.ᵃ They took possession of the land of Sihon, the land of the king of Heshbon, and the land of Og, king of Bashan. ²³ You made their children as numerous as the stars of heaven, and brought them to the land which You told their fathers to go and possess. ²⁴ The sons came and took possession of the land: You subdued the Canaanite inhabitants of the land before them; You delivered them into their power, both their kings and the peoples of the land, to do with them as they pleased. ²⁵ They captured fortified cities and rich lands; they took possession of houses filled with every good thing, of hewn cisterns,

seems closest to Exod. 9.16. **11:** In Nehemiah's recounting of the splitting of the sea, Moses' role is limited, as in Ps. 78.13. In the exodus narrative Moses plays a much more active role (Exod. 14.16, 21, 27). **12:** The language here is almost a verbatim quotation from Exod. 13.21. **13–14:** Giving of the Torah at Sinai. This is lacking in the shorter historical retellings in Deut. 26.5–9; Josh. 24.2–13. **13a:** Here Nehemiah preserves, side by side, two different accounts of the Sinai theophany. *You came down on Mount Sinai* reflects the tradition in Exod. 19.11, 20 where God is said to have come down on Mount Sinai. *And spoke to them from heaven* reflects the tradition in Exod. 20.19 that God communicated to Israel from the heavens and not from an earthly location. **13b:** See Mal. 2.6; Ps. 119.137, 142. **16–21:** The prayer emphasizes God's compassion despite Israel's continued transgression. **18:** Nehemiah's retelling of the golden calf episode omits the role played by Aaron. Cf. Exod. 32.1–4, 21–24. **22–25:** Conquest of Israel and settlement. **22:** See Num. 21.21–35; Deut. chs 2–3.

a-a *Meaning of Heb. uncertain.*

vineyards, olive trees, and fruit trees in abundance. They ate, they were filled, they grew fat; they luxuriated in Your great bounty. 26 Then, defying You, they rebelled; they cast Your Teaching behind their back. They killed Your prophets who admonished them to turn them back to You; they committed great impieties.

27 "You delivered them into the power of their adversaries who oppressed them. In their time of trouble they cried to You; You in heaven heard them, and in Your abundant compassion gave them saviors who saved them from the power of their adversaries. 28 But when they had relief, they again did what was evil in Your sight, so You abandoned them to the power of their enemies, who subjugated them. Again they cried to You, and You in heaven heard and rescued them in Your compassion, time after time. 29 You admonished them in order to turn them back to Your Teaching, but they acted presumptuously and disobeyed Your commandments, and sinned against Your rules, by following which a man shall live. They turned a defiant shoulder, stiffened their neck, and would not obey. 30 You bore with them for many years, admonished them by Your spirit through Your prophets, but they would not give ear, so You delivered them into the power of the peoples of the lands. 31 Still, in Your great compassion You did not make an end of them or abandon them, for You are a gracious and compassionate God.

32 "And now, our God, great, mighty, and awesome God, who stays faithful to His covenant, do not treat lightly all the suffering that has overtaken us—our kings, our officers, our priests, our prophets, our fathers, and all Your people—from the time of the Assyrian kings to this day. 33 Surely You are in the right with respect to all that has come upon us, for You have acted faithfully, and we have been wicked. 34 Our kings, officers, priests, and fathers did not follow Your Teaching, and did not listen to Your commandments or to the warnings that You gave them. 35 When they had their own kings and enjoyed the good that You lavished upon them, and the broad and rich land that You put at their disposal, they would not serve You, and did not turn from their wicked deeds. 36 Today we are slaves, and the land that You gave our fathers to enjoy its fruit and bounty—here we are slaves on it! 37 On account of our sins it yields its abundant crops to kings whom You have set over us. They rule over our bodies and our beasts as they please, and we are in great distress.

26–31: Repeated transgression of Israel in the land, following a pattern already established in the desert (v. 18). Nehemiah recounts the period of the judges and the kings. The main theme is God's continued forgiveness and forebearance, which Nehemiah is invoking as paradigmatic for his own situation. (Ps. 106 has a similar function and structure.) 32–37: Returnees confess their sins. 32: The words *and now* mark a transition. Nehemiah turns his attention from the past to the present. This is common in many other biblical prayers, e.g., Num. 14.17; Dan. 9.15; Ezra 9.10. 34–35: List of people who are guilty and responsible for the exile. Cf. Jer. 24.1–10; 44.17; Dan. 9.6, 8; 2 Chron. 36.14–16; Zech. 1.5–6; 7.8–14.

10 "In view of all this, we make this pledge and put it in writing; and on the sealed copy [are subscribed] our officials, our Levites, and our priests.

2 "On the sealed copy[a] [are subscribed]: Nehemiah the Tirshatha son of Hacaliah and Zedekiah, 3 Seraiah, Azariah, Jeremiah, 4 Pashhur, Amariah, Malchijah, 5 Hattush, Shebaniah, Malluch, 6 Harim, Meremoth, Obadiah, 7 Daniel, Ginnethon, Baruch, 8 Meshullam, Abijah, Mijamin, 9 Maaziah, Bilgai, Shemaiah; these are the priests.

10 "And the Levites: Jeshua son of Azaniah, Binnui of the sons of Henadad, and Kadmiel. 11 And their brothers: Shebaniah, Hodiah, Kelita, Pelaiah, Hanan, 12 Mica, Rehob, Hashabiah, 13 Zaccur, Sherebiah, Shebaniah, 14 Hodiah, Bani, and Beninu.

15 "The heads of the people: Parosh, Pahath-moab, Elam, Zattu, Bani, 16 Bunni, Azgad, Bebai, 17 Adonijah, Bigvai, Adin, 18 Ater, Hezekiah, Azzur, 19 Hodiah, Hashum, Bezai, 20 Hariph, Anathoth, Nebai, 21 Magpiash, Meshullam, Hezir, 22 Meshezabel, Zadok, Jaddua, 23 Pelatiah, Hanan, Anaiah, 24 Hoshea, Hananiah, Hasshub, 25 Hallohesh, Pilha, Shobek, 26 Rehum, Hashabnah, Maaseiah, 27 and Ahiah, Hanan, Anan, 28 Malluch, Harim, Baanah.

29 "And the rest of the people, the priests, the Levites, the gatekeepers, the singers, the temple servants, and all who separated themselves from the peoples of the lands to [follow] the Teaching of God, their wives, sons and daughters, all who know enough to understand, 30 join with their noble brothers, and take an oath with sanctions to follow the Teaching of God, given through Moses the servant of God, and to observe carefully all the commandments of the LORD our Lord, His rules and laws.

31 "Namely: We will not give our daughters in marriage to the peoples of the land, or take their daughters for our sons.

32 "The peoples of the land who bring their wares and all sorts of foodstuff for sale on the sabbath day—we will not buy from them on the sabbath or a holy day.

"We will forgo [the produce of] the seventh year, and every outstanding debt.

33 "We have laid upon ourselves obligations: To charge ourselves one-third of a shekel yearly for the service of the House of our God—34 for the rows of bread, for the regular meal offering and for the regular burnt offering, [for those of the] sabbaths, new moons, festivals, for consecrations, for sin offerings to atone for Israel, and for all the work in the House of our God.

10.1–40: The covenant of Nehemiah and the returnees. 1–28: There is considerable overlap between this list and the priests listed in 1 Chron. ch 24. **29:** *The rest of the people* do not sign the covenant, but take part in the oath to keep the law. **30:** Josiah's covenant, like Nehemiah's, is preceded by a public reading of the text of the covenant, the Torah (2 Chron. 34.30–32). Hezekiah's covenant, like Nehemiah's, follows a communal confession (2 Chron. 29.5–10). **31:** Intermarriage, mentioned first, is a major theme in Ezra-Nehemiah. **32:** The Sabbath, mentioned second, became especially significant in the exilic period. This v. represents one of many attempts to develop and establish a coherent definition of the type of work that is prohibited on the Sabbath. (See also Ezek. 20.12, 16, 20, 24; Isa. 56.1–8; 58.13–14; Jer. 17.21–24.) *We will forgo [the produce of] the seventh year,* see Exod. 21.2–6; 23.10–11; Lev. 25.1–7; Deut. 15.1–18. **33–34:** This is related to Torah law, which requires every Israelite to pay half a shekel (Exod. 30.1–16; 38.25–26). See also 2 Kings 12.2–16; 2 Chron. 24.4–14, where payment is required for repair of the Temple.

a Heb. plural.

35 "We have cast lots [among] the priests, the Levites, and the people, to bring the wood offering to the House of our God by clans annually at set times in order to provide fuel for the altar of the LORD our God, as is written in the Teaching.

36 "And [we undertake] to bring to the House of the LORD annually the first fruits of our soil, and of every fruit of every tree; 37 also, the first-born of our sons and our beasts, as is written in the Teaching; and to bring the firstlings of our cattle and flocks to the House of our God for the priests who minister in the House of our God.

38 "We will bring to the storerooms of the House of our God the first part of our dough, and our gifts [of grain], and of the fruit of every tree, wine and oil for the priests, and the tithes of our land for the Levites—the Levites who collect the tithe in all our towns ᵃ·subject to royal service.·ᵃ 39 An Aaronite priest must be with the Levites when they collect the tithe, and the Levites must bring up a tithe of the tithe to the House of our God, to the storerooms of the treasury. 40 For it is to the storerooms that the Israelites and the Levites must bring the gifts of grain, wine, and oil. The equipment of the sanctuary and of the ministering priests and the gatekeepers and the singers is also there.

"We will not neglect the House of our God."

11 The officers of the people settled in Jerusalem; the rest of the people cast lots for one out of ten to come and settle in the holy city of Jerusalem, and the other nine-tenths to stay in the towns. 2 The people gave their blessing to all the men who willingly settled in Jerusalem.

3 These are the heads of the province who lived in Jerusalem—in the countrysideᵇ of Judah, the people lived in their towns, each on his own property, Israelites, priests, Levites, temple servants, and the sons of Solomon's servants, 4 while in Jerusalem some of the Judahites and some of the Benjaminites lived:

Of the Judahites: Athaiah son of Uzziah son of Zechariah son of Amariah son of Shephatiah son of Mahalalel, of the clan of Periz, 5 and Maaseiah son of Baruch son of Col-hozeh son of Hazaiah son of Adaiah son of Joiarib son of Zechariah son of the Shilohite. 6 All the clan of Periz who were living in Jerusalem—468 valorous men.

7 These are the Benjaminites: Sallu son of Meshullam son of Joed son of Pedaiah son of Kolaiah son of Maaseiah son of Ithiel son of Jesaiah. 8 After him, Gabbai and Sallai—928.

35: Torah laws concerning support of the Temple do not mention this tax. However, there is a requirement that the priests keep the fire burning continuously for the sacrifices in the sanctuary (Lev. 6.2–23). It may have been understood at the time of Nehemiah that this requirement could not be fulfilled unless a supply of wood was guaranteed. (See 13.31; *m. Ta'an.* 4.5; *b. Ta'an.* 28a.) **37:** As in the case of the prohibition against intermarriage, the laws of tithing and priestly support are given in more detail than in the Torah. The claim that these laws are *as is written in the Teaching* ("torah") should be understood to mean that the authoritative interpretation of Torah has the same authority as Torah itself. These stipulations of their covenant are violated by the people, and Nehemiah must reinforce them in 5.1–5; 13.1–3, 10–12, 15–17, 19–22, 23–28.

11.1–24: The list of those who settled in Jerusalem. 2: *Who willingly settled:* Despite its status as "the holy city," for economic reasons settlement in Jerusalem was not attractive, as recognized by the Rabbis (*b. Ketub.* 110b).

a-a *For this sense of* 'abodah, *"service," cf. 5.18.*   b *Lit. "towns."*

9 Joel son of Zichri was the official in charge of them, and Judah son of Hassenuah was the second-in-command of the city.

10 Of the priests: Jedaiah son of Joiarib, Jachin, 11 Seraiah son of Hilkiah son of Meshullam son of Zadok son of Meraioth son of Ahitub, chief officer of the House of God, 12 and their brothers, who did the work of the House— 822; and Adaiah son of Jeroham son of Pelaliah son of Amzi son of Zechariah son of Pashhur son of Malchijah, 13 and his brothers, heads of clans—242; and Amashsai son of Azarel son of Ahzai son of Meshillemoth son of Immer, 14 and their brothers, valorous warriors—128. Zabdiel son of Haggedolim was the official in charge of them.

15 Of the Levites: Shemaiah son of Hasshub son of Azrikam son of Hashabiah son of Bunni, 16 and Shabbethai and Jozabad of the heads of the Levites were in charge of the external work of the House of God. 17 Mattaniah son of Micha son of Zabdi son of Asaph was the head; at prayer, he would lead off with praise; and Bakbukiah, one of his brothers, was his second-in-command; and Abda son of Shammua son of Galal son of Jeduthun. 18 All the Levites in the holy city—284.

19 And the gatekeepers: Akkub, Talmon, and their brothers, who stood watch at the gates—172.

20 And the rest of the Israelites, the priests, and the Levites in all the towns of Judah [lived] each on his estate.

21 The temple servants lived on the Ophel; Ziha and Gishpa were in charge of the temple servants.

22 The overseer of the Levites in Jerusalem was Uzzi son of Bani son of Hashabiah son of Mattaniah son of Micha, of the Asaphite singers, over the work of the House of God. 23 There was a royal order concerning them, a stipulation concerning the daily duties of the singers.

24 Petahiah son of Meshezabel, of the sons of Zerah son of Judah, advised the king concerning all the affairs of the people.

25 As concerns the villages with their fields: Some of the Judahites lived in Kiriath-arba and its outlying hamlets, in Dibon and its outlying hamlets, and in Jekabzeel and its villages; 26 in Jeshua, in Moladah, and in Beth-pelet; 27 in Hazar-shual, in Beer-sheba and its outlying hamlets; 28 and in Ziklag and in Meconah and its outlying hamlets; 29 in En-rimmon, in Zorah and in Jarmuth; 30 Zanoah, Adullam, and their villages; Lachish and its fields; Azekah and its outlying hamlets. They settled from Beersheba to the Valley of Hinnom.

31 The Benjaminites: from Geba, Michmash, Aija, and Bethel and its outlying hamlets; 32 Anathoth, Nob, Ana-

11.25–36: The distribution of village settlements in Judah. Eleven of the listed settlements are said to be in territory known to be under Edomite-Arab control after the destruction of the First Temple, and scholars have questioned the historical reliability of this source. Some scholars have suggested that the settlement list reflects the conquest list in Josh. chs 14–15.

niah, 33 Hazor, Ramah, Gittaim, 34 Hadid, Zeboim, Neballat, 35 Lod, Ono, Ge-harashim. 36 Some of the Judahite divisions of Levites were [shifted] to Benjamin.

12 These are the priests and the Levites who came up with Zerubbabel son of Shealtiel and Jeshua:
Seraiah, Jeremiah, Ezra, 2 Amariah, Malluch, Hattush, 3 Shecaniah, Rehum, Meramoth, 4 Iddo, Ginnethoi, Abijah, 5 Mijamin, Maadiah, Bilgah, 6 Shemaiah, Joiarib, Jedaiah, 7 Sallu, Amok, Hilkiah, Jedaiah. These were the heads of the priests and their brothers in the time of Jeshua.

8 The Levites: Jeshua, Binnui, Kadmiel, Sherebiah, Judah, and Mattaniah, in charge of thanksgiving songs,ᵃ he and his brothers; 9 and Bakbukiah and Unni [and] their brothers served opposite them by shifts.

10 Jeshua begot Joiakim; Joiakim begot Eliashib; Eliashib begot Joiada; 11 Joiada begot Jonathan; Jonathan begot Jaddua.

12 In the time of Joiakim, the heads of the priestly clans were: Meriaiah—of the Seraiah clan; Hananiah—of the Jeremiah clan; 13 Meshullam—of the Ezra clan; Jehohanan—of the Amariah clan; 14 Jonathan—of the Melicu clan; Joseph—of the Shebaniah clan; 15 Adna—of the Harim clan; Helkai—of the Meraioth clan; 16 Zechariah— of the Iddo clan; Meshullam—of the Ginnethon clan; 17 Zichri—of the Abijah clan . . . of the Miniamin clan; Piltai—of the Moadiah clan; 18 Shammua—of the Bilgah clan; Jehonathan—of the Shemaiah clan; 19 Mattenai—of the Joiarib clan; Uzzi—of the Jedaiah clan; 20 Kallai—of the Sallai clan; Eber—of the Amok clan; 21 Hashabiah—of the Hilkiah clan; Nethanel—of the Jedaiah clan.

22 The Levites and the priests were listed by heads of clans in the days of Eliashib, Joiada, Johanan, and Jaddua, down to the reign of Darius the Persian. 23 But the Levite heads of clans are listed in the book of the chronicles to the time of Johanan son of Eliashib.

24 The heads of the Levites: Hashabiah, Sherebiah, Jeshua son of Kadmiel, and their brothers served opposite them, singing praise and thanksgiving hymns by the ordinance of David the man of God—served opposite them in shifts; 25 Mattaniah, Bakbukiah, Obadiah, Meshullam, Talmon, and Akkub, guarding as gatekeepers by shifts at the vestibules of the gates.

26 These were in the time of Joiakim son of Jeshua son of Jozadak, and in the time of Nehemiah the governor, and of Ezra the priest, the scribe.

12.1–26: Lists of priests, Levites, and gatekeepers of the Temple. This list supplements 11.10–24. It postdates Nehemiah and is dated to the 4th century BCE. **1–7:** This list of priests overlaps significantly with the list of priests who signed the covenant document in ch 10. **23:** *The book of the chronicles* is not the book of Chronicles included in the Tanakh, but rather a collection of genealogical lists that was presumably preserved among the Temple documents. **24:** *David the man of God:* Cf. Ezra 3.10, where David, who is traditionally viewed as the author of Psalms, is considered the author of the Temple liturgy. The title *the man of God* may reflect a tradition that David was a prophet, since he composed parts of the Bible. In rabbinic traditions David is listed as one of ten figures (e.g., Moses, Elkana, Elisha, Micha), each of whom is said to be a "man of God," "Ish Elohim" (*Sifre Devarim*, piska 342 on Deut. 33.1; *'Avot R. Nat.*, version B, ch 37).

---

a Meaning of Heb. uncertain.

27 At the dedication of the wall of Jerusalem, the Levites, wherever they lived, were sought out and brought to Jerusalem to celebrate a joyful dedication with thanksgiving and with song, accompanied by cymbals, harps, and lyres. 28 The companies of singers assembled from the [Jordan] plain, the environs of Jerusalem, and from the Netophathite villages; 29 from Beth-hagilgal, from the countryside of Geba and Azmaveth, for the singers built themselves villages in the environs of Jerusalem.

30 The priests and Levites purified themselves; then they purified the people, and the gates, and the wall.

31 I had the officers of Judah go up onto the wall, and I appointed two large thanksgiving [choirs] and processions. [One marched] south on the wall, to the Dung Gate; 32 behind them were Hoshaiah and half the officers of Judah, 33 and Azariah, Ezra, Meshullam, 34 Judah, Benjamin, Shemaiah, and Jeremiah, 35 and some of the young priests, with trumpets; Zechariah son of Jonathan son of Shemaiah son of Mattaniah son of Micaiah son of Zaccur son of Asaph, 36 and his brothers Shemaiah, and Azarel, Milalai, Gilalai, Maai, Nethanel, Judah, and Hanani, with the musical instruments of David, the man of God; and Ezra the scribe went ahead of them. 37 From there to the Fountain Gate, where they ascended the steps of the City of David directly before them, by the ascent on the wall, above the house of David, [and onward] to the Water Gate on the east.

38 The other thanksgiving [choir] marched on the wall in the opposite direction, with me and half the people behind it, above the Tower of Ovens to the Broad Wall; 39 and above the Gate of Ephraim, the Jeshanah Gate, the Fish Gate, the Tower of Hananel, the Tower of the Hundred, to the Sheep Gate; and they halted at the Gate of the Prison Compound. 40 Both thanksgiving choirs halted at the House of God, and I and half the prefects with me, 41 and the priests Eliakim, Maaseiah, Miniamin, Micaiah, Elioenai, Zechariah, Hananiah, with trumpets, 42 and Maaseiah and Shemaiah, Eleazar, Uzzi, Jehohanan, Malchijah, Elam, and Ezer. Then the singers sounded forth, with Jezrahiah in charge.

43 On that day, they offered great sacrifices and rejoiced, for God made them rejoice greatly; the women and children also rejoiced, and the rejoicing in Jerusalem could be heard from afar.

44 At that time men were appointed over the chambers that served as treasuries for the gifts, the first fruits, and the tithes, into which the portions prescribed by the Teaching for the priests and Levites were gathered from

12.27–43: The dedication of the wall. Scholars note that this section resumes the Nehemiah memoir from 7.5. After a long interruption from the Ezra memoir, which is inserted into the book of Nehemiah, the dedication of the Jerusalem wall provides closure. **27:** Cf. Ezra 3.10–13; 2 Chron. 23.18; 29.26–30; 30.23. For additional mention of these musical instruments, see the postexilic 1 Chron. 13.8; 15.16; 25.1, 6; 2 Chron. 5.12; 29.25. **43:** *And the rejoicing in Jerusalem could be heard from afar:* As at the beginning of the rebuilding, the sound of joy can be heard from afar. See Ezra 3.13.

12.44–47: Ensuring support of Temple clergy through tithing. 45: The Temple staff are authorized to dedicate, sacrifice, and continue the Temple service. Nehemiah emphasizes direct continuity with David and Solomon. **47:** Zerubbabel and Nehemiah are treated as contemporaries, which is historically inaccurate.

the fields of the towns; for the people of Judah were grateful to the priests and Levites who were in attendance, [45] who kept the charge of their God and the charge of purity, as well as to the singers and gatekeepers [serving] in accord with the ordinance of David and Solomon his son—[46] for the chiefs of the singers and songs of praise and thanksgiving to God already existed in the time of David and Asaph. [47] And in the time of Zerubbabel, and in the time of Nehemiah, all Israel contributed the daily portions of the singers and the gatekeepers, and made sacred contributions for the Levites, and the Levites made sacred contributions for the Aaronites.

13 At that time they read to the people from the Book of Moses, and it was found written that no Ammonite or Moabite might ever enter the congregation of God, [2] since they did not meet Israel with bread and water, and hired Balaam against them to curse them; but our God turned the curse into a blessing. [3] When they heard the Teaching, they separated all the alien admixture from Israel.

[4] Earlier, the priest Eliashib, a relative of Tobiah, who had been appointed over the rooms in the House of our God, [5] had assigned to him[a] a large room where they used to store the meal offering, the frankincense, the equipment, the tithes of grain, wine, and oil, the dues of the Levites, singers and gatekeepers, and the gifts for the priests. [6] During all this time, I was not in Jerusalem, for in the thirty-second year of King Artaxerxes of Babylon, I went to the king, and only after a while did I ask leave of the king [to return]. [7] When I arrived in Jerusalem, I learned of the outrage perpetrated by Eliashib on behalf of Tobiah in assigning him a room in the courts of the House of God. [8] I was greatly displeased, and had all the household gear of Tobiah thrown out of the room; [9] I gave orders to purify the rooms, and had the equipment of the House of God and the meal offering and the frankincense put back.

[10] I then discovered that the portions of the Levites had not been contributed, and that the Levites and the singers who performed the [temple] service had made off, each to his fields. [11] I censured the prefects, saying, "How is it that the House of God has been neglected?" Then I recalled [the Levites] and installed them again in their posts; [12] and all Judah brought the tithes of grain, wine, and oil into the treasuries. [13] I put the treasuries in the charge of the priest Shelemiah, the scribe Zadok, and Pedaiah of the Levites;

13.1-3: Prohibition against intermarriage with an Ammonite or Moabite. Cf. Ezra chs 9-10. **2:** Cf. Deut. 23.3-5. *Balaam*, see Num. 22-24. **3:** As in Ezra chs 9-10, not just Moabites and Ammonites are separated, but all foreigners.

13.4-9: Tobiah the Ammonite compromises the purity of the Temple and Nehemiah resolves the crisis. **6:** Nehemiah returned to Artaxerxes for an unknown time, during which problems arose. Cf. 2.6.

13.10-14: Reestablishing the tithes.

a I.e., Tobiah.

and assisting them was Hanan son of Zaccur son of Mattaniah—for they were regarded as trustworthy persons, and it was their duty to distribute the portions to their brothers.

14 O my God, remember me favorably for this, and do not blot out the devotion I showed toward the House of my God and its attendants.

15 At that time I saw men in Judah treading winepresses on the sabbath, and others bringing heaps of grain and loading them onto asses, also wine, grapes, figs, and all sorts of goods, and bringing them into Jerusalem on the sabbath. I admonished them there and then for selling provisions. 16 Tyrians who lived there brought fish and all sorts of wares and sold them on the sabbath to the Judahites in Jerusalem. 17 I censured the nobles of Judah, saying to them, "What evil thing is this that you are doing, profaning the sabbath day! 18 This is just what your ancestors did, and for it God brought all this misfortune on this city; and now you give cause for further wrath against Israel by profaning the sabbath!"

19 When shadows filled the gateways of Jerusalem at the approach of the sabbath, I gave orders that the doors be closed, and ordered them not to be opened until after the sabbath. I stationed some of my servants at the gates, so that no goods should enter on the sabbath. 20 Once or twice the merchants and the vendors of all sorts of wares spent the night outside Jerusalem, 21 but I warned them, saying, "What do you mean by spending the night alongside the wall? If you do so again, I will lay hands upon you!" From then on they did not come on the sabbath. 22 I gave orders to the Levites to purify themselves and come and guard the gates, to preserve the sanctity of the sabbath.

This too, O my God, remember to my credit, and spare me in accord with your abundant faithfulness.

23 Also at that time, I saw that Jews had married Ashdodite, Ammonite, and Moabite women; 24 a good number of their children spoke the language of Ashdod and the language of those various peoples, and did not know how to speak Judean. 25 I censured them, cursed them, flogged them, tore out their hair, and adjured them by God, saying, "You shall not give your daughters in marriage to their sons, or take any of their daughters for your sons or yourselves. 26 It was just in such things that King Solomon of Israel sinned! Among the many nations there was not a king like him, and so well loved was he by his God that God made him king of all Israel, yet foreign wives caused even him to sin. 27 How, then, can we acqui-

13.15–22: Observance of the Sabbath day. The closest parallel to this prohibition of business on the Sabbath day is Jer. 17.21–24 (cf. Amos 8.5). For other exilic and postexilic discussion of Sabbath observance, see Isa. 56.1–8; Ezek. ch 20. As is clear from the covenant in ch 10 and the discussion here, Sabbath observance is seen as inextricably linked to the fulfillment of the covenant between God and Israel. Violation of the Sabbath would result in the loss of Jerusalem and Judah again, as it did earlier, according to Jer. 17.1–24. **15:** The Rabbis explain that this v. reflects an early stage in the application of Sabbath law, when lax observance demanded a strict response, and the use of all but three utensils on the Sabbath day was forbidden. Later on, as reflected in *m. Shab.* 17.4, the Rabbis were more lenient (*b. Shab.* 123b and Rashi ad loc.).

13.23–27: Prohibition against intermarriage. 23: Though the book draws to a conclusion by restating one of its main themes, the dangers of intermarriage, the conception here is quite different from Ezra 9.2. **26:** See 1 Kings 11.1–13.

esce in your doing this great wrong, breaking faith with our God by marrying foreign women?" 28 One of the sons of Joiada son of the high priest Eliashib was a son-in-law of Sanballat the Horonite; I drove him away from me.

29 Remember to their discredit, O my God, how they polluted the priesthood, the covenant of the priests and Levites. 30 I purged them of every foreign element, and arranged for the priests and the Levites to work each at his task by shifts, 31 and for the wood offering [to be brought] at fixed times and for the first fruits.

O my God, remember it to my credit!

13.28–31: Purification of the returnees and concluding prayer. The final vv. in Nehemiah reemphasize the careful exclusion of any person who compromised the purification of the returnees and the rebuilding of the Temple. **28:** The perceived vulnerability of the newly constituted Jewish community in Jerusalem; even someone with authentic lineage must be banished because of a relation through marriage to Sanballat the Horonite. **29:** Here there is an emphasis on the inextricable link between the defilement of the priesthood and the vulnerability of the renewed covenant with the recent returnees. The reestablished community still perceives itself to be vulnerable to destruction and defilement. **30–31:** The final vv. are a repeated expression of the hope that the purification and the sacrifices will continue to be received as genuine and authentic by God and, furthermore, that God will consider the reestablished community to be genuine and authentic. Thus, the concluding vv. seem intended to link the reforms inextricably to the figure of Nehemiah. While the ending is certainly abrupt and arguably anticlimactic, it nevertheless seems to fit with the overall themes and focus of Ezra-Nehemiah.

דברי הימים א

I Chronicles

THE TITLE "THE BOOK OF CHRONICLES," a reflection of the Hebrew *divrei hayamim* (e.g., 1 Kings 14.19, "Annals"), is a misnomer. The book is neither a dry chronicle nor an analytic work, but a complex theological-historical composition beginning with Adam and concluding with the Cyrus declarations (538 BCE). Chronicles should not be identified with the Annals of the Kings of Israel or the Annals of the Kings of Judah which are frequently mentioned in Kings, since Chronicles was written after Kings. Furthermore, even though in English Bibles, following the tradition of the Septuagint (the ancient Greek Bible translation), Chronicles is divided into two books like Samuel and Kings, in the Hebrew tradition, it is a single book. It is thus proper to speak of the book rather than the books of Chronicles.

Rabbinic tradition (*b. B. Bat.* 15a) assigns authorship of part, but not all, of Chronicles to Ezra the scribe; medieval Jewish commentators differed over the scope of the Ezran material. Modern scholarship remains divided over the book's relationship to Ezra; through most of the 19th and 20th centuries scholars accepted the rabbinic position, based on several considerations, including linguistic similarities between Ezra-Nehemiah and Chronicles, similarity in outlook and theology, and the fact that the conclusion of Chronicles is identical to the introduction of Ezra. These scholars used the term "the Chronicler" to refer to the single author of Chronicles-Ezra-Nehemiah. Most scholars now reject this position, arguing that the two works, though similar because they were written in approximately the same period, differ substantively in matters of outlook and theology. Three key examples of this difference in outlook are: (1) the uncompromising stance of Ezra-Nehemiah regarding all forms of exogamy (marrying outside of the clan), as opposed to Chronicles' relatively liberal attitude on the matter; (2) Chronicles' inclusive definition of the true Israel, which contrasts sharply with Ezra-Nehemiah, in whose view only those Jews returning from the Babylonian captivity are viewed as the true Israel; and (3) the heightened place of the Davidic covenant in Chronicles, in contrast to the emphasis on the exodus-Sinai traditions found in Ezra-Nehemiah. In addition, there are significant linguistic and stylistic differences between the two corpora. Most scholars now use the term "the Chronicler" to refer to the author of Chronicles only and believe that he was likely a member of Levitical circles. Some suggest that the Chronicler was aware, and made use, of Ezra-Nehemiah in formulating his own positions.

The book's date of composition has also been the subject of considerable debate, with estimates ranging from approximately 500 (the early Persian empire) through the early 2nd century BCE (i.e., the Hellenistic age). All in all, the late middle or, possibly, early 4th century—i.e., mid-late Persian period (375–325)—appears the most likely. As for the literary growth of Chronicles—that is, the number of authors responsible for the book's final form—most scholars maintain that the main body of the book is the product of one author or circle. Nonetheless, some passages are commonly viewed as later additions to the book's basic stratum; therefore Chronicles probably reached its final form after the 4th century. Awareness of the Second Temple provenance of Chronicles has significant implications for understanding the purpose and methods of its author(s). The bulk of Chronicles is a retelling of the books of Samuel and Kings. The material selected or omitted, however, along with the new formulations and literary "spins" given to older material, indicate that the author imbues this material with new perspectives and meanings, in order to address the needs of his audience. In addition, the book's relatively late date of composition means that its author was familiar with the (completed, redacted) Torah in a form essentially identical to that preserved to our own day, and almost all of the prophetic, historical, and lyric works (e.g., Psalms) which comprise the present canon of the Bible. Accordingly, the author's understanding of a given subject or passage is likely to reflect not only the developed belief systems of his own period, but the influence of relevant passages from the earlier biblical corpus, as they were understood in his time. Indeed, the author's interest in harmonizing various biblical passages informs much of the author's novel, if perhaps idiosyncratic, reformulation of earlier texts.

Despite the large mass of material common to Chronicles and earlier biblical sources, particularly Samuel and Kings, there are many differences, both stylistic and substantive, between the two blocks of material. These may be the result of several factors. First, a deliberate change in the text may either be the creation of the author, reflecting his own tendentious concerns and perspectives or, alternatively, may indicate that the author has reformulated his text on the basis of source material not preserved in the canonical biblical corpus. On the other hand, the differences between the synoptic portions of Chronicles, namely those portions which have parallels elsewhere in the Bible, and the earlier compositions may simply indicate that the version of the older sources known to the author differed from that preserved in today's Bible (the Masoretic Text) or one of the ancient translations, such as the Septuagint. This latter scenario now seems more likely in light of the fluid and diverse textual forms displayed by the biblical texts found among the Dead Sea Scrolls. A somewhat different approach has been proffered by scholars who maintain that Chronicles and Samuel-Kings are wholly independent works which draw on a common source, but this remains a minority position. While the relationship of Chronicles to its sources has important implications for understanding the nature of Chronicles and its approach to its sources—i.e., its author's willingness to rework older sources—the book's final form presents a well-defined, and independent, view on a whole range of subjects.

Thus, any discussion of Chronicles must look at it as a complete and unified work as well as considering the sources that were likely utilized by the Chronicler.

Chronicles affords us evidence of the ways in which biblical authors utilized, interpreted, supplemented, and reformulated earlier source materials, evidence which has far-reaching implications for our understanding of biblical "historiography" and, more generally, inner-biblical exegesis (how later parts of the Bible interpret earlier parts). The numerous and substantive differences between Chronicles and earlier sources have led to widely divergent views concerning the quintessential nature and purpose of Chronicles. Many earlier scholars labeled Chronicles a tendentious falsification of Israel's past. More recent students have viewed Chronicles as a kind of edifying fiction or "exegetical" companion to Samuel-Kings. Others, noting that the presence of much nonsynoptic and wholly rewritten material does not allow for application of the term "exegesis," have argued that the work is an independent, genuine piece of historical writing—presented, like all "history," through the (idiosyncratic) prism of its author. Each of these perspectives has some merit.

The existence of many discrepancies between Chronicles and Samuel-Kings was noted already by Jews living shortly after the book's composition. Ancient readers of the Bible, as well as virtually all premodern exegetes, assumed as a matter of course that there could be no substantive contradictions between Chronicles and its earlier biblical sources. The Jewish translators responsible for the Septuagint translation, living in the pre-Christian era, thus called Chronicles "Paraleipomenon," i.e., a "supplement to things omitted." This title implies an exegetical stance, according to which the additional material of Chronicles is not the literary creation of the author of Chronicles; rather, it represents a genuine "historical" tradition which, for one reason or another, was not included in Samuel. While this approach is incorrect, it does reflect the fact that at points Chronicles presupposes the reader's familiarity with earlier sources (see, e.g., 1 Chron. ch 10). Rabbinic tradition, which clearly indicates awareness of the numerous differences between Chronicles and its sources, tends to view the earlier biblical compositions as historically veracious, while viewing Chronicles as a kind of midrash to these works. (On the genre midrash, see "Midrash and Jewish Interpretation," pp. 1863–75.) At the same time, it is important to note that the Rabbis of antiquity produced no systematic commentary to Chronicles, and there is little way to determine how they resolved the many discrepancies—or, for that matter, what they viewed as a true "discrepancy"—between Chronicles and its sources. This state of affairs improved only marginally in the post-talmudic and medieval periods, during which time this work was largely neglected. Indeed, one prominent medieval exegete openly acknowledged that he had never read the book prior to composing his commentary to Samuel (Isaac Abravanel's *Introduction to Samuel;* see also Radak's *Introduction to Chronicles*). In general, the available evidence suggests that, at least with respect to historical traditions, Jews of antiquity accepted the version of the accounts as preserved in the earlier Deuteronomistic sources of Samuel and Kings over that of Chronicles. The relative unimportance of Chronicles is also reflected by the fact that only a handful of copies of Chronicles have been uncovered among the literary finds of the Second Temple community at Qumran (the Dead Sea Scrolls).

Chronicles advances several major themes and religious perspectives. In some cases Chronicles has merely reworked and highlighted positions addressed, in different form, in other biblical books; in other instances, Chronicles charts a wholly new course. A brief overview of some of the salient issues follows. Other issues will be addressed in the commentary.

The central topic in Chronicles is the Temple cultus (service), the institution that lies at the center of Jewish/Israelite life, and around which Chronicles weaves its view of Israel's history. This position reflects the religio-political reality of Second Temple life, in which the cultus, rather than the (defunct) Davidic monarchy, occupied center stage. For much of this period the Temple remained a modest structure, and support for its personnel was not always forthcoming; accordingly, Chronicles' formulations reflect a call for rejuvenating the national cultus.

One of the principles long viewed as a hallmark of Chronicles is its strict notion of divine providence and retribution. On this view, virtuous deeds lead to a reward (wealth, children, etc.), while bad deeds bring punishment and suffering. Similarly, so it is held, Chronicles rejects the notion of vicarious punishment and/or reward; an individual is neither punished nor rewarded for the actions of another individual. This theodicy has generally been understood as largely, but not exclusively, retrospective in nature, accounting for national (and personal) misfortunes of the past, but also offering Jews of the Second Temple period theological guidance in their day-to-day lives. Indeed, some have argued that this position is Chronicles' raison d'etre. However, there is inconsistency in Chronicles' application of this principle. This fact has led some scholars to suggest that Chronicles does not differ fundamentally from other biblical books in its understanding of vicarious punishment and retribution. Rather, the book's uniqueness lies in its view of divine compassion or grace as the operative principle. It is this quality, so it is argued, which allows for repentance and forgiveness of transgressions, thereby conveying the message of eternal hope. Chronicles' approach is thus seen as primarily forward-looking and hope-inspiring, rather than retrospective.

A potentially related issue concerns Chronicles' realpolitik and the place of messianic or eschatological expectations in the work. Scholarly views differ widely, largely as a result of differing uses of the term "eschatology." To be sure, Chronicles—perhaps because of its nature as a rewriting of First Temple material, perhaps out of fear of upsetting the contemporary hegemony—contains no explicit statement on either matter. This has led to the view that the author of Chronicles was a "pragmatist" who saw contemporary Jewish society, with its functioning cult, as the fulfillment of Israel's role; Persian hegemony is accepted with no monarchic or royalist expectations. However, Chronicles' glorified and expanded depiction of the Davidic dynasty—and denigration of all other monarchs, including David's predecessor, Saul—along with the book's emphasis on "all Israel" may suggest that anticipation of a Davidic, messianic figure is a central feature of Chronicles.

Indeed, some see this messianic/eschatological yearning as the driving force behind Chronicles' forward-looking notion of grace: Proper conduct, together with divine compassion, can bring about Israel's restoration with a Davidic king at its head.

Chronicles' view regarding the northern monarchy is quite clear: Its very existence is illegitimate, since the Davidic kings alone constitute the earthly expression of the LORD's kingdom. For this reason, Chronicles discusses the fortunes of the northern monarchy only to the extent that they impact on Judah. Positions differ, however, regarding the importance of the populace of the northern tribes. Many scholars now acknowledge that the book's frequent use of the expression "all Israel," and its references to "pan-Israelite" participation in various passages (both synoptic and otherwise) indicate that Chronicles' author, in contrast to that of Ezra-Nehemiah, viewed the unification of (northern) Israel and Judah as an issue of paramount importance. This contrasts with the view of earlier scholars, who understood these same passages to mean that the true claim to the title "Israel" rests with Judah and those northern tribes aligned with her or living within her borders, yielding a position close to that of Ezra-Nehemiah.

A notable feature of Chronicles is its reticence concerning several pivotal events in the nation's history, e.g., the exodus from Egypt, the theophany at Sinai, and the "conquest" of Canaan. Many scholars see in these omissions Chronicles' expression of the eternal connection between the people of Israel and its land as an unbroken chain, having no real starting point, nor involving a hiatus after the First Temple period. At the time of Chronicles' composition, Jews constituted only one part of a heterogeneous population in their ancestral land, while a significant proportion, perhaps even a majority, of Jews lived in foreign lands. Chronicles makes a clear statement regarding the true owners of the land as well as the need for all Jews to return to their homeland.

Several aspects of Chronicles' worldview are reminiscent of views encountered in rabbinic literature. Two examples are the importance of intention (e.g., joy, sincerity) as opposed to concrete deeds alone in the service of the LORD, and the view that people are legally culpable for wrongdoing only if duly warned prior to commission of the offense. In light of this, some scholars have described Chronicles as a bridge between the "classical period" of the Bible and later rabbinic society. While there is some truth in this depiction, the points of similarity between Chronicles and rabbinic thought may have other explanations. Chronicles' frequent insistence on warning the king and/or people of Israel as a sine qua non for religious culpability may simply be part of the book's view of grace, with its repeated attempts to steer Israel in the right path. Similarly, the importance of joy, appearing mostly in connection with the cultus, may be the author's way of highlighting the centrality of the cultus, rather than constituting a general theological principle regarding the importance of intentions. Hence, while Chronicles certainly reflects positions differing from those of other biblical works, the scope of views common to Chronicles and earlier biblical works places it squarely within the biblical matrix, rendering the depiction of Chronicles as a "bridge" somewhat exaggerated.

The following is a schematic description of Chronicles' structure.

[DAVID ROTHSTEIN]

1 Adam, Seth, Enosh; [2] Kenan, Mahalalel, Jared; [3] Enoch, Methuselah, Lamech; [4] Noah, Shem, Ham, and Japheth.

[5] [a] The sons of Japheth: Gomer, Magog, Madai, Javan, Tubal, Meshech, and Tiras. [6] The sons of Gomer: Ashkenaz, Diphath, and Togarmah. [7] The sons of Javan: Elishah, Tarshish, Kittim, and Rodanim.

[8] The sons of Ham: Cush, Mizraim, Put, and Canaan. [9] The sons of Cush: Seba, Havilah, Sabta, Raama, and Sabteca. The sons of Raama: Sheba and Dedan. [10] Cush begot Nimrod; he was the first mighty one on earth.

[11] Mizraim begot the Ludim, the Anamim, the Lehabim, the Naphtuhim, [12] the Pathrusim, the Casluhim (whence the Philistines came forth), and the Caphtorim.

[13] Canaan begot Sidon his first-born, and Heth, [14] and the Jebusites, the Amorites, the Girgashites, [15] the Hivites, the Arkites, the Sinites, [16] the Arvadites, the Zemarites, and the Hamathites.

[17] The sons of Shem: Elam, Asshur, Arpachshad, Lud, Aram, Uz, Hul, Gether, and Meshech. [18] Arpachshad begot Shelah; and Shelah begot Eber. [19] Two sons were born to Eber: the name of the one was Peleg (for in his days the earth was divided), and the name of his brother Joktan. [20] Joktan begot Almodad, Sheleph, Hazarmaveth, Jerah, [21] Hadoram, Uzal, Diklah, [22] Ebal, Abimael, Sheba, [23] Ophir, Havilah, and Jobab; all these were the sons of Joktan.

[24] Shem, Arpachshad, Shelah; [25] Eber, Peleg, Reu; [26] Serug, Nahor, Terah; [27] Abram, that is, Abraham.

[28] [b] The sons of Abraham: Isaac and Ishmael. [29] This is their line: The first-born of Ishmael, Nebaioth; and Kedar, Abdeel, Mibsam, [30] Mishma, Dumah, Massa, Hadad, Tema, [31] Jetur, Naphish, and Kedmah. These are the sons of Ishmael. [32] The sons of Keturah, Abraham's concubine: she bore Zimran, Jokshan, Medan, Midian, Ishbak, and

Chs 1–9: The genealogies. Genealogies are important in many societies, especially those structured on familial relationships. They should not always be understood literally and are used in the Bible, as elsewhere, to express the relationships between various clans and peoples as well as to highlight the place of prominent individuals or to give them a pedigree. They play an especially important role in Priestly thinking, and are reflected in postbiblical literature as well, for example in Matt. 1.1–17. Given the interests of the Chronicler, it is not surprising that the genealogies of David and the descendants of Levi, the Levites and priests, play a particularly prominent role in this section. Some of these chs have their source in other biblical material, while other parts do not, reflecting the fact that the Chronicler had access to sources beyond what is now found in the canonical Bible.

1.1–2.2: Adam to Israel. Although this material follows Genesis, its selection and arrangement (e.g., placing secondary lines of descent before the primary) emphasizes the line culminating in Israel. There is no elaboration concerning Abraham, a point which, together with other hints in Chronicles, suggests that Chronicles views Jacob/Israel (consistently referred to as Israel in Chronicles) as the central patriarch; see 16.13. This may be part of the book's "inclusivist," pan-Israel tendency.

a With vv. 5–23, cf. Gen. 10.1–30.   b With vv. 28–33, cf. Gen. 25.1–16.

Shuah. The sons of Jokshan: Sheba and Dedan. ³³ The sons of Midian: Ephah, Epher, Enoch, Abida, and Eldaah. All these were the descendants of Keturah.

³⁴ Abraham begot Isaac. The sons of Isaac: Esau and Israel. ³⁵ The sons of Esau: Eliphaz, Reuel, Jeush, Jalam, and Korah. ³⁶ The sons of Eliphaz: Teman, Omar, Zephi, Gatam, Kenaz, Timna, and Amalek. ³⁷ The sons of Reuel: Nahath, Zerah, Shammah, and Mizzah.

³⁸ The sons of Seir: Lotan, Shobal, Zibeon, Anah, Dishon, Ezer, and Dishan. ³⁹ The sons of Lotan: Hori and Homam; and Lotan's sister was Timna. ⁴⁰ The sons of Shobal: Alian, Manahath, Ebal, Shephi, and Onam. The sons of Zibeon: Aiah and Anah. ⁴¹ The sons of Anah: Dishon. The sons of Dishon: Hamran, Eshban, Ithran, and Cheran. ⁴² The sons of Ezer: Bilhan, Zaavan, and Jaakan. The sons of Dishan: Uz and Aran.

⁴³ᵃ These are the kings who reigned in the land of Edom before any king reigned over the Israelites: Bela son of Beor, and the name of his city was Dinhabah. ⁴⁴ When Bela died, Jobab son of Zerah from Bozrah succeeded him as king. ⁴⁵ When Jobab died, Husham of the land of the Temanites succeeded him as king. ⁴⁶ When Husham died, Hadad son of Bedad, who defeated the Midianites in the country of Moab, succeeded him as king, and the name of his city was Avith. ⁴⁷ When Hadad died, Samlah of Masrekah succeeded him as king. ⁴⁸ When Samlah died, Saul of Rehoboth-on-the-River succeeded him as king. ⁴⁹ When Saul died, Baal-hanan son of Achbor succeeded him as king. ⁵⁰ When Baal-hanan died, Hadad succeeded him as king; and the name of his city was Pai, and his wife's name Mehetabel daughter of Matred daughter of Me-zahab. ⁵¹ And Hadad died.

The clans of Edom were the clans of Timna, Alvah, Jetheth, ⁵² Oholibamah, Elah, Pinon, ⁵³ Kenaz, Teman, Mibzar, ⁵⁴ Magdiel, and Iram; these are the clans of Edom.

2 These are the sons of Israel: Reuben, Simeon, Levi, Judah, Issachar, Zebulun, ² Dan, Joseph, Benjamin, Naphtali, Gad, and Asher. ³ The sons of Judah: Er, Onan, and Shelah; these three, Bath-shua the Canaanite woman

---

a With vv. 43–50, cf. Gen. 36.31–43.

1.43–54: The list of Edomite rulers from Gen. 36.31–43 is seemingly superfluous. Chronicles' point may be that physical descent alone is not determinative of one's worthiness; alternately, the list appears for the sake of complete-ness. **2.1–2:** With the exception of Dan (the son of Bilhah), the children of Israel are listed according to their mothers, beginning with the children of Leah, then Rachel, then the concubines Bilhah and Zilpah.

2.3–9.1: The tribes of Israel and Judah. Although thought by some to be a later addition to the book, this listing of Israel's forebears is an integral part of Chronicles and its literary plan. It establishes the book's audience: pedigreed Jews of the Second Temple period, as the only genuine heirs to the ancestral covenant, which has its most tangible expression in possession of the land of Canaan and the functioning of the Temple cultus. The historicity of this list is far from certain. The issue is particularly acute in connection with several key figures, such as the priest Zadok, in ch 5, for whom Chronicles appears to have supplied an entirely new pedigree. The appearance in these chs of many otherwise unknown names was noted by the early Rabbis, who, consistent with their tendency attested elsewhere, employed midrash-type interpretations of these names in order to link them with individuals known from other biblical passages. In some cases the Rabbis' motive appears to have been to explain (away) the seemingly non-Israelite origin of many of these individuals; in other cases, the Rabbis are attempting to harmonize divergent traditions. The structure of this list has been variously explained. Two likely explanations follow. The list reflects geographical location; it begins with the southern tribe of Judah, the leading nonsacral tribe, and then proceeds in counter-clockwise fashion, moving to the east (trans-Jordan) before returning westward to address the northern and, then, central tribes. At the center of this list is the tribe of Levi, reflective of the tribe's central role in Chronicles. Because this geographical depiction is not fully accurate, some maintain that the author was primarily interested in Judah, Levi, and Benjamin, the tribes that remained loyal to the Davidic monarchy and the Jerusalem Temple. This accounts for the framework: Judah (at the beginning of the list), Benjamin (at the end), and Levi (in the middle). The order of the remaining tribes was deemed bore to him. But Er, Judah's first-born, was displeasing to the LORD, and He took his life. [4] His daughter-in-law Tamar also bore him Perez and Zerah. Judah's sons were five in all.

[5] The sons of Perez: Hezron and Hamul. [6] The sons of Zerah: Zimri, Ethan, Heman, Calcol, and Dara, five in all. [7] The sons of Carmi: Achar, the troubler of Israel, who committed a trespass against the proscribed thing; [8] and Ethan's son was Azariah.

[9] The sons of Hezron that were born to him: Jerahmeel, Ram, and Chelubai. [10] Ram begot Amminadab, and Amminadab begot Nahshon, prince of the sons of Judah. [11] Nahshon was the father of Salma, Salma of Boaz, [12] Boaz of Obed, Obed of Jesse. [13] Jesse begot Eliab his first-born, Abinadab the second, Shimea the third, [14] Nethanel the fourth, Raddai the fifth, [15] Ozem the sixth, David the seventh; [16] their sisters were Zeruiah and Abigail. The sons of Zeruiah: Abishai, Joab, and Asahel, three. [17] Abigail bore Amasa, and the father of Amasa was Jether the Ishmaelite.

[18] Caleb son of Hezron had children by his wife Azubah, and by Jerioth; these were her sons: Jesher, Shobab, and Ardon. [19] When Azubah died, Caleb married Ephrath, who bore him Hur. [20] Hur begot Uri, and Uri begot Bezalel.

[21] Afterward Hezron had relations with the daughter of Machir father of Gilead—he had married her when he was sixty years old—and she bore him Segub; [22] and Segub begot Jair; he had twenty-three cities in the land of

him as the youngest of either four or eight sons (see, e.g., 1 Sam. 16.7–11; 17.12–14, 17). Some scholars maintain that Chronicles reflects a mistaken understanding of 1 Sam. 16.10. More likely, placement as the seventh is meant to glorify David since the number "seven" signifies completion in the Bible. The literary (i.e., artificial) nature of this datum is buttressed by the typological number of seven generations from Ram to Jesse and by the use of a similar technique in connection with Solomon (see 3.5–6 n.). **9–13:** Cf. Ruth 4.18–22. **16–17:** Joab is listed as the son of David's sister, as are Abishai and Asahel. Neither Zeruiah nor Abigail is ever identified as David's sister in the earlier biblical sources. This datum prepares the reader for ch 11, which credits Joab with the capture of Jerusalem. The description of Amasa as the son of an Ishmaelite is significant (see 2 Sam. 19.13, which indicates that Amasa was related to David). The MT of 2 Sam. 17.25 refers to Yether as an "Israelite," a difficult reading, which is emended by some scholars. Some medieval exegetes adopted a harmonistic approach: Yithra was an Israelite who lived in Ishmaelite territory. Chronicles' text probably indicates that its author was not bothered by Amasa's Ishmaelite descent nor by Abigail's marriage to an Ishmaelite, a position which differs markedly from Ezra-Nehemiah (see introduction). Some scholars argue that Ezra's hard-line position may have applied only to members of his generation, and that the presence of non-Israelite ancestors in Israel's (distant) past was not problematic. Rabbinic tradents were clearly aware of the difficulties posed by passages such as these. They resolved such passages by claiming that the foreign spouse had undergone religious conversion, an institution which is not attested in the biblical period, or by applying some other legalistic exegesis. **18–20:** Bezalel was the most prominent member of Caleb's family, owing to his role as head

not particularly important. The tribes of Dan and Zebulun are missing from the list, possibly as the result of scribal error. Some maintain that Chronicles intentionally omitted Dan because of its association with apostasy (see Judg. chs 17–19; 1 Kings 12.29–30); this allows Chronicles to portray a religiously idealized Israel.

2.3–4.23: Judah. Judah was especially important since the majority of the Jews living in this period traced themselves to Judah, and because the Davidic king was descended from Judah. In addition to material preserved elsewhere, this list contains traditions without parallel; e.g., the claim that Caleb and Jerahmeel were brothers, and sons of Hezron. **2.3–4:** A condensation of the narrative of Gen.

ch 38. **7:** Chronicles' laconic formulation presupposes the reader's familiarity with the episode in Josh. 7.1–26—this suggests that Chronicles was not written to supplant the earlier Deuteronomistic History, but to offer a new interpretation of those events. The passage in Joshua expresses the importance of observing divine regulations, especially those pertaining to the realm of the sacred, and makes the point that possession of the promised land, one of Chronicles' central themes, is contingent upon compliance with biblical law. **10–17:** David's ancestors. Chronicles' emphasis on David's genealogy reflects the monarch's central role within the book's theology. **12–15:** David is the youngest of seven sons according to Chronicles, but 1 Samuel lists

Gilead. 23 But Geshur and Aram took from them Havvoth-jair, Kenath and its dependencies, sixty towns. All these were the sons of Machir, the father of Gilead. 24 After the death of Hezron, in Caleb-ephrathah, Abijah, wife of Hezron, bore Ashhur, the father of Tekoa.

25 The sons of Jerahmeel the first-born of Hezron: Ram his first-born, Bunah, Oren, Ozem, and Ahijah. 26 Jerahmeel had another wife, whose name was Atarah; she was the mother of Onam. 27 The sons of Ram the first-born of Jerahmeel: Maaz, Jamin, and Eker. 28 The sons of Onam: Shammai and Jada. The sons of Shammai: Nadab and Abishur. 29 The name of Abishur's wife was Abihail, and she bore him Ahban and Molid. 30 The sons of Nadab: Seled and Appaim; Seled died childless. 31 The sons of Appaim: Ishi. The sons of Ishi: Sheshan. The sons of Sheshan: Ahlai. 32 The sons of Jada, Shammai's brother: Jether and Jonathan; Jether died childless. 33 The sons of Jonathan: Peleth and Zaza. These were the descendants of Jerahmeel. 34 Sheshan had no sons, only daughters; Sheshan had an Egyptian slave, whose name was Jarha. 35 So Sheshan gave his daughter in marriage to Jarha his slave; and she bore him Attai. 36 Attai begot Nathan, and Nathan begot Zabad. 37 Zabad begot Ephlal, and Ephlal begot Obed. 38 Obed begot Jehu, and Jehu begot Azariah. 39 Azariah begot Helez, and Helez begot Eleasah. 40 Eleasah begot Sisamai, and Sisamai begot Shallum. 41 Shallum begot Jekamiah, and Jekamiah begot Elishama.

42 The sons of Caleb brother of Jerahmeel: Meshah his first-born, who was the father of Ziph. The sons of Mareshah father of Hebron. 43 The sons of Hebron: Korah, Tappuah, Rekem, and Shema. 44 Shema begot Raham the father of Jorkeam, and Rekem begot Shammai. 45 The son of Shammai: Maon, and Maon begot Bethzur. 46 Ephah, Caleb's concubine, bore Haran, Moza, and Gazez; Haran begot Gazez. 47 The sons of Jahdai: Regem, Jotham, Geshan, Pelet, Ephah, and Shaaph. 48 Maacah, Caleb's concubine, bore Sheber and Tirhanah. 49 She also bore Shaaph father of Madmannah, Sheva father of Machbenah and father of Gibea; the daughter of Caleb was Achsah. 50 These were the descendants of Caleb.

The sons of Hur the first-born of Ephrathah: Shobal father of Kiriath-jearim, 51 Salma father of Bethlehem, Hareph father of Beth-gader. 52 Shobal father of Kiriath-jearim had sons: Haroeh, half of the Menuhoth. 53 And the families of Kiriath-jearim: the Ithrites, the Puthites, the Shumathites, and the Mishraites; from these came the Zorathites and the Eshtaolites. 54 The sons of Salma: Bethlehem, the Netophathites, Atroth-beth-joab, and half of the

craftsman of the Tabernacle; this explains the juxtaposition of vv. 18, 19 with v. 20. **42–49:** Many of the children mentioned here (e.g., Hebron) are known as geographical locations in Judah; the genealogical language here connects the founding of these cities to descendants of Caleb (cf. Josh. 14.12–14; Judg. 1.10), emphasizing the role of this important Judean in the foundation of important cities throughout Judah. In Torah tradition, Caleb attains prominence as a loyal spy (see Num. chs 13–14), but as noted, Chronicles deemphasizes the exodus and "conquest," and thus his significance is given a different reason here.

Manahathites, the Zorites. ⁵⁵ The families of the scribes that dwelt at Jabez: the Tirathites, the Shimeathites, the Sucathites; these are the Kenites who came from Hammath, father of the house of Rechab.

3 These are the sons of David who were born to him in Hebron: the first-born Amnon, by Ahinoam the Jezreelite; the second Daniel, by Abigail the Carmelite; ² the third Absalom, son of Maacah daughter of King Talmai of Geshur; the fourth Adonijah, son of Haggith; ³ the fifth Shephatiah, by Abital; the sixth Ithream, by his wife Eglah; ⁴ six were born to him in Hebron. He reigned there seven years and six months, and in Jerusalem he reigned thirty-three years. ⁵ These were born to him in Jerusalem: Shimea, Shobab, Nathan, and Solomon, four by Bath-shua daughter of Ammiel; ⁶ then Ibhar, Elishama, Eliphelet, ⁷ Nogah, Nepheg, Japhia, ⁸ Elishama, Eliada, and Eliphelet—nine. ⁹ All were David's sons, besides the sons of the concubines; and Tamar was their sister.

¹⁰ The son of Solomon: Rehoboam; his son Abijah, his son Asa, his son Jehoshaphat, ¹¹ his son Joram, his son Ahaziah, his son Joash, ¹² his son Amaziah, his son Azariah, his son Jotham, ¹³ his son Ahaz, his son Hezekiah, his son Manasseh, ¹⁴ his son Amon, and his son Josiah. ¹⁵ The sons of Josiah: Johanan the first-born, the second Jehoiakim, the third Zedekiah, the fourth Shallum. ¹⁶ The descendants of Jehoiakim: his son Jeconiah, his son Zedekiah; ¹⁷ and the sons of Jeconiah, the captive: Shealtiel his son, ¹⁸ Malchiram, Pedaiah, Shenazzar, Jekamiah, Hoshama, and Nedabiah; ¹⁹ the sons of Pedaiah: Zerubbabel and Shimei; the sons of Zerubbabel: Meshullam and Hananiah, and Shelomith was their sister; ²⁰ Hashubah, Ohel, Berechiah, Hasadiah, and Jushab-hesed—five. ²¹ And the sons of Hananiah: Pelatiah and Jeshaiah; the sons of [Jeshaiah]: Rephaiah; the sons of [Rephaiah]: Arnan; the sons of [Arnan]: Obadiah; the sons of [Obadiah]: Shecaniah. ²² And the sons of Shecaniah: Shemaiah; and the sons of Shemaiah: Hattush, and Igal, and Bariah, and Neariah, and Shaphat—six. ²³ And the sons of Neariah: Elioenai, and Hizkiah, and Azrikam—three. ²⁴ And the sons of Elioenai: Hodaviah, and Eliashib, and Pelaiah, and Akkub, and Johanan, and Delaiah, and Anani—seven.

4 The sons of Judah: Perez, Hezron, Carmi, Hur, and Shobal. ² Reaiah son of Shobal begot Jahath, and Jahath begot Ahumai and Lahad. These were the families of the Zorathites. ³ These were [the sons of] the father of Etam: Jezreel, Ishma, and Idbash; and the name of their sister

3.1–24: David's descendants. See 2.10–17 n. **1:** 2 Sam. 3.3 states that Abigail's son was named Kileab. Rabbinic and medieval commentators (*Targum Chron.*, Radak; cf. *b. Ber.* 4a) maintained that the child bore both names; his given name was Daniel, meaning "God has judged me (innocent of any guilt in the death of Abigail's husband, Nabal)"; the name Kileab, meaning "like the father" (or "entirely the father"), was given later, when it became clear that the son bore a striking resemblance to David, thereby removing any suspicion of Nabal's paternity. (Note that this tradition views Chronicles as maintaining the original name.) The actual "facts" remain uncertain. Chronicles nowhere records the circumstances surrounding David's marriage to Abigail (1 Sam. ch 25), possibly because they present a less than flattering picture of David or because the author may not have been interested in purely personal aspects of David's life. **2:** The author does not hesitate to mention David's marriage to a foreign woman, Maacah; see 2.12–15 n. Such marriages often served political purposes in antiquity. **5:** Solomon appears as the fourth son born to David in Jerusalem, and the fourth son of Bath-shua (= Bathsheba). According to 2 Sam. 12.24, Solomon is the second of as many sons born to Bathsheba. Chronicles' version glorifies Solomon, by claiming that despite having three older brothers, he alone was chosen to be king. The "three-four" number scheme, where the fourth is climactic (as in Judah, the fourth son of Jacob), is common in the Bible. **17–24:** Exilic and postexilic line, until Chronicles' time. This passage contains many otherwise unknown traditions, and there are substantive differences among the ancient versions. The updating of the genealogy of David likely reflects hopes that one of his descendants would again assume the throne.

4.1–20: Sons of Perez. The line which eventually produced David;

was Hazlelponi, [4] and Penuel was the father of Gedor, and Ezer the father of Hushah. These were the sons of Hur, the first-born of Ephrathah, the father of Bethlehem. [5] Ashhur the father of Tekoa had two wives, Helah and Naarah; [6] Naarah bore him Ahuzam, Hepher, Temeni, and Ahashtari. These were the sons of Naarah. [7] The sons of Helah: Zereth, Zohar, and Ethnan. [8] Koz was the father of Anub, Zobebah, and the families of Aharhel son of Harum. [9] Jabez was more esteemed than his brothers; and his mother named him Jabez, "Because," she said, "I bore him in pain."[a] [10] Jabez invoked the God of Israel, saying, "Oh, bless me, enlarge my territory, stand by me, and make me not suffer pain from misfortune!" And God granted what he asked. [11] Chelub the brother of Shuhah begot Mehir, who was the father of Eshton. [12] Eshton begot Bethrapha, Paseah, and Tehinnah father of Ir-nahash. These were the men of Recah. [13] The sons of Kenaz: Othniel and Seraiah; and the sons of Othniel: [14] Hathath and Meonothai. He begot Ophrah. Seraiah begot Joab father of Ge-harashim,[b] so-called because they were craftsmen. [15] The sons of Caleb son of Jephunneh: Iru, Elah, and Naam; and the sons of Elah: Kenaz. [16] The sons of Jehallelel: Ziph, Ziphah, Tiria, and Asarel. [17] The sons of Ezrah: Jether, Mered, Epher, and Jalon. She[c] conceived and bore Miriam, Shammai, and Ishbah father of Eshtemoa. [18] And his Judahite wife bore Jered father of Gedor, Heber father of Soco, and Jekuthiel father of Zanoah. These were the sons of Bithiah daughter of Pharaoh, whom Mered married. [19] The sons of the wife of Hodiah sister of Naham were the fathers of Keilah the Garmite and Eshtemoa the Maacathite. [20] The sons of Shimon: Amnon, Rinnah, Benhanan, and Tilon. The sons of Ishi: Zoheth and Benzoheth. [21] The sons of Shelah son of Judah: Er father of Lecah, Laadah father of Mareshah, and the families of the linen factory at Beth-ashbea; [22] and Jokim, and the men of Cozeba and Joash, and Saraph, who married into Moab and Jashubi Lehem (the records are ancient). [23] These were the potters who dwelt at Netaim and Gederah; they dwelt there in the king's service.

[24] The sons of Simeon: Nemuel, Jamin, Jarib, Zerah, Shaul; [25] his son Shallum, his son Mibsam, his son Mishma. [26] The sons of Mishma: his son Hammuel, his son Zaccur, his son Shimei. [27] Shimei had sixteen sons and six daughters; but his brothers had not many children; in all, their

this genealogy continues the end of ch 2, which has been disrupted by the insertion of the genealogy of David. **10:** Such short notices, which interrupt the genealogies, are found throughout the introduction of Chronicles; this notice outlines a vow, a popular sign of biblical religiosity (see Judg. 11.30–31; 1 Sam. 1.11). **21–23:** The presentation of Shelah's descendants suggests that Shelah and his descendants remained in Canaan and were not subjected to Egyptian bondage, a datum which contradicts Gen. 46.12; Num. 26.20; see 7.20–29 n. **22:** The Hebrew text behind "married into Moab" is opaque and variously translated. The present translation follows the Aramaic Targum. LXX renders "settled in Moab"; others, "ruled in Moab" or "worked for Moab." **24–43:** Simeon. This tribe was traditionally associated with Judah (so, e.g., Judg. 1.3), a fact which explains its position in the list.

---

a Heb. 'oṣeb, connected with "Jabez."
b Lit. "the valley of the craftsmen."
c Apparently Bithiah; cf. v. 18.

families were not as prolific as the Judahites. 28 They dwelt in Beersheba, Moladah, Hazar-shual, 29 Bilhah, Ezem, Tolad, 30 Bethuel, Hormah, Ziklag, 31 Beth-marcaboth, Hazar-susim, Beth-biri, and Shaaraim. These were their towns until David became king, 32 together with their villages, Etam, Ain, Rimmon, Tochen, and Ashan—five towns, 33 along with all their villages that were around these towns as far as Baal; such were their settlements.

Registered in their genealogy were: 34 Meshobab, Jamlech, Joshah son of Amaziah, 35 Joel, Jehu son of Joshibiah son of Seraiah son of Asiel. 36 Elioenai, Jaakobah, Jeshohaiah, Asaiah, Adiel, Jesimiel, Benaiah, 37 Ziza son of Shiphi son of Allon son of Jedaiah son of Shimri son of Shemaiah—38 these mentioned by name were chiefs in their families, and their clans increased greatly. 39 They went to the approaches to Gedor, to the eastern side of the valley, in search of pasture for their flocks. 40 They found rich, good pasture, and the land was ample, quiet, and peaceful. The former inhabitants were of Ham; 41 those recorded by name came in the days of King Hezekiah of Judah, and attacked their encampments and the Meunim who were found there, and wiped them out forever, and settled in their place, because there was pasture there for their flocks. 42 And some of them, five hundred of the Simeonites, went to Mount Seir, with Pelatiah, Neariah, Rephaiah, and Uzziel, sons of Ishi, at their head, 43 and they destroyed the last surviving Amalekites, and they live there to this day.

5 The sons of Reuben the first-born of Israel. (He was the first-born; but when he defiled his father's bed, his birthright was given to the sons of Joseph son of Israel, so he is not reckoned as first-born in the genealogy; 2 though Judah became more powerful than his brothers and a leader came from him, yet the birthright belonged to Joseph.) 3 The sons of Reuben, the first-born of Israel: Enoch, Pallu, Hezron, and Carmi. 4 The sons of Joel: his son Shemaiah, his son Gog, his son Shimei, 5 his son Micah, his son Reaiah, his son Baal, 6 his son Beerah—whom King Tillegath-pilneser of Assyria exiled—was chieftain of the Reubenites. 7 And his kinsmen, by their families, according to their lines in the genealogy: the head, Jeiel, and Zechariah, 8 and Bela son of Azaz son of Shema son of Joel; he dwelt in Aroer as far as Nebo and Baal-meon. 9 He also dwelt to the east as far as the fringe of the wilderness this side of the Euphrates, because their cattle had increased in the land of Gilead. 10 And in the days of Saul they made war on the Hagrites, who fell by their hand;

5.1–22: Reuben, Gad, Transjordan. The author explains (vv. 1–10) why it is that Reuben, Jacob's firstborn according to Genesis, did not occupy a leading role; see Gen. 35.22; 49.3–4. The formulation of vv. 1–2 highlights Judah's central role, while recognizing the significant role of the Joseph tribes (Ephraim and Manasseh). This picture neatly summarizes Chronicles' depiction of the true (i.e., pan-) Israel. Chronicles' emphasis on Judah is the reason that the genealogies do not begin with Reuben.

and they occupied their tents throughout all the region east of Gilead.

¹¹ The sons of Gad dwelt facing them in the land of Bashan as far as Salcah: ¹² Joel the chief, Shapham the second, Janai, and Shaphat in Bashan. ¹³ And by clans: Michael, Meshullam, Sheba, Jorai, Jacan, Zia, and Eber—seven. ¹⁴ These were the sons of Abihail son of Huri son of Jaroah son of Gilead son of Michael son of Jeshishai son of Jahdo son of Buz; ¹⁵ Ahi son of Abdiel son of Guni was chief of their clan, ¹⁶ and they dwelt in Gilead, in Bashan, and in its dependencies, and in all the pasturelands of Sharon, to their limits. ¹⁷ All of them were registered by genealogies in the days of King Jotham of Judah, and in the days of King Jeroboam of Israel.

¹⁸ The Reubenites, the Gadites, and the half-tribe of Manasseh had warriors who carried shield and sword, drew the bow, and were experienced at war—44,760, ready for service. ¹⁹ They made war on the Hagrites—Jetur, Naphish, and Nodab. ²⁰ They prevailed against them; the Hagrites and all who were with them were delivered into their hands, for they cried to God in the battle, and He responded to their entreaty because they trusted in Him. ²¹ They carried off their livestock: 50,000 of their camels, 250,000 sheep, 2,000 asses, and 100,000 people. ²² For many fell slain, because it was God's battle. And they dwelt in their place until the exile.

²³ The members of the half-tribe of Manasseh dwelt in the land; they were very numerous from Bashan to Baal-hermon, Senir, and Mount Hermon. ²⁴ These were the chiefs of their clans: Epher, Ishi, Eliel, Azriel, Jeremiah, Hodaviah, and Jahdiel, men of substance, famous men, chiefs of their clans. ²⁵ But they trespassed against the God of their fathers by going astray after the gods of the peoples of the land, whom God had destroyed before them. ²⁶ So the God of Israel roused the spirit of King Pul of Assyria—the spirit of King Tillegath-pilneser of Assyria—and he carried them away, namely, the Reubenites, the Gadites, and the half-tribe of Manasseh, and brought them to Halah, Habor, Hara, and the river Gozan, to this day.

²⁷ᵃ The sons of Levi: Gershom, Kohath, and Merari. ²⁸ The sons of Kohath: Amram, Izhar, Hebron, and Uzziel. ²⁹ The children of Amram: Aaron, Moses, and Miriam. The sons of Aaron: Nadab, Abihu, Eleazar, and Ithamar. ³⁰ Eleazar begot Phinehas, Phinehas begot Abishua, ³¹ Abishua begot Bukki, Bukki begot Uzzi, ³² Uzzi begot Zerahiah,

5.23–26: Half-tribe of Manasseh. Significantly, Chronicles limits mention of the northern exile to the Transjordan, never alluding to that suffered by the Cisjordanian tribes of northern Israel. The implication is that the Assyrian exile of the northern tribes was limited in scope; cf. 2 Kings ch 17. This passage is an example of the intimate bond between Israel and its land in Chronicles; see 2 Chron. 30.1 n. For the expression "they trespassed," see 9.1. Pul is a late Babylonian variant of the name Tiglath Pil(n)eser III, the great Assyrian expansionist king who reigned 745–727 BCE.

5.27–41: The high priestly line. Zadok's Aaronide pedigree does not appear in Samuel; many scholars thus assume that he was of foreign, possibly Jebusite, origin. The motive behind Chronicles' position is that Torah (Priestly) law requires that all priests be descendants of Moses' brother, Aaron (see esp. Num. ch 18). Since, according to Chronicles, David is the archpatron of all matters pertaining to Israel's sacrificial cult, Zadok had to be provided with an acceptable pedigree.

---

a In some editions, chap. 6 begins here.

Zerahiah begot Meraioth, ³³ Meraioth begot Amariah, Amariah begot Ahitub, ³⁴ Ahitub begot Zadok, Zadok begot Ahimaaz, ³⁵ Ahimaaz begot Azariah, Azariah begot Johanan, ³⁶ and Johanan begot Azariah (it was he who served as priest in the House that Solomon built in Jerusalem). ³⁷ Azariah begot Amariah, Amariah begot Ahitub, ³⁸ Ahitub begot Zadok, Zadok begot Shallum, ³⁹ Shallum begot Hilkiah, Hilkiah begot Azariah, ⁴⁰ Azariah begot Seraiah, Seraiah begot Jehozadak; ⁴¹ and Jehozadak went into exile when the Lord exiled Judah and Jerusalem by the hand of Nebuchadnezzar.

6 The sons of Levi: Gershom, Kohath, and Merari. ² And these are the names of the sons of Gershom: Libni and Shimei. ³ The sons of Kohath: Amram, Izhar, Hebron, and Uzziel. ⁴ The sons of Merari: Mahli and Mushi. These were the families of the Levites according to their clans. ⁵ Of Gershom: his son Libni, his son Jahath, his son Zimmah, ⁶ his son Joah, his son Iddo, his son Zerah, his son Jeatherai. ⁷ The sons of Kohath: his son Amminadab, his son Korah, his son Assir, ⁸ his son Elkanah, his son Ebiasaph, his son Assir, ⁹ his son Tahath, his son Uriel, his son Uzziah, and his son Shaul. ¹⁰ The sons of Elkanah: Amasai and Ahimoth, ¹¹ his son Elkanah, his son Zophai, his son Nahath, ¹² his son Eliab, his son Jeroham, his son Elkanah. ¹³ The sons of Samuel: his first-born ᵃ Vashni, and ᵃ Abijah. ¹⁴ The sons of Merari: Mahli, his son Libni, his son Shimei, his son Uzzah, ¹⁵ his son Shimea, his son Haggiah, and his son Asaiah.

¹⁶ These were appointed by David to be in charge of song in the House of the Lord, from the time the Ark came to rest. ¹⁷ They served at the Tabernacle of the Tent of Meeting with song until Solomon built the House of the Lord in Jerusalem; and they carried out their duties as prescribed for them. ¹⁸ Those were the appointed men; and their sons were: the Kohathites: Heman the singer, son of Joel son of Samuel ¹⁹ son of Elkanah son of Jeroham son of Eliel son of Toah ²⁰ son of Zuph son of Elkanah son of Mahath son of Amasai ²¹ son of Elkanah son of Joel son of Azariah son of Zephaniah ²² son of Tahath son of Assir son of Ebiasaph son of Korah ²³ son of Izhar son of Kohath son of Levi son of Israel; ²⁴ and his kinsman Asaph, who stood on his right, namely, Asaph son of Berechiah son of Shimea ²⁵ son of Michael son of Baaseiah son of Malchijah ²⁶ son of Ethni son of Zerah son of Adaiah ²⁷ son of Ethan son of Zimmah son of Shimei ²⁸ son of Jahath son of Ger-

a-a *Some ancient vv. read "Joel, and the second"; cf. 1 Sam. 8.2.*

6.1–81: Levi. The descendants of Gershom, Kohath, and Merari are each divided into "Levites" (vv. 1–15) and musicians/singers (vv. 16–31). Kohath contains a third group, the high priests, descended from Amram. The placement of this last group in the middle position (fourth among seven) reflects its central role. **13:** The appearance of Elkanah and the prophet Samuel in the list of Levites is unparalleled in other sources. 1 Sam. ch 1 indicates that Samuel was of either Ephraimite or, less plausibly, Judahite origin. Chronicles' revised position is informed by the fact that 1 Sam. chs 2–3 present Samuel as having ministered in the Shiloh Tabernacle, an activity typically identified with (later) Levitic service. Inasmuch as Torah law (e.g., Num. ch 18) proscribes cultic service by anyone not of Levitic descent, the author felt compelled to attach an explicit Levitic pedigree to Samuel. Some argue that 1 Samuel views Samuel's family as a Levitical family hailing from Ephraim or Judah. **16–17:** Outside of Chronicles, there is no indication that Levites were responsible for cultic music in the First Temple, and many scholars maintain that this institution is a Second Temple innovation. On this view, Chronicles' claim is part of its broadly attested tendency to attribute the cultic practices of its day to hoary antiquity; antiquity implies authenticity and greater sanctity, and allows the Jews of Chronicles' time to see their (modest) Temple as part of an illustrious tradition requiring their continued support. Scholars who hold this view also suggest that this section is to be connected to the narrative sections later in Chronicles (much of chs 15–29) that tendentiously suggest that David established the basic institutions and framework for the Temple though only Solomon his son built the actual structure. Other scholars, however, accept as authentic Chronicles' tradition regarding a First Temple Levitical musical guild. In support of this position shom son of Levi. ²⁹On the left were their kinsmen: the sons of Merari: Ethan son of Kishi son of Abdi son of Malluch ³⁰son of Hashabiah son of Amaziah son of Hilkiah ³¹son of Amzi son of Bani son of Shemer ³²son of Mahli son of Mushi son of Merari son of Levi; ³³and their kinsmen the Levites were appointed for all the service of the Tabernacle of the House of God.

³⁴But Aaron and his sons made offerings upon the altar of burnt offering and upon the altar of incense, performing all the tasks of the most holy place, to make atonement for Israel, according to all that Moses the servant of God had commanded. ³⁵These are the sons of Aaron: his son Eleazar, his son Phinehas, his son Abishua, ³⁶his son Bukki, his son Uzzi, his son Zerahiah, ³⁷his son Meraioth, his son Amariah, his son Ahitub, ³⁸his son Zadok, his son Ahimaaz. ³⁹ᵃThese are their dwelling-places according to their settlements within their borders: to the sons of Aaron of the families of Kohathites, for theirs was the [first] lot; ⁴⁰they gave them Hebron in the land of Judah and its surrounding pasturelands, ⁴¹but the fields of the city and its villages they gave to Caleb son of Jephunneh. ⁴²To the sons of Aaron they gave the citiesᵇ of refuge: Hebron and Libnah with its pasturelands, Jattir and Eshtemoa with its pasturelands, ⁴³Hilen with its pasturelands, Debir with its pasturelands, ⁴⁴Ashan with its pasturelands, and Bethshemesh with its pasturelands. ⁴⁵From the tribe of Benjamin, Geba with its pasturelands, Alemeth with its pasturelands, and Anathoth with its pasturelands. All their cities throughout their families were thirteen.

⁴⁶To the remaining Kohathites were given by lot out of the family of the tribe, out of the half-tribe, the half of Manasseh, ten cities. ⁴⁷To the Gershomites according to their families were allotted thirteen cities out of the tribes of Issachar, Asher, Naphtali, and Manasseh in Bashan. ⁴⁸To the Merarites according to their families were allotted twelve cities out of the tribes of Reuben, Gad, and Zebulun. ⁴⁹So the people of Israel gave the Levites the cities with their pasturelands. ⁵⁰They gave them by lot out of the tribe of the Judahites these cities that are mentioned by name, and out of the tribe of the Simeonites, and out of the tribe of the Benjaminites.

⁵¹And some of the families of the sons of Kohath had cities of their territory out of the tribe of Ephraim. ⁵²They gave them the cities of refuge: Shechem with its pasturelands in the hill country of Ephraim, Gezer with its pasturelands, ⁵³Jokmeam with its pasturelands, Beth-horon

are the following considerations: (1) David is elsewhere portrayed as having a personal connection with music (1 Sam. chs 16–18; 2 Sam. 6.5; 23.1); (2) the evidence of other ancient Near Eastern cultures that suggests that music was an important part of the cult, often under royal patronage, from an early period. Chronicles' list suggests data differing from those reflected in the superscriptions to Psalms, suggesting different (possibly preexilic) traditions. Cf. Ezra ch 2; Neh. ch 7. **54–81:** The list of dwelling places parallels Josh. 21.5–39, though there are several differences with respect to sequence. The chronological relationship between the passages is debated.

a With vv. 24–51, cf. Josh. 21.3–42.   b Josh. 21.13, "city."

with its pasturelands, ⁵⁴Aijalon with its pasturelands, Gath-rimmon with its pasturelands; ⁵⁵and out of the half-tribe of Manasseh: Aner with its pasturelands, and Bileam with its pasturelands, for the rest of the families of the Kohathites.

⁵⁶To the Gershomites; out of the half-tribe of Manasseh: Golan in Bashan with its pasturelands and Ashtaroth with its pasturelands; ⁵⁷and out of the tribe of Issachar: Kedesh with its pasturelands, Dobrath with its pasturelands, ⁵⁸Ramoth with its pasturelands, and Anem with its pasturelands; ⁵⁹out of the tribe of Asher: Mashal with its pasturelands, Abdon with its pasturelands, ⁶⁰Hukok with its pasturelands, and Rehob with its pasturelands; ⁶¹and out of the tribe of Naphtali: Kedesh in Galilee with its pasturelands; Hammon with its pasturelands, and Kiriathaim with its pasturelands. ⁶²To the rest of the Merarites, out of the tribe of Zebulun: Rimmono with its pasturelands, Tabor with its pasturelands; ⁶³and beyond the Jordan at Jericho, on the east side of the Jordan, out of the tribe of Reuben: Bezer in the wilderness with its pasturelands, Jahaz with its pasturelands, ⁶⁴Kedemoth with its pasturelands, and Mephaath with its pasture lands; ⁶⁵and out of the tribe of Gad: Ramoth in Gilead with its pasturelands, Mahanaim with its pasturelands, ⁶⁶Heshbon with its pasturelands, and Jazer with its pasturelands.

7 The sons of Issachar: Tola, Puah, Jashub, and Shimron—four. ²The sons of Tola: Uzzi, Rephaiah, Jeriel, Jahmai, Ibsam, Shemuel, chiefs of their clans, men of substance according to their lines; their number in the days of David was 22,600. ³The sons of Uzzi: Izrahiah. And the sons of Izrahiah: Michael, Obadiah, Joel, and Isshiah—five. All of them were chiefs. ⁴And together with them, by their lines, according to their clans, were units of the fighting force, 36,000, for they had many wives and sons. ⁵Their kinsmen belonging to all the families of Issachar were in all 87,000 men of substance; they were all registered by genealogy.

⁶[The sons of] Benjamin: Bela, Becher, and Jediael—three. ⁷The sons of Bela: Ezbon, Uzzi, Uzziel, Jerimoth, and Iri—five, chiefs of clans, men of substance, registered by genealogy—22,034. ⁸The sons of Becher: Zemirah, Joash, Eliezer, Elioenai, Omri, Jeremoth, Abijah, Anathoth, and Alemeth. All these were the sons of Becher; ⁹and they were registered by genealogy according to their lines, as chiefs of their clans, men of substance—20,200. ¹⁰The sons of Jediael: Bilhan. And the sons of Bilhan: Jeush, Benjamin, Ehud, Chenaanah, Zethan, Tarshish, and Ahishahar. ¹¹All

7.1–12: Issachar and Benjamin. The Benjamin list occasions surprise: (1) It opens with the word "Benjamin" instead of "the sons of Benjamin" (NJPS supplies "The sons of"); (2) the detailed list of Benjamin appears in ch 8; and (3) there is little shared material with Torah sources (Gen. 46.21; Num. 26.38–42). These data suggest that this passage draws on a source that is no longer extant outside of the Torah.

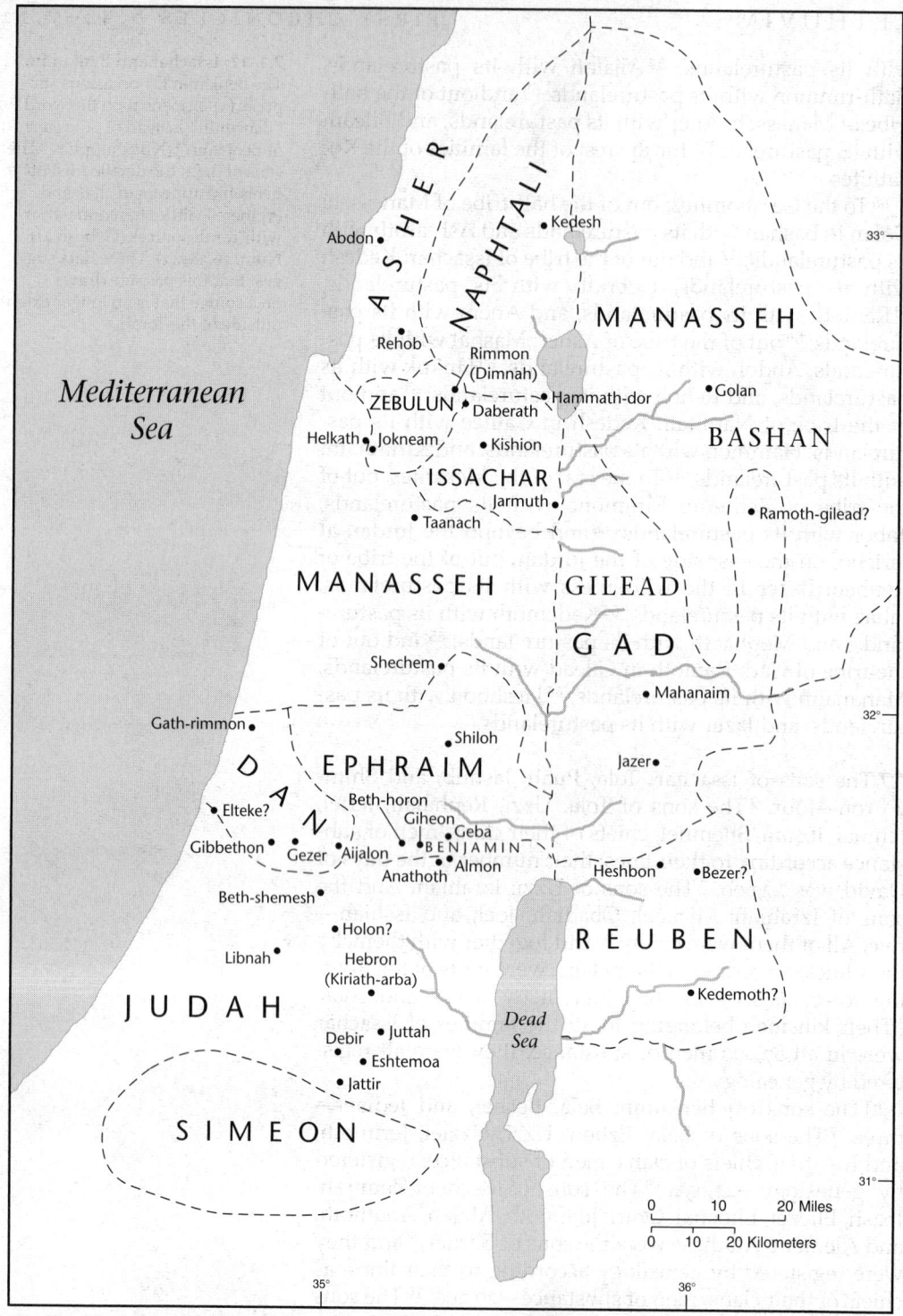

The Levitical cities according to First Chronicles. The dashed lines show the approximate boundaries of the tribes.

these were the sons of Jediael, chiefs of the clans, men of substance—17,200, who made up the fighting force. ¹² And Shuppim and Huppim were the sons of Ir; Hushim the sons of Aher.

¹³ The sons of Naphtali: Jahziel, Guni, Jezer, and Shallum, the descendants of Bilhah.

¹⁴ The sons of Manasseh: Asriel, whom his Aramean concubine bore; she bore Machir the father of Gilead. ¹⁵ And Machir took wives for Huppim and for Shuppim. The name of his sister was Maacah. And the name of the second was Zelophehad; and Zelophehad had daughters. ¹⁶ And Maacah the wife of Machir bore a son, and she named him Peresh; and the name of his brother was Sheresh; and his sons were Ulam and Rekem. ¹⁷ The sons of Ulam: Bedan. These were the sons of Gilead son of Machir son of Manasseh. ¹⁸ And his sister Hammolecheth bore Ishhod, Abiezer, and Mahlah. ¹⁹ The sons of Shemida were Ahian, Shechem, Likhi, and Aniam.

²⁰ The sons of Ephraim: Shuthelah, his son Bered, his son Tahath, his son Eleadah, his son Tahath, ²¹ his son Zabad, his son Shuthelah, also Ezer and Elead. The men of Gath, born in the land, killed them because they had gone down to take their cattle. ²² And Ephraim their father mourned many days, and his brothers came to comfort him. ²³ He cohabited with his wife, who conceived and bore a son; and she named him Beriah, because it occurred when there was misfortune^a in his house. ²⁴ His daughter was Sheerah, who built both Lower and Upper Beth-horon, and Uzzen-sheerah. ²⁵ His son Rephah, his son Resheph, his son Telah, his son Tahan, ²⁶ his son Ladan, his son Ammihud, his son Elishama, ²⁷ his son Non, his son Joshua. ²⁸ Their possessions and settlements were Bethel and its dependencies, and on the east Naaran, and on the west Gezer and its dependencies, Shechem and its dependencies, and Aiah and its dependencies; ²⁹ also along the borders of the Manassites, Beth-shean and its dependencies, Taanach and its dependencies, Megiddo and its dependencies, Dor and its dependencies. In these dwelt the sons of Joseph son of Israel.

a *Heb.* bera‘ah.

7.13: Naphtali. This passage's brevity may indicate that material has been lost.

7.14–19: Manasseh. This passage claims that Manasseh and his son, Machir, were born in trans-Jordanian territory (with no indication that either ever left Egypt), consistent with the Chronicler's ideological de-emphasis of the exodus, whereas Torah tradition (Gen. 41.51–52; Num. 27.1–4; 32.39–42; Deut. 3.14–15) records their birth in Egypt. Similarly, the claim that Asriel was Manasseh's son contradicts Num. 26.31, which mentions Asriel as Manasseh's great-grandson. Some medieval commentators argued that the Asriel mentioned here is, in fact, consistent with Numbers, and that Chronicles mentions him first because only he was born to a full wife, whereas Machir was born to Joseph's concubine. The difficulties are plain; note, e.g., that the brothers of Asriel (according to Numbers) are not mentioned here. Recent attempts at textual reconstruction of the passage remain speculative.

7.20–29: Ephraim. This passage maintains that Ephraim and his family remained in Canaan, in contradiction to Gen. chs 41–50, which states that Ephraim and his brother, Manasseh, were born, and died, in Egypt. The Aramaic Targum along with several rabbinic sources (*Mek. de R. Ishmael, beshallaḥ* (introduction); *b. Sanh.* 92b) resolved this contradiction by claiming that some members of Ephraim left Egypt and infiltrated Canaan before the divinely "appointed time" of redemption had arrived; their failure was a sign (especially for later generations) that one ought not to "play God" and try to expedite (messianic) redemption. Other traditional sources (*b. Sanh.* 92b; *Tg. Ps.-J.* and *Frg. Tg.* to Exod. 13.17) claim that the fiasco was the result of faulty computation of the period of enslavement imposed by Gen. 15.13, while some sources conflate the two explanations (*Song Rab.* to 2.7). Some medieval exegetes (Radak) argued that the words "born in the land" refer to the people of Ephraim and that the event described herein took place in either the desert or Transjordan. Some modern scholars simply emend the text, viewing the word "Ephraim" as a gloss, or maintain that the name refers to a later descendant. Others argue against emendation, claiming that this passage is part of Chronicles' portrayal of the eternal bond between Israel and its land.

30 The sons of Asher: Imnah, Ishvah, Ishvi, Beriah, and their sister Serah. 31 The sons of Beriah: Heber and Malchiel, who was the father of Birzaith. 32 Heber begot Japhlet, Shomer, Hotham, and their sister, Shua. 33 The sons of Japhlet: Pasach, Bimhal, and Ashvath. These were the sons of Japhlet. 34 The sons of Shemer: Ahi, Rohgah, Hubbah, and Aram. 35 The sons of Helem his brother: Zophah, Imna, Shelesh, and Amal. 36 The sons of Zophah: Suah, Harnepher, Shual, Beri, Imrah, 37 Bezer, Hod, Shamma, Shilshah, Ithran, and Beera. 38 The sons of Jether: Jephunneh, Pispa, and Ara. 39 The sons of Ulla: Arah, Hanniel, and Rizia. 40 All of these men of Asher, chiefs of the clans, select men, men of substance, heads of the chieftains. And they were registered by genealogy according to fighting force; the number of the men was 26,000 men.

8 Benjamin begot Bela his first-born, Ashbel the second, Aharah the third, 2 Nohah the fourth, and Rapha the fifth. 3 And Bela had sons: Addar, Gera, Abihud, 4 Abishua, Naaman, Ahoah, 5 Gera, Shephuphan, and Huram. 6 These were the sons of Ehud—they were chiefs of clans of the inhabitants of Geba, and they were exiled to Manahath: 7 Naaman, Ahijah, and Gera—he exiled them and begot Uzza and Ahihud. 8 And Shaharaim had sons in the country of Moab after he had sent away Hushim and Baara his wives. 9 He had sons by Hodesh his wife: Jobab, Zibia, Mesha, Malcam, 10 Jeuz, Sachiah, and Mirmah. These were his sons, chiefs of clans. 11 He also begot by Hushim: Abitub and Elpaal. 12 The sons of Elpaal: Eber, Misham, and Shemed, who built Ono and Lod with its dependencies, 13 and Beriah and Shema—they were chiefs of clans of the inhabitants of Aijalon, who put to flight the inhabitants of Gath; 14 and Ahio, Shashak, and Jeremoth. 15 Zebadiah, Arad, Eder, 16 Michael, Ishpah, and Joha were sons of Beriah. 17 Zebadiah, Meshullam, Hizki, Heber, 18 Ishmerai, Izliah, and Jobab were the sons of Elpaal. 19 Jakim, Zichri, Zabdi, 20 Elienai, Zillethai, Eliel, 21 Adaiah, Beraiah, and Shimrath were the sons of Shimei. 22 Ishpan, Eber, Eliel, 23 Abdon, Zichri, Hanan, 24 Hananiah, Elam, Anthothiah, 25 Iphdeiah, and Penuel were the sons of Shashak. 26 Shamsherai, Shehariah, Athaliah, 27 Jaareshiah, Elijah, and Zichri were the sons of Jeroham. 28 These were the chiefs of the clans, according to their lines. These chiefs dwelt in Jerusalem.

29 The father of Gibeon dwelt in Gibeon, and the name of his wife was Maacah. 30 His first-born son: Abdon; then Zur, Kish, Baal, Nadab, 31 Gedor, Ahio, Zecher. 32 Mikloth begot Shimeah. And they dwelt in Jerusalem opposite

7.30–40: Asher. The numbers reflect a dramatic decrease when compared to Num. 1.40–41; 26.47.

8.1–40: Benjamin. Structural features have led some scholars to argue that this list portrays the period of Josiah (late 7th century) or the postexilic period. Indeed, the Saulide genealogy may reflect the socioethnic background of Gibeon at the end of the monarchy (see below). If so, the term "son" in much of the ch refers to clan, rather than immediate family affiliations. The present list of Jonathan's descendants, comprising twelve generations, represents the family lineage until the Babylonian exile. This suggests that despite Chronicles' heavily pro-David (and anti-Saul) slant, remnants of a positive attitude toward the Saulides lingered on. Note that 10.6 (cf. 1 Sam. 31.6) states that Saul died together with all of his household, a position which makes the present list impossible. Some scholars see this point as evidence that Chronicles has undergone several editions, and that the genealogical lists of chs 8 and 9 are of later provenance than the main body of the work; see 10.6 n. **6:** A difficult verse. It may mean that part of Benjamin was exiled to Manahath in Edom; alternatively, Benjamin expelled the indigenous population to Manahath in Judah. **33:** Eshbaal appears in Samuel as Ishbosheth (2 Sam. 2.8) and Yishwi/Ishvi (1 Sam. 14.49). The name Eshbaal means "man of Baal" (or, perhaps, "Baal exists"). The "revised" form Ishbosheth, meaning "man of shame," reflects the ongoing threat posed by Canaanite religion in the preexilic period and the attempt by biblical authors and/or scribes to deprecate anything reminiscent of Baal worship. Chronicles preserves the original form of the name, since at this time the potential influence of Baal worship no longer constituted a threat. Some scholars argue that Chronicles' preservation of a Baalistic name here is part of the book's criticism of Saul, but this is unlikely, since their kinsmen, with their kinsmen. ³³ Ner begot Kish, Kish begot Saul, Saul begot Jonathan, Malchi-shua, Abinadab, and Eshbaal; ³⁴ and the son of Jonathan was Merib-baal; and Merib-baal begot Micah. ³⁵ The sons of Micah: Pithon, Melech, Taarea, and Ahaz. ³⁶ Ahaz begot Jehoaddah; and Jehoaddah begot Alemeth, Azmaveth, and Zimri; Zimri begot Moza. ³⁷ Moza begot Binea; his son Raphah; his son Eleasah, his son Azel. ³⁸ Azel had six sons, and these are their names: Azrikam, Bocheru, Ishmael, Sheariah, Obadiah, and Hanan. All these were the sons of Azel. ³⁹ The sons of Eshek his brother: Ulam his first-born, Jeush the second, and Eliphelet the third. ⁴⁰ The descendants of Ulam—men of substance, who drew the bow, had many children and grandchildren—one hundred and fifty; all these were Benjaminites.

9 All Israel was registered by genealogies; and these are in the book of the kings of Israel. And Judah was taken into exile in Babylon because of their trespass. ^{2a} The first to settle in their towns, on their property, were Israelites, priests, Levites, and temple servants, ³ while some of the Judahites and some of the Benjaminites and some of the Ephraimites and Manassehites settled in Jerusalem; ⁴ Uthai son of Ammihud son of Omri son of Imri son of Bani, from the sons of Perez son of Judah; ⁵ and of the Shilonites: Asaiah the first-born and his sons. ⁶ Of the sons of Zerah: Jeuel and their kinsmen—690. ⁷ Of the Benjaminites: Sallu son of Meshullam son of Hodaviah son of Hassenuah, ⁸ Ibneiah son of Jeroham, Elah son of Uzzi son of Michri, and Meshullam son of Shephatiah son of Reuel son of Ibneiah; ⁹ and their kinsmen, according to their lines—956. All these were chiefs of their ancestral clans.

¹⁰ Of the priests: Jedaiah, Jehoiarib, Jachin, ¹¹ and Azariah son of Hilkiah son of Meshullam son of Zadok son of Meraioth son of Ahitub, chief officer of the House of God; ¹² and Adaiah son of Jeroham son of Pashhur son of Malchijah, and Maasai son of Adiel son of Jahzerah son of Meshullam son of Meshillemith son of Immer, ¹³ together with their kinsmen, chiefs of their clans—1,760, men of substance for the work of the service of the House of God.

¹⁴ Of the Levites: Shemaiah son of Hasshub son of Azrikam son of Hashabiah, of the sons of Merari; ¹⁵ and Bakbakkar, Heresh, Galal, and Mattaniah son of Mica son of Zichri son of Asaph; ¹⁶ and Obadiah son of Shemaiah son of Galal son of Jeduthun, and Berechiah son of Asa son of Elkanah, who dwelt in the villages of the Netophathites.

the same phenomenon is attested in connection with David's sons and, possibly, Solomon's officials (see 14.7 || 2 Sam. 5.16; 2 Chron. 10.18 || 1 Kings 4.6; 12.18).

9.1–44: Identity of the community. 1: Note the key word "trespass" (Heb "ma'al"). In Priestly texts from the Torah, the term denotes encroachment upon (personal use of) sacred items; in Second Temple sources its semantic field expands to cover more general offenses. It appears frequently as part of Chronicles' theology, e.g., 10.13 (Saul's death); 2 Chron. 36.14 (Judah's exile). **2–17:** Though parallel to Neh. 11.3–19, there are many differences; some may be the result of variant traditions, while others reflect Chronicles' revisions. **2:** The opening words may refer to Second Temple society, requiring the translation "The first to settle again. . . ." On this reading, the v. emphasizes that First Temple Israel, with all of its tribes, is still alive and has its direct continuation in Second Temple society centered in Jerusalem, i.e., the Babylonian exile effected little change in the nation's structure. This is part of Chronicles' inclusivist approach to Israel's identity, as opposed to Ezra-Nehemiah, which privileges the returnees from the exile. Alternatively, the v. has been translated "The former settlers," referring to the (early) preexilic settlement in Jerusalem. On this approach, the concluding words of v. 1 (And Judah was taken into exile . . .) are a gloss added to restore the reality of exile which the original Chronicles had tried to avoid. **3:** See Neh. 11.4, which makes no reference to Ephraim and Manasseh. Chronicles' version (if understood as referring to Second Temple society) underscores the inclusivist tendency of Chronicles vis-à-vis Ezra-Nehemiah.

a With vv. 2–17, cf. Neh. 11.3–19.

17 The gatekeepers were: Shallum, Akkub, Talmon, Ahiman; and their kinsman Shallum was the chief 18 hitherto in the King's Gate on the east. They were the keepers belonging to the Levite camp. 19 Shallum son of Kore son of Ebiasaph son of Korah, and his kinsmen of his clan, the Korahites, were in charge of the work of the service, guards of the threshold of the Tent; their fathers had been guards of the entrance to the camp of the LORD. 20 And Phinehas son of Eleazar was the chief officer over them in time past; the LORD was with him. 21 Zechariah the son of Meshelemiah was gatekeeper at the entrance of the Tent of Meeting. 22 All these, who were selected as gatekeepers at the thresholds, were 212. They were selected by genealogies in their villages. David and Samuel the seer established them in their office of trust. 23 They and their descendants were in charge of the gates of the House of the LORD, that is, the House of the Tent, as guards. 24 The gatekeepers were on the four sides, east, west, north, and south; 25 and their kinsmen in their villages were obliged to join them every seven days, according to a fixed schedule. 26 The four chief gatekeepers, who were Levites, were entrusted to be over the chambers and the treasuries of the House of God. 27 They spent the night near the House of God; for they had to do guard duty, and they were in charge of opening it every morning.

28 Some of them had charge of the service vessels, for they were counted when they were brought back and taken out. 29 Some of them were in charge of the vessels and all the holy vessels, and of the flour, wine, oil, incense, and spices. 30 Some of the priests blended the compound of spices. 31 Mattithiah, one of the Levites, the first-born of Shallum the Korahite, was entrusted with making the flat cakes. 32 Also some of their Kohathite kinsmen had charge of the rows of bread, to prepare them for each sabbath.

33 Now these are the singers, the chiefs of Levitical clans who remained in the chambers free of other service, for they were on duty day and night. 34 These were chiefs of Levitical clans, according to their lines; these chiefs lived in Jerusalem.

35 The father of Gibeon, Jeiel, lived in Gibeon, and the name of his wife was Maacah. 36 His first-born son, Abdon; then Zur, Kish, Baal, Ner, Nadab, 37 Gedor, Ahio, Zechariah, and Mikloth; 38 Mikloth begot Shimeam; and they lived in Jerusalem opposite their kinsmen, with their kinsmen. 39 Ner begot Kish, Kish begot Saul, Saul begot Jonathan, Malchi-shua, Abinadab, and Eshbaal; 40 and the son of Jonathan was Merib-baal; and Merib-baal begot Micah. 41 The sons of Micah: Pithon, Melech, Taharea;

18–33: These verses, which have no extant source, outline various functions of the gatekeepers, who may have attained added significance in the Second Temple period. 34–44: A repetition (with variations) of part of the Benjaminite genealogy of 8.28–38; it here serves to introduce King Saul, a Benjaminite.

42 Ahaz begot Jarah, and Jarah begot Alemeth, Azmaveth, and Zimri; Zimri begot Moza. 43 Moza begot Binea; his son was Rephaiah, his son Eleasah, his son Azel. 44 Azel had six sons and these were their names: Azrikam, Bocheru, Ishmael, Sheariah, Obadiah, and Hanan. These were the sons of Azel.

10 ᵃThe Philistines attacked Israel, and the men of Israel fled before the Philistines and [many] fell on Mount Gilboa. 2 The Philistines pursued Saul and his sons, and the Philistines struck down Jonathan, Abinadab, and Malchi-shua, sons of Saul. 3 The battle raged around Saul, and the archers hit him, and he ᵇ-was wounded-ᵇ by the archers. 4 Saul said to his arms-bearer, "Draw your sword and run me through, so that these uncircumcised may not come and make sport of me." But his arms-bearer, out of great awe, refused; whereupon Saul grasped the sword and fell upon it. 5 When the arms-bearer saw that Saul was dead, he too fell on his sword and died. 6 Thus Saul and his three sons and his entire house died together. 7 And when all the men of Israel who were in the valley saw that theyᶜ had fled and that Saul and his sons were dead, they abandoned their towns and fled; the Philistines then came and occupied them.

8 The next day the Philistines came to strip the slain, and they found Saul and his sons lying on Mount Gilboa. 9 They stripped him, and carried off his head and his armor, and sent them throughout the land of the Philis-

a With vv. 1–12, cf. 1 Sam. 31.1–13.
b-b Meaning of Heb. uncertain.   c I.e., Israel.

10.1–14: Saul's death and transfer of the monarchy to David. 1 Samuel devotes approximately twenty chs to the reign of Saul; Chronicles deems one ch, focusing on Saul's death, sufficient. This fact, in itself, is a clear statement of Chronicles' primary interests, viz., David and the Davidic dynasty, and of the author's negative assessment of Saul. In addition to the paucity of material, Chronicles' overall depiction of Saul is decidedly different from that reflected in Samuel. The latter contains a block of material sympathetic to Saul, which emphasizes his courage and leadership and the esteem in which he was held. Overall, Samuel portrays Saul as a multi-dimensional,

tragic figure. Chronicles knows none of this; Saul is a one-dimensional figure, whose demeaning death is just desert for a host of offenses he committed. Chronicles' version of the circumstances of Saul's death and the readiness of some of the population to bury his mutilated corpse presents a far less flattering picture than that in Samuel. **6:** See introductory comment to ch 8. In addition to the contradictions noted therein, the present v. clashes with 15.29, which indicates that (at the least) Saul's daughter Michal remained alive. Some scholars explain 10.6 as a compositional oversight on the author's part. Others argue that this inconsistency is the

price that Chronicles had to pay in order to promote two distinct positions: The Chronicler wanted to show that David fulfilled his promise to Saul and his household concerning the continued well-being of Saul's descendants (1 Sam. 20.15; 24.22–23), but at the same time Chronicles was concerned that David not appear as a usurper—thus the notice that David ascended an heirless throne following Saul's death (vv. 1–3). **7:** The words "they had fled" are ambiguous; the present translation understands them to refer to the Israelite forces, while others take them to mean that Saul and his sons first fled, before giving up all hope. This offers a sharp contrast to David's valor; see 14.8 n. Saul's demoralizing defeat, resulting in whole tracts of Israel's land being overrun by the enemy, must be seen against the backdrop of Chronicles' "land-theology" which, as noted, portrays a picture of continuous Israelite settlement in its land and, moreover, maintains that the entire territory of Canaan had already been settled by the patriarchs (see 13.5 n.). The message is thus clear: Saul's rule was disastrous. **8:** For the connection between Saul and the people of Jabesh, see 1 Sam. ch 11. 1 Sam. ch 31 claims that Saul's corpse, with his head attached, was taken from the battlefield and impaled on the wall of Beth-shan. Retrieving the corpse entailed a dangerous operation: The people of Jabesh, operating by night, would have had to penetrate enemy territory under the very noses of the Philistine guards, suggesting that Saul was truly venerated by the people of Jabesh. By contrast, Chronicles states that Saul's head was taken to the temple of Dagon while the rest of his corpse was left at the battle site. According to this scenario, the people of Jabesh were willing to attend to Saul's corpse left on Mount Gilboa, but they were not prepared to endanger their own lives by approaching the (Philistine) temple of Dagon. Additionally, Saul was never buried fully and properly, a sign of distines to spread the news to their idols and among the people. [10] They placed his armor in the temple of their god, and they impaled his head in the temple of Dagan. [11] When all Jabesh-gilead heard everything that the Philistines had done to Saul, [12] all their stalwart men set out, removed the bodies of Saul and his sons, and brought them to Jabesh. They buried the bones under the oak tree in Jabesh, and they fasted for seven days. [13] Saul died for the trespass that he had committed against the LORD in not having fulfilled the command of the LORD; moreover, he had consulted a ghost to seek advice, [14] and did not seek advice of the LORD; so He had him slain and the kingdom transferred to David son of Jesse.

11 [a] All Israel gathered to David at Hebron and said, "We are your own flesh and blood. [2] Long before now, even when Saul was king, you were the leader of Israel; and the LORD your God said to you: You shall shepherd My people Israel; you shall be ruler of My people Israel." [3] All the elders of Israel came to the king at Hebron, and David made a pact with them in Hebron before the LORD. And they anointed David king over Israel, according to the word of the LORD through Samuel.

[4] David and all Israel set out for Jerusalem, that is Jebus,

a With vv. 1–9, cf. 2 Sam. 5.1–10, and with vv. 11–41, cf. 2 Sam. 23.8–39.

grace. This reflects Saul's diminished image in Chronicles.
13–14: Chronicles routinely explains death as punishment for sins, and so here, unlike in 1 Samuel, attributes Saul's death to his sins. To do so, it must rewrite some of the material that is known from Samuel (e.g., 1 Sam. 28.8–23). Chronicles highlights Saul's failure to seek advice (Heb "darash") of the LORD before going to battle, in contrast to 1 Sam. ch 28, where Saul was prevented from receiving divine guidance. This also creates a clear contrast with David's conduct (see 14.10, 14). The concluding words emphasize that the transfer of power to David was both immediate and decreed in heaven, a point restated several times in the ensuing chs. For trespass, see 9.1 n.

Chs 11–29: David's rule. The portrait of David is greatly enhanced. Many unflattering episodes found in Samuel are deleted, while posi-

tive aspects of David's career are embellished. There is, however, no attempt to whitewash all of David's misdeeds. The most striking change in Chronicles' portrayal concerns David's role in the religious cultus. Whereas Samuel describes the political and personal experiences of David the warrior, Chronicles' David is, first and foremost, the patron of the cultus. This portrayal, together with David's association with (parts of) the book of Psalms, casts him as a spiritual figure, leading to the rabbinic depiction of David as a Torah scholar. This transition is also attested in the Dead Sea Scrolls of Qumran, where David is credited with the composition of more than 4,000 psalms.

11.1–3: David's ascension to the throne. The formulation conveys the unmistakable impression that the transition between Saul's demise and David's rule was both

immediate and smooth; there was no void nor period of political instability. David's ascension to the throne was the result of divine decree and unanimous popular support. This differs dramatically from 2 Sam. chs 1–4, which describe the power struggle following Saul's death. Additionally, Chronicles never mentions David's having been a local chieftain; he is instead portrayed as going from private citizen to monarch over a united Israel-Judah. This, too, contradicts Samuel, which presents David as a local, Judahite leader, whose leadership over a united confederation of tribes comes about gradually, following years of friction between him and the regnant Saul. Chronicles thus avoids portraying David as a usurper since for the Chronicler, the "true" or "ideal" Israel consists of a unity of all the tribes headed by one legitimate monarch. **1:** Whereas 2 Sam. 5.1 speaks of all the tribes coming to Hebron, Chronicles says that all Israel came, reflecting the outpouring of unanimous support for David. This point is reiterated at 12.24–41. The participation by the entire nation in important events is a recurring motif in Chronicles. **4–9:** The conquest of Jerusalem. The appearance of this passage at this juncture is prompted by literary, rather than chronological, considerations—its placement conveys the impression that David's first official act consisted of capturing Jerusalem. It is true that, according to Chronicles, Jerusalem attains its special status only later (see 1 Chron. chs 21–22). Still, the centrality of Jerusalem was so deeply rooted by the time of Chronicles that his readers would probably have seen this story as suggestive of David's (prophetically) inspired leadership. According to biblical tradition, Jerusalem had been a Jebusite city, so that no Israelite tribe had any stronger claim to it than another—a sort of Washington, D.C. Viewed in the context of 2 Samuel, David's decision to establish Jerusalem as his new capital was designed to con-

The kingdom of David according to First Chronicles. The dashed line shows the approximate boundary of the kingdom at its greatest extent.

The following labels appear on the map:

Inset map:
Baal-hazor
Gilgal
Gezer
Gibeon
Geba
Ekron
Jerusalem
Gath?
Giloh
Tekoa
Hebron

Main map:
Mediterranean Sea
ZOBAH
ARAM (SYRIA)
Damascus
GESHUR
Tyre
Abel-beth-maacah
ISRAEL
AMMON
Mahanaim
Rabbah
Ashdod
Jerusalem
Ashkelon
PHILISTIA
JUDAH
Gaza
MOAB
Valley of Salt
AMALEK
EDOM

Scale:
0   25   50   75 Miles
0   40   80   120 Kilometers

where the Jebusite inhabitants of the land lived. [5]David was told by the inhabitants of Jebus, "You will never get in here!" But David captured the stronghold of Zion; it is now the City of David. [6]David said, "Whoever attacks the Jebusites first will be the chief officer"; Joab son of Zeruiah attacked first, and became the chief.

[7]David occupied the stronghold; therefore it was renamed the City of David. [8]David also fortified the surrounding area, from the Millo roundabout, and Joab rebuilt the rest of the city. [9]David kept growing stronger, for the LORD of Hosts was with him.

[10]And these were David's chief warriors who strongly supported him in his kingdom, together with all Israel, to make him king, according to the word of the LORD concerning Israel.

[11]This is the list of David's warriors: Jashobeam son of Hachmoni, the chief officer; he wielded his spear against three hundred and slew them all on one occasion. [12]Next to him was Eleazar son of Dodo, the Ahohite; he was one of the three warriors. [13]He was with David at Pas Dammim when the Philistines gathered there for battle. There was a plot of ground full of barley there; the troops had fled from the Philistines, [14]but they took their stand in the middle of the plot and defended it, and they routed the Philistines. Thus the LORD wrought a great victory.

[15]Three of the thirty chiefs went down to the rock to David, at the cave of Adullam, while a force of Philistines was encamped in the Valley of Rephaim. [16]David was then in the stronghold, and a Philistine garrison was then at Bethlehem. [17]David felt a craving and said, "If only I could get a drink of water from the cistern which is by the gate of Bethlehem!" [18]So the three got through the Philistine camp, and drew water from the cistern which is by the gate of Bethlehem, and they carried it back to David. But David would not drink it, and he poured it out as a libation to the LORD. [19]For he said, "God forbid that I should do this! Can I drink the blood of these men who risked their lives?"—for they had brought it at the risk of their lives, and he would not drink it. Such were the exploits of the three warriors.

[20]Abshai, the brother of Joab, was head of another three. He once wielded his spear against three hundred and slew them. He won a name among the three; [21]among the three he was more highly regarded than the other two, and so he became their commander. However, he did not attain to the other three.

[22]Benaiah son of Jehoiada from Kabzeel was a brave soldier who performed great deeds. He killed the two

solidate his hold over a newly united entity (Israel and Judah), which emerged only after a lengthy period of political instability. In Chronicles, however, David's ascension to the throne receives unanimous support; there is no need to seek a capital that will give stability to his regime. Accordingly, the conquest of Jerusalem takes on a different meaning in Chronicles: David intuitively sensed Jerusalem's (future) importance. Chronicles again claims that all Israel participated in this venture, whereas 2 Sam. ch 5 states that David was accompanied by "his men"; David's venture in 2 Sam. is a private one, whereas Chronicles views it as a religious priority, involving the entire nation. **5:** Chronicles deletes 2 Sam. 5.6b, 8, either because that passage was deemed incomprehensible or because it was seen as attributing to David a degrading prejudice toward the blind and lame. **6–8:** The role of Joab in capturing and providing for Jerusalem does not appear in 2 Samuel. The mention of Joab here foreshadows the following chs, which list David's warriors and their achievements, requiring that Chronicles establish Joab's credentials. While it is unclear whether this datum is based on historical records or is the Chronicler's invention, the net result is a more positive image of Joab than that in the Deuteronomistic History (see 20.1; 21.3–6; cf. 1 Kings 2.5–6). The glorification of David's closest officers adds to David's glorification. In addition, Chronicles' version enhances the importance of Jerusalem: He who captures Jerusalem attains glory and leadership. Chronicles further claims that the name "City of David" was given to Jerusalem by the people of Israel, another sign of public support for David. 2 Samuel, however, suggests that David, who alone (without Joab) was responsible for the capture of Jerusalem, introduced the new name. This fits the personal nature of David's venture, according to Samuel, and also makes for a less modest David.

[sons] of Ariel of Moab. Once, on a snowy day, he went down into a pit and killed a lion. 23 He also killed an Egyptian, a giant of a man five cubits tall. The Egyptian had a spear in his hand, like a weaver's beam, yet [Benaiah] went down against him with a club, wrenched the spear out of the Egyptian's hand, and killed him with his own spear. 24 Such were the exploits of Benaiah son of Jehoiada; and he won a name among the three warriors. 25 He was highly regarded among the thirty, but he did not attain to the three. David put him in charge of his bodyguard.ᵃ

26 The valiant warriors: Asahel brother of Joab, Elhanan son of Dodo from Bethlehem, 27 Shammoth the Harorite, Helez the Pelonite, 28 Ira son of Ikkesh from Tekoa, Abiezer of Anathoth, 29 Sibbecai the Hushathite, Ilai the Ahohite, 30 Mahrai the Netophathite, Heled son of Baanah the Netophathite, 31 Ittai son of Ribai from Gibeah of the Benjaminites, Benaiah of Pirathon, 32 Hurai of Nahale-gaash, Abiel the Arbathite, 33 Azmaveth the Bahrumite, Eliahba of Shaalbon, 34 the sons of Hashem the Gizonite, Jonathan son of Shageh the Hararite, 35 Ahiam son of Sacar the Hararite, Eliphal son of Ur, 36 Hepher the Mecherathite, Ahijah the Pelonite, 37 Hezro the Carmelite, Naarai son of Ezbai, 38 Joel brother of Nathan, Mibhar son of Hagri, 39 Zelek the Ammonite, Naharai the Berothite—the armsbearer of Joab son of Zeruiah—40 Ira the Ithrite, Gareb the Ithrite, 41 Uriah the Hittite, Zabad son of Ahlai. 42 Adina son of Shiza the Reubenite, a chief of the Reubenites, and thirty with him; 43 Hanan son of Maacah, and Joshaphat the Mithnite; 44 Uzziah the Ashterathite, Shama and Jeiel sons of Hotham the Aroerite; 45 Jedaiael son of Shimri, and Joha his brother, the Tizite; 46 Eliel the Mahavite, and Jeribai and Joshaviah sons of Elnaam, and Ithmah the Moabite; 47 Eliel, Obed, and Jaassiel the Mezobaite.

12 The following joined David at Ziklag while he was still in hiding from Saul son of Kish; these were the warriors who gave support in battle; 2 they were armed with the bow and could use both right hand and left hand to sling stones or shoot arrows with the bow; they were kinsmen of Saul from Benjamin. 3 At the head were Ahiezer and Joash, sons of Shemaah of Gibeah; and Jeziel and Pelet, sons of Azmaveth; and Beracah and Jehu of Anathoth; 4 Ishmaiah of Gibeon, a warrior among the thirty, leading the thirty; 5 Jeremiah, Jahaziel, Johanan, and Jozabad of Gederah; 6 Eluzai, Jerimoth, Bealiah, Shemariah, and Shephatiah the Hariphite; 7 Elkanah, Isshiah, Azarel,

ᵃ *Meaning of Heb. uncertain.*

11.10–46: Warriors who joined David. This material is largely similar to that of 2 Sam. ch 23, often viewed as part of an appendix to Samuel; this is one of several places where the Chronicler has rearranged his source material. Its placement at the end of Samuel allows for the reasonable inference that these warriors joined David over the course of his forty-year rule, while the Chronicler's sequence implies that these elite fighters joined the king at the very outset of his rule, supporting the notion that David enjoyed unanimous support. The historicity of the sixteen warriors in vv. 41b–47 added by Chronicles to the list in 2 Samuel has been the subject of differing views. **13–14:** In contrast to 2 Sam. 23.10, the Masoretic Text of Chronicles indicates that the Philistines were routed by Eleazar and David; cf. Saul's conduct in 10.7 and see n. there. LXX and other ancient versions of Chronicles read the singular form, indicating that it was Eleazar alone who defeated the enemy. Both readings accomplish the same goal, namely, exaltation of David. The Masoretic reading does so by stressing that David's valor was a crucial factor in the victory, the other versions do so by highlighting the truly extraordinary abilities of the warriors who saw fit to join David. **16–19:** Realizing that his actions needlessly endangered his men, and that drinking the water would be tantamount to drinking blood—an act proscribed by Lev. 17.11–12; Deut. 12.23–25—he offers it as a libation (offering) to God. **23:** Chronicles' reformulation of 2 Sam. 23.21 includes elements patterned after 1 Sam. 17.4, 7, which describes the defeat of the Philistine hero Goliath. Chronicles' version magnifies Benaiah's ("Benayahu's") military prowess, a fact which ultimately exalts David's status.

12.1–23: Warriors who joined David at Ziklag. This nonsynoptic section emphasizes the broad-based support which David enjoyed among all tribes and seg-

Joezer, and Jashobeam the Korahites; ⁸Joelah and Zebadiah, sons of Jeroham of Gedor.ᵃ ⁹Of the Gadites, there withdrew to follow David to the wilderness stronghold valiant men, fighters fit for battle, armed with shield and spear; they had the appearance of lions, and were as swift as gazelles upon the mountains: ¹⁰Ezer the chief, Obadiah the second, Eliab the third, ¹¹Mashmannah the fourth, Jeremiah the fifth, ¹²Attai the sixth, Eliel the seventh, ¹³Johanan the eighth, Elzabad the ninth, ¹⁴Jeremiah the tenth, Machbannai the eleventh. ¹⁵Those were the Gadites, heads of the army. The least was equal to a hundred, the greatest to a thousand. ¹⁶These were the ones who crossed the Jordan in the first month, when it was at its crest, and they put to flight all the lowlanders to the east and west. ¹⁷Some of the Benjaminites and Judahites came to the stronghold to David, ¹⁸and David went out to meet them, saying to them, "If you come on a peaceful errand, to support me, then I will make common cause with you, but if to betray me to my foes, for no injustice on my part, then let the God of our fathers take notice and give judgment." ¹⁹Then the spirit seized Amasai, chief of the captains:

> "We are yours, David,
> On your side, son of Jesse;
> At peace, at peace with you,
> And at peace with him who supports you,
> For your God supports you."

So David accepted them, and placed them at the head of his band.

²⁰Some Manassites went over to David's side when he came with the Philistines to make war against Saul, but they were of no help to them, because the lords of the Philistines in council dismissed him, saying, "He will go over to the side of his lord, Saul, and it will cost us our heads"; ²¹when he went to Ziklag, these Manassites went over to his side—Adnah, Jozabad, Jediael, Michael, Jozabad, Elihu, and Zillethai, chiefs of the clans of Manasseh. ²²It was they who gave support to David against the band,ᵇ for all were valiant men; and they were officers of the force.

a Or, "the troop," reading Heb. gedud with several mss.
b I.e., the band of Amalekite raiders; cf. 1 Sam. 30.8, 15.

out or, put differently, why David suspected them more than the others. Some note that this group parallels the one that remained loyal to the Davidic dynasty at the time of its schism; see 2 Chron. 10.16; 1 Kings 12.16. Because of this and other similarities and contrastive elements shared with those passages (see also, 2 Sam. 20.1), it is argued that this passage is Chronicles' way of reinforcing the divine election of David and his successors. Perhaps this section highlights the fact that even Benjaminites, of Saul's tribe, followed David (see v. 2). **19:** This reflects Chronicles' innovative view on prophets and prophecy. Whereas many biblical books view prophecy as the exclusive prerogative of "professional" prophets whose activity centers on the monarchy, Chronicles maintains that any individual, even a non-Israelite, may, under the proper circumstances, serve as a conduit for conveying the divine will; hence, Amasai, a military man, experiences ad hoc prophecy. The possession formulae (the spirit seized) introduce the speeches of "non-prophets" only, indicating that Chronicles differentiates between this group and "professional" prophets.

12.24–41: Fighting forces at Hebron. Chronicles again stresses that the selection of David was by divine decree, both explicitly in v. 24, "in accordance with the word of the LORD," and through the structure and contents of the narrative. **25–39:** The total number of the fighting men who arrived at Hebron, 340,822, does not take into account other (male) Israelites who supported David from afar. The incredible size of this number, and others in Chronicles, has led some scholars to argue that the Heb word "'elef" in these passages does not mean "thousand," but denotes, rather, a clan-based militia unit consisting of perhaps fifteen members. Closer examination of the relevant passages, however, reveals that Chronicles did, in fact, have the meaning "thousands" in mind. The passage emphasizes the

ments of the people, including Saul's kinsmen. Indeed, the fact that these many warriors joined David before his accession to the throne attests to the depth of David's popularity. The list highlights two qualities of these warriors: unusual martial qualifications and extreme eagerness to join David at all costs, without delay. It is likely that this ch is based at least in part on older sources. **17–18:** It is not immediately apparent why this group is singled

23 Day in day out, people came to David to give him support, until there was an army as vast as the army of God.

24 These are the numbers of the [men of the] armed bands who joined David at Hebron to transfer Saul's kingdom to him, in accordance with the word of the LORD:

25 Judahites, equipped with shield and spear—6,800 armed men; 26 Simeonites, valiant men, fighting troops—7,100; 27 of the Levites—4,600; 28 Jehoiada, chief officer of the Aaronides; with him, 3,700; 29 Zadok, a young valiant man, with his clan—22 officers; 30 of the Benjaminites, kinsmen of Saul, 3,000 in their great numbers, hitherto protecting the interests of the house of Saul; 31 of the Ephraimites, 20,800 valiant men, famous in their clans; 32 of the half-tribe of Manasseh, 18,000, who were designated by name to come and make David king; 33 of the Issacharites, men who knew how to interpret the signs of the times, to determine how Israel should act; their chiefs were 200, and all their kinsmen followed them; 34 of Zebulun, those ready for service, able to man a battle line with all kinds of weapons, 50,000, giving support wholeheartedly; 35 of Naphtali, 1,000 chieftains with their shields and lances—37,000; 36 of the Danites, able to man the battle line—28,600; 37 of Asher, those ready for service to man the battle line—40,000; 38 from beyond the Jordan, of the Reubenites, the Gadites, and the half-tribe of Manasseh, together with all kinds of military weapons—120,000.

39 All these, fighting men, manning the battle line with whole heart, came to Hebron to make David king over all Israel. Likewise, all the rest of Israel was of one mind to make David king.

40 They were there with David three days, eating and drinking, for their kinsmen had provided for them.

41 And also, their relatives as far away as Issachar, Zebulun, and Naphtali brought food by ass, camel, mule, and ox—provisions of flour, cakes of figs, raisin cakes, wine, oil, cattle, and sheep in abundance, for there was joy in Israel.

13 Then David consulted with the officers of the thousands and the hundreds, with every chief officer. 2 David said to the entire assembly of Israel, "If you approve, and if the LORD our God concurs,ᵃ let us send far and wide to our remaining kinsmen throughout the territories of Israel, including the priests and Levites in the towns where they have pasturelands, that they should

ᵃ *Meaning of Heb. uncertain.*

enormous number of Israelites who not only supported David but traveled from afar in order to demonstrate support for him. It is striking that the largest contingents hail from the most distant regions, indicating complete and far-reaching support for David.

13.1–14: Transferring the Ark: the failed attempt. 1 Chron. ch 13 reflects 2 Sam. ch 6, while 1 Chron. ch 14 reflects 2 Sam. ch 5, another example of the Chronicler's rearrangement of his source material (see 11.10–46 n.). The reason for this rearrangement is explored below (14.1–17 n.). **1–4:** In 2 Sam. ch 6, David's transfer of the Ark to his new capital is intended to consolidate his position as leader of the newly unified nation; accordingly, he is accompanied by thirty thousand "picked men." Historically, this is a reasonable motive, inasmuch as the establishment of a functioning cultus was, in the ancient Near East, a measure of a monarch's success and stability. By contrast, Chronicles presents David's act as expressing genuine concern for the cultus (see Ps. 132), requiring the support and participation of the entire nation. Moreover, Chronicles' David seeks the nation's consent. This portrays Israel's only legitimate monarchy in a "democratized" fashion; David consults with his subjects or, more precisely, his kinsmen (v. 2). This utopian depiction may be an expression of Chronicles' messianic yearnings. In addition, the author again makes the claim that important historical events were approved, and attended, by the population at large—a clarion call to his contemporaries for similar support. **2:** Heb "p-r-tz," lit. "to break forth," (here rendered "far and wide") recurs in various forms in this and the following ch. Its use in the present v. is particularly unusual, serving to alert the reader that David has "broken forth/out," i.e., acted impetuously. As emerges in ch 15, David's intentions were sincere, but his rash decision, which ignored critical cultic norms, resulted in disaster. See gather together to us ³in order to transfer the Ark of our God to us, for throughout the days of Saul we paid no regard to it." ⁴The entire assembly agreed to do so, for the proposal pleased all the people. ⁵David then assembled all Israel from Shihor of Egypt to Lebo-hamath, in order to bring the Ark of God from Kiriath-jearim. ⁶ᵃDavid and all Israel went up to Baalah, Kiriath-jearim of Judah, to bring up from there the Ark of God, the LORD, Enthroned on the Cherubim, to which the Name was attached. ⁷They transported the Ark of God on a new cart from the house of Abinadab; Uzza and Ahio guided the cart, ⁸and David and all Israel danced before God with all their might— with songs, lyres, harps, timbrels, cymbals, and trumpets. ⁹But when they came to the threshing floor of Chidon, Uzza put out his hand to hold the Ark of God because the oxen had stumbled.ᵇ ¹⁰The LORD was incensed at Uzza, and struck him down, because he laid a hand on the Ark; and so he died there before God. ¹¹David was distressed because the LORD ᶜhad burst outᶜ against Uzza; and that place was named Perez-uzzah, as it is still called.

¹²David was afraid of God that day; he said, "How can I bring the Ark of God here?" ¹³So David did not remove the Ark to his place in the City of David; instead, he diverted it to the house of Obed-edom the Gittite. ¹⁴The Ark of God remained in the house of Obed-edom, in its own abode, three months, and the LORD blessed the house of Obed-edom and all he had.

14 ᵈKing Hiram of Tyre sent envoys to David with cedar logs, stonemasons, and carpenters to build a palace for him. ²Thus David knew that the LORD had es-

a With vv. 6–14, cf. 2 Sam. 6.2–11.   b Meaning of Heb. uncertain.
c-c Heb. paraṣ . . . pereṣ.   d With vv. 1–16, cf. 2 Sam. 5.11–25.

comments to ch 15. **4–6:** Chronicles' version reflects its portrayal of Solomon and David as parallel or continuous figures; David is in no way inferior to Solomon. This was important since only Solomon constructed the Temple itself, and thus he might be seen as more significant than David. Thus, since 1 Kings ch 8 (compare 2 Chron. 5.2) states that the elders and tribal heads participated in the relocation of the Ark into the Temple, the author provided a similar scene for David. **5:** This v. conveys two important views. First, as understood by most scholars, Chronicles

maintains a position attested only rarely in the Bible (see Josh. 13.3), that Israel's southern border extends to the easternmost branch of the Nile (*Shihor*), i.e., Pelusium, located on the western coast of the Sinai peninsula. Second, in contrast to the early history, which portrays a gradual expansion of Israelite control culminating in the conquests of David, Chronicles claims that all of Canaan had already been populated by Israelites at an early stage in the nation's history. This is another expression of Chronicles' position regarding Israel's continuous presence in its

land. Most scholars identify Lebo-hamath with Lebweh in modern Syria. These borders are ideal; it is doubtful that Israel ever controlled such an extensive area. **6:** *Cherubim:* Traditional Jewish sources, using an Aramaic wordplay, tend to view the cherubs as angel-like figures, having the face of a child (*b. Sukkah* 5b); several medieval exegetes, however, reject this position (e.g., Rashbam; Hezekiah ben Manoah ["Ḥizzequni"]). The cherubs were actually griffinlike or sphinxlike, composite creatures, similar to those attested in other cultures of the ancient Near East. Their role was twofold: to protect sacred or important precincts by warding off evil forces, and to serve as a throne for gods and/or kings (see Exod. 25.18–22; 26.31; Ezek. 1.5–27; 10.1–22; see notes to these vv.). This latter role explains why it is that the LORD is referred to as *Enthroned on the Cherubim,* as well as the Ark's unique status: It symbolizes the presence of the LORD. **9–14:** Obed-edom is a Gittite, probably hailing from the city of Gath, in Philistine territory. Nothing in 2 Sam. ch 6 suggests that he was a Levite. Nonetheless, the ample attestation of Levitical guards and musicians bearing this name in 1 Chronicles (e.g., ch 16) implies that Chronicles views him as a Levite. Some scholars defend this pedigree, arguing that Chronicles understood Gath to refer to Gath-rimmon, a Levitical city (Josh. 19.45; 21.24). It is more likely, however, that Chronicles could not portray David as abandoning the Ark in a house of a foreigner which just happened to be close to the site of Uzza's death. Thus, the Chronicler reworked the genealogies to suggest that David placed the Ark in the hands of a person formally charged with this cultic task.

14.1–17: David's palace, family, and battles. The material found in this ch appears in 2 Samuel in a different arrangement. 2 Sam. ch 5 places this material between David's coronation and his capture of Jerusalem, allowing the infertablished him as king over Israel, and that his kingship was highly exalted for the sake of His people Israel.

3 David took more wives in Jerusalem, and David begot more sons and daughters. 4 These are the names of the children born to him in Jerusalem:ᵃ Shammua, Shobab, Nathan, and Solomon; 5 Ibhar, Elishua, and Elpelet; 6 Nogah, Nepheg, and Japhia; 7 Elishama, Beeliada, and Eliphelet.

8 When the Philistines heard that David had been anointed king over all Israel, all the Philistines went up in search of David; but David heard of it, and he went out to them. 9 The Philistines came and raided the Valley of Rephaim. 10 David inquired of God, "Shall I go up against the Philistines? Will You deliver them into my hands?" And the LORD answered him, "Go up, and I will deliver them into your hands." 11 Thereupon David ascended Baal-perazim, and David defeated them there. David said, "God ᵇ-burst out-ᵇ against my enemies by my hands as waters burst out." That is why that place was named Baal-perazim. 12 They abandoned their gods there, and David ordered these to be burned.

13 Once again the Philistines raided the valley. 14 David inquired of God once more, and God answered, "Do not go up after them, but circle around them and confront them at the bacaᶜ trees. 15 And when you hear the sound of marching in the tops of the baca trees, then go out to battle, for God will be going in front of you to attack the Philistine forces." 16 David did as God had commanded him; and they routed the Philistines from Gibeon all the way to Gezer. 17 David became famous throughout the lands, and the LORD put the fear of him in all the nations.

15 He had houses made for himself in the City of David, and he prepared a place for the Ark of God,

---

a With the list in vv. 4–7, cf. also 1 Chron. 3.5–8.
b-b Heb. paraṣ.   c Meaning of Heb. uncertain.

---

ence that David occupied himself with personal matters (e.g., construction of his palace) before attending to the Ark. Chronicles, by placing this material between the two attempts at transferring the Ark, conveys the impression that the delay in attending to the Ark was not due to lack of motivation; rather, David was occupied with other matters. Chronicles deletes 2 Sam. 6.12, which indicates that David renewed his efforts only after being informed that Obededom had prospered as a result of the Ark's presence because this portrayal reflects poorly upon David and his veneration of the cultus—two important emphases of the book. Chronicles offers no clear explanation regarding the timing behind David's decision to again attend to the Ark; this implies that David returned to this task at the first opportunity following the activities described in

ch 14. **1–2:** The placement of this passage in Chronicles may indicate that, despite David's culpability in the failure of the first attempt to relocate the Ark and Uzza's death, he was still the object of divine favor, since his intentions concerning the cultus were sincere. **3–7:** Having many wives and children is a sign of success and divine favor in Chronicles; hence the passage's juxtaposition to the preceding vv.

14.8–17: David defeats the Philistines. These vv. convey a fundamental difference between David and Saul: Unlike Saul, David inquires of God in time of need (war), thereby assuring victory. They also anticipate the reason (given in ch 15) for the disastrous results of David's first attempt to move the Ark. The Heb root "p-r-tz" in v. 11 serves to connect this ch with chs 13 (vv. 2, 11) and 15 (v. 13), indicating that when Israel follows the divine lead, all goes well; when they act rashly ("p-r-tz") and without due concern for the law, punishment follows. **12:** Cf. 2 Sam. 5.21. The latter states that David and his men "carried off" the enemies' idols. Chronicles' formulation is designed to reconcile David's conduct with Deut. 8.25, which demands that such paraphernalia be burnt. Deuteronomy in its final form was not authoritative for the author of Samuel, but was for the Chronicler; given his interest in depicting David as righteous, the v. needed to be adjusted so David would follow "Mosaic" law. It is unclear whether the Chronicler simply changed his text or, as some aver, he interpreted the Heb term in 2 Samuel, "vayisaʾem" "he carried them off," to mean "burnt them"; evidence from the Dead Sea Scrolls may also suggest that this particular change predated the Chronicler.

15.1–29: The Ark successfully moved to Jerusalem. The primary purpose of this ch is to explain, in theological terms, the reason(s) behind David's ultimate success in and pitched a tent for it. [2] Then David gave orders that none but the Levites were to carry the Ark of God, for the LORD had chosen them to carry the Ark of the LORD and to minister to Him forever. [3] David assembled all Israel in Jerusalem to bring up the Ark of the LORD to its place, which he had prepared for it. [4] Then David gathered together the Aaronides and the Levites: [5] the sons of Kohath: Uriel the officer and his kinsmen—120; [6] the sons of Merari: Asaiah the officer and his kinsmen—220; [7] the sons of Gershom: Joel the officer and his kinsmen—130; [8] the sons of Elizaphan: Shemaiah the officer and his kinsmen—200; [9] the sons of Hebron: Eliel the officer and his kinsmen—80; [10] the sons of Uzziel: Amminadab the officer and his kinsmen—112.

[11] David sent for Zadok and Abiathar the priests, and for the Levites: Uriel, Asaiah, Joel, Shemaiah, Eliel, and Amminadab. [12] He said to them, "You are the heads of the clans of the Levites; sanctify yourselves, you and your kinsmen, and bring up the Ark of the LORD God of Israel to [the place] I have prepared for it. [13] a-Because you were not there the first time,-a the LORD our God burst out against us, for we did not show due regard for Him."

[14] The priests and Levites sanctified themselves in order to bring up the Ark of the LORD God of Israel. [15] The Levites carried the Ark of God by means of poles on their shoulders, as Moses had commanded in accordance with the word of the LORD. [16] David ordered the officers of the Levites to install their kinsmen, the singers, with musical instruments, harps, lyres, and cymbals, joyfully making their voices heard. [17] So the Levites installed Heman son of Joel and, of his kinsmen, Asaph son of Berechiah; and, of the sons of Merari their kinsmen, Ethan son of Kushaiah. [18] Together with them were their kinsmen of second rank, Zechariah, Ben, Jaaziel, Shemiramoth, Jehiel, Unni, Eliab, Benaiah, Maaseiah, Mattithiah, Eliphalehu, Mikneiah, Obed-edom and Jeiel the gatekeepers. [19] Also the singers Heman, Asaph, and Ethan to sound the bronze cymbals, [20] and Zechariah, Aziel, Shemiramoth, Jehiel, Unni, Eliab, Maaseiah, and Benaiah with harps a-on alamoth;-a [21] also Mattithiah, Eliphalehu, Mikneiah, Obed-edom, Jeiel, and Azaziah, with lyres to lead a-on the sheminith;-a [22] also Chenaniah, officer of the Levites in song;b he was in charge of the songb because he was a master. [23] Berechiah and Elkanah were gatekeepers for the Ark. [24] Shebaniah, Joshaphat, Nethanel, Amasai, Zechariah, Be-

transporting the Ark. Two issues inform the Chronicler's reformulation of 2 Samuel: (1) the author's need to account for the failure of the first attempt at relocating the Ark, a point not addressed in 2 Samuel, and (2) the author's unwillingness to accept material concerning cultic norms which Samuel's version contains because these conflict with Torah texts and Second Temple practices. **2–11:** The second attempt at bringing the Ark to Jerusalem is successful because David observes the cultic norms of the Torah; see Deut. 10.10 and Num. 7.9, which suggest that Levites and priests must lead all cultic events and ceremonies. **12:** The holiness of the Ark requires that those handling it sanctify themselves; cf. Josh. 3.5–6. **13–15:** David complies with Torah legislation; see Num. 6.9. **16, 19:** The cymbals, like the trumpets, were not used for musical accompaniment; rather, they announced the beginning of a song; see 23.5 n.

a-a Meaning of Heb. uncertain.   b Meaning of Heb. uncertain.

naiah, and Eliezer the priests sounded the trumpets before the Ark of God, and Obededom and Jehiah were gatekeepers for the Ark. [25a]Then David and the elders of Israel and the officers of the thousands who were going to bring up the Ark of the Covenant of the Lord from the house of Obed-edom were joyful. [26]Since God helped the Levites who were carrying the Ark of the Covenant of the Lord, they sacrificed seven bulls and seven rams. [27]Now David and all the Levites who were carrying the Ark, and the singers and Chenaniah, officer of song of the singers, [b]were wrapped[-b] in robes of fine linen, and David wore a linen ephod. [28]All Israel brought up the Ark of the Covenant of the Lord with shouts and with blasts of the horn, with trumpets and cymbals, playing on harps and lyres. [29]As the Ark of the Covenant of the Lord arrived at the City of David, Michal daughter of Saul looked out of the window and saw King David leaping and dancing, and she despised him for it.

16 [c]They brought in the Ark of God and set it up inside the tent that David had pitched for it, and they sacrificed burnt offerings and offerings of well-being before God. [2]When David finished sacrificing the burnt offerings and the offerings of well-being, he blessed the people in the name of the Lord. [3]And he distributed to every person in Israel—man and woman alike—to each a loaf of bread, [b]a cake made in a pan, and a raisin cake.[-b] [4]He appointed Levites to minister before the Ark of the Lord, to invoke, to praise, and to extol the Lord God of Israel: [5]Asaph the chief, Zechariah second in rank, Jeiel, Shemiramoth, Jehiel, Mattithiah, Eliab, Benaiah, Obed-edom, and Jeiel, with harps and lyres, and Asaph sounding the cymbals, [6]and Benaiah and Jahaziel the priests, with trumpets, regularly before the Ark of the Covenant of God. [7]Then, on that day, David first commissioned Asaph and his kinsmen to give praise to the Lord:

a Vv. 25–29 are found also in 2 Sam. 6.12–16.
b-b Meaning of Heb. uncertain.
c With vv. 1–3, cf. 2 Sam. 6.17–19.

25: The recurring use of "joy" in Chronicles emphasizes the importance of the occasion. 2 Sam. 6.12 also mentions this element, but assigns it only to David. Chronicles apparently sought to apply 2 Chron. 8.1, which states that the elders and heads of tribes participated in the dedication of Solomon's Temple, to David's celebration; see 13.4–6 n. **26–27:** In contrast to the wording of 2 Sam. 6.13, Chronicles' listing of sacrificial animals reflects the influence of Priestly formulations in the Torah. **28–29:** Since Chronicles has deleted references to David's excessive ecstasy and the subsequent confrontation between Michal and David (see 2 Sam. 6.20–23), the reference to Michal's response might seem out of place. In fact, it is Chronicles' way of saying that Michal resented David's immense joy in attending to the Ark, a depiction which indicates that Saul's disregard for the cultus was shared by other members of his family. Thus, the theme of Saul's illegitimacy is continued.

16.1–6: The Ark is placed in the tent. 4–6: Following the Priestly tradition incorporated in the Torah (contrast Deuteronomy's Levitical priests; see Deut. 17.9), Chronicles, here and elsewhere, insists on a strict separation between the roles of Levites and priests. The Levites are assigned the duties of singing, guarding the sacred precincts, and generally assisting the priests. The role of blowing the cultic trumpets is reserved for priests, in accordance with Num. 10.8. The trumpets have several functions: to proclaim the presence of the Lord/Ark (here and 15.24, 28), to call for the people to prostrate themselves (2 Chron. 29.27, 28), and to give the signal for prayer (2 Chron. 13.14). For a different function, see Num. 10.9–10. The role of Levites in connection to Temple song is very prominent in Chronicles, but is not clearly attested in earlier sources; it is thus unclear whether this is a new role developed during the Second Temple period.

16.7–36: A medley of parts of Pss. 96, 105, and 106. The exact relation between Chronicles and these psalms has been debated, though it is most likely that Chronicles had the book of Psalms more or less in the form we have it, and here copied out sections of psalms that were relevant to this occasion and were popular among Jews of his time. **7:** Asaph is one of the leading Levitical figures and appears (as does Korah) in many superscriptions in the book of Psalms. Some consider him to be a founder of a guild of Temple singers, while others doubt that he was a historical figure; see

8ª   "Praise the LORD;
call on His name;
proclaim His deeds among the peoples.

9   Sing praises unto Him;
speak of all His wondrous acts.

10   Exult in His holy name;
let all who seek the LORD rejoice.

11   Turn to the LORD, to His might;ᵇ
seek His presence constantly.

12   Remember the wonders He has done;
His portents and the judgments He has
     pronounced,

13   O offspring of Israel, His servant,
O descendants of Jacob, His chosen ones.

14   He is the LORD our God;
His judgments are throughout the earth.

15   Be ever mindful of His covenant,
the promise He gave for a thousand
     generations,

16   that He made with Abraham,
swore to Isaac,

17   and confirmed in a decree for Jacob,
for Israel, as an eternal covenant,

18   saying, 'To you I will give the land of Canaan
as your allotted heritage.'

19   You were then few in number,
a handful, merely sojourning there,

20   wandering from nation to nation,
from one kingdom to another.

21   He allowed no one to oppress them;
He reproved kings on their account,

22   'Do not touch My anointed ones;
do not harm My prophets.'

23ᶜ   "Sing to the LORD, all the earth.
proclaim His victory day after day.

24   Tell of His glory among the nations,
His wondrous deeds among all peoples.

25   For the LORD is great and much acclaimed,
He is held in awe by all divine beings.

26   All the gods of the peoples are mere idols,
but the LORD made the heavens.

27   Glory and majesty are before Him;
strength and joy are in His place.

6.16–17 n. **8–22:** These vv. (= Ps. 105.1–15) describe the LORD's covenant with Abraham. Significantly, Chronicles deletes the subsequent vv. of the psalm, in which Joseph and then the Israelites are in Egypt. This excision is part of Chronicles' reticence concerning periods during which Israel was absent from its land. **23:** Taken from Ps. 96.1–13a, these vv. invite the nations to recognize the LORD's glory and His actions on behalf of Israel. The "universalistic" approach is seen by some as a late biblical (i.e., Second Temple) phenomenon, reflecting the contact between Jews and other peoples; it is unlikely that such an appeal would have been made during David's days.

a With vv. 8–22, cf. Ps. 105.1–15.
b I.e., the Ark; cf. Pss. 78.61; 132.8.
c With vv. 23–33, cf. Ps. 96.1–13.

28   "Ascribe to the LORD, O families of the peoples,
       ascribe to the LORD glory and strength.
29   Ascribe to the LORD the glory of His name,
       bring tribute and enter before Him,
       bow down to the LORD majestic in holiness.
30   Tremble in His presence, all the earth!
       The world stands firm; it cannot be shaken.
31   Let the heavens rejoice and the earth exult;
       let them declare among the nations, "The LORD is
         King!"
32   Let the sea and all within it thunder,
       the fields and everything in them exult;
33   then shall all the trees of the forest shout for joy
       at the presence of the LORD,
       for He is coming to rule the earth.
34   Praise the LORD for He is good;
       His steadfast love is eternal.
35   ᵃDeclare:
       Deliver us, O God, our deliverer,
       and gather us and save us from the nations,
       to acclaim Your holy name,
       to glory in Your praise.

36 Blessed is the LORD, God of Israel, from eternity to eternity." And all the people said, "Amen" and "Praise the LORD."⁻ᵃ

37 He left Asaph and his kinsmen there before the Ark of the Covenant of the LORD to minister before the Ark regularly as each day required, 38 as well as Obed-edom with their kinsmen—68; also Obed-edom son of Jedithun and Hosah as gatekeepers; 39 also Zadok the priest and his fellow priests before the Tabernacle of the LORD at the shrine which was in Gibeon; 40 to sacrifice burnt offerings to the LORD on the altar of the burnt offering regularly, morning and evening, in accordance with what was prescribed in the Teaching of the LORD with which He charged Israel. 41 With them were Heman and Jeduthun and the other selected men designated by name to give praise to the LORD, "For His steadfast love is eternal." 42 Heman and Jeduthun had with them trumpets and cymbals to sound, and instruments for the songs of God; and the sons of Jeduthun were to be at the gate. 43 Then all the people went every one to his home, and David returned to greet his household.

17 ᵇWhen David settled in his palace, David said to the prophet Nathan, "Here I am dwelling in a house of cedar, while the Ark of the Covenant of the LORD

34: A common postexilic liturgical refrain; see v. 41; 2 Chron. 5.13; 7.3, 6; 20.21. Praise or "give thanks" (Heb "hodu") forms an inclusio with the opening, v. 8. **35–36:** Conclusion of prayer (= Ps. 106.47–48). V. 35 is anachronistic: In Chronicles' time most Jews found themselves living in foreign lands, but in David's time all of Israel resided within the borders of its promised land, as understood by Chronicles; see 13.5. (Ps. 106 is generally viewed as an exilic or postexilic composition.) It is possible that the author was willing to allow for this inconsistency in order to tell his contemporaries that the rightful place of every Israelite/Jew is in the land of Israel. The entire medley is traditionally recited as part of the "pesukei dezimrah" ("verses of song"), the opening section of the daily morning prayers. **36–39:** The reference to Gibeon is part of a tradition unique to Chronicles, though it may be based on 1 Kings chs 3, 4–5. In the earlier books, one finds either the Tabernacle or the Ark as the focus of cultic concern, but not both. Moreover, one hears nothing of the Tabernacle after its destruction in Shiloh. Chronicles maintains that both Ark and Tabernacle were concurrently important, with the Ark located in one place and the Tabernacle in another. No explanation is given as to how this situation came about. Some argued that this tradition is Chronicles' way of claiming that Lev. 17.8–9 was observed in every generation, but this explanation entails various difficulties (see vv. 1, 2). See also 2 Chron. 1.3–6.

17.1–15: Rejection of David's request to build an edifice for the Ark and the "dynastic oracle." This is a revision of 2 Sam. 7.1–17, often seen as the culminating center of Samuel. Many differences exist among the Masoretic Text of Samuel, the corresponding LXX, and Chronicles. Some explain Chronicles as reflecting an underlying Heb text different from Masoretic 2 Samuel; others claim that Chronicles used a proto-Samuel

---

a-a Cf. Ps. 106.47–48.   b With this chapter, cf. 2 Sam. 7.

is under tent-cloths." [2]Nathan said to David, "Do whatever you have in mind, for God is with you."

[3]But that same night the word of God came to Nathan: [4]"Go and say to My servant David: Thus said the LORD: You are not the one to build a house for Me to dwell in. [5]From the day that I brought out Israel to this day, I have not dwelt in a house, but have [gone] from tent to tent and from one Tabernacle [to another]. [6]As I moved about wherever Israel went, did I ever reproach any of the judges of Israel whom I appointed to care for My people Israel: Why have you not built Me a house of cedar?

[7]"Further, say thus to My servant David: Thus said the LORD of Hosts: I took you from the pasture, from following the flock, to be ruler of My people Israel, [8]and I have been with you wherever you went, and have cut down all your enemies before you. Moreover, I will give you renown like that of the greatest men on earth. [9]I will establish a home for My people Israel and will plant them firm, so that they shall dwell secure and shall tremble no more. Evil men shall not wear them down anymore as in the past, [10]ever since I appointed judges over My people Israel. I will subdue all your enemies.

And I declare to you: The LORD will build a house[a] for you. [11]When your days are done and you follow your fathers, I will raise up your offspring after you, one of your own sons, and I will establish his kingship. [12]He shall build a house for Me, and I will establish his throne forever. [13]I will be a father to him, and he shall be a son to Me, but I will never withdraw My favor from him as I withdrew it from your predecessor. [14]I will install him in My house and in My kingship forever, and his throne shall be established forever."

a I.e., a dynasty; play on "house" (i.e., Temple) in v. 4.

source, and that 2 Samuel is secondary. At least some of the differences should be attributed to Chronicles' creative reworking of its sources; Chronicles' version of 2 Sam. ch 7 is consistent with its emphases in other parts of Chronicles. (LXX to 2 Samuel, while different from Chronicles, agrees with the latter on many substantive points, further suggesting that both result from tendentious reworking.) **1:** 2 Sam. 7.1 concludes "the LORD had granted him [David] safety from all the enemies around him." Chronicles' deletion

is informed by two considerations: David's alacrity, leading to the request to build a Temple immediately and, second, the fact that David will have more battles to wage, a fact which contradicts 2 Sam. ch 7. See v. 10 n.; 22.9. **4:** *You are not the one to build a house for Me:* Chronicles' reformulation indicates that the construction of a Temple (by someone) is not in doubt (as in 2 Sam. ch 7; see below, v. 15) but that David will not be the builder. **10:** 2 Sam. 7.11 reads: "I will give you safety from all your enemies";

Chronicles' reading again avoids the idea of David's safety. **13:** Most scholars understand the dynastic promise in 2 Sam. 7.14–16 to be absolute; should David's successors sin they will be chastised, but the dynasty will remain intact. (This is a clear reference to the sins committed by Solomon and, perhaps, later Judahite kings; Chronicles omits any mention of such potential sins, so as to avoid even the hint of Solomon's sinning.) Chronicles, by contrast, elsewhere explicitly adopts the position that the dynastic promise is contingent upon fidelity to the commandments (e.g., 28.9; 2 Chron. 7.17–20). The present passage, by its omission of part of 2 Sam. 7.14, 15, allows for the possibility that the promise is granted conditionally. The unconditional dynastic promise is seen by most scholars as chronologically prior; later biblical thinking, reflecting the reality of the cessation of the Davidic dynasty, claims that the divine promise was contingent upon proper religious conduct (e.g., 1 Kings 2.3–4). Some scholars, however, argue that the conditional and unconditional views of the dynastic promise are coeval. They argue that the present passage, with its deletion of part of 2 Sam. 7.14, 15, adopts the unconditional view, while other Chronicles passages endorse the opposing position. See also Pss. 89, 132. **14:** Kingship (Heb "malkhut") may refer generally to Solomon's role as representative of the LORD's kingdom or, more likely, to Solomon's palace; see 2 Chron. 1.18; 2.11. Chronicles views the establishment of a dynasty as directed primarily toward Solomon, since he gives complete expression to divine rule in both cultic and political spheres. (Cf. 2 Sam. 7.16: "your house . . . your kingship . . . your throne.") Chronicles claims that David's dynasty is not his own; rather, he and his descendants sit on the LORD's throne, i.e., they are His representatives on earth (see 1 Chron. 28.5; 29.11; 2 Chron. 13.8). 2 Sam. ch 7, however, views the dynasty as being David's possession or grant, given

15 Nathan spoke to David in accordance with all these words and all this prophecy. 16 Then King David came and sat before the Lord, and he said, "What am I, O Lord God, and what is my family, that You have brought me thus far? 17 Yet even this, O God, has seemed too little to You; for You have spoken of Your servant's house for the future. *·You regard me as a man of distinction,·* O Lord God. 18 What more can David add regarding the honoring of Your servant? You know Your servant. 19 O Lord, *·for Your servant's sake, and of Your own accord,·* You have wrought this great thing, and made known all these great things. 20 O Lord, there is none like You, and there is no other God but You, as we have always heard. 21 And who is like Your people Israel, a unique nation on earth, whom God went and redeemed as His people, winning renown for Yourself for great and marvelous deeds, driving out nations before Your people whom You redeemed from Egypt. 22 You have established Your people Israel as Your very own people forever; and You, O Lord, have become their God.

23 "And now, O Lord, let Your promise concerning Your servant and his house be fulfilled forever; and do as You have promised. 24 Let it be fulfilled that Your name be glorified forever, in that men will say, 'The Lord of Hosts, God of Israel, is Israel's God'; and may the house of Your servant David be established before You. 25 Because You, my God, have revealed to Your servant that You will build a house for him, Your servant has ventured to pray to You. 26 And now, O Lord, You are God and You have made this gracious promise to Your servant. 27 Now, it has pleased You to bless Your servant's house, that it abide before You forever; for You, O Lord, have blessed and are blessed forever."

18 *b*Sometime afterward, David attacked the Philistines and subdued them; and David took Gath and its dependencies from the Philistines. 2 He also defeated the Moabites; the Moabites became tributary vassals of David.

3 David defeated Hadadezer, king of Zobah-hamath,

a-a Meaning of Heb. uncertain.   b With this chapter, cf. 2 Sam. 8.

All successful dynasties in the ancient Near East were expected to establish and maintain a functioning cultic establishment. Accordingly, David is rebuffed and told that he has it backwards: It is the Lord who will grant him a stable dynasty. In other words, David cannot use God to further his own political ambitions; the Temple will be built only when the Lord deems fit. This explanation, as noted, will not suffice for Chronicles, for which tending to the cultus was paramount. Moreover, Chronicles' David has little reason to be concerned over lack of stability, since (in contrast to Samuel's David) he has never been the object of opposition and, indeed, was accepted by the entire nation. The reason that David cannot build the Temple is supplied by the Chronicler only at 22.8, 9: The Temple could not be built by one whose hands were sullied with the blood of human beings.

17.16–27: David's response. The unambiguous reference to the sojourn in Egypt (vv. 21–22) is relatively rare in Chronicles; see introduction. Chronicles, like other biblical texts, is not fully consistent in its editing or its incorporation of earlier traditions. Cf. Solomon's reticence concerning this issue and his emphasis on the Davidic covenant (2 Chron. ch 6), suggesting that the latter has surpassed the former in significance.

18.1–17: David's victories. This ch presents David's military victories and the extension of his empire, particularly to the north/northeast. **1:** 2 Sam. 8.1 states "David attacked the Philistines and subdued them; and David took Metheg-Ammah from the Philistines." Chronicles' shorter version may indicate that its author found Samuel incomprehensible. **2:** The Chronicler shortens the parallel v. at 2 Sam. 8.2, perhaps because David's orders that two-thirds of the Moabites be killed appear to be both ruthless and arbitrary. **3:** Setting up a monument was a means of fixing the boundaries of

to him and his descendants. Stated differently, Chronicles views the Davidic monarchy as a vehicle for the theocratic kingdom, and therefore, anyone who challenges (or does not await the renewal of) the Davidic dynasty rejects the Lord;

see, e.g., 2 Chron. 13.8, 12. **15:** A close reading of 2 Sam. ch 7 suggests David's request is rejected because it stems largely from personal motives (2 Sam. 7.5: "Are you the one to build a house for Me to dwell in?"; cf. v. 4, above).

who was on his way to set up his monument at the Euphrates River. ⁴David captured 1,000 chariots and 7,000 horsemen and 20,000 foot soldiers of his force; and David hamstrung all the chariot horses except for 100, which he retained. ⁵And when the Arameans of Damascus came to the aid of King Hadadezer of Zobah-hamath, David struck down 22,000 of the Arameans. ⁶David stationed [garrisons] in Aram of Damascus, and the Arameans became tributary vassals of David. The LORD gave David victory wherever he went. ⁷David took the gold shields[a] carried by Hadadezer's retinue and brought them to Jerusalem; ⁸and from Tibbath and Cun, towns of Hadadezer, David took a vast amount of copper, from which Solomon made the bronze tank, the columns, and the bronze vessels.

⁹When King Tou of Hamath heard that David had defeated the entire army of King Hadadezer of Zobah, ¹⁰he sent his son Hadoram to King David to greet him and to congratulate him on his military victory over Hadadezer—for Hadadezer had been at war with Tou; [he brought with him] all manner of gold, silver, and copper objects. ¹¹King David dedicated these to the LORD, along with the other silver and gold that he had taken from all the nations: from Edom, Moab, and Ammon; from the Philistines and the Amalekites.

¹²Abshai son of Zeruiah struck down Edom in the Valley of Salt, 18,000 in all. ¹³He stationed garrisons in Edom, and all the Edomites became vassals of David. The LORD gave David victory wherever he went.

¹⁴David reigned over all Israel, and David executed true justice among all his people. ¹⁵Joab son of Zeruiah was commander of the army; Jehoshaphat son of Ahilud was recorder; ¹⁶Zadok son of Ahitub and Abimelech son of Abiathar were priests; Shavsha was scribe; ¹⁷Benaiah son of Jehoiada was commander of the Cherethites and the Pelethites; and David's sons were first ministers of the king.

a Or "quivers."

2 Sam. ch 8. This passage again suggests continuity between David and Solomon as Temple builders, and furthers David's image as the archpatron of the Temple, and as one whose personal wealth was of secondary importance. **10:** Hadoram's name appears at 2 Sam. 8.9 as Joram. Hadoram means "Had(d)u (i.e., Baal) is exalted." Such a name would be natural among Arameans. By contrast, the typically Israelite Yoram, meaning "the LORD is exalted," is surprising. Samuel reflects a "censored" form of the name, whereas Chronicles retains the original form; see 8.33 n. **14:** True justice (Heb "mishpat u-tzedakah") refers, in the Bible and the ancient Near East, to the establishment of social order ("law and order"), the sine qua non of any society. This, together with the establishment and maintenance of a functioning sacrificial cult, was the sign of a successful monarch who was fulfilling his divinely given mandate. **17:** The Cherethites and the Pelethites were mercenary troops whose origin probably lay in the Aegean Sea. Sons . . . first ministers: 2 Sam. 2.18 states that "the sons of David were priests (Heb "kohanim"). Since Torah (Priestly) sources mandate that only descendants of Aaron, Moses' brother, could be priests, commentators have labored to explain the term "kohanim" in 2 Samuel as referring to some office other than priesthood, e.g., (leading) court officials or military advisers; others emend the text of 2 Samuel. The simplest explanation is that the Chronicler could not accept the idea that the sons of David, a Judean, functioned as priests, so he revised the tradition. This explanation also accounts for another difference between Chronicles and Samuel. 2 Sam. 20.26 refers to "Ira, the Yairite . . ."; no such notice appears in Chronicles. The gentilic "Yairite" probably refers to a clan within the Transjordanian tribe of Manasseh, or, possibly, to the town of Kiriath-jearim (see 13.6). Some traditional sources (Targum to 2 Samuel; Tosafists to b. 'Eruv.

a ruler's sovereignty. The second half of this v. (in Heb) is syntactically ambiguous; it is unclear if David or Hadadezer was going to set up his monument. If Hadadezer is the subject of the second half of the v., it then describes David's response to Hadadezer's attempt to free himself from David's subjugation. **4:** Hamstringing horses

rendered them unusable for military (or other) purposes. This v. fits nicely with Chronicles' view of military success as determined by religious merit, not military prowess; see also Deut. 17.16, 20. **8–9:** Chronicles' claim that the copper taken by David was used by Solomon in fashioning Temple appurtenances does not appear in

19 [a]Sometime afterward, Nahash the king of the Ammonites died, and his son succeeded him as king. [2]David said, "I will keep faith with Hanun son of Nahash, since his father kept faith with me." David sent messengers with condolences to him over his father. But when David's courtiers came to the land of Ammon to Hanun, with condolences, [3]the Ammonite officials said to Hanun, "Do you think David is really honoring your father just because he sent you men with condolences? Why, it is to explore, to subvert, and to spy out the land that his courtiers have come to you." [4]So Hanun seized David's courtiers, shaved them, and cut away half of their garments up to the buttocks, and sent them off. [5]When David was told about the men, he dispatched others to meet them, for the men were greatly embarrassed. And the king gave orders, "Stay in Jericho until your beards grow back; then you can return."

[6]The Ammonites realized that they had incurred the wrath of David; so Hanun and the Ammonites sent 1,000 silver talents to hire chariots and horsemen from Aram-naharaim, Aram-maacah, and Zobah. [7]They hired 32,000 chariots, the king of Maacah, and his army, who came and encamped before Medeba. The Ammonites were mobilized from their cities and came to do battle.

[8]On learning this, David sent out Joab and the whole army, [including] the professional fighters. [9]The Ammonites marched out and took up their battle position at the entrance of the city, while the kings who came [took their stand] separately in the open. [10]Joab saw that there was a battle line against him both front and rear. So he made a selection from all the picked men of Israel and arrayed them against the Arameans, [11]and the rest of the troops he put under the command of his brother Abishai and arrayed them against the Ammonites. [12]Joab said, "If the Arameans prove too strong for me, you come to my aid; and if the Ammonites prove too strong for you, I will come to your aid. [13]Let us be strong and resolute for the sake of our people and the towns of our God; and the LORD will do what He deems right."

[14]Joab and the troops with him marched into battle against the Arameans, who fled before him. [15]And when the Ammonites saw that the Arameans had fled, they too fled before his brother Abishai, and withdrew into the city. So Joab went to Jerusalem.

[16]When the Arameans saw that they had been routed by Israel, they sent messengers to bring out the Arameans

63a) understood Ira to be a court official or military adviser, a position adopted by some moderns. Another view found in traditional sources maintains that Ira's father, but not his mother, was a descendant of Aaron. Chronicles' omission of this datum indicates that its author probably understood 2 Samuel as maintaining that Ira was a priest.

19.1–19: More victories for David. This passage is a light reworking of 2 Sam. ch 10. **1–2:** Nahash respected the terms of his treaty (performed "ḥesed," faith) with David and, for that reason, David saw fit to send his condolences. Rabbinic tradents, who understood the Heb term "ḥesed" to mean "acts of kindness," were perplexed by the absence of any unusual expressions of friendship on the part of Nahash. Accordingly, they claimed that David's family members had been killed while in the custody of the king of Moab, save for one brother; the brother found refuge with Nahash, who refused Moab's request to extradite him (*Num. Rab.* 14:3; *Yelammedenu, Va-Yera*). **13:** The formulation of this v., like its parallel in 2 Samuel, expresses the generals' trust in God, the key factor, according to Chronicles, in assuring victory over the enemy. This is a good example of an idea that appears in the sources of Chronicles but gains new importance in Chronicles.

a With this chapter, cf. 2 Sam. 10.

from across the Euphrates; Shophach, Hadadezer's army commander, led them. ¹⁷David was informed of it; he assembled all Israel, crossed the Jordan, and came and took up positions against them. David drew up his forces against Aram; and they fought with him. ¹⁸But the Arameans were put to flight by Israel. David killed 7,000 Aramean charioteers and 40,000 footmen; he also killed Shophach, the army commander. ¹⁹And when all the vassals of Hadadezer saw that they had been routed by Israel, they submitted to David and became his vassals. And the Arameans would not help the Ammonites anymore.

20 ᵃAt the turn of the year, the season when kings go out [to battle], Joab led out the army force and devastated the land of Ammon, and then besieged Rabbah, while David remained in Jerusalem; Joab reduced Rabbah and left it in ruins. ²David took the crown from the head of their king; he found that it weighed a talent of gold, and in it were precious stones. It was placed on David's head. He also carried off a vast amount of booty from the city. ³He led out the people who lived there and ᵇhe hacked them·ᵇ with saws and iron threshing boards and axes;ᶜ David did thus to all the towns of Ammon. Then David and all the troops returned to Jerusalem. ⁴After this, fighting broke out with the Philistines at Gezer; that was when Sibbecai the Hushathite killed Sippai, a descendant of the Rephaim, and they were humbled.

⁵Again there was fighting with the Philistines, and Elhanan son of Jair killed Lahmi, the brother of Goliath the Gittite; his spear had a shaft like a weaver's beam. ⁶Once

a With vv. 1–3, cf. 2 Sam. 11.1; 12.30–31.
b-b Meaning of Heb. uncertain. 2 Sam. 12.31 has "set them to work."
c Heb. megeroth; cf. 2 Sam. 12.31 magzeroth, "axes."

18–19: The Chronicler expands the number found in 2 Sam. 10.18 to glorify David and to emphasize the power of divine assistance.

20.1–8: Defeating Ammon and the Philistines.

20.1–3: Capture of Rabbah.
2 Sam. 12.26–30 states that Joab sent a message reminding David that if he remained in Jerusalem, he would be denied the glory accompanying the impending capture of Rabbah. David then joins his troops and takes part in the conquest. 2 Samuel's version portrays David as a monarch guilty of adultery with Bathsheba and of the abuse of power (leading to the death of Uriah), who also takes the credit for a military victory whose groundwork has been laid by someone else. Chronicles presents a more flattering picture; it makes no mention of Joab's message or David's motive in joining his troops, and states simply that Joab captured and then destroyed Rabbah. See 11.7 n. Following v. 1, 2 Sam. 11.1 presents the story of David and Bathsheba. Chronicles deletes the entire episode, because of its damaging portrayal of David. The disturbing implications of 2 Sam. chs 11–12 were not lost upon rabbinic tradents and medieval exegetes who offered various attempts at mitigating the severity of David's deeds (see *b. Shab.* 56a-b; Isaac Abravanel to 2 Samuel). Some scholars maintain that, as in other instances of deletion, Chronicles is not attempting to deny the tradition of 2 Samuel, which would have been known to his readers; rather, the author has simply selected the material that best suited his interests and goals. **2:** In place of Heb "malkam," "(the crown of) their king," several versions read "Milkom," i.e., the (crown of) the national god of Ammon. (The early Heb text was written without vowels, so the consonantal text may be read either way. Cf. Zeph. 1.5.) Rabbinic sources (*b. A. Z.* 44a) reflect the same understanding. Similar uncertainty attends 2 Sam. ch 12. *A talent of gold:* The immense weight, approximately 34 kg (75 lbs), has been variously explained. **3:** The words *he hacked them* have been variously interpreted, e.g., "he ruled over them, placing upon them hewing of stones."

20.4–8: Battles with the Philistines. 2 Sam. 21.18–19. The term *Rephaim,* in various Semitic languages and biblical Heb, bears several meanings; here the reference is to "giants" or "megaliths." The Bible frequently ascribes Transjordanian provenance to these beings. This v. discusses one whose origin lay in the city of Gath (v. 8, below), along the coastal plain. **6:** 2 Sam. 21.19 states: "Elhanan son of Jaare-oregim the Bethlehemite killed Goliath the Gittite, whose spear had a shaft like a weaver's bar." This seems to contradict 1 Sam. ch 17, which states that David killed Goliath. Although it is likely that Samuel preserves two variant traditions, a rabbinic tradition (Targum to 2 Sam. 21; *Ruth Rab.* 2.2) claimed that David and Elhanan were one and the same. A similar position is adopted by some again there was fighting at Gath. There was a giant of a man who had twenty-four fingers [and toes], six [on each hand] and six [on each foot]; he too was descended from the Raphah. [7] When he taunted Israel, Jonathan son of David's brother Shimea killed him. [8] These were descended from the Raphah in Gath, and they fell by the hands of David and his men.

21 [a]Satan arose against Israel and incited David to number Israel. [2] David said to Joab and to the commanders of the army, "Go and count Israel from Beersheba to Dan and bring me information as to their number." [3] Joab answered, "May the LORD increase His people a hundredfold; my lord king, are they not all subjects of my lord? Why should my lord require this? Why should it be a cause of guilt for Israel?"

[4] However, the king's command to Joab remained firm, so Joab set out and traversed all Israel; he then came to Jerusalem. [5] Joab reported to David the number of the people that had been recorded. All Israel comprised 1,100,000 ready to draw the sword, while in Judah there were 470,000 men ready to draw the sword. [6] He did not record

a With vv. 1–26, cf. 2 Sam. 24.

modern commentators, who argue that David was a throne name, while Elhanan was the king's given name. One medieval exegete (Isaiah of Terrani) argued that Goliath of 2 Sam. ch 21 was not the same warrior referred to in 1 Sam. ch 17. Chronicles' formulation probably reflects the author's attempt to reconcile the two different traditions preserved in Samuel; thus, David killed Goliath, while Goliath's brother was slain by Elhanan. Alternatively, Chronicles may result from textual corruption, or a different underlying text, of 2 Sam. 21.17.

21.1–26: David's census and consequences. The differences between Chronicles' version and 2 Sam. ch 24 are numerous and substantive, leading to divergent views regarding the textual history of both passages. Chronicles shares many features with 4QSam[a] (one of the Dead Sea Scrolls from Qumran), yet still differs from it in fundamental re-

spects. The following remarks relate to the Masoretic Text alone. In 2 Samuel this episode appears in a closing addendum or appendix to the book. It concludes with the notice that the plague has come to a close, with no hint of a logical nexus between this incident and the opening chs of 1 Kings. Indeed, the first chs in Kings deal with David's last days and the rocky transition to Solomon's rule. Finally, 2 Samuel does not indicate when in David's career this episode took place. In Chronicles this story, which takes place while David is relatively young (see 23.1), serves as a prelude to the choice of the Temple site. In the last century, several scholars saw the divinely guided selection of the Temple site as part of the book's polemic—and that of Second Temple Judaism, generally—against the Samaritans, who maintained that Mt. Gerizim (in Shechem), rather than Jerusalem, constituted the "chosen place." This position is unlikely, since ten-

sions between Samaritans and Jews reached their height during the Hasmonean period and the establishment of the cultic site on Mt. Gerizim can be dated no earlier than the early 2nd century BCE, well after the accepted date(s) of Chronicles' composition. More likely, Chronicles' point is that all aspects of the Israelite/Jewish Temple and cultus are determined by the divine will, not human caprice, a theme repeated elsewhere. **1:** 2 Sam. 24.1 states that "the anger of the LORD again flared up against Israel" and, consequently, incited David to sin so as to bring (further) guilt upon the people. There is no hint as to the cause of this state of affairs, however. Chronicles resolves some of the difficulty by eliminating reference to the LORD's anger. Furthermore, Chronicles mitigates the difficulties created by 2 Samuel by claiming that David was incited by an intermediary, Satan. Many scholars understand the Heb "satan" to refer to the infamous heavenly being, but it is more likely that it here refers to a human adversary. The ascription of David's incitement to a divine being accomplishes little, since he is submissive to the divine will; ultimately, then, the LORD stands behind David's offense. For these reasons, the term has been interpreted as referring here to a human (possibly, military) adversary, who sought to cause David harm by inciting him to execute the census. **3–5:** Israel, like other ancient societies, viewed census taking, unless given explicit divine sanction, as taboo (e.g., Exod. 30.11–16). While the reasons for this taboo are not clearly explained in biblical texts, it is likely that Chronicles opposed this practice, frequently associated with military preparations, because it implies that martial strength, rather than religious merit and divine providence, is primarily responsible for victory in battle. **6:** 2 Samuel makes no reference to the exclusion of Levi and Benjamin. The common denominator between the two tribes is their intimate connecamong them Levi and Benjamin, because the king's command had become repugnant to Joab. [7] God was displeased about this matter and He struck Israel.

[8] David said to God, "I have sinned grievously in having done this thing; please remit the guilt of Your servant, for I have acted foolishly." [9] The LORD ordered Gad, David's seer: [10] "Go and tell David: Thus said the LORD: I offer you three things; choose one of them and I will bring it upon you." [11] Gad came to David and told him, "Thus said the LORD: Select for yourself [12] a three-year famine; or that you be swept away three months before your adversaries with the sword of your enemies overtaking you; or three days of the sword of the LORD, pestilence in the land, the angel of the LORD wreaking destruction throughout the territory of Israel. Now consider what reply I shall take back to Him who sent me." [13] David said to Gad, "I am in great distress. Let me fall into the hands of the LORD, for His compassion is very great; and let me not fall into the hands of men."

[14] The LORD sent a pestilence upon Israel, and 70,000 men fell in Israel. [15] God sent an angel to Jerusalem to destroy it, but as he was about to wreak destruction, the LORD saw and renounced further punishment and said to the destroying angel, "Enough! Stay your hand!" The angel of the LORD was then standing by the threshing floor of Ornan the Jebusite. [16] David looked up and saw the angel of the LORD standing between heaven and earth, with a drawn sword in his hand directed against Jerusalem. David and the elders, covered in sackcloth, threw themselves on their faces. [17] David said to God, "Was it not I alone who ordered the numbering of the people? I alone am guilty, and have caused severe harm; but these sheep, what have they done? O LORD my God, let Your hand fall upon me and my father's house, and let not Your people be plagued!" [18] The angel of the LORD told Gad to inform David that David should go and set up an altar to the LORD on the threshing floor of Ornan the Jebusite. [19] David went up, following Gad's instructions, which he had delivered in the name of the LORD. [20] Ornan too saw the angel; his four sons who were with him hid themselves while Ornan kept on threshing wheat. [21] David came to Ornan; when Ornan looked up, he saw David and came off the threshing floor and bowed low to David, with his face to the ground. [22] David said to Ornan, "Sell me the site of the threshing floor, that I may build on it an altar to the LORD. Sell it to me at the full price, that the plague against the people will be checked." [23] Ornan said to David, "Take it and let my lord the king do whatever he

tion to Israel's cultic worship. The Levites were central to the cultus, and, according to Jewish tradition, the southern edge of Benjamin included part of Jerusalem. Moreover, Gibeon, the site of the Tabernacle (see 16.39), was also in Benjamin. Thus, Chronicles distances these tribes from any involvement in David's misdeed. Some see Chronicles' position as related to its view of theodicy: Jerusalem was spared because the Levites and Benjamin had no part in the census. The Jewish historian Josephus (late 1st century CE) claims that the exclusion of these two tribes was the result not of Joab's refusal, but of David's regret (over his decision) during the course of the census (*Ant.* 7.320). **6–17:** David's request that he and his household alone be punished is surprising, if one attributes to Chronicles a strict view of retribution and personal accountability. What sin have the family members committed, not to mention the seventy thousand citizens who perished? It is possible that the taboo associated with census taking is sui generis. Alternatively, this passage may indicate that Chronicles, in principle, accepts the prevalent biblical notion of vicarious punishment; see introduction. The description of the angel in v. 16 is more detailed than that of Samuel, and may reflect more developed notions of angelology in Second Temple times. **18–27:** 2 Sam. ch 24 states that David paid fifty shekels of silver. Chronicles' version may reflect a different economic system; alternatively, Chronicles is making the point that no amount is too great concerning the cultus. **28–30:** This is part of Chronicles' view that the locus for sacrifice was the altar (made in Moses' day) located in the Tabernacle. See 16.36–39 n.

22.1: Selection of the Temple site. The heavenly fire pinpoints the precise location chosen by the LORD for construction of the Temple and also serves as a sign of divine favor; see Lev. 9.24; 1 Kings 18.38; 2 Chron. 7.3 n., in connecsees fit. See, I donate oxen for burnt offerings, and the threshing boards for wood, as well as wheat for a meal offering—I donate all of it." ²⁴ But King David replied to Ornan, "No, I will buy them at the full price. I cannot make a present to the LORD of what belongs to you, or sacrifice a burnt offering that has cost me nothing." ²⁵ So David paid Ornan for the site 600 shekels' worth of gold. ²⁶ And David built there an altar to the LORD and sacrificed burnt offerings and offerings of well-being. He invoked the LORD, who answered him with fire from heaven on the altar of burnt offerings. ²⁷ The LORD ordered the angel to return his sword to its sheath. ²⁸ At that time, when David saw that the LORD answered him at the threshing floor of Ornan the Jebusite, then he sacrificed there—²⁹ for the Tabernacle of the LORD, which Moses had made in the wilderness, and the altar of burnt offerings, were at that time in the shrine at Gibeon, ³⁰ and David was unable to go to it to worship God because he was terrified by the sword of the angel of the LORD. ¹ David said, "Here will be the House of the LORD and here the altar of burnt offerings for Israel."

22

² David gave orders to assemble the aliens living in the land of Israel, and assigned them to be hewers, to quarry and dress stones for building the House of God. ³ Much iron for nails for the doors of the gates and for clasps did David lay aside, and so much copper it could not be weighed, ⁴ and cedar logs without number—for the Sidonians and the Tyrians brought many cedar logs to David.

⁵ For David thought, "My son Solomon is an untried youth, and the House to be built for the LORD is to be made exceedingly great to win fame and glory throughout all the lands; let me then lay aside material for him." So David laid aside much material before he died. ⁶ Then he summoned his son Solomon and charged him with building the House for the LORD God of Israel.

⁷ David said to Solomon, "My son, I wanted to build a House for the name of the LORD my God. ⁸ But the word of the LORD came to me, saying, 'You have shed much blood and fought great battles; you shall not build a House for

David's image by suggesting that he did everything allowable for building the Temple short of constructing the structure itself. The Chronicler thus presents the construction of the Temple as a two-part venture, begun by David and completed by Solomon, again suggesting strong continuity between David and Solomon. **22.2–19:** Chronicles repeatedly makes the point that, although David was denied the honor of building the Temple, he did everything in his power to lay its groundwork (see below, vv. 11–16). Accordingly, David prepares the labor force and raw materials which, because of the magnitude and majesty of the Temple, are described as being without limit (v. 16). This is a recurring theme in Chronicles. Since the Second Temple, for most of its duration, was a modest structure, this theme is Chronicles' clarion to his contemporaries to "recreate" the Temple's grandeur. **2:** The term "gerim," aliens, here refers to the indigenous peoples of Canaan who had been subdued, but retained a distinct identity. Chronicles does not address their legal status; their use as forced laborers may reflect Deut. 20.10–18 and, especially, Josh. 9.27. The claim that the arduous work was carried out by the labor of aliens may indicate that the ideal king spares his own people from such labor; see 2 Chron. 2.16–17; 8.8, 9. **4:** For a similar statement concerning Tyrians and Sidonians, see 2 Chron. 2.1–15. The present v. implies that these northern neighbors donated their services and materials, a sign of their admiration for David or the importance that they attached to the Temple project; cf. 14.1. **5–10:** This explanation of David's disqualification from building the Temple, put in the form of a divine oracle (v. 8), is unique to Chronicles; Temple and bloodshed do not go hand in hand. True, David's wars were justified and, moreover, a sign of David's righteousness and success; still, tainted hands cannot build the Temple. Whereas 1 Kings 5.17

tion with Solomon's dedication of the Temple. Chronicles again views David and Solomon as two parallel, continuous personalities. David's reasoning here is simple: Since the altar and Tabernacle built in Moses' day were located in Gibeon, the divine instruction concerning the locus for David's offering (along with the heavenly fire)

proves that Gibeon is merely a temporary phase; the permanent "chosen" site is in Jerusalem.

22.2–29.25: David's preparations for the Temple, its service, and transfer of power to Solomon. This entire section has no parallel in other biblical sources. The Chronicler composed it to bolster

My name for you have shed much blood on the earth in My sight. [9] But you will have a son who will be a man at rest, for I will give him rest from all his enemies on all sides; Solomon[a] will be his name and I shall confer peace[b] and quiet on Israel in his time. [10] He will build a House for My name; he shall be a son to Me and I to him a father, and I will establish his throne of kingship over Israel forever.' [11] Now, my son, may the LORD be with you, and may you succeed in building the House of the LORD your God as He promised you would. [12] Only let God give you sense and understanding and put you in charge of Israel and the observance of the Teaching of the LORD your God. [13] Then you shall succeed, if you observantly carry out the laws and the rules that the LORD charged Moses to lay upon Israel. Be strong and of good courage; do not be afraid or dismayed. [14] See, [c-]by denying myself,[-c] I have laid aside for the House of the LORD one hundred thousand talents of gold and one million talents of silver, and so much copper and iron it cannot be weighed; I have also laid aside wood and stone, and you shall add to them. [15] An abundance of workmen is at your disposal—hewers, workers in stone and wood, and every kind of craftsman in every kind of material—[16] gold, silver, copper, and iron without limit. Go and do it, and may the LORD be with you."

[17] David charged all the officers of Israel to support his son Solomon, [18] "See, the LORD your God is with you, and

a Heb. Shelomoh.　　　*b Heb.* shalom.　　　*c-c With Targum; or "in my poverty."*

claims that David was engaged in warfare throughout his life, leaving no time for Temple building, Chronicles claims that David's wars came to a close well before his demise (see 22.18). It was therefore necessary to account for David's failure to establish a Temple. Deut. 12.9 indicates that the Temple is to be built only after Israel arrives at its "allotted haven." Whereas Deuteronomy and the Deuteronomistic History mean by this "rest for the nation," Chronicles emphasizes the notion that the LORD finds rest among His people. **9:** This v. puns on Solomon's name: "Shelomoh" expresses the idea that in his day peace ("shalom") and quiet will prevail (see translators' notes *a, b*). Chronicles employs this literary technique elsewhere. By calling

Solomon a man at rest, Chronicles shifts the rest required for the Temple's construction from David's reign (as in 2 Samuel) to Solomon. Chronicles' description, here and elsewhere, ignores 1 Kings chs 1–2, which states that Solomon's accession involved subterfuge and elimination of competitors and other "undesirables." Chronicles' reformulation expresses the view that the two earthly expressions of divine sovereignty—the Temple cultus and the Davidic dynasty—were divinely determined, leaving no room for dissent. **10:** The terms *father* and *son* here denote covenantal relationships between the two parties. The term *son* may also signify legal adoption, in which the son represents the interests of the family (Ps. 2.5–7). **11–16:** This

literary unit is framed by the words *the LORD be with you.* The use of such devices is common in Chronicles. David encourages Solomon, reminding him that success in executing construction of the Temple hinges on God's granting him wisdom and on his observance of God's Torah. Whereas Kings' Solomon is renowned for his judicial wisdom and general knowledge, Chronicles focuses on Solomon's wisdom as manifest, primarily, in connection with organization of all aspects of the Temple's construction; see, e.g., 2 Chron. 2.11. This section anticipates many of the qualites of Solomon that are depicted in 1 Kings and 2 Chron. **12:** The phrase *observance of the Teaching ("torah") of the LORD your God* is reflective of Chronicles' era, in which proper conduct was defined exclusively in accordance with the laws of the (authoritative form of the) Torah; cf. the less legal formulation at 1 Kings 8.25. These vv., especially 12–13, employ a Moses-Joshua typology in their depiction of the relationship of David and Solomon (see Deut. 3.28; 31.7–8; Josh. 1.5–9). This Moses-Joshua typology expresses the view that David, like Moses, laid the groundwork for Israel's future life, though he himself did not live to see its realization. In addition, the smooth transition from Moses to Joshua, decreed by God and warmly endorsed by the people (Josh. 1.16–18), parallels Chronicles' depiction of the transfer of power from David to Solomon. Finally, the days of Moses and Joshua constitute Israel's classic "golden age," much as the reigns of David and Solomon form the golden age of Judah's monarchy. For Moses-David typology, see 2 Chron. chs 13–14. **14–16:** David again claims that he has prepared building materials, as well as workers and craftsmen. This formulation is reminiscent of Exod. 31.1–6; 35.10ff. Chronicles, here and elsewhere, draws an analogy between the Mosaic Tabernacle and the First Temple, in order to accentuate the continuity, authen-

He will give you rest on every side, for He delivered the inhabitants of the land into my hand so that the land lies conquered before the Lord and before His people. ¹⁹ Now, set your minds and hearts on worshiping the Lord your God, and go build the Sanctuary of the Lord your God so that you may bring the Ark of the Covenant of the Lord and the holy vessels of God to the house that is built for the name of the Lord."

23 When David reached a ripe old age, he made his son Solomon king over Israel. ² Then David assembled all the officers of Israel and the priests and the Levites. ³ The Levites, from the age of thirty and upward, were counted; the head-count of their males was 38,000: ⁴ of these there were 24,000 in charge of the work of the House of the Lord, 6,000 officers and magistrates, ⁵ 4,000 gatekeepers, and 4,000 for praising the Lord "with instruments I devised for singing praises." ⁶ David formed them into divisions:

The sons of Levi: Gershon, Kohath, and Merari. ⁷ The Gershonites: Ladan and Shimei. ⁸ The sons of Ladan: Jehiel the chief, Zetham, and Joel—3. ⁹ The sons of Shimei: Shelomith, Haziel, and Haran—3. These were the chiefs of the clans of the Ladanites. ¹⁰ And the sons of Shimei: Jahath, Zina, Jeush, and Beriah; these were the sons of Shimei—4. ¹¹ Jahath was the chief and Zizah the second, but Jeush and Beriah did not have many children, so they were enrolled together as a single clan. ¹² The sons of Kohath: Amram, Izhar, Hebron, and Uzziel—4. ¹³ The sons of Amram: Aaron and Moses. Aaron was set apart, he and his sons, forever, to be consecrated as most holy, to make burnt offerings to the Lord and serve Him and pronounce blessings in His name forever. ¹⁴ As for Moses, the man of God, his sons were named after the tribe of Levi. ¹⁵ The sons of Moses: Gershom and Eliezer. ¹⁶ The sons of Gershom: Shebuel the chief. ¹⁷ And the sons of Eliezer were: Rehabiah the chief. Eliezer had no other sons, but the sons of Rehabiah were very numerous. ¹⁸ The sons of Izhar: Shelomith the chief. ¹⁹ The sons of Hebron: Jeriah the chief, Amariah the second, Jahaziel the third, and Jekameam the fourth. ²⁰ The sons of Uzziel: Micah the chief and Isshiah the second. ²¹ The sons of Merari: Mahli and Mushi. The sons of Mahli: Eleazar and Kish. ²² Eleazar died having no sons but only daughters; the sons of Kish, their kinsmen, married them. ²³ The sons of Mushi: Mahli, Eder, and Jeremoth—3.

²⁴ These are the sons of Levi by clans, with their clan chiefs as they were enrolled, with a list of their names by

ticity, and antiquity of Israel's sacrificial cult. **17–19:** David employs the same terms, used in the previous vv., when addressing the nation's officers; compare Moses' charge in Deut. 30.6–8. **19:** *Worshiping* (Heb "lidrosh"), specifically, attending to the Temple cultus. As in Deuteronomy (e.g., 12.11), God's name rather than God resides in the Temple.

23.1–27.34: David's administration. On the basis of repetitions and contradictions, many scholars argue that parts of this section are secondary, disagreeing only on the particulars. Others, however, maintain that these chs are an integral part of the original, and explain the repetitions and contradictions as either intentional literary flourishes or the result of Chronicles' incorporation of variant traditions. **23.1–2:** David takes a census of the Levites. The Levites, who were not included in David's earlier census, are now counted. This census was probably carried out in order to assess the organization of the Temple, not for David's own sake; hence, there is no criticism of David. This separate census parallels the practice of Moses' day; see Num. 3.14–39. The introduction to the ch suggests a smooth transition between David and Solomon, in sharp contrast to the end of 2 Samuel and the beginning of 1 Kings. **5:** Chronicles credits David with another feature of Temple worship: fashioning the instruments; see 2 Chron. 7.6; 29.26, 27. Ch 29.25 claims that the use of these instruments was, ultimately, divinely ordained. **13:** The end of this v. is reminiscent of Deut. 10.8 which, however, applies to the entire tribe of Levi (the "Levitical priests"); following Priestly norms found in the Torah, it is applied to priests only. The first part of Deut. 10.8 has informed the Levites' role at 1 Chron. 15.2. **23–32:** This passage involves a shift from v. 2, leading some scholars to posit different authorship for the vv.; this argument, however, is not compelling. David introduces an innovation by allow-

heads, who did the work of the service of the House of the
LORD from the age of twenty and upward. 25 For David
said, "The LORD God of Israel has given rest to His people
and made His dwelling in Jerusalem forever. 26 Therefore
the Levites need not carry the Tabernacle and all its various service vessels." 27 Among the last acts of David was
the counting of the Levites from the age of twenty and upward. 28 For their appointment was alongside the Aaronites for the service of the House of the LORD, to look
after the courts and the chambers, and the purity of all the
holy things, and the performance of the service of the
House of God, 29 and the rows of bread, and the fine flour
for the meal offering, and the unleavened wafers, and the
cakes made on the griddle and soaked, and every measure
of capacity and length; 30 and to be present every morning
to praise and extol the LORD, and at evening too, 31 and
whenever offerings were made to the LORD, according to
the quantities prescribed for them, on sabbaths, new
moons and holidays, regularly, before the LORD; 32 and so
to keep watch over the Tent of Meeting, over the holy
things, and over the Aaronites their kinsmen, for the service of the House of the LORD.

24 The divisions of the Aaronites were:
The sons of Aaron: Nadab and Abihu, Eleazar and
Ithamar. 2 Nadab and Abihu died in the lifetime of their
father, and they had no children, so Eleazar and Ithamar
served as priests.
3 David, Zadok of the sons of Eleazar, and Ahimelech of
the sons of Ithamar divided them into offices by their
tasks. 4 The sons of Eleazar turned out to be more numerous by male heads than the sons of Ithamar, so they divided the sons of Eleazar into sixteen chiefs of clans and
the sons of Ithamar into eight clans. 5 They divided them
by lot, both on an equal footing, since they were all sanctuary officers and officers of God—the sons of Eleazar and
the sons of Ithamar. 6 Shemaiah son of Nathanel, the
scribe, who was of the Levites, registered them under the
eye of the king, the officers, and Zadok the priest, and
Ahimelech son of Abiathar, and the chiefs of clans of the

functioning cultic establishment
demanded more personnel or, as
indicated by biblical sources, that
the number of Levites living in
postexilic and Second Temple
Judah was quite small (see Ezra
8.15–20); accordingly, it was necessary to enlist all those of adult age.
David is presented as a legislator,
again signaling a role parallel to
that of Moses. **26:** *Need not:* The
Aramaic Targum understands this
v. to mean that Levites were no
longer allowed to move the cultic
vessels. **28:** The duties assigned to
the Levites include tasks wholly
unattested in earlier sources, as
well as tasks mentioned in these
sources but not assigned to any
specific group (see, e.g., Lev.
24.5–9). Numbers (3.5–9; 18.2–6)
does state that the Levites shall
guard the Tabernacle and serve the
priests, but the precise nature of
their service is not explained; the
Chronicler fills in this gap, most
likely attributing practices of his
period to that of David. The net result is that the Levites perform
most of the Temple duties and
make the daily Temple service
possible. The priests are limited to
sacrificing, blowing the trumpets,
and "blessing" in the LORD's
name. **30–31:** The cultic songs accompany the morning and afternoon or evening services together
with the burnt offering, i.e., they
have no independent role. They
are also performed on the Sabbath,
new moon, and pilgrimage festivals; 2 Chron. 2.4; 8.13; 31.3. In
Psalms, we only have a single
psalm attributed to one of these
occasions, to the Sabbath (Ps. 92),
though liturgical texts found
among the Dead Sea Scrolls reflect
a more extensive liturgy. **32:** Service (Heb "'avodah") as a generic
term for Levitical responsibilities
is unattested in Torah texts,
where it refers to physical labor
(portage). This development continues in postbiblical Heb, where
"'avodah" means "prayer."

24.1–19: Sons of Aaron. Chronicles claims that the existence of
twenty-four priestly divisions, a
familiar part of Second Temple

ing (or, perhaps, requiring) Levites
to assume their duties at the age of
twenty, rather than the age of
thirty or twenty-five, as set forth in
the Torah (Num. 4.3, 23, 39, 47).
The rationale is that the age of
thirty was necessary in the wilderness period, when carrying the
Ark required stronger or more re-

sponsible and experienced cultic
personnel; a permanent cultus
made such age restrictions unnecessary. This is apparently an example of Chronicles attributing contemporary cultic norms to hoary
antiquity and, in particular, to
David. Historically, the change in
policy may reflect the fact that a

priests and Levites—ᵃ one clan more taken for Eleazar for each one taken of Ithamar.ᵃ

7 The first lot fell on Jehoiarib; the second on Jedaiah; 8 the third on Harim; the fourth on Seorim; 9 the fifth on Malchijah; the sixth on Mijamin; 10 the seventh on Hakkoz; the eighth on Abijah; 11 the ninth on Jeshua; the tenth on Shecaniah; 12 the eleventh on Eliashib; the twelfth on Jakim; 13 the thirteenth on Huppah; the fourteenth on Jeshebeab; 14 the fifteenth on Bilgah; the sixteenth on Immer; 15 the seventeenth on Hezir; the eighteenth on Happizzez; 16 the nineteenth on Pethahiah; the twentieth on Jehezkel; 17 the twenty-first on Jachin; the twenty-second on Gamul; 18 the twenty-third on Delaiah; the twenty-fourth on Maaziah.

19 According to this allocation of offices by tasks, they were to enter the House of the LORD as was laid down for them by Aaron their father, as the LORD God of Israel had commanded him.

20 The remaining Levites: the sons of Amram: Shubael; the sons of Shubael: Jehdeiah; 21 Rehabiah. The sons of Rehabiah: Isshiah, the chief. 22 Izharites: Shelomoth. The sons of Shelomoth: Jahath 23 and Benai, Jeriah; the second, Amariah; the third, Jahaziel; the fourth, Jekameam. 24 The sons of Uzziel: Micah. The sons of Micah: Shamir. 25 The brother of Micah: Isshiah. The sons of Isshiah: Zechariah. 26 The sons of Merari: Mahli and Mushi. The sons of Jaazaiah, his son—27 the sons of Merari by Jaazaiah his son: Shoham, Zakkur, and Ibri. 28 Mahli: Eleazar; he had no sons. 29 Kish: the sons of Kish: Jerahmeel. 30 The sons of Mushi: Mahli, Eder, and Jerimoth. These were the sons of the Levites by their clans.

31 These too cast lots corresponding to their kinsmen, the sons of Aaron, under the eye of King David and Zadok and Ahimelech and the chiefs of the clans of the priests and Levites, on the principle of "chief and youngest brother alike."

25 David and the officers of the army set apart for service the sons of Asaph, of Heman, and of Jeduthun, who prophesied to the accompaniment of lyres, harps, and cymbals. The list of men who performed this work, according to their service, was:

2 Sons of Asaph: Zaccur, Joseph, Nethaniah, and Asarelah—sons of Asaph under the charge of Asaph, who prophesied by order of the king. 3 Jeduthun—the sons of Jeduthun: Gedaliah, Zeri, Jeshaiah, Hashabiah, Matti-

life, was David's innovation. This passage is viewed by many as secondary. **7:** Order established by lot. The Maccabees trace their lineage to Jehoiarib, which has led some to argue that the list is of 2nd-century provenance; this is unconvincing.

24.20–31: More sons of Levi. This list is frequently thought to reflect an updated version of 23.6–23.

25.1–31: The musicians/singers. The placement of this group following the Levites reflects their related roles in the cultus. **1–3:** Another facet of Chronicles' views on prophecy. It is possible that the Levitical prophecy of these vv. is a kind of cultic and musically inspired prophecy, but more likely Chronicles viewed the musical performance itself as a form of prophecy, i.e., written or performed under prophetic inspiration. Chronicles claims that the musical aspects of the Levites' activity are, like other features of Israel's cultic service, the product of divine inspiration. (Even so, precisely what is intended by this position, viz., the "lyrics" or musical arrangement, etc., is uncertain.) For earlier examples of music as part of prophetic ecstasy, see 1 Sam. 10.5. **1:** Asaph, Heman, and Jeduthun (elsewhere: Ethan) appear in the superscriptions (introits) to several compositions in the book of Psalms (e.g., 50, 88, 39). These figures, about whom little (historically reliable) information is known, are viewed here as the founders of the cultic guilds bearing their names.

---

a-a *Meaning of Heb. uncertain.*

thiah—6, under the charge of their father Jeduthun, who, accompanied on the harp, prophesied, praising and extolling the LORD. ⁴Heman—the sons of Heman: Bukkiah, Mattaniah, Uzziel, Shebuel, Jerimoth, Hananiah, Hanani, Eliathah, Giddalti, Romamti-ezer, Joshbekashah, Mallothi, Hothir, and Mahazioth; ⁵all these were sons of Heman, the seer of the king, [who uttered] prophecies of God for His greater glory. God gave Heman fourteen sons and three daughters; ⁶all these were under the charge of their father for the singing in the House of the LORD, to the accompaniment of cymbals, harps, and lyres, for the service of the House of God by order of the king. Asaph, Jeduthun, and Heman—⁷their total number with their kinsmen, trained singers of the LORD—all the masters, 288.

⁸They cast lots for shifts on the principle of "small and great alike, like master like apprentice."

⁹The first lot fell to Asaph—to Joseph; the second, to Gedaliah, he and his brothers and his sons—12; ¹⁰the third, to Zaccur: his sons and his brothers—12; ¹¹the fourth, to Izri: his sons and his brothers—12; ¹²the fifth, to Nethaniah: his sons and his brothers—12; ¹³the sixth, to Bukkiah: his sons and his brothers—12; ¹⁴the seventh, to Jesarelah: his sons and his brothers—12; ¹⁵the eighth, to Jeshaiah: his sons and his brothers—12; ¹⁶the ninth, to Mattaniah: his sons and his brothers—12; ¹⁷the tenth, to Shimei: his sons and his brothers—12; ¹⁸the eleventh to Azarel: his sons and his brothers—12; ¹⁹the twelfth, to Hashabiah: his sons and his brothers—12; ²⁰the thirteenth, to Shubael: his sons and his brothers—12; ²¹the fourteenth, to Mattithiah: his sons and his brothers—12; ²²the fifteenth, to Jeremoth: his sons and his brothers—12; ²³the sixteenth, to Hananiah: his sons and his brothers—12; ²⁴the seventeenth, to Joshbekashah: his sons and his brothers—12; ²⁵the eighteenth, to Hanani: his sons and his brothers—12; ²⁶the nineteenth, to Mallothi: his sons and his brothers—12; ²⁷the twentieth, to Eliathah: his sons and his brothers—12; ²⁸the twenty-first, to Hothir: his sons and his brothers—12; ²⁹the twenty-second, to Giddalti: his sons and his brothers—12; ³⁰the twenty-third, to Mahazioth: his sons and his brothers—12; ³¹the twenty-fourth, to Romamti-ezer: his sons and his brothers—12.

26

The divisions of the gatekeepers: Korahites: Meshelemiah son of Kore, of the sons of Asaph. ²Sons of Meshelemiah: Zechariah the firstborn, Jediael the second, Zebadiah the third, Jathniel the fourth, ³Elam the fifth, Jehohanan the sixth, Eliehoenai the seventh. ⁴Sons of Obed-edom: Shemaiah the first-born, Jehozabad the sec-

4: This difficult v. has been emended and reconstructed by many scholars, resulting in a song of praise, rather than the present list of sons. **5:** The description of Heman as the seer of the king (LXX: royal musicians) is an expression of the inspired nature of the cultic music and the activity of the leaders of the Levitical singers/musicians (see v. 1 n.). Contrary to some opinions, Chronicles does not portray all Levites as prophets. For abundance of children as sign of divine favor, see 14.3–7. **6–8:** Some scholars understand v. 6 to mean that Heman's daughters were part of the Temple orchestra (cf. Ezra 2.65; Neh. 7.67); the v. probably refers only to the sons listed in v. 4, however. **9–31:** Chronicles again credits David with establishing cultic norms. Division of the Levites into twenty-four watches appears only in Second Temple sources. The Levites are assigned by Num. 18.4–6 to guard the Tabernacle against encroachment by outsiders, an act which unleashes the divine wrath. Chronicles assigns the Levite clans specific locations, but does not indicate whether their primary role is to prevent encroachment or simply as a kind of "honor guard," a notion which appears in later Jewish sources (*Sifre Zuta*, Korah, Num. 18.4; Maimonides, *Book of Commandments,* 22). The Rabbis (*Sifre Num.* 116, b. ʿArak. 11b) understood the division of labor to be absolute, such that a Levite may not perform the task(s) assigned to another Levitical clan.

26.1–19: Gatekeepers. The gatekeepers follow the cultic singers.

ond, Joah the third, Sacar the fourth, Nethanel the fifth, ⁵ Ammiel the sixth, Issachar the seventh, Peullethai the eighth—for God had blessed him. ⁶ To his son Shemaiah were born sons who exercised authority in their clans because they were men of substance. ⁷ The sons of Shemaiah: Othni, Rephael, Obed, Elzabad—his brothers, men of ability, were Elihu and Semachiah. ⁸ All these, sons of Obed-edom; they and their sons and brothers, strong and able men for the service—62 of Obed-edom. ⁹ Meshelemiah had sons and brothers, able men—18. ¹⁰ Hosah of the Merarites had sons: Shimri the chief (he was not the first-born, but his father designated him chief), ¹¹ Hilkiah the second, Tebaliah the third, Zechariah the fourth. All the sons and brothers of Hosah—13.

¹² These are the divisions of the gatekeepers, by their chief men, [who worked in] shifts corresponding to their kinsmen, ministering in the House of the LORD. ¹³ They cast lots, small and great alike, by clans, for each gate.

¹⁴ The lot for the east [gate] fell to Shelemiah. Then they cast lots [for] Zechariah his son, a prudent counselor, and his lot came out to be the north [gate]. ¹⁵ For Obed-edom, the south [gate], and for his sons, the vestibule. ¹⁶ For Shuppim and for Hosah, the west [gate], with the Shallecheth gate on the ascending highway. Watch corresponded to watch: ¹⁷ At the east—six Levites; at the north—four daily; at the south—four daily; at the vestibule—two by two; ¹⁸ at the colonnade on the west—four at the causeway and two at the colonnade. ¹⁹ These were the divisions of the gatekeepers of the sons of Korah and the sons of Merari.

²⁰ And the Levites: Ahijah over the treasuries of the House of God and the treasuries of the dedicated things. ²¹ The sons of Ladan: the sons of the Gershonites belonging to Ladan; the chiefs of the clans of Ladan, the Gershonite—Jehieli. ²² The sons of Jehieli: Zetham and Joel; his brother was over the treasuries of the House of the LORD.

²³ Of the Amramites, the Izharites, the Hebronites, the Uzzielites: ²⁴ Shebuel son of Gershom son of Moses was the chief officer over the treasuries. ²⁵ And his brothers: Eliezer, his son Rehabiah, his son Jeshaiah, his son Joram, his son Zichri, his son Shelomith—²⁶ that Shelomith and his brothers were over all the treasuries of dedicated things that were dedicated by King David and the chiefs of the clans, and the officers of thousands and hundreds and the other army officers; ²⁷ they dedicated some of the booty of the wars to maintain the House of the LORD. ²⁸ All that Samuel the seer had dedicated, and Saul son of Kish, and Abner son of Ner, and Joab son of Zeruiah—or

26.20–32: Officers and judges. The listing of officials most removed from cultic responsibilities appears toward the end of the block extending from ch 23 through ch 27, following priests and Levites. It offers a bridge to the following ch that outlines non-cultic functionaries. **28:** This passage offers a more positive view of Saul than that encountered earlier, suggesting that the author here may have drawn on popular tradition. More likely, the author means to say that if a person like Saul was aware of the importance of the cultus, it follows that any self-respecting Jew must do no less. Abner was the commander of Saul's army; Joab was the commander of David's.

[what] any other man had dedicated, was under the charge of Shelomith and his brothers. ²⁹ The Izharites: Chenaniah and his sons were over Israel as clerks and magistrates for affairs outside [the sanctuary]. ³⁰ The Hebronites: Hashabiah and his brothers, capable men, 1,700, supervising Israel on the west side of the Jordan in all matters of the LORD and the service of the king. ³¹ The Hebronites: Jeriah, the chief of the Hebronites—they were investigated in the fortieth year of David's reign by clans of all their lines, and men of substance were found among them in Jazer-gilead. ³² His brothers, able men, 2,700, chiefs of clans—David put them in charge of the Reubenites, the Gadites, and the half-tribe of Manasseh in all matters of God and matters of the king.

27 The number of Israelites—chiefs of clans, officers of thousands and hundreds and their clerks, who served the king in all matters of the divisions, who worked in monthly shifts during all the months of the year—each division, 24,000. ² Over the first division for the first month—Jashobeam son of Zabdiel; his division had 24,000. ³ Of the sons of Perez, he, the chief of all the officers of the army, [served] for the first month. ⁴ Over the division of the second month—Dodai the Ahohite; Mikloth was chief officer of his division; his division had 24,000. ⁵ The third army officer for the third month—Benaiah son of Jehoiada, the chief priest; his division had 24,000. ⁶ That was Benaiah, one of the warriors of the thirty and over the thirty; and [over] his division was Ammizabad his son. ⁷ The fourth, for the fourth month, Asahel brother of Joab, and his son Zebadiah after him; his division had 24,000. ⁸ The fifth, for the fifth month, the officer Shamhut the Izrahite; his division had 24,000. ⁹ The sixth, for the sixth month, Ira son of Ikkesh the Tekoite; his division had 24,000. ¹⁰ The seventh, for the seventh month, Helez the Pelonite, of the Ephraimites; his division had 24,000. ¹¹ The eighth, for the eighth month, Sibbecai the Hushathite, of Zerah; his division had 24,000. ¹² The ninth, for the ninth month, Abiezer the Anathothite, of Benjamin; his division had 24,000. ¹³ The tenth, for the tenth month, Mahrai the Netophathite, of Zerah; his division had 24,000. ¹⁴ The eleventh, for the eleventh month, Benaiah the Pirathonite, of the Ephraimites; his division had 24,000. ¹⁵ The twelfth, for the twelfth month, Heldai the Netophathite, of Othniel; his division had 24,000.

¹⁶ Over the tribes of Israel: Reuben: the chief officer, Eliezer son of Zichri. Simeon: Shephatiah son of Maaca. ¹⁷ Levi: Hashabiah son of Kemuel. Aaron: Zadok. ¹⁸ Judah:

29–32: These vv. occasion surprise because they refer to secular duties of the Levites, a phenomenon which elsewhere appears only in the late biblical period (2 Chron. 19.8–11; Neh. 11.16). This section's historicity is debated.

27.1–34: Non-cultic arrangements. This ch deals with general organizational features of David's reign; it is likely of secondary origin. David's reign is depicted as one of order, with the nation centered on the Jerusalem cultus. **1–15:** The monthly shifts. Chronicles' notion of monthly shifts is probably inspired by 1 Kings 4.7, which details the monthly arrangements for Solomon's household. Note the typological number twenty-four (thousand) in this passage. **16–24:** A listing of tribal chiefs. The tribes of Asher and Gad are missing, perhaps in order to keep the number of tribes at twelve. The census of ch 21 is here presented in terms more favorable to David, less favorable to Joab. **25–31:** Stewards of David's holdings. Like most kings in the ancient Near East, David acquired large tracts of property. The description of these holdings is part of Chronicles' glorification of David. **32–34:** Important figures in the king's entourage; some but not all of these are known from the lists and narratives in Samuel.

28.1–21: David encourages Solomon and the people.
2: The footstool refers to the Ark. The expression reflects the belief that the LORD was seated upon a throne created by the (wings of the) cherubs—situated above the Ark—so that His feet rested on the Ark itself (cf. Lam. 2.1). **3–7:** Davidic kings "sit on the LORD's throne"; see 17.14.

Elihu, of the brothers of David. Issachar: Omri son of Michael. ¹⁹Zebulun: Ishmaiah son of Obadiah. Naphtali: Jerimoth son of Azriel. ²⁰Ephraimites: Hoshea son of Azaziah. The half-tribe of Manasseh: Joel son of Pedaiah. ²¹Half Manasseh in Gilead: Iddo son of Zechariah. Benjamin: Jaasiel son of Abner. ²²Dan: Azarel son of Jeroham. These were the officers of the tribes of Israel.

²³David did not take a census of those under twenty years of age, for the LORD had promised to make Israel as numerous as the stars of heaven. ²⁴Joab son of Zeruiah did begin to count them, but he did not finish; wrath struck Israel on account of this, and the census was not entered into the account of the chronicles of King David.

²⁵Over the royal treasuries: Azmaveth son of Adiel. Over the treasuries in the country—in the towns, the hamlets, and the citadels: Jonathan son of Uzziah. ²⁶Over the field laborers in agricultural work: Ezri son of Chelub. ²⁷Over the vineyards: Shimei the Ramathite. And over the produce in the vineyards for wine cellars: Zabdi the Shiphmite. ²⁸Over the olive trees and the sycamores in the Shephelah: Baal-hanan the Gederite. Over the oilstores: Joash. ²⁹Over the cattle pasturing in Sharon: Shirtai the Sharonite. And over the cattle in the valleys: Shaphat son of Adlai. ³⁰Over the camels: Obil the Ishmaelite. And over the she-asses: Jehdeiah the Meronothite. ³¹Over the flocks: Jaziz the Hagrite. All these were stewards of the property of King David. ³²Jonathan, David's uncle, was a counselor, a master, and a scribe: Jehiel son of Hachmoni was with the king's sons. ³³Ahitophel was a counselor to the king. Hushai the Archite was the king's friend. ³⁴After Ahitophel were Jehoiada son of Benaiah and Abiathar. The commander of the king's army was Joab.

28 David assembled all the officers of Israel—the tribal officers, the divisional officers who served the king, the captains of thousands and the captains of hundreds, and the stewards of all the property and cattle of the king and his sons, with the eunuchs and the warriors, all the men of substance—to Jerusalem. ²King David rose to his feet and said, "Hear me, my brothers, my people! I wanted to build a resting-place for the Ark of the Covenant of the LORD, for the footstool of our God, and I laid aside material for building. ³But God said to me, 'You will not build a house for My name, for you are a man of battles and have shed blood.' ⁴The LORD God of Israel chose me of all my father's house to be king over Israel forever. For He chose Judah to be ruler, and of the family of Judah, my father's house; and of my father's sons, He preferred to make me king over all Israel; [5] and of all my sons—for many are the sons the LORD gave me—He chose my son Solomon to sit on the throne of the kingdom of the LORD over Israel. [6] He said to me, 'It will be your son Solomon who will build My House and My courts, for I have chosen him to be a son to Me, and I will be a father to him. [7] I will establish his kingdom forever, if he keeps firmly to the observance of My commandments and rules as he does now.' [8] And now, in the sight of all Israel, the congregation of the LORD, and in the hearing of our God, [I say:] Observe and apply yourselves to all the commandments of the LORD your God in order that you may possess this good land and bequeath it to your children after you forever.

[9] "And you, my son Solomon, know the God of your father, and serve Him with single mind and fervent heart, for the LORD searches all minds and discerns the design of every thought; if you seek Him He will be available to you, but if you forsake Him He will abandon you forever. [10] See then, the LORD chose you to build a house as the sanctuary; be strong and do it."

[11] David gave his son Solomon the plan of the porch and its houses, its storerooms and its upper chambers and inner chambers; and of the place of the Ark-cover; [12] and the plan of all that he had by the spirit: of the courts of the House of the LORD and all its surrounding chambers, and of the treasuries of the House of God and of the treasuries of the holy things; [13] the divisions of priests and Levites for all the work of the service of the House of the LORD and all the vessels of the service of the House of the LORD; [14] and gold, the weight of gold for vessels of every sort of use; silver for all the vessels of silver by weight, for all the vessels of every kind of service; [15] the weight of the gold lampstands and their gold lamps, and the weight of the silver lampstands, each lampstand and its silver lamps, according to the use of every lampstand; [16] and the weight of gold for the tables of the rows of bread, for each table, and of silver for the silver tables; [17] and of the pure gold for the forks and the basins and the jars; and the weight of the gold bowls, every bowl; and the weight of the silver bowls, each and every bowl; [18] the weight of refined gold for the incense altar and the gold for the figure of the chariot—the cherubs—those with outspread wings screening the Ark of the Covenant of the LORD. [19] "All this that the LORD made me understand by His hand on me, I give you in writing—the plan of all the works."

[20] David said to his son Solomon, "Be strong and of good courage and do it; do not be afraid or dismayed, for

7: Continuity of the monarchy is here contingent upon observance of the divine commandments; see 17.13 n. **8–9:** The importance of serving the LORD wholeheartedly; see 29.9–19. **12:** Spirit here refers to prophetic inspiration, as clarified in v. 19. **19:** Chronicles' David is not explicitly labeled a prophet or seer, but is the recipient of prophetic revelation or inspiration. This v. is consistent with Chronicles' glorification of David, as well as the recurring theme of the divine source of all things pertaining to the Temple. David's prophetic status is explicitly acknowledged in the writings of the Dead Sea Scrolls (11QPs[a]) and some traditional Jewish sources (Tg. Chron.; Isaac Abravanel). Even so, other sources (y. Meg. 1.1 [70a], Rashi ad b. Sukkah 51b) claim that the Temple plans were given to David via the prophets Samuel, Gad, or Nathan; see above, 9.22, and 2 Chron. 29.25. Radak averred that David experienced not prophecy but, rather, a lesser degree of divine inspiration (Heb "ruah hakodesh"; compare y. Meg.). **20:** Reminiscent of Moses' exhortation to Joshua (Deut. 31.7, 8); David and Solomon are viewed like Moses and Joshua (22.12 n.).

the Lord God my God is with you; He will not fail you or forsake you till all the work on the House of the Lord is done. 21 Here are the divisions of the priests and Levites for all kinds of service of the House of God, and with you in all the work are willing men, skilled in all sorts of tasks; also the officers and all the people are at your command."

29 King David said to the entire assemblage, "God has chosen my son Solomon alone, an untried lad, although the work to be done is vast—for the temple^a is not for a man but for the Lord God. 2 I have spared no effort to lay up for the House of my God gold for golden objects, silver for silver, copper for copper, iron for iron, wood for wooden, onyx-stone and inlay-stone, stone of antimony and variegated colors—every kind of precious stone and much marble. 3 Besides, out of my solicitude for the House of my God, I gave over my private hoard of gold and silver to the House of my God—in addition to all that I laid aside for the holy House: 4 3,000 gold talents of Ophir gold, and 7,000 talents of refined silver for covering the walls of the houses 5 (gold for golden objects, silver for silver for all the work)—into the hands of craftsmen. Now who is going to make a freewill offering and devote himself today to the Lord?"

6 The officers of the clans and the officers of the tribes of Israel and the captains of thousands and hundreds and the supervisors of the king's work made freewill offerings, 7 giving for the work of the House of God: 5,000 talents of gold, 10,000 darics, 10,000 talents of silver, 18,000 talents of copper, 100,000 talents of iron. 8 Whoever had stones in his possession gave them to the treasury of the House of the Lord in the charge of Jehiel the Gershonite. 9 The people rejoiced over the freewill offerings they made, for with a whole heart they made freewill offerings to the Lord; King David also rejoiced very much.

10 David blessed the Lord in front of all the assemblage; David said, "Blessed are You, Lord, God of Israel our father, from eternity to eternity. 11 Yours, Lord, are greatness, might, splendor, triumph, and majesty—yes, all that is in heaven and on earth; to You, Lord, belong kingship and preeminence above all. 12 Riches and honor are Yours to dispense; You have dominion over all; with You are strength and might, and it is in Your power to make anyone great and strong. 13 Now, God, we praise You and extol Your glorious name. 14 Who am I and who are my people, that we should have the means to make such a

29.1–9: The call to support Solomon in building the Temple. Chronicles describes the grandeur of the Temple, requiring participation of the entire population; for similar description, see 2 Chron. 2.3–8. The willing participation of the people mirrors the construction of the Tabernacle in Exod. 35.4–29.

29.11–19: David's thanksgiving prayer. This prayer is structurally and thematically similar to the Psalms anthology in ch 16; together they form an inclusio of David's cultic activity. Both passages contain the following themes: transition from landless patriarchs to landed society, the Lord's kingship, and a closing petition. Another significant element now appears: Deeds are truly virtuous only if accompanied by proper intentions. Humans cannot gloat in the act of contributing to the Lord's Temple, since all human success and wealth come from Him. But people can take pride in the fact that their donations are given with joy and not as a result of coercion; see introduction. This prayer, however, seems to be an original composition of the Chronicler, and it does not have any parallels in Psalms. Like 16.8–36, vv. 10–13 are traditionally recited as part of the "pesukei dezimrah" of the morning prayers.

a Lit. "fortress."

freewill offering; but all is from You, and it is Your gift that we have given to You. [15] For we are sojourners with You, mere transients like our fathers; our days on earth are like a shadow, with nothing in prospect. [16] O LORD our God, all this great mass that we have laid aside to build You a House for Your holy name is from You, and it is all Yours. [17] I know, God, that You search the heart and desire uprightness; I, with upright heart, freely offered all these things; now Your people, who are present here—I saw them joyously making freewill offerings. [18] O LORD God of Abraham, Isaac, and Israel, our fathers, remember this to the eternal credit of the thoughts of Your people's hearts, and make their hearts constant toward You. [19] As to my son Solomon, give him a whole heart to observe Your commandments, Your admonitions, and Your laws, and to fulfill them all, and to build this temple[a] for which I have made provision."

[20] David said to the whole assemblage, "Now bless the LORD your God." All the assemblage blessed the LORD God of their fathers, and bowed their heads low to the LORD and the king. [21] They offered sacrifices to the LORD and made burnt offerings to the LORD on the morrow of that day: 1,000 bulls, 1,000 rams, 1,000 lambs, with their libations; [they made] sacrifices in great number for all Israel, [22] and they ate and drank in the presence of the LORD on that day with great joy. They again proclaimed Solomon son of David king, and they anointed him as ruler before the LORD, and Zadok as high priest. [23] Solomon successfully took over the throne of the LORD as king instead of his father David, and all went well with him. All Israel accepted him; [24] all the officials and the warriors, and the sons of King David as well, gave their hand in support of King Solomon. [25] The LORD made Solomon exceedingly great in the eyes of all Israel, and endowed him with a regal majesty that no king of Israel before him ever had.

[26] Thus David son of Jesse reigned over all Israel; [27] the length of his reign over Israel was forty years: he reigned seven years in Hebron and thirty-three years in Jerusalem. [28] He died at a ripe old age, having enjoyed long life, riches and honor, and his son Solomon reigned in his stead. [29] The acts of King David, early and late, are recorded in the history of Samuel the seer, the history of Nathan the prophet, and the history of Gad the seer, [30] together with all the mighty deeds of his kingship and the events that befell him and Israel and all the kingdoms of the earth.

24: Chronicles is oblivious to 1 Kings chs 1–3. **25:** Some scholars argue that this formulation indicates that Chronicles viewed Solomon as no less important a figure than David; others reject this, noting that David is Chronicles' king, par excellence. Alternatively, this formulation may reflect Chronicles' use of a Solomonic typology in its depiction of Hezekiah. 2 Kings 20.13 describes Hezekiah's magnificent wealth; accordingly, Chronicles applied this artificial note to Solomon in order to allow for this literary parallel. **26–27:** Whereas 1 Kings 2.11 states that David ruled over Judah in Hebron, and over a united Israel in Jerusalem, Chronicles avoids this dichotomy. Chronicles' position carries a price: If David ruled from Hebron over all Israel for seven years, then his move to Jerusalem has no clear motive. Since Chronicles presents the capture of Jerusalem as a national-religious issue, one wonders why the move was postponed seven years; see 11.1–3, 4–9 n. **28–30:** A recurring feature of Chronicles is the claim that the official royal chronicles were composed by prophets. This is another example of the changed role and nature of prophets in Chronicles; they are, among other things, historians who record, study, interpret, and assess past events. In addition, Chronicles' claim implies that everything contained in these official accounts—and, by implication, the book of Chronicles itself—is fully accurate and credible. Many modern scholars, however, doubt that these works, typically mentioned at the end of the kings' reign, ever existed.

a Lit. "fortress."

דברי הימים ב

2 Chronicles

AN INTRODUCTION TO THE BOOK of Chronicles precedes 1 Chronicles.

[DAVID ROTHSTEIN]

1 [a]Solomon son of David took firm hold of his kingdom, for the LORD his God was with him and made him exceedingly great. ²Solomon summoned all Israel—the officers of thousands and of hundreds, and the judges, and all the chiefs of all Israel, the heads of the clans. ³Then Solomon, and all the assemblage with him, went to the shrine at Gibeon, for the Tent of Meeting, which Moses the servant of the LORD had made in the wilderness, was there. (⁴But the Ark of God David had brought up from Kiriath-jearim to the place which David had prepared for it; for he had pitched a tent for it in Jerusalem.) ⁵The bronze altar, which Bezalel son of Uri son of Hur had made, was also there before the Tabernacle of the LORD, and Solomon and the assemblage resorted to it. ⁶There Solomon ascended the bronze altar before the LORD, which was at the Tent of Meeting, and on it sacrificed a thousand burnt offerings.

a With vv. 3–13, cf. 1 Kings 3.4–15; with vv. 14–17, cf. 1 Kings 10.26–29.

1.1–9.31: Solomon's reign. Chronicles presents a much more favorable depiction of Solomon than the books of Samuel and Kings, omitting any passages which reflect poorly upon him. In general, Chronicles portrays Solomon as a near mirror-image of David. Solomon's reign is marked by the realization of David's cultic preparations and economic growth. Thus, the continuity between David and Solomon in Chronicles is greater than in Samuel-Kings.

1.1–13: Solomon travels to Gibeon. In the "incubation" story of 1 Kings 3.4–14 Solomon makes a private pilgrimage to Gibeon in the hope of receiving divine communication. Chronicles views this pilgrimage as a sign of Solomon's devotion to the cultus and, thereby, having national-religious significance. In line with the ten-dency to create greater continuity between David and Solomon, Solomon's actions parallel those of David; see 1 Chron. 11.4–8 and esp. 13.1–5. **1:** David's prayers on behalf of Solomon have materialized (1 Chron. 28.20). **3:** 1 Kings (3.2–3) acknowledges that Israel offered local sacrifices prior to the construction of Solomon's Temple; Chronicles consistently avoids mention of any such possibility. The Tabernacle and altar were, for Chronicles, the mobile "chosen place" for cultic activity, in accordance with Lev. 17.8; Deut. 12.4–28. For this reason Chronicles claims that Gibeon was the site of the Mosaic Tabernacle (and sacred appurtenances), whereas 1 Kings 3.4 states only that the "great altar"—i.e., one of many—was there (see 1 Chron. 16.39). For Chronicles, but not for Kings, Leviticus as well as Deuteronomy was authoritative; this explains the revision here. Rabbinic tradition (m. Zevaḥ. 14.4–7; t. Zevaḥ. 13.19) reconciles the divergent biblical traditions (Lev. ch 17, Deut. ch 12, 1 Kings, Chronicles) by arguing that prior to the construction of the Temple, local cultic slaughter was permitted so long as there was no central tabernacle housing both the "great altar" and the Ark (as in Chronicles' description of Gibeon); when such existed, as in the rab-

[7] That night, God appeared to Solomon and said to him, "Ask, what shall I grant you?" [8] Solomon said to God, "You dealt most graciously with my father David, and now You have made me king in his stead. [9] Now, O LORD God, let Your promise to my father David be fulfilled; for You have made me king over a people as numerous as the dust of the earth. [10] Grant me then the wisdom and the knowledge [a-to lead this people,-a] for who can govern Your great people?" [11] God said to Solomon, "Because you want this, and have not asked for wealth, property, and glory, nor have you asked for the life of your enemy, or long life for yourself, but you have asked for the wisdom and the knowledge to be able to govern My people over whom I have made you king, [12] wisdom and knowledge are granted to you, and I grant you also wealth, property, and glory, the like of which no king before you has had, nor shall any after you have." [13] From the shrine at Gibeon, from the Tent of Meeting, Solomon went to Jerusalem and reigned over Israel.

[14] Solomon assembled chariots and horsemen; he had 1,400 chariots and 12,000 horses that he stationed in the chariot towns and with the king in Jerusalem. [15] The king made silver and gold as plentiful in Jerusalem as stones, and cedars as plentiful as the sycamores in the Shephelah. [16] Solomon's horses were imported from Egypt and from Que; the king's traders would buy them from Que at the market price. [17] A chariot imported from Egypt cost 600 shekels of silver, and a horse 150. These in turn were exported by them[b] to all the kings of the Hittites and the kings of the Arameans.

[18] Then Solomon resolved to build a House for the name of the LORD and a royal palace for himself.

2 [c]Solomon mustered 70,000 basket carriers and 80,000 quarriers in the hills, with 3,600 men supervising them. [2] Solomon sent this message to King Huram of Tyre, "In view of what you did for my father David in sending

---

a-a Lit. "that I may go out before this people and come in."
b That is, Solomon's dealers.   c Cf. 1 Kings 5.

---

a "political" one, intended to consolidate his position; only after this stability is assured does Solomon, according to 1 Kings, go to Gibeon. Chronicles, however, maintains that Solomon's rule was divinely ordained and had never been in doubt; hence, the diplomatic motive behind this marriage was irrelevant. **13:** Chronicles omits Solomon's sacrifice before the Ark upon his return to Jerusalem; cf. 1 Kings 3.15. This probably reflects Chronicles' slant concerning cult centralization even before the construction of the Temple; see, however, 1 Chron. 16.2.

1.14–17: Economic growth. Almost identical wording appears at the close of Solomon's life in 2 Chron. 9.27–28 (= 1 Kings 10.23–28); it is not unusual for Chronicles to rearrange source material for literary or ideological reasons. While some scholars see this use of inclusio (2 Chron. 1.14–17 || 2 Chron. 9.27–28) as nothing more than a literary device, others maintain Chronicles here portrays God's promise as being realized without delay, such that the entire period of Solomon's reign was marked by economic prosperity. There is no hint here of the hardships endured during the course of this economic boom; see 10.1. Note that Chronicles omits 1 Kings 3.16–28, Solomon's first successful adjudication, because Chronicles maintains that Solomon's wisdom was manifest, first and foremost, in executing the Temple project; see 2 Chron. 2.11.

1.18–2.17: Preparation of work force and Solomon's negotiations with Huram. There are many differences between this ch and 1 Kings ch 2. Kings calls the king Hiram, while in Chronicles he is Huram. In Kings Hiram establishes diplomatic contact with Solomon, to continue the beneficial (and lucrative; see below) relations which he had enjoyed with David; he therefore does this only after Solomon's rule has been fully stabilized. By contrast, Chronicles claims that Solomon initiates the

---

binic understanding of the Shiloh Tabernacle (see Josh. 18.1; 1 Sam. 3.3), sacrificial activity was permitted only at the central site. This accounts for David's sacrifices, in Jerusalem, at 1 Chron. 16.2. As previously noted, Chronicles omits reference to the dynastic struggle during David's old age. Chronicles

also defers mention of Solomon's marriage to Pharaoh's daughter (1 Kings 3.1) until 8.11. The reasons are twofold. First, Chronicles seeks to convey the impression that Solomon's first act as monarch pertained to religious, Temple-related matters. Second, Solomon's marriage to Pharaoh's daughter is him cedars to build a palace for his residence—[3] see, I intend to build a House for the name of the LORD my God; I will dedicate it to Him for making incense offering of sweet spices in His honor, for the regular rows of bread, and for the morning and evening burnt offerings on sabbaths, new moons, and festivals, as is Israel's eternal duty. [4] The House that I intend to build will be great, inasmuch as our God is greater than all gods. [5] Who indeed is capable of building a House for Him! Even the heavens to their uttermost reaches cannot contain Him, and who am I that I should build Him a House—except as a place for making burnt offerings to Him? [6] Now send me a craftsman to work in gold, silver, bronze, and iron, and in purple, crimson, and blue yarn, and who knows how to engrave, alongside the craftsmen I have here in Judah and in Jerusalem, whom my father David provided. [7] Send me cedars, cypress, and algum wood from the Lebanon, for I know that your servants are skilled at cutting the trees of Lebanon. My servants will work with yours [8] to provide me with a great stock of timber; for the House that I intend to build will be singularly great. [9] I have allocated for your servants, the wood-cutters who fell the trees, 20,000 *kor* of crushed wheat and 20,000 *kor* of barley, 20,000 *bath* of wine and 20,000 *bath* of oil."

[10] Huram, king of Tyre, sent Solomon this written message in reply, "Because the LORD loved His people, He made you king over them."

[11] Huram continued, "Blessed is the LORD, God of Israel, who made the heavens and the earth, who gave King David a wise son, endowed with intelligence and understanding, to build a House for the LORD and a royal palace for himself. [12] Now I am sending you a skillful and intelligent man, my master[a] Huram, [13] the son of a Danite

---

a Lit. *"my father."*

---

diplomacy shortly after his visit to Gibeon and his conscription of Temple workers; his alacrity demonstrates his commitment to executing the construction of the Temple. Second, the negotiations in 1 Kings are based on a quid pro quo; Solomon pays for needed services, while the terms of payment are dictated by Huram. In Chronicles Solomon unilaterally dictates the terms, while Hiram is presented as a "believing," monotheistic Gentile, whose motive for assisting Solomon is largely, or even exclusively, religious. Third, the cost in Kings involves yearly provisions for Hiram's household; Chronicles speaks of a one-time payment. Fourth, in 1 Kings Solomon's description of the planned Temple is terse and businesslike; Chronicles' Solomon describes the magnitude of the Temple project in superlative terms and spells out the specific cultic activities (integrating Priestly perspectives) to take place in the Temple. Fifth, by having Huram use the expression "my lord" to Solomon (v. 14), Chronicles portrays Solomon as the dominant monarch; see 8.1–6 n. Finally, according to 1 Kings 5.26, the wisdom that God bestowed upon Solomon is demonstrated by Solomon's execution of a treaty with Hiram. Chronicles makes no reference to this treaty nor to its constituting the realization of Solomon's wisdom. As noted above, Chronicles maintains that Solomon's wisdom was manifest primarily in connection with the Temple building, and only secondarily in other spheres. Chronicles' omission of the treaty reflects two factors. Since Chronicles presents Solomon as the most powerful and wealthy monarch in the region, there is no reason for Solomon to limit himself by a political treaty. Second, Chronicles' omission reflects an ideological stance of Chronicles, according to which a truly believing individual must trust in the LORD's ability to provide for all needs, making treaties with foreigners (and wicked Israelites) superfluous and even improper. **2.3:** The addition of details of the sacrifices reflect Chronicles' incorporation of the Priestly perspective found in Leviticus and elsewhere. **5:** Chronicles expresses the divine transcendence; the Temple does not actually "house" the LORD (contrast 1 Kings 8.13). This formulation may be informed by Deuteronomy's "name theology," according to which only the LORD's name is localized at the Temple (see, e.g., Deut. 12.5, 11). **10–13:** Huram's reply: The implication of Huram's readiness to assist Solomon is that if a foreigner—albeit righteous—recognizes the importance of the Israelite Temple, how much more so should be the response of all Israelites/Jews. **11:** A patent formulation of the view that the wisdom granted Solomon was realized primarily in the building of the Temple, not in domestic and international leadership. **12–14:** The materials listed are reminiscent of the Tabernacle account in Exod. 25.3–7; 35.5–9; see the "continuity theme" in 1 Chron. ch 21. This motif also explains the woman, his father a Tyrian. He is skilled at working in gold, silver, bronze, iron, precious stones, and wood; in purple, blue, and crimson yarn and in fine linen; and at engraving and designing whatever will be required of him, alongside your craftsmen and the craftsmen of my lord, your father David. [14] As to the wheat, barley, oil, and wine which my lord mentioned, let him send them to his servants. [15] We undertake to cut down as many trees of Lebanon as you need, and deliver them to you as rafts by sea to Jaffa; you will transport them to Jerusalem."

[16] Solomon took a census of all the aliens who were in the land of Israel, besides the census taken by his father David, and they were found to be 153,600. [17] He made 70,000 of them basket carriers, and 80,000 of them quarriers, with 3,600 supervisors to see that the people worked.

3 [a]Then Solomon began to build the House of the LORD in Jerusalem on Mount Moriah, where [the LORD] had appeared to his father David, at the place which David

a With vv. 2–17, cf. 1 Kings 6; 7.1–22.

name and tribal background of the chief Temple craftsman. Whereas 1 Kings 7.14 assigns his mother to the northern tribe of Naphtali, Chronicles claims that his mother was from the northern tribe of Dan, while his father was a Tyrian; the (half-)Danite lineage of Huramabi thus parallels the Tabernacle account in Exodus, wherein one of the head artisans, Oholiab, was a Danite (Exod. 31.6). The Tyrian origin of the craftsman's father troubled Jewish exegetes. Josephus (Ant.) and some medieval commentators argued that his father was Jewish, by taking "Tyre" to refer to the mainland Tyre, apportioned to Asher (Josh. 19.29), rather than the Phoenician city. Others suggested that his father was originally from the fort-city of Ser, which formed part of Naphtali, but subsequently moved to Tyre. The Chronicler's statement here reflects his relatively moderate position on intermarriage and lineage; see introduction. **16–17:** Solomon again prepares the work force. Significantly, he uses only *aliens* for the work force; Kings is ambivalent on this matter (cf. 1 Kings 5.27; 9.21). In addition,

Chronicles has omitted the covenant between Solomon and Hiram (1 Kings 5.26).

3.1–2: The Temple site. The "Land of Moriah" appears elsewhere only at Gen. 22.1 in connection with the 'Akedah, Abraham's binding of Isaac. Chronicles claims that David's altar was erected on the very spot on which Abraham prepared to sacrifice Isaac. Other allusions to Gen. ch 22 include the words "who was seen/appeared to David," (Heb "r-ʾ-h"), reminiscent of Gen. 22.4, 8, 13 and, esp. v. 14. Chronicles thus emphasizes the "chosen" nature of the Temple site, which reaches back to Israel's earliest forebear, suggesting that the site's uniqueness is almost ontological. This may also be another expression of the fulfillment of the divine promise to Abraham; see 1 Chron. 16.8–18. A rabbinic tradition (*Pirqe R. El.* 31; see, also *y. Naz.* 7.2 [56a]; *Gen. Rab.* 34; *b. Zevaḥ.* 62a) further maintains that the locus of the Temple altar was the place from which Adam was created, and where Cain and Abel made their respective offerings (Gen. 4.3–4), suggesting that

the locus of humankind's creation is also the locus of atonement (i.e., "rejuvenation"). The Samaritan community preserves a parallel tradition, wherein the binding of Isaac took place on Mt. Gerizim, the religious center of the Samaritans. **2:** The delay in building the Temple at 1 Kings 6.1 is reasonable, since Solomon had been forced to first secure his throne. Chronicles, however, omits the entire episode (see 1.3 n.); indeed, Chronicles implies that Solomon's negotiations with Huram took place immediately upon his return from Gibeon, i.e, within days of Solomon's accession to the throne. Furthermore, David had already laid most of the groundwork. Nevertheless, Chronicles depicts Solomon as waiting until the fourth year perhaps because the period of three years in Chronicles is typological, signifying a (relatively) short period (see 11.7; 17.7) and the magnitude of the Temple project, emphasized repeatedly in Chronicles, required two to three years of preparation. Note that Chronicles omits 1 Kings' reference to 480 years from the exodus (6.1); this omission is another instance of Chronicles' reticence concerning Israel's sojourn in, and deliverance from, Egypt (see introduction).

3.3–5.1: Solomon's Temple. Chronicles' description of the Temple and appurtenances differs considerably from that found at 1 Kings chs 6–7, in two respects. First, Chronicles' account is much shorter than that of 1 Kings. Second, Chronicles' version brings Kings' description into closer harmony with the Mosaic Tabernacle described in the Priestly source of the Torah, another example of the "continuity theme." Beginning with v. 8, and with the exception of 4.11–16, the syntactic subject of these vv. is Solomon, thus emphasizing Solomon's role as executor of David's preparations. **3.4:** For the use of *gold* inlay, see 1 Kings 6.22, 30. **6:** *Parvaim* is most likely a place name (so LXX and Targum), possibly located in northeastern had designated, at the threshing floor of Ornan the Jebusite. ² He began to build on the second day of the second month of the fourth year of his reign. ³ These were the dimensions Solomon established for building the House of God: its length in cubits, by the former measure, was 60, and its breadth was 20. ⁴ The length of the porch in front [was equal] to the breadth of the House—20 cubits, and its height was 120. Inside he overlaid it with pure gold. ⁵ The House itself he paneled with cypress wood. He overlaid it with fine gold and embossed on it palms and chains. ⁶ He studded the House with precious stones for decoration; the gold was from Parvaim. ⁷ He overlaid the House with gold—the beams, the thresholds, its walls and doors; he carved cherubim on the walls. ⁸ He made the Holy of Holies: its length was [equal to] the breadth of the house—20 cubits, and its breadth was 20 cubits. He overlaid it with 600 talents of fine gold. ⁹ The weight of the nails was 50 shekels of gold; the upper chambers he overlaid with gold. ¹⁰ He made two sculptured cherubim in the Holy of Holies, and they were overlaid with gold. ¹¹ The outspread wings of the cherubim were 20 cubits across: one wing 5 cubits long touching one wall of the House, and the other wing 5 cubits long touching the wing of the other cherub; ¹² one wing of the other [cherub] 5 cubits long extending to the other wall of the House, and its other wing 5 cubits long touching the wing of the first cherub. ¹³ The wingspread of these cherubim was thus 20 cubits across, and they were standing up facing the

Arabia. Others understand the term to mean "finest gold" (thus, apparently, Vulgate and Peshitta). Postbiblical and rabbinic sources understood the term as denoting either a mythical location or quality. **7:** 1 Kings 6.22 makes no mention of *cherubim* being engraved on the walls of the Temple. Chronicles' position, informed by Exod. 26.1, 31, appears to be an artificial construct. In Exodus the curtain encloses the portable walls of the Tabernacle, but the permanence of the Temple made a curtain unnecessary. **8:** The *600 talents*, mentioned only in Chronicles, recalls the price paid by David for the Temple site (1 Chron. 21.25). This may be intended to highlight the central role of the "most holy," in which the Ark was housed. This number (= 12 × 50) may also be Chronicles' way of saying that the Temple site, along with the "most holy," is the rightful possession of all of Israel's tribes. **11–13:** The winged *cherubim:* In Exodus 25.20 the cherubim in the Tabernacle faced one another. The Rabbis reconciled the positions by claiming that when Israel obeyed the LORD's will the cherubim faced one another, signaling harmony; when Israel veered from the path,

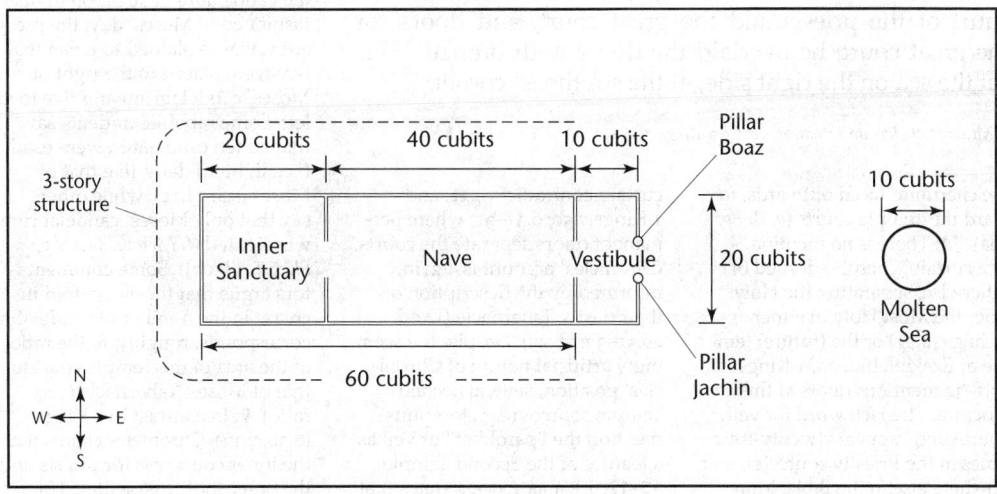

The Temple of Solomon according to Second Chronicles

House. ¹⁴He made the curtain of blue, purple, and crimson yarn and fine linen, and he worked cherubim into it. ¹⁵At the front of the House he made two columns 35 cubits high; the capitals^a on top of them were 5 cubits high. ¹⁶He made chainwork in the inner Sanctuary and set it on the top of the columns; he made a hundred pomegranates and set them into the chainwork. ¹⁷He erected the columns in front of the Great Hall, one to its right and one to its left; the one to the right was called Jachin, and the one to the left, Boaz.

4 ^bHe made an altar of bronze 20 cubits long, 20 cubits wide, and 10 cubits high.

²He made the sea^c of cast metal 10 cubits across from brim to brim, perfectly round; it was 5 cubits high, and its circumference was 30 cubits. ³Beneath were figures of oxen set all around it, of 10 cubits, encircling the sea; the oxen were in two rows, cast in one piece with it. ⁴It stood upon twelve oxen: three faced north, three faced west, three faced south, and three faced east, with the sea resting upon them; their haunches were all turned inward. ⁵It was a handbreadth thick, and its brim was made like that of a cup, like the petals of a lily. It held 3,000 *bath*.

⁶He made ten bronze lavers for washing; he set five on the right and five on the left; they would rinse off in them the parts of the burnt offering; but the sea served the priests for washing. ⁷He made ten lampstands of gold as prescribed, and placed them in the Great Hall, five on the right and five on the left. ⁸He made ten tables and placed them in the Great Hall, five on the right and five on the left. He made one hundred gold basins. ⁹He built the court of the priests and the great court, and doors for the great court; he overlaid the doors with bronze. ¹⁰He set the sea on the right side, at the southeast corner.

a Meaning of Heb. uncertain.   *b Cf. 1 Kings 7.23–50.*   *c I.e., a large basin.*

icles implies that Solomon was responsible for them. The position of these pillars—on either side of the entrance to the sanctum, a point not specified in the Kings account—corresponds to archeological evidence afforded by the sanctuaries at Hazor and Arad. **4.1:** The *altar of bronze* is missing in 1 Kings. Some scholars explain the reference here as a scribal error, while others maintain that Chronicles has added it under the influence of Exod. 27.1; 38.1. The dimensions probably describe the altar base, from which steps led to the altar itself. **2–5:** *The sea:* The differences between this v. and 1 Kings 7.23–26 have generated many explanations. The difference in size may reflect a cylindrical shape (Chronicles) versus a hemisphere (Kings). Chronicles' reference to *oxen* may result from Chronicles' difficulty in understanding the Kings passage. Some postbiblical sources (Josephus, *Ant.*) maintained that production of the oxen violated the anti-iconic position of Deut. 4.16–18; see 9.18–19. **6–8:** The purpose of the *lavers*, not found in 1 Kings, reflects the influence of Exod. 30.17–21; here too the Priestly description of the Tabernacle is used to fill in the depiction in Kings. **4.7:** Cf. Exod. 25.31–39; 37.17–24. Rabbinic sources maintain that there were ten candelabra in addition to that fashioned in Moses' day; the present v. was explained to mean that five were placed to the right of Moses' candelabrum and five to its left. Some rabbinic tradents say that all ten candelabra were used (i.e., lighted) daily, like that of Moses (see 13.11), while others say that only Moses' candelabrum was lighted (*t. Menaḥ.* 11.10; *y. Shek.* 6.3 [50b]). Some commentators argue that the elevenfold increase in the number of candelabra corresponds, roughly, to the ratio of the area of the Temple court to that of Moses' Tabernacle (12:1 ratio). **9:** In contrast to 1 Kings (6.36; 7.12), Chronicles claims that the inner court was for priests and the outer for lay Israelites. This position, informed by Ezek. chs

the cherubim faced outwards, toward the Temple courts (*b. B. Bat.* 99a). **14:** There is no mention of a curtain, cherub-adorned or otherwise, separating the Holy from the Most Holy in either 1 Kings (6.21) or the (future) temple of Ezekiel. Indeed, 1 Kings 6.31–32 mentions doors at this juncture. The Heb word for veil, "parokhet," appears twenty-four times in the Priestly source[s], and nowhere else in the Bible. Moreover, the very existence of such a

curtain contradicts 4.22, and 1 Kings 7.50; 6.31–32, where permanent doors separate the courts. Chronicles' account is, again, informed by the description of the Priestly Tabernacle (Exod. 26.31–37; 36.35). Despite the seemingly artificial nature of Chronicles' position, several Second Temple sources (e.g., Josephus) mention the "parokhet" or veil as a feature of the Second Temple. **15–17:** 1 Kings 7.15–22 states that Hiram had the pillars built; Chron-

¹¹ Huram made the pails, the shovels, and the basins. With that Huram completed the work he had undertaken for King Solomon in the House of God: ¹² the two columns, the globes, and the two capitals on top of the columns; and the two pieces of network to cover the two globes of the capitals on top of the columns; ¹³ the four hundred pomegranates for the two pieces of network, two rows of pomegranates for each network, to cover the two globes of the capitals on top of the columns; ¹⁴ he made the stands and the lavers upon the stands; ¹⁵ one sea with the twelve oxen beneath it; ¹⁶ the pails, the shovels, and the bowls.ᵃ And all the vessels made for King Solomon for the House of the LORD by Huram his master were of burnished bronze. ¹⁷ The king had them cast in molds dug out of the earth, in the plain of the Jordan between Succoth and Zeredah. ¹⁸ Solomon made a very large number of vessels; the weight of the bronze used could not be reckoned. ¹⁹ And Solomon made all the furnishings that were in the House of God: the altar of gold; the tables for the bread of display; ²⁰ the lampstands and their lamps, to burn as prescribed in front of the inner Sanctuary, of solid gold; ²¹ and the petals, lamps, and tongs, of purest gold; ²² the snuffers, basins, ladles, and fire pans, of solid gold; and the entrance to the House: the doors of the innermost part of the House, the Holy of Holies, and the doors of the Great Hall of the House, of gold.

5 ᵇ When all the work that King Solomon undertook for the House of the LORD was completed, Solomon brought the things that his father David had consecrated—the silver, the gold, and the utensils—and deposited them in the treasury of the House of God.

² Then Solomon convoked the elders of Israel—all the heads of the tribes and the ancestral chiefs of the Israelites—in Jerusalem, to bring up the Ark of the Covenant of the LORD from the City of David, that is, Zion.

³ All the men of Israel assembled before the king at the Feast,ᶜ in the seventh month. ⁴ When all the elders of Israel had come, the Levites carried the Ark. ⁵ They brought up the Ark and the Tent of Meeting and all the holy vessels that were in the Tent—the Levite priests brought them up. ⁶ Meanwhile, King Solomon and the whole community of Israel, who had gathered to him before the Ark, were sacrificing sheep and oxen in such abundance that they could not be numbered or counted.

⁷ The priests brought the Ark of the LORD's Covenant to

40–48, is reflected in postbiblical and rabbinic sources. The "Temple Scroll" from Qumran (11QTemple) speaks of three courts, the outermost being designated for women and minors under the age of twenty. **10–22:** This passage is very similar to 1 Kings 7.39–50. The many apparent contradictions between it and other aspects of Chronicles' description have led many scholars to view this passage as a late addition to the book. **11:** The wording is reminiscent of the completion of the Tabernacle at Exod. 39.32, again emphasizing the continuity theme. Similarly, the following vv. here parallel Exod. 39.33–41, which list the Tabernacle vessels.

5.1: For David's role, see, e.g., 1 Chron. 18.8, 10–11; 22.3–4, 14, 16; 29.2–9.

5.2–7.11: Dedication of the Temple. The culmination of all that has transpired since 1 Chron. ch 11. Patterned after 1 Kings 8.1–66, this section consists of three parts: (1) transfer of the Ark into the Temple, (2) Solomon's dedicatory prayer, (3) descent of divine fire and concluding ceremonies. Chronicles adds, at several points, descriptions of the Levitic choral rite, indicative of the enhanced role of Levitic service in Chronicles.

5.2–6.11: Transfer of the Ark. This section may also be titled "The Consecration of the Temple," since the placement of the Ark in the Temple constitutes the latter's consecration.

---

a Or "forks."   b Cf. 1 Kings 7.51–8.11.   c I.e., of Tabernacles.

its place in the inner Sanctuary of the House, in the Holy of Holies, beneath the wings of the cherubim; [8] for the cherubim had their wings spread out over the place of the Ark so that the cherubim covered the Ark and its poles from above. [9] The poles projected beyond the Ark and the ends of the poles were visible from the front of the inner Sanctuary, but they could not be seen from the outside; and there they remain to this day. [10] There was nothing inside the Ark but the two tablets that Moses placed [there] at Horeb, when the LORD made [a Covenant] with the Israelites after their departure from Egypt. [11] When the priests came out of the Sanctuary—all the priests present had sanctified themselves, without keeping to the set divisions—[12] all the Levite singers, Asaph, Heman, Jeduthun, their sons and their brothers, dressed in fine linen, holding cymbals, harps, and lyres, were standing to the east of the altar, and with them were 120 priests who blew trumpets. [13] The trumpeters and the singers joined in unison to praise and extol the LORD; and as the sound of the trumpets, cymbals, and other musical instruments, and the praise of the LORD, "For He is good, for His steadfast love is eternal," grew louder, the House, the House of the LORD, was filled with a cloud. [14] The priests could not stay and perform the service because of the cloud, for the glory of the LORD filled the House of God.

6 [a]Then Solomon declared:
　"The LORD has chosen
　To abide in a thick cloud;
[2]　I have built for You
　A stately House,
　And a place where You
　May dwell forever."

[3] Then, as the whole congregation of Israel stood, the king turned and blessed the whole congregation of Israel. [4] He said,"Blessed is the LORD God of Israel, [b]who made a promise to my father David and fulfilled it.[-b] For He said, [5] 'From the time I brought My people out of the land of Egypt, I never chose a city from among all the tribes of Israel to build a House where My name might abide; nor did I choose anyone to be the leader of my people Israel. [6] But then I chose Jerusalem for My name to abide there, and I chose David to rule My people Israel.'

[7] "Now my father David had wanted to build a House

5.11–14: Based upon 1 Kings 8.10–11. Immediately upon transferral of the Ark, the Levites perform, whereupon the LORD's glory appears, veiled in a cloud and hidden from the people's sight. The coincidence of the sacred song with the divine cloud has been explained in several ways. Some see it as indicating divine approval of the choral song; others argue that it is the choral service, specifically mentioning the divine name and His virtuous acts, that evokes the divine Presence. This latter approach sees the daily recital of the choral service as serving to announce, and procure, the LORD's protective presence in the Temple. See 7.1–3. On the phrase *For He is good, for His steadfast love is eternal,* see 1 Chron. 16.34 n.

a Cf. 1 Kings 8.12–53.
b-b Lit. "who spoke with His own mouth a promise to my father David and has fulfilled with His own hands."

for the name of the LORD God of Israel. [8] But the LORD said to my father David, 'As for your wanting to build a House for My name, you do well to want that. [9] However, you shall not build the House; your son, the issue of your loins, he shall build the House for My name.' [10] Now the LORD has fulfilled the promise that He made. I have succeeded[a] my father David and have ascended the throne of Israel, as the LORD promised. I have built the House for the name of the LORD God of Israel, [11] and there I have set the Ark containing the Covenant that the LORD made with the Israelites."

[12] Then, standing before the altar of the LORD in front of the whole congregation of Israel, he spread forth his hands. [13] Solomon had made a bronze platform[b] and placed it in the midst of the Great Court; it was 5 cubits long and 5 cubits wide and 3 cubits high. He stood on it; then, kneeling in front of the whole congregation of Israel, he spread forth his hands to heaven [14] and said, "O LORD God of Israel, there is no god like You in the heavens and on the earth, You who steadfastly maintain the Covenant with Your servants who walk before You with all their heart; [15] You who have kept the promises You made to Your servant, my father David; You made a promise and have fulfilled it—as is now the case. [16] And now, O LORD God of Israel, keep that promise that You made to Your servant, my father David, 'You shall never lack a descendant in My sight sitting on the throne of Israel if only your children will look to their way and walk in the [path] of My teachings as you have walked before Me.' [17] Now, therefore, O God of Israel, let the promise that You made to Your servant, my father David, be confirmed.

[18] "Does God really dwell with man on earth? Even the heavens to their uttermost reaches cannot contain You; how much less this House that I have built! [19] Yet turn, O LORD my God, to the prayer and supplication of Your servant, and hear the cry and the prayer that Your servant offers to You. [20] May Your eyes be open day and night toward this House, toward the place where You have resolved to make Your name abide; may You heed the prayers that Your servant offers toward this place. [21] And when You hear the supplications that Your servant and Your people Israel offer toward this place, give heed in Your heavenly abode—give heed and pardon.

[22] "If a man commits an offense against his fellow, and an oath is exacted from him, causing him to utter an imprecation against himself, and he comes with his impreca-

6.12–42: Solomon's dedicatory prayer. This section, together with 7.1–11, may also be titled the "Consecration of the Altar." Though fundamentally similar to 1 Kings 8.22–53, two differences stand out: 2 Chron. 6.12–42 contains fewer references to the exodus (it is omitted from 1 Kings 8.21, 51) and places greater emphasis on the role of the Davidic covenant. **16:** 1 Kings 8.25 reads "to walk before me." Chronicles expresses the "Torah-centered" perspective, wherein proper service of God is defined, exclusively, by observance of the commandments. The Heb word "torah," in this and other contexts, has been rendered by some commentators *teachings* (as here) and by others as "the Torah (i.e., Pentateuch)"; in Chronicles, the latter is more likely.

a Lit. "risen in place of."   b Meaning of Heb. uncertain.

tion before Your altar in this House, [23] may You hear in heaven and take action to judge Your servants, requiting him who is in the wrong by bringing down the punishment of his conduct on his head, vindicating him who is in the right by rewarding him according to his righteousness.

[24] "Should Your people Israel be defeated by an enemy because they have sinned against You, and then once again acknowledge Your name and offer prayer and supplication to You in this House, [25] may You hear in heaven and pardon the sin of Your people Israel, and restore them to the land that You gave to them and to their fathers.

[26] "Should the heavens be shut up and there be no rain because they have sinned against You, and then they pray toward this place and acknowledge Your name and repent of their sins, because You humbled them, [27] may You hear in heaven and pardon the sin of Your servants, Your people Israel, when You have shown them the proper way in which they are to walk, and send down rain upon the land that You gave to Your people as their heritage. [28] So, too, if there is a famine in the land, if there is pestilence, blight, mildew, locusts, or caterpillars, or if an enemy oppresses them in any of the settlements of their land.

"In any plague and in any disease, [29] any prayer or supplication offered by any person among all Your people Israel—each of whom knows his affliction and his pain—when he spreads forth his hands toward this House, [30] may You hear in Your heavenly abode, and pardon. Deal with each man according to his ways as You know his heart to be—for You alone know the hearts of all men—[31] so that they may revere You all the days that they live on the land that You gave to our fathers.

[32] "Or if a foreigner who is not of Your people Israel comes from a distant land for the sake of Your great name, Your mighty hand, and Your outstretched arm, if he comes to pray toward this House, [33] may You hear in Your heavenly abode and grant whatever the foreigner appeals to You for. Thus all the peoples of the earth will know Your name and revere You, as does Your people Israel; and they will recognize that Your name is attached to this House that I have built.

[34] "When Your people take the field against their enemies in a campaign on which You send them, and they pray to You in the direction of the city which You have chosen and the House which I have built to Your name, [35] may You hear in heaven their prayer and supplication and uphold their cause.

[36] "When they sin against You—for there is no person

who does not sin—and You are angry with them and deliver them to the enemy, and their captors carry them off to an enemy land, near or far; [37] and they take it to heart in the land to which they have been carried off, and repent and make supplication to You in the land of their captivity, saying, 'We have sinned, we have acted perversely, we have acted wickedly,' [38] and they turn back to You with all their heart and soul, in the land of their captivity where they were carried off, and pray in the direction of their land which You gave to their fathers and the city which You have chosen, and toward the House which I have built for Your name—[39] may You hear their prayer and supplication in Your heavenly abode, uphold their cause, and pardon Your people who have sinned against You. [40] Now My God, may Your eyes be open and Your ears attentive to prayer from this place, and now,

[41]   Advance, O LORD God, to your resting-place,
        You and Your mighty Ark.
        Your priests, O LORD God, are clothed in triumph;
        Your loyal ones will rejoice in [Your] goodness.
[42]   O LORD God,
        do not reject Your anointed one;
        remember the loyalty of Your servant David."

7 [a]When Solomon finished praying, fire descended from heaven and consumed the burnt offering and the sacrifices, and the glory of the LORD filled the House. [2] The priests could not enter the House of the LORD, for the glory of the LORD filled the House of the LORD. [3] All the Israelites witnessed the descent of the fire and the glory of the LORD on the House; they knelt with their faces to the ground and prostrated themselves, praising the LORD, "For He is good, for His steadfast love is eternal."

[4] Then the king and all the people offered sacrifices before the LORD. [5] King Solomon offered as sacrifices 22,000 oxen and 120,000 sheep; thus the king and all the people dedicated the House of God. [6] The priests stood at their

a Cf. 1 Kings 8.54-9.9.

present consecration of the altar. Citation of Psalms in Chronicles, but not in Kings may suggest that some form had become known by the time of the Chronicler; since Ps. 132 addresses many topics central to Chronicles (e.g., the dynastic promise, David's devotion to the cultus), it is especially suitable for quotation. The phrase *mighty Ark* (v. 41) reflects the Ark's function as divine throne-footstool (see 1 Chron. 13.6) and the view that the divine warrior, seated upon the Ark/cherubs, would lead His people in (victorious) battle (e.g., Num. 10.35; 1 Sam. 4.3-8; see also Ps. 78.61). Chronicles has left its mark on traditional Jewish prayer, in that it is customary in many congregations to recite the Psalms version of these vv. when returning the Torah scroll to the synagogue "ark," its "resting place."

7.1–11: Descent of divine fire and concluding ceremonies. 1–3: The divine Presence fills the Temple, in response to Solomon's prayer; these vv. are absent in 1 Kings. Vv. 1 and 3 echo the dedication of the Mosaic Tabernacle at Lev. 9.24; in both passages a divine fire consumes the sacrifice in the presence of the people, who then prostrate themselves and sing the LORD's praise. (See also the reference to the divine Presence three times in these three verses and in Lev. 9.23.) The Chronicler thus also establishes a continuum between the Tabernacle and Temple, including, by implication, the Second Temple of his own day; see 1 Chron. 21.26, which forms the connecting link between Lev. ch 9 and the present v. The recurring refrain, "for He is good . . . eternal" (see 1 Chron. 16.34 n.) expresses the belief in the beneficence and protection of Him whose glory resides in the Temple. The present passage complements the appearance of the divine glory at 5.11–14: The former marks the dedication of the Temple, accomplished by placement of the Ark within it, the latter the dedication of the altar. **6:** Chronicles stresses the Davidic origin of Levitic praise and music, which Solomon ap-

41–42: These vv. appear (with some variation) in Ps. 132.8–10; since they are contextually appropriate, Chronicles places them here, in Solomon's mouth. The concluding words (*the loyalty of Your servant David*) in Heb are ambiguous, referring either to David's acts of steadfast love toward the LORD or the LORD's

steadfast love toward David (see Isa. 55.3); here they emphasize the fulfillment of David's role in establishing the cultus. These vv. differ from the concluding part of Solomon's prayer in 2 Kings (8.54–61). There, Solomon petitions the LORD to accept Israel's future prayers in the Temple; here, Solomon's words form part of the

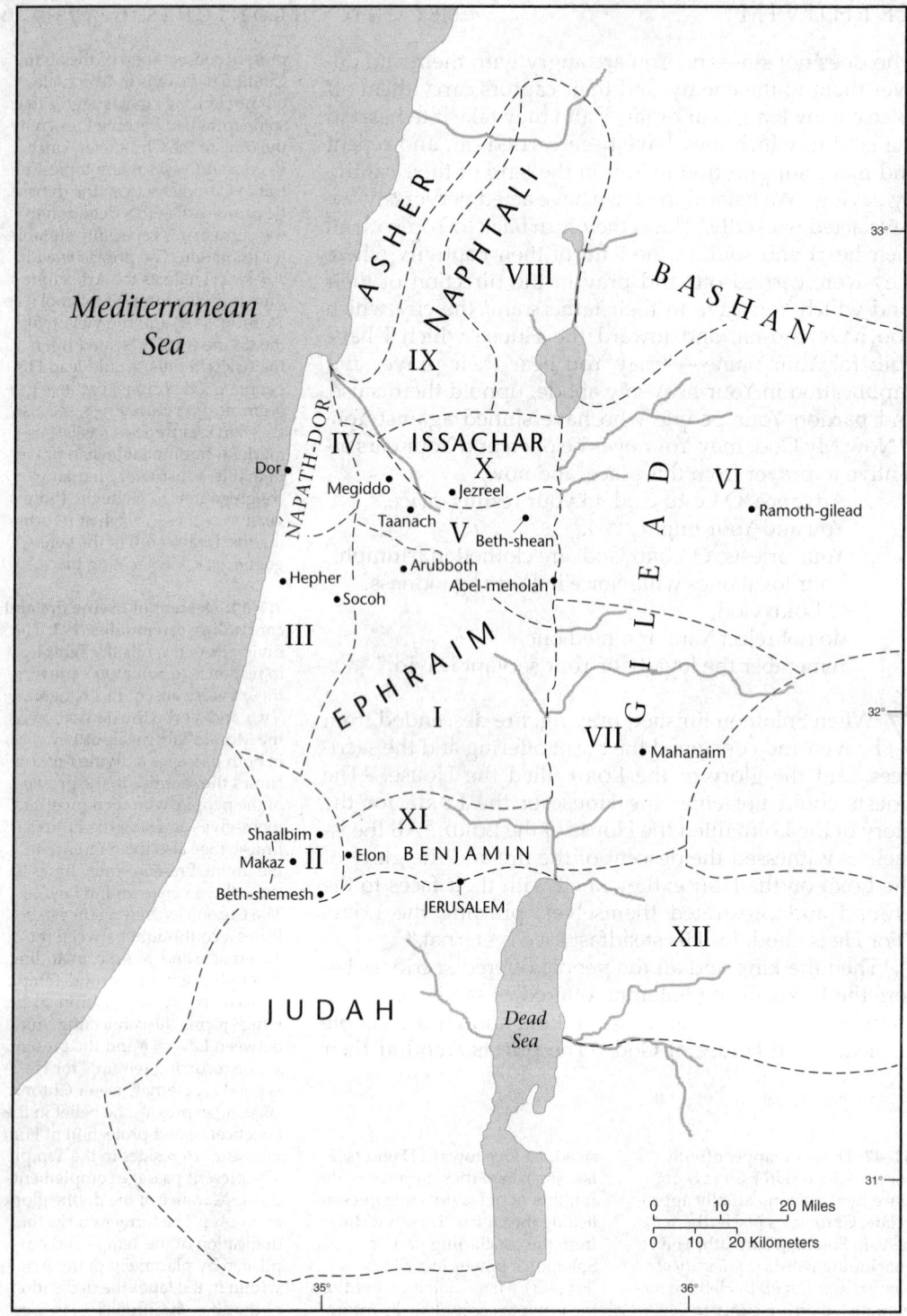

Mediterranean
Sea

A S H E R

N A P H T A L I

VIII

B A S H A N

IX

NAPATH-DOR

IV

ISSACHAR
X

• Dor

Megiddo •

• Jezreel

VI

G I L E A D

• Ramoth-gilead

Taanach •

V

• Beth-shean

• Hepher

• Arubboth

• Socoh

Abel-meholah •

III

E P H R A I M

I

VII

• Mahanaim

Shaalbim •

XI

Makaz • II

• Elon

B E N J A M I N

Beth-shemesh •

JERUSALEM

XII

J U D A H

Dead
Sea

33°

32°

31°

0   10   20 Miles

0   10   20 Kilometers

35°

36°

The kingdom of Solomon according to Second Chronicles

watches; the Levites with the instruments for the LORD's music that King David had made to praise the LORD, "For His steadfast love is eternal," by means of the psalms of David that they knew. The priests opposite them blew trumpets while all Israel were standing.

7 Solomon consecrated the center of the court in front of the House of the LORD, because he presented there the burnt offerings and the fat parts of the offerings of well-being, since the bronze altar that Solomon had made was not able to hold the burnt offerings, the meal offerings, and the fat parts. 8 At that time Solomon kept the Feast for seven days—all Israel with him—a great assemblage from Lebo-hamath to the Wadi of Egypt.

9 On the eighth day they held a solemn gathering; they observed the dedication of the altar seven days, and the Feast seven days. 10 On the twenty-third day of the seventh month he dismissed the people to their homes, rejoicing and in good spirits over the goodness that the LORD had shown to David and Solomon and His people Israel.

11 Thus Solomon finished building the House of the LORD and the royal palace; Solomon succeeded in everything he had set his heart on accomplishing with regard to the House of the LORD and his palace. 12 The LORD appeared to Solomon at night and said to him, "I have heard your prayer and have chosen this site as My House of sacrifice. 13 If I shut up the heavens and there is no rain; if I command the locusts to ravage the land; or if I let loose pestilence against My people, 14 when My people, who bear My name, humble themselves, pray, and seek My favor and turn from their evil ways, I will hear in My heavenly abode and forgive their sins and heal their land. 15 Now My eyes will be open and My ears attentive to the prayers from this place. 16 And now I have chosen and consecrated this House that My name be there forever. My eyes and My heart shall always be there. 17 As for you, if you walk before Me as your father David walked before Me, doing all that I have commanded you, keeping My laws and rules, 18 then I will establish your royal throne over Israel forever, in accordance with the Covenant I made with your father David, saying, 'You shall never lack a descendant ruling over Israel.' 19 But if you turn away from Me and forsake My laws and commandments that I set before you, and go and serve other gods and worship them, 20 then I will uproot them[a] from My land that I gave them, and this House that I consecrated to My name I shall cast out of my sight, and make it a proverb

plied to the newly built Temple. **8–11:** The conclusion of the ceremony. 1 Kings 8.65–66 seems unaware of both Yom Kippur (Day of Atonement/Purgation), which falls on the tenth of the seventh month (Lev. 23.26–32; Num. 29.7–11), and the eighth-day assembly, following the seventh day of Sukkot (Lev. 23.36; Num. 29.35–38). Kings' text is generally understood to reflect the festival cycle of Deut. ch 16, which recognizes only three pilgrimage festivals. Chronicles harmonizes Kings with all of the relevant Torah sources, especially the Priestly calendar, by claiming that the people returned on the twenty-third of the month, i.e., the day following the eighth-day assembly. The lack of mention of Yom Kippur remains surprising. Some scholars think that Chronicles, in opposition to 1 Kings, maintains that the two seven-day celebration periods (Sukkot and the Temple dedication) overlapped. This period would have extended from the fifteenth through the twenty-second of the month, i.e., after the fast and purgation rites of Yom Kippur. Alternatively, and less likely, Chronicles' terse style may reflect an attempt to simply skirt the issue. Rabbinic sources claim that Yom Kippur was not observed that year owing to the unique nature of the occasion (*Gen. Rab.* 35; *b. Mo'ed Kat.* 9a).

7.12–22: The LORD's reply to Solomon. Similar to 1 Kings 9.2–9, Chronicles' formulation creates a "tighter" correspondence between Solomon's prayer and the divine response through the addition of vv. 13–15. **17–18:** Chronicles' formulation (cf. 1 Kings 9.5) highlights the assurance of an eternal dynasty, assuming Solomon's fulfillment of the necessary conditions. V. 18, *ruling over Israel* ("moshel 'al yisra'el"), echoes Mic. 5.1, highlighting the dynastic promise.

---

a I.e., Israel; cf. 1 Kings 9.7.

and a byword among all peoples. [21] And as for this House, once so exalted, everyone passing by it shall be appalled and say, 'Why did the LORD do thus to this land and to this House?' [22] And the reply will be, 'It is because they forsook the LORD God of their fathers who freed them from the land of Egypt, and adopted other gods and worshiped them and served them; therefore He brought all this calamity upon them.' "

8 [a]At the end of twenty years, during which Solomon constructed the House of the LORD and his palace— [2] Solomon also rebuilt the cities that Huram had given to him,[b] and settled Israelites in them—[3] Solomon marched against Hamath-zobah and overpowered it. [4] He built Tadmor in the desert and all the garrison towns that he built in Hamath. [5] He built Upper Beth-horon and Lower Beth-horon as fortified cities with walls, gates, and bars, [6] as well as Baalath and all of Solomon's garrison towns, chariot towns, and cavalry towns—everything that Solomon desired to build in Jerusalem and in the Lebanon, and throughout the territory that he ruled. [7] All the people that were left of the Hittites, Amorites, Perizzites, Hivites, and Jebusites, none of whom were of Israelite stock—[8] those of their descendants who were left after them in the land, whom the Israelites had not annihilated—these Solomon subjected to forced labor, as is still the case. [9] But the Israelites, none of whom Solomon enslaved for his works, served as soldiers and as his chief officers, and as commanders of his chariotry and cavalry. [10] These were King Solomon's prefects—250 foremen over the people. [11] Solomon brought up Pharaoh's daughter from the City of David to the palace that he had built for her, for he said, "No wife of mine shall dwell in a palace of King David of Israel, for [the area] is sacred since the Ark of the LORD has entered it."

a Cf. 1 Kings 9.10–28.   b Lit. "Solomon."

8.1–16: Other projects. 1–6: Solomon expands Israel's territory. 1 Kings 9.11–13 states that Solomon relinquished twenty cities to Hiram in payment for materiel. Hiram there addresses Solomon as "my brother," a technical term used in the ancient Near East between sovereigns of equal stature, and then reproves him for having made payment with land of poor quality. Some medieval and modern commentators adopt a harmonistic approach to the parallel passages, arguing that Kings and Chronicles complement each other. This view may be buttressed by the fact that Israel's northern frontier shifted during the early monarchy between Israelite and Phoenician rule. Others argue that Chronicles' text is tendentious. Chronicles could not accept the fact that Solomon, the wealthiest of kings, would be forced to relinquish land in payment. This is especially problematic for Chronicles, given its maximalistic approach to Israel's borders and its view that the entirety of Israel's territory had been settled before David's time (see 1 Chron. 13.5; cf. the critique of Saul at 1 Chron. 10.7). In addition, the absence of any apparent motive for Huram's (unilateral) gesture suggests that Chronicles' position is tendentious. Furthermore, Huram's reproof of Solomon as depicted in Kings is unacceptable to Chronicles (see 2.1–15 n.). Vv. 3–6, which have as their theme "Solomon as successful builder of Israel," then form a seamless continuation of v. 2. Indeed, this passage mentions only Solomon's achievements; setbacks mentioned in 1 Kings, e.g., Pharaoh's incursion into Israel and capture of the city of Gezer (9.16), are omitted by Chronicles. **3–10:** *Lebanon,* the mountains of anti-Lebanon. **10:** *250:* 1 Kings 9.23 reads "550." Medieval commentators (Rashi, Radak) averred that the present v. refers only to Israelites, whereas 1 Kings ch 9 includes the foreign officials. Some have observed that the differential of "300" corresponds to a similar difference between 2.17 (3,600 overseers) and 1 Kings 5.30 (3,300 overseers); thus the total number is the same in each book. This explanation is problematic; Chronicles plainly states that Gentile overseers are involved at 2.17, Israelites here. The present v. may simply be the result of scribal error. **11:** 1 Kings 9.10–13, Chronicles' source, functions as part of the "Solomon as builder" theme; he fortifies cities throughout his domain, including Jerusalem, and suggests that his wife's move was the result of personal motives. Chronicles gives the incident a religious motive; he moves his wife into another domicile, because her presence in the sacred precincts is improper. The juxtaposition of this v. to the following (reworked) passage, along with the shared Heb term "he'elah" *(brought up, offered),* suggests a shared theme: Solomon as guardian and patron of the Temple and its environs. Chroni-

12 At that time, Solomon offered burnt offerings on the altar that he had built in front of the porch. 13 What was due for each day he sacrificed according to the commandment of Moses for the sabbaths, the new moons, and the thrice-yearly festivals—the Feast of Unleavened Bread, the Feast of Weeks, and the Feast of Booths. 14 Following the prescription of his father David, he set up the divisions of the priests for their duties, and the Levites for their watches, to praise and to serve alongside the priests, according to each day's requirement, and the gatekeepers in their watches, gate by gate, for such was the commandment of David, the man of God. 15 They did not depart from the commandment of the king relating to the priests and the Levites in all these matters and also relating to the treasuries. 16 And all of Solomon's work was well executed from the day the House of the LORD was founded until the House of the LORD was completed to perfection.

17 At that time Solomon went to Ezion-geber and to Eloth on the seacoast of the land of Edom. 18 Huram sent him, under the charge of servants, a fleet with a crew of expert seamen; they went with Solomon's men to Ophir, and obtained gold there in the amount of 450 talents, which they brought to King Solomon.

9 ^aThe queen of Sheba heard of Solomon's fame, and came to Jerusalem to test Solomon with hard questions, accompanied by a very large retinue, including camels bearing spices, a great quantity of gold, and precious stones. When she came to Solomon, she spoke to him of all that she had on her mind. 2 Solomon had answers for all her questions; there was nothing that Solomon did not know, nothing to which he could not give her an answer.

3 When the queen of Sheba saw how wise Solomon was and the palace he had built, 4 the fare of his table, the seating of his courtiers, the service and attire of his attendants, his butlers and their attire, and the procession with which he went up to the House of the LORD, it took her breath away. 5 She said to the king, "What I heard in my own land about you and your wisdom was true. 6 I did not believe what they said until I came and saw with my own eyes that not even the half of your great wisdom had been described to me; you surpass the report that I heard. 7 How fortunate are your men and how fortunate are these courtiers of yours who are always in attendance on you and can hear your wisdom! 8 Blessed is the LORD your

cles' depiction of Solomon is at polar odds with that of Kings. The latter has Solomon tolerating and even supporting the foreign worship of his many wives (11.1). Chronicles not only omits this entire issue—Solomon's numerous wives as well as their cultic offenses—but stresses that Solomon exhibited cultic zeal precisely by "cracking down" on his wife. For discussion of Solomon's marriage to a foreigner, see introduction.
12–16: Chronicles elaborates on 1 Kings 9.25, bringing it into harmony with Num. chs 28–29 and Deut. ch 16. In general the Chronicler "updates" his sources by bringing them in conformity with Priestly and Deuteronomic Torah material; the Chronicler assumes that righteous kings such as Solomon certainly followed these laws. **14:** *Man of God,* a title also applied to Moses (Deut. 33.1; Ps. 90.1) as well as to several other biblical figures. Its purpose here is to highlight the parallel between David and Moses as founders of Israel's cultus and its norms.

8.17–9.31: Solomon's grandeur. 8.17–18: Solomon is again depicted as the dominant monarch. That Huram's ships were transported either by land or by a canal connecting the Red Sea and the Nile is historically improbable. **9.1–12:** Queen of Sheba visits. This passage is largely identical to 1 Kings 10.11–13; it furthers Chronicles' depiction of Solomon's success and majesty. **8:** This v. forms an inclusio with the blessing uttered by Huram at 2.11. (Kings mentions this only once; see 1 Kings 10.9.) Huram, a northern neighbor of Israel, and the queen of Sheba, from a country to the south, together symbolize universal recognition of Solomon's importance and, specifically, that the Davidic monarch is a concrete sign of the LORD's love for Israel. This is another expression of Chronicles' messianic aspirations. Note that Chronicles again claims that the Davidic monarchs are the earthly representatives of divine rule; see 1 Chron. 17.14.

a Cf. 1 Kings 10; 11.41–43.

God, who favored you and set you on His throne as a king before the LORD. It is because of your God's love for Israel and in order to establish them forever that He made you king over them to execute righteous justice."

⁹ She presented the king with 120 talents of gold, and a vast quantity of spices and precious stones. There were no such spices as those which the queen of Sheba gave to King Solomon—¹⁰ also, the servants of Huram and Solomon who brought gold from Ophir brought algum-wood and precious stones. ¹¹ The king made of the algum-wood ramps for the House of the LORD and for the royal palace, and lyres and harps for the musicians, whose like had never before been seen in the land of Judah—¹² King Solomon, in turn, gave the queen of Sheba everything she expressed a desire for, exceeding a return for what she had brought to the king. Then she and her courtiers left and returned to her own land.

¹³ The gold that Solomon received every year weighed 666 gold talents, ¹⁴ besides what traders and merchants brought, and the gold and silver that all the kings of Arabia and governors of the regions brought to Solomon. ¹⁵ King Solomon made 200 shields of beaten gold—600 shekels of beaten gold for each shield, ¹⁶ and 300 bucklers of beaten gold—300 [shekels] of gold for each buckler. The king placed them in the Lebanon Forest House. ¹⁷ The king also made a large throne of ivory, overlaid with pure gold. ¹⁸ Six steps led up to the throne; and the throne had a golden footstool attached to it, and arms on either side of the seat. Two lions stood beside the arms, ¹⁹ and twelve lions stood on the six steps, six on either side. None such was ever made for any other kingdom. ²⁰ All of King Solomon's drinking vessels were of gold, and all the utensils of the Lebanon Forest House were of pure gold; silver counted for nothing in Solomon's days. ²¹ The king's fleet traveled to Tarshish with Huram's servants. Once every three years, the Tarshish fleet came in, bearing gold and silver, ivory, apes, and peacocks.

²² King Solomon surpassed all the kings of the earth in wealth and wisdom. ²³ All the kings of the earth came to pay homage to Solomon and to listen to the wisdom with which God had endowed him. ²⁴ Each brought his tribute—silver and gold objects, robes, weapons, and spices, horses and mules—in the amount due each year. ²⁵ Solomon had 4,000 stalls for horses and chariots, and 12,000 horsemen, which he stationed in the chariot towns and with the king in Jerusalem. ²⁶ He ruled over all the kings from the Euphrates to the land of the Philistines and to the border of Egypt. ²⁷ The king made silver as plentiful in Je-

12: *Gave [her] . . . everything she expressed a desire for:* The exchange of gifts is a mark of cordial relations between sovereigns; Chronicles probably did not view it as signifying a formal treaty; see 2.16–17. **13–28:** Miscellaneous notices. Following 1 Kings 10.14–28, with minor differences. **18–19:** The use of *twelve lions* probably reflects the unity of Israel's tribes. Rabbinic sources deal extensively with the design and significance of Solomon's throne. Although the reticence of rabbinic sources implies no criticism of Solomon's use of iconography, Josephus (*Ant.*) states that Solomon's production of the lion images was sinful; see 4.2–5. **21–23:** Solomon's commercial ventures. Elsewhere the Bible identifies *Tarshish* as a source of silver, iron, and lead—not gold, ivory, apes, etc. 1 Kings 10.22 refers to "Tarshish vessels," with no reference to the vessels' destination. Some scholars locate Tarshish in Africa, along the Red Sea, and historical sources indicate that Tarshish lay in the Mediterranean basin, not along the Red Sea, as emerges from Chronicles. Chronicles' text may reflect an ancient misunderstanding of a technical term, a phenomenon attested in LXX to 1 Kings 10.22, as well. *Tarshish fleet* or Tarshish ships originally denoted a type of maritime vessel, not the ship's destination or route; see 20.36–37. **25–28:** Solomon's extreme wealth would seem to be in violation of Deut. 17.17 and may have led the translators of LXX to 1 Kings to bring Solomon's depiction more in line with Deut. ch 17. Indeed, rabbinic sources are critical of the excessive number of horses, in violation of the same v. (see *b. Sanh.* 21b). Some medieval Jewish scholars maintained that Deuteronomy's limitation on royal wealth refers only to wealth gained by levying of taxes (R. Meir Abulafia, Nissim Gerondi, *b. Sanh.* 21b). Alternatively, some explained that the monarch was prohibited only from amassing wealth for purely personal glory, whereas wealth used to bring honor to the king-rusalem as stones, and cedars as plentiful as sycamores in the Shephelah. ²⁸ Horses were brought for Solomon from Egypt and all the lands. ²⁹ The other events of Solomon's reign, early and late, are recorded in the chronicle of the prophet Nathan and in the prophecies of Ahijah the Shilonite and in the visions of Jedo the seer concerning Jeroboam son of Nebat. ³⁰ Solomon reigned forty years over all Israel in Jerusalem. ³¹ Solomon slept with his fathers and was buried in the city of his father David; his son Rehoboam succeeded him as king.

10 ª Rehoboam went to Shechem, for all Israel had come to Shechem to acclaim him king. ² Jeroboam son of Nebat learned of it while he was in Egypt where he had fled from King Solomon, and Jeroboam returned from Egypt. ³ They sent for him; and Jeroboam and all Israel came and spoke to Rehoboam as follows: ⁴ "Your father made our yoke heavy. Now lighten the harsh labor and the heavy yoke that your father laid on us, and we will

a Cf. 1 Kings 12.1–19.

dom was permitted (Maimonides, *Laws of Kings and their Wars*, Menahem ha-Meiri, *b. Sanh.* 21b). **29–31:** No mention is made of Solomon's offenses; cf. 1 Kings ch 11. Following a model established with David, Solomon's official biography was composed by prophets; see 1 Chron. 29.28–30. Solomon's reign of forty years parallels that of David, a further example of the way these monarchs mirror each other for the Chronicler. Many scholars maintain, with Josephus's *Ant.*, that Iddo (Jedo), the seer, is to be identified with the anonymous prophet of 1 Kings 13.1–10; see 12.15; 13.22. The mention of the prophet *Ahijah the Shilonite* is especially surprising, since according to 1 Kings 11.29–30; 12.15, sources omitted by Chronicles, he tells Solomon of the dissolution of the united monarchy.

10.1–36.23: From Rehoboam to the exile. This section builds on the parallels in Kings, but offers much new information and many differing assessments of monarchs. The literary forms (topoi; sg. topos) in this section are: building reports, military stock and capabil-

ities, sickness and death, military victories and defeats. With regard to each of these, arguments have been made in support of both their (purported) fictional character as well as their (purported) factual nature, based on authentic sources that Chronicles, but not the author of Kings, had. Perhaps the most salient topos of this section is that of war accounts. Fifteen such reports appear, all without parallel in Kings. Some scholars see the novel features of Chronicles' formulation as the creation of its author, who sought to portray the first four post-Solomonic kings positively, so as to establish the legitimacy of Judah over its northern neighbor, the Samaritans. It is further argued that the battles reported here reflect Second Temple reality, when Judah was surrounded by neighbors who posed a territorial and religious threat. The message of these reports is understood to be that salvation lies in cultic fidelity. Other scholars counter by noting that Chronicles' treatment of the first four post-Solomonic kings is not uniformly positive in nature. With regard to the battle accounts, these scholars

acknowledge that they are all characterized by Chronistic style and moralizing, but argue that the numerous details (of geography, proper nouns, etc.) point to a genuine historical basis. In addition, it is argued that most of the battles involve Israelite military activity, such that Israel's victories cannot be attributed, exclusively, to religious fidelity. The bulk of this section, 10.1–28.27, describes a divided "house." Judah, and parts of the other tribes who identify with Judah, remain faithful to the Davidic monarchy and the Jerusalem Temple. The bulk of the northern tribes follow the illegitimate kings of (northern) Israel. As noted in the introduction, Chronicles focuses exclusively on Judah (and its supporters), mentioning the northern empire only where it affects Judah's fortunes. Though some scholars see the "anti-northern" critique as applying to the populace of the north, namely the Samaritans who were contemporaries of the Chronicler, most agree that the Chronicler inveighs only against the northern monarchs and their supporters.

10.1–11.4: Rehoboam's coronation and division of the monarchy. Shechem was an ancient religious center of the northern tribes. The choice of this northern site, rather than Jerusalem, for Rehoboam's coronation indicates that there was opposition among the northern tribes to Rehoboam's accession, most likely because they feared that he would continue Solomon's policies of conscription for forced labor. Thus, although Chronicles' description of Solomon's reign creates the impression of prosperity and almost utopian social harmony, this passage, along with the ensuing episode, indicates that the actual situation was quite different. **10.2–3:** These vv. are problematic in Chronicles, since the relevant background material in Kings has been omitted. 1 Kings 11.29–40 relates the story of Jeroboam as told by Ahijah the prophet: Owing to Solomon's role in his wives' cultic offenses, the serve you." [5] He answered them, "Come back to me in three days." So the people went away.

[6] King Rehoboam took counsel with the elders who had served during the lifetime of his father Solomon. He said, "What answer do you counsel to give these people?" [7] They answered him, "If you will be good to these people and appease them and speak to them with kind words, they will be your servants always." [8] But he ignored the counsel that the elders gave him, and took counsel with the young men who had grown up with him and were serving him. [9] "What," he asked, "do you counsel that we reply to these people who said to me, 'Lighten the yoke that your father laid on us'?" [10] And the young men who had grown up with him answered, "Speak thus to the people who said to you, 'Your father made our yoke heavy, now you make it lighter for us.' Say to them, 'My little finger is thicker than my father's loins. [11] My father imposed a heavy yoke on you, and I will add to your yoke; my father flogged you with whips, but I [will do so] with scorpions.' "

[12] Jeroboam and all the people came to Rehoboam on the third day, since the king had told them, "Come back on the third day." [13] The king answered them harshly; thus King Rehoboam ignored the elders' counsel. [14] He spoke to them in accordance with the counsel of the young men, and said, ᵃ-"I will make-ᵃ your yoke heavy, and I will add to it; my father flogged you with whips, but I [will do so] with scorpions." [15] The king did not listen to the people, for God had brought it about in order that the LORD might fulfill the promise that He had made through Ahijah the Shilonite to Jeroboam son of Nebat. [16] When all Israel [saw] that the king had not listened to them, the people answered the king:

> "We have no portion in David,
> No share in Jesse's son!
> To your tents, O Israel!
> Now look to your own house, O David."

So all Israel returned to their homes.ᵇ [17] But Rehoboam continued to reign over the Israelites who lived in the towns of Judah. [18] King Rehoboam sent out Hadoram, who was in charge of the forced labor, but the Israelites pelted him to death with stones. Thereupon, King Rehoboam hurriedly mounted his chariot and fled to Jerusalem. [19] Israel has been in revolt against the house of David to this day.

a-a *Some mss. and printed editions read "my father made"; cf. 1 Kings 12.14.*
b *Lit. "tents."*

northern tribes will be taken away from Solomon and Jeroboam will rule over these tribes. Thereafter, Jeroboam flees to Egypt and returns to the land of Israel following Solomon's demise. Chronicles deletes all of this material, for two reasons. First, it indicates that the period of Solomon's rule was not quite so idyllic, nor was his personal conduct exemplary. Second, Kings offers explicit legitimization for the existence of a northern, non-Davidic dynasty, provided that it observe God's laws. As already noted (introduction), Chronicles views the very existence of a non-Davidic dynasty as both treasonous and rebellion against God. Chronicles' omission of this material results in several problems. First, the reader of Chronicles has no prior acquaintance with Jeroboam, unless he has previously read 1 Kings. Many scholars therefore argue that Chronicles, here and elsewhere, presumes the reader's familiarity with the earlier sources. Indeed, v. 15, contains a clear allusion to 1 Kings 11.29–39. If correct, the Chronicler assumes that his readers know 1 Kings, but seeks to recast the information found there. **18:** The name *Hadoram* appears in 1 Kings (12.18) as Adoram. This is another instance in which Chronicles has preserved the original form of a name; see 1 Chron. 18.10 n. **19:** It is unclear whether Chronicles views Rehoboam as culpable for the division of the monarchy or, rather, as a victim of inexperience and bad counseling. Given Chronicles' view of retribution, and the fact that Chronicles makes no mention of Solomon's offenses and the punishment pronounced in 1 Kings, one would expect that the secession of the northern tribes would be attributed to Rehoboam's wrongful conduct. But v. 15 indicates that the entire episode was divinely guided so as to allow for fulfillment of Ahijah's royal oracle. Moreover, as explained below, Chronicles seems to exonerate Rehoboam by claiming that his miscalculations were the result of youthful inexperience in handling

11 ^aWhen Rehoboam arrived in Jerusalem, he mustered the house of Judah and Benjamin, 180,000 picked fighting men, to make war with Israel in order to restore the kingdom to Rehoboam. ²But the word of the LORD came to Shemaiah, the man of God: ³"Say to Rehoboam son of Solomon king of Judah, and to all Israel in Judah and Benjamin: ⁴Thus said the LORD: You shall not set out to make war on your kinsmen. Let every man return to his home, for this thing has been brought about by Me." They heeded the words of the LORD and refrained from marching against Jeroboam. ⁵Rehoboam dwelt in Jerusalem and built fortified towns in Judah. ⁶He built up Bethlehem, and Etam, and Tekoa, ⁷and Beth-zur, and Soco, and Adullam, ⁸and Gath, and Mareshah, and Ziph, ⁹and Adoraim, and Lachish, and Azekah, ¹⁰and Zorah, and Aijalon, and Hebron, which are in Judah and in Benjamin, as fortified towns. ¹¹He strengthened the fortified towns and put commanders in them, along with stores of food, oil, and wine, ¹²and shields and spears in every town. He strengthened them exceedingly; thus Judah and Benjamin were his.

¹³The priests and the Levites, from all their territories throughout Israel, presented themselves to him. ¹⁴The Levites had left their pasturelands and their holdings and had set out for Judah and Jerusalem, for Jeroboam and his sons had prevented them from serving the LORD, ¹⁵having appointed his own priests for the shrines, goat-demons, and calves which he had made. ¹⁶From all the tribes of Israel, those intent on seeking the LORD God of Israel followed them to Jerusalem, to sacrifice to the LORD God of their fathers. ¹⁷They strengthened the kingdom of Judah, and supported Rehoboam son of Solomon for three years, for they followed the ways of David and Solomon for three years.

¹⁸Rehoboam married Mahalath daughter of Jerimoth son of David, and Abihail daughter of Eliab son of Jesse. ¹⁹She bore him sons: Jeush, Shemariah, and Zaham. ²⁰He then took Maacah daughter of Absalom; she bore him Abijah, Attai, Ziza, and Shelomith. ²¹Rehoboam loved Maacah daughter of Absalom more than his other wives and concubines—for he took eighteen wives and sixty concubines; he begot twenty-eight sons and sixty daughters. ²²Rehoboam designated Abijah son of Maacah as chief and leader among his brothers, for he intended him to be his successor. ²³He prudently distributed all his sons throughout the regions of Judah and Benjamin and

a With 11.1–4, cf. 1 Kings 12.21–24.

a northern "rebellion." Although a definitive answer is not possible, it is likely that Chronicles does not view the divine decree regarding secession and Rehoboam's own actions as mutually exclusive. **11.1:** Chronicles omits Jeroboam's election by the north (1 Kings 12.20), a point which typifies Chronicles' reticence on matters concerning the northern monarchy. **2–4:** Whereas v. 3 states that Shemaiah's prophecy was to be addressed to *all Israel in Judah and Benjamin,* 1 Kings 12.23 reads "the House of Judah"; Chronicles here integrates Benjamin into the Southern Kingdom.

11.5–12: Rehoboam's building projects. Building projects are a sign of a king's success and divine favor. This favorable evaluation of Rehoboam suggests that he is not the cause of the secession but, rather, its victim. In addition, the juxtaposition of Rehoboam's acceptance of the prophetic directive to refrain from warfare and his successful building ventures also expresses another Chronicles theme, viz., the importance of heeding the prophetic word. This section has no parallel in Kings.

11.13–17: Rehoboam's support for the Levites. This section has no parallel in Kings.

11.18–23: Rehoboam's family. This section has no parallel in Kings. Rehoboam's many wives are further evidence of Chronicles' positive evaluation of Rehoboam. Note that Kings focuses on Jeroboam, devoting only eleven vv. to Rehoboam (1 Kings 14.21–31); Chronicles devotes 11.5–12.16 to Rehoboam, a clear statement of its concern with Judahite kings at the expense of the northern monarchy. Many of the names appearing here are otherwise unattested (e.g., v. 19); others stand in tension with other passages, probably indicating that Chronicles has used an independent source. **20:** *Maacah,* see 13.2 and 1 Kings 15.2, 10.

throughout the fortified towns; he provided them with abundant food, and he sought many wives for them.

12 When the kingship of Rehoboam was firmly established, and he grew strong, he abandoned the Teaching of the LORD, he and all Israel with him.

² In the fifth year of King Rehoboam, King Shishak of Egypt marched against Jerusalem—for they had trespassed against the LORD—³ with 1,200 chariots, 60,000 horsemen and innumerable troops who came with him from Egypt: Lybians, Sukkites, and Kushites. ⁴ He took the fortified towns of Judah and advanced on Jerusalem. ⁵ The prophet Shemaiah came to Rehoboam and the officers of

12.1–12: Shishak's invasion. Chronicles expands upon the parallel passage found at 1 Kings 14.25–28. Chronicles' explanation, seen by many as part of its view on providence and retribution, is that Rehoboam's conduct was virtuous during the initial three years of his reign. During the fourth year he began to sin and, consequently, was punished in the following year. **1–8:** Chronicles specifies that the king, his officers, and the people were all guilty; hence, all were punished—the nation cannot be punished for the acts of the

The divided monarchy according to Second Chronicles. The dashed line shows the approximate boundaries between Israel, Judah, and Philistia.

Judah, who had assembled in Jerusalem because of Shishak, and said to them, "Thus said the LORD: You have abandoned Me, so I am abandoning you to Shishak." [6] Then the officers of Israel and the king humbled themselves and declared, "The LORD is in the right." [7] When the LORD saw that they had submitted, the word of the LORD came to Shemaiah, saying, "Since they have humbled themselves, I will not destroy them but will grant them some measure of deliverance, and My wrath will not be poured out on Jerusalem through Shishak. [8] They will be subject to him, and they will know the difference between serving Me and serving the kingdoms of the earth." King Shishak of Egypt marched against Jerusalem. [9] [a]He took away the treasures of the House of the LORD and the treasures of the royal palace; he took away everything; he took away the golden shields that Solomon had made. [10] King Rehoboam had bronze shields made in their place, and entrusted them to the officers of the guard[b] who guarded the entrance to the royal palace. [11] Whenever the king entered the House of the LORD, the guards would carry them and then bring them back to the armory of the guards. [12] After he had humbled himself, the anger of the LORD was averted and He did not destroy him entirely; in Judah, too, good things were found.

[13] King Rehoboam grew strong in Jerusalem and exercised kingship. Rehoboam was forty-one years old when he became king, and he reigned seventeen years in Jerusalem—the city the LORD had chosen out of all the tribes of Israel to establish His name there. His mother's name was Naamah the Ammonitess. [14] He did what was wrong, for he had not set his heart to seek the LORD. [15] The deeds of Rehoboam, early and late, are recorded in the chronicles of the prophet Shemaiah and Iddo the seer, in the manner of genealogy. There was continuous war between Rehoboam and Jeroboam. [16] Rehoboam slept with his fathers and was buried in the City of David. His son Abijah succeeded him as king.

13 In the eighteenth year of King Jeroboam, Abijah became king over Judah. [2] He reigned three years in Jerusalem; his mother's name was Micaiah daughter of

force suddenly departs, with no apparent loss of life. Chronicles offers no details, military or otherwise. This is an example of Chronicles' use of "one-dimensional" causality.

12.13–15: End of Rehoboam's reign. By mentioning Rehoboam's mother, v. 13 acknowledges (at least some of) Solomon's foreign wives. For prophetic court biographers, see 1 Chron. 29.28–30. Chronicles' overall evaluation of Rehoboam is not one-dimensional. The assessment here is essentially negative. Yet, the following ch offers an apologia on his behalf; see 13.7; 11.3–17. In contrast, 1 Kings 15.3 offers no hint that Rehoboam or the people repented from their idolatrous ways.

13.1–23: Abijah's reign. Chronicles' account of *Abijah* shares virtually nothing with the much briefer account (eight vv.) in 1 Kings ch 15 (where his name is Abijam). Furthermore, Chronicles contains not the slightest criticism of Abijah, whereas 1 Kings 15.3–4 states that Abijam was evil and that his rule was preserved merely for the sake of the Davidic dynasty. Chronicles' reworking may have been informed by its theology of retribution; since Kings does not indicate that Abijam was punished for his misdeeds, Chronicles concluded that Abijah could not have been so bad. Alternatively, the tradition concerning Abijah's victory over the north, which many view as authentic, may have led Chronicles to conclude that Abijah was an upright king. (The details of that victory, however, reflect the Chronicler's terminology and ideology, and were likely his creation.) Still, Chronicles does not depict Abijah in the same laudatory terms typical of other righteous kings; the assessments of Kings and Chronicles are therefore not radically different. This position is buttressed by the reference to reforms executed by his son (e.g., 14.2–4), suggesting some shortcomings on Abijah's part. **1–3:** The incredibly large military forces recorded here are typi-

a With vv. 9–16, cf. 1 Kings 14.26–31.   b Lit. "runners."

king alone. As soon as the king repents, he is forgiven. **9–12:** The claim that *good things* were also found among the people may mean either that the people, too, repented, or that they had to their

credit good deeds which offset their sins. Typically, Chronicles claims that contrition effects the LORD's immediate forgiveness, a sign of divine compassion or grace (see introduction). The invading

Uriel of Gibeah. There was war between Abijah and Jeroboam. ³ Abijah joined battle with a force of warriors, 400,000 picked men. Jeroboam arrayed for battle against him 800,000 picked men, warriors. ⁴ Abijah stood on top of Mount Zemaraim in the hill country of Ephraim and said, "Listen to me, Jeroboam and all Israel. ⁵ Surely you know that the LORD God of Israel gave David kingship over Israel forever—to him and his sons—by a covenant of salt. ⁶ Jeroboam son of Nebat had been in the service of Solomon son of David, but he rose up and rebelled against his master. ⁷ Riffraff and scoundrels gathered around him and pressed hard upon Rehoboam son of Solomon. Rehoboam was inexperienced and fainthearted and could not stand up to them. ⁸ Now you are bent on opposing the kingdom of the LORD, which is in the charge of the sons of David, because you are a great multitude and possess the golden calves that Jeroboam made for you as gods. ⁹ Did you not banish the priests of the LORD, the sons of Aaron and the Levites, and, like the peoples of the land, appoint your own priests? Anyone who offered himself for ordination with a young bull of the herd and seven rams became a priest of no-gods! ¹⁰ As for us, the LORD is our God, and we have not forsaken Him. The priests who minister to the LORD are the sons of Aaron, and the Levites are at their tasks. ¹¹ They offer burnt offerings in smoke each morning and each evening, and the aromatic incense, the rows of bread on the pure table; they kindle the golden lampstand with its lamps burning each evening, for we keep the charge of the LORD our God, while you have forsaken it. ¹² See, God is with us as our chief, and His priests have the trumpets for sounding blasts against you. O children of Israel, do not fight the LORD God of your fathers, because you will not succeed." ¹³ Jeroboam, however, had directed the ambush to go around and come from the rear, thus ᵃ the main body was ᵃ in front of Judah, while the ambush was behind them. ¹⁴ When Judah turned around and saw that the fighting was before and behind them, they cried out to the LORD, and the priests blew the trumpets. ¹⁵ The men of Judah raised a shout; and when the men of Judah raised a shout, God routed Jeroboam and all Israel

a-a Lit. "they were."

cal of Chronicles; see 1 Chron. 12.25–39 n. Note that some mss read 14,000 in place of 400,000. Some argue that the 800,000 of the northern forces is the same as the number of "warriors" mentioned at 2 Sam. 24.9, highlighting that Jeroboam mustered every available fighter and outnumbered the enemy but was, nonetheless, defeated. **4:** The location of *Mount Zemaraim* is uncertain, but a Benjaminite town of that name appears at Josh. 18.21–24. LXX reads "Mount Samaria." The use of oration as a rhetorical device in the non-synoptic passages is a ubiquitous feature of Chronicles. Like Herodotus and other Hellenistic historians, the author uses these speeches to express his position on a variety of subjects. **5–12:** This passage is a parade example of Chronicles' critique of the northern dynasty. The appeal to the populace of the north reflects the book's "inclusivist" slant; see introduction. This paradigmatic oration, with its emphasis on the Jerusalem cultus and Davidic monarchy, explains the basis for the divided kingdom and Judah's supremacy, as narrated through ch 28. **5–8:** The Chronicler expresses his view that any monarchy other than the Davidic one is illegitimate. Moreover, since the Davidides are God's proxies, opposition to, and armed struggle against, their rule is tantamount to rebellion against God (see 1 Chron. 17.14 n.). V. 7 indicates that the inexperienced Rehoboam fell victim to a more powerful group of scoundrels. **7–8:** Repetition (in Heb) of "become strong" at the end of v. 7 and the beginning of v. 8 (*stand up to . . . opposing*) is Chronicles' way of saying, "you are attempting to impose your monarchy upon God's representatives, just as you did at the inception of Rehoboam's rule"; see 12.13–15 n. **9–12:** The only true and proper cult is that observed in the Jerusalem Temple, in accordance with the Torah, especially the Priestly laws; treason against the Davidic monarchy and cultic apostasy thus go hand in hand. **13–14:** Chronicles is consistent that the *trumpets* are to be blown, in warfare and on religious occasions, by *priests* only; see 1 Chron. 16.4–6 n. The much larger Israelite force succumbs to Abijah's forces. Here, as in so many other instances, Chronicles jettisons any concrete physical description of the battle; what is recorded is not human military tactics, but the divine will, which responds to before Abijah and Judah. [16] The Israelites fled before Judah, and God delivered them into their hands. [17] Abijah and his army inflicted a severe defeat on them; 500,000 men of Israel fell slain. [18] The Israelites were crushed at that time, while the people of Judah triumphed because they relied on the LORD God of their fathers. [19] Abijah pursued Jeroboam and captured some of his cities—Bethel with its dependencies, Jeshanah with its dependencies, and Ephrain with its dependencies. [20] Jeroboam could not muster strength again during the days of Abijah. The LORD struck him down and he died. [21] But Abijah grew powerful; he married fourteen wives and begat twenty-two sons and sixteen daughters.

[22] The other events of Abijah's reign, his conduct and his acts, are recorded in the story of the prophet Iddo. [23] Abijah slept with his fathers and was buried in the City of David; his son Asa succeeded him as king. The land was untroubled for ten years.

14 Asa did what was good and pleasing to the LORD his God. [2] He abolished the alien altars and shrines; he smashed the pillars and cut down the sacred posts. [3] He ordered Judah to turn to the LORD God of their fathers and to observe the Teaching and the Commandment. [4] He abolished the shrines and the incense stands throughout the cities of Judah, and the kingdom was untroubled under him. [5] He built fortified towns in Judah, since the land was untroubled and he was not engaged in warfare during those years, for the LORD had granted him respite. [6] He said to Judah, "Let us build up these cities and surround them with walls and towers, gates and bars, while the land is at our disposal because we turned to the LORD our God—we turned [to Him] and He gave us respite on all sides." They were successful in their building.

[7] Asa had an army of 300,000 men from Judah bearing shields and spears, and 280,000 from Benjamin bearing bucklers and drawing the bow; all these were valiant men. [8] Zerah the Cushite marched out against them with an army of a thousand thousand and 300 chariots. When he reached Mareshah [9] Asa confronted him, and the battle lines were drawn in the valley of Zephat by Mareshah. [10] Asa called to the LORD his God, and said, "O LORD, it is all the same to You to help the numerous and the powerless. Help us, O LORD our God, for we rely on You, and in Your name we have come against this great multitude. You are the LORD our God. Let no mortal hinder You." [11] So the LORD routed the Cushites before Asa and Judah, and the Cushites fled. [12] Asa and the army with him pur-

human petition and trust in the divine. **19–21:** The expansion, as well as the development, of territory is a sign of success and divine favor; see 8.1–3; 11.5–12. **22–23:** *Story* (Heb "midrash," used only here and in 24.27): The term in postbiblical literature becomes a common term for exegesis and exposition; here it means simply "narrative." Still, the choice of this term reflects Chronicles' view that such stories are the product of prophetic exposition and interpretation; see 1 Chron. 29.29.

14.1–16.14: Asa's reign. Chronicles expands upon 2 Kings' version (15.9–24), dividing it into two periods: the period of fidelity (14.1–15.19) and the period of faithlessness (16.1–16.14). The reigns of Asa and Ahijah are bound by the shared motif of reliance upon the LORD. **14.1–8:** Reform and prosperity. An expansion of 1 Kings 15.11–12. Chronicles' presentation is, at this stage, unambiguously positive, as emphasized by the repeated reference to *his God* (vv. 1, 10). **2–4:** This passage is best viewed as an elaboration of Chronicles' independent source (but influenced by 2 Kings 18.4). Cf. 1 Kings 15.14 regarding shrines. The presence of paraphernalia of foreign cultic worship is assumed but never explained. Heb "hamanim" has been translated *incense stands* and *shrines*. **5–6:** For building cities as a sign of monarchic success and divine favor, see 11.5–12. **7–14:** Asa battles Zerah the Cushite. There is no extrabiblical evidence for this account, whose historicity is debated. Most of the scholars who see the account as factual agree that the expedition was led by a commander of Nubian extraction, supported by Nubian forces; others, less convincingly, maintain that the original confrontation involved Bedouin tribes south of Judah. The numbers of the enemy force are again fantastic, though. The Syriac translation (Peshitta) reads "thirty thousand chariots." On either reading, the point is the same: Asa's extremely large force, outsued them as far as Gerar. Many of the Cushites fell wounded beyond recovery, for they broke before the LORD and His camp. Very much spoil was taken. ¹³ All the cities in the vicinity of Gerar were ravaged, for a terror of the LORD seized them. All the cities were plundered, and they yielded much booty. ¹⁴ They also ravaged the encampment of herdsmen, capturing much sheep and camels. Then they returned to Jerusalem.

15 The spirit of God came upon Azariah son of Oded. ² He came to Asa and said to him, "Listen to me, Asa and all Judah and Benjamin; the LORD is with you as long as you are with Him. If you turn to Him, He will respond to you, but if you forsake Him, He will forsake you. ³ Israel has gone many days without the true God, without a priest to give instruction and without Teaching. ⁴ But in distress it returned to the LORD God of Israel, and sought Him, and He responded to them. ⁵ At those times, ᵃ no wayfarer ⁻ᵃ was safe, for there was much tumult among all the inhabitants of the lands. ⁶ Nation was crushed by nation and city by city, for God threw them into panic with every kind of trouble. ⁷ As for you, be strong, do not be disheartened, for there is reward for your labor."

⁸ When Asa heard these words, the prophecy of Oded the prophet, he took courage and removed the abominations from the entire land of Judah and Benjamin and from the cities that he had captured in the hill country of Ephraim. He restored the altar of the LORD in front of the porch of the LORD. ⁹ He assembled all the people of Judah and Benjamin and those people of Ephraim, Manasseh, and Simeon who sojourned among them, for many in Israel had thrown in their lot with him when they saw that the LORD his God was with him. ¹⁰ They were assembled in Jerusalem in the third month of the fifteenth year of the reign of Asa. ¹¹ They brought sacrifices to the LORD on that

a-a Lit. "one who goes out and one who comes in."

numbered nearly two-to-one and lacking a large chariot force, manages to defeat the enemy force by virtue of exclusive trust in, and supplication to, God. Chronicles does not explain the circumstances surrounding the incursion of the Cushites. **15.1–7:** Azariah's address. This Azariah is otherwise unattested. Since the situation described in vv. 3–7 does not correspond to events of Asa's reign, some commentators view these vv.

as a prophetic pronouncement regarding the future, a view reflected in LXX. The Aramaic Targum interprets these vv. as alluding to the conduct of Jeroboam and his supporters. Alternatively, they may allude to the reigns of Rehoboam and Abijah or, less plausibly, the period of the judges (e.g., Judg. 2.11–13). Others maintain that the passage may, indeed, have Asa's reign in mind; the rhetorical style reflects Chronicles'

thematic concerns, and need not refer to specific events of Asa's reign. Vv. 2–7 draw on several biblical passages; see Hos. 3.4 (v. 3); Amos 3.17 (v. 5b); Deut. 4.29–30 (vv. 2–4); and Zech. 8.9–11 (vv. 4–7). **1:** For similar use of the "possession formula," see 1 Chron. 12.19 n.; 2 Chron. 20.14; 24.20. This formula appears only in Chronicles' nonsynoptic passages and only in connection with "nonprofessional prophets." Chronicles distinguishes between professional prophets, who address the monarchy exclusively, and other "temporary prophets/messengers," whose messages are directed at the people at large (including the king). **3:** Some medievals (Radak, disciple of Saadia) interpreted Heb "ʾelohim," here rendered "God," to mean "magistrates"; hence, the phrase "without the true God" is to be rendered "without magistrates who judge honestly." **8–19:** Religious reform. This passage, an independent doublet of 14.2–4, was probably taken from an independent source, which has not been fully harmonized with the surrounding passages. Note, specifically, that the reference to Asa's capture of territory in Ephraim (v. 8) has no antecedent, since Asa's reign is depicted as peaceful. The covenant described in this passage is reminiscent of the theophany and lawgiving related in Exod. chs 19–20; both take place in the third month. The present passage probably informs the book of *Jubilees* and other writings of the Qumran community, the earliest sources that view the festival of Shavuʿot, celebrated in the third month, as the annual occasion for renewal of the covenant and acceptance of new members. The presence of Simeon, the southernmost tribe, together with northern tribes remains anomalous; 34.6–7 n. **8:** *Oded the prophet:* The words are syntactically problematic and have been variously rendered. In addition, attribution of the prophetic message to Oded contradicts v. 1. The ancient versions (LXX, Vulgate, Peshitta) harmonize with v. 1. The day; they brought 700 oxen and 7,000 sheep of the spoil. [12] They entered into a covenant to worship the LORD God of their fathers with all their heart and with all their soul. [13] Whoever would not worship the LORD God of Israel would be put to death, whether small or great, whether man or woman. [14] So they took an oath to the LORD in a loud voice and with shouts, with trumpeting and blasts of the horn. [15] All Judah rejoiced over the oath, for they swore with all their heart and sought Him with all their will. He responded to them and gave them respite on every side.

[16] [a] He[b] also deposed Maacah mother of King Asa from the rank of queen mother, because she had made an abominable thing for [the goddess] Asherah. Asa cut down her abominable thing, reduced it to dust, and burned it in the Wadi Kidron. [17] The shrines, indeed, were not abolished in Israel; however, Asa was wholehearted [with the LORD] all his life. [18] He brought into the House of God the things that he and his father had consecrated— silver, gold, and utensils. [19] There was no war until the thirty-fifth year of the reign of Asa.

16 [c] In the thirty-sixth year of the reign of Asa, King Baasha of Israel marched against Judah and built up Ramah to block [d] all movement[-d] of King Asa of Judah. [2] Asa took all the silver and gold from the treasuries of the House of the LORD and the royal palace, and sent them to King Ben-hadad of Aram, who resided in Damascus, with this message: [3] "There is a pact between me and you, as there was between my father and your father. I herewith send you silver and gold; go and break your pact with King Baasha of Israel so that he may withdraw from me." [4] Ben-hadad acceded to King Asa's request; he sent his army commanders against the towns of Israel and ravaged Ijon, Dan, Abel-maim, and all the garrison towns of Naphtali. [5] When Baasha heard about it, he stopped building up Ramah and put an end to the work on it. [6] Then King Asa mustered all Judah, and they carried away the stones and timber with which Baasha had built up Ramah; with these King Asa built up Geba and Mizpah.

[7] At that time, Hanani the seer came to King Asa of Judah and said to him, "Because you relied on the king of Aram and did not rely on the LORD your God, therefore the army of the king of Aram has slipped out of your hands. [8] The Cushites and Lybians were a mighty army

words may be a gloss. **16–19:** Cultic reforms. *Queen mother* (Heb "gevirah"): Some maintain that the "gevirah" held an official position within the monarchy, and wielded significant political power, perhaps second only to the king. Others have gone further, arguing that the "gevirah" regulated aspects of the official Temple cult, as suggested by the fact that *Maacah* had been responsible for the production of "the abominable thing," likely a (proscribed) cultic mask. Others believe that the "gevirah" enjoyed no formal status, and that the influence wielded by various queen mothers was a function of their personalities.

16.1–10: Asa's fateful alliance. A reversal of Asa's previous exclusive reliance on the LORD, and the resulting rebuke by the prophet Hanani. **7–10:** *Hanani,* the father of Jehu the prophet; see 1 Kings 16.1, 7; 2 Chron. 19.2; 20.34. Chronicles thus has Jehu's father prophesying during the reign of Jehoshapat's father. **7:** Some mss of LXX read "Israel" in place of *Aram,* probably a secondary reading. According to the Masoretic Text, had Asa remained faithful he would have conquered Baasha as well as his confederates, the Arameans.

---

a With vv. 16–19, cf. 1 Kings 15.13–16.   b I.e., Asa.
c Cf. 1 Kings 15.17–24.   d-d Lit. "one who goes out and one who comes in."

with chariots and horsemen in very great numbers, yet because you relied on the LORD He delivered them into your hands. [9] For the eyes of the LORD range over the entire earth, to give support to those who are wholeheartedly with Him. You have acted foolishly in this matter, and henceforth you will be beset by wars." [10] Asa was vexed at the seer and put him into the stocks,[a] for he was furious with him because of that. Asa inflicted cruelties on some of the people at that time.

[11] The acts of Asa, early and late, are recorded in the annals of the kings of Judah and Israel. [12] In the thirty-ninth year of his reign, Asa suffered from an acute foot ailment; but ill as he was, he still did not turn to the LORD but to physicians. [13] Asa slept with his fathers. He died in the forty-first year of his reign [14] and was buried in the grave that he had made for himself in the City of David. He was laid in his resting-place, which was filled with spices of all kinds, expertly blended; a very great fire was made in his honor.

17 His son Jehoshaphat succeeded him as king, and took firm hold of Israel. [2] He stationed troops in all the fortified towns of Judah, and stationed garrisons throughout the land of Judah and the cities of Ephraim which his father Asa had captured. [3] The LORD was with Jehoshaphat because he followed the earlier ways of his father David, and did not worship the Baalim, [4] but worshiped the God of his father and followed His commandments—unlike the behavior of Israel. [5] So the LORD established the kingdom in his hands, and all Judah gave presents to Jehoshaphat. He had wealth and glory in abundance. [6] His mind was elevated in the ways of the LORD. Moreover, he abolished the shrines and the sacred posts from Judah.

[7] In the third year of his reign he sent his officers Benhail, Obadiah, Zechariah, Nethanel, and Micaiah throughout the cities of Judah to offer instruction. [8] With them were the Levites, Shemaiah, Nethaniah, Zebadiah, Asahel, Shemiramoth, Jehonathan, Adonijah, Tobijah and Tobadonijah the Levites; with them were Elishama and Jehoram the priests. [9] They offered instruction throughout Judah, having with them the Book of the Teaching of the LORD. They made the rounds of all the cities of Judah and instructed the people. [10] A terror of the LORD seized all the kingdoms of the lands around Judah, and they did not go to war with Jehoshaphat. [11] From Philistia a load of silver

a *Meaning of Heb. uncertain.*

16.11–14: Conclusion of Asa's reign. 12: Some see Asa's affliction as punishment for his alliance with Benhadad, though the text does not quite say as much. The episode involves another instance of paranomasia (wordplay or punning), here based on the name Asa ("'asa'"), since the Aramaic root "'-s-y/'-s-'" means "heal." The use of Aramaic is hardly surprising in a book of the Second Temple period, given how widespread this language was throughout the Near East. The exact intent of the criticism leveled against Asa is not clear but certainly suggests that Asa failed to recognize God's power to cure illness. **14:** The burial description is fuller than that of 1 Kings 15.24, yielding a fundamentally positive assessment of Asa's reign.

17.1–20.37: Jehoshaphat's reign. Chronicles' portrayal of Jehoshaphat differs dramatically from that in 1 Kings. The latter (quite reasonably) views Jehoshaphat's northern counterpart, Ahab, as the more important of the two kings; accordingly, Kings contains only occasional notices concerning Jehoshaphat. Chronicles, however, devotes a total of four chs to Jehoshaphat, with only passing reference to his northern counterparts. Several features reflect a Solomon typology, where features of Jehoshaphat are modeled after those of his illustrious forebear, since in Chronicles all good and successful monarchs embody the qualities manifest by David and Solomon. Despite Chronicles' critique of Jehoshaphat's alliance with the wicked, which apparently reflects the book's understanding of the parallel passages in Kings, Chronicles' overall assessment of the king is positive, leading some scholars to argue that Chronicles has drawn on extrabiblical material. **17.3–4:** Chronicles presupposes the reader's familiarity with 1 Kings 17ff., which relate the prevalence of Baal worship in northern Israel. **5:** The wording of this v. is reminiscent of Solomon. **7–9:** *Levites* stand out was brought to Jehoshaphat as tribute. The Arabs, too, brought him flocks: 7,700 rams and 7,700 he-goats. ¹²Jehoshaphat grew greater and greater, and he built up fortresses and garrison towns in Judah. ¹³He carried out extensive works in the towns of Judah, and had soldiers, valiant men, in Jerusalem. ¹⁴They were enrolled according to their clans. Judah: chiefs of thousands, Adnah the chief, who had 300,000 valiant men; ¹⁵next to him was Jehohanan the captain, who had 280,000; ¹⁶next to him was Amasiah son of Zichri, who made a freewill offering to the Lord. He had 200,000 valiant men. ¹⁷Benjamin: Eliada, a valiant man, who had 200,000 men armed with bow and buckler; ¹⁸next to him was Jehozabad, who had 180,000 armed men. ¹⁹These served the king, besides those whom the king assigned to the fortified towns throughout Judah.

18 ªSo Jehoshaphat had wealth and honor in abundance, and he allied himself by marriage to Ahab. ²After some years had passed, he came to visit Ahab at Samaria. Ahab slaughtered sheep and oxen in abundance for him and for the people with him, and persuaded him to march against Ramoth-gilead. ³King Ahab of Israel said to King Jehoshaphat of Judah, "Will you accompany me to Ramoth-gilead?" He answered him, "I will do what you do; my troops shall be your troops and shall accompany you in battle." ⁴Jehoshaphat then said to the king of Israel, "But first inquire for the word of the Lord."

⁵So the king of Israel gathered the prophets, four hundred men, and asked them, "Shall I march upon Ramoth-gilead for battle, or shall I not?" "March," they said, "and God will deliver it into the king's hands." ⁶Then Jehoshaphat asked, "Is there not another prophet of the Lord here through whom we can inquire?" ⁷And the king of Israel answered Jehoshaphat, "There is one more man through whom we can inquire of the Lord; but I hate him, because he never prophesies anything good for me but always misfortune. He is Micaiah son of Imlah." Jehoshaphat replied, "Let the king not say such a thing." ⁸So the king of Israel summoned an officer and said, "Bring Micaiah son of Imlah at once."

a Cf. 1 Kings 22.

9.3, likely refers to the Torah. **10–19:** The offering of royal tribute by foreign kings, a clear statement of geopolitical dominance, is reminiscent of Solomon and David. **12:** The Heb words rendered *greater and greater* are virtually identical with those depicting Solomon; see 1.1.

18.1–34: Jehoshaphat joins forces with Ahab. The details are identical to 1 Kings ch 22, with a few notable exceptions. The primary difference concerns the episode's purpose in the context of Kings and Chronicles. Kings focuses on the question of true vs. false prophecy, while Chronicles' focus is on the impropriety of forging an alliance (military or political) with foreign or wicked entities (see 19.1–3). Thus the opening vv., unattested in Kings, explain that Jehoshaphat's error had its roots in the marriage between his son and Ahab's daughter. **1–2:** An implicit rebuke: Jehoshaphat has wealth and honor in abundance—what enticement could there be for creating a family bond with a wicked northern king? The harsh indictment is reaffirmed by v. 2, Ahab *persuaded* ("hesit," lit. "enticed/incited") Jehoshaphat. Heb "incite" has, throughout the Bible, a decidedly negative connotation, generally involving sedition to idolatry. Moreover, this same verb appears at a crucial point later in the story, indicating that Jehoshaphat has become the victim of sedition. The enticement was apparently the abundance of animals slaughtered in honor of Jehoshaphat. *Ramoth-gilead* (lit. "heights of Gilead") is located on the eastern bank of the Jordan, south of the present-day Golan Heights. **3:** In contrast to 1 Kings ch 22, Jehoshaphat here makes no mention of his horses joining the horses of Ahab, perhaps because Chronicles saw it as implying that victory is determined largely by one's military might, an unacceptable position in Chronicles' worldview, even for a king who has been "enticed." **4:** On inquiring of the Lord before warfare as a sign of righ-

among those sent to educate the people; Deut. 33.10 may inform the v. The historicity of this passage is debated; it may reflect Second Temple, rather than First Temple, reality. The itinerant instructors are sent only to the cities of Judah, not Ephraim; this may be the author's way of expressing Judah's religious superiority. *Book of the Teaching* ("torah") of the Lord: This term, used in 34.14 and Neh.

9 The king of Israel and King Jehoshaphat of Judah, wearing their robes, were seated on their thrones situated in the threshing floor at the entrance of the gate of Samaria; and all the prophets were prophesying before them. 10 Zedekiah son of Chenaanah had provided himself with iron horns; and he said, "Thus said the LORD: With these you shall gore the Arameans till you make an end of them." 11 All the other prophets were prophesying similarly, "March against Ramoth-gilead and be victorious! The LORD will deliver it into Your Majesty's hands."

12 The messenger who had gone to summon Micaiah said to him, "Look, the words of the prophets are unanimously favorable to the king. Let your word be like that of the rest of them; speak a favorable word." 13 "By the life of the LORD," Micaiah answered, "I will speak only what my God tells me." 14 When he came before the king, the king said to him, "Micah,a shall we march against Ramoth-gilead for battle or shall we not?" He answered him, "March and be victorious! They will be delivered into your hands." 15 The king said to him, "How many times must I adjure you to tell me nothing but the truth in the name of the LORD?" 16 Then he said, "I saw all Israel scattered over the hills like sheep without a shepherd; and the LORD said, 'These have no master; let everyone return to his home in safety.' " 17 The king of Israel said to Jehoshaphat, "Did I not tell you that he would not prophesy good fortune for me, but only misfortune?"

18 Then [Micaiah] said, "Indeed, hear now the word of the LORD! I saw the LORD seated upon His throne, with all the host of heaven standing in attendance to the right and to the left of Him. 19 The LORD asked, 'Who will entice King Ahab of Israel so that he will march and fall at Ramoth-gilead?' Then one said this and another said that, 20 until a certain spirit came forward and stood before the LORD and said, 'I will entice him.' 'How?' said the LORD to him. 21 And he replied, 'I will go forth and become a lying spirit in the mouth of all his prophets.' Then He said, 'You will entice with success. Go forth and do it.' 22 Thus the LORD has put a lying spirit in the mouth of all these prophets of yours; for the LORD has decreed misfortune for you."

23 Thereupon Zedekiah son of Chenaanah came up and struck Micaiah on the cheek, and exclaimed, "However did the spirit of the LORD pass from me to speak with you!" 24 Micaiah replied, "You will see on the day when you try to hide in the innermost room." 25 Then the king of

teousness, see 1 Chron. 10.14; 14.10. **27–28:** *Come home safe* (lit. "return in peace"): "In peace," Heb "beshalom," is a leading idea in this story. This v. anticipates v. 34, which states that the (basically) upright Jehoshaphat returned "in peace," whereas the wicked Ahab was killed, as prophesied by Micaiah. **27:** The words *Listen, all you peoples* appear at Mic. 1.2, possibly indicating that Chronicles identified Micaiah, the prophet of the present episode, with the prophet Micah, one of the twelve "minor prophets." **31:** 1 Kings reads "he cried out," which denotes either a shout of desperation or an attempt to muster the troops. Chronicles' text, which adds *and the LORD helped him,* explains this call as a shout of prayer, emphasizing that prayer and repentance are efficacious, even in seemingly hopeless situations. Jehoshaphat is thus implicitly contrasted with Saul who, in similar circumstances, chose to take his life, rather than engage in prayer. *God diverted them* (Heb "wayesitem," "he enticed them"): LXX's reading suggests the graphically similar "wayesirem," i.e., "he moved them away," but this is likely a secondary reading. The very strangeness of "wayesitem" however, is part of Chronicles' literary strategy. Chronicles applies a kind of talion (measure-for-measure) principle: He who was previously "enticed" to commit an egregious act by trusting in the might of alliances with the wicked (v. 2) is saved by the LORD, who "entices" the attacking force to suddenly desist, merely by virtue of his recognition that salvation comes only from trust in divine omnipotence. This is a further instance of Chronicles' one-dimensional perspective; there is no explanation of the military means by which Jehoshaphat's deliverance came about.

a *A shortened form of Micaiah.*

Israel said, "Take Micaiah and turn him over to Amon, the governor of the city, and to Prince Joash, 26 and say, 'The king's orders are: Put this fellow in prison, and let his fare be scant bread and scant water until I come home safe.' " 27 To which Micaiah retorted, "If you ever come home safe, the LORD has not spoken through me." He said further, ᵃ·"Listen, all you peoples!"·ᵃ

28 The king of Israel and King Jehoshaphat of Judah marched against Ramoth-gilead. 29 The king of Israel said to Jehoshaphat, ᵇ·"I will disguise myself and go·ᵇ into the battle, but you, wear your robes." So the king of Israel disguised himself, and they went into the battle. 30 The king of Aram had given these instructions to his chariot officers: "Do not attack anyone, small or great, except the king of Israel." 31 When the chariot officers saw Jehoshaphat, whom they took for the king of Israel, they wheeled around to attack him, and Jehoshaphat cried out and the LORD helped him, and God diverted them from him. 32 And when the chariot officers realized that he was not the king of Israel, they gave up the pursuit. 33 Then a man drew his bow at random and hit the king of Israel between the ᶜplates of theᶜ armor and he said to his charioteer, "Turn around and get me behind the lines; I am wounded." 34 The battle ᶜraged all day long,ᶜ and the king remained propped up in the chariot facing Aram until dusk; he died as the sun was setting.

19 King Jehoshaphat of Judah returned safely to his palace, to Jerusalem. 2 Jehu son of Hanani the seer went out to meet King Jehoshaphat and said to him, "Should one give aid to the wicked and befriend those who hate the LORD? For this, wrath is upon you from the LORD. 3 However, there is some good in you, for you have purged the land of the sacred posts and have dedicated yourself to worship God."

4 Jehoshaphat remained in Jerusalem a while and then went out among the people from Beer-sheba to the hill

a-a Cf. Mic. 1.2.

b-b Infinitives used for finite verb; cf. note at 1 Kings 22.30.

c-c Meaning of Heb. uncertain.

19.1–20.30: This entire section has no parallel in Kings. 19.1–3: Prophetic rebuke. 2: *Befriend* (Heb "teʾehav," root "ʾ-h-v") connotes treaty or covenant fidelity; the same idea is present in *give aid*. These vv. are not present in the Deuteronomistic version in Kings, since that source focuses on the person of Ahab and, more fundamentally, because the Deuteronomist sees no religious dilemma in joining forces with a northern king (or other wicked individual) so long as one does not adopt his sinful ways. Chronicles, however, takes the position that the mere act of displaying tolerance toward the wicked is wrong, since it countenances the LORD's enemies (see Ps. 139.21). Moreover, such tolerance and cooperation signals a lack of exclusive trust in the LORD and His ability to provide for one's every need. Chronicles' view of separation from the wicked informed postbiblical literature (see, e.g., *'Avot R. Nat.*, A, 16). Chronicles explains the absence of punishment for this breach of faith—for which no remorse is expressed—by the fact that Jehoshaphat has many good deeds to his credit that offset the present offense. For this reason, Chronicles prefaces this story with an account of Jehoshaphat's worthy acts in ch 17. Since the question of differentiating true from false prophecy is not at issue in Chronicles, it is quite natural that Jehoshaphat is not blamed for having gone to battle, per se.

19.4–11: Establishment of judiciary. Jehoshaphat responds to the prophetic rebuke by promoting justice throughout the land. The historicity of this passage, unattested in Kings, has been debated at length. The formulation and content of this ch are highly reminiscent of Deut. 1.13–17; 16.18; 17.8–12. Some scholars appeal to the use of paranomasia—the name Jehoshaphat means "the LORD has judged" (Heb "shafat")—as evidence of this passage's literary, rather than historical, value. They thus view the passage as a type of midrash on Jehoshaphat's name: The king whose name includes the root "to judge" established the judicial system in Judah. Others, pointing to various differences between Chronicles and Deuteronomy (e.g., the cities in which courts were established, the absence of vocabulary characteristic of Chronicles), have argued that Chronicles' story is factual, and draws on pre-Chronicles, non-Deuteronomic material. **4:** In contrast to ch 17, here Jehoshaphat's reform was applied not only to Judah but up through the hill country of Ephraim; he brought them back to the LORD God of their fathers. ⁵ He appointed judges in the land in all the fortified towns of Judah, in each and every town. ⁶ He charged the judges: "Consider what you are doing, for you judge not on behalf of man, but on behalf of the LORD, and He is with you when you pass judgment. ⁷ Now let the dread of the LORD be upon you; act with care, for there is no injustice or favoritism or bribe-taking with the LORD our God." ⁸ Jehoshaphat also appointed in Jerusalem some Levites and priests and heads of the clans of Israelites for rendering judgment in matters of the LORD, and for disputes. Then they returned to Jerusalem. ⁹ He charged them, "This is how you shall act: in fear of the LORD, with fidelity, and with whole heart. ¹⁰ When a dispute comes before you from your brothers living in their towns, whether about homicide, or about ritual, or laws or rules, you must instruct them so that they do not incur guilt before the LORD and wrath be upon you and your brothers. Act so and you will not incur guilt. ¹¹ See, Amariah the chief priest is over you in all cases concerning the LORD, and Zebadiah son of Ishmael is the commander of the house of Judah in all cases concerning the king; the Levitical officials are at your disposal; act with resolve and the LORD be with the good."

20 After that, Moabites, Ammonites, together with some Ammonim,ᵃ came against Jehoshaphat to wage war. ² The report was brought to Jehoshaphat: "A great multitude is coming against you from beyond the sea, from Aram, and is now in Hazazon-tamar"—that is, Ein-gedi. ³ Jehoshaphat was afraid; he decided to resort to the LORD and proclaimed a fast for all Judah. ⁴ Judah assembled to beseech the LORD. They also came from all the towns of Judah to seek the LORD.

⁵ Jehoshaphat stood in the congregation of Judah and Jerusalem in the House of the LORD at the front of the new court. ⁶ He said, "LORD God of our fathers, truly You are

a Probably for mᵉnym "Meunites" (1 Chron. 4.41); cf. Kimhi.

credible local tradition. Still others see the reference to *Meunites* in v. 1 (see translators' note *a*) as indicating that the attacking force involved Nabateans from Meun/Ma'anthe, near Petra, in the 4th or 3rd century BCE. Finally, some accept Chronicles' claim that the battle occurred in Jehoshaphat's time. Note that Chronicles does not offer any theological explanation for the outbreak of war during the reign of a (basically) righteous king. Chronicles thereby acknowledges that some wars come about not as punishments but, rather, as a means of testing the religious commitment of the king and his people, or for some other (unexplained) reason. This may be further proof that Chronicles does not maintain a rigorous theology of retribution. **20.1–2:** The redundant *some Ammonim* has prompted several exegetes to read "Meunim." On the basis of the biblical site Ma'on and Arabic Ma'an, it appears that the Meunites lived either in the southern Negev, i.e., west of the Arabah, or slightly to the Arabah's east, near Petra. LXX reads here "Minaeans." **2:** The Masoretic Text entails a geographical difficulty: Peoples coming *from beyond the sea* (whomever this might refer to) and Arameans, whose territory lay to the northeast of Israel, would not be expected to gather at Ein-gedi, located at roughly the middle of the length of the Dead Sea. The old Latin translation renders "Edomites" in place of Arameans, a reading adopted by many moderns, especially since the two words are graphically similar in Heb. **3–5:** These vv. again refer only to the cities of Judah, either because the impending battle was due to take place in Judah's territory or, once again, as a sign of Chronicles' preferential treatment of Judah, whose residents understand the importance of seeking out the LORD. **5:** *The new court*, a third (outer) court or, alternatively, a newly formed division within Chronicles' second (i.e., lay) court. **6–12:** Jehoshaphat's prayer contains a reprise of Israel's early history. V. 9 portrays this public gath-

country of Ephraim, as well. (This action is described as "returning" the people to the LORD.) This is another example of Chronicles' inclusivist position. This position may also reflect Deut 16.18, which refers to cities located in (all of) Israel's tribes. **6:** For similar phrasing and notions, see Deut. 1.17. **7:** See Deut. 10.17. **10:** See Exod. 18.16; Deut. 17.8.

20.1–21.1: Jehoshaphat defeats an eastern confederation. The historicity of this ch is, again, much debated. Some scholars argue that the entire account is a historical "midrash" on either 2 Kings ch 3 or Exod ch 14 and Isa 7.9b. Others accept a historical kernel to the account, seeing it as a magnified version of a local conflict (in the postexilic period) or drawing on a the God in heaven and You rule over the kingdoms of the nations; power and strength are Yours; none can oppose You. ⁷O our God, you dispossessed the inhabitants of this land before Your people Israel, and You gave it to the descendants of Your friend Abraham forever. ⁸They settled in it and in it built for You a House for Your name. They said, ⁹'Should misfortune befall us—the punishing sword, pestilence, or famine, we shall stand before this House and before You—for Your name is in this House— and we shall cry out to You in our distress, and You will listen and deliver us.' ¹⁰Now the people of Ammon, Moab, and the hill country of Seir, into whose [land] You did not let Israel come when they came from Egypt, but they turned aside from them and did not wipe them out, ¹¹these now repay us by coming to expel us from Your possession which You gave us as ours. ¹²O our God, surely You will punish them, for we are powerless before this great multitude that has come against us, and do not know what to do, but our eyes are on You." ¹³All Judah stood before the LORD with their little ones, their women-folk, and their children.

¹⁴Then in the midst of the congregation the spirit of the LORD came upon Jahaziel son of Zechariah son of Benaiah son of Jeiel son of Mattaniah the Levite, of the sons of Asaph, ¹⁵and he said, "Give heed, all Judah and the inhabitants of Jerusalem and King Jehoshaphat; thus said the LORD to you, 'Do not fear or be dismayed by this great multitude, for the battle is God's, not yours. ¹⁶March down against them tomorrow as they come up by the Ascent of Ziz; you will find them at the end of the wadi in the direction of the wilderness of Jeruel. ¹⁷It is not for you to fight this battle; stand by, wait, and witness your deliverance by the LORD, O Judah and Jerusalem; do not fear or be dismayed; go forth to meet them tomorrow and the LORD will be with you.' " ¹⁸Jehoshaphat bowed low with his face to the ground, and all Judah and the inhabitants of Jerusalem threw themselves down before the LORD to worship the LORD. ¹⁹Levites of the sons of Kohath and of the sons of Korah got up to extol the LORD God of Israel at the top of their voices.

²⁰Early the next morning they arose and went forth to the wilderness of Tekoa. As they went forth, Jehoshaphat stood and said, "Listen to me, O Judah and inhabitants of Jerusalem: Trust firmly in the LORD your God and you will stand firm; trust firmly in His prophets and you will succeed." ²¹After taking counsel with the people, he stationed singers to the LORD extolling the One majestic in holiness as they went forth ahead of the vanguard, saying,

ering as a fulfillment of Solomon's prayer at 2 Chron. 6.24–25, again linking Jehoshaphat and Solomon. **10:** This v. adopts the tradition regarding *Seir* preserved in Deut. 21.2–8; cf. Num. 20.14–21. **12:** *Punish them* (lit. "judge them," Heb "tishpot-bam") is another example of paranomasia. The LORD is asked to judge (Israel's enemies), precisely as the literal meaning of "Jehoshaphat" indicates. **13–14:** The leading role of the Levites is once again in evidence, as the critical oracle is delivered by one of the Temple minstrels. This v. should not be taken to indicate that "Levitic prophecy" always, or even generally, involved an oracular saying; instead it reflects the type of ad hoc prophetic activity favored by Chronicles. **15–17:** The wording of these vv. draws on earlier works, most notably Exod. 14.13–14. Like Moses in the latter instance, Yahaziel tells Judah that the war is the LORD's battle. This passage is perhaps the clearest example of Chronicles' one-dimensional approach to human endeavors. **20:** Jehoshaphat, the fundamentally good king, addresses his people, reminding them that trust in the LORD and his prophets brings success. Trust in God, along with proper cultic activity (including prayer) centered on the Temple, ensures victory. Indeed, in contrast to previous military encounters, this passage makes no mention of the number of the Judahite forces, for Israel's strength is not responsible for victory. True to form, the righteous monarch engages his people in the decision making, rather than dictating to them. The people's ready assent shows they are worthy of the LORD's intervention. *Trust firmly . . . and you will stand firm* ("ha'minu . . . vete'menu") reflects the similar paronomasia in Isa. 7.9. **21:** Note the refrain *"Praise . . . for His steadfast love is eternal."* *The One majestic in holiness:* Others render "in holy attire," "his holy splendor," or "the holy place of his appearing"; see 16.29. The "democratization" theme appears at 1 Chron. 13.1–4 (see n.); 2 Chron.

"Praise the LORD, for His steadfast love is eternal." [22] As they began their joyous shouts and hymns, the LORD set ambushes for the men of Amon, Moab, and the hill country of Seir, who were marching against Judah, and they were routed. [23] The Ammonites and Moabites turned against the men of the hill country of Seir to exterminate and annihilate them. When they had made an end of the men of Seir, each helped to destroy his fellow.

[24] When Judah reached the lookout in the wilderness and looked for the multitude, they saw them lying on the ground as corpses; not one had survived. [25] Jehoshaphat and his army came to take the booty, and found an abundance of goods, corpses, and precious objects, which they pillaged, more than they could carry off. For three days they were taking booty, there was so much of it. [26] On the fourth day they assembled in the Valley of Blessing—for there they blessed the LORD; that is why that place is called the Valley of Blessing to this day. [27] All the men of Judah and Jerusalem with Jehoshaphat at their head returned joyfully to Jerusalem, for the LORD had given them cause for rejoicing over their enemies. [28] They came to Jerusalem to the House of the LORD, to the accompaniment of harps, lyres, and trumpets. [29] The terror of God seized all the kingdoms of the lands when they heard that the LORD had fought the enemies of Israel. [30] The kingdom of Jehoshaphat was untroubled, and his God granted him respite on all sides.

[31a] Jehoshaphat reigned over Judah. He was thirty-five years old when he became king, and he reigned in Jerusalem for twenty-five years. His mother's name was Azubah daughter of Shilhi. [32] He followed the course of his father Asa and did not deviate from it, doing what was pleasing to the LORD. [33] However, the shrines did not cease; the people still did not direct their heart toward the God of their fathers. [34] As for the other events of Jehoshaphat's reign, early and late, they are recorded in the annals of Jehu son of Hanani, which were included in the book of the kings of Israel.

[35] Afterward, King Jehoshaphat of Judah entered into a partnership with King Ahaziah of Israel, thereby acting wickedly. [36] He joined with him in constructing ships to go to Tarshish; the ships were constructed in Ezion-geber. [37] Eliezer son of Dodavahu of Mareshah prophesied against Jehoshaphat, "As you have made a partnership with Ahaziah, the LORD will break up your work." The ships were wrecked and were unable to go to Tarshish.

1.2; 30.2; 32.3. **22–24:** In contrast to other passages, where the priestly trumpet blasts lead the army into victory (e.g., Josh. 6.8–10,16), here the Levitic choral rite dominates. The victory begins as soon as the Levites break forth in chant; Judah engages in no military activity. No explanation is offered for how the internecine fighting broke out in the enemy camp (cf. Judg. 11.19–22). Since the Jewish community of Chronicles' time was in no position to wage war, the message of the Levitic role here seems to be that it is their cultic chant, whether performed in battle or in the Temple, which invokes divine favor and protects Israel. **25–30:** All of the enemy force has been decimated, another feature appearing in Exodus (14.28). The only task left for Judah's "army" is scavenging and collection of the spoils. **35–37:** The story of Jehoshaphat's joint maritime venture differs markedly from 1 Kings 22.49–50, either because Chronicles' text reflects a different source or due to its own tendentious reworking. Kings states that Jehoshaphat prepared ships for sailing but these were destroyed in Ezion-geber (near present-day Eilat) and did not sail. Jehoshaphat then refused Ahaziah's offer of assistance. No reason is offered there for Jehoshaphat's refusal. Chronicles' version results in a second offense on the part of Jehoshaphat, one that appears to be identical to his wrongdoing in ch 18. It is possible that this latter episode teaches that any form of cooperation with the wicked is forbidden, i.e., even where the upright individual participates purely for his own benefit and with no regard for the welfare of the wicked. Chronicles claims that the ships were intended to sail for Tarshish, whereas 1 Kings states that the ships' destination was Ophir, located in Africa, at the mouth of the Red Sea; see 9.21. As elsewhere in Chronicles, a prophet not known from other sources appears to offer a short speech to the king.

---

a With vv. 31–37, cf. 1 Kings 22.41–49.

21

^{a}Jehoshaphat slept with his fathers and was buried with his fathers in the City of David; his son Jehoram succeeded him as king. ^{2}He had brothers, sons of Jehoshaphat: Azariah, Jehiel, Zechariah, Azariahu, Michael, and Shephatiah; all these were sons of King Jehoshaphat of Israel. ^{3}Their father gave them many gifts of silver, gold, and [other] presents, as well as fortified towns in Judah, but he gave the kingdom to Jehoram because he was the first-born.

^{4}Jehoram proceeded to take firm hold of his father's kingdom and put to the sword all his brothers, as well as some of the officers of Israel. ^{5}Jehoram was thirty-two years old when he became king, and he reigned in Jerusalem eight years. ^{6}He followed the practices of the kings of Israel doing what the House of Ahab had done, for he married a daughter of Ahab; he did what was displeasing to the LORD. ^{7}However, the LORD refrained from destroying the House of David for the sake of the covenant he had made with David, and in accordance with his promise to maintain a lamp for him and his descendants for all time. ^{8}During his reign, the Edomites rebelled against Judah's rule and set up a king of their own. ^{9}Jehoram advanced [against them] with his officers and all his chariotry. He arose by night and attacked the Edomites, who surrounded him and the chariot commanders. ^{10}Edom has been in rebellion against Judah, to this day; Libnah also rebelled against him at that time, because he had forsaken the LORD God of his fathers. ^{11}Moreover, he built shrines in the hill country of Judah; he led astray the inhabitants of Jerusalem and made Judah wayward.

^{12}A letter from Elijah the prophet came to him which read, "Thus says the LORD God of your father David: Since you have not followed the practices of your father Jehoshaphat and the practices of King Asa of Judah, ^{13}but have followed the practices of the kings of Israel, leading astray Judah and the inhabitants of Jerusalem as the House of Ahab led them astray, and have also killed your brothers of your father's house, who were better than you, ^{14}therefore, the LORD will inflict a great blow upon your people, your sons, and your wives and all your possessions. ^{15}As for you, you will be severely stricken with a disorder of the bowels year after year until your bowels drop out."

^{16}The LORD stirred up the spirit of the Philistines and the Arabs who were neighbors of the Cushites against Jehoram. ^{17}They marched against Judah, breached its defenses, and carried off all the property that was found in

21.2–20: Jehoram's reign. An expanded version of 2 Kings 8.16–24; some of Chronicles' added material probably draws on additional written sources. **2–4:** Jehoram establishes his rule. The placement of these vv. highlights the theme of the threat of extinction to the Davidic line which unites the following two chs (see 21.17; 22.8–9; 22.10–11). **5–11:** The passage, aside from v. 11, is taken from 2 Kings 17–22. **6:** Athaliah was probably a daughter of Omri, King of Israel, and hence sister of Ahab. **7:** Chronicles' reformulation of 2 Kings 8.19 highlights the divine promise to the Davidic dynasty. **8–11:** Chronicles suggests that Jehoram's troubles are the result of his religious infidelity. **10–19:** These vv. have no parallel in Kings. **12–15:** Letter from Elijah. The prevalent view maintains that this letter is Chronicles' creation. The choice of Elijah was probably informed by his role as zealous champion of the worship of YHVH against the influence of Baalism in northern Israel during the rule of Ahab and Ahaziah. Given Jehoram's marriage to Ahab's daughter, Elijah was the natural choice. Because of uncertainty surrounding the chronology of the period (see 2 Kings 1.17; ch 2; 3.11), it is unclear whether Chronicles thought that Elijah was still alive or had perished after composing the prophetic letter.

21.16–20: End of Jehoram's reign. The form "Jehoahaz" (v. 17) in place of the standard "Ahaziah" supports the likelihood that this v. is taken from an independent source. **17:** LXX reads "daughters" in place of "wives."

---

a Cf. 2 Kings 8.17–24.

the king's palace, as well as his sons and his wives. The only son who remained was Jehoahaz, his youngest. ¹⁸ After this, the LORD afflicted him with an incurable disease of the bowels. ¹⁹ Some years later, when a period of two years had elapsed, his bowels dropped out because of his disease, and he died a gruesome death. His people did not make a fire for him like the fire for his fathers. ²⁰ He was thirty-two years old when he became king, and he reigned in Jerusalem eight years. He departed unpraised,ᵃ and was buried in the City of David, but not in the tombs of the kings.

22 ᵇ The inhabitants of Jerusalem made Ahaziah, his youngest son, king in his stead, because all the older ones had been killed by the troops that penetrated the camp with the Arabs. Ahaziah son of Jehoram reigned as king of Judah. ² Ahaziah was forty-two years old when he became king, and he reigned in Jerusalem one year; his mother's name was Athaliah daughter of Omri. ³ He too followed the practices of the house of Ahab, for his mother counseled him to do evil. ⁴ He did what was displeasing to the LORD, like the house of Ahab, for they became his counselors after his father's death, to his ruination. ⁵ Moreover, he followed their counsel and marched with Jehoram son of King Ahab of Israel to battle against King Hazael of Aram at Ramoth-gilead, where the Arameans wounded Joram. ⁶ He returned to Jezreel to recover from the wounds inflicted on him at Ramah when he fought against King Hazael of Aram. King Azariah son of Jehoram of Judah went down to Jezreel to visit Jehoram son of Ahab while he was ill. ⁷ God caused the downfall of Ahaziah because he visited Joram. During his visit he went out with Jehoram to Jehu son of Nimshi, whom the LORD had anointed to cut off the house of Ahab. ⁸ In the course of bringing the house of Ahab to judgment, Jehu came upon the officers of Judah and the nephews of Ahaziah, ministers of Ahaziah, and killed them. ⁹ He sent in search of Ahaziah, who was caught hiding in Samaria, was brought to Jehu, and put to death. He was given a burial, because it was said, "He is the son of Jehoshaphat who worshiped the LORD wholeheartedly." So the house of Ahaziah could not muster the strength to rule.

¹⁰ When Athaliah, Ahaziah's mother, learned that her son was dead, she promptly did away with all who were

---

a Following Septuagint; cf. Arabic ḥamada, "praise."
b With vv. 1–6, cf. 2 Kings 8.25–29; with vv. 8–9, cf. 2 Kings 9.27–28; with vv. 10–12, cf. 2 Kings 11.1–3.

18–20: The king's disease is not recorded in Kings; it is unclear whether Chronicles draws on a genuine source or has created this account in fulfillment of v. 15. Chronicles' version highlights the ignominious nature of Jehoram's demise; cf. 2 Kings 8.23–24.

22.1–9: Ahaziah's reign. 1–9: This account, not preserved elsewhere, is reminiscent of 14.9–15 and may derive from the same source. Two features continue from Jehoram's reign to Ahaziah's: the influence of Athaliah and the threat to the Davidic line. The passage contains several allusions to the disastrous reign of Saul (1 Chron. ch 10); compare, esp., vv. 7 and 9 with 1 Chron. 10.6, 13–14. **1–3:** The age, *forty-two*, is impossible, since it would make Ahaziah older than his father. Many LXX mss read "twenty"; Peshitta reads "twenty-two," as does 2 Kings 8.26. **4–5:** Added by Chronicles; contacts with the north bring disaster. **7–9:** A condensed and reworked version of 2 Kings 9.1–28; 10.12–14, provided with an introductory sentence explaining that the events befalling the dynasty are the result of backsliding. Chronicles differs from 2 Kings in the following respects: The princes of Judah die before Ahaziah (cf. 2 Kings 10.12–14); the circumstances of his death are different (cf. 2 Kings 9.27); the circumstances surrounding his burial are different (cf. 2 Kings 9.28). Chronicles' text may be based on an independent source, or it may be the creation of its author. The emphasis on God's complete control of history (v. 7, *God caused the downfall of Ahaziah*) is consistent with Chronicles' theology, as is the emphasis on the impropriety of association with northern monarchs.

22.10–24.27: Joash's reign. With the possible exception of parts of ch 24, Chronicles is based on 2 Kings 11–12. Joash's reign consists of three periods: (1) the Davidic dynasty at its lowest point; (2) a period of revitalization, echoing the upswing upon Joash's as-of the royal stock of the house of Judah. ¹¹But Jehoshabe-ath, daughter of the king, spirited away Ahaziah's son Joash from among the princes who were being slain, and put him and his nurse in a bedroom. Jehoshabeath, daughter of King Jehoram, wife of the priest Jehoiada— she was the sister of Ahaziah—kept him hidden from Ath-aliah so that he was not put to death. ¹²He stayed with them for six years, hidden in the House of God, while Athaliah reigned over the land.

23 ᵃIn the seventh year, Jehoiada took courage and brought the chiefs of the hundreds, Azariah son of Jeroham, Ishmael son of Jehohanan, Azariah son of Obed, Maaseiah son of Adaiah, and Elishaphat son of Zichri, into a compact with him. ²They went through Judah and assembled the Levites from all the towns of Judah, and the chiefs of the clans of Israel. They came to Jerusalem ³and the entire assembly made a covenant with the king in the House of God. Heᵇ said to them, "The son of the king shall be king according to the promise the LORD made concern-ing the sons of David. ⁴This is what you must do: One third of you, priests and Levites, who are on duty for the week, shall be gatekeepers at the thresholds; ⁵another third shall be stationed in the royal palace, and the other third at the Foundation Gate. All the people shall be in the courts of the House of the LORD. ⁶Let no one enter the House of the LORD except the priests and the ministering Levites. They may enter because they are sanctified, but all the people shall obey the proscription of the LORD. ⁷The Levites shall surround the king on every side, every man with his weapons at the ready; and whoever enters the House shall be killed. Stay close to the king in his com-ings and goings." ⁸The Levites and all Judah did just as Je-hoiada the priest ordered: each took his men—those who were on duty that week and those who were off duty that week, for Jehoiada the priest had not dismissed the divi-sions. ⁹Jehoiada the priest gave the chiefs of the hundreds King David's spears and shields and quivers that were kept in the House of God. ¹⁰He stationed the entire force, each man with his weapons at the ready, from the south end of the House to the north end of the House, at the altar and the House, to guard the king on every side. ¹¹Then they brought out the king's son, and placed upon him the crown and the insignia. They proclaimed him king, and Jehoiada and his sons anointed him and shouted, "Long live the king!"

cension; (3) religious backsliding, including rejection of the pro-phetic word, leading to military defeat and the king's death.

22.10–23.21: Joash takes power. **22.10–12:** Following Kings, the standard opening and closing for-mulae are lacking, indicating that the period of Athaliah is not for-mally recognized. It is uncertain whether, as a matter of principle, Judah recognized female mon-archs. **23.1–21:** Joash's corona-tion and removal of Athaliah. Cf. 2 Kings 11.4–20. Two key alter-ations appear: (1) Joash's rule is welcomed and supported by the populace (it is a personal affair in Kings); this is reminiscent of Chronicles' depiction of David and Solomon. (2) Chronicles ad-justs the cultic details to its view of proper cultic procedure, as it pertains to priests and Levites. **1–16:** Blessings. The period focuses on restoration of the Temple.

a Cf. 2 Kings 11.4–20.   b I.e., Jehoiada.

12 When Athaliah heard the shouting of the people and the guards and the acclamation of the king, she came out to the people, to the House of the LORD. 13 She looked about and saw the king standing by his pillar at the entrance, the chiefs with their trumpets beside the king, and all the people of the land rejoicing and blowing trumpets, and the singers with musical instruments leading the hymns. Athaliah rent her garments and cried out, "Treason, treason!" 14 Then the priest Jehoiada ordered out the army officers, the chiefs of hundreds, and said to them, "Take her out between the ranks, and if anyone follows her, put him to the sword." For the priest thought, "Let her not be put to death in the House of the LORD." 15 They cleared a passage for her and she came to the entrance of the Horse Gate to the royal palace; there she was put to death.

16 Then Jehoiada solemnized a covenant between himself and the people and the king that they should be the people of the LORD. 17 All the people then went to the temple of Baal; they tore it down and smashed its altars and images to bits, and they slew Mattan, the priest of Baal, in front of the altars. 18 Jehoiada put the officers of the House of the LORD in the charge of Levite priests whom David had assigned over the House of the LORD to offer up burnt offerings, as is prescribed in the Teaching of Moses, accompanied by joyful song as ordained by David. 19 He stationed the gatekeepers at the gates of the House of the LORD to prevent the entry of anyone unclean for any reason. 20 He took the chiefs of hundreds, the nobles, and the rulers of the people and all the people of the land, and they escorted the king down from the House of the LORD into the royal palace by the upper gate, and seated the king on the royal throne. 21 All the people of the land rejoiced, and the city was quiet. As for Athaliah, she had been put to the sword.

24 aJehoash was seven years old when he became king, and he reigned in Jerusalem forty years. His mother's name was Zibiah of Beer-sheba. 2 All the days of the priest Jehoiada, Jehoash did what was pleasing to the LORD. 3 Jehoiada took two wives for him, by whom he had sons and daughters.

4 Afterward, Joash decided to renovate the House of the LORD. 5 He assembled the priests and the Levites and charged them as follows: "Go out to the towns of Judah and collect money from all Israel for the annual repair of

24.1–2: Joash's reign begins. Chronicles' depiction is more favorable than that of 2 Kings ch 12; it omits the notice about sacrifice at the local shrines or high places ("bamot"; 2 Kings 12.4).

24.4–14: Temple restoration. The passage differs substantially from 2 Kings 12.4–16 and conveys several of Chronicles' recurring themes. The claim that there was a surplus of money for other purposes (cf. 2 Kings 12.13–14) due to generosity of the people is to be expected; see 1 Chron. 29.11–19.

a Cf. 2 Kings 12.1–22.

the House of your God. Do it quickly." But the Levites did not act quickly. ⁶ The king summoned Jehoiada the chief and said to him, "Why have you not seen to it that the Levites brought the tax imposed by Moses, the servant of the LORD, and the congregation of Israel from Judah and Jerusalem to the Tent of the Pact?" ⁷ For the children of the wicked Athaliah had violated the House of God and had even used the sacred things of the House of the LORD for the Baals. ⁸ The king ordered that a chest be made and placed on the outside of the gate of the House of the LORD. ⁹ A proclamation was issued in Judah and Jerusalem to bring the tax imposed on Israel in the wilderness by Moses, the servant of God. ¹⁰ All the officers and all the people gladly brought it and threw it into the chest till it was full. ¹¹ Whenever the chest was brought to the royal officers by the Levites, and they saw that it contained much money, the royal scribe and the agent of the chief priest came and emptied out the chest and carried it back to its place. They did this day by day, and much money was collected. ¹² The king and Jehoiada delivered the money to those who oversaw the tasks connected with the work of the House of the LORD. They hired masons and carpenters to renovate the House of the LORD, as well as craftsmen in iron and bronze to repair the House of the LORD. ¹³ The overseers did their work; under them the work went well and they restored the House of God to its original form and repaired it. ¹⁴ When they had finished, they brought the money that was left over to the king and Jehoiada; it was made into utensils for the House of the LORD, service vessels: buckets and ladles, golden and silver vessels. Burnt offerings were offered up regularly in the House of the LORD all the days of Jehoiada. ¹⁵ Jehoiada reached a ripe old age and died; he was one hundred and thirty years old at his death. ¹⁶ They buried him in the City of David together with the kings, because he had done good in Israel, and on behalf of God and His House.

¹⁷ But after the death of Jehoiada, the officers of Judah came, bowing low to the king; and the king listened to them. ¹⁸ They forsook the House of the LORD God of their fathers to serve the sacred posts and idols; and there was wrath upon Judah and Jerusalem because of this guilt of theirs. ¹⁹ The LORD sent prophets among them to bring them back to Him; they admonished them but they would not pay heed. ²⁰ Then the spirit of God enveloped Zechariah son of Jehoiada the priest; he stood above the people and said to them, "Thus God said: Why do you transgress the commandments of the LORD when you cannot succeed? Since you have forsaken the LORD, He has

24.15–16: The death of Jehoiada. The burial notice indicates Chronicles' positive evaluation of Jehoiada, Joash's mentor.

24.17–27: Judgment. 2 Kings 12.17–21 states that Joash submitted to the Arameans and was assassinated, but offers no theological explanation. Chronicles provides it by claiming that Joash's death resulted from his refusal to heed the teachings of Jehohiada, who had just died. This passage exemplifies Chronicles' view of the divine capacity for forgiveness, and of the importance of prophetic forewarning before punishment. Much of the core material, especially that concerning Zechariah and the Aramean invasion, may be taken from earlier sources. **17–22:** Unknown from other sources. Zechariah here is a foil to Joash and highlights the difference between the several periods in Joash's reign. The sermonic style is typical of Chronicles.

forsaken you." ²¹ They conspired against him and pelted him with stones in the court of the House of the LORD, by order of the king. ²² King Joash disregarded the loyalty that his father Jehoiada had shown to him, and killed his son. As he was dying, he said, "May the LORD see and requite it."

²³ At the turn of the year, the army of Aram marched against him; they invaded Judah and Jerusalem, and wiped out all the officers of the people from among the people, and sent all the booty they took to the king of Damascus. ²⁴ The invading army of Aram had come with but a few men, but the LORD delivered a very large army into their hands, because they had forsaken the LORD God of their fathers. They inflicted punishments on Joash. ²⁵ When they withdrew, having left him with many wounds, his courtiers plotted against him because of the murderᵃ of the sons of Jehoiada the priest, and they killed him in bed. He died and was buried in the City of David; he was not buried in the tombs of the kings. ²⁶ These were the men who conspired against him: Zabad son of Shimeath the Ammonitess, and Jehozabad son of Shimrith the Moabitess. ²⁷ As to his sons, and the many pronouncements against him, and his rebuilding of the House of God, they are recorded in the story in the book of the kings. His son Amaziah succeeded him as king.

25 ᵇ Amaziah was twenty-five years old when he became king, and he reigned twenty-nine years in Jerusalem; his mother's name was Jehoaddan of Jerusalem. ² He did what was pleasing to the LORD, but not with a whole heart. ³ Once he had the kingdom firmly under control, he executed the courtiers who had assassinated his father the king. ⁴ But he did not put their children to death for [he acted] in accordance with what is written in the Teaching, in the Book of Moses, where the LORD commanded, ᶜ "Parents shall not die for children, nor shall children die for parents, but every person shall die only for his own crime." ᶜ

⁵ Amaziah assembled the men of Judah, and he put all the men of Judah and Benjamin under officers of thousands and officers of hundreds, by clans. He mustered them from the age of twenty upward, and found them to be 300,000 picked men fit for service, able to bear spear and shield. ⁶ He hired 100,000 warriors from Israel for 100 talents of silver. ⁷ Then a man of God came to him and said, "O king! Do not let the army of Israel go with you,

21–22: Jehoiada is killed in the very place where he crowned Joash; see also 23.14, where Jehoiada refuses to allow Athaliah's killing in the sacred precincts. **23–24:** Aramean invasion. Other than the mention of war spoil, this passage differs markedly from 2 Kings 12.7–18. There, the Aramean king, Hazael, is bought off and does not attack. Here, it appears that the Aramean force attacks while Hazael remains at home. Finally, the two versions of the battle differ substantively. Chronicles' text is probably a reformulation of earlier material. Note how Chronicles' formulation indicates that (only) those who sinned were now being punished. **25:** Chronicles explains the king's assassination as retribution for his treatment of Zechariah, highlighting the explanation through several key words shared by this v. and vv. 21–22; cf. 2 Kings 2.20. The problematic phrasing of 2 Kings 12.20 is replaced here by "on his bed," perhaps indicating that Chronicles no longer understood the reference in Kings. The "bed" may also be an allusion to the bedroom mentioned above (22.11), indicating a total lack of appreciation on Joash's part. Chronicles' statement regarding Joash's burial is likely tendentious, suggesting a more negative evaluation of Joash. **26:** Cf. the names at 2 Kings 12.21. The claim that two of the conspirators were foreigners may bear a talionic or measure-for-measure message: When Israel turns to foreign gods their (divinely ordained) punishment comes at the hands of foreigners. **27:** On *story*, "midrash," see 13.22 n.

25.1–28: Amaziah's reign. Amaziah's reign, like that of Joash and others, is divided into periods of fidelity and infidelity. As in other cases, divine forbearance and grace require that a prophet be sent to warn Amaziah, but to no avail. **1–4:** Chronicles' less than fully positive evaluation reflects the book's criticism of Amaziah's dependence on mercenaries. V. 4 is

---

ᵃ Lit. "blood."　　ᵇ Cf. 2 Kings 14.　　c-c Cf. Deut. 24.16.

for the LORD is not with Israel—all these Ephraimites. [8] But go by yourself and do it; take courage for battle, [else] God will make you fall before the enemy. For in God there is power to help one or make one fall!" [9] Amaziah said to the man of God, "And what am I to do about the 100 talents I gave for the Israelite force?" The man of God replied, "The LORD has the means to give you much more than that." [10] So Amaziah detached the force that came to him from Ephraim, [ordering them] to go back to their place. They were greatly enraged against Judah and returned to their place in a rage.

[11] Amaziah took courage and, leading his army, he marched to the Valley of Salt. He slew 10,000 men of Seir; [12] another 10,000 the men of Judah captured alive and brought to the top of Sela. They threw them down from the top of Sela and every one of them was burst open. [13] The men of the force that Amaziah had sent back so they would not go with him into battle made forays against the towns of Judah from Samaria to Beth-horon. They slew 3,000 of them, and took much booty.

[14] After Amaziah returned from defeating the Edomites, he had the gods of the men of Seir brought, and installed them as his gods; he prostrated himself before them, and to them he made sacrifice. [15] The LORD was enraged at Amaziah, and sent a prophet to him who said to him, "Why are you worshiping the gods of a people who could not save their people from you?" [16] As he spoke to him, [Amaziah] said to him, "Have we appointed you a counselor to the king? Stop, else you will be killed!" The prophet stopped, saying, "I see God has counseled that you be destroyed, since you act this way and disregard my counsel."

[17] Then King Amaziah of Judah took counsel and sent this message to Joash son of Jehoahaz son of Jehu, king of Israel, "Come, let us confront each other!" [18] King Joash of Israel sent back this message to King Amaziah of Judah, "The thistle in Lebanon sent this message to the cedar in Lebanon, 'Give your daughter to my son in marriage.' But a wild beast in Lebanon passed by and trampled the thistle. [19] You boast that you have defeated the Edomites and you are ambitious to get more glory. Now stay at home, lest, provoking disaster you fall, dragging Judah down with you." [20] But Amaziah paid no heed—it was God's doing, in order to deliver them up because they worshiped the gods of Edom. [21] King Joash of Israel marched up, and he and King Amaziah of Judah confronted each other at Beth-shemesh in Judah. [22] The men of Judah were routed by Israel, and they all fled to their homes. [23] King

a reformulation of 2 Kings 14.5–6, itself based on Deut. 24.16. Whereas Deuteronomy and Kings employ the Heb form meaning "execute" ("yumtu"), Chronicles employs the form meaning "die" ("yamutu"). This may be merely a textual or linguistic variant, although some see it as proof of Chronicles' strict theory of retribution: An innocent individual cannot be punished, whether in human court or divine justice, for the offense of another. **5–13: Campaign against Edom.** Chronicles expands greatly upon 2 Kings 14.7. **6:** The tradition regarding mercenaries may be historically authentic. **7:** The reference to Ephraimites probably indicates that the mercenaries were hired from territory bordering on Judah. **12–13:** Sela is identified by some as Petra, in southern Jordan, but this remains uncertain. **14–16:** Worship by a victorious Judean king of the gods of a defeated enemy is unparalleled elsewhere in the Bible and quite surprising. This is likely Chronicles' creation, intended to explain Amaziah's defeat at the hands of Joash; see v. 20. **17–24:** These are largely identical to 2 Kings 24.8–14, with the addition of the phrase *it was God's doing, in order to deliver them up because they worshiped the gods of Edom* (v. 20), which makes explicit the Chronicler's theology. This v. also anticipates 26.5, below; Chronicles stresses the difference between father and son, and, accordingly, the vastly different outcomes (cf. 26.6–8).

Joash of Israel captured Amaziah son of Joash son of Jeho-ahaz, king of Judah, in Beth-shemesh. He brought him to Jerusalem and made a breach of 400 cubits in the wall of Jerusalem, from the Ephraim Gate to the Corner Gate. [24] Then, with all the gold and silver and all the utensils that were to be found in the House of God in the custody of Obed-edom, and with the treasuries of the royal palace, and with the hostages, he returned to Samaria.

[25] King Amaziah son of Joash of Judah lived fifteen years after the death of King Joash son of Jehoahaz of Is-rael. [26] The other events of Amaziah's reign, early and late, are recorded in the book of the kings of Judah and Israel. [27] From the time that Amaziah turned from following the LORD, a conspiracy was formed against him in Jerusalem, and he fled to Lachish; but they sent men after him to La-chish and they put him to death there. [28] They brought his body back on horses and buried him with his fathers in the city of Judah.

26 Then all the people of Judah took Uzziah, who was sixteen years old, and proclaimed him king to suc-ceed his father Amaziah. [2] It was he who rebuilt Eloth and restored it to Judah after King [Amaziah] slept with his fathers.

[3] Uzziah was sixteen years old when he became king, and he reigned fifty-two years in Jerusalem; his mother's name was Jecoliah of Jerusalem. [4] He did what was pleas-ing to the LORD just as his father Amaziah had done. [5] He applied himself to the worship of God during the time of Zechariah, instructor in the visions[a] of God; during the time he worshiped the LORD, God made him prosper. [6] He went forth to fight the Philistines, and breached the wall of Gath and the wall of Jabneh and the wall of Ashdod; he built towns in [the region of] Ashdod and among the Phil-istines. [7] God helped him against the Philistines, against the Arabs who lived in Gur-baal, and the Meunites. [8] The Ammonites paid tribute to Uzziah, and his fame spread to the approaches of Egypt, for he grew exceedingly strong. [9] Uzziah built towers in Jerusalem on the Corner Gate and the Valley Gate and on the Angle, and fortified them. [10] He built towers in the wilderness and hewed out many cis-terns, for he had much cattle, and farmers in the foothills and on the plain, and vine dressers in the mountains and on the fertile lands, for he loved the soil.

[11] Uzziah had an army of warriors, a battle-ready force who were mustered by Jeiel the scribe and Maasseiah the

26.1–23: Uzziah's reign. The treat-ment of Uzziah's reign is divided into two parts: the king's lengthy reign and his affliction with skin disease. This division is an attempt to deal with the source material: 2 Kings 14.21–15.4 depict Uzziah in a positive fashion, while 15.5–7 describe his affliction. Perhaps using some additional sources, Chron. fills in both periods, and explains why the king is punished. 1–4: 2 Kings generally employs the name Azariah. This difference is explained either as a regnal, rather than personal, name; or, since the Heb roots "'-z-z" (the root of Uzziah) and "'-z-r" (the root of Azariah) both mean "strong," as an interchangeable alternate form of the name. 5: Zechariah, not oth-erwise attested, may have ap-peared in an earlier source avail-able to Chronicles. Some exegetes argued that he is synonymous with Azariah, the priest, of 26.17. 6–8: The literary features connect-ing these vv. with 25.20 have led some to doubt the historicity of 26.6–8; see above.

---

a Some Heb. mss. read byr't; compare ancient versions, "fear."

adjutant under Hananiah, one of the king's officers. 12 The clan chiefs, valiants, totaled 2,600; 13 under them was the trained army of 307,500, who made war with might and power to aid the king against the enemy. 14 Uzziah provided them—the whole army—with shields and spears, and helmets and mail, and bows and slingstones. 15 He made clever devices in Jerusalem, set on the towers and the corners, for shooting arrows and large stones. His fame spread far, for he was helped wonderfully, and he became strong.

16 When he was strong, he grew so arrogant he acted corruptly: he trespassed against his God by entering the Temple of the LORD to offer incense on the incense altar. 17 The priest Azariah, with eighty other brave priests of the LORD, followed him in 18 and, confronting King Uzziah, said to him, "It is not for you, Uzziah, to offer incense to the LORD, but for the Aaronite priests, who have been consecrated, to offer incense. Get out of the Sanctuary, for you have trespassed; there will be no glory in it for you from the LORD God." 19 Uzziah, holding the censer and ready to burn incense, got angry; but as he got angry with the priests, leprosy broke out on his forehead in front of the priests in the House of the LORD beside the incense altar. 20 When the chief priest Azariah and all the other priests looked at him, his forehead was leprous, so they rushed him out of there; he too made haste to get out, for the LORD had struck him with a plague. 21 King Uzziah was a leper until the day of his death. He lived in ᵃ-isolated quarters-ᵃ as a leper, for he was cut off from the House of the LORD—while Jotham his son was in charge of the king's house and governed the people of the land.

22 The other events of Uzziah's reign, early and late, were recorded by the prophet Isaiah son of Amoz. 23 Uzziah slept with his fathers in the burial field of the kings, because, they said, he was a leper; his son Jotham succeeded him as king.

27 Jotham was twenty-five years old when he became king, and he reigned sixteen years in Jerusalem; his mother's name was Jerushah daughter of Zadok. 2 He did what was pleasing to the LORD just as his father Uzziah had done, but he did not enter the Temple of the LORD; however, the people still acted corruptly. 3 It was he who built the Upper Gate of the House of the LORD; he also built extensively on the wall of Ophel. 4 He built towns in the hill country of Judah, and in the woods he built

18–19: The consequences of cultic infractions are severe. The punishment is equally severe, since this skin affliction (traditionally translated as leprosy, but actually relecting a range of skin lesions) renders the afflicted person so contaminated that he or she must dwell outside of the city (see Lev. 13.44–46). Another instance of retributive justice may be seen here: He who treads upon forbidden soil—the inner sanctum—is ultimately removed beyond the physical bounds of society (owing to skin disease). The theme of "trespass" (Heb "maʿal") recurs throughout the remainder of Chronicles. Some have noted similarities between this passage and the Korah rebellion of Num. ch 16. **23:** Instead of 2 Kings 15.7, "in the City of David," Chronicles here reads *in the burial field of the kings.* A burial inscription was found in Jerusalem describing the transport of Uzziah's bones. No similar inscriptions have been found for other kings, suggesting that the tradition found here that Uzziah was not buried with his ancestors is accurate.

27.1–9: Jotham's reign. Jotham's reign is depicted in decidedly positive terms. His religious obedience brings prosperity; even the notice at 2 Kings 15.37 concerning the military campaign by Aram and the northern king Pekah are omitted here, being diverted to the reign of Ahaz. This contrasts markedly with the reign of his son, Ahaz, whom Chronicles portrays as wicked in the extreme (see ch 28). This pattern may reflect the influence of Ezek. ch 18. **3–4:** Chronicles adds details to the terse description in 2 Kings 15.32–38.

ᵃ-ᵃ *Meaning of Heb. uncertain.*

fortresses and towers. [5] Moreover, he fought with the king of the Ammonites and overcame them; the Ammonites gave him that year 100 talents of silver and 10,000 *kor* of wheat and another 10,000 of barley; that is what the Ammonites paid him, and [likewise] in the second and third years. [6] Jotham was strong because he maintained a faithful course before the LORD his God.

[7] The other events of Jotham's reign, and all his battles and his conduct, are recorded in the book of the kings of Israel and Judah. [8] He was twenty-five years old when he became king, and he reigned sixteen years in Jerusalem. [9] Jotham slept with his fathers, and was buried in the City of David; his son Ahaz succeeded him as king.

28 Ahaz was twenty years old when he became king, and he reigned sixteen years in Jerusalem. He did not do what was pleasing to the LORD as his father David had done, [2] but followed the ways of the kings of Israel; he even made molten images for the Baals. [3] He made offerings in the Valley of Ben-hinnom and burned his sons in fire, in the abhorrent fashion of the nations which the LORD had dispossessed before the Israelites. [4] He sacrificed and made offerings at the shrines, on the hills, and under every leafy tree. [5] The LORD his God delivered him over to the king of Aram, who defeated him and took many of his men captive, and brought them to Damascus. He was also delivered over to the king of Israel, who inflicted a great defeat on him. [6] Pekah son of Remaliah killed 120,000 in Judah—all brave men—in one day, because they had forsaken the LORD God of their fathers. [7] Zichri, the champion of Ephraim, killed Maaseiah the king's son, and Azrikam chief of the palace, and Elkanah, the second to the king. [8] The Israelites captured 200,000 of their kinsmen, women, boys, and girls; they also took a large amount of booty from them and brought the booty to Samaria.

[9] A prophet of the LORD by the name of Oded was there, who went out to meet the army on its return to Samaria. He said to them, "Because of the fury of the LORD God of your fathers against Judah, He delivered them over to you, and you killed them in a rage that reached heaven. [10] Do you now intend to subjugate the men and women of Judah and Jerusalem to be your slaves? As it is, you have nothing but offenses against the LORD your God. [11] Now then, listen to me, and send back the captives you have taken from your kinsmen, for the wrath of the LORD is upon you!" [12] Some of the chief men of the Ephraimites—Azariah son of Jehohanan, Berechiah son of Meshille-

5–9: The historicity of this campaign, not recorded elsewhere, is debated. Some scholars emend "Ammonites" to "Meunites" (see 20.1), believing that Jotham continued his father's policy (see 26.7).

28.1–27: Ahaz's reign. The low point of the preexilic Judahite monarchy. Besides the sharp contrast with his father, Ahaz's wickedness creates a foil for his son, Hezekiah, the most righteous of the post-Solomonic Davidides. In many ways, this reign marks a complete reversal of 2 Chron. ch 13 and the lessons of Chronicles' Abijah. Thus, the present ch portrays the northern tribes in a most positive light, including a (veracious) self-reckoning of their sinful ways (cf. 2 Chron. 13.4–12). Chronicles maintains that the Northern Kingdom fell to Assyria during this reign. This paves the way for a single sovereign (Hezekiah) to reunify Judah and the northern tribes, another key theme of 2 Chron. ch 13. **1–4:** Ahaz's idolatrous ways are more pronounced than in 2 Kings 16.12–18; this leads to exile for much of the population. **5–7:** Chronicles' description of the Syro-Ephraimite war differs from other biblical versions (2 Kings 15.37; 16.5; Isa. ch 7; Hos. 5.8–6.6). Chronicles probably draws on earlier sources, but formulates them in accordance with its overall depiction of Ahaz; cf. 2 Kings 16.5. **5:** A complete reversal of 13.15–17. **6:** While the numbers and time frame may reflect literary embellishment, the defeat of Judah is quite plausible; see 2 Kings 16.5, where the confederation puts Jerusalem to siege. **8–15:** The names in v. 12, along with the (unexpected) mention of Jericho, further the likelihood that Chronicles has drawn on an earlier source. The description of the prophetic activity of Oded (v. 9) and its aftermath, however, comports with the theology of Chronicles and was likely composed for illustrative purposes, filling in gaps in the story line. **16–17:** An Edomite attack is consistent with historical evidence of Edomite expansion at moth, Jehizkiah son of Shallum, and Amasa son of Hadlai—confronted those returning from the campaign [13] and said to them, "Do not bring these captives here, for it would mean our offending the LORD, adding to our sins and our offenses; for our offense is grave enough, and there is already wrath upon Israel." [14] So the soldiers released the captives and the booty in the presence of the officers and all the congregation. [15] Then the men named above proceeded to take the captives in hand, and with the booty they clothed all the naked among them—they clothed them and shod them and gave them to eat and drink and anointed them and provided donkeys for all who were failing and brought them to Jericho, the city of palms, back to their kinsmen. Then they returned to Samaria.

[16] At that time, King Ahaz sent to the king of Assyria for help. [17] Again the Edomites came and inflicted a defeat on Judah and took captives. [18] And the Philistines made forays against the cities of the Shephelah and the Negeb of Judah; they seized Beth-shemesh and Aijalon and Gederoth, and Soco with its villages, and Timnah with its villages, and Gimzo with its villages; and they settled there. [19] Thus the LORD brought Judah low on account of King Ahaz of Israel,[a] for he threw off restraint in Judah and trespassed against the LORD. [20] Tillegath-pilneser, king of Assyria, marched against him and gave him trouble, instead of supporting him. [21] For Ahaz plundered the House of the LORD and the house of the king and the officers, and made a gift to the king of Assyria—to no avail.

[22] In his time of trouble, this King Ahaz trespassed even more against the LORD, [23] sacrificing to the gods of Damascus which had defeated him, for he thought, "The gods of the kings of Aram help them; I shall sacrifice to them and they will help me"; but they were his ruin and that of all Israel. [24] Ahaz collected the utensils of the House of God, and cut the utensils of the House of God to pieces. He shut the doors of the House of the LORD and made himself altars in every corner of Jerusalem. [25] In every town in Judah he set up shrines to make offerings to other gods, vexing the LORD God of his fathers.

[26] The other events of his reign and all his conduct, early and late, are recorded in the book of the kings of Judah and Israel. [27] Ahaz slept with his fathers and was buried in the city, in Jerusalem; his body was not brought to the tombs of the kings of Israel. His son Hezekiah succeeded him as king.

24–25: Chronicles repeats *every* to emphasize the extent of Ahaz's cultic sins, which go beyond those attested in 2 Kings ch 16.

a Some mss. and ancient versions read "Judah."

29 Hezekiah became king at the age of twenty-five, and he reigned twenty-nine years in Jerusalem; his mother's name was Abijah daughter of Zechariah. [2] He did what was pleasing to the LORD, just as his father David had done.

[3] He, in the first month of the first year of his reign, opened the doors of the House of the LORD and repaired them. [4] He summoned the priests and the Levites and assembled them in the east square. [5] He said to them, "Listen to me, Levites! Sanctify yourselves and sanctify the House of the LORD God of your fathers, and take the abhorrent things out of the holy place. [6] For our fathers trespassed and did what displeased the LORD our God; they forsook Him and turned their faces away from the dwelling-place of the LORD, turning their backs on it. [7] They also shut the doors of the porch and put out the lights; they did not offer incense and did not make burnt offerings in the holy place to the God of Israel. [8] The wrath of the LORD was upon Judah and Jerusalem; He made them an object of horror, amazement, and hissing [a] as you see with your own eyes. [9] Our fathers died by the sword, and our sons and daughters and wives are in captivity on account of this. [10] Now I wish to make a covenant with the LORD God of Israel, so that His rage may be withdrawn from us. [11] Now, my sons, do not be slack, for the LORD chose you to attend upon Him, to serve Him, to be His ministers and to make offerings to Him."

[12] So the Levites set to—Mahath son of Amasai and Joel son of Azariah of the sons of Kohath; and of the sons of Merari, Kish son of Abdi and Azariah son of Jehallelel; and of the Gershonites, Joah son of Zimmah and Eden son of Joah; [13] and of the sons of Elizaphan, Shimri and Jeiel;

a See note at Jer. 18.16.

29.1–32.33: Hezekiah's reign. Hezekiah is, after David and Solomon, the outstanding Judean monarch in Chronicles, equivalent in stature to Josiah in Kings. In addition to the bulk of material devoted to his reign, several features and lexical links suggest that Chronicles sought to portray him as a second Solomon or, possibly, a combination of David and Solomon. Most fundamentally, Hezekiah symbolizes the reunification of all Israel around the Jerusalem Temple, as in the days of David and Solomon. Other typo-logical features will be noted below. The high esteem in which Hezekiah was held is reflected in the rabbinic statement that, despite some failings, he had been worthy to be Israel's messiah (_b. Sanh._ 94a). The key difference between Kings' treatment of Hezekiah and that of Chronicles is that while the former concentrates on Hezekiah's military and geopolitical engagements, especially with Assyria, the latter minimizes these in favor of Hezekiah's religious achievements. (This is reminiscent of Chronicles' treatment of David.)

Chronicles' treatment may be divided into two units. Chs 29–31 address Hezekiah's religious reforms, a topic that Kings treats in one v. The remaining ch, 32, is a condensed, and radically rewritten, description of the fortunes of the faithful king. The form Jehezekiah, Heb "Yeḥizkiyahu," (lit. "the LORD is strong") is the standard form in Chronicles—which, in fact, preserves almost all of the attestations of this form—whereas Kings prefers the shorter form Hezekiah (Heb "Ḥizkiyahu" [lit. "the LORD is my strength"]). Cuneiform evidence, which preserves the vocalization "ḫa-za-qi-ya-u" and similar formulations, indicates that the form preserved in Kings is older. The form in Chronicles fits patterns of names in later Heb, and is secondary.

29.1–26: Purging and rededication of the Temple. Aside from the first two vv., there is no extant source for this account; it is unclear if Chronicles has drawn on an independent source. The beginning of this ch, claiming that Hezekiah attended to the cultus immediately upon ascending the throne, together with its conclusion, are part of the Solomonic typology applied to Hezekiah. **3–11:** Charge to the Levites. V. 3 contains two novel points. Chronicles claims that the king opened the doors to the Temple. No such datum appears in 2 Kings; the closest source is found at 2 Kings 18.16, though the reference there is quite different. (See also 2 Kings 16.18, in connection with Ahaz.) Second, Chronicles makes the highly improbable and tendentious claim that this action was undertaken during Hezekiah's _first year_—indeed, first day—of rule (see v. 17). Chronicles' date means that Hezekiah attended to the cult on the very day on which he ascended the throne and, moreover, that the priests gathered and sanctified themselves on this same day. Chronicles portrays Hezekiah as wasting no time in attending to cultic matters—a clear echo of David and Solomon. The first and of the sons of Asaph, Zechariah and Mattaniah;[14] and of the sons of Heman, Jehiel and Shimei; and of the sons of Jeduthun, Shemaiah and Uzziel—[15] and, gathering their brothers, they sanctified themselves and came, by a command of the king concerning the LORD's ordinances, to purify the House of the LORD. [16] The priests went into the House of the LORD to purify it, and brought all the unclean things they found in the Temple of the LORD out into the court of the House of the LORD; [there] the Levites received them, to take them outside to Wadi Kidron. [17] They began the sanctification on the first day of the first month; on the eighth day of the month they reached the porch of the LORD. They sanctified the House of the LORD for eight days, and on the sixteenth day of the first month they finished. [18] Then they went into the palace of King Hezekiah and said, "We have purified the whole House of the LORD and the altar of burnt offering and all its utensils, and the table of the bread of display and all its utensils; [19] and all the utensils that King Ahaz had befouled during his reign, when he trespassed, we have made ready and sanctified. They are standing in front of the altar of the LORD."

[20] King Hezekiah rose early, gathered the officers of the city, and went up to the House of the LORD. [21] They brought seven bulls and seven rams and seven lambs and seven he-goats as a sin offering for the kingdom and for the Sanctuary and for Judah. He ordered the Aaronite priests to offer them on the altar of the LORD. [22] The cattle were slaughtered, and the priests received the blood and dashed it against the altar; the rams were slaughtered and the blood was dashed against the altar; the lambs were slaughtered and the blood was dashed against the altar. [23] The he-goats for the sin offering were presented to the king and the congregation, who laid their hands upon them. [24] The priests slaughtered them and performed the purgation rite with the blood against the altar, to expiate for all Israel, for the king had designated the burnt offering and the sin offering to be for all Israel. [25] He stationed the Levites in the House of the LORD with cymbals and harps and lyres, as David and Gad the king's seer and Nathan the prophet had ordained, for the ordinance was by the LORD through His prophets.

[26] When the Levites were in place with the instruments of David, and the priests with their trumpets, [27] Hezekiah gave the order to offer the burnt offering on the altar. When the burnt offering began, the song of the LORD and the trumpets began also, together with the instruments of King David of Israel. [28] All the congregation prostrated themselves, the song was sung and the trumpets were

month of the Heb year (roughly April) marks not only the renewal of the festal cycle but, according to Exod. ch 40, also the time when Moses' Tabernacle was erected; thus, typologically, Hezekiah is depicted as a new Moses. **4–6:** The only sin cited in v. 6 is rejection of the cultus (not idolatry), succinctly expressing the central role of the cultus in Chronicles. **12–14:** The fourteen Levites fall into two groups. The first eight consist of *Kohath, Merari, Gershon,* and *Elizaphan;* a similar ordering appears at 1 Chron. 15.5–6. The second group consists of *Asaph, Heman,* and *Jeduthun;* this grouping appears in 1 Chron. chs 15–16 and 25.1. The message here is that all Levitic clans responded with equal alacrity. **16:** Informed by Torah law, Chronicles emphasizes that the innermost Temple precincts were accessible only to priests; Levites served in the other precincts. **17:** Completion of the Temple purification *on the eighth day* (of the first month) is unmistakably reminiscent of Exod. 40.17, which, together with Lev. 8.33–9.24, indicates that the Tabernacle dedication ceremonies lasted eight days. **18–29:** Chronicles' description of the purification and rededication reflects the terminology of the Priestly source. **21:** This evokes the Tabernacle dedication ceremony of Num. 7.9ff. A similar arrangement of cultic offerings appears at Ezra 8.35, which also echoes Num. ch 7 (see *b. Menaḥ.* 45a); see v. 31, below. **24:** This may contain an allusion to the ordination rites of Exod. 29.12, 36–37. *All Israel* may refer to those exiled as well as those remaining in the land, or may indicate that the king made the offerings on behalf of a wider group than that envisaged by the priests and Levites above. The reference to the cultic vessels here, following their desecration by Ahaz (28.24), may allude to the pristine conditions of Solomon's reign. **25–30:** Hezekiah's reestablishment of the choral rite casts him as a second David, who was, according to Chronicles, the composer of psalms and the fashioner

blown—all this until the end of the burnt offering.
29 When the offering was finished, the king and all who
were there with him knelt and prostrated themselves.
30 King Hezekiah and the officers ordered the Levites to
praise the LORD in the words of David and Asaph the seer;
so they praised rapturously, and they bowed and prostrated themselves.

31 Then Hezekiah said, "Now you have consecrated
yourselves to the LORD; come, bring sacrifices of well-
being and thanksgiving to the House of the LORD." The
congregation brought sacrifices of well-being and thanksgiving, and all who felt so moved brought burnt offerings.
32 The number of burnt offerings that the congregation

of musical instruments employed
in the Temple. **31:** The reference
to "consecration" and *all who felt
so moved* (lit. "those of a generous
heart") echoes the Tabernacle project; see Exod. 36.3–7. **34:** The author treats the Levites preferen-
tially. **36:** As with David (1 Chron.
29.9), cultic activity is synonymous
with joy.

**30.1–27: Celebration of the Pass-
over festival.** The historicity of
this ch, along with its literary development, is much debated. Some
scholars maintain that Chronicles

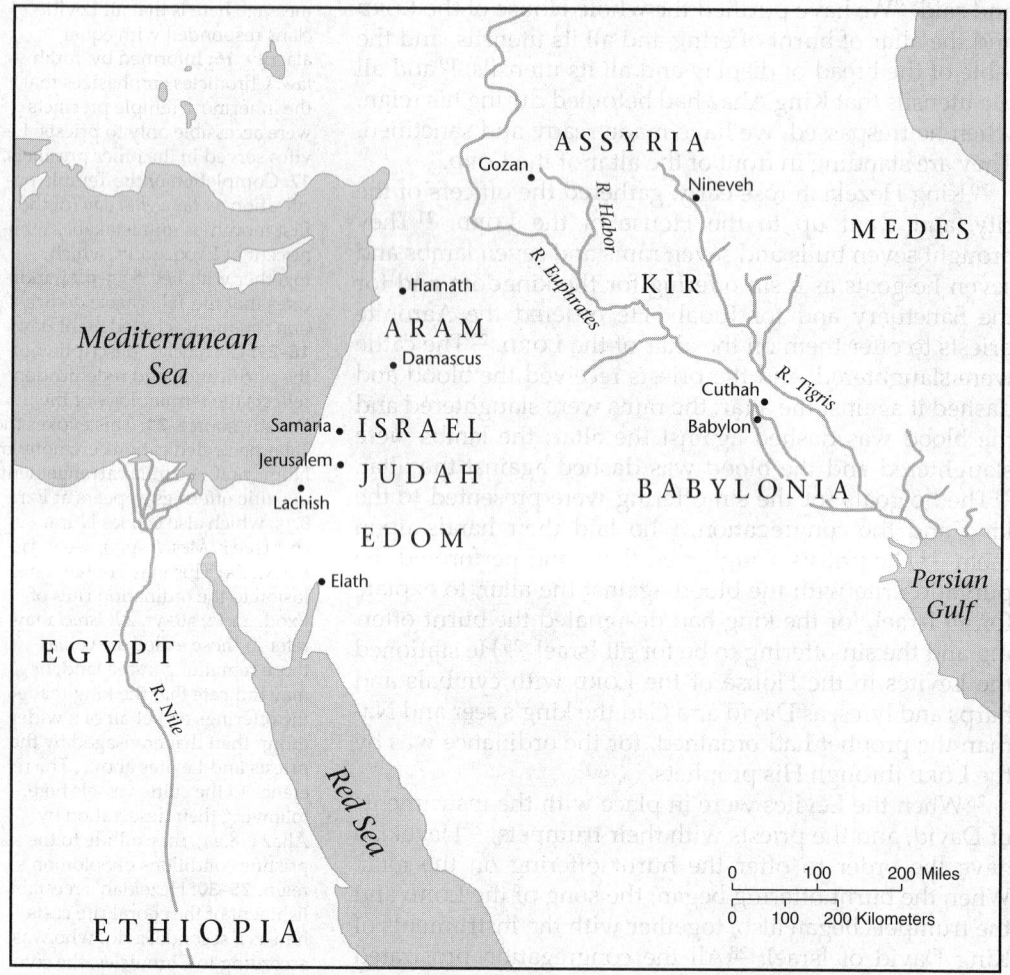

Assyria and Israel and Judah in the book of Chronicles

brought was 70 cattle, 100 rams, 200 lambs—all these for burnt offerings to the LORD. ³³ The sacred offerings were 600 large cattle and 3,000 small cattle. ³⁴ The priests were too few to be able to flay all the burnt offerings, so their kinsmen, the Levites, reinforced them till the end of the work, and till the [rest of the] priests sanctified themselves. (The Levites were more conscientious about sanctifying themselves than the priests.) ³⁵ For beside the large number of burnt offerings, there were the fat parts of the sacrifices of well-being and the libations for the burnt offerings; so the service of the House of the LORD was properly accomplished. ³⁶ Hezekiah and all the people rejoiced over what God had enabled the people to accomplish, because it had happened so suddenly.

30 Hezekiah sent word to all Israel and Judah; he also wrote letters to Ephraim and Manasseh to come to the House of the LORD in Jerusalem to keep the Passover for the LORD God of Israel. ² The king and his officers and the congregation in Jerusalem had agreed to keep the Passover in the second month, ³ for at the time, they were unable to keep it,ᵃ for not enough priests had sanctified themselves, nor had the people assembled in Jerusalem. ⁴ The king and the whole congregation thought it proper ⁵ to issue a decree and proclaim throughout all Israel from Beer-sheba to Dan that they come and keep the Passover for the LORD God of Israel in Jerusalem—not often did they act in accord with what was written. ⁶ The couriers went out with the letters from the king and his officers through all Israel and Judah, by order of the king, proclaiming, "O you Israelites! Return to the LORD God of your fathers, Abraham, Isaac, and Israel, and He will return to the remnant of you who escaped from the hand of the kings of Assyria. ⁷ Do not be like your fathers and brothers who trespassed against the LORD God of their fathers and He turned them into a horror, as you see. ⁸ Now do not be stiffnecked like your fathers; submit yourselves to the LORD and come to His sanctuary, which He consecrated forever, and serve the LORD your God so that His anger may turn back from you. ⁹ If you return to the LORD, your brothers and children will be regarded with compassion by their captors, and will return to this land; for the LORD your God is gracious and merciful; He will not turn His face from you if you return to Him."

¹⁰ As the couriers passed from town to town in the land of Ephraim and Manasseh till they reached Zebulun, they

has drawn upon earlier sources, based on the anomalous date and duration of the festival, along with various other details, which would hardly have been concocted by Chronicles, for whom proper cultic procedure was paramount. Some argue that Chronicles reflects a pre-Priestly tradition of the Unleavened Bread festival, as preserved in Exod. 34.18. Others view the ch as Chronicles' creation, which combines the Unleavened Bread festival with the Passover feast; this reflects Deuteronomic (hence, Josianic) influence. Accordingly, Chronicles' version cannot be historical; it is intended to highlight the cultus as observed in the postexilic era, and Hezekiah's status (cf. Chronicles' treatment of Josiah, below). Chronicles' pan-Israel orientation is evident at several points in the episode. While scholars disagree on the historicity of Hezekiah's attempt to unite north and south at this juncture, as well, there is good reason to accept this depiction. First, the Assyrians, following their conquest of the northern tribes, were occupied for a short period with other matters, thus creating a window for Hezekiah's expansion. Second, Hezekiah's son is named Manasseh; this name, together with the name Ephraim, forms a recurring pair which together connote the confederation of northern tribes in Chronicles. **1–3:** In addition to expressing Chronicles' pan-Israel view, this passage also conveys the importance of the cultus. The inclusion of all segments of the population in the decision-making process is typical of upright "democratic" kings; see 1 Chron. 13.1. **1:** *Sent word:* The use of letters for royal proclamations reflects the practice of the Persian period, and is thus anachronistic here. **5:** *From Beer-sheba to Dan,* i.e., the full expanse of Israelite settlement in the ancestral land; this is consonant with Chronicles' view of the ongoing Israelite presence in the land. **6:** Measure-for-measure reward is expressed: If the people *return to the LORD . . . He will return to the remnant.* V. 9 continues this motif

---

ᵃ I.e., on its proper date; cf. Num. 9.1–14.

were laughed at and mocked. [11] Some of the people of Asher and Manasseh and Zebulun, however, were contrite, and came to Jerusalem. [12] The hand of God was on Judah, too, making them of a single mind to carry out the command of the king and officers concerning the ordinance of the LORD. [13] A great crowd assembled at Jerusalem to keep the Feast of Unleavened Bread in the second month, a very great congregation. [14] They set to and removed the altars that were in Jerusalem, and they removed all the incense stands and threw them into Wadi Kidron. [15] They slaughtered the paschal sacrifice on the fourteenth of the second month. The priests and Levites were ashamed, and they sanctified themselves and brought burnt offerings to the House of the LORD. [16] They took their stations, as was their rule according to the Teaching of Moses, man of God. The priests dashed the blood [which they received] from the Levites. [17] Since many in the congregation had not sanctified themselves, the Levites were in charge of slaughtering the paschal sacrifice for everyone who was not clean, so as to consecrate them to the LORD. [18] For most of the people—many from Ephraim and Manasseh, Issachar and Zebulun—had not purified themselves, yet they ate the paschal sacrifice in violation of what was written. Hezekiah prayed for them, saying, "The good LORD will provide atonement for [19] everyone who set his mind on worshiping God, the LORD God of his fathers, even if he is not purified for the sanctuary." [20] The LORD heard Hezekiah and healed the people.

[21] The Israelites who were in Jerusalem kept the Feast of Unleavened Bread seven days, with great rejoicing, the Levites and the priests praising the LORD daily with powerful instruments for the LORD. [22] Hezekiah persuaded all the Levites who performed skillfully for the LORD to spend the seven days of the festival making offerings of well-being, and confessing to the LORD God of their fathers. [23] All the congregation resolved to keep seven more days, so they kept seven more days of rejoicing. [24] King Hezekiah of Judah contributed to the congregation 1,000 bulls and 7,000 sheep. And the officers contributed to the congregation 1,000 bulls and 10,000 sheep. And the priests sanctified themselves in large numbers. [25] All the congregation of Judah and the priests and the Levites and all the congregation that came from Israel, and the resident aliens who came from the land of Israel and who lived in Judah, rejoiced. [26] There was great rejoicing in Jerusalem, for since the time of King Solomon son of David of Israel nothing like it had happened in Jerusalem. [27] The Levite priests rose

with a slight twist: The captives will be returned to the land. **18–20:** This is a remarkable deviation from Priestly norms, which are punctilious concerning matters of ritual purity. Sincere prayer from a righteous king (v. 20) trumps typical concerns. **21:** Some exegetes take the words *kept the Feast . . . seven days* as an ellipsis for "consumed the festal offerings." **23:** Note the popular nature of this decision. **24–26:** The celebration of the festival in the second month (see v. 13), contrary to the first month legislated in Torah sources (e.g., Exod. 12.2–3; Deut. 16.1–8) is explained by some as reflecting a northern calendar, which lagged behind the Judahite calendar by one month. Others explain Chronicles as applying to the community the legislation concerning an individual in Num. 9.6–12, which addresses the "Second Passover," i.e., the paschal sacrifice offered by those unable to participate in the regular paschal offering due to ritual impurity or other legitimate reasons; see *t. Pisha* 8.4, where this point is debated. Some rabbinic sources (*m. Pes.* 4.9; *t. Pisha* 8.5) explain Hezekiah's controversial move as based on intercalation, in which an additional (i.e., thirteenth) month is added to the concluding year; thus he did not really change the month of the festival. Some Israelites accepted Hezekiah's intercalation, while others did not, and so refrained from participating. **25:** The reference to *resident aliens* recalls Num. 9.14; some medieval exegetes (Gersonides, pseudo-Rashi) averred that *aliens* refers to northerners who had relocated in Judah. The reference to Solomon's period is a clear example of Chronicles' Solomon typology (see 29.1–32.33).

and blessed the people, and their voice was heard, and their prayer went up to His holy abode, to heaven.

31 When all this was finished, all Israel who were present went out into the towns of Judah and smashed the pillars, cut down the sacred posts, demolished the shrines and altars throughout Judah and Benjamin, and throughout Ephraim and Manasseh, to the very last one. Then all the Israelites returned to their towns, each to his possession.

² Hezekiah reconstituted the divisions of the priests and Levites, each man of the priests and Levites according to his office, for the burnt offerings, the offerings of well-being, to minister, and to sing hymns and praises in the gates of the courts of the Lord; ³ also the king's portion, from his property, for the burnt offerings—the morning and evening burnt offering, and the burnt offerings for sabbaths, and new moons, and festivals, as prescribed in the Teaching of the Lord.

⁴ He ordered the people, the inhabitants of Jerusalem, to deliver the portions of the priests and the Levites, so that they might devote themselves to the Teaching of the Lord. ⁵ When the word spread, the Israelites brought large quantities of grain, wine, oil, honey, and all kinds of agricultural produce, and tithes of all, in large amounts. ⁶ The men of Israel and Judah living in the towns of Judah—they too brought tithes of cattle and sheep and tithes of sacred things consecrated to the Lord their God, piling them in heaps. ⁷ In the third month the heaps began to accumulate, and were finished in the seventh month. ⁸ When Hezekiah and the officers came and saw the heaps, they blessed the Lord and his people Israel. ⁹ Hezekiah asked the priests and Levites about the heaps. ¹⁰ The chief priest Azariah, of the house of Zadok, replied to him, saying, "Ever since the gifts began to be brought to the House of the Lord, people have been eating to satiety and leaving over in great amounts, for the Lord has blessed His people; this huge amount is left over!" ¹¹ Hezekiah then gave orders to prepare store-chambers in the House of the Lord; and they were prepared. ¹² They brought in the gifts and the tithes and the sacred things faithfully. Their supervisor was Conaniah the Levite, and Shimei his brother was second in rank. ¹³ Jehiel and Azaziah and Nahath and Asahel and Jerimoth and Jozabad and Eliel and Ismachiah and Mahath and Benaiah were commissioners under Conaniah and Shimei his brother by appointment of King Hezekiah; Azariah was supervisor of the House of God. ¹⁴ Kore son of Imnah the Levite, the keeper of the

31.1–21: Cultic arrangements. The cultic reform is executed by the entire population, both Judah and the northern regions. The overwhelming response of the people indicates the nation's worthy and upright nature. This state of affairs offers a theological explanation for the miraculous deliverance depicted in the following ch. This is summarized in the ch's final verse, which emphasizes that "he prospered" because of his concern for the Temple and for the "torah" (*Teaching*).

East Gate, was in charge of the freewill offerings to God, of the allocation of gifts to the LORD, and the most sacred things. [15] Under him were Eden, Miniamin, Jeshua, Shemaiah, Amariah, and Shecaniah, in offices of trust in the priestly towns, making allocation to their brothers by divisions, to great and small alike; [16] besides allocating their daily rations to those males registered by families from three years old and up, all who entered the House of the LORD according to their service and their shift by division; [17] and in charge of the registry of priests by clans, and of the Levites, from twenty years old and up, by shifts, in their divisions; [18] and the registry of the dependents of their whole company—wives, sons, and daughters—for, relying upon them, they sanctified themselves in holiness. [19] And for the Aaronite priests, in each and every one of their towns with adjoining fields, the above-named men were to allocate portions to every male of the priests and to every registered Levite. [20] Hezekiah did this throughout Judah. He acted in a way that was good, upright, and faithful before the LORD his God. [21] Every work he undertook in the service of the House of God or in the Teaching and the Commandment, to worship his God, he did with all his heart; and he prospered.

32 [a] After these faithful deeds, King Sennacherib of Assyria invaded Judah and encamped against its fortified towns with the aim of taking them over. [2] When Hezekiah saw that Sennacherib had come, intent on making war against Jerusalem, [3] he consulted with his officers and warriors about stopping the flow of the springs outside the city, and they supported him. [4] A large force was assembled to stop up all the springs and the wadi that flowed through the land, for otherwise, they thought, the king of Assyria would come and find water in abundance. [5] He acted with vigor, rebuilding the whole breached wall, raising towers on it, and building another wall outside it. He fortified the Millo of the City of David, and made a great quantity of arms and shields. [6] He appointed battle officers over the people; then, gathering them to him in the square of the city gate, he rallied them, saying, [7] "Be strong and of good courage; do not be frightened or dismayed by the king of Assyria or by the horde that is with him, for we have more with us than he has with him. [8] With him is an arm of flesh, but with us is the LORD our God, to help us and to fight our battles." The people were encouraged by the speech of King Hezekiah of Judah.

a Cf. 2 Kings 18–20; Isa. 36–39.

32.1–33: Assyrian invasion and Hezekiah's faithfulness. A highly revised version of 2 Kings chs 18–19 and Isa. chs 36–39. The negative features of Hezekiah's conduct, e.g., pride and removal of Temple vessels, surrender to the Assyrians, are omitted. Similarly, Hezekiah's military preparations, severely criticized by Isaiah, are here presented as being accompanied by the king's hortatory speech stressing trust in the LORD; this results in a positive assessment of Hezekiah's preparations. In v. 1, Chronicles omits the reference in 2 Kings 18.4 to the bronze serpent fashioned by Moses—which later became a source of cultic offense—presumably out of respect for Moses and Mosaic law. **1–6:** 2 Kings 18.13 and Isa. 36.1 state that Sennacherib's invasion took place in the fourteenth year and that the Assyrians managed to capture (many of) the cities of Judah, but not Jerusalem (see v. 10 n.). Chronicles omits the date; in its place it employs a connective link, *after these faithful deeds*, whose function is to explain theologically the reason for the Assyrians' defeat. The invasion by a foreign army at this juncture would appear to undermine Chronicles' strict view of retribution. This passage's purpose may be to teach what should be the proper response to "trials": Trust and piety are more potent than military might. Cf. 14.9–15. **3:** The democratization principle at work. Rabbinic sources differ over the propriety of the decision to stop the springs: *m. Pes.* 4.9 expresses criticism, while *'Avot R. Nat.* A, 2, informed by v. 30, below, lauds the move (see, also, *Pirqe R. El.* 9). **7–8:** The words *be strong and of good courage* are highly reminiscent of David and Solomon; see 1 Chron. 22.13. These vv. are a potent expression of one of Chronicles' main themes, a theme that would have resonated deeply with his audience in the postexilic period, when Israel lacked military power. **10:** As noted above, some understand Chronicles' text to mean that the Assyrian forces did

⁹ Afterward, King Sennacherib of Assyria sent his officers to Jerusalem—he and all his staff being at Lachish—with this message to King Hezekiah of Judah and to all the people of Judah who were in Jerusalem: ¹⁰ "Thus said King Sennacherib of Assyria: On what do you trust to enable you to endure a siege in Jerusalem? ¹¹ Hezekiah is seducing you to a death of hunger and thirst, saying, 'The LORD our God will save us from the king of Assyria.' ¹² But is not Hezekiah the one who removed His shrines and His altars and commanded the people of Judah and Jerusalem saying, 'Before this one altar you shall prostrate yourselves, and upon it make your burnt offerings'? ¹³ Surely you know what I and my fathers have done to the peoples of the lands? Were the gods of the nations of the lands able to save their lands from me? ¹⁴ Which of all the gods of any of those nations whom my fathers destroyed was able to save his people from me, that your God should be able to save you from me? ¹⁵ Now then, do not let Hezekiah delude you; do not let him seduce you in this way; do not believe him. For no god of any nation or kingdom has been able to save his people from me or from my fathers—much less your God, to save you from me!" ¹⁶ His officers said still more things against the LORD God and against His servant Hezekiah. ¹⁷ He also wrote letters reviling the LORD God of Israel, saying of Him, "Just as the gods of the other nations of the earth did not save their people from me, so the God of Hezekiah will not save his people from me." ¹⁸ They called loudly in the language of Judah to the people of Jerusalem who were on the wall, to frighten them into panic, so as to capture the city. ¹⁹ They spoke of the God of Jerusalem as though He were like the gods of the other peoples of the earth, made by human hands. ²⁰ Then King Hezekiah and the prophet Isaiah son of Amoz prayed about this, and cried out to heaven.

²¹ The LORD sent an angel who annihilated every mighty warrior, commander, and officer in the army of the king of Assyria, and he returned in disgrace to his land. He entered the house of his god, and there some of his own offspring struck him down by the sword. ²² Thus the LORD delivered Hezekiah and the inhabitants of Jerusalem from King Sennacherib of Assyria, and from everyone; He provided for them on all sides. ²³ Many brought tribute to the LORD to Jerusalem, and gifts to King Hezekiah of Judah; thereafter he was exalted in the eyes of all the nations.

²⁴ At that time, Hezekiah fell deathly sick. He prayed to the LORD, who responded to him and gave him a sign. ²⁵ Hezekiah made no return for what had been bestowed

not reach Jerusalem, a position which comports with 2 Kings 19.32–33 (= Isa. 37.33–34). This v., however, does suggest that Jerusalem was under siege. Chronicles' depiction thus magnifies the miracle of Jerusalem's remaining unharmed. Extrabiblical data supports the historicity of a limited Jerusalem siege. **19:** An added summary v., accusing Sennacherib and his officials of blasphemy, thus justifying their defeat. **20:** Chronicles conflates 2 Kings 19.2–4 and 19.14, while omitting the specific content of Hezekiah's prayer and Isaiah's message at 2 Kings 19.15–33. Chronicles also omits 2 Kings 19.34, which implies that Hezekiah's own merit would not have sufficed to save Jerusalem and its environs. **21–23:** The LORD *provided for them* (the people) and *exalted* Hezekiah *in the eyes of all the nations*, acts that are reminiscent of Jehoshaphat and especially Solomon (1 Chron. 22.9) and David (1 Chron. 14.17). The stark contrast between Hezekiah's fate and that of Sennacherib could hardly be clearer: One is *exalted in the eyes* of the entire world, the other is murdered by *his own offspring*. **24–26:** This passage contains but a fleeting allusion to 2 Kings 20.1–11, which states that Hezekiah, stricken by illness, beseeched the LORD; he requested and was shown a portent signaling his recovery, and his life is extended by fifteen years. Chronicles' omission of the substance of this passage may indicate that Chronicles viewed Hezekiah's request for an explicit sign as indicating less than full trust in the prophetic word (2 Kings 20.8). Also, Hezekiah's petition contains self-descriptions that do not reflect the submissive stance that Chronicles requires. **25–26:** This may reflect an understanding of the previously narrated seige of Jerusalem as punishment for Hezekiah's arrogance, but as a result of proper penitence, the seige was not successful.

upon him, for he grew arrogant; so wrath was decreed for him and for Judah and Jerusalem. ²⁶ Then Hezekiah humbled himself where he had been arrogant, he and the inhabitants of Jerusalem, and no wrath of the LORD came on them during the reign of Hezekiah. ²⁷ Hezekiah enjoyed riches and glory in abundance; he filled treasuries with silver and gold, precious stones, spices, shields, and all lovely objects; ²⁸ and store-cities with the produce of grain, wine, and oil, and stalls for all kinds of beasts, and flocks for sheepfolds. ²⁹ And he acquired towns, and flocks of small and large cattle in great number, for God endowed him with very many possessions. ³⁰ It was Hezekiah who stopped up the spring of water of Upper Gihon, leading it downward west of the City of David; Hezekiah prospered in all that he did. ³¹ So too in the matter of the ambassadors of the princes of Babylon, who were sent to him to inquire about the sign that was in the land, when God forsook him in order to test him, to learn all that was in his mind.

³² The other events of Hezekiah's reign, and his faithful acts, are recorded in the visions of the prophet Isaiah son

27–29: Solomon typology: great wealth and honor. Chronicles' text presupposes the reader's familiarity with 1 Kings 1–2 Kings 19. **30:** This action guaranteed a constant water supply for Jerusalem. This may refer to the construction of the Siloam tunnel, though the inscription from the middle of that tunnel does not mention any king by name. See v. 3 n. **31:** Chronicles radically transforms 2 Kings 20.12–19. The entire episode is a test of Hezekiah's faith, made necessary by his faltering and repentance in vv. 25–26. Hezekiah's successful performance may have been suggested by the account of Hezekiah's confession at 2 Kings 20.19. **32:** Chronicles' note that the people *accorded him much honor* is unique to Hezekiah—he is exceptional even at his death.

33.1–20: Manasseh's reign. Chronicles' presentation of Manasseh is the subject of widely divergent views. Some maintain that vv. 11–19, the story of Manasseh's captivity and repentance, are the creation of Chronicles, intended to resolve the theological difficulties engendered by the Kings version. The portrayal of this monarch in 2 Kings ch 21 is unambiguously negative. He exceeded all previous Judahite kings (and the kings who lived in the land before Israel came there, as well) in his wickedness. His fostering of idolatry is cited as the reason for the ultimate destruction of Jerusalem (2 Kings 21.12–16; 24.3). Chronicles knows none of this. Chronicles' radical revision is generally explained as reflecting the author's theological stance; his view on retribution left no room for the notion that the most wicked of kings managed to rule longer than any other monarch—and, apparently, enjoyed a peaceful life, to boot!—or that Manasseh's egregious sins could be visited upon a later generation. Hence, Chronicles simply had to delete these troublesome issues, while creating a much more positive image of the king. According to others, however, Chronicles' portrayal is to be explained on the

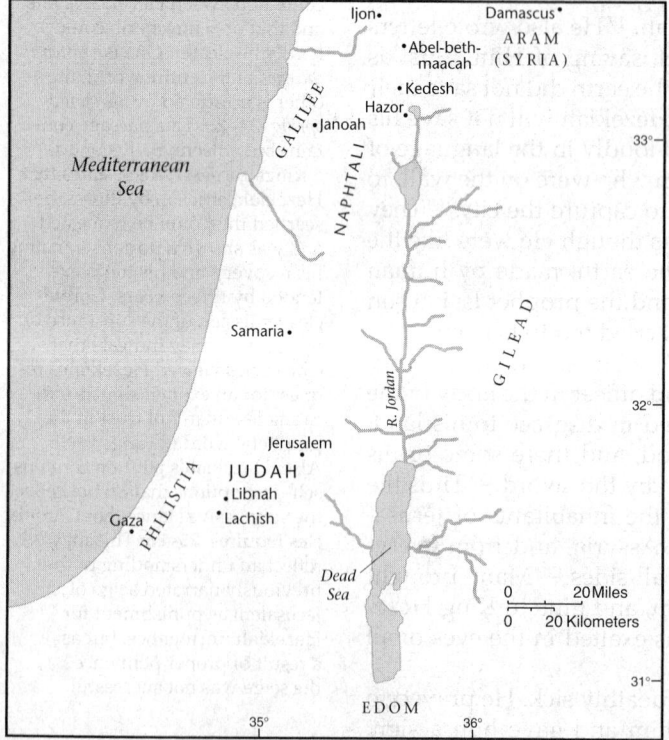

Places associated with Sennacherib's invasion of Judah

of Amoz and in the book of the kings of Judah and Israel. [33] Hezekiah slept with his fathers, and was buried on the upper part of the tombs of the sons of David. When he died, all the people of Judah and the inhabitants of Jerusalem accorded him much honor. Manasseh, his son, succeeded him.

33 [a]Manasseh was twelve years old when he became king, and he reigned fifty-five years in Jerusalem. [2] He did what was displeasing to the LORD, following the abhorrent practices of the nations that the LORD had dispossessed before the Israelites. [3] He rebuilt the shrines that his father Hezekiah had demolished; he erected altars for the Baals and made sacred posts. He bowed down to all the host of heaven and worshiped them, [4] and he built altars [to them] in the House of the LORD, of which the LORD had said, "My name will be in Jerusalem forever." [5] He built altars for all the host of heaven in the two courts of the House of the LORD. [6] He consigned his sons to the fire in the Valley of Ben-hinnom, and he practiced soothsaying, divination, and sorcery, and consulted ghosts and familiar spirits; he did much that was displeasing to the LORD in order to vex Him. [7] He placed a sculptured image that he made in the House of God, of which God had said to David and to his son Solomon, "In this House and in Jerusalem, which I chose out of all the tribes of Israel, I will establish My name forever. [8] And I will never again remove the feet of Israel from the land that I assigned to their fathers, if only they observe faithfully all that I have commanded them—all the teaching and the laws and the rules given by Moses." [9] Manasseh led Judah and the inhabitants of Jerusalem astray into evil greater than that done by the nations that the LORD had destroyed before the Israelites.

[10] The LORD spoke to Manasseh and his people, but they would not pay heed, [11] so the LORD brought against them the officers of the army of the king of Assyria, who took

a Cf. 2 Kings 21.

innocents could be forgiven so easily and continue his rule as a leading proponent of religious fidelity. **6:** Chronicles enlarges Kings' sin by changing "his son" to *his sons;* either is a violation of Deut. 18.10–13. **7:** Manasseh places the forms in the very Temple wherein the LORD has "placed" his name. **9:** Chronicles states that Manasseh and the people at large were guilty of foreign worship. Accordingly, both the king and the people are the object of the Assyrian assault. **10–13:** Some scholars view the story of Manasseh's exile as wholly artificial, while others accept the story's historicity, suggesting that it transpired between 677 and 648 BCE. The "true" reason for his presence in the Assyrian court is also debated, with some arguing that, in fact, Manasseh actually came to proclaim his fidelity to the throne. Whether true or not, the style of these vv., which ignore any attention to geopolitical and military details (e.g., who governed Judah in Manasseh's absence), is typical of Chronicles' one-dimensional perspective, which emphasizes only religious/theological factors. Finally, Chronicles implies that the people of Judah were not punished, despite their role in the foreign worship. It is possible that their eventual return to proper religious worship atoned for their misdeeds; cf. 2 Chron. 12.12. Chronicles' terse formulation of Manasseh's prayer and contrition, along with his seemingly immediate pardon, was problematic for Jews in antiquity. LXX traditions preserve an apocryphal "prayer of Manasseh"; the Dead Sea Scrolls preserve a different prayer attributed to him (4Q381). A rabbinic tradition states that Moses had prayed that Manasseh's prayer be accepted (*Sifre Deut.* 348). Similarly, rabbinic (and early Christian) sources attempt to explain the means by which Manasseh (miraculously) managed to return to Jerusalem. The detail that Manasseh was led off *to Babylon* by the Assyrian king is impossible; the Assyrian king would have led him to an Assyrian rather

basis of divine compassion, which allows even the most wicked of individuals to repent and start anew (see introduction). Later Jewish tradition understood the two accounts as complementary. See vv. 10–13 n. **1–6:** Unlike 2 Kings 21.16, Chronicles refers only to cultic offenses, and makes no reference to Manasseh's execution of inno-

cents. (Rabbinic sources [*y. Sanh.* 10.2; *b. Yebam.* 49b] state that, in addition to the offenses cited herein and at 2 Kings ch 21, Manasseh had the prophet Isaiah killed.) Chronicles' reticence may reflect its highlighting of cultic issues; it may also reflect discomfort with the notion that a Davidic monarch guilty of executing many

Manasseh captive in manacles, bound him in fetters, and led him off to Babylon. [12] In his distress, he entreated the Lord his God and humbled himself greatly before the God of his fathers. [13] He prayed to Him, and He granted his prayer, heard his plea, and returned him to Jerusalem to his kingdom. Then Manasseh knew that the Lord alone was God. [14] Afterward he built the outer wall of the City of David west of Gihon in the wadi on the way to the Fish Gate, and it encircled Ophel; he raised it very high. He also placed army officers in all the fortified towns of Judah. [15] He removed the foreign gods and the image from the House of the Lord, as well as all the altars that he had built on the Mount of the House of the Lord and in Jerusalem, and dumped them outside the city. [16] He rebuilt the altar of the Lord and offered on it sacrifices of well-being and thanksgiving, and commanded the people of Judah to worship the Lord God of Israel. [17] To be sure, the people continued sacrificing at the shrines, but only to the Lord their God.

[18] The other events of Manasseh's reign, and his prayer to his God, and the words of the seers who spoke to him in the name of the Lord God of Israel are found in the chronicles of the kings of Israel. [19] His prayer and how it was granted to him, the whole account of his sin and trespass, and the places in which he built shrines and installed sacred posts and images before he humbled himself are recorded in the words of Hozai.[a] [20] Manasseh slept with his fathers and was buried on his palace grounds; his son Amon succeeded him as king.

[21] Amon was twenty-two years old when he became king, and he reigned two years in Jerusalem. [22] He did what was displeasing to the Lord, as his father Manasseh had done. Amon sacrificed to all the idols that his father Manasseh had made and worshiped them. [23] He did not humble himself before the Lord, as his father Manasseh had humbled himself; instead, Amon incurred much guilt. [24] His courtiers conspired against him and killed him in his palace. [25] But the people of the land struck down all who had conspired against King Amon; and the people of the land made his son Josiah king in his stead.

34 [b] Josiah was eight years old when he became king, and he reigned thirty-one years in Jerusalem. [2] He did what was pleasing to the Lord, following the ways of his father David without deviating to the right or to the left. [3] In the eighth year of his reign, while he was still

than a Babylonian city. Some scholars therefore view the text symbolically, with Manasseh prefiguring the later exile of the Judeans to Babylonia. The story thus emphasizes the efficacy of repentance, for even the wicked Manasseh is returned to Judah after he is contrite. **14–17:** Signs of divine favor and monarchical success; see 2 Chron. 8.3–8; 11.5–12. **18:** Chronicles emphasizes the point that Manasseh had been forewarned by the Lord's messengers; hence, his failure to heed them justified his punishment. The claim that explicit warning is a sine qua non for punishment is seen by many scholars as a forerunner of the rabbinic view that courts may punish offenders only if the latter had been warned of the sinful nature of their actions prior to commission of their offense. More likely, Chronicles' position may be viewed as part of its notion of divine grace (see introduction). **19–20:** Chronicles' omission of Manasseh's culpability in Judah's exile demands an alternate explanation or justification for this national catastrophe. Chronicles addresses this point in ch 36.

33.21–25: Amon's reign. Humbling oneself (or not; see 1 Kings 21.29) is the theme that emphasizes the fundamental difference between Amon and Manasseh: Amon is killed in his palace, whereas Manasseh enjoyed an honorable burial in the same place. These vv. imply a retributive punishment.

34.1–35.27: Josiah's reign. Although Chronicles incorporates much material here from Kings, its depiction of Josiah differs in significant ways, both in detail and in overall assessment. Kings claims that Josiah ascended the throne at age eight; discovery of the "scroll" took place ten years later and was followed by Josiah's cultic and religious reforms, which were undertaken in response to the warnings of divine wrath and punishment that Josiah found in the discovered scroll. Chronicles,

a Or "seers."　　b Cf. 2 Kings 22; 23.1–20.

young, he began to seek the God of his father David, and in the twelfth year he began to purge Judah and Jerusalem of the shrines, the sacred posts, the idols, and the molten images. [4] At his bidding, they demolished the altars of the Baals, and he had the incense stands above them cut down; he smashed the sacred posts, the idols, and the images, ground them into dust, and strewed it onto the graves of those who had sacrificed to them. [5] He burned the bones of priests on their altars and purged Judah and Jerusalem. [6] In the towns of Manasseh and Ephraim and Simeon, as far as Naphtali, [lying] in ruins on every side, [7] he demolished the altars and the sacred posts and smashed the idols and ground them into dust; and he hewed down all the incense stands throughout the land of Israel. Then he returned to Jerusalem.

[8] In the eighteenth year of his reign, after purging the land and the House, he commissioned Shaphan son of Azaliah, Maaseiah the governor of the city, and Joah son of Joahaz the recorder to repair the House of the LORD his God. [9] They came to the high priest Hilkiah and delivered to him the silver brought to the House of God, which the Levites, the guards of the threshold, had collected from Manasseh and Ephraim and from all the remnant of Israel and from all Judah and Benjamin and [a]the inhabitants of Jerusalem.[-a] [10] They delivered it into the custody of the overseers who were in charge at the House of the LORD, and the overseers who worked in the House of the LORD spent it on examining and repairing the House. [11] They paid it out to the artisans and the masons to buy quarried stone and wood for the couplings and for making roofbeams for the buildings that the kings of Judah had allowed to fall into ruin. [12] The men did the work honestly; over them were appointed the Levites Jahath and Obadiah, of the sons of Merari, and Zechariah and Meshul-

a-a With kethib and ancient versions; qere, "they returned to Jerusalem."

however, offers a different chronology, portraying Josiah as having sought the LORD at the age of sixteen, *while he was still young,* and undertaking cultic purification at the age of twenty, prior to the discovery of the (missing) scroll. This version creates a more flattering image of this righteous king, employing motifs familiar from the David, Solomon, and Hezekiah episodes. Some scholars, in support of Chronicles' version, argue that the prophets Zephaniah and Jeremiah exerted influence on Josiah before 621 BCE, the year in which the scroll was found. Others have attempted to correlate each step of Josiah's reform in Chronicles with a corresponding wane in Assyrian influence. No consensus exists as to which version is more reliable, and whether or not Chronicles has rearranged these events for theological reasons. Chronicles' enhanced image of much of Josiah's reign highlights the ultimately less than positive assessment of Josiah, as indicated by Chronicles' description of his death. Overall, Chronicles' Josiah is a less significant monarch than Kings' Josiah. Whereas Josiah is the leading monarch in Kings, in Chronicles it is Hezekiah.

34.3: *The eighth year of his reign,* i.e., when Josiah was sixteen years of age. Some premodern commentators (Josephus, *Ant.;* Radak) maintain that Josiah began his reform at the age of eight, the age at which he ascended the throne. It is generally agreed that the scroll discovered by Hilkiah in 2 Kings is some form of the book of Deuteronomy. There is less unanimity regarding Chronicles' position. Some scholars maintain that Chronicles understands the referent to be the entire Torah; this would explain Chronicles' omission of 2 Kings' claim (22.8) that Shaphan read the scroll (see also 35.6). **6–7:** Chronicles' version entails a serious difficulty: Since Josiah had already purged the Temple and people of illicit practices, what remained for him to correct following discovery of the scroll? This passage provides the answer: Josiah now extended his reform even to more distant points within the northern tribes, following his illustrious ancestor Hezekiah. **8–13:** Cf. 2 Kings 22.3–7; there the Temple repairs simply set the stage for discovery of the scroll. Chronicles maintains that the repairs were part of Josiah's religious reform, already underway, during which the scroll was discovered. **8:** The date, *the eighteenth year,* marks one stage in the activities begun in v. 3. Chronicles' formulation suggests that discovery of the scroll was a reward for Josiah's cultic zeal, which the king displayed from an early age. Chronicles makes limited mention of Josiah's cleansing of the Temple, since Chronicles claims that such action had already taken place under Manasseh (33.15–16); cf. 2 Kings 23.4–6. **9:** The reference to *Manasseh, Ephraim,* et al., is another example of Chronicles' inclusivist slant; see v. 21. **12:** Chronicles expands the role of the Levites; cf. 2 Kings 22.7.

lam, of the sons of Kohath, to supervise; while other Levites, all the master musicians, [13] were over the porters, supervising all who worked at each and every task; some of the Levites were scribes and officials and gatekeepers.

[14] As they took out the silver that had been brought to the House of the LORD, the priest Hilkiah found a scroll of the LORD's Teaching given by Moses. [15] Hilkiah spoke up and said to the scribe Shaphan, "I have found a scroll of the Teaching in the House of the LORD"; and Hilkiah gave the scroll to Shaphan. [16] Shaphan brought the scroll to the king and also reported to the king, "All that was entrusted to your servants is being done; [17] they have melted down the silver that was found in the House of the LORD and delivered it to those who were in charge, to the overseers." [18] The scribe Shaphan also told the king, "The priest Hilkiah has given me a scroll"; and Shaphan read from it to the king. [19] When the king heard the words of the Teaching, he tore his clothes. [20] The king gave orders to Hilkiah, and Ahikam son of Shaphan, and Abdon son of Micah, and the scribe Shaphan, and Asaiah the king's minister, saying, [21] "Go, inquire of the LORD on my behalf and on behalf of those who remain in Israel and Judah concerning the words of the scroll that has been found, for great indeed must be the wrath of the LORD that has been poured down upon us because our fathers did not obey the word of the LORD and do all that is written in this scroll."

[22] Hilkiah and those whom the king [had ordered] went to the prophetess Huldah, wife of Shallum son of Tokhath son of Hasrah, keeper of the wardrobe, who was living in Jerusalem in the Mishneh,[a] and spoke to her accordingly. [23] She responded to them: "Thus said the LORD God of Israel: Say to the man who sent you to Me, [24] 'Thus said the LORD: I am going to bring disaster upon this place and its inhabitants—all the curses that are written in the scroll that was read to the king of Judah—[25] because they forsook Me and made offerings to other gods in order to vex Me with all the works of their hands; My wrath shall be poured out against this place and not be quenched.' [26] But say this to the king of Judah who sent you to inquire of the LORD: 'Thus said the LORD God of Israel: As for the words which you have heard, [27] since your heart was softened and you humbled yourself before God when you heard His words concerning this place and its inhabitants, and you humbled yourself before Me and tore your clothes and wept before Me, I for My part have listened, declares the LORD. [28] Assuredly, I will gather you to your fathers,

21: *Those who remain in Israel and Judah* replaces "all Judah" of 2 Kings 22.13, and *the word of the LORD* replaces "the words of this scroll" in 2 Kings 22.13. The first change reflects the inclusivist tendency of Chronicles. The "word of the LORD" refers in other biblical books to prophecy, but Chronicles employs it also in connection with Torah legislation (see 1 Chron. 10.13; 15.15; 2 Chron. 35.6). This probably indicates that for Chronicles, and the postexilic period generally, Torah replaced prophecy; stated differently, the prophet was a transmitter or interpreter of Mosaic law. **24:** Some explain Chronicles' reference to *curses* as an allusion to Deut. 29.20, thus indicating that Chronicles understood the discovered scroll to be Deuteronomy. **27:** 2 Kings 22.19b reads: ". . . I decreed against this place and its inhabitants—that it will become a desolation and a curse." The word "place" may refer to either Jerusalem or the Temple. In either case, Chronicles could not tolerate the "place" being cursed and so omitted these words. **30:** Chronicles reads *Levites* in place of 2 Kings' "prophets" (23.2). This change reflects the social makeup of Second Temple society and/or Chronicles' view of Levites as involved in prophetic activity; see 1 Chron. 25.1–4, 5.

---

a *A quarter in Jerusalem; cf. Zeph. 1.10.*

and you will be laid in your grave in peace; your eyes shall see nothing of the disaster that I will bring upon this place and its inhabitants.' " They reported this back to the king. [29] Then the king sent word and assembled all the elders of Judah and Jerusalem. [30] The king went up to the House of the LORD with all the men of Judah and the inhabitants of Jerusalem and the priests and the Levites—all the people, young and old—and he read to them the entire text of the covenant scroll that was found in the House of the LORD. [31] The king stood in his place and solemnized the covenant before the LORD: to follow the LORD and observe His commandments, His injunctions, and His laws with all his heart and soul, to fulfill all the terms of the covenant written in this scroll. [32] He obligated all the men of Jerusalem and Benjamin who were present; and the inhabitants of Jerusalem acted in accord with the Covenant of God, God of their fathers. [33] Josiah removed all the abominations from the whole territory of the Israelites and obliged all who were in Israel to worship the LORD their God. Throughout his reign they did not deviate from following the LORD God of their fathers.

35 [a]Josiah kept the Passover for the LORD in Jerusalem; the passover sacrifice was slaughtered on the fourteenth day of the first month. [2] He reinstated the priests in their shifts and rallied them to the service of the House of the LORD. [3] He said to the Levites, consecrated to the LORD, who taught all Israel, "Put the Holy Ark in the House that Solomon son of David, king of Israel, built; as you no longer carry it on your shoulders, see now to the service of the LORD your God and His people Israel, [4] and dispose yourselves by clans according to your divisions, as prescribed in the writing of King David of Israel and in the document of his son Solomon, [5] and attend in the Sanctuary, by clan divisions, on your kinsmen, the people—by clan divisions of the Levites. [6] Having sanctified yourselves, slaughter the passover sacrifice and prepare it for your kinsmen, according to the word of God given by Moses." [7] Josiah donated to the people small cattle—lambs and goats, all for passover sacrifices for all present—to the sum of 30,000, and large cattle, 3,000—these from the property of the king. [8] His officers gave a freewill offering to the people, to the priests, and to the Levites. Hilkiah and Zechariah and Jehiel, the chiefs of the House of God, donated to the priests for passover sacrifices 2,600

a Cf. 2 Kings 23.21–30.

35.1–19: The Passover celebration. With the exception of the last two vv., none of this material is found in Kings. When compared to 2 Kings 23.21–23, Chronicles' version involves two important developments: the prominence of Levites in cultic affairs and the transformation of the Paschal offering into a Temple sacrifice like all others. Chronicles' much extended treatment, which involves elements from various Torah sources (see below), reflects Chronicles' view that the scroll found by Hilkiah was the entire Torah (more or less), whereas Kings maintains that only "a scroll of the Teaching," which most scholars identify as an early form of Deuteronomy alone, had been discovered. **1:** Chronicles omits the words "as it is written in this book of the covenant" found in Kings, avoiding the inference that the religious reforms were based exclusively on the discovery of the scroll and, hence, that before that discovery such reforms had not taken place. **2–15:** Another example of inner-biblical legal interpretation, in which earlier legal texts are, in this case, harmonized. (The translations of the various texts somewhat obscure this harmonization.) Exod. 12.3–5 specifies that the Paschal offering may be brought only from sheep or goats and must be roasted, not cooked in water ("b-sh-l") or consumed raw. By contrast, Deut. 16.2 states that cattle, as well as sheep and goats, are acceptable. Furthermore, Deut. 16.7 specifies that the offering must be boiled ("b-sh-l"—the NJPS translation there, "cook," is imprecise). Chronicles reconciles the two sources. The result is that the Paschal offering must be either *lambs* or *goats*, following Exod. ch 12; Deuteronomy's reference to "cattle" is interpreted as denoting a distinct offering—which Chronicles calls simply *sacred offerings* (v. 13)—and is intended as an adjunct to the Paschal offering. Chronicles further claims that Deuteronomy's use of the term "boil" means "boiled [as in Deuteronomy] in fire [as in Exodus]." This incorporates [small cattle] and 300 large cattle. ⁹Conaniah, Shemaiah, and Nethanel, his brothers, and Hashabiah and Jeiel and Jozabad, officers of the Levites, donated 5,000 [small cattle] and 500 large cattle to the Levites for passover sacrifices.

¹⁰The service was arranged well: the priests stood at their posts and the Levites in their divisions, by the king's command. ¹¹They slaughtered the passover sacrifice and the priests [received its blood] from them and dashed it, while the Levites flayed the animals. ¹²They removed the parts to be burnt, distributing them to divisions of the people by clans, and making the sacrifices to the LORD, as prescribed in the scroll of Moses; they did the same for the cattle. ¹³They roasted the passover sacrifice in fire, as prescribed, while the sacred offerings they cooked in pots, cauldrons, and pans, and conveyed them with dispatch to all the people. ¹⁴Afterward they provided for themselves and the priests, for the Aaronite priests were busy offering the burnt offerings and the fatty parts until nightfall, so the Levites provided both for themselves and for the Aaronite priests. ¹⁵The Asaphite singers were at their stations, by command of David and Asaph and Heman and Jeduthun, the seer of the king; and the gatekeepers were at each and every gate. They did not have to leave their tasks, because their Levite brothers provided for them. ¹⁶The entire service of the LORD was arranged well that day, to keep the Passover and to make the burnt offerings on the altar of the LORD, according to the command of King Josiah. ¹⁷All the Israelites present kept the Passover at that time, and the Feast of Unleavened Bread for seven days. ¹⁸Since the time of the prophet Samuel, no Passover like that one had ever been kept in Israel; none of the kings of Israel had kept a Passover like the one kept by Josiah and the priests and the Levites and all Judah and Israel there present and the inhabitants of Jerusalem. ¹⁹That Passover was kept in the eighteenth year of the reign of Josiah.

²⁰After all this furbishing of the Temple by Josiah, King Necho of Egypt came up to fight at Carchemish on the Euphrates, and Josiah went out against him. ²¹[Necho] sent

Second Temple compositions (e.g., the book of *Jubilees*) as well as rabbinic circles (see the variant traditions in *Sifre Deut.* 129; *Mek. R. Ishmael, Pisha*, 4; *y. Pes.* 6.1 [33a]; *b. Pes.* 66b; *Tg. Onk.* and, especially, *Tg. Ps.-J.* to Deut. 16.2.) (For more on this type of inner-biblical interpretation, see "Inner-biblical Interpretation," pp. 1829–35.) **12–13:** *As prescribed in the scroll of Moses* and *as prescribed* signify Chronicles' claim of authentic legal interpretation. **16–19:** Summary of events. **18:** The phrase *no Passover like that one* cannot refer, as in 2 Kings, to cult centralization, since such had taken place during Hezekiah's reign. Rather, it probably refers to the prominence of the Levites or to the performance of the offerings in this precise fashion.

35.20–27: Josiah's death. 2 Kings 23.28–31 offers a laconic account, whose historical background and veracity are uncertain. Chronicles' longer text probably reflects an elaboration upon Kings or perhaps a slightly longer text of Kings that has not been preserved. Chronicles' formulation suggests that the incursion of the Egyptian forces took place shortly after the Passover celebration. The formulation of v. 20 is reminiscent of 32.1, appearing in connection with the Assyrian assault on Hezekiah's kingdom. By emphasizing the achievements of both monarchs in the cultic realm, and the polar differences in their respective fates, the author emphasizes that despite his many meritorious deeds, Josiah died because of his failure to heed the LORD's word conveyed by Necho. The episode is reminiscent of Ahab's death in ch 18: He died because of his failure to heed prophetic warning. Chronicles thus portrays Josiah, a symbol of piety in Kings, in a more negative fashion. He must do so to explain Josiah's surprising death. **20–21:** While the details of this incident are not certain, it is likely that Necho was on his way to assist his Assyrian allies who had been driven to Carchemish by the

the language of both Exodus and Deuteronomy, while the accompanying sacred offerings may, like most sacrifices, be boiled or poached, following Deuteronomy. (The beginning of v. 13, translated literally, is "They boiled the passover sacrifice in fire.") Chronicles'

formulation reflects a bold step: Chronicles has changed the simple, straightforward meaning of Deuteronomy and, moreover, his interpretation creates a heretofore nonexistent accompanying sacrifice. Chronicles' innovations were adopted, in varying form, in later messengers to him, saying, "What have I to do with you, king of Judah? I do not march against you this day but against the kingdom that wars with me, and it is God's will that I hurry. Refrain, then, from interfering with God who is with me, that He not destroy you." 22 But Josiah would not let him alone; instead, ªhe donned [his armor]ª to fight him, heedless of Necho's words from the mouth of God; and he came to fight in the plain of Megiddo. 23 Archers shot King Josiah, and the king said to his servants, "Get me away from here, for I am badly wounded." 24 His servants carried him out of his chariot and put him in the wagon of his second-in-command, and conveyed him to Jerusalem. There he died, and was buried in the grave of his fathers, and all Judah and Jerusalem went into mourning over Josiah. 25 Jeremiah composed laments for Josiah which all the singers, male and female, recited in their laments for Josiah, as is done to this day; they became customary in Israel and were incorporated into the laments. 26 The other events of Josiah's reign and his faithful deeds, in accord with the Teaching of the LORD, 27 and his acts, early and late, are recorded in the book of the kings of Israel and Judah.

36 ᵇThe people of the land took Jehoahaz son of Josiah and made him king instead of his father in Jerusalem. 2 Jehoahaz was twenty-three years old when he became king and he reigned three months in Jerusalem. 3 The king of Egypt deposed him in Jerusalem and laid a fine on the land of 100 silver talents and one gold talent. 4 The king of Egypt made his brother Eliakim king over Judah and Jerusalem, and changed his name to Jehoiakim; Necho took his brother Joahaz and brought him to Egypt.

5 Jehoiakim was twenty-five years old when he became king, and he reigned eleven years in Jerusalem; he did what was displeasing to the LORD his God. 6 King Nebuchadnezzar of Babylon marched against him; he bound him in fetters to convey him to Babylon. 7 Nebuchadnezzar also brought some vessels of the House of the LORD to Babylon, and set them in his palace in Babylon. 8 The other

a-a With Targum.
b With vv. 1–13, cf. 2 Kings 23.28–37; 24.1–20.

flected in Radak's commentary), while the Aramaic Targum (35.23) offers the generic formulation, "Josiah died because he did not seek instruction from the LORD." **22–24:** *He donned [his armor]:* Heb "hithapes" is the term employed at 18.29 with Ahab, where it means "disguise," so its use here may be intended to connect Josiah to Ahab's folly. 2 Kings 23.29 states that Josiah was slain at *Megiddo;* this is not repeated in Chronicles, perhaps in an attempt to minimize (but not resolve) the discrepancy between 2 Kings 23.29 and the prophecy of Huldah, which promised that the king would be gathered unto his grave in peace (2 Kings 22.20 ‖ 2 Chron. 34.28). **25–27:** The *laments* were understood by rabbinic tradents (*t. Ta'an.* 2:10) and, possibly, Josephus (*Ant.*), as referring to part of the book of Lamentations (in their view, composed by Jeremiah). Alternatively, the reference is to another (unknown) collection of laments. For *Teaching* ("torah") *of the LORD,* see 34.1–3.

36.1–21: Judgment and exile. Chronicles' depiction of the stages of Judah's exile differs in several significant respects from the Deuteronomistic version in Kings. Chronicles abbreviates the parent text (2 Kings chs 23–24), omitting the death notices of each king, while highlighting the everworsening state of the cultus. **1–4:** A condensed version of 2 Kings 23.30–34; Chronicles omits the negative appraisal of *Jehoahaz.* Chronicles also omits discussion of the fate of the kings and Temple spoils following their removal from the land; this may be another expression of the centrality of Israel's attachment to its land in Chronicles. **5–8:** The description of *Jehoiakim* being bound and led to Babylon in v. 6 contradicts 2 Kings 24.1. Some explain the Heb to mean that the king need not have actually been taken to Babylon, merely that he was bound and threatened with such a punishment. Others aver that he was taken to Babylon as a vassal to

Babylonians (cf. formulation of 2 Kings 23.29). The use of Necho as a conduit for the LORD's word constitutes the clearest statement of Chronicles' view on "spontaneous" prophecy: Even a foreign king may be chosen to convey the

divine message, putting him (temporarily) on the same footing as an Israelite prophet. The anomalous nature of this episode is reflected in postbiblical works. 1 Esd. 1.26 replaces *Necho's words* with "the words of Jeremiah" (a position re-events of Jehoiakim's reign, and the abominable things he did, and what was found against him, are recorded in the book of the kings of Israel and Judah. His son Jehoiachin succeeded him as king.

⁹Jehoiachin was eight years old when he became king, and he reigned three months and ten days in Jerusalem; he did what was displeasing to the LORD. ¹⁰At the turn of the year, King Nebuchadnezzar sent to have him brought to Babylon with the precious vessels of the House of the LORD, and he made his kinsman Zedekiah king over Judah and Jerusalem.

¹¹Zedekiah was twenty-one years old when he became king, and he reigned eleven years in Jerusalem. ¹²He did what was displeasing to the LORD his God; he did not humble himself before the prophet Jeremiah, who spoke for the LORD. ¹³He also rebelled against Nebuchadnezzar, who made him take an oath[a] by God; he stiffened his neck and hardened his heart so as not to turn to the LORD God of Israel. ¹⁴All the officers of the priests and the people committed many trespasses, following all the abominable practices of the nations. They polluted the House of the LORD, which He had consecrated in Jerusalem. ¹⁵The LORD God of their fathers had sent word to them through

a Viz., a vassal oath.

participate in the victory celebrations. On this approach, the removal of Temple *vessels* (v. 7), not mentioned in Kings, was carried out in order to serve as royal tribute. **9–10:** Chronicles' text is terse, focusing on the exile of *Jehoiachin* and the spoiling of the Temple; cf. 2 Kings 24.8–17. **11–23:** Zedekiah and Chronicles' justification of the destruction of Judah and the exile. As noted above, 2 Kings claims that the main cause of the destruction and exile of Judah was the foreign worship sponsored by Judah's kings, Manasseh in particular. Chronicles, however, minimizes the role of Manasseh's sins, claiming that the exile was (primarily) the result of the sins of Zedekiah's generation. **12–14:** Specific significant sins (not heeding prophets, false oaths) are attributed to Zedekiah, as well as the people as a whole—the king's sins alone cannot explain the national disaster. In v. 14, Chronicles places blame on the *priests* as well as laity, but notably omits reference to the Levites. **15–17:** Another instance of warn-

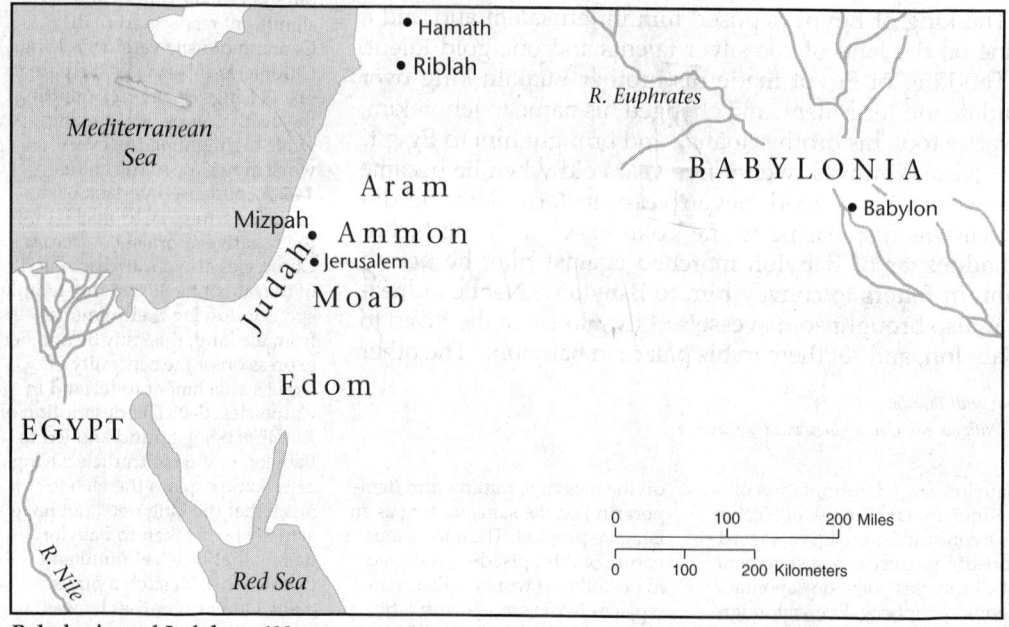

Babylonia and Judah ca. 600 BCE

His messengers daily without fail, for He had pity on His people and His dwelling-place. 16 But they mocked the messengers of God and disdained His words and taunted His prophets until the wrath of the LORD against His people grew beyond remedy. 17 He therefore brought the king of the Chaldeans upon them, who killed their youths by the sword in their sanctuary; He did not spare youth, maiden, elder, or graybeard, but delivered all into his hands. 18 All the vessels of the House of God, large and small, and the treasures of the House of the LORD and the treasures of the king and his officers were all brought to Babylon. 19 They burned the House of God and tore down the wall of Jerusalem, burned down all its mansions, and consigned all its precious objects to destruction. 20 Those who survived the sword he exiled to Babylon, and they became his and his sons' servants till the rise of the Persian kingdom, 21 in fulfillment of the word of the LORD spoken by Jeremiah, until the land paid back its sabbaths; as long as it lay desolate it kept sabbath, till seventy years were completed.

22 And in the first year of King Cyrus of Persia, when the word of the LORD spoken by Jeremiah was fulfilled, the LORD roused the spirit of King Cyrus of Persia to issue a proclamation throughout his realm by word of mouth and in writing, as follows: 23 "Thus said King Cyrus of Persia: The LORD God of Heaven has given me all the kingdoms of the earth, and has charged me with building Him a House in Jerusalem, which is in Judah. Any one of you of all His people, the LORD his God be with him and let him go up."

prophetic message. This likely reflects a situation in which prophetic books, along with Torah literature, were seen as authoritative for the Chronicler's community.

36.22–23: Conclusion. Chronicles' conclusion overlaps Ezra 1.1–3a. The numerous explanations proffered depend, to some extent, on the question of the unity of Chronicles and Ezra-Nehemiah. and their relative dates of composition (see introduction). Some scholars who accept the unity of the two works argue that these common vv. join the two works together. Others, rejecting the works' unity, argue that these vv. were added to the original conclusion to avoid ending on a pessimistic note. Unlike Ezra 1.3, which says "May his God be with him," Chronicles adds *the LORD*. The attribution of monotheism to foreign nations and their leaders is attested above (1 Chron. 16.23; 2 Chron. 1.18–2.15). Finally, the grammatical form of the concluding Heb word, *and let him go up,* is taken by some to indicate that the process of redemption is ongoing. Cyrus's edict is depicted as the fulfillment of prophecy; with it, Israel's sins have been requited and the brief period of Israel's rupture from its land has ended.

ing preceding divine punishment. Chronicles' formulation is intended to emphasize the extent of the people's sin: Despite the numerous opportunities for repentance, the people persist in their sinful ways. The absolute decadence is highlighted by the use of three verbs in v. 16 to express the people's disdain for the prophetic word. **21:** In a midrashic fashion, Chronicles' formulation of the exile is informed by combining Jeremiah (25.10–12; 28.3; 29.9) and Leviticus (26.19–21). Chronicles accepts Jeremiah's pronouncement that the exile will last seventy years, but explains the significance of this period on the basis of Leviticus's claim that exile will befall Israel because of its neglect of the sabbatical and jubilee years (Lev. 25.1–13). Whereas *seventy years* signifies in Jeremiah a lengthy stay in captivity, Chronicles views this period as a brief hiatus in Israel's history, which did not significantly alter the nature of Israel's bond, and claim, to its land. It does not repeat 2 Kings 25.21, which states that Judah was exiled from its land, referring instead to the destruction of Jerusalem and the fate of its exiled inhabitants, with no attention given to those who remained in Judah. Chronicles' reference to (the veracity of) Jeremiah's warning, along with Chronicles' depiction of the people as mocking the divine messengers, is another expression of the importance that Chronicles attaches to heeding the

Introduction to the Essays

THE TWENTY-FOUR ESSAYS in this section set the annotations to the biblical books in a broader context, enhancing our goal of representing Jewish academic scholarship on the Bible. They offer a wealth of supplementary material, not easily accessible elsewhere, and they represent the best of current scholarship. Inevitably, there is some overlap from essay to essay, but we view this as a positive feature. As in the case of the annotations, we have given our authors free rein to shape their material, and their essays manifest, as do the annotations, the variety of approaches that is typical of Jewish biblical interpretation.

The first set of essays, "Jewish Interpretation of the Bible," surveys, in chronological order, Jewish biblical interpretation in various periods, from earliest times to the present. These essays explain and model what is quintessentially Jewish about Jewish interpretation. They convey a flavor of each age, its distinctive modes of interpretation. Taken as a whole, they form a study in the continuities and discontinuities that mark the history of Jewish biblical interpretation.

The second set of essays, "The Bible in Jewish Life and Thought," gives some intimation of the importance of the Bible for Judaism and the Jewish community, an importance that cannot be overstated. The Bible is *the* key text of Jewish life. The essays in this section are largely arranged chronologically, from antiquity to the present. They describe the place of the Bible in different communities and intellectual contexts, from the Jewish community that composed and preserved the Dead Sea Scrolls through the modern State of Israel, and in the Jewish philosophical and mystical traditions as well as in the scholarly writings of contemporary Jewish women. No description of the Bible in Jewish life would be complete without a discussion of the role of the Bible in the synagogue and in the liturgy, or the making of Jewish translations of the Bible from antiquity to modern times.

The third set of essays, "Backgrounds for Reading the Bible," provides contemporary scholarly background material for understanding the Bible. Unlike the previous two sections, the emphasis here is not specifically Jewish. The topics addressed reflect the editors' sensibilities of what an informed reader might want to know about important biblical concepts and about how contemporary scholars study the Bible. About half of this material has been reworked by the editors from essays previously published in *The New Oxford Annotated Bible*. Newly commissioned essays are "The Religion of the Bible," "Concepts of

Purity in the Bible," "Languages of the Bible," "The Development of the Masoretic Bible," and "Reading Biblical Poetry."

In the final section of this volume, following "Tables and Charts," the "Translations of Primary Sources" and the "Glossary" are of particular importance. The Translations offer an introductory English bibliography of many primary sources mentioned in the annotations and the essays, including ancient Near Eastern, early postbiblical, classical rabbinic, medieval, philosophical, and mystical works. The Glossary explains both Hebrew and Jewish terms, as well as technical terms used in modern biblical scholarship. The material in all five sections following the annotated biblical books—the essays, charts, and other supplementary materials—is intended to inform the reader, concisely but without sacrificing high academic quality, about the Bible and its world, from both Jewish and academic perspectives.   [ADELE BERLIN AND MARC ZVI BRETTLER]

Inner-biblical Interpretation

The interpretation of the Bible begins in the Bible itself. Biblical authors frequently commented on other biblical texts; they revised them, they argued with them, and they alluded to them. In so doing, they conveyed an understanding of the texts they utilized—in short, they interpreted earlier biblical writings. This tendency became especially prominent at the end of the preexilic period and during the exilic and postexilic periods, in other words after an early protocanonical set of texts became sacred. These reader-writers understood older texts in original ways, applied their principles to new situations, or borrowed from their prestige. In this respect the biblical authors resemble later Jewish (and Christian) writers, who constantly look back to biblical models as they create new texts, ideas, and practices. Thus the religion that *generated* the Bible foreshadows the religions *generated by* the Bible: Israelite thinkers, like those of various forms of Judaism and Christianity, constructed their works by recasting language and themes found in earlier ones. Biblical authors bequeathed their successors not only a text, but ways of relating to that text, reacting to that text, recreating that text, and allowing that text to remain alive.

It will be helpful to discuss both the forms that inner-biblical revision takes and the effects of those revisions at the level of ideas—both *how* and *why* biblical authors borrow from their predecessors. In examining both these issues, this essay will also compare the ways biblical authors used biblical texts with the ways postbiblical authors did so.

To begin, then, with the rhetoric of reuse and rereading: Biblical authors utilized the work of their predecessors in several ways. Some biblical passages use a formula when they quote an older text, thus making the borrowing explicit. (This practice resembles the modern footnote.) 2 Kings 14.5–6 tells us of King Joash, "Once he had the kingdom firmly in his grasp, he put to death the courtiers who had assassinated his father the king. But he did not put to death the children of the assassins, in accordance with what is written (*kakatuv*) in the Book of the Teaching of Moses (*torat moshe*), where the LORD commanded, 'Parents shall not be put to death for children, nor children be put to death for parents; a person shall be put to death only for his own crime.'" The formula "in accordance with what is written" (or, more simply, "as it is written") introduces a nearly word-for-word quotation from Deut. 24.16. In other instances this formula introduces quotations or refers to ideas found elsewhere in the Torah (1 Kings 2.3; Ezra 3.2; 2 Chron. 23.18). This formula (*kakatuv* or *kemo shekatuv*) is also used to introduce quotations from Scripture in rabbinic literature, the Dead Sea Scrolls, and (in Greek translation) the New Testament.

In a much larger number of cases, however, biblical texts borrow phrasing or imagery without citing the source explicitly; rather, the shared items help the knowledgeable reader identify the source. The prophet responsible for the latter part of the book of Isaiah (see the introduction to Isaiah) comforted Judeans after the destruction of Jerusalem with these words:

The LORD comforts *Zion*, comforts all her ruins. He makes *Zion's* wasteland an Eden;

her desert, a garden of the LORD . . . Listen to Me, My *people*, and My nation, give ear! *For teaching goes forth from Me*, and I will give *My judgment* as a light of the peoples . . . My arms will *judge peoples*. Islands will look eagerly to Me, and in My arms they will have hope. *Lift up* your eyes towards heaven and look at the earth below! For the heaven can melt away like smoke, and the earth can wear out like a garment . . . But My salvation will endure forever (Isa. 51.3–6, author's translation).

In issuing this prediction, the exilic author borrows from a passage found in the work of two prophets who lived more than a century and a half earlier, (First) Isaiah and Micah:

In the future, the mountain of the LORD's House will be established as the greatest of mountains and *lifted up* above the hills. All nations will flow towards it, and many *peoples* will come and say, "Let us go up to the LORD's mountain, to the House of Jacob's God," . . . *For teaching goes forth from Zion*, and the LORD's word from Jerusalem. And God will *judge* the nations, . . . and they will beat their swords into plowshares and their weapons into pruning forks; nation will not lift up sword against nation, and they will learn war no more (Isa. 2.2–4, author's translation; Mic. 4.1–4 is almost identical).

The author of Isa. ch 51 borrowed the items printed in italics above. In addition, *ḥorvoteha* ["her ruins"] in Isa. ch 51 is an intentional pun, hinting at *ḥarvotam* ["their swords"] in Isa. ch 2 and Mic. ch 4, a word that has a different meaning but sounds nearly identical. The passages share several images as well. The idea of peoples gathering appears in both passages, and both predict that the LORD will teach nations and judge them at His mountain. In both passages agricultural images (plowshares and pruning hooks in Isa. ch 2 and Mic. ch 4, gardens in Isa. ch 53) take the place of figures of destruction. The new text reworks the old one. It repeats the earlier prediction, but it shifts attention from the nations

who come in pursuit of instruction and peace to the benefits that Jerusalem will gain from her newly exalted position. The later author does not use a citation formula to tell the reader that the new text depends on the older one, but the many items they share indicate their relationship. We may characterize this relationship as a literary allusion. A great many biblical texts utilized their predecessors in this way, and some postbiblical writers continued the tradition of allusion. Based on similarity of vocabulary and phraseology, it is clear that many of the Dead Sea Scrolls borrow and rework texts from the Bible; the same is true of the New Testament. On the other hand, the central works of rabbinic literature (the Talmuds and the midrashim) allude to the Bible much less frequently. They tend instead to cite the Bible explicitly by using citation formulas like "as it is written" or "as it was said." Other rabbinic works, however, often borrow vocabulary and images from the Bible in a style that recalls the Bible itself; these rabbinic works include prayers found in the Siddur (prayerbook), moralistic books, and some mystical texts. Allusions to the Bible continue throughout the development of Hebrew literature; they are very frequent in medieval Hebrew poetry and in the work of modern Israeli writers such as Bialik, Agnon, Amichai, and others.

Some biblical works borrow whole sections from older texts. For example, the book of Chronicles repeats, more or less verbatim, large parts of Samuel and Kings. The legal collection in Deut. chs 12–26 includes laws similar to those in Exod. chs 21–23. According to most modern source-critical biblical scholars, the books of Genesis through Numbers incorporate several older texts that are no longer available to us in their original form. In all these cases, the new works make small but highly significant changes in the borrowed material. Thus the theological and historical outlook of Chronicles differs from that of Samuel-Kings, even as Chronicles reports the same events using many of the same words (see the introduction to Chronicles). Some modern scholars maintain that a group of priests copied an older form of the festival law now found in Lev. ch 23, but they added verses 9–22 and 39–44 when they did so (see notes there). By making the additions, these priests radically altered the religious outlook of the original document. They acknowledged the validity of popular ritual observances deliberately shunned by the more elite priests responsible for the older version of the chapter. Revising a text by copying it with significant variations or additions remained a common form of Jewish writing in the period immediately following the completion of the Bible. Works such as *Jubilees* and some of the Dead Sea Scrolls retold the stories of the Torah or repeated and modified laws found there. These works were not preserved by later Jewish groups, however, and they did not continue to be studied, read, or chanted in Jewish communities. The Rabbis did not incorporate large sections of the Bible into new works that they wrote; instead, they typically compiled collections of interpretive comments on the Bible (known as midrashim), included interpretive comments in legal works (such as the Talmud), and, beginning with the Middle Ages, wrote verse-by-verse commentaries on the Bible.

Finally, some later comments on biblical passages occur within those passages themselves, at least in the text of the Bible that has been in use for the past two millennia. Like modern readers, ancient readers penned explanations or reactions to the text they were reading in margins or between the lines. Some of these marginal comments were subsequently inserted into the text itself by scribes who copied the scroll containing the marginal comment. (It is also possible that some of these comments were inserted to begin with by scribes who made them as they were copying a scroll.) For example, 1 Kings 15.5 originally limited itself to a comment praising King David, and one important manuscript of the ancient Greek translation of Kings preserves that original text. A later scribe found the fulsome praise of David inconsistent with the

story in 2 Sam. ch 11. That story is exceedingly critical of David for committing adultery with the wife of Uriah the Hittite (one of his own soldiers) and for having Uriah murdered to ensure that the adultery was not discovered. Therefore, the scribe added a qualification in 1 Kings 15.5: "except in the matter of Uriah the Hittite." These words became part of the Masoretic Text, which thus contains both the original author's evaluation of David and a later reader's reaction to that evaluation. Similarly, Exod. 22.24 originally read, "If you lend money to My "'am,' do not act toward them as a creditor; exact no interest from them." Now, the Hebrew word "'am" usually means "people," but it can also mean "the poor" or "common folk, peasantry" (see Isa. 3.15; Ps. 72.2; Neh. 5.1). To make clear that in this case the second of these meanings was to be understood, a later scribe added the words "to the poor among you" immediately after "'am." Since the meaning of "'am" as "people" was more common, the scribe worried that without clarification the verse would be misread.

The goals of other biblical authors and scribes who borrowed material from older biblical texts were varied. As we can see from the scribal insertion in Exod. ch 22 just discussed, they sometimes wanted to explain a passage that seemed ambiguous, problematic, or somehow relevant to their own situation. In other words, they wrote an interpretation. A famous example occurs in Dan. 9.2: "I, Daniel, consulted the books concerning the number of years that, according to the word of the LORD that had come to Jeremiah the prophet, were to be the term of Jerusalem's desolation—seventy years." In this verse the author of Daniel cited a passage from the book of Jeremiah explicitly. Jeremiah wrote that passage shortly after the Babylonians deported many of Jerusalem's leaders in 597 BCE: "Thus said the LORD: When Babylon's seventy years are over, I will take note of you, and I will fulfill to you My promise of favor—to bring you back to this place" (Jer. 29.10). The author of Daniel wrote at a time when the Second Temple was being desecrated and Jerusalem's status as a holy city was in peril (in the middle of the 2nd century BCE.) Therefore, that author felt that the redemption and favor promised in Jer. 29.10 had still not materialized, even though seventy years had long passed. How, then, to understand Jeremiah's prophecy as a true prophecy? Daniel reports that the angel Gabriel answered this question: "Seventy weeks have been decreed for your people and your holy city until . . . eternal righteousness [is] ushered in; and prophetic vision ratified" (Dan. 9.24). According to Gabriel's interpretation, Jeremiah's words were really a sort of code. When Jeremiah said "seventy (shiv'im) years" he meant "seventy weeks" or "seventy sevens" (shavu'im shiv'im) of years; the consonants shv'ym had to be read twice, with slightly different vocalization each time. As a result what seems like one word is really two. The redemption would occur not seventy years after Jeremiah issued the prophecy, but four hundred and ninety years afterwards. This interpretation of Jer. ch 29 confirms the prophecy as a true one, and makes it applicable to a current situation. The interpretation is certainly a novel one, and not what Jeremiah himself meant; it makes it seem that Jeremiah was speaking for the benefit of the audience at the time of Daniel, not for Jeremiah's own audience. Nevertheless, Daniel's reading of Jeremiah follows a recognizable logic. The word of God is not like the word of a human; divine speech is infinitely more meaningful. When a human utters the consonants of the word shiv'im, it means only one thing ("seventy"), but when God does so they have (at least) another layer of meaning, and thus they can be read twice in two different ways (shavu'im shiv'im), to mean seventy sevens. Precisely the same theory of divine language as supercharged with meaning underlies biblical interpretations found in postbiblical Jewish literature, such as the midrashim (see "Midrash and Jewish Interpretation," pp. 1863–75). Indeed, this passage in Daniel is an early case of classical Jewish scriptural interpretation. Midrash, then, is not just a postbiblical invention used by the Rab-

bis to revise the Bible as they saw fit. It is a biblical means of relating to the Bible, which the Rabbis inherited from the biblical authors themselves.

One more case in which a biblical author explicitly interprets older biblical texts: Both Exodus and Deuteronomy provide regulations concerning the Passover sacrifice, but these regulations differ in several respects. According to Deut. 16.7, the Passover sacrifice should be boiled. The law concerning the Passover sacrifice in Exod. 12.9 takes issue with Deuteronomy on this point, warning its audience, "Don't eat it raw or boiled in water; rather, [eat it] roasted in fire" (author's translation; the NJPS translation obscures this point by translating the verb "cook" in Deuteronomy). That such a disagreement (maḥloket) occurs in this ancient Jewish literature is not surprising: Two groups in the biblical period agreed that the Passover sacrifice was important but disagreed on its precise details. Such disagreements over the precise requirements of a ritual are a regular feature of Jewish law in all ages. Classical rabbinic authorities, for example, agree that one should not eat dairy products for some time after eating meat but disagree concerning the exact length of the waiting period (some say it should be three hours; others, six); contemporary Jewish groups agree that communal prayers are important but disagree concerning whether women should be allowed to lead them. The authors of the book of Chronicles, however, cannot tolerate disagreement between two texts in the Torah; unlike most modern scholars, they view the Torah not as an anthology of differing opinions (comparable to the Talmud), or as a compendium of different sources, but as a single work, written by Moses (comparable to a law code such as Maimonides' *Mishneh Torah*). Consequently, they deny that a legal disagreement or *maḥloket* can occur in the Torah. When narrating the Passover observances during the reign of the righteous King Josiah, Chronicles tells us that "they slaughtered the Passover sacrifice . . . according to what is written in the Book of Moses . . . and they boiled the Passover sacrifice in fire, in accordance with the law" (2 Chron. 35.11–13, author's translation). Precisely what Chronicles means by the phrase "boiled in fire" is not clear. What is evident, however, is that Chronicles insists the sacrifice was performed in accordance with the Torah *as a whole*: somehow the priests simultaneously *boiled* it (as per Deuteronomy) and roasted it *in fire* (as per Exodus). The interpretive principle that the book of Chronicles advocates here is shared by classical rabbinic commentators: The Torah is a single document, and therefore what seem to be contradictions within it must be explained away through harmonization. (Rabbinic interpreters on these passages in Exodus and Deuteronomy devised several ways of showing that they do not really disagree with each other; see, for example, the Talmud's explanation in *b. Pes.* 70b.)

In the cases just examined, the goal of the later passage is to illuminate the earlier one. In many other instances of inner-biblical borrowing, however, the new text presents an innovative variation of the older text's ideas or even argues against it. Instead of saying, "Here is how you ought to understand the older text," the new composition tells the reader, "There are some ideas in the older text that need to be revised or extended or discarded. Here's my proposal for a replacement." Exod. 34.6–7 informs us that God sometimes punishes children for their parent's sin—indeed, even grandchildren and great-grandchildren can be punished:

> The LORD! the LORD! a God *compassionate and gracious, slow to anger, abounding in kindness* and faithfulness, *extending* kindness to the thousandth generation, forgiving iniquity, transgression, and sin; yet He does not remit all punishment, but visits the iniquity of parents upon children and children's children, upon the third and fourth generations.

According to this formulation (which appears in condensed form in Exod. 32.1–6, 34; Num.

14.1–20; 2 Kings 20.12–19; Ps. 99.8), God punishes children for the sins of their parents, apparently as a sign of mercy to the parents: When sinners repent, their punishment is deferred to their offspring. Other biblical writers, however, rejected this notion. Ps. 103.8–10, for example, notes: *The LORD is compassionate and gracious, slow to anger, abounding in kindness.* He will not *extend* his anger forever, nor will He fight for all time (author's translation).

The psalmist quotes the text from Exod. ch 34, which was already an authoritative and holy text, but revises the morally troubling part: Where the older text informed us that God punishes a sin for generations, the psalm maintains that God does not contend forever. A similar quotation-with-revision occurs in Deut. 7.9–10, Jonah 4.2, and Joel 2.12. These texts do not attempt to tell us how to read Exod. ch 34; that is, they do not argue that Exod. ch 34 somehow means something other than what it seems to say. Rather, they repeat it while also disagreeing with part of it. The same phenomenon occurs in rabbinic liturgy. During the introduction to the Torah service on festivals and throughout the Yom Kippur service, the first part of the statement from Exod. ch 34 is quoted, but the section at the end describing the intergenerational punishment is omitted. In purposefully misquoting the scriptural passage, then, the Rabbis who created the festival liturgy follow a scriptural precedent.

Sometimes it is difficult to be sure whether a later biblical author means to interpret an earlier text or to revise it. Exod. 23.9 reads, "Do not oppress *the foreigner*. You experienced the life of the foreigner, *for you were foreigners in the land of Egypt*" (author's translation). Deut. 10.19 echoes but amplifies the verse from Exodus: "Love *the foreigner, for you were foreigners in the land of Egypt.*" Does Deuteronomy intend to explain that "not oppressing" really means "loving," and that Exod. 23.9 at a deeper level commands us to love the foreigner? Or does Deuteronomy rather mean to say that not only is what Exodus commanded right, but we should go further and actively love the foreigner? It is difficult to be sure, but given the many other cases in which Deuteronomy clearly disagrees with Exodus (for example, the law of the Passover sacrifice discussed above, or the law of the slave in Deut. 15.12–18, which revises Exod. 21.2–7), the latter explanation seems more likely.

Biblical writers often use older texts to bolster their own writing or to help make some claim in a particularly clear or lively fashion. According to Jer. 2.3,

> Israel is the LORD's *holy item,* the *first-fruits* He produced. All who *consume* Israel will *incur guilt;* disaster will befall them (author's translation).

In making this assertion, Jeremiah relies on the ritual law found in Lev. 22.14–16:

> If a man *consumes* a *holy item* by mistake he must give a *holy item* to the priest plus one fifth of its value. The priests must not let the *holy items* donated to the LORD by the Israelites be defiled, nor may they allow the Israelites to *incur punishment* by *consuming holy items* (author's translation).

Jeremiah suggests an analogy in order to make his own point more vivid: According to ritual law, certain agricultural products (especially *first-fruits,* according to Num. 18.11–13) are holy items. They belong to the Temple and cannot be consumed (i.e., eaten) as regular food; those who do so incur guilt. So too the nation Israel is sacred to the LORD; the nation is, metaphorically, a holy item. Therefore, any who would consume (i.e., attack or destroy) that nation will incur guilt and suffer disaster. This sort of literary allusion differs from the examples of inner-biblical interpretation and revision we saw above. Jeremiah neither explains the passage from Leviticus nor repeats it while modifying its message. He does not claim that the older passage is really a geopolitical warning to Israel's enemies rather than a law concerning the sacrificial rites. Nor does he suggest that the text ought to be such a warning and needs to be rewritten. In fact, Jeremiah's statement does not affect the meaning of the older text at all. Rather, Jeremiah evokes the law from Leviticus in order to make his own message readily understood by analogy. In so doing, he also aligns himself with an authoritative text and thus bolsters his own status as prophet.

The following case of inner-biblical allusion, on the other hand, at once enriches the text that makes the allusion and illuminates the source. When two Israelite spies venture into Jericho at the outset of the book of Joshua, the Canaanite harlot Rahab allows them to hide in her house, thus disobeying an edict of her own Canaanite king. She explains her reasons to the Israelite spies:

> I know that the LORD has given you the land. Indeed, *fear* of you has *overtaken* us, and *all the inhabitants of* the land *are trembling* because of you (Josh. 2.9, author's translation).

Rahab's words closely resemble a line from the song Moses and the Israelites sang at the Reed Sea after they escaped from Egypt:

> *All the inhabitants of* Canaan *will tremble; fear* and terror will *overtake* them (Exod. 15.15–16, author's translation).

The allusion in Joshua (which was written after the poem in Exod. ch 15) works on several levels. It establishes a link between the events described in the first chapters of Joshua and the exodus from Egypt, a link that other passages in Joshua strengthen. (For example, the crossing of the River Jordan in Josh. chs 3–4 reenacts the crossing of the Red Sea in Exod. chs 14–15.) This brief allusion helps the author make a central point: The grand act of salvation that the LORD performed for Israelite slaves in the past was not the last such act; in each and every generation Jews should see themselves as participating in that miracle, because similar miracles may well save them, too. By repeating vocabulary from Exod. ch 15, the author of Joshua forges a parallel between two moments in time and hence expresses a philosophy of history: History repeats itself, and the activities of earlier generations are a sign for what will happen to their offspring. At the same time, this allusion also tells us something about the song in Exodus. It is possible to read that poem as prophetic, and to view the line describing the Canaanites' fear as a prediction made by Moses well before the Canaanites actually heard of the Israelites' good fortune. By paraphrasing that line in the past tense, the author of Joshua confirms the accuracy of the older prediction and thus reinforces Moses' prestige. Allusions to biblical texts occur with enormous frequency in later Jewish literature. One cannot move through a page of the Dead Sea Scrolls' *Community Rule*, a paragraph from the rabbinic liturgy, a poem by Yehudah Halevi or Nathan Zach or Dan Pagis, or a novel by A. B. Yehoshua or Amos Oz without finding vocabulary and images that evoke particular passages from the Bible. Indeed, the constant reworking of biblical material is a hallmark of Jewish literature, a hallmark that is already prominent in the Bible itself.

It is often stated that postbiblical Judaism is a religion of the Book, and that interpretation and debate are quintessentially rabbinic activities. In light of the phenomenon of inner-biblical exegesis and allusion, it becomes evident that these characteristics of Jewish creativity did not begin with the Rabbis. Biblical authors themselves regarded older biblical texts as authoritative, sacred, and worthy of study. Close examination of some biblical documents, especially those composed toward the end of the biblical period but including some from the preexilic era, shows something extraordinary: Priests and prophets, psalmists and scribes composed Scripture by recycling Scripture, by turning it and turning it to find new truths in it. For many biblical writers, new words from God emerged from intense examination and reordering of old ones. The interpretation of a sacred text could yield revelation, as much as revelation yielded a sacred text. If this is so, then the gulf that separates the Bible or *Torah shebikhtav* ("Written Torah") from rabbinic tradition or *Torah shebeʿal peh* ("Oral Torah") is smaller than one might think. The Rabbis stand alongside their biblical forebears when they interpret the Bible, even when they interpret the Bible in surprising or radical ways. It is perhaps for this reason that they portrayed biblical figures as the first biblical commentators. "Moses wrote many things in an obscure way [in the Torah], and then came King David [in the book of Psalms] who explained them," we read in a midrash on Exodus (*Exod. Rab.* 15:22). By reading and revising, explaining and debating, the authors of the Bible as well as those who follow them demonstrate that many different texts, biblical and otherwise, contain the living words of God.

[BENJAMIN D. SOMMER]

Early Nonrabbinic Interpretation

A variety of extrabiblical texts preserve ancient interpretations of biblical law and narrative. Many motifs from these interpretations are found in later rabbinic (as well as Christian and Islamic) sources. But the interpretive texts were, for the most part, not preserved within rabbinic corpora and libraries, and they often represent legal and theological views that diverge sharply from those found within rabbinic Judaism. Scholars use these texts—recovered from Christian libraries and from the Dead Sea Scrolls at Qumran—both to reconstruct the diverse character of the Second Temple community before the emergence of rabbinic Judaism and Christianity, and to illuminate later interpretations. (For an explanation of the Dead Sea Scrolls and the ways in which they are named and referenced, see "The Bible in the Dead Sea Scrolls," pp. 1920–28.)

These interpretive texts vary greatly in the way they present their relationship to the biblical texts they interpret. At one extreme are interpretive texts that efface themselves, presenting themselves as nothing more than editions, retellings, or translations of biblical passages. Translations and interpretations that claim divine authority are less self-effacing, but claim to present nothing but the one true meaning of biblical passages. At the opposite extreme are the interpretive writings of individuals such as Josephus and Philo of Alexandria, who self-consciously occupy particular points of view, which they know to be at some distance—perspectively, historically, linguistically—from the biblical passages they interpret.

Biblical Retellings

Examples of self-effacing texts, which present themselves as editions or retellings of biblical texts, include *Jubilees*, the *Genesis Apocryphon* (1QapGen^{ar}), *Reworked Pentateuch* (4Q158, 4Q354, 4Q365, 4Q366, 4Q367), and the *Temple Scroll* (11QT). These texts are often characterized as "pseudepigrapha"—as writings falsely attributed to earlier authoritative figures, such as Moses, Ezekiel, or Ezra. However, this term is misleading and anachronistic. It is misleading because it presupposes that, in contrast to these extrabiblical texts, the biblical texts are authentically attributed to certain authors—a presupposition that biblical scholars no longer maintain. In addition, the term is anachronistic, because it assumes a conception of authorial attribution—as marking a historical and proprietary fact—which was operative in some Greek-speaking circles in late antiquity, long after the last scriptural works had been written and, indeed, canonized. There is no evidence, however, that this conception was operative for Second Temple writers and readers.

Self-effacing texts rewrite traditions familiar from the Bible, sometimes in strikingly unfamiliar ways, in order to resolve interpretive questions and to serve particular theological and legal agendas, of which there were many in the diverse atmosphere of Second Temple

Judaism. Since their authors do not identify themselves, they seem more like inner-biblical than like rabbinic interpretations (which generally ascribe interpretations to a named Rabbi). In fact, it is anachronistic to apply the distinction between inner-biblical and extra-biblical interpretations to Second Temple reworkings because, when these works were composed, there was no rigidly defined and universally accepted biblical canon. These works aspired not to replace, but rather to accompany traditions already regarded as authoritative, and thus to provide those traditions with their proper interpretive contexts. Just as the Deuteronomic law collection came to be accepted within the Torah alongside the earlier Covenant Collection in Exod. chs 20–23, so it is possible to see the aforementioned extrabiblical works as accompanying the Torah texts at Qumran, where they have been found.

It was in this spirit that *Jubilees*, a work written in the land of Israel during the first third of the second century BCE, rewrote Genesis and the first part of Exodus. These sections of the Torah appear to be concerned exclusively with narratives about the patriarchs and matriarchs and about Israel's sojourn in Egypt. The absence of legal significance was problematic for *Jubilees*, as it would be, centuries later, to Rashi, the great medieval commentator (see "Medieval Interpretation," pp. 1876–1900). Rashi's solution was the suggestion, derived from classical rabbinic sources, that the initial, nonlegal sections of the Torah serve to establish the Jewish people's right to the land of Israel. In contrast, the solution of *Jubilees* was to rewrite the narratives as stories with legal implications. These implications were explained in accordance with a particular (nonrabbinic) view of law, especially regarding the calendar, which *Jubilees* insists should be solar. For example, *Jubilees* was bothered—like many other ancient, medieval, and modern interpretations—by a narrative in Genesis ch 38 in which Judah, son of Jacob, has sexual relations with his daughter-in-law, Tamar. To make matters even worse, according to Ruth ch 4, the line of David springs from this illicit union! *Jubilees* offers an exegetically ingenious solution. In its version of the story, neither of Judah's sons, Er and Onan, consummated his marriage with Tamar (*Jub.* 41.2–5):

> He hated (her) and did not lie with her because his mother was a Canaanite woman and he wanted to marry someone from his mother's tribe. But his father Judah did not allow him. That Er, Judah's firstborn, was evil, and the Lord killed him. Then Judah said to his brother Onan: "Go in to your brother's wife, perform the levirate duty for her, and produce descendants for your brother." Onan knew that the descendants would not be his but his brother's, so he entered the house of his brother's wife and poured out the semen on the ground. In the Lord's estimation it was an evil act, and He killed him.

Consequently, although Judah transgressed, he did not, strictly speaking, commit the serious sin of adulterous union with his daughter-in-law. He therefore did not deserve the death penalty, and was able to achieve atonement through his remorse and through his expression of commitment to the law (*Jub.* 41.27–28):

> We told Judah that his two sons had not lain with her. For this reason his descendants were established for another generation and would not be uprooted. For in his integrity he had gone and demanded punishment because Judah had wanted to burn her on the basis of the law which Abraham had commanded his children.

Interpretations of this kind were not presented by *Jubilees* merely as plausible solutions to exegetical problems, which would have allowed them to compete with other possible solutions. Instead, *Jubilees* purports to be a text dictated to Moses, at God's command, by the angel of the Presence at Sinai. In some ways, this is similar to the notion of an authoritative Oral Torah that would be-

come so central to rabbinic theology (see "Classical Rabbinic Interpretation," pp. 1844–63). Here is the prologue to the book of *Jubilees:*

> These are the words regarding the divisions of the times of the law and of the testimony, of the events of the years, of the weeks of their jubilees throughout all the years of eternity as He related (them) to Moses on Mt. Sinai when he went up to receive the stone tablets—the law and the commandments—on the Lord's orders as He had told him that he should come up to the summit of the mountain.

Toward the end of the first chapter Moses receives his command to record what is dictated to him (*Jub.* 1.26):

> Now you write all these words which I will tell you on this mountain: what is first and what is last and what is to come during all the divisions of time which are in the law and which are in the testimony and in the weeks of their jubilees until eternity—until the time when I descend and live with them throughout all the ages of eternity.

Many of the laws expounded in *Jubilees* were also said to be inscribed on heavenly tablets (following Mesopotamian models), and to have been transmitted by angels to a select line of humans, beginning with Enoch. Clearly, the stakes were very high in Second Temple contests of biblical interpretation. How else may we explain the need for so many modes of self-authorization?

In addition to solving exegetical problems, another function of ancient reworkings was to spell out in detail what older traditions had expressed with great concision. For example, in Genesis 12.11, Abram briefly acknowledges his wife's beauty: "[*Hineh na*] I know what a beautiful woman you are." The first two words are left untranslated by NJPS, but may be translated as "now." This immediately raises the question: What event had brought about Abram's recognition *now*? To answer this question the *Genesis Apocryphon*, a Dead

Sea text written in Aramaic, expands the biblical passage as follows (column 20.1–12):

1 ... [...] How ... and pretty is the shape of her face, and how [l]ovely and how smooth the hair of her head! How lovely are her eyes; how pleasant her nose and all the blossom of her face ... How graceful is her breast and how lovely all her whiteness! How beautiful are her arms! And her hands, how perfect! How alluring is the whole appearance of her hand[s]! How pretty are the palms of her hands and how long and supple all the fingers of her hands! Her feet, how lovely! How perfect her thighs! No virgin or wife who enters the bridal chamber is more beautiful than her. Above all women her beauty stands out; her loveliness is far above them all. And with all this beauty there is in her great wisdom. And everything she does with her hands is perfect. When the king heard the words of Hirqanos and the words of his companions, which the three of them spoke in unison, he desired her greatly and sent immediately for her to be fetched. He saw her and was amazed at all her beauty, and took her for himself as a wife. He wanted to kill me, but Sarai said to the king: He is my brother, so that I could profit at her expense. I, Abram, was spared on her account and I was not killed. But I wept bitterly that night, I, Abram, and my nephew Lot with me, because Sarai had been taken away from me by force.

The language of praise used here is from the Song of Songs. Use of traditions from other biblical books, which presupposes that all the biblical books bear one on the other, is characteristic of ancient reworkings, as well as of later rabbinic interpretations. But the above passage does more than expand Abram's remark. It justifies Abram's lying to Pharaoh, while also providing the careful reader of Genesis with a more complete picture of Abram's own inner spiritual struggles. The continuation of the passage challenges God to "do justice for me against him and show your

mighty arm against him." Such boldness is not out of character for Abram, as his challenges to God in Gen. chs 15 and 18 show. But it is not to be found in Gen. ch 12. Motifs are thus moved from one section to another where they might appropriately belong. Clearly, one motive for the reworking is to emphasize central features of Abram's personality. Thus ancient reworkings seek to explain not only the legal, but also what we might call the literary aspects of the text, giving insights into character and plot.

Translations

Ancient translations of the Torah into Greek, Aramaic, and Latin are governed by the original texts in ways that reworkings are not. Nevertheless, these translations were often interpretive; they solved interpretive problems, took sides in theological and legal controversies, and expanded narrative and legal material, while purporting merely to convey the meaning of the texts they translate. That this phenomenon was originally connected to the linguistic and cultural difficulties facing those who returned from Babylonia to reconstruct the Temple is suggested by Neh. 8.1–8:

All the people gathered together ... They asked Ezra the scribe to bring the book of the Torah of Moses ... Ezra the priest brought the Torah before the assembly, men, women, and all who could hear with understanding ... He read aloud from ... dawn until midday facing the men, women, and the interpreters, and ... all the people were attentive to the book of Torah ... Ezra the scribe opened the book before the eyes of the entire people ... When he opened it all of the people stood. Ezra blessed the Lord, the great God and the entire people answered: "Amen, Amen" while raising their hands, bowing down, and prostrating themselves before the Lord with their faces upon the ground ... Those interpreting the Torah ... read aloud from the book of the Torah of God, explaining, applying insight, and making the reading comprehensible (author's translation).

Evidently, the audience could not understand the text without some help, and translators (later called *meturgemanim*) continued to provide such help in rabbinic times. The Rabbis dated the earliest Targumim (plural of "Targum," Aramaic "translation") to the time of Ezra (*b. Meg.* 3a and *b. Ned.* 37b) and, in even the earliest rabbinic sources, refer to the public reading of Targum alongside the recitation of the weekly Torah portion. Thus, for example, the halakhot associated with reading and translating are discussed in the Mishnah (*Meg.* 4:4): "The reader of Torah is not to read less than three verses. He is to read to the *meturgeman* not more than one verse at a time, or in a reading from the Prophets [i.e., haftarah] not more than three." It was the responsibility of the *meturgeman* (translator) not only to translate the text, but to render it comprehensible. The Aramaic Targumim (e.g., *Targum Onkelos, Targum Neofiti, Fragmentary Targum, and Targum Pseudo-Jonathan*) often supplement and gloss biblical narratives, and they take special pains to avoid any suggestion of inappropriate anthropomorphism. For example, in Exod. ch 33, Moses asks God to see His Presence (33.18). Here is the NJPS translation of God's response (Exod. 33.19–23):

> And He answered, "I will make all My goodness pass before you, and I will proclaim before you the name LORD, and the grace that I grant and the compassion that I show. But," He said, "you cannot see My face, for man may not see Me and live." And the LORD said, "See, there is a place near Me. Station yourself on the rock and, as My Presence passes by, I will put you in a cleft of the rock and shield you with My hand *(kapi)* until I have passed by. Then I will take My hand away and you will see My back; but My face must not be seen."

Here *kapi* is translated "My hand." For the Targumim, however, such a translation would

have been problematic, because it suggested that God is embodied and anthropomorphic. Accordingly, the Targumim wanted to emphasize that *kapi* is used metaphorically to mean "my instrument." They differ, however, in their views about the instrument used. Thus *Targum Onkelos* writes, "I will shield you with My *Memra*," understanding *Memra* (Aramaic for "word" or "utterance") to be a mediating power through which God communicates with human beings. In other Targum traditions (*Targum Neofiti, Pseudo-Jonathan, and the Fragmentary Targum*) *kapi* is translated as "the group of angels who stand and minister before Me."

Commentary

Some ancient interpretations are more forthright about what they are doing than these reworkings and translations, such as the *pesharim* found at Qumran, e.g., *Pesher Habakkuk* [1QpHab]; *Pesher Psalms* [4Q171]; *Pesher Nahum* [4Q169]; *Pesher Hosea* [4Q166 and 4Q167]; *Pesher Isaiah* [4Q161–165]. These compositions clearly distinguish between the biblical texts and their interpretations. In this respect, they differ from *Genesis Apocryphon, Jubilees, 1 Enoch, 4 Ezra*, and many other Second Temple interpretive texts, and they anticipate later rabbinic midrash. To describe themselves, they use the word (*p-sh-r*), which has a biblical precedent in Daniel, where this verb is used (Dan. 2.5 ff.) to refer to the authorized interpretation of dreams. Consider, for example, this passage from *Pesher Habakkuk* (1QpHab VII, 1–8):

> And God told Habakkuk to write what was going to happen to the last generation, but he did not let him know the consummation of the era. *Blank* And as for what he says: "So that /may run/ the one who reads it." (Hab. 2.2) Its interpretation concerns the Teacher of Righteousness, to whom God has made known all the mysteries of the words of His servants, the prophets. (Hab. 2.3) For the vision has an appointed time, it

will have an end and not fail. *Blank* Its interpretation: the final age will be extended and go beyond all that the prophets say, because the mysteries of God are wonderful.

Note that the authority of divine revelation is claimed, not only for the prophetic text, but also for its interpretation, which has been given to the Teacher of Righteousness, a figure of great importance to the Qumran community. In Second Temple biblical interpretation, even when interpretation and text were distinguished, interpretations were not presented as personal opinions, or as plausible solutions to exegetical problems. Instead they were presented as having an authority based on divine revelation, thus as originating in the very same source as the text itself. Thus it might be most appropriate to refer to Second Temple writings not as extrabiblical, but rather as authoritative literature. To be sure, many of the interpretive texts which are contemporaneous with some of the exilic texts in the Bible, although not ultimately included in the Jewish canon, were considered to be inspired and to have assumed scriptural stature in various late Second Temple Jewish communities. However, this cannot be stated as a general characterization of all of the materials from Qumran or from Greek-speaking Jewish communities of the late Second Temple period.

Inspired Interpretive Texts by Named Individuals

Philo of Alexandria (ca. 20 BCE–50 CE) left behind a rich legacy of writings including theological essays, allegorical interpretations, explications of biblical laws, and questions and answers on Genesis and Exodus. Composed in Greek within the Hellenized community of Alexandria, which never recovered from its decimation in the 2nd century CE, his works, which interpret the Septuagint (Greek) rather than Hebrew texts, were apparently lost to later Jewish exegetes and philosophers. Indeed, he was appropriated so completely by

some Christians that he was retrospectively regarded as a Christian. Only centuries later, during the Reformation, was it recalled that Philo Christianus had in fact been Philo Judaeus. This recognition generated renewed interest by Jewish scholars and repudiation by some Christian theologians. To this day, some scholars interpret Philo as a proto-Christian, while others view him as a proto-rabbinic Jew.

Philo's challenge was different from the challenge confronting the authors of *Jubilees* or the *Genesis Apocryphon*. They had to authorize, to an exclusively Jewish audience, what they took to be authentic Judaism, in the face of rival practices and interpretations. Philo, in contrast, had to authorize Judaism itself to both Jews and non-Jews, within the relatively new context of the Hellenistic competition of cultures, a competition that was at the same time political, especially in light of the even newer Roman empire's quest to authorize itself through the appropriation of the Greek philosophical and literary heritage.

The place of Judaism within this new Roman world was far from clear. On the one hand, the significance of the Greek heritage was now as universal as the empire itself sought to be. Near Eastern cultures, which enjoyed the mystique of antiquity and exoticism, could legitimize themselves by identifying their gods with Greek gods and their teachings with Greek teachings. On the other hand, religious syncretism did not cohere easily with Jewish monotheism, and the Mosaic law, which seemed primarily to address Jews alone, was in danger of appearing parochial, thus rendering it potentially threatening to Rome and potentially insignificant to Hellenized Jews.

Thus, in Philo's world, the authority of Mosaic law itself was a live issue. One of his primary objectives was to show through interpretation that biblical texts have universal significance. Philo claimed (*Mos.* 2:12):

That Moses himself was the best of all lawgivers in all countries, better in fact than any that have ever arisen among either the Greeks or the barbarians, and that his laws are most excellent and truly come from God . . .

To be sure, Mosaic law is particular in the sense that it is binding in all its details only for the particular people of Israel. This law does, however, have universal significance in virtue of its special relation to natural law (*Mos.* 2:14):

> But Moses is alone in this, that his laws, firm unshaken, immovable, stamped, as it were, with the seals of nature herself, remain secure from the day when they were first enacted to now, and we may hope that they will remain for all future ages as though immortal, so long as the sun and moon and the whole heaven and universe exist.

Philo used a variety of methods to demonstrate this point. For example, he read the creation story in Genesis as a treatise on philosophical cosmology, akin to Plato's *Timaeus*, and he interpreted many laws and rituals as having an allegorical level of meaning, at which they signify philosophical doctrines of importance to Gentiles as well as Jews. Philo's immediate influence seems to have been greatest upon Christian interpreters, such as Origen and Clement of Alexandria. But his methods and ideas, transmitted through various intermediaries, resurfaced among medieval Jewish philosophers, for whose biblical interpretation his works serve as a paradigm, although it is likely they did not directly know his writings.

As in *Jubilees*, Philo perceived the need to explain why the Torah begins not with the revelation of the law at Sinai, but with the stories of creation and the ancestors (*Abr.* 5):

> First he [Moses] wished to show that the enacted ordinances are not inconsistent with nature; and secondly that those who wish to live in accordance with the laws as they stand have no difficult task, seeing that the first generations before any at all of

the particular statutes was set in writing followed the unwritten law with perfect ease, so that one might properly say that the enacted laws are nothing else than memorials of the life of the ancients, preserving to a later generation their actual words and deeds.

The point of the narratives was not to convey laws written on heavenly tablets, as it was for *Jubilees*. Instead, their point was to convey the unwritten law of nature, which was embodied in the exemplary lives of the ancestors. Indeed, the enacted laws peculiar to Israel had to be understood solely as memorials of the lives of these sages. This universalistic interpretation was intended to emphasize, not to undermine, the need for Jews to preserve their particular traditions and observances. But it implied that Jews could only observe the law properly if they understood it not only legally, but also philosophically.

In this spirit, Philo found in biblical narratives a meaning that was both cosmological and psychological. For example, he read the conflict between Cain and Abel as a conflict between the archetype of evil and the archetype of holiness, hence as an allegorical representation of moral conflict within a single human soul. Every detail related about the brothers—their names, their chosen professions, their conceptions of God and their actions—conveyed a moral lesson about the impression of vice or virtue. Thus Cain's name, which Philo derives from the Hebrew verb meaning "to possess," shows that the root of all evil is the belief that humans are possessors of what properly belongs to God. In contrast, Abel's "name means 'one who refers (all things) to God' " (*Sacr.* 2). Similarly, Cain chose to till the soil, a profession that involved him with earthly and inanimate objects, not with preparation for a future life. In contrast (*QG* 1:59): "Abel's choice of work as a shepherd is understood as preparatory to rulership and kingship." It is hardly surprising, then, that God preferred Abel's sacrifice. Cain's reaction—the jealous fratricide—only exacerbated his problem by removing the possibility of coming under Abel's virtuous influence (*Det.* 68):

> It would have been to the advantage of Cain, the lover of self, to have guarded Abel; for had he carefully preserved him, he would have been able to lay claim only to a mixed "half and half" life indeed, but would not have drained the cup of sheer unmitigated wickedness.

Thus vice is self-destructive. To be sure, Abel died while Cain survived (*Post.* 39):

> But in my judgement and in that of my friends, preferable to life with impious men would be death with pious men; for awaiting those who die in this way there will be undying life, but awaiting those who live in that way there will be eternal death.

But hope never perishes. When God asks Cain, "Where is your brother?" this shows, according to Philo, that repentance is always possible and that we are consequently responsible for our actions (*QG* 1:68):

> Why does he who knows all ask the fratricide, "Where is Abel, your brother?" He wishes that man himself of his own will shall confess, in order that he may not pretend that all things seem to come about through necessity. For he who killed through necessity would confess that he acted unwillingly; for that which is not in our power is not to be blamed. But he who sins of his own free will denies it, for sinners are obliged to repent. Accordingly he (Moses) inserts in all parts of his legislation that the Deity is not the cause of evil.

Philo's philosophical approach to biblical narratives differed significantly from the approach of *Jubilees* and kindred works. But Philo also repeatedly connected these narratives to laws mentioned later in the Torah. For example, he connected the story of Cain and Abel to the law that requires that first fruits be brought as an offering. The point was not to show, as *Jubilees* intended, that the narratives were implicitly legal texts, but that Mosaic law provided solutions for the moral problems confronting all humans. The law is designed to implant healthy theological convictions, to efface evil impressions and to reinforce good ones. Thus, for example, the tiller of soil is commanded to bring the first fruits as an offering to God, and to profess God's dominion over a land to which the farmer is ultimately foreign. Philo's analysis of Cain brings out the wisdom of this law, which is shown to manifest a deep understanding of the human soul.

Thus Philo's interpretations are not wholly unlike the reworkings of biblical traditions found in *Jubilees* and similar works. But Philo does not present his interpretations as versions of the texts they interpret. Indeed, he could not "rewrite the Bible," since he accepted the story told by the *Letter of Aristeas* to authorize the Septuagint (see "Jewish Translations of the Bible," pp. 2005–20). According to the *Letter*, Ptolemy Philadelphus had commissioned a Greek translation of the Bible, which was then produced by seventy Jewish elders who worked in isolation on the island of Pharos, but miraculously produced a single text. Thus, in his relationship to the biblical texts, Philo was more like interpreters after canonization than like his Second Temple contemporaries in the land of Israel.

Philo occasionally presented his interpretations as results of his own insight, but he did this only on occasion, and more frequently appealed to other sources of authority. He invoked "the traditions of the fathers" and claimed divine inspiration. He even insisted, when he interpreted the creation story in Genesis as a philosophical cosmology, that "it is Moses who lays this down, not I" (*Opif.* 24–25). On the one hand, Philo's self-conscious use of the first-person pronoun exhibits his sense of his own independent activity as an interpreter. On the other hand, he continues to efface himself.

Another important source for pre-rabbinic Jewish interpretations is the voluminous writings of Flavius Josephus, or Joseph bar Matthias (37–100 CE). From the age of 30, Josephus spent his life in Rome during the reigns of Vespasian, Titus, and Domitian. He devoted his life to retelling the history of the Jewish people from the creation of the world (i.e., retelling the history of the Jews beginning with the beginning of Genesis) until the destruction of the Second Temple and the Roman conquest, focusing on the Jewish war with Rome, in which he had participated. At a time when the Jews were under severe attack and criticism, he sought to explain and glorify those who lived in accordance with the law of Moses.

Josephus himself was a member of the priestly aristocracy and was well educated in the traditions of Jewish interpretation. Scholars have noted his extensive supplementation and interpretation of biblical passages. Yet he claimed only to present Scripture itself (*Ant.* 1.17):

> The precise details of our Scripture records will, then, be set forth, each in its place, as my narrative proceeds, that being the procedure that I have promised to follow throughout this work, neither adding nor omitting anything.

This self-effacing claim is, perhaps, best understood in light of Josephus's understanding of what it means to "read" Scripture, i.e., interpret the authoritative texts in the context of the wealth of authoritative interpretation. It is clear that, by the time of Josephus, there was already an extant body of interpretive material that shaped the way Jews read and transmitted the books of Tanakh. When Josephus promised neither to add nor to omit, he did not mean that he would convey only the letter of these books, without also conveying the expansions and interpretations which he considered authoritative.

For example, while in Gen. ch 18 we are told only of Sodom's wickedness, Josephus provides his readers with an extensive gloss on the nature of that wickedness (*Ant.* 1.194–95):

Now, about this time the Sodomites, overweeningly proud of their numbers and the extent of their wealth, showed themselves insolent to men and impious to the Divinity, insomuch that they no more remembered the benefits that they had received from Him, hated foreigners and avoided any contact with others. Indignant at this conduct, God accordingly resolved to chastise them for their arrogance, and not only to uproot their city, but to blast their land so completely that it should yield neither plant nor fruit whatsoever from that time forward.

Other Second Temple texts—e.g., Wisd. 19.14 and Sir. 16.8—reflect the tradition that arrogance was the principal sin of the Sodomites. In addition, Josephus often explains and justifies actions that may have seemed morally questionable. So, for example, Josephus explained or even justified Joseph's concealment of his own identity (*Ant.* 2.99):

It was in order to discover news of his father and what had become of him after his own departure that he so acted; he moreover desired to learn the fate of his brother Benjamin, for he feared that by such a ruse as they had practiced on himself, they might have rid the family of him also.

This expansion resembles other Second Temple attempts to explain the characters and motivations of biblical personalities. But, living in Rome immediately after the Roman conquest, Josephus had an additional reason to cast Jewish tradition in a light that was morally favorable.

Like Philo, Josephus sometimes claimed divine authority for his writings. Thus he claimed to be a divine messenger who had to present the inspired word of God (*J.W.* 3.392–408; *Ant.* 10.78–79). Indeed, as an eyewitness to the destruction of the Second Temple, he implicitly and repeatedly identified himself with the prophet Jeremiah, who both prophesied and witnessed the destruction of the First Temple. Like Josephus, Jeremiah was also a priest—hence one of those entrusted with the faithful preservation of the records of the history of the Jewish people, which, as Josephus adds, "will continue to be preserved with scrupulous accuracy" (*Ag. Ap.* 1.29). Clearly, Josephus understood himself to be exercising this priestly and prophetic office, carrying on the work of Scripture transmission through his own inspired interpretations.

Conclusion

While nonrabbinic interpretive texts of the Second Temple period varied significantly in form, they shared two basic assumptions: a commitment to render the Scriptures relevant to the communities they addressed, and a belief in the inspired status of their own interpretations.   [HINDY NAJMAN]

Classical Rabbinic Interpretation

By the 1st century CE, Jewish interpretation was beginning a long process of standardization and development. The Rabbis who carried out this program clearly believed that sacred texts contain timeless wisdom; but when preserved in writing, this timeless wisdom becomes in time obscure or difficult to understand, and must therefore be explained. This necessity is the origin of commentary, which can run along a continuum between "pure" types: from the effort to explain the text as it is in itself—what might be called the "original intent" or "plain sense" of the writing—to the effort to interpret the text in contemporary terms in the commentator's day—the "application" or "practical intent" of the writing. In this sense, rabbinic interpretation functions much as other interpretation does.

The Classical Rabbinic Period

Covering nearly a millennium (1st century–11th century), the rabbinic period is a lengthy and complex era, during which exegetical approaches and traditions developed that link up with inner-biblical and early post-biblical interpretation at one end and with medieval interpretation at the other. Rabbinic tradition developed primarily in two centers: the land of Israel and Babylonia, with the latter gradually becoming more important and influential. In many ways the rabbinic approach to interpretation—comparison of

texts, inference according to established procedures, and intense argument over approaches and outcomes—established the "ground rules" for most of subsequent Jewish exegesis until the modern era.

The Historical Background

The Roman empire ruthlessly put down two Jewish efforts at rebellion, in 70 and 135 CE. These events were not the sole cause of the increasing emphasis on study in Judaism, but the first put an end to Temple worship and the second crushed any hope of its restoration. Thereafter, Jewish religious practice was marked to an even greater extent by study of the Bible, and comment on it, as a major religious activity. There had been study before, of course; rabbinic tradition had been handed on. The concerns and universe of discourse of MMT, the halakhic letter from Qumran, indicate that such debates date back to the 2nd century BCE, even in detail and language. Hillel and Shammai and their schools (1st c. BCE to 1st c. CE) argued points of law during the late Second Temple period, up to the time of the Temple's destruction in 70. That date is a convenient marker for the start of the classical rabbinic era, which is conventionally divided into four periods, with overlapping beginnings and endings for each. Periods are subdivided into generations, with a "generation" generally indicating the passing of a school of teaching from master to student.

SOME TANNAITIC RABBIS

First generation
>Gamaliel (sometimes called "the Elder"; late 1st century BCE)
>Shimeon ben Gamaliel (1st century CE)
>Yoḥanan ben Zakkai (1st century CE)

Second generation
>Elder
>>Gamaliel II (of Yavneh; son of R. Shimeon; born ca. 50 CE)
>>Eliezer ben Hyrcanus (pupil of R. Yoḥanan ben Zakkai; 1st–2nd century)
>>Yehoshua ben Ḥananiah (pupil of R. Yoḥanan ben Zakkai; 1st–2nd century)
>Younger
>>Akiva ben Yosef (ca. 40–135)
>>Ishmaʿel (or Yishmaʿel) ben Elisha (early 2nd century)

Third generation
>Students of Akiva
>>Meir (2nd century)
>>Shimeon bar Yoḥai (2nd century)
>>Yose ben Ḥalafta (2nd century)
>>Yehudah bar Ilai (2nd century)
>>Shimeon ben Gamaliel II (2nd century)

Fourth generation
>Judah ha-Nasi ("Rabbi"; ca. 135–220)
>Eleazar bar Shimeon (2nd century; son of Shimeon bar Yoḥai)

Fifth generation
>Gamaliel III (2nd century)

Rabbinic Periods

The early period, beginning from the followers of Hillel, is that of the *tanna'im*. A *tanna'* is one who "repeats" [traditions], i.e., a transmitter or tradent of oral teaching. This period began around 70 CE and extended into the early 3rd century. Prominent in the tannaitic period are Rabbis Gamaliel, Akiva, and Judah ha-Nasi (the last being the rabbi credited with the redaction of the Mishnah; see below). There are five generations of *tanna'im*, beginning with the schools of Hillel and Shammai and extending to the era of Gamaliel III.

The second period is that of the *'amora'im*. An *'amora'* is a "speaker" or interpreter. This period, beginning in the 3rd century, lasted until about the 6th. The amoraic period was the talmudic era (see below). The Babylonian *'amora'im* are divided into seven "generations" and the land of Israel *'amora'im* into five.

The third, little-known period is that of the *savora'im*. A *savora'* is an "expositor." These rabbis were members of academies in Babylonia in the 6th century.

The fourth period, which at its end crosses over into medieval interpretation, is that of the *ge'onim*. A *ga'on* is the leader of one of the academies in Babylonia; *ga'on* means "pride" and is a short form of the title *ro'sh yeshivat ga'on Ya'akov* "head of the academy [that is] the pride of Jacob." The geonic period extends from the mid-6th century to the 11th century, and saw the first efforts at systematic legal commentary of the Talmud. The greatest among these Rabbis was Saadia ben Joseph Gaon (10th century), who began rabbinic study of philosophy and literature, as well as

SOME AMORAIC RABBIS

Land of Israel	Babylonia
First generation	
Elder	
Ḥiyya (2nd–3rd century)	
Bar Kappara (3rd century)	
Levi bar Sisi (3rd century)	
Ḥaninah bar Ḥama (2nd–3rd century)	
Younger	
Yannai (known as Rabbah, "the Great,"	Rav (Abba Arikha, "the Tall"; died ca. 248)
or Sabba, "the Elder"; 3rd century)	
Yehoshua ben Levi (of Lydda; 3rd century)	Mar Shemuel (died ca. 254)
Second generation	
Yoḥanan (ca. 240–279)	Yehudah ben Yeḥezkel (d. 291)
Simeon ben Lakhish (d. ca. 275)	
Third generation	
Yosi bar Ḥanina	Rabba bar Naḥmani (d. ca. 321)
Abbahu (ca. 300)	Yosef (d. 333)
Eleazar ben Pedat (3rd century)	
Ammi bar Natan (ca. 279)	
Assi (3rd century)	
Ze'era (3rd century)	
Fourth generation	
Ḥaggai	Abbayei (ca. 278–338)
Yirmiyahu ben Abba (4th century)	Rava (Abba ben Yosef bar Ḥama; 4th century)
Yonah (4th century)	
Yosa	
Aḥa	
Fifth generation	
Mana	Papa (d. 376)
Yose bar Abin	
Ḥizkiya	
Sixth generation	
	Ashi (ca. 335–427)
Seventh generation	
	Yemar
	Mar bar R. Ashi

study of the Bible (rather than only study of the Talmud).

The Texts of the Rabbinic Periods

The major works of the rabbinic period are of two types: those arranged topically, of which the main ones are the Mishnah and the Talmud; and those arranged around the biblical text, Midrash, including the ten collections in the so-called *Midrash Rabbah*. We will describe these works, noting their types and approximate dates of composition or compilation.

Works arranged topically. The Mishnah is a compilation of the written records of oral discussions of various laws. "Mishnah" means "oral instruction" (from Heb *shanah*, "repeat," equivalent to Aramaic *teni'*, from which *tanna'* is derived). It is divided into six "orders," each of which has numerous subsections, called "tractates." The orders are: *Zera'im,* "Seeds" (rules about agriculture); *Mo'ed,* "Appointed Times" (rules about Sabbaths and festivals); *Nashim,* "Women" (primarily marriage laws); *Nezikin,* "Damages" (rules about money and legal disputes); *Kodoshim,* "Holy Things" (Temple procedures); and *Teharot,* "Purities" (ritual impurities and purification). The Mishnah is believed to have been compiled in its final form by Rabbi Judah ha-Nasi ("the Prince," or more correctly, "the Patriarch," the title of the head of the Jewish community in the land of Israel; he is known as "Rabbi") around 200 CE, though it contains material from generations before Rabbi's time.

Other material from the same period, more or less, is contained in the Tosefta ("addition"), a collection of further rabbinic comments on most of the topics covered in the Mishnah. The structure of the Tosefta parallels that of the Mishnah, though it is composed of extra-Mishnaic material.

The Talmud, the major work of Jewish rabbinical interpretation, exists in two forms: "Talmud Yerushalmi," the Jerusalem Talmud (sometimes more accurately called the Talmud of the land of Israel or the Palestinian Talmud) and "Talmud Bavli," the Babylonian Talmud. In references these are abbreviated *y.* and *b.* respectively. The Talmud consists of pericopes of the Mishnah, accompanied by a commentary called the Gemara ("learning"). The Talmuds were compiled during the 3rd through the 6th centuries CE, first in Israel (until 370), and later in Babylonia (6th century).

Works organized around the biblical text. The *Midrash Rabbah* ("Great Midrash") is a collection of rabbinic comments on the biblical text, which in its final form (Venice, 1545) contains ten midrashim: the five books of the Torah, Genesis through Deuteronomy, and the Five Scrolls, Song of Songs, Ruth, Lamentations, Ecclesiastes, Esther. Individual sections are referred to by their biblical title, for instance, *Genesis Rabbah* (or *Bereshit Rabbah*), *Lamentations Rabbah,* and so on. Despite their final publication in one volume, however, these works arose at widely different times, with *Genesis Rabbah* generally regarded as the earliest (ca. 5th century CE), followed by *Leviticus Rabbah* (slightly later). The latest are *Exodus, Numbers,* and *Deuteronomy.* To complicate matters further, some of these works are composite arrangements of works from different periods.

Halakhah and Aggadah. Cutting across the categories of separate works are the two main descriptive types of rabbinic comment: halakhah, or legal comment, and aggadah, or non-legal comment. Halakhah (from *halakh,* "go, walk") refers to the "way" of Torah; halakhah itself is concerned with explicating, applying, and in general making sense of the legal materials in the Bible. Aggadah is a much more amorphous category: it includes theology, lore, legend, sayings, prayer and praise—in fact, it seems to be a catch-all for whatever is not halakhah.

Principles of Rabbinic Interpretation

Rabbinic interpretation is characterized by several methods, the principles and illustrations of which we will examine below. The Rabbis themselves proposed various descriptive lists of types of interpretation, of which the shortest and best-known is attributed to Hillel (1st century BCE). Hillel found seven types of interpretation:

• *Kal vaḥomer:* the deduction from a minor case to a major case.

• *Gezerah shavah:* drawing an analogy between texts based on a word in common

• *Binyan 'av mikatuv 'eḥad:* applying a principle derived from one verse

• *Binyan 'av mishenei ketuvim:* applying a principle derived from two verses

• *Kelal uferat uferat ukelal:* modification of a general principle derived from a particular principle; modification of a particular principle derived from a general principle

• *Kayotze' bo bemakom 'aḥer:* principles derived from similar passages

- *Davar halamed me'inyano:* deduction from context

Rabbinic method also included such ancient types as *notarikon,* where each consonant of a Hebrew word was taken as an abbreviation for a different word. The Rabbis, for example, parsed the first word of the Decalogue, *'anokhi,* "I," as an acronym of the (Aramaic) words *'ana' ketavit yehavit*—"I [God] wrote it [and] gave it." This method was employed by Babylonian and Assyrian scribes long before the rabbinic era.

The earliest texts containing rabbinic interpretation were edited after 200 CE, and the origins of the system that gave birth to these texts must be inferred from texts of earlier groups (see "Early Nonrabbinic Interpretation," pp. 1835–44).

For two reasons we will concentrate on halakhah rather than aggadah. First, the Talmuds were much more explicitly consistent in their presentation of such texts, their methods are easier to understand, and consequently their development is also easier to trace. Second, these texts and methods are relatively unexplored in modern academic discourse. Nevertheless, more purely homiletical methods will also be described at the end of this essay.

Broadly speaking, rabbinic exegesis may be explained in three ways: historically, phenomenologically, and functionally. The historical approach looks at the *development* of interpretation. The functional approach seeks to understand the *purposes* of interpretation. Finally, the phenomenological approach studies *methods* of interpretation. This study combines all these perspectives.

Omnisignificance

James Kugel has proposed the term "omnisignificance" to describe the essential stance of rabbinic interpretation. These interpreters assume that there is no detail of the text, however insignificant it may seem, that does not carry meaning. Further, this meaning is not merely a matter of emphasis or rhetorical variation; the text intends to teach, and it intends this with every part of itself. The interpreter must find the correct analytical tool to make the teaching clear.

This is a restatement of the rabbinic interpretation of Deut. 32.47: "'For it is not an empty thing for you, it is your very life,' and if [it appears] devoid [of moral or halakhic meaning]—it is you [who have not worked out its moral or legal significance]" (*y. Ketub.* 8:11 [32c]). In rabbinic terms omnisignificance has a sharply limited and highly focused range: It is restricted to moral, theological, or legal interpretations. A rabbinic comment attributed to the mid-3rd century scholar in the land of Israel, R. Simeon ben Lakhish, will illustrate this: "There are verses which are worthy of being burnt, but they are [after all, when properly understood,] essential components of Torah" (*b. Ḥul.* 60b). "Omnisignificance" is not only a fundamental assumption of the rabbinic view of Scripture, it also guides interpretation into well-defined channels and establishes a hierarchy of exegetical alternatives.

It also presents a challenge. Having claimed such profundity for *all* of Scripture, the rabbinic program should deliver on its promise. But the Bible contains a great deal of material which, by rabbinic standards, is not legal, ritual, moral, ethical, or theological: stories of Israelite ancestors, genealogies, poetry (not all of it religious), census lists, geographical and dynastic information of dubious interest to a legal scholar. Thus the *Mekhilta* (a halakhic midrash on Exodus) runs only from Exod. 12.1 to 35.3, and skips long passages about the construction of the Tabernacle in Exod. chs 25–40, except for brief sections relating to 31.12–17 and 35.1–3. There is no halakhic midrash on Genesis at all. A truly omnisignificant program would fit in all the non-legal and non-edificatory passages. It would also cover what is missing. For instance, the Torah lacks explicit mention of matters that the Rabbis—and most Jews—would consider essential, such as the obligation to pray regularly. True, Abraham, Isaac, and Jacob pray, Moses prays, Joshua prays, but regular prayer is not mandated, nor is its structure laid down. The Rabbis settled on Deut. 11.13, "serving Him with all your heart," as referring to prayer, which is "the service of the heart" (b. Ta'an. 2a), but this reference is very vague.

Thus the promise was never totally fulfilled. Omnisignificance is a rabbinic view of Scripture rather than a complete exegetical program, and an ideal which was never actually realized. Not every scriptural text has been interpreted as a strictly "religious" one. The available collections of classic rabbinic texts do not constitute an omnisignificant corpus; not only do they fail to deal with many verses, and even whole biblical chapters, but features which are considered significant—legally or morally—in one context are ignored in others. The rabbinic program or programs do not even attempt to provide a complete commentary, in whatever mode, to any biblical book, chapter, or passage, though in some heavily halakhic chapters in Leviticus something resembling a complete commentary could be composed (an attempt to do so was the Vilna Gaon, in 'Aderet 'Eliyahu). Indeed, the statement quoted above, "if [it appears] devoid [of moral or halakhic meaning]—it is you [who have not worked out its moral or legal significance]," which is reported in the name of the fifth-generation authority, R. Mana, is an admission of this failure and a rebuke to his colleagues or disciples.

There is another aspect to this problem. The doctrine of omnisignificance assumes a uniform narrative or expositional density in Scripture; the biblical text is presumed to be uniformly informative on some level. The preserved rabbinic exegetical materials available to us do not bear out this assumption, however. For example, the phrases 'ish 'ish, "every man," (Lev. 15.2; 17.3, 8, 10, 13; 18.6; 20.2, 9; 22.4, 18; 24.15; Num. 1.4; 4.19, 49; 5.12; 9.10) and 'ish, "a man," (Lev. 19.20) are sometimes interpreted as including women (b. Zevah. 108b), but at other times not, since the verse itself includes them within its purview when it employs the phrase, 'ish 'o 'ishah, "a man or a woman" (Lev. 13.29, 38). Why does Scripture employ these variations? The impression one receives is that rabbinic exegesis reflects a concerted effort to harmonize such expressions and level their applications. Women are included in the expression "every man," as they are in the expression "a man," and of course explicitly in the expression "a man or a woman." The Rabbis never raise these questions in a systematic way.

The omnisignificant imperative proceeds directly from the view of the Torah and the entire Bible as divine revelation; it serves to justify interpretive approaches to biblical texts. Nevertheless, in practice this principle was not universally applied to all biblical texts nor was the meaning restricted to narrow halakhic or moral categories. Indeed, plain-sense interpretations are not excluded, so long as they have legal, ritual, or edificatory value. At times, then, the interpretation borders on what we would consider the plain sense of the text, so long as it has omnisignificant ramifications.

Goals and Methods of Rabbinic Interpretation

Rabbinic interpretation was concerned to increase the understanding of the text and its acceptability. The Rabbis also aimed to define legal requirements more exactly. The resulting explanations were primarily concerned with interpreting biblical passages in terms that were more understandable or palatable to their contemporaries, and to provide exact definitions and interpretations for biblical verses that had legal or ritual significance.

An example of the first is found in the rabbinic dispute over whether the case of a "rebellious son" of Deut. 21.18–21 ever occurred, or whether it was presented as part of the Deuteronomic legislation merely as an object lesson.

R. Judah said: If [the "stubborn and rebellious" son's] mother is not like his father in voice, appearance and stature, he does not become a stubborn and rebellious son [and thus subject to the death penalty]. Why so? Scripture said: "he will not obey our voice" (Deut. 21.20), and since they must be identical in voice, they must also be [identical] in appearance and stature.... There never has been a "stubborn and rebellious" son, and never will be. Why then was the law written? That you may expound it and receive a reward.... [This may agree with R. Simeon, who said:] Because one [= the son] eats a *tartemar* (about 180 grams) of meat and drinks half a *log* (about a cup) of Italian wine, shall his father and mother have him stoned? But it never happened and never will happen. Why then was the law written? That you may expound it and receive a reward (*b. Sanh.* 71a).

R. Judah interprets the biblical description of the parents' complaint that their son does "not obey *our* voice" as mandating that their *voices* be identical, and the Talmud takes this as an impossible condition. How often will a father and mother have the same "voice, appearance and stature"?

Precise interpretation of a grammatical element is commonly used for legal or ritual texts which are intended to be carried out. Indeed, in other cases, the requirement that two elements of the act be identical is not absolute: for instance, the Mishnah prescribes that the sin offerings brought on the Day of Atonement be alike, but that requirement may be waived (*m. Yoma* 6:1). It is clear, however, that the imperatives of the two cases are different. Sacrifices must be offered, but executing a rebellious son for being a glutton and a drunkard seemed excessive to R. Simeon. This insistence on the exactitude of biblical expressions is typical of rabbinic interpretation of biblical texts, even when there is no apparent cultural disparity between the biblical and rabbinic worlds. It is bound up with the rabbinic view of Scripture's exceedingly precise mode of expression. While it was in all likelihood Scripture's divine origin that allowed such a mode of interpretation to gain sway, once established, this mode was adopted for rabbinic

texts as well, and we find 4th- and 5th-century Rabbis applying similar modes of interpretation to the Mishnah and other rabbinic texts, and later authorities doing the same to the Talmuds and later texts.

Duplications and Redundancies

Of particular concern to the Rabbis were two challenges to the omnisignificant view: duplications and contradictions. How could an omnisignificant text tolerate either of these departures from the precision posited of it? If every letter were weighed, how could Scripture seemingly contradict itself, repeat itself, or deal with matters that seemed not terribly significant to the Rabbis? We will examine their methods for dealing with duplications, which probably concerned them as much as contradictions, if only because, from their point of view, there were so many of them.

Generally speaking, redundancies and duplications are interpreted as they may be applied to actual cases, so as to draw distinctions between apparently similar, identical, or contradictory passages. While the Babylonian Talmud states this principle only for legal texts (as in *b. Bek.* 6b), it clearly also applies, though with different methods, to nonlegal passages. This method of dealing with redundancies expanded to include all sorts of interpretation, and became typical of the traditional approach to most of the problems outlined above. As the medieval tosafists (commentators on the Talmud during the 12th–14th centuries) noted, only when these methods fail should one fall back on the plain sense (see *Tosafot Sot.* 3a, s.v. *lo*).

Examples of the Rabbis dealing with duplicate passages are numerous in the interpretive material from the 2nd century onward. One example is found in the various Torah passages regarding the law of a "Hebrew slave." The *Mekhilta* on Exod. chs 21–22 includes a section on the laws pertaining to a "Hebrew slave" in Exod. 21.4–7, which must be coordinated with another passage relating to slavery in Lev. 25.39–46, and, ultimately, to

Deut. 15.12–18. It does so by distinguishing between the application of each of these passages.

> You say that Scripture here deals with one sold into servitude by the court for stealing, telling us that such a one must serve not only the one who bought him but also the latter's son after him. Perhaps however it deals only with one who sells himself? When it says: "And if thy brother be waxen poor with thee and sell himself unto thee" (Lev. 25.39), behold the one selling himself is here spoken of. Why then should Scripture say here: "If thou buy a Hebrew slave?" It must therefore deal with one sold into slavery by the court for stealing, telling that such a one must serve not only the one who bought him but also the latter's son after him. (*Mekhilta*, ed. Lauterbach, vol. III p. 3)

Since the Exodus passage does not specify the cause of the sale into slavery while the Leviticus passage does, the Rabbis might have simply harmonized the two. The essential difficulty, that Exod. 21.2 specifies a six-year term of servitude, while Lev. 25.40 mandates a variable term, depending on when in the jubilee cycle the sale took place, could perhaps have been reconciled in some way; for example, the six-year term could have been required, while serving until the jubilee would have applied to a case in which the slave wanted to continue with his master, as, indeed, the *Mekhilta* itself does suggest in the case of an Israelite sold by the court. No new category would have had to be created. But by creating a new distinction, the Rabbis accounted not only for the overlap between the two passages but the very existence of two separate passages ostensibly dealing with but one topic: the Hebrew slave.

Finally, there is the third passage, Deut. 15.12–18, which specifies a term of six years, with the slave going out in the seventh loaded down with gifts. *Sifre Deut.* 119 deals explicitly with the relationship of this passage to the two categories of Hebrew slave already estab-

lished, and to the Hebrew maidservant of Exod. 21.7–12.

> When you set him free, do not let him go empty-handed. Furnish him out of the flock, threshing floor, and vat. . . . Perhaps we only furnish the one who goes out in six years (Exod. 21.2); whence [do we know that this applies also] to the one who departs in the jubilee (Lev. 25.40) or with the death of the master (referring to Exod. 21.2–6) and the Hebrew maidservant with her displaying signs of puberty (Exod. 21.7–12)? Scripture says: "You shall set free" (Deut. 15.12), "when you shall set free" (Deut. 15.13), "when you shall set him free" (ibid.)—[thus applying to all three cases].

This passage thus harmonizes and distinguishes among the various Torah texts referring to Hebrew servitude. These texts display differing emphases and phraseology, and thus offer opportunities for both means of exegesis.

What then do the Rabbis do when the repetition or repetitions are identical? Such a problem is posed by the threefold appearance of the prohibition of seething a kid in its mother's milk in Exod. 23.19, 34.26, and Deut. 14.21.

> Why is this law stated in three places? To correspond to the three covenants which the Holy One, blessed be He, made with Israel: One at Horeb (Exod. 24.7–8), one in the plains of Moab (Deut. 29.11), and one on Mount Gerizim and Mount Ebal (Deut. 28.69). . . .
>
> R. Jonathan says: Why is this law stated in three places? Once to apply to domestic animals, once to apply to wild animals, and once to apply to fowl.
>
> Abba Ḥanin states in the name of R. Eliezer: Why is this law stated in three places? Once to apply to large cattle, once to apply to goats, and once to apply to sheep.
>
> R. Simeon ben Eleazar says: Why is this law stated in three places? Once to apply to large cattle, once to apply to small cattle, and once to apply to wild animals.

R. Simeon ben Yoḥai says: Why is this law stated in three places? One is a prohibition against eating it, one is a prohibition against deriving any benefit from it, and one is a prohibition against the mere cooking of it.

Here the threefold mention is interpreted by means of standard matrices involving three classes, either of animals or of prohibited actions (eating, drinking, or deriving benefit). In the nature of things, as we might expect, not all of these matrices are equally compelling. In rabbinic literature, the animal world is regularly divided into domestic animals, wild animals, and fowl, and domestic animals in turn are subdivided into large and small cattle, so that R. Simeon ben Eleazar's division into large and small cattle, and wild animals, while somewhat unusual, is certainly in line with convention (though Abba Ḥanin's statement dividing animals into large and small cattle, and then subdividing small cattle into goats and sheep, does seem simply to be an effort to use the three repetitions). Thus, rabbinic exegesis combines the attempt to relate scriptural texts with rabbinic categories (which are often based on Scripture in any case; e.g., Gen. 2.20 for domestic animals, wild animals, and fowl) with the modification of those categories to fit a particular distribution of verses. This can often result in an elaborate series of arguments designed to demonstrate that each verse, though seemingly redundant, is intended to counter a particular hypothetical argument.

Though it is not explicitly stated, these examples illustrate the use of a principle attributed to R. Ishmael, an authority of the first half of the 2nd century and colleague of R. Akiva: "Every passage that is said and repeated is repeated only for the sake of the new information [contained] in it." This principle underwent an interesting and characteristic metamorphosis in the course of time. Originally it seems to have been intended as a "cap" on expositions: In the case of the duplicate passages, only the *differences*, or more

precisely the pluses in the duplicate passage, are expounded, not the repetitions themselves, which by definition contain no new information. Thus, in the case of the duplicate lists of animals forbidden to be eaten in Lev. 11.1–28 and Deut. 14.3–21, the Babylonian Talmud first cites a view which explains the repetitive mention of the camel (in Deut. 14.7 as opposed to Lev. 11.4) as an animal which is forbidden to be eaten as coming to include as forbidden the offspring of a camel which resembles a clean animal. Later in the discussion, the following teaching is quoted:

Why is [the list of clean and unclean animals] repeated? Because of the *shesu'ah* [according to rabbinic interpretation, an animal with two backs and two spinal columns, which is mentioned only in the Deuteronomic passage]. Why with regard to birds? Because of the *ra'ah* [a bird mentioned only in Deut. 14.13].—Then, perhaps, [the repetition of] "camel," "camel" [in both books] comes for the same purpose [that is, the camel "comes along for the ride" in order to provide a context for the two additions, and not for any other purpose]?—Nevertheless, whenever we can derive [a lesson from the biblical text], we do so (*b. Bek.* 6b).

The ideal here is to derive a lesson *from every repetition*. Every part of it is subject to interpretation, if only we can interpret it. If we cannot, a lacuna exists, which may be filled later or in messianic times, in accord with R. Yoḥanan's fervent wish as expressed in *b. Menaḥot* 45a: "This passage will be interpreted by Elijah in the future [in the messianic era]." Maimonides (1135–1204), on the other hand, rejected such amplifications; he seems to have been of the opinion that post-talmudic authorities could not multiply "counts" on their own, but only when they had already been made by a talmudic source.

This is not to say that the Rabbis did not have other methods of dealing with such problems. But for all their ingenuity, a not insignificant amount of Scripture escaped their treatment, at least as we may judge from the surviving compilations of late antiquity. We may understand the well-known rabbinic story of *b. Menaḥot* 29b in this light.

> R. Judah said in the name of Rav: When Moses ascended on high he found the Holy One, blessed be He, engaged in affixing coronets [small strokes on the tops of certain letters in a Torah scroll] to the letters. Said Moses: "Lord of the Universe, who prevents You [from giving the Torah without these coronets]?" He answered: "There will arise a man at the end of many generations, Akiva ben Joseph by name, who will expound heaps and heaps of laws upon each stroke." "Lord of the Universe, let me see him." He said: "Turn around." Moses went and sat down behind eight rows [of R. Akiva's disciples and listened to his expositions of the Torah]. He was not able to follow the arguments and was depressed, but when they came to a certain subject and the disciples said to the master, "How do you know it?" and [R. Akiva] replied: "It is a law given to Moses at Sinai," he was comforted. He then returned to the Holy One, blessed be He, and said, "Lord of the Universe, You have such a man and you give the Torah through me?" He replied: "Be silent, for such is My decree." Moses then said, "Lord of the Universe, You have shown me his Torah [teaching], show me his reward." "Turn around," said He. Moses turned around and saw them weighing out [R. Akiva's] flesh in the market stalls [after his martyrdom in the Hadrianic persecutions]. "Lord of the Universe! Such Torah, and such a reward!" He replied: "Be silent, for such is My decree."

We have no legal expositions based on the coronets of the letters of the Torah in the name of R. Judah or Rav, or, indeed, any earlier or later authorities. Unless we posit a tremendous ("heaps and heaps") amount of lost interpretation, we must assume that this story refers to those parts of the Torah which still lacked a definitive rabbinic exposition.

Argument by Analogy and the *Ribbuy* ("Extension")

The argument by analogy is characteristic of rabbinic interpretation as a whole. For example, the common biblical Hebrew phrase *'ish 'ish*, "a man, a man," i.e., "every man," "each man," by extension "every person," is often interpreted as including classes of people other than males. This is because the phrase is considered redundant, since *'ish* alone may mean the same. From that phrase the Rabbis derive, in various contexts, the applicability of the relevant rule to women, children, proselytes, their wives, non-Jews, or, in some cases, people of indeterminate sex or hermaphrodites. The fact that all of these are derived by analogy does not mean that there is a uniformity of choice, though. The form the analogy takes depends on the context. Thus, the prohibition of incest (Lev. 20.2) includes non-Jews:

> "And say (*to'mar*) to the Children of Israel," "and speak (*tedaber*) to the Children of Israel," "say (*'emor*) to the Children of Israel," "speak (*daber*) to the Children of Israel," "instruct (*tzav*) the Children of Israel," "and you shall instruct (*tetzaveh*) the Children of Israel"—R. Yose says: "The Torah speaks in the human language in many expressions, and all must be expounded (*lehidaresh*): 'Israel'—this refers to Israel (i.e., male Jews); 'sojourner' (*ger*)—this refers to the proselyte (*ger*); "*the* proselyte"—this includes the wives of proselytes; 'in Israel'—this includes women and slaves. If so, why does [Scripture] say "*ish 'ish*'? To include non-Jews" (*Sifra Kodoshim* 10:1–2, ed. Weiss 91b).

Nevertheless, *'ish* is always taken to exclude minors, even when some other means is employed to bring them within the applicability of the rule in question. Thus, in regard to the skin diseases commonly rendered as "leprosy" in Lev. 13.44, we find the following:

> *'ish*, "a man"—From where [do we know this] to include a woman or a minor? Scrip-

ture states: *"tzaruʿa,"* "one suffering from a skin disease," whether a man or a woman or a minor. If so, why is *'ish* stated? For a matter [stated] below: a man unbinds his hair and undoes his clothes but a woman does not unbind her hair or undo her clothes (*Sifra Tzriʿa* 12:1, ed. Weiss, 67d).

Minors are included by means of an interpretation of the word *tzaruʿa,* despite the exclusion signalled by *'ish.* Note also that the definite article, which in Hebrew is registered by a one-letter prefix, may also be used as a hook on which to hang an analogical interpretation. The word *ha-ger,* "the sojourner," or rather the *"ha-"* prefix, is taken to include the wives of proselytes, while the word *be-Yisrael,* "in Israel" is taken to include women and slaves. Ordinarily, the category of "women" is included by the repetition of the word *'ish,* as in the expression *'ish 'ish* noted above. Here there is only one *'ish,* and, instead, women are included in this way.

Rava and the Omnisignificant Revolution

Over time these inconsistencies in the application of methods became a matter of concern to later scholars, especially the great fourth-generation Babylonian *'amora'* of the second quarter of the 4th century, Rava, and some of his predecessors in the land of Israel as well, particularly the third-generation *tanna'* R. Ilai. Both were concerned with inconsistent uses of analogy, but Rava was concerned with the inconsistent use of the omnisignificant principle itself. Rava's concern manifested itself in a systematic research program into the limits of the application of omnisignificance, motivated, it would seem, both by his own powers of systematization, his apparently strong interest in the subject of halakhic interpretation, and by challenges to rabbinic interpretation and authority in his own time and place. Unlike most other rabbinic authorities, he seems to have had wide communal responsibilities in the city of Mahoza, which was located on the west bank of the River Tigris directly across from the Persian capital of Ctesiphon. The political head of Babylonian Jewry, the Head of the Exile, who also had standing as a Persian nobleman, was headquartered there, and adjacent to Mahoza was the *catholicos,* the head of the Nestorian Church, in Seleucia, then known as Veh-Ardaxshir. The cosmopolitan population that Rava ministered to was skeptical of rabbinic authority and exegesis, and this undoubtedly helped lead him to searching examinations of its aims and methods.

Rava was concerned with why the Rabbis interpreted some words and phrases in certain texts but not in others. Beyond that, he was concerned with why Scripture itself expends greater effort in expositing certain matters while leaving others relatively unexamined. In all these ways, and others, Rava explores the limits of omnisignificant interpretation as it existed in his day. In ten passages in the Babylonian Talmud (nine attributed to Rava [*b. Kid.* 9a, *B. K.* 77b, *Mak.* 8a, *Tem.* 6b, *Yoma* 63b, *ʿArak.* 30b, *Ned.* 80b; the tenth, *Tem.* 28b, is anonymous and may be redactional]), and in four similar cases in the Talmud of the land of Israel (all attributed to R. Ilai [*y. Yoma* 3.6 (40c), *Meg.* 1:12 (72a) = *Hor.* 3.3 (47c–d), *Yebam.* 6.4 (7c)]), the inconsistency of the application of rabbinic exegetical principles to specific texts is examined. For example, in *b. Kid.* 9a we have the following:

Our Rabbis taught: [A woman is acquired in marriage] by a document: How so? If A writes for B on a paper or a shard, even if not intrinsically worth a *perutah:* "Your daughter be consecrated to me," "your daughter be betrothed to me," [or] "your daughter be my wife," she is betrothed.

R. Zera ben Memmel objected: But this document is unlike a deed of purchase: there the seller writes: "My field is sold to you," while here the husband [i.e., the "acquirer"] writes: "Your daughter be consecrated to me."

Rava replied: There [the form is determined] by scriptural context, and here [likewise it is determined] by scriptural context. There it is written, "and *he sell* some of his possessions" (Lev. 25.25), thus Scripture made it dependent on the seller; while here it is written "when a man [takes a woman]" (Deut. 24.1), thus making it dependent on the husband."

Thus, legal rules based on scriptural texts are expected to be consistent, and their inconsistencies must be accounted for.

This insistence on consistency extends to a demand for a minimally uniform density of scriptural interpretation even within one passage. For example, in Deut. 22.1, 3, Scripture states: "If you see your fellow's ox or sheep gone astray, do not ignore it; you must take it back to your fellow. . . . You shall do the same with his ass; you shall do the same with his garment; and so too shall you do with anything that your fellow loses and you find: you must not remain indifferent."

Said Rava: Why does the All Merciful mention "an ox, a donkey, a sheep and a garment" [in Deut. 22.1, 3]?

For had the All Merciful mentioned "garment" [alone], I would have thought [that] that applies only if the object [can be identified] by witnesses or the object itself has a mark [of distinction by which it may be identified], but not in the case of a donkey [for which these means of identification do not apply]. [That is,] if its saddle [can be identified] by witnesses or its saddle has a mark [of distinction by which it may be identified], I might think that it need not be returned to him. Therefore the All Merciful mentioned "a donkey" to show that even the donkey [too is returned] by virtue of the mark of the saddle.

Why did the All Merciful mention "ox" and "sheep"? "Ox"—that even the shearing of its tail, and "sheep"—that even its shearings [must be returned]. Then the All Merciful should have mentioned [only] "ox" for the shearings of its tail, and the shearings of a sheep would follow *a fortiori*!

But, says Rava, "donkey" mentioned in

connection with a pit [in Exod. 21.33: "And if a man should open a pit . . . and an ox or a donkey should fall therein. . . ."] on R. Judah's view [which rejects the rabbinic use of the term to exclude vessels damaged in such a case] and "sheep" in connection with a lost article [in Deut. 22.1, 3] on all views, are difficult [in that they do not seem to serve any exegetical purpose] (*b. B. M.* 27a).

Clearly, Rava's concern with the interface of rabbinic interpretation and the formulation of biblical laws borders onto questions involving the construction of the biblical text itself.

According to geonic tradition, Rava was the head of the combined Babylonian academy, so that most of the authorities of the fifth generation were his disciples and continued to carry on this program. The Babylonian Talmud contains long passages working out the details of Rava's concerns, passages that have almost no parallels in the Talmud of the land of Israel.

Other Developments in Rabbinic Interpretation

Taking Contradictory Verses into Account

Various passages in both Talmuds show methodological concerns that parallel those of Rava. For instance, there is the phenomenon of a sort of "round-robin" of queries designed to elucidate how an interpreter deals with the verses or phrases which seem to counter his own interpretation, or for which his own interpretation does not account. The Talmud of the land of Israel presents a dialogue between the schools of Shammai and Hillel. The school of Shammai maintains that not only is labor *on* the Sabbath prohibited, but one may not even initiate a process that proceeds automatically, on its own, *during* the Sabbath. The school of Hillel, however, permits this. The Talmud inquires into the scriptural support for the two positions.

Mishnah: The school of Shammai say: Ink, dyes and alkaline plants may not be steeped [in water in order to further the dyeing process] unless they can be dissolved while it is still daylight [before the Sabbath begins], but the school of Hillel permit it.

Talmud: And what is the reason of the school of Shammai [to prohibit]? "Six days shall you labor and do all your work" (Exod. 20.9)—complete *all* your work while it is still daylight [before the Sabbath, that is, during the six days of the week, and not on the Sabbath].

And what is the reason of the school of Hillel? "Six days shall you labor . . . and [the seventh] day" (Exod. 20.9–10)—[that is, you may complete your work on the seventh day—the Sabbath—so long as it is done as the automatic continuation of a process that began before the Sabbath] (y. Shab. 1:5 [3d–4a]).

How do the school of Hillel interpret the [verse used by the school of Shammai to justify] their reason? "Six days shall you labor and do all your work" [but not on the Sabbath]—this refers to working actually done by hand [and not automatically].

And how do the school of Shammai interpret the [verse used by the school of Hillel to justify] their reason? "Six days shall you labor . . . and on [the seventh] day"—this refers to [the following permitted process]: One may open a water-canal to a garden on the eve of the Sabbath [that is, before the Sabbath begins,] and [the garden] is watered [automatically] on the Sabbath.

Thus, each position must not only be justified on the basis of its own independent interpretation of the relevant biblical verses, but *it must account for the verses or phrases employed by its opponents.* This form of debate eventually made its way into nonlegal contexts, more often in the Babylonian Talmud. Ultimately, the legal point was seen to hinge on a methodological disagreement as to the proper interpretation of the biblical verse. This formal disagreement served to underline the essential biblical basis of these disputes.

Assessing Analogies

Since much of rabbinic interpretation is based on some form of analogy, there are cases in which the Rabbis were faced with competing analogies, and had to decide which to choose. When these choices were made early on, and appear later without explicit justifications, redactors must somehow account for them. Thus, for example, one midrashic text on Deut. 15.12 and Exod. 21.2 ("six years must he serve") proposes that a Hebrew slave may serve not only his master but his master's son, but not his master's heir.

Who whispered to you to include the son [in the "he shall serve" of the verse, as one whom the slave must serve] and to exclude the heir? I include the son who takes his father's place in regard to affiancing a Hebrew maidservant [as laid down in Exod. 21.9–10] and a field of inheritance [as per Lev. 25.25–28], and I exclude the heir who does not take the father's place [that is, the place of the master, who in this case is *not* the son of the father but merely his heir] and for a field of inheritance (Sifre Re'eh 118, ed. Finkelstein, pp. 177–178).

Thus, the rule regarding whom a Hebrew slave must serve may be likened to one in which only the son has a part, or to one in which (as in the case of Num. 27.6–11, which sets out the order of inheritance, though the son has priority) other heirs have a place. In this case, since the son has an exclusive right in the cases enumerated, he is assumed to have exclusive rights here too, and not merely priority as in the case of inheritance.

The Beginning of the End

Ironically, by the time Rava began his efforts at systematization, some of the options available were already being eliminated. A Babylonian version of an anecdote about the great second-generation 'amora' of the land of Israel, R. Yoḥanan, the most frequently cited authority in either Talmud, whose disciples made up the greater part of the third generation of 'amora'im, is depicted as declaring that the exposition of the letter vav was no longer possible.

R. Yohanan was [once] sitting and expounding: "Notar [a portion of a sacrifice left over beyond the prescribed time for eating it and which must be burnt on the third day, see Lev. 7.17] must be burnt in its [proper] time during the day; when not in its proper time, it may be burnt during the day or at night."

R. Eleazar [ben Pedat] raised an objection to R. Yohanan: " 'I only [know] that a child which must be circumcised on the eighth day must be circumcised during the day; how do I [know this of] a child circumcised on the ninth, tenth, eleventh or twelfth? It is stated: "And on the day" [Lev. 12:3].' And even one who does not expound a vav will expound a vav-heh ("and" and "the")."

[R. Yohanan] remained silent. After [R. Eleazar] left, R. Yohanan said to Resh Laqish: "Did you see [Eleazar] ben Pedat sitting and expounding like Moses in the name of the Almighty!"

Said Resh Laqish to him: "Is it then his [teaching]? It is really a baraita."

"Where is it taught?"

"In Torat Kohanim [= Sifra, the halakhic midrash on Leviticus]."

[R. Yohanan] went out, memorized it in three days and mastered it in three months (b. Yebam. 72b).

The parallel in the Talmud of the land of Israel is couched in different terms (y. Shab. 2:1 [4c]), but the essential point is that neither Talmud records any such exposition of a vav by any authority after R. Yohanan's time. (See b. Yebam. 68a,b for Rav and b. B. M. 8b, both first-generation Babylonian 'amora'im and senior to R. Yohanan.) R. Yohanan's decision thus seems to have marked a turning point in amoraic midrashic exposition.

This does not mean that 'amora'im abandoned the field of ribbuy—expounding extensions based on Hebrew particles or single let-

ters. Though we do not find the letter vav expounded for this purpose, R. Yohanan himself does expound other Hebrew prepositions and conjunctives: 'o, "or" (b. Shab. 63b), 'im, "if" (b. B. K. 43b), gam, "also" (b. 'Arak. 7a). But over time the 'amora'im did less and less of this type of exposition. On the other hand, we find authorities of the fourth generation, both in Israel and Babylonia, treating duplications in the Mishnah not too differently from the way they treated biblical verses. One example, which is expounded in both Talmuds, will illustrate the point.

Mishnah Shabbat 11:4: If one throws [an object over a distance of] four cubits in the sea, he is not liable [for transgressing the Sabbath law]. If there is a water pool and a public road traverses it, and one throws [an object] four cubits therein, he is liable. And what depth constitutes a pool? Less than ten handbreadths. If there is a water pool and a public road traverses it, and one throws [an object] four cubits therein, he is liable.

Gemara: One of the rabbis said to Rava: As for "traversing" [mentioned] twice, that is well, [as] it informs us this: (1) traversing with difficulty is designated "traversing" [for purposes of the Sabbath laws]; (2) use with difficulty is not designated use. But why state "pool" twice?—One refers to summer and one to winter, and both are necessary. For if only one were stated, I would say: That is only in summer, when people walk therein to cool themselves, but in winter [this is] not [the case]. And if we were told [this] of winter, [I would say that] they do not object [to wading through the pool], but not in summer.

The Talmud of the land of Israel on this Mishnah also adverts to this problem, and expounds the duplicate text in a similar way, and also in the name of a fourth-generation authority, R. Pinhas (y. Shab. 11:4 [13a]).

Why was it taught twice? R. Hanina in the name of R. Pinhas: [This text refers to a case in which there were] two pools, one through which people walked and one through which people did not walk, except when they were forced to, so that you do not say that since people do not walk through [it] except when they are forced to, it is not [considered] public ground but private ground; accordingly, you must say that it is public ground.

Thus, in the course of time, less and less recourse was made to the midrashic exposition of biblical verses, and more and more emphasis was given to extracting what information was available—even quasi-midrashically—from early rabbinic sources themselves. By the geonic period, under challenge from the Karaites, the system of halakhic midrash had closed down. Rava's work is to be dated closer to the beginning of this process than to its end, and he does make use of particular rabbinic exegetical principles. But, as we have seen, and as he admits, he cannot fill in every gap.

Nonlegal Interpretation

There is nothing like this systematic concern for nonlegal or "aggadic" interpretation in rabbinic literature, though here too the principle of omnisignificance holds sway. On the whole, the rabbinic collections of aggadic material were directed at the common people, and reflect their interests and concerns. Judging from this huge literature, theosophic and mystical concerns were then, as later, esoteric and limited to small numbers of adepts. Thus, the problems of interpreting the Bible as an omnisignificant text as described above were shaped by yet another concern: making the Bible relevant not only to rabbinic disciples but also to the nonscholarly audience who heard the Torah in synagogue rather than studying it in the bet midrash.

The Rabbis acknowledged the relative disproportion in the biblical text between rabbinic concerns and other material, as in this comment from R. Aḥa, perhaps the fourth-generation 'amora' in Israel of that name:

The conversation of the servants of the Patriarchs is more pleasing before the Holy One, blessed be He, than the Torah[-learning] of the[ir] descendants, for the passage [dealing with the journey] of Eliezer, [the servant of Abraham, in seeking a wife for Isaac takes up] two or three columns [of text in a Torah scroll], is said and repeated [i.e., the passage describes the journey and then quotes Eliezer describing the journey], while the [rule that] the blood of a [dead] creeping thing causes impurity as does its flesh, [which is] among the essential parts of the Torah (migupei Torah) [but is derived] from an inclusion [of one letter] (Gen. Rab. 60:32, ed. Theodor-Albeck, p. 650).

Later on another comment by the same sage is quoted, even more poignantly:

The foot-washing of the servants of the Patriarchs is more pleasing before the Holy One, blessed be He, than the Torah[-learning] of the[ir] descendants, for even the washing of [his] feet [in Gen. 24.32] must be recorded, [while the rule that] the blood of a [dead] creeping thing causes impurity as does its flesh, [which is] among the essential parts of the Torah (migupei Torah) [but is derived] from an inclusion [of one letter] (p. 651).

R. Aḥa's comment clearly calls attention to the disparity in Torah's treatment of halakhic matters versus the detail in the patriarchal narratives—and by extension, the non-halakhic parts of the Torah. But his intent is less clear. To his successors, the Torah could hardly be conceived as intending to devalue the halakhot derived by one letter, or the halakhic process in general. The case of the patriarchs, or the subjects of biblical narratives in general, must have an importance in God's scheme of things that warrants such attention to their doings.

This led, in later times, to the idea that the lives of the patriarchs prefigured the history of their descendants. The kernel of this idea may be seen in the Genesis narrative of the

Covenant Between the Pieces, where God informs Abram of the future Egyptian bondage, the exodus and the entrance into the land of Israel (Gen. ch 15). Thus, R. Aḥa (4th century), in describing the creation of Adam, concludes that God gives Adam his discharge after Adam's sin and says:

> This is a sign for you: just as you have come in judgment before Me and been discharged, so too your descendants will come in judgment before Me and I will give them their discharge. When? On Rosh Hashanah, [the Day of Judgment] (*Lev. Rab.* 29:1, ed. Margoliot, p. 669).

Without specifying this principle of patriarchal anticipation of the history of the people of Israel, R. Joshua of Sikhnin (4th century, a younger contemporary of R. Aḥa) comments on Abraham's battle with the Mesopotamian kings in Gen. ch 14:

> The Holy One, blessed be He, gave a sign to Abraham that whatever would befall him would befall his descendants. How? He chose Abraham from among his entire father's house . . . and he chose his descendants from the Seventy Nations (*Midrash Tanḥuma*).

On the whole, typical rabbinic midrash was intended to attract people and inculcate moral, ethical and religious values, particularly in preaching. In the process, a good deal of folkloric material was incorporated. At times, however, the folklore is brought in for its own sake, in order to appeal to the preacher's listeners. Thus, for example, in *Lev. Rab.* 19:6 (ed. Margaliot, p. 438), we find the following discussion regarding the name of Nebuchadnezzar's wife.

> What was the name of the wife of Nebuchadnezzar? R. Ḥananiah said: Semiram was her name; R. Abin said: Semiramis was her name; and the Rabbis said: Semiraʿam was her name, because she was born in *raʿam* during an earthquake [or, in thunder].

While the names come from Hellenistic sources, and at least one partly Hebrew folk-etymology was provided for one name, no moral lesson is drawn. The motive for the explanation of the names would seem to be the need to satisfy the curiosity of the listeners. In contrast, Noah's (scripturally anonymous) wife is identified with another biblical woman, and the name is expounded homiletically.

> "And the sister of Tubal Cain was Naamah" (Gen. 4.22). Said R. Abba ben Kahana: Naamah was the wife of Noah [the assonance of Noah and Naamah should not be overlooked], and why was she called Naamah? Because her deeds were pleasant (*neʿimim*). The rabbis said: [She] was another Naamah, who would play her tambourine sweetly for idol worship (*Gen. Rab.* 23:22, p. 224).

The purpose of this identification is more complex. It serves to connect two verses which are otherwise disconnected; it also serves to explain why Naamah is mentioned at all, since she plays no role in the events depicted by Scripture. And, finally, the identification allows the Rabbis to comment obliquely on the nature of the sinfulness of the generation before the flood. According to R. Abba ben Kahana, Noah, the righteous man, married a righteous woman, whose deeds were pleasant. According to the Rabbis, this Naamah was typical of her sinful generation, and her deeds helped bring on the flood. Needless to say, these identifications would also have satisfied the curiosity of the people who came to hear the scriptural portion expounded. Indeed, the Bible itself provides a precedent for such exegetical elaboration. The prophet Jehu ben Hanani is mentioned in 1 Kings 16.1–12, and his father, Hanani, appears only in his patronym. But in 2 Chron. 16.7, we find the father playing a more active role: "At that time Hanani the seer came to King Asa of Judah and said to him, 'Because you relied on the king of Aram and did not rely on the LORD your God, therefore the army of the king of Aram has slipped out of your hands.'" This then illustrates the rule expounded by R. Yoḥanan, that every prophet's father who is mentioned along with his son was also a prophet (*b. Meg.* 15a, *Lev. Rab.* 6:6, pp. 142–143). Such an assumption made sense in a society where sons most often followed their fathers' occupation. It also illustrates the idea that a person or family is to be judged as a whole: If a family is known for its piety, it (or, for that matter, a nation) is judged by its reputation. The result is the far-ranging rabbinic principle that "one attributes meritorious behavior to the meritorious (*megalgelin zekhut ʿal yedei zakai*), and sinful acts to the sinful" (*Sifre Num.* 114, p. 123) and its closely associated principle that if a person or nation performs a certain (minimally) meritorious or sinful deed, it is accounted as though she or they had performed a much greater one (*maʿaleh ʿalav/ʿalehen keʾilu*) (*Sifre Deut.* 253, p. 279).

In particular, when Scripture attributes a sinful act to an otherwise righteous character, or one whose reputation was considered, for one reason or another, sacrosanct, the Rabbis did not hesitate to reinterpret the relevant verse or verses. A case in point is David's adulterous relationship with Bathsheba and his plotting the death of her husband, Uriah the Hittite (a story omitted in Chronicles because it does not comport with David as an ideal king). A long disquisition on David is included as one of a long series of defenses of biblical characters to whom sin is imputed (*b. Shab.* 55b-56b).

R. Samuel ben Naḥmani said in R. Jonathan's name: Whoever says that David sinned is merely in error, for it is said, "And David behaved wisely in all his ways: and the LORD was with him" (1 Sam. 18.14). Is it possible that sin came to his hand, yet the divine Presence was with him? Then how do I interpret [the verse] "Wherefore have you despised the word of the LORD, to do that which is evil in His sight?" (2 Sam. 12.9)—he wished to do [evil] but did not.

Rav observed: Rabbi, who is descended from David, seeks to defend him! [Not so, for] the "evil" [mentioned] here is unlike any other evil [mentioned] elsewhere in the Torah. For of every other evil [mentioned] in the Torah it is written, "and he did," whereas here it is written, "to do"—this means that he desired to do, but did not (*b. Shab.* 56a).

The various verses that accuse David of adultery and murder are thereby reinterpreted; Uriah was guilty of disobeying the king's order to go home, and was therefore worthy of death as a rebel (see 2 Sam. ch 12). David was criticized for arranging his death in battle rather than having him arraigned before the Sanhedrin; again, his relationship with Bathsheba was not adulterous because all of David's soldiers gave their wives divorces before setting out to battle. Thus, Bathsheba was a divorced woman when David had his affair with her, and her husband was guilty of traitorous insubordination.

Unlike much of rabbinic midrash, which adds further layers of interpretation onto the plain meaning of the verse, the Rabbis' treatment of such incidents and verses run counter to that plain meaning. For the Rabbis and for the communities they represented, the stakes were simply too high to allow the plain sense to stand.

Similarly, at least for some Rabbis, the theological stakes were too high to maintain the plain sense of those verses which express an anthropomorphic view of God.

"And rested on the seventh day" (Exod. 20.11). But is He subject to such a thing as weariness? Has it not been said: "The creator of the ends of the earth is not faint or weary" (Isa. 40.28)? And it says, "He gives power to the faint" (Isa. 40.29). And it also says, "By the word of the LORD were the heavens made" (Ps. 33.6). How then can Scripture say, "And rested on the seventh day"? Rather, so to speak, God allowed it to be written about Him that He created His world in six days and rested on the seventh. Is it not an *a fortiori* argument? If He, for

Whom there is no weariness, allowed it to be written about Him that He created His world in six days and rested on the seventh, how much more should man, of whom it is written, "But man is born to toil" (Job 5.7), rest on the seventh day (*Mekhilta Yitro*, 7, end, ed. Lauterbach, vol. 2, pp. 255–256).

In this interpretation the Rabbis accomplish two objectives. First, any suggestion that weariness may be attributed to God is rejected, but, equally important, the verse in question is turned into one which stresses the importance of the Sabbath for humans.

Nevertheless, some Rabbis seem to have reveled in these anthropomorphic depictions of the Deity, and even added to them (*b. Ber.* 6a):

R. Abin son of R. Adda in the name of R. Isaac says: How do we know that the Holy One, blessed be He, puts on phylacteries (tefillin)? For it is said, "The Lord has sworn by His right hand, and by the arm of His strength" (Isa. 62.8). "By His right hand"—this [refers] to the Torah, for it is said, "At His right hand was a fiery law to them" (Deut. 33.2). "And by the arm of His strength"—this [refers] to the phylacteries, as it is said, "The Lord will give strength to His people" (Ps. 29.11). And how do we know that the phylacteries are a strength to Israel? For it is written, "And all the peoples of the earth shall see that the name of the Lord is called upon you, and they shall be afraid of you" (Deut. 28.11), and it has been taught: R. Eliezer the Great says: This refers to the phylactery of the head.

This is not meant as a metaphysical statement, however, for the Talmud goes on to inquire as to what verses are written on the parchments of God's phylacteries. According to R. Ḥiyya ben Abin, "And who is like Your people Israel, a unique nation on earth" (1 Chron. 17.21). The phylacteries become a visible symbol of the relationship of God and Israel, and God's love for His people.

God's love for Israel is one of the constant themes of aggadic interpretation. In a sense, we have seen it at work in the interpretation of the ancestral narratives as foreshadowings of the future history of the Jewish people. It also serves as a powerful exegetical tool for other nonlegal or nontheological passages. Any passage that has some relation to Israelite history, sociology, demography (as the various census lists), etc., may be viewed as a manifestation of God's love for His people. Such a love is expressed as a concern for anything that relates to the beloved.

"These were the marches of the Israelites" (Num. 33.1). A parable; to what may this be compared? To a king whose son was ill; he took him to one place to cure him, and on the way back, the father began to recount all the marches [they had undertaken], saying to him: Here we slept, here we were cold, here your head hurt. So too did the Holy One, blessed be He, say to Moses: Recount for them all the places they had angered Me. For that reason it is written: "These were the marches of the Israelites" (*Tanḥuma Mas'ei* 3).

Thus is a rather bare-bones list of camping places in the wilderness converted into an expression of God's love for Israel. This interpretive tool serves several functions: It explains the omnisignificant worth of many biblical passages by allegorizing them as reflecting in some way the relationship of God the Father to the Israelites; and in doing so, it responded to an urgent need for the reassurance of God's love for Israel and Israel's chosenness at a time when Christianity challenged both notions.

Conclusion

Scripture, according to the Rabbis, is the abiding evidence of God's presence and continued love for His people, but the rabbinic relationship to Scripture is not one of passive acceptance. Scripture provides the basic material and some of the ground rules for rabbinic interpretation, but the elements of

Scripture—passages, verses, words, even individual letters—are integrated in a way that is both scriptural *and* rabbinic. One consequence of this mutuality is the assumption that a reasoned argument has the force of a scriptural decree [*b. Pes.* 21b, *Ketub.* 22a, *B. K.* 46b, *Ḥul.* 114b, *Nid.* 25a]. The sovereignty of reason and of rabbinic authority is thereby affirmed.

It has been taught: On that day R. Eliezer brought forth every imaginable argument, but they did not accept them. [Finally, in frustration,] he said: If the law follows my opinion, let this carob-tree prove it! Thereupon the carob-tree was torn a hundred cubits out of its place—others affirm, four hundred cubits. No proof can be brought from a carob-tree, they retorted. Again he said to them: If the law agrees with my opinion, let the stream of water prove it! Thereupon the stream of water flowed backwards. No proof can be brought from a stream of water, they rejoined. Again he urged: If the law agrees with my opinion, let the walls of the schoolhouse prove it! Thereupon the walls inclined to fall. But R. Joshua rebuked them, saying: When scholars are engaged in a legal dispute, what have you to interfere? Hence [the walls] did not fall, out of deference to R. Joshua, nor did they resume standing, in deference to R. Eliezer, and they still stand inclined. Finally he said to them: If the law follows my opinion, let it be proved from Heaven! Thereupon a heavenly echo cried out: Why do you dispute with R. Eliezer, seeing that in all matters the law agrees with his opinion? But R. Joshua arose and exclaimed: "It is not in Heaven!" (Deut. 30.12).

What did he mean by that? Said R. Jeremiah: Since the Torah has already been given at Mount Sinai, we pay no attention to a heavenly echo, because You have long since written in the Torah at Mount Sinai: "After the majority must one incline" (Exod. 23.2).

R. Nathan met Elijah [the Prophet] and asked him, What did the Holy One, blessed be He, do at that time [in response to this statement]? He laughed [with joy], he replied, saying: My sons have defeated Me, My sons have defeated Me! (*b. B. M.* 59b.)

Appendix: The Orders and Tractates of the Mishnah

Zera'im ("Seeds"):
Berakhot
Pe'ah
Demai
Kil'ayim
Shevi'it
Terumot
Ma'aserot
Ma'aser Sheni
Ḥallah
'Orlah
Bikkurim
Mo'ed ("Season" or "Festival"):
Shabbat
'Eruvin
Pesaḥim
Shekalim
Yoma
Sukkah
Betzah
Rosh Ha-Shanah
Ta'anit
Megillah
Mo'ed Katan
Ḥagigah
Nashim ("Women"):
Yebamot
Ketubbot
Nedarim
Nazir
Sotah
Gittin
Kiddushin
Nezikin ("Damages"):
Bava Kamma
Bava Metzi'a
Bava Batra
Sanhedrin

Makkot
Shevu'ot
'Eduyyot
'Avodah Zarah
'Avot
Horayot
Kodoshim ("Sacred Things"):
Zevahim
Menahot
Hullin
Bekhorot
'Arakhin
Temurah
Keritot
Me'ilah
Tamid

Middot
Kinnim
Teharot ("Purifications")
Kelim
'Ohalot
Nega'im
Parah
Teharot
Mikva'ot
Niddah
Makhshirin
Zavim
Tevul Yom
Yadayim
'Uktzin

[YAAKOV ELMAN]

Midrash and Jewish Interpretation

It is often remarked that what is Jewish about the Bible is not the Bible itself, not even the Hebrew text of the Bible, but the Jewish *interpretation* of the Bible. And of all the types of Jewish biblical interpretation, none have been identified so closely with the Jewish Bible as midrash. Indeed, the two have been so closely identified that for some, midrash has become a virtual trope for Judaism, a figure for all that is distinctive and different about the Jews, their religion, and culture.

Midrash is the specific name for the activity of biblical interpretation as practiced by the Rabbis of the land of Israel in the first five centuries of the common era. The Hebrew word derives from the root, *d-r-sh*, which literally means "to inquire" or "to search after." In the earlier books of the Bible, the root is used to refer to the act of seeking out God's will (e.g., Gen. 25.22; Exod. 18.15), particularly through consulting a figure like Moses or a prophet or another type of oracular authority. By the end of the biblical period, the locus for that search appears to have settled on the text of the Torah where, it was now believed, God's will for the present moment was to be found. Thus the scribe Ezra, we are told in the book

by his name, "had dedicated himself to study the Teaching *(torah)* of the LORD so as to observe it" (Ezra 7.10). The Hebrew word for "study" used in the verse, *lidrosh,* has the same root as midrash. By late antiquity, midrash had come to designate Bible study in general. The Rabbis called their academy a *bet midrash,* literally "a house of study," and from such usage, midrash came to be the term the Rabbis themselves employed to designate the way they studied Scripture and interpreted its meaning.

In its primary sense, then, midrash refers to an *activity,* a mode of study. Somewhat confusingly, the same word is also applied to the products of that activity, namely, individual interpretations—a specific midrash of a verse or word, for example. These midrashic interpretations originally circulated and were transmitted orally, both in rabbinic schools and through synagogue sermons. Around the 3rd or 4th century CE, the oral traditions of the Rabbis began to be collected in literary anthologies, and these collections also came to be known as midrashim, as in *Midrash Rabbah,* the folio-sized collection of homiletical midrashim on the Torah which was first published in Constantinople in 1512. For the past hundred years, however, some scholars have appropriated the word "midrash" as a collective term to describe ancient biblical interpretation in general. For example, the French scholar Renee Bloch used the term "midrash" to describe any ancient "meditation on the sacred texts," an activity that could be found equally in the Aramaic translations of the Bible, in many of the books of the Apocrypha and Pseudepigrapha, and in the New Testament, as well as in later rabbinic texts. And still more recently, the term has passed into popular circulation as a name for all "creative" interpretations of the Bible that seek to move beyond the historical, "original" sense of the biblical text. In this usage, the word "midrash" stands for everything from novelistic retellings of biblical episodes to postmodernist essayistic explorations of Genesis and Exodus, New Age homilies, and contemporary poems that re-imagine the biblical text.

Language, of course, follows usage, not the strictures of scholars. Even if the latter (including myself) would prefer to restrict the use of the word "midrash" to the ancient biblical interpretations of the Rabbis—who, if they did not invent the term, nonetheless were the first ones to use it extensively—scholars do not control the fates of words. On the other hand, while contemporary efforts at "neo-midrash" are not direct descendants of the classical midrashic tradition of the Rabbis, it is also not entirely inappropriate to call these latter-day compositions living examples of the midrashic "spirit," motivated by some of the same desires that inspired the Rabbis to interpret the Bible. Yet precisely how to define that "spirit" is not an easy task. Perhaps the closest thing to a definition might be the classical midrashic statement attributed to the early sage Akiva (died ca. 135 CE), a comment on Deut. 32.47, "[This law] is no empty thing for you (lo' davar reik mekem)." Exploiting the fact that the preposition mekem literally means "from," not "for," you, Akiva explained: "If it seems empty, it is from you—on account of your own failure—for you do not know how

to study (lidrosh) its meaning properly" (Gen. Rab. 1:14). The imperative facing every Bible interpreter is, to paraphrase E. M. Forster, to connect, to find the text's significance for the present moment, to make it speak to us now. Nothing in the Bible is without such significance. If the interpreter can't find it, the fault is his or her own, not the Bible's. Akiva's elaboration might be called the credo of Jewish biblical interpretation.

In fact, the precise relation of midrash to other types of Jewish biblical interpretation and to Jewish tradition at large involves a truly complex set of questions, and these become even more complicated if the relationship of midrash is considered in connection with the competing traditions of Christian and Islamic interpretation. Ultimately, these questions boil down to some of the most fundamental issues that involve the study of biblical interpretation in general, and Jewish interpretation in particular. What does it mean to call a type of interpretation like midrash "Jewish"? Is there a distinctively or uniquely "Jewish" way of reading the Bible? Is a Jewish reading of the Bible distinguished merely by its content and by the theological beliefs it brings to its reading, or is there something intrinsically different about the very procedures of interpretation that Jews employ as opposed to those of, say, Christian readers of the Bible?

Within the context of this *Jewish Study Bible*, it would seem especially opportune to consider these questions even if there are no definitive answers to them. We may begin with a historical sketch of midrash's development. The origins of midrash lie in biblical tradition itself where many biblical passages self-consciously look back upon earlier passages and, in one way or another, reinterpret their meaning. The book of Chronicles, for example, consciously recasts the history of the earlier books of Samuel and Kings, adding some episodes and omitting others, and generally spinning the earlier narrative in the course of retelling it in a politically tendentious direction amenable to its author. Elsewhere, many "later" verses in the Bible recycle allusions and imagery from "earlier" biblical texts in order to apply them to new contexts and situations. The laws of marital divorce become the imagery to describe God's punishment of the people of Israel (cf., e.g., Deut. 24.1–4 and Jer. 3.1); the exodus from Egypt (Exod. chs 1–15), the paradigm for all future redemptions (see, for example, Isa. 43.16–20; 51.9–11; Ezek. ch 20).

In a very few cases it is possible even to see how certain textual "problems" are solved within the Bible itself. For example, in the year 605 BCE, some twenty years before the destruction of the First Temple and the exile of the Judeans to Babylonia, the prophet Jeremiah prophesied that Judea "shall be a desolate ruin, and those nations shall serve the king of Babylon seventy years" (Jer. 25.11). In a second prophecy, somewhat later, he went on to prophesy that "when Babylon's seventy years are over, I will fulfill to you My promise of favor—to bring you back to this place" (29.10). And some seventy years later, in 538 BCE, when the Judean exiles did indeed return to Judea from Babylonia, they must doubtless have believed that Jeremiah's prophecy had been fulfilled. Some 370 years later, however, around the year 165 BCE, in despair over the Hellenistic persecution of their religious practices, Jews had greater difficulty believing in the fulfillment of Jeremiah's promise of redemption even if they were physically living in the land of Israel. The author of the book of Daniel, in order to bolster faith in the apocalypse he believed was imminent, reinterpreted Jeremiah's earlier prophecy so that seventy years became seventy "weeks" of years—490 years, in other words—a date that brought the ancient prophecy close enough to his own time so as to convince his audience of its truth. Or to give a second example of a different type of "interpretation," here is a case where two earlier verses seemed to a later biblical author to contradict each other: Exod. 12.8 stipulates emphatically that the Passover sacrifice must be roasted (tzli 'esh). Speaking about the same sacrifice, however, Deut. 16.7 says, "You shall cook (uvishalta) it"—a verb

implying that the meat should be boiled (as in a stew). 2 Chron. 35.13, obviously troubled by the discrepancy between the two Torah verses, "solved" the textual problem (if not the culinary one) by maintaining both locutions: The Jews "cooked the paschal sacrifice in fire" (vayvashlu hapesah ba'esh)—"they boiled the paschal sacrifice in fire" (which probably means that they braised it).

The scholar Michael Fishbane, who has exhaustively studied these and similar cases in the Bible, has described them as part of a larger phenomenon which he calls innerbiblical exegesis (see "Inner-biblical Interpretation," pp. 1829–35). Although most of these examples are not, strictly speaking, exegeses (insofar as they do not explain or clarify anything about the earlier verse), they nonetheless exhibit certain tendencies—inner dynamics, as it were—that are, at the least, exegetical reflexes. These include the tendencies (as we have seen) to harmonize conflicting or discordant verses; to reemploy and reapply biblical paradigms and imagery to new cases; to reinvest "old" historical references with "new" historical contexts; and to integrate nonhistorical portions of the Bible within the larger context of biblical history (for example, by giving individual psalms historical superscriptions that "identify" the precise biblical episode during which David composed the psalm; e.g., Pss. 18 and 34).

Once the Bible was closed, Fishbane argues, these inner-biblical tendencies emerged as full-fledged, consciously applied interpretive techniques (demonstrating, if nothing else, the deep continuity of early postbiblical interpretation with the preceding tradition). Our earliest genuine commentaries on the Bible are the pesharim, or apocalyptic commentaries, found among the Dead Sea Scrolls at Qumran, and the allegorical treatises on the Bible written by Philo of Alexandria. The vast amount of early postbiblical interpretation is found, however, not in formal commentaries but in nonexegetical works that span the entire range of ancient postbiblical Jewish literature. These include the Aramaic Targumim (or translations); the various works of the Apocrypha and Pseudepigrapha which claim to "fill in" missing episodes or accounts from the Bible; and the various types of compositions sometimes called "the Re-Written Bible," works like the *Genesis Apocryphon*, the book of *Jubilees*, and Pseudo-Philo's *Biblical Antiquities*. These last works claim merely to "retell" the biblical narrative. They do so, however, by adding in, without comment, numerous details and events nowhere to be found in the Bible itself that are really implied interpretations, that is, solutions to "problems" ancient readers may have had with the biblical text.

Such is the context within which rabbinic midrash emerged in Roman Palestine as one type of Jewish exegesis among many others in the first centuries of the common era. We know very little about the inner history of midrash or about its practice, presumably in schools, academies, and synagogues. The one thing we do know is that, with a few scattered exceptions, the Rabbis did not explicitly theorize about their mode of interpretation or formally legislate its procedures. As a result, nearly everything we can say about midrash must be adduced from the texts themselves.

Generally speaking, the underlying interpretive assumptions that the Rabbis brought to midrash were not different from those of their nonrabbinic contemporaries, Jewish or Gentile. As scholars have shown repeatedly over the last century, the Rabbis shared hermeneutical techniques and procedures with their Greco-Roman neighbors as well as with the larger and more ancient Near Eastern culture into which ancient Judaism was born. Midrash dealing with halakhah, or legal matters, uses many of the same hermeneutical principles used by Greek and Roman jurists, and the Rabbis seem to have borrowed at least the names for some of those principles from their pagan contemporaries. In the realm of aggadah—narrative and lore—midrash applied to the Bible techniques known to be used in ancient literary and dream interpretation. Such, for example, seems to be the origin of *gematria*, perhaps the most "notorious"

type of hermeneutical technique in midrash wherein the numerical sum of a word's letters is used to decode its meaning. A good example of this type of technique is an interpretation attributed to R. Levi for the word *'ekhah* ("alas"), the first word in the book of Lamentations, a book that the Rabbis read not only as a lament but also as a prophecy of the destruction of the Temple. The numerical sum of the word's four letters (*alef* = 1; *yod* = 10; *kaf* = 20; *heh* = 5) is 36, and this number, according to R. Levi, points to the 36 transgressions punishable by excommunication that the Jews committed, thereby bringing upon themselves the destruction of the Temple. The unusual word *'ekhah*, with its archaic elongated form (rather than the shorter, more common *'ekh*) was understood, in other words, to be the hermeneutical key to the meaning of the entire scroll of Lamentations—the reason the Jews were forced to lament their fate. Along the same lines, in a related but different form of interpretation— *notarikon* (literally, stenographic interpretation), or interpretation by acrostics—ben Azzai used the same word's four letters as a key to showing that the Jews were not punished until they had denied the One (*alef*) God; transgressed all Ten (*yod*) Commandments; spurned circumcision (which was given after twenty [*kaf*] generations), and—on top of everything else!—rejected all the commandments in the Five (*heh*) Books of Moses. Both types of hermeneutical principles are attested in ancient handbooks for dream-interpreters.

Beyond these particular techniques, however, nearly all ancient readers of the Bible also shared four basic beliefs about the nature of Scripture, as James Kugel has cogently argued. First, they believed that the Bible was essentially a cryptic document—that its true meaning was not to be found on the surface but had to be discovered within the text, and that this discovery required special skills and wisdom. (In this, ancient readers of the Bible would have found themselves in agreement with ancient philosophers for whom it was no less axiomatic that all truth is obscure, never obvious or manifest to all; otherwise, anybody could be a philosopher or, for that matter, a scriptural exegete!) Second, the Bible was believed to be a perfect document, without contradiction, inconsistency, or superfluity. What might seem to be a contradiction or to be superfluous, even a word or phrase, was really an occasion—for some, a tip-off—for interpretation. Third, the Bible is always relevant—that is to say, its true meaning is always one that has import for the present moment. Nothing in the Bible— neither genealogies nor prophecies—is in Scripture for purely historical reasons, preserved for its antiquarian interest alone. Fourth, the Bible was believed to be of divine origin. As Kugel notes, however, this last feature was probably the least simple, since the Bible's divinity was not seen necessarily to preclude Moses' authorship. Furthermore, attributing divinity to the Bible means little if one does not define the nature of that divinity more closely. The God whom the Rabbis believed authored the Bible was hardly the same author as the God of an early Christian reader of the Bible like Origen.

Still, while the Rabbis shared these assumptions about the Bible with other ancient readers, Jews and Christians alike, they also brought some distinctive convictions of their own to their study. First and foremost, the Rabbis believed that the Bible—or what they called the Written Torah—was only one of two revelations God had given to the children of Israel at Mt. Sinai. Alongside the Written Torah, they believed, God had also revealed to the Israelites an Oral Torah which, as its name indicates, was delivered and transmitted orally. Precisely how to define the Oral Torah is one of the great debates among Jewish scholars. For our present purposes we may say that it comprises everything that the Rabbis believed was "Judaism" that is not *explicitly* written in the Torah; admittedly, this is a vast and heterogeneous body of material that encompasses everything from the many laws not spelled out in the Bible to the Rabbis' own beliefs and theology as well as all their folk wisdom and lore. Midrash itself is part of the Oral Torah, but the most important fact for understanding the role of the Oral Torah *in* midrash is that, for the Rabbis, these two Torahs—the Written and the Oral—were understood to be complementary. The "relevance" of the Written Torah for the Rabbis lay, we may say, in its application as Oral Torah; the two were not only in absolute agreement but deeply intertwined and mutually embedded. As a result, a great part of the Rabbis' midrashic efforts are devoted either to finding the roots of the Oral Torah in the Written Torah, or to elucidating the hidden truths of the Written Torah so as to make it yield the insights of what they already knew to be Oral Torah.

Nowhere is this more evident than in midrash halakhah, or legal exegesis. One passage will suffice to illustrate the point—a series of interpretations connected with the laws of kashrut, the dietary laws, and specifically the regulations pertaining to the separation of meat and milk products. Few laws are more closely associated with classical Judaism. Yet the source of these laws is a single injunction in the entire Bible, "You shall not boil a kid in its mother's milk" (Exod. 23.19) which, as we know today, was originally a cultic regulation, not a dietary rule. Curiously, that injunction also happens to be repeated verbatim twice more in the Bible (Exod. 34.26; Deut. 14.21), raising the additional problem of the verses' superfluity: Why say the same thing three times? Not surprisingly, the Rabbis exploited the multiple appearances of the injunction in order to expand the range of the single law. In the *Mekhilta* (*Kaspa* 5, Lauterbach III, 187–190), the earliest collection of midrashim on the book of Exodus, nine interpretations are offered to explain why the verse is repeated, and seven more simply to explain the full significance of the Exodus verse alone. Here is a small sampling of the interpretations:

R. Jonathan says: Why is this law stated in three places? Once to apply to domestic animals, once to apply to the beast of chase, and once to apply to fowl.

Abba Ḥanin said in the name of R. Eliezer: Why is this law stated in three places? Once to apply to large cattle, once to apply to goats, and once to apply to sheep. . . .

R. Simon ben Yoḥai says: Why is this law stated in three places? One is a prohibition against eating it, one is a prohibition against deriving any benefit from it, and one is a prohibition against the mere cooking of it . . .

R. Yosi the Galilean: Scripture says, "You shall not eat anything that dies a natural death" (Deut. 14.21), and in the same passage, it is said, "You shall not boil a kid in its mother's milk." [From this it follows that] the flesh of any animal which is forbidden to be eaten if the animal dies a natural death [and is not ritually slaughtered according to the laws of kashrut] is also forbidden to be cooked with milk. Now one might think that fowl, since it becomes forbidden to eat if it dies a natural death, should also be forbidden to be cooked with milk. Scripture, however, stipulates, "in its mother's milk." This excludes fowl because it has no mother's milk. And the unclean animal [an animal like pig that Scripture forbids one to eat in any case] is also excluded from the prohibition [of cooking it with milk] because it is forbidden to be eaten whether it is ritually slaughtered properly or whether it dies a natural death.

The first two opinions in the passage use "the extra verses"—the multiple occurrences of the verse—to extend its application from a goat, the actual subject of the verse, to other species of animals. R. Jonathan and Abba Ḥanin both adopt the same interpretive strategy, but they divide the animal kingdom in different cuts, as it were. The third opinion, of Rabbi Simon ben Yoḥai, uses the extra verses to extend the prohibition from cooking milk and meat together (which is itself already an interpretation, since the biblical verse prohibits only cooking a kid in its mother's milk) to eating it

and even deriving benefit from it (by, for example, selling meat and milk cooked together); this interpretation takes the biblical verse even closer to the complete dietary regulation in its full rabbinic form.

Now clearly, these opinions are being used to justify and to legitimate existing practices, which must have developed out of their own logic. The interpretations were not invented to derive the practices anew or for the first time. There is simply no way that any interpreter could have looked at the three identical verses and extrapolated from them the different prohibitions that, say, R. Simon bar Yoḥai proposes. With the fourth and final interpretation of R. Yosi the Galilean, however, the interpretations take a very different turn. The very form and style of Yosi's interpretation is of a very different nature than the first three—not only more expansive but also more academic in tone. The interpretation is based on the fact that Deut. 14.21 contains not only the prohibition against boiling a kid in its mother's milk but also the additional prohibition against eating an animal that has died a natural death and not been ritually slaughtered. From the fact that the two prohibitions are stated in the same verse, R. Yosi initially hypothesizes that all animals that fall under one prohibition should fall under the other one as well. This would seem to be a completely unexceptionable assumption, but R. Yosi himself immediately argues against it—and here the real gist of his interpretation emerges. For the verse prohibiting boiling a kid in milk explicitly states that the milk must be "its mother's," thereby excluding fowl from the prohibition since, as R. Yosi explains, they do not give milk. Similarly, he continues, an unclean animal—that is, an animal like pig that cannot be eaten under any circumstances—also does not fall under the prohibition, which is to say, it *could* be boiled in its mother's milk as long as one didn't eat it!

The structure of argument in this interpretation is very different from that in the first three. Essentially, R. Yosi builds upon the contiguity of the two prohibitions in the same verse to draw a general principle, and then uses that generalization to highlight a specific detail in the same verse ("its mother's milk") to prove an exception to the generalization. This technique (in Hebrew known as *kelal uferat*, a general rule followed by a particular) is one of the legal principles that the Rabbis share in common with ancient jurists in general. Yet even more striking about Yosi's interpretation, which *excludes* fowl from the prohibition, is the fact that it conflicts with that of R. Jonathan, who *did* include fowl under the prohibition. Exactly what is at stake in this disagreement is intriguing but unclear— whether their dispute really extends to practice (for some contemporary Jewish readers, it would be wonderful news to learn that a great sage like R. Yosi ate chicken with dairy products!), or whether it is a purely theoretical, academic argument. The more relevant observation to make is that the editor of the midrashic collection himself makes no note of the disagreement. He records the two interpretations along with the others as though there were absolutely no significant difference between them, no disagreement, no inconsistency.

This feature is common to the editing of many midrashic collections, but nowhere is it more the case than in midrash aggadah, that is, interpretations dealing with legend and lore, the vast terrain of nonlegal and homiletical material which effectively includes everything in rabbinic tradition from narrative to theology. In theory, midrash aggadah does not differ substantively or methodologically from midrash halakhah, and most midrashic collections mix halakhah and aggadah indiscriminately. As rabbinic literature developed, however, midrash became increasingly identified with aggadah, and it is for its aggadic interpretations that midrash has become most famous (or infamous, depending on your perspective) for its creative, playful, and multiple interpretations.

As a typical example of such multiple interpretations, consider the following passage. Gen. 25.19–36.42 is largely devoted to the story of Jacob and Esau and their rivalry from the time of their conception to their mature middle age. This rivalry began *in utero*. Rebekah, like all the matriarchs, cannot initially conceive, but once she does become pregnant with the two boys, Scripture tells us, *vayitrotzetzu habanim bekirbah*, "the children struggled in her womb" (Gen. 25.22). On this phrase, *Gen. Rab.*, the classical midrash on Genesis, offers the following four interpretations:

R. Yoḥanan and R. Shimon ben Lakhish [both offered opinions]. R. Yoḥanan said: This one ran (*ratz*) to kill the other, and the other ran (*ratz*) to kill the first one. [Namely, R. Yoḥanan associates the word *vayitrotzetzu* with the word for "run" (*ratz*).]

R. Shimon ben Lakhish said: This one permitted [what was forbidden] by command (*hitir tzivuyav*) to the other, and the other one permitted [what was forbidden] by command to the first [meaning, in other words, that from the beginning each one's laws and practices seem to have been diametrically opposed, in conflict with each other. The interpretation puns *vayitrozetzu* and *hitir tzivuyav*; say the two words quickly, and they'll begin to sound alike.]

R. Berechyah said in the name of R. Levi: Lest you think that it was only after they left the womb that the one attacked the other, [this verse teaches us] that even while they were in the womb [Esau] raised his fist (*zeirteih*) against [Jacob]. This is what is written, "The wicked are defiant (*zoru*) from the womb" (Ps. 58.4) [playing on the word *zoru* and the Aramaic word for fist. This interpretation seems to emphasize the word *bekirbah*, "in her womb" as the basis for its interpretation.]

"*Vayitrotzetzu habanim bekirbah*" ("the children struggled in her womb") means that they tried to run out of her womb. When Rebekah passed by a pagan temple, Esau would kick her to let him leave; this is what is written, "The wicked are defia (*zoru*) from the womb" (Ps. 58.4) [pla on the word *zoru* and the second hal term 'avodah zarah, literally "strange worship," i.e., idolatry]. And when Rebekah passed by a synagogue and a study-hall (bet midrash), Jacob would kick her to let him out, this is what is written, "Before I created you in the womb, I knew you (yedatikha)" (Jer. 1.5) [probably reading the last phrase as yidatikha, "I caused you to know"] (Gen. Rab., ed. J. Theodor and H. Albeck, 63:6, pp. 682–83).

Each of these four interpretations offers a slightly different though equally typical midrashic way of reading the word vayitrotzetzu: Some break it up into smaller words like ratz ("run"), or pun it with a similarly sounding phrase like hitir tzivuyav ("permitted the commands"), or connect the Genesis base-verse with another verse in Scripture (e.g., Ps. 58.4) which, through more punning interpretations, is enlisted to gloss the meaning of the base-verse. In the very last interpretation of Jer. 1.5, the anonymous Rabbi exploits the fact that the Hebrew text of the Bible in a Torah scroll records only consonantal letters, and no vowels—a fact that, somewhat ironically, now allows the midrashic reader to change the vowels of certain biblical words and thus their meaning, as here from the active form, yedatikha ("I knew") to the causative yidatikha ("I caused you to know").

What leads the Rabbis to base so many of their interpretations on phonetic puns, on associations between the sound of a word like vayitrotzetzu and other similarly sounding words and phrases? In part, this strongly aural dimension of midrash may derive from the Bible's own use of oral puns and sound-play—a habit facilitated by the very nature of spoken Hebrew—but it also probably reflects the way the Bible was learned by the Rabbis. Most likely, Jews in the land of Israel during the rabbinic period did not study the Bible by reading it directly in scrolls, which were doubtless scarce and, because of their size, rather unwieldy; rather, they learned Scripture from hearing it read aloud during the synagogue service or in classes in the acad-

emy. From such repeated auditory experiences, one assumes the Rabbis memorized the scriptural text and carried it around in their heads as a heard text. As we now know, a text learned this way is "known" differently than one learned from having read it on a page (or scroll). For one thing, the page itself does not figure as a primary unit in one's memory of the text. Another thing is that one "hears" the text rather than "sees" it (even in the mind's eye), and as a consequence, one is more likely to associate like-sounding words or phrases or verses (the latter probably having been the main units of memorization) rather than those connected by visual elements (either physical proximity in the written text or on a page, or matters of orthography). And while it may seem paradoxical, it is in fact perfectly explicable why the Rabbis tend to atomize verses or words into their constituent sounds, and simultaneously to associate otherwise unrelated verses or phrases on the basis of shared phonetic elements; in both cases, they are responding to the phonetic/aural element of the text. This is not to say that the Rabbis did not know the Bible as a written text; it was, in fact, the only text normatively written down in rabbinic culture. It was, however, also the only text in rabbinic culture to be regularly read aloud from the written scroll. Indeed, the Bible's most common name in rabbinic Hebrew is miqra', "that which is read aloud."

Midrash, then, is very much an exegesis of the heard text. This does not, of course, explain everything in midrash. For while they are willing to take the boldest liberties in interpreting Scripture, the Rabbis are also the closest "readers" of Scripture imaginable, with an almost preternatural sensitivity to the least "bump" in the scriptural text—an unnecessary repetition or superfluity, any kind of syntactical or lexical peculiarity, a mere hint at something unseemly in the way of behavior, or the smallest possibility of an inconsistency between verses or even between a verse and what the Rabbis believed must be the case.

Since we have been considering Jacob and Esau, let us look at an interpretation of another verse from their narrative, from the story in Gen. ch 27 of Jacob's deception of Isaac, where he fools his aged blind father into giving him the blessing intended for Esau, the first-born son. Jacob's wiliness (of which this episode was not the first case) may or may not have been in itself a cause for embarrassment to the Rabbis, but Gen. 27.19 posed a very concrete problem for them. In response to Isaac's question, "Which of my sons are you?" Jacob tells his father an outright lie, "I am Esau, your first-born." How does the midrash deal with this problem?

The answer is quite simple: By rereading the verse so that it no longer says, "I am Esau, your first-born" but "I am [that is, Jacob]; Esau is your first-born" (*Tanḥ.*, ed. S. Buber, Genesis, p. 131). Now this interpretation may seem overly clever, especially as an attempt to whitewash Jacob's reputation, but in fact the interpretation exploits a genuine "problem" in the verse. For why does Jacob need to tell his father that Esau is his first-born son? As an answer to Isaac's question, the detail is irrelevant; and as a piece of familial information, it is obviously something Isaac knows. Further, the Hebrew word that Jacob uses in the verse to identify himself, *'anokhi*, "I," is itself noteworthy as a somewhat archaic locution that every Rabbi would have instantly recognized as the opening word of the Decalogue—indeed, as the word with which God introduces Himself: "I am/*'anokhi* the LORD your God" (Exod. 20.2). (In fact, another, somewhat more expansive version of this midrash states that Jacob said, "I am he who will receive the Decalogue, but Esau is your first-born" [*Gen. Rab.* 65:18, p. 730].) Faced with all these textual "facts," along with the ethical problem raised by Jacob's outright lie, the midrashic reading might appear almost inevitable.

Almost, but not quite. Did the Rabbis believe that this was the "real" meaning of the verse, or what Jacob actually meant to say? This question takes us to the very heart of midrash and its hermeneutics. Some scholars have suggested that midrashim like this are midrashic "jokes," the humor lying in the self-conscious dissonance between what the Rabbis know the Bible is saying, and what they wish it to say. This is undoubtedly true: What midrash continually demonstrates is the possibility that Scripture may mean something other than what it says. But there is also a way in which the playfulness of midrash may be interpreted as the Rabbis' sense of the playfulness of Scripture itself. After all, could God have ever really allowed Jacob to mislead Isaac and let the blessing be given to the wrong son? Could Isaac, *our* ancestor, have been so easily misled? Must he not have known to whom he was giving the blessing? Were not Isaac and Jacob merely *pretending* to deceive and to be deceived? Isn't this pretence at deception the subtext of the story in which Isaac and Jacob act out their roles of deceiver and deceived so that providential history, the history of Israel and of the Jews, can take place despite history?

The Rabbis, after all, fully knew who Jacob and Esau *really* were—not just biblical figures, not merely their ancestors. They were also the progenitors of Israel and Rome—the latter was almost as ancient an identification as the former—and, in a certain sense, they *were* Judaism and Rome. "The voice is the voice of Jacob, yet the hands are the hands of Esau," Isaac announces as the disguised Jacob approaches (Gen. 27.22). On which the midrash comments: "Jacob attains domination through his voice [i.e., the power of language], and Esau through [the power of] his hands." R. Yehuda bar Ilai is said to have added that R. Judah the Prince interpreted the latter verse in even more contemporary terms: "The voice of Jacob cries out for what the hands of Esau have done to him" (*Gen. Rab.* 65:21, pp. 733–34, 740). The Rabbis knew that the story of Jacob and Esau and their rivalry was not simply biblical history. It was also their own history, the contemporary reality in which they had to struggle daily merely to survive.

With this understanding of the hermeneutical background behind midrash, let us return to the question with which we began this essay: What is Jewish about midrash? It would be tempting to say that interpretations like the preceding one, identifying Jacob with Judaism and Esau with Rome, point to the inherently Jewish nature of midrash. This is certainly true of the content of the interpretation, but it is worth recalling that ancient and medieval Christian students of the Bible used the same hermeneutical principle to identify Jacob with the church and Esau with Judaism. The same is true by and large of the ancient Jewish and Christian interpretations of the Song of Songs; both traditions interpret the poem as a love song between God and His chosen nation—the major difference being that in one case the beloved nation is Israel, in the other Christianity (or the church). Is the difference between Jewish and Christian interpretation then merely one of theological preferences?

Some scholars have posited the differences between the two interpretive traditions as being that between midrash and allegory. In fact, over the past twenty years, as they have awakened to the existence of midrash, literary theorists in particular have sought to see in rabbinic hermeneutics an alternative mode of interpretation to allegory. Where the latter is said to posit the existence of a reference or meaning "behind" the text as a kind of static metaphysical presence, midrash has been celebrated for seeing meaning "in front" of the text, in the intertextual play between verses, in the deferral of a single absolute meaning in favor of a multiplicity of provisional and possible meanings, and not least of all, for its far more open complicity between the interpreter and the act of interpretation as a subjective exercise whose interest lies less in the outcome of interpretation than in the process itself. Some scholars have even identified midrash with a kind of uniquely Jewish "ontology," or at least a mode of thinking whose difference from the so-called Greco-Christian logocentric tradition, usually identified with allegory, has been seen as closer to that of poststructuralism.

The difficulty with this comparison is not only that its view of midrash is overly romanticized but that it fails to take into account the fact that midrash is itself a form of allegory—not philosophical allegory, to be sure, but nonetheless a form of interpretation that seeks to show how the text means something other than what it says. In this, midrash is not different from other types of ancient interpretation. There is, in fact, much in early Christian interpretation from the New Testament itself through Augustine and the Antiochene fathers that is midrash-like. The main hermeneutical difference between the two is that Christian exegesis is far more systematic. Because of its greater intimacy with classical philosophical culture, Christian interpretation is heavily theorized and more programmatic (and to that extent, more obviously tendentious than rabbinic interpretation). It is also driven, as it were, by a different set of anxieties. The main anxiety for Christian interpreters is the knowledge that the New Testament is indeed a belated document, a late-comer, as it were, and hence the main challenge faced by Christian exegetes is to prove that the New Testament is in fact the key to understanding the Old Testament, and that the latter cannot properly be understood without the full knowledge afforded by the New Testament. In contrast, the anxiety driving the Rabbis is the worry that the Bible itself foresees their rejection and obsolescence; hence the constant challenge they face is to find through midrash a way for God to address them anew, to prove through the study of Scripture that they remain His chosen people, and that their interpretation, as embodied in the Oral Torah, is in fact the true and legitimate interpretation of the Bible's meaning.

The other feature that truly distinguishes rabbinic midrash is its singular literary form, the modes of discourse in which its hermeneutics are articulated. These literary forms show the close connection between rabbinic interpretation of the Bible and synagogue homilies. The most characteristic of all these forms is the proem or *petiḥta,* a form that may have served (as Joseph Heinemann has suggested) as a kind of mini-sermon that introduced the initial verse of the weekly Shabbat Torah reading. Instead of beginning with that verse, however, the proem opens with another verse taken from a completely different part of Tanakh; this verse is typically called the "remote" verse because it is, for all practical purposes, unrelated to the weekly Torah reading and its opening verse. It is this verse that the proem actually "interprets," building in the process a kind of exegetical bridge that eventually culminates in its true subject, the opening verse of the weekly reading.

As a brief example of the form, consider the following *petiḥta* for the weekly Torah reading that begins with Lev. 24.2, "Command the Israelite people to bring you clear oil of beaten olives for lighting, so as to maintain lights regularly."

> Bar Kapparah (d. 230 CE) recited a *petiḥta*: "It is You who light my lamp; the LORD, my God, lights up my darkness" (Ps. 18.29).
>
> The Holy One, blessed be He, said to man: Your lamp is in my hand, as it is said, "The lifebreath of man is the lamp of the LORD" (Prov. 20.27). And my lamp is in yours: [this is the meaning of the phrase] "so as to maintain lights regularly" (Lev. 24.2). To which the Holy One, blessed be He, added: If you light my lamp, I will light yours. That is the meaning of "Command the Israelite people . . ." (Lev. 24.2).

Perhaps the most remarkable thing about this particular *petiḥta* is the speech the author of the proem puts into God's mouth—a speech that is actually an interpretation of Ps. 18.29; God Himself confirms, as it were, the meaning of the verse in the psalm, but it is also through God's "interpretation" that the preacher or author of this sermon speaks to his audience. While the interpretation itself, as well as that of Prov. 20.27, are independent exegeses, the proem joins them in order to make its own point about Lev. 24.2. Contrary to how it looks in Scripture, this verse is not simply a commandment from God to the Isra-

elites to light a special candelabrum in the sanctuary. Rather, it is testimony to the reciprocity of the deeds of God and man: If Israel lights God's lamp in the sanctuary, then He will light man's lamp, namely, his soul. Or to put the same point in more general terms, human life is God's response to human observance of the commandments!

The *petiḥta* epitomizes the characteristic type of midrashic literary form that exists precisely in the gray area between pure commentary, on the one side, and an original, creative composition. Indeed, it is precisely in this gray area between the two separate realms of commentary and literature that midrash takes seed and grows, never crossing over entirely into either realm, flourishing in the space precisely in-between. The *petiḥta* is also only one among several literary forms of this kind that come into existence in midrash as the discourse of its exegesis. These relatively short literary units—which include the parable, the extrabiblical legend, pronouncement and fulfillment stories (in which interpreted biblical verses serve as punchlines or prophetic realizations of unusual narratives), and various types of lists and testimony forms—are the real literary units of rabbinic midrash.

Unlike their contemporaries, the Rabbis did not write treatises on the Bible and its meaning (as did Philo, for example), nor did they initially compose tracts in which they sought to "rewrite" the Bible (although such works do come into existence in the early post-rabbinic period). It is not even clear that they wrote commentaries as did the members of the apocalyptic community at Qumran. We know very little about the composition or process of editing of the various midrashic collections, but from their contents and overall skeletal style, it would seem that they were compiled to serve as source-books for "professionals"—that is, rabbinic preachers and teachers who used them to prepare sermons and lessons. There is little indication that they were originally meant to serve as commentaries to be studied alongside the Bible nor were they, as were a number of early Christian exegetical texts, transcripts of actual sermons or lessons in Scripture. As anthologies of interpretations, with multiple interpretations recorded side-by-side with no comments and few attempts to navigate between them, these midrashic collections embody the delight of midrash in always yet *another* additional interpretation. Yet unlike their postmodern descendants, in which polysemy signifies an indeterminacy that reflects the fundamental instability of meaning, multiple interpretation as found in midrash is actually a sign of its stability, the guarantee of a belief in Scripture as an inexhaustible fount of meaningfulness.

That the Rabbis preferred this type of anthological composition to systematic treatises or formal commentaries is in itself a revealing fact about the way they saw biblical interpretation. For them, Bible study was an ad hoc activity directed essentially to an audience hungry for a response to its immediate needs and to the desire to have Scripture speak in the present moment. This feature of midrash is also one that seems to have troubled some later rabbinic authorities and even led them to dismiss midrash as at best a poetic form of speech that need not be taken too seriously. Partly because of such ambivalence, midrash's fortunes following the rabbinic period decidedly waned. The high point of classical midrashic creativity was reached in the first five centuries in the common era, but while encyclopedias of midrash continued to be composed throughout the Middle Ages, original midrashic composition declined until, ultimately, the new forms of *peshat*-oriented exegesis—so-called contextual or plain-sense interpretation—emerged in the late 10th century in the Islamic world and the 11th century in Europe. What has survived in the popular Jewish tradition of Bible study from the classical midrashic traditions are primarily those interpretations that were selected by Rashi (R. Shlomo Yitzhaki, 1040–1105) for inclusion in his commentary to the Bible. Finally, in the 12th and 13th centuries, the literary forms of classical midrash were appropriated and

revived by the fledgling kabbalistic movement in such works as the *Sefer Bahir* and the *Zohar,* where they were infused with a new mystical content and thereby transformed into a medium for esoteric teachings. At this point, however, another literary tradition had begun.

For much of the past two centuries, since the beginnings of the Jewish Enlightenment and of modern critical study of the Bible among Jewish scholars, most interest in premodern Jewish biblical interpretation has centered upon the *peshat* interpreters of the Middle Ages, with their more contextual, grammatically informed, and rationalistic exegesis of the biblical text. And yet, as has become increasingly clear in the last half-century, *peshat* exegesis has been more of an exception, almost a blip, in the long history of Jewish biblical exegesis. If there has been a dominant mode of Jewish reading of the Bible, it has been more in the "spirit" of midrash—if not classical midrash itself—with its imperative to connect to the biblical text, its irrepressible playfulness, and its delight in multiple, polyvalent traditions of interpretation. And nowhere is this more visible than in the very page layout of what becomes the true Jewish study Bible—that is, the Rabbinic Bible, the *Miqra'ot Gedolot*—as it was first published in 1516 by the Christian printer Daniel Bomberg and then successively built upon and expanded by subsequent publishing houses. On this page, as one can see from Figure 1, the biblical text is surrounded by commentaries and para-exegetical works— the Aramaic Targum next to the biblical text, with the commentaries of Rashi, Ibn Ezra, Naḥmanides, Sforno, and others below. Although most of these commentaries are *peshat* commentaries, each one explicitly or implicitly insisting upon the univocal truth of its particular interpretation, here they all lie next to each other on the same page, as though there were no significant difference or disagreement between them, awaiting the reader who will study them all, gleaning each for its own contribution and added significance. In

A *Miqra'ot Gedolot* (RABBINIC BIBLE), VILNIUS 1907, FROM THE BEGINNING OF EXODUS 1
The page includes the biblical text, the standard Aramaic translation (*Targum Onkelos*), Rashi, a super-commentary on Rashi, Nahmanides, Ibn Ezra, Sforno, and two other commentaries.

its celebration of the possibilities of multiple interpretation, this very page layout is "midrashic"—and powerful testimony in itself to the supreme power midrash continues to wield in the Jewish study of the Bible.

[DAVID STERN]

Medieval Jewish Interpretation

The Way of the *Peshat*

The Bible has been the focus of a rich exegetical tradition, which began to evolve even before the canonization process was completed. The techniques of inner-biblical exegesis, *pesher*-type interpretation as practiced at Qumran, and rabbinic midrash are all examples of the application of the Bible to the changing spiritual needs of a faith-community. (See "Inner-biblical Interpretation," pp. 1829–35; "The Bible in the Dead Sea Scrolls," pp. 1920–28; and "Midrash and Jewish Interpretation," pp. 1863–75.) Rabbinic midrash treated the entire Bible as an organic whole, whose parts were infinitely significant and ripe for interpretation. This led to atomizing the text, reading words and verses out of context, and making connections between verses from various biblical books. Halakhic midrash attempted to anchor current practice in the biblical text, while aggadic midrash shed light on the character of biblical personalities and derived moral, educational, and theological lessons from biblical narrative through a variety of creative techniques, which often had little regard for the literary coherence or earlier meanings of the text. The midrashic method adequately satisfied the community's needs well into the early Middle Ages, when significant forces came to bear which called for new approaches to the biblical text and gave birth to the commentary genre. In contrast to midrashic collections, which are anthologies of comments by various sages, arranged either as a commentary on a biblical book or as a collection of sermons, the commentary bears the distinct stamp of a single author. From the 8th century onward, in Iraq, Judeo-Arabic paraphrases of biblical texts begin to appear, replacing Aramaic works of a similar nature. These are the precursors of the commentary genre. By the middle of the 9th century, a steady stream of commentaries begins to flow through the veins of the Jewish body politic, nourishing and invigorating it, and providing instruction and inspiration for each succeeding generation.

Karaites and *Geonim* (9th–11th Centuries)

Jewish scholars were doubtless aware of the importance of the Bible for Christians and its use as a source of inspiration and prooftexts. Indeed, Christians were already producing commentaries on biblical books in the 3rd century. However, only with the rise of Islam and the challenge posed by its claim of religious superiority did new approaches to the study of the biblical text seem imperative for Jewish scholars. The engagement of Muslim scholars in Quranic exegesis directly influenced the approach of their Jewish counterparts to the Hebrew Scriptures. The exposure to Islamic philosophy, especially rationalist Mutazilite Kalam, was also a powerful factor and left a distinct stamp of rationalism on the works of the period. Under the influence of Arabic philology and linguistics the serious study of the Hebrew language was undertaken, dictionaries were written, and rules, often derived from the Arabic grammarian's study of Quranic grammar, began to be defined for Hebrew grammar. One of the distinctive features of the commentary genre is the recognition that language follows specific rules and that these must be taken into account when explaining the text. Thus, although the message of the Bible is still seen as divine, the medium is human, and follows the conventions of human speech and communication.

It was at this time in Iraq, newly conquered by the Arabs from the Persians, that the Karaite movement began to take shape. By questioning the validity of the oral law and its supremacy over the written, and its sometimes idiosyncratic interpretations and occasional contradictions of the biblical text, this movement challenged the authority of the rabbinic leadership of the period. The Karaites advocated a return to Scripture and ridiculed the rabbinic readings of the text, which indeed were often difficult to justify on rational grounds. The movement's founding father, or better, precursor, was Anan ben David (mid-8th century), who according to recent scholarship, was not really the first Karaite, but rather the founder of a rival legal school which promoted a different interpretation of the halakhah, while using the same techniques of midrash halakhah as the Rabbis. Anan promoted an extreme ascetical form of religion, which he buttressed with midrashic exegetical methods, and many of his views were rejected by later Karaites. Anan, at least according to later tradition, seems to have coined the slogan "search diligently the Scriptures and do not rely on my opinion," thus inspiring an efflorescence of biblical scholarship in both the Karaite and Rabbanite (the term used for Rabbinic in Karaite contexts) camps that would reach its zenith in the 10th and 11th centuries.

The Karaites, who coalesced into a movement in the 10th century, were the first Jewish group to produce full-fledged scriptural commentaries. The earliest exegete seems to have been the Karaite Benjamin al-Nahawandi (first half of the 9th century), who wrote commentaries on the Torah and several other biblical books, of which only fragments remain. The earliest extant complete Jewish commentary is Daniel al-Qumisi's commentary on the Minor Prophets, the only part of his oeuvre to have survived intact. Al-Qumisi flourished in the last quarter of the 9th century, during which time he emigrated to Jerusalem where he helped found the Karaite community of Mourners of Zion. His commentary, written in Hebrew, bears a distinct authorial stamp, and presents a running verse-by-verse exposition of the biblical text, incorporating occasional Arabic and Persian glosses. Al-Qumisi demonstrates a distinct awareness of the literary nature of the biblical text, pointing out connections between verses and sections, and

offering philological analysis where necessary. On occasion he will apply certain prophetic statements to his own era, specifically engaging in polemics against the Rabbanites. But such interpretations are always offered as a second level of meaning after the verse has been subjected to philological and literary analysis. Take for example, Hos. 2.8–9: "Assuredly, I will hedge up her roads with thorns and raise walls against her, and she shall not find her paths. Pursue her lovers as she will, she will not overtake them; and seek them as she may, she shall never find them. Then she will say, 'I will go and return to my first husband, for then I fared better than now.' " After explaining the difficult words in the text and placing the verses in the general context of Hosea's prophecy, al-Qumisi then applies these verses to the Karaite-Rabbanite controversy, explaining that many will seek enlightenment through the teachings of the Rabbanites but will be disappointed ("seek them as she may, she shall never find them," 2.8) and as a result, there will be some who wish to "return to the first husband" (2.9), i.e., to the proper worship of God as prescribed in the Bible (the Karaite way), while there are those who "pursue their lovers" (ibid.), i.e., engage in improper acts, as did the early nations, in which men would marry their nieces and sisters-in-law and perform other forbidden unions, use candlelight on the Sabbath, etc., as did the Rabbanites. But the shepherds who mislead their flocks (i.e., the Rabbanites) will be dismissed and Israel will not find them, as it is written "I will dismiss them from tending the flock" (Ezek. 34.10). While this type of exegesis is somewhat reminiscent of the *pesharim* of the Dead Sea sectarians, there is a wide gap between the latter, which use the biblical text as a key for predicting the future, particularly the fate of their community, and those Karaites like al-Qumisi, who occasionally offer a midrashic type of gloss applying the text to their present situation. In general, in contrast with the Sages, who spoke of the multivalency of Scripture, al-Qumisi insisted that every word in the Bible had but one true interpretation. Unfortunately, this interpretation was not always immediately obvious. Therefore, multiple meanings could vie with each other, until the true meaning would be clarified at the End of Days when the Teacher of Righteousness (moreh tzedek), a messianic figure who is also prominent in Qumran pesher texts, would clarify ambiguities and decide on the one true interpretation.

The most prominent Rabbanite exegete of this period is Saadia Gaon (882–942), a polymath, who did pioneering scholarly work in many areas, including grammar and exegesis. Saadia was born in Egypt and later moved to Iraq, where he was eventually chosen to be gaon, or head of the Sura academy, the leading talmudic academy of his time. Saadia translated most of the Bible into Arabic and wrote commentaries on many books including the Torah, Isaiah, Proverbs, Job, and some of the Five Scrolls. He prefaced his commentaries with detailed introductions discussing grammatical, exegetical, and philosophical issues and polemicizing extensively against the Karaites. Saadia set down several principles of interpretation, which guided him in his work of translation and exegesis. These are most explicit in the introduction to his Torah commentary, where he affirmed the necessity of understanding the biblical text according to the plain meaning of the words, with the following exceptions: (1) if experience and sense perception contradict the plain meaning (e.g., that Eve was the mother of all living things [Gen. 2.20]); (2) if reason contradicts the plain sense (e.g., Deut. 4.24, that "the LORD your God is a consuming fire," which must be interpreted metaphorically); (3) when verses contradict each other (e.g., Mal. 3.10, "thus put me to the test," which must be interpreted so as not to contradict Deut. 6.16, "do not test the LORD, your God," which takes precedence); (4) when a verse contradicts established tradition (e.g., in the prohibition against seething a kid in its mother's milk [Exod. 23.19; 34.26; Deut. 14.21]). In the last case, an oral tradition (the complete separation of meat and milk products) was transmitted by the people, who saw how the prophets behaved in this matter. One of Saadia's key exegetical principles was maintaining a balance between the freedom of the interpreter and the authoritative tradition. This issue must have been heatedly discussed in Islamic circles as well, but for Saadia it was probably primarily motivated by the need to defend the oral tradition from the attacks of the Karaites. For Saadia unlimited freedom of interpretation, which the Karaites advocated, was unthinkable, since it would lead to religious anarchy. Exegetical freedom had to be limited by the dictates of tradition, which sometimes led to interpretations far from the plain sense.

Another important rabbinic exegete of this period was Samuel ben Ḥofni (d. 1013), gaon of Sura, who wrote an extensive commentary on the Torah in Judeo-Arabic, only part of which survives. This commentary follows in Saadia's footsteps but has its own unique features as well. It takes a rationalistic approach to the text and features extensive excursuses on various topics, which go far beyond the explication of the text and for which he was criticized by later exegetes. For example, his comment on Gen. 41.49 ("So Joseph collected produce in very large quantity, like the sands of the sea") includes a lengthy discourse on hoarding, and he appends to his commentary on the death of Jacob a long discussion of the laws of death and burial (Gen. 47.29).

One of the most prominent Karaite scholars of the period was Yaʻqub al-Qirqisani, a native of Iraq and a younger contemporary of Saadia, who wrote two major works in Arabic, a legal code called Kitab al-anwar waʼl maraqib (Book of Lights and Watchtowers), and a commentary on the Torah titled Kitab al-Riyad waʼl ḥadaʼiq (Book of Gardens and Parks). These two works constituted a unified exegetical project encompassing the legal and narrative portions of the Torah. In the latter work he sets down thirty-seven principles of exegesis and explains his exegetical aims and methods. Examples include the Mosaic authorship of the entire Torah and the necessity to interpret Scripture literally unless this would lead to a contradiction. Another important principle is that "Scripture addresses human beings in a manner accessible to them and about matters familiar to them from their own experience," which is reminiscent of the rabbinic principle "Scripture speaks in human language" (e.g., *b. Ber.* 31b). His works demonstrate a wide knowledge of contemporary philosophical and intellectual trends, as was typical for his time and environment.

In the 10th century Jerusalem became the spiritual center of Karaism. The greatest Karaite exegete was Japheth ben Eli, who flourished in the second half of the 10th century and was part of this Jerusalem school of Karaite scholars. He is the only exegete to have translated and commented on the entire Bible. He seems to have undertaken this task in order to provide the Karaite community with an adequate treatment of Scripture, which could hold its own against traditional rabbinic exegesis, especially the sophisticated treatment of his formidable Rabbanite opponent Saadia Gaon. While not as sophisticated and well developed in his understanding of Arabic linguistics and Mutazilite (rationalist Islamic) philosophy as his 11th-century successors, such as Yusuf al-Basir, Jeshuah ben Judah, and Abu'l-Faraj Harun, his originality and literary-contextual approach set the tone for succeeding generations of exegetes and were profoundly influential. Japheth's Karaite successors used his commentaries as the foundation for their remarks, expanding and elaborating upon them, and his comments also found their way into the rabbinic *peshat* tradition, mainly through the mediation of Abraham Ibn Ezra.

Japheth's commentaries are divided into two sections. Each biblical book begins with a programmatic introduction, followed by a section-by-section translation and commentary. The translation and commentary are intimately related: The translation represents the distillation of the exegete's understanding of the meaning of the text, while the commen-

tary discusses in depth the various options for its interpretation. Like Daniel al-Qumisi, Japheth also interpreted the text according to two methods, one the linguistic-contextual, the other, the *pesher*-like or prognostic, in which allusions are sought in the text to the exegete's own time, and to the struggle of the Karaite movement against its opponents. For Japheth and other Karaite members of the Mourners of Zion, such as Salmon ben Jeroham (mid-10th century), this second method, which had a strong messianic tone to it, replaced the rabbinic method of midrash, which they had rejected. However, this method was used selectively, only on works or verses deemed appropriate for such treatment (e.g., the poetic passages in the Torah and Early Prophets, Psalms, Daniel, Song of Songs).

In the late 10th century the Karaite Abu Ya'aqov Yusuf Ibn Nuh published a grammatical commentary on the Bible, the *Dikduk* (Grammar), which bears witness to an early Karaite tradition of Hebrew grammatical thought which originated in Persia and Iraq in the 8th to 9th centuries and was at first shared by Rabbanites and Karaites alike. The intention of this work was to use the tools of grammar and linguistics to elucidate the biblical text; it is thus distinguished from the grammars of Saadia and the Karaite Abu'l-Faraj Harun, which were more theoretical grammars arranged systematically. Ibn Nuh also wrote a long commentary on the Torah, only part of which survives.

The most important Karaite exegete of the 11th century is Jeshuah ben Judah, author of several exegetical works, including long and short commentaries on the Torah, and *Genesis Rabbah*, a theological commentary on the opening chapters of Genesis (not to be confused with the rabbinic midrash of the same name). His commentaries, scholastic in nature, are imbued with the teachings of Mutazilite Kalam and include lengthy halakhic discussions. They also include extensive quotations from rabbinic literature, some of them cited approvingly.

By the 11th century a Karaite community had taken hold in Byzantium, and soon Karaites from this community were traveling to Jerusalem to study at the feet of the great sages of the Jerusalem school. Led by Tobias ben Moses, these Byzantine sectarians translated into Hebrew and epitomized large portions of the Karaite exegetical and halakhic tradition of the time and brought them back to Byzantium. Thus were the Arabic works of Japheth, Jeshuah, and the great theologian Yusuf al-Basir salvaged and transmitted to new generations of students, albeit in rather inferior translations that did not do justice to the eloquence of their authors.

The *geonim* and their Karaite contemporaries are the pioneers of Jewish biblical exegesis, the first to produce systematic biblical commentaries. They influenced succeeding schools of interpretation, especially those in the Arabic sphere: e.g., exegetes such as Judah Ibn Bal'am and Abraham Ibn Ezra (Muslim Spain), Abraham Maimonides (Egypt) and the Yemenite midrashic commentaries such as *Midrash ha-gadol*.

The Spanish School (10th–11th Centuries)

In the late geonic period (10th–11th centuries), the intellectual and spiritual center of medieval Jewry moved to Muslim Spain, where the grammatical and exegetical work begun by Saadia Gaon and the Karaites was continued and reached new levels of sophistication. The first significant work to be produced in Spain was the *Maḥberet (Notebook)* of Menaḥem ben Jacob Ibn Saruq, (mid-10th century) the secretary of Ḥisdai Ibn Shaprut (ca. 915–ca. 970), a prominent minister in the court of the Caliph ʿAbd al-Raḥman. The *Maḥberet* is a Hebrew dictionary of biblical roots, the first of its kind to be produced in Hebrew. Though not a commentary, this work elucidated many difficult biblical verses, and represented the purest form of philological exegesis. The *Maḥberet* proved to be controversial and elicited a spirited response from Menaḥem's contemporary Dunash ben Labrat. The students of these

grammarians carried on the discussion in a series of exchanges. They focused on the basic meaning of biblical roots and verses, many of which had theological and doctrinal implications. For instance, Dunash accused Menaḥem of preferring Karaite interpretations to those of the Rabbanites. Indeed, Menaḥem is single-minded in his devotion to the biblical language and text, insisting that they needed to be understood on their own terms, without recourse to other sources. Thus, he avoids comparative philology as much as possible, even shunning Aramaic and Mishnaic Hebrew for the most part. Dunash is much more of a traditionalist, relying on the Masorah, comparative philology (Arabic, Aramaic), and traditional rabbinic interpretation. The works of these early grammarians would soon be surpassed by their successors, but the fact that they were written in Hebrew made them accessible to and extremely influential among the Northern French exegetical school of Rashi and his disciples.

One of the weaknesses of the grammatical theories of Menaḥem and Dunash was their adherence to the biliteral theory of "weak" Hebrew verbs (instead of the triliteral root theory that was later accepted). Indeed, in the case of some weak verbs, Menaḥem assigned them only one root letter. This understanding of the verbal root and other linguistic matters was improved considerably by the important grammatical work of Judah Ḥayyuj (ca. 945–ca. 1000) and Jonah Ibn Janaḥ (11th century), who raised the scientific study of Hebrew grammar to new heights. Ḥayyuj wrote three grammatical treatises, including *Sefer ha-Shorashim (Book of Roots),* and a grammatical commentary on the Prophets entitled *Kitab al-Nutaf (Book of Plucked Feathers).* These works contain a great deal of exegetical material, which greatly influenced subsequent exegetes. Ḥayyuj is credited with introducing the concept of the triliteral Hebrew root, which he applied to the weak verbs and which revolutionized the study of Hebrew grammar.

Ibn Janaḥ refined Ḥayyuj's theories in several grammatical treatises, including *Kitab al-Luma (Sefer ha-Riqmah, Book of Variegated Flowerbeds)* and *Kitab al-Usul (Sefer ha-Shorashim, Book of Roots)*. Much of the former deals with exegetical tools, including various kinds of substitutions, perhaps the most daring and controversial of his methods. For example at Eccl. 1.8, he explains *kol ha-devarim yege'im* (lit., "all things are weary") as *kol ha-devarim meyage'im* ("all things make one weary, are wearisome," substituting a verb for an adjective). At Exod. 21.8, "he shall not have the right to sell her to a foreign people (*'am nokhri*), he substitutes *'ish* (man) for *'am*. Similarly, when Abimelech pleads with God, "will you slay a nation (*goy*) though it be innocent?" (Gen. 20.4), Ibn Janaḥ insists that one must substitute *'ish* (man) for *goy* (nation). Many believe that Ibn Janaḥ is here anticipating the conjectural emendation, a significant tool of modern biblical scholarship, but it is more likely that these interpretations are based on established exegetical principles, many borrowed from Quranic exegesis. Most of these substitutions were accepted by his contemporaries, but some were criticized for exceeding the limits of the acceptable. For instance, Ibn Janaḥ proposes that in 1 Kings 2.28, "for Joab sided with Adonijah, and did not side with Absalom," Absalom should be replaced with Solomon, which makes more sense in the context. However, most of Ibn Janaḥ's critics accept the Masoretic Text and interpret the text as referring to Joab's lack of support for Absalom in the past. Ibn Janaḥ was also a pioneer in comparative philology and solved many an exegetical difficulty through recourse to Rabbinic Hebrew, Aramaic or Arabic. Some of his solutions have been proposed by modern Bible scholars who were unaware that Ibn Janaḥ had anticipated them. An example of his technique is his explanation of Num. 16.1: *vayikaḥ koraḥ*, "and Korah took." Exegetes throughout the ages, beginning with the Targumim and midrashim, have puzzled over what it was that Korah took and made various proposals for filling the gap. Ibn Janaḥ, on the basis of comparison with the Arabic equivalent of the

word *lakaḥ* (the root of *vayikaḥ*), suggests that the word here means "to begin" and does not require a direct object. It is rather connected to the verb in the following verse *vayakumu*, "they rose up," and means Korah and his men began to rise up against Moses.

In another important contribution, Ibn Janaḥ applied rhetorical principles to biblical usage, especially with regard to poetic repetition or parallelism. Thus, for example, one finds synonyms in Isa. 41.4, "Who has made and done?" and in Isa. 43.7, "I have created, fashioned and made him." Are these synonyms to be explained as having different meanings? The midrashic tradition and many medieval exegetes saw a distinct meaning in each word, assuming that since in the Bible no words are superfluous, each word had its own meaning. Ibn Janaḥ argued that the use of such synonyms and repetitions is rhetorical, to add elegance and beauty to the language; they do not add further meaning. If one should ask, then, why bother repeating the same idea in different words, Ibn Janaḥ would respond that in the art of rhetoric, elaboration is more elegant and artistic. This view was adopted by many Spanish and Provençal exegetes, especially Abraham Ibn Ezra and Radak, and was criticized by others who favored the midrashic method. In recent times, this question has again become a topic of dispute among interpreters of the Bible.

The two most important exegetes in Muslim Spain were Moses ben Samuel Gikatilla of Saragossa and Judah ben Samuel Ibn Bal'am of Toledo and later Seville, who were both active in the second half of the 11th century. Gikatilla translated the Arabic grammar books of Ḥayyuj into Hebrew and wrote a commentary on the Bible; most of it is lost. From the extant fragments of his commentary one can see that he was heavily influenced by Ibn Janaḥ in matters grammatical, but did not confine his exegesis to grammar and philology; he also commented on matters of content and general meaning. Notable is his severe rationalism, especially in dealing with miracles. He was also the first exegete to assign the second part of the book of Isaiah (chs 40–66) to a second prophet (called by modern scholars Second Isaiah or Deutero-Isaiah).

Judah Ibn Bal'am's works have fared better than Gikatilla's and most have survived, although, until recently, few had been published. His commentaries are very selective, focusing on verses about which he disagrees with his predecessors. In his introduction to the Prophets, he spells out his exegetical method, explaining that he will treat difficult words in three ways: by translating them into Arabic, by comparing them with cognate words in the Bible, and, wherever possible, by relating them to equivalents in Rabbinic Hebrew, Aramaic, or Arabic. Although some have considered him an epigone (a follower of lesser abilities) of Ibn Janah, he was clearly an independent thinker, who struggled with the text, rejected opposing views, and offered many innovative interpretations. In some cases, if he was not satisfied with previous solutions to a problem and could not provide a better solution of his own, he preferred to leave the problem unsolved. Only in matters of halakhah did he bow to tradition, as did most of the *peshat* (contextual) exegetes of the Middle Ages. Like his mentor Ibn Janah, he was concerned with identifying geographical names, objects, flora, and fauna.

Abraham Ibn Ezra (1089–1164)

The commentaries of Abraham ben Meir Ibn Ezra mark the culmination of the Spanish-Arabic period of exegesis. Ibn Ezra lived in Spain most of his life, but in 1140 he abandoned his homeland, probably for personal reasons, and set out on a journey that would take him to Rome and through much of France, arriving finally in England, where he died in 1164. As he traveled, he produced, often by commission, commentaries on various biblical books; in some cases, such as Exodus, Minor Prophets, Psalms, Esther, and Daniel, he produced two commentaries, one considerably longer and more detailed than the other. Ibn Ezra, in the Spanish tradition,

based his methodology on the twin pillars of grammar and reason. He argued that only an exegete thoroughly grounded in Hebrew grammar and lexicography could properly understand the meaning of the biblical text. For him the text had but one meaning, which could be obtained only through the application of the rules of grammar. Furthermore, an acceptable interpretation had to be logically consistent and stand up to the test of reason.

In the introduction to his Torah commentary, he discusses four earlier approaches to biblical exegesis which he found wanting: (1) the geonic, which tended to stray from the matter at hand and lapsed into lengthy discussions of matters not germane to the text; (2) the Karaite, which rejected the oral tradition of the Sages, allowing every exegete to interpret according to his own understanding, even in matters of halakhah, thus undermining rabbinic authority; (3) the Christian, which tended to allegorize the text, including matters of halakhah, thus robbing it of its basic meaning and calling into question the necessity for religious observance; and (4) the midrashic, the way of the Sages, whose interpretations defied logic and reason and ignored context. This lack of exegetical control was totally unacceptable.

Ibn Ezra then articulates his own methodology: he will explain the grammar of each word only once, at its first occurrence, and then explain its meaning in context. He also declares that he will ignore the comments of the Masoretes, which he claims have no exegetical value, though they provided much material for homilists.

Ibn Ezra's exegesis represents a distillation of the finest achievements of the Spanish philological school of exegesis, avoiding its more radical elements such as Ibn Janah's methods of lexical and consonantal substitution. He adopted Moses Ibn Ezra's stance (see below) that Scripture uses human language and therefore must conform to the rules of syntax and rhetoric; this led him to reject midrashim which tampered with the syntax, or interpretations based on plene or defective spellings since these had no effect on the meaning of the text. Furthermore, the Bible speaks of God and the elements of nature in human terms, so that human beings can understand what it is saying. Expressions such as the "mouth of the earth" (Num. 16.32) or "the heart of the sea" (Exod. 15.8) are figures of speech and should not be understood literally.

Ibn Ezra fully accepted the Spanish exegetical tradition that did not assign significance to changes in spelling or wording if the meaning was not affected. As a result, he paid little attention to textual nuance, unusual spellings, and stylistic variation, which are popular now among modern students of the Bible. He ignored the differences in parallel passages, e.g., the two versions of the Decalogue, or Pharaoh's two dreams, and, saw no significance in the unusual form 'oholoh (Gen. 9.21), instead of 'oholo, which Rashi as well as the midrash interpreted to refer to the fall of Samaria (called 'Oholah), brought down by drunkenness and depravity.

In his firm belief that Scripture could not contradict the demands of reason, he was a faithful follower of Saadia Gaon, invoking the method of tikun (correction or adaptation, based on the tawil of Quranic exegesis) in order to make a verse conform to reason by means of allegory or metaphor. But in order to avoid undermining the validity of the commandments, the historicity of the patriarchal narratives, or the truthfulness of the prophetic messages, he insisted, as did Saadia, that the method of tikun had to be applied only when absolutely necessary.

Ibn Ezra also followed Saadia in his steadfast defense of the oral tradition (kabbalah) of the Sages, particularly in matters of halakhah. In practical terms this meant that Ibn Ezra could not accept a peshat interpretation that contradicted halakhah, in contrast to other peshat exegetes, such as Rashbam, of the Northern French school, or Radak. Thus, for example, Exod. 13.9 and other passages which provide the scriptural basis for tefillin (phylacteries) are accepted as referring to the ha-lakhic requirement to actually bind copies of these passages on the arm and place them on the head in leather boxes (phylacteries, or tefillin). Ibn Ezra argues that since the literal interpretation does not contradict reason and that the commandment it entails can be carried out, it must be accepted, unlike the verse "and you should circumcise the foreskin of your heart" (Deut. 10.16), which cannot be interpreted literally. The Karaites and Rashbam, on the other hand, interpret both these verses metaphorically as merely urging constant vigilance in remembering the commandments. But while the oral tradition of the Sages, the vast body of halakhah gathered in the Mishnah and Talmud, was sacrosanct, the same authority was not ascribed to the midreshei ha-lakhah, the halakhic midrashim of the Sages meant to provide scriptural justification for the actual laws themselves. He felt no compulsion to defend these in the same way he defended the halakhic decisions of the Talmud (see, e.g., his short commentary to Exod. 21.8). Similarly, despite his respect for the halakhic decisions of the rabbinic Sages, Ibn Ezra feels no compulsion to accept their assignations of authorship to the various biblical books (e.g., he questions whether Jeremiah wrote Lamentations), or the midrashic identification of biblical characters (e.g., contra Rashi, he rejects the midrashic view that the prophet Joel was the son of the prophet Samuel).

Ibn Ezra had a very conservative view of the biblical text and rejected all attempts at emendation. On the other hand, he did have a penchant for higher criticism, pointing to later additions in the text (e.g., Gen. 12.6; 22.14; Deut. 3.11), and especially the last twelve verses of Deuteronomy ("the secret of the twelve"), which he claims were written prophetically by Joshua. Similarly, following Moses Gikatilla, he advocates the postexilic dating of the second part of Isaiah and of some of the psalms (e.g., Ps. 69).

Ibn Ezra was a serious philosopher, a Neoplatonist, heavily influenced by astrology. Although he never wrote any systematic theological or philosophical treatises, his thought may be gleaned from his biblical commentaries. Indeed, many of Ibn Ezra's allusions to secrets *(sodot)* refer to his views on central issues of Jewish theology, such as God's relation to the land of Israel, the people of Israel, and the role of the sacrificial cult, especially the scapegoat (Lev. 16.8) in determining the fate of the Jewish people. His referring to these views as secrets, and alluding to them obliquely, may be an indication that they might be threatening to the religious well-being of the Jewish masses and could only be tolerated and properly understood by the intellectual elite.

Ibn Ezra was one of the main conduits of Spanish-Jewish culture to the rest of Western Europe, and as such his legacy is of inestimable value. Despite the impression given by his "modern" critical allusions and his tendency to be overly critical of his predecessors and contemporaries, he was not a radical exegete. His importance lies in his position at the end of a productive period in Jewish intellectual history and his ability to summarize in Hebrew the exegetical achievements of this period clearly, succinctly, and judiciously. Nevertheless, his commentaries presented challenges to the reader because of their concise, difficult nature, and scattered cryptic comments, which stimulated the production of a whole corpus of super-commentaries that elucidate and elaborate upon them.

Interest in Ibn Ezra has continued down through the ages, making him one of the most influential cultural icons in Jewish history. In the Late Middle Ages, he was appropriated by nearly every intellectual school. Though he was a Neoplatonist, Maimonidean Aristotelians found common ground in him. Though he polemicized fiercely against the Karaites, these sectarians also claimed him as one of their own, perhaps because he often cited works by Karaite scholars. Baruch Spinoza cited him as the first biblical critic, making much of his so-called higher-critical comments and using his name to justify his own much more radical views. He was also much admired by the Christian Hebraists in the early modern period, who translated many of his works and quoted him approvingly. In the modern period, Jewish reformers and biblical critics saw him as a precursor of their views, as someone who was dedicated to the pursuit of truth but could not express his views openly, and as someone, who, like Maimonides, was open to the outside world, willing to accept the truth from whatever source it came.

Aesthetics and Philosophy

At the same time that grammarians were refining their tools to better explain the biblical text, another school of thought was approaching the Bible from a different direction. Scholars trained in philosophy were using their newfound knowledge to reexamine the biblical text and then reinterpret it in the light of their philosophical insights. While none utilized the commentary genre, their works are full of comments on the biblical text, which they attempt to harmonize with their philosophical teachings. (See "The Bible in the Philosophical Tradition," pp. 1948–75.) Although he did not write biblical commentaries as such, Moses ben Jacob Ibn Ezra (ca. 1055–1138), a relative and friend of Abraham Ibn Ezra, made an important contribution to biblical hermeneutics by developing a literary exegetical theory based on Arabic theories of aesthetics. His Arabic treatise, *Book of Discussion and Conversation,* provides guidelines for writing Hebrew poetry in the Arabic style. To illustrate his points Ibn Ezra brings examples from the Bible and thereby indirectly provides an analysis of biblical stylistics in comparison with the ideal of Arabic poetry. Applying his theory to prophecy, he portrayed biblical prophets as poets, who supplied the literary form for the divine message. The implications for exegesis are obvious, since this means that biblical prophecies can be analyzed like any other poetry. Furthermore, if the ideas expressed are paramount, then the stylistic embellishments of these ideas do not have interpretive significance and can be ignored. This leads to the principle, characteristic of the Spanish school of *peshat* exegesis, that the Bible may repeat the same idea in different words for stylistic, aesthetic purposes, and that such repetition is not exegetically significant. Thus, for example, in "Abraham breathed his last and died" (Gen. 25.8), "breathed his last" *(vayigva')* renders "and died" *(vayamot)* superfluous. As part of his theory, Ibn Ezra enumerates literary ornaments of poetry, known in Arabic as *badi*, which he proceeds to identify in the Bible. Some, such as metaphor, simile, and allegory, were commonly recognized; for others, he could not find good examples. Nevertheless, in the attempt, he revealed many characteristics of biblical style, which had hitherto not been recognized. Ibn Ezra's aesthetic exegesis, written in Arabic, towards the end of the Golden Age of Spanish-Jewish culture (10th–12th centuries, when Muslims controlled most of Spain), remained untranslated until recently, and thus had little impact on subsequent generations, living in Christian Europe with limited exposure to Arabic language and culture.

Bahya Ibn Pakuda (ca. 1100) in his *Duties of the Heart*, elaborates a theory of biblical exegesis in which he identifies several levels of understanding, from the basic linguistic to the lexical to the contextual and finally to the esoteric, which is only attainable by those who have intellect and understanding. Bahya was greatly influenced by the Sufi mystics of his time. Moses Maimonides (1138–1204) devoted much of his major philosophical work, the *Guide of the Perplexed*, to the interpretation of particular biblical texts. His primary purpose is to demonstrate that the inner meaning of the biblical text is compatible with Aristotelian philosophy. The whole first section is devoted to the elucidation of equivocal terms in the Bible, and sections of the Bible are interpreted or explained at various points in the work. Another major concern of his was the elucidation of parables, which he viewed as having two levels of meaning, revealed and hidden. Maimonides spends a great deal of ef-

fort in elucidating the biblical prophecies as well as the book of Job. For the former, a major concern was harmonizing the biblical text with reason and logic; the latter he read as a parable on divine providence and the problem of evil. He often uses midrashic interpretations as an aid for his exegesis, interpreting them philosophically as well. Maimonides' exegetical approach was very influential on succeeding generations of scholars. He was the prime representative and major spokesman for the Aristotelian school in Jewish philosophy, and subsequent Jewish philosophical exegesis shows strong signs of his influence.

Provençal School (12th–13th Centuries)

The lore of the Spanish *peshat* tradition was brought to Provence by the Kimhi family. The father Joseph (ca. 1105–1170) moved his family, which already included his elder son Moses, from Spain to Narbonne in Provence around 1150, in the wake of the Almohade persecutions. His second son David (ca. 1160–1235) was born in Narbonne. David lost his father at the tender age of ten years and was raised by his brother. The Kimhis were an impressive family, all steeped in the Sephardic tradition of philosophical rationalism and scientific study of the Hebrew language. All wrote biblical commentaries and grammatical works. Joseph is probably best known for his anti-Christian polemic *Sefer ha-Berit (The Book of the Covenant)*, which contains much material of an exegetical nature, Moses for his grammatical work, *Mahlakh shevilei ha-da'at (The Course of the Paths of Knowledge)*, which was translated into Latin in 1508 and became a favorite of 16th-century Christian Hebraists. Both Joseph and Moses left commentaries on Proverbs and Job; the latter's Proverbs commentary was attributed until recent times to Abraham Ibn Ezra. But the family's most distinguished exegete was David (better known by the acronym Radak), who surpassed his father and brother in celebrity. He produced commentaries on the

Torah, Prophets, Psalms, Proverbs, Job, and Chronicles. These commentaries along with his grammatical works, *Sefer ha-Shorashim (Book of Roots)* and *Sefer Mikhlol (Comprehensive Hebrew Grammar)*, became standard works in the field and epitomized the best of the Spanish *peshat* tradition. Growing up in Provence, with its history of midrashic exegesis, Radak was exposed to the positive aspects of this tradition; and in his commentaries he does justice to both *peshat* and midrash, quoting *derashot* (homiletical interpretations of the Sages) and also incorporating midrashic methods and sensibilities into his *peshat* exegesis. For instance, while Radak opposes the midrashic tendency to glorify the patriarchs and matriarchs, preferring to view them as having human strengths and weaknesses, he does derive moral encouragement and religious inspiration from their actions. For example, at Gen. 21.15, concerning Hagar and Ishmael, he teaches the lesson of patience and fortitude in the face of adversity, for if God can perform a miracle for Abraham's maidservants, anyone may benefit from such divine attention.

In similar fashion, Radak does not shy away from applying biblical prophecies and psalms to the situation of the Jews in their present exile and to the long awaited messianic salvation. Thus, in commenting on Isa. 52.1, "Awake, awake, O Zion! Clothe yourself in splendor; put on your robes of majesty, Jerusalem, holy city! For the uncircumcised and the unclean shall never enter you again," he explains "the uncircumcised and the unclean" as referring to the two nations of Edom (Christianity) and Ishmael (Islam) who have fought incessantly over Jerusalem, but who will eventually have to surrender it when the Messiah comes. In this contemporizing tendency he reacts against the extreme historicization of those exegetes such as Moses Gikatilla, who, perhaps for apologetic reasons, explained all the biblical prophecies as referring to past events.

A philosophically trained Maimonidean, Radak introduces philosophical ideas into his commentaries and vigorously defended the Maimonidean position both in writing and orally, participating in his later years in the first Maimonidean controversy. Radak also had a keen historical sense, which he applied judiciously to various biblical issues. For example, he explains the existence of variant readings for the same words, called *ketiv* (written) and *qere* (to be read) as the result of the confusion generated by the first exile (6th century BCE), when books were lost and traditions forgotten. In cases when the men of the Great Synagogue (a group believed by the Sages to have begun functioning in the early postexilic period) could not determine which of two variants was the correct one, they recorded both. In general, on matters concerning the transmission of the biblical text, he is relatively progressive.

The works of Radak, alongside those of Ibn Ezra, exerted tremendous influence in subsequent generations. His grammar books became the standard in the field, and were copied and printed numerous times. His grammatical works and his commentaries were very popular among Christian Hebraists of the 16th–19th centuries, and are consulted and cited by modern Bible scholars to this day.

Northern France (11th–12th Centuries)

During the heyday of the Spanish school (the second half of the 11th century), there developed in northern France another school of *peshat* exegesis, with similar goals and slightly different results. Anonymous glossators called *poterim*, who taught the Bible through the vernacular and are the school's precursors, were active during the early part of the century. In the middle of the century Menaḥem ben Ḥelbo (1015–1085) was writing complete commentaries on the Prophets and Writings, characterized by, among other things, a concern for the plain meaning, the interpolation of foreign words (*leʿazim*), and an attempt to show connections between various passages. Unfortunately very little of his work has survived. The true inspiration for this efflorescence in biblical scholarship was the 11th century scholar, R. Shlomo Yitzhaki (Rashi [an acronym for Rabbi Shlomo son of Isaac], 1040–1105). Rashi wrote commentaries on almost the entire biblical corpus as well as on the Talmud. They draw heavily on the rabbinic tradition and also display a newly discovered sensitivity to context, which influences his choice of midrashic material. The genius of Rashi's commentaries lies in their clarity, concision, felicity of expression, and skillful selection and editing of sources. On numerous occasions, Rashi modifies midrashic sources to accommodate his exegetical goals. In one of his few methodological statements (at Gen. 3.8), he states, "there are many aggadic interpretations, and our Sages have already arranged them in their proper place in *Genesis Rabbah* and other midrashic collections. I, however, am only concerned with the contextual meaning of Scripture (*peshuto shel miqra'*, from the same root as *peshat*) and with such *'aggadot* that properly explain the word and meaning of Scripture." Rashi is thus saying that he will be very selective in his choice of rabbinic material and will not include rabbinic comments which read the text out of context. One puzzling aspect of Rashi's commentaries is the double comment, in which he explains a verse according to context and then follows this with a citation from a midrashic source. It has been the generally accepted opinion that Rashi adds these rabbinic comments only if he is not completely satisfied with his *peshat* explanation. Thus, a weak midrash is used to strengthen a weak *peshat*. Recently, however, it has been suggested that each part of these double interpretations is actually complementary, representing a dualistic approach to the biblical text. The two interpretations when combined, produce a fuller, more satisfying picture, enabling the reader more fully to grasp the meaning of Scripture in all its complexity. Rashi was very sensitive to the nuances of biblical language, and though he lacked the training of his Spanish colleagues who read and wrote in Arabic, he knew the work of Menaḥem ben Saruq and

Dunash ben Labrat, whom he quotes in his commentaries. In addition his commentaries are replete with hundreds of *le'azim,* or word definitions in Old French. Although he does not reveal a great deal about himself in his commentaries, he does refer occasionally to realia or to social conditions in his own time. Rashi was a brilliant Hebrew stylist; this feature, as well as his ability to create a commentary with a didactic and moral thrust that had popular appeal, have helped assign his commentary pride of place in the Ashkenazi canon of classic Jewish texts which are still studied widely today. His commentary on the Torah became immensely popular, achieving near-canonical status, as an acceptable substitute for the required weekly reading of the Targum in preparation for the Torah reading on Sabbath mornings. Rashi's commentary also spawned an impressive number of super-commentaries, beginning with the commentary of Ramban (see below). Among the most famous are those of Judah Khalatz (Spain-Morocco, 15th century), Abraham Bukarat (late 15th–early 16th century, Spain, Tunis), Elijah Mizraḥi (Constantinople, ca. 1450–1526), Judah Loew ben Bezalel (Maharal) of Prague (ca. 1525–1609), and Shabbetai Bass (Prague, 1641–1718). Indeed the production of translations and super-commentaries continues to this very day. Rashi's blend of contextual exegesis and ethical homiletics was a winning combination. His reputation as a talmudist further strengthened his authority and assured that his Bible commentary would never be neglected.

Rashi's sense of *peshuto shel miqra'*, the plain or contextual sense of scripture, developed over the course of his lifetime. He reworked some of his commentaries and was constantly looking for new insights into the text. His grandson, Samuel ben Meir, relates that he admitted to him that if he had more time he would write new commentaries "based on the insights into the contextual meanings of Scripture which are being thought up every day" (commentary to Gen. 37.2). This indicates that there was a great deal of activity in biblical study at the time in the school of Rashi and the trend was away from the exclusive use of rabbinic material. For Rashi, *peshat* and *derash* coexisted in a state of tension and *derashot* that did not violate the integrity of the text and taught an important lesson were still favored.

With Rashi's students and younger contemporaries in the *peshat* school, the balance shifted away from the rabbinic in favor of the biblical. This can be seen already in the work of Joseph Kara (1050–1125), who applied the principles of contextual exegesis to the biblical text with greater rigor and consistency. The name Kara indicates that he dealt with the Bible *(miqra')* in his professional life, either as a teacher or an exegete, or both. Kara produced commentaries for most of the books of the Bible, of which the commentaries on the Former and Latter Prophets, Psalms, Job, and the Five Scrolls have survived. Recently significant portions of his Commentary on the Torah have been discovered. Kara was also an important exegete of religious poetry *(piyyut)*, his commentaries attaining great renown. In Kara, we find considerable progress away from the reliance on midrashic sources for exegesis, a fact which sets him apart from Rashi. In a lengthy programmatic statement in his commentary on 1 Sam. 1.17, Kara makes a strong case for the independent integrity of the text and its ability to stand alone without midrashic embellishment: "One should know that when the prophecies were written they were written complete, with nothing missing and with adequate interpretation, so that subsequent generations would not be led astray by them. It is not necessary to bring a proof from anywhere else, including the midrash, because the Torah was given and recorded in perfect form, lacking nothing. The purpose of the midrash of our Sages is to exalt and glorify the Torah." He compares someone who inclines towards the midrash to a drowning person desperately grabbing for something to hold on to. Had he heeded God's word and made the effort to grasp the contextual meaning, he would have been rewarded by deeper

insight. For Kara, then, the contextual meaning of the text has religious significance, in that it brings one closer to the true word of God. Kara was an independent thinker, not afraid to criticize his predecessors or to find fault with the interpretations of the Rabbis. He was concerned with methodology and his commentaries abound with statements proposing various hermeneutical rules. He was particularly sensitive to literary issues and pointed out instances of parallelism, metaphor and other aspects of biblical style. Kara was also noted for his rationalism, which manifests itself in his quest for reasons for the commandments, and rational explanations for characters' actions and for seemingly miraculous events.

The school of *peshat* exegesis reached the zenith of its achievements with the commentaries of Samuel ben Meir (Rashbam) (ca. 1080–ca. 1160), the grandson of Rashi. His greatest achievement was his Torah commentary, in which he diligently persevered in elucidating the contextual meaning of Scripture *(peshat)* without regard for the interpretations of the Sages. He took his grandfather Rashi to task for his deviations from the *peshat;* indeed, his commentary may be seen as a reaction and critical response to that of Rashi. In most cases, he provides a *peshat* explanation only if he feels that Rashi's comment does not do the job. In an interesting methodological statement, Rashbam makes it clear that his goal in his commentary is only to understand the text as it was written. This includes texts of a legal nature which supposedly govern Jewish practice.

Rashbam sees the halakhot (legal pronouncements) as primary, but recognizes that their connection with the text is often not that easy to justify. Nevertheless this does not detract from their primary importance: "All those with wisdom should know and understand that I have not come to explain halakhot, even though they are primary . . . Since from the superfluity of Scripture one derives halakhot and aggadot; some of these are found in the comments of R. Solomon, my mother's father. But I have come to explain Scripture contextually" (Exod. 21.1). In other words, Rashbam recognizes two legitimate modes of exegesis. The rabbinic mode is legitimate in its own right and does not need justification; in this context, it is noteworthy that Rashbam (in contrast, e.g., to Abraham Ibn Ezra) was an important halakhic scholar. But the *peshat* mode is also valid in and of itself and operates within its own methodological confines. The two are complementary. Rashbam was the most consistent exegete in insisting on a strict separation between the two. In some cases, he even interpreted the text in opposition to the halakhah. E.g., at Exod. 21.6 he explains that after having his ear pierced, the servant is bound to his master for life, even though the halakhah determines that he goes free in the jubilee year, following Lev. 25.40. At Exod. 21.34, in the case of an animal that falls into an open pit, Rashbam's interpretation is that the carcass should go, according to *peshat*, to the owner of the pit, while pointing out that the halakhah determines that it goes to the owner of the animal. Regarding the famous prohibition against seething a kid in its mother's milk (Exod. 23.19 and elsewhere), Rashbam offers a historical, cultural explanation: "Goats generally give birth to two kids at the same time. It was customary to slaughter one of them. Since goats produce much milk . . . it was the custom to boil the kid in its mother's milk. The text deals with the most likely case [which can be applied to other animals]. It is disgraceful, voracious and gluttonous to consume a mother's milk together with her offspring. . . . The intention of the text is to teach civilized behavior." At the end of his lengthy comment, he adds, however, that "this is the case for all meat and milk, as our Sages have explained in the Talmud Tractate Ḥullin."

Rashbam showed interest in linguistic and literary matters and had the most sophisticated approach to grammar of all the members of his school. He even wrote a book, called *Sefer Dayekut (Book of Precision)*, which deals with grammatical questions in the Bible.

But like other members of his school, his efforts were hampered by a lack of familiarity with the major Arabic works of grammar produced by the Spanish school. Only the works of Menaḥem and Dunash were available to him. Rashbam was the first medieval exegete to point out the literary technique of foreshadowing, providing information in anticipation of the later need for it. For example, Gen. 9.18, "Ham was the father of Canaan," is seemingly out of place in its context. However, it prepares the reader for the cursing of Canaan later on. Similarly, Num. 13.20 "Now it happened to be the season of the first ripe grapes," prepares the reader for the return of the spies with a cluster of grapes (Num. 13.23, 27). Rashbam points out many other instances of this feature of biblical stylistics.

The last major representative of the *peshat* school is Eliezer of Beaugency (mid-12th century), who may have been a student of Rashbam. He wrote commentaries on most of the books of the Bible, but only a few, on the Latter Prophets, have survived; therefore our knowledge of his methodology is scant. Eliezer is extreme in his avoidance of midrash; one finds few references to it in his writings. His style is paraphrastic, creating a seamless weave of text with his own words intermingled with the text of Scripture. He stressed the importance of context for explaining difficult words and passages (*davar lamed meˁinyano*, [the meaning of] a word is learned from its context). Like Joseph Kara, he proposed many rules for understanding the biblical text, and many of his comments deal with literary issues. He shows a sensitivity to nuance and devotes much more attention than his colleagues to matters of redaction and the ordering of the biblical books.

Joseph Bekhor Shor (1130–1200) was the last member of this school and his work already shows signs of a decline. He can be seen as a transitional figure situated between the most important members of the *peshat* school (Kara, Rashbam, Eliezer) and the tosafists (see below). His Torah commentary has characteristics of both schools. Although mainly devoted to *peshat* exegesis, his commentary includes more midrashic material than those of his predecessors. He also makes use of *gematria* (the numerical value of letters), which was in vogue among the Pietists in Germany. Among his most significant contributions was his psychological insights into the motivations of the characters in the Bible. He is also concerned with literary structure and connections between passages. His interpretations are often innovative, and even fanciful.

By the turn of the 13th century, just as the mini-renaissance of the 12th century died out and rationalism lost its luster, so too did the *peshat* school fade away. It may very well have been that the radical nature of the enterprise contributed to its lack of appeal to future generations of scholars and laity. The study of Scripture, as opposed to Talmud, was never primary in the curriculum in Ashkenaz, and an exegetical enterprise which could be seen as undermining the authority of rabbinic interpretation and halakhic rulings based on Scripture was simply not sustainable. The influence of this school, with the exception of Rashi, whose commentary managed to strike the right balance between *peshat* and *derash*, was minimal. The small number of surviving manuscripts of the commentaries of Rashbam and Eliezer bears this out. Joseph Kara fared slightly better, although much of his oeuvre was also lost. It seems that these types of commentaries had little appeal to the masses, and even among the intellectuals, changing currents in thinking and an anti-rationalist movement contributed to the neglect of the works of this school for the rest of the Middle Ages.

The Northern French School's Encounter with Christianity

Biblical exegesis among the Northern French was influenced by the Jewish encounter with Christianity in several ways. The interest in the biblical text shown by this school of Northern French exegetes has invited comparisons with similar trends in Christian scholarly circles at the time, notably the

School of St. Victor in Paris, where the canon, Andrew of St. Victor, pursued the *hebraica veritas* with the same assiduousness as Rashbam and his colleagues pursued the *peshat*. Though names are not mentioned, Andrew, who was not well-versed in Hebrew, consulted Jews regularly and cites Jewish exegesis frequently in his commentaries. Some of the sources he cites can be traced to members of the Northern French School. It is not unreasonable to assume that the winds of influence blew in the other direction as well. Indeed it has been argued convincingly that the focus of the exegetes of this school, especially Rashi, on the construction of a narrative that the Jewish people could identify with and be proud of was a primary concern, and was stimulated by the competing narrative presented by the Christian side in what was an ongoing debate and struggle for legitimacy. So, while there is definitely evidence of shared concerns and techniques, made possible by the atmosphere of tolerance and open rationalistic inquiry fostered by the 12th century renaissance, there is also evidence of competition, rivalry, and struggle for supremacy, which can be seen clearly in the polemical aspects of these exegetes' commentaries.

Indeed, it is likely that the exigencies of polemic and disputation stimulated study of the biblical text unencumbered by traditional non-literal interpretation. The New Testament interprets many verses in the Hebrew Bible christologically, as referring to the life or significance of Jesus of Nazareth. This method was continued in the writings of the Church Fathers and in the medieval Christian commentaries, and such comments loom large in the polemical works written by Jews and Christians in the later medieval period. One area which received special attention was the interpretation of the legal parts of the Torah. Christians argued that many of these laws, such as the dietary laws, were no longer applicable as they had been abrogated by the advent of Jesus as Messiah. Jews contended that all the laws remained valid, even if they lacked a rational explanation, since their fulfillment was an act of faith in God. Another issue was the status and interpretation of the words of the prophets, many of which the Christians applied to Jesus. Jewish exegetes tried to put these prophecies in their historical context, applying them to events in the past, either in the time of the prophet or immediately thereafter. Another important strategy of the Jewish polemicists was to argue from context, showing the indefensibility of the Christian interpretation if the context was considered. This approach, of course, militated against midrashic interpretation as well and contributed to the decline in its use during the Middle Ages. Many of the exegetes of the Northern French School were involved in polemics with Christians and these are alluded to in their commentaries either directly or obliquely. The impact of the Crusades is especially felt in Rashi's commentary on Psalms, written after 1096, in which he applies numerous verses to the struggle of the Jewish people in exile with Christianity (symbolized by Esau or Edom), in many cases reading these verses against the thrust of traditional commentary, in order to avoid any possible misuse of them by Christians. On the other hand his commentary on Song of Songs, in which on numerous occasions he uses the term *dugma'* in the sense of figure, shows the influence of contemporary Christian exegesis, where typology was an important exegetical tool. Joseph Kara's comments on the meaning and dates of prophecies of comfort, the meaning of the exile, and the continuing value of the observance of the commandments are apologetically motivated. He was also sensitive to comments that Christians might use for their own polemical purposes. Thus, he criticizes Rashi for explaining *ma'aseh merkavah*, the chariot vision in Ezek. ch 1, as wheels being held together by crossed bars, for fear that this explanation might be used by Christian polemicists to argue that God's chariot was supported by a cross (1 Kings 7.33). Another tendency evident in Kara, but especially in Rashbam and Joseph Bekhor Shor, is to explain the actions of the patriarchs

in as positive a manner as possible. Thus according to Rashbam, Abraham had given enough water to Hagar to last her and Ishmael until they reached the next inn. But because she lost her way in the desert, the water ran out (commentary to Gen. 21.14). Jacob dealt honestly with his brother and bought the birthright from him outright at its fair market value. He served him a meal of bread and lentil soup afterwards in order to confirm the transaction (commentary to Gen. 25.31–33). An especially sensitive topic was the despoiling of the Egyptians (Exod. 3.22). Rashbam explains that the Israelite women asked the Egyptians to give them the vessels as outright gifts, and adds that this is the literal meaning and an answer to the sectarians (*teshuvat ha-minim*). This last comment is a clear indication of the direct relationship between the contextual meaning and anti-Christian polemic. This type of interpretation was the best response to Christian allegorization, which tended to read a reference to Jesus and his life into every verse possible. Nevertheless, not all of these Jewish interpreters were equally engaged in anti-Christian polemic, and the development of *peshat* interpretation should not be seen entirely as a reaction to Christianity.

Ashkenaz in the Late Middle Ages

Biblical commentary in Ashkenaz in the later Middle Ages was produced by the tosafists, a school of students of the Talmud, which flourished between the 12th (from the time of Rashbam and his brother Jacob Tam) and 14th centuries, and German Pietists (Ḥasidei Ashkenaz), a pietistic school, which flourished from the mid-12th to the mid-13th centuries. The tosafist commentaries, mostly produced in the latter part of the tosafist period, were almost all anonymous and have only recently begun to be studied. Many were largely compilations. Very little attention was paid to linguistic matters. Rabbinic midrash was again favored, as were numerological techniques such as *gematria* (explaining a word or group of words according to the numerical value of the letters) and *notarikon* (interpreting every letter in a particular word as the first letter of a whole word, or interpreting a word by breaking it up into its components). The commentaries produced in this period were influenced by the methods of Talmud study of the tosafists, but did not neglect the *peshat* entirely. The best known is that of Hezekiah ben Manoaḥ (Ḥizekuni; mid-13th century), which incorporates a good deal of commentary by Joseph Bekhor Shor and other members of the *peshat* school. The commentaries of the German Pietists are of two types. Some, such as the commentary of Judah ben Samuel (ca. 1150–1217) as recorded by his son Zaltman, are rather undisciplined *peshat* commentaries intended for a wide audience; others, especially those of Eleazar ben Judah of Worms (ca. 1165–ca. 1230), are full of *gematriot, notarikonim,* and other esoteric methods of exegesis, and were intended for the small circle of initiates schooled in the particular brand of mysticism practiced by this group.

Naḥmanides (1194–1271)

Naḥmanides (Moses ben Naḥman; Ramban) marks a new stage in the history of exegesis, since he was the first scholar who wrote his commentaries under the influence of both the Sephardic Andalusian (the region of southern Spain) and Ashkenazic traditions. Naḥmanides was a product of Christian Spain, but he unquestionably felt himself to be in the line of the Andalusian exegetical tradition and indeed advanced the cause of *peshat* exegesis with many insightful comments. At the same time he had absorbed the work of Rashi and the Northern French school and held it in high regard. He also did not hesitate to utilize the vast resources of rabbinic literature—Talmudim, halakhic and aggadic midrashim, as well as geonic and mystical works. In his introduction he speaks of his attitudes to both Abraham Ibn Ezra and Rashi, the dean of Northern French exegetes. He shows respect for both of his predecessors,

but also is not afraid to criticize what he found wanting. Though certainly trained in grammar and philology, he found the Spanish approach as exemplified by Ibn Ezra to be excessively philological and therefore limiting. He was sympathetic to Rashi and his judicious selection of midrashic material, but here too, he did not hesitate to criticize a choice of midrash that he felt was too distant from the *peshat*. Thus he sought to strike a balance between the two approaches and to adopt a more holistic approach to the text. His commentaries are substantially longer than those of Rashi or Ibn Ezra, as he expanded the exegetical enterprise to encompass issues of theology, mysticism, ethics, history, or character analysis, thus weaving a particularly colorful and variegated tapestry which operated on several levels. His commentary is famous for its psychological insights and deep understanding of human nature. Although most Jewish exegetes avoided typology and pre-figuration, because of their extensive use by Christian exegetes and theologians, Naḥmanides uses them extensively in his Torah commentary, connecting the deeds and travels of the patriarchs with subsequent events in Jewish history. To a larger extent than most exegetes, he was concerned with problems of structure, order, and thematic unity, explaining the reasons for the sequence of the books in the Torah and also for sequences of sections, verses, or even items in lists. For instance he invests a great deal of effort in explaining the order of the verses and sections in the parashah of *Mishpatim* (Exod. chs 21–23), a section of laws in no apparent logical order. Scholars have identified at least fourteen categories of hierarchies in his Torah commentary, including birth order, order of importance, order of preference, and increasing or decreasing order of severity (for sins). In this tendency he follows the rabbinic mind-set for which nothing in the Torah is arbitrary or haphazard, but rather, as the word of God, has significance on multiple levels. Naḥmanides was also a kabbalist, steeped in mystical traditions of the Provençal school of kabbalah. He included in his commentary, which was intended for a popular audience, numerous allusions to hidden meanings of the verses of the Torah and interpretations of obscure, difficult midrashim, thereby stimulating kabbalistic activity and lending an aura of legitimacy to the esoteric understanding of the Torah as propounded by kabbalistic theosophy.

Kabbalistic Exegesis and *Pardes*

Nahmanides was active in Gerona, Spain, in the second half of the 13th century, in the generation preceding Moses de Leon and his circle who composed or compiled the zoharic corpus of mystical texts. (See "The Bible in the Mystical Tradition," pp. 1976–90.) While one can distinguish levels of interpretation in Nahmanides' commentary, it is in the last quarter of the 13th century, particularly in the *Zohar* and other writings often attributed by modern scholars to Moses de Leon that one first encounters the acronym *pardes* to refer to the four levels of interpretation of the biblical text, *peshat, remez, derash,* and *sod,* or historical, philosophical, homiletic, and mystical. This usage is primarily restricted to kabbalistic writings and did not achieve the almost universal application that the four senses achieved in medieval Christian exegesis. The first three methods of interpreting the text— the *peshat,* philosophical, and homiletical— already existed and were widely applied by exegetes of various persuasions up until that time. By introducing a fourth level and presenting it as the culmination of the exegetical process, the most profound understanding of the biblical text attainable, the kabbalists were validating the work of their predecessors while at the same time claiming pride of place for their own innovative approach to the text. The commentary of Nahmanides' student Bahya ben Asher (late 13th century) was more formally organized along the lines of the commentaries of the medieval Christian exegetes, with several levels of interpretation, although there are few verses which are interpreted on all four levels. But with the exception of Bahya, there are few examples of exegetes who analyze a book using all four methods consistently as did the Christians. Rather than being a methodology, *pardes* is a convenient way of describing the four approaches that medieval exegetes took in commenting on a biblical book. Some exegetes would use only one approach, some would combine two or three, but seldom would all four be consistently applied.

Eastern Post-Maimonidean School (13th Century)

Exegesis in the Middle East after Maimonides bears the unmistakable imprint of the thought of this greatly revered sage. Of great significance are the commentaries of Abraham, Maimonides' son (1186–1237), who was a great scholar, theologian and mystic in his own right. Abraham had hoped to fulfill his father's dream of producing a commentary on the Torah, but succeeded in completing only the first two books. His commentaries are eclectic, devoted in the main to *peshat* exegesis, in the tradition of scholars and grammarians of Andalusia, but also incorporating philosophical insights, and taking a critical stance vis-à-vis midrashic homilies. Abraham was greatly influenced by the pietistic Sufi (Muslim mystical) movement, which spread through Egypt in his day, and his commentaries are suffused with pietism. Indeed, he goes so far as to portray the patriarchs and the prophets as engaging in Sufi-style meditation and the pursuit of spiritual perfection. Abraham's commentaries, written in Judeo-Arabic, did not fare well, and survived in a single manuscript, published only in the mid-20th century.

The last significant *peshat* exegete in the Middle East was Tanhum ben Joseph Yerushalmi (ca. 1220–1291, originally from the land of Israel; died in Egypt). Tanhum was an anthologist, who compiled the best of the contextual exegesis of his predecessors, including Ibn Ezra, Radak, and Japheth ben Eli and other Karaites, often expressing his preferences. In his *Kitab al-Bayan (Book of Explanation)*, he commented on the entire Bible, but only sections on the Former Prophets, Latter Prophets (except Isaiah), Five Scrolls, Daniel, and parts of Psalms have survived. This work is preceded by an introduction which deals with many principles of scriptural exegesis, such as grammatical issues, textual difficulties, internal contradictions, and problems in chronology. In his commentaries he identifies many rhetorical devices, following in the tradition of Moses Ibn Ezra and other Spanish exegetes. Like Maimonides' son, Abraham, he too was profoundly influenced both by Maimonidean rationalism and by Sufi mysticism. Although primarily concerned with *peshat* exegesis, he often gives both exoteric and esoteric interpretations to specific passages. In the case of the book of Jonah, he deviates from his normal practice and interprets the entire book as an allegory of the soul.

The Fourteenth and Fifteenth Centuries

In the 14th and 15th centuries, commentaries tended to veer away from the *peshat* to follow homiletical, philosophical, or mystical lines. Nevertheless, *peshat* commentary was never completely abandoned. Jacob ben Asher (1270?–1340), who immigrated to Toledo, Spain, with his family in the early 14th century and was the author of a famous law code, *Sefer ha-Turim (The Book of Columns)*, wrote a lengthy *peshat* commentary in which he anthologized many of his famous predecessors, but also included many original comments. He prefaced each section with *gematriot* and explanations of the Masoretic tradition, in order to whet his reader's appetite. Ironically, it is these comments that proved to be most popular, and were frequently reprinted, while his long commentary languished in manuscript until 1806 and has never gained a wide readership. This is an indication of the low level of interest in *peshat* commentary in the later Middle Ages.

Exegetes of a philosophical bent tended to interpret Scripture through the prism of the philosophical school to which they adhered. (See "The Bible in the Philosophical Tradition," pp. 1948–75.) Two important examples are Levi ben Gershom (Ralbag; 1288–1344) and Joseph Ibn Kaspi (1279–1340), both Aristotelian rationalists, who followed the teachings of Maimonides. Ralbag was probably the most significant and original Jewish thinker of the later medieval period. He was also a prolific exegete, writing lengthy commentaries on the Torah, Early Prophets, Five Scrolls and Job. While his exegesis is certainly informed by his philosophical worldview, there is much in it that can be characterized as *peshat*. To give but one example of his rationalistic exegesis, he offers a daring interpretation of Joshua's miraculous victory at Gibeon (Josh. 10.12): the miracle that occurred was not that the sun actually stood still for Joshua and the Israelites, but that the Israelites enjoyed such a swift victory that it made it seem as if the sun stood still. In general, except for his commentary on Song of Songs, Ralbag did not engage in philosophical allegory. He typically divided his commentaries into three sections: (1) an explanation of the difficult words in a passage; (2) an expanded paraphrase of the text; and finally, at the end of the section, (3) a list of lessons, both moral and philosophical, which could be derived from it. Ralbag was the first exegete to provide such lessons in his commentaries, and in this he may have been influenced by Christian exegesis.

Ibn Kaspi, who hailed from Argentière in Provence (hence his name, meaning "silver"), wrote commentaries on almost the entire Bible. While primarily devoted to an understanding of *peshat*, these display his philosophical learning and his knowledge of Christian sources as well. He stresses numerous times in his commentaries the importance of a thorough knowledge of Hebrew grammar and a mastery of the science of logic in order to properly understand the Bible. For example, his entire commentary on the book of Esther is a critique of a comment by Ibn Ezra, which he refutes through logical analysis.

In this period, the Karaite community in Byzantium continued to develop biblical studies as it struggled to maintain its identity in the face of the overwhelming influence of the great medieval Rabbanite thinkers such as Maimonides and Ibn Ezra. The two great Karaite exegetes of the period were Aaron ben Joseph, the "elder" (ca. 1250–1320), and Aaron ben Elijah, of Nicomedia, "the younger" (ca. 1317–1369). Aaron ben Joseph produced commentaries on the Torah (Sefer ha-Mivḥar; The Book of the Most Select), on the Former Prophets, Isaiah, and Psalms (Mivḥar yesharim; The Most Select of the Righteous), and on Job (lost), while Aaron ben Elijah produced, inter alia, a commentary on the Torah (Keter Torah; The Crown of the Torah). Both authors cite Rabbanite sources extensively, including Rashi, Ibn Ezra, Maimonides, Radak, and Ramban. Ibn Ezra was especially popular, as he was among Rabbanite authors of the period. The commentaries of these exegetes follow in the Spanish tradition, relying on grammar and reason, rejecting aggadah, and, in halakhic matters, highlighting the differences between Rabbanites and Karaites.

In rabbinic circles, the sermons on the Torah ('Akeidat Yitzḥak; The Binding of Isaac) and the commentaries on the Five Scrolls of Isaac Arama (ca. 1420–1494) are exemplary models of homiletic exegesis, blending exegetical innovation and homiletic genius with psychological and philosophical insight. Arama was one of the first exegetes to use the method of problematization consistently, whereby the exegete raises a number of issues at the beginning of a passage, and then proceeds to solve the problems in the course of his discussion. This method was also followed by Don Isaac Abravanel (1437–1508), Arama's student, undoubtedly the greatest exegete of the 15th century. Abravanel produced voluminous commentaries on the Torah, Prophets, and Daniel, which are thoughtful, thought-provoking, and challenging. Abravanel was very much concerned with peshat exegesis, which he declared to be his primary focus. He also grapples seriously with the rabbinic midrashic tradition,

displaying a nuanced approach to midrashic interpretations, carefully selecting those that he found acceptable and rejecting others. More traditional in his theology than the rationalists of the later Middle Ages, he advocated a faith-based religious position which he considered to be more in line with the rabbinic tradition. For instance, he rejects Ralbag's rationalization of Joshua's miracle (10.12; see above) and declares that this was a divinely decreed deviation from the natural order. A true child of the Renaissance, he was open to the cultural innovations being articulated in his times and introduced much contemporary thought into his exegesis. He was particularly well-versed in Christian theological and exegetical literature, often quoting approvingly from Christian sources. Especially important are his ideas on the monarchy, expressed in his commentaries on Samuel and Kings. Drawing on his experience as a courtier and his deep familiarity with medieval history and political theory, he made a strong case against the monarchy, which he considered to be an inferior form of government.

Midrashic Exegesis

In the Middle Ages, the midrashic tradition was attacked on several fronts, especially by Karaites and Christians. As a result of these attacks, and because of the increased preference for peshat, many exegetes avoided rabbinic midrash as much as possible, while others incorporated it into their commentaries only sparingly, or else interpreted it philosophically or kabbalistically. Nevertheless, a strand of midrashic exegesis was maintained throughout the Middle Ages, quite possibly as a reaction to the elimination of such commentary from the medieval commentary tradition and out of a desire to hold up the standard of the rabbinic tradition and assure that it not be forgotten among Jews. Another reason could be the utility of midrashic material as a source for sermons, the demand for which seemed to increase as the Middle Ages waned. After the classical period of midrashic creativity during the late talmudic and geonic periods, the Middle Ages witnessed the production of many midrashic compilations. The largest and most comprehensive was the 13th century *Yalkut Shim'oni* (attributed to Simeon the Preacher of Frankfurt), an attempt at producing a comprehensive verse-by-verse midrashic anthology for the entire Bible. Others in this vein were *Midrash ha-Gadol (The Great Midrash)* by David Ha-Adani (Yemen, 14th century), *Yalkut (ha)-Makhiri* on the Latter Prophets and Writings by Makhir ben Abba Mari (Spain? 14th century?), and *Yalkut Re'uveni* (17th century), a kabbalistic-midrashic compilation by Reuben Ha-Kohen. There were also commentaries produced in the midrashic style, which included a great deal of *peshat* interpretation as well as midrashic material. Examples are the *Lekaḥ Tov (Good Instruction)* by Tobiah ben Eliezer (11th century, Byzantium) and *Sekhel Tov (Sound Understanding)* by Menaḥem ben Solomon (12th century, Italy?). Some anthologists had very ambitious goals for their work; for example, Jacob Sikili (Sicily, Damascus), stated in his anthology *Talmud Torah* (1366) that he included in it all halakhic and aggadic statements from all available sources, thus obviating the need to consult any other work.

Midrashic-style commentary was especially popular in Yemen, which witnessed the production of, among others, *Me'or ha-'afelah (The Luminary of the Darkness)* by Netanel ben Isaiah (1328–29), *Midrash ha-ḥefetz (The Midrash of Desire)* by Zekhariah ha-Rofe (1430), and *Midrash ha-be'ur (The Midrash of Explanation)* by Saadia ben David (1441). These editors were not mere compilers, but often edited their texts and added comments of their own, including many of a philosophical nature. Also unique to the Yemenite midrashim are numerous citations from Muslim lore and literature, as well as folkloristic material. Anthological commentaries such as these remained popular through the late Middle Ages and into the early modern period.

The Sixteenth Century

The upheaval of the expulsion from Spain (1492) and its aftermath scattered much of Spanish Jewry across Turkey, Greece, Italy, and North Africa. Biblical exegesis was produced in great abundance in all of these countries as well as in centers in Central and Eastern Europe. In Italy, the most famous exegete of the 15th century was Obadiah Sforno (ca. 1475–1550). He produced commentaries on the Torah and Psalms, which are dedicated above all to elucidating the *peshat*. Sforno, a rabbi, was also a trained physician and a cultured individual, a fine product of the world of Renaissance humanism, whose values infuse his exegesis. His Torah commentary became one of the mainstays of the biblical commentary tradition.

In the Ottoman Empire, important centers of study arose in Salonika and Constantinople. Rabbi Isaac ben Joseph Karo, a Spanish Jew, survived the Spanish and Portuguese exiles, ending up in Constantinople. In 1518 he published his commentary on the Torah, *Toledot Yitzḥak (The Story of Isaac)*, which proved to be one of the most popular and influential commentaries of the 16th century. The commentary is eclectic, incorporating comments in all four of the traditional modes of interpretation, and reveals the author's cultural sophistication. Its immense popularity is indicated by the fact that it went through four editions in fourteen years and is often quoted by later exegetes.

In Salonika, the yeshiva of Joseph Taitatzak flourished between 1525 and 1540, training many rabbis and scholars who produced vast quantities of biblical commentary, which far surpassed those produced in the Middle Ages in quantity if not in quality. For the book of Esther and other scrolls, for example, more commentaries were written in the 16th century than in all the centuries preceding. This surge in commentary production can be explained by the needs of the various communities for relevant biblical commentary; most arose out of sermons preached in public on the Sabbaths and holidays which were later committed to writing. Many of the commentaries produced are characterized by their prolixity, tendentiousness, inconsistencies, and homiletical nature. Yet there is still much of value that can be gleaned from them, and they deserve more attention than they have received in the past. Of particular interest is Eliezer Ashkenazi (1513–1586), a student of Joseph Taitatzak's who was one of the leading scholars of his generation. Ashkenazi was a talmudist and rationalist who knew many languages and was scientifically trained. He advocated the unfettered search for truth in Scripture. His greatest work is *Ma'asei 'Adonai (Acts of God)*, a four-part commentary on the narrative portions of the Torah. In this work, he urges the student to search diligently for the truth without regard for the opinions of the Sages or previous exegetes, especially the latter, since they may have become corrupted over time. He develops a theory concerning the nature and purpose of the biblical stories, according to which the events narrated in the Torah actually occurred, but the stories which relate these events are parables. The plain sense of the text can be found in the parables and not in the events themselves. In his commentary, Ashkenazi grapples with important theological issues, such as divine providence and the influence of astrology over Jewish destiny.

Other contemporary exegetes worthy of mention are Moses Alshekh (d. 1593) and Solomon ben Moses ha-Levi Alkabetz (ca. 1505–1584), both members of the Safed school of mystics. The exegetes of this period took a particular interest in the Kethuvim, especially the Five Scrolls, Psalms, and Job. Alshekh, a talmudist and kabbalist, had studied at Joseph Taitatzak's yeshiva in Salonika and later moved to Safed. Like many of his contemporaries, he preached on the Sabbaths and holidays on the weekly Torah readings and other biblical books and later edited his sermons for publication. He produced commentaries on almost the entire Bible. Solomon Alkabetz, another student of Taitatzak, and one of the

more important members of the kabbalistic circle of Safed, produced compendious commentaries on the Minor Prophets, Song of Songs, Esther, Ruth, Psalms, and Job, incorporating the comments of many of his contemporaries and predecessors. His commentaries are characterized by their extreme reverence for the words of the Sages, which he considered to be authentic traditions reflecting the true meaning of the text, and not mere homiletical interpretations, which could be accepted or rejected at will.

Meanwhile, in Aleppo, Syria, Samuel ben Abraham Laniado (d. 1605) was composing an impressive body of commentary, covering most of the Bible (Torah, Prophets, Psalms, Lamentations). Laniado's commentaries are especially noteworthy for their sensitivity to literary nuance and structural patterns in the text, thus making them quite "modern" in their orientation.

In Eastern Europe at this time, talmudic studies were dominant and biblical studies were in a state of decline. The output of biblical commentary, while significant, was dwarfed by the production in other fields. Even so, much of the commentary literature of this period was written in homiletic style, with constant recourse to rabbinic sources, and often to philosophical and mystical sources as well. Particularly popular as sources were the commentaries of Isaac Arama and Isaac Karo. *Peshat* commentaries were relatively uncommon. Among the better known commentaries was the *Gur Aryeh* by Judah Loew ben Bezalel of Prague (Maharal; 1525–1609), a super-commentary on Rashi, which combines concern with the *peshat* with reference to rabbinic sources as deep *peshat*, the true meaning of the text, which goes deeper than the literal. He also does not neglect mystical traditions. In general, however, Maharal and other exegetes of the period did not innovate methodologically and did not advance Bible study beyond the stage it was at by the end of the Middle Ages.

The Seventeenth and Eighteenth Centuries

In the 17th century, several noteworthy commentaries were produced. In Poland, Ephraim Solomon ben Aaron of Luntshits (1550–1619), a gifted *darshan,* or sermonizer, produced several collections of sermons and a commentary on the Torah in the homiletic style, called *Keli Yakar* (1st ed. Lublin, 1602), which enjoyed immense popularity and was included in many editions of the Rabbinic Bible. More than a century later, Ḥayyim ben Moses Ibn 'Attar (1696–1743), a rabbi and kabbalist of Moroccan origin, who led a group of rabbis and students to settle in the land of Israel in 1740, wrote a commentary titled *'Or ha-ḥayim,* first published in Venice in 1742. This commentary was often published alongside that of Ephraim of Luntshits in East European editions of the Rabbinic Bible (*Miqra'ot Gedolot,* see below) and was especially popular among the Ḥasidim.

In Jaworow, Galicia, David Altschuler began to produce a commentary on the Prophets and Writings in order to promote the study of the Bible. His work was continued by his son, Jehiel Hillel, who in 1780–82 published the entire commentary. It was divided into two sections, *Metsudat Tsiyon (Fortress of Zion)* and *Metsudat David (Fortress of David).* The former explains the meanings of individual words, the latter the meaning of the text. The commentary, based for the most part on the medieval *peshat* exegetes such as Radak and Ibn Ezra, was very popular and has been frequently republished. (It appears in most editions of *Miqra'ot Gedolot,* see below.)

This period also saw the production of vernacular commentaries on the Bible in various parts of the Jewish world. At the end of the 16th or beginning of the 17th century, Jacob ben Isaac Ashkenazi, of Janow (d. 1623), produced a Yiddish translation with commentary on significant liturgical portions of the Tanakh, namely the Torah, Haftarot (Prophetic Readings) and Megillot (Five Scrolls). The book, *Tzene-rene* (i.e., *Tze'enah u-re'enah,* or *Go Forth and Gaze* [based on Song of Songs 3.11, which is addressed to the daughters of Zion]), proved to be the most popular work in the history of Yiddish literature. Over 210 editions of this work have appeared to date. The oldest extant edition, which is not the first, appeared in Basel in 1622. At least three others had preceded it. The book was written in a popular style, intended for Yiddish-speaking Jewish men and women who lacked the education necessary for understanding the Bible in the original. In this work, the author does not provide a word-for-word translation of the text, but rather weaves together the biblical text, midrashim, medieval commentaries, elements of halakhah, and ethical admonition into a pleasing, harmonious whole. The author drew on a wide variety of rabbinic and medieval sources, not only commentaries, but also ethical (*Sefer Ḥasidim, Sefer ha-Mevakesh*), philosophical (Saadia, Ibn Gabirol, Maimonides), and mystical works (*Zohar,* Cordovero's *Palm Tree of Deborah*). The author's major medieval source seems to have been the commentary of Baḥya ben Asher. He also drew heavily on Isaac Karo's *Toledot Yitzḥak.* The work became especially popular with women, who would read it religiously every Sabbath. Its success can be attributed to the author's skill in selecting his material and finding those sources which would appeal to his unschooled readers. He was especially successful in selecting sources that would appeal to his female readers, injecting comments of a midrashic and moralistic nature, relating to marital relations and child-rearing. *Tzene-rene* went through numerous editions, first in Western, then in Eastern Europe, and some editions bore the ideological stamp of the maskilic rationalists or their Hasidic opponents. Editions, translations, and adaptations of this ever-popular work are still being produced. A similar work on the Prophets and Writings, called *Sefer ha-Magid (The Book of the Storyteller)* mistakenly attributed to Ashkenazi, also attained considerable popularity, but nothing approaching that of *Tzene-rene.*

In the 18th century, a parallel phenomenon to *Tzene-rene* was the publication in Constantinople of *Me'am Lo'ez (From a Foreign People)*, a Ladino (Judeo-Spanish) commentary on the Bible, which is considered to be the outstanding work of Judeo-Spanish literature. Conceived by Jacob Culi as a response to the havoc wrought by the Sabbatean heresy of the previous century (Shabbetai Tzevi was followed by many as Messiah, but converted to Islam in 1666, precipitating a great crisis), it was aimed at the masses who had strayed from observant Judaism and could no longer read the texts in Hebrew. Culi produced the volume for Genesis, which wove together in a pleasing and appealing manner a variety of sources dealing with the text, including much ancillary material such as anecdotes, ethical admonitions, folklore, and historical narratives. After Culi's death, his work was continued by others. The rest of the Torah was completed and published by 1772, and other volumes, published in a similar style, were produced over the following centuries. In recent years a Hebrew translation has been produced. It is difficult to overstate the importance of *Me'am Lo'ez* in Sephardic culture. It spread all over the Sephardic world and for many families it was the only literature that they read. Unlike *Tzene-rene,* it was never considered only suitable for women, and so was equally popular among men, women, and children.

By the mid-18th century, the winds of change were blowing through the Jewish communities of Europe, and the stage was being set for the Haskalah and the revolution in study that would follow in its wake. (See "Post-medieval Jewish Interpretation," pp. 1900–1908, and "The Bible in the Jewish Philosophical Tradition," pp. 1948–75.)

Miqra'ot Gedolot

The production of Bibles with the biblical text surrounded by a number of commentaries and translations began in the late Middle Ages, as scribes copied for themselves or patrons commissioned such works for their own use. With the introduction and spread of the printing press, commentaries were first produced individually, or accompanying the biblical text. The first Rabbinic Bible was published by Daniel Bomberg in 1516 in Venice and included the commentaries of Rashi, Ibn Ezra, and Ramban. Other editions soon followed (Venice, 1524–25, 1544). The second Rabbinic Bible (1524–1525), edited by Jacob ben Ḥayyim ben Isaac Ibn Adonijah (ca. 1470–ca. 1538), an apprentice of Bomberg's who converted to Christianity late in life, is especially important, because of the editor's attention to the accuracy of the text, seeking out manuscripts to help in this task, and his attempt to produce an edition faithful to the Masoretic tradition. (See "The Development of the Masoretic Bible," pp. 2077–84.) He also succeeded in printing more commentaries than had his predecessors. His edition set the standard for generations to come and served as the basis for many subsequent editions. Another important edition was *Kehilat Mosheh (The Congregation of Moses;* Amsterdam, 1724–1727), edited by Moses Frankfurter, which had sixteen commentaries never before included, such as those of Ralbag. In the 19th century in Eastern Europe, the production of such editions of the Bible became extremely popular and publishers in Warsaw, Vilna, and Cracow vied for customers' attention, competing for the distinction of having the greatest number of commentaries in their editions. It was early in the 19th century that the title *Miqra'ot Gedolot (Great Scriptures)* for such editions was first introduced. Besides the classical triumvirate of Rashi, Ibn Ezra, and Naḥmanides, the *Keli yakar (Precious Vessel)* by Ephraim of Luntshitz and *Or ha-Ḥayim (Light of Life)* by Ḥayyim Ibn 'Attar seem to have been immensely popular and gained a wide readership. For Prophets and Writings, the *Metzudot* of the Altschulers were constant companions of Rashi. Depending on the book, they were usually joined by Ibn Ezra, Radak, Ralbag, and Sforno. There can be no doubt that these editions had a tremendous influence on which commentaries were read and which were neglected. Inclusion in an edition of *Miqra'ot Gedolot* would ensure a wide audience. The juxtaposition of commentaries from different locations and periods also influenced how the Bible was studied (see p. 1875). Such editions facilitate a dialogue across generations and cultures mediated by the reader, who thus becomes another link in the ongoing tradition of biblical study and interpretation. [BARRY D. WALFISH]

Post-medieval Jewish Interpretation

The period between 1650 and 1900 forms a particularly rich and variegated chapter in the history of Jewish biblical interpretation, particularly within the European Ashkenazic communities. Over the course of these two and a half centuries, hundreds of Bible commentaries and super-commentaries were written and published, and although the vast majority have fallen into obscurity, a few have exerted considerable influence and continue to be studied to this day. The substantial scholarly output of this period was broadly due to three historically related factors: the growth and relative stability of communities in both Western and Eastern Europe, a flourishing religious and scholarly life, and an active Jewish printing industry.

The biblical scholarship of this period is particularly important because of the way in which it reflected and even shaped the far-reaching historical, religious, and cultural shifts taking place within European Jewry. Through most of the 17th and 18th centuries, the interpretation of the Bible was largely derivative of medieval exegesis, particularly the didactic and homiletical modes of late medieval scholarship. As the 18th century progressed, the textual and linguistic interests of medieval Spanish exegesis began to be revived, and by 1800 biblical interpretation was given new impetus by the Jewish Enlightenment and, to a lesser degree, by the reinvigorated scholarly circles that emerged in Lithuania in opposition to the spread of Hasidism. In the 19th century, as the cultural and religious insularity of traditional Jewish life gave way to the external pressures of emancipation, and as internal divisions weakened the authority of rabbinic Judaism, the interpretation of Scripture became a central factor in the struggle to determine the meaning and relevance of inherited Jewish traditions.

Despite the large numbers of Bible commentaries that appeared in the 17th and 18th centuries, almost all of them were methodologically unoriginal and substantively unremarkable. In the Sephardic communities of North Africa, the Middle East, and Western Europe (e.g., Amsterdam and Hamburg), there seems to have been some effort to maintain the study of the Bible and Hebrew language pioneered by medieval Spanish scholars, but with few linguistic or exegetical advances. Among the Ashkenazic communities of Western and Eastern Europe, the reality was more complex. On the one hand, biblical commentaries were a time-honored scholarly endeavor, and a great many of them centered around the careful parsing of midrashic texts and Rashi's commentary, which had attained near-canonical status. On the other hand, there was a pronounced ambivalence, if not indifference, toward Bible study, and especially any kind of scholarship that focused on the philological or grammatical aspects of the text. The study of rabbinic literature, both the Talmud and the long line of codes and commentaries that followed in its wake, was given intellectual and spiritual pride of place, and the study of the Bible was relegated to a respectful, honored, but distinctly secondary position. These realities are reflected in the fact that some of the best and most enduring writings of this era emerged from non-Ashkenazic Mediterranean communities: *Me'am Lo'ez*, the mid-18th-century popular

Ladino compilation of rabbinic writings (Constantinople, 1730–1772); Ḥayyim ben Moses Ibn ʿAttar's *'Or ha-ḥayim* (Venice, 1742) which became very popular among Ashkenazic Jewry; and David Samuel Pardo's *Maskil le-David* (Venice, 1761), a super-commentary to Rashi.

Modern students of the Bible have often credited a group of 17th-century thinkers, among them Benedict Spinoza (1634–1677), for anticipating the emergence of modern biblical criticism by eschewing traditional modes of interpretation and by raising questions concerning the reliability, authenticity, and even authorship of the Bible. In his *Theologico-Political Treatise* (1670) Spinoza set out to employ "the true method of scriptural interpretation," which would entail examining the Bible afresh "in a careful, impartial, and unfettered spirit, making no assumptions concerning it" (Benedict Spinoza, *Theologico-Political Treatise,* transl. R. H. M. Elwes, New York: Dover Publications, 1951; preface and pp. 98–119). Spinoza's intention was to undermine the presumption of a seamless, consistent text that could be ascribed to the hand of Moses and to convince his readers that the Bible was so confused and beset with problems that a clear understanding of its meaning was often beyond reach. A careful reading of the *Theologico-Political Treatise,* however, belies the scholarly value of his biblical insights by revealing the arbitrary nature of his methods and the capricious quality of many of his conclusions. Spinoza's discussion was far less interested in the interpretative difficulties and challenges of the Bible than in undermining the authority of Scripture for a variety of philosophical and political reasons. Moreover, since it was written in Latin, Spinoza's handling of the Bible had absolutely no impact on 17th- and 18th-century Jewish interpretation of the Bible. It is generally believed that European scholars who launched the serious critical study of the Bible drew upon Spinoza's writing, although a careful examination of their scholarship might suggest more limited influence.

The Ashkenazic ambivalence toward the Bible began to change slowly in the 18th century, as some rabbinic authorities and scholars increasingly complained about the neglect of Bible study, particularly the pedagogic inattention to sound grammatical and textual skills. A small number of new books, most notably those of Solomon Hanau (1687–1746), tried to revive interest in the study of Hebrew grammar and to recapture some of the vibrancy of earlier generations. There was a rediscovery of the *peshat*-oriented commentary of Rashbam, and later in the century, a renewed interest in the writings of David Kimḥi (Radak) and Abraham Ibn Ezra.

By far the most important development in this regard was the appearance of the Haskalah (Jewish Enlightenment) in late 18th-century Prussia and its impact on the culture of European Jewry. As part of their effort to promote the integration of Jews into European society, these Jewish Enlightenment figures, or maskilim as they came to be known, were highly attuned to the achievements of contemporary German culture and sensitive to the perceived deficiencies of Jewish education and scholarship. The maskilic interest in the study of Scripture was thus shaped by a double orientation. On the one hand, maskilim were attracted by some of the universalism and literary-aesthetic sophistication of the German and European Enlightenments, and they sought to infuse Jewish Bible study with the same textual sensibilities. On the other hand, embarrassed by the state of biblical scholarship within their own communities, they wanted to showcase the wealth of inherited textual traditions and advance the study of Scripture in distinctly Jewish terms.

Both tendencies were evident in the new edition of the Torah published by Moses Mendelssohn (1729–1786), a highly regarded German philosopher and man of letters who was also the most prominent individual associated with the Berlin Haskalah. Appearing in Berlin between 1780 and 1783 as *Sefer Netivot ha-Shalom,* Mendelssohn's Bible was a collaborative affair that came to include two of the finest scholars associated with the Haskalah, Naftali Herz Wessely (1725–1805) and Solomon Dubno (1738–1813). *Sefer Netivot ha-Shalom* included a new German translation, an extensive Hebrew commentary, and a series of highly technical Masoretic notes that attempted to fix the precise morphology and pointing of the text. The German translation, printed in Hebrew script and rendered into a good contemporary *Hochdeutsch* ("high," or "literary," German), served the same function as earlier Bible translations, namely, to make the text accessible to a growing number of Jews who felt less comfortable with Hebrew than with their native tongue. More importantly, the translation also set out to capture the prosaic and poetic qualities of the Hebrew original in order to offer Jews a text that was as aesthetically sophisticated as any German Bible in circulation, but without christologically-informed readings and interpretations, and without the textual emendations being introduced by contemporary German scholars. In this regard, Mendelssohn offered his co-religionists a Bible translation that conformed to both Jewish textual traditions and rabbinic interpretations.

The Hebrew commentary to this Bible embraced the same twofold orientation. On the one hand, the *Bi'ur* (Heb *b-'-r*) or "explanation," as this commentary was simply titled, culled the medieval exegesis of Rashi, Rashbam, Ibn Ezra, and Naḥmanides (see "Medieval Interpretation," pp. 1876–1900 and "Jewish Translations of the Bible," pp. 2005–20) for the best of their *peshat*-oriented interpretations, while also contributing its own linguistic and literary insights. In the face of broad European disregard for the scholarly value of rabbinic literature, on the other hand, Mendelssohn and some of his fellow commentators tried to demonstrate the exegetical acuity of midrashic interpretations by pointing to the sound philological, syntactical, and narrative insights exhibited by the Sages of late antiquity. This commentary, in fact, went out of its way to incorporate rabbinic literature, both midrash halakhah (legal interpreta-

tion) and midrash aggadah (interpretation of narratives), and to explain its relationship to *peshuto shel miqra'*—the "plain" sense of the text. Mendelssohn and his fellow contributors adopted differing strategies with regard to the articulation of this relationship: Mendelssohn viewed *peshat* (the plain sense) and *derash* (rabbinic-homiletical interpretation) as eliciting two hermeneutically distinct yet equally veracious layers of the text, while Wessely was more inclined to conflate the two by suggesting that the rabbinic reading represented nothing but the true depths of *peshat*. In either case, their commentaries displayed serious regard for the linguistic qualities of Scripture, using it to elicit fresh approaches to the biblical text as well as a better appreciation for the substantive exegetical legacy of rabbinic Judaism. The *Bi'ur* was reprinted in dozens of 19th-century editions, making it by far the most popular Jewish Bible and second only to the traditional texts published with Targum and Rashi.

In Eastern Europe, meanwhile, many Jewish communities had been swept up by the social and religious revivalism of Hasidism, and with it came a number of scholarly and popular commentaries to the Bible. The opposition to this movement, centered in the leadership of R. Elijah ben Solomon Zalman (the Vilna Gaon; 1720–1797) and his Lithuanian-based disciples, was no less intensely committed to the study of kabbalistic traditions, and they too incorporated these scholarly pursuits into their study of Scripture. R. Elijah and his followers, however, also cultivated an interest in the Bible that roughly paralleled, and may even have been informed by, maskilic developments in Western Europe. In his *'Aderet 'Eliyahu*, first published posthumously in an 1804 edition of the Torah, R. Elijah called attention to the importance of *peshat*-oriented readings of Scripture, while at the same time probing the nature of rabbinic exegesis. His expression of concern for the biblical text and its traditional rabbinic interpretation, however, was aimed at underscoring the far-reaching, even radical, nature of rabbinic *de-*

rashot (homiletical expositions). This commentary did not in itself set out to advance fresh approaches to the biblical text, nor did it substantively explicate the exegetical discernment of the Sages. With this emphasis on the distinction of *peshat* and *derash,* R. Elijah sought to highlight the interpretative creativity and profundity of rabbinic Judaism, an endeavor that would shape the intellectual and spiritual character of Lithuanian scholarship well into the 20th century.

The most significant developments in Jewish biblical scholarship, however, took place among 19th-century Jews concentrated in German-speaking Europe. As the Jews of these regions began their century-long struggle to gain civic equality and social integration, the contemporary study of the Bible came to reflect the cultural and religious vicissitudes of the age. One can discern three different though somewhat overlapping trends, all of them cognizant of the relationship of Bible study to the broader challenges of modernity, and all of them staking out a set of assumptions regarding Scripture and its religious and cultural meaning to contemporary Jews.

In the wake of the German Haskalah, there was a discernible revival of Hebrew and Bible study among European Jews. Within a decade after the publication of Mendelssohn's Bible, a group of younger maskilim had extended the project to cover the books of the Prophets and Writings. *Sefer Netivot ha-Shalom* was eagerly studied in some circles, and over the next half-century there appeared a number of super-commentaries to the *Bi'ur.* In 1810, Judah Leib ben Ze'ev (1764–1811), one of the last contributors to the German Haskalah before its dissipation, wrote a set of introductory essays to the Prophets and Writings that drew upon contemporary German scholarship, in which he laid out their respective historical and literary features, including some critical notions regarding authorship. More importantly, the interest in Hebrew and Bible study was also taken up by those not directly identified with the Haskalah, but who shared some

of its cultural predilections. Solomon Pappenheim (1740–1814), a rabbinic court judge in Breslau, wrote a multi-volume study of Hebrew synonyms, while Wolf Heidenheim (1757–1832), an important publisher and editor of liturgical texts, penned a series of commentaries on the Masorah and a super-commentary to Rashi.

As the Haskalah spread into other regions of Europe, a younger generation of traditionally trained yet maskilically oriented scholars also took up the study of the Bible. Much of this scholarship did not appear in the classical form of the commentary, but rather as essays and studies published in leading maskilic journals such as *Bikurei ha-Itim* and *Kerem Ḥemed.* In Galicia, Nachman Krochmal (1785–1840) addressed questions regarding Isaiah, Ecclesiastes, and Psalms, embracing the late dating of sections of this literature and arguing that such critical awareness was already evident in rabbinic literature. His one-time student and friend Solomon Rappoport (1790–1867) also included in his writings similar critical ideas regarding the books of Isaiah and Psalms. In Italy, Isaac Samuel Reggio (1784–1855) produced an extensive Hebrew commentary alongside his Italian translation of the Torah, as well as a number of essays on biblical issues. Samuel David Luzzatto (1800–1865), Reggio's contemporary and colleague, wrote at least two Hebrew grammars, a study of *Targum Onkelos,* and various articles on Hebrew philology. His lectures on the Torah, including introductions to issues regarding the biblical text and modes of interpretation, were collected and published posthumously. Paralleling but somewhat independent of these endeavors, there also emerged a group of Lithuanian maskilim who produced a number of commentaries, super-commentaries, and journal articles that took up various linguistic and exegetical issues pertaining to the study of the Bible.

Taken together, these writings exemplify the increased pedagogic and scholarly attention to biblical scholarship as part of an endeavor to expand the intellectual, religious, and cultural horizons of European Jews. This body of literature, however, was also largely traditionalist in its commitments and sensibilities, and did not broadly engage the critical-scholarly ideas emanating from the German universities. Critical notions regarding the text, its editing, and its historical context were raised only with regard to the non-Torah books of the Bible, and largely where medieval scholars had either opened the door to such notions or where there existed sufficient ambiguity to allow for new ideas. While these writings did not generally have enduring value, they did make the engagement with Scripture a far more central part of European Jewish culture.

The second salient trend that characterized the 19th-century study of Scripture emanated from a group of Jews far more receptive to the academic methods and intellectual discourse of contemporary German scholarship. Emerging in the 1810s, this group began to promote the *Wissenschaft des Judentums*, the critical-academic ("scientific") study of Jewish history and literature, with particular emphasis on texts, languages, and philosophical issues not generally studied in traditional settings. Two of the most important members of this movement, Leopold Zunz (1794–1886) and Abraham Geiger (1810–1874), contributed substantively to the scholarly study of the Bible. Zunz edited a German translation of the Bible and wrote critically about the books of Psalms and Chronicles, later even turning his attention to issues in the Torah as well. Geiger focused his *Urschrift und Übersetzungen der Bibel* (Breslau, 1857) on the originally fluid nature of the biblical text and the presence of competing versions, a phenomenon that he substantiated by pointing to the varying translations of Scripture that emerged in late antiquity.

Although Geiger's critical insights went beyond those of Krochmal, Rappoport, and Luzzatto, these scholars formed a broader circle in which the distinctions between maskil and proponents of *Wissenschaft* were considerably blurred. Still, those associated primarily with

Wissenschaft who had at the same time disencumbered themselves of traditional practices and beliefs had far more social and intellectual freedom to pursue a wide variety of questions regarding the Bible. In the case of Geiger, one of the most important and active Reform leaders, one might have expected a concerted effort to apply new historical-critical methods to the Bible to counter traditionalist beliefs and to help bolster some central historical assertions of the nascent Reform movement. In fact, proponents of *Wissenschaft des Judentums* engaged the Bible in a rather limited way; they appeared less interested in the development of new critical perspectives relating to the origins of the Bible or to the serious study of biblical history or philology, than in the textual and interpretative *reception* of the biblical text. This was evident in Geiger's *Urschrift* and its attention to early Bible translations. Underlying his scholarly thinking was the notion that the Bible was not a "sealed book of antiquity, whose meaning the student had to unlock in order to acquaint himself with the ideas of a day long past." Rather, "every age, every movement and every personality in history has brought its own ideas to bear upon the Bible" (Abraham Geiger, *Urschrift und Übersetzungen der Bibel*, Breslau, 1857, p. 72). This unobjectionable observation, a staple of intellectual history, was not merely a programmatic outline of an important subfield of biblical scholarship; Geiger's statement that the Bible was all things to all people was predicated upon his insistence that an objective interpretation of Scripture could not be achieved, and therefore was not a particularly valuable endeavor to pursue. For Geiger, as for other contributors to the *Wissenschaft des Judentums*, the cultural and religious needs of the moment manifested themselves in an almost exclusive focus upon the manifold ways in which the Bible had been read—pointing clearly to the possibility of other, more contemporaneous readings—rather than on the original meaning of the text. Jewish critical scholarship would eventually free itself of these constraints, but at this juncture the social and cultural bases upon which to develop such interests were as yet undeveloped.

The third trend that characterized the 19th-century study of the Bible arose out of the most traditionalist element of European Jewry, that which came to be identified by its orthodoxy. Traditionalist leaders were largely unwilling to deal with scholarly advances in biblical criticism, but they were acutely sensitive to other 19th-century developments that they perceived to be far more pressing: the growing abandonment of traditional Jewish practices, and the Reform eschewal of rabbinic authority in general, and ancient rabbinic readings of Scripture in particular. Alongside their communal and polemical activities against the burgeoning Reform movement, a number of these traditional defenders of rabbinic Judaism also sought to buttress their orthodoxy by turning to the Bible and trying to demonstrate the fundamental accord between Scripture and its rabbinic elucidations. The resulting commentaries, lengthy and extensive as they are, contributed an important and lasting corpus of traditional scholarship to the history of biblical interpretation.

The first of these commentaries, expressly written to address the relationship of the Oral Torah to Scripture, was *Ha-Ketav veha-Kabalah (The Written Text and [Rabbinic] Tradition)*, published in 1839 by R. Jacob Zvi Meklenburg (1785–1865) of Königsberg. This exegete exhibited an impressive scholarly range that included not only rabbinic and medieval texts, but also a rudimentary knowledge of classical languages and a familiarity with maskilic and *Wissenschaft* writings. Meklenburg was most concerned about the perceived inauthenticity of oral traditions, particularly the idea that rabbinic readings were foisted unnaturally upon Scripture. In response, he suggested that a refined grasp of the biblical language and idiom would demonstrate that "the Written Torah and the Oral Torah are twins, stuck one to the other such that they could not be sundered" (*Ha-*

Ketav veha-Kabalah, Leipzig, 1839, introduction, p. xiii). Meklenburg, however, did not intend to collapse the distinction between *peshat* and *derash*. His aim, rather, was to defuse any apparent tension between them and to legitimate midrashic and talmudic readings by grounding them in the biblical text with subtlety and sophistication.

In the body of the commentary itself, this particular concern for rabbinic exegesis actually played a secondary role. His explication of the rabbinic interpretations of Scripture was undertaken only on a selective basis, and his limited attempts at laying out a systematic approach to the problem relied substantially on Mendelssohn's writings. *Ha-Ketav veha-Kabalah* was devoted first and foremost to an explication of *peshuto shel miqra'* (the plain sense of the biblical text), drawing extensively and in an undifferentiated manner on Mendelssohn's *Sefer Netivot ha-Shalom*, the Vilna Gaon's *'Aderet 'Eliyahu*, and the scholarly contributions of Pappenheim, Heidenheim, Luzzatto, and others. In many ways, this commentary served as an excellent anthology of late 18th- and early 19th-century *peshat* exegesis, a collection that reflected the reinvigoration of Jewish Bible study. *Ha-Ketav veha-Kabalah* was published again in 1852 with a number of substantial additions and deletions, and material was again added to the edition that appeared in 1880; this latter edition was subsequently reprinted numerous times.

Responding to similar religious challenges and drawing upon some of the same scholarly traditions, R. Meir Leibush ben Yehiel Michel (1809–1879) also set out with the scholarly aim of joining the Written and Oral Torahs, but he approached the undertaking in a far more systematic and substantive fashion. More commonly known by his acronym, Malbim, he served as a communal rabbi in the Posen region of eastern Prussia through the 1850s, at a time when proponents of reform began to articulate their positions with greater forcefulness. By mid-century he had authored commentaries to Isaiah, Song of

Songs, and Esther, and in 1866 he produced a commentary to the Prophets and Writings. In 1860 he published an edition of the *Sifra*, the early rabbinic midrash to Leviticus, which interpolated the relevant biblical verses at the head of each midrashic segment, and to which he wrote a commentary titled *Ha-Torah veha-Mitzvah*. It is most significant, in terms of understanding Malbim's methods and aims, that it was this rabbinic commentary that appeared with the full text of the *Sifra* as the Leviticus section of his Bible commentary. Over the next two decades Malbim applied this approach to the other books of the Torah, producing a commentary to the *Mekhilta* (Exodus) and *Sifre* (Numbers and Deuteronomy); for sections of the Bible without midrash halakhah, Malbim posed a series of questions to which he supplied lengthy answers, somewhat reminiscent of the style employed earlier by Abravanel and other late medieval scholars. Judging by its numerous reprintings, this work proved to be one of the most popular Bible commentaries of late 19th-century European Jewry.

In his extensive two-part introduction to the original *Sifra* commentary, Malbim was unequivocal about his overarching objective: to develop tools that would demonstrate the veracity of rabbinic traditions. The Sages, he asserted, had a profound knowledge of Hebrew that included a firm grasp of grammatical principles, sensitivity to the subtlest of differences among apparently synonymous nouns and verbs, and an appreciation of biblical style and idiom, all of which he detailed in a separate section of the introduction. Malbim explicitly rejected the notion that rabbinic teachings were merely traditions that used scriptural verses as props or as a kind of subscript. Moreover, unlike Mendelssohn and Meklenburg, and more akin to the approach taken by Wessely, he insisted upon the linguistic profundity of rabbinic literature, which resulted in the blurring of the distinction between *peshat* and *derash*. After all, if the Sages were superb linguists and readers of texts, then all their interpretations could be identified with *peshuto shel miqra'*. The words of the Oral Torah, he wrote, "are compelled by and ingrained in the Scriptural *peshat* and in the depths of the language. *Derush* [sic] alone is the simple *peshat* that is based upon the true and clear rules of language" (Malbim, *Sifra devei Rav . . . im Peirush Ha-Torah veha-Mitzvah*, Bucharest, 1860, p. 2a).

The reawakened interest in Hebrew and Bible study and the need to reinforce the integrity of traditional Judaism shaped the writing of a number of other Bible commentaries worthy of note. In the late 1860s, R. Samson Raphael Hirsch (1808–1888) began publishing a translation and lengthy German commentary to the Torah (*Der Pentateuch, übersetzt und erläutert*, Frankfurt am Main, 1867–1878). As one of the most prominent and outspoken leaders of German Orthodoxy, Hirsch was no less committed to the defense of normative rabbinic Judaism than Meklenburg and Malbim, but he took an entirely different approach to the interpretation of Scripture. In his view, the corpus of rabbinic teachings could not—and for polemical purposes, should not—be derived from the biblical text. Although the Bible served as a kind of a mnemonic primer that elicited the particulars of the Oral Torah, this was possible only in the presence of a revealed tradition that Moses and the Israelites had already absorbed (see Hirsch's commentary to Exodus 21.2). Instead, highly sensitive to the prevailing European-Protestant depreciation of Judaism, Hirsch used his commentary to demonstrate the thoroughly integrated spiritual and ethical worldview of the Torah. Utilizing a mix of philology and homiletics, Hirsch produced what could best be described as a theosophical commentary which made heavy use of biblical symbolism and which mined biblical narratives and strictures for their sublime moral teachings. In tenor and substance, as in language and style, Hirsch's commentary remained a distinct contribution to 19th-century biblical interpretation.

More than a generation later, R. David Zvi Hoffmann (1843–1921), rector of the Orthodox rabbinic seminary of Berlin and an important leader of German Jewry in his own right, produced German commentaries to the books of Leviticus and Deuteronomy (*Das Buch Leviticus, übersetzt und erklärt*, Berlin, 1905–1906; *Das Buch Deuteronomium, übersetzt und erklärt*, Berlin, 1913–1922). His biblical commentaries combined overlapping traditionalist elements of Haskalah and *Wissenschaft* scholarship with the orthodox apologia of scholars like Meklenburg. Academically trained and well versed in contemporary European biblical scholarship, Hoffmann was as concerned with defending the integrity of the Bible as displaying its ultimate concordance with rabbinic oral traditions. Like Malbim, he devoted a considerable amount of scholarly attention to the study of midrash halakhah, but the methodological conclusions he drew were different. Hoffmann allowed that in many instances rabbinic traditions either preceded or appeared concurrently with their scripturally based articulation in midrashic literature and could not be independently derived from the biblical text. Nevertheless, the task of the modern exegete was to connect the Bible with tradition, even if retrospectively. Hoffmann's biblical writings, however, were not focused solely on this issue, and their scholarly range was broader than any other 19th-century commentary, incorporating linguistic and scientific insights alongside philosophy and comparative anthropology.

The revival of Bible study took root and flourished in Eastern Europe as well, and although the commentaries that emerged from there shared the traditionalist concern for the integrity of rabbinic interpretations, they tended to approach the problem in a more selective and discerning fashion. The head of the prestigious Volozhin yeshivah, R. Naftali Zvi Yehudah Berlin (1817–1893; known by his acronym as the Netziv), penned a commentary to the Torah titled *Ha-'Amek Davar* which first appeared in an 1879–1880 Vilna edition of the Bible. Like Malbim and Hoffmann, Berlin had elsewhere devoted significant scholarly energy to the study of early

rabbinic midrash, but his Bible commentary engaged both Scripture and rabbinic literature in ways that tried to develop an appreciation for their independent literary qualities. Berlin spoke incisively about the limitless interpretative possibilities that inhered in the biblical text, and at the same time allowed that earlier rabbinic modes of interpretation had been independently and creatively derived. At the end of the 19th century, Barukh Ha-Levi Epstein (1860–1942) also set out to show the fundamental accord between the Bible and the oral law in an edition of the Torah named *Torah Temimah* (Vilna, 1904). Epstein went about this task by anthologizing rabbinic uses of Scripture and appending a series of notes which proved to contain original and insightful comments regarding the rabbinic interpretation of Scripture. In many ways, the real scholarly achievement of this work may have been the anthology itself, in which Epstein culled a large corpus of rabbinic literature and edited and condensed his findings with masterful scholarship. Perhaps the most original of the late 19th-century traditionalist commentaries, however, was the posthumously published *Meshekh Ḥokhmah* (1927) of R. Meir Simhah Ha-Kohen of Dvinsk (1843–1926). Like Berlin, this exegete was an outstanding rabbinic scholar who appreciated not only the quality of rabbinic scriptural interpretation, but also its ongoing creativity. As such, he asserted the right of rabbinic scholars of all generations to venture beyond attested readings in order to derive new halakhah from scriptural *peshat*.

Conclusion

While the beginning of our survey clearly marked a new chapter in the history of Jewish biblical interpretation, the point we have reached here at the end of this overview does not represent its closing or conclusion. Rather, with the end of the 19th and beginning of the 20th centuries, we leave behind only the first stages of the Jewish encounter with modernity and its concomitant reengagement with the Bible. By the end of our period, to be sure, the traditionalist attempt to demonstrate the textually grounded nature—and hence presumed correctness—of rabbinic exegesis had effectively run its creative course. The 19th-century scholarship of the maskilim and the *Wissenschaft des Judentums*, which was groundbreaking and innovative for its time, nevertheless remained in many ways stunted and undeveloped. With few exceptions, the scholars we surveyed here did not seriously engage European biblical scholarship and some of its most challenging and critical developments (see "Modern Study," pp. 2084–96). As such, while Jewish biblical interpretation of the 18th and 19th centuries forms a distinct and historically important corpus, that time must also be seen as a period that cultivated new cultural and intellectual commitments that would express themselves fully only in the next century.

[EDWARD BREUER]

Modern Jewish Interpretation

The most distinctive feature of the modern study of the Bible is its emphasis on history: the attempt to uncover what the biblical texts meant at the time they were composed rather than what they came to mean in later tradition, or how they might inspire the believer. Although a number of premodern scholars pursued the "original sense," these practicing Jews and Christians were constrained by personal and institutional loyalty to limit the scope of their inquiries. For these reasons, what seem to us to be obvious contradictions and anachronisms within the texts were explained in ways that did not undermine the traditional authority of the Bible.

Among Jews, the return to serious study of the Bible is a modern phenomenon, having been neglected in many European Jewish communities during the medieval and early modern periods (see "Medieval Interpretation," pp. 1876–1900, and "Post-medieval Interpretation," pp. 1900–1908). Beginning with Saadia Gaon (882–942) and continuing for the next several centuries, medieval Jewish scholars had made the Bible a major focus of study. Sephardim (Jews of Spanish and Portuguese origin) and Italian Jews continued that tradition, but on the eve of modernity most Jews lived in Central and Eastern Europe. In contrast to the Sephardim who studied the Talmud only as a source of law, the Ashkenazim (Jews in Franco-German communities) viewed study of the Talmud as a religious end in itself, deserving undivided scholarly attention. Much like Catholics, Ashkenazim treated the Bible as a liturgical and homiletical text. Premodern Jewish communal life was based not on the Bible but on laws, customs, and traditions derived in the main from the Babylonian Talmud and codified in the 16th-century *Shulḥan 'Arukh* legal code and its commentaries. Although these documents of rabbinic Judaism derived their ultimate authority from the Bible, in practice, Rabbis, who served their autonomous communities more as judges than as spiritual leaders, required very little biblical learning. The 17th-century Rabbi Joseph Hahn of Frankfurt (d. 1637) wrote, "In our generation there are rabbis who never studied the Bible." Germany saw some improvement in the next century thanks to the Bible translation project initiated by Moses Mendelssohn (1729–1786), which was accompanied by contemporary commentaries *(Bi'ur)*. But even in Germany, and all the more in Russia and Poland, talmudical study carried greater prestige than biblical, and bright students were moved to Talmud by age seven or eight. (The small number of girls given schooling studied more Bible than did boys.)

If Bible study was largely ignored, "higher criticism" of the Bible (the identification of sources behind the biblical text; see "The Modern Study of the Bible," pp. 2084–96) as practiced in universities and some Christian seminaries beginning in the late 18th century was condemned. Pious Jews (and many of their Christian counterparts) were horrified that Bible "critics" questioned the reliability of the received biblical texts, denied the historicity of their contents, and detected numerous sources in books attributed by Jewish (and Christian) tradition to a single author. It is true that some features that characterize modern criticism had surfaced much earlier. Abraham Ibn Ezra (1092–1167) noted several anachronisms in the Torah; Joseph Bekhor Shor (12th century) observed contradictory parallel narratives in the Torah; some members of the Hasidei Ashkenaz (12th- to 13th-century German Jewish Pietists) challenged Davidic authorship of certain psalms and Mosaic authorship of sections of the Torah; and Jonah Ibn Janaḥ (ca. 990–ca. 1050) may have emended biblical texts. But none of these scholars, every one of them steadfast in the observance of the Jewish communal laws, developed a systematic critical approach. (The nascent biblical criticism of the excommunicate Baruch Spinoza [1632–1677] written in Latin had little influence on 17th-century Jews.) With the advent of Emancipation, adherence to Jewish law and membership in the Jewish community became voluntary. Just as the Protestant Reformation had made it possible for Christians to study the Bible directly without the authorized interpretations of the Church, Emancipation gave Jews an opportunity to study Bible outside of traditional circles. Those who began to study the Bible in the newer setting tended to sympathize with the Haskalah (Jewish Enlightenment) Movement or with Zionism rather than with old-style religious observance and belief.

Particularly odious to the faithful was the Documentary Hypothesis, especially as codified by Julius Wellhausen (1844–1918). The Wellhausen theory, which came to dominate biblical scholarship by the close of the 19th century, claimed that the Torah or Pentateuch (Genesis through Deuteronomy) had been written not by Moses but by authors who composed "documents" over a period of centuries. These documents, or sources, were combined to form the Torah, which owed its final shape to the priests of the Jewish "church" of the late first millennium BCE. Because of its priestly orientation, declared Wellhausen, the Torah, in contrast to the prophetic books of an earlier age, was a "legalistic" work obsessed with ritual purity and scrupulous observance of ceremonial minutiae. Wellhausen's view of the development of Judaism, therefore, saw it as inferior to the prophetic faith that scorned the legalistic requirements of Temple observance; this made it easier to embrace the New Testament polemic against "Judaism" (i.e., legalism) while still accepting the Old Testament (as recommending, in its highest development in the prophets, "faith," not ritual "works").

In the less-than-pious circles of *Wissenschaft des Judentums* (scientific study of Judaism) critical study of the Bible was also unpopular, but for different and sometimes contradictory reasons. Jewish scholars with university training sought to modernize Judaism, gain general acknowledgment of their own academic legitimacy, and secure broad rights of European citizenship for their people. As such, their research gave priority to Jewish intellectual creativity in the Gentile world. The study of the Jewish philosophers or of the great medieval poets demonstrated that Greek and Arabic speaking Jews had contributed to general intellectual life. Philo, Maimonides, and Judah Halevi could serve as models for 19th-century European Jews. The study of historic Israel in its own land, in contrast, underscored Jewish separateness. Certainly, the research agenda of the German reformer and scholar Abraham Geiger (1810–1874) was shaped by such concerns. Geiger's exemplary work on ancient translations of the Bible barely engages the literary history of the Bible proper. For his part, the eminent historian and Bible scholar Heinrich Graetz (1817–1891) was willing to study most of the Bible critically, but clung to a traditional view of the Torah's composition. Within some Zionist circles of the East European Haskalah, biblical criticism was unwelcome because it was too "European" and could lead to assimilation rather than to Zionism. The pleas of such spokesmen as Max Soloweitschik (1883–1957) and Zalman Rubashov [Shazar] (1889–1974; later president of Israel) that the study of the Bible was essential to Zionism went largely unheeded. Finally, it must be observed that many enlightened Jews including the American immigrants I. M. Wise (1819–1900), founder of the (Reform) Hebrew Union College in Cincinnati, and Solomon Schechter (1847–1915), the driving force at the (Conservative) Jewish Theological Seminary in New York, were deterred from serious study of the Bible by the triumphalist tone of Christian Bible criticism. Schechter, not without justification, referred to higher criticism as "higher anti-Semitism" (see discussion of J. Wellhausen, above). After all, Wilhem de Wette (1760–1849), the first to date the composition of Deuteronomy to the time of King Josiah (d. 609 BCE), thus providing a fixed date for the composition of a book of the Torah, had written that Judaism was a "misfortune" for which Christianity provided "consolation." The pioneering Semiticist and grammarian H. F. Wilhelm Gesenius (1786–1842) observed that the postexilic books Esther, Daniel, and Jonah were the products of "debased Jewish taste." Wellhausen himself had declared that the Torah's system of commandments turned God into the "manager of a petty scheme of salvation." The (Priestly) law, he asserted, "takes the soul out of religion and spoils morality." In studies on the Pentateuch in particular, Christian Bible scholars tended to denigrate "pharisaical" Jews and a "legalistic" Judaism so far removed from the elevated teachings of the great early Hebrew prophets that a completely new revelation was required in the advent of Jesus.

Nonetheless, there were Jewish scholars who saw the necessity for modern scientific Bible study. One such pioneer was the Italian Samuel David Luzzatto (acronym Shadal; 1800–1865). Luzzatto, who was schooled in the earlier Jewish and Christian translations of the Bible, suggested that the vowel points were secondary to the received Hebrew text. (He was here influenced by the earlier Italian Elija Levita [1468/9–1549].) He was the first modern Jewish scholar to propose textual emendations in biblical texts, so long as these were outside of the Torah. With regard to higher criticism he denied the attribution to David of many psalms and to Solomon the authorship of Ecclesiastes, while upholding Mosaic authorship of the Torah. As part of his philosophical program, Nachman Krochmal (1785–1840), an Eastern European Jewish intellectual, wrote *The Guide for the Perplexed of This Time (Moreh Nevukhei Ha-Zeman)* and accepted the view of general biblical scholarship that the latter half of Isaiah and the book of Koheleth (Ecclesiastes) were products of Diaspora Judaism in the latter first millennium BCE. In opposition to Christian scholarship, however, Krochmal held that lateness demonstrated not decay but rather continuing Jewish creativity and spiritual innovation. In further defense of Judaism, Krochmal asserted that the great Rabbis of the talmudic period (2nd–6th century) had reached the same conclusions about the lateness of some biblical books but concealed their findings out of concern that their laity had not reached the necessary level of sophistication.

Of particular interest is Markus M. Kalisch (1828–1885), who had rabbinical training and a degree from the University of Berlin *(Friedrich-Wilhems Universität)*. Thanks to his employment in England by the Rothschild family, Kalisch was able to devote himself to scholarship. Whereas most 19th-century Jewish scholars, even nonobservant ones, eschewed critical analysis of the "iconic" Torah, Kalisch wrote a two-volume commentary on Leviticus (1867, 1872), in which he examined the biblical sacrificial systems and determined that the document that was designated as the Priestly Code ("P") was later than Deuteronomy ("D"). He thus anticipated Wellhausen both in method and in some of his conclusions.

Leopold Zunz (1794–1886), founder of *Wissenschaft des Judentums*, had studied at the University of Berlin during the tenure there of Wilhelm de Wette. Zunz, though, did not direct his primary early research to the Bible, arguing that postbiblical literature as part of Jewish culture not shared with Christians was in need of scholarly attention, whereas the Bible had many Christian students. Nonetheless, his ground-breaking study of ancient Jewish preaching, *Die gottesdientlichen Vorträge der Juden, historisch entwickelt (The Worship Sermons of the Jews Historically Developed;* 1832) revealed the late date of many psalms, dated Ezekiel to the 5th century BCE, outlined the ideological concerns of Chronicles and argued for its shared authorship with Ezra-Nehemiah, and claimed that the Jewish canon had not been completed until shortly before 70 CE. In his old age Zunz turned to the central concerns of 19th-century biblical scholarship. He supported de Wette's 7th-century BCE dating of Deuteronomy with supplementary linguistic evidence. In agreement with Wellhausen, Zunz argued that Leviticus was written after both Deuteronomy and Ezekiel, under the influence of the Jewish priesthood of the later first millennium BCE.

Solomon Mandelkern (1846–1902), born in Russia, rabbinically educated and holding degrees in Semitics and law, provided the single most important scholarly tool for Bible study with his *Hekhal Hakodesh* (1896). This concordance was the standard work until the advent of computer concordances at the end of the 20th century. It took twenty years to complete, and made it possible to study every biblical word in context so that a scholar need not rely on memory or inadequate dictionaries.

The United States for most of the 19th century had a small Jewish population, with a correspondingly low level of Jewish knowledge. The major American Jewish contribution to biblical studies was the Bible translation written by Isaac Leeser (1806–1868). A Prussian immigrant, Leeser was employed as a *ḥazan* (cantor) in Philadelphia. Although Leeser's formal training was sparse, historical circumstances combined with his own sense of purpose and remarkable vision made him the primary architect of American Jewish institutional life. Leeser's Hebrew-English Bible (1853) was essentially a Jewish version of the King James with its christology removed and some Jewish traditional interpretation inserted. Despite the severe judgment rendered by some critics, the Leeser Bible met the needs of American Jewish life in the mid-19th century quite well (see "Jewish Translations of the Bible," pp. 2005–20).

The political revolutions that roiled Western and Central Europe in 1848, followed later in the century by the decline of the state of the Jews of Eastern Europe, encouraged Jewish immigration to the United States and raised the intellectual level of American Jewry. One such immigrant, Benjamin Szold (1829–1902), a rabbi in Baltimore, wrote a Hebrew commentary on Job (1886) drawing on the Jewish exegetical tradition and, conservatively, on 19th-century Christian scholarship. Szold attempted to resolve the controversy over the date of Job by arguing that an early form of the book was originally composed in the time of Moses, while our extant book is a much later reworking of the original.

Arnold B. Ehrlich (1848–1919), a younger contemporary of Szold, was a unique figure. Born in Wlodawa in Russian Poland and married at an early age, Ehrlich divorced his wife and moved to Leipzig in Germany. There he converted to Christianity and taught at the missionary Institutum Judaicum headed by the eminent biblicist Franz Delitzsch (1813–1890), helping to translate the New Testament into Hebrew for the purpose of converting Jews. In 1876 Ehrlich reached America and quickly returned to Judaism. Although unable to obtain a regular academic post, Ehrlich managed to produce two major scholarly works: the Hebrew *Miqra' Kifshuto (The Bible in its Plain Sense;* 1899–1901) and the seven-volume German *Randglossen zur hebräischen Bibel (Marginal Notes to the Hebrew Bible)*. Both works show their author's knowledge of philology and his ear for biblical language.

Although Ehrlich does not refer to the Documentary Hypothesis, he employs arguments based on linguistic usage, concepts, and institutions to assign relative "late" and "early" dates to specific passages. Numerous historical comments, such as his denial of the historicity of Egyptian enslavement and exodus are buried in notes to specific passages. Ehrlich wrote *Miqra'* in Hebrew for the express purpose of introducing Jews to the critical study of the Bible. His work has been highly influential on Jewish scholarship, as can be seen in the Bible translations produced by the Jewish Publication Society: the JPS Bible of 1917 and its replacement NJPS (1962–1982).

Because of the Christian orientation of Bible study in American colleges and universities, it was not easy for Jewish scholars with research interests in the Bible to find academic posts directly in that area. In addition, much biblical research at that time was done in the context of Protestant seminaries rather than in secular institutions. Departments of Semitic or Oriental Languages were more hospitable to Jewish scholars. For example, Morris Jastrow (1861–1922) received the Ph.D. in Semitics at Leipzig and then taught at the University of Pennsylvania from 1885 until his death. Although his primary fields were Assyriology and Mesopotamian religion, Jastrow published books on Ecclesiastes, Job, and Song of Songs. He served as editor of the Bible division for the twelve-volume *Jewish Encyclopedia* (New York, 1901–1906; most of the contributors to the Bible division were Christians). Jastrow served as the first Jewish president of the professional society, the Society of Biblical Literature, in 1916, and was an outspoken proponent of higher criticism.

Max Margolis (1866–1932) likewise earned a degree in Semitics. His doctoral thesis on text-criticism of the Talmud was written in Latin under Richard Gottheil at Columbia in 1891. Margolis began his scholarly career at Hebrew Union College (1893–1897) where I. M. Wise persuaded him to move into biblical studies. He left HUC for Berkeley and taught Semitics there until 1905, when he returned to HUC, which he once again left after a disappointing two years. In 1908 Margolis became editor-in-chief of the Jewish Publication Society's Bible translation. Published in 1917, the *JPS Holy Scriptures* became the quasi-official Bible of Jewish anglophones for the next half-century. An outstanding textual critic with special interest in the Septuagint (the ancient Jewish translation into Greek), Margolis was quite conservative in his attitude toward higher criticism. He served as president of the Society of Biblical Literature in 1923 and editor of its *Journal of Biblical Literature (JBL)* from 1914 to 1922. Margolis served as Professor of Biblical Philology at the non-sectarian Dropsie College (later the Annenberg Research Institute for Judaic and Near Eastern Studies and now the Center for Judaic Studies of the University of Pennsylvania) from 1909 until his death.

The first American Jewish Bible scholar to practice higher criticism systematically was the long-lived Julian Morgenstern (1881–1976). Morgenstern, ordained at HUC in 1902, earned the Ph.D. in Assyriology at Heidelberg. He not only championed the Documentary Hypothesis but expanded it by claiming to have identified an additional "document" in the Torah. As a professor at HUC from 1907 to 1960 and as its president from 1921 to 1947, he was the first Jewish scholar to make critical study of the Bible central to the curriculum of an American Jewish seminary. Over the years Morgenstern came to the conclusion that the Documentary Hypothesis, although necessary, was insufficient. In his presidential address to the Society of Biblical Literature in 1941, Morgenstern called for a synthesis of classical criticism with archeology, folklore studies, and religious phenomenology.

The modern Hebrew *Torah, Nevi'im Ukhetuvim im Perush Mada'i (The Bible with a Critical Commentary)*, edited by A. Kahana (1874–1946) in collaboration with scholars from all over the world, was a conscious product of the editor's Jewish nationalism. Although the full series was never completed, the seven volumes published over a period of twenty-six years (1903/04–1929/30) made use of the ancient versions, ancient Near Eastern sources unearthed by archeology, comparative Semitics, and the Documentary Hypothesis. Among the contributors were H. P. Chajes, F. Perles, Max Margolis and Kahana himself. Until 1990 the series was the only multi-volume critical Bible commentary in Hebrew.

The period between the First and Second World Wars had a great impact on Jewish Bible scholarship. The opening of the Hebrew University in 1925 meant that the Bible would be studied in Hebrew in the land of its origin. Zionist successes and the rise to power of the Nazis encouraged the immigration of European Jews to Palestine and the United States. The foundations of what was to become Israeli Bible scholarship were laid by such scholars as Tur-Sinai (Torczyner), Cassuto, Kaufmann, and Segal.

N. H. Tur-Sinai (Torczyner; 1876–1973) was an ingenious, sometimes overly ingenious, philologist who uncovered the meaning of many a biblical passage that had long eluded interpretation. Especially noteworthy are his three different commentaries on Job, in which he argues that most of the textual difficulties of the book can be solved by treating the Hebrew as a faulty translation from an Aramaic original. Rather than employing source-criticism, Tur-Sinai argued that our surviving biblical literature comes from compilations that were originally organized around the lives of ancient heroes, such as David, Moses, or Samuel. The title of Tur-Sinai's multi-volume *Peshuto shel Miqra'* (*The Plain Sense of the Bible*; 1962–1968) is an acknowledgment of the author's indebtedness to Ehrlich.

Umberto Moshe David Cassuto (1883–1951) was an Italian Jew trained as a rabbi at Collegio Rabbinico Italiano. His doctoral studies at the University of Florence brought him under the influence of the critical Bible scholar H. P. Chajes (1876–1927). Cassuto devoted his early scholarship to the history of the Jews of Italy. Appointment to the faculty at the University of Rome caused him to redirect his efforts into Semitics. Cassuto's studies of the Ugaritic literature of the late second-millennium BCE Syria led him to realize the cultural continuity between ancient Israel and the wider ancient Near East. A lover of Dante, Cassuto's background in literature impelled him to view the Documentary Hypothesis as unsound. Instead, Cassuto advocated what would later be called "synchronic" or "holistic" reading of the biblical text with an eye to its inner unity, an approach which has since become extremely popular in the "Bible as literature" movement. Cassuto moved to Israel (then Palestine) from Fascist Italy in 1939 and became a professor of Bible at Hebrew University. He was the founding editor of the *Entziklopediah Miqra'it* (*Encyclopaedia Biblica*; 9 volumes; 1950–1989).

Moses Hirsch (Zevi) Segal (1876–1968) was born in Lithuania, where he pursued a rabbinical education. His university studies in London and Oxford led to an appointment as lecturer at Hebrew University in 1926, where he became professor in 1939. Orthodox opposition to biblical study restricted the initial appointment to *Parshanut* (exegesis) rather than *Miqra'* (Bible) proper; this despite Segal's opposition to the Documentary Hypothesis. (H. P. Chajes, a stronger candidate, failed to get the post because of his critical stance.) Though rejecting most aspects of the critical study of the Torah, Segal clung to the newer tradition that biblical criticism was legitimate outside the Torah, and his commentary on Samuel (1956) is full of observations concerning the complex layers of composition of that book. In several articles and the book *The Pentateuch: Its Composition and Authorship and Other Biblical Studies* (1967), Segal attempts to demonstrate the essential Mosaic authorship of the Torah, but allows for numerous additions by later authors. Segal also wrote the widely read *Introduction to the Bible* (4 Hebrew vols. 1946–1950), and contributed much to the study of Mishnaic Hebrew, the Apocrypha, and the history of interpretation.

Yehezkel Kaufmann (1889–1963), best known for his opposition to Wellhausen, was, ironically, the most enthusiastic proponent of the Documentary Hypothesis among the pioneering Israeli biblicists. Kaufmann challenged the chronological order of the sources of the Torah proposed by Wellhausen. Tacitly accepting the view of Christian Bible scholarship that "earlier is better," Kaufmann argued that the P(riestly) source was a preexilic composition and not a late, inferior "Jewish" development. Kaufmann challenged as well Wellhausen's chronology of Israelite religion. From his dating of the sources Wellhausen had concluded that Israelite monotheism evolved out of polytheism over centuries as the teachings of the prophets finally took hold among the masses. Kaufmann in his magnum opus, *Toledot ha'Emunah ha-Yisra'elit* (8 vols. 1937–1957; English: *Religion of Israel*, translated and abridged by Moshe Greenberg, 1960), asserted that Israelite monotheism began as an original religious intuition in the time of Moses. Ancient Israelites, common folk and religious elite alike, were united by the monotheistic worship of the god YHVH. The Bible's repeated references to Israelite worship of "wood and stone idols" were to be explained as denunciations by religious zealots of what in reality were vestiges of superstition from pre-Mosaic times. Kaufmann's thesis stripped Torah criticism of its animus to Judaism and found eager acceptance among non-Orthodox Israelis and American religious moderates, particularly at the Conservative movement's Jewish Theological Seminary. Especially attractive was Kaufmann's description of monotheism as an original religious intuition, which supported Jewish claims to religious genius without appealing to supernaturalism.

During the 1st century of modern biblical scholarship, the field was largely restricted to source-critical examination of the biblical books themselves. The expansion of ancient Near Eastern archeology in the period between the World Wars heightened interest in comparative studies, both linguistic and cultural. To some extent the recovery of the world in which the Bible had been produced mitigated opposition to critical study by producing "positive" results. Through "biblical archeology" (as it used to be called, since it was done in conjunction with, and usually in support of, the biblical text), some textual emendations were vitiated by the discovery that a biblical text thought corrupt actually preserved a hitherto unknown word. Other discoveries substantiated the existence of biblical figures or provided background to biblical institutions. Jewish scholars such as the founder of Israeli archeology, Benjamin (Maisler) Mazar (1906–1995), learned from W. F. Albright (1891–1971) to combine field researches with biblical text-study. Nelson Glueck (1900–1971) was the only American Jew centrally involved in the "biblical archeology" movement. Glueck was president of HUC from 1947 to 1971 and the founder of its archeology school in Jerusalem, which now bears his name. Bold syntheses of text and archeology were also undertaken by a student of Margolis, E. A. Speiser (1902–1965) of the University of Pennsylvania, notably in his influential commentary on Genesis (Anchor Bible, 1964). Somewhat similar was the approach of Cyrus Gordon (1908–2001), a far-ranging comparatist who included the Aegean world within the purview of biblical and Near Eastern studies, and trained several generations of students. Within this same generation the most far-reaching comparative work was done by Theodor H. Gaster (1906–1992), whose *Myth, Legend and Custom in the Old Testament* (1969), based on the methods of the anthropologist James Frazer, attempts to gather "all that can be derived from comparative folklore and mythology for the interpretation of the Old Testament."

Perhaps the greatest of American Jewish biblicists trained between the wars was Harold Louis (or H. L.) Ginsberg (1903–1990). Born in Montreal, Canada, Ginsberg earned his doctorate at the University of London and moved to mandatory Palestine where he worked closely with Benjamin Mazar, concentrating on ancient Semitics. In 1936 he published a pioneering Hebrew translation and grammatical study of ancient Ugaritic tablets unearthed in Syria in 1929. Ginsberg was one of the first to employ Ugaritic to recover forgotten grammatical features and "lost" words in biblical Hebrew. He also demonstrated the value of Ugaritic in textual criticism of the Bible. Ginsberg's arrival at Jewish Theological Seminary in 1936 transformed the seminary's role in Jewish Bible studies. Although JTS had no Ph.D. program at that time, at least two generations of Jewish Bible scholars received their "basic training" and inspiration while studying Bible at JTS with Ginsberg. Ginsberg employed philology both for itself and as a clue to reconstructing inner-biblical literary and ideological development. For most of his scholarly career Ginsberg championed and publicized the view of Yehezkel Kaufmann that "D(euteronomy)" was later than "P(riestly Code)." As he began to concentrate on Torah, however, his research in biblical diction demonstrated to him that Wellhausen had been substantially correct. The results of much of Ginsberg's work are available to the larger public because he served as an editor and translator of the first two sections of the NJPS. He was also Bible editor of *Encyclopaedia Judaica* (1971), to which he contributed original articles far more documented and detailed than is usual in contemporary encyclopedias. These are characterized by brilliant intuitiveness and occasionally, by excessive ingenuity.

Another outstanding figure trained between the wars was Harry M. Orlinsky (1908–1992), likewise Canadian by birth. Orlinsky earned his Ph.D. at Dropsie and spent most of his teaching career at HUC in New York City (at the time the independent Jewish Institute of Religion). His 1967 study on the "Suffering Servant" in Deutero-Isaiah is a classic of modern scholarship, and is significant for its use of scholarly method to polemicize implicitly against Christian theological interpretation of the Bible. Most of Orlinsky's work, however, was in textual studies and translation. Especially noteworthy are his numerous articles on the Greek Septuagint

translation. Orlinsky crusaded for years in behalf of a Jewish translation to replace the 1917 JPS. His wishes were fulfilled when he served as editor-in-chief of the New *JPS Torah* (1961) and as an editor for the Prophets and *Megillot* (scrolls) sections (1985). Orlinsky was the only Jewish scholar involved in the Protestant Revised Standard Version translation of the Old Testament (1952) and its revision, the New Revised Standard Version (1989); no Christian scholars participated in the New Jewish Publication Society Bible (1985).

In the period between World War II and the late 1960s, Jewish scholarship became increasingly productive as a significant number of Jewish scholars entered the mainstream of biblical scholarship. The increased number of Jewish biblicists led to the emergence of a "Jewish School" with a common educational profile. At the time there were few university-supported programs in Judaic Studies. Almost all the scholars of this period (they were all men; no seminaries admitted women at that time), mostly now emeriti or deceased, had studied or taught at rabbinical seminaries, notably the Jewish Theological Seminary, and all were conversant with the Jewish exegetical tradition, even when they ignored it. Unlike Christian seminaries, the Jewish institutions emphasized historical method rather than theology. The Christian orientation of advanced biblical studies led most of these men to pursue their education in secular graduate schools, in Near Eastern Studies departments, where they studied the ancient languages and cultures of Western Asia, Mesopotamia, and Egypt. A crucial development unifying Jewish biblical scholarship was the rise of the State of Israel (1948), which led to interaction between American and Israeli scholarship. United in their common knowledge of modern Hebrew, Americans and Israelis studied and taught in each other's countries. A number of American scholars emigrated to Israel, most maintaining their American connections. A smaller number of Israeli biblicists settled in America, but maintained Israeli connections. Jewish Bible scholars on both sides of the globe were the foremost advocates of interpreting difficult biblical Hebrew texts in the light of other languages, particularly Ugaritic and Akkadian, and of interpreting biblical institutions, laws, and narratives in light of "parallels." In their approach to ancient Israelite religion, many were influenced by Yehezkel Kaufmann.

Of special note was the engagement of the Jewish scholars trained before the late 1960s in Torah-criticism, often avoided in earlier Jewish biblical scholarship, and absent from the curriculum of JTS until 1966. All the Torah volumes in the nonsectarian Anchor Bible are by Jews: E. A. Speiser (1902–1965; *Genesis*), Jacob Milgrom (b. 1923; *Leviticus*), Baruch Levine (b. 1930; *Numbers*), Moshe Weinfeld of Israel (b. 1925; *Deuteronomy*). The most recent volume, *Exodus,* is the work of a younger Jewish scholar, William Propp. In the JPS Torah Commentary, also all written by Jews, *Genesis* and *Exodus* are by Nahum Sarna, (b. 1923), *Leviticus* by Baruch Levine, *Numbers* by Jacob Milgrom, and *Deuteronomy* by Jeffrey Tigay. Both Milgrom and Levine are known for their studies of the Israelite cult.

Most influential have been Moshe Greenberg and Nahum Sarna. Greenberg, a student of E. A. Speiser, left the University of Pennsylvania, where he had been a young star, for Hebrew University. Greenberg was a pioneer in employing rabbinic midrash and medieval commentaries in pursuit of the original sense of the text. Over thirty years ago Greenberg called for emphasis on the individual books of the Bible as literary units. Greenberg's call heralded the new emphasis on "Bible as literature" and legitimated literary-aesthetic study among mainstream biblicists. In addition, his emphasis on the integrity of the Hebrew text offered an important corrective to much (German) biblical scholarship, which often corrects the Hebrew on the basis of the Greek Septuagint. Greenberg authored the Ezekiel commentary in the Anchor Bible (2 volumes published, a third to follow). He co-edited *Miqra' le-Yisra'el,* a multi-volume commentary in Hebrew designed to bring

biblical scholarship to the Israeli public as well as to scholars. Sarna, a student of Gordon, was originally interested in rabbinic literature; he thus shares with Greenberg a great appreciation of the rabbinic and medieval commentary tradition. Again like Greenberg, Sarna is a born teacher. His pedagogical skills, evident in all of his writing, come to the fore in the JPS Torah Commentary, particularly in Genesis, which masterfully synthesizes textual study, archeology and rabbinic tradition. A prescient essay on Psalm 89 (1963) brought the notion "inner-biblical exegesis" into scholarly consciousness. At Brandeis University Sarna trained large numbers of students, including Michael Fishbane, who has developed "inner-biblical exegesis" (see "Inner-biblical Interpretation," pp. 1829–35). Jeffrey Tigay has aptly written: "No scholar has done as much as Sarna to educate English-speaking Jewry about the Bible."

Another significant figure was the Israeli expatriate Moshe Held (1924–1984), who taught at Dropsie College and then at Columbia University. Held was an outstanding philologist and comparative Semiticist with a commanding personality. Held's years of teaching at nearby JTS brought "cuneiform-consciousness" to students in his Bible classes and attracted many of them into the advanced study of Bible and comparative Semitics. In Israel the figure of Menahen Haran (b. 1924) looms large. A student of Kaufmann, Haran's work has concentrated on biblical religion and cult within Kaufmann's model that the Priestly tradition is early. More recently his work has been on the formation of the biblical canon and its scribal transmission. Other highly influential Israeli figures are the late I. L. Seeligmann and the late S. E. Lowenstamm, as well as Abraham Malamat (b. 1922) and Moshe Weinfeld (b. 1925). Malamat has a comparative approach to Israelite institutions such as prophecy and monarchy. Weinfeld, a wide-ranging comparatist with a strong interest in institutions, was an early advocate of using Assyrian vassal treaties to understand the Bible, especially Deuteronomy; he is opening new vistas in his work comparing Israelite settlement patterns with ancient Greek colonization.

The last thirty years have been momentous for Jewish Bible scholarship in both numbers and diversification of approaches. In the United States the academic legitimation of ethnic studies enabled the creation of programs in Jewish Studies in private and public institutions of higher learning. Court decisions permitting the teaching of religion in publicly funded schools were an additional stimulus to growth. The influence of feminism brought women into a field that had been completely male. Women scholars regularly addressed questions that had been ignored, influencing men to do the same. Prominent women scholars of this first generation include: Adele Berlin, Tikva Frymer-Kensky, Susan Niditch, Carol Meyers, Tamara Eskenazi, and in Israel, Sara Japhet, Yaira Amit, and the late Sara Kamin. Some Jewish scholars, notably Jon Levenson at Harvard and the late M. H. Goshen-Gottstein (1925–1991) have engaged biblical theology, heretofore mostly restricted to Christians.

Additional diversity has come from Orthodox Judaism. In the past, Orthodox Jews were on the periphery of Jewish biblical studies. Their most important contributions were critical editions of medieval Jewish Bible commentators, famous and (undeservedly) obscure alike. An outstanding example is the ongoing M. Cohen (ed.) *Miqra'ot Gedolot Haketer* (Bar-Ilan University, 1992ff.) based on the Aleppo Codex of the Bible and accompanied by a comprehensive selection of medieval commentaries edited from the best texts. Notable exceptions are two Israeli scholars, Meir Weiss and Uriel Simon, who pioneered the literary study of the Bible. At the present time scholars personally affiliated with Orthodox Judaism engage the central questions of textual criticism, literary history, and historicity, applying critical method even to Torah literature.

The changing profile of the biblical field has implications for the future of Jewish biblical scholarship that are hard to predict. The founders of Jewish biblical scholarship had acquired much of their learning in Europe. The scholars who trained the current senior generation received a grounding in Jewish studies in seminaries. The experience of both groups differed significantly from that of more recent scholars whose background is more pluralistic. Precisely because the Jewish approach is not self-evident, and training in rabbinics and Talmud is not as strong, the newer crop has worked harder to articulate the ways in which their work is distinctively Jewish. At the same time the newer generations come with new disciplines and approaches, thereby moving the study of Bible beyond literary and historical criticism, and comparative philology. "Biblical archeology" has declined in popularity. The need to articulate the theoretical basis of one's approach became itself a trend beginning in the 1970s. Some of the newer approaches including ideological criticism, structuralism, deconstruction, and narrative criticism have come from comparative literature. Several younger Jewish scholars have also been involved in the serious application of sociological theory to biblical studies.

Jewish scholars have certainly benefited from the opportunity to study the Bible outside of departments with a Christian orientation, but the blessing is not unmixed. The earlier Christian orientation of biblical studies forced Jewish biblicists to earn degrees in the larger disciplines of text-criticism and ancient literary languages. This is no longer the case. Ironically, the attentive reading of a text as literature demands mastery of these disciplines. Fortunately, there have been countervailing trends. The American Michael Fox (b. 1940) has in particular broadened the application of Egyptology to biblical study. Jonas Greenfield (1926–1995) performed a similar service for Iranian languages. William Hallo (b. 1928), recently retired from Yale, and his student Peter Machinist (b. 1944) of Harvard have brought new sophistication to the study of the Bible in the light of Assyriology. Adele Berlin's (b.

1943) NJPS commentary on the book of Esther (2001) exemplifies the disciplined synthesis of philology, text, and historical criticism with the literary approach. In Israel, Alexander Rofé (b. 1932 in Pisa, Italy) makes extensive use of the ancient versions to combine classical source criticism with the literary-aesthetic approach. Emanuel Tov (b. 1941 in Holland) is the leading textual critic of the Hebrew Bible, and produced the indispensable *Textual Criticism of the Hebrew Bible* (first edition, 1992). He also spearheaded the completion of the standard scholarly publication of the Dead Sea Scrolls. The Hebrew University Bible Project, whose driving force was the late Moshe Goshen-Gottstein, has thus far (2003) provided the critical editions of Isaiah (1995) and Jeremiah (1997). Avi Hurvitz (b. 1936) has attempted to establish the history of biblical Hebrew on a solid linguistic basis.

In concluding this essay we turn our attention to a number of important collaborative projects, scholarly as well as popular, under Jewish sponsorship in the United States and Israel. The ongoing Hebrew University Bible Project has as its primary aim the publication, at long last, of a true critical text of the Hebrew Bible. HUBP is based on the authoritative 10th-century Aleppo Codex and its accompanying scribal notes (Hebrew: *masorah*). The base text is accompanied by variations attested in the Dead Sea Scrolls, the ancient translations, medieval Hebrew manuscripts, and in biblical citations in early rabbinic literature.

Several significant Israeli projects are aimed at larger audiences. In general the Israeli projects reflect the greater emphasis of Israeli scholarship on the realities of fauna, topography, and geography with which Israelis have direct experience. The *Miqra' leYisra'el* series (*A Bible Commentary for Israel*), begun in 1990, is the first multi-volume Hebrew language critical commentary on the Hebrew Bible in over fifty years. The target audience, like that of the American nondenominational Anchor Bible, is not only the scholar, but the educated nonspecialist. The members of the Israeli target audience come to the Bible with a general knowledge of its language and content. More popular is the *Entziklopedya 'Olam ha-tanakh* (*The World of the Bible*; 1982–1996), a 24-volume illustrated running commentary on the individual books of the Hebrew Bible, with particular attention paid to the realia of the ancient world in which the Bible was produced. The project combines the talents of biblicists and archeologists with those of specialists in such areas as ancient technology, military history, and the natural sciences.

The multi-volume *Da'at Miqra'* series (*Knowledge of the Bible*) is especially intriguing. Produced by the Rabbi Kook Institute, the Hebrew volumes written between 1970 and 2001 boldly walk the narrow line between solid popularized scholarship and commitment to Orthodox beliefs. "Corroborative" archeological data and numerous illustrations orient the reader to the material world of ancient Israel and its surroundings. Parallels between biblical and other ancient Near Eastern literature are often noted. Interestingly, the commentary on Ezra which inaugurated the series in 1970 included Gentile critical commentaries in its bibliography, a feature abandoned in subsequent volumes.

As is the case with its Israeli counterpart, American Jewish biblical scholarship has not neglected the Jewish public. The JPS Torah Commentary, completed in 1996 provides the New Jewish Publication Society translation of the Torah with running semi-popular commentaries by leading Jewish Bible scholars. Periodic references to earlier Jewish scholarship and discussions of relevant postbiblical Jewish beliefs and practices provide a Jewish flavor. The continuation of the series, the JPS Bible Commentary, edited by Michael Fishbane, will cover the Haftarot, Five Megillot (or scrolls)—Song of Songs, Ruth, Lamentations, Ecclesiastes, and Esther—as well as the book of Jonah, each of which is read within the liturgical cycle of the Jewish year. The commentaries to Jonah by Uriel Simon (1999) and Esther by Adele Berlin (2001) have also appeared in Hebrew in the *Miqra' leYisra'el* series.

More popular works have been produced with the needs in mind of the different Jewish denominations and synagogues. American Orthodoxy is less centralized than its Conservative and Reform counterparts, so one cannot speak of an official Orthodox Bible commentary. Nonetheless, one cannot ignore the beautifully produced Artscroll Series (1976–2001) edited by Rabbis Meir Zlotowitz and Nosson Scherman. Noteworthy more as a sociological and publishing phenomenon than as a Bible commentary, Artscroll is largely aimed at Jews without strong Jewish educational backgrounds seeking what they perceive to be "authentic" Judaism. Unabashedly obscurantist, Artscroll proudly eschews data drawn from archeology, Gentile scholarship, non-Orthodox scholarship, and suspect-Orthodox scholarship. As a result, the richness of traditional and Orthodox commentary is reduced in this series to harmonization, continuous apologetic, and pietistic moralizing.

The Union of American Hebrew Congregations (UAHC) of the Reform movement produced the *Torah: A Modern Commentary* in 1981. Written primarily by Rabbi Gunther Plaut, who completed the work several years before he was able to get it published, the UAHC commentary is an excellent synagogue Bible, less detailed than the JPS commentary. Though now a bit dated, "The Plaut," as it is popularly known, brings the results of scholarship through the early 1970s before a wide audience.

The *Etz Hayim: Torah and Commentary* edited by David Lieber of the University of Judaism was published in 2001 by the rabbinical and synagogal arms of Conservative Judaism. Long delayed, *Etz Hayim*'s appearance immediately generated controversy in the movement and outside of it. Although biblical criticism is taught at Jewish Theological Seminary, University of Judaism, in Conservative seminaries around the world and in Conservative Jewish day-schools, the de facto Bible in most Conservative synagogues has been the Hertz Pentateuch completed in 1936. Edited by Joseph Hertz (1872–1946), Chief Rabbi of the British Empire, this literate but apologetic commentary is theologically committed to the notion that Moses himself authored the historically accurate Torah, a notion which most Conservative congregational rabbis (though not all) had failed to dispel. As a result their congregants were shocked to learn, among other things, that the exodus from Egypt and the conquest of Canaan might have (p. 1342) "little or no historical basis." Outside the movement some ultra-Orthodox rabbis equated *Etz Hayim*'s questions about the Bible's factuality with the blood libel. A calmer perspective reveals *Etz Hayim* to be a highly useful digest of the JPS Torah Commentary in one volume, with the addition of homiletical comments, and notes and essays of special interest to Conservative Jews.

Thus, the status of Jewish Bible scholarship at the beginning of the 21st century is quite different from that at the beginning of the 20th century. A significant number of scholars at Israeli universities are part of the mainstream of biblical scholarship, and Jewish Bible scholars now teach in many North American academic departments that previously had strong Protestant biases. In addition, the methods of critical study of the Bible are no longer perceived as anti-Semitic, and are entering into the Jewish consciousness, even into the new Bibles used liturgically by some Jews. Jewish Bible scholarship, for its part, including concern with traditional Jewish interpretation, has likewise entered mainstream academic scholarship, and is studied by Jews and non-Jews alike. One can only ponder what further developments the coming century will bring. [S. DAVID SPERLING]

The Bible in the Dead Sea Scrolls

Until the discovery in the Judean Desert, near the Dead Sea, of more than 200 scrolls containing various parts of the Bible, historical and textual analysis of the biblical text relied on ancient translations and medieval manuscripts. The Judean Desert discoveries brought to light Hebrew manuscripts older by 1,000 years than the ones previously known, and document a period of pluriformity in the biblical text. Although no original copy of any biblical text has survived, these manuscripts not only greatly enhance our knowledge of textual features in general but also have a significant impact on central issues in biblical scholarship.

Before proceeding to a discussion of their effect on biblical scholarship, a brief aside to explain the conventional scholarly signs or sigla commonly used for Qumran and Judean Desert scrolls is in order. The elements included comprise the number of the cave (for Qumran, 1–11); identification of the site (Q = Qumran, Mas = Masada, Hev = Naḥal Ḥever); an abbreviated name of the biblical book (e.g., Gen = Genesis); number of the copy (in superscript; the first copy is ^{a}, the second is ^{b}, etc.). Other details sometimes indicated include the material on which the scroll is written (pap = papyrus), the language (gr = Greek; ar = Aramaic), the script (paleo = Paleo-Hebrew [the ancient Hebrew script]), or the literary genre (p = *pesher*). For example, 11QPs is a scroll from Qumran Cave 11 and contains material from the book of Psalms. A provisional list of documents from the Judean Desert, containing text numbers, sigla, and names is found in the *Encyclopedia of the Dead Sea Scrolls* (Oxford, 2000). For a categorized list of the biblical texts and an index list of all passages preserved in biblical manuscripts from the Judaean Desert, see *The Texts from the Judaean Desert: Indices* (DJD 39; Oxford 2002).

Finds

The story of the discovery of the Dead Sea Scrolls in the mid-20th century needs no retelling. What is significant are the large numbers of biblical and especially Torah books preserved in the Judean Desert. The bulk of these mainly fragmentarily preserved biblical scrolls come from caves located near Qumran, a site occupied from ca. 150 BCE to 68 CE. Smaller numbers of scrolls were found elsewhere in the Judean Desert: at Masada, Naḥal Ḥever, and Wadi Murabbaʿat. Of a total of 900 separate scrolls found at Qumran, 200 are biblical. At Masada, seven of the fifteen literary texts found, that is, nearly half, are biblical. Within the biblical corpus itself, proportionally more copies of Torah books were found: at Qumran they comprised 43.5 percent of the biblical corpus, and at other sites in the Judean Desert a full 64 percent of the biblical scrolls. Paleographical analysis shows that the script of the Qumran scrolls dates from 250 BCE (the earliest scroll is 4QExod^f) to the mid-1st century CE, with most of the manuscripts dating from the 1st century BCE to the 1st century CE. In addition, two types of Hebrew scripts were found at Qumran: Thirteen texts were written in paleo-Hebrew ("archaic" Hebrew, used mainly in the First Temple period and on Second Temple coins), but the overwhelming majority of the texts were written in square script (also called Assyrian or Jewish, borrowed during the Babylonian exile; used from the Second Temple period on). The non-Qumran Judean Desert scrolls were written exclusively in square script and date to the 1st and 2nd centuries CE.

The table on p. 1922 summarizes the data for the numbers of biblical scrolls found in the Judean Desert. A brief glance at the table not only reveals the prominence of Torah books in general, but also the greater popularity of specific biblical books, as evidenced, for example, by the relatively large number of copies of Deuteronomy, Psalms, and Isaiah. These latter works are also the ones most often cited in sectarian compositions at Qumran as well as in the New Testament and later rabbinic literature.

A small number of the scrolls found at Qumran contained more than a single book; thus two scrolls from Cave 4 contained Genesis and Exodus, one combined Exodus and Leviticus, and another Leviticus and Numbers. This perhaps suggests the writing of the books of the Torah on one scroll, but there is too little evidence to prove it. On the other hand, essential to any consideration of the Judean Desert finds is the rarity of a fully preserved text of any biblical work; fragmentary preservation is the rule. Most of the 200 biblical scrolls from the eleven Qumran caves contain no more than one-tenth of a biblical book; the complete Isaiah scroll (1QIsaᵃ) is the exception.

The table also indicates that, excluding Esther (but see discussion below), all the books of what was to become the Hebrew canon are represented in the Judean Desert corpus. Direct evidence for Nehemiah is also missing; however, as Ezra-Nehemiah was perceived as a single book in antiquity, scholars posit its presence at Qumran indirectly, from the Ezra scroll from Qumran Cave 4.

Text Type Classification

Although higher concentrations of biblical texts were found in Qumran Caves 4 and 11, almost without exception the finds in the caves are not homogeneous; thus no one cave contained the "biblical library shelf" at Qumran. Nor does it necessarily follow that a text found at Qumran was written or copied there; it is now widely held that many of the texts found at Qumran were imported from elsewhere. Thus, these finds have important implications for our general understanding of the biblical text and the canon in the late Second Temple period.

Even prior to the discovery of the Dead Sea Scrolls, scholars were aware of the existence of more than one biblical text type. Scholarly division of biblical texts according to three main types—the Masoretic Text (MT) as reflected in medieval manuscripts; the Septuagint (LXX), the ancient Greek translation of the Bible; and the Samaritan Pentateuch (SP), that is, the version preserved by the Samaritan community—received confirmation from Qumran finds. Ancient Hebrew exemplars of each of these three later text types were found at Qumran. As they predate the above-mentioned exemplars, in speaking of these text types at Qumran, they are more aptly labeled proto-Masoretic, proto-Septuagintal, and pre-Samaritan (or harmonistic; see below). The Qumran biblical texts shed light on the formation and the relationship between these types. They do not, however, represent the full variety of texts discovered at Qumran. A quarter of all of the biblical texts discovered there cannot be assigned to a type and are best referred to as independent or nonaligned texts, raising questions about the earlier scholarly tripartite division. Some Qumran texts display distinctive orthography (spelling), morphology (grammatical word formation), and scribal practices, and it has been suggested that they represent particular scribal habits or even a scribal school of the Qumran community itself.

Proto-Masoretic Scrolls

The largest group of biblical scrolls at Qumran, about 40 percent, resembles the consonantal text in medieval Masoretic manuscripts, as documented in some of the earliest medieval codices; for example, in Codex

BIBLICAL BOOKS FROM JUDEAN DESERT FINDS

Biblical Book (some scrolls contain two books)	Scripts at Qumran			Other Judean Desert Sites
	Qumran	"Square"	Paleo-Hebrew	
Genesis	19	16	3	4
Exodus	15	13	2	1
Leviticus	12	8	4	2
Numbers	5	4	1	4
Deuteronomy	30	28	2	3
Joshua	2	2		1
Judges	3	3		1
1–2 Samuel	4	4		
1–2 Kings	3	3		
Isaiah	21	21		1
Jeremiah	6	6		
Ezekiel	6	6		1
Minor Prophets	8	8		1
Psalms	36	36		3
Proverbs	2	2		
Job	4	3	1	
Song of Songs	4	4		
Ruth	4	4		
Lamentations	4	4		
Ecclesiastes	2	2		
Esther	0			0
Daniel	8	8		
Ezra-Nehemiah	1	1		
Chronicles	1	1		
Total	200	187	13	22

Leningrad (dated 1009) and the 10th-century Aleppo Codex. (Both of these codices are authoritative copies of the Bible with vocalization and cantillation traditions; all Qumran texts lack these signs, which developed in the late first millennium CE.) Some scholars prefer the label "proto-rabbinic" for this category. The high proportion of texts belonging to this type at Qumran, as opposed to the lesser representation of other text types there, evidently reflects their dominant, though not exclusive, status. The proportionate predominance of this text type perhaps reflects a crucial stage in the process that resulted in its emergence as the authoritative text (see below). Among the Qumran texts the ones that bear the most re-

markable affinity to medieval ones are 4QGen[b] and 1QIs[b]. Other closely related texts are 4QJer[a] and 4QJer[c].

Proto-Septuagintal Texts

A significant legacy of the discovery of the Dead Sea Scrolls is related to their attestation to the reliability of ancient translations. It is no longer possible to argue that differences from the MT preserved in the ancient translations all reflect intentional changes introduced by the translator rather than a different underlying text (Vorlage); it is clear that multiple text types circulated at the same time. One small group of texts found at Qumran, four in number, includes scrolls closely resembling the presumed Hebrew parent *(Vorlage)* of the Septuagint translation. Of the texts found at Qumran, 4QJer[b] and 4QJer[d] are closest to LXX, resembling both its shorter text and its verse arrangement. Other texts exhibiting close affinities to LXX are 4QDeut[q] and 4QSam[a]. Readings from the ancient translations hitherto regarded as questionable have now been shown to preserve authentic Hebrew ones.

Harmonistic Editing

A few texts are often called pre-Samaritan, since they share certain features of the Samaritan text, but lack the distinctive ideology of the Samaritans (references to Mount Gerizim, for example). This small group of five texts from Qumran—4QPaleoExod[m], 4QPaleo-Exod-Lev[f], 4QNum[b], 4QDeut[n], and 4Q364 *(Reworked Pentateuch[b]; see below)*—is better characterized by a different feature: the presence of harmonizing alterations, that is, changes or additions that create concord between two separate but parallel Torah texts. The two texts undergoing harmonization can be contextually close, such as the addition to Exod. 7.8 based on 7.15–18, or remote, such as the two versions of the Decalogue (Exod. ch 20 and Deut ch 5). Alterations can be of different kinds: additions of a "source" for a quotation, mostly insertions from Deuteronomy to the parallel sections in the earlier books of the Torah, or provision of a missing command or its fulfillment. Harmonistic editing is also found in some nonbiblical texts from Qumran, including quotations in *Reworked Pentateuch*, excerpts cited for liturgical purposes, phylacteries, and mezuzot.

As compared to some of the later Qumran biblical scrolls, the Samaritan Pentateuch (SP) itself reflects a limited degree of harmonization, a fact that has bearing on the question of its dating. SP includes, in addition to harmonizing alterations, particularistic changes introduced by the Samaritans—related mainly to the sanctity of Mount Gerizim—before the destruction of the Samaritan temple on Mt. Gerizim in 111 BCE. On this basis, it appears

that the specifically sectarian changes and additions now found in the SP were introduced during the 2nd century BCE to pre-Hasmonean Jewish harmonizing texts of the Torah. Although biblical texts continued to undergo harmonistic editing at Qumran, the Samaritans did not continue to update their texts with the more extensive changes attested in Qumran texts from the final two centuries of the Second Temple period.

Nonaligned Texts

The remaining texts, about 25 percent of the biblical corpus, may combine readings belonging to one or more traditional categories alongside independent variants; they are not easily assigned to a particular text type and are therefore classified as independent or nonaligned. To this group also belong the so-called vulgar (in the sense of popular) texts, exemplified by 1QIs[a], which exhibit a freer approach to the text. The scribal changes introduced into vocabulary and grammar reflect, on the whole, an attempt either to simplify the difficult biblical text, or to remove grammatical and contextual difficulties.

In addition, also related to this group are some texts of doubtful biblical nature, among them the so-called *Reworked Pentateuch*. This group is composed of six Hebrew manuscripts, in which a running biblical text is reworked by scribal intervention, characterized by omissions of, additions to, and rearrangements of biblical passages, and, in some cases, the introduction of nonbiblical passages as well. We must also bear in mind that no external features or headings distinguish between biblical and nonbiblical texts at Qumran. Scholars debate these texts' classification: Some assign them to the biblical corpus, others define them as *Reworked Pentateuch*, whereas still others view them as nonbiblical. These texts stand on the boundary between text and interpretation.

Translations

Also of notable importance as witnesses to the development of the biblical text during the late Second Temple period are the Greek and Aramaic translations of the Bible. Among the Qumran scrolls Greek translations were found: two scrolls of Leviticus and one scroll each of Exodus, Numbers, and Deuteronomy. These texts are reliable witnesses to an early stage of the transmission of LXX, preceding the one in which revisions bringing LXX into line with MT are attested. In addition, a Greek copy of the Minor Prophets was found in Naḥal Ḥever (8ḤevXII); it belongs however to the latter type, being the earliest extant revision bringing LXX into line with MT (mid-1st century BCE). Aramaic Targumim, of lesser importance than LXX as witnesses to an early stage of the Hebrew biblical text, were also found at Qumran. The oldest extant Targum texts (to Lev, 4QtgLev; and Job, 4QtgJob and 11QtgJob) are extremely literal in contrast to the exegetical expansions characteristic of later Targumim.

Quotation and Use of Scriptures

Other biblically related texts found at Qumran, which will not be discussed at length here, are excerpted and abbreviated texts probably used for liturgical purposes, such as phylacteries (tefillin) and mezuzot. (There is a significant amount of variation in the texts found in these, and many do not agree with the later rabbinic prescriptions concerning their content.) Texts such as 4QExod[d] which contains Exod. 13.15–16 and 15.1, and 4QDeut[n] where Deut. ch 8 precedes Deut chs 5–6, also belong to this category. Also found in Qumran texts, both sectarian and nonsectarian, are free quotations of and allusions to biblical texts. Another genre found at Qumran, pesher, also incorporates biblical quotations. The works in question take selected biblical texts and apply them to the contemporary sectarian setting. From the formal viewpoint they resemble later medieval commentaries; the basic structure includes citation of a biblical text (the lemma), an introductory formula containing the word pesher (actualized interpretation), and the interpretation, which is an application of the text to a contemporary real-

ity typically unrelated to its original context. Thus the lemmata of the pesharim also serve as witnesses to the biblical text of the mainly prophetic books they interpret. In some cases, more than one text to the same verse seems to be interpreted. In other cases, the biblical lemma may have been changed to fit the pesher interpretation. In addition to these obvious uses of biblical texts, there are, scattered throughout the sectarian writings of the Qumran community, many allusions to and citations of biblical verses or parts of verses. The Qumran community was "Bible-centric"; its literature was saturated with biblical phrases.

Literary Development and Textual Transmission

Higher Criticism

Of the contributions made by the discovery of the Qumran scrolls, one of the most telling belongs to the realm of higher criticism (see "Modern Study of the Bible," pp. 2084–96). The scrolls brought to light unambiguous witnesses to textual differences belonging to earlier stages of the literary growth of various biblical books; before their discovery, these differences were only attested indirectly, especially in the ancient translations or versions. The discovery of the Qumran scrolls has had a particularly significant impact on our understanding of the text of Judges, Samuel, Jeremiah, Esther, and Daniel. The examples below demonstrate how Qumran texts bear witness to what is believed to represent an earlier editorial stage of a biblical work. Qumran texts also support hitherto unattested variants or different readings found in LXX. Additionally, some texts found at Qumran are believed to represent possible sources for biblical books.

Additions Not Found in MT

As witnessed by MT (and Vulgate, Syriac, and the Targum), Nahash, king of Ammon, agreed to make a treaty with the people of Jabesh-gilead on condition that he gouge out their right eyes (1 Sam. 11.1–2). In the context of these textual witnesses this seems an unusually brutal act. An additional passage preserved in 4QSam^a, which unfolds the story of how Nahash oppressed the tribes of Gad and Reuben, inflicting terror by gouging out their right eyes, and how 7,000 men escaped mutilation by fleeing to Jabesh-gilead, provides a more natural link between the election of Saul as king in Mizpah (1 Sam 10.27a) and his Ammonite campaign (10.27b). Moreover, the reading found in 4QSam^a, "it was about a month's time" (k-m-ḥ-d-sh), provides a more logical connection between the additional passage and the one following than MT's "he pretended not to mind" (k-m-ḥ-r-sh, 11.1). (In Hebrew script, d and r are almost identical and easily confused.)

Although some scholars explain the additional passage in 4QSam^a as a secondary midrashic addition, it is more likely that 4QSam^a has preserved the original reading and that MT's reading is based on scribal error, that is, an accidental omission during an early stage of the book's literary development or transmission. In general, the text of Samuel as reflected by MT is problematic, and LXX and the fragments discovered at Qumran reflect a better-preserved text.

Witness to an Earlier Editorial Stage

Judg. 6.7–10 is missing from a text found at Qumran, 4QJudg^a. Evidently not the result of scribal error, this omission can be seen as reflecting an earlier stage in the editing of the book of Judges. The section found in MT, in which a prophet tells the Israelites that God will save them even though they have sinned in the past, has clear parallels to vv. 11–24, in which the angel of the LORD appears to Gideon; it is also very similar to other texts found in Deuteronomy and related literature. It appears, then, that Judg. 6.7–10 was a later addition by the so-called Deuteronomistic Historian, the editor of Deuteronomy, Joshua, Judges, 1–2 Samuel, and 1–2 Kings, who focused on the centralization of the cult in Jerusalem.

Attestation to LXX

The organizational complexity of Jeremiah and the relationship between MT and other ancient versions, especially LXX, enhances the importance of the Qumran finds. Two of the six fragmentary manuscripts of Jeremiah found there (4QJer^b and 4QJer^d) are close in nature to the so-called original Septuagint version of Jeremiah (to be distinguished from later revisions correcting the translation to reflect MT and from Syriac, Vulgate, and the Targumim). LXX to Jeremiah differs from MT in two ways: first, in chapter and verse order; second, in the length of the text, where the Septuagint is one-eighth shorter than MT, missing words, phrases, or even entire sections. Evidently, the Septuagint was translated from a Hebrew text close in nature to these two manuscripts, which reflects a first, short edition of the book of Jeremiah that differs from the longer, differently ordered text documented in MT and other related versions. The Qumran texts support the view that LXX reflects an authentic Second Temple period variant tradition of the biblical text.

Possible Sources for Biblical Books

As opposed to the above examples, the following ones do not reflect stages in the editing of a biblical work; rather they relate to possible sources for biblical books.

Esther. As mentioned earlier, all the books of the Hebrew canon were represented among the Qumran scrolls, with the exception of Esther. The different explanations for its absence range from the vagaries of chance, to suggestions that the Qumran community did not observe the holiday of Purim and/or the book had not yet achieved "canonical" status. The exact nature of a text from Cave 4 labeled Proto-Esther (4Q550–550e) is also a matter of debate. Some identify it as an Aramaic prototype or source underlying the various Hebrew, Greek, Latin, and even Armenian versions of Esther, while others find only a general resemblance between the book of Esther and this composition, and still others argue that this text has very little in common with the Hebrew story of Esther, and is simply a hitherto unknown Aramaic text. Even if this Qumran text has no direct relationship to Esther, it is another example of a story with a Persian court setting.

Daniel. Cave 4 at Qumran contained some Hebrew and Aramaic texts exhibiting varying degrees of connection to Daniel. The most clear-cut link is that between Daniel and 4QPrayer of Nabonidus (4Q242). Long before the latter text's publication, the resemblance between the story of Nabonidus's illness while in exile at Teima and the legend of Nebuchadnezzar's madness in Dan. ch 4 was noted. The author of Dan. 4 adapted this material to his worldview, most significantly by changing the name of the king to that of the better-known one—Nebuchadnezzar—and by identifying the anonymous Jew who assisted the king with Daniel.

Another fragmentary text found at Qumran, labeled 4QHistorical Text A (4Q248), resembles Dan. ch 11. This text mentions, in an extremely condensed manner, a number of events pertaining to Antiochus IV Epiphanes, also referred to in Daniel. These chronologically arranged events start with Antiochus IV's first invasion of Egypt (170–169 BCE) and end with his second inroad into Egypt in 168. Following the last event mentioned in the Qumran text, which is the second invasion of Egypt, words parallel to Dan. 12.7 appear: "and when the shattering of the power of the ho[ly] people [. . . comes to an end, then shall all] these things [be fulfilled]." The absence of references to Antiochus's religious persecutions, as compared with ample references of this nature in Daniel (7.25; 11.30–33; 12.1), makes it clear that 4Q248's composition preceded 167 BCE. If so, this work was composed before the completion of the final edition of Daniel, commonly dated to ca. 165 BCE, and may have been part of an apocalyptic work that served as a source for this book.

Finally, another possible source for Daniel is found in the throne-theophany of the *Book*

of Giants (4Q530, col. ii). Comparison of this text to Daniel 7.9–10 shows that the book of Daniel preserved a more expanded form of the vision.

Text Criticism

Another important aspect of the contribution of biblical Dead Sea Scrolls to biblical studies belongs to text criticism (sometimes called "lower criticism"). As opposed to the literary-historical bent of higher criticism, this field relates to the technical aspect of establishing the best readings of the wording of the text. The examples demonstrate how the scrolls enhance our understanding of the development of variants created in the course of textual transmission. On occasion the Qumran texts preserve superior readings; in other instances, they represent vulgarization of the text.

Haplography

1QIsa[a], which is the oldest manuscript of Isaiah that has been preserved, dated ca. 125 BCE, is of a vulgar or popular text type (see above). Its fifteen surviving fragments contain about forty, mostly minor, variants from MT, some of which shed light on the development of variants in the biblical text.

1QIsa[a] usually has the secondary variant, that is, scribal changes and "corrections" made to proto-MT not based on ancient witnesses. Two instances of haplography (an erroneous omission of one or two identical or similar adjacent letters or words) include the omission by the original copyist of 1QIsa[a] of part of Isa. 40.7–8 because of the double repetition of "grass withers, flowers fade," or Isa. 26.3–4, where 1QIsa[a] has reduced the double occurrence of *trust* to a single one. In both these cases MT has the superior reading.

Nevertheless, 1QIsa[a] also provides an example where MT's reading reflects haplography. MT (Peshitta and Vulgate) reads Isa. 40.12 as: "Who measured *the waters (mayim)* with the hollow of his hand, and gauged the sky with a span?" This question seems out of place in the context of a rhetorical list with negative answers. 1QIsa[a] has a slightly different but superior reading: "Who measured *the waters of the sea (mei yam)* with the hollow of his hand. . . ." A similar reading is also attested in a paraphrase found in an apotropaic prayer, 4Q511, which reads: "Can *the waters of the sea (mei rabah)* be gauged in the hollow of a man's hand?"

Another original reading preserved in the Dead Sea Scrolls comes from 4QSam[a]. MT to 1 Sam. 1.24 has the double reading *ve ha-na'ar na'ar*: "And though the boy was still very young" whereas 4QSam[a] has an expanded reading: ". . . and *the boy (ve ha-na'ar)* [with] them. And they went before the LORD, and his father slaughtered the sacrifi[ce as] it happened [every year to the LORD. And she brought *the boy (ha-na'ar)*]. . . ." MT reflects a case of parablepsis (or homoioarcton), that is, the identical beginning ("the boy") caused the erroneous omission of a section.

Matres Lectionis

In its most ancient form the Hebrew alphabet contained only consonants. It is well known that *matres lectionis,* literally "mothers of reading," that is consonants used to indicate vowel length and quality, were secondarily introduced into the text, sometimes relatively late in its development. Variants in the use of *matres lectionis* usually do not affect the biblical text, but in some cases they provide evidence for a different scribal understanding. Such is the case in 1 Sam. 1.24, where MT reads three bulls *(parim sheloshah),* while 4QSam[a] reads: three-year-old bull *(be par meshulash).* Both MT and 4QSam[a] presumably derive from the same common consonantal source: *b-p-r-m-sh-l-sh,* with a difference of opinion about where to divide the words. The Qumran scroll's variant seems more reasonable contextually, as the following verse refers only to an offering of one bull. When *matres lectionis* were later introduced, 4QSam[a] (and LXX and the Peshitta) were in a better position to indicate the proper reading, while MT (Targum and Vulgate), lacking *matres lectionis,* have a corrupt reading.

Original Reading Preserved in a Qumran Text

4QTestimonia (4Q175) is one of the few almost completely preserved texts found at Qumran. Written on one sheet of skin (parchment), this text is a collection of quotations directly linked to each other without quotation formulas or interpretations.

A superior reading is documented in the quotation of Deut. 33.9 in 4QTestimonia. Where MT has the singular "him" following a reference to mother and father, a reconstructed reading of 4QTest restores the original parallel structure: "Who said of his father, 'I consider you not' and to his mother 'I ignore you.' His brother he disregarded, ignored his own children."

Canon at Qumran

The discoveries at Qumran, while shedding light on the pluriformity of biblical texts in the Second Temple period, do not provide the means to definitively establish which books the sect held sacred. Nor do the finds of large numbers of copies of particular biblical alongside other apocryphal (*Jubilees, Enoch,* etc.) or sectarian works necessarily indicate their sanctification in the eyes of the Qumran sect. Moreover, as not all of the texts found at Qumran were copied there and it is impossible to establish who wrote or copied them, we cannot determine their canonical status.

Nonetheless, the biblical scrolls found at Qumran do bear on the question of the growth of the Hebrew canon, which was, according to many scholars, fixed only at a later period. The presence at Qumran of all of the books found in the Hebrew canon (with the exception of Esther) may support the inference that these books already had canonical status. What was not yet agreed upon was the *exact* boundaries of the canon as well as the final textual form of the individual works. Thus it is that we find proto-Septuagintal and harmonistic texts alongside the prevailing proto-Masoretic type. In the course of less than a century after the scrolls were hidden, however, the proto-Masoretic text type emerged as the accepted one.

On the other hand, using the multiformity of the biblical texts found at Qumran as evidence, some scholars argue that the canon was not yet fixed and even postulate a broader canon. Some claim that the examples of *Reworked Pentateuch* reflect a free approach to the Bible. Others base their argument against a fixed canon at this date on the existence of various editions of Psalms at Qumran, including some with additional psalms (some of which are attested in the LXX and other versions), submitting that this indicates the fluidity of the collection at that time. However, many of these psalm texts may have been liturgical rather than biblical texts, and reflect a different order for this reason, just as we find a different ordering of psalms in the present-day *siddur*. We must also bear in mind that multiple copies of a text can testify to alternative uses: liturgical, for study, for copying, and so on. Therefore, notwithstanding the variety of text types preserved in the Qumran library, it seems that at that period the canon itself, that is, the identity and number of biblical books it encompassed, was already well on the way to becoming fixed.

The Emergence of MT as the Authoritative Text

There is no scholarly consensus regarding the history of the biblical text. Some argue for a gradual development between the 5th and 1st centuries BCE in three geographical areas: the land of Israel, Egypt, and some third locality, in all probability Babylonia. Others suggest that the Rabbis, the Samaritans, and the Christians each preserved a particular collection of biblical texts, derived from a larger variety of text forms, which were lost with the disappearance of the groups that had presumably saved them.

The presence of diverse texts and text types at Qumran led other scholars to argue for a paradigm reflecting textual variety, based on three main text types but including texts with a free approach to the biblical one. Clearly, based on the Qumran evidence, plurality of texts was the rule from the 3rd to the 1st century BCE. The additional finds from the Judean Desert document a shift in this state of affairs, however. At Masada, the much more limited number of biblical finds represents only the so-called proto-Masoretic (or proto-rabbinic) type, as is the case for the later finds from the Bar Kokhba Revolt refuge caves. This supports the view that this text type achieved authoritative status during the period between the Great Revolt and the Bar Kokhba Revolt (between 70 and 135 CE), pushing the other variants out. Thus, by the end of the Bar Kokhba Revolt, the textual pluriformity attested in the pre-destruction period gave way to the exclusive choice of the already prominent proto-Masoretic text type as binding. Thus, the destruction of the Temple and its aftermath served as a strong impetus for creating a more unified text. Given the lack of evidence for the biblical libraries in the possession of the different groups in Second Temple Judaism—with the Qumran library serving as perhaps only a sampling of biblical texts circulating among various groups—it is impossible to establish a definite link between particular groups and specific text types. The sole known exception is the Samaritan community, which chose harmonistic texts for its Holy Writings at a date preceding the acceptance of MT as the authoritative text version. It is possible that, in the absence of a tradition similar to rabbinic oral law, the Samaritans preferred a text relatively free of internal contradictions as the basis for their Holy Writings.

In sum, the discovery of biblical texts in the Judean Desert has been of inestimable value for biblical scholarship. By significantly enlarging the number of ancient witnesses to the biblical text, the finds shed light on manifold aspects of the development of the biblical canon and text as represented by MT and the other variants and facilitate better understanding of when MT emerged as the authoritative witness to the biblical text.

[ESTHER ESHEL]

The Bible in the Synagogue

During the period of the Second Temple (from the return to Zion [538 BCE] until the destruction of the Temple [70 CE]), and in particular after the conquest of the entire Near East by the armies of Alexander the Great (ca. 330 BCE), numerous upheavals occurred in the religious-spiritual world of the Jewish people. Two of the fundamental changes caused by these upheavals are important for our discussion, having left their mark on Judaism, in all places, in every era, and upon the various forms of Jewish expression, up to the present day: the growth and establishment of the synagogue, and the central role played by the Bible in the religious and spiritual existence of the Jewish people. Since then, a Jewish community without a synagogue at its center is unimaginable, nor could one conceive of a synagogue in which a central place was not reserved, both physically and in terms of its activities, for the three sections of the Tanakh: the Torah, the Prophets, and the Writings.

During the era of the First Temple (until its destruction in 586 BCE), and to some extent during the ensuing two or three centuries, the word of God was perceived to be revealed to humanity in numerous ways. First and foremost, it came through the prophet through whom God revealed His will or His plans. God also answered the people's questions, both by way of the priests, using the Urim and Thummim, as well as through dreams (see 1 Sam. 28.6: "But the LORD did not answer him, either by dreams or by Urim or by prophets"). Thus the prophet, the priest, and the interpreter of dreams served as intermediaries between God and human beings. In this respect, a major upheaval occurred when it was believed that prophecy had departed from Israel after the prophets Haggai, Zechariah, and Malachi (b. B. Bat. 14b), that the Urim and Thummim had disappeared (y. Mak. 5:2), and that dreams are not divine messages from heaven but a result of human

self-reflection (b. Ber. 55b). All of these methods of discovering the divine will were then replaced by texts, the Holy Scriptures. The nation of Israel became what was later termed the "People of the Book." The intermediary between God and humanity was henceforth the Rabbi, the wise man who knew how to read Scriptures and to hear through them God's voice. Instead of one-time divine revelations through dreams or prophets or priests, the Jewish people were given a book which was understood to contain God's revelation for all time. The era of revelation to individuals at appointed times came to a close, and was replaced by a new era with continuous revelation for all, by way of the Holy Scriptures. From this point on, the religion and culture of Israel developed around the twenty-four books of the Tanakh: in Houses of Study and in schools, at particular events such as eulogies or festive religious celebrations, but first and foremost in the synagogues.

It would appear that, as the prestige of the Temple began to decline, the need to continue hearing the word of God was among the central factors leading to the ascent of the synagogue as an institution, or perhaps even to its creation. Parallel to the sacrificial service which was practiced in the Jerusalem Temple only, it became necessary to create an institution in which Jews, wherever they might be, could gather on special occasions, to listen together to the word of God and to discover what it implies (as is described in the Bible itself, in Neh. ch 8). In the course of time these gatherings became formalized in fixed, obligatory forms, but the exact process through which they took shape is for the most part unknown, due to the dearth of extant sources from the Second Temple period. However, aided by the Jewish philosopher Philo (De Somnis 2:127), by the historian Josephus Flavius (Against Apion 2:175), and by early Christian literature (Acts 15.21), we can pinpoint some early stages of this process in the 1st century CE, though the origin of the synagogue may be several centuries earlier. We may reasonably assume that slowly and gradually, the idea of the synagogue began to crystallize. That which eventually coalesced during the period of the rabbinic Sages (from the first century CE until the Islamic conquest [ca. 640 CE]) attained its ultimate form in the geonic period (which ended just beyond 1000 CE). It was at that time that the first Jewish prayer books were compiled. Despite all the social and cultural metamorphoses that the Jewish people have undergone subsequently, the position of the Bible in the synagogue has remained basically unchanged. There are regular readings from the Torah, fixed readings from the Prophets, reading of the Five Scrolls on specific days, explication of Scriptures during or close to their public reading, including their translation into different languages, and extensive use of Scripture in the liturgy. Liturgical use includes the recitation of various psalms, reading of additional scriptural excerpts such as the Song of the Sea (Exod. ch 15) or the story of the binding of Isaac (Gen. ch 22) in the daily morning prayer, recitation of *piyyutim* (liturgical poetry) that draws on Scripture in various ways, as well as extensive use of biblical Hebrew and its expressions within the prayers (see "The Bible in the Liturgy," pp. 1937–48).

Reading from the Torah

According to a tradition recorded in the Talmud (*b. B. K.* 82a), a custom had already been established during the time of Moses—and later re-affirmed by Ezra the Scribe—to read from the Torah every Monday, Thursday, and Sabbath, so that the Jewish people would not remain without Torah for three consecutive days. This tradition, even if it cannot be substantiated, confers great antiquity and considerable importance on the custom of reading from the Torah. It seems likely that initially people gathered for the reading and study of

selected sections of the Torah on festivals or other special days, but that during the Second Temple period the custom of a weekly reading from the Torah, in order, from beginning to end, was gradually established.

The reading of the Torah in most Jewish communities (at least until the 19th century, when some modern movements introduced changes) follows the custom consolidated by Babylonian Jewry during the period of the Sages and the *geonim*. There is some indication that this custom originated in the land of Israel, but even if this is so, it was the Babylonian Jewry that granted it pivotal status. According to this custom, the Torah is read in an annual cycle, divided into 54 fixed sections, called "parashiyot" (singular: "parashah"). The full parashah is read in the synagogue on Sabbath morning, between the *Shaharit* and *Musaf* prayer services. On Sabbath afternoon (during the *Minhah* service) and during *Shaharit* on Monday and Thursday mornings, the beginning verses from the parashah that will be read in full on the following Sabbath are read. Designated sections of the Torah whose themes are appropriate are also read on special days such as festivals, Rosh Hodesh (the new moon), and public fast days, as well as other special occasions. For example, the passage describing the religious precept of blotting out the remembrance of Amalek (Deut. 25.17–19) is read on the Sabbath preceeding Purim, due to the connection between Haman and the Amalekites (Esth. 3.1). Most of these special excerpts were already selected for this purpose during the rabbinic period (*b. Meg.* 31a–b, etc.).

The division of the Torah into 54 parashiyot (instead of the expected 52) stems from the fact that in certain years there are 54 Sabbath days. This is possible only in a leap year, which contains 13 lunar months, and even then provided that hardly any festivals occur on Sabbath. (When a festival does occur on Sabbath, the passage which is read from the Torah is one associated with that festival rather than the weekly parashah.) In a year that has fewer Sabbath days, as is the case in most years, two consecutive parashiyot are joined in accordance with predetermined rules (e.g., *Mattot* and *Mas'ei* from the book of Numbers [30.2–32.42 and 33.1–36.13], or *Nitsavim* and *Va-yelekh* from Deuteronomy [29.9–30.20 and 31.1–30]), so that the entire reading will be concluded within one year and by a fixed date in the calendar. This date is the day after the Sukkot festival, which is called *Simḥat Torah* (Rejoicing of the Torah); on the following Sabbath, referred to as *Shabbat Bereshit* (the sabbath of the parashah of Bereshit, the first parashah), the Torah reading recommences with Genesis. The division of the Torah into parashiyot and the assignment of each parashah to a given week are essentially identical in all Jewish communities throughout the world. They are predictable and follow a fixed routine.

The Torah is read in the synagogue from a parchment scroll and seven (or more) people are called up to the Torah for the reading, one after the other. The parchment scroll contains the unvocalized text of the Torah without the diacritical marks (for chanting), so that the reading requires skill and preparation. In antiquity, each person called to the Torah would read his own passage (*b. Kid.* 49a), but as time passed, it became customary for each person called up to the Torah (who had an 'aliyah) to recite only the blessings before and after the reading, while another individual designated for this task, and who had prepared himself for it, would read the parashah. The regulations for reading from the Torah were fashioned by halakhah and custom into clear rules: the order of those called to the Torah, their number, the passages apportioned to each of them, the blessings recited by those called up, the manner in which the congregation congratulates them, etc. The blessings recited by each honoree before and after the reading are noteworthy (*b. Ber.* 11b). Their main emphasis is on the choosing of the Jewish People, expressed among other things, in the giving of the Torah, the "Torah of truth" with its promise of "everlasting life."

It becomes apparent that in the land of Is-

rael during the period of the Rabbis or Sages and that of the *geonim* (as well as in some communities outside the land of Israel that assumed its custom), a different mode of reading from the Torah was widespread, referred to inaccurately as the "triennial cycle" (cf. *b. Meg.* 29b). Here, too, the Torah was read in sequence, but it was divided into a greater number of readings (called "sedarim" [singular: "seder"]). The length of each seder and the overall number of sedarim in the Torah varied from one synagogue to another. That which was read in one synagogue on Sabbath was not necessarily identical to that read on the same Sabbath in another synagogue. Moreover, even the seder read in a particular synagogue on a certain Sabbath did not have to be identical in length with what would be read in later years in the same synagogue when the same Torah portion was reached.

Each synagogue and community on each Sabbath would determine for itself the length of the Torah reading, according to its custom or requirements: the desire to honor more people with the Torah reading, the presence of a groom in the synagogue, the time available, and so forth. The earliest halakhah (*m. Ber.* 4:4) requires that each reader recite at least three verses from the Torah, but it does not specify the maximum number permitted. The Mishnah (ibid., 4:1) further requires that at least seven people should read from the Torah every Sabbath, but it allows additional participants. In other words, at least twenty-one verses were read on each occasion, but apparently the reading would often be extended, in accordance with the desires of the readers and their number, or in order to conclude the reading at an appropriate point, rather than in the middle of a subject. If we assume that eight or nine peo-ple read from the Torah each Sabbath, and that each of them would read about four or five verses, we can conclude that at this pace each synagogue completed its Torah reading in approximately three years. The evidence we possess (mostly from discoveries over the past century, primarily from the Cairo Genizah) indicates numerous Torah reading cycles that extended over 141–175 Sabbaths. Thus, it is also clear that it would have been impossible to set any fixed date in the annual calendar at which the Torah reading would either conclude or recommence. The festival we now call *Simḥat Torah* was celebrated in the land of Israel at the very most on the Sabbath on which the Torah reading was concluded, approximately once in three years, and at a different time in each synagogue because in the land of Israel there was no fixed date to conclude the Torah reading in the annual calendar.

A person attending a synagogue in the land of Israel in ancient times, who had not been present there on the previous Sabbath, could not know beforehand which seder he was about to hear. Reading over a cycle of three years resulted in a particular story in the Torah being read at one time in winter and at another in the summer; or in a legal portion such as our parashah of *Mishpatim* (Exod. chs 21–24) being subdivided in different ways in different years. A preacher who came to the synagogue to give a sermon on a subject arising from the Torah reading and who had not previously enquired as to where the congregation stood in their Torah reading cycle would likely find himself more than surprised or even totally unprepared—a situation not entirely unknown (see *Lev. Rab.* 3:6). A person who wandered from one synagogue to the next would read about the birth of Moses on one Sabbath, mourn his death with another congregation on the following Sabbath, and then hear of Moses walking upon the face of the earth if he came the next Sabbath to a synagogue in the process of reading from Leviticus or Numbers. Flexible reading systems like these may possibly fit the customs of smaller congregations permanently located in one place, but it would be most difficult to utilize them to construct a national religious system extending over distant locations. This, then, would seem to be the reason why the Babylonian custom eventually won out, replacing the customs of the land of Israel in a process which reached its final stages around the 12th

century. From then on, all those attending synagogue would hear the entire Torah every year, and this undoubtedly was sufficient to forcefully instill the Torah into the cultural agenda.

The Haftarah

The last of those called up to the Torah on Sabbath and festivals remains on the podium after the reading has concluded, and then reads (usually from a printed vocalized text, not a scroll) an additional portion from Scripture, taken from the Prophets. This reading is termed "haftarah" (a word that means conclusion), as it brings the readings from Scripture on Sabbath and festivals to their end.

The haftarah section is often connected either linguistically or in content with the weekly parashah, e.g., the haftarah which begins with the verse "King David was now old and advanced in years" (1 Kings 1.1) is read on the Sabbath when the passage "Abraham was old and advanced in years" is read (Gen. ch 24); or the Prophet Isaiah's mention of the flood (ch 54) is read on the Sabbath when the story of the flood is read from the Torah. At other times, however, the haftarah has a particular connection with the occasion upon which it is read, such as the haftarah beginning with the words "Comfort, oh comfort my people" (Isa. ch 40), which is always recited on the Sabbath after Tishʿah beʾav (a day of national mourning), or the haftarah which begins "Return, O Israel, to the LORD your God" (Hos. 14.2ff.), which is read in the Sabbath preceding Yom Kippur.

It is most likely that the institution of the haftarah was created at the close of the Second Temple era, during the great dispute between the Jews and the Samaritans, the latter deeming the Torah to be holy, but not accepting the sanctity of the prophetic books. The decision to read something from the Prophets every Sabbath was apparently part of the polemic against the Samaritans, as though the Jews wished to state: The books of the Prophets are also holy, and are also the word of God, so it is appropriate to read them publicly and to recite a blessing upon their reading. The blessings recited before and after the haftarah ("... Who has chosen good prophets, and desires their words, which are spoken in truth ...," "... Who has chosen the Torah and His prophet Moses and His people Israel and prophets of truth and righteousness") clearly emphasize this point. Evidence for the reading of the haftarah may already be found in the Apocrypha (2 Macc. 15.9) and in the New Testament (Luke 4.16–30). The subject is also discussed extensively in various contexts in the literature of the Sages (e.g., *m. Meg.* 4:1–3; 3:5–6).

It seems that initially the choice of passage to be read from the Prophets and its precise length was made by the the reader of the haftarah himself (called the *maftir*), or according to the custom of his congregation. As time passed, however, these readings also became formalized, attaining permanent status. Here, too, halakhah and custom brought about orderly, fixed lists of haftarot. But certain differences are notable even today among the various communities of the Jewish people—Ashkenazic, Sephardic, Yemenite, and Italian Jews—being the heritage of those flexible and dynamic times in antiquity. Needless to say, in ancient times in the land of Israel, where the extent of the Torah readings was irregular and flexible, there were numerous alternative customs for the haftarot. (A modern commentary on the haftarot is *Haftarot: The Traditional Hebrew Text with the New JPS Translation*, commentary by Michael Fishbane [Philadelphia: The Jewish Publication Society, 2002].)

Thus, with regard to the manner in which reading from the Torah and the haftarah were consolidated, the land of Israel and Babylonia reveal two opposite conceptions concerning uniformity and permanence, the quantity of Torah and prophetic readings to which the synagogue congregation was exposed on Sabbath and festivals, and the total annual extent.

The Five Scrolls

On five occasions during the year, one of the five scrolls is read in the synagogue: The Song of Songs (during the week of Passover); the Scroll of Ruth (Shavuot); Lamentations (Tish'ah be'av); Ecclesiastes (during the week of Sukkot); and the Scroll of Esther (Purim). Evidence shows that during the geonic period some parts of the scrolls were also read on the Sabbaths prior to these occasions, in preparation for them.

The reading of the Scroll of Esther on Purim appears to be the most ancient of all (see *m. Meg.* 1:1). This is self-evident, since the whole story of the origin of Purim is contained in this scroll. The second scroll to be introduced into the synagogue would appear to be Lamentations, which relates to the story of the destruction of the Temple. Evidence of its recitation on Tish'ah be'av may already be found in the writings of the Sages (e.g., *Lam. Rab.*, petiḥta 17). The other three scrolls, which are read on the three pilgrimage festivals, apparently were not read liturgically in the synagogue until the end of the period of the Sages, or even until the geonic period (see *Tractate Soferim* 14:3). An adequate explanation has yet to be offered as to why a certain scroll is read on a given festival. The links between the scrolls and the festivals on which they are recited are vague and mainly of a homiletic nature. Apparently, once Esther and Lamentations came to be read in the synagogue, because of their close ties with the occasions on which they were read, a need was felt to grant the other three scrolls a similar status. Thus, for reasons we cannot fully discern, they slowly entered the world of the synagogue. The result was that those attending synagogue on the three festivals were exposed to all portions of Scriptures (Torah, Prophets, Writings), which marked the synagogue activities in an especially vigorous and emphatic manner.

The Bible in "The Literature of the Synagogue": Translation, Sermon, *Piyyut*

The regular reading of Torah, Prophets, and the Scrolls served as a permanent basis for relating to Scriptures within the framework of synagogue life. We can point to three types of literary activities which accompanied the Bible as it reached the synagogue congregation (as noted, besides the prayers): (1) translation of Scripture into the vernacular (in the ancient context, primarily into Aramaic); (2) homilies and explication of the passages read; (3) extensive use of their themes and content for composition of *piyyutim* (liturgical poems).

The Translation

Once part of the synagogue congregation had a limited command of Hebrew, and especially once the Rabbis began to find multiple and varied halakhic and aggadic meanings in Scriptures, it became impossible to separate the reading of the holy texts (the Torah and probably the haftarot and scrolls as well) from their fixed companion: the translation into Aramaic (in its various dialects) in the land of Israel and Babylonia, or into Greek in Hellenistic centers such as Alexandria. The Aramaic translations (the Targumim), as described below, preserved the vitality of the ancient texts and prevented them from becoming merely a fossilized heritage of the past (regarding the translation of Scripture, see also "Jewish Translations of the Bible," pp. 2005–2020).

Based on the sources (e.g., *m. Meg.* 4:6), it appears that next to the readers of the Torah a man stood translating the reading into Aramaic: the *meturgeman* (translator). The reader and the translator alternated, verse following verse (but in the haftarah several verses could be translated together). They were required to respect each other by not beginning to speak before the other had concluded his words (*b. Sot.* 39b). This ensured that there was no overlap or confusion between the Torah text and its translation. The *meturgeman* may possibly have been a professional who earned his living from this work, but he could also have been a learned member of the congregation who knew how to fulfill the religious duty of translation.

In the same way that there was a difference between the land of Israel and Babylonia regarding the customs of Torah and haftarah readings, there was a difference concerning the translations into Aramaic that were customary in both places. The Targum that was customary in Babylonia (*Targum Onkelos* on the Torah and the Targum by Yonatan ben ʿUziʾel on the Prophets) tended to be a literal translation, adhering as closely as possible to the biblical text. In passages containing poetry (such as Gen. ch 49), in ambiguous verses, and in a few other cases, the Babylonian Targum permitted minor additions or even deviations from the Scriptural source, for exegetical or theological purposes, such as the removal of what seemed to be contradictions in the biblical text and anthropomorphic expressions relating to God or the need to preserve the honor of the fathers of the nation. But even more important is the fact that these two translations were the exclusive, authorized translations of Scripture, and on every Sabbath those attending the synagogue would be exposed to their single, fixed text. Although there was a clear risk of monotony and routine, this was the way in which the Babylonian rabbis sought to present the biblical text to its listeners.

Such was not the practice of Jews in the land of Israel. The *meturgeman* wove into the words of the Torah a long series of exegetic, literary, haggadic, and halakhic traditions, remonstrations or words of encouragement for the congregation. He thus brought to their ears the biblical text, readapted and refashioned in many ways, in accordance with the intellectual competence of different congregations, current and local occurrences, and the *meturgeman's* own tendencies. It is also worthy to note that in the land of Israel—as opposed to Babylonia—no single biblical verse was translated in an identical, uniform manner in every place or at all times. The *meturge-*

man was permitted to choose the manner of translation that seemed proper to him, to add his own comments to the traditions he had imbibed from his teachers, to omit or to expand on words, and thus to emphasize one or other aspect of the translated text. This picture of variation and flexibility is clearly reflected in the Aramaic translations of the Torah and Prophets that have come down to us from the land of Israel. They are referred to by name, such as the "Targum Yerushalmi," "Targum Yonatan ben 'Uzi'el on the Torah" (even though its composer is not the same person of similar name who composed the Targum on the Prophets), and so on. If we recall that in the land of Israel a reading of about forty verses was deemed adequate for any occasion, it would seem that ample time remained for the *meturgeman* to expand on the passage. Indeed, the amount of material inserted by the *meturgeman* is often greater than the text itself. The translator would sometimes even weave a long poem into his translation, if he thought that it would add majesty and beauty to his words and enhance their dramatic potential (e.g., within the narrative of the Parting of the Red Sea [Exod. chs 14–15], or the Binding of Isaac [Gen. ch 22]). The aggadic traditions embedded in the various translations are frequently colorful and exciting, with a distinct educational and popular tone, and shed new light on the text that was just read. These traditions stress the importance of prayer or extol the patriarchs of the nation, describe in bold colors the days of redemption or emphasize the principle of reward and punishment, and so forth. Not only was the length of the passages read from the Torah and Prophets variable and flexible, but even the manner in which these passages were presented to the congregation by way of the Aramaic translation was constantly changing. The audience in the land of Israel could not then be lulled by feelings of familiarity and routine.

The Sermon

Besides the Torah reading and its translation, there was often a public sermon, given on various occasions, festivals, and Sabbaths, usually during the *Shaḥarit* (morning) prayer or in the afternoon, sometimes prior to the Torah reading and sometimes afterwards. The preacher, either a local sage or a guest, an elder of the congregation or one of their teachers, dealt with various and sundry topics, educational, academic, and issues of contemporary concern, according to his understanding of the task at hand.

Naturally, the sermons differed from one Sabbath to the next and from festival to festival, adding another dimension to the use of the Bible in the synagogue. In nearly every case the preacher dealt with the subject of the Torah reading, together with the haftarah or the scroll for that day, contributing his part to what the congregation had learned from the reading and its Aramaic translation.

There are thousands of literary units in the literature of the Sages, especially in midrashic literature (e.g., *Gen. Rab.* or *m. Tanḥ.*) that originally served as public sermons offered prior to scriptural readings. These literary units demonstrate the remarkably rhetorical character of the public sermon, relating various topics that would be of concern to its audience: the reason for suffering, the nature of religious life without the Temple, relations between Jews and Gentiles, the difficulty of observing the commandments, the hope for redemption, and others. Such sermons were studded with innumerable biblical verses, together with their explication, so that the realm of Scriptures was broadened to include excerpts from texts that were not read on that Sabbath or festival.

In the land of Israel—but seemingly hardly ever in Babylonia—the preachers would often expound on an issue arising from the biblical reading, through the use of a widespread literary pattern referred to as *petiḥta* (usually translated as "proem"). According to this pattern the preacher would first choose a verse from the Prophets or the Writings, a verse that appeared to have no connection whatsoever with the topic in the Torah, haftarah, or scroll read that day. He would then spiral from this verse, from topic to topic, until he arrived at the opening verse of the reading and by that gave closure to his sermon. This pattern, which connected two unrelated verses, allowed the preacher to illuminate different issues while piquing the congregation's curiosity. The listeners knew from the outset what the preacher's concluding verse would be, and they must certainly have attempted to surmise how the preacher would eventually make the connection between the opening and the concluding verses of his sermon. The choice to open the sermon with verses from books that were usually not read in the synagogue (those Prophets that were not used as haftarot, the book of Proverbs, the book of Job, etc.) was another way to expose all portions of Scripture to the synagogue congregation, and to emphasize that the entire Bible is interconnected. On Sabbath and festivals they would then read from the Torah and the Prophets, and would hear a sermon based to a large extent on the Writings. Thus all portions of Scripture would be reviewed once again, and the audience would see the full extent of Scripture.

The Piyyut

Piyyut refers to the poetical religious compositions, nearly all in Hebrew, recited in liturgical contexts in the synagogue or outside it, such as at wedding ceremonies or at festive meals. These compositions maintain the various characteristics of poetry in general, such as rhythm, meter, refrains, and acrostics of various kinds.

During the era of the Sages and the geonic period, the *piyyut* blossomed primarily in the land of Israel, mainly for use in the synagogue. The *piyyutim* were not composed as adornments for the prayers or as supplements to them, but rather, first and foremost, as lyrical alternatives for the fixed and obligatory prayers. If the congregation or its leaders desired, the standard prayer would be recited by the cantor in prose (as it is recited to this day), but if they wished to vary the expression of their feelings through a *piyyut*, this option

was also open to them. For this reason hundreds and even thousands of *piyyutim* were composed by many poets, only some of whom are known to us by name: Yose ben Yose (4th to 5th century); Yannai (5th to 6th century); Rabbi Elazar Ha-Kalir (6th to 7th century); and others. Those attending synagogue could occasionally hear, for example, a one-time lyrical substitution for the 'Amidah or for the blessings enveloping the reciting of the Shema. At times, the poet was accompanied by a small choir, contributing a further dimension to the experience the *piyyutim* brought with them.

Since the *piyyut* was essentially a lyrical substitute for prayer, its themes were primarily drawn from that realm, but it appears that the poets frequently dealt as well with the topics of the Torah reading, the haftarah, or, when appropriate, one of the five scrolls. Thus we can also view their words as a kind of poetic sermon on the themes associated with that day. For example, through his poetic substitute for the second blessing of the 'Amidah, the blessing of "He who revives the dead," the poet could relate in his own way to the story of the Binding of Isaac, who according to a rabbinic tradition was slain by Abraham, but revived; or through his poetic version of the blessing before reciting the Shema, the blessing of "Who creates the heavenly lights," he could relate to the story of the creation of the world and the heavenly lights in his own way. Within the *piyyutim*, the poet was also permitted to introduce explicit quotations of verses from the entire Bible, as many did. Since the number of poets and *piyyutim* was virtually unlimited, the person listening to them in the synagogue could on nearly every occasion sample another new composition, different from those he recognized, and in this way he would also come to know many varied scriptural passages.

As time went on, and in no small part due to the opposition of Babylonian Sages to the use of the *piyyut* in the synagogue, the status of the *piyyut* as a substitute for prayers was reduced to a mere embellishment, recited in various Jewish communities primarily on Rosh Ha-Shanah and Yom Kippur, and in a minority of congregations on festivals and other occasions as well. We see, therefore, another example of the triumph of the Babylonian view over that of the land of Israel in regard to the reading of Scripture in the synagogue and to matters associated with it (Targum, sermon, and *piyyut*).

Conclusion

It is difficult to know whether on any given Sabbath or festival, the Targum, sermon, and *piyyut* would all have been heard together in the synagogue. It would seem logical that when one was expanded, the others would have been curtailed. But needless to say, the existence of these three components in prox-imity to the scriptural texts that were read in the synagogue made Scripture into a magnet, which attracted various literary forms through which it was presented to the community .

No synagogue lacks a central and impressive place designated to house the Torah scroll(s), or a special spot assigned for the reading of the Torah, haftarah, and the five scrolls. There is no Sabbath or festival when the congregation does not hear portions of Scripture, as the focus of synagogue activity and its climax. In the light of what we have seen, there is no way whatsoever to comprehend the history of the synagogue and what was taking place within its walls without fully comprehending that the foundation of all synagogue activity is the Bible.

[AVIGDOR SHINAN]

The Bible in the Liturgy

For much of Judaism's history, one of its central means of liturgical expression has been the traditional rabbinic prayerbook or Siddur. The Siddur (understood in the sense of prayerbooks from many times and places) deserves close attention when considering the role of the Bible in Jewish religious thought and practice, since biblical texts figure prominently in it. While the reading, translation, and interpretation of biblical texts in the synagogue are also integral parts of Jewish liturgical practice, they receive attention elsewhere in this volume (see "The Bible in the Synagogue," pp. 1929–37); this article concentrates on biblical texts found in the Jewish prayers.

The word *siddur* ("order") refers to the established "order [of prayer]" in any prayerbook. Such "orders" were created from as early as the 9th century CE, and efforts to create a standard book continued during the succeeding centuries, but there is no "standard" Jewish prayerbook. Nevertheless, those in use contain certain common elements, and these form the basis of this discussion.

The prayers described here are those recited in the morning, afternoon, and evening on a daily basis. They consist primarily of the Shema (Deut. 6.4–9; 11.13–21; Num. 15.37–41, recited morning and evening), with its introductory and concluding benedictions; the weekday 'Amidah ("standing prayer") with its nineteen benedictions of praise, entreaty, and thanksgiving; and a set of varied items that are prefixed and appended to these two central pieces. Brief reference is also made to the Sabbath and festival prayers, which abbreviate some of the central weekday prayer-texts and expand others to take account of the special nature of these days, and to communal, domestic, and personal rituals that have gradually been incorporated into the medieval and modern liturgies. The essay focuses on how the rabbinic tradition relates to the Bible and how the prayerbooks of the various periods engaged the problem of this relationship. There are sections on the language and theology of the prayers vis-à-vis their biblical connections, and on some of the best known biblical passages included in the liturgy. The importance of mysticism and the needs of contemporary prayer also feature briefly.

Is Jewish Liturgy Biblical?

Biblical texts are so prominent in many parts of the Siddur that the immediate impression is that the Jewish liturgy is borrowed directly from the Tanakh. A mere glance at the traditional prayers confirms that the language is predominantly Hebrew, that the theology rings biblical bells, and that the relationship presupposed is that between God and Israel. Following biblical models, gratitude is expressed, praise offered, and supplication made, and there is no lack of special requests for divine assistance in matters mundane as well as spiritual. The names of biblical heroes frequently occur and topics such as sacrifice, Temple, priest, and Levite are also to be found. Yet it must be emphasized that the quotations and citations of the Bible in liturgy are not fully representative of the Bible. For example, the reason why a verse such as Ps. 51.7, "Indeed I was born with iniquity; with sin my mother conceived me," was not included is perhaps because it was regarded as too close to Christian notions. Liturgical tradition does not favor the rather complex notions of theodicy and retribution found in Job. Thus, although the use of the Bible in the liturgy is extensive, it is also selective. There is a partial tendency to favor late biblical texts that are closer temporally and conceptually to rabbinic theological notions.

The index to the use of the Psalms appended to the edition of the Anglo-Jewish *Authorised Daily Prayer Book*, edited by Simeon Singer and first published in London in 1890, indicates that no less than 74 out of a total of 150 biblical psalms occur in the context of the standard prayers. Might we not suppose that the Siddur is the direct continuation of trends represented by Abraham's entreaty for Sodom (Gen. 18.23–25), Jacob's bargaining with God (Gen. 28.16–22), Moses' request for

the healing of Miriam (Num. 12.13), Samson's appeal for vengeance through his death (Jud. 16.30), Hannah's prayer for a child (1 Sam. 1.10–16), the Temple ritual, and the composition of psalms? Some of the roots of the Jewish prayers are indeed to be found in the biblical soil, but historical accuracy forces us to draw a distinction between the notions of "liturgy in the Bible" and "the Bible in Jewish liturgy." Both historically and thematically, the story is a more complicated one.

Pre-rabbinic Traditions

The biblical passages just cited, and many similar to them, indicate that the earliest biblical sources provide later Jewish practice with the inspiration for personal, improvised prayer, in prose format, with patterns using common speech forms. This type of prayer constituted a democratic and egalitarian way of approaching God, not at all similar to the formal, sacrificial cult of the Jerusalem Temple. During the Second Temple period, the tendency developed to link the personal prayer and the formal liturgy. From prayers incorporated into Hellenistic apocryphal and pseudepigraphical sources, it is apparent that there was an increasing number of benedictions, hymns and praises, mystical formulations of considerable variety, a concern for the absorption of Torah knowledge, and a growing use of the Temple precincts on special liturgical occasions.

The Hellenistic Jewish authors Philo and Josephus make clear that Jews prayed and studied in various contexts, at times with priestly guidance and involvement, especially on the Sabbath, and that biblical texts played a part in such rituals. Though unquestionably devoted to the Temple cult in the 2nd century BCE, ben Sirach (author of the Wisdom book of that name, also called "Ecclesiasticus") linked Torah and wisdom with prayer. He also used words and phrases that are essentially biblical but take on special forms and meanings. The Qumran scrolls provide clear evidence of a practice, at least among some groups, to recite regular prayers at specific times. Some of these were linked to the calendar, some to special events, and some to penitential themes, but there is no obvious consistency of text and context.

Rabbinic Innovation and Development

Rabbinic prayer incorporated material from a broad set of prayer traditions known at Qumran, as well as from various other contexts of the Second Temple period, among them the Temple, the priesthood, communal gatherings for Biblical readings (ma'amadot), pietistic and mystical circles with eschatological and angelological interests, and popular practice. Among the themes that they shared with earlier Jewish groups were the election of Israel, the status of Zion, the holiness of Jerusalem, the return of the Davidic dynasty, and the manifestation of God's great power now and in the future. The Rabbis imposed upon inherited traditions a fresh order, style, and distinctive formulation, and they transmitted them in oral form until the compilation of the first written texts of the Siddur in the 9th century. They absorbed the earlier elements but effectively created a new structure that represented a *formal* liturgy. In essence, this constituted a collection of personal prayers and benedictions, which had been given a communal flavor and dimension, and a preferred synagogal context.

There was never total agreement about the precise place of prayer in the theological hierarchy of Judaism, but there certainly existed a universal consensus about the need for the observant Jew to pray. As the rabbinic tradition progressively committed its liturgical traditions to short and simple codices, to larger and more elegant manuscripts, to printed volumes, and ultimately to the contemporary formats of photocopies and digitized images, so the Siddur grew in its independence, authority, and centrality for the practitioners of the faith. Use of the Bible was always part of these developments but found its expression

in the traditional Jewish liturgy in a number of interesting and novel ways.

By the time that the talmudic Rabbis of the early common era were debating the matter of the inclusion of biblical verses and chapters in their standard prayers for daily, Sabbath, and festival use, a number of these verses were well established by popular tradition within the liturgical context. Minor examples are the sets of verses that were included in the *Musaf* ("additional") 'Amidah for Rosh Ha-Shanah and illustrated the three themes of kingship, remembrance, and shofar (ram's horn) that stand at the center of that prayer. More common and more major examples are the Shema, the Ten Commandments, the Hallel ("praise"), the Passover *Haggadah*, the Song at the Sea, the Priestly Benediction, and the *Kedushah,* and these will shortly be examined in more detail. This examination will indicate that the issue of the role of biblical material in the liturgy was a lively and controversial one.

There is evidence that rabbinic formulations were regarded as preferable to biblical precedents, and that biblical verses were to be differentiated from rabbinic prayers (y. Ber. 1:8, 3d). Could, for instance, the verses from Isa. 12.6 and/or Ps. 22.4 be employed at any point in the *Kedushah* benediction of the 'Amidah without valid halakhic objection being raised? The early Rabbis sometimes even made changes in liturgical formulations out of polemical considerations. A good example is the use of the biblical Hebrew word 'olam (meaning "world" as well as "eternity" in postbiblical Hebrew) in such a way as to ensure that the notion of a future world was not excluded (m. Ber. 9:5). Nevertheless, the liturgical preexistence of such specific items as the Shema, and others mentioned above, provides positive proof that earlier attitudes were more tolerant concerning the direct quotation of biblical texts. Perhaps the Rabbis feared the potential influence of some groups whom they regarded as sectarian and who had opted for the inclusion of biblical texts among their prayers. The Jews whose literary works were found at Qumran, by the Dead Sea, were of such an ilk, and medieval Karaites, whose prayers were exclusively composed of biblical texts, pursued a similar liturgical philosophy. The situation among the Rabbanite Jews changed from the beginning of the Islamic period when, instead of merely a few favorite verses (such as Pss. 51.17; 84.5; 144.15) and entire Psalms (such as Ps. 145), substantial blocks of biblical verses, groups of chapters, and individual verses came to be incorporated into the traditional daily prayers, and then into the first prayerbooks. Perhaps the popular urge to include biblical selections was so powerful that the halakhic authorities had to submit to it, or perhaps the authorities determined that this attractive religious practice should not be left exclusively to the theological opposition.

The Early Prayerbooks

In the early prayerbooks, therefore, the introduction of the morning prayers by the recitation of Pss. 145–150 (called the *pesukei dezimra*, or "biblical verses of praise"), a custom known in earlier times, was not the only use of that biblical book. Sets of psalms made up of such chapters as Pss. 19, 33–34, 90–93, 98, 100, 121–124, and 135–136 came to be added, in different groupings according to the various rites, for use on Sabbaths and festivals. Catenae ("chains" or selections) of verses were similarly used to preface the central liturgy. They included late biblical passages from 1 Chron. chs 16 and 29 and from Neh. ch 9, as well as from a variety of Torah, prophetic, and Kethuvim books. They were often strung together by a common theme such as God's salvation and protection or His gifts, including the revelation of the Torah. As the prayerbook and the synagogal ritual became progressively more formalized in the high and later Middle Ages, other biblical texts were introduced. An examination of the earliest known versions of the "grace after meals," for instance, reveals that some rites were eager to conclude the body of each benediction with a biblical verse while others preferred to restrict the content to rabbinic for-

mulations. In later texts of the same prayer, the passages appended to the final benediction include a significant number of biblical verses, especially at the conclusion.

Conscious as they were of these tendencies and of the need to stress that rabbinic Judaism was not in any sense rejecting the Bible in favor of the Talmud, leading scholars such as Saadia ben Joseph, the rabbinic leader *(gaon)* in the 10th-century Babylonian center of Sura, and Maimonides, his counterpart in 12th-century Cairo, made statements on the matter. Saadia (in his introduction to the Siddur) attempted to demonstrate that all the rabbinic prayers were merely formulations of liturgical genres that already appeared in the Bible. Maimonides, for his part, argued (in his code, *Mishneh Torah*) that it was only because the Jewish people's knowledge of Hebrew had deteriorated severely after the Babylonian Exile that they could no longer be left to their own liturgical devices, but had to be guided by being provided with rabbinic structures. Thus, these two leading authorities set about merging the two major sources of Judaism, the Bible and the Talmud, in theological terms, just as this had been achieved by practical religious custom in the ritual context.

Medieval Additions

It was decided that when the worshippers entered the synagogue, they should recite verses from such sources as Num. 24.5 ("How fair are your tents, O Jacob") and Pss. 5.8 ("I, through Your abundant love, enter Your house"), 26.8 ("O LORD, I love Your temple"), 55.15, 69.14, and 95.6. Similarly, biblical verses were added when the Torah scroll was taken out of the Ark for public reading, and when it was returned to the Ark. Some of these verses did not even appear in the text of the prayerbook until well after the invention of printing. The most common of these on a weekday were Num 10.35 ("Advance, O LORD") and Isa. 2.3 ("Come, Let us go up to the Mount of the LORD") before the biblical reading, and Ps.

148.13–14 ("Let them praise the LORD") and Num. 10.36 ("Return, O LORD") after it. Among other verses introduced in connection with the synagogal use of the Torah scroll were Pss. 86.8 and 132.8–10, Prov. 4.2 and 3.16–18, Lam. 5.21, and Deut. 4.35. Many of these make no direct reference to the Torah (e.g., Prov. 4.2, "I give you good instruction"), but were understood by postbiblical Judaism as referring to the Torah. Later (more voluntary) additions to the conclusion of the formal service were the Binding of Isaac (Gen. ch 22) and the Manna (Exod. ch 16). One of the contributions of the early modern mystics was to champion the recitation of the entire Song of Songs as an introduction to Friday evening prayers and to follow that by the recitation of Pss. 95–99 and 29 and of Prov. 31.10–31 before the Sabbath meal. The early Reform movement was more attached to biblical passages than to rabbinic texts, and they consequently removed the rabbinic benedictions that talmudic tradition had attached to the reading of the lectionaries and to the recitation of such items as Hallel.

The Language of the Liturgy

The Hebrew of the Siddur is very reminiscent of its biblical counterpart but by no means identical with it. The basic vocabulary and phraseology of praise and supplication is borrowed from Psalms, and there are occasionally linguistic usages that are characteristic of biblical rather than rabbinic Hebrew. The overall style, syntax, and linguistic flow are, however, very much dependent on rabbinic literature, and there is no doubt that the early talmudic leaders were anxious not to confuse the two forms of the language. Perhaps one of the ways in which rabbinic Judaism created its own identity was by rejecting a preference for the biblical Hebrew style in the formulation of its traditions and committing itself to its own linguistic usage.

Throughout its history of almost two millennia, the language of rabbinic prayer underwent a long and complicated development from a format that may well have been oral in origin, through a process of literary improvement and linguistic selection, toward the establishment of independent parameters. It achieved a status that ultimately exercised a formative influence on the reemergence of contemporary, spoken Hebrew in the modern period. The process was always accompanied by a tension between those who were anxious to reforge the link with the Bible and those who saw the need for the language of rabbinic prayer to grow independently, whatever its deepest roots. The "biblicizers" of each generation made their stand. They fought off the challenges of Greek, Aramaic, and later vernaculars and expressed preference for wording the prayers in a style that followed the biblical precedent more closely. When the ben Asher text of the Bible became the standard in the second millennium CE, it was their circles that fought valiantly to apply its principles to the language of the liturgy. They were not averse to the employment of strange strategies to achieve their aims.

The 16th-century Polish rabbinic scholar Solomon Luria argued that the Sabbath day should be termed *shabbat* and not *manoaḥ* in Hebrew, because Manoaḥ in the Bible is not used for "rest" but as the name of Samson's father, about whom the Talmud makes derogatory remarks. Similarly, the verse in Num. 24.5 should not be used in the synagogue because it originates in the words of the Gentile pseudo-prophet, Balaam. Though leaving an impact, particularly at times and places that had a need for a stronger identification with the Bible (as, for instance, in Central and Western Europe immediately after the Reformation or during Jewish emancipation), their efforts were neither intended nor destined to remove parts of the rabbinic liturgy from their place in traditional Jewish literature. Such a result was achieved only by the nontraditional movements beginning in the late 18th and early 19th centuries.

The Theology of the Siddur

A similar situation pertains to the theology of the Siddur. The common prayers undoubtedly reflect, for example, the religious ideology of rabbinic Judaism. They reflect postbiblical, rabbinic notions of the world to come. The divine authority of Oral Torah is presupposed in many contexts, and the obligation to perform the 613 *mitzvot* (religious precepts), as formulated by rabbinic interpretation, underlies various texts. There is a conviction that goodness will be rewarded and evil punished and that repentance brings forgiveness. The study of Torah makes its appearance both as one of the observant Jew's duties and in the form of texts that are cited from rabbinic literature. Torah study is so successfully welded into the body of the prayerbook that it is effectively treated as liturgy rather than education. The ideology underlying its inclusion is that the absence of the Temple ritual prescribed in the Torah (since the Temple was destroyed) can be compensated for by the recitation of the biblical and talmudic passages that describe its detailed requirements (so *b. Ta'an.* 27b).

Having first been formulated in the period following the destruction of the Temple, the expulsion from the holy city of Jerusalem, and the loss of the independent Jewish homeland, the rabbinic prayers lay powerful stress on Israel's appeal to God for the restoration of these religious and national symbols. Much is made of God's choice of Israel for a special religious role, and there are polemical undertones in some prayers that appear to be aimed at Christianity or Islam. At the same time, there is an enthusiasm for the "righteous proselyte" and a fervent hope (following biblical eschatological models) that the whole world will ultimately come to recognize God's sovereignty. The ultimate redemption, like that of Israel from Egypt, will be an impressive manifestation of God's power and will include the arrival of the Messiah and the resurrection of the dead. The assumption is frequently made that the worshipper can enjoy a close relationship with God and that practical matters in human life require God's blessing for them to flourish. Formal catechisms are not a feature of rabbinic prayer although there are certainly texts such as the Shema that include the relevant theological principles. A poetic summary of Maimonides' "Thirteen Principles of Faith," known from its opening word as the *Yigdal* hymn, is included for recitation before formal prayer in the morning and for singing after the Friday evening service, but this is late, optional, controversial, and an exception rather than the rule. In some communities, Maimonides' thirteen principles of faith were also recited in their prose form at the conclusion of the morning prayers.

Most of the religious ideology just charted is either represented in an earlier form in the Bible or has a basis in some of its texts. Sometimes, the only change in a phrase is the adjustment of the singular to the plural to take account of the change from individual request to communal petition. The notions of a special relationship between God and Israel, of direct access to His favor, and of revelation and redemption from the divine source, are all familiar features of the biblical books. By the same token, the nature of rabbinic theodicy, eschatology, and religious law is largely shaped by ideas to be found in the Written Torah.

Shema and Decalogue

What is widely regarded as rabbinic Judaism's most famous prayer, the Shema, is in fact a section borrowed from Deut. 6.4–9, with a second paragraph from Deut. 11.13–21 and a third from Num. 15.37–41. In the Bible, these are prose passages that are not marked as prayers. In a Hebrew papyrus inscription from the 2nd century BCE named the Nash Papyrus after W. L. Nash, who purchased it in Egypt in 1903, the text of the first two verses of the Shema appears after the Decalogue in a formulation that corresponds closely to the Greek translation of the Exodus version.

Whether that papyrus is to be identified as an amulet or as a piece of liturgy, it testifies to a Jewish use of these two biblical texts as something other than a direct quotation, since they do not occur together in the Torah. Such a use was therefore being made before the earliest manifestation of either Christianity or rabbinic Judaism, and further evidence is provided by the Hellenistic Jewish writers, as well as from the Mishnaic traditions of the 2nd century CE. They indicate that both the Shema and the Decalogue had already by then a special and well-established liturgical significance, apparently because they gave expression to the most central religious ideas of the Jews. Attempts were indeed made to draw parallels between the occurrences of such ideas in the two passages.

In the case of the Shema, there appears to have been a gradual development from the use of one paragraph to the acceptance of three, and to its recitation, in some (as yet unclear) form of special chant, in both the morning and evening prayers. On the other hand, the independent status of the Decalogue led to controversy and a diminution of its liturgical function. It was once so central to liturgical use that it was often included among the biblical texts inserted in the tefillin ("phylacteries") boxes by such sects as those who lived by the Dead Sea. Later, it came to be regarded with suspicion when it was polemically cited by groups that rabbinic Judaism regarded as heretical. Their argument was that such a central liturgical use permitted the conclusion that only such *parts* of the Torah were authoritative. Such a challenge encouraged the Rabbis to rule against the liturgical recitation of the passage in spite of its impressive pedigree, a ruling that was widely followed at least in Babylonian Jewry. The finds from the Cairo Genizah, however, document a continuing use of the Decalogue among the Jews in the land of Israel, in a place of honor in the prayerbook just before the commencement of the Shema benedictions. Having apparently brought the practice with them from the Holy Land when they fled the Crusades, they were loath to abandon it in favor of the dominant Babylonian custom, but their rite ultimately all but disappeared. Some authorities in Spain proposed its inclusion but it was not until the early modern period that the passage was again included in the Siddur on a regular basis, and then not as an integral part of the prayers but as an appendix to the morning service for those few Jews who might wish to add voluntarily to their daily recitation of biblical passages.

For its part, the Shema was, by the end of the talmudic period, already surrounded by rabbinic benedictions and liturgical poems, and inextricably bound together with the ʿAmidah both evening and morning. (The texts of these prayers, however, were not yet fixed in this period.) Given that its recitation in the communal context might not therefore take place immediately after rising in the morning, or just before settling down to sleep at night, which had been part of the original intent (see Deut. 6.7; 11.19), a secondary use of the prayer for those purposes was adopted. Its two manifestations were referred to respectively as the "Shema of Rabbi Judah the Patriarch" and the "Shema by the Bedside" and they were inserted into the prayerbook. The custom of remaining seated for the Shema, which was initially that of the Babylonian communities, in contradistinction to the requirement to stand for the ʿAmidah, was perhaps a way of expressing the conviction that rabbinic prayers still had a higher liturgical status than the recitation of Scripture. Moreover, the 13th-century controversy in Spain about whether to recite the Shema aloud or silently might again have had to do with approaches to its communal liturgical significance. The earliest Reform prayerbooks retained the Shema in Hebrew, but there were some more radical versions in which it was severely truncated. In the more recent versions produced by the progressive movements, various options are offered. Since its recitation does not require a *minyan* (quorum of ten men), Orthodox women's prayer groups include it in their services without major controversy.

Hallel

Tracing in the rabbinic prayerbook the fate of other pieces of Scripture that have a Jewish liturgical history going back for at least two millennia may also be profitable for seeing the overall picture. Although the word "Hallel" does occur with reference to other biblical passages, its oldest liturgical definition relates to the recitation of Pss. 113–118. Such a collection of Scripture is reported by the Mishnah to have been part of the Temple ritual during the offering of the paschal lamb (*Pes.* 10.6–7). Whether or not the custom is, from a critical, historical perspective, as ancient as Temple times, it was incorporated into the domestic ritual on the first night of Passover in post-Temple times, and the nature of its recitation is the subject of early rabbinic discussion. Three teachers from the tannaitic period compared its declamation with that of the Song at the Sea (Exod. ch 15), namely, responsively by prayer-leader and community, but each had a different concept of the precise form taken by such an exchange (*Mekhilta of R. Ishmael* on Exod. 15.1). Such a fluidity of view about the precise nature of the recitation of Hallel had its equivalent in the later rules about its use in the standard prayers. In spite of its more than respectable origins, it was limited to certain festivals, and even then with an abbreviated format for the new moon. Even with regard to the first night (or, according to some rites, first two nights) of Passover, some communities incorporated it into the synagogal services while others restricted it to domestic use in the *Haggadah* (the Exodus story and exposition recited at home, at the Passover seder). It was, however, important enough for a benediction to be formulated (perhaps not in early talmudic times) to precede and to follow it and, consequently, for some of the 19th-century Reform prayerbooks to allow its retention as a biblical passage but without such a benediction.

Passover *Haggadah*

The earliest rabbinic sources take for granted that there is a domestic liturgy on the first Passover night, but its earliest format was not lengthy. It constituted the usual festival benedictions relating to the wine and the meal, some references to the unleavened bread, the paschal lamb and the bitter vegetables of Exod. 12.8, the exposition of the passage from Deut. 26.5–8 summarizing the Egyptian bondage and the exodus, and ending with a special redemption blessing and the Hallel. This domestic celebration generated a large number of additional liturgical and pedagogical offshoots, many of them with biblical content. Already in talmudic times, the early rabbinic interpretations of the Exodus story and of the requirement to relate it (Exod. 12.26; 13.8, 14; Deut. 6.20) were incorporated and expanded, as were the references to the meal and the special foods. In the Middle Ages, the persecution of the Jews elicited a liturgical response in the form of the recitation of biblical verses calling for divine retribution, as in Pss. 79.6–7; 69.25 (and other verses in that chapter); and Lam. 3.64–66. The secular Zionists of the 20th century created novel texts that stressed the themes of springtime and of national freedom, already recorded in the Exodus story, but with a contemporary application.

Song at the Sea

Talmudic discussion of the antiphonal recitation of the Song at the Sea revolved around what the Rabbis presupposed to have been its original format in the mouths of Moses and the Children of Israel. One is led to wonder whether the authors of these comments had in mind a liturgical use in their own day. If there was such a use, it was evidently a ritual originally reserved for the Sabbath afternoon service and only in post-talmudic times made its way into the Sabbath morning and even the daily prayers. It then took a place of honor at the conclusion of the block of Psalms known as the *pesukei dezimra* (Pss. 145–50; see above), that linked the morning benedictions and readings with the Shema and its benedictions.

Priestly Benediction

A silver amulet dating from the 7th-century BCE contains a version of the Priestly Benediction closely resembling that recorded in Num. 6.24–26 and demonstrates that even at that early period some special liturgical significance was already attached to the benediction. It certainly played a role in the worship performed in the Second Temple, and there is no doubt that elements of priestly liturgy were absorbed into the proto-rabbinic prayers. At the same time, the extensive talmudic sources record tensions about whether priests are to retain their privileged position or are to be succeeded by the Rabbis. For the *tanna'* R. Simeon, it was not priesthood but a good reputation that had maintained an attractive religious standing (*Eccl. Rab.* 7.1.3), and a Mishnaic statement (*Ber.* 5:4) seems to regard the Priestly Benediction as separate from the standard prayer context. Other teachers, however, preferred a compromise to such a categorical differentiation. What is clearly attested (*b. Sot.* 37b–39b) are changes in the use of the divine Name, the custom of raising the hands in blessing, the nature of the accompanying ritual, and the Jewish constituency to whom the Priestly Benediction is addressed. Although biblical privileges were to a large extent retained, and the priestly genealogy and role continued to be recognized, intellectual and halakhic leadership became more democratically available.

As the rabbinic liturgy became more formal in the early medieval period, the congregational recitation of the Priestly Benediction was permitted only in restricted circumstances to the priests (that is, descendents of the priestly line who had almost no function and little status after the destruction of the Second Temple), and there were some arguments for weakening even that privilege, especially among the Jewish communities in Christian lands. The Benediction even came to be part of the biblical readings of the daily "morning benedictions" that were originally recited by every pious individual at home and were later absorbed into the synagogal ritual. The halakhic authorities in the Middle Ages generally maintained the biblical restrictions and some of the special honor that applied to the priests, but they were content to leave the matter of the restoration of their total power to the messianic age. The priests did at times mount counterattacks in attempts to restore their earlier authority but generally with only limited success. The recitation of the Priestly Benediction by the father (not necessarily a priest) to bless his children in the domestic service preceding the Friday evening meal was promoted by the 16th-century mystics and amounted to a further process of democratization. With the rise of the modern progressive movements, even those last few ceremonial roles and restrictions left to the priests were abolished in all but Orthodox communities. In the latter, there were doubts about the priestly role in the 19th and early 20th centuries, but these seem to have been widely overcome in more recent decades, as reflected in current editions of Orthodox prayerbooks.

Kedushah

Although the recitation of the *Kedushah*, or *trisagion* (Gk., "thrice holy"), from Isa. 6.3 ("*kadosh, kadosh, kadosh*") is accorded importance in the Talmud, it is not clear precisely what piece of liturgy is intended by the term and on which occasions and at what time it was employed in the prayers. In the post-talmudic period, however, it was certainly used regularly in a number of different contexts in the prayers, especially together with such verses as Ezek. 3.12 ("Blessed is the Presence of the LORD"), Ps. 146.10 ("The LORD shall reign forever"), and Isa. 5.16 ("the LORD of Hosts is exalted"). It was employed in connection with the study of Torah, as well as in the prayer-leader's repetition of the 'Amidah and in the first benediction preceding the morning Shema, as a description and emulation of the angelic choir praising God. Since there are precedents in the Qumran literature, the custom might well have been transmitted by pietistic groups, at that time and later, and thus incorporated into the rabbinic liturgy. They found the close description of what they regarded as the heavenly liturgy as a mystical activity that extended their religious experience and sharpened their spiritual sensitivity.

Whether or not such groups were initially based in the land of Israel, there is a report from Pirqoi ben Baboi in the 9th century that the communities there did not recite the pre-Shema' Kedushah on a daily basis until the Babylonian Jews living in Jerusalem and some other cities created contention about its omission. In the 10th century, Saadia ben Joseph made a point of including the Kedushah only in the communal, and not the individual, context, but gradually it became the widespread custom to allow its recitation even by the individual in at least the non-'Amidah contexts. It need hardly be pointed out that the 19th-century rationalists were no happier with this mystical item than they were with any others.

Mystical Input

Later mystics also played a part in the expansion of the biblical dimension in the rabbinic Siddur. The major impact was made by those of the city of Safed in the 16th century, but they had predecessors in North Africa, Spain, and Germany two and three centuries earlier, as well as successors in Eastern Europe several centuries later. The achievement of blissful communion with God required special levels of devotion and these could be reached by the recitation of special prayers and of biblical verses. These latter were often borrowed from the Psalms, but it was not always the actual content and simple sense that was being recalled. The number, the enunciation, and

the special combination of certain letters was held to have a mystical effect and the belief was that the first letter of each verse recited could contribute to this effect. If, for example, verses from Lam. 3.56, Pss. 119, 106, 122, 162, 66, and 108 were recited before the sounding of the shofar, the relevant letters (kr' stn) made up a Hebrew phrase that invited a diminution of Satan's powers. Similar uses of verses were made as additions to prayers and in amulets to protect the living and to entreat for the souls of the dead.

Psalms for Special Days

The Siddur also contains biblical chapters and verses which, though not as central as those noted earlier, were placed there for more contextual reasons. On the Sabbath, an obvious choice was Ps. 92 (see v. 1, "for the sabbath day"), on Hanukkah it was logical to opt for Ps. 30 (see v. 1, "for the dedication of the House"), the sounding of the shofar could be introduced by Ps. 47 (see v. 6), and the themes of Pss. 24, 27, and 130 matched the mood of the days before and after New Year and the Day of Atonement. Since there was a rabbinic tradition that claimed that certain psalms (Pss. 24, 48, 82, 94–95, 81, and 93) had been recited in the Temple on particular days, it was natural to follow such an alleged precedent, although it is not clear that such a ritual had been adopted in the daily version of the earliest talmudic liturgy (m. Tamid 7:4). Some authorities, such as the early medieval Seder Rav Amram, recorded objections to the tendency to extend the use of these psalms beyond the morning services.

Miscellaneous Addition of Verses

The study (subsequently no more than the recitation) of passages from talmudic literature, to which was appended a special doxology titled "kaddish," inevitably provided an opportunity of citing verses that stressed the importance of Torah and the eternal bliss its study was said to guarantee. Among such texts were Deut. 33.4, Isa. 42.21, 60.21, and Ps. 29.11. When the custom arose of inserting supplicatory prayers after the recitation of the morning 'Amidah, there were many verses, especially from Psalms, that were regarded as suitable for such a context, and both Ps. 6 and the Thirteen Divine Attributes (Exod. 34.6–7) were pressed into service. At nightfall, God's protection was invoked by the recitation of such verses as Pss. 20.10; 46.8; 78.38; and 84.13. Verses from Exod. ch 15 (e.g., 11 and 18) were obviously appropriate for the theme of the redemption from Egypt. The domestic rituals that preceded the Sabbath meals and marked its conclusion (kiddush and havdalah), though they began as purely popular rabbinic customs, fairly distinct from anything in the Bible, eventually attracted to themselves the addition of verses regarded as relevant to the topic or to the atmosphere.

New Prayers

One of the trends that was typical of the Jewish communities of the land of Israel in the pre-Crusader period was to follow up references to past events in the Jewish religious experience with hopes for similar developments in the future. Although such a liturgical expansion met with the opposition of those authorities who preferred the prayers to deal with one discrete theme at a time, it was broadly adopted in a number of instances, and in those cases the hope for the ideal future was tied to the citation of a biblical verse that predicted it. Examples are to be found in the various rites at the conclusion of the ge'ulah (redemption) benediction before the 'Amidah, the relevent verse being Ps. 147.2. Where novel prayers were introduced into the liturgy in the late medieval and early modern period, biblical verses were added to them in order to give them a more authentic flavor and an additional degree of authority. In the case of the prayer for the secular ruler, use was made of Pss. 144.10; 145.13; Isa. 43.16; and Jer. 23.6, but a glance at the total original

contexts of each of these verses reveals an emphasis on God's supreme power and the ultimate kingdom of David rather than on their temporal, secular equivalents.

The English Chief Rabbinate's prayerbook of 1890 included a number of new prayers for such events as childbirth, charity collection, the house of mourning, and taking up residence in a new house, as well as some for young children to recite. All of these were richer in psalms and other scriptural quotations than they were in traditional liturgical phraseology. The same philosophy was adopted by those in the progressive movements when they formulated new pieces of liturgy for events and circumstances that had previously lacked them. Twentieth-century prayers introduced in communities of various religious hues for the State of Israel and its Defense Forces, though less biblically dominated, also incorporate such verses as Deut. 20.4 and 30.3–5, and the last part of Isa. 2.3. Here too, the earlier tension between subservience to biblical quotations and the use of newer liturgical language and forms is evident. The clear indication, however, is that the biblical quotation, though by no means ubiquitous, continues to be indispensable.

Addendum: Some Liturgical Uses of Psalms in Jewish Tradition

Ps. 1: unveiling of tombstone
Ps. 3: recitation of the Shema before going to sleep
Ps. 6: vv. 2–11 are in Taḥanun
Ps. 8: daily evening service
Ps. 15: dedication of a new house; unveiling of a tombstone
Ps. 16: funeral; unveiling; in a house of mourning
Ps. 19: introductory prayers (pesuqei de-zimra) in the morning service for Sabbath and festivals
Ps. 20: daily morning service
Ps. 23: for the sick; funeral; unveiling
Ps. 24: psalm for Sunday; on festivals when the Torah is returned to the Ark

Ps. 27: from 1 Elul through Hoshana Rabbah

Ps. 29: Friday evening service; on Sabbath when the Torah is returned to the Ark

Ps. 30: introductory prayers for the daily, Sabbath, and festival morning service; dedication of a new house

Ps. 33: introductory prayers for the Sabbath and festival morning service

Ps. 34: introductory prayers for the Sabbath and festival morning service

Ps. 39: house of mourning

Ps. 47: before the blowing of the shofar (ram's horn) on Rosh Ha-Shanah

Ps. 48: psalm for Monday

Ps. 49: house of mourning; funeral

Ps. 63: consecration of a cemetery; funeral

Ps. 67: evening service at the conclusion of Sabbath

Ps. 81: psalm for Thursday

Ps. 82: psalm for Tuesday

Ps. 83: daily morning service when *Taḥanun* is recited

Ps. 90: introductory prayers for the Sabbath and festival morning service

Ps. 91: recitation of the Shema before going to sleep; before going on a journey; introductory prayers for the Sabbath and festival morning service

Ps. 92: Friday evening service; introductory prayers for the Sabbath and festival morning service

Ps. 93: psalm for Friday; Friday evening service; introductory prayers for the Sabbath and festival morning service

Ps. 94: psalm for Wednesday

Ps. 95–99: Friday evening service

Ps. 100: introductory prayers for the daily morning service

Ps. 102: consecration of a cemetery

Ps. 103: for the sick; consecration of a cemetery

Ps. 104: new moon; Sabbath afternoon service (fall and winter); consecration of a cemetery

Ps. 113–118: Hallel on new moon, festivals, and Hanukkah

Ps. 120–134: Sabbath afternoon service (fall and winter)

Ps. 126: introduction to grace after meals on Sabbath and festivals

Ps. 130: morning service of Ten Days of Repentance

Ps. 135–136: introductory prayers for the Sabbath and festival morning service

Ps. 137: introduction to grace after meals on weekdays

Ps. 139: for the sick

Ps. 144: evening service at the conclusion of Sabbath

Ps. 145–150: introductory prayers for the daily, Sabbath, and festival morning service

[STEFAN C. REIF]

The Bible in the Jewish Philosophical Tradition

Understanding what the Bible says and means has been the central concern of the Jewish philosophical tradition. Jewish philosophers have assumed that the biblical text, as God's revealed word, is true. In principle, then, what is true in the Bible must cohere with what is known to be true from other sources of knowledge. Given the limitations of human knowledge, however, no one philosophical reading of the Bible can be definitive; all readings are necessarily partial, incomplete, and amenable to correction. Committed to the pursuit of truth, Jewish philosophers "translated" the Bible into other languages, composed commentaries on the Bible, expounded the particularly difficult or significant sections of the Bible, and theorized about the relationship between knowledge discovered by human reason and knowledge revealed by God. All of these activities were regarded as expressions of the religious obligation to love God.

Although the Bible played an important role in all phases of Jewish philosophy, the philosophical tools for reflections about the Bible have changed over time, reflecting the transformation of Jewish culture as influenced by its general surroundings. In ancient Alexandria, medieval Spain, Provence, and Italy, modern Germany, and contemporary America, Jewish philosophers have engaged diverse philosophical schools, including Platonism, Stoicism, Kalam, Aristotelianism, Enlightenment, Kantianism, Existentialism, Phenomenology, and Post-Structuralism. By thinking about Judaism in light of these philosophical traditions, Jewish philosophers not only fathomed the depth of the Bible anew but also acted as cultural mediators between Judaism and surrounding cultures.

The Greco-Roman World

The Bible itself laid the foundation for the pursuit of wisdom in Judaism, even though the Bible is not a philosophical text. Fusing ancient Israelite wisdom with covenantal theology, the book of Deuteronomy stated that the laws given to Israel are wisdom that the people of other nations can appreciate and the *torah* or teaching (understood in postbiblical Judaism as the Torah) is wisdom proper to Israel (4.5–8). The identification of Torah and wisdom meant that the scholar of Torah is also the carrier of the sapiential tradition and that to stand in a proper relationship with God, the wise person must fathom the truth of the Torah. As attested in the Wisdom of Ben Sirach, by the 2nd century BCE, the fusion of Torah and wisdom was fully in place: The Torah was understood to contain not only divine commands that regulate social relations and Israel's relationship with God, but also information about God's created world. Since Torah is revealed wisdom, the pursuit of wisdom about the world, which is the task of philosophy, would have to be linked to the interpretation of the divinely revealed text.

Jewish philosophy began in earnest during the Hellenistic period, when Diaspora Jews encountered Greek philosophy. As Greek-speaking Egyptian Jews lost their facility in Hebrew, they translated the Bible into Greek—the Septuagint—and began to study it in light of Greek philosophy. The first Jewish philosopher known by name, Aristobulus (ca. 180–145 BCE), wanted readers to understand the Torah philosophically in order to demonstrate the rationality of the Jewish religion. (A few extant fragments of his work are in *The Old Testament Pseudepigrapha* [ed. James Charlesworth, Garden City: Doubleday, 1985], pp. 831–42.) Writing in Greek to Jews and Gentiles, Aristobulus presented Judaism as a type of philosophical school. He did not wish to assimilate the Jewish religion into Greek philosophy, but rather to argue that Judaism is superior to other philosophical schools because "Plato and the philosophers borrowed from Moses." Though Aristobulus equated the God of the Jews and the God of the Gentile philosophers, his teachings were thoroughly Jewish because he also identified the rational wisdom of the philosophers with "Torah." Precisely because the Torah teaches philosophical truths, it must *not* be taken literally. Through allegorical reading of the Septuagint, Aristobulus and other educated Jews could explain to themselves and to non-Jews the meaning of Jewish practices, beliefs, and sacred texts that kept the Jews a people apart in the Greco-Roman world. Allegory would typify much of the early Jewish Hellenistic philosophical tradition.

Another typical example of Judeo-Hellenistic philosophical writing was the author of the Wisdom of Solomon, who was conversant in Middle Platonism (a philosophical school that flourished from 80 BCE to 220 CE and was steeped in Stoicism), as well as in Israelite Wisdom tradition. The Wisdom of Solomon was an attempt to place the Jewish religion within a broad philosophical text, intelligible to educated contemporaries who are at home in Hellenistic philosophy. The author identifies himself with King Solomon and, on the basis of 1 Kings ch 3, presents King Solomon as achieving a union with Wisdom through searching and praying (7.7–9; 9.1–8). For the duration of Jewish philosophy, the belief that King Solomon was the prototype of the sage and patron of arts and sciences would legitimize the study on philosophy and science and would make Ecclesiastes and the Song of Songs, two works attributed to him, central texts for philosophical commentaries.

The most important and prolific Jewish philosopher of the Hellenistic period was Philo of Alexandria (15 BCE–50 CE). At home in the culture of the Greek polis and thoroughly proficient in the philosophy of the major Greek schools of Plato, Aristotle, the Stoics, and the Pythagoreans, Philo's allegiance to Scripture was never in question. He rejected a radical allegorical reading of the Bible and argued that those who advocated it merely wished to assimilate into Hellenistic Roman society and abandon Judaism. For Philo true philosophical life is to be found in the divine law of Moses, which leads its adherents to the attainment of the ultimate end of human life—the seeing of God. Philo's exposition of Scripture's truths was meant to prove the uniqueness and epistemological superiority of the Jewish tradition over other intellectual and religious traditions.

The prophecy of Moses plays an important role in establishing the perfection of the Hebrew Scriptures. For Philo, Moses was the most perfect of men with reference to his priestly piety (Mos. 2:66) and his constant and unbroken nobility of life and other virtues (Mos. 1:24; 29; 2:58). With no sin and imperfection, Moses was "king, lawgiver, high priest, prophet," and "in each function he won the highest place" (Mos. 2:292). Philo provides a highly idealized account of Moses' life, illustrating his outstanding moral and religious qualities. Moses' prophecy itself proved his intellectual perfection since he comprehended the incorporeal, intelligible world of Ideas. Using the language of allegory to do it, Moses wrote down what he had seen of the incorporeal world of real essences. The intellectual study of "mental things and real existences" is the allegorical study of Scripture. In accordance with the Platonic schema of the *Repub-*

lic, Philo portrays Moses as the philosopher-king who "attained the very summit of philosophy," and he is credited with discoveries wrongly attributed to others (*Mos.* 2:2). While Moses was not God, he was not merely human either. Philo applies to Moses the same title—*theos*—that he applies also to the Logos. Indeed, Moses receives a "divine communication," meaning that "all that follows in the wake of God is within the good man's apprehension while he himself is beyond it." As the embodiment of Logos, Moses is called "the law-giving Word," by which humanity could be rescued from the bondage of matter. Thus Moses is the supreme high priest, who bestows "a blessing which nothing in the world can surpass" (*Mos.* 2:67). Moses rescued mankind from the bondage of matter.

Philo adapted to Scriptures the same method that the Stoics used to interpret Homer and Greek mythology. The Hebrew Scriptures for him are the inspired word of God. Moses' utterances were "absolutely and entirely signs of the divine excellence, conduct and particularly the nation of his worshippers, for whom he opens up the road which leads to happiness" (*Mos.* 2:189). The Bible was composed in a state comparable to that of the philosopher when he is inspired to recall intelligible ideas beyond the world of sense and matter. That means that for Philo, the Torah is inspired, but Moses and not God was its author, a daring notion indeed as far as later rabbinic Judaism is concerned. The same inspiration also filled the Septuagint translators who preserved the true meaning of the mysteries conveyed by Moses.

At Sinai Moses' purified soul was engraved or inscribed by God. By virtue of this divine impression of knowledge, Moses was a "living law" even before he composed the written laws. In his own person Moses functioned as a kind of seal designed to impress the law in the shape of his life on those who would become his followers (*Mos.* 1:158–59). Moses expressed his extraordinary knowledge through the act of writing (rather than speaking) when he composed the Torah, which contains laws of proper conduct and facts about the structure of the cosmos. The language at his disposal, however, was post-lapsarian; it was no longer the original Adamic language, which had been mimetic. Whereas Adamic language presented reality by giving names to things on the basis of direct apprehension of the essences of things, Moses could only use an imperfect language. Moreover, since Moses addressed all Israelites, who by definition were imperfect and ill prepared, he had to use audio-visual aids to convey his conceptual message. The result was the anthropomorphic language of the Bible, which requires allegorical interpretation.

The upshot of Philo's analysis is that only the Mosaic law enables those who follow it to live by the Stoic mandate of life in accordance with nature. The zenith of the well-lived life is an individual, ecstatic, unmediated experience of coming to know the transcendent and immaterial God. This is a contemplative, mystical experience in which the "eye of the mind" or the soul comes "to see God." As the goal of human life, this mystical experience governs the direction of the happy life, organizing all human activities to attain it. Since for Philo the revealed law of Moses is the ideal law, which God implanted in nature at creation, the universal goal of "seeing God" is achievable only for those who live by the law of Moses, since it alone guides humanity in accordance with nature. Hence the experience of "seeing God" constitutes the community of "Israel" which for Philo is a nonethnic intellectual-religious category ("those who see God") rather than an ethnic or national category. This view would enable Christian readers to adapt Philo for their own needs, making him into a Church Father, and explains why the works of Philo were preserved in the church rather than in the synagogue.

Philo illustrates the extent to which a Jewish intellectual in 1st-century Alexandria could creatively reconcile the Greek philosophical tradition with Scripture-based religion. Yet Philo did not chart the future devel-opment of Judaism. Instead, the Rabbis of the land of Israel and Babylonia articulated what became normative Judaism. Although the Rabbis reflected on the same themes of concern to Philo, they did not adopt his allegorical method of interpretation. Similarly, while the rabbinic academy shared many features with Greco-Roman philosophical schools, including the total commitment to the love of wisdom (which the Rabbis equated with Torah), and the life-long cultivation of moral and intellectual virtues, rabbinic speculations about God, the universe, the problem of evil, and the purpose of human life proceeded hermeneutically and homiletically rather than systematically and demonstratively. In addition, rabbinic views developed from the Hebrew text, rather than from the Septuagint. These views, found in a wide variety of early and late rabbinic texts, are extremely diffuse and diverse and are extremely difficult to categorize and to compare to the oeuvre of a single individual like Philo.

Medieval Jewish Philosophy

The Greco-Roman period in Jewish history ended with the redaction of the Talmud, the Jerusalem Talmud (ca. 400 CE) and the Babylonian Talmud (after 500 CE). Soon afterwards, with the rise and expansion of Islam, the life of Jews in the Middle East radically changed. The new religion recognized the Bible as revealed Scripture and granted Jews the status of protected subjects (dhimmi). As a monotheistic religion, Islam did not pose a theoretical challenge to Jews. But when Greek and Hellenistic philosophy and science were translated into Arabic during the 8th and 9th centuries, Islamic civilization gave rise to a new systematic philosophy (falsafah) and speculative theology (kalam). The latter two did pose an intellectual challenge to which Jewish thinkers, who were conversant in Arabic language and culture, had to respond. In the new rationalist climate, which sets up reason as a judge of religion, Judaism had to be proven to be a rational religion.

Most problematic were the anthropomorphic depictions of God in the Bible and in rabbinic texts. In the ecstatic and visionary strand of rabbinic thought, known as the Hekhalot and Merkavah literature (see "The Bible in the Jewish Mystical Tradition," pp. 1976–90), God was not only imaged as a king seated on the Throne of Glory as in the Bible, but the limbs of God's body were given precise (albeit fantastic) measurements. In the new intellectual climate of the 9th century, the corporeal depiction of God in rabbinic Judaism became an intellectual embarrassment and a target of severe criticism from rationalist skeptics such as Hiwi al-Balkhi (whose "Two Hundred Questions concerning Scripture" are known only through Saadia's response to them). The most scathing critique of rabbinic Judaism came from the Karaites, who denied the validity of the oral tradition and regarded only Written law as sacred. But how is Scripture to be interpreted without the rabbinic tradition? Following the Kalam theologians of the Mutazilite school, the Karaite thinkers posited human reason and the sciences of grammar and philology as the way to fathom the meaning of divinely revealed Scripture. The Karaites' exposition of the biblical text would give rise to their articulation of the dogmas of Judaism and to the formal distinction between ceremonial and rational commandment. The Karaites were thus the first Jewish philosophers in the Middle Ages. Their critique of rabbinic Judaism put them outside normative Judaism, but their influence on the way normative Judaism formulated its philosophical beliefs was profound.

It was the great foe of Karaism, Saadia Gaon (882–942), who articulated the philosophic defense of rabbinic Judaism. Like the Karaite philosophers, Saadia Gaon's theology was shaped by the Mutazilite Kalam, but he applied its claim that human reason is compatible with a divinely revealed religion not only to Scripture but to the entire rabbinic tradition. There is nothing in rabbinic Judaism that is contradictory to reason, provided the written law and the oral law are properly interpreted. To prove the first claim, Saadia translated almost the entire Bible into Arabic. This literal translation (*Tafsir*) was accompanied by an extended paraphrastic commentary on the biblical text (*Sharh*) intended for the more learned reader. To prove the latter claim, Saadia composed thematic monographs on rabbinic law. In his main theological treatise, *Kitab al Amanat wa'l itiqadat (Book of Doctrines and Beliefs)*, Saadia delineated the circumstances that legitimized a nonliteralist understanding of the biblical text.

Saadia's *Book of Doctrines and Beliefs* had a clear polemical intent: to reject all forms of Jewish skepticism and disbelief rife in his time and to place rabbinic Judaism on a firm rationalist foundation. Saadia's method of reasoning was not significantly different from that of the Karaites, but his conclusions were. Like the Karaites, he regarded the rationalist inquiry into the meaning of the received tradition by the tools that God implanted in humans (namely, human reason) to be a religious obligation. Saadia believed that his method of exposition could help turn religious belief, affirmed on the basis of tradition, into firmly held convictions that are corroborated by rational proofs. For Saadia, the revealed tradition is a source of valid knowledge that complements what can be known through the other three sources: sense perception, self-evident truths, and logical inference. A revelation from God is necessary because human beings are not intellectually equal; some are more gifted than others. Furthermore, the pursuit of truth by natural human reason is very arduous, time-consuming, and prone to errors. Divine revelation is necessary to compensate for human limitations, making truth available to all, including women and children.

A superb close reader of the Bible, Saadia found scriptural support for almost every detail of rational argument. Saadia's rationalist exposition of Scripture demanded that whenever Scripture appears to be in conflict with what is known to be true from the other three sources of knowledge, it is necessary to submit the text to careful examination and interpret the scriptural text in question allegorically. This is especially necessary in regard to the corporeal depiction of God in the Bible. Since reason independently demonstrates that God is the creator of the universe and that, therefore, God is not corporeal, it follows that the literal meaning of the biblical text cannot be true. Saadia proposes how to decode the corporeal language of the Bible. For example, when the term *head* is applied to God it must mean "excellence and elevation"; *eye* means "supervision"; *ear* "denotes acceptance"; *mouth* and *lip* mean "teaching and command"; *heart* "signifies wisdom"; *bowels* "denote amiability;" *foot* denotes "coercion." Since these words are used in the Bible also in nonanthropomorphic senses, it is most appropriate that the nonanthropomorphic sense will be used in scriptural utterances about God. Thus the rationalist conception of God recommended the allegorical interpretation. After Saadia, the allegorical interpretation of the text was applied not only to divine attributes but also to human agents in biblical narratives.

The intellectualization of rabbinic Judaism reached its zenith in Muslim Spain during the 11th and 12th centuries. The unique cultural symbiosis between Judaism and Islam flourished under the Ummayad Caliphate in Cordoba and its successor petty kingdoms, where outstanding Jews rose to power in the administration of the Muslim state, creating a Jewish culture suffused with the sensibilities and ideals of *adab*, namely, the broad scientific and rhetorical learning that made one courteous and urbane. The *adib* (the man schooled in *adab*) was a highly refined person who was expected to know a little about many topics in order to add brilliance to the court. The key for success in the court was possession of rhetorical skills, poetic eloquence, and calligraphic excellence, all of which were cultivated through the study and production of prose and poetry. The *adib* culled his knowledge from prose books that encompassed tales, fables, anecdotes, practical advice, and popularization of scientific information, all gleaned from the philosophical-scientific heritage of the Hellenistic world, interspersed with some material from India.

Jewish culture in Muslim Spain changed profoundly as Jewish courtiers absorbed the *adab* program, but without compromising their Jewish identity or their conviction about the spiritual superiority of Judaism. Indeed, the Bible anchored the Jewish response to the attraction of the dazzling Islamic civilization in Andalusia. Fully aware of Islamic claims about the Quran's divinity and perfection, including the superiority of Quranic Arabic to all other languages, Jewish scholars asserted the uniqueness of the Tanakh and its pure language and applied the sciences of grammar and philology to prove the perfection of the Bible. This perfection was not merely linguistic or rhetorical; it was scientific and philosophic as well. The linguistic analysis of the Bible by grammarians such as Judah ben David Ḥayyuj (ca. 950–ca. 1000), Isaac ben Levi Ibn Mar Shaul, Samuel Ibn Naghrella (933–1056), Judah ben Samuel Ibn Bal'am (d. ca. 1090), Moses ben Samuel Ibn Gikatilla (or Chiquitilla) (d. ca. 1080), Jonah Ibn Janaḥ (ca. 985–c. 1040) and Shmuel Alkanzi (1050–1130), enabled a deeper philosophical understanding of the Bible to emerge. It was through the literal meaning of the text (later called *peshat*) that the deeper philosophical meaning could be accessed.

The most outstanding exponent of the link between the linguistic analysis of Hebrew and the philosophical exposition of the Bible was Abraham Ibn Ezra (1089–1167). A poet, liturgist, grammarian, translator, mathematician, astronomer, astrologer and philosopher, Abraham Ibn Ezra's interpretation of Judaism was naturalist and rationalist. Regarding the Jews as unique mediators between cultures, Ibn Ezra was committed to imparting knowledge of Greek and Arabic cultures to his Jewish audience and even wrote scientific works in Latin to make the work of Jews known to Christians. He began to comment on the biblical canon rather late in life after migrating from Muslim Spain to Italy with the intention of teaching the correct reading of the Bible to Jews who were not yet familiar with the Jewish rationalist tradition and Judeo-Hispanic biblical exegesis. Though Ibn Ezra composed commentaries to the entire Bible, the extant texts include commentaries (some preserved in two versions) on the Torah, Isaiah, the Twelve Minor Prophets, Psalms, Job, the Five Scrolls, and Daniel. The style of the commentary is terse and cryptic, full of allusions to philosophical and scientific (especially astrological) theories, purportedly contained in the Bible, but which should not be expounded in full in the context of the biblical commentary.

Ibn Ezra claimed that the Bible itself attests to the fact that ancient Israelites were versed in the sciences, so that the study of the sciences is an inherently Jewish activity. Therefore, only a scholar who is deeply proficient in the sciences, especially astronomy and astrology, can properly understand the meaning of the biblical text. For Ibn Ezra the exposition of the text by means of astrological references does not mean imposing science on the Bible, but rather showing how the biblical text itself actually enlarges the scope of the scientific discourse known to him from extrabiblical, Muslim and Hermetic sources. At times the biblical text is used by Ibn Ezra to address questions that are raised by other sciences or resolve tensions between various scientific theories, for example between the assumption of astrology that ascribes to celestial bodies the physical properties such as hot and cold, and the Aristotelian views according to which the celestial bodies are made of a refined substance that does not carry physical properties. The Bible can also remove a contradiction between the assumptions of astrology and the physical view that Ibn Ezra accepted as correct. For example, Ps. 148 teaches not only about the cosmological differentiation between the lower and supernal worlds, but also about the physical composition of objects in the supra-lunar world and the fixed cyclical motion.

For Ibn Ezra, the science of astrology captures the fixity of natural laws, even though he maintained that the predictive power of astrology is not perfect. Although Ibn Ezra did not consider astrology to be practically useful, he made many allusions to astrological theories when he explained animal sacrifices, the festivals, the scapegoat ritual, and the uniqueness of the Holy Land, among other aspects of Israelite religion. The prevalence of astrology in the exposition of the biblical text, however, should not obscure the main claim of Ibn Ezra about the relationship between astrology and the Torah. Precisely because Israel is in possession of the revealed Torah, Israel alone can be free from the influences of astral forces, provided Israel studies the Torah and observes its commandments. As Ibn Ezra teaches in the commentary on Exod. 3.21, the very commitment to Torah study and the life that flows from it ensures that Israel is not subject to astrological influence.

Ibn Ezra's naturalism went hand in hand with his esoteric style of biblical commentaries and, in turn, with his intellectual elitism. He made a clear distinction between the masses, who lack the capacity to engage in philosophy and science, and the few who possess the "heart," which is the seat of reason in Ibn Ezra's psychology. Only the very few who are scientifically educated can attain the ultimate end of human life and enjoy the bliss of immortality reserved to the individual soul. For the educated reader, laconic allusions are sufficient to direct him to the deep philosophic and scientific matters taught by the Torah. These are the "secrets" (sodot) of the Torah that remain obscure to the masses. In the 14th century, as we shall see below, several Jewish philosophers composed supercommentaries on Ibn Ezra's commentaries, spelling out (not always correctly) the precise meaning of these secrets.

Until the second half of the 14th century it was Moses Maimonides, Rambam (Rabbi Moses son of Maimon; 1138–1204), rather than Abraham Ibn Ezra who dominated the Jewish philosophical approach to the Bible. Although Maimonides perpetuated many ideas of Ibn

Ezra, Maimonides also vigorously rejected the science of astrology, highlighted the limitation of human knowledge in metaphysics, and recognized naturalist causality only as far as the sublunar world is concerned. At the heart of Maimonides' approach to the Bible stood his theory of prophecy, which is remarkably similar to that of Philo, even though the immediate source of inspiration for Maimonides was not Philo but the Muslim philosopher Abu Nasr Alfarabi (d. 950). Adopting Plato's political theory to the case of Islam, Alfarabi portrayed the founder of the true religion as a philosopher-prophet-legislator-imam whose perfect law contains the translation of philosophic truths into figurative speech.

Following Alfarabi, Maimonides understood prophecy as a cognitive activity by an intellectually perfect person. All prophets must be philosophers, though not all philosophers are endowed with the imaginative faculty that can translate philosophic knowledge into figurative speech characteristic of prophecy. Maimonides, however, took pains to differentiate between the prophecy of Moses and the prophecy of all other prophets: Moses received his prophecy in broad daylight, and he prophesied whenever he wished, without fear or trembling, and without any input from his senses or the imagination. Moses' prophecy was qualitatively different because he transcended human corporeality and "attained the angelic." Suppressing his senses, appetites, and desires to the utmost minimum, Moses transcended human embodiment, and his body no longer functioned as a "veil" between him and God. Mosaic prophecy was, therefore, purely intellectual, the result of the conjunction between Moses' perfected intellect and the Active Intellect. In knowing what the Active Intellect knows, Moses apprehended the pattern of the law of nature. Therefore, the Torah of Moses "enters into what is natural" (*Guide* II:40), that is to say, it fits the structure of reality. The perfection of the Torah is thus completed in the perfection of the agent that received the Torah—the prophet Moses.

Moses was not only cognitively perfect; his imaginative faculty was also the most perfect. While Moses' prophecy was itself strictly conceptual or cognitive, the transmission of its content to the Israelites required the use of the imagination, since this faculty is the difference between philosopher and prophet. Because of Moses' perfect imagination, the Torah of Moses is the most perfect poetic text, one in which there is a perfect fit between the cognitive, esoteric core of the philosophic truths and figurative language of Torah narratives, a fit that justifies *allegoresis*. In Aristotelian language this is to say that the narratives, poetic imagery, and laws of the Torah function as Matter for the cognitive truths that are their Form. In its figurative language, the Torah teaches the sciences of physics and metaphysics. The task of the philosophic reader of the Bible is to remove the figurative veils of the Torah in order to fathom its philosophic content.

For the philosophically inclined reader, Maimonides composed *The Guide for the Perplexed*, whose first part contains a philosophical dictionary of the most problematic terms in the Bible. For example, Scripture uses the terms *image* and *likeness* to refer to God. These terms, Maimonides explains, are equivocal terms: When applied to natural things they refer to shapes of natural bodies, but when applied to God they mean something altogether different, because God is noncorporeal. Maimonides proceeds to explain the meaning of other terms such as *figure, shape, place, throne, to descend, to ascend, sitting, standing, rising, to stand, to approach, to rise,* and others, all in order to teach the reader how to read the Bible correctly in a manner that does not violate the radical otherness of God.

Maimonides held that there is an unbridgeable ontological gap between God, the Necessary Existent, and all other things. It is therefore impossible for humans to know the essence of God. Human beings can only know who God is not, although from the observation of the natural world and the science of physics, human beings can know a lot about the actions of God. The radical negative theology of Maimonides entails that all terms applied to God in the Torah are either equivocations or absolute equivocation, which would suggest that the term "prophecy" as applied to Moses and any other prophet is also absolutely equivocal. Maimonides, however, does not go that far, because he could not make Moses into a deity; Moses can only be a unique human being. Because Maimonides insisted that Moses remain a human being and the Torah rationally intelligible, he had to explain in what sense the Torah of Moses is from God. This is the purpose of talking about "divine ruse" (Heb: "*'ormah*" Arabic: "*talattuf*") in the *Guide* III:30 and 32.

The "divine ruse" was to give Israel the Torah through the intermediacy of Moses who communicated with Israel at a level that Israel could accept. Since God is an absolute unity, in God will and wisdom are the same: What God wills and what God knows are the same, and both are manifested in the way God governs the world. And since God governs through natural causes, divine management of human affairs takes into consideration the particular conditions of humanity. Given the prevalence of idolatrous practices and beliefs, the "divine ruse" was evident both in forcing Israel to live in the desert in order to improve its character, and in using Moses as the intermediary to address Israel at a level at which it could comprehend God's word. Concomitantly, in order to make sure that we will not conclude erroneously that the Torah of Moses is merely contingent, the Eighth Principle of Maimonides' Thirteen Principles of Jewish Faith specifies dogmatically that the Torah cannot change.

The cognitive perfection of Moses yielded a perfect text, but the divinity of the Torah can also be determined by an examination of its function. The Torah is divine because it can be shown that the Torah brings about the perfection of the body (*tikun ha-guf*) and perfection of the soul (*tikun ha-nefesh*). The Torah is a prescription for human well-being, because the inner meaning of the Torah corresponds to the structure of reality. By living according to the regimen articulated in the Torah, human beings can attain well-being of body and soul, when the former is understood as a means to the attainment of the latter. By observing the commandments of the Written Torah as interpreted by the Oral Torah, one ensures physical health, the acquisition of the requisite virtues, culminating in the perfection of the intellect. It is the perfection of the intellect through cognition of intelligibles that constitutes the immortal life that the Jewish tradition denotes as "world-to-come." Whether this cognitive state constitutes personal immortality and whether this is the correct interpretation of rabbinic Judaism would become a major theme in the debate about Maimonides's legacy during the 13th century.

Maimonides did not compose a linear commentary on the Bible, but only articulated general hermeneutical principles. The application of Maimonides' hermeneutical principles to the Bible was carried out by his followers, beginning with Samuel Ibn Tibbon (d. 1232), who translated the *Guide* from Arabic into Hebrew, composed a glossary of philosophical terms in the *Guide*, explained the esoteric meaning of Ecclesiastes, and composed a systematic exposition of the biblical creation narrative in light of Aristotle's physics. To master the latter and make it accessible to Jewish seekers of wisdom, Ibn Tibbon also translated Aristotle's *Meteroa* into Hebrew in 1210. Samuel Ibn Tibbon inaugurated the tradition of philosophical biblical commentaries that read the Bible as an encoded Aristotelian, philosophical text.

Jewish philosophers in 13th century Spain vacillated between two conflicting goals: On the one hand, the philosophers wished to teach philosophy to the many in order to raise the intellectual level of Jews and enable them to perfect their soul so as to attain immortality. On the other hand, the philosophers believed that ordinary Jews lacked the intellectual preconditions to engage in philosophy; they may misunderstand philosophic teachings and harbor erroneous views. The followers of Maimonides attempted to bridge the gap between the philosophers and the public by composing summaries of philosophical texts, popularizing philosophy in prose studded with rhymed poetry, and by writing philosophical commentaries on the Bible in which they made clear what Maimonides only hinted at in the *Guide*. With the treatment of the Bible as a philosophic-scientific text, opposition to rationalist philosophy was unavoidable. Throughout the 13th century, Jewish communities in Spain, Provence, France, Italy, the land of Israel, Egypt, and Iraq were engaged in a bitter controversy about the status of philosophy within Jewish traditional society.

R. David Kimḥi (Radak; 1160–1235), a biblical exegete, grammarian, and translator, whose family migrated from Muslim Spain to Provence, played a major role in what we now call the Maimonidean Controversy of the 1230s. He is an example of a militant rationalist commentator on the Bible for whom the Torah was intentionally written by Moses with a "double meaning, one obscuring the other . . . the exoteric for the masses and the esoteric for the Sages" (Frank Talmage, *David Kimhi: The Man and the Commentaries* [Cambridge, MA: Harvard University Press, 1975], p. 120). Although Radak retains the *peshat* level of the biblical text and contributed greatly to its understanding, his commentaries also provided an elaborate allegorical reading. For example, "the Garden of Eden represents the Active Intellect and the Tree of Life the human Intellect, while the Tree of Knowledge of Good and Evil symbolized the material intellect" (Talmage, p. 121). Radak goes on to interpret biblical personae allegorically. Cain, for example, was a farmer and devoid of intellectual accomplishments, whereas Abel was occupied with the vanities of life, even though he was endowed with material intellect. In Radak's reading, it was the third son, Seth, who ate from the Tree of Life and was created in the image of Adam. It was he who shared with Adam the human intellect. Seth was the good seed and the true founder of mankind. In this allegorical fashion

Radak explicates the two main bodies of esoteric teachings in the Torah, the Account of Creation (*ma'aseh bereshit*), based on the creation narrative of Genesis, and the Account of the Chariot (*ma'aseh merkavah*), based on the first chapter of Ezekiel. Based on Maimonides's reading of the latter, Radak was even more elaborate and specific than was Maimonides in reading this chapter as expression of Aristotelian cosmology whose principles are explained in "chapter headings" in the *Guide*.

The rationalist philosophers insisted that to worship God correctly Jews must know philosophy. Therefore, the controversy during the 13th century concerned the cultural boundaries of Judaism and the degree to which the Bible contains truths articulated in other sources. Yet, if the Torah is indeed divine Wisdom, as the philosophers argued, then one could argue that there is no need to consult philosophy and science at all since Scripture already contains all the knowledge necessary for its correct interpretation. Kabbalists (see "The Bible in the Mystical Tradition," pp. 1976–90) such as Jacob Ibn Sheshet (13th century) advanced that claim and rejected the Maimonidean interpretation of the creation narrative. Yet the kabbalists too developed their ideas and exegetical strategies through familiarity with Jewish philosophy, and like the philosophers the kabbalists endorsed the distinction between the exoteric (*nigleh*) and esoteric (*nistar*) levels of the biblical text. Likewise, the kabbalists accepted Maimonides' claim that the Torah is the prescription for human well-being, or happiness, culminating in personal immortality. For this and other reasons, the impression often given of an absolute difference between the medieval philosophical and kabbalistic tradition is incorrect.

The primary difference between the rationalist philosophers and the kabbalists concerned the nature of the Hebrew language. Whereas to the Maimonidean philosophers Hebrew was a conventional, human language, the kabbalists maintained that Hebrew is literally the language of God whose elements—the Hebrew letters—are the "building blocks," so to speak, of the created universe. The revelation of the Torah and the creation of the universe are two sides of the same coin. For the kabbalists, then, *ma'aseh bereshit* and *ma'aseh merkavah* refer not to the physical universe of the sublunar and supra-lunar worlds, respectively, but to processes within the Godhead. In other words, Scripture, according to the kabbalists, is a symbolic manifestation of God's essence, the very thing that Maimonides claimed lies beyond the ken of human knowledge. Although both rationalist philosophers and kabbalists asserted that the Hebrew Scriptures contain salvific truths about God, for the philosophers these truths concern the created world and its relationship with God, whereas for the kabbalists these truths are of God's very essence.

The final phase of the Maimonidean Controversy took place in 1303–1305 and ended on July 31, 1306, when R. Solomon Ibn Adret imposed a ban on the study of philosophy for men under twenty-five years of age. The ban signaled the complex status of philosophy within traditional Jewish society, but it by no means ended the philosophical interpretation of the Bible. In the first half of the 14th century, especially in Provence, additional philosophical commentaries on the Bible were composed in which rationalist philosophers, such as Joseph Ibn Kaspi (1279–ca. 1331) and Nissim ben Moses of Marseilles (active 1320s), expounded the philosophic import of the biblical text and attempted to solve various exegetical problems that arise by reading the Bible in light of Aristotelian philosophy. The most extensive and philosophically sophisticated of these commentaries are those composed by Rabbi Levi ben Gershom, known as Ralbag or Gersonides (1288–1344).

Gersonides was a first-rate scientist, specializing in astronomy, who mastered the Aristotelian corpus by writing supercommentaries on commentaries of Averroes (1126–1198). Intimately versed with the legacy of Maimonides, Gersonides took issue

with his Jewish predecessor on many points, radicalizing the intellectualist tenor of Jewish rationalist naturalism. Most importantly, Gersonides rejected Maimonides' esoteric method of teaching philosophy. Philosophy need not and must not be kept secret from the masses but must be taught openly, systematically, and without allusions and hints. Accepting Aristotelian philosophy wholeheartedly, Gersonides was determined to teach the Jewish public at large the correct meaning of the doctrines of creation, prophecy, providence, miracles, and the chosenness of Israel in his systematic philosophical work *Milḥamot ha-Shem (The Wars of the Lord)* as well as in his biblical commentaries. Like Ibn Ezra, Gersonides launched his philosophical exegesis only after composing scientific-philosophic works; proficiency in philosophy was a necessary condition to the proper understanding of the revealed text.

In agreement with Maimonides, Gersonides held that "the Torah is the written record of Moses' prophetic revelation, and, therefore, its value for guiding the Israelites to perfection is determined by the nature and quality of Moses' prophetic capabilities" (Robert Eisen, *Gersonides on Providence, Covenant, and the Chosen People: A Study in Medieval Jewish Philosophy and Biblical Commentary* [Albany: State University of New York, 1995], p. 73). But unlike Maimonides, Gersonides considered the prophet's ability to predict the future as the major difference between philosophers and prophets. The predictive capacity of the prophets follows from their perfect knowledge of causal relations in the natural world governed by astral forces. Contrary to Maimonides, who vehemently rejected the science of astrology, Gersonides, like Ibn Ezra, was an expert astrologer who attempted to shed light on the remote past on the basis of his astrological and astronomical knowledge. This knowledge is especially relevant to the interpretation of the commandments, whose allegorical meaning Gersonides spells out. Contrary to Maimonides, for whom the masses at the time of Moses were incapable of philosophical sophistication, Gersonides held that Moses taught the entire nation of uneducated Israelites the full range of philosophical doctrines, natural science, and metaphysics after their exodus from Egypt.

The pedagogic function of the Torah and the need to teach philosophy openly do not mean that Gersonides renounced the elitism characteristic of the Jewish philosophical tradition. He too believed that different audiences understand the Torah on different levels in accord with their level of intellectual perfection. Because of their lack of philosophical training the masses cannot appreciate the deep philosophical meaning of the Torah. Yet Gersonides was much more optimistic than Maimonides and Ibn Ezra about the ability of the philosopher to bring the masses to a higher level of knowledge. His philosophical commentaries accomplished that task for the general Jewish reader, but they did not simply rehash his philosophical-scientific views. Sometimes the exposition of the biblical text provided Gersonides an opportunity to offer new insights and revisions of what he said in his earlier philosophical text *The Wars of the Lord*.

Gersonides' commentaries on the Torah were written to be accessible, and followed a rigid structure: He first explained the meaning of the words, then provided a statement of the import of the section under consideration, and concluded the discussion with a summary of the "lessons" (*to'aliot*) to be derived from the Torah portion. In his *Commentary on the Song of Songs* Gersonides departed from that style. Writing for a generally educated reader who has just embarked on the study of philosophy, Gersonides presented the Song of Songs as a philosophical allegory about the path toward ultimate felicity. From Abraham Ibn Ezra, through Joseph Ibn Aqnin (ca. 1150–1220), Moses Ibn Tibbon (active 1240–1270), and Immanuel of Rome (ca. 1261–ca. 1328), Jewish philosophers read the Song of Songs as a philosophical allegory about the human path of spiritual improvement. But unlike his predecessors, who interpreted the Song of Songs as an intellectual process culminating in the conjunction between the human rational soul and the Active Intellect, Gersonides interpreted the text to refer to internal processes, namely, the relationship between the human rational soul and the imagination. Reviewing the fundamentals of philosophy for his reader, Gersonides instructs the reader of the Song to understand the obstacles to the attainment of felicity and the ways to overcome them. Though relatively few could reach the lofty goal of spiritual perfection by which humans attain personal immortality, the goal is in principle attainable by the students of science and philosophy.

Gersonides' commitment to the dissemination of scientific knowledge was shared by Jewish philosophers in Spain and Provence during the second half of the 14th century. By then, however, what were considered sound scientific theories included not only the teachings of Aristotle, but also Neoplatonic and Hermetic theories about the natural world. This syncretistic mixture was used as a new interpretative grid for the Bible, deriving its inspiration from Abraham Ibn Ezra. In Spain during the second half of the 14th century, Samuel Ibn Motot, Joseph Tov Elem, Ezra Gatingo, Shlomo Franco, and Shem Tov Ibn Shaprut composed super-commentaries on Ibn Ezra's biblical commentaries, openly using astrology and astral magic to decode the hints of Ibn Ezra so as to explain ancient Israelite practices such as the tabernacle, the sacrifices, and the priestly vestments.

The main claims of their astral theology include the following: The Torah was given at Sinai on the basis of astrological calculation. Biblical events reflect the influences of the stars, and biblical personalities and rabbinic sages were expert astrologers. Prophecy is predicated on knowledge of astrology. Miracles are understood to be the results of the prophet's intellectual perfection. Moses was able to overcome Egyptian magicians because he was a superior astrologer. His intellectualist perfection included the knowledge of astrology, culminating in the conjunction of his intellect with the Active Intellect. He was a practicing magician who correctly understood the link between earthly and celestial powers. The knowledge of astrology enables the intellectually perfect to extricate themselves from astral causality. Moreover, the uniqueness of the people of Israel is explained in its ability to transcend the impact of astral influences through Israel's mastery of the astrological sciences. Most importantly, the commandments themselves function as tools in the manipulation of astral forces. The commandments either manifest the influence of a given celestial body, or were given as techniques to draw spiritual energy from the celestial spheres into the corporeal world. In this regard, the commandments are effective tools in the attempt to prosper in this world. The performance of the commandments mitigates the destructive forces of the corporeal world that are regulated by the celestial bodies. Observance of the commandments thus has an instrumental value, for the more consistently one performs them the more one can extricate oneself from the impact of astral forces.

In short, by the turn of the 15th century the scientists-philosophers proposed a strictly naturalistic interpretation of Torah on the basis of astral determinism. As Judah Halevi in the 12th century rejected such a naturalist approach to the Bible, so in the early 15th century did Hasdai Crescas (d. ca. 1412), who set out to extricate Judaism from the clutches of philosophy. Crescas himself was a well-trained philosopher, but he was convinced that the intellectualization of Judaism by the rationalists was responsible for the mass conversion of Jews to Christianity during and after the anti-Jewish riots and massacres of 1391. To rejuvenate Iberian Jewish life, Crescas subjected Aristotle's physics to minute critique, manifesting familiarity with contemporary scholastic critique of Aristotle's conception of motion. If Aristotle's philosophy can be proven to be either nondemonstrative or patently mistaken, Aristotle's philosophy could not constitute the true meaning of the Torah. Crescas, however, advanced his critique of Aristotle by using Aristotelian logic so that the novelty and full implications of it were either not fully understood by Jewish philosophers, or dismissed outright as evidence of his philosophical limitations.

Crescas was not alone in his displeasure with the naturalist exposition of the Bible, in which the Torah was viewed as a means to an end. Similar claims were voiced by other Jewish thinkers in Spain and Portugal in an attempt to rethink the relationship between Torah and philosophy. Continuing to uphold the Aristotelian worldview, Jewish philosophers in the 15th century increasingly acknowledged that the Torah is not identical with philosophy, but is rather superior to it. Whereas philosophy is grounded merely in knowledge of created things, Torah is revealed knowledge that can be explained by reason but not exhausted by it. Thus Simon ben Tzemach Duran (1361–1444), who was well versed in Aristotelian philosophy, maintained that it only serves to shed light on the meaning of Torah and that philosophy alone could not possibly lead to the attainment of ultimate felicity. A similar position was espoused by Joseph Ibn Shem Tov (ca. 1400–ca. 1460), who composed commentaries to Aristotle and who interpreted the ultimate end of human life in terms of Averroes's theory of cognition.

The philosophers' own admission that knowledge of philosophy alone fails to secure personal immortality and that it must be complemented by revealed knowledge gave 15th century Jewish philosophy its conservative posture as much as this viewpoint served an important polemical purpose against Christianity. As Spanish Jewry was fighting for its physical and spiritual survival, Jewish intellectuals were increasingly engaged in philosophical polemics against Christianity either through systematic exposition of Jewish dogmas, or through philosophical examination of Christian readings of the biblical text. The gist of this defense was that Judaism is superior to Christianity because Judaism is a rational religion. The God of Judaism does not do what is logically impossible; only what is naturally impossible. Whether rational arguments sustained Jewish believers is hard to determine; what is clear is that by the 15th century in Spain allegiance to Judaism became harder and harder.

In the 15th century, the philosophical defense of Judaism became more difficult because the opponents were often Jewish apostates with illustrious rabbinic backgrounds. Thus the Jewish delegation to the forced disputation in Tortosa (1413–1414) performed rather poorly against the apostates Jeronimo de Santa Fe and Pablo de Santa Maria who presented the Christian understanding of the messianic meaning of biblical and rabbinic texts. The rivalry between the two religions in Spain ended with the mass expulsion of Jews from Spain and the possessions of the Spanish Crown (1492), whose main goal was to end any contacts between professing Jews and *conversos* (Jewish converts to Christianity), to make Spain a unified, Catholic kingdom.

The Early-modern Period

The traumatic expulsion from Spain, and soon thereafter from Portugal, did not extinguish Jewish culture. In the Sephardi diaspora in North Africa, Italy, and the Ottoman Empire, Jewish culture continued to flourish and even experience a Renaissance of sorts. The interpretation of the Tanakh stood at the center of the cultural renewal, although there were two distinctive approaches to the Bible. On the one hand, there was the growing familiarity with Renaissance humanism and a willingness to adopt its historical sensibility to the interpretation of the Bible. The science of history was added to the list of sciences relevant to tease out the true meaning of Scriptures. On the other hand, the historical approach of kabbalah influenced Jewish philosophers who were seeking to fathom the infinite, eternal meanings of the canonical text, which could be penetrated but not exhausted by human reason.

The most innovative interpreter of the Bible in the generation of the expulsion from Spain was Isaac Abravanel (1437–1508), the illustrious diplomat, financier, and royal adviser to the kings of Portugal, Spain, and Naples. Familiar with Renaissance humanism (which had penetrated Iberia in the 1440s and flourished under the patronage of Queen Isabella during the 1480s), Abravanel introduced historical sensibility to the exposition of the Bible, while defending the inviolability of the rabbinic tradition. Abravanel's biblical commentaries are replete with quotations from Greek, Roman, Christian, and Muslim sources along with references to medieval Jewish biblical interpreters such as Rashi, Ibn Ezra, Radak, Gersonides, Naḥmanides, and Ibn Kaspi, and philosophers such as Maimonides and Crescas. Paying due respect to his predecessors, Abravanel also criticizes Maimonides for harmonizing the Torah with Aristotelian philosophy, chides Ibn Ezra for speaking in riddles, and rebukes Gersonides for deducing moral lessons from the Bible. The Torah must not be read reductively or allegorically.

Under the influence of contemporary humanists, Abravanel was the first to ponder the historical process that brought about and shaped the making of the biblical texts qua texts. He began his commentaries with extensive introductions in which he discussed the character of the book, the author, the date of composition, the content, and the structure of the book under consideration. Abravanel also noted textual problems such as inconsistencies and discrepancies in a given biblical text or between biblical books. Abravanel's novel literary criticism of the Bible broke new ground in regard to questions about the structure and divisions of the biblical canon as a whole and the interrelationship of its parts. Thus Abravanel attempted to account for divergences between the books of Samuel and Chronicles, suggested that the author of Chronicles was Ezra, paid attention to the human dimension of biblical narratives, assessed the stylistic differences between various prophetic books against the psychological makeup of the prophets as reflecting their particular historical circumstance, discussed biblical geography, investigated chronological quandaries, and examined the actual political circumstances at a given time in order to shed light on the narrative. Abravanel's astute historical observations yielded many insights that anticipated the biblical criticism of Spinoza in the mid-17th century. But unlike Spinoza, Abravanel remained deeply committed to the tradition and was aware of the potential danger that critical thinking could pose to Judaism. To address this danger Abravanel developed the construct of the "Torah of Moses" as a "central theological prop" (Eric Lawee, *Isaac Abrabanel's Stance toward Tradition: Defense, Dissent, and Dialogue* [Albany: SUNY Press, 2001, p. 185]), often endorsing views that were even more conservative than those of his medieval predecessors.

Similarly, Abravanel's exposure to humanism did not come at the expense of his familiarity with scholastic philosophy. He quotes directly from Thomas Aquinas (ca. 1225–1274), Albertus Magnus (1206–1280), and Nicholas de Lyra (ca. 1270–1340), and from the Christian scholastics Abravanel derived the distinction between human government and divine government which parallels the scholastic distinction between temporal and spiritual authorities. The scholastic philosophers developed their political theory on the basis of Aristotle's *Politics,* though most Jewish thinkers did not use it. Abravanel, by contrast, made massive use of the third book of the *Politics* in his commentary on 1 Sam. ch 8, although he did not quote the text directly. With Aristotle's analysis of political regimes and his own experience in European courts, Abravanel could read the biblical text as a political document, but without concluding that the Bible as a whole is a human document.

The inquiry into the literary and historical dimensions of Scriptures continued throughout the 16th century, especially in Italy. The Hebrew grammarian Elija Levita (d. 1549) was the first Jew to show that the vocalization of the biblical text and the system of accents were the work of the Masoretes of Tiberias, after the Talmud had been completed in the 6th century. The Masoretes concretized the tradition of how the Bible should be read, how it should be transmitted in writing, and, concommitantly, how the Bible should be understood. Since prior to the Masoretes the biblical text was handed down without vocalization, punctuation, or other signs, the lateness of the Masoretic text indicates that the biblical text itself has a history. Levita's grammatical studies added yet another rationale for studying the Bible as any other ancient, human, literary text.

The best example of the historical awareness of Italian Jewish intellectuals was Azariah di Rossi (1512–1575). Familiar with classical and Renaissance historiography, Azariah composed his *Ma'or 'Einayim (Light of the Eyes)* "to advance the legitimacy of objective historical inquiry into the Jewish past by establishing the total adequacy of religious tradition for purposes of moral edification, independent of any outside sources" (Lester A. Segal, *Historical Consciousness and Religious Tradition in Azariah de Rossi's Me'or Einayim* [Philadelphia: Jewish Publication Society, 1989], p. 30). Committed to the pursuit of truth, which Azariah regarded as "the seal of the truthful God, the quality of the beautiful soul, and it is well that all pursue it" (Segal, p. 32), Azariah moved to examine some of the problematic aspects of biblical chronology, such as "the uncertain duration of the First Temple period" (Segal, p. 31). Azariah did not intend to challenge the validity of the rabbinic tradition but rather to provide new evidence to prove the uniqueness of the people of Israel and their spiritual superiority in all aspects of human culture. Along with other Jewish apologists who argued for the doctrine of the divine election of Israel by showing that the Jews were the creators of music, di Rossi claimed that Moses was the author of the book of Job and the composer of the first known dialogue. While Azariah (like Abravanel before him) validated the authority of rabbinic tradition, his examination of the rabbinic past with references to non-Jewish texts and his observation about the historical origins of Jewish philosophy in the Greco-Roman world gave rise to a heated public controversy. Other contemporaries of di Rossi, such as Abraham ben David Portaleone (1542–1612), also affirmed the authority of the rabbinic tradition and the ideals of Torah study while at the same time providing rich historical and scientific information about aspects of the biblical text.

Awareness of the history of the biblical text itself was common among Jewish thinkers exposed to Renaissance humanism, especially in Italy. In the Ottoman Empire, however, most Sephardic intellectuals shared the kabbalistic notion that the revealed Torah is the manifestation of a supernal, primordial Torah that has infinite meanings. The task of the Jewish philosopher was to fathom the endless meaning of the Torah, knowing full well that it cannot be exhausted. In the Ottoman Empire, even more than in 15th century Spain, the Bible became the focus of philosophical midrash. Applying the analytic procedures of talmudic scholars to the biblical text, the philosopher-preachers attempted to penetrate the meaning of Scripture with scientific precision. The homilies of Isaac Karo (1458–1535) illustrate this tendency.

Assuming that his audience was fully familiar with the biblical text, Karo did not provide a running commentary but aimed at explicating Scripture in its complexity. In accord with the medieval assumption that Scripture is a scientific text, Karo held that the role of the commentator is to elucidate the practical and theoretical wisdom in the Bible because such understanding enables the soul of the learner to cling to God and to enjoy the bliss of immortality. Other contemporaries and successors of Karo, such as Joseph Taitatzak (ca. 1477–1545), Moses Almosnino (ca. 1515–1580), Isaac Aderbi (16th century), Isaac Arroyo (16th century), and Moshe Alshekh (d. after 1593) also considered the scrutiny of the Bible a religious activity par excellence leading to the attainment of immortal life. The

philosophical exegesis of sacred texts reflects the theological postures that the exiles brought with them from Iberia, namely, that revealed religion perfects natural human reason and that the divinely revealed Torah contains all human wisdom because it is identical with the infinite wisdom of God.

The exegetical unveiling of the infinite meanings of Scripture required linguistic sophistication and rhetorical versatility. The Sephardic philosophers in the Ottoman Empire selectively adopted the Renaissance cult of rhetorica. Though the exiles did not boast a recovery of the ancient sources, living either in the land of Israel itself or merely getting closer to it did inspire the Jewish exegete to present the Bible as a perfect text, aesthetically, morally, and intellectually, measuring or surpassing the achievements of the classics. Thus Moses Almosnino (ca. 1515–1580), for example, presented King Solomon as the embodiment of Renaissance *homo universalis* and the wisest of all ancient sages, and the religious poetry of King David was favorably compared to Greek and Roman poetry. By the same token, the moral teachings of King David and King Solomon recorded in Psalms, Proverbs, and Ecclesiastes, and interpreted by the rabbinic sages, were claimed to have surpassed the moral wisdom of Aristotle, Cicero, and Seneca, along with other ancient moral philosophers.

During the 16th century, then, the historical-literary investigation of the Bible coexisted with the philosophical-homiletical approach. If the first approach regarded the Bible as a text like all others, the second approach accentuated the exceptionality of the Bible and its divine perfection. In the mid-17th century, especially in the Dutch Republic, the tension between the two approaches could not be glossed over, but resulted in open doubts about the divinity, authority, and exceptionality of the Bible. The most consistent and radical critic of the Bible and of the Jewish philosophical exposition of the Bible was Baruch (Benedict) Spinoza (1632–1676). A child of ex-*conversos* who received traditional Jewish education, Spinoza was familiar with the biblical commentaries of Abraham Ibn Ezra and Maimonides' *Guide.* Spinoza praised Ibn Ezra's linguistic insights, but vehemently rejected the philosophical hermeneutics of Maimonides. It is doubtful that Spinoza was informed of the biblical commentaries of Isaac Abravanel or that he was familiar with Azariah di Rossi's work. Yet Spinoza's challenge appears less radical if it is viewed in light of his Jewish predecessors.

Spinoza argued that the Bible could not be proven to be a divinely revealed text, and even if the Bible was revealed by God, its meaning is accessible only through human interpretation. Spinoza applied the historical-philological method to demonstrate inconsistencies—logical and temporal—in the Bible. The Bible, according to Spinoza, is a human document that must be studied like any other ancient text, a product of the imagination of its human authors. With a thorough knowledge of the Hebrew language and an understanding of the historical past, the Bible can be seen precisely for what it is: a book that teaches morality and politics rather than philosophy and science.

Rejecting Maimonides' claim that the Bible contains philosophical truths expressed in figurative language, Spinoza argued that the Bible has nothing to do with philosophy and science because it is a product of prophetic imagination. The prophets were neither scientists nor philosophers; they were people with limited knowledge of nature who were endowed with vivid imaginations, very much like poets. Unlike natural knowledge, prophecy cannot be taught and cannot be imitated; it is a special gift. Prophecy must not be regarded as the "highest degree of men" or the "ultimate term of perfection," as Maimonides held, for which reason prophecy requires an external "sign" to verify its authenticity. With his critique of prophecy Spinoza not only denied the epistemic superiority of the biblical text, which has been presupposed by all Jewish philosophers since Philo, he also rejected the Maimonidean attempt to interpret the

Bible esoterically. Because there is no hidden truth behind the surface of the Bible, Spinoza charged Maimonides and his followers with an attempt to make Scripture present the same teachings as pagan philosophers.

For Spinoza truth is not a property of Scripture, as Jewish philosophers since Philo had maintained, but a characteristic of the method of interpreting Scripture. Differentiating between the meaning of Scripture and its truth, Spinoza asserted that the meaning must be found solely from the usage of language, for which mastery of Hebrew grammar is absolutely necessary. The Bible does not accommodate itself to human limitations; rather, radicalizing earlier ideas found in rabbinic literature, the Bible speaks the only language it can speak, namely, a human language. To the extent that the Bible does have a universal message, it has nothing to do with philosophy or science but with morality, namely, the commandment to love one's neighbor. This message, Spinoza believed, is the reason why the Bible is still politically relevant, even though the political order established by Moses in the Bible no longer exists. The Bible teaches against religious intolerance and persecution, and in this regard the Bible is the basis of universal ethics; yet the Bible is not an exceptional, or privileged text. To treat the Bible as such is itself the result of "prejudice," a harmful habit of thought that hinders clear thinking. In short, the Bible has no cognitive significance or authority. It rather reflects the ordinary conception of God as imagined by common people of the time, among whom were the prophets.

Spinoza regarded the editorial work of the Bible, which he ascribed to Ezra, as far from perfect, because the text of the Bible was put together at a considerably later time from the events recorded. Through close reading of the text, Spinoza attempted to show that biblical religion developed over time. Spinoza portrayed Moses strictly as a legislator and political leader who single-handedly ruled a mass of ex-slaves who were incapable of self-governance. The law that Moses gave Israel left no free choice for individuals, and Moses could induce the Israelites to observe the law only by promising material benefits. Spinoza then rehashed some of the Christian arguments about the nature of Mosaic law, which highlighted its earthly nature of biblical rewards and the absence of spiritual rewards. Biblical religion then deals only with temporal matters and has nothing to do with ultimate felicity, even though biblical religion provided a universal, ethical basis to a society.

Spinoza's devastating critique of the Bible undermined the foundation of rabbinic Judaism. Though Spinoza articulated his biblical criticism after he was excommunicated on July 27, 1657, his challenge was correctly assessed by the leaders of the Jewish community who expelled him. Refusing conversion to Christianity, Spinoza socialized with the Collegiants, an offshoot of a radical Calvinist group whose liberal theological and political views had been condemned by official Calvinism early in the century and who were hospitable to people alienated from their own religious communities. Spinoza also rejected a post at the University of Heidelberg in order to maintain his intellectual freedom, preferring to correspond with contemporary scientists such as Henry Oldenburg, the secretary of the Royal Society in London. Spinoza's critique of the Bible became known in England and inspired the English Deists of the late 17th and early 18th centuries. Some Deists attacked the Bible for its lack of a doctrine of immortality, whereas for others the dubious moral character of the prophets and other biblical heroes was a sign of the inferior quality of the Bible.

Spinoza's challenge to traditional Judaism would continue to reverberate throughout the modern period as biblical criticism became prevalent, especially among Protestant scholars. That challenge of biblical criticism, on the one hand, and the determination of Jews to integrate into European society, on the other hand, necessitated a reinterpretation of Judaism. The traditional belief in the revealed status of Scripture would have to be rethought

with new philosophical tools during the modern period. Modern Jewish philosophy would be articulated on the basis of Judaism's conversation with the Enlightenment, Kantianism, Hegelianism and Romanticism, affecting the approaches to the Bible. In modern times, as in the Middle Ages, the Bible continued to serve as the bridge between the particularistic beliefs of Judaism and non-Jewish cultures.

Modern Jewish Philosophy

Moses Mendelssohn (1729–1786) captures the transition from premodern to modern philosophy. Although he was a staunch advocate of Jewish emancipation and a proponent of the Jewish Enlightenment (Haskalah), Mendelssohn remained deeply committed to traditional Jewish life. At the same time, he also socialized with the leading intellectuals in Germany, who regarded him as spokesman of the German Enlightenment. Mendelssohn's views were shaped by German philosophers such as Gottfried Wilhelm Leibniz (1646–1716), Christian Wolff (1679–1754), and Gothold Ephraim Lessing (1729–1781) no less than by Maimonides and Spinoza.

Endorsing the Enlightenment concept of natural religion, Mendelssohn maintained that reason alone can prove that God exists, that God governs the universe through providence, and that the human soul is immortal. These three universal propositions are accessible to the human mind without a special revelation from God. In contrast to Jewish medieval philosophers, Mendelssohn held that revelation does not disclose any ideas that cannot be discovered by human reason. In terms of truth, there is only one source (viz. reason) rather than two (viz. reason and revelation). If natural religion requires no additional revelation, what then is Judaism? Mendelssohn answers that Judaism is not a revealed religion but a "revealed legislation." At Sinai God did not reveal any truths or doctrines, but only laws. Prior to the Sinaitic event, the ancient Israelites already reached a level of intellectual development resulting in the knowledge of three pillars of natural religion. What distinguishes Jews from non-Jews is not religion, which is common to all humans endowed with reason, but a specific legislation obligatory to Jews only. The revealed legislation charts the particular path that Israel alone must follow in order to attain the felicity to which all human beings aspire. And since the laws were revealed by God rather than discovered by humans, they could neither be changed nor abrogated. In Mendelssohn's mind, loyalty to the laws of Judaism was fully compatible with the rationalist universalism of the Enlightenment.

The Bible stood at the center of Mendelssohn's attempts to modernize the Jews and prepare them for integration into European society. He translated parts of the Bible into German but printed the translation in Hebrew characters in order to make it accessible to Yiddish-speaking Jews whom he wished to wean away from the language that symbolized Jewish cultural backwardness. In additional to the translation of the Bible, Mendelssohn composed and edited commentaries in Hebrew in order to offer Jews an alternative to Protestant biblical commentaries. Like his medieval predecessors, Mendelssohn began his exegetical endeavor by composing a commentary on Ecclesiastes (1768–1769), but in contrast to them Mendelssohn saw Ecclesiastes in a philosophical light that attributed its skepticism to imagined conversation partners. On the basis of medieval commentaries, especially by Rashi, Radak, and Abraham Ibn Ezra, Mendelssohn focused on the literal meaning of the biblical text and on the accent marks of the Masoretic Text in order to clarify Ecclesiastes' philosophical stance. Ecclesiastes, Mendelssohn argued, taught no theoretical knowledge but only practical knowledge conducive to moral improvement and in accord with contemporary science. Nonetheless, Mendelssohn still defended the traditional Jewish view that King Solomon was the author of Ecclesiastes and perpetuated the notion that the ancient king was the source of all known sciences. Hence, there is

no surprise that even Harvey's theory of blood circulation (1628) is alluded to, according to Mendelssohn, in Eccl. 12.6: "Before the silver cord snaps and the golden bowl crashes, the jar is shattered at the spring and the jug is smashed at the cistern" (David Sorkin, *Moses Mendelssohn and the Religion of Enlightenment* [Berkeley and Los Angeles: University of California Press, 1996], p. 43). While few Jews paid attention to Mendelssohn's commentary on Ecclesiastes, German biblical scholars translated it into German and published it in 1771.

During the 1770s Mendelssohn worked on the German translation of the Psalms, which he regarded as a seminal biblical text for moral and spiritual edification. Familiar with the aesthetic theories of the 18th century, Mendelssohn considered the Psalms the highest exemplar of the sublime and believed that the Psalms illustrate how theology and aesthetics are intertwined. He translated the Psalms into German in order to show the glory of Hebrew lyric poetry alongside classical and Nordic poetry and also in order to replace existing German translations of the Psalms, especially Luther's, even though Mendelssohn held that translation in great esteem and retained some of its most elegant parts. The translation of the Psalms was published in 1785 and was well received by Jews throughout Europe.

The crown of Mendelssohn's biblical studies and educational activities was the translation of the Torah into German with an accompanying Hebrew commentary (known as *Bi'ur*, 1780–1783). With the help of the grammarian Solomon Dubno (1738–1813), Mendelssohn focused on the literal meaning of the text *(peshat)*, often relying on the commentary of Abraham Ibn Ezra, in an attempt to respond to the challenges of contemporary biblical criticism. While Mendelssohn considered the literal meaning to be primary, he still defended the legitimacy of rabbinic homiletical exegesis *(derash)*. Mendelssohn's translation and commentaries on the Torah was a true group effort. Dubno departed from the project before completing the assigned commentary on Genesis, but other Jewish Enlightenment figures joined it. Naphtali Hertz Wessley (1725–1805) wrote the commentary on Leviticus, and Hertz Homberg (1749–1841) and Aaron Jaroslav commented on Numbers and Deuteronomy. When the five volumes were reissued as one volume, under the title *Sefer Netivot ha-Shalom (The Book of the Paths of Peace)*, Mendelssohn composed a new introduction, titled *'Or Netivah (Light for the Path)*, spelling out the principles of the entire enterprise.

According to Mendelssohn the Bible is not about revealed truth but about "trust and faith that result in Israel's obedience through the Commandments, which are the preeminent form of practical knowledge" (Sorkin, p. 55). Since Mendelssohn understood the Bible as a record of the unique covenantal relationship between God and Israel, his views were closer to Judah Halevi's than to Maimonides's. With Halevi, Mendelssohn held that Sinai was a historical, collective event in which Moses directly heard God's speech and wrote it down. Contrary to Maimonides, Mendelssohn regarded the Hebrew language not as a conventional human language but as a divine language. Even the accents of the Masoretic texts, said Mendelssohn, have a divine source. Moses could transmit divine communication to Joshua so accurately because of the unique features of the Hebrew language: It is the only language whose written form retains the oral nature of all languages. The task of the translator and commentator is to capture the sense of the text, and Mendelssohn took as his model the ancient Aramaic translator of the Bible, Onkelos, regarded as authoritative by the rabbinic tradition. The emphasis on the unique orality of the biblical text was Mendelssohn's best proof against the Documentary Hypothesis, which was based on the lateness of the Masoretic Text. In Mendelssohn's view the oral tradition preserved the way God had spoken, which Moses duly recorded. Mendelssohn was not oblivious to the historical study of the Bible, but he believed that it could only help establish the traditional Jewish faith.

Mendelssohn's idiosyncratic blend of Jewish traditionalism and Enlightenment rationalism was difficult to perpetuate to the next generation. Traditional Jews, suspicious of the Emancipation and its perils, were critical of his biblical translation and commentaries; and the more radical disciples who desired full integration into German culture found his observance of Jewish law a hindrance to their goal. Even Mendelssohn's own children failed to reconcile the two worlds of their father; all but one of his six children converted to Christianity. Ironically, Christian contemporaries of Mendelssohn understood his claim that Judaism is a revealed legislation to mean that Judaism is a legalistic, obsolete fossil of an ancient era, a ceremonial law that has no vitality. This view was accepted by Immanuel Kant and through him became commonplace among German intellectuals of the 19th century.

For Jews in Germany and Central Europe, the 19th century consisted of the relentless struggle to gain civil rights and social acceptance, the rise of *Wissenschaft des Judentums* (the scientific study of Judaism), and the drive to reform Judaism from within. Whereas the emancipation of the Jews was possible because of the French Revolution, the defeats of Napoleon rolled the process back as anti-Jewish fulminations swept through Germany. The violence against Jews in Bavaria during the Hep!Hep! riots of 1819 accentuated Jewish insecurity and manifested the unwillingness of German society to see Jews as equals. In response, a group of Jewish scholars convened in Berlin in November 1819 to found the Society *(Verein)* for the Culture and Scientific Study of the Jews. Its agenda was to examine the entire records of the Jewish past—biblical and rabbinic—from a scientific perspective and aided with new tools of contemporary science, especially history and philology. The members of the society had different interests and agendas: Some wished to show how Judaism contributed to Western civilization, in order to secure a position in German academia, while others were mostly interested in ameliorating the situation of the Jews and improving Jewish education. Still others were primarily concerned with determining what is subject to change in Judaism, and hence obsolete, as opposed to the eternal essence of Judaism that is not subject to change. Although their research into the Jewish past was of highest academic quality, it did not lead to university posts. In frustration, the Jewish scholars created their own institutions of higher learning, that is, rabbinical seminaries in which Jewish students studied the entire gamut of Jewish literary heritage scientifically and objectively.

The critical stance of *Wissenschaft des Judentums* scholarship was mainly directed toward postbiblical Judaism, but the Bible could not remain immune to it. In 1810 a student of Mendelssohn, Yehuda Leib ben Ze'ev, published his *Mavo' 'el Mikra'ey Kodesh (Introduction to Holy Scriptures)*, which was modeled after J. C. Eichhorn's study by the same title, in which he established the composite nature of the book of Isaiah, among other critical observations. Leopold Zunz (1794–1886) in his *The Religious Teachings of the Jews, Historically Developed (Die gottesdienstlichen Vortraege der Juden, historisch entwickelt* [1832]) advanced daring new theses regarding the books of Chronicles and the Psalter. Isaac Samuel Reggio (1784–1855) and Shlomo Yehudah Rapoport (1790–1867) also advanced critical theses regarding Isaiah and Psalms. What was commonplace among Protestant biblical critics of the 19th century was beginning to make inroads in Jewish scholarship. A new Jewish philosophy was needed to integrate contemporary historical research into a new schema. It was provided by Nachman Krochmal (1785–1840).

Krochmal was the first modern Jewish philosopher to make not only the Jewish religion but also the Jewish people a subject for philosophic investigation, thereby providing a philosophic explanation of Jewish history. His philosophic model was Georg Wilhelm Friedrich Hegel (1770–1831), though he was also deeply influenced by Giambattista Vico (1668–1744), Johan Gottfried Herder (1744–1803), and the German Idealists, Friedrich von Schlegel (1772–1829) and Friedrich Wilhelm Joseph von Schelling (1775–1854). No less central to Krochmal's reinterpretation of Judaism were the views of Maimonides, Ibn Ezra, Spinoza, and Mendelssohn, as well as the teachings of kabbalah. Krochmal's *Moreh Nevukhei Ha-Zeman (The Guide for the Perplexed of This Time)* was written in 1840 and published posthumously in 1851, edited by Leopold Zunz. The title, a play on Maimonides' great work, was no accident: Krochmal wished to accomplish for the Jews of his generation what Maimonides did for his contemporaries: a comprehensive reconciliation of Judaism with the reigning philosophy. Since the Aristotelianism of Maimonides was now obsolete, and Maimonides' emphasis on God's radical otherness was religiously unsatisfying, a reconceptualization of Judaism in terms of the reigning Idealist philosophy was now in order. The Neoplatonic ontology of Ibn Ezra's philosophy and the teachings of kabbalah served Krochmal to prove that Judaism is a metaphysical system that is not only compatible with German Idealism, but that Judaism is the most refined expression of the Absolute Spirit.

Writing in Hebrew to the proponents of Jewish Enlightenment in Galicia, Bohemia, Moravia, and Italy, who were disoriented by modernity but who had not lost their Jewish commitment, Krochmal introduced the post-Kantian understanding of the relationship between religion and philosophy. For Krochmal "religion and philosophy are essentially identical, in that both represent processes of speculation, which are equal in their apprehension of truth" (Jay M. Harris, *Nachman Krochmal: Guiding the Perplexed of the Modern Ages* [New York: New York University Press, 1991], p. 26). But whereas philosophy conceives of Spirit in the form of concepts, religion does so through representations *(Vorstellungen)*. The representation is a form of consciousness higher than that of sensation and observation but lower than that of concept. The representations of religion (i.e., the metaphors and symbols) "are not expressions of poetic genius and creativity; rather, they are rooted in the universal mind—the essence of human spirituality—and therefore virtually all metaphors are equivalent in many different languages" (Harris, p. 27). Krochmal's view of prophetic activity would thus place him between Maimonides and Spinoza. While agreeing with Maimonides that there is a relationship between theology and truth, Krochmal also was in agreement with Spinoza that prophets and theologians cannot be considered philosophers.

For Krochmal, who defined religion as the belief in spiritual powers, biblical religion is the highest form of religion; it contains the same faith in the Absolute Spirit which is present in the ultimate truth of philosophy. Krochmal's biblical studies and his philosophy of history were to document this claim. Krochmal was fully aware that much of biblical criticism was at odds with prevailing Jewish traditional ideas, but he believed that proper understanding of the Bible and postbiblical history could show both the continuity of Jewish faith and its evolution over time. With detailed knowledge of rabbinic Jewish exegesis and modern biblical criticism, Krochmal was intent to prove that the Rabbis in fact shared the assumptions of the modern critics. Thus in regard to the book of Isaiah, Krochmal argues that the Rabbis themselves were aware of the composite nature of the book and its rather late date of composition. To his satisfaction, he manages to prove that critical conclusions about Isaiah are compatible with traditional sensibilities.

Similarly, Krochmal uses the rabbinic debate about the doubtful sanctity of Ecclesiastes (*m. Yad.* 3:5) to prove that "wisdom, and especially Solomon's wisdom, is acknowledged to be a gift from God, and therefore the Rabbis could not have denigrated Qohelet [Ecclesiastes] for being simply a product of Solomon's mind, for this would, in fact, confer upon it sufficient status to be worthy of canonization" (Harris, p. 176). The very fact that the Rabbis debated it proved to him that they entertained the possibility that the book was not authored by Solomon but by a later author. The Rabbis, Krochmal maintains, were equally aware of the late date of composition of some of the psalms, even as late as 2nd century BCE, notwithstanding the fact that the tradition ascribed them to King David. Traditional Jews, then, should not ignore contemporary biblical scholarship but rather incorporate it into their own understanding of the tradition since it is in many ways consonant with earlier traditions. Krochmal believed that contemporary modern biblical scholarship proves his philosophy of history: Jewish creativity and vitality is eternal and ever-evolving. Unlike any other nation that exhibits the finite cycle of growth, maturation, and disintegration, the Jewish people is eternal. Due to its special relationship with God, the Absolute Spirit, the Jewish people repeatedly renews its national life, manifesting the eternal Absolute Spirit.

Whereas Krochmal articulated a Jewish philosophy that addressed the perplexity of East European Enlightened Jews who wished to remain loyal to Judaism, in Germany the dominant secular philosopher who shaped Jewish thinking was not Hegel and other Idealist philosophers, but Immanuel Kant (1724–1804). His claim that human beings are in principle unable to have certain knowledge about God, the soul, and the origin of the universe was intended not to abolish faith, but to make room for it. For Kant, faith was rational, an apprehension of the greatest good and striving toward it. Although Kant denied the possibility of metaphysics and limited the scope of theoretical, demonstrative knowledge to the phenomenal world of sense perception, he did not deny the existence of God. Indeed, reason must postulate the existence of God, but the "only content we can ascribe to our idea of God is moral." God is not the giver of the moral law but the "necessary condition for the possibility of the summum bonum," i.e., for the "distribution of happiness in exact proportion to morality" (*Critique of Practical Reason*, trans. Beck [1956], p. 129). The existence of God is postulated in order to fulfill a fundamental requirement of the moral law, namely, that the virtuous man is worthy of happiness. True religion, in contrast to clericalism, is, therefore, an ethical religion in which the kingdom of God is nothing else than the ethical commonwealth: "If God is to be found at all, it is not behind nature but behind moral law" (Kenneth Seeskin, *Jewish Philosophy in a Secular Age* [Albany: State University of New York Press, 1990], p. 58). So long as we think about God as a moral agent, we cannot be accused of anthropomorphism, since morality has no empirical content. God cannot do otherwise than act as is morally required. Yet Kant also showed that historical religion did not develop in ignorance of the moral law. He wants to claim that actual religions have in one way or another approached the ideal of the pure founded on a universal conception of humanity and a commitment to its moral improvement. Unless actual religion approached this ideal it would be impossible for Kant to argue that it is engraved on each of our hearts. Not surprisingly, Kant's depiction of Judaism was anything but complimentary. Following Spinoza and Mendelssohn, Kant viewed Judaism as a mere national-political entity, contending that it fails to satisfy the essential criteria of religion in that it fails to inculcate the appropriate inner morals, demanding only external obedience to statutes and law. Judaism, Kant said in accord with traditional Christian perception, is concerned only with things of this world and lacks any formulation of the concept of immortality.

Kant's philosophic formulation of religion accorded with the orientation of modern liberal Judaism. Seeking to distill the essence of Judaism that remained constant throughout the process of change over time, Reform theologians defined the essence of Judaism as ethical monotheism. Kant's understanding of the moral law as rational self-legislation was believed to be totally congruent with the biblical emphasis on "duty" and "right." The Jewish followers of Kant reinterpreted Judaism in such a way that it would conform to Kant's formulation of religion, while at the same time rejecting Kant's critique of Judaism.

Hermann Cohen (1842–1918), the towering Jewish philosopher of the late 19th century, was able to show how a Neo-Kantian reading of Judaism leads to universalizing the revealed message of the Bible. Benefiting from the final success of the Emancipation in Germany, Cohen held a regular academic post at the University of Marburg, reformulating the principles of Kantian philosophy. While rethinking Kant during the 1870s, Cohen also witnessed the rise of modern anti-Semitism as a backlash to the Emancipation. In his *A Public Declaration Concerning the Jewish Question* (*Ein Bekenntnis zur Judenfrage* [1880]), Cohen called for the total integration of German Jewry into German society, but while calling Jews to take their religion seriously. Cohen got involved in a public defense of Judaism against anti-Semitic charges that according to the Talmud the laws of the Torah apply only to Jews and not to relations between Jews and Christians. He rejected this reading and published his view that Israel's chosenness by God from the outset had universal scope: Since God is the one who loves the stranger, Israel is chosen as a mission to mankind.

Cohen did not write a commentary on the Bible, but his main exposition of Jewish philosophy—*Religion of Reason out of the Sources of Judaism*—takes most of its data from the Bible. Rejecting Kant's portrayal of Judaism, Cohen argued that when properly understood "the ancient sources and their received interpretation are much closer to a morally pure faith than Kant thought" (Seeskin, *Jewish Philosophy*, p. 160). Cohen does not say that Judaism is the religion of reason, but rather that the ideas of a purely rational faith can be found in Jewish sources, first among them the Bible. At the University of Marburg, Cohen's colleagues included Julius Wellhausen, the most important biblical scholar of the time. Cohen's reformulation of biblical religion could be viewed as an attempt to reject some of the claims of Wellhausen and his followers. Cohen's religion is strictly ethical religion or religion of ethics. Morality is an infinite task of self-sanctification, precisely as Lev. 11.44 ("For I the LORD am your God: you shall sanctify yourselves and be holy, for I am holy") teaches. For Cohen, however, the laws of ancient Israel are of universal scope. Precisely because there is only one God, there can be only one law applicable to all people who share a common dignity (Lev. 19.34; 24.22). The social legislation of the Bible is not restricted to Jews only but applies to the "stranger," namely to all humans. Cohen interpreted the command to love the stranger along the lines of Kantian philosophy: It is not a commandment forced on us by a supernatural being but a duty that we in our better moments would impose on ourselves. The Bible itself, especially the book of Deuteronomy, spells out the need to bridge the gap between what is and what ought to be.

Following a Protestant model, in the teachings of prophets Cohen found the most refined expression of the relationship between humanity and God. The prophets made pity and sympathy for others the cornerstone of their moral teachings. Through empathy with the suffering of my neighbor I am able to encounter the person as a Thou rather than merely as an instance of humanity. The main challenge to humanity is not impending death but the experience of poverty, about which the prophets were deeply concerned (Cohen, *Religion of Reason*, tr. Kaplan [New York, 1972], pp. 135–136). Ethics, then, needs the idea of a perfect being to guarantee that our effort to perfect the world has some hope of succeeding. God does not only sustain the world but shows compassion for those who suffer and forgives those whose quest for self-sanctification falls short. The forgiveness of sin brings God into relation with each person, who remains a sinner in constant need of God. Thus, religion goes beyond ethics; religion does not negate our duties as moral agents but provides us with a richer conception of the task of fulfilling them.

Hermann Cohen influenced an entire class of German Jewish philosophers, including Ernest Cassirer (1874–1945), Julius Guttmann (1880–1950), Leo Baeck (1873–1956), Joseph B. Soloveitchik (1903–1993), and Steven Schwarzchild (1924–1989), as well as the work of the biblical scholar Yehezkel Kaufmann (1889–1963). After resigning from his post in Marburg, Cohen joined the *Academie für die Wissenschaft des Judentums* in Berlin, calling on Jewish scholars not to divorce scientific study from inner piety. His aim was to encourage Jewish scholars to establish an intimate bond between their scholarly and spiritual interests. Cohen's disciple Franz Rosenzweig would later perpetuate the fiction that in later life Cohen renounced his commitment to religion of reason; in truth Cohen remained consistent throughout his life, advocating the idealization of Judaism through a correct reading of the Bible.

After Cohen's death in 1918, Jewish philosophy in Germany would be dominated by two main figures—Martin Buber (1878–1965) and Franz Rosenzweig (1886–1929)—who also collaborated on a new translation of the Bible into German. The goal of that translation was precisely the opposite of Mendelssohn's enterprise a century and a half earlier: Whereas Mendelssohn wanted the Jews of his day to master the German language in order to integrate into German society, the Buber-Rosenzweig translation of the Bible intended to Hebraicize the Bible for German Jewish readers who had been thoroughly integrated into German culture and who had been emotionally and practically distanced from Judaism. The translation begun in 1925 was completed in 1961 by Buber alone after many intermissions, and long after Rosenzweig's untimely death in 1929. Tragically, when that new translation of the Bible into German was completed, German Jewry, for whom it was intended, was no longer in existence.

Despite their collaboration and deep respect for each other, Buber and Rosenzweig did not share the same understanding of the Bible. For Buber the language of the Bible was inseparable from the living Hebrew language and the foundational stratum of Jewish culture. Along with other Jewish biblical scholars such as Simon Bernfeld (1860–1940), Abraham Kahana (1874–1946), Benno Jacob (1862–1945), Moses David Cassuto (1883–1951), Yehezkel Kaufmann (1889–1963), Moses Hirsch Segal (1877–1968), and Naphtali Herz Tur-Sinai (1886–1973), Buber rejected the dominant readings of the Bible by Protestant theologians. Instead of theologizing the Bible, these scholars attempted to listen to the Bible's own unique voice, emphasize the rhythm of living utterance reflected in it, trace the associative elements that lead the attentive listener to the original meaning of the living utterance, and explore the concrete meaning and original dynamics of basic words. Unlike some of his Jewish cohorts, Buber had no difficulty maintaining a critical distance from the biblical text or sorting out the seeming contradictions and inconsistencies of the Bible without feeling apologetic about it. At the same time, Buber developed distinctive linguistic tools that enabled him to wrest the lived experience from the biblical text.

With Rosenzweig, Buber introduced the search for key-words (Leitwörter) repeated in a given text with stubborn consistency, conveying its meaning. The key words force the listener not only to concentrate in a particular manner but also to participate in the experience evoked by the biblical text. Buber's translation attempted to retain the identity of each Hebrew root without blurring its manifold associations; if the semantic field of German words was too narrow in scope, Buber created new compound words in which the added word or root explained the particular development of a basic root. Through this message, Buber attempted to penetrate the primordial life of the spoken word as it reflected the unique otherness of the speaker. In this regard, Buber's translation/interpretation of the Bible stood in diametrical opposition to medieval philosophical commentaries that highlighted the abstract, philosophical content of the Bible.

Buber's attempt to recapture the concrete, living, unique human utterance of the biblical text differed from the approach of his collaborator, Franz Rosenzweig. For him, the goal of the translation was to break through the linguistic particularity of the text to the supra-linguistic language without word. He did not compose a commentary on the Bible but his philosophical magnum opus, Der Stern der Erlosung (The Star of Redemption), presented his biblical theology as an alternative to Western philosophy. For Rosenzweig, not only is revelation an encounter with the Other, revelatory speech is dialogical. Rosenzweig states: "The ways of God are different from the ways of man, but the word of God and the word of man are the same. What man hears in his heart as his own human speech is the very word which comes out of God's mouth" (The Star of Redemption, trans. William W. Hallo [Boston: Beacon Press, 1972], p. 151). Accordingly Rosenzweig reinterpreted the prophetic speech: "The prophet does not mediate between God and man. He does not receive revelation in order to pass it on; rather, the voice of God sounds forth directly from within him, God speaks as 'I' directly from within him." (Star, p. 178). In the Bible Rosenzweig found the "I" addressed by God. Biblical literature is unique because it authenticates the renewal of the divine word.

Buber, by contrast, did not believe that through the Bible one can still hear the voice of the living God, because he considered the Bible itself to be a human response to the encounter with God. Though we cannot hear the voice of God, we can hear the voice of those who were in the presence of God. In doing so, the listener/reader stands again in the presence of God. The encounter with God, according to Buber, is a content-less experience that cannot be rendered propositionally. Developing Cohen's emphasis on correlation, Buber highlighted the relational nature of reality. All existence has two relational modalities: an I-It or an I-Thou. In Kantian terms, the former modality treats the other as a means to an end, whereas the latter treats the other as an end for its own sake. The I-Thou is the ideal relationship that, alas, cannot be maintained over time, since it necessarily disintegrates into I-It, objectifying the other. The only Thou that cannot be objectified is God, the Eternal Thou. Revelation, for Buber, is not a single event in the remote past, but an ongoing encounter with the presence of God. Similarly, the revelation at Sinai did not signify the disclosure of a legal code but a living experience of God's immediate presence. The spokenness (Geschprochenheit) of the Bible captures that direct encounter between God and the people of the time. The intent of the new German translation was to come as close as possible to the raw spokenness of the Bible. For Buber the engagement in biblical studies in Nazi Germany was an act of spiritual resistance. He finally departed from Germany in 1938 and settled in Israel (then called Palestine) where he continued the translation enterprise and went on to compose various essays on the Bible, the most important of which was *Moses*, written in 1944 and published in 1946. These midrashic essays illustrated Buber's own dialogical relationship with the biblical text, attempting to retrieve the past experience in order to stand once again in the presence of God.

In 1937, just a year before he departed from Germany, Buber appointed Abraham Joshua Heschel (1907–1972) to succeed him as supervisor of adult education in Germany and director of the *Jüdisches Lehrhaus* at Frankfurt am Main, the main institutional context for the revitalization of Jewish life in Germany since the 1920s. The Nazis, however, deported Heschel (who was a Polish Jew) back to Poland in 1938, and after several months of teaching in Warsaw he was able to emigrate to England and from there to the United States in 1940. What Buber attempted to accomplish for the Jews of Germany, Heschel attempted to accomplish, with partial success, for American Jews. It was a dialogical reinterpretation of Judaism that addressed the predicament of modernity, its gnawing doubts and rootlessness. The tragedy of the modern person is the loss of the ability to ask the right questions to

which the Bible is the answer. Heschel powerfully stated the challenge facing humanity in the second half of the 20th century: "Our problem . . . is how to share the certainty of Israel that the Bible contains that which God wants us to know and to hearken to; how to attain a collective sense for the presence of God in the biblical words. In this problem lies the dilemma of our fate, and in the answer lies the dawn or the doom" (*God in Search of Man: A Philosophy of Judaism* [New York: Farrar Straus and Giroux, 1955], p. 246). In the return to the Bible lies the solution to the modern predicament of Jews and non-Jews alike.

In continuity with Buber, Heschel denied that the Bible is a philosophical text or that the God of the Bible is a philosophical abstraction or a psychological projection. Rather, God is a living reality who takes passionate interest in the life of His creatures, or as Heschel's celebrated title put it, God is in search of man. Indeed, "the Bible is not primarily man's vision of God, but God's vision of man" (*Man Is Not Alone: A Philosophy of Religion* [New York: Farrar Straus and Giroux, 1951], p. 129). Heschel then placed God at the center of the divine-human drama told in the Bible, a long story of God's active pursuit of a rebellious Israel. The biblical text itself came into being as a response to God's revealing power. In Heschel's understanding of the Bible, the question of authorship, which exercised so much of modern biblical scholarship, is a moot point. The Bible is a product of divine and human authorships.

Heschel viewed attachment to the Bible to be essential to continued Jewish existence. The destiny of the Jewish people is to be a "community in whom the Bible lives on." Israel must remain dedicated to the Bible in order for the Bible to remain "a sublime challenge and source of illumination for the world." Since the Bible is "the frontier of the spirit" that "shows the way of God with man and the way of man with God, "had the Bible not been preserved, an invaluable pathway to God would be lost. The current spiritual poverty throughout the world is due largely to a "growing alienation from the Bible" (*God in Search of Man*, pp. 252, 238). Heschel viewed the Bible as the deepest alternative to the spiritual malaise of the 20th century, the only hope for the revival of divine wisdom, justice and compassion. Heschel was committed to reengagement with the Bible in order to preserve the Jewish faith for the future.

In his doctoral dissertation at the University of Berlin, *Die Prophetie* (1933), which was later published in an expanded form in *The Prophets* (1962), Heschel articulated the doctrine of divine pathos according to which "God does not reveal himself in an abstract absoluteness, but in a personal and intimate relation to the world. . . . God is also moved and affected by what happens in the world, and reacts accordingly" (Heschel, *The Prophets* [New York: Harper and Row, 1962], pp. 223–224). "It is precisely because God is filled with pathos for human beings that they may respond with sympathy to God. . . . The prophetic faith is thus a sympathetic response to divine pathos" (John C. Merkle, "Heschel's Theology of Divine Pathos," in John C. Merkle (ed.), *Abraham Joshua Heschel: Exploring His Life and Thought* [London and New York, 1985], p. 81).

Heschel's uncanny ability to present the biblical faith as the answer to the modern predicament was partially responsible for the spiritual revival of Judaism in America during the 1960s and 1970s. Yet it is hard to gauge whether Heschel's enormous fame as a cultural icon actually led American Jews in search of Jewish renewal back to the study of the Bible. Jewish Studies programs began to sprout in the 1970s at the same time that Religious Studies departments were established in secular universities. Courses in the Bible were then offered as part of the academic study of religion, and the Bible was now studied either as an ancient Near Eastern document, or as sophisticated "literature" that illustrated many of the linguistic subtleties of contemporary literary theories, or as a source of information about the socio-cultural setting of the framers of the biblical canon. For Jewish

Studies professors in American universities, the philosophic import of the Bible has become neglected, presumably because taking the biblical text as Scripture, namely, as an existentially meaningful text, is perceived as belonging in the denominational seminaries but not in the secular university.

Three contemporary Jewish philosophical theologians—Norbert M. Samuelson (b. 1936), David R. Blumenthal (b. 1938) and Judith Plaskow (b. 1947)—challenge this convention, illustrating the continued relevance of the Bible for contemporary Jewish thought and the indebtedness to Buber and Heschel. Samuelson illustrates how the Bible is engaged in the context of the dialogue between science and religion. Though his academic training was in analytic philosophy and medieval Jewish philosophy, Samuelson regards the task of Jewish philosophy to be predominantly constructive rather than historical or analytical. Since what is true in the Bible must be in accord with what is known to be true in contemporary science, if the literal meaning of the biblical text is in conflict with contemporary science, it could not be the correct reading of the text. Samuelson's reading of the creation narrative shows how the biblical story of creation accords with contemporary physics. (See Norbert M. Samuelson, *The First Seven Days: A Philosophical Commentary on the Creation of Genesis* [Atlanta: Scholars Press, 1992]; *Judaism and the Doctrine of Creation* [Cambridge: Cambridge University Press, 1994].) Samuelson's theory of revelation is very much in accord with Buber's, but his approach to the biblical text is similar to medieval biblical exegesis, in that it pays close attention to contemporary science.

Like Samuelson, David Blumenthal was trained as a historian of medieval Jewish philosophy, but has devoted his efforts to writing constructive Jewish philosophy. If for Samuelson contemporary science is the main challenge to the meaning of the Bible, for Blumenthal the point of departure is the trauma of the Holocaust. Applying post-Structuralist strategies to the Psalms, Blumenthal attempts to construct a post-Holocaust Jewish theology by therapeutically confronting the personal God of Israel as an abusive deity (David R. Blumenthal, *Facing the Abusing God: A Theology of Protest* [Louisville: Westminster/John Knox Press, 1993], esp. pp. 57–192). Selecting Pss. 128, 44, 109, and 27 for close reading, Blumenthal offers not only his own new translation of the psalms but also four simultaneous commentaries. The first commentary is a philological commentary based on existing biblical scholarship. The second commentary is written under the influence of Heschel, Blumenthal's teacher, in an attempt to capture the spiritual tradition of Hasidism. The third commentary focuses "on the emotional attitudes which the psalmist tradition wishes us to cultivate," and the fourth commentary attempts "to respond to Jacque Derrida, Michel Foucault, Sigmund Freud, Alice Miller, Carol Gilligan, Jessica Benjamin, Elie Wiesel and others in the calling-reading-proclaiming of the psalms" (pp. 58–60). By writing four simultaneous glosses on the biblical text, Blumenthal intentionally mimics the medieval Jewish exegetical tradition, clearly implying that he sees his work in continuity with medieval predecessors no less than an attempt to respond to psychoanalysis, deconstruction, feminism, and the Holocaust. It remains to be seen whether this reading will catch the imagination of American Jews.

At present the one contemporary Jewish theologian who has succeeded in influencing how some American Jews approach the Bible is Judith Plaskow, perhaps the best-known Jewish feminist (see "Women's Scholarly Writings," pp. 2000–2005). She has argued that Judaism is in need of healing not because of the Holocaust but because of the systematic and pernicious exclusion of women from the activity of scriptural interpretation. (See Judith Plaskow, *Standing Again at Sinai* [San Francisco: Harper and Row, 1990].) Women were present at Sinai but it was the male-centered rabbinic tradition that ignored, silenced, and marginalized women. A new reading of the Bible is necessary if Jewish women are to be restored to their rightful place within the tradition and become creative readers of their own sacred texts. Plaskow inaugurated an insightful feminist engagement with the Bible and rekindled a feminist midrashic discourse, but since most of those who engage in this enterprise are not philosophically trained, feminist biblical interpretations to date lack philosophical rigor.

Conclusion

In sum, our survey of the Bible in the Jewish philosophical tradition makes it clear that the Bible stood at the center of the Jewish philosophical enterprise. Through translations, interpretations, and commentaries, Jewish philosophers were able not only to negotiate the differences between Judaism and other cultures, but also to rethink Judaism anew by using new philosophic tools and theoretical paradigms. As each generation of Jewish philosophers asked, "What does the Bible say and what does it mean?" they were able to respond flexibly to changing historical circumstances and ponder the meaning of Judaism. Premodern and modern Jewish philosophers approached the Bible quite differently. Whereas the former presupposed that the Bible contains abstract, universal truths that are either identical to philosophy or can be explicated by philosophy, most (though not all) modern Jewish philosophers regarded the Bible as the record of divine-human direct, unmediated encounter. Accordingly, whereas the premodern Jewish philosophers composed philosophical commentaries on the Bible, modern Jewish philosophers have regarded the Bible as the source from which springs their Jewish theology. For all Jewish philosophers the pursuit of wisdom to which Israel is called by God can be accomplished through the encounter with the Bible itself.

[HAVA TIROSH-SAMUELSON]

The Bible in the Jewish Mystical Tradition

Background to the Jewish Mystical Tradition

Early Sources

The mystical tradition in Judaism is a multi-faceted phenomenon whose early roots reach back to the time of the Rabbis and that exerted religious influence well past the medieval era, when its full flowering occurred. It is not possible here to survey this tradition fully; it is a complex and by no means completely unified movement. Rather, this essay will concentrate on how the medieval mystical tradition, referred to as kabbalah, used the text of the Bible both as source and as guide for the mystical path. It is necessary first to define "mysticism," particularly as it developed in Judaism. Mysticism can be seen as the quest, either by individual adherents to a religious tradition or by groups of the like-minded, to experience the presence of God directly. The yearning to know God sometimes takes the form of an effort to recover such experiences believed to have been given to earlier figures in the tradition—Moses, the prophets—who were granted direct access to God. It can also be an effort to "see" the imageless God without the aid of images, in keeping with the commandment that God may not be represented by any image. Finally, the goal of this quest is sometimes the direct experience of God, while remaining oneself; sometimes, however, it is the individual's effort to return to the source of being to reunite with the Godhead even to the point of subsuming one's individuality in the infinite being of God. Mystical movements often arise when God is seen as most transcendent, and therefore most removed from ordinary human life: separate from the natural and human world, unknowable, incomprehensible.

Although specific influences on Jewish mysticism are often uncertain, one philosophical school did provide some of its leading ideas (as it did also for some forms of Christian and Islamic mysticism). That philosophy was Neoplatonism, especially as expressed in the writings of Plotinus (ca. 204–70 CE) who taught that there were three realms of being, designated by the technical term hypostases: the One, the unknowable, utterly simple, and self-sufficient source of all being; Mind (*Nous*), the determinative foundation of all existents that, by virtue of contemplating the One, manifests the unified power in the multiplicity of intelligible objects or Ideas; and Soul, the potency that contemplates Mind and thereby extends by acting upon its own ideas into the realm of difference and indeterminacy, the location within which the cosmos takes shape as a determinate, physical form. Soul mediates between the intelligible world, the world of Mind, and the material world. Physical matter, at the furthest remove from the One, is the lowest form of existence, and is the eternally receptive substratum in and by which all determinate existents receive their discrete form. The universe is balanced between emanation, or movement outward from the One, and contemplation or return, movement back toward the One. The One itself is indescribable, beyond all thought and transcending all efforts to speak of it. The individual soul, by the practice of contemplation, can attain union with the One, but this involves a series of purifications and renunciations to detach the soul from matter, from images, from ideas, and finally from all discursive reason, until it is able to achieve a vision of the invisible and union with the One. The stages of contemplation are often pictured as ascents or steps away from the world of matter and toward the One, and the process itself is described as "apophatic," literally, "speaking-away," that is, achieving an understanding of the One through negation—the One is not this, the One is not that—until every possible identification has been eliminated and the contemplative is left only with a void of thought in which the One can be indescribably experienced. This "apophatic" or negative way is contrasted with the affirmative, "kataphatic" way in which positive attributes are ascribed to the deity: God is good, loving, merciful, just, and so on.

The first major expression of mysticism within postbiblical Judaism can be found in the writings that make up the so-called *merkavah* ("chariot") or *heikhalot* ("palace") corpus. These terms are used to designate those texts, composed and redacted over a period of several centuries, that describe in detail the ascent of an individual through the heavenly realms, culminating with an ecstatic vision of the luminous form on the throne located in the seventh palace of the seventh heaven. The details of a vision of the divine chariot were first recorded in the book of Ezekiel, a prophet living in Babylonia in the sixth century BCE. The first use of the technical term *merkavah* to refer to Ezekiel's vision of the enthroned glory is found in the apocryphal Ecclesiasticus 49.8: "It was Ezekiel who saw the vision of glory, which God [*lit.* he] showed him above the chariot of the cherubim" (NRSV). While many of the themes in the biblical prophecy served as the exegetical basis for the visionary experiences elaborated in the *Merkavah* corpus, the essential difference between the prophetic theophany and mystical vision is evident. Closer to the spirit of the *Merkavah* works are remnants of heavenly ascents recorded in Jewish and Christian apocalyptic literature from the second century BCE to roughly the third century CE. It has been argued by some scholars that *Merkavah* mysticism is an outgrowth of Jewish apocalypticism, though some important differences are found as well. Another important link in this chain is the so-called *Angelic Liturgy* of the Qumran sectarians, otherwise known as the *Songs of the Sabbath Sacrifice*, as well as other liturgical fragments found among the Dead Sea Scrolls. While there is some uncertainty regarding the appropriateness of the term "mystical" to refer to the poetic descriptions of the angelic realm and the throne contained in these documents, there can be little doubt that the motifs discussed in these sources bear a striking resemblance to the main concerns of the *Heikhalot* literature.

One work that specifically had a deep and lasting influence on the development of the mystical tradition is *Sefer Yetzirah, Book of Formation*, which is dated anywhere from the third to ninth centuries. Properly speaking, the work should not be described as a single composition but rather as a composite of distinct literary strands that have been woven together through a complicated redactional process whose stages are not clearly discernible. (The title is derived from the verb *yatzar*, "form," in Gen. 2.7, 8, 19.) According to *Sefer Yetzirah*, the creation of the world was based on the "thirty-two paths of wisdom," the ten numbers and twenty-two letters of the Hebrew alphabet. According to one section in *Sefer Yetzirah* the *sefirot* ("ciphers" or numbers) are interpreted as the ten dimensions of the universe: north, south, east, west, up, down, beginning, end, good, evil. The individual letters of the alphabet each control various aspects of the creation, in the cosmos, in time, and in the body.

Sefer Yetzirah is a short work—less than 2,000 words—but it had great influence, especially because of commentaries on it, both scientific and mystical. Among those who wrote a scientific commentary on it was Saadia Gaon, in the 10th century (see the essay "Medieval Jewish Interpretation," pp. 1876–1900). Later, in the 12th century, mystics would take up many of its ideas and develop them.

Another seminal work, of uncertain date, is *Shi'ur Komah*, a mystical writing that consists of a physical description of God as a being of immense size. Although later writers, particularly Maimonides, condemned the work because of its anthropomorphic treatment of God, its defenders maintained that it was not meant to be taken literally, but was rather trying to convey a sense of God's infinite majesty.

The Medieval Period

Beginning in the 12th century, the kabbalistic movement grew within the Jewish communities in northern Spain and southern France, particularly in Provence. Kabbalah is a system of hidden or secret tradition that is seen as handing on from teacher to student the inner meaning of the biblical text. (The word "kabbalah" means "tradition.") It is not strictly speaking a mystical tradition; rather it is an esoteric one, meaning by that a teaching that is intended for only a small group, and thus one that is difficult to understand and master. (The opposite of esoteric is exoteric, teaching intended for a general audience.) Nevertheless, since the goal of kabbalah involves achieving a contemplative vision of divine reality, and therefore a closer approach to God, it has many elements of mystical thought as well. Rather than seeking an ascent to the divine throne, as the earlier mystics of the *heikhalot* and *merkavah* schools did, the kabbalists are now concerned with discovering the hidden nature of the divine reflected in the meaning of sacred texts. Along with this emphasis, the activity too has changed: from the mystical praxis of visual ascent to esoteric hermeneutics or scriptural interpretation. This leads to an intensified concentration on the text, even on its individual words and letters, that is unique to Jewish mysticism.

An influential work that began to circulate in the late 12th century, *Sefer ha-Bahir* or *Book of Brightness*, is generally regarded as the first work of kabbalistic symbolism. It bases itself partly on *Sefer Yetzirah*, in which the ten *sefirot* were seen as constitutive of the order of creation. In some sections of *Sefer ha-Bahir*, these ten attributes are expressive of the divine *pleroma* or fullness: They are emanations of the divine nature, and are expressive of the balance and harmony within the divine being. God contains various attributes, even opposites; and God contains both male and female aspects. The female aspect is the *shekhinah* or "Presence" of God; this Presence is where the divine realm and creation meet, the "Gate of Heaven" that permits contact with God. God's fullness or completeness includes the union between masculine and feminine aspects.

The most influential mystical writing, however, is *Sefer ha-Zohar, Book of Splendor*. This text, written largely in medieval Aramaic, purports to be biblical midrash from the 2nd century; it was actually written in the late 13th century, largely by Mosheh de Leon (d. 1305) and other kabbalists from the region in northern Spain known as Castile. It is therefore akin to an anthology, a collection of writings, rather than a work with a single author. The *Zohar* is presented as a mystical commentary on the Bible and fictional depictions of scenes from the life of the 2nd century Rabbi Shimeon bar Yoḥai and his disciples, whose discussions present the biblical interpretations. It also contains other material of a speculative nature.

The *Zohar* develops the idea of the *sefirot* or divine emanations into a full-fledged presentation of the nature of God and creation, and the relationship between them. The mysterious Godhead, *'Ein Sof* ("no end," the infinite, unknowable divine being) manifests itself through the ten *sefirot*, the realms of the divine world. These are: *Keter* ("crown"), the unknowable Godhead; *Hokhmah* ("wisdom"), the first stirring of creation, primal Torah; *Binah* ("understanding"), creation's first form; *Ḥesed* ("benevolence," "mercy," "loving-kindness"), divine love; *Gevurah* ("might"), the strength to control and punish; *Tif'eret* ("beauty"), the balance of opposites; *Netzaḥ* ("victory"), God's loving action; *Hod* ("majesty"), God's judging action; *Yesod* ("foundation"), the divine principle within creation; and *Malkhut* ("sovereignty"), the link between God and creation that is also called *Shekhinah* ("presence"). An additional aspect of these realms is the differentiation amounting to opposition between the left side (*Binah, Gevurah, Hod*), God's judgment, and the right side (*Hokhmah, Ḥesed, Netzaḥ*), God's love. God descends through these realms until the final manifestation in the *Shekhinah*. This Presence of God, the feminine aspect of the divine being, is also the ideal representation in the divine realm of the people Israel. The differing aspects of God, as represented in the *sefirot*, must come into balance—for instance, *Ḥesed* and *Gevurah* must reconcile with each other—and when they do the feminine *Shekhinah* can be in harmony with the masculine, higher *sefirot* and the fullness of God pours out into the world.

[THE EDITORS]

The Glorious Name and the Incarnate Torah

The place occupied by the Bible in the mystical imagination cultivated by various fraternities of kabbalists in the high Middle Ages, is, as one can imagine, enormous in scope, thematically, chronologically, and geographically speaking. Although one must be careful not to offer a definition of mysticism that would obscure the complexity and multifaceted nature of the phenomenon of Jewish mysticism, it is valid to suggest that a current that runs through the mystical landscape in Jewish history has been the quest to see God. Within the aniconic tradition of Judaism, this quest took the form of the paradoxical imagining of the imageless. The iconoclastic reverberations of biblical faith fostered a prodigious imaginative representation of the non-representable in Jewish mystic circles through the centuries where specific meditational practices were cultivated for the stated aim of attaining a vision of the invisible, the locus of that vision situated in the heart/imagination of the visionary, the site where the normative epistemic divisions between external and internal dissolved in the play of double mirroring.

A unique feature of Jewish mysticism in all of its historical manifestations has been the convergence of light and letter symbolism: The emanation of God's light coincides with the revelation of the divine name. It follows, moreover, that the experience of God's presence consisted of both an ocular and auditory dimension, that is, seeing and hearing are intertwined in mystical envisioning, to behold the invisible is to heed the ineffable. Even

within the Bible—see Deut. 28.58 and Ps. 72.19, for instance—the idea of "glory," *kavod* (lit. "weighty," that which impresses), was merged with the notion of the "name" *(shem)*, that is, the most sacred of names, YHVH. Hence, in place of the indwelling of the glory in the Tabernacle, *mikdash*, or Tent of Meeting, *'ohel mo'ed* (Exod. 25.8; 29.44–45; 40.34–35), there are references to God causing His name to dwell, *leshaken shemo* (Deut. 14.23; 16.2, 11; 26.2; see also 12.11: *lasum et shemo sham leshikhno*), in the place *(makom)* of his choosing, the Jerusalem Temple. In these biblical contexts, *shem* represents the divine Presence by metonymy, and thus *shem* and *kavod* were virtually synonymous: To speak of God causing His name to dwell is effectively to speak of God causing His glory to dwell. Nevertheless, the change in locution was not lost on subsequent mystical writers, for whom the substitution of terms meant a convergence of realities: a conception of the name that is embodied, the body that is the name.

The phrase *kevod* YHVH, accordingly, is read esoterically not as a genitive phrase (i.e., the X of Y), "the glory of the LORD," but as an appositive, "the glory [that is] the LORD." Just as the concept arose during the Second Temple period that the God of Israel had no visible, manifest form, so YHVH became the ineffable name, the name that cannot be vocalized as it is written, the name that demarcates the Presence that cannot be represented. The metaphysical assumption behind this mythopoeic belief—a belief that was expressed in *Heikhalot* texts, *Shi'ur Komah* fragments, early Jewish Neoplatonic writings, and kabbalistic works—is that body is letter, and letter body. This premise knits together the disparate strands of Jewish esotericism. The kabbalistic tradition, particularly by the 13th century, goes a step further and identifies the name with Torah. Moreover, since kabbalists assumed that the Tetragrammaton (YHVH) comprises within itself the twenty-two letters of the Hebrew alphabet, the mystical identification of Torah as the name, *ha-Shem*, incorporates the older notion that Torah consists of a polyphony of names that effectively make the divine present in the text. By assuming the identity of these different ideas, it is possible to substitute one for another: If the name is the glory, and the Torah is the name, it follows that the glory is the Torah. For kabbalists, the interchangeability of these terms meant that Torah was the incarnate form of divine Presence, which, at the height of prophetic vision, assumes a human shape (anthropos) in the heart of the visionary. This is the hermeneutical foundation for the kabbalistic understanding of Scripture: The scroll, rendered hyperliterally, constitutes the scriptural body of the divine.

The equation of the name and Torah thus yielded the notion of the textual body in which, or from which, those who read were led toward the text of the body. This incarnational theme, very significant for understanding the mystical approach to Scripture, is quite ancient, though the precise formulation is not attested until the 12th and 13th centuries. By the late Middle Ages, moreover, Neoplatonic influence had impacted the Jewish religious philosophies promulgated by elitist rabbinic circles throughout Europe, North Africa, and the Mediterranean countries, to the point that it was no longer tenable to conceive of presence and absence as antithetical; on the contrary, since God was widely conceived as the existence whose essence could not be fathomed by the human mind, the apophatic (negative) and kataphatic (positive) responses could not be credibly dissociated: The "absence" of all positive attributes, including "presence" itself, was the manifestation of the divine, and thus "absence" equals "presence," presence signifies absence in the absence of presence.

The unique contribution of medieval kabbalists is to view YHVH, the most sacred of divine names, as comprising all the letters of the Hebrew alphabet. In line with the philosophical stance articulated by Judah Halevi (see "The Bible in the Jewish Philosophical Tradition," pp. 1948–75), kabbalists considered Hebrew to be the one "natural" or "essential"

language in contrast to all other languages, which are "conventional" or "contingent." One of the better known, and surely most lucid, formulations of this idea is offered by the 13th-century Castilian kabbalist Joseph Gikatilla (1248–ca. 1325), a likely member of the fraternity responsible for the zoharic anthology, in the introduction to his *Sha'arei 'Orah,* a systematic delineation of the symbolic names associated with each of the ten emanations progressing from the bottom to the top of the sefirotic ladder: The twenty-two letters are portrayed as branches stemming from a tree whose trunk is inscribed with YHVH, the root-word of the "original" language, the mystical essence of Torah. Thus Torah is the blueprint of creation, and furthermore by studying Torah one can gain knowledge, both historical and natural, of all that takes place in the world. From the vantage point formulated textually by kabbalists beginning in earnest in the 13th century, everything that exists in the cosmos may be perceived as a permutation of the name, elicited from the linguistic matrix of Torah. The permutation both says and unsays the ineffable name, as a garment both hides and reveals the body it clothes.

Inner and Outer Meaning are Ultimately Identical

In great measure, as scholars have long noted, the kabbalistic approach to Scripture takes its cue from the analogy in the introduction to the *Guide for the Perplexed* by Maimonides. Maimonides utilizes the image of the apples of gold covered in the lattice of silver (Prov. 25.11) to convey the idea that there are two levels of meaning in Torah, the external *(zahir)* and internal *(batin)*. In Maimonides this approach is not applied to every verse of Scripture. Rather, it is limited to those where the literal meaning contradicts natural reason and it becomes necessary to interpret the text figuratively so that the potential conflict is resolved. To be sure, Maimonides uses an image that conveys a sense of an organic whole, an indissoluble bond between inner and outer: Just as the golden apples encased in silver settings appear from a distance as silver but from up close as gold, the literal and the figurative must both be preserved even though one comes to discern that the literal meaning is but appearance cloaking a reality embedded within the text. This hermeneutic, therefore, is decidedly hierarchical, clearly privileging the internal over the external as the more appropriate articulation of truth. The external meaning is but a shell that covers and thereby shows the internal meaning.

Many kabbalist exegetes similarly begin by presuming Torah encompasses two layers of meaning, the exoteric and esoteric. In contrast to Maimonides, however, for kabbalists the *entirety* of Tanakh must be read in this way, not just words or verses that ostensibly conflict with the dictates of reason. In other words, all Scripture yields a twofold meaning irrespective of conformity with what is considered to be rational truth. In content there is clearly a distinction between what is called prophetic kabbalism and theosophic kabbalism. The secret (*sod*) for prophetic kabbalists is the inner life of God, believed to have been made known to the prophets, reached through the scriptural language contained in the letters of the name, which constitute the ideational forms of the Active Intellect, the repository of the intelligible forms that govern the sublunar world. For theosophic kabbalists the secret is the inner meaning of the text, in which each word has a literal and symbolic sense, the literal dealing with matters of the mundane realm, the "world of differentiation" (*'olam ha-perud*), and the symbolic expressing the sefirotic realm, the "world of unity" (*'olam ha-yihud*).

Although at times kabbalists do seem to be articulating a hierarchical view akin to that of Maimonides, privileging the figurative over the literal, in fact the mystical perspective is predicated on discerning that exoteric and esoteric, *peshat* and *sod*, are indistinguishable. In the philosophical esotericism espoused by Maimonides, the two must be set in binary opposition, for the inner truth might under-

mine the literal meaning; in kabbalism, there is overlap or convergence of the two and thus the hermeneutic path of kabbalah is more like a circular journey than a linear process, although at times linear language is inevitable. The influence of sequential language is no doubt indebted in part to the well-known motif of the hierarchy of sciences in medieval scholasticism (shared alike by Muslims, Jews, and Christians): Logic and mathematics are preparatory disciplines at the base, followed by physics or the science of natural phenomena, and culminating with metaphysics, the science of ideal forms (in the Platonic view) or of being as such (in the Aristotelian view). In kabbalah which followed the Platonic tradition, in which the world of unity was perceived to be superior to the world of particularity, the esoteric meaning, corresponding to the world of unity, is privileged since it discloses the truth compared to the exoteric sense, dealing with the world of ephemeral appearance. In kabbalah influenced by the Aristotelian approach, God was the necessary Being and all else is contingent. Whether this influence was present or not, the kabbalists, even when they used linear language, portrayed the goal of the linear process as coming full circle; when one reaches the core at the end and returns thereby to the surface from the beginning, one realizes that where one ended up was where one had begun, and consequently one comes to see that the innermost secret was folded within the initial allusion, leading to the hermeneutical maxim that *peshat* is *sod*, the literal spiritual, the exoteric esoteric.

Nahmanides (Ramban, 1194–1220; see "Medieval Jewish Interpretation," pp. 1876–1900), the Spanish rabbinic leader, talmudic and halakhic scholar, biblical exegete, and kabbalist, states in the introduction to his commentary on the Torah that the Torah given to Moses had two aspects. The first was the written text (the rabbinic term is *miqra'* from the root *q-r-'*, "to call out," "to invoke," "to read," whence the word *qeri'ah*, "recitation"), which relates to the "way of our reading," *derekh qeri'atenu*, also described as the "division according to the ritualistic reading," *derekh ḥilluk qeri'at ha-mitzvah*. The second was the oral text, which is not a reference to the standard rabbinic Oral Torah but an occult reading by "way of the names," *derekh ha-she-mot*. There are thus two ways of reading Scripture anchored in the Sinaitic epiphany, the mystical way of *shemot* transmitted orally and the ritual way of *torah* and *mitzvah* inscripted in written form; the textual ground of both is the primordial Torah, which as Naḥmanides describes, citing an ancient tradition (kabbalah), was written in black fire on white fire. This aggadic image conveys the underlying unity of the literal and symbolic, a theme to which Naḥmanides returns on several occasions in his commentary when he discusses the kabbalistic intent marked by his signature *al derekh ha-'emet*, "by way of truth."

The kabbalist strategy of reading relies on the recognition that signifier discloses the nature of signified, and signified the nature of signifier, precisely because the two are, though different, identified with one another. Even Abraham Abulafia (13th century kabbalist of Spain)—who contrasts the Written Torah as a compendium of commandments with the Oral Torah as the names of God that are all contained in the Tetragrammaton, which is further identified as the Active Intellect—makes a point of emphasizing that the truth of both the revealed (*nigleh*) and concealed (*nistar*) dimensions of Torah must be upheld. Thus, Abulafia articulates the matter after attempting to affirm, in a blatantly acknowledged challenge to the Aristotelian law of contradiction (*Sitrei Torah*, MS Paris, Bibliothèque Nationale, fol. 149b), the veracity of both the traditional account of creation and the philosophically sanctioned view of eternity, the former conveyed by the literal sense of Scripture and the latter by the allegorical: "With regard to the Torah its revealed aspects without doubt are completely true (*'emet gamur*) and its concealed aspects are absolutely true (*'emet muḥlat*), and both of them are one unified matter in truth" (ibid., fol.

150b). Reiterating the dual meaning of the text at the conclusion of this section, Abulafia writes that it would be a "complete heresy" (*kefirah gemurah*) if one were to deny the literal facticity of Torah on account of the figurative interpretation (the example he gives is the splitting of the Reed Sea). The assault on the law of contradiction maintains the paradox that both the exoteric and esoteric meanings are true even if they seem to be in conflict. In Abulafia's own words:

> The truth is, as I have indicated to you in the secret previous to this, the secret of the creation of the world, that the Torah in its truth comprises two types of existence, and the two of them are equally good, and they are the revealed and the concealed, and both are true. And this you may understand from the matter of the existence of the body [and the soul] together, for they are two, the one created and the other eternal, the one revealed and the other concealed, and it is as if the one is the exemplar (*mashal*) and the other the exemplum (*nimshal*), but the two are found together (ibid., fol. 151a).

In other treatises, Abulafia employs different exegetical classifications. For example, in *'Igeret Zo't li-Yehudah* and *'Otsar 'Eden Ganuz*, he distinguishes seven paths of interpretation (literal, halakhic, homiletical, and allegorical, letter-permutation, restitution of letters to their primary matter, and prophecy or the way of the divine names), whereas in *Mafteaḥ ha-Ḥokhmot*, he demarcates three levels of meaning (literal, allegorical, and prophetic, which correspond respectively to the righteous, pious, and prophets). As he states in *'Igeret Zo't li-Yehudah*, in the final analysis, scriptural reading is not possible unless one minimally possesses both "knowledge of how to read" the written text, *yedi'at ha-mikhtav*, that is, the "literal reading," *ha-keri'ah ha-peshutah*, and "knowledge of how to interpret," *yedi'at ha-perush*, "for this is like a matter of the dream itself, as a dream needs an interpretation, and any dream that is not interpreted is like a parable and an enigma that are written and not explicated" (Adolph Jellinek, *Philosophie und Kabbala: Erstes Heft* [Leipzig: Heinrich Hunger, 1854], p. 13). The meaningfulness of the text resides in the interstices between the literal and figurative, the document that is to be read and the reading that is to be interpreted. Tellingly, in the description of the seven paths, Abulafia resorts to the image of the sphere to describe the relationship of one path to another, beginning with the "sphere of the literal," *galgal ha-peshat*, and culminating with the seventh path, which is compared to the "all-encompassing sphere," *galgal ha-makif* (ibid., pp. 2–4). The use of the standard medieval image of the concentric heavenly spheres to describe the hermeneutical paths is meant to convey that the linear progression of the paths and the hierarchical stratification that they imply gives way in the end to the mystical insight that breaks the binary opposition between literal and figurative, exoteric and esoteric, revealed and hidden.

The matter is similarly expressed in the *Zohar*:

> Come and see: The supernal world and the lower world are balanced on one scale. Israel below and the angels above. Concerning the supernal angels it is written, "He makes his angels into spirits" (Ps. 104.4). When they descend below they are garbed in the garment of this world, and if they were not garbed in the garment that is in the likeness of this world, they could not exist in this world and the world could not endure them. If this is so with respect to the angels, how much more so with respect to the Torah, which created them and all the worlds, and they exist on account of it, when it descends to this world, if it were not garbed in the garments of this world, the world could not endure. Thus the narrative of Torah is the garment of Torah. The one who thinks that the garment is the Torah itself, and not another matter, let his spirit deflate, and he will have no share in

the world to come. Therefore, David said, "Open my eyes that I may perceive the wonders of your Torah" (Ps. 119.18), what is beneath the garment of Torah (*Zohar* 3:152a).

In the continuation of the passage, the exegetical layering of Scripture is expanded from two to four levels: garment, body, soul, and soul of souls, which correspond respectively to stories, laws, esoteric wisdom, and messianic secrets. The standard reference to this idea was by the acronym PaRDeS: *peshat* (contextual sense), *remez* (allegorical sense), *derash* (homiletical sense), and *sod* (mystical sense). *Pardes* was apparently first used by Mosheh de Leon but applied more systematically by Baḥya ben Asher (d. 1320) in the second part of the 13th century. It was formulated as an elaboration of the principle of dual meaning, the internal and external, esoteric and exoteric, revealed and concealed, the garment and what is beneath it. The hermeneutical principle of dual meaning in the text is based on the parallel between the supernal and lower worlds. In the zoharic idiom, the image of two worlds "balanced on one scale," *be-ḥad matkela 'itkalu*, conveys the notion of similitude through difference, that is, two dissimilar things rendered equal in their incongruity. The zoharic kabbalists maintained that the spiritual is discerned through the physical, the invisible through the visible, a cosmological principle that shaped their hermeneutical disposition. The hidden meaning of the text, the "mystery" *(raz)* or "light" *('or)*—an equivalence of terms that was substantiated on the basis of their numerical equivalence, both equaling 207—was discoverable through its literal body, the letter; mystical cognition thus entails a seeing of the secret "through the garment" *(migo levusha)* rather than by removing the garment (*Zohar* 2:98b). In inverse emulation of the dissimilitude of Torah to conceal in the charade of revealing, the master of esoteric gnosis reveals in the display of concealing. The capacity to divulge secrets, attributed in the zoharic passage to Simeon ben Yoḥai, is traced to the "skilled tongue," *leshon limudim* (Isa. 50.4), which is identified as the "holy tongue," *leshon ha-kodesh*, or the "holy spirit," *ruaḥ ha-kodesh*. In the divine outpouring to the world through *Shekhinah* (compare *Zohar* 1:228a and 2:236b), the lower wisdom *(ruaḥ)* receives the overflow from the upper wisdom *(kodesh)* and is thereby transformed from passive female to active male *(Zohar* 3:60b–61a). This suggests that the word *leshon*, "tongue," is to be interpreted phallically; indeed the phallus empowers the "skilled tongue" of the holy spirit to talk.

The intent of the passage above comes into sharper focus when seen with another text from the *Zohar*, a dramatic section that chronicles the discourse of the elderly donkey driver focused on the mystery of conversion and the doctrine of transmigration of souls (metempsychosis), the voyage of the soul from one embodiment to another. The old man lures other members of the fraternity (and, by implication, the reader) onto his path with three seemingly incomprehensible parables. In time, through the unfolding of the narrative—which presents the tension between the urge to reveal and the need to conceal—the donkey driver, outwardly foolish, discloses himself to be a true master. The point of the narrative is that by plumbing the depths of the mystery of conversion of the Gentile (which implies for these thinkers the existence of a Jewish soul in a non-Jewish body), one is led to a mystical understanding of the ontological identification of God and Torah, two seemingly disparate realities, one delimited and beyond semantic demarcation and the other comprised of the twenty-two letters that are the names branching off the root YHVH. Conversion suggested to the Castilian kabbalists a crossing of the boundaries of being that seemingly challenged the overtly dualistic view that Israel was aligned with the holy right side of God, mercy, and the nations of the world (Gentiles) with the unholy left side, judgment.

Part of the text *(Zohar* 2:98b) articulates the assumption regarding the Torah and mystical secrets, an assumption that is, at once, onto-logical and hermeneutical (the two cannot be separated in the thinking of these kabbalists). The explanation of the garbing of a Jewish soul in a non-Jewish body, the key factor to understanding the mechanics of conversion, is interrupted, so it seems, by the observation of the old man that God hides secrets in the garments of Torah. Only the wise that are replete with eyes are capable of apprehending these secrets, a vision that is designated as seeing through rather than discarding the garment. Shortly after the reader encounters this principle, the old man offers a parable of the beautiful maiden in a castle, which recounts the erotic relationship that pertains between Torah and the mystical exegete *(Zohar* 2:99a–b). Four levels of meaning are delineated: *remizu*, "sign"; *derashah*, "homily"; *ḥidah*, "allegory," or *hagadah*, "narrative"; and *razin setimin*, "hidden mysteries." These four levels are presented sequentially as stages of ever-increasing disclosure: In the first meaning is offered through the barrier of the wall, in the second from behind a curtain, in the third through a more subtle veil, and, finally, in the fourth the reader encounters the text face to face, which, in the zoharic vernacular, signifies union of a most intimate and erotic sort. When the Torah removes her veil and exposes her face fully to her lover, he comes to realize that the secret was already present in the first stage when the initial hint was offered. At that moment he understands that *peshatei dikera'*, the literal sense of the text—the text in its literal embodiment, the mien of the letters—must be as it is, no word added or subtracted, precisely in accord with the halakhic ruling. To discern the initial insinuation at the end confirms the point that the secret can be seen only through the garment of the letters, the body of the text, the face unmasked in effacing the mask. The uncovering of the innermost meaning at the culmination of the journey is thus a recovery of the overt sense allusively disclosed in the beginning.

The somewhat curious choice of the term *remizu* ("sign") to denote the *peshat* in the initial delineation underscores that in the mystical understanding of the revealed word, the literal is metaphorical and the metaphorical literal. To be sure, on the face of it, the final disclosure—the fourth level—bears the intimacy of the face-to-face encounter, a showing that ostensibly does away with the previous barriers, the wall, curtain, and veil; but when one understands that the secret exposed at the end was contained in the hint offered at the beginning, it then becomes apparent that the face itself is a veil, indeed the greatest of veils, since it can be unveiled—appear in the flesh—only by being veiled—remaining enfleshed. What is revealed in the final hermeneutical disclosure, therefore, is the veil of presuming there is an unveiling that results in a vision of the divine without the veil of the text, to apprehend the essence of God without the shibboleth of the name, which is the Torah. As the matter is expressed in another zoharic context, "The letters are inscribed in the supernal mysteries, for they all emerge from the mystery of the supernal Wisdom by way of the thirty-two paths that come forth from Wisdom. . . . All the letters are inscribed in a mystery and they are the bodies of Torah (*gufei torah*) for they exist to instruct and to notify about the supernal mysteries" (*Zohar Ḥadash*, 73b). The author of this comment appropriates the rabbinic expression *gufei torah*—which in the older sources that use *guf* (body) metaphorically denotes the rudiments of law—to formulate the idea of a mystical body of God, taking *guf* literally, a body that is composed of letters, which are at one and the same time linguistic signs and numeric ciphers of divine wisdom.

Poetic Incarnation and the Embodied Text of Textual Embodiment

In the kabbalistic tradition, the anthropomorphic shape of God refers not to humanity in general but specifically to the Jew, a point often expressed in the relevant texts in terms of the rabbinic dictum (linked exegetically to Ezek. 34.31) that the title *'adam* ("person") applies to Israel and not to the nations of the world. In particular, the ethnocentric dimension of the incarnational myth, which has profoundly informed the kabbalistic orientation, is captured in the symbolic identification of God, Torah, and Israel implied in the zoharic comment that "there are three gradations bound one to the other, the holy One, blessed be He, Torah, and Israel" (*Zohar* 3:73a). The full implication of this symbolism is shown in the obligation incumbent upon every male Jew to write his own Torah scroll, a theme found in other kabbalistic texts such as the anonymous *Sefer ha-Yiḥud*:

The reason for this commandment by way of kabbalah alludes to the fact that the Torah scroll is the holy of holies . . . for the entire Torah is the name of the holy One, blessed be He . . . and His Torah is within the holy One, blessed be He, and within Him is His Torah, and this is what the kabbalists say the holy One, blessed be He, is in His name and His name is in Him. "His name" is His Torah and the Torah is made through the pure and holy chain in the supernal image, and it is verily the shade of the holy One, blessed be He . . . Therefore He commanded that each man should make a Torah scroll for himself to discern and to know that he cherishes the Torah and to allude to the unity and to demonstrate the pattern of the Creator, blessed be He. When the holy One, blessed be He, sees that each and every one in Israel has a Torah scroll that is precisely in the likeness of His pattern, blessed be He, the holy One, blessed be He, immediately causes His Presence to dwell upon Israel, verily in his pattern, in the Torah scroll. Therefore God, blessed be He, commanded each and every man from Israel to make a Torah scroll for himself . . . this alludes to the fact that all of Israel is one form, as the sages, blessed be their memory, said all Israel is one body. . . . Since all of Israel is one supernal pattern, and each and every one from Israel is a limb of the chariot, each and every man from Israel must take a Torah scroll for himself so that the limb will cleave to the limb in the pure and holy chain (*Sefer Ta'amey ha-Mizvot*, pp. 78–80).

The incarnational theology that informs the kabbalistic standpoint is predicated on a distinctive understanding of corporeality. "Body" does not denote physical mass that is quantifiable and measurable, but the phenomenological sense of the corporeal as lived presence. Medieval kabbalists, due to the influence of philosophical thinking that had informed the general cultural trends of European societies in the high Middle Ages, adopted a negative view toward the corporeal body (indeed, according to some passages in zoharic literature, for example, 3:170a, the physicality of the human is linked to the demonic "left" side) and thus considered the contemplative life as a way to escape the bonds of carnality. (There are many other strong connections between the philosophical and mystical traditions; these traditions should not be depicted as opposites, as they often are.) This explains the adoption of ascetic forms of piety on the part of kabbalists with special emphasis placed on sexual abstinence. On the other hand, the positive value accorded the body in kabbalistic symbolism, reflected in the repeated use of anthropomorphic images to depict God, images that on occasion embrace an intense erotic tone, is related to the textual nature of bodiliness, which, in turn, rests on an assumption regarding the bodily nature of textuality. The linguistic aspect of embodiment accounts as well for the kabbalistic understanding of ritual as participation in divine energy, epitomized in the saying "limb strengthens limb"; that is, the performance of ceremonial acts by human limbs fortifies the divine attributes, which are envisioned as bodily limbs. Alternatively expressed, insofar as Torah is the name YHVH, and the latter takes the form of an anthropos (an idea buttressed by the numerical equivalence of the four letters of the name written out in full and the word *'adam*, "person"), it follows that each commandment can be represented as a limb

of the divine body. The kabbalistic representation of Torah as body is supported by the idea that the 248 positive commandments correspond to the 248 limbs and the 365 negative commandments to the 365 sinews. This formulation is a modification of the tradition attributed to R. Simlai (*b. Mak.* 23b) according to which the 248 positive commandments correspond to the limbs and the 365 negative commandments to the days of the year. The kabbalistic perspective reverses the generally assumed allegorical approach to scriptural anthropomorphisms promoted by medieval rabbinic exegetes, for instead of explaining anthropomorphic characterizations of God as a figurative way to accommodate human understanding, the attribution of corporeal images to an incorporeal God indicates that the real body, the body in its most abstract tangibility, is the letter, which is the principle of poetic incarnation. Anthropomorphism in Scripture therefore indicates that human and divine corporeality are entwined in a mesh of double imaging through the mirror of the text that renders the divine body human and the human body divine. For kabbalists, life revolves about the axis of the embodied text of textual embodiment.

Flesh Made Word and the Body as Text

There is no escaping the incarnational implications of the esoteric identification of Torah and the name, since the latter is the divine essence, a point made explicitly in several zoharic passages (2:60b, 87a, 90b, 3:13b, 19a, 21a, 35b–36a, 73a, 89b, 98b, 159a, 265b, 298b) and confirmed by other kabbalists contemporary with the *Zohar*, for instance, Gikatilla. Thus, in one zoharic passage we read, "It has been taught that the holy One, blessed be He, is called Torah" (2:60b). In a second passage, the matter is laid out in more detail based on the symbolic correspondence between the ten commandments revealed at Sinai, which contain the whole Torah, and the ten divine utterances, the emanations comprised within the Tetragrammaton (YHVH):

The Torah is the name of the holy One, blessed be He. Just as the name of the holy One, blessed be He, is inscribed in ten utterances so Torah is inscribed in ten utterances; these ten utterances are the name of the holy One, blessed be He, and the Torah is entirely one name, verily the holy name of the holy One, blessed be He. . . . The one who is meritorious with respect to Torah is meritorious with respect to the holy name. R. Jose said that he is indeed meritorious with respect to the holy One, blessed be He, because He and His name are one (2:90b).

The Castilian kabbalists whose views are preserved in the zoharic homilies make even more explicit the assumption of their predecessors. The equation of Torah and the name implies that God is embodied in Torah and, consequently, engagement in study and fulfilling the commandments serve as the means by which one is conjoined to the divine. In the words of another zoharic homily: "He who is occupied with Torah it is as if he were occupied with the holy One, blessed be He, for Torah is entirely the name of the holy One, blessed be He" (3:89b). But how can we speak of God being embodied in the text? Can light that is without limit be contained in letters that are limited by their very shape? The mystery that is basic to zoharic kabbalah (though by no means unique to its fraternity) is that God is absent from the text in which God is present, since for God to be present in the text God must be absent.

The Significance of the Single Letter

Kabbalistic interpretation sees every unit of the text as significant, including individual letters; this builds upon a method of interpretation of some of the classical Rabbis (see "Classical Rabbinic Interpretation," pp. 1844–63). As an example, an explanation (attributed to R. Ḥiyya) is offered for why the first letter of Torah is bet, ב, the second letter of the alphabet, a query that appears in classical rabbinic literature: This letter signifies the

dual Torah, oral and written, a doctrine that is also used in this context to explain the plural in "Let Us make Adam in Our image," that is, Adam was created by means of the oral and written Torah, reflected in the mentioning of image and likeness in tandem with his creation, the former correlated with the masculine and the latter with the feminine. According to R. Isaac, the orthographic structure of bet as the letter that is opened on one side and closed on three sides, already attested in older mystical sources, is interpreted as a sign that Torah receives those who seek to be conjoined to her but she is closed from the other side in relation to those who close their eyes and turn away from her. It is at this point in the homily that, for our purposes, the critical passage appears:

R. Judah said: Bet has two sides and one that connects them. What do they come to teach? One for heaven, one for earth, and the holy One, blessed be He, connects and receives them. R. Eleazar said: These are the three holy, supernal lights bound as one, and they are the totality of Torah, and they open an opening to everything. They open an opening to faith and they are the abode of everything. Thus they are called bet for they make up the dwelling (beita'). And thus the beginning of Torah is bet, for it is the Torah, the remedy for the world. Therefore, whoever is occupied with Torah it is as if he were occupied with the holy name . . . for Torah is entirely the one supernal holy name. And since it is the holy name, it begins with bet, for it is the totality of the holy name in three knots of faith. Come and see: all those occupied with Torah are conjoined to the holy One, blessed be He, and they are crowned in the crowns of Torah, and they are beloved above and below (Zohar 3:36a).

According to R. Judah, bet means heaven, earth, and God who unites them. The further, theosophic explication is offered in the name of R. Eleazar. The three lines of bet refer to three holy, supernal lights that are bound as one, and they are the totality of Torah (kelala' de'oraita'). Insofar as the three potencies are the opening for faith, which may here denote the lower seven emanations, they are characterized as the abode (beita') of all that exists, and hence they are the three lines that make up beit, the letter that is the "totality of the holy name in three knots of faith" (kelala' dishema' kadisha' bitelat kishrei meheimanuta'). All of Torah is the name and thus its first letter must encompass the totality of the name; the three lines by which the letter is drawn are the knots of faith. The three knots of faith—faith is the fourth side that is the opening created by the three closed sides—may be the three letters, YHV, contained in the four-letter name, YHVH. Alternatively, the knots of faith may allude symbolically to Ḥokhmah, Binah, and Tif'eret, "Wisdom," "Understanding," and "Beauty," three configurations of the divine that are imaginally depicted in some zoharic passages as father, mother, son and demarcated as YHV; the last letter of the name, the fourth party of the quaternity, the daughter, Malkhut ("Sovereignty") or Shekhinah, is represented by the second he, the letter that has already appeared, a duplicate of the second.

The beginning of Torah, therefore, is the letter that marks the mystery of the threefold unity, the totality of the name, the secret abode of faith. The trinitarian resonance in the zoharic locution telat kishrei meheimanuta, "three knots of faith," has been noted by Yehuda Liebes. Reinforcing this, the author of the homily has combined the motif of Torah as the incarnation of the divine name and the trinitarian symbol of the three knots of faith. In this matter, as with regard to a number of crucial themes, the kabbalists whose ideas and interpretations are preserved in zoharic literature reflect a complex relationship to Christianity, which was viewed as the major competitor in the arena of salvation history: This is an instance of the perennial struggle between synagogue and church, Jacob and Esau, with its concomitant attraction and repulsion. On one hand, zoharic kabbalists adopted a harsh stance and portrayed Chris-

tianity as an earthly manifestation of the demonic potency, the idolatrous religion that seduces Jews (men are especially vulnerable) both in the form of spiritual enticement (particularly in the guise of magic) and sexual temptation. On the other hand, these kabbalists were duly impressed with aspects of this faith, including trinitarian and incarnational symbols, as well as imagery derived from devotions to Mary, the mother of Jesus, and attempted to appropriate them as authentic esoteric tradition, perhaps even modeling the fraternity of Simeon ben Yoḥai and his comrades on the pattern of Jesus and his disciples. Medieval kabbalists sought to divest christological symbols of their Catholic garb and re-dress them as the mystical truths of Judaism. The zoharic understanding of text as body, which provides the mechanism by which the body is understood as text, is a stunning illustration of this strategy.

One final zoharic text demonstrates the subtle and complex relationship that pertains between kabbalistic and christological symbolism:

"As for the tabernacle, make it of ten strips of cloth" (Exod. 26.1). Here is the mystery of unity, for the arrayment of the tabernacle was from several gradations, as it is written with respect to it "and the tabernacle was one" (ibid., 6). This is to illustrate that all the parts of the body are all the mystery of one body. In a man, there are several upper and lower parts, the ones interior and the others revealed on the outside, and all of them are called one body, and the man is called one composition. So here, all the parts of the tabernacle are in the pattern of what is above and when all of them are joined as one, then it is written "and the tabernacle was one." The commandments of Torah are all parts and limbs in the mystery above, and when all of them are joined together, then all of them add up to one mystery. The mystery of the tabernacle, which consists of the parts and limbs, all compute to the mystery of Adam in the manner of the commandments of Torah, for the commandments of Torah are all of them the mystery of Adam, male and female. When they are joined together, they are one mystery of Adam (*Zohar* 2:162b).

In this homily, the images of the Tabernacle, the human body, the androgynous Adam (created "male and female," Gen. 1.27), and the Torah are linked together like pearls in a necklace of symbolic equivalences. The thread that ties these images together is the linguistic conception of embodiment, that is, what the four compositions share in common is the assumption that they are constructed from the letters of the Hebrew alphabet. In older rabbinic sources, one can find the notion that the Tabernacle, the earthly residence of the divine glory, which is depicted as a microcosm of the universe, was built by means of the letters (*b. Ber.* 55a). What the zoharic author has added is that the Tabernacle assumes the shape of an anthropos. The Tabernacle symbolically stands for the totality of the divine pleroma, a secret alluded to in the hyperliteral rendering of the verse that dictates the making of the Tabernacle from ten strips of cloth, which correspond to the ten emanations. The mystery of the Tabernacle's construction, therefore, imparts the wisdom that the multiplicity of divine powers cohere in a unified whole, that is, God's unity may be represented organically, as a composite of discrete elements the infinity of which denies the possibility of fixed enumeration.

The organic unity of the Tabernacle is illustrated further by comparing it to the human body. The anthropomorphic representation is illumined by a similar characterization of Torah, for the commandments are the limbs of the body of Torah, which is envisioned as the mystery of the androgynous Adam, the positive commandments being masculine aspects and the negative commandments feminine ones. The conjunction of the two facilitates the constitution of the mystery of the divine anthropos, which is envisioned both as the textualization of the Tabernacle and the material-

ization of Torah: Parallel processes in the hidden disclosure of the divine name. The secret of poetic incarnation imparted by masters of Jewish esoteric lore, beholding the luminous flesh from the word, may be seen as a countermyth to the Christian image of the word/light made flesh in the prologue to the Gospel of John, which played an inestimable role in fashioning the hermeneutical aesthetic of medieval Christendom. In the history of Christian devotion the incarnational theme also expressed itself in terms of textual embodiment, but the basis for this form of embodiment in Christianity is always the incarnation of the Word in the person of Jesus. As a consequence, medieval Christian piety has been informed by the exegetical supposition that incarnation of the word in the flesh had the effect of removing the veil of the letter, the literal meaning that kills the spirit, the carnal law that obstructs the true knowledge of the Last Things. By contrast, in the kabbalistic wisdom that materialized in the course of the 12th, 13th, and 14th centuries, incarnation of the flesh in the word preserved the veil of the letter. The only credible means to apprehend the inner meaning of the law was thought to be through its outer covering, to behold the mysteries of Torah underneath the garment, to see the image of God embodied iconically in the text that is the textual embodiment of the name. The ultimate secret of Scripture in the kabbalistic imagination embraces the paradox that the revealed word is the mirror whose visibility consists precisely in its invisibility, and, as such, the task of revisioning remains constant, as the invisible can never be seen once and for all. Since the task of scriptural reading is presented primarily as the eye-centered image of lifting the veils to see the face hidden beneath, it can be said that this task is never complete, as the mandate to lift the veils does result in discarding all possible veils; indeed, there can be no "final" veil to lift as there is always another veil through which the nonmanifest will be made manifest. Therein lies the soteriological hope (the hope concerning salvation) fostered by the soteric approach to Scripture advocated by kabbalists. The uncovering of secrets by their recovery, and their recovery by uncovering, infuses the act of reading with the redemptive mandate to see again and hear anew, interpretive gestures that have the potential to transform text and reader to the point that the latter may adopt the mantle of writer and study provides the quill, ink, and tableau for rewriting the text that is yet to be scripted through the hermeneutical glance.

[ELLIOT R. WOLFSON]

The Bible in Israeli Life*

The Bible, once at the center of the cultural scene in Israel, has become marginalized; its magic has faded. A new Israeli generation no longer believes that, to be considered educated, one must be well-versed in the canonical national literature; to a greater or lesser degree, it rejects Bible study as a required subject. Pride in the greatness of the Bible is giving way to alienation; instead of proficiency in Scripture one finds unashamed ignorance of its content. Before we can measure the depth of the change and trace its causes, we must examine the situation as it was until recently, when the Bible proudly held sway over the Israeli scene.

Early Days: The Holy Scripture of Secular Zionism

The Zionist endeavor defined itself from the start in biblical language, as the "return to Zion" (Ps. 126.1), and by placing Bible study at the center of the school curriculum made it an integral component of national rebirth, rebuilding the ancestral land, and revival of its language. The return to the land, cultivation of the land, national independence, military valor, speaking the tongue of Amos and Isaiah, received quasi-religious inspiration from the Bible; it embodied that generation's tasks and visions as if the present were recapturing the past. Leaders, authors, and teachers all believed that the Bible legitimized Zionism: It testified to Jewish ownership of the land and foretold the return, the rebuilding, and the ingathering. Conversely, Zionism enhanced Scripture: It was realizing prophecy and thereby confirming the Bible's eternal truth. The Bible was an inspiring commentary on the present, and the present was a concrete interpretation of the Bible. The immediacy and reality of the biblical saga—from the immigration of individuals in obedience to the command, "Go forth from your native land" (Gen. 12.1) and the mass exodus from the house of bondage, through the frailty of the "desert generation" and the virility of the conquerors of Canaan, culminating in the defensive wars waged by the Judges and the establishment of the monarchy—invested the present with an aura of ancient splendor. Biblical history gave the Zionist endeavor roots in time; geography, with its memory-laden sites, confirmed its ties to place; and archeology provided the newcomers with material proof of their "nativity" in this old-new land.

Literature, particularly poetry, played a major role in this two-way association of Zionism with the Bible. The power of poetry can be seen in two poems about Saul's heroic death by Natan Alterman and Amir Gilboa, both published in the first decade of the State of Israel. Alterman's ballad, "The Day of Battle and Its Eve are Ended" ('Ir ha-Yonah, Tel Aviv, 1957, pp. 184–185) begins with a brief reference to the biblical story of the overthrow of Israel's army on Mount Gilboa: defeat, flight, and King Saul's suicide. The poet then goes on to describe in detail how the

* A longer version of this article appeared in Hebrew in Yeri'ot 1, 1999; an English translation by Mr. David Louvish was published in Modern Judaism, 19.3, 1999, pp. 217–239. This adaptation is published with the kind permission of Modern Judaism.

wounded herald rides a whole night from the battlefield to the queen mother's home and, upon arriving, falls to the ground, speechless. His blood, staining her feet, and the news of the king's death implied by his silence, have brought the battlefield to her doorstep. Her heroism is no less impressive than Saul's in this struggle for the national spirit. "Rise, my son," she commands the herald, and upon hearing his tearful description of the king's falling on his sword, she responds, expressing the heroism of mothers:

> Then spake she to the youth: Blood
> Will cover mother's feet,
> But the nation will rise seven times
> If it be defeated on its own land.
> Judgment has been visited upon the
>   king,
> But a successor will arise in due time,
> For it was upon his own land that
> He leaned the sword upon which he
>   died.
> Thus she spake and her voice trembled.
> And so it was. And David heard.

She neither weeps nor holds her tongue, but her voice trembles. David, and with him the readers, heard in her words the essence of Zionism: A defeat in Exile is final, but a defeat in the homeland is temporary. The blood-soaked soil of the land strengthens the resolve of its sons and their mothers: Vanquished in exile by death and its terror, here they will prevail over both.

Alterman speaks through the mouth of a fictitious biblical character, whereas Amir Gilboa in his poem "Saul" (*Keḥullim va-Adummim*, Tel Aviv, 1963, p. 216) bridges the time gap by having a contemporary speak to Saul. While the courage of Saul's mother is super-human (in a sense even inhuman), Gilboa's narrator expresses amazement at Saul's awe-inspiring death by describing his own weaknesses and doubts:

> Saul! Saul!
> I do not know whether it was shame
> or fear of a bodiless head—

> But upon passing by the wall of Beth-
>   Shean
> I turned my head away.

> Then, when your arms-bearer refused
>   you the sword you commanded,
> I stood dumb, speechless,
> and my blood flowed from my heart.
> I really cannot say what I would have
>   done in his place
> had I been your arms-bearer.

> And you are the king.

> And it is your honor as king when you
>   command.

> I really cannot say what I would have
>   done in his place.

> Saul, Saul, come!
> In Beth-Shean the Children of Israel now
>   live.

Saul's head is impaled upon the (Roman) wall of Beth-Shean at this day (1952), and the speaker, averting his gaze, admits that he does not know whether he did so out of shame at what the Philistines did to his king or out of fear of the terrible sight. Uncertainty as to the real reason for his behavior is also expressed in a further, even more heartrending, quandary: He is present at Gilboa when Saul's arms-bearer disobeys the king's command to bring him his sword so that he can commit suicide. The speaker does not know whether he himself would have been brave enough to disobey his monarch, or whether he would have obeyed, recognizing that the king's honor required him to obey even unto death. The solemnity of the biblical scene is expressed through the narrator's insignificance and doubts: It does not occur to him to identify with the king, and while he is identifying with the arms-bearer, he is still no more than a silent observer, his heart bleeding at the gravity of the dilemma. Only toward the end of the poem does a new certainty seize him, enabling him to address the live Saul and inform him of the great Zionist message of comfort; the story of Israel's defeat on Mount Gilboa and the abuse of Saul's body has a happy ending: Beth-Shean is being rebuilt and settled by new immigrants!

Alterman delivers the message in loud, resonant tones; Gilboa whispers: By virtue of national continuity, geographic identity, and Scripture's eternal truth, we are living in the Bible and the Bible lives in us. Thus the Bible had become the Holy Scriptures of Zionism, but there was a profound difference between those who considered it a heroic *epos,* to be released from the heavy shackles of prophetic ethics, and those for whom it was a source of ethical lore and Jewish spiritual life. The latter considered the ethical values underlying the laws of the Torah, as well as the courageous social censure and vision of national redemption pronounced by the prophets, as a firm basis for a new version of Judaism: neither halakhic, traditional, nor exilic; but authentic by virtue of being neo-biblical.

In addition to these groups of writers, however, there were radical discreditors of Judaism, for whom clinging to the national heritage and accepting authority, excess spirituality, moral scruples, the claim to national uniqueness, were obstructions on the path to a natural, free life. They rejected the Bible entirely, or expressed their adoption of alternative values by such means as giving poetic expression to the false prophets or explicitly rejecting David.

Method of Interpretation:
Derash Claiming to Be *Peshat*

Accompanying the return to the Bible was an enthusiastic devotion to *peshat* (contextual and philological interpretation). *Peshat* alone would reveal the text's authentic meaning, extricating it from talmudic midrash (homiletics) and medieval commentaries, and from the confining authority of the Rabbis. Part of the magic of *peshat* was that it extended the secular hegemony (already effective in society, politics, and culture) to the realm of Bible commentary, freeing it from religious tradition. David Ben-Gurion does not say this ex-

plicitly in his article, "The Bible Shines with Its Own Light" (*Iyyunim ba-Tanakh,* Tel Aviv, 1969, pp. 41–45) but conveys it indirectly by three examples of the superiority of *peshat:* "an eye for an eye" cannot possibly refer to payment of damages, as taught by the Rabbis; the biblical David was no scholar, poring night after night over the oral law, but an intrepid warrior-king, capable of committing grave sins; and "the truth obliges us" to recognize that "The Song of Songs is (in its plain meaning, as a love song) one thing, while the midrash of the Song of Songs is another." But then Ben-Gurion declares, "The books of the Bible declare the glory of Israel. As to the glory of God—that is declared by the heavens, and the 'heavens' belong not to our nation only, not even to humankind, but to infinity. . . . The Bible is our own creation. . . . The Holy One, blessed be He, does not need an identity card." With that he abandons a contextual, philological reading of innumerable passages that speak in God's name or magnify and glorify Him; through radical midrash, he ignores the active, clearly manifest deity, and replaces Him by the spirit of the nation or the soul of the universe.

Indeed, although Zionism promoted understanding of the Bible (through biblical realia and analogy between the two periods), it also obstructed understanding (since the modern Return responded to a national, not divine, imperative). The secular generation, eager to find its reflection in the text and guide itself by its light, could ardently embrace such verses as "doing work with one hand while the other held a weapon" (Neh. 4.11), but was puzzled and repelled by "you shall be holy, for I, the LORD your God, am holy" (Lev. 19.2). To bridge the gap, they had to resort to quasi-midrashic interpretation, which sanctified biblical values while rejecting the plain meaning of divine revelation. "Thus says the LORD" and "I the LORD am your God, who brought you out of the land of Egypt" (Exod. 20.1), were metaphorical, archaic expressions that actually represented a psychological reality: an ethical imperative emerging from the depths of the soul, or the national spirit inspiring the liberators. But since midrash was considered invalid, contrary to *peshat,* and identified with the disparaged *pilpul* (hair-splitting, legalistic reasoning), such naïve explanations had to obscure their remoteness from *peshat.*

By using one of the most characteristic tools of midrash, metaphor, the authors of the Declaration of Independence of Israel could substitute for the transcendent "God of Israel" the national "Rock of Israel" (this too purged of its plain religious meaning, as in 2 Sam. 23.3: "The God of Israel has spoken, the Rock of Israel has said . . ."). Similarly, midrashic license divorced the words "the guardian of Israel neither slumbers nor sleeps" from their context in Ps. 121 (where the name of God occurs five times), interpreting "guardian of Israel" not as the omnipotent heavenly guardian but as the brave human guards on earth. One popular Hanukkah song used the quite radical technique of *al tikre* (substitution of one word for another) to transform "Who can tell the mighty acts of the LORD" (Ps. 106.2) into "Who can tell the mighty acts of Israel." A song for the fifteenth day of Shevat (the New Year for trees) took the first phrase of the verse "When you enter the land and plant any tree for food, you shall regard its fruit as forbidden . . ." (Lev. 19.23) and made of it a separate commandment by cutting the verse in half, the syntax in Hebrew allowing the remaining words to be understood as: "When you enter the land, you shall plant every tree. . . ." The song then added a rhyme in biblical Hebrew: ". . . / And the tree shall give its fruit and the land its yield." Even the injunction to donate money to the Jewish National Fund was traced to the Torah by a kind of modern halakhic midrash, so convincing that everyone was sure that the words "redemption shall be granted to the land" (Lev. 25.24) are an imperative to purchase Gentile land by peaceful means; the context of the phrase, however, calls for restoring a family's ancestral holdings, sold to strangers because of poverty, to the family's ownership. Similarly,

the emblem of the Reali School in Haifa urged its students, "Walk modestly," dropping the words, "with your God" (Mic. 6.8); and the words "Let My people go" were likewise taken from the ritual context "that they may worship Me in the wilderness" (Exod. 7.16), thereby severing them from context, detaching them from their history, and obscuring the identity of the divine speaker. Anyone could thus claim that the rousing challenge to a tyrannical government had sprung from the nation's spirit, uttered by its heroic fighters.

One might think that this Zionist midrash had no place in academia, which is committed to philological and historical study of the biblical text. Nevertheless, despite the detachment of the academy from the social world and its resistance to any ideological manipulation of the Bible, scholars also have reinforced the Zionist-worldly conception of the Bible. Engagement in critical study of the Bible in itself is an expression of the Zionist ambition to normalize all aspects of our life and resume our place in the family of nations. Owing to these efforts, the Bible is studied in Israel, too, in light of scientific criteria developed in the last few centuries, mainly by Protestant scholars, thus breaking free of the Jewish study tradition (which subordinates the written law to the oral). Bible research in Israel has become an active partner in international Bible study, as noted with pride by the editors of the Hebrew-language *Encyclopedia Biblica* (preface, Vol. I, 1950): "The nation that created the Bible is gradually taking its rightful place in the study of its eternal book" (p. 9). The critical study of Scripture, with no prior assumption of sanctity or overt superiority, makes its own contribution to the national midrash, undermines the perfection of Scripture, and considerably dims its brilliance; but it also provides a scientific-rationalistic justification for the secular view of the Bible as a human, national creation. Moreover, the academic definition of Bible studies agreed with the spirit of the times, treating the oral law as irrelevant to understanding the Bible. In the early 1950s, when I was pursuing my studies in the Hebrew University's Bible Department, one could not study midrashic exegesis there, as it ran counter to *peshat*. Nor was any course devoted even to those of the medieval commentaries that were based on *peshat*, as they were not sufficiently critical (the situation has since changed quite radically). The spirit of the times also molded the scientific principles guiding the *Encyclopedia Biblica*; it, too, reinforced the secular-material view. The encyclopedia was indeed committed to "the original meaning of the texts, in accordance with the intentions of the authors, as they were understood at the time of writing and by the audiences for whom they were originally written" (preface, p. 11). But the editors' understanding of *peshat* was so one-sided that the ancient authors would probably have been amazed at the extraordinary emphasis on realia, archeology, and the world of the ancient Near East, and the utter neglect of theological, ideological, and literary aspects (as evident, for example, in the almost complete disregard for the writings of the Israeli scholars Yehezkel Kaufmann and Martin Buber). As the times changed, this distortion, too, was somewhat mitigated in the last volumes; but the encyclopedia still lacks entries on memory, labor, property, peace, and remnant, on the one hand, and speech, humor, satire, and narrative, on the other. In sum: Bible scholars, high in their ivory towers, who had no part in the creation of the national midrash, were influenced by it unawares and indirectly helped to buttress it.

The secularizing national midrash also gave schoolchildren a social motive to study the Bible: it prepared them for "life," because minimal knowledge of the Bible was necessary for participation in the collective discourse. The Bible was not only one of the founts of Israel's literary and artistic creation, its inventory of associations (as it still is to some extent), but also the key to the values and ideas current in society. Incoming immigration is referred to in Hebrew, contrary to geography, as *'aliyah*, "coming up," while outgoing emigration is

yeridah, "going down," to take one example; and native-born Israelis, looking down upon the so-called primitive culture of the new immigrants, could invoke the term "desert generation" to justify their attitudes (and their budgetary priorities). A person who did not study the Bible was a stranger in Israeli society.

Religious Zionism, too, was an integral part of this collective discourse. Children in religious schools also "granted redemption to the land" with their mothers' pennies; they marched on the fifteenth of Shevat, holding saplings and singing "When you enter the land"; and at Hanukkah parties they sang "Who can tell the mighty acts of Israel," entertaining no doubts that the words had religious validity. Clearly, despite religious Zionism's efforts to contend with the predominantly secular bent of Zionism, it, too, was charmed by the national midrash. Perhaps this was because of the remarkable ability of that midrash, on the one hand, to provide biblical confirmation for the truth of Zionism, and, on the other, to guarantee on behalf of Zionism that the Bible would continue to occupy a central position in Jewish society. Thus, a fierce controversy raged as to the religious sanctity of the Bible, but at the same time no one denied that it belonged to the entire nation—a shared, unifying, and inspiring possession.

The Crisis of Secular Zionism Undermines the Validity of the National Midrash

One does not have to be a "post-Zionist" to realize that Zionism, as an ideology and a mass movement, is in deep trouble, and this has implications for the place of the Bible in contemporary Israeli society.

The establishment of the State of Israel brought about major changes in the country: Voluntarism gave way to state-run action, donations to taxation; governmental relief labor made tree-planting on the fifteenth of Shevat an anachronism, and the Land Administration took over "redemption of the land" from the Jewish National Fund. Manual labor has become the province of foreign workers. Finally, the Yom Kippur War (1973) revealed for all to see that the institutionalized Israel Defense Forces could no longer be compared to the Israelite army of the time of the judges and the early monarchy.

Along with social, economic, and political change has come a mental revolution: Romantic dreams and utopian aspirations have given way to concrete, short-term realism; a self-assured ideology, ignoring anything that clashed with its all-embracing concepts and not averse to shallow conformism, has become unfashionable. There is a strong bias for skepticism and open-mindedness, avoiding bombastic phraseology (embellished with biblical quotations) and preferring understatement—a descent from declamation to stammering; a systematic demythologization of Zionism is underway in the name of one's right—and obligation—to know the complex truth underlying appearance and pretension. The cult of heroism, with its implied contempt for human weakness and disregard for the enemy's suffering, has been discredited. The collective vision, which demanded bravery and self-sacrifice, has been supplanted by personal goals, in which individuals make their own choices and decide what demands to make on themselves. Spontaneity and permissiveness are preferred to normativity and moderation; education has shifted from nurturing values to developing aptitudes, advocating extracurricular studies rather than youth-movement activities. The humanities and natural sciences are neglected in favor of social and applied sciences, law, and business administration. The ambition of the second-generation *sabra* [native Israeli] is no longer to put down roots in this country but to spread his or her wings and explore the world.

Some consider this crisis to be the beginning of the end of Zionism, for better or for worse. I, however, see the process not as disintegration but as maturation, which is a precondition for any new growth. At any rate, Zionism is gradually losing its power as a secular religion, and the Bible is no longer the Scripture of that religion. The allure of romantic Zionism has dimmed, the sensation of miracle in Israel's revival has faded, and feelings of national pride have weakened; the abyss between the real present and the mythological past has deepened. As a result, the national midrash has lost its potency, no longer able to bridge the chasm between life and the Book. We increasingly lack a link with the Bible; it is no longer a source of inspiration and guidance. It has lost its magic.

A brief hermeneutic excursion will explain. The interpretive power of *peshat* derives not from religious common ground but only from philological credibility. In contrast, the interpretive validity of a midrashic system, the confidence that the content attributed to the text is indeed concealed between its lines, is limited a priori to believers. For the members of that audience to embrace the proposed midrashic commentary as an authentic, binding interpretation, they must agree on:

1. The overall truth of the values, ideas, and ideals that they are supposed to believe: Zionism as renaissance and redemption; Eretz Israel as the promised land; the duty of self-sacrifice to pioneering and security goals; and so on.

2. The supreme position of the Book in the community, its ability to reinforce the beliefs, precepts, and hopes to which it is committed: the Bible as the peak of creativity in the era of our national splendor and an embodiment of eternal truths.

3. The capacity of quasi-homiletical exegesis—despite its relative methodological freedom—to reveal an inner truth behind the linguistic exterior.

The first two assumptions taken together—the truth of the values the audience embraces and their acceptance of the eternal truth of the Book—clearly justify an interpretive technique flexible enough to adapt those eternal truths to the needs of the times: The secularizing national midrash is indeed revealing and faithfully representing the message of Scripture to our generation, which is once again implementing, "for the first time in two thousand years," the injunction to return to Zion and to rebuild the land. But once the force of Zionist values has faded, their brilliance dimmed, with the concomitant weakening of the need to connect with the Bible as the values' source of inspiration, the methodological weakness of the national midrash is clear: It is artificial, empty, meaningless. Interpretive flexibility, tolerated because it was necessary to bridge the gap between the Bible and its readers, is now seen as illusion, repugnant manipulation. Once the national midrash has lost its allure, it has also lost its creative power.

These days, appeals to the Bible for inspiration or motivation are rare indeed, and they are generally low-key; perhaps the only instance in recent years was the use of the anti-pharaonic call "Let my people go" as a unifying slogan in the struggle for liberation of the Soviet Jews. Another echo of biblical language is the Hebrew name of the Israeli association for the protection of human rights in the Occupied Areas, Be-Tzelem, "in the image" ("in the image of God," Gen. 1.27), implying that the association's work is a true expression of the biblical ethic. The secular nature of this midrash is brought out by divorcing the word from its context—whose "image"?—but the link with the Bible is highlighted by printing the word with the traditional vowel points and cantillation accents. A similar technique is employed on the title page of Arieh (Lova) Eliav's anthology, On Peace in Jewish Tradition (Heb.: Tel Aviv, 1975), where the word shalom is printed in the same way. In this book, however, even the sympathetic reader senses that the author is seeking in the Bible not inspiration but "proofs" for his values. Similarly— though the differences are greater than the comparison—Member of Kenesset (Israel's Parliament) Yael Dayan's attempt to anchor her campaign for gay rights in David's lament for Jonathan was seen not as authentic, merely provocative. On the other hand, Meir Shalev's humorous midrash, The Bible Now (Heb.: Jerusalem and Tel Aviv, 1985), was received enthusiastically and widely circulated

because, in contrast to the traditionally adulatory attitude, he has brought the Bible down to our own level. His readers willingly swallow even his entirely imaginary additions (such as the idea that Abigail poisoned her husband Nabal in order to marry David) because the humorous midrash provides us with a kind of biblical confirmation for a realistic, forgiving view of ourselves.

In contrast to Ben-Gurion's ideals, not only has the Bible lost its hold on young people but Israeli youth has rallied to the Diaspora's characteristic issue: the Holocaust. This may be an attempt to atone for early condescending sabra-Zionist attitudes to the Diaspora and the hasty judgment of the millions of victims as "lambs led to slaughter"; it may also represent a desire to exchange the imperative of Return implicit in the biblical promise, grounds for fervent, ideological Zionism, for the imperative of preventing a further Holocaust, grounds for pragmatic Zionism. Perhaps it also expresses a craving for a national ideal protected by a universal, unchallenged taboo, uniting the entire nation in the face of a calamity whose uniqueness and exclusiveness are vehemently defended.

None of these revolutionary developments have affected the ḥaredi [ultra-Orthodox] community. One component of that community's opposition to Zionism is a firm refusal to detach the Bible from the oral law and make it shine "with its own light" in the center of national existence. The talmudic worldview considers the written law first in sanctity but not in authority. That privilege is reserved for the oral law, which, as the authoritative interpretation of the Bible, also determines which of its contents are effective today. The hierarchy is also reflected in the curriculum of the ḥaredi schools: The Bible is studied by children, both boys and girls, but when the boys are ready to study Talmud they no longer study the Bible (except for the weekly Torah portion). The Talmud itself, it is true, lists the Bible as a subject for study in its own right, binding for adults: "Man should always divide his time into three: a third [spent] studying Bible, a third Mishnah, a third the Talmud" (b. Kid. 30a). In the Middle Ages, however, it was ruled that that injunction is fulfilled—in all three parts—by studying the Babylonian Talmud, since it includes all three.

With the Talmud occupying center stage, contextual, philological interpretation of the text, *peshat,* is not a challenge (except for the two centuries between Rashi and Ḥizkuni, the Golden Age of the French school of *peshat,* which flourished in the explicitly talmudic culture of northern France); besides, over the last few generations, the creativity of homiletic interpretation in general has declined. As a result, contemporary *ḥaredi* society has raised the exclusivity of Talmud study to an unprecedented level, and accordingly has not been affected by the changing attitudes to the Bible in the Zionist camp. One cost of this stability has been a loss of creativity: There are among this group no new commentaries on the Bible; they prefer instead to publish anthologies of classical commentaries. Examples are the eclectic commentaries published in English in the United States by the *ḥaredi* Art-Scroll Publishing House, and the popular book by Yehudah Nashoni, *Hagut be-Parshiyot ha-Torah,* i.e., *Meditation on the Portions of the Torah,* subtitled "Original Exegesis according to *Pardes,* as directed by Early and Late Authorities, with the Addition of Innovations and Insights" (2nd ed., Benei Berak, 1979).

The national-religious public, too, believes in the unity of the oral and written law, while insisting that this principle in no way bars its participation in the Zionist return to the Bible. On its face this should be easy: it requires a clear differentiation between *peshat* and midrash, as taught by the great exponents of *peshat,* mainly in medieval Spain and northern France. Since both modes of exegesis are legitimate, each can be considered for its specific purpose: midrash explains the written law in accordance with the oral, while *peshat* extracts the primary meaning of the biblical text. In fact, however, the paths blazed by the medieval commentators cannot simply be re-

sumed, for in modern biblical studies the *peshat* method is immeasurably more critical than in the medieval period: It challenges not only the unity of the written and oral law but even the sanctity of the Bible itself—at least, in the traditional definition.

Orthodox Bible scholars, therefore, who teach at Bar-Ilan University and other academic institutions, must contribute to the development of *peshat* while meeting the double criterion of scientific method and religious faith. In answering this challenge they are motivated, among other things, by the belief that the quest for truth is a religious duty—a *mitzvah*—and that intellectual integrity is an ethical-religious virtue. In this endeavor they indeed require no little courage to face opposition from both right and left.

The great majority of religiously observant Bible teachers, however, prefer not to confront the tension between *peshat* and *derash,* or the critical bent of modern *peshat,* instead adopting various pragmatic solutions. Quite typical, for example, is the inclusion of Bible lessons in almost all the yeshivah high schools, in the category of "secular" rather than "sacred" studies. Moreover, most Bible teachers in these schools—and in the parallel girls' *ulpenot*—are not university graduates with degrees in Bible studies, but yeshivah graduates whose studies have centered on the Talmud. Not only are they unqualified, having professionally studied neither the Bible itself nor the related tools; but, lacking the aptitude to explain the *peshat* consistently and systematically (particularly as they sometimes view it contemptuously as overly "simple" and superficial), they tend to offer their own fanciful interpretations in the spirit of *derash.* Even when teaching the Torah with the standard commentators, they generally fail to distinguish between *peshat* and *derash,* preferring to present their students with a harmonistic hodgepodge of "pretty" explanations, unsystematic and uncontrolled.

Observant Jews are exposed in the synagogue to signficant sections of the Bible: the weekly Torah portions, the haftarot, and the

Five Scrolls; and a good many psalms in the prayers. They regard study of the Torah (including the Written Torah) as a major religious duty (mitzvah). Consequently, their sons and daughters rival each other in the worldwide Bible Quiz for Youth, with no secular competitors on the scene. Nevertheless, whether they are slowly edging to the right and adopting ḥaredi ways, or maintaining their involvement in society as a whole, they cannot evade their part in the process of the deterioration of the Bible's status.

Now that the Bible has been divested of the colorful cloak created by the national midrash, it emerges in its primary light, as a religious document. As long as the national midrash ruled, the secular public thought it understood the Bible better than did the religious public, which was still shackled by the bonds of rabbinic midrash. Now, however, with the religious nature of the Bible rediscovered, secular Israelis have seemingly renounced such pretensions, and are perhaps even willing to relinquish possession, and restore the Bible to the believers in its sanctity. The latter, for their part, are quick to cite the relative short-livedness of the secular interpretation as historical proof of its illegitimacy; intoxicated by this newfound power, they are inclined to arrogate to themselves the exclusive right to interpret and explain the Bible. Moreover, as religiosity is generally perceived today from the outside and from a distance, in its fundamentalist-nationalist guise, secular Israelis are increasingly distancing themselves from the Bible. This has been reinforced by yet another development: As the secular-national midrash has lost its cogency, it has been supplanted by a new national midrash, which places the values of a maximalist—at times brutal—religious Zionism on what seems like the plain meaning of the biblical text. Thus, exclusive Jewish ownership of the land is justified by Rashi's comment on the first verse of the Torah; commitment to the territorial integrity of Greater Israel is derived from Abraham's "Covenant of Pieces" with God in Gen. ch 15; triumphalist isolationism

is substantiated by Balaam's blessing, "A people that dwells apart, not reckoning itself among the goyim" (Num. 23.9); and the taking of excessive political and military risks is based on "Israel, trust in the LORD! He is their help and shield" (Ps. 115.9); not to mention the Kahanist glorification of Simeon's and Levi's killing in Shechem (Gen. ch 34) and the topical espousal of the book of Joshua and the war against Amalek. If this is indeed the true message of the Bible, little wonder that many secular Israelis, who believed with all their heart that justice and humanity, if applied only to our own people, are no better than injustice and inhumanity, draw back and reject the Bible. It has lost its universality; once a unifier, it has become divisive.

Existential Peshat as a Possible Response to Current Needs

The time is not ripe for a new collective midrash. We have only just emerged from an era of collective certainties, and a time of searching may follow the current transitional period of alienation. Peshat is essentially an open-ended quest. While derash is generally founded on a priori acceptance of certain truths, peshat depends on the credibility of method. The seeker of peshat is not supposed to know in advance what may be found in the text; the only prerequisites are philological exactitude, common sense, intellectual honesty, an open mind, and an awareness of the distinctiveness of the ancient text. If its religious nature, which can no longer be denied, is not to erect a barrier between an avowed nonbeliever and the Book, he or she must be on guard against secular arrogance toward religious faith, and perhaps also overcome the fear of being bewitched by its charms, and listen with an open mind and heart to the direct voice of the text. Intelligence, imagination, and empathy will help to understand the meaning of the words "says the LORD" when uttered by a prophet, as well as their implications for the messenger's attitude to his Master and to his mission. On the other hand, one can understand a biblical passage properly without having to accept it as factual truth or normatively binding. One must refrain from negating the text a priori, enter into a dialogue with the text, and thereby enhance one's ability to listen to it on its merits.

The national midrash built an educational analogy between past and present, but the seeker of *peshat*, in the quest for the primary meaning of the text, does not ignore the differences between past and present. A heightened awareness of passing time teaches one that even religious values and institutions are dependent on historical context. This historical sense can protect us from the fundamentalism that uncritically embraces biblical norms (such as political violence) in utterly changed circumstances. The seeker of *peshat* must also scrutinize the Bible against the background of its environment, gaining a broad perspective that indicates the limits of our national uniqueness, the relationship between adoption (say, of Canaanite language and poetics) and rejection (for instance, of Babylonian ethical and legal norms). Identification with biblical heroes, too, is no longer romantic but critical, in the spirit of the fervent inner criticism discernible in the Bible itself. This sober realism of *peshat* is accompanied by the quest for truth, and this may enhance the attraction of *peshat* for those who have lost trust and interest in the high-flown idealism of the national midrash.

Peshat is inconceivable without methodological awareness: It is relative, derived from scant information (because of the extreme brevity of biblical historiography and the scarcity of contemporary extrabiblical documentation), and constrained by the scholar's scientific school and personality. This methodological awareness must go hand in hand with hermeneutic awareness that a text may tolerate more than one interpretation. The time of arrogant *peshat*, professing to be the supreme, exclusive, scientific truth, is over; the time has come for *peshat* which, though conscious of its advantages—rigorous discipline, rationality, consistency, independence,

immediacy—is also acutely aware of the attendant disadvantages—clinging to the past, exclusive attention to the rational, and aversion to ambivalence. This *peshat*, far from disdaining midrash, recognizes its contribution. It is therefore vital that departments of biblical studies at universities and high schools introduce the thorough, systematic study of rabbinic midrash. Students at all levels should be capable of evaluating the nature of creative, nonphilological exegesis and thereby of understanding the sterling value of midrash down through the generations, from those remote times when religious creativity shifted from revelation to interpretation, to the recent times when a modern national movement found it necessary to connect with its ancient source of inspiration. The attraction of Bible studies will be enhanced if students realize that they demand not only proficiency and understanding of the text, but also methodological sophistication. One cannot simply say anything that comes to mind; but differences of opinion and variant exegetical methods are legitimate, each generation having its own interpreters.

Existential *peshat* is based on critical *peshat*, but the two are not identical. While many scholars must keep the text at a distance, behind a barrier, an interpreter seeking to make the Bible relevant to his or her personal existence is thereby regarding him- or herself as one of those to whom it is addressed. The Bible's role as the foundation text of the Jewish people is not dissimilar to the role of parents: One can develop relationships of all kinds toward them, but one cannot relate to them as strangers. Just so, a member of the Jewish people may respect the Bible, love it, obey it; but may equally well disobey it, rebel against it, or feel estranged from it. Whatever the case, that person cannot view the Bible as "just another book." This is aptly demonstrated by a recent show, *"Va-yo'mer va-yelekh"* ("And he said, and he went"), staged by the *Ittim* ensemble under the direction of Rina Yerushalmi, who writes in the program notes that, after staging two Shakespeare plays, "we felt that the time had come to reach out to our own text, and the Bible is our primeval text." As a prodigal son returning to his parents, this powerful show comes back to the Bible, with admiration, love, anger, bitter mockery, and pain.

Existential *peshat* will never be able to place the Bible at the center of public life. Instead of struggling in vain to recreate a bygone situation, it is more realistic to promote understanding of the Bible as it is, with its beliefs, inner tensions, and chronological and geographical contexts; and, at the same time, to bring out the relevance of the Torah, the Prophets, and the Writings for our own time. No exegetical technique, however, can create unassisted the motivation for its use. Lacking

thirst, there is no sure need for the well or the pump. Good teachers are capable of provoking thirst, but their numbers are steadily decreasing for lack of a supportive public atmosphere. Nevertheless, if we can believe the many signs that herald the beginning of a new era, marked by reaction to the prevalent cynicism and nihilism, by growing awareness of the benefit inherent in a definition of personal and collective identity, in a commitment to norms and values, and in the awe confronting spiritual greatness—if we can trust these signs, there are good prospects that all these will be sought first and foremost in that wonderful book which rests, well-nigh forgotten, on the bottom shelf of the "Jewish bookcase."

[URIEL SIMON]

Jewish Women's Scholarly Writings on the Bible

Recent biblical scholarship has been witness to the growing visibility of women scholars, and the profound impact of feminist criticism. Jewish women have participated actively in these trends, and there now exists a corpus of Jewish women's biblical scholarship, some of which also partakes of and contributes to the area of feminist criticism. What follows is a brief survey that outlines its range of subject matter and methodologies, examines its presuppositions, and assesses its place in the field of biblical studies in general and feminist biblical criticism more specifically. The works cited are only a small sample of an ever-growing library, but they illustrate the diversity of current approaches and interests that are addressed in Jewish women's writing on the Bible.

Subject Matter

The studies undertaken by Jewish women address a range of topics similar to that found in women's biblical scholarship more generally. First and foremost, Jewish women's writing on the Bible had focused on the representation

of women both within and outside of their family contexts. *Countertraditions in the Bible: A Feminist Approach*, by Ilana Pardes (Cambridge, MA: Harvard University Press, 1992), for example, analyzes stories about women as well as the female imagery in the Song of Songs, while *Taboo or not Taboo: Sexuality and Family in the Hebrew Bible*, by Ilona N. Rashkow (Minneapolis: Fortress, 2000) explores incest and other aspects of sexuality within the family unit. Athalya Brenner's study, *The Intercourse of Knowledge: On Gendering Desire and "Sexuality" in the Hebrew Bible* (Leiden: Brill, 1997), examines both the semantics and the narratives of gender and sexuality, including the broad range of what she refers to as "deviations from socio-sexual boundaries." Yet not all books by women scholars pay special attention to issues of gender and the representation of women. For example, *From Father to Son: Kinship, Conflict, and Continuity in Genesis*, by Devora Steinmetz (Louisville, KY: Westminster John Knox Press, 1991), focuses primarily on male relationships and pays little attention to the presence and absence of women in the Genesis narratives.

By contrast, other works incorporate a strong emphasis on gender issues into their treatments of topics that extend beyond women, family, and female imagery. Susan Niditch's study, *War in the Hebrew Bible: A Study in the Ethics of Violence* (New York: Oxford University Press, 1993), is not explicitly a feminist reading of the Bible; indeed, it is much more concerned with addressing the anti-Jewish interpretations in which biblical Israel, and, by extension, Judaism, are viewed as war-mongering and parochial. Nevertheless, Niditch examines such female figures as Jael (Judg. chs 4–5) and Esther, and addresses issues such as the fate of women in time of war. Adele Reinhartz's *Why Ask My Name? Anonymity and Identity in Biblical Narrative* (New York: Oxford University Press, 1992) focuses on the unnamed characters in the Bible, both male and female, but it too pays special attention to issues related to gender, particularly because so many of the Bible's anonymous figures are women.

Whereas the above studies focus primarily on biblical texts as such, others place them within the broader context of the ancient Near Eastern world. Tikva Frymer-Kensky's *In the Wake of the Goddesses: Women, Culture, and the Biblical Transformation of Pagan Myth* (New York: Fawcett, Columbine 1992) examines the biblical transformation of ancient Near Eastern goddess mythology and its impact on sexuality, gender, and wisdom as expressed in the Bible. Other writers look at biblical women as a starting point for a broader discussion of the role of women in Judaism or in Jewish literature. Nehama Aschkenasy's book, *Eve's Journey: Feminine Images in Hebraic Literary Tradition* (Philadelphia: University of Pennsylvania Press, 1986), for example, traces the ongoing influence of female archetypes back to the "otherness" of women in ancient Hebrew literature. Helena Zlotnick's *Dinah's Daughters: Gender and Judaism from the Hebrew Bible to Late Antiquity* (Philadelphia: University of Pennsylvania Press, 2002) looks at the ways in which Judaism contrasts Jewish and Gentile women in the context of national

identity. Leila Leah Bronner's *From Eve to Esther: Rabbinic Reconstructions of Biblical Women* (Louisville, KY: Westminster John Knox, 1994) examines the treatment of key biblical women in rabbinic literature. These studies are based on the assumption that the biblical portrayal of women has profoundly informed the ways in which women are described in later Jewish literature, and in the laws and customs that have determined women's roles in postbiblical Jewish law and everyday life.

Finally, there is a growing body of literature that takes biblical narratives about women as a basis for more personal responses, in the form of meditations and creative retellings. For example, Alicia Suskin Ostriker's book, *The Nakedness of the Fathers* (New Brunswick: Rutgers University Press, 1994), combines poetry, biblical interpretation, and autobiography in a uniquely refreshing and illuminating way. In doing so, she also exhorts Jewish women to do their own interpretations of biblical texts, thereby engaging in their own acts of discovery and creativity. Such works mark the intersection of scholarship and creative literature. They do not so much elucidate the possible meanings of the Bible in its original context as they explore its possibilities for contemporary Jewish women. Yet in the very process of doing so, they often draw attention to the ways in which, and the degree to which, these narratives themselves reflect a particular time and place.

Methodologies

In contrast to the field of biblical studies more generally, Jewish women's biblical scholarship does not focus very much on source analysis and other historical-critical issues, nor is there much concern about "what really happened," an issue that is of great interest in feminist New Testament scholarship (for example, concerning the role of female disciples of Jesus, and the role of women as deacons in early Christian worship). One exception is the work of Savina Teubal (*Sarah the Priestess: The First Matriarch of Genesis* [Athens, OH: Swallow Press, 1984]; *Hagar the Egyptian: The Lost Tradition of the Matriarchs* [San Francisco: HarperSanFrancisco, 1990]), which attempts to treat Hagar and Sarah as historical figures and account for their biblical representations on the basis of the history, politics, and demographics of Israelite society. Most scholars, however, refrain from such specific historical reconstructions, due to the paucity of evidence (but see the discussion below on social-scientific methodologies).

If the Bible does not provide a clear window into Israelite history, it does provide ample basis for other types of approaches. Most prevalent among women writers on the Bible have been literary-critical methodologies, either on their own or in combination with other methods. From Adele Berlin's *Poetics and Interpretation of Biblical Narrative* (Sheffield: The Almond Press, 1983) to Yairah Amit's introduction, *Reading Biblical Narratives: Literary Criticism and the Hebrew Bible* (Minneapolis: Fortress, 2001), a central concern has been to explore the workings of biblical narrative by employing the categories and methods applied to the genres of narrative and poetry. Such works consider the fundamental building blocks of narrative, including plot, character, and setting, as well as more subtle dimensions such as narrative point of view and linguistic elements such as morphological and syntactical parallelism (e.g., Adele Berlin, *The Dynamics of Biblical Parallelism* [Bloomington: Indiana University Press, 1985]).

In most cases, literary approaches are seasoned with a strong dose of historical consciousness. Exemplary in this regard is the work of Susan Ackerman (*Warrior, Dancer, Seductress, Queen: Women in Judges and Biblical Israel* [New York: Doubleday, 1998]). While Ackerman does not assume a historical reality for the stories or characters of the book of Judges, she does take seriously the historical reality of the authors and their audiences. In analyzing Judges' stories about women, she discerns six character types and compares their stories to others from the ancient Near East in order to discern the ways in which

they were imagined and developed over the thousand-year period of Israelite history.

Other scholars explicitly combine literary approaches with social-scientific methodologies. Athalya Brenner (*The Israelite Woman: Social Role and Literary Type in Biblical Narrative* [Sheffield: JSOT Press, 1985]) draws on biblical narratives in order to examine the social roles available in ancient Israelite society outside of the family and household contexts. Carol Meyers (*Discovering Eve: Ancient Israelite Women in Context* [New York: Oxford, 1988]) uses a socio-historical method that draws upon archeology, feminist criticism, anthropology, and social-scientific theory more generally to discern the social world of ancient Israel, in particular women's lives within the household in relation to the larger community.

Another fruitful combination has involved literary studies and psychoanalysis. For example, Ilona N. Rashkow draws on psychoanalysis in *The Phallacy of Genesis: A Feminist-Psychoanalytic Approach* (Louisville, KY: Westminster John Knox Press, 1993) and, more recently, *Taboo or not Taboo: Sexuality and Family in the Hebrew Bible*. In a category all its own is the work of Aviva Gottlieb Zornberg (*Genesis of Desire: Reflections on Genesis* [Philadelphia: Jewish Publication Society, 1995]; *Particulars of Rapture: Reflections on Exodus* [New York: Doubleday, 2001]), which draws both from traditional Jewish sources and from a broad range of philosophical, literary, and psychoanalytical works in her struggles with the meaning of the biblical text.

On the whole, these varied approaches and areas of investigation coexist amicably within the field of biblical studies. This state of affairs may reflect not only the desire of women to be supportive of women's study of the Bible generally, but also a postmodern ethos that validates the notion that a given text may be subject to a plurality of interpretations. Nevertheless, there is one contentious issue that also makes its way, at least occasionally, into the literature, and that is the extent to which Jewish women's writings on the Bible may confirm rather than resist or subvert the biases of mainstream biblical criticism, whether of "secular" scholars or traditional Jewish interpretation. In particular, the literary critical enterprise is sharply criticized by Esther Fuchs in her book *Sexual Politics in the Biblical Narrative: Reading the Hebrew Bible as a Woman* (Sheffield: Sheffield Academic Press, 2000). Fuchs argues that literary-critical works are often fundamentally androcentric; by admiring "the virtuosity of the biblical narrator" they "ignore the patriarchal ideology that inspires so much of what they glorify" (Fuchs, p. 7). She is similarly dismissive of postmodern approaches that, in her view, implicitly or explicitly condone patriarchal readings (p. 9). Fuchs advocates a resistant reading that "questions the ways in which the biblical narrative universalizes and legislates its hierarchical endorsement of the power relations between male and female characters" (p. 9). Despite these views, her own approach is literary, in that it focuses on the Bible as a literary text or texts, at the same time as it is also ideological, in that it exposes the ideological tendencies within these literary texts.

The questions raised in these works, the approaches they take, and the audiences that they address, all place them firmly within the spectrum of biblical studies more generally, including feminist biblical criticism. The participation of Jewish women in the larger enterprise is illustrated by the multi-volume anthologies titled *A Feminist Companion to the Bible* (edited by Athalya Brenner, first series, 11 volumes [Sheffield: Sheffield Academic Press, 1993–1997], second series, 7 volumes [Sheffield: Sheffield Academic Press, 1998–2000]), in which chapters by North American and European authors—Christian, Jewish, and neither—sit side by side and often engage in dialogue with one another. These collections provide readers from many different social locations and levels of knowledge with access to the range of feminist scholarship, including the European and Jewish voices that are often not well known to North American and non-Jewish readers.

In keeping with this broad range of approaches, Jewish women's writings on the Bible draw upon a wide variety of sources, from the classics of biblical scholarship, to works in other fields that develop the methodologies that women apply to the Bible, to a range of religious and other literature from which parallels can be drawn and to which connections can be made. While some women situate their work firmly within the spectrum of critical biblical scholarship, others draw liberally from traditional Jewish sources. This is apparent not only in the apologetic works, in which traditional Jewish exegesis is often seen as the key to the meaning of the text, but in a number of other creative works, including the work of Elyse Goldstein (*ReVisions: Seeing Torah through a Feminist Lens* [Woodstock, VT: Jewish Lights, 1988]), Norma Rosen (*Biblical Women Unbound* [Philadelphia: Jewish Publication Society, 1986]), Alicia Ostriker (*The Nakedness of the Fathers*), and Ellen Frankel (*The Five Books of Miriam: A Woman's Commentary on the Torah* [San Francisco: HarperSanFrancisco, 1996]).

All four of these books evoke the genre of midrash, that is, classic Jewish biblical interpretation, as a resource for their own creative approaches. Goldstein and Frankel both intend their books as contributions to the Jewish commentary genre that has its roots in rabbinic midrash and is exemplified in medieval Jewish interpretation. Frankel's book reflects this genre not only in its content but also in its formal structure, in which biblical passages are quoted, and then the imagined responses of a range of collective ("our daughters," "our mothers," "our bubbes," "the rabbis") and individual (such as Lilith, Sarah, Hagar, Dinah, and Miriam) commentators are recorded, in a way that imparts a sense of lively dialogue. Books that fall more squarely into the genre of critical biblical scholarship, however, draw much less frequently upon classic Jewish sources such as midrash or medieval exegesis. Some refer occasionally to specific midrashim (Reinhartz, Steinmetz, Pamela Tamarkin Reis, *Reading the Lines: A Fresh Look at the Hebrew*

Bible [Peabody, MA: Hendrickson, 2002]), or discuss midrash as a genre (Berlin, Meyers, Steinmetz), but their primary frame of reference is critical biblical scholarship.

Basic Assumptions

Despite these diverse interests and approaches, Jewish women's writings on the Bible share a number of presuppositions. Most important is the need to include women and gender issues in the overall study of the Bible. Implicit in this assumption is the view that biblical scholarship, while not ignoring women entirely, has generally overlooked the presence and importance of women. Thus to some extent women's biblical scholarship aims to correct a bias in mainstream scholarship. Second, while few of these works concern themselves directly with textual or literary reconstruction, many of them, with the exception of those taking a very traditional stance, do presume the results of standard source criticism, that is, they agree that the Bible in its present form took shape over a number of centuries and drew upon several written sources. They also agree that it is important to situate biblical writings within their context in the ancient Near Eastern world, and to consider social and historical circumstances to the extent that these can be ascertained.

Most controversial, perhaps, is the degree to which Jewish women writers accept or reject the fundamental assumptions of feminist biblical scholarship more generally: that the society reflected in the Bible was patriarchal in that it privileges men, and that the Bible itself is an androcentric text, written from the perspective of male interests, concerns, and activities. On one end of the spectrum we find apologetic works, often written by Orthodox women (e.g., Tamar Frankiel, *The Voice of Sarah: Feminine Spirituality and Traditional Judaism* [San Francisco: HarperSanFrancisco, 1990]) with the intention of affirming the traditional separation of gender roles according to which women are relegated to the pri-

vate, domestic sphere and hence excluded from public roles, particularly within the synagogue service. Such works reflect the influence of feminism insofar as they focus on the role of women in a way that is not usually apparent in traditional Jewish men's writings on the Bible, but they reject the feminist emphasis on liberation due to its implied critique of traditional Judaism. Such works will argue that traditional women's roles stem from the Torah and hence are divinely mandated; furthermore, they do not oppress women or imply their secondary status, but, on the contrary, affirm their elevated spiritual status.

Many other works, whether written by secular women (e.g., Pardes) or by women who affiliate themselves with the established Jewish denominations (Goldstein, Reinhartz), either implicitly or explicitly accept the feminist argument regarding the Bible's androcentrism and patriarchy. Rashkow (*Taboo or not Taboo*), for example, views biblical patriarchy and androcentrism as mechanisms by which heterosexual males defined themselves as the norm (p. 10). Niditch ("Portrayals of Women in the Hebrew Bible," in Judith R. Baskin, ed., *Jewish Women in Historical Perspective* [Detroit: Wayne State University Press, 1991], p. 28) and Pardes both acknowledge the Bible as patriarchal and androcentric, but argue for the presence of "nuances" (Niditch) or "countertraditions" (Pardes) that subtly subvert or undermine the predominant patriarchal ideology.

Context in Biblical Scholarship

Jewish women writers on the Bible differ fundamentally from non-Jewish women to the extent that they relate in some way to classical Jewish sources as being part of their own heritage; that they in some way or another incorporate Jewish sensibilities or experiences, however these may be defined, into their scholarship and writing; and that they envisage Jews, or more specifically Jewish women, as an important part of their audiences. In other ways, however, the concerns and perspectives of Jewish women parallel those of non-Jewish women, particularly women who explicitly identify themselves as Christian, who examine issues that arise in Christian contexts and address their studies primarily to Christian women. In both cases there are interpreters who read the Scriptures with a "hermeneutics of suspicion" (Elisabeth Schüssler Fiorenza) in order to identify patriarchal and androcentric tendencies, those who creatively fill the gaps of the text to create new texts, those who find "countertraditions" in the Bible that can be used as a basis for subverting or correcting the text's patriarchal biases, and those who believe that the Bible is beyond redemption. These similarities exist because of mutual influence, but also because Jewish and Christian women are engaged in parallel struggles against the ways that the biblical text has been used to restrict women's activities and possibilities.

The value of Jewish women's writings on the Bible as scholarship can be measured by their contributions to the understanding of the Bible, its narrative, theology, ideology, and all other aspects. In the context of feminist scholarship, however, their value can be measured in terms of their liberative potential. The latter can be seen most clearly in those works that draw on the creative imagination of the author. These works may fall at or outside the margins of the scholarly world, but as personal reflections that attempt to address contemporary women through ancient texts, they have the potential to reach a general audience that may also be open to a new way of reading the Bible. Nevertheless, the proliferation of Jewish women's writing on the Bible, in its very diversity, is a force for liberation and transformation. It exemplifies women's access to education and to the institutions of higher education and publication, and allows women's views to stand alongside those of male scholars in shaping the field of biblical studies. Whether they do or do not view the Bible as a positive force in women's lives, women writers on the Bible themselves model the possibilities for Jewish women to become engaged and make strong contribution in the form of works that will be read and have influence both within the academy and in the broader community.

[ADELE REINHARTZ]

Jewish Translations of the Bible

Jews first translated the Bible approximately 2,300 years ago, and Jews continue—as individuals and as members of committees—to translate the Bible to the present day. The first translation was the Septuagint or Old Greek version of the Bible, produced in Alexandria for use by Greek-speaking Jews. Translations such as the Jewish Publication Society's new Tanakh, therefore, on which this study Bible is based, have a considerable lineage.

In spite of a rich and varied heritage, Jewish translations have not received the attention accorded to Christian versions. This has only partly to do with the relative sizes of the Jewish and Christian communities. It has much more to do with the role of translation in the history of Christianity. Translation was present from the beginning: Although Jesus (presumably) primarily spoke Aramaic, his words were preserved and disseminated in Greek. Translation, therefore, as a function of mission, was present in Christianity from the beginning.

In Judaism, by contrast, respect for the original Hebrew wording has been maintained through the intervening centuries. Even when substantial numbers of Jews have not understood Hebrew—as occurred during the Hellenistic period, when many adopted Greek as their primary language—those who translated the Hebrew text produced a version that was markedly influenced by Hebrew phrasing, idiom, and syntax. This points to a distinctive feature of Judaism: the desire to preserve some familiarity with the Hebrew text and language in at least some part of the community. Thus, for instance, chanting of the Bible in Hebrew remains a part of liturgical practice in almost all contemporary synagogues—whether or not most worshippers can understand the text in its original tongue.

Thus for Jews a translated Bible is an accompaniment to, not replacement for, the original Hebrew. This helps explain the prominence of Jewish versions that display the Hebrew and English (or other foreign language text) on facing pages. Even when the Hebrew text is not physically present in its entirety, it is typically brought to the reader's attention through numerous notations and references.

On the other hand, another tradition attempted to make the Bible available in more idiomatic versions to the increasing number of Jews who had little or no acquaintance with Hebrew and no desire to learn it. These two impulses have continued in the history of Jewish translation to the present.

From these remarks it can be deduced that for many in the Jewish community Bible translations have had an ambivalent status: The Bible has needed to be translated so it would be understood; at the same time, this translation typically pointed to the importance of the original Hebrew. These translations have followed the Jewish tradition in terms not only of contents and order, but with familiar divisions into weekly Torah portions, inclusion of haftarot (the readings from the Prophets that accompany the weekly Torah readings), and other features associated with synagogue usage. Moreover, such a version reflects the richness of the exegetical traditions, both halakhic and midrashic; christological interpretations have no place in such editions.

Early Versions

The earliest Jewish Bible translation, the Torah translated into Greek, dates to approxi-

mately 275 BCE in Alexandria, the Egyptian capital city. As recorded in the *Letter of Aristeas*, which was composed at least a century after the events it purports to narrate, the second ruler of Hellenistic Egypt, Ptolemy II Philadelphus, was persuaded by his librarian to initiate and support a Greek translation of the Jewish laws or *torah*. This text was to occupy a place of honor at the great library Ptolemy was assembling at Alexandria. Ptolemy arranged for seventy-two elders—each renowned for his scholarship and unblemished morality—to be brought in from Jerusalem to ensure that the translation would meet the highest standards of both Hellenistic and Jewish scholarship. Ptolemy welcomed them with lavish entertainment, after which they set about their task. They finished their work in seventy-two days, dividing themselves into subcommittees and consulting with each other. This story has parallels, with variants and embellishments, in rabbinic literature, as well as in Josephus, Philo, and other ancient Jewish sources.

The last part of the *Letter of Aristeas* narrates a formal ceremony during which the Jews of Alexandria accepted this Greek translation of the Torah as Sacred Writ. Details of this ceremony call to mind, intentionally so, the account of Moses' giving of the law in the biblical book of Exodus. To underscore the seriousness of this action, a curse was uttered against anyone daring to alter the wording of this Greek version.

It is unlikely that this lofty view of translation accords with what its translators actually had in mind. If we examine the Septuagint version of the Torah, we find a fairly literal reflection of its Hebrew *Vorlage* (underlying text). It is not difficult to see in this approach the desire to produce something on the model of a Hebrew-Greek interlinear version, which would presuppose at least rudimentary knowledge of both languages on the part of its originally intended audience.

Such a Greek text, especially when it circulated independently among people who had little or no knowledge of Hebrew, could well become a substitute for the original, as the *Letter of Aristeas* envisions. That is not necessarily the case, however. In fact, numerous revisers of this earliest version of the Greek, of whom Aquila (2nd century CE), Theodotion (2nd century CE), and Symmachus (2nd–3rd century CE) are the best known, regularly displayed their acceptance of the subservience of the Greek to the Hebrew when they "corrected" older Greek texts to accord with the Hebrew wording in use within their community. In this way they reflected the view, described above, of the foreign-language text as at most the next-best thing to the Hebrew. At the same time, the care with which they fashioned their Greek version demonstrates the seriousness with which they carried out their craft.

We cannot know for certain what led the author of the *Letter of Aristeas* to promote the Septuagint as a document with sanctity and authority equal to the original. The fact that Jewish revisers, presumably active before and during the period when the *Letter* was composed, continued their work in spite of the threats of anathema might lead to the conclusion that the *Letter*'s author was an idiosyncratic or at least ineffective proponent of his point of view. But that is certainly not so. The 1st-century CE Jewish philosopher Philo, himself a native of Alexandria, equated the Septuagint translators with the biblical prophets, thus according their words—and especially the differences between the Greek and the Hebrew texts—the status of inspired revelation. Philo knew no Hebrew; for such an individual, the Bible in translated form assumed preeminent importance.

While Philo was undoubtedly not the sole Jew to feel this way, his point of view is more characteristic of early Christians. It was in their communities that the relatively sober account of Aristeas acquired its miraculous characteristics: Each scholar worked alone to produce, under divine intervention, exactly the same text as his colleagues. And until Jerome (ca. 345–420 CE), hardly any church leader studied Hebrew or sought to learn the language so as to read the Old Testament in its original formulation. The Greek text served that purpose, as it continues to do for Orthodox Christians to this very day.

Was this earliest Greek version the result of internal Jewish concerns about the need for authoritative interpretation as the Hebrew grew increasingly foreign to the community? Or was the impetus, as asserted in the *Letter of Aristeas*, external, the result of intellectual curiosity on the part of the Ptolemaic leadership? As is so often the case, the response need not be either/or. Rather, it is perfectly understandable that a convergence of compatible motives led to this development.

The *Letter of Aristeas* deals only with the translation of the Torah. In the absence of external evidence, even sources as problematic as the *Letter of Aristeas*, it is difficult to speak with certainty about the order, provenance, and *tendenz* (ideological slant or general orientation) of other books or blocks of material for the Septuagint. We can note, nonetheless, that some later translators consciously modeled their renderings on the generally literal approach taken by the translators of the Torah, while other translators apparently felt free to modernize, harmonize, and otherwise modify the underlying Hebrew text, presumably to accord with their perception of audience needs. Among revisers such as Theodotion and Aquila, there is a noticeable tendency toward more literal representation of the Hebrew, not only in quantitative terms, but also qualitatively, whereby even the fairly limited freedom of lexical and stylistic variation in the Torah yielded to standardization. No matter what we may think of the literary value of the resultant Greek, such texts were popular, as witnessed by the continued use and development of the extremely literal version of Aquila by Greek-speaking Jews throughout the Byzantine period.

The sources cited above witness to differing views about the value of the Greek version, but none condemns translation per se. Such condemnations are found in rabbinic sources, along with positive statements, often directed specifically at the Greek text, about biblical versions in languages other than Hebrew. Such divergent opinions likely reflect deep divisions among rabbinic authorities, linked to factors such as chronology (pre- or post- 70 CE), geography (in the land of Israel or the Diaspora), and ideology. Although Christians disputed—sometimes heatedly, as in the case of Jerome and Augustine—about which text to translate, the question of whether to translate never arose.

In the formal sense the Septuagint does represent the earliest recorded enterprise aimed at producing a written version of Scripture in a language other than Hebrew. But it is likely that Bible translation or interpretation is several centuries older. As depicted in Nehemiah ch 8, Ezra, standing before the people at Jerusalem's Water Gate, read from the Book of the Law (essentially the Torah) in Hebrew, with others providing an explanation. (The exact meaning of the Hebrew terminology used in Neh. 8.8 is debated; see notes there.) It is likely that this explanation or interpretation was in Aramaic, by then the lingua franca of the Middle East, for the benefit of the populace, who were no longer fluent in Hebrew. If this scenario is correct, interpreters were utilizing Aramaic to supplement and explain, but not replace, the Hebrew original, and in an oral rather than scribal context.

At some point in the pre-Christian era, scribes put Aramaic renderings of the Bible into written form; the term Targum (plural: Targumim or Targums) designates such texts. Traditional Jewish sources identify the Torah as the earliest portion translated into Aramaic. Among the Dead Sea Scrolls are indeed two small Aramaic Leviticus fragments, alongside a far longer Targum of Job. The most important Targumim date from the early centuries of the Christian era, although the materials they contain are often much older. There are several important Targumim for the Torah, the Former Prophets, the Latter Prophets, and the Writings. The most influential Targumim were composed in Babylonia.

It is often asserted that the texts of the Targumim, which initially functioned liturgically as supplements to the Hebrew, were essentially paraphrases. This is not so. For the most part, translators into Aramaic were relatively restrained in parting from whatever underlying Hebrew text they had. When they did depart from it, however, it is the case that they exercised considerably more freedom than most Septuagint translators in introducing extensive blocks of "nonbiblical" material in both narrative and legal sections. Among the techniques they adopted were circumlocutions for the name of God. They also incorporated a broad range of updatings to conform to their perceptions of both communal needs and the Oral Tradition. Parallel to developments in the transmission of the Septuagint, later Targumists allowed fewer and fewer paraphrases.

As part of Christian Scripture, the books of the Old Testament also circulated in Syriac, or Eastern Aramaic, and Latin. Jews may well have been responsible for some of the early (3rd century CE and before) Syriac versions that played a part in the later development of the standard Syriac Bible or Peshitta. On the other hand, there is no sure evidence that Jews produced Latin versions of the Bible, in spite of their presence in North Africa, where Christians prepared their earliest biblical texts in Latin. As noted above, Jerome made a point of learning Hebrew and of consulting Jewish teachers to produce the Latin text ultimately adopted by the Catholic Church as the Vulgate. For this, he was roundly attacked on philological, theological, and religious grounds; in terms of the latter, he was almost universally condemned for consorting with Jews who would infect him with their perverse interpretations (or rather misinterpretations) of sacred Scripture. It is nonetheless true that almost all subsequent translators (for example, Martin Luther) and translation committees (such as those responsible for the King James Version) made use, often extensive use, of Jewish sources.

The Medieval and Renaissance Periods

The preeminence of the Arabic language accompanied the rapid rise of Islam in the mid-7th century CE. Jews living in the East and in North Africa quickly adopted it, as they had earlier Latin, Greek, and Aramaic. Several centuries passed before Saadia ben Joseph, a *gaon* (head of a Babylonian rabbinic academy) in the early 10th century, took it upon himself to prepare an Arabic translation of the Bible. Originally written in Hebrew characters (as was most Judeo-Arabic), Saadia Gaon's version was destined to be the standard biblical text for Arabic-speaking Jews—a status it still retains for certain Yemenite communities. Saadia's goal, which he magnificently achieved, was to produce a clear, unadorned Arabic rendering of what he understood the Hebrew original to mean. Where this practice came into conflict with the presentation of distinctive features of Hebrew grammar or syntax, he readily jettisoned the latter.

As Jews settled throughout Europe, they did not at first translate the Bible. Their adherence to the Bible in Hebrew ran parallel to, albeit at some distance from, the aversion of the Catholic Church to vernacular versions (the official Bible of the Roman Catholic Church is the Latin Vulgate). In fact, Jewish translations of the Bible were rarely among the earliest literary achievements of European Jewry.

In the case of the Spanish Jews, for example, the most influential version, the Ferrara Bible, postdates the expulsion of 1492 by half a century, taking its name from the northern Italian city to which many prominent Jews had fled. Although this text ultimately formed the basis for other Spanish-language Bibles in wide use among Catholics, its Jewish origins are securely fixed by a number of distinctive features: use of Hebrew characters in its first printings, close adherence to Hebrew grammar, transcription of proper names, and its division according to traditional synagogal practice.

Among German-speaking Jews translation of the Hebrew Bible goes back to the 1200s. These early exemplars, shaped primarily for the home and school, were often excruciatingly literal representations of a single book or block of biblical material. The implicitly "female" orientation of such versions—after all, women had charge of the home and elementary education, but no public role in the synagogue—became explicit in the *Teutsch Ḥumash* of Jacob ben Isaac of Yarnow, from the mid-1600s. Better known as the *Tzena Ure'ena* or "Women's Bible" (see "Post-medieval Jewish Interpretation," pp. 1900–1908), this rendering incorporated an enormous amount of extra-biblical, largely aggadic, material. This development seems to support the prevailing view of the time that women could comprehend the Bible only when it was augmented with stories and concrete examples; men, on the other hand, could be trusted with the Hebrew original.

A century before Jacob ben Isaac, and unnoted by him, Martin Luther had produced his landmark German version of the Bible, laboring on the Old Testament from 1522 to 1534. As part of his efforts to reform Christianity, he shaped a German text characterized by forceful language and direct diction. A literary masterpiece against which all subsequent German Bibles would be measured, Luther's version, like Jerome's some 1,100 years earlier, reflected the Jewish interpretive tradition—in Luther's case, Rashi, as refracted through Christian sources, influenced him more than he would probably have been comfortable admitting.

Early Modern Translations

Two and a half centuries later, it was to Luther, or at least to the language of Luther, that the Jewish intellectual Moses Mendelssohn (1729–1796; see "Post-medieval Jewish Interpretation," pp. 1900–1908) turned. He was not happy with the simpler German used in Jewish Bible translations and, more generally, in Jewish society. He looked to language, in this case the higher form of German that prevailed in cultured circles, as a means to bring his fellow Jews into closer contact with German society, its ideas and ideals. To achieve this end, he adopted the language, but not the theological outlook or presuppositions, of Luther. Only Jews, Mendelssohn argued, could produce a proper version for Jews. Moreover, in common with Saadia Gaon and the Ferrara Bible, Mendelssohn's text at first circulated in Hebrew characters. From his perspective, it was a singular mark of success that the Mendelssohn translation was soon thereafter printed in German script, facilitating for Jews even greater familiarity with that language and for Christians a firsthand acquaintance with an elevated Jewish view of Scripture.

Successive editions of Mendelssohn's translation bear witness to a growing market that he both reflected and stimulated. The rise of Reform and neo-Orthodox communities among German-speaking Jews was a further impetus to the preparation and publication of biblical versions in German and Judeo-German or Yiddish. While Orthodox constituencies favored renderings that adhered to traditional Jewish sources, others were receptive to editions that incorporated the fruits of the new, critical schools then taking hold among Protestants. Increased sales also resulted from the packaging of some editions as family Bibles.

Mendelssohn's efforts, like those of many translators before and after him, resulted in a translation that in effect brought the biblical text to the contemporary reader. For Mendelssohn, this movement from antiquity to the modern world served to acquaint both Jews and non-Jews with traditional Jewish interpretation in a style that was already familiar to Christians and, it was hoped, in which cultured Jews would also immerse themselves.

Other Translations

The 20th century witnessed another major Jewish translation into German that took a decidedly different approach to the entire enter-

prise of Bible translation. This version grew out of a collaboration between the philosophers Martin Buber (1878–1965) and Franz Rosenzweig (1886–1929) (see "The Bible in the Jewish Philosophical Tradition," pp. 1948–75). The resultant text, begun before World War I but completed only after World War II and the Holocaust, did not read like anything else in German literature—and this was precisely the point. The Bible was a product of an ancient society, chronologically and geographically far removed from 20th century Europe. In order to experience it in an authentic way, the reader needed to be transported, as it were, back into antiquity. For those without the knowledge of Hebrew, precisely the audience for a Bible translation, the best way to do this was to experience a modern language text that sounded, looked, and functioned as much as possible like the ancient original. Reading Buber-Rosenzweig was not intended to be an easy task, but the rewards—in terms of discovering many literary and theological features otherwise obliterated through translation—were well worth the struggle, at least for some.

By the time Buber-Rosenzweig appeared in its entirety, most of European Jewry, including the Jews of Germany, had been destroyed. A similar, though not identical circumstance occurred in connection with Yiddish translation, in that perhaps its most notable achievement did not appear until well after the high point of Yiddish cultural and linguistic dominance. In this case it was one individual, Solomon Bloomgarden—better known by his pen name Yehoash—who was responsible for the text. Beginning in 1910, he published his version in serialized form, revising and perfecting it until he died in 1927. It was the eve of World War II, however, before his work appeared as a whole. By that time, Yiddish had lost or was soon to lose its prominence as a living language.

Jews had been preparing Yiddish translations long before Yehoash's time. But Christians, or more precisely Jews who had converted to Christianity, were also active in this field during the 19th century. Supported by the British and Foreign Bible Society, among others, such individuals produced Yiddish-language Old Testaments compatible with Christian theology that missionary societies distributed widely throughout Eastern Europe and among immigrant Jewish communities in the West. Together with Yiddish versions of the New Testament, these Yiddish Bibles were intended to provide the Good News in an attractive and accessible format. Bible Society records indicate that such theological motivations were accompanied by the desire to raise the quality of Yiddish from jargon to a standardized, recognized language.

English Translations

The history of Jewish translation of the Bible into English shares many of the features of Jewish versions in other modern languages. At the same time, distinctive elements mark its development, culminating in the proliferation of texts during the past several decades.

In some ways, the King James Version (KJV) of 1611 functions for English speakers as Luther's version has for those who speak German. Although not the earliest English rendering, KJV is by far the most influential. The members of its translation committee resemble Luther's individual effort in two other respects: They were deeply indebted to Jewish scholarship, in their case the work of David Kimḥi (Radak); but they themselves had no recorded contact with Jews who, having been expelled from England several centuries earlier, were not officially welcomed back until the mid-1600s.

The cadence, vocabulary, and overall structure of KJV strongly resemble the Hebrew original. Any number of memorable turns of phrases ("tender mercies," Ps. 25.6 and elsewhere) or lingering verbal pictures ("the face of the waters," Gen. 1.2, and "the LORD make his face shine upon thee," Num. 6.26) we associate with KJV are in fact quite literal renderings of the Hebrew lost in freer translations into English or other modern languages.

Whether through recognition of this indebtedness, a desire to fit in, a lack of interest in making a new English translation, or a combination of such factors, KJV apparently served the needs of England's growing Jewish community for the first century of its post-expulsion existence.

The first Jewish versions of the Bible in English appear in the 1780s and are limited to the Torah. They are not in fact new translations: A page of Hebrew text faces the corresponding version of KJV, with a scattering of notes (in English and Hebrew) from traditional Jewish sources such as Rashi. Such editions may represent a reaction to Hebrew-English texts published in the preceding decades under Protestant auspices. In any event, the materials in these versions, consciously shaped as they are for English-speaking Jews, represent an important step—and not an isolated one.

Earlier in this essay, both internal and external causes or stimuli were identified for the Greek translation of the Torah (the Septuagint). A similar complex of concerns was operative in England at the turn of the 19th century. It is clear that by that time most Jews, those who immigrated from Spanish-speaking lands as well as those from German and Yiddish backgrounds, were becoming increasingly familiar and comfortable with English. Synagogues established by both German and Spanish communities made use of prayerbooks with some English, and it was not uncommon to hear at least a few sermons in English. Under such circumstances the appearance of "Jewish Bibles" that combined English with Hebrew (and some traditional Jewish exegetical annotation) is not surprising.

External forces were active that would slowly propel the Jewish community in the same direction. Missionary societies had existed for some time, but by the early 1800s their number, and especially their focus on the conversion of Jews, increased considerably. Most notable in this respect was the London Society for Promoting Christianity among

Jews, generally referred to simply as the London Jews Society. Their proselytizing was in turn greatly abetted by the British and Foreign Bible Society, founded in 1804. Although not a missionary society per se, this organization (and others founded throughout the world, including the American Bible Society), had as one of its principal goals the mass production of inexpensive Bibles that were useful in acquainting non-Christians with the New Testament gospel and the Old Testament as Christian texts. (Yiddish Bibles of this sort were noted above.) In what might appropriately be termed a measure of self-defense, the Jewish community would come to see the value of producing its own English-language versions.

An additional feature marks the introduction of English Bibles into London's Jewish community and from there throughout the Empire and to North America: the few known pre-1800 editions came not from the Jewish establishment, but from individuals on the periphery of the organized community or even at odds with its leadership. Perhaps Jewish leaders of this period thought it imprudent to challenge, if only implicitly, the unique status of KJV. On the other hand, they may have been resisting the incursion of English into precincts where Hebrew and German (Yiddish) or Spanish had previously reigned unchallenged.

In any case, by the mid-1800s, individuals well connected by profession, relation, or both were preparing English versions, typically of the Torah or specific books rather than the entire Bible, for Jews. In an unmistakable sign that these versions had "arrived," the Chief Rabbi of the British Empire sanctioned two of them. Perhaps the better parallel is the term "authorized," as in the Authorized Version, another name for KJV. We must, nonetheless, be careful to distinguish the procedures, and especially the goals, envisioned in these two cases. When the Church of England "authorizes" a translation of Scripture, it signifies its suitability for liturgical use in a church. When the Chief Rabbi "sanctioned" Jewish versions,

he pointedly did not refer to the synagogue, but to their use in schools and homes. It was not conceivable that the Chief Rabbi would have bestowed similar recognition for liturgical usage, where the Hebrew text retained its central role. Still, it is worthy of note that he at least tacitly recognized the increasing role of the home and school in transmitting and inculcating Jewish values as enshrined in the Bible.

By the end of the 19th century, the Jews of England had their choice of more than a dozen English-language versions specifically marketed to them. The translations themselves are admittedly not distinguished nor do they differ markedly from KJV. Efforts were made to excise christological language and to (re-)introduce traditional Jewish interpretations. Nevertheless, at the very time Protestants themselves were beginning to experiment with rather radical (for Victorian society) departures from KJV, Jews departed but rarely from its linguistic heritage and overall format. This may have stemmed from the desire "to be more English than the English," or (as noted above for the 18th century) from the recognition of KJV's "Jewish" roots. It was left to the Jews of the United States, and then not until the middle of the 20th century, to devise new approaches to Bible translation.

Even with communal recognition, Jewish translators in England had, as had Jews in German-speaking lands, worked as individuals—unlike the committees that produced KJV and its successors (or the Septuagint, for that matter). This pattern prevailed throughout most of the 19th century in the United States as well. One man, Isaac Leeser, is responsible for the most influential English-language translation on either side of the Atlantic. Like Saadia, Leeser was a communal leader of prodigious accomplishment and not a little controversy. Despite his notoriety in some circles, Leeser's Torah translation of the 1840s, followed a decade later by his rendering of the entire Bible, attracted considerable interest and resulted in a series of new editions and republications over seven decades.

Unlike Saadia's flowing Arabic, Leeser's English was rather wooden and at many points essentially devoid of literary distinction. It is perhaps the existence of Leeser's work rather than its merits that marks it as a noteworthy achievement.

By the end of the 19th century, the American Jewish community had become sufficiently sophisticated to support a growing number of cultural organizations in addition to synagogues and other communal structures. Among the most important organizations is the Jewish Publication Society (JPS) of America. Founded in Philadelphia in 1888, JPS attracted the financial support of some of America's wealthiest Jews and the involvement of some of the country's leading Jewish intellectuals and writers. In 1917, JPS organized and published the first committee-produced English-language version of the Bible for Jews. The idea for such a version, which was to function as a replacement for Leeser, originated with the Central Committee of American Rabbis, made up of Reform clergy. Their plan, put into action in the 1890s, was to enlist individual rabbis and scholars to work on a given book or block of biblical material. An editorial committee was to ensure some measure of consistency and quality. But these procedures were difficult to implement, and by the early 20th century little progress had been achieved.

At that point JPS took charge, having secured the cooperation and support of most of those involved in the earlier project. Rather than farming out sections of the text to individuals, they established a committee that would be responsible for the translation. This committee was composed of six men, two each from the three major Jewish institutions of higher learning: Hebrew Union College (HUC) in Cincinnati, affiliated with the Reform movement; the Jewish Theological Seminary (JTS) in New York City, part of the Conservative movement; and Dropsie College in Philadelphia, which was not a rabbinical seminary but a nondenominational graduate school that provided instruction in fields, such as biblical studies, that were not readily accessible to Jews elsewhere. No representative from an Orthodox institution was part of the committee. In terms of their ideological or theological stances, these men ranged from quite liberal to fairly traditional. None of the six, however, was a biblical scholar of any distinction.

In addition to these six translators, JPS selected as editor-in-chief the biblical scholar Max L. Margolis, who was among the best qualified, in terms of temperament as well as training, for the task at hand. He had taught at HUC in Cincinnati as well as at the University of California at Berkeley before being selected in 1908 as one of the original faculty members at Dropsie. He was thoroughly grounded in traditional Jewish learning, as might be expected, but was also well trained in the classics and in the critical approaches to biblical study then in vogue (in terms of the latter, he was generally skeptical, although appreciative). In one respect, the choice of Margolis was unusual: He had been born in Eastern Europe, educated there and in Berlin, and came to the United States only in the late 1880s. As it happened, the selection of an immigrant rather than a native speaker of English helped shape both the process that produced this version and the translation itself.

As an immigrant, Margolis was acutely aware of distinctions in English diction and the negative effects of improper language or slang as a newly arrived populace sought to improve its status in America. To Margolis, the language of King James, albeit lexically antiquated and stylistically out-of-date, was nonetheless the best possible model for his fellow immigrants. In his desire to inculcate the best of English, along with a Jewish understanding of the Bible, Margolis consciously emulated Moses Mendelssohn, whom he greatly admired.

Margolis's efforts were entirely consistent with the approach prescribed by JPS. Although most readers of its 1917 English translation did not know it, this version adhered quite closely to the (British) Revised Version of 1885, which constituted the first major revision of the 1611 KJV. Verse-by-verse comparisons between the Jewish Version of 1917 and the Revised Version reveal agreement, typically word-for-word agreement, in most passages. Where it was necessary to incorporate materials not found in KJV or its revision, Margolis deliberately chose KJV-sounding language, so as to achieve a text that seamlessly combined the "new" with the "old."

Margolis, of course, excised overtly christological renderings and introduced some traditional Jewish exegesis. But a well-educated early 20th-century Protestant would in no way have been put off by the JPS translation, and the same might well have been true for any Jewish reader of the Revised Version. This harmonious picture, which carried over to formatting and even binding, was surely consistent with the goals of the JPS leadership. Margolis, like Mendelssohn over a century earlier, could also derive considerable satisfaction from the recognition that one could learn to be a better Jew and a good citizen through one and the same process.

It was biblical scholar Harry M. Orlinsky who aptly remarked that the shelf life of translations for English-speaking Jews has averaged half a century. That was the case with Leeser and also, so it turns out, for the JPS version of 1917. That JPS itself initiated the project which resulted in a replacement for its earlier translation is due primarily to the energetic advocacy and leadership of Orlinsky. A long-time faculty member at New York City's Jewish Institute of Religion, later merged with Hebrew Union College, Orlinsky was singularly well placed to head the new translation project. He had been selected in the 1940s as the first Jewish member of the Revised Standard Version translation committee; in fact, he was the first Jew to serve on any committee to prepare a mainstream (that is, Christian) Bible translation. His experience in this regard led to his subsequent selection as the only Jewish editor for the New Revised Standard Version. By the late 1950s, when he began to lobby for a new Jewish translation, Orlinsky was well known and respected among a wide range of rabbis and Jewish scholars.

Moreover, Orlinsky had a clear vision of what a Jewish translation should look and sound like, a vision that marked a definite departure from the King James-type language characteristic of earlier Jewish versions. For Orlinsky, the effectiveness of any Bible translation was linked to its easy intelligibility by contemporary readers, who can be readily put off by antiquated or obscure words and stilted or foreign-looking syntax. The question translators should always have before them is this: What did the original authors intend to say to their audience and how can we convey that meaning to our audience? In short, this approach to translation seeks to bring the text to the reader. Although an admirer of Mendelssohn and Margolis, Orlinsky's model from within Judaism itself was Saadia Gaon. More broadly, Orlinsky was allying himself with a number of (mostly Protestant) scholars associated with the American Bible Society, who promoted and practiced a dynamic or functional equivalence approach to translation in two popular versions of the post–World War II era: Today's English Version (*The Good News Bible*) and the Contemporary English Version.

Orlinsky of course approached his task from what he understood to be a thoroughly Jewish stance. In his opinion, sensitivity to distinctively Jewish interpretations and exegetes produced a text that was not only more suitable for the Jewish community, but that often presented a more accurate rendering than those offered by other translations. When published in a volume that dispensed with hard-to-read type and the two-column-per-page format traditionally associated with Bibles, the New Jewish Publication Society translation (NJPS) was positioned to take its place among the other accessible, readable, and attractive English Bibles of the mid- to late 20th century.

Orlinsky served as editor-in-chief of the committee that prepared the NJPS translation of the Torah, which initially appeared in the mid-1960s; he was also part of the group that worked on the Prophets. Other scholars from North America and Israel composed the committee for the Writings. Their efforts were first published as separate volumes, 1962 (first edition of Torah, revised 1967), 1978 (Nevi'im), and 1982 (Kethuvim). It was 1985 before the entire Tanakh appeared, incorporating in revised form the efforts of all three translation committees. Until 1999, volumes of the Tanakh contained only the English version; in that year, a Hebrew-English language edition first came out, thereby facilitating comparison between text and translation.

It is instructive to compare the two JPS versions, 1917 and 1985, in order to gauge both the distance that separates them and the features they hold in common:

Genesis 1.1–2
1917: **In the beginning God created** the heaven and the earth. . . . And **the spirit of God hovered** over the face of the waters
1985: **When God began to create** heaven and earth. . . . And **a wind from God sweeping** over the water

The 1917 version retains the wording of KJV; it parts company with the Protestant text by replacing the upper case "s" of Spirit, a reference to the Trinity, with a lower case "s." In addition to rendering Hebrew "ruaḥ" with "wind" rather than with a form of "spirit," Orlinsky (in the 1985 version), in keeping with one line of Jewish exegesis, renders the notoriously difficult wording of Genesis' (and the Bible's) beginning as "When God began to create." In so doing, he excludes the theological doctrine of *creatio ex nihilo*, to the extent that this belief is dependent on the traditional English text. Moreover, it reflects the opening of the Babylonian creation story, *Enuma Elish*, which also begins with a "when" clause. It is also characteristic of Orlinsky's approach that the literal "face of the waters" yields to the simpler, more modern-sounding "the water."

Genesis 11.5 (Tower of Babel)
1917: And the LORD came down to see the city and the tower, which the **children of men builded.**
1985: The LORD came down to look at the city and tower that **man had built.**

It is characteristic of almost all post-World War II versions to update archaic verb forms, such as "had built" for "builded" in this passage. More noteworthy is the use of the generic "man" (but not "human" or "humankind" as in gender-neutral texts like the roughly contemporary New Revised Standard Version or NRSV) for the literal, but perhaps misleading, "children of men." In like manner, "Israelites" consistently replaces "children of Israel" in the 1985 version.

Exodus 21.15
1917: **And he that smiteth his** father, or **his** mother, shall be surely put to death.
1985: **He who strikes his** father or **his** mother shall be put to death.

"He who strikes" sounds far more natural to today's readers than "he that smiteth." The retention of the third singular masculine pronoun, a precise reflection of the Hebrew wording, is avoided in certain other modern translations, most notably the NRSV. As mentioned above, Orlinsky played a role in the development of the NRSV as well as the JPS version of 1985. Although his sympathies in such passages lay with the gender-neutral approach taken by the NRSV, in these instances the NJPS Torah tended to resist any innovation. An important innovation, from Orlinsky's perspective, is found at the beginning of this verse (as in Gen. 11.5 and many other places), where the conjunction *vav*—typically translated as "and" in traditional English versions (esp. KJV)—is omitted. Elsewhere, its presence is signaled through the use of subordination where the paratactic structure of Hebrew favored coordination.

Deuteronomy 24.16
1917: The **fathers** shall not be put to death for the children, neither shall the children be put to death for the **fathers; every man** shall be put to death for **his** own sin.

1985: **Parents** should not be put to death for children, nor children be put to death for **parents: a person** shall be put to death only for **his** own crime.

In this case, NJPS shows considerable, although not consistent, sensitivity to gendered language. The version understands that "fathers," although a literal translation of the Hebrew, does not reflect the more inclusive meaning of the term here, hence "parents." In like manner, "every man" is more accurately rendered by "a person." The NRSV, although not the NJPS, manages to eliminate all vestiges of male-oriented language by the use of "their own" after "persons." Although more consistent in terms of gender language, such an approach involves more restructuring of the Hebrew than the NJPS Torah editors apparently found desirable.

Judges 12.9
1917: And he had thirty sons, and thirty daughters he sent **abroad,** and thirty daughters he brought in from **abroad** for his sons.
1985: He had thirty sons, and he married off thirty daughters **outside the clan** and brought in thirty girls from **outside the clan** for his sons.

In his own distinctively insightful way, Orlinsky used to point out how misleading the traditional rendering "abroad" is here. It is not that the judge Ibzan sought foreign spouses for his sons and daughters, but that he went "outside the clan" for prospective sons- and daughters-in-law. A small point perhaps, but instructive for showing what were, for Orlinsky, some of the benefits of the approach he championed.

Isaiah 7.14
1917: **Behold, the young woman shall conceive, and bear** a son.
1985: **Look, the young woman is with child and about to give birth to** a son.

With the rendering "a virgin," the KJV translation of this passage has been central to a christological interpretation of the Old Testament. In keeping with a long-standing Jewish understanding and with the philologically more correct meaning, both JPS and NJPS have "the young woman." For the rest, JPS 1917 retains the traditional KJV rendering, which places conception and child-bearing in the (distant) future. Although such a rendering of Hebrew present participles is possible, NJPS is surely on more solid ground, syntactically and contextually, when it portrays the women as pregnant and soon to give birth. It is noteworthy that the Revised Standard Version (RSV) Old Testament of 1952 was the first mainstream Christian translation to place "the young woman" in the text itself, relegating "a virgin" to the margins. Orlinsky's presence as an RSV editor did not go unnoticed by that translation's conservative critics.

Jeremiah 31.29–30 (similar expression found in Ezekiel 18.14)
1917: In those days they shall say no more: The **fathers** have eaten sour grapes, and the children's teeth are set on edge. But every one shall die for **his** own iniquity; **every man** that eateth the sour grapes, **his** teeth shall be set on edge.
1985: In those days they shall no longer say: The **parents** have eaten sour grapes, and the children's teeth are set on edge. But **all** shall die for **their** own sins; the teeth of **everyone** who eats sour grapes shall be set on edge.

It is instructive to compare the NJPS text here with a passage from the Torah, such as Deut. 24.16 above. In the earlier example, NJPS retained the singular (with "person"; cf. "man" in traditional English versions), leading to the retention of the masculine singular pronoun "his." In the Prophets, NJPS, in a move that could be characterized as quite bold if nonetheless consistent with NRSV, eliminates all exclusively male references. Such a practice, while less literal than the 1917 JPS version, does more accurately reflect the meaning of the Hebrew original, as understood by the committee responsible for the Prophets.

Ezekiel 2.1 (and frequently elsewhere in the book of Ezekiel)
1917: **Son of man**
1985: **O mortal**

Ben 'adam is the characteristic way in which God addresses the prophet Ezekiel throughout his book. The literal translation of this Hebrew phrase is "son of man," which the 1917 JPS version shares with many traditional and even modern English-language versions. The NJPS editors responsible for the Prophets determined that the main point of this appellation was not Ezekiel's maleness, but his humanness or mortality, vis-à-vis the divinity and immortality of the Lord. Hence, they decided to dispense with tradition, a decision found in several other contemporary versions as well.

Proverbs 31.10
1917: **A woman of valour** who can find? For her price is far above rubies.
1985: What a rare find is **a capable wife!** Her worth is far beyond that of rubies.

The expression "a woman of valour" is one of the few memorable phrases coined by the JPS 1917 translators. To this day, it is used to describe women of noteworthy achievement within the Jewish community. It is a rather literal rendering of the Hebrew, *'eshet ḥayil*. The NJPS editors for the Writings discarded this expression in favor of "a capable wife," which is to be sure a possible rendering of the Hebrew. Nonetheless, in this case it is difficult to see this newer wording as either a closer reflection of the Hebrew or a sensitive application of the ancient text to the modern world.

Other English Versions

The post-World War II period has witnessed the proliferation, some might call it explosion, of new, often competing English-language versions, especially among Protestants. The number of such versions is in effect multiplied by the seemingly endless variety of editions, often aimed at niche markets (recent widows, virgin teenagers, recovering alcoholics, for example) in which these translations appear. In comparison, the corresponding market for Jewish versions is quite limited, even when interested non-Jewish scholars, ministers, and laity are taken into account. Nonetheless, the NJPS is far from alone in finding supporters (as well as detractors!) in the contemporary English-speaking Jewish community, or better, communities.

Among the most widely advertised and beautifully produced versions is the ArtScroll's Tanach (Tanach, an alternate spelling of Tanakh, is an acronym reflecting the traditional tripartite Jewish division of the Bible: Torah, Nevi'im [Prophets], Kethuvim [Writings]), a product of Mesorah Publications of Brooklyn, New York. It is aimed primarily at more traditional or Orthodox segments of the Jewish community, but its appeal has gone beyond that market, in common with many of Mesorah's other publications in the ArtScroll series. For the Torah, its translators relied on the interpretations of the medieval exegete Rashi; elsewhere, they are more eclectic—but they never range beyond traditional sources. This leads to a number of distinctive English renderings, among which are:

Genesis 2.2: **By the seventh day** God completed His work which He had done, and **He abstained on the seventh day.**

For the first prepositional phrase, the Hebrew reads "on the seventh day," which is contextually difficult, given the fact that creation is elsewhere portrayed as a six-day event.

Exodus 12.15: For a seven-day period shall you eat matzos, but **on the previous day** you shall nullify the leaven from your homes.

The highlighted prepositional phrase is, literally in the Hebrew, "on the first day," which creates confusion when compared to other biblical passages in which the leaven was to be "nullified" before the Passover began.

Exodus 20.7: You shall not take the Name of **HA-SHEM,** your God, in vain, for **HA-SHEM** will not absolve anyone who takes His Name in vain.

Here, as frequently elsewhere, the tetragrammaton ("Yhvh")—which in most English-language versions is represented by the title, the LORD—is replaced by an expression that literally means "the Name," reflecting the ineffability of God's proper name. *Ha-Shem* as a surrogate for Yhvh is frequently used in Orthodox contexts.

Exodus 22.24: **When** you lend money to My people . . . do not lay interest upon him.

The Hebrew word rendered here as "when" is the common Hebrew conjunction, *'im,* which in the vast majority of instances is translated literally as "if." The use of "when" here, paralleled in two other places in the Torah, is in accordance with the tradition that in Judaism charity is not a matter of "if," but "when."

Leviticus 23.11: He shall wave the Omer before HA-SHEM to gain favor for you; on the morrow **of the rest day** the Kohen shall wave it.

This verse describes a ceremony, still maintained among traditional Jews, in which the days from Passover to Shavuot (the Festival of Weeks or Pentecost) are enumerated by an offering called the Omer. The Hebrew text specifies that the counting of the Omer starts with the day after "the Shabbat." But rabbinic Judaism understands "Shabbat" here not in its usual sense, but as "the day of rest," that is, the first day of Passover. As in several examples above, the ArtScroll Tanach follows rabbinic interpretation rather than a more literal rendering of the biblical text itself, especially when the more literal rendering might create confusion on halakhic matter.

Another version intended primarily for Orthodox and other traditional Jews is *The Living Torah,* by Rabbi Aryeh Kaplan, and the *Living Nach,* three successive volumes covering the Prophets and the Writings, translated by Kaplan's followers after his death. Kaplan was a prolific writer on Jewish topics and often emphasized mystical elements in Jewish thought and practice. The volumes influenced by Kaplan reflect traditional Jewish sources—for legal interpretation especially the philosopher Maimonides—and also display a demonstrable interest in matters of spiritual import. Among characteristic Kaplan renderings are:

Exodus 20.8–10: Remember the Sabbath to keep it holy. You can work during the six weekdays and do all your tasks. But **Saturday** is the Sabbath to God your Lord.

Lest there be any doubt about when the "seventh day" falls, Kaplan explicitly introduces the modern-sounding expression "Saturday" into the ancient text.

Leviticus 17.14: Tell the Israelites not to eat any blood, since the **life-force** of all flesh is in its blood. Whoever eats it shall be cut off **[spiritually].**

The translation of this passage, along with Kaplan's rendering of Deut. 12.23 below and elsewhere, explicitly introduces a spiritual element into the biblical text that is, at best, implicit in the literal wording of the Hebrew text.

Leviticus 18.7: Do not **commit a sexual offense against** your father or mother. If a woman is your mother, you must not **commit incest with her.**

There is no specific Hebrew word for "incest" as opposed to the more general term translated here as "sexual offense." As in other examples, Kaplan's practice leads to modification of the literal text in the direction of specificity or explicitness.

Leviticus 19.14: Do not place a stumbling block before the **[morally]** blind.

Leviticus 19.29: Do not defile your daughter with **premarital sex.**

As elsewhere, Kaplan renders a fairly general term with a specific one; in this instance, "premarital sex." In a sense, he may be responding to those who, with some justification, make statements like, "there is no specific prohibition against premarital sex in the Old Testament." While that may otherwise be quite true, the explicit prohibition does appear in *The Living Torah!*

> *Deuteronomy 12.23*: Be extremely careful not to eat the blood, since the blood is associated with the **spiritual nature,** and when you eat flesh, you shall not ingest the **spiritual nature** along with it.

Working on his own, the Jewish scholar Everett Fox has produced an English-language version of the Torah that draws its distinctive inspiration from the German translation of Buber-Rosenzweig. Like them, Fox endeavors to draw the contemporary reader into the world of antiquity through a modern-language version that incorporates many aspects of the ancient Hebrew text absent in most other English renderings. The flavor, as it were, of his *Schocken Bible: The Five Books of Moses,* can be appreciated through the following examples:

> *Genesis 1.1–2*: **At the beginning of God's creating** of the heavens and the earth, when the earth was wild and waste, darkness rushed over the face of Ocean, **rushing-spirit of God hovering** over the face of the waters—
>
> *Genesis 1.8*: God called the dome: **Heaven!**
>
> There was **setting,** there was **dawning:** second day.
>
> *Genesis 17.5*: No longer shall your name be called **Avram,** rather shall your name be **Avraham,** for I will make you *Av Hamon Goyyim*/**Father of a throng of Nations!**

Fox chooses to present the biblical names in their Hebrew form, thereby allowing English readers to hear more clearly what the ancient listener would have heard and to enjoy something of the wordplay hitherto accessible only to readers of Hebrew.

> *Genesis 25.30–31*: *Esav* said to **Yaakov: Pray give me a gulp of the red-stuff, that**

red-stuff, for I am so weary! Therefore they called his name: **Edom/Red-One. Yaakov** said: Sell me your **firstborn-right here-and-now.**

Although other versions note wordplays, here and elsewhere, in their notes, Fox presents wordplays associated with names in the text itself. It is also characteristic of Fox to use dashes to indicate that what takes more than one "word" to say in English required only one word in Hebrew.

> *Genesis 27.36*: He [Esav] said: Is that why his name was called **Yaakov/Heel-Sneak?** For he has now **sneaked against me** twice.
>
> *Genesis 30.24*: She [Rahel] became pregnant and bore a son. She said: God has **removed/*asaf* my reproach!** So she called his name: **Yosef,** saying: May **YHWH add/ *yosef*** another son to me!
>
> *Genesis 42.7*: When **Yosef** saw his brothers, he **recognized** them, but he **pretended-no-recognition** of them and spoke harshly with them.
>
> *Genesis 43.10*: The man [Yosef] **warned, yes, warned us,** saying: You shall not see my face unless your brother is with you.

Where the Hebrew uses the same root (here, "warn") twice in proximity, most English translations either ignore it or paraphrase, as "surely" or "really warned us." Here and elsewhere, Fox represents this verbal repetition as literally as possible.

> *Genesis 45.12–13*: Here, **your eyes see, as well as my brother Binyimin's eyes,** that it is **my mouth** that speaks to you. So tell my father of all **the weight I carry** in Egypt, and of all that you have seen, and **make haste,** bring my father down here!
>
> *Exodus 5.17*: But he [Pharaoh] said: **Lax you are, lax.**
>
> *Exodus 12.42–43, 48:* It is a night of **keeping-watch for YHWH. . . . YHWH** said to **Moshe** and **Aharon:** This is the law of the **Passover-meal.** Any **foreign son** is not to eat of it. . . . But any **foreskinned-man** is not to eat of it.

Exodus 13.1: **Hallow to me** every first-born, **breacher of every womb** among the **Children of Israel,** of man or of beast, it is mine.

These are among the most important English-language Jewish versions available today. They are by no means the only ones. Especially among Orthodox Jews, individual rabbis or groups of rabbis are preparing their own translations, reflecting both distinctive elements in their teaching and the need for instruction in English even within the most traditional communities. In many ways, the production of such versions parallels developments within the far larger Protestant communities, where distinctive theologies stimulate an ever increasing number of translations.

In today's world there are many factors that promote the production and publication of Bible translations. Theological, literary, social, even fiscal forces have come to play their role in this phenomenon, which is as old as the Septuagint and as new as the latest version. For Jews, the questions that arise are ancient and perennial, modern and immediate: What is it that makes a Bible translation Jewish? Should a Jewish translation ever supplant, rather than supplement, the Hebrew original? Who, if anyone, should determine which mode of translation, or presentation, or annotation is best? Do differing versions serve to divide Jews, and, if so, should there be one unifying version? In the past, diverse responses have met such queries, giving rise to present circumstances. For the future, even greater diversity is likely. Nonetheless, it is possible to be optimistic that Jewish Bible translators will remain true to their task of finding and perfecting distinctive ways to link their communities with the sacred text of the Torah, the Prophets, and the Writings.

[LEONARD J. GREENSPOON]

The Religion of the Bible

We must first understand that biblical religion is not, strictly speaking, "biblical" because, unlike Judaism and Christianity, it is not a religion based on the Bible—i.e., the canonized record of past divine revelation—but on that revelation itself. Also, it is not a "religion" in the sense of the beliefs and practices of an actual community. Rather, biblical religion was a minority, dissident phenomenon, always at odds, as the Bible itself states, with the actual religions of the small kingdoms of Israel and Judah. The religion of the latter might better be termed Israelite-Judean religion. For more than a century the difference between biblical and Israelite-Judean religion has been an axiom of modern biblical studies (see discussion below).

Moreover, biblical religion is not a unity but rather a congeries of differing and often competing opinions and traditions. Historical scholarship has isolated at least three major forms of biblical religion in the Bible:

1. Deuteronomic-covenantal religion, based on the legal form of a treaty between Israel and its deity, emphasizing Israelite loyalty and the performance of divine commandments, viewed as stipulations of the treaty.

2. Priestly religion, centering on the cult and emphasizing purity and punctilious observance of rituals.

3. Wisdom religion, focusing on understanding the cosmos and the laws of human nature, and dealing with such general problems of human existence as suffering and theodicy.

Despite considerable mutual influence and interpenetration, these three major types of biblical religion are best examined individually.

We shall first summarize the little that is known, or surmised, about Israelite-Judean religion, and then take up each of these major streams of biblical religion in turn.

Israelite-Judean Religion

The actual religion of the states of Israel and Judah from ca. 900 to 600 BCE can be partially reconstructed from archeological and inscriptional evidence and from some evidence in the biblical text, which must be interpreted with caution, because the Bible stands in a polemical relationship to the contemporary religions of Israelites and Judeans, consistently distorting the real meaning of such features as the "high places" (*bamot*, translated "open shrines" in NJPS [e.g., 1 Kings 3.2]). Northern, Israelite religion was especially misrepresented by the propaganda of the predominantly southern, Judean authors and editors of most of the Tanakh. For these reasons the following sketch is conjectural, but represents the generality of current scholarly opinion.

There is no question that the national deity of both Israel and Judah was YHVH (LORD in NJPS), but the relationship to this deity might be better called monolatrous, the worship of one god without denying the existence of others, rather than strictly monotheistic. YHVH is the name regularly, but not exclusively, appearing as the theophoric or divine element in Israelite-Judean names. YHVH's attributes, as expressed in the oldest examples of Israelite poetry, such as the Song of Deborah (Judg. ch 5) and the Blessings of Jacob (Gen. ch 49) and Moses (Deut. ch 33) seem to be a mixture of features attested in Canaanite and Ugaritic religions for the ancient creator god El, the "old god" (*'ilu du 'alami* = Heb *'el 'olam*, "Everlasting God" [Gen. 22.33]) and the young vigorous fertility-storm god, Baal. YHVH is usually portrayed as seated on His heavenly throne, surrounded by the angelic host waiting in attendance, like Canaanite El; or, like Baal, either mounted in the divine chariot, or riding on the "wings of the wind/cherubim." Derived from the latter deity is the pervasive theophanic imagery, namely depictions of the deity appearing with storm clouds, thunder, lightning, earthquake, etc., so familiar to Bible readers. Holy war themes, in which YHVH leads His hosts in battle, are also similar to those elsewhere in the ancient Near East. YHVH is often portrayed as setting out for battle, armed with the divine spear, bow and arrows, against Israel's foes (Ps. 18.7–16; Deut. 32.22–25, 41–42; Hab. 3.3–13; etc.).

Perhaps mingled with, and partially absorbed by, YHVH was a type of god reflecting an older type of religion centering on a familial deity, often referred to simply as the "god of X" (X being the name of an ancestor of the family or clan) or, more generally, as the "god of the fathers." Evidence for this kind of religion comes mainly from the patriarchal narratives of Genesis ("God of Abraham, Isaac and Jacob") and is otherwise attested in the Near East from Mesopotamia in the second millennium BCE to, much later, the region of the Nabatean Arabs (centered in Jordan) in Roman times.

In sum, the major attributes of YHVH that continued in biblical religion were already found in Israelite-Judean religion: king, creator, father, warrior, provider of fertilizing rain. Since many of the oldest texts (e.g., Judg. 5.4) refer to YHVH as "coming from the south" (Seir, Paran, Sinai/Horeb), He originally may have been a god of one of the regions south of Judah. But even in old texts He has already absorbed the attributes of several kinds of an-

cient Near Eastern deities, to become a kind of over-arching deity. The name YHVH may be attested in pre-Israelite documents from the Amorite region of upper Mesopotamia. In the Bible the name is explained as referring to His ability to protect Israel (*'ehyeh asher 'ehyeh*, "I shall be what I shall be" [Exod. 3.14]) interpreted in context as "I shall be with you." The original sense of the name may refer to God as creator (taking "YHVH" as causative *hiphil*, "He brings into being") or it may have some other, lost connotation.

One of the most discussed issues in recent years is whether YHVH had a female consort, the ancient Canaanite mother/fertility goddess Asherah, identified with the tree of life. Two Hebrew inscriptions contain benedictions in the name of "YHVH and his Asherah." Scholars are divided in opinion whether Asherah here referred to the goddess herself, or whether the term has been reduced to an abstract hypostatization of YHVH's power to provide fertility. More evidence is needed, but in any case it is certain that biblical religion, in possible contrast to Israelite-Judean religion, viewed Asherah simply as a Canaanite deity and her symbol, reduced to a wooden pole, as idolatrous.

YHVH was worshipped at "high places" scattered around the country, which varied from simple hilltop shrines with stone or earthen altars, cultic pillars (*matzevot*), and wooden poles (*'asherot*), to larger structures such as the main high places in the Northern Kingdom, Dan and Bethel, where YHVH was worshipped as a calf. In biblical religion the high places are viewed propagandistically as totally idolatrous from the time of Solomon on, since all "legitimate" worship was to be confined to the Jerusalem Temple. Ironically, the latter itself was a typical Canaanite shrine, built by the Phoenicians, with three divisions, the last of which was the "Holy of Holies," with altar, cultic pillars, elaborate decoration of palmettes, lotus, bulls, and cherubim. According to the main traditions of the Bible, the Holy of Holies contained no divine image, as in typical ancient shrines, but only the Ark of the Covenant containing the stone tablets given by Yhvh to Moses. The Ark seems to have had its origin in the kind of box-like palladium still used by some Bedouin tribes. Mounted on a camel, it leads their migrations, as the Israelite Ark is said to have led Israel in the desert (Num. 10.33). The Ark also led the army into battle according to texts describing the early period. Its capture by the Philistines caused a major religious crisis (1 Sam. chs 4–6). According to the Bible, the Ark was brought to newly conquered Jerusalem by David and was placed by Solomon in the Temple, where it was viewed by many as the throne of Yhvh. It is not mentioned thereafter, and its later fate is unknown.

Israelite-Judean religion seems to have had aniconic tendencies; it avoided depicting Yhvh through any image or icon. Later biblical religion condemns images of deities vehemently, and has suppressed all evidence of their legitimate use, except for the cryptic reference to human-like statues called teraphim, attested in a few places, like Gen. 31.34 and 1 Sam. 19.13, which seem to have been family deities, or talismans. It is possible that the strange story in Judg. chs 17–19 of the image stolen by the Danites, which became the center of a cult served by a priesthood descended from Moses, preserves the memory of an image of Yhvh worshipped in some circles. Archeological evidence has as yet turned up no divine images in an excavated shrine, though of course such valuable objects probably would have been removed or looted in antiquity. Israelite-Judean sites do contain large numbers of different types of female figurines, some of which probably represent the fertility goddess Asherah. Such images are usually viewed by scholars as amulets, and as belonging to "popular," not "official," religion (see below).

Worship of Yhvh consisted of sacrifices, the oldest of which seem to have been the "whole offering" (ʿolah), the "communal offering" (shelem) and, probably, the "sin (or purification) offering" (ḥataʾt). Pilgrimages were made to local shrines on sacred occasions. Old biblical texts show that the three major festivals, two in the spring, one in the fall (later called Passover-Matzot, Shavuot, and Sukkot), along with the new moon and Sabbath were occasions for such visits, though it is unclear if in Israelite-Judean religion the Sabbath was already associated with the seven-day week. A yearly pilgimage is also attested at which a communal offering was made and consumed by the family (1 Sam. ch 1). The elaborate cultic establishment described in the Torah, especially in Leviticus, is held by most scholars to be a development of later biblical religion projected back into the past, but it undoubtedly contains elements reflecting the actual cults of Israel and Judah, such as the scapegoat ritual on the Day of Atonement, itself probably originally a shrine-cleansing rite.

Curiously, the Bible contains no reference to a New Year festival (the references in Lev. 23.24 and Num. 29.1, later taken to refer to the New Year festival, do not mention that name); yet it is scarcely likely that Israel was the only Near Eastern people without such an event, so crucial to ancient thinking and the actual lives of people. It is likely that biblical religion has expunged all reference to the New Year festival, except for an enigmatic reference to a "Day of Acclaim" (yom teruʿah). Some scholars have hypothesized a New Year festival based on the evidence of some biblical psalms, especially the so-called "enthronement psalms" (Pss. 93, 96–98), and comparative evidence, primarily the Babylonian akitu festival. The event might have proclaimed Yhvh's victory over cosmic chaos (see below), and His kingship as creator. Certainly, the themes of creation and kingship survive in the later Jewish Rosh Ha-Shanah; but that Israel also had such a festival remains conjectural. If the new year rituals were as close to those of the ancient Near East as suggested by some scholars, biblical religion may have edited the festival out as too redolent of idolatrous practices. Some scholars have also suggested a festival celebrating covenant renewal, held every seven years, based on Deut. 31.10–11; but the existence of such a cultic event is even more conjectural than that of a New Year festival.

Prophets played a prominent role in both Israel and Judah. Prophecy of various kinds is attested in practically all ancient cultures. In the ancient Near East prophets are found in Egypt and Mesopotamia, where their function was secondary to the dominant oracular means employed. But in western Asia ecstatic prophecy seems to have had a more central significance. The closest parallels to biblical prophecy are found in the Mari texts (in modern Syria on the Euphrates) of the middle second millennium BCE, reflecting an Amorite (West Semitic) culture related to Israel in many respects. There, as in the Bible, prophets, both men and women, are sent to kings to deliver messages, and sometimes rebukes, from deities. Prophets are well attested from areas around Israel, from Phoenicia to Transjordan, where texts have been found mentioning a seer Balaam, evidently the prophet described in Num. 22–24.

But in Israel and Judah prophets seem to have been even more important than in neighboring cultures. Mechanical forms of divination played a less significant role; there is reference to what were probably a sort of sacred dice, the Urim and Thummim, which could give a simple yes-or-no answer to questions. Later, they are said to be stones set in the breastplate of the high priest. There are also references to consulting the spirits of the dead, such as Saul's visit to the woman of Endor, who raised the ghost of Samuel (described as a "god" [*elohim*]) (1 Sam. ch 28). But from an early period, the standard means of "inquiring of God" was through a prophet (*navi'*), also called "seer" (*ro'eh*), "visionary" (*hozeh*), and "man of God" (*'ish ha-'elohim*).

Prophets were characterized by a non-normal psychological state, ecstasy. When the "spirit of God" entered them they fell (sometimes literally) into a trance and received messages from God. They might appear to be asleep, or babble uncontrollably. Prophecy might be stimulated by music (1 Sam. 10.5; 2 Kings 3.15) and was always related to music

through the art of poetry, because much biblical prophecy was composed in rhythmical parallelistic discourse, that is, poetry. The early prophets traveled in bands with a leader in their midst, who might be called their "father"; they themselves were "sons of the prophets." They delivered oracles on everything from lost asses (1 Sam. ch 9) to campaigns in war to the appointing of kings. It is likely that groups of cultic prophets were found at shrines, and royal prophets at the courts of kings. In all of this the role of prophets was probably similar to that in surrounding cultures.

However, some prophets took on a more exalted, and isolated, function in Israel and Judah. Prophecy, represented by the seer Samuel, seems to have been centrally involved in the founding of the monarchy, in the transition from charismatic to royal leadership in the 10th century BCE. The Bible attests to prophetic figures who claim to be empowered to appoint kings, and who presume to remain censors of monarchy and state. They deliver unbidden oracles, often unwelcome to rulers, on state policies, both religious and military. They criticize the people for lack of social concern and for oppressing the poor. Such independent prophets, great figures like Samuel and Nathan in the 10th century, Elijah and Elisha in the 9th, Amos, Hosea, Isaiah in the 8th, Jeremiah, Ezekiel and others in the 7th and 6th centuries, far surpass the prophets in the surrounding cultures and are of great importance in the biblical tradition.

The prophets' dominant literary form was the "messenger speech," a discourse purporting to be the direct words of the deity—in structure these were often similar to the message a messenger might deliver on behalf of a king. Many genres were used: laments, parables, hymns, etc., but the central type of speech was the "lawsuit" (*riv*), which used legal forms to excoriate Israel. The basic outline was a statement of the crime, of an individual, like a king or priest, or of the people as a whole, followed by the sentence passed by the divine court in heaven (of which prophets seem to have been viewed as human members, transported there in their visions). One often finds also a call to "heaven and earth" to serve as witnesses. Lawsuit oracles were delivered not only against Israel and Judah, but also against surrounding peoples (sometimes called "oracles against the nations"). Although the implied audience is the other nations, the actual audience was Israel-Judah, who were to learn a lesson from these speeches. Most prophets also gave "salvation oracles," predictions of weal and assurances of divine protection, a function that may originally have belonged to cult prophets at shrines. It has also been suggested that many psalms reflect an oracle of salvation delivered by priests, or cult prophets, at the shrine. We shall see below that it was the independent, fearless brand of prophecy that provided the stimulus for the growth of biblical religion out of Israelite-Judean religion, but that prophecy itself eventually became effectively outlawed by later biblical religion.

Did Israelite-Judean religion practice child sacrifice, as surrounding Canaanite religions did? To be sure, the Bible condemns "passing children through the fire to Molech" (probably a form of Baal), but Israelites were acquainted with the practice, and recognized its numinous terror when performed by others (2 Kings ch 3). The prophets condemn those who sacrifice their children at the tophet outside Jerusalem, a place of such horror that it gave its name, Gehenna (ge' ben hinom), to the later concept of hell. Biblical religion recognized that the first-born "belong" to YHVH and must be "redeemed." The story of Abraham's binding of Isaac implies that child sacrifice has been superseded, but it also recognizes the significance of the rite as the supreme test of loyalty to YHVH. The story of the unhappy fate of Jephthah's daughter (Judg. ch 11) suggests that the practice of child sacrifice in connection with a strong oath was not unknown in Israel. Certain prophetic texts as well suggest that it was practiced (see, e.g., Mic. 6.7).

Very little is known about the official cult of the Northern Kingdom, beyond the establishment of two royal shrines in Dan and Bethel by Jeroboam I in the 9th century, where worship centered on the images of two calves set up by him, mentioned above. Jeroboam is also said to have established a festival in the eighth month to replace the festival in the seventh month (the New Year festival?) in Judah (1 Kings 12.33).

More is known about the state cult of Judah, which centered in the shrine on Mt. Zion in Jerusalem. Judean religion seems to have reflected a royal theology, or ideology, based on a covenant (berit), an unconditional divine promise to David that his dynasty would rule forever, "as long as the sun and moon exist" (Ps. 89.37–38). The king was viewed as the "son" of God (Pss. 2.7; 89.27; 2 Sam. 7.14), though whether this implied actual royal divinity is questionable. There is little doubt that this royal religion was imported into Judah from primarily Egyptian and Phoenician sources. The terms used to describe the king in the biblical texts that most directly reflect Judean royal tradition, the "royal psalms" (Pss. 2, 20, 21, 45, 72, 89) are used elsewhere only of God. Also prominent in this royal cult were notions of unconditional divine protection of Zion and Jerusalem, amounting to what has been termed a doctrine of the "inviolability of Zion." (This notion is also expressed in Isa. chs 1–39.) It was believed that no enemy could capture the city in which was located God's sacred house, the Temple built and maintained by the king, which was viewed as the royal chapel. The "Zion Psalms" (Pss. 46, 47, 48) are possibly early expressions of this doctrine, which also figures prominently in later prophetic messianic visions (see below). The aim of this political, religious, and cultic complex was undoubtedly to strengthen the claim of the monarchy to legitimacy. It seems to have succeeded, because Judean dynastic kingship remained stable for over three centuries (the brief usurpation by Athaliah is the only exception, and she was a northerner, the daughter of Phoenician Jezebel). Northern Israel, by contrast, probably lacking such a royal ideology, saw the rise and fall of many ruling houses. The main ideas of royal religion became transmuted in biblical religion into messianic eschatology (see below).

What can reasonably be conjectured about the belief system of ancient Israel and Judah? If one relies only on the biblical evidence, very little can be extrapolated that is not dependent on the dating of the texts—a highly debated enterprise—so that any interpretation must remain to some extent circular. For example, was covenant already a feature of early Israelite religion, or did it rise to prominence only later, in biblical religion? The answer to this question depends on how one dates the biblical covenantal traditions, a topic with little scholarly consensus. The only religious complex of ideas that is more or less unanimously accepted for ancient Israel is the "monomyth" of the primeval battle between YHVH and the dragon-like Sea (Yam, also called Rahab, Serpent, Leviathan, River[s], etc.). This myth is found throughout biblical literature and is usually connected with creation (cf. Pss. 74.13–15; 89.10–11; Isa. 51.9–10; Job 26.12–13, etc.; chapter 1 in Genesis reflects biblical religion and has been largely demythologized, with the exception of a reference to sea monsters in 1.21). But what did the myth mean to ancient Israel? Was it reflected, even reenacted in the cult? Had it been reduced to merely a literary motif? We have no answer for such questions.

The extrabiblical archeological and epigraphic evidence points to little overt difference between Israelite-Judean religion and the religions of surrounding peoples. The religious picture that emerges from the great Moabite inscription of the mid-9th century BCE does not differ from what is described in, and may reasonably be extrapolated from, the older texts of the Bible; except that it is Chemosh, national deity of Moab, who wages holy war on YHVH and puts Israel itself to the ban of extermination (ḥerem). Iconography points in the same direction. Israel and Judah made unrestrained use of the typical Levan-

tine Egypto-Phoenician and Mesopotamian repertoire of motifs: winged sun discs, scarabs, moon god symbols, sacred trees of life, paradise imagery, cherubim (a composite beast with the body of a lion, the wings of eagles, and a human head), winged cobras (seraphim?), etc. Many of these symbols were used on seals, the most personal representation of individual identity, and it is therefore difficult to dismiss them as mere "art." But it is a mystery what such things meant to the Israelites. The full significance of the amulets, especially female figurines, abundant at Israelite sites also escapes us.

Amulets and "pagan" visual symbols are commonly ascribed to "popular" rather than to "official" religion, which supposedly shunned them. Worship at the high places and consultation with the spirits of the dead (ʾovot veyidʿonim) are similarly ascribed to "folk religion." But the opposition of "popular or folk vs. official" is inherently polemical and is dependent on individual interpretation; this dichotomy may not reflect the reality of Israelite-Judean religion. For example, it is well known that the Bible presents only a gloomy picture of the afterlife in Sheol, as a shadowy, listless realm cut off from contact with God. But it is becoming ever clearer that the high places, and especially the cultic pillars (matzevot) associated with them, point to a belief in some kind of active contact with long-dead ancestors, perhaps even a cult of dead heroes. The communal marzeaḥ drinking bouts, condemned by the prophets as "pagan," may also have been thought to enable one to commune with ancestors. Is one to label such things as reflecting only "popular religion"? Or is it more likely that developed biblical religion has edited these practices out and declared them to be "idolatrous?" Similarly, biblical religion reduced the heavenly assembly of divine beings, called "sons of God" (Ps. 29.1), "holy ones" (Ps. 89.6–7) and even "gods" (Ps. 82.1) in older biblical texts, to colorless and nameless "messengers" (angels). But there is every reason to suspect that in Israelite-Judean religion the angels were the same type of potent, named heavenly forces so prominent in postbiblical religion, especially apocalyptic, and also in rabbinic midrash.

The general picture of Israelite-Judean religion that emerges is of a cult along the same pattern of other cults in the ancient Near East. If the surface conceals some "elusive essence" of an already totally monotheistic, covenantal, Torah-oriented faith, scholarship has not yet discerned it with certainty (see below). It is likely not in Israelite-Judean, but rather in biblical religion—what might be termed the Biblical Revolution—that the essential developments lie.

Biblical Religion

Revolution or Reform?

The complexes of traditions in edited texts that form the evidence for biblical religion date, for the most part, from the 7th to 5th centuries BCE: the Torah, the historical works, the beginnings of the compilation of the prophetic books, the chief wisdom books. Embedded in these works are materials that reflect older stages of biblical religion—its prehistory, as it were—and many traditions of Israelite-Judean religion that have, in the main, been altered to reflect later viewpoints.

A key question is whether biblical tradition is merely a later, more developed stage of Israelite-Judean religion, continuing the same basic religious ideas and tendencies, a viewpoint that posits essential continuity; or whether, conversely, biblical religion marks a basic shift in religion, a reinterpretation of older traditions so radical as to be revolutionary. Continuity or revolution?

The Bible claims continuity from Moses on, with no meaningful development. This single authentic tradition was constantly violated by apostasy, but was also restored in a series of "reforms" by figures such as Josiah and Ezra. Modern critical scholarship overturned the traditional viewpoint by emphasizing the principle of change and development. The classic late 19th century synthesis of Julius

Wellhausen posited discontinuity between older Israelite and later biblical traditions. The former was a "nature" religion, not essentially different from the cults of surrounding ancient peoples; the latter was a new kind of faith, rooted in prophetic inspiration. Later, according to Wellhausen, it became a fossilized text-centered religion dominated by Priestly ritual and petty legalism. Such value judgments, reflecting Social Darwinist prejudices, seemed to invalidate Wellhausen's synthesis to many 20th century scholars. William F. Albright and his students tried to show that archeology could demonstrate substantial continuity between Israelite and biblical religions. For example, the covenant traditions were held to go back to recently discovered second millenium models. Some of the patriarchal traditions were demonstrated to have had early roots. Monotheism was related to trends in the late Bronze Age Near East, and so on. A similar attempt at demonstrating essential continuity was made by the Israeli scholar Yehezkel Kaufmann, who attacked Wellhausen's synthesis and tried to show that Israel's religion reflected the same basic ideas from beginning to end. By the end of the 20th century a revisionist reaction against the claims of continuity set in, with claims of discontinuity much stronger than those made by Wellhausen. Some claimed that biblical religion was mainly a product of the Persian and even Hellenistic eras, and that the existence of Israelite-Judean religion, and even of "Israel" itself was chimerical. Some revisionist scholars were justly accused of having political goals.

Which approach is the most justified, on the basis of the biblical and extrabiblical evidence, including archeology? This is not a matter in which one can simply allow the "facts" to speak for themselves, because interpretation plays a key role at every stage of the discussion. But it is possible to list a few major differences between what scholarship generally considers to be typical of earlier vs. later religion:

1. *Monotheism.* Older, especially poetic, texts portray the deity as seated among the as-

sembly of divine beings, who are sometimes, as noted above, called *bene 'el(im)*, ("sons of gods"), *kedoshim* ("holy ones"), among other terms. Statements of divine incomparability echo those commonly found also in extra-biblical hymns; for example "Who is like you among the gods?" (Exod. 15.11). Now, monotheism is really a complex philosophical idea that is very hard to express in biblical language, but later texts, especially Deuteron-omy, do seem to be struggling to make overt statements about God's oneness and unique-ness, most famously in Deut. 4.35: "It has been clearly demonstrated to you that the LORD alone is God; there is none beside Him." and (depending on one's interpretation) in the Shema: "Hear, Israel, the LORD, our God, the LORD is one" (Deut. 6.4). In the Bible, key ideas are generally expressed peripherally, es-pecially by concrete, often ritual actions. A probable sign of real monotheism is the active polemic against idolatry one finds in Deutero-nomic texts and in late prophets, like Jeremiah and, especially, Second Isaiah. It (mis)rep-resents other ancient religions as mere fetish-ism, the foolish worship of images of "wood and stone."

2. *Centralization of worship.* A potent ritual expression of absolute monotheism is the at-tempt to reflect God's oneness by insisting on one legitimate shrine, the Jerusalem Temple. This is a cultic development of the Deutero-nomic movement, perhaps first attempted by Hezekiah in the late 8th century (1 Kings ch 18), and later effected by Josiah in his famous "reform" in 621 BCE (2 Kings chs 22–23). Ear-lier religion tolerated a multiplicity of altars, a fact obscured by the Deuteronomic editing of most of the historical books. But actions speak louder than words. The fact that Josiah, the paragon of militant piety, did not kill the priests of the "high places" (except for Bethel, the main rival of Jerusalem), but rather al-lowed them to share the Priestly income of the Jerusalem shrine (2 Kings 23.9) is a tacit ad-mission that local shrines had been consid-ered quite legitimate before. In the context of ancient religion, centralization of worship,

which is also reflected in the contemporary Priestly writings (despite some signs of earlier decentralization), was an extremely radical step that deserves to be viewed as revolution-ary in the extreme.

3. *Myth vs. history.* It is often said that bibli-cal religion broke with the kind of mythical thinking characteristic of the religions of the ancient Near East in favor of history. God was praised for His great acts of national redemp-tion, such as the exodus from Egypt and the conquest of Canaan ("salvation history"). It is true that biblical religion has ousted most of the mythology of the ancient world, with the exception of a few stock themes, like creation, the garden of Eden and YHVH's cosmic battle in primeval times with the sea. Especially the sexual aspects of mythology, involved with the birth and procreation of the gods, have been eliminated (except for a few relics like Gen. 6.1–4). Indeed, it can fairly be stated that the processes of demythologization and de-sexualization of religion are related to each other and go hand-in-hand in biblical reli-gion.

But it is less certain that biblical religion broke with the concept of myth itself. If one defines myth as narrative that expresses a culture's deepest attitudes and emotions about the origin and nature of the world in which it lives, it is correct to say that biblical re-ligion created new but potent myths of its own. And it is certainly incorrect to hold that biblical religion is historical in any modern, scientific sense. Rather, the unique creation of biblical religion is a blend of history and myth that might best be termed typology, the cycli-cal recurrence of a few historical patterns, such as national apostasy and repentance, which serve as the basis of a vital historiography. Events are made to reflect, anticipate, and ex-plain each other typologically. For example, the patriarchal narratives foreshadow later Is-raelite settlement in many ways (a fact the Rabbis recognized and expressed in the princi-ple that "the deeds of the fathers prefigure what will occur to their descendants" (*ma'ase 'avot siman levanim*). Disparate events are united by extended and intertwining typologies of creation and redemption. So, the return from exile in Babylonia is viewed as a second exodus from Egypt; the exodus itself is described in such a way as to evoke creation typology, as is the Sinai theophany, and so on. History is valued not for the unique, but for the recurrence of these repeated patterns. It is in this sense that biblical religion may be termed a historical faith.

Was Israelite-Judean religion already historical in this sense? The answer depends on the dating of the texts. Numerous typical ancient Near Eastern mythological themes are, however, prevalent in creation accounts outside Gen. ch 1. Moreover, texts that reflect the royal theology of Judah, which are mostly very old, are also replete with language and themes drawn from ancient mythology. Indeed, that tradition does not even shrink from calling the king the "son of God" (albeit adoptive). Such facts lead one to suspect that the characteristic use of historically rooted typology is likely a feature of biblical, not earlier, religion.

4. *Individualism.* Older religion viewed the individual as a member of society: family, clan, tribe, and nation. Corporate, transgenerational responsibity for sin was the rule, as in the Decalogue ("punishing children for the crime of their fathers to the third, even the fourth generation" [Exod. 20.5]). This notion is often evident even in Deuteronomy, where the Hebrew text often refers to the plural rather than the singular Israelite, suggesting that he or she will be punished or rewarded with the larger group (see e.g., Deut. 11.13–21). Evidence of an overt challenge to this doctrine first appears in the prophets of the late 7th and 6th centuries BCE, Jeremiah and, especially, Ezekiel (Ezek. ch 18). In late texts individual responsibility for sin has become the standard doctrine, as in the book of Chronicles. The belief in individual responsibility for sin went along with an elevated position for women and a new formulation of the nation Israel as a community of committed believers (ʿedah, kahal).

The change was also reflected in new models of piety. Older psalms remain more or less on the level of similar compositions from the ancient Near East. But a new inwardness, focused on individual relationship to God, appears prominently in later psalms, like Pss. 139 and 119. A new concept of the religious individual, totally devoted to God, is especially a feature of developed Deuteronomic religion, and is linked to the new emphasis on the oneness of God. It will be remembered that the Shema continues: "You shall love the LORD, your God, with all your heart, and all your life" (Deut. 6.5). Another sign of the new individualism is a much heightened concern with the problem of individual suffering and the concomitant theological issue of theodicy. It finds expression mainly in later texts such as the "confessions" of Jeremiah (e.g., Jer. 11.18–12.6) and, above all, the book of Job.

5. *Text religion and canon.* The older forms of Israelite religion probably were mainly oral, especially prophecy (at least before the 7th century). But Deuteronomic religion introduced a new text-centeredness by insisting on the unchangeability of the written form of the *torah* ("instruction") given to Moses on Horeb (Sinai). More than any other Torah book, Deuteronomy emphasizes the *sefer* or written document. Nothing may be added or taken away (Deut. 4.2; 13.1). This is the beginning of the notion of immutable canon, an approach to sacred texts quite at variance with the liberal attitude toward textual transmission of most ancient cultures. Indeed, despite this injunction, even biblical traditions remained astonishingly fluid for several centuries after Deuteronomy. But eventually the process of codification, standardization, and canonization set in, beginning with the Torah (probably in the 5th century) and extending gradually to the Prophets and the Writings, a development that was completed by the 1st century CE (or several centuries earlier, according to several scholars). Along with the increasing textualization and literariness of biblical religion went an intertextual aspect of internal commentary and inner-biblical interpretation.

6. *Forms of piety.* A new kind of piety also arose, fostered especially by Deuteronomy, focused on prayer and study. Ritual was not ignored, but it became secondary to teaching and meditation. Attitudes and themes native to the older wisdom tradition were adapted to this new piety, which emphasized study of the written record of divine revelation. It should be noted that biblical religion makes no claim for Mosaic authorship of the Torah as a whole, but only of Deuteronomy (Deut. 31.9). In addition, the older liturgical tradition was revised to make it compatible with strict monotheism, resulting in the type of prayer found in most of the book of Psalms (see discussion below).

These developments fit the general historical and cultural context of the centuries between about 800 and 400 BCE. It was a time of extreme change and uncertainty in the Near East, marked by the rise of a radically new form of political organization, the empire, first of the Assyrians, later of the Neo-Babylonians and the Persians. These world empires made imperial religious as well as political claims, and the policies of mixing of populations through exile and resettlement weakened the old polities of the region. The chief gods of the imperial states were raised to supremacy over other deities. Henotheism, if not true monotheism, and syncretism were tendencies of the age. But uncertainty led to its opposite: cultural, including religious, conservatism, a focus on ancient traditions, and an attempt to present the new as authentically old. The typical literary production of the time is the pseudonymous *fraus pia*, a document that claims to have been written by a sage in hoary antiquity, but which actually fulfills some current need. The "finding" of the book of Deuteronomy in the Temple in 621 BCE, corresponds nicely to this contemporary model. In sum, biblical religion fits the period in question in a general way, and sometimes very specifically.

To return to the original question: Do all of these new developments of the 7th to 5th centuries BCE mark a radically new departure, or only a later stage in the development of Israelite religion? The explosion of new features in the period in question is undeniable, from the scholarly point of view. But at what point does a difference in degree become a difference in kind? At what point is one justified of speaking of something as revolutionary, as radically new, especially if the tradition in question keeps insisting it is really very old, and merely being stripped of later accretions, "reformed"? Probably the claims of continuity vs. discontinuity cannot be judged only on the basis of logic. Rather, one must choose the answer one judges to be best supported by the evidence one accepts, and, it must be admitted, one's private religious convictions. To me, it seems clear that biblical religion possesses such a cohesiveness, even in its disparity of traditions; so clearly reflects the needs of its times; and, above all, so evidently represents a heightening and sharpening of traditional ideas, that it deserves to be viewed as revolutionary. The following discussion reflects this judgment.

The Development of Biblical Religion: From Prophecy to Text

Whether biblical religion marks a radical break with older Israelite-Judean religion, or only a new, heightened phase, its formative stimulus seems to have been in the Northern Kingdom of Israel in the 9th century BCE. The attempt of Jezebel to import the worship of Tyrian Baal, along with its rites and coterie of prophets, into Israel stirred the violent opposition of the prophets of the native deity YHVH. The leaders of the "YHVH-only" party, as Morton Smith called it, Elijah and his disciple Elisha, inspired a military coup against the northern monarchs, the Omrides. Elijah was filled with exclusive "zeal" *(kin'ah)* for God, an intolerance of other deities, that remained one of the hallmarks of biblical religion. The struggle with Baalism in the North continued into the 8th century, as evidenced by the activity of Hosea, who seems to have introduced a number of other key ideas, such as the use of pungent sexual terminology to describe apostasy ("whoring after foreign gods"). Biblical religion was thus Northern in origin, which explains why, as a religious reference (as opposed to political and cultural), the name of the community that accepted biblical religion was to remain "Israel" long after the late 8th-century demise of the historical kingdom of Israel.

After the fall of the Northern Kingdom in the 8th century, this prophetically rooted, exclusive faith migrated south to Judah, perhaps already at the end of the 8th century, when it may have inspired the reforming efforts of King Hezekiah. By the late 7th century biblical religion had become consolidated into the Deuteronomic "movement," probably a loose confederation of priests, prophets and their disciples, and royal officials. King Josiah was induced, by the "finding" of a "Book of the Instruction" (*sefer* hatorah—probably a form of Deuteronomy) in the Temple, and by political motives (the weakening of Assyria) to undertake the great revolutionary "reform" of 621 BCE. The traditional high places were proscribed, worship was centralized in Jerusalem; images, stelae *(matzevot),* wooden poles *('asherot),* and the other paraphernalia of "idolatry" were destroyed (2 Kings chs 22–23); and the worship of the "Queen of Heaven" (Astarte) was forbidden (Jer. 44.18).

The reform, or revolution, lapsed after Josiah's ignominious death in battle, which could hardly have been interpreted by most contemporaries other than as divine judgment on his impiety in uprooting so many traditional forms of worship (see Jer. 44.15–19). But the ruling classes of Judah were soon exiled to Babylonia. The exile community of the 6th century BCE, centered near Nippur in southern Babylonia, was a crucible of religious activity: prophetic (Ezekiel, Second Isaiah) and historical (the work of the Deuteronomistic Historian, editor of the first edition of the Former Prophets, the historical books from Joshua to Kings). The basic theological ideas of the Deuteronomic and Priestly tradition began to take their classic written forms,

as did the first editions of some of the prophetic writings.

The most active period in the establishment of biblical religion thus took place in the exile, and it was this religion that was transplanted back into the tiny Judean community of returned exiles in the late 6th and mid-5th centuries BCE. The first attempts at return were feeble and indecisive. The final reforms of Ezra and Nehemiah (after 450 BCE) imposed the standards of developed biblical religion on the community, with the Torah, probably in more or less its present form, as the constitution. The development of biblical religion was therefore gradual, stretching from at least the late 9th or 8th to the 5th centuries. In its final form it marks an attempt to restore pre-exilic Judah, reinterpreted as a religious community of Israel, by restructuring old institutions and formulating new theological ideas projected back into a Mosaic age that was now viewed as uniquely authoritative. Contemporary prophecy was demoted and all but abolished in favor of the written documents that contained past revelation, so that biblical religion became a completely textual religion, requiring a body of approved interpreters, the scribes. Interpretation of the old revelation displaced the new revelations of contemporary prophets. The final form of biblical religion was supported by the Persian state, which may have stimulated the formation of the Torah, a compromise document of the two major ongoing traditions of biblical religion, the Deuteronomic-covenantal and the Priestly-cultic, both of which will now be briefly described.

Deuteronomic-covenantal Religion

The dominant stream of biblical religion is the Deuteronomic, or covenantal tradition. It conceives of the relationship between God and Israel as a legal form, a *berit* or *'edut,* a covenant, i.e., a contract, or treaty, made between God and the escapees from Egypt at Horeb (in other traditions, Sinai) with the mediation of the prophet Moses. The people had a direct mass revelation of the divine Presence for the announcement of the Decalogue; the rest of the laws, the terms of the covenant, were transmitted privately to Moses on the mountain and read to the people later. The people agreed to the treaty freely, binding themselves and their descendants by an oath and covenant ceremony. By this treaty YHVH became Israel's God, with an obligation to give them the land of Canaan and otherwise protect them and provide for their needs; and Israel became God's people, with a permanent obligation to fulfill the divine commandments, the laws of the covenant. Horrendous curses are threatened for Israel's breach of the contract (see esp. Deut. 28.15–68). The Horeb/Sinai covenant is therefore conditional, unlike the covenant with David, which is strictly promissory. The most explicit and complete form of the covenant is in the book of Deuteronomy, whose core is a work of the 7th century BCE. Fragmentary and perhaps older covenantal traditions are found in Exod. chs 19–24 and 32–34.

It is now known that the conditional covenant between God and Israel generally follows the form of the treaty between a suzerain and his vassals, attested from the second millennium on. The covenant patterns of Deuteronomy have been shown to follow most closely later, Assyrian, treaty forms of the first millennium. Whether other covenant traditions can be shown to go back to earlier forms, attested among the Hittites of the late Bronze Age, is a matter of scholarly dispute. It is possible that covenant (berit) was first applied in the Judean royal tradition to the divine promise of protection to the House of David, as the unconditional, promissory type of covenant (itself based on ancient royal grants by kings to favored vassals). It was later said to have been prefigured by a similar "covenant," a promise to the national patriarch Abraham (Gen. chs 15, 17). Finally, the covenant idea, in its conditional form, was extended to the whole nation as a unique mass divine revelation. It is also possible that some traditions of the conditional type of national covenant pre-

cede the monarchy, and that the two types of covenant, conditional and unconditional, competed with each other already in Israelite-Judean religion. But the virtual absence of references to the Horeb/Sinai event in definitely old, especially poetic, texts, suggests the greater likelihood of the sequence described above.

Whatever its age and provenance, the covenant idea, as expressed in the Deuteronomic tradition, now dominates the Bible, not only the Torah, but also the work of the historical books, which have undergone a Deuteronomic edition, and some of the prophets, especially Hosea and, above all, Jeremiah (though, curiously, the covenant with Israel is hardly mentioned at all outside the Torah). The leading religious ideas of this tradition, in their classic Deuteronomic form, may be summarized as follows:

Deuteronomic religion is strictly monolatrous and probably monotheistic; i.e., not only insisting on the worship of one God, but positing the effective existence only of this deity. Other gods are mere breaths, nothings (hevel); all idols are but material objects. Monotheism was an abstract idea difficult to express in ancient language, but it is palpable in Deuteronomic theology, if only by inference. As noted above, the abstract notion of monotheism is manifested in the strong Deuteronomic insistence that God be worshipped at only one shrine.

Deuteronomic religion places central stress on the name of God, and for this reason has been called by scholars a "name theology." The name (rather than the deity!) is said to "rest" (shakan) on the place God has chosen, i.e., the sole legitimate shrine (Jerusalem). It is a religion that implies divine transcendence. Direct divine contact with the world is strongly denied, except for the Horeb/Sinai revelation (and Deut. ch 4 seems to deny that God appeared on earth even then). Rather, God remains in heaven, from which He hears human prayer (1 Kings 8.30–49). This type of religion placed great stress on the word, both as name and prayer; and concomitantly on the sense of hearing, as manifested not only in God's hearing of prayer, but also in human hearing of the words of the covenant and transmitting them to the young through teaching. The divine instruction *(torah)* must be the sole topic of human religious thought and meditation; it is Israel's true "wisdom" (Deut. 4.6). Deuteronomy places great emphasis on mind and inner thought. It contains a certain rationalizing, even rationalistic tendency, often offering reasons and explanations for the commandments of the covenant (Deut. 5.15; 15.18; etc.).

The focus on the oneness of God, shrine, and thought, extends also to emotion. Israel is enjoined not only to fear and obey, but also to love God, with total, singular inner devotion. The commandment to love, a seeming paradox, has its roots in the legal language of the ancient Near East, as an expression of volition, insuring that the terms of an agreement are entered into freely; for example, a vassal king may be commanded to "love" his overlord. But in Deuteronomy, loving God has become more than a legal metaphor. It is a total commitment, expressive of the emotion of *kin'ah,* which not only means "zeal," but also "jealousy." Stemming from this deep emotional bond between deity and individual (for Deuteronomic religion has a pronounced focus on the individual in the group) is a certain tendency toward intolerance and even totalitarianism, which has manifested itself often in later, biblically-based religions. But it is also true that covenant religion is the locus of an implicit doctrine of free will, because Israel is always confronted with the choice to obey or not obey, even if the promised reward for the former is life and the threatened punishment for the latter is death (see esp. Deut. 30.15–20).

Covenant faith is also a militant religion. It draws upon and reinterprets the holy war traditions of the ancient Near East and of Israelite-Judean religion, but focuses them not on any actual national foe but on what must be regarded, in Deuteronomy's day, as a quite fictitious enemy, the Canaanites, demanding their complete destruction (see esp. Deut. 20.16–18). Since the latter no longer existed as a group in the period in question, it is difficult to escape the impression that by "Canaanites" is meant an inner foe, Canaanizers, as it were, most likely adherents of older Israelite-Judean religion.

Covenant religion is a text religion, limiting itself to the written record of the contract between God and Israel. Creation themes are practically absent; reference to nature as "heaven and earth" is limited to invoking them as witnesses to the covenant, a literary survival of the list of gods in ancient treaties. Although it has prophetic roots, and reveres Moses as a unique super-prophet, Deuteronomic religion all but abolishes future prophetic revelation, lest new divine communications compete with the single authoritative written revelation at Horeb/Sinai (see below).

Deuteronomic religion has little interest in the cult, apart from insisting that it be limited to one spot. Otherwise, its major interest in ritual is in linking observance with the exodus, as it does with the Sabbath (Deut. 5.15), or in highlighting the Passover, by its nature already linked with the exodus. Passover seems to have played a key role in Deuteronomic-covenantal religion, since the "reforms" of Hezekiah and Josiah are described as being accompanied by special Passover ceremonies.

Priestly-cultic Religion

The Priestly tradition, the core of which is the mass of cultic legislation including the end of Exodus, all of Leviticus, and parts of Numbers, represents a type of religion that, like Deuteronomic faith, is also monotheistic and centered on one place of worship. It, too, presents itself as the result of revelation in a covenant, which it also terms *berit,* although, unlike Deuteronomic texts, it does not avoid adding the word "eternal" *(berit 'olam).* It views the sacrificial cult as an unconditional and permanent establishment, like the Davidic covenant, and unlike the Sinai/Horeb covenant, which was dependent on Israel's obedience and was therefore conditional. Like the Deuteronomic tradition, the Priestly tradition uses the term "rest" *(shakan)* to describe God's link to the shrine *(mishkan)*, but what "rests" on it is not the divine name, but the "glory" *(kavod)*. For this reason it is often said that the Priestly texts reflect a "glory" theology, in opposition to Deuteronomic "name" theology, expressive of an implied idea of divine immanence rather than transcendence. *Kavod* is the term already used in Israelite-Judean religion to describe the manifestation in theophany of the divine presence as storm cloud, lightning, earthquake, and, above all, as refulgent radiance. These ideas are rooted in the ancient Near East; a similar light surrounded the gods (a late relic of this belief is the halo around saints' heads in Christian art, prefigured by the light that streamed from Moses' face [Exod. 34.30]). But in Priestly thinking the ancient concepts and images have become more systematic. The divine glory, which was the main manifestation of the Sinai experience (Exod. 24.16–18) in the Priestly worldview, is said to have entered the completed Mosaic Tabernacle, model of future shrines, at its dedication (Exod. 40.34–35) and to return each year on the Day of Atonement to the Holy of Holies in the Temple, where it appeared over the cherub lid of the Ark (Lev. 16.2) (an alternative interpretation is that it was always immanent in the shrine but became visible only on that day). To be sure, it was seen only by the high priest on that day, but Priestly religion is nevertheless in general a religion of seeing, not hearing, like Deuteronomic religion. It is also a religion of touching, and smelling of the propitiating odor *(reah nihoah)* of sacrifice and of the sweet savour of incense and spices. In other words, it is a religion of the physical, in which language, even prayer, plays little role, being quite absent from Torah texts reflecting this tradition. The contrast with Deuteronomic religion on this point could not be greater.

The Priestly tradition includes not only cul-

tic texts dealing with sacrifice and ritual, but also the Priestly narrative source, responsible for the creation account of Gen. 1.1–2.4 and other key stories in Genesis and later in the Torah. If the narrative materials are viewed in conjunction with the cultic ones, it is possible to extrapolate an implicit Priestly theology that blends ritual and theology. The central ritual substance is the blood of sacrifice, and the central religious idea is atonement. The only explicit statement of the connection between the two is Lev. 17.11, where it is said that the blood of sacrifice effects atonement for the lives of Israelites. The underlying theology is not explained, since, unlike Deuteronomy, the Priestly authors eschew explanation and rationalization; but in the preceding chapter, Lev. ch 16, it is said that the high priest is to attain atonement for Israel by entering the Holy of Holies and sprinkling sacrificial blood before the divine presence. The link between atonement and blood is therefore quite firm. According to another Priestly text, Gen. ch 9, avoiding consumption of blood is part of a complex of themes, in which the eating of the meat of animals is presented in the context of a divine concession to inherent human sinfulness. But the preceding chapter (Gen. ch 8) contains an eternal divine promise never to allow human sin to lead to another catastrophic flood. It may perhaps be extrapolated that blood is a reminder to God both of human sin and of His promise to forgive. Perhaps it is safer to say that the link between sacrificial blood and forgiveness for sins is a mystery, because the Priestly tradition cultivates mystery and a sense of the immanently numinous. The Priestly complex of blood and atonement was to have a great effect on Christian theology. After the destruction of the Temple, the Rabbis stated that prayer, rather than blood, attains forgiveness for Israel; this reflects a melding of Deuteronomic and Priestly worldviews.

Priestly religion has reinterpreted the old cult of Israelite-Judean religion to focus less on the ancient whole, communal, and thank offerings *('olah, shelem, todah)*, than on the expiatory sacrifices, the "sin offering" (*ḥaṭa't*) (better translated "purification offering") and "trespass offering" ("guilt offering") (*'asham*). Old festivals were reinterpreted, the ancient probable New Year, as noted above, all but disappearing in the process.

The Priestly tradition also continues the ancient insistence that worshippers be morally as well as ritually pure. It has been suggested that some psalms, especially Pss. 15 and 24, reflect ancient "entrance liturgies," declarations of moral purity pilgrims were obliged to make before they could enter the sacred precincts of the shrine. The moral aspect finds expression in the Priestly tradition of later biblical religion primarily in the "Holiness Collection" (Lev. chs 17–26), especially in Lev ch 19 (the command to "love thy neighbor as thyself" comes from Lev. 19.18). In these chapters, worshippers are enjoined to be "holy as the LORD, your God is holy." To the developed Priestly tradition holiness means not just the numinous "other," or moral perfection, but physical and spiritual separation from the impure: clean from unclean, sinner from wicked, Israel from the nations. Gen. ch 1 represents creation itself as a series of separations and distinctions by means of which primeval chaos became ordered. Similarly, the Temple consists of a complex of precincts of increasing holiness. This reclusive, segregating notion of the holy is derived from ancient Near Eastern, ultimately mythically rooted models, like much of Priestly thinking. But in its final form this definition of holiness as separation and exclusion fits especially well with the milieu of postexilic Judah in the 5th century BCE, in which, as the books of Ezra and Nehemiah show, separation from other groups was the key issue. Gone is the broad view of holiness as the divine presence that fills the whole earth (Isa. 6.3). Also reflecting postexilic circumstances is the ritual prominence in the Priestly codes of the Sabbath as a weekly day of rest memorializing creation, and the rite of circumcision as a sign of the Abrahamic covenant, distinguishing Jews from their neighbors.

Other Traditions of Biblical Religion

The Liturgical Tradition

As noted above, the Deuteronomic tradition exalts prayer (though mainly in the deuteronomistic historical books of Former Prophets), while the Priestly tradition seems to all but ignore it (the high priest's confession on the Day of Atonement is a notable exception). Prose prayer plays a prominent role in the historical works edited by the Deuteronomic school, as well as in the later book of Chronicles. Poetic prayer is mainly found in the book of Psalms, the history and development of which is very complex and poorly understood. Chronicles states that liturgical pieces, such as hymns and petitions, were composed by Levitical guilds in Second Temple times (1 Chron. chs 15–16). This may also have been true in earlier periods as well, but the only liturgical situation that can definitely be reconstructed for Israelite-Judean religion is the one associated with the large genre of the "petitions of the individual." A worshipper in distress vowed to make a sacrifice of thanksgiving (*todah*) if rescued by God, and to declare God's praise to those assembled for the communal sacrificial meal. There is evidence that in some cases the prayer and praise would be written down, sometimes on a stele. This form of prayer is also attested elsewhere in the ancient Near East, but is most highly developed in the book of Psalms. Doubtless the cult of Israelite-Judean religion included hymns to the deity, of which old psalms like Pss. 29 and 68 may be examples. Prayers were also offered at the Jerusalem Temple on behalf of the king, of which the small number of "royal psalms" are probable survivors (Pss. 20, 21, 45, 72, 89).

The canonical book of Psalms reflects biblical religion and was collected in the postexilic period of the 5th and 4th centuries. Many psalms are assigned pseudepigraphically to David, others to Levitical figures such as Asaph, Ethan, and Korah. Many are unascribed. The work is divided into five "books," likely on the model of the Torah. The old traditions of Israelite-Judean prayer have been reinterpreted and reworked to supply models of approved monotheistic piety. Prayers are addressed only to YHVH; there is no mention of the mediating angelic figures that seem to have played a role in "popular" religion (Job 33.23; Ps. 91.11). Numerous genres are represented: petitions of the individual (the largest group), communal petitions and complaints, historical hymns, nature hymns, "enthronement psalms" (describing God as king), "royal psalms" (praise and petition for the Davidic king), "Zion psalms" (hymns about Jerusalem and the Temple mountain), "songs of ascent" (for pilgrimages), wisdom and Torah psalms. There is a scholarly debate about the extent to which the canonical psalms represent actual liturgical pieces written for and used in the cult. Opinions range from the view that practically all of the psalms, except for wisdom and Torah, were used in the cult, to the view that almost all psalms have been freed from their cultic roots and have become "spiritualized" literary expressions of a dominantly individual, Temple-focused piety. There is little doubt the "royal psalms" are intended by the editors to be taken eschatologically, as referring to the future messianic (not, as they originally did, the current Davidic) king. It is likely that the other genres had many functions; as is often the case with liturgical texts, actual usage and inner meaning are not always apparent from the bare text, because the same words can be applied to many, and ever-changing, circumstances. This fact, though inconvenient for scholarship, no doubt partially accounts for the great popularity of the book of Psalms to this day.

Prophetic Tradition in Biblical Religion

The role of prophets in Israelite-Judean religion was sketched above, as well as the prophetic background to the development of biblical religion, specifically, the Deuteronomic-covenantal tradition. Strangely enough, however, biblical religion has a divided attitude toward the phenomenon of prophecy. On the one hand, prophecy was exalted in the figure of Moses, and revelation, by origin a purely prophetic phenomenon and limited to individuals, was made a constitutive national experience at Horeb/Sinai, albeit limited to that one occurence. On the other hand, prophecy as a living phenomenon was discouraged. Future prophets had to prove they were "true" and not "false" by producing prophecies that came true before their messages would be heeded (Deut. 18.21), a tautologous condition that effectively abolished prophecy as a living institution after the 5th century BCE, at least in "official" religion. No future revelation could compete with Moses or amend what he had said.

The books of the Latter Prophets (Isaiah, Jeremiah, Ezekiel, the Twelve), which purport to be a record of the great literary prophets of the past, were composed and edited in such a way that the viewpoint of developed biblical religion was dominant. The ecstatic aspect of the prophetic experience was downplayed, and visions were usually reported in some detail only for the inaugural of the prophet. Otherwise, the visual aspect, while definitely present, is secondary to the auditory. This produces the impression that the prophets were motivated by some vague kind of "inspiration" akin to that experienced by artists or writers, and that they were mainly preachers of morality, rather than the strange, antisocial, conflicted, and—if we can judge from the "Confessions" of Jeremiah—doubt-tortured individuals they often were. Jeremiah rails against his prophetic mission, but feels an irresistible inner compulsion ("a burning fire imprisoned within my bones, which I struggle to contain but cannot") to deliver God's words (Jer. 20.9). Biblical religion has flattened the prophets (a process continued by later tradition) but could not obliterate all evidence of their powerful personalities.

The Latter Prophets were also edited with much interpolation of later tradition, so that it is often difficult to tell in a book like Isaiah which speeches go back to the prophet himself (chs 24–27, 40–66 are definitely non-

Isaianic). Many of the later additions are eschatological and messianic. Eschatology, "the doctrine of the end," is the prophetic tradition that expresses hopes for the coming of an era of perfect peace, often brought about by a messianic ruler. The ancient Near Eastern background seems to have been in a type of oracle that predicted the coming of such a ruler after a time of troubles and disorder. The royal tradition of Judah (and perhaps even of Northern Israel) may already have contained such visions of a future king, but the attestations of messianism are in the literary prophets, especially Isaiah of Jerusalem, who seems to have been the first to introduce eschatology in a major way. The oracles in Isaiah from chs 7–11 predict the birth of several royal or royal-like children. The paradigmatic oracle is Isa. ch 11, which describes the reign of the future king in terms of a return to paradise. Peace will reign over the whole earth; even predatory animals will lose their urge to harm. Edenic themes dominate the developing messianic tradition in the later prophets, so that messianic oracles have been said to express an underlying belief in the cyclical, or at least circular nature of history, reflected in the dictum that "the end of time will be like the beginning of time" (Hermann Gunkel, the great German biblical scholar active in the late 19th and early 20th centuries). The messianic age will witness the submission of the nations to Israel, its king and its God, the cessation of war, the exaltation of the Temple on Mount Zion, and so on. The eschatological tradition became the focus of the hopes of an exiled and subjected people. This accounts for its popularity after the exile, and the fact that the prophetic books were edited with many eschatological additions. Contemporary prophecy after the 5th century may have been viewed as dangerous, but the prophets of the past, now made into canonical texts, could be studied for their glowing predictions, actual or interpolated, of the reversal of Israel's lowly state among the nations. Some scholars have tried to find a social milieu for the development of messianism, and posited an opposition in the postexilic period between conservative and privileged Priestly circles, who eschewed messianic enthusiasm, and oppressed circles of "visionaries," who cultivated it as a form of protest. In fact, messianism is entirely absent from the Torah, the central document of postexilic official religion; but it is uncertain that one is justified in positing a societal opposition of the type just described to explain the cultivation of messianic themes. Even the rich can long for the coming of the messiah.

By the 3rd to 2nd centuries BCE eschatology had developed into apocalyptic (a Greek term meaning "to uncover"), a form of literature combining many strands of tradition. The only representative of apocalyptic in the Bible is Dan. chs 7–12, but it was the subject of a vast literature from the 3rd century BCE to the 3rd century CE, eventually becoming a Christian genre. The Dead Sea community is held by most scholars to have been the Essenes, an apocalyptic sect; and Christianity grew from apocalyptic roots as well. Apocalyptic differs from earlier prophetic eschatology in being deterministic, hermetic, and systematic; it typically also uses an intermediary angelic figure as a conduit for its revelations. The pattern of history was fixed by God at creation; free will is therefore an illusion. A great crisis, in the form of the persecution of the righteous, viewed as a small group of the faithful who are "in the know" and who can interpret the meaning of the strange and wild imagery that fills apocalyptic texts, will trigger divine intervention and the final cosmic battle between good and evil, waged on an earthly and angelic plane. The holy war traditions of the ancient world find their apotheosis in Armageddon. Apocalyptic literature has a definite concept of an afterlife, linked to reward and punishment, unlike biblical religion: The dead will be resurrected on the Day of Judgment, some for eternal punishment, others for eternal bliss in paradise. The apocalyptic concept of resurrection and judgment was accepted by the Rabbis and by Christians as a dogma.

The Wisdom Tradition

The wisdom tradition is found in many places in the Bible, but it especially dominates the Writings, not only "proper" wisdom books like Proverbs, Job, and Ecclesiastes, but also some psalms (1, 19, 37, 119, etc.) and other texts. Wisdom (*ḥokhmah*) is the term used to describe the intellectual and educational tradition of the ancient Near East, the province of scribal schools, teachers and students, but also elders, wise fathers and mothers. Wisdom was a determinedly international and humanistic tradition. The wise of all nations communicated with each other; genres, themes, and even language crossed boundaries freely. Parts of the book of Proverbs are virtually translations of an Egyptian work of wisdom; and biblical wisdom texts are replete with themes and language drawn from foreign wise men. The themes of traditional wisdom were the training of the young, expressed in maxims for correct living that would produce prosperity and esteem, so called "practical wisdom." But there also was so-called "speculative wisdom," which dealt with philosophical and religious issues, above all the problem of suffering and theodicy, the justifying of the ways of God: Why do the righteous often suffer and the wicked prosper? There are Babylonian and Egyptian "Jobs" as well as the biblical figure; and even the latter, in consonance with the international focus of wisdom, is portrayed not as an Israelite but as an Aramean from Uz. Wisdom was also a tradition interested in creation, in the workings of nature. Natural imagery abounds in wisdom texts, like proverbs and fables; and Solomon is said to have delivered parables about plants, animals, fish, and trees (1 Kings 5.13).

Many scholars hold that there was a kind of incipient natural philosophy in the ancient world shared also by Israel. The world was created by wisdom, and reflects an underlying unity of natural and moral orders, called *ma'at*, "truth," in Egypt, *mesharum*, "right," in Mesopotamia, and by various terms in Israel, among them *'emet*, "stability, truth," and *tzedek*, "righteousness, order." In Israel, it was believed that the world was created by God with the help of wisdom (Job ch 28, Prov. ch 8), so that His plan is manifested in the order of the cosmos.

Up to the 7th century the wisdom tradition seems to have shown little interest in the particular religious traditions of Israel-Judah (though the prophets make increasing use of wisdom themes, especially Jeremiah, Second Isaiah, and Ezekiel); this explains the absence of references to cultic worship and to covenant in wisdom books. The development of full biblical religion, in the form of the Deuteronomic-covenantal complex, created a crisis of the wise. Deuteronomy rejects wisdom that does not concern itself with revelation and covenantal law. In the exile and afterwards, some of the wise began to accommodate their views to biblical religion, in varying degrees. Some refused all but superficial adherence to the new order. Although it is a very late book, Ecclesiastes remains almost wholly on the level of traditional old wisdom, except for the last verses (probably added by an editor). The book shows no concern for covenant religion and in its gentle cynicism is close to the ancient Near Eastern wisdom tradition (especially in regard to its *carpe diem* philosophy) and also to contemporary Epicurean philosophy.

But much of wisdom compromised with biblical religion by combining themes of traditional wisdom with the new faith. A strange deterministic theology of retribution developed that dominates much of Proverbs, some Psalms (especially 37) and, most strikingly, the speeches of Job's "friends": The righteous are always rewarded, the wicked always punished. Combined with this belief in strict reward and punishment was a doctrine of absolute cause and effect, derived from the nature interest of old wisdom, but now distorted into this new deterministic theology. Since only the wicked suffer, Job's friends say, Job must have committed some crime since he is clearly suffering. This doctrine is really a hybrid wisdom-covenantal faith, though it avoids explicit mention of covenant and presents itself as a form of natural law.

The greatest rebel against this deterministic and pitiless pseudo-piety was the author of Job, who rejects the arguments of the friends. Job is a radical rebel, who refuses to admit he is being punished for sin. With astounding hubris he demands that God appear to justify His ways. Job forces the deity to intervene to save His reputation. In a set of great speeches (Job chs 38–41), some of the most magnificent poetry of the Bible, God challenges Job to explain the works of creation. The problem with the divine "answer" is that God does not seem to address Job's challenge that He must explain why He is making Job suffer. Interpretations of the meaning of the book are numerous. Some maintain that God is simply overwhelming Job by confronting him with his human ignorance of the ways of God. Who are you to challenge the deity? A more modern reading holds that God is confirming the lack of congruence between natural and moral realms, a total rejection of traditional wisdom philosophy. A more positive interpretation is that God, even as He reminds Job of his human weakness, rouses him to awe and wonder at the greatness of nature, so that human suffering, even Job's, sinks into relative insignificance, at least temporarily. Probably the meaning of the book, like the meaning of *Hamlet* or any great work of literature, will always remain a riddle. Eventually wisdom's focus on nature gave way entirely to a focus on covenant, with results we see in the "Torah psalms," of which Ps. 119 is the longest, if not the most stirring, example.

Conclusions and Synthesis

Can one summarize biblical religion in a way that will organize its disparate traditions? The Bible is the most unsystematic of sacred texts, representing 1,000 years of textual development from different areas and social and religious groups. The several traditions of biblical religion we have listed, and the added complication of their superimposition on an earlier, and in many ways quite different, stage and type of religion, are so complex and confusing that one despairs of finding meaning in the whole, rather than in the parts. The historical discipline of source criticism has isolated the traditions and strands, without explaining their presence combined in the same work, often next to each other, in a way that seems intended to bewilder the reader. The traditional Jewish strategy in dealing with the multifariousness of the Bible is midrash, with its joyously insouciant ability to connect both the similar and the contradictory with a leap of imagination. However, historical scholarship, more limited in its agility than midrash, seems to be faced with two stark choices: to renounce interpretation of the whole and consider only the parts; or, conversely, to overlook the diversity and deal only with the whole on the canonical level. Indeed, canonical criticism, which views the Bible in the light of the communities that regard it as their Scripture, is one of the most important hermeneutical developments of recent years.

Yet there is a middle way: to recognize in the multiplicity of viewpoints not the result of incompetent editing, but the intent to express new religious insights in a culture that had as yet developed no theological, philosophical language adequate to describe them—a culture that, in addition, was conscientious about preserving old texts and traditions. In place of a harmonized, systematized theology, the Bible presents conflicting traditions, often next to each other: two creation narratives in Gen. chs 1–3; two forms of covenant tradition in the Torah, Deuteronomic and Priestly; two forms of prophetic speech, excoriating *riv* and comforting eschatology, and so on. Since biblical religion is textual, the believer is also necessarily a reader and an interpreter. Therefore a literary approach, a reading of God, as it were, may be preferable to a systematic theological approach that seeks to reconcile contradictions. Sympathy, not sophistry or scholasticism is required. The Bible must be read with the same freedom one has in all literary, especially poetic, interpretation, with concern for language and nuance, with awareness of the device of the juxtaposition of opposites, with delight in the kind of ambiguities that give texts deeper meaning. The later Rabbis recognized this freedom in midrash, and even in matters of halakhic disagreement sometimes allowed that both opinions were the "words of the Living God," a God made living precisely by the play of debate.

Indeed, biblical religion seems to go out of its way to cultivate and display disunity, to express religious ideas in terms of paired themes in tension, even opposition. For example, it can speak of God in one verse in a way that emphasizes the austere transcendence of the Deity; in the next verse it can use the most earthy and explicit anthropomorphism. The Bible is the least ecclesiastical, scholastic, and dogmatic of texts. As a transitional form of religion, biblical traditions had the luxury not to systematize, which is precisely what made the Bible the fertile ground from which its daughter religions could grow.

Yet there is an underlying unity in the varying traditions: the development of the characteristically biblical notion of faith in God. Faith is a much more complex idea than it is commonly held to be, so accustomed are we to speaking of "simple" faith. In fact it is a very complicated concept, the result of a long process of development. Its roots are probably in the ancient institution of holy war. Warriors were commanded to have confidence in God's protection, not to fear or let their hearts become weak (Deut. 20.3). This idea of trust or confidence in God's protection in battle did not become the truly biblical concept of faith until it was taken over by prophecy, from which it passed into the Deuteronomic-covenantal tradition and from thence into the other major traditions of biblical religion. Diagnostic of the idea of faith in its biblical form is that it has not only a primary object, God, but also a secondary one, the prophet. Moreover, the trust it demands is total and unconditional. This is the sort of faith Isaiah demanded of King Ahaz (Isa. 7.9): "If you do not have faith you will not be established!" (The Hebrew is a play on words, and says literally, "If you do not display firmness you will not be made firm.") The faith demanded here is not only that God will rescue Judah in a time of grave peril, but that Ahaz must also believe Isaiah is a true, not a false prophet. The sign of Immanuel (Isa. 7.14–17) that Isaiah gives Ahaz is unique, a test rather than a confirmation of confidence. Biblical faith involves absolute trust in the prophet as well as in God. This was later transmuted into faith in the authenticity of the textual record of past revelation. This mediated type of faith is the essential uniting core of all forms and all major traditions of biblical religion, and the unique contribution of biblical religion to world religion.

Faith, in the sense just described, pervades the whole Bible. Genesis has been edited to represent a struggle for faith on the part of the patriarchs, especially Abraham, who proves his faith only with the binding of Isaac. The narratives of the rest of the Torah record the people's struggle to maintain absolute trust in God, a test they repeatedly fail, despite the prevalence of overwhelming miracles. The prophets wrestle with faith constantly, especially with faith in the fact that they themselves are true and not deluded false prophets. Job, whatever the exact meaning of the book, certainly implies faith in divine Providence, despite all evidence to the contrary. The Psalms, especially the petitions of the individual, represent the struggle for firm, if not unquestioning, conviction despite suffering, doubts, and inner weakness. This biblical faith has as its locus a new kind of religious individual, the believing self, united in its devotion to the Deity. The tension between the faith-filled self, its own doubts, and the new type of community of believers posited by biblical religion as the true "Israel," is what gives the Bible its paradoxical unity in disparity, and its great religious power.

[STEPHEN A. GELLER]

Concepts of Purity in the Bible

As in many religious traditions past and present, ancient Israelites categorized persons, places, and other things as "holy" (kodesh) or "common" (ḥol) and as "pure" (tahor) or "impure" (tame᾽) (Lev. 10.10). These sets of categories are not identical: What is pure is not necessarily holy, nor is the common necessarily impure. Moreover, ancient Israel had multiple conceptions of purity, each of which developed over time, possibly under the influence of distinct religious ideologies. One notion of impurity, moral impurity, concerned the dangers of defilement associated with grave sins such as idolatry, incest, and murder. Another notion of impurity, ritual impurity, concerned contact with various natural substances relating to birth, death, and genital discharges. Contact with ritual impurity had serious consequences in one's religious life, rendering one temporarily unfit to encounter holy space and objects. To understand and appreciate these distinctions is a challenge for modern readers who are accustomed to looking down on hierarchy in general and to scoffing at seemingly irrational avoidances, especially when they pertain to death and sex.

In the early days of modern biblical scholarship, conceptions of defilement were treated with outright scorn. James Frazer (1854–1941) and William Robertson Smith (1846–1894), two founders of modern anthropology, could barely conceal their disgust for the avoidance behaviors of the Bible. Smith, Frazer, and others approached purity rules as if they were a random collection of primitive taboos. Their origin lay in savage fears of blood and demons; their preservation by Israel was simply a matter of perpetuating ancient custom. Making matters worse, Sigmund Freud (1856–1939) in Totem and Taboo famously compared religious avoidances with the obsessive behavior of psychotics. Whether they were seen as the products of primitive fears or primeval obsessions, ritual-

ized avoidances were dismissed by many as irrational, pointless, and just plain foolish.

The situation changed dramatically only in the 1960s. Under the influence of structural anthropology in general and the works of Mary Douglas (b. 1921) in particular, biblical scholars began approaching purity rules in new ways. Scholars came to recognize that avoidance behaviors could no longer be dismissed as something inherently or distinctly primitive. Many societies draw boundaries around certain behaviors (especially when it comes to death and sex), and these boundaries are certainly not always rational. Second, scholars also began to recognize that the avoidances of any religious tradition or culture had to be treated systemically or structurally. While earlier scholars would collect and analyze taboos in an encyclopedic fashion—comparing, for instance, various cultures' attitudes toward blood or hair—scholars would now focus on how the avoidance rules of any single culture work together to form a coherent conception of things permitted and prohibited, of things sacred and defiled.

A third important development was the willingness of scholars to recognize that a system of avoidance behaviors may be symbolic in nature. Where earlier scholars had assumed that the laws must be connected to primitive notions of health or hygiene, scholars now recognize that there might be more to these rules than a simple desire to avoid dirt or disease. In line with this perspective, scholars are increasingly translating the Hebrew terms tame᾽ and tahor as "impure" and "pure," instead of as "unclean" and "clean."

Yet some interpretive challenges remain. One error introduced under the influence of some anthropologists is the assumption that the ancient Israelite purity system was put in place in order for priests to subordinate Israelites and for Israelite men to subordinate their wives and daughters. Yet it is increasingly recognized that the ancient Israelite purity system affects men and women, priests and Israelites. While Israelite society was hierarchical and patriarchal, the ritual purity system did little to enforce these social demarcations; in any case, this certainly was not the system's primary purpose. Another common error is the identification of ritual impurity with sinfulness. The distinction between ritual and moral purity—also increasingly recognized by scholars—allows us to see better the complex relationship between impurity and sin.

Ritual Impurity

The bulk of the biblical purity laws concerns the situations and substances that render one ritually impure, and therefore temporarily unfit to encounter the sacred. Ritual impurity results from direct or indirect contact with any one of a number of natural sources or processes including childbirth (Lev. 12.1–8), certain skin diseases (13.1–46; 14.1–32), funguses in clothes (13.47–59) and houses (14.33–53), genital discharges (15.1–33), the carcasses of certain impure animals (11.1–47), and human corpses (Num. 19.1–22). Paradoxically, ritual impurity also comes about as a byproduct of some sacrificial procedures (Lev. 16.28; Num. 19.7–8). The durations of these impurities differ, as do the requisite cleansing processes. In general, however, there are three distinct characteristics of ritual impurity: (1) The sources of ritual impurity are natural and more or less unavoidable. (2) It is not sinful to contract these impurities. (3) These impurities can convey an impermanent contagion to people (priests and Israelites) and to many items within close proximity.

That the sources of ritual impurity are natural is really quite clear. Birth, death, sex, disease, and discharge are part of life. Ritual impurity is also generally unavoidable. While certain defiling substances are relatively avoidable (e.g., touching carcasses), others are inescapable (discharge, disease, and death). Some ritual impurities are not just inevitable,

but obligatory. All Israelites (priests included) are obligated to reproduce (Gen. 1.28; 9.7). All Israelites (except the high priest) are required to bury their deceased close relatives (Lev. 21.10–15; cf. 21.1–4). Priests are also obligated to perform cultic procedures that result in their defilement (Lev. 16.28; Num. 19.8).

It is not a sin to contract these ritual impurities. This idea proceeds logically from the observations drawn above. While priests must limit their contact with corpse impurity (Lev. 21.1–4), they are not prohibited from contracting other impurities (22.3–7). To be sure, priests and non-priests alike are sternly warned against eating sacred food or entering sacred precincts when in a state of ritual impurity (Lev. 7.19–21; 22.3–7), lest they defile holy food or space. Yet the primary concern incumbent upon the priests is not to avoid ritual impurity at all times, but to safeguard the separation between ritual impurity and purity (Lev. 10.10; cf. Ezek. 44.23). By extension, Israelites are obliged to remain aware of their ritual status, lest they accidentally come into contact with the sacred while in a state of ritual impurity (Lev. 15.31). Because ritual impurity is contagious, the danger here is that defilement if left unchecked will accumulate and defile the Tabernacle or Temple, rendering it impure and unfit for divine habitation. It is for this reason that the refusal to purify oneself would constitute a transgression (Num. 19.20). But this does not make being ritually impure sinful in and of itself. As long as Israelites remain aware of their status and avoid contact with the Temple and holy objects while impure—and do what is necessary to ameliorate the situation—there is little chance of danger or transgression.

A few biblical narratives nevertheless view at least one form of ritual defilement as a punishment for moral shortcomings. Miriam was afflicted with a "leprous" or "scale" ailment when she spoke against Moses' Cushite wife (Num. 12.10); the Judean King Uzziah was similarly afflicted when he sinfully asserted priestly prerogatives (2 Chron. 26.16–21). But viewing one particular skin disease as a possible punishment for sin is not tantamount to viewing ritual impurity as sinful in and of itself. If it were, the sinner would be defiling even without the manifestation of a defiling affliction. Thus the following claim still stands: It is not sinful to be ritually impure, and ritual impurity does not result directly from sin.

The third characteristic of ritual impurity is that it conveys to persons (priests and Israelites, men and women) an impermanent contagion. This is obviously true of the ritual impurity that Israelites contract from direct or indirect contact with a ritually impure carcass or another ritually impure Israelite. In such a case, the period of defilement can be as brief as less than one day, until the setting of the sun (Lev. 11.24; 15.7; Num. 19.22). The same holds for persons who engage in permitted sexual relations (Lev. 15.16–18). A man who has sexual contact with a menstruant or a person who comes into contact with a corpse will be ritually impure for a week (Lev. 15.24; Num. 19.11). Other defiling conditions can result in even longer periods of defilement; for example, the ritual impurity following childbirth lasts, in its less severe form, either thirty-three or sixty-six days (Lev. 12.1–8). Finally, irregular genital flows (for both men and women), scale disease, and house funguses last an unspecified amount of time. But even these forms of impurity are conceived of as impermanent—that is why the biblical tradition records purificatory procedures for all of them. There is no form of ritual impurity that does not have purificatory procedures; they may include waiting until sundown, bathing, washing clothes, and performing sacrificial rites. Even when long-lasting, the status of ritual defilement is an impermanent one.

Clearly, ritual impurity cannot be understood simply as a concern with health or hygiene. There is no direct correspondence between what is unhealthy or unclean and what is impure. Some sources of impurity (such as a pig's carcass) may strike some as dirty in some way. But some things that even ancient Israelites considered to be dirty were not nec-

essarily ritually defiling: Excrement, human and animal, is not impure according to the Priestly system described in the Torah, despite the fact that it was recognized to be dirty and contrary to holiness (Deut. 23.13–15; but cf. Ezek. 4.12–15).

The idea that ancient Israelites viewed what is unhealthy as impure finds only scant support in Lev. chs 13–14, which discuss the ritual impurity that results from various obscure skin diseases and other funguses. Other biblical texts suggest that ancient Israelites knew about all sorts of diseases. If the concern with purity were the concern with health, we would expect all known diseases to be defiling. Yet only one kind of illness is defiling, and it defiles even when it affects a house or clothing, without affecting people. The concern in Lev. chs 13–14 is not with the spreading of the disease so much as with the spreading of impurity. All who come into contact with what is deemed "leprous" are impure, and are so for a day, whether or not they show signs of the disease.

It is also commonly believed that the dietary prohibitions extend from rules concerning health. (This view can be traced back, in part, to the medieval Jewish philosopher and physician Moses Maimonides.) This is nowhere explicit in biblical texts. Furthermore, while this is arguably true of certain defiling foods (e.g., pork), there is no known health risk associated with the majority of defiling land animals and birds. On the other hand, there are many known health risks associated with the consumption of various plants, but not even poisonous plants are viewed as defiling. There is, in the end, no direct association between health and purity, or between disease and defilement.

It can also be clearly seen now that ritual impurity is not a system put into place in order for priests to subordinate Israelites or for men to subordinate women. The subordination of classes—where it exists—needs to be supported by permanent or at least long-lasting social stigmas that are selective in such a way as to support the intended social agenda. Ritual impurity, however, is impermanent and applies to all Israelites—men and women, priests and laypersons. The system is therefore not well suited to reinforce any specific social hierarchies.

Traditional Judaism—in both the medieval and modern periods—has been primarily interested in the ritual impurity associated with menstruation. For a variety of reasons, this remains the only aspect of the biblical ritual impurity system that was maintained for very long after the destruction of the Second Temple in 70 CE. But the Bible knows of no such selective focus. In Leviticus, genital flows from both men and women are sources of ritual defilement. "Leprous" impurities affect men and women equally, and the corpses of men and women equally constitute the most severe form of ritual defilement.

Even in the case of defilements pertaining to women, it is difficult to understand the rules as intending to subordinate them or exclude them. One must bear in mind that women would only experience menstrual impurity after puberty, before menopause, and when not pregnant or lactating. For most ancient Israelite women, periodic ritual defilement was probably not a monthly affair. Moreover, the procedures of ritual purification require women to come into the sanctuary and to actively participate in sacrificial procedures (Lev. 12.6–8). If the rules were meant to exclude women, one should wonder why rituals of purification serve to bring women into the sanctuary.

If ritual impurity is not directly related to sin, health, or hygiene, or the desire to subordinate laypersons or women, what then is its basis?

The common denominators of the varied sources of ritual defilement are death and sex. Concerns with death-avoidance explain the defilements associated with corpses, carcasses, and the loss of reproductive genital fluids. Death-avoidance can also explain the concern with the skin disease, which is explicitly described as decomposition of the flesh (Num. 12.12). Yet death-avoidance on its own

does not explain why sex and birth defile. The only substances that flow from the body and defile are sexual/genital in nature. (Even blood flowing from the veins of a dying person is not ritually defiling.) The dual concerns with death and sex provide the basis for understanding all of the ritual purity rules.

The ritual purity system of ancient Israel serves to force a separation between the experience of encountering God's sanctity and matters pertaining to death and sex. Because God is eternal, God does not die. Because God has no consort, God does not have sex. Therefore, by separating from sex and death—by following the ritual purity regulations—ancient Israelites separated themselves from what made them least God-like. Only a heightened God-like state—the state of ritual purity—made one temporarily eligible to approach the sanctuary, God's holy residence among the Israelites (Exod. 24.8). Following the ritual purity laws is yet another way of behaving in accordance with the theological underpinning of the Holiness Collection: imitatio Dei (Lev. 11.44–45; 19.2; 20.7, 26).

Ritual impurity is for these reasons diametrically opposed to holiness. And as noted, ritual purity—the established absence of any ritual defilement—is the prerequisite for encountering God's holy presence, as manifest in the tabernacle or the Temple. But this formula is not reversible: The lack of holiness does not necessarily constitute ritual impurity. There are in fact four possible states. At either end of the spectrum are the diametrically opposed statuses of ritual impurity and holiness. In between the extremes are two intermediary—and in many cases, overlapping—positions. Working in from one end, in the absence of impurity one can be considered to be pure (tahor). Working in from the other end, in the absence of holiness one can be considered to be "common" (ḥol) (Lev. 10.10). It has been emphasized that the prohibitions related to ritual impurity primarily involve the dangers associated with bringing what is impure into contact with what is holy. It remains permitted for pure and impure persons and things to commingle in non-holy, "common" space. For instance, when Israelites consumed food that was permitted but not sacrificial (and thus not holy), ritually pure and impure persons were permitted to consume such food together (Deut. 12.15).

It is difficult to know how widely these regulations were followed in ancient Israel. They are reflected in detail only in Priestly literature, and in related texts such as Ezekiel. Priestly material is particularly concerned with these issues, since priests were responsible for the ritual purity of the Temple. References to ritual impurity can nonetheless be identified in a variety of other texts (e.g., Deut. 23.11–12; 2 Sam. 11.4; Isa. 52.11). Ritual purity should not therefore be understood as an issue of concern only to priests.

Moral Impurity

As noted above, the Bible is concerned with another form of purity and impurity, often referred to as "moral." (Some scholars draw this distinction in different terms, speaking of "permitted" [ritual] and "prohibited" [moral] impurities.) Moral impurity results from committing certain acts so heinous that they are considered defiling. Such behaviors include certain sexual sins (e.g., Lev. 18.24–30), idolatry (e.g., 19.31; 20.1–3), and bloodshed (e.g., Num. 35.33–34). These "abominations" bring about an impurity that *morally*—but not *ritually*—defiles the sinner (Lev. 18.24), the land of Israel (Lev. 18.25; Ezek. 36.17), and the sanctuary of God (Lev. 20.3; Ezek. 5.11). This defilement, in turn, leads to the expulsion of the people from the land of Israel (Lev. 18.28; Ezek. 36.19). The bulk of the references to these ideas can be found in Priestly traditions (especially the Holiness Collection) and in the most Priestly of prophetic books, Ezekiel. Additional articulations of the notion or echoes of it can be found in various strands of biblical tradition, including Gen. 34.5; Deut. 24.1–4; 1 Kings 14.24; Jer. 2.7, 23; 3.1; Hos. 5.6; 6.10; and Ps. 106.34–40.

There are seven important differences between moral and ritual impurity.

1. While ritual impurity is generally not sinful, moral impurity is a direct consequence of grave sin.

2. A characteristic feature of moral impurity is its deleterious effect on the land of Israel. Ritual impurity, in contrast, may threaten the sanctity of the Temple, but poses no threat to the land.

3. While ritual impurity often results in a contagious defilement, there is no personal contact-contagion associated with moral impurity. Moral impurity does defile the sinners themselves (Lev. 18.24; 19.31; cf. Gen. 34.5; Deut. 24.1–4). But one need not bathe subsequent to direct or indirect contact with an idolater, a murderer, or an individual who committed a sexual sin.

4. While ritual impurity results in an impermanent defilement, moral impurity leads to a long-lasting, if not permanent, degradation of the sinner and, eventually, of the land of Israel.

5. While ritual impurity can be ameliorated by rites of purification, that is not the case for moral impurity. Moral purity is achieved by punishment, atonement, or, best of all, by refraining from committing morally impure acts in the first place.

6. Since moral impurity does not produce ritual defilement, sinners—in contrast to those who are ritually impure—are not excluded from the sanctuary. In the case of the suspected adulteress (Num. 5.11–31), the woman is brought into the sanctuary itself in order to determine her moral status. It also appears that Israelite murderers sought sanctuary *in the sanctuary* (Exod. 21.14; cf. 1 Kings 1.50–53; 2.28–30). Moral impurity does indeed defile the sacred precincts (e.g., Lev. 20.3), but the effect of moral impurity does not penetrate the holy realm by the entrance of sinners into it. Moral impurity is a potent force unleashed by sinful behavior that affects the sanctuary even from afar, in its own way.

7. In addition to these phenomenological differences between ritual and moral defile-

BIBLICAL IMPURITIES

Type	Source	Effect	Resolution
Ritual	Bodily flows, corpses, etc.	Temporary, contagious defilement of persons and objects	Bathing, waiting
Moral	Sins: idolatry, sexual transgression, bloodshed	Long-lasting defilement of sinners, land, and sanctuary	Atonement or punishment, and ultimately, exile

ments, there are also terminological distinctions drawn in the texts themselves. Although the term "impure" *(tame')* is used in both contexts, the terms "abomination" *(to'evah)* and "pollute" *(ḥanaf)* are used with regard to the sources of moral impurity, but not with regard to the sources of ritual impurity. For all of these reasons, it is imperative to distinguish between moral and ritual impurity.

Ritual and Moral Impurities

For reasons that are not entirely clear, the passages that articulate the idea of moral impurity are often understood as metaphors. Metaphor is a complex phenomenon; even its definition is still debated by linguists and philosophers. According to some, metaphor is so pervasive that it could accurately be argued that all rituals involve metaphor on one level or another. But when scholars refer to moral impurity in particular as metaphorical, the implication is that the passage is not to be taken literally: The defilement in question is not real. There is, however, no reason why the defilement of the land by blood shed upon it (Num. 35.33–4) ought to be a metaphor, while the defilement of a person who merely enters a tent in which a corpse lies is real (Num. 19.14). Though the sources and modes of transfer of moral and ritual impurity differ, we are dealing, nonetheless, with two analogous *perceptions of contagion,* each of which brings about effects of religious, legal, and social consequence. There are indeed differences between ritual and moral defilements. But the difference between ritual and moral defilement is not accurately understood by describing one (ritual impurity) as literal and the other (moral impurity) as metaphorical.

The ritual impurity rules constitute a set of avoidances that symbolically express the notion of *imitatio Dei.* The moral impurity rules constitute a set of danger beliefs, and the symbolism involved here works differently. When ancient Israelites believed that the land and sanctuary were defiled by idolatry, sexual sin, and murder, they believed that God finds these behaviors so abhorrent that He would not and could not abide on a land that is saturated with residue left by their performance. It is precisely this ramification of moral defilement that is depicted quite dramatically in Ezek. chs 8–11. Upon Israel's performance of grave sins, God's "glory" departs from the sanctuary and Israel's exile then ensues. The doctrine of moral defilement underscores the fact that grave sins affect not only their perpetrators and victims, but also Israelite society as a whole. If God cannot abide in His earthly sanctuary because it has been defiled, then all Israel will suffer exile together.

Purity Disputes in Ancient Judaism

Disputes among Jews with regard to the nature and force of the purity laws are in evidence throughout the Second Temple period. Purity debates among Pharisees and Sadducees are preserved in the Mishnah (*m. Yad.* 4:6–7), and heightened concerns with purity are also characteristic of the sectarian literature discovered at Qumran. In the Dead Sea Scrolls we find stricter rules concerning ritual impurity in the *Temple Scroll,* and stricter rules concerning moral impurity in, especially, the

Community Rule. Early Christianity was characterized, among other things, by a heightened interest in certain aspects of moral purity over and against a reduced focus on ritual purity (e.g., Mark 7.1–23). The Rabbis, in contrast, exerted much more effort in discussing the rules of ritual purity (to which much of the Mishnah is devoted), while exhibiting relatively little interest in moral defilement (but see *Sifra* on Lev. 18.24–30).

One purity dispute in particular is already reflected in the early Second Temple period, and the documents pertaining to the dispute can be found within the Bible. During the Persian period, both Ezra and Nehemiah confronted situations in which a number of the Jews had married local non-Jewish women. Both Ezra and Nehemiah urged the dissolution of these marriages (Ezra 9.1–10.44; Neh. 13.23–31). It is rather clear that purity in some form was at issue. Terms of defilement are used with reference to the problem (Ezra 6.21; 9.1, 11–14), and the proposed solution—divorce—is referred to as a purification (Neh. 13.30). This has led many scholars to the view that these books considered the foreign wives to be ritually impure, presumably as the result of their status as Gentiles. The passages in question, however, echo not the Priestly traditions relating to ritual impurity, but the Holiness Collection traditions relating to moral impurity: What is being said here by Ezra, Nehemiah, and their supporters is that the foreign women are in an inherent state of moral defilement and that inevitably the defilement will be passed to their progeny as well.

The view of Ezra and Nehemiah met with considerable opposition. The book of Ruth, according to some interpretations, effectively counters the prejudiced perspective of Ezra-Nehemiah, as do various Second Temple prophetic passages (Isa. 56.3–8). When one looks back at the Priestly traditions on these matters, it also becomes clear that Ezra's position is by no means clearly articulated there. One can find in the Torah limited prohibitions of intermarriage (e.g., Deut. 7.1–5) and even passages ascribing moral impurity to foreigners (e.g., Lev. 18.24). Yet one cannot find a clear, Priestly prohibition of intermarriage, justified by appeal to the notion of moral defilement (cf. Ezra 9.11–12). This may reflect the fact that the prohibition only emerged in the Second Temple period. Alternatively, this may reflect the continuing influence of Ezra's Priestly opponents, who certainly had a more welcoming attitude toward foreigners. Looking back on the Torah from the vantage point of Ezra ch 9, one can imagine a group of priests maintaining strong systems of ritual and moral purity while at the same time establishing a society with relatively open social boundaries.

The biblical traditions, from Leviticus to Ezra, leave a legacy that is not only challenging to contemporary scholars, but was likely equally challenging to ancient Jews themselves—giving rise to the purity disputes of the Second Temple period. When evaluating purity disputes among various ancient Jewish groups (early Christians included), it is imperative to understand well the complex and symbolic character of the purity systems, and it is equally important to appreciate the distinct natures of the ritual and moral purity systems. The purity rules are often disparaged as blunt instruments of social control, put in place by the priestly few to enforce their hegemony over laypersons and women. Alternatively, some still see purity rules as vestiges from primitive times. The challenge is to recognize purity rules (of the ritual and moral sort) as meaningful and yet nuanced ways of highlighting issues of social and theological significance.   [JONATHAN KLAWANS]

Historical and Geographical Background to the Bible

Some Methodological Considerations. It is not easy to reconstruct the history of ancient Israel. Although many of the texts in the Bible have been characterized as historical texts, they certainly are not historical in our sense. The biblical authors, unlike modern professional historians, made no attempt to be objective or complete in recording events from the past; instead, they constructed narratives of the past for religious and/or didactic purposes. Certainly, these narratives incorporated many facts, but it is often difficult to disentangle fact from fiction, truth from myth or legend. Unfortunately, relatively little writing outside the Bible has been preserved that might help us confirm what is historically accurate or fill in historical gaps. Though much archeological effort has gone into studying ancient Israel, the evidence is often ambiguous and open to different interpretations. In some cases, a careful combination of analysis of biblical texts, archeological finds, and records about ancient Israel from its neighbors may yield a detailed description of a period or an event. This, however, does not occur as often as we would like. For this reason, much of the history summarized below, though based on the best information currently available, should be considered tentative.

Beginnings

By the time Israel appeared on the stage of the ancient Near East, civilization and the patterns of empires and of the larger shared culture of the Levant were already well established. Before the end of the fourth millennium BCE, full urbanization had developed in the great river valleys of Egypt and Mesopotamia. The development of sophisticated technology to exploit the flooding of the Nile and to channel the waters of the Euphrates and Tigris enabled the production of regular food supplies and led to regional hegemonies. In Egypt, oriented about the south-to-north direction of the Nile's flow, this culminated in the unification of Upper (southern) and Lower (northern) Egypt, at the onset of the Early Dynastic Period toward the end of the fourth millennium. In southern Mesopotamia the kings of Sumer ruled that region (now southern Iraq) from a succession of dominant city-states beginning at about the same time.

The stages that had preceded urbanization are prehistoric in the sense that they antedate the development of writing. Archeologists have been able to trace the slow, and often independent, progress from hunter-gatherer economies throughout the Near East to stable cultures that relied on domesticated crops and animals for their sustenance. Dependable supplies of food led to increases of population, and ultimately competition for resources. These factors combined to necessitate specialization of tasks, centralized control, and record-keeping. For these purposes, writing was invented, again toward the end of the fourth millennium, and once introduced, was widely adopted in different systems in Egypt and Mesopotamia. By 3000 BCE, then, written history may be said to have begun.

As a result of nearly two centuries of discovery, excavation, and deciphering of ancient texts, a detailed chronology of the ancient Near East has been established. While there are occasional gaps in the sequence of rulers for Egypt and for the various Mesopotamian city-states, those sequences are relatively complete. For regions peripheral to the centers of power the historical record is more spotty, but still substantial. Allowing for minor scholarly disagreements, the chronology is secure and is the framework for the history of the entire ancient Near East, including Israel. Nor is the knowledge of the historical record restricted to kings and princes. Hundreds of thousands of non-elite texts have been found. These are not great myths and royal inscriptions, but mundane business and commercial records which shed valuable light on the lives of ordinary men and women and have begun to make possible a reconstruction of the social world of the ancient Near East.

Ancient cultures were as intrigued as we are by beginnings, and they constructed elaborate myths to explain their own prehistory. The establishment of the natural and social orders is typically presented in these myths as the work of a deity, usually the principal god or goddess of the political entity in which they were written. Both Egyptian and Mesopotamian literatures have a large number of such creation myths, many features of which have parallels in biblical traditions. It should not be surprising that Israel, a latecomer to the area, would be influenced so significantly by the older, more dominant cultures of its neighbors. Israel's accounts of its origins were ultimately collected and edited in the book of Genesis. The early chapters of Genesis deal with prehistory. In these Israelite expressions of the origins of the world, of society, and of civilization, the principal agent is the god of Israel. And, although intended as the prologue to a larger historical narrative, they are not historical in any modern sense, that is, they do not accurately represent what the archeological record shows to have taken place, whether in terms of chronology, or the origin of species, or a universal flood.

Egypt and Mesopotamia have their own complex histories during the third millennium, now relatively well known thanks to textual and archeological data. In the Levant this is the period known as the Early Bronze Age, when northern Syria was largely in the orbit of Mesopotamia, and Egypt exercised direct control over Canaan. For complex reasons not fully understood, toward the end of the third millennium Egypt experienced some internal disruption, reflected in the decline of city-states in Canaan but not farther to the north. By 2000 BCE, however, centralized control had been reestablished, and the textual and artifactual evidence is abundant. Trade flourished, as is indicated by both the archeo-logical record and commercial and diplomatic correspondence among larger urban centers, and between them and Mesopotamia and Egypt. The Levant was spanned by a cultural continuum, with Syria and northern Canaan being more closely linked with Mesopotamia, and southern Canaan with Egypt. Canaan itself had a relatively homogeneous culture, and its inhabitants, especially in rural and village settings, went about their lives with relatively few changes despite the struggles of the urban centers with each other. From as far back as the end of the fourth millennium, and into the first, there appears to have been continuity of population, whose patterns of material culture develop rather than being replaced by successive waves of invaders, as earlier historical reconstructions suggested.

It is in this larger context that Israel placed its own beginnings, centered on the lives of four generations of ancestors: the families of Abraham and Sarah, of Isaac and Rebekah, and of Jacob and Leah, Rachel, Bilhah, and Zilpah, and their offspring.

The Historicity of the Ancestral Narratives in Genesis

In the biblical account of the origins of Israel, narratives concerning Israel's ancestors in Gen. chs 12–50 follow the mythic material in chs 1–11. The chronology of the narratives themselves is set in the early second millennium BCE, but there are no direct connections between the biblical traditions and nonbiblical sources. No person or event known from Egyptian, Mesopotamian, or other sources is even mentioned in the biblical narrative. At the relatively few points where the Bible does name rulers (as in Gen. ch 14; 20.2; 26.8), none of them are found in any nonbiblical sources. Moreover, at many points in the narrative the Bible is tantalizingly vague. If the biblical writers had just named, for example, the pharaoh who took Sarah into his house (Gen. 12.15), or the pharaoh in whose court Joseph rose to power (Gen. ch 41), we would at least know when the biblical writers thought those events took place, and could correlate them with Egyptian chronology.

The biblical narratives themselves are the result of a lengthy and complicated process of the formation, transmission, and editing (see the Introduction to the Torah, pp. 1–7). Although the reconstruction of that process is hypothetical, there is no doubt that the process itself has led to the inclusion of a large number of anachronisms. The stories reached the written form in which we have them long after the purported events that they recount, and they often reflect the times when they were written or edited rather than the times in which their stories are set. For this reason, it is unlikely that these stories can be useful in reconstructing any particular period in the second millennium. The ancestral stories in Gen. chs 12–50 may preserve some authentic historical memories, but these have been so refracted by the processes of transmission and the idealization of the ancestors that it is impossible to designate any of the individuals mentioned in Genesis as historical or to establish anything resembling a precise chronology.

The Historicity of the Exodus from Egypt

As with the ancestral narratives in Genesis, there is no direct connection between biblical traditions in Exodus and other ancient sources. Egyptian records contain no mention of the major individuals and events of the narrative in Exod. chs 1–15: Moses, Aaron, the plagues, and the defeat of the Egyptian army at the sea are completely absent from the extensive documentation we have for ancient Egypt. Again, the biblical sources are frustratingly unspecific and at places contradictory. Neither the pharaoh "who did not know Joseph" (Exod. 1.8) nor the pharaoh of the exodus itself (Exod. chs 5–15) is named. The only precise detail in the narrative is the store cities named in Exod. 1.11, but both their precise location and the dates when they were founded and occupied are uncertain, and their inclusion could also be anachronistic. As with the

ancestral narratives in Gen. chs 12–50, the exodus narrative has been shaped by centuries of transmission and redaction, and should not be taken at face value as a historical record, although it is clearly central to the self-identity of Israel.

The first fixed datum, one of great importance, is a victory stele of Pharaoh Merneptah (1213–1203). In it he claims to have defeated various enemies in Canaan, including the identifiable cities of Gezer, Yanoam, and Ashkelon, and in the same geographical region, a group identified as Israel. Though it is doubtful that the victory celebrated on the stela is as complete as claimed, it is clear that by the end of the 13th century BCE the Egyptians knew of the existence of a geopolitical entity called Israel in the land of Canaan.

That some type of exodus took place may be a reasonable inference, given the persistence of the exodus tradition in the Bible and its presence in the earliest biblical poetry (notably Exod. ch 15), and some smaller details, such as the Egyptian names of Moses, Aaron, and Phinehas. The event must have involved fewer people than the exaggerated biblical numbers (see Exod. 12.37) indicate, and may have constituted little more than the escape of a relatively small group of Hebrews from forced labor in the eastern Nile delta, most likely in the 13th century. Given the lack of historical data, it is impossible to say more.

That group, whatever its size, interpreted its escape as the direct intervention of its god YHVH on its behalf, to be celebrated in hymns and magnified in importance as it was told and retold. When the group eventually entered Canaan, at a time when there was no centralized power to oppose it, it joined with others and eventually became the twelve-tribe confederation of Israel.

The Early History of Israel in the Land of Canaan

The beginning and end of this era are framed by two synchronisms: the mention of Israel in the Merneptah Stele in the late 13th century (see above), and the campaign of the Pharaoh Shishak in Western Asia in 925 (see below), an event documented both in Egyptian sources and in the Bible. During the intervening three centuries, according to the chronology accepted by the majority of scholars, Israel developed from a loose confederation of tribes into a relatively stable dynastic monarchy. But of the principal events and individuals that figure in biblical narratives, none occurs in other sources.

One reconstruction of the beginning of this period, following the biblical narrrative, is that of conquest. Much of the book of Joshua describes how the large group of Israelites crossed the Jordan under the leadership of Joshua and in a series of swift and relentless campaigns defeated the kings of the major Canaanite cities and annihilated most of the indigenous population. In the first part of the 20th century, this view seemed to be confirmed by the presence of destruction layers at key sites, all dated to the very end of the Late Bronze Age.

Reexcavation of many of those sites and more refined ceramic chronology, however, made it clear that some of the sites had not in fact been occupied at that time, and that the destructions were not all contemporaneous. Moreover, the opening chapters of the book of Judges, which also describes Israel's conquest of Canaan, presented a very different picture. While some Israelite tribes were apparently successful in defeating their Canaanite neighbors, many others coexisted alongside them. This is apparently confirmed even in the book of Joshua, where such Canaanite groups as the family of Rahab (Josh. 6.25) and the Gibeonites (Josh. ch 9) were incorporated into Israel. Thus the conquest model has largely been abandoned by scholars, but no other reconstruction has gained general acceptance.

One plausible scenario is to combine elements of various models to suggest that Israel as we know it emerged in the land of Canaan, and was comprised of diverse groups. One of these was the exodus group, whose allegiance to the god who had brought them out of Egypt, Yhvh, would become the central religious tenet of the confederation. They were joined by others, some who were apparently their kin who had never gone down to Egypt, and some who may have been Canaanites disaffected from the centers of power. These disparate elements eventually united in a confederation or league, whose primary principles of worship of Yhvh and mutual support were expressed in a social compact or covenant. The elements are called tribes, and they are associated with specific subregions in the land. While the number of twelve tribes is constant, both the names of the tribes and the territories with which they were associated shifted in response to historical vicissitudes. The religious symbol of the confederation was a moveable shrine, the Ark of the Covenant, which seems to have been based at different tribal centers at different times. The confederation was decentralized, with no overarching authority, and the tribes were relatively independent. In time of crisis, however, tribes were expected to come to the assistance of a beleaguered member, as in the very ancient poem in Judg. ch 5, or to punish one of their own for breach of the compact, as in the account of the Benjaminite war in Judg. chs 19–21. In situations like these a volunteer militia was mustered.

This reconstruction takes into account a variety of biblical data which are admittedly embedded in a later historical work, the Deuteronomistic History (see the Introduction to the Nevi'im, pp. 451–61). It also incorporates recent archeological evidence, including both significant elements of cultural continuity between the Late Bronze Age and the Iron Age, and the proliferation of small rural settlements in the hill country both west and east of the Jordan. Not all of these settlements would have been Israelite, nor would tribal territory necessarily entail complete control.

At the beginning of the Iron Age (ca. 1200 BCE), shortly after the likely date for the pattern of settlement described in the previous paragraph, another group arrived in Canaan. These were the Philistines, one component of the "Sea Peoples" well documented in Egyptian sources and in the archeological record. Of Aegean origin, they had repeatedly failed in their attempts to invade Egypt, and one or more of these Sea Peoples, including the Philistines, settled in Canaan along the Mediterranean coast. According to the biblical account, they formed a pentapolis in the five cities of Gaza, Ashkelon, Ashdod, Gath, and Ekron, and the four of these cities that have been securely identified (Gath is the exception) show a remarkably homogenous material culture at this time.

The broad outline of the biblical account, in Judg. chs 13–16 (the Samson stories) and in 1 and 2 Samuel (the stories of Samuel, Saul, and David), and the archeological record are in considerable agreement. The Philistines had a superior technology, especially in metallurgy (see 1 Sam. 13.20) and military hardware, and a professional standing army. By the mid-11th century they had considerably expanded their territory to the north and east, and their presence is evident at important centers beyond it, including Beth-shan in the Jordan Valley, and at military outposts in the heart of Judah, the dominant southern tribe, and in the north as well. The Philistines and the Israelites were thus on a collision course, both vying for control of the same region.

The United Monarchy (ca. 1020–928 BCE)

The emergence of Israel as a nation-state is part of a larger pattern of the development of regional geopolitical and ethnic entities throughout the region, such as those of the Edomites, Moabites, and Ammonites in Transjordan, the Arameans in Damascus and other centers in central and northern Syria, and the Phoenicians in Tyre. In the case of Israel, there was an additional stimulus. At least in part because of the Philistine threat, toward the end of the 11th century Israel profoundly changed its form of government from a loose confederation of tribes to a monarchy. The first ruler, Saul, seems to have been more a military chief than a full-fledged king (and he

is thus a transitional figure from the "judges" to the monarchy). And despite initial successes, he was unable to check the Philistine advance, and died in a battle with them deep in Israel's territory in the Jezreel Valley. He was succeeded by a former commander in his army, David, who moved swiftly to contain the Philistines within their original territory and to unite Israel around himself and a newly chosen capital, Jerusalem.

Biblical historians describe additional military successes, which enabled David, and his son and successor Solomon, to subject kingdoms adjacent to Israel to vassal status, including the Edomites, the Moabites, the Ammonites in Transjordan, and the Arameans in Damascus. Whether the extent of the territory controlled by David and Solomon is as large as biblical sources suggest is questionable. Clearly the biblical historians have magnified the period of the United Monarchy, the reigns of David and Solomon, viewing them in many respects as an ideal age, made possible by divine favor. Underlying the sometimes hyperbolic and often ideologically motivated biblical accounts, however, is authentic historical memory of increasing centralized control and concomitant administrative complexity, a picture indirectly confirmed by the archeological record.

The most important synchronism between biblical and extrabiblical sources for this period comes just after the death of Solomon. The Egyptian pharaoh Shishak (Sheshonq I) undertook a campaign in Western Asia in 925, a date based on established Egyptian chronology. Mentioned in 1 Kings 14.25–26 (cf. 2 Chron. 12.2–9), this campaign is further documented in Egyptian sources and is confirmed by destruction layers at key cities in Israel. This synchronism is the basis for the chronology of the first three kings of Israel, Saul (ca. 1025–1005, the exact length of his reign is unclear), David (1005–965), and Solomon (968–928, allowing for a coregency with David at the beginning of his reign).

To be sure, the biblical account of the reigns of these three kings, found in 1 and 2 Samuel and 1 Kings chs 1–11, is shaped by theological and ideological concerns, and also displays a pervading interest in the characters of the narrative—the tragically inadequate Saul, the heroic David, the ambitious but flawed Solomon—and in the intrigues of the royal court. But it is also significantly different from narratives about earlier periods in Israel's history. Divine intervention is minimal, with most events taking place largely on the human plane. Moreover, a careful reading of the biblical text discloses some archival and other details that can be correlated with the archeological record and are consistent with the framework of events presupposed by the narrative. Thus, the skepticism of some modern historians, who argue that the biblical accounts of the United Monarchy are totally fictional retroversions from a much later time, seems unwarranted.

David also seems to have initiated the transformation of the monarchy into a dynastic kingship, which, consistent with other Near Eastern models, was understood to be the result of divine choice. With the establishment of the monarchy came social and religious innovation. The older structures of the decentralized premonarchic confederation were now coopted by royal institutions. The Ark of the Covenant was enshrined in the Temple in Jerusalem built by Solomon, providing in effect divine sanction for the monarchy. Priests became royal appointees, and there was a growing movement toward centralization of worship in the capital. Yet this centralized administration formed a kind of overlay, a veneer, on the social systems of the nation as a whole. Individuals still identified themselves as members of a family, clan, and tribe, and disputes between them were usually settled at the local level. Apart from the requirement of paying taxes and providing personnel for royal projects (corvee) and for the army, life in the villages probably proceeded much as it had for centuries.

The establishment of the monarchy, however, had entailed the formation of an elite, wealthy class. Life in the capital of Jerusalem,

and after the split of the kingdom into two, in the northern capital of Samaria as well, was characterized by conspicuous consumption. This is evident in accounts of Solomon's court (1 Kings 4.22–28; 10.14–22) and in the description of the Temple and royal palace complex he constructed (1 Kings chs 6–7). That the extravagances documented in these accounts are not entirely an exaggeration is evident from archeological data at Samaria, and at royal cities such as Megiddo, Hazor, Gezer, and Dan. With the concentration of political power in the hands of a ruling aristocracy came abuse. One of the constants of the biblical traditions is opposition to the exploitation of the poorer classes. This opposition was frequently expressed in prophetic rebukes of the aristocracy, as in the admittedly legendary traditions concerning Elijah (2 Kings ch 20), and in the books of the prophets themselves. While their own relationship to the centers of power was not always antagonistic, prophets such as Amos, Isaiah, and Micah in the 8th century and Jeremiah in the late 7th to early 6th centuries were harsh in their denunciation of social injustice. In a sense they were conservatives, even perhaps reactionaries, insisting that the older premonarchic tradition of covenant was still binding, a tradition that commanded not only exclusive worship of YHVH but also fair treatment of every Israelite.

The Divided Monarchies
(ca. 928–the Late 7th Century BCE)

The split into the Northern and Southern Kingdoms is based on geographical distance and differences. The union of north and south had been fragile, even during the United Monarchy, and it disintegrated at Solomon's death. The reason implied in 1 Kings ch 12 is the northerners' anger at the cost of the extravagances of the capital, and this must have been at least part of the motivation. Solomon's son and successor Rehoboam was unable to gain the allegiance of the ten northern tribes, who seceded and formed a separate kingdom. This inaugurates the period called the Divided Monarchy, with the kingdom of Israel in the north and the kingdom of Judah in the south. The dynasty that David had established remained in power in Judah for nearly four centuries, while Israel (the Northern Kingdom) was ruled by a succession of royal families, many of whose rulers came to power in military coups. The parts were less than their sum had been, and the two kingdoms had mixed relations, sometimes friendly, sometimes hostile. Neither was able to control effectively the regions that bordered them, and the Davidic-Solomonic empire, such as it was, ceased to exist.

Changes on the larger international scene would increasingly affect these two kingdoms. Pressure from a revived Egypt is already evident in the above-mentioned campaign of Shishak to the north in 925. Meanwhile, in northern Mesopotamia, the kingdom of Assyria had consolidated its control over Babylonia in the south and adjacent regions to the north and east, and by the 9th century was poised to expand into the west. At this point the fairly complete Assyrian annals enable the construction of a relatively exact chronology and provide numerous synchronisms with biblical texts. Beginning with Ahab, king of Israel in the mid-9th century, many of the rulers of both Israel and Judah are mentioned in Assyrian sources, an indication of the growing Assyrian interest in the region that was of ominous significance.

The Assyrians were establishing an empire, a process which reached its zenith with the Assyrian king Esarhaddon's subjugation of Egypt in 671. They accomplished this by virtue of a technologically sophisticated army which in relatively rapid advance overwhelmed the smaller kingdoms to its west, usually incorporating their territories into the empire as provinces and deporting the elite of their populations to other regions, destroying their national identity and thereby suppressing their desire to rebel. By the late 8th century this subjugation was virtually complete. The Aramean kingdoms had been taken, including that of the Arameans in Damascus in

732. In 722 Samaria fell, its ruling class was exiled to Assyria, and the Northern Kingdom of Israel became an Assyrian province. Judah's territory was curtailed, and in part because of the remote location of Jerusalem, was allowed to exist in vassal status. Toward the end of the 8th century the Judean king Hezekiah attempted to reassert Judean independence, but was ruthlessly quashed by the Assyrian king Sennacherib in a campaign (701) which is well documented in both biblical and Assyrian sources. Most of the cities and towns of Judea were razed; Jerusalem avoided destruction only by payment of a heavy tribute, and the Davidic dynasty survived.

Beginning with Amos and Hosea in the mid-8th century, the prophets and the later authors of the Deuteronomistic History (Joshua–2 Kings) interpreted these events as a deserved punishment inflicted by YHVH on his rebellious people. For them, the repeated experiences of attack, siege, and exile were ultimately caused not by the inexorable progress of the Assyrian armies, but by divine agency, imposing the fulfillment of the curses attached to the covenant. Yet, other prophets, especially Isaiah, focused on the preservation of Jerusalem and advocated the notion of Jerusalem's inviolability.

The End of the Kingdom of Judah (Late 7th–Early 6th Centuries BCE)

By the late 7th century the Assyrian empire was overextended, and was unable to prevent first independence and eventually overthrow by a resurgent Babylonia to its south. The Babylonians captured the Assyrian capital of Nineveh in 612, and in effect took over the Assyrian empire. In the initial years, Egypt and Judah attempted to take advantage of the transfer of power by reasserting their independence. This was the time of the reign of the Judean king Josiah (640–609), whom Kings compares to David and whose accomplishments are magnified like those of his illustrious predecessor. It seems likely that

Judah was able to reestablish control over some of the territory to the north and west that had been under direct Assyrian rule; Josiah's religious reforms of 621 (see 2 Kings chs 22–23) should be understood in this context. This autonomy, such as it was, was short-lived. After Josiah's death in battle at Megiddo in 609, in a failed attempt to prevent the Egyptians from moving north to reinforce the tottering Assyrians, Judah was again reduced to the status of a vassal, first to Egypt, and then, by the end of the 7th century, to Babylonia. Caught between two greater powers, the Judean kings Jehoiakim and Zedekiah successively allied themselves with Egypt, which proved to be the weaker partner. Under Nebuchadrezzar (also called Nebuchadnezzar) II, the Babylonians laid siege to Jerusalem in 597 and 586, in the second instance destroying the city, burning down the Temple, and ending the Davidic dynasty. Thus came the demise of the kingdom of Judah.

It was the end of an era. Despite the extravagant propaganda of the royal establishment, neither the Davidic dynasty nor its capital city were impregnable. Jerusalem was destroyed, its Temple burned, and its population decimated by death and exile. Although a significant number of Judeans remained in Judah, autonomous control of the promised land became only a memory. And despite partial restoration later in the 6th century, exile in Babylonia transformed the religion of Judah into what would later be called Judaism. From this point on, a significant proportion of Jews would be living outside of the land of Israel, without king, Temple, or priesthood. The Torah and other texts that would eventually comprise the Bible gained new importance in this period, filling the vacuum left by the destruction of these core institutions. The preservation and compilation of older texts, and the creation of new ones during and after the exilic period, preserved and developed the national identity of the Jews. It may not be putting it too strongly to say that had it not been for the cataclysmic event of the destruction of Judah, there would be no Bible.

The Persian Period (539–333 BCE)

The Babylonian exile and the period of Persian domination that followed was a time of great transformation for Judean institutions, religious practices, and culture; but it was equally a time in which the fundamental continuity with preexilic traditions was reaffirmed and secured. When Nebuchadnezzar put down the rebellion of Judah in 586 BCE, he exiled to Babylonia a portion of the population, especially the ruling class and the skilled artisans. Most, however, remained in Judah, where a subsistence economy was soon reestablished. Although the system of regular sacrifices at the Temple was disrupted, the ruined Temple remained a focus for religious observances. The book of Lamentations may preserve liturgical poems used on days commemorating the destruction of Jerusalem and its Temple. Little is known about the circumstances of those who went into exile, although it appears that the exiles were settled in a number of local communities in Babylonia, where they were able to oversee their own internal and cultural affairs under the leadership of Jewish elders and prophets (see Ezekiel; Isa. chs 40–55). Other exiles, it would seem, viewed the exile not as a sign of God's displeasure, but of divine weakness, and likely assimilated into the mainstream Babylonian culture (see Jer. ch 44).

The conquest of Babylon by the Persian king Cyrus the Great in 539 BCE brought significant changes. In keeping with his policy of respecting the various deities worshipped throughout the empire, a decree by Cyrus in 538 (see Ezra 1.1–4; 6.1–5) authorized the rebuilding of the Temple in Jerusalem and the return of the Temple vessels captured by Nebuchadnezzar. In addition, Cyrus allowed any of the exiles who wished to return to Judah to do so. Within the exilic community in Babylonia the anonymous prophet known as "Second Isaiah" (Isa. chs 40–55) strongly supported Cyrus and urged the exiles to return to Judah. Although historical sources are few and not always easy to interpret, it appears that only a small minority of the exiles and their descendants returned to Judah, most choosing to remain in Babylonia. This latter group became the nucleus of a large and highly significant Jewish Diaspora community (Jews of "the dispersion," that is, living voluntarily outside the land of Israel), which strongly influenced the development of Judaism and Jewish culture during the following centuries. A less numerous Diaspora community also developed in Egypt, formed originally of Judeans who fled during the last days of Judah.

Despite the decree of Cyrus, the Temple in Jerusalem was not rebuilt until 520–515 BCE. The reasons for the delay were various. Persian control over the western territories may actually have been tentative until after the Persians conquered Egypt in 525. The economy of Yehud (the name by which the Persian province of Judah was known) was weak, and there appears to have been friction between the population that had remained in the land and the small but powerful group who returned from exile with the authorization and financial backing of the Persian king. Conflicts with the neighboring territories of Samaria and Geshur and Ammon in Transjordan also complicated the situation. Within the Bible the prophetic books of Haggai and Zechariah and portions of Ezra chs 1–6 refer to this period, but these sources have to be read and interpreted critically, for they are neither consistent with one another nor easy to understand on their own terms. At least during the early part of Persian rule the governors of Judah appear to have been prominent Jews from the Diaspora community, one of whom, Zerubbabel, was a member of the Davidic royal family. Davidic kingship, however, was not reinstituted because Yehud was not an independent country but a province of the Persian empire. The province of Yehud itself was very small, consisting of Jerusalem and the territory surrounding it within a radius of about 24–32 km (15–20 miles).

Once the Temple was rebuilt, it became the nucleus of the restored community, and con-

sequently a focus of conflict (Isa. chs 56–66; Malachi). The high priestly family, which had also returned from the Diaspora, became very powerful, and at least on occasion was in conflict with the governor appointed by the Persian king. Although the details are often unclear, there appears to have been continuing conflict during the 5th century between those Jews whose ancestors had been in exile and those whose ancestors had remained in the land. Those who returned from the Diaspora styled themselves the "children of the exile" and referred rather contemptuously to the rest as "people of the land," as though their very status as Jews was in question. In fact, the question of the limits of the community was one of the most contentious issues of the period, reflected both in the controversy over mixed marriages between Jewish men and ethnically foreign women (Ezra ch 10; Neh. ch 13) and also in conflicts within the Jewish community over who had the right to claim the traditional identity as descendants of "Abraham" and "Israel" (see Isa. 55–66, esp. 63.16). Although the conflicts between various contending groups in early Persian period Yehud are largely cast in religious terms, there is no question that they were also in part socioeconomic (see Neh. ch 5). All of these conflicts and efforts toward redefinition of the community, however, took place within the reality of Persian imperial control. Thus it is not by accident that the two most prominent figures involved in various reforms of mid-5th century Yehud, Ezra and Nehemiah, were Diaspora Jews of high standing, carrying out tasks that had been specifically authorized by the Persian kings.

Because this was a period of self-conscious reconstruction, it was also a time of immense literary activity, as traditional materials were collected, revised, and edited, and new works composed. Although much of the Torah may have existed in various forms during the time of the monarchy, it was probably reworked during the Persian period into something close to its final form. Indeed, some have suggested that this revision may have been undertaken under the sponsorship of the Persian government, reflecting Persia's interest in achieving stability throughout its empire by means of religious and legal reforms in the provinces. Although a history of Israel and Judah called by modern scholars the Deuteronomistic History (Deuteronomy through 2 Kings) had been composed during the latter years of the monarchy and updated during the exile, a new version of that history, 1–2 Chronicles, was prepared during the Persian period (ca. 350 BCE). It clearly reflects the concerns of the postexilic community, focusing almost exclusively on the history of Judah and giving particular emphasis to the institution of the Temple. The book Ezra-Nehemiah interprets events from the decree of Cyrus in 538 until the late 5th century.

In addition to the prophetic books composed at this time (Isa. chs 56–66, Haggai, Zechariah, Malachi, and perhaps Joel), there is evidence that the texts of older prophets were also edited and reinterpreted. Psalmody had been an important element of worship at the First Temple, but appears to have taken on an even more significant role in the Second Temple. Although the expansion and revision of the book of Psalms may have continued into later periods, an important shaping of the psalter, perhaps including its division into five "books," was part of Persian period activity. Wisdom writing, too, flourished during this time. The book of Job, parts of the book of Proverbs, and perhaps Ecclesiastes were likely composed then.

The Hellenistic Period (333–63 BCE)

The westward expansion of the Persian empire into the area of Asia Minor had brought it into conflict with Greece, since many of the cities of Asia Minor which came under Persian control had been founded and populated by Greeks. Twice the Persians had even invaded the Greek mainland, but were defeated on both occasions. Eventually, Philip of Macedon developed a plan to free the Greek cities of Asia Minor from Persian domination. Al-

though he died before he could undertake the campaign, it was taken up by his son Alexander the Great in 334 BCE. Alexander, however, did not stop with the accomplishment of that initial goal. In 333 he continued down the Phoenician coast, subduing any city that resisted, conquered Egypt, then turned to the Persian heartland, defeating Darius III, the last Persian emperor, in 331. Alexander continued his conquest into the eastern reaches of the Persian empire before returning in 324 to Babylon, which he apparently intended to establish as the capital of the empire he now controlled. He died in 323, however, before he could successfully organize his enormous territory. After Alexander's death, his generals fought for control of portions of the empire. By 301 an agreement gave Egypt to Ptolemy and Mesopotamia and the Levant to Seleucus. Ptolemy, however, occupied most of the Levant. Through a series of five wars extending over more than 100 years the Ptolemaic kings managed to hold onto their Levantine territory, finally losing it to the Seleucids in 198 BCE.

Jerusalem had surrendered to Alexander in 333 and was relatively undisturbed by the events of his conquest. Samaria, too, surrendered, but rebelled in 332 and was severely punished, its inhabitants killed or sold into slavery, and the city refounded as a Macedonian military colony. Documents belonging to a group of Samaritans who fled and were later tracked down and killed by Alexander's troops have been excavated from the Wadi Daliyeh in the Jordan Valley. In contrast to the relatively settled conditions following Alexander's conquest, however, the dispute between the Ptolemies and the Seleucids over territorial control had serious consequences for Jerusalem and Judea. Not only did the wars sometimes affect Judean territory, at the border between the two, but the nation's leaders had to make difficult choices concerning which power to support. The conflict between pro-Ptolemaic and pro-Seleucid factions within the Judean community was a significant factor in internal politics during the 3rd century BCE.

Although the high priest was the primary

representative of the Judeans, the Ptolemaic system of government and taxation had significant effects on the power structure of the country. The Ptolemies considered their territories primarily as a source of revenue. Rather than collecting funds directly, they employed "tax farmers," often local persons who bought the right to collect taxes for a specified area. Their profit was the difference between the amount they raised and the amount they had pledged to the government. Some of these positions were quite lucrative. Moreover, the Ptolemies also engaged prominent landowners to keep the peace as the heads of locally organized military villages. The 1st-century CE Jewish historian Josephus preserves a long account of the Tobiad family, which served the Ptolemaic government in both capacities. From his lively narrative one has a sense not only of the power and wealth such positions could afford but also of the dangers and conflict they often entailed.

Culturally, the most significant effect of Ptolemaic rule was the establishment of a large Jewish Diaspora community in Egypt, centered in the new city of Alexandria, founded by Alexander the Great. Jews had often migrated to Egypt during times of economic or political trouble (see Jer. chs 42–44). In the 5th century a Jewish military colony in the service of the Persian army was established at Elephantine (Hebrew: Yev; near modern Aswan). They had their own temple, though they did not offer animal sacrifices there, and remained in correspondence with Jerusalem concerning various religious matters, including the proper celebration of Passover and assistance in securing Persian permission for the rebuilding of the Elephantine temple after it was destroyed by local Egyptians. The various Aramaic documents found there (letters, contracts, marriage documents, records of legal disputes, etc.) provide an important glimpse into the daily life of this Jewish community in Egypt. Among the papyri was a copy of the book of Ahikar, a legendary story about an official in the Assyrian court at the time of Sennacherib and Esarhaddon (late 8th to early 7th

century). Although the story was not Jewish in origin, it became popular among the Jews. The book of Tobit in the Apocrypha makes reference to Ahikar, even calling him Tobit's nephew (Tob. 1.21–22).

The Hellenistic-era Egyptian Diaspora, however, was much larger and more influential than the previous small communities of Jews living in Egypt. Its origins are not clear, but during the initial Ptolemaic conquest of the eastern Mediterranean territory, Ptolemy I apparently captured Jerusalem and took many prisoners back to Egypt, where they settled. Later many other Jews migrated there, presumably for economic reasons. The community continued to grow, both in numbers and in prosperity, until in the Roman period the Jewish population numbered in the hundreds of thousands, including many wealthy and prominent families.

By the middle of the 3rd century BCE the Jewish community in Egypt had translated the books of the Torah into Greek, and over the next century or so, the other books of the Bible were also translated. A legendary account of this project is contained in the *Letter of Aristeas*. According to that narrative, the impetus for the project came from the king himself, Ptolemy II Philadelphus (285–246 BCE), who wished to have a copy for the library of Alexandria. Seventy-two Jewish translators were brought to Egypt from Jerusalem for the task; hence the translation came to be known as the Septuagint, from the Greek word for "seventy." All the translators miraculously agreed on the wording of the translation. Similar stories about the origin of this important translation are found in rabbinic literature. Scholars largely reject these accounts as unhistorical and maintain that the translation was undertaken for the religious needs of a Jewish community that no longer understood Hebrew. The stories do show, however, that the first translation of the Torah needed justification, both in terms of its being of no less literary merit than Greek literature and in terms of its accuracy and authority. (See "The Canonization of the Bible," pp. 2072–77, and "Jewish Translations of the Bible," pp. 2005–20, for more information about the Septuagint.) In addition to the translation of the Scriptures, the Jewish Diaspora in Egypt produced a rich and varied literature in Greek. One should not assume, however, that every Jewish writing in Greek originated in Alexandria, for during the Hellenistic period Greek became the most important international language. Educated Jews in the land of Israel and in the eastern Diaspora were nearly as likely to speak Greek as their counterparts in Egypt, as the language and customs of the Greeks influenced much of the Jewish community in profound ways. Nevertheless, Alexandria remained unparalleled in the richness of its intellectual culture.

Less is known about the Jews of the eastern Diaspora who remained under Seleucid control than about the Jews of Egypt and the land of Israel, but it appears that peoples of various ethnic groups had access to economic and political advancement within the Seleucid empire. Several writings from this time—Tobit and Dan. chs 1–6—suggest something of the outlook of Jews in the eastern Diaspora. Written originally in Hebrew or Aramaic, and later translated into Greek, these books are works of fiction, edifying entertainments that tell the stories of Jews who achieved high status in foreign courts, were threatened by jealous rivals, and yet succeeded in securing personal power and the good will of the king. Though the stories are all set in the pre-Hellenistic period (Tobit in the Assyrian empire, Daniel in the Babylonian exile), they were probably written during the Seleucid period. While they acknowledge that faithful Jews may be vulnerable because of their religion, on the whole these are optimistic stories with a positive view of the Gentile kings.

The eastern Diaspora was also the conduit for important religious developments that arose from the contact between Judaism and the religions of Babylonia and Persia. This influence is most clearly seen in the development of apocalyptic literature. Although it is more difficult to trace the path of influence in its earliest stages, the dualistic religious beliefs of Persian Zoroastrianism almost certainly contributed to the development of Jewish apocalyptic and to some of the ideas of the later sectarians at Qumran.

The eventual triumph of the Seleucid kingdom over the Ptolemies in the fifth Syrian war (198 BCE) obviously had a greater significance for the Jews of Judea than for those of Egypt. The Seleucid ruler Antiochus III treated the Judeans generously in appreciation for the support he received from the pro-Seleucid faction, granting an allowance for the Temple and various tax concessions, as well as confirming the Judeans' right to live "according to the laws of their country." Although relations began well, the difference in the way the Seleucid empire governed its territories set the stage for a terrible conflict. Unlike the Ptolemaic system of centralized government administered with the cooperation of local leaders, the Seleucid regime was more decentralized. It derived some unity, however, from a network of Greek cities established throughout the empire. These were not necessarily ethnically Greek but were cities that had received a charter to organize as a *polis*, the Greek form of city government. Cultural prestige and economic advantages often led the leadership of Near Eastern cities to request such a charter.

The events leading up to the conflict between Judea and the Seleucid king Antiochus IV Epiphanes (175–164 BCE) are complex and not fully understood. In part they involved a struggle for succession to the high priesthood and the attempts of various contenders to secure the support of the king by paying him large sums of money. The first of the contenders, Jason, also paid to have Jerusalem established as a Greek *polis*, Antioch at Jerusalem. Neither of these acts in itself seems to have aroused much opposition in Jerusalem. The conflict was not a cultural conflict between Judaism and Hellenism, for Jews had already incorporated significant elements of Hellenistic culture, which they considered quite compatible with their religious identity.

The crisis was sparked by the attempt by another contender, Menelaus, to buy the office of high priest. When he promised the king more than he could pay, he attempted to raise the money by taking golden vessels from the Temple. At this, a riot broke out in Jerusalem. Subsequent fighting between the forces of Jason and Menelaus convinced Antiochus that Judea was in revolt, and he retook the city and plundered the Temple, either in 169 or 168. Sometime later there were further disturbances, and Antiochus sent Syrian troops, which remained garrisoned in Jerusalem. Whether the status of Jerusalem at this point was a *polis* or a military colony is uncertain, but in either case in 167 the Temple was reorganized to accommodate the religious needs of the Syrian troops. A dedication was made to Zeus Olympius, the Greek name for the Syrian god Baal Shamem, and an altar established for sacrifice. Though Menelaus continued to preside as high priest, most Jews considered these actions to have profaned the Temple. In addition, the traditional practices of Judaism such as circumcision and observing the Sabbath were suppressed by Antiochus, perhaps with the cooperation of Menelaus. Since religious persecution was virtually unknown in antiquity, it is difficult to know how Antiochus understood this repression and what he hoped to accomplish by it. Its actual result was to ignite the resistance known as the Maccabean revolt. Knowledge of this period is reflected in Dan. chs 7–12, most likely the latest composition in the Tanakh.

The Hasmoneans, Mattathias and his sons Judas Maccabeus, Jonathan, Simon, John (Hebrew: Yoḥanan), and Eleazar, were the leaders of the revolt. Although Judas managed to retake control of the Temple in 164 (its rededication being the occasion for the institution of the festival of Hanukkah), it was not until 142 that the last of the Seleucid army was expelled and actual independence was secured by Simon. From then until the Roman conquest of Judea in 63 BCE the small kingdom was ruled by the Hasmonean family, who in addition to ruling as kings also assumed the office of high priest. The Romans would destroy the Second Temple in 70 CE, in response to a series of Jewish revolts.

The Geographic Background

The geographical territory encompassed by the Bible (if one includes all identifiable places that are at least mentioned) includes most countries that border the Mediterranean Sea as well as those to its east. The majority of the narratives of the Bible are set in that subregion of the Middle East known as the Levant and now governed by Lebanon, Syria, Jordan, Israel, and the Palestinian Authority. Egypt to the southwest and Mesopotamia (largely modern Iraq and parts of Syria) and Persia (Iran) to the northeast are also part of the biblical landscape.

In Mesopotamia—the Greek term for the region between the Euphrates and Tigris Rivers (Color Maps 1 and 3)—as in Egypt, urban civilization developed by the fourth millennium BCE in the river valleys that provided the essential water for a region where rainfall was at best seasonal. The regular summer flooding of the Nile Valley enabled the early and continuous existence of a remarkably long-lasting culture in Egypt. In Mesopotamia the inhabitants had harnessed the two rivers to provide, by means of an elaborate irrigation system, sufficient water for agriculture as well as for consumption. The several successive imperial powers that originated in Mesopotamia were able to use this productive region as a base for expansion, especially to the west, over which they exercised control throughout most of the first millennium BCE, until the Hellenistic period.

Although surrounded by vast deserts, there is a narrow stretch of land where agriculture can flourish that extends from the Nile Valley around to the Persian Gulf. The western part of this "Fertile Crescent," the Levant is characterized by almost ideal growing conditions for grapes and olives and for raising sheep and goats; grains and legumes and other fruits can also be grown in much of the region.

Its climate is moderate, without excessively high or low temperatures for the most part, and with abundant rainfall that occurs mainly during the winter months. Jerusalem, for example, receives on average about 550 mm (22 in) of rain annually, almost all of it falling between November and February, with January being the rainiest month. Higher elevations to the north receive still more rainfall, and the southern and easternmost regions considerably less.

Within the Levant itself, the primary focus of biblical narratives, there is a wide variety of environments, the result of the geological substructure of the region, which presents dramatic changes in a relatively small area. Moving from west to east, the Mediterranean coast is occupied by a coastal plain that is about 25 km (15 mi) wide in the south but narrows as one moves north. It is interrupted by Mount Carmel, which juts into it, and virtually disappears in northen Israel and Lebanon. The coast itself has several excellent harbors in the north, from which the Canaanites and their successors the Phoenicians conducted a flourishing maritime trade. Farther south, the coast is relatively even, and there are few natural harbors. Phoenician influence eventually extended to such port cities as Acco, Dor, Joppa, and Ashkelon. Along the coastal plain was a major route, known as "the way of the sea" (Isa. 9.1), used by traders and by armies of conquest between Egypt and Damascus. This route ran to the point where the coast narrows below Mount Carmel, from which passes led from the coastal plain to the Jezreel (Esdraelon) Valley; from there, several routes could be taken to the northeast. To the north of the Jezreel Valley lies the Galilee. Because of its abundant springs, Galilee was dotted by settlements from prehistoric times, but it plays little role in biblical narratives.

Adjacent to the coastal plain in the south is an uplift of smaller, gentler hills called "the Shephelah" ("lowland"). As the natural western boundary of the kingdom of Judah in the Iron Age, and of other entities in the same region before and after, it was protected by a number of important cities, including Lachish and Gezer. The Shephelah forms the foothills of the mountainous region immediately to its east. This is the "hill country" of the biblical writers, with higher elevations to the north. For example, Jerusalem, about 55 km (35 mi) east of the Mediterranean, is some 760 m (2,500 ft) above sea level, and many mountains in northern Galilee have elevations of over 1,000 m (3,300 ft). The highest peak in the region is Mount Hermon, which is some 2,800 m (9,200 ft) high and for that reason is snow-covered year round. The hill country is the setting for many of the key locales in biblical narrative, including the relatively inaccessible sites of Jerusalem, the capital of the kingdom of Judah (later Judea), and Samaria, the capital of the Northern Kingdom of Israel and later of the province with the same name. This central mountainous ridge is bisected by the broad, fertile Jezreel Valley, the major route to the interior and hence the location of a number of important ancient cities, including Jokneam, Megiddo, Taanach, Ibleam, and Jezreel.

Just east of the central mountainous region is the Rift Valley. This major depression in the earth's crust extends from southern Turkey into East Africa, and in Israel and Jordan is almost entirely below sea level. Included in it are the Huleh Basin in northern Galilee, some 70 m (230 ft) above sea level, where the site of Hazor was a major fortified city from early in the 2nd millennium BCE until its destruction by the Assyrians in 732 BCE. Some 20 km (12 mi) south of Lake Huleh (now drained) is the Sea of Kinneret, or the Sea of Galilee (also called the Sea of Tiberias), a large lake about 20 km (12 mi) long that fills the valley. It lies some 210 m (700 ft) below sea level and is fed by the Jordan River, which flows into it from the north. It is habitat to nearly two dozen species of fish, and the fishing industry has been an important part of the local economy since prehistoric times.

The Jordan River continues its flow south from the Kinneret some 105 km (65 mi) to the Dead Sea. The valley itself is about 20 km (12 mi) wide, and is entirely below sea level, with a semi-tropical climate that produces lush vegetation, even though it receives relatively little rain. Important cities in the valley include Beth-shan in the north and Jericho in the south.

The Dead Sea, lying some 400 m (1,300 ft) below sea level, is the lowest point on the land mass of the earth. Because of evaporation due to the high temperatures (a record 51° C [124° F] was measured here), the composition of the water is about 25 percent salt and other minerals, making organic life impossible and giving this lake its ancient Hebrew name, *yam ha-Melaḥ*, "the salt sea" (Num. 34.3, 12; NJPS "Dead Sea"). The desolate region that surrounds it is the narrative setting for the legendary cities of Sodom and Gomorrah. On its western shore are Qumran, where the Dead Sea Scrolls were found, and Masada, a palace constructed by Herod that was the last Jewish outpost to be captured in the First Jewish Revolt.

East of the Rift Valley there is a rapid rise to the relatively level Transjordanian plateau to the east, with the elevation of modern Amman (ancient Rabbah) at ca. 820 m (2,700 ft) about average. This region too receives sufficient rainfall to sustain agriculture, and moreover is watered by two tributaries of the Jordan, the Yarmuk and the Jabbok, and by the Arnon, which flows into the Dead Sea. The northern part of the plateau, biblical Bashan, was famous for its cattle and for its oak forests. Traversing the Transjordanian plateau

from south to north is a major route, called in the Bible the "King's Highway" (Num. 20.17), used throughout antiquity as a conduit for the incense and spice trade from Arabia to Damascus. East of the plateau is a vast desert region, a continuation of the Arabian desert that extends northward to the Euphrates Valley, and thus limits the Fertile Crescent on both east and west. Apart from a few oases, especially Tadmor (later Palmyra) northeast of Damascus, this desert was essentially uninhabited in historic times.

South of the hill country of Judah lies the Negev, a region of limited rainfall and hence marginal agriculture. The city of Beer-sheba is located in the extreme northern Negev, just south of the Judean hill country. The Negev merges into the Sinai peninsula, which is formed by the two northern arms of the Red Sea, separating the Sinai from the North African desert to its west and the Arabian desert to its east.

The size of Israel, approximately the same as that of the state of Vermont, is inversely proportionate to its importance in ancient times. Israel found itself in a strategic position between the two great powers of Egypt and Mesopotamia. It would thus be influenced by these great powers, and in later times, Israel's central location on major sea and land routes would allow rapid dissemination of ideas to and from the outside world.

[*Adapted by* ADELE BERLIN
AND MARC ZVI BRETTLER]

Languages of the Bible

Hebrew and the Semitic Languages

The bulk of the Bible was originally composed in Hebrew, the language of the biblical Israelites, and the language that was spoken in the land of Israel until the end of the tannaitic period (the time of the Mishnah, ca. 200 CE). During the amoraic period (the time of the later talmudic Rabbis, ca. 200–500 CE) it ceased to be

a living language, although for Jews it remained the language of liturgy and literature until its revival as a spoken tongue at the end of the 19th century. Hebrew is a member of the Semitic family of languages, which on the basis of geography can be divided into three groups: Northeastern Semitic (Akkadian and its dialects of Assyrian and Babylonian, and Eblaite), Southern Semitic (Old South Arabian and its modern descendants, Ge'ez and the modern Ethiopic dialects, and Classical Arabic and its pre-classical and modern dialects), and Northwest Semitic (Ammonite, Aramaic, Deir Alla, Edomite, Hebrew, Moabite, Phoenician and Punic, and Ugaritic).

Within the Northwest Semitic family of languages, Hebrew is part of the "Canaanite" branch of languages. Other members of the Canaanite branch include Ammonite and Edomite, both of which are attested in a few poorly preserved inscriptions; Moabite, the language of the Mesha Stele erected by King Mesha, which boasts of Moab's victory over Israel (see 2 Kings 3.4–27 for the biblical account); and Phoenician and Punic (the form of Phoenician in the western Mediterranean), which are attested in inscriptions and in Greek and Latin transcriptions. These languages share several linguistic features that distinguish them from the other branches of Northwest Semitic: Aramaic, Ugaritic, and Deir Alla (attested in a text from biblical Succoth that mentions Balaam the Seer).

Alphabet

The earliest Hebrew inscriptions are written in a consonantal script that was probably borrowed from the Phoenicians at the beginning of the 1st millennium BCE. This script, like its Phoenician ancestor, was at first purely consonantal and did not mark vowels. The use of a script that does not indicate vowels can create ambiguity for the reader since a sequence of consonants can often be read in different ways with different meanings, e.g., *km* can represent *kam* "he arose," *kama* "she arose," *kamu* "they arose," *kum/kumi/kumu/kuma* "arise!," *kom/kum* "arising." Inscriptions from different centuries show that certain letters known as *'amot keri'ah*, *matres lectionis*, or vowel letters (*alef*, *heh*, *vav*, and *yod*) were gradually employed to represent vowels, at first at the end of words, and then in the middle, too. In the consonantal text of the Bible one can find both final and medial *matres lectionis*.

The Hebrew script that developed from the Phoenician is known as the Paleo-Hebrew script. Sometime in the centuries before the Common Era it was replaced by a descendant of the Aramaic square script, which also originally developed from the Phoenician. It is known as the Jewish square script or *ketav 'ashuri* (Assyrian script), the latter name pointing to its origins in the Aramaic speaking East. By the time of the Dead Sea Scrolls (mid-3rd century BCE to 1st century CE), almost all manuscripts were written in the square script, though a few were still written in the Paleo-Hebrew script, and in some documents the Tetragrammaton (YHVH) alone was written in Paleo-Hebrew. The Jewish square script is used today in printing modern Hebrew, and the Paleo-Hebrew script continues to be used by the Samaritan community.

There is evidence of graphic confusion of consonants in the Bible. Some of the confusion can be attributed to the similarity in form of letters in the Paleo-Hebrew script, and some is due to the similarity of letters in the square script. For example, it appears that *resh* and *dalet*, which are similar in the square script, have been confused in two parallel passages: *'adikem* "(Like dirt of the streets) I crushed them" (2 Sam. 22.43) vs. *'arikem* "(Like dirt of the streets) I cast them out" (Ps. 18.43).

Pronunciation of Biblical Hebrew

Evidence for the pronunciation of Hebrew during the biblical period comes from three main sources:

Transliterations of Hebrew into Akkadian, Greek, Latin, and Arabic. Some Hebrew proper nouns are transliterated into cuneiform in Akkadian tablets, e.g., Ha-za-qi-a-u Ya-u-da-ai "Hezekiah the Judean" in Sennacherib's annals from the very beginning of the 7th century BCE. The Septuagint (3rd century BCE) is a rich source for transliteration of proper nouns, though, as is the case with all transliterations, there are many unknown variables including the lack of a one-to-one correspondence between the Hebrew alphabet and the

Greek alphabet and the possibility that the Hebrew tradition underlying the transliteration into Greek differs chronologically and possibly dialectically from the Hebrew of the Tiberian tradition that is found in Bibles currently used. See, e.g., the difference in pronunciation between the Greek transliteration *Rebekka* and Tiberian Hebrew *Rivka*. The Hexapla of the church father Origen, a six-column work from the 2nd to 3rd centuries CE, is also of importance since column two (the "Secunda") contains the Biblical text (not only proper nouns) transliterated into Greek. Unfortunately, only fragments from the Psalms have survived. Transliteration of Hebrew into the Roman alphabet is attested in the 5th century in the Latin works of Jerome. Biblical Hebrew transcribed into Arabic can be found in medieval Karaite works.

Vocalized Manuscripts. The oldest extant manuscripts of the Bible are the Dead Sea Scrolls from Qumran, which are purely consonantal and have no vowel signs. The oldest manuscripts with vowel signs (and cantillation signs that serve as musical notes and also mark word stress and punctuation) are attested only about a thousand years later toward the end of the first millenium. Four different vocalization systems were in use during the Middle Ages. The most prestigious system and the one that is still used today is that of the Tiberian Masoretes (see "Masoretic Bible," pp. 2077–84), who devised vowel and cantillation signs in order to preserve an ancient tradition of reading that had been passed down orally for centuries. There were also Masoretes in Babylonia who developed a separate graphic system of pointing, which reflects a slightly different pronunciation. The discovery of the Cairo Genizah at the end of the 19th century revealed another system, known today as the "Palestinian," which appears to be the ancestor of the Sephardic pronunciation of Hebrew (both the *kamatz* and the *patah* are pronounced as *a,* and both the *tzere* and *segol* are realized as *e*). A fourth system known as "the expanded Tiberian" or "Tiberian-Palestinian" makes use of Tiberian vowel signs to represent a "Palestinian" pronunciation.

Oral Traditions of the Recitation of the Bible. The oral traditions of the recitation of the Bible that have survived into the present also deserve mention, in particular that of the Yemenite Jews, whose reading tradition preserves many old features, e.g., the hard/soft (stop/fricative) pronunciation of all six consonants *bgdkpt* (in contrast to Modern Hebrew where one finds an alternation of *b/v, k/kh,* and *p/f,* but not *g/gh, d/dh,* and *t/th*). Additional phenomena in the Yemenite reading tradition conform to what is described in the medieval treatises of the Tiberian Masoretes and thus demonstrate the antiquity of the tradition.

Dialects

It is widely assumed that there were different dialects of Hebrew during the biblical period. The biblical narrator at Judg. 12.6 notes a difference between the Gileadites and Ephraimites in pronouncing the sibilant (sh/s) in *shibbolet/sibbolet.* Scholars have suggested that stories that take place in the north (e.g., the Elijah and Elisha narratives in Kings) sometimes display dialectal forms that differ from the biblical norm, which is thought to reflect southern Hebrew, i.e., the Hebrew of the Judean kingdom. See, e.g., the spelling of the second feminine singular independent pronoun "you" *'ty* (= *'atti*) in northern stories as opposed to normal biblical *'at* (see, e.g., 2 Kings 4.16). The Samaria ostraca from the 8th century BCE provide clear extrabiblical evidence of a northern Hebrew dialect. "Year" is written as *sht* (= *shat*) as against *shanah* in Judea, and "wine" spelled *yn* reflects *yen* as against southern *yyn* (*yayin*). On the basis of the contraction of *ay* to *e* in *yn,* scholars have suggested that the prophet Amos, who prophesied in the north, makes a linguistic pun (8.1–2) that is understandable only if one realizes that northern Hebrew contracted *ay* to *e*: He rhymes *kayitz* "summer fruit" and *ketz* "end" (probably pronounced the same).

Chronology and Periodization of Biblical Hebrew

All spoken languages develop over time and thus it is only natural that Hebrew too underwent changes during the lengthy biblical period, which stretches from sometime in the second millenium BCE almost down to the destruction of the Second Temple in 70 CE. In addition to differences in style and language between some biblical books, and between the literary sources (J, E, P, and D) that make up the Torah, scholars are able to discern four linguistic periods:

Early Biblical Hebrew. It is not known when Hebrew was first spoken and when it developed into a language that was distinct from other Canaanite languages. The earliest stories in Genesis, e.g., the account of creation and the flood, are not datable linguistically, since they are written in the same language as other stories from the First Temple period. The earliest datable Hebrew is an agricultural calendar found at Gezer, which is assigned to the latter part of the 10th century BCE. There are two sources from the 15th to 13th centuries BCE that hint at what proto-Hebrew may have looked like—the language of the Ugaritic tablets from Ras Shamra in Syria and the Canaanitisms in the El-Amarna tablets found in Egypt. The former tablets include mythological stories of Canaanite gods that are echoed in motifs and language in the Bible. The latter include letters written by Canaanite-speaking scribes in the area of modern-day Lebanon, Syria, and Israel to the Pharoah in Egypt; the language of the tablets is Akkadian, yet the scribes inadvertently inserted features of their own Canaanite tongue and sometimes deliberately glossed Akkadian words with their Canaanite equivalents. Neither Ugaritic nor El-Amarna Canaanite, however, is a linear ancestor of Hebrew.

The oldest Hebrew in the Bible is found in several poems that are replete with archaic-looking features of morphology (e.g., the remains of case endings such as the final *o*-vowel in *ḥayto 'eretz* "wild beasts" [Gen. 49.11]), syntax (the frequent absence of the definite article and the relative pronoun), and vocabulary. Among the most striking archaic poems are the Blessing of Jacob (Gen. ch 49), the Song of the Sea (Exod. ch 15), the Balaam parables (Num. chs 23–24), the Song of Moses (Deut. ch 32), the Blessing of Moses (Deut. ch 33), the Song of Deborah (Judg. ch 5), as well as some psalms (e.g., Ps. 29). Many terms in these poems occur only once in the entire Bible *(hapax legomena)* and thus it is often difficult to pinpoint their precise meaning.

Classical Biblical Hebrew. This language, which includes most of the books of the Bible from Genesis through Kings as well as portions of the Latter Prophets and the Writings, is the Hebrew of the First Temple period. In general, when one talks of biblical Hebrew, one refers to the language of this period. Perhaps the most salient feature of the language is the use of verbal forms with the *vav conversive (vav ha-hipukh)*, e.g., *va-yakom va-yelekh* "and he arose and went" (Gen. 24.10), *ya'aleh . . . ve-hishkah* "would go up . . . and water" (Gen. 2.6). Other noteworthy features include lengthened and shortened modal forms, e.g., *'eshmera* "I want to keep, allow me to keep" as opposed to regular *'eshmor* "I shall keep," *yehi* "let there be" as opposed to regular *yihyeh* "there will be."

Transitional Period between Classical and Late. The destruction of the First Temple and the Babylonian Exile are a watershed in the history of biblical Hebrew. Postexilic Hebrew differs markedly from preexilic Hebrew. The language of the books of Jeremiah and Ezekiel demonstrates features of Hebrew from both the First and Second Temple periods, and thus reflects a period of linguistic transition, e.g., Ezekiel's use of both classical Hebrew *shesh* and late biblical Hebrew *butz* for the cloth "byssus." One of several grammatical peculiarities of this period that is particularly noticeable in the language of Jeremiah and Ezekiel is the frequent spelling in the consonantal text of the 2nd-person feminine perfect ending in *-ty*, e.g., *lmdty* (= *limmadti*) "you taught" (Jer. 2.33) as opposed to regular -*t*: *lmdt* (= *limmadt*).

Late Biblical Hebrew. The Hebrew of the Second Temple period, the language of Esther, Ezra, Nehemiah, Daniel, and Chronicles, clearly reveals a late composition. The contrast in language is apparent when comparing passages in Chronicles to parallel passages in Samuel and Kings. The verbal system of Late Biblical Hebrew is marked by the gradual disappearance of the classical verbal forms with *vav conversive* and the lengthened and shortened verbal forms. The language is also characterized by the adoption of loanwords from Aramaic (e.g., *zman* "time" as opposed to classical Hebrew *mo'ed; madda'* "knowledge" as against classical *da'at*) as well as some from Persian (e.g., *pardes* "park," *pitgam* "decree"). The Hebrew of the period also evidences features that reflect Tannaitic Hebrew, the early stratum of Mishnaic Hebrew, e.g., *nulledu* "they were born" (1 Chron. 20.8) reflecting the stem *nuf'al*, a combination of *nif'al* and *pu'al* as against classical biblical *noledu (nif'al)*.

Extrabiblical Hebrew Sources

Our knowledge of the Hebrew of the biblical period is limited almost entirely to what is attested in the Bible. There is a relatively small corpus of Hebrew inscriptions from different sites in the land of Israel (e.g., Gezer, Samaria, Jerusalem, Arad, and Lachish) whose grammar corresponds to that of biblical Hebrew. These inscriptions have also slightly enriched our knowledge of the vocabulary of the biblical period. The Siloam inscription (8th to 7th centuries BCE) describing the digging of a water tunnel (also mentioned in 2 Kings 20.20 and 2 Chron. 32.30) contributes a previously unattested word *zdh,* whose pronunciation is unknown since there is no internal *mater lectionis* to inform us what the medial vowel was (the final *heh* probably represents *a*). The word seems to mean "crack, fissure" since it occurs in a context in which something in a rock allowed masons wielding picks on either side of the rock to hear each other. A Lachish ostra-

con (6th century BCE) also reveals a new form *tsbh* (= *tesibbah?*) "course" (from the root *s-b-b*, "to turn") in the phrase *tsbt hbkr* (= *tesibbat ha-boker*) "during the course of the morning."

In addition to inscriptions, archeological digs have turned up seals and bullae (seal impressions on clay) that contain names known from the Bible, e.g., *lbrkyhw bn nryhw hspr* "belonging to Berekhyahu son of Neriyahu the scribe" (the amanuensis of Jeremiah known as *Baruch ben Neriyahu* in Jer. 36.32). A few seals bear the title *'asher 'al ha-bayit,* "who is over the house," an official in charge of the royal palace mentioned several times in the Bible, e.g., 1 Kings 4.6; 16.9; 18.3. Many of the seals and bullae reveal names from the ancient Hebrew onomasticon (inventory of names) that are not attested in the Bible.

The Qumran caves next to the Dead Sea have yielded hundreds of Hebrew documents. Multiple copies of biblical texts have been discovered (all books are attested except for the book of Esther) as well as sectarian writings of the Qumran community. (See "The Bible in the Dead Sea Scrolls," pp. 1920–28.) The linguistic contribution of the Dead Sea Scrolls is considerable. Frequently one witnesses the linguistic modernization of biblical texts: Older, archaic forms found in the Masoretic Text are replaced by more modern ones, e.g., the archaic case ending on the first word of the Masoretic *ḥayto ba-saday* "beasts in the field" (Isa. 56.9) has been deleted in the Great Isaiah Scroll from Qumran (1QIsaᵃ), and the archaic form of the second word *(saday)* has been changed to the classical *sadeh*. Some features in the language of the Dead Sea Scrolls are representative of Late Biblical Hebrew, e.g., the expression *beshel she-* "so that," and even Tannaitic Hebrew phenomena crop up, e.g., the idiom *nasa' ve-natan* "carried and took" (= "traded"). From the slightly later period of the Second Jewish Revolt one finds that the Hebrew of the Bar Kokhba letters from nearby Naḥal Ḥever and Wadi Murabba'at no longer reflect biblical Hebrew, but rather a Tannaitic-like Hebrew, e.g., the use of final *nun* and the negative particle *loʾ* in *wlʾ dʾgyn lʾhykhn (ve-loʾ doʾagin le-ʾahekhon)* "you do not care for your brethren" as against what in biblical Hebrew would have final *mem* and the negative particle *ʾen (ve-ʾen doʾagim le-ʾahekhem)*.

Aramaic in the Bible

There are a few passages in the Bible that were written in Aramaic and not Hebrew. Aramaic is attested in the Bible in two words in Gen. 31.48, *yegar sahaduta* (glossed into Hebrew as *gal ʿed* "the heap of witness"), one verse in Jer. 10.11, four chapters in Ezra (4.8–6.18 and 7.12–26) and six chapters (2.4–7.28) in Daniel. The use of Aramaic in each of these sources is not surprising. In Gen. ch 31 Aramaic is put into the mouth of Laban, who is an Aramean. The biblical narrative explicitly links the patriarchal families with the Arameans. By the time of Jeremiah, Aramaic had already become a language of trade and diplomacy in the Neo-Assyrian and Neo-Babylonian empires. During the time when Ezra and Daniel were composed, Aramaic had become the undisputed lingua franca of the ancient Near East. Biblical Aramaic belongs to the period of Aramaic known as "Official" or "Imperial" Aramaic (ca. 700 BCE–200 BCE), the latter term emphasizing that Aramaic was used throughout the Achaemenid Persian empire for communication and administration. Documents written in the Aramaic of this period have been found in Egypt (Elephantine, Hermopolis), Mesopotamia, and even farther afield (Spain, Afghanistan, India). Although belonging to Official Aramaic, the one Aramaic sentence in Jeremiah reveals a sign of older Aramaic in the form *ʾarkaʾ* "land" alongside the Official Aramaic form *ʾarʿa*. The Aramaic of Ezra shows signs of being older linguistically than the Aramaic of Daniel (the pronouns with final -*m* in Ezra are older than the corresponding pronouns with final -*n* in Daniel).

The use of Aramaic in the land of Israel spread with the return of the exiles from Babylonia, where Aramaic was in the process of replacing Akkadian. Even when using Hebrew, scribes of this period typically employed the Aramaic script rather than the paleo-Hebrew script, as noted above. During the Second Temple period it was spoken and written together with Hebrew, as evidenced by the Dead Sea Scrolls and the Bar Kokhba letters, both of which were written in Hebrew and in Aramaic. Aramaic completely supplanted Hebrew as the spoken language by the end of the tannaitic period.

[STEVEN E. FASSBERG]

Textual Criticism of the Bible

No original manuscript of any biblical book has ever been discovered. This situation, which may seem surprising, is actually quite common for ancient writings, and even for those from only a few centuries ago. For instance, none of Shakespeare's plays is available in the original manuscript from Shakespeare's hand, and for most of them there are two or more early printed versions with many differences between them. For the biblical books, numerous copies or partial copies, varying greatly in age and quality, have been preserved in various parts of the world. Occa-sionally, as with the discovery of the Dead Sea Scrolls in the mid-20th century, new copies come to light (see "The Bible in the Dead Sea Scrolls," pp. 1920–28). Nevertheless, for the entire text of the Bible, scholars are faced with a situation in which they have multiple manuscripts that have been copied by hand so that each is a unique product, unlike a modern printed book, and therefore the copies differ among themselves in many places, some differences trivial and some important. The differences among manuscripts range from a single letter to words or lines, to the absence or presence of entire sections, or to the presentation of the same material in a different order. Some of these differences are of little consequence for meaning; others have significant impact on the meaning. Some of the latter may have been intentional changes or may have arisen through an error, and been preserved over time. Given this situation, scholars have had to develop a methodology for comparing and accounting for the differences in wording in cases where the copies disagree. This methodology is called textual criticism.

Textual criticism involves, first of all, the collection of all the differences between copies of any text. The manuscripts may be in several forms. The earliest were scrolls (like those found at Qumran, near the Dead Sea), long strips of parchment (animal skin) or papyrus rolled up. Scrolls can accommodate a book or a few books, but not the entire Bible. In the late first millennium CE, collections of biblical books in book form, called codices (the plural of codex), came into use. Another source for the biblical text is citations, or quotations in ancient writings, such as the Dead Sea Scrolls or rabbinic literature. These sources, taken all together, are called witnesses or authorities, and the differences among them are called variant readings or simply variants. The ancient translations, or versions, of the Bible, which provide indirect evidence for the Hebrew text on which the translation was based, are a final important source for variants.

There is no unanimity concerning the theoretical goal of textual criticism. Some, following the older school, aim to reconstruct the original text of the Bible, what it looked like when it was first written. Others are less certain that we can or should speak of an "original" text, since the evidence suggests that some biblical books may have circulated in different editions (or recensions) from a very early period. Texts, even once written, may have been fluid, with sections being added or subtracted. In addition, ancient copyists may have had a very different notion from ours of what it meant to copy a text; for example, it was acceptable to update the spelling of a word, to substitute a synonym for a word, or to gloss a word with a brief explanation. Thus, the "best" text in a certain time and place may not have been the "original" text. Those who espouse this second approach do not consider the task of textual criticism to be the reconstruction of the original text, but rather the analysis of differences among texts, the investigation of the significance of those differences, and in some cases, the determination of which textual variant is better or preferable, though it may not be original.

Reasons for Variants

Variants can be of several kinds. The copyist may have misseen or misheard a word, producing a simple spelling error, or perhaps a different word. For example, in Gen. 22.13 the Hebrew text, which reads *'ayil 'ahar*, "a ram afterwards" or "behind," is almost certainly an error for *'ayil 'ehad*, "one ram"; the two letters *resh* and *dalet* are nearly identical and are easily confused, and many of the ancient versions translate this phrase as "one ram" or "a ram." Scribes may also accidentally skip a line or two, omitting a phrase from their manuscript. This was done, for example, by the scribe of the Great Isaiah Scroll from Qumran, who skipped the end of Isa. 40.7 and the beginning of 40.8; this was facilitated by the phrase "grass withers, flowers fade," which is repeated in these two verses. Conversely, the copyist may inadvertently have written a phrase twice, producing a repetition. Both internal evidence from the Hebrew text, and comparison of that text to the versions, has suggested that many variants are of this kind.

It is also likely, as noted above, that the attitude of early copyists of biblical texts was fundamentally different from ours. They probably did not feel the need to transcribe exactly, letter for letter. This explains why many ancient manuscripts and versions reflect a range of minor variants, where, for example, synonyms are used. Thus, one manuscript might use the word *'eretz* for land, and another its synonym, *'adamah*. The order in which phrases might be copied was also somewhat flexible in this period. "Variant" traditions which the author knew might also have influenced his copying. For example, it is clear that in antiquity there were two traditions concerning the number of descendants of Jacob who went down to Egypt: 70 and 75. While the number 70 is preserved in what crystallized as the Masoretic Text to Exod. 1.5, the variant 75 is found in the Septuagint and in two Qumran manuscripts.

Sometimes copyists seem to have tried to improve the text they were reproducing. They might have done this in several ways. They may have tried to "correct" a word or phrase that was unacceptable for one reason or another, by substituting a more acceptable word or phrase. This might be related to what the Rabbis later called *Tikunei Soferim*, "corrections of the scribes," where a locution that might be read as offending God was corrected so it would not be understood as offensive. Early copyists might also have tried to make the text support a particular theological view or belief. For instance, at Deut. 32.8, some versions and a Dead Sea Scroll fragment read "according to the number of the sons of God," while the Masoretic Text reads "in relation to Israel's numbers." There is general agreement that the second variant was introduced by a scribe trying to avoid a polytheistic wording. Copying a manuscript, then, was not necessarily just a mechanical process, but could involve deliberate changes.

Ancient Translations

Another source of information that scholars turn to is very early translations of the Bible. These early translations are called versions, and they were in use among Jews or Christians who could no longer understand the Bible in its original languages. (See "Jewish Translations of the Bible," pp. 2005–20.) They include translations of the Bible into Greek (for instance, the Septuagint), Syriac (the Peshitta), Aramaic (the Targumim [singular "Targum"]), and Latin (the Vulgate).

These versions are useful in ascertaining what early Hebrew texts of the Bible might have looked like. The earliest complete manuscripts of the Septuagint are centuries earlier than our first complete Hebrew manuscripts of the Bible, and it is clear that the Septuagint was translated from a Hebrew text that differed in significant ways from the Masoretic Text. (There are many cases where this is now confirmed, where the Septuagint agrees with a Dead Sea scroll fragment against the Masoretic Text.) The versions can therefore be consulted, with care, for determining an earlier stage of the biblical text or an alternate tradition of its wording. In many modern translations, including the NJPS Tanakh, these ancient versions are sometimes cited in the footnotes to provide explanations or alternate solutions to difficulties in the Masoretic Text. The translators' notes in NJPS call attention to many of these matters. These notes are keyed to the text by superscript letters, and can be found at the bottom of the translation. The abbreviations used in these notes are listed on pp. xix–xx. NJPS, however, on principle follows the Hebrew Masoretic Text, which is discussed, along with the versions, in the section below, "The Bible: Texts and Versions," and in greater detail in "The Development of the Masoretic Bible," pp. 2077–84.

While not all scholars approach textual criticism in the same way, there are some guidelines that are generally agreed upon. First is the importance of collecting all the significant variants and information about the manuscripts in which they occur. Manuscripts must be evaluated as to their reliability and age. When it comes to choosing among different readings, in general, shorter readings are preferable to longer ones, since scribes are more likely to add to a text than to delete materials (though, in the case of offensive or theologically challenging texts, deletion must be considered); difficult readings, including awkward phrases, coarse words, and poor grammar, are preferable to smoother ones, since scribes might try to "correct" such difficulties; and stylistic considerations can help judgments about how a particular author would have written. There are cases where none of the variants seem to be satisfactory, or where the text does not make sense as far as current scholarship can determine. In such cases scholars must assume that the wording of the text has been lost or distorted in the course of the copying process. They then have several options open to them. One (called conjectural emendation) is to conjecture, based on the text as it now stands, what the lost or corrupted wording might have been. This can often be based on a scholar's general knowledge of the ancient languages, just as an English speaker can notice, and mentally correct, a typographical error in a modern book without having access to the author's manuscript. Finally, scholars may have to admit defeat and acknowledge that, given the current state of our knowledge, it is impossible to determine what the wording might have been. For instance, at 1 Sam. 13.1, the translation shows, by the use of ellipsis, that a word (the age of Saul when he began to reign) is missing; the Hebrew text literally translated would read: "Saul was one year old when he became king," a chronological impossibility. In this case, unfortunately, the Septuagint does not include any part of the verse, and there are no Dead Sea Scrolls which preserve the missing data. It is therefore impossible to recover the lost words.

The Bible: Texts and Versions

The Masoretic Text

The basic text for the Bible in both the Jewish and scholarly communities today is the Masoretic Text (MT), an edition of the Hebrew that was standardized in the second half of the first millennium CE by rabbinic scholars (called "Masoretes," from *masorah*, probably "what is handed down," that is, "tradition"). The Masoretic Text accomplished two main things: It settled upon a consonantal text, that is, it established specific choices for the letters of the Hebrew words in the text; and it pointed those consonants with a system of markings that indicated which vowels should be read with the Hebrew consonants. It also offered cantillation and accentual marks, showing how words were to be sung or chanted and grouped together into phrases; and it included a set of marginal notes to assure that the text would be copied properly. (See "The Development of the Masoretic Bible," pp. 2077–84.) The decision to add vowel points was necessary because biblical Hebrew writing was in effect a system of consonants, with only a few ways of indicating vowel sounds. Words with the same consonants but different vowels would look the same, as would the English words "untrained" and "interned" if they were both spelled "ntrnd." Modern text critics are sometimes less hesitant to emend the vocalization of the text, on the theory that the vowel points are more recent than the consonants, and therefore less venerable, even though they may represent an ancient tradition of pronunciation.

All Hebrew copies of the Tanakh that were known until recently reflected the Masoretic Text. With a few exceptions (most notably biblical texts found in the Cairo Genizah), this remained the case until the discovery of the Dead Sea Scrolls (the documents of the Qumran community) in 1947. Among the scrolls were manuscripts of most books of the Bible that were over a thousand years older than the oldest manuscripts available up to that point. These more ancient copies of the Hebrew text have shed light on some passages in the traditional form of the biblical text. For example, at 1 Sam. 10.27–11.1 in the MT there is no indication of the background to the conflict between king Nahash of Ammon and the men of Jabesh-gilead. But in a Qumran manuscript of 2 Samuel (4QSam[a]) there is a continuation of 10.27 and an opening phrase for 11.1 that explains the context. The New Revised Standard Version (NRSV) translates this as follows:

> Now Nahash, king of the Ammonites, had been grievously oppressing the Gadites and the Reubenites. He would gouge out the right eye of each of them and would not

grant Israel a deliverer. No one was left of the Israelites across the Jordan whose right eye Nahash, king of the Amorites, had not gouged out. But there were seven thousand men who had escaped from the Ammonites and had entered Jabesh-gilead. (11.1) About a month later, . . .

This text, which most scholars believe to be more original than the preserved MT, is found in the NRSV, but is absent from NJPS, which follows the MT.

The Ancient Versions

The ancient versions are used in several ways by biblical scholars. Particularly in cases where these versions are not translating literally, they provide important evidence for the early interpretation of biblical texts. In addition, because these versions predate the creation of the Masoretic Text, they are suggestive about the earlier state of the Hebrew text, and even choices of wording at the time of their translation. Of course, these ancient translations are themselves preserved only in copies, so that all of the considerations that apply to the original language texts of the Bible also apply to them: it is necessary to establish a critical text for them by comparing variant readings, and they must therefore be used with caution. This is, of course, a standard of comparison at one remove from the text itself: scholars must look at the Greek, for instance, in the Septuagint, and conjecture or assume what the Hebrew text before the translator (the *Vorlage*) would have been ("retrovert") in order to result in a particular rendition into Greek. Nevertheless, it is a valuable source of clues.

Names and Character of the Ancient Versions

The ancient versions of the Bible are referred to in a variety of ways by scholars. Following is a list, by language, of the chief versions (see also "Jewish Translations of the Bible," pp. 2005–20).

Greek. The most prominent Greek version, and the oldest surviving translation of the

Bible, is the Septuagint, which was translated for use of Greek-speaking Jews who were living in the Diaspora in Alexandria, Egypt, and other places around the Mediterranean in the centuries after the conquests of Alexander the Great. The Septuagint, from a word meaning "seventy" because of a legend that seventy or seventy-two scholars worked on it, is abbreviated LXX (the Roman numeral for seventy). Three later Greek versions—by Aquila, Symmachus, and Theodotion—were produced for the use of Jews after Christians had taken over the Septuagint and the increasing conflict between Jews and Christians about the interpretation of the Jewish Scriptures had led Jews to stop using the Septuagint. These versions are also sometimes used by translators, though none of them has survived in its entirety.

Aramaic. The Aramaic language was the official language of the Persian empire, and the Jews who lived under Persian domination spoke Aramaic, which eventually largely supplanted Hebrew as the ordinary language of Jews. Aramaic is a Semitic language, like Hebrew, and shares some vocabulary with it, but Aramaic speakers cannot easily understand Hebrew. It was therefore necessary to provide translations of the Bible for Aramaic speakers. Read aloud in liturgical contexts, after the Hebrew had been read (see Neh. 8.7 for an early example), these translations, called Targumim (sg. Targum), reflect a wide variety of translation styles (See "The Bible in the Synagogue," pp. 1929–37 and "Jewish Translations of the Bible," pp. 2005–20.) Some, like *Targum Onkelos*, are relatively literal, while others, like the Targumim of the Torah from the land of Israel, or the late Targum to Song of Songs, are much freer.

Syriac. The Syriac language is a form of Aramaic, and was spoken by Jews in northern Syria. The Peshitta (which means "simple," that is, a plain translation) was prepared for the use of these Jews and later taken over by Syriac-speaking Christians.

Latin. Two Latin translations are used by scholars. The first, the "Old Latin" version, was actually a Latin translation of the Septuagint and of the New Testament dating from before the 4th century CE. More useful is the Vulgate, the translation prepared in the 4th century by the great biblical scholar and early church father Jerome. Jerome worked directly from the Hebrew text of the time, and his version therefore can be helpful in determining how his Hebrew text might have read.

It cannot be emphasized sufficiently that textual criticism is as much an art as a science. For this reason, and because the Masoretic Text has been the favored Jewish text for the Bible for over a millennium (the consonantal basis for this text is clearly ancient—it is the predominant text-type found at Qumran), the translators of the NJPS have based their translation on the MT. Yet the MT is not perfect, nor is it the only ancient reflection of the text that has come down to us. Therefore at times notes to the NJPS text and various annotations call attention to other possible ancient readings that deserve the reader's attention.

[ADELE BERLIN AND MARC ZVI BRETTLER]

The Canonization of the Bible

Canonization, broadly construed as the process through which the Bible became the Bible, is only vaguely understood. We do not know exactly how various books were chosen to be part of the Bible to the exclusion of others, how these books were put into a particular order, and how their text was established. Since there are no contemporaneous documents that describe this process, it needs to be reconstructed from indirect evidence, namely, from the variety of biblical texts from different periods and places that have survived, and from later traditions in rabbinic and other sources that discuss canonization. Thus, the reconstruction suggested below should be viewed as tentative.

Definitions

"Canon" is a Greek word meaning "reed," and came to refer to any straight stick that could be used for measuring. This basic meaning was extended to refer to any rule or standard by which things could be compared or judged. The Alexandrian grammarians, classical Greek writers who were not simply grammarians but also what we would call literary critics, used "canon" as their term for the list of standard or classic authors who were worthy of attention and imitation. This was not a closed category, and there were dis-putes about adding or removing works from the list. Furthermore, inclusion on the list merely recognized a work's quality; it did not confer upon it any new status. Nevertheless, a canon of writings came to denote those texts that were of central importance to a given group. The term is used somewhat imprecisely for the Bible, since the earliest evidence we have for understanding the development of the Tanakh does *not* come from book lists. Furthermore, when used in reference to the Bible, canon has an even stronger significance: Not only is a given set of texts included, but all other texts—no matter how worthy otherwise—are excluded. This sense is expressed in a rabbinic comment on Eccl. 12.12. The biblical text reads:

> Of anything beyond these [Heb *mehemah*], my child, beware. Of making many books there is no end.

The rabbinic comment states:

> Those who bring more than twenty-four books [the standard number in the Tanakh; see below] into their house introduce confusion [Heb *mehumah*] into their house (*Eccl. Rab.* 12:12).

This suggests not only that the works in the canon are important, but that they, along with their authoritative interpretation, are sufficient in and of themselves. Once the biblical canon was fixed, there could be no additions to it or subtractions from it. More important, books in the biblical canon, unlike those in the canons of the Greek grammarians, came to be thought of as divinely inspired.

The Tanakh

It is extremely difficult to trace how this conception of canon developed, and how it is connected to related notions, such as the eventual stabilization of the biblical text. Until the mid-20th century, many scholars thought that the canon of the Tanakh was established at Yavneh (Jamnia), a city near the Mediterranean coast, west of Jerusalem, that was a center of Jewish learning after the destruction of the Second Temple (70 CE). According to this theory, a group of Rabbis met there in about 90 CE and voted on whether or not certain books are canonical; at the end of this meeting, the official contents of the Bible were supposedly established. It is now acknowledged that this overly neat reconstruction is wrong and was based on a misunderstanding of rabbinic texts. The rabbinic texts that tell of this are no longer understood as granting canonical status, but are now viewed as reflecting certain ambivalences toward particular biblical books, such as Song of Songs, which were already in the canon, and whose canonical presence needed to be justified. Unfortunately, evidence is not available to offer a clear picture of how the canon of the Bible was formed, since much of the material from early Jewish sources (including the Dead Sea Scrolls, rabbinic texts, and the 1st century CE historian Josephus) and Christian sources, is ambiguous or biased.

This much is clear: the canon of the Bible did not develop at a single moment in time but rather in stages. There is general agreement that the Torah was the first section of the Bible to be canonized, that is, to be recognized as central by the community. Exactly when this happened is uncertain. Many scholars had associated this development with Ezra,

and they saw the "law of your God" (Ezra 7.14), with which Ezra was entrusted in the 5th century BCE, as the Torah. We now recognize, however, that this assertion goes beyond the evidence of the text. Though the Jewish community had recognized the Torah as central to its identity by the Persian period (6th to 4th centuries), a conclusion suggested by citations of Torah material as authoritative in biblical books from this period (for example, Chronicles, Ezra-Nehemiah), it is unclear exactly how this happened, or whether this development should be associated primarily with a single individual such as Ezra, or should be seen as part of a larger, more complicated process that likely began during the Babylonian exile.

According to rabbinic tradition, the Torah is the first part of a tripartite (three-part) canon, followed by Nevi'im (Prophets) and Kethuvim (Writings), forming a work that much later was known by the acronym Tanak(h), Torah, Nevi'im, Kethuvim. Nevi'im is composed of Joshua, Judges, Samuel (seen as one book), Kings (seen as one book)—historical works known as "the former prophets"—and "the latter prophets," consisting of Isaiah, Jeremiah, Ezekiel, and the twelve minor prophets (Hosea through Malachi, seen as one book). The order of these eight books has been relatively stable. Kethuvim is composed of the following eleven books, which, by contrast, appear in a wide variety of orders in various book lists and biblical manuscripts: Psalms, Proverbs, Job; the "five scrolls," whose order has been especially variable, Ruth, Song of Solomon, Ecclesiastes, Lamentations, and Esther; Daniel, Ezra-Nehemiah (seen as one book), and Chronicles (seen as one book). The number of canonical books according to traditional Jewish sources is thus twenty-four (five in the Torah, eight in Nevi'im, eleven in Kethuvim).

The time of origin of the name "Tanakh" is not clear. Rabbinic texts recognize a tripartite canon, where the names we know of, Torah, Nevi'im and Kethuvim, are used for each part of the canon. Their Aramaic equivalent 'oraita, *nevi'ei ukhtivei* (b. *Kid.* 49a) could be used as a general term for the Bible as a whole though in classical rabbinic literature this cumbersome locution is not generally employed for the Bible. (Rabbinic literature prefers the terms *miqra'* [that which is read] and *kitvei hakodesh* [the holy writings].) The acronym Tanakh is first found in Masoretic literature in the form of 'n"k (from the Aramaic *'oraita, nevi'ei ukhtivei*—Masoretic notes are typically in Aramaic). Tanakh, a Hebrew reflection of this Masoretic term, is also found in Masoretic literature. It would thus seem that the term originates in the late first millennium, with the flourishing of the "Masoretic movement." In contrast to earlier Jewish terms for the Bible which did not explicitly distinguish between different parts of the canon, the term Tanakh may be understood as creating clearer dividing lines between the canonical sections, in some cases even (explicitly) suggesting priority of Torah over Nevi'im and Nevi'im over Kethuvim.

The origin of the tripartite canon has been a topic of recent dispute, with several scholars suggesting that a two-part canon, the Torah and other works, was the original form, and that only later was it divided into three parts. It is more likely, however, that the tripartite canon is primary, and evidence for it appears in such sources as the prologue to the Wisdom of Jesus ben Sirach, which says that "many great teachings have been given to us through the Law and the Prophets and the others (or, other books) that followed them" and Luke 24.44, which refers to "the law of Moses, the prophets, and the psalms," and in parallel expressions in the Dead Sea Scrolls. The tripartite canon likely reflects the gradual nature of the canonization process, with Nevi'im canonized before Kethuvim. This would explain why the Kethuvim contain the book of *the prophet* Daniel (dating from the 2nd century BCE), and several late historical books, such as Ezra-Nehemiah and Chronicles, which would seem more appropriately to belong with similar works such as Joshua and Kings. The tripartite canon most likely suggests, therefore,

that Torah was canonized in the Persian period, followed by the canonization of Nevi'im in the late Persian or early Greek period, while the Kethuvim were canonized last, around the time of the destruction of the Second Temple (70 CE).

The tripartite order is not the only one known in antiquity, nor is the number of twenty-four books the only number mentioned in ancient Jewish sources. Josephus, the Jewish historian of the 1st century CE, refers to twenty-two biblical books (*Against Apion* 1.42). It is not clear if he simply had a smaller canon or if, instead, his canon had the texts in a different order, combined in different ways. Some traditions put Ruth after Judges and Lamentations after Jeremiah, treating these smaller books as appendices to the ones they follow, rather than as independent works. Such an arrangement would yield twenty-two books, a number which conveniently corresponds to the number of letters in the Hebrew alphabet; some early Christian sources also cite this as the number of books in the Bible. The arrangement of Ruth and Lamentations mentioned above is found in the Septuagint, the Greek translation of the Bible begun in Alexandria, Egypt, in the 3rd century BCE (see "Jewish Translations of the Bible," pp. 2005–20). According to this originally Jewish tradition, mentioned in some early church fathers and reflected in the arrangement of the earliest comprehensive Septuagint manuscripts (4th century CE), the Hebrew Bible is divided into four parts: Torah, Histories, Poetical and Wisdom books, and Prophets. This order continues to be used by Christians in their organization of the Hebrew Bible (Old Testament) materials (see chart at the end of this essay). Older scholarship spoke of this four-part, twenty-two book arrangement as the Alexandrian canon, in contrast to the tripartite, twenty-four book Palestinian canon, but scholars now recognize that such a clear dichotomy never existed and therefore avoid the use of those terms.

Scholars also now recognize that even when canonization took place, the contents of the Bible did not absolutely freeze. Yet, some evidence suggests that by the 2nd century CE the text had largely stabilized—this is reflected in the (few) manuscripts we have from this period, as well as the development of early rabbinic midrash, much of which presupposes a stable text. The destruction of the Second Temple and the Hadrianic persecution of the early 2nd century CE may have also caused a type of conservatism which was responsible for establishing "the" biblical text. These were gradual processes. It is important to remember that other groups, too, had their ideas about the canon; for instance, it is unlikely that the Qumran community, most of whose texts date from a century or so immediately before and immediately after the Common Era, viewed Esther as canonical, since no manuscript of that biblical book has been found among the thousands of fragments discovered. In contrast, many manuscripts of *Jubilees,* a work similar to Genesis and Exodus, have survived, and given this work's affinities with the practices of the Dead Sea community, it was probably a canonical text for them. Within rabbinic literature, the Wisdom of Jesus ben Sirach (Sirach or Ecclesiasticus) is sometimes cited with the same formula used for biblical texts and was thus, in some sense, canonical for some Rabbis. Therefore, although we may speak of "the" canon forming in the 1st century CE, there was a certain amount of flexibility or variability around the fringes.

This flexibility may also be seen in the extensive divergence with respect to the wording of the biblical text as shown in manuscripts from Qumran, in translations of the Bible in the Septuagint and elsewhere, and to a lesser extent in early rabbinic citations (see "Textual Criticism of the Bible," pp. 2067–72). These differences are not just small, such as a variant spelling here or there, but are often major, and affect the meaning of the text. There are cases where the text is found in two or more different recensions—identifiably different versions, revisions, or critical texts, not merely two different copies of the same original with minor variants—which may simply vary the order of materials or may exhibit fundamentally different text-types (for example, short types versus expansive types, as with the text of Jeremiah; see the introduction to Jeremiah). This evidence suggests that, at least in the early stages of the canonization process, it was quite acceptable for a book to circulate in different versions and that different communities may have canonized different versions of the same book.

The most basic question is why particular texts were canonized while others were not. Canonized texts within Jewish tradition were considered part of *miqra'*—"that which is read (aloud)" or *kitvei ha-kodesh*—"the holy Scriptures" (to use rabbinic designations). Excluded texts in some cases had been translated in the Septuagint and were therefore canonized in the Christian community; others were lost, or survived as pseudepigrapha (writings falsely attributed to major biblical figures), or were preserved only in fragmentary form in the Dead Sea Scrolls. Some of these excluded texts date from after the Persian period (later than 332 BCE), and thus were seen as too recent to be eligible for inclusion in the canon.

In various ways, canonical status for a book or group of books has to do with the community's views of their centrality, authority, sacredness, and inspiration. Over time these characteristics have become connected, inseparably so in some traditions; yet they are not identical, and though they overlap, they must still be viewed distinctly. The Song of Songs, for instance, was originally an erotic love poem; by the early rabbinic period, it came to be interpreted allegorically as a love poem between God and Israel. It was also seen as the inspired composition of Solomon himself. Why was it canonized? Was it canonized before it was seen as a holy, allegorical text? In that case, its canonization might reflect a central role that it held in culture or ritual. Or was it canonized only after it was viewed as allegorical and as a composition of Solomon? In that case its significance, whether of author-

CANONS OF THE BIBLE

Jewish Canon	Protestant Canon	Roman Catholic/Orthodox Canon
Torah (LAW)	PENTATEUCH	PENTATEUCH
Genesis	Genesis	Genesis
Exodus	Exodus	Exodus
Leviticus	Leviticus	Leviticus
Numbers	Numbers	Numbers
Deuteronomy	Deuteronomy	Deuteronomy
Nevi'im (PROPHETS)	HISTORIES	HISTORIES
FORMER PROPHETS	Joshua	Joshua
Joshua	Judges	Judges
Judges	Ruth	Ruth
Samuel (1 and 2)	1 and 2 Samuel	1 and 2 Samuel
Kings (1 and 2)	1 and 2 Kings	1 and 2 Kings
	1 and 2 Chronicles	1 and 2 Chronicles
LATTER PROPHETS	Ezra	Ezra
Isaiah	Nehemiah	Nehemiah
Jeremiah	Esther	Tobit
Ezekiel		Judith
The Twelve	POETICAL/WISDOM BOOKS	Esther
Hosea	Job	1 and 2 Maccabees
Joel	Psalms	
Amos	Proverbs	POETICAL/WISDOM BOOKS
Obadiah	Ecclesiastes	Job
Jonah	Song of Solomon	Psalms
Micah		Proverbs
Nahum	PROPHETS	Ecclesiastes
Habakkuk	Isaiah	Song of Solomon
Zephaniah	Jeremiah	Wisdom of Solomon
Haggai	Lamentations	Sirach
Zechariah	Ezekiel	
Malachi	Daniel	PROPHETS
	Hosea	Isaiah
Kethuvim (WRITINGS)	Joel	Jeremiah
Psalms	Amos	Lamentations
Proverbs	Obadiah	Baruch
Job	Jonah	Ezekiel
(Five Scrolls)	Micah	Daniel
Song of Songs	Nahum	Hosea
Ruth	Habakkuk	Joel
Lamentations	Zephaniah	Amos
Ecclesiastes	Haggai	Obadiah
Esther	Zechariah	Jonah
Daniel	Malachi	Micah
Ezra-Nehemiah		Nahum
Chronicles (1 and 2)	THE APOCRYPHA	Habakkuk
	1 and 2 Esdras	Zephaniah
	Tobit	Haggai
There is no Apocrypha	Judith	Zechariah
in the Hebrew Bible	Esther (with additions)	Malachi
	Wisdom of Solomon	
	Ecclesiasticus (Sirach)	
	Baruch	Orthodox canons generally include
	Letter of Jeremiah (Baruch ch 6)	1 and 2 Esdras
	Prayer of Azariah and Song of Three	Prayer of Manasseh
	Daniel and Susanna	Psalm 151
	Daniel, Bel, & Snake	3 Maccabees
	Prayer of Manasseh	4 Maccabees (as an Appendix)
	1 and 2 Maccabees	

ship or of ideas, could have played a more important part. There is no way to judge between these two paths to canonization, and the resulting difficulty is characteristic of the problems in dealing with issues of canonization in general.

Despite such major uncertainties in our understanding of the process of canonization, however, several points seem fairly certain. First, it is likely that the final stages of canonization were a reaction to the destruction of the Second Temple in 70 CE and its aftermath. This crisis intensified a development which had begun over half a millennium earlier, with the destruction of the First Temple (586 BCE). Through this development Israel gradually became the People of the Book (a term first found in the Quran in reference to Jews and Christians). Second, it is unlikely that

canonization represents a purely top-down process, through which a small group of leaders (Rabbis) determined the canon; instead, the designation of certain works as canonical was more like the official recognition of the works that a large segment of the community had already held to be central, holy, or authoritative. Finally, the act of canonization was remarkably inclusive, creating a body of works richly textured by a wide variety of genres, ideologies, and theologies. This is, fundamentally, a typical ancient Near Eastern process: Instead of creating a small, highly consistent text, as we perhaps would now do, those responsible for the process made efforts to include many of the viewpoints in ancient Israel, incorporating differing and even contradictory traditions into this single, and singular, book.   [MARC ZVI BRETTLER]

The Development of the Masoretic Bible

The transmission of the Bible may be divided into four broad periods: (1) the era of Qumran (3rd century BCE–1st century CE); (2) the era of the Sages until the Masoretic codices (2nd century–8th/9th century); (3) the era of the Masoretic codices (9th/10th century–15th century); (4) the era of the printed editions (15th/16th century–21st century). We will survey these periods below, briefly summarizing the first two eras, and concentrating on the latter two.

The Era of Qumran

Our knowledge of the early history of the transmission of the Bible was greatly expanded with the discoveries in the mid-20th century in the Judean Desert (Qumran and other sites) of Bible manuscripts ranging from the 3rd century BCE to the 1st century CE (and beyond); there are no extant manuscripts before this era, though some manuscripts predate the actual Qumran community. (See "The

Bible in the Dead Sea Scrolls," pp. 1920–28.) All the books of the Bible (except Esther) were found, typically in fragmentary manuscripts, with the books of Genesis, Exodus, Deuteronomy, Isaiah, and Psalms most frequently represented. These discoveries caused a reexamination and reevaluation of other early witnesses of the biblical text, such as the text of the Septuagint (LXX; the Greek translation of the Bible) and the Samaritan Pentateuch. Hebrew variants which had been surmised on the basis of the Greek in LXX were now shown to have actually existed. Many scholars tried to categorize the Qumran material in its relationship to these known versions, as well as to the current standard Bible text, MT (Masoretic Text). Some noted that the Qumran material does not always fit into the categories of the previously known witnesses. The Qumran era reflects a multiplicity of texts (i.e., of variants), with witnesses for all three of the previously known text-types (MT [at that time: the proto-Masoretic text-type, which seems to have been the dominant text-type then, and which later attained exclusivity among the Hebrew texts], LXX, SP), as well as other previously unknown variants. It is this era that preserves substantial variants in the reading of a word, a phrase, a verse, or larger units.

Notwithstanding the multiplicity of texts, it seems that within the Jerusalem Temple circles there was a clear preference for the one textual tradition that we call the proto-Masoretic text-type (because of its close affinities to the later Masoretic Bibles). Thus, the consonantal text of fragments of biblical manuscripts found at Masada (brought there by the fighters) conform closely to MT. Some rabbinic evidence may substantiate this conclusion (see *y. Ta'an.* 4:2 [fol. 68a] and *b. Ketub.* 106a).

The current text of the Bible (MT) preserves evidence of variant texts from an early period. This can be seen especially in the transmission of parallel texts in the Bible, which preserve early variants of the same text (e.g., in the list of names of David's warriors [2 Sam. 23.8 ff.; 1 Chron. 11.11 ff.], or in various parallel psalms [e.g., Pss. 14 || 53]). Another phenomenon that preserves early variants is "double readings," where two variants appear consecutively in the text (e.g., 1 Sam. 28.3, lit. "they buried him in Ramah and in his city"); this phenomenon also occurs in LXX and the Aramaic Targumim.

The Era of the Sages till the Masoretic Codices

It is especially difficult to reconstruct this period because we lack direct witnesses to the Hebrew text; i.e., we do not have Hebrew Bible manuscripts from most of this period. (We have some evidence from the Bar-Kokhba period, found in Wadi Murabba'at and Naḥal Ḥever, and perhaps some from its end.) Instead, the vast literature of the Sages serves as a significant secondary witness to the Bible text in this period, both in its constant citations of biblical texts and its various statements about the text. For example, *b. 'Eruv.*

13a/*Sot.* 20a admonishes to be careful while copying biblical texts, for even one letter added or omitted can destroy the world. We also have many statements of R. Naḥman ben Yitzḥak, noting explicitly "x *ketiv*," that a word in the Bible is to be spelled in a specific way (usually defective spelling; this spelling, e.g. without a *yod* or a *vav*, serves as the basis for his midrashic re-vocalization of the word); e.g., *b. Shab.* 28b; 55b.

Once we enter the era of the Sages, the quality and quantity of variants of the Bible, as known from the prior period, disappear almost entirely. This is due to the fact that the Sages rejected both the Septuagint and the Samaritan text (accepted by the Christians and the Samaritans, respectively), and accepted the proto-Masoretic text-type as their Bible text. So, in effect, we are now left with only one text-type for the Bible. Although within this text-type there still remains a range of variants, they are minor; they are almost never of the substantial type known from the earlier era.

During this period the Sages continued to develop the concept of the sanctity of the biblical text which included the details of its spelling (including whether it was plene or defective, that is, written, e.g., with a *vav*, or without it). This can be seen in the numerous *derashot*, or expositions, both halakhic (legal) and aggadic (nonlegal), that hinge on the details of the spelling, and which assume only one correct way of spelling. (For examples, see *Gen. Rab.* 12:6 [Theodor-Albeck edition, Jerusalem 1965, pp. 101–102, 104], on the exact spelling of *toldot* in the Bible and *b. Menaḥ.* 34b/*Zevaḥ.* 37a/*Sanh.* 4b on the plene/defective spellings of *(u)le-totafot* in Exod. 13.16; Deut. 6.8; 11.18.)

According to the conception of the Sages there was one accurate text—in all its details. Nevertheless, a range of (minor) variants in the texts that circulated continued to exist, though these now all belonged to one text-type. Occasionally, these variants are reflected in the literature of the Sages itself (see, e.g., the list of R. Akiva Eiger in his Gilyon Hashas to *b. Shab.* 55b; V. Aptowitzer, *Das Schriftwort in der Rabbinischen Literatur;* and the apparatus in the Hebrew University Bible).

The Era of the Masoretic Codices

The third period differs from the earlier ones in a number of ways. First, the form of transmission changed. Previously, all Hebrew texts were written in scroll format; now, in addition to the continued use of scrolls for ritual reading (e.g., the Torah scroll), the codex—a manuscript in book form—was introduced. The earliest extant dated Hebrew biblical codex is from 916 CE; however, the Hebrew codex format had apparently been in use since the 8th century CE (when it was mentioned by R. Yehudai Gaon).

Second, *nekudot* (vowel points) and *te'amim* (cantillation marks) were introduced into the text. These signs—reflecting the pronunciation and accentuation that had previously been transmitted orally—were the work of the Masoretes. Scholars in the 19th and 20th centuries have shown, especially based on manuscripts in the Cairo Geniza, that in addition to the well-known system of vocalization and accentuation currently in use, which was developed in Tiberias, there were two other systems that were developed, but which were later abandoned. All three systems differ in the choice of signs. One was developed in Babylonia, and the other in the land of Israel, though perhaps not in Tiberias. Both of these latter systems (which place their signs on top of the letters) reflect a slightly different pronunciation than that of Tiberias. For example, the other systems have only five, and not seven, vowels; i.e., only one sound for *pataḥ-qamatz; tzere-segol;* akin to current "Sephardi" pronunciation. In addition to these three major systems, other subsystems, variants of the major systems, developed.

The introduction of the different systems of signs in different geographical areas at about the same time (apparently the 7th–8th centuries CE) seems to reflect the need felt by various experts to preserve in written form the oral tradition of pronunciation and accentuation of the biblical text before it would be lost. It is possible that the upheavals associated with the Arab conquests in this period served as a major impetus for this development.

The third difference between the third period and the previous ones was the introduction of the Masorah, an extensive system of notes intended to preserve the written text of the Bible. This Masorah was recorded in both biblical codices and in independent works. The scholars who composed these notes, and who are also responsible for the introduction of the vocalization and cantillation marks, are called Masoretes. Here, too, as in the case of the systems of vocalization, different Masorahs developed in different locations; in addition to the Tiberian Masorah, there was an independent development of Masorah in Babylonia. These Masorahs have as their goal the preservation of a sanctified text, accurate in all its details, including plene-defective spelling (as noted above, this view developed in the second era, with roots in the Temple circles in the first era). In short, the goal of the Masorah apparatus is to preserve the one correct or authoritative biblical text.

Two stages were usually involved in producing a Masoretic codex: First a scribe would write the biblical text, and then the Masorete would add the vocalization, accentuation, and the Masorah. The Masorah on the page was of two types. The first type was the Masorah Parva or small Masorah—short notes in between the columns (usually three) of the page, which referred to specific words in the text (those words were marked by a little circle above them). The note would often just note "*l*" (Aramaic "leita" = there is no other; it is unique), opposite a given word. At other times, it would note the number of times a word occurs in a particular form, e.g., "*b*"; "*d*" (it occurs twice; it occurs four times). As a rule, the Masorah would take note of the exceptions in any given case, preventing a copyist from normalizing an odd form to a more common one. The second type was the Masorah Magna—longer notes on the top and/or bottom of the page, repeating select phenomena marked in the Masorah Parva, and adding the references to the verses involved. This was done by quoting a few words of the given verses, since verse and chapter numbers were not yet used. Due to space limitations, there were many more Masorah Parva notes on the page than there were Masorah Magna notes.

Two main types of masoretic lists were compiled: (a) elaborative Masorah *(masorah mefaretet)*—this is the type noted above, e.g., elaborating how many times a word occurs in a given form, e.g., six times with defective spelling; (b) collative (or cumulative) Masorah *(masorah metzarefet)*—which collates the various unusual forms or words that appear (but not plene-defective spelling), and arranges them according to the alphabet or the order of biblical books. For example, a well-known list organizes all cases of words in the Bible that occur once without, and once with, a *vav* at their beginning (for example, *'okhlah* [1 Sam. 1.9], *ve'okhlah* [Gen. 27.19]). As the lists of the collative Masorah are sometimes very long, they cannot be copied in full on a given page in a Bible codex, but are usually copied there only in part (in those codices that bring these types of lists). In addition, the lists of the collative Masorah were edited early-on as a separate work, sometimes called *'Okhlah ve-'Okhlah*, based upon the first example of the first list.

The sources available to the Masorete were sometimes different from those of the original scribe who wrote the consonantal text. If the Masorete found a contradiction between his source (Bible manuscript or Masorah note) and the Bible codex he was working on, he would correct the codex (sometimes adding a corresponding Masorah Parva note). At first, both the Masorah Parva and the Masorah Magna played a role in the correction of the codices, and were copied diligently. With time, however, the Masorah Magna took on a formalistic function, with the scribe filling up a set number of lines, e.g., two lines on top and three lines on the bottom, with Masorah Magna, thereby giving the codex the "mas-

oretic codex format"—but without using it for correcting the biblical text. (In fact, in some manuscripts the copyist would on occasion simply cut off the list to fit the space available). Occasionally, the Masorah Magna was written in micography, using the letters of the Masorah Magna decoratively to form different shapes, both geometrical (Sepharad) and even zoomorphic (animals and other shapes; Ashkenaz). At this later stage of transmission, then, the Masorah Parva was still often used for text-critical purposes, but the more complex Masorah Magna had, in effect, lost its original purpose, and had become decorative.

The medieval Masoretic codices may be divided into various groups based on geographical areas: (1) accurate Tiberian manuscripts (10th–11th centuries); (2) Sephardi manuscripts (13th–15th centuries); (3) Ashkenazi manuscripts (12th–15th centuries); (4) Italian manuscripts (12–15th centuries); (5) Yemenite manuscripts (15th–16th centuries). Most of these manuscripts are now held in state and university libraries around the world.

The accurate Tiberian manuscripts (manuscripts from the land of Israel and Egypt, with Tiberian Masorah) form a group whose text accurately reflects the Bible as reflected in the Tiberian Masorah. The most accurate manuscript among this group is the Aleppo Codex (= A) (ca. 930), whose Masorete was Aharon ben Asher, the last and most famous of the renowned ben Asher family of Masoretes. The other manuscripts in this group are close to this text.

The Sephardi manuscripts can be subdivided into three subgroups: those whose text is very close to A; those close to A (these were called "accurate Sephardi manuscripts" in the Middle Ages); those further away from A.

The Ashkenazi manuscripts can generally be divided into two groups: those whose text is far from A; those whose text is very far from A. (At least in the Torah, however, there are some that are close to A.)

The Italian manuscripts show somewhat

similar characteristics to those in the Ashkenazi manuscripts.

The Yemenite manuscripts are very accurate in the Torah text, as they reflect A, because they conformed to the rulings of Maimonides, who followed A.

The Bible text in any medieval ms depended on the sources available to the scribe and to the Masorete; i.e., on the Bible manuscripts and on the Masorah. Throughout the Middle Ages, there were often minor differences between the various sources available. There is clear evidence of places where manuscripts are corrected (usually differences in plene-defective spelling) based upon another Bible manuscript or upon a Masoretic note; we can still see in the manuscripts cases where a letter is erased and an adjacent letter is extended to fill in, or a letter is erased by crossing it out, or a letter is added above the line. This is seen most often in Ashkenazi manuscripts, where the original text represents an alternate subtradition in spelling, whereas the Masorah represents the "accurate" tradition. The extant evidence points to the second half of the 13th century as the beginning of the awareness among certain Ashkenazim that the Sephardi manuscripts are accurate and differ from their own. These adaptations continued until the era of the printed Bible, and all reflect minor variants, very rarely affecting meaning.

The Torah was always regarded with special care and attention. In addition to the Masoretic codices, Torah scrolls continued to be written for ritual use. Special halakhic regulations legislated issues, such as where different types of paragraph spaces should be inserted (*parshiot petuḥot u-setumot*) and song layout (Exod. ch 15; Deut. ch 32). Indeed, Maimonides legislated in his Code (*Hilkhot Sefer Torah* 10:1) that deviations in spelling, in section division, and in song layout render a scroll unfit for ritual use.

Given the many variants that Maimonides was confronted with, he had to decide what, in fact, was the accurate Torah text; i.e., what should be the standard text that others must copy. Maimonides chose the Aleppo Codex. He wrote a Torah scroll based upon it, and he included in his Code (*Hilkhot Sefer Torah* 8:4) a list of the sections and the layout of the songs based upon it. As we now know, he chose wisely; for the Aleppo Codex is, in fact, the most accurate among the accurate manuscripts in that it reflects the Tiberian Masorah most accurately. The Yemenites followed Maimonides, first basing themselves upon his Code, and then apparently making a model based upon his Torah scroll. Therefore, their Torah scrolls by and large reflect the Aleppo Codex in the text, sections and songs (excluding some minor variants).

Others, however, followed different options. R. Jacob Tam (France; 12th century), a significant French halakhist, wrote a work that determined the sections and song layout based on French sources (he also attended there to unique letters and special *tagim* [tittles]). Ramah, R. Meir ha-Levi ben Todros Abulafia (d. 1244), a major Spanish halakhist, though he mostly followed Maimonides in the layout of sections and songs, decided on a different tactic for the text. He chose to follow the well-known halakhic rule of following the majority, and thus followed a selective majority of Sephardi manuscripts (using only ancient "accurate" ones, rather than a single manuscript). In addition, he made use of the Masorah. In the 13th century, we have evidence of Ashkenazi scholars coming to Spain (1250; 1273) to make an accurate copy based on Ramah's work, in order to serve as a model in Ashkenaz. R. Menaḥem ha-Meiri, a significant Provencal halakhist, also used the method of majority when determining the text in his *Kiryat Sefer* (1306), but allowed a wider selection of sources. (In addition, he attended to unique letters and special *tagim*.) He also allowed himself to deviate from Maimonides in various section divisions, basing himself on French/Ashkenazi sources as well as logic. Later, R. Yom Tov Lipman Muelhausen (15th century; Ashkenaz) reverted to exclusively following Maimonides concerning the sections and the layout of the songs.

Thus, we see that there were different tactics used by different decisors in determining the proper text, sections, and song layout. Some followed a single manuscript, while others decided on the basis of several manuscripts. Regional variation was significant. The net result was that there was no absolute unity during the Middle Ages concerning the details of the Torah scrolls, even though the halakhah required unity.

The Era of the Printed Editions

The fourth era differs from the previous three by the change in medium—from handwritten manuscripts to print. This eventually gave rise to a major change in the transmission of the text, as totally identical volumes could be printed in multiple copies and distributed to diverse geographical areas. At the outset of printing, different Bible editions reflected the different types of sources available to the editors. Thus, for example, the first dated edition of the complete Bible in Hebrew, Soncino 1488, reflected Ashkenazi sources (e.g., with many variants in the text, mostly plene-defective variants, but also other types of variants).

Printing proceeded apace, each editor relying on the sources at hand, until the first edition of the Rabbinic Bible (*Miqra'ot Gedolot*), Venice 1517 (referred to as RB1517), edited by the convert Felix Pratensis for the Christian publisher Daniel Bomberg. This edition not only included the complete Bible (there had previously appeared four or five other complete editions and over fifty partial editions, e.g., just Torah), but also the Aramaic Targum to each book (excluding Ezra, Daniel, Chronicles), and one or two commentaries to each book. The editor also often listed in the margin variants in the biblical text or vocalization that he found in the manuscripts. He also listed in the margin cases of *qere* (where a word is to be read differently than it is written), but omitted the term *qere*; this made it impossible to distinguish between cases of *qere* and cases of other variants. The introduc-

tion and the closing remarks to the work highlight that the editor and publisher were very proud of this edition and felt that it reflected the accurate Bible text. In reality, the editor created a new hybrid biblical text, of the Sefardi tradition mixed with certain Ashkenazi phenomena.

Eight years after this first edition of the Rabbinic Bible, Bomberg issued a second edition of the Rabbinic Bible, this time edited anew by Jacob ben Ḥayyim Ibn 'Adoniyahu, a Jew (who later converted to Christianity) learned in Talmud, halakhah, and kabbalah. This Venice 1525 edition (referred to as RB1525) differed from the first in a number of areas. First, it presented two or three commentaries on each book. Second, it presented for the first time the apparatus of the Masorah on every page: Masorah Parva and Masorah Magna; it presented the masorah finalis—over 5,000 masoretic lists at the end of the edition, arranged alphabetically, and cross-referenced to the lists in the edition; it also included at the end of the edition the variants between various Masoretic schools, namely between ben Asher and ben Naphtali, and the textual variants between the West and the East (Eretz Israel and Babylonia; beginning with the Prophets). Third, this edition was more accurate in its marking of the *qere-ketiv*, adding *q'[ere]* to the variant, thus clearly identifying it as such; and was more accurate in marking other phenomena, such as majuscular (large) and minuscular (small) letters, etc. Fourth, this edition differed from the first in details of the text, vocalization, and accentuation.

This edition is based upon Sephardi manuscripts; unlike the first Rabbinic Bible, it does not reflect a hybrid edition. RB1525 was the initiative of Jacob ben Ḥayyim Ibn 'Adoniyahu who convinced Bomberg that the first edition, RB1517, could not serve as a model edition, unlike other editions of basic works undertaken by Bomberg, e.g., the Babylonian Talmud; Maimonides' *Mishneh Torah*. Jacob ben Ḥayyim felt that the first edition contained inaccuracies in the text, vocalization, and accentuation. Furthermore, it was not accurate enough concerning Masoretic issues. These matters were important to him especially because of his kabbalistic background. Though at first glance these were minor variants (e.g., plene-defective spelling), which did not affect the meaning of the text, in kabbalistic terms these were often of major importance. The kabbalists envisaged the Torah text as the name(s) of God, and any variant would thus cause damage to the name. Therefore, they venerated the work of the Masoretes in preserving the accurate text. So, too, the various unique phenomena of the biblical text, e.g., majuscular and minuscular letters, all had kabbalistic import; it was therefore, important to reproduce these, too, accurately in the Bible edition.

Using these kabbalistic arguments, Jacob ben Ḥayyim was able to convince Bomberg of the importance of undertaking a new Bible edition with the Masorah. Bomberg, as a Christian Hebraist (he had learned Hebrew from Pratensis), was aware of the newer phenomenon of Christian kabbalah (using the kabbalah for Christian purposes), and in fact wished to promote it. A few vestiges of the kabbalistic factor can be found in RB1525 itself. Thus, we find that Jacob ben Ḥayyim in his introduction to the edition explained the qere-ketiv in a kabbalistic vein; we find him bringing a few references to kabbalistic issues in the Masorah Parva; and we even find one note in the Masorah Magna (Exod. 10.5) where Jacob ben Ḥayyim uses the kabbalah as a criterion to decide between two conflicting masoretic notes.

RB1525 together with its Masoretic apparatus became the standard for the accurate Bible text for the next four centuries. This edition was reproduced again in Venice in 1548; 1568; 1618, and Basel 1618; and later in Amsterdam 1724; and still later in Warsaw 1860–1866.

The medium of print allowed this text to become the standard text *(textus receptus)*, for now there was the ability to distribute one text in many copies among many geographical areas. Furthermore, now it was possible to refer to this work as a standard, even when

suggesting that it must be modified. For example, Menahem di Lonzano's *'Or Torah* (in: *Shtei Yadot;* Venice 1618) was devoted to corrections in the Torah, and Yeididya Norzi's *Minḥat Shai* (Mantua 1626; first published Mantua 1742–1744; and later republished e.g., in RB1860–1866; introduction—Vienna 1876) was devoted to corrections in the whole Bible. Both of these critics, following the lead of Ramah (Abulafia), and somewhat similar to Jacob ben Ḥayyim, used Sephardi manuscripts and Masoretic notes as their criteria of accuracy. Using these criteria they corrected various cases of textual variants, mostly plene-defective spelling, and certain cases of vocalization and accentuation. This corrected text, Jacob ben Ḥayyim-(Ramah)-Lonzano-Norzi, then became the *textus receptus.*

With time, this text also became the standard in Torah scrolls both for Sephardim and Ashkenazim. Only the Yemenites continued to follow the tradition of Maimonides (i.e., the Aleppo Codex). As it turned out, these two crystallizations (the joint text; the Yemenite text) are very close in the Torah, with only a few variants between them.

A new era in the printed Bible began with the Stuttgart 1937 edition of the *Biblia Hebraica*. Here P. Kahle abandoned the RB1525 text (which had still served C. D. Ginsburg in his London 1926 edition), and in its place used the text of manuscript Leningrad B19a (1008 CE), which belongs to the accurate Tiberian manuscripts. This manuscript is quite close to the Aleppo Codex, and in some cases is corrected to agree with it. (Kahle had wanted to reproduce the Aleppo Codex, *the* manuscript of Aharon ben Asher, then still in Aleppo, Syria, but was unable to do so.) Kahle also printed there for the first time the Masorah Parva (but not the Masorah Magna) of manuscript L.

The Aleppo Codex arrived in Israel in 1958 and became the spur for renewed activity in this field. It was chosen as the base text for the Hebrew University Bible Project's Bible edition, a critical edition of the Bible incorporating variants from the ancient translations,

Dead Sea Scrolls, and rabbinic literature. So far, only a small part of this important edition, which also reproduces the Masorah Parva and the Masorah Magna in A, has appeared. In addition, various complete Bibles have appeared that are based on A (edited by M. Breuer); so, too, M. Cohen's CD Rom of the Bible (with vocalization and accentuation searchable; to be augmented in 2003 with both Masorahs of A, as well as a selection of medieval Jewish commentators), and his *Miqra'ot Gedolot Ha-Keter* (which will encompass the complete Bible [8 vols. to date], and which also reproduces the Masorah Parva and the Masorah Magna of A). All of these editions involve some reconstruction and conjecture, since the Aleppo Codex is now missing almost all of the Torah (except for the last eight chapters), as well as the end of the manuscript, and several leaves in between. This material is filled in by using Yemenite Torah manuscripts, which are believed to represent the Aleppo Codex closely, and the extant Mas-

oretic notes from the Aleppo Codex. After 500 years of printing the Bible, we can thus turn back from the *textus receptus* based on Sefardi manuscripts to the accurate Tiberian manuscripts, and indeed to the most accurate of these manuscripts, the Aleppo Codex.

Using the many manuscript sources available today, it is now possible to trace the vicissitudes of the Bible from the era of Qumran to today. The earliest period shows significant textual variation, but by the second period, once one text-type was accepted, the many variants in the Bible manuscripts that continued to circulate were mostly of a minor nature. By the third period, the sanctity of the Bible text, as well as the apparatus of the Masorah, kept the biblical variants in a minor mode. This was even more the case in the fourth period, under the influence of printing, but most especially in the modern period, where ancient reliable manuscripts can be reproduced with great accuracy and disseminated widely.   [JORDAN S. PENKOWER]

The Modern Study of the Bible

The Historical-Critical Method

General philosophical developments of the 17th and 18th centuries prompted an approach to the Bible that is often characterized as "critical." It was critical in the sense that it was free of presuppositions, especially those derived from either theology or tradition. To fully understand the Bible, scholars increasingly adopted an inductive approach, interpreting the Bible as they interpreted secular literature, setting aside received views of its authority and authorship. By and large, Jews, who continued to work within a traditional framework, did not participate in this early stage of critical scholarship. This critical approach, an outgrowth of attitudes fostered during the Enlightenment, was very much in the spirit of the times, and was, like other legacies of the Enlightenment, influenced by

larger intellectual currents, such as Romanticism and the theory of evolution.

The overriding goal was historical: to determine what had actually taken place, and to recover the actual persons and events of the Bible as they had been preserved in the various stages of biblical tradition. The nature and development of these stages were to be understood through the historical-critical method. This was the aim of "higher criticism," as distinguished from "lower," or textual criticism (see "Textual Criticism," pp. 2067–2072). With its many subdisciplines, the historical-critical method dominated biblical interpretation through the mid-20th century and continues to be influential. The scholars whose work is surveyed in the following pages were immensely learned, often experts in a variety of fields, including philology, textual criticism, comparative literature, and the study of ancient Near Eastern cultures contemporaneous with the biblical traditions. Moreover, also in keeping with the intellectual mood of the 19th and early 20th centuries, they were optimistic, in retrospect even overconfident, operating on the assured conviction that with sufficient data and careful analysis of the data an objective, accurate, and complete understanding of the Bible was possible.

Source Criticism

The critical study of the Bible began in the 17th century with Hobbes, Spinoza, and Richard Simon, and continued to gain momentum during the Enlightenment. The emphasis was on history, and the way to get at history was to begin with a careful analysis of the sources. This was done, first of all, in the analysis of the Pentateuch (the term used by Christian scholars) into several literary strands. Jean Astruc had proposed in 1753 that the different names used for God in different parts of the book of Genesis were evidence of different sources that antedated the final composition of the book. Astruc's insight was elaborated and refined mainly by German scholars, especially W. M. L. de Wette and K. H. Graf, who extended the analysis of sources to the rest of the Pentateuch (and in some cases to the book of Joshua, leading to the term "Hexateuch"; see below).

The results of more than a century of this source criticism were brilliantly synthesized in 1878 by the German scholar Julius Wellhausen, in his book *(Prolegomena to) The History of Israel*. Wellhausen's goal, which he never completed, was to write a history of ancient Israel, especially its religion. He followed an evolutionary model, arguing that the religion of Israel had developed in three stages, from a primitive, spontaneous phase in the era before the monarchy, to its high point in an ethical monotheism, from which it degenerated into a sterile legalism (this reflected a Christian view of rabbinic Judaism). To support this reconstruction he engaged in a careful analysis of the biblical traditions,

and, drawing especially on the earlier work of de Wette and Graf, gave the classic formulation to what is called the Documentary Hypothesis. According to the Documentary Hypothesis as elaborated by Wellhausen, the Hexateuch was an unreliable source for reconstructing the history of the time periods it narrated, but the "sources" that comprised it, identified as J, E, D, and P, were datable and important evidence for the periods in which they were compiled. These "documents," reconstructed from the Hexateuch in its current form, were hypothetical constructs, that is, they did not now exist as separate documents, but they were the best explanation of the evidence—the parallels, repetitions, and inconsistencies in the final form of the Hexateuch.

Wellhausen's historical reconstruction is clearly a product of its time, and reflects the biases of the late 19th century. His view of early Israel as a fresh, undefiled religious spirit has a Romantic flavor, and his characterization of postexilic Judaism as a decline into dead legalism has an anti-Semitic cast, which caused Jewish scholars to ignore it or to polemicize against it. But his formulation of the Documentary Hypothesis became a classic statement, the theory that subsequent scholars up to the present have built upon, accepted, modified, or rejected. Though the exact contours of the sources identified by Wellhausen and his simplistic reconstruction of their development are rejected by many, the general picture that he popularized—the image of the Hexateuch developing through the combination of different strands from different periods—is widely accepted by biblical scholars.

Source criticism was not an end in itself, but a method to be used in historical reconstruction for the entire Bible. It recognized the inherent complexity of biblical traditions, and attempted to disentangle the prior stages of their development. Among the many significant results of source criticism was the recognition that the book of Isaiah is a composite work. The isolated insights of earlier scholars, including Rabbi Abraham Ibn Ezra in the 12th century, and J. G. Eichhorn and others in the 18th, were expanded and elaborated in the commentary on Isaiah by Bernhard Duhm in 1892, who argued that the book of Isaiah was in effect an anthology spanning several centuries. A similar argument was developed concerning Jeremiah, suggesting that a poetic core by the prophet was supplemented by prose sections authored under the influence of Deuteronomy. The same was found to be true of other biblical books, such that almost all of the traditional authorship ascribed by rabbinic and church tradition was questioned.

The Recovery of the Ancient World

The recovery of extensive written remains from the ancient Near East coincided with the development of the disciplines of anthropology, sociology, linguistics, and folklore. Both new data and new methods were applied to the Bible, resulting in works of extraordinary insight, and, in retrospect, often of a certain naïvete. As a result of these discoveries, which helped to place ancient Israel within the ancient Near Eastern world, Biblical studies, however labeled, became a subject not just in theological curricula, but a discipline recognized in larger university contexts as well, often as part of religious studies or ancient Near Eastern studies, and later, also as part of Jewish Studies.

The process of recovery began with the deciphering of ancient Egyptian hieroglyphic writing in the early 19th century, made possible when a member of Napoleon's army, in Egypt in 1799, discovered the Rosetta Stone. The vast literature of Egypt was opened up, including valuable historical texts that provided synchronisms with biblical data relating especially to the first millennium BCE, and provided the basis for what would eventually be a comprehensive absolute chronology of the ancient Near East. Egyptian literature also provided parallels to such biblical genres as love poetry and wisdom literature.

In the mid-19th century, British and French explorers began to unearth hundreds of thou-sands of cuneiform texts in Mesopotamia, and these too were rapidly deciphered, giving access to the literature and written remains of ancient Babylonia, Assyria, and Persia. Like the Egyptian texts, they could often be correlated with biblical history. But their impact on biblical studies was more profound. In 1872, George Smith, working in the British Museum, discovered on one of the tablets that had been sent to London a flood narrative remarkably similar to the account in Genesis. While some took this as a simple historical confirmation of the flood, it soon became clear that the biblical account was a literary descendant of earlier Mesopotamian accounts. Further discoveries provided many other parallels between Babylonian and Israelite literature, law, institutions, and beliefs, and in most cases Babylonia again appeared to be the source. Sparked by a series of lectures by the German Assyriologist Friedrich Delitzsch in 1902–1904, a heated controversy developed, pitting "Babel" against the Bible. Ultimately many of the simplistic conclusions concerning the priority, and the superiority, of the traditions of "Babel" were rejected, and in retrospect they seem clearly anti-Semitic. But the controversy not only marks the emergence of Assyriology (the study of the cultures of ancient Mesopotamia) as an independent discipline, but also established the importance of a wide variety of nonbiblical materials for the understanding of the Bible.

Form Criticism

While source criticism became a dominant interpretive method, the influx of nonbiblical data, along with the rise of folklore and a growing awareness of oral literature, prompted a more nuanced investigation of the prehistory of the written biblical traditions. The pioneer in this work was the German scholar Hermann Gunkel (1862–1932), perhaps the most influential biblical interpreter of the 20th century. While accepting Wellhausen's analysis as valid, Gunkel incorporated evidence both from Babylonian literature and from comparative folklore to propose a shift in emphasis from history to the history of literature. Prior to the formation of the Hexateuchal "documents" there was discernible a long process of development and transmission of "forms," or genres, which both had parallels in nonbiblical sources, and, coincidentally, were vehicles for preserving very ancient traditions. These forms have their own history and diachronic continuity, and similarities across cultures.

Central to form-critical method was the identification of the *Sitz im Leben* ("setting in life"), the original and subsequent contexts in which the forms were developed and used. Gunkel applied form criticism himself to the book of Genesis, in his commentary first published in 1901, where he isolated such forms as saga, legend, taunt, curse, hymn, etiology, and proverb. His studies on the Psalms (1928–1933) were also groundbreaking, setting the terms of the discussion for the rest of the century by his classification of the various genres (hymn, individual and communal laments, individual and communal thanksgivings, royal psalms, wisdom psalms, etc.). Although there is a kind of idealism about the definition of the forms, parallels from outside the Bible confirmed their applicability and enhanced the understanding of the particulars of biblical traditions.

Archeology

Serious exploration of the Levant began in the early 19th century, and notable advances were made in mapping the region and in identifying ancient sites. In the decades before World War I extensive, and by the standards of the time scientific, excavations were undertaken by British, German, French, and American archeologists. Attention was focused on the major cities of ancient Israel, and Jerusalem, Samaria, Megiddo, Shechem, Jericho, Taanach, and Gezer were all partially excavated. An overriding preoccupation of the excavators was historical, even apologetic: to verify, by independent data, the historicity of biblical traditions.

In the 1920s and 1930s many more projects were initiated, and excavation techniques were improved. Greater accuracy in dating excavated remains became possible through the refinement of ceramic typology, especially as elaborated by the American scholar W. F. Albright in his excavations at Tel Beit Mirsim. But very little of the vast amount of material that was excavated and published could be related directly to the Bible, and debates often ensued about how to synthesize archeological and biblical data. When work resumed in the 1950s and 1960s, new projects were undertaken and many sites that had been earlier, and fortunately only partially, excavated were redug, especially by British, American, and Israeli archeologists. In part because of the flood of material from periods long before and after biblical times or with little direct relevance to the Bible, archeology began to develop as an independent discipline, as had already happened in the study of the classical world. More attention was given to what archeology actually produced, the material culture of the region in various periods, and in some circles there developed a theoretical tension between archeology and biblical studies.

Many earlier archeologists were also biblical scholars. Now, more and more archeologists were acquiring interest and expertise in periods and regions not directly relevant to biblical history, and in methodologies (like urban planning and soil analysis) that were far removed from the methods for studying the Bible. The result, by the late 20th century, was that some archeologists lacked sufficient textual and historical expertise to connect what they excavated with the written sources, and in any case, they considered it a virtue to work independently of biblical scholarship. On their part, many biblical scholars simply ignored the potential contributions of archeology to the interpretation of the Bible, a situation exacerbated by the fact that, at the end of the 20th and the beginning of the 21st centuries, several archeologists, in a reversal of the Albrightean school, became interested in showing how the archeological record conflicts with the Bible. Thus, a century after the beginning of serious archeological study of ancient Israel, the relation between the biblical text and archeological finds remains problematic.

Ethnography, Sociology, and Anthropology

As explorers and archeologists began to make the ancient Near East known, they also observed those living there in the present. While many of the descriptions published were little more than naïve catalogues of perceived parallels between Arab customs and details of life in biblical times, there were serious works of scholarship, including W. Robertson Smith's *Lectures on the Religion of the Semites* (1889) and Gustaf Dalman's extensive survey of Palestinian social life and customs (*Arbeit* [work] *und Sitte* [customs] *in Palestina*, 1928–1939). At the same time, the disciplines of sociology and anthropology were becoming more sophisticated. An early sociological interpretation of the Bible was Max Weber's *Ancient Judaism* (1917–1919), though sociological studies of the Bible began to proliferate only in the late 20th century.

Anthropological research had an earlier impact. Typical of early efforts was the encyclopedic work of James G. Frazer. In *The Golden Bough: A Study in Comparative Religion* (1890; revised and abridged by Theodor Gaster in 1959), and subsequent works, such as *Folklore in the Old Testament* (1919), Frazer organized a staggering amount of data in support of his understanding of the evolution of society from primitive beginnings to civilization. His principal focus was on myth and rituals, especially the essential role of the king in the welfare of the larger society, and he included both the Hebrew Bible and the New Testament in his analysis.

While Frazer's work was subsequently criticized for its failure to pay sufficient attention to specific cultural contexts and for its cavalier treatment of the data to fit his theories, his influence was considerable. In particular, both in Britain and in Scandinavia, many scholars developed and refined his approach, developing what has been characterized as a "myth and ritual" school. The work of Sigmund Mowinckel of Norway is representative. Using form criticism as a method (he had been a student of Gunkel) and the function of the king as an organizing principle, and drawing heavily on Babylonian sources, his study of the Psalms (1921–1924) focused on their use in what he suggested was an annual enthronement festival of God, like the Babylonian New Year festival. Most scholars now find Mowinckel's reconstruction overly conjectural.

Redaction Criticism

The impression left by source criticism was that the final forms of the Pentateuch and other biblical books or collections for which multiple sources were hypothesized were pedestrian compilations with little literary merit. Beginning in the 1930s, again mainly in Germany, attention began to be paid to the larger units as creative works in their own right. In a number of influential essays, and in his commentaries on Genesis and Deuteronomy, Gerhard von Rad argued that the Hexateuch (the Pentateuch plus Joshua) was itself a literary form. This observation was extended at the end of the 20th century, as a variety of scholars posited structural and thematic patterns that were used by redactors to create a finely crafted, aesthetic final product. Ultimately these discoveries helped to influence a branch of biblical scholarship called Canonical Criticism (see below), which emphasized the role of the text in its final form within the canon as a whole. They also bore some relationship to the newly developing literary approaches to the Bible, which also emphasized the final form of the text, its coherence, and its aesthetic merits.

Discoveries of Texts between the World Wars

The discovery and deciphering of cuneiform texts of ancient Assyria and Babylonia during the second half of the 19th century had profoundly changed the understanding of the

Bible. On the historical level, the repeated references especially in Assyrian annals to kings of Israel and Judah and to events mentioned in the Bible enabled the construction of a detailed chronology. But for the most part connections between the cuneiform texts and biblical traditions were indirect. This is not surprising, given the distance and often the time that separated those Mesopotamian cultures from ancient Israel. And apart from a scattering of inscriptions in Hebrew, Phoenician, Aramaic, and Moabite, there were no significant written remains from Israel itself or its most immediate neighbors. That changed in the 1920s and 1930s, as excavations uncovered more collections of ancient texts, and further deciphering shed light on more distant groups such as the Sumerians, the Hittites, and the Hurrians. While there were seldom direct correlations with the Bible, the tablets from Nuzi in northern Iraq and Mari and Ugarit in northern Syria were especially important in expanding the knowledge of the larger world to which ancient Israel belonged.

In many respects the mythological texts from Ugarit are the most important because of their geographical proximity to ancient Israel and the direct light they shed on the Bible. Written in a previously unknown Semitic language belonging to the same subfamily as Hebrew, they are composed in poetry that is often remarkably close in diction and in form to biblical poetry. The myths feature gods and goddesses such as El, Baal, and Asherah, all frequently mentioned in the Bible but hitherto incompletely known, largely because of the biblical writers' antagonism toward other gods. Moreover, similar motifs—for example, the childless patriarch, the theophany of the storm god, the council of the gods, the sacred mountain—and innumerable smaller details illustrate the shared commonalities between the culture of Israel and those of its neighbors. Despite undeniable chronological and geographical discontinuities, the literary, religious, and institutional traditions of the Levant, including ancient Israel, are best understood as part of a cultural continuum that, allowing for local particularities, is remarkably consistent and pervasive.

The Dead Sea Scrolls

Another discovery that sent scholarship in new directions was that of a cache of manuscripts in caves near Qumran at the northwest corner of the Dead Sea (see "The Bible in the Dead Sea Scrolls," pp. 1920–28). Over the course of several years, beginning in 1947, the remains of hundreds of manuscripts were discovered, first by local Bedouin and subsequently by archeologists. Some of the manuscripts were largely intact, including an almost complete scroll of the Hebrew text of the book of Isaiah, and others were preserved only in fragments. Written mostly in Hebrew and Aramaic, with a few in Greek, they are generally agreed to have been a library deposited in the caves for safekeeping during the First Jewish Revolt (66–73 CE) by the inhabitants of the nearby settlement. Most scholars identify these inhabitants as Essenes, one of the major groups within Judaism in the Roman period, according to the 1st-century CE Jewish historian Josephus. Among many important aspects of the scrolls, three may be highlighted here. First are the manuscripts of the Bible, more than a thousand years older than any previously known, giving new evidence concerning the history of the biblical text and greater impetus to text criticism and the history of canonization (see above). Second is their contribution to the understanding of both Hebrew and Aramaic in the Roman period, and the histories of these two biblical languages. And third is the glimpse they provide of one community within Judaism around the turn of the era. Through what have been termed "sectarian documents," that is, various community regulations, hymns, eschatological texts, and biblical commentaries (*pesharim*; see "The Bible in the Dead Sea Scrolls," pp. 1920–28)—we learn the beliefs and practices of this one group and we get insight into how they used and interpreted various books of the Bible. It turns out that the variety of early Judaisms and the early history of the textual transmission and interpretation of the Bible are much more complex than earlier imagined.

The Historical-Critical Method through 1950

Various aspects of the historical-critical method, which aimed to reconstruct the history of ancient Israel and the history of the biblical text, were immensely influential through much of the 20th century, and they continue to serve as the basis of much scholarship. However, with the change in intellectual currents at the end of the second millennium, the consensus that the historical-critical method was the only legitimate method began to fragment, and it ultimately shattered with the proliferation of new methods and approaches for investigating biblical texts. Beginning in the 1970s many biblical scholars have questioned the adequacy of an almost exclusive orientation to questions with a historical focus. Also, in keeping with a trend characteristic of most of the humanities and social sciences, there has been a strong movement toward interdisciplinary conversation. Although it is difficult to give a simple overview of the proliferating approaches to biblical studies since the 1970s, they can be roughly grouped under the categories of literary, social-scientific, and cultural hermeneutical approaches.

Literary Approaches

A popular appreciation of the narrative art of the Bible has always existed. Its stories were represented in the sculpture and stained-glass windows of medieval churches, and Western literature has been profoundly influenced by its characters, themes, and symbols. In both Judaism and Christianity the reading and retelling of the stories in devotional and liturgical contexts made them deeply familiar. Yet even though biblical Hebrew poetry had been the subject of academic study since the 18th century (most notably in Bishop Robert

Lowth's *Lectures on the Sacred Poetry of the Hebrews*), little attention had been paid to the poetics of biblical narrative. One impetus to the interest in biblical narrative that developed in the 1970s can be traced to a development in American higher education: the creation of departments of religious studies in nondenominational colleges and public universities in the 1960s and 1970s. In such contexts the study of the Bible "as literature" was deemed especially appropriate to a secular curriculum. Such interest was not restricted to scholars in secular contexts, however. In 1968 James Muilenberg, who for much of his career had been a professor at Union Theological Seminary, delivered a presidential address to the Society of Biblical Literature titled "Form Criticism and Beyond." In this lecture he called for a type of literary-theological approach to the poetry and prose of the Bible which he referred to as "rhetorical criticism." Giving further impetus to literary study of the Bible was the work of several scholars of English and comparative literature, who extended their expertise in the analysis of literature to biblical texts. Most prominent were Northrop Frye (*The Great Code: The Bible and Literature*) and Robert Alter (*The Art of Biblical Narrative and The Art of Biblical Poetry*). Much work was done in this area in Israel, especially by Meir Weiss in Jerusalem (*The Bible from Within*) and his students, as well as scholars who were influenced by the work of Meir Sternberg (*The Poetics of Biblical Narrative*) and his circle at Tel-Aviv.

This literary approach differed from historical study in significant ways. Whereas historical study tended to be concerned with the prehistory of the text (oral traditions and written source materials) and with its development through successive redactions, literary study focused on the final form of the text. Whereas historical study was interested in the world referred to *by* the text, literary study directed its attention to the world constructed *in* the text. Nevertheless, there were certain historical dimensions to this early work in biblical literature. Both Alter and Meir Sternberg attempted to isolate distinctive features of ancient Israelite narrative art (e.g., modes of characterization, the use of type-scenes, techniques of repetition, forms of plot development) which set the Bible apart from modern Western narrative.

Much of the early literary study of the Bible was influenced by the "New Criticism," an approach that had dominated Anglo-American literary scholarship from the 1930s through the 1950s. In New Criticism the literary text was considered an autonomous work of art, an "artifact," to be studied independently of its author's intentions and of the sociopolitical currents of the time in which it was produced. New Criticism was a reaction both to a methodology arising out of the history of literature, in which new literary movements are seen as developing from those of previous eras, and to biographical criticism, which reads literary texts as expressions of the life experiences of the writers. The focus in New Criticism is rather on the way in which the text itself is structured so as to produce the observed or expected effects and understandings. Thus, the plot, characters, setting, point of view, and other aspects of the story's rhetoric are analyzed. As the literary study of the Bible was gaining ground, however, rapid changes were taking place in the larger field of literary study, changes that were quickly reflected in biblical studies.

Structuralism was the first of these new movements to make its impact. The origins of structuralism are in the work of the early 20th-century linguist Ferdinand de Saussure, who attempted to analyze the system of relationships within a language that make acts of speech possible. In particular, he stressed that meanings are produced not so much by simple definition as by a network of contrasts (e.g., a tree is a woody plant that is *not* a bush or a shrub). The anthropologist Claude Lévi-Strauss argued that symbolic structures within human societies, including their kinship systems and their mythologies, could be analyzed in the same way, as systems of differences structured according to binary oppositions (e.g., life/death; male/female; hunting/farming; outside/inside). In a parallel development A. J. Greimas attempted to use Saussure's insights to develop a "grammar" of narrative in much the same way as Saussure attempted to develop a grammar of sentences. Biblical scholars, anthropologists, and literary theorists were quick to apply these approaches to the Bible. The mythic narratives and genealogical accounts of Genesis, and the legal material in the Torah offered opportunities for analyzing the patterns of binary opposition that structuralists argued were the key to the meaning of the texts.

Even as structuralism was being adapted for the study of biblical literature, its assumptions and claims were being challenged in the wider world of philosophical and literary studies. Structuralism claimed that the binary oppositions that structure human thought are essentially universal and unaffected by culture or history. Though the surface features of texts might vary with different societies and over time, the underlying structures did not. Such claims proved difficult to sustain. Just as structuralism dispensed with history, so it also had no place for the individual reader in the production of meaning. Structuralism understood itself as a kind of scientific method. Yet different readers regularly reached different understandings of the same text. Finally, though structuralism seemed to lend itself well to myths, folktales, laws, and highly formulaic narratives, it seemed unable to deal with more complex narratives.

Against the focus on a supposedly objective and stable text in narrative criticism and against structuralism's focus on impersonal and universal codes, reader-response criticism argued for the essential role of the reader in the process of making meaning. Structuralism tended to display its results in terms of charts, an implicitly spatial understanding of the text. But reader-response theory insisted that reading is essentially a temporal affair. In reading, one only gradually gathers information that is progressively organized and reorganized by the reader to produce meaning.

Moreover, the text often contains "gaps" which the reader, consciously or unconsciously, fills in (e.g., details concerning characters, aspects of motivation or causality, connections between events). As the reader becomes actively involved in the process of reading, what the reader engages is not simply the issues of plot and character but also matters of norms and values, which the reader may embrace or resist. Reader-response criticism thus accounts for the different understandings of and reactions to the "same" text by different readers by claiming a necessary place for the subjective element in reading. Personal subjectivity is limited, however, by what the reader's community considers to be a plausible or implausible inference. Thus it is not so much individual readers as "interpretive communities" who set the parameters according to which interpretation takes place. Although a number of reader-response studies of Hebrew Bible texts have been produced, the method found its most enthusiastic reception in the study of the New Testament Gospels, where texts can be dated with greater precision, and we know more about the early communities that produced them.

If reader-response criticism represented one reaction to the limitations of traditional narratology and to structuralism, a more pervasive criticism emerged under the rubric of post-structuralism, or deconstruction. This movement, associated with the French philosopher Jacques Derrida, is above all a critique of the metaphysical assumptions of Western philosophy, and only secondarily an analysis of the nature of texts and the interpretive process. Derrida noted the attempt of philosophy to posit a central term (God, reason, the human being) in relation to which all of reality can be organized. This organization characteristically takes place by means of binary oppositions (e.g., rational/irrational, oral/written, presence/absence), in which the first term is accepted as superior to the second. Deconstruction attempts to dismantle such structures in order to show their artifi-

ciality and the inevitable ways in which any such structure of thought implicitly "decenters" its central term and undermines itself through internal inconsistency and contradiction. When applied to texts, deconstruction begins with the perception that language is inevitably incomplete and surprisingly fluid. (In this respect it resembles rabbinic midrash.) It then analyzes how even a text's ostensible argument is rendered problematic and even self-contradictory by extraneous details or slippages in meaning which at first appear peripheral and unimportant. For deconstruction the point of reading is not to restate the meaning intended by the author but, like many midrashic texts, to engage the text in creative thought, often by means of punning play with the text. Deconstruction's very style serves to undermine the binary opposition serious/frivolous, for its aim is in part to uncover the ways in which various forms of thought attempt to inscribe power and privilege.

The perspectives of deconstruction have been combined with other intellectual currents (most notably Freudianism and Marxism) to produce a variety of related approaches that are often referred to comprehensively by the term postmodernism. Along with Derrida's deconstruction, Michel Foucault's study of the complex nature of power and truth and Fredric Jameson's neo-Marxist analysis of ideology have been deeply influential on postmodernism in biblical studies. For an overview of these trends as well as other forms of postmodernism, see The Postmodern Bible by The Bible and Culture Collective.

Since one of the features of postmodernism is its tendency to dissolve boundaries, it is scarcely surprising that its characteristic approaches have combined with a wide variety of other impulses within biblical studies, most notably feminist criticism, but also various forms of ideological criticism (see below under cultural hermeneutics). Similarly, postmodern analysis is not restricted to narrative but employed in relation to all sorts of texts. Indeed, the self-conscious study of the literary artistry of the Bible, such a controversial novelty in 1970, has been all but put aside in the rapidly shifting mix of methods and approaches that have been developed alongside the classical forms of biblical interpretation.

Social-scientific Criticism

Social-scientific criticism, another form of biblical criticism that has arisen in more recent years, applies insights and methods from the fields of sociology, anthropology, and ethnography to describe aspects of ancient social life manifested in the biblical texts and to reconstruct the social worlds behind the text. To a certain extent historical criticism has always had a social dimension, since the objects of its interest included nations, states, social groupings, and religious movements. Yet self-conscious social-scientific investigation, though not unknown in earlier stages of biblical studies, has come into its own since the 1960s.

As early as the Renaissance, students of the Bible were concerned to make cross-cultural comparisons between ancient Israel and the nations of the ancient Near East. With the development of critical biblical study in the 19th century, this interest in cross-cultural study focused particularly on the comparison between Israel and the pre-Islamic Bedouin Arabs, as well as with contemporary Bedouin society, especially in the work of Julius Wellhausen and William Robertson Smith. Similarly, Martin Noth compared Israel's premonarchical tribal confederacy with ancient Greek tribal leagues. In retrospect, these early attempts at social-scientific analysis were hampered by a lack of rigorous method, by erroneous assumptions about the economic and social organization of ancient Israel, and by an overly static model of ancient culture. More sophisticated was the work of the sociologist Max Weber, whose *Ancient Judaism* (compiled from lectures given in 1917–1919) attempted to incorporate the dimensions of historical and institutional change in his account of the social organization of ancient Is-

rael. Certain features of Weber's analysis, such as viewing some prophets as "charismatic" figures, continue to be influential within biblical studies.

These early attempts at social-scientific criticism were largely displaced by interest in other questions and methods, and for almost forty years little was published in this field. By the 1960s and 1970s, however, interest in it revived. The first issue to be examined, and one still sharply debated, is that of the socioeconomic and political nature of the formation of the Israelite tribal confederacy. Social historians rejected the conquest model of Israel's entry into Canaan as it is described in the biblical narrative. Both George Mendenhall and Norman Gottwald argued that Israel's origins were to be sought instead in a peasant revolt against urban Canaanite overlords. The peasant movement was a revolt against the hierarchical socioeconomic structure and developed as a retribalization along egalitarian lines in the central highlands. What differentiated Mendenhall and Gottwald, however, was Gottwald's explicit use of Marxist social theory. Although both of their proposals have been sharply criticized for reliance more on presupposed models than on textual or material evidence, they served to open the question of Israel's origins for fresh investigation. Since the 1970s archeology has also generated increasing information concerning population patterns, forms of domestic architecture, agricultural practices, and trade patterns for the period preceding the monarchy. This information, together with a wider array of possible comparative models for the development of noncentralized peasant societies, has begun to generate new ways of understanding early Israel, though none has yet achieved consensus. Unlike the earlier studies, which concentrated on comparisons with Middle Eastern peoples, these newer studies looked at a variety of groups that were distant from Israel, but believed to have similar social structures.

Similarly, attempts to understand the movement from a loose tribal confederation to the eventual formation of royal states has been aided by comparative social analysis. Social anthropologists have documented the development of chieftanships as an intermediate stage between these two forms of social organization. A chiefdom is a hierarchically organized society that lacks the strong central governmental apparatus characteristic of a true state. Though some aspects of the process are still debated, it is now generally thought that Saul's "kingship" and at least the early stages of David's rule should be thought of as chieftainships.

Prophecy is another area of Israel's religious and social life that has proven fruitful for social-scientific analysis. In addition to looking at prophetic oracles recovered from neighboring nations, the biblical texts have been analyzed in light of sociological models and comparative ethnographic evidence. Though the limited evidence makes many conclusions elusive, it has proven possible to clarify to a certain extent the social location of the prophets and their relationship or nonrelationship to established religious institutions and to the monarchy. How a prophet secures legitimation, the role of ecstasy and other phenomena of abnormally heightened consciousness, and the relation of oral and written communication have all been examined in social-scientific perspective. The later development of apocalypticism and the question of its social location—whether it was, for example, an outgrowth of prophecy, a scribal phenomenon, or a movement of the social margins or of the priestly elite—has been debated as the biblical texts are reread in light of apocalyptic and millenarian movements in the medieval and modern periods.

The biblical text also contains significant information about purity laws and kinship and family patterns, topics which lend themselves to comparative social analysis. In the 1960s the anthropologist Mary Douglas pioneered such studies with her analysis of the food laws in Leviticus and Deuteronomy, interpreting them as a symbolic system for organizing the world and correlating purity laws in general with the social concern for boundaries. There is currently a growing interest in purity and impurity, especially as it pertains to women, and in general as it relates to the social and religious dimensions of ancient Israel. More recently the narratives in Genesis, the family laws in Deuteronomy, and the reports on the postexilic community in Ezra-Nehemiah have been investigated in an attempt to discern the basic structures of family organization, as well as changes over time in the patterns of family life. As modern interest in gender constructs and roles has grown, so has the investigation of such issues in ancient Israel. Through the application of social-science theory, especially theories of gender, to the texts of the Bible, and in some cases also calling on the findings of archeology, we are learning more about the patterns of life and activity characteristic of males and females in biblical times.

Cultural Hermeneutics

Modern biblical studies, as it emerged from its Enlightenment roots, understood itself as a form of critical analysis that was objective, disinterested, and even "scientific." Though biblical theology might make normative claims, even those claims were based on a preliminary act of interpretation that was grounded in objective scholarship. In recent years the claim of biblical scholarship to be a quasi-scientific enterprise has been questioned by those who insist that the enterprise of historical criticism of the Bible is unconsciously shaped and informed by cultural assumptions specific to the time and place in which that method was developed. Pure objectivity is an illusion. In the interpretation of texts and cultures there is no "view from nowhere." All interpreters, whether or not they are aware of it, frame their questions and perceive the data from some perspective, which helps to shape their understanding of the text or culture in question. Rather than seeing the influence of the interpreter's social and cultural location as a problem, some have claimed it as a positive value. Thus the term "cultural hermeneutics" serves as an umbrella term for a variety of approaches to biblical interpretation (e.g., liberationist, feminist, postcolonial) in which the social location of the interpreter is not only made explicit but serves as a normative principle in interpretation. The primary categories which have figured in such interpretation are those of class, ethnicity, and gender.

The earliest and most methodologically self-conscious of these approaches is that of Latin American liberation theology, which emerged in the 1960s and 1970s. This approach did not begin as an academic perspective but rather emerged out of the concrete experience of the poor and of those pastors and other religious professionals who lived and worked with them. They insisted that the starting point for reading and interpreting the Bible must not be a stance of "objectivity" but rather the experience of the crushing poverty and oppression of the lowest social classes. Interpreted from the perspective of material poverty, the Bible discloses itself as a text of liberation and serves to further a revolutionary process of emancipation. The exodus narrative and various prophets have been key texts within this movement. In the wake of Latin American liberation hermeneutics, religious communities and academics in the various countries of Africa and Asia have developed analogous forms of biblical interpretation that work from the particular experiences of those nations. These are sometimes grouped under the rubric of postcolonial hermeneutics. Much of this work has taken place within the Christian community, and it has not had a widespread impact on general or specifically Jewish biblical studies. However, in light of the trend to validate the ways in which different ethnic or racial communities read the Bible, Jewish scholars are looking to their traditional modes of biblical interpretation. Traditional Jewish exegesis, examined from a scholarly perspective, is increasingly appearing on the interpretive scene, and has gained some attention among non-Jewish scholars.

Whereas, for the most part, the various perspectives discussed so far under the rubric of cultural hermeneutics are distinctively Christian, the same cannot be said for feminist biblical hermeneutics. Here, although Christian feminist biblical interpretation emerged slightly earlier, Jewish and Christian feminist interpretation has largely developed in tandem, and the critical conversation between Jewish and Christian feminists has been one of the distinctive features of this movement (see "Jewish Women's Scholarly Writings on the Bible," pp. 2000–2005). In the 1950s and 1960s Protestant seminaries began to admit women in significantly larger numbers than before, followed soon after by an increase in the number of Catholic and Jewish women pursuing seminary education. The emergence of the women's movement in the 1960s and its criticism of the role of the Bible in the oppression of women posed a challenge to those who identified themselves as both Christian or Jewish and feminist. One early position is to affirm that the Bible, when correctly interpreted, affirms women's full humanity. Other feminists, more critical of the Bible itself, have attempted to expose and analyze the patriarchal elements in the biblical text itself in order to show how the patriarchal values can be separated from the essentially liberating values that form its primary message. More radical feminists, however, have attempted to show that the biblical traditions are thoroughly and irredeemably antifeminist.

Feminist interpretation of the Bible has embraced a variety of methodologies. Some of it utilizes the approaches of historical-critical and sociological biblical scholarship, since it attempts to recover and reconstruct the historical reality of women's lives in ancient Israel.

Not all feminist interpretation has been concerned with historical reconstruction, however. A significant strand of feminism has used literary methods, exploring the ways in which biblical texts construct and represent an image of women that may function in the service of particular ideologies. In many instances this literary approach has involved reading against the grain of the text. For instance, a character whom the text treats as a subsidiary character may become for feminist analysis the central character of the text (e.g., Jephthah's daughter in Judg. ch 11 or the Levite's concubine in Judg. ch 19). Of particular concern to feminists has been the issue of women and violence, for many of the biblical texts do represent violence against women, and a smaller but significant number represent women engaged in violence. The influence of these various types of feminist approaches to the Bible has been significant, and has had an important impact on how both scholars and the laity approach biblical texts.

Finally, canonical criticism, which often describes itself as a theological mode of interpretation, may also be considered as a form of cultural hermeneutics, since it also puts the community context within which the text was created and from which it is to be read into the foreground. Though the forms of canonical criticism developed by its two major proponents, Brevard Childs and James Sanders, differ, one can identify common elements. Specifically, canonical criticism is concerned with how Scripture's final form was created within a believing community and how the meanings created by that final form continue to guide the reading practices of the community. The canonical shaping of the Jewish Bible, for instance—which places the writings in the final position and concludes in many editions with the call of 2 Chronicles for the exiles to go up to Jerusalem to rebuild the Temple—tells a different story from that produced by the shaping of the Christian Old Testament, which places the prophets last and concludes with Malachi's reference to the return of the prophet Elijah to announce the coming Day of the Lord.

In one sense canonical criticism is an extension of historical criticism's interest in the development of traditions. But in contrast to historical criticism's tendency to investigate the earliest stages of development, canonical criticism explicitly privileges the latest stage, the canon in its final form. This concern with reading the text of Scripture in its final form gives canonical criticism some similarity to the literary approaches of the "New Criticism." Thus, where historical criticism, reading the book of Isaiah, tries to distinguish which materials come from the 8th-century prophet, the 6th-century prophet, and the 5th-century prophet, literary and canonical critics focus on how the final form of the book has created the context within which all of its materials are now to be read, as a movement from destruction to hope. While canonical criticism's self-conscious attention to what it means to read Scripture as a member of a religious tradition links it with cultural hermeneutics, it also differs from some of the other forms of cultural hermeneutics discussed above. Just as those forms of interpretation make repeated reference to the specific experience of the reader as a guide to interpretation, canonical hermeneutics finds the clues to a proper reading in the ways in which the text of Scripture was shaped by the believing community at the time its canon was fixed.

If anything ties together the various strands of newly developing approaches to biblical interpretation, it is a concern for the relationship of language, meaning, and power. More historically oriented literary and social methods increasingly examine the ways in which issues of conflict and access to power can be traced, as there is a new awareness that people, typically elites functioning within a power-group, are responsible for writing and preserving biblical texts. Cultural hermeneutics, though not uninterested in historical reconstruction, also focuses on the ways in which access to the power to interpret the text and construe its meaning serves to empower those who have traditionally been marginalized. And postmodernism has attempted to underscore the ironies of all such strategies, since in its view a stable and definitive meaning always eludes the interpreter.

[*Adapted by* ADELE BERLIN
AND MARC ZVI BRETTLER]

Reading Biblical Poetry

Most literary works from the ancient Near East are in the form of poetry. Prose narrative, which dominates in the Torah and the Former Prophets, as well as in several books in Kethuvim (the Writings), is a distinguishing feature of biblical literature. Yet while biblical narrative is mainly in prose (there are a few narrative poems, e.g., Ps. 136), biblical hymns, laments, victory songs, love poems, wisdom instruction, prophetic speeches, and several other types of discourse are in poetry. About one-third of the Bible is poetry, including the books of Psalms, Proverbs, Job, Song of Songs, Lamentations, and Ecclesiastes. Modern scholars also consider most of the speeches of the Latter Prophets (Isaiah, Jeremiah, Ezekiel, the Twelve) to be poetry. In addition to these large blocks of text, poems are interspersed in the prose narrative; examples are the Testament of Jacob (Gen. ch 49), the Song of the Sea (Exod. ch 15), the Sayings of Balaam (Num. 23.7–10, 18–24; 24.3–9, 15–24), the Song of Moses (Deut. ch 32), the Testament of Moses (Deut. ch 33), the Song of Deborah (Judg. ch 5), the Prayer of Hannah (1 Sam. ch 2), the Elegy over Saul and Jonathan (2 Sam. ch 1), and David's Song in 2 Sam. ch 22 (= Ps. 18). Shorter poems or fragments of poems have been identified in, for example, Gen. 4.23–24; 1 Kings 8.12–13; Ruth 1.16–17.

Poetry is a form of elevated discourse that differs in certain formal properties from prose (which is also somewhat elevated discourse, not a record of everyday speech). Some argue that these differences are a matter of degree rather than of kind, but at a certain point quantitative difference becomes qualitative difference. The attributes of poetry will be discussed below.

The identification of biblical poetry and the definition of what constitutes poetry in the Bible has been a vexed issue since early postbiblical times. Each generation of scholars has applied its own criteria, usually drawn from its own vernacular poetry, be it the classical meters of Greek and Latin poetry, the medieval Arabic systems of rhyme and meter, or the accentual meter of English poetry—but none of these fit biblical poetry. The Bible itself has little to say about its poetry, other than offering some terms that may indicate types of poems.

The most general term is *shir* or *shira*, "song." *Shir* may stand alone, as in Judg. 5.12; Ps. 65.1, or may be qualified, as in *shir hamaʻalot*, "song of ascents" (Pss. 120–134); *shir yedidot*, "a love song" (Ps. 45.1); *shir ḥanukat habayit* "a song for the dedication of the House" (Ps. 30.1); *shir tziyon*, "Zion song" (Ps. 137.3); *shir tehilah*, "song of praise" (Neh. 12.46). The feminine form, *shira*, is found in Exod. 15.1; Deut. 31.30; Num. 21.17; Isa. 5.1; and elsewhere, and appears to be synonymous with *shir*. Another frequent term is *mizmor*, "psalm, a song sung to the accompaniment of a stringed instrument," commonly found in the superscriptions to psalms, sometimes in combination with *shir* (e.g., Pss. 67.1; 68.1). A third term, *qinah*, "lament, dirge" is known from 2 Sam. 1.17; Amos 8.10; etc. These terms are suggestive of ancient notions of poetic genres, but they do not occur in every passage that a modern reader would consider poetry.

Aside from these terms, a suggestive feature of the Masoretic Text is the traditional scribal convention of stichography, whereby certain passages are written in verse-like lines (e.g., Exod. ch 15; Deut. ch 32; Judg. ch 5; 2 Sam. ch 22). This scribal convention, discussed in rabbinic literature, sets off certain sections from the blocks of surrounding text. There are two forms, called by the Rabbis "small brick over large brick, large brick over small brick" and "small brick over small brick, large brick over large brick." Small brick over large brick looks like

Small brick over small brick looks like

The stichographic writing, too, is not a sufficient criterion by which to identify poetry by today's standards because it was used for only a fraction of passages that we would consider poetry (for example, most manuscripts do not use this stichography for Psalms); moreover, it is occasionally used for nonpoetic lists (Josh. 12.9–24; 1 Sam. 6.17; Esth. 9.7–9).

A third potential indicator of poetry, in the Masoretic Text, is the system of accents (tropes, or cantillation marks) used in the Tiberian Masorah, whereby the books of Psalms, Proverbs, and most of Job are given a different system of accents from the other twenty-one books of the Bible. These three books are referred to as *sifrei 'emet*, *'emet* (meaning "truth") being an acronym from the initials of *'iyov* (Job), *mishlei* (Proverbs), and *tehilim* (Psalms). Again, while we consider these three books to be poetic, there are additional poetic books and passages for which these accents are not used. It seems that this system of accents indicates only the cantillation and says nothing about poetry per se.

Since the Bible does not define or describe its poetry, scholars have offered their own descriptions. Most would accept the following description: Biblical poetry is a type of elevated discourse, composed of terse lines, and employing a high degree of parallelism and imagery. Other tropes and figures may also be present, most commonly, word and sound repetition and patterning. There is no scholarly consensus regarding meter (see below).

Terseness is a feature of many of the world's poetries, whether or not there are metrical constraints on the length of lines; lines of poetry tend to be shorter and more concise than prose clauses. Lines of biblical poetry are generally no longer than three or four words. Their terseness is further en-

hanced by the omission of the definite article, the accusative marker *'et,* and the relative pronoun *'asher.* This tendency toward terseness operates both within a single line and over the composition as a whole. Biblical poems are relatively short, about thirty verses or less on average; there are no epic-length poems in the Bible. (The longest single poem is Psalm 119, with 176 verses. The book of Job is poetry from 3.2 to 42.6, but is actually a series of poems set in a prose frame.) Accompanying the terseness of the lines is the paratactic style by which lines are joined together. In parataxis, the connectives between lines may be missing altogether or may consist of the multivalent conjunction *vav,* "and, but, or." Thus the relationship between lines is often not explicit, opening up both difficulties and opportunities for interpretation. Terseness and parataxis make poetry seem more intense; they give the impression that each word is heavily laden with meaning.

Biblical poetry is characterized most of all by its binary form of expression known as parallelism. Parallelism is the pairing of a line (or part of a line) with one or more lines that are in some way linguistically equivalent. The equivalence is often grammatical—that is, both parts of the parallelism may have the same syntactic structure, as in

> The LORD is my light and my help;
>   whom should I fear?
> The LORD is the stronghold of my life,
>   whom should I dread? (Ps. 27.1).

Often, though, the grammatical structure is not identical, at least on the surface, as in

> . . . before I created you in the womb . . .
> Before you were born (Jer. 1.5).

In this example, "you" (the prophet) is the grammatical object in the first line and the subject in the second. In Prov. 6.20, a positive clause is paired with a negative clause.

> My son, keep your father's
>   commandments,
> Do not forsake your mother's teaching.

Grammar has many facets and any one of them can be brought into play in parallelism.

Another form of equivalence is semantic equivalence; the meaning of the lines is somehow related: perhaps synonymous, perhaps reflecting the converse or reverse (sometimes called antithetical), or perhaps extending the meaning in any one of a number of ways. Equivalence does not imply identity. The second line of a parallelism rarely repeats exactly the same words or exactly the same thought as the first; it is more likely to echo, expand, or intensify the idea in the first line in any one of a number of ways. For example,

> Women in Zion they raped;
> Maidens in the towns of Judah (Lam
> 5.11).

The parallelism intensifies from "women" (women in general) to "maidens" (women of marriageable age), making the second line a more poignant image of rape. It expands from "Zion" to "towns of Judah," making the atrocity more widespread—not only in the capital but throughout the country. Such intensification of the first line by the second is common.

Grammatical and semantic equivalence account for most parallelisms (both are present in Lam. 5.11), but because there are so many equivalent permutations for any given line, the number of potential parallelisms is enormous, if not infinite. By shaping the parallel line, that is, by narrowing the potential choice to a single statement, the poet clarifies the first line and moves the poem forward. Compare, for example, two couplets that differ in only one word:

> But you, O LORD, are enthroned forever,
> Your *fame* endures throughout the ages
> (Ps. 102.12)

> But you, O LORD, are enthroned forever,
> Your *throne* endures through the ages
> (Lam. 5.19).

Both verses open with the image of God enthroned as a king. The slight difference in their second lines changes the thrust of the thought in their first lines. Ps. 102 is concerned with God's permanence, which it contrasts with the fleeting life of humans; it therefore focuses on God's fame, literally, the mention of His name, symbolizing His being. Lamentations has a different concern: the existence of God when He has no Temple, no earthly locus for divine worship, no earthly throne to symbolize His kingship. The author of Lamentations claims that God's throne is independent of the Temple and continues to exist despite the loss of the Temple. In parallelisms like these, the first line presents a picture and the second line shines a spotlight on a certain part of it.

Parallelism helps to bind together the otherwise paratactic lines. In this sense it works as a counterweight to the parataxis, creating a relationship between the lines that is otherwise unexpressed. The basic structuring unit of the poem is not a single line, but a set of parallel lines (a two-line set is sometimes called a couplet or a bi-colon, and a three-line set is a tri-colon), as these examples demonstrate.

Another by-product of parallelism is the balance that it creates. Scholars have long sought metrical regularity in biblical poetry, but no metrical system—be it syllable counting, stress counting, thought-rhythm, or constraints on the number of syntactic units in a line—has met with unanimous acceptance. If biblical poetry has a metrical system, it has been eluding us for 2,000 years. More likely, the ancient Hebrew poets embraced a looser system—one in which many lines of a poem are more or less the same length and partake of the rhythm of their parallelism, but without the requirement of precise measurement.

Beyond the level of sets of parallel lines it is possible to find larger structural units, sometimes called strophes or stanzas. These are not units of a required number of lines, but merely a subdivision of a poem, not indicated formally, that modern readers make on the basis of the poem's contents or its structural or lexical repetitions. Some translations indicate subdivisions by leaving space between sections. The strophe is less well-defined than a couplet, and less basic to the overall poetic structure. The principles whereby couplets are combined into longer segments or entire poems is not well understood, but it is clear that poems have movement and development, and that their lines and couplets cohere as unified compositions. A dramatic example is the "scene" at the end of the Song of Deborah (considered to be one of the oldest poems in the Bible), with a dialogue in which Sisera's mother answers her own question (Judg. 5.28–30).

> Through the window peered Sisera's
>   mother,
> Behind the lattice she whined:
> "Why is his chariot so long in coming?
> Why so late the clatter of his wheels?"
> The wisest of her ladies give answer;
> She, too, replies to herself:
> "They must be dividing the spoil they
>   have found:
> A damsel or two for each man,
> Spoil of dyed cloths for Sisera,
> Spoil of embroidered cloths,
> A couple of embroidered cloths
> Round every neck as spoil."

In these verses some words repeat while others are echoed by words related in meaning. Redundancy is raised to an art-form. The terse lines—snapshots, as it were—grow into a larger moving picture as we imagine, through the eyes of Sisera's mother, that Sisera is bedecking himself with damsels and beautiful cloths obtained as the spoils of war (even as we know all the while that he lies dead in Jael's tent).

The unity of a poem is sometimes, but far from always, promoted by a formal device like an acrostic, an inclusio, or a refrain. Occasionally, an alphabetic acrostic forms the unifying structure of a poem, marking it as ordered and complete, from A to Z. Acrostics may have served also as a pedagogic or mnemonic device. Alphabetic acrostics (sometimes incomplete) are present in Pss. 9–10, 25, 34, 37, 111, 112, 119, 145; Prov. 31.10–31; Lam.

chs 1–4. A more common unifying device is "inclusio" (also called inclusion, frame, envelope, or ring-composition), in which the poem begins and ends with a similar line, as in Ps. 104.1 and 35: "Bless the LORD, O my soul." Compare also Ps. 8.2, 10: "O LORD, our LORD, how majestic is Your name throughout the earth." Inclusio provides a strong sense of closure to a poem. Less common is refrain, the repetition of a chorus-like line which, in the case of psalms, may have been sung antiphonally (e.g., Ps. 136); sometimes refrains are not repeated exactly.

We can see terseness and parallelism in operation, as well as larger structuring devices, in a segment of Psalm 136. The segment also illustrates how poetry differs from prose, since it is a poetic rendering of a prose narrative in the Torah.

> Who made the heavens with wisdom
>   His steadfast love is eternal;
> Who spread the earth over the water,
>   His steadfast love is eternal;
> Who made the great lights,
>   His steadfast love is eternal;
> the sun to dominate the day,
>   His steadfast love is eternal;
> the moon and the stars to dominate the
>   night,
>   His steadfast love is eternal (Ps.
>   136.5–9).

Immediately evident is the refrain, which unambiguously separates each line of poetry, and also gives cohesion to the whole, as well as rhythm. Even in English translation (and more so in Hebrew) each line seems terse, and about the same length, so that reading the lines one after another creates a rhythm, although not a precise meter. Compare the Genesis account of the creation of the celestial bodies that the psalm encapsulates in vv. 7–9: "God made the two great lights, the greater light to dominate the day and the lesser light to dominate the night, and the stars" (Gen. 1.16). The prose account also has parallelism, but it is not as obvious or as pervasive as in the psalm. The psalm has broken up the prose verse into poetic lines, by the use of, and clearly marked by, the refrain.

In addition to terseness and parallelism, biblical poems may employ the repetition and patterning of words and sound clusters, sometimes producing word- or soundplay. An ABBA or chiastic word pattern occurs in Song of Songs 2.14:

> Let me see your *face*, let me hear your
> *voice*;
> for your *voice* is sweet, and your *face* is
> comely.

A classic example of soundplay is found in Isa. 5.7:

> *vayekav lemishpat vehineh mispaḥ litzdakah ve-hineh tzeʿakah*, "And he hoped for justice, but behold injustice; for equity, but behold, iniquity."

(Cf. also Isa. 61.3; Zeph. 2.4.) Repeated words may be key words, words that recur often and point to the message of the poem; for example, in Ps. 121 the word "guard/guardian" occurs six times within the eight verses of the psalm, and indeed the psalm is about God as Israel's guardian. In Ps. 122 the topic is Jerusalem, and the name of the city occurs three times. In addition, combinations of the letters that make up the name "Jerusalem" occur frequently throughout the poem; many words in the poem echo Jerusalem's name.

These are a few samplings of the myriad repetitions of words and sounds that enhance the poeticalness of biblical poetry, and often its rhetorical force as well. Poetry is an auditory medium. Sound—be it the repetition of sounds or the rhythm of lines—and the nexus of sound and meaning contribute to the heightening of the discourse and to the effect on the listener. Poetry is related to music. The psalms were probably recited or sung to musical accompaniment, as were other poems (cf. Exod. 15.20–21; Ps. 137.2). Musical instruments are called *kelei shir*, "instruments of song/poetry" (Neh. 12.36). David, the psalmist par excellence (according to tradition), is a musician (1 Sam. 16.23). At the same time, po-

etry *(shir)* is associated with "speaking, reciting" (Ps. 137.3; Judg. 5.12.) The combination of music and words, sound and meaning, is epitomized in poetry.

No discussion of poetry can omit imagery, or metaphor, often thought to be the essence of poetry. It is not merely a question of inserting metaphors here and there for decoration; imagery, like parallelism, is pervasive in poetry. Poetry envisions the world metaphorically; it offers an alternative way of seeing reality. As medieval Jewish scholars put it, "The best part of poetry is its falseness (that is, its figurativeness)." (They got this idea from Arabic sources, who in turn got it from Aristotle.) Poetry, in this view, is not only elevated language, it is elevated vision.

A small example is in Ps. 136.6. We looked at this psalm earlier, noting how it poeticizes the creation story in Gen. ch 1. But the poetry of Ps. 136 is not merely a matter of breaking up prose sentences into terse, parallelistic poetic lines; it is a matter of re-envisioning the account of creation. Ps. 136.6 says that God "spread (Heb *rokaʿ*) the earth over the water." Genesis does not say this; in fact, according to Gen. 1.9, the water was gathered to one place so the dry land could appear—the land was actually under the water, visible when the water was removed. Moreover, the word that the psalm uses for "spread" is the same word that Genesis uses for "firmament." The psalmist has a different conception, or a different interpretation, of how the world was created. He sees the earth being spread, like a firmament, upon the water. The earth is a firm expanse set permanently in place over the waters (the forces of chaos, which cannot now escape); the earth is made analogous to the firmament of Genesis that separates the upper and lower waters. The psalm's conception of the creation of the earth is more mythological than that of Genesis, more like, for instance, Ps. 24.2: "He founded it [the world] upon the ocean, set it on the nether-streams." Poetry can retain more mythological concepts than prose, not because it is earlier or more primitive (Ps. 136 is probably exilic, after 586 BCE), but because it is free to call upon more imaginative views of the universe than can be tolerated in the "logical" or "theological" discourse of prose.

Metaphor, rather like parallelism, juxtaposes similarities and differences in such a way that a relationship between them is created. In metaphor, two things that do not generally occur together are brought together; they collide, or explode, leaving in their wake a new way of seeing. Metaphors come in many shapes and sizes. Some take but a line, others inform an entire poem. Some are deeply embedded in the culture of Israel, like the parent-child relationship or the husband-wife relationship used to portray the relationship between God and Israel; others may be the new creation of the poet; and still others may be "dead metaphors," commonplace idioms that have lost their impact. Much of the difficulty in understanding poetry arises from the difficulty in recognizing what is metaphoric (and what is not) and in perceiving the meaning of the metaphor.

Ps. 133.1: "How good and pleasant it is that brothers dwell together," contains a metaphor that is often overlooked. The verb "dwell together," *shevet yaḥad*, is a legal term that means to live in joint tenancy; that is, to hold land in joint ownership without dividing it up among separate owners (cf. Gen. 13.6; 36.7; Deut. 25.5). The psalm is not about harmonious family life (a common reading based on a misunderstanding of the verb and adverb), but is about brothers holding land together. This is a metaphor for the (re)unification of Israel and Judah, as observed in *Metzudat David*, an 18th century commentary written by David Altschuler (and printed in most editions of *Miqra'ot Gedolot*), which explains:

How very good and how very pleasant is the thing when the whole house of Israel will dwell on its land; they are called "brothers" for the great affection that is among them. . . . And they will be together in one kingship and will not be divided into two kingdoms any more.

Metaphors, again like parallelisms, can have many permutations. A common metaphor for human beings is a tree, with its leaves and fruit. The water that nourishes the tree/person is God's *torah* or trust in God. Prov. 11.28 and 30 capture the idea in pithy statements: "The righteous shall flourish like foliage" and "The fruit of the righteous is a tree of life." More embellishment is found in the following examples.

The righteous bloom like a date-palm;
they thrive like a cedar in Lebanon;
planted in the house of the LORD,
they flourish in the courts of our God.
In old age they still produce fruit;
they are full of sap and freshness (Ps. 92.13–15).

The image is of beauty and stature; the date-palm has beautiful flowers and the cedars of Lebanon are tall and massive. They are also long-lived trees, and the righteous will be similarly long-lived, vigorous in old age.

More famous is the tree imagery in Ps. 1.3, applied to the man who delights in God's teaching *(torah)*.

He will be like a tree planted beside
water channels,
which produces its fruit in its season,
and whose foliage does not wither;
And all that he does will succeed (author's translation).

Just as the tree is nourished by water, more specifically, by irrigation canals that provide a constant supply of water, so the man is continually nourished by God's teaching *(torah)*, a constant source of life, which he studies day and night (v. 2). Just as the tree flourishes and accomplishes its purpose in life, so will the man succeed in his purpose. The rootedness and productiveness of the righteous man is contrasted with the transience and worthlessness of the wicked, who are like the chaff, the husks that are blown away in the winnowing process.

There may be a further implication in the description of the tree's fruit and foliage, if they are taken not merely as an enhancement of the tree image but as part of the analogy between the man and the tree. The man, like the tree, will have fruit (= children) in its season (year after year) and unwithering foliage (= a long life). Children and long life are the ideal blessing in ancient Israel (cf. Job 42.16–17), and that blessing is achieved, says the psalm, through devotion to God's teaching.

Often compared to Ps. 1 is Jer. 17.5–8, which contrasts the man who trusts in humans with the man who trusts in God. The former will be like a tamarisk, a desert shrub with small, narrow leaves.

> He shall be like a tamarisk in the desert,
> which does not sense when good
>   (= rain) comes.
> It dwells in the parched wilderness,
> in salt-lands, without inhabitants.
> As for the man who trusts in God,
> He will be like a tree planted beside
>   water,
> sending forth its roots by a stream.
> It does not sense when heat comes,
> Its leaves remain fresh,
> And in a drought year it does not worry;
> It does not cease to produce fruit.
>   (author's translation)

The man who trusts in humans lives in a permanent desert, without nourishment; even when a bit of water reaches him, he cannot make use of it. On the other hand, the man who trusts in God is constantly nourished, and because he has sunk his roots deep into water sources, he can easily survive a drought with no loss of productivity.

These tree metaphors show how the same basic image may be altered or embellished to fit different contexts. Now let us see how the same concept may be conveyed through different images. Wisdom is an abstract concept that is expressed metaphorically in different ways in Proverbs and in Job. Prov. 1.20–33 personifies Wisdom as a woman calling aloud in the public square, scolding those who reject her and warning them that she will be gleeful when they fail in life (cf. also Prov. chs 8–9).

Lady Wisdom, while not quite a prostitute, is certainly advertising her availability and urging everyone to pay heed to her. This is firmly in keeping with the main purpose of the book of Proverbs, to provide Wisdom to everyone so that all may prosper.

Job, on the other hand, has a very different notion of Wisdom. Wisdom is desirable but elusive, unattainable. Job ch 28 compares it to precious metals and gems hidden in deep mines, showing that Wisdom is more precious than metals and gems and more difficult to find. Like the other poems in Job, this chapter employs difficult language and develops its images in detail. It opens with a picture of metal mining, deep in the dark earth, far from human habitation, where men dig shafts to retrieve ore. Especially evocative are vv. 5–6:

> Earth, out of which food grows,
> Is changed below as if into fire.
> Its rocks are a source of sapphires;
> It contains gold dust too.

The world below the surface is a very different place from the world above. Above is the soil that provides bread, below is a hot colorful fantasy-world of potential riches. The poem moves on to its main point, that, unlike any other creature—even the sharp-eyed birds of prey and the hunter par excellence, the lion—humans are capable of finding these sources of wealth; and by prodigious construction projects—overturning mountains and carving out channels through rock (vv. 10–11)—they extract these precious ores and bring them to the surface, "so that hidden things may be brought to light" (v. 11). This last phrase is, of course, suggestive of more intangible "hidden things" that need to be brought to light, and it leads directly to the main topic: Wisdom.

> But where can wisdom be found?
> Where is the place of understanding?
>   (v. 12).

Humans may be able to bring hidden treasures from under the ground to light, but they are not able to find wisdom, the greatest treasure of all. The link between the first section (v. 1) and the second section (v. 12) is forged by the repetition of two words.

There is a source *(motza')* for silver
And a place *(makom)* where gold is
    refined (v. 1).

But where can wisdom be found
    (timatze');
Where is the place *(makom)* of
    understanding? (v. 12).

Verses 13–19 echo the first section by saying that no one can put a price on wisdom; its value is beyond all the precious materials in the world. Moreover, its location is not anywhere in the natural world, nor even in the mythological world of the "deep" and the "sea" (the primordial waters).

Where, then, does wisdom come from? asks the third section of the poem (vv. 20–28).

It is hidden from the eyes of all living,
Concealed from the fowl of the sky.
Abbadon and Death say,
"With our ears we have heard a rumor
    of it" (vv. 21–22, author's
    translation).

A number of parallels are invoked: earth, sky, and the netherworld; the living and the dead; eyes and ears and seeing and hearing—to the effect that no creature, earthly or not, alive or dead, anywhere in the cosmos, has perceived Wisdom.

Only God knows where it is and how to reach it, for He is all-seeing, and in the course of creating the world He saw and gauged Wisdom. The poet here borrows the well-known idea that Wisdom was present at creation—compare Prov. 8.22–31. But the picture of creation in vv. 25–26 is not at all like Gen. ch 1, or like Ps. 136, or even like Prov. ch 8.

When He fixed the weight of the winds,
Set the measure of the waters;
When He made a rule for the rain
And a course for the thunderstorms.
    (Job 28.25–26)

This description focuses on God's power over meteorological, or mythological forces. The creation is not centered on the earth, or below the earth where the mines are (where men can penetrate to), or in the watery deep, or in the realm of Death (below the ground), but far above the earth, the place of wind and water. Wisdom was and remains in the domain of God, not in the domain of human beings. How, then, can humans achieve wisdom? Only through the fear of the Lord (v. 28). "Fear of the Lord" is the essence of wisdom according to most biblical conceptions, but Job ch 28 puts that principle in a special light.

It is not easy to sum up what biblical poetry is. More than just a set of formal features or structures, poetry is sound and vision compressed for intensity and expressed with potency. Biblical poetry struggles to probe and stretch the important cultural concepts and issues of ancient Israel in exquisitely distilled Hebrew. In that sense, it is the purest, most rarefied, expression of biblical thought.

[ADELE BERLIN]

Weights and Measures

Modern equivalents for biblical weights and measures are presented in the following tables.

WEIGHTS

HEBREW	NJPS	EQUIVALENCE	U.S. AVOIRDUPOIS	METRIC UNITS
kikar	talent	60 minas	75.558 pounds	34.3 kilograms
maneh	mina	50 shekels	20.148 ounces	571.2 grams
shekel	shekel	2 bekas	176.29 grains	11.42 grams
pim (or payim)	pim	.667 shekel	117.52 grains	7.61 grams
beka'	half-shekel	10 gerahs	88.14 grains	5.71 grams
gerah	gerah		8.81 grains	.57 gram

The practice of weighing unmarked ingots of metal used in commercial transactions prior to the invention of money explains that the names of the units of weight were used later as indications of value, and as names for monetary standards.

LENGTH MEASURES

HEBREW	NJPS	EQUIVALENCE	U.S. MEASURES	METRIC UNITS
'amah	cubit	2 spans	17.49 inches	.443 meter
zeret	span	3 handbreadths	8.745 inches	.221 meter
tofaḥ, tefaḥ	handbreadth, hand's breadth	4 fingers	2.915 inches	.074 meter
'etzba'	finger		0.728 inch	.019 meter

The cubit described in Ezekiel 40.5; 43.13 is equal to seven (not six) handbreadths, namely 20.405 inches.

CAPACITY: LIQUID MEASURES

HEBREW	NJPS	EQUIVALENCE	U.S. MEASURES	METRIC UNITS
kor	kor	10 baths	60.738 gallons	230 liters
bat	bath	6 hins	6.073 gallons	23 liters
hin	hin	3 kabs	1.012 gallons	3.829 liters
kav	kab	4 logs	1.4349 quarts	1.276 liters
log	log		0.674 pint	.32 liter

CAPACITY: DRY MEASURES

HEBREW	NJPS	EQUIVALENCE	U.S. MEASURES	METRIC UNITS
ḥomer	homer	2 lethechs	6.524 bushels	229.7 liters
kor	kor	2 lethechs	6.524 bushels	229.7 liters
letekh	lethech	5 ephahs	3.262 bushels	114.8 liters
'efah	ephah, measure	3 seahs	20.878 quarts	22.9 liters
se'ah	seah	3.33 omers	6.959 quarts	7.7 liters
'omer	omer	1.8 kabs	2.087 quarts	2.3 liters
'isaron	tenth of a measure	.1 ephah	2.087 quarts	2.3 liters
kav	kab		1.159 quarts	1.3 liters

Timeline*

DATE	PERIOD	EGYPT
Ca. 3300–2000 BCE	EARLY BRONZE AGE	
3300–3100	Early Bronze I	Earliest forms of writing
3100–2700	Early Bronze II	Political unification; Early Dynastic period
2700–2300	Early Bronze III	Old Kingdom; Dynasties 3–5
2300–2000	Early Bronze IV	First Intermediate Period
Ca. 2000–1550 BCE	MIDDLE BRONZE AGE	
2000–1650	Middle Bronze I–II	Middle Kingdom; Dynasties 11–12
1650–1550	Middle Bronze III	Second Intermediate/ Hyksos Period
Ca. 1550–1200 BCE	LATE BRONZE AGE	New Kingdom; Dynasties 18–19: Thutmose III (1479–1425), Akenhaten (1352–1336), Seti I (1294–1279), Rameses II (1279–1213), Merneptah (1213–1203); Sea Peoples (groups including Philistines) invasions begin
Ca. 1200–586 BCE	IRON AGE	
Ca. 1200–1025	Iron I	Rameses III (1184–1153)**
Ca. 1025–586	Iron II	
Ca. 1025–928	Iron IIA	
Ca. 928–722	Iron IIB	Shishak I invades Palestine (925)

* Many dates before 1000 BCE are highly uncertain.
** For a more complete list of rulers, see "Chronological Table of Rulers," pp. 2110–2113.

LAND OF ISRAEL	MESOPOTAMIA, ASIA MINOR
	Earliest forms of writing; Full urbanization; Sumerian culture develops
In Egyptian sphere	High point of Sumerian culture
Flourishing city-states	Sargon of Akkad; Naram-Sin of Akkad; Gudea of Lagash
Decline/abandonment of city-states	Third Dynasty of Ur
Revival of urbanism; Invention of alphabet	Amorite kingdoms: Shamshi-Adad of Assyria (ca. 1813–1781); Hammurabi of Babylon (ca. 1792–1750); Rise of Hittites
In Egyptian sphere; Rise of Mitanni in north; Ugarit flourishes; Presence of Israel in land of Israel	Hittites challenge Egypt for control of Western Asia
Collapse of city-states	Hittite empire collapses; Trojan War
Israel emerges in Canaan; Philistines settle on SW coast; Small city-states develop in Phoenicia, Aram, Transjordan	Resurgence of Assyria: Tiglath-pileser I (1114–1076)
United monarchy in Israel: Saul (1025–1005); David (1005–965); Solomon (968–928)	

Divided monarchy:

JUDAH:	ISRAEL:	
Rehoboam (928–911)	Jeroboam I (928–907)	Rise of Neo-Assyrian empire
	Omri (882–871); Capital at Samaria	Shalmaneser III (858–824); Battle of Qarqar (853)
	Ahab (873–852)	
Jehoshaphat (867–846)	Prophet Elijah (mid-9th century)	
	Prophet Elisha (mid- to late 9th century)	
Athaliah (842–836)	Jehu (842–814)	
Jehoash (836–798)	Jehoash (800–788)	Adad-nirari III (811–783)
	Jeroboam II (788–747)	
	Prophet Amos (mid-8th century)	
	Prophet Hosea (mid-8th century)	Tiglath-pileser III (745–727); Assyrian conquest of the Levant
Ahaz (743/735–727/715)	Hoshea (732–722)	Shalmaneser V (727–722) Samaria captured (722)

DATE	PERIOD	EGYPT
Ca. 722–586	Iron IIC	
		Egypt conquered by Assyria (671) Psammetichus I (664–610)
		Neco II (610–595)
Ca. 586–539	NEO-BABYLONIAN	

		GREECE AND ROME
539–333	PERSIAN	Greeks repel Persian invasions
		Peloponnesian War (431–404)
333–63	HELLENISTIC	Alexander the Great (336–323); Defeats Persians at Issus (332); Occupies the Levant and Egypt
		Rome gains control over Greece (ca. 188–146)
		Sack of Carthage and Corinth (146)
63 BCE–330 CE	ROMAN	Julius Caesar named dictator (49); assassinated (44) Octavian (Augustus) defeats Antony at Actium (31); (Emperor 27 BCE–14 CE) Tiberius (14–37 CE) Gaius (Caligula) (37–41) Claudius (41–54) Nero (54–68) Vespasian (69–79) Titus (79–81) Domitian (81–96) Nerva (96–98) Trajan (98–117) Hadrian (117–138)

LAND OF ISRAEL	MESOPOTAMIA, ASIA MINOR
JUDAH: Prophet Isaiah (late 8th to early 7th centuries) Prophet Micah (late 8th century) Hezekiah (727/715–698/687) Manasseh (698/687–642) Josiah (639–609) Prophet Zephaniah (late 7th century) Prophet Jeremiah (late 7th–early 6th centuries) Jehoahaz (609) Jehoiakim (608–598) Jehoiachin (597) Prophet Ezekiel (early 6th century) Zedekiah (597–586); Capture of Jerusalem (586)	Sargon II (722–705) Sennacherib (705–681); Attack on Judah and seige of Jerusalem (701) Esarhaddon (681–669) Ashurbanipal (669–627) Rise of Babylonia Assyrian capital of Nineveh captured (612) Nebuchadrezzar II (604–562) of Babylonia

Nabonidus (556–539)

EASTERN MEDITERRANEAN	
Some exiles return from Babylonia (538) Second Temple built (520–515) Prophet Haggai (520); Prophet Zechariah (520–518) Nehemiah governor of Judah (ca. 445–430) Mission of Ezra the scribe (mid-5th [or early 4th] century)	Cyrus II (the Great) (559–530); Capture of Babylon (539) Cambyses (530–522); Capture of Egypt (525) Darius I (522–486) Xerxes I (486–465) Artaxerxes I (465–424) Artaxerxes II (405–359)

Seleucus I (312/311–281) controls Syria and Mesopotamia
Ptolemy I (323–282) controls Egypt, Palestine, Phoenicia
Antiochus III (223–187) gains control of southern Syria,
  Phoenicia, and Judea from Ptolemy IV (202–198)
Ben Sira (Sirach) (early 2nd century)
Antiochus IV Epiphanes (175–164)
Revolt of the Maccabees (167–164)

HASMONEAN RULE OF JUDEA (165–37):
John Hyrcanus (135–104); Alexander Janneus (103–76);
Salome Alexandra (76–67)

Pompey conquers the Levant (66–62); Enters Jerusalem (63)
Herod the Great king of Judea (37–4);
  Rebuilds Second Temple

First Jewish Revolt in Judea against Rome (66–73);
Jerusalem is captured; Second Temple destroyed (70)

Jewish revolts in Egypt, Libya, Cyprus (115–118)
Second Jewish Revolt in Judea against Rome (132–135)

Chronological Table of Rulers

DATE	EGYPT	ASSYRIA	BABYLONIA
1300 BCE	DYNASTY 19 (1295–1186): Seti I (1294–1279) Rameses II (1279–1213) Merneptah (1213–1203)		
1200	DYNASTY 20 (1186–1069)		
		Tiglath-pileser I (1114–1076)	
	DYNASTY 21 (1069–945)		
1000			
	DYNASTIES 22–24 (945–715): Shoshenq I **(Shishak)** (945–924)		
		Shalmaneser III (858–824)	
		Shamshi-Adad V (824–811)	
	DYNASTY 25 (780–656):		
800		Adad-nirari III (811–783)	
		Shalmaneser IV (783–773)	
		Ashur-dan III (773–755) Ashur-nirari V (755–745) **Tiglath-pileser III (Pul)** (745–727) **Shalmaneser** V (727–722) Sargon II (722–705) **Sennacherib** (705–681) **Esarhaddon** (681–669) Ashurbanipal (669–627) Ashur-etil-ilani Sin-shum-lishir } (627–612) Sin-shar-ishkun Ashur-uballit II (612–609)	Marduk-apal-iddina II **(Merodach-baladan)** (721–710, 703)
700	Taharqa **(Tirhakah)** (690–664)		
	DYNASTY 26 (664–525):		
	Psammetichus I (664–610) Neco II (610–595) Psammetichus II (595–589) Apries **(Hophra)** (589–570) Amasis II (570–526) Psammetichus III (526–525)		Nabo-polassar (625–605) **Nebuchadrezzar** II **(Nebuchadnezzar)** (605–562) Amel-Marduk **(Evil-merodach)** (562–560) Neriglissar (560–556) Labashi-Marduk (556) **Nabonidus** (556–539) **Belshazzar** (co-regent 553–543)
400			

325 BCE

Note: Names in boldface occur in the Tanakh. Overlapping dates indicate co-regencies. Date ranges are reigns, not life spans. Many dates are uncertain or approximations.

DATE	PERSIA	ISRAEL
1300 BCE		
1200		

UNITED MONARCHY:
Saul (1025–1005); **David** (1005–965); **Solomon (Yedidiah)** (968–928)

DIVIDED MONARCHY:

	JUDAH:	ISRAEL:
1000	**Rehoboam** (928–911)	**Jeroboam I** (928–907)
	Abijam (Abijah) (911–908)	**Nadab** (907–906)
	Asa (908–867)	**Baasha** (906–883)
	Jehoshaphat (870–846)	**Elah** (883–882); **Zimri** (882)
		Omri (882–871)
	Jehoram (Joram) (851–843)	**Ahab** (873–852)
		Ahaziah (852–851)
	Ahaziah (Jehoahaz) (843–842)	**Jehoram (Joram)** (851–842)
	Athaliah (842–836)	**Jehu** (842–814)
800	**Jehoash** (Joash) (836–798)	**Jehoahaz** (817–800)
	Amaziah (798–769)	**Jehoash (Joash)** (800–784)
	Azariah (Uzziah) (785–733)	**Jeroboam II** (788–747)
		Zechariah (747); **Shallum** (747)
		Menahem (747–737)
		Pekahiah (737–735)
	Jotham (759–743)	**Pekah** (735–732)
	Ahaz (743/735–727/715)*	**Hoshea** (732–722)
	Hezekiah (727/715–698/687)*	
700	**Manasseh** (698/687–642)*	
	Amon (641–640)	
	Josiah (640–609)	
	Jehoahaz (Shallum) (609)	
	Jehoiakim (Eliakim) (608–598)	
	Jehoiachin (Jeconiah, etc.) (597)	
	Zedekiah (Mattaniah) (597–586)	
	Cyrus II (559–530)	
	Cambyses (530–522)	
	Darius I (522–486)	
	Xerxes I **(Ahasuerus)** (486–465)	
	Artaxerxes I (465–424)	
	Darius II (423–405)	
400	Artaxerxes II (405–359)	
	Artaxerxes III (359–338)	
	Artaxerxes IV (338–336)	
	Darius III (336–330)	
325 BCE		

*Data are inconsistent for the dates of the reigns of Ahaz, Hezekiah, and Manasseh.

DATE	EGYPT	SYRIA
	HELLENISTIC PERIOD	Alexander (the Great) (336–323)
300 BCE	Ptolemy I Soter (305–282)	Seleucus I Nicator (305–281)
	Ptolemy II Philadelphus (285–246)	Antiochus I Soter (281–261)
		Antiochus II Theos (261–246)
	Ptolemy III Euergetes (246–221)	Seleucus II Callinicus (246–225)
	Ptolemy IV Philopator (221–204)	Seleucus III Soter Ceraunos (225–223)
	Ptolemy V Epiphanes (204–180);	Antiochus III (the Great) (223–187)
	Cleopatra I (180–176)	Seleucus IV Philopator (187–175)
		Antiochus IV Epiphanes (175–164)
	Ptolemy VI Philometor (180–145);	Antiochus V Eupator (164–162)
	Cleopatra II (175–116)	Demetrius I Soter (162–150)
	Ptolemy VII Neos Philopator (145)	Alexander Epiphanes (Balas) (150–145)
	Ptolemy VIII Euergetes II Physcon (170–116)	Demetrius II Nicator (145–141 and 129–125)
		Antiochus VI Epiphanes (145–142)
		Trypho (142–138)
		Antiochus VII Sidetes (138–129)
		Cleopatra Thea (126–121)
		Antiochus VIII Grypus (125–121 and 121–96)
	Cleopatra III (116–101)	Seleucus V (125)
	Ptolemy IX Soter II (116–107 AND 88–80)	Antiochus IX Cyzicenus (115–95)
100 BCE	Ptolemy X Alexander I (107–88)	Seleucus VI (95)
		Antiochus X Eusebes (95–83)
		Antiochus XI Philadelphus (95)
	Cleopatra Berenice (101–88)	Demetrius III Eukairos (95–88)
		Philip I Epiphanes Philadelphus (95–84)
	Ptolemy XI Alexander II (80)	Antiochus XII Dionysus Epiphanes (87–84)
		Philip II (67–66)
	Ptolemy XII Auletes (80–59 and 55–51)	Antiochus XIII Asiaticus (69–68 and 65–64)
50 BCE	Cleopatra VII (51–30)	
	Ptolemy XIII (51–47)	
	Ptolemy XIV (47–44)	
25 CE		
50 CE		
100 CE		

DATE	ROMAN EMPIRE	LAND OF ISRAEL

— 300 BCE

— 100 BCE

— 50 BCE

— 25 CE

— 50 CE

— 100 CE

*In 41 Judea was made part of the kingdom of Herod Agrippa I,
grandson of Herod the Great (see Herodian Dynasty, above). At
his death in 44 it became a province again.

Calendar

The year was composed of twelve lunar months (beginning on the day of the new moon), with an intercalary month added periodically (see perhaps 1 Kings 12.33). In some traditions, and perhaps originally, the year began in the fall, at the autumnal equinox (see Exod. 23.16; 34.22). In others, following Babylonian practice, the new year was celebrated in the spring. The fall new year became standard in postbiblical Judaism.

Months in the Bible are usually identified by ordinal numbers, beginning with the spring new year. Some months (in boldface in the following list) are also designated with names derived either from a Canaanite calendar or, in postexilic texts, from a Babylonian one; the names of months not found in the Bible are known from other ancient sources.

	CANAANITE NAME	BABYLONIAN/ARAMAIC NAME	MODERN EQUIVALENT
First	**'Aviv**	**Nisan**	March–April
Second	**Ziv**	'Iyar	April–May
Third		**Sivan**	May–June
Fourth		Tamuz	June–July
Fifth		'Av	July–August
Sixth		**'Elul**	August–September
Seventh	**'Etanim**	Tishri	September–October
Eighth	**Bul**	Marḥeshvan	October–November
Ninth		Kislev	November–December
Tenth		**Tevet**	December–January
Eleventh		**Shevat**	January–February
Twelfth		**'Adar**	February–March

The Jewish calendar is based on the lunar month, which is a bit longer than 29½ days, so Jewish lunar months are 29 or 30 days long. Twelve lunar months usually amount to 354 days, 11 days short of a solar year. In order for the festivals to stay in the correct season in relation to the solar year, an extra month is added every few years. Following ancient Babylonian models, the calendar runs on a 19-year cycle: years 3, 6, 8,11, 14, 17, and 19 of the cycle are intercalated or "leap" years, containing an extra month of Adar, sometimes called *Adar Sheni* (second Adar). Adar was chosen for intercalation because it is the last month of the Babylonian year and of the biblical year beginning in Nisan (an alternate calendar, the one now in use, begins the year in Tishri with Rosh Ha-Shanah). The next 19-year intercalation cycle will begin in 5768 (2007–2008 CE).

Observances fall within the calendar as follows:

Rosh Ha-Shanah (the New Year)	1-2 Tishri
Yom Kippur (the Day of Atonement)	10 Tishri
Sukkot (Booths) begins	15 Tishri
Hanukkah begins	25 Kislev
Purim	14 Adar (15 Adar in Jerusalem and other ancient walled cities)
Passover begins	15 Nisan
Shavuot (Weeks) begins	6 Sivan
Tish'ah be' av	9 Av

Table of Biblical Readings

	TORAH		NEVI'IM

WEEKLY SABBATH READINGS

Genesis

בראשית	Bere'shit	1.1–6.8	Isaiah 42.5–43.10 (42.5–21)*
נח	Noaḥ	6.9–11.32	Isaiah 54.1–55.5 (54.1–10)
לך לך	Lekh Lekha	12.1–17.27	Isaiah 40.27–41.16
וירא	Va-yera'	18.1–22.24	2 Kings 4.1–37 (4.1–23)
חיי שרה	Ḥayyei Sarah	23.1–25.18	1 Kings 1.1–31
תולדות	Toledot	25.19–28.9	Malachi 1.1–2.7
ויצא	Va-yetse'	28.10–32.3	Hosea 12.13–14.10 (11.7–12.12)
וישלח	Va-yishlaḥ	32.4–36.43	Hosea 11.7–12.12 (Obadiah 1.1–21)
וישב	Va-yeshev	37.1–40.23	Amos 2.6–3.8
מקץ	Mikkets	41.1–44.17	1 Kings 3.15–4.1
ויגש	Va-yiggash	44.18–47.27	Ezekiel 37.15–28
ויחי	Va-yeḥi	47.28–50.26	1 Kings 2.1–12

Exodus

שמות	Shemot	1.1–6.1	Isaiah 27.6–28.13; 29.22, 23 (Jeremiah 1.1–2.3)
וארא	Va-'era'	6.2–9.35	Ezekiel 28.25–29.21
בא	Bo'	10.1–13.16	Jeremiah 46.13–28
בשלח	Be-shallaḥ	13.17–17.16	Judges 4.4–5.31 (5.1–31)
יתרו	Yitro	18.1–20.26	Isaiah 6.1–7.6; 9.5, 6 (6.1–13)
משפטים	Mishpatim	21.1–24.18	Jeremiah 34.8–22; 33.25, 26
תרומה	Terumah	25.1–27.19	1 Kings 5.26–6.13
תצוה	Tetsavveh	27.20–30.10	Ezekiel 43.10–27
כי תשא	Ki Tissa'	30.11–34.35	1 Kings 18.1–39 (18.20–39)
ויקהל	Va-yakhel	35.1–38.20	1 Kings 7.40–50 (7.13–26)
פקודי	Pekudei	38.21–40.38	1 Kings 7.51–8.21 (7.40–50)

Leviticus

ויקרא	Va-yikra'	1.1–5.26	Isaiah 43.21–44.23
צו	Tsav	6.1–8.36	Jeremiah 7.21–8.3; 9.22, 23
שמיני	Shemini	9.1–11.47	2 Samuel 6.1–7.17 (6.1–19)
תזריע	Tazria'	12.1–13.59	2 Kings 4.42–5.19
מצרע	Metsora'	14.1–15.33	2 Kings 7.3–20
אחרי מות	'Aḥarei Mot	16.1–18.30	Ezekiel 22.1–19 (22.1–16)
קדשים	Kedoshim	19.1–20.27	Amos 9.7–15 (Ezekiel 20.2–20)

Local practice may differ from the selections listed.   *Parentheses indicate Sephardi ritual.

TORAH			NEVI'IM

Leviticus *(continued)*

אמר	'Emor	21.1–24.23	Ezekiel 44.15–31
בהר	Be-har	25.1–26.2	Jeremiah 32.6–27
בחקתי	Be-ḥukotai	26.3–27.34	Jeremiah 16.19–17.14

Numbers

במדבר	Be-midbar	1.1–4.20	Hosea 2.1–22
נשא	Naso'	4.21–7.89	Judges 13.2–25
בהעלתך	Be-ha'alotekha	8.1–12.16	Zechariah 2.14–4.7
שלח לך	Shelaḥ-Lekha	13.1–15.41	Joshua 2.1–24
קרח	Koraḥ	16.1–18.32	1 Samuel 11.14–12.22
חקת	Ḥukat	19.1–22.1	Judges 11.1–33
בלק	Balak	22.2–25.9	Micah 5.6–6.8
פינחס	Pinḥas	25.10–30.1	1 Kings 18.46–19.21
מטות	Matot	30.2–32.42	Jeremiah 1.1–2.3
מסעי	Mase'ei	33.1–36.13	Jeremiah 2.4–28; 3.4 (2.4–28; 4.1, 2)

Deuteronomy

דברים	Devarim	1.1–3.22	Isaiah 1.1–27
ואתחנן	Va-'etḥanan	3.23–7.11	Isaiah 40.1–26
עקב	'Ekev	7.12–11.25	Isaiah 49.14–51.3
ראה	Re'eh	11.26–16.17	Isaiah 54.11–55.5
שפטים	Shofetim	16.18–21.9	Isaiah 51.12–52.12
כי תצא	Ki Tetze'	21.10–25.19	Isaiah 54.1–10
כי תבוא	Ki Tavo'	26.1–29.8	Isaiah 60.1–22
נצבים	Nitzavim	29.9–30.20	Isaiah 61.10–63.9
וילך	Va-yelekh	31.1–30	—
האזינו	Ha'azinu	32.1–52	2 Samuel 22.1–51
וזאת הברכה	Ve-zo't Ha-berakhah	33.1–34.12	Joshua 1.1–18 (1.1–9)

READINGS FOR SPECIAL SABBATHS

Sabbath coinciding with Rosh Ḥodesh
    Weekly portion and Numbers 28.9–15   Isaiah 66.1–24

Sabbath immediately preceding Rosh Ḥodesh   Weekly portion   1 Samuel 20.18–42

Shekalim   Weekly portion and Exodus 30.11–16   2 Kings 12.1–17 (11.17–12.17)

Zakhor   Weekly portion and Deuteronomy 25.17–19   1 Samuel 15.2–34 (15.1–34)

Parah   Weekly portion and Numbers 19.1–22   Ezekiel 36.16–38 (36.16–36)

Ha-Ḥodesh   Weekly portion and Exodus 12.1–20   Ezekiel 45.16–46.18 (45.18–46.15)

Ha-Gadol   Weekly portion   Malachi 3.4–24

First Sabbath Hanukkah   Weekly portion plus the verses
          relating the prince (nasi') of the day   Zechariah 2.14–4.7
          corresponding to the day of Hanukkah

Second Sabbath Hanukkah   Weekly portion and Hanukkah   1 Kings 7.40–50
          portions as above

READINGS FOR THE DAYS OF AWE

Rosh Ha-Shanah

First Day	Genesis 21.1–34; Numbers 29.1–6	1 Samuel 1.1–2.10
Second Day	Genesis 22.1–24; Numbers 29.1–6	Jeremiah 31.2–20

TORAH	NEVI'IM
Sabbath Shuvah Weekly portion	Hosea 14.2–10; Micah 7.18–20; Joel 2.15–27 (Hosea 14.2–10; Micah 7.18–20)

Yom Kippur

	TORAH	NEVI'IM
Morning	Leviticus 16.1–34; Numbers 29.7–11	Isaiah 57.14–58.14
Afternoon	Leviticus 18.1–30	Jonah 1.1–4.11; Micah 7.18–20

READINGS FOR THE FESTIVALS

Sukkot (Tabernacles)

First Day	Leviticus 22.26–23.44; Numbers 29.12–16	Zechariah 14.1–21
Second Day	Leviticus 22.26–23.44; Numbers 29.12–16	1 Kings 8.2–21
Sabbath during the Middle Days Exodus 33.12–34.26;	Ezekiel 38.18–39.16
	Daily portion from Numbers 29	
Eighth Day	Deuteronomy 14.22–16.17 (15.19–16.17);	1 Kings 8.54–66
	Numbers 29.35–30.1	

Simḥat Torah	Deuteronomy 33.1–34.12; Genesis 1.1–2.3;	Joshua 1.1–18 (1.1–9)
	Numbers 29.35–30.1	

Pesaḥ (Passover)

First Day	Exodus 12.21–51; Numbers 28.16–25	Joshua 5.2–6.1; 6.27
Second Day	Leviticus 22.26–23.44; Numbers 28.16–25	2 Kings 23.1–9, 21–25
Sabbath during the Middle Days Exodus 33.12–34.26;	Ezekiel 37.1–14
	Numbers 28.19–25	
Seventh Day	Exodus 13.17–15.26; Numbers 28.19–25	2 Samuel 22.1–51
Eighth Day	Deuteronomy 15.19–16.17;	Isaiah 10.32–12.6
	Numbers 28.19–25	

Shavuot (Pentecost)

First Day	Exodus 19.1–20.23; Numbers 28.26–31	Ezekiel 1.1–28; 3.12
Second Day	Deuteronomy 15.19–16.17;*	Habakkuk 3.1–19 (2.20–3.19)
	Numbers 28.26–31	

READINGS ON WEEKDAY OCCASIONS

Purim	Exodus 17.8–16	—

Ninth of Av

Morning	Deuteronomy 4.25–40	Jeremiah 8.13–9.23
Afternoon	Exodus 32.11–14; 34.1–10	Isaiah 55.6–56.8

Public Fast Days

Morning	Exodus 32.11–14; 34.1–10	—
Afternoon	Exodus 32.11–14; 34.1–10	Isaiah 55.6–56.8

READINGS OF THE FIVE MEGILOT

The Song of Songs	Sabbath during Pesaḥ (Passover)
Ruth	Shavuot (Pentecost)
Lamentations	Ninth of Av
Ecclesiastes	Sabbath during Sukkot (Tabernacles)
Esther	Purim

* On the Sabbath, 14.22–16.17.

Chapter/Verse Differences

Chapter/verse differences between standard English numbering and Hebrew text numbering used in NJPS. Books are listed in Hebrew canonical order.

ENGLISH	HEBREW	ENGLISH	HEBREW	ENGLISH	HEBREW
Gen. 31.55	Gen. 32.1	Jer. 9.1	Jer. 8.23	Ps. 13.1–5	Ps. 13.2–6a
Gen. 32.1–32	Gen. 32.2–33	Jer. 9.2–26	Jer. 9.1–25	Ps. 13.6	Ps. 13.6b
Exod. 8.1–4	Exod. 7.26–29	Ezek. 20.45–49	Ezek. 21.1–5	Ps. 14. title	Ps. 14.1a
Exod. 8.5–32	Exod. 8.1–28	Ezek. 21.1–32	Ezek. 21.6–37	Ps. 15. title	Ps. 15.1a
Exod. 22.1	Exod. 21.37	Hos. 1.10–11	Hos. 2.1–2	Ps. 16. title	Ps. 16.1a
Exod. 22.2–31	Exod. 22.1–30	Hos. 2.1–23	Hos. 2.3–25	Ps. 17. title	Ps. 17.1a
Lev. 6.1–7	Lev. 5.20–26	Hos. 11.12	Hos. 12.1	Ps. 18. title	Ps. 18.1–2a
Lev. 6.8–30	Lev. 6.1–23	Hos. 12.1–14	Hos. 12.2–15	Ps. 18.1–50	Ps. 18.2–51
Num. 16.36–50	Num. 17.1–15	Hos. 13.6	Hos. 14.1	Ps. 19. title	Ps. 19.1
Num. 17.1–13	Num. 17.16–28	Hos. 14.1–9	Hos. 14.2–10	Ps. 19.1–14	Ps. 19.2–15
Num. 26.1a	Num. 25.19	Joel 2.28–32	Joel 3.1–5	Ps. 20. title	Ps. 20.1
Num. 29.40	Num. 30.1	Joel 3.1–21	Joel 4.1–21	Ps. 20.1–9	Ps. 20.2–10
Num. 30.1–6	Num. 30.2–17	Jon. 1.17	Jon. 2.1	Ps. 21. title	Ps. 21.1
Deut. 12.32	Deut. 13.1	Jon. 2.1–10	Jon. 2.2–11	Ps. 21.1–13	Ps. 21.2–14
Deut. 13.1–18	Deut. 13.2–19	Mic. 5.1	Mic. 4.14	Ps. 22. title	Ps. 22.1
Deut. 22.30	Deut. 23.1	Mic. 5.2–15	Mic. 5.1–14	Ps. 22.1–31	Ps. 22.2–32
Deut. 23.1–25	Deut. 23.2–26	Nah. 1.15	Nah. 2.1	Ps. 23. title	Ps. 23.1a
Deut. 29.1	Deut. 28.69	Nah. 2.1–13	Nah. 2.2–14	Ps. 24. title	Ps. 24.1a
Deut. 29.2–29	Deut. 29.1–28	Zech. 1.18–21	Zech. 2.1–4	Ps. 25. title	Ps. 25.1a
1 Sam. 20.42b	1 Sam. 21.1	Zech. 2.1–13	Zech. 2.5–17	Ps. 26. title	Ps. 26.1a
1 Sam. 21.1–15	1 Sam. 21.2–16	Mal. 4.1–6	Mal. 3.19–24	Ps. 27. title	Ps. 27.1a
1 Sam. 23.29	1 Sam. 24.1	Ps. 3. title	Ps. 3.1	Ps. 28. title	Ps. 28.1a
1 Sam. 24.1–22	1 Sam. 24.2–23	Ps. 3.1–8	Ps. 3.2–9	Ps. 29. title	Ps. 29.1a
2 Sam. 18.33	2 Sam. 19.1	Ps. 4. title	Ps. 4.1	Ps. 30. title	Ps. 30.1
2 Sam. 19.1–43	2 Sam. 19.2–44	Ps. 4.1–8	Ps. 4.2–9	Ps. 30.1–12	Ps. 30.2–13
1 Kings 4.21–34	1 Kings 5.1–14	Ps. 5. title	Ps. 5.1	Ps. 31. title	Ps. 31.1
1 Kings 5.1–18	1 Kings 5.15–32	Ps. 5.1–12	Ps. 5.2–13	Ps. 31.1–24	Ps. 31.2–25
1 Kings 18.33b	1 Kings 18.34a	Ps. 6. title	Ps. 6.1	Ps. 32. title	Ps. 32.1a
1 Kings 20.2b	1 Kings 20.3a	Ps. 6.1–10	Ps. 6.2–11	Ps. 34. title	Ps. 34.1
1 Kings 22.22a	1 Kings 22.21b	Ps. 7. title	Ps. 7.1	Ps. 34.1–22	Ps. 34.2–23
1 Kings 22.43b	1 Kings 22.44	Ps. 7.1–17	Ps. 7.2–18	Ps. 35. title	Ps. 35.1 (1st word)
1 Kings 22.44–53	1 Kings 22.45–54	Ps. 8. title	Ps. 8.1	Ps. 36. title	Ps. 36.1
2 Kings 11.21	2 Kings 12.1	Ps. 8.1–9	Ps. 8.2–10	Ps. 36.1–12	Ps. 36.2–13
2 Kings 12.1–21	2 Kings 12.2–22	Ps. 9. title	Ps. 9.1	Ps. 37. title	Ps. 37.1 (1st word)
Isa. 9.1	Isa. 8.23	Ps. 9.1–20	Ps. 9.2–21	Ps. 38. title	Ps. 38.1
Isa. 9.2–21	Isa. 9.1–20	Ps. 11. title	Ps. 11.1a	Ps. 38.1–22	Ps. 38.2–23
Isa. 63.19	Isa. 63.19a	Ps. 12. title	Ps. 12.1	Ps. 39. title	Ps. 39.1
Isa. 64.1	Isa. 63.19b	Ps. 12.1–8	Ps. 12.2–9	Ps. 39.1–13	Ps. 39.2–14
Isa. 64.2–12	Isa. 64.1–11	Ps. 13. title	Ps. 13.1	Ps. 40. title	Ps. 40.1

ENGLISH	HEBREW	ENGLISH	HEBREW	ENGLISH	HEBREW
Ps. 40.1–17	Ps. 40.2–18	Ps. 73. title	Ps. 73.1a	Ps. 124. title	Ps. 124.1a
Ps. 41. title	Ps. 41.1	Ps. 73.1	Ps. 73.1b	Ps. 124.1	Ps. 124.1b
Ps. 41.1–13	Ps. 41.2–14	Ps. 74. title	Ps. 74.1a	Ps. 125. title	Ps. 125.1a
Ps. 42. title	Ps. 42.1	Ps. 74.1	Ps. 74.1b	Ps. 125.1	Ps. 125.1b
Ps. 42.1–11	Ps. 42.2–12	Ps. 75. title	Ps. 75.1	Ps. 126. title	Ps. 126.1a
Ps. 44. title	Ps. 44.1	Ps. 75.1–10	Ps. 75.2–11	Ps. 126.1	Ps. 126.1b
Ps. 44.1–26	Ps. 44.2–27	Ps. 76. title	Ps. 76.1	Ps. 127. title	Ps. 127.1a
Ps. 45. title	Ps. 45.1	Ps. 77. title	Ps. 77.1	Ps. 127.1	Ps. 127.1b
Ps. 45.1–17	Ps. 45.2–18	Ps. 77.1–20	Ps. 77.2–21	Ps. 128. title	Ps. 128.1a
Ps. 46. title	Ps. 46.1	Ps. 78. title	Ps. 78.1a	Ps. 128.1	Ps. 128.1b
Ps. 46.1–11	Ps. 46.2–12	Ps. 78.1	Ps. 78.1b	Ps. 129. title	Ps. 129.1a
Ps. 47. title	Ps. 47.1	Ps. 79. title	Ps. 79.1a	Ps. 129.1	Ps. 129.1b
Ps. 47.1–9	Ps. 17.2–10	Ps. 79.1	Ps. 79.1b	Ps. 130. title	Ps. 130.1a
Ps. 48. title	Ps. 48.1	Ps. 80. title	Ps. 80.1	Ps. 130.1	Ps. 130.1b
Ps. 48.1–14	Ps. 48.2–15	Ps. 80.1–19	Ps. 80.2–20	Ps. 131. title	Ps. 131.1a
Ps. 49. title	Ps. 49.1	Ps. 81. title	Ps. 81.1	Ps. 131.1	Ps. 131.1b
Ps. 49.1–20	Ps. 49.2–21	Ps. 81.1–16	Ps. 81.2–17	Ps. 132. title	Ps. 132.1a
Ps. 50. title	Ps. 50.1a	Ps. 82. title	Ps. 82.1a	Ps. 132.1	Ps. 132.1b
Ps. 51. title	Ps. 51.1–2a	Ps. 82.1	Ps. 82.1b	Ps. 133. title	Ps. 133.1a
Ps. 51.1–19	Ps. 51.2b–21	Ps. 83. title	Ps. 83.1	Ps. 133.1	Ps. 133.1b
Ps. 52. title	Ps. 52.1–2a	Ps. 83.1–18	Ps. 83.2–19	Ps. 134. title	Ps. 134.1a
Ps. 52.1–9	Ps. 52.2b–11	Ps. 84. title	Ps. 84.1	Ps. 134.1	Ps. 134.1b
Ps. 53. title	Ps. 53.1	Ps. 84.1–12	Ps. 84.2–13	Ps. 138. title	Ps. 138.1a
Ps. 53.1–6	Ps. 53.2–7	Ps. 85. title	Ps. 85.1	Ps. 138.1	Ps. 138.1b
Ps. 54. title	Ps. 54.1–2	Ps. 85.1–13	Ps. 85.2–14	Ps. 139. title	Ps. 139.1a
Ps. 54.1–7	Ps. 54.3–9	Ps. 86. title	Ps. 86.1a	Ps. 139.1	Ps. 139.1b
Ps. 55. title	Ps. 55.1	Ps. 86.1	Ps. 86.1b	Ps. 140. title	Ps. 140.1
Ps. 55.1–23	Ps. 55.2–24	Ps. 87. title	Ps. 87.1a	Ps. 140.1–13	Ps. 140.2–14
Ps. 56. title	Ps. 56.1	Ps. 87.1	Ps. 87.1b	Ps. 141. title	Ps. 141.1a
Ps. 56.1–13	Ps. 56.2–14	Ps. 88. title	Ps. 88.1	Ps. 141.1	Ps. 141.1b
Ps. 57. title	Ps. 57.1	Ps. 88.1–18	Ps. 88.2–19	Ps. 142. title	Ps. 142.1
Ps. 57.1–11	Ps. 57.2–12	Ps. 89. title	Ps. 89.1	Ps. 142.1–7	Ps. 142.2–8
Ps. 58. title	Ps. 58.1	Ps. 89.1–52	Ps. 89.2–53	Ps. 143. title	Ps. 143.1a
Ps. 58.1–11	Ps. 58.2–12	Ps. 90. title	Ps. 90.1a	Ps. 143.1	Ps. 143.1b
Ps. 59. title	Ps. 59.1	Ps. 90.1	Ps. 90.1b	Ps. 144. title	Ps. 144.1 (1st word)
Ps. 59.1–17	Ps. 59.2–18	Ps. 92. title	Ps. 92.1	Ps. 145. title	Ps. 145.1a
Ps. 60. title	Ps. 60.1–2	Ps. 92.1–15	Ps. 92.2–16	Ps. 145.1	Ps. 145.1b
Ps. 60.1–12	Ps. 60.3–14	Ps. 98. title	Ps. 98.1 (1st word)	Song of Songs 6.13	Song of Songs 7.1
Ps. 61. title	Ps. 61.1	Ps. 100. title	Ps. 100.1a	Song of Songs 7.1–13	Song of Songs 7.2–14
Ps. 61.1–8	Ps. 61.2–9	Ps. 100.1	Ps. 100.1b	Eccl. 5.1	Eccl. 4.17
Ps. 62. title	Ps. 62.1	Ps. 101. title	Ps. 101.1a	Eccl. 5.2–20	Eccl. 5.1–19
Ps. 62.1–12	Ps. 62.2–13	Ps. 101.1	Ps. 101.1b	Dan. 4.1–3	Dan. 3.31–33
Ps. 63. title	Ps. 63.1	Ps. 102. title	Ps. 102.1	Dan. 4.4–37	Dan. 4.1–34
Ps. 63.1–11	Ps. 63.2–12	Ps. 102.1–28	Ps. 102.2–29	Dan. 5.31	Dan. 6.1
Ps. 64. title	Ps. 64.1	Ps. 103. title	Ps. 103.1 (1st word)	Dan. 6.1–28	Dan. 6.2–29
Ps. 64.1–10	Ps. 64.2–11	Ps. 108. title	Ps. 108.1	Neh. 4.1–6	Neh. 3.53–58
Ps. 65. title	Ps. 65.1	Ps. 108.1–13	Ps. 108.2–14	Neh. 4.7–23	Neh. 4.1–17
Ps. 65.1–13	Ps. 65.2–14	Ps. 109. title	Ps. 109.1a	Neh. 9.38	Neh. 10.1
Ps. 66. title	Ps. 66.1a	Ps. 109.1	Ps. 109.1b	Neh. 10.1–39	Neh. 10.2–40
Ps. 66.1	Ps. 66.1b	Ps. 110. title	Ps. 110.1a	1 Chron. 6.1–15	1 Chron. 5.27–41
Ps. 67. title	Ps. 67.1	Ps. 110.1	Ps. 110.1b	1 Chron. 6.16–81	1 Chron. 6.1–66
Ps. 67.1–7	Ps. 67.2–8	Ps. 120. title	Ps. 120.1a	1 Chron. 12.4	1 Chron. 12.4–5
Ps. 68. title	Ps. 68.1	Ps. 120.1	Ps. 120.1b	1 Chron. 12.5–40	1 Chron. 12.6–41
Ps. 68.1–35	Ps. 68.2–36	Ps. 121. title	Ps. 121.1a	2 Chron. 2.1	2 Chron. 1.18
Ps. 69. title	Ps. 69.1	Ps. 121.1	Ps. 121.1b	2 Chron. 2.2–18	2 Chron. 2.1–17
Ps. 69.1–36	Ps. 69.2–37	Ps. 122. title	Ps. 122.1a	2 Chron. 14.1	2 Chron. 13.23
Ps. 70. title	Ps. 70.1	Ps. 122.1	Ps. 122.1b	2 Chron. 14.2–15	2 Chron. 14.1–14
Ps. 70.1–5	Ps. 70.2–6	Ps. 123. title	Ps. 123.1a		
Ps. 72. title	Ps. 72.1 (1st word)	Ps. 123.1	Ps. 123.1b		

Translations of Primary Sources

ANCIENT NEAR EASTERN DOCUMENTS

Coogan, Michael David, ed. *Stories from Ancient Canaan*. Philadelphia: Westminster, 1978.

Dalley, Stephanie. *Myths from Mesopotamia: Creation, the Flood, Gilgamesh, and Others*. Oxford: Oxford University Press, 1989.

Foster, Benjamin R. *Before the Muses: An Anthology of Akkadian Literature*. 2 vols. Bethesda, Md.: CDL Press, 1993.

———. *From Distant Days: Myths, Tales, and Poetry of Ancient Mesopotamia*. Bethesda, Md.: CDL Press, 1995.

Hallo, William W. and K. Lawson Younger, eds. *The Context of Scripture*. Vol. 1, *Canonical Compositions from the Biblical World*. Vol. 2, *Monumental Inscriptions from the Ancient World*. Vol. 3, *Archival Documents from the Biblical World*. Leiden: E. J. Brill, 1997; 2000; 2002.

Lichtheim, Miriam. *Ancient Egyptian Literature: A Book of Readings*. 3 vols. Berkeley: University of California Press, 1973–1980.

Parker, Simon B., ed. *Writings from the Ancient World*. A series produced by the Society of Biblical Literature (Atlanta, Ga.), with each volume devoted to a particular genre and language. Volumes include: *Ugaritic Narrative Poetry* (ed. S. B. Parker; 1997); *Law Collections from Mesopotamia and Asia Minor* (M. F. Roth; 2nd ed., 1997); *Hittite Myths* (H. A. Hoffner, Jr.; 2nd ed., 1998); *Hittite Diplomatic Texts* (G. M. Beckman; 2nd ed., 1999); *Hittite Prayers* (I. Singer, 2002); *Ritual and Cult at Ugarit* (D. Pardee, 2002).

Pritchard, James B., ed. *Ancient Near Eastern Texts Relating to the Old Testament*. 3rd ed. Princeton, N. J.: Princeton University Press, 1969.

ANCIENT TRANSLATIONS OF THE BIBLE

Greek

Brenton, Lancelot C. L. *The Septuagint with Apocrypha: Greek and English*. 1851. Reprint, Peabody, Ma.: Hendrickson, 1986.

International Organization for Septuagint and Cognate Studies. *A New English Translation of the Septuagint*. New York: Oxford University Press, 2000– .

Aramaic

McNamara, Martin J.; Kevin Cathcart; Michael Maher. *The Aramaic Bible: The Targums*. Collegeville, Mn.: Liturgical Press, 1987– .

DEAD SEA SCROLLS

Abegg, Martin, Jr.; Peter Flint; and Eugene Ulrich, eds. *The Dead Sea Scrolls Bible: The Oldest Known Bible*. San Francisco: HarperSanFrancisco, 1999.

Charlesworth, James E., ed. *The Dead Sea Scrolls: Hebrew, Aramaic, and Greek Texts with English Translations*. Vol. 1, *Rule of the Community and Related Documents*. Vol. 2, *Damascus Document, War Scroll, and Related Documents*. Vol. 4A, *Pseudepigraphic and Non-Masoretic Psalms and Prayers*. Vol. 4B, *Angelic Liturgy: Songs of the Sabbath Sacrifice*. Vol. 6B, *Pesharim, Other Commentaries, and Related Documents*. Louisville: Westminster/John Knox Press, 1994– .

García Martínez, Florentino, ed. *The Dead Sea Scrolls Study Edition*. 2 vols. Leiden: E. J. Brill, 1998.

Vermes, Geza. *The Complete Dead Sea Scrolls in English*. New York: Penguin Press, 1997.

APOCRYPHA AND PSEUDEPIGRAPHA

Charles, R. H., ed. *The Apocrypha and Pseudepigrapha of the Old Testament*. 2 vols. Oxford: Clarendon Press, 1913.

Charlesworth, James H., ed. *The Old Testament Pseudepigrapha*. 2 vols. New York: Doubleday, 1983–1985.

PHILO OF ALEXANDRIA

Colson, F. H. and Whitaker, G. H., trans. *Philo*. Loeb Classical Library. 10 vols. Cambridge, Ma.: Harvard University Press, 1961–1991.

BIBLIOGRAPHY

Williamson, Ronald. *Jews in the Hellenistic World: Philo.* Cambridge, Eng.: Cambridge University Press, 1989.

Yonge, C. D., trans. *The Works of Philo.* 1854. New updated edition. Peabody, Ma.: Hendrickson Publishers, 1993.

JOSEPHUS

Thackeray, H. St. J. and Ralph Marcus, trans. *Josephus.* Loeb Classical Library. 9 vols. Cambridge, Ma.: Harvard University Press, 1976–1981.

Whiston, William, trans. *The Works of Josephus Complete and Unabridged.* 1736. New updated edition, Peabody, Ma.: Hendrickson Publishers, 1987.

Williamson, G. A., trans. *Josephus: The Jewish War.* New York: Penguin Books, 1984.

RABBINIC TEXTS

Mishnah

Danby, Herbert. *The Mishnah: Translated from the Hebrew with Introduction and Brief Explanatory Notes.* Oxford: The Clarendon Press, 1933.

Neusner, Jacob. *The Mishnah: A New Translation.* New Haven: Yale University Press, 1988.

Talmud

Epstein, I. *The Babylonian Talmud.* 30 vols. London: Soncino Press, 1935–48.

Steinsaltz, Adin. *The Talmud.* New York: Random House, 1989– .

Midrash

Bialik, Hayyim N. and Y. H. Ravinsky. *The Book of Legends: Sefer Ha-Aggadah.* New York: Schocken Books, 1992.

Freedman, H. and M. Simon, eds. *Midrash Rabbah.* 10 vols. London: Soncino Press, 1961.

Ginzberg, Louis. *The Legends of the Jews.* 8 vols. Philadelphia: Jewish Publication Society, 1968.

Hammer, Reuven. *Sifrei Deuteronomy: A Tannaitic Commentary on the Book of Deuteronomy.* New Haven: Yale University Press, 1986.

Kasher, Menahem. *Encyclopedia of Biblical Interpretation, A Millennial Anthology.* 9 vols. New York: American Biblical Encyclopedia Society, 1953–1979.

Lauterbach, J. Z. *Mekhilta of Rabbi Ishmael.* Philadelphia: Jewish Publication Society of America, 1976.

Medieval Jewish Commentaries

Baker, Joshua and Ernest Nicholson, trans. *The Commentary of Rabbi David Kimhi on Psalms 120–150.*

TRANSLATIONS OF PRIMARY SOURCES

Cambridge: Cambridge University Press, 1973.

Chavel, Charles B., trans. *Ramban (Nachmanides): Commentary on the Torah.* 5 vols. New York: Shilo Publishing House, 1971–1976.

Gruber, Mayer, *Rashi's Commentary on the Psalms.* Atlanta: Scholars Press, 1998.

Japhet, Sara and Robert B. Salters, *The Commentary of R. Samuel ben Meir, Rashbam, on Qoheleth.* Jerusalem: Magnes, 1985.

Lockshin, Martin I., trans. *Rashbam's Commentary on Genesis: An Annotated Translation.* Jewish Studies, vol. 5. Lewiston, N. Y.: E. Mellen Press, 1989.

———. *Rabbi Samuel ben Meier's Commentary on Exodus: An Annotated Translation.* Brown Judaic Series, no. 310. Atlanta: Scholars Press, 1997.

———. *Rabbi Samuel ben Meier's Commentary on Leviticus and Numbers; An Annotated Translation.* Brown Judaic Series, no. 330. Providence, R. I.: Brown Judaic Studies, 2001.

Silbermann, A. M. and M. Rosenbaum, trans. *Pentateuch with Targum Onkelos, Haphtaroth and Rashi's Commentary.* 5 vols. New York: Hebrew Publishing Co., 1969.

Strickman, H. Norman and Arthur M. Silver, trans. *Ibn Ezra's Commentary on the Pentateuch.* 5 vols. New York: Menorah Publishing Co., 1988– .

Medieval Jewish Philosophy

Feldman, Seymour, trans. *Levi ben Gershom: The Wars of the Lord.* 3 vols. Philadelphia: Jewish Publication Society, 1999.

Frank, Daniel H., trans. *The Book of Doctrines and Beliefs.* Indianapolis: Hackett Publishing Co., 2002.

Lewy, Hans. *Three Jewish Philosophers: Philo, Saadya Gaon, Jehuda Halevi.* New York: Macmillan Publishing Co., 1972.

Pines, Shlomo, trans. *The Guide of the Perplexed.* Chicago: University of Chicago Press, 1963.

Mystical Texts

Cohen, Martin Samuel. *The Shi'ur Qomah: Texts and Recensions.* Tübingen : Mohr, 1985.

Kaplan, Aryeh. *The Bahir : An Ancient Kabbalistic Text Attributed to Rabbi Nehuniah ben HaKana, First Century, C. E.* New York : S. Weiser, 1979.

Matt, Daniel C., trans. *Zohar: Annotated and Explained.* Woodstock, Vt.: SkyLight Paths Publishing Co., 2002.

Sperling, Harry and Maurice Simon. *The Zohar.* London: Soncino Press, London, 1931–34.

Glossary

Abarbanel an alternative pronunciation of **Abravanel.**

Abraham Ibn Ezra see **Ibn Ezra, Abraham.**

Abravanel, Isaac (1437–1508) a medieval philosopher and biblical commentator. He fled from Portugal to Spain to escape a sentence of death in a supposed plot against the king; in 1492, with the expulsion of Jews from Spain, he was forced to flee again and lived in Venice. His works include commentaries on the Torah and the Prophets, as well as philosophical works that followed, and were partly intended to correct, Maimonides. His biblical commentaries were, unlike most medieval commentary, not verse-by-verse or word-by-word, but were concerned with larger passages united by a single theme; he opens each unit with a set of questions that he answers in great detail. In philosophy he insisted on the primary importance of religion and wrote against efforts to explain biblical events in naturalistic terms; he also opposed efforts to formulate a set of dogmatic principles for Judaism.

Abravanel, Judah (1460–1521) physician, poet, and philosopher, and son of Isaac Abravanel. His *Dialogue on Love* (published posthumously) argued that love was the structural principle of the universe, and that the soul therefore sought and could reach God through love.

Abulafia, Abraham ben Shemuel (13th century) a leading kabbalist and mystic of Spain. Abulafia taught a method of mystical insight that involved contemplating the letters of the Hebrew alphabet, seen as the elements of the names of God. His method was therefore called "The Path of the Names" (*Shemot*), in contrast to other kabbalistic methods called "The Path of the Numbers" (*Sefirot*).

acrostic a literary device in which the first letter of each line of poetry occurs according to a predetermined pattern. In the Bible acrostics only occur as alphabetical acrostics, in which the individual lines of a poem (or occasionally small groups of lines) begin with the twenty-two letters of the Hebrew alphabet in order. (This would be equivalent to the first line of an English poem beginning with A, the second with B, etc.) The acrostic form, besides giving the aesthetic pleasure of a pattern, may have been intended to make memorization easier. It may also have been intended as a way of expressing completeness: In Lamentations, for instance, the acrostic format of the individual chs might have been used to express both the completeness of the outpouring of grief and its finality. The following poems in the Bible are acrostics: Pss. 9–10, 25, 34, 37, 111, 112, 119, 145; Prov. 31.10–31; Lam. chs 1, 2, 3, 4; Nah. 1.2–8 (or 9) (incomplete).

Active Intellect in mystical thought, the repository of the intelligible forms that govern the sublunar world.

Adar the twelfth month (February–March) in the Jewish year. In order to bring the lunar calendar into alignment with the solar year, a leap year, in which there are two months of Adar, occurs seven times during each nineteen-year cycle of years (see p. 2114). This added month is called either *'adar sheni*, "second adar," or *ve'adar*, "and adar."

Adonai (Heb "my Lord") a divine title and the word generally substituted for the **Tetragrammaton**, YHVH, when the Bible is read aloud.

aggadah (or "haggadah,"possibly from Heb *huggad*, "things said" or "what is told") the nonlegal portions of the Talmud and Midrash (see **halakhah**). Aggadah is concerned with explicating the meaning of Scripture in the moral sense, and with elaborating on the stories in the Bible. As such it is more akin to preaching than to legal analysis, and many aggadic collections are homiletical in character. The legal sections, **halakhah,** are concerned with understanding the obligations placed on the believer by the biblical text; aggadah, by contrast, contains ethical teaching as well as illustrative narrative, prayers, legends, and folklore.

Aḥad Ha'Am (Heb "one of the people" or "the people are one") pen-name of Asher Ginzberg (1856–1927), Zionist writer.

Ahikar the hero of an ancient Near East court story who is deprived of his position through a false accusation.

'Akedah (Heb "binding") the story of the binding of Isaac (Gen. ch 22).

Akiva (Aqiba) ben Yosef, R. (ca. 50–135 CE), rabbi at Lydda, martyred in the Hadrianic persecutions. He played an instrumental role in the task of beginning to assemble and organize the oral law, which was continued by his pupil R. **Meir** and concluded by R. Judah *ha-Nasi'* **(Judah the Prince)**, resulting in the **Mishnah** (see).

Akkadian the language of the Assyrian and Babylonian empires. Akkadian is a Semitic language related to Hebrew, and is written in cuneiform, wedge-shaped writing, typically on clay tablets.

'aliyah (Heb "ascent") pilgrimage or emigration to the land of Israel; being given the honor of "ascending" to read the Torah in synagogue worship.

allegory an extended comparison in which an author, while speaking directly of one reality, intends to mean, and is understood by the reader to be speaking indirectly about, something entirely different. Allegory uses action, setting, and character to point to a symbolic level. Some texts, e.g., the "Song of the Vineyard" in Isa. ch 5, expressly mark themselves as allegorical. "Allegorical interpretation," such as that used by Philo to draw out the meaning of the Bible, is an effort to make an allegory out of a writing that was not originally intended to be one, but that is, in the view of the interpreter, presenting a hidden meaning that the allegorical interpretation will reveal.

Amarna Letters Akkadian cuneiform tablets from the period of 1350 BCE or slightly earlier, containing diplomatic correspondence from the reigns of Pharaohs Amenophis III and Akhenaton and providing scholarly insight into the language of and the situation in Canaan in the period preceding the rise of the Israelite tribal confederation.

'Amidah (Heb "standing") the main prayer in Jewish worship. Also called the *Shemonah 'Esrei* (eighteen [blessings]), although on regular weekdays (not Shabbat or festivals), it now consists of nineteen blessings: three at opening, followed by thirteen petitions and three at closing. For Shabbat and festivals, the three initial and final blessings frame a special blessing that focuses on the special day.

'amora' (Aram. "speaker"; pl. *'amora'im*) a rabbinic teacher of the talmudic period. The name is used in both Babylonia and the land of Israel.

Amorites according to the Bible, one of the native nations of Canaan. Amorites are attested in other ancient Near Eastern documents from the third millennium and onwards as residents of Western Asia who migrated to Mesopotamia and other areas. They spoke a language related to Hebrew.

amphictyony a social organization in ancient Greece where tribes are united around a central sanctuary and service this sanctuary on a rotating basis. Some scholars believe that a similar system existed in Israel in premonarchic times.

anaphora the repetition of a word or phrase at the beginning of successive lines or sentences. "As the eyes of slaves follow their master's hand, / as the eyes of a slave-girl follow the hand of her mistress, / so our eyes are toward the LORD our God, awaiting His favor" (Ps. 123.2).

anastrophe the repetition at the beginning of one line of the word or phrase concluding the previous line. "The voice of the LORD convulses the wilderness; / the LORD convulses the wilderness of Kadesh" (Ps. 29.7).

Anat a Canaanite goddess often depicted as a warrior.

anthropomorphic (Gk "human form") language that presents God in human or human-like terms. "Your right hand, O LORD, glorious in power, / Your right hand, O LORD, shatters the foe!" (Exod. 15.6).

antithesis the contrast of ideas through closely contrasted words. "A gentle response allays wrath; / A harsh word provokes anger" (Prov. 15.1). See **parallelism**, "Reading Biblical Poetry" (pp. 2097–2104).

antithetic parallelism two parallel lines related to one another by opposition, e.g., Prov. 10.4, "Negligent hands cause poverty, / But diligent hands enrich."

apocalypse (Gk *apokalypsis*, "revelation") a narrative literary genre in which an angel or other heavenly being communicates to a human being the divine plan for history and the arrangement of the supernatural order. Many apocalypses are a series of visions of heaven and earth that are then explained. Apocalypses are a feature of late biblical religion.

apocalyptic a worldview that assumes the disclosure of heavenly secrets, most typically to or for a community that perceives itself as suffering or victimized. Communities that espouse this worldview often interpret biblical passages (especially in the Prophets) as pertaining to their own time.

Apocrypha (Gk "hidden things") a group of about 20 mostly Jewish writings (e.g., Ben Sirach, 1 Maccabees), many of which were included in the **Septuagint**, but that were ultimately not included in the Bible. They are, however, part of the canon of the Orthodox Christian churches, and most (though not all) of them are included in the canon of the Roman Catholic church.

apodictic law law stated absolutely, as in the Decalogue's "you shall not," rather than casuistically, "if a person" (see **casuistic law**).

apophatic (from Gk for "deny") the theology that works by denying likenesses between God and anything that can be conceived, since God transcends all human thought and experience; the nature of God is thus inferred only negatively, by what God is not.

apostrophe an address to an absent person or personified object. There is an apostrophe to Assyria in Isa. 10.5.

Aquila (lived 2nd century CE) a Jewish reviser of the Greek Bible; Aquila tried to make the text, which had become the Bible of the early Christian church, less favorable to some christological exegesis. The translation follows the Hebrew very closely. According to tradition, he was a convert and a student of Akiva.

Aramaic a Semitic language used widely in Mesopotamia and the land of Israel during the Persian period, though it developed earlier. In the mid-first millennium, it eventually replaced Akkadian as the lingua franca of the ancient Near Eastern world. It became the ordinary language of Jews and is the language of much rabbinic literature. The Aramaic translation of the Bible is the **Targum.**

Arameans a Semitic people living in the area of modern Syria from the second millennium onwards. Some biblical texts suggest particular kinship between Israel and the Arameans (see esp. Deut. 26.5). Damascus was their main city.

Ark (for the Torah) a box or cabinet, typically of wood, in which the Torah scrolls are stored at the front of the synagogue. It is often finely decorated, reflecting the centrality of the Torah scrolls to Judaism.

Ark of the Covenant the chest (Heb *'aron*) in the Tabernacle or Temple that contained the Pact (Heb *'edut*) (Exod. 40.20), or the tablets (Deut. 10.2), or that served as the throne of the LORD (1 Sam. 4.4).

Asherah (pl. Asherim) Canaanite goddess, wife or consort of El; her sacred symbol, a pole or tree, was the object of prophetic condemnation.

Ashi, Rabbana (ca. 335–427) Babylonian *'amora'* of the Sura academy; one of the primary editors of the Babylonian Talmud.

Ashkenazi the name Ashkenaz appears in Gen. 10.3, as a descendant of Gomer, son of Japheth, son of Noah. In geonic tradition (ca. 9th century CE) Ashkenaz became identified with Germany, and Jews living in the Rhineland, and their descendants in France and Bohemia, were called Ashkenazi(m). See **Sephardim.**

Ashtoreth the Canaanite goddess of love and fertility; worship of Ashtoreth is condemned in Judg. chs 2 and 10.

Assyria a Mesopotamian world power, in addition to Babylonia. Its capital cities included Ashur and Nine-

veh. The Assyrian empire conquered the Northern Kingdom of Israel in 722 and exiled its people. The Assyrians were well-known for their massive building projects and for their cruelty in war.

Astarte see **Ashtoreth.**

'atbash a form of cipher in which a word is transformed into a code by letter substitution, in which the last letter of the alphabet is substituted for the first, the next-to-last for the second, and so on: *alef* becomes *tav, bet* becomes *shin, gimel* becomes *resh,* etc. (In English, A would become Z, B would become Y, etc.) Using this method, Jeremiah transforms Babylon into Sheshach (Jer. 25.26; 51.41): *b-b-l* or *bet-bet-lamed* becomes *sh-sh-k* or *shin-shin-kaf.*

atonement the expiation for sin, or reparation for an injury committed against another. Heb *kapparah* (with possible root meaning "to cover") refers to ritual cleansing of the Temple precincts.

Atrahasis hero of the Mesopotamian epic of Atrahasis, who survives the god Enlil's efforts to destroy humankind by, among other means, a flood (with some parallels to the story of Noah in Gen. chs 6–9). Sections of the epic are reworked in tablet 11 of the Gilgamesh Epic, which also recounts a flood story.

'Avot (Heb "fathers") the name of the first blessing in the **'Amidah,** from its reference to "the God of Abraham, the God of Isaac, and the God of Jacob"; also the name of a tractate in the **Mishnah;** see *Pirkei 'Avot.*

'Avot de Rabbi Nathan A rabbinic midrash on the mishnaic tractate of **'Avot;** see *Pirkei 'Avot.*

Baal the Canaanite storm god; also a word meaning "lord" or "master, owner."

Babylonia a Mesopotamian world power. It often competed against Assyria, which it conquered in 612 BCE. Its major city was Babylon, Akkadian for "gate of the gods." Its main god became Marduk, and its religion and literature were extremely influential, even on its arch-rival Assyria. Babylonia destroyed the First Temple in 586, and was conquered by Cyrus the Great in 539.

Babylonian exile the forced relocation of some of the population of Judah, perhaps the ruling portion of it, after the conquest by Babylonia in 597–586 BCE. The exile ended with the permitted return to the land under Cyrus (beginning ca. 538 BCE).

Babylonian Talmud see **Talmud.**

Baḥya ben Asher (d. 1320) biblical commentator of Spain. He used the *Zohar*'s method of distinguishing four levels of meaning in Scripture: *peshat* (contextual sense), *remez* (allegorical sense), *derash* (homiletical sense), and *sod* (mystical sense). These were known by the acronym *pardes.*

ban (Heb *ḥerem*) the devotion of war booty (including people) in its entirety to the deity (see esp. Deut. 20.17), or the forfeiture of goods (e.g., idols) from which no benefit is permissible. See *ḥerem.*

Baraita (Aram. "outside," i.e., external to the Mishnah) a section of rabbinic material with a ruling or interpretation like that in the Mishnah, that is from the tannaitic period but not contained in the Mishnah.

Bar Kappara 3rd century CE scholar; he lived in the land of Israel.

Bar Kokhba, Shimeon (Aram. "son of a star") sobriquet of Shimeon Bar Kosiba (d. 135 CE), leader of the second Jewish revolt against Rome.

Bavli, Talmud the Babylonian Talmud; see **Talmud.**

BCE Before the Common Era, an alternative to BC.

Bedouin an Arab nomad; in general, a member of a nomadic desert tribe.

Bel Akkadian "master," (cognate to Baal) alternative name for **Marduk,** head of the Babylonian pantheon.

ben Asher, Aaron (9th–10th centuries) Masorete of Tiberias. Ben Asher was one of the primary scholars who established the Hebrew Masoretic Text.

berit (Heb "treaty") a term that may be used of a treaty between two individuals, groups, or nations, or between God and Israel (see **covenant**).

bet midrash (Heb "house of study") a place with a traditional Jewish library where people study Jewish texts together and listen to classes on these texts. Along with the synagogue, to which it is often connected, this is the central Jewish institution.

bicolon unit of Heb poetry composed of two *cola,* or lines (sometimes called a *distich*).

binding (of Isaac) see ʿAkedah.

Bonfils, Joseph 11th century rabbi of Limoges, France; **tosafist,** biblical scholar, and author of liturgical poetry who introduced such poetry *(piyyutim)* into the synagogue service.

Booths, Festival of see **Sukkot.**

bulla a clay seal with the impression of a signet ring or other symbol of authority.

Cairo Genizah the storeroom (see **genizah**) of the synagogue of Fostat in Old Cairo (built 882 CE). In it were discovered many thousands of fragments of texts, including a portion of Ben Sirach (Ecclesiasticus) in Heb, and many early rabbinic documents, translations of the Bible, liturgical texts, poetry, letters, and other writings.

calendar see chart on p. 2114.

Cambyses son of Cyrus and king of Persia 529–522 BCE. He conquered Egypt in 525.

Canaan a designation for the area roughly equivalent to the land of Israel in prebiblical Mesopotamian and Egyptian documents. In the Bible, it most often refers to the pre-Israelite land of Israel.

canon (Gk "reed" or "measuring stick") the group of writings considered to be holy or authoritative by a particular community. The canon of the Bible is the list of books in the Tanakh.

cantillation the practice of chanting or intoning the biblical text in public reading, according to traditional systems of tone, pitch, and length; also, the written system of marks in the biblical text that serves as a guide to the systems of recitation.

casemate wall a double wall, usually the outside of a larger house or of a city wall, that is filled up with dirt or rubble.

casuistic law (also called "case law") the form of law dealing with the treatment of specific cases. It is frequently in the form of "if/when ... then" formulae. Most ancient Near Eastern law collections are formulated this way.

CE Common Era; equivalent to the christological term AD.

charismatic (Gk "gifted, graced") characterized by the ability to influence or lead others; personally magnetic; talented.

Chemosh the chief god of **Moab.**

cherubim (pl. of *kerub*) composite, winged creatures; two carved cherubim guarded the Ark in the Temple, where they may have served as guardians of sacred places and attendants on YHVH.

chiasm, chiasmus (from Gk *chi,* the letter that resembles an "X") inverting the second pair of terms in a parallel structure, so that the corresponding terms, if laid out in a square, would make an X. The resultant pattern is ABBA, ABCBA, ABCCBA, etc. For example: "Truthful speech (A) wins the favor of kings (B); / They love those (B) who speak honestly (A)" (Prov. 16.13). Chiasmus can also describe the structure of an entire passage, and it can involve several terms or parts of a passage, each of which has an analog that occurs in the reverse order of the original list of terms or sequence of parts.

Christian Hebraists Christian scholars, inspired by the examples of Origen and **Jerome,** who taught the importance of returning to the Hebrew text of the Christian Old Testament, and who therefore studied Hebrew with rabbinic scholars and influenced Christian Bible translation and commentary to rely on the Hebrew and not on the Latin Vulgate text. The beginnings of Christian Hebraism are generally traced to Andrew of St. Victor (d. 1175), a monk at the Abbey of St. Victor in Paris, where Hugh of St. Victor (d. 1141) had established a school specializing in biblical exposition. There was a significant renaissance of Christian Hebraism during the Renaissance.

citadel a stronghold or fortress, whether standing alone or serving as the inner fortification of a city.

Classical Biblical Hebrew the main dialect of biblical Hebrew, reflected in over half of the Bible. This dialect was used in Judah through the Babylonian exile of 586. Classical Hebrew was then replaced by Late Biblical Hebrew, comprised of Exilic and Postexilic Hebrew. Both of these latter forms were significantly influenced by Aramaic.

colon, (pl. *cola*) a single line of poetry (also known as a *stich*).

colophon (Gk "summit," by extension "finishing touch") an inscription at the end of a writing giving information about authorship.

Community Rule (or *Rule of the Community*) a scroll from the Dead Sea community, 1QS, that sets out the communal arrangements under which the community functioned, or at least those that they held up as an ideal: holding property in common; eating, blessing, and advising one another in unity; preparing for the eschaton; and training new members of the community in their responsibilities. Also called *The Manual of Discipline.*

concordance a word index to a given text, listing each occurrence of a given word along with a context line so that scholars may better see how a particular word is used.

concubine a woman who is the sexual partner of a man, and is legally recognized as such, but who does not have the full status of a wife.

Cordovero, Moses ben Jacob (Moshe ben Ya'akov; 1522–1570) kabbalist, of Spain. Cordovero wrote commentaries on the Bible and on kabbalistic works; his interests were philosophical, but ultimately his views were mystical and esoteric.

corvée forced labor for the state

cosmology any account (mythical or otherwise) of the origin of the world.

covenant (Heb *berit*) a treaty between God and Israel. Some covenants have specific conditions or treaty stipulations, while others are covenants of grant. The biblical notion of covenant between God and Israel, especially as it appears in Deuteronomy, may reflect a theologized reworking of treaties between Assyrian kings and their vassals.

cult, cultus the religious ritual and practice of a particular group; the rules governing worship, sacrifice, etc.

Cyrus king of Persia (559–530 BCE). He defeated Media in 550 and conquered most of the ancient Near East, including Babylonia, allowing the Jewish exiles in Babylonia to return to the land beginning ca. 538.

Cyrus Cylinder an Akkadian inscription describing the conquest of Babylon by Cyrus.

D the Deuteronomic source, which covers almost the entire book of Deuteronomy (except for sections of the last few chapters).

Davidic dynasty the direct descendants of King David, who reigned in Jerusalem from the 10th century through the 6th. An attempt to reinstitute this dynasty after the return from exile was not successful.

Day of Atonement (Heb **Yom Kippur**) commemorated on the tenth day of the seventh month in the fall. It was a day of fasting and abstinence, as well as performance of certain key Temple rituals (see Lev. ch 16).

Day of the Lord a time mentioned in many prophetic books where God appears as a warrior, sometimes fighting against Israel, sometimes against Israel's enemies. The earliest text to mention this Day is Amos 5.18.

Dead Sea Scrolls a group of texts, mostly from the 2nd century BCE through the 1st century CE found in the area of the Dead Sea. Most are from eleven caves at Qumran. These scrolls, mostly preserved in fragmentary form, include biblical texts, ancient texts which were known in translation before the scrolls were discovered, and new texts. Often the nonbiblical texts are divided into sectarian documents, namely those unique to the group that lived in this area, and nonsectarian documents that were in the group's library, but were not unique to this group, often understood as the ancient Essenes (see essay, "The Bible in the Dead Sea Scrolls," pp. 1920–28).

defective spelling the form of a word in the Heb text that is missing one or more optional vowel letters. See **plene spelling.**

defilement a state of ritual impurity caused by contact with a corpse or other impure object. Priestly literature in the Torah is especially concerned with defilement and removing defilement (see essay, "Concepts of Purity," pp. 2041–47).

derash (Heb *d-r-sh,* "inquire") interpretation (see **midrash**).

derashah (pl. *derashot*) interpretation, particularly in a homiletic context; a sermon.

Deutero-Isaiah the general term for the portion of Isaiah beginning with ch 40. Most scholars consider Deutero-Isaiah to consist of chs 40–55 (or 40–54). These chapters are primarily concerned with the promise of return from exile and the events leading up to the decree of **Cyrus** (538 BCE) permitting the exiles to return to Judah and rebuild their city and Temple. See **Trito-Isaiah.**

Deuteronomistic History the account in the books Deuteronomy, Joshua, Judges, Samuel, and Kings, that portrays the history of Israel as a partial failure to keep the covenant faithfully, and the consequences of that failure in the subsequent history of the people. These books show significant theological and linguistic similarities, suggesting that they have a common editor or editors.

Deuteronomistic having the qualities or the theology of the **Deuteronomistic History.**

Diaspora (Gk "dispersion") the places outside the land of Israel where Jews live.

diatribe an argument against a position or critical of a person holding it. Diatribe often includes an imagined dialogue between opposing viewpoints.

dittography (Gk "twice written") a copying error in which a word or phrase is written twice; see **haplography.**

divination the effort to learn about the future or the current situation, particularly such an effort undertaken by occult means, such as consulting mediums.

Documentary Hypothesis the theory that the Torah (Pentateuch) is a combination of sources or documents from different eras and different geographical or social groups: **J** or the Yahwist source, possibly reflecting the traditions of Judah during the monarchic period; **E** or the Elohist source, possibly from the Northern Kingdom; **D** or the Deuteronomistic source, possibly from a group involved in the reforms undertaken by Josiah and his successors; and **P** or the Priestly source, the groups that maintained Temple worship and the ritual and other practices, and who assembled these materials during or after the exile (see "Torah," pp. 1–7).

Dov Baer (1710–72) a Hasidic leader and follower of Isaac Luria; he became well known as a preacher (*maggid*) and is therefore known as "the Maggid."

E one of the four sources or traditions in the Torah, which characteristically refers to God as *'elohim.* More recently, as scholars have examined the texts more closely, they speak of a JE tradition, since E as a separate source is difficult to isolate entirely. It may represent the traditions and practices of the inhabitants of the northern areas of Israel.

Edom/Edomites the territory and people to the southeast of Judah, first attested in late second millennium texts. Edom is identified in Gen. ch 36 with Esau, Jacob's brother. The enmity between these brothers and between Judah and Edom mirror each other.

El a Canaanite deity popular in the second millennium. In the texts from **Ugarit,** he is a significant deity,

but is often depicted as old and is largely supplanted by Baal.

Elephantine Papyri Aramaic documents, mostly from the 5th century BCE, found on the island of Elephantine, near Syene (modern Aswan) in Egypt. The papyri show that among those who inhabited the colony on Elephantine were Jews who kept up religious observances, such as Passover, and had their own temple.

Eliezer, Rabbi two *tanna'im* are named Eliezer: Eliezer ben Hyrcanos (1st–2nd century), teacher of R. Akiva ben Yosef; and Eliezer ben Yosei ha-Galili (2nd century), a pupil of R. Akiva.

Elijah a biblical prophet and miracle worker living in the 9th century in northern Israel. Much postbiblical folklore collected around Elijah, who is depicted as ascending to heaven rather than dying in 2 Kings ch 2. He was later thought of as the forerunner or announcer of the messiah.

Elijah ben Solomon Zalman (1720–1797) the "Vilna Gaon," scholar of Vilna, Lithuania. He studied religious and secular subjects (such as mathematics and philosophy), arguing that knowledge in these areas was necessary for Torah study. For eight years he wandered throughout Europe, meeting with and teaching local rabbis and establishing his reputation for learning. He then returned to Vilna, where he spent the rest of his life expounding the Talmud. He strongly opposed the nascent Hasidic movement.

Elohim the Heb word *'elohim* is usually translated "God," though its plural form is sometimes translated "gods" (e.g., Gen. 6.2, "sons of elohim," NJPS "divine beings"). It is originally a common noun (a god), though it is often used as a proper noun for The God of Israel, even though it is a plural form.

Elohist the putative author of the E source (see **E**).

Enki the Mesopotamian god of wisdom.

Enlightenment the philosophical movement that flourished in the 18th century in continental Europe (primarily Germany and France) and England. It was characterized by an emphasis on the importance of human reason and reflection on actual experience, a tendency to favor materialist as opposed to religious views, optimism about human progress, and pragmatic approaches to politics and ethics. The movement within Judaism corresponding to the Enlightenment, and influenced by it, is called Haskalah.

Enlil a chief Mesopotamian god, ruler of earth and sky; he also decreed the fate of human beings and the other gods.

Enoch, books of writings dating from the 3rd century BCE to the 6th century CE, attributed to Enoch (Gen. ch 5). They contain apocalyptic visions, describe visits to the heavenly places, and make use of the character of

Enoch (who, according to the Genesis account, was believed to have been taken directly to heaven without dying) as a guide to and interpreter of the meaning of history. Portions of some of these works have been discovered among the Dead Sea Scrolls.

Enuma Elish a Babylonian creation epic, in which the god Marduk becomes king of the gods after creating the cosmos from the body of the goddess of the deep, Tiamat.

ephod the priestly garment similar to a tunic. It held the breastplate that contained the lots Urim and Thummim, used in casting lots to determine the divine will; this led to the use of the term *ephod* to mean the agency of divination.

eponym the use of a representative figure to stand for an entire group; the "Table of Nations" in Gen. ch 10 contains eponyms such as Canaan (v. 6).

eschatological, eschatology (Gk *eschata,* "last things") a concern with the end time, or the end of the world as we know it, whether that involves a new historical era radically discontinuous from this one, or an entirely new cosmos after the destruction of the current one.

Essenes a Jewish group that flourished from around the 1st century BCE to the 1st century CE. They kept the Jewish law with utmost rigor, living apart from other Jews in their own communities. Most scholars believe that the members of the Qumran community (where the Dead Sea Scrolls were discovered) were Essenes.

etiology (Gk *aition,* "cause") an explanation for a word, an event, or a natural phenomenon. An etiological story is one that posits a particular cause (not necessarily the right cause) for some event. For example, the story at the end of Gen. ch 32 explains why Israelites do not eat the thigh muscle.

euphemism the substitution of an inoffensive word for one that is too explicit. The word "legs" in Isa. 6.2; 7.20 is a euphemism for "genitals."

exegesis (Gk "lead into") the explanation or interpretation of the meaning of a written text, especially a biblical text.

exilarch (Heb *resh galuta'*) the title of the head of Babylonian Jewry.

exile the forced removal of a people from its land, and the community in which they lived in the foreign land. The Israelites of the Northern Kingdom were exiled by the Assyrians in the late 8th century, and the Judeans were exiled by the Babylonians in the early 6th century. Specifically, "the exile" is the period from 586 to approximately 539 BCE. During this time the ruling classes of Judah were forced to leave Judah and live in Babylonia. See **Babylonian exile.**

exodus the journey that Israel took from Egypt toward the land of Israel, according to the book of Exodus.

fable an illustrative story in which animals or plants have speaking parts. Judg. 9.8–15 is a fable told against the proposal to establish a monarchy in Israel.

Fertile Crescent the agriculturally fertile areas of Egypt, Israel, and Mesopotamia, forming a rough arc from the Nile through the coastal regions of Israel to the Tigris-Euphrates basin.

Festival of Weeks see **Shavuot.**

First Temple the Temple in Jerusalem from Solomon's time (10th century) until the destruction of Jerusalem by the Babylonians in 586 BCE. The First Temple period extends from the 10th to 6th centuries BCE.

form criticism a method of studying biblical texts that developed in Germany in the late 19th and early 20th centuries. This method isolates structures or forms of particular types or genres of biblical literature, and attempts to connect these forms to a particular social setting *(Sitz im Leben)* (see "Modern Study," pp. 2084–96).

Former Prophets the subdivision of the **Nevi'im** section of the Bible that includes the books of Joshua, Judges, Samuel, and Kings (Heb title *nevi'im ri'shonim*). See also **Latter Prophets.**

Galilee the northernmost geographical area of Israel.

galut (Heb "exile") most often used of the **Babylonian exile** (see).

gaon, pl. *geonim* title of heads of rabbinic academies in Babylonia from the mid-6th to 11th centuries. The title is taken from the phrase, *ro'sh yeshivat ga'on Ya'akov,* "head of the academy [that is] the pride of Jacob."

Gehenna Gk spelling of Heb *ge'hinnom,* "valley of Hinnom," the area outside Jerusalem where trash was burned. By metaphoric extension it came to mean a place of torment, and in postbiblical literature meant "hell."

Gemara (Aram. "completion") the commentary on the **Mishnah** that supplemented and extended the Mishnaic material, although not all of the Mishnah is treated in the Gemara. The **Mishnah** and the Gemara together form the **Talmud.**

gematria, pl. *gematriot* (*gimatriya,* likely from Gk *geometria*) a procedure for interpreting a word or phrase by its numerical value. Heb letters may represent numbers (*alef* = 1; *bet* = 2, etc.), and the letters of a word or phrase are added up and equated with other words having the same total. For example, according to Gen. 14.14, Abraham musters 318 retainers. Some rabbinic commentaries suggest that he merely mustered Eliezer, since the numerical value of Eliezer's name is 318 (ʾ-l-y-ʿ-z-r is 1+30+10+70+7+200).

genizah a storeroom in a synagogue used for keeping old books and objects, especially those that are too sacred to be thrown away. See **Cairo Genizah.**

geonic period the period characterized by the teachings of the academies in Babylonia that extended from roughly the mid-6th to the mid-11th century CE. See *gaon.*

ger (Heb) in biblical usage, a resident alien, a foreigner who sojourns in Israel. In rabbinic literature, the word means a convert; conversion did not exist in the biblical period.

Gersonides see **Ralbag.**

Gikatilla, Yosef ben Abraham (1248–ca.1325) kabbalist of Spain. He was a student of **Abraham Abulafia,** and later was associated with **Moshe de Leon,** author of much of the *Zohar.* Gikatilla was one of the main formulators of the kabbalistic view that the divine name, YHVH, implicitly contained all the letters of the Hebrew alphabet.

Gilgamesh the Babylonian and Assyrian epic whose hero, Gilgamesh, travels the world in search of immortality. Among the characters he encounters is Utnapishtim, whose tale of the flood has parallels with the biblical account of Noah (Gen. chs 6–9).

God, names for see **Adonai, Elohim, YHVH.**

God, titles for see **Tzevaot, Melekh ha-ʿOlam, ha-Shem** (see **Shem**).

Graf-Wellhausen Hypothesis the hypothesis developed in the 19th century (primarily by the German biblical scholar J. Wellhausen) that the Torah is comprised of four more or less complete documents, J, E, D, and P, in that order. See **Documentary Hypothesis.**

Greek Bible a general term for the variety of ancient translations of the Bible into Greek in antiquity, including the Septuagint and the translations of **Aquila, Symmachus,** and **Theodotion.**

Guide of the Perplexed (*Moreh Nevukhim*) the philosophical work by Maimonides **(Rambam)** that interpreted the Torah mainly in the light of Aristotelian philosophy with the aim of removing contradictions between the teaching of Torah and the understandings of philosophy.

H the Holiness Collection (imprecisely called the Holiness Code), the ritual and ethical laws found in Lev. chs 17–26. The author of these laws was affiliated with the Priestly school, but was probably writing after that school penned the bulk of its material that now appears in the Torah. The authors of the Holiness Collec-

tion likely wrote small sections dispersed throughout the first four books of the Torah. The collection is so named from the exhortation, "You shall be holy, for I, the LORD your God, am holy" (Lev. 19.2).

haftarah (Heb "conclusion") the reading from a prophetic book that follows the Torah reading in the Sabbath or festival service.

Ḥag Sameaḥ good wishes for a holiday: "joyous festival."

Ḥag festival, particularly one of the three Pilgrim Festivals (*shalosh regalim:* Passover [pesaḥ], Shavuot, Sukkot).

Haggadah of Pesaḥ ("telling of Passover") the liturgical recitation used at the Passover **Seder;** also the book that contains the recitation and instructions of the Seder.

haggadah see **aggadah.**

halakhah (Heb "way," from *halakh* "go"; pl. *halakhot*) the legal portions of the Talmud, or any legal ruling according to Jewish law.

Halevi, Judah (ca. 1075–ca. 1141; also Yehudah ha-Levi) Hebrew poet, of Spain, and author of the Arabic philosophical work, *The Kuzari,* a defense of Judaism.

Hallel (Heb "praise") Psalms 113–118, which are recited on major Jewish festivals.

Hammurabi Babylonian monarch (reigned 1792–1750 BCE), responsible for the formulation of a legal collection (the Code [or Laws] of Hammurabi) that is one of the earliest collections of case law on various subjects.

haplography (Gk "writing once") the unintentional omission of a repetition—letter, syllable, word, or phrase—from a written text because the scribe's eye went to the second occurrence; see **dittography.**

ha-Shem see **Shem.**

Hasidic, Hasidim (Heb. *Ḥasid,* "pious one") a renewal movement that began in the mid-18th century in Eastern Europe under the influence of the Baʿal Shem Tov ("master of the good Name"), R. Yisrael ben Eliezer (ca. 1700–1760).

Haskalah see **Enlightenment.**

Hasmonean Revolt the uprising led by the family of Mattathias Heshmon against the Seleucid ruler Antiochus IV Epiphanes beginning in 166 BCE, particularly by Mattathias's son Judah (or Judas) Maccabeus ("the hammer"), which succeeded in liberating Jerusalem and the surrounding territory from Seleucid rule in 164. When the Temple, which had been desecrated by Antiochus, was retaken by the Jews it was rededicated, an event commemorated in the festival of Ḥanukkah ("dedication").

Hebrew Bible a term used to refer to what Christians call the Old Testament. Though the two terms refer to basically the same body of writings, the order of books in the Hebrew Bible (that is, the Jewish Bible) differs from that found in the Old Testament.

heikhalot rabbati ("greater halls") mystical writings probably dating from the 3rd to 7th centuries CE. The "halls" (or "palaces, temples") are heavenly realms through which the narrative moves.

heikhalot zutarti ("lesser halls") mystical writings of the same type as the *heikhalot rabbati*.

Hellenism a general term for the spread of Greek culture, politics, and language around the Mediterranean in the period after the conquests of Alexander the Great (d. 323 BCE).

hendiadys figure of speech that expresses a compound idea by two words linked by a conjunction. E.g., "pain and childbearing" (Gen. 3.16) means "pangs in childbearing."

ḥerem (Heb **"ban"**) the total dedication of conquest to God; later, the exile or suspension of someone from the community ("excommunication").

hermeneutic principles the rabbinic types of interpretation. A list attributed to Hillel (1st century BCE) includes: *kal vaḥomer* (deduction from minor to major); *gezerah shavah* (analogy between texts based on a common word); *binyan 'av mikatuv 'eḥad* (applying a principle derived from one verse); *binyan 'av mishenei ketuvim* (applying a principle derived from two verses); *kelal uferat uferat ukelal* (modifying the general from the particular; modifying the particular from the general); *kayotze' bo bemakom 'aḥer* (principles developed from similar passages); *davar halamed me'inyano* (deduction from context). See "Classical Rabbinic Interpretation" (pp. 1844–63.)

Hexapla the compendium of six Bible versions (in columns: 1. Hebrew, 2. Hebrew transliterated into Greek, 3. Greek [**Aquila**], 4. Greek [**Symmachus**], 5. Septuagint, 6. Greek [**Theodotion**]) compiled by the early Christian scholar Origen (d. 254). The original Hexapla, which ran to 7,000 pages, was lost, but quotations from it exist in various early writings and a Syriac translation of column 5 (known as the Syriac Hexapla or Syro-Hexapla), prepared by a Christian bishop, Paul of Tella (who held office in 618–619), is an important witness to the transmission of the text of the Septuagint.

Hexateuch (Gk "six scrolls") a grouping of the first six books in the Bible—Genesis through Joshua—to complete the Torah narrative with the conquest of the land that is in Joshua. See **Pentateuch, Tetrateuch.**

high places places of worship or sacrifice, often at the top of a hill or mountain. Under the influence of the centralization of worship in Jerusalem at the Temple, particularly in the Deuteronomic reform carried out under Josiah, the high places were vilified as idolatrous, though in earlier writings, and even in the narratives in Kings, there are clear indications that sacrifice and worship took place in numerous locations throughout the land of Israel.

higher criticism the effort to distinguish among the sources of biblical documents, and to trace them back to their origins, so far as that is possible; distinguished from textual criticism ("lower criticism"), which is concerned with establishing the most accurate text in its final form. See **Documentary Hypothesis.**

Hillel an important early rabbinic sage of the 1st century BCE; according to tradition, he migrated from Babylonia to Israel. Tradition also suggests that he set up a "house" or scholarly school. The House of Hillel often differs with the House of Shammai in halakhic rulings, and is typically more lenient.

Holiness Collection see **H.**

homoioteleuton (Gk "similar ending") a copying error in which the scribe omits words or phrases between a word that is repeated or between words with similar endings.

hortatory characteristic of writing or speech that aims at changing the behavior of the hearers or inspiring them to a particular course of action.

ḥumash (from *ḥamishah ḥumshei Torah*, "five fifths of Torah") a synonym for the Torah, or the book used by a synagogue congregation to follow the Torah reading.

Hyksos the mostly Semitic rulers of Egypt during the period 1665–1560 BCE (approximately).

hyperbole exaggeration for effect. "Would the LORD be pleased with thousands of rams, / With myriads of streams of oil?" (Mic. 6.7).

hypostasis (Gk "that which stands under," i.e., the real nature or essence of anything; pl. *hypostases*) a Greek philosophical term, meaning both "essential being" or what defines a thing as a member of a class of things and "individual being" or what a thing is in itself. It was used by, among others, the neoplatonist mystics. It refers to the three constitutive orders of reality, the One, Mind, and Soul, each of which is an hypostasis. See "The Bible in the Jewish Mystical Tradition" (pp. 1976–90).

Ibn Aknin, Yosef ben Yehudah (ca. 1150–1220) philosopher and biblical commentator, of Spain and Morocco. His commentary on the Song of Songs treated it as an allegory of the soul's effort to free itself from matter and unite with the intellect that emanates from God.

Ibn Bal'am, Yehudah (11th century) biblical commentator and grammarian, of Spain. His commentary on the Torah and the Prophets is a link between the work of **Saadia Gaon** and Abraham **Ibn Ezra.**

Ibn Daud, Abraham (ca. 1110–1180) philosopher and historian, of Spain. His work was concerned to show the consonance of science and religion, and particularly of Aristotelianism and Judaism.

Ibn Ezra, Abraham (1089–1164) poet, biblical commentator, translator, philosopher, who lived in Spain, N. Africa, Italy, France, and England. His biblical commentaries cover large portions of the text, and provided Hebrew readers with their first chance to read the comments of **Saadia Gaon,** which Ibn Ezra translated from Arabic.

Ibn Ezra, Moshe (1070–1138) philosopher and poet of Spain. He wrote on philosophical matters such as the nature of the divine, the intellect, and nature, but his best-known works are poems, particularly those sacred poems in the Sephardic prayer book.

Idumea Gk form of the name "Edom"; province in the land of Israel during Persian, Hellenistic, and Roman times, located south of Judah (Yehud), between the Dead Sea and the Mediterranean.

impurity a ritual state which forbade the impure individual to partake in Temple rituals (see **defilement,** and "Concepts of Purity," pp. 2041–47).

Inanna Sumerian goddess of fertility and war; equivalent to the Babylonian **Ishtar.** She was similar to the Greek Persephone in being captive in the underworld, later released.

inclusio the use of the same word or phrase at the end of a passage as appeared at the beginning, thus rounding off or completing it. Inclusio may have been used to mark subsections of a work. It is also called inclusion, frame, and envelope structure.

incubation the practice of sleeping in a particular place, or in contact with particular things (animal skins, the ground) in order to induce dreams that might provide divine guidance.

Ingathering (*kibutz galuyot*, "ingathering of the exiles") the belief that the people will ultimately return to the land of Israel from their places of exile.

intercalation adding an extra time unit (day or month) to a calendar to compensate for the inexact fit between the solar year and the daily or lunar cycle. In the Jewish calendar, an extra month (a repetition of Adar) is intercalated in seven years of the nineteen-year cycle. See **Adar;** see also p. 2114.

interpolation an insertion of material into a previously existent text. In the absence of textual evidence—e.g., differing forms of a manuscript for a given text—interpolation must be inferred and is often the subject of scholarly disagreement.

interregnum an interruption or gap between the end of one reign or dynasty and the beginning of the next.

intertextuality the interrelationship between one part of a text (or collection of texts) and other parts. Intertextuality can take the form of recurrent images (the vineyard in Isa. 5.1–10 and 27.2–4), quotation and/or inner biblical interpretation (Jer. 25.11–12 is partly quoted in Dan. 9.2 before it is reinterpreted), or allusion (Isa. 54.8 alludes to the promise made to Noah in Gen. 9.11).

Ishtar the Mesopotamian goddess of fertility and war (the Gk spelling was Astarte); the Canaanite version of her name is Ashtar. See **Inanna.**

Isis the Egyptian mother-goddess, wife of Osiris, the god of vegetation and hence of regeneration.

J the posited document or narrative tradition that is one of the constituent parts of the Torah (Pentateuch), according to a scholarly hypothesis codified by J. Wellhausen and subsequently developed by numerous biblical researchers. J is usually understood to be the earliest source, and is Judean; it frequently depicts God, for whom it uses the **Tetragrammaton** (YHVH, misvocalized Jehovah, thus J), in very anthropomorphic terms. See introduction to the Torah (pp. 1–7).

Jerome (ca. 340–420) Christian theologian and translator. Beginning in 382, he produced a Latin version of the Bible, the Old Testament of which was based not on a previous Latin version nor on the Greek text (**Septuagint**) but on the Hebrew. In order to do this Jerome studied Hebrew with rabbis of the time, an unusual step for a Christian. His version, which became known as the **Vulgate** ("common") because it was the translation into commonly used Latin in the Western world, was completed in 405.

Jerusalem Talmud also called the Palestinian Talmud or the Talmud of the land of Israel, although none of these titles is fully accurate. This **Talmud,** mostly reflecting traditions of the Galilean *'amora'im* of the 3rd and 4th centuries CE, is a commentary on several tractates of the **Mishnah.** It was ultimately seen as less authoritative than the longer, more comprehensive, and more carefully edited Babylonian Talmud. See **Talmud.**

Josephus Hellenistic Jewish historian (ca. 37–ca. 100 CE). Four of his writings have survived: *The Jewish War* (an account of the rebellion against Rome in 66–70 CE, with background information starting at about 200 BCE); *The Antiquities of the Jews* (a history from creation up to the start of *The Jewish War*); *Against Apion,* a defense of Judaism; and an autobiography. Josephus provides invaluable historical information about Judaism and its background from 200 BCE to 100 CE; his account of the rebellion, in which he was a participant, is partly that of an eyewitness. He also provides first-hand information about the Essenes and the Pharisees (he was at one time or another associated with both), as well as information about the Sadducees. Josephus is important in understanding Second Temple Judaism and the context in which rabbinic Judaism developed.

jubilee (Heb *yovel*, perhaps "ram" from the sounding of the ram's horn to mark the beginning of the observance) the year of release for slaves and return of ancestral lands to their original owners (or descendants of the owners), to occur every fifty years (after seven sabbaths of years) (Lev. ch 25). It is a cornerstone of Priestly ideology, but it is uncertain if it was ever practiced.

Jubilees, **book of** a pseudepigraphic book, retelling much of Genesis and Exodus, representing itself as a hidden revelation to Moses. It was most likely written in the 2nd century BCE in the land of Israel. The book gets its name from its concern with cycles of time. *Jubilees* was apparently considered authoritative by the Qumran community. It is attributed to Moses and purports to be a revelation to him from the angel of the Presence.

Judah the area of southern Israel. According to the biblical text, after the death of Solomon, the kingdom was divided into two, with Judah in the south and Israel in the north. The capital of Judah was Jerusalem.

Judah Halevi see **Halevi, Judah.**

Judah the Prince R. Judah ha-Nasi, the prince or patriarch (Heb *nasi'*) of the community in Israel in the late 2nd century CE. He was very powerful, and had close relation with the Roman rulers. He played a central role in editing the Mishnah, and tradition sees him as *the* editor of that work.

Judea the Roman name for the area of Judah.

kabbalah "what is received," i.e., matter handed to one. In the 12th century and later, however, kabbalah came to mean esoteric or in some sense mystical teaching. Kabbalah taught that God was inaccessible by direct experience, and could only be apprehended through emanations of the Godhead; Torah in kabbalistic teaching had a hidden meaning, and meditation on texts was a method of ascent to a mystical vision.

kaddish (Aram. "holiness, sanctification") prayer in praise of God that is recited at the conclusion of a principal section of the synagogue service; a special type of kaddish is also recited in memory of the deceased.

Kalam (Arabic "speech, reason") Islamic scholasticism, dating from the 8th century CE, a theology that developed in response to the rediscovery of Aristotelian philosophy in the Islamic world. The earliest proponents of this school were called Mutazilite ("separatist") because they were seen as separate from orthodox Islamic teaching. The Kalam movement influenced both Karaite and rabbinic teaching, including among the latter the work of **Saadia Gaon.**

kapparah see **atonement.**

Karaites (lit. "Scripturists"; from Heb *Miqra'*) the theological movement in Judaism dating from Babylonia in the 8th century CE. Karaites claimed to be restoring an original form of Judaism from the Second Temple period, and were opposed by the rabbis of their time, particularly **Saadia Gaon.** Karaite calendars, festivals, dietary restrictions, and other practices differed in various ways from rabbinic norms. The movement reached its height around the 11th century though a small Karaite community is still in existence today in Israel.

kashering the process of making a permissible food **kosher** or fit for consumption, esp. soaking and salting meat to remove blood.

kashrut the system of dietary laws and restrictions; see **kosher.**

kataphatic (from Gk for "affirm") the theology that works by ascribing positive attributes to God, through which one understands the divine nature.

Kedushah (Heb "holiness") prayers of sanctification of God, especially the third blessing of the *'amidah,* including the words "Holy, holy, holy" from Isa. 6.3.

kere see *qere.*

ketiv ("what is written") the biblical text in its written form, in contrast, in certain cases, to the way it is to be read aloud. See *qere.*

Kiddush short for *kiddush ha-yom,* "sanctification of the day," both the ceremony and the prayer that proclaims the holiness of the Sabbath (or festival), recited over wine before the Sabbath (or festival) meal.

Kimḥi a family of grammarians and exegetes in medieval France (originally from Spain); the three great scholars of this family were Yosef Kimḥi (ca. 1105–1170), who defended Jewish interpretation against Christian criticism in *Sefer ha-Berit,* and his two sons, Moshe and David. The latter, a prolific biblical commentator and grammarian, was known as **Radak.**

kitvei hakodesh (Heb "holy writings") a rabbinic term for the Bible; the Holy Scriptures.

kohen (Heb "priest") a member of the hereditary group within the Levites, traditionally supposed to be descended from Aaron or Zadok, who alone were allowed to serve as Temple priests.

kosher (Heb "fit" or "proper") a general term used in postbiblical texts for dietary laws; usually applied to food, but also to other ritual objects and practices. Most dietary laws apply to meat: It may not be consumed with blood in it, certain kinds of internal fat are not to be eaten, it may not be consumed along with dairy products, and some meats (e.g., pork), sea creatures (e.g., shellfish), and "creeping things" (e.g., snails) are not permitted.

Latter Prophets the canonical division of Nevi'im that includes the books of Isaiah, Jeremiah, Ezekiel, and the Twelve (Heb title *nevi'im aḥaronim*).

Laws of Eshnunna the legal collection of a Mesopotamian city-state, about 50 km (30 mi) from present-day Baghdad, that flourished in the early part of the 2nd millennium BCE. These laws include parallels to those found in the legal collections in the Torah.

LBH Late Biblical Hebrew, the dialect spoken during and after the Babylonian exile, when Aramaic influenced Hebrew significantly.

Lekha Dodi the mystical 16th-century hymn or song that is sung at the beginning of the Sabbath. The title means "Come, my friend," and the first line is: "Come, my friend, to meet the bride; let us welcome the presence of the Sabbath."

Letter of Aristeas an apocryphal work, the supposed eyewitness account of the translation of the Torah into Greek. It is the origin of the story that the translators numbered 72 (rounded off to 70 and therefore the reason that this Greek translation of the Bible is called the **Septuagint** [Gk "seventy"] and is abbreviated LXX).

Levi ben Gershon, R. see **Ralbag.**

Leviathan the monster of the sea in Canaanite mythology, who is defeated by Baal. This has echoes in Ps. 74.14–17 and elsewhere.

levirate marriage (from Latin *levir,* "husband's brother") the provision that if a man died without an heir to carry on his name, his brother would marry the widow, and the first son she bore would be regarded as the dead brother's heir. This practice is dealt with in Deut. 25.5–10, but it is unclear whether it was actually carried out to any extent; by rabbinic times *ḥalitzah,* the ceremony that released the levir from this obligation, was preferred.

lex talionis (Latin "law [of retribution] in kind") punishment fitting the crime; see **talion.**

liminal (Latin *limina,* "threshhold") the term for rites or practices that governed life passages, such as entry into puberty or marriage.

lingua franca a common tongue or shared language that enables people with different native languages to converse, carry on commercial relationships, etc. In the Persian period Aramaic replaced Akkadian as a lingua franca around the Near East; during the Hellenistic period Greek did the same for the lands surrounding the Mediterranean.

littoral a region lying along the shore of a large lake or sea.

liturgy the form or rite for communal, public worship.

lower criticism, textual criticism, as distinguished from source criticism ("higher criticism"). See "Textual Criticism of the Bible" (pp. 2067–72).

Luria, Itzḥak (1534–1572) halakhic and kabbalistic teacher, active in Safed, Israel. Though he wrote little or nothing himself, his followers after his death produced a large amount of writing presenting his teaching, which basically stated the goal of all creation to be the gradual perfection of all realms, divine and human. This perfection was to be sought not just individually, but communally, and therefore fit with messianic expectations and other movements for renewal.

Lurianism the teachings of Itzḥak Luria or based on the writings of his followers.

LXX the Roman numeral 70, the standard abbreviation for the **Septuagint.**

Ma'ariv (from *'erev,* "evening") the evening prayer service, held after nightfall. See *Minḥah, Shaḥarit.*

Ma'at Egyptian goddess of reason and order; her name literally means "truth."

maftir (Heb "completer") the reader who completes the Torah portion by repeating the last three or so verses of it, reciting the Torah blessing, and reading the **haftarah** (see).

"Maggid, the" see **Dov Baer.**

Maimonides, Moses (also Moshe ben Maimon) see **Rambam.**

malediction curse; opposite of benediction, "blessing."

manumission release from servitude.

Marduk chief god of Babylon; according to *Enuma Elish,* a Babylonian epic of creation, he formed the cosmos from the corpse of **Tiamat,** goddess of the deep.

maskil, maskilim (lit. "knowledgeable") a title for an educated person; later, a kabbalist; still later, an adherent of Haskalah **(Enlightenment).**

Masorah the system of markings (vowel signs, marginal notes, cantillation and accent marks, etc.) that were added to the consonantal Hebrew text by scribal scholars **(Masoretes)** in the early Middle Ages.

Masorete a scholar of the scribal schools that in the early Middle Ages established the basic Heb text for the Bible, fixed its accepted pronunciation, and ensured its accurate copying and transmission by a system of markings **(Masorah).**

Masoretic Text (MT) the Heb text as established by the Masoretes.

matrilineal tracing descent through female ancestors; see **patrilineal.**

matzah, matzot unleavened bread, associated with Passover, but also used with certain sacrifices.

Megillot (Heb "scrolls") the five books of Kethuvim that are read during various festivals: Song of Songs in **Pesah,** Ruth on **Shavuot,** Lamentations on **Tish'ah be'av,** Ecclesiastes on **Sukkot,** and Esther on **Purim.**

Meir, R. 2nd century pupil of Akiva who helped to reconstitute the Sanhedrin after the second (Bar Kokhba) revolt. R. Meir's teachings were partly aimed at organizing the oral law, and led to the compilation of the Mishnah under R. Judah ha-Nasi **(Judah the Prince).**

Mekhilta two halakhic midrashic commentaries on sections of Exodus, one attributed to R. Ishmael and the other to R. Shimeon bar Yohai.

Melekh ha-'Olam Heb "ruler of the universe," a title for God.

Mendelssohn, Moses (1729–1786) German scholar, defender of Judaism against Christian argument, and leader of the Haskalah or **Enlightenment** movement. He led the efforts of a team of scholars to translate the Bible into German (printed in Hebrew characters).

merism a figure of speech in which opposing terms, e.g., "good and bad," are combined to convey the idea of including both terms and everything in between. The "tree of knowledge of good and bad" (Gen. 2.17), therefore, may mean the tree of knowledge of everything.

merkavah a name for mystical writings, inspired by Ezek. ch 1, in which the visionary is conducted through the heavenly realms by a chariot *(merkavah).*

Merneptah Stele an Egyptian inscribed stone that includes the first mention of Israel outside the Bible. It celebrates the victories of Pharaoh Merneptah (ca. 1200 BCE) in the area of **Canaan.**

Merodach Heb version of **Marduk,** chief god of Babylon (Jer. 50.2).

Mesha Stele (also called the "Moabite Stone") a commemorative stone dating from about 830 BCE with engraved text celebrating the reign of King Mesha of Moab (2 Kings 3.4–5). Besides an account of the dealings of Mesha with the descendants of Omri, king of Israel, the text deals with the god of Moab, **Chemosh,** and the favor that Chemosh has shown to Mesha in contrast to his predecessors in allowing Mesha to reclaim territory from Israel. It also contains a reference to the **herem** or **ban,** indicating that this idea was not unique to Israel.

Mesopotamia (Gk "between the rivers") the area between the Tigris and Euphrates rivers.

messiah (Heb *mashiah,* "anointed [one]") a title for the king or other servant or agent of God (priest, prophet, or even non-Israelite Cyrus in Isa. 45.1). In the Tanakh, *mashiah* never refers to the future ideal king.

metaphor a direct comparison between two unlike things: "The LORD is my shepherd" (Ps. 23.1). See **simile.**

metonymy a figure of speech in which a word is used in place of another word to which it is closely related. In Isa. 41.5 "the coastlands" is a metonymy for "the inhabitants of the coasts," i.e., foreigners.

meturgeman (Aram. "interpreter"; cf. **Targum**) the one who provided a running translation into the language of the congregation—Aramaic, in the origin of the practice—of the Torah reading (and other Scripture readings) in the synagogue service.

mezuzah (Heb "doorpost") a parchment on which are written the paragraphs of the Shema (Deut. 6.4–9; 11.13–21), and on the back of which *sh-d-y* ("Shaddai," "Almighty") is written, often so as to be visible through a small opening in the case. *Sh-d-y* is interpreted as an acronym for *shomer delatot Yisra'el,* "guardian of the doors of Israel."

midrash, midrashic (Heb *derash,* "inquire") interpretation to draw out meanings from a text that are other than, or go beyond, the "plain sense" (see **peshat**).

Milcom Heb form of the name of the god of Ammon. See **Molech.**

Minhah (Heb "offering") the second of the daily prayer services. It occurs during the period between noon and sunset. See *Shaharit, Ma'ariv.*

miqra' ("that which is read [aloud]") the standard rabbinic way of referring to the biblical text.

Miqra'ot Gedolot the Rabbinic Bible, an edition of the Masoretic Text accompanied by the Aramaic translation (Targum) and various commentaries such as Rashi, Ibn Ezra, Ramban, and Rashbam.

Miqsat Ma'aseh ha-Torah ("matters of the Torah") one of the Dead Sea Scrolls (4QMMT), in the form of a letter from the Qumran sect to its opponents, explaining, among other things, the differences in legal interpretation and application between the Qumran community and the Jerusalem establishment of the time.

Mishnah (Heb "oral instruction," from *shanah,* "repeat") the compilation of oral law and rabbinic commentary, edited ca. 200 CE, that is the basis of the **Talmud.** The Mishnah in its final form is generally attributed to R. Judah ha-Nasi **(Judah the Prince,** ca. 135–220), though it contains material that may go back centuries before R. Judah's time.

Mishneh Torah the first codification of Jewish law, by Maimonides **(Rambam).**

mitzvah (Heb "commandment") a religious obligation; by extension, any good deed.

MMT see *Miqsat Ma'aseh ha-Torah.*

Moab/Moabites the territory and inhabitants southeast of the Dead Sea.

Moabite Stone see **Mesha Stele.**

Molech the title—"king"—of the Ammonite god. The worshippers of this god were accused of child sacrifice.

Moshe ben Maimon, R. see **Rambam.**

Moshe ben Naḥman, R. see **Ramban.**

Moshe de Leon (ca. 1240–1305) kabbalist of Spain. He wrote kabbalistic books in Hebrew, but also wrote (in Aramaic) large parts of the *Zohar*, a purported compendium of 2nd-century rabbinic teachings that is the main work of kabbalistic commentary.

Mot the Canaanite god of death.

motif an image or character type that recurs throughout a literary work. The Servant motif occurs in Isa. at 42.1–4; 49.1–6; 50.4–11; 52.13–53.12.

Musaf ("addition") the extra service on a Sabbath or festival, after *Shaḥarit* (see).

Musar Movement a 19th-century Lithuanian movement to promote piety and ethical behavior; its founder was R. Yisrael Salanter (1810–1883). Its practices continue in yeshivas influenced by followers of the movement.

Mutazilite Kalam see **Kalam.**

Naḥmanides Moshe ben Naḥman, known as **Ramban** (see).

narrative a connected account of an incident, or a longer account including many incidents. Narratives can be historical, fictional, legendary, mythical, or a combination of types.

necromancy the practice of divination by communication with the dead, who are presumed to have knowledge of the future.

Negev the high plateau south of the central hill country of Israel.

Neoplatonism the philosophical movement, originating with Plotinus (ca. 204–270), that saw the universe as a series of emanations flowing out from the One, the causeless, unknowable source of all that is. The emanations, Mind *(nous)* and Soul, are, along with the One, called **hypostases.** The individual's task is to return to the One by contemplation, involving a progressive detachment from the world of matter and sense and ultimately from all categories of thought until the One can be grasped in an indescribable void of thought.

new moon see **Rosh Ḥodesh.**

Ninth of Av see **Tish'ah be'av.**

Noahide laws the basic commandments laid upon Noah, and therefore seen as binding upon all human beings, Jews and Gentiles alike: They prohibited blasphemy, idolatry, sexual immorality, murder, robbery, and eating blood; and they commanded justice.

notarikon, pl. *notarikonim* (from Gk *notarikon,* "shorthand") a method of interpretation that takes each letter of a word as the initial letter of another word, thereby creating a phrase that is treated as the full meaning intended by the word; also breaking a word into constituent parts and interpreting those parts in order to reveal a hidden meaning within the original word. For example, rabbinic interpretation treated the first word of the Decalogue, *'anokhi* (the longer word for "I"), as an acronym for the Aramaic sentence *'ana' ketavit yehavit,* "I [God] wrote it [and] gave it."

obelisk a four-sided stone shaft, usually tapered and topped with a pyramid, characteristic of ancient Egypt.

'Olam the biblical Heb term for unending (time), extended in postbiblical Heb to mean all space, i.e., the world or universe.

oracle a unit of prophetic speech; usually translates *masa'* ("burden").

Oral Torah a synonym for the **Mishnah** and **Talmud.** According to traditional rabbinic belief, the oral law was given to Moses on Mount Sinai along with the written law, the Torah. The oral law was, however, as its name suggests, originally transmitted orally alongside the Torah, as the authoritative interpretation of the Torah. As a result of historical exigencies, it was committed to writing by the Rabbis, in stages, in the first millennium CE.

Ovadiah of Bertinoro (ca. 1450–1509) commentator on **Mishnah,** from Bertinoro (Italy). By treating the Mishnah itself, in isolation from its treatment in the **Talmud,** Ovadiah encouraged the study of Mishnah independently of the Talmud.

P the Priestly document in the Torah, comprised of both narratives and laws. It is concerned, among other things, with laws and regulations, ritual practices, the proper conduct of Temple worship, holiness and purity, and genealogies. P may also have had a hand in the shaping or redaction of the Torah. See introduction to the Torah (pp. 1–7).

Palestine a name derived from the Roman designation *Provincia Syria Palaestina,* "Syro-Palestinian Province," which replaced *Provincia Judaea* after the revolt of 135 CE; *Palaestina* was the Roman spelling of "Philistine," and the designation was probably intended as a derogation of Jewish claims to the territory.

Palestinian Talmud the **Jerusalem Talmud** or Talmud Yerushalmi; see **Talmud.**

parallelism a characteristic feature of biblical Hebrew poetry in which the second line of a unit in some way echoes the meaning or grammatical structure of the first line. This can take the form of a repetition of the meaning, or of a statement of opposites, or of a further statement that serves to extend or modify the first line in some way. See "Reading Biblical Poetry" (pp. 2097–2104).

parashah the portion of Torah designated to be read publicly for each week of the year. There are 54 parashiyot, to provide for the maximum possible number of Sabbaths in a year (that can only occur in an intercalated or leap year). In years with fewer Sabbaths, the readings are combined to produce fewer portions. The weekly portion is also sometimes improperly called the *Sidrah*, "arrangement."

pardes a Late Biblical Hebrew word borrowed from Persian, meaning "park, garden, orchard." It was later employed as an acronym for the four levels of meaning in Scripture according to the *Zohar: peshat* (contextual sense), *remez* (allegorical sense), *derash* (homiletical sense), and *sod* (mystical sense).

Paschal pertaining to the Passover (ultimately from the Gk *pascha*, derived from Heb *pesaḥ*).

Passover *Haggadah, Haggadah of Pesaḥ* the "telling" of the Passover story in the context of the household liturgy of Pesaḥ, which accompanies the ritual meal, the **Seder.**

Passover see **Pesaḥ.**

patriarchs the founding fathers (*'avot*) of Israel: Abraham, Isaac, and Jacob.

patrilineal tracing one's descent through male ancestors; see **matrilineal.**

Pentapolis the five cities of the **Philistines** (see): Ashdod, Ashkelon, Ekron, Gath, Gaza.

Pentateuch (Gk "five scrolls") the first five books of the Bible—Genesis through Deuteronomy—regarded as a unit after its final editing during or after the exile. The traditional term in Judaism for this collection of books is Torah, "teaching." Although these five books are traditionally grouped together, they contain markedly different kinds of writing—prehistory, narrative, law, ritual instruction, etc.—and scholars have investigated the materials of which they are composed. Deuteronomy is largely a separate work that was probably attached to the first four books at a later stage, leading some scholars to speak of a **Tetrateuch** consisting of Genesis through Numbers; and it is also the case that the actual narrative climax of the story, the conquest of the land of Israel, is given in the book of Joshua, leading other scholars to speak of a **Hexateuch** consisting of Genesis through Joshua. See introduction to the Torah (pp. 1–7).

Persian period ca. 539–333 BCE, from the time of Cyrus the Great until the Greek conquest by Alexander.

Pesaḥ (probably "protection"; others "pass over") the name of the festival commemorating the exodus from Egypt. The first day involves the sacrifice of the lamb, which took place on the eve of the exodus (14 Nisan); the rest of the festival, *Ḥag ha-Matzot* or "festival of unleavened bread," was probably originally a festival marking the beginning of the spring barley harvest. Pesaḥ is the first of the **shalosh regalim** or "three pilgrim festivals."

peshat (Heb "simple") the "plain sense" or "contextual sense" of a text, often contrasted with *derash,* the homiletical meaning.

pesher, pesharim (Heb "interpretation") a type of commentary on the Bible from the Qumran community in which the biblical text is understood to be actualized or fulfilled in the interpreter's time period. Some are comments on verses in biblical order, while others group verses by subject; typically, the comment contains the word *pesher.*

Peshitta (Syriac "simple") a translation of the Bible into Syriac (a dialect of Aramaic) for the use of Syriac-speaking Jewish communities; it was largely taken over by Syriac-speaking Christians, who added a Syriac translation of the New Testament.

Pesikta de Rav Kahana and **Pesikta Rabbati** (Aram. *pesikta', "section"*) two collections of midrash that deal with selected biblical passages, the first dating from the 5th–7th century, the second from the 9th–13th.

petiḥta ("opening") an introduction to a midrashic unit, often begun with a verse unconnected to the biblical text being interpreted. Sometimes termed "proem."

Pharisees a movement among Jews in the 1st century CE, according to Josephus and the writings in the New Testament. The Pharisees were concerned to extend Jewish practice into all areas of life, and followed the tradition of interpretation **(Oral Torah)** associated with the schools of **Hillel** and Shammai. They were thus proponents of a Jewish identity separate from the larger non-Jewish culture that surrounded Judea, but were also opponents of the more conservative Sadducees, who did not accept their traditions of oral law. See **Sadducees.**

Philistines a group from the **Sea Peoples,** who invaded and settled on the coastal region of Canaan. They had been repulsed from an invasion of Egypt (ca. 1190 BCE). The five major Philistine cities (the **Pentapolis**) were Ashkelon, Ashdod, Ekron, Gath, and Gaza.

Philo Judaeus (ca. 20 BCE–50 CE) Hellenistic Jewish philosopher of Alexandria, Egypt. Philo worked out a system that tried to interpret biblical concepts and beliefs in terms of the philosophy of Plato and his followers. In this system, God cannot be known directly, but only through intermediate beings; the soul, the higher element in the human person, is always attempting to return to God, its origin, although if this task is not far enough along at the time of the individual's death, the soul may have to transmigrate into another body and try again. In trying to make this philosophy compatible with Judaism, Philo developed a highly allegorical exegesis of the Bible.

Phoenicians the people who lived in the area north of Israel, in part of what is present-day Lebanon. Their chief cities were Tyre and Sidon. The Phoenicians were known throughout the eastern Mediterranean region as merchants, and for producing a reddish-purple dye, from which they apparently got their name (*phoinix* is the Gk word for the color of the dye).

phylacteries see **tefillin.**

pilpul dialectical argument; superseded in talmudic study in some locations by logical argument promoted by the followers of the Vilna Gaon.

Pirkei 'Avot ("chapters of the Fathers") a tractate of the **Mishnah** (called *'Avot*) that begins by tracing the transmission of the oral law from Moses to the Rabbis; emphasizes the strong link between Torah study and ethical behavior; and contains non-legal, moralistic sayings of various Rabbis. *'Avot* is included in the traditional prayerbook and is made part of the liturgical recitation in many communities.

piyyut (formed from *payyetan,* the creator of a liturgical poem; from Gk *poietes,* "thing made," "poem") a liturgical poem accompanying the prayers in the synagogue service. *Piyyutim* began to be composed around the 5th century in the land of Israel, and new ones continued to be created up until the 18th century.

plene spelling (from Latin "full") the form of a word in the Heb text that includes all of the vowel letters. See **defective spelling.**

primogeniture the social arrangement by which the eldest son inherits a father's title or the bulk of the father's property.

proem a short introduction or preface to a literary text. See *petihta.*

proleptic anticipatory; literary device of foreshadowing or anticipating a later development in a narrative, or anticipating and answering an argument from an opponent.

prophet (Gk *prophetes,* "speak out" or "speak forth") the LXX translation of *navi'* ("one who is called"), the standard Heb term for prophet. Synonyms include "seer," "man of God," and "visionary." See the introduction to Nevi'im (pp. 451–461).

prophetic lawsuit see *riv.*

Pseudepigrapha (Gk "things falsely attributed") the name for a class of writings not included in the canon, many of which are ascribed to figures of antiquity like Enoch, Moses, and Solomon. Most of these works, which were not canonized by any community, were written by Jews in the Hellenistic period.

Purim the festival that commemorates the delivery of the Jews in Persia from destruction, as recounted in the book of Esther. It is celebrated on 14 or 15 Adar.

qere ("what is read") a biblical word as it should be pronounced, in contrast to what is written in the text. See *ketiv.*

qinah Heb "lament."

qinah meter a metrical pattern consisting of a line with three stresses followed by a line with two stresses; it is primarily used in psalms of lament or complaint, and in the book of Lamentations, though it can also express joy (Ps. 65).

Qumran community the settlement near Wadi Qumran at the Dead Sea, most likely composed of Essenes. The Qumran group was a sectarian Jewish community that kept its own practices in opposition to the established community in Jerusalem and Judea; the library of this group was discovered in 1947 and is known as the Dead Sea Scrolls.

Rabbanite an adherent of the rabbinic teaching tradition, in contrast to the **Karaites,** who questioned or denied many halakhic interpretations of the Rabbis.

Radak acronym for Rabbi David Kimhi (ca. 1160–1235), son of Yosef Kimhi, biblical commentator, of France. He wrote commentaries on Genesis, Psalms, Proverbs, Chronicles, and the Prophets, as well as a Hebrew grammar and lexicon.

Ralbag acronym for R. Levi ben Gershon, Gersonides (1288–1344), medieval talmudic scholar of France. Ralbag wrote on philosophy, astronomy, and mathematics, in addition to his biblical exegesis and talmudic explications; his conception of God was philosophical, particularly Aristotelian. He wrote commentaries on most of the books of the Bible.

Rambam acronym for Rabbi Moshe ben Maimon (Moses Maimonides) (1135–1204), a philosopher and rabbi—also a practicing physician—was probably the greatest medieval Jewish philosopher. His writings include *Sefer ha-Mitzvot* ("Book of the Commandments"), *Mishneh Torah,* a code of Jewish law, and the philosophical work *Guide of the Perplexed.* Originally from Spain, he lived part of his life in Egypt.

Ramban acronym for Rabbi Moshe ben Nahman (1194–1270), or Nahmanides, rabbi and scholar, of Spain. He defended Judaism against Christian arguments so effectively that he was persecuted and fled to

Israel (Acre); his writings on the Torah and on early kabbalistic works were influential in the later kabbalistic movement.

Rashbam acronym for Rabbi Shemuel ben Meir (ca. 1080–1160), talmudic and biblical commentator, of France. His biblical commentaries concentrated on explicating the literal sense of the text; he often disputed the commentary of his grandfather, Rashi.

Rashi acronym for Rabbi Shlomo ben Isaac (ca. 1040–1105), French talmudic and biblical scholar. He was the author both of a commentary on the whole Bible and of a commentary on the Talmud Bavli **(Babylonian Talmud),** both of which became extremely popular. His scriptural interpretation, largely taken from earlier sources, favored the contextual sense of the text rather than a set of atomistic interpetations to each phrase; his talmudic commentary was part of a greater effort to interpret Jewish law for an increasingly far-flung population.

Rav a 3rd century Babylonian 'amora' whose real name was 'Abba ben 'Aivu. "Rav" means "great" and is a tribute to the regard in which he was held by his students at the academy in Sura, which he founded. Rav and Mar Samuel are seen as the main teachers in the tradition that became the Babylonian Talmud. Rav's specialty was issues relating to religious law and interpretation.

redaction criticism the study of how already existing textual units—narratives of incidents, laws, proverbs, or other isolatable pieces that can be disentangled by **source criticism**—were combined into larger texts by the activities of editors, called "redactors." Redaction criticism concentrates on the perspective of the editor, trying to deduce what editorial intentions can be understood from the way smaller units are arranged, expanded, and combined.

redactor an editor who works with already existing units to combine them into larger wholes.

riv (pronounced "reev") the literary form in the Prophets and elsewhere of a "covenant lawsuit."

Roman period the period from 63 BCE onwards, marking the beginning of Roman rule of Judea.

Rosh Ha-Shanah (Heb "head [i.e., beginning] of the year") the fall New Year in the Jewish calendar, 1 Tishri. (Rosh Ha-Shanah is now observed for two days.) The beginning of the religious calendar is 1 Nisan.

Rosh Ḥodesh (Heb "new moon") the beginning of the month, celebrated as a festival in biblical times (e.g., Isa. 1.13–14).

Saadia Gaon Saadia ben Joseph (882–942) was the *gaon* (head of the academy) of Sura in Babylonia and the greatest of the *geonim*. He translated the Torah and other books of the Bible into Arabic, along with a short commentary.

Sadducees a movement among Jews in the 1st century CE, according to Josephus and the New Testament. They held to a strict application of Torah and to maintaining Temple worship according to its mandate; in order to continue the Temple practices without interference, the Sadducees were apparently willing to collaborate with the occupying Roman power to some extent, including accepting Roman interference in the choice of high priest. They were opposed to the Pharisees in not accepting the traditions of oral law as a guide to Torah practices, and they were also opposed to the political activists who wished to rebel against Roman rule, fearing that any rebellion would bring an end to the limited autonomy under which they could maintain Temple worship. See **Pharisees.**

Samaritan Pentateuch a text of the Torah in Hebrew used by the **Samaritans.** This text disagrees with the **Masoretic Text** at many points. Some of these disagreements reflect Samaritan beliefs (e.g., in the religious importance of Mt. Gerizim), but others are supported by the **Dead Sea Scrolls** and reflect an alternate textual tradition.

Samaritans the descendants of the population of Samaria (Northern Kingdom) after the invasion of that kingdom and the deportation of the inhabitants in 722 BCE. The Samaritans regard themselves as descended from the Jewish remnant after the deportation, but the returning exiles from the Southern Kingdom (after the Babylonian exile) did not regard them as Jews, seeing them rather as descendants of foreigners who had been settled there after the Jewish population had been removed. Therefore, beginning with Ezra and Nehemiah, the leadership forbade intermarriage between Samaritans and Jews. The Samaritans maintained worship (with a temple on Mt. Gerizim) and the Torah (but not the rest of the Bible), although their calendar is not the same as the Jewish calendar.

Samuel ben Ḥofni (also Shemuel ben Ḥofni) **gaon** of the **Sura** academy in Babylonia from ca. 997 until his death in 1013. He wrote commentaries in Judeo-Arabic on parts of the Torah (including a translation), and also philosophical and theological works.

Samuel, Mar 2nd–3rd century Babylonian 'amora', a contemporary of Rav and founder of the other great Babylonian academy at Nehardea. Samuel and Rav are the two sources of the teaching that became the Babylonian Talmud; Samuel specialized in issues related to civil law.

Sanhedrin (ultimately from Gk *synedria* from *syn-* and *hedra*, "with seat," i.e., "council") the religious court that held ruling authority over the Jewish people during the Roman period and into the Byzantine era; also, a tractate of the **Mishnah** dealing with issues of the law courts in general.

scroll a long strip of parchment (treated leather) or papyrus (reeds split, moistened, and pressed together), on which a text was written in columns. The scroll was read by unrolling one side while rolling up the other, to expose successive columns of text.

Sea Peoples remnants of the Mycenean or Aegean civilizations, which collapsed towards the end of the second millennium BCE. Some of these people sailed eastward on the Mediterranean and attacked those living along the **littoral;** they were repulsed from Egypt (ca. 1190) and settled along the coast of Canaan at about the same time the Israelites were entering the land from the other direction. The biblical **Philistines** are among the Sea Peoples.

Second Isaiah see **Deutero-Isaiah.**

Second Temple the Temple constructed ca. 515 BCE by the returning exiles, and continued and expanded over the course of time, until its destruction by the Romans in 70 CE.

Seder, Sedarim (Heb "order") the ritual meal and recitation of Passover eve. Also, the major divisions of the **Mishnah.**

Seder 'Olam ("order of the world") a rabbinic history of the world and the Jewish people up to the 2nd century CE.

Sefirot ("ciphers" or numbers) the ten numbers that formed part of the basis of creation in mystical thought; primarily the emanations from the Godhead that correspond to these numbers.

Seleucid empire the political entity that ruled over Syria and (at times) Judea after the death of Alexander the Great. The Seleucid ruler Antiochus IV "Epiphanes" desecrated the Temple in 167 BCE, leading to the Maccabean revolt and the rededication of the Temple in 164 BCE, an event commemorated in the festival of Ḥanukkah.

Sephardim based on Sepharad, the early Jewish name for Spain (based on a misunderstanding of Obad. 1.20, which refers to Asia Minor, specifically Lydia); by extension the name of Jews living in Iberia or descended from those who did.

Septuagint the Gk translation of the Heb text of the Bible, begun with the Torah in Alexandria in the 3rd century BCE. According to a legend repeated in the *Letter of Aristeas,* 72 scholars gathered to translate and finished their work in 72 days; this number, rounded to 70 and represented in Latin as LXX, became the standard symbol for the Septuagint.

Sforno, Ovadiah ben Yaakov (1475–1550) philosopher and Bible commentator of Italy. Sforno was concerned to explicate the plain meaning of the text, and was opposed to kabbalistic interpretation.

Shabbat (Heb "cessation") the Sabbath day; also, a Tractate in the **Mishnah** (order Mo'ed), in the **Tosefta** and in the **Talmuds,** dealing with the laws of Shabbat.

Shaḥarit (Heb "morning") the morning prayer service. See *Minḥah, Ma'ariv.*

shalosh regalim "three pilgrimages," the three Pilgrim Festivals—Pesaḥ, Shavuot, Sukkot, when all Israelite males were expected to go up to the Jerusalem Temple.

Shavuot the festival of "Weeks" (also "Pentecost," Gk for "fiftieth" [day]), the spring harvest, occurring according to Priestly texts fifty days (seven full weeks) after Pesaḥ. It is the second of the *shalosh regalim.*

Shekhinah a postbiblical term for the "dwelling" or "presence" of God with Israel; by extension, the divine manifestation in the community's life, or the sense of divine immanence within the world. In kabbalistic thought, Shekhinah is the feminine aspect of God that must be reconciled with the masculine, higher aspects so that God's love can be manifested in the world.

Shem, ha-Shem "name" or "the Name," a locution for YHVH to avoid saying the actual name of God (see Deut. 28.58).

Shema the first word, used as a title, of the exhortation (Deut. 6.4), "Hear, O Israel, the LORD our God is one LORD" (or, "the LORD our God, the LORD is one"); also the name of perhaps the most important and best-known prayer in Judaism, comprised of Deut. 6.4–9; 11.13–21; Num. 15.37–41.

Shemini 'Atzeret "eighth [day] of assembly," following the seven days of Sukkot; in the Diaspora it is celebrated as two days, the second of which is *Simḥat Torah.*

Shemoneh 'Esrei "the Eighteen," rabbinic name for the *'Amidah,* from the number of benedictions in the original prayer.

Shemuel ben Meir see **Rashbam.**

Sheol the underworld or abode of the dead. In the Bible, all deceased descended to Sheol; there is no concept of a separate heaven and hell.

Shephelah the foothills leading to the central hill country of the land of Israel.

Shimeon bar Yoḥai (also Simeon ben Yoḥai) a 2nd century Rabbi, pupil of R. Akiva ben Yosef and teacher of R. Judah *ha-Nasi'* **(Judah the Prince).** R. Shimeon began the classification of **halakhah.** He was the subject of legendary tales based on the period of his life in which he was in hiding from Roman persecution, reportedly living in a cave. The medieval kabbalists claimed that during this sojourn in the cave the doctrines of mysticism were revealed to him, and thus the **Zohar** is presented as teachings of, and tales about, R. Shimeon.

Shi'ur Komah mystical work from the 10th century CE or earlier, which tries to convey a sense of God's infinite greatness by a description of God's immense size.

Shiv'ah (Heb "seven") the seven days of mourning following the death of a near relative.

Shlomo ben Isaac, R. see **Rashi**.

shofar the ram's horn for ceremonial use. In ancient Israel it was sounded to announce the anointing of a king or as a summons to war or to sound an alarm; today, in the synagogue, it is sounded on the High Holy Days.

Siddur (Heb "order") the traditional Jewish prayerbook.

signet ring a ring bearing a personal seal or impression, used to make an indentation in clay as a sign of authenticity of authorship.

Simḥat Torah "rejoicing of Torah," the second day of *Shemini 'Atzeret,* marking the completion of the annual Torah reading cycle.

simile a comparison between two unlike things in which one is compared with the other on the basis of a posited similarity, usually using the terms *like* or *as:* "My heart is like wax, melting within me" (Ps. 22.15).

sod (Heb "secret") in mystical interpretation, the hidden or inner meaning of a text; the hidden or inner life of God.

source criticism the effort to discover the written sources or documents behind a text and to explore how the sources were combined into larger units. See **Documentary Hypothesis.**

Spinoza, Baruch (Benedict) (1632–77) philosopher. Spinoza was born a Jew, but as his philosophy developed he became increasingly at odds with traditional Jewish teaching, and he was excommunicated at the age of 24. Besides his philosophical writings, Spinoza engaged in biblical criticism (see esp. his "Of the Interpretation of Scripture" in his *Theological-Political Tractate*), and in some respects anticipated critical findings that did not become established until well after his death, including the assertion that someone other than Moses wrote the Torah.

Sukkot (Heb "booths") the autumn harvest festival (*ḥag ha-'asif,* "festival of ingathering"), during which it is customary, following Lev. 23.42–43, to dwell in temporary booths. It is the third of the *shalosh regalim.*

Sumer the civilization that arose in southern Mesopotamia during the late 4th millennium BCE. Organized around city-states, the Sumerian culture held sway for most of that time until it was finally superseded by Hammurabi in 1750 BCE. The Sumerians developed cuneiform writing, which involved using a wedge-shaped reed to press marks into wet clay. The clay was then baked and the resulting tablet could be stored. Many cuneiform tablets have been recovered from archeological sites in Mesopotamia, from Sumer and from later civilizations, such as Babylonia, that adopted the cuneiform method of writing.

Sura the southern Babylonian city that was the site of one of the two academies (the other was in Pumbedita) that were centers of rabbinic and geonic study. Sura was founded by **Rav** in the 3rd century CE and continued in existence for more than 800 years.

suzerain the lord or ruler to whom loyalty is due in a covenant relationship. (Although the term is actually Old French for "sovereign," and originally applied to the feudal relationship of lord to peasant or subsidiary, it has been adapted for the ancient Near Eastern covenant system.)

Symmachus a 2nd–3rd century translator of the Bible into Greek, whose translation was included in Origen's **Hexapla** (a compendium of six Bible versions). Most of the Hexapla, and therefore most of Symmachus's translation, has been lost, and nothing is known about Symmachus as a person.

syncretism the incorporation into one religion of practices and teachings derived from another, or the effort to combine two different religious traditions into a third, composite religion.

synecdoche figure of speech in which a part of a thing or concept is used to represent the whole—e.g., "hand" for "worker"—or the larger whole is used to represent the part—e.g., "the law" for "police."

synonymous parallelism an imprecise term used for the type of parallelism (see **parallelism**) where the second line or *colon* of a *bicolon* echoes the meaning of the first in different terms, e.g., Isa. 1.3, "An ox knows its owner, An ass its master's crib: Israel does not know, My people takes no thought." See "Reading Biblical Poetry" (pp. 2097–2104).

Tabernacle the temporary sanctuary for containing the Ark of the Covenant, and for worship and sacrifice in the wilderness according to Priestly tradition. Exod. chs 25–30 contain instructions for building it; the construction is narrated in Exod. chs 35–40.

tablet a slab, typically of clay, with a smoothed surface that can be inscribed with a text.

talion (Latin *talio,* "in kind" from *talis,* "like," "such like") a punishment that is of the same kind as the crime: exacting an equivalent penalty, such as an equal economic loss for theft, or death for murder, or "an eye for an eye." Talion is well-attested in Mesopotamian law, and in some biblical legal collections.

tallit four-cornered fringed shawl worn during prayer; also called *tallit gadol,* "large tallit," in contrast to *tallit katan,* "small tallit," worn throughout the day beneath the clothing by observant Jewish men (see Num. 15.38–39; Deut. 22.12).

Talmud (Heb "teaching") the title of the two great collections of rabbinic teaching, the Jerusalem Talmud or Talmud Yerushalmi and the Babylonian Talmud or Talmud Bavli. The Talmuds were compiled beginning after 200 CE, as an extensive commentary on the **Mishnah;** they consist of comments on, and extensions of, the Mishnah sections to work out the application of Jewish teaching to everyday life, but they also include much other material, and information and teaching on a wide range of topics. The form of the Talmuds is that passages of the Mishnah are commented on by rabbinic teachings (called **Gemara**). The Mishnah is not treated in its entirety. At the beginning of the Talmud's formation, the two centers of rabbinic study (the land of Israel and Babylonia) were in contact with each other and the commentary therefore reflected a common effort; later, especially with the completion of the Talmud in Israel (ca. 400 CE), the Babylonian effort continued to refine and extend the applications, and it was the Talmud developed in Babylonia (completion after 500 CE) that was distributed worldwide, under the auspices of the academies that continued to work in Babylonia until the beginning of the second millennium CE.

tanna' (Aram. "repeat" [traditions]) a rabbinic teacher during the period from the destruction of the Second Temple (70 CE) to the final form of the **Mishnah** (ca. 200 CE).

Targum, Targumim Aramaic translations of the Bible. There are two main texts on the Torah: *Targum Onkelos,* used by Babylonian Jews, and *Targum Yerushalmi* or the Jerusalem Targum (often mistakenly called Targum Jonathan), used in the land of Israel.

tefillin small black leather boxes containing biblical passages from Exod. 13.1–10; 13.11–16; Deut. 6.4–9; 11.13–21. Two are worn during weekday morning prayer: one on the head (above the space between the eyes, just below the hairline) and one on the (left) arm (see, e.g., Deut. 6.8).

tel a mound formed by repeated occupation and destruction on a particular site.

teshuvah (Heb "return") repentance.

Tetragrammaton (Gk "four letters") the divine name, YHVH (see).

Tetrateuch the first four books of the Bible, Genesis through Numbers, regarded by some scholars as an edited collection to which Deuteronomy was then attached. See **Pentateuch.**

textual criticism the effort to establish, by scholarly assessment of manuscript copies and other sources, an accurate version of a text. See "Textual Criticism of the Bible" (pp. 2067–72).

Textus Receptus (Latin "received text") the standard text in a tradition. For the Hebrew text the "received

text" is understood to be the Masoretic Text, particularly that in the Rabbinic Bible *(Miqra'ot Gedolot)* in the 1525 edition published in Venice.

theodicy the theological effort to justify the goodness of God in the face of suffering.

Theodotion (ca. 2nd century CE) a translator of the Bible into Greek and reviser of the **Septuagint.**

theophany (Gk "appearance of god") the temporary appearance or manifestation of a divine being in a form that can be apprehended by the human senses.

Third Isaiah see **Trito-Isaiah.**

threshing floor a location where the usable portion of grain is separated from its outer covering. Grain is threshed by being beaten to crack the husks and separate the grain from the stems. It is then winnowed by being tossed in a flat basket in a breeze, allowing the husks (chaff), which are lighter, to blow away. A good location for this process is a flat area on a hilltop; this was also an ideal spot for offering sacrifice (see 1 Chron. 21.18–27).

Tiamat goddess of the deep and mother of the Babylonian pantheon; she is sometimes portrayed as a dragon.

Tish'ah be'av 9 Av, the day of mourning commemorating the destruction of the two Temples. 2 Kings 25.8–9 says that the First Temple was burned (by the Babylonians) on 7 Av, while Jer. 52.12 dates it on 10 Av; the **Talmud** places it on 9 Av. The Second Temple was destroyed (by the Romans) on 10 Av.

tosafist author of **tosafot** (see).

tosafot brief commentaries on the Talmud (12th–14th century) by rabbis in France and Germany, which are printed in the outer columns. The tosafot carry on the talmudic traditions of conversation and interaction with the text and with previous commentators, including resolving contradictions, extending applications, and revisiting matters previously discussed.

Tosefta (Aram. "addition") a compilation of oral law, of uncertain provenance and date, that follows the arrangement of the **Mishnah.**

tradition criticism the investigation of the development of a text from its earliest stages (oral or original source documents) to the latest (canonical) stage.

Transjordan the area to the east of the Jordan River.

Trito-Isaiah the scholarly term for chs 56–66 (or 55–66) of Isaiah. These chs are primarily concerned with the life of the returned exiles in the province of Yehud (the Persian name for Judah) after 538 BCE. Some scholars doubt the separate existence of Trito-Isaiah; others maintain that it is not the product of one author, but a collection of diverse oracles by different members of a "school of Isaiah" collected during the Persian period.

Tzevaot, Yhvh "Lord of Hosts," a title for God as leader of the heavenly armies (Ps. 89.6–9).

tzitzit the fringes attached to the four corners of a garment (Num. 15.38); also the entire garment that has such fringes, usually identical to the *tallit katan* (see **tallit**).

Ugarit city near the Mediterranean coast (Ras-Shamra in present-day Syria), source of an important store of Canaanite myths. Beginning in the 1920s archeological excavations in and around the area led to the discovery of a large number of cuneiform tablets in **Akkadian**, and others in a previously unknown language (subsequently named Ugaritic) which was related to Hebrew. The tablets also provided an archive of the political and economic activities of the rulers of Ugarit during the second half of the second millennium (1500–1200 BCE).

unleavened bread (Heb *matzah*, pl. *matzot*) bread made without yeast; also the festival, *Ḥag ha-Matzot*, that follows **Pesaḥ** (see).

Urim and Thummim a method of divination (the details of which are unclear) that the high priest used to discover God's response to yes-or-no questions.

Vassal Treaty of Esarhaddon an Assyrian treaty document from the reign of the Assyrian king Esarhaddon (681–669 BCE), with parallels to parts of Deuteronomy.

vassal the underlord in a covenant relationship, who is granted power and control over people in a particular area in return for loyalty to the suzerain.

Vilna Gaon see **Elijah ben Solomon Zalman.**

Vorlage (German "preceding position," i.e., pattern) the underlying text of a translation.

Vulgate (Latin "common") the Bible translated by **Jerome** (completed 405 CE). The Old Testament of the Vulgate was translated directly from Hebrew, unlike that of the previous Latin version (the "Old Latin" or "Vetus Latina"), which was translated from the **Septuagint.**

wadi a seasonal watercourse, dry in the summer and full of water during the winter rainy period.

Weeks, Festival of see **Shavuot.**

Wisdom literature modern scholarship has identified the books of Proverbs, Ecclesiastes, and Job, and certain Psalms (e.g., Ps. 37) as examples of a type of literature with analogues in other ancient Near Eastern literatures. Wisdom is concerned with matters of insight and meditation on the meaning of life, moral exhortation, and the identification of recurrent patterns in nature and human life. Wisdom generally focuses on the individual rather than the nation, and therefore does not examine many of the events and teachings central to biblical literature, such as the exodus, Temple worship and sacrifice, the covenant, the monarchy, or prophecy.

Yehud designation of the province of Judah during Persian times.

Yerushalmi, Talmud the Jerusalem (sometimes called Palestinian) Talmud. See **Talmud.**

Yhvh the name of God, which conventionally remains unpronounced and is represented in the text by the Heb letters *yod-he-vav-he* and the vowels for the title *Adonai*, "my Lord." In standard English translations, including NJPS, Yhvh is represented by the word Lord written in capital and small capital letters. The original vocalization and meaning of this name is unknown, though it is connected to the verb *h-y-h*, "be" or "become," most likely in a causitive sense, "he who causes to be."

Yom Kippur (Heb "day of atonement") the solemn fast observed each year on 10 Tishri, according to the command recorded in Lev. 23.26–32. The observance involves abstention of various kinds and focuses on personal and communal repentance **(teshuvah).** The prayer services begin with the evening service and continue through the next day, with a morning service, an additional service, an afternoon service, and a concluding service.

Yose (Yosi, Yossi) ben Ḥalafta mid-2nd century *tanna'.* He was a pupil of R. Akiva and one of the Rabbis frequently quoted in the **Mishnah.**

ziggurat a temple-tower in ancient Mesopotamia. Ziggurats are presumed to represent a mount, on the top of which the earthly and divine realms merged.

Zohar ("Splendor") kabbalistic writing of the late 13th century, partly the work of **Moshe de Leon** (d. 1305).

Index

This index contains entries to important, extended, or recurring persons, places, and subject matter in the study material.

A

Aaron: communication of ritual laws to, 229, 234, 247; death of, 324–25, 339, 350, 352; denial of entry to promised land, 323–24; Exodus, 109, 112, 114, 117, 140, 147–48, 162, 165, 182, 185; Ezekiel, 1055; genealogy, 338; God speaking directly to, 319; Korah rebellion, 288, 315–19, 336, 338–39; Leviticus, 222–28; Moses, speaking against, 308–9; Nadab and Abihu consumed by fire, 225, 227, 288, 317, 338; Numbers, 288; Psalms, 1412, 1414, 1432

Aaronide priesthood, 5 (see also individual high priests); Chronicles, 1724, 1756–57; Exodus, 162, 171; Ezra-Nehemiah, 1674, 1680, 1686; high priest and governor/king sharing power in postexilic period, 1432; Leviticus, 203, 222–28; Numbers, 288, 334, 335

Abaddon, 1471, 1491

abandonment by God, 1049, 1056–76, 1108, 1305, 1598

Abarbanel, Isaac, see Abravanel (Abarbanel, Abrabanel), Isaac

Abel and Cain, 18–19, 57, 209, 248, 1059, 1264, 1526

Abiathar, 566, 604, 605, 634, 646, 654, 672, 676, 679, 917, 921

Abigail, 608–10, 621, 1719, 1721

Abijah/Abijam (son of Rehoboam), 706, 707, 1785–87, 1806

Abimelech, 31, 42–43, 45, 54, 55, 60, 637, 1318, 1399

Abiram and Dathan, rebellion of, 315–16, 336, 389, 1402

Abishag the Shunammite, 671, 675–76

Abishai, 611, 626, 648, 654, 659

Abner, 622–25, 657, 1760

abominations, see idols and idol-worship

abortion, 25, 154

Abraham: 1 Chronicles, 1717; Deuteronomy, 359; Ezra-Nehemiah, 1, 1666, 1701; Genesis, 8, 10, 30–52, 54, 92; Isaiah, 864, 887; Jeremiah, 932, 990; Job more virtuous than, 1505; Leviticus, 207, 251, 270, 276–77; Psalms, 1399

Abram's name changed to Abraham, 8, 37–38

Abravanel (Abarbanel, Abrabanel), Isaac: biblical interpretation and study, 1895, 1906; Chronicles, 1714; Hosea, 1144; Jeremiah, 1008; Joel, 1168; Judges, 554; Kings, 672, 676, 707, 771; Obadiah, 1197; philosophy, 1961–62, 1964; Psalms, 1299; Samuel, 606, 626

Absalom, 638–53, 656, 671, 1287, 1335

abstinence, see fasting and abstinence

Abulafia, Abraham ben Shemuel, 1982–83

Abulafia, Rabbi Meir (Ramah), 1780, 2081, 2083

"accidental" or every-day occurrences, God's will manifested in (providence), 575, 577, 705, 724

Achan, sin of, 474–75, 502

Achsah, 462, 490, 492, 511

acrostics, 2100; Lamentations, 1588; Proverbs, 1497; Psalms, 1291, 1293, 1309, 1310, 1318, 1319, 1322, 1409, 1415

Adam and Eve, 9, 14–18, 30, 851, 1276, 1507, 1717

Adonai, 112, 137, 1206

Adonijah, 638, 671–76

adoption, 94–95, 100

adultery: Deuteronomy, 377, 417; Esther, Haman believed to be attempting to seduce, 1634–35; Exodus, 149, 150, 156; Ezekiel's allegory of, 1067–71, 1084–86; Genesis, 78; Hosea, 1143–52; Isaiah, 897; Jeremiah, marriage motif in, 923, 926–28, 952–54, 958, 963, 971, 973, 988, 990, 995; Jeremiah's false prophets attempting to commit adultery with Nebuchadnezzar's daughters, 984; Job, 1536, 1544–1545; Leviticus, 254; Numbers, 294–95; Proverbs, 1452, 1456, 1458–60, 1496; 2 Samuel, David and Bathsheba, 635–39

Adversary, the (Satan/ha-Satan), 329, 665, 698, 1253, 1502–6

African-American understanding of exodus, 107

afterlife/personal resurrection: Daniel, 1665; Ecclesiastes, 1610, 1621; Ezekiel, valley of dry bones in, 1114, 1665; Isaiah, 834; Job, 1523; Proverbs, 1452, 1468; Psalms, 1289, 1292, 1314, 1337, 1369; Rabbinic Judaism, 834, 1114, 1665; 1 Samuel, 563

afterworld, see Sheol

Agag, 333, 589, 590, 1624, 1629

age at death/life span, 20, 72, 100, 438, 1385, 1562 (see also elders/elderly)

aggadah, 1847, 1848, 1858–62, 1876, 1895, 1934, 2009

agricultural festivals, 159–60, 263, 703, 1156–57 (see also specific festivals)

Ahab: Chronicles, 1790–93, 1797, 1822, 1823; Kings, 710–26, 741, 743, 745, 772; Micah, 1216; Psalms, 1332; Samuel, 635

Ahasuerus, 1245, 1623–39, 1659, 1676

Ahaz, 757, 771, 797–802, 1806–7, 1809

Ahaziah of Israel, 725–27, 741

Ahaziah of Judah, 742, 744, 745, 747, 1797–98

Ahijah, 699, 701, 705, 708

Ahimelech, 529, 530–34, 602–4, 611

Ahithophel, 647, 648, 649, 650

Ai, destruction of, 474–78, 552

'Akedah (binding of Isaac), 45–47, 54, 1768, 1936

Akitu or New Year Festival, Babylon, 877

Akiva (Aqiba) ben Yosef, R., 1845, 1852–53, 1864; Malachi, 1272; Zechariah, 1257

alcohol and intoxication (see also wine, grapes, vineyards, vines, and winepresses): Amos, 1181; cup of God's wrath/water of bitterness, 185.295, 977, 1347, 1365, 1532, 1596; Daniel, 1643;

God and religion by, 1624, 1631; principles and themes, 1279; Purim, 1276, 1279, 1933; text and annotations, 1625–39
eternity, *see* afterlife/personal resurrection; Sheol
Ethan the Ezrahite, 1282, 1381, 1757
ethical monotheism, 1186
ethics and morality: Amos, 1176, 1185–86; David and Bathsheba, depiction of, 636; Deuteronomic moral responsibilities, 415–16, 419–23; liturgy and prayers, morality as necessary accompaniment to, 1471; Malachi, 1271–72; Micah, 1205, 1208–9; neighbors, moral duties towards, 415; pattern and repetition in nature applied to moral life in wisdom literature, 1277; Psalmic theme, 1297, 1308, 1360, 1382; purity/impurity, moral vs. ritual, 2045–46; ritual actions, morality's primacy over, 955; sacrifice, morality's primacy over, 590, 785, 871, 914, 1153, 1176, 1186, 1215, 1287, 1338, 1471; theological foundation for, 389
Ethiopia, *see* Cush
ethnography, 2088, 2093–96
eunuchs, 418, 575, 896
Eve and Adam, 9, 14–18, 30, 851, 1276, 1507, 1717
evil and good, knowledge of, 16–18
evildoers of Psalms, 1288, 1293, 1321, 1350, 1388, 1407, 1438
Evil-merodoch, 779
excavations, *see* archeological evidence
exclusivist nature of later Israelite identity: Chronicles, 1731, 1819, 1820; exilic descent as sign of Jewish pedigree in Diaspora, 1628; Ezra-Nehemiah, 1673, 1676, 1701, 1711; purity/impurity issues, 2047; Ruth, 1579, 1585
exile: Amos, 1183; Assyrian exile of northern tribes, 758–60; Assyrian threat to and siege of Judah, 764; Babylon (*see* Babylonian exile); common Near Eastern practice of, 430; Moses in Midian, 109–10; objectives of, 776–77
Exodus (book): date, composition, authorship, and sources, 104–5; Genesis, transition from, 107; history and historiography, 103–4, 452, 2050; introduction, 102–7; Jewish tradition rooted in, 106–7; law and legal material, 102, 103, 105, 106–7; Leviticus and Numbers as direct continuation of, 204, 281; narrative structure and focus, 102–3; origins of names, 102; Psalms quoting, 1396; text and annotations, 107–202
exodus from Egypt (*see also* enslavement in and redemption from Egypt; wilderness, Israelites' wandering in): Chronicles' reticence regarding, 1716, 1720, 1729, 1744, 1747; dating of, 683; death of exodus generation, 367, 370, 374, 379; Ezekiel, 1063, 1077, 1079, 1089, 1103; Ezra-Nehemiah, 1681, 1701–2; historicity, 2050; Isaiah, 852, 871, 882, 888, 890, 972; Jeremiah, 944, 960, 964, 972, 986, 1010, 1013, 1016, 1017 (*see also* wilderness, Israelites' wandering in); Jordan, echoes of exodus in crossing of, 468–71; march through the desert from Sinai to Moab, 282–83; metaphorical use of, 1172–73, 1217; Philistines' knowledge of, 570, 571; Psalmic theme, 1283, 1307, 1308, 1352, 1353, 1354, 1366, 1367, 1368, 1373, 1374, 1400, 1411, 1433, 1434, 1435; Song of Deborah echoing elements of, 517; Song of Songs tied to events of, 1565; story of, 124–30, 274, 277, 377; undoing of, 431–32
exogamy, *see* intermarriage
exposure of corpses, 415, 482, 813, 1117
"eye for an eye," *see* talion
eyes, gouging out of, 580
Ezekiel: authorship, 1043; calculation of years of punishment of Israel in, 1051; chronological scheme, 1044, 1098; composition, compilation, and redaction, 1043; dating, 1043; Deutero-Isaiah, 1103; Deuteronomy, 407, 1054; divine throne chariot and attendant creatures, 1043, 1045–48, 1059–60, 1119; "dry bones," valley of, 834, 1042, 1113–14, 1117, 1665; Ezra compared to, 1680; Gog and Magog, 115–18, 1043; introduction,

1042–45; Isaiah, use of, 1067, 1100, 1101, 1103; Jeremiah influencing, 1061, 1062; Josiah's reforms of priesthood confirmed, 773; Leviticus, 207, 259, 1042; moral purity/impurity, 2045; Moses, compared to, 1042, 1043, 1050, 1059; Numbers, 303, 320, 341; people of the land, 748; priesthood and (*see* priesthood); reputation of God as theme of, 1112, 1293; scroll eaten by, 1049; structure and divisions, 1044–45; Temple (*see* Temple); text and annotations, 1045–1138; theologically challenging nature of, 1042, 1043, 1045; wife of Ezekiel, death of, 1088
Ezion-geber (Gulf of Eilat), 133, 161, 695, 698, 724, 1798
Ezra (person): Aaronide priesthood, inclusion in, 1680, 1686; apocryphal works attributed to, 1667–68; Chronicles, Ezra as author of, 1712; Ezekiel, compared to, 1680; Malachi, identified with, 1684; Moses, compared to, 1669, 1680–81; reading of Torah to people by, 1699–1700; return to Jerusalem by, 341, 1672, 1680–84; Torah knowledge of, 1672, 1680
"Ezra, Apocalypse of," 1668
Ezra-Nehemiah (book): Aramaic and Hebrew, use of both, 1668, 1676, 1681, 1700; authorship, 1667, 1668, 1669; Chronicles, as continuation of, 1666, 1667; Chronicles, authorship of, 1667; Chronicles, relationship to, 1667, 1712, 1716, 1731, 1825; dating, 1667, 1689; division into two books, 1667; early sources underlying, 1668; foreigners, 896; Haggai and Zechariah associated by, 1249; intermarriage crisis, 1669, 1682, 1684–86, 1704, 1709–11, 2047; introduction, 1666–71; Malachi, 1268; memoirs, 1668–69; narrative structure, 1669, 1670–71, 1688–89; Psalms, 1675; purity issues, 2047; single book, viewed in Jewish tradition as, 1276, 1667, 1689; text and annotations, 1671–87, 1689–1711; title, 1667; Torah, understanding of (*see* Torah); unity/separateness of Ezra and Nehemiah, debate over, 1667–68, 1689

F

fabric laws in Leviticus, 237–38, 254
fairness and justice, *see* divine justice; justice, human
faith and faithfulness (*see also* ḥesed; trust/confidence in God; unfaithfulness, punishment, repentance, and return to the Lord): Exodus, 136, 137, 189; Lamentations, 1596–97; Psalms, 1287, 1332, 1339, 1349, 1350, 1367, 1371, 1394; unity of religious traditions in Bible regarding, 2040
fallow land, 399–400 (*see also* sabbatical year)
false gods, *see* idols and idol-worship
false prophecy, *see* true and false prophecy
falsehood and lying, *see* honesty/dishonesty
family idols (household idols or teraphim), 64–65, 88, 547, 599–600, 1260, 1346, 2022
family life (*see also* children; gender roles/differences; marriage; parents): basic social unit, family as, 475; patriarchal family structure, 1269, 1271–72; Proverbs on family and friends, 1490; punishment of whole family for actions of male head, 1655; Ruth, family continuity as principle of, 1279; social-scientific analysis, 2094
famine: Amos, 1183–84, 1190; Exodus, 139; Ezekiel, 1052, 1054, 1055; Genesis, 82–94; Jeremiah, 956; 2 Kings, 734, 738, 740, 763, 777; Lamentations, 1599; Leviticus, 275–76; Proverbs, 1466; Psalms, 1318, 1400; Ruth, 1578, 1580; 2 Samuel, 658
farce, Esther viewed as, 1279
fasting and abstinence: Daniel, 1659; Esther, 1632, 1638; Exodus, 127, 159, 191; Ezra-Nehemiah, 1683, 1685, 1686, 1689, 1701; Gedaliah, Fast of, 1009, 1257; Isaiah, 899–900; Joel, 1168; Judges, 553; Leviticus, 246, 265; Malachi, 1275–76; Psalms, 1394; rain, fasting tradition associated with, 954; 1 Samuel, 618; 2 Samuel, 625; Temple destruction (*see* Tish'ah be'av); Zechariah, 1256–57
fat/suet, 210–11, 221, 229

X

Y

THE NEW OXFORD

BIBLE MAPS

JEWISH STUDY BIBLE

Prepared by Oxford Cartographers
and based on the Oxford Bible Atlas

MAP 1

The Land of Israel:
Genesis–Deuteronomy

GAD, etc.   Tribes of Israel
EDOM, etc.   Kingdoms said to have been
                       encountered by the Israelites
                       at the time of the settlement
                       (13th century B.C.E.)

0   10   20 Miles
0   10   20 Kilometers

MEDITERRANEAN

SEA

(Sea of Philistia)

Sidon

Damascus

A R A M
(SYRIA)

Mt. Lebanon

Mt. Hermon
(Sirion, Sion, Senir)

Ijon

Tyre

Uzu

Abel

Laish
(Dan)

Kanah

Beth-anath?

MAACAH

Kedesh

GESHUR

ARGOB

Achzib

Hazor

Aduru

BASHAN

Janoah   Merom

Acco

Chinnereth

Sea
of
Chinnereth

Golan

Karnaim
Ashtaroth

Mt. Carmel

Hannathon
Achshaph?

Madon

Beth-yerah
(Philoteria)

Yanoam

HAVVOTH-JAIR

Edrei

Shimron
Japhia

Jokneam

Shunem   Anaharath?

Ramoth-gilead

Dor

Megiddo

Taanach

Aruna

Beth-haggan
(En-gannim)

Beth-shean
Rehob

Pehel
(Pella)

Ham

Ibleam

Migdal

Gath of
Sharon

Dothan

Arubboth   Yehem

Socoh

Tirzah

Succoth

Penuel R. Jabbok

Mt. Ebal
Shechem

Mt. Gerizim

Mahanaim

Aphek

Joppa

Ono

Jazer

Jogbehah

Beth-dagon

Lod

Beth-nimrah
(Nimrah)

Rabbah

AMMON

Bethel
(Luz)   Ai

Jericho   Gilgal

Plains
of Abel-shittim
Moab   (Shittim)

Beth-horon

Gezer

Ajalon

Gibeon

Jerusalem
(Salem)

Beth-
jeshimoth

Heshbon

Elealeh

Ashdod

Ekron

Beth-shemesh

Timnah

Bethlehem
(Ephrath)

Mt.
Pisgah

Mt. Nebo

Bezer?

Gath?
Socoh

Ashkelon

Chezib

Adullam

Medeba

Kiriathaim

Keilah

Baal-meon
(Beon)

Gaza

Lachish

Eglon?

Beth-tappuah

Mamre
Hebron
(Kiriath-arba)

Ataroth

R. Nahaliel

Mattanah

Beth-eglaim
(Eglaim)

Kedemoth?

Yurza

Gerar

Ziklag?

Debir

Dibon
(Dibon-gad)

Aroer

Sharuhen

Wadi Arnon

Beer-sheba

Moladah

ARAD?

Hormah

Arad?

Bab ed-Dra

Ar

Aroer

Rehoboth

Ziph

Hazazon-tamar
(301 451N)

Zoar
es-Safi

Numeira

M O A B

The   N e g e b

Ascent of
Akrabbim

(Khanazir)

Feifa

E D O M
(S E I R)

Wadi zered

© Oxford University Press

Possible location of the cities of Sodom,
Gomorrah, Admah, Zeboiim, and Zoar
in the Valley of Siddim

R. Jordan

The Arabah

River Jordan

G I L E A D

M A N A S S E H

G A D

A M O R I T E S

R E U B E N

Hill Country of Israel

Plain of Sharon

The Shephelah

Hill Country of Judah

Dead Sea
(Salt Sea, Valley of Siddim)

Hills of Abarim

OUTER BORDER SHOWS 10 MILE SUBDIVISIONS

MAP 2

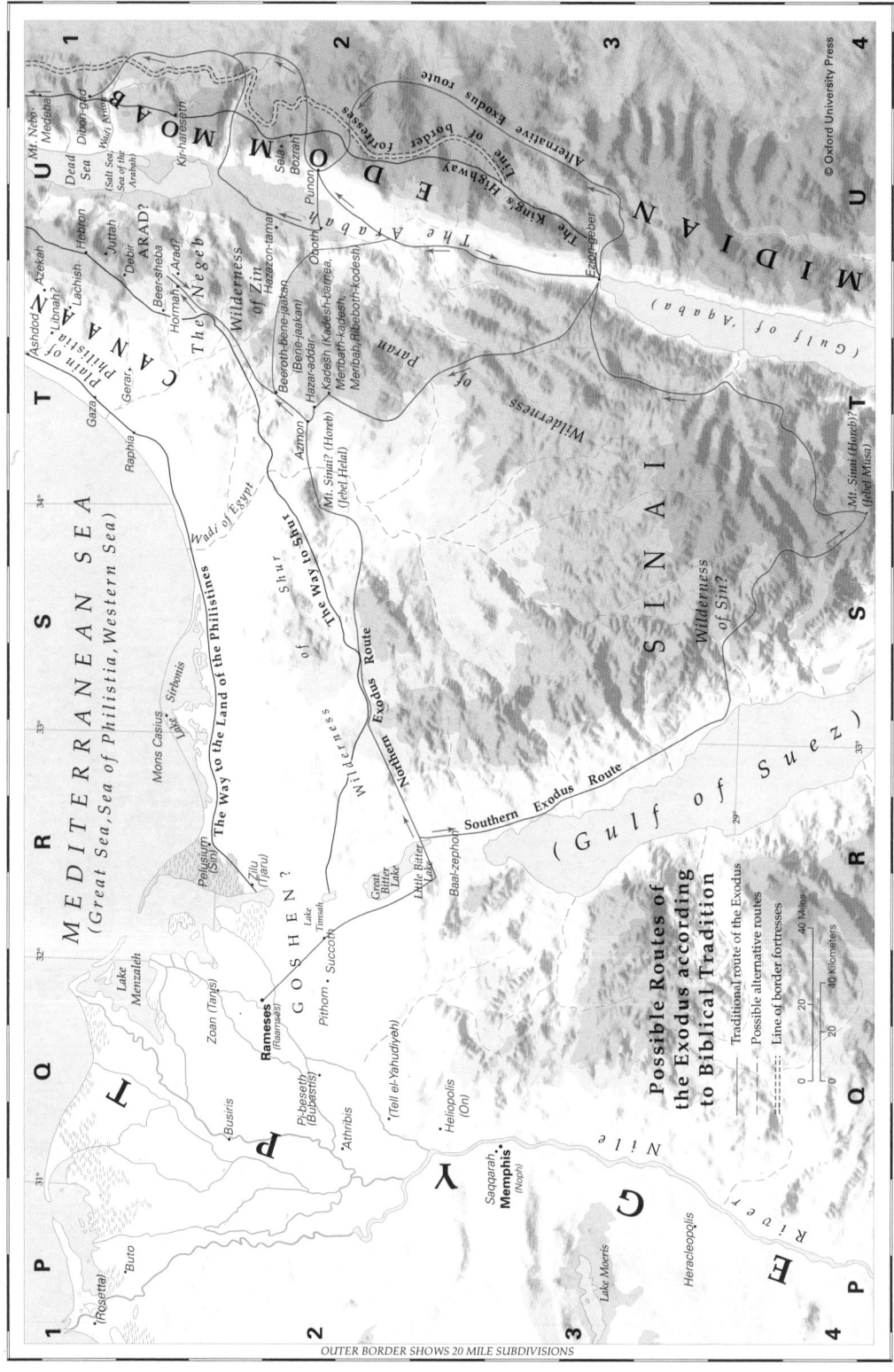

OUTER BORDER SHOWS 20 MILE SUBDIVISIONS

© Oxford University Press

Possible Routes of
the Exodus according
to Biblical Tradition

Traditional route of the Exodus
Possible alternative routes
Line of border fortresses

MEDITERRANEAN SEA
(Great Sea, Sea of Philistia, Western Sea)

CANAAN

EDOM

MOAB

MIDIAN

SINAI

EGYPT

GOSHEN?

The Way to the Land of the Philistines

The Way to Shur

Wilderness of Shur

Northern Exodus Route

Southern Exodus Route

(Gulf of Suez)

(Gulf of 'Aqaba)

The Arabah

The King's Highway

Line of border fortresses

Alternative Exodus route

Wilderness of Paran

Wilderness of Sin?

Wilderness of Zin

The Negeb

Plain of Philistia

Dead Sea
(Salt Sea, Sea of the Arabah)

Mt. Nebo?
Medeba
Dibon-gad
Wadi Arnon
Kir-hareseth
Sela
Bozrah
Punon

Ashdod?
Azekah
Libnah?
Lachish
Hebron
Juttah
Debir
Beer-sheba
Hormah? Arad?
ARAD?

Ezion-geber

Gaza
Gerar
Raphia

Wadi of Egypt

Azmon
Hazar-addar
Kadesh (Kadesh-barnea,
Meribath-kadesh,
Meribah Ribeboth-kadesh)
Beeroth-bene-jaakan
(Bene-jaakan)
Oboth
Hazazon-tamar

Mt. Sinai? (Horeb)
(Jebel Helal)

Mt. Sinai (Horeb)?
(Jebel Musa)

Mons Casius
Lake Sirbonis

Pelusium
(Sin)

Zilu
(Tjaru)

Baal-zephon
Little Bitter Lake
Great Bitter Lake
Lake Timsah

Lake Menzaleh

Zoan (Tanis)

Busiris

P-beseth
(Bubastis)
'Athribis

Rameses
(Raamses)
Pithom   Succoth

'(Tell el-Yahudiyeh)

Heliopolis
(On)

Saqqarah
Memphis
(Noph)

Rosetta?

Buto

Heracleopolis

Lake Moeris

Nile River

31°   32°   33°   34°   33°   29°   33°

40 Miles
40 Kilometers
20
20
0
0

MAP 3

OUTER BORDER SHOWS 10 MILE SUBDIVISIONS

MAP 4

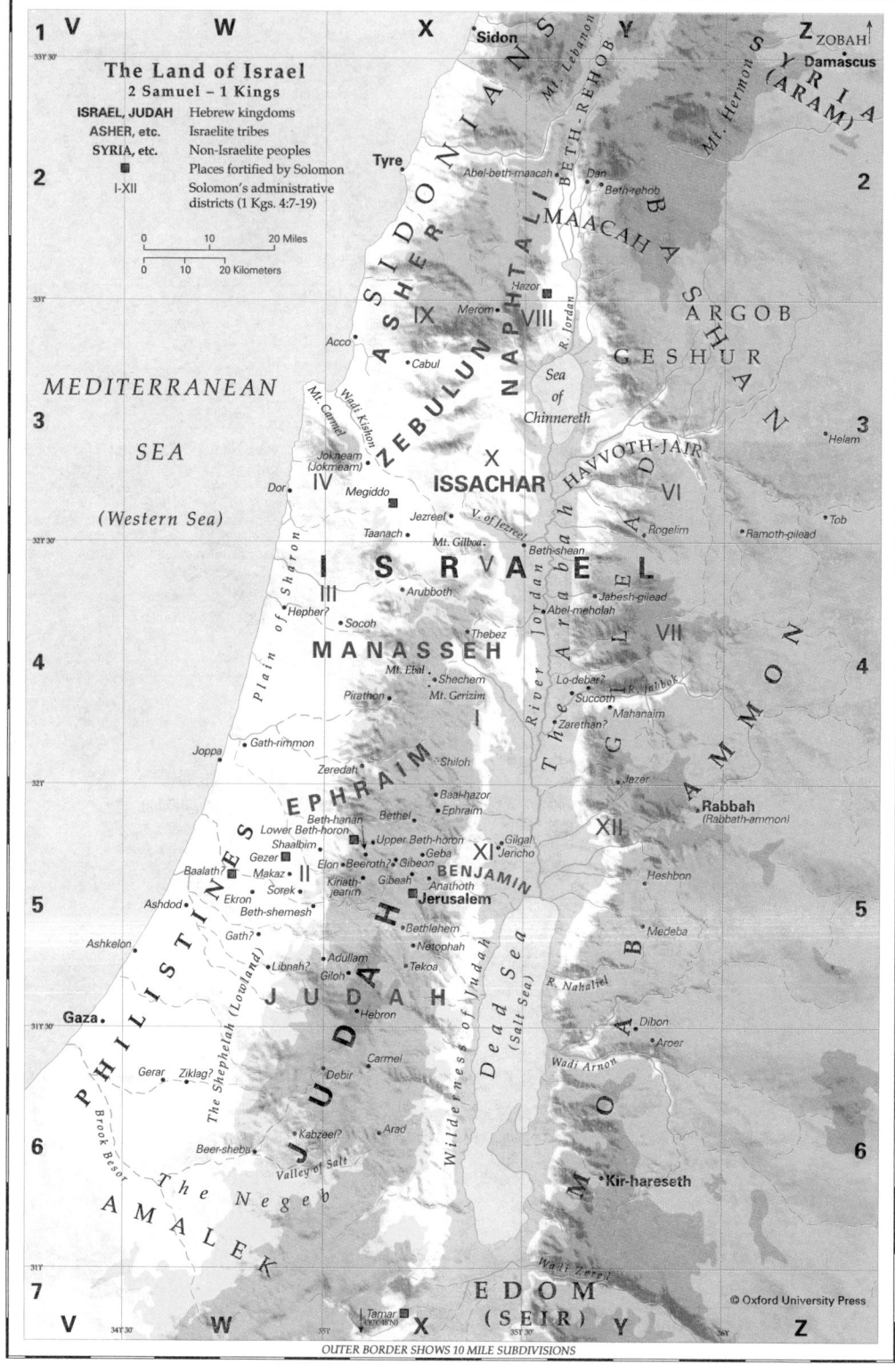

The Land of Israel
2 Samuel – 1 Kings

ISRAEL, JUDAH   Hebrew kingdoms
ASHER, etc.   Israelite tribes
SYRIA, etc.   Non-Israelite peoples

■   Places fortified by Solomon
I–XII   Solomon's administrative
districts (1 Kgs. 4:7-19)

0   10   20 Miles
0   10   20 Kilometers

MEDITERRANEAN

SEA

(Western Sea)

Sidon
Tyre
ZOBAH
Damascus
SYRIA (ARAM)
Mt. Lebanon
Mt. Hermon
SIDONIANS
ASHER
BETH-REHOB
Abel-beth-maacah
Dan
Beth-rehob
MAACAH
ARGOB
GESHUR
Hazor
Merom
VIII
Acco
Cabul
IX
NAPHTALI
R. Jordan
Sea of Chinnereth
Helam
ZEBULUN
Mt. Carmel
Wadi Kishon
Jokneam (Jokmeam)
IV
Megiddo
Dor
X
ISSACHAR
HAVVOTH-JAIR
VI
Tob
Ramoth-gilead
Jezreel
V. of Jezreel
Taanach
Mt. Gilboa
Beth-shean
Rogelim
Plain of Sharon
I S R A E L
Jabesh-gilead
Abel-meholah
GILEAD
VII
Arubboth
III
Hepher?
Socoh
Thebez
Lo-debar?
Succoth
Mahanaim
AMMON
MANASSEH
Mt. Ebal
Shechem
Pirathon
Mt. Gerizim
Zarethan?
R. Jabbok
Joppa
Gath-rimmon
Zeredah
Shiloh
Jezer
Baal-hazor
Ephraim
XII
Rabbah (Rabbath-ammon)
EPHRAIM
Beth-hanan
Bethel
Lower Beth-horon
Upper Beth-horon
Gilgal
Jericho
Heshbon
Shaalbim
Gezer
Elon
Beeroth?
Gibeon
Geba
XI
Baalath?
Makaz
Kiriath-jearim
Gibeah
Anathoth
BENJAMIN
II
Sorek
Ekron
Jerusalem
Ashdod
Gath?
Beth-shemesh
Bethlehem
Medeba
PHILISTINES
Libnah?
Giloh
Natophah
Tekoa
R. Nahaliel
MOAB
Ashkelon
Adullam
Dibon
Gaza
JUDAH
Hebron
Aroer
Gerar
Ziklag?
Debir
Carmel
Wadi Arnon
The Shephelah (Lowland)
Wilderness of Judah
Dead Sea (Salt Sea)
Kir-haresheth
Beer-sheba
Kabzeel?
Arad
Brook Besor
Valley of Salt
The Negeb
AMALEK
Wadi Zered
EDOM (SEIR)
Tamar
© Oxford University Press

V   W   X   Y   Z

MAP 5

The Land of Israel
2 Kings

ASHER, etc.   Tribal areas
SYRIA, etc.   Non-Israelite peoples
- - - -   Approximate boundary
between Israel, Judah
and Philistia

0   10   20 Miles
0   10   20 Kilometers

MEDITERRANEAN

SEA

(Western Sea)

© Oxford University Press

OUTER BORDER SHOWS 10 MILE SUBDIVISIONS

SIDONIANS
Sidon
Zarephath
Tyre
Abel-beth-maacah
(Abel-maim)
Ijon
Dan
Kedesh
Yiron
Hazor
Janoah
Merom
Acco
ASHER
GALILEE
NAPHTALI
Chinnereth
Sea of
Chinnereth
R. Jordan
Mt. Carmel
Wadi Kishon
Rumah
Hannathon
Gath-hepher
ZEBULUN
Mt. Tabor
ISSACHAR
Jokmeam
Dor
Megiddo
Shunem
Jezreel
V. of Jezreel
Taanach
Beth-haggan
Borim
Ibleam
Dothan
Socoh
Yazith
Samaria
Tirzah
Siphtan
MANASSEH
Mt. Ebal
Shechem
Mt. Gerizim
Pirathon
Baal-shalishah
Tappuah
Joppa
Zeredah
Shiloh
Jeshanah
EPHRAIM
Baal-hazor
Bethel
Ephron
Gath
(Gittaim)
Gimzo
Beth-horon
Zemaraim
Mizpah
Jabneel (Jabneh)
Gibbethon
Aijalon
Ramah
Geba
Mount Baalah
Shikkeron
Gibeah
Anathoth
BENJAMIN
Baalath?
Timnah
Zorah
Jerusalem
Ekron
Beth-shemesh
Middin
Ashdod
Azekah
Socoh
Bethlehem
Etam
Ashkelon
Gath?
Adullam
Beth-zur
Tekoa
Libnah
Mareshah
Zair
Lachish
JUDAH
Hebron
Adoraim
Ascent of Ziz
Gaza
Ziph
PHILISTIA
Carmel
En-gedi
(Salt Sea,
Eastern
Sea)
Gerar
Yurza?
The Shephelah (Lowland)
Raphia
Sharuhen
Brook Besor
Beer-sheba
Valley of Salt
Gurbaal
Great Arad
Arad of Beth-yeroham?
SIMEON
The Negeb
Dead
Sea
Middin
Secacah?
Nibshan?
City of Salt?
Br. Kidron
Wilderness
Judah
V. of Berach
V. of Achor
EDOM
Hazazon-tamar
(30? 48?)

SYRIA
(ARAM)
ZOBAH
R. Abana
Damascus
Mt. Lebanon
Lebo-Hamath
Mt. Hermon
R. Pharpar
BASHAN
MANASSEH
Karnaim
Ashtaroth
Aphek
HAURAN
HAVVOTH-JAIR
Beth-arbel
Edrei
Ramoth-gilead
Tishbe
Brook Cherith
Abel-
meholah
River Jordan
The Arabah
GILEAD
R. Jabbok
Lo-debar?
Penuel
Mahanaim
AMMON
Rabbah
Heshbon
Baal-peor
Bezer? (Bozrah?)
Nebo
Kiriathaim
Medeba
Beth-meon (Baal-meon)
Beth-diblathaim
Jahaz?
Ataroth
Dibon
R. Nahaliel
MOAB
Aroer
Wadi Arnon
Kir-haresheth
Waters of
Nimrim
Wadi Zered
Zoar

MAP 6

D   E   30°   F   35°   G

2

B l a c k   *S e a*

40°

R. *Sangarius*

PHRYGIA   Gomer

Gordion   (Gimarrai)

Meshech

R. *Hermus*   **LYDIA**

Sardis   R. *Halys*

(Sepharad)   *Usiana*

R. *Maeander*

Tubal

Togarmah

(Til-garimmu)

Milid

(Malitene)

3

J A V A N   **Musri**

COMMAGENE

(KUMUKHU)

CILICIA   Kue

(KHILAKKU)

Amanus Mts.   *Sam'al*

Carchemish

Crete   *Rhodes*   *Calno*   Haran

(Caphtor)   *Arpad*   Beth-

35°   Cyprus   *Aleppo*   (Bit-

(Isles of the Kittim)   *Tiphsah*

Rezeph

Arvad   *Hamath*   *Tadmor*

Riblah   *Qarqar*   (Tadmar)

Gebal (Byblos)   *Kadesh*

Berytus   *Lebo-Hamath*

M e d i t e r r a n e a n   *S e a*   R. *Helbon*

25°   (Western Sea)   **Sidon**   *Libanon*

4   **Tyre**   **Damascus**

Acco   *Ushu*

Hauran

Samaria   *Salecah*   **Ked**

ISRAEL   (Qid

Jerusalem   AMMON

30°   *Raphia*   JUDAH   MOAB

Zoan   *Pelusium*   *Gaza*

Sais   (Tanis)

Tahpanhes   *Migdol*   *Sela*   **A**

Athribis   EDOM

L i b y a   **Memphis**   *Heliopolis*

(Noph)   (On)

S i n a i   *Ezion-geber*

(Elath)

5

E G Y P T

Hermopolis   R. *Nile*   *Tema*

Lycopolis   *Dedan*

(Siut)   *R e d*

Thebes   *S e a*

35°   25°

6

Syene

© Oxford University Press

ETHIOPIA

(NUBIA)

E   F   G

MAP 6

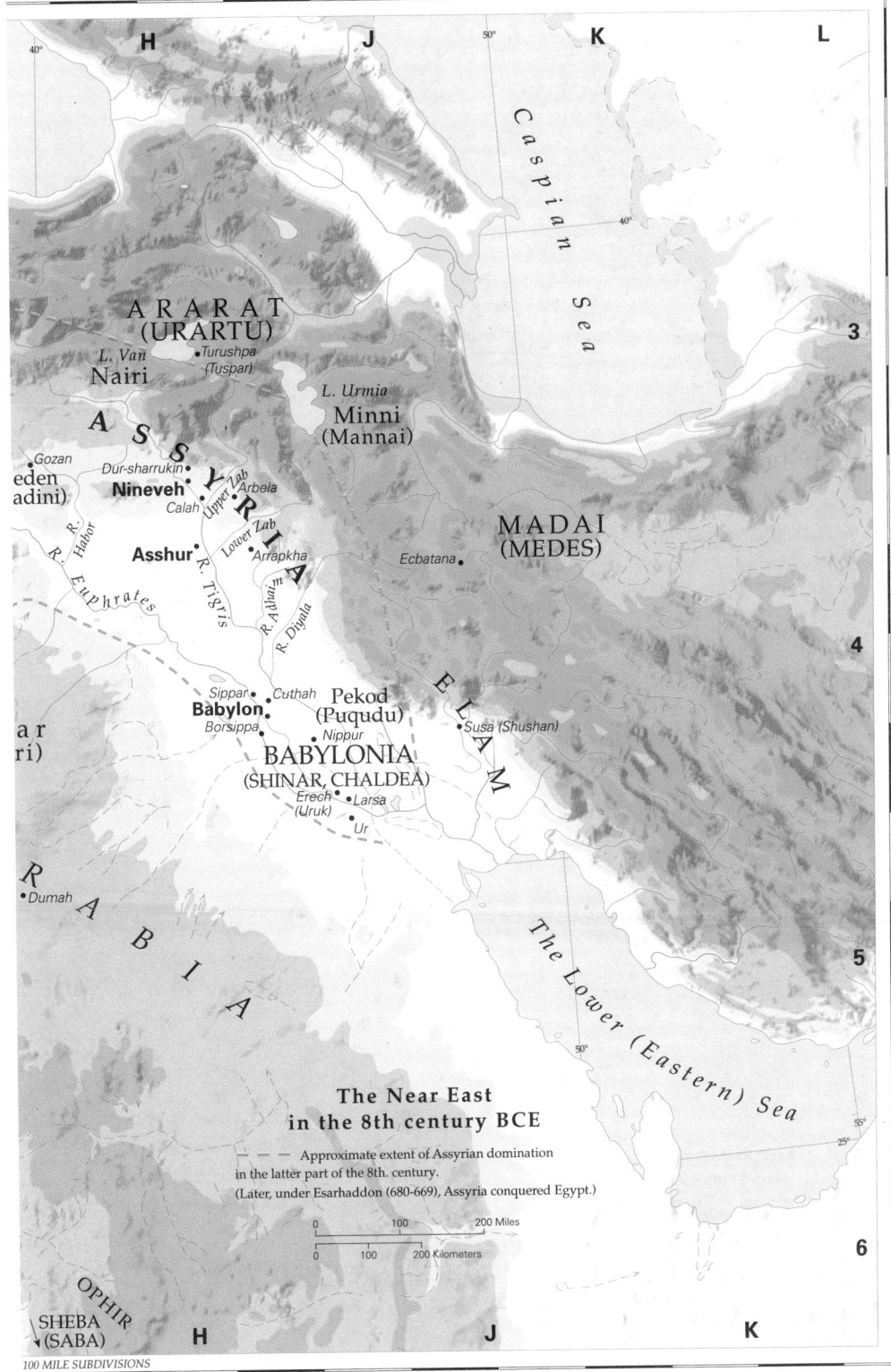

ARARAT
(URARTU)
L. Van • Turushpa
(Tuspar)
Nairi

A S S Y R I A

Gozan
Dur-sharrukin •
Nineveh
Calah • Upper Zab
• Arbela
Lower Zab
Asshur • • Arrapkha

eden
adini)

R. Habor
R. Euphrates
R. Tigris
R. Adhaim
R. Diyala

L. Urmia
Minni
(Mannai)

MADAI
(MEDES)

Ecbatana •

ar
ri)

Sippar • Cuthah
Babylon • Pekod
Borsippa • (Puqudu)
• Nippur
BABYLONIA
(SHINAR, CHALDEA)
Erech • Larsa
(Uruk)
• Ur

Susa (Shushan) •

E L A M

Caspian Sea

• Dumah

A R A B I A

The Lower (Eastern) Sea

**The Near East
in the 8th century BCE**

– – – Approximate extent of Assyrian domination
in the latter part of the 8th. century.
(Later, under Esarhaddon (680-669), Assyria conquered Egypt.)

0   100   200 Miles
0   100   200 Kilometers

OPHIR
SHEBA
(SABA)

MAP 7

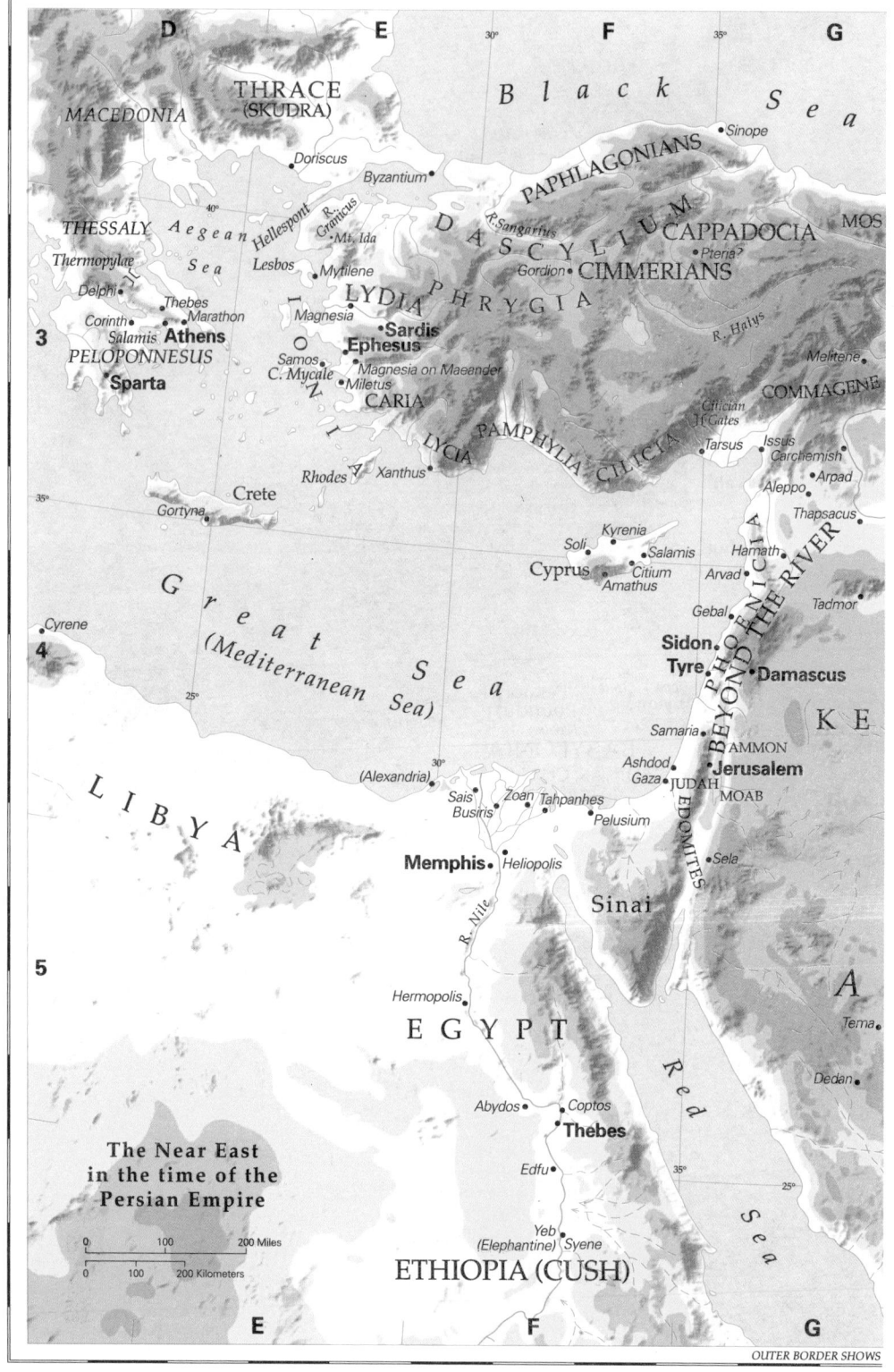

THRACE
(SKUDRA)

MACEDONIA

Doriscus

B l a c k   S e a

Byzantium

PAPHLAGONIANS

Sinope

MOS

THESSALY

Aegean

Hellespont

R. Granicus

R. Sangarius

D A S C Y L I U M

CAPPADOCIA

Thermopylae

Sea

Lesbos

Mt. Ida

Gordion•

CIMMERIANS

Pteria

Delphi

Mytilene

LYDIA

PHRYGIA

R. Halys

Thebes *Marathon*

Magnesia

Sardis

Melitene

Corinth

Athens

Ephesus

COMMAGENE

3

Salamis

Samos

Magnesia on Maeander

PELOPONNESUS

C. Mycale

Miletus

Cilician

Sparta

CARIA

Gates

Tarsus

Issus

PAMPHYLIA CILICIA

Carchemish

Arpad

Rhodes

LYCIA

Xanthus

Aleppo

Thapsacus

Crete

Kyrenia

Gortyna

Soli

Salamis

Hamath

Arvad

Tadmor

G r e a t

Cyprus

Citium

Amathus

Gebal

Cyrene

4

Sea

(Mediterranean Sea)

Sidon

Tyre

Damascus

K E

Samaria

AMMON

Ashdod

Jerusalem

(Alexandria)

Gaza JUDAH

Sais *Zoan* *Tahpanhes*

MOAB

Busiris

Pelusium

EDOMITES

Sela

L I B Y A

Memphis *Heliopolis*

Sinai

A

5

Hermopolis

Tema

E G Y P T

Dedan

Abydos *Coptos*

Thebes

Red

**The Near East
in the time of the
Persian Empire**

Edfu

Sea

0   100   200 Miles

0   100   200 Kilometers

Yeb
(Elephantine) *Syene*

ETHIOPIA (CUSH)

MAP 7

H   J   K   L

COLCHI

Caucasus Mountains

2

40°

Trapezus

CHI (MESHECH)

R. Cyrus

Hyrcanian

Sea

R. Araxes

40°

(Caspian Sea)

L. Van

ARMENIA
(URARTU)

3

HYRCANIA

Astrabad
(Gorgan)   Zadrakarta
(Turang Tepe)
(Damghan)

L. Urmia

Haran

ASSYRIA

M
E
D
I
A

PARTHIA

Nineveh   Arbela

Asshur   Arrapkha

Rages
(Rhagae)

R. Euphrates

R. Tigris

Ecbatana
(Achmetha)

SAGARTIA

Behistun
(Bisutun)

Eshnunna

Der

E
L
A
M

Gabae
(Isfahan)

4

Sippar

BABYLONIA

(SUSIANA)

DAR

Babylon

Nippur

Susa
(Shushan)

Borsippa

Erech (Uruk)

Larsa   Ur

Anshan
(Tall-i Malyan)

Parsagarda
(Pasargadae)

Persepolis

Dumah

P E R S I S
(P E R S I A)

R A B I A

5

Lower Sea (Persian Gulf)

50°

25°

6

© Oxford University Press

H   J   K

100 MILE SUBDIVISIONS

MAP 8

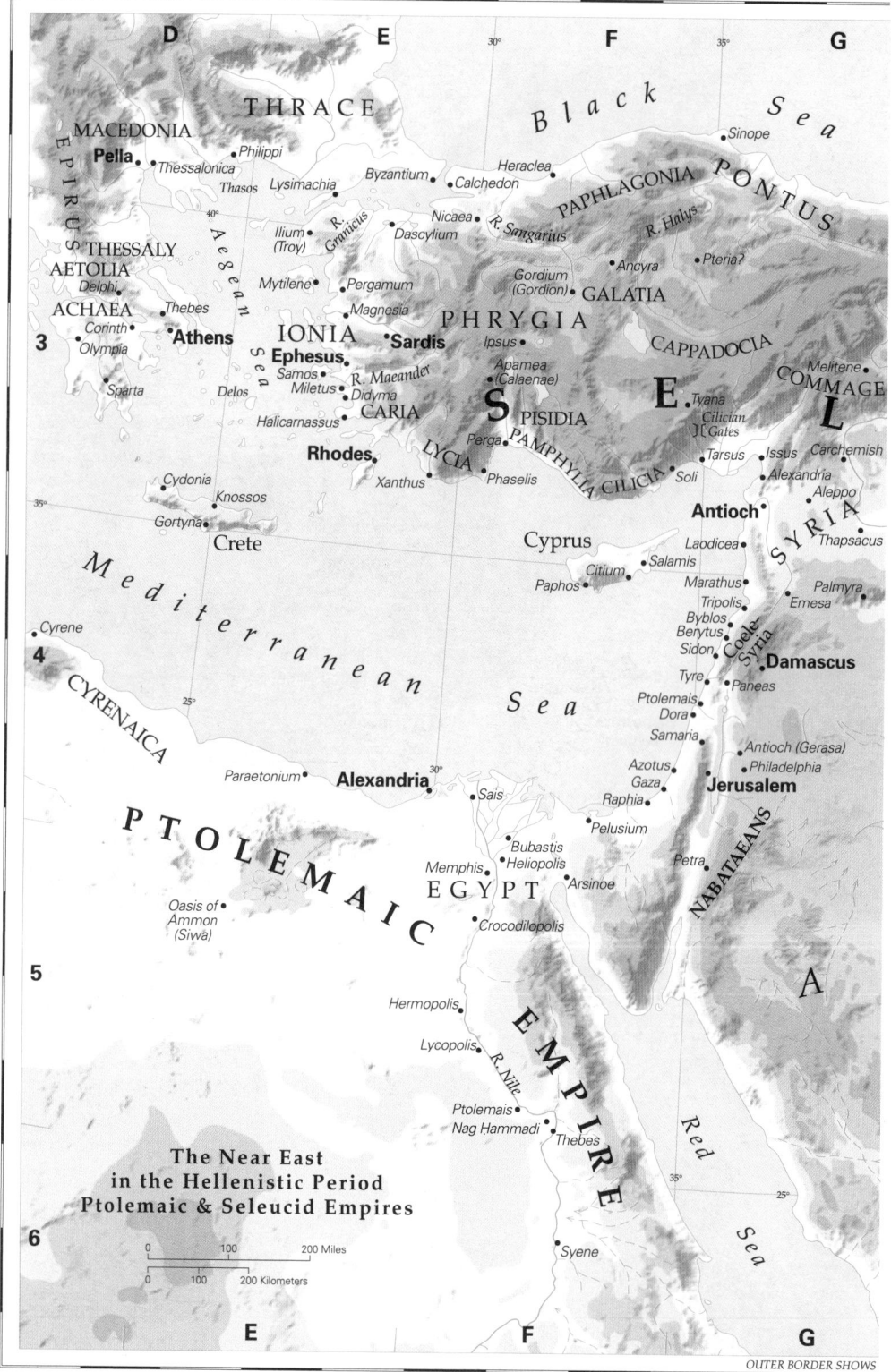

THRACE

MACEDONIA
Pella•
•Philippi
•Thessalonica
Thasos• Lysimachia
Byzantium• Heraclea
•Calchedon
Black Sea
•Sinope
PAPHLAGONIA
PONTUS
EPIRUS
Aegean Sea
Nicaea• R. Sangarius
Dascylium
R. Halys
•Pteria?
THESSALY
AETOLIA
Delphi•
Ilium• R.
(Troy) Granicus
•Ancyra
Gordium
(Gordion) •GALATIA
ACHAEA
•Thebes
Mytilene•
Pergamum•
Magnesia•
PHRYGIA
CAPPADOCIA
COMMAGE
Melitene•
Corinth•
•Athens
IONIA
•Sardis
Ipsus•
S
Olympia•
Ephesus•
Apamea
(Calaenae)
E
•Tyana
L
•Sparta
Samos•
Delos•
Miletus•
R. Maeander
Didyma•
Cilician
Gates
Carchemish•
CARIA
PISIDIA
•Tarsus
•Issus
Halicarnassus•
Perga•
•Alexandria
•Cydonia
LYCIA
PAMPHYLIA CILICIA
•Soli
•Aleppo
Knossos•
Xanthus•
Phaselis•
•Antioch
SYRIA
Gortyna•
Crete
Cyprus
Laodicea•
•Thapsacus
Mediterranean
Citium•
•Salamis
Marathus•
Palmyra•
Paphos•
•Emesa
•Cyrene
Tripolis•
Byblos•
Berytus•
Sidon•
Coele
Syria
•Damascus
CYRENAICA
Sea
Tyre•
•Paneas
Ptolemais•
Dora•
Paraetonium•
•Alexandria
Samaria•
•Antioch (Gerasa)
•Philadelphia
Azotus•
Gaza• •Jerusalem
Sais•
Raphia•
•Pelusium
Bubastis•
Memphis• •Heliopolis
•Arsinoe
Petra•
NABATAEANS
PTOLEMAIC
Oasis of•
Ammon
(Siwa)
EGYPT
•Crocodilopolis
A
Hermopolis•
Lycopolis•
R. Nile
EMPIRE
Ptolemais•
Nag Hammadi• •Thebes
Red
Sea
**The Near East
in the Hellenistic Period
Ptolemaic & Seleucid Empires**

•Syene

0   100   200 Miles
0 100   200 Kilometers

MAP 8

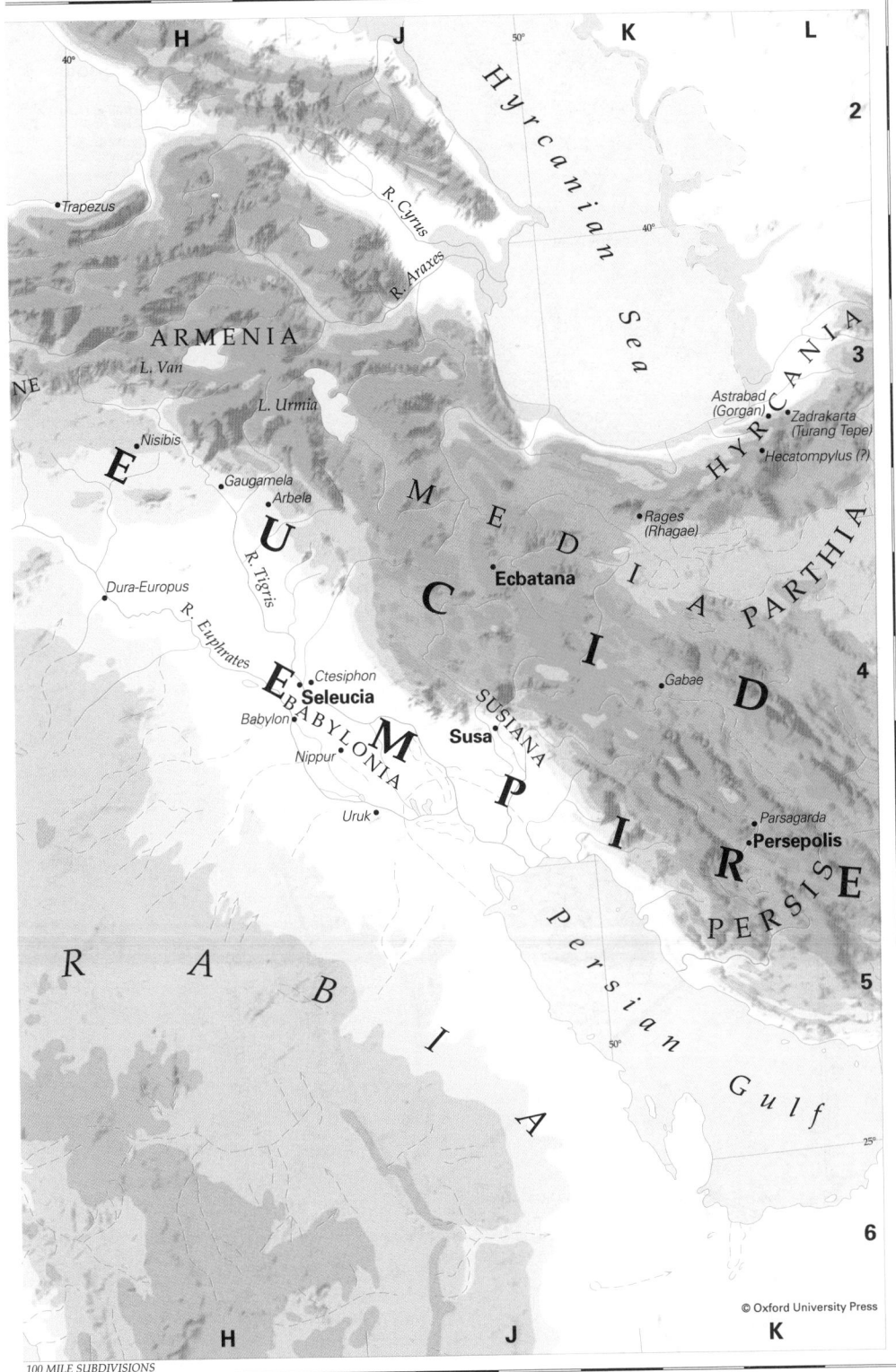

40°

2

H y r c a n i a n

• *Trapezus*

R. Cyrus

S e a

40°

R. Araxes

ARMENIA

L. Van

3

Astrabad (Gorgan)•

•*Zadrakarta (Turang Tepe)*

L. Urmia

H Y R C A N I A

•*Hecatompylus (?)*

NE

•*Nisibis*

E

•*Gaugamela*

•*Arbela*

M

E

D

•*Rages (Rhagae)*

I

PARTHIA

U

R. Tigris

Ecbatana

A

D

•*Dura-Europus*

C

R. Euphrates

I

4

•*Gabae*

E

•*Ctesiphon*

B **Seleucia**

SUSIANA

Babylon•• *BABYLONIA*

M

Susa

•*Nippur*

P

•*Parsagarda*

Uruk •

P

Persepolis

I

R

PERSIS

E

R

A

P e r s i a n

B

I

A

5

50°

G u l f

25°

6

© Oxford University Press

H   J   K

100 MILE SUBDIVISIONS

MAP 9

Jerusalem in First and Second Temple Periods

The Old City of Jerusalem
(medieval and Turkish city)
Approximate lines of City Walls:
of original Zion (2 Sam 5:7)
extended under the Kings
extended after the Exile
(by Maccabees, 2nd Cent. B.C.E.?)
Eastern wall of Nehemiah's city
Modern roads
Original Rock Contours are shown.

0   300 Meters
0   300 Yards

Tower of Hananel
←Baris

TEMPLE ☐ ALTAR

Solomon's Wall

? PALACE

Post-exilic
Jewish tombs
Monument of
Benei Hezir

TURKISH WALL

Tombs

Central (Cheesemaker's) Valley

(LOWER CITY)

Solomon's Wall

UPPER
CITY

?MISHNA
(SECOND QUARTER)

CITY OF DAVID

OPHEL

Manasseh's Wall

Wall of Zion

Gate

Water
shaft

Conduit

Gihon Spring

Upper
Pool

Old Conduit

Wall of Hezekiah (Manasseh) ?

Hezekiah's

Lower Pool

SILOAM

Old Pool

Gate

Mount of Olives

Kidron Valley

Pre-exilic Judean tombs

?

The lines of the
southern walls of the city
after the Exile are uncertain

Ben Hinnom Valley

En-rogel
Spring

© Oxford University Press